Britannica Book of the Year

Encyclopædia Britannica, Inc.
Chicago • London • New Delhi • Paris • Rome • Seoul • Sydney • Tokyo

1999 Britannica Book of the Year

As 1998 unfolded, it became increasingly clear that two major events dominated the news. The first, the Asian financial crisis that began in Thailand in 1997, affected everything in 1998 from the purchase of fur pelts and the seesawing world stock markets to the restructuring of national economies. This story is featured in the *1999 Britannica Book of the Year* in the Spotlight "The Troubled World Economy" by Robert J. Samuelson, *Newsweek* magazine correspondent. The role of the International Monetary Fund in dealing with the ongoing crisis is showcased in a special report by William Glasgall, *Business Week* magazine senior financial editor. The second recurring theme in the *Book of the Year* is the rising popularity of the Internet, which, with its millions of World Wide Web sites, is fast becoming a trusted destination for information retrieval—for example, www@eb.com—and emerging as the world's largest shopping centre. A sidebar on electronic retailing in "Business and Industry Review" provides a revealing look at these "netrepreneurs." The worldwide dependence on computers has become only too clear; many worried governments and companies spent billions of dollars coping with the potentially devastating "millennium bug," often referred to as the "year 2000" or "Y2K" problem. This potential bugaboo is discussed in a sidebar that complements the "Computers and Information Systems" article.

During the year there were other stories that captured the imagination. Harvard University professor Stephen Jay Gould explores the giant strides made in genetic understanding and electronic technology of information processing in his commentary "Tragic Optimism for a Millennial Dawning." Gould examines the growth of technology and the stagnation of morality against the backdrop of 1998 events, using as points of reference such films as *Armageddon, Deep Impact, Antz,* and *A Bug's Life.* Although the approaching millennium held fascination for many, the events of the past continued to mesmerize detectives searching for clues pertaining to the evolution of dinosaurs. The latest discoveries about these creatures are illuminated in a sidebar in "Life Sciences."

Whereas the special report "Senior Citizen Housing" discloses that the goal of most of the nation's elderly population is to age in place—that is, in the dwellings to which they have become accustomed—77-year-old American astronaut Sen. John Glenn blasted off into space, proving that not all seniors were content to stay at home. Back on Earth, baseball heroes Mark McGwire and Sammy Sosa aimed for the stars too, with a home-run duel that rekindled for fans the romance in America's favourite pastime. Earlier in the year other athletes gave star performances at the XVIII Olympic Winter Games in Nagano, Japan, and their records and achievements are detailed in a special report on the Winter Games.

The year was marked by devastating natural disasters, with Hurricane Georges battering Florida, Cuba, and the Dominican Republic; Hurricane Mitch pummeling Honduras and Nicaragua; and severe flooding inundating China and Eastern Europe. The specifics are found in the article "Disasters" and in relevant articles throughout the book. Political storms made headlines too, with U.S. Pres. Bill Clinton under investigation by Special Prosecutor Kenneth Starr. The role of the special prosecutor and the power he wields is featured in a "Law, Crime, and Law Enforcement" sidebar.

I invite you to turn the pages of this thought-provoking and fact-filled volume and discover why the editors at Encyclopædia Britannica found the events of 1998 so compelling. Our readers' comments are always appreciated; you can contact us at yearbook@eb.com.

Karen Sparks, Managing Editor

Contents

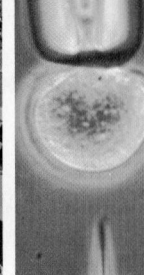

Tragic Optimism for a Millennial Dawning

by Stephen Jay Gould

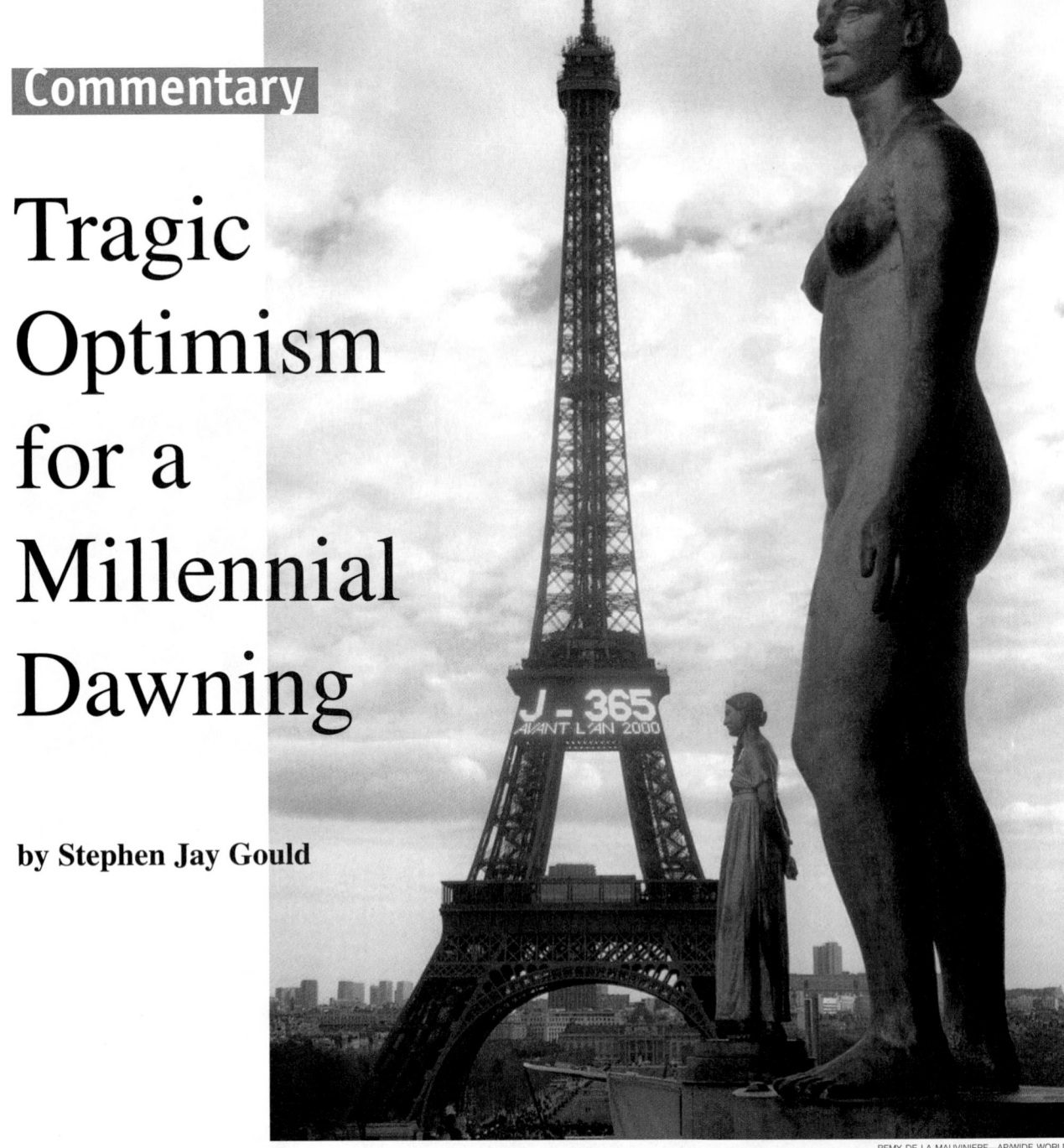

REMY DE LA MAUVINIERE—AP/WIDE WORLD

Stephen Jay Gould, Professor of Geology and Curator of Invertebrate Paleontology at Harvard University since 1973, has gained worldwide renown as a paleontologist, evolutionary biologist, and, not least, as a gifted writer on scientific subjects. With Niles Eldredge he developed in 1972 the theory of punctuated equilibria, a revision of Darwinian theory that proposes that evolution occurs not at slow constant rates over millions of years but rather in rapid bursts over periods as short as thousands of years followed by long periods of stability. His books, many of which deal with controversies in evolutionary biology, intelligence testing, and paleontology, include Ontogeny and Phylogeny *(1977),* The Mismeasure of Man *(1981),* Time's Arrow, Time's Cycle *(1987),* Dinosaur in a Haystack *(1995), and* Questioning the Millennium *(1997). Beginning in 1974, he has regularly contributed essays to* Natural History *magazine. He has won many awards for his teaching and research.*

WALLACE'S PARADOX

As 1998 unfolded in the homestretch of our millennial countdown, I remembered that, exactly 100 years ago, the leader in my profession of evolutionary biology, then a new science dedicated to explaining the causes and pathways of life's ancient history, wrote a book to mark the end of the last century. Charles Darwin died in 1882, so leadership had fallen to Alfred Russel Wallace, who also had recognized the principle

of natural selection in an independent discovery made before
Darwin's publication.

In *The Wonderful Century: Its Successes and Failures,* published in 1898, Wallace presented a simple thesis combining
both joy and despair: The 19th century had witnessed such a
spectacular acceleration of technological progress that innovations made during this mere hundred years had surpassed the
summation of change in all previous human history. This
dizzying pace, however, may do more harm than good because
human morality, at the same time, had stagnated or even ret-
rogressed—thereby putting unprecedented power (for good or
evil) into the hands of leaders inclined to the latter alternative.
Wallace summarized his argument:

> A comparative estimate of the number and importance of these
> [technological] achievements leads to the conclusion that not
> only is our century superior to any that have gone before it, but
> that it may be best compared with the whole preceding histori-
> cal period. It must therefore be held to constitute the beginning
> of a new era in human progress. But this is only one side of the
> shield. Along with these marvelous Successes—perhaps in con-
> sequence of them—there have been equally striking Failures,
> some intellectual, but for the most part moral and social. No im-
> partial appreciation of the century can omit a reference to them;
> and it is not improbable that, to the historian of the future, they
> will be considered to be its most striking characteristic.

As the 20th century (and an entire millennium) draws to its
close, we can only reaffirm Wallace's hopes and fears with increased intensity—for our century has witnessed even greater
changes, with special acceleration provided in recent years by
two great revolutions—in genetic understanding and the electronic technology of information processing. Our century has
also, however, experienced the depths of two world wars, with
their signatures of senseless death in the trenches of Belgium
and France, in the Holocaust, and at Hiroshima. How dizzy-
ingly fast we move, yet how stuck we remain.

History will not remember the following items as particularly memorable or defining features of 1998, but two pairs of
remarkably similar films, released by two rival companies,
epitomize Wallace's paradox as applied to our time. The summer of 1998 featured two disaster movies, one about a comet,
the other about an asteroid, on track to strike and destroy the
Earth and how courageous heroes divert the menace with nuclear weapons, thus saving our planet: *Deep Impact* by
DreamWorks and *Armageddon* by Disney. A few months later
the same companies fought another round by releasing, nearly
simultaneously, moral fables about insects (standing in for human values, of course) done entirely by computer animation:
Antz and *A Bug's Life,* respectively.

Consider the dizzying spiral of upward scientific and technological advance illustrated in these pairings. The intellectual
basis for these disaster films—the theory that an extraterrestrial impact triggered the catastrophic mass extinctions that
wiped out dinosaurs (along with half the species of marine organisms) 65 million years ago and gave mammals their lucky
and golden opportunity—was first proposed (and dismissed as
fanciful nonsense by most of my paleontological colleagues)
in 1980. Late in 1998 a published report that a tiny fragment
of the impacting asteroid had been recovered from strata deposited at the time of the hypothesized blast pretty much sealed
the continually improving case for this revolutionary scenario.

Few hypotheses that begin in such controversy can progress
to accepted fact in a mere 20 years. Even fewer ideas ever pass

from the professional world of science into hot themes for
mass markets of our commercial culture. (The popular resonances are not hard to identify in this case: if extraterrestrial
impact caused mass extinctions millions of years ago, why not
again? And why not use our nuclear weapons, heretofore imbued with no conceivable positive utility in saving life, to fend
off such a cosmic threat?) Consider also the equally accelerating spiral of technological advance illustrated by the manufacture of these films—60 years from Disney's first animated
full-length feature, *Snow White and the Seven Dwarfs,* where
each frame had to be drawn and painted by hand, to orders of
magnitude more complexity based on orders of magnitude less
handwork, as computers interpolate smooth action between
end points of human design in *A Bug's Life.*

And yet, to invoke the other side of Wallace's paradox, these
films, for all their technical wizardry, remain mired in the same
conventions, prejudices, and expectations that keep our social
relations (and moral perceptions) so far behind our material
accomplishments. Both *Antz* and *A Bug's Life* feature young
male heroes who are reviled and misunderstood by a con-
formist multitude but who eventually save their colonies by
their individualistic ingenuity—and, of course, then win the
(anthropomorphic) hand of the young queen. But true ant societies are matriarchies. Males are rare and effectively useless,
and all the so-called workers and soldiers (including the proto-
types for the two male heroes of the recent movies) are sterile females. In *A Bug's Life* the worthy ants have four limbs
and look human; only the villainous grasshoppers have—as all
insects truly do—six legs (and a resulting sinister appearance
in their two pairs of arms, at least to human observers; good
guys must look like us).

The transitions between centuries and millennia fall at precise, but entirely arbitrary, boundaries of human construction.
No astronomical or biological cycle works at a repeat frequency
of exact tens, hundreds, or thousands. Yet we imbue these
purely conventional boundaries with our own decreed meaning,
and parse time into decades (the Gay Nineties, the Roaring
Twenties, the Complacent Fifties). We have even coined a
phrase to mark our anxiety and stocktaking at major boundaries—the fin de siècle (or "end of century") phenomenon.

We are now about to face, for the first time in the history
of most nations and traceable family lines, the largest of all
human calendric boundaries in a millennial transition. And
who can possibly predict what the first years of the new millennium will bring? Wallace's paradox—the exponential
growth of technology matched by the stagnation of morality—
implies only more potential for instability and less capacity for
reasonable prognostication. But at least we might find some
solace in the sharply decreasing majesty of our fear. At the
last millennial transition of year 1000, many European
Christians awaited (either with fear or ecstasy) the full apoc-
alyptic force of Christ's Second Coming to initiate his thou-
sand-year reign of Earthly bliss. At the turning in 2000, we
focus most dread upon the consequences of a technological
glitch that may make our computers read a two-digit year code
as 1900 rather than 2000.

TRAGIC OPTIMISM

Human rationality, that oddest of all unique evolutionary inventions, does confer some advantages upon us. This most distinctively human trait does grant us the capacity to analyze the
sources of current difficulty and to devise (when possible)
workable solutions for their benign resolution. Unfortunately,
as another expression of Wallace's paradox, other all-too-
human traits of selfishness, sloth, lack of imagination, fear of
innovation, moral venality, and old-fashioned prejudice often
conspire to overwhelm rationality and to preclude a genuine

resolution that good sense, combined with good will, could readily implement under more favourable circumstances.

The lessons of history offer no guarantees but only illustrate the full range of potential outcomes. Occasionally, we have actually managed to band together and reach genuine solutions. Smallpox, once the greatest medical scourge of human civilization, has been completely eradicated throughout the world, thanks to coordinated efforts of advanced research in industrialized countries combined with laborious and effective public health practices in the developing world. On a smaller but still quite joyous note, during 1998 the bald eagle reached a sufficient level of recovery—thanks to substantial work by natural historians, amateur wildlife enthusiasts, and effective governmental programs—to become the first item ever deleted for positive reasons from the American Endangered Species List.

Just as often, unfortunately, we have failed because human frailty or social circumstances precluded the application of workable solutions. (Cities become buried by volcanoes viewed as extinct only because they haven't erupted in fallible memory. Houses built on floodplains get swept away because people do not understand the nature of probability and suppose that, if the last "hundred-year flood" occurred in 1990, the next deluge of such intensity cannot happen until 2090—thus tragically failing to recognize the difference between a long-term average and a singular event. In 1998 did India or Pakistan do anything but increase their expenditures, decrease their world respect, and endanger their countrymen by matching atomic tests, with both nations remaining at exactly the same balance after their joint escalation?)

I do, however, think that one pattern—the phenomenon that engenders what I have called "tragic optimism" in setting a title for this essay—does emerge as our most common response, and therefore as the potential outcome that should usually attract our betting money in the lottery of human affairs. We do usually manage to muddle through, thanks to rationality spiced with an adequate dose of basic human decency. This capacity marks the "optimism" of my signature phrase. But we do not make our move toward a solution until a good measure of preventable tragedy has already occurred to spur us into action—the "tragic" component of my designation.

To cite an example from the hit movie of 1998—James Cameron's gloriously faithful (and expensive) re-creation of the greatest maritime disaster in our civil history—we do not equip ships with enough lifeboats until the unsinkable *Titanic* founders and drowns a thousand people who could have been saved. We do not develop the transportation networks to distribute available food, and we do not overcome the social barriers of xenophobia until thousands have died needlessly by starvation. (As pointed out by Amartya Sen, winner of the 1998 Nobel Memorial Prize in Economic Science, no modern famine has ever been caused by a genuine absence of food; people die because adequate nourishment, available elsewhere, cannot reach them in time, if at all.) We do not learn the ultimate wisdom behind Benjamin Franklin's dictum that we must either hang together or hang separately, and we do not choose to see, or to vent our outrage in distant lands beyond our immediately personal concerns, until the sheer horror of millions of dead Jews in Europe or Tutsi in Africa finally presses upon our consciousness and belatedly awakens our dormant sense of human brotherhood.

To cite a remarkable example from 1998 on the successes of tragic optimism, many people seem unaware of the enormously heartening, worldwide good news about human population growth—a remarkable change forged by effective research, extensive provision of information, debate, and political lobbying throughout the planet, and enormous effort at local levels of village clinics and individual persuasion in almost all nations—mostly aimed at the previously neglected constituency of poor women who may wish to control the sizes of their families but had heretofore lacked access to information or medical assistance.

In the developing countries of Africa, Latin America, and Asia—the primary sources of our previous fears about uncontrollable population explosions that would plunge the world into permanent famine and divert all remaining natural environments to human agricultural or urban usages—the mean number of births per woman has already been halved from a previous average of about six to a figure close to three for the millennial transition. In most industrialized nations birthrates have already dropped below replacement levels to fewer than two per woman.

But, as the dictates of tragic optimism suggest, we started too late once again. Today's human population stands at about 5.9 billion, arguably too high already for maximal human and planetary health. Moreover, before stabilization finally gains the upper hand, the momentum of current expansion should bring global levels to about 10.4 billion by 2100. Most of this increase will occur in maximally stressed nations of the developing world. We have probably turned the tide and gained the potential for extended (and even prosperous) existence on a stable planet, but we dithered and procrastinated far too long and must bear the burden of considerable, and once preventable, suffering (and danger) as a result.

> ... the duration
> of human life
> on Earth represents
> only an eyeblink
> of cosmic time ...

DIFFERING SCALES OF TIME

In most of my writings on evolutionary biology, I emphasize the unity of humans with other organisms by debunking the usual, and ultimately harmful, assumptions about our intrinsic self-importance and domination as the most advanced creatures ever evolved by a process predictably leading in our direction. All basic evidence from the history of life leads to an opposite interpretation of *Homo sapiens* as a tiny, effectively accidental, late-arising twig on an enormously arborescent bush of life.

Fossil evidence for life on Earth dates back to bacterial cells more than 3.5 billion years old. For more than half this history, no other creatures existed except these simplest single-celled organisms of bacterial grade. These indestructible bacteria have always dominated, and still rule, life on Earth by criteria of numbers, diversity of biochemistry, range of inhabited environments, and prospects for continued prosperity. The number of *E. coli* cells (just one of many bacterial species that inhabit the human gut) carried by each person alive today exceeds the total number of humans who have ever existed.

In 1998 fossil embryos of the most ancient animals of modern design were discovered in China in rocks more than 570 million years old. By contrast, the duration of human life on Earth represents only an eyeblink of cosmic time, a millisecond in the Earth's geological history. The entire human lineage began with the evolutionary split from our closest relatives (chimpanzees and gorillas) in Africa only six to eight million years ago. *Homo sapiens,* the modern species to which all humans belong, represents a truly new kid on the evolutionary block, having originated, presumably in Africa, only about 250,000 years ago.

In the context of this essay, however, I need to emphasize the flip side of this chronology by pointing out the extraordinary impact of human existence during such an utterly insignificant amount of geological time. During the 3.5-billion-year tenure of life on Earth, no other species has left so strong an imprint upon our planet's surface in such a geological instant. We cannot attribute this influence to any novelty of merely physical form. (We are a large mammalian species, rather frail of body, and endowed with no special gift of brawn.) Our extraordinary achievements, for better or worse as only the future can tell, arise from an unparalleled increase and remodeling of neuronal tissue in our brains and from the attendant power of emerging consciousness, to unleash an entirely novel force upon the history of this planet: the power of cultural transmission, a much stronger and more rapid process of change than Darwinian physical evolution.

Only about 30,000 years have passed from the first European Paleolithic cave paintings at Chauvet (showing a mastery of style fully comparable with the skill of a Picasso) to the blockbuster art shows of America in December 1998 (Jackson Pollock in New York City, late Monet in Boston). Fewer than 10,000 years have elapsed since several human societies independently developed agriculture and unleashed the phenomena of accumulating wealth and dwellings in fixed places that serve as a prerequisite to the ever-growing social and material complexities called "civilization" (as opposed to the nomadic style of our previous lives as hunter-gatherers). The people who painted at Chauvet, and who first planted and reaped, belonged to our species and did not differ from us in any feature of bodily form, including size and structure of the brain. In other words, all the technological change that marks the full impact of human presence upon this planet has been forged by the power of cultural transmission among humans of unaltered evolutionary form and capacity.

Cultural change gains both its extraordinary power and its quirky unpredictability by operating under different principles than those regulating the slower Darwinian history of physical evolution. To cite the two most important differences, human cultural change works by the Lamarckian mechanism of inheritance of acquired characteristics (while evolutionary change must follow the vastly slower Mendelian and Darwinian route of natural selection upon genetic variation). Whatever we learn or invent in one generation we pass directly to the next by writing and teaching. Change, therefore, can accumulate and accelerate with unparalleled rapidity, leading us either to dizzying and disruptive success or into the abyss of gargantuan failure. As a second difference, biological evolution yields permanent separation on the tree of life. Once a species branches off from an ancestral lineage, it must follow its own distinctive pathway forever. Nature cannot make a new all-purpose mammal by mixing 80% of a bat with 20% of a dolphin. (Genetic engineering may be on the verge of breaking these age-old rules, but such fracturing would only represent a feedback from human invention upon biological history.) By contrast, cultural change proceeds largely by amalgamation and imitation. One distant traveler, gaining one look at a wheel invented by other peoples, can return to transform his own society forever.

Essential unpredictability, as a matter of principle (based on the unique complexity of most parts and the partial randomness of many processes, not on the limitations of our own ability to understand a genuinely deterministic universe), ruled the natural world long before humans made their boisterous and accidental entrance in the history of life on Earth. But the special principles of human cultural change only enhance the volatility and quirkiness of our own impact. At its own time scale, where a million years represents but a cosmic day, the Earth may wink at our hubris. Species come and species go, but the Earth endureth forever (or at least for many billion years more until the Sun explodes).

Yes, we may wipe out a large percentage of species (including ourselves), but Earth will recover, at its own time scale, several million years from now, as hardy survivors repopulate a temporarily battered planet. (After all, five major mass extinctions have occurred during the 600 million years of animal life on Earth. The biggest, 225 million years ago, wiped out about 95% of all marine species. Yet evolution always restores full diversity, though the process requires several million years.) Yes, we may unleash a powerful greenhouse effect, melt the polar ice caps, and raise sea levels sufficiently to drown most of our major cities (built at or near sea level for primary function as ports and harbours). But the Earth will prosper, though we may die. (At many past times during the history of continental drift, both poles lay over open oceans, no ice caps existed, sea level stood much higher, and life prospered.)

These claims are surely correct, but we make a terrible and tragic mistake—the classic error of mixing time scales—if we argue that the Earth's ability, at its own time scale, to heal the effects of potential human malfeasance should give us any solace or lead us to a position of "why worry" about environmental deterioration or anthropogenic extinction. The Earth's time scale, however majestic, cannot be the appropriate ruler for our own legitimately parochial interest in our lives (measured in decades or, at most, a century), our nations and bloodlines (measured, at best, in millennia), our cultures with all their magnificent achievements (and their gruesome failures), and the immediate environments and fellow creatures that now share the planet with us at the only time scale we can know, at least in crucial moral and psychological senses.

The Earth will survive if we unleash the dark side of Wallace's paradox, but our own glorious and tentative experiment in consciousness will fail, and we will (albeit temporarily) take much of the Earth's present splendour with us. We must care intensely, and at the appropriate scale of human existence—the scale now so palpably before us as we prepare for the first and only millennial transition (our longest measuring rod) in any living organism's memory (except for a few unconscious trees).

With tragic optimism we may place our bets on survival. Consciousness does give us the capacity to prevail along with the ability to destroy. John Playfair, the great Scottish scientist who explicated deep time by writing a famous book in 1802 on the immensity of geological cycles, ended his *Outlines of Natural Philosophy* (1814) with a wonderfully succinct description of tragic optimism, and its moral implication that we must never abandon the struggle. He wrote, using the old subjunctive mood (where his "were" equals our "would be"): "About such ultimate attainments, it were unwise to be sanguine, and unphilosophical to despair."

> No other species but humans has left so strong an imprint upon our planet's surface in such a geological instant.

Earthquake in China:
January 10

At the stroke of the new year, the Russian ruble is worth a thousand times less than before, as three zeros are removed from its value; about six new rubles equal one U.S. dollar.

•

Foreign Minister David Levy threatens to resign from the government of Israel because of differences regarding the state budget; he quits on January 4.

•

A rebel group allegedly led by Hutu forces based in Rwanda attacks a military camp outside the Burundian capital, Bujumbura, killing at least 150 civilians and 10 soldiers.

The new caretaker government of Prime Minister Josef Tosovsky, which was formed after the resignation in 1997 of Vaclav Klaus, takes office in Prague.

•

Following elections in November 1997, Toronto and five surrounding municipalities amalgamate to form a new metropolis of Toronto with a population of 2.4 million people.

Mexican Pres. Ernesto Zedillo reshuffles his Cabinet, replacing Interior Minister Emilio Chuayffet, who had been involved in negotiations with the rebel Zapatista National Liberation Army; the governor of Chiapas state, the rebels' stronghold, leaves office on January 7.

Valdas Adamkus, a citizen of the U.S. and former federal government official, is elected president of Lithuania by a narrow margin in a runoff election.

•

At the media preview of the North American International Auto Show in Detroit, the newly redesigned Chevrolet Corvette is named the Car of the Year and the Mercedes ML 320 the Truck of the Year; the show, which opens to the public on January 10, also showcases fuel-efficient vehicles and Volkswagen AG's new Beetle.

Several days of fierce ice storms, followed by freezing cold, sweep across Ontario, Quebec, and New Brunswick, Canada, as well as several New England states in the U.S.; damages are in the billions of dollars, and as many as three million people are without power, many for two weeks or more.

Daniel arap Moi is sworn in as president of Kenya for his fifth consecutive term following his win in contested elections in December 1997.

6

One of Denmark's most famous tourist attractions, the bronze statue of Hans Christian Andersen's heroine the Little Mermaid, which rests on a rock in Copenhagen Harbour, is decapitated by vandals; the missing head is returned two days later.

•

Lunar Prospector, a 300-kg (660-lb) unmanned spacecraft, is launched from Cape Canaveral, Florida (*see* March 5).

Apple Computer acting chief executive Steve Jobs announces that the company will show a $45 million profit for the first quarter of fiscal year 1998, astounding industry analysts.

7

The government of Canada formally apologizes to its indigenous peoples for having instituted assistance programs over the past 150 years that did more harm than good to the native communities; Canada also promises a $245 million "healing fund" to help victims.

8

Ramzi Ahmed Yousef, convicted of involvement in the 1993 bombing of the World Trade Center in New York City, is sentenced to life in prison by a U.S. district judge in New York.

•

International health officials announce that some 450 recent deaths originally feared to have been caused by the Ebola virus in Somalia and Kenya were due to an epidemic of Rift Valley fever.

9

Philippine Pres. Fidel Ramos rejects a proposal that would have returned to the people much of the billions of dollars taken from them by former ruler Ferdinand Marcos and his family; the money would have been returned in exchange for a general amnesty for the Marcos family.

•

Prime Minister Lionel Jospin of France says he will create an emergency relief fund totaling F 1 billion ($166 million) to assist the country's hard-core unemployed (*see* January 17).

•

Anatoly Karpov of Russia soundly defeats Vishwanathan Anand of India, defending his title as Fédération Internationale des Échecs champion in a match in Lausanne, Switz.

10

An earthquake of magnitude 6.2 hits Hebei province, China, killing at least 50 people and leaving tens of thousands homeless in freezing temperatures.

•

Shamil Basayev, the field commander whose troops shamed the Russian army during the Chechen secession struggle, assumes leadership of the government of Chechnya.

•

American figure skater Michelle Kwan wins the U.S. women's championship in Philadelphia; Todd Eldredge wins the men's title on January 8.

11

Torrential rains and flooding overcome Townsville, Queen., Australia; at least one person is killed and 120 are homeless.

12

UN Secretary-General Kofi Annan announces the appointment of Louise Fréchette, Canada's deputy defense minister, to the newly created post of deputy secretary-general of the United Nations.

•

The government of Iraq again prevents UN arms inspectors, led by U.S. personnel, from continuing their search for chemical and biological weapons.

Ronaldo, the star striker for the Inter Milan association football (soccer) team, wins the Fédération Internationale de Football Association's World Player of the Year award for the second year in a row, a first.

13

Scientists led by Andrea G. Bodnar of Geron Corp., Menlo Park, Calif., and Michel Ouellette of the University of Texas Southwestern Medical Center, Dallas, announce that they have genetically altered human cells to defeat the cells' programmed self-destruction due to aging, which could possibly lead to the extension of the human life span; their results are published in the January 16 issue of *Science.*

•

The government of Guyana bans street demonstrations following weeks of public protests by parties opposed to Pres. Janet Jagan.

•

Officials of the National Football League and four U.S. television networks, CBS, ABC, Fox, and ESPN, sign agreements on fees for coverage of NFL football games during eight seasons beginning in 1998–99 for the record amount of $17.6 billion; on January 14 the NBC

Statue of the Little Mermaid vandalized: January 6

network agrees to pay Warner Brothers Television $13 million per episode for the popular "ER" series.

14

With Japan as the 26th signatory state, a 50-year treaty banning mining and mineral extraction on the Antarctic continent and surrounding seabed enters into force.

•

The American Academy of Arts and Letters announces that the first recipient of its new Charles Ives Living Prize, which provides $75,000 a year for three years so that a composer can devote his full time to his work, is Martin Bresnick of Yale University.

15

President Suharto accedes to the demands of the International Monetary Fund and signs an agreement to enact reforms, including divesting himself and his large family of some of their accumulated wealth, in order to stabilize Indonesia's economy, which was unsteady in late 1997.

•

As the 5,000-member United Nations peacekeeping force departs from the city of Vukovar and its hinterland, sovereignty of the Eastern Slavonia region reverts to Croatia; the area had been occupied by the Serbs since 1991.

16

Turkey's highest court bans the Welfare Party, saying that the country's largest political party has a subversive agenda to replace Turkey's secular democracy with an Islamic regime; the ban enters into effect in February.

•

The Greek-owned freighter *Flare* breaks up off the coast of Newfoundland, killing at least 15 crewmen; 4 persons are rescued.

•

Sen. John Glenn of Ohio, at age 77, is selected by NASA to make a space shuttle flight in October 1998 to test the effects of space travel on aging; Glenn was one of the original team of U.S. astronauts and in 1962 was the first American to orbit the Earth (*see* October 20).

17

Pres. Bill Clinton spends six hours in the office of his attorneys formally answering questions from the lawyers representing Paula Corbin Jones in connection with her sexual harassment suit; this is the first time a sitting U.S. president has been a defendant in a civil court case (*see* April 1).

•

Mass demonstrations in Paris and other cities call for France's Socialist government to do something about the legions of unemployed, said to number three million (*see* January 9).

18

Pope John Paul II appoints 22 new cardinals, including 2 Americans and 2 whose names will be kept secret for fear of political reprisals; investiture will take place on February 21.

•

Serb nationalists boycott elections to the Bosnian Serb parliament and lose their majority to a pro-West moderate, Social Democrat Milorad Dodik; Dodik is sworn in on January 31.

•

In The Hague, Pakistani Zia Mahmood and Briton Tony Forrester win the Cap Gemini world top pairs competition in contract bridge by 21 victory points.

19

At a meeting in Rio de Janeiro, Ecuador and Peru agree to begin peace talks to end more than 50 years of hostile relations between the two countries (*see* October 26).

•

Food riots break out in Harare, the capital of Zimbabwe, and the government of Pres. Robert Mugabe, under increasing economic pressure, deploys national troops for the first time since independence.

•

Two large oil companies in Russia, AO Yukos and AO Sibneft, announce that they are merging to form AO Yuksi, the 11th largest oil company in the world.

20

Vaclav Havel is reelected president of the Czech Republic by the national legislature to serve a second five-year term.

•

The government of Nigeria seizes and closes 26 banks that have been on the brink of bankruptcy or have already ceased operations.

21

Pope John Paul II arrives in Havana for a five-day visit, his first to Cuba; extraordinary preparations are made by the Cuban government for the pontiff's stay, during which he criticizes the U.S. embargo policy and Cuba's communist government's long suppression of religion.

22

Theodore Kaczynski pleads guilty to charges that he is the "Unabomber," the man who led a terrorist mail-bomb campaign aimed against high technology in American society; in the agreement with the court, Kaczynski is to be sentenced to life imprisonment without the possibility of release or appeal (*see* May 4).

•

In a ceremony at Muela, Lesotho, King Letsie III of Lesotho and Pres. Nelson Mandela of South Africa formally inaugurate the Lesotho Highlands Water Project and mark the delivery of the first water from the project to South Africa.

•

The space shuttle *Endeavour* lifts off for the 12th time, carrying a crew of seven, including Australian-born Andrew

Paris police during mass demonstrations by jobless: January 17

JOEL ROBINE—AFP PHOTO

S.W. Thomas, to the space station *Mir;* Thomas is the last American scheduled to work on the Russian-built station.

23

P.W. Botha, the former president of South Africa (1978–89), appears before a court in George, S.Af., to answer charges that he refused to testify before the country's Truth and Reconciliation Commission about his role in abuses during the final years of the apartheid system; he pleads not guilty on February 24.

•

On the island of Bougainville in Papua New Guinea, the rebel forces and the local and national governments agree on a cease-fire to take effect on April 30 and end the savage nine-year conflict.

•

The largest and the third largest banks in Canada—the Royal Bank of Canada and the Bank of Montreal—announce plans to merge and thereby create the second largest bank in North America when measured by assets (*see* April 17).

24

In a gesture aimed at reopening talks with the rebel Zapatista National Liberation Army, the government of Chiapas state in Mexico releases 300 persons from jail in Chiapas; most, however, are not political prisoners.

•

Three human rights activists appear in court in Mauritania on charges that they participated in the filming of an illegal documentary about the slave trade in this West African country.

•

The Pro Football Hall of Fame in Canton, Ohio, announces that five former players will be inducted: linebacker Mike Singletary, tackle Anthony Muñoz, centre Dwight Stephenson, wide receiver Tommy McDonald, and safety Paul Krause.

25

Three suicide bombers kill themselves and eight others at the Temple of the Tooth in Kandy, the holiest Buddhist shrine in Sri Lanka; the act is ascribed to the Liberation Tigers of Tamil Eelam, who

Nuns awaiting arrival of Pope John Paul II in Cuba: January 21

have waged a secessionist war for 15 years (*see* February 4).

•

The Denver Broncos, led by star quarterback John Elway, upset the Green Bay Packers by a score of 31–24 in Super Bowl XXXII in San Diego, Calif.

•

In Karlsruhe, Ger., Haile Gebrselassie of Ethiopia runs the 3,000-m race in 7 min 26.14 sec, breaking his previous indoor world record by 4.58 sec.

•

The Sundance Film Festival ends in Park City, Utah (opened January 15); the Grand Jury Prize for a dramatic film goes to *Slam* by Marc Levin, and the Grand Jury Prize for a documentary is shared by *The Farm* by Jonathan Stack and Liz Garbus and *Frat House* by Todd Phillips and Andrew Gurland.

26

President Clinton asserts, "I did not have sexual relations with that woman, Miss Lewinsky," his bluntest and most direct denial of the accusations being made about his relationship with the former White House intern.

•

A comprehensive law banning nearly all handguns enters into effect in Great Britain.

In the second largest merger in Canadian history, two of the nation's biggest energy firms, TransCanada PipeLines Ltd. and Nova Corp., announce plans to form a company with Can$21 billion in assets.

27

Carlos Flores Facussé is sworn in as president of Honduras.

•

German Roman Catholic bishops announce that they will accede to the instruction of Pope John Paul II and stop counseling pregnant women about abortion.

•

Gro Harlem Brundtland, a physician and former prime minister of Norway, is elected director general of the World Health Organization by the WHO executive body; she succeeds Hiroshi Nakajima of Japan.

28

Japanese Finance Minister Hiroshi Mitsuzuka resigns in the wake of a bribery scandal and in the midst of a growing financial crisis; Vice Minister Takeshi Komura follows suit on January 29.

•

Major banks in South Korea agree to extend the payment schedule on a number of short-term loans totaling some $24 billion, an impor-

tant boost to the restructuring plans of the new government.

•

The Amoco Corp. announces that it has made the most important new find of crude oil in the past quarter century; the company estimates the reserves in the new field southeast of Trinidad at as much as 70 million bbl.

29

British Poet Laureate Ted Hughes's new collection, *Birthday Letters,* detailing the years of his marriage to poet Sylvia Plath, who committed suicide in 1963, is published; Hughes wins the Whitbread Book of the Year Award on January 27 for his *Tales from Ovid* but succumbs to cancer on October 28.

30

The U.S. Department of State issues its annual human rights report; the most important change is a notable moderation in U.S. criticism of the human rights situation in China.

31

Martina Hingis easily defends her Australian Open women's tennis title with a 6–3, 6–3 victory over Conchita Martínez.

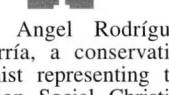

Miguel Angel Rodríguez Echeverría, a conservative economist representing the opposition Social Christian Unity Party, is elected president of Costa Rica.

•

Petr Korda of the Czech Republic trounces Marcelo Rios of Chile 6–2, 6–2, 6–2 to win the men's title at the Australian Open tennis competition.

Bianca Jagger (right) and Amnesty International director Sam Jordan at a rally for Death Row inmate Karla Faye Tucker: February 3

A Cebu Airlines DC-9 jetliner on an internal flight in the Philippines crashes in Mindanao, killing all 104 persons aboard.

•

U.S. Pres. Bill Clinton proposes a balanced federal budget to Congress; the country has not had a balanced budget in almost three decades.

•

In a federal court in Phoenix, Fife Symington, the former governor of Arizona, receives a sentence of 2½ years in prison after being convicted of fraud in real estate dealings in the 1980s and 1990s.

A cable car at a ski area near Cavalese, Italy, falls 80 m (260 ft), killing 20 persons aboard, after a U.S. Marine Corps training jet from the NATO air base at Aviano cuts the cable while flying too low.

•

Pres. Levon Ter-Petrosyan of Armenia is forced to resign by the country's military leaders; the prime minister, Robert Kocharyan, is made acting president.

•

Despite extraordinary international appeals and protests, Karla Faye Tucker, convicted of the pickax murder of two persons in Houston 15 years ago, becomes the first woman to be executed in the state of Texas since the Civil War.

•

Farmers and civil servants in Greece take part in several days of protests and rallies brought about by the government's stringent economic measures.

Sri Lanka officially celebrates the country's 50th anniversary in Colombo, the capital; the ceremonies were originally planned for Kandy but were hurriedly moved in light of the recent terrorist bombing incident there (see January 25, March 5).

•

Alfred E. Mann, the founder of a number of medical device companies, announces that he will give $100 million each to the University of Southern California and the University of California, Los Angeles, for the purpose of establishing biomedical research institutes.

Eight African states—Burkina Faso, Chad, Egypt, Libya, Mali, Niger, The Sudan, and Tunisia—meeting in Tripoli, Libya, agree to form the Sahara-Sahelian Community States Rally to promote multilateral cooperation; Algeria, Mauritius, Morocco, Nigeria, and Senegal do not participate.

•

The government of Sweden announces that it plans to close one of the two nuclear reactors at Barseback in conjunction with the nation's total phaseout of nuclear energy by 2010.

The exhibit "China, 5,000 Years" opens at the two Guggenheim museums in New York City.

•

President Clinton signs a bill to rename Washington, D.C.'s National Airport in honour of former president Ronald Reagan.

The Winter Olympic Games open in Nagano, Japan; featured in the ceremony is a

Policeman at the site of a cable car accident in Italy: February 3

performance of the "Ode to Joy" from Beethoven's Ninth Symphony sung simultaneously by choruses in Australia, China, Germany, South Africa, and the U.S.

•

The Rev. Jesse Jackson, special U.S. envoy for the promotion of democracy and human rights in Africa, begins a five-day tour of Kenya, the Democratic Republic of the Congo, and Liberia.

•

In another failed attempt at an around-the-world balloon flight, a three-man European crew lands the *Breitling Orbiter II* in a rice paddy north of Yangon (Rangoon), Myanmar (Burma), after an 8,525-km (5,294-mi) flight; the craft did, however, set a number of records.

8

Claude Erignac, the top government official in the French territory of Corsica, is shot and killed outside a theatre in Ajaccio, apparently by two members of a separatist group that opposes his policy of encouraging tourism on the island.

•

Chicago Bulls superstar Michael Jordan is presented the Most Valuable Player award, his third, at the 48th annual National Basketball Association All-Star Game in New York City.

•

Within a few minutes of each other, three speed skaters—Bart Veldkamp (Belgium), Rintje Ritsma, and Gianni Romme (both of The Netherlands)—all using the newly adopted clap skates, set successive world records for the 5,000-m race at the Winter Olympic Games.

•

The Council of Fashion Designers of America holds its annual award ceremonies in New York City; Narciso Rodriguez and Sandy Dalal win the Perry Ellis Award for new talent in the women's and men's fashion categories, respectively, and Elizabeth Taylor is recognized for a lifetime of glamour.

9

A terrorist attack using antitank grenades on the motorcade of Georgian Pres. Eduard Shevardnadze in the capital, Tbilisi, kills one bodyguard and injures two.

Israel's chief rabbinate, historically controlled by the Orthodox Jewish movement, strongly rejects a proposal from the Conservative and Reformed Jewish movements to cooperate in determining policies on conversions and religious rites.

10

In a deal valued at $2.4 billion, the Canadian National Railway Co. announces it will buy the Illinois Central

Corp., creating a network spanning Canada and running from Chicago to New Orleans.

•

David Satcher, director of the Centers for Disease Control and Prevention, Atlanta, Ga., is confirmed by the U.S. Senate as surgeon general.

11

The U.S. Senate defeats a bill, introduced by leading

Republicans, that would ban human cloning.

•

Gambling casinos are closed in Turkey at midnight following a vote by the Grand National Assembly in June 1997 aimed at controlling crime and illegal activities in the country.

•

A U.S. district judge in Oregon rules that the Professional Golfers' Association may not prevent Casey Martin, who suffers from a partial disability in one leg, from using a cart during PGA tournaments; nonhandicapped players must walk.

12

The first vice president of The Sudan, Maj. Gen. az-Zubayr Muhammad Salih, and at least 12 other officials are killed in an airplane crash in Nasir, in the southern part of the country.

•

U.S. District Judge Thomas F. Hogan rules that the line-

item veto, passed by Congress and signed by President Clinton in 1996, is unconstitutional; the provision will be forwarded to the U.S. Supreme Court for consideration.

•

Claudio Abbado, chief conductor of the Berlin Philharmonic since 1989, announces that he will not seek a renewal of his contract when it expires in 2002.

13

Nigerian-led forces take Freetown and capture dozens of senior Sierra Leonean junta officials who have fled the country to Liberia.

•

A constitutional commission votes 89–52, with 11 abstentions, to make Australia a republic before the end of the millennium, severing formal ties with Great Britain; a referendum on the issue is planned for 1999.

•

A tentative agreement is announced between United Auto Workers and Caterpillar Inc. to end 6½ years of disagreement, the longest major labour dispute in U.S. history; the workers reject the agreement in a vote on February 22.

14

Two men, Larry Wayne Harris and William Job Leavitt, Jr., are arrested in Las Vegas, Nev., for possession of what is at first believed to be deadly anthrax toxin for use as a weapon.

•

A series of bomb explosions during election campaigning in Coimbatore, Tamil Nadu state, India, kills between 30 and 50 people.

•

Te Papa Tongarewa, New Zealand's grand and costly new national museum, opens in Wellington amid much fanfare.

•

The Picture Makers, a play by Swedish playwright Per Olov Enquist and directed by Ingmar Bergman, premieres at the Royal Dramatic Theatre in Stockholm.

15

Voters in Greek Cyprus narrowly reelect Glafcos

Speed skater Gianni Romme at the Winter Olympics: February 8

Clerides to his second five-year term as president.

•

Mexico wins the Gold Cup, the championship of the Confederation of North American, Central American, and Caribbean Association Football, in a 1–0 contest over the U.S.

The 40th running of the Daytona 500 automobile race is won by Dale Earnhardt; this race is his 20th attempt to win the title.

16

All 197 persons aboard a China Airlines flight from Bali, Indon., are killed, as are at least 7 persons on the ground, when the plane crashes upon landing at Taipei, Taiwan.

•

The Biswa Ijitema, a yearly three-day mass gathering of the Muslim faithful, second in size only to the hajj, begins in Tongi, Bangladesh; an estimated two million people, including the president and prime minister of Bangladesh and pilgrims from 70 other countries, participate.

•

The 22nd annual Laurence Olivier Awards for excellence in theatre are presented in London; Richard Eyre is tapped as best director, Ian Holm and Zoë Wanamaker are named best dramatic actor and actress, and Philip Quast and Ute Lemper are named best actor and best actress in a musical.

17

Voyager 1 becomes the man-made object farthest from the Earth; the spacecraft was launched on Sept. 5, 1977, and is still functioning.

•

A group of wrestlers from the U.S., the first Americans to visit Iran officially since 1979, arrive in Tehran to participate in an international tournament.

18

Former Zambian president Kenneth Kaunda is charged with concealing information about a coup attempt against the government of Pres. Frederick Chiluba in October 1997; Kaunda led his nation to independence and was president for 27 years.

In Sweden the official inquiry into the worst maritime disaster in European history, the sinking of the ferry *Estonia* off the coast of Finland in September 1994, is closed; no charges are pressed against anyone.

19

Japan reports its first monthly trade deficit with the countries of Asia in eight years, although its trade surplus with the U.S. grew again to a total of $3 billion.

•

Seventy groups active in the campaign to ban land mines meet in Frankfurt to decide how to divide their half of the 1997 Nobel Peace Prize award and who will coordinate the movement; Jody Williams, the recipient of the other half of the prize, announces her resignation as coordinator of the International Campaign to Ban Land Mines on February 6.

•

For the first time in history, a Canadian senator, Andrew Thompson, is suspended without pay for his poor attendance record.

20

With three cables already out, the fourth of the main cables that supply power to Auckland fails, and nearly all of New Zealand's largest city is left without electricity.

•

Tara Lipinski, 15, becomes the youngest athlete ever to win a gold medal in an individual event in the Winter Olympics when she emerges ahead of favoured Michelle Kwan in the women's figure-skating event.

•

Danish choreographer Peter Martins's new ballet *Stabat Mater,* to music by Giovanni Battista Pergolesi, is premiered by the New York City Ballet in New York.

21

In Moscow, Russia and Japan sign an agreement that regulates fishing quotas for Japan in the waters off the disputed Kuril Islands.

•

Longtime American civil rights activist Julian Bond is elected chairman of the National Association for the Advancement of Colored People to replace Myrlie Evers-Williams.

22

The United Nations announces the terms of the agreement reached by Secretary-General Kofi Annan with Iraqi Pres. Saddam Hussein, saying that Iraq will now permit UN arms inspectors unconditional access to possible weapons sites.

•

An internal U.S. Central Intelligence Agency report on the 1961 Bay of Pigs invasion of Cuba is released to the public; the report is highly critical of the agency itself, citing its institutional arrogance and incompetence.

•

Central do Brasil, by the young Brazilian director Walter Salles, wins the Golden Bear award, the top film honour at the Berlin Film Festival, and Neil Jordan of Ireland wins the best director award for his work in *The Butcher Boy.*

23

Tornadoes rip through several counties in central Florida, causing at least 42 deaths and a record amount of tornado damage for the state.

24

Prime Minister Khamtay Siphandon is elevated to the post of president of Laos by the National Assembly; Vice Pres. Sisavath Keobounphanh is named prime minister.

•

Danny Yatom, the head of Mossad, Israel's intelligence agency, resigns in the wake of criticism of the agency, once considered among the best in the business, for a series of humiliating failures, notably a botched 1997 assassination attempt in Jordan and another in Switzerland in mid-February 1998.

•

The motion picture *Titanic* surges past *Jurassic Park* to become the highest-grossing motion picture in U.S. history, with box-office receipts of $919.8 million worldwide; the trade magazine *Variety,* however, calculates that in ticket prices adjusted to 1998 levels, *Titanic* still lags far behind number one

movie *Gone with the Wind* (1939), which grossed almost $1.3 billion in domestic theatres alone.

25

Kim Dae Jung, a former dissident and longtime opposition leader, is formally inaugurated as president of South Korea.

•

In a referendum more than 90% of the residents of Anjouan approve a new constitution that grants the Indian Ocean island independence from the Comoros Islands.

•

The 40th annual Grammy awards ceremony of the National Academy of Recording Arts and Sciences is held in Radio City Music Hall, New York City; record of the year and song of the year awards go to Shawn Colvin's "Sunny Came Home," and veteran Bob Dylan's *Time out of Mind* wins the album of the year and contemporary folk album awards.

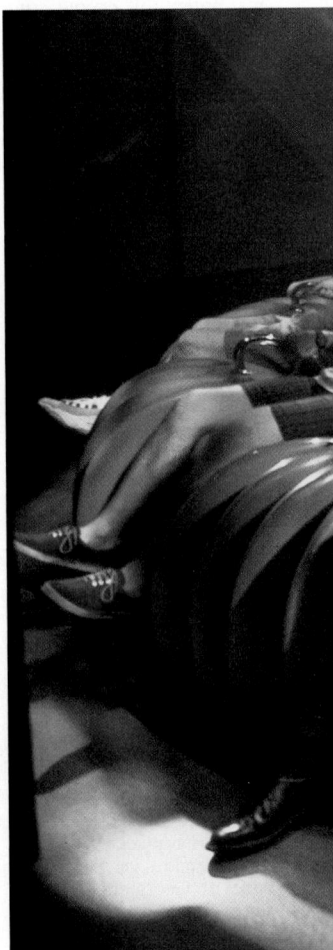

The $40,000 Neustadt International Prize for Literature is awarded to novelist Nuruddin Farah of Somalia; the award is given every other year by the journal *World Literature Today* and the University of Oklahoma.

26

Oprah Winfrey is exonerated by a federal jury in Amarillo, Texas, from charges by a Texas cattlemen's group; the group had charged that remarks she made on her popular television program about the relationship of "mad cow" disease to the American beef industry were slanderous and had caused a drop in cattle prices, costing the cattlemen millions of dollars.

•

In the area of the former Yugoslav federation, for the first time in six years, obstacles to rail transportation are removed and a freight train moves through territory controlled by the Serbs, the Croats, and the Muslims.

27

Queen Elizabeth II tells Parliament that she approves of plans to change the law of primogeniture, by which the eldest son of the reigning monarch is first in line to ascend to the throne; such a change would give the eldest child, male or female, of a British king or queen that right.

•

The International Court of Justice in The Hague rules that it has jurisdiction to settle the dispute over the venue for the trial of the two Libyan nationals accused of the bombing of Pan American Flight 103 over Lockerbie, Scot., in 1988 (*see* August 26).

•

HarperCollins Publishers Inc., apparently concerned about an adverse reaction from the Chinese government, announces that it will not publish the memoir of former British Hong Kong governor Chris Patten as planned.

28

The governments of Hungary and Slovakia agree on plans to build a large hydroelectric dam across the Danube River, putting new life into the controversial Gabcikovo-Nagymaros project and precipitating vocal protests in Budapest, the Hungarian capital.

•

The Russian government votes to bury the remains of Tsar Nicholas II and his family in the royal crypt in St. Petersburg.

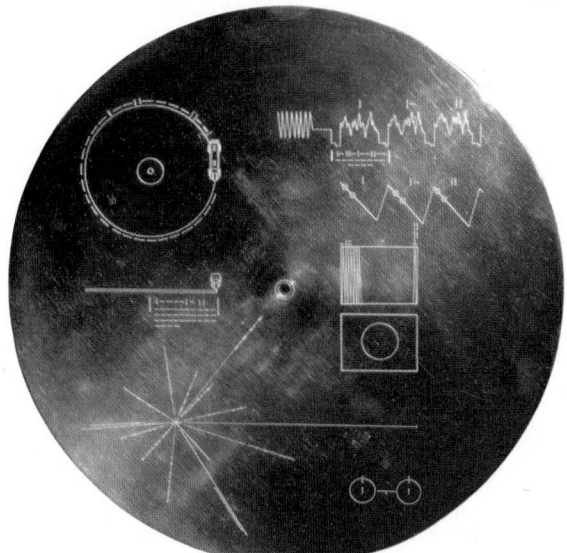

JPL/NASA

Gold-plated copper disk on *Voyager 1* containing recorded sounds and images of life on Earth: February 17

The Time Warp exhibit at New Zealand's new national museum, Te Papa Tongarewa: February 14

MUSEUM OF NEW ZEALAND TE PAPA TONGAREWA; PHOTOGRAPH, MICHAEL HALL (F.4554/46)

1

The Social Democratic Party of Germany (SPD), led by Gerhard Schröder, premier of Lower Saxony, wins comfortably in elections in the German state and clinches Schröder's position as SPD candidate to run against Chancellor Helmut Kohl in the federal election (*see* September 27).

•

Owens-Illinois, one of the largest manufacturers of glass and plastic containers in the Americas, announces plans to acquire BTR PLC, a British company whose holdings include a top supplier of glass containers in Australia, New Zealand, and Great Britain, for $3.6 billion in cash.

2

A protest demonstration by some 30,000 ethnic Albanians in Pristina, the capital of Serbia's province of Kosovo, is forcefully broken up by Serbian police; 24 civilians have died at the hands of Serbian police and paramilitary forces.

•

Kim Jong Pil, the choice of South Korea's Pres. Kim Dae Jung for prime minister, is rejected by the National Assembly but is appointed anyway in an acting capacity; meanwhile, the government of North Korea admits that the country is facing a severe famine and that food stocks have been all but exhausted.

•

For the first time, a single chef is the recipient of six stars from France's Michelin guide to restaurants; Alain Ducasse wins the top three-star rating for the Alain Ducasse restaurant in Paris as well as his Louis XV in Monte-Carlo.

3

The U.S. Federal Trade Commission votes to block the planned mergers of two pairs of wholesale drug sellers—McKesson Corp. with Amerisource Health Corp. and Cardinal Health Inc. with Bergen Brunswig—on antitrust grounds.

•

Time, an American weekly news magazine, celebrates its 75th anniversary with a gala party at Radio City Music Hall that brings together 1,190 guests from among the powerful, rich, and famous.

4

Ruling in *Oncale* v. *Sundowner Offshore Services, Inc., et al.,* the U.S. Supreme Court finds that same-sex harassment in the workplace is a violation of federal civil rights law, just as is male-female harassment.

•

Sir Sigmund Sternberg, a British businessman and philanthropist, is named as the recipient of the 1998 Templeton Prize for Progress in Religion; Sternberg, who is Jewish, has been active in promoting interfaith understanding.

5

At the opening of the National People's Congress in China, Premier Li Peng announces a major reduction in the central bureaucracy; the cutback includes, among other measures, a reduction in the number of ministries from 40 to 29.

•

Some 32 people are killed and more than 300 injured when at least two shrapnel bombs explode on a bus in Colombo, Sri Lanka; terrorists of the Liberation Tigers of Tamil Eelam are suspected (*see* February 4). ·

•

Scientists at the Lunar Research Institute in Gilroy, Calif., report that the U.S. *Lunar Prospector* spacecraft, launched on January 6, has discovered evidence of the existence of water at the Moon's north and south poles in the form of ice crystals mixed with soil (*see* January 6).

6

Cécile, Annette, and Yvonne, 63, the three surviving members of the Dionne quintuplets, accept from the Ontario government a settlement of $2.8 million and promises of an inquiry into their treatment during their childhood, when they were made wards of the state and used by the government for promotional purposes.

•

Elisabeth Gehrer, Austrian minister of culture, breaks rank with museum officials in Europe and America when she announces that Austria is prepared to return art treasures taken by the Nazis from Jews during World War II and kept in state-run museums (*see* April 14).

•

The government of Ecuador passes the Galápagos Conservation Law, which includes provisions for the expansion of a marine sanctuary extending 65 km (40 mi) out to sea and the banning of "industrial-scale fishing" from the area around the ecologically unique island group.

7

An avalanche in the Salang region of Afghanistan 110 km (68 mi) north of Kabul kills as many as 70 persons.

•

Hermann Maier of Austria wins the men's title in Alpine skiing World Cup competition at Kvitfjell, Nor.; Germany's Katja Seizinger wins the women's title on March 13 at Crans Montana, Switz.

•

And now for something completely different—the original Monty Python group is reunited, for the first time since the death of troupe member Graham Chapman in 1989, at the United States Comedy Arts Festival in Aspen, Colo.

8

Legislative elections in Colombia return the incumbent Liberal Party to power despite a succession of scandals over corruption charges.

•

In ceremonies at the National Academy of Sciences in Washington, D.C., Christopher Mihelich of Carmel, Ind., is named the winner of the annual Westinghouse Science Talent Search for high-school students; Mihelich wins a $40,000 college scholarship.

9

The Aluminum Company of America (Alcoa), the largest producer of aluminum in the U.S., announces it will purchase the third largest aluminum company, Alumax Inc., for $2.8 billion in cash and stock.

10

The elected president of Sierra Leone, Ahmad Tejan Kabbah, returns from 10 months in exile; his return follows the ejection, by an international military force led by Nigeria, of the military government formed after a coup by Maj. Johnny Paul Koromah.

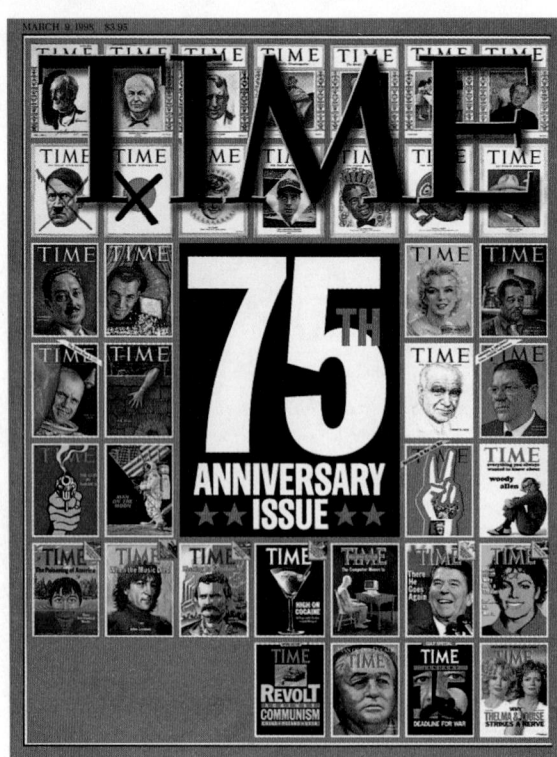

Time magazine's 75th anniversary issue: March 3

Indonesian President Suharto is reelected by the People's Consultative Assembly for a seventh term of office and is given additional powers to deal with economic and security problems in the country (*see* May 21).

•

Viswanathan Anand of India clinches a victory at the Linares Supertournament chess championship in Spain.

11

Legal authorities raid the Bank of Japan, the country's central bank, and arrest a top official on charges of accepting bribes; the bank's director, Yasuo Matsushita, resigns on March 12 and is replaced by Masaru Hayami on March 20.

•

In Denmark Prime Minister Poul Nyrup Rasmussen and his centre-left coalition partners win a narrow victory in legislative elections, controlling the Folketing (parliament) by one vote.

•

Brian Marsden of the Smithsonian Astrophysical Observatory in Cambridge, Mass., makes news when he announces that there is a chance that the Earth will be hit by an asteroid in the year 2028; a day later NASA announces that additional calculations suggest there is no risk at all.

12

A government official says that fires burning out of control in the Amazonas area of Brazil since mid-January have consumed more than 51,780 sq km (20,000 sq mi) and are threatening the reservation of the Yanomami, a Stone Age people, in Roraima state.

The U.S. Congress passes the African Growth and Opportunity Act, which will exempt exports from the nations of sub-Saharan Africa from U.S. duties and trade quotas for 10 years and promote the creation of a U.S.–sub-Saharan free-trade zone.

•

The Houston (Texas) Ballet premieres the $1.2 million, three-act ballet *The Snow Maiden* in Houston.

13

President Kim of South Korea, himself a former political prisoner, declares a general amnesty affecting the police records, mostly for minor offenses, of 5.5 million people and frees a number of political prisoners.

•

Astronomers at the Keck Observatory in Hawaii announce that they have observed light from an object located 12.2 billion light-years from Earth, the most distant object yet discovered.

14

King Hassan II appoints a new coalition government for Morocco headed by Prime Minister 'Abd ar-Rahman al-Youssoufi.

15

An unusually strong and long-lasting *khamsin* (sand and dust storm) engulfs a portion of the eastern Mediterranean area from Egypt to Syria.

•

The Columbus Quest defeats the Long Beach StingRays 86–81 to win the second American Basketball League championship for women in Columbus, Ohio.

16

The giant national health insurance provider Aetna Inc. announces a $1,050,000,000 deal to buy the health care division of the New York Life Insurance Co.

•

Obeid ibn Saif an-Nasiri of the United Arab Emirates is named head of OPEC.

•

Sonia Gandhi, the Italian-born widow of former prime minister Rajiv Gandhi, is unanimously elected to lead India's Congress Party.

17

During the March 5–17 session of the Chinese National People's Congress, Vice-Premier Zhu Rongji is elected to the post of premier, replacing Li Peng.

•

Washington Mutual, Inc., the largest savings and loan in the United States, buys H.F. Ahmanson, the second largest savings unit, in a $9.9 billion stock merger; the purchase creates a new company with $149.2 billion in assets, making it the seventh largest firm in the industry.

•

For the third time Jeff King of Denali Park, Alaska, wins the 1,790-km (1,110-mi) Anchorage-to-Nome Iditarod Trail Sled Dog Race ; his time is 9 days 5 hours 52 minutes.

18

A Formosa Airlines airplane with 12 people aboard disappears and is presumed crashed into the sea off Taiwan.

19

Atal Bihari Vajpayee of the Bharatiya Janata Party is sworn in as Indian prime minister; he will lead a coalition government comprising 20 parties.

•

The sale of the Los Angeles Dodgers professional baseball team to media magnate Rupert Murdoch's Fox Group for $311 million is approved by the major league baseball owners at their annual meeting.

•

The Promise Keepers, an all-male evangelical Christian group, reports that for financial reasons it will lay off its entire paid staff.

20

The government of Botswana announces the completion of the last 600-km (370-mi) stretch of the 1,600-km (1,000-mi) Trans-Kalihari Highway; the highway runs

(From left) Annette, Yvonne, and Cécile, the three surviving members of the Dionne quintuplets: March 6

Sonia Gandhi, new leader of India's Congress Party: March 16

from Windhoek, Namibia, to Maputo, Mozambique, and is the first direct link between the Atlantic Ocean and Indian Ocean coasts of Africa.

•

For the first time, the intelligence budget of the U.S. is made public; Director of Central Intelligence George Tenet reveals that the U.S. plans to spend $26.7 billion on intelligence activities in fiscal year 1998.

21

Pope John Paul II begins a three-day visit in Nigeria.

22

Voting informally and, the Serbians say, illegally, the residents of Kosovo decide to elect a legislature and a president for their break-away region of Yugoslavia.

23

Russian Pres. Boris Yeltsin abruptly fires his entire Cabinet, including Prime Minister Viktor Chernomyrdin, and proposes former minister of energy Sergey Kiriyenko as the next prime minister (*see* August 22).

•

President Clinton arrives in Accra, Ghana, beginning a 12-day sojourn in six countries of Africa.

•

Bertelsmann AG, which already owns Bantam Doubleday Dell and other American media companies, announces that it will buy Random House Inc. for about $1.5 billion, which will make the German publishing

giant the largest publishing company in the U.S. (*see* October 6).

•

Juan Somavía, Chile's chief delegate to the United Nations, is elected director general of the International Labour Organisation.

24

Prime Minister Apas Jumagulov of Kyrgyzstan resigns and is replaced on March 25 by Kubanychbek Jumaliyev.

•

Two boys, aged 11 and 13, are taken into custody in Jonesboro, Ark., after 4 students and a teacher are killed and 11 people are wounded by gunshots as they leave a school building following a false fire alarm.

•

In the first awards of the National Book Critics Circle to allow non-American entries, British author Penelope Fitzgerald wins for her novel *The Blue Flower;* other laureates are James Tobin in biography for *Ernie Pyle's War: America's Eyewitness to World War II,* Anne Fadiman in general nonfiction for *The Spirit Catches You and You Fall Down,* and Charles Wright for poetry with his *Black Zodiac.*

25

The first award ceremony for the "Eisies," the Alfred Eisenstaedt Awards for Magazine Photography in 20 categories, is held in New York City.

•

Kruger National Park in South Africa celebrates 100 years of wildlife conservation.

Viagra impotence drug: March 26

26

Viagra, a drug developed by the pharmaceutical firm Pfizer Inc. to treat male impotence, is approved by the U.S. Food and Drug Administration; the drug is an immediate best-seller.

•

Switzerland's three major banks agree to negotiate plans for a global settlement with Holocaust victims and vow to organize a compensation fund in the U.S. to make restitution for World War II atrocities; the fund could reach $3 billion (*see* June 19).

Imelda Marcos, the widow of former president Ferdinand Marcos of the Philippines, reveals for the first time the amount of her personal wealth held in foreign banks: $800 million.

27

At a meeting of the National Security Council in Ankara, Turkish generals demand that Prime Minister Mesut Yilmaz take action against religious-oriented movements in an effort to separate religion and politics.

28

Cyber Promotions, Inc., the biggest sender of junk mail on the Internet, agrees to pay $2 million in reparations to settle lawsuits filed by Internet service providers.

•

Venus Williams of the U.S. defeats Russian-born Anna Kurnikova to clinch the Lipton Championship tennis tournament in Key Biscayne, Fla.

•

Silver Charm, the 1997 Kentucky Derby and Preakness Stakes winner, noses past Swain to win the Dubayy

Grieving students
in Jonesboro, Ark.:
March 24

World Cup horse race and its $2.4 million prize, more than doubling his previous earnings.

29

Pat Hurst wins the Nabisco Dinah Shore golf tournament at Mission Hills Country Club in Rancho Mirage, Calif.; Lee Trevino finishes two strokes ahead of Mike McCullough and captures his first golf title since 1996 at the Southwestern Bell Dominion Professional Golfers' Association Senior tour event in San Antonio, Texas.

In Kansas City, Mo., the University of Tennessee defeats Louisiana Tech 93–75 to win the NCAA women's basketball championship for the third straight year.

•

In Reno, Nev., the Vanderbilt Knockout Team Championship in contract bridge is won for the second year in a row by a team led by Richard Schwartz.

30

Prime Minister Robert Kocharyan is elected president of Armenia in the sec-

ond stage of an election process that is marked with irregularities.

•

Former prime minister Norodom Ranariddh returns to Cambodia from exile to run for reelection against Hun Sen, the coup leader who ousted him in June 1997.

•

Donald Kalpokas is elected prime minister of Vanuatu.

•

Prime Minister Victor Ciorbea of Romania resigns; Gavril Dejeu is appointed to replace him in a caretaker role.

31

Reacting to the violent suppression of dissidence in the province of Kosovo by Serbian authorities, the United Nations Security Council votes 14–0 to impose an arms embargo on Yugoslavia (*see* March 2, May 9).

•

Six European countries— Cyprus, the Czech Republic, Estonia, Hungary, Poland, and Slovenia—begin negotiations with the European Union in Brussels for membership in the union.

April

Michelle Kwan at the World Figure-Skating Championships: April 4

Citing a lack of evidence to prove sexual misconduct, Judge Susan Webber Wright of Federal District Court dismisses the lawsuit filed by Paula Corbin Jones against Pres. Bill Clinton (*see* January 17).

•

Festus Mogae is sworn in as president of Botswana, replacing Sir Ketumile Masire.

The Japan Prizes are awarded in ceremonies in Tokyo; Leo Esaki, president of the University of Tsukuba, Sakura, Japan, wins in the area of materials science, and two Belgians, Jozef Schell of the Max Planck Institute, Cologne, Ger., and Marc Van Montagu of the Flanders Interuniversity Institute for Biotechnology, Ghent, Belg., win in the area of agricultural biotechnology.

The 57th annual George Foster Peabody Awards for excellence in radio and television broadcasting are announced; the ABC comedy series "Ellen" and the CBS news program "60 Minutes" are among the recipients.

•

The U.S. Food and Drug Administration approves Sucralose, a new no-calorie sweetener 600 times as sweet as sugar and the only artificial sweetener made from sugar.

Douglas F. Groat, former veteran officer of the U.S. Central Intelligence Agency, is arrested for espionage and accused of having revealed U.S. secrets to two foreign nations.

Maurice Papon, former member of the collaborationist government in Vichy, France, is convicted of war crimes for having turned Jews over to the Nazis during World War II.

•

Jean-Marie Le Pen, leader of the far right in France, is convicted of having assaulted an opponent while campaigning in France; Le Pen was later declared ineligible to run in European parliamentary elections in 1999.

Leaders of 10 Asian nations and 15 member states of the European Union gather in London for the second Asia-Europe Meeting (ASEM); discussions focus on the Asian economic crisis.

•

The Swiss National Bank, Switzerland's central bank, announces its intention to fight an American lawsuit accusing the bank of having aided Nazi Germany in the acquisition of looted assets during World War II (*see* August 12).

Approximately 280 people are believed dead when a boat en route to Gabon capsizes in rough waters off the coast of Nigeria.

•

American figure skater Michelle Kwan wins her second world figure-skating championship in Minneapolis, Minn.; Russian Aleksey Yagudin had won the men's title two days earlier.

Earth Summit wins the Grand National steeplechase in Liverpool, Eng.

The world's longest suspension bridge, the 3.9-km (2.4-mi) Akashi Kaikyo Bridge linking Japan's Shikoku and Honshu islands, is officially opened; the bridge has been built to withstand earthquakes of magnitude 8.5.

•

Charlotte Bacon receives the 1998 Hemingway Foundation/PEN Award for her short-story collection, *A Private State,* at the John F. Kennedy Library in Boston.

President Clinton imposes a permanent ban on importing 58 types of military-style assault weapons.

•

The World Trade Organization orders the U.S. to cease prohibiting imports from countries that do not try to preserve endangered sea turtles by keeping them out of shrimp nets, which the WTO considers a restriction on free trade.

•

Citicorp Bank and Travelers Group Insurance, two of the largest companies in the U.S., agree to a $70 billion stock merger.

•

Gramophone magazine, perhaps the most respected voice in classical music journalism, celebrates its 75th anniversary in ceremonies in London.

Tara Lipinski, U.S. figure skater and gold medalist at the 1998 Winter Olympics, announces that she will turn professional.

•

At Barbican Hall in London, British composer Andrew March receives the first Masterprize at the conclusion of an 18-month international competition designed to encourage new classical works; the prize, supported by a number of British cultural organizations, is valued at £25,000.

The Swiss pharmaceutical company Novartis Pharma announces that it has earmarked $250 million for the creation of the Novartis Institute for Functional Genomics in La Jolla, Calif., to track down and record the function of genes as they are discovered.

•

American architect I.M. Pei is named the recipient of the Edward MacDowell Medal for his contributions to the arts; Pei is the first architect to receive the award in its 38-year history.

•

The results of a survey conducted for more than 20 years by botanists and conservationists around the world are announced in Washington, D.C.; the study finds that 12.5% of the 270,000 known plant species are at risk of extinction.

More than 100 Muslim pilgrims die in a stampede in Mecca, Saudi Arabia, while participating in a religious event known as "stoning the devil" during the last day of the annual hajj.

•

Powerful tornadoes rip through Alabama, Mississippi, and Georgia, killing 39 people and leaving many homeless.

•

A federal jury in New York City awards Sandra Ortiz-Del Valle $7,850,000 in damages for sex discrimination at the hands of the National Basketball Association, which prevented her from becoming a referee.

•

The National Prisoner of War Memorial Museum, situated on the grounds of the Civil War prison at Andersonville, Ga., is officially dedicated.

10

The Northern Ireland peace talks in Belfast produce an agreement between Catholic and Protestant representatives that will allow members of both religions to govern jointly in a 108-seat national assembly in Northern Ireland (*see* May 22).

11

Talks between North and South Korea about the provision of agricultural assistance by Seoul open in Beijing; the meeting collapses with no resolution regarding relief aid needed by North Korea or the South's desire to reunite family members split by the 1945 division of the Korean peninsula.

12

Girija Prasad Koirala is appointed prime minister by King Birendra of Nepal; Koirala assumes his duties on April 15.

•

Heavy rains flood mine shafts at the Mererani tanzanite mines in Tanzania, killing 100 workers.

•

Some of the worst storms and flooding of the century hit eastern England and cause at least four deaths.

•

The first emergency shipment of American water-purification equipment arrives in the Marshall Islands, which have experienced a severe shortage of freshwater because of freakish El Niño-related weather.

•

American Mark O'Meara wins the Masters golf tournament in Augusta, Ga., his first major title, by one stroke and finishes nine under par.

13

Nationsbank Corp. of Charlotte, N.C., and BankAmerica Corp. of San Francisco, in a merger worth an estimated $60 billion, create the nation's first coast-to-coast banking institution.

•

The celebrity sheep Dolly, the first mammal to be cloned, gives birth—naturally; the lamb is named Bonnie.

14

Russian Pres. Boris Yeltsin signs a law prohibiting the return to Germany of art objects that were looted by the Red Army during World War II (*see* March 6).

The Hindu ceremony of Mahakumbh, held every 12 years, brings more than 10 million pilgrims to Hardwar, Uttar Pradesh state, India, to bathe in the holy Ganges River; the ceremony, believed to be the largest convocation in the world, has often been the scene of sectarian violence in the past.

•

The Pulitzer Prizes are announced in New York City; among the winners are Philip Roth's *American Pastoral* for fiction and Aaron Jay Kernis's *String Quartet No. 2, Musica Instrumentalis* for music.

•

The Gillette Co. introduces the Mach 3, a shaver featuring three blades rather than two; Gillette's $300 million marketing budget is one of the largest advertising campaigns ever.

15

The trial on contempt charges of the former president of South Africa, P.W. Botha, opens in George, Western Cape province.

Economist Radu Vasile is confirmed as prime minister of Romania; Vasile is the nominee of the Christian Democratic National Peasants' Party of Romania.

•

Pol Pot, the leader of the Khmer Rouge revolutionary movement in Cambodia, who is held responsible for the murder of a million civilians in his country, dies of a heart attack in captivity.

16

In what may be an attempt to disrupt peace talks between Chechnya and Moscow, gunmen kill Russian Lieut. Gen. Viktor Prokopenko in North Ossetia, a republic in the north Caucasus region of Russia.

•

Tornadoes ravage Arkansas, Tennessee, and Kentucky, killing 10 and injuring more than 110 people.

17

It is reported that a 40 × 5-km (25 × 3-mi) chunk of the Larsen B ice shelf in Antarctica has broken off; scientists are concerned that global warming will cause additional crumbling of the ice shelves.

•

Ambassador to the UN Bill Richardson receives a cordial welcome in Kabul, Afg., on the first high-level visit by a U.S. official in 25 years; Richardson meets with Taliban leaders in the capital and with the opposition Northern Alliance in the town of Sheberghan.

The Canadian Imperial Bank of Commerce and the Toronto-Dominion Bank, two of Canada's largest banking institutions, propose a $15.9 billion merger; the merger will consolidate Canada's already-compressed banking system, leaving just four major national banks (*see* January 23).

•

Israeli violinist Pinchas Zukerman is named conductor of the National Arts Centre Orchestra in Ottawa; he succeeds Briton Trevor Pinnock.

18

In Kilbuye, Rwanda, two Roman Catholic priests, the Rev. Jean-François Kayiranga and the Rev. Edouard Nkurikiye, are sentenced to death for their collaboration with Hutu militants in the deaths of 2,000 Tutsi during the 1994 genocide.

The Shroud of Turin, believed by some to be the burial cloth of Jesus Christ and by others to be a medieval hoax, is placed on public

OWEN FRANKEN—CORBIS

Architect I.M. Pei:
April 8

April

display; some three million pilgrims view the cloth before the exhibit closes on June 14.

The Shroud of Turin on display in Rome: April 18

19

Chinese dissident Wang Dan, a leader of the 1989 Tiananmen democracy movement, is exiled to the United States by the Chinese government.

•

Thomas Klestil is reelected president of Austria in a landslide vote.

•

Italian Renzo Piano, designer of the Pompidou Centre in Paris and the new Kansai Air Terminal in Japan, is named the winner of the 1998 Pritzker Architecture Prize.

•

Fire destroys the 9th-century Taktsang Monastery, the oldest Himalayan Buddhist shrine in Bhutan.

20

The Cabinet of Prime Minister Armen Darbinyan (who was appointed on April 10) is approved by Armenian Pres. Robert Kocharyan.

•

Moses Tanui of Kenya wins the 102nd annual Boston Marathon, for the second time in three years, with a time of 2 hr 7.34 min; Ethiopian Fatuma Roba wins the women's division for the second year in a row with a runaway time of 2 hr 23.21 min.

21

American astronomers working in Chile and Hawaii report having observed a complete planetary disk, the best evidence yet of the formation of planets around a young star.

•

The 1997 Heinz Awards are presented to John Harbison for arts and humanities, Amory Lovins for the environment, Carol Gilligan for the human condition, Ernesto Cortés, Jr., for public policy, and Ralph Gomory for technology, the economy, and employment.

22

Animal Kingdom, an $800 million theme park from the Disney Co., officially opens in Lake Buena Vista, Fla.;

there is some criticism of the operation in mid-May when it is revealed that at least 29 of the animals died in transit or in the park.

•

The new Berlin Prize fellowships are awarded to 16 American scholars by the American Academy in Berlin; playwright Arthur Miller is designated the distinguished inaugural senior fellow.

•

The Red Army Faction, the terrorist organization of the 1970s, announces its dissolution because their cause is "now history."

•

The National Academy of Sciences disassociates itself from a statement and petition circulated by former NAS president Frederick Seitz, which attacks the theory of global warming and enjoins the U.S. government to reject the 1997 Kyoto Protocol.

23

Konstantinos Karamanlis, a prominent politician in Greece for more than half a century, dies at age 91.

•

James Earl Ray, convicted killer of civil rights leader Martin Luther King, Jr., dies in Nashville, Tenn.

24

The Russian Parliament approves Sergey Kiriyenko, President Yeltsin's choice for prime minister, with a vote of 251 to 25; a government restructuring ensues (see August 23).

•

In Rwanda 22 people convicted of genocide during

the nation's civil war are executed by firing squads.

25

A pyrite mine reservoir at Los Frailes mine on the Guadiamar River in Spain ruptures, flooding the valley with contaminated mine wastes and threatening the Coto Doñana National Park, the largest nature preserve in Europe.

•

Upon releasing the results of a poll of its members, the Sierra Club announces that it will not endorse any policy on federal limits on immigration; the issue had radically split the environmental group's membership.

26

A prominent Guatemalan bishop, Juan Gerardi Conedera, is beaten to death with a concrete block in the garage of his home two days after he delivered a report on human rights violations during the country's 36-year civil war.

•

In an effort to restore civilian rule, Nigeria holds parliamentary elections; fear of violence and distrust for Gen. Sani Abacha, however, keeps 50 million registered voters from the polling places (see June 8).

27

U.S. Surgeon General David Satcher releases a report on the dangers of tobacco use among minority groups; American Indians and Alaskan natives are found to be especially vulnerable.

The Actors Studio of New York celebrates its 50th anniversary (through May 18).

28

Over U.S. and Turkish opposition, Russia agrees to deliver S-300 advanced anti-aircraft missile systems to the Greek Cypriot government in August.

29

Russian financial mogul Boris Berezovsky is appointed chief executive of the Commonwealth of Independent States at the organization's summit meeting.

•

Brazil agrees to set aside about 25 million ha (62 million ac), approximately 10%, of the Amazon rain forest for conservation (*see* June 17).

•

Vickers PLC, owner of the British Rolls-Royce Motor Cars, accepts a $566 million takeover offer from German car manufacturer BMW.

•

It is revealed in Oslo that in experiments conducted for decades until 1994, Norwegian and American researchers used mentally ill or retarded Norwegians in tests of the biological and genetic effects of X-ray radiation on the body.

30

A cease-fire agreement is signed at Arawa, capital of the island of Bougainville, potentially ending the decade-long movement of many islanders to secede from Papua New Guinea.

•

It is announced that the Art Gallery of Ontario in Toronto will become the only site in North America to exhibit what many consider to be the rarest collection of Impressionist and Postimpressionist paintings; the show, from June 10 to September 21, will include works by Manet, Monet, Renoir, Cézanne, van Gogh, Degas, Gauguin, and Seurat.

•

Four hundred years ago Don Juan de Oñate of Spain crossed the Rio Grande and entered what is now New Mexico, introducing the first Spanish settlements to the Southwest; the anniversary is celebrated by Hispanics in New Mexico and Texas.

Amazon rain forest in Brazil: April 29

At the UN War Crimes Tribunal in Arusha, Tanz., Jean Kambanda, a former prime minister of Rwanda, pleads guilty to charges of genocide in connection with the 1994 massacres in his country.

Tisseel, the nation's first commercial surgical glue for the control of bleeding caused by surgery or trauma, is approved for use in the U.S. by the Food and Drug Administration.

•

Folkways Records, a pioneer in recording folk music of the U.S. and the world, celebrates its 50th anniversary with a concert at Carnegie Hall in New York City.

Real Quiet wins the Kentucky Derby in Louisville, Ky., defeating Victory Gallop by half a length; the win marks horse trainer Bob Baffert's second consecutive win in the derby.

•

King Hussein celebrates the 45th anniversary of his reign; the day is celebrated as a national holiday in Jordan.

Natasha Gelman, widow of film producer Jacques Gelman, dies in Cuernavaca, Mex., and bequeaths her collection of 85 works of modern art valued at more than

$300 million to New York City's Metropolitan Museum of Art.

In London *The Sunday Times* newspaper reports that Foreign and Commonwealth Secretary Robin Cook allegedly had known that a British company, Sandline International, sent arms to Sierra Leone earlier in the year despite a UN arms embargo; a government flap ensues.

•

"The Sèvres Road" by the 19th-century French landscape painter Camille Corot is stolen from the Louvre in Paris.

•

The opening of the American Ceramic Society's annual meeting in Cincinnati, Ohio, commemorates the 100th anniversary of the society's founding.

Lionel Jospin, prime minister of France, arrives in New Caledonia to sign an accord allowing the French colony to form a government; a vote on sovereignty is to be postponed for 20 years.

•

Confessed "Unabomber" Theodore J. Kaczynski receives four life sentences plus 30 years in prison for four of the bombings he car-

ried out during his 17-year bombing spree, which killed 3 people and injured 22 (*see* January 22).

•

In Vatican City State, hours after being appointed commander of the pope's Swiss Guards, Col. Alois Estermann and his wife are shot to death by another guard, who then takes his own life.

•

Combating its worst drought in its recorded history, Fiji imposes water-usage restrictions across the nation.

A series of mud slides on Mt. Sarno in Italy kills at least 135 people and leaves thousands homeless.

•

More than 50 years after the last prisoners were freed from Austria's biggest Nazi death camp in Mauthausen, the nation holds its first-ever national day of remembrance for Holocaust victims.

•

The Ronald Reagan Building and International Trade Center on Federal Triangle in Washington, D.C., is formally dedicated; designed by James Ingo Freed, it is the second largest U.S. government building (after the Pentagon) ever built.

It is announced in Washington, D.C., that astronomers have detected evidence of a huge explosion, unpredicted in cosmic theory, that took place at the farthest reaches of the universe about 12 billion years ago and is thought to have been second in magnitude only to the theoretical "big bang" that created the universe.

Pres. Nursultan Nazarbayev of Kazakstan signs a decree formally changing the name of Aqmola, the capital since 1997, to Astana, which means *capital* in Kazak.

Daimler-Benz AG, the German manufacturer of Mercedes-Benz autos, and the American Chrysler Corp. announce plans to merge in a $36 billion deal that would create DaimlerChrysler, with combined 1997 sales of about $131 billion.

The U.S. Senate votes unanimously in favour of a bill to overhaul the Internal Revenue Service and create a board to oversee the tax-collecting agency.

8

Prime Minister Adrien Houngbedji of Benin resigns; Pres. Mathieu Kérékou appoints a new government, without filling the prime minister post, on May 14.

•

A study published in the *American Journal of Human Genetics* suggests that a specific gene mutation, occurring only in people of European descent, may provide complete immunity to the AIDS virus.

•

Wired magazine is purchased by Condé Nast, a unit of Advance Publications Inc., which publishes magazines such as *Vogue, Vanity Fair,* and *GQ* for an upscale market.

9

The G-8 group of industrialized countries, with the exception of Japan and Russia, imposes a ban on investment in Serbia and freezes that country's overseas assets because of the failure of Serbian troops to withdraw from the province of Kosovo (*see* June 29).

•

Roman Catholic Bishop Zeng Jingmu, who had been imprisoned in China for holding illegal religious services, is released by the government.

10

Paraguay goes to the polls and reelects the Colorado Party, which has ruled the country for 51 years, and elects its candidate for president, Raúl Cubas Grau.

•

It is announced that the Stone Container Corp. will be bought by Jefferson Smurfit Corp. for $2 billion in stock, creating a giant in the paper-based packaging industry.

•

Louis Luyt, the president of the South African Rugby Football Union, resigns in Johannesburg under intense pressure and charges of racism and corruption in the management of the sport.

"Unabomber" Ted Kaczynski sentenced: May 4

11

India detonates three nuclear devices at a test site in the northwest of the country; in the face of strong international objections, two more underground tests are conducted on May 13 (*see* May 28).

•

SBC Communications Inc. announces that it plans to acquire Ameritech Corp. in a $62 billion deal that would create the largest local telephone company in the U.S.

•

The Sunbeam Corp., reeling from huge losses and questionable business strategies, announces plans to lay off 40% of its workforce, or 6,400 employees (*see* June 15).

12

At the annual pageant, in Honolulu, Hawaii, Wendy Fitzwilliam of Trinidad and Tobago is crowned the 47th Miss Universe.

•

American soul singer Ray Charles and Indian sitar virtuoso Ravi Shankar are awarded the Swedish Academy of Music's Polar Music Prize for 1998.

•

American violinist Axel Strauss wins the Walter W. Naumburg International Violin Competition; in addition to a cash prize, the award includes two recitals at New York City's Lincoln Center and a recording contract.

13

The Environmental Protection Agency issues a license to the federal Department of Energy authorizing the burial of Cold War-era nuclear waste in the $2 billion Waste Isolation Pilot Plant (WIPP) situated in excavated salt beds near Carlsbad, N.M.

•

Gro Harlem Brundtland, former prime minister of Norway, is confirmed as the new director general of the World Health Organization; she will assume the post July 21.

14

Popular American entertainer Frank Sinatra dies in Los Angeles at age 82.

•

Yemen's Pres. 'Ali Abdallah Salih names 'Abd al-Karim al-Iryani prime minister.

•

A group of scientists working in London and publishing in *Psychological Science* has discovered for the first time a gene that is linked to high intelligence.

15

Leaders of the G-8 nations, the world's largest industrial countries (and for the first time officially including Russia), gather at an estate outside Birmingham, Eng., and discuss international crime and additional finan-cial support for the world's poorest nations.

16

Real Quiet, the winner of the Kentucky Derby, comes from behind to beat Victory Gallop by 2¹/₄ lengths in the Preakness Stakes in Baltimore, Md., the second win in thoroughbred racing's Triple Crown.

•

In the English Football Association Cup final played in London's Wembley Stadium, London Arsenal defeats Newcastle United 2–0; having earlier won the Carling Premier League championship, Arsenal achieves a "double," a rare accomplishment.

•

Rafi Zabor is awarded the PEN/Faulkner Award for Fiction; the prize is valued at $15,000.

17

The outspoken Gen. Aleksandr Lebed, a candidate for the presidency of Russia in the last (and possibly the future) election, wins the governorship of Krasnoyarsk *kray,* a vast, sparsely populated area in Siberia.

•

A deal is struck whereby the education division of American publisher Simon & Schuster will be acquired from Viacom by Pearson PLC, the largest publisher in Great Britain and owner of the Penguin group, for $3.6

Japanese protest against nuclear tests in India: May 11

Kentucky Derby and Preakness Stakes winner Real Quiet: May 16

billion, and Hicks, Muse, Tate & Furst Inc., a Texas investment firm, will buy the reference, business, and professional divisions for $1 billion.

•

David Wells of the New York Yankees pitches a perfect game (no opposing player gets on base), only the 15th such feat in the history of major league baseball.

•

South Korean golfer Pak Se Ri, a rookie on the professional circuit, wins the McDonald's Ladies Professional Golf Association championship at 11 strokes under par for the tournament at the DuPont Country Club in Wilmington, Del. (*see* July 6).

18

The U.S. government indicts three large Mexican banks and a host of banking officials on charges of laundering money from cocaine and marijuana trafficking.

The greats of golf gather in St. Augustine, Fla., to celebrate the induction of Johnny Miller and Nick Faldo into the new Golf Hall of Fame and to inaugurate a luxurious new golf complex, World Golf Village.

19

Three armed men subdue the guards at Rome's National Gallery of Modern Art and make off with three masterpieces valued at $34 million: "Le Jardinier" and "L'Arlésienne" of Vincent Van Gogh and "Le Cabanon de Jourdan" of Paul Cézanne; the paintings are later recovered (*see* July 6).

•

The murder trial of Patrizia Reggiani, called the "Black Widow" in the Italian press, opens in Milan; Reggiani is convicted of having contracted for the death of her ex-husband, Maurizio Gucci, heir to the high-fashion leather goods company, and sentenced to 29 years in prison on November 3.

20

After celebrating its 100th anniversary on May 16, the American Academy of Arts and Letters inducts 14 new members and awards 4 honorary memberships to foreign notables; the academy's gold medals are awarded to artist Frank Stella and playwright Horton Foote.

•

Retired electrician Frank Capaci and his wife, Shirley, of Streamwood, Ill., win the largest-ever lottery jackpot in the U.S., $195 million, in the Powerball lottery.

21

Suharto, Indonesia's president for 30 years, steps down following weeks of growing economic, social, and political unrest; a close associate, Bacharuddin Jusuf Habibie, immediately replaces him (*see* March 10).

•

Marion Barry, the controversial mayor of Washington, D.C., announces that he will not seek a fifth four-year term.

•

Daniel arap Moi, president of Kenya, fires David Western, the director of the Kenyan Wildlife Service; no explanation is given, but Western believes it is because he refused to permit mining in the parks (*see* September 24).

•

The Seagram Co., originally a spirits and wine firm, announces that it plans to acquire Polygram NV, a music company, for $10.6 billion in cash and stock; Seagram, which also owns Universal Studios, stands to become a leading force in the entertainment industry.

22

Voters in both the Republic of Ireland and Northern Ireland overwhelmingly support the so-called Good Friday agreement of April 10.

•

The World's Fair opens to the public in Lisbon, with pavilions from 146 nations and a general theme of protecting the world's oceans.

23

The ruling Lesotho Congress for Democracy wins a lopsided election victory, taking 78 of 80 seats in the National Legislature; party leader Bethuel Pakalitha Mosisili is sworn in as prime minister on May 29.

At the Queen Elizabeth Stadium in Hong Kong, the Chinese women's badminton team wins its record sixth Uber Cup; on May 24 the Indonesian men's team wins the Thomas Cup for the third consecutive year and gains its 11th championship.

24

Hong Kong holds elections for the 60-seat Legislative Council; the vote is the first since Hong Kong reverted to Chinese control in 1997.

•

The Swedish yacht *EF Language,* with an international crew of 12, arrives in Southampton, Eng., the winner of the Whitbread Round the World Race.

•

At the Cannes International Film Festival, Greek director Theo Angelopoulos wins the Palme d'Or, the top prize, for his *Eternity and a Day;* Italian comedian and director Roberto Benigni wins the Grand Prize for *Life Is Beautiful.*

•

Eddie Cheever, in his first major racing victory, wins the 82nd running of the Indianapolis 500 auto race.

25

In Spain a former interior minister and 11 other top government officials begin their trial on charges of having waged a "dirty war" in the 1980s against ETA, the Basque separatist organization.

•

Egypt officially celebrates the conclusion of a 10-year, multimillion-dollar restoration of the Great Sphinx.

•

William J. Ivey, a folklorist and ethnomusicologist who had been director of the Country Music Federation in Nashville, Tenn., is confirmed as chairman of the National Endowment for the Arts, succeeding actress Jane Alexander.

26

Australia marks its first National Sorry Day to remember the hundreds of thousands of Aboriginal children, the so-called stolen generations, who were forcibly taken from their families in the past in an attempt to integrate them into white society.

27

The Russian central bank raises its Lombard rate (the interest rate for loans to commercial banks) from 50% to 150% in an attempt to relieve pressure on the ruble and avert a devaluation.

•

Thousands of workers in South Korea strike to protest layoffs and the replacement of regular workers with temporaries.

•

The *Grand Princess,* the world's largest and most expensive cruise ship ever built (approximately $450 mil-

World's Fair in Lisbon: May 22

lion), departs from Istanbul's Golden Horn on its maiden voyage.

28

Pakistan becomes the world's seventh nuclear power just 17 days after India joined the nuclear club, detonating five nuclear devices at its Chagai Hills test site in Baluchistan (*see* May 11).

•

Jody-Anne Maxwell of Kingston, Jam., wins the 71st annual Scripps Howard National Spelling Bee in Washington, D.C.

The world premiere performance of David Del Tredici's cantata *The Spider and the Fly*, written to commemorate the New York Philharmonic Orchestra's 150th anniversary in 1992, takes place in Avery Fisher Hall in New York City.

29

Joseph Estrada is declared the winner of the presidential election in the Philippines; he formally takes over from Fidel Ramos on June 30.

•

It is reported that Comoros Pres. Mohamed Taki Abdoulkarim has dismissed the entire government and Prime Minister Nourdine Bourhane; antigovernment rioting had broken out in Moroni, the capital, earlier in the month.

30

A magnitude-6.9 earthquake shakes Takhar and Badakhshan provinces in northeastern Afghanistan, leaving an estimated 5,000 people dead and 50,000 homeless.

•

The Social Democratic Party announces that it will leave the coalition that has governed Japan since 1994.

31

The U.S. pledges support for an international plan to stabilize the Russian ruble; the International Monetary Fund has intervened to bail out the Russian economy on four occasions in recent months.

•

Geri Halliwell (Ginger Spice) of the Spice Girls announces that she has resigned from the popular British singing group (*see* October 20).

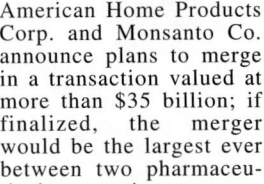

June

Death of Nigerian
strongman Gen.
Sani Abacha:
June 8

1

American Home Products Corp. and Monsanto Co. announce plans to merge in a transaction valued at more than $35 billion; if finalized, the merger would be the largest ever between two pharmaceutical companies.

•

In Chicago the John D. and Catherine T. MacArthur Foundation announces the 29 recipients of this year's MacArthur fellowships.

•

Susie Maroney of Australia becomes the first person to swim from Mexico to Cuba, across the Yucatán Channel, a distance of about 200 km (125 mi); the swim, most of it in a shark cage, took 38 hr 33 min.

2

The first Friedrich Kiesler Prize for Architecture and the Arts, a new $60,000 award to honour the memory of the Austrian-born architect, is presented to Canadian-born American architect Frank O. Gehry, designer of the Guggenheim Museum in Bilbao, Spain, the Samsung Museum of Modern Art in South Korea, and the American Center in Paris, among many other buildings.

3

Near Eschede, Ger., the high-speed InterCity Express (ICE) train crashes into an overpass at a speed of about 200 km/h (125 mph), killing at least 100 persons; a faulty wheel is later determined to have been the cause of the crash.

•

VaxGen Inc. announces that the U.S. Food and Drug Administration has granted it permission to begin full-scale human trials of its vaccine Aids Vax, which may completely prevent HIV infections.

4

The U.S. Supreme Court rejects a request from independent counsel Kenneth Starr to speed its review of legal privilege claims advanced by Pres. Bill Clinton and members of his administration in Starr's investigation into alleged presidential misdeeds.

The U.S. space shuttle *Discovery* docks with the Russian space station *Mir* and retrieves American astronaut Andrew Thomas; the station is being shut down and will be destroyed in December 1999.

5

Workers at a General Motors metal-stamping plant in Flint, Mich., go on strike; employees at other GM facilities in North America follow suit in the days to come.

•

A group of Japanese and American scientists meeting at the Neutrino '98 conference in Takayama, Japan, announces that for the first time they have found firm evidence that the neutrino, a subatomic particle with a neutral charge, has mass.

6

The president of Burundi, Pierre Buyoya, signs into law the Transitional Constitutional Act, an interim constitution to replace the decree imposed when Buyoya took over the country in a military coup in July 1996.

•

Victory Gallop wins the Belmont Stakes, barely nosing out Real Quiet and spoiling that horse's bid to win thoroughbred racing's Triple Crown (*see* May 2, May 16).

7

A referendum proposed by the Green Party and a variety of other environmental and consumer groups in Switzerland to restrict research in genetic engineering is soundly rejected by the electorate; the referendum is believed to be the first ever on genetic engineering.

•

Art, by Yasmina Reza, is declared the best play at the Tony award ceremonies at New York City's Radio City Music Hall; *The Lion King* wins in six categories, including best musical, and *Ragtime,* another musical, takes home Tonys in four categories.

•

Spanish tennis players dominate the French Open tournament as Carlos Moya defeats countryman Alex Corretja 6–3, 7–5, 6–3 for the men's title; on June 6 Arantxa Sánchez Vicario defeated Monica Seles of the U.S. for the women's title.

8

The U.S. space shuttle *Discovery* undocks from the Russian space station *Mir,* ending three years of cooperative research by scientists and astronauts from the two countries.

•

Strongman Gen. Sani Abacha dies suddenly in the Niger-

ian capital, Abuja; Gen. Abdulsalam Abubakar, the defense minister, is swiftly sworn in as Abacha's replacement (*see* April 26).

•

European fisheries officials meeting in Luxembourg agree to a ban on drift-net fishing in the Atlantic and the Mediterranean beginning in 2002; conservation organizations have sought a ban on huge drift nets because of the damage they cause to marine mammals and noncommercial fish populations.

•

In the latest of a series of large bank mergers, Norwest Corp. of Minneapolis, Minn., and the San Francisco–based Wells Fargo & Co. agree to merge, forming Norwest–Wells Fargo, the seventh largest bank in the U.S., holding some $191 billion in assets.

•

A Swiss, Joseph ("Sepp") Blatter, is elected president of the Fédération Internationale de Football Association, the governing body of world professional soccer, replacing long-time incumbent João Havelange of Brazil.

9

The Southern Baptist Convention, the largest Protestant denomination in the U.S., adopts a change to its basic document on the structure of the family, asserting

APTV/AP/WIDE WORLD

that the husband should "provide for, protect and lead his family," whereas the wife should "submit herself graciously" to his leadership.

10

The World Cup soccer tournament opens in Paris after an Air France strike is settled and following a noisy and colourful evening of festivities; the games will be played in 10 locations throughout France.

•

The Supreme Court of Wisconsin rules that the city of Milwaukee may use tax revenue to pay for pupils to attend parochial or other religious schools; the decision is regarded as the most significant test yet of the trend toward school vouchers, a form of financial aid.

11

The genome, or DNA structure, of the tuberculosis bacterium, which comprises 4,411,529 elements, is successfully decoded by a team of French and British scientists, as reported in the journal *Nature*.

•

About 1,000 Ukrainian miners, on strike for back pay, conclude a march from the coal-producing region in eastern Ukraine to Kiev, the capital, and demand government action.

•

Mitsubishi Motors Corp. agrees to pay $34 million, a record amount in a sexual harassment settlement, in a suit brought by the U.S. Equal Employment Opportunity Commission on behalf of employees at the Mitsubishi auto plant in Normal, Ill.

12

In Manila, Pres. Fidel Ramos leads the celebrations of the 100th anniversary of Philippine independence from Spain; the Philippines came under U.S. hegemony following the Spanish-American War and gained full independence in 1946.

•

An important exhibition of the work of Civil War–era photographer Mathew Brady opens at the International Center of Photography Midtown, New York City.

13

Billed as the largest benefit concert since Live Aid in 1985, the two-day Tibetan Freedom Concert opens in Washington, D.C.'s RFK Stadium; although the first day is aborted because of weather, on Sunday fans enjoy a lineup of top rock groups assembled to protest China's occupation of Tibet.

•

The International IMPAC Dublin Literary Award for 1998, at $150,000 believed to be the largest prize for a single work of fiction, is presented to Herta Müller, a native of Romania who writes in German, for her novel *The Land of Green Plums*.

14

The Chicago Bulls win the National Basketball Association championship for the third year in a row, defeating the Utah Jazz 87–86 in the final game; Michael Jordan is named Most Valuable Player of the series.

JOHN BAZEMORE—AP/WIDE WORLD

A Canadian long-distance telephone company, Teleglobe Inc., announces it will buy Excel Communications Inc., the fifth largest U.S. telecommunications company, for $3.5 billion.

15

The board of the Sunbeam Corp. decides to fire its chairman, Albert J. Dunlap; Dunlap earned the nickname "Chain Saw Al" for his technique of radically downsizing companies that he was called in to rescue from financial peril (*see* May 11).

Billy Ray Cyrus is the big winner (five awards, including best single) at the TNN/Music City News Country Awards ceremony in Nashville, Tenn.; Neal McCoy is named Entertainer of the Year, and Porter Waggoner is identified as a "living legend."

16

The Detroit Red Wings defeat the Washington Capitals in Washington, D.C., to win the Stanley Cup of the National Hockey League for the second consecutive year; Detroit's captain, Steve Yzerman, wins the Conn Smythe Trophy for most valuable player in the tournament.

•

The government of North Korea acknowledges publicly for the first time that it has sold missiles abroad and intends to continue doing so; the founder of South Korea's Hyundai Group, Chung Ju Yung, leads a convoy of trucks delivering 500 head of cattle to the hard-pressed North.

The ruling Council of the Lutheran World Federation approves the "Joint Declaration on the Doctrine of Justification," aimed at bridging a doctrinal difference and repairing relations with the Roman Catholic Church, which have been strained for some 400 years.

•

The Islamic fundamentalist Taliban group that controls Afghanistan announces the closing of 100 more schools for girls, which the UN tried to keep open despite the proclaimed policy that women and girls are to remain in the home.

17

In London, Amnesty International releases its annual report detailing human rights abuses in 141 countries; 1998 is the 50th anniversary of the adoption of the Universal Declaration of Human Rights.

•

The government of Suriname announces that it is setting aside about 10% of the country's area for the creation of a huge Central Suriname Wilderness Nature Reserve in order to conserve the Amazon rain forest (*see* April 29).

•

An antitobacco bill before the U.S. Congress that would have raised the price of a pack of cigarettes by more than a dollar in an attempt to discourage teenagers from smoking is jettisoned in the Senate when support proves insufficient to pass certain procedural hurdles.

18

Pres. Leonel Fernández of the Dominican Republic begins a visit to Haiti, with which the Dominican Republic uneasily shares the Caribbean island of Hispaniola; this is the first overnight visit by a Dominican head of state since 1936.

•

President Clinton announces that he is appointing Richard C. Holbrooke, the chief U.S. negotiator of the Dayton peace accords for Bosnia and Herzegovina, as ambassador to the United Nations; Holbrooke replaces Bill Richardson, who becomes secretary of energy.

Country singer Neal McCoy: June 15

19

An attempt by the Organization of African Unity to mediate the growing discord between Ethiopia and Eritrea and promote a U.S.-backed peace plan ends in failure in the Ethiopian capital, Addis Ababa.

•

Warren Buffett's Berkshire Hathaway Inc., an investment holding company, acquires General Re Corp., a reinsurance company, for $22 billion; Berkshire Hathaway thereby becomes the largest insurance company in the world.

ERIC GAY—AP/WIDE WORLD

The battleship USS *Missouri* at Pearl Harbor, Hawaii: June 21

Three of the largest banks in Switzerland agree to set up a $600 million fund for the victims of the Holocaust who had deposited money in the banks but were unable to retrieve it after World War II; Jewish groups were generally not impressed (*see* March 26).

20

Pres. B.J. Habibie indicates that the government of In-

donesia might be willing to release rebel leader José Xanana Gusmão from custody if the disputed East Timor area is recognized as Indonesian property.

•

The U.S., Great Britain, Germany, Japan, France, and other countries announce that they will withdraw diplomats from Minsk; the withdrawals come after the government of Belarusian Pres. Alyaksandr Luka-

shenka tried to force the diplomats from their homes in the diplomatic compound by using various tactics, including shutting off utilities.

21

Andrés Pastrana Arango of the Social Conservative Party and former mayor of Bogotá easily defeats Horacio Serpa, the candidate of

incumbent Ernesto Samper's Liberal Party, for the presidency of Colombia.

•

At even par, Lee Janzen edges past Payne Stewart to win the U.S. Open golf tournament at the Olympic Club in San Francisco by one stroke.

•

The battleship USS *Missouri,* the ship on which the Japanese surrender was accepted by the United States

at the end of World War II, is towed into Pearl Harbor, Hawaii, where it will be turned into a museum.

22

The government of Bosnia and Herzegovina introduces its new currency, the marka, to replace an assortment of banknotes in circulation in various parts of the country; the marka is pegged 1:1 to the Deutsche Mark.

Scientists at a meeting in Victoria, B.C., report that they have discovered a planet orbiting the low-mass red-dwarf star Gliese 876, which, at a distance of only 15 light-years, is very near the Sun.

•

The Learning Company announces that it will purchase Brøderbund Software Inc., another manufacturer of computer software, for some $420 million in stock.

23

The Bangabandhu Jamuna Multipurpose Bridge across the Jamuna River, at 4.8 km (2.9 mi) the longest bridge in South Asia, is formally opened by Bangladesh Prime Minister Sheikh Hasina Wajed.

•

Scientists report at a press conference at the National Geographical Society in Washington, D.C., that recent fossil finds in northeastern China provide a definitive link between carnivorous dinosaurs and birds.

24

AT&T Corp. announces that it will acquire Tele-Communication Inc. (TCI), a cable television company, for $37 billion.

•

In a major setback in Chinese-American cultural relations, negotiations between the directors of the Lincoln Center Festival in New York City and Ma Bomin, director of the Bureau of Culture in Shanghai, fail to secure Ma's approval for the staging of the classic Chinese opera *Peony Pavilion*.

•

In Århus, Den., two new agreements to control and reduce long-range air pollu-

tion caused by heavy metals and persistent organic pollutants are signed by 33 countries.

25

The U.S. Supreme Court rules 6–3 that the line-item veto, whereby the president vetoes selected items from a bill passed by Congress, is unconstitutional.

Windows 98, the upgrade of the popular Windows 95 personal computer operating system of Microsoft Corp., goes on sale.

26

The U.S. Supreme Court hands down two decisions that significantly clarify the responsibility of employers and the rights of employees in regard to sexual harassment.

•

In the small town of Lens, France, police, some in riot gear, arrest or expel some 400 football hooligans before England's match against Colombia in the World Cup football (soccer) play-off.

27

President Clinton meets with Pres. Jiang Zemin in Beijing; Clinton arrived in China on June 25 for a state visit.

•

The National Steinbeck Center, a museum to honour popular novelist and native son John Steinbeck, opens in Salinas, Calif.

28

The government of Thailand announces that henceforth every March 13 will be Na-

tional Elephant Day to honour the gentle endangered beast that has been Thailand's national animal since 1963.

•

Two statues designed by Robert Shure to commemorate the famine in Ireland in the 1840s and 1850s are dedicated in Boston.

29

Following weeks of unrest in the Serbian province of Kosovo, which is dominated by ethnic Albanians, the government inaugurates a major attack on positions

occupied by the secessionist Kosovo Liberation Army (*see* May 9 and July 19).

•

Slavko Dokmanovic, a Serb and former mayor of the town of Vukovar, who is on trial for a mass murder in former Yugoslavia, commits suicide in his cell at the UN War Crimes Tribunal in The Hague (*see* July 6).

•

The U.S. government informs the family of Lieut. Michael J. Blassie, who was killed in action in Vietnam in 1972, that the remains of a previously unknown serviceman that had lain in the Tomb of the Unknowns in Arlington, Va., has been identified as their son.

30

A new constitution for The Sudan is signed into law by Pres. Omar Hassan Ahmad al-Bashir on the ninth anniversary of the coup that brought him to power.

•

The new Congolese franc is entered into circulation, exchanging at 1.40 to the U.S. dollar.

National Elephant Day announced in Thailand: June 28

The coffin of Lieut. Michael J. Blassie at the Tomb of the Unknowns in Arlington, Va.: June 29

1

Ace-K, an artificial sweetener, is approved for use in soft drinks by the Food and Drug Administration; shortly after the announcement, PepsiCo Inc. announces plans to introduce a new soft drink containing the sweetener in October.

The tax-evasion case against Webster L. Hubbell, longtime friend of Pres. Bill Clinton who is believed to hold incriminating evidence against Clinton and his wife, Hillary, in the Whitewater case, is thrown out by a Federal District Court judge citing independent counsel Kenneth W. Starr's abuse of authority.

At the Tchaikovsky music competition in Moscow, Russian musicians finish with top honours in piano, violin, and cello.

David Trimble, leader of the Protestant Ulster Unionist Party, is elected chief minister of Northern Ireland, and Seamus Mallon is chosen deputy minister at the inaugural meeting of the Northern Ireland Assembly.

The Star Banc Corp. announces plans to buy Firstar Corp. for $7.2 billion in stock, creating a banking company with $38 billion in assets and locations in 10 states.

At the 33rd Karlovy Vary International Film Festival in the Czech Republic, Michael Douglas receives the Special Prize for Outstanding Contribution to World Cinema, and Lauren Bacall and Rod Steiger are honoured with Life Achievement Awards.

The 42nd season of the Santa Fe (N.M.) Opera begins with a production of Puccini's *Madama Butterfly* in a new theatre building designed by James Stewart Polshek and Associates.

Jana Novotna of the Czech Republic beats Nathalie Tauziat of France 6–4, 7–6 for the women's title at the All-England championships at Wimbledon; on July 5 American Pete Sampras ties Björn Borg's record of five wins at Wimbledon, defeating Goran Ivanisevic of Croatia in five sets.

The 12th World AIDS Conference ends in Geneva, Switz., still offering little hope for the 34 million persons worldwide who are infected with HIV or who have developed AIDS.

The Lewis and Clark National Historic Trail Interpretive Center, a museum that focuses on the Native American cultures encountered by the pioneering expedition in 1804–05, officially opens in Great Falls, Mont.

Archaeologists excavating at the historic Tintagel Castle in Cornwall in southwestern England, reputedly the birthplace of King Arthur, find a stone bearing the Latin inscription *Pater Coliavi ficit Artognov*, which they connect to the legendary king.

5

The *Observer* newspaper publishes a report that lobbyists with ties to the Labour Party have been receiving money in exchange for privileged communications with government officials in what is called the "cash for access" scandal.

Americans win four of the Henley Royal Regatta trophies in rowing; Jamie Koven captures the single-sculling title, Harvard University's heavyweight varsity squad wins the Ladies Challenge Plate, the U.S. national quadruple-sculling team wins the Queen Mother Challenge Cup, and doubles team Steve Tucker and Greg Ruckman clinch the Double Sculls Challenge Cup.

6

Pak Se Ri of South Korea wins the U.S. Women's Open golf tournament in Kohler, Wis., the second major win for the 20-year-old rookie in two months (*see* May 17).

Two van Gogh paintings and a Cézanne are recovered on the outskirts of Rome seven weeks after they were stolen from the National Gallery of Modern Art in Rome (*see* May 19).

7

Moshood ("MKO") Abiola, Nigeria's most famous political prisoner, suffers a heart attack while meeting with American and Nigerian officials in Abuja and dies in a hospital shortly afterward; Abiola's family and associates express suspicion of government involvement in his death (*see* June 8).

In a transatlantic crossing from New York City to Lizard Point, England, French yachtsman Christophe Auguin breaks the record for monohull yachts with a time of 9 days 22 hr 59 min 30 sec, beating the previous record by more than a day.

The last turbine of the Yacyretá Hydroelectric Station on the Paraná River, which serves as the border between Argentina and Paraguay, is dedicated by those countries' respective presidents, Carlos Menem and Juan Carlos Wasmosy.

8

After a 10-year legal battle, the Dow Corning Corp. and lawyers for tens of thou-

REMY DE LA MAUVINIERE—AP/WIDE WORLD

sands of women who claim to have been injured by silicone breast implants made by Dow agree to a $3.2 billion settlement.

•

Poet, translator, and environmental activist W.S. Merwin is named the winner of the 1998 Ruth Lilly Poetry Prize, which carries an award of $75,000; he is honoured by the Modern Poetry Association July 28 at the Arts Club of Chicago.

Jeffrey P. Koplan, president of Prudential Health Care Research in Atlanta, Ga., is chosen by the Clinton ad-

ministration to be director of the Federal Centers for Disease Control and Prevention; he will assume the post October 5, replacing David Satcher.

•

The 10th annual Praemium Imperiale prizes for outstanding lifetime achievement in the arts are awarded by the Japan Arts Association in Munich, Ger.; the prizes of ¥15 million (about $110,000) go to Robert Rauschenberg of the U.S. for painting; Dani Karavan of Israel in sculpture; Alvaro Siza, Portugal, architecture; Sofia Gubaidullina, Russia, music; and Sir Richard Attenborough, Great Britain, theatre and film.

10

Russian Pres. Boris Yeltsin appeals to Western leaders to support a multibillion-dollar aid package to uphold Russia's deteriorating currency.

•

The Three Tenors (Luciano Pavarotti, Plácido Domingo, and José Carreras) give a concert in Paris in connection with the association football (soccer) World Cup.

11

Polish composer Krzysztof Penderecki's *Credo* receives its world premiere at the Oregon Bach Festival in Eugene.

12

In Ballymoney, N.Ire., three Roman Catholic boys are burned to death in their home after a flaming gasoline bomb is thrown into a downstairs window; the arson attack is believed to be the work of Protestants.

In the championship match of the World Cup soccer tournament in Saint-Denis, Fr., France wins its first World Cup title, defeating the favoured Brazilians 3–0.

•

Japanese Prime Minister Ryutaro Hashimoto says he will resign, citing his inability to "live up to the people's

The Three Tenors in Paris: July 10

35

expectations"; he does so on July 13.

13

An accord is reached between the Russian government and international lenders under which $17.1 billion will be advanced over the next two years, principally by the International Monetary Fund.

•

Italian media tycoon and former prime minister Silvio Berlusconi receives a sentence of two years four months and a $5.6 million fine for making illegal political donations only a week after receiving convictions for bribery and tax fraud; because Berlusconi is a member of Parliament, however, he has immunity and is not required to serve a jail sentence.

•

Stephen G. Smith is named to replace James Fallows as editor of *U.S. News & World*

14

Zhu Lilan, China's minister of science and technology, arrives in Taipei, Taiwan, to discuss official science and technology exchanges; he is the highest-ranking Chinese official to visit since the establishment of the nationalist Chinese government on the island.

•

At the Golden Gala track meet in Rome, Moroccan runner Hicham al-Guerrouj sets the world record for 1,500 m with a time of 3 min 26 sec.

15

A three-month cease-fire is declared between the Islamic government of The Sudan and Christian rebels in the southern part of the country to allow food shipments to reach hundreds of thousands of starving people.

replace the country's 49 provinces with 16 larger, stronger ones.

17

The remains of the last tsar of Russia, Nicholas II, and most of his family are laid to rest in St. Petersburg, the former imperial capital, in a ceremony without the participation of Patriarch Aleksey II of the Russian Orthodox Church but supported by Pres. Boris Yeltsin.

•

At the Tour de France bicycle race, all nine members of Festina from Italy, the world's top team, are disqualified after their coach admits to issuing illegal performance-enhancing drugs to the riders (*see* August 2).

•

Following a magnitude-7.0 earthquake 20 km (12 mi) offshore, a tsunami washes away several beach villages on the northern coast of

19

Ethnic Albanians in the Serbian province of Kosovo announce the capture of the town of Orahovac from Yugoslav forces; the town is recaptured on July 22.

•

Professional American golfer Mark O'Meara clinches his second major championship of the year at the British Open in Southport, Eng.

•

In celebration of the 150th anniversary of the first women's rights convention in the U.S., which convened on this date in 1848, the Women's Rights National Historical Park opens in Seneca Falls, N.Y.

20

Nigerian ruler Gen. Abdulsalam Abubakar promises to hold elections in the first three months of 1999 and ultimately hand over power to a civilian president.

•

PepsiCo announces that it will buy the Tropicana juice business from Seagram Co. in a $3.3 billion cash purchase, PepsiCo's largest acquisition to date.

•

James Joyce's *Ulysses* is voted by a panel of scholars and writers the finest English-language novel published this century.

21

In a $3.5 billion cash deal, health care manufacturer Johnson & Johnson Inc. agrees to buy DePuy Inc., maker of orthopedic mechanisms, which will make Johnson & Johnson one of the largest makers of artificial joints and devices.

•

A group of scientists reports in *The Proceedings of the National Academy of Sciences* that they have identified a new fungus that they believe may be causing the massive die-offs of frog populations in Australia, Panama, and elsewhere.

22

Ryuzo Yanagimachi and Teruhiko Wakayama, biologists at the University of Hawaii, announce the creation of more than 50 cloned mice.

Food shipments to
The Sudan:
July 15

BRENNAN LINSLEY—AP/WIDE WORLD

Report, and David Remnick is named editor of *The New Yorker,* replacing the controversial Tina Brown, who resigned on July 8 to join the Disney Corp.

•

Chris Smith, culture secretary of Great Britain, announces the appointment of David Puttnam as chairman of Britain's new National Endowment for Science, Technology, and the Arts.

The Clinton administration imposes trade sanctions on nine Russian companies and institutions believed to be aiding Iran's missiles and weapons programs.

16

After a long and contentious debate, the Polish Sejm (parliament) votes in favour of a compromise plan that would

Papua New Guinea, killing at least 2,500 people and leaving 4,500 homeless.

18

Pres. Nelson Mandela of South Africa observes his 80th birthday and marries Graça Machel, his longtime companion and the widow of former Mozambique president Samora Machel.

Ukrainian Pres. Leonid Kuchma and U.S. Vice Pres. Al Gore sign a five-year agreement that will establish the International Radioecology Laboratory in the city of Chernobyl, near the site of the nuclear power station accident in 1986, to study the effects of radiation on the environment and humans.

23

Gholamhossein Karbaschi, the mayor of Tehran and a major supporter of moderate Iranian Pres. Mohammad Khatami, is sentenced to five years in prison on corruption charges; he was arrested on April 4.

•

Iran successfully tests a medium-range missile believed to have been purchased from North Korea; experts worry that Iran's acquisition of such devices could significantly alter the balance of power in the Middle East.

•

Pope John Paul II releases an apostolic letter intended to increase Rome's control over the 108 bishops' conferences worldwide.

24

The foreign ministers of the ASEAN nations of the Asian and Pacific region gather for their annual meeting in Manila, amid gloomy forecasts for the economic health of their area.

•

Russell Weston, Jr., opens fire in the United States Capitol, killing Officer Jacob J. Chestnut and Detective John M. Gibson, before he himself is shot to death by Capitol guards.

•

The U.S. defeats Canada by a score of 15–14 in the International Lacrosse Federation world championships in Baltimore, Md.; Australia beats the Iroquois Nation for third place.

•

The Alte Pinakothek, a major art museum in Munich, Ger., specializing in the Old Masters, reopens after a 52-month, $41.7 million renovation of its physical plant.

25

President Clinton is subpoenaed by Whitewater inde-

pendent counsel Kenneth Starr to testify before the federal grand jury regarding his relationship with Monica Lewinsky; this makes Clinton the first incumbent president ever to appear before a federal grand jury.

•

Seven for Luck, John Williams's song cycle for soprano and orchestra, receives its world premiere in a performance by the Boston Symphony Orchestra at the Tanglewood Music Center in Massachusetts.

26

Despite accusations of fraudulent voting by opponents, the Cambodian People's Party, led by Second Prime Minister Hun Sen, easily wins in Cambodia's first parliamentary election in five years.

•

The AT&T Corp., the largest American communications company, and British Telecommunications PLC, Great Britain's leading telecommunications provider, announce plans to merge most of their international operations into a new company worth $10 billion.

27

The new constitution of Fiji enters into force; the document enhances the rights of the non-Melanesian portion of the population, mostly persons of Indian descent.

•

The boards of Bell Atlantic Corp., which provides local telephone service in the northeastern U.S., and GTE Corp., the largest indepen-

DOUGLAS C. PIZAC—AP/WIDE WORLD

dent local and long-distance company, agree to Bell Atlantic's acquisition of GTE for $52.8 billion in stock.

28

The United Automobile Workers union agrees to end its eight-week strike, which has shut down General Motors plants across North America and affected hundreds of thousands of workers.

29

In Madrid, José Barrionuevo and Rafael Vera, two officials in the 1980s government of Spanish Prime Minister Felipe González, are sentenced to 10 years in prison for the kidnapping of a French furniture dealer whom they mistook for a Basque terrorist.

In a $19 billion deal, Brazil sells control of most of its telephone system, Telebrás, to Telefónica SA of Spain, Portugal Telecom, and MCI Communications Corp.

•

On Little Galloo Island in Lake Ontario, New York, state biologists discover the bodies of more than 800 cormorants believed to have been executed by people whose livelihood depends on the aquatic life in the lake.

30

The Japanese Diet (parliament) elects Keizo Obuchi of the Liberal Democratic Party as prime minister; he served as foreign minister in the previous government.

•

A single ticket purchased by 13 assembly-line workers from Westerville, Ohio, wins them $295.7 million from the Indiana Powerball, the biggest American lottery jackpot ever.

31

Commercial Bank of Korea and Hanil Bank announce their intention to merge and thereby create the largest bank in South Korea.

•

Astronomers in Australia report in *Science* the discovery of strongly polarized radiation in a star-forming cloud 1,500 light-years away; the radiation may be similar to the type responsible for the twisting of molecules in living organisms.

The biggest American lottery jackpot ever: July 30

DOUG MILLS—AP/WIDE WORLD

Tribute to U.S. Capitol guards killed on July 24

ERIC GAILLARD—REUTERS

Tour de France victor Marco Pantani of Italy (center): August 2

1

Milan Kovacevic, a Bosnian Serb medical doctor and civic leader who ran three detention camps near Prijedor, dies of an apparent heart attack in his cell at The Hague; on July 6 Kovacevic became the first defendant at the UN War Crimes Tribunal to be charged with genocide (*see* June 29).

•

After meeting in Kiev, Ukrainian officials and representatives of the International Monetary Fund report that the way has been cleared for the IMF to pay the first of three tranches of a $2.2 billion loan to Ukraine.

2

Disturbances against the central government of Pres. Laurent Kabila break out in several towns in eastern Democratic Republic of the Congo near the Rwandan border (*see* August 13).

•

Fifteen years after his troops fled a U.S. invasion in Grenada, Cuban Pres. Fidel Castro visits the Caribbean island, the last of three stops on a six-day tour of the region.

•

Marco Pantani wins the Tour de France, the first victory by an Italian since 1965; festivities are subdued, however, because of the drug scandal that haunted the year's running of the world's most important cycling race (*see* July 17).

3

The Indian Cabinet approves a proposal to create three new states: Uttarakhand from the existing Uttar Pradesh state, Vananchal from Bihar, and Chattisgarh from Madhya Pradesh; the measure later runs into opposition from the affected states, however.

•

Albertson's Inc., a grocery store chain, announces that it will acquire American Stores Co. for $8.3 billion in stock, forming the largest supermarket corporation in the U.S.

•

Figures released by the Department of Justice indicate that the prison population in the U.S. has grown by more than 60% since 1990 and by 1997 totaled 1,250,000 in state and federal institutions.

4

The Dow Jones industrial average drops almost 300 points, reflecting, experts believe, a delayed reaction to the Asian economic crisis (*see* August 31).

•

The government of Canada and the Nisga'a Indian Nation sign an agreement that would give the Nisga'a title to 2,000 sq km (770 sq mi) of land and a cash settlement of some $100 million over 15 years in return for their renouncing any other present or future land claims; this is the first such agreement between the Canadian government and a native people.

5

At the United Nations in New York City, Indonesia and Portugal initial a settlement of the problem of the island of Timor that would give the secessionist Portuguese province of East Timor self-government and limited autonomy within Indonesia.

•

Iraqi leader Saddam Hussein announces that his country is ceasing all cooperation with the United Nations arms inspectors; criticism from the UN and elsewhere is quick and sharp.

•

In Canterbury, Eng., the Lambeth Conference, a gath-

ering of Anglican bishops from 160 countries held every 10 years, adopts a resolution against the ordination of homosexuals.

6

Monica Lewinsky admits to having had an affair with Pres. Bill Clinton; she had denied this in earlier sworn testimony (*see* August 17).

•

Swimmer Michelle Smith-de Bruin, the first Irish swimmer and first Irish female athlete to win an Olympic gold medal, is banned from further competition for having tampered with a urine sample in a test for illegal drugs she may have used.

7

Bombs explode nearly simultaneously in the U.S. embassies in Nairobi, Kenya, and Dar es Salaam, Tanz.; about 270 people, mostly local citizens, are killed.

•

In Colombia, Andrés Pastrana Arango is sworn in as president together with his Cabinet; Santafé de Bogotá is under heavy security during the ceremonies.

8

Forces of the Islamic Taliban overrun the city of Mazar-e Sharif, the last major stronghold of the United Islamic

ROBERTO BOREA—AP/WIDE WORLD

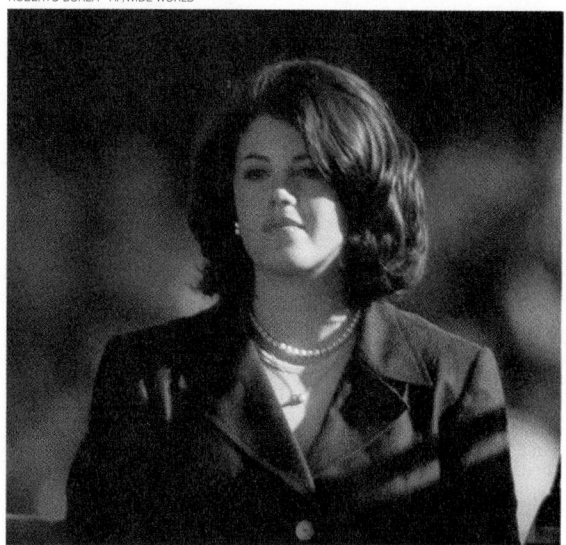

Monica Lewinsky testimony: August 6

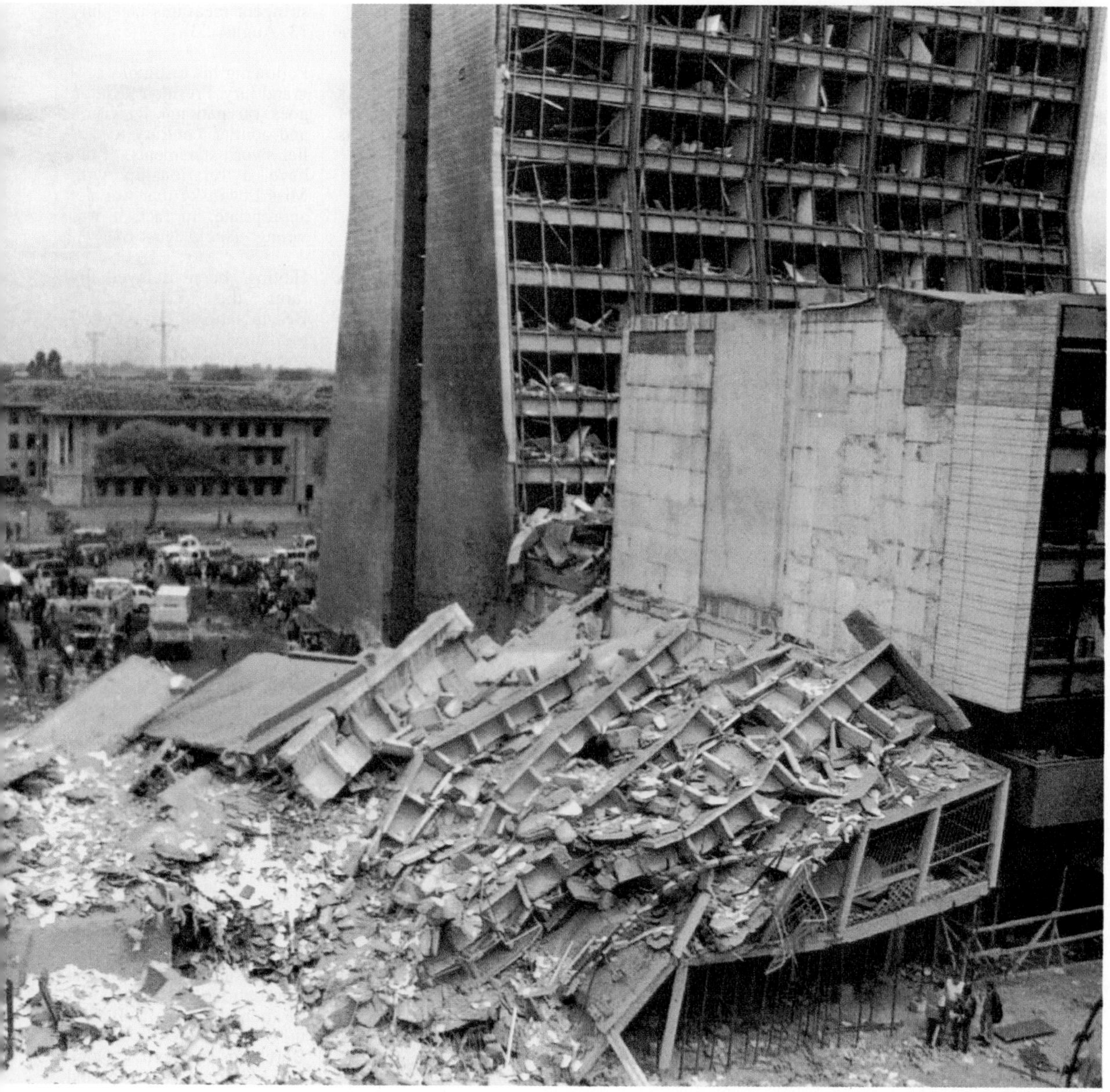

SAYYID AZIM—AP/WIDE WORLD

Bomb site in Nairobi, Kenya: August 7

Front for the Salvation of Afghanistan.

It is announced in China that the worst floods in 40 years are threatening major cities in the central part of the country; more than 3,000 people have died and 5,000,000 homes have been destroyed to date.

9

The government of Brazil announces a reform of the country's labour laws; the reform is designed to introduce greater flexibility into labour contracts and to make part-time employment more common.

10

In a colourful ceremony in the capital, Bandar Seri Begawan, Prince al-Muhtadee Billah, the eldest son of the sultan of Brunei, is officially installed as crown prince.

The partners of the private investment bank Goldman, Sachs & Co., valued at $28 billion, vote to offer the company to public trading.

In Chicago two boys aged 7 and 8 are charged with the sexual molestation, robbery, and killing of an 11-year-old girl; the boys apparently wanted the girl's bicycle; the charges were later dropped.

11

Garth H. Drabinsky, cofounder of Livent Inc., which has produced several successful Broadway theatrical productions in recent months, is suspended after the discovery of what the *New York Times* calls "serious accounting problems involving millions of dollars."

Twenty years to the day after the first crossing of the North Atlantic in a helium-and-hot-air balloon, adventurer Steve Fossett becomes the first to cross the South Atlantic in a flight from Mendoza, Arg., to the southern tip of Africa; Fossett continues his second attempt of the year to circumnavigate the globe but fails again on August 17 when his balloon, *Solo Spirit,* is punctured and plunges 9 km (5.6 mi) into the Coral Sea.

The Mashantucket Pequot Museum & Research Center, a high-tech facility to promote knowledge of the history and culture of the Mashantucket Pequot Tribal Nation, opens near Mashantucket, Conn.; the $135 million facility is funded with receipts from the Foxwoods Resort Casino owned and operated by the tribe.

12

Two large Swiss banks, the World Jewish Congress, and lawyers representing 31,500 survivors of the Holocaust announce in New York that they have reached an agreement on compensation for the survivors' claims; the banks agree to pay the claimants $1,250,000,000 over three years, and the Holocaust survivors will drop claims against the banks and other Swiss institutions.

Myanmar (Burma) opposition leader Daw Aung San Suu Kyi is halted by police outside Yangon (Rangoon) and prevented from meeting with supporters; in protest, she refuses to leave the minibus she is traveling in until August 24, when she is finally forced to return home (*see* September 6).

13

Rebels press in on Kinshasa, capturing the strategically important Inga Hydroelectric Dam and cutting power to the capital (*see* August 2).

14

The government of Thailand announces a series of measures involving outlays of $7,240,000,000 to put the country's financial institutions back on a sound footing.

15

A car bomb explodes in the town of Omagh, N.Ire., west of Belfast, killing 28 persons and injuring more than 200 in the worst terrorist incident since the signing of the Ulster peace agreement (*see* April 10).

Raúl Cubas Grau assumes the office of president of Paraguay and swears in his Cabinet.

16

It is announced in Amman that King Hussein of Jordan, currently undergoing treatment for cancer at the Mayo

VINCENT THIAN—AP/WIDE WORLD

Prince al-Muhtadee Billah of Brunei during proclamation ceremony: August 10

Clinic in Rochester, Minn., has delegated significant responsibilities for the conduct of state business to his brother and heir to the throne, Crown Prince Hassan.

Vijay Singh, a native of Fiji, wins the championship of the Professional Golfers' Association of America with a score of 271, 9 under par, at the Sahalee Country Club near Seattle, Wash.

17

Under increasing economic pressures, the Russian government effectively devalues the ruble by more than one-third until the end of 1998, places a 90-day moratorium on repayment of foreign debts, and institutes other stringent measures (*see* July 13, August 23).

Following his testimony to a grand jury, President Clinton goes on national television and admits, contrary to earlier sworn statements, "I did have a relationship with Miss Lewinsky that was not appropriate. In fact, it was wrong" (*see* August 6).

Having been delayed by rains, the AT&T Pebble Beach National Pro-Am golf tournament is completed six and a half months after it began; Phil Mickelson wins with a score of 14 under par.

18

Winston Peters leads his New Zealand First Party out of the centre-right coalition four days after he was dismissed as deputy prime minister by Prime Minister Jennifer Shipley.

As she tacks her 36-ft yacht into San Diego, Calif., Karen Thorndike of Washington state becomes the first woman to have sailed solo around the world; the 61,116-km (33,000-naut mi) trip has taken two years and two weeks.

19

The 1998 Fields Medals for achievement in mathematics are awarded at the International Congress of Mathematicians in Berlin; the winners are Richard E. Borcherds, William T. Gowers, Maxim Kontsevich, and

Curtis T. McMullen; a special award goes to Andrew Wiles of Princeton University, and Peter Shor of AT&T Laboratories in Florham Park, N.J., receives the Nevanlinna Prize.

An official of the Taliban indicates that the Islamic fundamentalist organization would be willing to talk to U.S. officials about granting access to Osama bin Laden, the Saudi Arabian businessman suspected of having masterminded the Nairobi and Dar es Salaam embassy bombings, if hard evidence of his involvement can be produced (*see* August 7, 20).

20

Missiles fired from U.S. warships and a submarine in the Indian Ocean destroy a chemical factory believed to be producing components of nerve gas in The Sudan and terrorist training camps in Afghanistan thought to be used by bin Laden for refuge.

The Supreme Court of Canada rules that the province of Quebec does not have the constitutional right to secede from Canada but that the confederation must negotiate with Quebec if secessionists in the largely French-speaking province win a referendum on the issue.

21

Former South African president P.W. Botha is convicted on contempt charges for refusing to testify before the country's Truth and Reconciliation Commission (*see* April 15).

A court in Hattiesburg, Miss., finds Sam H. Bowers, former imperial wizard of the Mississippi White Knights of the Ku Klux Klan, guilty of murder in the Jan. 10, 1966, firebombing of the house of Vernon Dahmer, Sr., near Hattiesburg.

22

Leaders of the 16 countries of the Caribbean Community, including Cuba's Pres. Fidel Castro, sign a free-trade agreement in Santo Domingo, the capital of the Dominican Republic; the accord will eventually remove all tariffs among the signatories.

Gen. Abdulsalam Abubakar, military ruler of Nigeria, swears in a new Federal Executive Council (Cabinet); Nigeria has been without a government since the earlier FEC was dissolved on July 8.

23

Frustrated and disgusted with their inability to halt the growing economic crisis, Russian Pres. Boris Yeltsin fires all his top government economic officials and invites former prime minister Viktor S. Chernomyrdin to assume the top post again.

The Nepali Congress Party (NCP) and the United Communist Party of Nepal–Marxist and Leninist agree to form a coalition government; the country has been led by a minority NCP government since April 1998.

24

Workers who walked off their jobs on July 20, in protest against plans by South Korean automaker Hyundai to lay off more than 1,500 employees, return to work after a compromise solution is found.

Plans by the U.S. Bureau of the Census to use statistical sampling to enhance the efficiency of the 2000 census run aground when a federal court declares the plan a violation of federal law.

25

Marco Aurelio Días Alcántara, a former policeman in Rio de Janeiro, is convicted of complicity in the murder and attempted murder in the killings of eight street children in 1993.

A group of conservation organizations publishes the World List of Threatened Trees, which finds that more than 8,750 of the 80,000–100,000 known species of trees are at risk of extinction, 1,000 of them critically so.

26

The government of Libya conditionally accepts an offer from the U.S. and Great Britain to try two Libyan nationals alleged to have been involved in the bombing of Pan Am Flight 103 over Lockerbie, Scot., in 1988.

William S. Ritter, Jr., the longest-serving U.S. official on the UN arms inspection team to Iraq, resigns, claiming that lack of support from the UN secretary-general and the Clinton administration undercuts the team's efforts.

Previously unknown text from the diary of Anne Frank, the Dutch girl who perished at the hands of the Nazis after the occupation of The Netherlands in World War II, are published in the Amsterdam newspaper *Het Parool;* five pages were removed from the manuscript by Anne's father because they contained unflattering descriptions of the Frank family's relations with each other.

27

Investors desert Russia in droves after its central bank stops supporting the ruble; it is announced in New York that the investment company owned by financier George Soros has lost $2 billion in Russian markets during the crisis (*see* August 17).

An intense blast of cosmic radiation—gamma rays, X-ray radiation, and high-energy particles—from a magnetic flare on a star 20,000 light-years away strikes Earth's upper atmosphere and causes perturbations in radio transmissions and Earth satellites.

28

In the Pakistani National Assembly, Prime Minister Nawaz Sharif proposes a constitutional amendment to introduce Islamic law throughout the country; the proposal is quickly criticized by the opposition and human rights leaders.

Boris Yeltsin goes on national television to assure his countrymen that he will finish his term as president, which is scheduled to expire in 2000; many observers believe that politics, economics, or ill heath will intervene.

29

The Air Line Pilots Association goes on strike against Northwest Airlines, underlining a long history of differences between pilots and management in this industry.

The baseball team from Toms River, N.J., defeats the team from Kashima, Japan, 12–9 to capture the 52nd annual Little League Baseball World Series.

30

Only 8 of the 22 Formula One autos entered in the Belgian Grand Prix at Spa finish in an unusually accident-ridden race.

The September issue of *The American Psychologist* carries a report by a team of scientists at Carnegie Mellon University, Pittsburgh, Pa., that home Internet use adversely affects social involvement and personal well-being, with those who use the Internet more reporting higher levels of depression and loneliness.

31

The Angolan National Assembly, dominated by the Popular Movement for the Liberation of Angola, expels the opposition National Union for the Total Independence of Angola (UNITA), the former rebel movement, because UNITA has not disarmed as prescribed in the 1994 peace accord.

A German court finds Rolf Glaeser, a swimming coach in the former East Germany, guilty of causing bodily harm by administering performance-enhancing drugs to women team members; this is the second such court decision in Germany.

Japan protests a violation of its airspace and suspends food-aid deliveries after North Korea tests what is first believed to be a ballistic missile; North Korea replies on September 4 that the event was not a missile launch but rather the country's first launch of an artificial Earth satellite.

The Dow Jones industrial average drops 512 points, or 6.4%, the largest fall since October 1987 (*see* August 4).

September

Russian and U.S. heads of state confer at a restrained summit meeting in Moscow; both men are under enormous domestic pressures, Bill Clinton politically and Boris Yeltsin both economically and politically.

•

The death penalty is abolished in Poland when a new penal code comes into effect.

•

The Houston Comets defeat the Phoenix Mercury 80–71 to win the Women's National Basketball Association championship for the second year in a row.

Anwar Ibrihim, deputy prime minister of Malaysia, who had been widely expected to become prime minister, is abruptly fired by Prime Minister Mahathir Mohamad; Ibrahim is arrested on charges of sexual indecency on September 20.

•

Malaysia fixes the ringgit's exchange rate indefinitely at 3.80 to the U.S. dollar, a point it had not reached since May.

•

A Swissair jetliner trying to make an emergency landing crashes off the coast of Nova Scotia, killing 229 persons.

•

The UN tribunal convened in Arusha, Tanz., to investigate mass killings in Rwanda finds Jean-Paul Akayesu, the former mayor of a small town, guilty of genocide, the first time an international court has delivered such a verdict; on September 4 former Rwandan prime minister Jean Kambanda is sentenced to life in prison for genocide (*see* May 1, August 1).

3

Pressures on Brazil's economy increase after Moody's, an American financial ratings agency, downgrades the country's sovereign debt rating from B1 to B2.

•

The 12th summit conference of the Non-Aligned Movement ends its two-day session in Durban, S.Af.; most of the discussions of the 113-member organization concern regional conflicts and disputes.

Jean-Paul Akayesu of Rwanda convicted of genocide: September 2

4

Reacting to a statement on September 3 by Sen. Joseph Lieberman that the president's actions in the Monica Lewinsky scandal were "immoral" and "disgraceful," President Clinton, on a visit to Ireland, acknowledges that he "basically" agrees with the senator.

•

A report from the U.S. Office of Management and Budget indicates that seven government agencies are expected to have exceptional difficulties dealing with the "millennium bug," or "year 2000 (Y2K) problem" (the inability of some computers to recognize the year 2000), and that expenses involved in combating the problem will run to about $5.4 billion.

5

North Korea declares Kim Il Sung, who died four years ago, "eternal president" and names his son, Kim Jong Il, "great leader," the highest post of the state but one that apparently is something less than "president."

•

Support beams give way, and the roof of the Universal Church in Osasco, a suburb of São Paulo, Braz., collapses, killing at least 20 people and injuring about 500.

6

The government of Myanmar (Burma) cracks down on the National League for Democracy, the opposition party of human rights and political activist Daw Aung San Suu Kyi, arresting 110 members (*see* August 12).

Former Maltese prime minister Eddie Fenech Adami returns to that office following a victory over Alfred Sant in elections on September 5 in the Mediterranean island republic.

7

Sergey K. Dubinin, the leader of Russia's central bank, resigns under pressure over his handling of the country's financial crisis; meanwhile, the State Duma rejects Viktor S. Chernomyrdin, President Yeltsin's candidate for prime minister, for a second time (*see* September 11).

•

Students in Indonesia demonstrate in large numbers for the first time since the fall of President Suharto; about 1,000 students enter the grounds of the legislature in Jakarta and demand the resignation of Pres. B.J. Habibie and the reduction of food prices.

8

Mark McGwire of the St. Louis Cardinals breaks Roger Maris's 1961 record for most home runs hit in a regular professional baseball season by hitting his 62nd of the season; ironically, the record-breaking homer comes in a game against the Chicago Cubs, whose Sammy Sosa has also been in contention to break Maris's record (*see* September 27).

•

The Great Silk Road Conference, an international trade gathering, convenes in Baku, Azerbaijan, bringing together representatives of Asian countries, the European Union, and Central

Asian and Black Sea trade and economic promotion groups.

9

Special Prosecutor Kenneth W. Starr sends to Congress the long-awaited 445-page report on his investigation into the actions of President Clinton in the Whitewater affair and subsequent matters; the report, with indications of perjury and obstruction of justice on Clinton's part, notably concerning Clinton's improper sexual relationship with Lewinsky, is made public on September 11 and is said by Starr to provide grounds for impeachment (*see* September 12).

•

A team of scientists at a fertility center in Fairfax, Va., announces in the journal *Human Reproduction* that they have devised a method, involving sorting sperm according to the amount of genetic material they contain (Y chromosomes, which produce a male, have less genetic material), to determine the sex of a baby at conception.

10

Burkina Faso becomes the 40th state to ratify the international treaty banning land mines; this was the last signature required for the treaty to enter into effect in March 1999.

•

In recognition of the contribution of his film *Schindler's List* to an understanding of the Holocaust, American filmmaker Steven Spielberg receives the Officer's Cross of the Order of Merit from German Pres. Roman Herzog in ceremonies in Berlin.

11

Foreign Minister Yevgeny M. Primakov is confirmed by the Russian State Duma as prime minister by a comfortable margin; the Duma had twice previously rejected President Yeltsin's nomination of Chernomyrdin for the post (*see* September 7, 22).

•

Pres. Liamine Zeroual of Algeria announces that he will not serve out his full term, which runs until 2000, but will call elections before March 1999.

JEAN-MARC BOUJU—AP/WIDE WORLD

42

The Emmy-winning cast of NBC's "Frasier": September 13

Volkswagen AG, the largest employer in Germany, announces plans to set up a DM 20 million (U.S. $11.2 million) fund to compensate survivors of workers who were employed under forced-labour conditions by the auto manufacturer during the Nazi era; another large German firm, Siemens, follows suit on September 23.

12

Attorneys for President Clinton fiercely attack the report of Special Prosecutor Starr as a "hit-and-run smear campaign" without substance and refute, point by point, the 11 grounds for possible impeachment adduced by Starr (*see* September 9).

•

Lindsay Davenport of the U.S. unseats favoured Martina Hingis of Switzerland 6–3, 7–5 to win the women's title in the United States Open tennis tournament; on September 13 Patrick Rafter of Australia defeats his countryman Mark Philippousis 6–3, 3–6, 6–2, 6–0 to win the men's competition for the second year in a row.

13

Ultranationalist Serb Nikola Poplasen wins the presidency of Republika Srpska,

the Serb-controlled entity in Bosnia and Herzegovina, in the two-day elections, ousting the moderates led by Biljana Plavsic, the clear favourites of the Western powers.

•

The Venice Film Festival closes as Gianni Amelio's *The Way We Laughed* wins the Gold Lion and Warren Beatty is honoured for lifetime achievement.

•

ABC's "The Practice" and NBC's "Frasier" win recognition for the best drama series and best comedy series, respectively, at the 1998 Emmy award ceremonies in Los Angeles; the award for "Frasier" is the show's fifth in a row, a record.

14

The Northern Ireland Assembly holds its first working meeting in Belfast, N.Ire.; discussion involves mostly procedural matters, such as which flags will fly over the assembly and what languages will be official (*see* July 2).

•

Top economic officials from the last Soviet communist government of Mikhail Gorbachev, including Leonid Abalkin, Nikolay Petrakov, and Oleg Bogomolov, are recalled to the Kremlin to ad-

vise President Yeltsin on the current economic crisis.

15

Scientists at several institutions who have been studying the rings around the planet Jupiter announce that they are made of dust from the impacts of cosmic bodies that crashed into Jupiter's moons.

•

The John F. Kennedy Center for the Performing Arts in Washington, D.C., announces the creation of the Mark Twain Prize for American humour and names as its first recipient comedian Richard Pryor; the award ceremony is held on October 20.

16

ETA, the secessionist Basque terrorist organization in Spain, declares an "indefinite and total" truce.

•

Toys "Я" Us, a toy retailer, announces plans to close 90 stores internationally and eliminate up to 3,000 jobs.

17

The Kurdish Democratic Party and the Patriotic Union of Kurdistan, two feuding factions in northern Iraq, say

they have agreed to unite their efforts against Iraqi leader Saddam Hussein.

•

The French government blocks plans by the Coca-Cola Co. to acquire Orangina, a French soft-drink brand, fearing excessive dominance by Coca-Cola in the French market.

•

A remote-controlled research submersible owned by Odyssey Marine Exploration films the remains of what is believed to be a Phoenician merchant ship from the 5th century BC in 900 m (3,000 ft) of water east of Gibraltar; the ship, named *Melkarth* (the Phoenician god of sailors) by the crew, is the oldest deep shipwreck discovered to date.

18

The Swiss police have determined that Raúl Salinas, brother of former Mexican president Carlos Salinas, was deeply involved in the Mexican cocaine trade, using his contacts to arrange protection for drug dealers and diverting drug revenues to his brother's campaigns.

19

A ferry with 453 persons aboard sinks in heavy

September

Record-setting marathoner Ronaldo da Costa of Brazil: September 20

weather in Manila Bay; at least 43 people die.

Great Britain launches HMS *Vengeance,* the last of its four planned Trident missile-carrying submarines.

20

Voters in Sweden keep the coalition government led by the Social Democratic Labour Party under Göran Persson in power by a slim margin.

In a strategic business shift for the defense-contract company, Lockheed Martin Corp. announces that it will acquire the Comsat Corp., a communications satellite company, for $2.7 billion.

Brazilian Ronaldo da Costa breaks the 10-year-old world record for the marathon by 45 seconds with a time of 2 hr 6 min 5 sec in the Berlin Marathon.

Cal Ripken, Jr., third baseman for the Baltimore Orioles, who in 1995 broke Lou Gehrig's record for most consecutive games played, sits out his first major league baseball game since 1982; the new record stands at 2,632.

21

Before devastating the Dominican Republic and Haiti, Hurricane Georges, the strongest storm in 70 years, slams into Puerto Rico, causing an estimated $2 billion in damage; at least 300 people in the Caribbean area are killed (*see* September 25).

The videotapes of President Clinton being interrogated by Special Prosecutor Starr and his associates before a grand jury on August 17 are broadcast on television to the nation.

22

South African troops invade the kingdom of Lesotho, a state that is completely surrounded by South African territory, to put down a rebellion against the government; the rebels resist stoutly, casualties on both sides rise to more than 65, and the Lesotho capital, Maseru, is devastated.

Russian President Yeltsin restructures his government and creates an inner Cabinet comprising the prime minister and six other top officials (*see* September 11).

23

Sagging under heavy debts and losses of revenue and unable to resolve a labour dispute, Philippine Airlines (PAL) ceases operations.

Philanthropist Joan Kroc, widow of the founder of the McDonald's fast-food chain, announces that she will donate $80 million to the San Diego, Calif., chapter of the Salvation Army, the largest single gift ever to the religious organization.

24

The government of Iran announces that it no longer supports the fatwa, or sentence of death, on British author Salman Rushdie; the U.K. responds by reinstating full diplomatic relations with Iran, which it had broken in 1989.

In an unusual twist, Kenyan Pres. Daniel arap Moi reinstates as head of the Kenya Wildlife Service anthropologist Richard Leakey, who resigned the post in 1994 over disagreements with Moi (*see* May 21).

The journal *Nature* reports that two specimens of the coelacanth, a fish with antecedents older than the dinosaurs, were caught in July off Celebes (Sulawesi) island, Indonesia; the rare species had previously been seen only off the coast of southern Africa.

25

Hurricane Georges reaches the Florida keys, bringing winds of over 160 km/h (100 mph), traverses the Florida Gulf coast, and then slams into the area between Panama City, Fla., and New Orleans on September 27 (*see* September 21).

The Albert Lasker Medical Research Awards of the Albert & Mary Lasker Foundation are presented in a ceremony in New York City to Lee Hartwell, Toshio Masui, Paul Nurse, Alfred G. Knudson, Jr., Peter C. Nowell, and Janet D. Rowley; the foundation's special achievement award goes to Daniel E. Koshland, Jr., of the University of California, Berkeley.

26

Some 34 persons are reported massacred by Serbian military and police officials in three villages around Gornje Obrinje as violence continues unabated in the province of Kosovo.

The *New York Times* reports that Cornell University is investigating allegations of falsification of scientific data in the research of John L. Ho, a leading immunologist and AIDS investigator in the university medical school laboratories in New York City.

27

Social Democrat Gerhard Schröder leads his party to a stunning victory in German elections, unseating Christian

son in style, hitting two more home runs for a new record total of 70 during a regular season (*see* September 8).

28

Continuing the political and economic confusion in the country, Russian President Yeltsin fires his main economic adviser and chief tax collector, Boris G. Fyodorov.

•

The Gillette Co., anticipating poor third-quarter business results, announces that it will cut 4,700 jobs, 11% of its workforce around the world (*see* April 15).

•

California Gov. Pete Wilson signs a bill to move the primary elections in the state three weeks earlier to the first Tuesday in March; earlier primaries will increase the importance of the nation's most populous state in the selection process for presidential candidates.

29

The U.S. Federal Reserve reduces interest rates by one-quarter point, to 5.25%, to help insulate the economy against pressures of the international financial crisis; this is the first reduction in rates since January 1996.

•

The ruling Socialist Party in Albania selects 31-year-old Pandeli Majko to replace Fatos Nano, who resigned as prime minister on September 28.

•

New Zealand scientists report that the size of the hole in the ozone layer of the atmosphere over Antarctica has increased by 5% in the past two years and is now the largest it has ever been.

30

At the end of the country's fiscal year, the U.S. Treasury reports a surplus of $70 billion, the first budgetary surplus in 29 years and the largest ever.

•

Following a week of pitched battles in Sri Lanka, Red Cross officials report more than 1,300 dead on both sides in the government's continuing battles against the Tamil rebels in the northern part of the country (*see* March 5).

Democrat Helmut Kohl, who has occupied the chancellorship for 16 years, Europe's longest-ruling politician.

•

The Adelaide Crows win their second championship in a row in the Australian Football League grand final match at the Melbourne Cricket Ground; they defeat the favoured North Melbourne Kangaroos 15.15 (105) to 8.22 (70).

•

The Vietnam Era Educational Center, believed to be the first museum dedicated solely to the Vietnam War, opens in Holmdel, N.J.; the facility, which cost $3.8 million, is funded largely by donations from casinos in Atlantic City, N.J.

•

McGwire ends the 1998 National League baseball sea-

Wreckage in
Puerto Rico from
Hurricane Georges:
September 21

Pandeli Majko,
new prime minister
of Albania:
September 29

October

New York City's
Grand Central
Terminal: October 1

1

With attacks by the rebel Sudan People's Liberation Army on the increase, the government of The Sudan imposes a ban on relief flights to the southern part of the country where the SPLA is based (*see* July 15).

•

New York City's Grand Central Terminal, an architectural landmark dating from 1913, is rededicated after an extensive $196 million renovation.

2

Sanjaasurengiyn Zorig, a minister in the Mongolian government and a leading candidate to become prime minister, is brutally murdered in his home in Ulaanbaatar; the motive for the killing is not immediately clear.

•

NASA, the U.S. space agency, announces that it will purchase thousands of hours of cosmonaut time in space aboard the International Space Station from the financially straitened Russian Space Agency for $60 million.

•

Cleveland, Ohio's, Allen Theater reopens after a yearlong, $15 million reconstruction; the theatre is the last of four historic buildings to undergo refurbishment in Playhouse Square Center, a large performing arts facility.

3

The conservative-led coalition government of Prime Minister John Howard wins reelection in Australia; Pauline Hanson's One Nation Party does unexpectedly poorly, taking only 8.4% of the vote.

•

Qatar begins voter registration for municipal elections, the first in this or any of the other five Persian Gulf states.

•

In connection with general elections, Latvians vote to ease regulations for ethnic Russians to acquire Latvian citizenship; the existing laws were criticized as unduly harsh and were seen as a barrier to Latvian integration into Europe.

4

Pres. Fernando Henrique Cardoso of Brazil is comfortably reelected to office in the first round with 53% of the vote; his nearest rival, the Workers Party's Luiz Inácio Lula da Silva, wins 31.7%.

•

Ethnic violence, fueled by conflicting claims to potentially oil-rich lands in southern Nigeria, break out between the Ijaw people and the Ilaje clan of the Yoruba.

•

The blockbuster art exhibition "Van Gogh's Van Goghs," comprising some 70 paintings on loan from the Van Gogh Museum in Amsterdam, opens to the public at the National Gallery of Art in Washington, D.C.

5

The Judiciary Committee of the U.S. House of Representatives recommends impeachment hearings against Pres. Bill Clinton; by a vote of 258 to 176, on October 8 the full U.S. Congress decides to hold such hearings.

•

With no end in sight to the labour dispute between owners and players that began with a lockout of players on July 1, officials of the National Basketball Association cancel all preseason exhibition games; on October 13 the NBA announces cancellation of the first two weeks of the 1998–99 season, which was to begin on November 3 (*see* December 5).

6

Amnesty International, the London-based human rights organization, publishes a report highly critical of the United States, which, according to the report, has "a persistent and widespread pattern of human rights violations," notably in the criminal justice system.

•

The Philippine Supreme Court overturns the 1993 conviction of Imelda Marcos, wife of former dictator Ferdinand Marcos, on fraud charges; she expresses relief that "justice prevailed."

•

German publishing giant Bertelsmann AG acquires a 50% stake in the on-line bookselling operations of Barnes & Noble and an-

nounces that it is discontinuing its plans to set up a competing on-line service in the U.S.

•

The winners of the 1998 Lannan Literary Awards, totaling $850,000 and including a lifetime achievement award to author John Barth, are announced.

Pakistani Prime Minister Nawaz Sharif accepts the resignation of army chief Gen. Jehangir Karamat and replaces him with another top general; the incident is significant because the generals have generally exercised supreme power in Pakistan.

•

Drivers on the Paris Métro strike, demanding improved protection against violent passengers.

8

Pres. Kim Dae Jung of South Korea, on an official visit to Japan, hears Japanese Prime Minister Keizo Obuchi express "remorseful repentance and heartfelt apology" for the damage and pain Japan inflicted upon the Korean people earlier in the 20th century.

•

The Swedish Academy in Stockholm announces that Portuguese novelist José Saramago is the recipient of the 1998 Nobel Prize for Literature.

•

Following several weeks of rising tensions, shots are exchanged between the Islamist Taliban forces of Afghanistan and Iranian troops on the border between the two countries; heavy casualties are reported.

•

Robert Wilson, theatre producer and designer, receives the 1998 Harvard Excellence in Design Award from the Harvard Graduate School of Design in recognition of the continuing influence of design in the work of an artist celebrated for vision and creativity in avant-garde theatre.

9

Meeting in Lusaka, Zambia, the Commonwealth lifts sanctions imposed against

Nigeria because of its human rights record and partially readmits Africa's most populous state to the organization.

•

A court in London rules in favour of Yemen in its dispute with Eritrea over control of the Hanish islands in the Red Sea.

•

John Cripton, director of the National Arts Centre in Ottawa, resigns because of differences with the government over arts funding in Canada.

10

David Sheldon Boone, a longtime employee of U.S. Army Intelligence and the National Security Agency, is arrested in Arlington, Va., and later charged with having spied for the Soviet Union against the U.S. in the late 1980s and early 1990s.

11

Pres. Heydar Aliyev of Azerbaijan is returned to office, easily defeating five contenders in presidential elections.

ANDREW MEDICHINI—AP/WIDE WORLD

Edith Stein, a Jewish woman who became a Carmelite nun and was killed by the Nazis in the Auschwitz concentration camp, is pronounced a saint and martyr of the Roman Catholic Church by Pope John Paul II in a ceremony in Vatican City.

•

An airliner with 40 people aboard is shot down by a missile fired by rebels near Kindu in the eastern Democratic Republic of the Congo; all aboard are believed to have died.

12

Americans Robert Furchgott of the State University of New York Health Science Center in Brooklyn, Louis J. Ignarro of the University of California School of Medicine in Los Angeles, and Ferid Murad of the University of Texas Medical School in Houston are named as winners of the Nobel Prize for Physiology or Medicine for their studies of the effect of nitric oxide in the human organism.

•

The Japanese Diet (parliament) approves new regula-

tions for banks in the country that permit the government to intervene and provide support for failing banks.

•

Matthew Shepard, a gay student at the University of Wyoming, dies in a hospital in Colorado, the victim of a brutal beating and exposure after being tied to a fence in near-freezing temperatures.

13

The winners of the 1998 physics and chemistry Nobel Prizes are announced: the physics award goes to Americans Robert Laughlin of Stanford University and Daniel Tsui of Princeton University and German Horst L. Störmer of Columbia University, New York City; the chemistry prize is awarded to Americans Walter Kohn of the University of California, Santa Barbara, and John Pople of Northwestern University, Evanston, Ill.

•

After a lengthy standoff and under threat of NATO air strikes, Pres. Slobodan Milosevic agrees to withdraw Yugoslav troops and police forces from the province of Kosovo (*see* December 24).

•

"Mary Cassatt: Modern Woman," the first major retrospective of the work of the American Impressionist painter in three decades and featuring nearly 100 of her paintings, pastels, drawings, and prints, opens to the public at the Art Institute of Chicago.

14

Indian Amartya Sen, master of Trinity College, Oxford, wins the Nobel Memorial Prize in Economic Science for his work on famines and the ethical aspects of economic decision making.

•

Nigeria's leading literary figure, Nobel Prize winner Wole Soyinka, returns home after nearly four years of self-imposed exile.

•

The new German coalition government announces that it will press for a revision of the country's tough citizenship laws to permit automatic citizenship for children born in Germany of foreign-born parents if one parent has lived in Germany since age 14.

Edith Stein pronounced a saint: October 11

A 27,000-km (17,000-mi) overland fibre-optic cable, the longest in the world, is opened along the route of the ancient Silk Route, from Shanghai to Frankfurt, Ger., linking 20 countries in Central and West Asia and Eastern and Central Europe.

15

The final touches are put on a $1.7 trillion U.S. budget, and the bill is approved by President Clinton and Congress; the budget includes the largest peacetime increase in military spending since 1985 (see October 20).

In an unexpected move, the U.S. Federal Reserve Board cuts interest rates by a quarter of a point, which suggests a pessimistic view as to whether the economic boom in the country will continue.

Youth unrest in France, which has been growing for two weeks and which involves half a million secondary-school students, breaks into violence after large numbers demonstrate in Paris and some of their number begin looting and burning cars.

A major exhibition of the American painter John Singer Sargent opens in London's Tate Gallery.

16

Gen. Augusto Pinochet is detained in London at the request of Spain, which seeks to try him for the murder of a number of Spanish and Chilean citizens during the 17 years that he led a right-wing military regime in Chile.

John Hume, leader of Northern Ireland's Roman Catholic Social Democratic and Labor Party, and David Trimble, leader of the Protestant Ulster Unionists, are jointly awarded the Nobel Peace Prize in recognition of their efforts to bring peace to the British province.

The 20th anniversary of the ascendancy to the papacy of Karol Cardinal Wojtyla of Poland as Pope John Paul II on Oct. 16, 1978, is commemorated; a papal encyclical, *Fides et Ratio,* is issued on October 15, and a high mass is celebrated in St. Peter's Square in Vatican City.

17

An oil pipeline catches fire in Warri, southern Nigeria; sabotage is suspected in the incident, which leaves more than 700 people dead.

Kaji Sherpa of Solukhumbhu, Nepal, reaches the summit of Mt. Everest (8,848 m, or 29,029 ft) in a record time of 20 hours 24 minutes, starting from his base camp at 5,350 m (17,552 ft).

18

Rebel insurgents are blamed for the explosion and fire on a pipeline near Segovia, Antioquia province, Colom., that kills at least 45 people.

A train jumps the tracks in a railway station near Alexandria, Egypt, killing dozens of people.

19

The antitrust trial of the U.S. government against Microsoft Corp. opens in Washington, D.C.

The Kroger Co., the second largest grocery dealer in the U.S., announces that it will buy Fred Meyer Inc., with $4.3 billion in debts, for $8 billion in stock, a transaction that will give the new company the top slot again (see August 3).

Ernesto Bazan, who resides in Brooklyn and Cuba, is awarded the 1998 W. Eugene Smith Grant in Humanistic Photography; the award, given annually, is valued at $20,000.

Heavyweight Mike Tyson is granted a boxing license by the state of Nevada; his license had been revoked after he bit the ear of Evander Holyfield in a World Boxing Association title bout in June 1997.

20

As part of the U.S. budget bill Congress approves a subvention of $18 billion to the International Monetary Fund; passage had been delayed, largely by Republicans who were unhappy with the IMF's handling of the global financial upheavals.

Geri Halliwell, the British pop music star formerly known as Ginger Spice of the Spice Girls, is named cultural ambassador for the United Nations Population Fund (see May 30).

21

Following the confidence-vote loss by Italian Prime Minister Romano Prodi on October 9, Massimo D'Alema of the Democrats of the Left Party is sworn in as prime minister; he is the first ex-communist to lead a government in Western Europe.

President Clinton abolishes the U.S. Arms Control and Disarmament Agency and the U.S. Information Agency and places their activities under the U.S. Department of State; the U.S. Agency for International Development, formerly an independent agency, is now to report to the State Department.

The Newell Co., a manufacturer of housewares with brands such as Mirro and Wearever cookware and Anchor Hocking glassware, announces that it will purchase Rubbermaid Inc., a well-known brand name in the kitchen accessories market, for about $5.8 billion.

In the fourth game of a clean best-of-seven sweep, the New York Yankees beat the San Diego Padres to capture their 24th World Series victory.

22

The largest stockbrokerage company in Japan, Nomura Securities Co., announces that it has posted a loss of $1,780,000,000 for the first half of 1998, largely because of reverses in its American real-estate repackaging business.

Bankers Trust Corp. posts a hefty loss, $488 million, much of which is attributed to losses in Russian and other international markets (see November 30).

The Fisher-Price Co. recalls 10 million toy vehicles in

Pipeline fire in Nigeria: October 17

CLEMENT NTAYE—AP/WIDE WORLD

their Power Wheels line because certain models can catch fire or fail to stop when a child is riding on them; the recall is one of the largest ever in the toy industry.

23

Israeli Pres. Benjamin Netanyahu and Palestinian Authority (PA) Pres. Yasir Arafat sign an agreement in the White House—soon dubbed the Wye Memorandum, after the Maryland estate at which the two sides negotiated for more than a week—that is expected to reenergize the Middle East peace process and essentially restate the terms of the 1993 and 1995 Oslo agreements whereby the PA would gain full control over additional territory in Palestine in exchange for the Palestinians' commitment to give up their anti-Israel activities.

Elections to Iran's Majlis-e Khobregan (Assembly of Experts) result in a clear victory for the conservative supporters of the ruling ayatollahs, but their win seems inconsistent with the election just 17 months earlier of a moderate president, Mohammad Khatami.

In Amherst, N.Y., Barnett Slepian, a doctor known for providing abortions, is shot dead in his kitchen by a sniper; police suggested this killing could be linked to similar murders of abortion doctors in New York and Ontario dating back to 1993.

24

Germany's Green party agrees to the terms of a coalition agreement with the Social Democrats forming the first ruling "Red-Green" coalition in the country's history.

The transatlantic sailing record is broken by nearly two and a half days by the 44.5-m (146-ft) Mari-Cha II, skippered by Bob Miller of Great Britain and Jef d'Estivaud of France, who sailed the two-master from New York Harbor to Britain in just under nine days.

25

The European Union institutes a law that prohibits the buying and selling of personal financial data, such as

is commonly done in the United States for marketing purposes.

The Chicago Fire defeats D.C. United by a score of 2–0 for the U.S. Major League Soccer championship in Pasadena, Calif.; the victory is the first by any professional sports expansion team in its first year.

26

Presidents Alberto Fujimori of Peru and Jamil Mahuad of Ecuador sign a peace accord in Brasília, Braz., ending decades of squabbling and three wars over the border between the two countries through the rugged Cordillera del Condór region.

The Yokohama BayStars defeat the Seibu Lions by a score of 2–1 to claim professional baseball's Japan Series; this was the BayStars' first win in the series since 1960.

27

In Great Britain the secretary of state for Wales, Ron Davies, resigns from the government to avoid potential embarrassment to the government and his family after being robbed at knifepoint at the home of a man he met at a park in south London known to be a homosexual meeting place.

Hurricane Mitch strikes Honduras and Belize with 190-km/h (120-mph) winds.

Ian McEwan is named recipient of the Booker Prize for fiction for his novel Amster-

dam; the Booker Prize, considered Britain's top literary award, is celebrating its 30th anniversary in 1998.

Toronto's fourth English-language daily newspaper, Conrad Black's National Post, publishes its first issue.

The Cathedral of Hope, a gay and lesbian congregation based in Dallas, Texas, brings suit against WGN-TV, a television station in Chicago whose programs are rebroadcast nationally via satellite, for breaking an agreement to air an infomercial prepared by the church intended to attract homosexual members.

28

The government of Brazil introduces a three-year, $84.5 billion plan, including tax increases, government spending cuts, and fiscal reorganization, to shore up its sagging economy.

Because of continuing violence at the hands of the opposition National Union for the Total Independence of Angola rebels, their leader, Jonas Savimbi, is stripped of his "special status" in the Angolan legislature, which allowed him to operate as the leader of an opposition political party (see August 31).

Archaeologist S. Thomas Parker of North Carolina State University tells the press that a church he discovered in 1997 near the Red Sea at Al-'Aqabah, Jordan, has been dated older than A.D. 300, which makes it the earliest-known existing Christian church.

29

Traveling aboard the U.S. space shuttle Discovery, 77-year-old American astronaut John Glenn returns to Earth orbit after having been the first American to orbit the Earth, in 1962.

South Africa's Truth and Reconciliation Commission releases its final report, precipitating controversy for its findings that nearly every political group as well as the apartheid government had been involved in violence, torture, and murder.

The U.S. Food and Drug Administration approves the use of the drug tamoxifen, manufactured by Zeneca Pharmaceuticals, in treating women who have a high risk of developing breast cancer.

The German chemical company Hoechst AG sells paint manufacturer Herberts to the American chemical giant DuPont Co. for about $1.9 billion; the new company, with estimated sales of $3.7 billion, will be the largest manufacturer of automotive coatings.

30

After more than a month of political jockeying in Bratislava, Slovakia, a four-party coalition government under Prime Minister Mikulas Dzurinda of the Slovak Democratic Coalition is sworn in.

At least 60 young people are killed and 190 injured in a fire in a discotheque in Göteborg, Swed.

31

The first of 42 television stations throughout the continental U.S. begins broadcasting in digital high-definition television (HDTV); HDTV has been mandated as a federal standard and will replace current technologies in several years.

The Tech Museum of Innovation, a $96 million, 12,250-sq m (132,000-sq ft) facility, opens to the public in San Jose in California's Silicon Valley, the location of many high-technology companies.

Peace accord signed by Peru and Ecuador: October 26

Rock singer Billy Joel:
November 10

1

A peace accord signed in the Nigerian capital, Abuja, calls for Pres. João Bernardo Vieira of Guinea-Bissau to set up a government of national unity and then leave the country; peace with the rebel forces under Asumane Mane is to be monitored by troops provided by the Economic Community of West African States (ECOWAS).

•

John Kagwe of Kenya wins the New York City Marathon with a time of 2 hr 8 min 45 sec, his second victory in a row; Franca Fiacconi of Italy is the fastest woman in the race, with a time of 2 hr 25 min 17 sec.

•

Mika Hakkinen wins the Japanese Grand Prix auto race at the Suzuka International Racing Course and with it the Formula One title for 1998.

•

Jeff Gordon wins the AC Delco 400 National Association for Stock Car Auto Racing race at the North Carolina Speedway in Rockingham, clinching his third NASCAR Winston Cup.

2

Local officials in Central America estimate that the number of dead from Hurricane Mitch, which lashed Honduras and other countries with 320-km/h (200-mph) winds as well as the rains and mud slides that followed, will exceed 7,000.

•

It is announced in New York City that the National Association of Securities Dealers Inc. (Nasdaq) and the American Stock Exchange (Amex) have completed all the requirements for their planned merger.

•

Tenor Plácido Domingo is named artistic director of the Los Angeles Opera; he will retain his job as artistic director of the Washington (D.C.) Opera and begin the new assignment in 2000.

3

Americans go to the polls; results of the U.S. congressional and local elections prove disappointing for the Republican Party.

•

China's Xinhua news agency announces that a previously unknown 25-km (15.5-mi) segment of the Great Wall of China has been discovered in Mu Us desert, Ningxia province, about 700 km (435 mi) west of Beijing.

4

The government of Russia admits that it cannot pay its foreign debts and plans to renegotiate its international loans.

•

In Bangladesh, according to *Ittefaq,* the newspaper of the Islamist party Jamaat e Islami, a reward is being offered for the delivery of Taslima Nasrin, an author and women's rights advocate; Nasrin, who has been living in exile, returned to Bangladesh secretly on September 13 to visit her mother, who is seriously ill.

5

The journal *Nature* publishes a report that DNA testing confirms that, as has long been alleged, Thomas Jefferson, the third president of the U.S., fathered at least one child by his slave Sally Hemings.

TONY DEJAK—AP/WIDE WORLD

6

Newt Gingrich, speaker of the U.S. House of Representatives, announces that he will not stand for reelection to the post and will leave Congress at the end of his term in January 1999 (*see* November 3).

•

Rwandan Vice Pres. Paul Kagame admits for the first time that troops from his country are assisting the rebellion against Pres. Laurent Kabila in the Democratic Republic of the Congo.

7

The Breeders' Cup Classic, with a purse of $5.2 million, horse racing's richest prize, is won by Awesome Again, trained by Patrick Byrne and ridden by Pat Day.

8

Sarah Fitz-Gerald defeats fellow Australian Michelle Martin 3–2 to win the World Open squash championship in Stuttgart, Ger.

•

Jeff Gordon wins the NAPA 500 race, the final event in the NASCAR season, at the Atlanta Motor Speedway in Hampton, Ga.

•

Placing second (after Venezuelan Gilberto González) in the Australian round of the men's Triathlon World Cup at Noosa, Australia, Hamish Carter of New Zealand wins the overall 1998 men's title; Australian Loretta Harrop wins the women's title.

9

In Bermuda the Progressive Labour Party, led by Jennifer

Jennifer Smith, new premier of Bermuda: November 9

LYNNE SLADKY—AP/WIDE WORLD

Smith, wins 26 of the 40 seats in the parliament, the party's first victory in 30 years.

•

Candidates of the ruling Institutional Revolutionary Party in Mexico win the governorships of three states, bringing the total victories in state elections in 1998 to 7 of 10 states.

•

Kerry Wood, a right-handed pitcher for the Chicago Cubs baseball team, is named the National League's Rookie of the Year for 1998.

10

It is reported that the Chinese government has cracked down on Christian "house churches," unofficial congregations that worship in private homes, arresting at least 140 church members in recent weeks.

•

In France Paule Constant is awarded the Prix Goncourt for her novel *Confidence pour confidence;* Dominique Bona wins the Prix Renaudot for her novel *Le Manuscrit de Port-Ébène.*

The Rock and Roll Hall of Fame in Cleveland, Ohio, names its 1999 inductees, who include performers Bruce Springsteen, Paul McCartney, Del Shannon, Curtis Mayfield, Dusty Springfield, Billy Joel, the Staple Singers, Charles Brown, and Bob Wills and the Texas Playboys as well as record producer George Martin; induction ceremonies will take place in March 1999.

•

Two English cricketers, Graham Thorpe and Mark Ramprakash, set a record for the most runs for a partnership in a single match, 377, against South Australia in Adelaide.

11

The Israeli Cabinet ratifies the Wye Memorandum, but not without intense debate and a number of caveats (*see* October 23).

•

It is announced that the Jack S. Blanton Museum of Art at the University of Texas at Austin will receive the Old Masters collection of William Suida and Bertina Suida-Manning, some 700 works valued at $30 million.

12

The three groups contending for power in Cambodia come to an agreement brokered by King Norodom Sihanouk that would retain Hun Sen as prime minister and make the king's son, Prince Norodom Ranariddh, National Assembly president.

•

Abdullah Ocalan, leader of the secessionist Kurdistan Workers Party, is arrested in Rome; the government of Turkey, where Ocalan is considered a criminal terrorist, files for extradition, but Italy declines because of a constitutional prohibition on extradition to countries that apply the death penalty.

•

Paleontologist Paul Sereno of the University of Chicago reports the finding in the desert in Niger of a previously unknown species of dinosaur, *Suhcomimus tenerensis,* that was about 10.5 m (35 ft) in length and had crocodile-like jaws.

13

Student protests in Indonesia turn violent, and at least eight persons are killed in clampdowns by police.

•

The International Monetary Fund and a group of lender countries announce a loan package for Brazil totaling $42 billion.

•

Pres. Bill Clinton agrees to a settlement with Paula Corbin Jones whereby he will pay her $850,000 but without any admission or apology, and she will drop charges that he made an indecent proposition to her in 1991.

14

Charles, prince of Wales, celebrates his 50th birthday.

•

England defeats The Netherlands 110–0 in the qualifying match for the European World Cup in rugby; the lopsided score is a record.

15

President Clinton announces that Pres. Saddam Hussein has unconditionally agreed to cooperate completely with UN arms inspectors, averting air and missile attacks within

Orthodox Jews praying in opposition to the Wye Memorandum: November 11

hours of being launched by the U.S. and its allies.

•

Allison Fisher of the U.K. defeats Franziska Stark of Germany 11–3 to win her third consecutive World Pool–Billiard Association title, the first time this has happened.

American wrap artists Christo and his wife, Jeanne-Claude, expend 55,000 sq m (592,000 sq ft) of fabric and 22.5 km (14 mi) of rope to cover up 178 trees on the grounds of the Beyeler Museum in Riehen, near Basel, Switz.; the "Wrapped Trees" exhibit opens to the public on November 21.

16

Monica Lewinsky chooses among the many opportunities to tell her side of her affair with President Clinton,

announcing that she will be interviewed by Barbara Walters for the ABC television show "20/20" and has agreed to a $600,000 advance from St. Martin's Press for a book with the working title *Monica's Story*.

•

Roger Clemens of the Toronto Blue Jays and Tom Glavine of the Atlanta Braves win the annual Cy Young Awards for pitchers in the American League and National League, respectively.

17

Earth witnesses the Leonid meteor storm.

•

The Indianapolis (Ind.) Museum of Art announces that it has purchased a major collection of paintings and prints by French artist Paul Gauguin.

18

The Asia-Pacific Economic Cooperation forum ends its session in Kuala Lumpur, Malaysia; the meeting was tarnished somewhat by a diplomatic uproar over a speech by U.S. Vice Pres. Al Gore in which he spoke favourably of pro-human rights forces opposing the host government and because of a disagreement between the U.S. and Japan over a trade pact.

•

Winners of the 1998 National Book Awards are named in New York City: Alice McDermott in the fiction category for her novel *Charming Billy* and Edward Ball in nonfiction for his *Slaves in the Family*.

•

Livent Inc., the Canadian theatre production company that brought a string of

blockbuster hits to Broadway, files for bankruptcy (*see* August 11).

19

Hearings in the U.S. House of Representatives over the impeachment of President Clinton begin; congressmen hear Special Prosecutor Kenneth W. Starr present his case.

•

Congressional Republicans confirm their selection of Robert L. Livingston of Louisiana to succeed Newt Gingrich as speaker of the U.S. House of Representatives (*see* December 19).

•

For the first time since the country was divided in two, a group of tourists from South Korea enters North Korea; 826 mostly elderly people arrive in the port of Chanjon aboard a luxury tour boat.

20

Russia launches the 24-metric ton unmanned Zarya command and control module, the first stage in the International Space Station, from the Baikonur Cosmodrome in Kazakstan; the space station will be assembled over the coming five years (*see* December 4).

•

Galina Starovoytova, a prominent liberal politician and deputy in the Russian State Duma (legislature), is found shot to death in the entryway of an apartment building in St. Petersburg.

•

American tobacco companies sign an agreement with the governments of 46 states to settle the states' claims for reimbursement of Medicaid funds they had expended to treat smoking-related illnesses; the settlement costs the tobacco manufacturers $206 billion beyond the $40 billion they agreed to pay four other states in 1997.

•

German publishing giant Bertelsmann AG buys an 82% share of Springer-Verlag GmbH, the leading German scientific and technical publisher (*see* October 6).

21

Talks begin in San Cristóbal de las Casas, the capital of Chiapas state, between rep-

Paleontologist Paul Sereno's new discovery: November 12

DENNIS COOK—AP/WIDE WORLD

resentatives of the Mexican government and the rebel Zapatista National Liberation Army, but the meetings do not go well (*see* January 24).

•

Speaking in Seoul, S.Kor., President Clinton calls on the leaders of North Korea to help strengthen ties to South Korea and the U.S. and to put aside their aspirations to nuclear technology.

22

Riots break out in Jakarta, Indon., between Muslim residents and Catholic settlers from the island of Amboina and later involve attacks on ethnic Chinese.

AFP PHOTO

Dariush Farouhar, a prominent opposition leader, civil rights advocate, and former Iranian government official, and his wife are found murdered in their home in Tehran.

•

A 5-m (16-ft)-high white marble stone, the foundation of the Khalsa Heritage Memorial Complex, is officially dedicated in Anandpur Sahib, Punjab state, India; the site will commemorate the 300th anniversary of the founding of the Sikh religion on April 13, 1699.

23

Siebe PLC of Great Britain, a large company manufacturing industrial controls and automation equipment, announces plans to acquire for $6,130,000,000 in stock rival BTR PLC.

•

Two large disability insurance companies, Maine-based UNUM Corp. and the Provident Companies of

Tennessee, agree to merge in a deal that values the latter at $4,750,000,000.

•

The B.F. Goodrich Co. announces it will buy Coltec Industries for $2.2 billion to form the largest supplier of aircraft landing gear.

•

Tyco International, a manufacturer of security alarms and systems, announces it will buy AMP Inc., a manufacturer of electrical connectors, for $11.3 billion.

24

Queen Elizabeth II, speaking at the annual ceremonies opening Parliament, announces that the right of hereditary peers to vote in the House of Lords will end; almost two-thirds of the membership of the upper house of Parliament have hereditary titles.

•

The Gaza International Airport opens at Rafah, Gaza Strip, providing Palestinians their first direct international transportation link with the rest of the world.

•

Yugoslav strongman Slobodan Milosevic fires Army Chief of Staff Momcilo Perisic, the latest in a purge of close aides and political cronies, which observers interpret as a sign of Milosevic's growing isolation and desperation.

•

America Online Inc., a giant among Internet service providers, announces that it will buy Netscape Communications Corp., owner of the Netscape Navigator World Wide Web browser software, for $4.2 billion; also involved in the far-reaching new alliance is Sun Microsystems.

25

The British House of Lords rejects the claims of former Chilean president Augusto Pinochet for immunity from arrest (*see* October 16).

•

The centrist government of Turkish Prime Minister Mesut Yilmaz, long under attack from both the military and Islamists, falls after a vote of no confidence.

•

Jack Kevorkian, a physician and assisted-suicide activist, is charged with first-degree murder in Oakland county, Mich., after he administers a lethal injection to a terminally ill patient; the event was videotaped and shown on national television on November 22.

26

Tony Blair, in the first speech ever by a British prime minister before the Irish Parliament, declares an end to the historic enmity between the two countries.

•

A court in Harare, Zimb., finds Canaan Banana, a former president of the country, guilty of sodomy; Banana, a Methodist minister, denied the charges but fled the country and has reportedly asked for political asylum in Botswana.

•

The government of Singapore lifts all restrictions it had placed on the political activities of Chia Thye Poh, an opposition leader, since his arrest and incarceration in 1966.

27

The large German utility company Viag AG announces that it is buying Algroup AG of Switzerland for $8.7 billion in stock.

•

Science magazine reports that a team of American and Chinese scientists working at a site 415 km (250 mi) northeast of Beijing has discovered the fossil remains of a 142 million-year-old plant believed to be the world's oldest flower.

28

President Clinton responds to 81 questions submitted to him in connection with the

impeachment hearings by the House Judiciary Committee.

•

On the country's Independence Day, Pres. Rexhep Meidani signs into law Albania's first constitution since the collapse of communism in 1991.

29

Returns from local elections in India show heavy reverses for the Hindu nationalist Bharatiya Janata Party, notably in the city of Delhi and Rajasthan state, and significant gains for the formerly dominant Congress Party.

•

In papal bull *Incarnationus Mysterium,* Pope John Paul II announces a revival of the time-honoured practice in the Roman Catholic Church of granting indulgences, the early elimination of punishment for sins for persons who are judged truly penitent and perform a charitable act.

•

The Musée d'Art et d'Histoire du Judaïsme formally opens in Paris's Marais district, the historical Jewish quarter, after 50 years of planning and controversy; the museum opens to the public on December 6.

30

Deutsche Bank AG of Germany announces it will acquire Bankers Trust Corp. of the U.S. for $10 billion, which will make the new Deutsche Bank the largest banking company in the world (*see* October 22).

•

Voters in Canada's mostly French-speaking province of Quebec narrowly return the pro-secessionist Parti Québécois and its leader, Lucien Bouchard, to the provincial assembly.

•

American Olympic gold-medal gymnast Dominique Moceanu, 17, is granted a temporary protective order from a court in Texas against her father, whom she accuses of mismanaging the money she made in her sports career as well as harassment of her and her friends; on October 28 the court awarded Moceanu adult status in order that she may manage her own financial affairs.

Leonid meteor shower: November 17

New president of
Venezuela Hugo
Chávez Frías:
December 6

The two largest oil companies in the world, Exxon and Mobil, say they will merge in an $80 billion deal that would create Exxon Mobil, the world's largest corporation, with some $200 billion in annual sales.

•

The French petroleum company Total SA announces plans to acquire the Belgian petrochemical firm Petrofina SA in a stock swap valued at $13 billion.

•

Two of Europe's largest chemical and pharmaceutical companies, Rhône-Poulenc SA of France and Hoechst AG of Germany, announce they are beginning a process of merging; a new company, called Aventis, will become the second largest pharmaceutical firm in the world and number one in agricultural chemicals.

Gen. Radislav Krstic is arrested by Western troops in Bosnia and Herzegovina; he will be tried by the International Criminal Tribunal in The Hague on charges of genocide for his leadership of the brutal attack on Srebrenica in 1995.

•

Sanofi SA and Synthélabo SA, two large French pharmaceutical companies, announce they will merge to form a new entity, Sanofi-Synthélabo, in a deal valued at $10.4 billion.

In anticipation of the introduction of the euro, the common European currency, and in response to the depressing effects on their economies by the Asian financial crisis, central bank authorities in 11 countries drop their lending rates to a uniform 3%, except for Italy, which drops to 3.5% (*see* December 31).

A team of six American astronauts and a second piece of an international space station are launched into Earth orbit from Florida aboard the *Endeavour; Endeavour*'s payload, the American-built Unity module, will be joined with a portion placed in orbit earlier by Russia (*see* November 20).

•

Bill Bradley, former Rhodes scholar, professional basketball player, and Democratic senator from New Jersey, announces his interest in running for the presidency in 2000.

•

The body of Mohammad Mokhtari, a prominent Iranian poet and anticensorship activist who had been reported missing, is found on the outskirts of Tehran; no cause of death is given, but suspicions fall on the ruling circles in the country.

James P. Hoffa, son of James R. Hoffa, who led the International Brotherhood of Teamsters from 1957 to 1971 and disappeared under murky circumstances in 1975, is elected to lead the labour union.

Hugo Chávez Frías, who led a coup attempt in 1992, sweeps to victory over the establishment candidate, Henrique Salas Römer, in the Venezuelan presidential elections.

•

Playing in Milan, Italy, Sweden defeats Italy four matches to one to win the Davis Cup men's professional tennis championship for the second year in a row.

Differences between Islamic fundamentalists and those eager to promote a greater economic role for women result in violent clashes in Bangladesh.

•

Americans begin voting for one of six designs for a new gold-coloured one-dollar coin featuring Sacajawea, a 16-year-old Shoshone woman who traveled with the Lewis and Clark expedition through the Northwest in 1804–05, that will be introduced in 2000.

8

The severed heads of one New Zealand and three British telecommunications engineers who had been working on a Russian telephone-installation project with the support of the local Chechen authorities are found 40 km (25 mi) south of Grozny, the Chechen capital; the bodies are recovered some weeks later.

•

The AT&T Corp. announces that it will acquire the global data network of the International Business Machines Corp. for $5 billion in cash.

9

The British pharmaceutical firm Zeneca Group PLC plans to merge with the large Swedish firm Astra AB to form AstraZeneca, the world's fourth largest drug company, with an estimated $14 billion in sales.

•

Commemorating the 50th anniversary of the international convention against genocide, the United Nations General Assembly resolves for the first time to consider anti-Semitism as a form of racism.

•

Ruth Dreifuss is elected president of Switzerland by the Swiss Federal Assembly, the first woman and the first Jew to hold the position.

•

It is announced in Johannesburg, S.Af., that a virtually complete 3.5 million-year-old skull and skeleton of an *Australopithecus* has been discovered at Sterkfontein by Ronald J. Clark of the University of the Witwatersrand, Johannesburg.

•

Spanish poet José Hierro is awarded the Cervantes Prize for lifetime achievement in literature.

10

On the 50th anniversary of the Universal Declaration of Human Rights, the United Nations Human Rights Prizes go to activists on five

continents: Sunila Abeyesekera of Sri Lanka, Angelina Acheng Atyam of Uganda, former president Jimmy Carter of the U.S., José Gregori of Brazil, and Anna Sabatova of the Czech Republic.

•

During its 50th anniversary assembly in Harare, Zimbabwe, the World Council of Churches rejects the membership application of the Celestial Church of Christ, established in Nigeria in 1947 and claiming more than five million members, because some of the church's longer-serving clergy have more than one wife.

11

The Judiciary Committee of the U.S. House of Representatives votes in favour of impeachment of Pres. Bill Clinton on three counts; a fourth count is approved on December 12, and the recommendation is forwarded to the full House (*see* December 19).

•

Science magazine reports that researchers at the Sanger Centre, near Cambridge, Eng., and Washington University, St. Louis, Mo., have successfully transcribed the complete genetic code of an animal; the genome of the microscopic worm *Caenorhabditis elegans* reportedly contains 97 million chemical units and 19,099 genes.

•

Science also prints a report by scientists at Kinki University, Nara, Japan, stating that they have successfully cloned eight calves from cells gathered from a single adult cow (*see* December 16).

•

The Mars Climate Orbiter spacecraft is launched from Cape Canaveral, Florida; the craft and its mate, the Mars Polar Lander (scheduled for launch in January 1999), will study Martian weather and look for evidence of water on the planet.

12

Marc Hodler, a longtime International Olympic Committee official, alleges that four agents acting for a few of the 115 IOC members had for many years been "selling" blocs of votes to city organizations eager to win the fiercely competitive bidding to host the Olympic Games; Salt Lake City, Utah, site of the 2002 Winter Games, for example, reportedly paid $400,000 to several IOC officials in such a scheme.

•

Saving Private Ryan is chosen best film of the year by the Los Angeles Film Critics Association and its director, Steven Spielberg, best director; on December 16 the New York Film Critics Circle also chooses *Saving Private Ryan* as best picture but gives the director's award to Terrence Malick for *The Thin Red Line*.

13

The United States is defeated soundly by the International team 20½–11½ in the Presidents Cup professional golf tournament at the Royal Melbourne Golf Club in Australia.

•

Ty Murray of Stephenville, Texas, wins a record seventh world all-round cowboy title at the National Finals Rodeo in Las Vegas, Nev.

14

The Canadian Ministry of Finance announces that it will not approve two planned major bank mergers that would have left the country's financial industry concentrated in too few institutions (*see* January 23, April 17).

•

The General Motors Corp. announces that it has appointed Cynthia M. Trudell chairwoman and president of its Saturn operations, the first woman in any auto company to head a car division.

15

Günter Dreyer, director of the German Archaeological Institute in Egypt, announces the discovery in the tomb of Egyptian King Scorpion I about 500 km (310 mi) south of Cairo of clay tablets containing what is believed to be the earliest example of writing.

•

British magazine publishing firm Emap PLC says it will acquire the American Peterson Companies Inc., publisher of magazines for young men, for $1.2 billion.

16

President Clinton calls for air strikes against Iraq, citing the continued refusal of that country to permit UN arms inspectors to do their work; the operation, called Desert Fox, is joined by Great Britain and continues for four days.

•

Because of the attacks on Iraq, Republican leaders in the U.S. Congress postpone the vote to impeach President Clinton that was to have begun on December 17.

•

Researchers at Kyunghee University, Seoul, S.Kor., report that they have taken the first step toward cloning a human being by combining an egg and a cell from an infertile woman and creating a four-cell embryo (*see* December 11).

17

The World Meteorological Organization reports that in 1998, for the 20th year in a row, the surface temperature of the Earth has been higher than the average of recent years; 1998 is the warmest year on record.

•

Without changing its claims to sovereignty over the Falkland Islands, Great Britain eases the arms embargo against Argentina that it imposed in April 1982 at the time of the Argentine invasion of the islands, known as the Islas Malvinas in Spanish.

•

The nomination of Jacques-Édouard Alexis as prime minister of Haiti is ratified by the Chamber of Deputies; final approval of his program and his government is still required.

18

It is announced in Lusaka, Zambia, that the Anglo American Corp. of South Africa mining company will purchase three large state-owned copper mines in the country.

19

The U.S. House of Representatives impeaches President Clinton on two articles of perjury and obstruction of justice; two other articles do not pass.

AP/WIDE WORLD/GERMAN ARCHAEOLOGICAL INSTITUTE

Ancient Egyptian clay tablets: December 15

Pres. Bill Clinton
and Democratic
leaders:
December 19

Speaking during the impeachment hearings in the House of Representatives, Robert L. Livingston announces that he will not stand for the post of speaker of the House and will leave Congress in six months' time; on December 17 Livingston had admitted having had past extramarital affairs.

20

Nkem Chukwu, a native of Nigeria, completes her delivery of octuplets—two boys and six girls with a total weight of 4.45 kg (9.8 lb)—in a hospital in Houston, Texas; this is the first case of octuplets' being born alive, but the smallest girl dies on December 27.

21

Israeli Prime Minister Benjamin Netanyahu yields to pressure from within his party and from the opposition, acknowledges the end of his government, and agrees to call early elections in 1999.

•

Four days of icy temperatures grip southern California, destroying as much as one-third of the valuable citrus crop.

22

Unable to compete with the better-funded and better-publicized Women's National Basketball Association, the American Basketball League terminates its schedule partway through the third season and says it will file for bankruptcy.

23

The Belgian Supreme Court finds some of the best-known names in Europe's military-industrial sector, including French military aircraft manufacturer Serge Dassault, the Belgian former secretary-general of NATO, Willy Claes, and former officials of the Belgian Defense Ministry, guilty of corruption in connection with military contracts.

•

Trade and Industry Minister Peter Mandelson, a close adviser of British Prime Minister Tony Blair, resigns after it is revealed that he improperly accepted a large personal loan from a wealthy businessman whose activities came under investigation by Mandelson's ministry.

•

The government of the U.S. expels three Cuban diplomats for spying; the three were linked to the arrests of 10 suspected Cuban agents in Miami, Fla., in September.

24

A two-month cease-fire in the Serbian province of Kosovo goes up in flames as Serbian units mount a concerted attack on Kosovo Liberation Army positions in the northern part of the province (*see* October 13).

25

Presidents Boris Yeltsin of Russia and Alyaksandr G. Lukashenka of Belarus agree to begin integrating the two countries' economies closely and work toward a common currency in 1999.

Yet another attempt at a nonstop circumnavigation of the globe in a hot-air balloon fails as the *ICO Global Challenge,* with American balloonist Steve Fossett, British businessman Richard Branson, and Per Lindstrand of Sweden aboard, dips into the Pacific near Hawaii.

26

A UN-chartered plane carrying 14 people crashes near Huambo, Angola; Angolan government spokesmen claim it was shot down by rebel National Union for the Total Independence of Angola guerrillas.

•

A storm with 145-km/h (90-mph) winds devastates the Sydney-to-Hobart yacht race off Australia's southeast coast, killing six sailors; the race continues, however, and the American 24.4-m (80-ft) maxi *Sayonara* finishes first on December 29.

27

In a clampdown on human rights activities in the country and in the fourth such ruling in a week, a court in China condemns an activist to a 10-year prison term for having provided information about antigovernment demonstrations to Radio Free Asia, a U.S.-financed radio station.

28

The 25th anniversary of the Endangered Species Act is noted; some 1,135 species of animals remain on the Endangered Species List.

Preliminary data released by the Boston Consulting Group and shop.org, which monitored Internet retail sales during the holiday season, indicate shoppers made purchases of $5 billion via their computers, a figure more than two times higher than predicted and four times higher than during the corresponding period in 1997.

•

The market value of Charles Schwab Corp. has reached $25.5 billion, which puts it in second place among stock brokerages, behind Morgan Stanley Dean Witter & Co.; Schwab's dramatic rise is attributed to its successful Internet trading strategy.

•

In a matter of a few hours, five coaches of National

Football League teams are fired: Dom Capers of the Carolina Panthers, Ray Rhodes of the Philadelphia Eagles, Dennis Erickson of the Seattle Seahawks, Dave Wannstedt of the Chicago Bears, and Ted Marchibroda of the Baltimore Ravens.

29

Cambodian Prime Minister Hun Sen welcomes Khieu Samphan and Nuon Chea, two top Khmer Rouge leaders who abandoned their opposition movement on December 26, back into Cambodian life; many in the country feel the Khmer Rouge leaders should be tried for crimes against the people, especially during the period when they ruled the country in the late 1970s.

•

Russia fails to pay the $362 million due on a loan from a group of commercial banks; many fear that the country may simply begin defaulting on other financial obligations (*see* November 4).

•

Four British and Australian citizens are killed—but it is not clear by which side—as Yemeni government forces attack the headquarters of an Islamic militant gang that had kidnapped them and 12 other tourists on December 28.

30

Rebels in Sierra Leone take two important towns in the northern part of the country and approach Freetown, the capital; some reports claim the rebels now control the entire northern province (*see* March 10).

•

Several days of fighting between the left-wing Revolutionary Armed Forces of Colombia and a right-wing paramilitary United Self-Defense Forces of Colombia in northern Colombia have resulted in at least 30 people dead, including noncombatants.

•

Several days of religious violence between radical Hindu organizations and evangelical Christian congregations in India's Gujarat state lead to the destruction of a church in Madalbari village.

31

In Brussels officials of the European Union fix the final rates of exchange for the currencies of 11 countries that will adopt the euro as official tender on Jan. 1, 1999.

•

According to estimates published by the U.S. Bureau of the Census on December 29, the country's population stands at 271,645,214, an increase of 2,500,000 over the year.

•

The year 1998 becomes slightly longer than 1997 as one "leap second" is added to the old year at the stroke of midnight Universal Time (7:00 PM, U.S. Eastern Standard Time).

A Christian woman in front of a burned Christian church in India: December 30

57

Disasters

The loss of life and property from disasters in 1998 included the following:

Aviation

January 13, Southwestern Pakistan. An Afghan cargo plane carrying 51 persons, including members of the Islamic Taliban militia, ran out of fuel and slammed into a mountainside in a remote area; there were no survivors.

January 28, Thandwe, Myanmar (Burma). A passenger plane spun out of control during take-off and crashed; 14 persons were killed.

STEVE SENNE—AP/WIDE WORLD

A trio of Canadian Army soldiers combs the rocky shore near Blandford, Nova Scotia, in search of debris from the crash of Swissair Flight 111. The airliner went down in the Atlantic Ocean off the coast of Nova Scotia on September 2.

February 2, Southern Philippines. An airliner en route to Cagayan de Oro crashed on a mountain about 45 km (28 mi) northeast of its destination; all 104 persons aboard the craft, including 5 crew members, perished.

February 3, Cavalese, Italy. A low-flying U.S. military jet cut the cable of a ski lift on a resort in the Dolomite Mountains, sending a cable car hurtling some 80 m (260 ft) to the ground; all 20 passengers aboard the cable car were killed; it was later determined that the jet had strayed off course during a training flight and was flying at far below the approved minimum altitude.

February 12, Southern Sudan. At least 13 persons, including First Vice Pres. Al-Zubeir Mohammed Saleh and other Sudanese senior government officials, died when their plane went down in bad weather during a tour of southern war zones.

February 16, Taipei, Taiwan. While attempting to land in heavy fog, an airliner slammed into several houses and erupted in flames; all 197 persons aboard the craft were killed, along with at least 9 persons on the ground.

March 20, Near Kabul, Afg. Bad weather was blamed when a Boeing 727 crashed into a mountain, killing all 45 persons aboard.

March 29, Piura, Peru. An air force plane transporting civilians fleeing El Niño-driven floods lost power in one of its engines and crashed into a canal; at least 28 persons died.

April 20, Bogotá, Colom. A Boeing 727 carrying 52 persons hit a fog-shrouded mountain shortly after takeoff; there were no survivors.

May 5, Northeastern Peru. An air force plane being used to transport workers to an oil camp in a remote Amazon jungle plummeted into a swamp about five kilometres (three miles) short of its destination; of the 87 persons aboard, 13 survived.

May 12, Southeastern Mauritania. A military transport plane crashed during a sandstorm; 36 of the 38 persons aboard were killed.

May 26, Northern Mongolia. A passenger plane carrying 28 persons crashed shortly after takeoff; there were no survivors.

June 4, East Timor. An Indonesian military helicopter crashed on a mountain in conditions of poor visibility; of the 12 persons aboard, one survived.

June 18, Near Montreal. A commuter plane caught fire after takeoff, then exploded while attempting to make an emergency landing; all 11 persons aboard were killed.

July 30, Off the coast of Quiberon, France. A collision between two small planes, one of which had deviated from its flight plan to fly over the giant cruise ship *Norway,* claimed the lives of all 15 persons aboard the two craft.

August 23, Dominica. A charter plane carrying 11 persons crashed in bad weather in the northeastern part of the island; there were no survivors.

August 24, Northern Laos. An airliner crashed on a mountain during bad weather; at least 33 persons were believed dead.

August 29, Quito, Ecuador. After bursting into flames on takeoff, an airliner plowed through airport fences and into a nearby field where children were playing football (soccer); of the 90 persons aboard the plane, 69 perished, and 10 on the ground were killed.

September 2, Off the coast of Nova Scotia. An airliner en route to Geneva with 229 persons aboard crashed into icy waters after the pilot reported smoke in the cabin; the plane had been attempting to make an emergency landing at Halifax International Airport when it disappeared from radar screens; there were no survivors.

September 4, Southern Nevada. Two air force helicopters collided during a nighttime training mission over a remote mountainous area; all 12 crew members aboard the two choppers were killed.

September 25, Northern Morocco. A Spanish passenger plane crashed into a hillside near the Mediterranean coast, killing all 38 persons on board.

November 1, Southwestern Guatemala. A plane flying through heavy rain crashed into a mountain, killing 12 doctors who were on their way to perform medical relief work in the aftermath of Hurricane Mitch; six persons survived the crash.

December 11, Southern Thailand. An airliner attempting to land in bad weather went down in a flooded rubber plantation; at least 44 persons perished.

Fires and Explosions

Mid–late January, Abuja, Nigeria. At least 28 persons were killed by explosions of adulterated fuel; a mixture of kerosene and gasoline (petrol), the fuel was sold on the black market to unwitting residents of Abuja's shantytowns, who attempted to use it for cooking and lighting; another 80 persons suffered severe burns from the blasts.

January 24, Hebei province, China. In separate incidents fireworks vendors demonstrating their wares in outdoor markets before the Chinese New Year celebration inadvertently set off two huge explosions that killed 47 persons and injured dozens of others.

February 15, Yaoundé, Cameroon. An explosion at the site of a derailed train that had spilled its oil cargo claimed the lives of 120 persons and injured more than 150 others; the blast was thought to have occurred after someone lit a cigarette.

March 22, Miles township, Pa. An early-morning fire engulfed a mountain cabin where 11 youths on a weekend outing were sleeping; there were no survivors; the cause of the fire was undetermined.

March 26, Mombasa, Kenya. A blaze sparked by an electrical fault at a girls' boarding school claimed the lives of 26 students.

May 5, Central Mexico. A forest fire blamed on dry weather conditions brought on by El Niño claimed the lives of 19 volunteer firefighters who were battling the blaze.

May 14, Jakarta, Indon. A fire set during violent street riots swept through a five-story shopping mall; at least 110 persons were killed.

May 16, Near Islamabad, Pak. Material used to manufacture fireworks exploded during a fire and caused the collapse of the three-story building where the material was stored; at least 13 persons were killed.

June 8, Palembang, Indon. A fire that started on the second floor of a shopping mall quickly swept through the building; at least 50 persons were believed dead.

October 17, Southern Nigeria. Hundreds of people were scavenging gasoline from holes in a state-owned pipeline when the pipeline exploded, igniting a huge fire that burned for several days; more than 700 persons died, and some 300 were injured.

October 30, Göteborg, Swed. A fire raced through an overcrowded discotheque where hundreds of young people had gathered for a Halloween party; 63 persons were killed, and some 190 were seriously injured.

December 3, Manila. A fire believed to have been caused by faulty electrical wiring engulfed a wooden building that housed an orphanage and child-care centre; at least 30 persons, mostly children, were killed.

Marine

January 16, Off the coast of Newfoundland. A freighter registered in Cyprus broke in half for unknown reasons and sank near the islands of St. Pierre and Miquelon; 15 persons lost their lives, but 4 men survived the disaster by clinging to an overturned lifeboat until rescue helicopters arrived.

January 21, Lake Victoria, Uganda. A boat loaded with fishermen and traders overturned near the Buvuma Islands; 17 persons drowned, and 13 were missing and feared dead.

March 15, Southeastern Bangladesh. Two overcrowded ferries capsized on a river after being caught in a storm; at least 50 persons perished.

March 31, Off the coast of Yemen. A boat crowded with Somali refugees sank in the Gulf of Aden, killing some 180 persons; 2 passengers and the 6-man crew survived.

April 3, Near Kwamouth, Democratic Republic of the Congo. Two barges overloaded with passengers and cargo collided on the Kasai River; nearly 40 persons drowned.

April 4, Off the coast of Nigeria. An overcrowded ferry capsized in rough waters; as many as 280 persons were feared dead.

April 24, Southern Nicaragua. A boat carrying a group of U.S.-bound Ecuadorians capsized in rough waters in Lake Nicaragua and sank; of the 20 persons aboard, one survived.

May 30, Northern India. At least 22 persons drowned when their boat capsized in the Chenab River about 122 km (75 mi) north of Jammu.

June, California. An overabundance of melting snow in the Sierra Nevadas turned rivers into dangerous torrents; 11 whitewater rafters lost their lives.

June 5, Guangdong province, China. An overcrowded ferry capsized in the middle of a river, killing at least 20 persons.

June 8, Bermuda. A boat overloaded with Haitian refugees capsized when passengers rushed to one side of the vessel after police fired warning shots over the bow, and at least 30 persons drowned; reports that police had hit the boat were unconfirmed.

July 5, Comoros. A makeshift boat overloaded with refugees from Anjouan who were attempting to reach the French-governed island of Mayotte capsized, killing 16 persons.

July 26, Off the coast of Tamil Nadu, India. A boat carrying Sri Lankan refugees capsized after developing a leak; 45 persons were feared dead.

Late August, Bihar, India. A boat capsized after being caught in a whirlpool on the Lakhandei River; at least 35 persons drowned.

September 19, Manila Bay, Philippines. A large Philippine interisland ferry sank in stormy weather, possibly after its heavy cargo shifted and caused the vessel to tilt to one side; 43 persons were killed, and 48 were missing and feared dead.

Early October, Northern Nigeria. An overloaded ferry capsized on a river and sank, killing 73 persons.

October 8, Northern Spain. A tour boat loaded past capacity sank in Lake Banyoles; 20 persons, most of them French retirees, perished.

October 23, Northern India. An overcrowded boat capsized on a swiftly flowing river; 10 persons were killed, and 27 were missing.

Mining

January 16, Southern Yugoslavia. A methane gas explosion at a coal mine claimed the lives of 29 miners and injured 19.

January 18, Vorkuta, Russia. A methane gas explosion at a coal mine caused a tunnel to collapse and sparked an underground fire; 27 miners were presumed dead.

January 24, Liaoning province, China. A powerful gas explosion at one of China's largest coal mines killed 77 miners and injured 8.

February 11, Western Bolivia. A mud slide attributed to heavy rain brought on by El Niño buried a gold mine in the Tipuani Mountains near the Peruvian border; at least 50 persons were killed.

April 4, Donetsk, Ukraine. A buildup of methane gas was the cause of an explosion at a coal mine; 63 miners lost their lives.

April 6, Henan province, China. A series of gas explosions at a coal mine killed at least 59 miners and left 25 missing.

April 12, Mbuguni, Tanz. Flash floods induced by heavy rains caused 14 shafts at the Mererani tanzanite mines to collapse; at least 100 miners were feared dead.

May 13, Sichuan province, China. A gas explosion at a coal mine killed at least 14 miners and injured more than 10.

June 14, Southern Niger. Heavy rains were the apparent cause of a cave-in at a gold mine about 60 km (35 mi) southwest of Niamey; more than 30 miners were killed.

July 17, Lassing, Austria. A mud slide snapped the cable of an underground elevator in a talc mine, stranding 10 men who were attempting to rescue a miner who had been trapped by an earlier mud slide; the 10 rescuers perished, but the miner trapped earlier was pulled out alive on July 26.

August 16, Luhansk, Ukraine. A powerful methane gas explosion ripped through a coal mine, killing at least 24 miners and injuring 4.

Late October, Guangxi province, China. A flash flood swept through two coal mines that had been closed for the rainy season but illegally reopened; 36 miners perished.

November 29, Yunnan province, China. A gas explosion at a state-run coal mine killed at least 38 miners and injured 18.

November 30, Northern Vietnam. A gold mine collapsed after heavy rainfall; at least 25 miners died.

Natural

January 2, Northern Spain and western France. Powerful storm winds were responsible for blowing cars off roads, toppling buildings, interrupting electricity, and creating high waves along coastlines; at least 18 persons lost their lives.

Early January, Northern Bangladesh. An unusual cold spell claimed the lives of more than 130 persons, many of whom were homeless.

Early January, Western Canada and Montana. At least 10 persons were killed by avalanches in the Rocky Mountains.

January, Peru. The worst flooding in Peru in 50 years left some 70 persons dead and 22,000 homeless; the torrential rain that caused the floods was blamed on El Niño.

January 5–11, Eastern Canada and northeastern U.S. A severe ice storm swept through Quebec, Ontario, and New Brunswick and parts of Maine, New Hampshire, Vermont, and New York; more than three million homes were without power, some for two weeks or more, and at least 20 persons died.

January 10, Hebei province, China. An earthquake of magnitude 6.2 claimed the lives of at least 50 persons and injured more than 10,000.

Mid-January, Kenya. Floods triggered by unseasonal downpours killed at least 86 persons and caused extensive damage across the country.

January 20, Central Mozambique. A landslide brought on by heavy rains destroyed mountain settlements in Zambezia province; at least 26 persons were killed, and some 60 were missing.

January 23, Near Les Orres, France. An avalanche in the French Alps claimed the lives of 11 persons on a school outing.

February 4, Northeastern Afghanistan. An earthquake of magnitude 6.1 and subsequent tremors killed some 4,500 persons and left 30,000 homeless.

February 23, Central Florida. Tornadoes killed at least 42 persons, injured more than 260, and left hundreds homeless.

February 23, Tajikistan. An avalanche buried a house in a mountainous area about 100 km (60 mi) east of Dushanbe; of the 12 persons inside the house, only one survived.

February 27, Aobamba, Peru. About 40 workers digging a canal in the Andes were swept to their death by a mud slide brought on by weeks of heavy rain.

March 3–4, Baluchistan, Pak. Flash floods claimed the lives of 300 persons; 1,500 were missing and presumed dead, and some 25,000 were left homeless.

March 4, Rio Cana, Ecuador. A mud slide that followed days of torrential rain buried a mountain village; at least 17 persons were killed.

March 7, Near Kabul, Afg. An avalanche near the Salang Pass in the Hindu Kush Mountains killed at least 70 persons.

March 20, Georgia and North Carolina. Tornadoes killed at least 14 persons and injured 80 in northern Georgia; 2 persons were killed and at least 22 injured by a tornado in North Carolina.

Late March, Eastern India. A cyclone devastated several villages in the states of West Bengal and Orissa; at least 200 persons died, and some 10,000 were left homeless.

March 31, Thangu, India. Strong wind triggered an avalanche that buried an army camp in northern Sikkim state; 19 soldiers were killed.

Early April, Iran. Floods across the country claimed the lives of 100 persons.

Early–mid-April, Southern U.S. Tornadoes ripped through parts of Mississippi, Alabama, and Georgia on April 8–9, leaving 39 persons dead; on April 16 two tornadoes claimed the lives of at least 10 persons in Kentucky, Tennessee, and Arkansas.

Mid–late April, Argentina and Paraguay. Massive flooding along the Paraná basin caused extensive damage and forced some 100,000 persons to evacuate their homes; at least 18 persons lost their lives.

Early May, Southern Italy. A river of mud swamped the mountain town of Sarno and nearby villages after torrential rains; at least 135 persons were killed.

May–early June, India. A severe heat wave, India's worst in 50 years, claimed the lives of at least 2,500 persons; more than 1,000 deaths occurred in Orissa.

Mourners gather at a funeral for Ukrainian miners killed on April 4 in an explosion at a coal mine in Donetsk. In what was described as the worst mining disaster in Ukraine since the breakup of the Soviet Union, 63 miners perished.

May 20, Central Bolivia. An earthquake of magnitude 6.8 destroyed the towns of Aiquile and Totora and killed at least 105 persons.

May 22, Southeastern Bangladesh. A cyclone struck coastal areas, killing at least 25 persons and injuring more than 100.

May 30, Northern Afghanistan. A magnitude-6.9 earthquake destroyed some 60 villages and killed at least 5,000 persons.

June–July, Texas. A blistering heat wave claimed the lives of 110 persons.

June–August, Northeastern China. Widespread flooding along the Chang Jiang (Yangtze River) caused $20 billion in damage and claimed the lives of 3,656 persons, according to a senior government official; the floods affected an estimated 230 million residents.

June 9, Western India. The most powerful cyclone to hit India in 25 years struck the coast in Gujarat state; according to an official report, more than 100 persons were missing and feared dead.

Mid–June, Northern Romania. Floods triggered by heavy rain were responsible for the deaths of 21 persons.

June 27, Southern Turkey. An earthquake of magnitude 6.3 claimed the lives of at least 129 persons and injured more than 1,000.

Late June, Midwestern and eastern U.S. Thunderstorms, floods, and tornadoes occurred from Wisconsin to West Virginia and along the Appalachian Mountains as far north as Vermont; at least 21 persons lost their lives, including 11 in Ohio.

July, Uzbekistan and Kyrgyzstan. Massive flooding claimed the lives of at least 115 persons.

July–August, South Korea. Floods brought on by record rainfalls left 234 persons dead and 91 missing; more than 121,000 persons were homeless.

July 9, Azores. A magnitude-5.8 earthquake rocked the Portuguese islands in the North Atlantic Ocean; 10 persons were killed, and 90 were injured.

In the town of Yueyang in China's Hunan province, a man gazes out at houses flooded by the overflowing Chang Jiang (Yangtze River). In 1998 epic floods occurred throughout northeastern China from June–August.

Mid-July–mid-September, Bangladesh. Extraordinarily heavy monsoonal rains left more than two-thirds of the country under water; at least 1,000 persons died, and more than 30 million persons lost their homes.

July 17, Papua New Guinea. A tsunami struck the northern coast, killing at least 2,500 persons and destroying several villages.

Late July, Eastern Slovakia. Floods triggered by severe storms claimed the lives of at least 21 persons.

Early August, Cyprus. A severe heat wave was responsible for the deaths of 48 persons, many of whom were elderly.

Early–mid-August, Yemen. Floods produced by torrential rains killed at least 30 persons across the country.

Mid-August–early September, Northern and eastern India. Floods and landslides claimed the lives of at least 1,000 persons.

August 23–24, Southern Texas and northern Mexico. Flooding along the rain-swollen Rio Grande left 16 persons dead and more than 60 missing.

August 26, Northern Guatemala. A mud slide that swamped several mountain villages killed at least 25 persons and forced 4,000 from their homes.

Late August, Northern Japan. Landslides and floods related to Typhoon Rex left 11 persons dead and 5 missing; 40,000 persons were forced to evacuate their homes.

Early September, Southern Mexico. Floods produced by days of heavy rain killed at least 185 persons in the state of Chiapas; some 25,000 were left homeless.

September–October, The Sudan. Heavy flooding along the Nile River destroyed more than 120,000 homes and left at least 200,000 persons homeless; at least 88 persons died, including 63 Sudanese herdsman who were swept away in a flash flood on October 12 in the state of Kordofan.

September 21–28, Carribean and U.S. Gulf Coast. With winds of up to 193 km/h (120 mph), Hurricane Georges devastated the region, causing extensive damage and at least 300 deaths in the Caribbean, including some 250 in the Dominican Republic and at least 27 in Haiti; the hurricane also pounded parts of Louisiana, Mississippi, Alabama, and Florida, dumping heavy rain and causing 4 deaths.

Late September–early October, South Korea. According to government officials, Tropical Storm Yanni flooded a quarter of the country's cropland and left at least 27 persons dead and 28 missing.

October 1, Tenextepango, Mex. A week of heavy rain in central Mexico triggered a mud slide that killed 12 persons.

Mid-October, Philippines, Taiwan, and Japan. Typhoon Zeb wreaked havoc on its sweep through Asia, killing at least 74 persons in the Philippines, 25 in Taiwan, and at least 12 in Japan.

October 17–18, Texas. Heavy rain left one-quarter of the state under water; at least 22 persons died in the floods, including 6 in San Antonio.

October 20–22, Central Vietnam. Floods caused by heavy downpours claimed the lives of 52 persons and caused extensive damage.

Late October, Central America. Powerful Hurricane Mitch tore through the region, producing torrential rain and creating winds as high as 240 km/h (150 mph); considered the worst Atlantic basin hurricane in 200 years, Mitch caused extensive damage and left more than 1.5 million persons homeless; the number of confirmed deaths reached 6,500 in Honduras, 1,845 in Nicaragua, 239 in El Salvador, 253 in Guatemala, 8 in Costa Rica, and 2 in Panama; an additional 12,000 persons in the region had disappeared.

Late October, Philippines. Typhoon Babs cut a destructive swath through the country, triggering landslides and floods and claiming the lives of at least 132 persons; some 320,000 persons were left homeless.

Mid-November, Western Ukraine. Floods in the Carpathian Mountains destroyed some 30 villages and forced at least 8,000 persons from their homes; at least 12 persons died.

Mid–late November, Europe. An intense cold wave claimed the lives of at least 71 persons across the continent, including 36 in Poland.

November 19–23, Central Vietnam. Typhoon Dawn, the worst storm to hit the region in 30 years, triggered devastating floods that forced some 200,000 persons from their homes; more than a hundred persons were killed.

Mid-December, Central Vietnam. At least 22 deaths were blamed on Tropical Storms Faith and Gil, which dumped heavy rain on the region; thousands were displaced.

December 15, Umtata, S.Af. A tornado killed at least 17 persons and injured at least 162.

Railroad

January 5, Near Lucknow, India. A passenger train sped through a red light in thick fog and plowed into the back of an express train, which had stopped after hitting a nilgai (Indian antelope); 54 persons were killed, and 64 were injured.

March 6, Central Finland. An express passenger train derailed as it was slowing before a station stop; 11 persons were killed, including an engineer, and 39 were injured.

April 24, Near Bombay. Several cars of a freight train detached from the main body and rolled to hit a stationary passenger train; at least 24 persons lost their lives.

May 10, Eastern Bangladesh. A passenger train crashed into a cargo train stopped at a station; 17 persons were killed, and 26 were injured.

May 22, Near Blantyre, Malawi. A passenger train derailed on a steep hill after a brake failure; 20 persons were killed, and more than 200 were injured.

June 3, Near Eschede, Ger. A high-speed Inter-City Express (ICE) train traveling at 200 km/h (125 mph) derailed and slammed into a concrete overpass, and at least 100 persons were killed; a faulty wheel was determined to have caused the derailment.

August 13, Near Karur, India. At a railway crossing a train rammed into a crowded bus that apparently had stalled on the tracks after crashing through a warning gate; 19 persons were killed.

October 18, Kafr ad-Dawwar, Egypt. A passenger train derailed when its driver changed tracks at high speed, and the train then plowed into a crowded market square; 47 persons were killed.

November 26, Northwestern India. A collision between two trains claimed the lives of at least 205 persons.

Traffic

January 3, Near Jhelum, Pak. A multiple pileup involving an oil tanker, a truck, and an overcrowded bus claimed the lives of at least 50 persons.

January 7, Central Kenya. A bus plunged off a bridge into a river after the driver lost control of the vehicle; at least 54 persons were killed.

January 13, West Bengal, India. A school bus skidded off a road and plummeted into a river after the driver lost control of the vehicle in a thick fog; at least 66 persons died.

January 14, Near La Paz, Bol. A truck carrying farmers headed to La Paz to sell coca leaves overturned while crossing the Andes, possibly because of brake problems; 28 persons lost their lives.

February 14, Near Amritsar, India. A minibus carrying members of a wedding party fell from a road into a canal; at least 28 persons died.

February 21, Nagoan, India. A collision between a bus and a truck claimed the lives of at least 16 persons.

February 26, Near Lokoja, Nigeria. A bus crashed into a ditch after losing a tire; 40 persons were killed.

March 2, Binh Dinh province, Vietnam. An overcrowded bus crashed through the railings of a bridge and fell into a lake, apparently after it attempted to pass a truck; some 50 persons were feared dead.

April 3, Southern Turkey. A collision between a bus and a fuel tanker near the Syrian border claimed the lives of at least 32 Iranians who were making the annual pilgrimage to Mecca.

April 15, Near Newcastle, S.Af. A multiple pileup involving a school bus, horse and trailer,

Rescue workers near Eschede, Ger., search for survivors of a railroad disaster on June 3. The incident occurred when a faulty wheel caused a high-speed train to derail.

minibus, car, and taxi occurred in rainy weather on a stretch of open road; 31 persons were killed, and at least 50 were injured.

April 26, Near Villafranqueza, Spain. A tour bus full of senior citizens overturned while trying to stop on a rain-slickened bridge, then rolled off the side and slid down an embankment; 10 persons were killed, and 38 were injured.

May 3, Northern Tanzania. An overcrowded bus attempting to cross a flooded bridge was swept away by a rain-swollen river; 72 persons perished.

May 7, Near Kishtwar, India. A bus skidded off a road and fell into a gorge; at least 17 persons were killed.

May 26, Near Tehran. A bus plunged into a reservoir after the driver lost control of the vehicle; 18 persons died.

June 27, Near Lima, Peru. A crowded bus traveling in fog plummeted off a steep cliff; 18 persons were killed.

July 5, Northern India. A truck overloaded with worshipers returning from a prayer meeting at a Hindu temple fell 100 m (330 ft) into a ravine; at least 27 persons died.

July 9, Near Tibba Sultanpur, Pak. A head-on collision between two buses claimed the lives of 18 persons and injured 50.

July 19, Near Catulaca, Honduras. A fire aboard a bus claimed the lives of at least 17 passengers and injured 18; reports that the fire was sparked by fuel inside the bus or by a short circuit were unconfirmed.

July 26, North West province, S.Af. A collision between a bus and a truck on a sharp curve claimed the lives of 19 persons and injured more than 60.

August 6, Northeastern Brazil. Before dawn a bus plowed into a group of passengers from another bus as the group stood on a highway after its vehicle had broken down; 12 persons died.

August 11, Near San Salvador, El Salvador. A collision between a bus and a truck claimed the lives of at least 16 persons and injured 20.

August 17, Near Jakarta, Indon. A crowded bus skidded off a highway and plunged into a ditch; at least 26 persons were killed.

August 29, Near Papallacta, Ecuador. A truck carrying 50 persons fell over a cliff; 33 persons were killed.

September 8, Southeastern Brazil. A fuel tanker overturned on a highway and was hit from behind

by a truck transporting liquor, which ignited a fire that engulfed the vehicles as well as two charter buses; at least 57 persons were killed, and dozens were injured.

September 18, Northeastern Egypt. A collision occurred between a tourist bus and a truck on a desert road between Cairo and Suez; 14 persons were killed, and 36 were injured.

September 24, Northern Peru. An overcrowded truck went over a cliff high in the Andes, apparently after its motor failed on a steep mountainside and the vehicle rolled backward out of control; 26 persons, mostly schoolchildren, were killed, and 15 were injured.

October 4, Eastern Ghana. A bus collided head-on with a fuel tanker; 15 persons perished.

October 14, Central India. A bus plummeted from a bridge into the Karam River in the state of Madhya Pradesh after the driver lost control of the vehicle; at least 45 persons died.

October 17, Southern Brazil. A head-on collision between two buses on a winding highway in the state of Parana claimed the lives of at least 14 persons.

November 5, Near Cuttack, India. A crowded bus careened off a bridge into a river after the driver of the bus attempted to pass another vehicle on the bridge; at least 43 persons were killed.

November 8, Southern Thailand. A van carrying a Thai dance troupe crashed into a roadside utility pole in the province of Prachub Khirikhan; all 12 persons in the van were killed.

Early December, Near Dhangai, India. A collision between a bus and an oil tanker claimed the lives of at least 26 persons.

December 26, Anhui province, China. An explosion occurred following a collision between a bus and a truck loaded with detonators and fuses; at least 18 persons died.

Miscellaneous

April 9, Mina, Saudi Arabia. At least 118 persons died in a stampede on the last day of the hajj, the annual pilgrimage to Mecca; the stampede occurred as tens of thousands of Muslims made their way across a bridge to perform the sacred rite known as "stoning the devil."

Mid-April, Bangladesh. At least 72 persons died after drinking contaminated homemade liquor during Bengali New Year celebrations.

April 28, Panama City, Pan. An elevator plummeted 25 floors to the ground at the construction site of a high-rise building, and all 13 workers inside the elevator were killed; mechanical failure and overloading were blamed for the accident.

May 4, Northern India. At least 20 persons were electrocuted when a bicycle tied to the roof of the bus on which they were traveling touched a high-voltage electric wire.

June 25, Nalchik, Russia. A balcony collapsed onto the crowded floor of an indoor sports stadium during a wrestling tournament; 23 people were killed.

July 6, Mpumalanga province, S.Af. A bridge under construction collapsed when one of its supporting pillars buckled for unknown reasons; 25 persons were feared dead.

July 13, Western Kenya. Villagers near the site where a fuel tanker overturned on a road were looting the vehicle's liquid when someone's lit cigarette ignited an explosion; 10 persons were killed, and more than 50 suffered serious burns.

August 3, Bombay (Mumbai). The collapse of a seven-story apartment building claimed the lives of at least 30 persons.

Late August, New Delhi. At least 40 persons died and hundreds were hospitalized after they ate food cooked in contaminated mustard oil.

September 5, Osasco, Braz. The roof of a church collapsed during an early-morning vigil attended by some 1,300 worshipers; at least 20 persons were killed, and more than 500 were injured.

Mid-September–Mid-November, Cabo Delgado province, Mozambique. At least 33 persons died after they ate fish contaminated with pesticides; authorities said the contamination occurred when unscrupulous fishermen dumped pesticides into waters where they fished to increase their catch.

October 28, Kasai province, Democratic Republic of the Congo. During a football (soccer) match a lightning bolt killed all 11 members of one team but left members of the opposing team unharmed, which led local investigators to conclude that witchcraft was responsible for the incident; more than 30 spectators were also injured, though none seriously.

December 16, Rome. A five-story apartment building collapsed during the night, apparently because of a structural fault; 23 persons were killed.

People of 1998

NOBEL PRIZES

Prize for Peace

In October 1998 the Norwegian Nobel Committee awarded its Nobel Prize for Peace to the two architects of the peace agreement that had been signed on April 10, 1998, in Northern Ireland—John Hume, the Roman Catholic leader of the nationalist Social Democratic and Labour Party (SDLP), and David Trimble, the Protestant leader of the Ulster Unionist Party (UUP). Thirty years of violence, short-lived cease-fires, and spasmodic secret negotiations had given way to a deal that held out the hope of sustained peace for the troubled British province. For most of those 30 years, Hume and Trimble had been enemies; eventually, however, they came to trust each other and ended up sharing the same platform as they campaigned for peace—something that would have been inconceivable for most of their political lives.

Hume, who was born Jan. 18, 1937, was brought up in poverty in Londonderry. He trained to be a priest but was attracted to politics by the civil rights movement in the late 1960s, when Northern Ireland's Catholic minority adopted the nonviolent tactics of the U.S. civil rights movement to protest against the discriminatory policies of the (mainly Protestant) Unionist rulers of the province. The violent suppression of this movement provoked hard-line nationalists to revive the Irish Republican Army (IRA). Hume, believing always in only peaceful and constitutional action, joined the SDLP; in 1973 he served briefly as commerce minister in the short-lived power-sharing assembly that was headed by the leader of the UUP and that collapsed in 1974. Five years later Hume became leader of the SDLP.

In 1988, after 20 years of violence and with no end in sight, Hume took an enormous risk by opening a private dialogue with Gerry Adams,

leader of Sinn Fein—the political wing of the IRA and the bitter rival of the SDLP in the contest to win the support of Northern Ireland's nationalist voters. Hume was frequently attacked by members of his own party for speaking to "the men of violence," but he persisted, believing that peace would come only when Adams could be persuaded to end the IRA's armed struggle—and when Adams could in turn persuade the rest of Sinn Fein and the IRA.

Trimble's trajectory toward peace was rather different. Born Oct. 15, 1944, into a middle-class Belfast family, he first ventured into politics in 1973 when he joined the Vanguard Party, which was established following the abolition of Northern Ireland's provincial parliament at Stormont. The party provided more militant opposition to British direct rule than that offered by the official UUP. As an active member of Vanguard, Trimble supported the strikes by Protestant workers that brought down the power-sharing assembly in which Hume had served.

In the mid-1970s Vanguard split, and Trimble, as part of its relatively moderate faction, joined the UUP. His opposition to any concession to Irish nationalism persisted, however; in 1985 he joined a newly formed organization, Ulster Clubs, which was dedicated to militant tactics to derail the 1985 Anglo-Irish accord designed to bring peace to the province. When the IRA called a cease-fire in 1994, Trimble opposed negotiations with Sinn Fein and warned his party not to make concessions to terrorism. In 1995 his record as a hard-liner helped him win a surprise victory in the contest to succeed James Molyneaux as leader of the UUP.

Once elected leader, however, he proved to be more thoughtful and less strident than expected. He agreed to take part in peace talks chaired by

former U.S. senator George Mitchell. The talks—which progressed slowly, primarily because the IRA in February 1996 had resumed violent struggle before agreeing to a "permanent" cease-fire in July 1997—embraced every political group in Northern Ireland, from Sinn Fein to the Protestant paramilitary groups and to the British and Irish governments. It was the dialogue between Hume and Trimble that was crucial, however. In the end, both men had enough credit with the more militant members of their communities to deliver the compromises that were inevitable to secure the agreement that became known as the "Good Friday" peace pact.   (PETER KELLNER)

Prize for Economics

Amartya Sen was awarded the 1998 Nobel Memorial Prize in Economic Science for his contributions to welfare economics and social choice and for his interest in the problems of society's poorest members. Sen was best known for his work on the causes of famine, which led to the development of practical solutions for preventing or limiting the effects of real or perceived shortages of food. The Royal Swedish Academy of Sciences noted that Sen's work "restored an ethical dimension to the discussion of vital economic problems." In recognizing his work on the social underpinnings of economics, the Nobel Committee broke with its tradition of the previous few years of awarding its prize to those researchers, most of them conservative, working in the field of market economics.

Welfare economics is the branch of economics that seeks to evaluate economic policies in terms of their effects on the well-being of the community. Sen, who devoted his career to such issues, had been called the "conscience of his profession." His influential monograph *Collective Choice and Social Welfare* (1970), which addressed problems such as individual rights, majority rule, and the availability of information about individual conditions, inspired many researchers to turn their attention to issues of basic welfare. Sen devised methods of measuring poverty that yielded information useful to improving economic conditions for the poor. His theoretical work on inequality provided an explanation for why there are fewer women than men in some poor countries in spite of the fact that more women than men are born and infant mortality is higher among males. Sen claimed that this skewed ratio results from the better health treatment and childhood opportunities afforded boys in those countries.

Sen's interest in famine stemmed from personal experience. As a nine-year-old boy, he witnessed the Bengal famine of 1943, in which three million people perished. This staggering loss of lives was unnecessary, Sen concluded, given that there was, he believed, an adequate food supply in India at the time. Its distribution was hindered, however, because particular groups of people—in this case rural labourers—lost their jobs and therefore their ability to purchase food. In his book *Poverty and Famines: An Essay on Entitlement and Deprivation* (1981), Sen revealed that in many cases of famine, food supplies were not significantly reduced. Instead, a number of social and economic factors, such as declining wages, unemployment, rising food prices, and poor food-distribution systems, led to starvation in certain groups in society.

David Trimble (left) and John Hume

Governments and international organizations handling food crises were influenced by Sen's work. His views encouraged policy makers to pay attention not only to alleviating immediate suffering but also to finding ways to replace the lost income of the poor, as, for example, through public-works projects, and to maintain stable prices for food. A vigorous defender of political freedom, Sen believed that famines do not occur in functioning democracies because their leaders must be more responsive to the demands of the citizens. In order for economic growth to be achieved, he argued, social reforms, such as improvements in education and public health, must precede economic reform.

Sen was born in Santiniketan, Bengal, India, on Nov. 3, 1933, and was educated at Presidency College in Calcutta. He went on to study at Trinity College, Cambridge, where he received his B.A. (1955), M.A. (1959), and Ph.D. (1959). While at Trinity he was awarded the Adam Smith Prize (1954), the Wrenbury Scholarship (1955), and the Stevenson Prize (1956). He taught economics at a number of universities in India and England, including the Universities of Jadavpur (1956–58) and Delhi (1963–71), the London School of Economics, University of London (1971–77), and the University of Oxford (1977–88), before moving to Harvard University (1988–98), where he was professor of economics and philosophy. In 1998 he was appointed to his current position as master of Trinity College, Cambridge. Sen was the sixth Indian to win a Nobel Prize and the first to be awarded the economics prize.

(MARY JANE FRIEDRICH)

Prize for Literature

Although Portuguese author José Saramago did not begin writing in earnest until his mid-50s, some critics believed that his reception of the 1998 Nobel Prize for Literature was long overdue. Heralded as an achievement for the language and culture of Portugal, it was only the second Nobel awarded to a Portuguese (neurologist António Egas Moniz won the 1949 Prize for Physiology or Medicine). Saramago came of age as a writer in the 1980s with a series of inventive, multilayered novels that ruminated on human fate and foibles. Often presented as allegory, his stories balanced the gravity of his political skepticism and historical knowledge with the lightness of magic realism, experimental grammar, and compassion for his characters. In addition to authoring 10 best-selling novels, Saramago wrote poetry, plays, short stories, and essays.

Saramago first earned international fame at age 60 with *Memorial do convento* (1982; published in the U.S. as *Baltasar and Blimunda*, 1987), widely considered his finest novel. Set in the early 18th century during the Inquisition, it was an intricate historical fantasy about a romance between war veteran Baltasar and clairvoyant Blimunda, who with the help of an adventurous priest, build a flying machine powered by human will. Central to the plot was the epic construction of the Convent of Mathra (1717–35), outside Lisbon. Saramago adapted the novel into a libretto for the opera *Blimunda* (1990), with a score by Italian composer Azio Corghi. The novel's satire was unflinching in its litany of class differences between the haves and the have-nots:

"The heat is unbearable and the spectators refresh themselves with the customary glass of lemonade, cup of water or slice of water-melon, for there is no reason why they should suffer from heat prostration just because the condemned are about to die. And should they feel peckish, there is a wide choice of nuts and seeds, cheeses and dates. The King, with his inseparable Infantes and Infantas, will dine at the Headquarters of the Inquisition as soon as the auto-da-fé has ended. Once free of the wretched business, he will join the Chief Inquisitor for a sumptuous feast laden with bowls of chicken broth, partridges, breasts of

veal, pâtés and meat savouries flavored with cinnamon and sugar, a stew in the Castilian manner with all the appropriate ingredients and saffron rice, blancmanges, pastries, and fruits in season."

Saramago was born on Nov. 16, 1922, into a farming family in the village of Azinhaga, Ribatejo province. He left high school early to begin work, eventually entering publishing as a journalist and editor, though he wrote little on his own. Stifled by the repressive cultural atmosphere during the dictatorship of António de Oliveira Salazar, Saramago joined the Communist Party in 1969, but, following the revolution of April 1974, an anticommunist backlash forced him from his job at the newspaper. At that time he began writing. In 1977 he published his first novel, *Manual de pintura e caligrafia* (1976; *Manual of Painting and Calligraphy*, 1994), about an idealistic portrait painter who makes sacrifices to defend his integrity as an artist and a critic. His themes turned to politics in a collection of short stories,

Walter Kohn

Objecto Quase (1978) and the follow-up novel *Levantado do chão* (1980), set during the Salazar regime.

In 1986, as Spain and Portugal were joining the European Community, Saramago published *A jangada de pedra* (1986; *The Stone Raft*, 1994–95), a surreal tale of the Iberian peninsula physically breaking apart from Europe and floating out into the Atlantic Ocean; chaos reigns until a band of ordinary citizens takes control. When a proofreader inserts the word "not" into a sentence of a book about Portugal, history is literally rewritten in *A história do cerco de Lisboa* (1989; *The History of the Siege of Lisbon*, 1996), one of the author's most contemplative works. *O evangelho segundo Jesus Cristo* (1991; *The Gospel According to Jesus Christ*, 1994) raised some hackles in its well-crafted depiction of an earthy Jesus set in conflict with a ruthless God. After moving to the Canary Islands, Saramago wrote *Ensaio sobre a cegueira* (1995; *Blindness*, 1998), a sharp-edged social commentary about how an epidemic of blindness speeds civilization toward self-destruction. His most recent novel, *Todos os nomes,* was published in 1997.   (TOM MICHAEL)

Prize for Chemistry

"As we approach the end of the 1990s, we are seeing the result of an enormous theoretical and computational development, and the consequences are revolutionizing the whole of chemistry." So stated the Royal Swedish Academy of Sciences in its award of the 1998 Nobel Prize for Chemistry to "the two most prominent figures in this process," Walter Kohn and John A. Pople. Kohn, a British citizen and a physicist at the University of California, Santa Barbara, and Pople, an Austrian-born U.S. mathematical chemist at Northwestern University, Evanston, Ill., were widely acknowledged pioneers in devising computational methods to study the properties of interactions of molecules.

The development of quantum mechanics in physics in the early 1900s offered chemists the potential for a deep new mathematical understanding of their science. Nevertheless, describing the quantum mechanics of large molecules, which are very complex systems, involved what appeared to be impossibly difficult computations. Chemists remained stymied until the 1960s, when computers for solving these complex equations became available. Quantum chemistry, the application of quantum mechanics to chemical problems, emerged as a new branch of chemistry. "Quantum chemistry is used nowadays in practically all branches of chemistry, always with the aim of increasing our knowledge of the inner structure of matter," the Swedish Academy said. "The scientific work of Walter Kohn and John Pople has been crucial for the development of this new field of research."

Kohn and Pople made contributions as closely related as the two faces of a coin. The Swedish Academy cited Kohn for development of the density-functional theory in the 1960s. It simplified the mathematical description of bonding between atoms that make up molecules. Pople was cited for having developed computational methods, based on quantum mechanics, which he packaged in 1970 in the computer program Gaussian. Gaussian later became the basic tool used by thousands of scientists worldwide for modeling and studying molecules and chemical reactions.

Before Kohn's and Pople's work, chemists thought that a description of the quantum mechanics of molecules required precise knowledge of the motion of every electron in every atom in a molecule. In 1964 Kohn showed that it is sufficient only to know the average number of electrons at any one point in space—i.e., the electron density. For determining that information Kohn introduced a computational method that became known as the density-functional theory. Years of additional research, however, were needed before chemists were able to apply the theory to large-scale studies of molecules. By the late 1990s the theory had become widely used as the basis for solving many problems in chemistry—for example, calculating the geometrical structure of large molecules such as enzymes.

Pople's research in the 1960s led to the discovery of a new approach for analyzing the electronic structure of molecules, based on the fundamental laws of quantum mechanics. He put the approach, called theoretical model chemistry, into a computer program that allowed chemists to create computer models of chemical reactions that were difficult or impossible to run in a laboratory. One use of such information was, in the development of new drugs, to determine how a molecule would react inside the body. In the early 1990s Pople incorporated Kohn's density-functional theory into the program, making possible the analysis of more complex molecules. The original program, Gaussian 70, was updated and improved over the years. Its commercial version, marketed by Gaussian Inc., Pittsburgh, Pa., was one of the most widely used quantum chemistry programs.

Kohn was born on March 9, 1923, in Vienna and received a Ph.D. in physics from Harvard University in 1948. He developed his density-functional theory while at the University of California, San Diego (1960–79). In 1979 he became founding director of the Institute for Theoretical Physics at the University of California, Santa Barbara, where he later served as a professor (1984–91). Pople was born in Burnham-on-Sea, Somerset, Eng., on Oct. 31, 1925. He received a Ph.D. in mathematics in 1951 from the University of Cambridge. He became a professor at Carnegie Mellon University, Pittsburgh, in 1964 and a professor at Northwestern in 1993.   (MICHAEL WOODS)

Prize for Physics

The 1998 Nobel Prize for Physics was awarded to three scientists, a German and two Americans,

who discovered that electrons in semiconductors placed in very strong magnetic fields at extremely low temperatures demonstrate bizarre behaviour. Under such conditions electrons condense to form a quantum fluid similar to the quantum fluids that occur in superconductivity and liquid helium. Electrons in the fluid act, seemingly impossibly, as if they have only a fraction of a whole electron charge. "What makes these fluids particularly important for researchers is that events in a drop of quantum fluid can afford more profound insights into the general inner structure and dynamics of matter," stated the Royal Swedish Academy of Sciences in its prize announcement. "The contributions of the three laureates have thus led to yet another breakthrough in our understanding of quantum physics and to the development of new theoretical concepts of significance in many branches of modern physics."

The prize was shared by Horst L. Störmer of Columbia University, New York City, Daniel C. Tsui of Princeton University, and Robert B. Laughlin of Stanford University. Störmer was born on April 6, 1949, in Frankfurt am Main, Ger., and received a Ph.D. in physics in 1977 from the University of Stuttgart. Tsui, a naturalized U.S. citizen, was born in Henan, China, on Feb. 28, 1939, and earned a Ph.D. in physics in 1967 from the University of Chicago. Laughlin, born on Nov. 1, 1950, in Visalia, Calif., received his Ph.D. in physics in 1979 from the Massachusetts Institute of Technology.

Störmer and Tsui were cited for the discovery in 1982 of a new aspect of a phenomenon first demonstrated in an 1879 experiment by Edwin H. Hall, a U.S. physicist. Hall found that when a conductor carrying an electric current is placed in a magnetic field that is perpendicular to the current flow, an electric field is created that is perpendicular to both the current and the magnetic field. This phenomenon, called the Hall effect, occurs because the magnetic field deflects the flow of electrons toward one side of the current-carrying material. The electric field gives rise to a voltage, called the Hall voltage, and the ratio of this voltage to the current is called the Hall resistance. The Hall effect, which occurs in both conductors and semiconductors, later became a standard measurement tool in physics laboratories around the world.

In 1980 the German physicist Klaus von Klitzing discovered a variation of the Hall effect, which came to be called the integer quantum Hall effect. For moderate applied magnetic fields, the Hall resistance changes smoothly with changes in the strength of the field. Klitzing, however, used high-magnetic fields and temperatures near absolute zero to study the Hall effect in a semiconductor device in which electron motion was confined to two dimensions. Under those conditions he found that varying the magnetic field causes the Hall resistance to change not smoothly but rather in discrete steps, a behaviour physicists described as being quantized. Klitzing won the 1985 Nobel Prize for Physics for his work.

In 1982 Störmer and Tsui, then at Bell Laboratories, Murray Hill, N.J., carried out a similar experiment using even lower temperatures and stronger fields. To their surprise they found more steps in the Hall resistance, some of them lying between Klitzing's integer steps. Whereas the integer quantum Hall effect could be understood in terms of the behaviour of individual electrons, the new effect suggested that the involved particles had fractional electric charges—one-third, one-fifth, or one-seventh that of an electron. The finding mystified and excited physicists, who searched for an explanation.

A year later Laughlin, at Bell Labs and then Lawrence Livermore National Laboratory, Livermore, Calif., in the early 1980s, solved the mystery with a theoretical explanation. He proposed that the low temperature and intense magnetic field made the electrons condense into a new kind of quantum fluid. Earlier researchers had observed other quantum fluids at very low temperatures in liquid helium and in superconductor materials. Laughlin's quantum fluid exhibited many bizarre properties, including one in which the participating electrons behaved as fractionally charged "quasiparticles." Laughlin showed that such quasiparticles had exactly the right electric charges to explain Störmer and Tsui's findings.

The Swedish Academy stated that the laureates' work in 1982–83 represented "an indirect demonstration of the new quantum fluid and its fractionally charged quasiparticles." Verification came only in the late 1990s thanks to "astonishing developments in microelectronics" that made it possible to obtain more direct evidence for the existence of quasiparticles.   (MICHAEL WOODS)

Prize for Physiology or Medicine
Three American scientists, Robert F. Furchgott of the State University of New York (SUNY) Health Science Center in Brooklyn, Ferid Murad of the University of Texas Medical School in Houston, and Louis J. Ignarro of the University of California School of Medicine in Los Angeles, won the 1998 Nobel Prize for Physiology or Medicine for discovering that a gas, nitric oxide (NO), acts as a signaling molecule in the cardiovascular system. Their work, the bulk of which was performed in the 1980s, uncovered an entirely new mechanism for how blood vessels in the body relax and widen. It led to the development of the anti-impotence drug Viagra (see HEALTH AND DISEASE: Sidebar) and potential new approaches for understanding and treating other diseases.

The Nobel Assembly of the Karolinska Institute in Stockholm, which presented the prize, said that the identification of a biological role for NO was surprising for several reasons. Nitric oxide was known mainly as a harmful air pollutant, released into the atmosphere from automobile engines and other combustion sources. In addition, it was a simple molecule, very different from the complex neurotransmitters and other signaling molecules that regulate many biological events. No other known gas acts as a signaling molecule in the body.

Nitric oxide's role began to emerge in the 1970s and '80s. In 1977 Murad, then at the University of Virginia, showed that nitroglycerin and several related heart drugs induce the formation of NO and that the colourless, odourless gas acts to increase the diameter of blood vessels in the body. Murad was born on Sept. 14, 1936, in Whiting, Ind., and received his M.D. and Ph.D. degrees from Western Reserve University (later Case Western Reserve University), Cleveland, Ohio, in 1965. Murad was also cited by the committee for work that he accomplished at Stanford University in the 1980s and later at Abbott Laboratories in Illinois.

Around 1980 Furchgott, in an ingenious experiment, demonstrated that cells in the endothelium, or inner lining, of blood vessels produce an unknown signaling molecule. The molecule, which he named endothelium-derived relaxing factor (EDRF), signals smooth muscle cells in blood vessel walls to relax, dilating the vessels. Furchgott was born on June 4, 1916, in Charleston, S.C. In 1940 he earned a Ph.D. in wbiochemistry from Northwestern University, Evanston, Ill., and he joined SUNY-Brooklyn's Department of Pharmacology in 1956.

The Nobel Committee cited Ignarro for "a brilliant series of analyses" that demonstrated that EDRF was nitric oxide. Ignarro's research, conducted in 1986, was done independently of Furchgott's own work to identify EDRF. It was the first discovery that a gas could act as a signaling molecule in a living organism. Ignarro, who was born on May 31, 1941, in Brooklyn, gained a Ph.D. in pharmacology from the University of Minnesota. Before making his significant discovery at UCLA, he was professor of pharmacology (1979–85) at Tulane University's School of Medicine, New Orleans.

Furchgott and Ignarro first announced their findings at a scientific conference in 1986 and triggered an international boom in research on nitric oxide. Scientists later showed that NO is manufactured by many different kinds of cells in the body and has a role in regulating a variety of body functions. The Nobel Assembly said that the scientists' research was key to the development of the highly successful drug Viagra, which acts to increase NO's effect in penile blood vessels. Researchers expected that other medical applications of knowledge about NO would come in treating heart disease, shock, and cancer. Tests that analyze production of NO also could improve the diagnosis of lung diseases such as asthma and intestinal disorders such as colitis.

The Nobel Assembly cited one irony about the award. When Alfred Nobel, inventor of dynamite, became ill with heart disease, his physicians advised him to take nitroglycerin. Dynamite consists of nitroglycerin absorbed in a material called kieselguhr, which makes nitroglycerin less likely to explode accidentally. Nobel, however, refused, unable to understand how the explosive could relieve chest pain. It took science 100 years to find the answer in NO, the Assembly said.

(MICHAEL WOODS)

Horst L. Störmer

MIKE DERER—AP/WIDE WORLD

BIOGRAPHIES

Abubakar, Abdulsalam

On June 9, 1998, following the sudden death of Nigerian military ruler Gen. Sani Abacha the previous day, Maj. Gen. Abdulsalam Abubakar, Nigeria's defense chief of staff, was sworn in as the country's head of state. Although Abubakar had never before held public office, his appointment by Nigeria's ruling military junta was not unexpected. A high-ranking career soldier from the country's northern region, Abubakar fit the profile of former rulers of Nigeria, which for 28 of its 38 years of independence had been controlled by military regimes.

Abubakar was born June 13, 1942, in Minna in north-central Nigeria and went to secondary school in the neighbouring town of Bida. In 1963 he attended the Kaduna Technical Institute. He served in the air force and then joined the army in 1975 but received his formal training in the United States. Rising steadily through the ranks of the Nigerian army, he commanded Nigeria's contingent of the UN peacekeeping forces in Lebanon in 1981. By the late 1980s he had become a senior officer, and in 1993 he was named defense chief of staff by Abacha.

As the new head of state, Abubakar inherited a host of long-standing problems, including ethnic and regional strife, political corruption, widespread poverty, and mismanagement of the country's oil industry. In his first address to the nation in June, he stated that "all hands must be on deck to move this nation forward," but he provided no detailed plan of action. By July, Abubakar had announced that he would follow a program that would restore the country to democracy. He had freed a number of political prisoners and announced the dissolution of the political parties and structures set up by Abacha. Abubakar also addressed economic issues, promised to assemble a Cabinet that would represent Nigeria's ethnic diversity, and outlined a plan for multiparty elections, setting May 29, 1999, as the swearing-in date for a new civilian president.

By October, Abubakar had succeeded in convincing the European Union and the United States of his commitment to a transition to civilian rule—a step that was crucial for the restoration of much-needed aid for Nigeria's crippled economy. Support from Nigerians was more difficult to obtain; promises of democracy made by previous military rulers had often been broken. Abubakar's standing with his countrymen, however, improved substantially when Nigerian author Wole Soyinka, winner of the 1986 Nobel Prize for Literature, returned home on October 14 after a four-year exile. The fact that Soyinka, a highly regarded advocate of democracy and a fierce critic of Nigeria's military governments, would return was viewed as a major vote of confidence for Abubakar. (ELIZABETH LASKEY)

Adamkus, Valdas V.

In 1997 Valdas Adamkus retired from his post at the U.S. Environmental Protection Agency (EPA) after nearly 30 years—the longest tenure of any senior executive at the agency—with the expressed intention of working on his golf game. Soon afterward, however, it seemed that golf would have to wait, because in February 1998 the unassuming 71-year-old career bureaucrat, a citizen of the United States for the past half century, became a European head of state. A month earlier, after a closely contested election, he had won a five-year term as president of his native country, Lithuania, where he had only recently regained citizenship. His candidacy had generated considerable controversy; opponents painted him as an interloping American-made carpetbagger, whereas supporters viewed him as a prodigal son, long an exile in a foreign land, completing his odyssey back home.

His absence during the Soviet era may have helped Adamkus gain his victory. "I don't carry any political baggage," he declared. "I don't represent any old systems." His winning margin during the election, decided by a runoff, was less than 1%, only a few thousand votes, but it was enough to defeat Arturas Paulauskas, who was backed by the popular outgoing president, Algirdas Brazauskas, a former communist. As president, Adamkus announced his intention to give up his U.S. passport but not his ties to the West. In fact, he worked to strengthen those bonds by continuing in force the two main objectives of Lithuanian foreign policy: eventual membership in NATO, in order to improve national security, and in the European Union, to improve the economy. All the while, Adamkus was careful not to alienate his nation from Russia and its Baltic neighbours; he met with Polish and Ukrainian leaders in May and with the other presidents of Eastern and Central Europe in June.

Adamkus was born with the surname Adamkavecius in Kaunas, Lith., on Nov. 3, 1926. During World War II he fought with Lithuanian insurrectionists against Soviet rule, published an underground newspaper during the Nazi occupation, and then resumed the fight against the returning Soviet army before fleeing in 1944 to Germany, where he attended the University of Munich. In 1949 he immigrated with his family to the United States, settling in a Lithuanian-American community in Chicago, where in 1960 he graduated from the Illinois Institute of Technology with a degree in civil engineering. Adamkus was active in émigré politics in the 1950s and 1960s, promoting Lithuanian independence and cultural heritage and achieving high positions in such organizations as the liberal Santara-Sviesa ("Accord-Light"), the Lithuanian Community in America, and the American Lithuanian Council.

Adamkus began his career with the EPA upon its inception in 1970, and in 1971 he was picked to be the deputy regional administrator of Region V, in the Midwest. Ten years later he was appointed to the position of regional administrator. Adamkus distinguished himself by improving the water quality of the Great Lakes with a model program that gained international repute, by crafting groundbreaking agreements with Native American tribes, and by refusing to participate in an EPA cover-up regarding the unlawful emission of chemical toxins. Most far-reaching perhaps was his work in helping to address and solve environmental protection issues in Eastern Europe by supplying consultation and infrastructure.

(TOM MICHAEL)

Valdas Adamkus

MINDAUGAS KULBIS—AP/WIDE WORLD

Badu, Erykah

By 1998, just one year after the release of her phenomenally successful debut album, *Baduizm,* singer-songwriter Erykah Badu had become one of the fastest-rising American recording artists. The phrasing and emotive qualities of her smooth, jazz-inflected vocals were sometimes reminiscent of the style of Billie Holiday, an artist to whom she was often compared. Badu's follow-up album, *Erykah Badu Live,* debuted at the top spot on the pop charts. The combined sales of the two albums exceeded three million copies, and both efforts were certified as platinum. She then went on to capture two NAACP Image Awards, four Soul Train Awards, an American Music Award, and two Grammys.

Badu was born Erica Wright, the eldest of three children, c. 1971 in Dallas, Texas. Of her adopted stage name, Badu explained, "I spell [my name] with a 'y' because it stands for origin and 'kah' is [ancient Egyptian] meaning 'inner light that shines and cannot be contaminated.' . . . Badu . . . means 'to manifest' in Arabic." Never formally trained in music, Badu majored in dance and theatre at Grambling (La.) State University after graduating from the High School for the Performing and Visual Arts in Dallas. She dropped out of Grambling in 1993 to pursue a singing career and formed the group Erykah Free with her cousin, while also working as a waitress and a drama teacher to support herself. In 1995, while opening for singer D'Angelo, Badu was singled out of the band by Kedar Massenburg, who was just starting his own record company. He offered her a solo contract, which she accepted because she felt that she would receive more individual attention at a smaller label. In January 1997 "On & On," Badu's first single, was released and quickly became a hit. The next month *Baduizm,* for which she wrote all but one of the songs, was released, and the album solidified her popularity.

Distinguished by her elaborate Afrocentric attire, in particular her signature head wraps, or geles, Badu lit a candle and incense onstage to focus herself before beginning each performance. With a sound built upon the roots of her heritage, she cited among her early influences Miles Davis, Al Jarreau, Chaka Khan, Stevie Wonder, and Marvin Gaye. A spiritual person whose lyrics concentrated on the more positive aspects of life, Badu said, "I never get tired of writing inspirational words." She spoke of the need for artists to have a plan and said of her own, "I'll start as a singer, so I can be individually recognized . . . then I'll go on to acting, because everyone wants to see a recording star on film. Then after film, I'll direct . . . write movies and have my own corporation . . . and ultimately a whole arts foundation." It was clear that Badu was well on her way.

(ANTHONY L. GREEN)

Barad, Jill E.

On Jan. 1, 1998, Jill Barad celebrated her first anniversary as chairman and CEO of Mattel, the world's largest toy manufacturer. In January 1997, after 16 years with the company, Barad joined the small number of female executives who head major U.S. businesses. During her tenure at Mattel she experienced everything ranging from the company's near bankruptcy in the 1980s to its transformation into a thriving, $4.8 billion operation, whose brands included Barbie dolls, Hot Wheels and Matchbox cars, Fisher-Price, Tyco Toys, and Cabbage Patch Kids.

Barad's path took several turns on her way to the top of the El Segundo, Calif.-based Mattel. Born Jill Elikann on May 23, 1951, in New York City, she received (1973) her B.A. from Queens College in New York City. Following graduation she worked as an assistant to the Italian producer Dino De Laurentiis and landed a nonspeaking role in his 1974 film *Crazy Joe.* After deciding not to pursue an acting career, she worked for Coty Cosmetics as a cosmetician-trainer. Even at this

early job, her innovative nature shone through—when she realized that Coty's products were not being placed well in the stores she visited, she designed a wall display that the company would use for the next two decades. She married Thomas Barad in 1979 and left the workforce when she became pregnant with their first child.

By 1981 she felt corporate America beckoning her back, and she began her career with Mattel as a product manager. Her first assignment was an ill-fated rubbery product called A Bad Case of Worms, but she gained recognition for her initiative in promoting the product. In 1982 Barad was put in charge of the Barbie line. Launched in 1959, by the early 1980s Barbie was experiencing unspectacular sales. Barad brought new life into the line, overseeing the expansion of the Barbie collection by packaging different versions of the doll, each with its own accessories, so that children would want to own more than one. The results were astounding—annual sales of the Barbie brand grew from $200 million in 1982 to $1.9 billion in 1997. By 1998 the average girl in the U.S. owned nine Barbies, and the brand amounted to some 40% of Mattel's sales.

She was named president and chief operating officer of Mattel in 1992, and by 1997 she was primed to take over as CEO. Barad planned to put Mattel toys in the hands of even more children around the world. In early 1998 she announced plans to pursue the international market aggressively. In December, amid reports of disappointing earnings, Barad announced that Mattel would acquire the Learning Company, an educational software maker.   (SANDRA LANGENECKERT)

Berners-Lee, Tim
As the World Wide Web grew in social and economic significance in 1998, heated debate ensued on such related issues as censorship, monopolization, and privacy rights, and the industry looked increasingly toward hypertext pioneer Tim Berners-Lee for a vision of the electronic future. As the Web's creator, he saw it grow into an interactive, dynamic global medium where ideas were exchanged, goods and services were purchased, and virtual communities were born at a previously unimaginable pace. In 1998 the unassuming innovator was also the recipient of the John D. and Catherine T. MacArthur Foundation grant and the Eduard Rhein Foundation prize for technology.

Born on June 8, 1955, in London to two computer scientists, Berners-Lee became fascinated with computers at an early age. He built toy computers from cardboard and later constructed his first working computer from a television set and a variety of spare parts. He graduated with an honours degree in physics from Queen's College, Oxford, in 1976 and worked for several technology firms in England before being hired in 1980 as a software developer for CERN, the European Laboratory for Particle Physics, in Geneva. It was there that he struggled with the problem of integrating and exchanging information held on different computers in often widely scattered places. His solution, a program he dubbed "Enquire," incorporated the use of hypertext, a system that links documents from different sources, forming an electronic path that users follow to obtain related information. Although he quickly envisioned its potential, it was not until 1989 that he was able to gain support to develop the system. By the end of that year, Berners-Lee had developed software to edit and view documents and the protocol to transfer them. In 1990 his system, the World Wide Web, was made available to the CERN community. It was released to the public on the Internet in the summer of 1991. With its ability to transfer text, sound, images, and even video in a simple, straightforward manner, the World Wide Web grew from a resource used by researchers to exchange information to an international communications medium, commercial tool, and social phenomenon used by millions of people. Already a multibillion-dollar industry in 1998, the Web was expected to continue its exponential growth over the next several years.

Although Berners-Lee could have parlayed his invention into incredible wealth—and he did receive many lucrative commercial offers—he in-

stead became (1994) the director of the newly formed World Wide Web Consortium (W3C) at the Massachusetts Institute of Technology Laboratory for Computer Science. As the W3C director, he worked with quiet diligence to improve the Web's technological capabilities and help set the design standards for more than 275 member organizations and companies, such as IBM, Microsoft, and Netscape. As the Web continued to grow, Berners-Lee remained an advocate for its easy, inexpensive, and unrestricted use as a communications tool into the next millennium.
(CHRISTOPHER CALL)

Bin Laden, Osama
When bombs ripped through American embassies in Kenya and Tanzania on Aug. 7, 1998, the United States was quick to suspect that Saudi-born millionaire Osama bin Laden was the orchestrator of the explosions. Since 1996 he had been described by the U.S. State Department as "one of the most significant financial sponsors of Islamic extremist activities in the world today." There was no doubt that bin Laden had advocated terrorist activities and had a significant number of followers; he issued a call to arms in February 1998 that stated: "We—with God's help—call on every Muslim who believes in God and wishes to be rewarded to comply with God's order to kill the Americans and plunder their money wherever and whenever they find it." Though he was accused by U.S. intelligence sources of having masterminded a number of terrorist attacks—notably deadly 1995 and 1996 bombings in Saudi Arabia that were aimed at U.S. military personnel—proof

camps. By 1991 bin Laden's hatred of the United States had crystallized; he viewed the U.S. troops stationed in Saudi Arabia during the Gulf War as armed infidels and denounced the House of Saud for allowing the troops into the country. In 1991 the Saudi government expelled bin Laden (he was deprived of his citizenship in 1994), and he fled to The Sudan, where he operated several businesses and also, reportedly, a number of clandestine terrorist training camps. The Sudan forced bin Laden to leave in mid-1996, and he returned to Afghanistan, where he allegedly established at least two training facilities, including one that the U.S. termed a "terrorist university."

Several weeks after the embassy bombings, the U.S. fired missiles at bin Laden's "terrorist university" in Afghanistan and at a Sudan pharmaceutical plant thought to be manufacturing nerve gas on bin Laden's orders. He continued to deny his involvement in terrorist activities. The U.S. charged bin Laden with inciting violence against American citizens and requested his deportation to the U.S. to face trial. By year's end, however, Afghanistan's ruling Islamic militia, the Taliban, had said that bin Laden was a guest in their country and that he would be prosecuted in Afghanistan only if the U.S. could supply convincing evidence of his involvement in terrorist acts.   (ELIZABETH LASKEY)

Bourne, Matthew
In October 1998 Broadway audiences finally got the chance to see British choreographer Matthew Bourne's controversial restaging of Tchaikovsky's *Swan Lake* and judge for themselves what the crit-

Tim Berners-Lee

of his role in any of the incidents remained, like bin Laden himself, elusive.

Osama bin Mohammad bin Laden was born *c.* 1957 in Riyadh, Saudi Arabia. As the son of a self-made construction billionaire, he inherited a large fortune. The same year that he graduated (1979) from King Abdul Aziz University in Jiddah, the Soviet Union invaded Afghanistan, and bin Laden, a devout Muslim, traveled there to aid the mujahideen in their jihad (holy war) against the Soviets. He recruited many of the so-called Arab Afghans—volunteer resistance fighters from the Persian Gulf nations—to aid the U.S.-backed mujahideen fighters. Drawing from his personal wealth and funds raised from other wealthy Muslims, he also financed training

ical buzz was all about. For more than 100 years, the swans in the ballet had been portrayed by ethereal young women in romantic white costumes. For his updated reinterpretation of the classic, however, which placed the prince in a dysfunctional family that reminded many audience members of current British royalty, Bourne looked not only to the power of Tchaikovsky's music but also to nature for his inspiration. Seeing swans as large, aggressive, and powerful creatures with wings shaped like male dancers' muscular arms, he had his swans danced by bare-chested men clad only in knee-length shorts made with layers of shredded silk that resembled feathers. Adventures in Motion Pictures (AMP), the London-based dance company that Bourne cofounded in 1987 and

served as artistic director, premiered the ballet in late 1995 and a year later reopened it in London's West End. It won the 1996 Laurence Olivier Award for the best new dance production and was presented to sold-out audiences in Los Angeles in 1997 before opening on Broadway.

Radical reinterpretation of classic ballet was not new to Bourne. In 1992 he set the Christmas Eve scene of *The Nutcracker* in a Victorian orphanage reminiscent of a workhouse in a Charles Dickens novel, and *Highland Fling,* his 1994 version of *La Sylphide,* took place in a housing project in modern-day Glasgow, Scot. His follow-up to *Swan Lake,* in 1997, was another new look for an old story, this time the ballet *Cinderella.* Bourne's staging was set in World War II London during the Blitz, and the prince was portrayed as a fighter pilot.

Matthew Bourne

Born on Jan. 13, 1960, in Hackney, London, Bourne entered the world of dance relatively late. Although he had been a fan of musical films and theatre since childhood (when he created his own versions of shows he had seen), he began studies at London's Laban Centre at age 20 and did not begin dance classes until he was 22. Bourne received a bachelor's degree in dance theatre in 1985 and then toured for two years with Transitions, the centre's dance company. His number of dance appearances diminished as he took on more and more choreographic work—for television, theatre, and other dance companies as well as for AMP—but he still performed such roles as the Private Secretary (his production's counterpart to the villainous Rothbart) in *Swan Lake.* Bourne, having choreographed the London revival of *Oliver!* in 1994, was slated to do the same for that musical's North American performances in 1999.

(BARBARA WHITNEY)

Brown, Gordon

When Tony Blair became the U.K.'s prime minister on May 2, 1997, he appointed his long-standing friend and ally Gordon Brown chancellor of the Exchequer. Brown swiftly established himself as the Cabinet's second most important member, both by taking control of almost all policies concerned with the U.K.'s domestic economy and by sustaining close, personal links to Blair that no other Cabinet minister could match. In October 1998, as chairman of the Group of Seven's subgroup of finance ministers, Brown extended his influence and played a key role in helping to establish new international mechanisms to stabilize world financial markets.

Born in Glasgow, Scot., on Feb. 20, 1951, Brown was the son of a Church of Scotland minister. At 16, Brown was the youngest person since World War II to win a scholarship to the University of Edinburgh, where he immersed himself in student politics. He also played rugby until he lost the sight in one eye, the delayed result of an accident in a school rugby game. In 1974 Brown helped organize the campaign to elect Robin Cook to Parliament. By the time the two men entered the Cabinet together 23 years later (with Cook as foreign secretary), they had become rivals. Their hostility dated from the ill-fated 1979 campaign for limited self-government for Scotland, when Brown supported a "yes" vote in that year's referendum, and Cook opted for a "no" vote. In 1998, after a successful vote on devolution, Brown campaigned against the extreme Scottish Nationalists.

Brown entered Parliament in 1983 as MP for Dunfermline East, an industrial constituency near Glasgow. He became friends with Tony Blair, an-

other new MP, and the two soon found themselves at the forefront of the campaign to modernize Labour's political philosophy, replacing the dream of state socialism with a more pragmatic, market-friendly strategy. Brown, two years older than Blair, was widely regarded as the senior half of the partnership and the one more likely eventually to become party leader. By the time then-Labour leader John Smith died in 1994, however, Blair had overtaken Brown as the favoured candidate of party activists and the wider public.

Brown reluctantly agreed to step aside and allow Blair to run as the "modernizer" candidate. After Blair won, he reappointed Brown Labour's shadow chancellor (a post that Smith had first given him two years earlier). Labour's landslide victory in the 1997 general election propelled Brown into the treasury, where he immediately made his mark by ceding the power to set interest rates to the Bank of England. Brown set out to establish a reputation for prudent economic management. He disappointed many Labour supporters by largely retaining for the first two years the strict public-spending policies he inherited from the Conservatives, but by July 1998 he had drawn up new plans that allowed for significantly more spending on health, education, and overseas aid, starting in 1999.

(PETER KELLNER)

Cameron, James

It was full speed ahead for James Cameron in 1998 as the Canadian filmmaker defied critics and logistics by building a *Titanic* that refused to sink. His screen adaptation of the doomed ocean liner's 1912 maiden voyage sailed into the record books, grossing more than $1.5 billion worldwide and tying *Ben-Hur* (1959) for most Academy Awards won (11). Skillfully blending special effects with a fictional love story between a penniless artist (played by American actor Leonardo DiCaprio) and an unhappily engaged first-class passenger (British actress Kate Winslet), *Titanic* stood atop the American charts for an unprecedented 15 weeks, earning well over $500 million in North America to become the highest-grossing movie in U.S. history.

Bringing the luxury liner to the big screen, however, proved anything but smooth sailing. Written, directed, and co-produced by Cameron, *Titanic* experienced production delays and budget overruns—at a cost of $200 million, it became the most expensive movie ever made—as detailed sets and a model of the ship's exterior, 90% to scale, were built. As rumours circulated about Cameron's legendary perfectionism and demanding direction, many predicted disaster. Instead, Cameron and *Titanic* glided into cinematic his-

tory. After collecting Oscars for best picture and best director, it seemed only fitting when he declared himself "king of the world."

Born on Aug. 16, 1954, in Kapuskasing, Ont., Cameron studied art as a child and later provided the drawings that figured prominently in *Titanic*. In 1971 his family moved to California. After studying physics at California State University at Fullerton, Cameron worked at a series of jobs, including machinist and truck driver, before a viewing of *Star Wars* (1977) inspired him to try his hand at moviemaking. In 1980 he was hired as a production designer, and the following year he made his directorial debut with *Piranha II: The Spawning*. A flop at the box office, the movie encouraged Cameron to write his own material. The result was *Terminator* (1984), an action thriller about a robot hit man that made actor Arnold Schwarzenegger a star and established Cameron as a bankable filmmaker. A series of high-tech and big-budget pictures followed, including *Aliens* (1986) and *The Abyss* (1989), both of which received an Oscar for best visual effects, *Terminator 2: Judgment Day* (1991), and *True Lies* (1994). In 1992 Cameron formed his own production company, Lightstorm Entertainment, and the following year he cofounded Digital Domain, a state-of-the-art effects company.

Although his films met with success at the box office, many complained that they lacked substance, relying too heavily on visual effects. With *Titanic* Cameron demonstrated his ability not only to tell a story but, as was the case in 1998, to be the story.

(AMY TIKKANEN)

Charest, Jean

In March 1998 charismatic Canadian politician Jean Charest abandoned the federal government and the Progressive Conservative Party (PCP) to assume the leadership of the Quebec Liberal Party (QLP). His move into provincial politics was made in an effort to wrest political control of Quebec from the separatist Parti Québécois (PQ), headed by Lucien Bouchard, prior to a referendum on Quebec independence. Although Charest's popularity in Quebec had been expected to propel the QLP to a victory in the November 30 provincial election, his party won only 48 seats in the Quebec National Assembly, compared with 75 seats for the PQ. The QLP gained a slight majority (44%) over the PQ (43%) in the popular vote, however, an outcome that would delay the referendum on independence.

John James Charest was born June 24, 1958, in Sherbrooke, Que., and grew up speaking both English and French. He earned a law degree from the University of Sherbrooke and was called to the Quebec bar in 1980. He practiced criminal law in Sherbrooke before entering politics. He was elected to the House of Commons in 1984 and represented the riding of Sherbrooke for 14 years.

His rise in federal politics was meteoric. The same year that he was elected to the Commons, Charest was named assistant deputy speaker. In 1986 he made Canadian history when he assumed the portfolio of minister of state for youth—he became the youngest MP to be named to the Cabinet. He was appointed minister of state for fitness and amateur sport in 1988 and deputy leader of the government in 1989. In 1990, however, his career suffered a setback. He was cited for interfering with the judicial process after he telephoned a judge about a case. Although forced to resign from the Cabinet, Charest did not remain a backbencher for long. In 1991 he returned to the Cabinet as minister of the environment and a member of the Priorities and Planning Committee. When Prime Minister Brian Mulroney retired in 1993, Charest made an unsuccessful bid for leadership of the PCP. Thereafter, he served in the Cabinet of Prime Minister Kim Campbell as deputy prime minister until the 1993 election, which swept the PCP from power; Charest was one of only two PCP candidates to be elected to Parliament. After succeeding Kim Campbell as PCP leader in December 1993, he worked to rebuild the party and achieved some success. In the 1997 general election, the PCP won 20 seats in the House of Commons.

Charest rose to national prominence as chairman of the parliamentary Special Committee to

Study the Proposed Companion Resolution to the Meech Lake Accord 1990, a proposed constitutional amendment that would have given Quebec special status. After the 1993 election he campaigned vigorously in Quebec against separation and was credited with helping to defeat the proposition in the October 1995 vote.

(DIANE LOIS WAY)

Chow Yun-Fat

After having conquered the Asian film world, Chinese actor Chow Yun-Fat set his sights on the U.S. in 1998, making his Hollywood debut in *The Replacement Killers*. Starring opposite American actress Mira Sorvino, Chow played a professional assassin who refuses to complete an assignment and thus becomes a target himself. The role—that of a suave, sullen killer with a conscience—was reminiscent of ones that had made the veteran actor a screen legend to millions of Asian moviegoers. *The Replacement Killers* earned praise as a sophisticated thriller, and critics lauded Chow's understated performance. Moreover, the movie's success at the box office seemed to indicate that Western audiences were warming to the idea of an Asian leading man in mainstream films.

Chow was born on May 18, 1955, on Lamma Island, Hong Kong. After dropping out of high school at age 17 and holding a number of menial jobs, he began taking acting lessons. Eventually he earned a contract to perform on television, and by the mid-1970s he was a soap-opera star. His success on television landed him movie roles. His first acclaimed film was *The Story of Woo Viet* (1981), in which he played a Vietnamese refugee struggling to reach the U.S. He won a Golden Horse Award (the Taiwanese equivalent of an Academy Award) for best actor for his work in *Hong Kong, 1941* (1984), a poignant war drama.

In 1986 Chow teamed up with action-film director John Woo in *A Better Tomorrow*. The movie made Chow a box-office superstar in Asia and launched a series of Chow-Woo pairings that included *A Better Tomorrow II* (1987), *The Killer* (1989), *Once a Thief* (1990), and *Hard Boiled* (1992). Chow also made several popular action films with director Ringo Lam, including *City on Fire* (1987), *Wild Search* (1989), and *Full Contact* (1992).

After Woo and other notable figures in the Asian film world went to work in Hollywood in the 1990s, Chow decided to follow in their footsteps. He made his last Chinese film, *Peace Hotel*, in 1995 and moved to the U.S. that year. Determined to be successful, he was careful about the transition. Rather than rushing into a project, he spent two years studying English, honing his acting skills, and waiting for the right script to come along. His patience paid off. After the release of *The Replacement Killers*, Chow was flooded with movie offers. By year's end he had begun filming a police drama and was working on a remake of the 1946 classic *Anna and the King of Siam*.

(TOM MICHAEL)

Clinton, Bill

On Dec. 19, 1998, the U.S. House of Representatives approved two of the four articles of impeachment against U.S. Pres. Bill Clinton. The president was charged with two counts of perjury and one count each of obstruction of justice and abuse of power. The tally of 228–206 for the first article, with only 5 Republicans voting no, reflected the partisan nature of the action. Although Republicans would hold a 55–45 edge in the Senate trial convening in January 1999, conviction required approval by a two-thirds majority, and it seemed unlikely that Clinton would be removed from office.

The drive toward impeachment grew out of testimony the president had given in January in a deposition in a lawsuit charging him with sexual harassment. The suit had been brought against him by Paula Corbin Jones, a state employee when Clinton was governor of Arkansas. (The case was later dismissed, but in November Clinton agreed to an $850,000 payment to Jones.) In the deposition the president testified that he had not had sexual relations with former White House intern Monica Lewinsky. Special Prosecutor Kenneth Starr (*q.v.*), who had been investigating the president and his

Chow Yun-Fat

wife, Hillary Rodham Clinton, in the Whitewater land deal and other matters, expanded his probe to investigate the Lewinsky affair. Thus began an inquiry that consumed the attention of the media and of politicians throughout the year. Starr eventually subpoenaed Clinton, who on August 17 testified before a grand jury and admitted to an "inappropriate" relationship with Lewinsky. On September 9 Starr submitted his report to the House, and the Judiciary Committee approved the four articles of impeachment on December 11–12. With the vote of the full House, Clinton became the second president in U.S. history, the other being Andrew Johnson in 1868, to have had articles of impeachment brought against him.

Despite Clinton's perilous political position during the year, he retained a high approval rating among voters and remained active in both domestic and foreign affairs. In budget negotiations with Republicans, for example, the president was successful in winning additional spending for education and farm aid as well as additional U.S. contributions to the International Monetary Fund. He failed, however, to secure legislative approval for a number of other programs. Among foreign trips were a meeting at the end of June with Chinese Pres. Jiang Zemin in Beijing, a visit to many countries in Africa (*see* Spotlight: *Clinton's Trip to Africa*), and meetings in the Middle East with Israeli and Palestinian leaders in December, the latter an attempt to shore up agreements that the president had earlier helped the two sides reach at talks in the U.S. The president played a low-key role in the November congressional elections, but Mrs. Clinton was successful in a number of personal appearances on behalf of Democratic candidates.

William Jefferson Blythe IV (he later took the name of his stepfather) was born on Aug. 19, 1946, in Hope, Ark. He received a bachelor's degree from Georgetown University, Washington, D.C., and was a Rhodes scholar at the University of Oxford. Both he and his wife gained law degrees from Yale University. After teaching, practicing law, and holding elective office in Arkansas, including five terms as governor, he won the U.S. presidency in 1992 and was reelected in 1996.

(ROBERT RAUCH)

Close, Chuck

In February 1998 the Museum of Modern Art in New York City mounted a retrospective of some 120 portraits, most of them large-scale, by American artist Chuck Close. The exhibit, which moved to Chicago in June and Washington, D.C., in October and was scheduled to finish in Seattle,

Wash., in 1999, documented the evolution of Close's style and highly inventive techniques. Visually, his body of work was diverse—his earliest work consisted of meticulously detailed hyperrealistic studies in gray, whereas his later works were colourful gridded abstractions. Yet all his work was remarkably similar in some respects; his subject was always the human face, he painted only from photographs he took of his friends and family, and his fascination with the process of creating a work of art was always evident.

Charles Thomas Close was born on July 5, 1940, in Monroe, Wash. When he was 14, an exhibition of Jackson Pollock's abstract paintings helped influence him to become a painter. Close studied at the University of Washington School of Art (B.A., 1962) and at the Yale University School of Art and Architecture (B.F.A., 1963; M.F.A., 1964). In 1964 he won a Fulbright scholarship to study in Vienna. Close taught (1965–67) at the University of Massachusetts at Amherst, where he gradually rejected the elements of Abstract Expressionism that had initially characterized his work.

Close's first solo exhibition in 1970 was a series of enormous black-and-white portraits painstakingly transformed from small photographs to colossal paintings. He reproduced and magnified both the mechanical shortcomings of the photograph—blurriness and distortion—and the flaws of the human face: bloodshot eyes, broken capillaries, and enlarged pores. To make his paintings, Close superimposed a grid on a photograph and then transferred a proportional grid to his gigantic canvases. He then applied acrylic paint with an airbrush and scraped off the excess with a razor blade to duplicate the exact shadings of each grid in the photo.

During the 1970s and '80s, Close began using colour and experimenting with a variety of media and techniques. Using only red, yellow, and blue, he simulated the printing process, applying only one layer of colour at a time. He developed one of his most innovative techniques for his "fingerprint series," in which he inked his thumb and forefinger and pressed them to the canvas to achieve a subtle range of grays. Viewed up close, the whorled patterns of his fingerprints could be easily seen; from a distance the method was unidentifiable.

In 1988 a spinal blood clot left Close almost completely paralyzed and confined to a wheelchair. A brush-holding device strapped to his wrist and forearm, however, allowed him to continue working. In the 1990s the minute detail of his earlier paintings was replaced by a grid of tiles daubed with elliptical and ovoid shapes. Viewed

Chuck Close

MARK LENNIHAN—AP/WIDE WORLD

up close, each tile was in itself an abstract painting; when seen from a distance, the vividly multihued tiles became a dynamic deconstruction of the human face. Close was called a photo-realist, a minimalist, and an Abstract Expressionist, but such labels were probably premature, as the 1998 retrospective clearly proved that his style was still evolving. (ELIZABETH LASKEY)

Dæhlie, Bjørn

Norwegian cross-country skiing legend Bjørn Dæhlie rocketed into the record books in 1998 by shattering the previous marks for gold medals and total medals won by an individual in Winter Olympics competition. With victories at the 1998 Games in Nagano, Japan, in the 10-km race, 50-km race, and 4 ×10-km relay, he established himself as one of the greatest Nordic skiers of all time. "The Rocketman," as his adoring fans referred to Dæhlie, also claimed a silver medal in the 15-km race, which increased his impressive inventory to 8 gold medals and 12 overall.

Born on June 19, 1967, in Råholt, Nor., Dæhlie was involved in several sports while growing up and did not focus on competitive Nordic skiing until his mid-teens. Despite his rather late entry into the sport, he rapidly ascended to the top of the World Cup circuit. Hailing from a country with a long history of success in cross-country ski racing, Dæhlie proved able to maintain the ferocity and mastery of his Norwegian predecessors, gaining 35 career World Cup victories, including 5 overall World Cup titles, and 14 world championship gold medals. His achievements in the Winter Olympics included three gold medals and one silver at the 1992 Games in Albertville, France, and two gold and two silver at Lillehammer, Nor., in 1994, in addition to the four

medals at Nagano. His dominance in international competition led some in the cross-country world to confer upon him the moniker "King Bjørn."

Dæhlie achieved superstar status in Norway, where he was featured in a top-selling autobiography, a line of sportswear, and a popular television show, "Men on Adventure," on which he traveled to exotic locations around the world and engaged in two favourite pastimes—hunting and cooking. There was even speculation that a new Oslo airport would be named in his honour.

After his dramatic finish in the 50-km race at Nagano, in which he overtook the leader with eight kilometres (five miles) to go and then collapsed face-first in the snow at the finish line, Dæhlie stated, "Right now I feel I have finished my ski career. I've no motivation." One month later, however, he had apparently found motivation in the opportunity to share in the record for most overall Olympic gold medals (nine) or even to set a new mark. Though he planned on reducing his appearances at World Cup and other events over the next four years, Dæhlie was expected to go for the gold—and the record books—one last time at the 2002 Winter Olympics in Salt Lake City, Utah.

(LAURA RODNITSKY)

Dench, Judi

In January 1998 British actress Judi Dench lit up London's West End in David Hare's play Amy's View, in which she portrayed an actress who over a period of overwhelming loss never loses her passion for the theatre. The part, which she first played at the National Theatre in 1997, was tailor-made for the indomitable Dame Judi. During most of her 40-year career, Dench's fame resided mostly in her native Great Britain, where she was best known for her numerous and quite varied stage roles, a few television series, and supporting parts in motion pictures. American audiences recognized her mainly as James Bond's boss, M, in the two most recent 007 films, GoldenEye (1995) and Tomorrow Never Dies (1997), and as one of the stars of the British romantic comedy series "As Time Goes By" on public television. Dench's performance as the recently widowed Queen Victoria in the 1997 film Mrs. Brown moved her into the ranks of international stars, however, and in early 1998 earned her an Academy Award nomination for best actress and the Golden Globe Award for best actress in a drama.

Judith Olivia Dench was born on Dec. 9, 1934, in York, Eng., and studied at the Central School of Speech Training and Dramatic Art in London. She made her stage debut in 1957 as Ophelia in Hamlet, and Shakespearean works became her specialty, both on the stage and on television. Her performance as Lady Macbeth in the Royal Shakespeare Company's Macbeth earned her the best actress award from the Society of West End Theatres in 1977—the first of her many SWET awards—and her lead role in Antony and Cleopatra brought her Evening Standard, Plays and Players, and Drama Magazine awards in 1987.

Dench, who was also at home in musical roles, starred as Sally Bowles in the London premiere of Cabaret in 1968. In 1996, for her performance

as Desirée in a revival of A Little Night Music, she won the Laurence Olivier Award for best actress in a musical, one of two Olivier awards she captured that year (the other, for best actress in a play, honoured her work in Absolute Hell).

Among Dench's other notable credits were the 1981–84 TV series "A Fine Romance," in which she starred with her husband since 1971, Michael Williams, and such films as 84 Charing Cross Road (1986), A Room with a View (1986), and A Handful of Dust (1988). In late 1998 she appeared in the comedy Shakespeare in Love—this time portraying Queen Elizabeth I—and she was planning to follow that with The Last of the Blonde Bombshells. The stage remained Dench's first love, however, and after starring in a revival of Eduardo de Filippo's Filumena, she was scheduled to take Amy's View to Broadway in 1999. Dench was created O.B.E. in 1970 and advanced to D.B.E. in 1988. (BARBARA WHITNEY)

Diller, Barry

As the so-called telecommunications superhighway continued to develop at breakneck speed during 1998, U.S. entrepreneur Barry Diller remained one of its prime movers by consolidating the string of acquisitions he began to make in the mid-1990s. In 1995 he bought Silver King Broadcasting, which included a number of local television stations, and in 1996 merged it with his newly acquired Home Shopping Network. In 1997 he took control of two cable networks, USA and the Sci-Fi Channel. That same year Diller also acquired assets of the production company Universal Television and became part owner of Ticketmaster. By 1998 his holdings included TV stations, cable systems, and TV production facilities, and he announced plans for a new type of high-quality local news and entertainment programming on his station in Miami, Fla. A tough and demanding boss, he had in the past successfully guided companies through financial difficulties while putting his mark on American pop culture. Analysts were waiting to see what he might now do with his new media holdings.

Diller was born in San Francisco on Feb. 2, 1942. He dropped out of college and in 1961 took a job as a mail clerk at the William Morris Agency. In 1966 he began working as a programming assistant at ABC, where he rose in the ranks to become a vice president of the company. There, he gained acclaim for his successful programming innovations such as the TV miniseries, notably Roots, and the made-for-TV movie of the week. In 1974 he moved to Paramount Pictures, where he served as chairman and chief executive. Under his leadership Paramount became the most successful of the Hollywood studios in the late 1970s and the early '80s, producing such movies as Saturday Night Fever and Raiders of the Lost Ark and the popular television series "Cheers." In 1985 he became chairman and chief executive of Twentieth Century-Fox and later, under new owner Rupert Murdoch (q.v.), was given the job of creating a fourth television network. With programs like "Married . . . with Children" and "The Simpsons" delivered by satellite to a hastily assembled group of affiliates, the Fox Network succeeded against all odds.

In 1992 Diller left Fox and purchased QVC, a home-shopping cable network. Two years later he was defeated in his attempt to buy his old employer, which had been renamed Paramount Communications. That same year QVC and CBS announced a merger, but it was quickly squelched by QVC investors. Diller then sold QVC and started on the series of acquisitions and mergers that by 1998 once again made him a power broker in telecommunications. (ROBERT RAUCH)

Duchovny, David, and Anderson, Gillian

In 1998 the motion picture The X-Files: Fight the Future—released in June and becoming the number one box-office hit, with a take of over $30 million in its first weekend—brought to the big screen one of the hottest television shows and hottest couples of the 1990s. FBI Special Agents Fox ("Spooky") Mulder and Dana Scully, played by David Duchovny and Gillian Anderson, respectively, on the TV series "The X-Files," had

never so much as kissed in the five years the program had been on. Nonetheless, to the show's 20 million weekly viewers there was no denying the chemistry between Mulder (a believer in space aliens and government conspiracies) and his partner, Scully (a skeptical scientist and doctor), as they pursued the truth behind the odd, usually paranormal cases described in the X-file dossiers. The movie also added to the electricity between Scully and Mulder but still brought them only to the brink of a kiss, and the kiss that took place in an episode early in the series' sixth season, because of its context, was not "official."

David William Duchovny was born Aug. 7, 1960, in New York City. He was educated at Princeton University, where he received a B.A. degree, and Yale University, where he earned an M.A. in English literature and began working on a Ph.D. Duchovny added acting classes in New York City to his schedule and began getting work, including a TV commercial for beer and some Off-Broadway plays. He left Yale in 1987 to live in New York City and later that year moved to Hollywood, where his first movie roles were in *Working Girl* (1988) and the independent film *New Year's Day* (1989). Other credits followed, notably *Julia Has Two Lovers* (1991), *The Rapture* (1991), *Chaplin* (1992), and *Kalifornia* (1993). In the early 1990s he added such TV roles as Jake on "The Red Shoe Diaries" and the memorable transvestite detective Dennis/Denise on "Twin Peaks." Duchovny's "X-Files" popularity led to TV guest appearances as himself on "The Larry Sanders Show" and as the voice of Mulder on the animated series "The Simpsons." In 1997 he starred in the motion picture *Playing God*.

Anderson was born Aug. 9, 1968, in Chicago. When she was in high school, entertaining thoughts of becoming a marine biologist, community theatre participation whetted her appetite for acting. She earned a B.F.A. degree at the Goodman Theatre School at DePaul University, Chicago, and attended the National Theatre of Great Britain's summer program at Cornell University, Ithaca, N.Y., before pursuing a theatre career in New York City. Anderson appeared in the Off-Broadway production *Absent Friends,* winning a 1991 Theatre World Award, and in *The Philanthropist* at the Long Wharf Theatre in New Haven, Conn., before moving to Los Angeles. After a few motion-picture and television appearances, she auditioned for the part of Scully and in 1993, at "The X-Files" creator Chris Carter's insistence, landed her first starring role. In 1998 Anderson could be seen in two additional films, *Chicago Cab* and *The Mighty,* and in the autumn she and Duchovny headed into their sixth television season, more certain than ever that "the truth is out there."   (BARBARA WHITNEY)

Duisenberg, Wim

Europe made a great stride toward achieving economic and monetary union, one of the primary goals set out in the Maastricht Treaty of 1991, with the establishment on July 1, 1998, of the European Central Bank (ECB). At the helm was Dutch banker Wim Duisenberg, who had been chosen two months earlier at the European Union (EU) summit meeting in Brussels on May 1–3. Duisenberg's immediate task was to shepherd in the arrival of the euro, the EU's new single currency, on Jan. 1, 1999.

Although not well known outside banking circles, the tall, silver-haired Dutchman was considered eminently qualified to manage this historic transition. During his 15-year tenure as president of the Dutch central bank—a post he accepted in 1982—Duisenberg helped build The Netherlands into a nation with a vigorous economy that boasted a strong currency, low inflation and interest rates, and decreasing unemployment. In 1997 Duisenberg was elected president of the European Monetary Institute—the forerunner of the ECB—with the assurance that he would be a leading candidate for the position of president of the central bank. His candidacy did not go unchallenged, however, and his confirmation was anything but smooth. French Pres. Jacques Chirac led the battle over his appointment. In a politically charged maneuver, Chirac nominated the

governor of the French central bank, Jean-Claude Trichet, to oppose Duisenberg. The dispute was resolved when Duisenberg agreed that he would step down after serving only four years of the eight-year term stipulated by the Maastricht Treaty—to make way for Trichet to take over.

For the remainder of 1998, Duisenberg worked with a five-member board of the new central bank, which was based in Frankfurt, Ger., to address a number of key issues in preparation for the euro's introduction to 11 of the EU member states—Germany, France, Italy, Spain, The Netherlands, Belgium, Ireland, Portugal, Luxembourg, Austria, and Finland.

Born Willem Frederik Duisenberg on July 9, 1935, in Heerenveen, Neth., he spent a portion of his early career in academia. After receiving a doctorate degree in economics from the State University of Groningen for his thesis on the economic results of disarmament, he served a four-year stint as a teaching assistant at the school. He left to join the International Monetary Fund in Washington, D.C., in 1965, and from there, in 1969, went on to serve briefly as an advisor to the Dutch central bank. From 1970 to 1973 he was a professor of macroeconomics at the University of Amsterdam. At the age of 38, Duisenberg was appointed Dutch finance minister, a post he held until 1977 when he entered politics for a year as a Labour Party MP. He joined the board of the Dutch cooperative banking group Rabobank Nederland and remained there until 1982, when he returned to the Dutch central bank.

(MARY JANE FRIEDRICH)

Duvall, Robert

American actor Robert Duvall had known he "wanted to play a preacher" for nearly 30 years, ever since the day he observed two evangelists sermonizing in the small town of Hughes, Ark. His fascination with the styles and cadences of Pentecostal preachers led him to visit many churches across the U.S., and he eventually used the notes he took on those visits to write a screenplay, *The Apostle,* about a volatile Southern minister. Hollywood studios uniformly balked when approached with the project, however, in part because the film failed to indict the religious views of the title character. Deciding to finance *The Apostle* himself, Duvall proceeded to both direct and star in the film, which not only became a box-office success in early 1998 but won accolades from critics and earned Duvall his third Academy Award nomination for best actor.

Born on Jan. 5, 1931, in San Diego, Calif., where his father, a career navy officer, was stationed at the time, Duvall grew up in Fairfax county, Va. Although his mother was a talented amateur actress, Duvall gave little thought to a career in acting until he began taking theatre classes at Principia College, Elsah, Ill. Upon graduation he entered the army and served two years (1951–53) in the Korean War before moving to New York City to study acting at the Neighborhood Playhouse. To support himself, he worked at various jobs and shared an apartment with other aspiring actors, among them Dustin Hoffman. Duvall first attracted attention with his portrayal of a longshoreman in a one-night studio production of *A View from the Bridge* (1957) and made a memorable film debut in the role of Boo Radley, the enigmatic neighbour of lawyer Atticus Finch (Gregory Peck) in the 1962 classic *To Kill a Mockingbird.*

In the more than 60 movie appearances that followed, Duvall demonstrated a remarkable versatility. Among his roles were the outlaw Ned Pepper, John Wayne's nemesis, in *True Grit* (1969), the prudish Maj. Frank Burns in *M*A*S*H* (1970), the consigliere Tom Hagen in *The Godfather* (1972) and *The Godfather Part II* (1974), and the maniacal Lieut. Col. Bill Kilgore in *Apocalypse Now* (1979). He received Academy Award nominations for best supporting actor for his work in *The Godfather* and *Apocalypse Now,* and he earned his first Oscar nomination for best actor for his portrayal of a troubled U.S. Marine Corps pilot in *The Great Santini* (1979). He won the best actor Oscar for his riveting performance as a washed-up country singer in *Tender Mercies*

(1983). Duvall also appeared on television, most notably in the miniseries *Lonesome Dove* (1989).

Between 1993 and 1997 he acted in 13 feature films, and, with prominent roles in *Deep Impact* and *A Civil Action,* two 1998 blockbuster motion pictures, the "Apostle" seemed poised to convert a new generation of fans.

(SHERMAN HOLLAR)

Elway, John

On Jan. 25, 1998, National Football League (NFL) quarterback John Elway of the Denver Broncos added a much-anticipated credential to his already impressive resume: Super Bowl champion. Three previous Super Bowl appearances (1986, 1987, 1989) had ended in defeat, and it seemed that Super Bowl XXXII—against the defending champion Green Bay Packers—would be Elway's final chance for a victory. Having acknowledged before the game that his future was uncertain, the 38-year-old star left thousands of longtime Broncos fans praying for both their first Super Bowl championship and the return of their revered quarterback. The Denver devotees were joined by football fans and players throughout the country in support of Elway, whose illustrious career almost certainly guaranteed him a place in the Football Hall of Fame. With the fans and media behind him, Elway became the hero of Super Bowl XXXII long before the first snap was even taken.

Born on June 28, 1960, in Port Angeles, Wash., Elway excelled at football and baseball in high school and was drafted by the major league baseball Kansas City Royals in 1979. He instead attended Stanford University, where he received a B.A. in economics and set several football passing and other offense records. He was the number one draft pick of baseball's New York Yankees in 1981 and played on a Yankees farm club the following summer. In 1983 he was chosen by the Baltimore Colts as the number one pick in the NFL draft. Elway was set to play baseball, but when he was traded by Baltimore to the Denver Broncos later in 1983 he headed for the "Mile High City" instead.

Elway wowed fans in the NFL with his throwing precision, cool leadership, and rushing ability. By the end of the 1997–98 season he was the winningest starting quarterback in league history, was tied for the most seasons (12) with at least 3,000 passing yards, and led the NFL with 45 fourth-quarter game-winning drives. Elway received the Mackey Award from the NFL Players Association as the top American Football Conference quarterback of the 1997–98 season and was voted to his eighth Pro Bowl appearance (his fifth as a starter). His well-known scrambling and comeback abilities were used most notably in Denver's 31–24 win over Green Bay in Super Bowl XXXII. In the third quarter Elway dove headfirst between two much larger Green Bay defenders to gain a first down that set up a Bronco touchdown. The play revealed Elway's intense desire to achieve the one honour missing from his storied career, and it came to symbolize Super Bowl XXXII. Months later Elway rewarded his legions of fans with another division title and seemed to be well on his way to a record fifth Super Bowl in January 1999.

(LAURA RODNITZKY)

Estrada, Joseph

On May 11, 1998, Joseph ("Erap") Estrada, a former star of B movies, was elected president of the Philippines. Despite lacking the support of outgoing president Fidel Ramos, the country's business community, and the influential Roman Catholic Church, Estrada captured nearly 40% of the vote, handily defeating his nearest rival, House Speaker José de Venecia, who garnered only 15.9%. The margin of victory was the largest in a free election in the history of the Philippines. Estrada, whose charisma and populist platform helped win him a devoted following among the country's poor, was officially declared president by Congress on May 29.

Estrada was born Joseph Ejercito on April 19, 1937, in Manila. The son of a government engineer, he entered the Mapua Institute of Technology with the intention of following in his

John Elway

father's footsteps but eventually dropped out to become a film actor. Forbidden by his parents from using the family name, he adopted the screen name Erap Estrada. He played the lead in more than 100 movies, usually portraying a swashbuckling tough guy who defends the poor against the corrupt establishment. He also produced some 75 films.

He entered politics in 1968, successfully running for the mayorship of the Manila suburb of San Juan, in which office he remained until 1986. The following year he was elected to the Senate. In 1992 he ran for vice president on the National People's Coalition ticket. Although the party's presidential candidate, Eduardo Cojuangco, Jr., lost the election to Ramos, Estrada won the vice presidential contest.

Barred by the Philippine constitution from running for a second term, Ramos supported the candidacy of de Venecia. Businessmen, who had benefited from the economic reforms of Ramos and who were fearful of Estrada's populist proposals, supported the candidacy of Renato de Villa, who had served as secretary of defense under Ramos.

Joseph Estrada

The Roman Catholic Church denied Estrada its support because he had admitted to having fathered four children by women other than his wife. He had, however, the support of Imelda Marcos, the widow of former president Ferdinand Marcos and a member of Congress, who withdrew from the race on April 29 after courts upheld her 1993 conviction and sentence on charges of graft. Moreover, Estrada was able to persuade at least some key business leaders that his administration would not hamper free-market reforms.

After the results of what were described as generally peaceful elections were affirmed, Estrada was inaugurated on June 30. Having promised to crack down on crime and political corruption and to develop agriculture, he vowed to live up to the title he had given himself during the campaign, "president of the masses."   (ROBERT RAUCH)

Farah, Nuruddin

In 1998 the Somali writer Nuruddin Farah won the Neustadt International Prize for Literature. Although his primary languages were Somali, Amharic, and Arabic, Farah chose to write in English. By his own admission, this decision was a practical one: "Because I could find a typewriter in English"; nevertheless, his choice gave him an international audience. The Neustadt—awarded every two years by the University of Oklahoma and its literary publication, *World Literature Today*—entailed an award of $40,000 and a cast silver replica of an eagle feather. Farah was the second African writer to receive the prize; Algeria's Assia Djebar was the first in 1996.

The son of a merchant and the well-known Somali poet Aleeli Faduma, Farah was born in 1945 in the city of Baidoa in what was then Italian Somaliland. He was educated in Ethiopia and at the colonial-era Institutio Magistrale in Mogadishu, where he learned English as well as Italian and published an apprentice novella, *Why Die So Soon?* (1965). After working for the Somali Ministry of Education, he studied literature and philosophy at Panjab University, Chandigarh, India. While there, he wrote his first full-fledged novel, the feminist *From a Crooked Rib* (1970). The novel portrayed the determination of one woman to maintain her dignity in a society that believed "God created Woman from a crooked rib; and anyone who trieth to straighten it, breaketh it"; it would not be the last of Farah's feminist works.

In his next novel, *A Naked Needle* (1976), Farah used a slight tale of interracial and cross-cultural love to reveal a lurid picture of postrevolutionary Somali life in the mid-1970s. He next

wrote a trilogy—*Sweet and Sour Milk* (1979), *Sardines* (1981), and *Close Sesame* (1983)—about life under a particularly African dictatorship in which ideological slogans barely disguise an almost surreal society and human ties have been severed by dread and terror. His unblinking portrayal of life under the dictator Muhammad Siad Barre eventually forced him into exile. During this period he taught for a time in Europe, North America, and elsewhere in Africa, writing in 1998, "My novels are about states of exile; about women shivering in the cruel cold in a world ruled by men; about the commoner denied justice; about a torturer tortured by guilt, his own conscience; about a traitor betrayed." *Secrets,* the third novel of his second trilogy—which includes the novels *Maps* (1986) and *Gifts* (1992)—was published in 1998. Farah's rich imagination and his refreshing and often fortuitous use of his adopted language made him the most significant Somali writer in any European language.

(KATHLEEN KUIPER)

Folkman, (Moses) Judah

"If you have cancer and you are a mouse, we can take good care of you," remarked cancer researcher Judah Folkman in 1998. He was referring to a new treatment that he and his colleagues had discovered that completely eliminated essentially any type of cancerous tumour in mice. Folkman, however, was cautious about predictions regarding the success of the therapy in humans, since the path to a cure for cancer was strewn with once-promising treatments that had not proved effective.

Folkman's findings were the result of nearly four decades of persistence to an idea. As a young navy surgeon, he began to investigate the relationship between the growth of malignant tumours and angiogenesis, the process of blood vessel development. He was intrigued by the fact that cancer does not progress from a small, harmless mass of cells to a large, deadly tumour unless tiny capillaries develop to provide each cancerous cell with the nutrients and oxygen necessary for its growth. Folkman started to search for factors that trigger angiogenesis in tumours, reasoning that if he could determine how blood vessel development begins, he might be able to halt it and thereby arrest tumour growth. Folkman and others found that tumours themselves produce substances that both stimulate and inhibit angiogenesis and that it is the balance between them that determines if and when the tumour grows. The substances that shrink tumours by limiting their blood supply and preventing new blood vessel growth are called angiogenesis inhibitors. One of them, called angiostatin, was isolated in 1994 by Michael O'Reilly, a researcher in Folkman's laboratory. Using angiostatin in combination with another angiogenesis inhibitor called endostatin, Folkman's team was able to eradicate any type of cancerous tumour in mice.

Folkman was born Feb. 24, 1933, in Cleveland, Ohio. After graduating from Ohio State University (B.A., 1953), he entered Harvard Medical School (M.D., 1957). While at Harvard Folkman developed the first atrioventricular pacemaker, a discovery for which he won the first of many awards. He worked as an intern and assistant resident at Massachusetts General Hospital from 1957 to 1960, leaving to serve at the National Naval Medical Center. There he not only began his tumour-growth studies but also discovered, with David Long, a polymer that facilitated the sustained release of drugs that came to be used in implantable contraceptives. Folkman returned to his surgery residency at Massachusetts General in 1962. He became an instructor of surgery at Harvard three years later and associate director of the Sears Surgical Laboratory at Boston City Hospital a year after that. From 1967 to 1981 he served as surgeon in chief and chairman of the department of surgery at Children's Hospital Medical Center of Harvard, where he later became director of the surgical research laboratory. In 1981 Folkman resigned as pediatric surgeon to focus on angiogenesis research.

(MARY JANE FRIEDRICH)

Gracida, Memo
When Guillermo ("Memo") Gracida, Jr.'s Isla Carroll team lost the 1998 U.S. Polo Open, it ended Gracida's six-year Open winning streak and led to speculation that the 42-year-old legend may have finally passed his peak. Talk of Gracida's retirement had been unthinkable only a year earlier when he won his 15th U.S. Open in 20 years and was inducted into the Polo Hall of Fame. As one of only a dozen or so top 10-goal-handicap players in the world, Gracida had an instinct for the game that had long seemed infallible—almost inhuman. Although his retirement still could be years away, in 1998 some polo fans already spoke of him as the greatest ever to have played the game.

Gracida may have seemed the quintessential "natural" polo player, but his mastery of the game was neither a fluke nor casually achieved. Born in Mexico City in 1956, Gracida grew up on polo—his father, Guillermo ("Memo") Gracida, Sr., and uncles won the U.S. Open in 1946, and his cousins and younger brother Carlos all became distinguished professional polo players. The young Gracidas played on a rough polo practice field they nicknamed "La Luna" for its pockmarked surface, and the dedicated, almost obsessive Memo Jr. rarely traveled far from it. Such a polo-centred upbringing not only honed Gracida's considerable talent but also instilled in him the desire to keep vital the future of the sport. Later in his career he sought to pass along this desire, generously giving his time and expertise to the education of young polo players and the sponsorship of children's tournaments.

In 1976 he and his father helped Mexico upset the U.S. in the Camacho Cup, and later that same year the younger Gracida moved to the U.S. One year after his American polo debut, he won his first U.S. Open, and by 1982 he was a 10-goal player. For the next 15 years he dominated the sport with a combination of smooth riding, seemingly effortless strokes, and, most of all, the sort of intangible, innate sense of the game exhibited by players who reach their sport's pantheon. During this period his titles included six World Cups, three USPA Gold Cups, two Camacho Cups, and the 1982 Argentine Open.

The U.S. Open loss in 1998 may have been merely an off match for Gracida. If it did signal the beginning of a decline in his skills, it was clear that his record-breaking achievements and dignified sportsmanship—as well as his efforts to educate young polo players—had guaranteed that the mark he left on the game of polo would remain for generations. (LOCKE PETERSEIM)

Gray, John
With his 1992 book *Men Are from Mars, Women Are from Venus,* relationship guru John Gray managed to parlay the rather obvious observation that men and women are different into a series of phenomenally successful books that spawned videotapes, motivational seminars, counseling franchises, and even a Broadway show. In 1998 he added to his rapidly growing empire a magazine and a board game that pitted Martians (men) and Venusians (women) against each other and that also, according to Gray, provided a "vehicle to talk about relationships in a casual setting."

Gray was born in Houston, Texas, in 1951. As a teenager he became involved in the Transcendental Meditation (TM) movement and eventually became the personal assistant of TM founder Maharishi Mahesh Yogi. Taking a vow of celibacy, Gray traveled with the guru for nine years and learned firsthand the necessary attributes of a charismatic leader. In 1979 he left the movement and moved to California, and in 1982 he married Barbara DeAngelis (who also became a best-selling self-help author). Together they began a business that specialized in weekend sex-and-relationship workshops. The marriage ended in 1984, the same year Gray self-published his first book, *What You Feel You Can Heal.*

Throughout the 1980s he worked as a "spiritual counselor" and conducted relationship seminars. His credentials as a professional psychologist were questionable to some—he held degrees from the Maharishi International University and obtained his Ph.D. through correspondence courses. In 1990 he self-published a second book, *Men, Women and Relationships,* which he described as "a thick book of my research into the differences between men and women." In 1992 *Men Are from Mars, Women Are from Venus* was released and became a best-seller. It was based on Gray's premise that men and women have different emotional requirements and that a misunderstanding of the differences leads to the breakdown of relationships. The book's lighthearted tone as well as its ample selection of examples, anecdotes, remedies, and peculiar metaphors and analogies ("men are like blowtorches, women are like ovens") had immense appeal. It remained on best-seller lists for more than four years and on paperback best-seller lists even longer. Gray followed up with successful variations, including *Mars and Venus in the Bedroom* (1995), *Mars and Venus in Love* (1996), and *Mars and Venus on a Date* (1997).

The popularity of the Mars-Venus formula was undeniable, and Gray took credit for revitalizing scores of foundering relationships. A number of people criticized his view of contemporary relationships, claiming his work was little more than an exhaustive reworking of age-old gender stereotypes. Such judgments, however, failed to deter Gray, whose future plans included a Mars-Venus parenting book and a television sitcom and who, with characteristically blithe egotism, claimed, "I feel it's in me to help negotiate peace in the world." (ELIZABETH LASKEY)

Hackl, Georg
By winning the gold medal in the men's singles in luge at the Winter Games at Nagano, Japan, in February 1998, Georg Hackl of Germany established himself as the greatest Olympic luger of all time. With his triumph Hackl became the first luger and only the sixth athlete to win a Winter Olympics event three consecutive times. He accomplished that feat at Nagano by winning all four runs of the two-day competition—the first time that had ever been done in the Olympic Games—to finish with a time of 3 min 18.436 sec, more than half a second ahead of the silver medalist, Armin Zoeggeler of Italy.

Hackl was born Sept. 9, 1966, in Berchtesgaden, Ger., a resort town in the Alps where grammar-school students could luge in physical education class. Hackl, who never considered himself much of an athlete, took to the sport immediately. He did not develop any real advantage, however, until he served an apprenticeship as a metalworker and learned the essential sled-building skills that lugers must possess. He built his first sled at age 16, and from then on his unmatched ability to adjust his sled to the conditions of the race helped carry him to success. Along with his metalworking expertise, Hackl was credited with possessing nerves of steel. Total concentration is essential to winning in a sport in which the difference between winning and losing is only a fraction of a second. Racers must stay relaxed while guiding a sled at speeds of up to 130 km/h (80 mph) while using only their toes to steer. Hackl used his uncanny powers of concentration time and again to thwart his rival, Markus Prock of Austria.

The favourite at the 1988 Winter Olympics at Calgary, Alta., Prock performed poorly on the choppy ice. Hackl, however, adjusted to the conditions and finished with a silver medal. Although Hackl finished first at the world championships in 1989 and 1990 and second in 1991, Prock was once again the favourite at the 1992 Winter Olympics at Albertville, France. Hackl and Prock stood first and second, respectively, after the first day of competition, but snow fell the next day. Hackl tinkered with his equipment and came away with his first gold medal, beating Prock by 0.3 sec. Two years later, at the Winter Olympics at Lillehammer, Nor., Prock again was favoured, and he led the field after three runs; Hackl, however, turned in the second best run of the day on his final try and won the gold. Prock took the silver.

Despite winning the world championships again in 1997, Hackl went back to the workshop to find a way to improve his chances in the Nagano Games. With smaller, better runners on his sled, he was able to dominate the field and win the gold medal once again.
(ANTHONY G. CRAINE)

Harada, Masahiko
On Feb. 17, 1998, 15,000 jubilant spectators jammed Central Square in Nagano, Japan, to witness the medal ceremony in which the members of Japan's Olympic ski-jumping team received gold medals. Fans had witnessed the Japanese team's failure four years earlier at the Winter Games at Lillehammer, Nor., when the celebrated Masahiko ("Happy") Harada, needing to jump only a little more than 100 m (1 m=3.3 ft) to secure the win, launched prematurely and completed the shortest jump of the competition—97.5 m—and thereby handed first place to Germany. After that disappointing jump Harada's inconsistency became well known, and so, although Japan entered the 1998 Games as a heavy favourite in team ski jumping, an entire country seemed to be letting out a collective sigh of relief as the medals were awarded.

Harada was born May 9, 1968, in Kamikawa, Japan. He became a national hero when he took first place in the normal-hill jump at the 1993 world championships. The following year, as Japan appeared poised to take its first gold in ski jumping since the 1972 Games at Sapporo, Japan, his failure at Lillehammer caused the man nicknamed "Happy" to become best known for collapsing in the snow in tears. Harada's misfortune carried over into the 1995 season, and he finished 59th overall in the World Cup competition. In 1996 he began to return to the form that had brought him acclaim in 1993. With four wins in World Cup events, he finished fifth overall for the season. He continued to excel in 1997. Leading up to the Nagano Winter Games, Harada performed as though he meant to erase what had happened at Lillehammer and bring gold to Japan. In an Olympic warm-up meet in Sapporo held on the course used in the 1972 Games, he set a course record with a jump of 140.5 m and won the event.

Harada seemed to return to 1994 form during his two individual events at Nagano. In the 90-m competition he led the field after the first of two jumps, but a poor showing on the second dropped him to fifth place. His first jump in the 120-m left him in sixth place and all but eliminated any hope of a medal. Then his fortune changed. With nothing to lose on his final jump, Harada sailed 136 m—by far the longest distance in that event—and won the bronze.

In the team competition Harada hit rock bottom again, posting a 79.5-m performance, one of the worst of the competition, on his first jump. His second effort, for 137 m, matched the best mark of the team event, and Japan went on to win the gold. Soon after the contest ended, Harada once again broke down into tears. This time, however, Happy Harada was truly just that.
(ANTHONY G. CRAINE)

Hasek, Dominik
In 1998 Dominik Hasek, "the Dominator," borrowed a page from the comic books and turned in his own performance as the Masked Marvel. The goaltender for the National Hockey League (NHL) Buffalo Sabres won his fourth Vezina Trophy as the league's best netminder and became the first goalie to win consecutive Hart Memorial trophies as the NHL's most valuable player (MVP). These awards complemented the gold medal that Hasek earned in February at the Winter Olympics in Nagano, Japan—the first Games to feature NHL players. There he led the surprising Czech Republic team past the favoured American and Canadian squads to the country's first gold in the sport. With his unorthodox style (highlighted by spectacular flopping saves) and lightning-quick reflexes, Hasek proved that he was one of the game's best goalies. The Sabres agreed, rewarding their star netminder with a new three-year, $26 million contract extension that made Hasek the highest-paid goaltender in NHL history.

Born in Pardubice, Czech., on Jan. 29, 1965, Hasek began playing ice hockey as a child, skating on shoes with blades screwed into the bottom. Incredibly flexible, he quickly became a standout in the net and was named the country's League Player of the Year three times (1987, 1989, and 1990). In 1983 he was selected by the Chicago Blackhawks in the NHL draft, but it was not un-

Masahiko ("Happy") Harada
CHARLES PLATIAU—REUTERS/ARCHIVE PHOTOS

til after Czechoslovakia's "Velvet Revolution" in 1989 that he left his homeland and joined the team. Following a rookie season (1990–91) largely spent on the bench, Hasek was traded to the Sabres in 1992. Faced with little playing time in Buffalo, he contemplated leaving the league. During the 1993–94 season, however, an injury to a teammate gave Hasek the chance to play regularly. He responded by turning in one of the best performances by an NHL netminder. With a 1.95 goals-against average (GAA)—the lowest GAA posted by a goalie in two decades—Hasek won the first of his four Vezina trophies (1994, 1995, 1997, and 1998) and secured his position as the team's starting goaltender. In 1998 he became the first goalie in 35 years to receive the Hart Memorial Trophy.

The 1997–98 season began with a shaky start as teammates continued to question Hasek's decision during the previous season's play-offs to remove himself from the lineup because of an injury. Furthermore, fans blamed the goaltender for the departure of the Sabres' popular coach in the off-season. Faced with the turmoil, Hasek struggled in the net as his GAA rose to more than three. In December, however, he returned to form, tying an NHL record for most shutouts in a month (six). He went on to post a 2.09 GAA with 13 shutouts and led the Sabres on an unexpected postseason run, advancing to the Eastern Conference finals. By then, everyone knew who the masked man was.   (AMY TIKKANEN)

Holbrooke, Richard Charles Albert

June 1998 was an eventful month for American diplomat Richard Holbrooke. His book *To End a War*, an account of the 1995 Balkan peace negotiations, was published. Then, six days after his name was announced as Pres. Bill Clinton's choice for the U.S. ambassadorship to the UN, Holbrooke undertook a diplomatic mission to the Serbian province of Kosovo to attempt to negotiate a cease-fire between Serbs and the ethnic Albanian majority seeking autonomy.

Described by many in Washington as an ambitious self-promoter, Holbrooke had enjoyed a number of careers, including magazine editing, investment banking, and writing. He was born April 24, 1941, in New York City to a European Jewish couple who had fled the Nazis in the 1930s. After receiving a bachelor's degree from Brown University, Providence, R.I., in 1962, he joined the Foreign Service and was posted to Vietnam until 1966. His experience there and in Washington on Pres. Lyndon Johnson's Vietnam staff led to his being named a junior member of the U.S. delegation to the Paris Peace Talks in 1968–69. After serving as Peace Corps director in Morocco from 1970 to 1972, he edited the controversial quarterly magazine *Foreign Policy* (1972–76). He returned to the government in 1977 when Pres. Jimmy Carter appointed him assistant secretary of state for East Asian and Pacific affairs. From 1981 to 1985 Holbrooke was both

vice president of Public Strategies, a Washington, D.C., consulting firm, and senior adviser to the New York investment firm Lehman Brothers; he then served as managing director of Lehman Brothers from 1985 until 1993. In 1996 he became vice chairman of Crédit Suisse First Boston.

Holbrooke served the Clinton administration as ambassador to Germany (1993–94) and assistant secretary of state for European and Canadian affairs (1994–95). The 1995 Dayton accords, achieved through his unorthodox mix of diplomacy, bluffing, and bullying, gained what continued to be a fragile peace in Bosnia and Herzegovina. Considered briefly in late 1996 as a possible candidate for secretary of state, Hobrooke lost the position to Madeleine Albright but in 1997 was appointed special envoy to Cyprus, where he attempted to broker a settlement of the two-decade-old dispute over that island between Greece and Turkey.

From June through August, Holbrooke's shuttle diplomacy did little toward achieving a cease-fire in Kosovo, where both sides continued fighting. In September Congress postponed discussing Holbrooke's nomination to the UN post until the new year because of allegations of conflict of interest. Despite some progress made in October with Serbian strongman Slobodan Milosevic, disunity between rebel factions, NATO's failure to use force against the Serbs, and a shifting U.S. policy in the region hampered negotiations. It remained to be seen whether Holbrooke, if appointed to the UN, would effect a peaceful settlement.   (REBECCA RUNDALL)

Humphries, (John) Barry (Dame Edna Everage)

In the spring of 1998, after a lengthy absence from the theatre, self-proclaimed international megastar Dame Edna Everage returned to the live stage in Guildford, Eng.—courtesy of her "manager" and alter ego, Australian writer, actor, and comic performer Barry Humphries—in the world premiere of *Edna: The Spectacle*. On stage a pink-bewigged, outrageously bespectacled Humphries gave life to his much-beloved, self-absorbed, and often acid-tongued character, affectionately known as simply Dame Edna. Costarring with Edna in her autobiographical musical revue was another of Humphries's popular characters, Sir Les Patterson, who was comically referred to as Australia's chief emissary of culture. Not one to neglect her international fans, or "possums" as Edna referred

to her audiences, later that fall she took the show to the United States.

Humphries was born on Feb. 17, 1934, in Melbourne, Australia. He attended Melbourne University, made his theatrical debut in 1953 at the Union Theatre in Melbourne, and subsequently toured with a theatre company. His London stage debut was in *The Demon Barber* (1959), and he later appeared in various productions of the musical *Oliver!* as well as in several one-man stage shows. In 1955 the character of Edna Everage was created for a skit he was performing. Humphries said that Edna's character arose out of his desire to lampoon the people and standards of his parents' generation. What evolved was a character that could at times be condescending, insulting, and intrusive while still likeable and always sincere.

According to Humphries's biographical accounts of Everage, she was "born" Edna Beasley and began performing anecdotal material at small venues in her hometown of Moonee Ponds, a Melbourne suburb. She was left a widow after the death of her husband, Norman Everage. She made her film debut in *The Naked Bunyip* (1970) and later had a role in the film *Sgt. Pepper's Lonely Hearts Club Band* (1978). Edna achieved superstar status at lightning speed when she was made a dame on television in the 1970s in a spontaneous gesture by Australian Prime Minister Gough Whitlam. She made numerous television appearances, among them "The Dame Edna Experience" (1987), "Dame Edna's Hollywood" (1991), and "Dame Edna Kisses It Better" (1997). Among the books that she authored were *Dame Edna's Coffee Table Book: A Guide to Gracious Living and the Finer Things in Life by One of the First Ladies of the World Theatre* (1976) and *My Gorgeous Life: The Life, the Loves, the Legend* (1989). Humphries himself also wrote several books, including *Barry Humphries' Treasury of Australian Kitsch* (1980). After more than 40 years of success with Dame Edna, Humphries said, "It entertains me to think a character I invented for a one-night stand in Melbourne in 1955 should still be entertaining people."   (ANTHONY L. GREEN)

Dame Edna (Barry Humphries)

ARCHIVE PHOTOS

Hunt, Helen

It seemed that everyone was mad about Helen Hunt in 1998. The year began with the American actress winning a Golden Globe for her performance as a lonely waitress in the surprise hit film *As Good as It Gets* (1997). A Screen Actors Guild Award soon followed, and in March she received an Academy Award, which completed her sweep of the major American film honours for best actress. Her first Oscar came just hours after NBC had agreed to pay Hunt $1 million per episode to return for a seventh season on television's "Mad About You" and six months before she won her third Emmy award for the series. For Hunt, 1998 was as good as it gets.

Born on June 15, 1963, in Culver City, Calif., Hunt was introduced to acting by her father, a director and drama coach. At the age of six, she decided she wanted to become an actor, and within three years she had hired an agent and made her television debut, appearing on "The Mary Tyler Moore Show." Other small-screen parts soon followed, including a recurring role on "St. Elsewhere" and numerous made-for-television movies. After several failed TV series, Hunt was offered the role of Jamie Buchman on "Mad About You" in 1992. Developed by and costarring Paul Reiser, the comedy followed the ups and downs of a married couple. The show was an instant hit, and Hunt, with her caustic wit and easy charm, became a star. In addition to acting, for which she received four Golden Globes (1994–95, 1997–98) and those three Emmys (1996–98), Hunt also spent time behind the camera, producing and directing several episodes.

Although Hunt had found fame on television, big-screen success remained elusive. After making her film debut in *Rollercoaster* (1977), she appeared in a string of movies, including *Peggy Sue Got Married* (1986), *Mr. Saturday Night* (1992), and *Bob Roberts* (1992). Though Hunt earned praise for her performances, the films failed to ignite at the box office. That changed in 1996 with *Twister*. The special-effects-driven movie about tornado chasers was a blockbuster, grossing more than $200 million. As offers for other big-screen ventures poured in, Hunt chose the unlikely romantic comedy *As Good as It Gets*. Playing opposite Jack Nicholson, a neurotic and bigoted writer, Hunt charmed viewers with her sympathetic and humorous turn as Carol, a single parent struggling with bills, an ill child, and an intrusive mother. She next appeared on stage as the cleverly disguised Viola in Shakespeare's *Twelfth Night*. It was a fitting choice for Hunt, who revealed in 1998 that behind the image of the girl next door was actually one of the most sought-after actresses in Hollywood. (AMY TIKKANEN)

Iyengar, B.K.S.

In 1998 B.K.S. Iyengar, unlike most octogenarians, celebrated his 80th birthday year at the height of his fame and in outstanding physical and mental health. Generally regarded as the world's foremost teacher and practitioner of yoga, he was also its most influential popularizer. From his Shrimati Ramamani Iyengar Memorial Yoga Institute—named in honour of his late wife and run with the assistance of his daughter and son—in Pune, India, he surveyed a steadily expanding empire of more than 200 Iyengar-style yoga centres, more than 10,000 teachers, and some 2,000,000 students worldwide.

Iyengar regularly taught hatha yoga—an orchestration of numerous postures, controlled breathing, and meditation that relaxes and develops mind, body, and spirit—to classes in Pune and

Helen Hunt
FRED PROUSER—REUTERS/ARCHIVE PHOTOS

throughout the world. His appearance and method of teaching were both unforgettable, and his flexible body belied his age. He wore his long gray hair drawn back from a brow bisected from hairline to bridge of nose by a red painted line. His bushy eyebrows shaded deep-set, luminous eyes. Iyengar spoke nonstop during his classes and used a personal approach characterized by sensitivity to his students' unique physiques. His method was sympathetic to the difficulty of trying to meditate and relax while at the same time trying to control one's breathing while twisted in an improbable posture. He introduced the use of various props—for example, blocks, chairs, and blankets—to make yoga less daunting, especially to Westerners.

Iyengar was born into a large, impoverished family on Dec. 14, 1918, in Bellur, Kolar district, Karnataka, India. He was a sickly child with a distended belly and an inability to hold his head up straight. His physical condition made him a laughingstock among his peers, and his friendlessness hindered his academic achievement. While still in his teens, he turned to yoga for relief, although not without suffering great physical pain in his effort to master the 200 yoga postures (asanas). The pain paid off when, by an arrangement with his brother-in-law, he began to attract some measure of attention by demonstrating the asanas. In 1952 he met and taught the violinist Yehudi Menuhin. Subsequently, Menuhin rewarded him with an introduction to the West and also wrote a foreword to Iyengar's treatise *Light on Yoga* (1965). This

seminal work featured some 600 photographs of Iyengar demonstrating the asanas and proved to be a great success in Europe and the U.S. Iyengar later wrote *Light on Pranayama* (1981), *The Art of Yoga* (1985), *The Tree of Yoga* (1988), and *Light on the Yoga Sutras of Patanjali* (1993).
(LAWRENCE KOWALSKI)

Jagan, Janet Rosenberg

When she was sworn in on Dec. 19, 1997, American-born Janet Jagan made history on two fronts—becoming the first elected female president in South America and the first white president of Guyana. Jagan had been elected December 15 in a bitterly fought campaign to succeed her husband, Cheddi Jagan, as Guyana's president after his death in March 1997. Following the election, hundreds demonstrated in the capital city of Georgetown, charging Jagan with fraud and an inability to lead the country on the grounds that she was not a natural-born citizen and was too old. Less than a week after her inauguration, police defused two bombs found near Jagan's official residence.

Jagan was born Oct. 20, 1920, in Chicago into a middle-class Jewish family. In 1942, while working as a student nurse, she met Cheddi Jagan in Chicago, where he was studying dentistry. The following year they were married and returned to Georgetown in what was then the colony of British Guiana, where he set up a dental practice. By 1950 they had both become active in politics, and during that year they joined with Linden Forbes Burnham to found the People's Progressive Party (PPP), with a goal of gaining independence for the colony (which it achieved in 1966). In 1953 the colony was granted home rule, and Cheddi Jagan became its first prime minister. He subsequently headed governments from 1957 to 1964, and during that time Janet Jagan held several Cabinet posts and served in the parliament.

Having been stripped of her U.S. citizenship more than 20 years earlier because of her Marxist political views, Jagan in 1966 officially became a citizen of Guyana. In addition to her government positions, she served as the PPP's secretary general for nearly 20 years. Hesitant at first to run for the presidency, Jagan accepted her party's nomination on Aug. 31, 1997, in order to carry forward her late husband's agenda. Her main opposition came from People's National Congress leader Desmond Hoyte, who had been defeated in 1992 by Cheddi Jagan. After the election Hoyte's supporters demanded a recount and protested so vehemently that, in an effort to quell the unrest, Jagan and Hoyte reached an agreement on Jan. 17, 1998, to hold new elections in 2000, two years earlier than required. Furthermore, reforms would be made to the constitution that would achieve more balanced power between the nation's two main ethnic groups: blacks and those of Asian Indian descent. Continuing political protests and violent demonstrations pushed Jagan and Hoyte to sign another agreement in July. In her inaugural address Jagan stated, "I intend to be a president of all the people." It remained to be seen whether all of the people would allow her to do so.
(ANTHONY L. GREEN)

Jiang Zemin

On June 27, 1998, Chinese Pres. Jiang Zemin met with U.S. Pres. Bill Clinton for formal talks in Beijing. The summit, a follow-up to Jiang's state visit to the U.S. in October 1997, yielded few major accords but broke new ground for public discussion of China's human rights practices. In an unprecedented move, Jiang allowed his press con-

ference with Clinton to be broadcast live on state television and thereby gave Chinese viewers a chance to hear an argument for American-style democracy. Although Jiang defended Beijing's crackdown on the 1989 student-led pro-democracy demonstrations in Tiananmen Square, his willingness to debate human rights and other sensitive subjects in an open forum signaled the Chinese leader's growing comfort with talk of political change.

Jiang was born Aug. 17, 1926, in Yangzhou, Jiangsu province. He joined the Communist Party of China (CPC) in 1946 and earned a degree in electrical engineering from Jiaotong University, Shanghai, in 1947. He received further technical training in Moscow in the mid-1950s and subsequently held various mid-level posts in a number of ministries. He was elected to the 12th Central Committee of the CPC in 1982, and he served (1983–85) as minister of the electronics industry. He was named mayor of Shanghai in 1985 and became a member of the powerful Political Bureau in 1987.

Jiang endeared himself to China's paramount leader, Deng Xiaoping, by supporting Beijing's forcible suppression of the Tiananmen Square demonstrations. When the Chinese leadership was reshuffled following the crackdown, Jiang was made general secretary of the CPC. By combining a commitment to continue Deng's free-market reforms with a determination to preserve the CPC's political monopoly, he was able to consolidate his power. He succeeded Deng as chairman of the CPC's Central Military Commission in 1989 and became state president in 1993.

Under Jiang's leadership the state began to reduce ownership and control of some of its 300,000 industries. China aggressively promoted exports and actively sought foreign investment, and as a result, the Chinese economy began to grow at spectacular rates. Observers noted, however, that the overwhelming majority of industries continued to be owned and operated by the state and were notoriously inefficient. A thoroughgoing reform of the Chinese economy, many argued, would require massive restructuring, and it was not clear how the Chinese leadership would handle the political changes that would accompany a free-enterprise economy.

In this context the visits of Jiang to the U.S. and of Clinton to China were important to both countries as they worked to forge a new relationship. Although many of the accords reached during the Clinton visit were of a general nature, China promised to resume the dialogue on human rights, and the two nations pledged not to target strategic nuclear weapons at each other. In addition, Jiang and Clinton agreed on plans for exchanges of scholars, students, and publications.

(ROBERT RAUCH)

Keïta, Seydou

Although Malian photographer Seydou Keïta had not actively practiced his art for more than 20 years, his captivating black-and-white images received international attention in the late 1990s. Rediscovered by a French collector, Keïta's portraits were the focus of exhibitions at the Cartier Foundation in Paris and the San Francisco Museum of Modern Art, as well as gallery shows in New York City and Los Angeles. The 1997 publication of a coffee-table book dedicated to his photography and a 1998 exhibit at the St. Louis (Mo.) Art Museum further broadened the interest in his work.

Born in 1923, Keïta grew up in the bustling capital city of Bamako in what was then the French Sudan. He began taking photographs in 1945 when his uncle gave him a camera, and he quickly developed a passion for the art. Self-trained, Keïta displayed a gift for formal portraiture that was recognized by the residents of Bamako. They flocked to his studio to have their pictures taken, and a portrait by Keïta became a status symbol among the middle class. His flattering studio portraits of both individuals and groups followed a simple formula that focused attention on the figures. He posed his subject facing forward in front of a backdrop, the first of which was his patterned bedspread.

His portraits documented a unique period of transition in Mali's history as the country adjusted to its newly won independence from France. Like Mali itself, the subjects of Keïta's portraits displayed the trappings of modern European culture as well as a loyalty to native African traditions. Often the figures were posed with props of their own selection, items such as a sewing machine and radio, suggesting a desire to adopt the styles and technologies of the modern world. The dress similarly reflected European tastes of the period. Interestingly, the clothing was often provided by the photographer, who kept a complete wardrobe for his clients' use. Closer examination revealed the lasting influence of the native African culture that underlaid the new modernity of the Malians. Traditional hair styles were favoured, and the marks of ritual scarification were frequently evident.

Keïta continued to operate his studio in Bamako until 1960, when he was appointed state photographer for Mali. At that time he closed his business and carefully stored his collection of negatives. He worked as the official government photographer until his retirement in 1977. He later cooperated with those interested in reviving his work, providing access to his negatives. The photographs taken during his 17-year career as the state photographer remained the property of the government, however, and were not exhibited.

(BETH KESSLER)

Kelley, David E.

As creator of three different successful shows airing on three competing networks during the 1997–98 TV season, writer and producer David E. Kelley was unique in the world of television. He had begun this string of hits, each of which featured unusual scenarios and quirky characters, with "Chicago Hope" (CBS), a medical drama series set in Chicago that premiered in 1994. Debuting in the 1997–98 season to critical acclaim were two shows about lawyers (Kelley's area of expertise): "Ally McBeal" (Fox), which popularized the computer-generated "dancing baby" phenomenon and introduced TV's first unisex bathroom, won a Golden Globe award for best comedy in 1998, while the more serious "The Practice" (ABC) won the Emmy award for best drama.

Kelley's achievement was a follow-up to his past successes with such long-running shows as "L.A. Law," "Picket Fences," and "Doogie Howser, M.D." Perhaps Kelley's most distinguishing characteristic was his ability to write dozens of scripts in succession, often completing an entire year's episodes of a show. During the 1997–98 season, he single-handedly wrote all 23 episodes for "Ally McBeal" and most of the 22 for "The Practice" at a standard length of 60 pages per script.

Kelley was born c. 1956 in Waterville, Maine, and attended Princeton University. After graduating in 1979, he enrolled at Boston University Law School. In 1983 he received a J.D. degree and joined a Boston law firm. That same year he began working on a feature film, *From the Hip,* which explored the ethics of a young lawyer and was moderately successful at the box office. When the script was brought to the attention of television producer Steven Bochco, who at the time was looking for writers with legal backgrounds for his new show, Kelley was hired almost immediately as the story editor of "L.A. Law" in 1986. He quit the law firm and moved to California, and, at the age of 33 and after the show's third season, he became executive producer. "L.A. Law" won the Emmy award for outstanding drama series four of the years Kelley worked on the show.

Kelley left "L.A. Law" at the end of the 1991–92 season and created "Picket Fences," which debuted in 1992. The show was a popular and critical success and won three Emmys in 1993. In 1994 he created "Chicago Hope." Juggling the scripts for "Chicago Hope" and "Picket Fences" became a difficult task, however, and by the end of the 1994–95 season, Kelley was exhausted. He had written 40 one-hour scripts for the two shows over an eight-month period and decided to relinquish his position as executive producer to two new producers. This time away from TV allowed him to write and produce the feature film *To Gillian on Her 37th Birthday* (1996), which starred his wife, actress Michelle Pfeiffer, and to develop new projects for his company, David E. Kelley Productions. In 1998, Kelley began production on two more movies, *Mystery Alaska* and *Lake Placid.* (HEATHER A. BLACKMORE)

Kim Woo Choong

In March 1998 Kim Woo Choong, founder and chairman of the Daewoo Group, among the four largest conglomerates in South Korea, took over as chairman of the Federation of Korean Industries (FKI). The FKI, which represented the interests of 418 companies, was considered South Korea's most powerful business organization. Kim used his new position to help combat South Korea's worst economic slump since the end of the Korean War; he spearheaded nationwide campaigns to boost exports and increase foreign currency reserves.

It was not Kim's first brush with economic woes. Born on Dec. 19, 1936, in Taegu, Korea, he came of age during the Korean War and at age 14 found himself responsible for supporting his family. He sold newspapers to make ends meet and managed to graduate from the prestigious Kyunggi High School in Seoul. In 1960 he graduated from Yonsei University with a B.A. in economics.

Kim's business career began in 1961 at Hansung Industrial Co., Ltd., a company owned

David E. Kelley (right), with "Ally McBeal" star Calista Flockhart

Kim Woo Choong

by one of his relatives. Six years later he borrowed $10,000 to establish Daewoo Industrial Co., Ltd., a textiles trading business. The firm received a boost in 1976 when the South Korean government introduced state-led economic policies. Kim was asked to take over a debt-ridden heavy industry company. Within a year that company was making a profit, and Daewoo had a firm foundation in heavy industry as well as textiles. Kim went on to take over a shipyard company in 1978 and a home appliance business in 1983.

In the 1980s South Korea's economic growth hit a snag owing to maturing markets and rising wages, and so Kim made daring investments in such far-flung countries as Libya, Poland, Pakistan, and The Sudan. As a result, the Daewoo Group emerged as a global corporation. During this time Kim became a noted philanthropist, using his personal holdings in Daewoo to establish the Daewoo Foundation, a nonprofit organization that operated rural hospitals throughout South Korea and funded research in various fields.

By 1998 the Daewoo Group, with 320,000 employees worldwide and $44 billion in assets, ranked 18th on *Fortune* magazine's Global 500 List of the world's largest corporations. The widely diversified conglomerate was involved in construction, shipbuilding, automobile manufacturing, telecommunications, electronics, textiles, and heavy industry. Kim was also a successful writer. His autobiography, *Every Street Is Paved with Gold* (1989), which he wrote primarily for young people, was a runaway best-seller and was listed in the Korean edition of the *Guinness Book of Records* for having sold one million copies in five months.   (JOOHEE CHO)

Komar, Vitaly, and Melamid, Alex

The Russian-American artistic team of Vitaly Komar and Alex Melamid gained considerable attention in the art world in 1998 for *Painting by Numbers,* a book that documents their international survey of aesthetic tastes in painting. The project began in late 1993 when Komar and Melamid hired a professional market research firm to poll Americans about their preferences in art. On the basis of the opinions reflected in the poll, the two artists then created the Most Wanted and the Most Unwanted paintings. The project was later expanded to cover other countries. The results were surprisingly similar throughout the world. Although some minor variations existed, the majority of people worldwide preferred a painting of a realistic landscape with blue as the predominant colour. Abstract paintings in hot colours like fuchsia and yellow were almost universally disliked. Although the publication of the book brought new attention to the project, the re-

sults of the poll and images of the paintings had been available since 1995 on the World Wide Web. Interestingly, the opinions of those polled through the Web site deviated most from the worldwide consensus, expressing a taste for more abstract, modern works.

Komar and Melamid's project was a humorous and insightful comment on the contemporary art world, as well as a critical look at a culture that relied heavily on opinion polls to determine public policy. The disparity between the preferences suggested by the poll and the contemporary paintings lauded by most museums and galleries called into question the size of the audience for the contemporary works.

The impact of the project was enhanced by the artists' origins in the Soviet Union, where the government endorsed Socialist Realism as the art of the people. Both artists were born in Moscow, Komar on Sept. 11, 1943, and Melamid on July 14, 1945. Their educations followed the same path: they attended the Moscow Art School from 1958 to 1960 and then the Stroganov Institute of Art and Design, where they began their collaborative work in 1965. Rather than exemplifying the dictates of the official style, their career in the Soviet Union was marked by dissident tendencies. Together they launched in 1967 the SOTS Art movement, a Soviet version of Pop art. In 1978 Komar and Melamid immigrated to the United States. Even while living in the more democratic American culture, they managed to maintain a dissident and critical edge, as demonstrated by projects such as the construction of a 4.9-m (16-ft) tower on which they sacrificed Komar's suitcase and the ongoing Most Wanted and Most Unwanted survey.   (BETH KESSLER)

Koolhaas, Rem

In 1998 Rem Koolhaas, hailed by many as "the architect for the new millennium," was selected as the winner of the design competition for a new campus centre at the Illinois Institute of Technology in Chicago. The proposed 9,300-sq m (100,000-sq ft) building—scheduled to be completed in the spring of 2000—would act as a bridge between the academic and residential areas of the school and would accommodate student organizations, dining and entertainment facilities, a bookstore, and a tribute to the campus's original designer, Ludwig Mies van der Rohe.

The legacy of Mies presented a unique challenge to those who participated in the competition. Any proposed addition to the campus could not ignore its strict Modernist style, nor could it follow the same model exactly. Koolhaas's plan acknowledged Mies by using simple geometric forms but was not constrained by Modernism's rigidity. For example, the one-story structure would contain crisscrossing passageways that would replicate the present-day flow of pedestrian traffic at the site. The plan quite literally embraced the urban setting with a stainless steel tunnel that would encircle the existing elevated train tracks and thereby allow trains to run directly above the building.

With its decidedly urban character and its focus on integrating the new into an existing space, the IIT project meshed well with Koolhaas's career-long interest in cities and the urban environment. He was born in Rotterdam, Neth., in 1944 and worked as a journalist before becoming an architect. He studied at the Architectural Association School in London, worked for three years in the United States, and then in 1975 formed the Office for Metropolitan Architecture (OMA) with Elia and Zoe Zenghelis and Madelon Vriesendorp, his wife. The firm had its headquarters in Rotterdam and offices in Berlin and London.

Koolhaas first achieved recognition not as an architect but as a theorist when his book *Delirious New York: A Retroactive Manifesto for Manhattan* was published in 1978. It profiled the architectural development of Manhattan, suggesting that this was an organic process created through a variety of cultural forces. For Koolhaas the city functioned as a metaphor for the contemporary experience. In 1994–95 his designs were the subject of a show at New York City's Museum of Modern

Art. OMA and Koolhaas frequently operated at this theoretical and conceptual level, conceiving of several works that as of 1998 remained unbuilt. Their best-known completed projects were large-scale structures: the Kunsthal in Rotterdam; the Grand Palais, an exhibition hall, in Lille, France; and a master plan for the MCA/Universal Studios site in Los Angeles. Appropriately, Koolhaas's second book addressed the theme of size. Entitled *S, M, L, XL* and published in 1996, it chronicled the accomplishments of OMA and architecture at the end of the 20th century.   (BETH KESSLER)

Lee, Ang

During 1998 Taiwanese-born film director Ang Lee, the creative hand behind such masterfully made films as *Sense and Sensibility* (1995) and *The Ice Storm* (1997), surprised many by choosing to direct a Civil War-era western, *To Live On,* and a war drama, *The Berlin Diaries.* Moviegoers, however, were coming to expect the unexpected from his films. Aspiring to make each movie different from the last, Lee moved effortlessly through various genres, time periods, and cultures in the transition from his early Chinese films to major English-language productions.

Lee was born on Oct. 23, 1954, in P'ing-tung county, Taiwan. After high school he enrolled in the Taiwan Academy of Art, where he became interested in acting. In 1978 he moved to the United States to study theatre at the University of Illinois at Urbana-Champaign and cinema at New York University, where his master's project, *Fine Line,* received best film and best director awards. After graduating in 1984, Lee spent the next six years unsuccessfully pitching ideas to Hollywood studio executives. Frustrated and depressed by the stagnancy of his film career in the U.S., he entered two scripts in a Taiwanese screenplay contest and placed first and second. This honour inspired two independent film production companies to fund and produce his movies.

His first three features, which he co-wrote and directed, were comedies that poignantly examined intergenerational conflicts in Chinese families: *Tui Shou* (1992; *Pushing Hands*), *Hsi Yen* (1993; *The Wedding Banquet*), and *Yinshi nan nu* (1994; *Eat Drink Man Woman*). Looking back, he jokingly referred to these movies as his "father knows best" trilogy, in which the characters "find a new energy in life" in the confrontation between tradition (represented by the father) and personal freedom. As Lee explained, this emphasis on family drama, which also dominated his next two films, reflected his role as a cultural observer: "Seeing how a family changes has made me sensitive to how life and society and values change."

After earning international acclaim for *The Wedding Banquet* and *Eat Drink Man Woman,* Lee was chosen to direct a screen adaptation of the Jane Austen novel *Sense and Sensibility.* This film marked a turning point in his career, with Lee proving that he could handle a British period piece. Despite his admittedly clumsy English, Lee worked with the actors—sometimes even employing t'ai chi chuan exercises—to evoke poignant performances, a hallmark of his directorial style. The movie was a stunning success, garnering seven Oscar nominations.

Having shied away from Hollywood for years because of his first negative experience there, Lee finally returned to make his next film, *The Ice Storm,* a tragic drama set in the 1970s about two spiritually empty upper-middle-class American families. This artfully made film dispelled any fear that Hollywood would stamp out his individual touch. It also held the promise that, as Lee's career progressed, he would inhabit the world of Hollywood corporate moviemaking while maintaining the creative freedom of the independent film movement.   (AFRODITE MANTZAVRAKOS)

Lipinski, Tara Kristen

The tiniest American competitor at the 1998 Winter Olympic Games in Nagano, Japan, was a powerhouse when it came to both competing and breaking records. In winning the women's figure-skating title at the age of 15 years 255 days, the 1.47-m (4-ft 10-in), 37.2-kg (82-lb) Tara Lipinski broke Sonja Henie's 70-year-old world record by

Ang Lee

60 days to become the youngest female to capture Olympic figure-skating gold. This was not her first world record, however. In 1994 Lipinski was the youngest female Olympic Festival gold medalist; in 1996 she was the first skater to successfully land a triple loop–triple loop combination in competition; and in 1997 she became the youngest world champion ever, a record that—because of new International Skating Union age limits—might never be broken.

Lipinski, born on June 10, 1982, in Philadelphia, had been planning for Olympic gold for most of her life. Watching the 1984 Summer Games on television when she was two, she was quite taken with the awards ceremonies and conducted her own by singing the national anthem atop a Tupperware podium as her father draped a homemade gold medal around her neck. At age three she began roller-skating classes and soon was taking private lessons; she won her age group's gold medal at the national championships when she was nine. By that time Lipinski had been ice skating for about three years, and when her family moved to Houston, Texas, in 1991, she focused on that sport. Most mornings she was on the ice by four, and she spent her summers training with coaches in Delaware. She and her mother moved there in 1993 so that she could get the coaching she needed for competing at the highest levels; her father visited on weekends. The move paid off with her Olympic Festival victory the following year. In late 1995 Lipinski and her mother moved to the Detroit suburbs, and Richard Callaghan became Lipinski's coach. Six weeks later, competing at the senior level at the U.S. championships, she placed third. Though she was only 15th in the world championships the following month, a year later she came in first.

Following her Olympic victory in February 1998, Lipinski decided not to participate in the 1998 world championships in March, and in early April she announced that she was turning professional so that her family could be together. Later that month she won her first professional competition, Skate TV, with a score of all 10s. Among Lipinski's future plans were the Stars on Ice tour and TV specials on CBS. (BARBARA WHITNEY)

Maier, Hermann

Just two years after leaving his job as a bricklayer to join the Austrian national ski team, Hermann Maier stormed into the Winter Olympic Games in February 1998 at Nagano, Japan. His astonishing rise to the heights of his sport, along with the power and size that put him there, had earned him the nicknames "Monster," "Beast," and "Herminator." Despite a harrowing spill that had the potential to inflict a career-threatening injury, Maier stuck with his gutsy, straight-ahead style and emerged from the Olympic Games with two gold medals.

Maier was born Dec. 7, 1972, in Flachau, Austria. As a child he idolized the great World Cup skiers of the day, including fellow countryman Franz Klammer. His father, also named Hermann, owned a skiing school, and the boy developed superior technique at a young age. Maier was accepted into the Austrian national ski academy at age 15 but was dropped from the program within a year because of knee problems and his small size (50 kg; 110 lb). He took a job as a bricklayer's apprentice and worked as a skiing instructor during the winters.

In 1995, at the age of 22 and bigger and stronger after seven years of manual labour, Maier quit his job and tried once more to become a World Cup skier. He attracted enough attention on the Europa Cup circuit to earn three World Cup starts late in the 1995–96 season, finishing 11th in a giant slalom competition in Norway. During the 1996–97 season he was hampered by a wrist injury, so it was not until 1997–98, the season leading up to the Nagano Olympics, that Maier was truly a regular on the World Cup circuit, and he took full advantage of his shot at skiing glory. Through January 1998 he had won eight World Cup races—including five straight—and had finished among the top three in 13 of 17 races.

At Nagano disaster struck when, just 17 seconds after starting his downhill run, Maier crashed and suffered shoulder and knee injuries that forced him out of that race and the following day's slalom competition. Three days later, however, he returned to action and won the gold medal in the supergiant slalom (super G) with a time of 1 min 34.82 sec. Three days after that victory Maier crashed again during his first run in the giant slalom, but he returned for the second run to post a gold-medal-winning time of 2 min 38.51 sec. A week later Maier clinched the overall World Cup title. For the 1998–99 World Cup season, he picked up where he left off, still dominating the sport he almost did not get the chance to try. (ANTHONY G. CRAINE)

Marty, Martin E(mil)

Despite reaching the age of 70 in February 1998 and retiring from his teaching post at the University of Chicago in March, American church historian Martin Marty continued apace of his masterwork, *Modern American Religion*. A pro-

posed four-volume study of national religious tradition over the past century, as of 1998 it comprised three books: *The Irony of It All, 1893–1919* (1986), *The Noise of Conflict, 1919–1941* (1990), and *Under God, Indivisible, 1941–1960* (1996). During his 35 years as professor of the history of Christianity at the university's Divinity School, Marty wrote some 50 books and 4,300 articles, was awarded 57 honorary degrees, and trained more than 100 doctoral students. At his birthday celebration, the university announced the establishment of a theological research institute in his name—the Martin E. Marty Center—in honour of his strong history of public ministry. Though rarely acting in a political role, Marty accepted in the autumn of 1997 the appointment to head the Lutheran-Episcopalian Concordat, an ecumenical program almost 30 years in the making.

Academic in thought but accessible to a wide readership, Marty's writings examined contemporary religion against the institutional infighting and growing secularity of the 20th century. An ordained minister in the Evangelical Lutheran Church in America, he wrote much on Protestantism, but he also wrote with authority on Catholicism and other traditions. Marty was admired for his ability to explain trends in terms of their broader cultural and historical context. In 1997 he was named director of the Public Religion Project, which interprets American religious issues, and was awarded the National Humanities Medal and the inaugural Martin E. Marty Award in the Public Understanding of Religion.

Marty was born Feb. 5, 1928, in West Point, Neb., and was educated at Concordia Seminary in St. Louis, Mo., where he studied theology and church history (B.A., 1949) and, in 1952, received a master's degree in divinity. Ordained in 1952, he served as assistant pastor in River Forest, Ill. (1952–56), while working toward his master's degree in sacred theology at the Lutheran School of Theology (1954) and his doctorate in American religious and intellectual history at the University of Chicago (1956).

While serving as the founding pastor of a church in Elk Grove Village, Ill. (1957–63), he began his career in publishing, writing books and moonlighting as an editor of *Christian Century,* where he was a weekly columnist and, later, senior editor. Marty wrote several primers of religious history, beginning with *A Short History of Christianity* (1959) and continuing with *Pilgrims in Their Own Land: Five Hundred Years of Religion in America* (1984) and *A Short History of American Catholicism* (1995). In 1972 he won a National Book Award for *Righteous Empire: The Protestant Experience in America* (1971), which describes how Protestantism shaped early American culture and then, except for brief revivals, waned after the Civil War.

(TOM MICHAEL)

Ma, Yo-Yo

One of the most publicized events in classical music in 1998 was the release of Chinese-American superstar Yo-Yo Ma's recording of the six suites for unaccompanied cello by Johann Sebastian Bach along with six related films created with artists in other media. Ma collaborated on the project with, among others, landscape architect Julie Moir Messervy, director François Girard, choreographer Mark Morris, director Atom Egoyan, Kabuki actor Tamasaburo Bando, and ice dancers Jayne Torvill and Christopher Dean. The films were partly documentaries of the collaborations between Ma and fellow artists and partly interpretations of Bach's music.

Ma was born in Paris to Chinese parents on Oct. 7, 1955. A child prodigy, he gave his first public recital at the age of five and made his debut in New York City at Carnegie Hall at age nine. Ma studied at the Juilliard School in New York City under Leonard Rose and Janos Scholz before graduating from Harvard University with a degree in humanities. In 1991 his alma mater bestowed on him an honorary doctorate in music. Praised for his extraordinary technique and rich tone, Ma was celebrated for performances and recordings of the standard cello repertoire and for receiving an un-

usually large number of commissions from contemporary composers. A champion of chamber music, he also recorded unconventional repertoire with bluegrass musicians (*Appalachia Waltz*) and recorded the tangos of Astor Piazzolla (*Soul of the Tango*). Ma appeared regularly at major world festivals as both a performer and a teacher, received many Grammy awards, and was the sole recipient of the Avery Fisher Prize in 1978.

At a time when classical recordings were accounting for a shrinking market share and crossover artists were dominating sales with releases often of dubious quality and sometimes with embarrassing results, Ma represented perhaps the best of the attempts to expand the reach of the classical tradition and audience. His willingness to search for collaborators in other musical and artistic traditions and to try new approaches was often a hit with critics and listeners. The Bach project clearly was the most ambitious of these attempts. Long revered as one of the supreme achievements of the Western musical tradition, the Bach suites remained a touchstone by which cellists demonstrated their mastery of the instrument. Ma first recorded the suites when he was in his 20s, but critics agreed that his second recording showed greater maturity and insight. The judgments on the films were mixed, however. Some, like the collaboration with Morris, *Falling Down Stairs,* which was paired with *Suite No. 3,* received generally positive notices, but others less so. Some people complained that the films were superfluous to the appreciation of the music, but no one could deny that the undertaking was vastly more creative and interesting than the usual crossover project.

(ROBERT RAUCH)

McCarthy, Cormac

With the publication of *Cities of the Plain* in 1998, American novelist Cormac McCarthy completed his Border Trilogy, the series of metaphysical westerns that began with *All the Pretty Horses* (1992), winner of the National Book Award. Known for his virtuoso use of language and dense tales suffused with violence and evil, the reclusive McCarthy was the focus of numerous articles, dissertations, and symposia, yet the details of his life remained sketchy. Although McCarthy's earlier books did not sell well and critics once referred to him as "America's best unknown major writer," the Border Trilogy succeeded in finally securing for him a wide readership.

Born on July 20, 1933, in Providence, R.I., Charles McCarthy, Jr., later adopted the name Cormac, the Gaelic equivalent of "Charles." When he was four, his family moved to Knoxville, Tenn. There he came into contact with the colourful mountain people who would populate much of his fiction. He attended the University of Tennessee at Knoxville for two years before joining the air force in 1953. While stationed in Alaska he became a voracious reader and began to write.

He returned to the University of Tennessee in 1957 but left without graduating. He worked in an auto-parts store in Chicago while writing his first novel, *The Orchard Keeper.* Published in 1965, the book won him immediate critical acclaim. After receiving a Rockefeller Foundation grant, he traveled throughout Europe (1966–68), beginning what would become a characteristically spartan and nomadic lifestyle.

Working in the Southern Gothic literary tradition, McCarthy wrote about spiritually troubled characters, outcasts constantly confronted by—and often engaged in—evil. Set primarily in Tennessee, his early novels rendered internal and external landscapes in language that was both evocatively naturalistic and mythopoeic. After *The Orchard Keeper,* he published *Outer Dark* (1968) and *Child of God* (1974). Written over 20 years, *Suttree* (1979), McCarthy's most autobiographical work, was considered the finest of his Tennessee novels.

In 1982 McCarthy moved to El Paso, Texas. Abandoning his Southern rhetoric in favour of a leaner, more lucid style, he began to write westerns, in which philosophical themes showed a deepening concern for humankind's struggle with spiritual desolation. Based on extensive historical research, *Blood Meridian,* set in the U.S. Southwest and Mexico, appeared in 1985. Thereafter McCarthy produced the Border Trilogy; *All the Pretty Horses* spent 21 weeks on the *New York Times* best-seller list, and *The Crossing* (1994) and *Cities of the Plain* received mostly positive reviews.   (JEFF WALLENFELDT)

McGwire, Mark David

On Sept. 8, 1998, Mark McGwire hit his shortest home run of the year but the biggest one of his career. With a 104-m (341-ft) line drive, the first baseman for the major league baseball St. Louis Cardinals shattered Roger Maris's 37-year-old single-season home-run record (61) and capped one of baseball's most exciting seasons. Millions witnessed not only history but also the revival of a sport that had been tarnished by labour disputes and player scandals. With his strength and unassuming manner, McGwire gave fans reason to cheer. Backed by standing ovations and light shows of camera flashes, he finished the year with 70 home runs and a place in the record books.

Mark David McGwire was born in Pomona, Calif., on Oct. 1, 1963. As a senior in high school, he attracted more attention with his arm than with

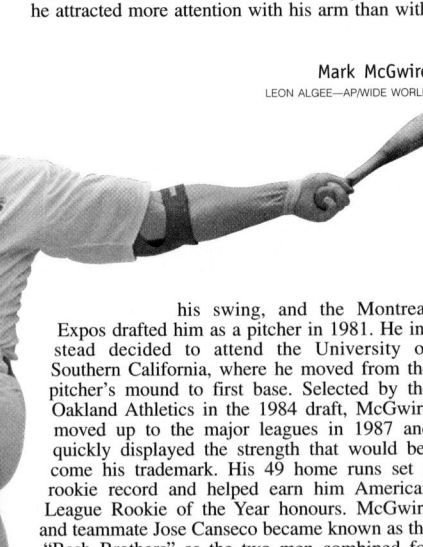

Mark McGwire
LEON ALGEE—AP/WIDE WORLD

his swing, and the Montreal Expos drafted him as a pitcher in 1981. He instead decided to attend the University of Southern California, where he moved from the pitcher's mound to first base. Selected by the Oakland Athletics in the 1984 draft, McGwire moved up to the major leagues in 1987 and quickly displayed the strength that would become his trademark. His 49 home runs set a rookie record and helped earn him American League Rookie of the Year honours. McGwire and teammate Jose Canseco became known as the "Bash Brothers" as the two men combined for 154 home runs during the 1987 and 1988 seasons. In 1988 McGwire made his first World Series appearance but managed only one hit, a home run, as the A's lost to the Los Angeles Dodgers. The following year his .343 postseason batting average paced

Oakland to victory in the World Series. Injuries, however, soon plagued him, and from 1993 to 1995 he missed 290 games. In 1996, after briefly contemplating retirement, McGwire became only the 13th player to hit 50 home runs in a single season. Traded to the Cardinals the following year, he posted 58 homers and elected against free agency to sign a three-year, $30 million deal with St. Louis, $1 million of which he used to help abused children.

Talk of Maris's record dominated the start of the 1998 season. The 1.96-m (6-ft 5-in), 133-kg (250-lb) McGwire responded with a grand slam on opening day and months later hit the longest homer of his career (166 m [545 ft]). Midway through the season the quest for 61 home runs became a race as McGuire was joined by Chicago Cub Sammy Sosa (*q.v.*). On Sept. 1, 1998, McGwire broke Hack Wilson's 68-year-old National League record (56). Six days later, on his father's 61st birthday, McGwire tied Maris's mark.   (AMY TIKKANEN)

McLachlan, Sarah

After a decade in which her music reached a relatively limited number of devoted fans, Canadian singer and songwriter Sarah McLachlan surfaced in 1998 as the acclaimed leader of a musical revolution. She was hailed for her role as organizer and headliner of the phenomenally successful Lilith Fair, a traveling summer concert tour that featured female musicians and amassed over $25 million in its second year. Earlier in the year, McLachlan had won two Grammy awards for her introspective album *Surfacing*.

Born Jan. 28, 1968, in Halifax, N.S., McLachlan received classical training in guitar, piano, and voice. Rebelling against a conservative upbringing, she focused her musical talents on the popular punk and new-wave music movements of the 1980s. She was discovered by an executive at a Canadian record label when she was 17 and the lead singer of the October Game. After two years at the Nova Scotia College of Art and Design, McLachlan moved to Vancouver, B.C., signed a recording contract, and released her debut album, *Touch,* in 1988. The critically acclaimed recording was followed by such other albums as *Solace* (1991), *Fumbling Towards Ecstasy* (1993), and *The Freedom Sessions* (1995), all showcasing McLachlan's talents as a singer, guitarist, and songwriter. Her fans were immediately drawn to her vocal range and the intense emotion that came to define her music.

These qualities were evident in *Surfacing* (released in late 1997), an extremely personal album that was written after months of soul searching. The candidness of such songs as "Sweet Surrender" and "Building a Mystery," about artists' creation of new identities, earned McLachlan Grammy awards for best female pop vocal performance and best pop instrumental. She also received Juno (Canadian Music) Awards for best album, best female vocalist, single of the year, and songwriter of the year and East Coast Music Awards for female artist of the year, songwriter of the year, and video of the year. Her good fortune continued into the summer of 1998, when Lilith Fair, which she had founded in 1997, outsold all other collaborative tours. By bringing together some of the most talented and popular women artists in the music industry, including Jewel, Tracy Chapman, and Paula Cole, McLachlan proved to wary record executives that women artists were as marketable as their male counterparts.   (LAURA RODNITZKY)

Moi, Daniel Toroitich arap

On Jan. 5, 1998, Daniel arap Moi was sworn in for a fifth term as president of Kenya after being declared the winner of national elections held in December 1997. Although the elections were marred by riots and demonstrations, and although Moi's opponents charged the ruling Kenya African National Union (KANU) party with widespread electoral fraud, an independent commission found the elections to have been legitimate. Charges of fraud and corruption were nothing new to Moi; similar accusations had been leveled against him during previous campaigns. In any

event, Moi responded to critics in the manner to which they had become accustomed during his 20-year rule—he ignored them. A favourable new biography published in November raised as many questions as it answered.

Moi was born in 1924 in Sacho, in what was then Britain's Kenya colony. A member of the Sudanic Kalenjin people, an ethnic minority in the predominantly Bantu nation, he was educated at mission and government schools. At the age of 21 he became a teacher. In the early 1950s the Mau Mau rebellion broke out in the colony. As a Kalenjin, Moi was not involved in the rebellion, which was almost solely the work of the Bantu Kikuyu people. The revolt was the harbinger of Kenyan independence, and Moi's teaching background led to his appointment as minister of education in a transition government in the early 1960s. Although Moi had originally been chairman of the Kenya African Democratic Union, a party composed of minority peoples, he joined the Kikuyu-dominated KANU in 1964. That same year Kenya became an independent nation, and Moi was appointed minister of home affairs. In 1967 he was appointed vice president.

With the death of Jomo Kenyatta in 1978, Moi became president. He promoted his Kalenjin countrymen to positions of authority in his government at the expense of the Kikuyu and curried the favour of the army, which proved loyal to him in suppressing a coup attempt in 1982. Moi also continued Kenyatta's pro-Western policies, which ensured significant sums of development aid during the Cold War. Although corruption was endemic and civil rights more of an abstract concept than a reality, under Moi's stewardship Kenya emerged as one of the most prosperous and stable African nations.

As Moi consolidated his power, he consistently refused to consider constitutional reforms. Dissent grew, and the 1997 elections were the greatest challenge of his political career. A disorganized opposition (there were about a dozen other presidential candidates) and an electoral system that

overwhelmingly favoured the ruling party ensured his reelection. Violence continued after the election, and hundreds of Kenyans, mainly Kikuyu, were killed.   (JOHN H. MATHEWS)

Morimura, Yasumasa

One of the most provocative events in the world of art in 1998 was a retrospective of the work of Yasumasa Morimura, held at the Museum of Contemporary Art, Tokyo. "The Museum of Daydream and Disguise: Self-Portrait as Art History" highlighted the series of large-scale self-portraits for which Morimura was best known. Incorporating photography, painting, and computer digital imaging, the series showed the artist posed playfully in scenes that re-created famous masterpieces by Rembrandt, Édouard Manet, and Vincent van Gogh, among other renowned Western artists. Whereas some critics were puzzled by the self-portraits and wondered whether they amounted to art or simply humorous imitations, others saw them as the work of a clever cultural commentator interested in reinterpreting and parodying Western subjects from an Asian point of view. Although critics debated the significance of Morimura's art, they were unanimous in recognizing his contributions to a new global art movement, one that was based on the collapse of cultural boundaries and the free exchange of artistic influences.

Morimura was born in Osaka, Japan, in 1951. After graduating (1978) from Kyoto City University of Arts, he served as an assistant at the university and devoted himself to painting, drawing, photography, and woodblock art. He first attracted international attention in 1988, when a number of his self-portraits were included in the Venice Biennale's "Aperto" exhibition for young artists. Solo exhibitions at the Museum of Contemporary Art, Chicago (1992), and the Cartier Foundation for Contemporary Art, Paris (1993), earned him further high marks. He was also one of 60 artists whose work was selected for the influential show "Japanese Art After 1945: Scream Against the Sky," which opened at the Yokohama Museum of Art in 1994 before traveling to the Solomon R. Guggenheim Museum in New York City.

In the 1990s Morimura broadened his range of parody. Besides re-creating masterworks of Western art, he used computer technology to manipulate photographs of Western pop-culture icons, in some cases superimposing portions of his image over those of celebrities such as Marilyn Monroe, Madonna, and Michael Jackson. At a number of exhibitions, he took this technique to extremes by installing instant-photo booths alongside his self-portraits. The devices allowed any spectator to superimpose an image of his or her face over Morimura's. The artist explained his intentions by saying he believed all people had a common desire for transformation.

In recent years Morimura had demonstrated his versatility by designing clothing for Japanese fashion designer Issey Miyake and gaining attention as a lecturer, author, and singer-songwriter. In 1998 another major exhibition of his artwork, held at the Melbourne (Australia) Festival, helped solidify his reputation as one of Japan's most innovative contemporary artists.

(TEIJI SHIMIZU)

Murdoch, (Keith) Rupert

In 1998 one of the most talked-about conflicts in baseball took place off the field and in the boardroom. Australian media mogul Rupert Murdoch revealed

Sarah McLachlan

HEINZ RUCKEMANN—UPI

in late 1997 that he planned to purchase the Los Angeles Dodgers for a record-high price of $350 million. Despite the protest of media giant and Atlanta Braves owner Ted Turner, a longtime critic of Murdoch, on March 19, 1998, the sale was approved by all but two major league team owners.

Born on March 11, 1931, in Melbourne, Australia, Murdoch received an M.A. (1953) from Worcester College, Oxford. Upon the death of his father, a renowned Australian war correspondent and publisher, he was left with two small Adelaide newspapers, the *Sunday Mail* and *The News*. With little experience in the publishing field, he returned to Australia in 1954 to take them. Focusing their content on scandals, sex, sports, and crime, Murdoch watched as circulation numbers for the revamped journals increased dramatically. Having discovered the marketability of "soft news" and scandal, he spent the next four decades acquiring and reworking other publications. He built a media empire that included such newspapers as the *News of the World, The Sun, The Star*, and the *New York Post;* magazines such as *TV Guide* and *Seventeen;* radio and television stations; and Twentieth Century-Fox Film Corp. His diverse assets also included such properties as *The Times* of London and Harper & Row Publishers.

In 1987 Murdoch launched the Fox television network to compete with "The Big Three"—NBC, CBS, and ABC. Though much of its programming was considered in poor taste, the network proved to be a viable competitor with such innovative shows as "In Living Color," "The Simpsons," and "The X-Files," and Fox repeatedly outbid its stunned competitors in the 1990s for shares in the broadcasting rights to National Football League, National Hockey League, and major league baseball games. Though many of his colleagues respected Murdoch's ability to create a fourth television network and to turn fledgling newspapers into commercial successes, Turner consistently focused on negative aspects of Murdoch's achievements, referring to him as "the schlockmeister." In 1996 Murdoch further infuriated Turner when he inaugurated the Fox News Channel to compete with the Turner-owned Cable News Network. By purchasing the Dodgers, Murdoch intensified the rivalry—this time in yet another direction.   (LAURA RODNITZKY)

Niemann-Stirnemann, Gunda

Competing in the second-to-last pairing in the 5,000-m race at the 1998 Winter Olympic Games held in Nagano, Japan, German speed skater Gunda Niemann-Stirnemann broke her own world record and became the first woman ever to post a 5,000-m time under seven minutes when she crossed the finish line in 6 min 59.65 sec. As the crowd roared its approval, Niemann-Stirnemann put a finger to her lips to quiet the crowd. She knew that her rival—and teammate—Claudia Pechstein would be racing in the final pairing, and she also knew that the new clapskates used during these Games left no record unthreatened. Pechstein did indeed shatter the new world record—by 0.04 sec—but Niemann-Stirnemann still had plenty to celebrate: by taking the silver medal in the race, she tied an all-time record for most individual medals won in the Winter Games, and she erased the memory of a disappointing Olympic performance four years earlier at Lillehammer, Nor.

Born Gunda Kleeman on Sept. 7, 1966, in Sonderhausen, East Germany, she left home for a sports school when she was 12 years old, originally playing volleyball but soon taking up track and field. Although mildly successful as a hurdler, she shifted her focus to speed skating at age 17. Her first appearance in the Olympics came in 1988 at Calgary, Alta., where she finished seventh in both the 1,500 m and the 5,000 m. It was at the 1992 Winter Games at Albertville, France, that she began to display her command of the sport; she won the gold medal in the 3,000 m and the 5,000 m and the silver in the 1,500 m. This performance made her the favourite two years later at Lillehammer, but she failed—relatively speaking—when she took the bronze in the 1,500 m,

the silver in the 5,000 m, and appeared headed for the gold in the 3,000 m before falling and being disqualified. Despite the letdown, the 1.7-m (5-ft 7-in), 67-kg (148-lb) skater had five Olympic medals in her possession.

In the ensuing years Niemann-Stirnemann dominated speed skating, finishing first in nearly every major event from 1995 through 1997. At the same time her popularity in Germany soared. Dubbed the "ice queen" by the media, she earned more than $300,000 in endorsements in 1997 alone. In April 1997 she underwent knee surgery and spent the summer in-line skating to rehabilitate herself. Any doubts about her condition for Nagano, however, were quelled when she set a world record in a 3,000-m race just two months before the Games. At Nagano she won the 3,000 m and took the silver in the 1,500 m and 5,000 m. Her total of eight tied her with East German speed skater Karin Enke-Kania (who dominated in the early 1980s) and Norwegian cross-country skier Bjørn Dæhlie (*q.v.*) for the most individual medals ever won in the Winter Games.
(ANTHONY G. CRAINE)

Obuchi, Keizo

On July 30, 1998, Japan's Diet (parliament) named Keizo Obuchi the country's new prime minister. He replaced Ryutaro Hashimoto, who was forced to resign as prime minister and as president of the ruling Liberal Democratic Party (LDP) following the LDP's stunning losses in elections in the upper house of the Diet earlier in the month. On July 24 the LDP had elected Obuchi its new president over two other candidates and thus all but assured his approval as prime minister, since the LDP held a majority in the powerful lower house. The selection of Obuchi as party president was seen as a triumph for the LDP's veteran power brokers over younger party members, who had called for more dynamic leadership. An undistinguished, mild-mannered foreign minister whom pundits had dubbed "Mr. Average" and described as "about as exciting as cold pizza," Obuchi was nevertheless considered a competent politician who headed the largest of the five LDP factions. After prevailing in the Diet's first split vote for prime minister since 1989, he acknowledged being the candidate least popular with the general public and moved

Keizo Obuchi

ITSUO INOUYE—AP/WIDE WORLD

quickly to win the confidence of Japanese citizens, assembling a credible Cabinet and vowing decisive action to pull the country out of its worst economic crisis in decades.

Obuchi was born on June 25, 1937, in Nakanojo, Japan. The son of a politician, he resolved to become a politician himself after his father died in 1958. At Waseda University, Tokyo, he joined the university's oratory club to hone his speaking skills and, believing that a politician should also be physically strong, practiced bodybuilding and aikido. He earned a degree in English literature in 1962. The following year, at age 26, he was elected to the seat his father had held in the lower house of the Diet.

Retaining his seat in 11 subsequent elections, Obuchi built a reputation as a congenial party functionary adept at forging behind-the-scenes compromises between competing political factions. In 1973 he served as deputy director general in the prime minister's office, and in 1987 he was named chief Cabinet secretary. He also rose steadily through the ranks of the LDP, serving as deputy secretary-general (1984) and secretary-general (1991). Hashimoto appointed him foreign minister in 1997.

As prime minister, Obuchi had as his first order of business the need to address the formidable problems facing Japan's banking sector. After a frustrating two months, his administration was able to win parliamentary approval of crucial bills to bail out banks saddled with bad loans. In other efforts to jump-start the Japanese economy, he planned to cut taxes by more than $41 billion and to seek a significantly expanded 1999 budget. Although some observers doubted Obuchi's ability to implement effective proposals, his experience in striking deals and his strong power base within the LDP were reassuring to others.
(TEIJI SHIMIZU)

Pak Se Ri

The Associated Press called her "the rookie sensation"; *Time* magazine hailed her as the "Tigress Woods" of golf; and the *New York Times* claimed she was the best product South Korea had ever exported to the U.S. In 1998 there seemed to be no superlative too great for Pak Se Ri, the most exciting rookie to appear in women's golf since Nancy Lopez made her Ladies Professional Golf Association (LPGA) debut in 1978. In her first year on the LPGA circuit, Pak won two major tournaments, became the second highest money winner on the tour, and carded the lowest 18- and 72-hole scores in LPGA history. She also captured the hearts of an entire nation; one year after leaving South Korea for the U.S. as a virtual unknown, Pak was given a hero's welcome in October when she returned to her homeland to accept the Blue Dragon, South Korea's top sports award.

In the first nine events of the 1998 LPGA season, Pak had finished no better than 11th place, but by May she had shifted her game into high gear. At the McDonald's LPGA championship in May in Wilmington, Del., she jumped out to an early lead and never looked back. She finished with an 11-under-par 273 to win by three strokes and take the $195,000 prize. Only 20 years old, she was the youngest golfer ever to win the event and the second youngest to win a major women's tournament.

On July 6 Pak won the U.S. Women's Open in Kohler, Wis. In one of the Open's most memorable finishes, she outdueled amateur Jenny Chuasiriporn in a 20-hole play-off after both golfers had tied in regulation play. The victory made her the youngest woman golfer to win two majors and the first rookie to win two majors since Julie Inkster in 1987. Nearly eight million South Koreans stayed up late to watch Pak's historic achievement on television.

Just six days after her U.S. Open triumph, Pak won another tournament, the Jamie Farr Kroger Classic. Her stunning second-round score of 61 and her four-round total of 261 were both LPGA records. By season's end she had added one more tournament victory, at the Giant Eagle LPGA Classic, and captured the LPGA's Rookie of the Year award.

Pak was born on Sept. 28, 1977, in Daejon, S.Kor. Her father introduced her to golf when she was 14 years old, and she soon took up the sport avidly. She won 30 tournaments in South Korea as an amateur. She turned professional in 1996 and moved to the U.S. the following year to train under noted golf coach David Leadbetter. In October 1997 she joined the LPGA.

(WANG HEE SOO)

Pastrana Arango, Andrés
The election of Andrés Pastrana Arango as Colombia's new president on June 21, 1998, inspired cautious hope for a peaceful resolution to more than three decades of leftist guerrilla warfare. Backed by the Conservative Party, Pastrana won over 50% of the vote in a second-round runoff to defeat Liberal candidate Horacio Serpa Uribe. Acting immediately on his campaign promise to initiate peace talks, President-elect

Pastrana held an unprecedented secret meeting with the leader of the country's largest insurgent group. Just days prior to his August 7 inauguration, however, guerrillas engaged in coordinated attacks on police and army bases and other targets across the country, killing some 130 persons and wounding scores. Although the rebels claimed that the bloodshed was a send-off for outgoing Pres. Ernesto Samper Pizano, some political analysts suspected that it was a show of strength before the start of formal negotiations. Nonetheless, Pastrana remained determined to lead the peace process.

Born on Aug. 17, 1954, in Bogotá, Colom., Pastrana was the son of Misael Pastrana Borrero, Conservative president of Colombia from 1970 to 1974. Pastrana earned a graduate degree in public law from San Carlos College in Bogotá and later studied at the Center of International Affairs at Harvard University. During the 1980s he

Pak Se Ri

Andrés Pastrana
JOHN MOORE—AP/WIDE WORLD

worked as a television journalist and a city councilman. From 1988 to 1990 Pastrana served as Bogotá's first popularly elected mayor, and in 1991 he won a seat in the Senate.

Pastrana first ran for president in 1994 but lost to Samper. Shortly afterward, he publicly released audio recordings of Samper campaign officials soliciting donations from the Cali drug cartel. Although Samper was eventually exonerated, the allegation tarnished his administration and led to further civil unrest and economic disintegration. The situation also produced a backlash against Pastrana for having brought the charge to light, forcing him to spend much time outside Colombia as a consultant to the UN. Pastrana's success in the presidential race four years later was, therefore, thought to be a personal vindication as well as a signal of the public's growing intolerance with the scandal-plagued Liberal Party.

The change of government seemed to promise a turning point for Colombia on several fronts. Pastrana pledged not only to end the guerrilla war but also to crack down on political corruption, institute reforms to bolster the faltering economy, and combat drug trafficking. Still, many political observers were apprehensive. Pastrana inherited a country with a volatile brew of aggressive and well-financed left-wing rebel groups zealously opposed by the military and right-wing paramilitary organizations. He also faced a powerful narcotics industry, whose drug money infiltrated almost every level of society.

(AFRODITE MANTZAVRAKOS)

Pippen, Scottie
When the Chicago Bulls met the Utah Jazz in Game 6 of the 1998 National Basketball Association (NBA) finals, Bulls forward Scottie Pippen staged perhaps the most courageous performance of his career. Back spasms kept him from playing most of the first half of the game, but his relentless defensive play in the second half helped his team win the game and clinch their sixth championship in eight seasons. Pippen's effort went largely unnoticed, however, as teammate Michael Jordan scored the winning basket. Such had been the case throughout Pippen's career; his

MORRY GASH—AP/WIDE WORLD

finest moments were often overshadowed by his legendary teammate.

Pippen was born on Sept. 25, 1965, in Hamburg, Ark. He played high school basketball but stood just 1.85 m (6 ft 1 in) upon graduation. However, he had grown 5 cm (2 in) by the time he entered the University of Central Arkansas, where he initially served as manager of the basketball team before earning a spot on the roster. By his senior year, he stood 2 m (6 ft 7 in) and was the team's best player. In 1987 the Seattle SuperSonics selected Pippen in the first round of the NBA draft, then traded him to Chicago. A year later he was a regular in the Bulls' starting lineup. His size and strength served him well under the basket, while his ball-handling skills and shooting touch made him a threat from the outside. On defense, his long arms and quick footwork made him an imposing force.

A reputation for coming up short in big games dogged Pippen's early career, however. In 1994 this criticism was revived after he refused to reenter a crucial play-off game with 1.8 seconds remaining because he disagreed with coach Phil Jackson's play-calling strategy. Despite the bad publicity, no one doubted that Pippen's stellar play—most notably his workmanlike approach to defense—was a key factor in the Bulls' championships. Jordan was often quoted as saying he would not play for the Bulls without Pippen on his team.

Through the end of the 1998 season, Pippen had won six NBA titles, secured two Olympic gold medals (1992, 1996), and been named to the All-NBA First Team three times and to the All-Defensive First Team seven consecutive seasons. He had also participated in seven NBA All-Star Games, starting in six of them and winning the game's Most Valuable Player award in 1994. Pippen joined basketball's elite ranks in 1996 when he was honoured as one of the "50 Greatest Players in NBA History." He was perhaps the only man on that list to be considered the second-best player on his own team, but Pippen's future was likely to be bright even if Jordan followed through on his rumoured retirement.

(ANTHONY G. CRAINE)

Primakov, Yevgeny Maksimovich
Russian Pres. Boris Yeltsin's appointment of Foreign Minister Yevgeny Primakov as prime minister in September 1998 was greeted with a mixture of relief and skepticism. Forced to compromise on a candidate acceptable to both the impatient reformers and hard-core Communists in the Duma (the lower house of parliament), Yeltsin had tapped Primakov, many felt, for his acceptability rather than his qualifications. The idea of a former intelligence chief as prime minister rang warning bells in the West owing to Primakov's tough pro-Russian, anti-NATO, and pro-Arab positions.

Primakov was born in Kiev, Ukrainian S.S.R., on Oct. 29, 1929. He kept his early years cloaked in secrecy and would neither confirm nor deny reports that his parents were Jewish, that his father had vanished in a Stalinist purge, and that he had changed his surname from Finkelshteyn to avoid anti-Semitic unpleasantries. He grew up with his mother in Tbilisi, Georgia. Showing a flair for the Arabic language, Primakov went to Moscow, graduating from the Institute of Oriental Studies in 1953 and receiving a candidate degree in economics from the M.V. Lomonosov Moscow State University in 1956. He joined the Communist Party of the Soviet Union in 1959. From 1962 to 1970 Primakov worked for *Pravda*, the party's daily, as a Middle East specialist, columnist, and deputy editor. During this period he developed close relations with numerous influential Arab leaders.

In 1970 Primakov was named deputy director of the Institute of World Economy and International Relations (IMEMO), the top foreign policy think tank, and in 1977, director of the Institute of Oriental Studies. He became director of IMEMO in 1985. A leading architect of perestroika (restructuring), he worked closely with Pres. Mikhail Gorbachev and continued to rise in the government and the Communist Party, be-

Puff Daddy

coming a candidate member of the Politburo in 1989. As his political standing rose, however, Primakov suffered personal setbacks, losing both his son and his first wife to heart disease in the 1980s. Serving as a special envoy, he spearheaded Gorbachev's efforts to help Iraqi leader Saddam Hussein in the Persian Gulf War standoff, and in the fall of 1991 he was made first deputy to the director of the State Security Committee (KGB) and head of its First Directorate (foreign intelligence). The KGB was disbanded a few months later, but Primakov went on to head its successor, the Russian Foreign Intelligence Service, until Yeltsin appointed him foreign minister in 1996.

The skepticism accompanying Primakov's confirmation as prime minister intensified to concern as Russia's economy continued spiraling downward and Primakov failed to map out a concrete economic plan. Moreover, well before the end of the year, the frequently indisposed Yeltsin had relinquished most of his day-to-day tasks to the new prime minister.   (LOCKE PETERSEIM)

Puff Daddy
To the delight of his fans and the dismay of his critics, music mogul-producer-rapper Sean ("Puffy") Combs, aka Puff Daddy, remained in the forefront of the music industry in 1998. Although hip-hop devotees derided the self-aggrandizing showman for his creation of hit singles through the liberal "borrowing" of entire choruses of classic songs, most fans and many fellow musicians appreciated the young entertainer's Midas touch as a producer and performer.

Combs was born Nov. 4, 1970, and raised in Harlem in New York City, where the city streets claimed the life of his father when Combs was three but also fostered Combs's hip-hop sensibilities. Nine years later the family moved to suburban Mount Vernon, N.Y., where Combs attended prep school and supposedly received the nickname "Puffy" for his habit of puffing up his chest during football practice. Combs attended Howard University, Washington, D.C., but his interest lay in promoting dance parties. He left college after two years to become an intern at Uptown Records in New York City and within a year had moved up to vice president. Tragically, in December 1991 nine people were crushed to death as crowds pushed into a charity basketball game Combs had promoted at City College of New York.

In 1993 Combs was fired from Uptown, and he turned his energies to his own label, Bad Boy Entertainment. He soon discovered and befriended a street hustler named Christopher Wallace, who rapped as Biggie Smalls and recorded as the Notorious B.I.G. By 1994 Wallace was a rising rap star, and Combs had negotiated a $15 million deal to move Bad Boy to Arista Records, which gained him a growing industrywide reputation as a rap impresario and entrepreneur.

In the spring of 1997 the Notorious B.I.G. was murdered, and his death made Combs's first album, *No Way Out,* released that summer, less a celebratory debut and more a mournful tribute to his friend. The first single was "I'll Be Missing You," a musical eulogy featuring the voice of Wallace's widow and the melody from the Police's "Every Breath You Take." Several more singles from *No Way Out* dominated the pop charts in 1997, and in December Combs presented Wallace's children with a check for $3 million in proceeds from "I'll Be Missing You" and pledged to donate future profits from that single to them as well.

In 1998 Combs toured in support of *No Way Out* and maintained his presence on the airwaves; for the movie *Godzilla* he enlisted guitarist Jimmy Page to concoct the single "Come with Me," a thunderous reworking of Page's Led Zeppelin song "Kashmir." His hold on pop music seemingly secure, Combs signed deals to create a clothing line and co-write his autobiography and tried, unsuccessfully, to become a professional sports agent.   (LOCKE PETERSEIM)

Putman, Andrée
From the interior elegance of Air France's Concorde jet to the prosaism of the toothbrush, French designer Andrée Putman had by 1998 firmly put her stamp on late-20th-century style. She had long been known for her minimalist, avant-garde furniture and interior designs that were issued through her Paris companies Écart S.A. and Écart International. In 1997, however, she opened a new company under her own name and published a second edition of *Andrée Putman.* Written by Paris-based journalist Sophie Tasma-Anargyros, the monograph presented a comprehensive analysis of Putman's influential oeuvre from 1979 to 1996.

Born Andrée Christine Aynard in Paris on Dec. 23, 1925, she was educated at the Collège d'Hulst

and studied piano at the Paris Conservatoire, winning the school's highest award at the age of 20. Although she turned her back on a career in music, her training would later serve her well—the balance, harmony, and rhythm of musical composition would be reinterpreted in her designs in the restraint of simple lines, monochromatic colours, and unique combinations of materials.

Putman began her professional life as a journalist in 1950 at *Femina* magazine; she moved to *Elle* in 1952, where she was a design columnist until 1958, and then to *L'Oeil* (1960–64) as the interiors editor. Self-taught in design, she was also stylist for the Prisunic department stores in Paris from 1958 to 1967. After working with various publicity agencies and designer groups from 1968 until well into the '70s, she founded her own furniture and interior design business in 1978. Through Écart, she reissued classic Modernist furnishings from 1930s designers Eileen Gray, Mariano Fortuny, and Pierre Chareau, and she began creating boutiques for well-known fashion designers—Thierry Mugler (Paris, 1978), Yves Saint Laurent (*q.v.;* 15 throughout the U.S. from 1980–84), and Karl Lagerfeld (Paris, New York City, Toronto, and Melbourne, Australia, from 1980–85).

Commissioned in 1984 to refurbish, on a tight budget, New York City's Morgans Hotel, she shunned what she called the "vulgarity" of traditional luxury and opted instead for a streamlined yet opulent comfort. Her signature black-and-white checkerboard tiles were featured throughout the hotel's hallways and bathrooms, along with lobby and guest room interiors in shades of gray. Other interiors included the Orchid Club House in Kobe, Japan (1992), and the circular Wasserturm Hotel in Cologne, Ger. (1989), converted from a water tower built in 1868. She also redesigned the interior of the 1916 Villa Turque in Switzerland, an original by architect Le Corbusier.

Putman received numerous prizes, among them the Interior Design Hall of Fame Award (New York, 1987), the Grand Prix National de la Création Industrielle (Paris, 1995), and an honorary doctorate from Parsons School of Design (New York, 1996). Her later work included sets for Peter Greenaway's 1996 film *The Pillow Book* and, in 1998, for the Lagerfeld Gallery in Paris. She also continued to create original designs in home furnishings, such as lighting, tableware, and fabrics.

(REBECCA RUNDALL)

Ramazzotti, Eros
Having mesmerized European and South American audiences with his yearning ballads of love, Italian pop superstar Eros Ramazzotti hoped to croon his way into the hearts of North Americans in 1998. Since its 1997 release, almost four million copies of *Eros,* his ninth album, had been sold worldwide. To promote *Eros* in the United States, the handsome balladeer embarked on a national tour in March 1998, accompanied by Tina Turner, a collaborator on "Cosas de la vida" ("Things of Life"), one of his songs from the album. Ramazzotti opened the tour with a sold-out performance at Radio City Music Hall in New York City followed by appearances on such television shows as "The Tonight Show with Jay Leno," "Good Morning, America," and popular Hispanic radio and television shows.

Ramazzotti was born on Oct. 28, 1963, in an impoverished suburb of Rome and was named after the Greek god of love as a symbol of luck. Encouraged by his father, an aspiring singer and musician, Ramazzotti began to play the guitar at the age of seven. Owing to a lack of musical background, however, he was refused entry into the Roman Musical Conservatory. In 1981 he made his singing debut at the Castrocaro Voci Nuove talent-hunt competition, where he signed a recording contract. "Ad un amico," his first single, was released the following year. Ramazzotti enrolled in the San Remo Festival of Italian Song, a highly regarded pop-music competition in Italy, in 1984 and won with the song "Terra promessa"; it was featured on his album *Cuori agitati,* released in 1985. His second album, *Nuovi eroi* (1986), proved to be an even bigger success and was followed by *In certi momenti* in 1987. With the re-lease of each album, his popularity soared and catapulted him to greater international stardom. The 1990 release of his album *In ogni senso* was the groundbreaker for Ramazzotti in the U.S. By 1998 it had sold more than seven million copies worldwide.

In 1991 Ramazzotti made his first world tour and performed at Radio City Music Hall. After the performance, however, he expressed disappointment that his audience consisted largely of Italian-Americans. To give his sound a more international flavour on his next album, he employed the talents of musicians and vocalists who had backed up such well-known performers as Sting, Pink Floyd, Celine Dion, and Stevie Wonder. Although there was some speculation as to whether Ramazzotti, who did not speak English, could find a following in the U.S., the success of Julio Iglesias, Gloria Estefan, and Selena was testimony to the impact being made in the U.S. by foreign-language performers. Ramazzotti, who wrote much of his own material, was also expanding his role in the music business by producing albums for up-and-coming talent.

(HEATHER A. BLACKMORE)

Roy, Arundhati
In 1998 Indian author Arundhati Roy rocked the literary world with the Booker Prize-winning debut novel, *The God of Small Things,* which was released in paperback and quickly climbed the charts. Published in 1997 to critical acclaim, the semiautobiographical work departed from the conventional plots and light prose that were typical among best-sellers. Writing in a lyrical language about South Asian themes and characters in a narrative that wandered through time, Roy proved to the publishing industry that readers were willing to be challenged. The biggest-selling book by a nonexpatriate Indian author, Roy's novel heralded the arrival of a promising and uncompromising new voice.

Born in 1961 in Bengal, India, Arundhati Roy was raised in Kerala. Her father was a tea planter, and her mother would later help alter India's inheritance laws by successfully suing for Christian women to receive an equal share of their fathers' estates. Though trained as an architect, Roy had little interest in design, but dreamed instead of a writing career. After a series of odd jobs, including artist and aerobics instructor, she wrote and costarred in the film *In Which Annie Gives It To Those Ones* and later penned scripts for the film *Electric Moon* (1992) and several television dramas. The films earned Roy a devoted following, but her literary career was interrupted by controversy. In 1995 she wrote two newspaper articles claiming that Shekhar Kapur's film *Bandit Queen* exploited Phoolan Devi, one of India's most wanted criminals in the early 1980s and heroine of the oppressed. The columns caused an uproar, including a court case, and Roy retreated from the public and returned to the novel she had begun to write.

In the works for more than four years, *The God of Small Things* vividly depicted a family's tragedy. Following fraternal twins Estha and Rahel, it explored jealousies, social prejudices, and forbidden love. Though the novel was an instant sensation, some critics panned it. Within five months of release, more than 350,000 copies had been sold worldwide; the book would eventually appear in 30 countries and 24 languages. It won the Booker in 1997, making Roy the first Indian woman to receive the honour. Controversy, however, continued to dog her, as some critics in India charged that passages in the novel dealing with sex were obscene. Though Roy stated that she might never write another book, her legions of fans clearly hoped otherwise.

(AMY TIKKANEN)

Saint Laurent, Yves
To celebrate his 40th year as a designer, French fashion legend Yves Saint Laurent staged a fashion show of unprecedented scale on July 12, 1998, at the grand Stade de France in Paris, the site of the final match of the World Cup soccer competition. Before the start of play, some 300 models outfitted with Saint Laurent ensembles presented a retrospective of his work before 80,000 spectators. The show was also broadcast on 176 television channels worldwide and marked the end of a year of special tributes, including a photographic exhibition of his work and the opening of the Yves Saint Laurent Gallery—housing a collection of 16th- and 17th-century French paintings—in the restored wing of London's National Gallery.

Yves-Henri-Donat-Mathieu Saint Laurent was born on Aug. 1, 1936, in Oran, Alg. He went to Paris at the age of 17 and briefly attended fashion school before becoming Christian Dior's protégé after the latter saw some of his sketches. Following Dior's death in 1957, the 21-year-old Saint Laurent, on Jan. 30, 1958, was placed in charge of designing couture for the House of Dior, which had become the most respected French fashion house. Soon, this shy designer became a star. He was also romantically linked with Pierre Bergé, an outspoken part-time political raconteur.

Arundhati Roy

KARAN KAPOOR—CORBIS

Yves Saint Laurent

Two years after Saint Laurent's stellar Dior debut, he was fired from his post, and he suffered the first of several nervous breakdowns. With Bergé he set up his own fashion house, and although their personal relationship fizzled sometime in the 1980s, their strong, successful—though often stormy—partnership remained intact. Besides earning a fortune—his personal net worth has been estimated at £94 million—Saint Laurent was the originator of a number of fashion firsts and was foremost remembered for popularizing women's trousers for all occasions. He introduced a "little girl" look, the A-line silhouette, and see-through blouses. His styles for skirts ranged from sophisticated, longer ones to drastically shorter skirts. During the 1960s turtlenecks and black leather jackets edged in fur ushered in the beatnik look, and he featured metallic and transparent fabrics in his collections of that era. A decade later Saint Laurent introduced the haute peasant look.

Though branching out into ready-to-wear lines, accessories, household linens, fragrances, and men's clothing, during recent years Saint Laurent seemed content to perfect his classics rather than initiate any groundbreaking trends. In June Bergé announced that the increasingly reclusive Saint Laurent would concentrate on his haute couture designs and that the duties for the ready-to-wear line would be assumed by Alber Elbaz. Speculation about the fate of the Yves Saint Laurent Groupe had begun in 1993 when it was purchased by Elf Sanofi, which on Jan. 1, 2000, would take full control of the house.

(BRONWYN COSGRAVE)

Satcher, David

On Feb. 12, 1998, David Satcher was sworn in as the 16th surgeon general of the U.S. Public Health Service; his confirmation by a wide margin (65–35) in the U.S. Senate two days previously ensured that the post would be filled for the first time in four years. Although some Republican senators attempted to derail voting by citing Satcher's refusal to support legislation against late-term abortion, he was generally considered an ideal choice because of his years of public health experience. Confirmation included concurrent service for Satcher as assistant secretary of health in the Department of Health and Human Services. Together, these positions provided a forum to emphasize public health issues and shape biomedical research policy.

Born March 2, 1941, near Anniston, Ala., Satcher nearly died of whooping cough at the age of two. Although a vaccine was available at the time, his poor African-American family had little access to medical care. He was attended by the only black physician in the area, and from an early age Satcher resolved to become a doctor. Valedictorian of his racially segregated high school, he was one of only three graduates to go on to college, earning a B.S. from Morehouse College in Atlanta, Ga., in 1963. In 1970 he became the first African-American to earn both an M.D. and a Ph.D. (cytogenetics) at Case Western Reserve University in Cleveland, Ohio.

During the 1970s Satcher held administrative and teaching posts in Los Angeles at the Charles

David Satcher

F. Drew Postgraduate Medical School and its affiliated hospital, the King-Drew Sickle Cell Center, and UCLA's School of Public Health. He returned to Morehouse in 1979 to chair the department of community medicine and family practice, and from 1982 to 1993 served as president of Meharry Medical College in Nashville, Tenn. When he assumed the presidency, Meharry was on the verge of losing its accreditation; before he left, he had recruited new faculty members, strengthened its academic standing, and ensured the financial security of both the school and its teaching hospital.

In 1993 Satcher was appointed director of the Centers for Disease Control and Prevention (CDC). During his tenure the CDC instituted initiatives that increased childhood immunization rates from 55% in 1992 to 78% in 1996, improved the nation's ability to respond to emerging infectious diseases, laid the foundation for a system to detect and prevent food-borne illnesses, and increased the emphasis on disease prevention. He caused controversy by enlisting the CDC in the research and prevention of violence, calling it a problem for public health as well as for criminal justice.

The recipient of numerous national and professional awards, including the American Medical Association's Nathan Davis Award (1996), Satcher eagerly embraced his role as the nation's chief doctor. In April he presented a report to the president on tobacco use, which focused especially on the health risks it poses to minorities and minority teenagers. He also commissioned a report on suicide, sought to eliminate race-based health-care disparities, and urged the nation to open an "honest debate" on mental health.

(REBECCA RUNDALL)

Schrempp, Jürgen

When two stars collided in May 1998, the news piqued the interest of the business community rather than the scientific world. This was because the astral collision was not an actual astronomical event but a symbolic one that represented the merger between Daimler-Benz, the German luxury automaker whose trademark was the three-pointed star, and the Chrysler Corp. of the U.S., whose five-pointed trademark graced the hoods of a more downscale line of vehicles. Spearheading this deal—one of the biggest industrial takeovers in history—was German businessman Jürgen Schrempp, the brash and unconventional executive who turned Daimler-Benz around when he took over as chairman in 1995. Schrempp agreed to run the new company, called DaimlerChrysler, jointly with Chrysler's chief executive, Robert Eaton. In spite of this dual stewardship, Daimler-Benz was the dominant partner, and Schrempp was expected to become the sole leader of DaimlerChrysler in three years.

The takeover was the latest event in Schrempp's overhaul of Daimler-Benz, the largest industrial concern in Europe. When promoted to chairman in 1994, Schrempp faced the formidable task of restructuring the company, which had diversified rapidly but not necessarily wisely, and turning it into a profitable business once again. Although car sales were profitable, subsidiary businesses such as aerospace, software, and electronics were not.

Schrempp wasted little time in paring down the company. By selling more than a dozen subsidiary companies and severely reducing the workforce, he refocused attention on the core automotive business and reversed the outward flow of money. For his efforts, some dubbed him "Neutron Jürgen" after General Electric chief executive Jack Welch, whom critics derided as "Neutron Jack"—a sobriquet that likened Welch's strategy of eliminating numerous jobs in the interest of saving his company to the way a neutron bomb destroys lives while leaving buildings intact. Although Schrempp's approach appeared similar to Welch's, Schrempp saw himself as a hybrid that wedded American concern with profitability to a German tradition of responsibility to employees. As he said, "Only profitable companies can be socially responsible."

Schrempp was born on Sept. 15, 1944, in Freiburg im Breisgau, Ger. His association with

Daimler-Benz spanned his career. After completing his education, he served as an apprentice motor mechanic at the Mercedes-Benz plant in his hometown and qualified as a graduate engineer. In 1982 he became president of Euclid Inc., a Daimler-Benz subsidiary based in Cleveland, Ohio, and in 1985 he was appointed president of Mercedes-Benz of South Africa. He left South Africa in 1987 to serve as head of the commercial vehicle division of Daimler-Benz. He was named chief executive of the newly founded Deutsche Aerospace AG (now Daimler-Benz Aerospace) in 1989, a position he held until he became chairman of Daimler-Benz in 1995.

(MARY JANE FRIEDRICH)

Schröder, Gerhard

History was made in Germany on Sept. 27, 1998, when Gerhard Schröder led the Social Democratic Party (SPD) to power, ending 16 years of conservative rule under Helmut Kohl. The Social Democrats had mounted Germany's first U.S.-style media-driven campaign, marketing Schröder chiefly on his appealing image. His energy and vitality were made to contrast favourably with Kohl's long-winded speechifying and fatigued appearance. The substance behind his energy was unclear, however, and many discerned little difference on the issues between the incumbent Christian Democrats and the SPD challengers. Schröder seemed evasive on topics such as Germany's role in the European Union and lacked concrete proposals for economic revival, notably in the eastern part of the country. His message was pragmatic and domestic: continue Germany's social welfare programs while encouraging a probusiness agenda. In this way, he sought to please the party faithful and reach out to small-business owners and young professionals, while reinventing himself as a left-leaning centrist.

Comparisons with U.S. Pres. Bill Clinton and British Prime Minister Tony Blair were inevitable—Schröder too was a young, vigorous left-centrist taking over after years of conservative rule. As chancellor he faced a fractious coalition with the Greens, the difficulty of filling Kohl's very large shoes in the foreign arena, and troublesome unemployment at home. By the year's end he had already encountered challenges—from legislators over his plan for new taxes on energy and from businessmen because of his proposal to close corporate tax loopholes.

Schröder was born on April 7, 1944, in Mossenberg, near Detmold, Lower Saxony. Shortly after Gerhard's birth, his father was killed in action in World War II, and the family's reduced circumstances led his mother to take cleaning jobs to support her family. Schröder left school at age 14 to work in a number of odd jobs. He later enrolled in night classes and received his secondary school diploma. In 1963 he joined the SPD and was politically active in the Young Socialists. As a law student at Göttingen University he participated in the student protests of 1968.

Schröder set up a law practice in Hanover. In 1980 he was elected to the Bundestag (parliament) and served there until 1986, when he lost a campaign for premier of the state of Lower Saxony. He led the SPD opposition in the state parliament until he was elected to the premiership in 1990. The SPD joined with the Greens, the ecological party, in a "Red-Green" coalition government until 1994, when the Social Democrats won a clear majority. Schröder's strong showing in the March 1998 state elections effectively clinched his nomination as the party's candidate for federal chancellor. (CATHERINE KEICH)

Shandling, Garry

Although the television series "The Larry Sanders Show" was not as popular as "Seinfeld," many critics felt its end, in May 1998, was the greater loss. Like most great satire, the series—which chronicled the behind-the-scenes neuroses, vanities, and backstabbings among members and guests of a fictional television talk show—blurred the line between art and reality and between the show's cocreator and star, Garry Shandling, and his character, the shallow, insecure talk-show host, Larry Sanders.

Shandling was born Nov. 29, 1949, in Chicago. After receiving a degree in marketing from the University of Arizona, he moved in 1978 to Los Angeles, where he wrote for the TV series "Sanford and Son" and "Welcome Back, Kotter." Frustrated by the situation comedies' formulaic writing, he began doing stand-up comedy featuring his whining self-deprecation and self-absorption. Shandling made his television stand-up debut on "The Tonight Show" in 1981, and by 1983 he was a frequent guest host and considered a possible successor to regular host Johnny Carson.

DARRYL ESTRINE—HBO/ARCHIVE PHOTOS

Garry Shandling (right)

"It's Garry Shandling's Show" appeared on the Showtime pay cable channel in 1986. The innovative and subversive series starred Shandling as a character named Garry Shandling who knew he was on a television sitcom and often broke the "fourth wall," addressing the audience while he strolled from one set to another. The show ran until 1990 and won the CableACE award four times, including twice for best comedy series.

In 1992, instead of becoming the host of his own "real" talk show, Shandling became the host of "The Larry Sanders Show" for the HBO pay cable channel. Though the program itself was fictional, the series was set in the real entertainment world, offering a razor-sharp look at the siege mentality of television production, including narcissistic celebrities, greedy agents, misanthropic writers, and long-suffering staff. Shandling convinced his show-business friends to appear on the series as themselves, and over the next six seasons about 200 celebrities accepted his invitation to deflate their images with self-mockery.

"The Larry Sanders Show" received numerous Emmy nominations but won only three awards. In early 1998 Shandling became caught up in the sort of real-life Hollywood battle of egos and lawsuits that his show often skewered when he sued his former longtime friend and manager for conflict of interest. Sanders followed suit on the fictional show by firing his agent.

Although on the final episode of the series guest Sean Penn told Larry Sanders how awful it had been to work with the talentless actor wannabe Garry Shandling on the real, soon-to-be-released film *Hurlyburly,* Shandling was reportedly considering the possibility of a genuine post-"Sanders" film career. *Confessions of a Late Night Talk Show Host,* Sanders's autobiography "as told to Garry Shandling," was published in November.

(LOCKE PETERSEIM)

Skármeta, Antonio

In 1998 the award-winning Chilean novelist Antonio Skármeta was chosen to write the screenplay for the movie adaptation of Isabel Allende's novel *Eva Luna.* The choice of Skármeta was not really surprising. The author of *Ardiente paciencia* (1985; *Burning Patience,* 1987)—the source novel of the 1995 Academy Award–nominated Italian motion picture *Il postino* (*The Postman*)—was himself an accomplished screenwriter and the director of several films, including a 1983 award-winning version of *Ardiente paciencia.*

Skármeta was born on Nov. 7, 1940, in Antofagasta, Chile, the grandson of Yugoslav immigrants. While attending the University of Santiago, from which he graduated in 1963, he produced plays by Edward Albee, William Saroyan, and Eugène Ionesco with the university drama group. He published his first book, a collection of short stories entitled *El entusiasmo* (1967), the year after he graduated with a master's degree from Columbia University. It was followed by *Desnudo en el tejado* (1969), which won the Casa de las Américas de la Habana Prize and was the first of his works to be widely translated, and *El ciclista del San Cristóbal* (1973). He finished another collection, *Tiro libre* (1973), and the novel *Soñé que la nieve ardía* (1975; *I Dreamt the Snow Was Burning,* 1985) while living in Argentina in exile from Chile's military regime. In 1975 he moved to Berlin, where he lived until 1988, when he returned to Santiago. During this period he wrote *Ardiente paciencia,* as well as *Novios y solitarios* (1975), *No pasó nada* (1980), and *La insurrección* (1980; *The Insurrection,* 1983).

Ardiente paciencia, Skármeta's best-known work, is the story of an extraordinary friendship that develops between the Chilean poet Pablo Neruda, living in exile, and his postman; it has been translated into 20 languages. The book's title was inspired by a quote from the French poet Arthur Rimbaud—"A l'aurore, armés d'une ardente patience, nous entrerons aux splendides villes." ("At dawn, armed with burning patience, we shall enter the splendid cities.") Skármeta wrote that he wanted "to say to all men of good faith, to the workers, and to the poets, that the entire future was expressed by Rimbaud in that one sentence: only with burning patience shall we conquer the splendid city that will give light, justice, and dignity to all men. Thus poetry will not have sung in vain." Skármeta's other books included *Match Ball* (1989) and *Watch Where the Wolf Is Going* (1991), an anthology of his short stories in English translation. He also wrote several film scripts, hosted a successful television program on books, and translated a number of English-language works into Spanish.

(KATHLEEN KUIPER)

Smith, Will

By the time he won the 1998 Grammy award for best rap solo performance for "Men in Black," charismatic rapper, actor, writer, and producer Will Smith, though not yet 30 years old, had already accomplished the rare feat of achieving critical and financial success across a variety of media: film, television, and recordings. First making a name for himself as the second half of the duo billed as DJ Jazzy Jeff and the Fresh Prince (winning several duo Grammy awards), Smith then starred in his own successful television comedy series, appeared in several high-grossing Hollywood movies, and, in the process, made himself

a multimillionaire and a major player in the entertainment industry.

Willard Smith, Jr., was born on Sept. 25, 1968, in a middle-class section of Philadelphia. He adopted the stage name "Fresh Prince" when he altered a school nickname, "Prince Charming," to reflect a more hip-hop sound and formed an alliance with schoolmate and deejay Jeffrey Townes, whom he met in 1981. They began recording as DJ Jazzy Jeff and the Fresh Prince and released their first single, "Girls Ain't Nothing but Trouble," in 1986, later followed by the album *Rock the House*. In 1988 the group released the groundbreaking single "Parents Just Don't Understand," which went on to win a Grammy award (the first Grammy ever presented in the rap performance category).

Smith's act, notable for its wide crossover appeal, was sometimes characterized as "light rap" owing to the lack of hard-core lyrics and themes in his compositions. Platinum-certified recordings and accompanying videos subsequently brought him to the attention of television producers. The TV situation comedy "The Fresh Prince of Bel-Air," loosely based on Smith's real-life persona (and occasionally featuring Townes in guest spots), ran on NBC for six successful seasons, ending in 1996 at the star's request. During the series' run Smith garnered two Golden Globe nominations and enhanced his resume by producing several episodes.

Buoyed by his small-screen success, Smith expanded into cinema in *Where the Day Takes You* (1992). His first dramatic role was in the film version of the successful stage play *Six Degrees of Separation* (1993). The action comedy-thriller *Bad Boys* (1995), however, proved to be the turning point in his film career. While the movie was not a critical success, it made well over $100 million worldwide, proving Smith's star power. In 1996 he starred in that year's number one film, *Independence Day*. He again broke box-office records the next year in the science-fiction comedy *Men in Black*, for which he also recorded the Grammy-winning title song. As 1998 wrapped, Smith enjoyed the success of his first solo album, *Big Willie Style*, and his starring role in the dramatic thriller *Enemy of the State*.

(ANTHONY L. GREEN)

Sosa, Sammy
In 1998 Sammy Sosa borrowed the line "Baseball's been very, very good to me" to describe his season. Many would argue, however, that it was major league baseball that should offer thanks to the Chicago Cubs right fielder. Sosa's pursuit of Roger Maris's single-season home-run record (61) helped revitalize a sport that had experienced dwindling interest in recent years. Millions tuned in and showed up to watch Sosa battle St. Louis Cardinal Mark McGwire (*q.v*) for a place in the record books. Though he finished behind McGwire (70) with 66 homers, Sosa's all-around performance was second to none. With a .308 batting average, 198 hits, and 158 runs batted in, he was named the National League's Most Valuable Player. Sosa also displayed heroics off the field as he provided assistance to his native country, which had been devastated by Hurricane Georges.

Born on Nov. 12, 1968, in San Pedro de Macoris, Dom.Rep., Samuel Sosa Peralta worked at a number of jobs, including shining shoes, to help support his family following his father's death. At the age of 14, using a mitt made from a milk carton, he began playing organized baseball, and in 1985 he signed with the Texas Rangers. In 1989 he made his professional debut but was traded weeks later to the Chicago White Sox. After struggling at the plate, Sosa was sent across town to the Cubs in 1992. The following year he became the team's first player to hit 30 home runs and steal 30 bases in one season, an achievement he repeated in 1994. In 1995 he made his All-Star Game debut, and during the 1997 season he recorded his 1,000th career hit. Midway through the year the Cubs signed him to a $42.5 million, four-year contract extension. It was not a popular move. Though Sosa was a powerful hitter, he was undisciplined—his strikeouts

(174) outnumbered his hits (161) that season. Many believed he was more concerned with personal statistics than team success.

The 1998 season, however, marked a turnaround for Sosa. He became more patient at the plate and displayed a modesty and enthusiasm that endeared him to fans. After a slow start, he hit 20 home runs in June to set a major league record for most four-baggers in a single month. Though not expected at first to threaten Maris's record, he was soon battling McGwire for the home run lead. On September 13, five days after McGwire had passed Maris, Sosa hit his 61st and 62nd homers. His efforts helped the Cubs make the play-offs for the first time in nine years, though they were swept in the first round by the Atlanta Braves.

(AMY TIKKANEN)

Springer, Jerry
In 1998, amid flying fists and bleeped-out epithets, "The Jerry Springer Show" continued its ascent to the top rung of the talk-show ladder. While so-called trash TV had flourished earlier in the 1990s, by the later part of the decade many other

KHUE BUI—AP/WIDE WORLD

Kenneth W. Starr

daytime talk shows had cleaned up their acts or disappeared altogether. "The Jerry Springer Show" had, however, headed in the opposite direction; what had begun seven years earlier as a relatively tame talk show had mutated over the years to become a program whose outrageous topics had included "I'm pregnant by my brother" and "I'm a breeder for the Klan."

"Springer" had enjoyed only a modest following, but a pivotal change occurred in 1996 following a transfer in the show's ownership; scenes of physical fighting among the guests, which had previously been edited out, were now included, and the ratings soared. Allegations that many of the battles had been staged seemed to have little effect on the show's popularity, and many political and community leaders publicly condemned the show and its brawls. Critics scored a brief victory in mid-1998 when the show's producers, perhaps to appease detractors or to draw advertisers, announced that they would take the fighting off the air. On June 8 the first show with the physical violence edited out was aired. It took only a month of declining ratings (the show's audience decreased by 14% during this time) before the fights were resumed.

For someone so enmeshed in the world of the absurd, Springer had taken a fairly conservative early path. He was born Feb. 13, 1944, in London, and his family immigrated to the U.S. when he was five years old, taking up residence in New York City. He graduated (1965) with a political science degree from Tulane University, New Orleans, and he earned (1968) a law degree from the Northwestern University School of Law, Chicago. Following graduation he worked on the presidential campaign of Robert F. Kennedy. In the early '70s he embarked on his own political career in Ohio, serving on Cincinnati's city council, and in 1977 he became the city's mayor. A failed attempt at the governor's office led to his departure from politics, after which he turned to television journalism. In the early 1980s he began work as a reporter at a local television station; he later became anchor and was the recipient of seven Emmy awards for commentaries during his tenure. He cast his hat into the talk-show ring in 1991 with the launch of "The Jerry Springer Show," and by 1998 it was being seen by millions of viewers in more than 40 countries.

(SANDRA LANGENECKERT)

Starr, Kenneth W.
On Sept. 9, 1998, Special Prosecutor Kenneth Starr reported to the U.S. Congress grounds for finding that Bill Clinton (*q.v.*) had committed perjury, obstructed justice, tampered with a witness, and abused his power as U.S. president. In the report, which was accompanied by voluminous evidence that included a semen-stained dress, tapes of telephone conversations, and grand jury testimony, Starr charged that Clinton had lied under oath about a sexual relationship with former White House intern Monica Lewinsky and had taken steps to cover it up. The report was both legalistic in its tone and salacious in its explicit descriptions of sexual encounters between the two. On October 8 the full House voted 258–176, with 31 Democrats joining the Republican majority, to conduct impeachment hearings, and on December 11–12 the House Judiciary Committee reported four articles of impeachment against the president. On Decemebr 19 the full House approved two of the charges, perjury and obstruction of justice.

Starr was born July 21, 1946, in Vernon, Texas. His father was a minister, and during one summer Starr sold bibles door-to-door to earn money for college. He graduated from George Washington University, Washington, D.C. (B.A., 1968), and Brown University, Providence, R.I. (M.A., 1969), and earned a J.D. (1973) from Duke University, Durham, N.C.. He held government positions, serving as a law clerk (1975–77) to Chief Justice Warren Burger, as a counselor to the U.S. attorney general (1981–83), as an appellate judge (1983–89), and as U.S. solicitor general (1989–93). In August 1994 he took over the investigation of the so-called Whitewater affair, which involved a land deal in Arkansas during the time Clinton was that state's governor. As a result of the investigation, 11 people—including Clinton associates James and Susan McDougal—were convicted of crimes. Starr later investigated the suicide of Vincent Foster, a longtime friend of the Clintons and White House counsel, but the matter was eventually closed. He subsequently was directed to investigate what came to be known as Travelgate, involving the firing of longtime White House workers, and Filegate, pertaining to FBI files on Republicans that were found in the White House. In 1998, however, the Clinton-Lewinsky relationship consumed Starr's attention.

Controversy surrounded Starr's investigation, which included the media's relentless reporting of lurid information, and both Starr and the White House were charged with making improper leaks. There were accusations that the investigative ac-

tivities of Starr, a fervid Republican, were politically motivated. Starr also was criticized for continuing to represent clients of his law firm, Kirkland & Ellis, and he was eventually forced to take an unpaid leave from the firm. As the inquiry progressed, the president's and the prosecutor's approval ratings moved in opposite directions: Clinton's rose and Starr's fell. This seemed partly to reflect much of the public's distaste for the Starr investigation, which many saw as an attempt by congressional Republicans to topple the president over a matter of private rather than public conduct. Some observers even called for abolition of the role of special prosecutor, an office established in the 1970s, or for its modification when authorization expired in 1999. (ROBERT RAUCH)

Sternberg, Sir Sigmund

On March 4, 1998, Sir Sigmund Sternberg, British businessman and philanthropist, was named winner of the Templeton Prize for Progress in Religion, the world's largest annual monetary award—$1,230,000—for having "advanced public understanding of God and spirituality." The prize was established by Sir John Templeton in 1972 to complement the Nobel Prizes, which he felt neglected humanity's spiritual dimension.

Sternberg was born in Budapest on June 2, 1921. The seeds of his interest in improving interfaith relations were sown during his childhood through his early awareness of the absence of dialogue between Roman Catholics and Jews. Owing to quota restrictions for Jews at the University of Budapest and to the rise of Nazism, he left Hungary for Great Britain in 1939. At the outbreak of World War II in September 1939, he was classified by the British government as a "friendly enemy alien"; Hungary was not at war with Britain, but it was not an ally. Because of the classification, he could not attend school and so began to work in metal recycling. He established his own business in that industry, became a member of the London Metal Exchange (1945), and was naturalized as a British citizen (1947).

Sternberg's involvement in business, civic life, and charitable causes paved the way for his interfaith work and resulted in his knighthood by Queen Elizabeth II in 1976. In 1979 he joined the International Council of Christians and Jews, an umbrella organization created to fight anti-Semitism, racism, and xenophobia, and in 1981 he founded the Sternberg Centre for Judaism, Europe's largest Jewish cultural centre. The recipient of honours bestowed by many nations, he was in 1985 named a Knight Commander of the Pontifical and Equestrian Order of St. Gregory the Great at the request of Pope John Paul II, only the second Jew so named in the United Kingdom. His many accomplishments included helping to arrange the first-ever papal visit to a synagogue (Rome, 1986); helping to establish diplomatic relations between the Vatican and Israel (1993); and assisting in the creation of the Three Faiths Forum to promote mutual understanding between Islam, Christianity, and Judaism (1997).

During recent years Sternberg became best known for his facilitation of the Geneva Declaration, an agreement calling for the removal of a Carmelite convent that had been established in the mid-1980s at the site of the World War II Nazi death camp at Auschwitz in Poland.

Although the nuns' intent was to pray for the camp's victims, many considered their presence an intrusion in a setting where nearly two million Jews were killed during the Holocaust. Prior to Sir Sigmund's intercession in 1989, relations between the Roman Catholic Church and the Jewish people had deteriorated. He negotiated with Poland's Jozef Cardinal Glemp, who subsequently agreed to the move, which was eventually completed in 1993.

Sir Sigmund was the second Jew—and the first Reform Jew—to receive the Templeton Prize. The prize money was to be used by the Sternberg Charitable Foundation to support its interfaith causes. (REBECCA RUNDALL)

Suharto

Ending 32 years of autocratic rule, Suharto stepped down as president of Indonesia in 1998. His resignation came after months of student-led pro-democracy demonstrations, which grew in size as the Asian economic crisis plunged Indonesia into desperate financial straits. Equally responsible for his resignation, however, was the nation's increasing disgust with the corruption and cronyism that had characterized the Suharto regime.

Suharto was born on June 8, 1921, in Kemusu Argamulja, Java, Dutch East Indies (now Indonesia). Like many Javanese, he used only his given name. After finishing high school, he joined the Dutch colonial army and graduated from its noncommissioned officers school. In 1942, when the Japanese wrested control of the colony from the Dutch, he joined the Japanese-run defense corps, where he trained to become an officer. Although he initially welcomed the occupying forces, by 1945 he was involved in the anti-Japanese rebellion. After Japan's surrender to the Allies, he fought in the guerrilla forces resisting Dutch efforts to regain control. By the time Indonesia became a republic in 1950, he had risen to the rank of lieutenant colonel. Suharto led the army in putting down an allegedly communist coup d'état attempt on Sept. 30, 1965. In the following months he directed a purge of communists and leftists, during which the army massacred more than 500,000 ethnic Chinese.

Suharto took control of the Indonesian government in 1966 under an emergency powers act. He

was elected president in 1968. His modernization programs brought roads, electricity, and irrigation systems to the most remote areas of the country, and his family-planning programs drastically cut Indonesia's high birthrate. Suharto ruled with an iron hand, however. In 1975–76 his government forcibly incorporated East Timor into Indonesia. In the process some 200,000 Timorese were killed, and an equal number were tortured or imprisoned.

Although Suharto's modernization programs helped turn Indonesia into a regional economic and political powerhouse, serious problems were brewing by 1998. A small group of Suharto cronies had profited enormously from lucrative noncompetitive government contracts. Even more blatant was the favouritism shown to members of his own family. Four of his six children sat on the People's Consultative Assembly, Indonesia's highest legislative body, and all of them had grown wealthy through extensive business interests. Cronyism and nepotism were tolerated in relatively stable economic times, but when the Asian economic crisis hit Indonesia, riots erupted on May 12 throughout the country, resulting in the deaths of more than 500 people. Suharto strove to remain in power, but public opposition had grown too strong. Faced with the possibility of revolution and no longer able to count on the army to maintain order, he stepped down on May 21. In December he was questioned by state prosecutors about his wealth, which he maintained was earned not stolen. (JOHN H. MATHEWS)

Summitt, Pat Head

In 1998 American basketball coach Pat Summitt reached the apex of women's basketball after guiding the University of Tennessee Lady Volunteers to an unprecedented third consecutive National Collegiate Athletic Association (NCAA) championship, capping a perfect season (39–0). It was her sixth title and came just days after she received the Associated Press's Coach-of-the-Year award. Second only to John Wooden's 10 championships on the college hard court, Summitt had amassed an .823 winning average and made a record 15 trips to the Final Four. The athletes she coached have gone on to play in the Olympics and at the professional and international level. In more

Sir Sigmund Sternberg

Pat Summitt

than 24 years as head coach at Tennessee, Summitt rejected numerous coaching offers from other schools in an effort to climb to new heights with the Lady Vols.

Born on June 14, 1952, in Henrietta, Tenn., Patricia Head grew up on a dairy farm, where she developed the toughness that would become her trademark. She first played basketball in a hayloft, and her aggressive and instinctive play at the University of Tennessee at Martin (B.S., 1974), earned her spots on national teams. In 1975 she won gold at the Pan-American Games and the following year overcame a serious knee injury to co-captain the U.S. Olympic team to a silver medal in Montreal. Soon afterward, she retired as a player to concentrate on coaching. Named head coach of the Lady Vols at the University of Tennessee at Knoxville in 1975 while pursuing a master's degree in physical education (1975), she posted a 16–8 record in her inaugural season. In 1987, months after earning her 300th win, she guided the Lady Vols to their first NCAA championship. With Summitt at the helm, the university's team went on to claim five more titles (1989, 1991, 1996–98), and since 1986 won at least 20 games each season. In 1996 Summitt notched her 600th victory, becoming only the second woman to tally that many wins on the court. In addition to collegiate basketball, she also coached on the international level, leading the U.S. women's team to gold at the 1984 Olympics in Los Angeles.

Driven and uncompromising, Summitt demanded the best from her players and, armed with the threat of strenuous practices and the legendary "look" that would send athletes for cover, she was rarely disappointed. The recipient of numerous coaching honours, including the Naismith award (1987, 1989, and 1994), Summitt was the first woman to receive (1990) the John Bunn trophy from the Basketball Hall of Fame. A master motivator, she released two self-help books, *Reach for the Summit* and *Raise the Roof* (each with Sally Jenkins), soon after the 1998 championship. The books covered a subject quite familiar to Summitt—achieving success.   (AMY TIKKANEN)

Taniguchi, Yoshio
In late 1997 the Museum of Modern Art (MOMA) in New York City selected the design of Japanese architect Yoshio Taniguchi for the museum's planned expansion. Taniguchi, the least known of the 10 architects whose designs were considered by MOMA officials, proposed a dramatic reconfiguration of one of the world's most important cultural institutions. His plans called for doubling the museum's exhibition space, adding large skylights to galleries, moving the main entrance, and creating an extensive research and education complex. Announcing the museum's selection, MOMA Chairman Ronald S. Lauder praised Taniguchi's "exceptional creative vision" and his sensitivity to the museum's complex needs. A model of the winning design was included in an exhibition at the museum in March–April 1998.

Taniguchi, who was born on Oct. 17, 1937, in Tokyo, was the son of Yoshiro Taniguchi, a noted figure in the modern architectural movement in Japan. He earned a B.A. (1960) in mechanical engineering from Keio University, Tokyo, and an M.A. (1964) in architecture from Harvard University's Graduate School of Design. Taniguchi did design work for the Kenzo Tange Studio (1964–72) and taught architecture at the University of Cape Town, S.Af., and at the University of California, Los Angeles, before cofounding an architectural firm in Tokyo in 1975.

Heeding his father's advice to handle each of his assignments with care and not to take on too many projects at one time, Taniguchi built up a successful practice, specializing in museums and other public buildings. He won numerous awards, including the 1987 Japan Academy of Art Prize for the Ken Domon Museum of Photography, Sakata City, and the 1990 Mainichi Art Award for the Tokyo Sea Life Park, a popular aquarium. In 1995 he designed the Toyota Municipal Museum of Art, Toyota City, and in 1998 construction began on his Gallery of Horyuji Treasures at the Tokyo National Museum.

Because of his belief that architecture should be an outgrowth of dialogue between architect and client, Taniguchi had never entered a competition before submitting his proposal to MOMA, and he was somewhat surprised to succeed over his more famous competitors. His deceptively simple design to maximize space and light and his refined, delicate sense of beauty had greatly impressed the selection committee, however. Although the commission—Taniguchi's first outside Japan—thrust him suddenly into the international spotlight, he seemed eager for the challenge. He elaborated on his goal to transform MOMA into "a bold new museum," one very much in harmony with midtown Manhattan and better equipped than the old structure to facilitate visitors. Construction on the project was expected to begin in 2000 or 2001.
    (TEIJI SHIMIZU)

Testino, Mario
The publication of the book *Any Objections?*, Peruvian-born photographer Mario Testino's personal look behind the fashion scene, was eagerly anticipated in 1998. Testino, dubbed the "Super Mario" of the fashion industry, had published his work in some of the world's top fashion monthly magazines, including American, French, and British *Vogue, Vanity Fair, W, Allure, The Face,* and *Dutch Magazine.* He also had been widely sought after to shoot advertisements for such fashion companies as Versace, Missoni, Sonia Rykiel, Yves Saint Laurent, Ralph Lauren, and Gap.

In the May/June issue of *American Photo,* Testino was ranked number 12 among the industry's 100 most influential people of 1998. His images for Gucci's 1995/96 autumn/winter collection helped Tom Ford relaunch the then-lagging multimillion-dollar-generating Italian luxury leather goods line. Celebrities, too, coveted the chance to work with the photographer. In 1997 Diana, princess of Wales, requested that Testino shoot her image for a *Vanity Fair* cover story, and in 1998 Testino's photo of the Spice Girls graced the cover of American *Vogue.* In addition, Madonna's album *Ray of Light* featured Testino images of her.

As a permanent fixture on the international fashion-show circuit, Testino was easily recognized. Always seated in a front row at the best shows, he wore natty, colorful clothes and was ac-companied by Carine Roitfeld, the striking Parisian fashion stylist who was his most frequent collaborator. Testino's bright, sharp style of photography put an end to the fashion industry's love affair with heroin chic and the accompanying dark, murky images that dominated magazine pages in the early 1990s. "Fashion photography is all about making an image that people desire—so they want to buy the clothes," he maintained. According to the London *Telegraph* newspaper, Testino's work also helped mute the supermodel trend.

Testino was born in 1954 in Lima, Peru, of Irish, Spanish, and Italian descent. He found his inspiration, however, in the work of British celebrity and fashion photographer Cecil Beaton and since 1976 has made his home in London. Though Testino had studied law and economics at the University of Lima and international affairs at the University of California, San Diego, he made portfolios for up-and-coming models during the day and worked as a waiter at night. Although he made influential friends quickly, including fashion designer Jasper Conran and celebrity shoemaker Manolo Blahnik, Testino claimed that it was hard work and discipline that propelled him into his position of power. "I made a rule with myself that no matter what time I went to bed, I'd be up at eight and in the office by nine whether I had any work to do or not."
    (BRONWYN COSGRAVE)

Vajpayee, Atal Bihari
In May 1998 India exploded five nuclear bombs in quick succession, reminding the world that the nuclear era was far from over. Though condemnation for the acts was nearly universal in the West, India's newly elected prime minister, Atal Bihari Vajpayee, struck a defiant tone. Undaunted by the economic sanctions imposed by the U.S. and Japan and supported by his countrymen, Vajpayee declared that "India has the sanction of her own past glory and future vision to become strong." Prior to elections in early 1998, Vajpayee had been viewed by many as the moderate face of the Hindu-nationalist Bharatiya Janata Party (BJP).

Vajpayee was born on Dec. 25, 1926, in the town of Gwalior, Madhya Pradesh. He became politically active as a teenager and was briefly jailed by the British colonial administration. Though initially attracted to communism, he became disillusioned when the communists supported the creation of Pakistan in the 1940s. Vajpayee dropped out of law school and became editor of a publication run by the Hindu-nationalist Rashtriya Swayamsevak Sangh, a self-

Atal Bihari Vajpayee

defense force created in 1925 to protect Hindus in riots and promote Hindu culture.

Vajpayee was first elected to Parliament in 1957 as a member of the Jan Sangh, a forerunner of the BJP. During Indira Gandhi's rule as prime minister under a state of emergency (1975–77), he was jailed along with thousands of opposition members. In the late '70s Vajpayee served as foreign minister and earned a reputation for improving relations with Pakistan and China. He helped found the BJP in 1980, but his moderation was overpowered by hard-liners. Vajpayee—one of the few Hindu leaders to speak out against the 1992 destruction of the historic Muslim mosque at Ayodhya—was sworn in as prime minister in May 1996 but served only 13 days in office, failing to attract needed support from other parties. In 1998 the BJP won a record number of seats but was forced to make a shaky alliance with regional parties, many of which were opposed to Hindu nationalism.

Though Vajpayee had campaigned on the promise of international "peace and reconciliation" and been praised for his eloquence, integrity, and conciliatory gestures toward India's 120 million Muslim minority, relations with Pakistan deteriorated in the months following the nuclear explosions. Despite pleas from the international community urging India and Pakistan to hold peace talks, Vajpayee and Prime Minister Nawaz Sharif of Pakistan found it difficult even to agree on the topics open for discussion.   (BENJAMIN SCHALET)

Weill, Sandy

When the proposed merger of the Travelers Group financial giant and banking's Citicorp was announced in April 1998, the news stunned the financial industry; involving some $76 billion in stock, it was at the time the largest merger in history. For Wall Street's latest superstar, Travelers chairman and CEO Sanford "Sandy" Weill, not only was the merger a step closer to the creation of the huge international diversified financial services institution he had been dreaming about for over a decade, but its audacity and risk was in step with Weill's reputation as a corporate visionary who was as savvy as he was fearless.

Weill was born March 16, 1933, in Brooklyn, N.Y., to Polish immigrants and was the first in his family to earn a university degree, graduating from Cornell in 1955. Afterward, he worked his way up from Wall Street messenger to stockbroker to cofounder of a firm in 1960. During the next two decades Weill aggressively bought securities houses and amassed his first financial services network, Shearson Loeb Rhoades. His steady rise came to a halt, however, in the 1980s, when he sold Shearson to American Express. At the time of the sale Weill had hoped to become chief executive of American Express, but in 1985 he left the company.

At that time, in his 50s and financially secure, Weill would not have been begrudged his retirement. Instead he started over, buying the Commercial Credit division of Control Data Corp. in 1986. It was not an auspicious rebirth of an empire—the small division was a faltering reject of its parent company. Weill, however, displayed a talent for rebuilding such organizations through cost cutting and employee motivation, and two years later he was expanding again, merging Commercial Credit with the larger, but struggling, Primerica, and acquiring the securities firm Smith Barney in the process. The acquisition of Travelers and the repurchase of Shearson from American Express followed during 1992–93.

In October 1997 Weill gained widespread attention for the $9 billion purchase of Salomon Inc., parent company of the prestigious Salomon Brothers investment bank. It was at the time the second-largest acquisition in Wall Street history. But even as Weill's comeback was hailed on Wall Street, his dream was far from complete. Driven either by ego or vision, or perhaps both, he still sought the greater size and diversity that the merger with Citicorp would bring. As Weill awaited approval of the deal, which faced the problem of banking regulation laws that prohibit a bank from selling insurance, the financial industry waited to see if he had again grabbed too much too fast, or if he would now finally see his grand vision become a reality.

(LOCKE PETERSEIM)

Zinedine Zidane

Zidane, Zinedine

Hollywood fiction could hardly have improved on World Cup reality for Zinedine Zidane. Starting the France 98 tournament as the best hope of the host nation in its campaign to win the gold medal, the Marseille-born association football (soccer) star quickly showed his class and outstanding ability, inspiring France to beat South Africa in the opening match in front of adoring fans in his home city. Then came disaster. He was sent off the field in the match against Saudi Arabia for the uncharacteristic act of stamping on an opponent. In addition, he was banned for two matches and disgraced, and there were even rumours that he might be dropped from the French team completely. France, however, needed him, and so he returned and in the final against Brazil became the hero everyone in the country had wanted him to be, scoring two goals and giving France its first major trophy. They were his 10th and 11th international goals. In the *World Soccer* poll he was voted player of the year.

Zidane was born on June 23, 1972, the son of Berber immigrants from Algeria. After playing for minor teams Castellane and Septimes-les-Vallons, he joined Cannes and soon developed as a rangy looking, 1.85-m (6-ft, 1-in)-tall midfield player with great upper body strength and a somewhat ungainly gait that masked exceptional vision, a deft sleight of foot, and an ability to outwit the most determined defenders. He made his debut for Cannes on May 20, 1989, at Nantes. Operating behind the two main strikers, "Zizou" (as he was known to all) became the focal point of the attack. In 1992 he was transferred to Bordeaux. Two years later, when voted Best Young Player in France, he played in his first full international competition for France, scoring both goals in a 2–2 draw with the Czech Republic.

In 1995 he played an incredible 57 matches overall for club and country and helped secure a place in the UEFA Cup final for his Bordeaux club. The exhausting year took a toll on his stamina, however, and worse followed: he narrowly escaped serious injury in a car crash. Despite performing below his usual form, he played in the finals of the 1996 European Championship, in which France reached the semifinals. That summer the Italian club Juventus paid Bordeaux a transfer fee of £3.2 million for Zidane's services, starting in September 1996. In Italy he soon became as much of a favourite as he had been in France, appearing on Juventus's winning team at the World Club Championship and European Super Cup as well as on its 1997 Italian league-winning squad. Juventus also reached the European Champions League final in 1997 and 1998, and Zidane finished third in the European Player of the Year vote in 1997. In January 1998 he scored the only goal when France beat Spain 1–0 in a match to inaugurate the Stade de France, the new stadium that was to be the scene six months later of France's—and Zidane's—World Cup triumph.   (JACK ROLLIN)

OBITUARIES

Abacha, Sani, Nigerian military leader (b. Sept. 20, 1943, Kano, Nigeria—d. June 8, 1998, Abuja, Nigeria), participated in the overthrow of three successive military governments before gaining control of the country himself in 1993. Having entered the army at age 18, Abacha was educated at military schools in Nigeria, England, and the United States and rose to brigadier by 1980. He participated in the ouster of Pres. Alhaji Shehu Shagari (December 1983) and was chosen to announce the new leadership of Mohammed Buhari, who named Abacha to the Supreme Military Council. In August 1985, however, Abacha helped to overthrow Buhari's government and install Ibrahim Babangida, who named Abacha army chief of staff (1985), chairman of the Joint Chiefs of Staff (1989), and minister of defense (1990). When Babangida annulled the 1993 general election—in which Moshood Abiola (*q.v.*) was the apparent winner—Abacha took advantage of public outrage to depose Babangida. In late 1993 Abacha declared himself president and promised restoration of democracy. His presidency, however, soon turned into a ruthless dictatorship. Under his rule Nigerians saw profits from the country's vast oil supply dwindle as their leader's own wealth grew. Abacha siphoned off as much as $4 billion, and those who spoke out against him were either executed or jailed. He eliminated all elected institutions and assemblies, fired a significant portion of the military, hired a personal security force of approximately 2,000 men, and took control of the press. Though he sent troops to restore democracy in Liberia and Sierra Leone, he was unwilling to support it at home. The elections he had promised for 1996 did not take place. One by one the parties contesting the elections scheduled for August 1998 declared Abacha their candidate for president. He died following an apparent heart attack.

Abiola, Moshood Kashimawo Olawale, Nigerian executive, financier, and politician (b. Aug. 24, 1937, Abeokuta, Nigeria—d. July 7, 1998, Abuja, Nigeria), was one of the richest magnates in Africa and popularly regarded as the leader of the pro-democracy movement in Nigeria. He had been imprisoned since 1994 after winning the 1993 presidential election. Abiola, who was born in poverty, attended the University of Glasgow, Scot., on scholarship. He became an accountant for ITT Nigeria in 1968; by 1971 he was its chief executive and chairman, posts he held until 1988. During that time he amassed an immense private fortune and became owner of a publishing house, a newspaper syndicate, and an airline. With his luxurious, flamboyant lifestyle—which included marrying more wives (21 at the time of his death) than sanctioned by Islam—Abiola became a popular public figure; he also made generous donations for building schools. After decades of nearly uninterrupted military rule, democratic elections were held in Nigeria in 1993. Abiola, running as the presidential candidate of the Social Democratic Party, won almost 60% of the vote. The ruling junta, threatened by Abiola's popularity, annulled the election at the instigation of Gen. Ibrahim Babangida. This provoked a political crisis that remained unresolved. Abiola agitated publicly for the presidency he had won, which led to his 1994 arrest on a charge of treason. During his imprisonment Abiola was deprived of outside news and subjected to solitary confinement and abuse that included negligent medical care. His release seemed imminent following the death of Gen. Sani Abacha (*q.v.*) in June 1998 and a visit to Nigeria by UN Secretary-General Kofi Annan made largely on Abiola's behalf. However, Abiola died suddenly under mysterious circumstances. Although heart attack was officially declared to be the cause of death, that conclusion was greeted with skepticism by many.

Abrahams, William Miller, American writer and editor whose three-decade-long editorship of the annual volumes of O. Henry Award–winning stories brought the short story a steady growth in interest and respect (b. Jan. 23, 1919, Boston, Mass.—d. June 2, 1998, Hillsborough, Calif.).

Abzug, Bella (BELLA SAVITZKY), American lawyer and politician (b. July 24, 1920, New York, N.Y.—d. March 31, 1998, New York), variously identified as "Battling Bella" and "Mother Courage," was a quintessential progressive known for her groundbreaking roles as peace activist, feminist, environmentalist, and early advocate for gay rights. Abzug was the daughter of Russian-Jewish immigrants. She earned degrees from Hunter College of the City University of New York (B.A., 1942) and Columbia University Law School, New York City (LL.B., 1947). It was during her years as an attorney (1947–70), when few women were practicing law, that she began wearing her signature wide-brimmed hats to ensure that her clients and colleagues did not assume she was a secretary. She acted as chief defense attorney for Willie McGee, an African-American man convicted and eventually executed for raping a white woman in Mississippi, defended victims of Sen. Joseph McCarthy's anticommunist witch-hunts, and helped draft legislation for the 1954 Civil Rights Act and the 1965 Voting Rights Act. To fight the U.S. government's plans to resume nuclear-weapons testing, she founded the Women Strike for Peace in 1961, and to protest the Vietnam War, she led the Democratic Party's "Dump Johnson" movement and supported Sen. Eugene McCarthy in his 1968 bid for the presidency. Along with Gloria Steinem and Betty Friedan, Abzug was in the forefront of the feminist movement and was an early advocate for equal rights for women, abortion rights, and child-care legislation. She successfully ran for Congress in 1970 from Manhattan's 19th district with the slogan "This woman's place is in the House—the House of Representatives." On her first day in Congress (Jan. 21, 1971), she introduced a motion calling for the withdrawal of U.S. troops from Vietnam, and she later used a little-known procedural tactic to force Pres. Richard Nixon's administration to release the top-secret Pentagon Papers. She was also the first member of Congress to call for Nixon's impeachment. After serving three terms in the House, she lost a Senate race to Daniel P. Moynihan in 1977. Firmly committed to women's empowerment, she founded several or-

ganizations, including the National Women's Political Caucus and the International Women's Environment and Development Association, and she participated in the UN's Fourth World Conference on Women in 1995. Her book *Bella!* was published in 1972, and *Gender Gap: Bella Abzug's Guide to Political Power for American Women,* co-written with Mim Kelber, appeared in 1984.

Addison, John Mervyn, British composer who specialized for more than 40 years in writing effective, lightly orchestrated scores for motion pictures and television programs and incidental music for the theatre. Among Addison's most admired films were *Seven Days to Noon* (1950), *Tom Jones* (1963), for which he won an Academy Award, the Oscar-nominated *Sleuth* (1971), and the Bafta-winning *A Bridge Too Far* (1977). His television work included the 21-hour miniseries "Centennial" and "Murder, She Wrote," the theme for which earned him an Emmy award (b. March 16, 1920, Cobham, Surrey, Eng.—d. Dec. 7, 1998, Bennington, Vt.).

Ajit (HAMID ALI KHAN), Indian actor whose charming villainy and outrageous double entendres made him a national folk hero during a film career that spanned several decades in Bollywood, the nickname for Mumbai (Bombay), India's film capital (b. Jan. 27, 1922, Golconda, India—d. Oct. 21, 1998, Hyderabad, India).

Alfaro, Emilio, Argentine actor and director whose highly regarded career lasted nearly 50 years; from 1989 he served as director of the Teatro General San Martín in Buenos Aires (b. Jan. 20, 1933, Buenos Aires, Arg.—d. July 18, 1998, Buenos Aires).

Allin, the Right Rev. John Maury, American religious leader who was the Episcopal Church's 23rd presiding bishop, serving from 1974 to 1986; he was active in efforts to raise money for the rebuilding of over 100 firebombed black churches but was unwilling to support the ordination of women (b. April 22, 1921, Helena, Ark.—d. March 6, 1998, Jackson, Miss.).

Ambler, Eric, British author and screenwriter (b. June 28, 1909, London, Eng.—d. Oct. 22, 1998, London), drastically transformed the traditionally

Bella Abzug

musty spy thriller with a series of six novels. In contrast to earlier British spy stories, in which xenophobic, romantic heroes defeated vast conspiracies to dominate the world, Ambler wrote of ordinary educated Englishmen thrust by chance or innocent curiosity into danger; Ambler's villains, too, were realistically drawn and were frequently violent fascists and Nazis. The novels, which were set in continental Europe, were permeated with the emotional atmosphere of the impending world war. Ambler's careful writing, intricate plots, and growing skill at creating vivid characterizations culminated in the sustained tension of *The Mask of Dimitrios* (1939; U.S. title, *A Coffin for Dimitrios*) and *Journey into Fear* (1940), both later made into memorable films. Ambler, the son of music-hall entertainers, studied engineering at the University of London and completed his first novel, *The Dark Frontier* (1936), while employed as an advertising writer. During World War II he wrote training films for the British army, a job that led to a postwar career as a screenwriter, adapting films from novels; he was nominated for an Academy Award for his script *The Cruel Sea* (1953). A onetime Marxist sympathizer, he later attacked Stalinism in *Judgment on Deltchev* (1951), which marked his return to thrillers. He also began traveling widely, and subsequent novels were often set in the Middle East or East Asia, including *The Light of Day* (1962), which was adapted to the big screen as *Topkapi* (1964), and *The Levanter* (1972), a film about a terrorist plot against Israel; his much-praised *Doctor Frigo* (1974) was set on a Caribbean island. For a time Ambler lived in the U.S., where he met his second wife, film producer Joan Harrison, before finally settling in the late 1960s in Switzerland. His fiction was a major influence on other writers, including Graham Greene, John le Carré, and Len Deighton.

Ametistov, Ernest Mikhaylovich, Russian judge who from 1991 was a member of the Constitutional Court, Russia's highest court, and as such was a liberal champion of human rights and democratic freedoms (b. May 17, 1934, Leningrad, U.S.S.R.—d. Sept. 7, 1998, near Moscow, Russia).

Amory, Cleveland, American writer and animal rights advocate (b. Sept. 2, 1917, Nahant, Mass.—d. Oct. 14, 1998, New York, N.Y.), was the author of a number of best-selling books and founder (1967) of the Fund for Animals, a New York–based animal-protection agency, which he served as unpaid president for 31 years. Amory's writing career began in his senior year in college when he became president of the *Harvard Crimson.* He graduated in 1939 and, after a brief term as a newspaper reporter, became the youngest editor ever hired by the *Saturday Evening Post.* During World War II he served in army intelligence. After the war he produced three humorous social histories: *The Proper Bostonians* (1947), *The Last Resorts* (1952), and *Who Killed Society?* (1960). In the early 1950s Amory began an 11-year term as a social commentator on "The Today Show." From 1963 to 1976 he was the chief critic for *TV Guide* and also wrote a column for the *Saturday Review* and a daily radio essay, "Curmudgeon at Large." In his book *Man Kind? Our Incredible War on Wildlife* (1974), Amory detailed inhumane hunting practices. Inspired by his cat Polar Bear, he wrote a trilogy: *The Cat Who Came for Christmas* (1988), *The Cat and the Curmudgeon* (1990), and *The Best Cat Ever* (1993). His most recent book, *Ranch of Dreams* (1997), detailed the lives of abused and unwanted animals at the Black Beauty Ranch in Texas, an animal sanctuary that he was instrumental in establishing.

Ashmore, Harry Scott, American editor who, as executive editor of the *Arkansas Gazette,* won a Pulitzer Prize for editorials he wrote in support of integration of a Little Rock high school in 1957; he later served as editor in chief of the *Encyclopædia Britannica* and as president of the Center for the Study of Democratic Institutions (b. July 27, 1916, Greenville, S.C.—d. Jan. 20, 1998, Santa Barbara, Calif.).

Aury, Dominique (ANNE DESCLOS), French writer and translator who was a respected member of the literary establishment but gained her greatest fame in 1994 when it was confirmed that she was the author, under the pseudonym Pauline Réage, of the sensational erotic best-seller *Histoire d'O,* published in 1954 and later translated into at least 20 languages (b. Sept. 23, 1907, Rochefort, France—d. April 30, 1998, Paris, France).

Autry, (Orvon) Gene, American entertainer (b. Sept. 29, 1907, Tioga, Texas—d. Oct. 2, 1998, North Hollywood, Calif.), gained fame in motion pictures as the first American singing cowboy and used his earnings to amass a fortune in a business empire that comprised hotels, oil wells, broadcasting stations, a cattle ranch, a flying school, music-publishing companies, and the California Angels major league baseball team. Rivaled only by Roy Rogers (*q.v.*), he appeared in nearly 100 "horse operas," often accompanied by his horse, Champion, and recorded more than 600 songs— a great number of which he wrote or co-wrote and among which were his signature "Back in the Saddle Again"; his first gold record, "That Silver-Haired Daddy of Mine"; and the enduring hits

AP/WIDE WORLD

Gene Autry

"Here Comes Santa Claus," "Frosty the Snowman," and "Rudolph the Red-Nosed Reindeer." Autry began singing when he was a young boy, and when he was 17 and working as a railway telegrapher in Oklahoma, he happened to meet Will Rogers in the office, sang for him, and was encouraged to pursue a singing career. He became Oklahoma's yodeling cowboy on a Tulsa radio station in 1928 and in the early 1930s performed on the weekly radio show "The National Barn Dance." From 1939 he appeared on the "Melody Ranch" radio show. Autry's first movie appearance was in 1934 in a small role in *In Old Santa Fe,* and he followed that with the serial *Phantom Empire* the same year. His first starring role came the next year in *Tumbling Tumbleweeds.* In 1937 Autry became the top-ranked western star, and he retained that spot through 1943; he was a top-10 box-office favourite in 1940–42. Following military service in World War II, he formed his own production company and resumed his filming career, and from 1950 to 1956 he starred on a weekly television show. Autry then began concentrating more on his business interests. In 1988 he opened the Gene Autry Western Heritage Museum in Los Angeles to house his collection of western art and memorabilia.

Badgro, Morris Hiram ("RED"), American football player and coach who was an offensive and defensive end for the New York Giants from 1930 to 1935, during which time he was on four All-Pro teams, and played for the Brooklyn Dodgers in 1936; he was inducted into the Pro Football Hall of Fame in 1981 (b. Dec. 1, 1902, Orillia, Wash.—d. July 13, 1998, Kent, Wash.).

Ballestrero, Anastasio Alberto Cardinal, Italian Roman Catholic priest who served as archbishop of Turin from 1977 to 1989 and as such was custodian of the Shroud of Turin; he allowed scientific dating tests to be performed on the shroud and later made the announcement that it dated from the Middle Ages and thus was not the burial cloth of Jesus Christ (b. Oct. 3, 1913, Genoa, Italy—d. June 21, 1998, La Spezia, Italy).

Barker, Louisa Dupont ("BLUE LU"), American blues singer whose trademark style combined her innocent girlish voice with bawdy songs (b. Nov. 13, 1913, New Orleans, La.—d. May 7, 1998, New Orleans).

Barton, Sir Derek Harold Richard, British chemist (b. Sept. 8, 1918, Gravesend, Kent, Eng.—d. March 16, 1998, College Station, Texas), altered the landscape of modern chemistry by originating the fields of conformational analysis and stereochemistry. He showed how differences in the spatial structure, or conformation, of molecules relate to differences in their reactivity and how the differences can be calculated by analyzing the conformation of the molecules. In 1950 Barton presented a theory that described organic molecules as having preferred three-dimensional forms that determine their chemical properties, a revolutionary concept that soon became a basic principle of modern chemistry. For this he was awarded the 1969 Nobel Prize for Chemistry, along with Odd Hassel of Norway, who had earlier shown how chemically identical molecules can have different conformations. Barton left the family carpentry business to study chemistry at Imperial College of Science and Technology, University of London (B.S., 1940; Ph.D., 1942). After wartime service in military intelligence, he returned to Imperial College to teach physical chemistry, publishing calculations of the preferred three-dimensional shape of organic molecules. While a visiting professor (1949–50) at Harvard University, he presented a landmark four-page paper on conformational analysis, *The Conformation of the Steroid Nucleus* (1950), which explained the unusual reaction rates of steroids and related isomers. His findings won quick acceptance and were soon incorporated into basic science curricula. He returned to London as a reader at Birkbeck College (1950–55), where he uncovered the properties of phenol oxidative coupling and investigated how poppies produce morphine. During his career he also examined new chemical reactions and syntheses, experimenting with santonin, aldosterone, sulfur, photochemistry, fluorination, penicillin, and free radicals. After a brief stint at the University of Glasgow, Scot. (1955–57), he returned (1957) to Imperial College as chemistry chairman and remained there until 1978, when he became director of the Institute for the Chemistry of Natural Substances, Gif-sur-Yvette, France. In 1986 he joined the faculty at Texas A&M University, and at the time of his death, he was working on the oxidation of saturated hydrocarbons. Barton, who was knighted in 1972, was the author of more than 1,000 scientific papers, owner of many patents, mentor to hundreds of students, and a valued scientific consultant.

Bassett, John White Hughes, Canadian journalist and broadcasting executive who at various times owned the *Toronto Telegram,* was part owner of the Toronto Maple Leafs hockey team and the Toronto Argonauts football team, and was granted Canada's first license for a privately owned television station, CFTO; he later helped form and became chairman of Baton Broadcasting Inc., and CFTO became the flagship of the CTV network (b. Aug. 25, 1915, Ottawa, Ont.—d. April 27, 1998, Toronto, Ont.).

Bates, Clayton ("PEG LEG"), American tap dancer who, despite having lost a leg in an accident when he was 12 years old, enjoyed a performing career that lasted some seven decades and saw him in vaudeville, clubs, stage musicals, and motion pictures and on television, including 21 appearances on "The Ed Sullivan Show," a record for tap dancers (b. Oct. 11, 1907, Fountain Inn, S.C.—d. Dec. 6, 1998, Fountain Inn).

Belanger, Mark Henry ("BLADE"), American baseball player who won eight Gold Gloves and played in four World Series during his 16 seasons (1965–81) as a fielding shortstop with the Baltimore Orioles (b. June 8, 1944, Pittsfield, Mass.—d. Oct. 6, 1998, New York, N.Y.).

Beriosova, Svetlana, Lithuanian-born British ballerina (b. Sept. 24, 1932, Kaunas, Lithuania—d. Nov. 10, 1998, London, Eng.), was one of the Royal Ballet of England's major ballerinas for more than 20 years. Known for her eloquent and elegant classical style, she created such leading roles as the Fairy in Kenneth MacMillan's *Le Baiser de la fée,* Princess Belle Rose in John Cranko's *The Prince of the Pagodas,* the title role in Cranko's *Antigone,* and Lady Elgar in Frederick Ashton's *Enigma Variations* in addition to dancing such traditional classical roles as Odette-Odile in *Swan Lake,* Aurora in *The Sleeping Beauty,* and the title role in *Giselle.* Beriosova was the daughter of Lithuanian State Opera dancer and ballet master Nicolas Beriosoff and grew up in the various companies for which he worked. In 1941 she began appearing in children's roles with the Ballet Russe de Monte Carlo, including Clara in *The Nutcracker,* and in 1947 she made her professional debut with the Ottawa Ballet. Later in 1947 she joined the Cuevas Grand Ballet de Monte Carlo as an apprentice, and the following year she moved to England and joined the Metropolitan Ballet. Upon that company's closure at the end of 1949, Beriosova was invited to join the Sadler's Wells Theatre Ballet as a principal dancer. In 1952 Beriosova transferred to the Sadler's Wells company at Covent Garden (later the Royal Ballet) as a soloist, and she was made a principal dancer in 1955. In one of her more unusual parts, the title role of Ashton's *Persephone* (1961), she recited André Gide's poetry in French in addition to dancing to the music of Igor Stravinsky. Although Beriosova retired from the stage in 1975, becoming a much-valued teacher and coach, she made onstage appearances in 1978 and 1980 as the ballet mistress in Maina Gielgud's demonstration piece *Steps, Notes and Squeaks.*

Bernardino, Minerva, Dominican feminist and public servant who in 1945 was one of only four women signers of the UN Charter and went on to be the driving force behind the founding of the UN Commission on the Status of Women (b. 1907, Seibo, Dom.Rep.—d. Aug. 29, 1998, Dominican Republic).

Bettmann, Otto L., German-born American photograph archivist who fled from Germany in the 1930s with two trunks full of photographs and went on to found the Bettmann Archive and build it into the world's largest image collection (b. 1903, Leipzig, Ger.—d. May 1, 1998, Boca Raton, Fla.).

Bing, Ilse, German-born avant-garde photographer whose images featured an inventive use of oblique angles and patterns; she was dubbed "queen of the Leica" for her use of that new lightweight camera in the 1930s (b. March 23, 1899, Frankfurt, Ger.—d. March 10, 1998, New York, N.Y.).

Bird, Florence Bayard, American-born Canadian broadcaster, journalist, politician, and author who, as chairman of the Royal Commission on the Status of Women, helped launch Canada's contemporary feminist movement; she also served in the Senate (1978–83) and wrote under the name Anne Francis (b. Jan. 15, 1908, Philadelphia, Pa.—d. July 18, 1998, Ottawa, Ont.).

Salvatore ("Sonny") Bono

Bono, Salvatore ("SONNY"), American entertainer, restaurateur, and politician (b. Feb. 16, 1935, Detroit, Mich.—d. Jan. 5, 1998, South Lake Tahoe, Calif.), enjoyed a political career that culminated in service in the U.S. House of Representatives but was better remembered as a performer and the driving force behind the singing duo Sonny and Cher. The two had a number of hits on the pop charts in the 1960s and '70s and were the hosts of a successful television variety show in the '70s. Bono moved to California in the early 1950s and began trying to sell his songs. After working in a succession of jobs that included meat delivery truck driver and construction worker, he became a record packer at Specialty Records, where he worked his way up to writer and producer. He released a few records under a variety of pseudonyms and was co-writer (1962) of "Needles and Pins," which became a hit for Jackie DeShannon and later for the Searchers, before meeting (1963) and marrying (1964) Cherilyn Sarkisian. The couple began (1964) recording Bono's songs and in 1965 had their first—and the best known—of several major hits, "I Got You Babe." They starred in "The Sonny and Cher Comedy Hour" from 1971 to 1974, and although they were divorced in 1974, they appeared as cohosts of another television show in 1976–77. Bono then left show business, except for a few guest appearances on TV series, and became (1982) a successful restaurant owner. His opposition to zoning regulations in Palm Springs, Calif., inspired him to enter the 1988 mayoral election there, which he won. Bono's success in that post prompted him to run for the U.S. Senate in 1992, but he lost in the Republican primary. He ran for the House of Representatives in 1994, this time successfully, and was reelected in 1996. His sense of humour was especially prized, and he was one of the most sought-after fund-raising speakers. Bono was killed in a skiing accident.

Bradley, Owen, American musician and business executive who was credited with having been a major force in the establishment of Nashville, Tenn., as the centre of the country music industry; in 1974 he was elected to the Country Music Hall of Fame (b. Oct. 21, 1915, Westmoreland, Tenn.—d. Jan. 7, 1998, Nashville, Tenn.).

Bradley, Thomas, American politician (b. Dec. 29, 1917, Calvert, Tex.—d. Sept. 29, 1998, Los Angeles, Calif.), transformed Los Angeles into a bustling business and trading centre during his five terms (1973–93) as the city's mayor. The son of a sharecropper, Bradley moved to Los Angeles when he was seven and faced economic hardship after his father abandoned the family. He attended the University of California, Los Angeles, on a track scholarship but left before graduation to serve on the Los Angeles police force; he earned a law degree (1956) from Southwestern University School of Law in Los Angeles, attending night school. After reaching the rank of lieutenant, with little chance of further promotion owing to his African-American heritage, Bradley retired in 1961 to pursue a career in politics. In 1969, at a time when the city was still reeling from the 1965 Watts riots, Bradley staged his first mayoral campaign. Though narrowly defeated, he ran again in 1973 and won. During his tenure as mayor Los Angeles experienced massive growth

Thomas Bradley

and became the second largest city in the U.S., and Bradley was instrumental in forging alliances between business and government sectors. With his stately bearing and soft-spoken demeanour, he enjoyed great popularity that reached a zenith when the city hosted the 1984 Olympic Games. The first privately funded Olympics, they produced a huge profit for Los Angeles. Bradley's approval rating began to fall in the late 1980s, however. Complaints arose over the city's increasing pollution, traffic, and crime, and in 1989 he was fined for improper financial dealings. Trouble continued in 1991 when four white policemen were captured on videotape beating Rodney King, an African-American. Hours after the policemen's acquittal in 1992, the city erupted in riots and more than 50 people were killed. The violence was, in part, blamed on Bradley's mishandling of the situation and his acrimonious relationship with police chief Daryl Gates. Deeply disturbed by the course of events, he decided not to run for reelection.

Brickhouse, John Beasley ("JACK"), American radio and television broadcaster who, as the voice of the Chicago Cubs (1941–81) and White Sox (1940–67) baseball teams, combined exuberance and colourful storytelling with his signature home-run call, "Hey-hey! Hey-hey!"; a member of the Baseball Hall of Fame (inducted 1983), he also announced football, basketball, golf, and boxing contests as well as numerous political events (b. Jan. 24, 1916, Peoria, Ill.—d. Aug. 6, 1998, Chicago, Ill.).

Bridges, Lloyd Vernet, Jr., American actor (b. Jan. 15, 1913, San Leandro, Calif.—d. March 10, 1998, Los Angeles, Calif.), was cast in a wide range of supporting roles on the big screen, including a conniving deputy (*High Noon*), a space pilot (*Rocketship X-M*), an ex-Nazi and mountaineer (*The White Tower*), a brutal kidnapper (*The Sound of Fury*), and a malevolent cowboy (*Colt .45*), before achieving crossover success on television as the daring skindiver on "Sea Hunt" (1957–61). Although Bridges attended the University of California, Los Angeles, with the intention of becoming a lawyer, he grew interested in acting and after graduation went to the East Coast to perform in theatrical productions. He made his Broadway debut in 1937 in *Othello*, in which he had a walk-on role. Bridges soon drew the notice of Hollywood and in 1941 signed with Columbia Pictures. Although many of his early performances were in forgettable movies, he won critical praise for his supporting roles in the classics *High Noon* and *A Walk in the Sun* (as a GI during World War II). Bridges's career stagnated when he was blacklisted in the 1950s during the McCarthy era, largely for his membership in the Communist Party and the Actors' Lab, a radical theatre group. Even though he felt that he was typecast in the role of U.S. Navy frogman Mike Nelson in the immensely popular television series "Sea Hunt," he remained with the show for 156 episodes. Until his death Bridges continued to appear in film and television, branching into comic roles, including memorable performances in the film *Airplane!* and the television comedy "Seinfeld." Bridges's sons, Jeff and Beau, became successful actors.

Brimsek, Francis Charles ("FRANKIE"), American ice hockey goaltender for the Boston Bruins who gained renown during the first weeks of his 10-year career for a series of shutouts, which earned him the nickname "Mr. Zero"; he was an All-Star eight times and in 1966 was inducted into the Hockey Hall of Fame (b. Sept. 26, 1915, Eveleth, Minn.—d. Nov. 11, 1998, Virginia, Minn.).

Brinnin, John Malcolm, American biographer, critic, and poet (b. Sept. 13, 1916, Halifax, N.S.—d. June 26, 1998, Key West, Fla.), shepherded the boisterous Welsh poet Dylan Thomas throughout his U.S. speaking tours and wrote freely of the experience after Thomas's death. At the age of four Brinnin moved from Canada with his American parents to Detroit. He attended Wayne

(later Wayne State) University, the University of Michigan (B.A., 1941), and Harvard University (1941–42). His first book of poems, *The Garden Is Political,* was published to considerable acclaim in 1942; his seventh and last, *Skin Diving in the Virgins and Other Poems,* was published in 1970. He also began a long teaching career in 1942. Although he once had defeated the better-known poet John Berryman for a poetry prize, Brinnin eventually came to prefer other genres. While serving as director of the Poetry Center of the Young Men's and Young Women's Hebrew Association (YM-YWHA), Brinnin arranged for Thomas's first performance in the United States in 1949. Brinnin's sympathetic response to the alcoholic poet led to a relationship that lasted until Thomas's death of "insult to the brain" (a fatal mix of cortisone and whiskey) some four years later. Brinnin's description of his experiences, *Dylan Thomas in America: An Intimate Journal* (1955), presented in detail the greater poet's womanizing and drinking. Brinnin found the relationship disquieting, and he quit his post at the YM-YWHA. In the following years he wrote a number of books, including *The Third Rose: Gertrude Stein and Her World* (1959), a biography of Gertrude Stein; *Sextet: T.S. Eliot & Truman Capote & Others* (1981), a series of vignettes on T.S. Eliot, Truman Capote, Elizabeth Bowen, and others; and three histories of North Atlantic steamships (he was an inveterate traveler). He also edited three anthologies of 20th-century American and British poetry and *Emily Dickinson: Poems* (1960).

Brown, Raymond Edward, American theologian (b. May 22, 1928, New York, N.Y.—d. Aug. 8, 1998, Redwood City, Calif.), was a highly regarded Roman Catholic biblical scholar. His rigorous examination of the Gospels resulted in the publication of such works as the two-volume *The Gospel According to John* (1966, 1970), *The Birth of the Messiah* (1977), and *The Death of the Messiah* (1994) as well as more than 35 other books. Brown's centrist stance sometimes angered conservative Catholics, especially in 1971, when he questioned whether Mary's virginal conception of Jesus could ever be proven historically. After receiving both a B.A. (1948) and M.A. (1949) from the Catholic University of America, Washington, D.C., Brown entered (1951) the Society of St. Sulpice for seminary teaching and was ordained (1953) in the St. Augustine, Fla., diocese. In Baltimore, Md., he earned doctorates in sacred theology (1955) from St. Mary's Seminary and in Semitic languages (1958) from Johns Hopkins University. While a fellow at the American Schools of Oriental Research in Jerusalem, Brown worked on a Dead Sea Scrolls concordance, and in 1963 he was an adviser to Bishop Joseph Hurley at the Second Vatican Council. Brown taught at St. Mary's Seminary from 1959 until 1971, then spent the majority of his teaching career at Union Theological Seminary in New York City until his retirement in 1990. He was the first Roman Catholic professor given tenure at the historically Protestant institution and built a reputation as an erudite and spellbinding lecturer.

Brugger, Kenneth C., American amateur naturalist who on Jan. 2, 1975, discovered the long-sought winter home of the monarch butterfly in the mountains of Mexico (b. 1918?—d. Nov. 25, 1998, Austin, Texas).

Bryden, Beryl Audrey, British jazz singer whom Ella Fitzgerald dubbed "Britain's queen of the blues"; of the more than 100 songs she recorded during her half-century-long career, she was especially remembered for her washboard accompaniment on Lonnie Donegan's "Rock Island Line" (b. May 11, 1920, Norwich, Eng.—d. July 14, 1998, London, Eng.).

Bunting-Smith, Mary Ingraham, American scientist, educator, and administrator (b. July 10, 1910, New York, N.Y.—d. Jan. 21, 1998, Hanover, N.H.), as president of Radcliffe College (1960–72), created the Radcliffe Institute for

Independent Study (later Bunting Institute), which sought to advance women's role in society. After graduating from Vassar College (B.A., 1931), she attended the University of Wisconsin, where she earned a doctorate (1934) in agricultural bacteriology. She married in 1937 and divided her time between raising a family and conducting research at Yale University. Following the death of her husband in 1954, Bunting-Smith was forced to find full-time employment. Unable to obtain a faculty position at Yale (then an all-male college) because she was a woman, she became dean of Douglass College, the sister school of Rutgers University, where she also served as professor of bacteriology. In 1960 she became the fifth president of Radcliffe College. Believing there was a "climate of unexpectation" for women, Bunting-Smith founded the Radcliffe Institute of Independent Study in 1961. The centre examined the forces affecting women's position in society and provided fellowships to female scholars and artists, particularly those whose careers had been interrupted by family obligations. Alumnae of the institute include author Alice Walker and psychologist Carol Gilligan. Bunting-Smith also sought a fuller integration of the college with Harvard University, and it was during her tenure that Radcliffe students first received Harvard degrees and were granted admission to the university's graduate and business schools. In 1964 Bunting-Smith became the first female member of the U.S. Atomic Energy Commission.

Burney, Leroy Edgar, American physician who, as surgeon general of the U.S. Public Health Service from 1956 to 1961, became the first federal official to name smoking as a cause of lung cancer (b. Dec. 31, 1906, Burney, Ind.—d. July 31, 1998, Arlington Heights, Ill.).

Buscaglia, (Felice) Leo(nardo) ("DR. HUG"; "DR. LOVE"; "LOVE MERCHANT"; "HUG DOCTOR"), American guru to self-help aficionados who, by means of books, lectures, and recordings, was a tireless advocate of the power of love; he often reinforced his message by physically embracing members of his audiences (b. March 31, 1924, Los Angeles, Calif.—d. June 12, 1998, Lake Tahoe, Nev.).

Caccialanza, Gisella, American ballet dancer who was a charter member of George Balanchine's first company in the U.S., danced in musical films Balanchine choreographed, and was a member of the New York City Ballet's forerunner, Ballet Society, before joining the San Francisco Ballet in 1951; she later taught at the latter company's school (b. Sept. 17, 1914, San Diego, Calif.—d. July 16, 1998, Daly City, Calif.).

Calderone, Mary Steichen, American physician who, as cofounder (1964) and head (1964–82) of the Sexuality Information and Education Council of the United States, crusaded for the inclusion of responsible sex education in the public-school curriculum (b. July 1, 1904, New York, N.Y.—d. Oct. 24, 1998, Kennett Square, Pa.).

Campanis, Alexander Sebastian (ALESSANDRO CAMPANI; "AL"), Greek-born American baseball executive whose 44-year career with the Dodgers (in both Brooklyn, N.Y., and Los Angeles), which included the 1981 World Series championship, was ended in 1987 by televised comments in which he opined that blacks did not have managerial ability (b. Nov. 2, 1916, Kos, Greece—d. June 21, 1998, Fullerton, Calif.).

Caray, Harry (HARRY CHRISTOPHER CARABINA), American baseball announcer whose exuberant coverage of major league games made him a favourite of fans for over 50 years; his trademark expression "Holy cow!" and his raspy seventh-inning-stretch renditions of "Take Me Out to the Ball Game" became legendary, and he was inducted into the Baseball Hall of Fame in 1989; Caray's son and grandson also became baseball announcers (b. March 1, 1919?, St. Louis, Mo.—d. Feb. 18, 1998, Rancho Mirage, Calif.).

Carmichael, Stokely (KWAME TURE [OR TOURE]), Trinidadian-born civil rights leader and black nationalist (b. June 29, 1941, Port of Spain, Trinidad—d. Nov. 15, 1998, Conakry, Guinea), originated the slogan "black power," urged African-Americans in the United States to abandon nonviolent protests in favour of more radical—even revolutionary—tactics, and advocated Pan-Africanism. Carmichael immigrated to the United States at the age of 11 and attended the predominantly white Bronx High School of Science in New York City. While a student at Howard University, Washington, D.C., he joined the Freedom Riders, activists who traveled by bus throughout the South to challenge segregationist transportation laws. After graduating (A.B., 1964) he led a Student Nonviolent Coordinating Committee (SNCC, popularly pronounced "snick") voter-registration drive in Lowndes county, Ala., that raised the number of registered black voters from 70 to 2,600. Although candidates of the newly created Lowndes County Freedom Organization were defeated in the November 1966 election, the political party and its panther logo served to inspire the creation of the militant Black Panther Party. After witnessing the brutality inflicted upon nonviolent civil-rights demonstrators, Carmichael supported more aggressive methods of protest. Within weeks of being chosen in 1966 as chairman of SNCC, he electrified and alarmed the nation with calls for black power, and he was seen as an indirect contributor to the fiery riots that burned through U.S. inner cities that summer. His essay "What We Want," published in the *New York Review of Books* in September 1966, defended black power as a philosophy "because this country does not function by morality, love, and nonviolence, but by power. Thus, we determined to win political power, with the idea of moving on from there into activity that would have economic effects." He argued for social upheaval and the "liberation" of the country's black ghettoes, and he staunchly defended his militancy: "No one ever talked about 'white power' because power in this country is white . . . the furor over 'black power' reveals how deep racism runs and the great fear which is attached to it." While his writings focused on the community-building aspects of black power, his rhetoric became more inflammatory. He was ousted from SNCC leadership in 1967 but then was made honorary prime minister of the Black Panthers. Opposing a decision by the Black Panther leadership to seek support among white groups, Carmichael left the U.S. for Guinea in 1969, urging other African-Americans to follow him. He adopted the name Kwame Ture after the Guinean president Ahmed Sékou Touré and the deposed Ghanian leader Kwame Nkrumah—both early proponents of Pan-Africanism—and redirected his efforts toward Pan-Africanism through leadership in the All-African People's Revolutionary Party. He blamed "imperialistic forces" for the prostate cancer that eventually claimed his life, but his spirit remained unbowed—he continued to answer the telephone with the emphatic pledge "Ready for the revolution!" He was coauthor, with Charles V. Hamilton, of *Black Power: The Politics of Liberation in America* (1967) and compiled his speeches in *Stokely Speaks: Black Power Back to Pan-Africanism* (1971).

Carter, Betty (LILLIE MAE JONES), American jazz singer and songwriter (b. May 16, 1929, Flint, Mich.—d. Sept. 26, 1998, Brooklyn, N.Y.), sang with energy, swing, and a freewheeling vocal range that marked her as one of the most vivid and original vocalists of her time. She studied piano and singing at the Detroit Conservatory of Music, and, by the age of 16, she was singing in Detroit clubs with bebop musicians, notably Charlie Parker. As Lorraine Carter, she toured (1948–51) with the Lionel Hampton big band and developed her scat-singing skills; Hampton nicknamed her Betty Bebop and reportedly fired her several times, but each time, his wife and manager, Gladys Hampton, rehired Carter. During the 1950s and '60s Carter's career faltered, she had occasional popular successes, such as her 1961 album of duets with Ray Charles and a

handful of tours. Unhappy with record producers' attempts to make her a more conventional singer, she formed Bet-Car Productions. Her third self-produced album, *The Audience with Betty Carter* (1979), was a hit with jazz fans, and she became a favourite on the international jazz club–concert circuit. Carter's artistry was marked by her selection of unusually fast or slow tempos, complex melodic interpretations that usually strayed far from the composers' themes, and an expressive face, which matched her pliable range of vocal sounds. A demanding leader, she was accompanied by trios of gifted young bop musicians, including pianists Benny Green, Cyrus Chestnut, and Stephen Scott and drummer Lewis Nash, who themselves went on to highly successful careers. Her 1988 album *Look What I Got* won a Grammy award, and in 1997 U.S. Pres. Bill Clinton awarded her a National Medal of Arts.

Carter, Helen (HELEN CARTER JONES), American singer and musician who was a member of the Carter Family band—considered the "first family" of country music—and, after it disbanded, of Mother Maybelle and the Carter Sisters, who toured, recorded, performed on radio and television, and were members of the Grand Ole Opry (b. Sept. 12, 1927, Maces Springs, Va.—d. June 2, 1998, Nashville, Tenn.).

Casaroli, Agostino Cardinal, Italian Roman Catholic priest and diplomat who from the 1960s served as the Vatican's liaison to the communist bloc and from 1979 to 1990 was secretary of state and thus second in command under Pope John Paul II (b. Nov. 24, 1914, Castel San Giovanni, Piacenza, Italy—d. June 9, 1998, Rome, Italy).

Cassilly, Richard, American Wagnerian opera singer whose physical presence and mastery of heldentenor roles delighted audiences for some 30 years (b. Dec. 14, 1927, Washington, D.C.—d. Jan. 30, 1998, Boston, Mass.).

Castaneda, Carlos, Peruvian-born anthropologist and writer (b. Dec. 25, 1925/31?, Cajamarca, Peru—d. April 27, 1998, Westwood, Calif.), was considered a father of the New Age movement for his series of books based on the mystical secrets of a Yaqui Indian shaman. Though critics claimed the works were more fiction than fact, they became international best-sellers, translated into some 17 languages. An enigmatic figure who refused to be photographed or recorded, Castaneda offered conflicting autobiographical information, and much of his early life was unclear. Though he claimed to have been born in São Paulo, Braz., U.S. immigration records listed his birthplace as Cajamarca. It was known, however, that in 1951 he moved to the U.S., where he studied anthropology at the University of California, Los Angeles (Ph.D., 1973). During a trip to Arizona in the early 1960s, he met Don Juan Matus, a Yaqui who allegedly could manipulate time and space. Castaneda became his apprentice, and the two men embarked on a series of drug-fueled adventures. In 1965 Castaneda returned to Los Angeles and began writing about his experiences. *The Teachings of Don Juan: A Yaqui Way of Knowledge* was published in 1968 and quickly became a best-seller. With its eloquent descriptions of "non-ordinary reality," it proved particularly popular with American youth disillusioned with the Vietnam War. A series of books followed, including *A Separate Reality: Further Conversations with Don Juan* (1971) and *Journey to Ixtlan: The Lessons of Don Juan* (1972). His

growing fame made Castaneda increasingly reclusive, and his death was not revealed for nearly two months.

Celebrezze, Anthony J., Italian-born American politician who served as mayor of Cleveland, Ohio, from 1953 to 1962, as secretary of health, education, and welfare from 1962 to 1965, and as an appellate judge from 1965 to 1995; in his Cabinet position he helped guide a number of important New Frontier and Great Society bills to passage by Congress (b. Sept. 4, 1910, Anzi, Italy—d. Oct. 29/30, 1998, Cleveland).

César (CÉSAR BALDACCINI), French sculptor (b. Jan. 1, 1921, Marseille, France—d. Dec. 6, 1998, Paris, France), was one of Europe's most controversial contemporary artists. He was at the forefront of the New Realism movement with his radical compressions (compacted automobiles, discarded metal, or rubbish), expansions (polyurethane foam sculptures), and fantastic representations of animals and insects. The son of Italian immigrants, César quit school at the age of 12 in order to work, but three years later he en-

FRANCOIS MORI—AP/WIDE WORLD

César

rolled in evening classes at a local art academy. In 1943 he won a scholarship to the École des Beaux-Arts in Paris. With his artistic vision shaped by poverty, he utilized the most economical of materials for sculptures and became a founder of the New Realism movement, which blended elements of the Arte Povera movement of Italy—which emphasized raw and unprocessed materials—and the French Matiéristes, who focused on "found objects." His first solo art show was in 1954 at the Galerie Lucien Durand in Paris, and his first compression appeared in 1958. César used a hydraulic press to form many of his compressions, and he occasionally used a welding torch or sledgehammer. One composition featured thousands of crushed counterfeit Cartier watches that had been seized by customs officials. His sensational gigantic "Sein" was modeled on a cabaret dancer's breast and molded in pink polyester resin. In 1968, during a black-tie reception in London at the Tate Gallery, César created a stir by producing, from a mixture of chemicals, a liquid foam expansion onto the floor. One of his more widely available works, reproduced in many

sizes for commercial sale, was a representation of his thumb; "Le Pouce," a 12-m (40-ft-)-tall version of his digit, was placed in the skyscraper-strewn Parisian quarter of La Défense. César's most massive work was a 520-ton barrier of compressed automobiles erected at the Venice Biennale in 1995. His work bore influences of Pablo Picasso, French sculptor Germaine Richier, Swiss artist Alberto Giacometti, and the loosely geometric abstract creations of British artist Anthony Caro. Because his creations were often interpreted as critiques of consumerism, César's consumer-waste sculptures were sometimes compared to Andy Warhol's Pop art. César, however, refused to be grouped or unduly influenced by the categorizations of the art world. He also became an emblem for filmmaking. In 1975 the French film industry commissioned him to design its annual award, the César, a compression-styled gold statuette bearing (by intent) absolutely no resemblance to its American cousin, the Oscar. In 1976 César was made a Chevalier of the French Legion of Honour.

Chatichai Choonhavan, Thai politician (b. April 25, 1922, Bangkok, Thai.—d. May 6, 1998, London, Eng.), served as prime minister of Thailand during an economic boom in the late 1980s and was known for his carefree, flamboyant style. Chatichai—the only son of Phin Choonhavan, a prominent army officer and head of a powerful Thai family—became one of the country's youngest generals as a result of his father's influence. A 1951 coup led by his father gained Chatichai a Cabinet post, but when the government was ousted in 1957, he was sent on a diplomatic assignment to Argentina—tantamount to exile. After other diplomatic postings in Switzerland, Austria, Yugoslavia, and the Vatican, during which he developed Western tastes for wine, cigars, and sports cars, Chatichai returned to Thailand in 1972. He then formed the Thai Nation Party, rebuilding his family's old coalitions in preparation for the 1975 national elections. No party won a majority, and a succession of temporary governments followed, in which the charismatic, popular Chatichai was often prominent, holding a number of Cabinet posts. He became prime minister in 1988, with the goal of expanding Thailand's role in the Asian economy. His government deregulated business and promoted capital speculation, helping to produce unprecedented rates of economic growth and property development. Amid accusations of corruption, he was ousted in 1991. Chatichai maintained a base of power in the 1990s, however, by forming the Chart Pattana Party, a major opposition party. A quintessential wheeler-dealer whose popularity was unaffected by the taint of corruption that attended his entire political career, Chatichai maintained a breezy attitude that was symbolized by his slogan "no problem," a phrase he used repeatedly to answer his many critics.

Chey Jong-Hyon, Korean business executive who, as chairman of the SK Group (formerly the Sunkyong Group) of Korea, fostered the group's development and helped it become the fifth largest business conglomerate in South Korea; he also served as chairman of the Federation of Korean Industries (b. Nov. 21, 1929, Suwon, Kyonggi province, S. Kor.—d. Aug. 26, 1998, Seoul, S. Kor.).

Chiles, Lawton Mainor, Jr., American politician who gained the nickname "Walkin' Lawton" by walking the length of Florida in 1970 in his successful campaign for a U.S. Senate seat, which he held until 1989; from 1991 he served as Florida's governor, and, in addition to continuing to pursue the concerns that had marked his years in public service—environmental protection and government fiscal responsibility—he sued the tobacco industry and won an $11.3 billion settlement on behalf of the state (b. April 3, 1930, Lakeland, Fla.—d. Dec. 12, 1998, Tallahasee, Fla.).

Clancy, Patrick ("PADDY"), Irish singer who, with his brothers and a friend, formed the Clancy Brothers and Tommy Makem singing group,

which was credited with the Irish folk music revival in the 1950s and '60s (b. 1922, Carrick-on-Suir, County Tipperary, Ire.—d. Nov. 11, 1998, Carrick-on-Suir).

Clark, Dane (BERNARD ZANVILLE), American actor on stage, on television, and especially in motion pictures, where he was most memorable in roles as a tough but sympathetic down-to-earth "Joe Average" in such World War II–era films as *Destination Tokyo* (1943), *God Is My Co-Pilot* and *Pride of the Marines* (1945), and the 1948 film *Whiplash* (b. Feb. 18, 1913, Brooklyn, N.Y.—d. Sept. 11, 1998, Santa Monica, Calif.).

Cleaver, Eldridge, American author and activist (b. 1935, Wabbaseka, Ark.—d. May 1, 1998, Pomona, Calif.), was a leading member of the 1960s African-American militant group the Black Panthers and author of the prison memoir *Soul on Ice,* an angry commentary on race relations in the U.S. The book made him a symbol of radical black consciousness in the late 1960s. Cleaver spent most of his early life in California reform schools and prisons on charges ranging from theft and marijuana possession to assault and rape. While in prison he expressed remorse for the rapes and became a Black Muslim and a follower of Malcolm X. Eldridge's prison writings, first published in the radical journal *Ramparts,* garnered attention and helped him obtain parole in December 1966. These writings were collected and published in 1968 as *Soul on Ice.* A sequence of essays influenced by Thomas Paine, Karl Marx, Vladimir Lenin, and, especially, Malcolm X, *Soul on Ice* achieved great celebrity and was acclaimed as one of the best books of the year. One of Cleaver's slogans made famous in the book was, "You're either part of the problem or part of the solution." Soon after his parole, he joined the Black Panthers, eventually becoming their "minister of information." His parole was rescinded after a 1968 confrontation between the Panthers and the Oakland, Calif., police. Later that year it was reinstated, which allowed Cleaver to run for the U.S. presidency (he received 30,000 votes) and to give lectures at the University of California, Berkeley; efforts to stop the lectures led to student demonstrations. In November of the same year, his parole was again revoked; instead of returning to jail, Cleaver fled the country, first to Canada, then to Cuba, Algeria, and Paris, and finally to the French Riviera. He returned to the U.S. voluntarily in 1975, saying that he had undergone a religious transformation, and spent an additional eight months in prison. In later years he campaigned for the U.S. Senate (as a Republican), designed men's trousers, ran an Oakland recycling centre, experienced various spiritual conversions (his only other book, *Soul on Fire,* was dedicated to Jesus Christ), had minor drug-related scrapes with the law, and, at the time of his death, was involved with environmental issues.

Clifford, Clark, American lawyer (b. Dec. 25, 1906, Fort Scott, Kan.—d. Oct. 10, 1998, Bethesda, Md.), was a knowledgeable and savvy adviser to four U.S. Democratic presidents and as such served a number of public and private interests. After graduating (1928) with a degree in law from Washington University, St. Louis, Mo., Clifford began work as an attorney. During World War II he enlisted in the navy and served as an aide to Pres. Harry S. Truman. Clifford became special counsel to the president in 1946, and in that capacity he assisted in the formulation of the Truman Doctrine, created the whistle-stop campaign that helped Truman win the 1948 election, and was instrumental in persuading Truman to recognize the nation of Israel. In 1950 he left politics to open a law firm and was reportedly the first Washington lawyer to achieve a million-dollar income. He was John F. Kennedy's attorney while the latter was still a senator, and Kennedy continued to seek his advice during his campaign and presidency. Clifford returned to government in 1968 to become Pres. Lyndon B. Johnson's secretary of defense, a post that he occupied for less than a year. One significant action during his brief

tenure was to advise the president to commence action to end the war in Vietnam. His guidance was also sought by Pres. Jimmy Carter, who consulted Clifford regarding difficulties involving his budget director. In his later years Clifford was plagued by accusations of involvement in the Bank of Credit and Commerce International scandal, although he denied any misconduct.

Commager, Henry Steele, American historian and teacher (b. Oct. 25, 1902, Pittsburgh, Pa.—d. March 2, 1998, Amherst, Mass.), regarded the United States as the best example of a nation

Eldridge Cleaver

based on a system of rational law, in the form of the U.S. Constitution, which he held to be a perfect blueprint for a political system. Commager first gained attention in 1930 as coauthor, with the distinguished Harvard historian Samuel Eliot Morison, of *The Growth of the American Republic,* long a standard textbook, in which he first displayed his ability to record history in a clear, cogent narrative style. Among his many other books were *The American Mind* (1951), a meditation on what Commager perceived to be the American character, often considered his finest work; and *The Empire of Reason* (1977), in which he rejected economic determinism as an explanation of American history, arguing that through conscious, rational will the Founding Fathers brought into being a state based on the principles of the Enlightenment. On several occasions Commager's reverence for the Constitution led him to confront contemporary political issues. In 1947, at the beginning of the McCarthy era, Commager published an article in *Harper's* magazine attacking loyalty oaths as a violation of constitutional rights, and in 1966 he objected to the Vietnam War on the grounds that the congressional prerogative of waging war had been usurped. Commager's emphasis on reason led some to suggest that he overlooked the role of religion in American history; others criticized him for ignoring the history of women, blacks, Native Americans, workers, and other nonestablishment groups. Commager earned bachelor's, master's, and doctor's degrees in history from the University of Chicago, the last in 1928. He was a history professor at New York University (1929–38), Columbia University, New York City

(1938–56), and Amherst (Mass.) College (1956–92); he also held short appointments at the University of Cambridge (twice in the 1940s) and the University of Oxford (1952). Commager was a member of the National Academy of Arts and Letters and was awarded its gold medal for history in 1972.

Conein, Lucien E., French-born American intelligence agent whose exploits during his service in the CIA and its World War II forerunner, the Office of Strategic Services, made him a CIA legend; from 1973 to 1984 he was the U.S. Drug Enforcement Administration's head of covert operations (b. 1919, Paris, France—d. June 3, 1998, Bethesda, Md.).

Cookson, Catherine (DAME CATHERINE ANN MCMULLEN COOKSON), British author (b. June 20, 1906, Jarrow, Durham, Eng.—d. June 11, 1998, Jesmond Dene, near Newcastle upon Tyne, Eng.), penned almost 100 popular novels, which she set in the industrial region of northeastern England, frequently dubbed "Cookson Country." She was intimately familiar with the physical and emotional lay of this land, having been raised in the Tyneside docks area in poverty. Her early experiences lent an edge to her work, which was marked by an earthiness and sincerity that spoke to many readers. Early life was hard for Cookson, who was the illegitimate daughter of an alcoholic mother and a father she never knew. To escape her grim situation, she left school at age 13 and found work in a laundry. In 1940 she married Thomas Cookson, a teacher who encouraged her to write. In 1950 she published her first book, *Kate Hannigan.* From this time on, in spite of ill health—she suffered from bouts of severe depression and a lifelong blood disorder—Cookson wrote constantly. Although not the recipients of high literary praise, her books were some of the most well-worn volumes in British libraries. Popular beyond British shores, Cookson's novels were translated into 17 languages and sold in some 30 countries. Many of her stories, such as the Mallen trilogy, which chronicled the lives of a wealthy family from Victorian times to the 20th century, were adapted for television. Other tales were brought to life on radio, film, and stage. Cookson wrote two autobiographies, *Our Kate: An Autobiography* (1969) and *Catherine Cookson Country* (1986), as well as nine children's books, and a collection of poems, paintings, and meditations, *Let Me Make Myself Plain* (1988). She was created O.B.E. in 1985 and was advanced to D.B.E. in 1993.

Cormack, Allan MacLeod, South African-born American physicist (b. Feb. 23, 1924, Johannesburg, S.Af.—d. May 7, 1998, Winchester, Mass.), formulated the mathematical algorithms that made possible the development of the cross-sectional X-ray imaging process known as computerized axial tomography (CAT) scanning, for which he was awarded a share of the 1979 Nobel Prize for Physiology or Medicine. A lecturer in physics at the University of Cape Town, Cormack was hired for a part-time job at Cape Town's Groote Schuur Hospital in 1955 because of a regulation requiring that trained physicists calculate radiation doses for cancer therapy, even though he had no medical training and knew nothing about medical diagnostics. Cormack observed the inadequacies of X-ray technology, whose imprecise images made diagnosis haphazard. He determined that much greater precision could be achieved by taking many X-ray images of the same body part from different perspectives and then integrating the data to produce a single image. Recognizing that the problem was fundamentally mathematical, Cormack published the results of his work in two papers in 1963 and 1964, documenting a technique that represented a vast improvement over conventional X-ray imaging methods and permitted a much more precise differentiation of soft tissues. Cormack never attempted to build a working tomographic scanner that would demonstrate the technique he had formulated, and his papers attracted little notice. His work was reproduced independently in the early 1970s by the British engineer Godfrey Newbold Hounsfield, whose CAT scanning machine gained worldwide attention, and with whom Cormack shared the Nobel Prize. After his tenure (1950–56) at the University of Cape Town, Cormack held a one-year research fellowship at Harvard University, then moved to Tufts University, Medford, Mass., where he remained until his retirement in 1980, studying the interaction of subatomic particles and refining the mathematics of tomographic imaging methods. Cormack became a member of the American Academy of Arts and Sciences in 1980.

Costa, Lúcio, Brazilian architect (b. Feb. 27, 1902, Toulon, France—d. June 13, 1998, Rio de Janeiro, Braz.), was the creator of the master plan for Brasília, the capital of Brazil, and helped to establish the modern architectural aesthetic in the country. Six years after graduating (1924) with a degree in architecture from the National School of Fine Arts in Rio de Janeiro, Costa was appointed director of his alma mater. Although his tenure was brief—lasting only a year—he introduced young Brazilian architects to the Modernist style, especially the Functionalism espoused by Swiss architect and urban planner Le Corbusier. In 1939 Costa invited Le Corbusier to consult with him on the design of the Ministry of Education and Health Building in Rio de Janeiro. Costa also collaborated on that project with one of his students, Oscar Niemeyer, and the pair worked together again in 1939 to design the Brazilian Pavilion for the New York World's Fair. Costa completed several noteworthy projects on his own over the next decade, among them the award-winning Eduardo Guinle Apartments (1948–54) in Rio de Janeiro. In 1957 he won an international competition with his futuristic design of Brasília, which replaced Rio de Janeiro as the government centre, and asked Niemeyer to design many of the city's major buildings. The undertaking was part of Pres. Juscelino Kubitschek's campaign to encourage Brazilian development, and Brasília, which had been an arid savanna, was constructed in only four years. The realization of Costa's plan was often likened to an airplane with a central axis for government and public buildings and wings on either side for the residential districts. Some critics, however, viewed Brasília as too sterile in character. Costa, who spent the final years of his life in Rio de Janeiro, collected and published his letters, sketches, and writings in the book *Lúcio Costa: registro de uma vivência* (1995), his last major project.

Coulter, Wallace Henry, American scientist and entrepreneur who redefined the field of hematology and cellular biology with his numerous inventions, the most significant of which was the Coulter principle, a method of counting and measuring microscopic particles such as blood cells immersed in liquid; in 1958 he cofounded Coulter Corp., a leading producer of medical diagnostic equipment (b. 1913, Little Rock, Ark.—d. Aug. 7, 1998, Miami, Fla.).

Craine, John Thornton ("JACK"), Canadian broadcasting executive who was a pioneer in public radio and television, guiding their growth and shaping their output (b. April 24, 1928, Lethbridge, Alta.?—d. March 16, 1998, London, Eng.).

Crichton Smith, Iain (IAIN MAC A'GHOBHAINN), Scottish poet, novelist, and playwright who was one of Scotland's most important writers and lyric poets; writing prolifically in both English and Gaelic, he produced a dozen novels, 11 volumes of short stories, and 17 books of poetry, in addition to stage and radio plays and literary criticism (b. Jan. 1, 1928, Glasgow, Scot.—d. Oct. 15, 1998, Taynuilt, Argyll, Scot.).

Cudlipp of Aldingbourne, Hugh Cudlipp, Baron (HUBERT KINSMAN CUDLIPP), British journalist who in 1968 became chairman of the International Publishing Corp., the parent company of the Mirror newspapers; because of innovations he introduced to give the papers a more populist tone, he was said to have created the modern British tabloid (b. Aug. 28, 1913, Cardiff, Wales—d. May 17, 1998, Chichester, Eng.).

Davis, Donald, Canadian actor who was adept in both classical and modern roles and was admired as one of the most outstanding interpreters of Samuel Beckett's works; his signature role was the title character in Beckett's *Krapp's Last Tape,* for which he won an Obie award in 1960 (b. 1928?, Toronto, Ont.—d. Jan. 23, 1998, Toronto).

Davis, Fred, British snooker and billiards player who was world professional snooker champion eight times (1948–49, 1951–56) and world billiards champion twice (1980–81); Davis carried on the tradition of his renowned older brother, Joe, who held the snooker title for 20 years (1927–46), and remained a formidable player well into his 60s, reaching the snooker semifinals as late as 1978; he did not retire until 1992 (b. Aug. 13, 1913, Whittingham Moor, Derbyshire, Eng.—d. April, 15, 1998, Denbigh, Clwyd, Wales).

Denevi, Marco, Argentine writer and political journalist whose first published novel, *Rosaura a las diez* (1954), won a Kraft award, given by an Argentine publisher, and went on to become a best-seller that was translated into a number of languages as well as being filmed, televised, and dramatized; another of his works, the short novel *Ceremonia secreta* (1960; *Secret Ceremony,* 1961), won a *Life* magazine prize and was the basis for a 1968 film (b. May 12, 1922, Sáenz Peña, Arg.—d. Dec. 12, 1998, Buenos Aires, Arg.).

Denning, Richard (LUDWIG ALBERT HEINRICH DENNINGER, JR.), American actor who played opposite Lucille Ball in the radio series "My Favorite Husband," portrayed the "other man" in a number of movies in the 1940s and '50s, and became a cult figure in the '50s by battling menacing creatures in such low-budget monster films as *The Creature from the Black Lagoon;* on television he starred in "Mr. and Mrs. North" from 1952 to 1954 and appeared as the governor on "Hawaii Five-O" from 1968 to 1980 (b. March 17, 1914, Poughkeepsie, N.Y.—d. Oct. 11, 1998, Escondido, Calif.).

Denson, William Dowdell, American lawyer who, as chief military prosecutor of Nazis accused of many of the most horrific of the atrocities committed in Germany at the Buchenwald, Mauthausen, Flossenberg, and Dachau concentration camps, was the most successful of the American prosecutors of World War II criminals; of 177 Nazis he prosecuted between 1945 and 1947, 97 were hanged and the rest went to prison (b. May 31, 1913, Birmingham, Ala.—d. Dec. 13, 1998, Lawrence, N.Y.).

Derek, John (DEREK HARRIS), American actor and director who, despite a number of notable film roles, became better known for his succession of beautiful wives—especially his fourth, Bo Derek—and the role he took in shaping their careers (b. Aug. 12, 1926, Hollywood, Calif.—d. May 22, 1998, Santa Maria, Calif.).

Dickson, (Robert George) Brian, Canadian jurist who was named to the Supreme Court of Canada in 1973 and served as chief justice from 1984 to 1990; he was a champion of individual rights and became an important interpreter of the Charter of Rights and Freedoms (b. May 25, 1916, Yorkton, Sask.—d. Oct. 17, 1998, near Ottawa, Ont.).

Diemer, Walter E., American businessman who was working as an accountant for the Fleer Chewing Gum Co. when in 1928 he accidentally invented bubble gum while experimenting during his spare time with recipes for a chewing gum base; he later became senior vice president of Fleer (b. 1904?—d. Jan. 8, 1998, Lancaster, Pa.).

Diggs, Charles, Jr., American politician whose service (1954–80) as a Democratic representative from Michigan helped pave the way for future

African-American lawmakers but ended in disgrace after a conviction in a kickback scheme led to his resignation; in 1969 he helped form the Congressional Black Caucus (b. 1922, Detroit, Mich.—d. Aug. 24, 1998, Washington, D.C.).

Donegan, Dorothy, American jazz pianist who was known for her flamboyant showmanship, her outrageous humour, and the mixture of musical styles she incorporated into her performances (b. April 6, 1922, Chicago, Ill.—d. May 19, 1998, Los Angeles, Calif.).

Douglas, Marjory Stoneman, American author and environmentalist (b. April 7, 1890, Minneapolis, Minn.—d. May 14, 1998, Miami, Fla.), helped dispel the centuries-long revulsion that many had for the Everglades wilderness in southern Florida through her writings and environmental activism. In 1915, when Douglas arrived in southern Florida, the young Wellesley College graduate first encountered those negative attitudes, views that had little changed since the first Europeans set eyes on the region in the 16th century. In her influential 1947 book, *The Everglades: River of Grass,* she wrote of the beauty and the environmental usefulness of what had been described as "a series of vast, miasmic swamps, poisonous lagoons, huge dismal marshes without outlet, a rotting, shallow, inland sea, or labyrinths of dark trees hung and looped about with snakes and dripping mosses, malignant with tropical fevers and malarias, evil to the white man." Since its publication, *The Everglades* has been continuously in print. Before her death at age 108, Douglas witnessed a reversal of these attitudes, largely brought about by her own work. The daughter of the founding editor of the *Miami Herald,* Douglas wrote books and magazine articles with the intention of changing public perceptions of the attractiveness of the Everglades and of its ecological function as a vast recharge zone for southern Florida's freshwater supplies. Not content to watch the battle for the future of the Everglades from the sidelines, Douglas was a leading member of the committee that lobbied for the establishment of Everglades National Park in the 1940s. In 1969, to fight a proposal to build a jetport in the park, she helped to found Friends of the Everglades, a conservation group now numbering some 5,000 members. In the 1970s, when developers and farmers threatened to drain 622 sq km (240 sq mi) of the Everglades, an unflappable Douglas, dressed in her signature straw hat and formal string of pearls, defended the Everglades before a hostile audience. Almost deaf and already in her 80s, she boldly prefaced her remarks by urging the crowd to "Boo louder." The recipient of numerous honours, Douglas was referred to as Mother Nature by Pres. Bill Clinton during a 1993 White House ceremony in which her work on behalf of the Everglades was honoured with the Medal of Freedom.

Driftwood, Jimmy (JAMES CORBETT MORRIS), American folksinger and songwriter (b. June 20, 1907, Mountain View, Ark.—d. July 12, 1998, Fayetteville, Ark.), wrote more than 6,000 folk songs but was best remembered for his recording "The Battle of New Orleans," which won a Grammy award when Johnny Horton's 1960 version made the song a smash hit. The son of folksinger Neil Morris, Driftwood learned to play guitar on an instrument his grandfather made from a fence rail, an ox yoke, and the headboard of a bed. He performed at regional folk festivals after graduating from Arkansas State Teachers College and while teaching high school. After Driftwood received his second Grammy for "Tennessee Stud," a hit for Eddy Arnold, he accepted an offer to perform with the Grand Ole Opry in Nashville, Tenn. He garnered additional Grammys for songs and albums, but his lifelong passion was the preservation of folk music and culture. In the early 1950s, under the aegis of RCA Victor, he compiled the album Newly Discovered Early American Folk Songs. During the 1950s and '60s he worked successfully to prevent damming of the Buffalo River in northern Arkansas, now known as the Buffalo National River. Driftwood obtained

$3.4 million in state funding to create the Ozark Folk Center, near Mountain View, and founded the annual Ozark Folk Festival. With his wife, Cleda, he opened the Driftwood Barn, where he performed free of charge; he passed the hat, however, to help defray expenses. Requesting that the space be used to study folk music, he later deeded it to his alma mater, now the University of Central Arkansas. He performed throughout the U.S. and Europe but remained close to his roots, living on his farm in the Ozark Mountains.

Drury, Allen Stuart, American journalist and writer whose first and most famous novel, *Advise and Consent* (1959), won a Pulitzer Prize and became a Broadway play in 1960 and a motion picture in 1962; he wrote 19 additional novels and 5 nonfiction books (b. Sept. 2, 1918, Houston, Texas—d. Sept. 2, 1998, San Francisco, Calif.).

Dudintsev, Vladimir Dmitriyevich, Russian dissident writer whose controversial novel *Ne khlebom yedinim* (1957; *Not by Bread Alone,* 1957), a condemnation of Soviet bureaucracy, caused a sensation when it was serialized in the mid-1950s and denounced by the government (b. July 29, 1918, Kupyansk, Ukraine—d. July 23, 1998, near Moscow, Russia).

Duncan, (Robert) Todd, American baritone who was the first to perform the role of Porgy in George Gershwin's *Porgy and Bess,* was the first black to sing with the New York City Opera, and was a noted teacher and recitalist; he presented some 2,000 recitals in 56 countries during his 25-year career (b. Feb. 12, 1903, Danville, Ky.—d. Feb. 28, 1998, Washington, D.C.).

Dundee, Chris (CRISTOFO MIRENA), American fight promoter who was responsible for the rise of Miami Beach, Fla., as a boxing centre; the eight world championship fights he promoted during his six-decade-long career included the world heavyweight bout in which Cassius Clay (now Muhammad Ali) knocked out Sonny Liston to capture the title (b. Feb. 27, 1907, Philadelphia, Pa.—d. Nov. 16, 1998, Miami).

Dunnett, Sir Alastair MacTavish, Scottish journalist who served as editor of the *Daily Record* from 1946 to 1955 and of the *Scotsman* from 1956 to 1972 and turned the latter paper from dull to lively and vital; he was also active in the arts and public affairs and in 1972 became an oil industry executive (b. Dec. 26, 1908, Kilmacolm, Scot.—d. Sept. 2, 1998, Edinburgh, Scot.).

Dunphy, Don, American radio and television sports announcer known especially as the voice of boxing; during his 50-year career he broadcast more than 2,000 fights, 200 of which were title matches, including 50 heavyweight championships, and also appeared as a boxing announcer in six motion pictures (b. July 5, 1908, New York, N.Y.—d. July 22, 1998, Roslyn, N.Y.).

Dutton, Geoffrey Piers Henry, Australian writer, critic, publisher, and activist (b. Aug. 2, 1922, Anlaby, Australia—d. Sept. 17, 1998, Canberra, Australia), was one of the country's leading literary figures and helped revive support for the republican movement. Dutton studied at the University of Adelaide until the outbreak of World War II, when he joined the Royal Australian Air Force as a flying instructor. After the war he graduated (1949) from Magdalen College, Oxford, and published his first novel, *The Mortal and the Marble,* in 1950. He soon returned to Australia and Adelaide, where he taught English (1954–62) while pursuing his writing career. An elegant and versatile author, Dutton penned more than 40 works, including children's books, poetry, biographies, travel writings, and five novels, most notably *Queen Emma of the South Seas* (1976). He also contributed lively and incisive criticism to newspapers and magazines and was known for encouraging new literary voices. A key figure in the country's publishing industry, Dutton was a co-founding editor of *The Australian Book Review* and the *Australian Literary Quarterly* and helped

create Penguin Books Australia and Sun Books. Following a brief professorship (1963) at Kansas State University, Manhattan, Dutton returned home and wrote a blistering article that maintained that Australia could not achieve its potential under a monarchy. The resulting furor reignited the republican movement, a cause for which Dutton wrote and lectured until his death. He was made an Officer of the Order of Australia in 1976, and his autobiography, *Out in the Open,* appeared in 1994.

Edmonds, Walter Dumaux, American writer of historical novels that explored the lives of "ordinary" characters; his best-known book, *Drums Along the Mohawk* (1936), chronicled the struggles of pioneer farmers during the American Revolution and was filmed in 1939 (b. July 15, 1903, Boonville, N.Y.—d. Jan. 24, 1998, Concord, Mass.).

Elias, Edward George ("EDDIE"), American lawyer and celebrity representative who in 1958 founded the Professional Bowlers Association and went on to help establish bowling's presence on television, where its longevity as a sports series is second only to that of college football (b. Dec. 12, 1928, Akron, Ohio—d. Nov. 15, 1998, Naples, Fla.).

Ellis, Larry Thomas, American track coach at Princeton University from 1970 to 1992 who was also head coach of the 1984 Olympic men's track and field team and from 1992 to 1996 served as president of USA Track & Field, the sport's national governing body (b. Sept. 29, 1928, Englewood, N.J.—d. Nov. 4, 1998, Skillman, N.J.).

English, Sir David, British journalist whose editorship of London's *Daily Mail* from 1971 to 1992 transformed it into a successful and influential tabloid that was must reading for the country's middle class; in 1992 he became editor in chief and chairman of Associated Newspapers, publisher of the *Daily Mail* and a number of other papers (b. May 26, 1931, Oxford, Eng.—d. June 10, 1998, London, Eng.).

Epelbaum, René de, Argentine human rights activist who helped found the Mothers of the Plaza de Mayo to protest the disappearance of their children during the dictatorship of the military regime and to campaign for information about their missing relatives (b. 1920, Entre Rios province, Arg.—d. Feb. 7, 1998, Buenos Aires, Arg.).

Etchells, E(lwood) W(idmer) ("SKIP"), American boat builder and yachtsman who helped build navy destroyers and icebreakers during World War II, won numerous national and international yachting championships, and in the 1960s designed the popular Etchells 22—a one-design yacht (so-called because the boats are built to a specific design so the crew's skill rather than the boat's builder determines a race's outcome)—which became known as the International Etchells Class (b. July 5, 1911, Philadelphia, Pa.—d. Dec. 20, 1998, Easton, Md.).

Evans, Roy, Welsh table tennis player and official who, as president of the International Table Tennis Federation, in 1971 initiated what, to his chagrin, became known as "ping-pong diplomacy," which led to the thawing of relations between China and the U.S.; he also helped get table tennis accepted as a sport in the 1988 Olympic Games (b. Oct. 8, 1909, Cardiff, Wales—d. May 18, 1998, Cardiff).

Ewbank, Wilbur Charles ("WEEB"), American football coach of the Baltimore Colts from 1954 to 1962 and of the New York Jets from 1963 to 1973, he led each team to pro football championships, the Colts in 1958 and 1959 and the Jets in 1968–69, and thus became the only coach to win championships in both the National and the American football leagues; he was inducted into the Pro Football Hall of Fame in 1978 (b. May 6, 1907, Richmond, Ind.—d. Nov. 17, 1998, Oxford, Ohio).

Falco (JOHANN HÖLZEL), Austrian rock singer and songwriter who was the number one national pop star and achieved international fame in the 1980s with the hits "Der Kommissar" and "Rock Me Amadeus" (b. Feb. 19, 1957, Vienna, Austria—d. Feb. 6, 1998, Puerto Plata, Dom. Rep.).

Farber, Viola, German-born American modern dancer and choreographer who was a founding member (1953–65) of the Merce Cunningham Dance Company, formed the Viola Farber Dance Company and choreographed most of its works (1968–85), and from 1988 directed the dance program at Sarah Lawrence College, Bronxville, N.Y.; she also taught and choreographed throughout the U.S. and in Great Britain and France (b. Feb. 25, 1931, Heidelberg, Ger.—d. Dec. 24, 1998, Bronxville).

Farlow, Talmadge Holt ("TAL"), American jazz musician who began playing guitar in 1943, inspired by jazz great Charlie Christian, and later performed during the early–mid-1950s as a professional with the innovative Red Norvo Trio and with Artie Shaw's Gramercy Five, establishing a national reputation as a fluent improviser of melodic bop lines. While leading small groups in the New York City area and on recordings such as *The Artistry of Tal Farlow* (1954), he showcased his lyric artistry. He was noted for his outstanding technique and his electric guitar sound, which was uniquely soft, the result of playing with his thumb instead of a plectrum and of using a unique fingerboard of his own design. After 1958 Farlow performed and recorded only irregularly, meanwhile earning a living by painting signs. He was the subject of the 1981 documentary film *Talmadge Farlow* (b. June 7, 1921, Greensboro, N.C.—d. July 25, 1998, New York, N.Y.).

Fashanu, Justin, British association football (soccer) player who was hailed as a promising young striker with Norwich City (1978–81); Nottingham Forest (1981–82), which paid £1 million for him in 1981 (then a record fee for a black player); and Notts County (1982–85). His career foundered, however, after a debilitating knee injury and a public profession of his homosexuality (b. Feb. 19, 1961, London, Eng.—found dead May 2, 1998, London).

Faye, Alice (ALICE JEANNE LEPPERT), American singer and actress who from the mid-1930s to the mid-1940s made 32 films, among them *In Old Chicago, Alexander's Ragtime Band,* and *Hello, Frisco, Hello;* she later starred with her husband on the popular radio program "The Phil Harris–Alice Faye Show" (b. May 5, 1915, New York, N.Y.—d. May 9, 1998, Rancho Mirage, Calif.).

Fell, Norman, American character actor in motion pictures and on television who was known especially for his role as the nosy and cranky landlord Stanley Roper on the TV sitcom "Three's Company" (1977–79) and its spin-off, "The Ropers" (1979–80); *The Graduate* (1967), *Bullitt* (1968), and *Catch-22* (1970) were among his more than 30 films (b. March 24, 1924, Philadelphia, Pa.—d. Dec. 14, 1998, Woodland Hills, Calif.).

Ferragamo, Fiamma di San Giuliano, Italian designer who helped turn her family's shoe business into one of the most famous in the world of high fashion; her Vara model, a low-heeled pump that sported grosgrain ribbon and a gold buckle embossed with the family signature, was created in the 1960s and became a classic (b. 1941, Florence, Italy—d. Sept. 28, 1998, Florence).

Feuillère, Edwige (EDWIGE CAROLINE CUNATI), French actress whose long career as a much loved and respected star of the French stage and screen saw her shine in a variety of roles, including classical, comedic, and sensual; among her most acclaimed stage performances was in the 1947 *Partage de midi* (b. Oct. 29, 1907, Vesoul, France—d. Nov. 13, 1998, Paris, France).

Flock, (Julius) Timothy ("TIM"), American stock-car racing driver who counted the 1952 and 1955 National Association for Stock Car Auto Racing Winston Cup series championships among his numerous triumphs; in 1998 he was named one of NASCAR's 50 greatest drivers (b. May 11, 1924, Fort Payne, Ala.—d. March 31, 1998, Charlotte, N.C.).

Flowers, Thomas Harold ("TOMMY"), British engineer who led the developers of Colossus, one of the first electronic digital computers, which broke complex codes used by the Germans during World War II and thus enabled the Allies to gain valuable military information; the use of Colossus was said to have shortened the war by two years (b. Dec. 22, 1905, London, Eng.—d. Oct. 28, 1998, London).

Franz, Marie-Louise von, German-born Swiss analytic psychologist and fairy-tale expert who collaborated with Carl Jung for more than 30 years; her research revealed the similarities between tales from many cultures and connected the tales' themes with situations in daily life (b. Jan. 4, 1915, Munich, Ger.—d. Feb. 16/17, 1998, Küsnacht, Switz.).

Frawley, Patrick Joseph, Jr., Nicaraguan-born American corporate executive who, though he was a high-school dropout, made a fortune through his creation of the Paper Mate leakproof pen and the Schick stainless steel razor blade; he went on to become an avid supporter of anticommunist causes and was prominent in the fight against alcohol and drug addiction (b. May 26, 1923, León, Nic.—d. Nov. 3, 1998, Santa Monica, Calif.).

Freij, Elias, Palestinian politician who served as mayor of Bethlehem for 25 years, from 1972 to 1997, and during those years worked to bring about Palestinian-Israeli coexistence and peace (b. 1918, Bethlehem, Palestine—d. March 29, 1998, Amman, Jordan).

Elias Freij

Friendly, Fred W. (FERDINAND FRIENDLY WACHENHEIMER), American broadcast journalist, educator, and executive (b. Oct. 30, 1915, New York, N.Y.—d. March 3, 1998, New York), teamed with reporter Edward R. Murrow to formulate television journalism. The two men developed the news documentary and pioneered the use of original footage and unrehearsed interviews. Their partnership began in 1948 when they collaborated on *I Can Hear It Now,* an album series of oral history covering the years 1932–45. Encouraged by its success, they created the weekly radio news digest "Hear It Now" (1950–51) and in 1951 moved to television with "See It Now" (1951–58). With Murrow as host and Friendly as producer, the program set the standard in television journalism with its innovative and hard-hitting reporting. It featured the first live hookup between the two coasts and helped end Sen. Joseph McCarthy's anticommunist campaign. In 1959 "CBS Reports" debuted with Friendly as executive producer. The show aired landmark documentaries on migrant workers, illegal gambling, and racial conflict. Friendly became the president of CBS News in 1964 but resigned two years later when the network refused to air live Senate hearings on the Vietnam War. As Edward R. Murrow professor of journalism at Columbia University, New York City (1966–79), Friendly lectured that freedom of the press must be tempered with integrity and honesty. In 1984 he created the Columbia University Seminars on Media and Society (also known as the Fred Friendly Seminars), a public television series that featured discussions on a wide range of topics. Friendly won 10 Peabody Awards and wrote several books, including *Due to Circumstances Beyond Our Control* (1967), a chronicle of his career at CBS. In 1994 he was inducted into the Television Hall of Fame.

Fujita, Tetsuya ("TED"), Japanese-born meteorologist who was known as "Mr. Tornado" and "the Tornado Man" as a result of the Fujita scale, which he and his wife, Sumiko, developed for measuring tornadoes on the basis of their damage; he also discovered microbursts and their role in some airplane crashes (b. Oct. 23, 1920, Kitakyushu City, Japan—d. Nov. 19, 1998, Chicago, Ill.).

Fukui, Kenichi, Japanese theoretical chemist (b. Oct. 4, 1918, Nara, Japan—Jan. 9, 1998, Kyoto, Japan), applied a variety of concepts in physics to research that revolutionized the understanding of how chemical reactions take place. His work was based on a mathematical analysis of the actions of electrons as they are exchanged between atoms and molecules during a chemical reaction. Applying principles of quantum physics and using related mathematical treatments, he analyzed the properties that these electrons exhibit during and after reactions. Fukui theorized that in many chemical reactions it is the electrons in the outer orbitals—those regions of space occupied by electrons farthest from the atomic nuclei—that determine the pathway of the reaction and its final products. To the crucial configurations in which electrons in these outer orbitals participate during reactions, Fukui gave the name frontier orbitals. Although he had first set forth his theory in a 1952 paper and went on to publish more than 270 papers on frontier orbitals, his work received little initial notice, owing to the obscurity of the English-language journals that carried most of his papers and the extremely complex nature of his calculations. He and Roald Hoffmann shared the 1981 Nobel Prize for Chemistry for their independent work on the theoretical analysis of chemical reactions. Fukui's theories have enabled scien-

AP/WIDE WORLD/UNIVERSITY OF CHICAGO

Tetsuya Fujita

tists to predict chemical reaction pathways more precisely and have led to many advances in the pharmaceutical and chemical-synthesis industries. Fukui was awarded (1948) a doctorate from Kyoto University, where he served as a professor of physical chemistry (1951–82). He was the president of the Kyoto Institute of Technology from 1982 to 1988. In 1981 Fukui was elected a foreign associate of the U.S. National Academy of Sciences, and he was also the recipient of the Japanese Order of Culture.

Gable, Christopher Michael, British ballet dancer and actor (b. March 13, 1940, Hackney, London, Eng.—d. Oct. 23, 1998, near Halifax, Yorkshire, Eng.), was a popular star of the Royal Ballet, and his strong dramatic ability paved the way for him to make a smooth transition to theatre and motion pictures. When he was a young boy, Gable, having seen dance numbers in films, asked for lessons. His mother consented, if he also studied piano, and by the time he was 11, he had been accepted into the Sadler's Wells (now Royal) Ballet School. After graduation (1956) Gable joined the Sadler's Wells Opera Ballet, and a year later he entered the Covent Garden Opera Ballet. Not satisfied with this outcome, he arranged to get himself noticed by the director of the Royal Ballet's touring company and before long was asked to join. His big break came when company member Lynn Seymour—herself a dramatic dancer and well aware of Gable's talent for bringing a story to life—suggested that choreographer Kenneth MacMillan cast him opposite her in his ballet *The Invitation* (1960). The value of their partnership was proved a year later when they danced together in the premiere of Frederick Ashton's *The Two Pigeons*. Gable continued to dance leading roles, and in 1963 he joined the Royal Ballet at Covent Garden, where he added even more ballets to his repertoire. In 1965, however, although MacMillan's *Romeo and Juliet* had been choreographed on Gable and Seymour and was exquisitely suited to their style, the honour of dancing the premiere was given to Margot Fonteyn and Rudolf Nureyev for box-office reasons. Disappointment over this, in addition to foot troubles caused by arthritis, led him to leave the company within two years. After guest appearances with Ballet Rambert, Gable spent a season with the Royal Shakespeare Company, where his most notable role was Lysander in Peter Brook's production of *A Midsummer Night's Dream,* and several seasons with the Royal Exchange Theatre in Manchester. Gable also found work in television and motion pictures, especially under the direction of Ken Russell. He was acclaimed for his role as Eric Fenby in the BBC television film *Song of Summer* (1968) and for his performance

in the title role, opposite Twiggy, in the film *The Boy Friend* (1971). In 1982 Gable cofounded the Central School of Ballet in Clerkenwell, London, and in 1987, after having danced once again—in Northern Ballet Theatre's *A Simple Man*—he became NBT's artistic director. Through his efforts NBT, then based in Manchester (now in Leeds), was transformed from a financially endangered company into one of major stature, imprinted with Gable's dramatic style. He was the subject of a BBC television documentary in 1989 and was appointed C.B.E. in 1996.

Gaddis, William Thomas, American writer of complex satiric works who was considered one of the most important post–World War II modernist novelists and whose first novel, *The Recognitions* (1955), became an underground classic; he published only three more novels—*JR* (1975), *Carpenter's Gothic* (1985), and *A Frolic of His Own* (1994)—and had finished another, *Agape Agape,* which was to be published posthumously (b. Dec. 29, 1922, New York, N.Y.—d. Dec. 16, 1998, East Hampton, N.Y.).

Gallagher, John Patrick ("SMILIN' JACK"), Canadian geologist and industrialist who founded (1950) Dome Petroleum Ltd., built it into a large, successful oil and gas company, and pioneered in exploration in the Beaufort Sea area; he left the company in 1983 as accumulated debt threatened it, and it was taken over in 1988 (b. July 16, 1916, Winnipeg, Man.—d. Dec. 16, 1998, Calgary, Alta.).

Gandar, Laurence Owen Vine ("LAURIE"), South African newspaper editor whose antiapartheid articles in 1965 introduced investigative journalism to South Africa by revealing the dreadful prison conditions faced by blacks; he crusaded for economic integration and took the then revolutionary step of referring to blacks as "Africans" instead of as "natives" (b. Jan. 25/28, 1915, Durban, S.Af.—d. Nov. 14, 1998, Pietermaritzburg, S.Af.).

Garro, Elena, Mexican writer whose novels, plays, and short stories revealed an intelligence and lyric intensity that made her one of the country's leading literary voices; she became politically active during her marriage to writer Octavio Paz (*q.v.*) and spent more than 20 years in exile after being accused of instigating a 1968 student riot in which hundreds of protesters were killed (b. Dec. 12, 1920, Puebla, Mex.—d. Aug. 22, 1998, Cuernavaca, Mex.).

Gary, John, American singer who was a regular on Don McNeill's "Breakfast Club" on radio and television in the 1950s, hosted his own TV show for three years in the 1960s, and recorded a total of 49 albums, the most successful of which was *Catch a Rising Star;* he also invented a scuba-diving device (b. Nov. 29, 1932, Watertown, N.Y.—d. Jan. 4, 1998, Dallas, Texas).

Gellhorn, Martha Ellis, American journalist and novelist (b. Nov. 8, 1908, St. Louis, Mo.—d. Feb. 15, 1998, London, Eng.), as one of the first female war correspondents, candidly described ordinary people in times of unrest. Though often remembered for her brief marriage to American author Ernest Hemingway, Gellhorn refused to be a "footnote" to his life; during a career that spanned some six decades, she covered a dozen wars and drew praise for her fictional work. Gellhorn attended Bryn Mawr (Pa.) College but left in 1927 to begin a career as a writer. After contributing to several publications, including *The New Republic* magazine, Gellhorn took a job with the Federal Emergency Relief Administration,

touring the U.S. to report on the Great Depression. *The Trouble I've Seen* (1936) is an account of her experiences. In 1937 she accepted her first war assignment, covering the Spanish Civil War for *Collier's Weekly,* and it was during this time that she began an affair with Hemingway. He dedicated *For Whom the Bell Tolls* (1940) to her, and they married in 1940 (divorced 1946). Gellhorn traveled the world to report on such events as the Nürnberg trials, the Arab-Israeli wars (1967), and the Vietnam War. In 1944 she impersonated a stretcher bearer to witness the D-Day landings during World War II. Always distrustful of politicians, Gellhorn eloquently championed the cause of the oppressed. Her fictional work, noted for its lean prose, includes the novels *A Stricken Field* (1939) and *The Lowest Trees Have Tops* (1967) and a collection of novellas, *The Weather in Africa* (1978).

Gerardi Conedera, Juan José, Bishop, Guatemalan religious leader who, in his campaign for human rights, led the Recovery of Historical Memory project; two days after the project's findings were published, documenting the abuses that took place during 36 years of civil conflict, Gerardi was beaten to death (b. Dec. 27, 1922, Guatemala City, Guat.—d. April 26, 1998, Guatemala City).

Godden, (Margaret) Rumer, British writer (b. Dec. 10, 1907, Eastbourne, Sussex, Eng.—d. Nov. 8, 1998, Dumfries, Scot.), published scores of works—novels, plays, poetry, children's books, memoirs, and anthologies among them—during her more than 60-year career. Her lyrical, evocative writing often reflected the influence of a childhood spent in India and the impression that the sights, sounds, and smells of that country made on her, and her psychological portraits revealed her observations of societal conflicts. Godden was less than a year old when her family moved to India, where her father worked for a shipping company. She and her sisters grew up in river towns and were for the most part educated at home. Godden showed an early interest in writing and even wrote a fictitious autobiography when she was a young child. In 1920 she was sent back to England—against her wishes—to finish her education; after trying a succession of schools, she ended up at Moira House in Eastbourne. There she was encouraged to continue writing, and she later took up the study of dance. From 1928 to 1934 she ran the Peggy Godden School of Dance in Calcutta, welcoming—despite the customs of the time—both Indian and English pupils. Godden's first novel, *Chinese Puzzle,* was published in 1935, but it was her third novel, *Black Narcissus* (1939), that gave her her first big success. It became a best-seller and, in 1947, was filmed. In 1945 Godden moved back to Great Britain permanently, and a year later *The River,* considered by some to be her best work, was published. It too was filmed (1951), as were a number of other of her books, including *The Greengage Summer* (1958; filmed as *Loss of Innocence,* 1961), *The Battle of the Villa Fiorita* (1963; film, 1965), and *In This House of Brede* (1969; filmed for television, 1975). In 1947 Godden wrote the first—and one of the best-known—of her nearly two dozen children's books, *The Doll's House;* another, *The Diddakoi* (1972), won a Whitbread Award. Godden collaborated with her sister Jon, also a successful writer, on a number of works, notably the memoir *Two Under the Indian Sun* (1966). Among Godden's later works were two volumes of autobiography, *A Time to Dance, No Time to Weep* (1988) and *A House with Four Rooms* (1989). Godden was named O.B.E. in 1993, and in 1994 she made a final trip to India to participate in a television documentary. Her last book, *Cromartie v. the God Shiva: Acting Through the Government of India,* was published in 1997.

Goldman, James, American novelist, playwright, and screenwriter (b. June 30, 1927, Chicago, Ill.—d. Oct. 28, 1998, New York, N.Y.), probed the lives of historical couples, most notably King Henry II and his wife, Eleanor of Aquitaine, in

The Lion in Winter (1968), a film for which he won an Academy Award for best screenplay. After earning (1950) an M.A. from the University of Chicago, Goldman studied music criticism at Columbia University, New York City. In 1952, however, he was drafted into the army; after his discharge (1954) he pursued a career as a playwright. In 1961 *They Might Be Giants* made its stage debut in London, and a movie version followed in 1971. A comedy about army life, *Blood, Sweat and Stanley Poole* (co-written with his brother, William), premiered on Broadway in 1961. Neither play, however, was a success. In 1966 Goldman's dramatization of the 12th-century succession fight over the English throne opened on Broadway. Though *The Lion in Winter* had only a brief run, his film adaptation was a box-office smash hit and was highlighted by light comedy and Katharine Hepburn's Oscar-winning performance as Eleanor. Goldman then produced a series of screenplays that focused on such historical couples as *Nicholas and Alexandra* (1971) and *Robin and Marian* (1976). In 1971 he wrote the book for Stephen Sondheim's *Follies,* a musical about the reunion of former Ziegfeld Follies–type showgirls. Goldman also penned several novels and adapted literary classics, such as *Anna Karenina,* for the small screen.

Goldwater, Barry Morris, American politician (b. Jan. 1, 1909, Phoenix, Ariz.—d. May 29, 1998, Phoenix), was considered the founder and icon of the modern conservative movement in the U.S. He served (1953–64 and 1969–87) as a U.S. senator and in 1964 was the Republican Party's presidential candidate. He lost to Lyndon Johnson in a landslide, however, after his statement that "extremism in the defense of liberty is no vice" caused him to be portrayed as a dangerous warmonger; one Democratic television commercial began with a small girl counting daisy petals as she plucked them, and ended with a missile-launch countdown and a mushroom cloud. Goldwater dropped out (1929) of the University of Arizona after his freshman year, went to work for Goldwater's, Inc., the family department store chain, and in 1937 became the company's president. There he instituted a number of progressive policies, such as health and life insurance plans and profit sharing. During World War II he served in the Army Air Force, and after the war he organized the Arizona Air National Guard, serving as chief of staff until 1952. By the time he retired from the reserves, he had attained the rank of major general. Goldwater entered politics in 1949 with a successful run for the Phoenix City Council. In an upset, he won (1952) the U.S. Senate seat of Majority Leader Ernest MacFarland. In 1954 Goldwater was one of only 22 senators who voted against the censure of Sen. Joseph McCarthy in the aftermath of the Army-McCarthy hearings, an action that was popular in Arizona and helped him gain reelection in 1958. His book, *The Conscience of a Conservative* (1960), reflected his philosophy—that the government should not interfere with individuals' lives and that communism should be vanquished. After his defeat in the 1964 presidential race, Goldwater returned to Arizona, but he won his Senate seat back in 1968. In later years his support of abortion rights and the service of homosexuals in the armed forces upset many conservatives, but he steadfastly maintained his belief in the right of individuals to be free from government interference.

Gonzalves, Nelson (ANTÔNIO GONZALVES SOBRAL), Brazilian crooner who recorded over 1,000 romantic songs during a successful career that lasted 56 years (b. June 1919, Rio Grande do Sul state, Braz.—d. April 18, 1998, Rio de Janeiro, Braz.).

Goulding, Cathal, Irish political activist who became chief of staff of the Irish Republican Army (IRA) in 1962 and whose relatively moderate stance helped trigger the 1969 split between his Official IRA, which called a cease-fire in 1972, and the more militant Provisional IRA (b. Dec. 30, 1922, Dublin, Ire.—d. Dec. 26, 1998, Dublin).

Barry Goldwater

Grade of Elstree, Lew Grade, Baron (LOUIS [OR LEWIS] WINOGRADSKY), British impresario (b. Dec. 25, 1906, Tokmak, Ukraine, Russian Empire—d. Dec. 13, 1998, London, Eng.), was a flamboyant, indefatigable motion picture, theatrical, and television producer who was one of the most influential personalities in British popular entertainment. Equipped with his signature "security blanket," a huge Havana cigar, he brought to the public such films as *The Return of the Pink Panther* (1975), *On Golden Pond* (1981), and *Sophie's Choice* (1982) and such television series as "Robin Hood," "The Saint," "The Avengers," "Coronation Street," "Sunday Night at the London Palladium," and, perhaps most memorably, "The Muppet Show." Grade dropped out of school at age 14 to help his father in his business. In 1926, however, he won a dance contest and began touring Europe as the world Charleston champion. After alerting show business agents to other acts he deemed talented, he went into the business himself, first with his friend Joe Collins and then, in 1943, after World War II army service, with his brother Leslie. Lew and Leslie Grade Ltd. booked acts at the London Palladium, among them such American imports as Judy Garland, Danny Kaye, and Jack Benny, and by the early 1950s had become Great Britain's largest talent agency. In the mid-1950s Grade invested in Associated Television (ATV), which was in competition with the BBC, and soon joined the company. Presenting light, wholesome entertainment, ATV flourished, and Grade expanded the fare to include lavish historical dramas about Moses and Jesus and productions by the National Theatre and the Royal Shakespeare Company. In addition, Grade ventured into producing motion pictures. Most were successful, but in 1980 *Raise the Titanic,* which had cost more than $30 million to make, was a disaster at the box office. This failure prompted one of Grade's most famous quotes, "It would have been cheaper to lower the Atlantic." He had to sell his Associated Communications Corp., which comprised ATV and a number of other entertainment ventures, to Robert Holmes à Court in 1982. Grade thereupon became chairman of Embassy Communications International, a position he held until 1985, when he formed the Grade Co., of which he served as chairman until his death. Grade was knighted in 1969 and made a life peer in 1976.

Green, Julien Hartridge, French-American writer (b. Sept. 6, 1900, Paris, France—d. Aug. 13, 1998, Paris), was the author of numerous novels, plays, and essays that reflected his lifelong conflicts emanating from his attempts to reconcile his sexual desires and spiritual side. Born in Paris to American parents from the South, Green spent most of his life in France. Although Protestant by birth, he converted to Roman Catholicism as an adolescent. During this time he also recognized his homosexuality, an event that precipitated in his writings evidence of his struggles and the parallel themes of spiritual devotion and carnal desire. After serving in World War I as both a soldier and an ambulance driver, Green entered (1919) the University of Virginia, Charlottesville, and studied there until 1921. After a year of teaching (1921–22) at the university, he returned to France. His first novel, *Mont-Cinere* (1926; *Avarice House,* 1927), was melancholic and infused with disturbing sexual undertones, like many of his novels, and written in French, the language in which he wrote all but a few of his works. He claimed that writing in English was for him like "wearing clothes that were not made for me." Although most of his novels were set in France, two of his most highly regarded works, *Moira* (1950; translation, 1951) and *Chaque homme dans sa nuit* (1960; *Each in His Darkness,* 1961), took place in the United States. His most acclaimed play, *Sud* (1953; *South,* 1955), which served as the basis of a 1973 opera by Kenneth Coe, was also set in the U.S. Among his other works were his multivolume *Journals,* which he kept from 1926 until 1996. In 1971 Green, who never relinquished his American citizenship, was elected to the Académie Française; he was the first American to receive this honour.

Green, Marshall, American diplomat and leading East Asia expert who advised a series of officials on foreign policy during various international crises in the 1960s and '70s; he had just become ambassador to Indonesia in 1965 when violent uprising that ousted Sukarno and brought Suharto into that country's presidency began (b. Jan. 27, 1916, Holyoke, Mass.—d. June 6, 1998, Washington, D.C.).

Griffith Joyner, (Delorez) Florence ("FLOJO"), American sprinter (b. Dec. 21, 1959, Los Angeles, Calif.—d. Sept. 21, 1998, Mission Viejo, Calif.), was considered the world's fastest woman, and she created a sensation on the track with her speed and flamboyant style. Griffith started running at the age of seven and attended the University of

Florence Griffith Joyner

California, Los Angeles, (B.A., 1983) to train with Bob Kersee. At the 1984 Olympics in Los Angeles, she won a silver medal in the 200-m race and quickly became a media celebrity with her 15-cm (6-in) decorated fingernails and eye-catching racing suits. In 1987, after a brief retirement, she undertook an intense weight-lifting program, altered her starting technique, and married Al Joyner, winner of the 1984 gold medal in the triple jump and brother of Jackie Joyner-Kersee, a heptathlon champion. The changes produced dramatic results. At the 1988 Olympic trials, Griffith Joyner set a world record in the 100-m sprint (10.49 sec), beating the old mark by 0.27 sec and improving her previous best by more than half a second. Later that year at the Olympics in South Korea, she captured three gold medals (100 m, 200 m, and 4 × 100-m relay) and a silver (4 × 400-m relay). Her world-record time in the 200 m (21.34 sec) and her earlier 100-m record still stood at the time of her death. In 1988 Griffith Joyner received the Sullivan Award as the nation's top amateur performer. Her remarkable prowess, however, sparked rumours of drug use. Though tests revealed no banned substances, her retirement in 1989, shortly before the introduction of mandatory random drug testing, fueled further speculation. From 1993 to 1995 she served as the cochair of the President's Council on Physical Fitness and in 1996 attempted a comeback, but sustained an injury. That same year she suffered a heart seizure; her death was attributed to a brain seizure.

Haggart, Robert Sherwood ("Bob"), American jazz bassist, arranger, and bandleader who per-

formed and cocomposed such hit songs as "Big Noise from Winnetka," "What's New," and "South Rampart Street Parade" for Bob Crosby's 1930s swing band; he then recorded with leading traditional jazz, swing, and bop musicians before forming a popular 1950s Dixieland band with trumpeter Yank Lawson. Haggart and Lawson then led the World's Greatest Jazz Band, a swing band that performed (1968–78) Haggart's arrangements at jazz festivals, in clubs, and on records (b. March 13, 1914, New York, N.Y.—d. Dec. 3, 1998, Venice, Fla.).

Hamming, Richard, American mathematician who discovered mathematical formulas and techniques that made it possible for computers to correct their own errors, thus paving the way for the creation of a number of devices that employ microprocessors and digital signal processors, such as modems, compact discs, and satellite communications; several of these techniques were named for him (b. Feb. 11, 1915, Chicago, Ill.—d. Jan. 7, 1998, Monterey, Calif.).

Hampton, Henry, American documentary filmmaker whose 1987 television series "Eyes on the Prize," which won a Peabody Award and four Emmys, told the story of the American civil rights struggle with an emphasis on the strength and leadership of African-Americans (b. Jan. 8, 1940, St. Louis, Mo.—d. Nov. 22, 1998, Boston, Mass.).

Hampton, Mark Iredell, Jr., American interior designer (b. June 1, 1940, Plainfield, Ind.—d. July 23, 1998, New York, N.Y.), decorated the homes of such luminaries as George and Barbara Bush,

Jacqueline Kennedy Onassis, and Estée Lauder, using 18th- and 19th-century American and English antiques and furniture upholstered in flowery chintz. In the 1980s Hampton became a household name, putting his imprint on interior design with his comfortable English country style. His popularity was further fueled by books, personal appearances and lectures, and the addition of his name to a collection of furniture. Born and raised on a farm in rural Indiana, Hampton displayed an early affinity for design, but after graduating (1962) from DePauw University, Greencastle, Ind., he entered law school at the University of Michigan. By 1964 he had changed his major to art history, eventually earning (1967) a master's degree from the New York Institute of Fine Arts. Hampton then began working for British designer David Hicks in 1967. Priding himself on giving the public whatever it wanted at the moment, under Hicks, Hampton adopted a modern Pop-art style that would greatly contrast with his later traditionalism. After leaving Hicks, Hampton worked for New York City society decorators McMillen Inc. for six years before starting his own company in 1975. He assisted in the restoration of Gracie Mansion, the mayor's residence in New York City; the governor's mansion in Albany, N.Y.; and the Treaty Room of the White House, although Hampton regretted having turned that room, at President Bush's request, from high Victorian style into a lacklustre private office. In 1989 Hampton wrote and illustrated *Mark Hampton on Decorating,* a collection of conversational, opinionated essays on interior design.

Handler, Milton, American lawyer and teacher who helped draft a number of well-known laws, among them the Federal Food, Drug, and Cosmetic Act of 1938, the National Labor Relations Act, and the GI Bill of Rights; he later was a noted antitrust litigator (b. Oct. 8, 1903, Bronx, N.Y.—d. Nov. 10, 1998, New York, N.Y.).

Häring, Bernhard, German Roman Catholic liberal theologian whose beliefs in pacifism, ecumenism, and freedom of conscience were set forth in some 80 books and 1,000 articles; his 1954 three-volume *The Law of Christ* was a best-seller in Germany and was translated into more than 12 languages (b. Nov. 10, 1912, Böttingen, Ger.—d. July 3, 1998, Gars am Inn, Ger.).

Harsch, Joseph Close, American newspaper and broadcast journalist who, during his 60-year career with *The Christian Science Monitor,* was noted for his presence at many of the period's most historic events and for his vivid reporting of those events; Great Britain's Queen Elizabeth II made him an honorary C.B.E. in 1965 (b. May 25, 1905, Toledo, Ohio—d. June 3, 1998, Jamestown, R.I.).

Hartman, Phil (Philip Edward Hartmann), Canadian-born American actor-comedian who, in his eight seasons on the "Saturday Night Live" TV show, built up a huge repertoire of impersonations; he also did voices for the TV cartoon series "The Simpsons," appeared in several films, and became a regular on the TV sitcom "NewsRadio"; he was shot by his wife, who then killed herself (b. Sept. 24, 1948, Brantford, Ont.—d. May 28, 1998, Encino, Calif.).

Hatfield, (William Rukard) Hurd, American actor whose long distinguished stage, screen, and television career was overshadowed by his brilliant portrayal of the handsome, aristocratic, but ultimately corrupt title character in the 1945 film version of Oscar Wilde's *The Picture of Dorian Gray* (b. Dec. 7, 1918?, New York, N.Y.—d. Dec. 25, 1998, Monktown, Ire.).

Hayes, Peter Lind (Joseph Conrad Lind), American entertainer who was best known for his appearances with his wife, Mary Healy, in nightclub acts, in several television series, on radio, in films, and on Broadway (b. June 25, 1915, San Francisco, Calif.—d. April 21, 1998, Las Vegas, Nev.).

Heino, Viljo Akseli, Finnish athlete who was the last of the "Flying Finns," track stars who dominated long-distance running from the 1920s through the '40s; he set a world record in the 10,000 m in 1944, also getting credit for a world 6-mi record, and set another 10,000-m world record in 1949 (b. March 1, 1914, Iitti, Fin.—d. Sept. 15, 1998, Tampere, Fin.).

Herbert, Zbigniew, Polish poet, essayist, and playwright (b. Oct. 29, 1924, Lwow, Pol. [now Lviv, Ukraine]—d. July 28, 1998, Warsaw, Pol.), revealed his lifelong opposition to communism in dissident poetry that was characterized by irony, historical allusion, restraint of language, and moral authority. Born into a wealthy, well-educated family, he served during World War II in the underground Polish Home Army, which fought against the Germans. Herbert later studied humanities, law, economics, and philosophy at the Universities of Krakow, Torun, and Warsaw. After his first poems appeared in 1950, he was declared an enemy of the people for refusing to cooperate with Poland's Stalinist regime and was expelled from the Writers' Union. Following a liberalization of the political climate, he was reinstated in the union and was coeditor (1955–65 and 1965–68, respectively) of the literary magazines *Twórczość* ("Creation") and *Poezja* ("Poetry"). Herbert's first collection of poems, *Struna światła* (1956; "A String of Light"), included writings from his years of enforced silence. As a writer, he traveled freely, and his trips in Europe resulted in a book of essays, *Barbarzyńca w ogrodzie* (1962; "A Barbarian in the Garden"). After publishing *Selected Poems* (1968), his first poetry translated into English, he taught (1970) modern European literature at California State College, Los Angeles. An ardent supporter of the pro-democracy Solidarity movement, he published *Raport z oblężnego miasta* (1983; "Report from the Besieged City") from an underground press. The book was an allegory of life under the martial law that was imposed to block the movement. Recognized by critics as one of Poland's greatest postwar poets, he was the recipient of numerous literary prizes. Herbert published his final collection, *Epilog burzy* ("Epilogue of a Storm"), several months before his death.

Hicks, David Nightingale, British interior decorator known for his use of bold, vibrant colours, for his mixture of antique and contemporary furnishings and modern art, and for the large number of aristocrats on his list of clients (b. March 25, 1929, Coggeshall, Essex, Eng.—d. March 29, 1998, Britwell Salome, Oxfordshire, Eng.).

Hickson, Joan, British actress who, after a distinguished career in more than 80 motion pictures and dozens of plays, gained international celebrity in her late 70s, playing what her admirers considered the definitive Miss Marple in a series of BBC television programs (1984–92) based on the Agatha Christie detective novels. Hickson also won the 1979 Tony award for best performance by a featured actress in a play, and she was appointed O.B.E. in 1987 (b. Aug. 5, 1906, Kingsthorpe, Northampton, Eng.—d. Oct. 17, 1998, Colchester, Essex, Eng.).

Higginbotham, A(loysius) Leon, Jr., American lawyer, judge, and scholar whose nearly 30 years as an influential federal judge included service as chief judge of the U.S. Court of Appeals for the Third Circuit from 1989 to 1993; referring to himself as a "survivor of segregation," he energetically championed integration and civil rights and in 1995 was awarded the Presidential Medal of Freedom, the highest civilian honour in the U.S. (b. Feb. 25, 1928, Trenton, N.J.—d. Dec. 14, 1998, Boston, Mass.).

Hillis, Margaret, American chorus and orchestra conductor (b. 1921, Kokomo, Ind.—d. Feb. 4, 1998, Evanston, Ill.), founded the Chicago Symphony Orchestra (CSO) Chorus and for 37 years served as its director. Under her leadership the chorus made almost 600 appearances with the orchestra, participated in the recording of 45 works, and won nine Grammy awards. It also sparked the formation of choruses elsewhere in the U.S. Hillis began her musical education, on piano, at the age of five and could play a number of instruments by the time she was in high school, but from the age of eight she knew that what she really wanted was to conduct orchestras. Following her graduation (1947) from Indiana University, Hillis attended the Juilliard School in New York City. Aware of the limited opportunities for women in her field, she heeded advice to concentrate on choral conducting and studied with Robert Shaw. She went on to serve as Shaw's assistant, found the Tanglewood Alumni Chorus, conduct choruses for the New York City Opera and the American Opera Society, teach at Juilliard and the Union Theological Seminary, and form the American Choral Foundation. In 1957, at the invitation of Fritz Reiner, the CSO's musical director, Hillis formed the CSO Chorus. It made its debut the next year and within a decade had become one of the country's best professional choirs. Hillis also conducted the CSO several times, spent a few seasons on the conducting staff of the Civic Orchestra of Chicago, appeared as guest conductor with a number of other American orchestras, and served as the choral director of the Cleveland (Ohio) Orchestra and the San Francisco Symphony. In addition, she worked with smaller regional and community orchestras, among them the Kenosha (Wis.) Civic Orchestra and the Elgin (Ill.) Symphony.

Hitchings, George Herbert, American pharmacologist (b. April 18, 1905, Hoquiam, Wash.—d. Feb. 27, 1998, Chapel Hill, N.C.), was a medical research pioneer who was awarded the Nobel Prize for Physiology or Medicine in 1988 for the development of important disease-fighting drugs. He shared the prize with colleague Gertrude B. Elion and with Sir James W. Black. Hitchings made great strides in the fields of chemotherapeutics and immunology, and his drug discoveries brought him international repute and secured the success of his employer, Burroughs Wellcome Co. (now part of Glaxo Wellcome PLC). He graduated cum laude from the University of Washington (B.A., 1927; M.A., 1928) and gained his Ph.D. in biochemistry (1933) from Harvard University, where he taught until 1939, when he transferred to Western Reserve University (now Case Western Reserve University), Cleveland, Ohio. In 1942 Hitchings founded the biochemical department at the American laboratories of Burroughs Wellcome in Tuckahoe, N.Y. (In the late 1960s the company moved to Research Triangle Park in North Carolina.) He was joined in 1944 by Elion, who first worked as his assistant before becoming his research partner. Their discovery of cancer-fighting drugs led in turn to the development of important immunosuppressants. Much of this success could be attributed to their unique methodology, which eschewed the prevailing tactics of trial and error and pointedly examined the biochemical differences between the development of normal cells and diseased cells. The investigation of purines and pyrimidines, the nucleotide bases of DNA, revealed that compounds could be introduced to stop the spread of the cancer, bacteria, or virus by tricking the pathogen (disease-causing agent) into believing that the compound was necessary for replication; once the compound was metabolized, however, it would in fact suppress the growth of the diseased cell. Among the valuable drugs Hitchings and Elion helped create to treat diseases were pyrimethamine (Darapin) for malaria, 6-mercaptopurine (6MP) for leukemia, azathioprine (Imuran) for rheumatoid arthritis and to facilitate organ transplants, trimethorpim (Septra) for urinary and respiratory tract infections, acyclovir for viral herpes, and azidothymidine (AZT) for AIDS. Hitchings, who later headed charitable organizations, wrote or co-wrote more than 300 scientific papers.

Hodgkin, Sir Alan Lloyd, British physiologist (b. Feb. 5, 1914, Banbury, Eng.—d. Dec. 20, 1998, Cambridge, Eng.), shared (along with his countryman Sir Andrew Huxley and Australian scientist Sir John Eccles) the 1963 Nobel Prize for Physiology or Medicine for the discovery of the chemical processes involved in nerve conduction. After graduating (1936) from Trinity College, Cambridge, he worked (1937–38) at the Rockefeller Institute in New York City and spent some time at the Woods Hole (Mass.) Marine Biological Laboratory. It was there that he first dissected squid nerve fibres, structures that, owing to their comparatively large size, were ideally suited to his research. Because of his expertise in physics and mathematics, the British government called upon him to work on the development of airborne radar during World War II. In 1945 he joined the faculty at Cambridge. The central focus of his studies was the biomedical process by which nerve impulses travel along individual fibres. With Huxley, he elucidated the complementary roles of sodium and potassium ions in the transmission of nerve impulses, work for which they received the Nobel Prize. Hodgkin was elected a fellow of the Royal Society in 1948 and served as the society's president from 1970 to 1975. He held the posts of master of Trinity College (1974–84) and chancellor of the University of Leicester (1971–84). Among his many awards and honours were the Royal Medal (1958) and the Copley Medal (1985). He was knighted in 1972. In addition to his scientific papers, Hodgkin wrote an autobiography, *Chance & Design: Reminiscences of Science in Peace and War* (1992).

Holub, Miroslav, Czech writer and immunologist (b. Sept. 23, 1923, Pilsen, Czechoslovakia—d. July 14, 1998, Prague, Czech Rep.), conducted advanced research in immunology with over 150 papers on the subject and was noted at home and in the West for his poetry, which was often infused with scientific imagery and vocabulary. During World War II Holub was conscripted to work on the railroad. After the war he earned (1953) a medical degree from Charles University in Prague and then worked as an immunologist at the Microbiology Institute of the Czechoslovak Academy of Sciences. In 1958 he was awarded a Ph.D. for the development of, and work with, "nude mice" as immunological test animals for various diseases. In 1958 Holub finished his first book of poems, *Denní služba* ("Day Shift"), and *Selected Poems,* his first volume in English, was published in 1967. From 1970 to 1980 his politically charged poetry was banned from publication in his homeland by the communist regime, and many of his works were published first in English. Other well-known titles include *Ačkoli* (1969; "Although"), *Notes of a Clay Pigeon* (1977), *Sagitální řez* (1980; "Sagittal Section"), *Sindrom mizející plíce* (1990; "Vanishing Lung Syndrome"), and *Poems Before and After* (1990), all of which featured subtle and surreal humour. In addition to his poetry and scientific papers, Holub wrote essays, notably the collection *Shedding Life: Disease, Politics and Other Human Conditions* (1998). His works have been translated into 37 languages.

Holzman, William ("RED"), American basketball coach who led the New York Knicks to their only National Basketball Association championships, in 1970 and 1973 (b. Aug. 10, 1920, Brooklyn, N.Y.—d. Nov. 13, 1998, New Hyde Park, N.Y.).

Huddleston, the Right Rev. (Ernest Urban) Trevor, British clergyman who was a leader in the campaign against apartheid in South Africa and helped bring that struggle to the world's attention; a founder of Great Britain's Anti-Apartheid Movement, he was knighted in 1998 (b. June 15, 1913, Bedford, Eng.—d. April 20, 1998, Mirfield, West Yorkshire, Eng.).

Huebner, Robert Joseph, American virologist whose theory that certain genes, which he called oncogenes, are involved in cancer focused researchers' attention on finding them; during his years as chief of the Laboratory of Infectious Diseases at the National Institute of Arthritis and Infectious Diseases, National Institutes of Health, Bethesda, Md., his investigations paved the way

for the discovery of viral causes of cancers and several other serious diseases and for the development of a number of vaccines and treatments (b. Feb. 23, 1914, Cheviot, Ohio—d. Aug. 26, 1998, Coatesville, Pa.).

Hughes, Edward James ("TED"), British poet (b. Aug. 17, 1930, Mytholmroyd, Yorkshire, Eng.—d. Oct. 28, 1998, London, Eng.), was renowned for over four decades for his powerful poetry—much of it featuring evocative images of nature and the violence of animals—and from 1984 served as Great Britain's poet laureate. Any celebration for his own accomplishments, however, was largely overshadowed by the notoriety that attended his having been the husband of the emotionally troubled American poet Sylvia Plath and, on the basis of her writings, blamed by many for her suicide. Hughes read English at Pembroke College, Cambridge, for two years and then switched to the study of anthropology and archaeology, graduating in 1954. In 1956 he met Plath at a party at Cambridge, where she was then a student, and four months later they married. Hughes had begun writing poetry, and in 1957 his first collection, *The Hawk in the Rain,* was published to great acclaim. Another volume, *Lupercal* (1960), brought him more success. Plath's emotional difficulties, which had led her to attempt suicide before she met Hughes, increasingly plagued her; the marriage deteriorated, and Hughes left her for poet Assia Wevill. In 1963 Plath gassed herself to death, but the fame of her pain-filled poems and journals—most of them published by Hughes after her death—grew, and Plath came to be seen as a legend, martyred by the callous treatment of her husband. Her tombstone was repeatedly defaced to remove Hughes's name. (In 1969 Wevill, too, committed suicide by gassing herself and her daughter by Hughes.) In 1970 Hughes remarried, moved to the countryside, and wrote prolifically, not only poetry but also prose for both children and adults. In addition, he translated the works of others, edited Plath's writings, wrote plays, campaigned to protect the environment, and served as executor of Plath's literary estate. His collections

Ted Hughes

Moortown (1979; reissued as *Moortown Diary,* 1989), *The Remains of Elmet* (1979), and *River* (1983) were among his finer works of that period. In 1997 Hughes published *Tales from Ovid,* adapted from Ovid's *Metamorphoses;* it won the Whitbread Book of the Year Award and a W.H. Smith prize. In 1998, aware that he was dying of the cancer that had afflicted him for several months, he finally told his story of his relationship with Plath. The intense *Birthday Letters* became a best-seller in both the U.S. and the U.K. and won the Forward Poetry Prize. Less than two weeks before his death, Hughes received the rare honour of being given the Order of Merit by Queen Elizabeth II.

Hunt of Llanfairwaterdine, (Henry Cecil) John Hunt, Baron, British soldier and mountaineer who was the leader of the 1953 British expedition during which Sir Edmund Hillary and Tenzing Norgay became the first persons to climb to the top of Mt. Everest; he was created C.B.E. in 1945, knighted in 1953, made a life peer in 1966, and named a Knight of the Garter in 1979 (b. June 22, 1910, India—d. Nov. 7/8, 1998, Henley-on-Thames, Eng.).

Innes, Hammond, British writer (b. July 15, 1913, Horsham, Sussex, Eng.—d. June 10, 1998, Kersey, Suffolk, Eng.), cultivated his thrill for adventure and travel while conducting research for his popular novels, in which the Arctic Ocean and other exotic locales set the stage for epic battles between man and nature. His most famous novel, *The Wreck of the "Mary Deare"* (1956; filmed 1959), is a maritime thriller involving conspiracy and insurance fraud. Innes wrote his first novel, *The Doppelgänger,* at the age of 17. It was published four years later, by which time he had begun work as an industrial correspondent (1934–40) for the *Financial News.* He then wrote the novels *The Trojan Horse* (1940) and *Wreckers Must Breathe* (1940). His experience as a volunteer with the British Royal Artillery (1940–46) provided material for *Attack Alarm* (1941), written between air raids during the Battle of Britain, and other military works. After the war Innes became a full-time novelist and children's book author (writing under the pen name Ralph Hammond), and he began contributing regularly to *Holiday* magazine, which funded many of his travel adventures. Sailing on his own boat (aptly named the *Mary Deare*), Innes spent six months each year visiting sites in Europe and Asia that were later featured in books, notably *Harvest of Journeys* (1960). His passion for sea travel was matched only by his environmental consciousness. Novels such as *The Blue Ice* (1948) and *The White South* (1949), for which he spent some time living and working with Norwegian whalers, reflected his concern for the humane treatment of animals. A member of the Timber Growers Association, Innes planted an estimated 1,500,000 trees. He was made a C.B.E. in 1978.

Johnson, Ian William, Australian cricket player who was a reliable, slow off-spin bowler for Victoria and in 45 Test matches, including 17 as captain (1954–57). Johnson played first-class cricket for Victoria briefly in 1935, but he served as a fighter pilot in World War II before making his Test debut against New Zealand in 1946. In his 11-year career Johnson achieved a Test-career double, scoring 1,000 runs in Tests (average 18.51) out of a total of 4,905 first-class runs (average 22.92) and taking 109 Test wickets (average 29.19) out of a first-class total of 619 (average 23.30). Johnson was appointed M.B.E. in 1955 and was advanced to O.B.E. in 1977 and C.B.E. in 1983 (b. Dec. 8, 1917/18, North Melbourne, Australia—d. Oct. 9, 1998, Melbourne, Australia).

Jones, Louis Marshall ("GRANDPA"), American singer and banjo player who for over half a century was a popular member of the Grand Ole Opry and from 1968 to 1993 was featured on the "Hee Haw" television program; he was inducted into the Country Music Hall of Fame in 1978 (b. Oct. 20, 1913, Niagara, Ky.—d. Feb. 19, 1998, Nashville, Tenn.).

Julien, Pauline, Canadian singer, actress, songwriter, and feminist activist who specialized in songs that championed the cause of Quebec separatism and independence (b. May 23, 1928, Trois-Rivières, Que.—d. Sept. 30, 1998, Montreal, Que.).

Jünger, Ernst, German novelist and essayist (b. March 29, 1895, Heidelberg, Ger.—d. Feb. 17, 1998, Wilflingen, Ger.), wrote works early in his career that were marked by a pervading interest in the depersonalization of man and the glorification of war, but in midcareer he became equally impassioned about peace, European federation, and individual dignity. Jünger, who studied philosophy and natural sciences at the Universities of Leipzig and Naples, served in both World War I and II. Wounded several times in combat, he was granted Germany's top military honour for his exemplary service in World War I. Jünger abandoned his militaristic attitude, evident in such works as *In Stahlgewittern* (1920; *The Storm of Steel,* 1929), after his son was forced to join a suicide mission in the mid-1940s. *Der Friede* (written 1943, pub. 1948) illustrated his conversion to pacifism. Though lauded throughout his literary career, Jünger was continually tormented by accusations that he was a Nazi sympathizer. In *Auf den Marmorklippen* (1939; *On the Marble Cliffs,* 1947), a loosely disguised allegory of Germany under Nazi control, Jünger foretold the horrors of such a regime. Although he ended the novel with "So I swear to myself in the future to fall alone in freedom rather than to accompany the servants on the path to triumph," Jünger later fought in the armed forces of the Third Reich. His youthful nationalism, expressed both in his early writings and in his military service, had attracted the attention of the Nazi Party, which offered him a seat in the Reichstag and membership in the nazified German Academy. Though he rejected both offers and was later associated with a group that plotted to kill Adolf Hitler, Jünger's relationship with the Nazi Party was never clarified and remained controversial.

Kane, Bob (ROBERT KAHN), American cartoonist who, with his partner, Bill Finger, created the comic-book characters Batman the Caped Crusader and Robin the Boy Wonder, Batman's sidekick, as well as a collection of those crime fighters' enemies, including the Joker, the Riddler, and the Penguin (b. Oct. 24, 1915, New York, N.Y.—d. Nov. 3, 1998, Los Angeles, Calif.).

Karamanlis, Konstantinos, Greek statesman (b. March 8, 1907, Proti, near Serrai, Macedonia, Ottoman Empire [now in Greece]—d. April 23, 1998, Athens, Greece), had a political career that spanned nearly 60 years—including six terms as prime minister and two as president—and was credited with restoring democracy following the collapse of a seven-year military junta in 1974. Born when Macedonia was under Turkish rule, he became a Greek citizen in 1913 after the Turks were expelled following the Second Balkan War. He graduated from the University of Athens law school in 1932 and first entered politics when he was elected to Parliament, representing the conservative royalist Populist Party in 1935. During the dictatorship of Gen. Ioannis Metaxas (1936–41) and the Axis occupation of Greece (ended in 1944), Karamanlis was politically inactive. He was reelected to Parliament in 1946, and in 1955 he became Greece's youngest prime minister and began modernizing the Greek economy through industrialization and foreign investment. He resigned in 1963, citing the difficulty of working under a separation of powers in a constitutional monarchy. From his exile in Paris, he witnessed the takeover of Greece by army colonels

in 1967, and when that repressive junta collapsed in 1974, he was called home to shore up the crisis-ridden country. He quickly reestablished democratic rule and reorganized the military command. Creating the New Democracy Party, which won elections in November 1974, he called a plebiscite that resulted in a 70% vote to end the monarchy. A new republic was established on Dec. 8, 1974, and a new constitution was drafted. Resigning as prime minister in May 1980, Karamanlis assumed the mostly ceremonial position of president. He secured Greece's place in the European political and economic family and, in 1981, full membership in what became the European Union. In 1985 he resigned the presidency after an uneasy five-year alliance with Andreas Papandreou's Panhellenic Socialist Movement, which had won national elections in 1981; Karamanlis took office again in 1990, however, and served until 1995.

Karff, Mona May Ratner, American chess player who reigned as the national women's chess champion seven times between 1938 and 1974 and was one of the first four Americans to qualify for the rank of international woman master (b. 1911?, Bessarabia, Russia—d. Jan. 10, 1998, New York, N.Y.).

Katsh, Abraham Isaac, Polish-born American educator and researcher who was a scholar of Judaica and was credited with the addition of modern Hebrew to the curricula of American colleges; during the Cold War he persuaded Soviet officials to allow him to study and microfilm— and thus make available to scholars—thousands of Jewish documents they had seized and hidden away (b. Aug. 10, 1908, Poland—d. July 21, 1998, New York, N.Y.).

Kazin, Alfred, American teacher and critic (b. June 5, 1915, Brooklyn, N.Y.—d. June 5, 1998, New York), was considered one of the most eloquent and influential literary critics of the 20th century; his seminal work, *On Native Grounds* (1942), was a sweeping historical study of modern American literature and set the standard in the field. The son of Russian immigrants, Kazin began his career as a critic in 1934 after a confrontation with a *New York Times* book reviewer led to a job at *The New Republic* magazine. It was while attending Columbia University, New York City (M.A., 1938), that he began writing *On Native Grounds.* Constructed in passionate and simple prose accessible to the general reader, it established Kazin as a perceptive critic with a distinctive point of view. A prolific writer, he contributed reviews and essays to a number of publications, including *Harper's, The New Yorker,* and *Partisan Review,* and penned more than a dozen books. His criticism, both severe and generous, also provided insight into the personalities of authors and their motivation to write. Unlike traditional reviewers who concentrated on style and form, Kazin was more concerned with a novel's relationship to the era in which it was written. While the development of American literature was a common topic of his works, Kazin also wrote extensively on New York City and Judaism. His memoirs include *A Walker in the City* (1951) and *New York Jew* (1978). In addition, Kazin taught at several universities and edited a number of works.

Kelly, William Russell, American businessman who in 1965 became chairman of Kelly Services, Inc., which he had founded in 1946 to provide businesses with personnel for temporary assignments; the company grew from providing the services of a few "Kelly Girls" during its early years to finding placement for more than 700,000 employees in 1997 (b. Nov. 21, 1905, Koksilah, Victoria, B.C.—d. Jan. 3, 1998, Fort Lauderdale, Fla.).

Kendal, Geoffrey (GEOFFREY BRAGG), British actor-manager whose Shakespeareana Company, which included his wife and eventually their daughters, toured India and the Far East for nearly 20 years, performing the works of Shakespeare and other classics; the film *Shakespeare Wallah*

(1965) was based on the company (b. Sept. 7, 1909, Kendal, Westmorland, Eng.—d. May 14, 1998, England?).

Kilgore, Thomas, Jr., American religious leader who led two prominent national Baptist organizations and played an important role in the Civil Rights Movement, working with the Rev. Martin Luther King, Jr., and helping organize the 1963 March on Washington (b. Feb. 20, 1913, Woodruff, S.C.—d. Feb. 4, 1998, Los Angeles, Calif.).

Kimbrough, David ("JUNIOR"), American blues musician who performed in Mississippi juke joints and at parties for over 30 years before attracting national attention when the 1992 documentary *Deep Blues* featured his music; he later released three albums on the Fat Possum label (b. July 28, 1930, Hudsonville, Miss.—d. Jan. 17, 1998, Holly Springs, Miss.).

Kinoshita, Keisuke (SHOKICHI KINOSHITA), Japanese motion picture director (b. Dec. 5, 1912, Hamamatsu, Shizuoka prefecture, Japan—d. Dec. 30, 1998, Tokyo, Japan), directed nearly 50 feature films, many of them social satires that emphasized the frailty and beauty of the human condition. Kinoshita wrote the screenplays for many of his films and was thrice awarded the prestigious Kinema Jumpo Award for excellence in Japanese cinema. After graduating (1930) from Hamamatsu Technology School, he enrolled in the Oriental Photography School and later worked at the Shochiku Motion Picture Co. under director Yasujiro Shimazu, first as cameraman, then as scriptwriter, and finally as assistant director. His first film, *Hanasaku minato* (1943; *The Blossoming Port*), was followed by those framed by patriotic doctrine but also including creative— and even controversial—touches. Kinoshita was awarded the Kinema Jumpo Award for *Osone-ke no asa* (1946; *A Morning with the Osone Family*), the story of a family's wartime vicissitudes. Japan's first colour film, *Karumen kokyo ni kaeru* (1951; *Carmen Comes Home*), was a popular satire revolving around a stripper with a heart of gold and was followed by a successful sequel, *Karumen junjosu* (1952; *Carmen's Pure Love*). Kinoshita also presented tales of familial breakdown, profound sacrifice, and wrongful violence. In *Nihon no higeki* (1953; *A Japanese Tragedy*) newsreel footage is interspersed with the story of a widow who prostitutes herself in order to support her ungrateful children. *Nijushi no hitomi* (1954; *Twenty-four Eyes*), another Kinema Jumpo Award–winner, focuses on the lives of 12 students and their beloved teacher in the years leading up to World War II. His third Kinema Jumpo Award–winner, *Narayama-bushi ko* (1958; *Ballad of Narayama*), centres on an elderly woman who smashes her teeth on a grinding wheel in order to persuade her impoverished son to carry her to Mt. Narayama, where villagers customarily abandon their decrepit forebears. Later films include *Kono ko o nokoshite* (1983; *The Children of Nagasaki*) and *Yorokobi mo kanashima mo ikutoshitsuki* (1986; *Times of Joy and Sorrow*). Though Kinoshita's works were often compared to those of Akira Kurosawa (*q.v.*) in their technical sophistication, Kurosawa usually favoured tales of strength and action, whereas Kinoshita preferred sentimentality.

Kudsi, Nazim al-, Syrian political leader who served as president for 18 months in 1961–63 before being ousted in a coup (b. Feb. 14, 1906— d. Feb. 6, 1998, Jordan).

Kulenkampff, Hans-Joachim, German film, radio, and television actor and game-show host, whose wit and charm made him one of the most beloved personalities on TV and earned him a reputation as Germany's master showman (b. April 27, 1921, Bremen, Ger.—d. Aug. 14, 1998, Seeham, near Salzburg, Austria).

Kurosawa, Akira, Japanese film director (b. March 23, 1910, Tokyo, Japan—d. Sept. 6, 1998, Tokyo), became one of the giants of world cin-

Akira Kurosawa

ema after introducing such Japanese films as *Rashomon* and *Seven Samurai* in the early 1950s. Kurosawa worked briefly and unsuccessfully as a commercial artist before landing a job as an assistant director with the PCL film company in 1936, becoming a director in 1943. His films revealed a strong Hollywood influence, particularly in their vigorous narrative drive; he spoke openly of his admiration for American films, especially those of John Ford. International notice came with *Rashomon* (1950), a study of the relativity of truth as demonstrated by four widely varying accounts of the same incident. Playing the leading role in the film was Toshiro Mifune, who reigned as Japan's greatest film star through his many collaborations with Kurosawa. Kurosawa's masterpiece, *Seven Samurai* (1954), was an epic account of a group of warriors who were greatly outnumbered while defending a rural village against pillaging bandits. Celebrated for its gallery of memorable characters, its masterful orchestration of physical movement, the stirring intensity of its action, and the poetry of its images of peace and life amid the savagery of violence and death, *Seven Samurai* was consistently ranked among the greatest films ever made. Some of Kurosawa's other notable credits include *Ikiru* (1952), *Throne of Blood* (1957), *The Hidden Fortress* (1958), *Yojimbo* (1961), *High and Low* (1963), *Dersu Uzala* (1975), and *Kagemusha* (1980). By the mid-1960s Kurosawa's films had declined in both popular and critical appeal, and he found it difficult to find financial backing for his ambitious projects; the negative reception of *Dodeskaden* (1970) led to a suicide attempt. Kurosawa made films only sporadically over the rest of his career but realized an artistic dream with *Ran* (1985), an extensive treatment of the King Lear story set in Japan's Shogun era. Known as "the Emperor" for his autocratic manner on the set, Kurosawa was one of the greatest masters of storytelling through physical action—the Hollywood style par excellence. Several of his samurai films were remade in the West as westerns, notably *Seven Samurai* as *The Magnificent Seven* (1960) and *Yojimbo* as *A Fistful of Dollars* (1964).

Lambert, William G., American journalist who shared a 1957 Pulitzer Prize for revealing Teamsters Union corruption and who in 1969, in a *Life* magazine article, disclosed U.S. Supreme Court Justice Abe Fortas's acceptance of a $20,000 fee from financier Louis Wolfson, who later was convicted of stock fraud; Fortas resigned shortly after the magazine article appeared (b. Feb. 2, 1920, Langford, S.D.—d. Feb. 8, 1998, Bryn Mawr, Pa.).

Lamoureux, Lucien, Canadian politician whose service as speaker of the House of Commons, from 1966 to 1974, was the longest in Canada's

history; he later was ambassador to Belgium and Luxembourg and to Portugal (b. Aug. 3, 1920, Ottawa, Ont.—d. July 16, 1998, Waterloo, Belg.).

Lang, Charles Bryant, Jr., American cinematographer whose stunning mastery of both black-and-white and colour photography and imaginative, flattering lighting graced such films as *A Farewell to Arms* (1932), for which he won an Academy Award, and *The Magnificent Seven* (1960); he was given the American Society of Cinematographers' Lifetime Achievement Award in 1991 (b. March 27, 1902, Bluff, Utah—d. April 3, 1998, Santa Monica, Calif.).

Laxness, Halldór (HALLDÓR KILJAN GUDJÓNSSON), Icelandic novelist (b. April 23, 1902, Reykjavík, Ice.—d. Feb. 8, 1998, Leikjalundur, Ice.), was awarded the Nobel Prize for Literature in 1955 and the Sonning Prize in 1969. At the time of his death, Laxness was his nation's only Nobel Prize winner. Though he initially rejected the literary tradition of his native country, Laxness later embraced the medieval Icelandic saga and was credited by the Swedish Academy, which awards the Nobel Prize, with having "renewed the great narrative art of Iceland." The nationalistic trilogy *Íslandsklukkan* (1943–46) established him as the country's leading writer. Laxness grew up on the family farm, from which he took his pen name, and from the age of 17 journeyed throughout Europe. During these travels he was introduced to French Surrealism and German Expressionism; the influences of both movements were evident in his early work. Yet, as was characteristic of Laxness throughout his life, he soon found inspiration in other movements and philosophies. A convert to Roman Catholicism in the early 1920s, he wrote about a young man torn between his religious faith and the pleasures of the world in *Vefarinn mikli frá Kasmír* (1927); it signaled the beginning of his dissociation from Christianity. During the 1930s and '40s, Laxness concentrated on the plight of Iceland's lower classes in such controversial works as *Sjálfstætt fólk* (1934–35; *Independent People,* 1946) and *Heimsljós* (1937–40; *World Light,* 1969), both of which criticize Icelandic society. His long-standing belief in Taoism was reflected in works after 1955, including *Brekkukotsannáll* (1957; *The Fish Can Sing,* 1966) and *Paradísarheimt* (1960; *Paradise Reclaimed,* 1962). Toward the end of his literary career, Laxness focused mainly on plays, translations, and memoirs.

Leandro (JOSÉ LUIZ COSTA), Brazilian singer who, as half of the brother team Leandro and Leonardo, helped popularize *sertanejo* (country music) in Brazil and inspired the use of cowboys

Leandro

as an advertising image; his adoration was such that his death was publicly mourned throughout the country (b. Aug. 15, 1961, Goiânia, Braz.—d. June 23, 1998, São Paulo, Braz.).

Lenz, Hermann, German writer whose greatest success came in the 1970s with his seven-part *Schwäbische Chronik* whose main character, based on Lenz, chronicled German life in the 20th century (b. Feb. 26, 1913, Stuttgart, Ger.—d. May 12, 1998, Munich, Ger.).

Lestor of Eccles, Joan Lestor, Baroness, Canadian-born British politician who was a Labour MP in 1966–83 and 1987–97, serving in the 1970s as a junior minister and as party chairperson; she was an outspoken advocate of children's rights and opponent of apartheid (b. Nov. 13, 1931, Vancouver, B.C.—d. March 27, 1998, London, Eng.).

Lewis, Janet, American writer and poet who produced short stories, children's books, such novels as *The Wife of Martin Guerre* (1941) and the libretto of the opera based on it (1956), and the librettos of four other operas in addition to hundreds of poems, her final collection of which, *The Dear Past* (1994), contained works covering most of the 20th century; with her husband, poet and critic Yvor Winters, she shared an interest in nature, a concern for Native Americans, and participation in a number of liberal causes (b. Aug. 17, 1899, Chicago, Ill.—d. Dec. 1, 1998, Los Altos, Calif.).

Lewis, Shari, American puppeteer and author (b. Jan. 17, 1933, New York, N.Y.—d. Aug. 2, 1998, Los Angeles, Calif.), entertained children for some 40 years as the creator and voice of a series of sock puppets, most notably a woolly character named Lamb Chop. Lewis studied acting, dance, and singing as a child and displayed a gift for ventriloquism, a skill her father encouraged by hiring a former vaudevillian as her coach. She performed in nightclubs and summer stock productions and in 1952 won top prize on the television program "Arthur Godfrey's Talent Scouts." In 1957 she appeared on "Captain Kangaroo" and introduced Lamb Chop, a hand puppet with long eyelashes, a squeaky voice, and an inquisitive manner. The duo's popularity led to "The Shari Lewis Show" (1957–63), a program that featured knock-knock jokes, singing, and humorous skits. She later added Charlie Horse and Hush Puppy to her cast of puppets, and other shows followed, including "Lamb Chop's Play-Along" (1989–95) and "Charlie Horse Music Pizza" (1998). Lewis sought to educate children in the role of an older playmate rather than that of a teacher. A vigorous supporter of quality children's programming, she won

12 Emmy awards for her television work. Among her 60 books for youths were *Things That Kids Collect!* (1980) and *One-Minute Bedtime Stories* (1986). A music aficionada, Lewis often played the piano on her shows, and she was a guest conductor for some 50 symphony orchestras.

Lighthill, Sir (Michael) James, British mathematician who was considered one of the greatest mathematicians of the 20th century; his innovative contributions to such fields as applied mathematics, aerodynamics, astrophysics, and fluid mechanics found such applications as the design of the supersonic Concorde jetliner and noise reduction in jet engines (b. Jan. 23, 1924, Paris, France—d. July 17, 1998, Sark, Channel Islands).

Limann, Hilla, Ghanaian politician who engaged in a seesaw battle with Lieut. Jerry Rawlings for the presidency of Ghana; Limann was elected president in 1979 when he defeated Rawlings, who had seized power in a coup; in 1981, however, Rawlings staged another coup and unseated Limann. When Limann ran for president again in 1992, he lost to Rawlings (b. Dec. 12, 1934, Gwollu, Gold Coast [now Ghana]—d. Jan. 23, 1998, Accra, Ghana).

Lippincott, J(oshua) Gordon, American engineer who helped create such designs as the labels for Campbell's soup and the logos for Coca-Cola, Betty Crocker, and FTD florists (b. 1908?—d. April 29, 1998, North Haven, Conn.).

Lloyd, George Walter Selwyn, British composer whose early success was followed by years of neglect after health problems caused by military service in World War II left him incapacitated for a time and his late Romantic style went out of fashion; in the late 1970s, however, his career underwent a revival, and he returned to serious composing (b. June 28, 1913, St. Ives, Eng.—d. July 3, 1998, London, Eng.).

Lord, Jack (JOHN JOSEPH PATRICK RYAN), American actor who was closely identified with the television character Detective Steve McGarrett, whom he portrayed for 12 years on the series "Hawaii Five-O," and with McGarrett's frequent closing line, "Book 'em, Danno" (b. Dec. 30, 1920, Brooklyn, N.Y.—d. Jan. 21, 1998, Honolulu, Hawaii).

Luckman, Sidney ("SID"), American football player and coach (b. Nov. 21, 1916, Brooklyn, N.Y.—d. July 5, 1998, North Miami Beach, Fla.), revolutionized American football in the 1940s by leading the National Football League (NFL) Chicago Bears to four championships (1940–41, 1943, and 1946) using the T formation, a system of offense that promoted passing and favoured quickness and deception over sheer strength. Following graduation from Columbia University, New York City, in 1939, Luckman was selected by Chicago in the NFL draft. The Bears, under owner and coach George Halas, had recently revived the T formation and added the man in motion. After learning the complex footwork and faking that were cornerstones of the offense, Luckman was named the team's starting quarterback in 1940. That year he led the Bears to the championship with a 73–0 victory over the Washington Redskins, the most one-sided title game in league history. In 1943 he set several passing records, including most touchdowns in a single game (7), in a season (28), and in a championship game (5) and was named the NFL's Most Valuable Player that year. With his spectacular throws and leadership skills, Luckman set the standard for the modern quarterback, and the T formation quickly became the offense of choice for both professional and collegiate teams. After retiring in 1950 he worked as a part-time assistant coach with the Bears and visited numerous colleges to teach the formation. A five-time All-Pro, Luckman was inducted into the Football Hall of Fame in 1965.

Lumley, Harry, American hockey goalie whose 16 seasons in the National Hockey League in-

cluded an important role in the 1950 Stanley Cup victory of the Detroit Red Wings as well as selection to the All-Star team three times; he was inducted into the Hockey Hall of Fame in 1980 (b. Nov. 11, 1926, Owen Sound, Ont.—d. Sept. 13, 1998, London, Ont.).

Lyotard, Jean-François, French philosopher, teacher, and writer who, influenced by the Paris riots of 1968, became a leader of the Postmodernists (b. Aug. 10, 1924, Versailles, France—d. April 21, 1998, Paris, France).

MacGregor, Sir Ian, British industrialist (b. Sept. 21, 1912, Kinlochleven, Scot.—d. April 13, 1998, Taunton, Eng.), gained a reputation for having a ruthless, no-nonsense approach to reducing costs in ailing businesses and was responsible for diminishing the power of British unions during the 1980s while presiding as chairman (1983–86) of the National Coal Board. In that post he stockpiled huge reserves of coal in anticipation of a 1984–85 strike and steadfastly rejected strikers' demands during the protracted walkout. As a result, the bitter yearlong British coal miners' strike collapsed, and the trade union movement in Great Britain was weakened. After earning a degree in metallurgical engineering at the University of Glasgow, he traveled (1940) with a British mission to the U.S. to advise on war production, specifically as an expert on Sherman tank design. Settling in the U.S., he began a 35-year career in the metal industry, working at American Metal Climax, Inc., where he served as president and chief executive (1966) and as chairman (1969–77). He was an investment banker for Lehman Brothers and at Lazard Frères and deputy chairman of British Leyland (1977–80) before signing a three-year contract with the British Steel Corp. (BSC) to revive the failing nationalized industry. As chairman and chief executive (1980–83), he reorganized, decentralized, and cut 100,000 jobs and thereby made the BSC both productive and profitable. MacGregor, who was knighted in 1986, served as director of several organizations and remained professionally active into his 80s.

Mahbub ul Haq, Pakistani economist who in 1990 created the Human Development Index, which the United Nations Development Programme used to produce annual reports that examined people's standards of living in order to determine their countries' wealth; he had previously served as the World Bank's director of policy planning and Pakistan's finance minister (b. Feb. 22, 1934, Jammu, India—d. July 16, 1998, New York, N.Y.).

Maher, Joseph, Irish-born American actor who, over the course of his more than 40-year career, filled a variety of character parts on television, in such motion pictures as *Heaven Can Wait* and *Sister Act,* and in live theatre, especially the black comedies of Joe Orton (b. Dec. 29, 1933, Westport, County Galway, Ire.—d. July 17, 1998, Los Angeles, Calif.).

Maia, Sebastião Rodrigues ("TIM"), Brazilian singer-songwriter whose mixture of samba and soul made him a major force in Brazilian pop music for over 30 years (b. Sept. 28, 1942, Rio de Janeiro, Braz.—d. March 15, 1998, Niterói, Braz.).

Malsed, Helen Herrick, American toy inventor who created a number of games and toys, most notably toys based on the already popular Slinky, such as the Slinky Dog and the Slinky Train (b. 1910?, Cincinnati, Ohio—d. Nov. 13, 1998, Seattle, Wash.).

Mankowitz, (Cyril) Wolf, British writer, playwright, and screenwriter who became an authority on and dealer in antique porcelain before gaining renown as the prolific author of such novels as *Make Me an Offer* (1952), which was filmed and later was staged as a musical, and *A Kid for Two Farthings* (1953), also filmed; he also wrote screenplays for such films as *The Day the Earth*

Caught Fire (1961) and *Casino Royale* (1967), as well as plays and TV dramas (b. Nov. 7, 1924, London, Eng.—d. May 20, 1998, Durrus, County Cork, Ire.).

Marais, Jean (JEAN-ALFRED VILLAIN-MARAIS; "JEANNOT"), French actor (b. Dec. 11, 1913, Cherbourg, France—d. Nov. 8, 1998, Cannes, France), appeared in more than 70 films as well as a number of stage productions and became one of France's most popular actors. He was especially noted for his performances in the works of the Surrealist poet and artist Jean Cocteau, his longtime partner and mentor, and it was as the beast in Cocteau's 1946 film *La Belle et la bête* (*Beauty and the Beast*) that he found his most memorable role. Though Marais had decided as a young child that he wanted to be an actor, drama schools rejected him, and he was able to win only small parts in stage and film productions. In 1937, however, Cocteau noticed Marais in his play *Oedipe roi* and later that year starred him in another of his plays *Les Chevaliers de la table ronde.* Although Marais's voice was considered weak, his good looks made him a screen idol; nonetheless, he worked to improve his acting skills and came to be respected for his performing abilities. Other Cocteau plays in which Marais starred included *Les Parents terribles* (1938), *La Machine à écrire* (1941), and *La Machine infernale* (1954). Among Marais's films for Cocteau were *L'Eternel Retour* (1943; *The Eternal Return*), *Les Parents terribles* (1948; *The Storm Within*), *Orphée* (1950; *Orpheus*), and *Le Testament d'Orphée* (1960; *The Testament of Orpheus*); films for other directors included *Le Comte de Monte-Cristo* (1953; *The Count of Monte-Cristo*), *Éléna et les hommes* (1956; *Paris Does Strange Things*), *Le notti bianche* (1957; *White Nights*), and the *Fantômas* series in the 1960s. In 1983, on the 20th anniversary of Cocteau's death, Marais presented a one-man show, *Cocteau-Marais,* and he made a notable cameo appearance in Bernardo Bertolucci's 1996 film *Stealing Beauty.*

Marasco, Robert, American playwright whose thriller *Child's Play* became a Broadway hit in 1970 and garnered four Tony awards; he also published the novels *Burnt Offerings* (1973; filmed 1976) and *Parlor Games* (1979) and had finished work on another play, *Our Sally* (b. Sept. 22, 1936, Bronx, N.Y.—d. Dec. 6, 1998, Manhasset, N.Y.).

Marshall, E(verett) G., American character actor whose resonant voice and authoritative demeanor made him particularly adept at portraying politicians, judges, and lawyers; notable among his work was the television series "The Defenders" (1961–65), for which he won two Emmys, the film *Twelve Angry Men* (1957), and the 1956 Broadway premiere of *Waiting for Godot* (b. June 18, 1910, Owatonna, Minn.—d. Aug. 24, 1998, Bedford, N.Y.).

Martin, William McChesney, Jr., American economist who served as chairman of the U.S. Federal Reserve from 1951 to 1970, under the administrations of five presidents; during his tenure the country enjoyed its longest period, 1961–69, of economic expansion to that time (b. Dec. 17, 1906, St. Louis, Mo.—d. July 27, 1998, Washington, D.C.).

Massey, Daniel Raymond, British actor in motion pictures, television, and—most notably—the theatre; his versatility was illustrated by the stylish performances he achieved in plays by William Shakespeare, Oscar Wilde, George Bernard Shaw, and Harold Pinter; such musicals as *She Loves Me* and *Follies;* and his last role, Wilhelm Furtwängler, the Berlin Philharmonic conductor accused of Nazi collaboration, in *Taking Sides* (b. Oct. 10, 1933, London, Eng.—d. March 25, 1998, London).

Mastroianni, Umberto, Italian sculptor who was celebrated especially for his large-scale abstract bronzes, notably a series of war monuments (b.

Sept. 21. 1910, Fontana Liri, Frasinone, Italy—d. Feb. 25, 1998, Marino, Italy).

Matoub, Lounés, Algerian singer and activist (b. Jan. 26, 1956, Taourirt-Moussa, Alg.—d. June 25, 1998, near Tizi-Ouzou, Alg.), celebrated in song the language and culture of the Berbers (Amazigh), an ancient North African people that represents about one-fifth of the Algerian population. Matoub was born in the northern mountainous region of Kabylia, an area steeped in Berber tradition. His mother introduced him to the folk music of the Berbers and nurtured his musical gifts. The young Matoub also was exposed to the vehement resistance his kinsmen raised against the policy of "arabization," which the new government introduced when Algeria won its independence in 1962. The Kabylie Berbers objected to this policy—which aimed to promote Arabic and Islamic cultural values throughout society—on the grounds that they would be forced to turn their backs on their own firmly entrenched and dearly loved traditions. Matoub poured these feelings into his songs. He became an activist in the Berber cultural movement, and in 1976 he co-founded the Algerian Human Rights League. Moving to France in 1978, Matoub played his protest songs in cafes and bars and soon recorded his first album, *Ay Izem* ("The Lion"), which became a success in France and Algeria. His politically charged music, however, raised the ire of pro-Arabic Muslim fundamentalists, and in 1994 a radical militant faction, the Armed Islamic Group, kidnapped Matoub and held him hostage for more than two weeks, an ordeal he detailed in his autobiography, *Rebelle* (1995). After his release Matoub lived mainly in France and returned only periodically to Algeria. On a recent trip there he was ambushed and murdered, an event that heightened the Berber anger toward the government's plan to make Arabic the official language of Algeria.

McCartney, Linda Louise Eastman (LADY MCCARTNEY), American-born British photographer and entrepreneur who overcame initial public skepticism and the pressures of a high-profile marriage to British singer-composer Paul (from 1997 Sir Paul) McCartney to achieve her own success as a champion of animal rights, the author of several photography collections and vegetarian cookbooks, and the founder (1991) of a popular line of vegetarian frozen foods; she was diagnosed with breast cancer in 1995 (b. Sept. 24, 1941, Scarsdale, N.Y.—d. April 17, 1998, Tucson, Ariz.).

McDonald, Richard, American restauranteur who designed the golden arches logo and the number-of-hamburgers-sold sign for the fast-food restaurant franchise that he and his brother started and gave the family name to; after being purchased by Ray Kroc, the business expanded into a large and well-known international chain (b. Feb. 16, 1909, Manchester, N.H.—d. July 14, 1998, Manchester).

McDougal, James B., American businessman whose revelations regarding real-estate dealings with Bill and Hillary Rodham Clinton led to the Whitewater investigation but also resulted in his being convicted of fraud in 1996 and imprisoned in 1997 (b. Aug. 25, 1940—d. March 8, 1998, Fort Worth, Texas).

McDowall, Roderick Andrew Anthony Jude ("RODDY"), British-born actor (b. Sept. 17, 1928, London, Eng.—d. Oct. 3, 1998, Los Angeles, Calif.), was a child star who defied the odds against continued success and went on to adult acclaim as a versatile performer. His career lasted more than 60 years, during which he made some 130 motion pictures, as well as stage and television appearances, and also became an accomplished photographer, with five books of his photos published. McDowall was encouraged to act by his mother, who had once had similar ambitions for herself, and he had already appeared in a number of movies by the time he moved with his mother and sister to the U.S. in 1940 during

Linda McCartney, with one of her photographs
GERALD PENNY—AP/WIDE WORLD

the London Blitz. Shortly thereafter he was screen-tested for a part in *How Green Was My Valley* (1941), which became his first big success and paved the way for prominent roles in such children's classics as *My Friend Flicka* (1943), its sequel, *Thunderhead—Son of Flicka* (1945), and *Lassie Come Home* (1943). His costar in the latter was Elizabeth Taylor, with whom he formed a lifelong friendship. Although McDowall appeared in the stage and film versions of Orson Welles's *Macbeth* in the late 1940s, directors still tended to think of him as a child. He therefore moved to New York City, took acting lessons, and performed onstage and on television. In 1957 he starred on Broadway in *Compulsion,* a drama based on the Leopold-Loeb murder case, in what became his favourite stage role, Artie Strauss (the Loeb counterpart), and in 1960 he won both a Tony award for *The Fighting Cock* and an Emmy for the TV drama "Not Without Honour." Later in 1960 he opened in the Broadway production of *Camelot,* portraying an effectively sneering Mordred. At about that same time, McDowall began making movies, appearing in such films as *The Longest Day* (1962) and *Cleopatra* (1963) before finding new fame as a talking ape in *Planet of the Apes* (1968) and three of its four sequels. His performance in those films and a TV series spin-off gained him a cult following. Other films included *The Poseidon Adventure* (1972), *Funny Lady* (1975), and *Fright Night* (1985).

McGlew, Derrick John ("JACKIE"), South African cricketer who was a mainstay for Natal (1947/48–67) and South Africa (1951–60). A tenacious defensive batsman (usually batting as an opener), McGlew scored 12,170 runs (average 45.92), including 2,440 (average 42.06) in 34 Test matches, 14 as captain. He made 27 career centuries (7 in Tests), including a marathon 255 not out against New Zealand in 1952/53 (b. March 11, 1929, Pietermaritzburg, S.Af.—d. June 8, 1998, Pretoria, S.Af.).

Médecin, Jacques, French politician who followed his father's 30-plus years as mayor of Nice by holding that office from 1966 to 1990; con-

sidered a virtual dictator by some, he escaped to Uruguay to avoid charges of corruption and fraud but later served a prison term in France before returning to Uruguay (b. May 5, 1928, Nice—d. Nov. 17, 1998, Punta del Este, Uruguay).

Merrill, Bob (HENRY ROBERT MERRILL LEVAN), American composer-lyricist (b. May 17, 1921?, Atlantic City, N.J.—d. Feb. 17, 1998, Beverly Hills, Calif.), wrote prolifically for both the pop music market and the Broadway musical stage. Although he could not read music and composed his tunes on a toy xylophone, 25 of his songs made it to the top-10 lists. Following army service during World War II, Merrill moved to Hollywood, eventually gaining employment as a radio writer. He went on to become (1948) a television casting director and at about that same time began writing songs. His early efforts were unsuccessful, but in 1950 his luck changed when he provided the lyrics for "If I Knew You Were Coming I'd've Baked a Cake," his first chart topper. He followed that with such hits as "My Truly, Truly Fair" (1951), "How Much Is That Doggy in the Window?" (1953), and "Mambo Italiano" (1954). Merrill's Broadway success began with *New Girl in Town* (1957), a musical adaptation of Eugene O'Neill's *Anna Christie*. Another O'Neill work, *Ah! Wilderness,* served as the basis for his next show, *Take Me Along* (1959), and the Leslie Caron film *Lili* provided the story for *Carnival* (1961), which featured the hit "Love Makes the World Go 'Round." His greatest Broadway success came with his collaboration with Jule Styne on *Funny Girl* (1964), for which Merrill wrote the lyrics; "People" and "Don't Rain on My Parade" became classics. His last Broadway musical was *Sugar* (1972), based on the film *Some Like It Hot. We're Home,* a four-character musical structured around a compilation of 37 of Merrill's songs, appeared Off-Broadway in 1984, and *Hannah . . . 1939* was produced there in 1990.

Jacques Médecin

JACQUES BRINON—AP/WIDE WORLD

Merrill also wrote screenplays, among them *Mahogany* (1975), and the book, music, and lyrics for an upcoming animated television musical, *Tom Sawyer.*

Middlecoff, (Emmett) Cary, American dentist turned golfer whose 40 wins on the Professional Golfers' Association Tour from 1945 to 1967 included the U.S. Open in 1949 and 1956 and the Masters in 1955; he was the top PGA Tour money winner in the 1950s (b. Jan. 6, 1921, Halls, Tenn.—d. Sept. 1, 1998, Memphis, Tenn.).

Mignone, Emilio Fermin, Argentine lawyer whose daughter's disappearance spurred him to found the Centre for Legal and Social Studies to document the abuses of the Argentine military during its 1976–83 dictatorship and to establish its accountability; he became the country's best-known human rights campaigner (b. July 23, 1922, Luján, Arg.—d. Dec. 21, 1998, Buenos Aires, Arg.).

Millar, Sir Ronald Graeme, British actor, playwright, and screenwriter who was a speechwriter for three prime ministers and provided one of Margaret Thatcher's most famous lines, "The lady's not for turning" (b. Nov. 12, 1919, Reading, Eng.—d. April 16, 1998, London, Eng.).

Minetti, Bernhard, German actor who was one of the giants of the German stage; during a career that spanned nearly 70 years, he was especially noted for his interpretations of roles by such intellectual playwrights as Samuel Beckett, Thomas Bernhard, Jean Genet, and Friedrich Dürrenmatt (b. Jan. 26, 1905, Kiel, Ger.—d. Oct. 12, 1998, Berlin, Ger.).

Mitchell, W(illiam) O(rmond), Canadian writer (b. March 13, 1914, Weyburn, Sask.—d. Feb. 25, 1998, Calgary, Alta.), created humorous, nostalgic works that evoked life on the farms and in the small towns of the prairies of western Canada. His works came to be considered classics, and he was said to be the country's most beloved writer. Mitchell studied (1932–34) at the University of Manitoba but dropped out to travel. After doing so and then working at a number of odd jobs upon his return to Calgary, he resumed his studies, receiving a B.A. degree from the University of Alberta in 1942; he then became a teacher and high-school principal. From 1948 to 1951 Mitchell was fiction editor of *Maclean's* magazine, and he later taught at the Banff (Alta.) Centre for the Arts and served as writer in residence at a number of Canadian universities. The first of Mitchell's 13 novels, *Who Has Seen the Wind* (1947; filmed, 1977), featured a young boy as he entered adolescence and brought the author instant acclaim. His fame spread when the Canadian Broadcasting Company began (1950) airing his series "Jake and the Kid," which ran weekly on radio until 1956 and was televised in 1961. Among Mitchell's other books were *The Vanishing Point* (1973), *How I Spent My Summer Holidays* (1981), and *Roses Are Difficult Here* (1990). He also wrote such stage plays as *The Devil's Instrument* (1972) and *The Black Bonspiel of Wullie MacCrimmon* (1979)—both of which had first been radio plays, in 1949 and 1955, respectively—as well as *Back to Beulah* (1974), *The Kite* (1981), and *For Those in Peril on the Sea* (1982). In addition, Mitchell's own performances of his works were treasured, and they brought him an even wider audience. Among his many honours were the Stephen Leacock Memorial Medal (1962 and 1990), the Order of Canada (1973), and membership in the Privy Council (1992). In 1997 a Can$15,000 W.O. Mitchell Literary Prize was announced.

Moore, Archie (ARCHIBALD LEE WRIGHT), American boxer (b. Dec. 13, 1913?, Benoit, Miss.—d. Dec. 9, 1998, San Diego, Calif.), won 194 of his estimated 228 bouts—141 by knockout—in a record 27-year professional career and held the world championship title for light heavyweight boxing from 1952 to 1962. His parents separated while he was an infant, and Moore went

to live with an aunt and uncle, taking on their name. After his uncle's death the teenaged Moore was arrested for stealing and sent to a reform school, where he learned to box. Moore turned professional as a middleweight in the mid-1930s, but few organizers during that era would give a black boxer a title shot. He finally captured the light heavyweight title on Dec. 17, 1952, by defeating Joey Maxim. During a bout in 1958 with Yvon Durelle, Moore was forced to the canvas several times but made an astonishing comeback, knocking out the contender in the 11th round. He defended his title eight times, but he was stripped of it in 1962 when he failed to answer a challenge by Harold Johnson. In two hard-fought attempts to become heavyweight champion, Moore was knocked out in 1955 by Rocky Marciano and in the following year by Floyd Patterson; in November 1962 he was defeated by the 21-year-old Cassius Clay (later Muhammad Ali). The self-monikered "the Mongoose" fought his last professional bout in 1963. After retiring from the ring, he founded and directed the Any Boy Can (ABC) Club, an organization for inner-city youth. He retained an interest in boxing, training Clay for a brief period and, later, George Foreman. In the 1980s he worked for the Los Angeles branch of the U.S. Department of Housing and Urban Development. Moore did a round in Hollywood, portraying the slave Jim in the 1960 motion picture *The Adventures of Huckleberry Finn*. His autobiography, *The Archie Moore Story*, was published in 1960.

Morgan, Dermot, Irish comedian, actor, and writer who was a stand-up comic and satirist for many years in Ireland before finding international fame as the title character in the irreverent and instantly successful comedy "Father Ted," which began in 1994 on British television's Channel 4 (b. March 3, 1952, Dublin, Ire.—d. March 1, 1998, Isleworth, Middlesex, Eng.).

Morris, Wright Marion, American writer and photographer (b. Jan. 6, 1910, Central City, Neb.—d. April 29, 1998, Mill Valley, Calif.), wrought careful examinations of the American character in novels, short fiction, essays, and photographs. Although his novels were set in many different parts of the country, Morris is best known for his portrayal of the bleak life on the Nebraska prairie, which was the setting for what many critics considered his most successful novel, *Ceremony in Lone Tree* (1960). Morris spent his adolescence in Chicago and with his father embarked on automobile trips between Chicago and California, journeys that inspired his first novel, *My Uncle Dudley* (1942). In 1930 he moved to Claremont, Calif., where he attended Pomona College. Morris dropped out of school to travel in Europe, returning to begin a career in writing. In 1940 he embarked on a photographic tour of the United States, capturing images of an agricultural America that was fading into the past; this work became the focus of *The Inhabitants* (1946). After living for many years in Pennsylvania, Morris returned to California and in 1963 began teaching creative writing at San Francisco State University, a post that he held until his retirement in 1975. During his career Morris published about 20 novels, 5 books of photographs, 4 compilations of essays, 2 short-story collections, and 3 memoirs. Despite being honoured with numerous awards, including the 1957 National Book Award for the novel *The Field of Vision,* the 1981 American Book Award for the novel *Plains Song,* and the Commonwealth Award for distinguished service in literature (1982), his work attracted less attention than many critics believed it deserved.

Moss, Jeffrey A., American writer and composer-lyricist who created the "Sesame Street" characters Cookie Monster and Oscar the Grouch, wrote such songs for the show as "Rubber Duckie" and "I Love Trash," won 14 Emmy and 4 Grammy awards, and received an Academy Award nomination for the music for *The Muppets Take Manhattan;* he also wrote a number of children's books (b. 1942, New York, N.Y.—d. Sept. 24, 1998, New York).

Motta, Sérgio Roberto Vieira da, Brazilian politician who, as minister of communications from 1995, devised the breakup and privatization of Brazil's telecommunications monopoly (b. Nov. 26, 1940, São Paulo, Braz.—d. April 19, 1998, São Paulo).

Muir, Frank, British comedy writer and broadcaster who exhibited his facility for wordplay, which figured prominently in his writing and in his participation on the radio shows "My Word!" and "My Music" and the television quiz show "Call My Bluff"; as a producer he worked on the influential BBC television shows "Till Death Do Us Part" and "Steptoe and Son," the models for the American TV series "All in the Family" and "Sanford and Son," respectively (b. Feb. 20, 1920, Ramsgate, Kent, Eng.—d. Jan. 2, 1998, Thorpe, Surrey, Eng.).

Murray, Jerome, American inventor of such varied items as the airplane boarding ramp, a television antenna rotator, and a pump that made open-heart surgery possible (b. 1912?, New York, N.Y.—d. Jan. 7, 1998, Dover, N.J.).

Mya Than Tint, Burmese writer who won a number of awards for his own works and translated into Burmese such Western classics as *War and Peace* and *Gone with the Wind* (b. May 23, 1929, Myaing, Burma [now Myanmar]—d. Feb. 18, 1998, Yangon [Rangoon], Myanmar).

Nanda, Gulzarilal, Indian politician who twice served briefly as interim prime minister, in 1964 following the death of Jawaharlal Nehru and in 1966 upon the death of Lal Bahadur Shastri (b. July 4, 1898, Badoki Gosain village, Gujranwala, India [now in Pakistan]—d. Jan. 15, 1998, Ahmadabad, India).

Narcejac, Thomas (PIERRE AYRAUD), French writer of best-selling crime novels who collaborated with Pierre Boileau on 43 thrillers, about 100 short stories, and 4 plays; their *Celle qui n'était plus* (1952) was filmed as *Les Diaboliques* (1954) by Henri-Georges Clouzot, and *D'entre les morts* (1954) became the 1958 Alfred Hitchcock film *Vertigo* (b. July 3, 1908, Rochefort-sur-Mer, France—d. June 7, 1998, Nice, France).

Newhouse, Theodore ("TED"), American publisher who with his brothers founded a publishing empire that grew to comprise such holdings as 26 newspapers, the Condé Nast magazine group, business journals, and cable television systems (b.

July 19, 1903, Bayonne, N.J.—d. Nov. 28, 1998, New York, N.Y.).

Newhouser, Harold ("HAL"), American left-handed baseball pitcher for the Detroit Tigers (1939–53) and the Cleveland Indians (1954–55) who was the only pitcher to win consecutive (1944–45) Most Valuable Player awards; he was elected to the Baseball Hall of Fame in 1992 (b. May 20, 1921, Detroit, Mich.—d. Nov. 10, 1998, Southfield, Mich.).

Newton, Sir (Leslie) Gordon, British journalist who, between 1950 and 1972, transformed the *Financial Times* into a highly regarded international newspaper while serving as its editor (b. Sept. 16, 1907, England—d. Aug. 31, 1998, Henley-on-Thames, Oxfordshire, Eng.).

Nguyen Van Linh (NGUYEN VAN CUC), Vietnamese politician (b. July 1, 1915, near Hanoi, Vietnam—d. April 27, 1998, Ho Chi Minh City, Vietnam), was a secretive guerrilla leader who operated under a number of aliases for many years before assuming a public political role after the Vietnam War ended. He served as general secretary of the Vietnamese Communist Party from 1986 to 1991 and during his time in office initiated a program of *doi moi* (renovation) and free-market reforms that encouraged international investment and helped free the country from its economic isolation. Nguyen Van Linh began his fight against French colonial rule when he was 14 and at 15 was imprisoned for his activities. Upon his release in 1936, he joined the Indochinese Communist Party and resumed his anti-French efforts, and he was jailed again from 1941 to 1945. He advanced in the party ranks, and after the division of the country following the French withdrawal (1954), he became an underground leader in South Vietnam. With the fall of the government of the south (1975) and the reunification of Vietnam, Nguyen Van Linh became party chief in Saigon (renamed Ho Chi Minh City); he was promoted to the party's Politburo the following year. He was dropped from the Politburo in 1982 but was reinstated in 1985, and in December 1986 he became party leader. Following his retirement from office in 1991, he remained an adviser to the party. Nguyen Van Linh later expressed regret over some of his reforms, claiming that they had led to corruption and exploitation.

Nitschke, Ray(mond) E., American professional football player who was a powerful middle linebacker for the Green Bay Packers from 1958 to

Ray Nitschke

Maureen O'Sullivan

1972, during which time the team won five National Football League championships and, in 1967 and 1968, the first two Super Bowls; he was elected to the Pro Football Hall of Fame in 1978 and was chosen for the NFL's 50th and 75th anniversary all-star teams (b. Dec. 29, 1936, Elmwood Park, Ill.—d. March 8, 1998, Venice, Fla.).

Nolan, Jeanette, American actress whose 70-year career encompassed numerous radio performances on such shows as "The March of Time" and "Mercury Theatre on the Air," roles in more than 20 films, including that of Lady Macbeth in Orson Welles's 1948 *Macbeth,* and more than 300 television appearances; she was especially noted for her roles in motion-picture and television westerns (b. Dec. 30, 1911, Los Angeles, Calif.—d. June 5, 1998, Los Angeles).

Norris, Kenneth Stafford, American marine naturalist and educator whose pioneering work with marine mammals, particularly dolphins, transformed their study into a modern science and led to the verification of echolocation, a process in which sound transmission is used by dolphins to see (b. Aug. 11, 1924, Los Angeles, Calif.—d. Aug. 16, 1998, Santa Cruz, Calif.).

O'Dwyer, (Peter) Paul, Irish-born American lawyer, liberal Democratic politician, and champion of the underdog who devoted his career to such causes as civil rights, the creation of Israel, an end to the Vietnam War, and a united and free Ireland (b. June 29, 1907, Bohola, County Mayo, Ire.—d. June 24, 1998, Goshen, N.Y.).

O'Sullivan, Maureen, Irish-born American actress (b. May 17, 1911, Boyle, County Roscommon, Ire.—d. June 22, 1998, Scottsdale, Ariz.), had a distinguished performing career that extended from the 1930s until the mid-1990s, but was perhaps best remembered for her film portrayal of the scantily clad Jane opposite Johnny Weissmuller in his title role as Tarzan in a half dozen jungle adventures. O'Sullivan, who attended convent and finishing school in London and Paris, was discovered in 1929 by director Frank Borzage in Dublin, was given a contract, and went to Hollywood. Her debut film, *Song o' My Heart,* opened the following year. After playing small parts in a few more films, among them *A Connecticut Yankee* (1931), O'Sullivan appeared in her first Tarzan adventure, *Tarzan, the Ape Man* (1932). She also was featured in such motion pictures as *The Thin Man* (1934), *The Barretts of Wimpole Street* (1934), *A Day at the Races* (1937), *A Yank at Oxford* (1938), and *Pride and Prejudice* (1940), before appearing in *Tarzan's New York Adventure* (1942), the last in the Tarzan series. After marrying writer-director John Farrow in 1936 and eventually becoming the mother of seven, she worked only intermittently, with Farrow's *The Big Clock* (1948) and *Where Danger Lives* (1950) among her few film appearances. In 1962 she began her Broadway career with *Never Too Late;* she also appeared in the 1965 film version. Other onstage successes included *The Subject Was Roses* (1965), the Broadway version of *No Sex Please, We're British* (1973), and the revival of *Morning's at Seven* (1980). O'Sullivan made a notable return to the silver screen in 1986 with fine performances in *Peggy Sue Got Married* and—playing mother to her real-life daughter, Mia Farrow—in *Hannah and Her Sisters.*

Ohain, Hans Joachim Pabst von, German aeronautical engineer (b. Dec. 14, 1911, Dessau, Ger.—d. March 13, 1998, Melbourne, Fla.), designed the HeS3b, the turbojet engine that powered the experimental first jet aircraft, the He178, on its historic maiden flight on Aug. 27, 1939, near the German port city of Rostock. Ohain conceived his theory of jet propulsion in 1933 while pursuing a doctorate in physics at the University of Göttingen. After graduating in 1935, he was recommended by the university to the German aircraft manufacturer Ernst Heinkel. Ohain joined Heinkel's firm in 1936, and by September 1937 he had built a factory-tested demonstration engine. Shortly afterward, Ohain directed the construction of the HeS3b, the first fully operational centrifugal-flow turbojet engine. Although the development of this technology did not pique the interest of the German High Command during World War II, it revolutionized postwar transportation and defense. After the war Ohain was recruited by the U.S. Air Force, and he became the chief scientist at Wright Patterson Air Force Base in Dayton, Ohio. After retiring in 1979, he served as a consultant to the University of Dayton Research Institute. Ohain, however, was not credited with being the first to invent the jet engine. Great Britain's Sir Frank Whittle registered a patent for the turbojet engine in 1930, though he did not perform a flight test until 1941. In 1991 Ohain (along with Whittle) was honoured by the U.S. National Academy of Engineering with the Charles Stark Draper Prize, recognizing him as a pioneer of the jet age.

Ordóñez Araujo, Antonio Jiménez, Spanish matador whose classical style and effortless grace in the bullring made him one of Spain's most admired bullfighters in the 1950s and '60s. Ordóñez's professional rivalry was with his more flamboyant brother-in-law, Luis Miguel Dominguín, and was chronicled by Ernest Hemingway in 1959 in a series of *Life* magazine articles, which were collected, edited, and published in 1985 as *The Dangerous Summer* (b. Feb. 16, 1932, Ronda, Spain—d. Dec. 19, 1998, Seville, Spain).

Ornes, Germán Emilio, Dominican journalist who served as publisher of the newspaper *El Caribe* and was a longtime campaigner for press freedom in Latin America (b. 1919?, Puerto Plata, Dom.Rep.—d. April 14, 1998, Santo Domingo, Dom.Rep.).

Ortese, Anna Maria, Italian writer of magic-realist fiction who was considered one of the 20th century's most important female Italian authors; *Il cardillo addolorato* (1993; *The Lament of the Linnet,* 1997) spent several weeks at the top of the Italian fiction lists (b. June 13, 1914, Rome, Italy—d. March 9, 1998, Rapallo, Italy).

Pakula, Alan J., American motion-picture director, producer, and screenwriter (b. April 7, 1928, Bronx, N.Y.—d. Nov. 19, 1998, Melville, N.Y.), evoked exceptional performances from actors and actresses in 16 films, most notably in 3 dark, foreboding psychological thrillers: *Klute* (1971), *The Parallax View* (1974), and *All the President's Men* (1976). Pakula examined complex emotions in his films, which often featured themes dealing with fear and the abuse of political power. After majoring in drama at Yale University, he moved to Hollywood, where he began working in the Warner Bros. cartoon department. Beginning in 1957, Pakula produced films in collaboration with director Robert Mulligan, most notably *To Kill a Mockingbird* (1962). In 1969 Pakula directed his first film, *The Sterile Cuckoo,* starring Liza Minnelli, who was nominated for an Academy Award. Pakula cemented his reputation as an important director when Jane Fonda won an Oscar as the protagonist of *Klute.* His moody film adaptation of the Carl Bernstein–Bob Woodward Watergate exposé, *All the President's Men,* was a

career high point—the film won four Oscars and Pakula earned an Oscar nomination for best director. He wrote the screenplays for four later films, including his Oscar-nominated adaptation of William Styron's novel *Sophie's Choice* (1982; Meryl Streep won an Oscar in the title role). Another Pakula screenplay, *See You in the Morning* (1989), featured a divorced man who, like himself, married a widow with several children. Later films included the legal thrillers *Presumed Innocent* (1990) and *The Pelican Brief* (1993). At the time of his death, resulting from an automobile accident, Pakula was working on a screenplay about Franklin D. and Eleanor Roosevelt's years in the White House.

Parker, Maynard Michael, American editor of *Newsweek* from 1982 who increased the magazine's readership by broadening the scope of its coverage from foreign events and politics to also include such topics as science and technology, social issues, medicine, and religion (b. July 28, 1940, Los Angeles, Calif.—d. Oct. 16, 1998, New York, N.Y.).

Parlá, Alicia, Cuban-born American dancer who in the early 1930s reigned as queen of the rumba, becoming an American and European sensation with her sensual dancing and attracting the attention of several members of European royalty (b. 1914, Havana, Cuba—d. Oct. 6, 1998, Miami, Fla.).

Patrick, Murray ("MUZZ"), Canadian hockey player who also served as coach and general manager of the New York Rangers; his family boasted several generations of professional hockey players (b. June 28, 1915, Victoria, B.C.—d. July 23, 1998, Riverside, Conn.).

Pawar, Lalita (AMBIKA SAGUN), Indian actress whose career of more than 600 films was most notably defined by her roles as a mean, domineering mother-in-law; her performances were enhanced by a permanent squint in one eye, the result of an accident on a film set (b. April 18, 1918, Indore, India—d. Feb. 24, 1998, Pune, India).

Paz, Octavio, Mexican poet and writer (b. March 31, 1914, Mexico City, Mex.—d. April 19, 1998, Mexico City), was Mexico's foremost man of letters and the winner of the Nobel Prize for Literature in 1990. He wrote poems that vividly celebrated sensual experience and essays that explored Mexico's history and national character. He was noted for his clear, concise writing style, a sharp contrast to the convoluted style that had predominated in Mexican letters. Although Paz studied law at National Autonomous University in Mexico City, his literary interests found early expression. He published his first poem at age 16, founded an avant-garde magazine (*Barandal*) at age 17, and published his first collection of poems, *Luna silvestre* (*Forest Moon*), before he was 20. Paz read widely, especially contemporary literature, and was particularly influenced by T.S. Eliot, Saint-John Perse, and surrealist André Breton. In 1937 Paz went to Spain to observe the civil war and became acquainted with Pablo Neruda, who influenced Paz's Marxist views; three years later Paz renounced communism and broke with Neruda. He was a political centrist for the rest of his life, often criticizing the repressive Mexican government. Paz's early poetry, gathered in the 1971 collection *Configurations,* was considered his best. Many of his poems dealt explicitly with sex, which Paz regarded as a transcendent force. His poetic reputation reached its height with the 1957 publication of *Piedra de sol* (*Sun Stone,* 1961). In the latter half of his career, Paz continued to experiment with poetry, but increasingly his attention was given to prose. His greatest prose work was considered *El laberinto de la soledad* (1950; *The Labyrinth of Solitude,* 1961), a rumination on the Mexican national character, particularly the tension between Mexico's native Indians and the colonizing Spaniards. Paz's father had been secretary to the Indian revolutionary Emiliano Zapata; Paz, himself partially of Indian descent, retained his father's sympathy for the

Indians. He also had a significant diplomatic career, beginning in 1945 and culminating with his 1962 appointment as Mexico's ambassador to India, a post he resigned in 1968 to protest the shooting of hundreds of demonstrating students at that year's Summer Olympic Games in Mexico City. Subsequently he edited the Mexico City journal *Plural* and accepted a number of visiting professorships at various universities in the United States. A series of literary honours climaxed with the Nobel Prize, in which he was cited for his "impassioned writing with wide horizons, characterized by sensuous intelligence and humanistic integrity."

Peña Gómez, José Francisco, prominent black Dominican politician whose lack of success in three presidential campaigns was attributed to racism (b. March 6, 1937, Valverde province, Dom.Rep.—d. May 10, 1998, Santo Domingo, Dom.Rep.).

Pencer, Gerald Norman, Canadian businessman who expanded his father's bottling business from a regional company into the Cott Corp., the world's fourth largest maker of soft drinks (b. April 26, 1945, Montreal, Que.—d. Feb. 3, 1998, Toronto, Ont.).

Pérez Martínez, (Gregorio) Manuel, Spanish-born priest (defrocked) and revolutionary who for some 20 years was the leader of the National Liberation Army, the second largest rebel group in Colombia (b. May 9, 1943, Alfamén, Spain—d. Feb. 14, 1998, Colombia).

Carl Perkins

MARK HUMPHREY—AP/WIDE WORLD

Perkins, Carl, American musician and songwriter (b. April 9, 1932, Tiptonville, Tenn.—d. Jan. 19, 1998, Jackson, Tenn.), was a pioneer of rockabilly, a fusion of blues, country, rhythm and blues, and gospel that gave rise to rock and roll; his single "Blue Suede Shoes" was the musical movement's anthem. Born the son of a sharecropper, Perkins was taught to play the guitar by a field hand and at the age of 14 began writing songs. He formed a band with his brothers Clayton and Jay, and after hearing the similar musical style of Elvis Presley, the trio moved to Nashville, Tenn., where they signed with Sun Records, Presley's label. Perkins soon began pro-

ducing regional hits and became the opening act for Presley. In 1955 he wrote "Blue Suede Shoes," which reached number two on the singles chart. The following year, en route to his first national television appearance, Perkins was seriously injured in an automobile accident. Though he recovered and resumed writing and recording other rockabilly standards, such as "Honey Don't" (1956) and "Matchbox" (1957), Perkins's career stalled, overshadowed by the popularity of Presley, whose version of "Blue Suede Shoes" had gone to the top of the charts, and plagued by personal problems, including alcoholism. His hard-rocking guitar play, however, proved influential to other musicians, and in the 1960s the Beatles covered several of his songs. From 1965 to 1976 he toured with Johnny Cash and performed on the country singer's television show. Perkins later formed a band with his sons. In 1987 he was inducted into the Rock and Roll Hall of Fame.

Piñeiro Losada, Manuel, Cuban government official and revolutionary who for over 30 years led security and intelligence operations and played a major role in the exportation of revolution to other Latin-American countries and the detection of political opposition at home (b. May 14, 1934, Matanzas, Cuba—d. March 12, 1998, Havana, Cuba).

Pires, José Augusto Neves Cardoso, Portuguese writer whose moralistic allegorical works reflected the alienation of both the well-off and those on the margins of society; his large number of national literary awards included the most prestigious, the Fernando Pessoa (b. Oct. 2, 1925, São João do Peso, near Vila de Rei, Port.—d. Oct. 26, 1998, Lisbon, Port.).

Pitts, Elijah, American football player who was a Green Bay Packers running back in the 1960s, when the Packers won the National Football League championship four times and the Super Bowl twice, and whose more than 20 years as an NFL assistant coach culminated in the position of assistant head coach of the Buffalo Bills (b. Feb. 3, 1939, Conway, Ark.—d. July 10, 1998, Buffalo, N.Y.).

Pol Pot, Cambodian political leader and dictator (b. May 1925, Kompong Thom province, Cambodia—d. April 15, 1998, near the Cambodia-Thailand border), was responsible, during a four-year reign of terror, for the deaths of 1.7 million people, nearly one-quarter of his nation's population, through starvation, torture, execution, and hard labour. Born Saloth Sar to landowning farmers, he was sent at age six to Phnom Penh to be educated at a Buddhist monastery and later at a Roman Catholic primary school. In the late 1940s and early '50s, he studied radio technology in Paris on a government scholarship, and it was there that he became involved in communist activities. While teaching in a private school in the mid-1950s and early '60s, he secretly formed the Khmer Workers' Party to resist Cambodia's ruler, Prince Norodom Sihanouk, and he disappeared into the jungle in 1963, where he adapted the charismatic revolutionary persona known variously as Pol Pot and Brother Number One. He spent the next years training his Khmer Rouge guerrillas; they first

clashed with the Cambodian army and police in 1968. Capitalizing on the U.S. bombing of Cambodia and Sihanouk's shifting loyalties, he led the Khmer Rouge—an army of 70,000—into Phnom Penh in 1975 and took control of the country. Ordering the city's entire population of two million to evacuate, he attempted to create an agrarian utopia without money or property; instead, he initiated Cambodia's destruction by such means as abolishing schools, religion, and family life and murdering those he deemed a threat—the educated, artists, technicians, former government officials, monks, and minorities. From 1975 to 1979 the newly renamed Democratic Kampuchea remained isolated from the world until his government was overthrown by the Vietnamese. Once again in hiding, he renounced communism and convinced the U.S. and other countries that his exiled government should retain political recognition; the Khmer Rouge occupied Cambodia's UN seat until two decades of civil war were ended in the early 1990s by a UN-mediated peace accord and elections. Although Pol Pot was not seen by outsiders for almost 20 years, he remained the guiding force of the Khmer Rouge until June 1997, when he was arrested by former Khmer associates, found guilty of treason during a show trial in July, and placed under house arrest. In the two weeks preceding his death, the Cambodian Government Army was closing in on Pol Pot's jungle retreat with plans to bring him before an international tribunal for crimes against humanity. Some were doubtful that Pol Pot was dead, whereas others harboured suspicions that he was killed to prevent his capture and a trial that could have implicated many others, including Prime Minister Hun Sen, for their actions in what notoriously became known as Cambodia's killing fields.

Porsche, Ferdinand Anton Ernst ("FERRY"), Austrian car designer and businessman who worked with his father on the design of the Volkswagen Beetle and later, after having taken over the vehicle-design firm that his father had founded and given the family's name, transformed the company into a renowned sports car manufacturer (b. Sept. 19, 1909, Wiener Neustadt, Austria—d. March 27, 1998, Zell am See, Austria).

Postel, Jonathan Bruce, American computer scientist (b. Aug. 6, 1943, Altadena, Calif.—d. Oct. 16, 1998, Santa Monica, Calif.), was lauded for his work as a creator and manager of the Internet. In the late 1960s, when correspondence was sent via "snail mail" rather than E-mail and no one had ever heard of a Web site, Postel was a graduate student at the University of California, Los Angeles, and was working to develop the ARPANET (Advanced Research Projects Agency Network), a forerunner of the Internet designed for use by the U.S. Department of Defense. During its development Postel took on some of the administrative functions of this system, and later of the Internet, a responsibility he continued for some three decades. He formed and served as director of the Internet Assigned Numbers Authority, which was responsible for, among other duties, allocating numerical addresses (IP numbers) and turning those into simpler written addresses (*i.e.,* <www.eb.com>). Postel's behind-the-scenes influence over the Internet was made more visible in early 1998 when, during a test, he redirected some of the Internet's directory-information computers to his own system. The Internet grew rapidly in the 1990s, and there was concern about its lack of regulation. Shortly before his death Postel submitted a proposal for review by the U.S. government for the acceptance of the Internet Corporation for Assigned Names and Numbers, an international nonprofit organization that would oversee the Internet. At the time of his death, Postel was also director of the computer networks division of the University of Southern California Information Sciences Institute.

Povich, Shirley, American sportswriter whose standard-setting columns, more than 15,000 in all, had graced the *Washington Post* since 1924, not only reporting the news in sports but also agitating for such causes as the racial integration of teams (b. July 15, 1905, Bar Harbor, Maine—d. June 4, 1998, Washington, D.C.).

Powell, (John) Enoch, British scholar and politician (b. June 16, 1912, Birmingham, Eng.—d. Feb. 8, 1998, London, Eng.), was an ardent nationalist noted for his early endorsement of monetarism, his staunch opposition to the European Economic Community, and his controversial rhetoric concerning Britain's nonwhite population. Arguably one of the most brilliant British politicians of his time, Powell never achieved office higher than minister of health (1960–63). His political demise began in 1965 when he captured an embarrassing 15 votes in his bid for the Conservative Party leadership. Three years later he lost his shadow cabinet post as a result of his infamous "Rivers of Blood" speech, in which he argued that Britain was building "its own funeral pyre" by allowing Indian, Pakistani, African, and West Indian immigrants to claim British citizenship through their Commonwealth status. He predicted violent clashes between races—quoting a famous statement by Virgil, "I seem to see the river Tiber foaming with much blood"—and, because he incited Britain's populace, created the atmosphere for such tensions. His bold opinions were also somewhat curious because, as minister of health, Powell had actively recruited Caribbean immigrants to fill hospital positions. Having been a Conservative Wolverhampton MP from 1950 to 1974, Powell ended his political career as an Ulster Unionist representing the Protestant Northern Ireland districts (1974–87). In addition to politics, he engaged in scholarly pursuits, including biblical and classical studies, and wrote poetry. At Trinity College, Cambridge, he was awarded every major classical prize available to undergraduate students, and he studied with the poet and scholar A.E. Housman, whose enormous influence on Powell was reflected in his published poetry. From 1934 to 1938 he was a fellow of Trinity College. A professor of Greek at the University of Sydney, Australia, at the age of 25 and one of the youngest brigadiers ever to serve in the British army, Powell experienced his only failing in the political arena; yet, as he once stated, "All political careers end in failure. No regrets."

Powell, Lewis Franklin, Jr., American lawyer and judge (b. Sept. 19, 1907, Suffolk, Va.—d. Aug. 25, 1998, Richmond, Va.), served as an associate justice of the U.S. Supreme Court for 15 years, during which he often provided a centrist viewpoint in an otherwise polarized tribunal. He cast the deciding vote on a number of landmark cases, most notably *Regents of the University of California* v. *Bakke* (1978), which opposed strict racial quotas but upheld affirmative-action programs, allowing race to be a consideration in university admissions. Powell graduated from Washington and Lee University, Lexington, Va. (B.S., 1929; LL.B., 1931; LL.D., 1960), was called to the bar in 1931, and earned an LL.M. from Harvard Law School in 1932. He then practiced law in Richmond, becoming a partner at the firm Hunton, Williams, Gay, Powell and Gibson in 1938 and staying with that firm, with the exception of his years of World War II military service, until he joined the Supreme Court. Prior to joining the court, he also served as president of the American Bar Association (1964–65), the Virginia State Board of Education (1968–69), the American College of Trial Lawyers (1969–70), and the American Bar Foundation (1969–71). In 1971 Powell, who had in 1969 refused an offer to take a seat on the Supreme Court, accepted Pres. Richard Nixon's plea, was quickly confirmed by the Senate, and was sworn in on Jan. 7, 1972. Although Powell was generally considered conservative, he voted with the liberal bloc on a number of social issues, siding with the majority on *Roe* v. *Wade* (1973), upholding abortion rights, and on a number of later cases concerned with attempts to add restrictions to those rights. Among the decisions on which Powell's vote was pivotal were those striking down programs to aid

Enoch Powell

parochial schools, *Aguilar* v. *Felton* (1985); rejecting the application of the right to privacy to consensual sex between homosexual adults, *Bowers* v. *Hardwick* (1986); and upholding the death penalty, *McCleskey* v. *Kemp* (1987). He later said that he regretted his votes on the latter two. Stating health concerns, Powell retired from the Supreme Court in June 1987, but he sat as a federal appeals court judge in Richmond until 1996.

Prelog, Vladimir, Swiss chemist (b. July 23, 1906, Sarajevo, Bosnia, Austria-Hungary [now in Bosnia and Herzegovina]—d. Jan. 7, 1998, Zürich, Switz.), pioneered research in several areas of molecular structure and function and made important discoveries about the way that atomic arrangements determine the chemical properties of many biological molecules. Along with John Warcup Cornforth, he was awarded the 1975 Nobel Prize for Chemistry for his work on the molecular architecture of cholesterol, antibiotics, and antimalarial alkaloids. Six years after earning a doctorate (1929) from the Institute Technical School of Chemistry in Prague, Prelog became a lecturer and later a professor of organic chemistry at the University of Zagreb, Croatia, but fled to Switzerland in 1942 to escape German occupation. There he accepted an offer to work at the Swiss Federal Institute of Technology, Zürich, with his mentor, 1939 Nobel Prize winner Leopold Ruzicka, whose research helped establish the field of stereochemistry, which examines the properties of chemical compounds on the basis of the three-dimensional arrangement of their atoms. Prelog focused on chirality—functional differences based on the mirror-image relationship, or left- and right-handedness, of otherwise identical chemical structures—and helped establish the chiral nomenclature system. His work with steroids, antibiotics, and antimicrobial chemical structures, including nonactins and rifamycin, facilitated a variety of pharmaceutical advances. A well-traveled and internationally acclaimed lecturer, Prelog was elected a foreign associate of the U.S. National Academy of Sciences in 1961 and became a member of the Royal Academy of Britain in 1962. He served as director (1957–65) of the Swiss Federal Institute of Technology's laboratory of organic chemistry, where he continued to teach until his retirement in 1976.

Prey, Hermann, German opera and concert singer (b. July 11, 1929, Berlin, Ger.—d. July 23, 1998, Berg, near Munich, Ger.), was a celebrated baritone who was one of the foremost contemporary interpreters of the songs of Franz Schubert; he was also noted for his charismatic stage presence and musical clarity. Prey's father was a merchant, and his mother was a talented amateur singer who encouraged his love for music. Prey briefly served in the army at the age of 15 during World War II but then sang with a band and began entertaining British and American troops. He enrolled (1949) in the Hochschule für Musik in Berlin to study under Günter Baum and in 1952 won a Meistersinger contest, which resulted in his American concert debut with the Philadelphia Orchestra, under the baton of Eugene Ormandy. That same year he made his stage debut in Wiesbaden, Ger., as Moruccio in Eugen Albert's *Tiefland*. He went on to the Hamburg State Opera, where he sang a large number of supporting roles, and in 1955 at the Vienna State Opera he sang Figaro in Gioacchino Rossini's *The Barber of Seville* to great acclaim. Though Prey received mixed reviews for his 1960 debut at the Metropolitan Opera in New York City as Wolfram in *Tannhäuser*, later appearances, including as Count Almaviva in *The Marriage of Figaro*, Eisenstein in *Die Fledermaus*, and Papageno in *The Magic Flute*, were more successful. Another of his unforgettable roles was as Beckmesser in *Die Meistersinger*. Whereas previous singers had turned the role of the town clerk into a caricature, Prey's portrayal was remarkably sympathetic and emotional. He also specialized in the songs (lieder)—from medieval to contemporary—of Robert Schumann, Gustav Mahler, and Carl Loewe.

Pyle, James T., American aviator who was considered the father of modern air traffic control systems (b. Nov. 8, 1913, New York, N.Y.—d. April 1, 1998, Oyster Bay, N.Y.).

Qabbani, Nizar, Syrian poet and diplomat (b. March 21, 1923, Damascus, Syria—d. April 30, 1998, London, Eng.), was one of the most widely read Arab poets of the 20th century. Written in simple but eloquent language, his verses, some of which were set to music, won him the hearts of countless Arabic speakers throughout the Middle East and Africa. Qabbani, who was born into a middle-class merchant family, was also the great-nephew of the pioneering Arab playwright Abu Khalil Qabbani. Such early experiences as the suicide of his sister, who was unwilling to marry a man she did not love, had a profound effect on the young poet, and he began to examine the experiences of women in traditional Muslim society. His first book of poetry, *Childhood of the Breast* (1954), which was financed by his unschooled mother, shocked conservative urban Muslims. Nevertheless, Qabbani continued to write love poetry and verses in defense of the social and sexual liberation of women while he studied law at the University of Damascus. Upon his graduation he worked in diplomatic service. From 1945 to 1966 he held postings in Cairo; Ankara, Turkey; London; Madrid; Beijing; and Beirut, Lebanon. The latter city became Qabbani's home when he left government service, and it was there that he established a publishing house, working as both a journalist and an editor. Following the Arab defeat in the Six-Day War of 1967, Qabbani's poetry took on a new sense of political and social urgency, as evidenced in the stinging *'Alā hāmish daftar al-naksa* (1967; "Marginal Notes on the Book of Defeat"). In 1981 Qabbani's second wife was killed by a car bomb, and thereafter he moved to Switzerland, France, and then London.

Quisenberry, Daniel Raymond ("DAN"), American baseball player who was known for his wit in addition to his submarine-style pitches as a star reliever for the Kansas City Royals; during his 12-year American League career, most of it with the Royals, he had 244 saves, was a five-time AL saves leader, and helped the Royals win two AL pennants and a World Series title (b. Feb. 7, 1953, Santa Monica, Calif.—d. Sept. 30, 1998, Leawood, Kan.).

Rabb, Ellis, American director and versatile actor who in 1960 founded the A.P.A. repertory theatre company and served as its artistic director; Rabb was hailed both for his performances in *The Royal Family* and *A Life in the Theater* and for his direction of *You Can't Take It with You* and *The Royal Family* (b. June 20, 1930, Memphis, Tenn.—d. Jan. 11, 1998, Memphis).

Rabbitt, Edward Thomas ("EDDIE"), American singer-songwriter-guitarist who in the 1970s and '80s reached the top of the charts with 26 country singles, among them "I Love a Rainy Night" (b. Nov. 27, 1944, Brooklyn, N.Y.—d. May 7, 1998, Nashville, Tenn.).

Raman, Bangalore Venkata, much-admired and respected Indian Vedic astrologer who challenged the Western scientific perception of astrology as a pseudoscience through international lectures and conferences and as editor of the monthly periodical *The Astrological Magazine*. In 1947 he was elected a fellow of the Royal Astronomical Society in London (b. Aug. 8, 1912, near Bangalore, India—d. Dec. 20, 1998, Bangalore).

Ramírez de León, Ricardo Arnoldo (COMANDANTE ROLANDO MORÁN), Guatemalan guerrilla leader and politician who in the 1990s, following decades of rebellion against the government, served as a leader in negotiations that resulted in a peace agreement in December 1996 (b. Dec. 29, 1930—d. Sept. 11, 1998, Guatemala City, Guat.).

Randolph, Jennings, American politician who served 14 years in the U.S. House of Representatives and 26 in the Senate and was the author of the 26th Amendment to the Constitution, which gave 18-year-olds the right to vote (b. March 8, 1902, Salem, W.Va.—d. May 8, 1998, St. Louis, Mo.).

Rasminsky, Louis, Canadian economist who helped form the post–World War II international finance and trade system; his half century of public service included the executive directorship of the International Monetary Fund, the deputy governorship and then the governorship of the Bank of Canada, and the chairmanship of the board of governors of the International Development Research Institute (b. Feb. 1, 1908, Montreal, Que.—d. Sept. 14/15, 1998, Ottawa, Ont.).

Ray, James Earl, American criminal who pleaded guilty to the 1968 assassination of the Rev. Martin Luther King, Jr., was sentenced to 99 years in prison, and spent the rest of his life demanding a trial, claiming that his confession had been coerced and that he had been a pawn in a larger conspiracy (b. March 10, 1928, Alton, Ill.—d. April 23, 1998, Nashville, Tenn.).

Rebozo, Charles Gregory ("BEBE"), American banker who for over 40 years was Richard Nixon's best friend and confidant, remaining loyal throughout the scandal that brought down Nixon's presidency (b. Nov. 17, 1912, Tampa, Fla.—d. May 8, 1998, Miami, Fla.).

Reiche, Maria, German-born Peruvian mathematician and archaeologist (b. May 15, 1903, Dresden, Ger.—d. June 8, 1998, Lima, Peru), was the self-appointed keeper of the Nazca Lines, a series of Peruvian ground drawings more than 1,000 years old. For five decades the "Lady of the Lines," as she was known, studied and protected the 60 km (35 mi) of desert near Nazca in southern Peru that served as the blackboard for etchings of animals and geometric patterns. Scratched into the ground and preserved by a lack of wind and rain, the figures are hundreds of feet in length and only fully recognizable from the air. Reiche, who emigrated to Peru in 1932 to escape the political situation in Germany, became fascinated with the mysterious lines after visiting the site in 1941. By 1946 she had moved to the desert and begun mapping and measuring the figures. Her work, the first serious study of the lines, led to the publication of *The Mystery on the Desert* (1949), in which she concluded that they represented an astronomical calendar; later experts, however, have suggested a ceremonial or community-building purpose. Reiche also funded several research projects and, as the region became a major tourist attraction, hired security guards to protect the drawings. UNESCO declared the Nazca Lines a World Heritage site in 1995 and in 1998 awarded Reiche a special medal for her work.

Reid, William Ronald, Canadian sculptor, carver, and goldsmith (b. Jan. 12, 1920, Victoria, B.C.—d. March 13, 1998, Vancouver, B.C.), helped spark a revival of interest in the traditions of the Haida of the Queen Charlotte Islands in British Columbia, with works that featured the influences of their culture. Partially of Haida ancestry, Reid had his interest in Haida culture aroused at age 24 by two gold bracelets made by his great-uncle, well-known Haida carver Charles Earnshaw. For the rest of his life, Reid served as a champion of the Haida in a number of ways: by becoming a spokesman for their political rights; by helping to protect their native lands from commercial interests; by leading the movement to preserve artifacts of Haida civilization, often resurrecting the traditional technology used to create totems, canoes, and other artifacts; and by creating original works in various media, using archetypal Haida imagery and symbolism. The most notable of Reid's sculptures include "The Spirit of Haida Gwaii," "The Raven and the First Men," and "The Chief of the Undersea World." Reid also inspired such artists as Robert Davidson and Jim Hart. In 1955 Reid participated in the salvage of totems from several abandoned Haida villages and took them for display to the University of British Columbia, where he was later commissioned to build two Haida-style houses. These efforts were not without controversy; many people felt that such objects should not have been disturbed and that approval by whites should not have been sought as a measure of the value of Haida culture. Reid coauthored several books, including

James Earl Ray

ALEJANDRO BALAGUER—AP/WIDE WORLD

Maria Reiche

Out of the Silence (1971), with photographs by Adelaide de Menil; *The Arts of the Raven* (1967), with Wilson Duff; *Form and Freedom* (1975), with Bill Holm; and *Haida Monumental Art* (1983), with George MacDonald. He also had a 16-year career as a broadcaster with the Canadian Broadcasting Corporation. Reid received an honorary doctorate from the University of British Columbia in 1976 and the Molson Prize in 1977.

Reines, Frederick, American physicist (b. March 16, 1918, Paterson, N.J.—d. Aug. 26, 1998, Orange, Calif.), was awarded the 1995 Nobel Prize for Physics for his detection in 1956 of neutrinos. The existence of these elusive subatomic particles, which have no electric charge and little, if any, mass, had been postulated by Wolfgang Pauli in the early 1930s but remained unproven until Reines and Clyde L. Cowan, Jr., used massive tanks of a water solution of cadmium chloride to observe signs of hydrogen nuclei being struck by the neutrinos from a nearby nuclear reactor. While a science undergraduate at Stevens Institute of Technology, Hoboken, N.J., Reines also took voice lessons at the Metropolitan Opera

in New York City. He eventually chose science over opera and received a B.S. (1939) and M.A. (1941) from Stevens and a Ph.D. (1944) from New York University. In later years Reines, a baritone, performed with the Cleveland (Ohio) Symphony Orchestra, and he could often be heard singing opera while working in the laboratory. Recruited to the Manhattan Project team at Los Alamos, N.M., after graduation, he also worked on atomic tests in the Marshall Islands after World War II. After finding the neutrino, Reines led pioneering research projects in neutrino astronomy and in 1959 became head of the physics department at Case Institute of Technology (now Case Western Reserve University) in Cleveland. In 1966 he was made the founding dean of physical science at the University of California, Irvine, where he worked until his retirement in 1988.

Rezzori d'Arezzo, Gregor von, Austrian-born writer whose works, the best known of which was *Memoiren eines Antisemiten* (1979; *Memoirs of an Anti-Semite,* 1981), chronicled the history of Europe from the time of the world wars and reflected loss of identity and disillusionment (b.

May 13, 1914, Czernowitz, Bukovina, Austria-Hungary [now Chernivtsi, Ukraine]—d. April 23, 1998, Donnini, Italy).

Ribicoff, Abraham Alexander, American politician who served as a U.S. representative, governor of Connecticut, secretary of health, education, and welfare, and U.S. senator but was best remembered by many for the reaction that he provoked from Chicago's Mayor Richard J. Daley at the 1968 Democratic national convention when he spoke out against police "Gestapo tactics in the streets" (b. April 9, 1910, New Britain, Conn.—d. Feb. 22, 1998, New York, N.Y.).

Richards, Gordon Waugh, British racehorse trainer who in 32 years was credited with some 2,000 steeplechase winners; one of his most memorable was the popular One Man, which captured a number of important races but was killed in a fall the day before the 1998 Grand National (b. Sept. 7, 1930, Bath, Eng.—d. Sept. 29, 1998, Carlisle, Eng.).

Ridenhour, Ronald L., American journalist whose investigation of the 1968 massacre of some 500 Vietnamese civilians at My Lai by U.S. troops led to public disclosure of the massacre in 1969 and the subsequent trial of some of the Americans involved; the incident shocked the public and reduced support for the war (b. April 6, 1946, Oakland, Calif.—d. May 10, 1998, New Orleans, La.).

Robbins, Jerome (JEROME WILSON RABINOWITZ), American choreographer and director (b. Oct. 11, 1918, New York, N.Y.—d. July 29, 1998, New York), was considered one of the premier choreographers of the 20th century and the best-ever of American-born ballet choreographers. He created such ballet classics as *Fancy Free, Dances at a Gathering,* and *The Goldberg Variations* and choreographed and directed such innovative Broadway musicals as *West Side Story* and *Fiddler on the Roof.* Robbins studied the violin and piano and accompanied his sister to dance classes when he was a child and, after attending New York University for a year, began to study dance and theatre seriously. He made his professional stage debut in 1937 with a walk-on role in a Yiddish Art Theater production of *The Brothers Ashkenazi* and began choreographing for summer shows at a resort in the Pocono Mountains. He danced (1938–40) in the choruses of several Broadway musicals before joining (1940) Ballet Theatre (later American Ballet Theatre), where he soon was dancing solo roles. His first choreography for a ballet company, *Fancy Free,* featuring a trio of sailors on shore leave dancing and cavorting to music by the then-unknown composer Leonard Bernstein, appeared in 1944 and was an instant success. Late that same year it was expanded into the Broadway musical *On the Town,* and that in turn was filmed in 1949. He choreographed such Broadway hits as *High Button Shoes* (1947), *Call Me Madam* (1950), *The King and I* (1951), and *Peter Pan* (1954) and *Gypsy* (1959), which he also directed. His two most successful musicals were *West Side Story* (1957), which he conceived, directed, and choreographed and for which Bernstein composed the music, and *Fiddler on the Roof* (1964), his last musical. The 1989 *Jerome Robbins' Broadway* was a compilation of numbers from shows Robbins had choreographed and/or directed. For the motion-picture version of *West Side Story* (1961), Robbins won two Academy Awards—for direction (shared with Robert Wise) and choreography. Although Robbins became associate artistic director for the New York City Ballet (NYCB) in 1949, he continued to choreograph ballets, among them *The Cage* (1951), *Afternoon of a Faun* (1953), and the comic masterpiece *The Concert* (1956). From 1958 to 1961 he had his own small company, Ballets: USA, and for that company he created *N.Y. Export: Opus Jazz* (1958) and his dance in silence, *Moves* (1959). From 1969 Robbins devoted his talents to NYCB, creating numerous works—such as *Dances at a Gathering* (1969), *In the Night* (1970), *The Goldberg Variations* (1971),

Jerome Robbins

Watermill (1972), *The Four Seasons* (1979), and *Glass Pieces* (1983)—and serving as ballet master until 1983, when he and Peter Martins became co-ballet masters in chief of NYCB shortly before the death of its director, George Balanchine. Robbins left that post in 1990 but continued to create new works for the company, notably *West Side Story Suite* (1995), which featured numbers from the stage musical adapted for ballet dancers, and *Brandenburg* (1997), his last new work.

Rodbell, Martin, American biochemist (b. Dec. 1, 1925, Baltimore, Md.—d. Dec. 7, 1998, Chapel Hill, N.C.), was corecipient (with Alfred G. Gilman) of the 1994 Nobel Prize for Physiology or Medicine for discovering that certain proteins—the so-called G proteins—play a crucial role in cell communication. The son of a grocer, Rodbell set out to fulfill his father's dream that he become a doctor, but he soon found that a career in the biological sciences was his true calling. After service in the Pacific as a U.S. Navy radio operator, which interrupted his undergraduate education, he earned a B.A. (1949) from Johns Hopkins University, Baltimore, and a Ph.D. (1954) in biochemistry from the University of Washington. As a researcher at the National Institutes of Health in Bethesda, Md., for nearly four decades, Rodbell investigated the effects of hormones on cells, especially fat cells. It was in the 1960s, after hearing a lecture by another future Nobel laureate, Earl W. Sutherland, Jr., about the latter's studies of the signaling action of hormones, that Rodbell began to elucidate the process of signal transduction—that is, how chemical messages from outside a cell are transmitted across the cell membrane to the interior. He showed that previously unknown molecules, which proved to be proteins, function in relaying chemical signals from the exterior to the interior. Because these proteins are activated by the energy-rich molecules guanosine diphosphate (GDP) and guanosine triphosphate (GTP), they were designated G proteins by Gilman and his associates. From 1985 until his retirement in 1994, Rodbell continued his work on signal transduction at the National Institute of Environmental Health Sciences, Research Triangle Park, N.C.

Rogers, Roy (LEONARD FRANKLIN SLYE), American cowboy actor-singer (b. Nov. 5, 1911/12, Cincinnati, Ohio—d. July 6, 1998, Apple Valley, Calif.), starred in some 90 motion pictures and over 100 episodes of a weekly television show from the late 1930s to the mid-1950s and reigned as king of the cowboys. The quintessential "good guy in a white hat," he subdued villains by shooting the guns from their hands instead of trying to kill them. During his childhood Rogers took up singing, guitar playing, and square-dance calling. He worked as a fruit picker in California and as a cowhand in New Mexico during the Depression, and, at the same time, he

and his cousin Stanley Slye began performing as the Slye Brothers. Rogers made radio and personal appearances with a succession of groups before helping form the Pioneer Trio, which, because of a radio announcer's mistake, became Sons of the Pioneers. They recorded such top hits as "Tumbling Tumbleweeds," their theme song, and "Cool Water"; were said to have put the "western" in country-and-western music; and by 1935 were appearing in motion pictures. Rogers was given his first starring role in the 1938 film *Under Western Stars,* which also featured Trigger, the horse that would be his costar until 1965, when Trigger died. Another favourite costar was his sidekick George ("Gabby") Hayes, who joined Rogers in *Southward Ho!* (1939). For *The Cowboy and the Senorita* (1944), Rogers was teamed with Dale Evans, and, in 1947, 14 months after the death of Rogers's first wife, he and Evans were married. They starred together in a number of films and from 1951 to 1957 in their own television series. At the end of each series episode, they signed off with the song "Happy Trails," which Evans had written and which also became the title of their 1979 autobiography. Rogers and Evans starred in a musical variety show on television in 1962–63 and thereafter made guest appearances on TV specials, series, and talk shows. Rogers also made state fair and rodeo appearances, marketed clothes and toys, ran a restaurant chain, and continued to record. He was elected to the Country Music Hall of Fame in 1988 and in 1991 released the album *Tribute,* which featured both old and new songs and included duets with current recording artists.

Rolle, Esther, American actress whose portrayal of Florida Evans in the 1970s television series "Maude" and "Good Times" brought her national recognition; long a campaigner against racial stereotyping, she temporarily left the cast of "Good Times" to protest the poor example set by her TV son in the series, and in 1990 she was awarded the NAACP Chairman's Civil Rights Leadership Award for her efforts to improve the image of blacks (b. Nov. 8, 1920, Pompano Beach, Fla.—d. Nov. 17, 1998, Los Angeles, Calif.).

Esther Rolle

Ronald, William (WILLIAM RONALD SMITH), Canadian painter (b. Aug. 13, 1926, Stratford, Ont.—d. Feb. 9, 1998, Barrie, Ont.), was the driving force behind the formation in 1953 of Painters Eleven, a group that introduced abstraction to Canadian art. Ronald studied with Jock Macdonald at the Ontario College of Art in 1951 before briefly attending Hans Hofmann's school in New York City the following year. Ronald embraced the contemporary, international style of Abstract Expressionism, and his monumental canvases were a striking departure from the then-prevailing approach of the Group of Seven, who painted folkloric subjects featuring Canadian themes in an earnest, traditional manner. Originally based in Toronto, Ronald visited New York City frequently before moving there in 1955. Several of his works were shown there in the Kootz Gallery, and others were purchased by the Guggenheim Museum in New York City and the Art Institute of Chicago. After a decade in New York City, he returned to Toronto. During a period of relative artistic inactivity, Ronald developed a flamboyant public persona and worked as an arts broadcaster on television and radio. He resumed painting in the early 1970s on a prolific scale, partly to fund his lavish lifestyle, but his extravagant self-hyped works of this period, featuring an increasing preoccupation with Action painting, did not enhance his reputation. Ronald's works from the middle and late 1950s were considered his most significant—large, ambitious panels of great spontaneity and exuberance, showing the influence of Willem de Kooning but featuring bold central images.

Rothermere of Hemsted, Vere Harold Esmond Harmsworth, 3rd Viscount, British media mogul (b. Aug. 27, 1925, London, Eng.—d. Sept. 1, 1998, London), was one of Great Britain's last press barons; he orchestrated a series of bold moves that revived his family's Associated Newspapers and made the company's flagship, the *Daily Mail,* a must read. After undistinguished academic and military careers, Vere Harmsworth joined (1951) the promotional department at Associated Newspapers. Once a dominating presence among British dailies, the company had already begun to lose money when he was made vice-chairman in 1963. He assumed control of his father's newspaper empire in 1970, when the elder Harmsworth began suffering with Alzheimer's disease. Nicknamed "Mere Vere," he quickly proved otherwise, with a number of daring and decisive moves. He closed down the *Daily Sketch* and changed the *Daily Mail* into a tabloid aimed at young professional women and the growing middle class. Within a year, circulation climbed, eventually surpassing the competition and forcing the rival *Express* to adopt a similar format. While other newspapers underwent cutbacks and layoffs, Rothermere—he succeeded his father as the 3rd Viscount Rothermere in 1978—hired more reporters and invested heavily in his papers. In 1982 he launched *Mail on Sunday* and four years later took control of the *London Evening Standard.* Rothermere exhibited an uncanny grasp of the newspaper market. When his monopoly of evening dailies was threatened in 1987 by Robert Maxwell, he revived the defunct *Evening News* and lowered its price until Maxwell's paper was forced to close. By the mid-1990s, Associated Newspapers' holdings were valued at $1.7 billion. Rothermere also headed the parent corporation, Daily Mail and General Trust PLC, which held educational publications and radio stations, among other interests.

Rowland, Roland Walter (ROLAND WALTER FUHRHOP; "TINY"), British business tycoon (b. Nov. 27, 1917, Belgaum, India—d. July 24, 1998, London, Eng.), was labeled "the unacceptable face of capitalism" by British Prime Minister Edward Heath in 1972, owing to his flamboyance and aggressive business practices. To other observers it seemed that in his 33 years as head of the Lonrho international conglomerate, the charming but contentious Rowland enjoyed making enemies as much as making money. Roland Fuhrhop was born to a German father and Dutch-Anglo

mother in a British internment camp in India during World War I and was thus guaranteed British citizenship. The family moved to England from Hamburg, Ger., in 1934, and during World War II Rowland (who by then had taken his uncle's surname) joined the Royal Army Medical Corps. He refused an officer's commission, reportedly out of reluctance to fight against his brother, who had enlisted in the German Army. Rowland later joined his parents in a British internment camp. After the war Rowland, disillusioned with Britain, moved to Southern Rhodesia (now Zimbabwe) and in 1961 took control of the London and Rhodesian Mining and Land Company (Lonrho). Although Rowland led Lonrho to its greatest strength in the 1960s, not all his financial dreams for Africa were realized, and in the early '70s he faced a series of boardroom battles to have him ousted from the company. In 1981 he bought the British newspaper *The Observer*, often using it as a bully pulpit in his long feud with his Egyptian-born rival, Mohammed al-Fayed, over ownership of Harrods department store, which Fayed purchased in 1985. Meanwhile, Lonrho spun increasingly out of Rowland's control, and in 1995 he retired after he was removed as its head.

Rybakov, Anatoly Naumovich, Russian author who was an acclaimed novelist and children's writer in the Soviet Union for many years before gaining international recognition when his long-suppressed semiautobiographical novel on the hardships of life under Joseph Stalin, *Deti Arbata* (*Children of the Arbat,* 1988), was finally published in 1987. With *Strakh* (1990; *Fear,* 1992) and *Prakh i pepel* (1996; *Dust and Ashes,* 1996), he expanded the novel into an Arbat trilogy (b. Jan. 1 [Jan. 14, New Style], 1911, Chernigov, Ukraine, Russian Empire [now Chernihiv, Ukraine]—d. Dec. 23, 1998, New York, N.Y.).

Rysanek, Leonie, Austrian operatic soprano whose nearly 50-year career, with over 2,100 performances, was distinguished by notable portrayals of Richard Strauss and Richard Wagner heroines; at one performance the applause lasted throughout an entire intermission (b. Nov. 14, 1926, Vienna, Austria—d. March 7, 1998, Vienna).

Sainsbury of Drury Lane, Alan John Sainsbury, Baron, British grocer who changed British food-shopping habits when he built the grocery business begun by his grandparents into a chain of supermarkets modeled on large American self-service stores; he served as chairman of Sainsbury's from 1956 to 1967 and president from 1967 to 1998 (b. Aug. 13, 1902, London, Eng.—d. Oct. 21, 1998, Toppesfield, Essex, Eng.).

Sanford, Terry, American politician who, as governor of North Carolina (1961–65), promoted racial equality at a time when it was unpopular to do so; he made unsuccessful attempts to be the Democratic Party's presidential nominee in 1972 and 1976 and served as a U.S. senator from 1986 to 1992 (b. Aug. 20, 1917, Laurinberg, N.C.—d. April 18, 1998, Durham, N.C.).

Sata, Ineko (SATA INO), Japanese writer and feminist whose semiautobiographical works reflected her concern with class struggle; she insisted on forming her own opinions and held fast to them, which twice led to her expulsion from the Japanese Communist Party (b. June 1, 1904, Nagasaki, Japan—d. Oct. 12, 1998, Tokyo, Japan).

Sayre, Anne Colquhoun, American writer whose book *Rosalind Franklin and DNA* (1975) helped reveal sexism in the scientific community and led to the acknowledgment of Franklin's contribution to the discovery of the structure of DNA (b. April 10, 1923, Milwaukee, Wis.—d. March 13, 1998, Bridgewater, N.J.).

Schnittke, Alfred, Russian composer (b. Nov. 24, 1934, Engels, Volga German Autonomous S.S.R. [now in Saratov oblast, Russia]—d. Aug. 3, 1998,

Hamburg, Ger.), created serious, dark-toned musical works characterized by abrupt juxtapositions of radically different, often contradictory, styles, an approach that came to be known as "polystylism." Schnittke's father was a Jewish journalist who had been born in Germany but was of Latvian descent, and his mother was a Catholic of German ancestry; he found inspiration for his music in his German origins and in his homeland. From 1946 to 1948 the family lived in Vienna, where Schnittke learned to play piano and studied music theory. His studies were completed at the Moscow Conservatory, where he later taught composition part-time until 1972. Like most Soviet composers, Schnittke was required to produce many works in easily digestible Socialist Realist style, particularly film scores, of which he wrote more than 60 between 1961 and 1984. His more demanding, experimental works were viewed with official disfavour, although Schnittke was spared the persecutions typical of the earlier, Stalinist era. His compositions embraced a wide range of genres and included symphonies, concertos, and choral and chamber music. His best-known works include the *Concerto Grosso No. 1*

Anatoly Rybakov

and the *Fourth Violin Concerto,* for which the violinist was instructed to mime the cadenza rather than actually play it. Like his great predecessor Dmitry Shostakovich, Schnittke intermingled disjointed elements within a single work, but his combinations were far more jarring—an offhand Beethoven quotation, a deconstructed folk song, fragments of medieval chant, and passages of ferociously dense, dissonant serialism might appear within the space of a few minutes. Virtually unknown outside the Soviet bloc until the mid-1980s, Schnittke rather suddenly acquired a large following in the West through the efforts of a number of prominent Russian musicians, including Gennady Rozhdestvensky, Gidon Kremer, Yury Bashmet, and Mstislav Rostropovich. Schnittke suffered a debilitating stroke in 1985 and endured ill health for the rest of his life.

Schreiber, R(aemer) E(dgar), American experimental physicist who during World War II was one of the scientists who worked on the Manhattan Project in Los Alamos, N.M., to develop the first atomic bombs and then helped assemble the two bombs that were dropped on Japan; after the war he stayed on at Los Alamos in the weapons division and helped develop the

hydrogen bomb, from 1955 led the nuclear rocket development division, and from 1972 to 1974 served as the laboratory's deputy director (b. Nov. 11, 1910, McMinnville, Ore.—d. Dec. 24, 1998, Los Alamos).

Schultz, Theodore William, American economist (b. April 30, 1902, near Arlington, S.D.—d. Feb. 26, 1998, Evanston, Ill.), popularized the study of agricultural economics, especially as it applied to less-developed nations. Using classical methods, he showed how farmers played an important part in the industrialization of their nation. He was best known for his recognition of "human capital"—education, incentive, and personal talent—as a leading factor of economic production, and he developed a theory of investment based upon it. In this regard he was viewed as a bridge to modern economists such as Gary S. Becker, who studied human behaviour. Owing to a labour shortage during World War I, Schultz never attended high school but matriculated at South Dakota State College (now University) in 1924. After receiving bachelor's and master's degrees in 1927, he attended the University of Wisconsin (Ph.D., 1930) under noted labour economist John R. Commons. After graduation Schultz joined Iowa State College (now University) in the department of economics, which he transformed into one of national renown, recruiting such talented faculty as John Kenneth Galbraith. During his tenure he successfully prevented the college administration from censoring a colleague's paper that angered a major business interest, but the bitter row prompted his decision to leave in 1943 for the University of Chicago. As head (1946–61) of Chicago's vaunted economics department, he unified the disparate group even as he simultaneously encouraged independent thinking. While on faculty he toured many agriculture-based countries and published *Agriculture in an Unstable Economy* (1945), *The Economic Value of Education* (1963), and *Economic Growth and Agriculture* (1968). In 1979 he was awarded the Nobel Prize for Economics, which he shared with Sir Arthur Lewis of Great Britain. Schultz remained active in academic life for two decades after his formal retirement in 1970. He continued to write books, among them *Investment in Human Capital* (1971) and *Investing in People: The Economics of Population Quality* (1981).

Schumann, Maurice, French politician and writer who was the inspirational radio spokesman of Gen. Charles de Gaulle and the French Resistance in broadcasts to Nazi-ruled France from London during World War II; he later served as a political party leader, foreign minister, and senator, and in 1974 he became a member of the French Academy (b. April 10, 1911, Paris, France—d. Feb. 10, 1998, Paris).

Seraphim, Archbishop (VISSARION TIKAS), Greek religious leader (b. Aug. 15, 1913, Artesianon, Greece—d. April 10, 1998, Athens, Greece), served as the head of the Orthodox Church in Greece from 1974. Conservative and anti-intellectual, he had a common touch that brought him great popularity. After receiving a degree in theology from the University of Athens in 1941, Seraphim was ordained a priest in 1942 and became active in the Greek resistance to the Nazi occupation. He established soup kitchens and or-

phanages and later fought with the Greek Democratic National Army resistance group. Seraphim became bishop of Arta in 1949 and of Ioannina in 1958. In the latter post he took up the cause of the ethnic Greek minority in southern Albania, whose religious practices were being suppressed by the government. He also supported guerrillas fighting for the union of Cyprus with Greece in the 1950s. Even though Seraphim was chosen archbishop in a controversial election during the final months of the military dictatorship in Greece, he was able to keep his post when democracy was restored. In the years that followed, he clashed with government leaders in his attempt to resist changes in society brought about by a lessening of the church's influence. Though his efforts were generally futile, he achieved a notable victory in the mid-1980s when he helped prevent the government from expropriating church landholdings. Seraphim's last years were marked by his opposition to Roman Catholic missionary activities in Eastern Europe and to other Orthodox leaders and by his resistance to his bishops' requests for his resignation.

Sharawi, Sheikh Muhammad Mutwali ash-, Egyptian Islamic cleric who delivered his religious messages by means of audiocassettes, videotapes, books, and especially his popular weekly lectures on television; from 1976 to 1978 he served as the country's minister of religious endowments (b. April 15, 1911, Daqadus, Egypt—d. June 17, 1998, al-Jizah, Egypt).

Sharif-Emami, Jafar, Iranian politician and close confidant of Mohammad Reza Shah Pahlavi who twice (1960–61 and August–November 1978) served as prime minister; during his second term, policies instituted to mollify the increasingly powerful Islamic fundamentalists failed, and after the shah's downfall in early 1979, Sharif-Emami fled to New York (b. Sept. 8, 1910, Tehran, Iran—d. June 16, 1998, New York, N.Y.).

Alan Shepard, Jr.

NASA/AP/WIDE WORLD

Shepard, Jr., Alan, American astronaut (b. Nov. 18, 1923, East Derry, N.H.—d. July 21, 1998, Monterey, Calif.), was the first American in space, riding in *Freedom 7,* the Mercury capsule, on May 5, 1961; his 15-minute suborbital flight included 5 minutes spent beyond Earth's atmosphere at a peak altitude of about 185 km (115 mi). He was also the fifth person to walk on the Moon as commander of Apollo 14 (Jan. 31–Feb. 9, 1971). After graduating (1944) from the U.S. Naval Academy, Annapolis, Md., Shepard began his military career aboard a destroyer in the Pacific during World War II. He earned his naval aviator wings in 1947, qualified as a test pilot in 1951, and ex-

perimented with high-altitude aircraft, in-flight fueling systems, and landings on angled carrier decks. In April 1959 Shepard was chosen by the newly created NASA as one of the seven top test pilots (dubbed "the Magnificent Seven") for the Mercury space project. He was selected from this original group of astronauts for the first American manned space mission. Although Shepard's flight came 23 days after the launch of Soviet cosmonaut Yury Gagarin, the first human to travel in space, it energized U.S. space efforts and made Shepard a national hero. He was later grounded due to an inner-ear problem until corrective surgery allowed him to return to full flight status in 1969. Two years later, at the age of 47, he embarked for the lunar highlands near the Fra Mauro crater on Apollo 14. Near the end of his Moon walk, Shepard—an avid golfer—swung at two golf balls with a makeshift six-iron club as a playful demonstration for live television cameras of the weak lunar gravity. After retiring from NASA and the navy in 1974 as a rear admiral, he went into private business. Shepard received numerous awards, including the NASA Distinguished Service Medal and the Congressional Medal of Honor. He also coauthored with fellow Mercury astronaut Deke Slayton, *Moon Shot: The Inside Story of America's Race to the Moon* (1994).

Sherer, Rabbi Moshe, American Orthodox Jewish leader who aided the right wing of Orthodox Judaism by helping build the Agudath Israel of America organization from a small group into an influential force (b. June 8, 1921, Brooklyn, N.Y.—d. May 17, 1998, Manhattan, N.Y.).

Shevchenko, Arkady Nikolayevich, Ukrainian-born Soviet diplomat who, as a UN undersecretary general, began passing secrets to the CIA in the 1970s and in 1978 sought asylum in the U.S., the highest-ranking Soviet official to have defected; his memoirs, *Breaking with Moscow* (1985), became a best-seller (b. Oct. 11, 1930, Horlivka, Ukraine—d. Feb. 28, 1998, Bethesda, Md.).

Shima, Hideo, Japanese engineer (b. May 20, 1901, Osaka, Japan—d. March 18/19, 1998, Tokyo, Japan), designed and supervised the construction of the world's first high-speed train. Shima, the son of a prominent railway engineer, graduated from Tokyo Imperial University in 1925. He joined the then state-run Japanese National Railways to design steam locomotives. By 1948 he had worked his way up to head of the rolling stock department, but he resigned three years later after taking responsibility for a fire at Yokohama station that killed more than 100 people. He worked for a time at Sumimoto Metal Industries but was asked by the president of the national railways to return as chief engineer. He soon began designs for the Shinkansen ("new trunk line"), a 515-km (320-mi)-long high-speed train line between Tokyo and Osaka. Shima oversaw the project until 1963, when he was forced to resign owing to escalating production costs. (The mostly straight tracks required construction of 3,000 bridges and 67 tunnels.) The project was completed just in time for the 1964 Summer Olympic Games in Tokyo, but Shima was not invited to the opening ceremony. The Shinkansen was the world's first train to reach top speeds above 209 km/h (130 mph). This bullet train, named after its aerodynamically shaped head, featured wide-gauge tracks, air suspension, and individually motorized cars instead of a sole front engine. Because the tracks were not shared with other trains, safety and punctuality were unprecedented. Despite the costs, Shinkansen rapidly expanded in the following years, and the train became a symbol of Japan's postwar economic prowess. After his resignation Shima continued to advise railway officials, especially on safety issues. In 1969 he began a new career as head of the National Space Development Agency. That same year he became the first non-Westerner to receive the James Watt International Medal of Great Britain's Institution of Mechanical Engineers. In Japan he was awarded the Order of Cultural Merit in 1994.

Shoemaker, Edwin J., American engineer and businessman whose invention of the recliner made the La-Z-Boy furniture company one of the most successful in the U.S. (b. 1907?, Monroe county, Mich.—d. March 15, 1998, Sun City, Ariz.).

Sinatra, Francis Albert ("FRANK"), American singer and actor (b. Dec. 12, 1915, Hoboken, N.J.—d. May 14, 1998, Los Angeles, Calif.), became the idol of squealing teenagers in the late 1930s and went on to serve as an object of fascination for several generations over a period of more than six decades. Known variously as "the Voice," "Ol' Blue Eyes," and "Chairman of the Board," he was celebrated nearly as much for his offstage activities—not only his brawling, womanizing (and four wives: Nancy Barbato, Ava Gardner, Mia Farrow, and Barbara Marx), and hobnobbing with both mobsters and prominent politicians but also his acts of extreme generosity—as for his performances on over 200 albums, in some 60 films, and in countless nightclub and concert appearances. A number of songs, among them "One for My Baby," "My Way," "Come Fly with Me," "New York, New York," and "My Kind of Town," were considered his signatures. Sinatra's start in show business began in the mid-1930s with a win for the Hoboken Four (Sinatra and three friends) on the "Major Bowes Amateur Hour" radio program. A period of touring followed, and in 1939 he became a vocalist with Harry James's band. A move to Tommy Dorsey's band came a few months later, and in 1942, having become the idol of bobby-soxers, Sinatra went solo. Concert and radio performances and appearances in such films as *Anchors Aweigh* (1945), *Take Me Out to the Ball Game* (1949), and *On the Town* (1949) enhanced his popularity. In the early 1950s, however, Sinatra's public image suffered because of his love affair with Gardner while he was still married to his first wife. Health problems followed, and his career seemed to be over. Nonetheless, he persevered and was given the role of Maggio in *From Here to Eternity* (1953), and his performance won him an Academy Award for best supporting actor. He followed that with strong performances in such films as *Suddenly* (1954); *Guys and Dolls* (1955); *The Man with the Golden Arm* (1955), for which he received an Academy Award nomination for best actor; *Some Came Running* (1959); and *The Manchurian Candidate* (1962). Lighter in tone were the motion pictures he made with his group of friends known as the Rat Pack (Dean Martin, Sammy Davis, Jr., Peter Lawford, Shirley MacLaine, and Joey Bishop). Sinatra's recording career also was reborn, especially when he began to take advantage of the long-playing record; such albums as *In the Wee Small Hours* (1955), *Only the Lonely* (1958), and *Come Dance with Me* (1959) were each built around a single theme or mood and earned him credit for the invention of the concept album. His most successful single came in 1966 with "Strangers in the Night." Sinatra announced his retirement in 1971, but in 1973 that retirement ended with the television special "Ol' Blue Eyes Is Back." He continued to record and tour until 1995. Among the most prestigious of his numerous awards were the Jean Hersholt Humanitarian Award (1971), a Grammy legend award (1994), and the Congressional Gold Medal (1997).

Skilling, John, American structural and civil engineer whose firm, Skilling Ward Magnusson Barkshire, designed over 1,000 buildings in 36 states and 27 countries; among his best-known work was the 110-story twin towers of the World Trade Center in New York City (b. Oct. 8, 1921, Los Angeles, Calif.—d. March 5, 1998, Seattle, Wash.).

Smith, Robert E. ("BUFFALO BOB"), American television personality (b. Nov. 27, 1917, Buffalo, N.Y.—d. July 30, 1998, Hendersonville, N.C.), was the creator and host of "The Howdy Doody Show" (1947–60), the theme song of which became an anthem for baby boomers who tuned in to Buffalo Bob and his wooden sidekick Howdy Doody for over 2,500 live broadcasts. Born Robert Schmidt, he learned to play piano and organ at an

Frank Sinatra

Sobek, Joseph George, American sportsman who, unhappy with the indoor racquet sports then available, invented racquetball in 1950; by the late 1990s there were 8.5 million racquetball players in 91 countries (b. April 5, 1918, Greenwich, Conn.—d. March 27, 1998, Greenwich).

Soper, The Rev. Donald Oliver Soper, Baron, British Methodist minister who preached in the open air every week for decades at Speaker's Corner in London's Hyde Park and at Tower Hill. An articulate, quick-witted orator, Soper made good use of his skills, and his denunciation of such wide-ranging enemies as alcohol, gambling, poverty, war, apartheid, blood sports, and capitalism, combined with his passionate support for such controversial issues as homosexual rights and the ordination of women, earned him throngs of listeners and, in 1965, a life peerage (b. Jan. 31, 1903, London, Eng.—d. Dec. 22, 1998, London).

Spilhaus, Athelstan Frederick, South African-born geophysicist who counted among his designs a device to measure deep-sea temperatures, a plan for covered walkways and tunnels for protection against severe weather, and some 3,000 varieties of toys; in 1954 he became the first U.S. ambassador to UNESCO (b. Nov. 25, 1911, Cape Town, S.Af.—d. March 29/30, 1998, Middleburg, Va.).

Spock, Benjamin, American pediatrician (b. May 2, 1903, New Haven, Conn.—d. March 15, 1998, La Jolla, Calif.), was the most influential child-care authority of the 20th century. His book *Baby and Child Care* sold over 50 million copies worldwide and was translated into 42 languages. Spock attended Yale University, where he rowed on a crew team that won an Olympic gold medal in 1924. He graduated from medical school at Columbia University, New York City, in 1929, and following his internship and residency, he entered (1933) private practice in New York City and taught pediatrics at Cornell University, Ithaca, N.Y. After service in the U.S. Navy during World War II, Spock accepted a teaching post at the University of Minnesota; he also taught at the University of Pittsburgh, Pa., and at Case Western Reserve University, Cleveland, Ohio. The first edition of his most famous work, *The Common Sense Book of Baby and Child Care,* was published in 1946. In his work Spock eschewed the strict discipline and emotional reserve promoted by other child-care experts, advising instead that parents allow their children to develop in an atmosphere of understanding and love. Although Spock was accused by some of having fostered the permissiveness and self-indulgence of the 1960s and '70s, his views were nevertheless regarded as mainstream by the time of his death. In addition to his status as a pediatrician, Spock became a leading figure in the anti-Vietnam War movement and was arrested several times for

early age and at 15 sang regularly on a local radio station. In 1947, as Robert Smith, he worked for the National Broadcasting Co. as a disc jockey on WEAF radio in New York City and as host for a children's radio quiz show, "The Triple B Ranch," on which Howdy was first introduced as the country bumpkin Elmer, whose catchphrase was "howdy doody." When the act moved to TV later that year, the simple wooden puppet was transformed into a grinning, freckled, red-haired, 69-cm (27-in)-tall marionette that sported blue jeans, a checked shirt, and a bandana around his neck. What began as a weekly program was soon expanded to a Monday–Friday format. Buffalo Bob opened every show with the question he posed to the studio audience he called the Peanut Gallery, "Say, kids, what time is it?"—and was met with a resounding "It's Howdy Doody time!" Buffalo Bob, in his fringed cowboy outfit, starred with Howdy and other residents of Doodyville, Texas, including Clarabell the Clown and Flubadub. When the show ended in 1960, Smith bought several businesses in Florida. He and Howdy made a comeback in 1970, however, when nostalgic students at the University of Pennsylvania invited him to reprise the program's 10th anniversary show. Following that appearance, Smith took his show on the road for another six years.

Smith, Thomas John ("T.J."), Australian racehorse trainer who was often considered to have been the country's most successful; among his credits were 34 Sydney trainers' premierships—33 of them successive—and two Melbourne Cups, four Caulfield Cups, six Golden Slippers, and seven Cox Plates (b. Sept. 3, 1918, near

Braidwood, N.S.W., Australia—d. Sept. 2, 1998, Sydney, Australia).

Smythe, Reg (REGINALD SMYTH), British cartoonist who created the comic strip "Andy Capp," reportedly basing its working-class subject on his father; the strip was syndicated internationally to hundreds of newspapers (b. July 10, 1917, Hartlepool, Eng.—d. June 13, 1998, Hartlepool).

Benjamin Spock

his participation in demonstrations. In 1972 he ran for the U.S. presidency as a candidate of the People's Party, a coalition of left-wing groups. Spock continued to engage in leftist activism in the 1980s, mainly protesting against nuclear weapons.

Squires, Dorothy (EDNA MAY SQUIRES), British popular singer who was considered one of the best in the 1940s and early '50s; a series of emotional and legal setbacks following her divorce from actor Roger Moore in the late 1960s left her destitute (b. March 25, 1915, Pontyberem, Wales—d. April 14, 1998, Llwynpia, Wales).

Stangerup, Henrik, Danish writer and film director whose internationally known works, influenced by the writings of Søren Kierkegaard, revealed his feelings of alienation and contempt for societal attitudes; *Manden der ville være skyldig* (1975; *The Man Who Wanted to Be Guilty,* 1983) and *Forføreren eller det er svært at dø i Dieppe* (1985; *The Seducer: It Is Hard to Die in Dieppe,* 1988) are among his most notable works (b. Sept. 1, 1937, Copenhagen, Den.—d. July 4, 1998, Langebaek, Den.).

Stans, Maurice Hubert, American accountant and politician whose fund-raising successes gained him the post of secretary of commerce during Pres. Richard M. Nixon's first term but led to his disgrace during the Watergate scandal (b. March 22, 1908, Shakopee, Minn.—d. April 14, 1998, Pasadena, Calif.).

Starovoytova, Galina Vasilyevna, Russian politician and member of the reformist party Democratic Russia who was an outspoken advocate of liberalization, tolerance, and reform and was intending to run for president; her honesty was considered a rarity in Russian politics, and her assassination was widely mourned (b. May 17, 1946, Chelyabinsk, U.S.S.R.—d. Nov. 20, 1998, St. Petersburg, Russia).

Stephens, Woodford Cefis ("WOODY"), American horse trainer (b. Sept. 1, 1913, Stanton, Ky.—d. Aug. 22, 1998, Miami Lakes, Fla.), was one of the most accomplished and respected trainers in thoroughbred racing in the United States and was best known for winning the Belmont Stakes five consecutive times, beginning in 1982 with the horse Conquistador Cielo and ending in 1986 with Danzig Connection. His other Belmont winners were Caveat (1983), Swale (1984), and Creme Fraiche (1985). Throughout his seven-decade-long career in racing, Stephens developed 11 national champions, including Swale, who captured both the 1984 Kentucky Derby and the Belmont Stakes. Born the son of a sharecropper, Stephens was raised in humble circumstances in Kentucky bluegrass country. He began his career in racing by breaking yearlings when he was 13. At age 16 he was apprenticed as a jockey and moved to New York. Astride a horse named Directly, he won his first race on Jan. 15, 1931, at Hialeah Park in Hialeah, Fla. A weight gain, however, foiled his career plans, and Stephens turned from riding horses to training them. Success as a trainer was achieved in 1940 when Bronze Bugle won at Keeneland Race Course in Kentucky. Stephens's first classic winner was Blue Man, who won the Preakness Stakes in 1952. Although he had a solid reputation as a trainer and was inducted (1976) into the National Museum of Racing and Hall of Fame, it was not until the 1980s—when he saddled some of his best runners—that his fame skyrocketed. In 1983 he received the Eclipse Award for outstanding trainer. Although his years of success made Stephens a wealthy man, he lived for his work and did not retire until 1997.

Stevens, Roger Lacey, American theatrical producer of such Broadway successes as *West Side Story, Cat on a Hot Tin Roof,* and *A Man for All Seasons* and fund-raiser who helped create and went on to lead Washington's John F. Kennedy Center for the Performing Arts (b. March 12, 1910, Detroit, Mich.—d. Feb. 2, 1998, Washington, D.C.).

Stickney, Dorothy Hayes, American actress who usually played eccentric character roles, but from 1939 to 1944 and again in 1947 starred as the mother—a role she created—in *Life with Father,* Broadway's longest-running nonmusical show; her costar was her husband, Howard Lindsay, who was also coauthor of the play (b. June 21, 1900?, Dickinson, N.D.—d. June 2, 1998, New York, N.Y.).

Strigler, Mordechai, Polish-born editor, poet, and essayist whose prolific writings included accounts of his experiences during the Holocaust; from 1987 he also served as the editor of the Yiddish-language socialist newspaper *Forverts* ("Forward") (b. Sept. 18, 1921/23?, Zamosc, Pol.—d. May 10, 1998, New York, N.Y.).

Susak, Gojko, Croatian government official who was instrumental in the attainment and preservation of Croatia's independence and from 1991 served as the country's defense minister (b. April 16, 1945, Siroki Brijeg, western Herzegovina, Yugoslavia—d. May 3/4, 1998, Zagreb, Croatia).

Suzuki, Shinichi, Japanese violinist and teacher (b. Oct. 17/18, 1898, Nagoya, Japan—d. Jan. 26, 1998, Matsumoto, Japan), devised a method by which millions of young children worldwide learned to play the violin. Instead of trying to teach them to read music, he emphasized listening, imitation, and repetition, theorizing that children could learn to play music the same way they learn language. Suzuki, the son of a violin maker, taught himself to play that instrument after hearing a recording by Mischa Elman. He studied commerce in a vocational school and after graduation went (1921) to Germany to further his musical studies. During much of his time there, Albert Einstein was one of his guardians. When he returned (1928) to Japan, Suzuki, with his three younger brothers, formed the Suzuki Quartet. Shortly thereafter, he became president of the Teikoku Music School, founded the Tokyo String Orchestra, and joined the faculty of the Imperial Music School. After World War II ended, Suzuki was invited to assist in the founding of a school in Matsumoto. He spent the remainder of his career there and more fully developed his theories regarding music education. By the 1950s his students were giving annual concerts, at which some 3,000 young students would perform together as a group. The Suzuki method gained attention in the U.S. when a group of 10 Japanese youngsters played their violins at music teachers' conferences in 1964, and teachers in Great Britain were adopting the method by the 1970s. To aid in the training of teachers in Europe, the European Suzuki Association was organized in the late '70s, and in 1983 the International Suzuki Association was created so that Suzuki could maintain contact with his method's teachers. By the late 1990s the number of those teachers had grown to over 8,000, and some 400,000 students in 34 countries were receiving instruction. Among Suzuki's numerous honours was his appointment to the Order of the National Treasure by the emperor of Japan.

Sviridov, Georgy Vasilyevich, Russian composer and pianist (b. Dec. 16, 1915, Fatezh, Russia—d. Jan. 5, 1998, Moscow, Russia), wrote music that paid tribute to Russian literature and folk traditions, achieving acclaim within the Soviet cultural system. Sviridov studied music under Dmitry Shostakovich at the Leningrad Conservatory, graduating in 1941. His talent was soon recognized, and his *Piano Trio* was awarded the Stalin Prize in 1945. Though Sviridov composed some additional chamber and orchestral music, vocal works were his greater contribution. They ranged from grandiose oratorios to simpler songs and, in later years, suites to accompany films. Sviridov's career blended a successful ascent in the Soviet musical hierarchy with his interest in Russian traditions and nationalism. Often he incorporated folk melodies into his pieces, arranging them according to 20th-century musical techniques. He also showed an interest in literature, setting to music the novels and poems of Russian authors such as Aleksandr Pushkin, Boris Pasternak, and

Sergey Yesenin. In 1959 Sviridov based his *Oratorio pathetique* on Vladimir Mayakovsky's tribute to Vladimir Lenin and was duly honoured with the Lenin Prize in 1960. Sviridov's rise within the official Soviet musical world soon followed. From 1962 to 1974 he served as secretary of the U.S.S.R. Union of Composers. For some of that time—from 1968 to 1973—he was also the secretary of the Russian Federation Composers Union. The much-honoured Sviridov was the recipient of the State Prize of the U.S.S.R. in 1968 for *Kursk Songs,* native folk melodies, and was named a People's Artist of the Russian S.F.S.R. in 1963 and a People's Artist of the U.S.S.R. in 1970. Despite changes in Russia's political leadership, during later years Sviridov's contributions continued to be acknowledged. In December 1997 he was given a prize for merit in culture and the arts by Russian Pres. Boris Yeltsin.

Tabarly, Eric Marcel Guy, French yachtsman who became a national hero when he won the 1964 *Observer* Single-Handed Transatlantic Race (OSTAR) in record time and, in a series of sailboats named *Pen Duick,* went on to win numerous other solo races, including the 1976 OSTAR; he drowned after falling from the original *Pen Duick* (b. July 24, 1931, Nantes, France—d. June 12, 1998, off the coast of Wales).

Taki Abdoulkarim, Mohamed, Comoros politician who from 1996 served as president of the country (b. Feb. 20, 1936, Mbeni, Grande Comore—d. Nov. 6, 1998, Beit Salam, Moroni, Comoros).

Taylor, Telford, American lawyer and writer (b. Feb. 24, 1908, Schenectady, N.Y.—d. May 23, 1998, New York, N.Y.), was best known for his role as the chief prosecutor during the Nürnberg war crime trials following World War II. In that capacity he helped establish the accountability of national leaders for their actions during wartime and the right of the international community to seek justice for crimes against humanity. Taylor graduated from Harvard Law School in 1932 and, after a clerkship with Judge Augustus Hand, served on the staffs of a number of government agencies before becoming (1940) general counsel to the Federal Communications Commission. When the U.S. entered the war, he joined Army Intelligence, eventually working on code breaking in England and attaining the rank of colonel. Taylor gained valuable knowledge of the German military in this assignment, and at the war's end he was asked to serve as an assistant prosecutor at the Nürnberg Trials. He helped ascertain that a standard of moderation prevailed so that the trials did not just become acts of vengeance; gradations of guilt were acknowledged, efforts were made to avoid guilt by association, and civil liberties were protected. After the first trial Taylor was promoted (1946) to brigadier general and made the chief prosecutor of the remaining trials. By the time the trials ended in 1949, nearly 150 Nazis had been convicted. Taylor later worked in the administration of Pres. Harry Truman for over a year during the Korean War and also entered private law practice and taught. He spoke out strongly against the tactics of Sen. Joseph McCarthy during his communist witch-hunts in the 1950s, and was an outspoken opponent of American conduct in the Vietnam War. Among Taylor's books were *Sword and Swastika* (1952), *Grand Inquest: The Story of Congressional Investigations* (1955), *Nuremberg and Vietnam: An American Tragedy* (1970), *Munich: The Price of Peace* (1979), and *The Anatomy of the Nuremberg Trials: A Personal Memoir* (1992).

Tazieff, Haroun, Polish-born French volcanologist whose fascination with volcanoes and knowledge of them, often obtained under extremely harrowing conditions, were enthusiastically shared by the French public through books and, especially, in films on television; he was considered one of the six most popular personalities in France (b. May 11, 1914, Warsaw, Pol.—d. Feb. 2, 1998, Paris, France).

Tennstedt, Klaus, German conductor (b. June 6, 1926, Merseburg, Ger.—d. Jan. 11, 1998, Kiel, Ger.), was known for uncommonly expressive performances of the Romantic and Postromantic repertory. Tennstedt attended the Leipzig (Ger.) Conservatory, where he studied violin, piano, and theory. Though he originally wanted to become a violinist like his father, Tennstedt was thwarted by a small growth on his left hand. He became a singing coach and later a conductor at the Halle Municipal Theatre, which in turn led to appointments in Germany at the opera in Karl-Marx-Stadt in 1954, the Dresden Opera (1958–62), and the Schwerin Orchestra (1962–70). In 1971 his visa was stamped in such a way that Tennstedt was able to defect from East Germany to Stockholm. One year later he was appointed general music director of the Kiel Opera in West Germany. Tennstedt's international career took off in 1974 when the manager of the Toronto Symphony Orchestra heard him conduct Anton Bruckner's *Seventh Symphony* and promptly invited Tennstedt to conduct an all-Beethoven concert in Toronto. That same year Tennstedt conducted the Boston Symphony Orchestra; after rehearsing Bruckner's *Eighth Symphony,* the orchestra spontaneously broke into applause during a coffee break. He soon conducted orchestras throughout the U.S. and Europe, including the Berlin Philharmonic Orchestra and the Orchestre de Paris. In 1976 Tennstedt began his long association with the London Philharmonic Orchestra, and in 1983 he became the ensemble's principal conductor. He conducted a substantial portion of the traditional repertory and was particularly noted for his treatment of Gustav Mahler and Bruckner. He was often praised for his expressive warmth and urgency, though some criticized him for being "inexact." Though a large and imposing figure, Tennstedt was shy and somewhat reluctant to be in the limelight. In 1985 he was diagnosed with cancer, and, having collapsed during a rehearsal in 1987, he relinquished his post at the London Philharmonic. In 1994 Tennstedt received an honorary doctorate from the University of Oxford and made his last public appearance at the university's orchestral rehearsal.

Thompson, Kay (KITTY FINK), American entertainer and writer (b. Nov. 9, 1902?, St. Louis, Mo.—d. July 2, 1998, New York, N.Y.), was a talented musician, singer, songwriter, musical arranger, vocal coach, and actress who also created a series of books about a precocious six-year-old girl named Eloise who called New York City's Plaza Hotel home. The character of Eloise was created when Thompson turned her voice into that of a child to apologize for arriving late for a cabaret act rehearsal. Her co-workers took to the character, and Thompson transformed her Eloise

Morris Udall

routine into a one-woman show at the Plaza in 1954; the book *Eloise: A Book for Precocious Grown-Ups* was published the next year. A record, a doll, clothing, a television special, and three more books—*Eloise in Paris* and *Eloise at Christmastime* (1958), and *Eloise in Moscow* (1959)—followed. Early in Thompson's career she was a pianist with the St. Louis Symphony, and she went on to sing with the Mills Brothers on radio and to arrange music and sing with Fred Waring's band. In 1935 she co-produced her own CBS radio show, "Kay Thompson and Company." In the mid-1940s Thompson became a musical arranger at the MGM film studios and served as vocal coach to Lena Horne and Judy Garland, and she performed (1947–53) in a nightclub act with Andy Williams and his brothers. It was during rehearsals for that act that Eloise sprang to life. Thompson performed in several motion pictures—among them *Manhattan Merry-Go-Round* (1937); *The Ziegfeld Follies* (1946), for which she also was a music arranger and songwriter; and *The Kid from Brooklyn* (1946)—before being cast in her most memorable role, the vivid fashion magazine editor Maggie Prescott, with her dictate to "think pink," in *Funny Face* (1957). Her last film was *Tell Me That You Love Me, Junie Moon* (1970).

Tippett, Sir Michael Kemp, British composer (b. Jan. 2, 1905, London, Eng.—d. Jan. 8, 1998, London), created a unique musical idiom with works over a long career that fused many different styles. Born to an educated but nonmusical family, Tippett decided to become a composer in 1923 despite having had no previous musical training. His studies at the Royal College of Music led to a gradual development from traditional, conservative composition to a personal approach that combined neoclassical counterpoint with echoes of popular music. Tippett's work reflected most of the styles prevalent in 20th-century music but maintained allegiance to none. In particular he rejected the folk song–based English nationalist school identified with Ralph Vaughan Williams. Among his major works were five operas, notably *The Midsummer Marriage* (composed 1946–52, premiered 1955); three large-scale choral works, including the mighty oratorio *A Child of Our Time* (composed 1939–41, premiered 1944); four symphonies; five string quartets; and five piano sonatas. Tippett also wrote the librettos for his operas and choral works. *A Child of Our Time,* which expressed the horrors of a world at war, was his first composition to gain recognition outside of Great Britain and is regarded as his masterpiece. Although by the end of his life he had achieved worldwide renown, Tippett's works were not performed regularly until the 1960s—perhaps being overshadowed by those of Benjamin Britten, the dominant

figure in postwar English music. Tippett was known for his political activism: a leftist and a pacifist, he was imprisoned for three months during World War II because of his status as a conscientious objector. He was knighted in 1966.

Townsend, Robert Chase, American business executive and writer who, as chairman and president of Avis Rent-a-Car from 1962 to 1965, gained the company its first profitability; his book *Up the Organization* (1970) was on the *New York Times* best-seller list for 28 weeks, 7 of them at the number one spot (b. July 30, 1920, Washington, D.C.—d. Jan. 12, 1998, Anguilla, West Indies).

Trease, (Robert) Geoffrey, British writer of more than 100 books, most of them children's historical novels that were translated into some 20 languages; his most notable in that genre was *Cue for Treason* (1940) (b. Aug. 11, 1909, Nottingham, Eng.—d. Jan. 27, 1998, Bath, Eng.).

Turner, Clyde ("BULLDOG"), American football player and coach who was a centre and linebacker for the Chicago Bears for the 13 seasons from 1940 to 1952, during which the team, nicknamed the Monsters of the Midway, won the National Football League championship four times; he was named All-Pro six times and in 1966 was elected to the Pro Football Hall of Fame (b. Nov. 10, 1919, Sweetwater, Texas—d. Oct. 30, 1998, Gatesville, Texas).

Udall, Morris King ("MO"), American politician (b. June 15, 1922, St. John's, Ariz.—d. Dec. 12, 1998, Washington, D.C.), was a liberal Democrat who served in the U.S. House of Representatives for 30 years and in 1976 was runner-up to Jimmy Carter for his party's presidential nomination. An advocate of environmental protection, campaign finance reform, national health insurance, and Food and Drug Administration control of tobacco products, he was also known for his self-deprecating humour and titled his 1988 book *Too Funny to Be President.* During World War II Udall interrupted his education at the University of Arizona to serve in the Army Air Corps, despite the fact that a childhood injury had cost him an eye. For two years he commanded an all-African-American squadron in Louisiana, and the discrimination they encountered proved to be influential in shaping his liberal outlook. Service in the South Pacific followed, and after the war, in 1946, Udall returned to the university. He was on the basketball team there and went on to play professionally for the Denver Nuggets. In 1949, however, Udall received an LL.B. with distinction, was admitted to the bar, and quit basketball to enter law practice with his brother Stewart, who later (1955) was elected to the U.S. House of Representatives. When his brother resigned (1961) to become secretary of the interior under Pres. John F. Kennedy, Udall won a special election and took his brother's seat in Congress. He immediately disclosed details of his finances and began pushing for legislation requiring reform of election financing, which eventually resulted in the passage of the Federal Election Campaign Act of 1971. Udall also succeeded (1977) in passing a law regulating strip mining, and in the 1980s he helped prevent oil drilling in Alaska in the Arctic National Wildlife Refuge. Udall was diagnosed with Parkinson's disease in 1980 but was able to continue serving in the House until 1991, when he resigned after suffering a fall in his home. In 1992 Congress established the Morris K. Udall Foundation, which promoted environmental education and mediation.

Ulanova, Galina Sergeyevna, Russian ballet dancer (b. Jan. 8, 1910, St. Petersburg, Russia—d. March 21, 1998, Moscow, Russia), was considered one of the greatest ballerinas of the 20th century. She possessed an excellent technique, a lyrical grace, and the ability to submerge herself in the characters she portrayed and communicate their humanity to audiences. Ulanova, the daughter of dancers, was taught first by her mother and afterward at the Leningrad State School of

Choreography, under Agrippina Vaganova. Graduating in 1928, she joined the Mariinsky Ballet (called the Kirov Ballet from 1935 to 1991) and soon began dancing the leading roles in such classic ballets as *Swan Lake, The Sleeping Beauty,* and *Giselle.* In 1934 Ulanova created the role that sparked her rise to fame—the tragic Maria in *The Fountain of Bakhchisaray.* In 1940 she starred as Juliet in Leonid Lavrovsky's *Romeo and Juliet.* It featured specially commissioned music by Sergey Prokofiev, who later wrote the score for *Cinderella* especially for her. Ulanova was transferred to Moscow's Bolshoi Ballet in 1944 and thereafter was associated with that company. Her first notable appearance outside the Soviet Union was in concert in Florence in 1951, but it was at London's Covent Garden in 1956, at the Bolshoi's first appearance in the West, that she sealed her status as an international legend. Her American debut came three years later. After Ulanova retired from the stage in 1961, she became a popular teacher and coach at the Bolshoi.

Vallières, Pierre, Canadian writer whose *Les Nègres blancs d'Amérique* (1968; *White Niggers of America,* 1971) reflected his anger at injustice, and became the Quebec separatist movement's call to action; at first favouring violence as a means of gaining independence, he came to prefer the political route but later grew disenchanted with the cause altogether (b. Feb. 22, 1938, Montreal, Que.—d. Dec. 22, 1998, Montreal).

Van Eps, George Abel, American jazz guitarist who played in a number of notable big bands and developed a seven-string guitar that allowed adding a bass line and made a wider range of chords possible (b. Aug. 7, 1913, Plainfield, N.J.—d. Nov. 29, 1998, Newport Beach, Calif.).

Villas Boas, Cláudio, Brazilian anthropologist and activist whose life was dedicated to the search for and protection of the country's indigenous people as their lands were taken over and developed; he and his brother Orlando aided in the creation of the Xingu National Park reservation in 1961 and the National Indian Foundation six years later (b. 1916, Botucatu, Braz.—d. March 1, 1998, São Paulo, Braz.).

Vivier, Roger-Henri, French shoe designer whose creations for many of the most famous French couture designers graced the feet of celebrities, members of high society, and royalty, including Queen Elizabeth II; he was credited with the invention of the stiletto heel (b. Nov. 13, 1903, Paris, France—d. Oct. 2, 1998, Toulouse, France).

Walker, Doak, American football player who won the 1948 Heisman Trophy, played for the Detroit Lions for six seasons, during which the team won two National Football League championships (1952 and '53), was picked for five Pro Bowl teams, was elected to the College Football Hall of Fame in 1959, and was selected for the Professional Football Hall of Fame in 1986; from 1990 the Doak Walker Award for the top college running back was given annually in his honour (b. Jan. 1, 1927, Dallas, Texas—d. Sept. 27, 1998, Steamboat Springs, Colo.).

Wallace, George Corley, U.S. politician (b. Aug. 25, 1919, Clio, Ala.—d. Sept. 13, 1998, Montgomery, Ala.), was a four-term Democratic governor of Alabama and a persistent presidential contender, notorious for his outspoken support of racial segregation. After earning (1942) a law degree from the University of Alabama and serving in World War II, Wallace was elected (1947) to the Alabama state legislature, where he served two terms. In 1958 he ran for governor but lost to his

Galina Ulanova

opponent, John Patterson, an extreme segregationist who had the official support of the Ku Klux Klan. Vowing never to be "out-segged" again, Wallace conducted his 1962 gubernatorial campaign with populist tirades against big government and blatant opposition to racial integration; he won in a landslide victory. In his 1963 inaugural speech, written by Klansman Asa Carter, Wallace proclaimed: "Segregation now, segregation tomorrow, segregation forever!" Later that year he attempted to make good his promise, as he barred the door to two black students trying to enroll at the University of Alabama. In 1968 Wallace ran for president as a candidate of the American Independent Party. With thinly veiled racist allusions and an anti-Washington platform, he snared 13% of the popular vote and five states. Wallace's 1972 bid for the Democratic presidential nomination was cut short on May 15, 1972, in Laurel, Md., when he was shot point blank by a would-be assassin, an action that paralyzed and confined him to a wheelchair for the rest of his life. He made one last unsuccessful attempt for the presidency in 1976. Wallace held his post as governor until 1978. By 1980, however, he had reversed his stance on segregation and even made public apologies for his former views. In 1982 he won an unprecedented fourth term as governor—a term he won with the support of black voters. Wallace retired from politics when his term ended in 1987.

Walsh, David Gordon, Canadian stock promoter whose company, Bre-X Minerals Ltd., sold shares on the basis of claims that the Busang gold deposit in Indonesia was the richest strike ever; although investors lost billions of dollars when it was discovered that there was little or no gold at the site and that reports had been falsified, Walsh and his family had previously sold stock worth millions of dollars and moved to The Bahamas (b. Aug. 11, 1945, Montreal, Que.—d. June 4, 1998, Nassau, The Bahamas).

Walsh, James Patrick ("J.T."), American actor whose roles in the David Mamet plays *American Buffalo* and *Glengarry Glen Ross* led to a successful motion picture career during which, in some 60 films, he specialized in villianous parts; one of the most recognizable character actors in the U.S., he had appeared most recently in such films as *Good Morning, Vietnam, A Few Good Men, Backdraft, Sling Blade,* and *Breakdown* (b. March 1, 1942, San Francisco, Calif.—d. Feb. 27, 1998, San Diego, Calif.).

Waters, Benjamin ("BENNY"), American tenor saxophonist and arranger who played for seven years with Charlie Johnson's early Harlem jazz band in New York City. A journeyman sideman, he later played woodwinds with American jazz and blues bands fronted by Fletcher Henderson, Jimmy Archey, and Roy Milton before moving (1952) to Paris and performing in Europe as a bandleader and soloist; after resettling in the U.S. in 1992, he continued to tour as a singer and alto saxophone soloist until shortly before his death (b. Jan. 23, 1902, Brighton, Md.—d. Aug. 11, 1998, Columbia, Md.).

Weese, Harry Mohr, American architect (b. June 30, 1915, Evanston, Ill.—d. Oct. 29, 1998, Manteno, Ill.), designed the subway system in Washington, D.C., considered one of the most remarkable public-works projects of the 20th century, and played a prominent role in the planning and architecture of Chicago. Following graduation (B.A., 1938) from the Massachusetts Institute of Technology, Weese studied city planning under Eliel Saarinen at the Cranbrook Academy of Art, Bloomfield Hills, Mich. Though Weese cofounded an architectural firm in 1941, his career was interrupted by World War II service in the navy. Two years after his discharge (1945), Weese opened his own Chicago-based firm and soon began shaping the city's skyline. He was one of the first major architects to foster historic preservation and renovated numerous landmarks, including Adler and Sullivan's Auditorium Theatre and the Field Museum of Natural History. In addition, he created designs for such buildings as the Metropolitan Corrections Center, a concrete tower whose irregularly spaced slit windows made it resemble a computer punch card, and helped redesign the city's lakefront. Rather than revealing a trademark style, Weese's work reflected his attention to setting, historical relations, and functional requirements. His design style was best evidenced in Washington's 160-km (100-mi) subway system, which, with spectacular concrete vaults and rippling lights at each station, had both awed and delighted commuters since its opening in 1976. Weese's other works include the Arena

Stage theatre in Washington, D.C., which featured the pioneering use of functional elements, such as lighting apparatus and catwalks as aesthetic features, and the Time and Life Building in Chicago.

Weidman, Jerome, American author (b. April 4, 1913, New York, N.Y.—d. Oct. 6, 1998, New York), created novels, short stories, and plays in which he presented a harsh and unapologetic view of New York City. The son of Jewish immigrants, Weidman grew up in New York City on Manhattan's Lower East Side. After graduating from high school, he worked in the garment district, where he gathered material for his writing. His first story, written at the age of 17, appeared in the *American Spectator.* Weidman attended the City College of New York (1930–33) and Washington Square College (1933–34) of New York University. While enrolled in New York University Law School, he penned his first novel, *I Can Get It for You Wholesale* (1937), which detailed the greed and amorality of the garment trade. The book received critical acclaim and commercial success (and later [1962] became a Broadway musical), but it also garnered criticism from the Jewish community for Weidman's unflattering character portrayals. Undaunted, he published a sequel, *What's in It for Me?* (1938), which was even more scathing than its predecessor. Although he was admitted to the bar, Weidman never practiced law, preferring to pursue a literary career. In addition to novels, he wrote numerous short stories, some of which were published in *The New Yorker* magazine, and many plays. He and George Abbott were corecipients of the 1960 Pulitzer Prize for drama for the book of the musical *Fiorello!*—the story of Fiorello Henry La Guardia, who served (1934–45) as mayor of New York City. *Fiorello!* also tied for best musical play with *The Sound of Music* for the 1960 Tony award. From 1969 to 1974 Weidman served as president of the Authors' League of America, and he published his memoir, *Praying for Rain,* in 1986.

Weil, André, French mathematician (b. May 6, 1906, Paris, France—d. Aug. 6, 1998, Princeton, N.J.), greatly influenced the course of mathematical research in the 20th century, most notably with his conjectures, in which he formulated the foundations of modern algebraic geometry. Weil developed an interest in numbers at an early age. He earned a Ph.D. (1928) from the University of Paris and accepted his first academic position as professor of mathematics (1930–32) at the Aligarh Muslim University in India. He then moved to the University of Strasbourg, France, and there (1933–40) Weil and a number of French mathematicians formed Nicolas Bourbaki, a group somewhat mischievously named after an imaginary Russian general. The Bourbaki group took on the responsibility of synthesizing the content of all major areas of mathematics, work that was published as a series of encyclopedic volumes called *Éléments d'histoire des mathématiques.* At the outbreak of World War II, Weil, a conscientious objector, fled to Finland to avoid the draft. He was sent back to France, however, and spent about six months in a French prison, a dangerous place for the son of Jewish parents and the brother of the mystic philosopher and French Resistance activist Simone Weil. While imprisoned, Weil formulated the Riemann hypothesis, which was named for a German mathematician and became a fundamental element of number theory. To secure his release from prison, he joined the French army but later managed to move to the United States, where he taught at Swarthmore and Haverford colleges in Pennsylvania. In 1945 Weil accepted a position at the University of São Paulo, Brazil, and in 1947 returned to the U.S. to serve (1947–58) on the faculty at the University of Chicago. From 1958 until his retirement in 1976, Weil taught at the Institute for Advanced Study, Princeton, N.J. In 1994 he was awarded the Kyoto Prize in Basic Science from the Inamori Foundation of Kyoto, Japan, for his lifelong contribution to mathematics.

Wells, Junior ("AMOS BLAKEMORE" OR "AMOS WELLS, JUNIOR"), American blues singer and harmonica player (b. Dec. 9, 1934, Memphis,

Tenn.—d. Jan. 15, 1998, Chicago, Ill.), was one of the musicians who introduced electric Chicago blues to international audiences and, from 1965, was one of the most popular of all blues performers. The son of an Arkansas sharecropper, Wells moved in 1946 with his mother to Chicago. There, in a pawnshop, he spied a harmonica priced at $2.00, left $1.50 on the store counter, and took the harmonica; arrested for theft, he played the instrument for a judge, who gave the store owner 50 cents and announced, "Case dismissed." At age 18 Wells joined the city's finest blues band, fronted by Muddy Waters, and led his own first recording session. Wells went on to success as a Chicago entertainer, had an early 1960s hit record "Messin' with the Kid," and was in the midst of an extended engagement at the Chicago nightclub Theresa's when in 1965 he recorded one of the first Chicago blues albums, the popular *Hoodoo Man Blues,* accompanied by guitarist Buddy Guy. The next year the Wells-Guy team first toured Europe; as white blues audiences grew larger, the pair made numerous recordings and played in many concert tours in the 1960s and '70s, including as the opening act for the Rolling Stones. Wells was noted for his elegant attire and his grand, energetic manner, both in his many performances with Guy and with the bands he led on his own. He selected his repertoire from senior bluesmen, including harmonica players Junior Parker and the first Sonny Boy (John Lee) Williamson, who had influenced him; both his singing and playing were uniquely dramatic and intense and punctuated with shouts, sexual moans, and humorous asides. His 1996 album, *Come On in This House,* won a W.C. Handy Blues Award. Before his final illness from cancer he appeared in the movie *Blues Brothers 2000;* days before his death his 1997 album, *Live at Buddy Guy's Legends,* was nominated for a Grammy award.

West, Dorothy, American writer (b. June 2, 1907, Boston, Mass.—d. Aug. 16, 1998, Boston), explored the aspirations and conflicts of middle-class African-Americans in many of her works and was perhaps the last surviving member of the prominent group of black artists, writers, and musicians who flourished in New York City's Harlem section during the period of sophisticated artistic creativity in the 1920s known as the Harlem Renaissance. She gained new renown in the 1990s with the publication of *The Wedding* (1995), her second novel, and its 1998 adaptation into a television miniseries by Oprah Winfrey's production company. West began writing when she was 7, and when she was 14 her stories began to be published in the *Boston Post.* In 1926 her short story "The Typewriter" won a prize in a national competition held by the Urban League's *Opportunity* magazine, and shortly thereafter she moved to New York and was taken under the wing of a group of Harlem literary figures. Among her circle—where, as the youngest member, she was known as "the kid"—were Langston Hughes, Zora Neale Hurston, Claude McKay, Wallace Thurman, and Countee Cullen. "The Typewriter" was included in *The Best Short Stories of 1926.* In 1932 West went with a group to the Soviet Union to make a film about American race relations, and though the film was never made, she and Hughes remained there for a year before returning to New York. To promote the efforts of young writers and attempt to rekindle the spirit of the Harlem Renaissance, which the Depression had snuffed, she started the literary magazine *Challenge* in 1934 and its short-lived descendant, *New Challenge,* in 1937. West then worked for a while as a welfare investigator and for the Federal Writers' Project and also began writing short stories for the *New York Daily News.* In 1947 she moved to Martha's Vineyard, Mass., where her family had a cottage. West's first novel, *The Living Is Easy,* was pub-

lished in 1948, and she began to write articles and stories for the *Vineyard Gazette* and also to formulate the book that was to become *The Wedding.* In the early 1990s Jacqueline Kennedy Onassis, who had seen West's work in the *Gazette* and who was working as an editor at Doubleday in New York, encouraged her to finish the book but did not live to see it published. West dedicated *The Wedding* to Onassis's memory. A collection of West's stories and essays, *The Richer, the Poorer,* was also published in 1995. At West's 90th birthday celebration in 1997, Hillary Rodham Clinton declared her a national treasure.

Wichterle, Otto, Czech chemist and educator who, in 1961, created soft contact lenses using a phonograph motor and a child's Erector set; by the mid-1990s some 100 million people used his alternative to eyeglasses (b. Oct. 27, 1913, Prostejov, Austro-Hungarian Empire [now Czech Republic]—d. Aug. 18, 1998, Stražisko, Czech Rep.).

Wieland, Joyce, Canadian artist (b. June 30, 1931, Toronto, Ont.—d. June 27, 1998, Toronto), was one of Canada's most influential woman artists and produced works in a variety of media, including sculptures, quilts, tapestries, paintings, and films, all celebrating her joy for life and reflecting her feminist leanings and passion for her beloved country. Wieland's parents were British immigrants and died when she was nine; she was raised by older siblings. Educated in the late 1940s at the Central Technical School in Toronto, she became an animator for Graphic Films. Wieland first exhibited her paintings at Toronto's avant-garde Isaacs Gallery in the 1950s and '60s, where she was the only woman in a white male Abstractionist milieu. Her work became anything but abstract as she incorporated quilting and embroidery into her increasingly intimate, earthy art. She turned to experimental filmmaking while living in New York City (1962–70). Her films—political, inventive, and infused with a newfound

ALISON SHAW—AP/WIDE WORLD

Dorothy West

sense of nationalism—included *Rat Life and Diet in North America* (1968), in which gerbils represented U.S. political prisoners who had escaped to Canada. Her only feature film, *The Far Shore* (1976), was considered unsuccessful. Wieland's 1971 exhibition, "True Patriot Love," the National Gallery of Canada's first retrospective of a living woman artist, featured "Water Quilt," a soft and lovely celebration of Canada's flora that was also a fiercely subversive statement about its exploitation. The Art Gallery of Ontario mounted a retrospective in 1987, again a first for a living female artist, and, appearing the same year was *Artist on Fire,* a documentary about her art and influence. She was a member of the Royal Academy of Arts (1973) and an officer of the Order of Canada (1987). Wieland returned to drawing and painting landscapes and figurative imagery in the '80s, her production waning only with the onset of Alzheimer's disease in the '90s.

Williams, Wendy Orlean, American punk rock singer and musician who was the leader of the shock-rock punk band the Plasmatics during the late 1970s and early '80s (b. 1949, Rochester, N.Y.—d. April 6, 1998, Storrs, Conn.).

Wills, Helen (HELEN NEWINGTON WILLS MOODY ROARKE), American tennis player (b. Oct. 6, 1905, Berkeley, Calif.—d. Jan. 1, 1998, Carmel, Calif.), dominated women's tennis in the 1920s and '30s, winning 31 major tournaments. Wills was encouraged to play by her father and at the age of 15 captured the girls national title. In 1923 she won the first of her seven U.S. singles championships (1923–25, 1927–29, 1931). Known for her stoic demeanor, Wills was dubbed "Little Miss Poker Face." Her steely concentration, combined with power, precision, and a strong baseline game, quickly established Wills as the premier player of her time. From 1927 to 1932 she won every set in singles play, including four French Open titles (1927–29, 1930). Her eight Wimbledon championships (1927–30, 1932–33, 1935, 1938) were unsurpassed until Martina Navratilova recorded her ninth title in 1990. In 10 Wightman Cup tournament appearances, Wills won 18 out of 20 matches. She also claimed 12 U.S., Wimbledon, and French doubles championships. At the 1924 Olympic Games in Paris, she captured gold medals in singles and doubles play. Wills, who was also known for her on-court rivalry with U.S. player Helen Hull Jacobs, retired from tennis in 1938. She wrote several books, including her autobiography, *Tennis* (1928), and coauthored the mystery *Death Serves an Ace* (1939). An accomplished artist, she also staged exhibits of her work. In 1959 Wills was inducted into the International Tennis Hall of Fame.

Wilson, Carl Dean, American guitarist, singer, and songwriter (b. Dec. 21, 1946, Hawthorne, Calif.—d. Feb. 6, 1998, Los Angeles, Calif.), was one of the founders of the Beach Boys rock band, which epitomized the California "surfin' sound." He performed with the group for over 30 years, was its lead guitarist, and was lead vocalist on many of its hits. Wilson and his older brothers, Brian and Dennis, began singing together when they were children. In 1961, with their cousin Mike Love and their friend Al Jardine, the brothers formed a group—with such names as Carl and the Passions, the Pendletones, and Kenny and the Cadets before they settled on the Beach Boys—fashioning their style on the close harmonies of groups like the Four Freshmen. Their first record, "Surfin'," a song by Brian, was released later that year and became only a minor success. After that, though, they launched a string of hits that included "Surfin' Safari," "Surfin' U.S.A.," and such examples of another favourite theme—cars, girls, and fun in the sun—as "Little Deuce Coupe," "I Get Around," "Help Me, Rhonda," "Barbara Ann," and "California Girls." By the end of 1965, they had released 10 albums. Brian then stopped touring because of health problems, and Carl assumed the leadership of the band. The album considered the group's best, *Pet Sounds,* was released in 1966, and a single from it, "God Only Knows," with Carl as lead vocalist, became one of the

REED SAXON—AP/WIDE WORLD

Flip Wilson

band's biggest hits. Later that year he sang lead vocals on another top hit, "Good Vibrations." The Beach Boys continued touring even after they had come to be seen as mainly a nostalgia act—though frustration with that emphasis led Carl to attempt a solo career in 1981—and even after Dennis's death in 1983. The 1988 film *Cocktail* introduced their last hit, "Kokomo," and the Beach Boys were inducted into the Rock and Roll Hall of Fame that same year.

Wilson, Flip (CLEROW WILSON), American comedian (b. Dec. 8, 1933, Jersey City, N.J.—d. Nov. 25, 1998, Malibu, Calif.), delighted audiences during the 1970s with his outrageous comedy routines. Wilson, one of 18 children in a destitute household, was placed in reform school and in foster homes at an early age, and he ran away from them several times. In 1950 he entered the Air Force by lying about his age (he was 16) and soon earned his nickname from the "flipped out" stories, jokes, and colourful dialects that he assumed to entertain his fellow servicemen. After leaving the Air Force in 1954, he worked as a bellhop at a San Francisco hotel, where he made his comedic debut during the intermission between two nightclub acts. In 1959 a Miami businessman sponsored him for $50 a week, giving Wilson the opportunity to develop his comedy routines, and in the 1960s he became a regular at the Apollo Theatre in Harlem in New York City. Wilson's big break in television came when Johnny Carson invited him to appear on "The Tonight Show." He also performed on such other TV shows as "The Ed Sullivan Show" and "Rowan and Martin's Laugh-In," from which his energetic announcement "Heah come de judge!" entered into the national lexicon. After hosting a successful television special in the late '60s, Wilson was catapulted to fame with his own program, the "Flip Wilson Show" (1970–74), for which he created such outlandish characters as the Rev. Leroy of the Church of What's Happenin' Now and the sassy ghetto queen Geraldine Jones, in whose personage Wilson sported a tight miniskirt or hot pants and made famous such one-liners as "When you're hot, you're hot; when you're not, you're not!"; "The Devil made me do it."; "I don't smoke and I don't do windows!"; and "What you see is what you get!"—lines that became instant African-American catchphrases. In many of his skits Wilson retold well-known biblical or historical tales with burlesque twists; Christopher Columbus selling Queen Isabella on his voyage, for example, because if he didn't discover America, "there's not gonna be a Ray Charles." In the film *Uptown*

Saturday Night (1974), Wilson delivered a show-stopping comedic sermon. He also appeared in the films *Skatetown, U.S.A.* (1979) and *The Fish That Saved Pittsburgh* (1979), hosted the unsuccessful television show "People Are Funny" (1984), and starred in "Charlie and Co." (1985–86). Notable among his comedy recordings were *Cowboys and Colored People* (1967), *Flippin'* (1968), *Flip Wilson, You Devil, You* (1968), and *The Devil Made Me Buy This Dress* (1971).

Wolf, Alfred Peter, American nuclear and organic chemist whose work led to advances in medical imaging, especially the development of positron emission tomography (b. Feb. 13, 1923, New York, N.Y.—d. Dec. 17, 1998, Port Jefferson, N.Y.).

Wood, Beatrice, American ceramicist who was dubbed the "mama of Dada" as a result of her relationship with the artist Marcel Duchamp; she gained celebrity for both her colourful lifestyle and her pottery and inspired a character in the book and film *Jules et Jim* as well as the 101-year-old Rose in the film *Titanic* (b. March 3, 1893, San Francisco, Calif.—d. March 12, 1998, Ojai, Calif.).

Wright, Stan, American track coach who served the sport for some 40 years, a number of them with the U.S. Olympic Committee and USA Track & Field, but was better remembered as the Olympic assistant coach who took responsibility for the disqualification of two sprinters in the 1972 Olympics when lack of notification of schedule changes caused them to be too late to run their races (b. Aug. 11, 1920, Englewood, N.J.—d. Nov. 6, 1998, Houston, Texas).

Wynette, Tammy (VIRGINIA WYNETTE PUGH), American singer (b. May 5, 1942, Itawamba county, Miss.—d. April 6, 1998, Nashville, Tenn.), was revered as the "First Lady of Country Music" from the 1960s to the '80s. Her powerful and tearful voice captivated listeners, who identified with her heartfelt songs. Wynette's life personified country music's rags-to-riches theme; after her father, a musician, died when she was an infant, her mother moved to Birmingham, Ala., to work in an aircraft factory, leaving her baby to be raised by grandparents on their cotton farm. Wynette, who married (1959) one month before her high-school graduation, worked as a beautician, sang in nightclubs, and appeared on Porter Wagoner's nationally syndicated country music television show. In 1966 she left her husband and moved with their three daughters to Nashville,

where she signed a contract with Epic Records. Renamed Tammy by producer Billy Sherrill, she scored her first hit in 1967 with the single "Apartment Number Nine," which was followed by "Your Good Girl's Gonna Be Bad," "I Don't Wanna Play House" (for which she won the first of three Grammy awards), and "D-I-V-O-R-C-E." With Sherrill she co-wrote her anthem, "Stand by Your Man," the 1968 number one smash hit. She married George Jones in 1969, and, known as "Mr. and Mrs. Country Music," they recorded many duet hits, chronicling their marital ups and downs. They continued recording together despite their divorce, and Wynette's last album, *One,* was recorded (1996) with Jones. Although plagued by personal problems—she was married five times, was abducted from a shopping mall and beaten, filed for bankruptcy, and was treated for pre-scription-drug addiction and a series of health problems that resulted in some 30 operations—she was the most successful female vocalist in the history of country music. Her recordings had sales of more than $100 million, and she recorded 39 top-10 hits between 1967 and 1988 and 20 number one hits throughout her career. The first female country music artist to sell a million albums, she eventually sold more than 30 million records. Of her 50 albums, 11 soared to number one. Wynette was a three-time winner of the Country Music Association's Female Vocalist of the Year award (1968–70) and was given the 1991 Living Legend Award by Music City News and TNN. During the 1980s her career stalled, but in 1992 she recorded the hit "Justified and Ancient" with the British pop group KLF. She also teamed up with Dolly Parton and Loretta Lynn to record the album *Honky-Tonk Angels* in 1993. Wynette's autobiography, *Stand by Your Man,* was published in 1979 and filmed in 1982.

Yang Shangkun, Chinese revolutionary figure and politician who was a veteran of Mao Zedong's Long March in 1934–35, in 1966 became a victim of Mao's Cultural Revolution and was sent to prison for 12 years, and then regained power, serving as president from 1988 to 1993; in 1989, under instruction from national leader Deng Xiaoping, Yang gave the order for the crackdown on the Tiananmen Square pro-democracy demonstrators that ended in a massacre (b. 1907, Shuangjiang, Sichuan province, China—d. Sept. 14, 1998, Beijing, China).

Yankovic, Frank John ("FRANKIE"), American musician who was known as the "polka king" for half a century of performing and brought nationwide attention to the Slovenian-style polka; in 1986 he won polka's first Grammy award (b. July 28, 1915, Davis, W.Va.—d. Oct. 14, 1998, New Port Richey, Fla.).

Yorty, Samuel William, American politician who gained national fame as mayor of Los Angeles from 1961 to 1973, a time of economic growth and civic improvement but also one of inner-city unrest that in 1965 erupted in riots in the Watts section; at first a liberal Democrat, he became increasingly conservative during his years in office and was especially controversial for his outspoken racial views (b. Oct. 1, 1909, Lincoln, Neb.—d. June 5, 1998, Los Angeles, Calif.).

Young, Frederick Archibald ("FREDDIE"), British cinematographer whose visual flair and artistry added immeasurably to British films for more than 70 years, beginning with his work as an assistant cameraman on the 1922 silent *Rob Roy.* He was particularly known for the stunning beauty of films he brought to a series of films by director David Lean, three of which—*Lawrence of Arabia* (1962), *Dr. Zhivago* (1965), and *Ryan's Daughter* (1970)—earned Young Academy Awards. He was made O.B.E. in 1970; his autobiography was scheduled to be published in 1999 (b. Oct. 9, 1902, London, Eng.—d. Dec. 1, 1998, London).

Young, Robert, American actor (b. Feb. 22, 1907, Chicago, Ill.—d. July 21, 1998, Westlake Village, Calif.), was best remembered for his portrayal of benevolent authority figures, starring in the title roles of such television classics as "Father Knows Best" and "Marcus Welby, M.D." When he was 10 years old, his family moved to Los Angeles, where he later performed in high school plays and community theatre. Signed by Metro-Goldwyn-Mayer in 1931, Young was loaned out to Fox Film Corp. for his debut in *The Black Camel,* a Charlie Chan mystery. During the 1930s and '40s he built a solid, prolific movie career, playing both comic and dramatic roles, usually as the leading man opposite such stars as Greta Garbo and Joan Crawford. His more than 100 films included *Northwest Passage* (1940), *Journey for Margaret* (1942), and *The Enchanted Cottage* (1945). In 1949 Young landed the role he reprised on TV from 1954 to 1960. He won two Emmy awards for the series and a third for his depiction of Marcus Welby (1969–76), the compassionate doctor who became personally involved in his patients' lives. Young's idealized TV roles were in sharp contrast to his life off the screen. He suffered for years from depression and alcoholism and attempted suicide in 1991. Despite these difficulties, he was respected in Hollywood for his professionalism, working consistently in television movies until his retirement in 1988.

Youngman, Henry ("HENNY"), American comedian (b. 1902/1906?, England—d. Feb. 24, 1998, New York, N.Y.), was heralded as the king of the one-liner. With his trademark violin and the catchphrase "Take my wife—please," Youngman became one of the leading comedic acts of the 1940s–1960s. He was born to Russian-Jewish parents who had immigrated to the U.S. but were living in England temporarily. Growing up in Brooklyn, N.Y., Youngman was an indifferent student who attended various public schools but spent most of his time at vaudeville performances. His father, hoping he would become a concert musician, had his son take violin lessons. Instead, Youngman formed a band that played the "Borscht Belt" vaudeville circuit. A club owner in the Catskill Mountains—more impressed by

Youngman's between-song stage banter—fired the band but retained Youngman as a comedian. In 1936 he made his first appearance on singer Kate Smith's popular radio show, and he soon became a regular. By the 1950s Youngman was also a popular television star and was featured in a number of variety shows. Although his act waned in popularity as the older vaudeville-trained comedians gave way to a younger, more sophisticated style of comic, Youngman still performed on a regular basis, working some 200 shows a year well into his 70s.

Zemro, Menashe, Ethiopian religious figure who was the last of the Ethiopian Jewish community's traditional spiritual leaders to have the authority that accompanied recognition as high *ques,* a position achieved through religious knowledge (b. c. 1905—d. Oct. 7, 1998, Qiryat Gat, Israel).

Zheng Zuoxin (CHENG TSO-HSIN), Chinese ornithologist who was considered one of the greatest ornithologists in the world and the founder of modern Chinese ornithology; his *A Synopsis of the Avifauna of China* was published in English in 1987 (b. Nov. 18, 1906, Fuzhou, China—d. June 27, 1998, Beijing, China?).

Zhivkov, Todor Khristov, Bulgarian politician (b. Sept. 7, 1911, Pravets, near Botevgrad, Bulg.—d. Aug. 5, 1998, Sofia, Bulg.) led the Bulgarian Communist Party from 1954 to 1989, a 35-year rule that was the longest of any communist dictator. Born into a peasant family, Zhivkov received a limited education. As an adolescent he moved to Sofia, where he trained and worked as a printer. During this time he became involved in Komsomol, the underground communist youth organization. Zhivkov's rise through the Communist Party ranks began in World War II. He helped organize the resistance movement known as the People's Liberation Insurgent Army, which was instrumental in overthrowing Bulgaria's regime in 1944 and allowing the Bulgarian Communist Party to become the country's dominant political force. After the coup Zhivkov was placed in charge of the newly created People's Militia, which arrested thousands of political enemies. In 1951 he became a full member of the party's governing Politburo and in 1954 was made first secretary of the Central Committee. Zhivkov served as prime minister from 1962 until 1971, when he was made chairman of a new Council of State, a position equivalent to that of president. Throughout his career he adhered closely to Soviet policy in both domestic and foreign affairs. His political savvy served him well until the 1980s, when the reform-minded Soviet leader Mikhail Gorbachev rose to power. At that time Moscow's confidence in Zhivkov began to erode not only because of Bulgaria's declining economy but also as a result of mass demonstrations precipitated by Zhivkov's campaign of forced assimilation of the country's Turkish population. At the end of 1989 Zhivkov was replaced as president of Bulgaria and ousted as head of the Communist Party. He was arrested in 1990 and in 1992 was found guilty of misappropriating state funds and was sentenced to seven years' imprisonment. Because of ill health he served his sentence under house arrest. Near the end of his sentence he was acquitted of embezzlement charges.

Zhuk, Stanislav Alekseyevich, Russian figure-skating coach who included many of the best-known Soviet pairs teams among his students; though a number of his pupils won Olympic gold medals, they later told about his tough and abusive tactics (b. Jan. 25, 1935, Ulyanovsk, U.S.S.R.—d. Nov. 1, 1998, Moscow, Russia).

Robert Young

Agriculture and Food Supplies

INTERNATIONAL ISSUES

World agricultural markets in 1998 were dominated by two events, the economic turbulence in Asia and the El Niño weather phenomenon. Asian problems lowered the value of world agricultural trade and raised concerns about the health of the global economy. The El Niño event, during which the waters in the Pacific Ocean off South America warm and alter global weather patterns, caused drought in some regions and floods in others but did not reduce total global food supplies compared with 1997. The combined effects of these forces, however, resulted in a difficult year for farmers in many parts of the world.

According to the Food and Agriculture Organization (FAO), world agricultural production rose 0.2% in 1998. (*See* TABLE I.) Even with the small increase, agricultural production reached a record level. For 1998 the growth in food production in the less-developed countries kept pace with the rise in population so that per capita food production was slightly higher. Developed countries experienced a decline in per capita production, which either reduced their surplus for export or increased their import needs.

Although at a global level food production rose, there were many differences by region, which reflected economic and weather problems. Among the developed countries, output in the United States and Canada increased 0.1% and 1.5%, respectively, while the European Union (EU) recorded another strong performance. Agricultural production in Russia had fallen during most of the 1990s, and there were production problems again in 1998. Reduced output was linked to the ongoing problems of the transition from central planning to a market economy. The agricultural sector experienced problems with obtaining adequate supplies of inputs, such as fertilizers and chemicals, as well as with tardy payments for products delivered and delayed wages. South Africa suffered greatly from El Niño, with 1997–98 corn production sharply lower. Although Australia suffered a reduced wheat crop due to El Niño, rain arrived at a critical time in the fall of 1997 and prevented a large crop loss.

For the less-developed countries location was critical to agricultural performance in 1998. Argentina and Brazil produced above-normal soybean crops owing to timely rains associated with El Niño. Other less-developed countries were not so fortunate. Indonesian agricultural production suffered from an El Niño-induced drought and the region's economic collapse. China also experienced some dryness induced by El Niño, which adversely affected its 1997–98 coarse

grain crops. By contrast, Mexico received excessive rains, which reduced its coarse grain output. Thailand and the Philippines were affected by both El Niño and economic problems, but Thailand was able to expand its rice output. Production problems in Central Africa were partly the fault of El Niño and partly man-made, as warfare erupted in the region.

Food Emergencies. A number of food emergencies occurred in 1998. The Sudan experienced one of its periodic droughts. Efforts to organize relief supplies were hampered because Sudanese government troops were fighting with rebel forces in the drought-stricken areas and regarded food aid as assistance to the rebels. North Korea experienced famine, as it had in 1997. During the spring of 1998 food supplies there shrank to very low levels, and millions, especially children and the elderly, were at risk. Large quantities of grain were delivered to that country during the spring, and, although the situation eased in the summer, the 1998 harvests were again poor. Drought in Indonesia and falling incomes due to the economic crisis produced a food emergency in that nation, but the international community provided billions of dollars in credits, allowing the purchase of large volumes of wheat and rice. In the fall of 1998 concern over food shortages in Russia emerged. Due to drought in the Volga River area and continued economic chaos, Russian grain production was at its lowest level since the

Table I. Selected Indexes of World Agricultural and Food Production															
(1989–91 = 100)															
Region and country	Total agricultural production					Total food production					Per capita food production				
	1994	1995	1996	1997	1998	1994	1995	1996	1997	1998	1994	1995	1996	1997	1998
Developed countries	**96.6**	**94.6**	**97.6**	**98.9**	**96.7**	**96.9**	**95.0**	**98.3**	**99.6**	**97.6**	**94.8**	**92.6**	**95.4**	**96.3**	**94.0**
Canada	108.7	111.2	115.4	114.2	116.1	108.4	110.7	115.3	114.1	115.6	103.5	104.7	108.0	105.9	106.4
European Union	97.7	97.5	101.7	103.7	101.4	97.6	97.4	101.8	103.7	101.3	96.2	95.7	99.7	101.4	98.9
Japan	99.4	97.3	95.4	95.3	94.5	99.9	97.8	96.0	95.8	95.0	98.9	96.6	94.6	94.2	93.2
Russia	73.1	65.4	68.2	67.6	56.5	73.4	65.8	68.7	68.2	56.9	73.2	65.7	68.8	68.5	57.2
South Africa	99.0	85.3	101.8	99.1	100.9	101.2	87.0	104.1	101.3	103.1	92.5	77.7	91.0	86.6	86.3
United States	116.4	109.5	114.7	118.5	117.1	116.1	109.4	114.5	118.4	118.3	111.5	104.1	108.0	110.8	109.8
Less-developed countries	**115.6**	**121.2**	**127.5**	**129.9**	**131.5**	**117.1**	**122.5**	**129.0**	**131.4**	**133.5**	**109.0**	**112.2**	**116.1**	**116.3**	**116.2**
Argentina	109.3	116.2	119.1	116.8	127.6	111.6	118.1	120.8	118.9	129.2	105.8	110.5	111.6	108.4	116.3
Bangladesh	100.5	103.4	110.0	111.1	111.9	99.9	103.7	110.2	111.2	111.7	94.1	96.2	100.7	100.0	98.8
Brazil	110.7	114.3	118.8	123.7	125.2	112.2	117.2	121.5	126.8	127.5	105.8	109.0	111.6	115.0	114.2
China	108.7	111.2	115.4	114.2	116.1	130.4	139.2	150.3	157.1	160.2	124.7	131.8	141.0	145.9	147.4
Congo, Dem. Rep. of the	105.7	107.5	99.2	96.5	94.6	106.3	108.3	100.4	98.1	95.9	90.7	89.2	80.3	76.5	73.0
Egypt	112.8	122.7	134.8	138.9	141.9	114.4	125.1	136.1	140.4	143.6	105.7	113.4	121.1	122.7	123.2
Ethiopia	107.2	118.0	126.5	115.7	119.5	107.7	118.5	127.7	116.1	120.9	94.9	101.2	105.6	93.0	93.7
India	112.3	116.6	119.8	121.7	121.2	111.9	115.6	118.8	121.2	120.4	104.2	105.9	107.0	107.4	105.0
Indonesia	112.3	119.6	121.8	119.7	118.7	112.6	120.1	122.0	119.8	118.9	105.8	111.2	111.3	107.7	105.2
Malaysia	113.2	114.7	117.8	120.0	118.4	119.7	121.4	125.3	128.0	126.1	108.8	107.9	109.0	109.0	105.2
Mexico	112.4	121.2	116.6	117.3	122.1	114.0	122.6	116.9	118.1	122.9	106.0	112.0	105.0	104.3	106.8
Nigeria	128.9	131.4	139.9	135.2	136.1	129.3	131.7	140.4	136.0	137.4	114.8	113.5	117.6	110.7	108.7
Philippines	113.9	117.0	120.9	124.0	121.8	114.9	119.3	122.8	126.0	123.7	105.3	106.9	107.8	108.3	104.2
Turkey	102.9	104.3	110.4	107.5	110.7	104.0	103.9	110.8	107.1	111.3	97.4	95.8	100.6	95.7	98.0
Venezuela	105.1	105.1	111.0	121.3	121.6	105.9	106.3	112.1	123.3	123.5	96.5	94.9	98.0	105.6	103.6
Vietnam	123.0	130.6	137.6	143.8	144.9	121.8	129.0	134.8	139.6	141.1	112.2	116.6	119.5	121.6	120.8
World	**107.0**	**109.1**	**113.9**	**115.9**	**115.7**	**107.7**	**109.8**	**114.8**	**116.7**	**116.7**	**101.5**	**102.0**	**105.2**	**105.4**	**104.2**

Source: World Wide Web site for the UN Food and Agriculture Organization: http//apps.fao.org (Nov. 19, 1998).

Table II. Shipment of Food Aid in Cereals
In 000-metric ton grain equivalent

Region and country	1994–95	1995–96	1996–97	1997–98[1]
Australia	258	181	169	240
Canada	602	436	373	349
China	0	1	171	90
European Union	2,488	1,731	1,073	861
Japan	398	821	281	302
Norway	34	14	32	44
Switzerland	54	35	43	41
United States	4,321	3,037	2,022	2,256
Others	1,288	1,141	1,134	1,161
Total	9,443	7,397	5,298	5,344
To LIFDC[2]	7,910	6,400	4,447	4,838
Sub-Saharan Africa	3,348	2,305	1,770	1,912
To other countries	1,533	997	851	3,232

[1]Estimate partly based on minimum commitments under the Food Aid Convention and budgetary allocations.
[2]Low-income food-deficit countries.
Source: UN Food and Agriculture Organization, October 1998.

Table III. World Cereal Supply and Distribution
In 000,000 metric tons

	1995–96	1996–97	1997–98[1]	1998–99[2]
Production				
Wheat	538	583	612	591
Coarse grains	802	908	889	883
Rice, milled	371	380	385	376
Total	1,711	1,872	1,886	1,850
Utilization				
Wheat	551	578	588	602
Coarse grains	840	879	881	880
Rice, milled	371	379	384	385
Total	1,762	1,836	1,853	1,867
Feed use	634	674	687	690
Food and other use	1,128	1,162	1,166	1,177
Exports				
Wheat	98	100	100	98
Coarse grains	88	93	87	86
Rice, milled	20	19	25	20
Total	205	212	212	205
Ending stocks[3]				
Wheat	106	111	135	124
Coarse grains	98	127	135	137
Rice, milled	50	51	52	43
Total	254	289	322	304
Stocks as % of utilization				
Wheat	19	19	23	21
Coarse grains	12	14	15	16
Rice, milled	13	13	14	11
Total	14	16	17	16
Stocks held by U.S. in %				
Wheat	9	11	14	19
Coarse grains	14	21	28	36
Stocks held by EU in %				
Wheat	10	14	12	14
Coarse grains	10	9	17	18

[1]Estimated.   [2]Forecast.   [3]Data not available for all countries.
Source: U.S. Department of Agriculture, December 1998.

early 1950s. With its political and economic problems Russia did not have the money to purchase food on world markets and was offered food assistance.

Some food emergencies were man-made. Ethnic warfare in Central and East Africa resulted in mass movements of people who did not have adequate food. Fighting in the Serbian province of Kosovo between Yugoslav forces and ethnic Albanians in the fall of 1998 drove the Albanians away from their villages and fields just before winter. An accord between the Yugoslav government and NATO provided humanitarian relief. Iraq continued to suffer food shortages as a result of the trade sanctions imposed by the UN.

The trend of decreasing food aid continued during the year. (*See* TABLE II.) In the early 1990s cereal food aid averaged more than 12 million tons. In 1996–97 the total dropped sharply to just over five million tons, and it remained at that level in 1997–98. A decline in cereal food aid was characteristic of most donor nations, but the major donors registered the largest declines. The U.S., the largest donor, had reduced cereal food aid by nearly five million tons, or 70%, since 1992–95. The second largest donor, the EU, had lowered its aid by three million tons, or 77%. These declines reflected changes in world grain markets, as government-owned surplus stocks were reduced by policy shifts as well as by the tight

global supplies of the mid-1990s. For example, in accord with a decision taken in 1996, the U.S. government no longer held large grain stocks accumulated under farm price support programs. In the past such stocks were often used for food aid. The trend of reduced cereal food aid was a concern to many food experts. Tighter world food supplies could be expected as production resources were being used to the maximum. There would be little to no growth in supply at a time when income and population growth would be boosting demand.

Asian Crisis. The Asian economic crisis affected world agriculture during 1998. Although the specific origins of the problems differed by country, all were related to unsound banking and financial systems. The crisis appeared in Thailand in July 1997 and by the end of that year had spread to Indonesia, Malaysia, South Korea, the Philippines, Singapore, and, to a lesser extent, Taiwan and Hong Kong. These nations devalued currencies, and the national economies suffered. In the case of Indonesia the downturn was extremely severe. For agricultural goods the economic problems resulted in reduced food imports and an incentive to increase domestic output and, when possible, increase agricultural exports.

The impact on agriculture was not as severe as many had feared, however. One reason was that the most affected nations were not large agricultural traders. Roughly 5–6% of world agricultural exports and imports were traded by South Korea, Indonesia, Thailand, Malaysia, Singapore, and Taiwan. Of the group South Korea was the most important to agricultural trade. A second reason was that sales contracts negotiated in late 1997 were shipped in 1998, and this delayed the impact of reduced incomes on agricultural trade. Furthermore, exporting nations and international agencies extended credit to Indonesia, South Korea, and Thailand.

Later in the year concern mounted that the economic malaise was spreading. Japan slid into recession. Growth in China slowed, but the nation managed to avoid serious difficulties in 1998. Reduced imports of primary commodities, from petroleum to metals to agricultural goods, put downward pressure on the export earnings of nations that relied heavily on primary commodity exports. In late summer Russia was forced to devalue and default on international payments. Soon afterward the currencies of Brazil, Venezuela, Chile, and Mexico came under attack.

For agricultural markets the possible spread of economic problems was a worrisome development. The countries originally affected were not large agricultural traders, but Japan was the world's largest agricultural importer. Also the countries of Latin America represented a large import market for some agricultural goods as well as being major exporters of others. The spectre of turbulence in Latin-American economies contributed to a sharp fall in agricultural prices.

El Niño. Agricultural markets in 1998 were influenced by the expectation of a strong El Niño and the realization, at least in part, of the worst fears. In the summer and fall of 1997 ocean temperature recordings confirmed that a strong El Niño was underway. With expectations of drought and flooding in some key agricultural producers, which would result in reduced global food supplies, prices rose during the fall of 1997.

El Niño did adversely affect a number of crops. Rice in Indonesia was badly damaged, as was corn in southern Africa. Excessive rains in California damaged vegetables, and crops on the western coast of South America were not spared. A number of important crops, however, escaped the full force of El Niño. The Australian wheat crop received timely rains, which reduced its decline. Rice production in Thailand rose, and Chinese crop production remained strong. Thus food production worldwide rose in 1998, despite El Niño.

AGRICULTURAL COMMODITIES

Prices. With economic difficulties in Asia and increases in the production of most agricultural goods, world market prices fell in 1998. For most commodities the decline in price was quite severe, and in many nations farm incomes were falling. In nations where farm prices were supported by governments, the budget costs of farm programs were rising.

Farm prices in the U.S. illustrated the extent of the decline. Prior to 1996 U.S. farm incomes were supported by payments that rose as crop prices fell. After 1996, however, farmers received a fixed payment regardless of the price. In 1995–96 the U.S. average farm price for wheat was $167 per ton. By 1997–98 the farm price dropped to $124 per ton, and the expected price in 1998–99 was $97 per ton. The U.S. farm price for soybeans dropped 26% from 1996–97 to 1998–99. Farm prices among the meats revealed a much different pattern. Beef and poultry prices at the farm level did not weaken greatly. Farm beef prices in the U.S. remained around $1,500–$1,600 per ton with poultry prices at about $1,300 per ton. Farm prices for pork, however, collapsed to levels unseen in recent decades. In 1997 the U.S. pork price at the farm level was slightly over $1,100 per ton, but in 1998 it had declined to $750 per ton.

Grains. World grain production in 1997–98 was 1,886,000,000 tons, up from 1,872,000,000 tons in 1996–97, despite production losses due to El Niño. (*See* TABLE III.) This increased production was achieved on 10 million fewer hectares (1 hectare= 2.47 acres). The expanded production reflected increased grain crops in the U.S., Canada, Europe, and Argentina. World wheat production registered a large increase from 1996–97 to 1997–98, rising from 583 million tons to 612 million. World rice production also rose, from 380 million tons on a milled basis to 385 million, the fourth consecutive year of record production. In contrast, world production of coarse grains— corn, barley, sorghum, millet, oats, and rye—was slightly lower, falling from 908 million tons to 889 million. Despite that decline, coarse grains output in 1997–98 was the second largest production level ever recorded. Economic upset in Asia kept world trade in grains stagnant in 1997–98, remaining at 212 million tons. The decline was due to less trade in coarse grains. World wheat trade was unchanged, but global coarse grains exports fell from 93 million tons to 87 million.

Although world trade declined, global consumption of wheat and coarse grains rose. Wheat use rose 10 million tons, or 1.8%. Consumption of coarse grains increased two million tons. At 25 million tons

world trade in rice in 1997–98 was six million tons above the 1996–97 total. With increased production resulting from the devaluation of the Thai baht and reduced domestic consumption because of declining incomes, rice exports from Thailand in 1998 increased to 6.1 million tons compared with 5.3 million in 1997. Indonesian and Philippine imports in 1997–98 rose sharply. Indonesia experienced a severe loss in rice output and rapidly rising food prices. This prompted a large increase in rice imports, from 800,000 tons in 1997 to 5.9 million tons in 1998.

Ending grain stocks at 320 million tons in 1997–98 equaled 17% of world consumption, or about 63 days worth of supply. That represented a marked increase over the much tighter global supplies of the middle 1990s.

Forecasts for 1998–99 saw a reduced, but still large, world grain crop of about 1,850,000,000 tons. World rice production was expected to fall to 376 million tons. Wheat production was forecast to fall to 591 million tons in 1998–99, as was the coarse grain output at 883 million tons. Continuing economic problems and abundant supplies were expected to cut world trade in 1998–99. Wheat, coarse grains, and rice exports were all forecast to decline. Worldwide grain consumption was expected to rise 14 million tons to 1,867,000,000 tons, most of

this increase was owing to expanded wheat use. Ending stocks for 1998–99 were expected to be lower, as output fell and use continued to rise.

Oilseeds and Products. World oilseed production in 1997–98 totaled 287 million tons, 26 million tons higher than the previous year. (*See* TABLE IV.) The U.S., the world's largest soybean producer, had a good crop in the fall of 1997 at 74 million tons, up 9 million from the previous year. The crops in Brazil and Argentina in the spring of 1998 increased 16% and 67%, respectively, owing to excellent growing conditions and stable economic conditions. Also contributing to the large expansion in Argentina was a shift to soybeans in some areas previously planted in wheat. Soybean production in China rose 11%. Oilseed production in Canada increased 25%, as farmers recovered from wet weather during the previous planting season. European oilseed output was 15% greater.

World oilseed trade rose sharply in 1997–98 to balance regional increases in demand for protein feed with the location of supplies. In 1996–97, 49 million tons of oilseeds were traded. For 1997–98 trade expanded to 53 million tons. With expanded oilseed production, outputs of oilseed meals and vegetable oils rose in 1997–98. Trade of oilseed meals and vegetable oils remained

Table IV. World Production of Major Oilseeds and Products			
In 000,000 metric tons			
	1996–97	1997–98[1]	1998–99[2]
Total production of oilseeds	**261.2**	**287.1**	**290.8**
Soybeans	**131.7**	**156.2**	**154.1**
U.S.	64.8	73.6	75.2
China	13.2	14.7	13.5
Argentina	11.2	18.7	17.0
Brazil	26.8	31.0	29.0
Cottonseed	**34.4**	**34.7**	**32.5**
U.S.	6.5	6.3	4.6
Former Soviet republics	2.8	3.1	2.8
China	7.6	8.3	7.4
Peanuts	**28.4**	**26.7**	**27.6**
U.S.	1.7	1.6	1.7
China	10.1	9.6	10.2
India	8.2	7.6	7.9
Sunflower seed	**23.9**	**23.9**	**26.2**
U.S.	1.6	1.7	2.1
Former Soviet republics	5.2	5.5	5.4
Argentina	5.2	5.5	6.7
European Union	3.9	4.1	3.8
Rapeseed	**31.6**	**33.3**	**36.8**
Canada	5.1	6.4	7.6
China	9.2	9.6	8.3
European Union	7.1	8.6	9.5
India	6.9	4.9	6.1
Copra	**5.8**	**5.6**	**5.4**
Palm kernel	**5.3**	**5.2**	**5.4**
Oilseeds crushed	**218.9**	**228.9**	**235.5**
Soybeans	115.5	126.9	128.3
Oilseed ending stocks	**16.4**	**22.2**	**25.4**
Soybeans	12.9	19.2	22.2
World production[3]			
Total fats and oils	**89.0**	**89.6**	**93.1**
Edible vegetable oils	74.5	75.4	78.6
Soybean oil	20.7	23.0	23.4
Palm oil	17.6	16.9	17.7
Animal fats	13.3	13.3	13.2
Marine oils	1.2	0.9	1.3
High-protein meals[4]	**149.3**	**155.8**	**161.1**
Soybean meal	91.8	100.8	102.4
Fish meal	6.4	5.1	6.4

[1]Preliminary. [2]Forecast. [3]Processing potential from crops in the year indicated.
[4]Converted, on the basis of product's protein content, to weight equivalent of soybeans of 44% protein content.
Source: U.S. Department of Agriculture, December 1998.

A farm worker picks fruit in a flooded lemon grove in Ventura, Calif. Several agricultural regions of the world, including southern California, sustained crop damage in 1998 due to either drought or heavy rain and flooding caused by the strong El Niño weather pattern.
DAMIAN DOVARGANES—AP/WIDE WORLD

TABLE VI.) In the U.S. higher prices and reduced feed prices helped boost milk yields to offset a decline in numbers of cows. Milk production in Canada was higher despite a reduced production quota, partly as a result of a mild winter in eastern Canada. Mexico also experienced an output increase, as some large dairies expanded animal inventories. With favourable prices compared to alternative outputs and lower feed prices, Australian production rose roughly 3% above the 1997 level. In contrast, dry weather in New Zealand limited the rise in production to about 1%.

Butter production also rose in 1998, but the Asian economic crisis contributed to a decline in butter trade. The Asian market represented the major market for traditional butter exporters Australia and New Zealand.

stable. Ending stocks of oilseeds grew from 16 million tons in 1996–97 to 22 million tons for 1997–98. The low level of ending stocks in 1996–97 reflected the high world market prices of that year, which discouraged stockholding.

Forecasts for world oilseed production in 1998–99 predicted a slight increase above the 1997–98 level. Soybean output in South America was expected to fall to more normal yields, but that drop would be offset by the large U.S. soybean crop harvested in the fall of 1998 and larger rapeseed crops in Canada and the EU. The composition of trade in oilseeds and products was expected to shift; for 1998–99 oilseed trade was forecast to weaken, and trade volumes of oilseed meals and vegetable oils were expected to rise. At a global level, oilseed stocks were forecast to continue to increase.

Livestock and Meat. World production of red meat in 1998 continued the recent trend of annual increases. (*See* TABLE V). In 1997 output totaled 136 million tons. For 1998 production was estimated at 141 million tons. With red meat trade totaling about eight million tons, consumption closely followed the production trend. Preliminary forecasts for 1998 indicated a slight decline in consumption due to falling incomes in Asian nations that traditionally import large quantities of beef and pork.

Poultry meat output in 1998 rose to more than 61 million tons from 60 million tons in 1997. Worldwide consumption kept pace with the expansion in output. Whereas world red meat production expanded 25% since 1989, world poultry meat production rose 62%. The faster rise in poultry meat production was owing to a number of factors. One was the shift in favour of poultry meats in developed countries because of health concerns associated with the consumption of red meat. Also, rising incomes in less-developed countries during the 1990s boosted the demand in those countries for meat, especially poultry. In addition, efficiency gains in poultry meat production kept prices relatively low compared with other meats.

Dairy. Milk production for 1998 was 548 million tons, or nearly 1% above 1997. (*See*

Table V. Livestock Inventories and Meat Production in Major Producing Countries

In 000,000 head and 000,000 metric tons (carcass weight)

Region and country	1997[1]	1998[2]	1997	1998[1]
	Cattle and buffalo[3]		Beef and veal	
World total[4]	**1,502**	**1,499**	**53.9**	**54.0**
Canada	13	13	1.1	1.1
United States	101	97	11.7	11.8
Mexico	26	25	1.8	1.8
Argentina	50	51	2.6	2.2
Brazil	145	143	6.1	6.1
European Union	85[4]	84[4]	7.8	7.6
Eastern Europe	13	12	1.4[4]	1.3[4]
Russia	32	28	2.3	2.0
Ukraine	14	12	0.9	0.9
Australia	26	25	1.9	1.9
India	303	307	1.4	1.6
China	147	NA[5]	5.4	5.8
	Hogs		Pork	
World total[4]	**937**	**956**	**81.7**	**86.6**
Canada	12	12	1.3	1.3
United States	61	62	7.8	8.5
Mexico	11	11	0.9	1.0
European Union	120[4]	119[4]	16.2	16.8
Eastern Europe	36	37	4.2[4]	4.8[4]
Russia	17	17	1.6	1.4
Ukraine	10	10	0.7	0.7
Japan	10	10	1.3	1.3
China	475	NA[5]	42.5	44.0
Taiwan	8	7	1.0	0.9
			Poultry Meat	
World total[4]	...	...	**59.9**	**61.4**
United States	...	...	15.0	15.1
Mexico	...	...	1.6	1.7
Brazil	...	...	4.6	4.6
European Union	...	...	8.2	8.4
Eastern Europe	...	...	1.7	1.7
Russia	...	...	0.6	0.6
Ukraine	...	...	0.2	0.2
Japan	...	...	1.2	1.2
China	...	...	11.2	11.7
			Sheep, goat meat	
World total[4]	...	...	**11.1**	**11.3**
			All meat	
Total[4]	...	...	**215.3**	**220.4**

[1]Preliminary. [2]Forecast. [3]Livestock numbers at year's end.
[4]UN Food and Agriculture Organization, December 1998. [5]Not available.
Sources: Country data: U.S. Department of Agriculture, December 1998; world totals: FAO, December 1998.

Table VI. World Production of Milk[1]
In 000,000 metric tons

Region and country	1996	1997[2]	1998[3]
Developed countries	**341**	**338**	**337**
United States	70	72	71
Canada	8	8	8
Western Europe	131	129	130
European Union	125	123	125
France	26	25	25
Germany	29	29	29
Italy	12	11	11
Netherlands, The	11	11	11
United Kingdom	15	14	15
Eastern Europe	29	29	29
Poland	12	12	12
Romania	5	5	5
Former Soviet republics	71	68	65
Russia	36	35	32
Ukraine	16	14	13
Australia/New Zealand[4]	19	20	21
Japan	9	9	9
Less-developed countries	**200**	**207**	**211**
Latin America	51	53	55
Brazil	18	19	20
Africa	23	24	24
Asia	138	142	144
China	10	11	11
India	70	72	72
World total	**541**	**544**	**548**

[1]Includes milk from cattle, buffalo, camels, sheep, and goats. [2]Preliminary. [3]Forecast.
[4]Year ended June 30 of year shown for Australia and May 31 for New Zealand.
Source: UN Food and Agriculture Organization, December 1998.

Table VII. World Production of Centrifugal (Freed from Liquid) Sugar
In 000,000 metric tons

Region and country	1996–97	1997–98[1]	1998–99[2]
North America	**11.5**	**12.9**	**12.5**
United States	6.5	7.3	7.3
Mexico	4.8	5.5	5.1
Caribbean	**5.3**	**3.9**	**4.0**
Cuba	4.2	3.0	3.2
Central America	**3.2**	**3.5**	**3.5**
Guatemala	1.6	1.8	1.8
South America	**21.0**	**22.3**	**23.7**
Argentina	1.4	1.8	1.8
Brazil	14.6	15.7	16.6
Colombia	2.1	2.2	2.2
Europe	**22.9**	**23.7**	**22.0**
Western Europe	18.4	19.5	18.2
European Union	18.2	19.3	18.0
Eastern Europe	4.5	4.2	3.8
Poland	2.4	2.3	2.2
Former Soviet republics	**5.2**	**4.0**	**3.9**
Russia	1.7	1.3	1.2
Ukraine	2.9	2.2	2.1
Africa and Middle East	**10.9**	**11.8**	**12.3**
South Africa	2.4	2.6	2.7
Turkey	2.0	2.4	2.6
Asia	**36.9**	**37.2**	**38.9**
China	7.8	8.6	8.7
India	14.6	14.5	16.8
Indonesia	2.1	2.2	1.7
Pakistan	2.6	3.8	3.6
Philippines	1.8	1.8	1.6
Thailand	6.0	4.2	4.2
Oceania	**6.2**	**6.0**	**5.6**
Australia	5.7	5.6	5.4
Totals			
Beginning stocks	26.6	26.7	25.2
As % of consumption	21.6	21.1	19.8
Production	123.1	125.4	126.5
Consumption	123.0	126.9	127.5
Exports	36.2	35.6	34.8

[1]Preliminary. [2]Forecast.
Source: U.S. Department of Agriculture, December 1998.

Production in the U.S. declined 3% from the 1997 total, while Canadian production remained at about the same level. EU output was slightly lower as were exports, which suffered from the economic dislocations in Russia, the major European butter market.

Cheese production rose about 2% in 1998, but trade remained unchanged. Output in the U.S. increased more than the world average—3%—and exports also rose. European cheese production remained about the same in 1998 as in 1997. European exports were weaker, as export subsidies were reduced according to an agreement by the World Trade Organization.

Sugar. World sugar production in 1997–98 reached a record 125 million tons as a result of production increases in many nations and regions, including Mexico, the U.S., Central and South America, China, Africa, the Middle East, Pakistan, and the EU. (*See* TABLE VII.) Cuba, other Caribbean nations, Eastern Europe, the nations of the former Soviet Union, India, and other Asian nations experienced stable or declining output. The expansion came on top of record production in 1996–97 of 123 million tons. Consumption in 1997–98 rose to 127 million tons from 123 million tons the previous year. With the production and consumption increases roughly the same, trade at the global level remained at 35.6 million–35.8 million tons.

For 1998–99 world production was expected to reach a record 127 million tons. With demand in South America and in Asia forecast to remain strong, world consumption was forecast to rise above the 1997–98 level to 128 million tons. World trade was forecast to fall slightly from 35.6 million tons to 34.8 million. Much of the production increase was owing to improved sugar output in India, Africa, and Brazil. The EU, Australia, and Thailand were expected to reduce exports; Brazil was expected to continue the large exports recorded in 1997; and exports were to be expanded in North African countries and South Africa.

Coffee. Coffee production worldwide in 1998–99 was forecast at a record 108 million bags, 14% above the 1997–98 figure. (*See* TABLE VIII.) The total reflected sharply increased production in Brazil—52%—and slightly increased output in Colombia—2%. Brazil experienced favourable weather, and prices for coffee were high in 1997, which created a positive climate for investment. Mexico produced a record crop of 5.6 million bags as a result of a larger planted area, new plants entering the production phase, and a rebound from the weather-reduced 1997–98 harvest. The opposite situation occurred in Indonesia, where production fell to 6.6 million bags, 6% below the 1997–98 output and 16% below the 1996–97 production of 7.9 million bags. Output in several Central and South American nations fell or remained unchanged. Guatemala, Costa Rica, and Ecuador experienced reduced production because of excessive El Niño–generated rainfall. In addition, Hurricane Mitch in October 1998 devastated coffee crops in Honduras and Nicaragua. By contrast, Peru and Venezuela recorded production increases. In Africa, Uganda registered a 15% increase in production with 3.8 million bags.

Expanded world production in 1998–99 led to increased world coffee trade, which was forecast at 81.1 million bags, 7% above

that of 1997–98. The sharply improved Brazilian output lowered the prices of Brazilian coffee in world markets and improved its competitiveness. Although Indonesia was a major coffee producer, domestic consumption was small and the bulk of that nation's production was exported. Exports in 1998–99 were forecast at 4,750,000 bags, compared with 4.9 million in 1997–98.

Cocoa. World cocoa production for 1998–99 was forecast at 2,690,000 tons, roughly the same as in 1997–98 and below the output of 2,717,000 tons of 1996–97. (*See* TABLE IX.) Within the global total several regional shifts occurred. For 1998–99 output in North and Central America returned to the level recorded for 1996–97, following a larger crop in 1997–98. South America exhibited the opposite pattern, as production was forecast to rebound in 1998–99 after a reduced 1997–98 crop. Despite continuous output gains in Africa's largest cocoa producer, Côte d'Ivoire, the regional total output was forecast to fall in 1998–99 because of smaller crops in Ghana and Nigeria.

Cotton. World cotton production continued its fluctuation of recent years. (*See* TABLE X.) The area planted to cotton in 1997–98 was just over 33 million hectares, slightly less than in 1996–97. Improved yields resulted in a small increase in production from 89 million bales to 91 million. With consumption of cotton stagnant at 88 million bales, world trade fell slightly, and approximately 3 million bales were added to world ending stocks. Weather caused reduced production in South Asia but boosted cotton output in the U.S. and China.

For 1998–99 these patterns were expected to continue. The area planted to cotton was forecast to fall just below 33 million hectares, with output declining to 84 million bales. Worldwide consumption was expected to remain at 88 million bales, so ending stocks should fall to just above the level of 1996–97, 38 million bales. The major cotton producers, the U.S. and China, were expected to reduce their 1998–99 crops, the large harvests in 1997–98 having put downward pressure on prices. The former Soviet republics were forecast to continue to reduce their production. Poor weather and the economic difficulties experienced by those nations created a negative outlook for their farmers.

(PHILIP L. PAARLBERG)

FISHERIES

The total world catch of fish in 1996, the latest year for which figures were available, increased significantly over that of 1995. The record total of 121 million metric tons represented a gain of 3.7 million metric tons over 1995.

China continued to be the leading producing nation, registering an increase of 7.5 million metric tons during 1996 for a total of 31,936,876 metric tons. The positions of the top 10 producing nations remained the same, with significant increases shown by Peru (up 578,752 metric tons over 1995), Iceland (up 447,821 metric tons), India (up 356,761 metric tons), Russia (up 354,803 metric tons), and Indonesia (up 283,940 metric tons). Nations registering decreases were Chile (down 680,391 metric tons), Denmark (down 318,188 metric tons), and the U.S. (down 240,289 metric tons).

Table VIII. World Green Coffee Production			
In 000,000 60-kg bags			
Region and country	1996–97	1997–98[1]	1998–99[2]
North America	**19.3**	**18.7**	**18.4**
Costa Rica	2.4	2.4	2.2
El Salvador	2.5	2.0	2.0
Guatemala	4.1	3.5	3.1
Honduras	2.3	2.6	2.6
Mexico	5.3	5.4	5.6
South America	**43.2**	**38.4**	**51.4**
Brazil	28.0	23.5	35.8
Colombia	10.8	10.8	11.0
Ecuador	1.8	1.3	1.0
Peru	1.6	1.8	1.9
Africa	**20.3**	**17.6**	**18.3**
Cameroon	1.0	1.1	1.0
Côte d'Ivoire	5.3	4.1	4.1
Ethiopia	3.8	3.5	3.7
Kenya	1.1	1.0	0.9
Uganda	4.4	3.3	3.8
Zaire	0.9	1.0	1.0
Asia and Oceania	**21.1**	**19.7**	**19.4**
India	3.4	3.8	3.5
Indonesia	7.9	7.0	6.6
Thailand	1.4	1.3	1.3
Vietnam	5.8	5.4	5.8
Total production	**103.9**	**94.3**	**107.5**
Beginning stocks	33.0	28.8	23.3
Exports	80.4	71.5	81.1

[1] Preliminary. [2] Forecast.
Source: U.S. Department of Agriculture, June 1998.

Table IX. World Cocoa Bean Production			
In 000,000 metric tons			
Region and country	1996–97	1997–98[1]	1998–99[2]
North and Central America	**109**	**119**	**100**
South America	**372**	**279**	**341**
Brazil	185	163	170
Africa	**1,765**	**1,842**	**1,797**
Cameroon	125	125	125
Côte d'Ivoire[3]	1,130	1,120	1,150
Ghana[4]	324	420	360
Nigeria[5]	155	145	130
Asia and Oceania	**470**	**455**	**452**
Indonesia	305	307	310
Malaysia	120	106	100
Total production	**2,717**	**2,695**	**2,690**

[1] Preliminary. [2] Forecast. [3] Includes some cocoa marketed from Ghana. [4] Includes some cocoa marketed from Côte d'Ivoire. [5] Includes cocoa marketed through Benin.
Source: U.S. Department of Agriculture, October 1998.

Table X. World Cotton Production and Consumption			
In 000,000 480-lb bales			
Region and country	1996–97	1997–98[1]	1998–99[2]
Production	**89.4**	**91.4**	**84.2**
Western Hemisphere	23.8	23.7	18.7
United States	18.9	18.8	13.5
Brazil	1.3	1.8	1.8
Europe	1.8	2.1	2.1
Former Soviet republics	8.6	7.2	6.6
Uzbekistan	4.8	5.3	4.6
Africa	7.5	8.2	7.6
Asia and Oceania	56.0	57.3	55.8
China	19.3	21.1	18.8
India	13.9	12.3	13.0
Pakistan	7.3	7.0	7.5
Consumption	**88.2**	**88.3**	**88.3**
United States	11.1	11.3	10.6
China	21.4	20.8	19.8
India	12.4	12.5	12.3
Pakistan	7.0	7.1	7.3
European Union	5.3	5.4	5.4
Southeast Asia	4.4	3.9	4.1
Turkey	4.7	5.0	4.4

[1] Preliminary. [2] Forecast.
Source: U.S. Department of Agriculture, December 1998.

Some interesting changes occurred among the top 20 species landed during 1996. Anchoveta remained in the top spot, increasing slightly from 8,664,576 metric tons in 1995 to 8,863,714 in 1996. Alaska pollock moved up to second place, even though it decreased from 4,687,718 metric tons in 1995 to 4,378,843 in 1996. A larger decrease, however, was registered by third-place Chilean jack mackerel, from 4,955,186 metric tons in 1995 to 4,378,843 in 1996.

The largest difference registered was that for Pacific cupped oysters, which rose from 17th place in 1995 with 1,020,969 metric tons to fourth place in 1996 with 2,948,605. The reason for this huge disparity was not a sudden massive increase in the number of oysters caught but instead was the result of a change in the way that China reported its production figures in order to conform with the standard reporting procedures of the UN Food and Agriculture Organization (FAO). China had been reporting production statistics for the blood cockle, Japanese carpet shell, and Pacific cupped oyster to the FAO as shelled or shucked weight. This method significantly understated its production of those species because the standard practice with the FAO and other international fishery organizations was to report aquatic production as "nominal catch," the liveweight equivalent. A major increase in the catch of capelin, mostly from waters surrounding Iceland, resulted in a move from 20th place with 748,796 metric tons in 1995 up to 11th with 1,527,065. Production of chub mackerel also increased significantly, rising from

World Fishery Production							
(million metric tons)							
	1990	1991	1992	1993	1994	1995	1996
Inland							
Capture	6.588	6.382	6.253	6.661	6.908	7.379	7.553
Aquaculture	8.172	8.422	9.391	10.592	12.109	13.860	15.607
Total Inland	**14.760**	**14.804**	**15.644**	**17.253**	**19.017**	**21.240**	**23.159**
Marine							
Capture	79.292	78.706	79.955	80.618	85.775	85.622	87.073
Aquaculture	4.956	5.345	6.129	7.334	8.666	10.416	10.778
Total Marine	**84.249**	**84.051**	**86.084**	**87.953**	**94.441**	**96.038**	**97.851**
Total Aquaculture	**13.129**	**13.767**	**15.520**	**17.927**	**20.775**	**24.276**	**26.385**
Total Capture	**85.880**	**85.088**	**86.209**	**87.279**	**92.683**	**93.001**	**94.625**
Total World Production	**99.009**	**98.855**	**101.728**	**105.206**	**113.458**	**117.277**	**121.010**

Source: UN Food and Agriculture Organization.

1,556,888 metric tons in 1995 to 2,167,881 in 1996.

The rises in production during the last few years were accounted for almost entirely by increases in output from aquaculture. (*See* Special Report.) The level of catch reported by the world's fishing fleets leveled off at about 85 million–87 million metric tons.

Despite the increases in production, the fishing industry was described during the year as "economically inefficient." The director of the FAO Fishery Resources Division commented in May 1998, "Although the problems of fishery management are now widely recognized and new international instruments such as the UN Agreement on Straddling and Highly Migratory Fish Stocks and the FAO Code of Conduct for Responsible Fisheries were adopted in 1995, fisheries management has generally failed to protect resources from being overexploited and fisheries from being economically inefficient." The main reasons for this failure, according to the FAO, were the "lack of political will to make difficult adjustments, particularly regarding the access to fishery resources and fishing rights," and the "success of industry lobbies in resisting changes" that would address the problems. Also mentioned was the persistence of direct and indirect subsidies and the lack of control of their fleets by flag states. Warnings were voiced that without "urgent intervention" to control or reduce fishing, the estimated 60–70% of global stocks that were currently fully exploited or overfished would continue to decline.

Although many of the world's fishery resources were heavily exploited, there did appear to be some limited scope for development. The FAO estimated that better management of marine fisheries would result in a catch totaling 93 million metric tons, a gain of 6 million–8 million metric tons over the present. Better management should include practices that reduce unwanted by-catch, as each year commercial fisheries discard about 20 million metric tons of fish.

The FAO concluded that a reduction of at least 30% of world fishing capacity would be required to allow the rebuilding of overfished resources. That message was taken up by the international environmental protection organization Greenpeace, which recommended a 50% reduction in the world's fishing fleets. In response, many countries began instituting controls on their fleets, although not as rapidly and extensively as Greenpeace wished. In the European Union the fisheries ministers agreed to cut the EU fishing fleet by up to 30% over five years as part of a fleet restructuring scheme.

(MARTIN GILL)

FOOD PROCESSING

Home meal replacements became a major trend in 1998, particularly in the U.S., and the popularity of ready-to-eat, carryout meals increased. Convenience was the main spur to product and package innovation. Package design focused on ease of opening and environmental benefits. The increase in vegetarianism prompted new products and market strategies in this field. Although consumers paid lip service to the importance of health-

Fishery Production and Trade by Principal Producers in 1996			
Country	Production (metric tons)	Imports ($000)	Exports ($000)
China	31,936,876	1,184,170	2,856,986
Peru	9,521,960	5,122	1,120,391
Chile	6,910,556	41,599	1,697,258
Japan	6,793,444	17,023,945	709,445
United States	5,394,130	7,080,411	3,147,858
India	5,260,420	9,902	978,352
Russia	4,728,630	418,977	1,686,162
Indonesia	4,401,940	113,427	1,678,222
Thailand	3,647,900	818,353	4,117,865
Norway	2,963,007	535,642	3,415,696
South Korea	2,771,772	1,057,511	1,512,992
Philippines	2,133,063	139,468	436,542
Iceland	2,063,854	42,540	1,425,837
North Korea	1,800,000	3,571	59,554
Denmark	1,722,945	1,618,669	2,698,976
Mexico	1,499,403	81,720	738,980
Spain	1,289,147	3,134,893	1,461,486
Bangladesh	1,264,435	619	255,366
Malaysia	1,239,691	344,655	326,692
Argentina	1,239,154	71,031	822,208
Taiwan	1,229,759	612,945	1,810,033
Vietnam	1,000,000	6,431	503,555
United Kingdom	977,674	2,065,025	1,307,859
Canada	971,199	1,158,864	2,291,261
Myanmar (Burma)	872,965	424	98,231
Brazil	850,000	481,552	133,876
France	827,846	3,194,133	1,003,460
Ecuador	793,891	16,224	924,596
Morocco	640,093	6,616	743,130
Italy	560,251	2,590,985	372,290
Pakistan	555,489	84	140,745
Turkey	554,856	60,975	101,510
New Zealand	493,004	58,763	816,495
Venezuela	490,194	17,421	84,091
Ghana	477,173	19,359	55,994
World Total	**121,009,900**	**56,863,709**	**52,452,015**

Source: UN Food and Agriculture Organization, *Yearbook of Fishery Statistics*, vol. 82 and 83.

ful eating, dieting for health reasons declined while demand increased for products containing natural and organically grown ingredients. Functional foods with claimed specific health benefits, once perceived as a fad confined to Japan, became increasingly important in many other countries.

Consumer resistance to genetic modification (GM) of food animals and plants grew markedly during the year. Consumers in Ireland were given official advice on whether GM resulted in foods that were safe to eat. Concerned that consumers were unaware of the growing use of GM in food and the constituents produced by GM and by the lack of legislation in this field, European trade bodies urged their members to label products that contained such constituents.

It was estimated that in the U.S. alone approximately 30 million people were affected by food poisoning, of whom some 9,000 died. Catering services accounted for about one-third of fatalities, and processing was thought to be responsible for the remainder. Fears over E. coli bacteria spurred the U.S. Food and Drug Administration (FDA) to order warning labels on containers of unpasteurized fruit juice. Sweden expressed concern that salmonella had been detected in food imported from other European Union countries under EU free trade rules. In the U.K. new cases of bovine spongiform encephalopathy, also known as "mad cow" disease, fell dramatically, but the British National Audit Office said that by the year 2000 the BSE crisis will have cost the country about $6 billion, making it Britain's most expensive peacetime catastrophe.

Business Trends. The economic crisis in Asia, a key emerging market for food products and machinery, had serious implications for the global food industry. Indonesia, Thailand, and South Korea, where the cost of imported goods doubled in six months, were most at risk, but there was optimism that China would emerge relatively unscathed. The New Zealand Dairy Board stood to lose annual sales to the region of powdered milk worth $1 billion.

Growth rates in most Latin-American countries, particularly Brazil, exceeded those in Europe, with demand for many food products, such as milk and meat, outstripping supply. Central and Eastern Europe provided opportunities for Western food companies and equipment suppliers, which increased their presence through exports, joint ventures, and new factories. Meanwhile, the consumer market for food in Western Europe reached saturation, but changes in the type of food consumed boosted the food ingredients market, worth $40 billion in the EU. The greatest growth was in non-nutritive sweeteners, a trend also seen in the U.S., where there was a general move toward more natural products and ingredients.

Company Developments. The British company Cadbury Schweppes joined with The Carlyle Group of the U.S. to set up the American Bottling Co., which bought two U.S. soft drink companies, Beverage America and Select Beverages, for $724 million. Cadbury also bought the Polish chocolate maker Wedel from PepsiCo Inc. for more than $70 million and spent $120 million on a chocolate factory in Novgorod, Russia.

In September French authorities blocked the acquisition by Coca-Cola Co. of Orangina of France, distributor of PepsiCo's two main brands, for about $850 million. The move was seen as an attempt by Coca-Cola to oust PepsiCo from France. Coca-Cola opened a $50 million plant in Shanghai, which was expected to increase the company's investment in China to over $800 million. PepsiCo announced the acquisition of the Tropicana fruit juice business from Seagram of Canada for $3.3 billion. Inchcape of the U.K. sold its Russian bottling plant to Coca-Cola for $87 million only days before the ruble was devalued in August.

Guinness PLC and Grand Metropolitan PLC of the U.K. were cleared to merge by the U.S. Federal Trade Commission (FTC), which gave its approval of the £24 billion ($40 billion) deal on condition that the new group, renamed Diageo, dispose of its Dewar's whisky and Bombay gin brands, together worth around £1,150,000,000 ($1,897,500,000). The sale of the global rights to the brands was the largest the FTC had ordered. The European Commission had already ruled that the Dewar's brand in Europe must be sold.

In other international deals, H.J. Heinz Co. of the U.S. chose Auckland, N.Z., as the headquarters of its newly merged Australia and New Zealand operations, with sales exceeding $500 million. The British dairy processor Colac International established a new division, Volactive, dedicated to the production of functional food ingredients based on U.S. technology.

A growth rate of about 6% was achieved by the world's top 50 food groups. The world's top 200 food groups had combined sales of some $750 billion and commanded 40% of the world's total food market. Nestlé SA of Switzerland, with food and drink sales of about $40 billion, remained the world's top food company.

New Products and Ingredients. The functional foods category presented the largest number of new product launches, as the market for healthful foods increased dramatically. In addition to products claiming to improve health, new products were formulated for their beauty benefits. Skin Beauty Drink from Pokka in Japan and Bio Aloe Vera yogurt from Danone in France were claimed to beautify the skin. Burgen Soy and Linseed Bread, introduced in the U.K. by Allied Bakeries and in Australia by Tip Top Bakeries, was claimed to alleviate menopause symptoms in women.

An appetite suppressor, Måvål yogurt from Skanemejerier of Sweden, was claimed to create a comfortable sated feeling lasting 3–6 hours and to contain no drugs or artificial digestion blockers. Despite concern among consumers over possible gastrointestinal side effects, snack chips containing the fat substitute olestra became available in the U.S.

An American company, McFarland's Food Co., launched Chicken Bacon, made by a patented process from ground chicken meat with the darker meat combined with lighter stripes to resemble traditional pork bacon, with natural smoke flavour and seasoning added. The company was looking for European licensees because of the EU embargo on U.S. poultry.

After 12 years of development, Tate & Lyle of the U.K. launched a new sweetener called Slite, described as having all the qualities of sugar but half the calories. It received clearance from the FDA, which also approved sweeteners developed by two U.S. companies, the sucrose-based Sucralose from McNeil Specialty Products and the calorie-free acesulfame potassium (called Sunett) from Nutrinova. Meanwhile, in mid-December an advisory group to the U.S. National Toxicology Program recommended that the artificial sweetener saccharin be removed from the U.S. government's list of suspected carcinogens. Three other groups had earlier studied the question; two had voted in favour and one against removal of saccharin from the list.

Technology. Uproar from environmentalists prompted the Joseph Co. of California with BOC in Britain to develop a self-chilling beverage can using carbon dioxide instead of the ozone-harming gas previously contemplated. The beverage was automatically chilled in two minutes when a button on the can was pressed. The National Food Research Institute of Japan developed a method of eradicating pests from farm produce by using low-energy electron beams, eliminating the need for fumigants.

A machine that sterilized meat without cooking it and which could be integrated into food-processing lines was developed by the U.S. Department of Agriculture's Research Service in Pennsylvania. It applied a vacuum to meat or poultry cuts followed by a burst of steam and then cooling. BTTG Biotechnology of the U.K. invented a DNA test method for identifying all types of meat and fish (whether raw, canned, or processed) contained in food products, even when present in very tiny amounts.

Packaging. LifeTop was the name of a package sealing system introduced by BioGaia Biologics AB of Sweden, allowing storage of beneficial bacterial cultures to be kept separate from short-life dairy products until the moment of consumption and thereby extending storage life from weeks to months. Chichiyasu of Japan launched a health drink using the system.

Combibloc of the U.S. launched cartons made by a laser-cutting process for creating an easily openable spout. The first user was Mexican processor La Costeña for its tomato products. In the U.K. researchers at Scientific Generics made an initial announcement on the development of a cardboard can strong enough to hold pressurized beverages.

Government Action. The World Health Organization ruled in favour of EU-member states setting health standards that exceed international minimal standards on the sale of products. This overturned a previous ruling that the EU import prohibition of beef treated with hormones violated international free trade.

An EU proposal that firms be allowed to state that their products "may contain genetically modified ingredients" was thrown out as being too confusing. It was replaced by a requirement that labels state either that products contain such ingredients or are guaranteed to be free from them.

The EU gave legal protection to certain traditional European meat, beer, and edible oil products to stop them from being produced outside their home regions and by the wrong methods. The EU threw out a European Parliament amendment to its chocolate directive and allowed British and Irish manufacturers to continue to describe their chocolate as "pure chocolate," despite its added vegetable fat.

(ANTHONY WOOLLEN)

Aquaculture: Fulfilling Its Promise

by Anne Platt McGinn

For 25 centuries fish farming (aquaculture) has been a mainstay of Asian agriculture. Throughout China, India, and Thailand, it prospered on traditional small-scale farms. In recent years, however, fish farming has begun to suffer from problems associated with rapid growth and careless stewardship. As the 20th century draws to a close, aquaculture must redefine itself in order to realize its full potential.

Early Aquaculture. The earliest-known documentation of fish farming is a Chinese book entitled *Fish Culture Classic,* written in 460 BC. The Chinese raised their fish, mainly carp, in small ponds to supplement other farm crops. Through experimentation, farmers discovered they could raise several species of fish together in one pond. This system, known as polyculture, proved highly productive and was taken to Thailand by Chinese immigrants in the early 20th century. Polyculture then evolved into "integrated" aquaculture—raising plants and fish together in the same pond. Up to this time, the fish farms had remained small operations, but in the mid-20th century fish farming became a serious commercial endeavour in Asia, Europe, and elsewhere.

Starting in the 1960s and '70s, international development agencies supported aquaculture as the ideal industry to provide food for less-developed countries. Fish has important dietary benefits. It is generally cheaper to raise than beef or mutton, and aquaculture has less impact on the environment than traditional farming. A dichotomy developed, however, between aquaculture's potential and its reality. Aquaculture had become a resource-intensive industry that failed to emphasize resource reuse and recycling. Many fish were raised for quick cash, with little thought given to where the inputs of water, feed, and land came from, where the fish went after leaving the farm, and what environmental costs were incurred in the process.

World Status. Aquaculture is one of the fastest-growing sectors in world food production. Industry output more than tripled from 1984 to 1996, when it was valued at $36 billion. Between 1990 and 1995, world aquaculture production expanded at an average annual rate of 11%.

China leads the world in aquaculture, providing two-thirds of total farmed fish in 1996. Between 1990 and 1995 alone, China's aquaculture output increased by 120%, and in 1998 it made up over half of total fish supplies in China. In 1995 India, Japan, Indonesia, and Thailand—the other leading aquaculture nations—together accounted for almost 17% of world production. In contrast, all the industrial countries combined produced 14% of the world's farmed fish in 1995. Worldwide, marine catches remained at 80% of global fish production, but fish farmers were quickly altering the balance. For instance, 40% of all salmon consumed have lived longer in captivity than in the wild, compared with 6% a decade ago. It is expected that by the year 2000 one out of every four fish eaten will come from a farm.

Aquaculture also affects the market for meat: for every 5 kg (11 lb) of beef produced globally, there are 2 kg (4 lb) of farm-raised fish. In the U.S. sales of farmed catfish exceed those of veal, mutton, and lamb combined. Aquaculture is expected to provide a growing share of dietary animal protein in the future; farmed fish requires fewer grain inputs than other types of animal protein for food, including pork and beef.

Environmental Issues. Aquaculture was originally touted as an alternative to marine fisheries, which themselves were under great pressure as harvests increased and stocks were depleting. Benefits may be imaginary, however, since marine fish are turned into high-protein feed pellets for the carnivorous cultivated species such as trout, shrimp, and salmon that make up 15% of all farmed fish and crustaceans. Demand for feed pellets actually increased pressure on marine fisheries and wild fish stocks. A net loss of fish protein occurred globally.

Water pollution is another major problem. Researchers estimate that each ton of cultivated fish can produce up to a ton of waste. Poorly managed fish farms can produce high volumes of biological waste, primarily from uneaten food and waste material, which can then leak into surrounding areas. In 1995, for example, salmon farms in British Columbia produced a volume of waste equivalent to sewage from half a million people. Though generally not toxic, these nutrient-rich wastes can trigger eutrophication (enrichment of a body of water with dissolved nutrients that stimulate often undesirable plant growth).

Aquaculture can also affect the land surrounding fish-cultivation waters. Shrimp farming is particularly notorious in this regard. Between 1985 and 1995, aquatic farmers in some 50 countries produced 7.2 million tons of shrimp. More than 150,000 ha (370,650 ac) of valuable coastal area—mangrove forests, tidal estuaries, and even farmland—were choked with waste and abandoned. In the Philippines alone, shrimp ponds accounted for one-half of the country's losses of mangrove forests. Thailand became the world's leading seafood exporter, thanks to an enormous leap in giant-tiger-prawn culture between 1970 and 1990. The coastline was so ruined by farming, however, that by the mid-1990s Thai aquaculturists had begun transporting salt water inland to convert productive rice fields to shrimp farms. The farms were profitable for a time but eventually became polluted and were then abandoned. In July 1998, fearing for the future of their vast rice-growing regions, the Thai government banned shrimp farming from all inland waters.

Raising fish in densely populated, highly contained environments can also trigger outbreaks of disease. In early 1998, at a cost of U.S. $10 million, more than one million diseased farm salmon in New Brunswick had to be slaughtered in their cages to prevent the spread of infectious salmon anemia (ISA). By mid-1998 Scotland had forced the closure of 40% of its salmon farms because of outbreaks of ISA. Diseases originating on fish farms sometimes spread beyond the confines of the farms and required drastic measures. Recently, over a period of several years, for example, Norwegian taxpayers have paid $100 million to contain diseases spread from farmed fish to wild stocks. Entire rivers in Norway had to be poisoned in order to kill the diseased fish. Still another environmental hazard is the possible escape of farmed fish. The fugitives can disrupt the gene pool of wild species by eating them, outcompeting them for food, or displacing them altogether. Norwegian scientists recently reported that one-fourth of salmon spawning in freshwater areas originally came from farms.

Directions. Some governments have finally realized the costs of unregulated fish farming and are enforcing regulations. To protect its coastal areas, Honduras implemented a one-year moratorium on new shrimp farms beginning in August 1998. India restricted all industrial shrimp farms

from operating within 500 m (one-third of a mile) of the high-tide line, and Norway banned floating metal-frame salmon net-cages from fjords and coastal areas.

Beyond government legislation, however, new approaches to aquaculture are being developed to capitalize on ancient and ecologically sound practices. Some studies indicate that by using aquaculture waste to feed the fish—by processing it into feed and thereby using the fish as a means of waste-water treatment—costs for the water treatment could be reduced by 30% to 90%. In addition, aquaculture waste output can be used as an input to another industry. Many aquaculture facilities in the U.S. cultivate hydroponic vegetables, fruits, and herbs together with fish. Plants are grown with their roots immersed directly in the fish pond or in a connected channel. The plants remove large quantities of nutrients from aquaculture effluent—essentially aquatic manure—and the water can be returned to the tank. The tech-

(Top) Salmon are harvested at a fish farm in New Brunswick. During the year the number of the world's farmed fish continued to grow. (Bottom) Unregulated shrimp farms, like this one in Dak Mui, Vietnam, may pollute surrounding areas. By 1998 some governments had begun to ban or restrict shrimp farms.

nical capability to recirculate water is a key to the success of such systems in areas where freshwater is in short supply. These systems have already been widely adopted in China, India, and Germany. Thousands of tilapia and carp are farmed in closed-pond systems—aquatic greenhouses—in the Israeli desert. Earlier flow-through systems that used continual flushing with water to remove wastes have given way to biofiltration, a natural cleansing process that utilizes bacteria to degrade the organic fish waste. The pH levels, temperature, and nutritional content in this type of facility are monitored and adjusted by computer. Tilapia here can grow to full size in about 12 months, compared with 17 months in traditional ponds.

Integrating pond systems with local resources is another beneficial approach that offers enormous potential for resource efficiency. Farmers in Southeast Asia report that raising fish in their rice paddies enables them to reduce fertilizer inputs and save money on herbicides and pesticides. The preferred species for such use are the noncarnivores—such as carp, tilapia, and catfish—and mollusks, both of which eat low on the food chain (*i.e.*, consume relatively little protein) and generate comparatively little waste. An estimated 10 million small-scale farmers in Asia could potentially raise small amounts of fish in rice paddies and improve the security of local food supplies.

The Future. The UN Food and Agriculture Organization estimates that under favourable conditions, aquaculture could supply the world with 39 million tons of fish by the year 2010—about 70% more than was produced in 1998. If aquaculture is to remain an important source of food and income in the 21st century, however, the industry must change its current practices to become more ecologically responsible. This includes cultivating less-resource-intensive fish species such as carp and tilapia, reducing water use and pollution, recirculating nutrients and water, and preserving coastal ecosystems.

Anne Platt McGinn is a research associate with Worldwatch Institute.

Anthropology and Archaeology

ANTHROPOLOGY

Physical Anthropology. In 1998 scientists described a fossil cranium from the northeast African country of Eritrea that possibly extends the earliest known appearance of the characteristic cranial form and structure of *Homo sapiens* back to approximately one million years ago, at least 300,000 years earlier than previous estimates. The nearly complete cranium, discovered in 1995 in the Northern Danakil (Afar) Depression about 50 km (30 mi) from the Red Sea, exhibits an interesting mixture of modern and ancient traits commonly attributed to different hominid species. The skull's long, ovoid braincase, massive browridge, and modest cranial capacity are ancient traits usually associated with *Homo erectus*. On the other hand, the skull is remarkably narrow and reaches its greatest breadth near the top, modern features that are more typical of *H. sapiens*. The Eritrean material remained to be allocated to a particular species, but the cranium's mosaic of ancient and derived features certainly blurs the morphologically defined boundaries between *H. erectus* and *H. sapiens*.

Observers inspect Site #3 at the Zhoukoudian cave site, located southwest of Beijing. A reanalysis of the cave by a team of experts in 1998 found no evidence that *homo erectus* used controlled fires there some 400,000 years ago as had been thought previously.

A startling discovery from the Indonesian island of Flores and a reanalysis of the evidence for the earliest controlled use of fire by *H. erectus* in China dramatically altered scientists' views about the cultural abilities of this species. Fission-track dates obtained from two fossil sites on Flores, one of which contained at least 14 stone artifacts, suggested that *H. erectus* inhabited the island at least 800,000 years ago. Even when sea levels were at their lowest during the Pleistocene Epoch, water crossings must have been necessary to reach Flores; thus, these findings implied that *H. erectus* may have used watercraft hundreds of thousands of years earlier than had been previously thought.

The Zhoukoudian cave site, about 50 km (30 mi) southwest of Beijing, had long been regarded to contain the only reliable evidence for the use of fire before about 400,000 years ago. Most researchers had believed that the site, littered with burnt mammal bones, was occupied by *H. erectus* between 500,000 and 200,000 years ago. A reanalysis of the Zhoukoudian site in 1998 by an international team of experts led to a different interpretation. No evidence for hearths, ash, or charcoal was found in the cave, suggesting that the burnt bones were the result of natural causes rather than the controlled use of fire by *H. erectus*.

An enlarged left planum temporale, a trait heretofore found only in humans, was discovered to be present in 17 of 18 chimpanzee brains. This tiny region of brain tissue located within the left temporal lobe of the brain is widely accepted to be associated with language, auditory processing of speech, and musical talent. The new findings suggested that the anatomical substrate for language may have been present in the last common ancestor of humans and chimpanzees five million to six million years ago.

The actual development of humanlike speech is a more recent event. New evidence hinted that it may greatly predate the appearance of anatomically modern humans. Scientists discovered that the hypoglossal canal, a small hole in the base of the skull that transmits nerves to the muscles of the tongue, is much wider in modern humans than it is in chimpanzees and our earliest hominid ancestors, the australopithecines. Researchers argued that the wider the canal, the greater the number of nerve fibres that can go through it and give greater motor control of the tongue, a precondition for articulate spoken language. The hypoglossal canals of Neanderthals, *Homo heidelbergensis,* and a very early modern *H. sapiens* specimen all fall within the size range of the canals of living humans, suggesting that our vocal capabilities may have been essentially modern by at least 400,000 years ago.

Based on genetic data, chimpanzees are the closest living relatives of humans. More than 20 years of genetic studies have consistently come to the same conclusion, namely, that at the level of nuclear DNA humans and chimpanzees are 98–99% identical. The distinctive anatomical and behavioural differences between the two species, therefore, must be due to only a small number of genetic differences, perhaps mostly in genes critical for determining the rate and timing of growth and development. The exact nature of these genetic differences was completely unknown until scientists discovered the first important ape-human difference

in gene product expression. Chimpanzees and other great apes possess a gene that codes for a hydroxylase enzyme, which adds an extra oxygen atom to form a particular kind of sialic acid, a type of sugar. The sugar is found on the surface of every body cell and is associated with intercellular communication and susceptibility to certain pathogens. Humans lack a piece of this gene due to a base-pair deletion and consequently make a different form of the acid. Although there were suggestions that sialic acid may be involved in brain development, the exact functional differences between the two forms of sialic remained to be identified.

In the 1990s the most popular hypothesis to explain the distinctive linguistic and genetic status of the Basque peoples of France and Spain was that they are direct descendants of the Upper Paleolithic Cro-Magnon peoples who came to Europe between 30,000 and 40,000 years ago. Genetic and linguistic data presented by investigators in 1998 questioned this model of Basque heritage. The new studies implied that the ancestors of the Basques first migrated from Central Asia to the Caucasus between 10,000 and 14,000 years ago, where they mixed with northern Caucasian peoples. Then, about 5,000 years ago, a Neolithic Caucasian group migrated to southern Europe. The new hypothesis was concordant with both genetic data and what is known about the distinctive Basque language, Euskera, which may be related to North Caucasian languages. Thus, the Basques may be much more recent colonizers of southern Europe than previously thought.

Exciting new confirmation of a possible pre-Clovis (*i.e.,* before about 11,200 years ago) maritime-based colonization of the Americas came from two sites in Peru. One site, Quebrada Jaguay 280, was inhabited shortly after 13,000 years ago and contains numerous stone tools and the remains of a variety of marine organisms. Another part of the site yielded knotted cordage that proba-

A human ovum is prepared for in vitro fertilization. The implications of such technological innovations offered new challenges to cultural anthropologists.

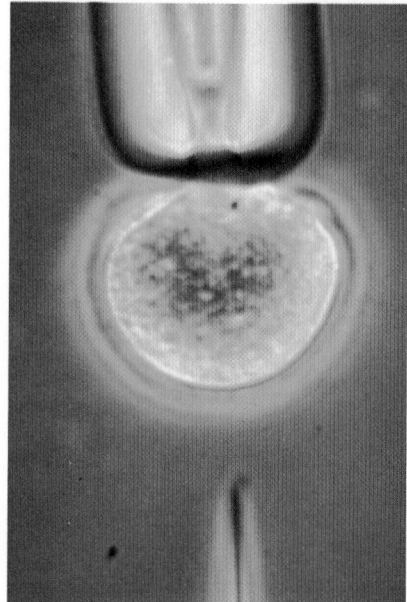

Recent research identified a small but significant genetic difference in the way humans and great apes, including this chimpanzee (above), synthesize sialic acid, a type of sugar thought to be associated with intercellular communication and brain development.

bly represents fishnets. The second site, Quebrada Tacahuay, dates to about 12,500 years ago and also indicates a reliance on marine fauna. The new sites suggested that the big-game hunting Clovis peoples of southwest North America may not have been the first Americans. The idea that early peoples colonized the Americas by migrating through the continental interior was also called into question. (*See* Spotlight: *The Peopling of the Americas.*) (STEPHEN L. ZEGURA)

Cultural Anthropology. Questions of culture continued to engage the attention of anthropologists everywhere in 1998. Debating the relative costs and benefits of involvement and detachment with the subjects and objects of their studies, anthropologists worked to develop more effective ways to describe culture while devising more productive modes of cultural interpretation. In *Culture: A Problem That Cannot Be Solved,* for example, ethnologist Charles W. Nuckolls of Emory University, Atlanta, Ga., critiqued anthropological schools of thought that defined culture as a means of resolving such contradictory human values as cooperation and competition. Rather, Nuckolls suggested, unresolvable contradictions creatively motivate cultural development. In *Envisioning Power: Ideologies of Dominance and Crisis,* City University of New York anthropologist Eric R. Wolf showed how 16th-century Aztec, 19th-century Kwakiutl, and 20th-century German National Socialist leaders employed power generated by cultural paradoxes to shape ideologies that often worked against the interests of many community members.

Anthropologists throughout the world increasingly worked in urban settings previously less studied by their discipline. In *The Future of Us All,* anthropologist Roger Sanjek of New York City's Queens College presented the findings of a 15-year ethnographic study of Elmhurst-Corona, a populous New York City neighbourhood and one of the most ethnically and racially diverse communities in the United States. Sanjek

and his students began fieldwork at a time when interracial tensions in urban communities were widely regarded as ominous portents of things to come. Instead, Sanjek's research suggested a more hopeful future. He found that older residents and newcomers responded to urban challenges by forming multiracial and interethnic community coalitions to overcome both internal conflicts and the indifference of city and state governments. Often led by women, these coalitions effectively opened lines of communication, helped people accept their differences, and built solidarity.

In *Exotics at Home* anthropologist Micaela di Leonardo of Northwestern University, Evanston, Ill., used examples from fieldwork conducted in New Haven, Conn., and Chicago to critically assess anthropology's impact upon Americans' attitudes toward themselves and others. Examining the roles Margaret Mead and other anthropologists played in shaping American identity by contrasting it with other cultures considered exotic, di Leonardo called on colleagues to consider more systematically the unique combinations of politics, economics, and history that both influence and bind all cultures. In the same vein, ethnologist Michael Jackson of Victoria University, Wellington, N.Z., encouraged anthropologists to use ethnography more effectively as a tool to help people see themselves as others see them.

Anthropologists also explored new cultural possibilities presented by technological innovations. In *Cyborg Babies: From Techno-Sex to Techno-Tots,* an interdisciplinary group of anthropologists, cultural critics, and historians of science weighed the potential impacts of Internet communication, artificial reproduction, and pre- and postnatal medical technology upon parents and children. Impressed by the rapidly expanding acceptance of in vitro fertilization, fetal ultrasound, amniocentesis, and other medical procedures by parents desiring healthy babies, the authors posed the ques-

tion of whether societies were creating the first generations of living cyborgs, symbiotic fusions of man and machine that had long existed in the domains of legend and science fiction.

Machine concepts also filtered into other aspects of culture study. In *Virtualism* another group of scholars explored how the virtual reality of globalized transnational economic models was compelling real societies to conform to idealized and potentially inappropriate abstractions. On a more positive note, ethnographer Robert Ibarra of the University of Wisconsin at Madison showed how distance-learning opportunities provided by "cyberschool" Walden University attracted an unusually diverse body of graduate students. Noting that over 35% of the university's 1,000 graduate students were members of minority groups, Ibarra suggested that phone and electronic mail (E-mail) communication with teachers allowed students to remain in their own communities, avoid economic and social dislocations, control the pace and intensity of their studies, and attain recognition for their intellect rather than their appearance or accent.

(ROBERT S. GRUMET)

ARCHAEOLOGY

Eastern Hemisphere. Evidence reported in 1998 from a project in Egypt suggested that humans living approximately 7,000 years ago enjoyed a social and spiritual life con-

siderably more complex than previously thought. In the Nubian Desert, about 800 km (500 mi) south of Cairo, researchers reported the discovery of numerous standing stones and megalithic structures aligned north to south, east to west, northeast to southwest, and approximately northwest to southeast. The alignments of the megaliths, dated to 6,000–7,000 years ago, reveal similarities to later Egyptian structures, such as the pyramids at Giza and Abusir, which are also laid out along a northeast-southwest axis. A stone circle, consisting of four sets of upright slabs, was also found and may have been used by the ancient nomadic peoples for sighting along the horizon. Project leaders speculated that the megaliths, which stand in a playa inundated by summer rains, might have formed a symbolic geometry that integrated death, water, and the Sun.

The French government succeeded in expropriating the land above Chauvet Cave, where hundreds of Paleolithic wall paintings were discovered in 1994. Researchers began a four-year program of study that had been on hold while the government and the principal landowner fought over rights to the cave. The project aimed to inventory and photograph completely the 30,000-year-old paintings.

In Ireland a stone tomb at the site of Carrowmore was dated to 7,400 years ago, which made it the earliest-known freestanding stone structure in Western Europe and the only one in all of Europe from the

Mesolithic Period before the introduction of agriculture. The discovery was greeted with some skepticism because agriculture had long been thought to have been the technological development that made much of complex civilization, including stone architecture, possible.

In the Mediterranean Sea southwest of Sicily, Italian fishermen netted a bronze statue of a nude young man, which researchers immediately compared to the Riace Bronzes, two remarkable sculptures found off the coast of Italy in 1972. The statue may represent Aeolus, the Greek god of the winds. Working from its style, scholars estimated that it dates to the 2nd or 3rd century BC.

In Rome excavations beneath the Trajan Baths uncovered a wall painting depicting a bird's-eye view of an ancient megalopolis. It was not clear to researchers what city was being portrayed in the fresco, which probably dates to the late 1st century AD. The new find was the largest-known Roman fresco with an image of a city in the entire corpus of Roman wall painting. One hypothesis was that the image represented ancient Rome before the Great Fire in AD 64. Nearby, part of the Museo Nazionale Romano, one of the world's greatest repositories of Roman art, reopened in its new home, the Palazzo Massimo, after 14 years of renovation.

Excavations in the Holy Land uncovered the earliest-known ruins of a synagogue and

A life-sized bronze statue of a young man thought to represent Aeolus, the Greek god of the winds, awaits inspection in March 1998. The badly damaged statue was retrieved from the Mediterranean Sea between the island of Sicily and Tunisia by Italian fishermen, who had netted a bronze leg a few days earlier. Scholars estimated that the work dated from the 2nd or 3rd century BC.

the remains of what may have been the oldest structure in the world designed for use as a church. Found outside Jericho, the synagogue, which dates from 50 to about 70 BC, was a mud-brick and stone construction that included a ritual bathing area, a small courtyard with seven or eight adjoining rooms, and a large rectangular main hall. The church, discovered in the Red Sea port of Al-'Aqabah, Jordan, was dated to the late 3rd or 4th century AD on the basis of pottery fragments found among its ruins.

A stone slab marked with the 6th-century Latin inscription *Pater Coliavi ficit Artognov,* meaning "Artognou, father of a descendant of Coll, has made this," was unearthed by archaeologists digging at Tintagel Castle, the legendary home of King Arthur on the Cornish coast of England. Some scholars rushed to claim that this was proof of the historicity of King Arthur, whereas others argued that *Artognov* was not close enough to *Arthur* to be conclusive.

In what was called the find of the decade in Japan, archaeologists recovered 33 Chinese bronze mirrors from a 3rd-century burial mound in the Yamato region of Honshu, Japan's main island. The discovery fueled a long-running debate over the location of the ancient Japanese kingdom of Yamatai, known only from the *Wei chih,* a Chinese historical text. According to the text, envoys of the Yamatai queen, Himiko, sent gifts to China in AD 239, and the return gifts included 100 bronze mirrors. Numerous Chinese mirrors had been recovered on the southern island of Kyushu, which led some Japanese historians to name it as ancient Yamatai. Other researchers, however, noting the similarity between the names, believed that the ancient civilization had been located in Yamato.

The year also was notable for two important legal developments in the ongoing debate between archaeologists, dealers, collectors, and museums for control of the past. In the United States a lawsuit before the Court of Appeals was to decide whether non-U.S. countries could claim national ownership of archaeological remains under the National Stolen Property Act to gain their return. A case in the 1970s set the precedent that artifacts covered by such laws do count as stolen as long as a country explicitly declares ownership. The case on appeal concerned a classical Greek gold phiale, a type of libation bowl, that was illegally exported from Italy and in 1991 sold to a New York collector for $1.2 million. In 1995, after the Italian government discovered the transaction, U.S. government officials seized the antique. Two years later a federal judge ruled that the phiale was to be returned to Italy. The collector subsequently appealed. Because of its implications for future repatriations of antiquities, the case had become an important test, with a coalition of museums supporting the collector's appeal and another alliance of scholars and preservation groups supporting Italy's side.

The 1995 Unidroit Convention on the Stolen or Illegally Exported Cultural Objects went into effect among the first five countries to ratify it: Romania, Lithuania, Paraguay, China, and Ecuador. Eighteen other countries had signed the convention, of which five were working toward ratification. The collecting of cultural artifacts by museums, preservation societies, and similar institutions was largely regulated by two international treaties, the 1954 Convention for the Protection of Cultural
Property in the
Event of
Armed
Conflict
and the 1970
Convention on the
Means of Prohibiting and Preventing the Illicit Import, Export, and Transfer of Ownership of Cultural Property. The Unidroit Convention was meant as a supplement to the 1970 convention and, as of late 1998, had not been signed by a number of countries, including the United States. Perhaps the most important feature of the Unidroit Convention was that it explicitly defined illegal excavation as theft, which could in theory eliminate the need for repatriation suits by foreign countries.

(ANDREW SLAYMAN)

Western Hemisphere. When Christopher Columbus explored the Caribbean islands in 1492, he encountered the Taino people, Arawak-speaking Native Americans who once flourished on the islands of Hispaniola, Puerto Rico, and Cuba. The Taino became extinct within 100 years after the Spanish conquest of the late 15th century, and little was known about their distinctive culture. Digging at the newly discovered underwater site of Los Buchillones in Cuba's Ciego de Avila province, archaeologists uncovered evidence for Taino history between AD 1220 and 1620, a period encompassing the first Spanish settlement. The excavations yielded a collapsed 400–700-year-old oval building more than 18 m (60 ft) in diameter that may have served as a community centre. Until this discovery Taino architecture had been known only from Spanish accounts.

Archaeologists had assumed that the Santa Cruz River valley in Tucson, Ariz., was largely uninhabited until the Hohokam people, a group of North American Indians who lived in the semiarid region of what is now central and southern Arizona, arrived about AD 600. Excavations in 1998, however, revealed seven riverside settlements dating between 800 BC and AD 150. The largest settlement, discovered at the Santa Cruz Bend site, was occupied between 760

This gold phiale, a type of Greek libation bowl, was at the centre of a U.S. court case between the American purchaser and the Italian government, which claimed the piece had been exported and sold illegally.

and 200 BC and contained at least 500 semisubterranean pit houses. Scientists agreed that the settlement was surprisingly sophisticated for such an early farming village in the southwestern desert. Nearby they found traces of simple water-control ditches dating to 800 BC, fragments of the earliest such communal structures in the Southwest. The inhabitants may have been the ancestors of the Hohokam culture, which flourished during the 1st millennium AD.

Researchers discovered evidence of a large farming settlement at a site called Cerro Juanaqueña in northern Chihuahua, Mex. It was believed that the site was inhabited at least 3,000 years ago, almost 2,000 years earlier than sites of such scale in the region. The village covers about 4 ha (10 ac) and is remarkable for its many hillside terraces, which extend over some eight kilometres (five miles). Archaeologists believed that the inhabitants lived on the terraces, where various kinds of occupation debris were found.

Important discoveries added new chapters to Maya history. Yaxuná is a Classic Maya site in northern Yucatán, Mex., dating to about AD 250. The ancient city was founded about 500 BC as a stopping point in a trade route that linked southern Maya cities with salt deposits on the northern coast. In 1996 archaeologists excavated the North Acropolis

A technician examines a mummy found in 1996 in an archaeological dig at Laguna de los Cóndores in the Peruvian Andes Mountains. The site yielded more than 200 well-preserved mummies, as well as clay pots and other artifacts of the pre-Incan Chachapoya culture.

and uncovered a sealed tomb. The nearly square burial chamber held burial 24, the archaeologists' code name for a collection of remains, which included the bones of a man about 55 years old who had been decapitated. An obsidian knife, perhaps used for ceremonial bloodletting, lay near his shoulders, and fragments of a polished white shell headdress worn by high lords were strewn at his feet. The bones of an adolescent girl and a young woman, also adorned with royal headdresses, flanked the male skeleton. Altogether archaeologists recovered the bones of 11 men, women, and children from the tomb. The city was sacked in the late 4th or early 5th century AD; thus, archaeologists believed that the remains represented the sacrifice of a royal family when the city was conquered by its enemies. Scientists were able to use deciphered Maya glyphs to reconstruct the events that accompanied burial 24. In a nearby temple they discovered a black stone ax and greenstone gems jammed in a black jar. It was believed that the artifacts commemorated a decapitation sacrifice, such as was often performed at change of leadership ceremonies.

In 1998 archaeologists reported the discovery of the oldest known ball court in the Americas, from a site called Paso de la Amada in the Soconusco area of Chiapas, Mex. When Spanish conquistadors came in contact with Maya communities in the Yucatán, they were impressed by the elaborate ball courts where players competed to knock a rubber ball through a wall-mounted hoop. Well-preserved courts were known from major Maya cities like Copán and Tikal, and the remains of latex balls and paintings of ball players indicated that the game had been established by at least the mid-13th century BC. The new ball court, unearthed in 1995, dates to about 1700 BC, which makes it at least five times older than any previously excavated ball court in Mesoamerica. The court is 79 m (260 ft) long and flanked on both sides by long mounds with benches built into them. The court lies among dwellings built by nobility, which suggests that the game was played by those of high status.

An examination of more than 200 well-preserved mummies discovered in Peru in 1996 and excavated in late 1997 revealed that they were members of an elite group called the "cloud people," the remote Chachapoya culture that dominated the Amazon River basin before the Inca conquered the area 500 years ago. In addition to the mummies, which were discovered high in the Andes Mountains at a place called Laguna de los Cóndores, scientists also recovered clay pots, baskets, decorated gourds, and carved wooden figures with stylized human faces. Unlike many Andean mummies in drier areas, the Chachapoya bodies had been deliberately mummified, the abdominal cavities emptied and the corpses embalmed. Ginned cotton was placed under the skin and in the mouth and nostrils to preserve the facial features. The people deliberately selected cold, dry areas that helped in the preservation of the dead. Archaeologists planned to study the mummies with modern medical technology and to excavate a 200-house settlement found nearby in an attempt to determine whether the burials were associated with that village.   (BRIAN FAGAN)

High-Tech Archaeology

More and more, archaeologists are moving aside their trowels, shovels, paper maps, and other traditional gear to make room for computers, mass spectrometers, chemical sensors, and global positioning systems. A number of new, high-technology science applications are now being utilized by archaeologists, dramatically revolutionizing the way these scientists date and analyze the past.

Radiocarbon (radioactive carbon-14) dating is well known for its use in establishing the antiquity of archaeological remains, including bone, shell, wood, and almost any other carbon-containing material of biological origin that formed in the past 40,000 years. A relatively new dating technique called accelerator mass spectrometry (AMS) radiocarbon dating, however, is now helping investigators look farther into the past, perhaps as far back as 75,000 years ago, and with much greater accuracy. The high-energy mass spectrometers work by counting the number of carbon-14 atoms in even the smallest of samples, such as tiny charcoal specks or single wheat grains. In 1997 archaeologist Bruce Smith of the National Museum of Natural History, Washington, D.C., demonstrated the use of AMS dating on domesticated squash seeds discovered in a Mexican cave. The seeds were dated to 8,000–10,000 years ago, and scientists were forced to rethink their views on when and where plant domestication first occurred in the New World.

In the past archaeologists relied heavily on the patterns of wear on teeth in order to make inferences about diet in prehistoric peoples. Today the isotopic analysis of ancient bone and hair is providing a much more complete picture of prehistoric diets. By analyzing the ratios of different carbon and nitrogen isotopes in bone, researchers can identify the main types of foods that people ate in the past. The technique is so sensitive that investigators may one day be able to pinpoint the moment at which a human population changed from a wild-plant diet to domesticated grains. In 1998 scientists reported the results of an isotopic analysis on an 11,000-year-old female skeleton found near Buhl, Idaho. They discovered that although the young woman had eaten a mostly meat-based diet, she also relied on a variety of fish and shellfish. This finding meshed well with other 1998 discoveries in Peru that suggested that the diet of early Americans was much more varied than previously thought.

Archaeologists are also using geochemical trace-element analysis on stone tools, metals, obsidian (volcanic glass), and other materials in order to learn more about the economics of past civilizations and to make inferences about prehistoric trade. For example, ancient South American hunters preferred to use obsidian for their knives and arrow points because of its predictable fracturing characteristics and sharp working edge. In 1997 researchers using spectrometers and other chemical analytic techniques discovered one of the primary sources of obsidian used by South American hunters. According to the scientists, the obsidian most likely originated from a quarry on the slopes of the Cotallalli volcano in the south-central Andes and was widely traded throughout Central and South America for a period of at least 4,500 years.   (BRIAN FAGAN)

Architecture and Civil Engineering

ARCHITECTURE

As the millennium neared its end, the buildings that were generating the most architectural excitement continued to be art museums and transportation centres, especially airports. The biggest, most ambitious airport of them all, Chek Lap Kok, opened during the year in Hong Kong. Indeed, at 51 ha (1 ha=2.47 ac), it was said to be the world's largest enclosed public space, with another 3 ha still under construction. British architect Sir Norman Foster, the principal designer, created a roof of lightweight steel vaults that allowed daylight to penetrate into the vast terminal. "It is a quest for calm spaces bathed in filtered light," the architect said.

Of the many remarkable new museums, perhaps the most notable was the small, remote Miho Museum near Kyoto, Japan, by American architect I.M. Pei that opened in late 1997. It housed a collection of Asian art owned by the Koyama family, leaders of a 350,000-person spiritual association, Shinji Shumeikai, a group for whom art and nature were the key to well-being. The museum was a modern glass-and-steel structure but with triangular roofs that recalled the shapes of traditional Japanese temples. It occupied a forested mountainous site that was often shrouded in mist. (See *Buildings,* below.)

The Miho was also noteworthy as an example of the increasing use of television to popularize architecture. A documentary by producer Peter Rosen, "The Museum on the Mountain," premiered on American television in October. Another example of the trend was a widely praised two-part biography of the American architect Frank Lloyd Wright, by noted filmmakers Ken Burns and Lynn Novick, that appeared in November, and still another was "Concert of Wills: Making the Getty Center," about the design and construction of the vast art complex in Los Angeles designed by Richard Meier.

Cultural Buildings. Besides the Miho, other museums included the Kiasma Museum of Contemporary Art in Helsinki, Fin.; by American Steven Holl, it was an experiment surfaced in zinc and glass, using the curving free-form shapes that had become common in the architecture of the late 1990s. Not yet open at the year's end was the long-awaited and controversial Jewish Museum in Berlin, an angular Z-shaped construction by avant-garde architect Daniel Libeskind. Libeskind's Felix Nussbaum Museum in Osnabrück, Ger., did open during 1998—the first work of the architect, then 52, to be built. It housed the paintings of a German Jewish artist murdered at the Auschwitz extermination camp in 1944. Its interior spaces, like those of the Jewish Museum, featured tilting walls and floors resembling those in such Expressionist films as *The Cabinet of Dr. Caligari.*

Spanish architect Rafael Moneo designed a new museum on an island in the harbour of Stockholm. The building was a modest villagelike assemblage of spaces gathered around a former drill hall that was used for exhibitions. In New Caledonia in the South Pacific, Italian architect Renzo Piano designed a cultural centre of swelling wooden egglike shapes, reminiscent of the architecture of the indigenous Kanak people. And in Basel, Switz., Piano designed the Beyeler Museum for a collection of French Impressionist masterpieces. It was an elegant high-tech pavilion of steel and glass. In Dallas, Texas, ground was broken for the Cathedral of Hope, which was to be the home of the world's largest gay and lesbian congregation. It was designed in a free-form style by American Philip Johnson.

Civic Buildings. Probably the most discussed new civic building of the year was the new British Library near St. Pancras Station in London. The architect, Sir Colin St. John Wilson, had worked on the structure since 1964, and ground was broken in

Critics continued to heap abuse on the new British Library in 1998. Located near St. Pancras Station in London, the library was called ill-conceived and overly expensive. The building's architect was Sir Colin St. John Wilson.

1982, but the project was held up by bickering among government agencies. The $800 million building was widely criticized as bland and uninspiring. In the U.S. a government building of comparable size was the $816 million Ronald Reagan Building and International Trade Center on Pennsylvania Avenue in Washington, D.C., by James Ingo Freed, a partner in the firm of Pei Cobb Freed & Partners. Freed, the designer of the U.S. Holocaust Memorial Museum nearby, wrapped the Reagan Building in a classical cloak of traditional limestone columns and domes and then exploded the interior as a spectacular contemporary glass-roofed atrium. In Boston a new federal courthouse by another partner in the same firm, Henry Cobb, featured a six-story glass curtain wall offering views across the harbour to the city's downtown.

The Lisbon World Exposition—EXPO '98—featured a ceremonial square designed by Portuguese architect Álvaro Siza Vieira that was shaded by an engineering marvel—a thin concrete canopy, spanning 65 m (1 m=3.28 ft), that looked as delicate as a tablecloth. The square was planned for conversion after the fair into a headquarters for the Portuguese Presidency and Council of Ministers. Also at the Lisbon fair was a new permanent aquarium by Peter Chermayeff of the U.S.

Commercial Buildings. The international rage for free-form architecture—an architecture of seemingly random curves and tilts, in which buildings often seem to be exploding or collapsing, as opposed to conventional vertical walls and right angles—was demonstrated in spectacular fashion with the opening of a new cineplex in Dresden, Ger., by the Viennese firm Coop Himmelblau. The building prompted one

The largest enclosed public space in the world, Chek Lap Kok Airport, built on an artificial island in Hong Kong, opened during the year. The principal designer of the new airport was British architect Sir Norman Foster.

critic to write, "Not since the Pompidou Centre in Paris has such a compelling building transformed and energized its urban environs. . . . The forms shoot off, and the eyes convince the body it is in the throes of a white-knuckle experience." Such structures became possible to design and construct only with the advent of the computer, the best-known example being the 1997 Guggenheim Museum in Bilbao, Spain, by U.S. architect Frank Gehry.

In the Napa Valley of California, the Dominus Winery was the first American building of the much-honoured Swiss partnership Herzog & De Meuron. The winery was a 91-m-long, two-story building that stretched like a wall across the vineyards, its exterior formed of piles of loose rocks that were held in place by the kind of steel-mesh screens normally used to prevent rockslides along highways. In Berlin the new Debis office tower on the Potsdamer Platz proved to be yet another remarkable building by Renzo Piano. Unlike the usual boxy office tower, the Debis was a bundle of vertical shafts, each containing a different function—either office space or elevators or exit stairs. Debis was also a sophisticated exercise in climate control. The glass wall of the office areas was really two walls. In the outer layer, glass panels were automatically operated by sensors, opening and closing to provide both ventilation and wind control. This outer layer also contained shades that could be operated by the tenants indoors, creating a varied appearance on the facade. Tenants could also open and close windows in the inner layer, set back about half a metre from the outer glass. In its use of a natural method of climate control rather than air-conditioning, the tower was typical of European and, especially, German architecture. Many German architects were going much farther, seeking the elusive goal of "zero-energy" by attempting to derive all the power used in their buildings from sunlight and soil.

Awards. Renzo Piano was named the 1998 winner of architecture's highest international honour, the Pritzker Prize. He first became known as the designer, with Richard Rogers, of the Pompidou Centre in Paris in 1976. Other works included the Kansai Air Terminal in Osaka, Japan, and the Menil Museum in Houston, Texas. Known for his interest in construction technology and his ability to collaborate with engineers to create inventive new building types, Piano avoided developing a personal style but instead searched for a unique solution to each building problem.

The Gold Medal of the American Institute of Architects, a lifetime achievement award, went to Frank Gehry, who was commended especially for his Guggenheim Museum in Spain. The AIA gave its 25-Year Award to the Kimbell Art Museum in Fort Worth, Texas, designed by Louis Kahn. The 25-Year Award was given to a building at least 25 years old that had stood the test of time. It was the fourth year in which the prize had gone to a work by Kahn. The AIA named Centerbrook Architects and Planners of Essex, Conn., as Firm of the Year. It also presented its annual Honor Awards for the best American buildings of the year. Among the more prominent of the 10 winners were the Chapel of St. Ignatius at the University of Seattle, Wash., by Steven Holl Architects and the renovation of the landmark U.S. Court of Appeals in San Francisco by Skidmore, Owings & Merrill.

At a ceremony in the historic Alhambra Palace in Granada, Spain, in October, attended by the Aga Khan and King Juan Carlos of Spain, the triennial Aga Khan Award for Architecture was presented to seven buildings scattered in countries from Malaysia to Israel. The Aga Khan, the wealthy spiritual leader of the Ismaili sect of Muslims, started the award program in 1977 to promote culturally appropriate architecture in the Islamic world.

Exhibitions. "Alvar Aalto: Between Humanism and Materialism" was on view at the Museum of Modern Art in New York City in the spring. It depicted the life work of the Finnish architect, who was known for combining Modernism with a love of nature. In the Guggenheim Museum in New York City, Frank Gehry jazzed up Frank Lloyd Wright's famous spiral ramp with chrome plating and neon lights for an exhibit of "The Art of the Motorcycle." At the Canadian Centre for Architecture in Montreal, an exhibit called "The American Lawn: Surface of Everyday Life" explored the near-mythical significance of lawns in American culture.

"At the End of the Century: One Hundred Years of Architecture," organized by the Los Angeles Museum of Contemporary Art, opened in Tokyo before traveling to Mexico, after which it was scheduled to visit Germany, Brazil, Los Angeles, and New York City. In 1,200 models, computer simulations, drawings, and photographs, the exhibit attempted to sum up all movements and trends of the entire century in a manner that would be easily understood by the general public. Sydney, Australia, was host to an exhibit called "Marion Mahoney and Walter Burley Griffin," the married team of architects who worked in the office of Frank Lloyd Wright in his early years and then designed the city of Canberra, capital of Australia.

New Commissions. Architects—in many cases quite avant-garde architects—were selected for several hotly contested new projects in the U.S. during the year. Zaha Hadid, London-based leader of the so-called Deconstructivist movement in architecture, who was known for designing computer-generated buildings that appeared to be freeze-framed at the moment of exploding, was chosen as designer of the Cincinnati (Ohio) Contemporary Arts Center, her first American building. Libeskind won the job of designing a new Jewish Museum in San Francisco. Dutch architect Rem Koolhaas (*see* BIOGRAPHIES), author of the classic book *Delirious New York,* was selected to design a new campus centre at the Illinois Institute of Technology in Chicago. Henry Cobb was chosen as architect for a new National Constitution Center near Independence Hall in Philadelphia.

Hardy Holzman Pfeiffer Associates of New York City won the job of converting the city's central post office into a new Pennsylvania Station, a replacement for the great Penn Station across the street that was demolished in 1963. In Edinburgh it was announced that Spanish architect Enric Miralles would design Scotland's new Parliament building, a structure made necessary by Scotland's recently granted status of home rule. Also in Scotland, Glasgow embarked on a year (1999) as "United Kingdom City of Architecture and Design," during which the city planned to restore the Glasgow Herald Building by the city's famed turn-of-the-century architect Charles Rennie Mackintosh.

Preservation. New York City's other great railroad landmark, Grand Central Station, reopened after years of meticulous restoration by architects Beyer Blinder Belle. Still another New York City icon, the main reading room of the Public Library, also reopened after renovation. A classic of the so-called Beaux-Arts style, the room was restored by architect Lewis Davis, who had to deal with such problems as windows painted black 50 years earlier, during World War II, because of the fear of air raids. In Philadelphia it was announced that the modernist classic PSFS Building, one of the first modern skyscrapers, would be converted to a hotel. Two of the most famous houses by Frank Lloyd Wright became preservation issues. Fallingwater in Pennsylvania, built over a waterfall, was found to be suffering severe structural weakening that would, if untreated, cause it to collapse into the river. And at Taliesin East, Wright's own home in Wisconsin, a centuries-old oak tree fell during a windstorm and crushed part of the roof. Plans were quickly made to repair both houses.

An international protest was mounted after the announcement that the 1972 Sho-Hondo Buddhist temple at the foot of Mt. Fuji in Japan, regarded as a classic of late modern architecture, would be demolished by the religious leaders who owned it. The

A spectacular glass-roofed atrium was one of the features of the new Ronald Reagan Building and International Trade Center in Washington, D.C. Architect James Ingo Freed, best known for the U.S. Holocaust Memorial Museum, designed the huge building.

The Akashi Kaikyo Bridge, which links the Japanese islands of Honshu and Shikoku, features a 1,991-m-long central span, the longest span in the world. The bridge opened in April.

World Monuments Fund announced its biennial list of the world's most endangered historic sites, ranging from the early-modern Russian Russakov Club theatre (1929) in Moscow to Fort Apache, a Native American village in Arizona. In New York City the nearly all-glass (including floors) penthouse apartment of the late architect Paul Rudolph, a modern classic, was placed at risk when the building it sat atop was offered for sale.

News Events and Controversies. In Washington, D.C., government agencies approved a revised design of the controversial proposed World War II Memorial, planned for a site on the Mall near the Washington Monument. Times Square in New York City continued its rebirth with several new projects. Architects Philip Johnson and Alan Ritchie unveiled a proposal for two towers, 40 and 49 stories, the entire facades of which would be changeable illuminated advertising. Also in New York City a 3,700-ton historic theatre, the Empire, was moved about 52 m along 42nd Street to make room for a new 25-screen cinema. City agencies had insisted that the old theatre be preserved. Ground was broken for a new theatre, the Second Stage, designed by Koolhaas and local architect Richard Gluckman.

The town of Seaside, Fla., gained notoriety when it was used as the setting for the film *The Truman Show,* which presented it, some thought unfairly, as a prettified prison. The movement that had created Seaside, the so-called New Urbanism, continued to spread rapidly throughout the U.S. and in other countries. It advocated closely knit, easily walkable "Main Street" towns, as op-

posed to the sprawl of highways and suburbs that had characterized development since World War II.   (ROBERT CAMPBELL)

BRIDGES

Even though much of Asia suffered a financial crisis in 1998, the world's longest bridge was completed there, and other major projects were underway. Foremost was the opening in April in Japan of the Akashi Kaikyo Bridge, a suspension bridge with a central main span of 1,991 m (1 m=3.28 ft). At year's end it was by far the world's longest span. The 3,911-m-long Akashi crosses a strait of the Inland Sea and links the Japanese islands of Honshu and Shikoku via Awaji Island. The bridge took 10 years to build and was affected by the 1995 Kobe earthquake, which moved the tops of the 283-m steel towers farther apart by 0.8 m. Engineers then recalculated the design.

A second noteworthy project in Japan was the Tatara cable-stayed bridge, which made up part of another bridge chain from Honshu to Shikoku. Crossing nine islands, the $800 million structure was to have a central span of 890 m when it opens in 1999 and a total length of 1,480 m. Cable-stay rather than suspension was chosen for this bridge because large suspension anchorages would have involved unsightly excavations in the middle of a national park.

In China construction was well advanced on the Jiangyin highway suspension bridge, one of the world's four largest. The superstructure team from Norwegian contractor Kværner, which built the 1,377-m Tsing Ma Bridge in Hong Kong, moved north to construct this 1,385-m central span suspension

bridge across the Chang Jiang (Yangtze River) near Shanghai. It was scheduled to be completed in mid-1999 as a symbol of the 50th anniversary of the Chinese Revolution.

Another landmark opening in Asia during the year was the Bangabandhu Jamuna Multipurpose Bridge in Bangladesh, one of the world's poorest nations and one regularly buffeted by typhoons and floods. The multispan concrete structure was the first major link between the two parts of the country separated by the Jamuna River, which can be up to 40 km wide in its floodplain and which frequently changes course (1 km=0.62 mi). When construction began, the bridge abutment could be fixed at only one end; the location of the other end could not be determined until the end of the next flood season. The bridge also needed extremely deep foundations, each of the concrete piers at 100 m spacings requiring 13-m-diameter tubes driven 105 m deep for stability.

In Europe another record holder, the Great Belt (Store Bælt) East suspension bridge opened in June. It was, at 1,624 m, the world's second longest span, and it carried a four-lane highway that extended onto multispan concrete viaducts on either side for a total crossing of 6.8 km. The bridge is part of an 18-km road-and-rail crossing between Funen and Zealand, Denmark's major islands. Another major bridge in Europe was to be the Rion-Antirion in Greece. Crossing the entrance to the Gulf of Corinth, it was to have three cable-stayed spans and total 2.9 km in length over water up to 62 m deep.

In the U.S., particularly in California, attention increasingly was focused on retrofitting and rebuilding bridges so that they

would be more resistant to earthquakes. Approaches to the Golden Gate Bridge in San Francisco were being strengthened, and the design for a single-tower suspension bridge and viaduct as the more than $1 billion replacement of the San Francisco–Oakland Bay Bridge was approved.

(ADRIAN LEE GREEMAN)

BUILDINGS

At the Jean-Marie Tjibaou Cultural Center in Nouméa, New Caledonia, which opened in 1998, fingerlike, laminated-wood ribs webbed with a fretwork of iroko wood and enclosing 10 shell-like exhibition pavilions reached toward the sky. Besides evoking the thatched structures of the native Kanak people, the pavilion's airfoil shape and double-wall construction, designed by the Renzo Piano Building Workshop (Genoa, Italy), served two purposes. The shape caused prevailing breezes to draw hot air out of the naturally ventilated structures, assisting the infiltration of cooler air from their base, and steel rods and connectors reinforced the two shells against typhoons.

In Berlin the Debis tower opened. A 22-story office building, also designed by Piano, it also featured a double-wall construction but one that was technologically sophisticated. Electronic sensors measured temperature, wind, and the Sun's intensity and instructed computerized controls to pivot open a glass outer wall when natural ventilation was needed. On cool days the window wall closed, sealing a 70-cm-wide airspace to insulate the interior (1 cm=0.39 in). Some areas of the building were shaded by specially fabricated, high-strength terra-cotta rods and panels. These innovations allowed occupants to have highly individualized control of heat, glare, and ventilation, while reducing energy consumption well below the strict European norms.

Rehabilitation of Berlin's 1894 Reichstag, which languished as a semi-ruin during the divided-city era, neared completion. It shared with the Tjibaou and Debis projects an increasing architectural focus on environmentally sustainable design and energy conservation. Within restored massive stone walls, the London-based firm, Sir Norman Foster & Partners, designed a glass box as the place where the German parliament will sit. Breezes wafting through a louvered-glass dome atop the Bundestag hall were designed to draw exhaust air up a funnel-like chimney. Mirrors on the exterior of the funnel would reflect daylight deep into the hall, reducing the need for electric light, while a track-mounted sunshade would revolve as the Sun moves, to reduce glare.

Exhibitions during the year showcased technological prowess. Portuguese architect Álvaro Siza Vieira, working with engineer Cecil Balmond of the Ove Arup Partnership, slung an inches-thin, curved-concrete roof spanning 65 m as a welcoming entrance to Lisbon's EXPO '98 (1 m=3.28 ft). The Millennium Dome, said to be the world's largest at 320 m in diameter, neared completion in Greenwich, east of London. Twelve outward-tilted, 90-m-high masts held tensioned-steel cables, stretching taut a coated, fibreglass roof. The designers were the Richard Rogers Partnership, architect (London), and Buro Happold (Bath, Eng.).

The site of the Miho Museum, near Kyoto, Japan, was adjacent to long-sacred landscapes. Pursuant to strict conservation criteria, architect Pei Cobb Freed & Partners placed 80% of the floor area underground, restoring on the roof preexisting landforms and native plantings. About 2,000 piles were driven for the 460-m-high Shanghai World

Financial Center, designed by architect Kohn Pedersen Fox of New York City and slated for completion in 2001. Primarily an office building of composite steel and concrete construction, it was to be topped by an observation deck and 10 floors of hotel guest rooms, both reached by double-decked, express elevators.

Technological advances in computers and telecommunications technologies began to affect commercial office building design in 1998. Data networking systems increasingly permitted roving workers to plug in phones and computers wherever desired within a building or complex of company facilities. Wireless networks also showed promise, though they remained limited in data capacity and sometimes entailed more wiring than conventional networks. Such technology advances promised a more mobile workplace, where employees increasingly eschew offices and desks for a variety of formal and informal work settings. (JAMES S. RUSSELL)

DAMS

Though often considered less valuable than claimed and in many cases environmentally harmful, in 1998 dams continued to be in demand to supply drinking water to the expanding population, for municipal and industrial purposes, and for agriculture. This was evidenced by the completion of 242 dams in 1997 and the 1,738 dams under construction in 1998. The less-developed countries continued to build the largest numbers: India (625), China (302), Turkey (236), and South Korea (145). In the developed nations dam construction slowed considerably, mostly because of the recognition that environmental impacts of the construction had often not been properly considered. *(continued on page 144)*

Among a number of notable building projects completed during the year was the Jean-Marie Tjibaou Cultural Center in Nouméa, New Caledonia, which featured 10 shell-like pavilions.

Notable Civil Engineering Projects (in work or completed, 1998)

Name	Location	Year of completion	Notes
Airports		Area (ha)	
Kuala Lumpur International	Sepang, Malaysia	10,000	1998	Includes high-speed rail link to Kuala Lumpur; opened June 30, 1998
Hong Kong International	Chek Lap Kok Island, Hong Kong	1,248	1998	World's largest artificial island; bridges + tunnel links
Seoul International	Inchon, S.Kor.	1,095	2001	Landfill between islands in Yellow Sea; includes seaport
Oslo International	Gardermoen, Nor.	?	1998	Opened October 8, 1998
Aqueducts		Length (m)	
Great Man-Made River	interior to coastal Libya (many sites)	1,900,000	2007	Begun 1991; 1,900,000-phase 1 pipeline; phase 3 begun 1998
Lesotho Highlands Water Project	Maluti Mountains, Lesotho–South Africa	82,000	2025?	Phase 1 (of 5) water transfer; inaugurated Jan. 22, 1998
Bridges		Length (main span; m)	
Akashi Kaikyo (Pearl)	Akashi–Awaji Island, Japan	1,991	1998	World record (suspension) upon completion on April 5, 1998
Great Belt (Store Bælt) East	Halsskov–Knudshoved, Den.	1,624	1998	World's second longest (suspension) upon completion on June 14, 1998
Jiangyin Yangtze	Jiangsu province, China	1,385	1999	Fourth longest in world (suspension) upon completion
Chesapeake Bay (#2)	Norfolk, Va.–Virginia's eastern shore	1,158	1999	New bridges/trestles parallel first C.B. link
Tatara Ohashi	Honshu–Shikoku, Japan	890	1998	World record cable-stayed; part of bridge chain
Rion Antirion	Pátrai, Greece (across Gulf of Corinth)	560	2003	Multicable-stayed; complex deepwater foundations
Øresund	Copenhagen, Den.–Malmö, Swed.	490	2000	16.4 km road/rail link; tunnel, artificial island, bridge
Ting Kau	Hong Kong mainland–Tsing Yi Island	475	1998	1 of 3 bridges to new airport; stunning cable-stayed design
Vasco da Gama	Libson, Port.	420	1998	Total length 17.2 km; Europe's longest road bridge; opened Feb. 29, 1998
Bangabandhu (Jamuna Multipurpose)	Sirajganj–Bhuapur, Bangladesh	99	1998	Total length 4.8 km; first link between NW & E Bangladesh
Buildings		Height (m)	
World Financial Centre	Shanghai, China	460	2002	Will be world's tallest; groundbreaking 1997, delayed 1998
Jin Mao ("Golden Prosperity")	Shanghai, China	420	1999	Topped out Aug. 28, 1997; grand opening January 1999
Plaza Rakyat	Kuala Lumpur, Malaysia	382	1999	World record reinforced-concrete complex with office tower
Millennium Dome	Greenwich, London, U.K.	50	1999	Will be world's largest dome; to open Dec. 31, 1999
Reichstag (reconstruction)	Berlin, Ger.	—	1999	Fire destroyed (1933); transparent cupola to be landmark
European Parliament building	Strasbourg, France	?	1998	Futuristic, dome-shaped deputy chamber
Frauenkirche (reconstruction)	Dresden, Ger.	—	2006	Baroque Lutheran church firebombed 1945
City		Area (ha)	
Putrajaya	near Kuala Lumpur, Malaysia	4,400	1999	Planned national capital; government transfer 2000
Dams		Crest length (m)	
Yacyretá Multipurpose	Paraná River, Argentina–Paraguay	69,600	1998	Hydroelectric power, navigation, irrigation; first stage July 7, 1998
Eastside Reservoir East/Domenigoni	Hemet, Calif., U.S.	3,380	1999	Reservoir=800,000 ac-ft
Eastside Reservoir West/Domenigoni	Hemet, Calif., U.S.	2,736	1999	Reservoir=800,000 ac-ft
Three Gorges	west of Yichang, China	1,983	2009	Stage 1: 1993–97; 2: 1998–2003; 3: 2004–09
Xiaolangdi	Huang Ho (Yellow River), China	1,667	2001	Flood, ice, silt control; irrigation; power
Lower Agno	San Roque, Luzon, Phil.	1,100	2003	Irrigation and flood control
Seven Oaks	Santa Ana River, Calif., U.S.	802	1999	Flood control
Longtan	Hongshui River, China	800	?	Pumped storage power facility
Ertan	Yalong River, China	775	2000	Second largest hydroelectric power project in China
Nam Theun 2	Upper Theun River, Laos	?	2004	Electricity to be sold to Thailand
Sardar Sarovar Project	Narmada River, Madhya Pradesh, India	?	?	Irrigation for Gujarat, electricity, extremely controversial
Highway		Length (km)	
M-1 Motorway	Karachi–Peshawar, Pak.	1,300	?	Islamabad–Lahore (1997), –Peshawar (begun 1998)
Railways (Heavy)		Length (km)	
South Xinjiang	Kashi–Korla, China	975	2000	Completes 1,470-km Turpan–Kashi Railway
Guangdong–Hainan	mainland China–Hainan	543	2001	First rail link to Hainan
Trans-Isthmus	Colón–Panama City, Panama	89	2000	Complete overhaul for container traffic
Railways (High Speed)		Length (km)	
Kyongbu	Seoul-Pusan, S.Kor.	431	2003	Connects two largest cities
Taiwan High Speed	Taipei-Kao-hsiung, Taiwan	345	2003	Connects two largest cities
Italy High Speed	Milan-Bologna, Italy (third line)	180	1998	8 lines (1992–2003)
German High Speed	Oebisfelde–Berlin, Ger.	152	1998	First link to Berlin; opened Sept. 27, 1998
Subways/Metros		Length (m)	
Oporto Metro	Oporto, Port.	70,000	2003	Europe's largest total rail system project
Madrid Metro	Madrid, Spain	37,500	1999	39 new stations
Kuala Lumpur Metro	Kuala Lumpur–Sepang, Malaysia	29,000	1999	Longest driverless metro system in the world
Manila Metro	Manila, Phil.	16,800	2000	Built over extremely congested auto routes
London Metro (Jubilee Extension)	London, Eng.	15,980	1999	Twin 12,390-m tunnels
Chongqing Metro: Line 1	Chongqing, China	15,000	1998	Line 2 planned 1996–2000
Paris Métro (Meteor Line)	Paris, France	7,500	1998	First new line since 1935; driverless
Tunnels		Length (m)	
Lærdal	Lærdal–Aurland, Nor.	24,500	2001	World's longest road tunnel
A86 Ring Road	around Paris	17,700	2005	Two tunnels; preserves Seine Valley beauty
Bosporus	Istanbul, Turkey	13,300	2003	Rail tunnel to ease bridge traffic pressure
Pinglin Highway	near Taipei, Taiwan	12,900	1999	Twin 11.8-m tunnels under Sheushshan Range
North Cape	Magerøy Sound, Nor.	6,820	1999	World's longest subsea road tunnel
Maynard Mountain (enlarged)	near Whittier, Alaska	4,000	2000	First roadway and new piggyback rail
Øresund	Copenhagen, Den.–Malmö, Swed.	3,750	2000	Twin tunnels; world-record immersed tube
Orelle	east of Frejus Tunnel, France	3,600	2000	
Central Artery/Tunnel	Boston, Mass., U.S.	330	2004	"One of the most complex construction challenges of this century"
Urban Development		Area (sq m)	
Potsdamer Platz	Berlin, Ger.	620,000	2000	19 buildings

1 m=3.28 ft; 1 km=0.62 mi; 1 ha=2.47 ac

(continued from page 142)
A particular focus in this regard was the resettlement of people from areas flooded by dam reservoirs.

In China the Three Gorges Dam continued to receive considerable attention because of the 1.3 million people that would be displaced from the reservoir area and the consequent economic damage to them, which had not been addressed adequately. After years of debate, however, the Chinese announced that they had made satisfactory arrangements for the displaced people. This was later confirmed in a report by the World Bank. The World Bank subsequently invited the World Conservation Union to hold a workshop to discuss and develop an agreement on international standards for deciding whether a dam should be built. The Union planned to conduct a review on the effectiveness of large dams in promoting social and economic development.

Worldwide in 1998 there were more than 45,000 dams, over 20,000 in China alone. About 80% of these dams were less than 30 m high, and only 1% had heights in excess of 150 m (1 m=3.28 ft). By type, 75% were earthfill dams, 10% gravity dams, 7% rockfill dams, 6% arch dams, and 2% masonry dams. As of 1998 only 80–85% of the hydroelectric potential had been tapped in the developed countries, and less than 20% had been exploited in the less-developed countries. Approximately 70–80% of the surface water in most less-developed countries was going to waste into the seas and oceans.

In Laos, near the Vietnam border, work proceeded on the Nam Theum 2 hydroelectric project. With a capacity of 680 MW, it was expected to generate $250 million per year in revenue from electricity sales. The reservoir was to be 70 km long, cover some 450 sq km, and store three billion cu m of water (1 sq km=0.386 sq mi; 1 cu m=35.3 cu ft). Its cost was estimated at $1.2 billion, and it would require the resettlement of 800 families in 17 villages.

Slovakia was pressing Hungary to build a dam on the Danube River so that the Gabcikovo hydroelectric project could be completed. Hungary stopped work on its Nagymaros Dam in 1989 after pressure from environmentalists. Nagymaros is 100 km downstream from Slovakia's Gabcikovo Dam and was needed to deal with river fluctuations caused by the Gabcikovo power output (1 km=0.62 mi).

The 165-m-high Sainte Marguerite 3 Dam was the largest under construction in Canada. An earthfill and rockfill dam 380 m long with a volume content of 6.3 million cu m and due for completion in 2001, it was to provide 882 MW of power.

In the U.S. the 168-m-high Seven Oaks Dam in southern California was scheduled for completion in 1999. In 1998 the U.S. Congress ordered that their effect on wildlife and recreation be considered rather than their power output alone, when existing dams needed to be relicensed.

(T.W. MERMEL)

ROADS

One of the biggest highway spending programs in history was approved by the U.S. Congress in 1998. The six-year infrastructure program, totaling $217 billion, would pay for new and reconstructed roads, bridges, and mass-transit systems across the nation and correct inequities in the formula for distributing highway funds by ensuring that no state would get back less than 91 cents for each dollar of gasoline taxes paid into the federal highway trust fund.

The International Road Federation (IRF) praised the U.S. investment, and Switzerland cautioned that if European Union (EU) countries failed to follow the U.S. example and unblock road spending programs, they risked falling to third place behind the U.S. and Southeast Asia in global competition. In June the EU approved more than $500 million for its Trans-European Networks, with 62% of the fund targeted for rail projects. Though the U.K. government planned to reduce road-building projects, it gave its consent for the construction of Great Britain's first private tollway, a $1 billion bypass of Birmingham. The project won legal clearance after protesters lost their suit, claiming that the government acted unlawfully in giving the go-ahead for the scheme. The IRF also made further progress in relaunching infrastructure development in Central Asia and the Caucasus, following the successful Silk Road Conference in Azerbaijan on Sept. 7–8, 1998.

Despite the economic crises in Southeast Asia, a huge road-building program in China appeared undisturbed. By 2010 an estimated 90 million more Chinese would be able to afford a car, and construction work was underway to complete two north-south and two east-west highways. In 1998 China became the largest borrower of investment loans ($2.6 billion) from the World Bank. China also slated $6 billion for new road projects in Hong Kong.

In Pakistan work started on the 154-km (1 km=0.62 mi) section of the M-1 expressway from Peshawar to Islamabad. The road, valued at $430 million, would form part of a 1,300-km expressway from Peshawar in the north to Karachi in the south. Another section of the $1 billion, 357-km Lahore-Islamabad expressway. In neighbouring India, where 80% of passenger and 60% of freight movement was by road, authorities were told by the World Bank that it would be prepared to allocate $1 billion to finance badly needed road construction. Following devastating floods, Bangladesh received $273 million, the largest-ever credit from the World Bank for road rehabilitation and maintenance projects.

Bangladesh also witnessed the opening of Bangabandhu Bridge—a 4.8-km, more than $900 million structure over the Jamuna River—which physically linked the east and west. Other highway bridge openings included the Akashi Kaikyo Bridge in Japan, part of a system of bridges linking the islands of Honshu and Shikoku (its main span of 1,991 m made it the longest suspension bridge in the world); the 17-km-long Vasco da Gama structure (including 12.3 km of viaducts) over the Tagus River in Lisbon; and the 6.8-km East Bridge in Denmark, which completed the $6.5 billion Great Belt (Store Bælt) project linking two islands. (See *Bridges*, above.)

See also Spotlight: *Latin America's New Transportation Links;* Transportation: *Sidebar.*

(PATRICK SMITH)

TUNNELS

Transportation created the greatest need for tunneling in 1998. Roads, railways, and urban mass transit systems throughout the world required tunnels, not as a last resort or only option through hills and mountains or under waterways but as the alternative of choice to satisfy a growing number of public and engineering concerns, including protection of the environment, a reduction of noise in urban and residential areas, and heightened awareness for security against the increased risk of terrorist attack.

The use of tunnels to protect the environment was best illustrated by the new road project in Paris, where two long tunnels totaling 17.7 km were to provide the final link in the A86 ring road around Paris and preserve the natural beauty of the Seine River valley and countryside near the palace of Versailles (1 km=0.62 mi). One of the two tunnels, at 10.1 km long and 11.6 m in outer diameter, would be the first to employ a double-deck design for the exclusive use of automobiles that would provide three lanes in each direction on each deck (1 m=3.28 ft). The second, 7.6 km long and 10.67 m in outer diameter, would provide a conventional two-lane interior, one lane in each direction, for trucks and other large vehicles. The project was expected to be completed by 2005.

Other outstanding road tunnels under construction during 1998 included the Lærdal Tunnel in Norway, the world's longest road tunnel to date at 24.5 km; the 14.2-m-diameter Elbe Tunnel under the Elbe River in Hamburg, Ger., which used the world's largest full-face soft-ground tunnel boring machine; and the 6.6-km twin-tube bored tunnel under the Westerschelde River in The Netherlands, which was chosen in preference to a bridge or an immersed-tube tunnel to replace ferry services across the busy waterway into the ports of Belgium. In Scandinavia 20 precast concrete elements 176 m long, 40 m wide, and 9 m high were floated out and lowered into a 10-m-deep trench on the seabed to form the 3.8-km immersed-tube tunnel section of the 16-km Øresund road-and-rail bridge-and-tunnel link across The Sound into the Baltic Sea between Kastrup near Copenhagen to Lernacken near Malmö in Sweden. Work started in 1995, and the project was expected to open to traffic in mid-2000.

Tunneling has increased significantly on high-speed railways, where trains need lines as straight and as flat as possible to maintain speeds of 300 km/h and more. The new high-speed 79-km line between Florence and Bologna in Italy, with 73 km in a tunnel, is an example. Other countries currently building or planning high-speed railways with large portions in tunnels included Germany, Switzerland, Taiwan, France, Spain, Sweden, Slovakia, and the Czech Republic. Tunneling for subways was underway in many cities in 1998, including Lisbon, Copenhagen, Los Angeles, London, Madrid, Athens, Paris, Rome, Toronto, Bangkok, Singapore, Shanghai, Beijing, and Delhi, India.

In Sydney, Australia, a new 10-km railway tunnel link from the airport to the city centre was to be completed and in operation before the start of the Olympic Games in 2000. In London the Jubilee Line extension of the Underground system was scheduled to open by the end of 1999 in time to carry thousands of visitors expected to celebrate the dawn of the new century at the Millennium Dome in Greenwich.

(SHANI WALLIS)

Art, Antiques, and Collections

The cautionary attitude that had prevailed among collectors and businesses since 1990, when a five-year boom in the art market ended abruptly, was reversed in 1998. Buyers were paying extraordinary prices for superior works of art when they were available. No major private collections were offered for sale, a factor that encouraged new business strategies among auction houses, including mergers and a revamping of the way they did business; Christie's, for example, reorganized its auction categories for 19th- and 20th-century artworks.

In an effort to become more global, several auction houses merged. Sotheby's formed a partnership with Leslie Hindman Auctioneers, Chicago (now Sotheby's Midwest); French retail magnate and art collector François Pinault bought a controlling interest in Christie's and privatized the firm; and Bonhams of London and William Doyle Galleries in New York City united in order to hold joint sales in those cities.

Blockbuster exhibitions showcasing the works of Édouard Manet, Claude Monet, Edgar Degas, and Jean Renoir deserved much of the credit for healthy attendance at shows. A survey conducted in 1997 by the National Endowment for the Arts found that during a 12-month period half of the United States' adult population—an increase of some 9% since 1992—had participated in at least one of seven arts activities, including musical performances, theatre productions, and museum exhibitions, which were the most popular.

A new international appreciation for Australian Aboriginal art resulted in high prices at an auction; some of the works brought as much as \$A200,000 (U.S. \$120,000) in June. The first North Asian

William Boyd's *Nat Tate: An American Artist* stirred controversy in 1998. Although many in the art world claimed to have known Tate, who purportedly jumped to his death from the Staten Island ferry in 1960, the memoir was eventually revealed to be a work of fiction.

Biennial was mounted in Taiwan at the Taipei Fine Arts Museum. The exhibit included works by artists from Japan, South Korea, Taiwan, and China and represented a reexamination of tradition and national identity.

An increase in prices for Latin-American art created a brisk market for forgeries, especially paintings by such Cuban masters as Mario Carreño, René Portocarrero, Victor Manuel, Mariano Rodríguez, and Esteban Chartrand. Copies of the paintings of Colombian artist Fernando Botero were also reportedly being turned out en masse in Asia by craftsmen working from photographs. As a result of a rash of forgeries, the works of Argentine artist Antonio Berni were being scrutinized by a newly established authentication committee. In another felonious act a rare book by Polish astronomer Nicolaus Copernicus was stolen in Kiev by a brazen thief at the Vernadsky Central Scientific Library of the National Academy of Sciences of Ukraine. British author William Boyd, with the help of his publisher, rock star David Bowie, perpetrated a literary hoax with the publication of a memoir of Nat Tate, who reportedly had been prone to depression and burned most of his paintings before jumping to his death from the Staten Island ferry. It was later revealed, however, following a New York City reception at which many in the art world claimed to have known him (but not very well), that *Nat Tate: An American Artist* was a work of fiction.

(REBECCA KNAPP ADAMS)

PAINTING AND SCULPTURE

During 1998 artistic practices and critical attention seemed to be divided between painting on one hand and photography, video, and installation work on the other. In New York City numerous galleries opened, and already-established names relocated from Soho to Chelsea to take advantage of the many large industrial spaces that could often easily accommodate large-scale installation work, such as that of Brazilian artist Tunga, who showed one of his characteristically complex pieces, "True Rouge," at Luhring Augustine Gallery. Installation art also became popular at international venues. German artist Thomas Hirschhorn filled the Kunstmuseum Bern with an array of glitter-covered objects, and Jason Rhoades—whose artfully cluttered and seemingly dangerous installations (comprising such objects as tables, chairs, electrical cords, and computers)—had a show at the Kunsthalle Nürnburg.

British artist Rachel Whiteread created a unique outdoor project for New York City's non-profit Public Art Fund. She cast a water tower from clear resin that was set atop a building in Soho, where rooftops were rather ubiquitously dotted with those structures. Some artists went beyond the mere casting or recasting of objects, creating pieces that commented on spatial relations or the environment inhabited by the viewer. Canadian Scott Lyall exhibited "Washington Square," a work composed of stacked plywood, fur, and polystyrene that was at once installation, sculpture, and monument while also resembling Modernist furniture. British artist Cornelia Parker made her New York solo debut with an installation of "Mass," a conceptual sculptural work made from the charred, strung-together remains of a church that had been struck by lightning. The use of destroyed objects was also seen else-

Jackson Pollock's "Gothic," an example of his unorthodox techniques of applying paint to canvas, was featured in a major retrospective of the artist's work at the Museum of Modern Art in New York City. The show consisted of 106 paintings, 49 works on paper, and 3 sculptures.

THE MUSEUM OF MODERN ART, NEW YORK; BEQUEST OF LEE KRASNER; PHOTOGRAPH ©1998 THE MUSEUM OF MODERN ART, NEW YORK

where, particularly in the recurring motif of the smashed or burned automobile. Sylvie Fleury showed smashed and enamel-coated cars, and Sarah Lucas's two burned autos (their interiors were also covered with cigarettes) were on view at Barbara Gladstone gallery in New York City. Los Angeles–based artist Charles Ray's life-size fibreglass version of a totaled Pontiac was included in the major traveling exhibition of his work.

The art world showed interest and quickly applied labels to two new approaches to painting; British artist Martin Maloney's Expressionistic figurative style was dubbed "new neurotic realism," and the so-called new colour field painting of Monique Prieto, Kevin Apell, and Ingrid Calame appeared in many galleries and in several art magazines.

Painting was conspicuously absent from the works of those nominated for the 1998 Hugo Prize. Pippiloti Rist of Switzerland produced pop-culture infused videos; Huang Yong Ping of China created ambitious installations; William Kentridge of South Africa was an actor, director, and theatre designer as well as an animated filmmaker; Bul Lee of South Korea did work that was largely performance based; and Lorna Simpson of the U.S. made photo- and text-based installations. The recipient of the prize, Scottish artist Douglas Gordon, specialized in video projections and conceptual text pieces. (MEGHAN DAILEY)

ART EXHIBITIONS

During 1998 long-awaited blockbuster shows were mounted of two important American painters from the 1950s: Abstract Expressionists Jackson Pollock (1912–56) and Mark Rothko (1903–70). In November the first retrospective devoted to the work of

Pollock since 1967 was presented at the Museum of Modern Art (MOMA) in New York City. This show of 106 paintings, 49 works on paper, and 3 sculptures reconsidered the work and legacy of one of the most explosive and influential figures in modern art. On view were some of his best-known paintings, including "One: Number 31, 1950," the rarely exhibited "Mural" (1943), and "Autumn Rhythm: Number 30, 1950." The exhibit was one of the most highly anticipated New York City events of the fall season. When Pollock first emerged on the scene in 1947, however, he had been largely denounced by the public and dubbed "Jack the Dripper" because of his technique of pouring, splattering, and dripping paint on canvas. The Tate Gallery in London planned to serve as host of the show in the spring of 1999. From May to August the work of Rothko was featured at the National Gallery of Art in Washington, D.C. Many of the 115 works shown were from the museum's own extensive collection and traced Rothko's development from early figuration to his distinctive, purely abstract paintings of ethereal floating bands of colour. The show was scheduled to travel to the Whitney Museum of American Art in New York City in September before moving to the Musée d'Art Moderne in Paris at the end of the year.

The National Gallery of Art, also mounted a major retrospective honouring the centenary of the birth of sculptor Alexander Calder (1898–1976), an innovator whose huge metal sculptures adorned corporate plazas in the U.S. during the 1960s and whose smaller sculptures (also called mobiles) featured thin wires that allowed movement in the pieces. In March more than 250 of his signature kinetic works fashioned from brightly coloured shapes, as well as supplemental works on paper and some paintings, went on view in both the interior and exterior spaces of the museum; included were some early pieces that had not been previously exhibited. In September the show went to the San Francisco Museum of Modern Art.

Although the works of African-American artist Norman Lewis (1909–79) were closely associated with the Abstract Expressionist movement, his contributions had often been overlooked. In April, however, the Studio Museum in Harlem in New York City opened an exhibition focusing on Lewis's "Black" paintings—displaying 65 works in all. The show was scheduled to travel nationally after its New York debut.

There were several significant museum exhibitions of the work of women artists in 1998. Two different shows of the work of British photographer Julia Margaret Cameron (1815–79) were mounted at Boston's Museum of Fine Arts (MFA) in March and the Art Institute of Chicago in September. Cameron, one of the most renowned portrait photographers of the

Julia Margaret Cameron's "Portrait of a Woman" is typical of the Victorian photographer's often allegorical images. Both the Museum of Fine Arts in Boston and the Art Institute of Chicago featured shows of her work during the year.

Victorian era, turned to photography at the age of 48 after her daughter presented her with a camera as a gift. About 85 of Cameron's Pre-Raphaelite-inspired images were on view at the MFA, including portraits of her family and friends and such famous literary and intellectual figures of the day as Robert Browning, Charles Darwin, and Alfred, Lord Tennyson. Most of the nearly 2,000 existing prints by Cameron were portraits of women. The Art Institute's exhibition concentrated specifically on these images, aiming to reveal the identity of her female subjects as well as to provide new insights into Cameron herself. The Chicago exhibition was scheduled to travel in 1999 to the MOMA and San Francisco's Museum of Modern Art.

In October the Art Institute of Chicago opened a show dedicated to the work of 19th-century American expatriate artist Mary Cassatt (1844–1926), a painter and printmaker. The exhibit, which showcased nearly 100 works, including paintings, prints, and pastels, was the first major consideration of Cassatt's work in nearly 30 years. She was a close associate of such French artists as Claude Monet, Camille Pissarro, and, particularly, Edgar Degas and the only American included in the Impressionist exhibitions in Paris. The curatorial objective, however, was to position Cassatt as a modern painter in her own right. The MFA and the National Gallery of Art in Washington planned exhibits in 1999.

The first full-scale consideration of the work of San Francisco Bay Area artist Joan Brown opened in September at two venues in California: the Berkeley Art Museum and the Oakland Museum of California. The show included 126 works by Brown, known

for her uniquely personal figurative style. Recognition of her talent came in the late 1950s, a particularly rich period of artistic activity in San Francisco that also saw the rise of the West Coast school of Abstraction and the Beat culture. Brown's significance for feminist art of the '70s and her importance as a major California artist were highlighted.

Several shows of Asian art opened during the year. In New York City the Solomon R. Guggenheim Museum staged "China: 5,000 Years." Organized in collaboration with the Ministry of Culture of China, this ambitious exhibition was the first attempt to bring together traditional artifacts and modern works from that nation. Hundreds of objects were shown, ranging from religious artifacts and examples from archaeological discoveries to the politically charged Socialist Realist paintings of the 1950s. Included were works in jade, porcelain, stone, and bronze, as well as landscape paintings, tapestries, calligraphy, and lacquerware. Works in these traditional media occupied the museum's uptown space, whereas the modern section was on display in the Guggenheim's larger downtown galleries. The focus there was on key developments in Chinese art from 1850 onward, particularly in woodcuts and painting. Although a section had been planned that would have considered work dating from 1965 to the present, the museum cited inadequate space and stated that the contemporary part of the exhibition would occur at a future date. The last-minute decision to eliminate this section set off a debate about the Chinese government's influence over the museum. Another exhibition of contemporary Chinese art, "Inside Out," was a welcome addition to the New York fall season. Critically successful and ambitious, the two-venue (P.S.1 Contemporary Art Center and the Asia Society) show included 80 works by more than 60 artists from Hong Kong, mainland China, and Taiwan in a range of media, including paintings in inks and oils, video, and installations.

The Kurtzman family collection of Japanese Hirado porcelains was seen at the Los Angeles County Museum of Art in the spring. It was the first exhibition to showcase a range of pieces (85 were on display), including many from the "golden age" of Hirado (1751–1843). The entire Kurtzman collection of more than 240 porcelains was a promised gift to the museum and would greatly enhance its holdings of Japanese art.

Another object-oriented show debuted at the Yale University Art Gallery in late 1997. "Baule: African Art/Western Eyes" was an exhibition of artifacts and objects made by the Baule artists of Côte d'Ivoire and was the first exhibition to concentrate on the significance of Baule art. The exhibit showcased over 125 examples taken from private collections worldwide and included sculptures, masks, and other objects rendered in gold, wood, ivory, and bronze. This important show was scheduled to travel to

Chicago, New York City, and Washington, D.C., through 1999.

The Tate Gallery's exhibition of French painter Pierre Bonnard (1867–1947) was one of the most popular of the year. After its London debut, the show traveled to the MOMA for the summer. The large crowds drawn to the show at both venues were testimony to the popular appeal of Bonnard's Impressionist legacy, evident in his bold use of colour, loose brushwork, and choice of subject matter: landscapes, gardens, still lifes, and warm interiors. Though Bonnard was known primarily as a colourist, the inclusion of his famous paintings of his wife, Marthe, in her bath provided an opportunity to consider his status as an important figurative artist in the context of his entire oeuvre. These important later nudes were considered the culmination of his career. The MOMA show was the first survey of Bonnard's work in New York in three decades.

Several exhibitions were devoted to 17th-century Dutch art. In September the Dulwich Picture Gallery, the United Kingdom's oldest purpose-built public art gallery, showed the work of painter Pieter de Hooch (1629–81). In December the show traveled to the Wadsworth Atheneum in Hartford, Conn.—the oldest free public art museum in the U.S. This first major exhibition of de Hooch featured 40 works drawn from museums and private collections. A contemporary of Jan Vermeer in Delft, Neth., although his stay there was brief, de Hooch remained best known for similarly intimate genre scenes depicting interiors and light-infused landscapes.

"Masters of Light: Dutch Painters in Utrecht During the Golden Age" featured 79 masterpieces that included landscapes, still lifes, and religious subjects by such 17th-century artists as Gerrit van Honthorst (1590–1656), Hendrik Terbrugghen (1588–1629), and Joachim Wtewael (1566–1638), who were influenced by the styles of Italian Mannerism and particularly by Caravaggio. "Masters of Light" opened in late 1997 at the Legion of Honor museum in San Francisco and traveled to the Walters Art Gallery in Baltimore, Md., in January 1998 before moving in May to the National Gallery in London.

In Germany the Kunstmuseum Düsseldorf offered a retrospective of more than 90 works by Angelica Kauffmann (1741–1807), an artist and personality in 18th-century Rome. Kauffmann was an accomplished historical painter and portraitist, her style embodying a fusion of the Neoclassical and the Rococo. Despite her significance as a historical and cultural figure—she was considered the most cultured woman of her time—Kauffmann had never been the subject of a large-scale exhibition.

On the occasion of French artist Eugène Delacroix's bicentennial birthday in April, the Grand Palais in Paris mounted an exhibition of the artist's late work. More than 70 paintings and works on paper were featured and were drawn from international collections, including works from his Moroccan journey and several paintings focusing on the subject of Christ on the Sea of Galilee, a theme that became something of a metaphor for the artist; these later works revealed a spiritual intensity not always evident in Delacroix's large public commissions. In September the show traveled to the

Philadelphia Museum of Art, its only U.S. venue.

"Monet in the 20th Century," organized by the MFA, brought together some 80 works by the French Impressionist for a comprehensive exhibition of his most important later works, including examples from the London series and the "Water Lily" paintings from 1903–08 and other works completed in the artist's gardens at Giverny. Co-organized by the Royal Academy of Arts, the show was to travel there in January 1999 after its September–December run in Boston.

The Guggenheim Museum captured New York's attention during the summer with its blockbuster "The Art of the Motorcycle." Enthusiasts and ordinary museum patrons flocked to see over 100 motorcycles (from 1868 to the present) parked in Frank Lloyd Wright's rotunda, which was transformed by blue neon, industrial steel, and rubber and wooden ramps designed by architect Frank Gehry. Among the technically innovative examples on view were an eight-valve Harley-Davidson from 1911 and an Aprilia Motò 6.5 designed by Phillipe Starck.

Work by several important contemporary artists was showcased at a variety of international venues. London's Hayward Gallery offered the first U.K. show of recent and new work by Indian-born sculptor Anish Kapoor. Known for his large-scale sculptures in stone, steel, and pigment, Kapoor often utilized the very spaces of the gallery to make works; the Hayward was no exception. The artist carved his "voids" directly into its walls and floors, creating negative spaces that were intended to invoke the spiritual and the sublime. The photographs of Japanese artist Yasumasa Morimura (*see* BIOGRAPHIES) were shown from April to June at Tokyo's Museum of Contemporary Art. The exhibition highlighted photographs from the "Art History" series, for which Morimura made unnerving realistic self-portraits of various figures from iconic Western paintings (*e.g.*, the "Mona Lisa" and Édouard Manet's "Fifer"). The show would

travel only within Japan. "An Unrestricted View of the Mediterranean," a group show organized by *Parkett* editor Bice Curiger at the Kunsthaus Zürich, featured 200 works by young Swiss artists, some well known (Pilpilotti Rist and Thomas Hirschhorn) and others more local (Fabrice Gygi). "Unrestricted" would travel later in the year to Frankfurt, Ger.

Stockholm was chosen as the Cultural Capital of Europe in 1998, an honour that had been bestowed upon one city each year since 1985. Among many cultural events offered in the Swedish capital was the opening of the newly renovated Moderna Museet in February. This new space was the venue for a subject new to Swedish museums—Joan Miró (1893–1983). The exhibition, subtitled "Creator of New Worlds," focused mainly on the Catalan artist's production from the '20s and his introduction to Pablo Picasso and the Surrealists in Paris. Among the 150 works on view from this period up until about 1950 were several well-known canvases, including "Landscape (The Hare)" (1927) and "The Tilled Field" (1923–24). The show would move in the fall to the Louisiana Museum of Modern Art near Copenhagen, Den.

The artist Marina Abramovic was the subject of an exhibition at the Museum of Contemporary Art in Sydney, Australia. This survey examined her earlier sound and performance pieces as well as more recent installation work and object-oriented pieces. In October in Canberra the National Gallery of Australia presented "Re-take," a show of contemporary Aboriginal and Torres Strait Islander photography highlighting the fascinating images taken by people who for so long had had the camera aimed at them.

The critically acclaimed "Out of Actions: Between Performance and the Object" opened in February at the Geffen Contemporary at the Museum of Contemporary Art in Los Angeles, its only U.S. venue. Focusing on the dialogue between visual art and performance, "Out of (continued on page 152)

A 1998 MV Agusta F4 motorcycle from the collection of King Juan Carlos of Spain was featured in the blockbuster exhibit "The Art of the Motorcycle," which opened at the Guggenheim Museum in New York City in June. The show opened at Chicago's Field Museum in November and was to travel to the Guggenheim in Bilbao, Spain, in 1999.

OUTSIDER ART MOVES IN

Works of art produced by amateurs unconnected to the conventional art world were long considered unworthy of serious attention, but in recent years these works, known as "outsider art," have gained a devoted following among many art critics and enthusiasts eager for a less-academic and more personal mode of representation. In 1998 some of the best examples of outsider art were featured in a traveling exhibition, "Self-Taught Artists of the 20th Century: An American Anthology," which enjoyed a successful debut at the Philadelphia Museum of Art. The Outsider Art Fair, staged annually since 1993 in New York City, also sparked much interest and, with 40 American and European dealers filling its booths, confirmed that outsider art was becoming a viable genre with a healthy market.

What characterizes outsider art? Its roots lie in the folk paintings of self-taught masters such as Grandma Moses, whose documentation of traditional farm life in the U.S. made her internationally popular, and Horace Pippin, celebrated for his primitivist depictions of African-Americans. Outsider art differs from folk art, however, in that it depicts the isolation of those living on the margins of society rather than reflecting the cultural traditions of a community. Among the most notable outsider artists are Henry Darger, a Chicago recluse whose fantasy-inspired watercolours and accompanying 15,000-page epic were discovered after his death, and Martín Ramírez, a Mexican-American who created large-scale surrealistic drawings during a life spent mostly in a mental institution.

After the 1972 publication of critic Roger Cardinal's influential book *Outsider Art*, interest in works of art unhampered by convention and created outside mainstream cultural influences grew at a steady rate. The British quarterly *Raw Vision* was established in 1989 exclusively to cover the genre. The American Visionary Art Museum, the first national museum dedicated solely to the work of self-taught artists, opened in Baltimore, Md., in November 1995. By 1998, with other specialist museums opening and an increasing number of collectors, the prospect that outsider art would find a wider audience seemed all but certain.

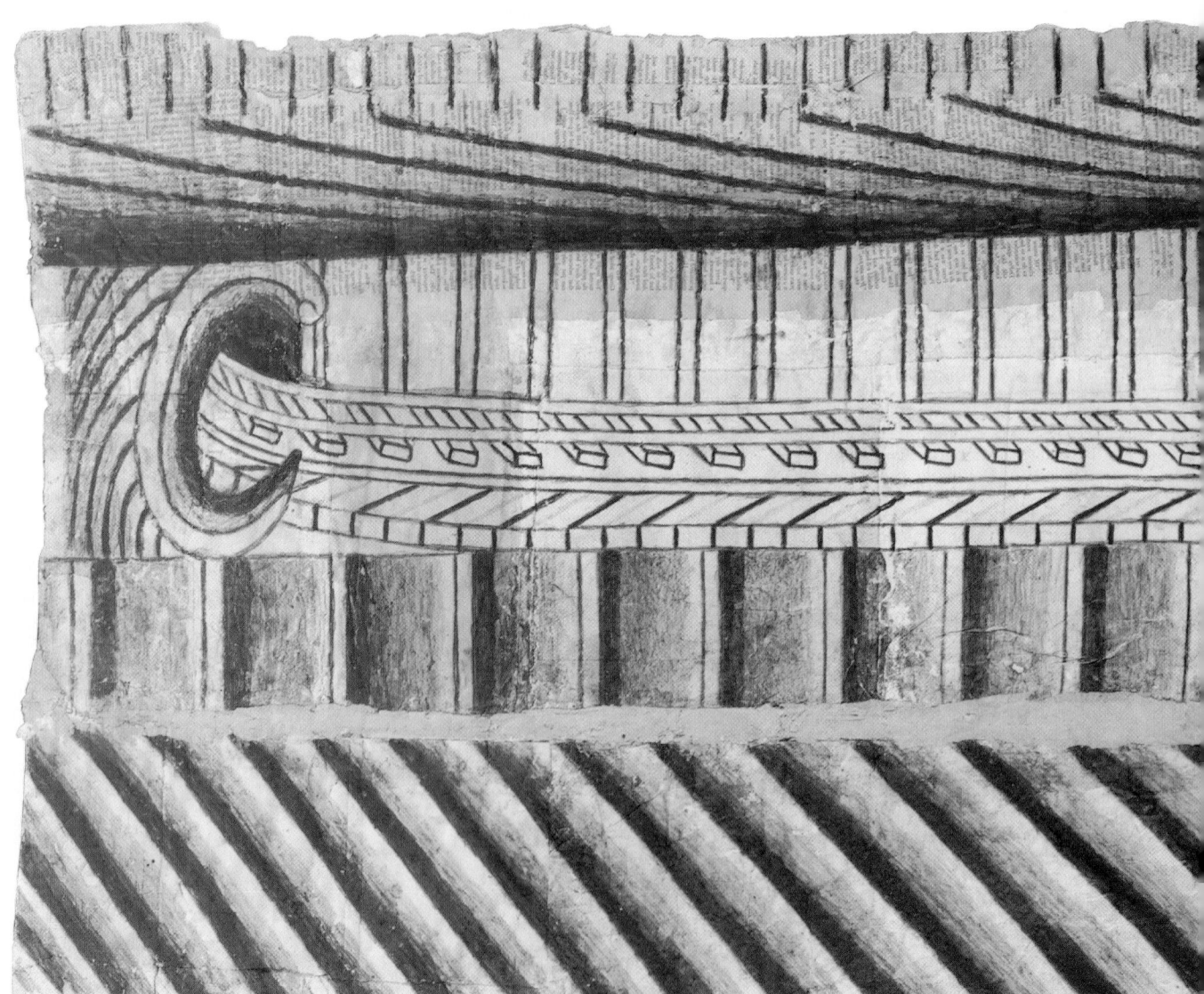

(Above) "Train" (c. 1948–60), by Martín Ramírez

(Top) "African Jungle Picture: If the
Ladies Had Knew the Snakes Wouldn't
Bite Them They Wouldn't Have Hurt
the Snakes; If the Snakes Had Knew
the Ladies Wouldn't Hurt Them They
Wouldn't Have Bit the Ladies"
(1989), by Thornton Dial (Below)
"Figure and Construction with Blue
Border" (c. 1941), by Bill Traylor

(Above) "Soldado with American Flag" (c. 1950–53), by Martín Ramírez
(Right) "Zebra Family" (1942), by Morris Hirschfield (Top left) "Crucifixion"
(c. 1932–37), by William Edmondson (Top right) "What Price Watermelon?"
(1981), by Nellie Mae Rowe

(continued from page 147)
Actions" featured works dating from 1949 to 1979 by artists and collaborative efforts from 20 countries, including the Viennese Actionists, Japan's Gutai Group, and Fluxus; individual artists shown included Lygia Clark, Otto Mühl, John Cage, Jim Dine, Adrian Piper, and Carolee Schneemann. Works in a variety of media were on view, including paintings by Robert Rauschenberg and Yves Klein, re-creations of famous installations such as Claes Oldenberg's "The Store" (1961–62) and Allan Kaprow's "Yard" (1961), and photographs, videos, and films documenting various performances or actions. The exhibition would continue its international tour in 1999 to Vienna; Barcelona, Spain; and Tokyo.   (MEGHAN DAILEY)

PHOTOGRAPHY

Photography's continuing enterprise of re-discovering its past and reinventing itself in the present produced a stimulating variety of exhibitions in 1998, and photographic galleries and auctions achieved record sales as they surfed the peak of a booming economy.

Two exhibitions in New York City explored the complex relationship between art and photography in the vision of two masters of both. At the Museum of Modern Art, "Aleksandr Rodchenko" for the first time provided an integrated view of this diverse artist's Constructivist work in painting, sculpture, and collage as well as his experimental, documentary, and propagandistic photography. "Edgar Degas, Photographer" at the Metropolitan Museum of Art delved into a lesser-known but brilliant aspect of this painter's creative vision. Degas made most of these photographs in 1895 during a brief but intense engagement with photography. The 40 rare images included portraits and figure studies recorded by the light of oil lamps and reflectors in Degas's studio.

A 1961 photograph shows Otto L. Bettmann, who fled Nazi Germany in the 1930s with two trunks filled with photographs and founded what became the multimillion-image Bettmann Archive of pictorial material. Bettmann died on May 1, 1998.

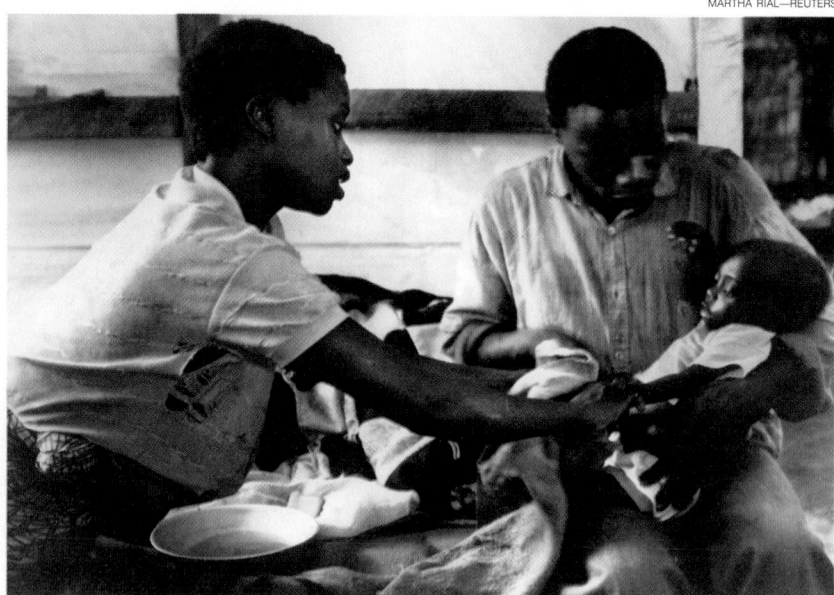

Martha Rial of the *Pittsburgh* (Pa.) *Post-Gazette* was awarded the 1998 Pulitzer Prize for spot news photography for her series of images depicting survivors of the Hutu and Tutsi massacres in east-central Africa. The photograph above shows a couple in Tanzania bathing their adopted son, a malnourished child whose mother had died.

Walker Evans, although best known for his Depression-era photographs of the rural American South, also produced less-familiar but powerful work recording New York City. The Getty Museum in Los Angeles selected some 100 of the urban images for its "Walker Evans: New York" exhibition. The show gave a richly diverse portrait of the city from 1927 to 1963, including some early large-camera work but mostly emphasizing Evans's later, dynamic street photographs taken with a small camera. In "A Practical Dreamer: The Photographs of Man Ray," the Getty exhibited more than 100 of the artist's works from its collection, including experimental photographs associated with the Dada and Surrealist movements and his cameraless photograms, which he called rayographs.

New York's Serge Sorokko Gallery exhibited examples of photographer-designer Marco Glaviano's giant Cubist-style images, which merged traditional photographic techniques with advanced digital imaging. Starting with a 35-mm camera and Ektachrome film, Glaviano generated as many as 70 layers on his computer to create the finished image, which was outputted onto four 76 × 112-cm (30 × 44-in) panels—obviously not for a cozy cabin.

Some of the first photographs to record an important American historical event were exhibited in "Silver and Gold: Cased Images of the California Gold Rush" at the Oakland Museum of California. Included were some 150 daguerreotypes and ambrotypes made from 1848 to 1860, the earliest less than 10 years after Louis-Jacques-Mandé Daguerre went public with his photography process. Although limited by technical necessity mostly to posed portraits and groups, they brought solace to lonely miners and the families that they had left behind and prefigured a revolution in visual reportage.

Photographic auction houses achieved record sales—more than $10 million for New York City's four major participants alone during their annual spring auctions. Prices paid for works by several photographers also broke auction records, including $226,500 for Edward Weston's "Circus Tent" at Sotheby's and $211,500 for Imogen Cunningham's "Magnolia Blossom" at Swann's.

A potential rival to established methods for merchandising art photographs emerged with Photography Auction's first on-line art-photography auction, held in May. Collectors could view works by Weston, Ray, Roman Vishniac, Alfred Stieglitz, and others over the Internet or by appointment at a gallery in New York City. Electronic bidding took place during an on-line "virtual auction," ringing up more than $100,000 in sales—enough to encourage a repeat of the event and give conventional auction houses something to ponder.

Notable photographers who died during the year included Ilse Bing, who recorded Paris during the 1930s in a distinctive, abstract style that made her known as "queen of the Leica" among the avant-garde, and Otto L. Bettmann, who fled Nazi Germany in the 1930s and founded the Bettmann Archive. (*See* OBITUARIES.)

The 1998 Pulitzer Prize for spot news photography was awarded to Martha Rial of the *Pittsburgh* (Pa.) *Post-Gazette* for her photographs of massacres in east-central Africa. Clarence Williams of the *Los Angeles Times* won the Pulitzer for feature photography with his photo-essay on the

plight of young children and their drug- and alcohol-addicted parents. At the 55th Annual Pictures of the Year competition, sponsored by the National Press Photographers Association and the University of Missouri School of Journalism, freelancer Eugene Richards was named Magazine Photographer of the Year and also received the Canon Photo Essayist Award. The contest's Newspaper Photographer of the Year award went to Nancy Andrews of the *Washington* (D.C.) *Post,* and Jacques Lowe received the Kodak Crystal Eagle Award for Impact in Photojournalism. At the 41st annual World Press Photo Contest, the World Press Photo of the Year award went to Algerian photographer Hocine of Agence France-Presse for his image of an Algerian woman grieving over her massacred children. The W. Eugene Smith Grant in Humanistic Photography was given to photojournalist Ernesto Bazan for "El periodo especial in Cuba," documenting the human condition in contemporary Cuba, and Lori Grinker received a fellowship grant for "After War: Veterans from a World of Conflict." The 1998 Howard Chapnick Grant for Leadership in Photojournalism was given to Shahidul Alam for his project of furthering photojournalism in South Asia. Winner of the 1998 Ernst Haas Award, presented at the Maine Photographic Workshops Golden Light Awards, was Dean Tokuno for his series of photographs of his dying father.

(ARTHUR GOLDSMITH)

ART AUCTIONS AND SALES

Building on renewed confidence in the art market, the 1998 auction market showed increased strength, and high prices were realized for works of exceptional quality. Both Sotheby's and Christie's auctions, driven by strength in the American and European sectors, experienced growth in the top and middle markets of the business. Despite turmoil in the worldwide stock markets, there were many new buyers; however, support from the Asian sector declined dramatically. Much of the growth could be attributed to strong sales of American, Old Master, Contemporary, Impressionist, and Modern paintings, drawings, and sculptures. In an interesting development French businessman François Pinault purchased Christie's and took the firm into the private sector.

In January Sotheby's posted phenomenal results of $53.3 million from the New York City sale of Old Master paintings, an auction record for this category. Twelve paintings sold for more than $1 million, and 12 individual artists' records were established. Among the highlights were Rembrandt's "Portrait of a Bearded Man in a Red Coat," selling for $9.1 million, and Rubens's "Head of John the Baptist Presented to Salome," which fetched $5.5 million. At the Old Master drawings sale in January, a record was set for Michelangelo's "Christ and the Woman of Samaria," which went to an anonymous buyer for $7.5 million. Christie's enjoyed similar success in New York at its January Old Master paintings sale, which totaled $21.7 million and set auction records for six of the represented artists. The high point of the sale was Francisco de Zurbarán's "Saint Dorothea," which brought $2,092,500. In January, Christie's New York sale of Old Master drawings realized $3.8 million, a record for that category.

American paintings, building on the momentum of 1997, enjoyed a healthy season at both auction houses. Christie's sale brought $42.4 million, their second highest total ever achieved for this category. Many of the top sellers came from the private collection of Thomas Mellon Evans, including Childe Hassam's "Flags, Afternoon on the Avenue," which commanded $7,922,500, a record for the artist. At Sotheby's New York the American paintings sale earned $42.3 million, their highest sale total for that category. Of particular note was Georgia O'Keeffe's "Calla Lily with Red Roses," which fetched $2.6 million, a record for one of her floral works. The Sotheby's auction was distinguished by the John F. Eulich Collection of Western art, which brought $25 million, a record for any single-owner collection of American works.

Contemporary art continued to be a strong contender across the board. Sotheby's May sale in New York totaled $32.9 million, the highest price for Contemporary works since 1990. The star was Andy Warhol's "Orange Marilyn," which went for a record $17.3 million. Lucian Freud's "Large Interior W11" realized a record $5.8 million. Christie's New York sale in June earned $16.2 million, with the Barbara Herbig single-owner collection from Germany reaching nearly $12 million.

The resoundingly successful November sales of Contemporary art exemplified the health of that market—the sale at Sotheby's totaled $32.9 million. A standout from the Reader's Digest corporate collection was Richard Diebenkorn's "Horizon—Ocean View," which fetched $3.9 million. November sales at Christie's totaled $9,297,350, and the star was Jean-Michel Basquiat's "Self-Portrait," which sold for $3,302,500, a record for the artist.

The strongest sales were found in Impressionist and Modern works of art, which brought extraordinary prices for exceptional works that were fresh to the market and carried a solid provenance. At Sotheby's May sale in New York, sales totaled $108 million, and the majority of purchases were made by private buyers. Claude Monet's "Le Grand Canal" was the top seller, fetching $12.1 million. Sotheby's June sale in London totaled $76.6 million, and Monet's "Bassin aux nymphéas et sentier au bord de l'eau" brought $33 million, the highest price for any work sold in Europe since 1990. At Christie's New York Impressionist highlights included another Monet, "Waterloo Bridge, brouillard," which went for $5,282,500, and an important work by Vincent van Gogh, "Bâteaux de pêches sur la plage à Saintes-Maries de la Mer, Mediterranée," which sold for $5,062,500. The most distinguished collection of 1998 was from the Reader's Digest Collection and was offered at Sotheby's in November. The sale of $86.6 million was the third largest single-owner paintings sale,

behind the John C. Dorrance Collection and the Victor and Sally Ganz Collection. The centrepiece of the Reader's Digest sale was a work of Amedeo Modigliani's mistress and later wife, "Portrait de Jeanne Hébuterne," which set a record for the artist at $15.1 million. Another Modigliani, also of Jeanne Hébuterne, went for $9.9 million. Paul Cézanne's "L'Estaque vu a travers les pins" sold for $11 million, and Monet's "Le Bassin aux nympheas" fetched $9.9 million. In another single-owner sale, Picasso's "Femme nue," from the collection of Morton G. Neumann, brought $11 million. In November at Christie's New York, van Gogh's "Portrait de l'artiste sans barbe" commanded $71 million.

The jewelry divisions also experienced robust sales. In April Christie's New York sold a brooch from the collection of Eva Perón for $992,500 at a sale that totaled $34.1 million. In Geneva Christie's hammered a blue heart-shaped 11.25-carat dia-

Vincent van Gogh's "Portrait de l'artiste sans barbe" brought $71 million at auction in November. Impressionist and Modern works did especially well in the market in 1998, with impressive amounts bid also for paintings by Monet, Modigliani, and Picasso.

mond for $1,423,600. The April sale at Sotheby's New York brought $17.1 million; a pair of diamond-pendant ear clips went for $1 million. The single-owner collection of jewels from the estate of Betsey Cushing Whitney was offered at Sotheby's in October and earned $11.8 million.

Decorative works of art continued to garner great prices for quality pieces. In January at Sotheby's the series of Americana sales totaled a record $25.8 million. An 18th-century Chippendale high chest and companion dressing table from the estate of Stanley Paul Sax sold for $1.2 million, the second highest price ever paid for American furniture. In its Americana series Christie's offered the Hollingsworth family suite of Chippendale furniture, which sold for $2,972,500, the highest price ever paid for Philadelphia furniture.

At the February nine-day sale of the collection of the duke and duchess of Windsor, 31,000 sale catalogues were sold; 44,000 objects were offered in 2,987 lots; and sales totaled $23.4 million. A painting by Sir Alfred Munnings, "H.R.H. the Prince of Wales on 'Forest Witch,'" fetched $2.3 million, the highest amount at the sale. The desk on which King Edward signed the instrument of abdication from the throne in 1936 sold for $415,000.   (AMY TODD)

ANTIQUARIAN BOOKS

A strong market for fine antiquarian books marked the 1997–98 season. The rapid rise of commerce on the Internet resulted in the publication of on-line book catalogs and a number of sales. In New York City, Sotheby's held its first on-line auction, selling a variety of books and manuscripts, notably from the Donald Stralem collection.

Important, rare, and beautiful books in a wide range of subjects fetched huge prices in a competitive international arena. Science, medical, travel, and colour-plate books all performed especially well, as did atlases and exceptional illuminated manuscripts.

The library of the duke and duchess of Windsor, which included over 600 lots of books, manuscripts, and related items, sold at Sotheby's New York for the astonishing price of $2.3 million. Winston Churchill's World Crisis, inscribed to the prince of Wales, fetched $145,500, and John F. Kennedy's Profiles in Courage, inscribed to both the duke and the duchess, made over $39,000.

In single-owner sales Christie's began its season with the Giannalisa Feltrinelli Library of Italian Books. The large library (over 1,800 lots) was dispersed over the year in sales at five venues. The highlight of the sales was a copy of Francesco Colonna's Hypnerotomachia Poliphili (1499, Venice)—with provenance dating back to the 17th century—which sold for $220,000. An early humanist illuminated manuscript of Virgil's Eclogues, Georgics, and Aeneid brought just over $1 million.

A piece of the duke and duchess of Windsor's wedding cake, contained in a silk-covered, ribbon-tied cardboard box, sold for $29,900 during a nine-day sale of the couple's collection in February. Some 44,000 objects were offered, and sales totaled $23.4 million.

SOTHEBY'S/REUTERS

Sotheby's New York sold for just over $2 million the Highly Important Americana from the Stanley Paul Sax Collection, which included 50 lots of books. Major works rising to record levels included George Catlin's North American Indian Portfolio ($107,000) and Yellowstone National Park ($140,000).

The collection of fine books in exquisite bindings and illuminated manuscripts owned by Jaime Ortiz-Patiño was offered by Sotheby's New York, and the top performer, at $3.3 million, was the superlative "Hours of St.-Lô," one of the finest recent examples of an illuminated manuscript to come on the market. Guillaume Apollinaire's Le Bestiaire, a presentation copy to artists Robert and Sonia Delaunay, sold for $220,000. Apollinaire's rare Case D'Armons, one of 25 copies, sold for $120,000. The magnificent Duchesse de Berry copy of Pierre Joseph Redouté's Les Roses (1817–24, Paris) brought $400,000.

In July Christie's London hammered down "the most expensive [printed] book ever sold" at the sale of English incunabula from the Wentworth Library. Chaucer's Canterbury Tales, printed in 1476–77 by William Caxton, brought £4.6 million ($7.6 million); the sale—which included seven other major early English printed books, including Caxton's Recuyell of the Historyes of Troye—yielded almost $10 million.

(KIMBALL HIGGS)

PHILATELY

Responding to a strong economy, the U.S. postage stamp market continued its modest but steady growth during 1998. In the face of an increasing number of new stamps, the worldwide new issue market remained highly competitive, which led many countries to increase their promotional efforts. The U.S. Postal Service (USPS) earmarked $100 million to promote its three-year "Celebrate the Century" program, in which customers' opinions were solicited to commemorate 15 of the most important events of the decades from the 1950s to 2000. The first four sheets appeared in 1998. France issued its first round stamp, a highly popular issue to publicize the World Cup of association football (soccer) championships. Great Britain offered chances to win an automobile with the purchase of a stamp booklet.

The United States experimented with reduced production quantities and limited regional distribution of new commemorative stamps, which led to criticism that some historic events were deemed less important than cartoon characters, which got national distribution. The USPS issued the first American semipostal stamp with a surcharge to benefit breast cancer research.

The death of Diana, princess of Wales, on Aug. 31, 1997, resulted in new issues from more than 70 countries. The

delay in the issue of stamps from Great Britain was due to the concerns about the emotional impact the issuance would have on Diana's sons. In July New Zealand postal authorities announced that they would not go forward with a planned memorial issue, citing overcommercialization and delay in receiving approval from Diana's Memorial Trust.

In January Krause Publications produced the first edition of its newly acquired Minkus U.S. stamp catalog. The catalog directly challenged Scott Publishing Co., the leading U.S. catalog publisher, by including Scott's numbers in a concordance with the Krause numbers. Scott responded with a lawsuit for infringement of copyright and misappropriation of property. By midsummer the highly charged legal battle had given way to private negotiations, with the prospect of settling the dispute in time for the next edition of the Krause-Minkus Catalog.

U.S. Postmaster General Marvin T. Runyon left office in May. The agency's chief operating officer and a career postal official, William J. Henderson, replaced him. Despite a projected profit of $1 billion, the USPS requested and received a postal rate increase of one cent for a 32-cent stamp effective in 1999.

Self-adhesive stamps continued to grow in popularity. The USPS announced that in 1997 sales of self-adhesives amounted to 81% of U.S. stamp sales. Late in 1997 Belgium issued its first self-adhesive stamp. The British Royal Mail announced additional self-adhesive stamp trials.

A venerable philatelic institution changed hands in April when Stanley Gibbons of London, the oldest and largest stamp dealer in the world, was acquired by a company that sold flowers by mail and was based on the island of Jersey.

New Zealand Post announced in May that it had purchased the only known example of the 4-penny pictorial from its 1903 series, with the centre, an image of Lake Taupo, inverted. The purchase price of $66,500 was a record in Australia for a single 20th-century stamp. In October the Robert A. Siegel Auction Galleries of New York sold the Robert Zoellner collection of U.S. stamps, the most complete collection of U.S. stamps ever to be offered for sale. One of two known copies of the one-cent blue Benjamin Franklin of 1868 with a Z grill was sold for $935,000, the highest price ever paid for a U.S. stamp. The entire collection brought more than $8 million. During the year the International Federación of Philately sponsored World Stamp Exhibitions in Tel Aviv, Israel; Granada, Spain; Luxembourg; Johannesburg, S.Af.; and Milan.

(ROBERT E. LAMB)

NUMISMATICS

In September 1998 the U.S. Federal Reserve released new 20-dollar notes that included an off-centre portrait of Andrew Jackson, colour-shifting ink, a watermark, and other anticounterfeiting devices. Like the 50-dollar bills that made their debut in 1997, the new 20s carried an enlarged numeral on the back side to help the sight-impaired. During 1998 government printers were expected to make about 2.2 billion 20-dollar notes, the denomination most often dispensed by automated teller machines. Meanwhile, a U.S.

Treasury official told Congress in March that although the government was testing several substitutes for paper, including plastic, there were no current plans to issue plastic notes. Some experts believed that plastic notes would help curtail counterfeiting achieved with personal computers and inkjet printers, a method that accounted for at least one-third of the relatively small number of fake U.S. notes passed into circulation in 1998.

Amid much debate, U.S. Treasury Secretary Robert Rubin announced in July that a circulating dollar coin would depict Sacajawea, Lewis and Clark's Indian guide. Some people said the gold-coloured coin—which was expected to debut in 2000—should portray the Statue of Liberty as a more easily recognized symbol. Rubin, however, accepted the recommendation of an advisory committee, which decided that the dollar should "bear a design of Liberty represented by a Native American woman, inspired by Sacajawea." Meanwhile, several governors reviewed state designs that would appear on the reverse side of circulating U.S. quarters. Under a 10-year program beginning in 1999, five states would be honoured each year in the order that they joined the union. Canadian citizens submitted more than 30,000 drawings for that country's circulating commemorative coin program of 1999 and 2000. Officials planned to issue 12 special quarter designs each year.

In 1998 the rare-coin market enjoyed perhaps its best showing of the decade. In May an 1845 U.S. proof set in its original case sold at auction for $756,250, and an 1838 10-dollar gold piece, also proof, brought $550,000. Both were part of the John J. Pittman collection. In another auction a series 1928 10,000-dollar Federal Reserve note fetched $126,500. In December an 1890 $1,000 U.S. Treasury note sold at auction for $792,000, believed to be a record for a bank note. Sales of gold bullion coins surged in 1998 as investors appeared to take advantage of a gold price that was below $300 per ounce for much of the year. During the first eight months of 1998, the U.S. Mint sold 942,000 oz of gold bullion coins, more than during all of 1997. The U.S. platinum bullion program, launched in September 1997, generated sales of 153,700 oz of metal in the program's first 11 months, surpassing the first-year goal of 100,000 oz. The U.K. introduced a one-ounce silver Britannia bullion piece, complementing its gold coin.

Some European nations made their first euro coins or bank notes, the currency of the European economic and monetary union (EMU). Eleven countries were scheduled to adopt the euro on Jan. 1, 1999, and euro-denominated coins and notes were scheduled to replace national currencies in those countries in 2002. Euro coins would have a common design on one side and a motif selected by the nation of issue on the other; euro notes would be uniform throughout EMU countries. In January the U.K. placed a new portrait of Queen Elizabeth II on its coinage, the fourth portrait of the queen to have appeared on circulating coins during her 46-year reign. The British Royal Mint released its first circulating two-pound coin in June.

It had a copper-nickel centre, a nickel-brass outer ring, and a latent-image security device on the reverse. In January the central bank of Russia distributed new currency, with one new ruble worth 1,000 old rubles. Israel marked its 50th year of statehood with various commemorative issues, and Canada and Australia each produced special coins featuring more than one colour.

(ROGER BOYE)

Newly minted coins in the United Kingdom bearing the likeness of Queen Elizabeth II circulated in 1998. Elizabeth's portrait had appeared on coins three times before since her coronation in 1953.

ANTIQUES AND COLLECTIBLES

Technology was rapidly changing the antiques and collectibles market in 1998. Items that sold well in shops, at shows, and at auctions were finding a niche on the Internet, with auctions there accounting for about 10% of all antiques and collectibles sales. Small items sold quickly, and some dealers reported that they could sell more on the Internet than at a show.

Though major auctions in New York and California attracted media attention, many records were set elsewhere at smaller sales and through mail-order auctions. In specialized sales many pieces sold for record prices; at a magic poster auction, a 1910 three-sheet lithograph poster by Strobridge & Co., Cincinnati, Ohio, "Thurston, the Great," a magician levitating a woman, fetched $13,800, and at a toy train auction, four record prices were set, including $7,700 for a set of four Lionel-scale freight cars and $5,170 for an American Flyer Empire Express set. At a mechanical bank auction, the Old Woman in the Shoe bank, which commanded $426,000, set a record for any toy or bank. Other banks at that auction selling for over $100,000 included Darkey and Watermelon ($354,500),

Freedman's ($321,500), Preacher in the Pulpit ($233,500), Zig Zag ($189,500), Roller Skating ($156,500), and Mikado ($123,500). At a videophone marble sale, a "Miller Swirl" Golden Rebel marble (c. 1927), with opaque yellow base and aventurine black and opaque red swirls, brought $2,993. At another sale the tall Architettura bureau designed in 1952 by Peiro Fornasetti fetched a record $140,000. At a special sale a head vase depicting Marilyn Monroe sold for $1,100.

Prices for bakelite jewelry remained high. The multicolour Art Deco style Philadelphia bracelet brought a record $17,600; a googly-eyed clown pin with ivory head, collar, and hat went for $7,700; and a pin with cigarette holder and match-shaped charms sold for $10,450. Other costume jewelry also sold at high prices. A Trifari Pearl Belly gilt metal clip shaped like a frog fetched $6,600, and a Boucher animated pelican pin with pull-chain movable mouth brought $5,500. California ceramics of the 1950s remained popular. A 51-cm (20-in) Kay Finch "Life-Size Lamb" made $5,170, and a 43-cm (17-in) Violet, a pink elephant with flowered ears, brought $4,400. Other records included a red-painted tin gooseneck toleware coffeepot (c. 1880) for $33,000 and a Cheyenne lattice cradle for $59,700.

Traditional favourites also sold well. The Pink Lotus Lamp with a bronze and mosaic base set a record for both Tiffany and for a 20th-century object when it commanded $2,807,500 in late 1997. In January a Tiffany Laburnum table lamp made $129,000; a 30-cm (12-in) cire perdue glass vase named "Roses" by René Lalique brought $409,500; and a 1.8-m (6-ft)-high cigar store figure of Corporal Joe (c. 1865) went for $46,750. Unusual collectibles that set records included a 1943 one-sheet movie poster of *Casablanca,* which sold for $21,850, and a 1793 book, reportedly the first written entirely about golf, for $80,500. A founder's stock certificate for Standard Oil Co. signed by John D. Rockefeller made $61,000.

Titanic memorabilia also made waves in the market. The enormous popularity of the movie made anything connected with the sunken ship a pricey collectible. Bits of chair caning from the original shipboard chairs fetched $3,000 or more, and small mounted pieces of wood recovered from the ship in 1912 were sold for $750. Costumes and dinnerware made as props for the film also sold for higher-than-expected prices.

Popular collectibles under $100 included toys and memorabilia from fast-food restaurants and kitchen accessories from the 1960s and '70s, especially salt and pepper shakers, condiment jars, and string holders. Firecracker labels, oilcans, face-powder boxes, pale-green jadeite glass, cigarette packs, and labels—especially tobacco ones—were selling well. Collectibles selling for more than $100 included radios, toasters, coffeepots, and early examples of old typewriters and telephones. Other sought-after items were Hot Wheels toy cars, Beanie Babies, farm equipment, garden statues and tools, Griswold pots, and Chintz china.

(RALPH AND TERRY KOVEL)

Business and Industry Review

The world economy prospered in 1997. Total world output rose by more than 3%, with manufacturing growing by almost twice that rate and, unusually, with the economies of the industrialized countries outpacing those of less-developed nations. Though there were some warning signs by the end of 1997 of the crisis that began in mid-1997 in Thailand and then spread to other Asian economies, the rest of the world financial market remained unaffected until August 1998, when the turbulence spread following Russia's declaration of a debt moratorium. As a result, the possibility of a more generalized slowdown in the world economy became real, and international industry observers feared that Western industrial economies, having failed to avoid the contagious ailing financial market, might also "catch" recession from Asia. (*See* Spotlight: *The World Economy in Trouble*.)

In North America, where production had enjoyed a six-year increase, output accelerated in 1997. Industrial production in the U.S. rose 5% and was boosted by capital formation, which reached a 19-year high. Canada experienced similar results, with soaring business investment driving a 4.9% rise in industrial production. The strength of the industrial North American powerhouse helped produce a year of record growth in South America, most notably in Argentina, Chile, and Peru, where total output rose 7–8%.

In continental Europe, where the fiscal consolidation imposed by the Treaty on European Union had been implemented, activity was recovering, particularly in the peripheral regions. Industrial production rose nearly 4% in Germany and France; at least 4% in Austria, Belgium, The Netherlands, and Portugal; nearly 7% in Spain; and more than 15% in Ireland. The relative strength of the core EU economies had beneficial

Table I. Annual Average Rates of Growth of Manufacturing Output, 1980–97

Area	Percent				
	1980–88	1989–93	1994	1995	1996	1997
World[1]	2.7	0.3	6.4	2.4	2.5	5.8
Developed countries	2.4	−0.7	6.9	1.6	2.0	6.1
Less-developed countries	4.5	4.3	4.9	5.6	4.4	5.3

[1]For definition, *see* Table IV.
Source: UN, *Monthly Bulletin of Statistics*.

Table II. Industrial Production in Eastern Europe[1]
1990=100

Country	1993	1994	1995	1996	1997	%[2]
Bulgaria	58	63	60	61	48	−22
Croatia	59	57	58	60	64	7
Czech Republic	68	70	76	77	81	5
Estonia	49	47	48	50	56	12
Hungary	77	84	88	91	101	11
Latvia	44	40	38	41	42	3
Poland	101	113	124	135	151	11
Romania	58	60	66	72	68	−6
Russia	65	51	49	47	48	1
Slovakia	70	74	80	82		
Slovenia	74	79	80	81		

[1]Former Soviet Union not available.
[2]% change, latest year shown from previous year.
Source: UN, *Monthly Bulletin of Statistics*.

Table III. Pattern of Output, 1994–97
Percent change from previous year

	World[1]				Developed countries				Less-developed countries			
	1994	1995	1996	1997	1994	1995	1996	1997	1994	1995	1996	1997
All manufacturing	6	2	3	6	7	2	2	6	5	6	4	5
Food, beverages, tobacco	3	3	2	3	3	1	1	2	5	6	6	6
Textiles	3	−1	−1	4	3	−2	−4	2	3	0	2	5
Clothing, footwear	0	−2	−4	−1	1	−2	−5	−1	0	−1	−2	−1
Wood, wood products	5	0	0	3	5	1	0	3	3	−2	−4	−1
Paper, printing, publishing	3	1	0	4	2	1	−1	4	6	4	1	3
Chemicals	15	−6	3	5	19	−9	2	4	5	4	6	6
Building materials, etc.	4	3	1	4	5	2	−1	3	3	6	5	8
Base metals	6	3	1	6	5	3	−1	5	7	5	7	8
Metal products	6	6	1	2	7	6	0	2	6	2	4	2
Electrical equipment	8	12	9	14	8	12	10	15	10	12	8	6
Transport equipment	4	3	2	8	4	1	2	8	1	15	4	7

[1]Excluding Albania, China, North Korea, Vietnam, former Czechoslovakia, former Soviet Union, and former Yugoslavia.
Source: UN, *Monthly Bulletin of Statistics*.

Table IV. Index Numbers of Production, Employment, and Productivity[1] in Manufacturing Industries
1990=100

Area	Production 1996	Production 1997	Employment 1996	Employment 1997	Productivity 1996	Productivity 1997	Area	Production 1996	Production 1997	Employment 1996	Employment 1997	Productivity 1996	Productivity 1997
World[2]	113	120	...	...	...	...	Denmark	117	123	...	...	...	...
Developed countries	108	115	...	...	...	...	Finland	121	133	82	83	147	160
Less-developed countries	133	140	...	...	...	...	France	98	102	...	...	...	...
North America[3]	121	132	...	...	...	...	Germany (1991=100)	96	100	...	...	...	...
Canada	112	119	93	96	121	124	Greece	98	99	...	...	...	...
United States	118	127	97	98	122	130	Ireland	176	205	116	...	151	...
Latin America[4]	115	118	...	...	...	...	Netherlands, The	109	114	...	...	...	...
Brazil	112	116	...	...	...	...	Norway	115	118	...	...	...	...
Mexico	117	127	...	...	...	...	Portugal	97	102	...	...	...	...
Asia[5]	113	118	...	...	...	...	Sweden	121	130	...	...	...	...
India	146	151	...	...	...	...	Switzerland	103	109	...	...	...	...
Japan	97	101	100	100	97	101	United Kingdom	103	104	...	...	...	...
South Korea	161	172	96	92	167	186	Rest of the world[7]	...	...	...	...	...	...
Europe[6]	94	97	...	...	...	...	Oceania	109	110	...	...	...	...
Austria	115	123	...	...	...	...	South Africa	103	106	98	...	105	...
Belgium	107	112	...	...	...	...							

[1]This is 100 times the production index divided by the employment index, giving a rough indication of changes in output per person employed.
[2]Excludes China and former U.S.S.R.
[3]Canada and the United States.
[4]South and Central America (including Mexico) and the Caribbean islands.
[5]Asian Middle East and East and Southeast Asia, including Japan, Israel, and Turkey.
[6]Excluding Albania, former Czechoslovakia, former Yugoslavia, and European countries of the former Soviet Union.
[7]Africa and Oceania.
Sources: UN, *Monthly Bulletin of Statistics*; ILO, *Yearbook of Labour Statistics*.

spillover effects in Eastern Europe, most obviously in those countries that were successfully making the transition to a market economy. In Poland industrial output rose more than 50% during the 1990s, but in countries that were struggling to make the transition from a centrally planned economy output declined by 50% during that same period.

The official data for Asia in 1997 showed few signs of the turmoil ahead. Across the region, healthy growth rates for the year as a whole were recorded—more than 7% for manufacturing in Asia, excluding Japan and Israel. Only in Thailand, where the troubles began, did output decline. Even in Japan, which of the major economies suffered most from the Asian crisis, industrial production rose more than 4%, although overall output rose less than 1%.

The changing pattern of activity was illustrated by patchy performances from some sectors. Even in a buoyant year output of clothing and footwear declined, whereas textiles recorded their first year of growth since 1994. At the opposite extreme, output of electrical equipment, including computers, rose 14%, faster than the 10% average of the previous three years.

The strength of activity in 1997 carried through into the first half of 1998, and for a time it was possible to believe that Western economies and financial markets would escape the worst of the Asian downturn. That view changed with the Russian debt moratorium, which produced a complete reassessment of the international economic outlook. It also became clear that the Japanese economy was even more severely affected than was previously thought—households increased their already very high rate of savings, knowing that, in a deflationary climate, goods in the shops would be falling rather than rising in price. There was a stark contrast between the 1994 Mexican crisis, when strong U.S. demand helped boost demand for Mexican exports, and the 1998 Asian crisis, in which Japan was unable to undertake the U.S. role.

As 1998 came to a close, a cloud hung over the global economy. Economic forecasts were downgraded, and there was a risk of recession. The Asian crisis stemmed from years of overinvestment and was compounded by a collapse in demand in that region. In addition an excess global supply of goods was forcing down prices.

(GEOFFREY R. DICKS)

ADVERTISING

Worldwide advertising on all media, including Yellow Pages and direct mail, was predicted to increase 5.3% to $418.7 billion in 1998 from $397.5 billion in 1997. Despite late-year jitters in the stock market, economic uncertainty in Asia, and doubts as to whether U.S. consumers would continue their robust spending habits, spending on U.S. advertising in 1998 was predicted to top the $200 billion mark for the first time in any given year. The expected total of $200.3 billion was a 6.8% increase over the revised figure of $187.5 billion in 1997, according to Robert J. Coen, McCann-Erickson Worldwide's senior vice president in charge of forecasting.

Advertising spending was closely watched because it was deemed a reliable indicator of the health of the economy. For instance, advertising as a percentage of gross domestic product peaked in 1987 and 1988 at 2.35% as the economy boomed. During the recession of the early 1990s it declined, bottoming out at 2.12% in 1992. Coen predicted that national advertising spending in 1998 would increase 7% to $118 billion, led by strong growth in cable television, broadcast television, and spot radio. Local advertising was expected to increase 6.5% to $82.3 billion.

Although countries such as Brazil, the U.K., and Mexico posted strong increases in advertising spending, the Asian financial crisis offset those gains. Spending outside the U.S. in 1998 was expected to increase only 3.6% to $218.4 billion from a revised figure of $210 billion in 1997.

General Motors Corp. rose to the rank of top U.S. advertiser in 1997, besting perennial leader Procter & Gamble Co., according to *Advertising Age*'s annual survey of the 100 leading national advertisers. The automaker became the first U.S. firm to spend more than $3 billion on advertising in one year, totaling $3,090,000,000 for an increase of 29.9% over 1996. Procter & Gamble's spending rose 6.3% to $2,740,000,000. According to the survey the 100 U.S. marketers in the report spent $58,030,000,000 in advertising in 1997, up 8.6% from 1996; the media portion rose an even stronger 9.9% to $33.4 billion. The substantial increase was attributed to the nation's healthy economy, government initiatives, and new technologies, such as the World Wide Web on the Internet.

The Web gained advertising ground in 1998, claiming 1.3% of overall ad budgets. Though technology companies continued to account for the largest percentage, 49.7%, of the Internet ads, governments, organizations, and retailers posted large gains. The percentage of companies advertising on-line rose to 68% in 1998, according to the second annual Web site survey conducted by the Association of National Advertisers. The survey also revealed that 47% of respondents were selling some product or service from their Web sites, up from 26% in 1997.

NBC held onto its title of broadcasting the most expensive show on prime-time television. With an average price per 30-second commercial unit of $565,000, NBC's medical drama "ER" was the costliest production of the 1998 fall season. The "ER" price, however, was $10,000 below the record-setting "Seinfeld" average of $575,000 per 30-second unit in the fall of 1997. When the final episode of "Seinfeld" aired, advertisers spent up to $1.7 million for 30-second spots. Based on the strength of "Monday Night Football" and "The Drew Carey Show," ABC was the most expensive of any broadcast network, with an average price per spot of $172,000, a 5.5% gain over 1997.

The "Big Four" networks—ABC, CBS, Fox, and NBC—sold approximately $6,050,000,000–$6,100,000,000 worth of commercial time during the 1998 "upfront" market, a media marketplace that occurs before a television season begins. At a time when broadcast television was besieged by viewer defections to cable networks, the Internet, and other entertainment outlets, it was considered a victory for the networks to sell about as much advance commercial time for the 1998–99 prime-time season as they did for 1997–98.

U.S. and European multinational firms continued during 1998 to pump marketing dollars into Asia, although consumer purchasing and ad spending tumbled as the economic crisis continued to ripple throughout the region. Some companies, such as Unilever and Philips Consumer Electronics, saw marketing opportunities amid the crisis, with lowered rates charged for media time. Unilever introduced new soaps and detergents under the Sunlight and Surf brand names in Indonesia and Thailand at discounts of up to 30%. In Indonesia, where inflation topped 80% during the year, Unilever began advertising sample-sized products at a fraction of the cost of a full-sized product. Philips in September 1998 launched an $80 million integrated marketing campaign in Indonesia for its state-of-the-art electronics equipment, taking advantage of dampened demand for media time.

In one of the largest agency switches of 1998, Compaq Computer moved creative duties on its entire $200–$300 million global advertising account to Omnicom Group's DDB Needham agency from Interpublic Group's Ammirati Puris Lintas, which held the account for only a year. Agencies also continued their brisk merger and acquisition pace. Interpublic Group acquired Carmichael Lynch, which had a reputation for feisty ads; Omnicom Group agreed to acquire GGT Group of London; and True North Communications began integrating its late 1997 acquisition of Bozell, Jacobs, Kenyon & Eckhardt.

In the U.S. the Association of National Advertisers (ANA) startled advertising executives by announcing that it would for the first time open its membership to regional and national agencies from all ends of the creative spectrum. The decision opened a potential rift between the ANA and the

The cast of NBC's popular medical drama "ER" is pictured below in a scene from the show. For 30 seconds of commercial time during "ER," advertisers had to cough up $565,000. In general, television advertising sales remained strong in 1998.

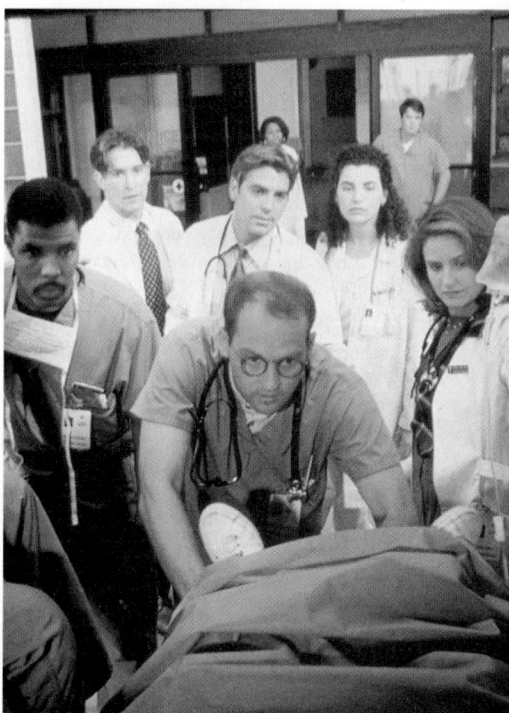

American Association of Advertising Agencies, the organization that such agencies had traditionally joined.

According to a study conducted by Roper Starch Worldwide Inc. consumers throughout the world were more similar than different, sharing attitudes and behaviour that advertisers and agencies could study to create more effective campaigns. The researchers interviewed 35,000 consumers in 35 countries to identify values and attitudes that crossed national borders. Consumers worldwide were found to belong to six basic groups: strivers, devouts, altruists, intimates, fun seekers, and creatives. The study was an example of recent efforts by advertisers to broaden consumer research beyond such traditional categories as demographics.

(LAURIE FREEMAN)

AEROSPACE

The improvement in the economic health of the world's airlines that began in 1995 continued in 1998, though growth in traffic and revenues often masked poor profit levels. The move toward ever-bigger alliances also continued. The emergence of the Star Alliance (United Airlines, Lufthansa, SAS, Air Canada, Varig, and Thai Airways) in 1997 was matched by rival Oneworld (American Airlines, British Airways, Canadian Airlines International, Cathay Pacific Airways, and Qantas), announced in September. Both groupings were of similar size, and both were expected to attract additional partners. KLM of The Netherlands and Italy's Alitalia announced a major European partnership. Meanwhile, the proposed British Airways–American Airlines link was contested by other airlines and by the regulatory authorities as being anticompetitive. PanAm, reborn in 1996, died yet again in February, but a revised business plan to restart the once-famous name with a handful of routes was under consideration.

The economic crisis in Asia, with the resulting loss of tourism and business traffic, jolted carriers in the region. Hong Kong's Cathay Pacific registered its first loss in 20 years; debt-laden Philippine Airlines temporarily ceased operations; Indonesia's national carrier Garuda had to return some of its aircraft, and its regional airline, Sempati, closed; Malaysian Airlines sold part of its fleet and deferred deliveries of new aircraft; and Korean Air shelved ambitious expansion plans.

Investigation of the 1996 TWA 747 crash off Long Island, New York, ended in July without a firm conclusion as to the cause, though fuel-tank ignition was suspected. In the year's worst accident a Swissair MD-11 crashed into the sea off Nova Scotia during September with the loss of all 229 lives after the crew radioed a flight-deck fire.

The airframe companies also continued their consolidation. Alliances between U.S. and European companies, once purely politically inspired, were seen as the most effective way of providing competitive economic solutions to future aerospace needs and sharing resources and business risks. But Lockheed Martin's proposed buyout of Northrop Grumman was blocked by the U.S. Department of Justice, which reasoned that the three existing industrial giants—Boeing, Lockheed Martin, and Raytheon—were already large enough. Boeing was busy digesting McDonnell Douglas following its

1997 acquisition of the California company, and the last of the latter's transport designs, launched by Douglas in 1995 as the MD-95, flew during September in Boeing colours as the 717-200. Not to be outdone, Airbus Industrie announced a rival for the 717, the 107-seat A318, a smaller version of the existing 124-seat A319. Boeing had earlier announced that, owing to poor sales, it would close the MD-11 trijet line.

Airbus in its 29th year worked to form a dual civil/military giant, dubbed the European Aerospace and Defense Co., from its four European partner companies (Aérospatiale of France, Daimler-Benz Aerospace Airbus GmbH of Germany, British Aerospace PLC, and Construcciones Aeronauticas SA of Spain). France's Dassault Aviation SA scorned a linkup with Aérospatiale, but, together with British Aerospace, announced the formation of European Aerosystems Ltd. to better exploit their combined military aircraft expertise. Boeing suffered from supply problems among its subcontractors as it endeavoured to increase production to meet demand, but late in the year the company announced that a loss of orders from Asia was forcing a cutback in production.

Taking advantage of a healthy regional airline market, Fairchild Dornier prepared to launch a family of jets seating 55–90. Similarly encouraged, new Dutch company Rekkof Restart (Rekkof is Fokker spelled backward) was negotiating to resurrect airframe builder Fokker, which went bankrupt in 1996, in order to resume its 70- and 100-seat regional aircraft production. Dassault continued to assess the market for its proposed Mach 1.8, eight-seat, 6,500-km (4,000-mi)-range SSBJ (supersonic business jet), while Lockheed Martin and Gulfstream in September unveiled a rival American SSBJ design. At a lower level the business and light aviation industry enjoyed a boom, with deliveries of new aircraft up 55% from 1997 and virtually no used aircraft available.

The problem of air turbulence came into focus when many passengers were injured and one died aboard a United Airlines 747, which subsequently had to be retired from service because of damage. The cost of turbulence to the airline industry because of injuries and damage since records began was estimated at $100 million.

The effort to choose and field new fighters continued; military experts claimed that while the Cold War threat from the Soviet Union had vanished, top Russian fighters such as the MiG-29 and Su-27 could be sold cheaply to Third World countries and could pose a formidable threat to the West. Indeed, cash-strapped Russia was endeavouring to sell Sukhoi Su-27s and Mikoyan MiG-29s on international markets along with advanced missiles. The risk of such high-class weapons being offered at cut-rate prices to pariah nations was viewed as likely to delay further NATO arms-reduction efforts. The U.S. Defense Department purchased 27 MiG-29 Fulcrum Cs from Moldova for technical and operational evaluation against its own F-15 Eagles and F-16 Falcons. The package also included AA-11 Archer air-combat missiles with performance probably superior to that of corresponding U.S. weapons. Russia's ongoing financial crisis paralyzed MiG-MAPO, the Russian company responsible for the MiG-29 and stopped production of the aircraft.

The increasing inadequacy of America's Tomahawk cruise missile against "hard" targets was demonstrated in August when a number of such weapons were launched from U.S. ships against a pharmaceutical factory in The Sudan that was allegedly making VX nerve-gas precursors and also against an Islamic terrorist/training camp in Afghanistan; the strikes were reprisals for terrorist bombing attacks on U.S. embassies in Kenya and Tanzania. The missile problem was ascribed to the inability of their nonnuclear warheads to penetrate thick bunkers.

There was accelerating development in the U.S. of UAVs (unmanned aerial vehicles) and UCAVs (unmanned combat air vehicles), both as a response to mounting public concern in recent decades over risks to aircrews of capture and because of their low cost. U.S. Predator UAVs continued to spy on Serbian army withdrawals from Kosovo in Yugoslavia. The U.S. aerospace industry was developing a family of microdrones, circular craft a few inches in diameter that could fly reconnaissance missions while being mistaken for birds by hostile forces.

(MICHAEL WILSON)

APPAREL

Clothing. After several years of lacklustre apparel sales, American consumers in 1998 decided to go shopping. By August 1998 sales had already surpassed those of 1997, and all indicators suggested that year-end sales figures would be at least double those of previous years. Static and declining prices helped fuel the boom, and consumers began making serious investments in their casual Friday wardrobe for work. Before the 1998 Christmas shopping season began, sales of both men's and women's tailored clothing, including suits, jackets, and overcoats, were up 10–15% over 1997. Jean sales for girls and boys also increased substantially, and the popularity of men's golf shirts continued unabated.

The crisis in the Asian economic markets dramatically affected apparel production and sales. With declining domestic sales Asian producers increased their exports, notably to the U.S. The most substantial import growth into the U.S., however, came from Mexico, where the effects of the North American Free Trade Agreement (NAFTA) were finally being realized. Hong Kong and China regained the market share they had lost in the early 1990s to Central American countries.

In an effort to address accusations that manufacturers were operating sweatshops, the American Apparel Manufacturers Association began developing a comprehensive factory monitoring and oversight program. The plan was created in conjunction with several large American accounting firms, which would monitor wage and employment data to ensure that all federal requirements were met.

The changing economics of apparel production prompted the industry, once again, to lobby for free trade status for Caribbean basin nations. Many U.S. apparel manufacturers—encouraged to invest in the region as part of a U.S. economic outreach policy formulated during the administration of Pres. Ronald Reagan—found themselves at a competitive disadvantage with companies that had moved their operations to Mexico after the passage of NAFTA. By granting

free trade status to Caribbean basin nations, companies would once again be on an economically level playing field. The proposed legislation, however, failed to survive the last-minute budget negotiations and impeachment frenzy that consumed the U.S. Congress.

On the domestic front, apparel manufacturers who had built their business by providing goods to the U.S. government found themselves losing even more ground to the Federal Prison Industries (FPI) program. FPI was created to teach prison inmates useful, marketable skills that would benefit them after their release. Although prisoners were paid, the rate was substantially lower than the federal minimum wage. The lower FPI wages also allowed FPI to bid for federal apparel contracts—usually for military apparel or specialty apparel, such as biohazard suits—at lower rates than conventional apparel manufacturers. The growth of the FPI program forced dozens of plant closures and created hundreds of job losses. Though generally supportive of the FPI program, U.S. lawmakers continued to work on a solution that would be economically equitable for the FPI and manufacturers.

(ALLISON WHEELER WOLF)

Footwear. By 1998 the financial crisis in Asia prompted both Nike Inc., which reported a more than 50% decline in future orders from the region, and Reebok International Ltd. to lower their earnings estimates for the first half of the year. Converse took a $4 million loss in the third quarter and reported that U.S. sales had dropped more than 50%, and Fila Holdings SpA also reported large losses. L.A. Gear expected to emerge from bankruptcy protection as a licensing operation by year's end. One bright spot in the athletics category, however, was Adidas America, which reported a 65.7% increase in sales in the third quarter.

Reporting substantial declines in earnings were Nine West in the women's fashion footwear market and Nike in its athletic sector, owing to the latter's increased competition from Adidas, among others, and a backlash over its overseas labour practices. As a result, Nike announced cost-cutting measures and a job reduction of 1,600 in its global workforce. Nine West planned to keep fewer than 100 stores open, compared with the 398 it had in 1997, and, despite poor earnings, agreed to acquire U.K.-based shoe chain Cable & Co. from British Shoe Corp. Florsheim Group also reported a shrinking retail business; it closed 23 specialty stores and 10 outlets.

Designer brand Kenneth Cole, on the other hand, posted double-digit gains during 1998. It was a good year for Stride Rite Corp., which produced Keds casual wear and Levi's and Tommy Hilfiger footwear, and for Jimlar Corp., owner of American Eagle and RJ Colt. Jimlar bought the century-old Frye footwear brand, which it had previously produced under license, and also became the exclusive footwear licensee for the upscale Coach leather-goods brand.

The comfort and outdoor footwear sectors also prospered. The "brown-shoe" trend put some muscle in the lines of rugged outdoor footwear brands Timberland, Hi-Tec, Wolverine, Caterpillar, and Sorel. Comfort brands, such as Rockport and Eurocomfort makers such as Birkenstock, Mephisto, Wolky of Holland, and Naot, featured up-

A model shows off a fur jacket at the Oscar de la Renta fall 1998 fashion show in New York City on April 2. Although fur retailers experienced some setbacks during the year, furs made a strong comeback in the fashion world. A number of top designers included them in their collections.
©JEFF CHRISTENSEN—ARCHIVE PHOTOS

dated styling and were welcomed into the realm of fashionable footwear. Action-sports shoe firm Vans Inc., however, closed its last U.S. plant in Vista, Calif., and shifted production of its vulcanized footwear to factories in Mexico and Spain.

Among retailers, Payless ShoeSource Inc. reported a 16.7% increase in earnings, opened 29 new stores in the U.S., and overhauled its 200 Parade of Shoes stores. The Venator Group Inc., the newly named parent company of the Kinney shoe chain, announced that it would shutter all of its 500 U.S. and 82 Canadian stores but would convert about 60 U.S. Kinney stores to Foot Locker specialty stores.   (BONNIE BABER)

Furs. The economic turmoil that disrupted international trade throughout much of 1998 also heavily impacted furs. Consumers in countries affected by economic downturns postponed purchasing luxury items, and continuing financial difficulties in such countries as Japan and South Korea—each of which had figured prominently in the international fur trade—forced them to the sidelines. After the Asian finan-

cial virus spread to Russia, which had recently emerged as a prominent new force in the fur trade, the country abruptly halted furskin purchases.

The financial crisis was further amplified by the resultant sharp fluctuations in the world securities markets, which tended to cloud the merchandising plans of North American and Western European fur retailers and manufacturers, who had been looking forward to a healthy season. Furs had been making a strong comeback in terms of fashion and were given favourable worldwide publicity in leading publications and other media. More than 200 international fashion designers—25% more than in 1997—showed collections that included furs either as full garments or as trimmings on textile or leather apparel. The El Niño weather phenomenon, which made the winter of 1997–98 the warmest on record in some areas, caused consumers to defer purchases of furs and other cold-weather apparel, but a reverse weather pattern, termed La Niña, was expected to spur fur sales in the 1998–99 season.

Production of ranched and wild fur skins was relatively stable, but prices soared in the first six months of 1998, owing to heavy Russian demand. When Russia's economic bubble burst and its ruble sank, Russian buying became severely restricted and skin prices began to drop. In recognition of Russia's problems, year-end auctions were either canceled or the offerings reduced in order to minimize an anticipated decrease in price.

Animal rights organizations, despite a further decline in support from the public and the media, nevertheless stepped up their activities. There was a marked increase in the number of break-ins at fur farms in North America and the U.K., where mink and foxes were released. Increased activity by local and government authorities resulted in the arrest and conviction of additional perpetrators.   (SANDY PARKER)

AUTOMOBILES

The automotive industry seesawed through 1998 with unexpectedly strong sales in some markets and surprisingly weak sales in others. During the year the industry was rocked with merger announcements that demonstrated the unmistakable march toward industrywide consolidation and led some automotive executives to predict that no more than nine automakers would survive the inevitable shakeout. Major corporate reorganizations and personnel changes took place, and labour strife paralyzed the world's largest automaker. It was also a year marked by significant outsourcing of work to suppliers by automakers.

The industry was stunned on May 6 to learn that Daimler-Benz AG and Chrysler Corp. would merge into one company, to be called DaimlerChrysler AG. Many industry analysts had predicted such consolidations, but few had foreseen this merger. The announcement was all the more surprising because Chrysler had begun to build an engine plant in Brazil jointly with Bayerische Motoren Werke AG (BMW) and was engaged in technical exchanges exploring other business opportunities with that company. Any thoughts Chrysler may have had about merging with BMW vanished, however, during a secret 17-minute meeting at Chrysler's headquarters in January when Daimler-Benz's chairman, Jürgen Schrempp (see BIOGRAPHIES), proposed the Daimler-Chrysler merger. When the public announcement was made four months later, it set off a furious debate as to whether this was truly a merger of equals or whether Daimler was simply taking over Chrysler. For the remainder of the year analysts, pundits, and competitors all tried to divine which company was gaining the upper hand as their operations were combined. Those arguing that it was a merger of equals pointed to the dual headquarters, dual chairmen, fifty-fifty split in automotive management, and the fact that English would be the official language. Those arguing that it was a takeover noted that the dual chairmanship would end in three years with Schrempp then taking charge, that there were more Germans on the management board, and that the new company was incorporated in Germany.

There was little doubt DaimlerChrysler would be a formidable competitor. It instantly became the world's fifth largest automaker in vehicle production and the third largest in revenue and profits. The two companies also identified first-year savings of about $1.5 billion through combined purchasing costs, a common finance department, and shared research and development. Analysts said they expected annual savings to reach $3.3 billion. Daimler-Benz planned to open up its distribution system to Chrysler in Europe and in less-developed countries where the American automaker was weak. Both companies, however, were adamant that they would keep their product brand identities separate. No Chrysler car would carry the famous three-pointed star that adorns the grille of every Mercedes, and no Mercedes would be sold in a Chrysler dealership. In 1997 Freightliner, a subsidiary of Daimler-Benz, had bought the heavy-duty truck operations of Ford Motor Co. in North America and renamed it Sterling.

Daimler and Chrysler were not the only automakers seeking consolidation. Volkswagen AG paid Vickers PLC about $700 million (£479 million) to buy British luxury carmaker Rolls-Royce Motor Cars Ltd., only to discover that it did not get the rights to the Rolls-Royce name or the famous insignia. Instead, VW was stuck with an old assembly plant and the rights to the venerable Bentley nameplate. It turned out that the jet engine maker Rolls-Royce PLC owned the rights to the name. Much to VW's embarrassment, BMW later bought the rights to use the Rolls-Royce name for only $66 million (£40 million) and then granted VW the use of the name until 2002. In an ongoing effort to corner the market on famous high-end automotive brands, Volkswagen bought Lamborghini and Bugatti and also held exploratory talks to buy Swedish automaker Volvo.

As the South Korean economy all but collapsed, automakers there scrambled to survive as best they could. Kia Motors Corp. was placed in receivership, and a round of bidding ensued to sell the troubled automaker. The sale went through three separate rounds of bidding before South Korea's Hyundai Motor Co. acquired a 51% stake both in Kia and in its truck-making subsidiary, the Asia Motors Co., for $951 million. Daewoo's chairman Kim Woo-Choong (see BIOGRAPHIES) publicly announced that General Motors Corp. was going to buy one-half of his company, but GM officials denied those claims. Meanwhile, Daewoo bought Ssangyong, which made vans, trucks, and a limousine based on an older design of the Mercedes-Benz E-class. Samsung completed building an assembly plant in South Korea capable of building 240,000 cars a year, but at the end of the year it decided to swap all of its automotive operations for Daewoo's electronics business.

Several multibillion-dollar mergers and acquisitions also took place in the automotive supplier industry in 1998. Dana bought Echlin for $4.3 billion and later purchased FMO for $434 million. German tire maker Continental AG bought the brake and chassis business of ITT Industries for $1.9 billion. French supplier Valeo SA purchased ITT's Electrical Systems for $1.7 billion. Federal-Mogul acquired Cooper Automotive for $1.9 billion. Du Pont Co. bought the Herberts group, which made automotive paints and finishes, for $1,890,000,000. The Lear Corp. purchased the seating operations from GM's parts-making operation, Delphi, for about $450 million. General Motors later announced that it would spin off Delphi as a stand-alone $32 billion company starting in 1999.

Canadian supplier Magna bought Steyr-Daimler-Puch AG for $398 million. The Steyr operations included two assembly plants in Austria that made the four-wheel-drive versions of the Mercedes-Benz G-class and E-class, as well as the Jeep Cherokee and Mercedes M-class. This acquisition cemented Magna's strategy to become a supplier with the capability to design, engineer, and manufacture entire vehicles.

Throughout the year automakers announced future contracts with suppliers that would employ modular design. Rather than build cars one piece at a time in their own assembly plants, automakers increasingly ordered suppliers to make modules, groups of parts that are assembled into one entity. "Corner modules," for example, emerged as a particular favourite among automakers. Such a module consisted of the brakes, suspension, and shock absorbers, which the supplier then delivered as a unit to a car company's assembly plant. All the automaker then had to do was bolt the modules onto a car, thus greatly simplifying the assembly process and reducing costs. Ford began building an assembly plant to make modular cars under a plan it code-named the Amazon project. GM, already underway with a Brazilian project it code-named Blue Macaw, also proposed to the United Automobile Workers (UAW) that it bulldoze four small car plants in North America and replace them with smaller modular plants.

Dana began supplying "rolling chassis" to a new Chrysler assembly plant in Campo Largo, Braz., signaling a new method for building vehicles. At a small, nearby plant of its own, Dana installed most of the components that comprise a truck chassis, including the axles, brakes, suspension, wheels, and tires. It then shipped the chassis to Chrysler's plant, where it was rolled to the assembly line. Chrysler then bolted the body to the chassis and installed the interior, and a new Dakota pickup truck was ready for sale. Other automakers announced their interest in the "rolling chassis" concept. Since a supplier would do a substantial part of the assembly work, it would allow the automakers to build smaller assembly plants with fewer workers. Analysts pointed out that the unions were likely to fight this move, viewing this outsourcing as a tactic to deplete their memberships by as much as 30%.

Ford announced significant management changes that resulted in a member of the Ford family being named to run the company once again. William Clay Ford, Jr., a great grandson of the founder of the company, was to become chairman of the board on Jan. 1, 1999. Jacques Nasser was promoted to president and chief executive officer. Ford moved the headquarters for its Lincoln-Mercury division out of Detroit to Irvine, Calif.

General Motors was dogged throughout the year by press reports detailing management friction between GM Europe (GME) and its International Operations (IO). GME argued that it was sacrificing too much of its engineering resources to satisfy the growing global needs of IO. GM's management reassigned the president of GME to Russia

and moved the headquarters of IO from Zürich, Switz., to Detroit. It later initiated a major corporate restructuring wherein it merged its North American Operations (NAO) with IO. Richard Wagoner, the former head of NAO, was named president.

The UAW went on strike against GM in June in what became the most severe work stoppage at the company in nearly 30 years. When General Motors was unable to persuade the UAW local at its Flint (Mich.) Metal Center to agree to work changes designed to improve productivity, it transferred stamping dies from that plant to another in Ohio. That triggered an immediate strike at the stamping plant in Flint, and the nearby GM Delphi Flint East plant that made spark plugs and oil filters initiated a sympathy strike.

In a matter of weeks the lack of crucial parts made by the plants on strike shut down almost all other GM manufacturing facilities. The strike lasted 54 days, idled more than 190,000 GM workers, and cost the company about 325,000 units and nearly $3 billion in net profits. GM executives said the company would be able to make up much of the lost production with heavy overtime, but by the end of the year GM was still struggling to recapture lost market share. In an effort to avoid another crippling strike, especially with its three-year labour contract due to expire in 1999, GM recalled Gary Cowger, an executive with extensive manufacturing and labour experience, back from GM Europe to run its Labor Relations department.

One of the year's most notable product developments included the much-anticipated debut of the new Volkswagen Beetle. Based on VW's Golf model and built in Mexico, it became an instant smash hit in the American market. VW soon began exporting limited quantities to Europe, where it also received rave reviews, prompting the company to explore adding manufacturing capacity to build the car there.

Toyota introduced the luxurious Lexus RX-300, known as the Harrier in Japan and other markets. This featured the body of a sport utility vehicle mated to a passenger-car platform. It represented a new entry in a new market segment that was dubbed "sport wagons," which many analysts expected to become a harbinger for the future.

Cadillac introduced the first automotive application of night vision. This was an infrared device that greatly enhanced a driver's vision in darkness, fog, or rain, thanks to a screen that sat above the dashboard. Developed by Delco Electronics and Raytheon, General Motors had been working on the device for almost a decade.

The California Air Resources Board announced that it would require large sport utility vehicles and pickup trucks to meet the same emissions standards as passenger cars by 2004. Automakers vehemently protested the ruling, arguing that these trucks were used for workloads, such as towing and hauling, that passenger cars could not accomplish. They also argued that they did not know how to meet those standards for trucks with large engines. The board countered that a large number of these vehicles were used for general driving purposes, and that their growing popularity forced the state to impose stricter standards in order to preserve its improvement in air quality. Automakers feared that if California

proceeded with the regulations they might be adopted by other states, eventually depriving the car companies of a popular line of vehicles.

Sales in Europe rose 6% to about 14.7 million units, as the passenger-car market continued to recover. The strength of the European market helped Volkswagen surpass Toyota to become the third largest automaker in sales volume behind GM and Ford. Sales in Japan, however, slid about 13% to about six million units for the year, as the economy failed to recover. Automakers in Southeast Asia and Brazil found themselves temporarily closing their assembly plants, as the economic crisis in those regions paralyzed their economies.

As truck-type vehicles accounted for nearly half of all new vehicles sold in the U.S., large sport utility vehicles came under increasing scrutiny by the National Highway Traffic Safety Administration. The government agency worried that the large vehicles posed safety hazards to passengers of small cars and began exploring ways to force changes in bumper heights to minimize the dangers that these trucks posed.

Strong vehicle sales in the U.S. market confounded the experts. Most automakers started the year fearing that the economic crisis in Asian and South American economies might cause the U.S. economy to slow. By early spring most automakers were increasing their sales incentives. GM, Ford, and Chrysler began offering "loyalty coupons" to former customers to lure them back into their showrooms. Most analysts pointed out that sudden surges in incentives that artificially increased demand usually resulted in a period immediately afterward when sales would dip below their normal trend and thus predicted that sales would slow later in the year. The market, however, continued to gain steam, and by the end of the year sales had reached 15.9 million units, a 4% increase and the second best year in the history of the industry.

(JOHN MCELROY)

BEVERAGES

Beer. Brewers did not just seek the right formulas for their products in 1998—they sought identities and purposes that would perk up sales and propel them toward a healthier sales environment in the first part of the new century. While Anheuser-Busch maintained its position as the world's preeminent beer marketer, it demonstrated an awareness that, despite the seemingly endless double-digit volume gains for Bud Light, its existing brand portfolio—most specifi-

cally, Budweiser—did not necessarily reflect the changing tastes of beer drinkers. Consequently, the firm began the aggressive testing of Tequiza, a tequila-flavoured brew with a hint of lime that was designed to lure U.S. drinkers away from the explosively popular Corona Extra. That Anheuser-Busch was a major stockholder in Mexico's Grupo Modelo, exporter of Corona Extra, revealed the complexity of the fight for market share. Corona's gain in the United States, while a plus for Anheuser-Busch's share in Modelo, came at the expense of its own products at home.

Meanwhile, Corona seemed to be making itself at home in more places in 1998, usurping the number one import ranking in the U.S. from Heineken and passing several competitors to become the fifth largest beer brand in the world. The momentum of Mexican beers was felt at Modelo rival FEMSA, where the brewer of Dos Equis and Tecate increased production to meet international demand.

Another noteworthy Corona-related development was the decision of one of its U.S. importers, Gambrinus, to buy one of the best-known American microbrewery labels, Pete's Wicked Ale. A few years ago craft beers such as Pete's were seen as the rising tide lifting imports from the U.S.; in 1998 that situation was reversed, as many U.S. consumers shifted to beers brewed abroad.

The beer of the 21st century may well be delivered to its drinkers in a plastic bottle. Several major brewers tested different resins to determine whether such packaging would retain the product's all-important freshness. They included Bass in the U.K. with its Carling Black Label brand and Miller Brewing, which offered Lite, Genuine Draft, and Icehouse in plastic in some U.S. markets.

(GREG W. PRINCE)

Spirits. In 1998 distillers sought relevance in a beverage market that, at times, appeared to have left them behind. No company in the spirits business looked more different at the end of the year from the way it did at the beginning than Seagram—and that had little to do with any of its alcohol beverages. When the conglomerate decided to discontinue producing orange juice, selling its Tropicana Products to PepsiCo in order to finance the purchase of music giant PolyGram, it meant that one of the bedrock firms of the spirits business was shifting once and for all to emphasize entertainment, but also that spirits would get a new look

What is different about these bottles of beer? It is not what is in them but the bottles themselves. In 1998 Miller Brewing offered bottles of its Genuine Draft, Lite, and Icehouse brands in plastic in some U.S. markets. As other major brewers prepared to follow suit, plastic beer bottles looked increasingly like the wave of the future.

MILLER BREWING COMPANY

from the suddenly juiceless company. Thus, Seagram announced the creation of a single senior management team based in New York City to streamline its spirits marketing. The new structure was headed by the new position of chief marketing officer, reporting directly to Seagram's CEO, and encompassed four brand groups: Crown Royal and Captain Morgan, based in New York City, and Chivas Regal and Martell, based in London.

The effects of the last realignment that shook the worldwide spirits business, the merging of Guinness and Grand Metropolitan into the newly christened Diageo in 1997, continued to be felt in 1998, as Bacardi acquired Dewar's Scotch whisky and Bombay gin for $1.9 billion from Diageo. The deal was necessitated by antitrust provisions of the transaction that created Diageo.

On the product front, spirits took two distinct roads. On one hand, old reliables often found new audiences. Brown-Forman reported its stalwart Jack Daniel's was meeting with increased success in Europe and Asia. Allied Domecq, meanwhile, resuscitated some previously stagnant brands like Beefeater gin, marketing them anew amid the "cocktail culture" of consumers aged 18–25. On the other hand, some firms searched for something new, different, and, increasingly, colourful. For example, Heaven Hill Distilleries released Fighting Cock Kentucky Straight Bourbon Whiskey, while Wein Brauer unveiled Bite, "the first and only sour apple liquor" distributed in the U.S.   (GREG W. PRINCE)

Wine. The quality of the vintage for 1998 was generally good in all wine-growing areas. The major developments took place in marketing, with prices continuing to rise. The only segment where prices softened was the auction market, where financial problems in East Asia continued to keep bidders away.

Because of the high quality of the 1997 vintage in Italy, prices there began to increase even before the wines were offered to the public. This trend spread to most of the other European growing areas. In Europe prices not including transportation costs and taxes were at their highest levels in recent memory. In California growers who in the past would sell their grapes to premium wine makers were releasing their own labels. These new small brands, many of which were expensive, removed sources of good grapes to other producers, thereby bidding up prices for dwindling resources.

New consumers entered the market during the year, keeping demand strong and providing an opportunity for the introduction of less traditional varieties and also products from new wine-growing areas. Champagne houses released *cuvées* (special-growth wines) for the millennium, causing fear that there would be a shortage of champagne during the upcoming celebrations. Consumers consequently rushed to lay in their own stocks for their celebrations so as not to be caught short. Southern Hemisphere producers continued to see their markets expand and responded with wines of greater quality and variety.   (HOWARD HERING)

Soft Drinks. The soft-drink industry, which had grown 43% in the U.S. since 1985 and was already competitive in nature,

became downright combative in 1998. There was no greater symbol of the rancor between Coca-Cola Co. and PepsiCo Inc. than a lawsuit filed by Pepsi against Coke, alleging unfair practices in certain sectors of the profitable U.S. fountain business. Coke argued that the charges did not reflect market reality, and at the year's end the issue remained unresolved.

In Europe Coke's major attempt at expanding its trade was thwarted by French regulatory authorities. In late 1997 Coke announced its intent to purchase France's leading homegrown soft drink, Orangina, from Pernod-Ricard. Pepsi, however, argued that the addition of Pernod's soda business would give Coke a near-monopoly on French distribution channels. French regulators ruled in Pepsi's favour but did give Coke a chance to revise its offer by the end of 1998.

PepsiCo also sought to widen its product base. A year after spinning off its restaurant division the company paid $3.3 billion to buy Tropicana Products from Seagram. Pepsi was immediately hit by a lawsuit from Ocean Spray, which claimed the acquisition was at odds with the distribution deal it had with Pepsi to deliver some of its products in the U.S. The suit, however, did not prevent the deal from being completed.

Amid these maneuvers of the industry leaders, middle-size beverage companies had to look out for themselves. Cadbury Schweppes PLC, whose Dr Pepper/Seven Up products could no longer count on being included on Coke and Pepsi bottler trucks, teamed with The Carlyle Group to buy two major U.S. bottlers and form American Bottling Co. In December Coke bought the overseas rights to the Cadbury brands for $1,850,000,000.

After waiting almost a decade soft-drink manufacturers were encouraged that U.S. regulators approved two new synthetic sweeteners for use in soda pop. Royal Crown immediately began using sucralose in a new version of Diet RC, and Pepsi blended acesulfame-k with aspartame and created a new diet cola, Pepsi One. The industry hoped that these additives would help perk up the sagging diet segment.

(GREG W. PRINCE)

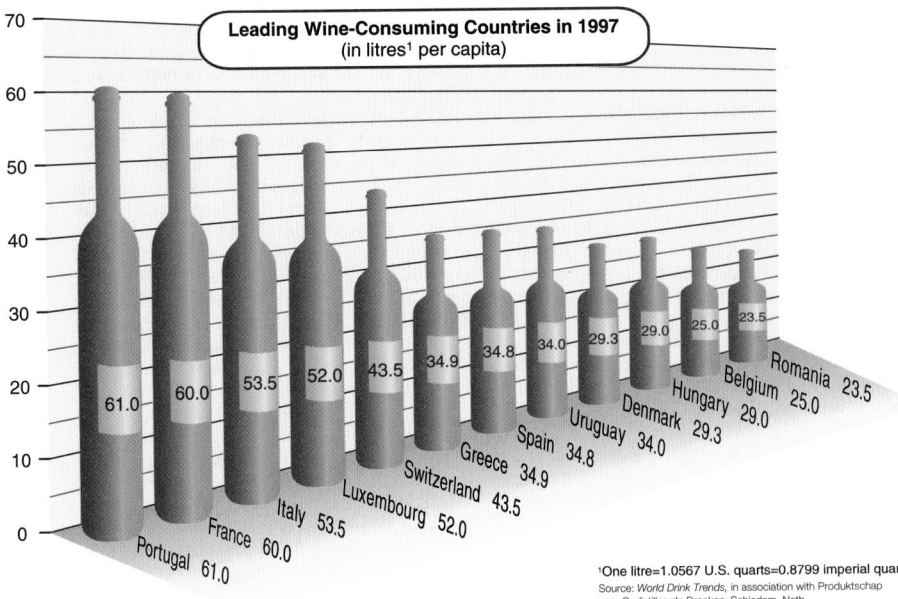

Leading Wine-Consuming Countries in 1997
(in litres[1] per capita)

Portugal 61.0
France 60.0
Italy 53.5
Luxembourg 52.0
Switzerland 43.5
Greece 34.9
Spain 34.8
Uruguay 34.0
Denmark 29.3
Hungary 29.0
Belgium 25.0
Romania 23.5

[1]One litre=1.0567 U.S. quarts=0.8799 imperial quart.
Source: *World Drink Trends,* in association with Produktschap voor Gedistilleerde Dranken, Schiedam, Neth.

BUILDING AND CONSTRUCTION

The U.S. government reported that a seasonally adjusted annual rate of $660.6 billion of construction had been completed in 1998 by September, a 6% increase over the September 1997 figure. The National Association of Home Builders reported in October an annual pace of 1.6 million housing starts, on track for a 7.9% increase over 1997.

Several large public works projects in the U.S. made significant progress during the year. Boston advanced its Central Artery Project, a multiyear, $10.8 billion effort to relieve downtown traffic congestion. Denver,

Colo., tried to improve airport access, opening two sections of E-470 in June. The privately financed toll road connected rapidly growing suburbs east and south of the city to Denver International Airport.

Los Angeles pushed forward with the long-awaited Alameda Corridor project, a plan to ease freight deliveries to downtown from the ports of Los Angeles and Long Beach 32 km (20 mi) away. The road-and-rail combination was designed to consolidate three freight routes into a single corridor by its 2001 completion date.

In Phoenix, Ariz., the Arizona Diamondbacks major league baseball team opened a 48,500-seat stadium in March. It was the first U.S. stadium with natural grass under a retractable roof, which was designed to open or close in five minutes. The $354 million stadium's air conditioning system was designed to cool the seating area from 110° F to 80° F (43° C to 26° C) in less than four hours. Other stadiums with retractable roofs were being planned in Seattle, Wash.; Milwaukee, Wis.; and Houston, Texas. In the November elections voters approved measures to fund new baseball parks in Cincinnati, Ohio, and San Diego, Calif., as well as a new football stadium in Denver.

In July Hong Kong opened Chek Lap Kok Airport, the heart of a $21 billion transportation system. For the passenger terminal British architect Sir Norman Foster designed the largest enclosed space ever constructed, big enough to house five Boeing 747s tip to tip. Despite problems with the baggage-handling system on opening day, the airport soon began to serve an estimated 35 million passengers a year. It was designed to handle up to 87 million passengers a year eventually.

Asia's financial crisis entered its second year, causing many large projects to be abandoned or scaled down. Hong Kong-based infrastructure entrepreneur Sir Gordon Wu Ying-sheung suspended work on the 1,320-MW Tanjung Jati B coal-fired power plant in central Java. The project was 70% completed, but Sir Gordon, chairman of Hopewell Holdings Ltd., said in September that Indonesia's economic depression had caused financiers to lose confidence. Hopewell paid $230 million to win the 30-year build-own-operate contract and could lose as much as $620 million. Another of Sir Gordon's high-profile projects, a railway in Thailand, was also on hold.

In May the European Parliament opened a new headquarters building in Strasbourg, France. The complex, designed by Paris-based Architecture Studio Europe, was supported by a 45,500-cu m concrete mat resting on piles driven 14 m deep. (1 cu m= 35.3 cu ft; 1 m=3.28 ft.) Walkways connected a 17-story cylindrical office building to the debating chamber, a 42-m-tall steel and concrete elliptical "egg" with an exterior covered with cedar and oak planks.

(ANDREW G. WRIGHT)

CHEMICALS

The value of the world's chemical production climbed almost 2% in 1997 to $1,586,000,000,000. It was an outstanding year for the industry in most parts of the world, particularly in view of the financial crisis in Asia that began in mid-1997. Concerning their prospects for 1998 and 1999, however, leaders of the industry were edgy, with their primary worry the continuing economic woes of several Asian countries, especially Japan, South Korea, Indonesia, and Malaysia.

Because of the problems generated by shifts in currency values and the fluctuations of chemical prices, some observers preferred to evaluate the industry in terms of production volumes. On that basis also, 1997 was a good year especially for most of the industrialized countries. The U.S. increased its production volume 4.3%, and Europe registered a 4.7% increase. Japan's Ministry of International Trade and Industry reported a 5% gain.

Viewed in product-value terms, Japan's chemical industry output was $202 billion in 1997 compared with $215.9 billion in 1996; this, in part, reflected its devalued currency. Japan was, nonetheless, second to the U.S. in the output value of its chemical industry. The U.S., buoyed by a strong dollar, totaled $392.2 billion in 1997. Europe at midyear anticipated growth near 3% for 1998, and the U.S. pointed toward a 3.5% increase. These estimates hinged on hopes for improvements in the economies of Japan and southeastern Asian nations.

Some parts of Asia were, however, prospering. China achieved an estimated $80 billion in output value in 1997, and India totaled more than $30 billion.

Latin America, with historic market ties to Japan, was affected by the latter's problems in 1998. Nonetheless, led by Brazil, the region had a strong performance of $93.4 billion in output value in 1997. As of 1998 it held a 6.6% share of world production (4.6% in 1990).

The European Union (EU) was by far the largest factor in world chemical trading. Its exports in 1997 totaled $278,821,000,000, and imports were $227,507,000,000. Germany was the largest element of the EU, shipping out chemicals worth $68,277,000,000 and importing $39,355,000,000. France's chemical exports were $41,064,000,000 and imports $31,311,000,000, and the U.K. exported $36,818,000,000 and imported $29,949,000,000. For the world as a whole exports and imports each grew 15% in 1997 compared to 1996.

For more than three decades the chemical industry emphasized petrochemicals—synthetic plastics, fibres, and related products derived or synthesized from oil and gas. Such products in the U.S., for example, comprised at least 30% of the product value of the industry in 1998 and were also produced in high volumes. In particular, ethylene and propylene-based petrochemicals (typically, the olefin plastics) were the products on which the Asian nations concentrated as they began to launch their chemical industries. No country, however, profited consistently from petrochemicals, and by 1998 in much of the world profits were nowhere near as large as they had been during the mid-1990s. Producers in many of the less-developed countries were competing for markets, which had the effect of forcing down profits. This was also true in the United States, where the profit margin for the chemical industry was above 8% in 1997 but was clearly not going to reach that level in 1998.

In an effort to diversify their product lines, many firms turned to specialty chemicals, by loose definition almost any high-cost, low-volume chemical ranging from pharmaceuticals to industrial gases to water

Pictured at left is the new headquarters building of the European Parliament in Strasbourg, France. Designed by Paris-based Architecture Studio Europe, the complex opened in May.

treatment chemicals. Sometimes specialties showed startling growth, as exemplified by a new development in producing silicon chips for computers. The high-purity compounds used to prepare ultrasmooth chips had a total market in 1995 estimated at just $25 million; it reached $85 million in 1997 and was expected to keep growing at a rate of 30% per year for the next decade.

A surge of interest in biotechnology was engaging the primary attention of management at many companies, including Hoechst AG, Bayer AG, and BASF in Germany; Rhône-Poulenc in France; and DuPont, Monsanto, and Dow in the U.S. Attracting considerable attention in 1998 were routes to the production of high-volume industrial compounds that use bioengineered bacteria and enzymes in processes that may challenge conventional chemical syntheses. Hoffmann-La Roche of Switzerland, for example, was replacing its chemical route to Vitamin B^2 by a new fermentation process. DuPont was testing a fermentation method to make a raw material used for a type of specialty polyester (polytrimethylene terephthalate) with high-end plastic and fibre uses.

(J. ROBERT WARREN)

ELECTRICAL

Although economic problems in Asia led to a downturn in the global market for electrical equipment in 1998, the leading multinational manufacturers reported an increase in revenues of about 13% in 1997 and remained optimistic for the long term. Indeed, General Electric (GE) reported in October 1998 that it was on target for a record financial performance with a double-digit increase in earnings. With Asia representing about 9% of the company's revenue, GE had a significant stake in this depressed market, but the firm's directors were confident that the current business uncertainty was manageable and that there was an opportunity to increase the company's presence in what they expected to be one of the great markets of the 21st century.

While admitting that turbulence in Southeast Asia's currency and financial markets would perceptibly damage growth in the region, Siemens AG, the world's largest electrical equipment manufacturer, forecast that growth rates in the world electrical market, particularly in Europe, would continue to outpace the global economy as a whole. Asea Brown Boveri (ABB), the third largest electrical manufacturer after Siemens and GE, forecast that Asia would begin to bounce back in the next two or three years and resume growth even faster than before. ABB claimed that it was among the first to recognize both the threats and opportunities of the Asian crisis, announcing a plan to accelerate its expansion in the region as early as October 1997. The plan also involved restructuring some of ABB's operations in Western Europe, involving the loss of 10,000 jobs to make the Western factories more competitive. In late 1998 financial difficulties in Russia and South America worried the world's banking systems, but the effect on the electrical equipment market had yet to be felt.

For the last 40 years there has been major restructuring of the electrical manufacturing industry. The past two years saw the demise of one of the most famous names in electrical engineering and the birth of a new multinational firm. With the $1,525,000,000 sale of its power plant business to Siemens in November 1997, Westinghouse Electric Corp. retired from its original role as an electrical engineering company to concentrate on broadcasting. The new multinational was Alstom, which became the fourth largest electrical manufacturing company in the world. Alstom was formed in June 1998 as a result of the flotation of 52% of GEC Alsthom, the joint venture business of the French telecommunications company Alcatel Alsthom and the General Electric Co. of the U.K. With headquarters in France, it employed 110,000 people in 60 countries.

Another milestone in 1998 was GE's achievement of meeting what was thought to be the "impossible" target of 15% operating margin. The company admitted that its operating margin, a critical measure of business efficiency and profitability, had hovered around 10% for decades. With its "Sigma Six—best practices" philosophy becoming more deeply involved in company operations, however, GE's operating margin passed the 14% barrier in 1997 and was approaching 15%. Groupe Schneider announced that the ambitious target of its "2000—continuous improvement" plan of 15% return on equity by the year 2000 was now within reach.

The electrical manufacturing industry was particularly affected by the year 2000 computer recognition problem in both its manufacturing systems and its products. In this regard GE said that compliance programs and information systems modifications had been initiated in an attempt to ensure that those systems and processes would remain functional. While there could be no assurance that all modifications would be successful, GE did not expect any material adverse effect on its financial position. Groupe Schneider estimated that it would cost the company approximately $53.3 million, which was only 0.63% of its 1997 revenue, to achieve year 2000 compliance. ABB was intensifying its review of all its products and systems to achieve year 2000 compliance, and, like other European companies, was devoting much effort in preparing for the introduction of the European common currency.

(T.C.J. COGLE)

ENERGY

Petroleum. The worldwide oil industry experienced a tumultuous year in 1998. One of the most dramatic price falls of recent times put intense financial pressure on countries that exported oil, and increased commercial competition caused some of the leading Western oil companies to join forces in the biggest industrial mergers yet seen.

The extent and speed of the price collapse caused surprise throughout the oil world. At the beginning of 1997 the price of Brent Blend oil futures reached a recent high of $24.25/bbl. By mid-December 1998, however, the price had fallen by more than $14, nearly 60%. Several factors were involved in the collapse. The first was the impact of a slow but steady buildup of oil stocks that had been taking place throughout the world since 1995. As long as demand remained healthy, this increase was hardly noticed and posed little threat to prices. Several relatively mild winters in Europe and North America, however, caused consumption in those regions to be less than had been ex-pected, thus reducing demand. A sharp rise in Iraqi oil exports under the UN oil-for-food program added to the growing surplus. The final factor was the East Asian financial crisis. It triggered a sharp fall in demand from a region that, until the crisis hit, had been the fastest growing oil market. Also, the impact of the Asian economic downturn began to affect other regions during the year.

In December the International Energy Agency (IEA), the Paris-based body that monitors the global oil market on behalf of the Western world's leading industrialized countries, reported that "growth in world oil demand appears to have stalled in September and October." The IEA said the demand weakness was not confined to Asia but was evident across much of the developed world, as economies began to slow.

The response of oil exporters to the price collapse was generally ineffectual for most of the year. In March three leading exporting nations, Saudi Arabia, Mexico, and Venezuela, met secretly in Riyadh, the Saudi capital. The three, which were also the main crude oil suppliers to the U.S., the world's single largest petroleum market, agreed to coordinate production cuts. Eventually other producers from the Organization of Petroleum Exporting Countries (OPEC) and some nations outside the group, including Norway and Russia, also agreed to take part in a worldwide round of production cuts to support prices. The effort was initially successful. Prices soon began to fall again, however, as the extent of the global supply surplus and the fall in demand in Asia and elsewhere became apparent.

The price collapse put intense pressure on the finances of many oil exporters. In November Bill Richardson, the U.S. secretary of energy, noted that in real dollars, "we are paying about the same for oil as we paid in 1920." He predicted that the 11 OPEC countries would see their collective oil revenues fall by about one-third, approximately $50 billion.

Even that level of financial pain, however, was not enough to induce all OPEC members to abide by their promised cuts. At its November meeting OPEC failed to agree on any further action, with Saudi Arabia, the dominant member and the world's biggest oil producer and exporter, demanding greater compliance with the first round of cuts before embarking on any new initiative. In mid-December new signs of price weakness prompted many OPEC governments to appeal for additional action to stem the renewed decline.

The oil price weakness was one of the reasons behind a sudden burst of merger activity among some of the biggest Western oil companies. In August British Petroleum Co. PLC ended more than a decade of stability in the ranks of the international integrated oil sector with its takeover of Amoco Corp. of the U.S. The deal propelled the combined company, known as BP Amoco, into the "super league" of the oil industry, which until then had been the exclusive preserve of Royal Dutch/Shell and Exxon Corp. of the U.S.

The BP Amoco deal triggered a wave of intense speculation about which companies would be next to merge or take over a competitor. Few, however, guessed that it would be Exxon that would be next to make a move. In December it confirmed that it was to take over Mobil Corp. in the world's

biggest industrial merger. At the same time the first sign of oil industry consolidation in Europe appeared when Total of France announced it was taking over PetroFina.

The logic behind the deals varied, although there were common themes. In each case the three dominant companies—BP, Exxon, and Total—were able to take advantage of relatively high share prices that allowed them to afford the takeover premiums required by the shareholders of their respective targets. All three companies also had a reputation for efficiency and cost-cutting that gave them credibility in arguing that the enlarged groups would produce substantial savings and operational synergies. Also, in the case of BP Amoco, it was argued that sheer size and financial firepower would be needed to tackle the big projects that were emerging as a result of the third dominant theme of the year, the opening of large OPEC countries to foreign investment.

Venezuela was the first of the large OPEC producers to seek foreign capital to expand its oil industry, which until several years ago was under the monopoly control of government-owned Petroleos de Venezuela. "La Apertura," or the "The Opening," attracted billions of dollars from international oil companies as part of Venezuela's ambitious strategy to boost output from 3.7 million bbl a day currently to 6.2 million bbl a day by 2009.

In July Iran, the world's third biggest exporter, announced a plan to open more than 40 projects to foreign participation. Although U.S. companies were barred from taking part because of unilateral U.S. sanctions on the country, European, Latin-American, and Asian companies responded with dozens of proposals.

Among the major OPEC producers only Saudi Arabia and Kuwait remained off-limits to foreign investment. Kuwait, however, was considering limited foreign participation, and in October Saudi Arabia summoned the heads of eight American oil companies to a meeting in Washington, D.C., during which they were asked to prepare "ideas" on ways in which their companies might take part more directly in the development of Saudi Arabia's energy potential.

(ROBERT CORZINE)

Natural Gas. Global demand for natural gas, the least polluting fossil fuel, continued in 1998 to grow faster than that for oil. The International Energy Agency estimated that demand for gas was rising by 2.6% a year, compared with 1.9% for crude oil.

During recent years gas captured a growing share in the power generation sector. Such growth was expected to accelerate, as converting to gas-fired power generation was regarded as one of the best ways for many countries to reduce emissions of carbon dioxide, a greenhouse gas, in line with commitments entered into at the Kyoto Conference in 1997. In Europe energy ministers formally adopted a directive forcing European Union nations to gradually open to competition one-third of the EU's natural gas supply industry, which in 1998 was dominated by national monopolies.

The Asian financial crisis and collapse in oil prices in 1998 affected some gas projects. Asia was the biggest market for liquefied natural gas, and several new projects to supply the region with LNG from the Middle East and elsewhere were likely to be delayed. Low oil prices took the edge off industry excitement about developing low-cost methods for converting natural gas into virtually pollution-free diesel and other middle-distillate fuels, including kerosene.

(ROBERT CORZINE)

Coal. Key events in 1998 signified a greater future reliance on coal as a fuel to generate electricity owing to worldwide requirements for an increase in electric power. Imported oil was used primarily for this form of energy until the 1973 oil embargo, but by 1998 world coal consumption had grown by the equivalent of 20 million bbl of oil a day. Germany's rejection of nuclear power, the U.K.'s move to diversify its energy sources by tentatively reintroducing coal, and the greater use of low-cost coal by U.S. producers over high-cost nuclear output all pointed toward a higher reliance on coal.

In 1997 U.S. utilities used a record 900 million short tons of coal for a record 57.2% of power. Preliminary figures for 1998 were somewhat higher. For the 12th consecutive year, worldwide coal consumption exceeded five billion short tons. The leading coal consumer was China followed by the U.S., India, South Africa, Russia, Poland, Japan, the U.K., Australia, and Ukraine; both China and the U.S. produced more than one billion short tons of coal annually. An ultra-advanced pulverized coal unit, reporting 47% thermal efficiency, began operating in Denmark. (RICHARD L. LAWSON)

Nuclear. The number of nuclear power reactors in operation throughout the world decreased in 1997, the first year in which a decline had been registered. International Atomic Energy Agency (IAEA) data for 1997, published in 1998, indicated that there were 437 operational nuclear units in 33 countries at the beginning of 1998 compared with 442 a year earlier. Total operating capacity was 351,795 MW, a net increase of 831 MW over the previous year. Worldwide, nuclear power units produced a total of 2,276.32 TWh, increasing the cumulative to-

tal of electrical energy produced by nuclear plants to 31,876.42 TWh (terawatt-hours; 1 TWh=1 billion kwh). A total of 36 units were under construction in 14 countries, including five new projects on which construction began and three that began production.

Countries with more than 50% of their national electricity production from nuclear power were Lithuania (81.5% from 2 nuclear units), France (78.2% from 59 units), and Belgium (60.1% from 7 units). The total number of commercial power reactors permanently shut down throughout the world reached 80.

The construction starts of 1997 were in China (three) and South Korea (two), and South Korea also had one of the units that began production. The other two, Chooz B2 and Civaux 1, were in France, where only one reactor, Civaux 2, remained under construction. This unit, due to start production in mid-1999, would mark the end of the massive French nuclear construction program. Japan, another country with a major nuclear power program, also had only one unit under construction, Onagawa 3, due to begin production in 2002. The situation was the same in most countries with large numbers of reactors in service. The Canadian provincial utility Ontario Hydro closed seven of its units and faced restructuring by the Ontario government. The only new generating plant of interest to Britain's nuclear utilities was gas fired. The election in Germany in the autumn resulted in victory for a left-of-centre coalition government that declared its intention to close down the country's nuclear power plants. In the U.S. some utilities looked for new partners or buyers to share or take over the operation of their nuclear plants.

Of the original U.S. vendors and developers of nuclear power, only General Electric Co. remained in the business. The nuclear operations of Westinghouse Corp., which pioneered the world's most popular reactor

Plans to make the Chernobyl nuclear power station environmentally sound were under way in 1998. The station near the town of Chernobyl, Ukraine, was the site of the worst accident in the history of nuclear power generation. After the accident occurred on April 25-26, 1986, the reactor core was enclosed in a concrete-and-steel sarcophagus that later was deemed structurally unsound.

type, the pressurized water reactor, were acquired by a consortium formed by the British nuclear fuel cycle company, BNFL, and Morrison Knudsen of Boise, Idaho. These acquisitions elevated BNFL and Morrison Knudsen into major firms in the nuclear industry. Together with Ukrainian industry partners, they signed a contract for the investigation and reconstruction of the Chernobyl sarcophagus so as to achieve an environmentally safe structure.

The delays in opening the Waste Isolation Pilot Plant in New Mexico and the construction of the spent fuel underground repository at Yucca Mountain in Nevada continued in 1998. On the other hand, progress was made in the industry's role in international nuclear disarmament, with an agreement signed by U.S. and Russian presidents Bill Clinton and Boris Yeltsin that increased the commitment of each country to convert nuclear weapons-grade materials into either nuclear power fuels or to forms that render them unusable in nuclear weapons.

Though the original major nuclear-power countries were reaching the end of their nuclear power construction programs and had produced no significant plans for expansion, in East Asia, particularly China and South Korea, comprehensive plans were announced and orders placed. South Korea's long-term development plan called for the completion of 18 new units with a capacity of 18,600 MW by 2015. Russia signed deals to supply two reactor units for China and two for India. Russia's Atomic Energy Ministry also announced plans for new nuclear stations at home and for decommissioning some of the oldest. Three partly built units at existing stations were scheduled to be completed by 2000 and six new units including a floating plant in the East Siberian Sea by 2005. An additional five units, including the BN-800 fast breeder, were planned for completion by 2010; by the same date, however, nine units were to have been decommissioned.

(RICHARD A. KNOX)

Alternative Energy. The long-term trend toward increased use of alternative energy sources continued in 1998, although it appeared that low prices for fossil fuels such as oil and natural gas might undermine some solar and wind power projects. The latest annual report from the Worldwatch Institute in Washington, D.C., noted that capacity for generating wind power and shipments of solar cells were growing at high rates throughout the world. Worldwatch estimated that in 1997 global wind power generating capacity grew by 25%, reaching 7,630 MW, compared with just 10 MW in 1980. Shipments of solar cells rose 43% in 1997 to 126 MW. The growth in both areas was, however, from a small base. The Paris-based International

Energy Agency (IEA) estimated that renewable energy (excluding hydroelectric power) accounted for only about 4% of the energy needs of its members, the world's industrialized countries. Renewable energy sources, mainly in the forms of hydroelectricity and biomass, such as firewood, agricultural by-products, animal waste, and charcoal, in 1997 supplied between 15%–20% of the world's energy demand, according to the IEA.

The speed with which renewable sources could grow depended in large part on government policies and technological progress. In many countries conventional fuels were subsidized, and governments offered insufficient financial incentives for companies or individuals to convert to renewable sources. As the IEA pointed out, "to achieve the substantial role expected of renewables in the future, enthusiasm needs to be harnessed to specific action."   (ROBERT CORZINE)

GAMBLING

In 1997 gross revenues from all forms of legal commercial gambling in the United States increased by 6.2% over the prior year to $50.9 billion, representing 0.74% of Americans' personal income. Between 1982 and 1997 revenues from legal gaming industries in the U.S. grew from a base of $10.4 billion, representing a compounded growth rate of 11.1%. Casinos, operating legally in more than 25 states in such diverse venues as resorts, riverboats, historic mining towns, and Indian reservations, accounted for more than half of the total. Lotteries, which operated in 36 states and the District of Columbia, were the second largest group, generating revenues after payment of prizes of $16.2 billion in 1997. Pari-mutuel wagering on races, both on-track and

off-track, finished a distant third with $3.8 billion in revenues.

The most visible centre of gambling in the world was Las Vegas, Nev. That city staged the opening of one of the world's most expensive hotels, the Bellagio, in October 1998. Modeled on an idyllic resort in the lake district of northern Italy, Bellagio opened with 3,025 guest rooms, an extravagant casino, and tastefully appointed shops, public areas, and grounds, not to mention a $300 million collection of fine art on display. Across the street rose other billion-dollar reproductions of Europe: the Paris, with an ersatz Eiffel Tower and Arc de Triomphe; and the Venetian, with a campanile and canals; also opening in 1999 was Mandalay Bay, featuring a tropical Pacific theme. Ceremoniously removed from the Strip were ghosts of gambling's recent past, the Aladdin, the Sands, the Landmark, and the Dunes, taken out by implosions needed to clear space for the next generation of casinos. Investors were apprehensive about the ability of Las Vegas to absorb the new casinos, and so most stock prices of publicly traded casino companies fell throughout 1998.

Though Las Vegas experienced growth and development during the year, Atlantic City, N.J., once again saw more promises than construction cranes. Political and legal battles over the financing of a road extension into a new casino area, and concern over the future potential for growth, made it difficult to develop new projects.

Riverboat casino gaming had become well-established in a number of Midwestern and Southern states since the early 1990s, but changing tax laws and operating rules, altered competitive circumstances, and constitutional challenges provided some of those new industries with anything but clear

One of the world's most expensive hotels, the Bellagio, opened in Las Vegas, Nev., in October 1998. The 36-story, 3,025-room resort, which was built to replicate an Italian village, sat on a hillside fronted by an expansive lake that featured 1,000 fountains. Nearly one million people visited the new resort in the first 20 days after it opened.

sailing. In Illinois the top percentage tax rate on gaming revenues was increased from 20% to 35% in 1997. In Missouri, the State Supreme Court in 1998 determined that the 1992 referendum authorizing riverboat casinos did not permit them to operate as "boats in moats," outside the actual channels of the state's navigable rivers. This ruling was rendered after the legislature and gaming commission had already authorized such facilities, affecting perhaps $1 billion in capital investment and most of the state's operating casinos. That led to an expensive but nonetheless successful initiative on the November ballot to alter the state's constitution to permit such venues.

Of all the states that legalized casinos in the 1990s, the one that encountered the greatest difficulties was Louisiana. In 1994 indictments were issued linking the distribution of video poker machines with members of various New York Mafia families; these later resulted in convictions. In 1998 former governor Edwin Edwards was indicted for allegedly soliciting bribes and kickbacks from potential riverboat casino operators in the granting of 15 licenses. Finally, the land-based Harrah's Jazz Casino in New Orleans, burdened by high taxes and strict operating constraints, went into bankruptcy in 1995 after operating for only five months.

South Carolina quickly became home to a 28,000-machine video poker industry scattered throughout the state in convenience stores and other retail outlets. The machines were introduced after the courts ruled that such devices were not illegal, and they quickly became a major presence in the state, generating revenues of approximately $2 billion.

Native American gaming continued its rapid expansion, with the most significant developments of 1998 occurring in California. In March a compact was negotiated between Gov. Pete Wilson and the nongaming Pala tribe that would have limited the extent of Native American gambling in the state. The governor then declared that the Pala compact would be the model for all other tribes, who were given the choice of going along or seeing their gaming operations shut down. A rebellion ensued as a consortium of tribes was successful in getting an initiative on the November ballot. Proposition 5 would give tribes substantial autonomy and control over the expansion of Native American gaming in the state. Following the most expensive campaign in the history of ballot issues in California and the U.S., an estimated cost for both sides of approximately $100 million, the proposition passed overwhelmingly.

Elsewhere, Native American casinos continued to have a strong presence in several states. Two of the largest and most profitable casinos in the world, Foxwoods and the Mohegan Sun, were Native American casinos in rural southeastern Connecticut. In 1998 the two casinos paid more than $250 million to Connecticut in exchange for a continuation of their exclusive right to operate casino gaming in the state. They generated gaming revenues in 1998 in excess of $1.5 billion. Besides Native American gaming, the only new U.S. jurisdiction to legalize casinos was the state of Michigan, which authorized three casinos for Detroit in a referendum in 1996. They would compete with a successful casino across the Detroit River in Windsor, Ont.

Casinos in other countries were also affected by economic and political events. The Asian crisis substantially reduced the amount of play at baccarat, which created difficulties for high-end casinos in Australia and the United Kingdom as well as Las Vegas. Some constraints on the British casino industry were relaxed, but these were offset by increases in the tax rate on earnings from gambling. South Africa moved forward in establishing a casino industry that would ultimately have 40 licensed casinos, primarily in or around the country's major cities. The first legal casino in Israel opened in Palestine-controlled Jericho in 1998. Operators there hoped to attract Israeli customers and take advantage of the closing of casinos in nearby Turkey earlier in the year.

Internet gambling continued to be a subject of vigorous debate. Some countries, such as Australia, decided to move forward with legislation that would legalize, regulate, and tax virtual casinos and World Wide Web sites offering betting on sports. The U.S., by contrast, remained opposed to such gambling. Legislation moved forward in Congress that would establish criminal penalties for offering commercial gaming and wagering opportunities over the Internet.

Generally, the racing industry suffered in competition with casino-style gambling. In some states, such as Iowa, Delaware, Rhode Island, and West Virginia, racetracks were successful in persuading legislatures to allow them to offer slot machines or other electronic gaming. The result was to turn those tracks into casinos. In 1998 Iowa's slot machines at tracks generated more than $250 million, and the slots at Delaware's tracks exceeded $350 million, more than ten times the revenues from pari-mutuel wagering. (WILLIAM R. EADINGTON)

GAMES AND TOYS

Despite some 5,000–6,000 items on retailers' shelves and efforts to spread sales more evenly throughout the year, the toy industry in 1998 again witnessed a year-end frenzy of a "must-have" holiday hit toy. Furby—manufactured by Tiger Electronics Inc., a company that was acquired by Hasbro Inc. earlier in the year—was a furry, animatronic pet with six built-in sensors that allowed it to react to the presence of other Furbys, to light and darkness, being turned right-side up or upside down, and being tickled or petted. Furby responded by slowly opening and closing its eyes, wiggling its ears, and speaking phrases from a vocabulary of 200 words and sounds in English and Furbish, an imaginary language. The toy became a hot-ticket item shortly after its October debut, selling out as quickly as the toys arrived in stores, despite the more than one million units that had been shipped by the manufacturer. As early as one month after its introduction, "Furbymania" struck the Internet, with on-line consumers offering up to $200 for the $30 retail item.

While some customers stood in lines for Furby and other hot holiday toys, others shopped from the convenience of their homes via the Internet, ringing up an estimated $13 million in toy sales. Polls indicated that nearly one-half of the 29 million American computer users utilized the information superhighway to purchase gifts during the 1998 holiday season. One of the most

popular and fastest-growing cyber toy shops was at <www.etoys.com>, which was launched in October 1997; acquired its largest competitor, <www.toys.com>, earlier in the year; and offered merchandise from 500 manufacturers. Besides toys, the Santa Monica, Calif.–based on-line retailer also included in its inventory books, videos, computer software, and video games. Toys "Я" Us also joined the race to capture market share of Internet toy sales, with its July debut into World Wide Web–based retailing at <www.toysrus.com>. The site boasted 1,500 products, including Feature Shop, which highlighted toys driven by timely events such as newly released films and links to toy manufacturers' Web sites. In November the industry's two largest toy companies, Mattel Inc. and Hasbro, also premiered new Web sites for collectors of their most popular brands. Barbie fans could go on-line at Mattel's <www.Barbie.com> and create a personalized Barbie doll—selecting hairstyle, hair colour, and doll name—and certificate of authenticity. The personalized My Design dolls were shipped within six to eight weeks of ordering, and retailed for $39.99 plus shipping. A key figure behind Mattel's successful marketing strategy was Jill Barad (see BIOGRAPHIES), the company's chairman and chief executive officer. For the millions of toy-collecting households, Hasbro developed <www.HasbroCollectors.com>, a Web site that provided information about this popular hobby and about Hasbro's col-

TIGER ELECTRONICS

Move over, Beanie Babies. A new "must-have" toy debuted in 1998—Furby. The cuddly stuffed animal from Tiger Electronics Inc. had holiday shoppers standing in line for hours. The interactive toy responded in numerous ways whenever it was tickled or petted.

lectible brands, including G.I. Joe and *Star Wars* action figures. In addition, collectors would be able to purchase a select number of products directly from the site. (See *Retailing:* Sidebar.)

Other popular toys included action figures based on hit films about little creatures—*Antz, A Bug's Life,* and *Small Soldiers.* From the small screen, "Teletubbies" captured the hearts of the littlest television viewers; the newest fab four from the U.K. were a hit on TV and in toy stores. The animated puppy Blue, from the cable TV hit "Blue's Clues," charmed kids ages two to five and spawned

a top-selling product line that had toy retailers happy about being blue.

In addition to Hasbro's acquisition of Tiger Electronics, the company in September purchased another top-10 toy manufacturer, Galoob Toys, Inc. This consolidation brought under one roof two best-selling *Star Wars* licensed toys—Galoob's small-scale vehicles and Hasbro's action figures—which were expected to drive toy sales when the first *Star Wars* "prequel" movie was released (scheduled for May 1999). The force was also with the LEGO Group in 1998, as the toy manufacturer announced in April that it had entered into an exclusive agreement to market *Star Wars* construction toys worldwide. It was the privately held, family-owned company's first venture into licensing, but not its last for 1998. In August LEGO announced that the company in 1999 would begin producing construction toys that featured Disney characters, including Mickey Mouse, among others.

Another acquisition in the toy industry was Mattel's purchase in June of The Pleasant Co., a Wisconsin-based direct marketer of books, dolls, clothing, accessories, and activity products bearing the American Girl brand, for approximately $700 million. In December Mattel announced that it planned to acquire The Learning Company, the largest U.S. publisher of educational software, in a $3.8 billion stock deal. Proving that hope springs eternal, in July POOF Products Inc. acquired the outstanding common shares of Slinky manufacturer James Industries Inc. Since the Slinky's debut in 1945, more than 250,000,000 have been sold.   (DIANE P. CARDINALE)

GEMSTONES

The Asian economic downturn in 1997 resulted in a decline in world gemstone trade, particularly in Thailand, but by 1998 the downward trend—while showing no sign of reversal—had slowed enough to allow leading gemstone firms to trade in the finest goods. Causes for continuing concern were the confused economy in Russia, which could affect trading in Germany, and signs of instability in South America, particularly in Brazil, one of the world's chief gem-producing countries. In Hong Kong and Shanghai, however, gem markets seemed to be operating satisfactorily despite fewer supplies from Thailand, and the traditional centre for gemstone dealing and jewelry making in Jaipur, India, was operating at normal levels.

News from gem-producing countries included the imposition of bans and controls on the mining industry in Tanzania. Only companies with a master dealer's license from the government would be able to export rough and cut material, whereas foreign companies would be allowed only to export finished products. In addition, both domestic and foreign firms were required to export annually at least $1 million worth of polished stones. The Tunduru deposit in Tanzania produced fine-coloured sapphire (blue, pink, orange, and purple), pink and orange spinel, cat's-eye alexandrite, fancy-coloured garnet, and a mint-green chrysoberyl. Sri Lanka reported a colour-change garnet (bluish-green to purplish-red), and in Brazil a deposit at Buriti in Paraíba produced a fire opal in which 80% of the material was cabochon quality. A new deposit of fine blue copper-bearing tourmaline was discovered in the

Brazilian state of Rio Grande do Norte. Stones from Madagascar, particularly blue sapphire, grew in importance.

A diamond look-alike, synthetic moissanite—a colourless transparent silicon carbide with a hardness of more than nine—was invading the jewelry world and causing considerable concern. Although there were simple instruments available for testing, it was feared that a widespread influx of stones could make testing difficult.

In the salesroom both Christie's and Sotheby's achieved good results, particularly in the Hong Kong jadeite sales. Selected items sold during the year included a 24.44 carat Sri Lanka padparadschah sapphire ($354,500, Christie's Los Angeles); a 11.25 carat heart-shaped fancy blue diamond ($1,420,000, Christie's Geneva); a ruby necklace with untreated stones ($403,000, Christie's London); and a rare Egyptian revival bracelet by Van Cleef and Arpels, with diamonds, rubies, sapphires, and emeralds (Sw F 234,500, Sotheby's, St. Moritz, Switz.).   (MICHAEL O'DONOGHUE)

HOME FURNISHINGS

Furniture. The residential furniture industry in 1998 reflected the adage, "What's new is old and what's old is new again." On the one hand, contemporary introductions were either "retro," harkening back to another era, or were new designs by Vladimir Kagan, John Mascheroni, and Fillmore Hardy, who also found that furniture designs they had created more than 20 years earlier were selling as "modern antiques." On the other hand, the best of traditional design was based on romantic re-creations, notably Widdicomb's V&A Museum collection inspired by the Victoria and Albert Museum in South Kensington, London, and Classic Leather's *Titanic* reproductions.

The most noteworthy change was the increase in the number of furniture collections tied to time-tested names or images that were identified as brands. Numerous licensing agreements were forged between manufacturers and entities from outside the industry. Previously, there had been arrangements between manufacturers and such fashion designers as Bill Blass, Ralph Lauren, and Alexander Julian and between manufacturers and historical museums in Williamsburg, Va., Charleston, S.C., and Natchez, Miss., among others. Diversity and an increased number of tie-ins abounded in 1998: there was a golf-inspired PGA Tour Home collection for Keller; a collection inspired by the paintings of Thomas Kinkade for Kinkade and La-Z-Boy; a fashion-inspired Bob Mackie collection for American Drew; and the massive theme collection devoted to writer Ernest Hemingway for Thomasville. Other design influences included an Asian "fusion" style and a West Indies and Caribbean island-inspired offering. Leather upholstery and furniture for the home office continued to expand market share.

On the basis of 1997 figures compiled by *Furniture/Today,* the top three manufacturers and retailers were Furniture Brands International ($1,808,300,000), which claimed first place, a position that had belonged in 1996 to LifeStyle Furnishings International ($1,693,600,000), now second, and La-Z-Boy ($1,074,000,000), which remained third. Among the top 10 manufacturers, only Ashley moved up significantly,

rising from 10 to 5. The American Furniture Manufacturers Association reported strong growth across the board; the 1997 wholesale total was $21,216,000,000, and the projected volume was $23,700,000,000 for 1998, a 12.1% increase.

In regard to retailing, Heilig-Meyers ($1,693,900,000), which now included Rhodes, recaptured first place. Levitz ($839.1 million) reclaimed second, and Office Depot ($779.2 million) edged out J.C. Penney ($747.2 million) for third place, which was occupied by Sears HomeLife in 1996. Both Levitz and tenth-place Montgomery Ward continued to operate under Chapter 11 bankruptcy protection. Although e-commerce and e-retail had not yet revolutionized the industry, electronic connections were being made—*Furniture/Today* offered a World Wide Web listing of over 1,000 furniture sites. Inducted into the American Furniture Hall of Fame were Henry Talmadge Link, Earl N. Phillips, Sr., and George Alden Thornton, Jr.   (ABBY CHAPPLE)

Housewares. The increased growth of retail supercentres and the impact of the Internet on how retailers and manufacturers marketed to consumers had a profound effect on the housewares industry in 1998. (See *Retailing:* Sidebar.)

In 1997 American consumers spent more than $58 billion on such items as cookware, small electronic appliances, heating and cooling equipment, cleaning goods, and personal-care products, representing a 6.1% increase over 1996. The average household spent $560 on housewares, a $38 rise over 1996. The largest increase in sales occurred in miscellaneous household appliances, which rose by 34.1%. A 14.1% increase in nonelectric cookware and a 13.9% boost in closet and storage accessories were also noteworthy. Sales of smoke alarms continued to rise, though the 10.4% increase was substantially less than the 1996 huge surge in all home-safety equipment. Decreased sales occurred mainly in silver serving accessories (39.5%), window coverings (6%), and clocks (2.8%).

The impact of the Internet continued to reshape the housewares market and affected the approach to sales. Many power retailers—*i.e.,* top discount stores and specialty stores—offered on-line retailing, and a few product manufacturers used the Internet to sell wares directly to consumers. Using current estimates, industry observers predicted that within 10 years households purchasing goods over the Internet would increase annually from 200,000 to 15–20 million. Other virtual retailers, including mail-order catalogs and television infomercials, made up 5% of domestic housewares sales.

(SUSAN DOLL)

INSURANCE

As the fourth consecutive year of record numbers of mergers and acquisitions in the insurance business, 1998 was most notable as the year of especially large-scale mergers in worldwide private insurance. Deregulation and the advent of the European Union's common currency spurred such changes, although economic downturns slowed the trend late in the year. Large insurers, including Allianz AG Holding Co. in Germany, Assurances Générales in France, and General Accident PLC in the U.K., became larger. Globalization of the U.S. market was

Residents of Tegucigalpa, Honduras, sort through debris left in the wake of Hurricane Mitch. The powerful hurricane, which contributed to the high weather-related uninsured losses during the year, caused extensive damage and left more than 1.5 million persons homeless in Central America.

evidenced by the fact that insurers headquartered outside the U.S. wrote 10% of the policies in 1998 and that one-third of U.S. reinsurance was written abroad. During the first half of 1998 Conning and Co. reported 263 U.S. insurance mergers with a value of $135 billion, led by the gigantic merger of Travelers Group into Citicorp ($70 billion) and by General Reinsurance Corp. into Berkshire Hathaway Inc. ($22 billion). The merger mania also affected the insurance brokerage business, as Aon Corp., J&H Marsh & McLennan, and Willis Corroon Group added smaller firms and became the three largest concerns in that field.

In addition to ordinary mergers, insurance company changes during the year featured many demutualizations and the formation of financial services conglomerates. (Mutualization is an insurance method in which the policyholders constitute the members of the insuring company.) Four of the largest life insurers, Metropolitan Life Insurance Co., Prudential Insurance Co. of America, John Hancock Life Insurance Co., and Mutual of New York, either had demutualized or intended to do so. Other smaller mutual insurers joined mutual holding companies in order to provide additional capital. Even mutual holding companies merged, as, for example, Acacia Mutual Holding Co. and Ameritas Mutual Insurance Holding Co. The merger trend for health maintenance organizations (HMOs) slowed because of low stock prices.

The potential benefits of combining financial services were being sought in many directions by insurers who were either buying or being bought. Examples included the GE Capital Services Inc. purchase of Kemper Reinsurance Co., Zurich Financial Services Group's merger with a unit of B.A.T. Industries PLC, American International Group's purchase of Sun America Inc. to form an insurance-retirement savings colossus with $200 billion in assets, and United Services Automobile Association's combination with a thrift bank and securities firm.

Swiss Reinsurance Co. research attributed the worldwide growth of life insurance to reductions in government pension systems. Sales of other types of insurance increased sluggishly. Among specific markets the U.K. appeared to be the best in Europe, with other markets showing slow premium growth. After the $2.5 billion bankruptcy of Nissan Mutual Life, life insurance sales in Japan dropped about 3%. In Japan's recessionary environment residential earthquake and compulsory automobile insurance rates also fell.

Major disasters in 1998 included the Swissair crash near Nova Scotia (estimated at $500 million in insurance costs), Hurricanes Georges ($2 billion) and Bonnie ($360 million), widespread fires in Florida, and ice storms and tornadoes in the southern and central U.S. In late October Hurricane Mitch, one of the most powerful storms of the century, devastated Honduras and Nicaragua. Damage in Honduras alone totaled at least $5 billion, but at year's end the insured losses were still being assessed.

In regard to specific types of insurance, comparison shopping for automobile and homeowners insurance became easier. As they competed with banks and securities brokers in the burgeoning pension rollover market, life insurers promoted the benefits of tax-deferred annuities. Variable annuity sales reached $50 billion during the first half of 1998, and variable life insurance sales rose 26%.

Among the fastest-growing types of insurance was that covering employment practices. Coverage by employers became both more essential and more expensive. Symptomatic of the rising costs of medical care were research studies that showed Alzheimer's disease affecting some four million Americans and costing businesses more than $33 billion a year. Health insurers were divided on the question as to whether or not to pay the claims made for the use of the new drug Viagra for both medically necessary treatment as well as for its general use. (*See* HEALTH AND DISEASE: *Sidebar.*)

The National Association of Insurance Commissioners approved a model bill for adoption by the states that would regulate the standards of conduct in replacing life insurance and annuities. New federal regulation was proposed for regulating HMO mergers, and policies that augmented Medicare coverage gained popularity, as HMOs restricted benefits in the face of much public criticism.

Among other developments, genetic and DNA research caused a flurry of proposed legislation to limit access to and use of such information in insurance underwriting. In August the largest insurance company in Italy agreed to pay $100 million to survivors and heirs of victims of the Holocaust as payouts for life insurance and annuity policies that it had refused to honour after World War II.   (DAVID L. BICKELHAUPT)

MACHINERY AND MACHINE TOOLS

According to preliminary figures released for 1997, the value of the worldwide production of machine tools amounted to about $38 billion. Japan was the leading country with production that totaled approximately $9,980,000,000; Germany was second with $6,790,000,000, followed by the U.S., $4.9 billion; Italy, $3,450,000,000; Switzerland, $1,990,000,000; Taiwan, $1,820,000,000; China, $1.7 billion; and the U.K., $1,380,000,000. France, South Korea, Spain, and Brazil each had production worth between $500 million and $1 billion. (All figures are for machines valued at approximately $3,000 or more.)

For reporting purposes machine tools are typically categorized as those that cut metal, such as drilling machines, lathes, and milling machines, and those that form metal, such as forging and stamping machines, bending machines, and shearing machines. The value of metal-cutting machines produced in a given year is typically three to four times the value of metal-forming machines produced. In 1997 worldwide production of metal-cutting machines was valued at about $28 billion, while that of metal-forming machines was about $10 billion.

Of the $4.9 billion total value of machine tools produced in the U.S. in 1997, just over 26% was exported to other countries. On a unit basis, nearly 32,000 units of the roughly 60,000 units produced in 1997 were shipped to customers in other countries. On a dollar basis, the biggest export markets for the U.S. in 1997 were, in order: Canada, which received machines having a total value of $360 million; Mexico, $232 million; and the U.K., $107 million. Worldwide, the largest exporters of machine tools in 1997 were, in order: Japan, with exports that were worth $6,650,000,000; Germany, $4,670,000,000; Italy, $2,090,000,000; Switzerland, $1,710,-000,000; Taiwan, $1,360,000,000; and the U.S., $1,280,000,000.

In regard to the consumption of machine tools, which consists of production plus imports minus exports, the U.S. headed the list in 1997 with a total value of $7,680,000,000. Germany was second with $4.5 billion, followed by Japan, $4,070,000,000; China, $3 billion; Italy, $2,420,000,000; the U.K., $1,790,000,000; South Korea, $1,550,-000,000; France, $1,430,000,000; Taiwan, $1,320,000,000; and Canada, $1,140,-000,000.   (JOHN B. DEAM)

MATERIALS AND METALS

Glass. During 1998 the Asia-Pacific region accounted for the fastest growth in the glass industry. The region's financial crisis did not discourage potential developers, as construction of new float and fibre plants began. Growth was also strong in Latin America and parts of Eastern Europe. Sales growth in North America, Western Europe, and Japan was slow. The glass industry in those areas had to contend with increased imports from less-developed countries, where production costs were lower and environmental regulations less stringent, and all three areas experienced some deterioration in their overall trade balance in glass products in 1997. In Russia the market remained severely depressed.

Float glass production in Asia-Oceania (excluding Japan) totaled one million metric tons in 1987. By 1997 this had increased to more than 6 million metric tons. By contrast, float glass production in Western Europe in 1987 was 4.8 million metric tons and increased to 6.7 million metric tons in 1997. While the float glass and fibreglass sectors experienced some deterioration in demand in Western Europe during the past few years, the industry managed to maintain its overall trade balance for container glass and glass tableware. Production in North America declined 3.5% from 5.7 million metric tons in 1987 to 5.5 million metric tons in 1997. Container glass production in Western Europe totaled just over 18 million metric tons in 1997.   (THERESA GREEN)

Ceramics. The ceramics industry demonstrated significant growth in 1998. Strong manufacturing economies in the U.S. and parts of Latin America generated double-digit growth rates for some segments of the industry, and recovering economies in the European Union brought about improved performance there compared with 1997. Difficulties continued in Asia (notably in Russia and other countries of the former Soviet Union), which accounted for nearly one-third of the global ceramic market, and in certain areas of Eastern Europe. In the U.S., where glass (q.v.) was considered part of the industry, total industry sales rose to nearly $95 billion, with glass accounting for 60% of sales, and the advanced ceramics segment continuing its growth to 28%.

Advanced ceramics, highly engineered materials that enable the operation of many industrial and consumer processes, grew strongly in 1998. Electronic materials dominated this category (about 75%), and the high growth rate of computers and communication equipment caused electronic ceramics to be the fastest-growing major product sector. Multilayer ceramic capacitors continued to gain market share through a reduction in thickness, and demand for these widely used components outstripped supply. A new automobile, for example, used 1,000 such capacitors on average. Explosive growth in wireless communication stimulated double-digit growth in the production of capacitors, piezoelectric crystals, varistors, thermistors, and similar ceramic components, many of which were used in mobile phone handsets. On the other hand, the growth of multilayer multicomponent electronic packages was disappointing, and the production of conventional ceramic packages for integrated circuits continued to stagnate because of competition from polymer composite packages with improved heat-removal capabilities.

Advanced structural and composite ceramics, historically limited to cost-insensitive aerospace and military applications, continued steady market penetration in industrial sectors due to lower costs and higher product reliability. The most successful approaches to achieving lower costs centred on dimensional control and net-shape fabrication to minimize machining and finishing expenses. Intrinsic reliability of materials moved incrementally forward via improved powder processing, although the unpredictable nature of ceramic strength and failure continued to limit applications. The use of silicon nitride ball bearings increased by more than 10% for a second year in a row owing to improved reliability, reduced costs, and greater customer acceptance. Ceramic turbochargers, valves, and valve-train elements, and assorted combustion chamber components were gaining acceptance and were being used by automotive manufacturers principally in Japan and Europe. Ceramic catalysts, a mainstay of automobile ceramics in the U.S. since 1975, were being used to clean factory smokestacks of pollutants. This market, as with automotive catalysts, was expected to be dominated by extruded ceramic honeycomb catalyst structures with wall thicknesses as small as 50 μm (0.002 in), a value thought impossible a decade ago.

The most notable examples of commercialized ceramic matrix composite materials were silicon carbide/alumina cutting tools that were used increasingly for machining cast iron and for high-velocity cutting of conventional metals. Silicon carbide/silicon carbide composites were found in specialty heat exchangers, and long-fibre composites continued to be developed for high-performance segments of advanced aircraft. The production of optical and electro-optic glass and ceramic materials, particularly devices that enabled optical switching and logic structures, was growing rapidly. The demand for these materials, which included optical fibres, sensors, and planar structures, was growing rapidly, particularly in telecommunications, automobiles, and data communication applications.

Whiteware ceramics—principally floor and wall tile, dinnerware, sanitary ware, artware, and a large miscellaneous group—showed steady growth during the 1990s, although year-to-year effects were difficult to forecast due to substantial flux in the markets and manufacturing environments. Demand in U.S. markets appeared to be stronger than in 1997, particularly in sanitary ware and giftware. A notable milestone was passed in 1998, when more than 60% of the ceramic tile sold in the U.S. was imported. Fast firing, a standard part of tile processing, was overcoming technical hurdles in the sanitary ware and dinnerware processes and contributed to higher productivity. A principal concern among whiteware manufacturers during the year was the conversion to leadfree glazes and decorations to reduce lead-related workplace risks and to skirt difficult marketplace regulations in some states. For dinnerware and "table-top" products the trend was to move away from heirloom-quality items toward less-formal products for daily use and casual entertaining.   (RICHARD L. LEHMAN)

Rubber. The Asian economic crisis had a serious impact on the rubber industry in 1998—almost 75% of the world's natural rubber production came from Southeast Asia. Currency devaluations, especially in Malaysia, prevented the stabilization of rubber prices as outlined in the International Natural Rubber Agreement (INRA). The INRA pact between producer and consumer countries contained a buffer stock mechanism, whereby the manager of the stock would attempt to stabilize prices through strategic purchases and sales of natural rubber. Price increases occurred, owing to currency devaluations in Malaysia and Singapore. Though the International Natural Rubber Organization (INRO), which implemented the agreement, was able to make rubber purchases late in the year, Malaysia, the third largest rubber-producing country, threatened to withdraw from the INRO. Thailand, second in production, indicated that it would soon follow. Political instability in Indonesia, however, prevented the world's top producer from addressing the issue.

Malaysia and Thailand began formulating a plan whereby the Association of Natural Rubber Producing Countries would oversee a production cut and set up a buffer stock to aid the producing countries. A cut in production, however, would be difficult to implement in many of these countries, owing to the dependence of small plantations on rubber production for their livelihoods.

Legislation and litigation in the U.S. was affecting natural rubber latex products, specifically powdered latex gloves used by the medical profession. As a result of a number of allergies to latex, eight states had introduced legislation to ban or regulate powdered latex gloves, and the U.S. Food and Drug Administration was drafting rules to regulate them. By mid-1998 more than 125 cases were pending in various state courts.

Evidence of the Asian crisis was reflected in the slowing of the growth rate in rubber consumption. The International Rubber Study Groups reported that natural rubber growth was only 2%, compared with the nearly 4% anticipated. The major consuming countries in Asia, Japan, and Malaysia, experienced declines of over 10% and 5%, respectively. World synthetic rubber consumption was 3.8% higher than in 1997 but lower than the 4.2% projected.

The major tire companies continued to expand globally and add production plants. Bridgestone Corp., which regained its number-one ranking in tire sales, announced expansions at plants in San José, Costa Rica; Hikone, Japan; Warren county, Tenn.; and Aiken, S.C. The company announced that it would build a plant in Poznan, Pol., that it purchased a 14% interest in Chile's Neumaticos San Martin LTDA, and that it was resuming construction, suspended earlier in the year, of tire plants in Indonesia and Thailand. Second-ranked Michelin North America Inc. expanded existing plants in Nova Scotia and Ardmore, Okla.; built new plants in Reno, Nev., and Brazil; and purchased Icollantes SA of Colombia for $73 million. Goodyear Tire & Rubber Co. began expansions of its plants at Tatsumo, Japan; Topeka, Kan.; Union City, Tenn.; and locations in Turkey. Goodyear was also building a new plant in Brazil.

The German-based company Continental AG announced plans to build a new tire facility in Brazil and expand three U.S. plants. In Slovakia, Continental set up a joint venture with Matador AS for truck tires. Dunlop

India Ltd. planned to add capacity at its passenger-tire facility in Tonawanda, N.Y., and Appolo Tyres of India said it would build a tire plant in northern India.

Bayer Corp. increased butyl capacity at its Sarnia, Ont., plant, announced plans to build a butyl plant in Russia and a polybutadiene plant in India, and closed its polychloroprene unit in Houston, Texas. Goodyear began construction of a multipurpose synthetic rubber plant in Beaumont, Texas, which was part of a $600 million investment plan and the largest one-time expansion of the chemical business in its history. Uniroyal Chemical doubled its nitrile capacity in Mexico, and DuPont Dow said it planned to open a synthetic rubber plant in The Netherlands.   (DONALD SMITH)

Plastics. World production of plastics in 1996–97 reached 286 billion lb and was projected to grow to 330 billion lb by the year 2000 (1 lb=0.454 kg). In the U.S., production of 78 billion lb valued at $275 billion made plastics the nation's fourth largest manufacturing industry, one that employed 1,340,000 workers.

World production of polyethylenes totaled 97 billion lb, projected to grow to 117 billion lb by 2000. U.S. production was 27 billion lb, and the fastest-growing segment was a new range of supersoft thermoplastic materials that provided increased comfort in sporting goods, shoes, and handles.

U.S. production of polyvinyl chloride totaled about 14 billion lb and of polypropylene, about 13 billion lb; output of the latter was growing rapidly due in part to its large-scale use in automobiles. Polystyrene, with U.S. production at 7 billion lb, was thought likely to benefit from new technology that would make it a valuable plastic for such engineering applications as gears and structural members. Demand for polyurethane for upholstery, clothing, carpet underlay, and thermal insulation was vigorous in the U.S. at 5 billion lb. Polyethylene terephthalate was used mainly in polyester fibre, but growth in carbonated beverage bottles and other packaging helped account for U.S. usage of 4 billion lb.

New plastic materials of special interest included liquid crystal polymers for electrical products, aliphatic polyketones for laser printers and fuel hoses, and cycloolefin copolymers for lenses, medical packaging, and colour toners. New additives to make plastics electrically conductive included very fine graphite filaments and inherently conductive polymers.

Manufacturing processes were being computerized to permit faster production, smaller parts, greater precision, and fewer rejects. Coextrusion of multilayer films, up to 11 layers thick, combined, at a reduced cost, softness, strength, scuff resistance, heat sealability, protection from ultraviolet radiation, and controlled semipermeability. Fibreglass blended with thermoplastic fibres was compression-moulded into high-performance reinforced thermoplastic composites of value in automobile doors and bumpers, stadium seats, kayaks, and helmets.

Leading applications of plastics in the U.S. in 1997 were packaging (29%), building (15%), transportation (5%), furniture (4%), and electrical products (4%). Packaging consisted primarily of bottles and films; major future growth areas for films were expected to be envelopes, grocery bags, and wrapping for fresh produce and snack foods. Building products included pipe, siding, windows, flooring, wall covering, wire and cable, insulation, carpet underlay, vapour barrier, panels, lighting, and bathroom fixtures. Electrical applications were primarily computers and communication equipment. Medical products worldwide used 4 billion lb of plastics, primarily polyvinyl chloride, polyethylene, polystyrene, and polypropylene. An area of potential growth was expected to be pallets, where replacement of wood by plastic resulted in easier cleaning, longer life, and improved recyclability.

In the U.S. in 1997 recycling of plastics from solid waste, primarily polyethylene and polyethylene terephthalate bottles, totaled 2 billion lb in 1,700 plants. Recent achievements included recycling 20,000 metric tons of nylon carpet and 3,000 metric tons of polycarbonate water jugs. Other major recycling efforts included computer housings, Kodak single-use cameras, and Saturn automobiles. Europe recycled 9 billion lb of plastics waste, primarily by incineration; the European Parliament hoped to recycle 15% of plastic packaging by 2001. Germany in 1998 recycled 65% of plastic packaging and targeted 85% recycling of junked cars by 2001.   (RUDOLPH D. DEANIN)

Advanced Composites. During 1998 the market for composite materials continued to grow. The Society of Plastics Industry's (SPI's) Composite Institute estimated that U.S. shipments for polymeric composites of all types (including glass-, carbon-, boron-, and organic-fibre-reinforced polymers) totaled 1,580,000 metric tons, an increase of about 2% over 1997 and 8% over 1996; it was the seventh consecutive year that shipments increased. The 1998 increases were most pronounced in the construction, consumer products, and transportation sectors, and were reflective of the growth in infrastructure applications, the continued strength of sporting goods applications, and the growing use of composites in automobiles and light trucks.

According to the Suppliers of Composite Materials Association, worldwide carbon-fibre shipments for 1997 were 11,800 metric tons, an increase of 25% over 1996. The industry operated at close to capacity in 1997, and materials were in short supply. It was estimated, however, that capacity would increase 80% by 1999. The industry transition from defense and aerospace applications to higher-volume, lower-cost applications led to the emphasis on the development of lower-cost tooling, materials, and manufacturing processes. For example, processes that produced lower-cost carbon fibres in bundles with increasing number of filaments (48,000–360,000 filaments) were finding applications in high-volume markets.

The industry continued to pursue aggressively two potentially large markets that would make use of lower-cost materials and processing methods—construction and automotive. The application of advanced composite technology in construction and infrastructure renewal continued to show promise. The SPI Composites Institute estimated that composite shipments to the construction industry in 1998 totaled 334,000 metric tons, an increase of 5% from 1997.

Composites, especially in the form of sheet molding compounds (SMCs), were becoming increasingly important in automobiles and light trucks. According to the SMC Automotive Alliance the amount of SMCs used by the automotive industry increased from 71,000 metric tons in 1993 to more than 107,000 metric tons in 1998. High-performance composites, however, were not finding significant applications in automotive structures, despite collaborative research and development efforts to develop continuous fibre-reinforced composite structures for lightweight, energy-efficient automobiles. The composites had to compete with the improved strength and toughness of metals.

The development of ceramic matrix composites (CMCs) continued to advance, particularly in the area of ceramic fibres and fibre coatings. Silicon carbide (SiC) fibres and dual-phase SiC/titanium diboride (TiB_2) fibres, essentially free from degradative impurities such as oxygen, free silicon, and free carbon, demonstrated improved property retention at elevated temperatures, but advances were needed to prevent oxidative degradation that plagued nonoxide CMCs.
                (THOMAS E. MUNNS)

Iron and Steel. After five consecutive years of growth, worldwide consumption of steel declined in 1998. Greatly reduced consumption of steel products in Japan, South Korea, and several other Asian countries was counterbalanced by growth in Europe and North America, so that world consumption in tonnage terms fell by little more than 1%. Large inventories and low prices, however, testified to the turnaround in the market after a buoyant 1997.

The Asian economic crisis that began in mid-1997 at first impacted relatively few countries, and they were not large consumers or producers of steel. By December 1997, however, the turmoil had spread to South Korea, the world's fourth largest consumer and sixth largest producer of steel, causing a 33% reduction in that country's consumption of steel products. During 1998 the "Asian flu" spread farther afield, to Russia and Brazil. Meanwhile, the Japanese economy had slipped into recession, reducing steel consumption in Japan in 1998 by about 12%. China's steel production continued to grow, but exports fell, and imports slowed by about 10%.

As the Asian region's markets plummeted in 1998, steel exports formerly sent to Asia were diverted to other destinations; at the same time, steel producers in Asian countries, helped by the sharp depreciation in their own currencies, diverted an increasing share of their output toward the rest of the world, mainly the still-buoyant markets in North America and Western Europe. U.S. imports in the first half-year rose to 16.5 million metric tons, 12% above the year-earlier figure; this included sharply higher shipments from Japan (+113%), South Korea (+89%), and Ukraine (+45%). The European Union's imports from Asia totaled about 294,000 metric tons per month, compared with only 40,000 metric tons per month during the previous year. With such levels of imports along with high domestic production, markets moved into oversupply, inventories swelled, and prices came under severe downward pressure. By the second half of 1998, steel producers across a range of developed and less-developed countries were seeking protection from low-priced imports.

A major development during the year was the introduction of the ULSAB (UltraLight Steel Auto Body). Following the completion of a $22 million four-year project, funded

by a consortium of 35 steel companies in 18 countries, body structures were exhibited throughout the world to demonstrate the weight reduction, increased performance, and affordability that could be achieved with modern steel products and technologies.

(ANTHONY TRICKETT)

Light Metals. The commercially important light metals, aluminum, magnesium, and titanium (and to a much lesser extent beryllium and lithium), were affected in 1998 by the very low prices in the entire base metals industry. This adversely impacted the financial performance of the producing firms. To a major degree this situation was directly related to the economic setbacks associated with the financial crises in East Asia, Latin America, and Russia.

A result of the economic events was a change in the world aluminum markets. Aluminum exports by such major producers as Australia and the Persian Gulf nations were redirected from the economically depressed areas to Europe and North America with a consequent negative impact on the price of the base metal. Aluminum pricing at the beginning of 1998 averaged 71 cents per pound, but it fell steadily to an average of 59 cents per pound by the end of the year, a 17% decline.

The world primary aluminum production (new metal) represented only a 0.5% increase over the 1997 total of 19 million tons. The United States was the largest-producing country with 3,550,000 tons of primary metal. The total U.S. aluminum output of 10 million tons consisted of domestically produced primary metal, substantial imports of primary metal, and metal reclaimed from scrap and recycling sources. Major markets for aluminum products included transportation applications, packaging (primarily the aluminum beverage can), and the construction industry. The relatively static market demand and sluggish near-term growth prospects created excess capacity in the primary metal production sector, and several firms idled facilities that had considerable production capacities.

The 1998 production of new magnesium totaled 356,000 metric tons, an 8% increase over 1997. (Russian and Chinese production is not included because quantity estimates are deemed unreliable.) The aluminum industry remained the largest customer, consuming 44% of the magnesium production for alloying purposes. The automotive market for magnesium alloy castings was static, as car builders continued alternating among steel, aluminum, magnesium, and plastics, depending on the price advantage offered.

After a growth spurt in 1997 a decline occurred in the titanium industry in 1998. This was associated with inventory adjustments and a slowdown in the commercial aircraft sector, as customers requested airplane manufacturers to delay deliveries of ordered aircraft. The earlier robust growth in golf club usage subsided to a level market, and its future was uncertain as alternate materials were being appraised as possibly offering better performance and lower prices. Other important titanium applications included the petrochemical industry, the chemical industry, and racing cars and bicycles.

(GEORGE BINCZEWSKI)

Metalworking. Market and governmental pressures in 1998 forced metalworking industries to develop and deploy manufacturing processes that would cut costs, shorten delivery time, and lessen the impact on the environment. Large enterprises, such as automakers, aerospace companies, and appliance manufacturers, invested in the necessary metalworking technology and enlisted the help of small and medium-size businesses in their supplier chains.

By compacting metal powder into nearly net-shape parts, manufacturers were able to eliminate many secondary machining and assembly processes and their associated by-products. Owing to advancements in materials, binders, and processing, the use of one such technology, metal injection molding, increased by about 20% and produced nearly $100 million in parts. Hot isostatic pressing was another technology that was increasingly used in making parts from specialty and high-technology metals, such as tool steels and superalloys.

Worldwide metal powder production exceeded one million tons, and parts made from the materials were estimated at more than $3 billion. North America was the largest market, shipping 486,000 short tons of powder in 1997; $2 billion of parts were produced from the powder. North American powder shipments increased almost 12% in 1997, and shipments were expected to grow another 4%–6% in 1998. In addition, the automobile industry was using 70% of powder metal parts. As a result, parts made by the more traditional casting and forging methods were being replaced.

To reduce weight for fuel efficiency, the automobile industry also continued looking for ways to use aluminum and other light-weight materials. The industry consumed 17% of U.S. aluminum shipments in 1997 and invested heavily in high-speed machining, welding, and other joining technologies used for working with the metal. Automakers and their suppliers sponsored original research into producing aluminum parts and adapted existing technology developed for the aerospace industry. The steel industry also worked with automakers to produce strong but lightweight components.

As a whole, the transportation sector was the largest domestic consumer of aluminum, using 29% of output. In 1997 U.S. aluminum consumption totaled 8.9 billion kg (19.6 billion lb), and based on third-quarter data from the Aluminum Association, that figure would increase in 1998 by 2.1% to an estimated 9.1 billion kg (20.1 billion lb).

(JAMES R. KOELSCH)

MICROELECTRONICS

Projected worldwide sales of semiconductors in 1998 dropped by 1.8% to $134.6 billion according to the Semiconductor Industry Association (SIA). The downturn, caused largely by Asia's economic problems, was expected to return to historic annual growth rates of 17% or more over the next few years, primarily because of growth in Internet usage. The SIA anticipated a growth rate of 17.2% in 1999, 18.5% in 2000, and 18.9% by 2001, resulting in sales of $222.3 billion in 2001. The SIA predicted that the products that would drive growth into the next millennium would be Internet-related communications and networking devices, digital signal processors (DSPs), systems-on-a-chip, microprocessors, and new consumer products, such as digital cameras and digital video (or versatile) discs (DVDs).

By the end of the first quarter of 1998, sales had declined 10.2% in the Americas (North and South), 11.5% in Japan, and 9.7% in the Asia-Pacific markets. Though Japan's market declined by $3 billion, the decline of the yen accounted for more than half of that amount. The Asia-Pacific market (including Singapore, South Korea, China, Taiwan, and India), which was forecast to increase 24% in 1998, grew only 3.2%, due mainly to South Korea's economic problems. The European market, with growth of 5%, posted the best single-year gain to $30.5 billion, followed by the Asia-Pacific region at 2.8% ($31 billion). The Americas decreased 4.1% to $43.9 billion, and Japan, at $29.1 billion, was down more than 9% from 1997. Estimates showed that by 2001 the Americas market would represent 33.1% of worldwide sales, followed by Asia-Pacific (25%), Europe (23.2%), and Japan (18.7%).

The one bright spot in the 1998 results was the continued growth of DSPs, which grew 23% in 1998 to $3.9 billion. It was estimated that DSP sales would reach $8.1 billion in 2001. In addition to digital cellular telephones, modems, and hard-disk drives, future uses for the DSPs included consumer electronics and home appliances, high-definition television, Internet telephony, and digital cameras.

Microchip manufacturers saw their profits all but disappear during the first half of 1998. Motorola Inc., with over 25% of its sales in Asia, suffered a revenue drop of 7% and barely avoided the company's first loss in 13 years. In June Motorola announced a 10% reduction in the workforce, eliminating 15,000 jobs. Including the charges for the layoffs, Motorola's loss was $1.3 billion for the quarter. Semiconductor manufacturer Advanced Micro Devices (AMD) experienced its fourth consecutive quarterly loss, while National Semiconductor Corp. announced a 10% reduction in its workforce. In January Motorola and Siemens AG announced a $1.6 billion joint venture for a chip manufacturing plant in Dresden, Ger., that would become Europe's largest semiconductor facility. In November, however, Siemens announced that it would divest itself of its semiconductor division.

Dynamic random access memory (DRAM) sales dropped 26.6% in 1998 due to oversupply problems. Hitachi Ltd. consolidated all of its DRAM manufacturing in its Singapore plant. In June Micron Technology, the last major manufacturer of DRAM in the U.S., announced an $801 million deal to acquire Texas Instruments Inc.'s memory business.

During the year almost every major manufacturer of microprocessors unveiled plans for new 64-bit microprocessors to be made available in mid-1999 for workstations and at the end of 2000 for personal computers (PCs). National Semiconductor planned to introduce a PC system-on-a-chip by mid-1999 that would replace more than 12 separate chips.

Using copper technology instead of aluminum in the manufacture of the next generation of chips was expected to increase the clock speed of the processors by up to three times, use less power, and need smaller dies in their manufacture. It was believed that with the copper technology processor speeds could reach 1 GHz (gigahertz) by the year 2000. In September IBM Corp. announced

shipments of a 400 MHz (megahertz) copper PowerPC microprocessor.

The use of smart cards, credit card-sized devices containing imbedded microprocessors, was projected to grow to 3.4 billion units by 2001. Holding up to 20,000 bytes of storage and costing anywhere from 80 cents to $15, these cards were popular in Europe and were being used in pay and wireless telephones, banking, health care, and pay-TV applications. In the U.S. their use had been limited to a few applications, and a major year-long trial undertaken by Citibank, Chase Manhattan Bank, Visa, and MasterCard was abandoned at the end of the year.

In May Craig Barrett, president and chief operating officer of Intel Corp., was named CEO, replacing Andrew S. Grove, one of Intel's founders and CEO for 11 years. Intel was also affected by the downturn in the industry and posted first-quarter revenues of $6 billion, down 7% from first-quarter 1997 and 8% from fourth-quarter 1997. A 3,000-person workforce reduction was announced. Intel faced an erosion of its PC market share, particularly in the below-$1,000 PC market. Late to market with its low-priced Celeron chip, Intel saw its chief rivals, AMD and National Semiconductor/Cyrix, increase their market share to 40%.

(THOMAS E. KROLL)

MINING

The Asian financial crisis had serious consequences for the mining industry in 1998. The demand for raw materials in that region had for years been a driving force in the industry, but in 1998 falling consumption there, owing to the financial crisis that began in Thailand in mid-1997 and then spread to Japan and China, gave rise to fears that a global surplus of metals and minerals was developing, resulting in a severe strain on prices. Several mines with high operating costs were either being forced to close or reduce their output, and by midyear the number of companies reporting losses or sharply decreased profits was increasing. The Asian crisis also served to exacerbate Russia's dire economic problems, and in the final months of 1998 it became apparent that the economies of the U.S. and Western Europe would not escape unscathed. (*See* Spotlight: *The World Economy in Trouble.*)

In the base metals sector the perception that demand would fall heralded a wave of selling on the principal market, the London Metal Exchange, an event that further aggravated the downward spiral on prices. By the end of October 1998 the price of nickel was 35% lower than it had been at the start of the year; zinc was down 14%, aluminum 13%, lead 8%, and copper 7.5%. Only tin managed an improvement, up about 2.3%. Compared with prices in mid-1997, those for nickel were 46% lower, copper 38%, and zinc 36%.

Companies that relied heavily on one metal were especially vulnerable. Inco Ltd., the leading Western nickel producer, was forced to reduce output at a number of its Canadian operations, and a leading U.S. copper producer, Phelps Dodge Corp., announced mine closures and a 10% cut in its global output. One of the world's largest and most efficient copper producers, Freeport-McMoRan Copper & Gold Inc., worried other producers when it announced that it

would combat depressed market conditions by stepping up copper and gold production at its giant Grasberg mine in Indonesia to lower unit costs.

Mining companies that produced a broad mix of commodities were not immune to the economic downturn either. Rio Tinto PLC reported that lower commodity prices had cost it $278 million in earnings during the first half of the year, in spite of production increases and improved efficiencies. The price of copper, it said, was the lowest in 65 years.

Countries that relied heavily on mineral exports as a source of revenue also suffered. Privatization plans were thwarted in Zambia, which attempted to sell off the Nchanga and Nkana divisions, the two biggest remaining assets of the Zambia Consolidated Copper Mine, when the consortium that had made a bid withdrew its offer, citing low copper prices and uncertain demand. Similarly, Venezuela also failed in its attempts to privatize its aluminum industry.

Among the industrialized nations, major mineral exporters Australia and Canada felt the pinch. The uncertain outlook for commodities was deterring investment, and the currencies in those countries were under constant pressure. That raised the cost of imported goods, but mining companies gained some advantage because commodities are traded internationally in U.S. dollars. For those companies producing commodities that were not traded on exchanges but sold under long-term contracts, exposure to the Asian crisis was not as critical to their operations. Big iron ore and bauxite producers in Australia and Brazil fared relatively well; however, negotiations for 1999 contracts were expected to favour buyers.

In the energy sector China remained by far the world's largest coal producer, with

annual output in excess of 1,300 million tons, or about 30% of world output. The U.S. ranked second (25%), followed by India (6.5%), Australia (6.1%), and Russia (4.7%). In Western industrialized countries concern over global warming meant that coal usage in power generation continued to come under fire, owing to the production of carbon dioxide emissions. U.S. coal producers argued that unilateral action to restrict usage and/or install expensive clean-coal technology would have only a limited impact on global carbon dioxide emissions, because less-developed countries, the largest coal consumers and producers, could not afford the cost of clean-coal technology.

Gold had another poor year, sinking to its lowest price level in 19 years. Prices remained depressed, owing to the Asian crisis and a sell-off in holdings by central banks. There were numerous casualties among producers, and in South Africa the impact of low prices was proving particularly painful. South African gold producers, along with those in Australia and Canada, benefited, however, from local currency weakness.

In recent years mining companies based in South Africa had been penalized by investors' growing disenchantment with emerging markets, and some of the largest mining houses had relocated to London in order to have better access to international capital. Billiton PLC moved there in 1997, and in 1998 Anglo American Corp. of South Africa Ltd. followed suit. The latter also announced a proposed merger with Minorco, its Luxembourg-based associate, making the combined entity potentially the world's largest mining and natural resources company.

Another South African company, De Beers Consolidated Mines Ltd., successfully

Indexes of Production, Mining, and Mineral Commodities (1990=100)

	1993	1994	1995	1996	1997	1998 1st qtr.
Mining (total)						
World	103.5	107.3	109.8	112.8	117.3	150.1
Developed market economies[1]	101.2	105.5	107.1	110.1	112.8	123.3
North America[2]	97.2	100.1	100.1	102.0	105.4	106.4
European Union[3]	101.7	108.3	111.2	113.3	111.7	126.4
Less-developed market economies[4]	105.3	108.6	111.8	114.9	120.8	170.6
Coal						
World	91.5	91.0	92.2	92.0	92.9	98.4
Developed market economies[1]	88.6	87.2	87.9	86.6	86.2	86.1
North America[2]	91.4	99.7	100.1	101.7	105.1	109.1
European Union[3]	80.4	71.4	70.7	66.2	63.2	60.0
Less-developed market economies[4]	99.2	101.1	103.7	106.5	110.6	131.1
Petroleum and natural gas						
World	107.2	111.1	113.3	116.6	119.5	163.5
Developed market economies[1]	106.0	112.2	114.2	119.5	123.1	141.0
North America[2]	97.5	99.4	98.3	100.5	103.9	107.1
European Union[3]	119.8	135.4	140.8	148.9	145.7	178.5
Less-developed market economies[4]	107.9	110.5	112.8	115.0	117.6	175.9
Metals						
World	90.0	93.0	99.7	105.0	127.9	153.2
Developed market economies[1]	99.9	98.6	97.9	98.4	100.7	100.2
North America[2]	102.0	101.6	105.1	106.5	109.0	109.5
European Union[3]	76.3	78.2	79.1	72.7	70.6	75.1
Less-developed market economies[4]	80.3	87.6	101.5	111.5	154.5	204.9
Manufacturing (total)	**101.0**	**107.5**	**110.1**	**112.9**	**119.5**	**128.5**

[1]Includes North America (Canada and the United States), Europe, Australia, Israel, Japan, New Zealand, and South Africa.
[2]Canada and the United States.
[3]Includes Austria, Belgium, Denmark, Finland, France, Germany, Greece, Ireland, Italy, Luxembourg, The Netherlands, Portugal, Spain, Sweden, and the United Kingdom.
[4]Includes Caribbean nations, Central and South America, Africa (excluding South Africa), Asia (excluding Israel and Japan), and Oceania (excluding Australia and New Zealand).
Source: UN, *Monthly Bulletin of Statistics*, August 1998.

negotiated a three-year extension for the diamond-trading agreement between its Central Selling Organization and the big Russian producer Almazy Rossii-Sakha. The agreement between the world's two biggest diamond producers was extended until December 2001 and was expected to help maintain stability in the world diamond market.

Elsewhere in Africa, developments in the mineral-rich Democratic Republic of the Congo, once a world leader in copper and cobalt production, were a major disappointment, owing to the civil war that threatened to destabilize the entire region. In neighbouring Angola the fragile peace accord between the government and the National Union for the Total Independence of Angola was shattered, and the latter was seeking to regain control of the country's rich diamond fields. On the positive side, mining investments continued apace for gold in Ghana, Mali, and Tanzania; farther south, Billiton's decision to proceed with the Mozal aluminum smelter in Mozambique marked one of the biggest-ever industrial developments for that country.

Exploration took a battering. Metals Economics Group of Canada estimated that global spending had declined by 31%. According to its survey, Latin America remained the most popular destination for exploration spending, accounting for 29% of the world total, followed by Australia and Africa (each 17.5%) and Canada (10.9%). A survey conducted by *Mining Journal,* which canvassed the opinions of senior executives from 100 mining companies, found that among the emerging-market countries—Argentina, Bolivia, Brazil, Chile, Mexico, and Peru—all ranked among the top-10 most favoured for exploration. The other countries were Ghana, Indonesia, Papua New Guinea, and South Africa.

Mining investment held up well in Latin America, especially in Chile, where the Collahuasi copper project was coming to fruition. Peru's piecemeal attempts to privatize the mining company, Centromin, progressed moderately well. Doe Run Co. of the U.S. purchased the La Oroya copper smelting and refining complex, Canadian companies acquired the Antamina copper-zinc property, and Centromin's largest zinc mine was offered for sale in December.

In Australia plans to develop the Jabiluka uranium mine in the Northern Territory continued to attract environmental and Aboriginal opposition in spite of government support. The Broken Hill Proprietary Co.'s large Cannington silver/lead/zinc mine reached full capacity in Queensland, and zinc producer Pasminco forged ahead with development of its Century deposit, which at its full capacity would contribute approximately 7% of world output. Initial production was expected in 1999.

Pasminco also made a hostile takeover bid for the Australian company Savage Resources. The latter's important Clarksville zinc smelter in Tennessee was the sought-after prize. Low metal prices also resulted in a reduction in the value of resource companies and presented a number of buying opportunities. Hostile bids, share buy-backs, and bids to buy up minority shareholders were common; QNI Ltd., another Australian company with major nickel interests, was the target of a takeover bid by its majority shareholder, Billiton.

In Canada the country's first diamond mine, Ekati in the Northwest Territories, was officially opened, and progress was under way for securing a permit for the development of a second mine, Diavik. Development of one of the world's largest nickel deposits, at Voisey's Bay in Labrador, continued to be delayed, however, and the Newfoundland government was threatening to withhold a mining permit unless Inco, the developer, committed to building a smelter near the mine.

In Europe mining was given a bad press from a tailings dam failure at the Los Frailes zinc mine in Spain. Waste from the mine spilled into a local river and threatened the Coto Doñana National Park, one of Europe's most important conservation areas. The owner of the mine, Boliden Ltd., had had an unblemished record and, although listed in Canada, had its origins in Sweden, a country extremely sensitive to environmental issues. An investigation into the cause of the spill was under way.

Russia's economic and political problems also shared the limelight. The crisis that developed in Russia's mining industry, owing to lack of investment, had long been predicted, and the country's coal miners protested unpaid wages and dangerous working conditions. Production of minerals for export had largely been maintained, but in 1998 questions were being asked about whether Russia had the ability to increase or even maintain its mineral exports in order to earn hard currency, or whether the situation was becoming so acute that production would fall or collapse. For some commodities, notably aluminum, much of the raw material—bauxite and/or alumina—had to be imported and transported great distances within Russia. Similarly, the weak ruble and lack of access to Western credit made importing modern mining and processing equipment a major problem.

In 1998 Russia was a major exporter of such metals as nickel and aluminum, an important contributor to world diamond output, and ranked as the world's biggest palladium producer. The country also had become an important contributor to supplies of world uranium based on huge stockpiles built up during the Soviet era. Reduced exports of some commodities would be welcomed by Western producers as this would help balance supply and demand, but if the Russian economy were to continue to deteriorate and civil unrest erupted, many questioned whether supplies of such commodities as natural gas, upon which the West was highly dependent, would be secure.

The mining industry also suffered from the effects of El Niño, with operations disrupted by mud slides in the Andes Mountains caused by torrential rains and with hydropower and river transportation hampered in Indonesia owing to low water levels. Although El Niño had disappeared, the virulence of the Asian economic flu remained, and with the Russian debt situation providing an added dimension, the mining industry faced an uncertain future.

(ROGER ELLIS)

PAINTS AND VARNISHES

Without doubt 1998 was the year of the megadeal, business realignments that struck at the heart of the paint industry and changed its global contours. Three acquisitions were especially significant: Akzo Nobel NV's purchase of Courtaulds for £1.8 billion (with Porter Paints in the U.S. and the worldwide packaging business sold separately to PPG Industries); Hoechst AG's sale of Herberts to DuPont Co. of the U.S. for $1,890,000,000; and the announced merger of Sigma Coatings of The Netherlands with the French Lafarge Group. (£1=$1.65.) The first resulted in the reemergence of Akzo Nobel as the world's largest paint firm; the second made DuPont the third largest paint company and brought it global preeminence in the automotive market with a 30% share; the third created in Lafarge a third ranking in the European architectural market. Lafarge also bought Max Meyer, Italy's market leader in architectural coatings, as well as U.S. traffic paint specialist Centerline.

Akzo Nobel also during the year acquired BASF's European architectural paints business, Reichhold's industrial coatings in Austria, nonstick coatings producer Lambda in Italy, Astral in Tunisia, and the architectural coatings business of Marshall Boya in Turkey and Oxylin in Brazil. ICI Paint spent $695 million on Acheson's electronic coatings business and £350 million for the bulk of Williams's European Home Improvement Division.

The year was also marked by the effects of the East Asian financial crisis. While paint output in the United States proceeded apace and most European countries enjoyed a recovery, the Asia/Pacific region did not fare well. Near zero growth was expected in the region's paint market in 1998, compared with 2% in the U.S., 1.5% in Europe, and 1–2% in Latin America; world paint output in 1998 was estimated at 17.8 billion litres. (1 litre=0.264 gal.)

Legislation restricting the use of ozone-generating volatile organic compounds (VOCs) continued to be the main driving force behind technical change. In 1998 the U.S. Environmental Protection Agency promulgated national VOC limits for automotive refinished and architectural and industrial maintenance coatings, effective from 1999. In Europe the long-awaited solvent directive was likely to be adopted early in 1999 but would not become operational for existing installations until 2007. Meanwhile, the government in The Netherlands set its own VOC limits for car refinishes.

(HELMA JOTISCHKY)

PHARMACEUTICALS

Pharmaceutical companies poured money into direct-to-consumer (DTC) promotions of prescription drugs in 1998, accelerating their efforts of 1997. Since late 1997, when the U.S. Food and Drug Administration (FDA) liberalized brand-specific advertising on television, the U.S. industry spent an estimated $1.8 billion on DTC advertising and related communications. Companies also expanded DTC promotion into more serious disease categories, such as cancer, heart disease, and AIDS. They reaped remarkable sales gains for DTC-promoted products, as patients and caregivers besieged physicians with product-specific requests. Products most heavily promoted on DTC—Schering-Plough's Claritin, Bristol-Myers Squibb's Pravachol, and Glaxo Wellcome's Zyban—all reaped U.S. sales growth of more than 35% for the year.

By the year's end, however, a backlash to DTC grew stronger among physicians, managed health-care organizations, and the FDA itself. The latter voiced concern that companies were soft-peddling the "fair balance" of product benefits as weighed against the risks and side effects. It announced that regulators would revisit the subject in early 1999.

Sales for the industry as a whole grew by an estimated 16% in the United States, 9% in Europe, and 7% worldwide. Asia and Latin America experienced growth of about 8%, and Japanese sales declined slightly. Leading companies scored comparable results through the third quarter, with some notable exceptions. Net income and earnings per share (EPS) grew by 14% for Bristol-Myers Squibb, 21% for Schering-Plough, and 6% for SmithKline Beecham. Merck's net income rose 14% and EPS by 15%. American Home Products (AHP) jumped 42% in income and 39% in EPS, compared with a previous year marred by the expensive withdrawal of its weight-reducer Redux. Pfizer fell short of expectations, doubling its income but boosting earnings by only 13%. Sales growth of its impotence pill, Viagra (see HEALTH AND DISEASE: *Sidebar*), declined in the second half. Warner-Lambert, riding high on its leading cholesterol product Lipitor, increased revenue by 44% and earnings by 49%. Johnson & Johnson registered an 11% increase and announced that it planned to reduce its workforce by 4,100 and close 36 plants worldwide during the next 12–18 months.

Large-scale mergers took a back seat to collaborative strategies in 1998. American Home Products scuttled two proposed mergers, with SmithKline Beecham and Monsanto, due to clashes of corporate cultures. Pharmacia & Upjohn, Hoechst Marion Roussel, and Wyeth-Ayerst/Lederle struggled to integrate their year-old mergers. Novartis, formerly Sandoz and Ciba-Geigy, and Glaxo Wellcome each made progress in integration but failed in their main goal of winning a greater world market share. Companies of all sizes turned increasingly to wide-scale partnerships to bolster their research, development, and marketing powers.

New therapies on the market in 1998 were developed from a landmark synthesis of traditional pharmacology, biotechnology, and breakthrough discovery methods such as "high-throughput screening" and "combinatorial chemistry." Genentech's Herceptin for breast cancer, Immunex's Enbrel for arthritis, and many other new products were developed through leaps in understanding the genetic basis of disease and cleverly combining old and new scientific tools. Vaccines, energized by DNA technology, took on new targets such as Lyme disease, hepatitis B, and meningitis.

Major product withdrawals also marked the year. AHP's painkiller Duract, Hoechst Marion Roussel's antihistamine Seldane, and Hoffmann–La Roche's antihypertensive Posicor were withdrawn because of side effects that emerged after they entered the market. The problems were blamed by some on FDA's new fast-track user-fee review program, which speeded up new-drug approvals. Companies and regulators each argued, however, that no safer practical alternative to the current system of clinical trials existed.   (WAYNE KOBERSTEIN)

PHOTOGRAPHY

Despite the stock market's roller-coaster ride and international financial turmoil in 1998, the photographic industry produced a variety of interesting products as it vigorously sought ways to exploit a changing market. The rapid growth of digitized electronic imaging in all its aspects—hardware, software, and applications—continued to attract much attention from photographic and electronic manufacturers.

Many of the new digital cameras were sleek, attractive models styled after popular film-using models. Prices dropped for high-resolution "megapixel" cameras (those with one million or more image-capturing pixels). Nikon's Coolpix 900, which featured three-mode metering, five-mode electronic flash, a Nikkor 3× optical zoom lens, and a 1.3 million-pixel charge-coupled-device (CCD) imaging sensor, was priced at less than $900. Kodak's DC220 zoom digital camera, with a 2× optical zoom lens, a Universal Serial Bus (USB) for faster transfer and downloading of images, and one million pixels per image, sold for less than $600. Retail prices for some entry-level digitals were as low as about $200.

Synergistic ways to combine digital and silver-halide technology were explored and promoted. Inexpensive scanners enabled silver-halide photographs to be digitized for computer viewing or transmission by E-mail or over the Web. State-of-the-art photofinishing equipment allowed photo labs to return customer's snapshots on floppy disks along with colour prints or download them directly onto home computers.

Manufacturers of film-using cameras introduced numerous new models. Canon and Minolta courted the advanced-amateur and professional markets with high-ticket 35-mm single-lens-reflex (SLR) cameras. Among its novel features the Canon EOS-3 provided a 45-segment autofocus system with a choice of auto, manual, or Eye Controlled Focus, in which an array of rectangles glowed red to indicate areas of sharp focus. A 21-zone evaluative metering system adjusted exposure accordingly as a moving subject shifted

its position in the viewfinder. Shutter speeds ranged from 30 seconds to 1/8,000 second. The ruggedly built Minolta Maxxum 9 had a stainless-steel, zinc, and aluminum die-cast body, user-friendly controls, a film advance as fast as 5.5 frames per second, and a top shutter speed of 1/12,000 second—fastest of any current autofocus SLR.

The so-far uncertain career of the Advanced Photo System (APS) received a boost from attractive new cameras in the 24-mm format. Nikon's Pronea S was a sleekly designed SLR hybrid that combined interchangeable-lens versatility and point-and-shoot simplicity with APS features. It came equipped with a compact zoom 30–60-mm *f*/4.5–5.6 Nikkor 1× lens for its Nikon F lens mount and a top shutter speed of 1/2,000 second. Ultracompact, stylish APS cameras inspired by Canon's popular ELPH included Fuji's diminutive Endeavor 1000ix MRC. Tiny enough to be covered by a credit card when folded, the titanium-finished Endeavor provided built-in flash, infrared autofocus, a choice of flash modes, and a 24-mm Super EBC Fujinon lens.

Hasselblad, long the most prestigious name in medium-format cameras, startled the industry by teaming with Fujifilm to introduce the 35-mm Hasselblad XPan. This rangefinder camera allowed conventional 24 × 36-mm or panoramic 24 × 65-mm format exposures on the same roll of film by using special *f*/4 45-mm or 90-mm lenses. Polaroid sought to invigorate slipping sales and profits with new models. An upscale version of its classic instant camera, the Polaroid 600, was restyled with sexy curves and a burnished silver-platinum outer covering. The compact, low-priced JoyCam used Captiva film but a manual system to pull out exposed film, thus eliminating an expensive electric motor. The intriguing Xiao! (its market name in Japan) was a compact instant camera for kids that put postage-stamp-sized sticker prints on a manual pull-out strip.

A bumper crop of more than a score of new or improved films were introduced by Kodak, Fuji, Agfa, and Imation. Agfachrome CT*precisa* 100 and 200 provided a very high

Visitors to the Comdex computer show at the Las Vegas (Nev.) Convention Center in November check out Kodak's latest digital point-and-shoot camera, the DC220. The camera features a 29–58 mm zoom lens, fast Universal Serial Bus interface, megapixel technology, and a built-in, multimode flash.

degree of pushability for colour transparency film—as much as four times their ISO ratings. Agfacolor HDC (High Density Color) print films were claimed to have better colour saturation, greater stability, higher definition, and finer grain than the previous generation of HDC emulsions. Another wide-latitude colour transparency film was Fujichrome MS 100/1000 professional, said to produce acceptable results with push-processing up to ISO 1000. Kodak brought forth four new colour negative Professional Portra films specifically for portrait photography, giving a choice of ISO 160 or 400 film speed and either natural colour (NC) or vivid colour (VC) saturation.

(ARTHUR GOLDSMITH)

PRINTING

Overall, the printing industry performed well in 1998, with record revenue levels reflected in increased investments by printing firms in advanced production technology. Manufacturing increased worldwide, with only minor ruffles related to Asian market problems.

IPEX, the annual international trade show, took place in Birmingham, Eng., in September 1998. It was the largest such event in history with more than 1,000 exhibitors and 100,000 visitors. The first digital colour presses premiered at IPEX '93 by Indigo (Israel) and Xeikon (Belgium), followed in 1996 by Canon (Japan) and Xerox (U.S.); by the end of 1998 some 19,000 such devices had been shipped worldwide.

Traditional static ink-on-paper printing advanced as well. Progress in press automation was led by the International Cooperation for the Integration of Prepress, Press and Postpress group, which seeks to make digital workflow a standard. New presses that integrate platemaking with the printing system were introduced by Heidelberger Druckmaschinen (Germany) and Dainippon Screen (Japan). The Heidelberg Speedmaster 74-DI, a six-colour press offering on-press or off-press platemaking, water or waterless printing, and a high level of automation, was introduced at IPEX '98. New processless thermal plates were introduced by Kodak Polychrome Graphics (U.S. and Japan), Imation (U.S.), and Presstek (U.S.). More than 3,000 computer-to-plate (CTP) systems had been installed worldwide since the introduction of the technology at IPEX '93.

The two largest stands at IPEX '98 were those of Heidelberg and Xerox, underscoring the pitched competition between traditional and electronic printing. A joint U.S.-German venture between Eastman Kodak (U.S.) and Heidelberg, NexPress Solutions, planned to introduce a high-capability toner-based printing system in 2000. Xerox advanced in all markets, from low-end three-page-per-minute office systems to colour printers churning out 40 pages or more per minute. The Xeikon web-fed 70- and 100-page-per-minute colour printer was being marketed as Chromapress by Agfa (Belgium), InfoColor by IBM (U.S.), DCP/32D and DCP/50D by Xeikon, and Docucolor 70 and 100 by Xerox.

The consolidation of printing and prepress services accelerated during the year as more printers adopted digital printing or CTP. It was predicted that 20% of U.S. printing services and more than half of prepress services would not exist as separate firms by 2001,

the losses due to mergers, acquisitions, and ceased operations.   (FRANK J. ROMANO)

RETAILING

Retailers in 1998 were speculating as to whether the boom was over. For much of the past decade, stores had been bustling with shoppers, their confidence buoyed by a robust economy and ever-rising stock market. As the year progressed, however, the outlook changed dramatically. Turmoil in the global economy, triggered by the 1997 Asian financial crisis, raised fears of recession in North America. The stock market bubble burst, and suddenly everyone from Wall Street traders to retired teachers was feeling less wealthy. (*See* Spotlight: *The World Economy in Trouble.*) Traditional retailers were also under pressure from the increasing use of on-line retailing, as busy consumers purchased more items, ranging from books to automobiles, on the Internet (*see* Sidebar).

With confidence ebbing, signs emerged that a retail downturn was imminent if not already under way. According to the U.S. Commerce Department, U.S. consumer spending slipped approximately 0.2% from June to July—the first drop in two years. Spending on big-ticket items such as automobiles and computers was especially weak, falling as much as 5.2%. Department stores were among the first to feel the pinch. J.C. Penney Co. suffered a 6.6% decline in sales in September, compared with 1997 September sales, and Sears, Roebuck & Co. saw sales drop 1.7%. Some discount and specialty retailers continued to post strong sales gains, but as the crucial Christmas season approached it was uncertain whether or not their holiday receipts would live up to expectations.

Toys "Я" Us Inc. worried about more than the economy. The U.S. toy retailer, saddled with bloated inventories and underperforming outlets, announced the biggest restructuring in its history. It planned to close 90 Toys "Я" Us stores—50 in Europe and the rest in the U.S. and Canada—along with 31 Kids "Я" Us clothing stores in the U.S. and an undetermined number of U.S. warehouses, resulting in a loss of some 3,000 jobs. The company also planned to slash prices to clear excess inventory and said it would remodel its stores to place the focus more on electronics and apparel, a move that was also designed to make it less reliant on Christmas sales and attract more year-round shoppers.

Despite the slowing global economy, mergers and acquisitions remained a prominent feature of the retail trade. The supermarket industry witnessed one big merger after another as grocers moved to bolster their size and increase their buying power with suppliers. In the U.S., Albertson's Inc. agreed to acquire American Stores Co. for $8.4 billion, creating what would have been the largest supermarket chain in the country, with sales of $36 billion. Months later, however, Kroger Co. agreed to buy Fred Meyer Inc. for $7.4 billion, forging an even bigger company, with sales of $43 billion. Safeway Inc. was also on the acquisition trail, buying Dominick's Supermarkets Inc. for $1.2 billion to create a $25 billion chain.

Such jockeying for dominance was not restricted to the U.S. In Canada, Loblaw Cos. Ltd., the country's biggest grocer, made a Can$1.6 billion bid for Provigo Inc. In another major deal, Empire Co. Ltd. swallowed Oshawa Group Ltd. for Can$1.4 billion. European grocers, which had started the consolidation trend several years earlier, continued to gobble up competitors at home and abroad. French supermarket operator Casino SA paid $200 million to acquire Argentina's Libertad SA. Another French retailer, Promodès SA, which in 1997 had failed in a hostile takeover bid for Casino, bought a minority stake in Belgium's largest grocer, owned by GIB SA, for $292.5 million.

The ongoing trend toward consolidation was being driven by several factors. Apart from increased buying power, companies that merged reduced their cost structures, which was crucial in an industry characterized by low profit margins. Another impetus for merging was that bigger companies would be better able to invest in ultramodern computerized inventory management systems that track consumer purchases.

DOUGLAS C. PIZAC—AP/WIDE WORLD

Customers enter an upscale, mini-grocery store inside the corporate headquarters of the American Stores Co. in Salt Lake City, Utah. In 1998 Albertson's Inc. agreed to acquire the supermarket giant for $8.4 billion.

The master of computerized inventory management, Wal-Mart Stores Inc., played a key role in forcing supermarket mergers. Wal-Mart, known primarily as a discount general merchandise retailer, was increasingly becoming a threat in the grocery business. It opened its first stand-alone supermarkets, complementing its growing chain of about 500 supercentres, which included a supermarket and discount store under one roof. Already the world's biggest retailer, Wal-Mart's rapid growth in groceries led one analyst to predict that it would become the biggest U.S. supermarket operator by the year 2004.

Wal-Mart's progress turned up the pressure on the third-leading discount retailer—Kmart Corp.—which was looking for potential merger partners in the grocery industry. In order to build on its 100 Super Kmart outlets, which sold general merchandise and groceries much like a Wal-Mart Supercentre, analysts stated that Kmart

Internet Retailing

In 1998 consumers could purchase virtually anything over the Internet. Books, compact discs, computers, stocks, and even new and used automobiles were widely available from World Wide Web sites that seemed to spring up almost daily. A few years earlier, skeptics had predicted that consumers accustomed to shopping in stores would be reluctant to buy items that they could not see or touch in person. For a growing number of time-starved consumers, however, shopping from their home computer was proving to be a convenient, cost-effective alternative to driving to the store.

The Massachusetts-based Forrester Research estimated that in 1998 U.S. consumers would purchase $7.3 billion of goods over the Internet, double the 1997 total, and the firm expected on-line sales to increase an additional 65% in 1999 to about $12 billion. Computers and software were the most frequent purchases, accounting for about one-third of all sales; travel services, compact discs, and books were also popular. Finding a bargain was getting easier,

owing to the rise of on-line auctions, such as the increasingly popular eBay, and Web sites that did comparison shopping on the Internet for the best deal.

For all the consumer interest, retailing in cyberspace was still a largely unprofitable business, however. Internet pioneer Amazon.com, which began selling books in 1995 and later branched into recorded music and videos, posted revenue of $153.7 million in the third quarter, up from $37.9 million in the same period of 1997. Overall, however, the company's loss widened to $45.2 million from $9.6 million, and analysts did not expect the company to turn a profit until 2001. Despite gushing red ink, Amazon.com had a stock market value of many billions, reflecting investors' unbridled optimism about the future of the industry.

Internet retailing appealed to investors because it provided an efficient means for reaching millions of consumers without incurring the cost of operating brick-and-mortar stores with their armies of salespeople. Selling on-

line carried its own risks, however. With so many companies vying for consumers' attention, price competition was intense and profit margins thin or nonexistent. In a demonstration of just how cutthroat the business had become, video retailer Reel.com sold the hit movie *Titanic* for $9.99, undercutting the $19.99 suggested retail price and losing about $6 on each copy sold. With Internet retailing still in its infancy, companies seemed willing to absorb such losses in a bid to establish a dominant market position.

Mergers and acquisitions were also common as competitors girded for the future. CDnow Inc. and N2K Inc., two of the largest on-line music retailers, agreed to merge, creating a formidable opponent to Amazon.com's compact disc business. Meanwhile, German media giant Bertelsmann AG agreed to buy 50% of Barnes & Noble Inc.'s on-line book business, providing yet another threat to Amazon.com. (*See* MEDIA AND PUBLISHING: *Book Publishing*: Sidebar.)   (JOHN HEINZL)

---

needed a partner with national distribution capabilities if it was to have any hope of competing with Wal-Mart, which had a huge lead in the race for supremacy.

(JOHN HEINZL)

SHIPBUILDING

In 1998 the world leaders among the principal shipbuilding countries were again Japan and South Korea; the only difference was that only 108,437 gross tons (gt) separated them in the world order book. According to figures released by Lloyd's Register of Shipping for the 1998 June quarter, Japan had 18,566,000 gt (33.4% of tonnage) and South Korea had 18,457,000 gt (33.2%). A comparison with the three area groupings of Western Europe 8,907,000 gt (16.0%), Eastern Europe 3,957,000 gt (7.1%), and the rest of the world 5,684,000 gt (10.2%) was not quite so one-sided as it might appear. The compensated gross tonnage (CGT) figures told a different story; CGT reflects the complexity of the structure and, therefore, the value. For Western Europe the CGT figure was calculated at 10,159,000; this was higher than Japan's calculated figure of 10,048,000 CGT, revealing that more sophisticated ships were being built in Western Europe.

Looking at the overall position, in 1998 there were 2,668 ships of 55.6 million gt in the world order book (ships currently under construction plus confirmed orders placed but not yet started). This represented an increase of 5 million gt over 1997. The cargo-carrying component of the order book was 1,962 ships of 53.6 million deadweight tons (dwt). Of those, the principal ship types (in dwt) were: oil tankers 30,880,000; dry bulk carriers 18,370,000; containerships 7,240,000; chemical carriers 3,660,000; general cargo

carriers 3,660,000; roll-on, roll-off cargo carriers 1,360,000; and liquefied gas ships 1,350,000.

Despite these numbers the shipbuilding industry entered 1998 with concern for the future. Though they enjoyed a 54% increase in orders, shipyards were unable to force up prices. The bulk carrier and containership markets started to cut back orders early in 1998, and, as the Asian financial crisis caused many tanker investors to reevaluate their plans, orders were likely to decrease and prices remain low.

Some ship types, however, continued to be in demand. During the past few years there was remarkable growth in high-speed ferry services. The first market was for fast ships to transport passengers and their cars, but the latest growth area was for rapid transport of cargo and containers. Hull designs included catamarans, hovercraft, hydrofoils, and monohulls.

The containership sector also continued to flourish. Contemporary containerships, with beams wider than 32.2 m (106 ft), had capacities of more than 6,000 TEU (20-ft equivalent units). Deliveries from AP Moller's Odense Steel Shipyard for the Maersk Line reported capacities of 7,060 TEU. The classification society, Germanischer Lloyd, performed seaway and strength analyses on a projected 8,000 TEU container carrier.

The cruise ship market remained upbeat, and vessels of 135,000 gt were projected. Many large ships were delivered during the past year, including the 77,000-gt cruise liner *Dawn Princess,* delivered from Fincantieri's Monfalcone yard to P&O Princess Cruises. The 74,140-gt cruise ship *Grandeur of the Seas* was delivered from Kvaerner Masa-Yards Inc., Helsinki, Fin., to Royal Caribbean Cruise Lines.   (EDWARD CROWLEY)

TELECOMMUNICATIONS

During 1998 the U.S. Federal Communications Commission (FCC) mandated the disclosure of price information for pay phones and other public telephones before a customer completed the call. To increase privacy, all telecommunications companies, including paging and cellular providers, were ordered to obtain customer permission before releasing personal information, including length and time of calls and who was called. Standards were adapted for v-chip technology to block sex, violence, and language content based upon a television rating system, and 50% of all new televisions had to be equipped with v-chips by July 1999. In April the FCC, after receiving over 1,400 complaints, fined a small long-distance provider, the Fletcher Companies, $5.7 million for "slamming" customers (switching their long-distance providers without permission). The FCC also revoked Fletcher's license for interstate service. Another goal of the FCC, its "e-rate" program designed to provide low-cost Internet connection to schools and libraries, met resistance when long-distance providers passed fees they were being charged to fund the program on to their customers.

Mergers were again prevalent in the telecommunications industry. During 1998 AT&T Corp. announced an $11.3 billion bid for Teleport Communications Group Inc., a provider of telephone services to businesses in 66 major U.S. markets. In June AT&T disclosed plans to buy the second largest U.S. cable-television provider, Tele-Communications Inc., for $32 billion, with the intent to upgrade and use TCI's cable to provide local phone service to their customers. The following month AT&T and British Telecommunications PLC an-

nounced they would merge their international operations into a jointly owned company. The newly appointed chairman of AT&T, C. Michael Armstrong, reported in January that the company would dismiss as many as 18,000 people, about 14% of its workforce, mostly through attrition and early retirement.

The regional Bell operating companies formed by the breakup of the old AT&T continued their consolidation. Bell Atlantic, the U.S.'s largest local phone company, announced a $67 billion merger with GTE Corp., a long-distance and wireless provider. SBC Communications Corp. announced its intent to acquire Ameritech in a $62 billion deal. Until the Bell Atlantic/GTE deal, this was the largest merger in U.S. telecommunications history and would create the largest local telephone company, second in size only to AT&T. In late October the FCC approved SBC's acquisition of Southern New England Telecommunications Corp. for $5.8 billion. The deal reduced the number of original "Baby Bells" from seven to four. At year-end 1998 almost all of these mergers were pending FCC, U.S. Justice Department, and state approvals.

In March Qwest Communications International Inc. bought the sixth largest long-distance provider, LCI International Inc., for $4.4 billion, thus becoming the fourth largest long-distance provider behind AT&T, MCI WorldCom, and Sprint. The MCI Communications Corp. merger with WorldCom Inc. was approved in July by European regulators and the U.S. Justice Department with the stipulation that MCI divest itself of its Internet assets, which it sold for $1.7 billion to Cable & Wireless PLC. The FCC approved the merger in September, and MCI WorldCom Inc. was formed. Within one week of the approval, former MCI chief executive Gerald H. Taylor resigned after 30 years with MCI.

In October Teligent, a new company led by a former AT&T top executive, was formed to provide wireless digital local, long-distance, and Internet services to business customers in 10 U.S. metropolitan areas. Using 30.5-cm (12-in) antennas on the roofs of office buildings, the company claimed savings of 30% over traditional providers. They were approved to operate in 31 states.

Two major service outages took place during the year. In April AT&T's high-speed frame relay network, the country's largest, was interrupted for almost 24 hours due to a problem caused by a software upgrade. In May a majority of the millions of pagers in the U.S. were rendered unusable when a PanAmSat satellite was knocked out of commission. Radio, TV, and ATM transmissions were also affected until a spare satellite could be moved into the malfunctioning one's orbit. Two labour disputes disrupted local telephone service, but the strikes by 73,000 Bell Atlantic workers and 34,000 employees from U.S. West were both settled without major incidents.

The shortage of available telephone numbers caused by the increased use of fax machines, modems, Internet access, cellular phones, pagers, and multiline households continued to generate the proliferation of area codes, access codes, and toll-free numbers. Many U.S. cities were committed to area code "overlays" in which existing customers could keep their old area codes but new customers would receive a different area code, even in the same geographic area. This resulted in the need always to dial at least 10 digits when making a local call instead of the traditional 7. A new toll-free area code 877 joined the 800 and 888 codes already in use, and long-distance access codes were increased from five digits to seven.

The Internet and World Wide Web continued to drive new technology and products to provide high-speed access to Web content over regular copper telephone lines and through cable television services (*see* COMPUTERS AND INFORMATION SYSTEMS). The use of the Internet for voice telephony also was being investigated by all the major long-distance providers. Called Voice-over-International Protocol (VoIP), it was estimated that calls could be placed using the traditional telephone, through VoIP services, for 7.5 to 9 cents per minute. Other innovations included Internet radio and voice access of Internet content.   (THOMAS E. KROLL)

TEXTILES

Worldwide growth in the textile industry leveled out to near zero in 1998, following high growth in 1997, when textile demand rose 6%, twice the 3% annual average. This correction created an excess of capacity at every level of the industry, and prices for fabrics and yarns fell dramatically. In addition, the fluctuation of exchange rates created winners and losers; South Korea improved its competitive edge, as did Indonesia, making Chinese exports more expensive relative to other Asian suppliers. Textiles from Asia were priced low, which caused textile mill activity to remain flat in Western Europe and increase only slightly in North America. Although most parts of Asia experienced a rise in exports, local demand was weak, resulting in a reduction in overall textile activity; production also fell in the Middle East. China registered a slight increase in production, and India boosted its output.

In such a volatile market, retailers tried initially to increase their profit margins by buying in volume, but competition rose for them, too, resulting in lower prices for the consumer. In 1998, 48,600,000 metric tons of textiles were produced, including 1,600,00 metric tons of wool, 19,200,000 metric tons of cotton, and 27,800,000 metric tons of manufactured fibres. Quality, however, suffered as a result of the price wars, and only toward the end of the year was there any sign of a return to more stable conditions.

Man-Made Fibres. Following a remarkable 9% growth in mill demand for manufactured fibres in 1997, a much flatter growth of only 1% was seen in 1998. The cellulosics (mainly acetate and rayon) fell slightly to 2.9 million metric tons of textile mill consumption. Acrylic also experienced a slight drop to 2.8 million metric tons, but nylon filament and staple products were unchanged at four million metric tons. Among the polyesters, filament was up 2.5% to 8.5 million metric tons and staple stayed level at 6.8 million metric tons. Polypropylene in its textile forms of filament and staple grew 4% to 2.9 million metric tons, benefiting from a strong carpet industry in the U.S. and additional gains in market share against all the other fibres.

A belief by many in the industry that future demand would be high was based on a long-term annual growth of just under 5% and was overoptimistic. The industry suffered from overcapacity, with worldwide production down by 3–4%. This situation applied particularly to nylon filament (running at 73% capacity worldwide), polyester filament (85%), and polyester staple (82%). International trade in fibres developed as efforts increased to off-load excess capacity from Asia into Europe and North and South America. As a result, filament and staple prices fell throughout the year, in most cases hitting bottom during the fourth quarter.

Courtaulds PLC settled its four-year dispute with Lenzing AG over the right to market Tencel, a lyocell fibre, and Formosa Chemical and Fibre Corp. of Taiwan became the first Asian producer of this relatively new product.   (PETER DRISCOLL)

Wool. The world wool clip in 1998 was 1,438,000 metric tons clean, down slightly from 1,471,000 metric tons in 1997. The 1998 wool production was the lowest since the 1960s. Australia ruled as the dominant producer (356,384 metric tons clean), followed by New Zealand (205,000 metric tons clean) and China (184,800 metric tons clean); these three countries accounted for over 54% of worldwide wool-fibre production.

Sheep populations in the U.S. continued to decline, resulting in production of 24,439 metric tons greasy, down 5% from 1997. U.S. wool consumption (90% for apparel and 10% for carpets) was 66,016 metric tons, down considerably from 74,197 metric tons in 1997.

Wool demand from much of Asia remained weak, especially from Japan, South Korea, and Taiwan. Orders from these three countries were at their lowest since 1995 and down 18% from 1997, primarily as a result of the Asian economic crisis. Increases in wool demand, however, were seen in China (11%) and Europe (5.3%). Worldwide wool demand rose 1.6%, but prices were very depressed for coarse wools and finer wools, the lowest in four and eight years, respectively. In New Zealand the average price of wool fell nearly 30% against the U.S. dollar. Overall, the wool market share had risen 40% over the past five years, and by the end of 1998 wool was expected to increase its share of the fibre market 20%, nearly double the 11% increase in 1997.

(EVERETT E. BACKE)

Cotton. Worldwide cotton production in 1998 fell to 18.6 million metric tons, down from 18.9 million metric tons in 1997. Most of the decline occurred in the United States and China, where production of cotton crops was down 24% and 9%, respectively. Production in such other major cotton-producing countries as India, Pakistan, and Uzbekistan remained essentially unchanged.

Fewer acres were planted in the U.S., owing to lower cotton prices and a change in government subsidy requirements. The Chinese crop suffered yield losses as a result of flooding and wet conditions in the Chang Jiang (Yangtze River) area. In Hubei (Hupeh) and Hunan provinces floods inundated up to one-third of the cotton fields. Some cotton warehouses were reported flooded in those provinces and in Jiangsu (Kiangsu) province.

Cotton consumption worldwide totaled 19.2 million metric tons, with the largest gains in Turkey, Pakistan, Mexico, and

Brazil; the increase in those countries slightly offset declines in China, Indonesia, and the U.S. A decline in consumption in the U.S. was attributed to slower growth in the economy and relatively cheap cotton textile and apparel imports from Asia.

Although the U.S. continued to dominate the export markets, volume was down 34.7% from 1997, when 1.5 million metric tons of cotton were exported. China's imports of raw cotton from the U.S. were down 56% from 1997. Behind the U.S. in the volume of exports were Uzbekistan, French-speaking Africa, Australia, India, and Pakistan. Combined, these countries exported 2.3 million metric tons of cotton.

(EVERETT E. BACKE)

Silk. After many years of relative stability, the silk industry entered a period of turbulence and uncertainty in 1998. China, the major producer and exporter of raw silk, tried to regulate raw-silk prices by curtailing production, notably through the closing and/or merging of some small and inefficient reeling mills. As a result 1997 raw-silk production reached only 52,700 metric tons, compared with 59,000 metric tons in 1996 and 76,400 metric tons in 1995. Although prices were expected to rise, they tended to decline instead.

Japanese raw-silk production continued to drop—from 3,228 metric tons in 1995 to 2,580 in 1996 and 1,980 in 1997. For many years Japanese authorities had conducted a skillful rear-guard action to preserve their raw-silk production through subsidies, but that maneuver ceased after Japan became a member of the World Trade Organization. As a result production over the past four years had declined 55%.

Demand for silk also suffered, owing to the financial difficulties of several Asian countries that were consuming less silk, the loss of appeal of silk as a high-end fashion fibre, and the decline in demand for printed fabrics. Although demand for yarn-dyed and jacquard designs was increasing, the rise was not enough to make up for the shortfall. Many silk industry observers felt that demand for silk would increase in the future, but they were uncertain as to when the turnaround would occur, owing to the unpredictable overall economic climate.

(EVERETT E. BACKE)

TOBACCO

The economic turmoil in East Asia resulted in increased cigarette prices in the United States and many European countries, factors that led to a decline in cigarette consumption in 1998. According to the 1998 edition of *World Tobacco File,* the decline began in 1997, when global consumption, at 5,195,800,000 cigarettes, fell by 0.4% as compared with an increase of 2.1% in 1990–97.

The three largest multinational tobacco manufacturers, Philip Morris Inc., R.J. Reynolds Tobacco Co., and B.A.T. Industries PLC, each reported reduced profits for the second quarter of 1998. By comparison, Japan Tobacco, the former state tobacco monopoly, after years of rising profits reported a 28% decline in consolidated net profits for its 1997–98 fiscal year, largely due to a 3% decrease in cigarette sales in its domestic market. The profits of the multinational manufacturers were adversely affected by the impact of million-dollar set-

tlements made in tobacco liability cases brought in the United States by Texas, Minnesota, and Mississippi. Three legislative issues in the U.S., however, were resolved in favour of the industry. The McCain bill, which would have imposed draconian measures on the manufacturers and forced up cigarette prices by at least $1.10 a pack, was unable to muster a majority of the Senate to bring the bill to the floor of the House of Representatives; and a North Carolina federal court ruled that the Environmental Protection Agency had wrongly classified secondhand smoke as a known carcinogen. In an even more important case, a federal appeals court decided that the U.S. Food and Drug Administration had no authority to regulate cigarettes as though they were drugs.

In September the new Russian prime minister, Yevgeny Primakov, announced that the government planned to restore the state monopoly for tobacco. It was too early to determine how this would affect the major Western tobacco manufacturers, which had invested millions of dollars in acquiring and modernizing 9 of Russia's 27 tobacco factories after they were privatized.

Because of the downturn in the fortunes of the tobacco industry, the two largest makers of cigarette-making machinery, Körber/Hauni in Germany and Molins in the U.K., were forced to lay off workers. Tobacco farmers suffered from lower prices that resulted from reduced purchases of leaf by the manufacturers. In Zimbabwe, a major supplier of flue-cured and burley tobacco, farmers boycotted the tobacco auctions in Harare for six weeks because of the low prices. In Brazil the crop was reduced by freak weather conditions caused by El Niño. The boom in premium cigars in the U.S. faded, as stock prices fell on Wall Street and the market was inundated with cheap imports.   (LAURENCE RIDGWAY)

TOURISM

Worldwide tourism posted positive results in 1998, with international travel increasing 1.5% for a total of 620 million arrivals. This compared with 2.8% growth in 1997 and 5.6% in 1996. Worldwide earnings from international tourism exceeded $450 billion. The lower growth rate for arrivals was mainly attributable to the Asian financial crisis, which resulted in five million fewer foreign tourists visiting East Asia and the Pacific during the year. The majority of the world's destinations, however, continued to experience an upward trend in arrivals.

In Africa devaluation of its currency allowed South Africa to offer competitive prices to tourists. Tanzania's wildlife-based tourism surged by 30% as Kenya's tourism operators sought government assistance to resuscitate an industry preoccupied with security. Arrivals in Morocco and Tunisia grew by 11% and 8%, respectively, and in West Africa, Côte d'Ivoire welcomed 10% more foreign visitors. Anticipating an end to UN sanctions, Libya prepared a five-year plan for tourism development.

In the Americas the U.S. hosted a record 24 million overseas visitors in 1997. During 1998 a modest slowdown was expected because of a decline in Asian tourists. In the absence of a federal tourism administration, U.S. states were obliged to invest heavily in travel promotion; Illinois led with $35 mil-

lion, followed by Hawaii, Texas, and Florida. The weakness of the Canadian dollar helped overnight trips to Canada to surge by 11% in 1998. Spending by U.S. travelers offset lower earnings from other visitors. Mexico, where tourism surpassed oil as a foreign currency earner, welcomed 20 million foreign visitors in 1998, investing $1,625,000,000 in new tourism facilities during the year. In Chile tourism increased by 7%. Caribbean destinations experienced mixed trends; Barbados (+10%) and Cuba (+11%) reported the best results. Nicaragua was among Central American tourism destinations adversely affected by the devastating Hurricane Mitch in November.

In East Asia and Oceania countries dependent on regional tourism were strongly affected by the aftermath of the financial crisis. They included Hong Kong (–13%), New Zealand (–10%), and Singapore (–16%). Civil unrest threatened Indonesia's five million-visitor market. Even in Bali, the country's most popular destination, hotel occupancy was down to 30%. Australia and the Philippines also reported a difficult year but experienced declines of only 5% and 1%, respectively, in overseas arrivals. Thailand, by contrast, reported a 6% increase in arrivals, a result of currency devaluation and a successful "Amazing Thailand" promotion, while in South Korea arrivals rose 7% as currency depreciation made shopping visits attractive. China welcomed 12% more tourists from overseas. Japan projected a 5% decline in overseas travel by its citizens, down to 16 million. In South Asia India planned to introduce new luxury tourist trains. Maldives tourism surged by 9%. In Myanmar (Burma) a new resort near Mandalay reflected the growing interest in ecotourism. (*See* Special Report.)

Europe continued to represent 60% of world tourist arrivals and half of global receipts. The region's prime tourist country, Germany, accounted for 56 million overseas trips and 50 million visits by tourists in 1998. The Lisbon World Exposition, which ran from May to September in the Portuguese capital, and the 32-nation association football (soccer) World Cup, which was held in nine cities across France

(continued on page 182)

World's Top 20 Tourism Spenders, 1997		
Rank	**Country**	**Expediture in $000,000**
1	United States	54,183
2	Germany	45,536
3	Japan	33,041
4	United Kingdom	28,215
5	France	16,755
6	Italy	16,000
7	Canada	11,284
8	Austria	10,992
9	Russia	10,401
10	Netherlands, The	10,232
11	Belgium	8,275
12	Taiwan	6,963[1]
13	Poland	6,900
14	Switzerland	6,731
15	Brazil	6,583
16	Sweden	6,441[1]
17	South Korea	6,262
18	Singapore	6,139[1]
19	Australia	6,129
20	Spain	4,440

[1]1996 figure is latest available.
Source: WTO Madrid.

Ecotourism: The New Face of Travel

by Carla Hunt

The latest trend in tourism is travel that combines preserving the natural world and sustaining the well-being of the human cultures that inhabit it. Known as ecotourism, the industry was unknown a decade ago yet now receives rave reviews from environmentally conscious travelers who immerse themselves in pristine places and authentic experiences. Unlike traditional tourism, ecotourism promotes environmentally responsible travel and seeks to ensure that visitors "take nothing but photographs and leave behind nothing but footprints."

An equally important part of the ecotourism equation is "sustainable" tourism that enables local people to protect their natural and cultural resources and profit from them at the same time. The truly "green" traveler also emphasizes the necessity for tours that strictly limit group size, coordinate with native guides, and donate a percentage of tour profits to community projects or research.

Varying interpretations and definitions of ecotourism currently exist. The ecotourism umbrella seems to shelter all kinds of outdoor travel-related products—from beach hotels that happen to be near a rain forest to a national park visit, guided bird-watching, or scientist-led Antarctic cruising. It also encompasses adventure expeditions, such as trekking and river rafting, as well as less rigorous trips to culturally exotic or archaeologically important locations.

The general concept of ecotourism arose when conservationists realized the potential benefits in combining people's interest in nature with their concern for the environment. An early model for ecotourism came from East Africa in the 1970s, when Kenya began collecting fees from safari-bound tourists heading into its national parks. Those revenues were earmarked to support conservation and park maintenance in its vast wildlife preserves.

According to the World Tourism Organization, Kenya developed a good thing. In an early national parks study, the organization determined that each lion in Kenya's Amboseli Park was worth $27,000 per year in tourism revenues to local tribes and an elephant herd about $610,000. A complementary investigation by Wildlife Conservation International showed that as a refuge the park was valued at $18 per acre per year compared with 36 cents per acre under the most optimistic agricultural returns. Certainly such dramatic figures contributed to the saying Wildlife Pays, So Wildlife Stays.

Ecotourism also flourished in the rain forests and nature lodges of Costa Rica and Belize, and the former was particularly successful in attracting ecotourists. Promoting itself as a destination with "no artificial ingredients," Costa Rica provided vacations rich in natural wonders and adventure, and the economic benefits were significant; in 1992 tourism surpassed bananas to become the primary source of foreign revenue.

As tourist figures increased by leaps and bounds in Costa Rica, however, so did the pressure to build larger hotels and other facilities to accommodate mainstream tourism. Charter planes began ferrying tourists straight to the coasts of the newly developing Guanacaste province, and the once-pristine zone around Manuel Antonio National Park became less tranquil. Another popular destination was the Galápagos Islands, perhaps the world's most renowned natural "laboratory" of flora and fauna unique to the region.

The high-profile islands were among the hundreds of world destinations battling the question: will success spoil ecotourism? Previously, limits on both the numbers of boats and

the numbers of visitors to the islands were weakly enforced. This was being changed, however, by implementing an itinerary system that set a precise schedule regulating quotas of boat visits for each island site allowed on any given day. Some island landings were closed to locally based ships and yachts, and, by law, international passenger vessels were not permitted to cruise anywhere in the Galápagos archipelago.

Similar practices were implemented in Antarctica, where the trickle of visitors turned into a steady stream. At the end of the 1980s there were some 3,000 travelers cruising in Antarctic waters; for the 1998–99 season the number approached 9,000. Though Antarctica could support this increase, the number of passengers landing on sites at any given time was closely monitored. The International Association of Antarctica Tour Operators, a group of travel companies concerned with the protection of wildlife and sites of historic and scientific interest, set guidelines, for example, that no more than 100 people may land at any one site at one time.

Australia demonstrated its leadership in the field, establishing guidelines to help developers protect the environment when planning projects. In addition, the Australian tourism ministry undertook to ensure that indigenous communities participate fully within the tourism industry. In some national parks, for instance, Aboriginal people were trained to operate tourism businesses and were closely involved in the development and interpretation activities at visitor centres.

Another positive result of ecotourism came from the ecotourists themselves, as they created a demand for smaller and greener lodgings worldwide. One of the pioneers in ecolodges was Stanley Selengut, whose Harmony Lodge on St. John in the U.S. Virgin Islands was the world's first resort to use materials fabricated from recycled trash and to operate exclusively on Sun and wind power. The lodge won the Condé Nast Global Ecotourism Award in 1995. With missionary zeal, Selengut advocated profitable and sustainable development of ecolodges that limit energy consumption, preserve the ecological balance, recycle waste, and avoid corrupting local cultures.

What will be the role for ecotourism in the new millennium? Ecotourism experts such as Megan Epler Wood, president of The Ecotourism Society, are confident that ecotourism is no longer a fringe part of the travel industry. "Major tour companies have bought into ecotourism, not just for bottom-line profits, but because they care about our en-

vironment," said Wood, "and their programs contribute greatly to its preservation." Concerns remain, she added, that "the lack of discipline of governments and the constant demand for growth will undermine efforts to create sustainable ecotourism economies that are small but beautiful."

In essence, preservation for tomorrow drives most of the discussion about a kinder and gentler tourism. For the future, balances need to be struck between our interest in visiting a place, the carrying capacity of the destination, and the well-being of all that live there.

Carla Hunt is a freelance journalist based in New York City.

(continued from page 179)
between June and July, each boosted tourism to the host countries. The Baltic Tourism Commission met in September in St. Petersburg to review the Baltic countries' marketing options; boating and culture were among the promising offerings. Visiting heritage sites was the most popular pastime of visitors to Great Britain, though tourists were also attracted by fashion, architecture, and the performing arts. The opening in June of Europe's longest suspension bridge linking eastern Denmark (where Copenhagen is located) with the Jutland Peninsula, increased tourism to Denmark by more than 40%. Other Nordic countries also fared well, with Norway's arrivals increasing 5% and Sweden's 8%. Despite Switzerland's strong currency the nation's hotels recorded 4% more tourist nights than in 1997. Europe's Mediterranean islands experienced a good tourist season; arrivals increased 7% in Cyprus and 5% in Malta. Among countries forming part of the former Yugoslavia, Croatia's tourism grew by 7%, as that Adriatic Sea nation drew up a long-term strategy to upgrade tourism facilities and services. Romania's hotels reported a 6% increase in occupancy. Although tourism had been among the fastest developing sectors during the 1990s, Russia's economic crisis left its travel sector badly crippled. Finally, Spain experienced a boom tourism year in 1998 with 10% more foreign tourists.

In the Middle East the political situation continued to affect tourism. Israel began the year below 1997 levels, though Jordan reported a recovery of 13% above the previous year. The opening in November of the new Gaza International Airport was seen as bringing tourism benefits to the Palestinian people.

Nearly 70% of users of the World Wide Web were said to have clicked onto a travel-related site in 1998. Information about airlines was especially popular.   (PETER SHACKLEFORD)

WOOD PRODUCTS

Wood. A continued strong housing market in 1998 allowed the wood products industry in the U.S. to begin the year on a positive note. As was normal, markets slowed in May and June for the summer holidays. A resurgence of demand for softwood lumber during the third quarter of the year was attributed to the continued strength of housing. For the first 10 months of the year housing sales were 9% over the same period in 1997, and, aided by low interest rates and strong consumer demand, they were expected to remain strong until early 1999.

During fiscal 1998 (Oct. 1, 1997–Sept. 30, 1998) the U.S. Forest Service sold 7,067,000 cu m (1 cu m=423.8 bd ft) of timber from the national forests, 20% less than during the previous fiscal year. Environmental objections to timber harvesting virtually stopped all new timber sales from national forests. Some were concerned

that the reduction in harvest would place the forests at a higher risk of catastrophic fires because dead or dying timber would generate a buildup of fuel.

U.S. lumber production maintained a strong pace in spite of the continued slowdown in sales from federal forests. For the first nine months of 1998 softwood lumber production was 61,731,000 cu m, down 1.3% from 1997. Production of structural panels, including plywood and oriented strand board, totaled 2,964,000,000 sq m (31.9 billion sq ft), 6.3% ahead of 1997. Hardwood lumber production was at a record pace of approximately 33 million cu m, and hardwood flooring production in

©JAMES SCHNEPF—GAMMA LIAISON

This paper manufacturing plant in Michigan was kept busy during the year. Despite mill strikes in Canada and a negative impact on the paper industry from the Asian economic crisis, North America remained the world leader in paper and paperboard production.

1998 was expected to reach 1,038,000 cu m, the highest level since 1968.

Affecting all parts of the U.S. wood products industry was the decline in exports, caused mainly by the Asian economic crisis. During the first nine months of 1998 softwood lumber exports overall declined 35.6%, but exports of softwood lumber to East Asia fell 60.3%. Hardwood lumber exports declined 15.8% during the same period, while shipments to Asian markets were down 41.4%. Imports into the U.S. of softwood lumber from Canada were slightly greater than in 1997, in spite of the quota agreement limiting the volume of lumber that could be shipped duty-free to the U.S.

Though exports declined in 1998, the long-term outlook was that more lumber from North America would be required to meet the world's demand. Eastern European production of lumber increased, but that region's forests were not expected to be able to meet the growing demands for housing, furniture, and flooring. China was forced to stop most of the logging in the Chang Jiang (Yangtze River) watershed because of heavy floods there during the summer. Environmental concerns in a number of tropical timber-produc-

ing countries led to reductions in harvests. Also, the unstable economy and widespread inefficiencies in Russia led to a decline in timber harvests and lumber production in that country.

During the third quarter of 1998 lumber exports began to improve, as the major Asian economies showed signs of improvement. The demand for hardwood lumber was growing, as high consumer confidence combined with strong housing markets led to increased furniture manufacturing.

(GEORGE BARRETT)

Paper and Pulp. The 300-million-metric-ton level of world paper and paperboard (P&B) production was almost reached for the first time in 1997 with a total of slightly over 299 million metric tons, an astonishing performance and an increase of 5.8% over 1996. The U.S. remained the largest P&B producer in 1997 with 28.9% (86.5 million tons) of the total and an increase of more than 5.3%, more than twice the 2.5% average annual growth during the previous 10 years. Including Canada, North America remained the leader in P&B production (105,446 million metric tons) in spite of the fact that strikes affected many of Canada's mills. An increase in 1998 seemed unlikely, however, in large part because of the financial crisis in East Asia.

The largest increases in P&B production and pulp production in 1997 were reported by Indonesia, with gains of 19.7% and 16.3%, respectively, over 1996. In 1998, however, the nation's economic and monetary crisis and a long dry season that resulted in major forest fires seemed certain to result in a sharp decrease in production. In Europe Finland turned in a 16.3% rise in P&B output and a 14.4% gain in pulp production. Sweden registered increases of 8.5% and 6.6%, respectively. Other large P&B increases in Europe were Germany (8.3%), France (7.2%), Italy (8.3%), and Belgium (12.3%).

Asia's P&B output increased 5.1% in 1997, with Japan and China as the continent's two top producers. It seemed unlikely, however, that this pace would be maintained in 1998. In Japan growth rates were slowing down, and the depreciation of the nation's currency resulted in an increase in exports and decrease in imports compared with the previous year. The Japan Paper Association estimated that domestic demand for P&B in 1998 would increase by 1.5%, a smaller growth than in 1997. In China, despite increased production, profits declined though the industry remained profitable.

Financial results worldwide in 1997 were well below the records set in 1995. Industry restructuring was underway in many areas. Sweden's giant Stora Kopparbergs Bergslags AB merged with Finland's Enso OY in midyear. Consolidation was taking place in the North American paper industry, as U.S. and Canadian firms sought to concentrate on a narrower range of products.

(H.-CLAUDE LAVALLÉE)

Computers and Information Systems

In 1998 information technology was dominated by a single event, the Microsoft Corp. antitrust trial, but although the outcome of that trial promised to have ripple effects throughout the computer and software industry, the year produced other notable events as well. These included the dramatic recovery of Apple Computer, Inc., the arrival of high-speed Internet access via telephone and cable television networks, the acquisition of Digital Equipment Corp. (DEC) by Compaq Computer Corp., the merger of America Online (AOL) and Netscape Communications Corp., and the introduction of high-definition television (HDTV). Throughout the year many people expressed growing concern about the approach of a new millennium and whether the world would be prepared to handle the attendant potential computer problems. (*See* Sidebar.)

Industry Developments. In May the U.S. Justice Department filed an antitrust suit against Microsoft, alleging that Microsoft had used monopoly power to restrict competition. Based on the contention that Microsoft improperly sought to dominate the market for Internet browser software—to the disadvantage of Netscape, maker of the most popular World Wide Web browser—the case grew to include allegations of broader anticompetitive actions to dominate the Internet software market. The broadened suit alleged that Microsoft, which in September passed General Electric to attain the highest market value in the nation, had used its influence as the maker of the Windows operating system (OS) for personal computers (PCs) to restrict competition. Among the actions at issue was the government's contention that Microsoft offered AOL, the world's largest on-line service provider, a prized spot for its software on the Windows "desktop" in exchange for AOL's decision to use Microsoft's Internet Explorer as its main Web browser. The federal suit was joined by 20 states (one of which later withdrew from the case) and after some delay went to trial in October before District Court Judge Thomas P. Jackson. Microsoft responded that the Justice Department's broadening of the case reflected desperation and that, whereas the company undeniably was a powerful player in the software market, it had done nothing illegal. It also asserted that, rather than trying to hurt competition by combining its Internet Explorer with Windows, as the government claimed, Microsoft had combined the products to improve Windows. Government lawyers introduced testimony by some of Microsoft's competitors and partners, internal memos and electronic mail (E-mail) messages, and excerpts from a videotaped deposition by Microsoft's founder and chairman, Bill Gates.

In late November AOL announced two startling deals: a $4.2 billion agreement to acquire Netscape and an alliance with Sun Microsystems, which had filed a separate suit against Microsoft over the alleged misuse of Sun's Java programming language. Government lawyers denied that the AOL-Netscape-Sun deal weakened their arguments against Microsoft, and the case was still pending at year's end. A lower-profile antitrust suit was filed by the Federal Trade Commission in June against computer chip giant Intel Corp. That suit accused Intel of using monopolistic practices when it stopped or threatened to stop providing vital information about Intel chips to three computer manufacturers that declined to license key patents to Intel. Intel maintained that it had the right to act as it did. A trial on that suit was set for February 1999.

Apple Computer staged an amazing recovery that became apparent in January when the firm returned to profitability and continued during the year with the introduction of successful new computer models, such as the Power Macintosh G3 and the iMac consumer computer. Apple introduced the iMac in August and promoted it on the basis of its ease of use and obvious physical differences from other machines, including a two-tone, "bondi blue"-and-white, semi-transparent case. By early in the Christmas season, Apple's iMac had become the top-selling PC in retail stores; in November the iMac made up about 7% of consumer PC sales through retail and mail-order outlets. The machine was described as Apple's reentry into the consumer market after an absence of six years. Along the way, however, some other hard choices had had to be made. In February Apple dumped its hand-held Newton, a pioneer in what had come to be called personal digital assistants that also had been the butt of many jokes about its initially limited handwriting-recognition capabilities. Apple said the Newton had not been profitable. Overseeing Apple's recovery was Steve Jobs, the cofounder and interim CEO, who had returned to the company in 1997 after having been ousted in 1985. During 1998 Apple consistently remained profitable, but the company remained a relatively small player in the industry, where its machines were overshadowed by computers that used Windows. Although sales of all of Apple's computer models combined to give it a 10% retail market share in late 1998, roughly double its position in July, Apple continued to trail the retail PC sales of Compaq, Packard-Bell NEC, Hewlett-Packard, and IBM.

In the biggest acquisition to date in the computer industry, Compaq announced in January that it would buy DEC for $9.6 billion in cash and stock. The purchase represented a sea change in computing history, since it entailed the takeover of an aging maker of minicomputers, a 1970s technology, by the largest manufacturer of PCs, an industry that began only in the 1980s. Once the world's third largest computer maker, DEC had lost billions of dollars and half its employees since the late 1980s. The purchase was expected to make Compaq the world's second largest computer manufacturer, behind IBM. While DEC had been financially ailing as interest in its proprietary computers and software waned, it still provided a doorway through which Compaq could enter the markets for higher-end computer workstations and computer networks. In 1997 Compaq had paid $2.8 billion for Tandem Computers, which manufactured computers used by banks and telecommunications firms.

Consolidation also occurred in the software industry. Mattel Inc., known primarily for its toys but also as a player in the entertainment software business, said that it would purchase educational software firm The Learning Company, Inc., based in Massachusetts, in an exchange of stock valued at about $3.8 billion. The Learning Company had been the world's second largest consumer software firm, after Microsoft. The acquisition followed The Learning Company's agreement earlier in the year to buy Brøderbund Software, another entertainment firm, for about $420 million in stock.

Despite a general trend toward good news in the high-technology world, several companies announced large layoffs. In June Motorola Corp. said it would eliminate 15,000 jobs because of depressed conditions in the computer chip industry. The firm cited slowed demand in Asia for cellular telephones, pagers, and other products that were heavy users of Motorola chips. It also said it faced tougher competition from Asian firms that could afford to cut prices because their currencies had been devalued in relation to the U.S. dollar. Following its acquisition of DEC, Compaq announced in June that it would cut 5,000 manufacturing jobs worldwide as part of the process of consolidating its operations. Most of the impact was outside the U.S. AMP, Inc., the world's largest supplier of electric and electronic connectors, said in July it would eliminate 3,500 jobs. The PC business got some good news late in the year. Inventory surpluses that had driven down prices in the first half of 1998 began to disappear as the PC market turned around. Worldwide sales, which grew 11% in the second quarter, were expected to grow 12.2% in the second half of the year. Strong sales in the U.S. and Europe were expected to offset economic instabilities in Asia and Russia. Strong sales by Apple in the second half of the year were thought likely to push Apple from the seventh-ranking PC supplier in the U.S. and the world to the fifth largest.

Technology Developments. Early in 1998 a barrier to achieving widespread use of 56,000 bits-per-second (56 kbps, or 56K) modems was overcome when a universal standard for the devices was adopted by the

Bill Neukom, a lawyer for Microsoft Corp., speaks to the media in front of the E. Barrett Prettyman U.S. Court House in Washington, D.C., after the first day of the Microsoft antitrust trial in October.

International Telecommunications Union, a standards-setting body in Geneva. Prior to that, 56K modem makers had been divided into two warring camps with modems that were so different and mutually incompatible that Internet service providers often had to choose between supporting one or the other. In 1997 U.S. Robotics Corp., which had developed one type of 56K modem, was acquired by 3Com Corp., and in October 1998 Hayes Corp., one of the original modem manufacturers, filed for Chapter 11 bankruptcy protection after losses of more than $12 million in the first half of the year.

Even as the 56K modem standard was being established, telephone and cable television companies were introducing high-speed Internet-access services in more cities. The telephone technology was called digital subscriber line (DSL), and the cable TV technology was described as a cable modem. While the speeds provided by the two technologies differed, both were substantially faster than a 56K modem. Some providers were promising speeds up to 125 times faster. Despite the growing shipments of cable modems, conventional analog computer modems still accounted for about 90% of the market. Two trends, however, appeared to favour cable modems: the increasing number of households with computers, and decisions by some PC makers to offer cable modems as an option on new home computers. Computer makers also gave DSL a boost. In January Intel, Microsoft, and Compaq announced plans to develop open standards for DSL. The high-speed Internet-access technologies had been slow in arriving because telephone and cable TV companies largely failed to live up to optimistic timetables. As consumers and businesspeople increasingly relied on information downloaded from the Internet—and became frustrated with slow conventional download speeds—they clamoured for high-speed Internet access. Some analysts predicted that there would be 500,000 cable-modem users in the U.S. and Canada by the end of 1998, up from about 200,000 at midyear. The promise of a budding cable-modem business also led to the rise of intermediary firms, such as @Home, that planned to provide high-capacity voice, video, and data transmission to cable-modem users via their cable companies.

HDTV, a long-awaited consumer product, was introduced as part of a government-ordered switch to the new TV technology. The first publicly broadcast program, the launch of the space shuttle *Discovery,* was presented in November. The major American TV networks (CBS, NBC, ABC, and Fox) would be required to provide HDTV signals in their top 10 markets by the end of the year. It was anticipated that by the year 2000, 50% of the country should be able to receive HDTV content. HDTV picture quality was sharper and brighter than conventional television and was expected to be akin to satellite TV or to the digital pictures produced by digital video (or versatile) disk (DVD). The downside of the switchover was that, according to the government's plan, nondigital TV signals would be phased out within 10 years. Since all broadcasts would be digital by the end of that period, consumers who wanted to watch television would have to buy a new set. Almost no one was watching in 1998, however, because although some television signals were avail-

Only a few days before Christmas, 15-year-old Stephanie Musso of Hammondsport, N.Y., uses a new Apple iMac consumer computer to give Santa Claus some gift ideas at one of Bloomingdale's on-line shopping kiosks. The popular iMac debuted in August.

able in digital format, few HDTV sets were available and those that could be found in stores cost about $7,000 each.

International Data Corp. (IDC), a computer-industry research firm, predicted that "mass market acceptance of digital TV is years away, despite 42 U.S. TV stations transmitting digital broadcasts as of November 1 [1998]. Consumer confusion, incomplete infrastructure, hardware costs, and technical questions will prevent digital TV—particularly HDTV—from growing as quickly as many have predicted." IDC predicted that more than 13 million HDTV units would be installed by the end of 2002 and that 138 million would be in use by the end of 2007.

Another milestone was passed in June when Microsoft finally delivered its Windows 98 OS software. The Justice Department had sought to block the shipment of Windows 98—which combined the Internet Explorer browser with the Windows OS—on antitrust grounds, but a federal appeals court ruled that antitrust restrictions placed on earlier versions of Windows did not apply to the new operating system. Although PC manufacturers quickly embraced Windows 98 and shipped it with new computers, the OS debuted to lacklustre reviews. Microsoft had described Windows 98 in much lower-key terms than Windows 95, and most reviewers labeled Windows 98 as merely an incremental upgrade to Windows 95 rather than the radical change that was evident between Windows 3.1 and Windows 95. That perception probably was reinforced by Microsoft's explanation that Windows 98 was the last in a line of Windows OS and that its successor would be more like the business-oriented operating system, Windows NT (the next version of which would be called Windows 2000). In August Microsoft issued an addition to Windows 98, which the company described as a multimedia enhancement, but some observers said it was designed mainly to fix software errors, or "bugs," in the just-released Windows 98 software. Despite the grumbling, Windows 98 sold as well as Windows 95 had when it was first released. It was estimated that at year's end about 376 million PCs in the world would be using some version of the Windows OS.

Despite the overwhelming success of Windows, several computer companies backed an alternative OS called Linux. Although Linux had a tiny market share compared with Windows, its use rose more than 200% in 1998. Linux, which resembled the better-known Unix, was created in Finland in 1991 and by 1998 was used as an OS for servers in local area networks. What made it unusual was that its computer code was available free to anyone willing to download it. It also could be modified to fit a user's particular needs. Still, Linux suffered from being an underdog OS. There was a lack of technical knowledge among corporate computer managers that made using Linux for key corporate functions, such as database management, a challenge. Even though makers of database software offered technical help with Linux versions of their products, the support was not as deep as it was with more conventional OS products.

There was yet another version of the world's fastest computer unveiled in 1998 when IBM introduced a new computer, called Blue Pacific, that could handle 3.9 trillion calculations per second. Blue Pacific contained more than 5,800 computer microprocessors and more than 25 trillion transistors. It was designed under a $96 million research contract from the U.S. Department of Energy and was used by the department's Lawrence Livermore National Laboratory to simulate nuclear weapons explosions without conducting actual nuclear tests.

PC prices continued their decline as consumers warmed to a new category of PCs, the under-$1,000 group. In late 1998 IBM introduced a $599 consumer PC (sold without a monitor), becoming the first of the major PC suppliers to drop the price below $600. At year's end the market was still awaiting what appeared to be the least-expensive PC ever, a $399 model (without a monitor) made in South Korea by a company named TriGem. Retailers were hoping the new low-priced machines would enable them to sell computers to the 55% of the U.S. households that did not own one. There was concern among retailers that even PCs at the $800 level had merely attracted second-time buyers who otherwise might have bought more expensive machines. Even at

the high end of the PC market, prices continued to decline. PCs with speeds as high as 450 MHz—about twice as fast as low-end models—sold for under $3,000.

A computer technology with both computing and entertainment aspects, the DVD player faced an uncertain future in 1998. DVD was a videocassette recorder (VCR) replacement technology that played movies on a TV with a picture and sound of much higher quality than VCR tapes. The DVD player's cousin, the DVD disc drive, became available on some PC models in late 1998. These computer DVD drives could store huge amounts of computer data and, in a crossover computing-entertainment application, also could play DVD movies on computer screens. DVD movie players for TVs were modestly popular in 1998, with about 600,000 sold within the first full year of marketing. DVD itself was threatened by a competing player technology called Digital Video Express (Divx). DVD discs, like VCR videotapes, could be played endlessly for the original purchase price. Divx discs cost only a fraction of their DVD counterparts but could be played for only two days unless an additional fee was paid. Late in 1998 some DVD players that incorporated Divx technology came on the market.

The Internet. On-line use continued to grow in popularity throughout 1998. An IDC survey predicted that 23% of all U.S. households would be using an on-line service provider by the end of the year. The prediction was based partly on lower prices for PCs; the use of more hybrid PC-TV products, such as WebTV, which allowed TV users to surf some parts of the Internet; and the growing availability of high-speed cable modems. The potential for WebTV-like products was clear. At year's end AOL was said to be seeking a manufacturer of TV set-top boxes so that it could compete with Microsoft's WebTV product. Yet another WebTV-related product emerged from an unlikely source. Sega, known for its computer game consoles, introduced in Japan its new Dreamcast game console, which would also function as a WebTV-like unit. Software to turn the game machine into a Web-browsing device was not expected to be available until mid-1999. In addition, Sony Corp., the leading competitor in home video-game machines, was expected to offer something similar in the future.

Retail sales on the Internet also increased as consumers began to take greater advantage of electronic commerce. (*See* BUSINESS AND INDUSTRY REVIEW: *Retailing:* Sidebar.) On-line sales lived up to expectations during the Christmas holiday season. AOL reported a 350% increase in on-line shopping. Analysts estimated that more than two million households shopped on-line for the first time and that sales in the fourth quarter of 1998 would hit about $3.5 billion, as expected. That was almost three times the 1997 total. The unanswered question was how many of those holiday shoppers would become regular Internet buyers.

The running battle between the computer industry and the federal government over Internet encryption software continued, even though the federal government relaxed its export restrictions. Encryption, or encoding, software was intended to protect the privacy of on-line data transmissions and help safeguard business transactions. The software-encryption industry and some of its key cus-

tomers had been battling the government for several years, claiming that encryption was important to the development of electronic commerce. In addition, American software companies had complained that export regulations made it difficult for them to compete in the world market for encryption. New rules from the Commerce Department allowed American firms to export products using the 56-bit Data Encryption Standard, the equivalent of an electronic lock with more than 70 quadrillion possible combinations. The government continued to limit exports of more powerful encryption software, although some could be sold in 46 countries to particular industries, such as insurance and health care. Despite relaxing export rules on encryption, the government continued to push for FBI access to computer-industry encryption experts so that potential criminal activity on the Internet would not be protected from government scrutiny. The government promised it would place no limits on the export of encryption products for which the government was provided with codes, or keys, for reading the encrypted messages.

In September the Internet played a role in the White House scandal of 1998. First it was chosen by Congress as the distribution medium for the text of Independent Counsel Kenneth Starr's report on his eight-month investigation into Pres. Bill Clinton's relationship with a former White House intern. Only days later it became one of the means of disseminating the video of Clinton's grand-jury testimony in the case. Because the streaming video technique used to deliver Clinton's testimony consumed much more bandwidth than the text-based report, there were concerns of gridlock on the Internet when many people tried to download the video at once. In the end the problem did not arise, because far fewer people downloaded the video than had downloaded Starr's report. The same news story helped boost the fortunes of the Internet's leading gossip columnist, Matt Drudge, who had helped break the White House scandal story in January by posting information on his Web site, the Drudge Report. Drudge, who had no journalistic training, maintained that the Internet opened up new opportunities for people who were not establishment journalists to present news information to a wide audience.

The makeup of that wide Internet audience also became a concern in 1998 when a scientific study suggested that African-Americans were being systematically excluded from the on-line world. In April a study published in the journal *Science* reported that whites in the U.S. with annual household incomes below $40,000 were six times more likely than African-Americans to have used the World Wide Web within the previous week. Among low-income households, whites were found to be twice as likely to own a home computer as blacks. The study contended that because a smaller percentage of black households than white households had incomes of more than $40,000, computer access in the U.S. was being restricted to a smaller portion of the African-American population than the white population. The Internet's role in rearranging American personal habits also was examined in 1998. A study showed that Americans were using the Internet to supplement TV news and newspapers, not to re-

place them, but it also found that 20% of Americans were going on-line at least once weekly to read the news, compared with 6% two years earlier.

Long-distance telephone service over the Internet, once a technical curiosity, showed signs of becoming a real business in 1998. Several phone companies offered a service in which phone calls were transmitted digitally over the Internet at reduced rates. The Internet was designed to carry data packets, not voice calls, and adapting phone calls to the Net had resulted in some complaints of spotty voice quality. By year's end the service had improved to the point that Internet telephony could compete on the basis of its lower price. Typically the service sold for far less per minute than conventional long-distance service—largely because Internet telephony bypassed much of the conventional telephone switching network but also because Internet telephone service providers were exempt from some fees that conventional long-distance companies had to pay. In a few cases Net phone service was sold for a flat monthly rate that covered unlimited long-distance calling privileges. While relatively few cities were covered by the service, some companies were planning national service introductions by early 1999.

In the U.S. Congress several bills favourable to the computer industry were pending in late 1998. One would expand the ability of American companies to hire skilled foreign workers. Corporations wanted to be able to hire more foreign workers because of a shortage of technology workers in the country. Another bill would benefit firms that sold products over the Internet by giving them a three-year period in which they would not have to charge customers sales tax. During that time the government would devise a tax plan for Internet sales. Legislation also was pending that would create penalties for commercial Web-site operators who offered material considered harmful to minors. This legislation was opposed by the American Civil Liberties Union and some companies with Internet Web sites. Other U.S. government actions affected many public schools and libraries that had hoped for improved Internet access. They were to be beneficiaries of federal telecommunications reforms that allocated money for telecommunications services, Internet access, and some high-tech wiring costs. The subsidy turned out to be less than expected when the Federal Communications Commission (FCC), under pressure from Congress, cut funding for the program by 42% and shifted the emphasis to helping the nation's poorest schools and libraries. The FCC's cuts were made after Congress heard complaints from long-distance telephone companies, which said they could not provide most of the $2,250,000,000 to fund the program without raising customers' rates.

Computer Crime. Computer security continued to be a major concern as outside electronic attacks by computer "hackers" on government and business computers reached new heights, sparking investigations into who was responsible. Those investigations led to a number of arrests but underscored the vulnerability of many computer systems connected to the Internet. The Computer Security Institute, a nonprofit research group in San Francisco, reported that 24% of corporations participating in its annual survey indicated that they had suffered an outside

computer break-in within the previous year. About 44% said they had experienced incidents of unauthorized access to their computer systems by employees. In March a boy was charged in Massachusetts with having caused airport-control-tower computers to be out of service for six hours. The boy accomplished the task by wiping out telephone access to the airport's control tower. The shutdown also affected the airport's fire department and security and weather services and the operations of several private airfreight firms. In April a Canadian man was arrested for having broken into a NASA Web site and caused more than $70,000 worth of damage. That same month the University of Minnesota was hit by a "smurf denial of service" attack on its computer systems, which shut down some computers, caused some data losses, and resulted in network slowdowns. (Such an attack floods the victim's computer network with replies to false tests of remote network computers.) Concern about computer attacks was also

heightened. In July two California teenagers pleaded guilty to juvenile delinquency charges after they accessed computers at the government's Lawrence Livermore National Laboratory and the U.S. Air Force. Although no classified computer systems were breached, the attack raised government fears because it indicated the effectiveness of a well-organized and systematic hacker attack. That same month flaws were discovered and corrected in two widely used E-mail programs that would potentially allow technically knowledgeable people to sabotage other people's PCs remotely. The unexpected flaws, which turned up in both Microsoft and Netscape E-mail programs, would enable an outsider electronically to crash or steal information from the computer that was using one of the affected E-mail programs.

Other types of computer crimes also attracted attention. In March more than 60 people were arrested as accused pedophiles who were trying to set up meetings with un-

suspecting children over the Internet. New Hampshire police posed as children on the Internet to set up meetings with the accused adults (most of whom lived in northern Europe) and then arranged for them to be arrested. In September police in the U.S. and 11 other countries arrested more than 100 people in a crackdown on the exchange of child pornography over the Internet.

A puzzling new computer virus struck near the end of the year, but experts were undecided about how big a threat it posed. Called the "Remote Explorer" virus, it was written by clever destruction-oriented programmers and was able to spread itself through corporate computer networks more rapidly than previously known viruses had. The virus attacked only computers using the Windows NT OS and only under certain conditions. Some experts said the virus had the ability to bring entire companies to a halt. It was unclear, however, whether the virus was a widespread phenomenon.

(STEVE ALEXANDER)

The Millennium Bug

When the year 2000 arrived, the future could be coloured by the mistakes of the past. Computer programming shortcuts taken as much as 30 years earlier had the potential to produce computer failures that could affect the critical underpinnings of society, such as government services, public utilities, banks, insurance companies, airlines, brokerage firms, telephone companies, and hospitals.

The reason was that many computer programs (especially those written in the early days of computers) were designed to abbreviate four-digit years as two digits in order to save memory space. These computers could recognize 98 as 1998 but would be unable to recognize 00 as 2000, perhaps interpreting it to mean 1900. This meant that when the clocks struck midnight on Jan. 1, 2000, many affected computers would produce wrong answers or fail to operate properly unless the computers' software was repaired or replaced before that date. Other computer programs that projected budgets or debts into the future could begin malfunctioning in 1999 when they made projections into 2000. In addition, some computer software did not take into account that the year 2000 was a leap year. And even before the dawn of 2000, some computers might fail on Sept. 9, 1999 (9/9/99), because early programmers often used a series of 9s to indicate the end of a program.

The situation became variously known throughout the world as the "Millennium Bug" (so-called because a programming flaw is generally called a "bug"), the "Millennium Bomb," the "year 2000 problem," or "the Y2K Bug" (so-called because in metric measurements K stands for thousand). Mainframe computers, including those typically used to run insurance companies and banks, were thought to have the most serious Y2K problems, but even

newer systems that used networks of desktop computers could be vulnerable.

The Y2K problem was not limited to computers running conventional software, however. Many devices containing computer chips, ranging from elevators to temperature control systems in commercial buildings to medical equipment, could also be affected. The computer chips in these "embedded systems" also needed to be checked to see whether they were sensitive to calendar dates.

In the U.S. business and government technology teams were working feverishly to correct the problem as 1998 drew to a close, with a goal of completing their work before the end of December 1999. Programmers with the necessary skills were able to demand ever-rising salaries and other perks. In some cases older programmers were even lured out of retirement. Although some industries were well on the way to solving the Y2K problem, most experts feared that the government was lagging behind. A Y2K preparedness survey commissioned in late 1998 by Cap Gemini America, a New York computer industry consulting firm, showed that among 13 economic sectors studied, government was the least ready for Y2K. Rated highest for preparedness was the software industry, followed by financial services, computer firms, manufacturing companies, telecommunications firms, aerospace companies, oil and gas firms, utility companies, pharmaceutical companies, distribution firms, transportation companies, and health care firms.

One of the most frequently cited fears associated with Y2K involved electric-power generation. Because the electric power utilities in the U.S. were interconnected, Y2K power-plant failures in one part of the nation conceivably could

affect people living elsewhere. In an effort to encourage companies to share critical information about Y2K, Pres. Bill Clinton in October signed the Year 2000 Information and Readiness Disclosure Act. The law was designed to encourage American companies to share Y2K data by offering them limited liability protection for sharing information about Y2K products, methods, and best practices. For example, businesses that shared information in good faith could not be sued if the information later proved to be confusing or misleading, but the new law would provide no protection from liability if a business deliberately lied or sold products that failed because of Y2K.

In Western Europe the European Commission issued a 25-page report warning that efforts to solve Y2K in many European Union members were insufficient, particularly in terms of the cross-border cooperation needed to be ready by 2000. The British government, with projected costs exceeding $656 million, announced that its armed forces would be prepared in time and would provide assistance to local police if utilities, transportation systems, or emergency services failed. Many other countries, notably Asian nations suffering from the ongoing economic crisis and small or geographically isolated countries, were thought to be less well prepared. It was uncertain how this would affect the tightly integrated world economy and physical infrastructure. In mid-December 1998 the UN convened its first international conference on Y2K in an attempt to share information and crisis-management efforts. Worldwide the year 2000 problem could cost as much as $300 billion to $600 billion, according to the Gartner Group, a Connecticut computer industry market research firm.

(STEVE ALEXANDER)

Earth Sciences

GEOLOGY AND GEOCHEMISTRY

The interrelatedness of Earth processes was a motif for 1998. The German Geological Society, under the leadership of Peter Neumann-Mahlkau, celebrated its 150th anniversary with a symposium on "The System Earth." Again, the role of convection in the Earth's interior geology and the geochemistry of lavas was elegantly illustrated in a physical model developed by Michael Gurnis (California Institute of Technology), R. Dietmar Muller (University of Sydney, Australia), and Louis Moresi (Australian Geodynamics Cooperative Research Centre, Nedlands) on problems related to the sedimentary rocks of Australia and properties of the oceanic spreading ridge between Australia and Antarctica.

The stratigraphic record of sedimentary rocks revealed that broad regions of Australia underwent vertical motion during the Cretaceous Period. These movements varied from a condition of maximum flooding by seas 120 million–110 million years ago to minimum flooding 80 million–70 million years ago. By the end of the Cretaceous (66 million years ago), Australia was about 250 m (820 ft) higher than it is today. These movements are out of phase with the global sea-level variations, because Australia was high and dry when the sea level throughout the world was at a maximum. The deepest part of the global oceanic ridge system is on the Australia-Antarctica spreading ridge. Its low elevation is believed to be due to an unexplained cold spot, possibly a downwelling. The basalts along this ridge have two distinct isotopic provinces, one to the west of the cold spot, characteristic of the Indian Ocean basalts, and one to the east, like the Pacific Ocean basalts.

The investigators developed a three-dimensional model of mantle convection, including the known history of plate tectonics near Australia. Two tectonic plates had been converging near eastern Australia through 100 million years before the Cretaceous. The model explored the consequences of the subduction beneath Australia of the cold lithosphere slab to the west, from 130 million years ago to the present, with the geometrical arrangement of the tectonic plates being adjusted in steps of 10 million years. The subducted slab passed beneath Australia during the Cretaceous, stagnated in the mantle near a depth of 670 km (415 mi), and is now rising up to the Southeast Indian Ridge. For a reasonable range of input values, the dynamic models explained the two unusual geologic and geochemical features, the inferred inundation and uplift of Australia, and the isotope geochemistry of the Australian-Antarctic ridge basalts. This successful modeling of the consequences of mantle convection, including plate motions, was a significant step forward in connecting the Earth's internal motions with surface geology and geochemistry.

New discoveries were made during the year concerning the exchanges that occur between the solid earth and seawater. The formation of continents begins, effectively, with the eruption of new basaltic lava from the Earth's mantle at the mid-oceanic ridges.

The northern Afghan village of Angaryan lies in ruins after being hit by an earthquake of magnitude 6.9 on May 30. The earthquake, one of two that rocked the Afghanistan-Tajikistan border in 1998, killed as many as 5,000 persons and injured thousands more.

The geology of the ocean floor and the geochemistry of the lavas are coupled with the convective motions occurring within the mantle beneath the ridges. The oceanic ridge system is the largest geologic formation on Earth, and the discovery in 1979 of submarine hydrothermal vents associated with the ridges revealed that they are probably also the most active formations in terms of hydrology. Circulation of ocean water through the rifted basalt, heated by the magma below, causes the exchange of many elements between the ocean and crust, and solutions heated to temperatures of up to 350° C (660° F) precipitate clouds of metallic sulfide minerals, giving them the appearance of "black smokers" as they emerge through fissures into the cold ocean. The chimneys of minerals and rock precipitated by the venting solutions contain geochemical and biological information that is difficult to sample from deep-ocean submersibles. During the summer of 1998, therefore, a team from the University of Washington and the American Museum of Natural History hauled four complete rock chimneys from the Juan de Fuca Ridge to a ship for study in the laboratory. A revisit two weeks later to install instruments at the site of one of the removed chimneys found that a new one had already grown 4.5 m (15 ft) high. The tallest chimney yet observed on the ocean floor was 43 m (140 ft) high.

The discovery of thriving sunlight-deprived bacterial colonies on these hot, lava-derived chemical precipitates, nourished by the chemosynthesis of sulfur, fostered the idea that life on the Earth and other planets may have begun in similar environments. John Holloway at Arizona State University constructed a large experimental apparatus to simulate the hydrothermal vents. In 1998 his pressurized experiments were producing a tiny black smoker in a tank of cool saltwater, precipitating sulfides and other minerals. The object of the experiment was to find out if the reactions, originally free of life-forms, produce organic chemicals, the ingredients of life.

The oceanic crust, partially hydrated by the circulating ocean water at the mid-ocean ridges, is eventually carried back into the Earth's interior at subduction zones, where the oceanic lithosphere penetrates to depths of at least 670 km (415 mi). The subducted rock is heated as it descends, and the water driven off participates in the generation of the explosive arc volcanoes associated with subduction, such as those in the Ring of Fire encircling the Pacific Ocean. *Geotimes* in 1998 reviewed some current experiments and ideas related to the experimental formation of hydrated minerals at high pressures and temperatures corresponding to 400 km (250 mi) or deeper within the Earth. Such minerals have the potential to store subducted water if any water escapes the melting process and volcanism and is carried deeper into the Earth. Maarten J. de Wit (University of Cape Town) outlined a process relating water at mid-ocean ridges and subducted slabs to the volume of ocean water. If more water is carried down in subduction than is released in arc volcanism, the sea level will fall. If the mid-ocean ridges are thus exposed, hydration of the ocean crust will be less efficient and less water will be available for subduction, which could later lead to a net flux of water from mantle back to the ocean. Such a mechanism could possibly regulate the volume of the oceans.

Study of the diversity and extinctions of species requires correlation between the geologic record containing fossils and the geochemical study of minerals that has made it possible to date the ages of rocks. Samuel A. Bowring (Massachusetts Institute of Technology) and Douglas H. Erwin (National Museum of Natural History, Washington, D.C.) reported in 1998 that the integration of detailed paleontology and

high-resolution uranium-lead geochronology "has revolutionized our knowledge of several important episodes in geological history." The geologic approach is to find fossiliferous sedimentary rocks interlayered with volcanic rocks, after which geochemists use mass spectrometers to measure the isotopic ratios of uranium and lead in zircons separated from the lavas or volcanic ash beds. The combination of high-precision geochronology and detailed field studies produced remarkable results. Uranium-lead dating of the mineral zircon can now define zircon ages with uncertainties of less than one million years. This precision is available for zircons in the age range of 200 million–600 million years, which includes the beginning of the Cambrian Period and the Cambrian explosion of life represented by the abrupt appearance of a wide range of fossils. On the basis of these studies, the age of the beginning of the Cambrian was determined to be younger than it had been according to the classical time scales. It was considered to be 590 million years in 1982 and 570 million years in 1983, and in 1998 it was reduced to 543 million years.

This precision in dating was also permitting the determination of the rates of evolution of species. It was demonstrated that the Cambrian explosion of life was much faster than previously recognized, lasting no more than 10 million years. Among the several known mass extinctions of life-forms, the disappearance of dinosaurs and many contemporary species from the fossil record 65 million years ago is the most familiar. Most scientists now believe that this extinction was caused by climatic changes associated with the impact of an asteroid, a meteorite, or a comet, about 10 km (6 mi) in diameter, into the ocean and underlying sedimentary rocks near Yucatán in Mexico.

There are, however, proponents for the argument that massive volcanic eruptions, as exemplified by the Deccan Traps of India, caused the climatic changes. The most severe mass extinction occurred at the end of the Paleozoic Era, now dated at 251 million years ago. At that time 85% of all marine species, about 70% of land vertebrates, and many plants and insects disappeared. Using high-precision mass spectrometry, researchers were able to show that the extinction occurred in less than one million years, a much shorter time than had previously been assumed. The cause of the extinction remained unresolved, but this discovery placed constraints on the kinds of processes that might have been responsible, such as the aggregation of the supercontinent of Pangaea, glaciation or global warming, volcanic eruption of excessive carbon dioxide into the atmosphere, or impact by an extraterrestrial body.   (PETER JOHN WYLLIE)

GEOPHYSICS

On Jan. 10, 1998, a magnitude-6.2 earthquake in northern China killed at least 50 people, injured at least 11,500, and left 44,000 homeless. Resulting fires added to the total destruction, reported to have been 70,000 houses destroyed or badly damaged. There was also some damage to the Great Wall in Hubei province. Two other shocks notable for their severity were one of magnitude 6.1, on February 4 on the Afghanistan-Tajikistan border, and one of magnitude 6.9, which struck the same area

on May 30. The first resulted in the deaths of more than 4,000 persons, injured 818, destroyed 8,094 homes, and killed more than 6,700 livestock. The second was even more destructive, killing as many as 5,000 and injuring many thousands. Extensive landslides contributed to the catastrophes.

These earthquakes were located in almost real time by the U.S. Geological Survey (USGS) in Golden, Colo. This service, which began in 1928, made a major leap forward in 1958 when a rudimentary program was developed to calculate earthquake epicenters by computer, and it made another in the early 1960s when the U.S. government developed and deployed standard seismograph systems to 125 sites around the globe. Although it had been continually upgraded and modernized, the network provided only a portion of the data used in the location process. One of the items tabulated was the number of station reports used in each determination. This number frequently reached 200 and for a very large shock exceeded 500. The USGS routinely located 15,000–20,000 events each year. The depth, seismic moment, several types of magnitude, and other factors were included with each epicentre.

In spite of the large number of active stations, there were areas of the Earth that were not well covered because its surface is about 70% water. To help alleviate this problem, the Scripps Institution of Oceanography, La Jolla, Calif., and the Woods Hole (Mass.) Oceanographic Institution formed an international group, the Ocean Seismic Network. They planned to install 20 permanent ocean-bottom seismometers in remote locations to augment data from existing stations. In 1998, with funding from the Ocean Drilling Program and the National Science Foundation, scientists successfully installed a pilot station south of Hawaii that included a seismometer in a borehole, a broadband seismometer on the ocean floor, and another in the bottom mud. The stations were designed to include magnetometers, acoustic arrays, climate and ocean current instruments, and tsunami (tidal wave) detectors.

Studies during the year were aimed at determining the nature of the upwelling of melt materials of the undersea mantle beneath the East Pacific Rise. The Mantle Electromagnetic and Tomography Experiment, funded by the U.S. National Science Foundation, engaged scientists from nine institutions from around the world. Fifty-one ocean-bottom seismometers were deployed in the region, where the plates were spreading at a rate of 15 cm (6 in) per year, among the fastest anywhere on the Earth. After researchers gathered seismic data for six months, an array of more than 40 instruments that measured the electromagnetic fields generated in the Earth by particle currents in the ionosphere was installed, and data from the instruments were gathered for another year. The detection of slow seismic velocities across the array indicated the existence and concentration of melt materials and passive, plate-driven flow, and the conductivity measurements revealed whether the melt areas were connected. The melt distribution was found to be asymmetrical, with a concentration to the west of the crest of the East Pacific Rise. This seemed to indicate that the magma forms over a relatively broad area and then is concentrated to go to the

surface along the narrow ridge to form crust. Investigators were not sure whether the asymmetry was due to thermal structure or geologic composition.

The well-defined seismic discontinuity at a depth of 410 km (255 mi) was widely believed to be due to a high-pressure phase change in olivine, but recent studies revealed that the increase in velocity in some areas was too large to be explained by that mechanism. Two scientists from Ehime University, Matsuyama, Japan, postulated that the problem was in the assumption of a fixed composition for olivine. They concluded that olivine must, in varying degrees, exchange its iron and magnesium in the mantle such as garnet majorite. In this manner the olivine would become denser and sustain a higher velocity.

Volcanoes had long been recognized as prone to landslides because of the relatively unconsolidated materials that form their slopes, but it was usually assumed that an eruption was required before the slopes would give way. Recently, however, researchers at Open University in the U.K. discovered that an eruption is not necessary. While studying a long-dormant volcano in Nicaragua, Benjamin van Wyk de Vries found that two conditions make a volcano susceptible to such slides. First, the crevices must be filled with hot acidic gas, which weakens the rocks. Second, the weight of the mountain tends to push the weakened material outward at the base. This is usually a gradual, evenly distributed ring of material around the base, but if the terrain is such that the force is directed asymmetrically, an avalanche may occur. Since dormant volcanoes were not monitored, de Vries feared that many populated areas of the world were in unrecognized danger of landslides.

The Tsunami Warning System, centred on Oahu in Hawaii, was founded by the U.S. Coast and Geodetic Survey after the devastating wave produced by the magnitude-7.8 Aleutian earthquake on April 1, 1946. The effectiveness of the system depended on the difference between the velocity of the sea wave, up to 965 km/h (600 mph), and the seismic wave velocities, ranging up to 29,000 km/h (18,000 mph). Through timely reporting of seismograph readings from stations of the international circum-Pacific network, large shocks could be located in minutes, and, if the epicentre was in an area where a tsunami might be generated, warnings could be issued to all points. This system worked well many times and saved hundreds of lives. Since only a small percentage of likely large shocks produce tsunamis, however, there was a problem with false alarms. To reduce this problem a network of tide stations was queried to determine whether a wave had actually been generated. This method was time-consuming, however, and its effectiveness was limited by communications difficulties.

The National Oceanic and Atmospheric Administration had by 1998 begun to set up a supporting network of ocean-bottom pressure recorders and seismic detectors in several areas believed likely to generate tsunamis. The data from these instruments were to be used to develop methods of detecting and locating tsunamis in real time and thus allow more warning time and the calculation of more exact arrival times and wave heights.

The Ocean Drilling Program (ODP) continued its long-term objectives of establishing the history of sea-level change and its influence on sedimentation. ODP Leg 174A began drilling 129 km (80 mi) east of Atlantic City, N.J. Some 800 cores were obtained and then submitted for laboratory studies. The information was then to be combined with the oxygen isotopic record. The coordinated analyses of these data were expected to provide a more accurate history of global sea-level change.   (RUTLAGE J. BRAZEE)

METEOROLOGY AND CLIMATE

The strong El Niño begun in 1997 continued into the first few months of 1998 before abruptly fading. A cold episode, La Niña, developed during the last half of the year. El Niño made an impact on weather over many parts of the world early in 1998, contributing to heavy winter rains in California and Florida, drought in Mexico and Central America, and floods and drought in South America. Widespread above-normal ocean temperatures contributed to the unusual warmth recorded over much of the globe. Preliminary data from land and ocean temperature observations through August indicated that 1998 would be the warmest year on record.

During winter 1997–98 numerous Pacific storms affected California, causing floods

and landslides. Heavy rains and severe weather struck the southeastern U.S., especially Florida, into the spring. A historic outbreak of tornadoes on February 23 took 42 lives in Florida. Another outbreak killed 39 in Georgia and Alabama on April 8–9, with the majority of deaths from one F5 twister (winds over 418 km/h [260 mph]) near Birmingham, Ala., killing 32. Northward displacement of the northern jet stream brought mild weather to the Midwest and Northeast, which resulted in a dearth of snow in low-elevation areas. Washington, D.C.'s 1997–98 snowfall total of 0.25 cm (0.1 in) tied that of 1972–73 as the lowest on record. The relative warmth contributed, however, to one of the worst ice storms of the century in upstate New York, northern New England, and eastern Canada during January. It left more than two million homes and businesses without power and caused tremendous damage to utilities and trees. The weather in the southern U.S. changed markedly in the spring as warm and dry conditions spread northward from Mexico. A severe drought contributed to a record number of wildfires in Florida from late May into early July. Despite scattered heavy rains in July, April–July rainfall was the lowest in more than 100 years in Florida. Texas and Louisiana also recorded the driest April–July ever. Extreme heat aggravated the drought, with June–July temperatures

High-voltage towers near St-Bruno, Quebec, show extensive damage from a severe ice storm that swept through eastern Canada and the northeastern U.S. in early January. At least 20 persons died in the storm, and more than three million homes were without power, some for as long as two weeks.

averaging the highest on record in Texas, Louisiana, and Florida. Tropical rains in August and September finally broke the drought in Texas and, to a lesser extent, Oklahoma, with agricultural losses estimated at $4 billion in those two states alone.

The 1998 Atlantic tropical cyclone season was active, highlighted by the rampage of Hurricanes Georges and Mitch through the Caribbean and eastern Gulf of Mexico. The Caribbean track of Georges on September 20–25 cost more than 400 lives and left more than 100,000 homeless, mainly on Hispaniola, where some mountainous locations recorded over 500 mm (20 in) of rain. Georges crossed the Florida Keys into the Gulf of Mexico on September 25, hitting the Mississippi coast three days later.

A scant month later Georges was dwarfed by Mitch, one of the deadliest hurricanes of the 20th century, which reached Category Five on October 26. Blocked from moving northward by a strong front, Mitch hung off the coast of Honduras for four days, causing torrents of rain (as much as 600 mm [2 ft] a day) that in turn caused catastrophic flooding and mudslides. End-of-the-year figures listed 9,021 dead in five Central American countries (most in Honduras and Nicaragua), one million homeless, another million persons affected, and the infrastructures of the worst-hit countries devastated.

In Mexico torrential rains, exceeding 400 mm (16 in) during September 6–12, triggered massive flooding in Chiapas. Mud slides and swollen rivers cut off 400,000 people. In contrast, during the first half of the year, fires abetted by drought consumed forests and grasslands on hundreds of thousands of hectares across Mexico and Central America. Drought affected northeastern Brazil during the first half of the year, but storms and floods killed hundreds and caused widespread damage in coastal Ecuador and Peru from November 1997 to May 1998. In February alone more than 700 mm (28 in) of rain inundated northern Peru's coast. Heavy rains from January to April caused major flooding in Argentina, Paraguay, Uruguay, and Brazil.

In South Asia the southwest monsoon produced catastrophic floods during the summer, killing more than 2,000 in India and over 1,000 in Bangladesh. In addition, a tropical cyclone packing 185-km/h (115-mph) winds and over 125 mm (5 in) of rain struck northwestern India on June 9, killing more than 600. In China heavy rains emptying into the Chang Jiang (Yangtze River) caused extensive flooding during July and August, resulting in more than 2,000 deaths. Along parts of the Chang Jiang from February 1 to August 18, over 2,000 mm (79 in) of rain fell, more than twice the normal amount. Summer floods struck northeastern China and South Korea; September typhoons battered Japan and flooded the Philippines. El Niño-related heat and dryness affected Indonesia, Malaysia, and the Philippines during the first part of the year, producing widespread smoke and haze. Summer drought hurt crops in Kazakstan and parts of Russia, and July–August heat and dryness led to a rash of fires in the Russian Far East, where August rainfall totaled less than 25% of the normal amount.

In Africa heavy rains in January caused flooding in Kenya. Drier weather early in the year, however, relieved flooding in Somalia, where torrential rains during

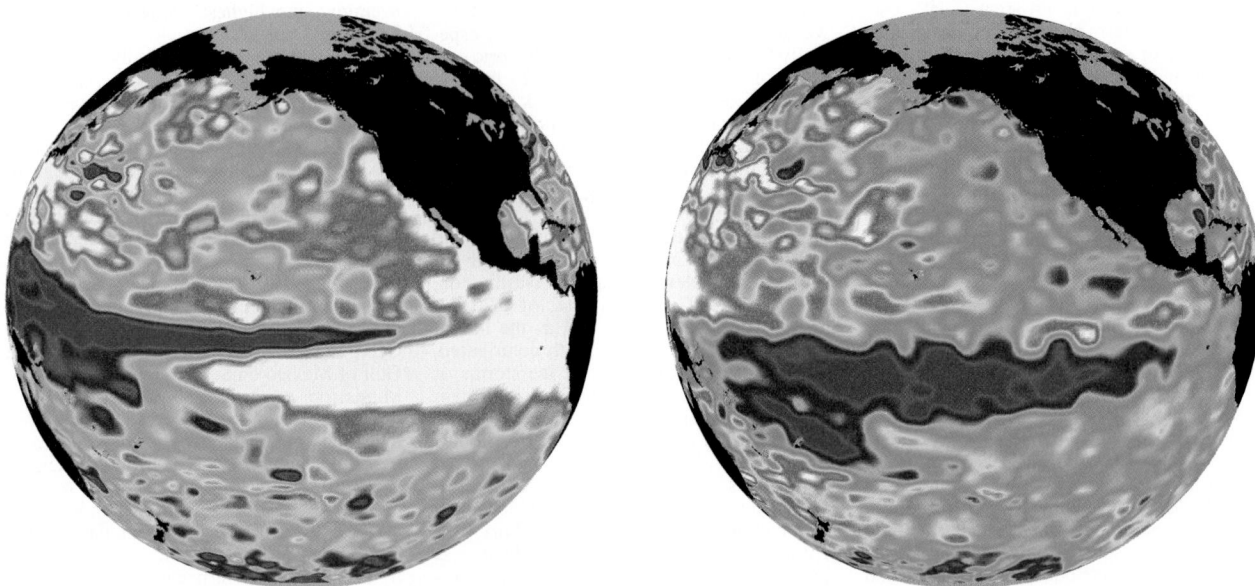

The signature of El Niño stands out in a November 1997 satellite image (left) depicting patterns of heat storage in the surface water of the Pacific Ocean. An abnormal warm-water pool in the eastern Pacific is delineated by the red and white areas. In a November 1998 satellite image (right) La Niña dominates, with the purple area indicating an abnormal cold-water pool.

JPL/NASA

October–December 1997 had inundated large parts of the south.

(JOHN J. KELLY, JR.)

OCEANOGRAPHY

After the strongest El Niño since 1982–83 in 1997, the equatorial Pacific upper ocean by early 1998 had begun to cool from the anomalously warm levels of the previous year. Instead of simply returning to normal conditions, however, equatorial Pacific sea-surface temperatures continued to decline until they were several degrees below the long-term average. El Niño thus was replaced by La Niña, a condition that is in many ways its reverse. As a result, climate-related matters continued to dominate oceanographic research as well as marine and coastal resource management during 1998.

Under normal circumstances Pacific equatorial trade winds blow from the east and are particularly strong in the eastern Pacific. On account of the Earth's rotation, these strong winds force surface waters both northward and southward away from the Equator. Colder water upwells from depths of many tens of metres to replace the poleward-flowing surface water, so that a tongue of cold surface water extends thousands of kilometres westward of South America along the Equator. The trade winds normally extend well into the western Pacific, but there they are usually weaker than in the east. The upper ocean is much warmer in the western than in the eastern Pacific, and the warm layer is thick, so that upwelling normally does not bring cold water to the surface. The result is that in the western Pacific the warm surface water evaporates into the atmosphere. When the warm and moist air reaches moderate elevations, the moisture condenses as rainfall. The far western Pacific is thus normally a region of widespread and intense rainfall.

During an El Niño the trade winds weaken or even reverse, and eastern Pacific

equatorial upwelling ceases so that the entire equatorial eastern Pacific Ocean is several degrees warmer than the long-term average. The region of rising moist air normally found in the western Pacific migrates eastward into the central tropical Pacific. The normally wet far western Pacific thus becomes a region of low rainfall and even drought, whereas the rainfall at normally temperate central tropical Pacific islands increases dramatically. Tropical storms in the Pacific are more frequent and occur over larger areas of the ocean during an El Niño.

In the La Niña that developed during 1998, the trade winds were strong, and the sea-surface temperature in the eastern equatorial Pacific was several degrees below the long-term mean. In Indonesia, in the far western Pacific, the drought and accompanying forest fires of 1997 were replaced by heavy rains that caused flash floods and mud slides.

Among the most important oceanic effects of an El Niño are changes in sea level. During much of 1997, for example, the sea level along the coasts of Peru-Ecuador and of southern California was 15–25 cm (6–10 in) above the long-term average. Part of this was attributable to the thermal expansion of the anomalously warm surface waters, but changes in the pattern of ocean currents also played a role. In 1998 researchers carried out a study spanning much of the eastern north Pacific to determine the relative importance of these two effects. The temperature of the water from top to bottom was monitored by measuring the time required for sound waves emitted from an acoustic transmitter located atop a seamount on the seafloor about 100 km (60 mi) west of San Francisco to reach receiving stations located across the Pacific to the west and southwest. Travel times were measured from December 1995 through March 1997. Because the speed of sound in water depends on the water temperature, such times could be used to estimate the heat content of the entire water column over

much of the northeastern Pacific during that time. Ocean currents were reconstructed from a combination of traditional measurements at sea and satellite measurements of the deviation of the sea surface from the shape it would assume if there were no currents (the geoid). Such measurements had been carried out routinely since 1992 by the Topex/Poseidon altimetric satellite. In order to make the best use of the physical understanding of the dynamics of ocean currents, all these observations were used as inputs into a numerical model of Pacific Ocean currents, and the model then constructed the current system that was most compatible with both the observations and physical theory. The result was that only about half of the seasonal and year-to-year changes in sea level are due to thermal expansion of the water; the rest result from shifts in the pattern of ocean currents.

During 1998 researchers continued to study possible oceanic effects on climate patterns over timescales of years to thousands of years. Deep-sea sediment cores revealed that millennial-scale climate shifts as documented in, for example, ice cores from Greenland were accompanied by changes in the rate of sinking of water from the surface in the far north Atlantic. A somewhat similar process may be important in modulating the strength and frequency of El Niño episodes. The temperature of surface waters in the northwestern Pacific and Atlantic is set by wintertime air-sea interactions. These waters sink below the surface and are carried to the Equator by the large-scale circulation, where, years afterward, they may affect the surface temperature and, consequently, the strength of the trade winds. Spurred by this possibility, researchers concentrated on reconstructing the pathways and travel times of such upper-ocean water masses, using numerical models of the circulation constrained by shipboard and satellite observations.

(MYRL C. HENDERSHOTT)

Economic Affairs

From the beginning of 1998, prospects for the world economy were marked by uncertainty as the Asian crisis that began in July 1997 with the collapse of the Thai baht deepened. (*See* Spotlight: *The Troubled World Economy*.) As the year progressed, it was clear that the effects of the recession in Japan and the repercussions of the financial crisis in East and Southeast Asian countries were worse than expected, although both Thailand and South Korea were showing strong signs of recovery. Because of the deterioration, the International Monetary Fund (IMF) revised its projections for world growth in 1998 to 2%, only half the level it was projecting a year earlier. (*See* Special Report.)

By September—in the wake of the August financial collapse in Russia, which caused a general retreat by investors from all emerging markets—the financial turbulence was spreading to the developed countries of the Organisation for Economic Co-operation and Development (OECD). Stock markets were falling, and trading losses were being made by some of the world's largest investment funds. Interest rates in the U.S., the U.K., and much of continental Europe were reduced. In Japan new legislation was adopted, supported by ¥60 trillion to recapitalize and reform the banking system. Many less-developed country (LDC) currencies came under severe pressure, which forced further drops in commodity prices. The lack of investor confidence created particular problems in LDCs, given their limited access to external capital.

During the year output in the major industrialized countries rose 2%, compared with 3.1% in 1997. The overall picture was distorted, however, by the recession in Japan, where a marked deterioration in the first half of the year led to a 2.5% decline, compared with a marginal rise in 1997. In

the newly industrializing economies such as South Korea, Taiwan, Hong Kong, and Singapore, there was an even sharper fall of 2.9% after a 6% increase in 1997. The American economy was extremely buoyant, particularly in the first half of the year, when it appeared to be overheating, and output increased 3.5%, which was only slightly below 1997 growth. Strong domestic demand provided the impetus for growth in the U.S. as it did in the European Union (EU), where output increased from 2.7% in 1997 to 2.9% in 1998. This included a 2.3% rise in the U.K., which was at a much more advanced stage in the economic cycle than France and Germany. Output in Central and Eastern Europe accelerated to 3.4% in 1998 from 2.8%, but only Poland, Slovenia, and Slovakia regained their 1989 levels of output; most were well below it. The 6% decline in Russia was the cause of a slight overall decline in output in the formerly centrally planned economies.

The growth rate of output in LDCs fell back from 8% in 1997 to 2.3% in 1998. Contributing to the increase was a 3.7% rise in Africa, where financial restructuring continued and good weather boosted agricultural output in some countries, whereas others benefited or suffered from falling

commodity prices and strengthening demand in Europe. Lower output in the Middle East (2.3%) and in Latin America (2.8%) was closely linked to the slump in oil prices. Holding down growth in output to 1.8% in Asia were Thailand, Malaysia, Indonesia, and the Philippines, where there was a decline of more than 10%. In Indonesia output in the third quarter was running at 17% below that of the same period a year earlier. By contrast, China, which retained its currency link with the U.S. dollar, and Taiwan showed more resilience.

The volume of world trade in goods and services grew more slowly in 1998—by 3.7%, compared with 9.7% in 1997. In value terms, export growth was similar to 1997, reflecting the fall in oil and other nonfuel commodities. Despite the difficult trading conditions, the trend toward opening up multilateral, regional, and unilateral markets was maintained. At the end of 1997, agreement was reached by 70 members of the World Trade Organization (WTO) to further liberalize financial services. The members, which represented 95% of global markets and included some of the East Asian countries most affected by the financial crisis, agreed to open up their financial markets. At the WTO meeting in May, the commitment to liberalization of markets was reinforced when governments rejected protectionism.

In much of the world, the problem and fear of inflation receded as the year progressed. In most advanced countries price rises eased gradually throughout the year. Although the average inflation rate for these countries was projected at 2%, compared with 3.1% in 1997, consumer prices were falling in several countries in the last months of the year. Concern about inflation was being superseded by the growing fears of deflation—and the associated risk of recession—over which governments could exercise little control.

In a crucial development that had as-yet-unclear implications for the world economy, 11 EU countries—Austria, Belgium, Finland, France, Germany, Ireland, Italy, Luxembourg, The Netherlands, Portugal, and Spain—were preparing their economies for the final stage of economic and monetary union (EMU). This was to culminate on Jan. 1, 1999, with the replacement of national currencies by a new currency, the euro. Monetary control was to move to the European Central Bank (ECB), which would set a single interest rate for the 11 countries. The four other members of the EU—Denmark, Greece, Sweden, and the U.K.—were not adopting the euro, at least for the time being.

Table I. Real Gross Domestic Products of Selected OECD Countries
% annual change

Country	1994	1995	1996	1997	1998[1]
United States	3.5	2.0	2.8	3.8	2.7
Japan	0.6	1.5	3.9	0.9	-0.3
Germany	2.7	1.8	1.4	2.2	2.7
France	2.8	2.1	1.5	2.4	2.9
Italy	2.2	2.9	0.7	1.5	2.4
United Kingdom	4.3	2.7	2.2	3.3	1.7
Canada	3.9	2.2	1.2	3.8	3.3
All developed countries	2.9	2.2	2.8	3.1	2.4
Seven major countries above	2.8	2.0	2.5	2.8	2.1
European Union	2.9	2.5	1.7	2.6	2.7

[1]Estimated.
Source: OECD.

Table II. Consumer Prices in OECD Countries
% change from preceding year

Country	1994	1995	1996	1997	1998[1]
United States	2.6	2.8	2.9	2.3	1.6
Japan	0.7	-0.1	0.1	1.7	0.4
Germany	2.7	1.8	1.5	1.8	1.0
France	1.7	1.7	2.0	1.2	0.7
Italy	3.9	5.4	3.8	1.8	1.7
United Kingdom	2.5	3.4	2.4	3.1	2.6
Canada	0.2	2.2	1.6	1.6	1.2
Austria	3.0	2.2	1.9	1.3	1.1
Belgium	2.4	1.5	2.1	1.6	1.0
Denmark	2.0	2.1	2.1	2.2	1.9
Finland	1.1	1.0	0.6	1.2	1.5
Greece	10.9	8.9	8.2	5.5	4.8
Iceland	1.6	1.7	2.3	1.8	2.2
Ireland	2.3	2.5	1.7	1.4	2.8
Luxembourg	2.2	1.9	1.4	1.4	1.6
Netherlands, The	2.8	1.9	2.0	2.2	1.8
Norway	1.4	2.5	1.3	2.6	2.3
Portugal	5.2	4.1	3.1	2.2	2.7
Spain	4.7	4.7	3.6	2.0	1.9
Sweden	2.4	2.9	0.8	0.5	0.5
Switzerland	0.9	1.8	0.8	0.5	0.1
Turkey	105.1	89.1	80.4	85.7	84.7
Australia	1.9	4.6	2.6	0.3	1.7
New Zealand	1.8	3.8	2.3	1.2	1.6
Total OECD	5.0	5.9	4.2	4.7	—

Sources: OECD, [1]World Bank.

NATIONAL ECONOMIC POLICIES

United States. Once again the U.S. led growth among the major industrial countries. For the seventh year in succession, the U.S. had exceeded by far the increase in output of most other advanced countries. The IMF projected rise in gross domestic product (GDP) was 3.5%, but with higher-than-expected third-quarter output, it could be slightly more. In any event, it was expected to be close to the 3.9% recorded in 1997. The strength of the economic performance was reflected in the achievement of the first balanced federal budget since 1960; it followed an unexpected fall in the 1997 deficit to $23 billion. The need to cut the deficit had become a political imperative since it peaked at $290 billion in fiscal 1992, but eliminating it before fiscal 2000 had not been thought possible.

The momentum continued to be driven by consumer spending, which accounted for some two-thirds of economic activity and showed few signs of slowing over the year. In the third quarter it was rising at an annual rate of 4.1%. The fact that spending was exceeding earnings in September and October raised some concerns. The personal savings rate (savings as a share of after-tax income) fell by 0.3% in those two months as Americans took advantage of falling interest rates through cheaper credit or drew on their savings or other assets. In the first quarter, when GDP was rising at an annual rate of 4.2%, retail sales advanced 3.3%, housing demand was buoyant, and cars and small trucks were selling at the rate of 14 million a year. The second quarter showed even more activity, with retail sales increasing by 6.3% over a year earlier. By November consumer spending had not fallen in any month since June 1996.

Consumer demand was being fueled by the strong growth in personal incomes, high employment, and low inflation. The tighter labour market forced employers to increase compensation at a faster rate than inflation in order to retain and attract employees. Wages and salaries rose by 4% in the year to end September, the fastest rate for seven years, easing back slightly to 3.1% in the three months to November before it rose again in December. New job creation was helped by the flexibility in the labour market; relative to labour conditions in Europe, American minimum wages and social benefits were low, and fewer members of the labour force were unionized. In 1998, for the first time, American manufacturing workers cost more than those in Spain while remaining ahead of Canada and Italy. There were, however, signs of an easing in the tight labour market during the second half of the year. The average rate of unemployment continued the annual downward trend that began in 1992 (7.5%). The unemployment rate edged up from a 29-year low of 4.3% in May and was holding at 4.6% through to October. It fell back again, to 4.4% in November and 4.3% in December, boosted by holiday recruitment in the retail sector and in the buoyant construction sector. The number of new jobs being created also declined from an average 244,000 a month in the first half of the year to 165,000 in the third quarter and in the fourth quarter.

Nevertheless, consumer confidence was only slightly dented. After falling for four months from the June peak, it recovered again in November (according to the Department of Trade Conference Board). The housing market remained buoyant, with construction in the third quarter rising at an annual rate of 9%. The amount of consumer credit was cause for some concern because Americans appeared to be living beyond their means. In September, when consumer installment credit was $8.4 billion and rising at an annual rate of 7.9%, spending exceeded saving for the first time since records began in the 1930s. Despite the strength of consumer demand, inflation was no longer considered a problem as the price stability achieved in 1997 (when the average inflation rate was 2.3%) continued. In November 1998 consumer prices were up only 1.5%, and the lower GDP deflator at 0.8% was the lowest for 35 years.

Although household expenditure remained buoyant, there were signs of a slowdown in areas affected by global trade. Industrial output rose by only 1.5% in the 12 months ending in November, although the latest three months showed some acceleration (up 2.4%). Factory orders for big-ticket goods declined in October for the first time in five months, a reflection of weaker demand for industrial hardware, railroad equipment, ships, and primary metals. The key indicator of spending on new equipment used in manufacture (nondefense capital goods excluding aircraft) fell 9.2% in October, the largest drop since November 1990, when the U.S. was in recession. The falloff in demand was also reflected in factory shipments of durable goods.

Because of the strength of the economy and the risk of its overheating, federal policy remained tight for the first three quarters. Until August policy makers had been ready to raise interest rates, but this changed as the impact of the global slowdown became apparent. For the first time in 40 years, export sales fell for three consecutive quarters while imports rose. The October deficit fell to $14.2 billion as export sales of farm products shot up. Nevertheless, the trade deficit with Pacific Rim countries in the first 10 months of the year was up by 34% to $134 billion. The uncertainty generated by the external factors and fears that the domestic economy could slow down led the monetary authorities to cut the target Fed Funds rate three times from September 29, each time by 0.25 percentage point, down to 4.75%.

United Kingdom. The economy started the year on a high note. Indicators reflected the buoyancy built up over the previous five years, when annual growth in output exceeded the long-term trend rate of 2.25%. During the year common EU statistical practices were being adopted, and—among other changes—all the national accounts were rebased. The revisions to historical economic indicators showed that the annual average increase in real GDP since 1991 was 0.25 percentage point higher than previously calculated. On this basis the 1997 increase output rose from 3.4% to 3.5%. As 1998 progressed, however, the economy lost momentum—not least because of the deterioration in the international economy—and the increase in 1998 output was expected to decline to 2.8%. By year's end business confidence had fallen, and a short period of recession was being widely predicted, with growth in 1999 not expected to exceed 1%.

Economic growth was led by the domestic economy, which was less vulnerable than the trade sector to the effects of the strong pound and the weak demand in Asian and other LDCs. Consumer demand and business investment provided the main impetus in the first half of the year. By the third quarter, however, it was clear that growth in consumer demand was slowing down. Retail sales growth eased over the year and in September and October fell compared with one year earlier, although it unexpectedly recovered in November. Turnover in the housing market declined further from the 1.4 million units in 1997, but prices remained high because of supply shortage. Business investment remained buoyant in the early part of the year and was likely to increase

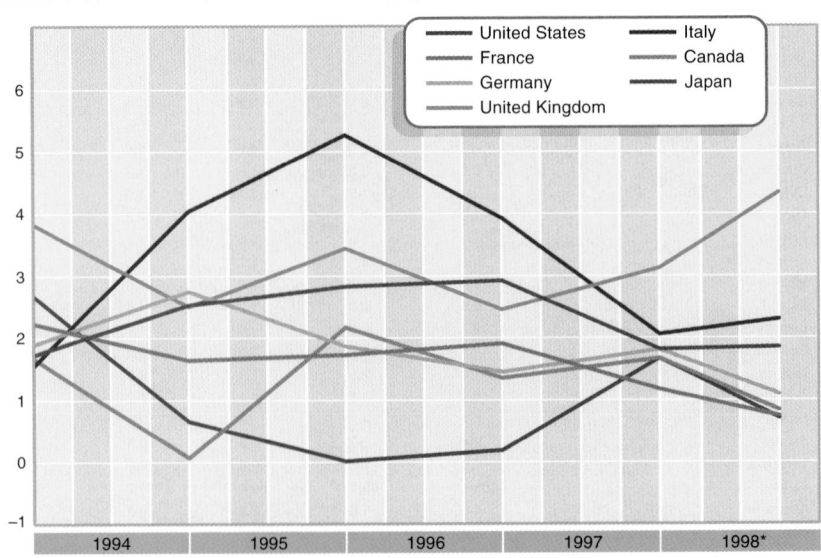

Inflation Rate
(percentage change from December to December)

Legend: United States, France, Germany, United Kingdom, Italy, Canada, Japan

1994   1995   1996   1997   1998*

*Percentage change from October 1997 to October 1998.
Source: International Monetary Fund, *International Financial Statistics.*

by up to 8% over the year. It was expected to slow down in response to lower profits. The dominant service sector, accounting for 60% of output, outperformed the rest of the British economy, but by the second quarter the growth rate had eased despite continuing strong demand in the transportation and telecommunications sectors. Manufacturing accounted for only 20% of output but was a major consumer of services. Demand for business services grew more slowly, a reflection of the slowdown in demand from manufacturers.

There were a number of positive developments during the year. The rate of inflation was more the result of external factors than actions by the Bank of England's Monetary Policy Committee (MPC), which was responsible for managing interest rates to facilitate an economic growth rate compatible with low inflation. The MPC benchmark was 2.25%, growth above which was perceived to be inflationary. Given the effect of the slowdown of global demand, however, this approach looked too simplistic. Fears of inflation were being superseded by uncertainty created by the less-familiar prospect of deflation.

Consumer prices were expected to have risen by 2.7% (excluding mortgage payments) in 1998, the same rate as in 1997. The annual rate rose above 3% in April and May as a result of increases in local tax and road-fuel excise duties and seasonal food prices. As the effects of indirect taxes diminished, the rate declined, helped by the impact of the Asian crisis and the strength of sterling, which, combined with falling exchange rates outside the euro area, resulted in lower year-on-year prices on a wide range of goods. The cost of services was continuing to rise around 5% a year.

Revisions to the average earnings data showed that growth in the first quarter fell

to an annual rate of 3.9%, compared with a peak of 5.3% in the same period a year earlier. By midyear the rate had accelerated to 5.4%, with most of the pressure coming from the private sector (6.2%) and more restrained growth in the public sector (2.5%). Over the year, average earnings were expected to rise by around 4% but to slow down in early 1999 in response to falling corporate profits. Despite signs of recession and the closure of a number of manufacturing plants, job creation was maintained at a brisk level, and unemployment fell by another 11,900 (to 1.3 million) in September. Additional job gains were recorded in the three months to October, when the number of employed rose to 27.2 million, up 259,000 on a year earlier. At around 6.2%, unemployment was at its lowest since 1980.

Japan. The year began on a weak note following signs of deepening recession and scandals and bankruptcies in the financial sectors, which had started at the end of 1997. International as well as domestic confidence in the Japanese economy had been badly damaged. Growth in output fell to a low 1% in 1997 following a real decline in the final quarter; this marked the start of the longest period of decline since World War II. In 1998 the economy continued to deteriorate despite government measures to shore it up, and by the end of the year the 2.5% decline predicted by the IMF seemed optimistic. In late December, however, the government predicted a fall of 2.2% in the year through March 1999.

The government's response to recession marked a reversal of policy. It announced at the end of 1997 a surprise ¥2 trillion in tax cuts and an acceleration of public investment planned for fiscal 1998. This did little to restore confidence or solve the country's problems. In the first quarter of 1998, industrial production fell for the third quarter

running. Inventories rose as consumers remained cautious, and exports fell to Asian countries suffering their own crises. At the same time, imports declined, which added to the already large current-account surplus. By April the unemployment rate, which had been rising slowly but steadily, rose to a record-high 4.1%. Nearly all the first-quarter indicators (in year-on-year terms)—including real consumption (down 4.9%), retail sales, new car registrations (down 20.4%), and machinery orders (down 5.8%)—reflected the continuing deterioration. Deflationary pressure was growing as both the overall and the domestic wholesale price indexes rose ever more slowly. In March, for the first time, each recorded declines of 1.1% and 0.1%, respectively. The next month the Bank of Japan presented a gloomy forecast of the economy that, among other things, reflected its concerns about the stability of the financial system.

On April 24 the government announced details of Japan's largest-ever economic stimulus package to pump prime the economy. Of the ¥16,650,000,000,000 involved, two-thirds was to go to new public-works spending, special income and residential tax cuts, and more central and local government spending on social infrastructure. The defeat of the Liberal Democratic Party in upper house elections on July 12 led to the resignation of Prime Minister Ryutaro Hashimoto and plunged Japan into more uncertainty. A major fear was that the planned reforms to stimulate the economy and measures to deal with the bad debt problems in the banking sector would be delayed. Concern also centred on whether bank reforms would address the problem adequately. If they dealt only with technically failed institutions and not the bad loans in apparently healthy banks, the reforms would be ineffective.

In fact, all three possible successors to Hashimoto were committed to such policies. The new government, led by former foreign minister Keizo Obuchi (*see* BIOGRAPHIES), announced a fiscal-stimulus package of ¥17 trillion in the form of tax cuts and more public spending. In October legislation was finally agreed for banking reforms to be put in place. To support them an exceptionally large sum of public funds (around ¥60 trillion, the equivalent of 12% of GDP) was made available, including ¥18 trillion for the nationalization of weak but essentially solvent banks and ¥17 trillion for the protection of depositors.

The government's fiscal package provided little relief, and economic conditions continued to deteriorate. In the April–June quarter real GDP contracted by 0.8%, and by the third quarter it was down 3.6% at an annual rate. Business and consumer confidence remained low, with corporate spending still falling. The continuing decline in consumer spending reflected the fall in incomes because of lower bonuses and less overtime (nonfarm incomes were down 3.8% on the year earlier) and offset the effect of tax rebates. Deflationary fears were realized, with consumer prices falling in both July and August. The unemployment rate increased to 4.4%, low by international standards but a postwar high for Japan.

The government announced another rescue package in November of a record ¥23.9 trillion. It included more spending on infrastructure as well as permanent income and

Industrial Production
semiannual averages: 1990 = 100

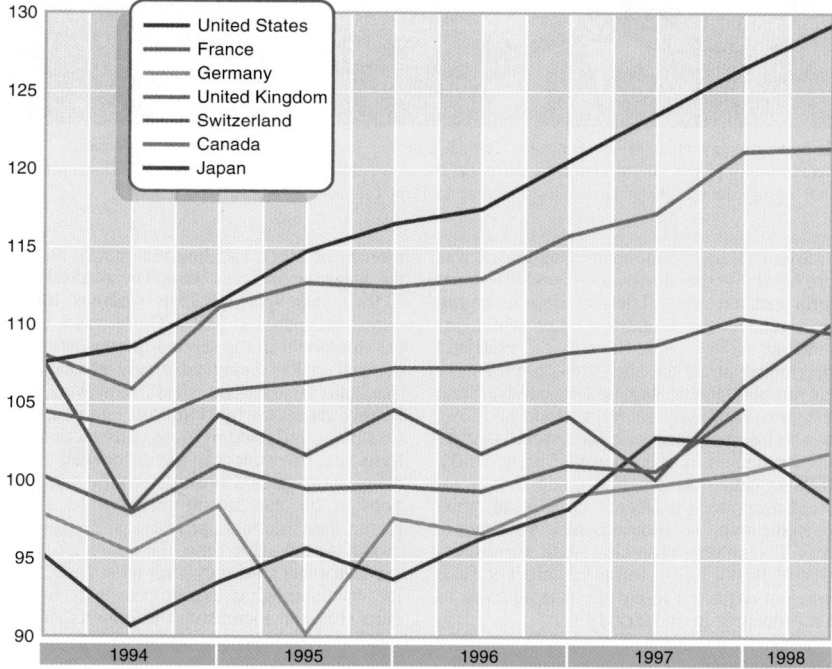

United States
France
Germany
United Kingdom
Switzerland
Canada
Japan

Source: International Monetary Fund, *International Financial Statistics.*

corporate tax cuts. Despite the stimulus being provided by the government and a hoped-for strengthening of the financial sector, the outlook remained uncertain. The weakness of the external sector was expected to continue, with increasing pressure on Japan's Asian operations and the prospect of shrinking demand from advanced countries. Output was not expected to recover until the year 2000.

Euro Area. By early 1998 the 11 EU countries scheduled to adopt the euro as a single currency on Jan. 1, 1999, were increasingly being viewed as one economy. The IMF designated these countries the euro area, but the new bloc was also known as euroland and the euro zone.

On May 2, 1998, formal approval was given for the 11 countries to participate in the third stage and final stage of the EMU. It was agreed that on December 31 the 11 national currencies would be converted into euros. The internal exchange rate of the euro to the 11 national currencies (Belgium and Luxembourg would have the same rate) was to be irrevocably fixed, whereas the market would determine its external value. The new currency was to be managed by the 17 governing members of the ECB, which was to become operational on January 1. A six-member executive board, led by Dutch banker Wim Duisenberg (*see* BIOGRAPHIES), was to share decision making with the central bank governors of the 11 member countries. The status of the ECB was one of strict independence and neutrality, and the central bank governors in turn had to preserve their independence regardless of pressure from their governments.

In the first few months of 1998, fiscal and monetary policy in the euro area continued to be influenced by the necessity to meet the convergence criteria set out by the Maastricht Treaty in order to qualify for the third stage of EMU. A flexible approach to achievement of the criteria was adopted so that countries qualified even if they failed to meet all the criteria. For example, the ratio of public debt to GDP in Belgium and Italy exceeded 120%, whereas the criteria stipulated a 60% "reference value." This was waived on the grounds that the ratio was declining.

In accordance with the stability and growth pact signed by the EU members in June 1997, most governments maintained a tight monetary policy in 1998. This was to keep fiscal deficits within the 3% of GDP limit that was one of the EMU qualification requirements and the maximum allowed under the pact. In 1998 the euro-area budget deficit was expected to meet its limit—for only the second time in 20 years—resulting in an improvement in the euro area's government finances. The ECB had to pursue price stability as a priority, and other objectives, such as employment and growth, could be pursued only if they were consistent with low inflation. A principal objective of the ECB was to maintain price stability. There were signs, however, that faced with the new threat of deflation rather than that of inflation, some euro-area governments wanted to relax fiscal policy and spend their way out of trouble in the short term rather than risk a return to recession. Significantly, the strong political swings to the left in France, Italy, and Germany, which were major influences in the euro area, were shifting emphasis away from austerity, and there was more likelihood that public spending would be used to boost demand.

THIERRY CHARLIER—AP/WIDE WORLD

Balloons are launched at the European Council building in Brussels to celebrate the official inauguration of the single European currency, the euro. Belgium was among the 11 EU countries that agreed to lock their currencies together to form the euro.

Some easing of monetary conditions was provided by the downward trend in short-term interest rates. These were converging in readiness for January 1, after which interest rates were to be fixed by the ECB and be binding on all the euro-area countries. By November 1998 it was widely believed that the rate would be set at a floor of 3.3%, which had been the rate for several months in France and Germany. Spain, Italy, Ireland, and Portugal had made moves toward this rate. On December 3, in an unexpected move, the Bundesbank cut its rate to 3%. The other currencies, with the exception of Italy (3.5%), followed suit. The ECB was not expected to cut the rate again at its first meeting in January 1999.

Export-led growth in output in the euro area accelerated in the first quarter to an annual rate of 3.2% from 3% in the last three months of 1997. Leading the growth among the larger economies were The Netherlands (3.9%) and Spain (3.7%), whereas Italy's output stagnated at 2.5%. There was a modest slowdown in the second quarter, with industrial orders being adversely affected by the Asia crisis. The slack, however, was largely taken up by domestic demand; this was being reflected in more construction activity and investment in plants, as well as increased car sales. Consumer confidence was boosted by the fall in inflation to 1.2%, faster real-income growth, and cheaper credit. At the same time, the appreciation of the European Currency Unit against the dollar was damaging export prospects in the euro area and increasing the imports. In the third quarter industrial output rose by an annual rate of less than 3%, compared with 6% in the first three months. As the year drew

Interest Rates: Short-term
three-month money market rates

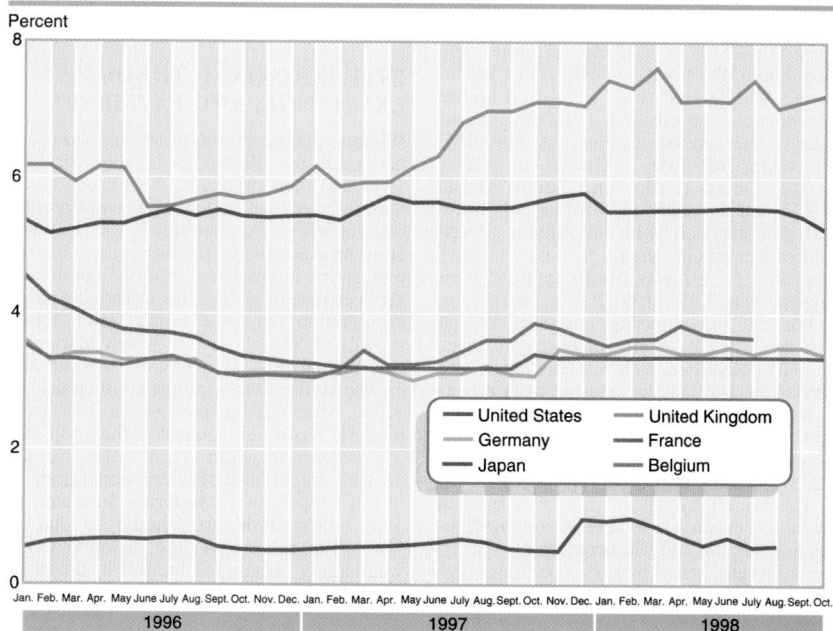

Percent

— United States — United Kingdom
— Germany — France
— Japan — Belgium

Jan. Feb. Mar. Apr. May June July Aug. Sept. Oct. Nov. Dec. Jan. Feb. Mar. Apr. May June July Aug. Sept. Oct. Nov. Dec. Jan. Feb. Mar. Apr. May June July Aug. Sept. Oct.

1996 1997 1998

Source: International Monetary Fund, *International Financial Statistics*.

to a close, business and consumer confidence was falling and the decline in unemployment had ceased.

The Former Centrally Planned Economies. In 1998 economic output in these countries was expected to decline by 1% or more. This followed an increase in output of 2% in 1997, the first regional rise after five consecutive years of decline and the first in Russia since 1989. The downturn was the result of several factors. These were led by the financial crisis in Asia, which prompted a fall in confidence in emerging markets generally and in the Russian financial system more specifically. Owing to financial market concerns the authorities took emergency measures. On August 17 Russia devalued its currency, defaulted on a large portion of its government debt, and stopped foreign credit repayments by companies and banks. The sharp depreciation of the ruble and the fall of Prime Minister Sergey Kiriyenko's government later the same month generated instability and uncertainty through much of the region.

In Russia output was expected to decline by around 6%, but elsewhere the overall picture was less gloomy. In Central Europe and Eastern Europe, real output was forecast to rise for the sixth consecutive year, accelerating from 3.1% in 1997 to 5.1% in 1988. Output was forecast to increase in Poland (5.8%) and in Hungary (5.2%), helped by strong domestic demand. The Czech Republic (up 1%) remained in recession because of policy mismanagement and the aftereffects of the May 1987 currency crisis. Only Romania and Ukraine experienced real declines (4% and 1%, respectively).

In the Transcaucasus and Central Asia, growth in output rose for the third straight year—4.1%, compared with 2.1% in 1997—with most countries experiencing faster growth. Against the trend, however, there was a marked turnaround in Turkmenistan, where, following several years of decline,

the economy was variously forecast to grow by 5–20%.

Despite the return to growth in many of the transition economies, only Poland, Slovenia, and Slovakia regained their 1989 levels of output. For all of the countries together the projection for real gross domestic

product in 1998 was an average 55% of the 1989 level. The output of the majority was well below half the 1989 level, with Georgia (35%) and Ukraine (37%) having the most ground to make up. Elsewhere, progress had been made, but most countries were still only three-quarters of the way or less to their 1989 levels.

There was a marked easing in inflationary pressures, but there was no room for complacency, as few countries had achieved the low inflation rates of most advanced countries. The International Monetary Fund projected an annual rise of 30% across the region, compared with 28% in 1997. The increase, however, obscured sharp falls in most of the 26 countries, and many were below or close to single-digit rates. In Central and Eastern Europe (excluding Russia), the rate fell from 15% to a projected 11%, with a dramatic dive in Bulgaria, where the rate fell from 1,082% to 27%. In the Transcaucasus and Central Asia, the inflation rate declined from 31% in 1997 to a projected 21%.

The notable exception to this trend was Russia, where the IMF projected an increase from 15% to 48%. By the year-end this looked too optimistic. The collapse of the ruble and crisis in the banking system resulted in spiralling price increases that were expected to exceed 100% year on year. At the same time, there were signs that Russian consumers were more willing to spend their devalued currency on products produced by domestic industries than on the more expensive products manufactured by foreign companies.

Restructuring suffered a setback in 1998. The numerical transition indicators of the European Bank for Reconstruction and

Interest Rates: Long-term

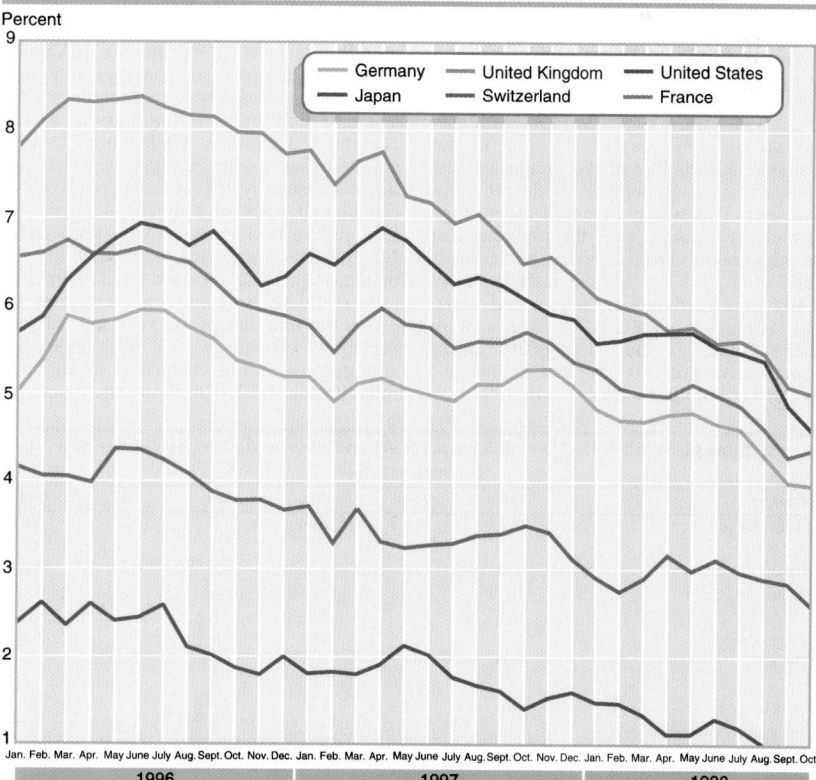

Percent

— Germany — United Kingdom — United States
— Japan — Switzerland — France

Jan. Feb. Mar. Apr. May June July Aug. Sept. Oct. Nov. Dec. Jan. Feb. Mar. Apr. May June July Aug. Sept. Oct. Nov. Dec. Jan. Feb. Mar. Apr. May June July Aug. Sept. Oct.

1996 1997 1998

Source: International Monetary Fund, *International Financial Statistics*.

Development provided a means by which the cumulative progress of the former centrally planned economies toward market economies since 1994 could be measured. Among the indicators being monitored were large- and small-scale privatization, price liberalization, corporate governance and restructuring, trade and foreign-exchange systems, competition policy, and financial-sector reforms. The indicators showed a much slower pace of reform in 1998 than in previous years, with progress that was made tending to reflect the catching up on long-delayed reforms. In Poland there was progress in the privatization of banking, and in Hungary private investors played a role in improving corporate governance. Progress in Russia slid backward in four areas: banking reforms, price liberalization, securities markets, and trade and foreign-exchange liberalization. Croatia tightened capital controls to contain the domestic credit growth stimulated by short-term capital inflows. Some countries—including Belarus, Turkmenistan, and Uzbekistan—continued to delay or deviate from the road to market economies.

Less-Developed Countries. At the end of 1997, the IMF projected that growth in the LDCs would be about 6% in 1998. At that time it was not realized how deep and widespread the contagion effect of the Asian and Russian crises would be on the global economy. Subsequent downward revisions were made, and LDC output was expected to increase by 2.3%, compared with 5.8% in 1997. On a per-head basis, GDP grew by 0.7%, a sharp decline following six consecutive years in which real GDP per head grew by 4% or more. The latest output projection for 1999 was for 3.6%, although the outcome would heavily depend on the movement of commodity prices, which remained uncertain.

For the first time, the Asian LDCs, which had averaged real growth of 7% annually in the 1980s and '90s, trailed the other regions. It was clear by mid-1998 that the recession in Asia was much deeper than expected. (*See* Spotlight: *The Troubled World Economy.*) Africa grew fastest in 1998, with output up by 3.7% despite the war in the Democratic Republic of the Congo and the civil unrest it generated in surrounding countries. This was in excess of the average annual performance over the previous two decades and produced a modest increase per head of 1.2%. The Middle East grew by 2.3%, falling slightly on a per-head basis. This compared with a 4.7% expansion in each of the previous two years. Latin-American output was expected to increase by 2.8%, compared with 5.1% in 1997.

Oil and nonfuel commodities were a major influence on the performance of Africa and the Middle East. In Africa the government oil revenues as a share of GDP in 1998 were 15–25% in Algeria, Angola, the Republic of the Congo, Gabon, and Nigeria. In the Middle East there were even higher dependencies on oil. In Kuwait the government relied on oil revenue as the GDP equivalent of 38%, followed by Qatar (27%), Oman (23%), and Saudi Arabia (19%). Latin-American governments were less reliant on oil, with the notable exception of Venezuela, where 58% of total revenue in 1996–97 was from oil; in 1998 oil revenue was 7.3% of GDP.

For the oil-importing countries in the Middle East, the benefits of lower oil prices were partially offset by lower remittances and investment and reduced demand from oil-exporting neighbouring countries. Nonfuel commodity price declines in 13 of the 43 oil-importing African countries were expected to offset the gains from lower oil prices.

The overall growth in Africa was boosted by strong expansion in several countries, including Algeria and Morocco (up 6%) in the north, where better weather conditions improved agricultural output following drought in 1997. No expansion was expected in South Africa following a 1.7% rise in 1997 and more than 3% in each of the previous two years. The country suffered financial contagion from the Asian crisis, and international investors were deterred. The fall in value of the rand (in dollar terms) brought inflationary pressure, and by November consumer prices were up 9.4% on a yearly basis.

In Latin America weaker oil prices and cutbacks in production contributed to lower-than-expected growth in Colombia, Mexico, and most of Venezuela. Most countries were forced to tighten monetary and fiscal policies because of the Asian crisis, which helped keep inflation down to an average 10.8%. Investor confidence remained strong until Russia devalued its currency in August. Given the region's low savings rate and heavy dependence on external funding, there was growing pressure on currencies. In September Colombia, Chile, and Ecuador adjusted their exchange rates. In Brazil political uncertainty led to heavy outflows of capital and fears of a financial crisis. An IMF rescue package that was approved in November was expected to stabilize the situation, depending on how quickly interest rates could be lowered. Argentina grew by 7% in the first half of the year and was expected to expand by 6% over 1998. Its strong credit rating enabled it to successfully launch a $250 million euro bond to-

ward the end of the year. The Mexican economy grew by 4.5% despite some peso volatility as a result of the Asia crisis and lower oil prices.

INTERNATIONAL TRADE, EXCHANGE, AND PAYMENTS

Whereas the economic problems being experienced by all regions of the world in 1998 had their origins in the financial system, international trade played an important role for individual countries in either alleviating or exacerbating the difficulties. In volume terms international trade of goods and services rose by 3.7%. This reflected a sharp deceleration from the much faster actual growth of 9.7% in 1997, which marked a new annual peak in international trade and exceeded the IMF's projected increase of 7.7%. Although the increase in 1998 was modest, it strongly outpaced the projected 2% increase in world output, reflecting the growing importance of international trade in global output. In value terms, however, at $6.6 billion trade was similar to that in 1997. The relative decline in value terms was largely because of the fall in the price of oil by nearly one-third over the year and nonfuel commodities by some 14%. Prices of manufactured goods continued to weaken but less steeply than in 1997.

The advanced countries overall provided the momentum in the market, which marked a decisive shift away from the LDCs, which for several years had provided the strongest growth markets for world exports. Whereas imports by the advanced markets rose 4.5% (9% in 1997), they increased only 1% in the LDCs (9.8% in 1997). Exports increased 3.6% (10.3%) from the advanced economies while rising a slightly faster 3.9% from the LDCs. In dollar terms total LDC exports and imports fell by 2.8% and 2%, respectively, compared with strong growth every other year since 1991.

The overall slowdown in the advanced countries' trade was skewed by Japan, which for the first time in decades experienced a drop in exports. In value terms these were down 8.5% in the first nine months, and weaker domestic demand pushed imports down 19% over the same period. In volume terms Japanese exports turned negative in the second and third quarters, when the buoyant demand from the U.S. and the EU was more than offset by the downturn in sales to its Asian markets. Export volumes were projected to fall 1.9%. The slowdown in the average rise in exports of goods and services of the advanced countries of 3.6%, however, was not influenced only by the recession in Japan. In the U.S. there was a dramatic deceleration in exports from the 12.8% rise in 1997 to only 3.1% in 1998, reflecting the drop in demand in its Asian markets. The U.S. nevertheless played a major role in sustaining global trade by raising the volume of its imports 11.5%, not far short of the 1997 level (13.9%).

Trade in goods and services from several EU countries reflected strong activity in the first half of the year, especially because of the buoyant conditions within the euro area. Lower inflation and continued economic recovery combined with the relative strength of European currencies and real increases in household disposable incomes. In the second half of the year, however, the effects of the global slowdown and increased compet-

Table III. Standardized Unemployment Rates in Selected Developed Countries						
% of total labour force						
Country	1993	1994	1995	1996	1997	1998[1]
United States	6.9	6.1	5.6	5.4	4.9	4.8
Japan	2.5	2.9	3.1	3.3	3.4	4.4
Germany	8.9	9.6	9.4	10.3	11.4	11.5
France	11.7	12.2	11.5	12.3	12.4	11.9
Italy	10.2	11.3	12.0	12.1	12.3	12.0
United Kingdom	10.3	9.4	8.6	8.0	6.9	6.8
Canada	11.2	10.4	9.5	9.7	9.2	8.6
All developed countries	8.0	7.9	7.6	7.5	7.2	7.1
Seven major countries above	7.3	7.2	6.9	7.0	6.8	6.7
European Union	11.1	11.5	11.2	11.4	11.2	10.9

[1]Projected.
Source: OECD.

Table IV. Changes in Output in Less-Developed Countries
% annual change in real gross domestic product

Area	1994	1995	1996	1997	1998[1]
All less-developed countries	6.7	6.1	6.6	5.8	2.3
Regional groups					
Africa	2.2	3.1	5.8	3.2	3.7
Asia	9.6	9.0	8.2	6.6	1.8
Middle East and Europe	0.7	3.8	4.7	4.7	2.3
Western Hemisphere	5.2	1.2	3.5	5.1	2.8
Countries in transition	−7.1	−1.5	−1.0	−2.0	−0.2

[1]Projected.
Source: International Monetary Fund, *World Economic Outlook*, October 1998.

Table V. Changes in Consumer Prices in Less-Developed Countries
% change from preceding year

Area	1994	1995	1996	1997	1998[1]
All less-developed countries	51.6	22.3	14.1	9.1	10.3
Regional groups					
Africa	37.5	34.1	26.7	11.0	7.7
Asia	15.0	12.8	7.9	4.7	8.3
Middle East and Europe	31.9	35.9	24.6	22.6	22.6
Western Hemisphere	208.3	35.9	20.8	13.9	10.8

[1]Projected.
Source: International Monetary Fund, *World Economic Outlook*, October 1998.

itiveness of Asian goods was beginning to be felt. EU exports were projected to rise 6.1% over the year (9.9% in 1997), whereas imports at 7.5% were maintained at close to the 1997 levels (8.8%). Germany, France, and Italy led trading activity of the major EU countries. In the U.K. the volume of exports rose only marginally (0.8%), compared with an 8% rise in 1997. The traded sector of the British economy was under severe pressure from the strength of sterling, both within and outside the euro area, and the fall in demand in LDCs. Imports (up 5.2%) became increasingly competitively priced as a result of the devalued Asian currencies and stronger pound sterling.

The most notable change in the trade picture of the 28 advanced countries was the group of four newly industrializing countries (NICs)—Hong Kong, Singapore, Taiwan, and South Korea. For the first time, these countries were a negative source of trade momentum. For most years in the last three decades, this group had registered close to double-digit export and import growth, but in 1998 the volume increase in exports from the NICs fell from 10.9% in 1997 to 0.7%. Imports fell sharply by 8.7% after a 7.3% rise in 1997.

The LDCs' trade performance in 1998 was as varied as that of the advanced countries. Overall, the volume rise in both exports and imports (3.9% and 1.3%, respectively) translated into declines (6.5% and 3.4%) in dollar-value terms from the 1997 peak, which reflected the decline in fuel and nonfuel commodity prices. Although Asia still accounted for the major share of LDC trade—nearly one-half—the region's 1998 exports were expected to rise marginally (0.4%) at best, with imports falling 9%.

The buoyant trading conditions in Latin America that had made it the most dynamic region in 1997 continued into 1998 but were soon dissipated. The value of exports, which had increased by more than 10% in 1997, stagnated in 1998. The dollar value of imports fell from 18% to under 9%. The decrease in commodity prices resulted in currency devaluations, with Chile, Colombia, and Ecuador adjusting their exchange rates in September, which further depressed rev-

enue from exports. Imports into Brazil fell by nearly 5% in the first nine months of 1998, compared with a rise in 1997.

The crises in emerging financial markets and the failure of Japan to move out of recession were the main influences on exchange-rate movements in the developed countries. In the first half of the year, both the U.S. dollar and sterling benefited from being perceived as safe havens as well as exhibiting strong economic growth accompanied by low inflation. The dollar appreciated by 2.7% between the start of the year and mid-July, with rates against sterling and the Deutsche Mark remaining steady at around $1.64 and $1.78, respectively. Later in the year, however, as the emerging countries' crisis took on global dimensions, the dollar weakened against the Deutsche Mark.

Against the yen the dollar appreciated strongly as the yen fell to new lows. Concerns that the problems in the Japanese banking system would not be quickly resolved pushed the yen to an eight-year low of 146 to the dollar in mid-June. There also were fears that the yen-to-dollar rate would put the Chinese fixed exchange rate under pressure, adding to the financial turmoil in the Pacific Rim. These concerns prompted the Fed and the Bank of Japan to intervene in the foreign exchange to try to prevent a further decline of the yen. Following a brief fall the yen strengthened through September and October, helped by the easing of U.S. interest rates. The dollar fell by 4.5% in October and ended the year at around 116 yen to the dollar. This compared with a 1998 high of 114.37 and a low of 147.25. The Australian and New Zealand dollars, which reached lows against sterling in September, stabilized in the last weeks of the year.

The pound sterling traded firmly against the dollar in the first three quarters of the year in the $1.64–$1.68 range. Although it appreciated toward the end of the year, it remained little changed over a year earlier. In Europe, however, sterling strengthened against the Deutsche Mark and euro currencies, mainly as a result of higher interest rates in the U.K. In early July sterling was trading at DM 3, but it fell on signs that the British economy was slowing and indica-

tions that interest rates had peaked. In October sterling fell to its lowest level against the Deutsche Mark in 15 months. By the end of the year, sterling was trading at around DM 2.80, close to the average for 1997. On December 31 the European Commission announced the 10 irrevocably fixed rates of the euro for the currencies in the euro area.

The balance on the current accounts of the advanced countries was expected by the IMF to narrow in 1998 to $39.6 billion from $69.4 billion in 1997. The deterioration was more than accounted for by the widening of the U.S. deficit by $81 billion to $236.3 billion. The strong domestic demand that was driving growth in the U.S. and the stronger buying power of the dollar encouraged imports, particularly from the crisis countries of Asia, which were extremely competitive in the first half of 1998. Exports were being held back by the deceleration of demand and reduced buying power in the Asian NICs and LDCs in general.

In the euro area strong domestic demand in the first half year, combined with currency weakening against the dollar, left the current-account surplus virtually unchanged at $111 billion. The current account of the U.K., however, moved into deficit ($18.7 billion) under pressure from the strong pound, which inhibited exports but encouraged purchases of competitively priced imports. In Australia the economy was expected to grow by 3.5% because of the buoyant domestic economy. This, combined with the decline in exports to the Asian markets on which Australia was heavily dependent, produced an increase in the deficit to around $19 billion. In New Zealand, where the economy was contracting, the deficit was expected to fall to $3.5 billion ($4.7 billion in 1997).

In Japan the surplus increased by more than a third, with the fall in demand from exports from its Asian neighbours being offset by the depreciation of the yen, reduced domestic demand, and lower commodity prices. The position of the NICs was similar, with Taiwan in particular moving into surplus.

Overall, the LDCs' current deficit was expected to increase by some $16 billion to $78 billion. The decline in oil prices pushed the Middle East into deficit from a small surplus in 1997, and in Africa the deficit grew to nearly $15 billion because of lower commodity prices. In Asian emerging countries the tighter financial conditions that resulted from the sharp depreciation in currencies, combined with much lower imports, pushed the surplus from $4.7 billion to $14.7 billion. The current-account balances of Indonesia, Malaysia, the Philippines, and Thailand were expected to move from a $15 billion deficit in 1997 to a combined surplus of $17.6 billion.

The total external debt of the LDCs rose more slowly in 1998 to $1,812,000,000,000, according to IMF predictions, compared with $1,774,000,000,000 in 1997. This was the equivalent of 148% of exports of goods and services, and although it was up on the 141.8% in 1997, it was well down on earlier years. The trend for the growth in export earnings to outpace the increase in indebtedness continued in Asia, where indebtedness was lowest as a percentage of exports, at 110%. External debt fell in

(continued on page 200)

The IMF's Changing Role

by William Glasgall

Even for an organization that had worked to alleviate its share of financial panics during more than five decades of existence, the International Monetary Fund (IMF) had an extraordinary year by any standard in 1998. As one tense month gave way to the next, the financial crisis that had begun the year before in Thailand spread to East Asia, Russia, and Latin America and was threatening to engulf the industrialized world as well. (*See* Spotlight: *The Troubled World Economy.*)

According to IMF Managing Director Michel Camdessus, the crisis had "already cost hundreds of billions of dollars, millions of jobs, and the unquantifiable tragedy of lost opportunities and lost hope for so many people, particularly among the poorest. . . . Even countries with well-managed economies have not been spared." Yet the traditional remedies the IMF had employed in the past to alleviate such global financial stresses—loans to troubled countries in return for pledges to restrict monetary expansion and rein in budget deficits—seemed curiously inadequate. It was not until the U.S. and other major economies took a series of striking steps that the crisis began to stabilize.

After months of rancorous debate, the U.S. Congress in October 1998 approved an $18 billion contribution to the IMF's capital base, giving the organization $90 billion for additional emergency loans and easing fears that it was about to run out of money. Indeed, the move enabled the IMF and other government leaders to pledge to make available $41 billion in credits for Brazil, where steep budget deficits left the nation's currency vulnerable to speculative attack.

The U.S. Federal Reserve and central banks in Japan and several European countries cut interest rates and helped ease the crisis further by shoring up global stock markets that had been falling precipitously for months amid fears of a worldwide recession. The Group of Seven (G-7) industrial countries agreed to set up a new IMF facility to provide emergency loans for countries affected by "contagion" from other distressed economies and called for more and better disclosure of emerging-market finances and flows of capital among hedge funds and other large international investors. At the same time, G-7 members called for improved supervision of financial flows from investment banks, hedge funds, and other lenders to emerging markets, the better to spot potentially destabilizing financial bubbles.

The fact that the IMF and the world financial system needed emergency assistance to get over the latest global crisis should have been no surprise. The size and scope of IMF-led financial-aid programs had increased in recent years, accelerating dramatically after the fall of the Soviet Union and other communist countries in 1989 thrust a new wave of emerging nations into the world economy. The organization itself, however, had not changed significantly since its creation in Bretton Woods, N.H., in 1944 by the U.S. and 43 allies as a critical element in the American-led Western post–World War II alliance.

Designed to foster monetary cooperation, the IMF sought to enforce strict rules of behaviour in a world based on the gold standard and fixed currency-exchange rates. To help bolster international trade, the IMF also provided short-term financing to countries encountering balance of payments problems. The U.S. abandonment of the gold standard in 1971, however, led to the collapse of the Bretton Woods system of fixed exchange rates two years later. The move to floating exchange rates in Western economies forced the IMF to end its role as traffic cop of the world monetary system and to concentrate instead on providing advice and information to its members, which in 1998 numbered 182 countries.

That role was key in helping nations in Latin America, Africa, Asia, and Central Europe restructure their economies following the 1982 debt crisis. Later the IMF sought a more ambitious role as an international lender of last resort to the world economy. It first assumed that position in the international bailout of Mexico in 1995. In return for the imposition of an economic austerity plan, the fund, along with the U.S. and other major countries' central banks, provided credit lines and other facilities totaling $47.8 billion. Although the assistance gave rise to criticism that the IMF was bailing out international investors and not the Mexican economy, the fund in 1997 and 1998 increased the amount each member contributed and expanded its lending activities further by establishing a $47 billion line of credit—called the New Arrangements to Borrow—with two dozen countries.

The increase in borrowing authority would allow troubled IMF members to draw well in excess of what would normally be allowed, a move that was well timed. In the 1990s capital had flooded into emerging economies—such as Thailand, Indonesia, and South Korea—with little attention to borrowers' creditworthiness. When economic problems started to occur, foreign and domestic investors alike rushed to get their money out of those countries. In the ensuing panic, currencies and stock and bond markets imploded, cutting off financing and swiftly throwing entire economies into recession. The crisis persisted, even amid billions of dollars in IMF and Western loan commitments. With the IMF estimating that world economic growth was only 2.2% in 1998, half what it had forecast in late 1997, it became apparent that more forceful moves would be required. Along with the IMF's fortified capital base and widened lending authority, it still was unclear whether widening the disclosure of emerging economies' foreign-currency reserve levels, publicizing their growth estimates, and announcing capital inflows and outflows would help forestall the next crisis—much less put a decisive end to the one that drew

IMF Managing Director Michel Camdessus (left) confers with director of external relations Shailendra Anjaria at the announcement in November of the IMF's multi-billion-dollar rescue package for Brazil.

headlines in 1998. This was because the entire face of international finance had changed since the IMF was created.

Financial flows were once controlled by a handful of major banks that could be easily corralled into restructuring problem loans in cooperation with relatively modest IMF assistance. In the late 1990s, however, flows were dominated by thousands of banks; securities firms; and mutual, pension, and hedge funds that could move capital in and out of countries with a click of a computer mouse. The number of countries seeking international investment, meanwhile, had proliferated, as had the diversity of debt, equity, and other financial instruments. This array of investors and instruments made coordinating any response to financial crises "extremely difficult," concluded Moody's Investors Service Inc., a major global credit-rating agency.

The IMF, meanwhile, continued to face criticism that it was secretive in its dealings, undemocratic in its makeup, and unresponsive to the needs of poorer members. Many critics noted that the economic austerity programs that were typically attached to any IMF assistance were not always appropriate. In some cases spending cuts only deepened local recessions and made the task of necessary financial and industrial restructurings all the more difficult.

Some economists, including Jeffrey D. Sachs, the director of the Harvard Institute for International Development, believed the IMF should permit countries to essentially go bankrupt, imposing formal suspensions of loan payments while creditors and debtors negotiated the value of the loans and determined whether any loans could be exchanged for equity. During the negotiations a troubled country could continue to obtain new financing and exporters could conduct business, selling their goods and earning foreign currencies vital to a country's economic revival.

Anti-IMF protesters in the U.S. march in front of the White House in October.

WILFREDO LEE—AP/WIDE WORLD

Suggestions such as these, if they were accepted, might require years to be put into practice. If the crisis of 1998 had one lesson, it was that nothing short of "a cooperative effort by the entire world community is needed to repair the major shortcomings in the global system," according to Camdessus. The question was whether the repairs would be performed quickly enough to enable the IMF and its backers to cope with the next financial implosion.

William Glasgall is senior editor of Business Week *magazine.*

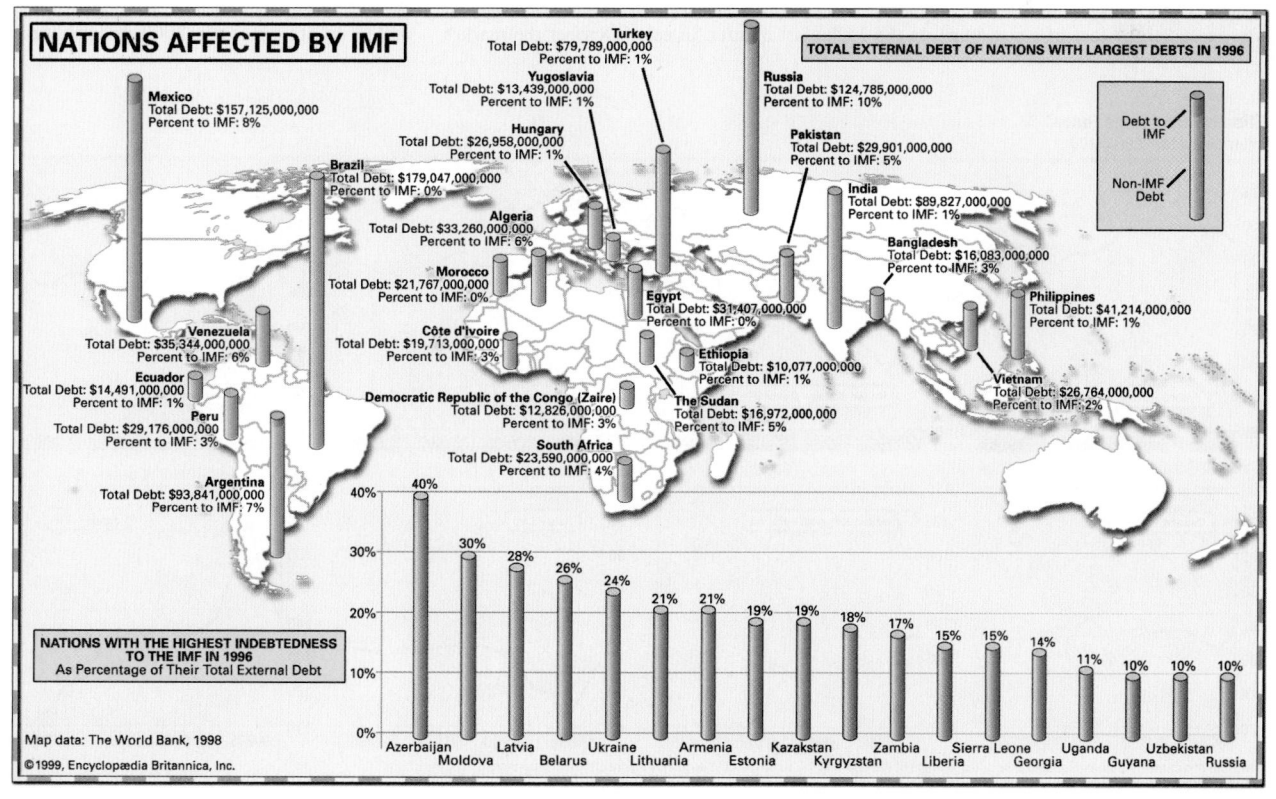

(continued from page 197)
absolute terms in both Africa and in Asia but rose slightly in the Middle East. In Latin America, which was the world's most indebted region in 1998, it rose slightly to $681 billion. The external debt of the former centrally planned economies reached a new peak at $45 billion, but as a proportion of exports of goods and services, it remained modest at 14.8%.   (IEIS)

STOCK EXCHANGES

By the end of 1998, world stock markets had formed two camps: the strong markets of Western Europe and North America and the weak markets of the rest of the world, particularly Asia. Lack of financial probity in Asia lay at the heart of this polarization. Following the collapse of Southeast Asian markets and currencies in summer 1997, investors largely abandoned debt-ridden emerging markets for the greater security of developed markets. By spring 1998 braver investors had been attracted back by the prospect of buying sound assets cheaply. Over the year to end November, the MSCI Emerging Markets Free Index fell 27.5% in U.S. dollar terms, but by year's end the stock market of one of the worst-affected Asian countries, South Korea, had risen by more than 49%.

The full implications of Asia's collapse were realized by midyear, when the gravity of Japan's financial plight and growing signs of economic stress in the hitherto strong markets of Latin America became plain. Until then investors' "flight to quality" had sent the markets of Europe and North America soaring, but by September successive economic shocks had undermined confidence. Fears surfaced that moves by banks to impose tougher lending criteria threatened a credit crunch that would stall investment and consumption in the U.S. and precipitate a global recession. Fear of inflation was overtaken by fear of a downturn. In the

U.S. short-term interest rates were reduced to ease liquidity concerns, but although American markets were volatile, the overall trend was upward.

In the rest of the world, investors' heightened fear of risk had driven down equity prices. The *Financial Times*/Standard & Poor's (FT/S&P) World Index had fallen nearly 12% from its July peak, and the *Financial Times* Stock Exchange 100 (FT-SE 100) had fallen by 20%. The slump in equity prices had lowered consumer-spending growth and lowered investment growth as firms reacted to the higher cost of capital. In the U.K. interest rates were cut in three successive months, by a quarter-percentage point in October and November and a half point in December, to stand at 6.25%.

Michel Camdessus, managing director of the International Monetary Fund, outlined plans for building a strong global financial system through the adoption of international standards of good practice. Even in the U.S., where financial systems were among the most robust, authorities were confronted in August by the $2 billion collapse of Long-Term Capital Management, a hedge fund that had extensive exposure to the international financial markets. The event was seen to have profound implications. Like the failed fund, nearly all major American banks and investment houses were trying to beat the market by using highly complex computer-aided trading strategies. These models failed to predict the sudden drying up of cash availability across markets. As Russia defaulted on its debts in August, Asia's crisis deepened and investors worldwide switched their money into safe securities such as U.S. Treasury bonds.   (IEIS)

United States. The American stock market was highly volatile in 1998, with wide swings in the averages. The general pattern was one of relatively steep increases in the first half of the year, followed by a sharp decline in the third quarter and a recovery in the last quarter. In early October the market

was locked in the grip of a near panic over whether the shaky world financial markets would push stocks into a major bear market. On October 8 the Dow Jones Industrial Average (DJIA) fell to a point more than 20% below its July peak, on the verge of what many securities analysts considered the technical onset of a bear market. The market lost $1.5 trillion between the end of July and the middle of October. Six weeks later the Dow broke new records, passing the 9000 mark as it surged more than 16% in just over a month.

The DJIA itself was particularly volatile during 1998. Beginning the year at 7908.25, it rose steadily to the 9000 level by the beginning of April, dipped in June, rose to 9337.97 in July, and then slid back in August. On August 31 the Dow fell 512.61 points, or 6.4%, to 7539.07, which left the bellwether index 4.7% below where it had started the year. The decline was the second largest in the Dow's history in point terms, trailing the 554-point drop in October 1997. There were numerous sharp swings on a daily basis, and less than two weeks later, on September 9, the DJIA had its biggest increase ever in point terms: 380.53, or 5%, to 8020.78. Although so-called blue-chip stocks fell more than 15% between the end of July and mid-October, the recovery that followed pushed the Dow into record territory, reaching the all-time high of 9374.27 on November 24. Amid continuing volatility, the DJIA finished 1998 at 9181.43, up 16.1% for the year.

Meanwhile, the over-the-counter stocks monitored by the National Association of Securities Dealers automated quotations (Nasdaq) index soared from an October low of 1419.12 to end the year at a record-high 2192.69, up 39.63%. The S&P index of 500 stocks (S&P 500) also finished well ahead of the Dow, up 26.67% for the year. Stocks of companies with low levels of capitalization (small-cap stocks), represented by the Russell 2000 index, were

Effective Exchange Rates*
average rates, 1990 = 100

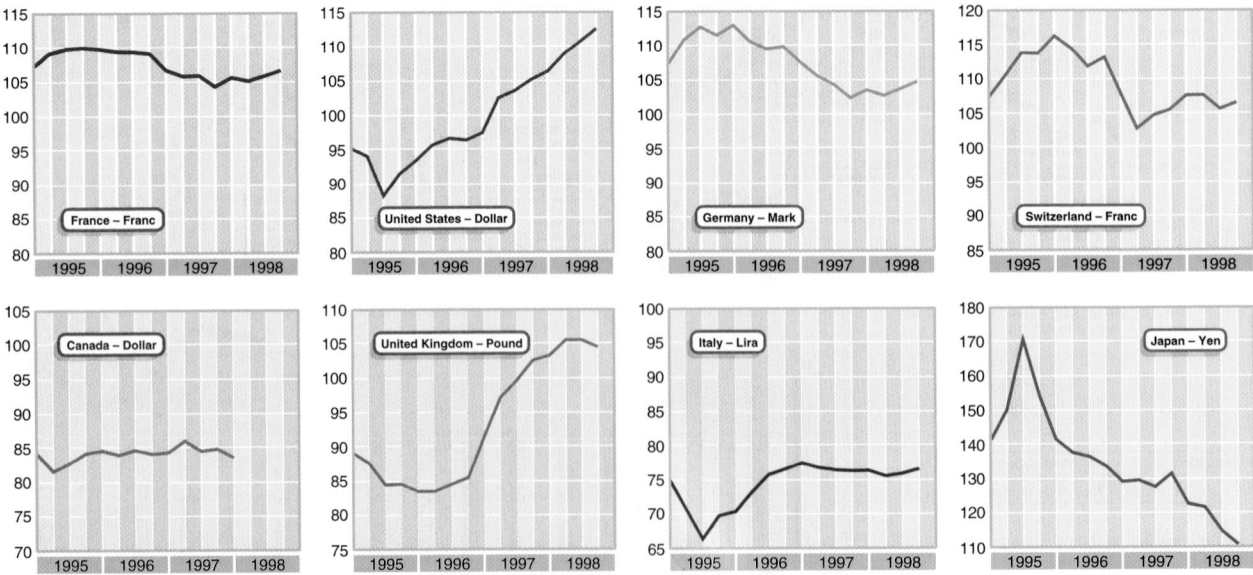

*Measure of a currency's value relative to a weighted average of the values of the currencies of the country's principal trading partners.
Source: International Monetary Fund, *International Financial Statistics*.

more vulnerable than the blue-chip stocks on the Dow, moving from 425 in January to a peak of 485 in late April before declining irregularly to under 350 by the end of September and ending the year down 3.45% at 421.96.

The near collapse of Long-Term Capital Management LP, the largest hedge fund, with capital of $1.5 billion leveraged to about $1 trillion, was rescued by a bailout by major financial institutions at the behest of the New York Federal Reserve. Using high-powered computers, some of the most profitable trading on Wall Street involved complex, innovative products known as derivatives. Such trading was designed to protect users from disadvantageous economic shifts such as currency devaluation or interest-rate risks.

August recorded one of the worst declines in stock market history. There was an erosion of consumer confidence, given that 60% of American households were invested in equities. Credit contraction in the financial system, partly because of losses suffered by its exposure to leveraged hedge funds and emerging market debt, added to investor uncertainty in the last quarter of the year.

In October investors' gloom deepened as international financial leaders meeting in Washington, D.C., failed to make tangible progress in sorting out the world's financial troubles. The flight to quality continued, pushing up Treasury bonds and some blue-chip stocks while trampling technology issues and smaller stocks on the Nasdaq.

Stock exchanges were consolidating worldwide. The National Association of Securities Dealers (NASD), parent of the Nasdaq, merged with the American Stock Exchange (Amex) in June, and the Amex acquired the Philadelphia Stock Exchange. The Pacific Stock Exchange and the Chicago Board Options Exchange also attempted to merge in 1998. The initial public offering (IPO) market started strong in the first quarter but then slowed remarkably as investors turned wary.

During the first nine months of 1998, 305 issues were announced, compared with 524 a year earlier, a decline of 14.7%. Some $30.7 billion were raised in 1997, compared with $20.9 billion in the first three quarters of 1998.

Analysts' strong optimism during 1998 was prompted by less worry about emerging markets and confidence in the Fed's cuts in interest rates. Bullish opinion was strong throughout the year. Americans had almost twice as much money invested in the stock market as in commercial banks during 1998. About 500 companies offered direct stock-purchase plans—up from 52 in 1994, and as many as five million investors participated in them. American investors had holdings in some 3,300 hedge funds around the globe with about $375 billion invested, up from roughly $145 billion a year earlier. Heavy losses were sustained, however, and the funds were under pressure as banks increased their margin requirements and investors fled to safer securities.

The third quarter was one of the slowest periods for IPOs in a decade. The total of 72 deals in the third quarter was the lowest since the first quarter of 1991 and the first time in over three years that fewer than 100 deals were completed in any single quarter. The $5.9 billion raised during the third quarter was the lowest since the first quarter of 1997 and about half the $10.8 billion raised a year earlier. Overall underwriting in the first nine months of 1998 was up sharply. In the first nine months, Wall Street raised nearly $1,410,000,000,000, surpassing the $1,310,000,000,000 raised in all of 1997.

The top underwriters of U.S. bonds and stocks during the first nine months of 1998 included Merrill Lynch & Co., $233,523,700,000 (for a market share of 16.5%); Salomon Smith Barney, $176,729,200,000 (12.5%); Morgan Stanley Dean Witter, $164,693,400,000 (11.6%); and Goldman Sachs, $156,561,900,000 (11%). As of mid-November the value of merger deals was more than $1,390,000,000,000, with many deals in the multibillion-dollar range. Among the biggest were the merger of Travelers Group Inc. with Citicorp for $72.6 billion, British Petroleum PLC's acquisition of Amoco Corp. for $43.2 billion, and Daimler Benz AG's $40.5 billion merger with Chrysler Corp. Exxon Corp. and Mobil Corp. announced a $78.9 billion merger in November. More than 10,000 deals were reported through mid-November, compared with 12,000 in all of 1997.

The yield on the 30-year bellwether Treasury bond plummeted to 4.713% in early October, the lowest yield for long-term government debt since April 1967. The Fed cut the Fed Funds rate, the lending rate on overnight funds between dealers, to 5.25% from 5.5% on September 29. The object was to cushion the effects on prospective economic growth in the U.S. of increasing weakness in foreign economies. On October 15 the Fed cut the target for the overnight lending rate by a quarter point to 5%. This cut was intended to encourage more lending and to bolster the economy by making it cheaper for consumers and businesses to borrow. They also lowered the discount rate for loans from the Fed to banks to 4.75%, the first change since January 1996.

Through October 20 volume on the New York Stock Exchange (NYSE) was 136,184,481,000, up from 105,184,933,000 during the corresponding period of 1997. During the third quarter, average daily trading volume rose 35% above the corresponding period of 1997. Forty-three new companies joined the list of stocks traded on the exchange, down from 65 a year earlier. A total of 4,285 issues traded on the NYSE, of which 1,850 advanced, 2,360 declined, and only 75 remained unchanged. High-tech companies dominated the most active list, including Compaq Computer Corp., America Online, Lucent Technologies, and IBM Corp. As an industry, oil-drilling companies fared the worst. Seat prices on the NYSE plummeted 32.5% from a record high of $2 million in February to $1,350,000, largely owing to the growth of on-line trading.

The NASD, hoping to use its technology and marketing muscle to boost the Amex's growing options business, completed its takeover by the end of October. Smaller companies were expected to favour Amex over Nasdaq because they had difficulty getting the market makers common to Nasdaq. The new organization, called the Nasdaq–Amex Market Group, had 6,178 listed companies with a combined market value of $2.2 trillion. By contrast, the NYSE had

New York Stock Exchange Composite Index, 1998 Stock prices (Dec. 31, 1965 = 50)

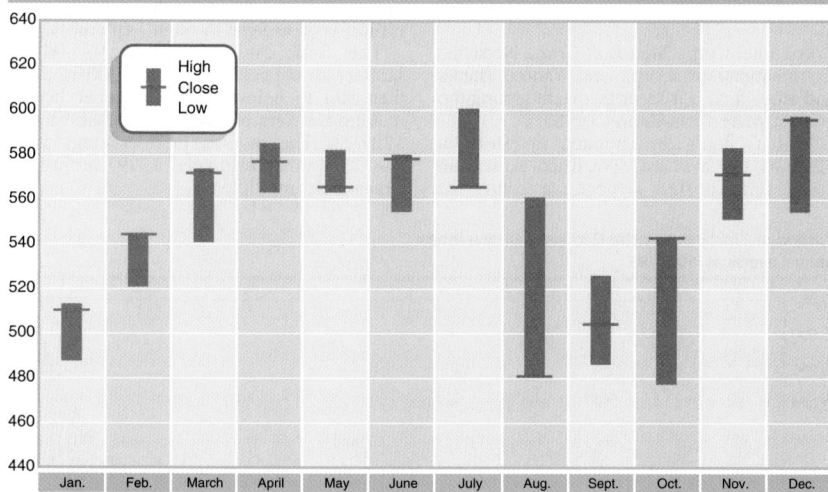

Average daily share volume in thousands of shares

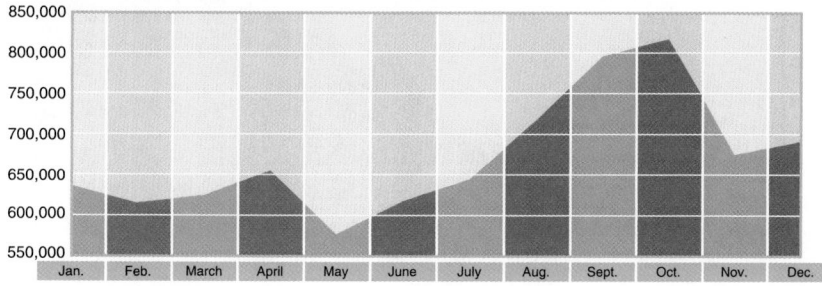

Sources: *Barron's National Business and Financial Weekly; The Wall Street Journal.*

A flag representing the new Nasdaq-Amex Market Group hangs from the ceiling of the American Stock Exchange in New York City in November.

OSAMU HONDA—AP/WIDE WORLD

−15.02%, with small stock funds sagging even worse (−21.52%) according to Lipper Analytical Services Inc. during the third quarter. It was the worst quarter for American stock funds since the third quarter of 1990, when the average fund delivered a −16.07% return, according to Lipper. The average stock fund was down −4.89% for the year through September. By contrast, bond funds and money market funds made money. The average taxable-bond fund posted a 4.98% return for the year to date. Value mutual funds (managers that specialize in out-of-favour stocks while steering clear of the fastest-growing, most glamorous growth companies) climbed 11.7% over the 12 months ended October 31, whereas an index of growth stocks climbed 32%. This was the widest disparity in 11 years between the S&P's growth and value indexes, which split the S&P 500 composite index between stocks with higher and lower ratios of price-to-book value. An unprecedented 9 out of every 10 American equity mutual funds performed worse in 1998 than the S&P 500 because most of the S&P's growth (22%) was due to a sharp rise in the 50 largest market capitalization firms, which were underweighted in the mutual fund portfolios. The largest mutual funds averaged one-year returns of 6.2%, but a few specialized groups—notably those invested in high-tech stocks—had returns for the year of more than 40%. Equity mutual funds recorded net new cash flow of $141 billion, versus $173 billion year to year through September.

The S&P 500 rose from 975.04 in January to a peak of almost 1200 in July, then slid to below 950 in October before making a strong recovery to end the year at 1229.23. The index's price-earnings ratio was 25.1 times estimated 1999 earnings, a near-record multiple.

3,090 listings with a market value of $11.6 trillion. The Nasdaq and Amex markets continued to operate separately. Through December 4 volume on the Amex was 6,758,536,000, up from 5,710,113,000 a year earlier, an increase of 18.4%. The Amex index ended the year less than 1% higher.

Through October 20 volume on the Nasdaq was 155,415,083,000, up 19% from 130,055,757,000 in the same period of 1997. A bear market in small stocks, coupled with tougher listing requirements, drove hundreds of companies off the Nasdaq stock market. Through August 564 companies had been delisted. At the beginning of the year, about 226 Nasdaq stocks, or 4.1% of the 5,500 on the market, were in the danger zone, priced below $1. By midyear nearly 600 additional stocks, or 10% of the market, traded under $1. Of the 6,584 total issues traded on the Nasdaq, 1,711 advanced, 2,898 declined, and 41 ended the year unchanged.

The NASD planned to pursue affiliations with eight international stock markets—including those in Tokyo, Paris, and Mexico City—in an effort to forge links that would let companies trade their shares around the world. Globalization was being pursued by all of the exchanges. Nasdaq volume through December 4 totaled 183,157,854,000, up from 151,593,495,000 a year earlier. The Nasdaq composite showed record highs for the year, led by computer, software, and telecommunications companies such as Dell Computer

Corp., Intel Corp., Microsoft Corp., Netscape Communications Corp., and Yahoo. Banks and other financial securities were among the poorest performers during 1998.

Mutual funds disappointed investors in 1998 as the average diversified American stock fund posted a negative return of

***Financial Times* Industrial Ordinary Share Index**
Annual averages, 1977–98

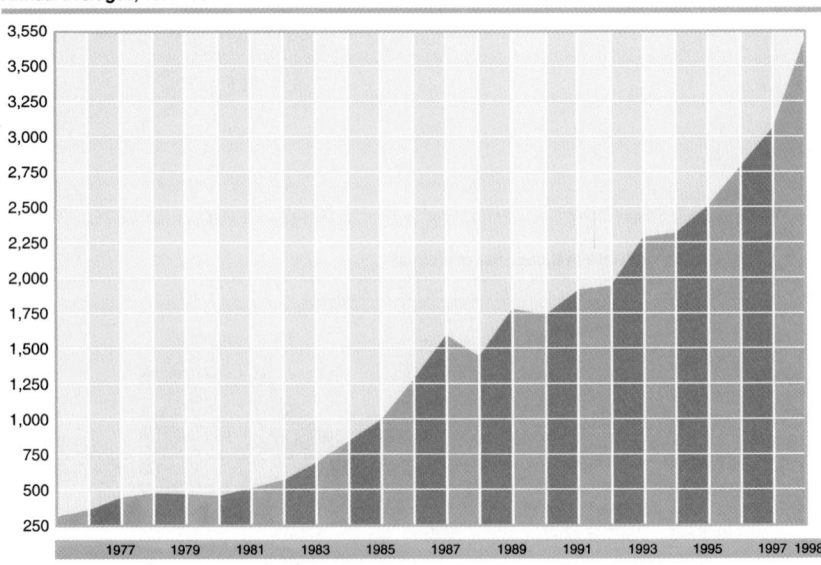

Source: *Financial Times.*

The bond market advanced with prices of Treasuries surging by the end of September to drive yields on the 30-year bonds below 5% for the first time in more than 30 years. U.S. Treasury securities, according to Lehman Brothers' indexes, rose across the board in 1998. Intermediate-term bonds were up 8.9%, long-term were up 14.96%, long-term (price) were up 8.29%, and the composite index was up 10.64%.

The bond market was capitalized at $12.5 trillion in 1998. American corporate debt issues, according to Merrill Lynch, gained during 1998. Bonds with maturities of 1–10 years climbed 8.75%, those with maturities of more than 10 years were up 10.19%, and high-yield bonds were up 3.73%.

The futures exchanges campaigned for the business of derivatives trading by citing clearinghouse protection against credit risk as a central reason futures exchanges offered greater safety than the over-the-counter market. The Dow Jones index of weekly closing prices of futures declined from a peak of 136 in January to a low of 120 in August

and September. The price of a seat on the Chicago Board of Trade (CBOT) plunged 52% from the year-earlier level, and a seat on the Chicago Mercantile Exchange sold for $312,500 in October. The Market Enhancement Committee, a group of option-trading firms that preferred the traditional open outcry system, lobbied against changes aimed at the development of computerized options trading. The CBOT voted against a move to electronic trading. The futures markets for grains and energy reached near historic lows in 1998. The Bridge Commodity Research Bureau Index of spot prices fell to 196.54 in November, just above the 21-year low of 195.35. Hog futures fell to an 18¹/₂-year low in December.

The international financial crisis, the move toward on-line trading by investors, and market uncertainties caused securities firms to take heavy losses. Massive layoffs in the securities industry began in October with Merrill Lynch laying off more than 1,000 representatives. Retail distribution of securities shifted increasingly toward the Internet on

the part of noninstitutional investors in 1998. Regulators were encouraging cybermarkets—on-line trading. The new electronic brokerage industry was projected to have 5.3 million customer accounts by the end of the year, and assets available for transactions in on-line accounts were $233 billion.

The Securities and Exchange Commission (SEC) focused on three principal areas in 1998: retail sales practices and supervision; municipal securities-market practices, including disclosure, pay-to-play, and "yield-burning" issues; and investment adviser abuses, including pricing, conflicts of interest, and "soft-dollar" issues. There were smaller investigations into insider-trading violations, false financial reporting, and small company "microcap" fraud and manipulations. The SEC proposed new rules to streamline stock offerings by public companies. Under the proposal, larger companies would no longer be subject to a monthlong review process after filing with the SEC to sell securities, companies would have fewer restrictions in communicating with potential investors, underwriters would have increased due diligence responsibilities, and investors would get more timely and better information. The SEC also went after yield-burning practices by underwriters, which occurs when investment banks slap excessive markups on bonds used to complete certain types of municipal bond refundings. By marking up the bonds, thus "burning" down the yields, underwriters pocket money that should have gone to the federal government and sometimes to the issuing municipality itself. Of the 5,600 brokerage firms required to file "year 2000" software-problem reports, some 37 firms were fined for failure to report on their plans for meeting the Y2K problem. (*See* COMPUTERS AND INFORMATION SYSTEMS: *Sidebar*.) In March the SEC required fund companies to replace unwieldy prospectuses with streamlined guides for investors and allowed them to issue even-more-brief fund profiles as well.

Canada. The Canadian markets were depressed because of languishing resource stocks and weak commodity prices. Commodities were down sharply most of the year, with gold stocks off about 36% and forestry stocks off 14%. Base-metal stocks were about even, whereas oil stocks rose about 9%. The overall market performance mirrored that of the U.S. Canada had its first budget surplus in 28 years.

Canada's economic growth rate dropped in the second quarter of 1998 to an annual rate of 1.8%, down from an annualized 3.4% rate in the first quarter. The Bank of Canada raised its bank rate a full point in August, which led to slower consumer and business spending. The Canadian economy grew at a rate of about 3% through the year, whereas consumer prices rose by only 1%. With the economy in its seventh year of expansion, GDP rose at an annual rate of 1.8% in the third quarter. The unemployment rate declined to a level of 8% in November, the lowest rate in 8¹/₂ years, with strong job growth. The Bank of Canada, matching the moves of the U.S. Fed, trimmed the bank rate to 5.75% from 6% and explained the move as a response to good inflation control and increased confidence in Canada's financial markets. On October 19 Canada reduced the bank rate a quarter point, paralleling the action of the Fed. The rate was dropped to 5.5% from 5.75%. Commercial banks lowered their

New York Stock Exchange Common Stock Index Closing Prices
Stock prices (Dec. 31, 1965 = 50)

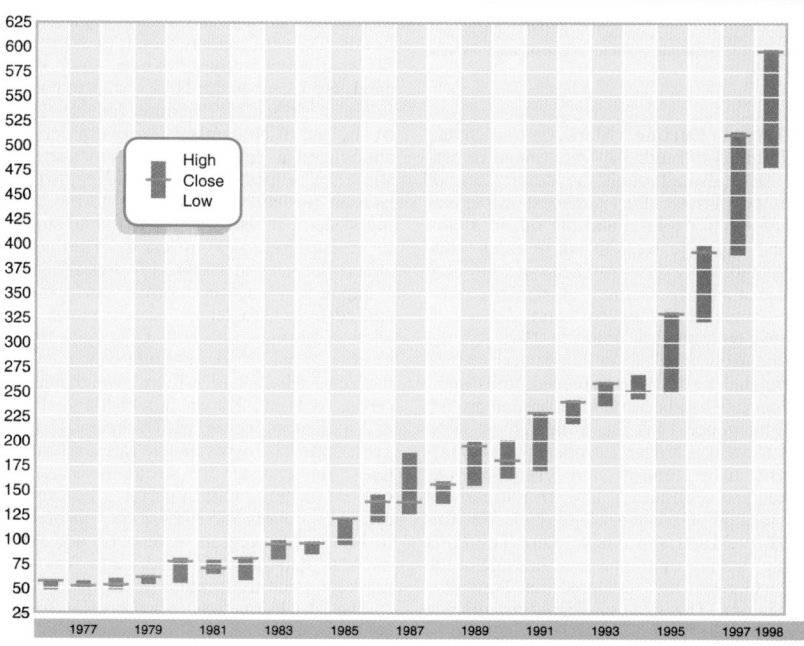

Number of shares sold
In billions of shares

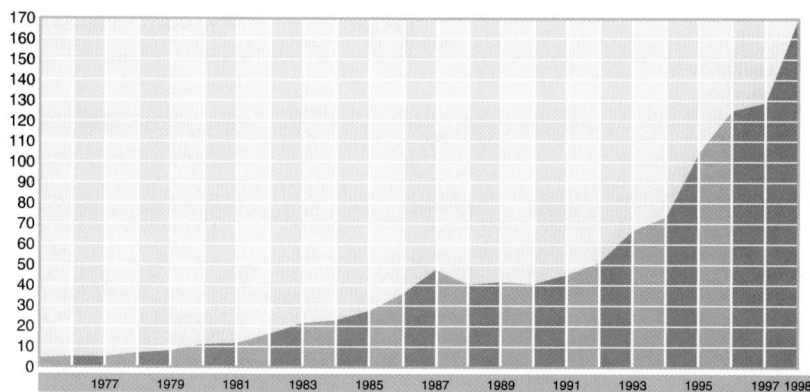

Sources: *Barron's National Business and Financial Weekly; The Wall Street Journal.*

Table VI. Selected Major World Stock Market Indexes[1]

Country and Index	1998 range[2] High	1998 range[2] Low	Year-end close	Percent change from 12/31/97
Australia, Sydney All Ordinaries	2881	2458	2813	7
Austria, Credit Aktien	584	345	382	−16
Belgium, Brussels BEL20	3632	2358	3515	45
Canada, Toronto Composite	7822	5336	6486	−3
Denmark, Copenhagen Stock Exchange	779	567	638	−6
Finland, HEX General	5799	3220	5565	69
France, Paris CAC 40	4388	2863	3943	31
Germany, Frankfurt FAZ Aktien	1941	1251	1594	15
Hong Kong, Hang Seng	11,811	6660	10,049	−6
Ireland, ISEQ Overall	5471	3745	4996	23
Italy, Milan Banca Comm. Ital.	1654	1064	1487	41
Japan, Nikkei Average	17,264	12,880	13,842	−9
Mexico, IPC	5204	2856	3960	−24
Netherlands, The, CBS All Share	845	548	735	19
Norway, Oslo Stock Exchange	2371	1360	1638	−22
Philippines, Manila Composite	2311	1082	1969	5
Singapore, SES All-Singapore	438	253	383	−10
South Africa, Johannesburg Industrials	9943	5247	6264	−16
South Korea, Composite Index	580	280	562	49
Spain, Madrid Stock Exchange	948	642	868	37
Sweden, Affarsvarlden General	3956	2412	3315	11
Switzerland, SBC General	5237	3311	4497	15
Taiwan, Weighted Price	9227	6251	6418	−22
Thailand, Bangkok SET	559	207	356	−5
United Kingdom, FT-SE 100	6179	4649	5883	15
United States, Dow Jones Industrials	9374	7539	9181	16
World, MS Capital International	1152	889	1149	23

[1] Index numbers are rounded. [2] Based on daily closing price.
Source: *Financial Times.*

prime rate to 6.75%. Corporate profits fell by 14% in the third quarter, and analysts expected a year-to-year decline of about 7.5%. For the first nine months of 1998, profits were down by 16%, according to a *Wall Street Journal* poll. Canada's mining companies suffered a sharp earnings downturn of 68% in the third quarter. Gold mining companies were up 25% in the quarter. Ten oil and natural gas companies reported earnings down 39% in the third quarter.

The Toronto Stock Exchange index of 300 stocks (TSE 300), which began the year at 6699.44, rose from January through April to reach the year's high of 7822.30. After slipping during the early summer, the TSE 300 followed the Dow on August 27, plunging 372 points in response to Russia's default. It closed at 5481.84 on October 9, down 18.17% from the corresponding date in 1997. After recovering somewhat in the fourth quarter, however, the TSE 300 finished 1998 at 6485.94 for an annual decline of 3.2%. The Montreal Stock Exchange index was down slightly less (2.1%) for the year, but the Vancouver Stock Exchange (VSE) index plummeted 35.9%. November recorded TSE record equity volume of 2.4 billion shares, with a November value of $39.2 billion. Year-to-date volume was 24.4 billion shares in 1998, compared with 23.4 billion a year earlier, a gain of 4.03%. The VSE, which traded smaller, more speculative issues, established an active Investigations and Enforcement Division concerned with manipulative trading and related abuses.

Canadian bond yields fell on expectations of strong economic growth in the world's largest trading partners. The benchmark 30-year Canada bond yielded 5.49% in early November and fell to 4.82% in December. Corporate bond yields were 6.26% in early December. Bank prime was 6.26% but ticked up to end the year at 6.75%.

(IRVING PFEFFER)

Western Europe. Markets that made steady gains through 1997 continued to perform strongly, although the contraction of Asian economies, the increased attractiveness of Asian exports, and the fall in global demand began to weaken the region's manufacturing base. The markets of the core euro-area bloc—France, Germany, and Italy—were buoyed by confidence in progress to monetary union in 1999. As the century drew to a close, substantial globalization had again been achieved, and financial markets had become far more integrated.

Convergence took on a new twist with steps toward a single European stock market. In July London and Frankfurt announced an alliance, and in November Madrid said it wished to join, closely followed by Milan and Amsterdam. The Paris Bourse, having first expressed outrage at the Anglo-German link, declared that Paris also would join. The London-Frankfurt alliance was scheduled to begin on Jan. 4, 1999. In

the U.S. the S&P announced the launch of two new euro-equity indexes to cover companies in the 11 countries of the European monetary union.

Interest rates moved down in several countries: Italy, Spain, Sweden, Denmark, and the U.K. On December 3 Germany's Bundesbank, the Bank of France, and all other euro-area central banks except the Bank of Italy brought down their base rates to 3%. European stock markets rallied on the news. Finland (up 69%) topped the euro area, but all continental markets ended the year higher, including those in France (31%), Germany (15%), Spain (37%), Belgium (45%), and Italy (41%). Outside the European Monetary Union, the FT-SE topped 5883 at year-end, a rise of 15%.

Other Countries. Whereas investor sentiment toward the U.S. remained benign, sentiment toward Japan continued to be negative despite the availability of stock on very attractive valuations. Little headway on banking reform and restructuring had been made by summer, and in August the seriousness of Japan's banking failures became clearer. Years of poor lending practices had left the country riddled with debt, estimates of which continued to rise. American officials put total banking industry debt at $1 trillion, double the estimate of Japanese officials. Concern remained high over the state of Japan's economy as the recession deepened. By October the Nikkei 225 index had fallen a further 13.2% since January 1, but by the end of November the government had announced a new package of measures to stimulate domestic demand and passed legislation to deal with problems in the banking system. It also pledged financial support to Asian countries in crisis. The Nikkei ended the year at 13,842.17, down 9.3%.

Japan's bleak economic performance spilled over into other Asian countries, exacerbating their problems. Contagion threatened to spread to Latin America's emerging markets, which had hitherto weathered the crisis. In South Korea and Thailand, financial indicators were positive for much of the year; appreciating exchange rates, falling interest rates, and very strong reserves signaled a turning point in performance and indicated recovery for 1999. Asia appeared set to be the first region to recover, and Asian markets had outperformed Latin-American markets since the middle of the year.

The stock markets of Europe's former centrally planned economies suffered de-

Table VII. Selected U.S. Stock Market Indexes[1]

	1998 range[2] High	1998 range[2] Low	Year-end close	Percent change from 12/31/97
Dow Jones Averages				
30 Industrials	9374	7539	9181	16
20 Transportation	3686	2345	3149	−3
15 Utilities	321	263	312	14
65 Composite	2961	2411	2871	10
Standard & Poor's				
500 Index	1242	928	1229	27
Industrials	1494	1077	1479	32
Utilities	267	226	260	10
Others				
NYSE Composite	601	477	596	17
Nasdaq Composite	2193	1419	2193	40
Amex Composite	754	564	689	1
Russell 2000	491	310	422	−3

[1] Index numbers are rounded. [2] Based on daily closing price.
Sources: *Financial Times, Wall Street Journal.*

clines ranging from 12% by Poland to a staggering 84.9% by Russia. Markets were shaken in August by Russia's unilateral decision to reschedule its debt, and fears were raised that other large debtors would do the same. Once that danger was seen to have receded, investors' attention moved elsewhere. Although there was political risk in the economic and social instability of the nuclear power, Russia's economy had become too small to have any significant impact on the progress of world markets. As the year ended, China faced increasing pressure to devalue its currency. Devaluation could cause American corporate profits to weaken further and stock prices to fall.

Commodity Prices. Commodity prices fell by 25% over the year and were at their lowest for more than 20 years. The price of North Sea Brent crude, used as a benchmark for global oil prices, averaged $13 a barrel, its lowest in real terms since the crisis of 1973–74, and dropped below $10 a barrel on December 10. It ended the year only slightly higher at $10.385. The root cause had been oversupply coinciding with mild weather and weak consumption in the winter of 1997–98. Oil stocks had been high throughout the summer. A number of producers agreed to cut production to help run down stocks and halt the slide in prices. Sluggish world economic growth was expected to hold prices well below the average $19 a barrel recorded in 1997.

The price of non-oil commodities was at its lowest since 1986, and the price of industrial materials was estimated to have fallen by more than 24%. Asia accounted for 25–30% of global consumption of industrial materials, and the slump in demand brought about by the contraction of these economies combined with a slowdown in developed economies to depress prices further.

Following a slump earlier in the year, demand for gold stabilized. Demand in the 25 countries monitored by the World Gold Council totaled 1,712 tons in the first nine months of the year, 20% down on the same period of 1997. Although the demand for gold had increased, the price continued to fall. An ounce of gold that cost $400 in early 1996 cost less than $300 by early December. *The Economist* Commodity Price Index showed the price to be down 3.9% over the year.

Foodstuff prices fell by 9% in the year to October. Good harvests in the U.S. and stagnant import demand were likely to hold down grain prices well into the first half of 1999. Short supply looked to be shoring up cocoa prices, and sugar prices appeared to stabilize. Downward pressure on coffee prices came from the marketing of a new Brazilian crop of around 35 million bags.

Low commodity prices eroded the revenues of countries dependent on the export of them but exercised a check on inflation in the developed economies. The decline in prices caused by the recession in Japan and the rest of East and Southeast Asia had been a factor in the spread of the Asia crisis. The wide range of affected prices had, in turn, further weakened equity markets.   (IEIS)

BANKING

Amid a global financial crisis and intense efforts to prepare for the introduction of the European Union common currency (the euro) and the computer problem caused by the year 2000 date change, industrywide consolidation both within and across national borders continued to reshape the financial services landscape in 1998. At the same time, 1998 was marked by ongoing efforts in the United States and other countries to modernize laws governing the affiliation of banks with other financial institutions.

In response to these pressures, consolidation within the American banking industry continued apace with the merger of major institutions such as NationsBank and BankAmerica. The merger of Citicorp and the Travelers Group—creating Citigroup—combined for the first time in the U.S. a major banking organization and an insurance company. Indicative of the extent to which the Depression-era barriers against combining banking and securities activities had been eroded by regulatory interpretations made by the Federal Reserve System during the past 10 years, the Citicorp-Travelers merger included one of the largest American investment banks, Salomon Smith Barney Inc. Without passage of financial modernization legislation, under existing law Citigroup would have to divest its insurance-underwriting activities within two years of the merger (under certain circumstances this divestiture period could be extended for up to an additional three years). Interestingly, no such requirement applies to its securities business.

Elsewhere around the world, Swiss Bank and Union Bank of Switzerland combined to form UBS AG, Fortis won the bidding to buy Generale de Banque of Belgium, Credito Italiano bought Unicredito, and Bayerische Vereinsbank AG merged with Bayerische Hypobank, to name but a few of the more notable transactions completed during 1998. Banks in several Latin-American countries were acquired by Spanish and other European banks, but proposed mergers among four of the largest Canadian banks were blocked by the government, which was concerned about their impact. As the year drew to a close, Deutsche Bank and Bankers Trust reached a merger agreement valued at approximately $10 billion, signaling that global competition in financial services was intensifying and that industry consolidation, including across borders, would continue in 1999.

Against this backdrop of market activity, legislative efforts in the U.S. Congress to lift the legal restrictions on the formation of financial conglomerates once again fell short. In May the House of Representatives passed financial-modernization legislation that would permit banks to affiliate with securities and insurance underwriters without limitation and expand merchant banking opportunities for their securities affiliates. Despite extensive efforts to secure the bill's enactment, the legislation failed to reach the floor of the Senate for a vote prior to Congress's adjournment late in the year. The legislation was to be reintroduced when the new 106th Congress convened in January 1999 and was expected to receive serious consideration, though significant policy differences, particularly between the Department of the Treasury and the Federal Reserve Board, remained to be resolved.

As the operations of financial institutions throughout the world became more complex and multifaceted, the functions and responsibilities of the supervisory authorities of financial services were being restructured, and increasing attention was being devoted to the exercise of "umbrella" supervision of financial institutions. In the wake of the Asian financial crisis, the default on Russian debt, and the repercussions those events had throughout the emerging markets, increasing attention also was being devoted to strengthening the organization of the international financial system as a whole.

At the national level Japan, South Korea, and the United Kingdom created new authorities and vested them with the responsibility for oversight of the financial system as a whole. Australia began implementing a comprehensive restructuring of its financial supervisory authorities that shifted supervisory responsibilities from the central bank to the new Prudential Regulation Authority. China was considering significant reform of its financial system, including restructuring the central bank along the lines of the U.S. Federal Reserve System. Questions about which governmental authority would exercise "umbrella" supervision of financial holding companies became a central part of the financial modernization debates in the U.S. Other countries, including Finland, Panama, South Africa, and Turkey, were either implementing or considering measures to enhance the effectiveness of their financial supervisory authorities without undertaking a wholesale restructuring of their financial systems.

Measures were also taken in 1998 to enhance the safety and soundness of financial institutions. Countries such as Belgium, China, Colombia, Latvia, and Uruguay strengthened the effectiveness of internal control and audit procedures, whereas Indonesia, Peru, Philippines, Turkey, and Venezuela adopted stricter rules relating to loan loss reserves and the classification of loans.

Preparations for the introduction of the euro in January 1999, meanwhile, extended well beyond the 11 countries that initially would constitute the Economic and Monetary Union (EMU). The magnitude of converting to a common currency was truly daunting, as the shift to a single currency necessitated the extensive reformulation of the systems used to conduct the myriad of transactions that occurred each day in the financial markets.

The year 2000 date change presented even greater technological and managerial challenges in 1998, and efforts to prepare for the new millennium were expected to intensify in 1999. It was clear that addressing the year 2000 issues was among the highest priorities within the international banking community and that it was being addressed through the concerted efforts of the regulators, banks, and banking associations. (*See* COMPUTER AND INFORMATION SYSTEMS: *Sidebar.*)

Throughout 1998 many countries continued to bolster their efforts to combat money laundering. These actions included imposing "know your customer" (KYC) requirements (in the U.S., for example, federal bank regulators in December published for comment proposed KYC regulations), expanding the types of institutions that would be subject to reporting requirements, creating special governmental agencies to investigate suspected money-laundering activities, and increasing penalties for money-laundering offenses.   (LAWRENCE R. UHLICK)

LABOUR-MANAGEMENT RELATIONS

The economic malaise in much of East Asia and in Russia continued in 1998, but for the economies of most Western industrial countries it was a modestly successful year. The unemployment situation, however, remained disappointing in many nations. For the world as a whole, the International Labour Organization (ILO) expected that the number of jobless would reach 150 million by the end of the year. Among the industrialized countries of the West, more than 10% of the workforce was unemployed in Belgium, Finland, France, Germany, Italy, and Spain.

Controversy continued as to whether observance of minimum labour standards should be made a condition of international trade agreements, with the United States and France among those arguing in favour of the proposition and others holding either that it was unnecessary or, particularly in the less-developed countries, that it was a protectionist device on the part of the advanced industrialized nations. In June the annual Conference of the ILO arrived at a declaration on fundamental labour standards, pledging member countries to uphold seven of the organization's key labour standards dealing with freedom to organize and bargain collectively and banning forced labour, child labour, and discrimination in the workplace. Juan Somavia of Chile was elected to be the next director-general of the ILO.

Europe. Of the 15 member countries of the European Union (EU), 11 were approved for membership in the European Monetary Union, requiring fixed rates of exchange to come into effect on Jan. 1, 1999, as a step toward the replacement of national currencies by the euro in 2002. Denmark, Sweden, and the United Kingdom did not request membership, and Greece did not satisfy the economic criteria needed for entry. While the present moves were not likely to produce Europe-wide collective bargaining, at least not in the short term, the expected economic transparency and the fact that control of economic levers was increasingly moving from national governments to the EU were bound to strengthen the international links in industrial relations, as was evidenced in September when trade unions from Germany, Luxembourg, The Netherlands, and Belgium met to discuss a common approach to collective bargaining.

In the U.K. the government moved to fulfill its election promises on low pay and union recognition. In May the Commission on Low Pay recommended that there should be a national minimum wage of £3.60 an hour from April 1999 (£1=$1.65). The government adopted this rate for workers 22 years old and over, coupling it with a rate of £3.00 an hour for those aged 18 to 22, subsequently to be increased to £3.20; no rate was fixed for those under 18. On May 22 the government announced its proposals on employment rights in a White Paper entitled "Fairness at Work." The most important proposal concerned an obligation for employers to recognize trade unions in cases when at least 40% of eligible employees voted in favour of having a union, with automatic recognition taking place when more than half of the relevant workforce belonged to a union. In disputed cases an existing body, the Central Arbitration Committee,

PAUL VATHIS—AP/WIDE WORLD

A tractor-trailer leaves a Caterpillar Inc. plant in York, Pa., after the United Automobile Workers union announced a tentative agreement with the earth-moving equipment company to settle a long-standing management-union dispute.

could grant recognition. The recognition procedure would not apply to firms employing up to 20 workers. Other noteworthy proposals in the White Paper concerned reducing the qualifying length of service for claims alleging unfair dismissal from two years to one year, giving an employee a statutory right to be accompanied by a fellow employee or trade union representative during grievance and disciplinary procedures, and introducing a right for time off for urgent family reasons. Statutory maternity leave would be increased from 14 to 18 weeks.

Unemployment continued to be particularly worrisome in Germany, but there the most significant event of the year was the election, in September, of a left-of-centre coalition government. It was announced that the new government would reverse the cuts in pensions and sick pay decided upon by its predecessor. It intended to work with the unions and employers in an alliance on jobs and training to attack unemployment. Strong voices among the unions quickly expressed the view that after years of union moderation in collective bargaining and acceptance of labour market flexibility, and in a buoyant economy, the time had come for workers to receive substantial improvements—the huge metalworkers' union spoke of a wage increase of 6.5% in the coming round of wage negotiations.

In France the centre of attention was the government's intention to ensure that the workweek be reduced to 35 hours by 2000 (2002 for firms employing fewer than 20 workers). A law to that effect was promulgated on June 14. Employers continued to deplore the measure and began trying to mitigate its damaging effects. Thus, in July the important metal employers' federation, covering employers of about 1.8 million workers, reached agreement with some—though not all—of its union counterparts, providing an actual working year of 1,645 hours for full-time workers (for some firms 1,610 hours). The agreement increased annual permitted overtime per worker from 94 to 180 hours (in some cases 150 hours),

those limits being extendable by 25 hours for the first two years of the life of the agreement. A possibility was provided for workers to offset overtime by extra days of leave. Companies introducing annualized working hours would have a daily limit per employee of 10 or 12 hours and a weekly limit of 48 hours or 42 hours, averaged over 12 weeks. These limits could be increased by negotiation within companies. The minister responsible for the law was angered by the agreement, which she considered did little to further the law's intention of reducing unemployment.

In Italy the government submitted its bill to reduce working hours to 35 a week, which had earlier been hotly contested but had led to an employer-union joint declaration on wider issues to the effect that the two parties should discuss new rules concerning concerted action, the government should discuss the operation of the 1993 inter-confederal agreement with them, and unions and employers should try to promote employment creation in southern Italy, where unemployment had long been high. It was agreed that collective bargaining should continue on a normal basis. It appeared at the year's end that the unions and employers had ensured that they would be fully involved in the discussions on the reduction of working hours in the wider context of Italian industrial relations.

Usually notable for industrial peace rather than conflict, Denmark in April, for the first time since 1985, suffered a major stoppage of work. Negotiations on a new two-year agreement had ended with the approval of a joint mediation proposal, which was put to a vote—regarded in advance as a formality. Voters, however, rejected the proposal, and a strike by more than 500,000 workers began on April 27. After 10 days of the strike and no progress in employer-union negotiations, parliament imposed a settlement based on the original mediation proposal but added some concessions, including an additional day's leave and extra leave after six months of service for workers with children under 14. Employers were given some tax concessions.

United States. A long-standing and often bitter period of management-union relations at Caterpillar Inc., the world's largest maker of earth-moving equipment, appeared to have ended in March, when the company and the United Automobile Workers union (UAW) arrived at a six-year agreement. The settlement was facilitated by the firm's undertaking to reinstate 160 workers dismissed for action related to strikes; the union, for its part, agreed to readmit to membership workers who had continued to work for the company and to drop unfair labour practice claims against the firm. The agreement allowed the company to engage new labour at lower wages, and changes were made in incentive arrangements, linking pay more closely to the performance of specific units. Caterpillar conceded pay raises and undertook to improve job security and pension entitlements. The UAW was also involved in a major dispute at General Motors Corp. (GM), which started in June with strikes in two parts plants in Flint, Mich., related to the firm's desire to improve productivity and make changes in workplace rules. The union was concerned about job security, fearing that the firm would move jobs to cheaper labour markets, and also about health and safety. The firm filed suit asking for arbitration, arguing that the strikes were illegal as they did not involve strikeable national issues. The dispute shut down the great majority of GM's facilities in North America, and settlement was only reached on July 29, when the company pledged not to sell its Delphi plant in Flint

before the end of 1999 and withdrew its legal suit and the parties agreed to work together on improving negotiating procedures.

Australia. In Australia the operation of the docks has long been regarded as one of the least efficient in any industrialized country, the unions exercising a stranglehold on working practices. In April, Patrick Stevedoring, one of the two largest stevedoring firms, withdrew financial support from its subsidiary labour-hire companies, resulting in their bankruptcy and the laying off of 1,400 dockworkers. Patrick then opened up dock work to nonunion labour. The union reacted strongly, receiving support from the International Transport Workers Federation, which said that it would boycott shippers using nonunion labour. A federal court required Patrick to reinstate the dockers. A deal was then struck, with Patrick undertaking to reinstate the dismissed workers and not use nonunion labour and the union agreeing not to proceed with further legal action and also to accept changes in working practices.

South Korea. In the summer South Korea's biggest car maker, Hyundai, was hit by strikes, and its production complex in Ulsan was occupied in protest against job cuts. A deal was reached on August 24, however, with the company agreeing to cut the number of workers dismissed to 277. Other workers the company had wanted to dismiss would have 18 months of unpaid leave and would receive training in the last six months of that period. (R.O. CLARKE)

CONSUMER AFFAIRS

International. Food concerns, world economic turmoil, and trade issues loomed large on the consumer agenda in 1998. As genetically modified (GM) food products reached supermarket shelves around the world, consumer organizations were concerned that consumers were being told far too little about the ethical and health implications of these products. Many foods made with GM organisms were not even required to be labeled as such. In May a committee of the Codex Alimentarius Commission—the UN body responsible for setting international food standards—held a meeting to discuss food labeling. At the meeting consumer groups and other nongovernmental organizations urged the Codex committee to require compulsory labeling of all GM food. Consumers International (CI), a federation of some 235 consumer organizations in more than 100 countries, ran a campaign exhorting people to fax the Codex committee directly and urge mandatory labeling. Hundreds of such faxes were sent, but the Codex committee, under heavy pressure from industry, rejected the call for mandatory labeling. Instead, it decided to seek further expert scientific opinion and take up the issue again in 1999.

Consumer issues became increasingly entangled with trade issues, due to the liberalization of global trade through such agreements as the 1994 General Agreement on Tariffs and Trade and the establishment of

Striking Hyundai Motor Company workers stage a rally on July 15 in Ulsan, S. Kor., to protest company layoffs. About 26,000 employees participated in the protest.

the World Trade Organization (WTO). Consumer groups grew increasingly concerned that such trade agreements, which in theory could mean lower prices and more products, could also mean lower standards in a variety of areas, from food to product safety.

Consumer organizations and other nongovernmental groups were also active in discussion on international trade and economic agreements. One of the successes exposed a little-known but potentially powerful trade deal called the Multilateral Agreement on Investment (MAI). The MAI was generated by the 29 member countries of the Organisation for Economic Co-operation and Development. Many organizations feared the MAI could give free rein to multinational companies in the area of foreign investment by weakening and perhaps overriding local and national consumer and environmental regulations. Progress toward passage of the MAI—scheduled for 1998—stalled under public opposition. In May, during the WTO's ministerial conference in Geneva, consumer organizations joined with other groups to demand greater transparency and accountability at the WTO.

Transatlantic trade between the European Union (EU) and the U.S. was a major issue for consumer organizations, which feared such relations were too heavily influenced by business and industry. In response, consumer organizations from the 15 EU countries and the U.S. met in September to discuss the launch of a transatlantic consumer dialogue to offset an already existing transatlantic business dialogue.

The Euro-Mediterranean Forum on Consumer Policy, held in October, included 12 Mediterranean countries or territories that were not part of the EU—Morocco, Algeria, Tunisia, Egypt, Syria, Jordan, Lebanon, the Palestinian Authority, Malta, Cyprus, Turkey, and Israel. The goal of the meeting was to promote the development of effective consumer policy in those places and to provide a forum for consumer organizations from the EU and the Mediterranean partner countries to exchange experiences and ideas.

Eastern and Central European consumer organizations and government consumer departments were involved in the process of harmonizing their laws with EU legislation in order to accelerate accession to membership in the EU. This included the regulation of marketing practices; consumer credit, guarantees, and after-sales services; and the regulation of package travel and time-share property. Consumer organizations also were campaigning to improve standards of health care and public utilities, which continued to deteriorate in many parts of the region. Economic turmoil in Russia brought the work of consumer groups to the forefront. Consumer organizations, through the media and other outlets, highlighted the critical need for consumer protection, particularly in the banking sector.

In Latin America the privatization of public utilities continued to be an important area of activity. The First Regional Conference on Consumers and Public Utilities, held in January, was the culmination of two years of research and lobbying work in Brazil, Peru, Chile, Mexico, and Colombia. Consumer groups in all five countries took important first steps to monitor the provision of basic services, such as electricity, water,

and telecommunications, and in participating in national regulatory agencies. Consumers in El Salvador and Guyana began organizing to press for more participation in the regulation of basic services. CI's office for Latin America and the Caribbean published seven reports on the state of consumer participation in public-utility regulation. Argentina launched new Consumer Defense Courts (three-member arbitration boards with consumer representation) for the settlement of consumer complaints and enacted reforms to its Consumer Defense Law. In Ecuador the new constitution adopted in 1998 included several articles devoted to consumer protection. In Brazil authorities decreed that consumer education be included in the national school curriculum for grades 5 through 8.

The ongoing economic crisis in Asia dominated the lives of consumers there. In Hong Kong the Consumer Council lobbied for legislative reforms on behalf of thousands of people who had lost millions of dollars on popular discounted prepaid coupons, which normally would be redeemed at a later date. Many consumers were left holding hundreds of useless coupons, however, when the businesses that had sold the coupons suffered financial troubles.

The most vulnerable consumers in Asia were the poor, who bore the brunt of the financial crisis. That was one of the reasons why the theme of 1998's World Consumer Rights Day was "Poverty: Rallying for Change." The day was commemorated on March 15 around the world in a variety of innovative ways, including a speech dedicated to the topic by Russian Pres. Boris Yeltsin. In Africa the consumer movement also was heavily involved with poverty issues, such as access to and quality of food, health services, and shelter. About 89 consumer organizations existed in 45 of Africa's 56 countries. The movement was gaining a foothold in the region, however, and the CI regional office had undertaken an ambitious three-year program called "Consolidating and Strengthening the Consumer Movement in Africa."   (ALINA TUGEND)

United States. Consumer affairs at the federal level in 1998 involved the continuing efforts to address information, safety, and fraud—with some attendant controversy. The Department of Agriculture delayed setting long-anticipated national organic-food standards; an extraordinary deluge of some 200,000 responses to its proposed regulations, issued in mid-December 1997, prompted the agency to make fundamental revisions. The standards were intended to govern the National Organic Program called for in the Organic Foods Production Act of 1990, which aimed to resolve the confusion created by a patchwork of private and state rules regulating organic-food production and labeling. The majority of the comments received opposed the proposal's inclusion of biotechnology-derived products as organic foods and the use of biosolids (municipal sludge) in their production and irradiation in their processing. One consumer group, however, warned that such concerns could backfire, with standards made too restrictive for the organic-food industry to expand into large-scale production.

With expansion of a new food-safety system called Hazard Analysis and Critical Control Points (HACCP) underway at the

beginning of the year, the Food and Drug Administration (FDA) in April called for retail food businesses to test the feasibility of the system in restaurants, grocery stores, and institutional food services. The FDA also proposed requiring food processors of packaged fruit and vegetable juices to implement HAACP. Following an outbreak of food-borne illness from apple cider the previous year, the agency issued final rules in July regarding warning labels on unpasteurized juices. The White House, meanwhile, established a President's Council on Food Safety to coordinate the various food-safety activities of the separate federal agencies into a comprehensive, strategic, federal food-safety plan. The General Accounting Office and National Research Council weighed in with reports suggesting coordination could entail streamlining safety laws and oversight in a single agency, rather than the existing 12 agencies and 35 different statutes.

Concerns about the risk that large vehicles, particularly sport utility vehicles, posed to people in smaller cars were highlighted when the National Highway Traffic Safety Administration (NHTSA) began crash testing light trucks and vans with passenger cars. The NHTSA reported on incompatibilities or mismatches in vehicle design, such as bumper heights, that might increase the consequences of crashes. The Insurance Institute for Highway Safety provided helpful perspective with its report, based on real-world crash data, that showed the relative importance of vehicle size in safety, but it also showed that other factors mattered, such as design, use patterns, and where and how vehicles were driven. The NHTSA proposed to increase the prominence of mandatory rollover warning labels in sport utility vehicles.

The Federal Trade Commission (FTC) reported a relatively new consumer problem known as cramming, in which unscrupulous billing firms added charges for unwanted products or services to consumers' local telephone bills without their knowledge. Sparked in part by the confusing complexity of local phone bills, cramming generated about 9,000 complaints to the FTC over a 12-month period and led to calls for federal or state intervention. Opponents of anti-cramming legislation wanted consumer safeguards for phone bills similar to those for credit card bills, which were developed successfully and voluntarily by the industry.

Stating that fraud could slow the growth of consumer business over the Internet, the FTC launched Consumer Sentinel, a secure consumer fraud and complaint database for use by law enforcement organizations in the U.S. and Canada. Following its report to Congress on Internet privacy, the FTC also suggested that legislative measures should be taken to protect consumer financial information, which prompted concern that overly rigid rules would hamper commerce.

As states cracked down on misleading and fraudulent sweepstakes pitches, 32 states and the District of Columbia reached a settlement with American Family Publishers, one of the largest sweepstakes outfits, over alleged misleading offers. The National Association of Attorneys General began to study whether additional specific laws were needed to protect consumers from abusive and deceptive sweepstakes activities.   (PETER L. SPENCER)

Education

Noteworthy educational events in 1998 concerned achievement testing, the expansion of information technology, educational policy controversies, cross-national cooperation in higher education, methods of financing schools, and student protests. In some predominantly Muslim countries, controversy arose over the schooling of girls and the teaching of the Qur'an.

Primary and Secondary Education. In a study of 34 nations by the Organisation for Economic Co-operation and Development (OECD), Norway and Belgium had the highest percentage of high-school students who graduated, each with 100%. The seven next highest were Japan (99%), Finland (98%), Poland (94%), New Zealand (93%), Portugal (91%), South Korea (91%), and Russia (88%). Germany ranked 11th (86%), France 13th (85%), Canada 22nd (73%), the United States 24th (72%), Argentina 32nd (34%), and Mexico 34th (26%). According to the study's director, Andreas Schleicher, rates in the U.S. had remained much the same over the years, whereas many other nations had rapidly increased their rates in recent times.

Test results were reported for students in the final year of secondary school who participated in the Third International Mathematics and Science Study, sponsored by the International Association for the Evaluation of Educational Achievement. The program's three tests focused on science-mathematics literacy, advanced mathematics, and physics. Among 21 nations represented in the science-mathematics literacy program, the highest average scores were in The Netherlands and Sweden, with Iceland, Norway, and Switzerland somewhat lower. Countries performing below the international average were, in descending order, Hungary, Russia, Italy, the U.S., Lithuania, Cyprus, and South Africa. In all 21 countries except South Africa, males had significantly higher average achievement than females. Students who made the greatest use of electronic calculators during the testing performed better than those who made less use of them. The nine nations in which more than 50% of students reported using computers weekly were Australia, Austria, Canada, Denmark, Iceland, The Netherlands, New Zealand, Switzerland, and the U.S.

Achievement tests for advanced mathematics and physics were administered in 16 countries. France ranked at the top in advanced mathematics, followed by Russia, Switzerland, Denmark, Cyprus, and Lithuania. The lowest average scores were in the Czech Republic, Germany, the U.S., and Austria. In physics Norway and Sweden were significantly higher than the other nations, followed by Russia and Denmark. The lowest physics scores were in France, the Czech Republic, Austria, and the U.S.

In the U.S. the school voucher and charter school movements continued to gain momentum. Typical voucher programs conducted by selected states and cities furnished parents a stipend ranging from $1,500 to $5,000 per year to help pay the cost of sending a child to a school of the parents' choice. Whereas in 1994 only 45% of respondents in a nationwide Gallup Poll endorsed voucher plans, in a 1998 survey 51% favoured full or partial government subsidies to pay tuition costs at any public,

First-grade students and their teacher (right) return from a visit to one of the 57 schools participating in a pilot school voucher program in Cleveland, Ohio. Supporters of the city's program were encouraged when they discovered that the U.S. Supreme Court had refused to hear a Wisconsin case opposing the voucher system.

private, or church-related school. Support for vouchers was also expressed in legal decisions and monetary contributions from nongovernmental sources. The U.S. Supreme Court accepted the Wisconsin Supreme Court's ruling that the state's voucher program did not violate the constitutional separation of church and state. This allowed Wisconsin to continue its voucher plan, under which many holders of vouchers enrolled their children in private schools. The growing list of donors offering voucher funds for poor families included officials of Gulfstream Aerospace and Wal-Mart Stores ($200 million), New York City's School Choice Scholarship Foundation ($11 million), and patrons of the Roman Catholic Archdiocese of New York ($10 million). Advocates of vouchers asserted that such plans improved education by allowing parents to decide where to have their children educated and by fostering healthy competition between schools. Opponents contended that vouchers not only breached the law separating church and state but also siphoned off the best students from public schools and allowed private schools to reject less-competent and handicapped pupils.

The first charter school in the U.S. opened in Minnesota in 1992. By the end of 1998, about 700 such schools were operating in 23 states and enrolling an estimated 165,000 students. The American version of a charter school was a primary or secondary institution financed by public funds but managed by either a nonprofit or a profit-making organization. The typical charter school was free to create its own curriculum, hire noncredentialed teachers, and monitor its own fiscal affairs. Such an arrangement, long practiced in other nations, was accompanied in the U.S. by heated debate. To evaluate the quality of charter schools, journalists visited dozens of them in the two states with the most charter institutions (Arizona and Michigan) and concluded that some of the schools were excellent but that many others displayed serious shortcomings—weak curricula, poor teaching, substandard buildings, and financial abuses.

A growing debate in the U.S. was concerned with whether students should hold jobs while attending school. A study conducted at the University of Massachusetts reported that in some communities as many as 80% of high-school students engaged in some sort of employment, with nearly half of them working 20 hours or more each week. Advocates of school-plus-work maintained that having a job builds self-confidence and teaches youths responsibility, economic self-reliance, and the ability to get along with customers and fellow employees. Critics worried that a job, particularly one that required more than 20 hours a week, deprived students of needed sleep and exercise, diverted their attention from school tasks, resulted in a shallow education, and left little time for social life.

In the U.S. the failure of educators to persuade teachers to enrich their lessons with

Muslim women stage a protest in downtown Istanbul over a ban on Islamic-style scarves in Turkish schools and public offices. The ban came at the behest of the military, which viewed the scarves as a symbol of radical Islam, and thus a threat to Turkey's secular educational system.

advanced technology motivated officials of the Olympia, Wash., school district to create an 18-week course for training secondary-school students in computer technology so that those students could then help teachers improve their use of technology to enhance instruction. News of the success of the Olympia program caused other school systems to adopt the plan.

In addition to forbidding students to carry guns or knives, American schools began to outlaw the laser pointer—a device in the shape of a pen or large bullet that could cast a red laser beam on anyone or anything within a quarter of a mile. Not only did teachers condemn laser pointers for disrupting classroom instruction, but critics also warned of likely damage to eyesight if the beam were directed into the eyes.

Disappointing test results among black secondary-school seniors caused South African officials to question the effectiveness of their postapartheid public-school system. Over a one-year period the percentage of blacks passing the national matriculation exam dropped from 58.5% to 52.2%. During the three years of postapartheid South Africa, the former black, white, and Coloured (mixed race) education systems were slowly being merged, with the hope that test results for blacks would gradually improve. The current condition of the education system's infrastructure suggested, however, that this hope would not soon be realized, as 51% of schools still lacked textbooks and 57% were without electricity.

Research in five countries (Mauritius, Namibia, Tanzania, Zambia, and Zimbabwe) of the 12-nation Southern African Consortium for Monitoring Educational Quality led to a variety of educational policy recommendations. Prominent among the suggestions were the proposals that parental support of children's schooling be increased through use of parent meetings, educational forums, and radio programs; that teachers

receive specific training in how best to work with parents; and that each government set a national policy concerning the frequency and amount of homework for different grades in its schools. A new study was launched for the 1998–2001 period to provide information about reading and mathematics achievement at the sixth-grade level that could guide governments' educational decisions in the 10 nations.

Teaching computer literacy became an increasingly high priority in much of the world. The British plan for a "national grid for learning" set the year 2003 as the time that all 32,000 U.K. schools would be linked to the Internet. By late 1998 more than 6,000 schools were already linked. The plan was supported by a private charity organization, UK NetYear, which offered free E-mail address services to pupils and teachers along with a multimedia program for teachers titled "Computers Don't Bite." Initial funding included £50 million (U.S. $82.5 million) from the central government and £50 million from local authorities, with an additional £230 million ($380 million) for teacher training derived from the national lottery.

Ireland's education minister, Michael Martin, announced his government's intention to establish Ireland as the "information services hub" for Europe by ensuring that all Irish children were computer literate by the end of their school career. In pursuit of this goal, the government planned to increase annual spending on education from $3.3 billion in 1997 to $4.6 billion by 2002. Of that amount, $71 million would be used to acquire information and communications equipment, training, curriculum manuals, and Internet connections for 4,000 schools.

A new national education policy in Botswana aimed to prepare students for an industrial economy driven by information technology. A key feature of the plan would be a computer awareness program in all sec-

ondary and tertiary institutions. The program, organized in a 10-year basic computer education curriculum, was designed to develop students' skills in word processing and the use of spreadsheets and databases.

China's new primary-school policies—introduced in Beijing, Tianjin, Shanghai, and selected provinces—reduced children's homework load by 50% and replaced the age-old 100-mark-exam tradition with a system that rated students' performance as excellent, good, pass, or fail. Sixty percent of a child's grade would be based on overall achievement and 40% on behaviour. Supporters of the change claimed it would improve children's mental health and allow them time for leisure reading, painting, and club activities. Critics worried that the change would make students lazy, decreasing their effort to work as diligently as they had under the 100-mark system.

In South Korea a new primary-school textbook came under fire from conservative forces for portraying life in North Korea in too favourable a light. Government officials charged the author, Lee Chang Hee, with violating South Korea's national security law, but Lee's supporters contended that his "open attitude" toward the North was necessary if the North and South were ever to be united.

Struggles between Japanese conservatives and liberals intensified over issues of teaching patriotism in the schools. In Tokorozawa High School students refused to participate in graduation ceremonies that involved the nation's flag and the national anthem, an act that reflected the national teachers union policy of resisting the use of the flag and anthem in schools. At the same time, the Ministry of Education directed all schools to fly the flag and sing the anthem. The new film *Pride* was lauded by conservatives for portraying Gen. Hideki Tojo, the architect of Japan's military conquests in World War II, as a gentle family man who was the victim of American bigotry.

Evaluators of a voucher system that had operated in Chile since 1980 concluded that allowing parents to use a government tuition coupon to send their children to any school of their choice did not result in private schools' providing better education than public ones. Competition between public and private schools also did not raise the overall quality of education or reduce its costs. Instead, the new instructional materials, technical assistance, and teacher in-service training provided by the government was credited with the improved test scores that students had achieved in recent years.

Afghanistan's Taliban Islamic fundamentalist government moved further in restricting educational opportunities for females by ordering the closing of private schools that had been teaching girls in defiance of the government's policy of keeping women and girls at home. Foreign-aid representatives reported that in 107 such schools in the nation's capital city of Kabul, half of the 6,500 children enrolled had been girls. Under a new set of rules, the schools could be licensed to reopen if they admitted girls no older than age eight and if the curriculum consisted solely of lessons about the Qur'an.

As a means of curbing Islamic activism in Turkey, the government closed dozens of Qur'an schools, banned weekend and summer Qur'an courses, and placed additional restrictions on religious instruction in the re-

maining Islamic institutions. Under the court ruling only children who had completed their eight years of required secular education could be taught about the Qur'an, and the lowest age at which students could enroll was raised from 12 to 15. In addition, the president of the University of Istanbul, Kemal Alemdaroglu, banned from the campus men with Islamic-style beards and women wearing head scarves. Alemdaroglu's edict resulted in protest demonstrations by 2,000 Muslim students.

Opinion questionnaires filled out by two million French secondary-school students revealed their overwhelming enthusiasm for sex education and for letting students grade themselves. The study also showed widespread concern among teenagers about finding a job in view of a national unemployment rate exceeding 12%.

Higher Education. In the U.S. controversy increased over colleges' affirmative-action practices introduced two decades earlier to admit students from disadvantaged minorities who had substandard entrance-test scores. After the University of California eliminated its affimative-action program, similar programs in the states of Texas, Michigan, and Washington came under attack by critics of preferential treatment for minority groups. In response to such attacks, students and professors at 25 colleges across the nation coordinated an array of rallies, lectures, and "walkout" strikes under the title "National Day of Action to Defend Affirmative Action." Advocates of affirmative-action programs contended that having more African-American and Hispanic students on campus was of educational value by introducing the white majority to minority students and their cultures. In defense of affirmative action, the University of Michigan's president, Lee Bollinger, asserted that "a classroom that does not have a significant representation from members of different races produces an impoverished discussion."

A pact aimed at reducing alcohol abuse among students on American campuses was signed by 24 colleges in the Boston area. Included among the 50 items in the pact were measures for encouraging first-year students to live in alcohol-free housing, for providing more alcohol-free social events, and for banning liquor at sororities' and fraternities' recruiting events. The colleges also planned regular meetings with police, community groups, and owners of liquor stores and nightclubs to improve the enforcement of laws prohibiting underage drinking. The pact was created in the wake of the binge-drinking deaths of three underage students at fraternity parties in separate institutions (the University of Iowa, Louisiana State University, and the Massachusetts Institute of Technology [MIT]). During 1998 an increasing number of national fraternities pledged to maintain alcohol-free housing after July 1, 2000.

At a rapidly increasing pace, American colleges were requiring each student to own a personal computer or to have one available. During 1998 in Georgia, Floyd College, in Rome, and Clayton College and State University, in Morrow, cooperated with local businesses to provide every student with a laptop computer, Internet access, and a student identity card that served as both a phone card and a credit card. At Dartmouth College, Hanover, N.H., each entering student was obliged to own a computer. Eighty

percent of first-year students at New York University brought computers with them when they arrived, and the remaining 20% gained access to them in computer laboratories, in the library, and in the student centre. At Wellesley (Mass.) College, as on most college campuses, every new student was furnished an E-mail address and access to World Wide Web services. Nearly 70% of all courses at Wellesley used Internet technology in some form, such as allowing students to E-mail completed homework assignments to their professors or to run virtual experiments in class. Cleveland (Ohio) State University and MIT allowed students to register for courses from home by means of a computer modem connection.

In late May France's oldest university, the Sorbonne, celebrated its 800th anniversary with seminars, celebrations, and an appeal for greater cooperation between European universities so as to provide more academic mobility for students and scholars. The festivities were attended by the education ministers of Britain, France, Germany, and Italy, who pledged to try "harmonizing" degree programs in Europe so that there would be just two principal cycles of study, undergraduate and graduate. All four ministers supported a proposal to award students credit in their home universities for studies they pursued in other European Union (EU) countries.

In the Erasmus program for the exchange of students between EU nations, Britain was the most popular recipient country, with 19,600 candidates from other European nations. France was second with 14,086 exchange students, and Germany third with 9,700. Among EU countries Germany provided the greatest number of exchange students, 13,000.

As part of the Chinese government's effort to simplify bureaucratic procedures, several key universities throughout the nation were given permission to set their own student selection and enrollment regulations, choose their own teaching materials, and establish graduation requirements. This devolution of power included permitting universities to enroll foreign students directly rather than relying on the central government to determine which applicants to ac-

cept from abroad. According to government figures, during the year China was host to 40,000 foreign students, many of them from less-developed countries.

The Malaysian government issued Australia's Monash University, Clayton, the first license to establish a branch of a foreign university on Malaysian soil. The Monash program was expected eventually to enroll as many as 5,000 students, offering them a comprehensive array of studies that included degree programs in business management, engineering, and information technology. The decision to accept foreign institutions was motivated by Malaysian officials' concern over the drain of currency and talent that resulted from 50,000 Malaysian students' studying abroad in 1998.

In a similar move Indonesian authorities for the first time allowed foreign institutions to establish programs in their country as joint ventures with Indonesian universities. The new policy was partly a result of the nation's economic crises that were preventing many students from carrying out their plans to study abroad. As a further step toward expanding the international scope of the country's higher-education system, all Indonesian universities could now teach a broad range of subjects in English, a practice limited in the past to language courses.

Enrollment in The Sudan's Ahfad University for Women, Omdurman, reached more than 4,500, despite efforts of the country's fundamentalist Islamic government to curtail the institution's operation. Ahfad was originally established in 1907 as a private girls' school by a reformist Muslim, Babiker Bedri, under the British-Egyptian colonial administration. In 1998 the university was headed by the founder's grandson, Gasim Bedri, who espoused a philosophy of increasing women's independence through education.

Administrators at Thailand's Chulalongkorn University, Bangkok, threatened to reduce the grades of women students who persisted in wearing miniskirts on campus. Authorities asserted that short skirts violated the Thai cultural expectation that women behave in a modest fashion so as not to entice sexual predators. To illustrate their concerns, offi-

Supporters of affirmative action congregate outside the Michigan Union building at the University of Michigan, Ann Arbor, to hear a speaker from the Coalition to Defend Affirmative Action by Any Means Necessary.

RICHARD SHEINWALD—AP/WIDE WORLD

cials displayed posters around the campus showing a crocodile salivating at the sight of a woman in a miniskirt.

Israel's finance minister, Yaakov Neeman, sought to abolish the government's half-century practice of subsidizing every man who wanted to study in a Jewish religious academy (yeshiva) for as long as the man wished. The approximately 30,000 yeshiva students not only received government grants but also were exempt from the military draft. Neeman's proposal was intended to pressure studious men to leave the yeshiva and take employment in the country's high-technology sector, which was very short of personnel.

The Israeli Ministry of Finance also launched an investigation of "excessive salary increases" in the nation's top universities. Salaries of several officials at Tel Aviv University surpassed those of the country's president and two senior judges on the Supreme Court. The term *excessive* was defined as at least five percentage points above the standard rate of increase set in collective-bargaining agreements between the government and public-employee labour unions.

The number of students at Al-Azhar University on the Gaza Strip rose from 10,500 in 1997 to 14,000 in 1998 as enrollments continued to rise in the region's Palestinian higher-education institutions. Officials attributed the rapid growth to the increased numbers of overseas Palestinians returning home in recent years and to Israeli security measures that prevented young people in Gaza from traveling to the West Bank to attend institutions there.

The Japanese government planned to combine the nation's Science and Technology

DMITRY LOVETSKY—AP/WIDE WORLD

A caricature of Russian Pres. Boris Yeltsin looms over a protest rally in St. Petersburg, where university students demanded that they and teachers receive the federal living allowances that were months in arrears. The demonstrations took place across the country on October 1.

Agency with the Ministry of Education, Science, Sports and Culture to form a new Ministry of Education. Supporters of the merger asserted that the new organization would strengthen both the funding and the quality of research.

Financial incentives to attract bright foreign students were offered in a variety of nations. As a means of encouraging students from other Asian countries to continue their higher education in Japan, the Japanese government established a fund to provide $390 per year for each student whose home nation's currency had declined in the recent recession. The plan applied to students from Cambodia, Indonesia, Laos, Malaysia, Philippines, South Korea, and Thailand. Canadian universities, facing declining enrollments, sought to draw more students from the U.S. by reducing tuition costs. For example, Windsor (Ont.) University lowered tuition for foreign students from Can$9,188 to Can$5,000 (Can$1=U.S. $0.67).

The favourite areas of study in Russia's higher-education system in 1998 contrasted dramatically with the favourites two decades earlier. In 1978 more than two-thirds of Russian college students had been in departments of engineering, medicine, agriculture, and pure and applied sciences. By 1998 fewer than one-quarter of students were in engineering, whereas more than 25% were enrolled in economics, up from 10% in the 1980s. In addition, increased numbers were enrolled in language courses and such new fields as environmental studies. A survey of 14-year-olds in Moscow revealed that the majority wanted to go into business as high-level professionals—21% as economists or accountants, 20% as lawyers, 18% as financiers, and 14% as entrepreneurs. About 2% chose each of the following occupations—politician, journalist, computer operator, physician, diplomat, bank teller, fashion model, car salesperson, translator, and hairdresser.

Higher-education institutions in many parts of the world struggled to operate with diminishing financial resources. During 1998 the German government spent only 0.92% of the gross national product on higher education, compared with 1.32% in 1978. Over the same 20-year period, enrollment in the 296 state-run institutions expanded from one million to 1.8 million students. The result was too few instructors, overflowing lecture halls, deferred maintenance projects, inadequate library resources, and deteriorating laboratory equipment. In order to help reduce overcrowded classrooms, proponents of reform recommended shortening the six years typically taken to earn a university diploma.

Universities in Canada, faced with one-third to one-quarter less public financing than five years earlier, increasingly generated funds through connections with

private corporations. At a growing rate faculties and buildings were renamed for donors, training programs were created for businesses, and research was designed to serve the needs of private industry. In 1997 the federal government encouraged this trend by agreeing to fund permanently the Can$47.4 million annual budget of the Centres of Excellence program that was designed to bring universities together with corporate partners and "accelerate the transfer of knowledge from universities to the private sector." Critics of close ties with corporations worried that schools were becoming too dependent on the whims of "unselected people with deep pockets" and that an injurious fiscal gap had developed between less-practical arts-oriented disciplines and business-friendly programs. As a further trend, over the period 1988–98 tuition had risen 134% so that in some universities students now paid nearly one-third of their school's operating costs.

Faculty and staff members in 51 of Brazil's 52 federal universities brought undergraduate education to a standstill in a strike over wages, leaving 420,000 students without classes to attend. Minister of Education Paulo Renato Souza refused to negotiate the strikers' demand for a 48% salary increase until they returned to work. Although more than half of Brazil's 1.6 million students attended private institutions, public universities were the source of most of the country's academic research and prestigious degree programs.

Across Russia thousands of students and staff members staged demonstrations to protest overdue faculty wage payments, tuition increases, and staff layoffs. By March the government owed nearly $10 billion in back wages to the nation's combined public workforce, of which higher-education personnel were a part.

Students' dissatisfaction with political events or campus conditions led to demonstrations in various nations. In India youths at the University of Delhi expressed their displeasure with the American criticism of India's nuclear tests by boycotting Coca-Cola and Pepsi products. Indonesian students were in the forefront of rallies that forced their nation's president, Suharto, to resign after 32 years in office. Kenyatta University, one of five national universities in Kenya, was shut down by antigovernment student demonstrators protesting ethnic violence in which more than 120 were killed. Later a mob of 3,000 students from Kenya's University of Nairobi demonstrated against a policy of lowering standards for medical school applicants; they chased off 24 riot police by throwing stones and chunks of wood.

In Belgrade police broke up a protest by several thousand students and faculty members who objected to the Serbian parliament's approval of a law that reduced university autonomy by giving the Yugoslav Education Ministry the power to appoint rectors and deans. In Oman food poisoning was the target of the first student protest in more than 30 years, as 300 youths from the Institute of Health Sciences marched with banners blaming the institute's catering personnel for serving tainted chicken in the cafeteria. Students at National Taiwan University staged a hunger strike to protest their university president's trip to the capital of China to attend Beijing University's centennial celebration.

(ROBERT MURRAY THOMAS)

The Environment

INTERNATIONAL ACTIVITIES

Kyoto Protocol on Climate Change. Greenhouse-gas emissions remained a major issue in 1998. In December 1997 representatives from 160 signatory nations to the UN Framework Convention on Climate Change had attended a meeting in Kyoto, Japan, and reached an agreement, called the Kyoto Protocol, to reduce global emissions by about 5.2% by 2012. The European Union (EU) agreed to reduce emissions by an average 8% below 1990 levels, followed by the U.S. (7%), Japan (6%), and 21 other industrial countries that would reduce emissions by varying amounts. Binding commitments were not required of less-developed countries (LDCs). Shortly before the meeting in Kyoto, it was reported that the World Bank had prepared a scheme, called the Global Carbon Initiative, that would allow developed countries to pay for low-cost, energy-efficient projects in LDCs. The saving in greenhouse-gas emissions could then be credited to the binding emissions target of the donor countries under a system called "joint implementation." Concerns that a reduction could have serious economic repercussions led to doubts over whether the U.S., which accounted for 20–25% of the world emissions total, would ratify the protocol; by the end of 1998, the U.S. had not yet done so.

Global Environment Facility. At their first assembly, held in New Delhi in April 1998, Global Environment Facility (GEF) managers agreed to review their policy on supporting environmental projects in LDCs. Funds would continue to be allocated to climate change (40%), biodiversity (40%), ozone depletion (10%), and water supplies (10%), but it was agreed that GEF activities should be more open to inspection and that there should be greater involvement from the private sector, the public, and environmentalist groups. The GEF fund was replenished by $2,750,000,000 over three years, although this figure included $680,000,000 brought forward from the first round of funding and $80,000,000 of unused funds.

Living Planet Report. On October 1 the World Wide Fund for Nature (WWFN), the New Economics Foundation, and the World Conservation Monitoring Centre at Cambridge, Eng., published the *Living Planet Report,* comparing the impact human activities were having on the global environment with the impact they had in 1960. The report stated that since 1960 use of freshwater had doubled, which was causing a decline in freshwater habitats. Carbon dioxide emissions had also doubled; consumption of wood and paper had increased by two-thirds; and consumption of sea fish had more than doubled. Most fish stocks were either fully exploited or declining, and few forests were being managed sustainably. The main cause of these increases was said to be rising consumption levels. In many parts of the world, there was heightened interest in ecological restoration. (*See* Special Report.)

Antarctica. The Madrid Protocol to the Antarctic Treaty came into force on Jan. 14, 1998, following its ratification by Japan, the last of the 26 parties to the treaty to do so.

SHIZUO KAMBAYASHI—AP/WIDE WORLD

EU Commissioner for the Environment and Nuclear Safety Ritt Bjerregaard ponders a question during a press conference in Tokyo on September 18. In Japan for a conference on global warming, Bjerregaard stressed the need for developed nations to lead the way in reducing global emissions.

The protocol required all explorers, tourist operators, and scientific expeditions to obtain permission to enter the region south of latitude 60° and to submit an environmental-impact assessment. Mining of any kind was banned within this area for 50 years, and environmental improvements were to be made at the sites of scientific stations. In April Australian workers started to clean up the abandoned Wilkes Station, which had been built by the U.S. military in 1957 and transferred to Australia in 1959. Australians had used it to study the atmosphere and weather, but in 1969 the researchers moved to Casey Station nearby, leaving years of accumulated garbage in the open.

Difficulties with waste disposal in the Antarctic climate were illustrated by a report in June that sewage from the U.S. McMurdo Station stretched at least one kilometre (0.6 mi) along the shoreline and for 300 m (985 ft) out to sea. Sewage from McMurdo, which housed about 1,000 people, was routinely macerated but not treated chemically or biologically before being discharged from an outflow pipe 50 m (165 ft) from the shore into 17 m (56 ft) of water. At a meeting held in Hobart, Tas., Australia, in late August, 50 Antarctic specialists agreed on proposals to reduce the risk of carrying pathogens to Antarctica, where they could cause disease among wildlife. The plan would involve briefing everyone visiting Antarctica on ways to avoid spreading pathogens—including proper cleaning of all equipment and clothing, especially boots, before and after visiting wildlife sites and certifying that poultry food products imported to Antarctica were free from dangerous pathogens. The scientists also proposed

that sewage be treated by boiling for five minutes. The scheme was to be presented to the next meeting of Antarctic Treaty nations, to be held in Lima, Peru, in 1999.

NATIONAL DEVELOPMENTS

Brazil. On February 12 Brazilian Pres. Fernando Henrique Cardoso signed a law imposing strict penalties for environmental offenses. Companies violating environmental regulations would be forbidden to bid for government contracts for 10 years and would lose tax breaks. Their owners would be fined in proportion to the company profits. Anyone caught illegally trading animals, burning trees, extracting minerals, or causing pollution could be imprisoned for up to three years.

Canada. In March Environment Minister Christine Stewart introduced a revised version of the Canadian Environmental Protection Act. This emphasized voluntary efforts by industry to achieve environmental improvement and increased cooperation between the federal and provincial governments. The act included the Canada-Wide Accord on Environmental Harmonization with three subagreements, signed at the end of January by Stewart and the provincial governments. It dealt with environmental assessment and the establishment of national environmental standards and inspections under federal law. The federal agency Environment Canada hailed the new act as a significant advance, but critics were concerned at the weakening of the role of the federal government.

It was reported in July that the Canadian government had reached agreement with the Inuit of the eastern Arctic on a Can$155 million (U.S. $105 million) deal to clean up 15 military radar sites. The sites were contaminated with polychlorinated biphenyls (PCBs), heavy metals, and other substances. A study by scientists from the Arctic Monitoring and Assessment Programme, based in Norway, reported in September that 48% of Inuit women living on Baffin Island were ingesting more of the pesticide chlordane than the World Health Organization (WHO) considered tolerable. In addition, 29% of the women exceeded the WHO limit for mercury, 21% for cadmium, and 16% for PCBs. Breast milk in Inuit women contained 10 times more chlordane and 5 times more PCBs than that from women in southern Canada. Most of the pollutants came from Russia, especially from farms and industrial complexes in the north.

Czech Republic. In May 45,000 salmon spawn from Germany were released into the Kamenice, Ploucnice, and Ohre rivers, three north Bohemian tributaries of the Elbe River. It was hoped the fish would migrate to the North Sea in two years and return four years later to the rivers from which they had migrated. The release marked the extent to which pollution had been reduced since the last salmon was caught in the Czech portion of the Elbe in 1950.

Germany. Elections to the German Bundestag (parliament) in late September led to the formation of a "Red-Green" coalition between the Social Democrats, led by Gerhard Schröder, and the Greens, led by Joschka Fischer. The Greens were already members of coalition governments in 4 of the 16 German states, but the federal election made the party influential at the national

Trucks loaded with nuclear-waste containers leave a power station near Neckerwestheim, Ger., on March 19. Police were on hand to deter environmental protesters, who, despite assurances from German energy authorities, claimed that the containers were not leakproof. The containers were put on a train in Walheim for shipment to a nuclear storage facility in Ahaus.

THOMAS KIENZLE—AP/WIDE WORLD

level for the first time, although they won less than 7% of the vote in the election.

On March 20 more than 30,000 police clashed with thousands of protesters who were trying to prevent a trainload of 60 tons of spent nuclear fuel from being delivered to a storage plant at Ahaus, north of Cologne. Demonstrations began on March 15, with more than 3,500 people protesting outside the Ahaus plant. In addition, about 1,000 protested in Neckerwestheim and about 250 in Günzburg, the two towns in southern Germany near the plants from which the waste was to be moved. The shipment set out on March 19, instead of March 23 as originally planned, in an attempt to outwit demonstrators, but near Stuttgart police found the road to the railhead weakened. A tunnel had been dug beneath it, and protesters were chained to one another inside it. There were demonstrations outside the plant and outside the Gundremmingen plant, near Munich, from which spent fuel was also being dispatched on March 19.

Spain. On April 25 the tailings dam containing a lagoon holding mining waste from the Los Frailes open-pit iron-pyrite mine operated by Boliden Apirsa Ltd., a Canadian-Swedish company, at Aznalcollar, near Seville, burst. A breach 50 m (165 ft) long appeared in the dike, and an estimated 5.7 billion litres (1.5 billion gal) of acid sludge spilled into the Agrio River. The sludge, which contained toxic metals, including cadmium, lead, zinc, and chromium, entered the Guadiamar River, contaminated farm-

land, and came within eight kilometres (five miles) of the boundary of the Coto Doñana National Park. Crop damage, covering 5,060 ha (12,500 ac), was estimated at $79 million.

Volunteers began clearing away dead fish on April 28. A series of dikes, hastily constructed from earth and sand, controlled the flow of the material, keeping it away from the park and diverting it into the Guadalquivir River and thence into the Atlantic. On May 3 bulldozers began removing the three million tons of contaminated mud. The plan was to dump the waste into a disused mine. By August delays in the cleanup were leading to fears that autumn floods would wash more poisoned water into the park. A task force of 1,600 workers promised by the regional government had failed to materialize, and the national and Andalucian governments had devised conflicting plans. This meant no agreed-upon plan had been submitted to Brussels, a condition for the release of an EU rescue fund, and the money could not be released before September, after autumn rains caused more flooding.

On September 22 the federal Environment Ministry announced the cleanup was almost complete. Millions of cubic metres of mud had been shifted, and heavy-metal contaminants were being removed by precipitation in a temporary reservoir. Spain requested ECU 96 million in structural funds for the cleanup and for the Doñana 2005 Programme to restore the Guadiamar River to its original

condition. On September 28, however, the WWFN and Adena, its Spanish counterpart, urged the EU to withhold funds for the central and Andalucian authorities responsible for the cleanup program. The WWFN released the results of a study that found that 30% of affected land was still untreated and that 1,600 ha (3,950 ac) in the Entremuros area, at the lowest part of the Guadiamar, had not been included in the program. This, the WWFN said, was an important winter habitat for birds, and it wanted the EU to conduct an independent quality-control study on the program before releasing funds.

Switzerland. Following a national referendum held on September 27, from the year 2001 heavy-goods vehicles using Swiss roads would be subject to an environmental tax calculated on the distance traveled. The law to impose the tax was passed in 1997, but it required referendum support before it could come into force. The referendum result showed 57% of people were in favour. The result also allowed the government to open Swiss roads to EU vehicles in transit, with an average charge of about 200 centimes (U.S. $1.35) per transit, and thus brought the country closer to finalizing a bilateral trade agreement with the EU.

United States. On June 17 it was announced that the Unocal Corp. had agreed to pay the $18 million cost of cleaning up sand and soil contaminated by gasoline, diesel fuel, and crude oil at Avila Beach, Calif., a town of 300 people northwest of Los Angeles. The cleanup required up to 20

homes and businesses to be dismantled or moved from the main commercial street while 1.5 million litres (400,000 gal) of contaminated sand was removed from beneath the street and beach. The operation was scheduled to take 18 months.

On July 14 the Natural Resources Defense Council published its annual survey of water quality at beaches. The survey covered 29 coastal and Great Lakes states and three U.S. territories and was conducted by the Council and the Enviromental Protection Agency (EPA). Beaches in Alabama, Georgia, Louisiana, Oregon, Texas, Washington, and Puerto Rico were awarded low marks. In 1997 there were 4,153 beach closings and pollution advisories on ocean, lake, river, and bay beaches, compared with 2,596 in 1996. This did not indicate an increase in pollution, however, because of the inclusion in the 1997 survey of Guam and some freshwater beaches omitted from the 1996 data.

In September a federal jury in Pittsburgh, Pa., found that the Babcock & Wilcox Co. and Atlantic Richfield Co., the successive operators of the Nuclear Materials and Fuels Corp., had been negligent in their running of a facility at Apollo, northeast of Pittsburgh, that processed uranium for nuclear reactors and submarines for about 20 years and had allowed radiation to escape from it. In the early 1990s the plant was demolished, and more than 2,265 cu m (80,000 cu ft) of soil and debris were moved to a radioactive-waste disposal site.

The trial, which began on August 10, was in regard to an action brought in 1994 by nearly 100 residents of Apollo, where there was an unusually high incidence of uterine, breast, and kidney cancer and leukemia. The court awarded them and their families $36.5 million. The case was a test for more than 90 personal injury cases, about 120 property damage cases, and a class-action law suit seeking medical monitoring for residents.

ENVIRONMENTAL ISSUES

Environmental Crime. On April 5 environment ministers from the U.K., the U.S., Japan, France, Italy, Germany, Canada, and Russia met at Leeds Castle, Kent, Eng., to discuss plans for combating the smuggling of hazardous waste, substances that damage the ozone layer, and endangered species. It was said that the trade in illicit drugs was the only illegal industry that generated more money than the $5 billion a year produced by the trade in endangered and rare species. The ministers agreed to increase public awareness of illegal trade that damages the environment and to provide more help to LDCs that complied with international environmental agreements and combat environmental crime.

Forest Fires. On March 4 the Indonesian Antara news agency reported that haze due to the fires on Borneo was blocking sunlight from crops and causing transport difficulties. In early April schools in one part of Borneo were closed for six successive days because of high air-pollution levels, and on April 12 it was reported that the Pollutant Standard Index (PSI) level on Borneo was 500. (A PSI value of 200 is considered "very unhealthy," above 300 is "hazardous," and above 400 is "very hazardous.") On April 13 the U.S. ambassador to Brunei said he had requested permission from Washington to evacuate embassy staff be-

cause of the potentially hazardous air pollution. On April 30 the Malaysian environment minister announced that Kuala Lumpur was to be hosed down from the roofs of skyscrapers to wash the smog from the air.

There were also severe fires in Central America. In May rural inhabitants burned land as usual in preparation for the planting season. Dry conditions caused by El Niño allowed the fires to spread, especially in the southern Mexican states of Chiapas, Oaxaca, and Guerrero; the eastern states of Yucatán and Campeche; and in Morelos state, near Mexico City. The fires covered about 485,600 ha (1.2 million ac), and their smoke spread through Mexico and into the southern U.S. Mexico City was badly affected. U.S. Southern Command forces helped fight the fires, supplying four helicopters and 21 crew members. On May 25 ozone levels in Mexico City reached 251 µg (micrograms)/cu m. (More than 100 is considered unsatisfactory, and more than 200 can cause health problems in children, the elderly, and people with respiratory and other illnesses.) Emergency measures to cope with the smog were imposed. Factories reduced production, schools kept children indoors, and almost 40% of the city's cars were ordered to remain parked for the following day; this ban was extended for several more days. On May 26 and 27, ozone levels exceeded 200 µg/cu m, and on May 28 the level reached 194. Two days later ozone levels fell below 180, and the pollution alert was lifted.

Air Pollution. Environment ministers from member states of the EU agreed on June 30 that from Jan. 1, 2000, permitted emissions from gasoline-engine cars and

A firefighter battles flames near Mexico City in April. Dry conditions brought on by El Niño resulted in forest fires in many parts of Mexico during the year.

vans would be reduced by 30–40% and from diesel-engine cars by 50%. The sulfur content of gasoline would be reduced by 70% and of diesel by 30%. These new emission limits would be reduced by an additional 50% from Jan. 1, 2005.

In the U.K. the results of a Department of Health study, published on January 13, said traffic fumes were causing the premature deaths of 12,000–24,000 people a year and causing 14,000–24,000 to be admitted to a hospital. Ozone, particulate matter, and sulfur dioxide were the principal pollutants involved.

Several steps to reduce air pollution were taken in China. It was announced in March that the Capital Steel Corp. had decided not to increase production at its main Beijing factory so that it would not increase the amount of air pollution it was causing. In 1997 the company had produced eight million tons of steel, 8% of the total national output. Later the same month it was reported that owners of cars and trucks in Beijing emitting more than the permitted amounts of exhaust gases would be required to fit catalytic converters to their vehicles. Up to 50,000 vehicles a year would be subjected to spot checks by police and environmental officers. Drivers whose vehicles exceeded permitted tailpipe-emission limits would have their licenses suspended. These would be reinstated once converters had been fitted.

On February 28 the Beijing local government started releasing weekly air-pollution reports, joining 27 other Chinese cities that had begun issuing such reports in 1997. The amount of information released varied from city to city. Shanghai issued levels of sulfur dioxide, nitrous oxides, and total suspended particulates; Beijing gave only the level of the worst pollutant among the three. The Beijing authorities also announced that over the next two years they would use 1.5 billion cu m (53 billion cu ft) of natural gas to discourage people from burning coal bricks and planned to establish 40 coal-free zones and encourage the use of higher-quality coal elsewhere. By 2000 half of all homes would be centrally heated. In the late 1990s, 27 million tons of coal were burned each year in Beijing, releasing a haze with a high sulfur dioxide content.

In the U.S. environmental administrators from northeastern states from Maine to New York met White House officials in July to lobby for an EPA proposal that would reduce emissions from Midwestern coal-burning power plants. The group presented the report of a study commissioned by the Northeast States for Coordinated Air Use Management that showed that the Midwestern plants could reduce emissions for $662 a ton; unless they did so, the northeastern states would have to impose controls at a cost of $3.9 billion a year to their own economy.

Ozone Layer. The ozone assessment produced every four years by more than 200 scientists on behalf of the World Meteorological Organization (WMO) and the UN Environment Programme (UNEP) was published in June. WMO Secretary-General Godwin Obasi said the report showed that the 1987 Montreal Protocol was working. Full recovery of the ozone layer was expected by the middle of the 21st century, but signs of recovery might not become apparent until about 2020 owing to natural variability.

In January the European Commission launched the Third European Stratospheric Experiment on Ozone, funded jointly by the EU and national agencies and involving more than 400 scientists, including workers from Canada, Iceland, Japan, Norway, Poland, Russia, South Africa, Switzerland, and the U.S. Due to run until the end of 1999, it had the task of gathering data on the long-term decline in ozone over Europe. Winter and early-spring ozone levels had already been found to be more than 10% lower than those of the 1970s. On October 1, scientists at the WMO in Geneva announced that in 1998 the Antarctic ozone depletion covered a surface area 5% larger than in previous years.

Nitrogen Cycle. It was suggested in February that the human contribution to the nitrogen cycle was threatening to overload the biosphere. It was calculated that the use of nitrogen fertilizer and the emission of nitrogen oxides by vehicles and factories produced 60% of all the fixed nitrogen deposited on land and that about 20% of the nitrogen fertilizer used on watersheds entered rivers. The excess nitrogen was polluting coastal and estuarine waters as well as rivers and lakes. Ragnar Elmgren, an aquatic ecologist at the University of Stockholm, attributed the collapse of the cod fishery in the Baltic Sea in the 1990s to nitrogen pollution. He said the nitrogen load in the Baltic had increased fourfold during the 20th century. Excess nitrogen was also said to be harming forests by encouraging tree growth that was unbalanced because of deficiencies in other nutrients, which thus made the trees weak and vulnerable to pests and diseases.

Marine Pollution. At a meeting held in Helsinki, Fin., on March 26, the EU and the nine countries bordering the Baltic Sea (Finland, Sweden, Denmark, Russia, Estonia, Latvia, Lithuania, Poland, and Germany) agreed on measures to reduce pollution. At their first Baltic port of call, all ships would be charged a dumping fee to encourage them to dispose of their wastes at port facilities. Nutrient discharges from farms, lead emissions from vehicle exhausts, and heavy-metal discharges from industry would also be reduced.

The 15 European members of the Ospar Convention met in Sintra, Port., in July. They agreed that emissions from nuclear installations would be reduced to "close to zero" by 2020. This would require British Nuclear Fuels to make modifications to the Enhanced Actinide Removal Plant at Sellafield, Eng., in order to reduce its discharges of technetium-99. It also meant all reprocessing of fuel from British Magnox reactors would end by 2020. To achieve this, eight Magnox reactors would have to close between 2007 and 2009.

The meeting also agreed that in principle all gas and oil rigs would be disposed of on land, although the large concrete platforms and their footings on 41 installations heavier than 10,000 tons could remain at sea temporarily while their final fates were decided on a case-by-case basis. This decision allowed the oil industry to divert the £1 billion (nearly U.S. $1.7 billion) cost of removing the stumps to a "green superfund," which would be used to address what the industry considered to be more urgent environmental problems. Certain sea areas would also be designated as "marine protected areas," within which activities, prob-

ably including fishing, would be restricted to allow the marine environment to recover.

On January 29 Shell Oil Co. announced that *Brent Spar,* the former oil-storage platform, would be used in the construction of a quay at a roll-on–roll-off ferry terminal at Mekjarvik, near Stavanger, Nor. The structure would be razed, the accommodation platform dismantled and disposed of on land, and the lower part sliced into six sections. These would then be carried on barges to Mekjarvik, filled with rubble, and have a concrete platform laid over them.

There was evidence that the condition of the Black Sea had improved. For the first time in 10 years, thousands of shellfish were found in April along the Romanian Black Sea coast, which suggested that the Black Sea Action Plan agreed upon in 1996 by all six Black Sea littoral states was having an effect.

Toxic Wastes. The fourth Conference of Parties to the Basel Convention on waste management, held under UNEP auspices in Kuching, Malaysia, in February, was attended by more than 300 environment officials from 117 countries. UNEP Executive Director Klaus Töpfer called for solidarity in ratifying the 1995 ban on the export of toxic waste from industrialized to industrializing countries. The meeting agreed on the content of the list of materials defined as hazardous and on a list of countries that were permitted to trade among themselves in toxic wastes.

UNEP also sponsored a five-day meeting in Montreal over June and July that was attended by delegates from more than 100 countries. Its aim was to reduce or ban the use of what were held to be the 12 most dangerous substances, with the hope of drafting a treaty reducing emissions of them from 2001. The 12 were PCBs, chlorinated furans, dioxins, aldrin, dieldrin, endrin, DDT, chlordane, hexachlorobenzene, mirex, toxaphene, and heptachlor.

Nuclear Waste. The British ship *Pacific Swan* left Cherbourg, France, on January 21 bound for Japan with a cargo of more than 24 metric tons of vitrified nuclear-reprocessing waste, on a route taking it through the Panama Canal. On February 5 the National Coordinating Council for Environmental Groups asked the canal authorities to prohibit the passage of the ship, but Franklin Castellon of the Panama Canal Commission refused, saying the ship met all the requirements for carrying nuclear cargo. Another official, Alberto Alemán Zubieta, said the *Pacific Swan* had passed through the canal 28 times without incident and 71 ships carrying radioactive waste had passed through the canal safely in 1997. He pointed out that other substances, such as petroleum, corrosive chemicals, and combustible fuels, were more dangerous than radioactive materials.

The *Pacific Swan* arrived at Rokkasho, Japan, on March 10, but Gov. Morio Kimura of Aomori prefecture refused to allow it to dock at Mutsu-Ogawara port until Japanese Prime Minister Ryutaro Hashimoto assured him progress was being made toward finding a permanent storage site for nuclear waste. Critics maintained that the Rokkasho Mura facility, selected to store waste for 50 years, was an unsuitable storage site because it was located on at least two seismically active faults. About 200 people demonstrated in the fishing village while the ship waited offshore. Late on March 12 Kimura partly

relented, allowing the ship into port so that its 26 crew members could rest and avoid rough seas but forbidding it to unload. Following a meeting with the prime minister, Kimura allowed the cargo to be unloaded. It was taken to the storage facility, where it would be held for 30–50 years.

On June 2 a bill to compel Nevada to accept nuclear waste for storage fell short in the U.S. Senate 56 votes to 39. The bill would have required more than 40,000 tons of waste being held at nuclear power plants in 31 states to be stored at an aboveground facility 160 km from Las Vegas, beginning in 2003. (*See* Special Report.)

(MICHAEL ALLABY)

WILDLIFE CONSERVATION

Orangutans (*Pongo pygmaeus*) were among the species that suffered the loss of habitat and death at the hands of humans as they fled the fires in Borneo (Kalimantan), Sumatra, and other parts of Indonesia in 1998. More than 30,000 sq km (11,580 sq mi) burned between January and May. Almost all of Kutai National Park was destroyed, as was the Wein River Orangutan Sanctuary.

In February the Truong Son muntjac deer from central Vietnam was described and named *Muntiacus truongsonensis* on the basis of 17 skulls and two tails obtained from hunters. In June the description of a new species of marmoset (*Callithrix humilis*) in Brazil was published. The marmoset, which did not appear to be endangered, had a known distribution covering some 250–300 sq km (95–115 sq mi), by far the smallest for any Amazonian primate. Another new species described in 1998 was a bird (*Scytalopus iraiensis*) found in an area that was to be flooded by a dam in Brazil. Work on the dam was suspended as a result of the discovery.

The cherry-throated tanager (*Nemosia rourei*) was rediscovered in Brazil in February, 47 years after the last sighting. Two other bird rediscoveries were reported in March; the forest owlet (*Athene blewitti*), not recorded since 1884, was found in India, and a population of the critically endangered bearded wood partridge (*Dendrortyx barbatus*) was discovered in Mexico, where the species was last seen in 1986.

A report published in March urged the protection of sharks and other elasmobranch fishes in North American waters. Shark fins had become one of the most valuable fisheries products in the world, and shark cartilage was also used in the growing Western health-food market. In August it was reported that not long after a commercial trawl fishery for rays started in the northwestern Atlantic Ocean, the largest species, the barn door skate (*Raja laevis*), was nearly gone. In the U.S. 27 leading chefs took North Atlantic swordfish (*Xiphias gladius*) off their menus in response to the finding that the fishery had crashed.

According to the Red List of Threatened Plants, published by the International Union of Conservation of Nature and Natural Resources in April, 12.5% of the world's plant species were threatened with extinction. The list of 33,798 species included 380 that were extinct in the wild and 371 that might be extinct. Of the species listed, 91% were endemic to a single country. Another report stated that many wild plants and an-

imals used in medicine were becoming scarce in East Africa and southern African countries; it identified 102 plant species and 29 animal species as priorities for conservation action, including the African rock python and the baobab tree (*Adansonia digitata*). Almost 9,000 of the world's tree species were threatened, according to research results published in September. At least 77 species were extinct, 8,753 were critically endangered, and 1,319 were endangered.

The 22nd meeting of the Parties to the Antarctic Treaty, held in Norway on May 25–June 6, failed to address the severe problem of illegal fishing for Patagonian toothfish (*Dissostichus eleginoides*) in the Southern Ocean. Illegal fishing was taking about 100,000 tons, compared with the 18,000 tons caught by the legal fishery, and the fish could soon become commercially extinct. The fishery also killed 5,000–154,000 seabirds annually, including threatened petrels and albatrosses.

Invasions by alien species, already a serious threat to biodiversity, were expected to worsen in the future as the world warmed, according to an international workshop held in San Mateo, Calif., in April. It was believed that the tropical alga (*Caulerpa taxifolia*) that invaded the Mediterranean Sea in the mid-1980s could move up the Atlantic coast of Europe if ocean temperatures rose. In Tonga an introduced species of long-legged ants (*Anoplolepis gracilipes*) killed hatchlings of the native Tongan incubator birds, and the little red fire ant (*Wasmannia auropunctata*) had invaded New Caledonia and the Solomon Islands, where it attacked native vertebrates and caused the loss of native invertebrates that had key functions in the natural community. The problem of marine-invading species in Australia was being tackled by a pilot community-monitoring program aimed at the early detection of new invasive species and the development of knowledge about introduced species already present. By 1998 more than 150 introduced species had been discovered in Australian waters, of which eight were considered pests. In the Hawaiian Islands there were once 750 species of native land snails, more than 99% of them endemic. Most had become extinct or severely threatened, largely owing to the introduction of predatory carnivorous snails.

The 1998 edition of the UN List of Protected Areas revealed a global network of more than 30,000 protected areas covering a total of 13.2 million sq km (5.1 million sq mi) designated under national legislation to conserve nature and associated cultural resources. One of the world's largest and most undisturbed tropical forests was permanently protected in June when Suriname created a 16,200-sq km (6,250-sq mi) reserve, covering some 10% of the country's land area.

An infectious agent was suspected in a mass mortality of Adelie penguin (*Pygoscelis adeliae*) chicks in Antarctica. Antibodies of the avian pathogen infectious bursal disease virus had been found in penguins from colonies near human activity. A possible source of the virus was humans' careless disposal of poultry products or contaminated clothing or vehicles. In January–February, 1,345 New Zealand sea lion (*Phocarctos hookeri*) pups and 85 adults died from septacaemia. Biopsies of

the sea lions, which lived only in the Auckland Islands, revealed salmonella and a second, unidentified bacterium. A new fungal disease was shown to be the cause of death in amphibians found dead at pristine rain-forest sites in Australia and Central America. The fungus, found in the keratinized cells of the skin of adult amphibians, appeared to be the same pathogen on both continents and probably caused death by interfering with supplementary water uptake or respiration through the skin. The disease was identified as the cause of death of frogs and toads belonging to nine genera, including *Taudactylus acutirostris,* an Australian species that might have become extinct.

In June conservationists celebrated the fact that 10 mountain gorillas had been born in the Virunga National Park in the Democratic Republic of the Congo since the onset of civil unrest 18 months previously,

but in September two mountain gorillas were killed by poachers in the park. In 1998 there were only about 600 mountain gorillas left.

(JACQUI M. MORRIS)

ZOOS

Release programs involving wildlife bred in captivity grew in numbers in 1998. For example, the endangered Mexican gray wolf, *Canis lupus baileyi,* had been extinct in the southwestern U.S. since the 1950s and unseen in Mexico since 1980. On March 29, 11 gray wolves in three family groups were let out of their acclimatization pens into the 18,000-sq km (7,000-sq mi) Blue Range Wolf Recovery area in the Apache and Gila national forests of Arizona and New Mexico. By late November, however, 5 of the 11 had been killed, one was missing, and 5 had been returned to captivity. Of the Mexican wolves *(continued on page 220)*

A worker at an animal refuge near Balikpapan, Indon., plays with three young orangutans rescued from forest fires that had devastated the island of Borneo. After more than 30,000 sq km (11,580 sq mi) in Indonesia burned between January and May, wildlife officials said that the orangutan population on Borneo had been almost completely wiped out.

RAMA SURYA—AP/WIDE WORLD

Ecological Restoration

by Stephanie Mills

Ecological restoration (the rapidly developing practice of healing damaged lands and waters) is grounded in the emerging scientific discipline of restoration ecology. The science and the practice are mutually informing. Restoration practices are as varied as natural communities themselves, but the basic idea is to return a particular place—be it a small nature preserve or a whole river basin—to a condition closely resembling its primal state. This may entail reestablishing the structures and functions of ecosystems as well as reintroducing native flora and fauna. The long-term objective is to foster the continuing existence, interaction, and evolution of the restored ecosystem's indigenous species of plants and animals (including humans). Because ecosystem dynamics are intricate, seldom obvious, and far easier to disrupt than to recreate, ecological restoration involves discovery, invention, and no little urgency.

As we approach the 21st century, scientists agree that we are in the most rapid extinction crisis in Earth's history. These mass extinctions are the result of habitat disturbance—ecosystem disruption—which is driven by dramatic increases in the human population and the consumption of natural resources that goes with economic activity. Ecological restoration endeavours to be a holistic means of arresting this loss of species. Many ecological restorationists hope through their work to bring humanity into a mutually sustaining relationship with the Earth's biodiversity. Although there are professional restorationists, many of them biologists or landscape architects, much ecological restoration is accomplished by volunteers. Since its first annual conference in 1989, the Society for Ecological Restoration (SER), headquartered at the University of Wisconsin at Madison, has fostered the growth, development, and vision of the international and interdisciplinary community of restorationists.

In the mountainous Pacific Northwest, citizen groups and governments from the local to the national levels have been working for 20 years to restore the salmon runs of their creeks and rivers, slowly regenerating their watersheds from ridgelines to river mouths. North Pacific salmon restoration spans the ocean. On the Japanese island of Hokkaido, Sapporo's schoolchildren have been promoting practices to improve water quality, hauling rubbish out of urban creeks and releasing hatchery-nurtured salmon fingerlings into the city's Toyohiro river. On Thailand's coasts villagers restore and manage their living resources, replanting mangrove trees to stabilize the shorelines and serve as nurseries for fish. In the waters off the Maldives, the Global Coral Reef Alliance has used solar-generated electric current to accrete minerals from ocean water to form anchorages for coral. The alliance's inventors have found that a continuing flow of the low-voltage current also stimulates the growth of coral transplanted to the anchorages. Thus, some of the devastation of coral reefs worldwide may be mitigated, and natural breakwaters, which help protect shorelines from erosion, may be created.

In Redwood National Park, California, watershed restoration has employed bulldozers and backhoes to remove logging roads and log-skidding trails. This resculpting is needed to check erosion on the slopes and sedimentation in the streams so that the terrain will once again be hospitable to giant redwoods and to the animal species requiring conditions unique to that region's ancient forests. The successes among such slow-growing species as redwoods may not be apparent for centuries, yet the auspicious beginnings are on the increase.

To heal the 20,000-ha (50,000-ac) man-made moonscape around the nickel mines and smelters of Sudbury, Ont., restorationists reduced the ground's pollution-caused acidity

(ABOVE) DRUZHININ—ITAR/TASS PHOTOS;
(BELOW) MICHAEL MULVEY—KRT PHOTOS

(Right, above) A "dead zone" around the city of Monchegorsk in northwestern Russia resulted from the pollution created by a local smelter. Around the world, scientists blamed rapid industrialization for the disruption of numerous ecosystems.
(Right, below) Bighorn sheep are released in a wilderness area in western Texas. Once common to the region, only about 320 bighorn sheep exist there today. The Texas Parks and Wildlife Department hoped to increase that number through its sheep restoration program.

by spreading crushed limestone by hand and from the air; then they sowed grasses and planted pine, larch, oak, and locust seedlings. With public and private funds, as well as thousands of paid and volunteer workers, Sudbury has, since the early 1970s, revegetated perhaps one-quarter of its most severely damaged surroundings and restored some natural beauty to the city and the region.

The widespread transport of plants and animals across formerly insurmountable geographic boundaries such as mountains and oceans has resulted in habitat-disturbing "alien invasion." For example, islands where the flora and fauna may have evolved with no need for defense against terrestrial predators or grazers such as house cats or goats may lose much of their endemic biodiversity within decades once these opportunistic domesticated animals come onshore. On Cuvier Island off the coast of New Zealand's North Island, the New Zealand Department of Conservation applied its effective methods of eliminating feral cats, goats, and rats. These introduced and stowaway animals had decimated the island's vegetation and consequently extirpated a number of Cuvier Island's birds, reptiles, and invertebrates. By the late 1960s and early '70s, it was possible to reintro-

duce some bird species that had vanished from Cuvier Island but had survived in populations on other islands nearby. In time the government hopes to reintroduce other missing bird species and a native reptile, the tuatara, which is being propagated in a captive-breeding program. Similar island-restoration projects have been under way throughout the New Zealand archipelago for the past 20 years.

In North America, alien vegetation—some deliberately imported for landscaping, range improvement, erosion control, or forestry, and some that hitchhiked—has proliferated wildly, especially in areas where there has been land disturbance, such as farming, grazing, or logging. In many settings a single weedy species has blanketed a landscape and displaced the more complex and varied mixes of trees, shrubs, grasses, or wildflowers that made up the original plant community, along with the specific pollinators upon which certain plants depend. Using elbow grease, "weed wrenches," cane knives, and sparing doses of herbicides, restorationists battle these alien species.

Many ecosystems depend on periodic localized disturbance for renewal, including hurricanes, floods, avalanches, earthquakes, lightning-set wildfires, and the light, cool fires set by aboriginal peoples as a subtle form of "cultivating" certain landscapes. Thus restoring an ecosystem may require some judicious disturbance. Occasional burning, restorationists have learned, is essential to the flourishing of prairies, savannas, and the conifer forests of arid and semiarid regions. Early experiments in prairie restoration in the U.S. demonstrated the necessity of controlled burning to maintain a healthy, diverse grass and wildflower community. Since these discoveries—or rediscoveries—in the 1940s, restorationists have been refining the techniques of reinstating fire to ecosystems in need.

Gathering and propagating the seed of endangered plants, hand-pollinating rare flowers for which insect or avian pollinators have become too scarce, clearing creeks and monitoring their recovery by counting aquatic invertebrates, pulling weeds, hacking brush, doing biological surveys of natural areas, setting fires, and even breaching dikes and dams (as is being done in Romania to restore the vast wetlands of the Danube Delta), as well as planting many millions of trees, are among the practices of ecological restoration. Altogether, as stated by U.S. Interior Secretary Bruce Babbitt, it is "an enormous act of the imagination."

Stephanie Mills is the author of In Service of the Wild: Restoring and Reinhabiting Damaged Land.

(Above) Newly hatched fish, or alevins, begin to emerge from salmon eggs in a hatchery aquarium. (Left) Flames engulf trees in Yellowstone National Park in 1988. That year a disastrous series of forest fires devastated large areas of the park. Restoration efforts followed. By 1998 experts were predicting that in another 10 years, vegetation would be 10 times as diverse as it was in 1988.

(continued from page 217)
that had remained in captivity, formation of 28 pairs (19 in the U.S. and 9 in Mexico) was planned by the American Zoo and Aquarium Association Species Survival Plan Management Group in July.

A management plan for the Mississippi sandhill crane, *Grus canadensis pulla,* was initiated in 1965 by the U.S. Fish and Wildlife Service. The subspecies was listed as endangered in 1973, after which a recovery plan was developed; releases began in 1981. In 1995 the managed flock was transferred to the Audubon Institute in New Orleans and the White Oak Conservation Center in Yulee, Fla. From 30 adult birds, about 14 chicks were produced in 1998, all but one on a rigorous artificial insemination schedule. The chicks were then transferred to the Mississippi Sandhill Crane National Wildlife Refuge in Gautier, Miss., for release. By late 1998 the wild population was about 100 birds, existing only on the refuge.

On June 16 more than 100 endangered razorback suckers, *Xyrauchen texanus,* that had been raised at the Phoenix (Ariz.) Zoo were returned to their original environment in the Colorado River. The suckers were originally released as juveniles into a lake on the zoo grounds. The objective was to raise the young fish in a quasi-natural environment and then return them to the wild after they were large enough to avoid predators.

Partnerships. The Columbus (Ohio) Zoo, in partnership with the University of Maryland, the Ohio Division of Wildlife, the Ohio Biological Survey, and the U.S. Fish and Wildlife Service, was cohost of a national meeting that addressed the conservation of native freshwater mussels. Papers and discussions focused on such issues as nutrition, rearing and propagation, rescue and reintroduction, physiology, and conservation of habitat of juvenile and adult mussels.

Cleveland (Ohio) Metroparks Zoo, Ogden/Silver Springs, Fla., and the Venezuelan organizations PROVITA and INPARQUES joined to support the Spectacled Bear Conservation Education Program in Venezuela. This program was presented to elementary-school children living within the spectacled bear's native habitat range. The Cleveland Zoo also established a partnership with INPARQUES and BIOANDINA (another Venezuelan organization) in a program aimed at reestablishing a breeding population of Andean condors in Venezuela.

Awards and Grants. The Board of Trustees of the Nature Conservancy Arizona Chapter selected the Phoenix Zoo as the 1997 recipient of its Morris K. Udall Award, given annually to an individual or group in the public sector that had demonstrated a sincere and consistent commitment to conservation in the state. The zoo was recognized for its efforts in leadership and commitment on behalf of Arizona's endangered or threatened wildlife populations.

Recipients of the 1997 Pittsburgh (Pa.) Zoo Conservation Fund grants included: Ecological Disturbance in Tropical Rain Forests; Health Screening as a Critical Component of Headstarting and Release Programs for Endangered West Indian Rock Iguanas; Test of Various Methods to Reduce Crop Raiding by Elephants Around Kibale National Park, Uganda; Determining Optimal Conditions for Cryobanking Semen for Artificial Insemination in African and Asian Elephants; Proposal to Preserve the Andean Mountain Tapir; and Assessment of Southern Right Whale Stock Identity and Population Health Using Genetic and Behavioral Data.

The Riverbanks Conservation Support Fund gave financial support for studying the following regional and international projects: Behavioral Ecology of the Micronesian Kingfisher in the Republic of Palau—The Use of a Surrogate Subspecies in the Recovery of Kingfishers from Guam; Western Giant Eland Ground Survey, Bafing Reserve, Mali; Phytochemistry of Forage and Browse Selection in a Group of Captive Hoatzins; Primate Survey of Monkey Bay National Park and Monkey Bay Wildlife Sanctuary, Belize; Subspecies Identification, Captive Management, and Conservation Education Programming for Spider Monkey Populations held in Mexican Zoological Institutions; Development of Artificial Insemination Technology for the Cinereous Vulture; and Determination of Migratory Routes of a Restored Population of Trumpeter Swans Using Satellite/Radio Telemetry.

(ALAN H. SHOEMAKER)

BOTANICAL GARDENS

The highlight of 1998 for botanical gardens was the fifth International Botanic Gardens Conservation Congress, held at Kirstenbosch National Botanical Garden in Cape Town and attended by more than 400 delegates from 55 countries. At the conference a two-year review process for the international Botanic Gardens Conservation Strategy was launched by Botanic Gardens Conservation International; the results were to be published at the sixth congress, scheduled to be held in Asheville, N.C., in June 2000. A new technical manual for botanical gardens presented at the congress outlined major aspects of their development and management.

An international conference on medicinal plant conservation took place in Bangalore, India, in February, convened by the Foundation for Revitalization of Local Health Traditions. The participants urged administrators of botanical gardens to create medicinal-plant-conservation programs and promote the development of medicinal gardens by local communities.

A meeting of the Latin American and Caribbean Association of Botanic Gardens was held in Mexico City in October. A dominant theme at the meeting was the need to strengthen national networks of botanical gardens in the region and focus gardens' efforts on the implementation of the Convention on Biological Diversity.

The Botanical Garden in Padua, Italy, was approved as a UNESCO World Heritage Site in 1997. Founded in 1545, it is the oldest existing botanical garden in the world. The John D. and Catherine T. MacArthur Foundation awarded a grant of $170,000 to support the U.S. Center for Plant Conservation (CPC) in Hawaii, where it worked with Hawaiian botanical gardens to conserve the critically endangered native flora of the islands. The CPC linked 28 U.S. botanical gardens and arboreta to maintain a collection of more than 500 of the nation's rarest plants.

Several initiatives in training botanical garden staff were undertaken in 1998. An International Diploma Course on Botanic Garden Management was held at Kew Gardens in London in July for students from more than 12 countries. In Africa a course on conservation techniques was organized at the National Museums of Kenya with the support of the British government, and in South Africa the British Council supported a course on environmental education.

A Conservation Action Plan for Botanic Gardens of the Caribbean Islands was published in May. Prepared in consultation with more than 50 individuals and institutions in the region, the plan outlined priorities for conservation and garden development in the countries of the Caribbean. During a meeting at the Bogotá (Colom.) Botanic Garden

Caribbean flamingos huddle together in a men's bathroom at Miami's Metro Zoo on September 24. The zoo sheltered the flamingos there temporarily as powerful Hurricane Georges swept through South Florida. Because the zoo provides its animals with a cageless environment, zoo officials were worried that many of the birds would attempt to flee before the storm hit.

in October, a national information-management strategy was developed for Colombian botanical gardens. Computer-based information systems were to be developed for use in each of the nation's 16 gardens.

In the Northern Territory of Australia, the Alice Springs Desert Park opened in March 1997. The goals of the 1,300-ha (3,200-ac) park included the conservation of native flora of the region and the interpretation of life in Australian desert ecosystems.

A meeting of the European Botanic Gardens Consortium was held in Denmark in June to review the preparation of a European botanical gardens action plan. The consortium included representatives of each of the national botanical garden associations in the European Union (EU). In May a workshop on information systems for botanical gardens in Kazakstan and the surrounding countries was held in Almaty, Kazakstan's former capital.

A new project to develop the botanical gardens of Morocco and Tunisia was funded by the EU. It included the creation of new plant-conservation facilities at gardens in Rabat, Mor., and Tunis, Tun., and was being carried out in partnership with Botanic Gardens Conservation International (BCGI) and Fauna & Flora International. The Stanley Smith Horticultural Trust (U.K.) sponsored a project for the Kisantu Botanic Garden, Democratic Republic of the Congo, to make available medicinal and other economic plants for local people. In February the National Commission for Wildlife Conservation and Development and BGCI undertook a feasibility study to develop a national botanical garden in Riyadh, Saudi Arabia, the first such garden in that country.

(PETER S. WYSE JACKSON)

GARDENING

The weather continued to have a global impact on gardening in 1998 as cool, wet conditions arising from an El Niño event in the eastern Pacific hurt spring and early-summer sales of both seed and nursery products in the U.S. Seed crops in the major production areas of Europe and Africa were also affected by wetter-than-normal weather leading up to harvest time, and shortages and a reduction in crops for many annual ornamentals resulted. In The Netherlands up to 35% of the bulb crop was lost.

A more sophisticated understanding of plant adaptation developed as gardeners and gardening experts in the media accepted more widely the notion of adding heat-tolerance data to the cold-hardiness information produced by American and Australian horticultural publishers and mail-order nurseries. Both countries began to include heat maps in their publications to assist gardeners in choosing plants adaptable to the full range of climatic conditions.

FLEUROSELECT

The *Zinnia* Profusion Cherry was awarded a Fleuroselect Gold Medal in 1998. A seed-propogated ornamental, the *Zinnia* Profusion Cherry featured stiff, hairy stems and lance-shaped leaves arranged opposite each other. Its cherry-red flowers with a yellow centre were borne only 60 days after seeding.

Horticulture continued its rapid expansion with publications in print, radio and television broadcasts, and Web sites; not every new media venture proved successful, however. In the U.K., BBC1 launched its first new garden show of the decade, and new, coordinated zone maps for the U.S. and Europe were developed so that plant culture from one location could be more successfully applied elsewhere. Vegetatively reproduced bedding plants and such container garden favourites as petunia, verbena, fuchsia, portulaca, and helichrysum became available in large quantities and, owing to their ease of propagation and inherent trueness to type, created significant competition with seed-grown crops. Many of the original stock plants used for these programs were introduced from Asia, Australia, and New Zealand and were quickly patented in the U.S. under existing plant patent laws. In Europe marketers formed a new organization, Fleuroprotect, which provided guidelines for the marketplace.

Among seed-propagated ornamentals, three new introductions were awarded the Fleuroselect Gold Medal. *Nemesia strumosa* Sundrops, recognized for its wide colour range (golden yellow, pink, red, orange, and white single flowers borne on compact plants), had both a diameter and a height of 25 cm (1 cm=0.4 in) and a bloom period from May to October in northern temperate climates. *Verbena* Quartz Burgundy was selected for its unusual wine-red flower umbels with a tiny white eye and the high resistance to powdery mildew of its dark, textured leaves. The plant spread to a diameter of 35 cm and reached a height of 30 cm. The interspecific hybrid *Zinnia* Profusion Cherry won a Fleuroselect Gold Medal for its uniform, compact habit (3 cm in diameter and height) and the outstanding mildew and bacterial leaf-spot resistance of its lance-shaped foliage. Its warm cherry-red 5-cm-diameter single flowers with a yellow centre were borne May to October only 60 days after seeding. Along with its sister line Profusion Orange, Profusion Cherry also won an All-America Selections (AAS) Gold Medal, the first gold medals to be awarded in 10 years. Other AAS award-winning flowers included the seed-grown tuberous *Begonia* Pin-Up Flame, a compact (25–30-cm-high) shade-loving plant with bright yellow 5–10-cm-high single flowers that shaded to edges of orange-red and dark, arrowhead leaves. The perennial *Tritoma* Flamenco (*Kniphofia uvaria*) convinced the AAS judges of its merit by producing 75-cm stems topped with spikes of tubular flowers in its first season from seed. The warm, yellow-to-red-orange flowers were recognized not only for their long vase life but also for their attractiveness to hummingbirds.

Four bedding plants were also named AAS award winners. Besides *Verbena* Quartz Burgundy, *Marigold* Bonanza Bolero was chosen for its exceptional earliness—it bloomed from seed in only 45 days—and for the irregular gold-and-red bicolour pattern on its 10-cm flowers. The plant had a height of 20–30 cm and a spread of 30–60 cm. *Osteospermum* Passion Mix, which was 30 cm tall and had a diameter of 40 cm, received recognition for its 5–7-cm pastel-to-white daisylike flowers with azure-blue centres that were less likely to close under low-light conditions. The final AAS bedding plant award went to *Portulaca* Sundial Peach, the first *Portulaca* to win such an award. Recognized for its increased petal count and the brilliant colour of its 5-cm flowers as well as their tendency to stay open even in low light situations, this creeping plant spread 20–30 cm and bloomed in only 65–70 days from seeding. AAS also bestowed four vegetable awards. Hybrid zucchini Eight Ball bore dark green 5–8-cm round fruits in only 40–50 days on compact 90-cm plants. Pumpkin Wee Be Little caught the attention of the judges by producing tiny round orange fruits only 225–450 g (8–16 oz) that were ideal for fall decorations; the plants grew to only 180–240 cm, which made them ideal for smaller gardens. Hybrid indeterminate tomato Juliet was an elongated cherry-type tomato recognized for the crack resistance and sweet flavour of the glossy red fruits that were ready for harvest only 60 days after transplanting. Finally, watermelon New Queen won for its 2.5–3-kg (5.5–6.5-lb) mottled green fruits that the AAS judges noted had both crisp texture and a sweet flavour. Plants were vigorous and grew to 270 cm, ripening their first fruits in only 75–80 days from seeding or 65 days from transplant, depending on weather conditions.

(SHEPHERD OGDEN)

Fashions

Casual luxury dominated international designer fashion in 1998. The style was a mix of classic yet flattering American tailored sportswear, with an emphasis on separates—loose trousers, sweaters, and knee- and ankle-length skirts—and costly couture fabrics such as cashmere. Though the "maximalism" style of luxury featured during 1997 had given way to a more casual look, some elements remained popular, including the use of strong colours such as red, petrol blue, winter white, purple, and gray, which, for both women and men, succeeded in eradicating the dominance of the basic black wardrobe. Real fur, too, was prevalent on the autumn-winter runways and was used for coats, skirts, shirts, and trim on shoes, collars, and handbags. Some of the most popular accessories were opulent, notably Fendi's beaded shoulder bag, which became a sought-after status item. Choker necklaces with dripping beads—like those featured in the film *Titanic* and created by British designer John Galliano and Belgian designer Olivier Theyskens—were completely sold out at American department stores. Increasingly, however, luxurious fashions seemed incompatible with the lives of women, most of whom were not willing to sacrifice comfort for fashion. Economic downturns in Russian and Asia also signaled a drop in sales of luxury goods.

Bernard Arnault—president and chairman of French luxury goods conglomerate LVMH Moët Hennessy Louis Vuitton—more than any designer, was the driving force behind fashion's new direction. In 1997 Arnault had appointed British designers Galliano and Alexander McQueen to head design at two LVMH fashion houses: Christian Dior and Givenchy, respectively. Their distinctly luxurious collections—including creations such as McQueen's razor-sharp tailored leather trouser suits and Galliano's lavish bias-cut lamé evening dresses—as well as their heavily stylized seasonal runway shows, continued to attract the attention and admiration of fashion critics and to create a stronger brand awareness worldwide.

In the 1990s fashion's chief modernist, Austrian designer Helmut Lang, pioneered the casual luxury look with what British *Vogue* summed up as "simple pieces . . . so authentically 'of the street' and yet utterly classic." By spring Lang had moved his business from Vienna to New York City and continued to lead fashion's modern direction. For his autumn-winter show, he chose the Internet instead of the runway to present his collection of predominantly spare, functional winter-white separates.

Meanwhile, Arnault's stable of new designers put their stamp on casual luxury with whimsical and lighthearted sartorial touches. Narciso Rodríguez at the Madrid-based leather house Loewe accessorized his own eponymous autumn-winter collection with cashmere Birkenstocks. For his first autumn-winter collection at Louis Vuitton, Marc Jacobs broke with tradition. Instead of using the company's recognizable signature gold-stamped-on-brown-leather LV insignia, he created "invisible luxury"—clothes and handbags that, though discreet, matched luxury with current street style. He created drawstring jogging-style trousers; a black

Halston was one of many designers who reintroduced fur in his fashion. His gown trimmed with a lynx collar was made of cashmere, an increasingly utilized fabric.

hooded, front-zipped sweatshirt wool jacket; and an LV-embossed white-on-white messenger bag.

Singaporean designer Andrew Gn explained to *Women's Wear Daily* that "the idea of the season is to take something simple, like jeans, and make them in a great fabric like cashmere." His collection for the house of Balmain, as well as the work of both Belgian designer Martin Margiela (who

debuted his first collection for the French luxury brand Hermès) and Cristina Oritz (who joined Lanvin after having served as design director for Prada), shared fashion's casual-luxury sensibility.

Spring-summer designer fashion introduced fashion's new feeling of ease. American *Vogue* described Belgian designer Anne Demeulemeester's "shrugged-on" style of jacket as "effortlessness." The best looks, however, presented on the runway and then copied by retailers around the world, were casual, feminine, and uncomplicated—like Capri pants ('50s-style pedal pushers), the pleated knee-length skirt, and the slide (a flat, open-toed shoe). The star of London Fashion Week was British designer Matthew Williamson, whose slip and sheath dresses appealed to the critics for their simple cut and bright colours, such as shocking pink and turquoise. Diane Von Fürstenberg's wrap dress, which had originally been introduced in 1973 and was reintroduced during the New York spring-summer collections, was sought after for the same reasons.

A more frivolous look was "hippie chic," a luxurious take on ethnic-inspired clothes. The style proved to be such a strong theme for summer that it reappeared on select autumn-winter runways as the bohemian look. The Italian labels Marni and Etro led the way at the spring-summer Milan collections, with drawstring trousers, sarongs, and collarless shirts made of bright ethnic-print fabrics such as linen, embroidered suede, and silk. American designer Anna Sui also captured the look with a spring-summer collection of print dresses, bandanna bikinis, and Liberty print sundresses, inspired, she claimed, by a "Tibetan surfer."

Meanwhile, a strong unisex trend among young urbanites was a casual look that American *Vogue* called "utility chic," the wearing of clothing originally designed for sports or to combat weather conditions on the street. At the forefront of the style was Vexed Generation, a London-based design duo of former music producers who created what they called "protective day wear," including fleece jackets with high zip-up collars and

Models, among them Kate Moss (second from right) and rocker Mick Jagger's daughter Jade (right), wait backstage at the Natural History Museum in London for their turn on the catwalk at the 1998 Spring-Summer Matthew Williamson Show.

jumpsuits made from Kevlar, a bulletproof fabric. Its most popular style was a messenger bag that, when slung over the shoulder, could be fastened with Velcro. Other popular utility-chic staples included Patagonia-style fleece jackets, Nike Air Max and New Balance trainers, and G-shock watches, colourful, indestructible digital watches designed by Kikuo Ibe in Japan for Casio.

High fashion also responded to the utility-chic trend. For autumn-winter several menswear designers, including Dolce & Gabbana and Gianfranco Ferre, incorporated a range of sportswear into their menswear collections. Miuccia Prada introduced functional elements to her autumn-winter menswear collection, adding such features as Velcro fastenings to shoes, formal suits, shirts, and cashmere coats. Prada also debuted for autumn-winter a "red stripe" collection, a complete athletic line that included the high-performance fabrics Gore-Tex and CoolMax lining.

The feeling of ease infiltrated other aspects of the fashion industry. The modeling industry and the fashion media advocated a stronger sense of individuality. On the runway and in magazines, the perfectly groomed blonde, blue-eyed models were eclipsed by a new generation of young women who shared a stereotypical exotic look. They had wide dusky eyes, olive skin, shapely figures, and full manes of long, dark hair. Emerging retail trends also pointed to a growing sense of individuality. Though such corporations as Gucci, Prada, Louis Vuitton, Tommy Hilfiger, and Ralph Lauren opened huge retail superstores, a growing number of women were drawn to a selection of female-owned boutiques like the Cross in London, Phare in New York City, and Colette in Paris. Instead of selling just one fashion label, these shops were set up like fashionable bazaars, offering eclectic merchandise, including high fashion and comfortable clothes, household goods, books, art, beauty products, and gift items.

Away from the catwalk, people seemed to share a relaxed attitude toward dressing. Former supermodel Cindy Crawford wore a simple short white slip dress and was barefoot when she wed Rande Gerber on a California beach. At the Academy Awards ceremony—the place where luxury dressing came to life every year—female celebrities opted for looks that were formal yet simple. Helen Hunt (*see* BIOGRAPHIES) wore a custom-made long ice-blue Gucci dress. Though it was strapless, Hunt left her shoulders and neck unadorned. Young women in the U.K. identified less with such past fashion icons as Diana, princess of Wales, and Carolyn Bessett Kennedy and more with Bridget Jones, the fictional chain-smoking, attractive-yet-disheveled 30-something single female character from British writer Helen Fielding's best-selling novel *Bridget Jones's Diary,* whereas teenage girls in the U.S. copied the look of All Saints, a British all-girl multiracial pop group who, for on-stage performances, favoured loose baggy jeans and athletic clothing like T-shirts, sweatshirts, and trainers.

Men's fashion produced relaxed looks through spring-summer and into autumn-winter. Labels Comme des Garcons and DKNY designed the casual men's mule, which was best described by the British men's magazine *Arena Homme Plus* as "slipper like soft (leather) shoes that, by

KEVORK DJANSEZIAN—AP/WIDE WORLD

Academy Award-winning actress Helen Hunt (right) wears a simple yet elegant Gucci dress to the Oscars ceremony. She eschewed the glitzy adornments and expensive jewelry that were typically arrayed at the Oscars.

willfully crushing the back, can be made to look like mules."

For summer suiting Giorgio Armani introduced the work-wear suit, featuring ideas from work clothes—exposed stitching, patch pockets, and concealed buttons on jackets. Designer denim appeared in several collections, including one by Gucci and Helmut Lang. For autumn-winter the fitted menswear cut gave way to more generous proportions and a longer, looser silhouette for suits and coats. Dolce & Gabbana, Raf Simons, Donna Karan, and Armani introduced '30s-style wide-leg trousers. Designers who focused on casual luxury for women also integrated that theme into autumn-winter menswear. Calvin Klein used ultralight leather for shirts and pullover tops and described his menswear as "wearable luxury." Tom Ford introduced fine-gauge and four-ply cashmere sweaters into his autumn-winter col-

lection for Gucci. During the year Yves Saint Laurent (*see* BIOGRAPHIES) celebrated 40 years as a designer, and designer Isaac Mizrahi left the business after Chanel terminated its partnership with him.

(BRONWYN COSGRAVE)

MIKE SEGAR—KRT PHOTOS

In October celebrated fashion designer Isaac Mizrahi stuns many in the fashion world when he announces that he will leave the business. Chanel terminated its contract with him, owing to lacklustre sales. Mizrahi was the third designer to abandon his trade; Kenar and Andrea Jovine declared bankruptcy and shuttered their doors earlier in the year.

Health and Disease

In 1998 antibiotic-resistant organisms were spreading rapidly in both less-developed and industrialized countries, a situation that was presenting an increasing threat to public health worldwide. The global scope of tuberculosis (TB) was highlighted by a World Health Organization (WHO) survey that found drug-resistant cases of the disease in 35 countries. The proliferation of resistant TB strains was largely attributable to weaknesses in TB-control programs. At the same time, however, there were disquieting signs that, at least in some locations, the tubercle bacillus, *Mycobacterium tuberculosis,* was becoming inherently more virulent.

Increasing drug resistance was seen in *Salmonella typhimurium,* a major agent of food poisoning. This prompted calls for stricter controls on the use of antibiotics in farm animals to promote growth and prevent disease. Particularly prevalent in England and Wales, multidrug-resistant *S. typhimurium* had also emerged in several European countries and the U.S. One American survey showed that the prevalence of salmonella strains unresponsive to five antibiotics (ampicillin, chloramphenicol, streptomycin, sulfonamides, and tetracyclines) had increased from 0.6% to 34% in only six years.

Researchers who analyzed more than 1,000 strains of *Streptococcus pneumoniae* (pneumococcus) from hospitals in the U.S. and Canada reported in the October issue of *Clinical Infectious Diseases* that the common bacterium had grown increasingly resistant to penicillin and cephalosporin antibiotics. *S. pneumoniae,* the bacterium most frequently responsible for infections of the bloodstream, pneumonia, and ear infections, was the third most common cause of bacterial meningitis in children.

The year was also one in which a number of long-term investments in basic scientific research bore fruit. American researchers succeeded in extending the life span of human cells grown in the laboratory. Most human cells divide in half a finite number of times before entering a condition known as senescence. As some types of cells age, their telomeres—protective caps at the ends of the chromosomes—shorten. This probably happens because telomerase, the enzyme that facilitates normal rebuilding of the telomeres, becomes less active. By incorporating the gene that gives rise to telomerase into senescent cells, however, scientists were able to reextend telomeres and thereby rejuvenate the cells. This achievement prompted speculation that it may one day be possible to maintain normal cells in a youthful state and thereby prevent many aging-related changes in the human body. There was, however, a catch-22 associated with telomerase (sometimes dubbed the "immortality enzyme"): the longer cells lived, the greater their chances were of becoming cancerous.

Equally dramatic was the isolation and growth in the laboratory of a key type of cell from human embryos and fetuses that gives rise to specialized tissues throughout the developing body. The cells, known as human embryonic stem cells, have the potential to be grown in the laboratory in large quantities and to replenish damaged tissues in patients suffering from an array of illnesses.

The new findings, reported independently in November by teams from the University of Wisconsin and Johns Hopkins University, Baltimore, Md., were viewed by most members of the scientific community as a breakthrough with enormous potential. Other groups, who were opposed to any kind of research on human embryos, were critical of the work.

Another exciting but surprising finding came from scientists in Sweden and California, who discovered for the first time that the adult human brain may be capable of producing new nerve cells, or neurons. This finding flew in the face of the long-held dogma that human brain cells do not regenerate. In the long run this new insight may lead to new means of treating the victims of stroke and certain degenerative brain conditions, including Alzheimer's disease and Parkinson's disease.

The medical event that arguably received the greatest publicity was the approval and subsequent marketing of the drug sildenafil (Viagra) for the treatment of male impotence. (*See* Sidebar.)

Asthma. In December two teams of researchers in the U.S. announced that they had identified a molecule, interleukin-13 (IL-13), which may be responsible for the airway inflammation characteristic of asthma. One group treated asthma-prone mice with a drug that blocks the action of IL-13 and then exposed the animals to a substance that normally triggers an asthma attack; the mice did not develop breathing problems. The other group treated the nasal passages of mice with a substance that blocks IL-13. When exposed to an asthma-triggering protein, these mice had few asthma symptoms.

In the U.S. the Centers for Disease Control and Prevention (CDC) issued a major report in April indicating that asthma rates had jumped 75% between 1980 and 1994, to an estimated 13.7 million sufferers nationwide. Increases in reported asthma cases and deaths affected all ages and racial groups, but rates of emergency room visits, hospitalizations, and deaths were consistently higher among African-Americans, as compared with whites.

On the global front international asthma experts met in December and launched an initiative aimed at reducing the burden of childhood asthma over the next five years. The goals were to reduce asthma death rates in children by at least 50%, to reduce the number of school days lost owing to asthma by 50%, and to cut asthma-related hospitalizations by at least 25%.

Cancer. Investigators in the U.S. called a halt to a large clinical trial of the hormonal drug tamoxifen 14 months earlier than originally planned when they found that women at high risk of breast cancer who took this drug had reduced their chances of developing the disease by 44%. U.K. researchers were critical of the decision to end the trial, pointing out that tamoxifen may simply have delayed the development of the breast cancer. The debate continued when the results of two smaller European trials published later in the year showed that the drug offered no protection against breast cancer in healthy women. The latter trials, however, may have included too few women for any benefit to have become apparent.

Despite these uncertainties, the U.S. Food and Drug Administration (FDA) approved tamoxifen for the prevention of breast cancer in otherwise healthy women who were at high risk for the disease. (Previously, the drug was approved only as a treatment for diagnosed cancer.) Cancer specialists

Recovering from tuberculosis, a young Portuguese woman sits in her hospital bed in Lisbon. Due in part to troubled health-care systems in many European countries, there was a rising incidence of tuberculosis on the continent. Portugal had the highest rate of tuberculosis among European Union nations.

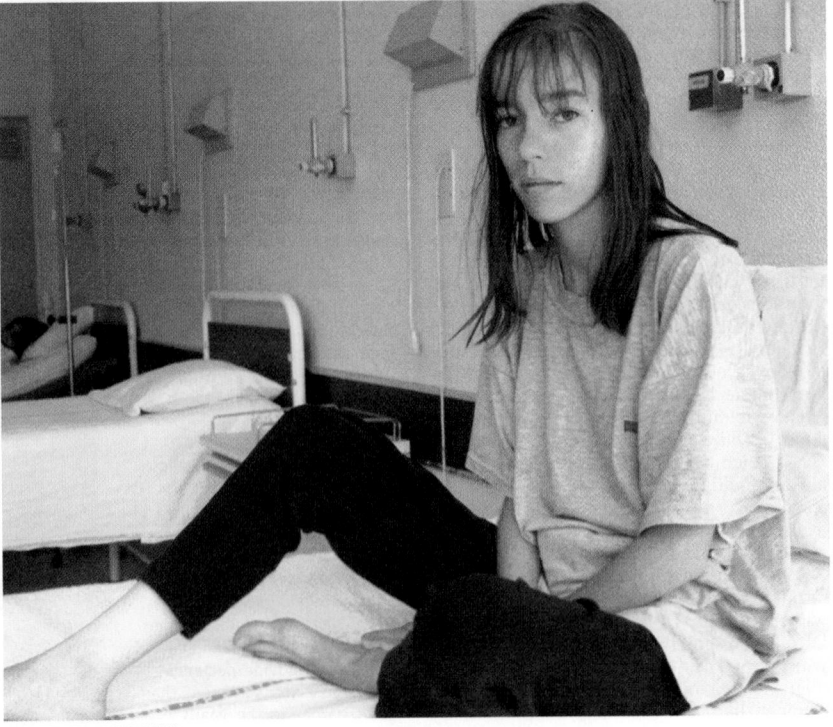

LUISA FERREIRA—AP/WIDE WORLD

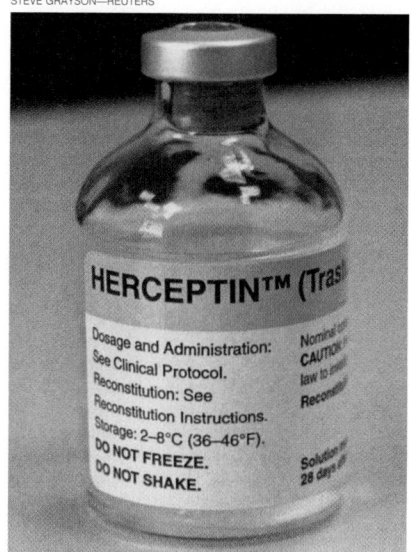

The breast-cancer drug Herceptin was tested at the University of California, Los Angeles, in 1998. The drug showed positive results in women with a form of breast cancer caused by an overabundance of a gene known as HER-2/neu.

stressed that benefits of the treatment for individual patients would have to be weighed carefully against the risks, since the drug was known to cause potential adverse effects, including uterine cancer and blood clots in the veins or lungs. Factors that put a woman at high risk of breast cancer included advancing age, personal history of abnormal breast changes, family history of the disease, birth of a first child at age 30 or older, or onset of menstruation before age 12.

Two studies found that a new biologically engineered weapon against breast cancer, Herceptin, boosted the benefits of chemotherapy in women with invasive breast cancer. Herceptin is a type of protein (a so-called monoclonal antibody) created from mouse cells and designed to bind to the receptors that control growth in breast cells. In September the FDA approved Herceptin for an especially aggressive form of breast cancer known as HER-2/neu.

The once-obscure work of Boston's Children's Hospital researcher Judah Folkman (see BIOGRAPHIES) became front-page news when his laboratory announced it had discovered two new drugs that had eradicated malignant tumours—even huge ones—in mice. For more than three decades, Folkman had been studying angiogenesis, the process by which localized blood-vessel growth feeds malignant tissues, enabling solid tumours to thrive and spread. Widespread publicity about the success of the drugs—endostatin and angiostatin—which had no apparent side effects, led to speculation that such an approach would work equally well in humans. Indeed, the National Cancer Institute (NCI) announced that getting the drugs into clinical trials was a top priority. Despite the promising prospects of the new drugs, experienced researchers, including Folkman himself, felt that the media coverage had raised premature hopes of a cure among cancer patients.

Cancer statistics for the U.S., released in March by the NCI, CDC, and American Cancer Society, showed that the rate of new

cases and deaths had declined overall. During the period 1990–95, the overall rates for new cases decreased about 0.7% annually, and overall cancer death rates declined about 0.5% per year. The good news, however, did not include all Americans. African-American men bore a disproportionate share of the cancer burden. The comprehensive survey had looked at 23 types of cancer in four ethnic/racial groups: whites, African-Americans, Hispanics, and Asian or Pacific Islanders. The prostate, lung, breast, and colon-rectum were the four leading cancer sites, accounting for nearly half of all newly diagnosed cases during the six-year period.

A study involving 29,000 male smokers, carried out by researchers from the NCI and the National Public Health Institute of Finland, suggested that long-term use of a vitamin E supplement significantly reduced subjects' risk of prostate cancer. The research found that men between the ages of 50 and 69 who took 50 mg a day of vitamin E in the form of alpha-tocopherol for five to eight years had 32% fewer cases of prostate cancer and 41% fewer deaths from the disease than men who did not receive the supplement. Experts urged that additional studies be carried out to confirm the beneficial effect.

Cardiovascular Disease. For many years medical researchers had suspected that women with heart disease did not respond as well as their male counterparts to existing therapies. A large-scale study carried out under the auspices of the U.S. National Heart, Lung, and Blood Institute put at least some of those doubts to rest. The study followed men and women who underwent either coronary artery bypass surgery or balloon angioplasty—procedures that promote blood flow to the heart. After five years 87% of the women patients were alive, a rate almost identical to that for men in the study.

Encouraging news for the early prevention of heart disease came from a U.S. government survey showing declines in total cholesterol levels in American adolescents between the late 1960s and the early 1990s. Elevated blood cholesterol levels early in life were known to increase the risk of heart disease in adulthood. Data from the survey showed that '90s teenagers had lower intakes of saturated fat and total fat than did their '60s counterparts. Previous surveys had shown that similar changes in the consumption patterns of American adults had contributed to a 50% decline in coronary heart disease deaths.

Lifestyle changes, including weight loss through diet and exercise and reduction of salt intake, can reduce, or possibly eliminate, the need for medication to control hypertension (high blood pressure) among elderly individuals. A clinical trial involving 975 men and women between the ages of 60 and 80 was the first of sufficient size and scope to confirm that older people who changed their behaviour could reduce their reliance on antihypertensive drugs.

In June a prescription drug for lowering blood pressure and treating angina pain, which had been available for less than a year, was taken off the market in 38 countries. The drug, Posicor (mibefradil), a calcium-channel blocker, was used by an estimated 400,000 patients worldwide. The reason for the swift withdrawal was that the drug was found to cause toxic—and sometimes lethal—reactions when taken in combination with certain other drugs.

Genetics. Researchers in the U.S. and the U.K. announced that they had completely sequenced the genome of the roundworm *Caenorhabditis elegans*. This was the first time scientists had sequenced the genetic instructions for a complete animal. Although the lowly roundworm is tiny (25 in one inch), it can shed light on many characteristics of humans. It has a relatively complex nervous system, and about 40% of its 19,099 genes match those of other organisms. Scientists around the world hailed the accomplishment, which they saw as an invaluable research tool for studying everything from embryonic development to aging.

The complete genomes of three important human pathogens—*M. tuberculosis, Treponema pallidum* (the syphilis spirochete), and *Chlamydia trachomatis* (responsible for the most common sexually transmitted disease)—were sequenced during the year. Having deciphered the complete sets of instructions that these microbes need to infect human cells and thrive therein, scientists

A microscopic image of *Caenorhabditis elegans,* a roundworm whose genome was completely sequenced by scientists, is shown below. Scientists working on the Human Genome Project in the U.S. and Great Britain performed the sequencing.

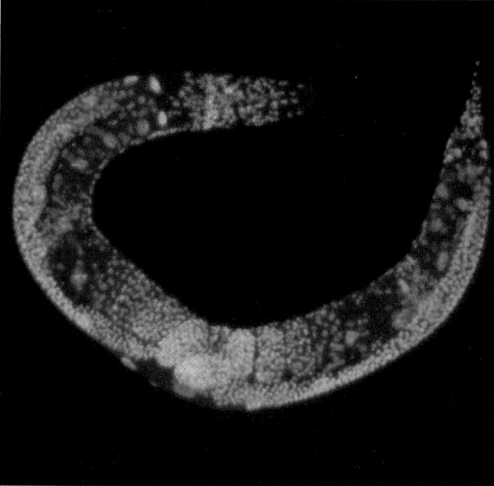

were now better equipped than ever before to find new ways to eliminate the diseases they caused.

In October a worldwide effort involving 64 scientists produced a new gene map, marking the chromosomal locations of more than 30,000 human genes, nearly half of the human genome. The compilation, called GeneMap'98, was accessible on the Internet (http://www.ncbi.nlm.nih.gov/genemap/) and was expected to help in the identification of numerous human disease-causing genes. Owing to this more-rapid-than-expected progress, American leaders of the Human Genome Project proposed that the goal of sequencing the entire three billion base-pair human genome could be accomplished by the end of 2003, two years ahead of schedule.

In January researchers reported the discovery of the first gene associated with human hair loss. The gene, called hairless, was found in a Pakistani family with the rare disorder alopecia universalis, in which those affected have no head or body hair, eyebrows, or eyelashes. Scientists speculated that this

During clinical trials of an experimental influenza vaccine carried out by the National Institute of Allergy and Infectious Diseases, a child receives the vaccine via nasal spray rather than a hypodermic needle.

discovery could lead to a new understanding of more common types of hair loss, including alopecia areata, an autoimmune disorder characterized by the loss of large patches of head hair and affecting as many 2.5 million people in the U.S. alone, and male-pattern baldness, a hormone-controlled disorder that causes some degree of hair thinning or baldness in up to 80% of men and women. If scientists were to discover a gene responsible for male-pattern baldness, it might be possible to prevent or treat the most common form of hair loss with gene therapy.

Infectious Diseases. Vaccines against the tickborne bacterial infection Lyme disease were developed by two pharmaceutical companies, one of which received FDA approval in late December to market its product LYMErix. Lyme disease can affect the skin, joints, heart, and nervous system and be highly debilitating. In clinical trials the vaccine demonstrated efficacy rates of 78% after three doses and 50% after two doses against symptomatic Lyme disease. Although the vaccine was approved for marketing, it was likely to be given only to very select individuals, such as those planning to travel to heavily tick-infested areas. Meanwhile, uncertainties remained over a number of issues, including the number of booster doses likely to be required for continued protection and the safety and efficacy of the vaccine in children, who represented 23% of Lyme disease cases.

An experimental influenza vaccine, given by nasal spray rather than hypodermic syringe, was found to be 93% effective in healthy American youngsters aged 15 months to 6 years. The nasal spray also proved to be highly protective against otitis media, a common flu-related ear infection of children. Healthy children were not routinely immunized against influenza, but public health officials were hopeful that the new product would be approved for use by the FDA in 1999 and that the availability of a safe, effective, and painless vaccine would lead to widespread vaccination of most children in schools and clinics.

In August the FDA licensed the first vaccine to prevent serious rotavirus infections,

the most common cause of severe diarrhea and vomiting among American infants. Prior to the development of the vaccine about 80% of children under age five experienced rotavirus symptoms annually, and about 55,000 were hospitalized for severe diarrhea and potentially life-threatening dehydration. The new vaccine was to be given orally at ages two, four, and six months. Authorities pointed out, however, that the new vaccine was too expensive to use in many countries, where rotaviral disease was responsible for about 870,000 deaths each year.

In the U.S. there were further signs of progress in the fight against AIDS, and the disease dropped off the list of the nation's top 10 killers. The CDC reported in October that HIV infection had dropped from the 8th leading cause of death to number 14; moreover, age-adjusted death rates from HIV infection dropped an unprecedented 47% between 1996 and 1997. The declining death rate was largely attributed to the success of combination drug therapies that included protease inhibitors. Health authorities noted, however, that the incidence of HIV infections—*i.e.,* the number of new cases reported per year—had not declined, which suggested that prevention efforts needed to be stepped up.

Internationally the HIV/AIDS news was much grimmer. A United Nations country-by-country survey found that there were 30 million people in the world infected with HIV and that 21 million of them were in Africa. About 90% of all AIDS deaths were in sub-Saharan Africa, where the vast majority of the victims had no access to the life-prolonging drugs available in the West.

Transplantation. Physicians reported that transplantation of bone marrow from an unrelated donor whose tissues were matched with those of the recipient was a safe and effective therapy for selected patients with chronic myeloid leukemia. Their results indicated that this procedure was potentially curative for most victims of the disease aged 50 or under. Previously the possibility of a cure was considered to be realistic for only a minority of young patients with this type of cancer of the blood cells.

Immunologists in the U.S. genetically modified bone marrow cells in mice in such a way that grafts of foreign tissues were no longer rejected, which suggested that the same method could be used to facilitate the transplantation of tissues from nonhuman donors into humans. Given that there were major shortages of human donor organs in most countries, this achievement could make xenotransplantation (animal to human transplants) a more acceptable and feasible prospect.

In September Clint Hallam, an Australian man who had lost his arm as the result of an industrial injury, received a transplanted forearm and hand. An international team of surgeons in Lyon, France, transplanted the donor arm in a 13$\frac{1}{2}$-hour microsurgical procedure that involved carefully attaching the patient's nerves, blood vessels, tendons, muscles, bones, and skin to those of the donor arm. A previous attempt at such a transplant, in Ecuador in 1964, had failed when the patient's body rejected the donor arm two weeks after the operation. The French doctors had high hopes that antirejection drugs would prevent such an outcome. In mid-November there were no signs of rejection in Hallam's new arm, and he was able to move each of the donor fingers. The surgeons estimated that it would be at least a year before they knew whether the recipient would be able to feel sensations in his new appendage.

Other Developments. A team of pediatricians and cardiologists in Italy may have discovered the underlying basis of a large proportion of cases of sudden infant death syndrome (SIDS), or cot death, as it was known in Britain. Electrocardiograph (ECG) testing of more than 33,000 infants a few days after birth revealed a developmental heart rhythm defect, indicated by a prolongation of the so-called QT interval, in more than one-third of those who eventually became SIDS victims. This suggested that routine neonatal ECG screening may allow physicians to identify babies at greatest risk; preventive measures could then be initiated.

Although previous surveys had shown that the "Back to Sleep" campaign launched in 1994 in the U.S. had been enormously effective at reducing the incidence of SIDS (by 38% between 1992 and 1996), three 1998 studies indicated that certain segments of the population were not heeding the public health admonition to put infants to sleep on their backs, not on their abdomens. New efforts were proposed to target groups that were not being reached by the advice.

The FDA announced that it would require new alcohol-warning labels on all nonprescription pain relievers and fever reducers, including aspirin, acetaminophen, and ibuprofen. Labels would advise those who consumed three or more alcoholic drinks daily to consult their doctors before taking such medications because their drinking could put them at increased risk of liver damage or bleeding in the stomach. The ruling was to take effect on April 23, 1999.

Scientists in Seoul, S.Kor., announced that they had combined an egg and a human cell from an infertile woman to produce an early-stage embryo. They allowed the cloned cell to grow only into a four-cell embryo and did not take the critical step of implanting it in the woman's uterus. If they had done so, it would have been theoretically possible for the embryo to grow into a

fetus that was genetically identical to the woman. In other cloning experiments during the year, scientists in Hawaii produced mice that were cloned from the cells of a single mouse, and Japanese scientists produced calf clones.

The Journal of the American Medical Association devoted an entire issue to alternative therapies, which, according to a Harvard Medical School survey, were used by 4 out of 10 American adults in 1997. The same survey found that women were more likely than men to try alternative treatments, as were higher-income, well-educated members of the baby-boom generation. Australian physicians reported that Chinese herbal medicines were helpful in relieving the symptoms of irritable bowel syndrome. A study from China found that moxibustion (the application of burning herbs to acupuncture points on the body) given to women in the 33–35th weeks of pregnancy stimulated fetal movements and helped alter the position of babies presenting in the breech position. Yoga was effective in relieving the hand and wrist pain of carpal tunnel syndrome. On the other hand, chiropractic spinal manipulation did not seem to relieve chronic tension headaches, and an Indian herbal product called *Garcinia cambogia* was of little or no help in promoting weight loss. Nor did acupuncture alleviate pain associated with HIV-related nerve damage.

Gro Harlem Brundtland, former three-term prime minister of Norway, was elected to a five-year term as director general of WHO. She pledged, among other things, to restore credibility to the beleaguered organization. She took the helm of the agency in late July when Hiroshi Nakajima, director general for a stormy 10 years, stepped down. Brundtland, who had a medical degree from the University of Oslo and a public health degree from Harvard, was highly respected for her political skills and had been recognized for her leadership in environmental health. She said that one of her goals was to make the governmental heads put the health needs of their people at the top of their political agendas.

(BERNARD DIXON; CRISTINE RUSSELL)

MENTAL HEALTH

A proposed new treatment for schizophrenia, based on neuroscience research in the U.S., lacked the disadvantages of currently used drugs. Investigators described an experimental compound that reduced levels of the chemical glutamate—one of the neurotransmitters that relays messages between nerve cells—in the brain. Given to rats with symptoms (such as incessant head turning) that paralleled the psychotic symptoms of human schizophrenia, it brought marked relief with no evidence of harmful side effects. The discovery stemmed from the finding that phencyclidine (PCP, or "angel dust") induced effects similar to schizophrenia in healthy individuals by altering glutamate transmission in the brain. Current treatments for schizophrenia worked by interfering with another neurotransmitter, dopamine. These, however, often failed to control all of the symptoms. The new approach might provide the alternative type of therapy that had been sought for many years.

A study in Manchester, Eng., established that intensive cognitive behaviour therapy can provide help for patients with chronic schizophrenia. Psychiatrists compared patients receiving medication and other routine care with those also given cognitive behaviour therapy (which aims to change thought processes, behaviour, and emotions). Those having the additional treatment were eight times more likely to show major improvements in their psychotic symptoms, which can be intensely disabling, than were the patients treated conventionally. Another Manchester team systematically reviewed six independent investigations on the value of cognitive behaviour therapy to combat childhood and adolescent depressive disorder. Their study of 208 patients (aged 8–19) treated in this way showed that cognitive behaviour therapy was indeed effective in helping those with moderately severe depressive disorders. The same approach, however, could not yet be recommended for those suffering from severe depression.

Research in Australia and the U.K. shed light on the underlying basis of major depression disorder in older people, which often has a poor prognosis. Brain scanning revealed that many such people often undergo changes known as deep white-matter lesions. Depression, it was discovered, is much more likely to relapse and to become chronic in individuals with the lesions than in those lacking them. Investigations now under way on the chemical basis of these changes could lead to improved therapies.

Depressive symptoms in older women were found to be associated with higher mortality. A seven-year study of white American women aged 67 or above showed that the mortality rate for those with six or more depressive symptoms was 24%, compared with 17% for those with three to five symptoms and 7% for women with no symptoms. The greatest increased risk was that of dying from cardiovascular disease.

Evidence continued to accumulate on the relationship between psychiatric illness and factors such as unemployment and poverty. Analyses of more than 7,000 British people established that both of these social factors were linked with the continuation, but not the onset, of most common mental disorders. Individuals suffering from more than a year's poverty and financial strain were more likely to develop a psychiatric illness.

Another U.K. survey, of more than 10,000 adults, showed that, independent of other influences, a low standard of living was associated with an increased prevalence of neurotic psychiatric disorders. The authors of this study observed that during the previous 20 years, one of the largest increases in income inequality in the Western world had taken place in the U.K., and they argued that this may have had adverse consequences for the mental health of the population.

American researchers pinpointed a gene that predisposes its carriers to psychiatric illness. Wolfram syndrome, characterized by diabetes mellitus and degeneration of the optic nerve and other parts of the nervous system, had previously been known to oc-

Clint Hallam (seated) poses on October 15 with French doctor Jean-Michel Dubernard (left) in Lyon, France, three weeks after undergoing a 13-hour operation to receive a transplanted forearm and hand. By mid-November Hallam was able to move each of his new fingers.

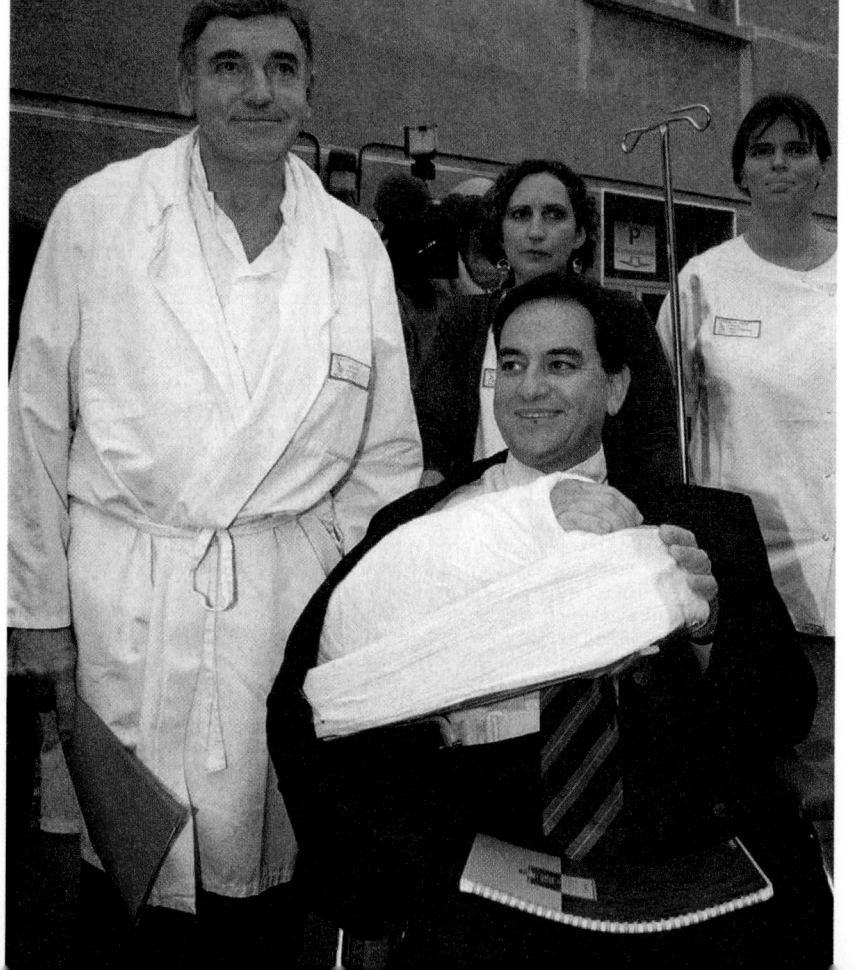

cur in people whose cells contained two copies of a particular mutant gene. The new findings concerned individuals who had one mutant and one normal gene. Although they did not suffer from Wolfram syndrome, they were 26 times more likely than average to develop psychiatric disease requiring hospital care. This discovery could explain the occasional reports that relatives of Wolfram syndrome patients were unusually likely to attempt suicide and to be admitted to a hospital for psychiatric reasons.

Researchers in The Netherlands implicated smoking in Alzheimer's disease. Contrary to previous studies, which implied that the habit might be protective, they reported that in a study of 7,000 individuals, smoking was associated with a doubling of the risk of dementia and Alzheimer's disease. Because the investigation was retrospective, following the subjects over time, the conclusions were likely to be more reliable than those of earlier studies based on less-rigorous methods.

Correlation of information regarding traffic accidents in the U.K. with information about drugs prescribed for the drivers showed that those taking benzodiazepines or zopiclone had an increased risk of experiencing an accident. The investigators concluded that users of those tranquilizers should be advised not to drive.

(BERNARD DIXON)

VETERINARY MEDICINE

Concerns arose during 1998 that the widespread use of antibiotics in farm animals could result in a loss of effectiveness when antibiotics were used to treat human infections. There had been suggestions that the use of products based on quinolone and fluoroquinolone could contribute to the creation of resistant strains of foodborne bacteria such as *Salmonella* and *Campylobacter,* which cause severe illness in humans as well as animals. A World Health Organization (WHO) meeting convened in Geneva in June recommended international cooperation to gather data, standardize testing methods, and develop a code of practice for the use of such products.

The biennial congress of the International Pig Veterinary Society, July 5–9, attracted more than 1,500 veterinarians to Birmingham, Eng. Delegates from 50 countries discussed problems in the production, health, welfare, and disease control of hogs. There was particular emphasis on porcine reproductive and respiratory syndrome, a viral disease that occurred worldwide and could cause serious losses among affected animals.

A symposium organized by the Office International des Epizooties on classical swine fever was held in conjunction with the conference. The disease had resisted international efforts to eradicate it and remained widespread, causing economic problems in Asia, Europe, and Latin America. A recent resurgence in Western and Central Europe affected pig breeding and called into question the effectiveness of prevention and control strategies. Recent developments in diagnostic and vaccine technology, however, were said to offer prospects for new approaches to controlling the disease.

A new variant strain of foot-and-mouth disease identified by the World Reference Laboratory, Pirbright, Eng., as originating in Iran and named A/Iran/96 had spread to

Viagra: A Second Honeymoon?

The approval in March 1998 of Viagra (sildenafil), the first oral drug for male impotence, brought new hope to the millions who suffered from this condition and revitalized the joke repertoire of late-night-TV talk-show hosts. The number of Viagra jokes was outpaced only by the number of prescriptions written: more than six million during the drug's first seven months on the market. Toward year's end, however, the enthusiasm was tempered by a cautionary note, as the U.S. Food and Drug Administration (FDA) warned of potentially serious side effects in some patients.

Viagra offered a novel way to treat male impotence, or erectile dysfunction, as it is known medically, a condition that affected an estimated 30 million men in the U.S. alone. Taken in pill form about an hour before sexual activity, Viagra improves blood flow to the penis and thereby allows a man to respond naturally to sexual stimulation. In clinical trials the drug was shown to restore sexual function in 7 out of 10 men. Previous treatments had involved surgical implants, suppositories, pumplike devices, and injection of drugs directly into the penis.

Doctors were immediately swamped with requests for the new drug, which cost $8–$10 a pill. The overwhelming demand created some unanticipated ethical, legal, and economic dilemmas. Although a full medical examination is recommended prior to taking Viagra, a controversial new industry sprang up, offering consumers prescriptions via the Internet. The high cost led some insurers, both private and public, to refuse to cover the drug, whereas others, including some state Medicaid programs, placed some limits on coverage.

Medical reports later in the year led the FDA to issue new warnings in November and prompted Pfizer, Inc., Viagra's manufacturer, to add them to its drug labeling for physicians. Although emphasizing that the drug was safe and effective for most users, the agency said that caution should be used in prescribing Viagra for some patients, including those who had recently suffered a heart attack or stroke and those with life-threatening arrhythmias, a history of heart failure or unstable angina, very low or very high blood pressure, or certain eye disorders. This warning was in addition to the original caution against Viagra use by people taking the drug nitroglycerin. The FDA also warned of the rare occurrence among some Viagra users of painful, prolonged erections requiring medical attention. As of mid-November the agency had received reports of 130 deaths among patients taking the drug, many from heart attacks, but there was no proof that the new medication itself caused the deaths.

(CRISTINE RUSSELL)

SANTIAGO LLANQUIN—AP/WIDE WORLD

Chilean pharmacist Jaime Zambrano displays the first boxes of Viagra to arrive at his drug store. As soon as the impotence drug hit the market in 1998, doctors around the world were immediately besieged with requests.

Turkey by 1998. Existing vaccines had proved ineffective, and so vaccines incorporating the new strain were produced.

Scrapie is a disease of sheep caused by a prion protein (PrP) that has links with Creutzfeldt-Jakob disease in humans; material from scrapie-infected sheep was also believed to be the origin of bovine spongiform encephalopathy ("mad cow" disease) in cattle. Attempts to eradicate scrapie would be greatly helped by the availability of a test to diagnose it before signs of the disease appeared. B.E.C. Schreuder and colleagues at The Netherlands Institute for Animal Science and Health devised a test that detected scrapie infection at 10 months of age, about halfway through the incubation period and well before clinical signs developed. The test was simple to perform and relatively noninvasive, using biopsies of material taken from the tonsil of the animal.

Knowledge of the weight of a horse is essential for calculating the dosage of medicines, formulating rations, and training for optimum condition. Methods of assessing the weight in the absence of a weighbridge (a platform scale flush with the roadway) included specially calibrated tapes, formulas based on body girth and length, precalculated tables, and visual estimation. J.M. Ellis of Warwickshire College, Moreton Morrell, Eng., and colleague Teresa Hollands endeavoured to establish the comparative accuracy of different methods by comparing the results in 600 horses of similar size and age against the actual weight. The accuracy of the results varied widely, the degree of error depending on the height of the horse. Most accurate, at 98.6%, was weight (kg) equals the square of the girth multiplied by the body length (cm) divided by 11,877.

(EDWARD BODEN)

Law, Crime, and Law Enforcement

LAW

Not only was 1998 notable as the 50th anniversary of the Universal Declaration of Human Rights, but it also marked the conclusion of a landmark agreement to establish an international criminal court to try war crimes, genocide, and crimes against humanity. This agreement, by 120 nations, reflected an increasing tendency to view human rights as a corollary to regional stability. This trend was also noticeable in ongoing efforts by the international community in former Yugoslavia, with the province of Kosovo presenting the latest challenge.

Contrasting with these positive developments, limited international resolve and comparatively scant resources were dedicated to problems far from Europe, such as Rwanda and the surrounding African countries. Major human rights violations in countries where civilians continued to suffer the aftereffects of conflict and associated human rights abuses, such as the Democratic Republic of the Congo (Congo [Kinshasa]), Algeria, and Indonesia, were given only cursory attention at the annual UN Human Rights Commission meeting. In June U.S. Pres. Bill Clinton's visit to China, where a policy of detention of dissidents continued, was notable for its low-key approach to human rights issues.

International Criminal Court. On July 17 in Rome, after discussions that lasted four years, a group of interested countries agreed by an overwhelming majority—120 in favour, 21 abstaining, and 7 against—to establish by treaty an international criminal court. The U.S. drew widespread criticism from human rights organizations by attempting to introduce amendments that would have considerably weakened the eventual powers of the court. It finally voted against the treaty, along with such unlikely bedfellows as Iraq, Libya, The Sudan, and China.

Crimes covered by the treaty included genocide, crimes against humanity, and war crimes; such contentious issues as terrorism and drug trafficking were not included. The court was not intended to be a substitute for a national judicial system and would intervene only when the national system did not investigate a possible crime or was "unable or unwilling" to do so. The real impact of the treaty was not expected to be felt for some time, as it required ratification by 60 nations before it came into force, a process that could take several years.

A serious limitation on the court's jurisdiction was that it could act only when the nation or territory or nationality of the accused had become a party to the treaty or had consented to do so. The decision by British courts to allow the extradition of Gen. Augusto Pinochet to Spain for crimes committed against Spanish citizens in Chile while president of that nation from 1973 to 1990 demonstrated a more robust approach to the issue of universal jurisdiction. The decision not to allow immunity for former heads of state for "crimes against humanity" revealed growing support for the legal enforcement of international human rights law.

Philip Kirsch (centre, standing), chairman of a UN committee organized to consider the idea of an international criminal court, speaks in Rome at the July 17 signing of a treaty to establish the court. The treaty was approved by 120 nations after four years of negotiations. The U.S. was among 7 nations that voted against ratification of the treaty.

The UN Security Council's role in the process of initiating investigations was limited by the treaty in favour of an independent and unfettered prosecutor. The power of the prosecutor to initiate an independent investigation was affirmed in the statute that established the court and was subject only to judicial approval prior to instituting a prosecution.

UN War Crimes Tribunals. The first verdict by the UN-established International Criminal Tribunal for Rwanda (ICTR) was handed down on September 4. Jean Kambanda, former prime minister of Rwanda during the genocide there in 1994, was found guilty. Cooperation by the states of former Yugoslavia with the International Criminal Tribunal for the Former Yugoslavia (ICTY) continued to be unsatisfactory, and both tribunals were hampered by a lack of resources.

War crimes trials by national courts in both former Yugoslavia and Rwanda often suffered from procedural deficiencies indicative of ethnic biases. Trials by the national courts in Rwanda resulted in the public execution of 22 persons in April for participation in the genocide, despite serious procedural inadequacies in the hearings. An estimated 130,000 persons detained in Rwandan prisons awaited trial.

Ethnic Conflict. Ethnic conflict continued to produce a cycle of revenge in Africa and former Yugoslavia. Despite a general return to stability in former Yugoslavia, a substantial return of refugees did not occur and ethnic discrimination and isolation continued to typify the climate in the region. At the end of February, the tension in the 90% ethnic Albanian province of Kosovo in Serbia finally led to the outbreak of a long-anticipated armed conflict between the Kosovo Liberation Army (KLA) and Serbian security forces.

The conflict continued throughout the spring and summer as the international community sought a diplomatic solution. In October Serbian Pres. Slobodan Milosevic agreed under threat of NATO air strikes to

allow in large numbers of unarmed representatives from the Organization for Security and Cooperation in Europe (OSCE) to monitor the implementation of UN Security Council resolutions providing for the withdrawal of Serbian forces from Kosovo and the return of the displaced population. Late in the year sporadic fighting continued in some areas, and the situation remained unstable.

Chaos continued to reign in the aftermath of the conflict in Rwanda. In Congo (Kinshasa), Pres. Laurent Kabila refused repeated requests by the UN and human rights groups to send missions to monitor the situation. Twenty-four soldiers were executed in October for treason following trial by a military tribunal. The executions were widely criticized by human rights organizations, in particular because of the lack of the right to appeal the death sentences.

Human Rights. Elections held in Cambodia on July 26 highlighted the limited success of the costly 1993 UN operation, when the first democratic election was held in that country. In the weeks preceding the 1998 vote, violence and intimidation encompassing illegal detention, torture, and extrajudicial killings increased. International observers pronounced the elections basically fair, which caused protests from human rights organizations such as Amnesty International, Funcinpec, and the Sam Rainsy Party, the main opposition groups. They alleged fraud and threatened to boycott the new National Assembly.

In September demonstrations in Phnom Penh, resulting from the postelection suppression of opposition parties, provoked a clampdown by the authorities, which led to further injuries and killings. In an anticlimactic episode in April, Pol Pot died in a jungle village near the Thai-Cambodian border, amid a growing clamour to establish an international tribunal to try Khmer Rouge leaders responsible for the 1979 genocide. The cause of his death was unverified but was said to have been a heart attack. (*See* OBITUARIES.)

The death of Nigerian leader Gen. Sani Abacha in June (*see* OBITUARIES) heralded positive changes in Nigeria's human rights climate. His successor, Gen. Abdulsalam Abubakar (*see* BIOGRAPHIES), released several prominent political detainees, introduced economic reforms, and initiated steps for Nigeria's readmission to the Commonwealth. A presidential election was scheduled for May 1999, marking the beginning of Nigeria's shift toward a more democratic system.

Changes in the political landscape in Iran indicated moves toward a more moderate policy by the regime. Rapprochement between Iran and the United States revealed the softening stance of the more liberal elements, represented by Pres. Mohammad Khatami. The internal struggle with the conservative Iranian religious establishment continued, however. Political repression was still commonplace, but the political shift gave new hope for the overall human rights environment.

Human Rights Watch reported in November on mass killings of 2,000 civilians by Afghanistan's ruling Taliban in the northern city of Mazar-e Sharif during fighting earlier in the year. Widespread repression of women living under the Taliban regime continued, including denial of education, employment, and freedom of movement; transgressors suffered beatings.

A peace deal concluded in Northern Ireland provided hope for a decrease in human rights abuses caused by the conflict. In the Middle East the peace process staggered along at a painfully slow pace threatened by continuing violence on both sides. The ultimate success of the negotiated agreements in both regions remained unclear.   (ANN MCMILLAN)

Court Decisions. The controversy involving U.S. President Clinton (*see* BIOGRAPHIES) dominated the American news media during the year and spawned several legal decisions handed down by the U.S. Supreme Court. The alleged wrongdoing that caused his troubles started in Arkansas while Clinton was governor there and involved a failed land deal, called "Whitewater," in which he and his wife, Hillary, were involved. Troubles continued for Clinton after he was elected president. In this connection one matter that later became important concerned the wholesale dismissal of White House travel office employees, allegedly done so that Clinton, through friends and colleagues, could take over this lucrative business. In view of these events and the charges and countercharges that they engendered in the media and the political arena, the Department of Justice appointed a special prosecutor, Kenneth Starr (*see* BIOGRAPHIES) to investigate the president's role in some of these activities.

Meanwhile, an employee of the state of Arkansas named Paula Jones brought an action in Arkansas charging Clinton with sexual harassment, allegedly committed while he was governor. As part of her proof, she sought to establish that Clinton had sexual affairs with many women and that this pattern of conduct was ongoing. In this connection Jones alleged that Clinton had engaged in sex with a young White House intern named Monica Lewinsky. In a deposition taken in the Jones case, Clinton denied under oath that he had a sexual relationship with Lewinsky.

Special Prosecutor Starr added the Lewinsky matter to his portfolio. His inquiry into this and the other charges falling within his jurisdiction went slowly, and he came under personal attack and was accused of delaying his work for reasons of personal political gain. He asserted that his investigation had been impeded by the refusal of Clinton and his staff to cooperate. Clinton replied that he was cooperating fully, but that many persons whom the special prosecutor wanted to interview or take before a grand jury were protected by various legal privileges that allowed them to refuse to give evidence. Starr then brought appropriate legal action to compel this testimony. It was this legal action and not the underlying facts or allegations making up the controversy that excited American legal scholars and produced two landmark decisions by the Supreme Court.

The first case involved the travel office dismissals. A deputy White House counsel, Vincent Foster, met with an "outside [the White House] attorney" to seek legal representation concerning the investigation of that matter. The outside attorney took three pages of handwritten notes of the meeting. Nine days later Foster committed suicide. Starr, through a grand jury subpoena, directed the outside counsel to produce the notes, but he refused. The Supreme Court held that the notes were protected by the attorney-client privilege, which survived Foster's death, and therefore could not be used in the ongoing investigation.

In a subsequent case, however, the Supreme Court limited the interpretation that some legal scholars were putting on the Foster decision. It let stand a lower court decision that Bruce Lindsey, a White House counsel, could not invoke the attorney-client privilege to refuse to testify before a grand jury regarding his conversations and other dealings with President Clinton. In that decision the court also held that Clinton had no "protective-function" privilege that would prevent his bodyguards from giving testimony to a grand jury concerning his activities.

At the same time, President Clinton agreed to testify before a grand jury empaneled by Starr, and his testimony given by video transmission from the White House was later telecast to the nation. This testimony was given under oath, and Starr subsequently alleged that some of it, particularly portions pertaining to Lewinsky, was untruthful and thus perjurious. Clinton denied the charge, but some Clinton supporters said that, even if it were true, no major importance should be attached to it, because most men deny sexual peccadilloes in an effort to protect their marriages and families.

By the year's end two important developments involving the Clinton controversy had occurred. Initially, the Jones case was settled out of court for $850,000 paid to her by Clinton with the explicit understanding that he had done no wrong. Second, Starr released his findings to Congress, and the House of Representatives impeached President Clinton.

The Court of Justice of the European Union ruled that an employer's refusal to allow travel concessions given by it to members of the opposite sex living with one another in a stable relationship could be denied to lesbians, even though they were living together in a meaningful relationship. The U.S. Supreme Court, perhaps, took a different view, holding that a same-sex harassment in the workplace was actionable under a federal statute prohibiting sexual harass-

ment. Additionally, the court showed its propensity to protect homosexuals by ruling that an employer of a person who sexually harassed a fellow employee could be held liable for that act without a showing of negligence.

In South Africa the abortion rights adherents gained a victory when the High Court ruled that a fetus is not a legal person under the constitution and therefore is not protected by its "right-to-life" provisions. The question arose in a lawsuit brought by pro-life adherents in which it was alleged that the Choice on Termination of Pregnancy Act of 1966, which allowed abortion, was contrary to the right-to-life provisions of the constitution.

The Supreme Court of Canada resolved a case that attracted national attention by holding that First Nations could sustain their claim to 58,000 sq km (22,400 sq mi) of land in northern British Columbia through proof of title by adducing oral history and tradition. They did not have to abide by common-law rules that allegedly had been made part of the basic law of Canada by an English Royal Proclamation of 1763.

The Supreme Court of the U.S. let stand a decision from the Supreme Court of Wisconsin that a school vouchers program did not violate the Constitution. School vouchers made government money available to economically disadvantaged students to attend private schools, including those affiliated with a religion. This program had been a key plank in the Republican Party's agenda and had been strongly opposed by advocates of public education, including teachers unions, most members of the Democratic Party, and President Clinton.

In 1998 Arizona, by means of a statewide initiative, amended its constitution to make "English the official language of the State of Arizona." The amendment further provided that the state and all its political subdivisions "shall act in English and no other language." This amendment, quite obviously aimed at a substantially large Spanish-speaking population in the state, was declared unconstitutional by the Arizona Supreme Court as a violation of the First Amendment of the federal Constitution, which preempts the constitutions of the various states.

A major dispute between the U.K. and Spain concerned General Pinochet, a former president of Chile in Great Britain for medical treatment. The Spanish government wanted to extradite him and prosecute him for the alleged serious violations of human rights he committed when he was president of Chile. His supporters claimed that he suppressed communism in Chile and left the country, after his resignation, incomparably better off than the one he had inherited. Early in December a British court granted Spain its request for extradition but later voided it and scheduled a new hearing in 1999.

In the Hague the ICTY sentenced Drazen Erdemovic to five years in prison for his part in an execution squad that allegedly murdered many Bosnian Muslims. It was alleged that Erdemovic himself had murdered 100 persons.

The European Court of Human Rights (ECH) held that a decision by the Constitutional Court of Turkey dissolving the Communist Party of Turkey was in violation of the Convention of the ECH. The International Court of Justice determined

that it had jurisdiction to deal with the merits of a case brought by Libya against the U.K. concerning Pan Am Flight 103; two Libyan nationals were suspected of having caused the destruction of the airplane and the death of its 270 passengers and crew members over Lockerbie, Scot., in 1988.

The constitution of Denmark sharply limited the right of a government to cede sovereignty to international organizations. Using this provision as their base, a number of citizens of Denmark sued their prime minister for signing the Treaty on European Unity in 1991. The Supreme Court of Denmark found no conflict between the constitution and the treaty but observed that if such a conflict should develop in the future, the Danish constitution would take precedence.

In India, in what the media considered a landmark decision, the Supreme Court held that courts are competent, in the absence of controlling legislation, to make law on the particular point in question. The decision was based on Article 142 of India's constitution to the effect that courts are required to do "complete justice" in cases they resolve. "Justice," the court said, must represent the will of the people on the particular matter in question, and the court opined that any court-made law would therefore be valid only until such time as the legislature passed legislation on the point in question.

The High Court of Australia decided an important case during the year involving secretly recorded evidence affecting the outcome of a criminal trial. The case had important implications for Australia's strict adherence to principles of human rights, including the right of one accused of a crime to remain silent. In the case at hand, the accused voluntarily admitted to a police officer, without knowledge that the confession was being tape-recorded, that he had committed the crime for which he was subsequently charged. When interrogated, he had not refused to answer questions or asserted any privilege in that regard. In a far-reaching decision the court ultimately resolved the matter by giving the trial court substantial discretion to admit or deny the confession into evidence. This discretion, however, was limited by a three-pronged test: (1) Was the confession voluntarily made? (2) Did the accused refuse to answer questions or stand on his right to remain silent? (3) Was the confession reliable or "bought at a price" that is unacceptable under contemporary community standards?

(WILLIAM D. HAWKLAND)

CRIME

Terrorism. On Aug. 7, 1998, terrorists launched coordinated and devastating attacks on U.S. embassies in Kenya and Tanzania. In the Kenyan capital of Nairobi, a massive truck bomb blast killed 257 people, 12 of them Americans, and left more than 5,000 persons wounded. An almost simultaneous blast in Dar es Salaam, Tanzania's capital, killed 11 people and injured hundreds more. The blasts provided a tragic reminder of just how vulnerable even the world's sole superpower remained to attacks of this type. They also precipitated an immediate and massive FBI investigation into the bombings, which were believed to have been committed by an Islamic terrorist network associated with Osama bin Laden, a wealthy Saudi businessman said to be living

in Afghanistan. (*See* BIOGRAPHIES.) On August 20 U.S. military forces, utilizing cruise missiles, delivered powerful surprise attacks against a number of sites in Afghanistan in an effort to destroy key bases used by the Islamic terrorists claimed to have been involved. An attack was also made upon an alleged chemical weapons factory located in Khartoum, the capital of The Sudan.

The military strikes, which were condemned by Russia and a number of other nations, were said to have signaled a shift to more aggressive counterterrorist tactics by the U.S. in order to respond to a new phenomenon, the privatization of terrorism, in which individuals such as bin Laden replaced government-sponsored terrorism groups. Bin Laden appeared to have survived the cruise missile strikes and remained at large, but the ongoing investigation resulted in a number of arrests of bombing suspects associated with his far-flung network. A reward of up to $2 million was also offered by the U.S. for information leading to the arrest of Haroun Fazil, a native of Comoros, who allegedly had played a leading role in the Nairobi attack.

In October U.S. federal authorities announced that they had charged Eric Robert Rudolph, one of the FBI's 10 most-wanted fugitives, with the long-unsolved bombing at the 1996 Olympic Games in Atlanta, Ga., in which one person died and more than 100 were injured. A reward of $1 million had al-

detonated. Worldwide, 304 acts of international terrorism were recorded, one of the lowest annual totals since 1971. The number of casualties remained large, however, with 221 deaths and 693 nonfatal woundings reported. Approximately one-third of all terrorist attacks were against U.S. targets, and most consisted of bombings of business-related targets such as oil pipelines and communication facilities.

A historic but fragile peace accord reached in April between Protestant and Catholic factions in the British province of Northern Ireland was placed in jeopardy on August 15 when a massive car bomb exploded in the centre of the town of Omagh, killing at least 28 people and injuring 220. The blast was the deadliest single atrocity in almost three decades of bloody conflict in Northern Ireland. Responsibility for the bombing was claimed by a hard-line terrorist splinter group, the Real Irish Republican Army, which had rejected the cease-fire announced during 1997 by the mainstream Irish Republican Army (IRA). In the wake of the Omagh bombing, both the Irish and the British governments introduced legislation giving new and wide-ranging powers to police to arrest, detain, question, stop, and search terrorist suspects.

On September 16 the Spanish Basque terrorist organization Euskadi Ta Askatasuna (ETA) announced an indefinite cease-fire

A rare interview with Islamic militant Osama bin Laden was granted to a group of reporters in December. The reporters met with the man accused of masterminding the bombings of U.S. embassies in Africa at his remote mountain hideout in southern Afghanistan. During the interview, bin Laden called it "a duty of Muslims to confront, fight, and kill [Americans]."

RAHIMULLAH YOUSAFZAI—AP/WIDE WORLD

ready been posted in May for information assisting with Rudolph's capture on charges involving a bombing of an abortion clinic in Birmingham, Ala., on Jan. 29, 1998, that killed one person. Final closure came in May in another bombing investigation and prosecution when Theodore Kaczynski, the so-called Unabomber, who killed 3 people and injured 22 in 16 attacks between 1979 and 1995, was sentenced to four terms of life in prison without parole.

In *Patterns of Global Terrorism,* the U.S. Department of State reported 13 international terrorist incidents in the U.S. during 1997, 12 involving letter bombs sent from the Middle East. None of the letter bombs

after 30 years of guerrilla attacks that were blamed for 800 deaths. Spanish political leaders in Madrid suggested that the cease-fire was the result of pressure on ETA from police arrests, large public street demonstrations demanding peace, and inspiration drawn from the peace accord reached in Northern Ireland.

War Crimes. In April, following the longest trial in French legal history, a jury in Bordeaux found Maurice Papon guilty of complicity in Nazi crimes against humanity while he was an administrator in German-occupied France during World War II. Papon, who was the highest-ranking French civilian official ever to be tried on war crimes

charges, was held responsible for the handing over to the Germans of more than 1,500 Jews in occupied Bordeaux. Following his conviction Papon was sentenced to 10 years in prison and deprived of his civil rights.

On April 15 Pol Pot, the leader of the radical communist Khmer Rouge and one of the most reviled figures of the 20th century, died in Cambodia. From 1975 to 1979 he presided over the party and regime whose paranoia and brutality resulted in the deaths of as many as two million Cambodians. (*See* OBITUARIES.) Despite the horrors inflicted by the Khmer Rouge, Pol Pot and his close colleagues in the party were never made accountable for their crimes. Pol Pot's death provided a stark reminder of the helplessness of the international community to try those accused of crimes against humanity in the face of the failure of a national criminal jurisdiction to protect its own people. In July the international community took a historic step toward redressing this situation when 120 countries voted in favour of a draft treaty setting out the fundamentals for an international court to prosecute war criminals and tyrants like Pol Pot. Though the conference approved the draft treaty, its implementation remained dependent upon ratification by at least 60 nations.

Meanwhile, the existing special tribunals set up by the UN to deal with crimes committed in former Yugoslavia and in Rwanda continued their work. In Arusha, Tanz., the UN International Criminal Tribunal for Rwanda handed down a landmark decision on September 2 finding Jean Paul Akayesu, a former mayor of a small commune in

Rwanda, guilty of nine counts of genocide and crimes against humanity. The verdict was the first of its kind, following a full trial, for the crime of genocide under international law. Akayesu, who was subsequently sentenced to the maximum penalty of life in prison for these crimes, was found by the court to have ordered fellow members of the Hutu tribe to kill their Tutsi neighbours, including children. He also encouraged and ordered the rape and murder of Tutsi women. In making rape part of Akayesu's genocide conviction, the tribunal's decision advanced the definition and punishment of sexual violence within the context of international law.

On October 16 British police arrested the former Chilean president, General Pinochet, who was in London seeking medical treatment. Pinochet's arrest was made at the request of a Spanish judge who sought Pinochet's extradition as part of an investigation into atrocities committed in the "dirty wars" in Latin America in the 1970s and 1980s. (See *Law,* above.)

Drug Trafficking. In February, as part of the annual antinarcotics certification process first required by the U.S. Congress in 1986, President Clinton's administration announced it had decided to waive economic sanctions imposed two years earlier against Colombia because of that nation's poor performance in combating drug trafficking. Although Colombia remained the world's leading producer and distributor of cocaine and a major supplier of heroin and marijuana, officials said the decision was based in part on the emergence of the Colombian national police as an effective force against narcotics. In addition to Colombia, Pakistan and Cambodia also received sanction waivers despite their poor records in dealing with the trade in narcotics. Critics of the certification process suggested that it was a clumsy tool for encouraging better narcotics enforcement, forcing the U.S. into difficult choices between papering over problems or offending otherwise friendly countries. Many of the nations subject to the evaluation also claimed that it was counterproductive. The root cause of the drug problem was, they said, the insatiable demand for narcotics in the U.S. and not lax enforcement by source countries.

In October retired general Barry McCaffrey, President Clinton's national drug policy director, warned on a visit to Haiti that the country had become the fastest-growing transit point for U.S.-bound cocaine shipments. Colombian and Dominican drug traffickers, sensing an opportunity in a nation weakened by a paralyzed government and an inexperienced police force, were said to be moving through Haiti up to 15% of all the cocaine consumed in the U.S., about four tons a month.

Murder and Other Violence. For the sixth consecutive year, the overall rate of serious crime in the U.S. fell in 1997, according to the FBI's annual survey of law-enforcement agencies. Murder and robbery showed the greatest decline, each down 9% from 1996. Serious crime also continued to fall in all of the largest cities, although a little more slowly than in 1996. A comparative study of crime and justice in the U.S. and the U.K., published in October by the U.S. Bureau of Justice, revealed that serious crimes rates were in general no higher in the U.S. than in the U.K. The major exception to the pattern was murder, with the U.S. murder rate in 1996 nearly six times higher than that of the U.K.

Americans were shocked in March by the bloody ambush killings of four young students and a teacher by a 13-year-old boy and his 11-year-old cousin outside the Westside Middle School in the small Arkansas city of Jonesboro. It was the fourth multiple shooting in less than six months at an American school by a person under the age of 17, and it prompted immediate debate about school safety and the pervasiveness of guns in U.S. homes. Some of the high-powered weapons used by the two boys were said to have been taken from the home of the grandfather of the 11-year-old suspect. In August, on his 14th birthday, Mitchell Johnson pleaded guilty, and Andrew Golden, 12, was found guilty at their trial on charges relating to the killing of four of their schoolmates and a teacher and the wounding of 10 others during the ambush. They were sentenced to be confined by state juvenile authorities until they turned 21, the maximum punishment available for children of their age. (*See* Special Report.)

The Vatican was stunned in May by the slaying of the commander of the Swiss Guard, the Holy See's private army, shortly after the pope had appointed Col. Alois Estermann to lead the 100-strong force. Estermann's corpse, together with that of his wife, Gladys Meza Romero, and a vice corporal in the Swiss Guard, Cedric Tornay, were found in the commander's apartment on May 4. It seemed that, in what a Vatican spokesman claimed was "a moment of madness," Estermann and his wife had been shot dead by Tornay, who then took his own life, after Tornay had received an official reprimand in February for breaking the Guard's midnight curfew. Tornay had also just learned that he was not to receive a medal he had anticipated being awarded.

In October the U.S. Department of Justice released a sketch of Eric Robert Rudolph (inset), a fugitive charged with a number of fatal bombings. In Nantahala National Forest in western North Carolina, a local bear hunter (below) assists federal agents in their search for Rudolph.

Police officers in the town of Omagh, Northern Ireland, inspect the debris left behind after a massive car bomb exploded on August 15, killing at least 28 persons and injuring 220 others. A hard-line terrorist splinter group that called itself the Real Irish Republican Army claimed responsibility for the bombing.

ALASTAIR GRANT—AP/WIDE WORLD

One of Russia's most admired and courageous advocates of democracy, Galina Starovoytova, was assassinated in St. Petersburg on November 20. A potential presidential candidate and virulent anticommunist critic, Starovoytova was gunned down as she climbed the stairs to her apartment with an aide, who was critically wounded in the attack. A liberal deputy in the State Duma (parliament), Starovoytova was the seventh deputy to be murdered since 1993 and the first woman. She had received threats from political enemies and was said to have prepared a dossier of evidence pointing to corruption in the Communist Party, which she was expected to have tabled shortly in the Duma. Her death came at a time when the Russian general prosecutor's office reported an increase of almost 18% in murder, rape, and other serious crimes in the first nine months of the year.

White Collar Crime, Corruption, and Fraud. The annual Corruption Perception Index (CPI), published by the Berlin-based global anticorruption organization Transparency International, ranked Colombia, Indonesia, and Nigeria as the world's most corrupt large countries. The CPI, a poll drawing upon many surveys of expert and general public views of the extent of corruption in 85 nations, listed Denmark, Finland, Sweden, New Zealand, and Canada among the least corrupt.

With billions of dollars' worth of foreign aid and investment in Asia disappearing as part of the economic collapse in the region, many countries began to deal with the rampant corruption that had fueled the crisis. In Vietnam in January three former businessmen convicted of corruption were executed in front of thousands of witnesses on the outskirts of Ho Chi Minh City. In China the government's policy of promoting capitalist economic reform without comparable change in the nation's closed political system was said by Western experts to be responsible for an epidemic of corruption among public officials, including the military. In July Chinese Pres. Jiang Zemin and Prime Minister Zhu Rongji unveiled plans to prosecute corrupt Communist Party, law-enforcement, and military officials and to create a national antismuggling force. China's military was mentioned as being heavily involved in smuggling activities, which were estimated to cost the government at least $12 billion each year in lost tax revenue.

LAW ENFORCEMENT

Policing experts remained uncertain about the role played by law enforcement in reducing rates of serious crime in the U.S. over recent years. The FBI admitted it could not readily explain why rates were falling so fast, and senior police officials expressed concern that the sharp drop in crime had produced new pressure on police departments to show ever-decreasing crime figures. Several charges of falsely reporting crime statistics led to the resignation or demotion of high-ranking police commanders, including the head of the New York City Police Department (NYPD) Transportation Bureau, who presided over an elaborate scheme to reclassify incidents on the city's subway as street crimes. The scheme underestimated crime in the subway by as much as 20%.

Despite such practices, other experts attributed the national decline in crime to the new "zero-tolerance" policing policies of the type adopted in New York City by Mayor Rudolph Giuliani. This concept was based on a theory, advanced by two criminologists in the 1980s, that authorities could create a climate in which serious crime would find it impossible to flourish if they refused to tolerate minor infractions of the law, such as painting graffiti on walls or dropping litter on the sidewalk. The criminologists termed this the "broken window" phenomenon—if one window in a building was broken, all the others would soon suffer a similar fate. If, however, one fixed the broken window rapidly, the situation would not deteriorate. In New York, Mayor Giuliani ordered crackdowns not only on graffiti writers and litterers but also on windshield cleaners, people who urinated in public, and jaywalkers. The policy seemed to work, as crime rates in the city dropped. Not everyone agreed that this was the reason for the fall in crime, however, and many critics suggested that zero-tolerance policing policies often resulted in the abuse of civil liberties.

Former NYPD police commissioner William Bratton attributed the declining (continued on page 235)

The funeral of slain Swiss Guard commander Alois Estermann and his wife takes place inside Saint Peter's Basilica in Rome on May 6. The two were shot to death by a Swiss Guard vice corporal, Cedric Tornay, who took his own life after the murders.

ARTURO MARI—AP/WIDE WORLD

Children Killing Children

by Elliott Currie

On March 24, 1998, two boys, aged 11 and 13, opened fire with rifles on a Jonesboro, Ark., middle school, killing four of their fellow students—all girls, aged 11 and 12—and one of their teachers. The Jonesboro tragedy was particularly shocking because the shooters were so young, but it was neither the first nor the last of a string of similar incidents that had begun more than two years earlier. In February 1996 a 14-year-old boy shot and killed two students and a teacher in Moses Lake, Wash. In October 1997 a Pearl, Miss., teenager stabbed his mother to death and then shot and killed two girls at his high school; in December a 14-year-old in West Paducah, Ky., sprayed a high-school prayer meeting with gunfire, killing three girls. In May 1998, just two months after the Jonesboro slayings, a 15-year-old killed two students and wounded 22 others at his Springfield, Ore., high school after having shot his parents to death at home; in September two teenagers in the Denver suburb of Aurora, Colo., gunned down four other teens and one adult.

Though experts were quick to point out that serious youth violence had actually declined somewhat overall in the United States during the past few years, these shootings were a grim confirmation of the deadly seriousness of the problem of youth homicide in the U.S. Because there was also a chilling suggestion that it could happen anywhere—in supposedly placid towns in the semirural or suburban heartland as well as on the streets of the inner cities, these shootings set off a national mood of self-searching about the roots of youth violence that a decade of inner-city carnage had not.

Many observers blamed the tragedies on a lenient juvenile justice system unprepared to cope with a new generation of hardened "predators." Most states, however, had already toughened their responses to teenage offenders. Between 1992 and 1995, for example, 41 states passed laws making it easier for teenagers to be tried as adults. Indeed, several of the youths involved in the recent spate of school killings received extremely severe sentences in adult courts—two consecutive life sentences plus 205 years for the Moses Lake youth, two life sentences plus seven consecutive 20-year terms for the youth convicted in Mississippi.

Seen in international perspective, moreover, the U.S. was, if anything, unusually harsh on many young offenders; an American juvenile was roughly 11 times as likely to be sent to adult court as his counterpart in Canada. The U.S. also remained the only advanced industrial society that imposed the death penalty for homicides committed by youths under 18. Yet, despite being relatively "tough" on young offenders, the U.S. also suffered the industrial world's highest levels of youth homicide. The most recent international figures (for 1995 and in some cases 1994) revealed that an American male aged 15–24 was 22 times as likely to die of homicide as a French or German youth, 34 times as likely as an English youth, and 94 times as likely as an Austrian. These differences persisted, if a bit less glaringly, for younger children and also applied, though less strikingly, to girls; at ages 5–14 an American girl was more than twice as likely to be murdered as a French boy and four times as likely as an English one.

What accounts for these disparities? The recent killings highlighted one of them—the prevalence of firearms in the U.S. and the ease with which children can find and use them. More than four out of five U.S. murder victims aged 12–17 are killed by firearms. Virtually all of the 116% rise in teen homicide deaths from 1985 to 1995 was accounted for by guns.

Guns, however, are only part of a more complex story. Homicide deaths among American children by means other than handguns remain much higher than the overall rates in many other advanced nations. Also, children in the U.S. typically had easy access to rifles and shotguns long before the shootings that stunned the nation in the 1990s. Beyond the sheer availability of the means of killing, therefore, part of the explanation for the U.S.'s tragic dominance in youth homicide must be sought in the broader social and cultural conditions that surround children and youth in the U.S.

One of these conditions is the unusual severity of economic inequality among American children and their families compared with their counterparts in most other industrial nations. An American child is roughly four times as likely to be poor as a French or German child and six times as likely as a Swedish or Dutch child, and although the gap between affluent and poor families and children has widened in many countries in recent years, the trend has been sharpest in the U.S. These differences involve more than money income alone; many of the other industrial societies also provide a broad array of other social supports, including child care. Criminological studies have found strong links between extremes of inequality and rates of homicide.

As with guns, however, the extremes of poverty and the social neglect do not fully explain the U.S.'s crisis of children killing children; the school killings during the past two years were not committed by the children of the very poor. It appears that some of the same forces that have bred high levels of youth violence in the inner cities may have been at work, in less-dramatic but still disruptive ways, in more mainstream American communities as well. Many such communities had, for example, suffered from long-term declines in public investment in activities and institutions that serve the young, including school counseling and adolescent mental health services. That decline, moreover, occurred just as other trends were eroding the capacity of families and communities to provide consistent support and guidance for their children. For example, stagnant wages for many American workers meant that parents often had to work longer hours to keep families afloat financially; others moved frequently in search of job opportunities, fracturing families and severing community ties.

By the same token, however, these troubling social deficits point to some of the elements of a more effective response to youth homicide. Some observers emphasize long-term improvements in social support services. Others stress the importance of more systematic strategies to keep guns out of childrens' hands—such as tougher laws mandating safe gun storage and trigger locks or other safety devices. During the 1990s a number of programs designed to work intensively with troubled youths have shown remarkable success, even with seriously violent children. Many experts agree that such programs can help, in many cases, to prevent the kinds of tragedies that have recurrently devastated American communities. The harder question is whether a nation suffused by an increasingly punitive mood toward juvenile offenders and skeptical of the value of social spending will be willing to commit resources to such preventive efforts on a scale to match the urgency of the problem.

Elliott Currie is a professor at the Center for the Study of Law and Society at the University of California, Berkeley.

(continued from page 233)
crime rates to a revitalized police department with better weapons and new personnel-deployment policies. Officers were removed from desk jobs and put back on the streets with increased discretionary powers. Precinct commanders were made personally responsible for reducing crime in their own areas, and those who failed were fired. Such policies were not unique to New York City. In most U.S. cities the number of police officers had increased during recent years, and in many locations officers were encouraged to work with the community to prevent crime and apprehend criminals. This community-policing philosophy was matched in many departments by the use of sophisticated computer mapping and intelligence systems to target high-crime areas.

In October the FBI opened a national computerized DNA database that, its proponents said, would help reduce rape and serious crimes by catching repeat offenders more rapidly. Similar to a database already in operation in the U.K., the FBI's new investigative aid allowed comparisons of a DNA sample from one state in the U.S. with all others in the system. From only a few cells, enough DNA could be obtained to identify the owner.

On October 1 Europe's cross-border police force, Europol, officially began operations with ambitious plans to target the illegal drug trade and terrorism across 15 European Union nations. Europol had worked in a more restricted capacity since 1995 as the European Drugs Unit. In this capacity, with only 155 staff members based in The Hague, it had assisted national police forces in combating illegal immigration networks, vehicle theft, and trafficking in nuclear and radioactive materials. After scandals in Belgium in 1996 concerning pedophilia and child murder, Europol was given responsibility for monitoring sexual exploitation, including trafficking in humans. It also collated information about money laundering. With this new role, Europol's staff was scheduled to rise to 350 by 2000.

The International Criminal Police Organization (Interpol) announced in January that it had brought its technological capabilities up to date, streamlined its operations, and tightened its security. More than 150 of the organization's 177 member nations were now linked by computer to the world's most extensive law-enforcement communications network.   (DUNCAN CHAPPELL)

PRISONS AND PENOLOGY

Hardening political and public attitudes on crime and punishment continued to be reflected by the rising numbers of untried and sentenced prisoners in many parts of the world in 1998. In this respect Russia and the United States held the lead with incarceration rates of approximately 690 and 645 prisoners per 100,000 population, respectively. Whereas the Russian figures declined slightly during the year, this was not the case in the U.S., where there had been an annual growth rate of about 6% since 1990. With the probable exception of China (where data were unavailable), reliance elsewhere upon imprisonment was mostly some 50–75% lower.

Excessively crowded conditions, dismal standards of sanitation, and a shortage of basic medical resources remained the norm for many prison systems. The conditions endured by prisoners awaiting trial remained

especially abysmal. In South Africa the number of children sentenced and remanded to prison had doubled since 1996, with many of them held 50 to a cell designed for half that number. In Russian prisons the rate of infection of tuberculosis was estimated to be 20–60% higher than the rate in the general community. Widespread deaths from infectious diseases were also reported among prisoners in Kenya and Uganda, and in Cambodia inmates frequently died of untreated diseases, exacerbated by malnutrition and overcrowding. In Venezuela, where 75% of prisoners were awaiting trial, 24,000 were held in facilities designed for 15,000. At the New-Bell prison in Douala, Cameroon, some 1,900 persons were crammed into a facility designed for 800. Severely crowded conditions were also by no means unknown to countries with more advanced economies. In Italy the Naples prison was housing twice its capacity, but even it compared favourably with Portugal's Oporto prison, which was designed for 500 prisoners but held 1,350.

Extensive prison-building programs were under way in the U.S., The Netherlands, and elsewhere but with problematic results. In England and Wales, where the prison population had risen from 42,000 to 67,000 since 1993, a huge capital investment in prisons was achieved in part at the expense of education and other services. Despite an expansion of the prison system in New York state, it was decided (contrary to the standards laid down by the American Corrections Association) to place two prisoners in cells measuring 4.2 sq m (45 sq ft) that had been designed for one person, a determination made necessary by cuts in staffing levels.

Elsewhere, imprisonment was made especially unpleasant as an explicit matter of public policy. It was reported in Chad that prisoners were bound with chains for the first three months of their detention. In China torture and ill-treatment of inmates remained widespread. With prisoners often denied protection from extreme temperatures, torture was also reported to be routine in Saudi Arabia. Torture and ill-treatment, including incidents of flogging and amputations, were widespread in prisons operated by the Taliban in Afghanistan. Deaths in custody remained widely reported by Amnesty International and other human rights organizations.

An opponent of the death penalty stands outside the prison building in Huntsville, Texas, where convicted killer Kenneth Allen McDuff was executed on November 17.

Prison riots and other serious incidents occurred in a number of countries. Sixteen prisoners died in a fire at the severely crowded Sabaneta prison in Venezuela, and seven inmates were killed during rioting at the Lurigancho prison in Peru, which at the time held 6,000 (mostly pretrial detainees) in 1,500 places.

Owing to increased prison populations, many commercial firms were becoming interested in the management of prisons. By 1998 such "private prisons" had been established in the U.S., the U.K., and Australia, with developments under consideration by governments in Canada and South Africa. The largest operator, Corrections Corp. of America, was responsible for some 62,500 prison beds worldwide.

Death Penalty. According to Amnesty International, 104 countries had by 1998 abolished the death penalty in law or practice. In 63 countries abolition was for all crimes, in 16 it was for all but exceptional crimes, and in 25 abolition was a matter of practice rather than law. In 91 other countries the death penalty was retained. Since 1976 each year an average of two countries had abolished the death penalty, and most recently the abolitionist majority was joined by Georgia and Poland.

Against this worldwide abolitionist trend, the scope of the death penalty was extended in 1998 by a number of countries. In Pakistan it covered gang rape. In Singapore it included the crime of trafficking in more than 250 g (8.8 oz) of crystal methamphetamine (during the first half of the year, at least six people were executed for drug offenses). It was reported in Tajikistan that the death penalty had been extended to cover "hooliganism." Executions for theft were reported under China's "Strike Hard" anticrime campaign.

In April the United Nations Commission for Human Rights strengthened its call for a moratorium on executions. A UN official also declared that capital punishment in the U.S. violated international law. He concluded that "race, ethnic origin and economic status appeared to be key determinants of who would and would not receive a sentence of death." There were 68 executions in the U.S. during 1998. The number of death sentences carried out seemed likely to increase under the Anti-Terrorism and Effective Death Penalty Statute, which imposed strict time limits on appeals, restricted access of prisoners to the federal courts, and empowered state courts to redress any constitutional violations.

Worldwide, at least 2,375 persons in 40 countries were known to have been executed during 1997. Of these, 1,644 were in China, 143 in Iran (which included 3 persons stoned to death), 122 in Saudi Arabia, and 33 in Nigeria. In South Korea 23 persons were reported to have been hanged in a single day.   (ANDREW RUTHERFORD)

Libraries and Museums

LIBRARIES

At the annual meeting of the International Federation of Library Associations and Institutions (IFLA), held in Amsterdam in August 1998, much of the attention of the approximately 3,300 attendees from 120 countries focused on political, social, and legal issues made more urgent by the breakneck pace of Internet growth. IFLA convened two new standing committees: one to focus on safeguarding freedom of access to information and freedom of expression and one to draft copyright laws appropriate to a publishing environment marked by great diversity. In Helsinki, Fin., at the fifth annual MetaData conference, work continued on developing conventions for describing and categorizing Internet resources.

Librarians in many countries faced more immediate challenges. In Guinea-Bissau soldiers seized the National Institute of Studies and Research to use as a garrison. Subsequent fighting and the troops' disregard for the institute's contents reportedly destroyed most of the institute's holdings, including unique materials that would have been primary sources for an as-yet-unwritten history of the country. A municipal library and a university were sacked and burned in Shkodër, Alb., during rioting in February. In Bosnia and Herzegovina efforts to resupply libraries destroyed by fighting continued, and in Cambodia Irish librarian Anthony Butler completed a three-year assignment to reorganize the library of the Royal University of Fine Arts in Phnom Penh, which had been ravaged by the Khmer Rouge and Pol Pot. Butler's progress report was dedicated to the librarians slain during the upheaval.

Economic woes staggered Asian libraries. Currency devaluations halved the buying power of acquisitions budgets in Philippine libraries in just four months. Malaysian government plans to build new libraries were shelved. Half a world away, the British Library was forced to propose a £300 (U.S. $495) annual fee to researchers. Public outrage persuaded officials to abandon the plan, but the budget shortfall remained. China, however, announced plans to build 50,000 new libraries over the next 11 years, and 63 new libraries were scheduled to open soon in Iran.

Censorship disputes continued unabated, but some were unusual enough to make news. A complaint about the "sickening violence" in a Punch and Judy book caused the public library in Marlborough, Eng., to pull the book from the shelves. In August Indian officials banned imports of the *Encyclopædia Britannica* on CD-ROM because they were unable to alter or obscure maps and text relating to the country's boundary dispute with Pakistan over Kashmir. The opening of a "video salon" in the library at Tsinghua University, where students could use the Internet and even watch American films, suggested that the Chinese government might be experimenting with relaxing long-standing limitations on access to information.

Theft remained as persistent as censorship. In 1997 and 1998 valuable works by

Ptolemy and Copernicus disappeared from French and Ukrainian libraries, respectively. Some 500 volumes stolen from a Vatican library in 1997 were recovered; however, 200 volumes remained missing. Hurricane Georges destroyed the entire collection of the Arecibo Regional Public Library in Puerto Rico in late September. The main library on the island nation of Montserrat was to be relocated to remove it from the danger of volcanic eruption.

The Eric Williams Memorial Collection at the Trinidad and Tobago campus of the University of the West Indies opened during the year. Williams, the first prime minister of Trinidad and Tobago and a respected scholar, was hailed by guest speaker Gen. Colin Powell as a tireless warrior against colonialism. The collection, which consisted of Williams's personal library and archives, was made available to the university by his daughter, Erica Williams Connell.

In the U.S. the increasing use of the Internet in libraries—a survey released in September showed that more than 73% of the nation's libraries offered public access to the Net—had not come without controversy. In many communities across the nation, libraries were being pressured to install filtering software designed to block access to World Wide Web sites that contained sexually explicit material. In November, how-

ever, in a decision with wide-ranging implications, a federal judge in Loudoun county, Va., ruled that public libraries cannot use filtering software on their computer terminals.

In another controversial trend a growing number of public libraries were contracting out their services to private companies. Following a 1997 agreement in which Riverside county, Calif., turned over the operation of its libraries to a Maryland-based firm, Jersey City, N.J., entered into a similar arrangement in July.

In the face of congressional opposition to its program to provide discounted telecommunications services to American libraries and schools, the Federal Communications Commission voted to scale back subsidies from $2,250,000,000 to $1,275,000,000 for 1998. The program received more than 30,000 applications in its first year.

As part of the ongoing $70 million renovation of its Center for the Humanities building on Fifth Avenue, the New York Public Library unveiled the restoration of its Main Reading Room in November. Flooding from a burst water main caused more than $10 million in damage at the Boston Public Library in August, destroying more than 300,000 government documents and damaging much of the sound and film archives. Muddy water that filled the basements of several Stanford University libraries during

a February rainstorm damaged about 120,000 books.

(GORDON FLAGG; THOMAS GAUGHAN)

MUSEUMS

It was a banner year in 1998 for the establishment of new museums. Te Papa, a new national museum on the Wellington waterfront, interpreted the dual influences of the Maori and European settlers in New Zealand. In the Philippines the Museum of the Filipino People, one of three museums that would eventually make up the new National Museum, was inaugurated in June. Two German museums designed by Polish-American architect Daniel Libeskind were completed—the Jewish Museum in Berlin opened in June, and the Felix Nussbaum Museum in Osnabrück, which was built to house some of the artist's 160 paintings, opened in July; Nussbaum, a local artist, had been killed at Auschwitz. In December the Museum of the Art and History of Judaism opened in Marais, the old Jewish quarter in Paris. Opening in the summer at the Spencer Estate in Great Britain were the shrine, museum, and souvenir stand honouring Diana, princess of Wales. In the U.S. the nation's first Vietnam War museum debuted in Holmdel, N.J., in September, following lengthy discussions regarding the presenta-

Library patrons enter the newly renovated Main Reading Room of the New York Public Library on November 12. Restored to its original splendour, the room was also outfitted for the next century, with new computers sitting on 90-year-old oak desks.

tion of historical and eyewitness accounts of the war. In Andersonville, Ga., the site of the Civil War's notorious Andersonville prison camp, the National Prisoner of War Museum was dedicated in April. The main exhibit, replete with bayonets and a variety of firearms imbedded into a black wall, re-created for museum patrons the feeling of captivity.

A year after its opening, the Guggenheim Museum in Bilbao, Spain, usurped the position of the Prado in Madrid as the country's most popular museum. The Louvre Museum in Paris completed its $1.2 billion renovation project with the completion of the 10,000-sq m (108,000-sq ft) Egyptian galleries. Outside London, Down House, where Charles Darwin penned *The Origin of the Species,* reopened to the public in the spring, following extensive renovations. The Van Gogh Museum in Amsterdam closed for eight months for extensive renovations and the construction of a new wing.

Museums were increasingly plagued by accusations that their collections contained artworks stolen from Jews and other Nazi victims or taken from museums of occupied countries during and after World War II. Countries dealt with the legalities differently. The Austrian parliament approved legislation that permitted works of art seized by the Nazis and later incorporated into state museums to be returned to their rightful owners. Although Germany identified 17 works in its museums that appeared in an Italian catalog of 1,500 works plundered by the Nazis, it had yet to return them. The Russian Ministry of Culture published the first 2 volumes of a planned 16-volume catalog of art stolen from museums near St. Petersburg during the Nazi occupation. After initially refusing to return any of the so-called trophy art looted from Germany and other countries by the Red Army, Russia later reported that it would return some of the booty. In The Netherlands a request by the heir of a Jewish art collector for the return of 160 paintings hanging in 17 Dutch museums was rejected on the grounds that the collector's widow had not pressed for the recovery of the art directly after the war. France returned one of the 2,000 art objects that were confiscated by the Nazis. The heirs to some 30 works held in Hungarian museums continued to lobby for the return of the collection, valued at between $8 million and $14.5 million. In an effort to encourage the return of more artworks, the U.S. Department of State was cohost of an international conference that dealt with the issue of

restitution of the remaining art and other goods looted during the war. Many U.S. museums were called upon to research the provenance of their collections, including objects from nations with strict patrimony laws as well as artworks that may have been looted during the Holocaust. The U.S. Congress held public hearings on the latter issue in February and later established a commission to investigate further steps. Despite all of the attention, few claims for restitution were actually lodged; all museums involved promised full cooperation.

Political movements were also afoot to aid museums. In Great Britain the Labour Party injected huge sums of money into the country's museums, with the goal of offering free admission by 2001. Iranian Pres. Mohammad Khatami, the nation's former minister of culture, spearheaded the exhibition of a treasure of Western masters hidden away in the vaults of the Museum of Contemporary Art in Tehran after the Islamic government forbade its display. In April an unprecedented meeting of museum professionals from across the Western Hemisphere gathered in Costa Rica to address the significant and positive role museums played in sustaining the culture of their communities.

Riding economic good times, American museums continued to prosper in 1998. The American Association of Museums reported that at least $4.3 billion would be spent on museum infrastructure during 1998–2000, with at least 55 new institutions planned. The public flocked to institutions both new and old—the new art museum at the Getty Center in Los Angeles attracted nearly twice as many guests as anticipated, and advance tickets for the Van Gogh exhibition in Washington, D.C., sold out within a few days.

Museums continued to affirm a primary role in American formal education—by year's end at least 19 public schools were located on museum grounds or run by museum personnel. Museums also moved steadily into the digital era, establishing hundreds of individual World Wide Web sites. Several major institutions formed consortia aimed at setting standards for design, research, reproduction, and financial and legal issues surrounding digitized collections.

(ANDREW FINCH; HELEN WECHSLER)

At the grand opening of the Vietnam Era Educational Center in Holmdel, N.J., in September, two Vietnam veterans pause to look over a wall of photographs and letters. The $3.8 million museum, which collected a wide range of historical artifacts relating to the Vietnam War, was the first of its kind in the U.S.

Life Sciences

ZOOLOGY

Scientists in 1998 uncovered intriguing new information about a number of critical stages in the life cycles of animals, including courtship (in oystercatchers), metamorphosis and development (in salamanders), and parental care and aging (in baboons and lions). A study of the association between hyenas and endangered African wild dogs offered insights that had application to conservation efforts, and an examination of fossil material resulted in a reinterpretation of the disappearance patterns of long-extinct trilobites. Fossil remains also provided support for Cope's rule that animals tend to increase in size during evolution and gave direct proof of the prey of a marine reptile.

The European oystercatcher (*Haematopus ostralegus*) is a wading bird in which breeding pairs are typically monogamous. Polygyny, in which a male mates with more than one female at one time, is rare among oystercatchers. Dik Heg and Rob van Treuren of the University of Groningen, Neth., investigated polygyny within a population of European oystercatchers to determine the reproductive consequences of the behaviour when it did occur. Using data from 14 years of study, the investigators determined that vacant breeding territories for which unmated females must compete for access are at a premium. Although females that participate in polygyny are less successful at breeding than monogamous females, observations indicated that when a pair of females share the breeding territory of a male, they can use it as a stepping-stone to a neighbouring territory and to an improved chance of a monogamous relationship during the next breeding season.

The Groningen study also revealed an unusual form of polygyny within the oystercatcher population. Among observed breeding trios (a male and two females), 57% involved the traditional form of polygyny, in which each of the females operates independently within the male's territory, aggressively defending her own portion. Among 43% of the trios, however, the researchers observed cooperative polygyny, in which both females laid their eggs in the same nest, helped the male brood eggs, and engaged in female-female copulations that mimicked male-female copulations.

A difficulty in understanding some evolutionary processes is that the target of natural selection—the trait upon which natural selection operates—is not always obvious. To address this issue in regard to the timing of metamorphosis and maturation, Travis J. Ryan and Raymond D. Semlitsch of the University of Missouri investigated the life history of the mole salamander (*Ambystoma talpoideum*). Larvae of this species can undergo metamorphosis before becoming mature, as amphibians typically do, or they can bypass metamorphosis and become mature while retaining most of the features of immature larvae. The researchers took pertinent body measurements and made determinations of maturity on 864 individuals raised at either high or low population densities in experimental ponds for periods of four to eight months. They found that salamanders that skipped metamorphosis matured sexually well before those that metamorphosed. Early maturation, which maximizes reproduction and is known to be advantageous in many natural populations, appears to necessitate the retention of the larval morphology (form and structure) in these salamanders. It previously had been assumed that both metamorphosing and nonmetamorphosing forms matured at the same rate and that larval morphology was the target of selection. The

experiment challenged the notion that morphological features are the chief targets, demonstrating instead that age of maturity is the principal target and that morphological changes are secondary effects.

Abrupt declines in female fertility at an advanced age are characteristic of many mammals, including dogs, whales, rabbits, and elephants. In humans cessation of reproduction, known as menopause, has been explained in terms of evolution as an adaptation that allows grandmothers an opportunity to invest in caring for their older offspring and grandchildren and thus increase their fitness (*i.e.,* their ability to transmit their genes successfully through successive generations). To examine such behaviour in long-lived mammals, Craig Packer of the University of Minnesota, Marc Tatar of Brown University, Providence, R.I., and Anthony Collins of Gombe Stream Research Centre, Tanzania, conducted a study of olive baboons (*Papio anubis*) and African lions (*Leo leo*), two species in which elderly females cease reproduction and engage in kin-directed behaviour. Using data from wild populations of baboons and lions that had been under continual observation for more than 30 years, the investigators examined ages of cessation of reproductive activity in females and compared infant survival patterns among young with and without interactions with grandmothers. They found no evidence that the fitness of grandchildren or older young of either species was enhanced by nurturing grandmothers. The researchers concluded that the loss of reproductive activity in older females is a nonadaptive by-product of senescence and confers no clear evolutionary advantage.

The population densities of an endangered species, the African wild dog (*Lycaon pictus*), and of spotted hyenas (*Crocuta crocuta*) appear to have an inverse relationship in most habitats—*i.e.,* wherever there are more hyenas, there are likely to be fewer dogs. One explanation is that hyenas steal food from the dogs, the risk of theft increasing in open habitats with high visibility, such as the Serengeti Plain, and decreasing in wooded habitats, where hyenas are rare and the killing of prey by dogs is harder to detect. Martyn L. Gorman and John R. Speakman of the University of Aberdeen, Scot., and Michael G. Mills and Jacobus P. Raath of South Africa's Kruger National Park, using an isotopically labeled water technique for measuring the metabolism of animals in the field, were able to determine the daily energy expenditure of dogs in their natural settings. From these estimates of the energy cost of hunting in real time, the researchers developed a model to determine the impact of food loss on energy balance. According to their calculations, a loss of only 25% of the dogs' food to hyena theft would more than triple their daily hunting time, which would approach the point of being physiologically untenable and thus threaten the dogs' survival. Because of the high energy cost to the dogs of food loss from theft, the investigators recommended that conservation efforts would be most effective in thickly wooded habitats, where theft was comparatively low.

Trilobites were among the most common animals of the early part of the Paleozoic Era (540 million to 245 million years ago), being noted for their explosive evolutionary development in the Cambrian Period (540

The African wild dog (*Lycaon pictus*), whose distinctively large ears amplify sound and dissipate heat, is an endangered species. During the year researchers studying the species worked to determine where conservation efforts would be most effective.

KENNAN WARD—CORBIS

million to 505 million years ago). After extensive diversification and specialization, trilobites appeared to falter by the middle of the succeeding Ordovician Period (505 million to 438 million years ago) such that about half of trilobite genus and family diversity was lost at the end of the Ordovician, followed by further decline of the remainder until their complete extinction near the end of the Paleozoic. An analysis by Jonathan M. Adrain and Richard A. Fortey of the Natural History Museum, London, and Stephen R. Westrop of the University of Oklahoma of 945 genera of trilobites in 56 families from the Ordovician demonstrated that scientists' impression of a steady decline of the entire trilobite group beginning in that period was simplistic. The researchers identified two major, phylogenetically distinguishable groups of trilobites that had dramatically different patterns of diversification and extinction. One group declined and completely disappeared by the end of the Ordovician, whereas the other flourished, with the surviving families showing a higher diversity of genera than did the families

JAMES L. AMOS—CORBIS

KEVIN SCHAFER—CORBIS

In 1998 trilobite fossils of Cambrian (left) and Ordovician (below) age were the focus of research by paleontologists attempting to understand the pattern of decline and extinction of the trilobites, which were among the most common animals during the early part of the Paleozoic Era.

that became extinct. Because understanding the pattern of decline and extinction of trilobites was critical to interpretations of the marine ecosystems of the times, paleontologists considered the discovery of two groups of trilobites with contrasting patterns of development an important advance.

An examination of fossil mammals on the North American continent provided strong support for a pattern named after the 19th-century paleontologist Edward Drinker Cope. Cope's rule, the observation that the average body mass of animal evolutionary lineages tends to increase with time because of its survival and reproductive advantages, had not been previously documented statistically with large sample sizes of mammals. In a more detailed look at the phenomenon, John Alroy of the Smithsonian Institution, Washington, D.C., reported that new animal species evolving within a genus were 9.1% larger on average than were older species. The pattern persisted throughout the Cenozoic Era (66.4 million years ago to the present), as revealed by estimates of body sizes of 1,534 species of fossil mammals analyzed in a manner to avoid sampling bias. Although the overall trend could be explained by within-lineage increases in body size, researchers concluded that several different evolutionary mechanisms may in turn be responsible for the increases.

Insight into the diet of a marine reptile from the Cretaceous Period (144 million to 66.4 million years ago) was provided by Tamaki Sato of the University of Cincinnati, Ohio, and Kazushige Tanabe of the University of Tokyo. Plesiosaurs had been assumed to have been marine predators, but most dietary evidence for this was based on morphology, particularly of the teeth. The two investigators described a plesiosaur fossil from Japan that was preserved in a way that allowed its fossilized stomach contents to be identified as ammonites, an extinct group of cephalopod mollusks. The direct evidence of prey in the diet of an extinct predator was useful in validating hypotheses of prey preference based on evidence from tooth morphology.   (J. WHITFIELD GIBBONS)

Entomology. Whereas inbreeding had been suspected to be a contributor, along with environmental and demographic factors, to the decline and ultimate extinction of small, isolated natural populations of organisms, in 1998 the first documentation of that link was provided by Ilik Saccheri of the University of Helsinki, Fin., and colleagues in studies of the Glanville fritillary butterfly (*Melitaea cinxia*) in Finland. In a region having more than 1,600 meadows suitable for small populations of the butterfly, the investigators found that the number of meadows in which butterfly larvae were present had decreased each year, from 524

to 320, between 1993 and 1996. In 1996, 42 populations were sampled for a determination of their genetic variability—specifically, their heterozygosity. For a given genetic trait, an individual is said to be heterozygous if the paired genes for the trait, one received from the mother and the other from the father, are different. By analyzing a sample of genes from the individual, researchers can estimate its level of heterozygosity—*i.e.*, the fraction of its gene pairs that differ. Low heterozygosity in the individuals of a population would imply a limited gene pool and indicate inbreeding. After eliminating the influence of a variety of ecological factors that could contribute to population decline or extinction, the researchers found that the probability of extinction of a butterfly population was significantly correlated with low heterozygosity. They identified larval survival, adult survivorship and longevity, and the hatching rate of eggs as the components of the insects' life cycle adversely affected by inbreeding. The findings were relevant to management considerations for populations living in fragmented habitats in which inbreeding was likely.

Previous evidence from fossil plants had confirmed that angiosperms, the flowering plants, were present in the Early Cretaceous Period (144 million to 97.5 million years ago), but uncertainty existed about earlier origins. The discovery in Liaoning province, China, of fossil short-horned flies, or orthorrhaphous Brachycera, in rocks of the preceding Late Jurassic (163 million to 144 million years ago) by Dong Ren of the National Geological Museum of China gave evidence of a pre-Cretaceous origin of angiosperms. Examination of the fossil flies revealed mouthparts and body hairs characteristic of those used by their modern counterparts to collect nectar and pollen. Modern members of the group are mostly flower feeders and pollinators. Confirmation of the existence of these pollinators during the Late Jurassic strongly implies that angiosperms originated during or prior to that time.

The discovery of fossil ants in amber deposits from New Jersey dating to 92 million years ago provided evidence that one major lineage of extant ants, the subfamily Ponerinae, is at least 50 million years older than previously documented. Uncertainty had existed about whether a specimen of *Sphecomyrma freyi* reported earlier from the New Jersey amber was actually an ant because the metapleural gland, located above the hind legs, was not identifiable. Within the insect order Hymenoptera, which includes ants, bees, wasps, sawflies, and other types, the metapleural gland is unique to ants. An examination of new specimens by Donat Agosti, David Grimaldi, and James M. Carpenter of the American Museum of Natural History, New York City, confirmed the identity of *Sphecomyrma* as an ant by the presence of a metapleural gland. The find was important in dating and defining phylogenetic relationships during the early

evolutionary origins of ants, which were estimated to have been about 130 million years ago, during the Early Cretaceous.

(ANNE R. GIBBONS)

Ornithology. Cuckoos are well known for their habit of brood parasitism, which consists of laying the eggs singly in the nests of certain other bird species to be incubated by the foster parents, which then rear the young cuckoo. In its foster home the cuckoo chick needs as much food as a brood of five original young—say, reed warbler chicks—would have consumed had they not been ousted from the nest by the cuckoo hatchling. Consequently, it might be expected that with only one begging gape rather than five, the foster parents would not be encouraged to deliver enough food. Experiments by Nick Davies and colleagues of the University of Cambridge, however, demonstrated that natural selection (ever an optimizing process) caused the young interloper to voice as many begging cries as would have the brood that it replaced. Thus, the young cuckoo fledges at about the same weight as the combined weight of the five juvenile reed warblers.

Another species of bird "cuckolded" by an avian brood parasite is the blue-grey gnatcatcher, in whose nests cowbirds lay their eggs. C. Groguen and N. Mathews of the University of Wisconsin discovered that some gnatcatchers recognize the egg as alien. Those birds avoid the role of surrogate parenting by dismantling the nest, leaving the cowbird's egg to addle, and then using the same materials to rebuild elsewhere.

Birds that feed on fermenting fruit run the risk of alcoholic inebriation and, as has been observed in some species, of incapacitation. This is not the case with the starling, however, even though it is a regular summer consumer of rotting apples. According to R. Prinzinger and G. Hakimi of the University of Frankfurt, Ger., starlings avoid the problem because the birds are equipped with powerful enzymes that steady their behaviour. The researchers fed an alcohol-laced diet to captive starlings and found that within two hours the birds had fully metabolized the alcohol.

Birds that forage on lawns—typically the song thrush in Europe and the robin in North America—characteristically run a short distance and then take up a noticeable stance in which the individual stops and appears to listen. In cocking its head, however, is the bird hunting for worms by ear or by eye? Two Canadian ornithologists, R. Montgomerie of Queen's University, Kingston, Ont., and P. Weatherhead of Carleton University, Ottawa, proved by experiment with American robins that the worm is detected not by smell, sight, or tactile means but by hearing.

In winter, a time when both sexes of the northern shrike regularly sing, they sing a different song from that of the male in summer. Eric Atkinson showed that cold-season singing by this predatory bird includes mimicry of the begging and alarm calls of small birds such as pine siskin and song sparrow and is given from bushy cover. Individuals of the copied species are attracted—lured by deception—toward the predating shrike, which may thus more easily attack them.

Species of living birds reported as new to science included, from Brazil, a particularly agile member of the ovenbird family named *Acrobatornis fonsecai* by its discoverers, José Pacheco and others of the University of

Rio de Janeiro. Another Neotropical bird new to the world list was the Chocó vireo, discovered in Colombia by Gary Stiles of the University of Bogotá and Paul Salaman of the University of Oxford. From Latin America came a species of antpitta, as yet unnamed, found by Robert S. Ridgely of the Academy of Natural Sciences in Philadelphia. Ridgely heard an unfamiliar birdsong in the forest, tape-recorded it, and played back the sound; down from the forest canopy came a male bird to investigate the apparent intruder. Robert B. Payne of the University of Michigan reported from Nigeria a new kind of firefinch, which he named the rock firefinch. The tiny bird was observed to be regularly and exclusively parasitized by the Jos Plateau indigo bird, which lays its eggs in the firefinch's nest.

(JEFFERY BOSWALL)

MARINE BIOLOGY

In 1998 American researchers working aboard the deep-sea submersible *Alvin* reported their discovery of the most temperature-tolerant eukaryotic (nucleated-cell) organism on record. The polychaete worm *Alvinella pompejana,* living near deep hotwater vents on the East Pacific Rise, experiences temperatures as high as 80° C (176° F) within its self-constructed protective tube, in contrast to 22° C (71.6° F) at the tube entrance. Its temperature tolerance exceeds that of other known multicellular organisms, which do not normally live at temperatures above 55° C (131° F). A German study of material collected by U.K. researchers described an unusual and abundant sea anemone new to science from the Porcupine Abyssal Plain in the northeastern Atlantic Ocean. The anemone, *Iosactis vagabunda,* exhibits unique behaviour by intermittently vacating its burrow rather than pursuing a completely sessile lifestyle.

Mass stranding of Cuvier's beaked whale (*Ziphius cavirostris*) is very unusual, but such stranding was reported in the eastern Ionian Sea of the Mediterranean. The event coincided with military acoustic tests for submarine detection, and an investigation of possible causal links was proposed. Scientists from Thailand, Spain, and Denmark presented encouraging findings for environmental managers who were concerned with halting an alarming decline of mangrove forests in Southeast Asia due to aquaculture and industrial and urban development. (*See* AGRICULTURE: *Special Report.*) Their examination of a 28-year record of aerial photographs and satellite images revealed undisturbed mangroves in Pak Phanang Bay, Thailand. The mangrove edge had advanced at nearly 39 m (128 ft) per year where sufficient propagules (structures that allow the plant to spread) were available for the pioneer colonizing mangrove species *Avicennia alba* and *Sonneratia caseolaris.*

A new technique for studies of plankton in natural habitats was developed in Sweden. Using an underwater video camera mounted at an oblique angle to a stroboscope, researchers produced dark-field images of plankton animals as small as 0.3 mm (0.01 in) in length, permitting detailed study of species interactions and distributions. Divers in the Atlantic off South Carolina and in the Pacific off the San Juan Islands, Washington state, made direct observations of aggrega-

tions of marine "snow," ubiquitous oceanic material comprising detritus, microbes, and phytoplankton embedded in mucus. These aggregations were visited, often in succession, by many types of zooplankton, probably to feed on microorganisms. Other American studies demonstrated a major source of dissolved organic nitrogen (DON) in the sea to be remnants of an organic molecule called peptidoglycan derived from bacterial cell walls. The finding suggested that predation on bacteria, and thus their removal as contributor of DON, may be an important control on the long-term cycling of nutrient organic nitrogen in the sea. A U.K. study demonstrated that the planktonic copepod *Pleuromamma* experiences a significant lowering of nitrogen content between dawn and dusk, the period when this minute crustacean migrates downward in the sea and then back to the surface. Quantification of such losses by defecation and excretion, which at depth release particulate organic nitrogen and dissolved nitrogen, should further increase scientists' understanding of nitrogen fluxes and so enhance models that describe nutrient flows in oceanic systems.

Molecular evidence demonstrated that the nine species of land crabs of the family Grapsidae found in Jamaica derive from a common marine ancestor that invaded terrestrial habitats only four million years ago. On an evolutionary time scale, this finding indicates a remarkably rapid diversification and specialization. A Canadian study of juveniles of the whelk *Nucella emarginata* assessed changes that the marine snail undergoes during development in its vulnerability to desiccation, susceptibility to predators, habitat distribution, and coloration. The study found marked changes in all four factors when juvenile whelks reach a shell length of 8 mm (0.3 in). This length demarcated a second "ecological shift," occurring later in development than the better-understood lifestyle changes that take place at metamorphosis from larva to juvenile. A joint Malaysian and Japanese study answered the question of how the mudskipper fish (*Periophthalmidae schlosseri*) and its eggs survive reduced oxygen conditions in what had been assumed to be water-filled burrows on tropical intertidal mudflats. The investigators observed fish on the surface gulping air into their mouths and then releasing it within the burrow to form an air store under the roof of the burrow, where developing eggs were situated.

Using sophisticated techniques for observing inside feeding oysters as they draw in water and filter the suspended particles, U.S. researchers showed that the oysters actively select living particles for ingestion and reject nonliving particles, evidently in response to chemical and particle-surface cues. Even greater selectivity was demonstrated by Italian workers who showed that the mussel *Mytilus galloprovincialis* feeds selectively on living dinoflagellates rather than diatoms, with a particular preference for the toxin-producing dinoflagellate *Dinophysis,* the main causative agent of diarrhetic shellfish poisoning in humans in the Gulf of Trieste region of Italy.

Global fisheries statistics from the UN Food and Agriculture Organization for 1950–94 revealed a marked change in the composition of catches over the period, attributed to overfishing. Initial catches were predominantly of long-lived, fish-feeding,

bottom-living fish positioned high in the food web, but recent catches were dominated by shorter-lived invertebrates and plankton-feeding, open-sea-dwelling fish located lower in the web. The changes indicated progressively increased fishing of organisms lower down the ocean food webs, a trend considered to be unsustainable. Urgent action by fisheries' managers was recommended to protect world marine fish stocks and the food webs in which they are embedded.

A German study highlighted a continuing decline in the numbers of coelacanth fish in the Comoro Archipelago in the western Indian Ocean. The need to prevent exploitation of this "living fossil," in the wider context of biodiversity conservation, was presented as a test case to measure the success or failure of "eco-ethics," as recently defined and called for by international ecologists.

(ERNEST NAYLOR)

BOTANY

Breakthroughs in genetic engineering continued at a staggering pace in 1998. For the first time, plants were engineered with a gene from a fungus to provide them with strong resistance to fungal diseases. Even more remarkable, potatoes were genetically engineered with a vaccine against *Escherichia coli* disease bacteria; this achievement heralded the dawn of edible vaccines produced and delivered by plants. Scientists at the University of Maryland School of Medicine, Baltimore, tested volunteers who, after eating the treated potatoes, achieved immunity lev-

els similar to those gained by people who underwent ordinary vaccinations by needle. Scientists were expected to place vaccines into other widely eaten foods.

Although much progress was being made in genetic engineering, once a foreign gene had been inserted into a crop plant, it was difficult to turn it on or off safely, and the process wasted much of the plant's energy. The only effective method was to use commanding genes called promoters, but they were usually activated only by applying toxic chemicals. Recently, however, researchers devised a way to turn on promoters by using an interesting substance—alcohol. Spraying crops with alcohol could be the first safe way for farmers to switch on genes, and the levels of alcohol would be far too low for anyone to become intoxicated.

The genetic engineering of plants was, however, becoming increasingly controversial. Fears for the safety of food derived from genetically modified crops led some protesters to dig up fields of test plants in Great Britain in illegal acts of sabotage. Concerns were also raised about the transfer of genes from modified crops to weeds; in a laboratory experiment weeds became resistant to herbicides when they acquired a gene for herbicide resistance from neighbouring genetically modified crops.

Two separate studies revealed that plants share with animals the same sort of defenses against diseases. A team from Rutgers University, New Brunswick, N.J., showed that tobacco plants infected with a disease virus use nitric oxide to turn on special

genes that attack the virus. A group at the Salk Institute, La Jolla, Calif., found that nitric oxide also plays a vital part in the hypersensitive disease response, whereby infected plant cells commit suicide in order to destroy pockets of disease before the entire plant is afflicted. The nitric oxide sets off a series of biochemical commands uncannily like that sparked off in mammals' white blood cells when they attack invading bacteria—strong evidence regarding the ancient origins of this form of disease immunity.

Additional evidence of the ancient links between plants and animals was uncovered in hormones and their receptors. G protein-coupled receptors, or GPCRs, had been found in mammals, but Richard Hooley and his colleagues at the Institute for Arable Crops Research, near Bristol, Eng., were amazed to find a counterpart of the mammalian gene for GPCRs in cress plants. The plant receptor seems to recognize an important group of plant hormones called cytokinins, which are involved in leaf, flower, and fruit growth and development. This discovery could have a major impact on agriculture by genetically improving crop yields and food quality.

The growth of plants also seems to be influenced by Earth's spin. Some conifer trees twist their growth in opposite directions in the Northern and Southern hemispheres, a mystery that may have been solved by Norwegian foresters. They noted that conifers tend to grow in the belt of prevailing westerly winds from latitudes 30° to 60° N and S. When the west winds buffet the trees, their trunks are stressed and the wood twists to compensate. In addition, trees grow more leaves toward the sunny side, which also helps explain the opposite twisting of some conifers in the Northern and Southern hemispheres.

An alarming report confirmed the high rate of plants headed for extinction. In the first fully worldwide survey, the World Conservation Union published results showing that one-eighth of the world's plant species—nearly 34,000 of an estimated 270,000 total species—were now threatened. Even worse, this figure may have underestimated the problem because many areas of the world, such as Brazil and central Africa, were difficult to survey. Of the species on the so-called Red List, 91% were endemic to just one country; those species growing on isolated islands, where they were often at the mercy of foreign plants and animals introduced by human settlers, were particularly at risk. Kerry Walter, one of the report's authors, expressed the hope that the Red List would "wake people up to the fact that we spend very little on conserving plants, yet there are many more threatened plants than threatened animals." For every dollar spent on animal conservation, only a dime was devoted to plants.

(PAUL SIMONS)

MOLECULAR BIOLOGY

A Promising Cancer Therapy. The sprouting and growth of new blood vessels is essential during embryonic development so that developing tissues can be supplied with oxygen, nutrients, and waste-disposal services provided by blood flow. At the same time, blood-vessel growth, or angiogenesis, must be limited so that an inordinate fraction of the mass of the organs will not be

The sensitive joint-vetch (*Aeschynomene virginica*) was among the nearly 34,000 species of plants worldwide that were under the threat of extinction in 1998. That figure, reported in a survey by the World Conservation Union, represented one-eighth of the world's plant species.

devoted to blood vessels. It follows that angiogenesis must be under the control of both natural stimulators and inhibitors such that the balance between them produces the proper degree of vascularity.

This same reasoning applies to the growth of a tumour as well as to the growth of an embryo. A solid cancer, or tumour, derives from a single cell that has mutated in a way that permits it to escape from the biochemical controls that limit the multiplication of normal cells. Once that cell fails to respond normally to growth inhibitors, it starts to proliferate. When the growing tumour reaches a diameter of about two millimetres (less than one-tenth of an inch), however, simple diffusion in and out of the tumour tissue no longer suffices to supply oxygen and nutrients and remove waste. Further growth depends on angiogenesis, and the small tumour must produce factors that stimulate the ingrowth of blood vessels.

In the early 1960s such considerations led Judah Folkman (*see* BIOGRAPHIES), then a U.S. Navy surgeon, to begin a search for angiogenic factors, a task he subsequently continued at Harvard University. An assay was essential to allow the detection of these factors and then to guide their purification, and over the years Folkman and his collaborators devised two assays that used living animal tissues to test the ability of a given substance to stimulate blood vessel growth.

Painstaking work over several decades resulted in the isolation of not one but several angiogenic factors, including angiogenin, vascular endothelial growth factor, vascular permeability factor, and basic fibroblast growth factor. Once these were available, it was easier to search for inhibitors of angiogenesis. That such inhibitors existed was surmised from the ability of a primary solid tumour to inhibit the growth of small offspring, or metastatic, tumours. During the past few years, a number of antiangiogenesis compounds were identified, and by 1998 some of them had been given clinical trials, the goal being a generally applicable treatment for solid cancers. Moreover, because factors that stimulate the growth of cells must bind to specific molecular receptors on the cell surface in order to function, a compound that can block those receptors will prevent the action of the growth stimulators. Several such blockers, or antagonists, of angiogenic factors were also under study.

During the year two recently isolated natural inhibitors of angiogenesis, called angiostatin and endostatin, were attracting particular attention. Folkman and his collaborators at Harvard showed that angiostatin given to mice prevented the growth of carcinoma in the lung. In a second approach they used genetic means in mice to cause their cells to overproduce angiostatin, which in turn resulted in long-lasting suppression of fibrosarcoma, ordinarily a fast-growing cancer. Importantly, there was no indication that the cancers could develop resistance to angiostatin. Researchers looked forward to conducting clinical trials of angiostatin and endostatin in cancer patients in the next year or two and, if these proved positive, to the widespread availability of this highly promising treatment.

Antifreeze Proteins. Certain species of fish routinely live in seawater cold enough to freeze their blood. Ocean water does not freeze at such temperatures because of its high salt concentration, but the fish blood has only a third the salinity of seawater. Why does it not freeze?

The answer lies in antifreeze proteins present in the fish blood. It is well known that highly purified water can be cooled below its freezing point (0° C, or 32° F) without freezing. If one adds the smallest crystal of ice to such supercooled water, it rapidly freezes. Water ordinarily freezes at 0° C because it contains minute particles that initiate the growth of ice crystals. The antifreeze proteins bind to ice crystals in the blood while they are still microscopic in size and prevent their further growth. In work extending back to the 1960s, scientists identified several types of antifreeze proteins from fish and determined their structures. Although all share the ability to bind to ice crystals, comparative study of their amino-acid sequences carried out in the past two years indicated that they can be grouped into four distinct families. It thus appeared that these antifreeze proteins, which have similar ice-binding functions and mechanisms, have independent evolutionary origins.

Silver Bullets for Parasitic Protozoans. Organisms that live in environments that are rich in some biologically essential compound can, through evolution, lose the ability to synthesize that compound themselves. For example, parasitic protozoans, including some that are important agents of human diseases, have lost the ability to synthesize purines, because they can obtain these essential organic compounds from their hosts. The enzyme, or protein catalyst, that the protozoans use to salvage purines from the host is named hypoxanthine/guanine phosphoribosyl transferase (HGPRTase). Mammals also use a form of HGPRTase but are not dependent on it, since their own cells can synthesize purines. Moreover, the protozoan enzyme differs from the mammalian one in specificity, which thus raises the possibility that a compound could be found to inhibit the protozoan HGPRTase but not the mammalian enzyme. Such a compound would constitute a specific poison, or "silver bullet," for the parasitic protozoans, without harming the human host.

The first step in this search was the determination of the three-dimensional structures of the protozoan and mammalian HGPRTases by X-ray crystallography. Next, computer-graphics methods were used to screen the molecular structures of known compounds for those specifically complementary to the active site of the protozoan HGPRTase. Compounds selected in this way were then evaluated in test-tube experiments for their abilities to inhibit the protozoan enzyme, and the best of these were then tested in infected animals. During the year researchers reported the results of this search: compounds that inhibit the HGPRTase from *Tritrichomonas foetus,* a protozoan parasite of cattle, 100 times more strongly than they inhibit the mammalian enzyme. The researchers' success offered hope that effective treatments for such protozoal diseases as sleeping sickness, leishmaniasis, and Chagas' disease, which afflicted millions of persons worldwide, would soon be developed.   (IRWIN FRIDOVICH)

The Genetics of Human Behaviour. One of the most complex and interesting of human characteristics is behaviour. Like many other characteristics, such as height or weight, behaviour has come to be understood to reflect a combination of influences, some genetic, others environmental. In recent years advances in a number of techniques have allowed researchers new and provocative glimpses into the genetic basis of human behaviour. As a result, a Pandora's box has been opened, spilling questions that by 1998 were cutting right to the heart of individual human identity and behaviour and the forces that control human destinies.

Despite its intrinsic interest, the genetic basis of human behaviour had until recently proved extremely difficult to study, as neither human genes nor the environment could be intentionally manipulated, for obvious ethical reasons. Studies aimed at dissecting the "nature or nurture" issues of human behaviour, therefore, had relied on quantitative assessments of correlation—between relatives; between biological, versus social, family members in adoption studies; and between identical and fraternal twins. Although these approaches could reveal the presence or absence of a heritable genetic component for a given behavioral trait, they provided little or no information about the actual gene or genes involved.

For example, it is undeniable that schizophrenia runs in families, with the children of schizophrenic parents demonstrating 13 times the risk of the general population for becoming schizophrenic themselves. How much of this increased risk, however, reflects genetic predisposition rather than the result of abnormal parenting? In a classic adoption study reported in the 1960s, investigators examined 97 offspring that were all given up for adoption at birth, one group (47) born to mothers with schizophrenia, the others (50) not. Of the 47 offspring of schizophrenic mothers, 5 were eventually diagnosed with schizophrenia, compared with none of the offspring born to mothers without schizophrenia. Indeed, the apparent risk (about 11%) of developing schizophrenia for the adopted offspring of schizophrenic mothers was statistically indistinguishable from the risk (about 13%) for offspring raised by biological schizophrenic mothers.

Subsequent evidence for a genetic component of schizophrenia came from twin studies in which the risk for schizophrenia in identical (one-egg) twins, whose genomes are identical, was compared with that for fraternal (two-egg) twins, who have no more genes in common (about half on average) than nontwin siblings. Of the sets of identical twins studied, if one twin was schizophrenic, the other had a 45% risk of also being schizophrenic. In contrast, of the fraternal twins, if one twin was schizophrenic, the other twin had only about a 15% risk of being so. Doubling the difference between these two values gives a statistical value called heritability, which for a given trait roughly describes how much of the variance seen in a population can be attributed to genetic influences. For schizophrenia, heritability is about 60%. Although the exact nature or identity of the relevant genes remained unclear from these studies, the conclusion that genetics contributes to schizophrenia was compelling.

Equally compelling, however, was the evidence from these same studies that genetics alone does not fully account for behaviour. After all, even for the genetically identical twins in the schizophrenia study, the second twin had a little less than a one-in-two chance of being schizophrenic like the first twin. Environment accounted for at

(continued on page 244)

Feathered Dinosaurs and Fractured Supercontinents

Dinosaur paleontologists would remember 1998 as a year filled with excitement, contention, and new insight spurred by a number of astonishing discoveries. The most publicized of the new finds related to the decades-old debate over the evolutionary link between dinosaurs and birds—specifically whether birds arose from small, light-boned theropod dinosaurs. (The bipedal theropods include nearly all the carnivorous dinosaurs, from species as small as chickens to the huge *Tyrannosaurus.*) In June scientists reported that fossils of two new theropod species from the Early Cretaceous Period of northeastern China, *Protarchaeopteryx robusta* and *Caudipteryx zoui,* had unmistakable feathers spreading out from the forearms and tails. (The Cretaceous Period lasted from 144 million to 66.4 million years ago.) The features described as feathers on these turkey-sized dinosaurs, which lived about 120 million years ago, were better preserved than the structures reported two years earlier as having been identified on the back of another Chinese theropod, *Sinosauropteryx.*

Although many paleontologists believed that the new discoveries clinched the case for the link between dinosaurs and birds, some continued to disagree about whether the structures represented true feathers, protofeathers, or something else. Others argued that the new-found fossil animals were not dinosaurs but primitive, flightless birds. If the evolution of feathers preceded the evolution of birds and bird flight, then feathers must have first served a different function. Some experts speculated that if feathers evolved for a purpose such as insulation, display, or camouflage, a downy coat or feathery patches on dinosaurs could have been fairly common, despite the meagre preservation of feathers in the fossil record.

Also reported during the year was the first known furcula—fused clavicles, also called the wishbone in birds—from a theropod in the tyrannosaurid family. Critics of the dinosaur-bird theory had long maintained that theropods could not have been the ancestors of birds because they lacked a furcula, and until recently the structure had been found in only a few dinosaurs. As of 1998, however, the furcula had been discovered in representatives of a number of theropod families, including the allosaurids, oviraptorids, and troodontids, in addition to the tyrannosaurids.

The very first dinosaur reported from Italy, *Scipionyx samniticus,* represented one of the best-preserved dinosaur specimens known. This exquisite specimen, of a small juvenile theropod, included impressions of preserved soft parts such as muscles and internal organs. Despite the preserved detail, however, the fossil showed no evidence of feathers.

Not only were new dinosaur discoveries shedding light on bird evolution, they were also providing insight into the way the Earth's ancient landmasses broke up to form the present-day continents and how these changes, in turn, affected dinosaur evolution and their distribution around the world. In May researchers described an especially well-preserved skull belonging to an unusual carnivorous dinosaur, *Majungatholus atopus,* from the Late Cretaceous of Madagascar. They assigned the new find to the theropod family Abelisauridae and judged it to be most similar to abelisaurs from South America. Typical theories of the Cretaceous breakup of the southern supercontinent Gondwana have Madagascar and the Indian subcontinent separating as one mass from Antarctica about 125 million years ago and South America separating from Africa before 100 million years ago, with Madagascar and India going their separate ways by 85 million years ago. However, because abelisaurs were known from South America, India, and now Madagascar but not from Africa, the findings suggested that Madagascar had land links with South America through India and Antarctica well into the Cretaceous, after it had severed any links to the African continent. This was consistent with a revised theory of Gondwanan breakup, in which Africa became completely isolated in the Early Cretaceous, whereas connections between the other southern landmasses were maintained until much later.

During the year researchers published an extensive work on the evolution and phylogeny of the sauropods, a group of large-to-gigantic quadrupedal herbivorous dinosaurs that includes *Brachiosaurus* and *Apatosaurus (Brontosaurus).* In addition to offering a detailed revision of the taxonomy of the sauropods, the study concluded that all of the major groups of sauropods had evolved before the Late Jurassic (163 million to 144 million years ago), prior to the separation of the supercontinent of Pangaea into the major landmass groups of Gondwana and Laurasia. Sauropods thus spread to all of the major continental regions before the Cretaceous, during which they suffered extinction in some areas and diversified in others.

The bevy of the year's important dinosaur discoveries extended even to the unborn. In November researchers reported finding numerous preserved sauropod embryos within a nesting ground comprising fragments of thousands of fossil eggs from the Late Cretaceous of Argentina. The remains represented the first identified embryos of sauropods and the first dinosaur embryos from a Gondwanan landmass. In addition to embryo bone, the specimens included large patches of fossilized skin casts, the first ever reported for dinosaur embryos. The detailed scale patterns preserved in the skin resembled those of modern-day reptiles. That the embryos were unequivocally sauropods discredited a controversial idea proposed by some paleontologists that this group of dinosaurs had been live bearers rather than egg layers.

(WILLIAM R. HAMMER)

This model depicts the possible appearance of *Caudipteryx zoui,* a theropod dinosaur from the Early Cretaceous Period. Fossils of the turkey-sized theropod, recently discovered in northeastern China, had feathers spreading out from the forearms and tails.

O. LOUIS MAZZATENTA—
NATIONAL GEOGRAPHIC
IMAGE COLLECTION

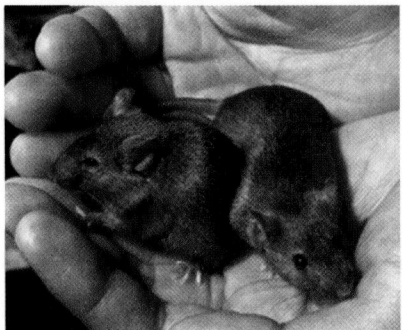

and processing speed) overlap markedly, which suggests that the same genes associated with one cognitive ability also influence others. Multivariate analysis studies also indicated that genetic contributions to scholastic achievement overlap completely with genetic contributions to general cognitive ability.

A third methodology, called extremes analysis, attempts to examine the genetic links between normal and abnormal behaviour. Specifically, this approach tests the hypothesis that if many different genes contribute to the genetic basis of behaviour, as seems likely, a given behavioral disorder

A pair of genetically identical mice (top) is shown at a news conference held in July. The cloned mice were produced by three scientists from the University of Hawaii (above, from left), Tony Perry, Ryuzo Yanagimachi, and Teruhiko Wakayama. The scientists' feat represented a significant step forward in the field of mammalian cloning.

©1998 PROBIO AMERICA, INC.

(continued from page 242)
least half of the nature-nurture pie. A better understanding of these nurture factors, therefore, appeared to offer the most hope for those seeking to treat or prevent undesirable behavioural outcomes in genetically "at-risk" individuals.

The power of these kinds of quantitative studies to explore the genetic basis of human behaviour was given a significant boost by three recently developed methodologies. One, called developmental genetic analysis, monitors change in genetic effects over a course of development, such as part or all of the human life span. For example, in research on general intelligence, many studies that did not follow their subjects over a long time (and that often involved young children) had estimated heritability at 40–50%. More recent studies that incorporated developmental genetic analysis, however, indicated that genetic contributions to intelligence become increasingly important throughout the life span, reaching heritabilities as high as 80% later in life.

A second quantitative advance, called multivariate genetic analysis, measures the genetic contributions to two or more traits as they vary together, rather than to individual traits. For example, with regard to human cognitive abilities, studies involving multivariate analysis demonstrated that genetic influences on all specific cognitive abilities (*e.g.,* memory, spatial reasoning,

may represent the extreme of a continuous dimension of genetic and environmental variability. The latest studies employing this technique to examine depressive symptoms, phobias, and reading disability, some of which were published during the year, produced results that seemed to support this hypothesis.

Once quantitative methods have identified behavioral traits, such as schizophrenia, that demonstrate a strong genetic component, the next step generally has been to identify and clone the gene or genes responsible. Although the potential benefits of having these genes in hand are great, not only for understanding normal behaviour but also for the diagnosis, prognosis, and treatment of abnormal behaviour, finding the correct genes can be extremely difficult. For traits that reflect principally the effects of one gene, identification of the gene usually has yielded to standard linkage approaches that track correlations between the inheritance of a given trait and the inheritance of specific regions of DNA. With few exceptions, however, most human behavioural traits appear to reflect the combined influences of many genes, which makes the standard approaches useless.

Fortunately, methods to identify candidate gene locations for so-called complex traits underwent major improvements during the 1990s. For example, so-called nonparametric approaches became available; these do not rely on traditional parameters, or as-

sumptions, but instead track correlations between siblings or other family members who share a given trait and also share specific regions of DNA. These and other methods, combined with continuing improvements in the available genetic and physical maps of the human genome, were expected to result in the identification and cloning of genes associated with a variety of human behaviours in the near future. Indeed, in the mid-1990s each of four different research groups implicated the same genetic locus, on the short arm of chromosome 6, in the cause of schizophrenia.

Perhaps one of the best measures of the fabric of a society is not how quickly new knowledge is uncovered but how it is used. Recent and future advances into the genetic basis of human behaviour were likely to test that fabric. By 1998 investigators had already reported evidence for strong genetic contributions to personality, vocational interests, alcoholism, and even sexual orientation. Yet another report used data collected from studies of identical twins reared apart to conclude that behavioural traits such as aggression, morality, and intelligence are substantially determined by genes. A major challenge for society will be to find ways to use this new genetic information to empower, rather than enslave, the individuals who might benefit from it.

Mammalian Cloning. In the year since Dolly the lamb ignited furor as the first mammal cloned from the DNA of a differentiated adult cell, the technique of mammalian cloning marched on. While scientists, politicians, religious leaders, and others debated ethics and possibilities, Dolly was joined by cloned mice, cloned calves, and another sheep that was not only cloned but also engineered with a human gene to produce blood-clotting factor IX in her milk. The cloned animal with the added gene, in particular, illustrated that practical applications of the technology were already under investigation.

Perhaps the most extraordinary application cited to date was revealed in July when scientists from China's Academy of Sciences announced a project to clone their endangered national symbol, the giant panda, by 2003. The proposed plan involved transfer of the cell nucleus of an adult giant panda into the enucleated egg of another species, perhaps the black bear. The hybrid egg would then be implanted into the uterus of a foster mother bear. Whether such transspecies cloning could actually work was the subject of considerable debate, but if it did, giant pandas would be only the first animals to benefit.

(JUDITH L. FRIDOVICH-KEIL)

PALEONTOLOGY

In the field of vertebrate paleontology in 1998, scientists described several significant discoveries from Madagascar. New evidence supporting the theory that birds evolved from theropod dinosaurs came from the remains of a raven-sized primitive Late Cretaceous bird, *Rahona ostromi,* found on that island. (The Cretaceous Period lasted from 144 million to 66.4 million years ago.) Other fossils from Madagascar—crocodiles, mammals, and dinosaurs, including one of the best-preserved and most complete dinosaur skulls known—suggested that a geographic link had been maintained between

that landmass and South America, perhaps through Antarctica, until late in the Late Cretaceous. Previously, it had been thought that connections between the southern landmasses emerging from the breakup of the supercontinent Gondwana had been severed by that time. (*See* Sidebar.)

Investigators reported from the Early Cretaceous of Australia a partial jaw of a shrew-sized mammal with tribosphenic molars—the kind of mammal from which both placental and marsupial mammals were thought to have evolved. About 115 million years old, the specimen was interpreted to be similar to jaws of primitive placental mammals from parts of Asia and North America. Previous to this discovery, paleontologists had assumed that both placental and marsupial mammals evolved in the Northern Hemisphere but that only the latter reached Australia near the end of the Cretaceous and thus attained dominance in the mammalian species of that continent. The discovery suggested that primitive placentals may have reached Australia from the north through South America and Antarctica much earlier in the Cretaceous. If true, these early placentals then became extinct in Australia before they could give rise to more advanced groups, as they did in other parts of the world.

Researchers at the University of Chicago published the results of a study on the origin of mammals, concluding that, unlike the origin of most other higher animal groups, the evolution of mammals was not linked to a major morphological change (such as the acquisition of feathers and wings in the hypothesized transition from theropod dinosaurs to birds). Instead, mammals evolved as a result of the gradual acquisition of a series of mammalian characteristics.

A new fossil whale genus and species described from the Late Eocene Period (43.6 to 36.6 million years ago) of Georgia was found in association with shallow-dwelling marine mollusks and plankton. This animal, named *Georgiacetus vogtlensis,* was the oldest known whale that did not have the pelvis articulated with (attached to) the vertebral column. The detached pelvis is an important feature that evolved in whales to better adapt them to a fully marine habitat.

The first record of fossilized amphibian eggs was reported during the year. The small oval-shaped eggs, 0.8 mm (0.03 in) in diameter, were discovered with fossil plants, invertebrates, and vertebrates in the Waggoner Ranch Formation of Texas. Because the eggs resembled those of modern amphibians and were of Early Permian age (286 million to 258 million years ago), it appeared likely that they were laid by dissorophoid amphibians, which belong to the order Temnospondyli. Dissorophoids were known from the Early Permian and were thought to be closely related to living amphibians.

A report of a fish-mass-mortality fossil bed discovered at the Cretaceous-Tertiary boundary (66.4 million years ago) on Seymour Island off Antarctica suggested that the fish may have been killed by the same asteroid impact event that had been proposed for the extinction of the dinosaurs. According to the report, however, the absence of ammonites (extinct cephalopods common in Cretaceous rocks) in the fossil-fish layer and the older, underlying clay layer indicated that other environmental factors already under way may have led to changing global biotic conditions near the end of the Cretaceous prior to the impact. It suggested that, if this was true, the impact was just the final blow to the remaining members of an ecosystem already depleted of life forms by other environmental factors.

Studies of microfossils were an important part of a major new project in the Antarctic. The Cape Roberts Project aimed to core 1,500 m (4,900 ft) of subsea sediment as much as 100 million years old near the coast of Antarctica over a period of several years. Scientists expected the study to improve their understanding of the geologic history of Antarctica prior to 40 million years ago through the use of marine microfossils, including foraminiferans, diatoms, calcareous nannofossils, and palynomorphs (fossil pollens). This project would also attempt to determine when permanent ice sheets first formed in the Antarctic.

Researchers reported on their investigations of an occurrence of unusually detailed microfossils preserved in chert from the Doushantuo Formation of China. These prokaryotes and protists, about 550 million to 600 million years old, provided a picture of biological diversity in the oceans just prior to the rapid diversification and specialization of marine organisms observed in the Cambrian Period (540 million to 505 million years ago). The presence of 12 species of cyanobacteria (prokaryotic photosynthesizers, also called blue-green algae), 31 species of acritarchs (eukaryotic algae), 8 species of multicellular algae, and compressed macrofossils of more than two dozen species of invertebrate animals indicated a much higher level of diversity for this early period than had been previously documented. The scientists also described microfossils interpreted as multicellular-animal embryos in various stages of division.

Notable advances in an understanding of fossil invertebrates included a major revision of the Athyridia order of brachiopods and a report on the discovery of brood pouches in trilobites of Cambrian and Ordovician age. (The Cambrian and Ordovician periods together cover from 505 million to 438 million years ago.) The later report proposed that large bulb-shaped structures on the head of these trilobites were used for sheltering larval trilobites to reduce the rate of larval mortality. The presence of the pouches in only some of the trilobites of a species suggested that they were an exclusive characteristic of females. This was the first good evidence that trilobites may have been sexually dimorphic—*i.e.,* that males and females may have differed in body form.

In paleobotany, studies of 400 million-year-old Rhynie Chert of the Early Devonian of Scotland provided the first conclusive evidence of lichens (cyanobacteria living symbiotically with fungus) in the fossil record. Researchers reported finding the fossil leaves, stems, and fruits of an angiosperm from the Upper Jurassic of China, the oldest known evidence for flowering plants.

(WILLIAM R. HAMMER)
See also Anthropology and Archaeology; The Environment.

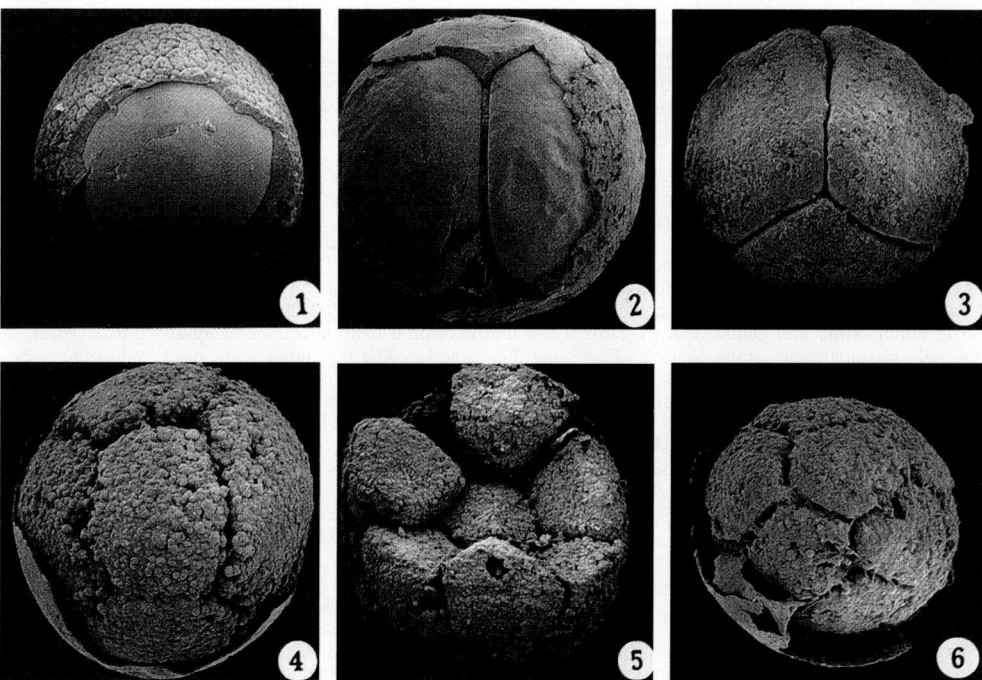

A composite of microscopic images shows fossil animal embryos at various stages of division. Discovered in China, these unusually detailed microfossils, about 550 million to 600 million years old, provided scientists with a more complete picture of an early stage in the evolution of animals.

Literature

The 1998 literary year was distinguished by a number of notable works from Eastern Europe, the Middle East, and Asia. The first-ever English version of Aleksandr Solzhenitsyn's *November 1916* appeared as the second "knot" in the Russian Nobel laureate's monumental epic *The Red Wheel,* a vivid and sweeping panorama of Imperial Russia at war on the eve of revolution. Victor Pelevin, perhaps the most gifted serious writer of post-Soviet Russia, published an English edition of his ironic and frequently grotesque prizewinning collection, *A Werewolf Problem in Central Russia and Other Stories.*

In *The Ultimate Intimacy* Czech novelist Ivan Klíma chronicled the illicit affair between a Protestant pastor and a beautiful and intelligent but unstable woman in his congregation. From the files of the late Serbian writer Danilo Kiš came *Early Sorrows,* a cluster of 19 linked stories that mixed childhood memories and fiction and centred on the prewar experiences of a young Jewish boy in a Yugoslav village.

From Israel came two taut, moving, and masterfully emblematic novels by Holocaust survivor Aharon Appelfeld. *The Iron Tracks* followed the peripatetic traveler Erwin Siegelbaum as he crisscrosses postwar Europe by train, buying up whatever remnants of Jewish culture he can find, and simultaneously searches for the former Nazi camp commandant who murdered his parents. *The Conversion,* a haunting tale of moral compromise and spiritual renewal, chronicled the representative yet complex fate of a provincial Austrian bureaucrat who converts from Judaism to Christianity in order to advance his career, improve his social acceptance, and survive.

The innovative fiction of Li Rui of China came to the West's attention with the publication of *Silver City,* a novel describing the "mountain-crumbling, earth-splitting events"—labour strikes, peasant revolts, Japanese occupation, student uprisings, political executions, the Communist takeover—of the era between the founding in 1912 of the Chinese Republic and the onset in 1966 of the Cultural Revolution. *The Sandglass,* the striking new novel by the young Sri Lankan author Romesh Gunesekera, recounted the saga of two feuding families whose lives are entwined by the changing fortunes of postcolonial Sri Lanka. South African Nobel laureate Nadine Gordimer commemorated the labours of South Africa's Truth and Reconciliation Commission with a weighty and complex novel about crime and punishment in transitional, postapartheid South Africa, *The House Gun.* One of French-speaking Africa's leading literary figures, Tahar Ben Jelloun of Morocco, broke a rather lengthy silence with *La nuit de l'erreur,* a shocking but stylistically brilliant novel of depravity and violence, tracking the ill-fated young heroine Zina's horrific series of trials and molestations. In *The Notebooks of Don Rigoberto* Peru's outstanding belletrist Mario Vargas Llosa produced a scandalously brilliant disquisition on true love and the imagination, full of elaborate, highly charged descriptions of sexual activity that may or may not be purely the fantasies of the eponymous Rigoberto and his adored but estranged second wife, Lucrecia.

In a relatively weak literary year in Western Europe, only a handful of new works were worthy of mention. Persian-born French dramatist Yasmina Reza brought her much-praised play *The Unexpected Man* from the stage to the printed page, presenting readers with a series of dazzling internal monologues by a man and woman sharing a compartment on a long train ride. In *Identity* Czech-born French novelist Milan Kundera produced "a twisting, teasing labyrinthine story of detection" that doubles as a set of speculations on topics such as identity versus anonymity and the preponderance of surveillance in both public and private life at the end of the 20th century. Finally, in *Todos os nomes* 1998 Nobel Prize winner José Saramago of Portugal chronicled the secret and wholly abstract infatuation of a bachelor bureaucrat for a deceased divorcée whose government file comes to his attention during a routine census.

(WILLIAM RIGGAN)

ENGLISH

United Kingdom. Ted Hughes, Great Britain's poet laureate, dominated the literary scene in 1998: as the year opened he won the Whitbread Book of the Year prize for his vivid *Tales from Ovid;* then a new collection of his poems, *Birthday Letters,* broke a 35-year silence about his stormy marriage to the almost legendary poet Sylvia Plath, who committed suicide in 1963; in the summer, their daughter Frieda Hughes astonished literary circles with the appearance of her first collection of poems, *Wooroloo;* and finally, in November—only a fortnight after receiving the Order of Merit—Ted Hughes died, leaving the royal position (an appointment for life) of poet laureate vacant and engendering much speculation as to who might succeed him. (*See* OBITUARIES.) Critics were divided on the artistic merit of *Birthday Letters.* Some found it overly confessional, imitative of Plath herself, and lacking in originality, whereas others found much to admire in the poems' tactile emotionality and passion. Frieda Hughes's work revealed influences of both of her parents, although some critics concluded that she was at her best when, like her father, she turned her attention to the natural world.

There were many other collections of major poets published. Foremost among them was Seamus Heaney's *Opened Ground: Poems 1966–1996* and D.J. Enright's *Collected Poems 1948–1998.* An exciting debut collection came from Paul Farley, whose *The Boy from the Chemist Is Here to See You* revealed a fresh talent for recapturing the mundane. The ingenious proficiency of Paul Muldoon's *Hay* prompted the *Guardian* newspaper to assert that "any year with a Muldoon book in it is a good year."

D.M. Thomas's major new biography of Aleksandr Solzhenitsyn was hailed as "the" book by A.N. Wilson, writing in the *Literary Review,* whereas the *Guardian* insisted that Michael Scammell's 1984 biography remained definitive. Other biographical subjects included Thomas More (by Peter Ackroyd), Matthew Arnold (by Ian Hamilton), Aubrey Beardsley (by Matthew Sturgis), and Francis Bacon (by Lisa Jardine and Alan Stewart). Richard Holmes's *Coleridge: Darker Reflections* reasserted Coleridge's stature as a writer of prose as well as verse, and Victoria Glendinning's *Jonathan Swift* painted Swift as a man obsessed with a feeling of unrealized ambition who had no idea that his *Gulliver's Travels* would be read for centuries to come.

The first volume of Ian Kershaw's vast biography of Adolf Hitler, *Hitler, 1898–1936: Hubris,* shed new and important light on its subject and distinguished itself from the plethora of some 120,000 existing biographies. By making intelligent use of previously unavailable Soviet sources, such as Joseph Goebbels's diaries, Kershaw renewed the debate about what had made Hitler possible.

Another major theme was war. Frank McLynn's *1066: The Year of the Three Battles* was a stirring portrait of the fraught year in which England was invaded by the Norwegians as well as the Normans. Several noteworthy books about World War I were published to mark the 80th anniversary of its conclusion. *The First World War* by John Keegan provided a successful introduction to this large and complex subject, and *The Pity of War* by Niall Ferguson challenged the notion held by many that World War I was "inevitable" and portrayed to devastating effect the intense suffering endured by its combatants. Lyn Macdonald's *To the Last Man: Spring 1918* was a carefully woven narrative of the eve of the final, bloody battles; based on surviving veteran accounts, it was the latest in a remarkable series of such in-depth testimony. *Letters from a Lost Generation,* edited by Alan Bishop and Mark Bostridge, charts the grim fortunes of Vera Brittain, her brother, fiancé, and two friends during the war—by 1918 only Brittain was still alive. *The Virago Book of Women and the Great War,* another collection of letters edited by Joyce Marlow, attempted to illuminate the largely forgotten role of women in the conflict.

The Eastern Front of World War II was examined in Richard Ovary's *Russia's War,* a masterly dissection of four years of appalling bloodletting, in which some 25 million people were believed to have died. Meanwhile, Noel Malcolm's *Kosovo: A Short History* could not have been more germane. The book, a scholarly history of the region, spanned centuries and rebutted the commonly held view that existing Balkan unrest stems from ancient ethnic rivalries and demonstrates, instead, how history and historical myths can be manipulated for political ends.

The stream of valedictory literature continued, with many farewells being made to the 20th century. Remarkable among these was Mark Mazower's *Dark Continent: Europe's Twentieth Century,* a 500-page documentation of discord. By now, he observed, Europe, which in 1900 was the main global power, has "ceased to matter." Cultural modernity was the theme of Peter Conrad's massive *Modern Times, Modern Places,* an attempt to "understand what it has meant to be alive in the twentieth century" by referring to the artistry that defined the era and providing some personal reflections as well.

The second volume of Martin Gilbert's *The Oxford History of the Twentieth Century* incorporated a more objective style of narration than *Modern Times, Modern Places*

and was arguably, owing to its single authorship, the most readable of such endeavours. This volume covered the years 1933–51, from the emergence of Hitler to the postwar era. The complete century was encapsulated in the rival *Oxford History of the Twentieth Century,* edited by Sir Michael Howard and W.M. Roger Louis. The volume, though more diffuse than Gilbert's volumes, was thematically broader in scope, examining as it did demographic changes, cultural development, and technology as well as the realm of high politics.

The year was also a lively and diverse one for fiction, with many noticeable debuts and several offerings from more established writers. Penelope Lively's *Spider Web: A Novel* followed the fortunes of a retired woman social anthropologist and was praised by the *Evening Standard* newspaper as a "wonderfully astute and quietly clever novel." Ben Okri's episodic *Infinite Riches* examined a fictionalized Nigeria that seemed to teeter in time between the present and the 1950s; the *Literary Review* hailed the book for its "powerful and righteous anger."

Many stories delved backward in time. Philip Hensher's fast-paced *Pleasured* examined Berlin just before the wall came down; Patrick McCabe's *Breakfast on Pluto* featured an Irish transvestite in the troubled Northern Ireland of the 1970s; Adam Thorpe's *Pieces of Light* recalled the author's 1920s childhood in Africa; and Beryl Bainbridge's *Master Georgie* was a Crimean War adventure and favourite for the Booker Prize. Real historical figures often cropped up in fictionalized settings. In *Casanova* by Andrew Miller, Casanova is let loose in London, with only a pedantic Dr. Johnson as a companion, and in Ferdinand Mount's *Jem (and Sam): A Revenger's Tale,* 17th-century diarist Samuel Pepys is the protagonist.

Jackie Kay's first novel, *Trumpet,* inspired by the true story of a jazz player who, once dead, was found to be a woman, and Derek Beaven's *Acts of Mutiny,* about a boy on a long sea voyage, were both cited by the *Guardian* as two of the year's most remarkable offerings from new voices. A debut novel—*The Restraint of Beasts* by bus driver Magnus Mills—was written between his work shifts and attracted intense media interest.

Julian Barnes, Martin Amis, and James Kelman were among those offering short-story collections; the *Guardian* suggested that neither Amis's *Heavy Water* nor Barnes's *England, England* revealed either man "writing at his best"; the stories in Kelman's *The Good Times,* however, were generally praised for their hilarity and deftness—one story, *Joe Laughed,* about a man who comes to see his life differently as he explores a derelict factory, was described as a "gem" by the *Literary Review.* Other Scottish novels included Irvine Welsh's *Filth: A Novel,* a portrait of a psychopathic detective, and Alan Warner's riotous and affecting *The Sopranos,* which featured the adventures of schoolgirls in Edinburgh.

In May the Orange Prize for Fiction, which was awarded only to women, went to a Canadian author for the second year in a row. Carol Shields traveled to London's Royal Festival Hall to collect her £30,000 prize for *Larry's Party,* a wry chronicle of the humdrum vicissitudes of a garden-maze designer.

The Booker Prize, which celebrated its 30th anniversary, was awarded in October to Ian McEwan for his short novel *Amsterdam.* McEwan collected a £21,000 check and said he felt as if he were "in a dream." Some were surprised at the choice; *Amsterdam,* a cautionary tale about the violation by the media of a senior politician's private life, echoed actual events in Great Britain and was acknowledged by reviewers as timely, witty, and readable. Many, however, found the novel less remarkable than his earlier works *The Comfort of Strangers, The Child*

©JERRY BAUER

Ethan Canin

in Time, and *Black Dogs.* Beryl Bainbridge, Julian Barnes, Patrick McCabe, and Magnus Mills were also short-listed for the prize, along with Martin Booth, whose *The Industry of Souls* was a sombre tale about a man held in a Soviet labour camp for 20 years. The chairman of the judges was Douglas Hurd, a former U.K. foreign secretary who commented that the decision had been easier than solving the war in Bosnia and Herzegovina, but harder than solving the war in the Persian Gulf.

Another novelist, Salman Rushdie, came into the news in September, when Pres. Mohammad Khatami of Iran, following a meeting with U.K. Foreign Secretary Robin Cook, announced that the government of

Iran would not seek to carry out the 1989 *fatwa* (decree) calling for Rushdie and his publishers to be killed and that it disassociated itself with any bounty money being offered on Rushdie's head. While security concerns about Rushdie necessarily remained, Rushdie professed satisfaction with Iran's statement, and his campaigners hailed it as a victory for freedom of expression.

There was also much excitement in September when Arden, the traditional arbiters of the Shakespearean legacy, announced that a 39th play would join the official repertory. *Edward III,* a five-act play thought to have been written mostly by Shakespeare *c.* mid-1590s, had been examined by a computer, which found the patterns of its language authentically Shakespearean; this conclusion was echoed by experts who believed that the play could have fallen out of favour when James VI of Scotland succeeded Elizabeth I, owing to its portrayal of a humiliating defeat of an earlier Scottish king.

Shakespeare himself, a lover of both neologisms and the vernacular, might well have approved *The Cassell Dictionary of Slang.* The 1,300-page book of 70,000 entries was the result of 25 years of research by its editor, Jonathon Green, and was hailed by the *Evening Standard* as surpassing Partridge's similar effort published more than 60 years ago and declared it a "learned, entertaining, funny, stimulating" book that "will afford countless hours of solitary pleasure."

Meanwhile, *The New Oxford Book of English Prose,* edited by John Gross, updated the original 1925 *Oxford Book of English Prose.* The former, a 1,100-page volume, contained a myriad of literary masterpieces from such authors as Shakespeare, John Donne, Sir Thomas Malory, Swift, Matthew Arnold, D.H. Lawrence, Anthony Trollope, H.G. Wells, Raymond Chandler, and Margaret Atwood, among many others, both famous and obscure. As a summation of nearly a millennium of literary talent, it could not have been more timely.   (SIOBHAN DOWD)

United States. The novel bounced back as the predominant form of popular narrative in 1998, displacing the memoir, which had seemed the genre of choice in 1997. Though the publishing industry continued its incremental downward slide toward ultimate "Hollywoodization," some major and important fiction writers came out with a number of successful works.

The most triumphant of these, in both critical reception and sales, was John Irving's *A Widow for One Year,* a charming, ribald, and enormously entertaining story of two writers drawn to each other by love and angst despite a large disparity in their ages. Veteran Robert Stone met with praise for his latest novel, the gripping *Damascus Gate,* a story of political apocalypse and the search for spiritual redemption in Jerusalem. ("In the main street of the Christian Quarter, a promiscuous babble of pilgrims hurried down the sloping cobbled pavement. One group of Japanese followed a sandaled

Japanese friar who held a green pennant aloft. There was a party of Central American Indians of uniform size and shape who stared with blissful incomprehension into the unconvincing smiles of merchants offering knickknacks. There were Sicilian villagers and Boston Irish, Filipinos, more Germans, Breton women in native dress, Spaniards, Brazilians, Quebecois . . . Palestinian hustlers hissed suggestively, offering guidance.")

Cormac McCarthy (*see* BIOGRAPHIES) published the third volume of his Border Trilogy, *Cities of the Plain,* in which his lyrical prose seemed more appealing than the overdone adolescent story of the romance between a cowboy and a Mexican woman in *All the Pretty Horses,* the first volume of the work. Tom Wolfe produced *A Man in Full,* another blockbuster in his signature style of larger-than-life pseudo-Dickensian prose on the subjects of money, race, ambition, and class in the new South. Like his first novel, *The Bonfire of the Vanities* (1987), his long-awaited second novel was seen as a major if flawed attempt to reflect the nation's character.

John Updike, springing back from the not terribly successful reception of his 1997 novel, *Toward the End of Time,* came out with the third volume of his wonderful Bech trilogy, *Bech at Bay,* in which his alter ego, the aging and not awfully gracious New York Jewish writer, grudgingly accepts the Nobel Prize for Literature. ("The page size was less than that of American typewriter paper; small sheets of onionskin thickness, and an elite typewriter had been used, and a blue carbon paper. The binding was maroon leather, with silver letters individually punched. The book that resulted was unexpectedly beautiful, its limp pages of blue blurred text falling open easily, with an occasional engraving, of Picassoesque nudes, marking a fresh chapter.")

Russell Banks published *Cloudsplitter,* arguably his best novel to date, a long and intriguing biographical fiction in the spirit of William Styron's *The Confessions of Nat Turner* based on the life of abolitionist John Brown. Novelist and storyteller T. Coraghessan Boyle began the year by offering his witty historical fiction *Riven Rock,* which was based on the actual case of a sexually demented American businessman and heir to the McCormick reaper fortune. Boyle ended the year by publishing *T.C. Boyle Stories,* a nearly 700-page book of 68 of his farcical short works, including 7 previously unpublished short stories. Norman Mailer won the battle of the pages with *The Time of Our Time,* an anthology of his work that was more than 1,000 pages long and that he edited himself.

In his meditative historical-biographical novel *Dreamer,* Charles Johnson carried readers back to the last years of Martin Luther King, Jr. Jane Smiley dared to write a historical novel set in bloody Kansas during the upheavals prior to the Civil War; the book was the very Huck Finn–like *The All-True Travels and Adventures of Lidie Newton.* Although Nobel Prize winner Toni Morrison came out with *Paradise,* which was perhaps her least successful novel, her highly regarded 1987 story of the traumas of slavery in postslavery Ohio, *Beloved,* gained new fans with the advent of the film version.

Philip Roth's latest novel, *I Married a Communist,* was set during the McCarthy era; it caused some gossip owing to its seeming allusions to his postdivorce quarrels with actress Claire Bloom, but it failed to garner much of a critical following. Gore Vidal's newest work was a science-fiction satire, *The Smithsonian Institution,* which seemed to lack his old spark. John Casey's tedious *The Half-Life of Happiness* improbably enjoyed a flurry of attention. Tim O'Brien's comic novel *Tomcat in Love* made some critics laugh and others moan, and Richard Bausch tried his hand at a thriller, *In the Night Season,* with interesting results.

Ethan Canin's second novel, *For Kings and Planets,* showed this prodigiously talented young writer working at the top of his powers in a novel of education set mainly in New York City in the 1970s: ". . . the weightless fretwork of the Chrysler Building a thousand feet above Lexington Avenue; the boasting spires of the Woolworth Building and the odd, saddened figure of Woolworth himself, cut in stone, counting dimes; the vertiginous lift he felt every time he rode to the top of the Empire State Building and paid to stand on the observation deck, the overpowering views filling him with fear not of falling but of flying upward." Jim Harrison's *The Road Home,* the sequel to his 1988 novel *Dalva,* showed one of the country's most serious talents in a deeply effective meditative mode as he dealt with several generations of a mixed-blood Nebraska family. Roxana Robinson wrote gracefully and powerfully about family matters in *This Is My Daughter.*

The Fall of a Sparrow, the second novel by Illinois writer Robert Hellenga, was a wrenching story about a father coming to terms with a murdered daughter. Susan Minot offered her evocative novel *Evening,* the fictive recollections of a dying New England woman in her late 60s who lived only for love. Howard Norman again took readers to Nova Scotia in *The Museum Guard.* Standing out among first fiction was C.S. Godshalk's *Kalimantaan,* a historical novel set in 19th-century Borneo.

The Shadow, written in the 1950s by Texas folklorist Américo Paredes, was finally published in 1998 and focused with great success on a crisis in the life of a Mexican farm foreman. *Yesterday Will Make You Cry,* a prison novel by Chester Himes, was reissued in the version originally approved by the late African-American writer; it was an event worth noticing.

Ann Beattie published *Park City,* her selected stories and eight new short pieces. Lorrie Moore's new story collection, *Birds of America,* was met with a great wave of praise, and Alan Cheuse published his third collection of stories, *Lost and Old Rivers.* George Garrett's miscellany, *Bad Man Blues,* was a welcome volume of stories, essays, and anecdotes.

("And I choose evening/ because the light clinging/ to the window/ is at its most reflective/ just as it is ready to go out.") Linda Pastan signed in with *Carnival Evening: New and Selected Poems, 1968–1998,* for which she was nominated for a National Book Award. A number of other poets of that generation also brought out new work, including W.S. Merwin in a book-length narrative of Hawaiian history, *The Folding Cliffs;* David R. Slavitt in *PS3569.L3;* Donald Hall in *Without,* his elegiac volume on his late wife, poet Jane Kenyon; and John Ashbery in *Wakefulness.* Gerald Stern also

published a new and selected volume, *This Time* ("I wanted to know what it was like before we/ had voices and before we had bare fingers . . . so I drove my daughter through the snow to meet her friend . . . and turned my head after them as an animal would . . . as they made their turn onto an empty highway.").

Blizzard of One was a volume of new poems from Mark Strand, and Edward Hirsch produced *On Love.* August Kleinzahler wrote *Green Sees Things in Waves,* and Brendan Galvin published the narrative poem *Hotel Malabar.*

Though poetry and dramatic criticism rarely make inroads on the public consciousness, the work of American poet laureate Robert Pinsky and Yale professor Harold Bloom provided interesting examples of such an occurrence. Pinsky produced a short volume, *The Sounds of Poetry,* a mixture of instruction and history in the tradition of Ezra Pound's *ABC of Reading.* His goal was to help the reader become more attuned to what was happening in poems and thereby provide greater enjoyment and understanding. Pinsky also edited *The Handbook of Heartbreak,* an anthology of various works ranging from an anonymous English lyric to contemporaries such as Robert Hass, Frank Bidart, C.K. Williams, and Louise Glück. Bloom's *Shakespeare: The Invention of the Human* was widely reviewed in the popular press and, as all good criticism should, made his subject something that thinking Americans had on their minds.

Elizabeth Hardwick in *Sight-Readings,* Michael Wood in *Children of Silence,* and Jay Parini in *Some Necessary Angels* published selections of their insightful newspaper and magazine articles and reviews. Poet J.D. McClatchy in *Twenty Questions* spoke to some of the interesting problems and pleasures of modern poetry. The essays by C.K. Williams in *Poetry and Consciousness* made for a deeply philosophical approach. Helen Vendler wrote lucid praise of the work of the Irish Nobel laureate in *Seamus Heaney. Trickster Makes This World,* a broad and suggestive study of the Dionysian in Western culture, came from Lewis Hyde, author of the much-praised *The Gift.* Critic Robert Scholes embraced the task of redefining the study of literature in *The Rise and Fall of English: Reconstructing English as a Discipline.* Short-story writer and essayist Grace Paley spoke out forthrightly on a wide range of topics in *Just as I Thought,* and short-story writer Andre Dubus mused on literature and life in *Meditations from a Movable Chair.* Barry Lopez traversed the globe in *About This Life: Journeys on the Threshold of Memory,* as did Alison Hawthorne Deming in *The Edges of the Civilized World.*

Memoirs displayed some of the sensationalism evidenced in 1997, notably in novelist Maria Flook's *My Sister Life,* the story of her relationship with a wayward sibling with whom she grew up in Delaware. A sense of a deep perspective on life, art, and culture was reflected in Frank Waters's posthumously published *Of Time and Change,* a series of autobiographical essays by the New Mexico writer. Doris Grumbach wrote about her mature sense of faith in *The Presence of Absence,* and Anne Lamott employed autobiographical material to the question of faith in *Traveling Mercies.* More

(continued on page 250)

Poetry for the People

Anyone who believed in 1998 that American poetry had perished or was clinging to life only among a small group of academics writing inaccessible verse for themselves alone might have been surprised by recent trends. Poetry as an art form was showing renewed vitality and was being celebrated by the people. Libraries, bookstores, and coffeehouses were holding poetry readings; people were flocking to see performance poets and join "poetry slams"; and there was poetry on the radio, on the Web, on city buses and subways, and even on refrigerator doors.

Poetry readings (usually dated to the historic 1955 event at San Francisco's Six Gallery, where Allen Ginsberg introduced his *Howl*) gradually became commonplace at bookstores—independents and large chains alike—eager to attract customers. Performance poetry—as much drama as literature—developed from more traditional readings and might have influenced rap music. The poetry slam, a competition between performance poets before an audience, was born in Chicago in the 1980s and spread rapidly. A slam circuit and an annual National Poetry Slam later came into existence. At the Arkansas Poetry Slam in November 1997, judged by Beat poet Gary Snyder and members of the audience, the first-prize winner, Daniel Roop, walked away with $1,000. Poets of the calibre of Ntozake Shange, Jimmy Santiago Baca, and Sherman Alexie crossed words in June 1998 at the Taos (N.M.) Poetry Circus.

Small journals and chapbooks, often self-published, had long been the staple of poetry publishing. Samples of such publications from 1960 to 1980 were on exhibit in July at the New York Public Library. Impetus to this movement came in the 1980s and '90s with the advent of desktop publishing. Small poetry journals also swiftly made the transition to electronic media, and " 'zines" and discussion groups proliferated on the World Wide Web (for example, *Poetry Daily* at http://www.poems.com/, *Gravity* at http://www.newtonsbaby.com/gravity/, or *Agnieszka's Dowry* at http://www.enteract.com/~asgp/agnieszka.html).

Poetry could be heard on National Public Radio, where popular radio-show personality Garrison Keillor served as host of a short feature called "The Writer's Almanac." In 1993 kitchens across the U.S. became workshops for do-it-yourself poets when Dave Kapell introduced the Magnetic Poetry Kit, words on individual refrigerator magnets that could be arranged into poems. Magnetic Poetry proved enormously popular for adults and children, and sales reached $6 million in 1997. In addition, the company erected "Mag Po" walls in public spaces in about 15 cities nationwide.

Institutions joined in the fun too. In 1996 the American Academy of American Poets designated April as National Poetry Month. In April 1998 U.S. Poet Laureate Robert Pinsky launched his widely publicized Favorite Poem Project, in which he invited people to send in a poem that had particular significance for them. Response was overwhelming, and at the end of the year 1,000 of the participants were chosen to read their choices for an audiotape archive.

Andrew Carroll, cofounder with the late Nobel laureate Joseph Brodsky of the American Poetry and Literacy Project, made headlines in the spring with "The Great APLseed Giveaway." Carroll traveled more than 9,650 km (6,000 mi), giving away 100,000 books of poetry at grocery stores, post offices, malls, diners, and bookstores. In 1998 the country truly seemed to be, as in the words of Walt Whitman, celebrating itself, singing of itself.   (AMANDA E. RICHARDS)

STEVEN SENNE—AP/WIDE WORLD; (BOTTOM) ©DON PERDUE 1998/PERDUE PHOTOGRAPHY

(Left) American Poetry and Literacy Project cofounder Andrew Carroll hands out volumes of poetry to theatregoers in New York City's Times Square. During the year Carroll distributed 100,000 poetry books across the nation. (Below) People arrange poems on a Magnetic Poetry Wall, one of a number of such walls erected in 15 U.S. cities during National Poetry Month in April.

(continued from page 248)
traditional autobiography came in Elizabeth Spencer's *Landscapes of the Heart* and Ted Solotaroff's *Truth Comes in Blows.* Mary Morris mixed autobiography and culture criticism in *Angels & Aliens.*

Jack Kerouac was the subject of two new biographies: *Jack Kerouac, King of the Beats* by Barry Miles and *Subterranean Kerouac: The Hidden Life of Jack Kerouac* by Ellis Amburn. Linda Simon focused on a sturdier American figure in *Genuine Reality: A Life of William James.* Scholar Lawrence Lipking went to 18th-century England for *Samuel Johnson: The Life of an Author.* Tim Page chose an American writer of the first half of the 20th century in *Dawn Powell.* James L.W. West III took on a living writer in *William Styron: A Life.* The gifted critic Joan Acocella edited a new translation of *The Diary of Vaslav Nijinsky.*

Southern history and culture emerged as the main subject in the work of a promising young scholar, Grace Elizabeth Hale's *Making Whiteness: The Culture of Segregation in the South, 1890–1940.* Taylor Branch continued his work on Martin Luther King, Jr., and the civil rights movement in *Pillar of Fire: America in the King Years, 1963–65.* Journalist and popular historian David Halberstam lavished a great deal of attention on the students who organized the first major civil rights demonstrations during this period in *The Children.*

Philip Roth won the Pulitzer Prize for fiction for his novel *American Pastoral.* Winners of the National Book Award in fiction and poetry, respectively, were Alice McDermott for *Charming Billy* and Gerald Stern for *This Time: New and Selected Poems.* MacArthur Foundation awards for 1998 went to fiction writers Ishmael Reed and Charles Johnson and poet Edward Hirsch. Among the winners of the Lannan Awards was the highly respected short-story writer Stuart Dybek.

Two deans of American letters died: novelist Wright Morris and literary critic Alfred Kazin (*see* OBITUARIES); fiction writer and critic Richard Elman also died during the year.   (ALAN CHEUSE)

Canada. The theme of escapism defined many of the literary works of 1998. In *Freedom's Just Another Word* Dakota Hamilton explored the paradoxes of liberty, and themes of guilt and innocence directed the course of this rambunctious novel of women on the lam. A teenager finds a mental hospital a temporary haven after giving birth and surrendering her baby for adoption in Lynn Coady's *Strange Heaven,* and Newfoundlander politician Joey Smallwood, the last "father of confederation," was featured in Wayne Johnston's biographical novel *The Colony of Unrequited Dreams.* Douglas Coupland's *Girlfriend in a Coma* was less an escape than a holiday of ideas; the coming-of-age tale was spun from the

rhythms of sleep and light. Two other novels embracing the same theme were André Alexis's *Childhood,* in which a reunion illuminates the necessary separation that preceded it, and Frances Itani's *Leaning, Leaning over Water: A Novel in Ten Stories,* which examined discovery and regret. Greg Hollingshead, far from escaping, created his own mind traps in *The Healer,* a quest for meaning that navigated through thickets of syntax and suspense and was assaulted by

©JERRY BAUER

Kerri Sakamoto

wild, strange concepts on every side. Even wilder was *Kiss of the Fur Queen,* Tomson Highway's foray into the magic of the North and the realism of the South, with language flaring like the aurora borealis, both illuminating and transforming. A sunnier mystical vision flickered through Gail Anderson-Dargatz's *A Recipe for Bees,* in which the natural and supernatural naturally coexist and, where least expected, blend into one another. In Barbara Gowdy's *The White Bone,* the action was described from an elephant's point of view as the pachyderm survivors of a massacre try to evade the humans who were laying waste to their land. Survivors of a different uprooting were caught in *The Electrical Field,* Kerri Sakamoto's meticulous depiction of a Japanese family's struggle to overcome the shame of their years spent in internment camps following their physical release.

Helene Littmann's short-story collection, *Peripheries,* followed those who fled to the West Coast and wound up staring out to sea. Alice Munro's tales in *The Love of a Good Woman* inextricably mingled goodness and

evil, and the ordinary dissolved suddenly into horror, notably when a bridal veil ignites in a candle's flame and a murderous complicity is exposed. Mark Sinnett's *Bull* abounded in beasts and blunders, whereas Dennis E. Bolen's *Gas Tank & Other Stories* delivered death in all of its rude, unintelligible reality.

Michael Ondaatje's poetry collection, *Handwriting,* deciphered many different scripts—ranging from superficial scratches to the calligraphic lettering on seals and certificates and to the deep bass lines of the drum—to convey messages from the heart of his Sri Lankan heritage. In *Alphabetical* P.K. Page played with the smallest bits of sense and nonsense, and in *How I Joined Humanity at Last* David Zieroth investigated his own mysterious character(s). Brian Brett's *The Colour of Bones in a Stream* was an evocation of appetites that was replete with metaphors of nourishment and slaughter cooked up in various tempting dishes. Louise Bernice Halfe celebrated survival in *Blue Marrow,* digging out toothsome truths with a finely pointed style. Patrick Friesen unhinged Winnipeg from the constrictions of fact in *St. Mary at Main,* and in *White Stone: The Alice Poems* Stephanie Bolster followed her muse into Wonderland, where anything can happen at any time. Kate Braid took historical liberties to bring two great artists together in her epic poem *Inward to the Bones: Georgia O'Keeffe's Journey with Emily Carr,* which meditated on the relationships between and among persons, places, art, and artifacts.

(ELIZABETH WOODS)

Other Literature in English. Among the most noteworthy literary works in 1998 were those by both promising new writers and established, internationally acclaimed authors from Africa, New Zealand, and Australia. Heading the list from Nigeria was Booker Prize winner Ben Okri's latest fictional offering, *Infinite Riches,* the third novel in his *Famished Road* series, which was set in the African ghetto. Also topping the list from Nigeria was 1986 Nobel laureate Wole Soyinka's collection of Harvard University lectures, *The Burden of Memory, The Muse of Forgiveness.* Other important contributions from the West African nation included works of fiction, such as Chinwe Okechukwu's *The Predicament* and Zakes Mda's *She Plays with the Darkness,* as well as Chimalum Nwankwo's 1997 verse collection *Voices from Deep Water.*

Benjamin Kwakye of Ghana explored the seductive power of corruption in *The Clothes of Nakedness;* Mary Karooro Okurut portrayed the traumas experienced by Ugandans since independence in *The Invisible Weevil;* and Zimbabwe's leading female writer, Yvonne Vera, presented her fourth work of fiction, *Under the Tongue* (1996), in which she continued to depict the sufferings of African women, this time by focusing on incest. Charles Mungoshi of

Zimbabwe added to his many laurels by winning the 1998 Commonwealth Writers Prize for the Africa Region for his 1997 short-story collection, *Walking Still.* Somali fiction standout and multilingual Nuruddin Farah (*see* BIOGRAPHIES) published his eighth novel, *Secrets,* and became the first sub-Saharan African writer to receive the $40,000 Neustadr International Prize for Literature. Distinguished Sudanese poet Taban Lo Liyong brought out *Homage to Onyame: An African God* (1997), which included a collection of 106 poems and a short article exploring man, his expectations, and cosmology.

In South Africa André Brink turned from writing fiction to commenting on it in *The Novel: Language and Narrative from Cervantes to Calvino,* and the 1991 Nobel laureate Nadine Gordimer examined postapartheid South Africa in her 12th novel, *The House Gun,* a spiraling story of love, murder, passion, and betrayal. Other highlights included the U.S. fiction debut of Achmat Dangor with his mythical novel *Kafka's Curse* (1997) and the release of Gomolemo Mokae's detective story *The Secret in My Bosom,* a publishing first for that genre in South African black literature. In nonfiction two outstanding works on Africa by non-Africans made their appearance—Philip Gourevitch's profound testament *We Wish to Inform You That Tomorrow We Will Be Killed with Our Families: Stories from Rwanda* and Adam Hochschild's riveting history *King Leopold's Ghost: A Story of Greed, Terror, and Heroism in Colonial Africa.*

From New Zealand veteran authors Maurice Gee (*Live Bodies*), Patricia Grace (*Baby No-Eyes*), and newcomer Elizabeth Know (*The Vitner's Luck*) saw their latest novels published in the West. Australian Neal Drinnan made an impressive fiction debut with *Glove Puppet,* and countryman Murray Bail received mixed reviews for his highly imaginative and provocative novel *Eucalyptus.* Other Australians with important new (1997) works included fiction writers Tim Winton (*Blueback*), Ken Levis (*The Adoration of Goanna and Other Stories: Explorations*), Gillian Mears (*Collected Stories*), and Alexis Wright (*Plains of Promise*). (DAVID D. CLARK)

GERMANIC

German. The year 1998 witnessed the successful fusion of the western and eastern German PEN clubs. The president of the newly unified club was the eastern German writer Christoph Hein. With the merger, a contentious issue that had plagued German writers since national reunification was largely settled; the German PEN club now turned its attention to helping oppressed writers in other countries and promoting freedom of speech and expression around the world.

Germany's most prestigious literary award, the Büchner prize, went to the Austrian feminist playwright Elfriede Jelinek, whose plays were harshly critical of patriarchal domination and the exploitation of nature. The Peace Prize of the German Book Trade was awarded to Martin Walser during the October Book Fair in Frankfurt, the world's largest literary trade fair. Walser's novel, the autobiographical *Ein springender Brunnen,* was an attempt to

portray a less dogmatic and more judicious representation of the German past. The novel told the story of his childhood and early adulthood in a small provincial town on Lake Constance during and shortly after the Nazi period. The novel's title comes from Nietzsche's *Also sprach Zarathustra,* where the human soul is described as a spouting fountain; for Walser, it is language that is the gushing source of wisdom.

Ingo Schulze's *Simple Storys,* greeted by many critics as the long-sought-after novel of German reunification, was probably the most important contribution of the year by a young writer. The 29 stories that made up the novel were loosely interconnected; all revolved around the Saxon town of Altenburg and its inhabitants, who were trying to live their lives in a world that had suddenly become foreign to them. Raised in the socialist German Democratic Republic, these characters had to remain afloat economically and emotionally in an insecure post-socialist East still haunted by the ghosts of the past. The prevailing tone was one of sadness and resignation. Schulze created a novel that added up to more than the sum of its parts; whereas any individual story may have seemed meaningless or even banal, all of the stories together formed a powerful picture of post-reunification eastern Germany.

The new eastern German writer Kathrin Schmidt published *Die Gunnar-Lennefsen-Expedition,* a feminist historical fantasy that recounted the expedition of the pregnant Josepha and her great-grandmother Therese into Germany's past. Like Günter Grass's *Der Butt* (1977), Schmidt's novel sought to retell history from a relatively anarchistic and fantastic female point of view so that the child in Josepha's womb would have a history/story when it was born. Another important novel came from Angela Krauß. Like Schulze's *Simple Storys,* Krauß's *Sommer auf dem Eis* dealt with problems in eastern Germany; set in the postindustrial wasteland of Bitterfeld in Saxony-Anhalt, the novel gave a powerful picture of people trying to cope with the historical changes around them.

Several fine short-story collections by young authors appeared during 1998. Judith Hermann's authorial debut, a collection of short stories entitled *Sommerhaus, später,* heralded the arrival of a major talent. Like Schulze's novel, Hermann's stories were unpretentious and relatively simple, but they created a compelling account of daily life in contemporary Germany for "Generation X." Another important short-story collection was Franz Dobler's *Nachmittag eines Reporters,* full of ironic observations about Germany today. The talented young writer Jakob Arjouni, author of several well-received detective novels, also produced a collection of short stories entitled *Ein Freund,* full of finely wrought characters and exciting action.

Among older writers, the 85-year-old Stefan Heym produced a major historical novel, *Pargfrider,* based on the life of a 19th-century Jewish businessman who went from great poverty to fantastic wealth by providing clothes for the Austrian army. An account of the role played by money, ethnic identity, aristocratic snobbishness, and democratic tolerance in Central European history, the novel was also a reflection on immortality and what one must do to attain it.

Peter Handke published a collection of diary entries, *Am Felsfenster morgens,* spanning the years 1982–1987. The Austrian writer Ulrike Längle published the novel *Vermutungen über die Liebe in einem fremden Haus,* a lyrical exploration of love and the Swedish landscape. Finally, 1998 witnessed the end of one of the most remarkable literary careers of the twentieth century: the novelist Ernst Jünger, author of the gripping World War I memoir *In Stahlgewittern* (1920), of the nonconformist and putatively anti-Nazi novel *Auf den Marmorklippen* (1939), and of many post–World War II memoirs and reflections, died in February at the age of 102. Jünger's life and work spanned the century and four different German states; the writer had embodied many of the contradictions and problems, as well as the brilliance shown by Germans during this period.

(STEPHEN BROCKMANN)

Netherlandic. In 1998 works by and about Anne Frank made headlines around the world. Two new biographies of Frank were published, and the existence of an additional five pages of text—that she had allegedly written for her diary and the discovery of which was known only to a very limited circle—were made public amid a flurry of debates and at least one lawsuit concerning their publication. The controversy centred around the authenticity, content, possible motive for suppression of the pages until the present time, and the potential to profit from the discovery.

In contemporary fiction semiautobiographical prose continued to reach new heights in popularity. Of the six finalists for the Libris Literatuur Prijs 1998, at least three of them could be termed autobiographical. The prize went to J.J. Voskuil for his novel *Plankton,* the third installment in his *Het Bureau* series. Another category that emerged was christened *weduwenproza* ("prose by widows") and referred to Connie Palmen's *I. M.* and Kristien Hemmerechts's *Taal zonder mij.* Both authors were established writers whose spouses were authors in their own right, and both works dealt with the loss of their respective partners. On the other hand, F. B. Hotz, known for his carefully crafted language, protested when he received the P. C. Hooftprijs award; he "had hoped that people had already forgotten him."

Poetry found new exposure and new audiences and was combined with music and other entertainment at various festivals. The Crossing Border Festival had presented various kinds of literature and music together in a lively context for a number of years, and Double Talk, where rap and poetry were combined, led to the publication of *Double Talk Too.* The literary form in that book was identified as "rapoëzie." In the preface to the book, Gerrit Komrij, established poet and scholar of poetry, declared "Rappers have saved poetry by mouth-to-mouth resuscitation at the last minute."

(JOLANDA VANDERWAL TAYLOR)

Danish. The standout author in Danish literature in 1998 was Jens Christian Grøndahl, who emerged as a dominant figure in Danish letters. He departed from his experimental style with the novel *Lucca,* which detailed, with deep insight and feeling, the unusual relationship between 32-year-old Lucca Montale, who had been seriously injured and blinded in an automobile

accident, and her doctor, Robert, recently divorced. In his book of essays, *Night Mail,* Grøndahl covered a wide scope geographically, historically, and intellectually. Carsten Jensen, too, stretched the imagination with *Jeg har hørt et stjerneskud* (1997), a work of cultural philosophy masquerading as a travelogue.

The epistolary novel made an appearance with Iselin C. Hermann's *Prioritaire,* a work about a young Danish woman who writes to thank a French artist for one of his works, an action that prompts an increasingly intense series of letters. When the two finally meet, their relationship takes an abrupt and tragic turn. Another tragic and intense work was Christina Hesselholdt's *Udsigten,* the final novel in the trilogy she began in 1996. Hesselholdt had already exhibited her mastery of the ultrashort but penetrating novel, providing readers with brief glimpses and hints of the action to come. At the other end of the spectrum was Michael Larsen's intellectual thriller set in Sydney, Australia; *Slangen i Sydney,* complex, bewildering, and spine-chilling, was infused with an encyclopedic knowledge of snakes and their poisons.

Greenland was the subject of two works. Hans Anthon Lynge's *Lige før der kommer skib* chronicled the conflict between the old and the new in a north Greenland community, while Kirsten Thisted published Jens Kreutzmann's *Fortællinger og akvareller* in English, using Kreutzmann's own translation. The Greenlandic legends thus appeared in a particularly fascinating form, with the author's point of view remaining intact.

In poetry, Morten Søndergaard's *Bier dør sovende* was filled with new insights intensified by a highly original use of language and metaphor. A determined use of a single metaphor—water—was at the centre of Pia Tafdrup's *Dronningeporten.* One of Denmark's internationally best-known authors, Henrik Stangerup, died in July. (*See* OBITUARIES.)

(W. GLYN JONES)

Norwegian. Epic novels that often dealt with realistic themes about dysfunctional families and problematic childhoods continued to dominate Norwegian literature in 1998. There was much discussion over the failure of the highly acclaimed novels by Linn Ullmann and Erik Fosnes Hansen to be nominated for the Brage Prize. Critic Ullmann, the daughter of Liv Ullmann and Ingmar Bergman, debuted with *Før du sovner,* a family chronicle spanning over 60 years. Hansen's long-awaited third novel, *Beretninger om beskyttelse,* was the 1998 Bookseller's prizewinner and included four separate, yet thematically connected stories that were set in present-day Norway, a remote Swedish island in 1898, and medieval Italy.

The Brage Prize nominees were Kjartan Fløgstad's winning *Kron og mynt,* a massive novel employing burlesque humour about money, art, work, and society; Geir Pollen's *Hutchinsons effekt,* which followed the protagonist's search for his roots; and Brit Bildøen's *Tvillingfeber,* about an orphan

who searches for a possible twin sister. Author Dag Solstad was the recipient of the award of honour for his accomplishments during his 30-year career.

Karl Ove Knausgård debuted with the critically acclaimed *Ute av verden,* a 700-page novel about a young substitute teacher who falls in love with a 13-year-old and then journeys back to his childhood home in search of truth. In prizewinning author Bjørg Vik's *Roser i et sprukket krus* a recent widow finds new love.

Noveller i samling, a collection of Liv Køltzow's stories written from 1970–89, showed Køltzow's talent for capturing the often invisible details of daily life. *Fantomsmerter,* a promising debut by Bjarte

Dominique Bona

Breiteig, offered a glimpse into the painful fate of the outsider.

Stein Mehren published his 22nd collection of poetry, *Nattmaskin,* which explored the theme of modern technology as a substitute for human contact. Torild Wardenær received the Halldis Moren Vesaas prize for *Døgndrift,* her fourth collection of poetry in five years.

Finn Benestad published *Brev i utvalg 1862–1907 I-II,* an annotated collection of over 1,500 letters by Edvard Grieg, and Inger Elisabeth Haavet profiled Grieg's wife, Nina, in *Nina Grieg-kunstner og kunstnerhustru.* Former Norwegian prime minister Gro Harlem Brundtland published the latest installment in her autobiography, *Dramatiske år. 1986–1996,* which was offset by *Statskvinnen,* a leftist view of Brundtland by Håvard Nilsen and Dag Østerberg. Two biographies of poet Rolf

Jacobsen also appeared: *Ord må en omvei* by Hanne Lillebo and *Rolf Jacobsen. En dikter og hans skygge* by Ove Røsbak.

(MARGARET HAYFORD O'LEARY)

Swedish. Publishing enjoyed a bountiful year in 1998 with many offerings in fiction and nonfiction. In fiction both established and first-time authors were well represented. Themes generally mirrored recent social and political debates. P.C. Jersild's *Sena sagor* showed a postmodern Stockholm with ruined monuments and a mysterious illness running rampant. Sigrid Combüchen's novel *Parsifal* was a futuristic description of a United Europe in dissolution, while Folke Isaksson's collection of poetry *Eldflugorna* contained powerful images of a self-destructing world. New poets also explored the last two decades, among them Anna Carlqvist with her bracing, ironic poems *Tribut till älskarinnan* and Peter Nordström in *Vulkaner på nappflaska eller Håll i evigheten en stund medan jag går in och köper gårdagens bröd.*

Fairy-tale motifs were also prevalent, and many books had the word *tales (sagor)* in their titles. Books that featured these motifs included Marie Hermansson's *Musselstranden,* Jersild's *Sena sagor,* and Birgitta Trotzig's *Dubbelheten-tre berättelser.* In one of the year's most acclaimed novels, *Och jag grep årorna och rodde,* author Birgitta Lillpers married myth and reality in a story of toil along a Swedish waterway.

Other novels revealed a nostalgia for childhood and a compassionate society. These included Stig Claesson's *Vad man ser och hedrar* and Björn Ranelid's work about a dying man and his last love, *Tusen kvinnor och en sorg.* Even young writers showed a sense of loss, as evidenced by Cecilia Davidsson's collection of short stories, *Utan pengar, utan bikini.* Strong nostalgia for 1920s Stockholm also ran through Heidi von Born's novel *Änglarnas stad.*

Johanna Ekström wrote compelling poems about love and loss in *Gå förlorad,* and Ylva Eggehorn returned with *Ett hemligt tecken.* Aging and death were explored in Göran Sonnevi's highly praised collection of sonnets, *Klangernas bok.*

Memoirs were published by Jörn Donner, Vilgot Sjöman, and Jan Myrdal, and Kerstin Thorvall came out with a semiautobiographical novel. Also noteworthy was Jacques Werup's collection of memoirs/travelogue/essays, *Människan är vem som helst,* that explored the issues of childhood and loss and paid homage to his colleagues who had consistently heard the voices of the marginalized and forgotten.

(ROSE-MARIE G. OSTER)

FRENCH

France. One of the most interesting literary trends of 1998 was the growing experimentation with genre, particularly the mixture of autobiography and fiction recently termed "autobiofiction." This was perhaps best exemplified by *Sujet Angot,* in which Christine Angot assumed the voice of her real-life ex-lover and wrote a hymn of love to herself

as well as a response to her critics' charges of rampant narcissism. A similar mixture of autobiography and fiction, including a philosophical treatise on the power of memory, marked Michel Braudeau's *Pérou*. This was the story of the author's voyage as a student to Peru, of the love he found there, and of the irreparable yearning he felt after losing that love forever.

Another autobiofiction book was Jean Pérol's *Un été mémorable,* a story about the author's coming of age as a 12-year-old amid the horrors of the Nazi occupation of France. Jean Rouaud also published *Pour vos cadeaux,* a novel about his mother. Widowed at 41 with three children, she held her family together with stern discipline until finally rediscovering life through laughter.

A related experiment in the blending of genres was Alain Corbin's biographical novel, *Le monde retrouvé de Louis-François Pinagot.* The author found a single name in a 19th-century population list of a provincial town and reconstructed the unknown man's entire world—from the sounds and smells in his life to the personal effects of insurrections raging in far-off Paris.

Besides the experimentation with genre, the year's novels also explored variations on two time-honoured themes: the dubiousness of memory and the struggle against despair. In Albert Bensoussan's *Le chant silencieux des chouettes* a man, guilt-stricken at the death of his ex-lover, obsessively attempts to revive their life together in his memory with all its excruciating and perhaps imaginary detail in order to understand his mistakes.

A similarly tentative process of resurrecting the past through memory was recounted in Marie Darrieussecq's *La naissance des fantômes,* in which a woman suddenly and inexplicably abandoned by her husband tries to discover the reasons for his disappearance. Fluctuating between fact and hallucination, the text emphasizes the unreliability of memory, especially when warped by neurotic remorse. The same uncertainty of memory formed the intrigue of Lorette Nobécourt's *La conversation,* a stream of consciousness monologue of a woman's life, tinged with all the contradictions of memory. She finally reveals that the death of a young man is the catalyst for her drunkenness, though the reader never learns whether she is guilty of murder or herself a victim.

Perhaps the most egregious example of the second prevalent theme, the struggle against despair, was Michel Houellebecq's *Les particules élémentaires,* in which two brothers, separated since childhood, reunite in adulthood only to find themselves completely isolated from the rest of the world. Both are embittered idealists. The first is a biologist who hopes to correct mankind through a genetic weeding out of desire. The second is forever seeking an ideal through sexual obsessions. The two wander hopelessly in an empty world, slowly sinking deeper into misery.

In Martin Winckler's best-selling *La maladie de Sachs* a doctor sets up practice in a provincial town. His patients realize that he is tormented and try to piece together the reasons for his despair. The doctor's writings reveal that he suffers from all the horrors he has seen and has become infused with humanity's misery.

The young protagonist of Sylvie Germain's *Tobie des marais,* based on the biblical book of Tobias, is also a victim of Existentialist despair, weighed down by his family's past: their plight as Jews in Poland and his mother's death in childbirth. Unlike the protagonists in Houellebecq's and Winckler's novels, however, Tobie finds a chance for redemption, reconquering life through friendship and love.

Essays dealt mainly with social issues. In *Le racisme expliqué à ma fille* Tahar Ben Jelloun tackled the problem of racism in a book written as a series of answers to his daughter's deceptively simple questions. Jean-Claude Guillebaud published *La tyrannie du plaisir,* which explored whether the sexual revolution actually freed relations between the sexes or if it was an outbreak of sexual militancy that subverted the preexisting order only to install hedonism as the supreme virtue. In *La domination masculine* the sociologist Pierre Bourdieu also examined the relation between the sexes, but from the viewpoint of domination. He suggested that although males have historically always dominated females, that hierarchy also victimizes men by continually forcing them to prove their manliness. The hierarchy of domination, though institutional rather than sexual, was also studied in François Bon's *Prison,* in which prisoners' own words were transcribed without commentary in order to produce a more true picture of their everyday life behind bars.

The Prix Femina was awarded to François Cheng's *Le dit de Tianyi,* a fictionalization of the author's spiritual and artistic quest within Chinese and Western cultures. The Prix Médicis was given to Homéric's *Le loup Mongol,* the lyric epic of Genghis Khan as told by his estranged childhood friend. The Prix Renaudot went to Dominique Bona's *Le Manuscrit de Port-Ébène,* which recounted the fictitious confessions of an 18th-century French woman, revealing her scandalous incestuous love against the backdrop of bloody slave revolts and the Haitian war of independence. Finally, Paule Constant won the Prix Goncourt for *Confidence pour confidence,* in which four women, reunited after a long separation, share their disappointments in love and life with a mix of despair and satire.

(VINCENT AURORA)

Canada. The premier event of 1998 in French-language literature was the Montreal Book Fair, or Salon du Livre, where an estimated 120,000 readers and writers gathered in November. Gaétan Soucy's 1997 *L'acquittement* captured the 1998 City of Montreal book prize of $10,000, and his new novel, *La petite fillequiaimait trop les allumettes,* enjoyed both critical and commercial success.

A best-selling book was produced from the popular French-language television program "La petite vie," a kind of theatre-of-the-absurd sitcom featuring an old couple, one of whom was a man who dressed like a woman. Though the book that was derived from the series was little more than a hodgepodge of dialogues from the show, readers lined up to buy it. In another television crossover popular small-screen personality Michel Desautel won the Prix Robert Cliche for best first novel with *Smiley,* a story about an Olympic sprinter.

A small but spirited publishing company, Les intouchables, made waves in 1998. The firm, headed by Michel Brûlé, provoked and challenged Quebec on political and literary grounds. Brûlé made a point of publishing young, performance-oriented poets like Stéphane Despatie. The 1998 Governor-General's Award for French-language poetry went to veteran writer Suzanne Jacob for *La part de feu.*

French Quebeckers also enjoyed new foreign-language literature written by their neighbours—English Quebeckers. Novels by "les Anglos" were translated into French and attracted media attention, disproving the tired myths about the two solitudes, at least in Quebec.   (DAVID HOMEL)

ITALIAN

The year 1998 was marked by celebrations of the bicentenary of the birth of Giacomo Leopardi, the great Romantic poet. Conferences, symposia, and public readings were held throughout Italy. Several new books appeared on the subject of Leopardi's slender poetry collection (the *Canti*) and his prose work (*Operette morali, Zibaldone*). In other nonfiction publications, an essay by Carla Benedetti, *Pasolini contro Calvino,* caused considerable controversy. It presented the writers Pier Paolo Pasolini and Italo Calvino as contrasting embodiments of Italian postmodernism: Calvino coldly experimenting within the boundaries of traditional literary institutions and Pasolini constantly, radically, and passionately in conflict with authority in both his work and his life.

The low number of Italian readers, especially among the young, was troubling. Best-sellers were, as usual, from the U.S. and included John Grisham, Patricia Cornwell, and Tom Clancy. The "American style" proved successful for Andrea Camilleri, who wrote several popular detective stories that suddenly invaded the Italian top-10 list. Set in Sicily and liberally sprinkled with Sicilianisms, most of Camilleri's novels were centred on the character of Montalbano. He was an ironic copy of the Manhattan sleuth: clever, hardworking, tenacious, and, with his appalling eating habits and difficult love life, captivatingly humane. Camilleri's newest Montalbano installment was *Un mese con Montalbano.*

Serious fiction, however, was not lacking. Sebastiano Vassalli reached a new level in his apparent progression toward mysticism with *La notte del lupo,* an ambitious rewriting of the life of Jesus as seen from Judas's point of view. Veering between the disturbingly profound and the plainly ludicrous, the novel linked Jesus and Judas across the centuries with Pope John Paul II and Mehmet Ali Agca (the young Turkish man who attempted to assassinate the pope in 1981). Vassalli's novel was inspired by the notion that Christ did not intend to found the church; therefore, Judas and Agca were the only two among his followers who did not betray him. Equally ambitious was *Adriatico* by Raffaele Nigro. Its focus was the recent spate of immigrants, mainly but not exclusively from Albania, into southern Italy—a problem debated almost daily in the Italian media. Though convincing in its portrayal of the early life of its protagonist—a journalist aboard an Italian coast guard ship—the novel was not as successful in integrating its various narrative strands.

Gianni Celati published *Avventure in Africa,* the diary of his journey across three African countries (Mali, Senegal, and Mauritania) whose people had recently begun migrating to Europe. Celati's minimal-

ist notes avoided any political or philosophical considerations unless lighthearted and self-deprecating. Two literary veterans returned to their favourite themes. In his short-story collection *Sentieri sotto la neve,* Mario Rigoni Stern told of a soldier's journey home at the end of a lost war; in a highly idyllic style, he wrote of a natural world and people from a past gone forever. Paolo Barbaro mused on his beloved Venice in *Venezia: la città ritrovata* and revealed, beyond the alleys worn away by tourists, the still-valid idea of a universal city designed for humans: the only unchanging city—beautiful, mysterious, and vulnerable.

Pulp fiction was still a hotly debated genre. Not all young writers, however, were its devotees. Gianni Riotta's accomplished novel of love and war, *Principe delle nuvole,* created the unusual character of a sophisticated military scholar who spends his life in Fascist Italy studying the great battles of the past. He proves himself as a strategist only when he chances to lead a group of Sicilian peasants against their landowners' paid gangs.

Notable new books by women writers included a reprint of *La vacanza* (1962) by Dacia Maraini—sun, sex, and war against the background of the fall of Fascism. In her book *Inventario,* Gina Lagorio compellingly distilled 50 years of memories about masters, books, music, and urban and rural landscapes from Piedmont to Israel. Particularly memorable was *L'isola riflessa* by Fabrizia Ramondino, a magical account of one year on the tiny island of Ventotene. First used as a prison by the Bourbons and later by the Fascists, the island had become an ambiguous microcosm of memories, corruption, and desires. Most disturbing were several novels that delved pitilessly into the darker side of Italian family life. *La bocca più di tutto mi piaceva* and *Due volte la stessa carezza* by Nadia Fusini were the stories of two young women caught in the deadly web of family affections. *Uffizio delle tenebre* by Fausta Garavini portrayed a mother-son relationship that disables the son while offering him an alibi, both for his inability to act and for his willingness to create an imaginary, though not less-distressing, world. The novel was a harrowing meditation on the devastating power of an obsessive mother's love that causes contempt and unbearable guilt in the loved one, crippling him even beyond her death.

(LINO PERTILE)

SPANISH

Spain. Centenary observances were held throughout 1998 in honour of Spain's most widely admired modern poet, Federico García Lorca (1898–1936). Also honoured was the memory of Spain's losses to the U.S. following the Spanish-American War, and a vast array of writing on both Lorca

and the war was published. The biggest event in Spanish publishing, however, was the release of a monumental critical edition of Cervantes's *Don Quijote de la Mancha,* prepared under the supervision of Francisco Rico and featuring a concordance of the novel on CD-ROM.

Miguel Delibes, one of the grand masters of contemporary Spanish fiction, published his 19th novel, *El hereje.* The book was a massive, meticulously researched narrative

©JERRY BAUER
Carmen Martín Gaite

set in 16th-century Valladolid that culminated in a historical *auto de fe* in the town's main square, where the Inquisition burned 28 Protestants at the stake in 1559. Through the experiences of his ill-fated protagonist, Delibes personalized the drama of faith versus heresy, the twin obsessions of Counter-Reformation Spain. Also grounded in dramatic historical events was Manuel Vázquez Montalbán's richly anecdotal novel, *O César o nada,* about the political and personal machinations of the infamous Borgias in 16th-century Italy.

In *Irse de casa,* Carmen Martín Gaite explored the psychic and sentimental dynamics of leaving home—that is, the centrifugal impulse of voluntary exile from one's roots—and the poignant inward journey of long-postponed return. Fanny Rubio published *El dios dormido,* an allegory of erotic love and spiritual redemption as told from the perspective of Mary Magdalene, and Manuel Rivas offered a moving, semi-historical love story, *El lápiz del carpintero,* suffused with painful memories of the Spanish Civil War. Critics seemed disappointed by Carmen Posadas's *Pequeñas in-*

famias, the Planeta Prize winner, while the opposite was true of *Beatriz y los cuerpos celestes,* a gritty postmodern story of rootlessness and lesbian desire by Lucía Etxebarría, who won the Nadal Prize. Also popular were several collections of short stories by well-established writers usually associated with novel-length fiction, including Rosa Montero (*Amantes y enemigos*), Lourdes Ortiz (*Fátima de los naufragios*), Marina Mayoral (*Recuerda, cuerpo*), Soledad Puértolas (*Gente que vino a mi boda*), and Antonio Gala (*El corazón tardío*).

Following a seven-year silence, the distinguished poet José Hierro published *Cuaderno de Nueva York,* a collection of 32 compositions hailed by many as his finest work to date; in December Hierro received the Cervantes Prize, the top award in Hispanic letters worldwide. The astounding success of Antonio Gala's *Poemas de amor* (1997) led the publisher to reissue the collection with an accompanying compact disc recording of 54 of its poems read by the author. Another accomplished poet, Jon Juaristi, who as a youth was briefly active in the Basque terrorist organization known as ETA, earned the National Essay Prize for *El bucle melancólico* (1997). Elegantly written and forcefully argued, Juaristi's devastating analysis of the key premises and principal advocates of radical Basque nationalism, from its 19th-century origins to the present, was the nonfiction blockbuster of the year.   (ROGER L. UTT)

Latin America. In 1998 women writers in Latin America and the Hispanic Caribbean continued to assert their presence as major players on the literary scene. Chilean novelist Isabel Allende, whose 1982 novel *La casa de los espíritus* (*House of the Spirits,* 1985) introduced her to the literary world, won the 1998 international Sara Lee Frontrunner Award. Mexican novelist Carmen Posadas's *Pequeñas infamias* won the 1998 Premio Planeta, and Mexican novelist Eladia González's *Quién como Dios* was declared the publisher's novel of the year after selling 25,000 copies in 30 days. Cuban poet Carilda Oliver Labra's *Sonetos* was awarded the National Prize of Literature.

Laura Esquivel, Mexican novelist and author of the 1989 novel *Como agua para chocolate* (*Like Water for Chocolate,* 1991), issued *Intimas suculencias,* a new collection of her writings, and Mexican-American novelist María Amparo Escandón published *Santos* (English title: *Esperanza's Box of Saints,* 1997). *¡Yo!,* the most recent novel of Dominican-American writer Julia Álvarez, appeared in English in 1997 and was published in Spanish in 1998 under the same title and distributed throughout Latin America. Other new literary works by women included Cuban novelist Daína Chaviano's *El hombre, la hembra y el hambre,* Dominican novelist Mélida García's *Laberinto,* Dominican poet Rosalina

García's *Poesía,* Dominican poet Angela Hernández's *Telar de rebeldía,* Chilean novelist Gloria Alegría Ramírez's *Mundo de cartón,* Argentine novelist Aurora Venturini's *Me moriré en París, con aguacero,* Mexican novelist Leticia Angélica Martínez y Castro's *Las señoritas de negro,* and Mexican writer Erma Cárdenas's *El canto de la serpiente,* a collection of short stories "for liberated men."

Many of the works of Latin-American women writers were characterized as belonging to the genre known as Magic Realism, and their literature clearly captured a reality historically experienced by women, including the daily events and routines of cooking, cleaning, and family life and the colours, flavours, passions, humour, intrigue, mystery, fantasy, and spirit that were evocative of their lives. The re-creation of historical reality through the eyes of a woman emerged as another theme in the works of contemporary women writers and added another facet of Magic Realism to the international literary canon. In González's *Quién como Dios,* for example, historical images of provincial life in 19th-century pre-Revolutionary Mexico are reenacted through the eyes of the female protagonist.

Patas arriba by Uruguayan writer Eduardo Galeano, a former winner of the Casa de las Américas Prize, parodied the dominant concept of historical reality by presenting actual news events and observations as bizarre reversals of traditional order, sensibility, and logic. Barbadian writer Kamau Brathwaite's major critical work *Magical Realism* won the coveted Casa de las Américas Prize in 1998 and was scheduled to appear early in 1999.

The world of history, politics, and life in general was the subject of several new novels, including: *¡México ardiente!* by Jorge Sayeg Helú, *Los colorados* by Mexican novelist Arturo Quevedo Rivero, *Juegan los comensales* by Mexican novelist and short-story writer Jesús Gardea, *Salteadores nocturnos* by Argentine novelist Agustín Barletti, *Memorial de la noche* by Chilean novelist Patricio Manns, *Crónica de fin de siglo,* a novel about Nicaraguan politics by Bayardo Tijerino Molina, *Juro que sabré vengarme* by Dominican novelist Miguel Holguín Veras, and *Morgan* by Dominican novelist and poet Cándido Gerón.

Other published literary works included Mexican novelist César Francisco Pacheco Loya's *La inexplicable especie humana,* Mexican novelist and playwright Carlo Còccioli's *San Benjamín perro,* Mexican writer Romeo Infante Córdova's adventure novel *Las islas perdidas,* Mexican novelist Alberto de Cisneros Villa's *Nunca, mañana es tarde,* Ecuadorian novelist Jaime Costales Peñaherrera's *¡La plaga!,* Chilean novelist Luis Alberto Tamayo's *La goleta Virginia,* and Puerto Rican poet Ramón Sánchez Cortés's first book, *Patria nuestra madre nuestra.*

Mexico continued to reign as Latin America's most prolific literary market, owing, perhaps, to the long history of successful editorial houses in that country. The panorama of activity included provincial and rural writers from Chihuahua in the north to Oaxaca in the south, representing a broad range of cultural, gender, and class perspectives. Throughout Latin America, however, it was the new writers who captured the attention of publishers, who culti-

José Saramago

vated works from the Hispanic diaspora—writers living in the U.S. and Europe—as well as translations of works from writers of the Anglophone and Francophone Caribbean who shared Latin America's historical and cultural experiences.

Upon the death of Mexican writer Elena Garro (*see* OBITUARIES), *Mi hermanita Magdalena* (written c. 1986) was published for the first time. The semiautobiographical story was a fictionalized detective adventure that chronicled the search from Mexico City to Europe for a kidnapped baby sister.

(M.J. FENWICK)

PORTUGUESE

Portugal. For the first time in its long history, the 1998 Nobel Prize for Literature was awarded to a Portuguese author: José Saramago. (*See* Nobel Prizes.) The news was welcomed by his many readers and admirers both at home and abroad. Saramago had been highly regarded as a favourite for the prize for the past few years. Translated into 25 languages, his novels were well-known and had a deep appeal. In his para-

bles and fables, Saramago explored the predicament of the individual and the question of human salvation, seeing history as passion and suffering that can be changed by hope. His latest novel, *Todos os nomes,* revealed these features. The Register Office, where births and deaths are recorded, stands as a symbol of power that disposes of every individual's life. In the cogs of this machinery, the civil servant who pursues the identity of a woman he loves but will never meet provides the note of human feeling that exposes the harshness of bureaucratic society.

The celebratory mood of the country was overshadowed by the deaths of José Cardoso Pires (*see* OBITUARIES) and David Mourão Ferreira. Cardoso Pires was a most distinguished novelist and winner of many literary prizes. His last work, *Lisboa, livro de bordo* (1997), was a literary gem—a collection of his impressions on wandering through Lisbon. He describes small streets, buildings, bars, and night spots, conveying their atmosphere. Contrary to what it may seem, the book had nothing to do with a tourist guide. It was as much a personal journey of the beloved city as an inner voyage that awakened reminiscences of places visited at different times. Sensations such as light and smells are evoked by prose of great sensitivity, permeated by Lisbon slang. Mourão Ferreira's death was another grievous loss for Portuguese letters. A poet and critic, he was also an accomplished fiction writer who had attained remarkable success with his novel *Um amor feliz—* a love story to appear soon in English translation.

The most original novel to appear in 1998 was published by Helder Macedo. *Pedro e Paula* was a story of male and female twins who stand as mythical representations of Portugal through the conflicts of the last 50 years. The author embraces with gusto the complexities of storytelling, becoming a character himself and engaging the reader's collaboration in the making of a narrative full of zest and fun. (L.S. REBELO)

Brazil. During 1998 eminent Brazilian playwright Plínio Marcos turned from his lifelong preoccupation with political themes. In his new play, *A dança final,* he detailed a couple's celebration of their 25-year marriage. *Videoclip Blues,* a play by Marcos's son, Leo Lama, also dealt with human concerns—specifically the lack of communication between a much younger couple. Also of theatrical note was Aracy Balabanian's one-woman show *Clarice Lispector-Coração selvagem,* which examined and tried to dispel the myth behind the supposed depressed state of Lispector, a short-story writer and novelist. A biography of theatrical director Ademar Guerra, best known for his agitprop productions of the 1970s, was written by his collaborator, Oswaldo Mendes.

Marly de Oliveira's volume of poems, *O mar de permeio,* dealt with themes of an-

guish and emptiness. Roberto Piva, one of the 1960s poets most influenced by the Beat Generation, published *Ciclones,* a volume of poems that centred on the sexual nature of young men. Heitor Ferraz's first collection of poetry, *A mesma noite,* provided isolation and frustration as its resounding themes.

New works of fiction included Marcelo Coelho's *Jantando com Melvin,* which might be considered a Rabelaisian critique of contemporary São Paulo high society; Luiz Alfredo García-Roza's *Achados e perdidos,* which found detective Espinosa immersed in contemporary life in Rio de Janeiro, where the city's social extremes were accepted as part of a normal existence; and Carmen L. Oliveira's *Trilhos e quintais,* a fictionalization of the life of Maria Lacerda de Moura (1887–1945), an early Brazilian feminist leader of the 1930s. Among other notable novels were Cristóvão Tezza's *Breve espaço entre cor e sombra* and Betty Milan's *O papagaio e o doutor.* New works of short fiction were published by Rubens Figueiredo and Eric Nepomuceno.

Antônio Cândido, Brazil's most highly regarded literary critic and scholar, was awarded the Camões Prize for his body of work. Poet Moacyr Félix published a biography of publisher Ênio Silveira, who, during the 1960s and '70s, issued works by the most controversial Brazilian and foreign writers despite recurrent harassment by the military regime. Finally, a new biography of film director Glauber Rocha was published by João Carlos Teixeira Gomes.

(IRWIN STERN)

RUSSIAN

The development of Russian literature in 1998 was set against the background of the gradual deterioration of the nation's economy. It was difficult to say exactly how the autumn crisis influenced Russian literature, but the painful effect of sharply increased prices and the bankruptcy of many banks that sponsored literary projects was certainly felt.

Literary life continued, nevertheless. Early in the year, when the economic situation was still relatively stable, several important literary prizes were awarded. Among these were the "anti-Booker" prizes awarded to authors dealing with themes related to the last years of the Soviet period. Recipients included Aleksandr Goldshteyn for his collection of essays, *Rasstavaniye s Nartsissom* ("Parting with Narcissus"), and Timur Kibirov for his latest collection of poems. Kibirov was also awarded the St. Petersburg-based "Northern Palmyra" prize for poetry. Inga Petkevich received the fiction prize for her autobiographical novel *Plach po krasnoy suke* ("Wake for a Red Bitch"), a brutal portrayal of the struggle for existence in Stalinist and post-Stalinist Russia. The prize for literary criticism was awarded to Yefim Etkind for his examination of Russian poetry. In a somewhat different vein, Ivan Zhdanov, a pure lyric poet of the metaphorical school, won the newly created Apollon Grigoryev prize.

Many books reflected two opposing tendencies: the growth of new genres (various types of nonfiction, ironic poetry, and the postmodern novel) and the persistent orientation toward the past. Yevgeny Popov's novella *Podlinaya istoriya "Zelyonykh muzykantov"* ("The True Story of the 'Green Musicians'") belonged to the latter category. The novella comprised a short story Popov wrote in 1976 with an ironic commentary appended. Anatoly Kim, considered by some a magic realist, published a rather traditional novel entitled *Moya zhizn* ("My Life") that described the fate of the Korean minority in Russia. Works that evoked a language and theme more reflective of 1990s Russia included Vladimir Makanin's novel *Andergraund, ili Geroy nashego vremeni* ("Underground, or A Hero of Our Time"), which was about a writer formerly belonging to the Soviet literary underground who commits a murder. Also prominent was the use of the macabre and various levels of reality in order to reveal the new Russia. This included prose from the poet Genrikh Sapgir, *Singapur* ("Singapore") and *Dyadya Volodya* ("Uncle Volodya"), and a posthumous publication from Andrey Sinyavsky, *Koshkin dom* ("Koshkin's House"). Even the hard-core realist Grigory Kanovich used a fantastic premise in his novel *Prodavets snov* ("The Dream Salesman"): A contemporary Lithuanian author earns money in America by selling stories to aged immigrants about their supposedly unchanged birthplaces.

The sheer variety of contemporary Russian literature was visible in the books nominated for the 1998 Russian Booker Prize. These included *Novy sladostny stil* ("The New Sweet Style") by the eminent Vasily Aksyonov; *Svezho predaniye* ("A Fresh Legend") by the nonagenarian author Irina Grekova, who was popular in the 1960s and '70s; Nina Sadur's *Nemets* ("The German"); Vladimir Gubin's *Ilarion i karlik* ("Hilarion and the Dwarf"); and *B.B. i drugiye* ("B.B. and Others") by Anatoly Nayman, a scandalous novel/memoir depicting the life of Russian literary scholars in the 1970s. The winner was Aleksandr Morozov for his novel *Chuzhoye pismo* ("A Foreign Letter").

The more well-known prose writers who published new works included Lyudmila Petrushevskaya (*Priklyucheniya utyuga i sapoga* ["Adventures of an Iron and a Boot"]), Dmitry Bakin (*Sny dereva* ["Dream of a Tree"]), and Dina Rubina (*Angel konvoyny* ["The Escort Angel"]). Viktor Pelevin, the most widely read serious prose writer of the 1990s, released a three-volume collection of works.

The most important single volume of poetry came from Yelena Shvarts, *Solo na raskalyonnoy trube* ("Solo on a Burning Trumpet"), a work marked by powerful human passion and pain. New books from several St. Petersburg poets (Olga Martynova, Nikolay Kononov, Yevgeny Myakishev, and Sergey Zavyalov) testified to their maturity and formal growth. Viktor Krivulin, Sergey Gandlevsky, Sergey Stratanovsky, Svetlana Kekova, Denis Novikov, and Dmitry Vodeynikov also published new works.

Several interesting books of literary criticism and scholarship also appeared, among them competing volumes from Vyacheslav Kuritsyn, the enfant terrible of Russian postmodernism, and the more traditional but no less authoritative Andrey Nemzer. The continuing fascination with the literary underground was evidenced by the publication of the poetry anthology *Samizdat veka* ("Samizdat of the Century") and, in the journal *Znamya,* a forum about unofficial literary activities of the 1960s that included Mikhail Ayzenberg, Boris Groys, and Olga Sedakova. Also memorable was Mikhail Epshteyn's intellectual mystification *Ivan Solovyov. Messianskiye rechi* ("Ivan Solovyov. Messianic Discourses"), a book based on the memoirs and defense of the works of an imaginary philosopher.

The best literary journals—*Znamya, Oktyabr, Druzhba Narodov,* and *Novoye Literaturnoye Obozreniye*—were published in Moscow, while the most prestigious publishers—Inapress, Pushkinsky Fond, Izdatelstvo Ivana Limbusa—were based in St. Petersburg.   (VALERY SHUBINSKY)

EASTERN EUROPEAN

Despite the ravages of war in Kosovo and the economic uncertainty throughout Eastern Europe, a number of excellent works were published in 1998. The death of Polish poet Zbigniew Herbert precipitated a great deal of interest in his poetry. His latest collection, *Epilog burzy* ("Epilogue to a Storm"), focused on his struggle with Parkinson's disease. His contemporary Tadeusz Rózewicz also published *Zawsze fragment* ("Always a Fragment"), in which he attempted to place the finishing touches on his biography and various bothersome fragments. His trademark wit and humour were most evident in the poem *Totentanz—wierszyk barokowy* ("Dance of Death—a Baroque Poem"), dedicated to his confidant, the Polish scholar Czeslaw Hernas. Stanislaw Baranczak continued his hold on the literary market with several new works and his latest collection, *Chirurgiczna precyzja* ("Surgical Precision"). With its emphasis on life's bearable irritations, Baranczak's poetry contrasted with the older poets' preoccupation with death and finality. Michal Głowinski's haunting reminiscences, *Czarne sezony* ("Black Seasons"), touched upon the darker side of man's nature. In a totally different vein, Irena Jurgielewiczowa, best known for her children's books, surprised readers and critics alike with her depiction of Polish society in the 1920s, *Byłam, byliśmy* ("I Was, We Were").

In the Czech Republic Václav Havel maintained his popularity. Celebrity turned statesman, his words carried weight with both intellectuals and the general public. His preface to *The Prague Spring, 1968,* compiled and edited by Jaromír Navrátil, was both authoritative and fair. The book was the first documented account of the Cold War crisis as seen from both sides of the Iron Curtain. Two important works appeared in English translation: *The Poetry of Jaroslav Seifert,* translated by Ewald Osers and edited by George Gibian, and *Karl Čapek: In Pursuit of Truth, Tolerance, and Trust,* by Bohuslava R. Bradbrook. A number of female writers made their mark on the literary scene: Iva Hercíková's *Vášeň* ("Passion"), a love story between two Czech émigrés set in a wealthy American suburb; Hana Belohradská's *Přestaštne manelství* ("A Very Happy Marriage"), a collection of 13 psychological stories based on contemporary life; and Miloslava Holubová's *Necestou cestou* ("Through Thick and Thin"), in which the writer reminisces about the philosopher Jan Patocka.

In Romania censorship continued to be a burning issue. *Censorship in Romania,* edited by Lidia Vianu, was a series of interviews with prominent Romanian literary

figures and a selection of their writings. Other publications included two poetry collections—Mihai Ursachi's *Nebunie di lumina* ("Craziness and Light") and Mircea Cartarescu's *Dublu CD* ("Double CD"). A number of excellent short-story collections were published, including Nicolae Breban's *Ziua di noaptea* ("Day and Night") and Gabriela Melinescu's *Copii radbarii* ("Children of Patience"). The novel form was well represented by Marius Tupan's *Coroana Izabelei* ("Isabela's Crown").

In Slovakia Marian Grupac made an auspicious debut, receiving numerous awards for poetry and short stories. His new collection of poems, *Audna noc v Paríži* ("Wonderful Night in Paris"), solidified his position as a significant presence on the Slovak literary scene.

The turmoil in Kosovo affected all areas of the former Yugoslavia. A number of writers had emigrated from the region, including Mario Suško, who continued to write in the U.S. His latest collection of poems in English translation, *Versus Exsul,* was highly praised. Josip Novakovich's collection of short stories, *Salvation and Other Disasters,* also first appeared in English. One of Croatia's finest writers, Petar Šegedin, died in 1998. His last novel, *Nema spasa od života* ("No Escape from Life"), was well-received by critics.

Bulgaria's vibrant literary and intellectual circle continued to surprise critics and observers. Among the outstanding poetry collections were Ivan Radoev's *Svurzvane* ("Bonding"), Edvin Sugarev's *Haiku ot Kamen Brjag* ("Haiku from Kamen Bryag"), and Binio Ivanov's *Chasut na uchastta* ("The Hour of Destiny"). Several interesting novels appeared, including one by Bulgaria's supreme prose stylist, Yordan Radichkov's *Myure* ("Sitting Duck"). Bulgaria's ambassador to Switzerland, Lea Cohen, published a highly personal novel, *Florida.*

Macedonia's literary scene continued to develop during the year, despite the political and social turmoil among its neighbours. Noteworthy novels included Slavko Janevski's *Cudotvorci* (1988; *Miracle Workers;* 1994), Slobodan Mičković's *Istorija na cmata ljubov* ("History of a Black Love"), and Petre Bakevski's historical novel *Vo senkata na mecot—Aleksandar Makadonski* (1994; *In the Shadow of the Sword—Alexander the Great;* 1996). Macedonia's finest poet, Ante Popovski, was lauded for his newest publication, *Arkanum II* (1996; "Arcanum II").

Slovenia continued to be a bright spot within a corridor of political chaos. A number of works were first published in the U.S., including Drago Jančar's novel *Mocking Desire* and Tomaz Šalamun's selected poems *The Four Questions of Melancholy.* Another Jančar novel, *Zvenenje v glavi* ("Ringing in the Head"), received accolades from Slovenian critics, along with Nina Kokelj's novel *Milovanje* ("Pity"). Two

collections of poetry stood out: Vladimir Kos's *Cvet ki je rekel Nagasaki: izbrane pesmi* ("The World, Which Uttered Nagasaki") and Uroš; Zupan's *Nasledstvo* ("Successor").   (EDWARD J. CZERWINSKI)

JEWISH

Hebrew. The main events in Hebrew literature in 1998 were S. Yizhar's new novel, *Malcomia Yefaifia* ("Lovely Malcomia") and Amos Oz's innovative novel *Ote hayan* ("The Same Sea"). Yizhar, considered one of the best Israeli novelists after S.Y. Agnon, had not published a work of fiction for almost 30 years until the early 1990s, when

©JERRY BAUER

Amos Oz

he began producing a new novel about every two years. Despite his long, self-imposed silence, these new works were of the same high quality as his early work. After a series of disappointing novels Oz surprised his readers with a poetic work whose imagery, rhythm, and occasional rhymes gave renewed force to his familiar themes.

Other notable novels by veteran writers included Yehoshu Kenaz's *Mahzir ahavot kodmot* (1997; "Restoring Former Loves"), Yonat and Alexander Sened's *Bamidbar melon orhim* ("In the Desert a Lodging Place"), Hayim Lapid's *Pesha haktiva* ("The Crime of Writing"), and Etgar Keret's *Hakaitana shel Kneller* ("Kneller's Happy Campers"). Some veteran novelists, however, did not match their previous achievements. Among them were Aharon Megged's *Dudaim min ha'aretz hakdosha* ("Love Flowers from the Holy Land"), David Grossman's *Shetiheyi li sakin* ("Words into Flesh"), Meir Shalev's *Beveito*

bamidbar ("In His Home in the Wilderness"), Savyon Liebrecht's *Ish ve'isha ve'ish* ("A Man, a Woman and a Man"), David Schütz's *Kemo nahal* ("Like a River"), and Yitzhak Laor's *Ve'im ruhi gviati* ("And with My Spirit, My Corpse"). Originality and promise could be found in the first novels of Binjamin Shvili (*Kastoria*) and Ori Rom (*Shemesh shehora* ["A Black Sun"]).

The premier publications in Hebrew poetry were the last two volumes of the collected work of Uri Zvi Greenberg as well as Yehuda Amichai's *Patuah sagur patuah* ("Open, Closed, Open"), Dalia Rabikovitch's *Hatzi sha'a lifnei hamonsoon* ("Half an Hour Before the Monsoon"), Hamutal Bar-Josef's *Halo* ("The No"), and Maya Bejerano's *Anase laga'at betabur bitni* ("Trying to Touch My Belly Button").

Among the works of literary scholarship were Ziva Shamir's study of Bialik stories, *Be'ein alila: sipurei bialik bemagloteihem* ("No Story, No History"), and Hanna Hertsig's examination of current trends in contemporary Israeli fiction, *Hakol ha'omer Ani* ("The Voice Saying I"). Pnina Shirav discussed female representations in the writings of Yehudit Hendel, Amalia Kahana-Carmon, and Ruth Almog in *Ktiva lo tama* ("Noninnocent Writing"), and Nili Levy studied the narrative of Joshua Kenaz in *Mirehov ha'even el ha'hatulim* ("From the Stone Streets to the Cats"). The Israel Prize was awarded to poet Dalia Rabikovitch and novelist Amos Oz.

(AVRAHAM BALABAN)

Yiddish.   Yiddish-language books were published in France, Israel, Japan, Lithuania, Poland, Ukraine, and the United States during 1998. The most prominent genres were poetry and memoirs, but short stories, books for children, and scholarly studies were also popular.

In observance of the 100th anniversary of the birth of poet Peretz Markish, identical collections of his *Yerushe: lider un poemen* ("Legacy: Poems and Verse") were published in Yiddish, Hebrew, and Russian. Rokhl Boymvol's *Treyst un troyer: hundert naye lider* ("Consolation and Grief: One Hundred New Poems") was a deftly crafted ensemble that exemplified her subtlety and lyrical fluency. Aleksander Shpigelblat's *In geiln tsvishn likht fun erev regn: lider* ("In the Yellow Twilight before the Rain: Poems") gathered all of his previously published Yiddish poems and provided translations in six languages.

Three remarkable books of children's verse appeared. Itzik Kipnis's *Yidishe mayselekh: far kleyne un groyse* ("Jewish Tales: For Small and Big") was a visually stunning achievement. Esther Himelstein's *Dos kleyne vekerl* ("The Little Alarm Clock") was a charming, imaginatively illustrated tale. Boris Khays's *Lakhenyu-veynenyu* ("Laughing-Crying") was an entertaining volume intended for Israeli children.

Two impressive collections of short stories were published. Aleksander Lizen's

Nevviim: emese un falshe: roman un balades ("Prophets: True and False: A Novel and Ballads") featured a tragicomic novel and prose ballads that were surrealistic in style, and Tsvi-Hirsh Smoliakov used an original and engrossing prose to chronicle his return to his roots in *Hintergeslekh* ("Back Alleys").

Four critically acclaimed memoirs were set in the former Soviet Union. Yoysef Goldkorn's *Navenad iber di shliakhn fun rusland* ("Wandering over the Roads of Russia") captured in dramatic and painstaking detail the heroism and drudgery of Jewish life under the Soviets; Yente Mash's *Besaraber motivn* ("Bessarabian Motifs") provided an evocative description of the complex universe—under the Nazis and Soviets—that constituted Jewish life in Bessarabia, a region rich in remarkable writers and critics of the 20th century; Avrom Meyerkevitch's memoir, *In di khvalyes fun yene zibn yor: a polet in Ratn Farband* ("In the Waves of Those Seven Years: A Refugee in the Soviet Union"), plunged into the shadows of Siberian exile under Stalin; and Dovid Volpe's *Ikh un mayn velt* ("Me and My World") was a harrowing odyssey that traced the author's experiences from a Lithuanian shtetl through Dachau to Munich.

Issaskhar Fater's *In der velt fun muzik un muzikers: likht un shotn* ("In the World of Music and Musicians: Light and Shadow") was an erudite and smoothly readable assemblage of essays, complete with scholarly apparatus about Jewish and other creators of music, and Moyshe Volf's *Hebreishe un Aramishe verter in yidish* ("Hebrew and Aramic Words in Yiddish") was an extensive and highly useful compendium. (THOMAS E. BIRD)

TURKISH

In the fall of 1998 Turkey celebrated its 75th anniversary, prompting much discussion of the country's literature that had emerged over the years. The major anthologies and critical analyses dealing with those literary works, however, would not appear until 1999. The literary "event" of 1998 was the removal of Istanbul's popular mayor, Recep Tayyip Erdoğan, for reciting part of a poem by Ziya Gökalp and reportedly attempting to incite a riot.

Although many volumes were published, few were impressive. Yashar Kemal's *Salman the Solitary* and Adalet Ağaoğlu's *Curfew,* copyrighted in 1997, were released in 1998. In mid-December Orhan Pamuk's long-awaited novel *Benim Adım Kırmızı* ("Call Me Crimson") made its appearance and was greeted with rave reviews; its first printing of 50,000 copies set a record. Critic Pethi Naci published a study of Kemal's fiction, which was also the topic for a book of critical essays by 10 Turkish and European writers. Naci, whose career spanned nearly half a century, was also named author of the

year. He published several new books, and all of his major works were reissued.

Two notable posthumous works appeared. The first was a biography of Nazım Hikmet by Aziz Nesin, who died in 1995, and the second was the publication of Oğuz Atay's final novel, *Eylembilim* ("Science of Kinetics"), which he had almost completed before his death in 1977.

Best-seller lists were dominated by Ahmet Altan's "late Ottoman novel," *Kılıç yarası gibi* ("Like a Sword Wound"); Ayşe Kulin's biographical work *Adı: Aylin* ("Her Name: Aylin"), which recounted the adventures and death of a Turkish psychiatrist in

ETIENNE GEORGE—SYGMA

Tahar Ben Jelloun

America; and Mina Urgan's *Bir dinozorun anıları* ("Memoirs of a Dinosaur"). Significant volumes of poetry included *Akşam şiirleri* ("Poems of Evening") by Hilmi Yavuz and poetry collections by İlhan Berk, Gülten Akın, Seyfettin Başçıllar, Enver Ercan, Ahmet Özer, and Ahmet Necdet. Notable fictional works were produced by Zeynep Aliye, Hıfzı Topuz, Nazlı Eray, Ahmet Ümit, Celâl Hafifbilek—winner of the Yunus Nadi Award—Leylâ Erbil, Hulki Aktunç, and Aslı Erdoğan. Also notable was Buket Uzuner's fascinating *Şehir romantiğinin günlüğü* ("Diary of an Urban Romantic"). Two prominent short-story writers, Erdal Öz and Orhan Duru, shared the Sait Paik Prize for their new collections. (TALAT S. HALMAN)

PERSIAN

The number of literary works published in Persian, both in Iran and in various Iranian

expatriate communities, increased considerably in 1998. Yet the high expectations generated by the election of Mohammad Khatami to the presidency remained largely unfulfilled. Little meaningful progress was made toward easing the censorship of literature, despite the rerelease of Mahmud Dowlatabadi's multivolume novel *Kelidar,* first published in the 1970s but long censored in the Islamic republic. Although a few other old titles were republished and some new works by certain dissident writers appeared, most of the incremental gains in freedom of expression were offset by the closure of several literary journals.

The year's literary sensation was the popular novel *Shab-i Sarab* ("The Night of the Mirage") by an author writing under the pseudonym Pejvak, meaning "echo." The book's title emphasized the ban on using the word *wine* in titles. As the Persian words *sharab* ("wine") and *sarab* ("mirage") are homographs, the poetic phrase the book echoes speaks of the night of wine-drinking. The story parallels, and responds to, the 1995 novel *Bamdad-e Khomar* ("Morning Hangover"), a cautionary tale of intoxicating youthful love gone sour by age. Hushang Golshiri's novella *Jen-Nameh* ("The Book of the Genie"), published in Europe, was noted as the outstanding work in prose literature.

Baha'eddin Khorramshahi's Persian translation of the Qur'an was also noteworthy. The translation presented Islam's holy book in an artistic prose considered inappropriate for the word of God and therefore absent from previous editions. In literary scholarship the year saw the publication of a complete edition of Hasan Mirabedini's *Sad Sal Dastan-nevisi-ye Iran* ("One Hundred Years of Fiction-Writing in Iran"), a descriptive history of fiction in 20th-century Iran.

Yadollah Roya'i's *Haftad Sang-e Qabr* ("Seventy Tombstones"), published in Cologne, Ger., was praised as the best collection of Persian poems. These innovative poems constituted a gigantic step forward for the poet and perhaps heralded the dawn of a new phase in contemporary Persian poetry. In Afghanistan and Persian-speaking Central Asia continued civil strife did not allow a glimpse into literary production. The death of Sadeq Chubak, a pioneering figure in the Persian fiction of Iran, left a void in the literary circles of the Iranian expatriate community. (AHMNAD KARIMI-HAKKAK)

ARABIC

In 1998 Arabic literature was characterized by two recurring themes: death and revival.

Several works, many reminiscent of the writings of the Jahili poet al-Khansā', eulogized writers and thinkers who were victims of tragic assassinations, especially in Algeria. The analogy to al-Khansā' was reinforced by the fact that many of these writers were women. Assia Djebar, who eulogized assassinated writers in *Le Blanc d'Algérie* (1995; "The Whiteness of Algeria"), produced a collection of short stories and prose, *Oran, langue morte* (1997; "Oran, Language Dead"), that was dedicated to other victims in Algeria. In *Leaving Beirut,* Mayy Ghaşşūb reflected on postwar Lebanon, and in *Baghdad Diaries,* Nuha Radi described the breakdown of society in post-Gulf War Iraq.

Of special importance, owing to the racial conflict between Arabs and Berbers in Algeria, was the publication, in Arabic, of *Al-Amāzīgh (al-Barbar), 'Arab 'aribah* (1996; "The Berber Amazigh, Pure Arabs") by 'Uthmān Sa'dī, a member of the Namamsha tribe, the largest of the Amazigh. In Egypt the complete collections of two journals were published: *Apollo,* which played a major role in promoting poetry in the 20th century, and *Al-Zuhur,* which featured both poetry and prose.

New and familiar writers in Morocco made their mark. 'Abd al-Karīm Ghallāb's latest collection of short stories, *Hādhā al-wajh a'rifuh!* (1997; "I Know This Face!"), probed the theme of social reform. Most prominent among the new Moroccan writers was Aḥmad Tawfīq, who in *Jārāt Abī Mūsā* (1997; "The Neighbours of Abi Musa") posed questions about the limits of authority and the interplay of religion and politics. A second novel, *Shujayrāt ḥinnā' wa-qamar* ("A Henna Shrub and a Moon"), explored the perils of political power.

Writings in French continued to be spearheaded by prolific writer Tahar Ben Jelloun, who published *Le Racisme expliqué à ma fille,* owing to his concern over the suffering immigrant Maghribi workers in France. The book received the first Global Tolerance Award.

Moving in synchrony with the transformation of her society, Palestinian novelist Sahar Khalīfah turned her attention to the inhabitants of the "liberated" territories in *Al-Mīrāth* (1997; "The Inheritance"), which ended on a pessimistic note.

Classical Arabic was the subject of several conferences and books, the most prominent of which was *Lughatunā al-'Arabīyah fī ma'rakat al-ḥaḍārah* (1997; "Our Language in the Battle of Civilization"), edited by Amīn al-'Alim. This feverish activity reflected a preoccupation with the future of classical Arabic in the new world order.

Poetry was the subject of similar concern. It was in that spirit that the Association Bayt ash-Shir ("House of Poetry") organized an international poetry conference that was held in Morocco in September. The occasion was marked by the publication of an anthology, *Dīwān ash-shir al-muaşir* ("The Collection of Contemporary Poetry"), edited by Salāḥ Bou Srīf.

Arab writers living in exile published several noteworthy works. Algerian Mohammed Dib, living in France, published the novel *Si Diable veut,* the theme of which was the impossibility of returning to one's homeland—a subject that was at the centre of most works by the children of North African immigrants. Tunisian Hédi

Bouraoui, living and working in Canada, published *Retour à Thyna* (1996), which featured Tunisian themes and won the prize of the city of Sfax. In *La Pharaonne* he raised the issue of Arab nationalism. Samar Attar, a resident of Sydney, Australia, evoked her native Syria in *The House on Arnus Square,* which she translated into English and published in 1998. Two well-known writers died in 1998: Syrian poet Nizār Qabbānī (*see* OBITUARIES) and Egyptian literary critic Ghālī Shukrī.

(AIDA A. BAMIA)

CHINESE

Chinese literature showed signs of renewed vitality in 1998. Brilliant works appeared one after another throughout the year.

One fervently discussed book was Liu Zhenyun's *Gu xiang mian he hua duo* ("Hometown Noodles and Flower"). The four-volume novel was the lengthiest Chinese literary work published since 1979. One of China's most accomplished young writers, Liu dedicated eight years to writing the novel, which employed a wide array of literary techniques, including stream of consciousness and magic realism, to explore the complexity of human nature as well as the absurdity of human society. In language that was extravagant, boisterous, and richly engaging, Liu unveiled an enigmatic and grotesque plot, in which the past and present were intertwined as modern-day characters encountered souls from ancient times while visiting the "hometown" of the novel. The end result was a remarkable work of literature that gave the creative imagination a free rein.

Wang Jiabing's *Bai nian hai lang* ("The Centennial Sea-Wolf") was an encyclopedic novel that discussed all matters relating to the sea, including maritime history, marine disasters, pirates, tsunamis, and sea gods and spirits. This ambitious undertaking attracted the attention of critics both in China and abroad, many of whom compared the novel to Herman Melville's *Moby Dick* and Ernest Hemingway's *The Old Man and the Sea.*

Another young writer, Zeng Weihao, published *Shi fu* ("Father Murdering"), a novel marked by a free and flowing prose style. Full of preposterous humour and hyperbolic expressions, the book was also philosophical, dealing with the themes of paradise and the fall of humankind from grace. Some critics referred to the novel as "an embodiment of life, death, love, and sorrow."

Veteran writer Cong Weixi published *Zou xiang hundun* ("Toward Chaos") after a decade of work on the novel. The book depicted the suffering of Chinese intellectuals and revealed the folly of those who had believed blindly in the government. A book of poignant soul-searching, *Zou xiang hundun* described the determination of individuals to keep a firm control over their own destiny. The novel was likened by some critics to Aleksandr Solzhenitsyn's *The Gulag Archipelago.*

During the year poet Lu Yuan won the Golden Wreath award at the 37th Struga Poetry Festival in Macedonia, one of the oldest and largest poetry festivals in the world. It was the first time that a Chinese poet had been awarded the honour. The *China Times* newspaper awarded Taiwanese novelist Zhang Guixing its 1998 prize for

best novel for Zhang's *Qun xiang* ("Mass Appearances"). Shi Shuqing's *Guo ke* ("The Passing Traveler"), a historical novel set in Hong Kong, was widely praised by critics and readers alike.

(QIAN ZHONGIVEN)

JAPANESE

In 1998 the Akutagawa Prize, Japan's top literary award for young writers, was shared by Shū Fujisawa, author of *Buenosuairesu gozen reiji* ("At 0 A.M. in Buenos Aires"), and Mangetsu Hanamura, author of *Gerumaniumu no yoru* ("Germanium Nights"). The Naoki Prize, presented to writers of popular fiction, went to Chōkitsu Kurumatani, who published *Akame-shijūyataki shinjūmisui* ("Double Suicides Committed at Forty-Eight Waterfalls in Akame").

Fujisawa's *Buenosuairesu gozen reiji* explored the relationship between a young man who works part-time at a small countryside inn and a senile old woman who was a prostitute after the war. Fujisawa's insightful work was a subtle explorationof feelings of hatred and sympathy and an impressive literary achievement. Hanamura's *Gerumaniumu no yoru* featured a young murderer on the lam who returns to the priory where he grew up. The book's hero was a complex character capable of both violence and self-sacrifice, and Hanamura deftly explored the themes of personal fury and the search for identity. Kurumatani's *Akame-shijūyataki shinjū misui* described double suicides, a familiar topic in contemporary Japanese popular fiction, but Kurumatani managed to bring a fresh perspective and depth of feeling to his story.

In the field of literary criticism, a major controversy was sparked by the work of prominent critic Norihiro Katō. In his 1997 work *Haisengoron* ("Story After the Lost Battle"), Katō examined the prewar, wartime, and postwar periods in Japan through the works and lives of respective Japanese authors. In a work published in 1998, *Sengo wo sengo igo kangaeru* ("Thinking About the Postwar Period After its End"), he declared that the postwar period was over, that enough had been written about the war's effect on Japan, and that it was time for a younger generation of writers to move on to other topics. The literary argument that followed the book's publication pitted those who claimed that the postwar period was not in fact over against those who agreed with Katō; that, with respect to the war, Japan had thoroughly digested its past.

Other literary works included Kiyoko Murata's short story "Shiomaneki" ("A Fiddler Crab"), about a group of old women who make money by faking automobile accidents, which claimed the Yasunari Kawabata Literary Prize. The Tanizaki Jun'ichirō Prize went to Yūko Tsushima's *Hi no yama* ("A Mountain of Fire"), a roman-fleuve set in modern Japan that interwove both dreams and memories. Best-selling works during the year included Hiroyuki Itsuki's essay *Taiga no itteki* ("A Drop in the Great River"), Kōji Suzuki's *Rūpu* ("Loop"), and Tawara Machi's *Midaregami: chokorēto goyaku* ("Disheveled Hair in Chocolate Language Version").

(YOSHIHIKO KAZAMARU)

Mathematics and Physical Sciences

MATHEMATICS

Major mathematical news in 1998 included the claim that a nearly 400-year-old conjecture finally had been proved. In 1611 the German astronomer and mathematician Johannes Kepler concluded that the manner in which grocers commonly stack oranges—in a square-based pyramid with each layer of oranges sitting in a square grid centred above the holes in the layer below—gives the densest way to pack spheres in infinite space. (Packing with oranges in each layer in a hexagonal grid is equally dense.). Thomas Hales of the University of Michigan, after 10 years of work, announced a proof of the conjecture. Nearly every aspect of the proof relied on computer support and verification, and supporting the 250-page written proof were three gigabytes of computer files. Mathematicians would need time to determine if the proof was complete and correct.

Kepler was set on the sphere-packing problem by correspondence with Thomas Harriot, an English mathematician and astronomer and an assistant to Sir Walter Raleigh. Raleigh wanted a quick way to determine the number of cannonballs in a pile with a base of any shape. Harriot prepared tables for Raleigh and wrote to Kepler about the problem in connection with their discussion of atomism. In 1831 the German mathematician Carl Friedrich Gauss showed that face-centred cubic packing, as the orange packing is known to mathematicians, could not be less dense than other lattice packings, those in which the centres of the spheres lie on a regular grid. Some nonlattice packings, however, are almost as efficient, and in some higher dimensions the densest packings known are nonlattice packings. It was thus possible that a denser nonlattice packing might exist for three dimensions.

Hales's work built on that of the Hungarian mathematician Laszlo Fejes-Toth, who in 1953 reduced the task of settling the conjecture to that of solving an enormous calculation. Hales formulated an equation in 150 variables that described every conceivable regular arrangement of spheres. This equation derived from a mathematical decomposition of the star-shaped spaces (decomposition stars) between the spheres. Hales had a computer classify the decomposition stars into 5,000 different types. Although each type required the solving of a separate optimization problem, linear programming methods allowed the 5,000 to be reduced to fewer than 100, which were then done individually by computer. The proof involved the solving of more than 100,000 linear programming problems that each included 100–200 variables and 1,000–2,000 constraints.

The analogue of the Kepler problem in two dimensions is the task of packing circular disks of equal radius as densely as possible. The hexagonal arrangement in which each disk is surrounded by six others—a lattice packing—was shown by Gauss to be the densest packing. For dimensions higher than three, it was not known if the densest lattice packings are the densest packings.

The mathematics of sphere packing is directly related to issues of reliable data transmission, including data compression and error-correcting codes, in such applications as product bar coding, signals from spacecraft, and music encoded on compact discs. Code words can be considered to correspond to points in a space whose dimension is the common length of a code word. The "Hamming distance" (named for pioneer coding theorist Richard Hamming) between any two given words, which can be code words or words to which they can become distorted by errors in transmission, is the number of positions in which the words differ. Around each code-word point, a sphere of radius r includes all words that differ in at most r places from the code word; these words are the distortions of the code word that would be corrected to the code word by the error-correcting process. The error-detecting and error-correcting capabilities of a code depend on how large r can be without spheres of different code words becoming overlapped; in the case of an overlap, one would know that an error had occurred but not to which code word to correct it.

An analogy is the task of packing into a box of fixed size a fixed number of same-size glass ornaments (the total number of code words) wrapped in padding, with the requirement that each ornament be padded as thickly as possible. This, in turn, means that the padded ornaments must be packed as closely as possible. Thus, efficient codes and dense packings of spheres (the padded ornaments) go hand in hand. The longer the code words are, the greater is the dimension of the space and the farther apart code words can be, which makes for greater error-detection and error-correction capability. Longer code words, however, are less efficient to transmit. A longer code word corresponds to using a bigger box to ship the same number of ornaments.

It remained to be seen whether Hales's result or the methods he used would lead to advances in coding theory. Mathematicians generally were skeptical of the value of proofs that relied heavily on computer verification of individual cases without offering new insights into the surrounding mathematical landscape. Nevertheless, Hales's proof, if recognized as correct, could inspire renewed efforts toward a simpler and more insightful proof.

(PAUL J. CAMPBELL)

CHEMISTRY

Physical Chemistry. Hydrogen is the lightest, simplest, and most plentiful chemical element. Under ordinary conditions it behaves as an electrical insulator. Theory predicts that hydrogen will undergo a transition to a metal with superconducting properties if it is subjected to extreme pressures. Until 1998, attempts to create metallic hydrogen in the laboratory had failed. Those efforts included experiments making use of diamond anvil cells that compressed hydrogen to 340 GPa (gigapascals) at room temperature, about 3.4 million times atmospheric pressure. Some theorists predicted that such pressures, which approach those at Earth's centre, should be high enough for the insulator–metal transition to occur.

Robert C. Cauble and associates of the Lawrence Livermore National Laboratory, Livermore, Calif., and the University of British Columbia reported the first experimental evidence for the long-awaited transition. They used a powerful laser beam to compress a sample of deuterium, an isotope of hydrogen, to 300 GPa. The laser simultaneously heated the deuterium to 40,000 K (about 70,000° F). In the experiments the sample began to show signs of becoming a metal at pressures as low as 50 GPa, as indicated by increases in its compressibility and reflectivity. Both characteristics are directly related to a substance's electrical conductivity. Cauble's group chose deuterium because it is easier to compress than hydrogen, but they expected that hydrogen would behave in the same way. Confirmation of the theory would provide new insights into the fundamental nature of matter and also lend support to an idea, proposed by astronomers, that giant gas planets like Saturn and Jupiter have cores composed of metallic hydrogen created under tremendous pressure.

Chemists long had sought methods for glimpsing the intermediate products that form and disappear in a split second as ultrafast chemical reactions proceed. These elusive reaction intermediates can provide important insights for making reactions proceed in a more direct, efficient, or productive fashion. A. Welford Castleman, Jr., and associates of Pennsylvania State University reported development of a new method to "freeze" chemical reactions on a femtosecond (one quadrillionth of a second) time scale. Their technique involved use of a phenomenon termed a Coulomb explosion to arrest a reaction and detect intermediates. A Coulomb explosion occurs when a particle, such as a molecule, has acquired many positive or negative electric charges. The like charges produce tremendous repulsive forces that tear the particle apart. A Coulomb explosion that occurs during a chemical reaction instantly halts the reaction. Fragments left behind provide direct evidence of the intermediates that existed in the split second before the explosion.

Castleman's group used a pulse from a powerful laser to ionize particles, and so trigger a Coulomb explosion, in a reaction involving the dimer of 7-azaindole. (A dimer is a molecule formed of two identical simpler molecules, called monomers.) When the dimer is excited by light energy, protons (hydrogen ions) transfer from one monomer to another in the system, allowing two dimers to combine into a four-monomer molecule, or tautomer. The explosion froze this reaction, which allowed a determination of exactly how the proton transfer occurs.

In the 1980s physicists developed laser and magnetic techniques for trapping individual atoms at ultracold temperatures, which allowed their properties to be studied in detail never before possible. At room temperature the atoms and molecules in air move at speeds of about 4,000 km/h (2,500 mph), which makes observation difficult. Intense chilling, however, slows atomic and molecular motion enough for detailed study. Specially directed laser pulses reduce the motion of atoms, sapping their energy and creating a cooling effect. The slowed atoms then are confined in a magnetic field. Chemists have wondered for years whether laser cooling techniques could be extended to molecules and thus provide an opportunity to trap and study molecular characteristics in greater detail.

John M. Doyle and associates at Harvard University reported a new procedure for

confining atoms and molecules without laser cooling. In their experiments the researchers focused a laser on solid calcium hydride, liberating calcium monohydride molecules. They chilled the molecules with cryogenically cooled helium, reducing their molecular motion, and then confined the molecules in a magnetic trap. The technique could have important implications for chemical science, leading to new insights into molecular interactions and other processes.

Inorganic Chemistry. Gold is somewhat unusual among its neighbours in the periodic table of elements. Whereas the transition metals platinum and palladium, for instance, have become important industrial catalysts, gold has long been regarded to be much less active catalytically. In the past few years, however, researchers reported that gold has extraordinarily high catalytic activity when dispersed as extremely fine particles on supports such as titanium dioxide. In that form gold is active in such processes as low-temperature catalytic combustion, partial oxidation of hydrocarbons, hydrogenation of unsaturated hydrocarbons, and reduction of nitrogen oxides.

During the year D.W. Goodman and associates at Texas A & M University at College Station reported a much-anticipated explanation for this unusual behaviour. They used scanning tunneling microscopy/spectroscopy and other techniques to study small clusters of gold atoms supported on a titanium dioxide surface. Gold's catalytic activity was found to be related to thickness of the layers, with maximum activity for clusters consisting of about 300 atoms. The findings suggested that supported clusters of metal atoms, in general, may have unusual catalytic properties as cluster size becomes smaller.

In past research Mika Pettersson and associates of the University of Helsinki, Fin., had synthesized a number of unusual compounds consisting of an atom of the rare gas xenon (Xe) or krypton (Kr), a hydrogen atom, and an atom or chemical group possessing enough affinity for electrons to allow it to bond with the rare-gas atom. The compounds included HXeH, HXeCl, HXeBr, HXeI, HXeCN, HXeNC, HKrCl, and HKrCN. During the year the chemists added to this list with their report of the synthesis of the first known compound containing a bond between xenon and sulfur (S). The compound, HXeSH, was produced during the low-temperature dissociation of hydrogen sulfide (H_2S) in a xenon matrix with ultraviolet light at specific wavelengths.

Organic and Applied Chemistry. Chemists have synthesized a wide variety of fullerene molecules since 1990, when the soccer-ball-shaped, 60-carbon molecule buckminsterfullerene (C_{60}), the first member of this new family of carbon molecules, was produced in large quantities. All of the fullerene molecules structurally characterized during the period, however, have had a minimum of 60 carbon atoms. Some chemists argued that C_{60} was the smallest fullerene stable enough to be synthesized in bulk quantities. During the year Alex Zettl and colleagues of the University of California, Berkeley, overturned that notion with the synthesis of the "minifullerene" C_{36}. They used the arc-discharge method, in which an electric arc across two graphite electrodes produces large quantities of fullerenes. The bonding in C_{36}, like that in C_{60},

comprises three-dimensional arrangements of hexagons and pentagons, with the minimum possible number of shared pentagon–pentagon bonds.

Nuclear magnetic resonance measurements indicated that the adjacent pentagons are highly strained in the fullerene's tightly bound molecular structure. Theorists speculated that the bond strain is so severe that C_{36} would likely prove to be the smallest fullerene to be made in bulk quantities. The extreme strain may also turn out to enhance the molecule's superconducting properties. Like C_{60}, C_{36} displays increased electrical conductivity when doped with alkali metals. Zettl speculated that C_{36} may prove to be a high-temperature superconductor with a higher transition temperature than that of C_{60}.

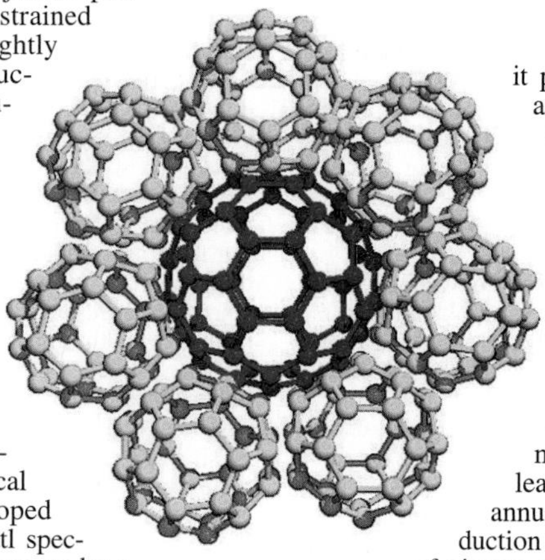

Polyethylene's great versatility makes it the single most popular plastic in the world. Although all polyethylene is made from repeating units of the same building-block molecule, the monomer ethylene, catalysts used in the polymerization process have dramatic effects on the physical properties of the plastic. Mixing ethylene with certain catalysts yields a polymer with long, straight, tough molecular chains termed high-density polyethylene (HDPE). HDPE is used to make plastic bottles, pipes, industrial drums, grocery bags, and other high-strength products. A different catalyst causes ethylene to polymerize into a more flexible but weaker material, low-density polyethylene (LDPE). LDPE is used for beverage-carton coatings, food packaging, cling wrap, trash bags, and other products.

American and British chemists, working independently, reported discovery of a new group of iron- and cobalt-based catalysts for polymerizing ethylene. Experts described the discovery as one of the first fundamentally new advances in the field since the 1970s. The catalysts were as active as the organometallic catalysts called metallocenes in current use for HDPE production—in some instances more active. They also had potential for producing a wider range of polymer materials at lower cost. In addition, the iron-based catalysts were substantially more active than current materials for the production of LDPE. Maurice Brookhart of the University of North Carolina at Chapel Hill headed the U.S. research team. Vernon C. Gibson of Imperial College, London, led the British group.

Adipic acid is the raw material needed for production of nylon, which is used in fabrics, carpets, tire reinforcements, automobile parts, and myriad other products. In the late 1990s about 2.2 million metric tons of adipic acid were produced worldwide each year, which made it one of the most important industrial chemicals. Conventional adipic acid manufacture involves the use of nitric acid to oxidize cyclohexanol or cyclohexanone. Growing interest in environmentally more benign chemical reactions, often called green chemistry, was making the traditional synthesis undesirable because

A computer graphic illustration shows C_{36} "minifullerenes" (yellow), which have fewer carbons than the original C_{60} molecule (blue).

it produces nitrous oxide as a by-product. Nitrous oxide was believed to contribute to depletion of stratospheric ozone and, as a greenhouse gas, to global warming. Despite the adoption of recovery and recycling technology for nitrous oxide, about 400,000 metric tons were released to the atmosphere annually. Adipic acid production accounted for 5–8% of nitrous oxide released into the atmosphere through human activity.

Kazuhiko Sato and associates at Nagoya (Japan) University reported development of a new, "green" synthetic pathway to adipic acid. It eliminated production of nitrous oxide and the use of potentially harmful organic solvents. Their alternative synthesis used 30% hydrogen peroxide to oxidize cyclohexene directly to colorless crystalline adipic acid under solvent- and halide-free conditions. Sato reported that the process was suitable for use on an industrial scale and could be the answer to the worldwide quest for a "green" method of synthesizing adipic acid. The major barrier was cost—hydrogen peroxide was substantially more expensive than nitric acid—but stricter environmental regulations on nitrous oxide emission could make the new synthetic process more attractive.

(MICHAEL WOODS)

PHYSICS

Particle Physics. Researchers in 1998 reported the most convincing evidence to date that the subatomic particle called the neutrino has mass. The standard model, science's central theory of the basic constituents of the universe, involves three families of observable particles: baryons (such as protons and neutrons), leptons (such as electrons and neutrinos), and mesons. Of those particles the neutrino has been the most enigmatic. Its existence was first postulated in 1930 by the Austrian physicist Wolfgang Pauli to explain the fact that energy appeared not to be conserved in nuclear beta decay (the decay of an atomic nucleus with the emission of an electron). Neutrinos interact so weakly with other matter that they are extraordinarily difficult to observe; confirmation of their existence did not come until a quarter century after Pauli's prediction. The assumption that neutrinos are massless particles is built into the standard model, but there is no theoretical reason for them not to have a tiny mass.

Three types of neutrinos were known: electron neutrinos, emitted in beta decay; muon neutrinos, emitted in the decay of a particle known as a pion and first observed in 1962; and tau neutrinos, produced in the

decay of an even more exotic particle, the tau. Although the existence of the tau neutrino had been supported by indirect evidence, it was only during 1998 that the particle was reported to have been observed for the first time. Physicists at the Fermi National Accelerator Laboratory (Fermilab), Batavia, Ill., carried out experiments in which they smashed a dense stream of protons into a tungsten target. Less than one collision in 10,000 produced a tau neutrino, but after months of taking data the Fermilab team claimed to have seen direct effects of at least three of these elusive particles.

That finding was overshadowed, however, by results from Super-Kamiokande, an experimental effort involving an international collaboration of physicists from 23 institutions and headed by the University of Tokyo's Institute for Cosmic Ray Research. The mammoth Super-Kamiokande detector, which was situated 1,000 m (3,300 ft) below the surface in a Japanese zinc mine to minimize the effect of background radiation, comprised a 50,000-ton tank of ultrapure water that was surrounded by 13,000 individual detector elements. Super-Kamiokande was able to observe electron neutrinos and muon neutrinos (but not tau neutrinos) that are produced continually in Earth's atmosphere by cosmic ray bombardment from space. Even that huge detector, however, was able to detect only one or two

The inner wall of the giant Super-Kamiokande detector, located 1,000 m (3,000 ft) beneath the Japanese Alps near Kamioka, is pictured below. The detector accumulated statistics on cosmic-ray-produced electron and muon neutrinos.

such neutrinos per day and required months of operation for researchers to accumulate sufficient data.

In 1998 Super-Kamiokande physicists reported a dramatic result. Whereas they found the rate of detection of electron neutrinos to be the same in all directions, they detected significantly fewer muon neutrinos coming upward through Earth than coming directly downward. Theory predicts that, if neutrinos have mass, muon neutrinos should transform, or oscillate, into tau neutrinos with a period depending on the mass difference between the two types. Those neutrinos traveling the longer distance through Earth to the detector had more time to decay. Results suggested a mass difference equal to one ten-millionth of the mass of the electron, giving positive evidence of the existence of neutrino mass and a lower bound for its value.

The result had two exciting consequences. First, because a nonzero mass for the neutrino is a phenomenon lying beyond the framework of the standard model, it may be the first glimpse of a possible new "grand unified" theory of particle physics that transcends the limitations of the current theory. Second, neutrinos with mass may be a solution to a major problem in cosmology. Present models of the universe require it to have a mass far in excess of the total mass of observable constituents. The presence in the cosmos of a total mass of billions of neutrinos may make up this deficit.

Solid-State Physics. In 1998 investigations of the physics of systems using single atoms and small numbers of electrons were making possible electronic devices that had been inconceivable just a few years earlier. These studies were being aided by the development of methods to manipulate single atoms or molecules with unprecedented precision and investigate their properties. In one example Elke Scheer and co-workers of the University of Karlsruhe, Ger., measured the electrical properties of a single atom forming a bridge across two conducting leads. Their achievement suggested the possibility of making even smaller, faster electronic switching devices.

Physicists from Yale University and Chalmers University of Technology, Göteborg, Swed., produced a variant of the field-effect transistor (FET)—a basic building block of modern computer systems—called a single-electron transistor (SET). In a FET a flow of electrons through a semiconducting channel is switched on and off by a voltage in a nearby "gate" electrode. In a SET the semiconducting channel is replaced by

an insulator, except for a tiny island of semiconductor halfway along the channel. In the device's conducting mode a stream of electrons crosses the insulator by "hopping" one at a time on and off the island. Such devices were highly sensitive to switching voltages and extremely fast.

The SET achievement was an example of the developing physics of quantum dots, "droplets" of electric charge that can be produced and confined in semiconductors. Such droplets, having sizes measured in nanometres (billionths of a metre), can contain electrons ranging in number from a single particle to a tailored system of several thousands. Physicists from Delft (Neth.) University of Technology, Stanford University, and Nippon Telegraph and Telephone in Japan used quantum dots to observe many quantum phenomena seen in real atoms and nuclei, from atomic energy level structures to quantum chaos. A typical quantum dot is produced in a piece of semiconductor a few hundred nanometres in diameter and 10 nanometres thick. The semiconductor is sandwiched between nonconducting barrier layers, which separate it from conductors above and below. In a process called quantum tunneling, electrons can pass through the barrier layers and enter and leave the semiconductor, forming the dot. Application of a voltage to a gate electrode around the semiconductor allows the number of electrons in the dot to be changed from none to as many as several hundred. By starting with one electron and adding one at a time, researchers can build up a "periodic table" of electron structures.

Such developments were giving physicists the ability to construct synthetic structures at atomic-scale levels to produce revolutionary new electronic components. At the same time, research was being conducted to identify the atoms or molecules that give the most promising results. Delft physicist Sander J. Tans and co-workers, for example, constructed a FET made of a single large molecule—a carbon nanotube—*i.e.,* a hollow nanometre-scale tubule of bonded carbon atoms. Unlike other nanoscale devices, the FET worked at room temperature. Future generations of electronics could well be based on carbon rather than silicon.

Condensed-Matter Physics. Whereas the properties of ordinary condensed gases were long familiar to physicists, quantum mechanics predicted the possibility of one type of condensate having dramatically different properties. Most condensed gases consist of a collection of atoms in different quantum states. If, however, it were possible to prepare a condensate in which all the atoms were in the same quantum state, the collection would behave as a single macroscopic quantum entity with properties identical to those of a single atom. This form of matter was dubbed a Bose-Einstein condensate after the physicists—Einstein and the Indian physicist Satyendra Bose—who originally envisaged its possibility in the early 20th century. There was no theoretical difficulty about producing such a condensate, but the practical difficulties were enormous, since it was necessary to cool a dilute gas near absolute zero (−273.15° C, or −459.67° F) in order to remove practically all its kinetic energy without causing it to condense into an ordinary liquid or solid.

Bose-Einstein condensates were first produced in 1995, but the condensate's atoms were trapped in a magnetic "bottle," which

An Athena II rocket carrying NASA's Lunar Prospector spacecraft lifts off (below) at Cape Canaveral, Fla., on January 6 and turns toward the Moon (right). The spacecraft, designed to provide NASA with the first global maps of the Moon's surface, entered lunar orbit on January 11.

PAUL KIZZLE—AP/WIDE WORLD

NASA

had a distorting effect. The removal of such distortions was made possible by the development of laser cooling devices in which kinetic energy is "sucked away" from the atoms into the laser field. Using such a device, physicists at the Massachusetts Institute of Technology succeeded in 1998 in producing a condensate of 100 million hydrogen atoms at a temperature of 40 millionths of a degree above absolute zero. Such a condensate exhibited macroscopic quantum effects like those seen in superfluids, and the interactions between individual atoms could be "tuned" by means of a magnetic field.

General Relativity. Although Einstein's general theory of relativity is generally accepted, physicists have suggested other possible theories of gravitation. Two observations gave results in confirmation of predictions made by Einstein. One was the result of an experiment using two Lageos laser-ranging satellites and carried out by physicists from the University of Rome, the Laboratory of Spatial Astrophysics and Fundamental Physics, Madrid, and the University of Maryland. It investigated the Lense-Thirring effect, which predicts that time as measured by a clock traveling in orbit around a spinning object will vary, depending on whether the orbit is in the direction of the spin or against it. The parameter that measures the strength of the effect was found to have a value of 1.1 ± 0.2, compared with general relativity's prediction of 1.

A second, more dramatic prediction of general relativity was observed by a team of astronomers from the U.S., the U.K., France, and The Netherlands. According to the theory, in the same way that light can be focused by a glass lens, light from a distant luminous object can be focused by the distortion of space by a massive foreground object such as a galaxy—a phenomenon called gravitational lensing. In a special case, called an Einstein ring, the image of the light source will smear out into the shape of a perfect ring around the foreground object. Using three radio telescopes, the group zeroed in on a possible Einstein ring, after which an infrared camera on the Earth-orbiting Hubble Space Telescope imaged to reveal the complete ring—the first unambiguous case in optical and infrared light and a dazzling demonstration of Einstein's theory.   (DAVID G.C. JONES)

ASTRONOMY

The year 1998 brought new discoveries about astronomical objects as close as the Moon and as far away as the most distant galaxies ever detected. More planets were detected orbiting other stars, and the total number found to date reached an even dozen. Powerful bursts of gamma rays were recorded from stars within the Milky Way Galaxy and from the remotest regions of space. The universe itself appeared to be accelerating in its rate of expansion, contrary to a requirement of the most widely held theoretical model of the cosmos.

Solar System. Perhaps the most electrifying astronomical announcement of the year was a prediction of a close encounter of an asteroid with Earth. In early March Brian Marsden of the Harvard-Smithsonian Center for Astrophysics, Cambridge, Mass., and director of the International Astronomical Union's Central Bureau for Astronomical Telegrams announced his calculations that a 1.6-km (one-mile)-wide asteroid, 1997 XF11, discovered the previous December, would pass within 48,000 km (30,000 mi) of Earth on Oct. 26, 2028. This would be the closest known approach of a body of such size since the asteroid that was

thought to have hit Earth 65 million years ago. The announcement made a powerful impression on the media, since it coincided with prerelease publicity for two major Hollywood movies, *Deep Impact* and *Armageddon,* both of which explored the consequences of the collision of a large body with modern Earth. Shortly after the original announcement, however, new orbital calculations based on 1990 "prediscovery" images of 1997 XF_{11} showed that Earth was not in imminent danger of a collision, with the asteroid expected to pass about 970,000 km (600,000 mi) from Earth.

Although humans had first walked on the Moon nearly 30 years earlier, many unanswered questions remained in 1998 concerning the origin and evolution of Earth's nearest neighbour. In January NASA launched Lunar Prospector, a small orbiter that carried a bevy of instruments to measure lunar gravity, magnetism, and surface chemical composition. In March William C. Feldman of Los Alamos (N.M.) National Laboratory and his collaborators announced that the craft had detected evidence of large quantities of water lying in the sunless craters of the lunar polar regions. The water was believed to have been carried to the Moon by comet bombardments in past aeons and to have survived only because the polar craters are in permanent shadow and cold. This resource would prove to be a great resource to any future human presence on the Moon.

Ever since Galileo Galilei first saw the rings of Saturn in the early 1600s, scientists and public alike had been fascinated by these beautiful astronomical apparitions. Beginning in the late 1970s, ring systems were discovered around the other giant gas planets in the solar system—first Uranus and then Jupiter and Neptune. The rings of Jupiter, first seen in photographs returned by the two Voyager spacecraft, are quite thin. The outermost one was shown by the Jupiter-orbiting Galileo spacecraft in 1998 to comprise two rings, dubbed gossamer rings. All of Jupiter's rings consist of very fine dust, a kind of reddish soot. Because of radiation from the Sun, these small particles should be dragged into Jupiter in a time that

is short compared with the age of the solar system. How then have the rings survived? The Galileo craft sent back data providing a likely answer: the dust is replenished with new material kicked off four of Jupiter's tiny inner moons by the continuing impacts of interplanetary meteoroids.

Stars. Since 1992, astronomers had been detecting the presence of planets around nearby stars by finding small periodic variations in the speeds of these stars caused by the gravitational tugs of their unseen planetary companions. By the end of 1998, the discovery of 12 planets around other stars had been reported, which made the number of known extrasolar planets greater than the number of planets within the solar system. In all cases the planets are very close to their parent stars, and most have masses measured to be several times that of Jupiter. These two factors combined to produce the relatively large tugs on the parent stars that made the gravitational effects of the planets detectable.

One of the planets detected during the year orbits the low-mass star Gliese 876, which at a distance of 15 light-years is one of the Sun's nearest neighbours. Geoffrey W. Marcy of San Francisco State University and his collaborators reported that the planet has a 61-day orbital period, placing it closer to Gliese 876 than Mercury is to the Sun. In spite of this proximity, the surface temperature of the planet is an estimated −75° C (−135° F). Calculations suggested that water might exist beneath the planet's surface in the form of liquid drops, one of the necessary conditions for life as it is known on Earth. In a second finding Susan Terebey of Extrasolar Research Corp., Pasadena, Calif., and her collaborators reported the first image of a possible extrasolar planet. Using the Hubble Space Telescope's Near Infrared Camera and Multi-Object Spectrometer, they detected a dim object in the constellation Taurus, about 450 light-years from Earth. Designated TMR-1C, the object appeared to be connected to two young stars by a gaseous bridge. At year's end its interpretation as a planet ejected by one of the stars was still being hotly debated.

Since the early 1970s sudden bursts of celestial gamma rays had been detected by instruments aboard Earth-orbiting and interplanetary spacecraft. Without seeing obvious optical counterparts, however, astronomers had found it difficult to say with certainty where the bursts were coming from. In 1997, following the discovery of X-ray and optical counterparts for several of the events, it was at last possible to argue convincingly that most of the gamma-ray burst events come from cosmological distances rather than from within or near the Milky Way Galaxy. Nevertheless, some events, called soft gamma-ray repeaters, were known to be associated with objects within the galaxy.

On August 27 a tremendous burst of gamma rays and X-rays lasting about five minutes pelted Earth. It was so powerful that it produced noticeable ionization in the Earth's upper atmosphere, comparable to that produced by the Sun in the daytime. The X-rays were found to vary with a 5.16-second period, exactly the same as that of an active X-ray source, SGR 1900+14, lying within the galaxy some 20,000 light-years from Earth in the constellation Aquila.

Such X-ray sources were thought to be rotating, magnetized neutron stars, and it was suggested that events like the August 27 burst are caused by a "glitch," or starquake, on a neutron star with an extraordinarily high magnetic field, possibly a million billion times larger than that of Earth. Such stellar objects were dubbed magnetars. According to one idea, the magnetar's enormous magnetic field occasionally cracks open the crust of the star, which leads in some way to the production of energetic charged particles and gamma rays.

Galaxies and Cosmology. More than 2,000 celestial bursts of gamma rays, each typically lasting some tens of seconds, had been detected by late 1998. On Dec. 14, 1997, one such burst, designated GRB 971214, was accompanied by an X-ray afterglow observed by the Italian-Dutch BeppoSAX satellite, which led to the subsequent observation of a visible afterglow. In early 1998 S. George Djorgovski of the California Institute of Technology and his colleagues, using the giant Keck II Telescope in Hawaii, were able to identify the host galaxy and found that it lies at a distance of about 12 billion light-years. The burst in the gamma-ray portion of the spectrum alone represented roughly 100 times the total energy of a typical supernova explosion, comparable to all of the energy radiated by a typical galaxy in several centuries. The most widely held theory of gamma-ray bursts—that they arise from the merger of two neutron stars—was called into question for being unable to generate sufficient energy to explain the event. Alternatively it was proposed that GRB 971214 was the result of a "hypernova," a kind of super-supernova, or that it was produced by a rotating black hole.

Astronomers continued scanning the skies for ever more distant galaxies. Their goal was not to add new entries to some

Earth Perihelion and Aphelion, 1999

Jan. 3	Perihelion, 147,096,800 km (91,404,200 mi) from the Sun
July 6	Aphelion, 152,098,500 km (94,509,500 mi) from the Sun

Equinoxes and Solstices, 1999

March 21	Vernal equinox, 01:46[1]
June 21	Summer solstice, 19:49[1]
Sept. 23	Autumnal equinox, 11:31[1]
Dec. 22	Winter solstice, 07:44[1]

Eclipses, 1999

Jan. 31	Moon, penumbral (begins 14:04[1]), the beginning visible in eastern Asia, Australia, New Zealand, the western United States; the end visible in Africa (excluding northwestern coast), Australia, western Alaska.
Feb. 16	Sun, annular (begins 03:52[1]), the beginning visible in southern Atlantic Ocean (southwest of South Africa); the end visible in the southern Pacific Ocean (northwest of Australia and southeast of Papua New Guinea).
July 28	Moon, partial (begins 08:56[1]), the beginning visible along the northeastern coast of Asia, Japan, Australia, New Zealand, North America (excluding the northeastern part), Central America, western South America; the end visible in eastern Asia, Australia, New Zealand, extreme western North America.
Aug. 11	Sun, total (begins 08:26[1]), the beginning visible in the northern Atlantic (south of Nova Scotia, Canada); the end visible in the Bay of Bengal (near Calcutta, India).

[1]Universal time.
Source: *The Astronomical Almanac for the Year 1999* (1998).

"Guinness Book of Cosmic Records" but to determine how long after the big bang the first galaxies formed and how they evolved at that time. The farther out one looks in space, the earlier one is seeing back in time. Because of the expansion of the universe, the more distant a galaxy, the faster it is receding from Earth. The red shift of a galaxy, or shift in the wavelength of its light toward the red end of the spectrum, is the measure of its recession velocity and therefore its distance. In 1997 a galaxy with a red shift of 4.92 was found, the most distant object reported at the time. In 1998 the record fell several times. In March a galaxy with a red shift of 5.34 was reported by Arjun Dey of Johns Hopkins University, Baltimore, Md., and colleagues. In May a group headed by R.G. McMahon of the University of Cambridge extended the record to 5.64, and in November the same group reported studies of another distant galaxy, this one with a red shift of 5.74. It formed when the universe was only 7% of its present age. The object appeared to be creating new stars at a rate of about 10 per year at that time.

Studies of objects with high red shifts were also the key to understanding the ultimate fate of the universe as a whole. In the 1920s astronomers began measuring the distances and velocities of galaxies, and in 1929 the American astronomer Edwin Hubble announced the discovery of a simple linear relationship between a galaxy's distance and its recession velocity. The relationship had been predicted (and even observed) earlier based on the idea that the universe had come into being in a violent explosion, leading to the expansion of space and the resultant recession of galaxies from one another. The future fate of the expansion depends on the competition between the initial expansion rate and the gravitational pull of the matter filling space, which should lead to a deceleration of the expansion. Whether the universe will expand forever or ultimately collapse depends on whether the mass density of the universe is greater or less than a critical value.

For decades astronomers had attempted to measure the expansion rate (called the Hubble constant) and the mean density of the universe (or, equivalently, its deceleration rate). In 1998 two teams of astronomers independently announced new results for those parameters. As their distance indicators, both teams used Type Ia supernovas, extremely bright exploding stars thought to have nearly identical intrinsic peak brightnesses, which makes them useful in comparing the distances to various galaxies. The Supernova Cosmology Project, headed by Saul Perlmutter of the Lawrence Berkeley National Laboratory in California, reported on measurements of the apparent brightnesses and red shifts of 42 Type Ia supernovas. The rival High-Z Supernova Search Team, headed by Brian Schmidt of the Mount Stromlo and Siding Spring Observatories in Australia, based their conclusions on a study of 16 Type Ia supernovas. Both teams came up with an astonishing result; not only is the rate of expansion of the universe not decelerating, but it also appears to be accelerating slightly.

The version of cosmology favoured by many theoretical physicists, the so-called inflationary big-bang universe, required in its simplest form that the universe have a rather

high mass density and that its expansion rate be slowing. An idea originally proposed by Albert Einstein in 1917, however, could account for the new observations. Having been told by observational astronomers at that time that the universe is static, Einstein reluctantly introduced a "cosmological constant," a kind of universal sea of repulsive mass and energy, into his general theory of relativity to counteract the attraction of gravity. After the discovery of the expansion of the universe, Einstein referred to the addition of this constant as his "greatest blunder." Nevertheless, if a new repulsive force turned out to exist, Einstein could be proved once again to have been the most prescient scientist of the 20th century.

(KENNETH BRECHER)

SPACE EXPLORATION

In sharp contrast to the previous year, Russia's orbiting space station *Mir* had a quiet 1998, whereas efforts to assemble the International Space Station (ISS) began under a cloud of management and budget problems. Exploration of the planets and Sun continued with new probes. The world also mourned the death of U.S. astronaut Alan Shepard, Jr. (*see* OBITUARIES), on July 21. Shepard was the first American in space (1961) and, as commander of Apollo 14 (1971), the fifth human to walk on the Moon.

Manned Spaceflight. The most watched space mission of the year was that of the space shuttle *Discovery* (STS-95, October 29–November 7), whose crew included U.S. Sen. John Glenn in a controversial decision by NASA. Glenn, who in 1962 was the first American to orbit Earth, had campaigned for a seat on a shuttle mission. (The *Discovery* flight was only Glenn's second trip into space; space-program observers generally believed that he had not been allowed to fly again in the 1960s out of concern that a national hero be put at undue risk.) NASA officials asserted that Glenn's presence on the shuttle mission would contribute to research on the aging process—Glenn was 77 at the time—but critics contended that the benefits would be minimal and that comparable data could be obtained from astronauts whom NASA was removing from flight status because they were almost as old as Glenn. The primary mission of STS-95 was to carry the Spacehab module, which contained an array of materials-sciences and life-sciences experiments.

The shuttle *Columbia* flew the last Spacelab mission, called Neurolab, during the year (STS-90, April 17–May 3). Spacelab, a reusable laboratory module, had been developed by the European Space Agency (ESA) as its first foray into manned spaceflight. The Neurolab mission performed a range of experiments on the way that nervous systems react and adapt to the effects of space travel. In addition to the human crew members, the experimental subjects included mice and rats (some pregnant), swordtail fish, snails, crickets, and cricket eggs. The results of the mission could have applications to neurological disorders such as Parkinson's disease.

Two shuttle missions concluded U.S. activities aboard *Mir. Endeavour* (STS-89, January 22–31) made the eighth shuttle docking with the Russian space station, and *Discovery* (STS-91, June 2–12) made the

ninth and last one. *Endeavour* replaced a U.S. astronaut who had been aboard *Mir* since the previous shuttle visit and carried experiments in protein crystal growth (for pharmaceutical studies) and low-stress soil mechanics (to understand how soil behaves when it liquefies during earthquakes). *Discovery* retrieved the American astronaut and delivered more supplies to the Russian crew staying aboard *Mir*. The shuttle crew also conducted microgravity-science and cosmic-ray experiments.

Operations aboard *Mir* included several space walks by the crew to repair the facility. Russia launched two manned spacecraft to *Mir*, Soyuz TM-27 on January 29 and TM-28 on August 13. Soyuz TM-26 (launched in 1997) returned to Earth on February 19 carrying two cosmonauts who had been aboard *Mir* since 1997 and a third who had launched with TM-27. A similar pattern was followed when TM-27 returned with three cosmonauts on August 25. One more manned launch to *Mir*, Soyuz TM-28 in February 1999, was scheduled to wrap up experiments and start shutting the systems down.

Assembly of the long-delayed and trouble-plagued ISS started on November 20 with the launch by Russia of the station's first element, Zarya ("Dawn," formerly called the FGB module), into an initial 350 × 185-km (220 × 115-mi) elliptical orbit and inclined 51.6° to the Equator. Engine firings over the next few days circularized the orbit and raised it to about 385 km (240 mi). Zarya was an unpiloted space "tugboat" providing early propulsion, steering, and communications for the station's first months in orbit. Eventually ISS was to comprise dozens of major elements, including pressure modules containing living and working spaces for a permanent crew of

(Below) Former U.S. senator John Glenn (centre), who in 1962 became the first American to orbit Earth, heads toward the launch pad with his fellow astronauts in late October for his return trip to space. (Inset) In a 1962 photograph Glenn poses while training for his first historic flight.

The Russian-built Zarya and U.S.-built Unity modules fly connected to one another after their release from the cargo bay of the *Endeavour* space shuttle in December. More joint space efforts between Russia and the U.S. were planned for 1999.

six persons and an open-latticework truss 108.6 m (356.4 ft) long supporting eight massive solar arrays for electrical power.

Zarya, which was built by Russia from the never-launched *Mir 2* station, was counted as a U.S. launch because NASA paid $240 million for it. The module would provide some working space, altitude control, power, and other services while the U.S. and its major partners—Russia, ESA, Canada, and Japan—developed and attached additional elements.

On December 4 *Endeavour* (STS-88) carried the second ISS element into orbit; this was the first connecting node, a U.S.-built element called Unity. After *Endeavour* rendezvoused with Zarya, astronauts grappled the Russian element with the shuttle's robot

Both the Earth (left) and the Moon appear as crescents in this image taken by Japan's Nozomi spacecraft, which made two flybys of the Moon during the year. Nozomi was set to orbit Mars in 1999.

arm. They then joined it with Unity and completed various connections inside and outside the nascent ISS core. Barring setbacks in space or on Earth, a series of U.S. shuttle and Russian rocket launches in 1999 would continue carrying up additional elements and equipment and assembly crews.

The program remained hobbled by a number of technical delays, mostly on the Russian side. U.S. officials claimed that Russia was not properly funding its commitments, and NASA was asked to bail out the Russian program with additional funds. In October NASA bought Russia's share of the research time aboard the station to provide a $60 million transfusion.

A potential stumbling block was the Service Module, a Russian element rescheduled for launch in March 1999. In addition to its function as an early station living quarters, it carried rocket engines and propellants to restore the altitude that the station would steadily lose to atmospheric drag. In 1998 Russia was so far behind in the development of the module that NASA started preliminary plans for a backup Interim Control Module derived from a classified U.S. Navy satellite. Assuming that one or the other country kept the program on schedule, the first permanent three-person crew would be taken to the ISS by a Soyuz launch in the summer of 1999. As with *Mir* missions, the Soyuz was to stay attached as a lifeboat. By late 1999 attachment of the U.S. Laboratory Module would allow limited science research to start.

Space Probes. While scientists continued to absorb the data from the successful Mars Pathfinder mission of 1997, other efforts to explore the red planet continued, and NASA sent its first probe to the Moon since Apollo 17 in 1972.

Mars Global Surveyor, which had achieved an initial elliptical orbit around Mars in September 1997, continued to work its way into a mapping orbit during the year, although progress was slowed by an incompletely locked solar array and other equipment problems. Scientists expected the satellite to be in its final mapping orbit by early 1999.

With its July 4 launch of Nozomi ("Hope") from Kagoshima Launch Center, Japan became only the third nation (after Russia and the U.S.) to reach for Mars. Nozomi made two flybys of the Moon in September and December to reshape its trajectory for arrival in a highly elliptical Mars orbit in October 1999. Unfortunately, the second maneuver was off target, and Japan had to alter the spacecraft's trajectory for a 2003 arrival. Nozomi's mission was to measure the interaction between the solar wind and Martian upper atmosphere.

Of NASA's two new Mars missions, the Mars Climate Orbiter was launched on December 11 for a September 1999 arrival, whereas the Mars Polar Lander was expected to launch on Jan. 3, 1999, and land in the south polar region the following December. During its descent the lander would release two microprobes designed to penetrate the surface and send back data about internal conditions.

NASA's Lunar Prospector was launched on January 6 by an Athena II vehicle. It entered lunar orbit on January 11 and achieved its final mapping orbit, 100 km (60 mi) high, four days later. It was equipped with a variety of radiation- and particle-measuring equipment to assay the chemistry of the lunar surface. Its major find, announced in March, was strong evidence for the presence of water in the Moon's south polar region—specifically, subsurface ice in areas protected from sunlight. If borne out by later low-level observations, the find would represent a major resource for future interplanetary missions. The water could be electrolyzed into oxygen (valuable as a rocket oxidizer and for crew air) and hydrogen (valuable as a rocket fuel).

The Jupiter-orbiting Galileo spacecraft, which had completed its primary mission to the giant gas planet in December 1997, started an extended mission of flybys of Jupiter's moon Europa. Earlier Galileo observations had hinted at the presence of an ocean of liquid water—and thus possibly conditions conducive to life—beneath Europa's icy surface. The Cassini mission to put a spacecraft in orbit around Saturn and

drop a probe into the atmosphere of Saturn's moon Titan continued smoothly after the craft's October 1997 launch. It flew past Venus for a gravity assist in April and was set to do the same with Earth in August 1999.

The Near Earth Asteroid Rendezvous (NEAR) mission approached its goal following a January flyby of Earth that reshaped its trajectory toward the asteroid Eros. On Jan. 10, 1999, NEAR was to go into an orbit around Eros that controllers on Earth would then reshape into a variable one for optimal observations of the irregularly shaped body. A crucial midcourse correction burn was missed in December, however, and the rendezvous was postponed a year.

The Deep Space 1 probe, launched on October 24, was designed to test a dozen new space technologies, including a low-thrust, high-efficiency ion engine, autonomous navigation, and superminiature cameras and electronics. Part of its mission—flybys of an asteroid and a comet—was threatened when the ion engine temporarily shut down unexpectedly November 11 only minutes after it was powered up for a test. Engineers soon determined the problem—apparently a common self-contamination effect—and started long-duration burns on November 24.

In June NASA formed an Astrobiology Institute to investigate the possibilities of life beyond Earth. The institute was to study the extreme conditions under which life exists on Earth and compare them with conditions on Mars, ice-covered Europa, methane-shrouded Titan, and even asteroids and meteors. It would also be concerned with planetary protection methods to ensure that alien life was not accidentally released on Earth.

Unmanned Satellites. Solar astronomy was given a powerful new tool with the launch on April 1 of the Transition Region and Coronal Explorer (TRACE) to study the mysterious region of the solar atmosphere where temperatures soar from 5,000 K (8,500° F) near the visible surface to about 10,000,000 K (18,000,000° F) higher in the corona. TRACE carried an extreme-ultraviolet telescope to monitor the plasma trapped by thin bundles of twisted magnetic force lines, which were presumed to contribute to coronal heating. TRACE soon provided a dazzling series of images of the transition region and corona.

The field of solar studies was dealt a major, though temporary, blow on June 25 when contact was lost with the Solar and Heliospheric Observatory (SOHO), positioned in a "halo" orbit around L-1, a gravitational balance point between Earth and the Sun about 1.5 million km (930,000 mi) away from Earth. Contact was reestablished in September, and by mid-October scientists were reactivating the science instruments.

The last spacecraft in the International Solar-Terrestrial Physics campaign was launched on Dec. 2, 1997, when Germany's Equator S spacecraft went into an equatorial orbit within the ring current of the Van Allen radiation belt. There was a complete data transmission failure in May 1998. The Advanced Composition Explorer, launched in 1997, reached its station in the L-1 halo orbit, where it was to sample the makeup of the solar wind before it struck the Earth's magnetosphere.

A new chapter in space studies opened with the February 25 launch of the Student Nitric Oxide Explorer, the first of three NASA-funded, student-built and student-operated satellites. The mini-satellite carried instrumentation built at the University of Colorado to measure how solar X-rays and auroral activity affect nitric oxide (a stratospheric-ozone–destroying gas) in the upper atmosphere. France launched the SPOT 4 remote-sensing and reconnaissance satellite on March 24. SPOT 4 carried instruments that could monitor vegetation at a one-kilometre (0.6-mi) resolution and other cameras that provided images at 10–20-m (33–66-ft) resolution.

Launch Vehicles. In October the U.S. Congress passed the Commercial Space Act to allow the Federal Aviation Administration to license firms to fly vehicles back from space. Since the 1980s private firms had been able to acquire licenses for commercial space launches, but until recently the return trip had been too expensive for any but government agencies. The Space Act also required the federal government to foster a stable business environment for space development.

NASA's X-33 moved ahead with testing of its rocket engines and heat shield and assembly of its first flight hardware. The X-33 was a subscale demonstrator of Lockheed Martin's proposed VentureStar Reusable Launch Vehicle (RLV) that would ascend from ground to orbit as a single unit and then fly back to Earth. No boosters or tanks would be shed along the way. One of the innovative elements of the X-33 was its linear aerospike engine, which comprised two lines of burners firing along a wedge between them. The outer "wall" of the engine was formed by shock waves from the vehicle's high-speed flight. A 2.8-second firing in October at NASA's Stennis Space Center, Bay St. Louis, Miss., initiated tests that would lead to full-scale testing of the engines.

NASA also moved to ensure complete testing of the X-34, a smaller RLV that was to be air-launched from a Lockheed L-1011 jetliner. NASA was buying parts to make a second vehicle in case the first was seriously damaged. The X-34 was a single-engine winged rocket, 17.8 m (58.4 ft) long and spanning 8.5 m (27.9 ft). It would fly as fast as eight times the speed of sound and reach altitudes as high as 76 km (250,000 ft) to demonstrate various RLV concepts, including low-cost reusability, autonomous landing, subsonic flights through inclement weather, safe abort conditions, and landing in strong crosswinds.

Several launches failed during the year, including the first attempt by amateurs to launch a satellite by "rockoon"—a rocket carried to high altitude by a balloon. It also was the first attempt by amateurs to launch a satellite. More spectacular failures came with the losses in August of a Titan 4 carrying a classified spy satellite and a Delta III launcher, on its first flight, carrying a Galaxy X communications satellite. A novel style of launch succeeded on July 7 when Russia orbited Germany's Tubsat-N and Tubsat-N1 remote-sensing microsatellites atop a submarine-launched ballistic missile. Russia hoped to market launch services using missile submarines that it otherwise could not afford to keep operable.

(DAVE DOOLING)

Media and Publishing

TELEVISION

Organization. AT&T stunned the telecommunications world in June 1998, agreeing to purchase the largest American cable operator, Tele-Communications Inc. (TCI), for $48 billion. The deal gave the long-distance telephone company what it most needed—direct access to millions of homes. Using the same technology that allowed several operators to begin offering high-speed access to the Internet, AT&T hoped to piggyback telephone service over cable's coaxial network.

Cable continued its inexorable rise. As of October 30, according to Paul Kagan Associates, cable subscribership reached 65.8 million, 66.3% of all U.S. homes with TV. As subscribership grew, however, so did cable rates—at two to three times the rate of inflation.

DirecTV and United States Satellite Broadcasting, which shared broadcast satellites and reception equipment, were the market leaders in satellite TV with 4.2 million subscribers as of October 30, according to SkyTRENDS. Primestar was second with 2.2 million homes and Echostar third with 1.7 million.

Pax TV debuted August 31 with a smattering of original programs and a heavy dose of family-friendly reruns such as "Dr. Quinn, Medicine Woman" and "Touched by an Angel." Along with those two shows from CBS, Pax also hired CBS's former entertainment chief, Jeff Sagansky, to head the network. Pax TV was the brainchild of Home Shopping Network cofounder Bud Paxson, whose business plan included running a "lean and mean" operation with much of the marketing, programming, and accounting handled not at the station level but from his West Palm Beach, Fla., headquarters. In that way, Paxson said, the network could be profitable with a relatively small rating—a 1 rating in prime time, compared with the 9.7 average of number one NBC in 1997–98.

Pax TV was generally ranked seventh among the broadcast networks, following ABC, CBS, NBC, Fox, the WB, and UPN. Some, however, placed it behind two Spanish-language networks, Univision and Telemundo. The former dominated the Spanish-language TV business in the U.S. and owned the top-rated TV station in Miami, Fla.

On Oct. 29, 1998, former U.S. senator and astronaut John Glenn was relaunched into space, and television was relaunched as a digital medium. A handful of television stations (24) broadcast Glenn's lift-off in high-definition television (HDTV) to the handful of sets that could receive a digital signal. It marked the beginning of the new digital broadcast TV service that most expected would gradually expand throughout the U.S. during the next several years.

With digital television (DTV), programs were delivered as bits of data. As a result, broadcasters could carry more information than with current analog technology. Most broadcasters planned to use that extra capacity to transmit HDTV, with its superior resolution. Others planned to deliver several channels and other information services. Still others sought to provide a mix of the two, broadcasting multiple channels for some part of the schedule and broadcasting prime-time shows, movies, or sports events in HDTV. At a minimum, broadcasters were required to deliver at least one stream of programming that was equal to or better than their current analog signal.

According to the Federal Communications Commission, which was overseeing conversion to digital, "most Americans will have access to DTV [programming] by 1999 and everyone in the country will have access by the year 2002." Traditional analog service would continue side-by-side with digital until 2006, after which broadcasts would be only in DTV. Affiliates of ABC, CBS, NBC, and Fox would have to be delivering a digital signal in the top 10 markets (about 30% of the country) by May 1, 1999, and in markets ranked 11–30 (another 53% of the country) by Nov. 1, 1999. All commercial stations would have to be delivering digital service by May 1, 2002. To receive a digital program, viewers would have the option of buying a converter for their existing sets or purchasing a digital set. By late 1998 some stations had launched digital channels, but the HDTV programming needed to fill them remained a scarce commodity.

As the year neared its close, delivering TV programming over World Wide Web sites (termed "streaming") was still in its infancy, with pictures often small and jerky, a function primarily of bandwidth limitations rather than underpowered computing. Most homes used telephone lines for Internet access at either 28.8 kbps (kilobits per second) or 56.6 kbps. Video optimally needed 500 kbps–2 megabits to run fluidly. Nonetheless, cable and telephone companies were working to provide high-speed digital lines to the home, and broadcast and cable executives continued to increase their Web output. An International Data Corp. (IDC) study revealed that 780,000 Internet-TV devices were activated in 1998. Using these devices, consumers could browse the Web or chat with friends while watching the Super Bowl.

Dutch TV production company Endemol entered the British market through Guardian Media Group (GMG), publisher of *The Guardian* newspaper. The partnership with GMG's Broadcast Communications, one of the largest independent producers in the U.K., was the latest move by Endemol to enter European countries outside its main markets of Germany and The Netherlands. A month earlier Endemol had bought 45% of the Italian entertainment group Aran. Exploiting entertainment formats in other markets by forming local partnerships with production companies accounted for 15% of the company's total revenues.

Italy's state broadcaster Radiotelevisione Italiana (RAI) changed its chairman and entire board of directors, appointing seasoned industry professionals rather than people with political connections. Pier Luigi Celli, formerly chief of personnel for ENEL, the Italian national electrical utility, became the new director general. The new leaders faced RAI's serious loss of audience to the private Mediaset networks of Silvio Berlusconi, Italy's former prime minister. For the first time, Mediaset Channel 5 overtook RAI's flagship evening news in the ratings war. RAI's lead weekend variety show

"Fantastico" was also overtaken by an old-fashioned Mediaset variety show.

BBC launched News 24, a 24-hour news service, in late 1997. BBC Worldwide's Rupert Gavin spearheaded the change (and increase in revenues) by recycling materials from the network's massive archives. Commercial broadcasters complained about the misuse of public funding and pointed out the unfair competition, as BBC was a public-sector, taxpayer-funded corporation.

The 20-strong European Commission unanimously vetoed on May 27 an alliance involving German media giants Bertelsmann and the Kirch Group, together with Deutsche Telekom. Karel Van Miert, the European Union's (EU's) competition commissioner, said that the merger would create in German digital TV a monopoly that newcomers would be unable to challenge, largely because of the three firms' control of the set-top decoders.

JSkyB, Rupert Murdoch's digital satellite multichannel service in Japan, merged with PerfecTV, a competitor. JSkyB, jointly owned by News Corp., Sony, Softbank, and Fuji TV, had yet to start services, and PerfecTV, whose shareholders included Japan's leading trade companies, had been struggling to gain more subscribers.

Programming. In the U.S. the broadcast networks and dozens of cable channels continued to fight for a fragmenting television audience in 1998. The combined prime-time viewership of the big three broadcast networks—ABC, CBS, and NBC—continued its precipitous slide, mustering 47% of the TV audience in the 1997–98 season, compared with 61% only five years earlier.

Skyrocketing programming costs and the decreasing audience shares caused network executives to ask their TV station affiliates for help in paying for sports rights; the networks also told the stations that they could no longer afford to pay them to carry their programming. Almost all network executives agreed that one of the keys to remaining competitive was to persuade the affiliates to allow "repurposing" of network shows. ABC, for example, was testing the delivery

of its soap operas on cable, where they could air in the morning, in prime time, and on weekends for viewers who could not watch them on weekday afternoons. Networks were also increasingly trying to produce more of the programs that they aired and to earn a greater share of the profits earned by programs produced for them by others.

A major reason behind the networks' cries for help was the almost $18 billion that broadcast and cable TV networks agreed to pay for rights to the National Football League for the eight years ending in 2005. The networks were even more concerned when the initial ratings for those football packages were less than stellar. For the month of September, ESPN's ratings were down 18% compared with former rights holder TNT; ABC was down 15%; Fox was down 3%; and CBS's ratings were flat compared with those of former rights holder NBC a year earlier. Disney Co. Chairman Michael Eisner said that broadcast affiliates of Disney-owned ABC had to share the cost of NFL football and give up "compensation" payments from the network. If they did not do so, he said, ABC might move its programming to cable.

One network that did not have to worry about paying for football was NBC, which lost the rights to the American Football Conference games to an aggressive bid by CBS. Also out of football was Time Warner's Turner Broadcasting System, which was outbid by rival cable network ESPN.

Although NBC was saving money on football, it was paying dearly to retain its Thursday-night anchor program, "ER." To keep the top-rated hospital drama on the schedule, the network agreed to pay the show's producers $850 million over the next three years. Consequently, each episode would cost the network $13 million, compared with the $1.5 million–$1.8 million the show had been commanding.

One reason that NBC was willing to pay so much for "ER" was that it was losing its other top Thursday night performer, "Seinfeld," after nine seasons and an esti-

mated $350 million–$400 million in earnings. The network had reportedly offered to boost Jerry Seinfeld's salary from $1 million-plus to $5 million per episode to keep the show on the air, but the star, who would collect hundreds of millions from the show's syndication run, chose to draw the curtain on "the show about nothing."

The show about fighting, also known as "The Jerry Springer Show," was another TV program much in the news in 1998. While critics and the producers of the syndicated talk show continued their tug-of-war over how much fighting the show featured and how much of it was staged, Springer (*see* BIOGRAPHIES) continued to achieve higher ratings than those of his competition. Thanks in part to its change to a no-holds-barred style that put more emphasis on action than talk, Springer had gone from not even cracking the top 50 shows in syndication in the 1996–97 TV season (according to Nielsen Media Research) to the 10th-most-watched syndicated show in 1997–98. For the first eight weeks (September through October) of the 1998–99 season, it was the top-rated talk show, surpassing longtime talk queen Oprah Winfrey, and was the seventh-ranked syndicated show.

NBC continued to dominate the ratings race in 1997–98, but its attempts to expand its power base beyond Thursday night were not so successful. The network had the top four shows: "Seinfeld," "ER," "Veronica's Closet," and "Friends"—but they were all on Thursday night, as was newcomer "Union Square," the eighth-ranked show of the season. CBS came in second in households, helped by shows, such as "Touched by an Angel," that appealed to older people. The network finished fourth, however, in the coveted 18–49-year-old demographic group. ABC placed third in households with sitcoms such as "The Drew Carey Show" and "Spin City." Fox finished fourth in households, but its edgy programming pushed it into second place in the 18–49 group for the first time. Helping it overtake ABC were the animated "King of the Hill" (*see* Photoessay) and the quirky hit "Ally McBeal." The WB got strong performances from "Dawson's Creek" and "Buffy the Vampire Slayer" to help push it past UPN into fifth place. It was the only network whose average rating did not decline compared with the 1996–97 season, posting a 12% increase on the strength of its programming and a station lineup bolstered by defections from rival UPN. By contrast, UPN was in a rebuilding year, repositioning itself with shows like "Love Boat: The Next Wave" from an urban-targeted to a more middle-American audience.

For the first five weeks of the 1998–99 season, the major networks continued their ratings slide. NBC was down 20% in household ratings, followed by ABC, down 4%, and CBS, down 3%. Of the big four, only Fox showed growth at 3%, although that was in part due to its coverage of the World Series. Although the series (a four-game blowout of the San Diego Padres by the New York Yankees) recorded its lowest ratings ever, they were enough to boost Fox's fortunes. Of the small networks, UPN was down an alarming 38%, whereas the WB continued in the plus column, up 14%. In the face of its ratings drop, NBC shook up programming executive suites in October, replacing NBC Entertainment's president,

Jerry Springer, the so-called king of trash TV, addresses his guests while taping a show in December. Outrageous topics, liberal doses of profanity, and physical fighting among the show's guests boosted ratings and stirred controversy in 1998. Allegations that many of the fights were staged had little effect on the show's popularity.

TODD BUCHANAN—JERRY SPRINGER NEWSMAKERS

Introduced in Britain in 1997, the "Teletubbies" children's show hit the air in the U.S. in 1998. Aimed primarily at 1–4-year-olds, the PBS show featured four chubby characters who lived in the green, rolling hills of Teletubbyland. Although the show proved to be wildly popular among kids, it also drew criticism from many adults who were worried about young children becoming addicted to TV.

Warren Littlefield, with station group head Scott Sassa.

U.S. Pres. Bill Clinton's relationship with intern Monica Lewinsky dominated TV news from its first reports in early January to the impeachment hearing that was being conducted at the year's end. In between, it powered cable news channels to some of their highest-ever ratings and filled the broadcast airways with subject matter that would have been unheard of—except on shock jock Howard Stern's radio and TV shows—only a few years earlier.

For the fourth year in a row NBC dominated the Emmy awards, winning 18, including 4 for "Frasier." ABC was second with 16, and HBO third with 14, including 3 for Tom Hanks's multipart epic "From the Earth to the Moon," and, finally, one for comedian Garry Shandling (*see* BIOGRAPHIES) after 19 nominations. One of the ceremony's biggest surprises was the three awards for ABC's "The Practice," which was produced by David E. Kelley. (*See* BIOGRAPHIES.) One was for best drama, in a category that included such critically acclaimed shows as "ER" and "NYPD Blue."

One cable program that became recognized as an innovator and ratings power featured four foul-mouthed third graders animated in a style that could best be described as early construction paper. Comedy Central's "South Park," described by *Broadcasting & Cable* editor John Higgins as a "twisted version of Peanuts," debuted in the summer of 1997, but it did not attract a large following until late in the year. In October 1997 it was averaging a 1.6 rating, but by February 1998 the show was the top-rated program on cable, with a 6.4 the week of February 2–8, and had become a cultural phenomenon. The catchphrase "Oh my God, they killed Kenny," a reference to the fact that the character Kenny died in almost every episode, was threatening to become a part of the vernacular.

Though it gained audience share, cable continued to demonstrate its greatest strength in a limited programming range. Aside from the big-ticket movies and occasional hit series, cable was dominated by major sports, wrestling, and childrens' shows, with those three programming types claiming 23 of the top 25 cable programs, according to the October 19 Nielsen ratings. Recognizing the need to broaden their programming base, the cable networks pledged to spend hundreds of millions on original programming with high production values. USA Network, for example, spent more on the two-part original "Moby Dick" ($20 million) than on any other program in its history, and the show returned the investment by achieving the highest-ever ratings for original entertainment on basic cable, an 8.1 (or an average 5.9 million households).

TV soap-opera addicts were cheered by University of Oxford professor Michael

(continued on page 273)

ADULTS 'TOON IN

By 1998 television cartoons aimed primarily at adults had reached an unprecedented popularity. Fox Broadcasting's "The Simpsons" not only was the longest-running animated program on TV but, after the show's ninth season on the air, had become the longest continually running prime-time series still releasing new episodes. The Cartoon Network was perhaps the most successful new cable channel. Another cable network, Comedy Central, attracted huge audiences and wowed critics with such animated hits as "South Park," "Dr. Katz, Professional Therapist," and the British-made "Bob and Margaret." At a time when the preponderance of television sitcoms featured generic characters, canned laughter, and pat story lines, adult viewers in search of intelligent humour and genuine, compelling characters were, ironically, turning increasingly to cartoons.

Adult-oriented TV cartoons had come a long way since 1960, when "The Flintstones" and "Mr. Magoo," the first prime-time animated programs, made their debuts. "The Flintstones" was based in part on Jackie Gleason's classic sitcom "The Honeymooners," and the antics of the nearsighted, crotchety Mr. Magoo recalled the comedy of W.C. Fields. These and other early animated shows, such as the popular "Peanuts" television specials, could be enjoyed equally by children and adults. By and large they avoided social and political criticism and, some would say, reflected a more wholesome era than today.

The cartoon landscape changed dramatically in 1990 with the appearance of "The Simpsons," the first animated prime-time series in two decades. Created by comic-strip artist Matt Groening, the show depicted the misadventures of the Simpson family, focusing particularly on Homer, the bickering, ineffectual husband and father, and Bart,

the sly, sarcastic 10-year-old son. A de facto revolt against idealized images of the American family promulgated by such well-known sitcoms as "Father Knows Best" and "The Cosby Show," "The Simpsons" instantly struck a chord with viewers and cleared the way for other adult-oriented cartoons. "King of the

(Opposite page, top) "Bob and Margaret."
(Opposite page, bottom) "South Park."
(Below) "The Simpsons."

Hill," developed by Fox as a companion show to "The Simpsons," debuted in 1997. Set in a Texas suburb and featuring another beleaguered working-class family, the cartoon was one of television's most successful new shows.

Other prime-time cartoons stirred controversy. MTV's "Beavis and Butt-head" and Nickelodeon's "Ren and Stimpy" tried hard to be obnoxious, but perhaps the most outrageous cartoon of all was "South Park." Although the series centred on the lives of four young boys, it carried a "mature audiences" rating for its liberal doses of profane language, gross humour, and graphic violence (one character, Kenny, was killed in almost every episode, sometimes more than once). Described by one critic as "Peanuts on acid," the cartoon's deadly satire helped it become the highest-rated show on cable. Like "The Simpsons," "South Park" also strove for an element of realism. "Most kids on TV are just projections of what adults think kids should be like," observed "South Park" cocreator Matt Stone. "Kids are not sweet and innocent. They're mean and vindictive . . . and that's what makes them so funny."

Although satire was sure to remain their emphasis, adult-oriented cartoons promised to continue breaking new ground. At year's end Groening was hard at work on "Futurama," an animated science-fiction series, scheduled to air in January 1999.

(Right) "King of the Hill." (Below) "Dr. Katz, Professional Therapist."

(continued from page 269)

Argyle's claim that people who watched soaps were happy people. The results of his 11-year study, analyzing thousands of questionnaires, were revealed late in 1998. The key to happiness, Argyle told the *Sunday Telegraph,* was to have one close relationship and a network of friends. Through TV watching, Argyle theorized, people made imaginary friends.

A Vietnamese soap opera with sympathetic HIV-positive characters was aired to reverse early propaganda and misconceptions about AIDS. Funded by the EU and provided with technical assistance by Australia, CARE International Vietnam taped several episodes of "Wind Blows Through Dark and Light" and aired them until mid-June.

"Mirada de mujer" ("A Woman's Gaze") became a hit for Mexico's TV Azteca in late 1997 despite protests from family-values groups complaining that the program promoted adultery. A petition drive to cancel it was welcomed by Ricardo Salinas Pliego, Azteca's chief executive. The controversy added to the 40% prime-time audience share taken from rival Grupo Televisa, Mexico's one-time TV monopoly and the world's largest producer of Spanish-language TV programming. Azteca in 1998 owned the top-rated evening news broadcast and crime newsmagazine show.

"Teletubbies" Tinky Winky, Dipsy, Laa-Laa, and Po from the hills of Teletubbyland were introduced in Britain in 1997 and began to air in the U.S. on the Public Broadcasting Service (PBS) in April 1998. Each Teletubby head carried an antenna, and the characters' stomachs beamed in video clips of real children in the real world, which triggered criticisms in both countries that viewing children were being hooked on TV before they had the language skills to protest. British creator Anne Wood referred to her work as a kind of "Sesame Street" primer.

A BBC documentary on the life of Field Marshal Lord Kitchener, turned out to be a bitter disappointment, especially to the members of the Kitchener family. Dwelling little on his achievements, "Kitchener—the Empire's Flawed Hero" portrayed him as obstinate and brutal, using snippets of interviews with relatives, veterans, and historians to debunk his reputation.

The French commanded and controlled TV coverage of all 64 matches of the 1998 World Cup. Broadcasting from Paris, "France 98" was watched by a cumulative worldwide audience of 37 billion people. Also in regard to soccer, England's Premier League rejected in May a proposal by BSkyB to televise the next season's games live on a pay-per-view basis. With soccer as a key attraction to subscription, BSkyB had hoped to use live pay-per-view matches to persuade customers to sign up for its new digital TV service.

Greece was singled out in May for immediate action by the World Trade Organization for having failed to crack down on rampant theft of TV programming. Some 150 Greek stations continued to broadcast American films and television programs without paying American copyright holders.

Technology. China planned to beam TV into every village in the nation by the end of the century, according to the State Administration of Radio, Film, and Television. Because of China's vast territory and complex terrain, satellite broadcasting was used by the government-controlled China Central Television as well as by 26 provincial-level TV stations. China's financial capital of Shanghai recently set up a new satellite TV station, Shanghai Broadcasting Network, to beam programs across China and Asia.

The Philips Flat TV—lightweight, totally flat, and only 11.4 cm (4.5 in) thick—was introduced during the year. Philips boasted that the set "duplicates every detail of the ultimate cinema experience." Sharp reportedly wanted to develop a way to give parents control over their children's TV-viewing habits by means of a View Timer switch, which restricted viewing time and controlled TV usage, and a Direct Access button that could set program restrictions.

RADIO

Five manufacturers, Bosch/Blaupunkt, Clarion, Grundig, Kenwood, and Pioneer, offered digital car radios for sale in Britain in 1998. They featured improved sound and stronger reception and, unlike bulkier early models, fit in the same space as standard car radio sets.

Providing radio broadcasts to China's 1.2 billion population was greatly assisted during the year by the government's investment in infrastructure. At the end of 1998, China had 1,630 radio stations, serving 86% of the people, according to the State Administration of Radio, Film, and Television.

In the U.S. the much-ballyhooed Telecommunications Act of 1996 seemed to have failed to spark the promised competition between local cable TV and telephone companies, but it triggered a major restructuring of the radio business. By eliminating the national restrictions of radio station ownership and drastically loosening the lo-cal ones, the law caused an unprecedented wave of buying and selling. The deal making was capped in October 1998 with the $4.4 billion merger of Clear Channel Communications and Jacor Communications. At the closing the surviving company, Clear Channel, had 454 stations in 101 markets. The deal was the second biggest in radio history, surpassed only by CBS's purchase of Infinity Broadcasting for $4.9 billion in 1996.

When the stock market began cooling and the transactions started slowing in the fall, Chancellor Media emerged as the U.S.'s largest radio group, with 488 stations and estimated annual revenue of $1.8 billion, according to *Broadcasting & Cable* and *Duncan's American Radio.* By revenue, CBS ranked second with $1.7 billion and Clear Channel third with $1.2 billion.

The large-station groups spawned their own programming services. In January Chancellor's AMFM Radio Networks signed one of radio's best-known personalities, Casey Kasem. His "American Top 40" show was a longtime radio staple. Although the signing gave AMFM a boost, it also landed the service in court. Westwood One, Kasem's former home, sued AMFM, claiming that Kasem had two years to go on its contract when he made the jump.

Howard Stern, the self-proclaimed "King of All Media"; Rush Limbaugh, the right-wing political pundit; and Dr. Laura

One of radio's biggest stars, talk-show host Dr. Laura Schlessinger smiles for the camera in February. Famous for dishing out moral advice to her listeners, Schlessinger was forced to defend herself later in the year when an online company posted 20-year-old nude photos of her on its Web site. She eventually dropped her lawsuit to have the photos taken down.

Schlessinger, radio's hard-edged answer to Ann Landers, were radio's biggest talk stars, drawing the largest national audiences. Art Bell, however, was the medium's most mysterious personality. His announcement in October that he was immediately quitting his overnight UFO-oriented show owing to a "threatening, terrible event" had millions of fans speculating that it was all due to some extraterrestrial plot. Within a fortnight, however, Bell was back on the air.

(RAMONA MONETTE S. FLORES; HARRY A. JESSELL; LAWRENCE B. TAISHOFF)

Juan Bautista, president of the Mexican Fraternity of Reporters, speaks to the media during a march in Tijuana in December 1997 to protest an attack on newspaper editor Jesus Blancornelas, who was seriously wounded by gunmen linked to a drug-trafficking organization. Violence against journalists continued to be a problem in Latin America in 1998.

DENIS POROY—AP/WIDE WORLD

Amateur Radio. In 1998 the amateur radio (ham) community in the U.S. was grappling with the most sweeping restructuring of amateur radio licensing since 1989. In July the American Radio Relay League proposed reducing the number of classes of licenses from six to four and streamlining the examinations needed to obtain the licenses. Instead of six license classes, there would be four: technician, general, advanced, and amateur extra. Lost in the reform would be the novice and technician-plus grades. In August the Federal Communications Commission (FCC) asked for comments on the four-class plan, noting that there "appears to be unnecessary overlap" between licenses in the existing six-class regime.

Just as it did with commercial AM and FM services, the FCC got tougher on amateur radio scofflaws. Acting on complaints from ham operators, the agency levied a $7,500 fine on a New Jersey licensee for operating an AM station that interfered with ham broadcasts. It fined a Florida ham $2,500 for causing "malicious interference" with business radio. In Connecticut a ham team led authorities to a man believed to be using ham equipment to jam local police and fire frequencies.

Throughout the year hams were on the scene of natural disasters and other trouble to lend a communications hand. They helped provide vital communications when the floodwaters rose in central and southern Texas, when Hurricane Georges threatened Florida, and when Hurricane Mitch struck with deadly and prolonged force in Honduras and Nicaragua. In early September a ham team in Arizona worked through the night with other volunteers to find a two-year-old boy who had wandered off. They contributed to a happy ending; after a 15-hour ordeal the boy was found in a cornfield just 3.2 km (2 mi) from home.

(HARRY A. JESSELL;
LAWRENCE B. TAISHOFF)

NEWSPAPERS

The *Independent,* the London newspaper founded in 1986 to provide an independent, nonpartisan voice on news issues, gained a new lease on life in 1998 as Anthony J.F. O'Reilly took control in March. O'Reilly, who headed Independent Newspapers, a chain of some 200 newspapers throughout the world, shared ownership with the tabloid Mirror Group. On March 13 Andrew Marr, reinstated as editor in chief, said in a letter to readers "[We] have been told in simple terms to make the paper steadily more intelligent and serious. During an era when most papers are dumbing down, it came as an unusual and exhilarating instruction." The *Guardian,* so

renowned for its misprints and typos it was dubbed "The Grauniad," introduced a column late in 1997 headed "Corrections and Clarifications." A runaway hit, it attracted a hard core of loyal fans who read it before they read anything else in the paper. The satirical magazine *Private Eye* noted, "The Grauniad's corrections are far, far more interesting than the original articles."

The *Financial Times* of London cut its newsstand price in the United States by one-third, from $1.50 to $1. The price cut was part of an effort by its owner, the Pearson group, to more than double its North American circulation to 100,000 readers by 2000.

In April Canada's Southam chain, controlled by Conrad Black's Hollinger International, Inc., announced plans to launch a new national daily newspaper. Southam in July agreed to trade four Ontario newspapers to Sun Media in exchange for Sun's 80% interest in the *Financial Post.* That paper was then merged into the *National Post,* which debuted in October. Based in Toronto, the *National Post* extended Black's newspaper empire across the country to a total of 57 of Canada's 105 dailies.

Journalism continued to be a risky business for reporters in Latin America. Between October 1997 and March 1998, 11 journalists were murdered, 5 in Colombia, 4 in Brazil, and 2 in Mexico. Because the reporters had written about the trade in illegal drugs, it was thought that drug traffickers were responsible for their deaths.

The addition of business news supplements boosted the earnings of many South American newspapers. The most successful was the *Wall Street Journal Americas,* a section of the *Wall Street Journal*'s business news translated into Spanish, or for Brazil, Portuguese. Some 20 South American papers published this supplement, which in 1998 reached approximately 2.2 million readers. Knight Ridder, Inc.'s *Miami Herald* became the top-selling English-language newspaper in Latin America, where it had 10 printing plants and appeared on newsstands in many cities. Ironically, the publisher of the *Herald,* David Lawrence, resigned in August because of eroding circulation numbers in Miami. He was succeeded by Alberto Ibarguen, publisher of the *Herald*'s Spanish-language newspaper, *El Nuevo Herald.* The growth of Miami's Spanish-speaking population, for whom *El Nuevo Herald* was designed, was thought to have hurt the *Herald*'s circulation.

Cuba allowed the Associated Press to reopen its news bureau there after a delegation of senior AP officials visited the country in November. The AP bureau in Havana had been closed since 1969, when Cuba expelled its last permanent correspondent. A rare public disturbance took place in Havana two weeks later when about a dozen protesters demonstrated against the trial of an independent journalist. Mario Viera, head of the tiny and unauthorized Cuba Verdad press agency, was charged with defaming a government official in an article posted on Cubanet, an Internet page based in Miami.

In Iran a pro-democracy newspaper defied two orders by the nation's Justice Department to shut down and continued publishing under a third name. Originally called *Jameah,* it was ordered to cease publishing on July 25. The editor, Mahmoud

Shams, renamed the paper *Tous* and continued publishing. Militants then assaulted Shams and threatened to kill him, and also attacked two AP reporters who arrived on the scene. Ordered to shut down *Tous,* Shams renamed the paper *Aftab'e Emrooz* ("The Sun Today") with the lead story being an account of the attack. In Nigeria the government-owned *Daily Times* announced it was cutting its staff by almost half because of financial difficulties. The Times group, one of the largest and oldest newspaper publishers in Africa, was heavily in debt, and efforts to increase circulation had not been successful.

China launched a new government newspaper in July. The *Beijing Morning Post* made its first appearance with the banner headline "China Will Clone Giant Panda." It sold out within hours.

In the U.S. the *Wall Street Journal* turned technicolor on March 20 with the addition of a new full-colour lifestyle section called *Weekend Journal.* Delivered every Friday, it focused on culture, travel, and personal finance. It featured columns on expensive houses and automobiles, home decorating, antiques, and fine wines, and even included a crossword puzzle. The U.S. circulation of the *Wall Street Journal* fell about 1% in 1998 to 1.8 million. On the Internet, however, in the last two years the newspaper picked up 250,000 subscribers, who paid $29 or $49 per year depending on whether they also subscribed to the print version. In 1998 the *Wall Street Journal* had the largest subscription base of any on-line publication and made additional gains by selling associated services from its World Wide Web site.

USA Today, part of the Gannett Co. chain, also changed its weekend format. The paper's Life section on Fridays expanded by 14 pages and split into two sections, Life Weekend and Life Destinations and Diversions.

The *Nashville* (Tenn.) *Banner,* an afternoon daily, announced in February that it was closing down after 122 years of publication because of declining circulation. Since 1937 the *Banner* had operated under a joint agreement with its main competitor, the Gannett-owned *Tennessean,* in which the latter, a morning daily, handled the business arrangements, including marketing, printing, advertising, and circulation for both newspapers; the editorial and reporting staffs, however, remained independent.

Another battle between morning and afternoon newspapers with joint business and production operations heated up in San Francisco. The morning *San Francisco Chronicle,* founded in 1865 by Michael H. de Young and still family-owned, was under siege by the Hearst-owned *San Francisco Examiner,* an afternoon daily, to merge, sell out to the *Examiner,* or face head-to-head competition in the morning. Although the *Chronicle* had a circulation of 484,000 compared to the *Examiner'*s 120,000, the Hearst Corp. was one of the country's largest and richest media companies with 12 daily and 7 weekly newspapers, a number of magazines such as *Esquire* and *Cosmopolitan,* and television stations and cable interests. As the conflict continued, chains Knight-Ridder, Inc., Gannett Co., McClatchy Newspapers Inc., Medianews Group Inc., and the New York Times Co. bought out newspapers in nearby towns and captured readership in the surrounding suburbs.

The *Boston Globe,* owned by the New York Times Co., lost two of its major columnists during 1998. In June Patricia Smith was forced to resign for having fabricated characters and quotations in her columns, and in August, 25-year veteran Mike Barnicle was ousted for wrongly using jokes by comedian George Carlin in his columns.

Mike Gallagher, a reporter for the *Cincinnati Enquirer,* was fired in June, accused of stealing voice mail messages from Chiquita Brands International Inc. during a yearlong investigation of the banana company's business practices. The *Enquirer* immediately retracted the report, and in September Gallagher pleaded guilty to two felony charges.

"If your mother says she loves you, check it out." This was the operating principle of the City News Bureau of Chicago, noted for its insistence on accuracy and fact verification. In October, however, the bureau announced that it would close down. This famous boot camp for reporters opened June 19, 1890, funded by 10 daily newspapers to provide round-the-clock coverage of police stations, city hall, and anywhere else there might be a story. Its alumni include Charles MacArthur, who wrote about it in the play *The Front Page;* Chicago columnist Mike Royko; and novelist Kurt Vonnegut. With only two newspapers, the *Chicago Tribune* and the *Chicago Sun-Times,* left to sustain it, the bureau planned to shut down in March 1999.

The *Grand Forks* (N.D.) *Herald* won the Pulitzer gold medal for public service for its coverage of the blizzard, flood, and fire that devastated the city, including its own presses. The *New York Times* won three Pulitzers: for beat reporting—Linda Greenhouse on the U.S. Supreme Court; for international reporting—the newspaper's staff for a series of articles on drug corruption in Mexico; and for criticism—Michiko Kakutani. The *Los Angeles Times* won two awards: for feature photography showing the plight of children whose parents are addicted to drugs—Clarence Williams; and for breaking news—the staff of the *Los Angeles Times* for its coverage of a spectacular shootout during a bank robbery. Bernard L. Stein of the *Riverdale Press,* Bronx, N.Y., won the honour for editorial writing. Other winners included: investigative reporting—Gary Cohn and Will Englund of the *Baltimore Sun* on the hazards involved in the dismantling of old ships; national reporting—Russell Carollo and Jeff Nesmith of the *Dayton* (Ohio) *Daily News* for their exposé of the military health care system; commentary—Mike McAlary of the *Daily News,* New York City, on the brutalization of a Haitian immigrant in a police station; explanatory journalism—

Paul Salopek of the *Chicago Tribune* on the Human Genome Diversity Project; feature writing—Thomas French of the *St. Petersburg* (Fla.) *Times* on the murder of a mother and two daughters vacationing in Florida; spot news photography—Martha Rial of the *Pittsburgh* (Pa.) *Post-Gazette* for her images of Hutu and Tutsi refugees in Tanzania; and editorial cartooning—Stephen P. Breen of the *Asbury Park Press,* (Neptune, N.J.).   (ANNE ROBY)

MAGAZINES

London's *Gramophone* magazine, the voice of classical music, marked its 75th year in April 1998 with a look back at some of its less-than-stellar reviews. Of renowned opera singer Maria Callas, the reviewer noted "I have no doubt that Maria Callas will do a great deal better than this in the future." The review of Leonard Bernstein's first Brahms recording concluded "He fails to give this symphony the greatness we know it to have." Like the subjects of those early reviews, the magazine achieved distinction as the best of its kind and in 1998 boasted 60,000 readers in 100 countries.

Germany's Bertelsmann, the largest media company in Europe, appointed a new chief executive. Thomas Middelhoff, who took over on November 2, was expected to make major changes. In contrast to U.S. media companies, which strove to use their content or product in as many ways as possible over the range of their media outlets, Bertelsmann's businesses had been run as independent entities concerned with their own profitability rather than that of the com-

A 1983 file photo shows Pulitzer Prize–winning newspaper columnist Russell Baker, who retired from the staff of the *New York Times* in December 1998. He began writing his nationally syndicated "Observer" column for the *Times* in 1962. His final column appeared on Christmas Day.

pany as a whole. Middelhoff vowed to change this practice. (*See* Sidebar.)

U.S. magazines were successful during the year in their expansion into Latin America. The greatest hit was *Seleções,* a new Portuguese-language edition of *Reader's Digest* for Brazil that followed the magazine's Spanish-language edition, *Selecciones.* Sales of both publications in Latin America by mid-1998 totaled 1.7 million copies per month. Surpassed only by *Veja,* a long-established Brazilian daily, *Seleções* became Brazil's second-best-selling magazine. The Spanish edition was the best-selling magazine in Chile with 150,000 copies per month and in Argentina with 250,000 copies. In addition to *Seleções,* Brazil embraced Portuguese-language editions of both *Time* and *Fortune* magazines, which were being distributed as newspaper supplements. Spanish-language editions of *Newsweek, Glamour, Discover, People, National Geographic,* and *Rolling Stone* also gained success.

In 1998 magazines in the United States continued to grow and proliferate, with more than 800 new titles covering a wide variety of subjects. *ESPN Magazine,* a joint venture of Disney Co. and Hearst Corp., owners of the popular ESPN sports cable TV channel, was a biweekly competing with *Sports Illustrated. Teen People,* a spin-off publication of *People* magazine, was aimed at teenagers. *More,* published by Meredith Corp., was targeted to women over 40. *Blaze,* published by Vibe/SPIN Ventures, catered to teenagers who liked hip-hop music. *Gear,* published by Guccione Media, was a fashion and pop culture magazine aimed at young male adults, and *Brill's Content,* published by Steven Brill, the founder and former owner of the *American Lawyer,* assessed the credibility of all media.

In addition to the new titles there were numerous mergers and acquisitions during the year. Among the most notable were the acquisition of *TV Guide* by the television-based United Video Satellite Group; the purchase of *Wired* magazine, one of the leading new media magazines, by Condé Nast Publications; and the purchase of Cowles Business Media and Cowles Enthusiast Media by PRIMEDIA Inc. (formerly K-III Communications).

Magazine advertising, the major contributor to profit for most magazines, continued to grow in 1998, with revenues up about 9% over 1997. Declines in major advertising categories such as automotive products, computers, and drugs were more than offset by strong growth in direct-response advertising, business and consumer services, and food products.

Magazine circulation continued to increase in 1998 at a modest rate consistent with the growth of the U.S. adult population. A new development during the year, however, threatened magazine subscription marketing. This was the attack on the use of sweepstakes offers in selling magazine subscriptions. A suit brought by 20 state attor-

AP/WIDE WORLD/MORE MAGAZINE

American actress Cybill Shepard appears on the cover of the debut issue of *More,* a bimonthly magazine for women over 40 that focused on fashion and beauty topics. *More* was one of more than 800 new magazines published in the U.S. in 1998.

neys general against the subscription agent American Family Publishers alleged that AFP and other agents misled consumers by causing them to think they were sweepstakes winners when in fact they were not. The suit was settled, but the negative publicity in the press caused a severe decline in responses to sweepstakes offers. Some magazines, most notably *Reader's Digest* and *TV Guide,* announced during the year that they would slash the circulation they guaranteed to advertisers—17% by *Reader's Digest* and about 8% by *TV Guide.*

Magazines continued to evolve into global enterprises, with dozens of U.S. titles launching foreign editions, usually in partnership with local magazine publishers. During the past year new foreign editions of American magazines included *National Geographic* in Italy, *Prevention* magazine in Poland, and *Harper's Bazaar* in Australia.

(DONALD D. KUMMERFELD)

BOOK PUBLISHING

The controversy over resale price maintenance (rpm) in Europe was not resolved in 1998. It resurfaced in Germany as a result of a complaint to the European Commission (EC) by Austrian retailing group Librodisk concerning the cross-border fixing of book prices in Germany and Austria, which was first introduced in 1993. The EC decided to open an investigation in January 1999, but even if it decides that the complaint is justified, the inevitable ensuing appeal to the European Court of Justice should serve to preserve the existing structure for as many as five years.

In the U.K. the issue was no longer rpm itself but sales over the Internet. U.S.-based Internet booksellers were supplying British customers with books licensed for sale in the U.S., and it was claimed by the U.K. Publishers Association that this was unfair (though clearly not to consumers, given widespread discounts) and illegal. The existence of the Internet also caused European publishers to publish in Europe at the same time as in the U.S. Interestingly, the boom in electronic selling coincided with a severe decline in electronic publishing, with publishers throughout Europe cutting back on plans to produce CD-ROMs. In the face of a worldwide trend toward increasingly fierce protection of rights, the New Zealand government surprisingly amended the 1994 Copyright Act in May 1998 so as to permit the parallel importation of copyrighted products lawfully produced elsewhere, regardless of who had acquired exclusive rights for New Zealand.

In March the year's largest proposed merger, between Reed Elsevier and Wolters Kluwer, was terminated. The merger was announced in October 1997, but the opening of a full inquiry by the EC in December, fueled by fears over potential dominance in the field of tax and legal titles, resulted in an unsuccessful attempt by Kluwer to renegotiate terms. Reed Elsevier did, however, finally rid itself of its remaining consumer book interests, including the sale of Reed Children's Books to Egmont of Denmark in April and of Octopus-Reed Illustrated to management in August. In April it offered to pay Times Mirror $1,650,000,000 for U.S. legal publisher Matthew Bender together with its 50% interest in Shepard's Co. In its turn, Wolters Kluwer successfully bid for Plenum Publishing, medical publisher Waverly, the Capitol Publishing Group, and Le Point Vétérinaire.

Also in March, Bertelsmann AG of Germany, the world's largest book publisher and third largest media group, offered roughly $1.5 billion for Random House. The purchase elicited fears in the industry that the new conglomerate, to be called Random House Inc., would emphasize glitzy best-sellers and doom the already-struggling midlist titles. Authors were concerned about another decline in the amount of places to sell their works. The Federal Trade Commission looked into possible antitrust violations but approved the acquisition in May. (*See* Sidebar.)

Pearson PLC, the British media group that owned the *Financial Times,* became the world's largest educational publisher in May by acquiring Simon & Schuster's education, reference, and business and professional divisions from Viacom for $4.6 billion, after which it sold all but the education division to Hicks, Muse, Tate & Furst of the U.S. for $1 billion. The education group joined Pearson's Addison Wesley Longman group and was called Pearson Education. Meanwhile,

HarperCollins lost credibility as a publisher of contemporary nonfiction by withdrawing its offer to publish Chris Patten's text on Hong Kong.

Approximately 30% of the output of French titles was accounted for by Havas (a subsidiary of Vivendi since March), which acquired Quotidien Santé and 51% of both La Découverte and Syros in May and Grupo Anaya in September; Hachette, which in August agreed to buy 70% of Orion; and Groupe Flammarion. In East Asia the economic crisis exacted a heavy toll on book publishers. In Indonesia, for example, 90% of them ceased operations.

The Internet during the year had a major impact on the way that books were sold. Amazon.com and BarnesandNoble.com, online bookstores, continued to grow, although there were concerns about their profitability; despite huge sales Amazon.com's operating loss for the first half of 1998 was more than $25 million. Borders, the national book chain, went on-line in May, and smaller on-line bookstores such as Books.com and Alt.Bookstore struggled to compete. Sales through the on-line sites rose so dramatically that independent book retailers complained that they were having problems stocking reorders of popular titles. The Intimate Bookshop, a small southern chain, filed a lawsuit against Barnes and Noble, Borders, and Amazon, claiming antitrust violations.

In July Modern Library caused a minor flap with the release of a list of 100 best English-language novels published in the 20th century. Even two of the judges, historian Arthur M. Schlesinger, Jr., and novelist William Styron, publicly expressed dismay with the final list. The most common criticism was that the list reflected the homogeneous nature of the judges, a predominantly elderly white male group. Modern Library promised to revamp its process when it picks the 100 best nonfiction books.

The sex scandal that threatened the presidency of U.S. Pres. Bill Clinton began with a book connection; literary agent Lucianne Goldberg urged friend (and government worker) Linda Tripp to start taping her phone conversations with White House intern Monica Lewinsky. The tapes led to the affair being revealed nationally. Pocket Books, PublicAffairs, and Prima Publishing all released books based on special prosecutor Kenneth Starr's behemoth investigative report of the scandal. All three publishers enjoyed good sales despite the fact that the full text of the report was readily available on the Internet. Jeffrey Toobin was signed by Random House to write a book on the scandal and its impact on the nation, while Lewinsky herself agreed to a $600,000 advance from St. Martin's Press in November for a book tentatively titled *Monica's Story.*

The 1998 Pulitzer Prize for fiction was awarded to Philip Roth's *American Pastoral* (Houghton Mifflin) and to Jared Diamond's *Guns, Germs, and Steel: The Fates of Human Societies* (W. W. Norton) for general nonfiction. Fiction bestsellers for 1997, as reported by *Publishers Weekly,* were *The Partner* by John Grisham (2,625,000 copies sold), *Cold Mountain* by Charles Frazier (1,458,280), and *The Ghost* by Danielle Steel (1,161,121). Nonfiction best-sellers were *Angela's Ashes* by Frank McCourt (1,650,000), *Simple Abundance* by Sarah Ban Breathnach (1,462,663), and *Midnight in the Garden of Good and Evil* by John Berendt (1,300,799). Total book sales in the U.S. increased 2.4% in 1997 to $21,280,000,000.

(PETER J. CURWEN; BETH LEVINE)
See also LITERATURE.

Bertelsmann—the German Giant

The announcement on March 23, 1998, that German media giant Bertelsmann AG would acquire venerable American publisher Random House sent shock waves—and several important messages—throughout the industry. The news astonished industry observers, especially because in recent years other large media companies had been trying to divest their trade-book operations. For the first time, more than half of the new U.S. trade books (general adult fiction and nonfiction) would be published by foreign-owned companies. In addition, Bertelsmann announced that it would merge Random House with Bantam Doubleday Dell, which it already owned, and thereby create a colossus with projected revenues two to three times those of its leading competitors.

The firm began in Germany in 1835, when Carl Bertelsmann founded a religious print shop and publishing establishment in the Westphalian town of Gütersloh. The house remained family-owned and grew steadily for the next century, gradually adding literature, popular fiction, and theology to its title list. Bertelsmann was shut down by the Nazis in 1943, and its physical plant was virtually destroyed by Allied bombing in 1945. The quick growth of the Bertelsmann empire after World War II was fueled by the establishment of global networks of book clubs (from 1950) and music circles (1958). By 1998 Bertelsmann AG comprised more than 300 companies concentrated on various aspects of media.

Led by Mark Wössner and, after November 2, by Thomas Middelhoff, Bertelsmann was also aggressively adding to its publishing interests. The Random House deal was quickly followed by an agreement in May to purchase Portuguese publisher and retailer Bertrand. Bertelsmann cemented its position as the world's largest book-club operator with the purchase in June of the outstanding 50% stake of Book Club Associates, Great Britain's largest book club. In July Bertelsmann successfully bid for Falken Verlag, an independent literary publisher, and later it obtained 50% of Doyma, the biggest medical publisher in Spain, adding it to its Argentine publisher Sudamericana. In Canada it was revealed in September that the German juggernaut had been quietly moving to take over Doubleday Canada Ltd. Bertelsmann also moved to become a major player in the on-line bookselling business in Europe and America.

Worldwide, Bertelsmann ranked third among media companies, lagging behind only the Walt Disney Co. and Time Warner Inc. It employed 58,000 people, of whom 24,000 worked in Germany. During fiscal year 1997–98, Bertelsmann earned more than $15 billion in revenue, with roughly 25% being generated by its music, book publishing/ book-club divisions and another 17.5% from magazines and newspapers.

(PETER J. CURWEN)

American publishing giant Random House, whose New York City headquarters are shown below, was acquired by German media conglomerate Bertelsmann AG in 1998, a move that surprised many industry observers.

Military Affairs

Among the major developments of 1998, the roster of acknowledged nuclear weapons nations jumped from five to seven in May when first India and then Pakistan conducted a series of nuclear weapons tests. UN inspectors continued to believe that Iraq had failed to provide all the details of its program to develop weapons of mass destruction. By ending cooperation with the inspectors in October, Iraq faced the prospect of punitive military strikes, and in December

Secretary of Defense William Cohen (left) and Gen. Hugh Shelton meet reporters after U.S. attacks in Afghanistan and The Sudan.

the U.S. and Britain launched a four-day air attack in the country. Many analysts suspected that North Korea had not given up its nuclear ambitions. Although the NATO-led force in Bosnia and Herzegovina kept the once-warring factions apart in that country, the war in the Balkans finally spread to the Serbian province of Kosovo. There Serbian military and police forces brutally suppressed efforts of the ethnic Albanian majority to gain greater autonomy within Serbia. NATO threats to use force against Yugoslavia angered Russia and further weakened the limited military cooperation between Russia and the alliance. In other parts of the world, few of the ongoing conflicts were settled, and new ones such as those between Turkey and Syria and between Iran and Afghanistan threatened to erupt. Africa, where the civil war in the Democratic Republic of the Congo threatened to expand into a regional conflict, remained a major victim of international and domestic military violence. A sad statistic of the continuing worldwide violence was a UN report that estimated that as many as 300,000 children under the age of 18 were

serving as combatants in either government armed forces or armed opposition groups. The UN set 18 as the minimum age for troops serving in its peacekeeping efforts and recommended that members provide only soldiers over 21.

Arms Control and Disarmament. The Indian and Pakistani nuclear tests dismayed the supporters of nuclear nonproliferation and disarmament, but there were also some positive developments in regard to this issue. Brazil, which had a covert nuclear weapons program in the 1980s, signed the Nuclear Non-proliferation Treaty, which left Israel, Cuba, India, and Pakistan as the only nations that had not signed. The U.K. and France became the first nuclear powers to ratify the Comprehensive Test Ban Treaty. For this treaty to enter into force, it had to be ratified by 44 nuclear or potential nuclear states. Although three of those nations, North Korea, India, and Pakistan, had not signed the treaty, the leaders of the latter two indicated that they might sign if the international economic sanctions imposed on them after their tests were lifted. Russia continued to balk at ratifying the 1993 Strategic Arms Reduction Talks II (START-II) treaty, as many legislators charged that the agreement to cut the Russian and U.S. strategic nuclear arsenal to no more than 3,500 warheads each was biased in favour of the U.S.

By late in the year 133 nations had signed the 1997 Ottawa Convention banning the use, stockpiling, production, and transfer of antipersonnel land mines, and 59 had ratified it; as a result the convention would enter into force on March 1, 1999. Some countries, including Germany and the U.K., had already unilaterally banned land-mine use or had eliminated their stockpiles. The U.S. continued to be a holdout, maintaining that antipersonnel mines were needed to defend the demarcation line between North and South Korea.

At the year's end 169 nations had signed or acceded to the Chemical Weapons Convention, which prohibited the development, production, possession, or use of chemical weapons (CW) and mandated the destruction of all CW stockpiles by 2008. The U.S. was in technical noncompliance for much of the year until Congress in October enacted the necessary implementing domestic legislation. Russia, which possessed 40,000 metric tons of CW agents and had the largest declared stockpile, indicated that it would not be able to meet the destruction deadline because of financial problems.

United States. Last-minute congressional legislation included in the October omnibus appropriations bill provided $9.2 billion in emergency funding for the Defense Department. This increased fiscal 1999 defense appropriations to $278.8 billion, the first real rise in 14 years. The nation's top military leaders had warned that the quick tempo of operations connected with the many U.S. military commitments worldwide was eroding military readiness. Among other worrisome developments, several of the services were unable to meet their reenlistment goals. The air force had 700 fewer pilots than it needed, a shortfall that was projected to grow to 2,000 by 2002. The navy fell 12% short of its fiscal 1998 recruiting goal, a deficit of nearly 7,000 recruits. The Joint Chiefs of Staff had objected that readiness funding in the fiscal 1999

budget was $27 billion too low. The supplemental bill provided an extra $1.1 billion for that category.

Once again Congress gave the Pentagon some weapons it had not requested and balked at endorsing two future rounds of base closings that Secretary of Defense William Cohen had urged as necessary to provide savings to help meet procurement and readiness needs. The administration's request for money to continue work on the army's Theater High Altitude Area Defense system was cut nearly in half, as the program continued to have problems. In May the missile failed for the fifth time to intercept a simulated target. Later in the year the army announced that the next test had been postponed until early in 1999. Perhaps signaling the end of the "megamergers" in the defense industry, Lockheed Martin Corp. in July called off its proposed $8.3 billion acquisition of Northrop Grumman Corp. in the face of government opposition.

The relative ease with which terrorists or foreign enemies might obtain biological weapons and the threat of nuclear proliferation prompted Pres. Bill Clinton to strengthen the nation's defense against such unconventional threats. U.S. military personnel deployed to the Persian Gulf region were vaccinated against anthrax beginning in March, and in May the program was expanded to cover the total force. National Guard units in 10 states with high urban densities were given special training to assist state and local authorities following a biological, chemical, or nuclear attack. In retaliation for the terrorist bombing attacks on the U.S. embassies in Kenya and Tanzania, navy warships on August 20 launched cruise missile attacks against two facilities thought to be connected with the organization responsible for the embassy bombings: a terrorist training compound in Afghanistan and a chemical factory in Khartoum, Sudan, that was believed to be producing precursors for nerve gas. During the buildup of U.S. forces in the Persian Gulf in November, the air force deployed one of its new air expeditionary forces, an integrated package of bomber, fighter, and support aircraft.

The new Defense Threat Reduction Agency became operational on October 1. It combined the several defense agencies and offices that had been concerned with arms control and the proliferation of weapons of mass destruction, such as the On-Site Inspection Agency and the Defense Special Weapons Agency. October's omnibus spending bill included a provision to end the independent status of the Arms Control and Disarmament Agency and to incorporate it within the State Department.

Sexual misconduct by instructors and fellow recruits against female recruits during basic training and allegations of adultery continued to be problems. Despite calls for the complete separation of men and women in all the services during basic training, Defense Secretary Cohen in June approved plans that would provide for separate sleeping facilities for men and women but would continue to integrate the sexes in army, navy, and air force basic training units. The marine corps was allowed to retain its established policy of separating the sexes during basic training. In July Cohen issued guidance to standardize the "good order and discipline" policies of the services and to

clarify the guidance regarding the offense of adultery.

In February a marine corps EA-6B Prowler electronic countermeasures aircraft struck a gondola cable while on a low-level training mission in the Italian Alps, causing the deaths of the 20 skiers who were riding in the gondola. The pilot and navigator of the jet faced a court-martial. In regard to gay rights, advocates charged that the government's "don't ask, don't tell" policy for homosexuals in the military was discriminatory; a federal appeals court in September, however, upheld the policy.

NATO. The process of bringing the Czech Republic, Hungary, and Poland into the alliance continued smoothly, and by the end of the year all of NATO's 16 members except The Netherlands had ratified the accession protocols. Plans continued to induct formally the three new members at a summit meeting in Washington, D.C., in April 1999. Twenty-nine nations, including Russia and Ukraine, participated in the NATO-led Stabilization Force (SFOR) in Bosnia and Herzegovina. In June the UN Security Council extended the mandate of SFOR until June 21, 1999, and NATO organized a slightly smaller follow-up force in which U.S. participation dropped from 8,500 to 6,900.

Disagreements over NATO policy in the Balkans led to a chilling of the alliance's relations with Russia. In June Russia recalled its military representative at NATO headquarters in Brussels and refused to allow NATO to establish a military mission in Moscow, as was called for in the 1997 Founding Act regulating NATO's special relationship with Russia. In October the Russians briefly recalled both their ambassador and military representative from Brussels and warned that Russia would abrogate the Founding Act and sever all relations with NATO should the latter carry out its threat to conduct air strikes against Yugoslavia.

The perennial tension between NATO members Greece and Turkey continued, exacerbated by the Russian commitment to provide sophisticated air defense missile systems to the Greek government on Cyprus and the brief deployment of Turkish F-16 jets to a new military air base on the Turkish Republic of Northern Cyprus. In May representatives from Germany, Italy, Spain, and the U.K. signed production contracts for the first batch of 148 Eurofighters, with the first deliveries expected in 2002. The export version of the plane was dubbed "Typhoon." Canada bought four surplus Upholder-class diesel submarines from the U.K. to replace its aging submarine fleet.

United Kingdom. In July Defence Secretary George Robertson announced the conclusions of the Strategic Defence Review. It placed emphasis on enhancing Britain's joint operations capabilities, including the creation of Joint Rapid Reaction Forces. Service modernization was to include two new large aircraft carriers for the Royal Navy, increasing the number of deployable army brigades from five to six, and modernizing the Royal Air Force's (RAF's) air transport fleet. To help pay for those programs, the ministry planned to sell off assets worth more than £2.2 billion.

During the year the Trident submarine-launched ballistic missile became Britain's sole nuclear weapons system; all RAF WE177 free-fall nuclear bombs were removed from service and dismantled. Only one missile submarine would be on patrol at any time, carrying a reduced load of 48 warheads. In a break with centuries of naval tradition, two women formally took command of Royal Navy warships in March.

France. Defense Minister Alain Richard presented a F 243.5 billion (U.S. $43.8 billion) 1999 budget proposal in keeping with the four-year defense spending plan he had unveiled in April. That plan was designed to cut F 20 billion ($3.5 billion) from the defense budget by 2002. To help meet this goal, France abandoned seven military programs, including the Horus radar satellite joint effort with Germany. Procurement under the 1999 budget plan was set at F 86 billion ($15.5 billion), which represented the first time since 1990 that this category had risen. It would provide 33 new Leclerc tanks for the army plus orders for 44 more as well as the start of production of the Franco-Germany Tiger helicopter.

Placing into service the nuclear aircraft carrier *Charles de Gaulle* topped the navy's priority list. The service also was to receive the first naval version of the Rafale fighter aircraft and the second E-2C Hawkeye maritime surveillance aircraft. The first production-series Rafale fighter was also to be delivered to the air force in 1999. In March Gen. Jean-Pierre Kelche was appointed chief of staff of the armed forces.

Germany. German officials continued in 1998 to show that they had overcome their previous reluctance to involve German forces in combat outside the nation's borders. In October the federal parliament approved a government offer to provide 14 jet planes and 500 troops to participate in any NATO campaign against Yugoslavia.

Rudolf Scharping, former leader of the Social Democratic Party (SPD) in the parliament, was named defense minister in the newly elected SPD government. A defense structures commission was appointed to review the tasks, structure, and equipment of the nation's armed forces.

The Rest of Europe. In February Yugoslav police began a crackdown on what they termed "terrorist" forces among the ethnic Albanian majority in the Serbian province of Kosovo. The effort escalated to include military units, and fighting occasionally spilled across the Albanian border. In April the UN Security Council imposed an arms embargo on Yugoslavia, and in September it demanded a cease-fire in Kosovo and the withdrawal from the province of Yugoslav security forces. NATO prepared for a bombing campaign against Yugoslavia but held off when Yugoslav Pres. Slobodan Milosevic in October agreed to remove his security forces from Kosovo and to allow a 2,000-strong Organization for Security and Cooperation in Europe observer force into the province to verify the pullout. In December, however, the cease-fire was broken when security forces attacked an ethnic Albanian stronghold.

The establishment of regional joint security or peacekeeping forces grew in popularity throughout Europe. These ranged in size from a planned Danish-German-Polish 50,000-strong mechanized corps to be headquartered in Szczecin, Pol., when Poland joined NATO to the small "Baltron" joint naval force composed of two minesweepers each from Estonia, Latvia, and Lithuania. In September defense ministers from Albania, Bulgaria, Greece, Italy, Macedonia, Romania, and Turkey signed an agreement to form a joint Balkan peacekeeping force of 4,000 troops. Hungary and Romania agreed to form a joint battalion, and a joint Polish-Lithuanian battalion was scheduled to become operational in January 1999.

Turkey. Continuing its long battle against the Kurdistan Workers' Party (PKK), the Turkish military made several incursions into northern Iraq during the year to attack suspected PKK bases. In October this struggle threatened to spill over into Syria. Turkish officials charged that Syria was harbouring PKK rebels, and Gen. Huseyin Kivrikoglu, who had been named chief of the general staff in August, said that Turkey was in "an undeclared war" with Syria.

In regard to domestic matters, Kivrikoglu pledged to continue the military's determined fight against Islamic fundamentalism. When the Supreme Military Council met in August, it decided to purge 25 officers suspected of links to Islamic extremist groups.

Commonwealth of Independent States (CIS). Buffeted by years of financial neglect, government indifference, and inept

Soldiers of Russia's Ministry of the Interior read the Russian national oath during a ceremony at the Sofrino Barracks in Moscow. Russia's faltering economy caused hardship for the military, including pay that was months in arrears.

leadership, the Russian armed forces continued to deteriorate. In September Defense Minister Marshal Igor Sergeyev stated that only the strategic rocket troops and the elite airborne forces were able to carry out their military tasks effectively. Earlier in the year he had admitted that it would be impossible to meet Pres. Boris Yeltsin's goal of reforming the armed forces by the year 2000, turning the military into an all-volunteer force. One of the few reform measures carried out in 1998 was the merger of the air force and air defense troops.

In August Yeltsin approved a UN Security Council defense policy document that established the concepts of military development until the year 2005. Although not made public, the plan was said to recognize that Russia would not be threatened by an all-out war during that period but would face small-scale conflicts along its borders and internal instability. The document also called for the administrative reorganization of the military districts and promoted the role of the armed forces proper at the expense of the military forces, such as the border and interior troops, that were subordinate to other ministries and departments. These were to be reduced in size. Security Council Secretary Andrey Kokoshin was clearly instrumental in preparing this policy document and had also been the driving force behind military reform when he served as first deputy defense minister. He was, however, abruptly dismissed from his duties on September 10.

Pay for the personnel in the military continued to be months in arrears despite repeated promises from the government to

Approximate Strengths of Selected Regular Armed Forces of the World

Country	Military personnel in 000s				Warships				Combat aircraft[1]				
					Submarines		Aircraft Carriers/ Cruisers	Destroyers/ Frigates	Bombers and fighter- ground attack	Fighters	Recon- nais- sance	Tanks[3]	Defense expenditure as % of 1997 GNP
	Total	Army	Navy	Air Force[2]	Nuclear	Diesel							
I. NATO													
Belgium	43.7[4]	28.2	2.6	11.6	—	—	—	3	100	—	—	155	1.6
Canada	60.6[4]	20.9	9.0	15.0	—	3	—	16	122	—	18	114	1.3
Denmark	32.1	22.9	3.7	5.5	—	5	—	3	69	—	—	337	1.7
France	358.8[4]	203.2	63.3[5]	78.1	10	2	2	39	400	104	68	548	3.0
Germany	333.5	230.6	26.7	76.2	—	14	—	15	288	175	58	2,716	1.6
Greece	168.5	116.0	19.5	33.0	—	7	—	16	265	115	28	1,735	4.6
Italy	298.4[4]	165.6	40.0	63.6	—	8	2	28	147	90	34	1,299	1.9
Netherlands, The	57.2[4]	27.0	13.8	12.0	—	4	—	16	170	—	15	600	1.9
Norway	28.9[4]	15.2	6.1	6.7	—	12	—	4	58	15	6	170	2.3
Portugal	53.6[4]	24.8	16.8	7.3	—	3	—	10	63	—	5	180	2.6
Spain	194.0	127.0	37.0[5]	30.0	—	8	1	17	41	149	21	725	1.4
Turkey	639.0	525.0	51.0[5]	63.0	—	16	—	21	354	47	39	4,205	4.2
United Kingdom	210.9	113.9	44.5[5]	52.5	15	—	3	35	311	106	71	545	2.8
United States	1,401.6	479.4	551.9[5]	370.3	84	—	31	97	3,613	270	231	8,239	3.4
II. NON-NATO EUROPE													
Albania	unk	unk	2.5	6.0	—	1	—	—	47	51	—	721	6.7
Armenia	53.4[4]	52.0	—	—	—	—	—	—	5	1	—	102	8.9
Austria	45.5	45.5	—	—	—	—	—	—	53	—	—	169	0.8
Azerbaijan	72.1[4]	55.6	2.2	10.3	—	—	—	2	16	19	2	270	4.0
Belarus	83.0[4]	43.0	—	22.0	—	—	—	—	129	135	12	1,778	2.9
Bosnia and Herzegovina	40.0	40.0	—	—	—	—	—	—	—	—	—	60+	5.0
Bosnian Serbs	30.0	30.0	—	—	—	—	—	—	20	—	—	570	n/a
Bulgaria	101.5[4]	50.4	6.1	19.3	—	2	—	1	112	84	21	1,475	3.4
Croatia	56.2	50.0	3.0	3.2	—	1	—	—	40	—	—	298	5.7
Czech Republic	59.1[4]	25.3	—	15.0	—	—	—	—	51	58	—	938	2.2
Finland	31.7	24.0	5.0	2.7	—	—	—	—	—	91	—	230	1.7
Georgia	33.2[4]	12.6	2.0	3.0	—	—	—	—	9	—	—	79	10.2
Hungary	43.3[4]	23.4	—	11.5	—	—	—	—	—	114	—	835	2.9
Poland	240.6[4]	142.5	17.1	55.3	—	3	—	2	127	182	16	1,727	2.3
Romania	219.6[4]	111.3	22.1[5]	46.3	—	1	—	7	74	267	21	1,373	2.3
Slovakia	45.4[4]	23.8	—	12.0	—	—	—	—	32	81	8	478	2.1
Sweden	53.1	35.1	9.2	8.8	—	10	—	—	211	151	—	537	2.4
Ukraine	346.4[4]	171.3	12.5[5]	124.4	—	4	—	9	403	455	112	4,104	2.7
Yugoslavia	114.2	90.0	7.5	16.7	—	4	—	4	121	79	38	1,270	7.8
III. RUSSIA													
Russia	1,159.0[4]	420.0	180.0[5]	359.0[6]	72	26	18	26	1,326	1,500	354	15,600	5.8
IV. MIDDLE EAST AND NORTH AFRICA; SUB-SAHARAN AFRICA; LATIN AMERICA													
Algeria	122.0	105.0	7.0	10.0	—	2	—	3	60	121	10	951	4.6
Egypt	450.0	320.0	20.0	110.0	—	4	—	9	165	400	20	3,700	4.3
Iran	545.6	450.0	45.6[5]	50.0	—	3	—	3	155	139	21	1,400	6.6
Iraq	429.0	375.0	2.0	52.0	—	—	—	2	166	180	—	2,700	7.4
Israel	175.0	134.0	9.0	32.0	—	3	—	—	450	—	22	4,300	11.5
Jordan	104.0	90.0	0.5	13.5	—	—	—	—	50	43	—	1,217	6.4
Lebanon	55.1	53.3	1.0	0.8	—	—	—	—	—	3	—	315	4.5
Libya	65.0	35.0	8.0	22.0	—	2	—	3	200	209	11	985	4.7
Morocco	196.3	175.0	7.8	13.5	—	—	—	1	70	15	4	524	4.2
Oman	43.5[4]	25.0	4.2	4.1	—	—	—	—	40	—	—	121	10.9
Saudi Arabia	105.5	70.0	13.5[5]	22.0	—	—	—	8	231	191	10	1,055	12.4
Sudan, The	94.7	90.0	1.7	3.0	—	—	—	—	45	6	—	280	5.6
Syria	320.0	215.0	5.0	100.0	—	3	—	2	240	335	14	4,600	6.3
Tunisia	35.0	27.0	4.5	3.5	—	—	—	—	44	—	—	84	1.8
United Arab Emirates	64.5	59.0	1.5	4.0	—	—	—	2	58	31	8	231	5.5
Yemen	66.3	61.0	1.8	3.5	—	—	—	—	29	20	—	1,320	7.0
Angola	114.0	106.0	2.0	6.0	—	—	—	—	31	4	10	300	8.8
Burundi	43.5[4]	40.0	—	—	—	—	—	—	4	—	—	—	5.7

remedy this situation. Many officers were forced to take illegal second jobs or borrow money from their parents in order to feed their families. The Ministry of Defense even suggested that the troops and their families be sent out into the forests and fields to forage for food. In these humiliating conditions the military suicide rate remained high.

With virtually no domestic contracts, Russia's defense industry continued to rely on foreign sales to survive. China and India continued to be the best customers, as the financial crisis in Asia forced the cancellation of a lucrative deal to sell jet fighters and combat helicopters to Indonesia. Following U.S. and Israeli charges that the Russians were supplying sensitive ballistic missile technology to Iran, a government commission in July began investigations of nine organizations suspected of violating the laws on the export of dual-use technology.

Russia lost one more link in the former Soviet chain of ballistic missile early-warning sites when Latvia refused to extend the lease on the radar at Skrunda, demanding instead that it be dismantled. Efforts to create a "common defense sphere" covering the territory of the former Soviet Union proceeded fitfully. The closest military ties were those between Russia and Belarus. Both parliaments ratified a loose military alliance, and there was talk of forming some joint forces. All the CIS members except Azerbaijan and Moldova participated to one degree or another in a united air-defense system. Russia continued to maintain peace-

Approximate Strengths of Selected Regular Armed Forces of the World (continued)

| Country | Military personnel in 000s | | | | Warships | | | | Combat aircraft[1] | | | | |
| | Total | Army | Navy | Air Force[2] | Submarines | | Aircraft Carriers/ Cruisers | Destroyers/ Frigates | Bombers and fighter-ground attack | Fighters | Recon-nais-sance | Tanks[3] | Defense expenditure as % of 1997 GNP |
					Nuclear	Diesel							
IV. MIDDLE EAST AND NORTH AFRICA; SUB-SAHARAN AFRICA; LATIN AMERICA													
Cameroon	22.1[4]	11.5	1.3	0.3	—	—	—	—	15	—	—	—	2.9
Chad	30.3[4]	25.0	—	0.3	—	—	—	—	4	—	—	60	4.1
Congo, Dem. Rep. of	10.0	8.0	0.8	1.2	—	—	—	—	12	—	—	40	2.5
Eritrea	47.1	46.0	1.1	—	—	—	—	1	15	—	—	unk	8.3
Ethiopia	120.0[4]	100.0	—	—	—	—	—	—	63	—	—	350	2.1
Kenya	24.2	20.5	1.2	2.5	—	—	—	—	30	—	—	76	2.4
Nigeria	77.0	62.0	5.5	9.5	—	—	—	1	91	—	—	200	4.0
Rwanda	47.0[4]	40.0	—	—	—	—	—	—	—	—	—	12	5.5
South Africa	82.4[4]	58.6	5.5	10.9	—	3	—	—	116	—	—	124	1.8
Tanzania	34.0	30.0	1.0	3.0	—	—	—	—	—	—	19	65	3.4
Uganda	40.0	40.0	—	—	—	—	—	—	4	—	—	50	2.4
Zambia	21.6	20.0	—	1.6	—	—	—	—	49	14	—	30	1.7
Zimbabwe	39.0	35.0	—	4.0	—	—	—	—	35	12	15	32	4.7
Argentina	73.0	41.0	20.0[5]	12.0	—	3	—	13	223	—	29	326	1.7
Bolivia	33.5	25.0	4.5[5]	4.0	—	—	—	—	32	18	—	—	2.0
Brazil	313.2	195.0	68.2[5]	50.0	—	6	1	18	284	16	30	60	2.3
Chile	94.5	51.0	30.0[5]	13.5	—	4	—	8	73	15	18	130	2.8
Colombia	146.3	121.0	18.0[5]	7.3	—	2	—	4	59	—	13	—	4.0
Cuba	53.0	38.0	5.0[5]	10.0	—	1	—	2	14	116	—	1,500	5.2
Dominican Republic	24.5	15.0	4.0[5]	5.5	—	—	—	—	10	—	—	—	1.2
Ecuador	57.1	50.0	4.1[5]	3.0	—	2	—	2	31	14	—	3	3.5
El Salvador	24.6	22.3	0.7[5]	1.6	—	—	—	—	18	—	11	—	1.9
Guatemala	31.4	29.2	1.5[5]	0.7	—	—	—	—	14	—	—	—	1.9
Mexico	175.0	130.0	37.0[5]	8.0	—	—	—	9	101	10	23	—	1.0
Peru	125.0	85.0	25.0[5]	15.0	—	8	2	5	77	41	7	300	2.2
Uruguay	25.6	17.6	5.0[5]	3.0	—	—	—	3	33	—	1	15	2.3
Venezuela	79.0[4]	34.0	15.0[5]	7.0	—	2	—	6	101	—	22	70	1.1
V. SOUTH AND CENTRAL ASIA; EAST ASIA AND OCEANIA													
Australia	57.4	25.4	14.3	17.7	—	4	—	11	103	—	23	71	2.2
Bangladesh	121.0	101.0	10.5	9.5	—	—	—	4	49	—	—	140	1.9
Cambodia	139.0[4]	90.0	2.0	2.0	—	—	—	—	5	24	—	100	7.3
China	2,820.0	2,090.0	260.0[5]	470.0	6	57	—	53	842	2,967	298	8,800	5.7
India	1,175.0	980.0	55.0[5]	140.0	—	19	1	24	406	379	64	3,414	3.3
Indonesia	476.0[4]	235.0	43.0[5]	21.0	—	2	—	17	67	12	61	—	2.2
Japan	242.6[4]	151.8	43.8	45.6	—	16	—	57	110	229	120	1,090	1.0
Kazakstan	55.1	40.0	0.1	15.0	—	—	—	—	79	32	12	630	2.3
Korea, North	1,054.0	923.0	46.0	85.0	—	26	—	3	607	—	—	3,000	27.0
Korea, South	672.0	560.0	60.0[5]	52.0	—	14	—	34	330	130	51	2,190	3.3
Laos	29.1	25.0	0.6	3.5	—	—	—	—	26	—	—	30	3.9
Malaysia	110.0	85.0	12.5	12.5	—	—	—	6	52	33	4	—	3.7
Myanmar (Burma)	434.8[4]	325.0	15.8[5]	9.0	—	—	—	—	85	36	—	126	7.7
Nepal	46.0	46.0	—	—	—	—	—	—	—	—	—	—	0.9
Pakistan	587.0	520.0	22.0[5]	45.0	—	9	—	10	163	228	19	2,120	5.8
Philippines	117.8	74.5	25.9[5]	17.4	—	—	—	1	12	6	29	—	1.7
Singapore	72.5	50.0	9.0	13.5	—	1	—	—	112	37	8	60	4.3
Sri Lanka	115.0	95.0	10.0	10.0	—	—	—	—	22	—	—	25	6.1
Taiwan	376.0	240.0	68.0[5]	68.0	—	4	—	36	529	—	31	719	4.7
Thailand	306.0	190.0	73.0[5]	43.0	—	—	1	14	167	50	44	277	2.1
Uzbekistan	80.0[4]	50.0	—	4.0	—	—	—	—	34	64	10	370	3.9
Vietnam	484.0	412.0	42.0[5]	30.0	—	2	—	7	77	124	4	1,315	4.1

Note: Data exclude most paramilitary, security, and irregular forces. Naval data exclude vessels of less than 100 tons standard displacement. Figures are for June 1998. Because of substantive changes in national forces and reassessments of evidence, data may not be comparable with previous editions.
[1] Includes combat aircraft from all services, including naval and air defense. Light strike/counterinsurgency aircraft are included in bomb/fighter—ground attack category. Reconnaissance includes maritime reconnaissance and antisubmarine warfare aircraft.
[2] Includes air defense troops.
[3] Main battle tanks (MBT), weighing at least 16.5 metric tons with gun of at least 75-mm caliber.
[4] Some countries have staffs, centrally controlled units, support services, military police, regular armed forces not responsible to Ministry of Defense, and the like, which means total armed forces are greater than the sum of the three armed forces.
[5] Includes marines or naval infantry.
[6] Includes strategic missile forces.
Source: International Institute for Strategic Studies, 23 Tavistock Street, London, *The Military Balance 1998–1999*.

Women in Baghdad demonstrate in support of Iraq's decision to stop cooperating with the UN Special Commission, which was overseeing inspections for weapons of mass destruction in Iraq.

had to stop. When Iraq continued to deny the inspectors access to some facilities, the U.S. and U.K. in December staged an air attack on selected targets in the country. At the year's end Iraq fired missiles at U.S. and British aircraft patrolling the "no-fly zones" in northern and southern Iraq; the U.S. and British retaliated by firing on an Iraqi air-defense battery.

In July Iran successfully tested the new Shehab-3 ballistic missile. With an estimated range of some 1,300 km (800 mi), it was based on a missile that Iran had purchased from North Korea. In Israel, Iranian-born Gen. Shaul Mofaz was named chief of staff in May. In an effort brokered by the U.S. to rejuvenate the Israeli-Palestinian peace process, the two sides signed another interim peace agreement in October. At the same time, the U.S. pledged to help protect Israel against the threat of ballistic missiles and weapons of mass destruction.

In Algeria the government continued to be unable to neutralize the extremist Islamic rebels, who had been conducting a terrorist campaign since 1992. In April the rebels killed 80 soldiers and seized large quantities of weapons in a raid on a military post south of Algiers.

South and Central Asia. The arms race between India and Pakistan escalated early in 1998 when Pakistan tested its new Ghauri medium-range ballistic missile. The new Hindu nationalist coalition government in India responded by conducting a series of nuclear tests, and Pakistan swiftly countered in kind. President Clinton immediately imposed economic sanctions on both countries.

The new Indian government's budget called for defense spending to be raised by 14%. At the end of July and in early August, India and Pakistan exchanged artillery fire across their border in disputed Kashmir. Tensions eased somewhat when the two parties met in October for peace talks, the first in more than a year. Although little progress was made, they pledged to meet again early in 1999.

The Taliban Islamic militia seemed during the year to be on the verge of occupying all of Afghanistan, but the success of this fundamentalist movement alarmed many of Afghanistan's neighbours, and so they supported an alliance that continued to defy the Taliban in the northeastern part of the country. Russia, Tajikistan, and Uzbekistan provided aid to the resistance groups, led by Ahmad Shah Masoud and Gen. 'Abd ar-Rashid Dostam. Iran also helped Masoud as well as the Shi'ite Hezb-i Wahdat faction. Following the murder of at least nine Iranians in Afghanistan in August, Iran was reported to have moved as many as 200,000 troops to the Afghan border. There was a brief border clash in early October.

In Sri Lanka the 15-year-old civil war between the government and the separatist Liberation Tigers of Tamil Eelam (LTTE) was no closer to resolution. In January the LTTE staged a daring suicide bombing of Sri Lanka's holiest Buddhist shrine. The two sides agreed to a brief cease-fire, which lasted only until April 19, when the LTTE blew up two government naval vessels. (*See* WORLD AFFAIRS: *Sri Lanka:* Sidebar.)

East and Southeast Asia, Oceania. North Korea's military activities continued to worry some of its neighbours. In June a North Korean miniature submarine thought

keeping troops in the Abkhazian region of Georgia, in Moldova, and in Tajikistan. In the latter, despite an agreement between the government and the opposition leadership to form a combined government of national unity, splinter opposition forces engaged government troops in heavy combat throughout the year. In early November a rebel group led by a former colonel in the Tajik army, Mahmud Khudoiberdiyev, invaded northwestern Tajikistan from bases in Uzbekistan. After capturing the country's second largest city, Khujand, the rebels were overwhelmed by government forces.

Concerned about the advances of the fundamentalist Islamic forces in neighbouring Afghanistan, Russia indicated that it might maintain a strong military presence in Tajikistan even after the civil war had ended. In Georgia about 100 soldiers mutinied in October and joined supporters of a deceased president, Zviad Gamsakhurdia. The insurgents marched on the city of Kutaisi with a force that included tanks and armoured personnel carriers. After a brief clash they returned to their barracks.

Middle East and North Africa. Iraqi Pres. Saddam Hussein repeatedly placed restrictions on the UN weapons-inspections teams in Iraq, provoking the U.S. and its allies to threaten retaliatory air attacks. In February Iraq refused to allow the teams to enter any of the many presidential palaces. UN Secretary-General Kofi Annan negotiated a compromise in which eight of the palaces could be inspected, provided UN diplomats accompanied the inspectors. At another location UN inspectors found traces of VX nerve gas on missile warheads despite assurances by the Iraqis that they had never loaded any weapons with chemical agents. The inspectors also suspected that Iraq was using its legal short-range missile program to conceal the continued development of banned long-range missiles. In August Iraq said it would no longer allow surprise inspections at new sites, and in October Hussein said that all inspections

to be on a mission to infiltrate agents into South Korea was caught in a fishing net just south of the border. The nine crewmen were found shot to death, and it was thought that four had killed the other five and then committed suicide. Three senior South Korean military commanders were fired several weeks later when evidence was found of another, successful, infiltration effort. In August North Korea attempted to place a small satellite in orbit, using a three-stage launch vehicle that overflew Japan. The attempt was first identified as a missile test and prompted Japan to postpone signing an agreement on sharing the cost of providing nuclear reactors to North Korea. The North Korean government refused a U.S. demand to inspect an underground facility suspected to be a nuclear weapons production plant under construction, but later said that if the U.S. paid it hundreds of millions of dollars it would allow the inspection to proceed. The four-power peace talks to end the Korean War officially broke down in March. When they resumed in October, North Korea once again demanded that the agenda focus on a U.S. troop withdrawal from South Korea.

During President Clinton's visit to China in June and July, he and Chinese Pres. Jiang Zemin announced that the two countries would no longer target each other with strategic nuclear missiles. The Chinese also agreed that they would not provide India or Pakistan with nuclear weapons or ballistic missile technology. President Jiang in July ordered the military to give up its huge commercial business empire.

The Asian financial crisis forced many countries in the region to abandon or postpone military modernization plans. In Indonesia the military did not block the ouster of President Suharto (*see* BIOGRAPHIES) but was accused of being ineffective in controlling the accompanying civil turmoil. Troops from Myanmar (Burma) were involved in skirmishes along that country's borders with both Thailand and Bangladesh. Although the Cambodian government believed that its troops had wiped out the last pockets of Khmer Rouge resistance forces

early in the year, Khmer Rouge guerrillas resumed their attacks on government positions in July. Fourteen senior Vietnamese military officers, including the chief of staff, were killed in a military plane crash in Laos in May.

Caribbean and Latin America. After 25 years in the post, Gen. Augusto Pinochet Ugarte retired as head of the Chilean army in March and was then sworn in as a senator for life in the Chilean legislature in line with a controversial constitutional provision enacted in 1980 while he headed the military junta ruling Chile. In October, however, while in London for medical treatment, Pinochet was arrested at the request of a Spanish magistrate. The Spanish judge wanted him extradited so that he could be tried for human rights violations against Spanish citizens during his military regime.

In October Peru and Ecuador settled a border dispute that had brought them to blows in 1941, 1981, and 1995. The Colombian government appeared to be losing ground in its struggle against the country's leftist guerrillas. Disturbed by a number of humiliating military setbacks, newly elected Pres. Andrés Pastrana replaced almost all the country's top military leaders in August.

Africa South of the Sahara. The Democratic Republic of the Congo (formerly Zaire) was again the scene of bitter fighting as troops from Angola, Chad, Namibia, and Zimbabwe aided the government of Pres. Laurent Kabila against disgruntled members of Kabila's army; the latter were supported by Uganda and Rwanda. Ethnic animosities again played a key role in the conflict. Kabila turned against the minority Tutsi soldiers who had helped bring him to power and embraced Hutu support, including that of the fugitive Rwandan Hutu soldiers who had been guilty of genocide against the Tutsi within their own country. In neighbouring Burundi, Hutu rebels clashed with the Tutsi-dominated army early in the year. The 17 parties involved in Burundi's long civil war began peace talks in Arusha, Tanz., in June. Two subsequent sessions were held, with a fourth planned for January 1999.

Nigerian military leader Gen. Sani Abacha died suddenly in June. (*See* OBITUARIES.) The military installed Gen. Abdulsalam Abubakar, the former defense chief of staff, as the country's new leader. (*See* BIOGRAPHIES.) The Nigerian-led West African peacekeeping force (ECOMOG) finally ended the civil war in Liberia, although conflict briefly erupted in Monrovia in September when a former faction leader sought refuge in the American embassy. ECOMOG was also successful in ousting the military junta in Sierra Leone and restoring Pres. Ahmad Tejan Kabbah to power. Rebel forces, however, continued to remain active in the north and east of the country. In October a military court in Sierra Leone found 34 persons, including two former chiefs of staff, guilty of treason for collaborating with the junta; 24 were executed. Also in West Africa, troops loyal to the head of Guinea-Bissau's military forces, Gen. Ansumane Mane, mutinied in June when Ansumane was dismissed. Senegal and Guinea provided troops to help the forces loyal to Pres. João Bernardo Vieira. A cease-fire agreement signed in July soon broke down, and rebel troops had approached the capital by mid-October. The two sides signed a peace agreement in November.

In February soldiers in Niger who had not been paid for four months also briefly mutinied. In October troops from Niger, Nigeria, and Chad launched a joint operation to clean out Chadian rebels operating in the region where the three countries had common borders.

In May Ethiopia and Eritrea clashed over disputed territory along their joint border. The fighting escalated during the next month to include air strikes by both sides. As the year ended, Eritrean forces continued to occupy territory claimed by Ethiopia. The long civil war in southern Sudan continued, with heavy fighting driving thousands from their homes in an area ravaged by famine. The rebel Sudan People's Liberation Army (SPLA) accepted a government cease-fire offer in August, but the truce was soon broken.

South Africa in April for the first time appointed a black general, Lieut. Gen. Siphiwe Nyanda, to head its armed forces. South Africa and Botswana encountered unexpected opposition in September when they sent troops to quell a military mutiny in Lesotho, an independent enclave surrounded by South Africa. This intervention surprised many, as South African Pres. Nelson Mandela had been a strong advocate of mediation in settling disputes between African nations.

New Technology. The U.S. Global Hawk unmanned reconnaissance aircraft made its first flight on February 28. With a 35.3-m (116-ft) wingspan, it was designed to operate with a range of 13,500 nautical miles at altitudes up to 19,800 m (65,000 ft) and with an endurance of 40 hours. The aircraft could carry radar, electro-optical, and infrared sensors and was able to transmit these data to ground stations via satellite link. At the other end of the size spectrum, Lockheed Martin unveiled the 12-cm (5-in)-wingspan Micro-Star air reconnaissance vehicle. Equipped with a day/night camera and a transmitter, the 85-g (3-oz) craft was designed to stay aloft for 20 minutes at an altitude of 60 m (200 ft), transmitting real-time intelligence to a laptop computer that would serve as a ground station.   (DOUGLAS L. CLARKE)

A Pakistani shopkeeper in the town of Chakoti cleans debris left after a bombardment in August by Indian troops from across the disputed Kashmir border.

Performing Arts

MUSIC

Classical. Throughout 1998 new operas were being composed and old ones were being revived at an accelerating pace. The new opera that attracted the most attention was *A Streetcar Named Desire,* commissioned and produced by the San Francisco Opera. The music was composed and conducted by André Previn, and Philip Little created a libretto based on the Tennessee Williams play. Renée Fleming sang the role of Blanche, and Rodney Gilfry played Stanley. Other notable premieres included Tan Dun's *Marco Polo* in New York City, Henry Mollicone's *Coyote Tales* in Kansas City, Mo., Mark Adamo's *Little Women* in Houston, Texas, Richard Wargo's *Ballymore* in Philadelphia and Milwaukee, Wis., and Eric Salzman's *The True Last Words of Dutch Schultz* in Amsterdam. Also premiered at the Lincoln Center Festival in New York City was *Patience and Sarah,* an opera by composer Paula Kimper and librettist Wende Parsons about a lesbian relationship between two women in Puritan New England.

Perhaps the most talked-about revival was *The Philosopher's Stone,* an opera written by three obscure contemporaries of Mozart, who also contributed several pieces of music. The libretto was written by Emanuel Schikaneder, author of the libretto for Mozart's *The Magic Flute.* Its first performance in more than two centuries was given in Boston by the Boston Baroque ensemble. Other notable revivals included Marvin David Levy's *Mourning Becomes Electra* by the Lyric Opera of Chicago and Kurt Weill's *Die Burgschaft.* The Spoleto Festival U.S.A. in Charleston, S.C., was host to the first American production of Francesco Cavalli's 350-year-old opera *Giasone.* The festival also premiered the new multimedia work *Hindenburg.* Described as a "meditation on humanity's hubris," the piece was a collaboration between composer Steve Reich and his wife, video artist Beryl Korot.

The effect of new technology was also evident. Some composers incorporated "created" sounds into their works, and several new productions employed various kinds of technology in their music. *Magic Frequencies* by Meredith Monk was a multimedia work dealing with folk art, outer space, and science fiction; the opera received its first performance in Munich, Ger. The Brooklyn (N.Y.) Academy of Music premiered *Chaos,* by the group Bang on a Can. The opera featured amplified singers, drum machines, synthesizers, and samplers. Matthew Maquire's libretto included elements of chaos theory in telling the story of two scientists who reach the "chaos zone" and encounter Pierre and Marie Curie.

Puccini's *Turandot* received its first performance in China when it was staged in an open-air format in Beijing's Forbidden City. Under the direction of Zubin Mehta, Sharon Sweet sang the role of Turandot, and Calaf was performed by Kristjan Johannsson. The producers claimed that at $15 million it was the most expensive opera ever produced.

New Yorkers were not so fortunate. The Lincoln Center Festival clashed with government officials in China when director Chen Shizheng attempted to stage a production of *The Peony Pavillion.* The classic Chinese opera runs for 20 hours and tells the story of a young woman who dies longing for the ideal love. Her ghost finds her soulmate, she is brought back to life, and the lovers marry. Written in 1598 by Tang Xianzu, the opera was considered a masterpiece of the venerated Kunqu Opera, a highly stylized, traditional form. Chen had revised the production to update and enliven the opera, but the Shanghai Bureau of Culture objected to his changes and refused to release the props, costumes, and sets. Intervention by high-level U.S. and French diplomats (the production was to travel later to France), and appeals by both Chen and Nigel Redden, the newly appointed director of the Lincoln Center Festival, proved futile.

Under the direction of Kurt Masur, the New York Philharmonic opened its season with a cycle of Beethoven and was joined by Isaac Stern as violin soloist. The orchestra went on to perform all nine Beethoven symphonies during a 10-week span. The Cleveland (Ohio) Orchestra had the distinction of performing perhaps the last premiere of a work by American composer Charles Ives, who died in 1954. David G. Porter, an Ives scholar, reconstructed the composer's "Emerson" Piano Concerto, using the Second Piano Sonata (subtitled *Concord, Mass., 1840–60*) and the Fourth Symphony as resources. The pianist was Alan Feinberg, with Christoph von Dohnanyi conducting.

GEORGE NIKITIN—AP/WIDE WORLD

In a rehearsal scene for Tennessee Williams's play *A Streetcar Named Desire*, Rodney Gilfrey, as Stanley Kowalski, plays opposite Renée Fleming's Blanche DuBois. The play made its world premeire as an opera at the San Francisco Opera on the weekend of September 19–20.

The music of American composer George Gershwin, who specialized in creating compositions for the Broadway musical theatre, was performed at numerous venues celebrating the 100th anniversary of his birth on September 26.

At Carnegie Hall the Violin Concerto of violinist and composer Ellen Taafe Zwilich was also premiered. In observance of Israel's 50th anniversary, the Israel Philharmonic Orchestra under Zubin Mehta spent three weeks touring throughout the U.S. with a series of fund-raising concerts.

The anniversaries of many composers and performers were observed in 1998. Hildegard von Bingen (1098–1179) was the earliest composer to be feted. Her *Ordo Virtutum* received a number of performances, including one for an audience of 5,000 in London's Royal Albert Hall. The Sequentia ensemble performed it in 1998 as part of its project to record all of her music on the Deutsche Harmonia Mundi label. The most lavishly celebrated anniversary—in classical, jazz, and popular circles—was George Gershwin's centennial. Also widely observed were the centennials of two close associates of Kurt Weill: Bertolt Brecht, librettist of *Die Dreigoschenoper* and *Aufstieg und Fall der Stadt Mahagonny,* and Lotte Lenya, Weill's wife and most noted interpreter. Luciano Pavarotti and Plácido Domingo both celebrated the 30th anniversaries of their debuts at the Metropolitan Opera in New York City. The avant-garde Kronos Quartet and the British early music choral group the Tallis Scholars both commemorated their 25th anniversaries.

The Vienna Boys' Choir celebrated its 500th anniversary in 1998 amid a maelstrom of controversy. Agnes Grossman, who was appointed in 1997 as the choir's first female artistic director, claimed that the young singers were overworked and announced plans to reduce the number of performances, which usually totaled 100 concerts a year. In addition, she wanted to establish a system of sponsorship for tours and concerts. Grossman was blocked by the governing board on both issues and resigned from her position in protest.

Inspired by the success of the Rock and Roll Hall of Fame and Museum in Cleveland, the American Classical Music Hall of Fame and Museum opened in Cincinnati, Ohio. The

first inductees included the U.S. Marine Band (also celebrating its bicentennial) as well as many individuals, including Ives, Leonard Bernstein, Igor Stravinsky, Fritz Reiner, Aaron Copland, Arturo Toscanini, Duke Ellington, and Gershwin.

Joanne Falletta, music director of the Richmond-based Virginia Symphony, was appointed music director of the Buffalo (N.Y.) Philharmonic. Masur announced his intention to take on the post of principal conductor of the London Philharmonic Orchestra, starting in 2000. New York Metropolitan Opera director James Levine was appointed to succeed Sergiu Celibidache as music director of the Munich Philharmonic, beginning in the fall of 1999. Andrew Davis, music director of the Glyndebourne Festival Opera in East Sussex, Eng., and chief conductor of the BBC Symphony Orchestra, announced that he would leave those positions to become music director and principal conductor of the Lyric Opera of Chicago in September 2000. Christoph Eschenbach announced that he would end his 10-year tenure as music director of the Houston Symphony when his contract expired in 1999. Christopher Hogwood renewed his contract with Boston's Handel and Haydn Society through the 1999–2000 season, after which he would become conductor laureate. Domingo announced that he would become the artistic director of the Los Angeles Opera in July 2000 in addition to his position as artistic director of the Washington Opera.

Several venues found themselves in need of refurbishment. Two venerable European opera houses, Venice's La Fenice and Gran Teatro del Liceu in Barcelona, Spain, had both been devastated by fire several years ago and were being rebuilt. Work on the Liceu neared completion, but the management still had to find other halls for its productions. London's Royal Opera House continued to struggle with financial problems. It was also under renovation but was forced to close, only partly because of problems related to its physical accommodations. New administrators were appointed after a parliamentary report sharply criticized its financial management. An opera season was held, using the Royal Albert Hall and the Sadler's Wells Theatre.

On the continent new concert halls were opened in Baden-Baden, Ger., and Lucerne, Switz. In the U.S. the Santa Fe (N.M.) Opera House was redesigned, with all seats now under a roof where part of its audience had previously sat in the open air. In September the Seattle (Wash.) Symphony opened its new facility, Benaroya Hall; the $188 million building had a 2,500-seat main auditorium and a 540-seat recital hall. The recently built New Jersey Performing Arts Center in Newark surpassed expectations and attracted half a million patrons. Despite the problems associated with expanding its season, the Washington (D.C.) Opera decided to remain in the John F. Kennedy Center for the Performing Arts after the cost of establishing its own opera house in the downtown area proved prohibitive.

Among the notable musicians who died in 1998 were German baritone Hermann Prey, American baritone Todd Duncan, American conductor Margaret Hillis, Russian composer Alfred Schnittke, and British composer Sir Michael Tippett. Shinichi Suzuki, founder of the Suzuki

method of teaching the violin, now used throughout the world, also died in 1998. (*See* OBITUARIES.) (JOSEPH MCLELLAN)

Jazz. Zoot suits, double-breasted suits, wide neckties, fedora hats, and other attire from Grandpa's trunk became the fashion again in 1998 as the swing revival, or neoswing, took off in jazz. The fad had had its beginnings in small nightclubs, especially on the U.S. West Coast, in the early 1990s and had quietly spread across the country. Couples began taking swing dance lessons, learning to jitterbug and also to hold each other while dancing, much as their ancestors used to do. With appearances by the Squirrel Nut Zippers on late-night television shows and popular recordings and tours by the Royal Crown Revue, Big Bad Voodoo Daddy, and Cherry Poppin' Daddies, the new swing music gained increased popularity in 1998. The music had little to do with the classic big-band jazz of the swing era; instead, simple arrangements and shuffle rhythms dominated, and the most important influences were black 1940s jump-rhythm and blues bands, western swing, and 1950s Las Vegas lounge acts.

More significant in strictly musical terms was the slowly but steadily increasing presence of gifted women jazz artists in the 1990s. College jazz programs and a gradual decline of sexist attitudes were contributing factors, and the three-day Mary Lou Williams Women in Jazz Festival at the Kennedy Center in Washington, D.C., held during Memorial Day weekend, was the most prominent gathering of jazz women yet, featuring performers such as vocalists Marlena Shaw and Nnena Freelon, violinist Regina Carter, the big band Maiden Voyage, and keyboard improvisers Renee Rosnes and Amina Claudine Myers. Williams had been an important arranger-pianist of the swing era; her fellow pioneer in breaking down gender barriers, Marian McPartland, was given an 80th-birthday tribute at New York City's Town Hall. Veterans such as pianist Barbara Carroll and trumpeter Harry ("Sweets") Edison and young pianists Rosnes and Benny Green were among those paying tribute and, as on her weekly radio program "Piano Jazz," pianist McPartland joined several of them in duets.

In 1939 Jelly Roll Morton composed his only swing-band works, which he hoped to sell to Benny Goodman, who had already made a pop hit of Morton's "King Porter Stomp." Unlike all previous Morton music, the works featured modern swing-band harmonies and no solos, a far cry indeed from the New Orleans ensemble style of Morton's early jazz masterpieces. Goodman did not buy the scores, and the compositions were never performed until 1998, when, 57 years after Morton's death, four of them were introduced by Don Vappie's Creole Jazz Serenaders, a New Orleans-based repertory band.

Unlike 1997, when New York City's two major jazz festivals were held simultaneously, in 1998 the upstart Texaco New York Jazz Festival, centred on late bop to free jazz, was held the first two weeks of June, and the long-standing JVC Jazz Festival, featuring more mainstream works, was held the following two weeks. Ornette Coleman brought a series of concerts titled *Civilization '98* to the Umbria (Italy) Jazz Festival, including Coleman's jazz trio joined by fellow alto saxophonist Lee

During a "Masters of Guitar" night at the Vienna Jazz Festival, American guitarist George Benson electrifies the audience. The festival, which ran for several days at the Vienna State Opera House in July, featured an eclectic mix of international jazz musicians.

Konitz; Coleman performed with Indian and Sardinian musicians, and his jazz-rock Prime Time band was joined by dancers and a video display. The 10th National Black Arts Festival, in Atlanta, Ga., was highlighted by a particularly daring concert series featuring international free-jazz notables, including, from the U.S., trumpeter Wadada Leo Smith, trombonist George Lewis, and saxophonists Roscoe Mitchell, Fred Anderson, Oliver Lake, and Dwight Andrews (the festival's music curator) and, from Europe, saxophonists Evan Parker (U.K.) and Peter Brötzmann (Germany) and pianists Alex von Schlippenbach and Gunter ("Baby") Sommers (Germany).

Tributes were prominent among the year's recordings. In the year of George Gershwin's 100th birthday, pianist Herbie Hancock's *Gershwin's World* (Verve), with guests including Kathleen Battle, Joni Mitchell, Stevie Wonder, and the Orpheus Chamber Orchestra, was notable. While Columbia/Legacy reissued Miles Davis's *The Complete Bitches Brew Sessions* as a four-compact disc (CD) set, *Yo Miles!*, by guitarist Henry Kaiser, Wadada Leo Smith, and guests that included the ROVA Saxophone Quartet and the World Saxophone Quartet's *Selim Sivad* appeared in tribute to Davis. The late-1997 reissue of Herbie Nichols's *The Complete Blue Note Recordings* (Blue Note, four CDs) was matched by, among others, the tribute CDs *Spinning Song* by guitarist Duck Baker and *Love Is Proximity* by the Herbie Nichols Project. Several significant saxophone-piano duet albums appeared, including Ornette Coleman–Joachim Kuhn *Colors* (Verve/Harmolodic), Ran Blake–Anthony Braxton *A Memory of Vienna* (hatOLOGY), and Lol Coxhill–Veryan Weston *Boundless* (Emanem). Branford Marsalis celebrated his appointment as creative consultant to Columbia Records by immediately signing tenor saxophonist David S. Ware; the first result was Ware's album *Go See the World*.

Among the year's odd events, an asteroid was named for soprano saxophonist Jane Ira Bloom, and Woody Allen, an amateur clarinetist, released *Wild Man Blues*, a film centred on his Dixieland playing. *The Bear Comes Home*, Rafi Zabor's novel about a saxophone-playing bear, won the 1998 PEN/Faulkner Award for Fiction. *The Playboy Guide to Jazz on CD* by Neil Tesser and *Jazz: The Rough Guide* by Ian Carr, Digby Fairweather, and Brian Priestley stood out among several new jazz CD guides. Other book highlights included *The History of Jazz* by Ted Gioia, a critical study; *Visions of Jazz*, a collection of essays by critic Gary Giddins; *New Dutch Swing*, a history of modern Dutch jazz by Kevin Whitehead; and *Such Melodious Racket*, a history of Canadian jazz by Mark Miller. The Canadian jazz magazine *Coda* celebrated its 40th year of continuous publication.

For many jazz listeners, 1998 would be remembered as the year Frank Sinatra, the master craftsman of emotion and the most popular of swinging postwar singers, died.

Jarvis Cocker of the rock group Pulp sings to a sold-out crowd assembled in RFK Stadium in Washington, D.C., in June for the Tibetan Freedom Concert.

The year's other deaths included singer Betty Carter, guitarist Tal Farlow, drummer Dennis Charles, jazz pianist–classical composer Mel Powell, saxophonist Benny Waters, pianists Dorothy Donegan and Walter Bishop, Jr., drummer Barrett Deems, blues singer Junior Wells, drummer Roy Porter, Hungarian guitarist Attila Zoller, Japanese bassist Yoshizawa Motoharu, and saxophonists Davey Schildkraut, Glenn Spearman, and Thomas Chapin. (*See* OBITUARIES.)   (JOHN LITWEILER)

Popular. In the U.K. the most impressive band of the year was Pulp, led by singer and songwriter Jarvis Cocker. Their new album *This Is Hardcore* continued Jarvis's quirky, bleak, and apparently confessional style in dealing with the more painful side of sex and relationships, but it also showed a new maturity and musical bravery that put the band ahead of such rivals as Blur and Oasis. Songs like "The Fear," "Dishes," and "Help the Aged" dealt with topics that other performers rarely dared tackle, ranging from fears of sexual inadequacy and loneliness to the pains of growing old. Despite such subject matter, the band proved highly successful. In a year during which several outdoor festivals and major concerts faced severe financial problems, Pulp proved that it could still attract large crowds for its clever, witty, and sometimes brutal songs.

Much of the best of the other new British music came from unexpected quarters, such as Wales—a part of the U.K. seldom renowned in the past for playing a major part in popular music. The best and most popular Welsh band, the Manic Street Preachers, followed the success of *Everything Must Go* with another best-selling set of passionate guitar-backed songs, *This Is My Truth Tell Me Yours*, which dominated the best-seller list during early autumn. Other successful Welsh bands included Catatonia, with its album *International Velvet*, and the Super Furry Animals.

Another unexpected influence on the popular music scene came from the British Asian community. The young band Cornershop, led by Tjinder Singh, mixed sitar-backed Indian styles with modern dance influences in its album *When I Was Born for the 7th Time*, which sounded like an Impressionist blend of all the sounds that a young Indian might have heard growing up in Britain during the 1980s and 1990s. It included a new version of the Beatles' Indian-influenced song "Norwegian Wood," originally recorded three decades earlier, as well as Cornershop's catchy and cheerful hit "Brimful of Asha." Another Anglo-Asian group, Asian Dub Foundation, created a distinctive blend of guitar rock and rap styles with an Asian edge on angry songs like "Naxalite." Both of these bands were nominated for the Mercury Music Award, the most prestigious British music prize.

British pop music traditionally thrived on novel and unexpected combinations of different, apparently unrelated styles. One other such musical surprise in 1998 was the new album from Billy Bragg, *Mermaid Avenue*. Bragg, from the East End of London, made his reputation in the 1980s as a solo electric guitarist who wrote highly political songs dealing with such topics as the miners' strike. During recent months, however, this most English of singers had been invited to look through the archives of the U.S.'s most famous folk troubadour,

Technology's New Spin on Music

Throughout the 20th century the music industry has been revolutionized by technology. This process, which accelerated in the 1980s and '90s, can be traced back to the invention of sound recording by Thomas A. Edison in 1877. Technological developments of this century have created a music culture unimagined even a few years ago.

By 1998 the challenges and opportunities brought about by technological change had become the most critical ever for musicians and music lovers. Crucial elements of this change included the advent of digital recording and the development of the Internet. By the late 1990s both of these technologies had reached a critical level of public acceptance and use for communication and data storage in general and music in particular. Digital recordings provided a high level of clarity and wide dynamic range, and the Internet had seemingly limitless space available for data storage.

The emergence of a new computer file format called MP3—which stands for MPEG-1, Layer 3—caused record companies to worry about their profits (competing schemes included Liquid Audio, a2b, and Madison Project). MP3 worked by compressing large amounts of information into small packages that could easily be sent over the Internet. The information could be anything that

could be transformed into digital information, such as video clips, art, or music. Once the information reached its destination, it was decompressed and used or stored as a computer file. Suddenly there was a completely new way to store and access music.

Electronic copyright quickly became important as a legal issue affecting all products on the Internet. The ease that digital recording provided in copying music from one format to another threatened the security of musicians' intellectual property rights to their compositions and performances. This risk was heightened by the development of a palm-sized MP3 player called the Rio from Diamond Multimedia that cost as little as $200 and stored up to an hour of digitally recorded sound. The Rio (as well as a number of similar devices) allowed the owner to upload a recording to the Internet or download music already available there onto a personal computer. The recording industry became alarmed by this trend, since individuals could now create their own collections of recordings without actually purchasing CDs. Whereas both the Rio and the Internet provided many advantages for musicians, if they were misused, the potential for worldwide high-tech violations of copyright was great.

On a more positive note, knowledge about and appreciation of good music

were much enhanced by the proliferation of World Wide Web pages devoted to music. Music organizations were no longer limited to the traditional print media to communicate their message. By the end of 1998, all the major musical organizations—symphony orchestras, chamber groups, music publishers, instrument manufacturers, and groups of aficionados with special musical interests, not to mention rock and pop music performers—had developed their own Web pages and established a solid presence on the Internet. Composers had home pages, as did national organizations such as the American Symphony Orchestra League and Opera America, reference publishers (e.g., the New Grove Dictionary of Music and Musicians), government agencies such as the National Endowment for the Arts, and magazines such as Opera News and Gramophone. One of the newest Web sites devoted to classical music was set up by Amazon.com, the third largest bookseller in the United States.

The technological curve established at the beginning of the century by record companies such as Deutsche Gramophone and EMI (both recently celebrated centennial anniversaries) was climbing sharply. As the music industry moved into the 21st century, the advantages and risks that new technologies represented were only beginning to be realized.   (JOSEPH MCLELLAN)

Woody Guthrie, and write new melodies for Guthrie song lyrics that he never recorded before his death and that had never been made public before. The resulting album, recorded with the American band Wilco, mixed country and folk influences on songs, like *Ingrid Bergman,* that showed a new side to Guthrie as an often playful as well as political songwriter.

Outside Britain the most successful new pop dance band of the year was Aqua. The band came from Denmark, a country with even less of a pop music history than Wales, and wrote novelty songs with a synthesizer backing. They were loathed by many pop music critics but were adored by young audiences and scored hits across Europe and beyond with "Barbie Girl" and "Doctor Jones." The more serious side of the new European popular music was shown by the success of Lo'Jo, a band from Angers, France. Led by keyboard player Denis Bean and two sisters of North African Berber origin, they mixed French balladry with influences from North Africa and the Arabic world and a dash of reggae from the Caribbean in their album *Mojo Radio.*

The other great success of the multicultural "world music" scene was Baaba Maal, a singer-songwriter from Senegal who emerged as arguably the finest vocalist in Africa. His new album *Nomad Soul* was a brave mixture of local African styles with influences from Jamaica and even Ireland, but with his concert at London's Festival Hall he proved that his passionate, semi-improvised style was best heard live. The

opening act at the concert was the veteran Jamaican guitarist Ernest Ranglin, who traveled to Senegal to record his new album *In Search of the Lost Riddim* with members of Maal's band. The result, in which Ranglin's rapid-fire reggae-tinged jazz guitar was backed by African acoustic instruments such as the kora, was one of the unexpected delights of the year.   (ROBIN DENSELOW)

The original soundtrack album for the motion picture *Titanic* dominated popular music in the U.S. during the early months of 1998, with sales driven by the movie's success and by the popularity of Celine Dion's romantic ballad "My Heart Will Go On." The song debuted at number one on *Billboard* magazine's "Hot 100" singles chart when it was released commercially.

Canadian singer Celine Dion, best known for her rendition of the romantic ballad "My Heart Will Go On," performs on February 25 at the 40th annual Grammy awards, held at New York City's Radio City Music Hall.

Lilith Fair organizer and headliner Sarah McLachlan (centre) completes her final encore after inviting other performers onstage at the University of British Columbia's Thunderbird Stadium in Vancouver, the last stop on the entertainers' summer tour.

Titanic was the first movie soundtrack to top the *Billboard* pop album chart since *Chariots of Fire* in 1982. *Titanic* held on to the top ranking in the face of competition from new releases by Madonna and Pearl Jam, among others. By the end of the year, it had sold more than 10 million copies, and a sequel, *Back to Titanic,* sold more than one million and rose to second on the *Billboard* pop album chart.

Another movie soundtrack, *Hope Floats,* with contributions from Garth Brooks, Sheryl Crow, the Rolling Stones, and the Mavericks, topped *Billboard*'s country album chart for several weeks. Movie soundtracks also dominated the pop charts during the summer, with five in *Billboard*'s top 10 for the week of July 11: *City of Angels* (with Alanis Morissette's "Uninvited"); *Armageddon: The Album* (with Aerosmith's "I Don't Want to Miss a Thing"); *Hope Floats; Godzilla, the Album;* and *Bulworth: The Soundtrack.*

Bob Dylan won the Grammy award for album of the year for his *Time Out of Mind,* and Shawn Colvin won record of the year and song of the year Grammys for "Sunny Came Home." Brooks made history when his album *Double Live* sold 1,085,373 copies in its first week of sales, more than any other album had sold in a single week since 1991, when SoundScan began computer tracking of album sales. In November he wrapped up a world tour with a concert in College Station, Texas. Over a three-year period, he played 348 concerts to more than five million people.

Canadian country star Shania Twain, who did not perform in concert while her 1995 release *The Woman in Me* amassed sales of 10 million copies, made her debut as a touring headliner on May 29 in Sudbury, Ont., in support of her third album *Come On Over.* Released at the end of 1997, the album had sold more than six million copies by the end of 1998 and topped the country album chart for more than 20 weeks. Twain's ballad "From This Moment On" became a major crossover hit, rising to fifth on the pop chart by early December.

The Spice Girls traveled to the U.S. in 1998, though without Geri Halliwell (Ginger Spice), who left the group on May 31. Notable summer tours included the all-women Lilith Fair (featuring Sarah McLachlan [*see* BIOGRAPHIES], Liz Phair, and Bonnie Raitt, among others); Dave Matthews Band; Pearl Jam; hard-rock's OzzFest (with Ozzy Osbourne, Tool, and Megadeth); the House of Blues Smokin' Grooves Tour (Public Enemy, Cypress Hill, Busta Rhymes); HORDE Fest (Blues Traveler, Barenaked Ladies, Ben Harper); and modern rock group Smashing Pumpkins, who donated their earnings to youth-oriented charities.

Hip-hop again proved its commercial viability as albums by Jay-Z, Snoop Dogg, DMX, Master P, and the Beastie Boys all topped the *Billboard* pop album chart. Lauryn Hill, a member of the hip-hop soul group the Fugees, made her solo debut with *The Mis-education of Lauryn Hill,* mixing hip-hop beats and soulful melodies. The album rose to first place on the pop chart, and a single from the album, "Doo Wop (That Thing)," entered the *Billboard* pop singles chart at number one in November.

Teenage singers Brandy and Monica jumped to the top spot on the pop charts with the single "The Boy Is Mine" and stayed there for 13 weeks, the longest-running chart topper of 1998. Monica later went to number one again with another single, "The First Night." Only Monica and Celine Dion had two number one pop hits during the year. Dion earned the honour for "My Heart Will Go On" and "I'm Your Angel," the latter a duet with R&B star R. Kelly. Though pop music usually dominated the music charts, shock rocker Marilyn Manson reached the top of the album chart with *Mechanical Animals,* and Korn did the same with *Follow the Leader.*

Deaths devastated the music world in 1998; among them were Frank Sinatra; country's first lady Tammy Wynette, rock and roll pioneer Carl Perkins, Beach Boy Carl Wilson, country producer Owen Bradley, pop star-turned-congressman Sonny Bono, singing cowboys Gene Autry and Roy Rogers, and jazz vocalist Betty Carter. (*See* OBITUARIES.)

The Canadian corporation Seagram purchased Dutch-owned Polygram for $10.6 billion. In a deal expected to be finalized in December, Polygram joined Seagram-owned Universal Music Group to create the largest record company in the world, with 23% of the worldwide market share, moving ahead of Time Warner and Sony. Retail sales of music on the Internet increased. Industry watchers predicted that on-line sales would amount to $2 billion–$5 billion by 2002.   (JAY ORR)

DANCE

North America. Throughout 1998 dance was challenged to be bigger on stage than it was in print. In March Oxford University Press published the *International Encyclopedia of Dance,* a six-volume, 4,000-page work that had been more than 20 years in the making. The publication was launched in New York City, still the world's unofficial dance capital despite a lessening of dance activities over the past few years. The city was still the place to be seen and reviewed.

New York City Ballet (NYCB) began the year with a revival of George Balanchine's *Jewels* (1967), the world's first "multiact abstract ballet." In July NYCB lost the last of its long-standing bedrock artistic forces when dancer and choreographer Jerome Robbins died. (*See* OBITUARIES.) American Ballet Theatre's (ABT's) first production of *Le Corsaire* proved to be very popular; the production was a reworking of the version created by Boston Ballet's Anna-Marie Holmes. ABT's staging of *The Snow Maiden,* however, was noted more for its shimmering, silvery costumes and settings than for its thin narrative and choreographic elements. ABT continued to draw sizable audiences throughout the fall at New York's more intimate City Center. Twyla Tharp's *Known by Heart* established itself as one of the company's most vivid and important new works.

City Center also offered performances by various international companies. The Eifman Ballet of St. Petersburg, performing only works by its artistic director, Boris Eifman, offered little more than a curious inversion of overwrought, old-style Soviet melodramatic ballet. The Universal Ballet of South Korea offered a remarkably good showing in a debut season for the young company. Both Argentina's Ballet Argentino and Ballet Ullate from Spain, however, had weak repertories and poorly attended performances. The National Ballet of Canada also drew sparse audiences and apparently lost money, despite much more impressive dancing and repertory. The San Francisco Ballet drew respectably sized audiences and offered further evidence of well-schooled dancers as well as glimpses of Lucia Lacarra, its newest impressive ballerina.

Lincoln Center's Festival '98, which coincided with a Dance Critics Association conference on popular culture, included seasons by both the Hamburg (Ger.) Ballet and Stuttgart (Ger.) Ballet. Eliot Feld's youthful Ballet Tech, the latest troupe to showcase his ballets, played in New York and at the John F. Kennedy Center for the Performing Arts in Washington, D.C. At year's end

Ballet Tech performed a season billed as "NotCRACKER," intended to buck the frequent all-*Nutcracker* tide found elsewhere. Alternative *Nutcracker* productions also included Donald Byrd's *Harlem Nutcracker* (1996), which returned to the Brooklyn (N.Y.) Academy of Music (BAM) for a two-week run.

BAM's other offerings included an appearance by the pupils of the renowned Vaganova Academy of St. Petersburg. From France the Next Wave Festival presented *Eclipse,* Zingaro's newest production of equestrian theatre. Capping the same festival was the first appearance in 10 years by the Frankfurt (Ger.) Ballet under the artistic direction of American-born William Forsythe.

Performances of *Fosse: A Celebration in Song & Dance* began in Toronto. The Broadway-bound production was co-directed by Ann Reinking and Richard Maltby, with assistance from Gwen Verdon. Matthew Bourne's (*see* BIOGRAPHIES) production of *Swan Lake* reached Broadway, where the debate of whether it was a show or ballet helped the production to gain attention and press coverage. *Swan Lake* was also fodder for a highly successful and zany season by Les Ballets Trocadero de Monte-Carlo. The Royal Winnipeg Ballet's presentations of *Giselle* included guest appearances by Canada's well-known Evelyn Hart. Mark Godden's *Dracula,* the latest in a series of works on this subject, opened its fall season. Former National Ballet of Canada ballerinas Veronica Tennant and Karin Kain collaborated on a film directed by Tennant and focused on Kain, entitled *Karin Kain: Dancing in the Moment.*

The San Francisco Ethnic Dance Festival commemorated its 20th anniversary with a world arts festival that ranged from hip-hop to clog dancing. Ella Baff was appointed director of Jacob's Pillow Dance Festival, whose summer season also included the collaboration between Postmodernism's Laura Dean and the American Indian Dance Theater for *Kotuwakan.* The American Dance Festival, Durham, N.C., capped its 65th-anniversary year by sharing in the "wealth" of the newly established funding of modern dance by the Doris Duke Charitable Foundation. Experimental dance venue Danspace at St. Mark's Church-in-the-Bowery in New York City celebrated its 25th anniversary with a grandly planned "Silver Series" starting in December. The Murray Louis and Nikolais Dance Company marked its 50th anniversary at New York's Joyce Theater with a mixed repertory of Alvin Nikolais and Louis works. Celebrating its 40th anniversary, the Alvin Ailey American Dance Theater continued to tour near and far throughout the year, culminating with its popular annual monthlong season at City Center. Geoffrey Holder's *Prodigal Prince* led the repertory's novelties. The 50th anniversary of the nation of Israel was observed with a series of dance company performances both in and around New York and at the Kennedy Center.

Publications also marked company anniversaries. Pacific Northwest Ballet crowned its silver-anniversary year by issuing *Let's Go On,* a record of the troupe's past work and future plans. NYCB eased into marking its golden anniversary with the publication of *Tributes,* an album of illustrations and text. The dance company also launched an interconnected two-season celebration on the theme "Fifty Years: One Hundred Ballets."

Merce Cunningham, Meredith Monk, and Bill T. Jones were each individually showcased in an "Art Performs Life" performance at the Walker Art Center of Minneapolis, Minn. Paul Taylor offered two new works—the sinister *The Word* and the sizzling *Piazzolla Caldera.* Mark Morris had a critical and popular success with his staging of the opera *Platee* in Berkeley, Calif. The dancer and choreographer enjoyed further acclaim with a repertory season at BAM that presented his farewell performances in his own production of Henry Purcell's *Dido and Aeneas.* Holder's *Dougla* filled out the repertory that Dance Theatre of Harlem (N.Y.) offered in its Kennedy Center season. New York-based Mark Dendy showed his wickedly witty "dance play" about the influences of the matriarchal Martha Graham at both the Kennedy Center and New York's Dance Theater Workshop. The butoh-based artistic team of Eiko & Koma presented their delicately chill and soft *Wind* at the Kennedy Center, which offered more modern-dance-based presentations than ballet-based ones under the recent direction of Charles and Stephanie Rhinehart.

News about individuals included the promotions at NYCB of both Monique Meunier and Charles Askegard to principal dancers as well as six men and two women from its corps de ballet to soloist level. Dancers also dominated newsworthy elements at ABT. Newcomer Giuseppe Picone and guest artist Yury Possokhov (from San Francisco Ballet) led the way, but new heights were also reached by the company's remarkable roster of men, including Vladimir Malakhov, Angel Corella, and newcomer Marcelo Gomes. Hartford (Conn.) Ballet's Kirk Peterson was fired in midyear, and his place was taken by modern-dance-based individuals. Ben Houk assumed the direction of Fort Worth (Texas) Ballet after Paul Mejia left; Houk's spot at Nashville (Tenn.) Ballet went to Paul Vasterling. Washington (D.C.) Ballet's venerable Mary Day retired from leading the company, and Septime Webre, of American Repertory Ballet, was chosen to replace her. Robert Weiss launched his own Carolina Ballet in Raleigh, N.C., with a March gala performance. After 31 years Harvey Lichtenstein announced his retirement from the directorship of BAM, to be succeeded by Joseph V. Melillo.

Preserve Inc., an organization dedicated to the art and science of preserving dance, marked its 10th anniversary with a special symposium in New York City. The Interpreters Archive of the George Balanchine Trust continued to document and record Balanchine's past work with videotaping sessions. These included one conducted by Cuban ballerina Alicia Alonso on *Theme and Variations* and another session by American premier danseur Frederic Franklin. In June the Library of Congress acquired the Martha Graham Dance Archives from the Martha Graham Trust. This arrangement preceded the action taken later in the year by the Graham organization, which sold the Martha Graham Dance Center's building in New York to acquire much-needed capital.

During a curtain call following the Ballet Nacional de Cuba's performance of *Cinderella* at New York City's City Center, Óscar Torrado (right), who portrayed Prince Charming, kisses the hand of Lorna Feijóo, who starred as Cinderella. The ballet was choreographed by Pedro Consuegra, with music composed by Johan Strauss.

Honours included the installation of Anna Sokolow in the Hall of Fame of Saratoga Springs (N.Y.) Museum of Dance. American dancers Rasta Thomas and Melissa Wishinski had medal-winning performances at the Jackson (Miss.) International Ballet Competition. The late Rudolf Nureyev made the news when the Rudolf Nureyev Dance Foundation won a suit brought by his family concerning the use of his assets. A detailed biography of Nureyev's life by Diane Solway was also published.

Besides the death of Robbins, the year's losses also included dancers Gisella Caccialanza, Clayton ("Peg Leg") Bates (*see* OBITUARIES), Gregg Burge, Bill Cratty, and Kyra Nijinsky; teachers Maria Grandy, Valentina Pereyaslavec, and Anatole Vilzak; choreographers Richard Bull and Nancy Topf; shoe manufacturer Alfred Terlizzi; writer P.W. Manchester; and philanthropist Howard Gilman.

(ROBERT GRESKOVIC)

Europe. Many ballet companies throughout Europe faced administrative challenges in 1998. In England the Royal Ballet reached its lowest ebb ever—its condition linked to the continuing cliff-hanging saga of resignations, mismanagement, and near bankruptcies in the Royal Opera House organization. The new chairman, Sir Colin Southgate, decided on the desperate money-saving measure of suspending all the opera company's outside performances during the Royal Opera House's current redevelopment (to be completed in December 1999). For Bernard Haitink, the theatre's music director, this was the last straw, and he resigned. Southgate had not yet demonstrated a radical reforming hand, although he announced his intention to create the new post of an artistic leader for the Royal Opera House. He also appointed as executive director Michael Kaiser, an American who had earned a formidable reputation for effecting miracle cures on troubled ballet companies such as ABT.

Never before had a company needed more help than the Royal Ballet. The company managed to maintain its performances at Sadler's Wells and elsewhere, yet morale and standards slumped. The recruitment of the Cuban Carlos Acosta (from Houston [Texas] Ballet) promised to add pep to the male ranks, but the sudden departure of popular Japanese virtuoso Tetsuya Kumakawa created shock waves when it became clear that five other prominent male dancers would join him as the core of a new large British-based classical company with generous financial backing. This left the director Anthony Dowell with a yawning soloist gap to fill and the fear that others might jump ship.

The good news in British dance was the opening of the rebuilt Sadler's Wells in London. The renovations included updated technology and a much larger stage. Companies such as William Forsythe's Frankfurt Ballet, which previously had been unable to arrange a suitable theatre, would now be able to perform in London. Other celebrations included the 100th birthday of Ninette de Valois, founder of the Royal Ballet. The Royal Ballet and the Birmingham Royal Ballet devised birthday programs that included revivals of de Valois's own *The Prospect Before Us.* The ballet, which had not been seen since the 1940s, was performed by the Birmingham Royal Ballet. In addition, the Royal Ballet presented her *The Rake's Progress.*

Germany's political reunification resulted in a surfeit of dance companies and theatres in Berlin. Gerhard Brunner, artistic director at Graz, was asked to streamline Berlin's three large ensembles—the Staatsoper Ballet, the Deutsche Oper Ballet, and the Komische Oper's modern Tanztheater—into the Berlin Ballet. The new company would consist of one classical and one modern ensemble. The appointment of Richard Wherlock as director and choreographer of the Komische Oper's Tanztheater, starting

British choreographer Matthew Bourne's unconventional version of *Swan Lake* featured an all-male cast of swans, including Adam Cooper (above) as the lead swan. The production opened on Broadway at the Neil Simon Theater on October 8.

with the 1999–2000 season, suggested that the Tanztheater would become the modern half of the Berlin Ballet.

Elsewhere in Germany former dancer Ivan Liska succeeded Konstanze Vernon as the head of the Bavarian Ballet, Daniela Kurtz became the director of the Nürnberg Ballet, and choreographer Rui Horta's Frankfurt-based SOAP closed in May because of budget cuts. The Frankfurt Ballet fared better, although Forsythe was engaged in tough contract-renewal negotiations. He secured agreement, however, that his company would henceforth be more autonomous and would manage its own budget. Forsythe also became artistic director of the TAT (Theater am Turm) in Frankfurt's Bockenheimer Depot, reopening in September 1999. He could use the TAT as an extra performing space for his own company and was now responsible for annual programming using outside artists. He also found time to create two masterful pieces: *Small Void* and *op.31 (erste Fassungen)*. Premiered in Frankfurt, both works returned to a balletic austerity that mirrored the questing compositional techniques of their respective scores by Thom Willems and Arnold Schoenberg.

John Neumeier celebrated 25 years with the Hamburg Ballet, as did Pina Bausch with the Tanztheater Wuppertal. The theatre was host to a festival with visitors such as Mikhail Baryshnikov and the Frankfurt Ballet, who donated their performances. There were also performances of Bausch's own work. Bausch created two new ballets; the first, *Masurca Fogo,* evoked the Portuguese fado tradition and themes of solitude and longing. The second work, *Duke Bluebeard's Castle,* was premiered at Aix-en-Provence, France, with Pierre Boulez conducting Bartok's score. This new ballet proved to be very different from Bausch's 1997 *Bluebeard.*

The Royal Swedish Ballet, the fourth oldest company in the world, reached its 225th birthday, an occasion coinciding with Stockholm's tenure as the 1998 cultural capital of Europe. The ballet company organized a conference about its history and performances that included the Bolshoi Ballet in *Raymonda,* a ballet never before seen in Sweden. There was also a program devoted to Les Ballets Suédois, the Paris-based company founded by Rolf de Maré with Jean Börlin as its single choreographer and star dancer. Ivo Cramér reconstructed Börlin's *El Greco* (1920), and the team of Millicent Hodson and Kenneth Archer re-created *Derviches* (1920), *Skating Rink* (1922), and *Within the Quota* (1923). The year also saw the 90th birthdays of Birgit Cullberg and Birgit Akesson, two grand ladies of Swedish dance.

The Batsheva Dance Company encountered problems with its intended contribution to Israel's 50th anniversary showcase, held in Jerusalem and involving hundreds of artists and worldwide television coverage. Haim Miller, the ultra-Orthodox deputy mayor of Jerusalem, demanded the withdrawal of Batsheva's piece, *Anaphase,* because of his objections to the dancers' stripping down to their underclothes. This was intended to be a gesture of rebirth and continuity that the choreographer, Ohad Naharin, had set to a Jewish song normally sung at the Passover seder, or festive meal. The result was a full-blown scandal involving both Israeli Prime Minister Benjamin Netanyahu and Pres. Ezer Weizman, who suggested the dancers wear long underwear as a compromise. The dancers refused and withdrew from the festival.

The headline news in France was Roland Petit's departure from the Marseille Ballet after 26 years. His successor was Marie-Claude Pietragalla of the Paris Opéra Ballet, who intended to keep up her Paris performances. Petit, insulted that his own candidate was not chosen, withdrew all his ballets from the Marseille repertory. His last new ballet for Marseille in 1998 was a revisionist *Swan Lake.* Entitled *Le Lac des cygnes et ses malefices,* Petit's ballet, in

American actor Kevin Spacey took to the British stage during the year in the lead role in Eugene O'Neill's *The Iceman Cometh* at the Almeida Theatre in London. Starring as Theodore Hickman ("Hickey"), Spacey received the critics' raves for his emotional portrayal.

(as the embryonic tyrant emperor Nero) in the second.

Financially bolstered by trend-spotting patrons and by Broadway interest, the Almeida also presented a bruised and brooding Liam Neeson as Oscar Wilde in Hare's *Judas Kiss* at the Playhouse and a wonderfully funny co-production with the Right Size of Bertolt Brecht's *Puntila and His Servant Matti* at the Edinburgh Festival on national tour and then at home and the West End. On its home stage and subsequently at the Old Vic, the Almeida presented a beautifully heartbreaking Juliet Binoche as the troubled heroine of Pirandello's *Naked*. The Donmar restored James Lapine and Stephen Sondheim's magically acid *Into the Woods* at the year's end.

Motion picture stars enjoyed great popularity in London during the year. Whereas in the old days the likes of Lauren Bacall, Jack Lemmon, Dustin Hoffman, or Charlton Heston would come to fill big theatres in musicals or revivals, the new Hollywood generation was playing it safe and trendy in sold-out small houses. Even the homegrown film stars did the same; among them, Ewan McGregor of *Trainspotting* fame led a fine revival at the tiny Hampstead Theatre of David Halliwell's 1965 student comedy *Little Malcolm and His Struggle Against the Eunuchs.*

The RNT under Trevor Nunn tried to maintain its prominence with a spectacular and truly glorious revival of Rodgers and Hammerstein's *Oklahoma!* (ES best musical) and dogged, if not uniformly successful, revivals of Jay Presson Allen's *The Prime of Miss Jean Brodie,* Harold Pinter's *Betrayal,* and Shakespeare's *Antony and Cleopatra.* In the latter Alan Rickman and Helen Mirren were framed in a production by Sean Mathias that received strongly mixed reviews.

Nunn unearthed an early, previously unperformed Tennessee Williams prison play, *Not About Nightingales,* that was graced by a fine central performance by Corin Redgrave. Other RNT highlights included Michael Frayn's new play about atomic scientists, *Copenhagen* (ES best play), and Sinead Cusack (ES best actress) as a dying heroine in Sebastian Barry's lyrical if disastrously undramatic *Our Lady of Sligo.* Best of all was Terry Johnson's new comedy about the very British vaudevillian "Carry On" films, *Cleo, Camping, Emmanuelle and Dick.*

In the smaller RNT Cottesloe theatre, which was host to the Frayn, Barry, and Williams dramas, the National could also boast Kevin Elyot's *The Day I Stood Still,* a cleverly arranged time-jumping meditation on the well of loneliness; an ebullient adaptation of Salman Rushdie's adventure fable *Haroun and the Sea of Stories;* and Jonathan Harvey's fine Liverpudlian domestic epic *Guiding Star.* Only average Shakespeare was produced by the RSC at Stratford, but this was balanced by a stunning, low-key, and wondrously atmospheric revival by Katie Mitchell of *Uncle Vanya* in an RSC–Young

which the character Siegfried was the swan, featured Altynai Asylmuratova as Odette. Asylmuratova had been dividing her time between the Mariinsky Ballet and Marseille. In anniversaries, Yvette Chauviré marked her 80th birthday with a celebratory gala from the Paris Opéra Ballet.

In Florence Davide Bombana replaced Karole Armitage as director and choreographer of the Teatro Communale. In Moscow Vladimir Vasilyev's new *Giselle* for the Bolshoi Ballet premiered at the end of 1997 and proved to be restrained compared with his controversially radical *Swan Lake.* The ballet provided more dancing for the characters Albrecht and Hilarion and boasted costumes created and donated by the retired French couturier Hubert de Givenchy.

Unlike ballet, contemporary dance did not benefit from state subsidies in the states of the former Soviet Union, and the art form was still in its infancy. Vitebsk, Belarus (artist Mark Chagall's hometown and an avant-garde centre in the 1920s), was an appropriate location for the 10th International Festival of Contemporary Choreography. The festival included a competition, master classes given by teachers from France, Germany, and the U.S., and performances by groups from all over the former Soviet Union. There were also performances from Sasha Pepelyayev's Kinetic Theatre, which also won a prize at the annual Bagnolet competition in France and appeared at London's Dance Umbrella festival.

Many celebrated dancers died, including Christopher Gable and perhaps the century's greatest ballerina, Galina Ulanova. Gable's death left Britain's Northern Ballet Theatre without a director. Other deaths included Svetlana Beriosova, Serge Golovine, William Louther, and Alexander Bogatyrev. (*See* OBITUARIES.)   (NADINE MEISNER)

THEATRE

Great Britain and Ireland. The dominance of the Royal National Theatre (RNT) and Royal Shakespeare Company (RSC), the

highly subsidized theatrical monoliths born in the early 1960s, began to fade in 1998. The best of London theatre changed around them to form new, and extremely potent, alliances of talent. The ensemble ideal in British theatre seemed to be as good as dead as various factions of writers, directors, and actors made arrangements to work in one place for shorter lengths of time. Much of this activity took place in London, at the Almeida Theatre in Islington and the Donmar Warehouse in Covent Garden.

The American film star Kevin Spacey won the Evening Standard (ES) best actor of the year award for his performance as Hickey in a magnificent revival of Eugene O'Neill's *The Iceman Cometh* at the Almeida. Nicole Kidman was the luminescent focus of attention at the Donmar in *The Blue Room,* Sir David Hare's brilliant rewrite of Arthur Schnitzler's famous fin de siècle comedy of sexual promiscuity, *La Ronde.* Former Royal Shakespeare Company director Howard Davies won the ES best director award for *The Iceman Cometh* and also during the year provided the RNT with a hit with his production in the Olivier Auditorium of Mikhail Bulgakov's radical classic *Flight.* Kidman's presence in *The Blue Room* highlighted the increasing prominence of director Sam Mendes at the Donmar as well as the important shift of Hare from his virtually in-house perch at the RNT to a commercially oriented father-figure position on the fashionable fringe.

The Almeida during the year sent productions to the Malvern Festival and the West End, where Dame Diana Rigg led Jonathan Kent's company in two unexpectedly successful productions of baroque tragedies by Jean Racine. *Phèdre* and *Britannicus* were translated, respectively, by the late poet laureate Ted Hughes (*see* OBITUARIES) and, in a much lighter vein, Robert David MacDonald. Both plays were performed in modern dress, and Dame Diana was memorably partnered by Toby Stephens as her incestuous object of desire in the first play and her flesh and blood son

Vic collaboration starring Stephen Dillane and Linus Roache as Vanya and Astrov.

The future of the Royal Court, home of new British theatre writing since John Osborne's *Look Back in Anger* in 1956 and of George Bernard Shaw and Harley Granville Barker 50 years earlier, remained precarious. The lease was sold back to the property owners, and the cost of the architectural adjustments to the Sloane Square headquarters outstripped the money available. At the year's end there was a tremendous row over whether the Jerwood Foundation, already a generous sponsor, could be allowed to include its name in that of the theatre itself—as in the Royal Jerwood Court—in exchange for a further donation of £3 million (about U.S. $5 million).

The Court's work itself continued unabated, with notable plays during the year from Phyllis Nagy (*Never Land*), Sarah Kane (*Cleansed*), and Rebecca Prichard (*Yard Gal*), all of them highly theatrical and full of energy and promise. Another Court highlight was the ubiquitous Hare appearing in his own abrasive and funny monologue about a first-ever visit to Israel, *Via Dolorosa*.

Dame Judi Dench (*see* BIOGRAPHIES) was engaged with Sir Peter Hall's company at the Picadilly, which completed a remarkable repertoire season of Shaw's *Major Barbara*, Eduardo De Filippo's *Filumena* (in which Dench played a reformed Neapolitan prostitute and broke all hearts), and a revival of Alan Bennett's *Kafka's Dick*.

Sir Ian McKellen announced that he would abandon the RNT for Leeds and lead a newly formed ensemble—in the face of the national trend—at Jude Kelly's ever-adventurous West Yorkshire Playhouse. The result was instant excitement and proud stirrings as Sir Ian and Clare Higgins shone notably among a fine group of actors in *The Seagull* by Chekhov and *Present Laughter* by Sir Noël Coward.

Australian-born American actress Nicole Kidman assumed five different personas for Sir David Hare's play *The Blue Room*, which opened in September at the Donmar Warehouse in London's Covent Garden.

Another Yorkshire house, the Sheffield Crucible, scored a huge popular hit with the stage version of *Brassed Off*, the British movie about the demise of the brass band culture in a decimated mining community. Michael Grandage directed a well-received *Twelfth Night* on the same stage, and Shakespeare received another boost at the Birmingham Rep, where Richard McCabe, an RSC associate, was an immensely fast and scabrously funny Hamlet in Bill Alexander's notable revival. Later in the year Charles Dance also went to the Birmingham Rep to lead a handsome production of Chekhov's *Three Sisters,* directed by Bill Bryden.

Chichester Festival Theatre recovered its dignity after financial mayhem in 1997 with a program that managed to be both sensible and refreshing: a sportive, non-Neapolitan revival of De Filippo's *Saturday Sunday Monday* starring David Suchet; a well-timed revival of Hare's *Racing Demon*, about crisis in the Church of England, with fine performances from Denis Quilley and Dinsdale Landen; Simon Callow and Keith Baxter in Orson Welles's version of Shakespeare's Henry IV plays, *Chimes at Midnight;* and *Katherine Howard,* a fine new historical play from William Nicholson about the least known of Henry VIII's wives. Richard Griffiths played the monarch superbly as a fat man with his thin Renaissance former self trying to get out.

The Edinburgh Festival was memorably devoted to an exploration of the links between Verdi and Schiller, and so the Glasgow Citizens produced Schiller's *The Robbers* (Verdi's basis for *I Masnadieri*), in which Benedick Bates, son of Alan, played both the good and bad brothers in a virtuoso performance. A visiting production from Germany by Peter Stein of Botho Strauss's *Die Ahnlichen* was a glorious occasion, and the ever-interesting Traverse Theatre presented several important new dramas, including Liz Lochhead's *Perfect Days* and David Greig's *Kill the Old, Torture Their Young.*

There was a veritable riot of musical theatre in London throughout the year, with competent revivals of such Broadway favourites as *Show Boat* (Harold Prince's production), *Sweet Charity, Annie, West Side Story* (supervised by the librettist Arthur Laurents, who took a few swipes at Jerome Robbins's posthumous reputation), and—in Regent's Park—*Gentlemen Prefer Blondes. Rent,* with at least eight superb songs, transferred from New York City to a mixed reception; something was lost in the passage of this new *Hair*-style phenomenon. *Doctor Dolittle* was a sumptuously designed translation of the Rex Harrison movie that attracted enthusiastic family audiences. *Saturday Night Fever,* directed and choreographed by Arlene Phillips at the Palladium, was a huge hit, catching a wave of nostalgia for disco dancing, flared trousers, John Travolta (superbly impersonated by Adam Garcia), and songs of the Bee Gees.

As usual, Lord Lloyd-Webber provoked a mixed critical reception when *Whistle Down the Wind,* with lyrics by Jim Steinman, opened at the Aldwych in the summer. This was a fiercely impassioned piece of work about the need for faith in a secular age. The story of how three young children in the English countryside mistake a runaway con-

Actor Alan Cumming, winner of the Tony award for best performance for a leading actor in a musical for his role in *Cabaret*, performs a number from the show at the Tony awards ceremonies in New York City.

vict for the Messiah was translated—as it was in the Washington, D.C., premiere directed by Harold Prince—to the Bible Belt in Louisiana. Gale Edwards's new production was, however, more minimally designed (by Peter J. Davison) under a great metaphoric freeway to nowhere, and the story had been honed and sharpened. The rock songs contained some of Lloyd Webber's best writing in years, and one of the sweetest numbers, "No Matter What," sung by the children to their mysterious saviour, became a chart-topping single for the pop group Boyzone.

In Ireland, not to be outdone by the Hollywood star casting in London, the Gate Theatre in Dublin invited Oscar winner Frances McDormand—the pregnant police officer in *Fargo*—to play Blanche DuBois in *A Streetcar Named Desire.* She packed a great punch and revealed a good voice but missed the key notes of psychological disintegration. Later in the year the Gate staged the highlight of the Dublin Festival, Niall Buggy's performance as Uncle Vanya in a new translation of the Chekhov play by Brian Friel.   (MICHAEL COVENEY)

U.S. and Canada. Adventurous new writing from young American playwrights, the importation to Broadway of a sensationally reconceived British staging of the musical *Cabaret,* and the arrival of promising, even visionary, new leadership at several major regional theatres were the highlights of an otherwise sketchy year in American theatre. Economically and artistically, 1998 was dominated by works that had debuted in 1997; on Broadway Disney's *The Lion King* and Livent's *Ragtime* held sway, and throughout the country Paula Vogel's provocative, Pulitzer-winning drama *How I Learned to Drive* became far and away the most-produced play of the year.

The critical attention afforded new works by such fledgling writers as Diana Son, Robert O'Hara, W. David Hancock, Kenneth Lonergan, Margaret Edson, and Warren Leight was the year's most promising sign, an indication that these next-generation playwrights had both significant messages to deliver and the sophistication to shape their medium inventively. Son's *Stop Kiss,* a seriocomic play about the blossoming romance between two women and a random act of violence that tragically interrupts it, opened late in the year at New York City's Public Theater to admiring notices and sold-out houses. O'Hara's *Insurrection: Holding History,* a free-form, time-tripping examination of slavery and its legacy, generated enthusiasm and controversy at San Francisco's American Conservatory Theatre. Experimentalist Hancock garnered awards and a virtual cult following in several cities for his menacing and poignant environmental works *The Convention of Cartography* and *The Race of the Ark Tattoo.*

Lonergan's *This Is Our Youth,* a sly, acerbic study of rudderless adolescents mounted by New York's New Group, was a dark-horse success Off-Broadway. Edson, a first-grade teacher from Atlanta, Ga., writing her first play, scored critically and commercially with *Wit,* an unlikely drama about a John Donne scholar dying of cancer (a breakthrough role for actress Kathleen Chalfant). Leight won kudos for the richly detailed memory play *Side Man,* about the dissolution of a family in the post-big-band era 1950s.

By contrast, better-known American playwrights turned out few works of note, and

---

Dramatic Cast Changes at Livent

On Nov. 18, 1998 Canada based Livent Inc., the first publicly traded company whose primary business was live theatre, filed for bankruptcy. Founders Garth Drabinsky and Myron Gottlieb were fired, and a $225 million civil damage suit alleging fraud and unjust enrichment was filed against the two. Originally established in 1989 as Live Entertainment Inc. by former Cineplex Odeon movie theatre executives Drabinsky and Gottlieb to produce lavish musicals for Cineplex's chain of legitimate theatres, the enterprise, renamed Livent, went public in 1993 on the strength of the hugely successful Toronto run of Andrew Lloyd Webber's *Phantom of the Opera.*

As spectacular production values escalated the costs of Broadway musicals during the 1980s, making it impossible for even sold-out shows to break even in less than a year, theatre owners began to join in partnership with producers in order to keep their theatres in use. Drabinsky and Gottlieb sought to surmount the big-budget jitters by selling shares in a chain of theatres and a roster of shows instead of expensive limited partnerships in individual shows. Elaborate revivals of *Joseph and the Amazing Technicolor Dreamcoat* and *Show Boat* (which opened in Toronto in October 1993) followed, complete with huge advertising campaigns beginning more than a year in advance of openings in some markets. Livent's new musicals won multiple Tony awards; *Kiss of the Spider Woman* took seven (including best musical), and *Ragtime* garnered four.

Livent's fortunes began to sour in 1997, when the company posted its first losses, largely due to heavy investments in theatre construction and renovation. By 1998 Livent's theatrical real estate included the 2,200-seat Pantages Theatre in downtown Toronto and several theatres seating more than 1,800—the Ford Center(s) for the Performing Arts in northern Toronto, Vancouver, B.C., New York City, and Chicago. Lacklustre performances by some *Show Boat* road companies also contributed to financial woes.

In the 15 months prior to June 1998, when Michael Ovitz, a $20 million investor, and New York investment banker Roy Furman assumed the top board positions, Livent lost $50 million. Drabinsky, however, remained as artistic director. While preparing second-quarter financial reports, auditors discovered serious accounting irregularities, including inflated earnings, expenses shuffled between productions, and unreported expenses. Canadian and American securities regulators suspended trading of Livent stock on August 10, and the new management team suspended Drabinsky and Gottlieb while a forensic audit was conducted. Standard & Poor's downgraded Livent's credit rating from B+ to BB−. After filing for bankruptcy Livent canceled one of its traveling productions of *Ragtime.* More than 100 employees in Toronto were laid off on November 25.

In the wake of the financial crisis, plans to develop a 1,400-seat theatre in a Toronto hotel-condominium complex south of the Pantages and a 500-seat theatre in New York City's Times Square were shelved. Todd Haimes of New York's Roundabout Theater, who specialized in producing on tight budgets, was named artistic director.

(BRUCE CANTWELL)

---

the New York theatre reached out for serious mainstream dramas to a dependable source from England, the recently knighted Sir David Hare, and a freshly celebrated (some would say notorious) one from Ireland, 27-year-old bad-boy dramatist Martin McDonagh. Hare, who had famously sworn off Broadway a decade ago following an angry set-to with then *New York Times* critic Frank Rich, was nevertheless represented there by back-to-back commercial successes—*The Judas Kiss,* a portrait of Oscar Wilde in decline featuring a game but miscast Liam Neeson in the leading role and *The Blue Room,* a sexually frank reworking of Arthur Schnitzler's *La Ronde* starring film actress Nicole Kidman. Neither play was up to the level of last season's *Skylight,* but the combination of celebrity wattage and sensationalism (Kidman and her *Blue Room* costar Iain Glen appeared briefly nude) assured an active box office.

The first two plays in Martin McDonagh's trilogy, set in Leenane, a backwater village in the west of Ireland, were imported to New York with great fanfare, much of it focusing on the dashing, argumentative young writer whose idea of theatre was, in his words, a "punk destruction of what's gone on before." Such aspirations notwithstanding, *The Cripple of Inishmaan,* a large-cast drama mounted in an uneven production at the Public Theater, and *The Beauty Queen of Leenane,* a tauter, funnier, and more sinister work handled with great delicacy by director Garry Hynes in an Atlantic Theatre Company production that moved to Broadway, proved straightforward, even conventional, in form. McDonagh, like his literary predecessors John Millington Synge and William Butler Yeats, made adept use of literary language and a strong narrative drive—even as he pessimistically surveyed the shattered fragments of Irish society riven by internal conflict and the pressures of modernity. In addition to acting awards for three of its principals, *Beauty Queen* earned Hines, head of Ireland's Druid Theatre, the first-ever Tony award to go to a female director.

That history-making moment at the June 7 Tony ceremony was followed in short order by a second win for a woman director,

Julie Taymor of *The Lion King*. The Disney-financed extravaganza earned six Tonys in all, beating out *Ragtime* for best musical (though Terrence McNally was cited for the latter show's book, and Lynn Ahrens and Stephen Flaherty won for original score). *Art,* French playwright Yasmina Reza's witty pas de trois for male actors about aesthetics in contemporary art and the demands of friendship, was a surprise win for best play of the year.

Director Sam Mendes's revisionist *Cabaret* swept the Tonys' musical-revival category and provided the New York season with indelible onstage images and a dramatic offstage survival story. Imported by the Roundabout Theatre Company from Mendes's increasingly vital Donmar Warehouse (after months of negotiation for a club-style venue in the theatre district where the show's Kit Kat Klub could be created environmentally), the production departed radically from the tone of Harold Prince's original 1966 stage production and Bob Fosse's landmark 1972 film. Mendes turned the gamine Sally Bowles (Natasha Richardson, later replaced by Jennifer Jason Leigh) into a desperate and self-deluded waif and the omnipresent Master of Ceremonies (Alan Cumming, in the role memorably played by Joel Grey as a tuxedoed German Expressionist marionette) into a gyrating, omnisexual creature spangled with glitter and scarred with needle track marks. Dark, erotic, and relentless, the production emphasized the economic desperation of late Weimar Germany rather than its honky-tonk gaiety and pointed to disturbing connections between the aesthetics of the Nazi era and those of current popular culture.

Ensconced in a 520-seat club on 43rd Street, the hit musical was forced to close down for several weeks when the scaffolding of a construction elevator attached to the nearby Condé Nast Tower in Times Square collapsed, making the neighborhood unsafe for pedestrians. The closing of *Cabaret* and two other Roundabout productions cost the theatre some $2 million, but producer Todd Haimes held out until the show could reopen and then announced plans to move it late in the year to refurbished quarters once occupied by the legendary discotheque Studio 54.

Haimes took centre stage in another financial drama when he was offered the reins of Livent, the Toronto-based production company founded by Garth Drabinsky and recently acquired by a team that included Hollywood power broker Michael Ovitz. Drabinsky was ousted amid allegations of bookkeeping irregularities, and Haimes assumed his duties while retaining his connections to the Roundabout. (*See* Sidebar.)

Other leadership changes at theatres around the U.S. bode well for the vitality of regional work. Director Michael Wilson slipped confidently into the shoes of long-time Hartford Stage Company director Mark Lamos, announcing his intention to devote the coming decade at the Connecticut theatre to examining the complete output of Tennessee Williams. Another Williams aficionado, Molly Smith, was selected as director of Washington, D.C.'s Arena Stage, on the basis of her years of progressive and community-sensitive work at the Perseverance Theatre of Alaska. At the debt-ridden Long Wharf Theatre in New Haven, Conn. (where Margaret Edson's *Wit* origi-

Actors Tom Hanks (right) and Tom Sizemore (left) prepare for combat in the film *Saving Private Ryan*, which garnered five Golden Globe Award nominations in December.

nated), second-season artistic director Douglas Hughes engineered an economic turnaround and steered a new creative team in inventive directions.

On the Canadian side of the border, Livent's business troubles—the management takeover was followed by bankruptcy and the decimation of the company's Toronto offices—engendered fears that Canadian tourism might be affected. The theatre community got more bad news in the form of continued government cutbacks in arts funding, although this was somewhat offset by a well-publicized gift of $1 million to small arts groups from Joan Chalmers, a prominent philanthropist.

A note of optimism was struck when leading Canadian actors joined forces to form a new classical company named Soulpepper, under the artistic directorship of Albert Schultz, with Broadway-certified musical-theatre actor Brent Carver (who also led the cast of the Livent-backed musical *Parade* at New York's Lincoln Center Theater) as its first-year guest artist. Among the year's most memorable productions was Shelagh Stephenson's wry confessional family drama *The Memory of Water* at Toronto's Tarragon Theatre.   (JIM O'QUINN)

MOTION PICTURES

If a single overall phenomenon could be identified in a generally uneventful cinema year, it was a surge in the worldwide relaxation of sexual taboos. Filmmakers as far afield as Switzerland, Africa, and Peru recognized that audiences were ready to accept alternative erotic relationships, and a startling number of the year's films depicted unconventional and same-sex matches as normal and undisturbing.

English-Speaking Countries. In the United States the year's big-budget "event" films—*Deep Impact, Armageddon,* and the resurrection of the Japanese 1950s B-picture monster *Godzilla*—paled after the 1997 blockbuster triumph of *Titanic.* Audiences seemed more ready to respond to "serious" themes. Two films about World War II were especially noteworthy. Steven Spielberg's ambitious *Saving Private Ryan* was set in

the Normandy campaign of 1944; after a compellingly realistic portrayal of the carnage during the D-Day landing on the beach, it chronicled the mission of a small group of soldiers to retrieve from behind enemy lines a soldier slated to be sent home because all his brothers had been killed in action. As meticulous in conveying the physical sense of combat but more philosophically reflective, Terrence Malick's *The Thin Red Line* adapted James Jones's novel about the battle of Guadalcanal.

Unsurprisingly, political disillusion found expression in satire. Barry Levinson's *Wag the Dog,* released late in 1997, was a dark horror-comedy about a war concocted by the White House to distract attention from a presidential sexual indiscretion. Mike Nichols's *Primary Colors,* coscripted with Elaine May and based on the book by Joe Klein, was a thinly disguised exposé of the first Clinton presidential campaign. In *Bulworth* director-star Warren Beatty offered an eccentric political morality tale about a liberal politician who disconcertingly takes to speaking the truth.

Television provided another ready target. Peter Weir's *The Truman Show* was a fable about the tyranny of the media, the story of a young man who suddenly discovers that since birth he has been the main character in a 24-hour-a-day soap opera. Gary Ross's *Pleasantville* was a satirical fantasy about two 1990s teenagers spirited into the black-and-white utopian small-town world of a favourite 1950s soap opera.

A revived taste for costume pictures sent filmmakers back to 19th-century literature. Alexandre Dumas's often-filmed swashbuckler *The Man in the Iron Mask* was intelligently adapted and directed by Randall Wallace (the writer of *Braveheart,* making his directorial debut) as a vehicle for Leonardo DiCaprio, supported by Jeremy Irons, Gérard Depardieu, Gabriel Byrne, and John Malkovich as the four musketeers. A low-budget version of the same subject, bravely directed, written, and even acted (in the role of Aramis) by William Richert was predictably no serious rival. The Danish director Bille August made an opulent and well-cast version of Victor Hugo's *Les*

INTERNATIONAL FILM AWARDS 1998

Golden Globes, awarded in Beverly Hills, California, in January 1998

Best motion picture drama	*Titanic* (U.S.; director, James Cameron)
Best musical or comedy	*As Good As It Gets* (U.S.; director, James L. Brooks)
Best director	James Cameron (*Titanic*, U.S.)
Best actress, drama	Judi Dench (*Mrs. Brown*, U.K.)
Best actor, drama	Peter Fonda (*Ulee's Gold*, U.S.)
Best actress, musical or comedy	Helen Hunt (*As Good As It Gets*, U.S.)
Best actor, musical or comedy	Jack Nicholson (*As Good As It Gets*, U.S.)
Best foreign-language film	*Ma vie en rose* (France; director, Alain Berliner)

Sundance Film Festival, awarded in Park City, Utah, in January 1998

Grand Jury Prize, dramatic film	*Slam* (U.S.; director, Marc Levin)
Grand Jury Prize, documentary	*The Farm* (U.S.; directors, Liz Garbus, Johnathan Stack) *Frat House* (U.S.; directors, Todd Phillips, Andrew Gurland)
Audience Award, dramatic film	*Smoke Signals* (U.S.; director, Chris Eyre)
Audience Award, documentary	*Out of the Past* (U.S.; director, Jeff Dupre)
Best director, dramatic	Darren Aronofsky (*P1*, U.S.)
Best director, documentary	Julia Loktev (*Moment of Impact*, U.S.)
Filmmakers Trophy, dramatic	*Smoke Signals* (U.S.; director, Chris Eyre)
Filmmakers Trophy, documentary	*Divine Trash* (U.S.; director, Steve Teager)

Berlin International Film Festival, awarded in February 1998

Golden Berlin Bear	*Central Station* (Brazil/France; director, Walter Salles)
Special Jury Prize	*Wag the Dog* (U.S.; director, Barry Levinson)
Best director	Neil Jordan (*The Butcher Boy*, Ireland)
Best actress	Fernanda Montenego (*Central Station*, Brazil)
Best actor	Samuel L. Jackson (*Jackie Brown*, U.S.)
Silver Berlin Bear, outstanding single achievement	Matt Damon (*Good Will Hunting*, U.S.)

Césars (France), awarded in March 1998

Best French film	*On connaît le chanson* (director, Alain Resnais)
Best director	Luc Besson (*Le Cinquième élément*)
Best actress	Ariane Ascaride (*Marius et Jeannette*)
Best actor	André Dussollier (*On connaît le chanson*)
Best first film	*Didier* (director, Alain Chabat)

Academy of Motion Picture Arts and Sciences (Oscars, U.S.), awarded in Los Angeles in March 1998

Best film	*Titanic* (U.S.; director, James Cameron)
Best director	James Cameron (*Titanic*, U.S.)
Best actress	Helen Hunt (*As Good As It Gets*, U.S.)
Best actor	Jack Nicholson (*As Good As It Gets*, U.S.)
Best supporting actress	Kim Basinger (*L.A. Confidential*, U.S.)
Best supporting actor	Robin Williams (*Good Will Hunting*, U.S.)
Best foreign-language film	*Character* (The Netherlands; director, Mike van Diem)

British Academy of Film and Television Arts, awarded in London in April 1998

Best film	*The Full Monty* (U.K.; director, Peter Cattaneo)
Best director	Baz Luhrmann (*William Shakespeare's Romeo and Juliet*, Australia)
Best actress	Judi Dench (*Mrs. Brown*, U.K.)
Best actor	Robert Carlyle (*The Full Monty*, U.K.)
Best supporting actress	Sigourney Weaver (*The Ice Storm*, U.S.)
Best supporting actor	Tom Wilkinson (*The Full Monty*, U.K.)
Best foreign-language film	*L' Appartement* (France; directors, Georges Benayoun, Gilles Mimouni)

Cannes International Film Festival, France, awarded in May 1998

Palme d'Or	*Eternity and a Day* (Greece; director, Theo Angelopoulos)
Grand Jury Prize	*La vita è bella* (Italy; director, Roberto Benigni)
Special Jury Prize	*La Classe des neiges* (France; director, Claude Miller) and *Festen* (Denmark; director Thomas Vinterberg)
Best director	John Boorman (*The General*, Ireland)
Best actress	Elodia Bouchez, Natacha Regnier (*La Vie revée des anges, France*)
Best actor	Peter Mullan (*My Name Is Joe*, U.K.)
Caméra d'Or	*Slam* (U.S.; director, Marc Levin)

Locarno International Film Festival, Switzerland, awarded in August 1998

Golden Leopard	*Mr Zhao* (China; director, Lu Yue)
Silver Leopard	*Dance of Dust* (Iran; director, Abolfazl Jalili) and *The Adopted Son* (Kyrgyzstan-France; director, Aktan Abdikalikov)
Best actress	Rossy de Palma (*Foul Play*, France)
Best actor	Three male leads (*Short Sharp Shock*, Germany)

Montreal World Film Festival, awarded in September 1998

Best film (Grand Prix of the Americas)	*The Quarry* (Belgium/France/The Netherlands/Spain; director, Marion Hansel) and *Full Moon* (Switzerland/Germany/France; director, Fredi M. Murer)
Best actress	Ingrid Rupio (*The Lighthouse*, Argentina/Spain)
Best actor	Hugo Weaving (*The Interview*, Australia)
Best director	Manon Briand (*2 Seconds*, Canada)
Special Grand Prix of the Jury	*Sun Bird* (China; directors, Wang Xueqi, Yang Liping)
Best screenplay	Rafa Russo (*The Man With Rain in his Shoes*, Spain/U.K.)
International cinematographic press award	Begging For Love (Japan; director, Hideyuki Hirtayama)

Toronto International Film Festival, awarded in September 1998

Best Canadian feature film	*No* (director, Robert Lepage)
Best Canadian first feature	*Last Night* (director, Don McKellar)
Best Canadian short film	*When Ponds Freeze Over* (director, Mary Lewis)
Metro Media award	*Happiness* (U.S.; director, Todd Solanz)
International cinematographic press award	*West Beirut* (Lebanon; director, Ziad Doueiri) and *Praise* (Australia; director, John Curran)
People's Choice Award	*La vita è bella* (Italy; director, Roberto Benigni)

Venice Film Festival, Italy, awarded in September 1998

Golden Lion	*Così ridevano* (Italy; director, Gianni Amelio)
Special Jury Prize	*Last Stop Paradise* (Romania; director, Lucian Pintilie)
Volpi Cup, best actress	Catherine Deneuve (*Place Vendôme*, France)
Volpi Cup, best actor	Sean Penn (*Hurlyburly*, U.S.)
Silver Lion, best direction	Emir Kusturica (*Black Cat, White Cat*, Yugoslavia)
International Film Critics' Prize	*The Powder Keg* (Yugoslavia/France; director, Goran Paskaljevic)

Chicago International Film Festival, awarded in October 1998

Best feature film	*The Hole* (Taiwan; director, Tsai Ming-Liang)
Special Jury Prize	*Wind With the Gone* (Argentina; director, Alejandro Agresti)
Best actress	Alessandra Martines (*Hasard ou coincidence*, France)
Best actor	Ensemble (*Friendly Fire*, Brazil)
Silver Hugo	*The Pear Tree* (Iran; director, Dariush Mehrjui)
International Film Critics' Prize	*The Outskirts* (Russia; director, Pyotr Lutsic)

San Sebastián International Film Festival, Spain, awarded in October 1998

Best film	*Wind With the Gone* (Argentina; director, Alejandro Agresti)
Special Jury Prize	*Gods and Monsters* (U.K./U.S.; director, Bill Condon) and *A la place du coeur* (France; director, Robert Guediguian)
Best director	Fernando Leon de Aranao (*Barrio*, Spain)
Best actress	Jeanne Balibar (*Late Autumn, Early September*, France)
Best actor	Ian McKellan (*Gods and Monsters*, U.K./U.S.)
Best photography	Rodrigo Prieto (*Under a Spell*, Mexico)
Jury Prize	*The Don* (Iran; director, Abolfazl Jalili)
New Director's Prize	*Fishes in August* (Japan; director, Yoichiro Takahashi)
International Critics' Award	*After Life* (Japan; director, Hirokazu Kore-eda)

Vancouver International Film Festival, Canada, awarded in October 1998

Federal Express Award	*Such a Long Journey* (Canada/U.K.; director, Sturla Gunnarson)
Air Canada Award	*La vita è bella* (Italy; director, Roberto Benigni)
Rogers Award	*Streetheart* (Canada; directors, Charles Binamé, Monique Proulx)
NFB Award (documentary feature)	*The Brandon Teena Story* (Canada; directors, Susan Muska, Greta Olafsdottir)
Telefilm Canada Award for Best Western Canadian Feature	*Dirty* (Canada; director, Bruce Sweeney)
Telefilm Canada Award for Best Western Canadian Short Film	*Keys to Kingdoms* (Canada; director, Nathaniel Geary)
Dragons and Tigers Award for Young Cinema	*Xiao Wu* (China/Hong Kong; director, Jia Zhangke)

Tokyo International Film Festival, Japan, awarded in November 1998

Grand Prix	*Open Your Eyes* (France/Spain; director, Alejandro Amenabar)
Special Jury Prize	*Leaf on a Pillow* (Indonesia; director, Garin Nugroho)

European Film Awards, awarded in London, December 1998

Best European film	*La vita è bella* (Italy; director, Roberto Benigni)
Best European actress	Elodie Bouchez and Natasha Regnier (*La Vie rêvée des anges*, France)
Best European actor	Roberto Benigni (*La vita è bella*, Italy)

Misérables, and stage director Des McAnuff presented a faithful adaptation of Balzac's chilly portrait of decadent 1840s Paris, *Cousin Bette.*

Woody Allen's *Celebrity,* Robert Altman's *The Gingerbread Man,* and the Coen brothers' comedy thriller *The Big Lebowski* fell short of their directors' best work, but other well-established artists were on form. Jonathan Demme directed an epic adaptation of Toni Morrison's Pulitzer Prize-winning novel *Beloved,* about the scars and aftermath of slavery. Robert Redford directed and starred, as a man who can communicate with horses, in a mature and visually splendid adaptation of Nicholas Evans's best-selling novel *The Horse Whisperer.* Spike Lee's *He Got Game,* the story of the relationship between a convict and his athletically gifted son, was the director's most human and least obviously didactic film. Steven Soderbergh made the wittiest and most sophisticated of several recent adaptations of Elmore Leonard crime thrillers, *Out of Sight.*

Independent production was prolific but for the most part conventional in choice of themes. Among the exceptions was David Riker's powerful and brutal *The City,* a neorealist film about Hispanic workers in New York City. Todd Solondz followed his debut success, *Welcome to the Dollhouse* (1995), with *Happiness,* a disturbing black comedy about sexual deviance and anxieties that lurk beneath polite social surfaces.

The first feature directed, written, acted, and co-produced by Native Americans, Chris Eyre's road movie *Smoke Signals,* sustained a light touch in its perceptive observation of the frustrations of the life of young people on reservations. The poet Maya Angelou directed a touching film about the problems of an inner-city Chicago African-American family, *Down in the Delta.* Among the year's remakes, Gus Van Sant incautiously attempted a near carbon copy of Alfred Hitchcock's classic 1960 thriller *Psycho,* and Brad Silberling transmuted

Television talk-show host and actress Oprah Winfrey appears with actor Danny Glover in a scene from *Beloved,* Jonathan Demme's film adaptation of Toni Morrison's Pulitzer Prize–winning novel.

Wim Wenders's philosophical fable *Wings of Desire* from Berlin to Los Angeles to become *City of Angels.*

Animation feature production was unusually prolific. The Disney studio's *Mulan,* set in ancient China, featured a feminist heroine who disguises herself as a man to fight in the Imperial army. The first animated feature by Warner Brothers, *Quest for Camelot,* turned to Arthurian legend. The computer-animated *Antz* by DreamWorks, about highly politicized insects, was answered by Disney's *A Bug's Life,* also computer-animated, and directed by John Lasseter. DreamWorks was also responsible for a much-publicized cartoon version of the saga of Moses, *The Prince of Egypt.*

The recurrent pattern of British filmmaking has always been to achieve a run of international successes (like the recent *Four Weddings and a Funeral* [1994], *Trainspotting* [1996], and *The Full Monty* [1997]) and then follow it with optimistic overproduction and imitation of the box-office winners. The same trend occurred in 1998. A sharp rise in production featured a rush of films about Glasgow lowlife in the style of *Trainspotting* (Paul McGuigan's *The Acid House,* written by *Trainspotting's* author, Irvine Welsh, and Genevieve Jolliffe's *Urban Ghost Story*) or featuring *The Full Monty*-type buddy groups of regional working men. This category included Sam Miller's *Among Giants* (scripted by *The Full Monty* writer Simon Beaufoy), about Sheffield men working on electric pylons; and Brian Gibson's *Still Crazy,* dealing with a group of middle-aged men who were reviving their 1970s rock band.

Glasgow working-class life more significantly provided the milieu of Ken Loach's *My Name Is Joe,* a multilayered portrait of a young former alcoholic. The film's gifted main actor, Peter Mullan, made his own directorial debut with *Orphans,* an absurdist comedy about a dysfunctional working-class Glasgow family dealing in its own bizarre fashion with the mother's death and funeral. Easily the most original British film of the year, John Maybury's *Love Is the Devil* was a ferocious and visually inventive re-creation of the personality of the painter Francis Bacon and his sadistic relationship with his working-class lover.

Some of the most successful films of the year reverted to the reliable British genre of historical costume pictures. Outstanding among these was *Elizabeth,* an unusually sharp, modern view of the court and per-

Actor Toby Maguire touches the face of actress Joan Allen in a scene from the movie *Pleasantville,* about a pair of modern-day teenagers who are magically transported into a 1950s black-and-white television show.

sonal intrigues of Queen Elizabeth I, by Indian director Shekhar Kapur. High production standards and fine casting did much for John Madden's *Shakespeare in Love,* wittily scripted by Tom Stoppard and Marc Norman and speculating on the theatrical, social, political, and amorous circumstances surrounding the writing of *Romeo and Juliet.* Re-creating a more recent era, playwright-director David Leland's *The Land Girls* was a perceptive study of an aspect of women's life in World War II.

Other creditable British movies included *The Nephew,* a first film by Eugene Brady, about local shock and subsequent adjustment when an Irish farmer's American nephew turns out to be black and dreadlocked; Simon Shore's accomplished *Get Real,* based on Patrick Wilde's play *What's Wrong with Angry?* and dealing lightly with the anxieties of a middle-class schoolboy adjusting to his homosexuality; and *Little Voice,* Mark Herman's bright adaptation of Jim Cartwright's play about the exploitation of an introverted provincial working-class girl with a gift for impersonating great pop singers.

From Ireland late in the year came writer-director Kirk Jones's lighthearted *Waking Ned Devine.* In this quirky film the title character has died of shock after learning his lottery ticket is a winner, and his fellow villagers plot to collect and split the money.

Among Canadian films that reached international festivals, Bruce Sweeney's *Dirty* was well described as "a walk on the wild side of human nature." Rodney Gibbons filmed *Louisa May Alcott's Little Men,*

based on the book *Little Men;* more sentimental than Alcott's *Little Women,* recently filmed by Gillian Armstrong, it had not survived as well.

The most extraordinary Australian film of the year was Rolf de Heer's affecting *Dance Me to My Song,* written by Heather Rose, a highly intelligent woman afflicted by severe cerebral palsy, who also played the principal role—an independent, sensitive, but severely handicapped woman who finds herself stirring the sexual jealousy of her unfeeling care-taker. Another noteworthy Australian picture was Ana Kokkinos's groundbreaking *Head On,* about a young Australian Greek battling to adjust to both his homosexuality and the problems of ethnic communities in Australia. George Miller directed a well-received sequel to the blockbuster sleeper success *Babe,* titled descriptively *Babe: Pig in the City.*

Continental Europe. It fell to veteran director Philippe de Broca to make one of the biggest French box-office successes of the year, the swashbuckling *Le Bossu* (1997; *On Guard*), the seventh screen adaptation of Paul Feval's 1857 picaresque novel. Another artist of the senior generation, Eric Rohmer completed the final film in his quartet dedicated to the four seasons: *Conte d'automne,* a gentle, touching tale of sporadic, middle-aged romantic intrigue.

From the middle generation of French filmmakers, Alain Corneau's *Le Cousin* was a literate and intelligent study of the relationship of a police detective and his informant, casting popular television comedians

Alain Chabat and Patrick Timsit in unaccustomed serious roles. The celebrated theatre director Patrice Chéreau presented *Ceux qui m'aiment prendront le train* (1997; *Those Who Love Me Can Take the Train*), an ambitious ensemble piece centred on a party of variously troubled personalities making the journey to the funeral of a common friend.

Younger directors favoured social themes. One of the year's most widely praised films, Erick Zonca's *La Vie rêvée des anges (The Dreamlife of Angels),* offered toughly realistic observation of the lives of two young women on the margins of society in a provincial town (Lille). Winner of the Jean Vigo Prize, Claude Mouriéras's *Dis-moi que je rêve* dealt with the problems of an inbred farming family in the Alps and their difficulties in coming to terms with their mentally handicapped children.

Italy's major directors were all prominently active. The comedian-director Roberto Benigni scored international success with *La vita è bella* (1997; *Life Is Beautiful*), a tragicomedy set in a Nazi concentration camp. Gianni Amelio took the Golden Lion of the Venice Film Festival with *Così ridevano (The Way We Laughed),* a chronicle of the long-term relationships of two Sicilian brothers. Giuseppe Tornatore made his first English-language film, the spectacular yet whimsical fable *La leggenda del pianista sull'oceano (The Legend of the Pianist on the Ocean).* Nanni Moretti's *Aprile* was a self-exploratory rumination on becoming a father during the political rise and fall of Silvio Berlusconi.

DreamWorks studio's computer-animated film *Antz* was a major box-office success in 1998. Some of Hollywood's biggest stars, including Woody Allen and Sharon Stone, provided the voices for the movie.

Among Italy's veterans, Ettore Scola used the claustrophobic setting of a restaurant as a microcosm of contemporary society in a finely orchestrated comedy, *La cena.* The Taviani brothers, Vittorio and Paolo, directed *Tu ridi,* based on two contrasting Luigi Pirandello stories. Pupi Avati was on form with *Il testimone dello sposo* (*The Best Man*), a romantic period comedy with deeper social resonances, about a fraught marriage at the beginning of the 20th century. At 78, the actor Alberto Sordi directed himself in *Incontri proibiti,* an elegant comedy about an old gentleman who finds love and a new lease on life.

Other interesting films of the year included Francesca Archibugi's *L'albero delle pere* (*The Pear Tree*), a keenly observed picture of an urban 14-year-old forced into premature responsibility by the fecklessness of his separated parents. Antonio Capuano's grotesque and sombre comedy *Polvere di Napoli* updated the characters and anecdotal structure of Vittorio De Sica's 1954 classic *L'oro di Napoli* to a less-optimistic present.

While many German directors revealed a developing skill for emulating Hollywood models of pace and production, Joseph Vilsmaier's *Comedian Harmonists* (*The Harmonists*) used the style of vintage Hollywood musicals to tell the real-life story of the famous 1930s musical group (whose original recordings were digitally restored for the sound track), which was broken up by the coming of Nazism because half of them were Jewish. One of the year's major successes, at home and abroad, Tom Tykwer's *Lola rennt* (*Run Lola Run*) combined technical brio with sensitive character observation as it explored three alternative scenarios to the heroine's race against the clock to save her boyfriend from a gangster boss. An Austrian-German co-production, Dani Levy's *Meschugge* (*The Giraffe*) was a political thriller about the exposure of events and people from the Nazi past. From Austria Florian Flicker's *Suzie Washington* was a compelling road movie about the flight of an illegal immigrant from Eastern Europe through picturesque but inhospitable Austria.

Among Spain's staple commercial production of sexy comedies, over-the-top farce, and thrillers, a few films stood out: veteran writer-director Manuel Gutiérrez Aragón's study of Cuban emigrés in Spain, *Las cosas que dejé en La Habana;* Fernando Trueba's stylish comedy *La niña de tus ojos* (*The Girl of Your Dreams*), about a Spanish film unit making an Andalusian musical in 1938 Berlin under a cultural agreement between Adolf Hitler and Gen. Francisco Franco; newcomer Fernando León de Aranos's *Barrio,* about street children; and José Luís Garci's *El abuelo* (*The Grandfather*), a 19th-century King Lear story that was the country's Oscar submission.

Greece's most eminent director, Theo Angelopoulos, won the Cannes Film Festival Palme d'Or for *Mia eoniotita ke mia mera* (*Eternity and a Day*), an elegiac tale of a middle-aged poet setting off on a mysterious journey during which an encounter with an illegal immigrant child changes his vision of life. Illegal Armenian immigrants in Greece were treated more realistically in *Mirupafshim* (1997; *See You*), coscripted and co-directed by Christos Voupouras and Giorgos Korras.

The Dutch director Orlow Seunke made *De Gordel van Smaragd,* a rich and ambitious chronicle of Indonesian history in the 1940s, viewing the succession of colonialism, Japanese occupation, and the independence struggle through the life and loves of a beautiful Indo-European; in *Felice...Felice...* Peter Delpeut skillfully blended antique photographs and dramatic reconstructions to tell the story of an imagined doomed romance between the 19th-century photographer Felice Beato and a Japanese woman.

From Sweden, Kjell Sundvall's *Sista kontraktet* (*The Last Contract*) offered a gripping and plausible speculative reconstruction of the 1986 murder of Sweden's prime minister, Olof Palme. Making a notable debut was Lisa Ohlin with *Veranda för en tenor,* the story of two middle-aged friends collaborating on a film that re-creates a traumatic moment of their own boyhood.

A group of four Danish filmmakers attracted attention with an aggressive manifesto, "Dogma 95," calling for a new cinema that would discard high-tech values in favour of simplicity and truth. Paradoxically, the handheld cameras and functional editing themselves became technical distractions in Dogma's showpieces—Thomas Vinterberg's *Festen* (*The Celebration*), an essentially conventional anecdote of a family gathering that collapses under the weight of home truths, and *Idioterne* (*The Idiots*) by Lars von Trier, the group's leader. Von Trier's film, written in four days and clearly involving much improvisation by the actors, focused on an informal commune whose members cultivate their "inner idiocy," to defy the restraints of social convention. The first feature to be shot on Greenland and in the local Inuit language, Jacob Grønlykke's *Lysets hjerte* (1997) intriguingly juxtaposed traditional myth and magic with the harsh social reality of Greenland as a poor, marginalized dependency of Denmark.

Finland's perpetual enfant terrible, Aki Kaurismäki turned back to film history to make a pure silent film, a new interpretation of Mauritz Stiller's classic *Johan.* August Gudmundsson, a leading figure in the emergent Icelandic cinema in the 1980s, returned after a 10-year absence with a haunting and mystical period piece, *Dansinn* (*The Dance*).

The best films from Russia dealt forthrightly with problems of contemporary living. A directorial debut by writer Pyotr Lutsik, *The Outskirts* related how a group of old peasants take revenge on New Russian entrepreneurs and gangsters who have stolen their land. In *Ménage à trois* Pyotr Todorovsky updated Abram Romm's silent classic *Bed and Sofa* to show a complex domestic relationship in contemporary Moscow. Todorovsky's son Valery showed people on the margins of the Moscow mafia in *The Land of the Deaf.* Vadim Abdrashitov revealed the veiled traumas of a group of people in a southern city recently emerged from civil war in *Vremya tantsyora* (*Time of the Dancer*).

Notable films came from now-independent former Soviet states. Tajikistan's first feature production, *Parvaz-e zanbur* (*Flight of the Bee*), was a touching humanist comedy-fable about feuding neighbours. From Latvia, Laila Pakalnina's *The Shoe,* a comedy set in Soviet times, was about the farcical furor among the military when a woman's shoe is found on an out-of-bounds beach.

Despite the acute problems of production in the new market economies, interesting films continued to emerge from Eastern Europe. Serbia was the location for two prestigious international co-productions: Emir Kusturica's frenetic folkloric comedy about the gypsies of the Danube banks, *Crna Macka* (*Black Cat, White Cat*), and Goran Paskaljevic's *Bure baruta* (*The Powder Keg*). One of the most extraordinary and timely films of the year, *Bure baruta* was a horror-comic tour of Belgrade during a single night, revealing a merry-go-round of violence, exploitation, and despair. Yugoslavia's entry for best foreign-language film Oscar, Mirjana Vukomanovic's *Three Summer Days* (1997), dealt gently with the intolerance of Serbs toward fellow Serbs uprooted by the wars.

The most original Hungarian film of the year was Gyorgy Feher's *Passion,* a highly visual black-and-white reworking of James M. Cain's three-times-filmed novel *The Postman Always Rings Twice.* The Czech Republic's major domestic and international successes were comedies: Petr Zelenka's eccentric *Knoflikari* (1997; *Buttoners*); Oskar Reifs's promising debut film, *Postel* (*The Bed*), the beyond-the-grave ruminations of a man whose life was dominated by women; and Vera Chytilova's *Pasti, pasti, pasticky* (*Trap, Trap, Little Trap*), improbably bringing humour to the story of a woman who castrates two macho officials who rape her.

A Romanian co-production with France, Belgium, and The Netherlands, Radu Mihaileanu's *Train de vie* was an original and poignant comedy about the inhabitants of a Central European village who in 1942 decide that the only way to escape Nazi deportation is to find a train and "deport" themselves via Russia to Israel.

Middle East. Turkey produced one of the year's rare truly poetic works, Nuri Bilge Ceylan's *Kasaba.* Made on a shoestring budget and photographed by the writer-director himself, it was imbued with a Chekhovian quality in its study of the relationships and concerns of an outsider family in a little town.

Iranian cinema continued to offer original and polished work. Dariush Mehrjui directed *Leila* (1996), a touching drama about the traumas of an infertile young married woman, and *The Pear Tree,* a warm chronicle of adolescent love. Mohsen Makhmalbaf's *Sokhout* (*The Silence*) was an enigmatic anecdote, set on the border with former Soviet Tajikistan, about a blind boy earning a pittance to support himself and his mother by tuning musical instruments. Makhmalbaf's 17-year-old daughter, Semira, made a momentous directorial debut with *Sib* (*The Apple*), which used real-life people to tell their own story of how, as a very poor family, they kept their twin daughters locked up from birth until they were discovered by the authorities.

Latin America. The Brazilian director Walter Salles, Jr., enjoyed worldwide success with *Central do Brasil* (*Central Station*), the story of a mean old spinster who unwillingly discovers her own resources of humanity through an encounter with an irresistibly appealing little orphan boy. In marked contrast was the visionary style of Djalma Limongi Batista's fantasy biography of an 18th-century Portuguese libertine poet, *Bocage, o triunfo do amor* (*Bocage, the Triumph of Love*).

From Argentina, Hector Babenco's *Corazón iluminado* (*Foolish Heart*) was a long-cherished autobiographical project, the story of a tragic first love affair. The veteran Fernando Solanas's *La nube* (*The Cloud*) was an end-of-the-millennium fable about rain and clouds overhanging a Buenos Aires in which the traffic and pedestrians move backward. In Peru Francisco Lombardi's *No se lo digas a nadie* treated what seemed the universal topic of the year, a young man coming to terms with his homosexuality.

Asia. The veteran Indian cinematographer Santosh Sivan made a striking first film, *The Terrorist,* which followed a 19-year-old woman suicide bomber in the days leading up to her planned assassination of a political figure, who is never seen. Deepa Mehta's Canadian-Indian production *Earth* viewed the trauma of Indian partition in 1947 through the eyes of an eight-year-old Parsee girl. A Pakistan-British co-production, Jamil Dehlavi's film biography of Mohammed Ali Jinnah, the creator of Pakistan, *Jinnah,* gave the British actor Christopher Lee a rewarding role.

Japan enjoyed its all-time box-office hit with Hayao Miyazaki's *Mononoke hime* (*The Princess Monokone*), an animated film based on a 14th-century fable; it grossed more than $150 million in the home market. Another national box-office success was Shunya Ito's provocatively titled *Unmei no toki* (*Pride*), a revisionist dramatization of the Tokyo war crimes trials of 1946–48. Nobuhiko Obayashi's stylistically inventive *Sada* meticulously retraced the story of Sada Abe, who gained notoriety in the 1930s for strangling and mutilating her lover in an excess of passion.

Chinese directors dramatically broadened the range of their themes with such films as debut director Zhang Yang's romantic comedy *Aiquing mala tang* (*Spicy Love Soup*); a touching portrayal of blue-collar problems in fast-changing contemporary Beijing, *Ingfu dajie* (*Happiness Street*), by a woman director, Li Shaohong; an acute and very modern portrait of a womanizing doctor, Yue Lu's debut film *Zhao Xiansheng* (*Mr. Zhao*); and an acute examination of the rigours of rural life in an undefined but not too distant past, Zhou Youchao's *Going to School with Dad on My Back.*

In Hong Kong a welcome variation from the staple diet of crime stories was offered by Jacob Cheung's *Ji sor* (1997; *Intimates*), a tender, poetic, and exquisitely played record of a 50-year lesbian love. From Vietnam, Le Hoang's *Ai xuoi van ly* (*The Long Journey*) recalled the Vietnam War from the viewpoint of a former Viet Cong soldier on a trek to retrieve the remains of a fallen comrade, and Vu Chao Nguyen's *Fated Vocation* filtered contemporary social and cultural problems through the colourful happenings in a touring opera company. A surprising black comedy from South Korea, *The Quiet Family,* directed by theatrical writer and director Kim Ji Un, focused on a family whose guest house becomes a morgue. From Cambodia, Rithy Panh's *Un Soir après la guerre* was a sober look at the state of the country through the eyes of three soldiers returning to civilian life after two decades of war.

Africa. A Franco-Belgian-Norwegian-Algerian co-production, Rachid Bouchareb's *Living in Paradise* was a tough and moving portrayal of the hardships of Algerian expa-

Actor Roberto Benigni kisses actress Nicoletta Braschi in a scene from the Italian movie *La vita è bella* (*Life Is Beautiful*). Benigni also directed the film, which became an international success in 1998.

triates in France in the early 1950s. In *Tunisiennes* Tunisian director Nouri Bouzid used the situations and relationships of three young women friends to expose the restraints still imposed on women's lives in modern North African societies.

From Senegal, Mohammed Soudani's *Waalo Fendo: Where the Earth Freezes* looked sympathetically at the urge of young villagers to emigrate and the tough fates that await them in cold northern cities such as Milan and Paris. A South African director, Katinka Heyns, attracted notice with *Paljas* (1997), about the magical effect produced upon an intolerant small town by the presence of a stranded traveling circus.

(DAVID ROBINSON)

Nontheatrical Films. Austrian filmmaker Kurt Mundl (Power of the Earth Productions) in 1998 created an amazing film about butterflies and moths, *The Messengers of the Gods—Butterflies.* The 49-minute gem was made from 18,000 minutes of film patiently photographed using special lenses. New findings about behaviour were brought to life. It won many awards, including Best of Festival at Chicago's U.S. International Film and Video Festival.

From Earth to the Moon reenacted the U.S.'s Apollo space program. Executive producer Tom Hanks and a team of talented associates relived key missions in 10 hours plus a special finale, a comparison with Georges Méliès's 1902 film *Le Voyage dans la lune* (*A Trip to the Moon*). Three Emmys and the Columbus Festival Presidents Award honoured the film.

In the zany *Writer's Block,* two screenwriters write a short film in which the characters come alive and go after the writers. This student film, made by Ari Taub at New York University, won a CINE Eagle award and top prizes in Hamburg, Ger.; Barcelona, Spain; and Prague. (THOMAS W. HOPE)

Population Trends

DEMOGRAPHY

At midyear 1998, world population stood at 5,926,000,000, according to estimates prepared by the Population Reference Bureau. This total represented an increase of 86 million over the previous year, firmly establishing that world population would reach the six billion mark during 1999. Given that the fifth billion was achieved as recently as 1987, global population was on track to add this next billion during the shortest time in history. The annual rate of increase declined to about 1.41% from about 1.47% in 1997, once again the result of birthrate declines in some less-developed countries (LDCs). The 1998 rate of increase, if maintained, would double world population in 49 years. Approximately 137 million babies were born worldwide in 1998, 2 million fewer than in 1997. Just over 90% of the births in 1998 occurred in LDCs. About 53 million people died in 1998; 78% of those deaths were in LDCs. The smaller percentage of the LDC share of deaths resulted from their much younger average age.

According to available survey data, 56% of married couples were using some form of contraception in 1998. The percentage using a "modern" form, which included such clinically supplied methods as the oral contraceptive and surgical methods such as sterilization, was 51%, slightly higher than in 1997. The number of couples using family planning in LDCs remained at 54% for all

methods and 49% for modern methods. The use of modern contraception in LDCs ranged from 58% in Latin America to as low as 11% in sub-Saharan Africa.

Worldwide, 32% of the population was below the age of 15 in 1998, but that figure was 37% in LDCs outside China. The more-developed countries (MDCs) continued to age in 1998; the population below age 15 fell one more point to 19%. This situation once again resulted from extremely low birthrates in Europe and in Japan, rates that showed little sign of rising despite growing concern in those countries over the societal effects of prolonged aging. The continuing youthfulness of the LDCs ensured that their populations would continue growing for many decades. Africa remained the youngest continent in 1998, with 44% of its population below age 15. Three MDCs—Finland, Italy, and Sweden—had the largest percentage of their population aged 65 and over, 17%.

The percentage of the world's population living in urban areas rose slightly in 1998, to 44% from 43% one year earlier. In the LDCs 36% of the population was classified as urban, the same as during the previous year, whereas 73% of the MDC population lived in urban centres. Urban population was

defined differently from country to country but generally included those living in towns of 2,500 or more inhabitants or in provincial and national capitals.

Life expectancy at birth was 64 years for males and 68 for females in 1998, the same as in the previous year. In the MDCs the same figures were 71 and 79 and in the LDCs, 62 and 65. The 1998 world infant mortality rate stood at 58 infant deaths per 1,000 live births, a slight decrease from 59 in 1997. The lowest infant mortality rates were in western and northern Europe, at 5 and 6 infant deaths per 1,000 live births, respectively. Finland reported the lowest rate of 3.5. Although there were small decreases in some LDCs, the overall rate remained at the high level of 64.

Less-Developed Countries. In 1998 the population of LDCs grew at 1.73% per year, 1.99% for LDCs outside China. These rates were slightly lower than in 1997, in part owing to a decline in the growth rate in India.

World's 25 Most Populous Urban Areas[1]				
Rank	City and country	City proper Population	Year	Metropolitan area Population	Year
1	Tokyo, Japan	7,966,195	1995 cen.	27,242,000	1996 est.
2	Mexico City, Mex.	9,815,795	1990 cen.	16,908,000	1996 est.
3	São Paulo, Braz.	9,393,753	1995 est.	16,792,000	1996 est.
4	New York City, U.S.	7,380,906	1996 est.	16,390,000	1996 est.
5	Bombay (Mumbai), India	9,925,891	1991 cen.	15,725,000	1996 est.
6	Shanghai, China	8,930,000	1993 est.	13,659,000	1996 est.
7	Los Angeles, U.S.	3,553,638	1996 est.	12,576,000	1996 est.
8	Calcutta, India	4,399,819	1991 cen.	12,118,000	1996 est.
9	Buenos Aires, Arg.	2,988,006	1995 est.	11,931,000	1996 est.
10	Seoul, S.Kor.	10,776,201	1991 est.	11,768,000	1996 est.
11	Jakarta, Indon.	9,160,500	1995 est.	11,500,000	1995 est.
12	Beijing, China	6,690,000	1993 est.	11,414,000	1996 est.
13	Lagos, Nigeria	1,518,000	1996 est.	10,878,000	1996 est.
14	Tianjin, China	5,000,000	1993 est.	10,687,000	1995 est.
15	Osaka, Japan	2,602,352	1995 cen.	10,618,000	1996 est.
16	Delhi, India	7,206,704	1991 cen.	10,298,000	1996 est.
17	Rio de Janeiro, Braz.	5,473,033	1995 est.	10,264,000	1996 est.
18	Karachi, Pak.	5,208,132	1981 cen.	10,119,000	1996 est.
19	Cairo, Egypt	6,849,000	1994 est.	9,900,000	1996 est.
20	Paris, France	2,156,766	1991 cen.	9,469,000	1995 est.
21	Manila, Phil.	1,654,761	1995 est.	9,280,000	1995 est.
22	Moscow, Russia	8,436,447	1996 est.	9,233,000	1995 est.
23	Dhaka, Bangladesh	3,839,000	1991 cen.	8,500,000	1996 est.
24	Istanbul, Tur.	7,774,169	1995 est.	7,817,000	1995 est.
25	Lima, Peru	5,706,127	1993 est.	7,452,000	1995 est.

[1]Ranked by population of metropolitan area.

Causes of Death in the United States (July–June)		
Rank in 1997	Rate per 100,000 population 1996	1997
1. Diseases of the heart	278.7	276.0
2. Malignant neoplasms	204.5	202.9
3. Cerebrovascular diseases	60.3	60.7
4. Chronic obstructive pulmonary diseases	39.2	41.4
5. Accidents and adverse effects	36.2	35.1
6. Pneumonia and influenza	31.2	33.4
7. Diabetes mellitus	22.9	23.5
8. Suicide	11.7	11.3
9. Nephritis, nephrotic syndrome, and nephrosis	9.0	9.6
10. Chronic liver disease and cirrhosis	9.6	9.3
11. Septicemia	8.0	8.5
12. HIV infection	15.1	8.5
13. Homicide and legal intervention	8.4	7.5
14. Atherosclerosis	6.3	6.2
15. Certain conditions of the perinatal period	5.0	4.7

Newborns crowd a nursery in Maternity Hospital in San Salvador, El Salvador's capital. Some 60 infants are born at the hospital daily. In 1998 Latin America's population totaled 500 million, with an annual growth rate of 1.8%.

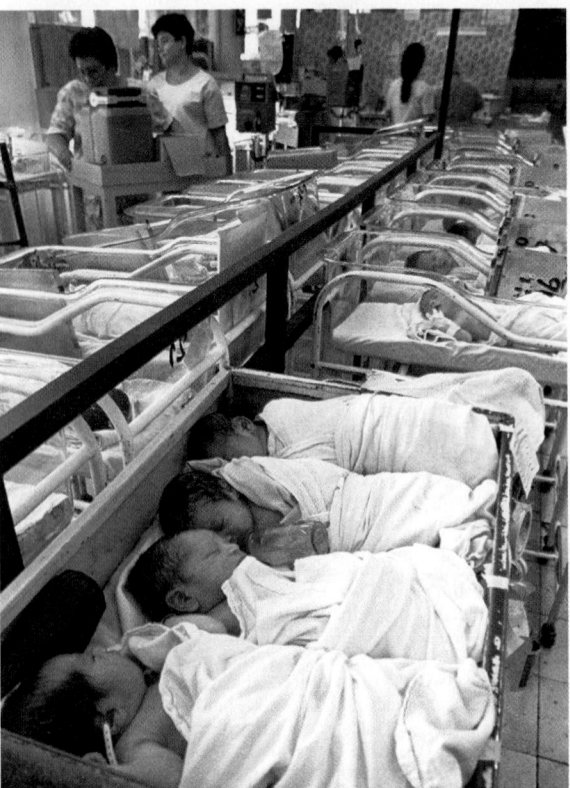

The total population of the LDCs was 4,666,000,000—82,000,000 more than in 1997. Their population constituted 80% of the world total. Of the 86,000,000 people added annually to the world population, 98% were in LDCs. In the LDCs women averaged 3.3 children each, down from 3.4 in 1997. In LDCs excluding China, however, women averaged 3.9 children each. This remained far from the "two-child family" essential to slowing population growth to zero and stabilizing world population size.

Fertility declines were noted in several LDCs, but others showed a tendency for fertility decreases to slow or to cease at moderately high levels. A major development was seen in Iran, where fertility fell to 3.5 children per woman, a result of a sharp turnaround in the national population policy, which was encouraging smaller families. Countries where fertility declines were reported to have slowed included Colombia, Jamaica, and Mali.

Africa's population in 1998 totaled 763 million, 20 million more than in 1997. The continent's annual growth rate was 2.5%, by far the world's highest and sufficient to double the population in only 27 years. In 1998 life expectancy at birth in Africa was the world's lowest at 50 years for males and 53 for females. Infant mortality was the world's highest at 91 infant deaths per 1,000 live births. Life expectancy in many African countries was severely affected by AIDS. In some areas of Africa in 1998, life expectancy was less than 40 years.

In 1998 Latin America's population totaled 500 million, with an annual growth rate of 1.8%, essentially the same as in 1997. Women averaged 3 children in 1998, unchanged from 1997; this ranged from 5.1 in Guatemala to 1.4 in Cuba. Life expectancy remained at 66 years for males and 72 for females. The infant mortality rate was 36 in 1998, down from 39 in 1997.

Asia's population totaled 3,604,000,000 in 1998, a gain of 54,000,000 over 1997. The region's growth rate declined from 1.6% in 1997 to 1.5% in 1998, largely owing to a small drop in the growth rate in India. Life expectancy in Asia in 1998 stood at about 64 for males and 67 for females. Women in Asia averaged 2.8 children in 1998, but the average was 3.3 in the countries outside China. In China women averaged only 1.8 children, a result of the national population program. In India women averaged 3.4 children, down slightly from 1997.

More-Developed Countries. The population of the MDCs was 1,178,000,000 in 1998. The growth rate during the year was an extremely low 0.1%. Much of that growth was in the U.S. In Europe in 1998 there were more deaths than births, as was also the case in 1997. The population of no fewer than 13 European countries experienced this

natural decrease in 1998, among them Germany, Italy, and Russia. The Czech Republic, Italy, Latvia, and Russia shared the world's lowest fertility in 1998, averaging only 1.2 children each.

Life expectancy at birth in Europe (including the European republics of the former Soviet Union) was 69 for males and 77 for females. Life expectancy in Russia continued to recover from its very low levels of the period immediately after the breakup of the Soviet Union, reaching 61 for males and 73 for females. This remained remarkably low by MDC standards. Infant mortality in the region continued at historically low levels. Western Europe in 1998 achieved the world's lowest, a rate of 5.

The resident population of the U.S. was 270,029,000 on July 1, 1998, up from 267,636,000 a year earlier. The National Center for Health Statistics (NCHS) reported that, during the 12 months ended in January 1998, natural increase—births minus deaths—amounted to 1,589,000, the net result of 3,891,000 births and 2,302,000 deaths. During that period the birthrate was 14.5 per 1,000 population, compared with 14.6 in the 12 months ended in January 1997. The fertility rate stood at about 2 as 1998 began. Data collected by the NCHS in 1998 revealed that the small decline in overall fertility since 1990, from 2.1 to 2 children, was largely accounted for by a drop in fertility among African-American women, from 2.5 in 1990 to 2.1 in 1996. The U.S. infant mortality rate continued to fall, reaching its lowest level ever at 7 for the 12-month period ended in January 1998. About 32.4% of births in 1996 were reported as occurring outside of marriage, 0.2% higher than in 1995.

The age-adjusted death rate for the 12-month period ended in June 1997 declined to 487.9 deaths per 100,000 population from 498.7 one year earlier. In 1998 the NCHS reported that in 1996 life expectancy at birth rose to a new high, 76.1 years. Female life expectancy was 79, a slight increase over the previous year, whereas male life expectancy rose a full half year, to 72.5. Life

expectancy for white females approached 80 years, at 79.6, whereas that of white males was 73.8. African-American men had the lowest life expectancy of all groups, 66.1 years, but gained almost one full year over the previous period. African-American women reached 74.2. During the 12 months ended in June 1997, there was also a major decline in the number of deaths due to AIDS reported to the NCHS, dropping that cause of death from 8th to 11th place.

(CARL V. HAUB)

REFUGEES AND INTERNATIONAL MIGRATION

In recent years complex ethnically based conflicts, mostly internal to one country and involving deeply divided communities, had resulted in increased numbers of displaced people. The total number of people of concern to the Office of the United Nations High Commissioner for Refugees (UNHCR) stood at 22.3 million as of Jan. 1, 1998. This figure, which represented one out of every 264 living persons in the world, included 12 million refugees, 3.5 million returning refugees in the early stages of their reintegration, more than 900,000 asylum seekers, and 5.9 million internally displaced persons (persons in a refugee-like situation but who had not crossed an international border) and others of concern, mainly victims of conflict. The resolution of long-standing conflicts in recent years permitted many millions of refugees to return home. In 1997 some 900,000 returned to their countries of origin, which highlighted the fact that repatriation is the preferred solution for many of the world's refugees. Often, however, they returned to countries either emerging from conflict or still embroiled in it.

Continued instability in the Great Lakes region of Africa caused protracted population movements both within the region and to surrounding countries. Refugees fleeing the conflict in the Democratic Republic of the Congo (formerly Zaire) arrived in Angola, Burundi, Republic of the Congo,

SAYYID AZIM—AP/WIDE WORLD

Burundian refugee children wave en route to the airport in Mwanza, Tanzania. A total of 228 Burundians and Rwandans left western Tanzania for the U.S. after their applications for refugee status were accepted. The estimated 260,000 Burundians in Tanzania constituted the largest single refugee group.

and Tanzania. Some 260,000 Burundians in Tanzania constituted the region's largest single refugee group.

The prospects for the repatriation and reintegration of refugees in West Africa became more promising as democratic processes and the rule of law began to be consolidated in the region in 1998. Hostilities in Sierra Leone early in the year, however, caused some 200,000 refugees to cross into Guinea and another 55,000 into Liberia. They joined those who had fled in previous years, bringing the total number of Sierra Leoneans living as refugees in neighbouring countries to some 450,000. In Guinea-Bissau unrest prompted tens of thousands of people to flee to the countryside, and late in the year most remained internally displaced. Since the presidential election and the end of the hostilities in 1997 in Liberia, a country that was devastated by one of the most brutal civil wars in Africa's history, some 50,000 refugees had returned to their homes by boat, truck, bus, and on foot, mainly from the two largest host countries, Côte d'Ivoire and Guinea. The repatriation of some 135,000 refugees to Mali and Niger marked the end of a displacement situation that had persisted since 1994.

The refugee situation in the East Africa and Horn of Africa regions continued to be complex, with several long-standing problems still unresolved. Despite the promising peace agreement of April 1997, The Sudan's civil war continued unabated. Nevertheless, the repatriation of some 70,000 Ethiopian refugees from The Sudan was concluded in June 1998. In 1998 some 30,000 persons returned to northwestern Somalia, primarily from Ethiopia; at the year's end, however, peace initiatives sponsored by various governments had not yet achieved their objectives, and the majority of those displaced remained so. In southern Africa the steady deterioration of the security situation in Angola generated new outflows of refugees, the majority of whom, an estimated 25,000, were going to Congo (Kinshasa).

The situation in Afghanistan did not improve during 1998. The absence of a political settlement, continued fighting between factions, related population displacements, and violations of basic human rights, especially those of women and girls, prolonged the human tragedy that the Afghan population had endured since 1980. Beginning in May 1997 the fighting in the northern part of Afghanistan caused serious disruptions in that region. Despite the continuing conflict, however, between January 1 and Nov. 30, 1997, 80,521 Afghans repatriated from Pakistan. During the same period 2,145 Afghan refugees returned from Iran, mainly to northwestern Afghanistan.

Four years after some 370,000 Cambodian refugees repatriated from neighbouring countries, political violence and the ensuing military conflict between opposing alliances in Cambodia resulted in an outflow of some 20,000 refugees to Thailand in August 1997. Further conflict erupted toward the end of September 1997 in western Cambodia and resulted in an additional estimated 35,000 Cambodians seeking refuge across the Thai border. In May 1998, following more military activity in the country, an additional 15,000 Cambodians fled into Thailand.

As a result of the 15 years of hostilities between the government of Sri Lanka and the Liberation Tigers of Tamil Eelam (LTTE), and especially owing to an escalation of the conflict since the second half of 1995, more than 800,000 persons in Sri Lanka were internally displaced and dependent on humanitarian assistance in 1998. Refugee flight to India, however, remained limited, with only 1,802 persons arriving in that country during the first five months of 1998. In spite of the ongoing conflict, increasing numbers of the internally displaced were returning to their home areas in the Jaffna Peninsula at the northern tip of Sri Lanka.

Between late 1991 and the middle of 1992, more than 250,000 people fled from Myanmar (Burma) to neighbouring Bangladesh. Since then some 229,000 persons had returned under a UNHCR-supported repatriation program, including some 10,000 refugees who voluntarily repatriated

Cambodian refugees ride atop a truck as they make their way to Thailand in order to escape fighting between opposing alliances in their country. An estimated 15,000 Cambodians fled into Thailand in May.

Ethnic Albanian refugees make camp in the village of Istinic in far western Kosovo, Yugos. The crisis in Kosovo dramatically worsened during 1998. By September the conflict, which had affected the civilian population with great severity, had led to the displacement of more than 270,000 persons.
MARCO DI LAURO—AP/WIDE WORLD

during 1997. At the same time, military activities in the eastern part of Myanmar displaced some 100,000 ethnic Karen and Karenni refugees. They were accommodated in 13 camps scattered along the Thai border with Myanmar, their return dependent on a resolution to the conflict across the border.

As of January 1998, 93,000 Bhutanese refugees were accommodated and assisted by UNHCR in seven camps in eastern Nepal. During 1997 and the first half of 1998, discussions between the governments of Bhutan and Nepal on the problem of the refugees continued but did not result in a resolution to the situation.

By early 1998 the Western Hemisphere had served as host to an estimated 1.4 million refugees and other persons of concern to UNHCR. In 1997 some 3,750

Guatemalan refugees, the only large single remaining group of refugees in Latin America, repatriated to their homeland, for the most part from Mexico, which brought the total number of returnees who had repatriated to Guatemala under UNHCR auspices since 1984 to approximately 38,000. During the year concern focused on the rise in the level of forced displacement related to the widening of the Colombian conflict and the implications of those developments for neighbouring countries. Border regions adjacent to Panama, Ecuador, and Venezuela were among those most affected by violence and displacement. More than 300,000 persons were estimated to have been internally displaced in those areas since 1996.

The U.S. continued to be the destination of the largest number of refugees resettled through UNHCR, with more than 70,000 re-

settled there in 1997. The number of asylum applications in North America fell in 1997 compared with the previous year, but the trend was reversed in Western Europe, where there was an overall increase of 10%. Government figures revealed that applications declined by 63,000 to 122,900 in the U.S. and by 3,500 to 22,600 in Canada. Whereas four European countries reported drops in applications, 15 European countries reported increased numbers of applicants, ranging from a 55% rise in The Netherlands to 171% in Italy and 225% in Ireland.

More than 1.8 million people remained displaced in and outside former Yugoslavia. UNHCR estimated that some 120,000 refugees repatriated to Bosnia and Herzegovina during 1997, mainly to areas where their ethnic group was in the majority. Elsewhere in the region of former Yugoslavia, the crisis in Kosovo dramatically worsened during 1998. By September the conflict, which had affected the civilian population with great severity, had led to the displacement of more than 270,000 persons. Of those, UNHCR estimated that some 200,000 were internally displaced inside Kosovo, 56,000 had moved into other areas of Serbia and to Montenegro, and 13,000 had taken refuge in Albania and the former Yugoslav republic of Macedonia. Of those displaced inside Kosovo, some 50,000 were thought to be living in the open in precarious conditions, which gave rise to concerns that another humanitarian catastrophe might be developing.

On Jan. 1, 1998, an estimated 4 million forced migrants were present in Russia, of whom some 1.2 million were registered with the nation's Federal Migration Services. Of that figure a total of 153,000 persons were registered as internally displaced persons from the Chechen Republic and were located in all regions of Russia. In Georgia the fighting that broke out in the Gali region of Abkhazia in May 1998 forced up to 40,000 of an original population of more than 50,000 returnees to become displaced again.

(UNHCR)

Refugees from the Georgian region of Abkhazia struggle to enter a bank in Tbilisi to collect their monthly government allowances. The U.S. offered $15 million to help the refugees return to Abkhazia. Fighting broke out in the region in May 1998 and forced up to 40,000 persons to become displaced.

SHAKH AIVAZOV—AP/WIDE WORLD

Religion

During 1998 religious groups worked to resolve contentious issues involving the Protestant Reformation and the Holocaust. Advocates of the rights of homosexuals, including same-sex marriages, challenged the policies of several churches. Christian women staged rallies to celebrate their faith, and a major denomination stirred debate with a statement on husband-wife relations. In addition, the U.S. Congress worked on bills to strengthen religious freedom both at home and around the world.

In June the Lutheran World Federation (LWF) and the Vatican approved a "Joint Declaration on the Doctrine of Justification," expressing common views on a subject that was a major source of conflict during the 16th-century Reformation. Although the declaration reflected a consensus that salvation is a free gift of God and cannot be earned by good works, and the LWF's Council voted to lift the historic condemnations of Roman Catholic teaching on the subject, several "clarifications" requested by the Vatican led the LWF to ask for more talks before the document was signed. (See *Lutheran Communion,* below.)

At its Eighth Assembly, meeting in December in Harare, Zimbabwe, the World Council of Churches set up a special commission to propose "necessary changes in structure, style, and ethos" of the ecumenical organization in response to Orthodox concerns. In a message to the assembly, Orthodox Ecumenical Patriarch Bartholomew said the WCC had taken "a critical turn" at its 1991 assembly, when a series of liberal theological and social positions were adopted. Earlier in 1998, the Bulgarian Orthodox Church left the 330-member organization.

The Vatican in March issued a long-awaited document on the Holocaust in which it expressed repentance for Roman Catholics who failed to oppose Nazi persecution of Jews. It made a distinction, however, between anti-Jewish sentiments that Christians have expressed historically and the secular anti-Semitic ideology of the Nazi regime and defended the activities and statements of Pope Pius XII, who had been criticized by many Jews for his silence on the Holocaust at the time. Although the document was welcomed by some Jewish leaders, several major Jewish groups said it was inadequate. In May Edward Idris Cardinal Cassidy, head of the Vatican agency that wrote the document, told a gathering of the American Jewish Committee in Washington that the Vatican was "amazed, almost distraught" because of the amount of negative Jewish reaction.

On a more positive note, Conservative Rabbi Mordecai Waxman of Great Neck, N.Y., a longtime leader in interfaith relations, became the first rabbi to be named a Knight Commander of St. Gregory by the Vatican. In April he became the fifth Jew to have received the papal honour, which was first awarded in 1831. In March Sir Sigmund Sternberg (*see* BIOGRAPHIES), chairman of the executive committee of the International Council of Christians and Jews, won the $1.2 million Templeton Prize for Progress in Religion. In other Christian-Jewish developments, Israel's two chief rabbis and the Latin patriarch of Jerusalem met for the first time in March in an attempt at reconciliation, and leaders of the National Council of Synagogues and the National Conference of Catholic Bishops in the United States issued in May a joint statement on the millennium, pledging to work for more mutual respect between the two faith traditions.

In August at the once-in-a-decade Lambeth Conference in Canterbury, Eng., the world's Anglican bishops declared homosexual activity to be "incompatible with Scripture," advised against the ordination of homosexuals, and called for sexual abstinence outside of marriage. The resolution, approved 526–70 with 45 abstentions, was adopted after a debate that highlighted differences on those issues between more liberal bishops in the West and their more traditional counterparts in many Third World countries.

In March in a church trial, the Rev. Jimmy Creech of Omaha, Neb., a United Methodist minister, was acquitted on charges of having violated church law by officiating at a ceremony that united two women. In August the United Methodist Judicial Council said the ban on homosexual unions in the denomination's statement of Social Principles had the status of church law in the nearly 10 million-member congregation. In October Bishop C. Joseph Sprague of the Northern Illinois conference filed a charge against Rev. Gregory Dell of Chicago for having performed such a ceremony for two men after the Judicial Council issued its ruling.

A proposal to replace Presbyterian Church (U.S.A.) ordination standards requiring fidelity in marriage and chastity in singleness with standards calling for fidelity and integrity in marriage or singleness was defeated in a vote by presbyteries. In June the denomination's General Assembly in Charlotte, N.C., decided to take no further action on the matter, which had divided the 2.6 million-member church for more than a

In 1998 Conservative Rabbi Mordecai Waxman, a longtime leader in interfaith relations, became the first rabbi to be named a Knight Commander of St. Gregory by the Vatican.

The Rev. Jimmy Creech (left), a United Methodist minister, appears with Pastor Richard Edens after a sermon. In March Creech was acquitted on charges of having violated church law by officiating at a ceremony that united two women.

decade. The Rev. James Callan was suspended by the Roman Catholic Diocese of Rochester, N.Y., in December for conducting same-sex weddings, serving Mass to non-Catholics, and allowing a woman to perform some priestly duties at the altar.

Trent Lott, a Republican senator from Mississippi and majority leader of the U.S. Senate, generated controversy in June when he declared homosexuality to be a sin. Subsequently, House Majority Leader Dick Armey, a Republican from Texas, said he agreed with Lott and that "the Bible is very clear on this." A few weeks later 15 conservative social and religious groups placed full-page ads in several major newspapers saying that men and women had converted from homosexuality to heterosexuality as a result of their Christian faith. The ad campaign was countered by a news conference in which former members of "ex-gay" organizations said that, on the basis of their experiences, such lasting change is rare if not impossible.

In the wake of its historic rally that drew hundreds of thousands of men to Washington, D.C., in 1997, Promise Keepers initially laid off hundreds of staff members from its Colorado Springs, Colo., headquarters and then recalled many of them after churches and individuals donated more than $4 million to maintain the organization. Meanwhile, such Christian women's movements as Women of Faith, Aspiring Women, and Time Out held their own stadium rallies and conferences in which speakers discussed such issues as overcoming a poor self-image, coping with marital problems, and dealing with financial matters. More than 600,000 women attended such events in 1998.

The nearly 16 million-member Southern Baptist Convention drew widespread attention in June when it added a section on fam-

ily to its doctrinal statement, saying that wives should "submit graciously" to their husbands' "servant leadership." The Lambeth Conference gave moral support to four U.S. Episcopal bishops who had refused to permit women priests in their dioceses, saying there should be no compulsion on any bishop in such matters. In August the Northern Province of the Moravian Church in America elected the Rev. Kay Ward of Bethlehem, Pa., its first female bishop.

A constitutional amendment to allow organized prayer in public schools fell short of the two-thirds vote necessary for passage in the U.S. House of Representatives in June. Congress passed a bill creating a State Department "ambassador-at-large for religious liberty" and giving the president several options, ranging from private communications to economic sanctions, for dealing with countries that permit religious persecution. Reversing two lower courts, the Wisconsin Supreme Court ruled 4–2 in June to uphold a plan that would allow low-income students in Milwaukee to use taxpayer-supported vouchers in order to attend religious schools. The ruling, which the U.S. Supreme Court declined to review, said the program did not "have the primary effect of advancing religion" but placed public and private school choice on an equal footing.

Widely accepted statistics on church attendance in the U.S. were challenged by an article in February in the *American Sociological Review.* Though the Gallup Organization and Barna Research Group had reported for years that about 4 in 10 Americans went to church each week, sociologists C. Kirk Hadaway, Penny Long Marler, and Mark Chaves said that if actual heads were counted each Sunday, closer to 25% of Americans would be found in church. A draft report from the Center for Applied Research in the Apostolate at Georgetown University, Washington, D.C., said that polls showing that between 40% and 50% of American Catholics attended mass weekly may have been overestimates. The report revealed that research based on actually counting churchgoers put the figure at between 26% and 33%.

(DARRELL J. TURNER)

PROTESTANT CHURCHES

Anglican Communion. The Lambeth Conference—a gathering of Anglican bishops from throughout the world held every 10 years—met at Canterbury, Eng., in July–August 1998. Its most publicized action was a resolution passed by a 526–70 vote rejecting homosexual practice as "incompatible with scripture." The lengthy resolution stated that the bishops "cannot advise the legitimising or blessing of same sex unions nor ordaining those involved in same gender unions" but committed bishops to listening "to the experience of homosexual people." Most of the dissenting votes on the resolution came from American bishops. The Episcopal Church's presiding bishop, Frank Griswold, abstained. In a later statement Griswold said that he took exception to some parts of the resolution and believed that "we must explore more fully the whole question of what is compatible and incompatible with scripture." The resolution was widely seen as a rebuke to American Episcopal Church bishops by representatives from Africa and Asia. Many American bishops had ordained practicing homosexuals, and the church's convention had only narrowly defeated a 1997 resolution that would have authorized a liturgy to bless same-sex unions.

Another Lambeth resolution was also seen as a reaction against the American church. Its 1997 General Convention had mandated the ordination of women in four dioceses that had not yet taken steps to do so. The Lambeth resolution urged mutual respect between bishops who did and those who did not ordain women, stating, "There is and should be no compulsion on any bishop in matters concerning ordination [of women]."

In January an African church leader called for a single church to unite all of Africa's Anglicans. Njongonkulu Ndungane, Anglican archbishop of Cape Town and successor to Desmond Tutu, made the proposal during a sermon in Uganda. Such an initia-

Charles, prince of Wales (second from left), watches as the Archbishop of Canterbury, George Carey (second from right), enters during the opening service of the Lambeth Conference in Canterbury Cathedral. More than 700 Anglican bishops from throughout the world attended the conference, which was held in July–August 1998.

tive would unite 11 Anglican provinces in Africa, comprising a majority of the world's 64 million Anglicans. The growth of the Anglican Church of Nigeria was cited in a July statement released by its bishops. They noted that the Church of Nigeria had doubled in membership to 17.5 million, seven times larger than the American church.

A Vatican Doctrinal Commentary released in July reaffirmed Pope Leo XIII's 1896 denunciation of Anglican ordinations as invalid. The Vatican's statement triggered a flurry of reactions throughout the Anglican Communion and was seen as a setback to ecumenical relations with Roman Catholicism. William Franklin, dean of Berkeley Divinity School at Yale University and a leader in Anglican–Roman Catholic dialogues, said that the commentary "seemed to end a fruitful era of ecumenical dialogue."

The Right Rev. John Maury Allin, 23rd presiding bishop of the Episcopal Church, died March 6 in Jackson, Miss. The former bishop of Mississippi led the church from 1974 through 1986. Stressing a theme of reconciliation, he successfully steered the church through turbulent years after it accepted the ordination of women in 1976 and a revised prayer book in 1979. (*See* OBITUARIES.)   (DAVID E. SUMNER)

Baptist Churches. The Southern Baptist Convention received wide media coverage in 1998 following its annual meeting. On June 9 messengers (delegates) met in Salt Lake City, Utah, and adopted a statement on the family that included their belief that a wife should "submit graciously" to her husband. According to reports, the majority of dele-

At the annual meeting of the Southern Baptist Convention, held in Salt Lake City, Utah, in June 1998, Paige Patterson was elected president of the 15.8 million-member denomination. Later in the year Patterson called for the resignation of Pres. Bill Clinton.

gates said it was time to declare to Baptists and society at large what they believed to be God's plan for the family.

In reaction to the media coverage, much of it negative, noted church historian Martin Marty (*see* BIOGRAPHIES) of the University of Chicago commented, "The denomination may pick up new members who are hungry for authority." Much of the support for the "submission" statement was based on a literal interpretation of Ephesians. Also at the meeting the denomination's traditional condemnation of homosexuality was reiterated.

Paige Patterson, one of the powers responsible for the conservative takeover of the 15.8 million-member denomination, was elected president. Patterson, president of Southeastern Baptist Theological Seminary in Wake Forest, N.C., ran unopposed. Early in September he joined the chorus calling for the resignation of Pres. Bill Clinton, a fellow Southern Baptist.

In March former U.S. president Jimmy Carter moderated a meeting of the feuding conservatives and moderates. He encouraged a declaration expressing mutual respect while acknowledging that, though "there are unresolved issues among us, the signatories to this declaration wish to overcome differences that may impede our mission."

Among African-American Baptists, the National Baptist Convention USA, Inc., was riven by charges against its president, Henry J. Lyons. Lyons had denied accusations in 1997 that he had used church funds to purchase a house, a car, and other personal items. In response the Rev. Calvin Butts III, minister of the influential Abyssinian Baptist Church in Harlem in New York City, repeated his criticism of the denomination's leadership: "The leadership is woefully inadequate, corrupt and untrustworthy."

In developments elsewhere, the Belgian government would no longer classify Baptists as a cult. On Dec. 6, 1997, the Baptists received unanimous acceptance from the nation's Protestant Synod. The acceptance was the result of other European Baptist groups' teaming up with the Baptist World Alliance to urge official recognition. Encouragement would now be offered to Austrian Baptists, who were also classified as a cult.

Milestones among Baptists in the U.S. included the appointment of R. Scott Rodin as the 11th president of Eastern Baptist Theological Seminary, an American Baptist school in Philadelphia. Rodin, a Presbyterian, was the first non-Baptist president in the seminary's 73-year history.

The Rev. Thomas Kilgore, Jr., one of the few men to lead two major national Baptist organizations (the Progressive National Baptists Convention and the American Baptists Churches, USA), died in February in Los Angeles. (*See* OBITUARIES.) Kilgore, pastor emeritus of the Second Baptist Church in Los Angeles, was a leader in the struggles for racial justice and served with the Rev. Martin Luther King, Jr.

(NORMAN R. DE PUY)

Christian Church (Disciples of Christ). Leadership changes, additional churchwide planning, and an effort to eliminate racism in church structures highlighted 1998 for the Christian Church (Disciples of Christ). The church's Northwest Region called the Rev. Jack Sullivan, Jr., as its new executive in March. Sullivan became the second African-American to head a regional body in the more than 900,000-member denomination. In 1998 the Northwest Region comprised 8,300 members in 77 congregations across Washington and northern Idaho and in Anchorage, Alaska.

In other action the General Board identified six "vital issues" to be addressed as the church fulfilled its four-year Mission Imperatives. They included evangelism and witness; spiritual vitality and faith development; leadership development; congregational hospitality, diversity, and inclusiveness; justice, reconciliation, service, and public advocacy; and strong worship life.

The General Board Administrative Committee in July endorsed a proposal to offer antiracism training to church members. This initiative stemmed from an ongoing churchwide examination of racism in North America, including within the church itself.

In late 1998 the Disciples of Christ celebrated the ministry of the Rev. Paul A. Crow, Jr. The church leader retired December 31 after nearly 40 years of global ecumenical ministry. In November Crow delivered the Peter Ainslie Lecture on Christian Unity, an annual celebration at which a world ecumenist is invited to share his or her vision of Christian unity.

(CLIFFORD L. WILLIS)

Churches of Christ. From 1979 to 1997 the Churches of Christ experienced only modest growth, but in 1998 their numbers increased markedly. New churches were established throughout the United States. Rhode Island led with a 72% growth rate, followed by Minnesota with 67% and Maryland with 60%. The largest numbers of churches continued to be in the southern states.

Also significant was the expansion of missions. In India membership was estimated at one million. Other nations showing growth were Ghana, Nigeria, Zambia, Zimbabwe, and Malawi. A largely indigenous movement also resulted in a large increase in Mozambique. The most noteworthy development in Asia was the reestablishment of contact between governments and church members in Laos, Vietnam, Cambodia, North Korea, and Lebanon.

During the first nine months of the year, Church of Christ Disaster Relief, headquartered in Nashville, Tenn., distributed $2.5 million in relief supplies to 26 disaster-stricken areas. Other organizations active in disaster relief were White's Ferry Road Church of Christ in West Monroe, La.; Manna International in Redwood City, Calif.; and Bread for a Hungry World in Fort Worth, Texas.

Universities operated by members of the church registered record enrollments. Among academies Coventry Christian School in Pottstown, Pa., led with a 25% enrollment increase.

"In Search of the Lord's Way," a television and radio program featuring Mack Lyon as host, expanded its coverage by 10%, adding 143 cable channels, the

Inspirational Network, the Odyssey Channel, and the Family Network. Among publications *The Christian Chronicle* continued to lead in circulation, with a total of approximately 100,000 households in 125 countries.   (GLOVER SHIPP)

Church of Christ, Scientist. In 1998 the 103rd annual meeting of the Mother Church focused on signs of significant change in theology. Featured were videotaped interviews with other religious leaders, including Harvey Cox of the Harvard Divinity School; the Rev. Tina Saxon, pastor of Disciples' Baptist Church in Boston; and John Fellers of the Institute of Religion at the Texas Medical Center in Houston. Their participation emphasized the widespread interest in Christian healing within the religious and medical communities. "We're at a point of historic change—a new birth in theology and practice," remarked incoming church president Jon G. Harder.

During the year interest in spiritual healing led many readers to *Science and Health with Key to the Scriptures* by Mary Baker Eddy. For the fourth year in a row it enjoyed sales of more than 100,000 copies, with the number purchased in the 1997 fiscal year up by 15%. First published in 1875, it was in 1998 carried by some 2,500 bookstores as well as by Christian Science reading rooms throughout the world.

On the 150th anniversary of the first Woman's Rights Convention in Seneca Falls, N.Y., the church was invited by the Women's Rights National Historic Park to cosponsor an exhibit on Eddy. It highlighted her accomplishments as pioneer, healer, author, leader, founder, and publisher.

In August the church was host to an International Conference titled "Pioneers of the Spiritual Millennium." Approximately 1,500 college students and faculty gathered at the church's Boston headquarters to explore ways to discuss the role of spirituality in the academic community. A redesigned *Christian Science Sentinel,* published weekly, increased its number of orders by 45% in 1998. Each month up to 13,000 Internet users visited the church's Web site (www.tfccs.com), and 450,000 accessed the electronic version of *The Christian Science Monitor* (www.csmonitor.com), logging over two million pages.

(GARY A. JONES)

Church of Jesus Christ of Latter-day Saints. During 1998 church president Gordon B. Hinckley exhibited marvelous powers of physical and mental endurance as he, in his 88th year, traveled to meet church leaders and members, heads of state, and other government officials in Nigeria, Ghana, Kenya, Zimbabwe, and South Africa in Africa; Ecuador, Venezuela, Uruguay, Paraguay, Brazil, and Chile in South America; all nations in Central America; the United Kingdom, France, Germany, and Switzerland in Europe; Samoa, American Samoa, Tonga, Fiji, and Tahiti in the South Pacific; Japan, the Philippines, and South Korea in the Far East; and several dozen communities in the United States, Canada, Australia, and New Zealand. Among his most notable appearances was an address to 24,000 Mormons at a special "fireside" at New York City's Madison Square Garden in April.

The church's worldwide building program continued. In late 1998 there were 52 temples operating in 24 countries and 46 new

Gordon B. Hinckley, president of the Church of Jesus Christ of Latter-Day Saints, is interviewed by television talk-show host Larry King on CNN. During the year Hinckley traveled around the world to meet with heads of state, government officials, and members of the media, as well as church leaders and members.

temples in various stages of design or construction. New temples were being built in Bolivia, Canada, Japan, Mexico, the U.S., and Fiji. With 200,000 attending an open house, the temple at Preston, Eng., was dedicated in August.

President Hinckley was honoured in the U.S. at the National Conference of Community and Justice for his tolerance and compassion, and he addressed a regional leadership meeting of the National Association for the Advancement of Colored People in April. He was interviewed during the year by Dan Rather for CBS and Larry King for CNN.

Continuing its vast humanitarian program, in 1998 the church assisted members and others after flooding, hurricanes, earthquakes, and other disasters in many locations throughout the world. In May the church was formally recognized as a centralized religious organization in Russia.

(LEONARD J. ARRINGTON)

Jehovah's Witnesses. During 1998 Jehovah's Witnesses highlighted their belief that the Bible is the word of God by means of a course of study that included textbooks such as *The Bible, God's Word or Man's?* They also volunteered their time to share with their neighbours information from a variety of sources, including *A Book for All People,* a brochure designed to build faith in the Bible.

Each year Jehovah's Witnesses schedule three-day instructional sessions in the form of conventions. In 1998 almost 200 were held in the United States, highlighting the theme "God's Way of Life." In the U.S. some 1.5 million people attended the conventions, where they were encouraged to strengthen their faith in the Bible and its teachings. These teachings included not only

doctrines but also standards of conduct. A handbook designed to build faith in the existence of a Creator was released to the audience at each of the conventions and had an initial distribution of five million copies in English, plus millions in 38 additional languages. The book, *Is There a Creator Who Cares About You?,* discusses the support that scientific evidence gives to the creation account.

As part of their work of getting the Bible and its message into the hands of people worldwide, Jehovah's Witnesses arranged for nearly 300,000 copies of the Bible to be printed in Russian for distribution throughout Russia and in other countries where Russian is spoken. This translation, the Makarios Bible, was the work of two 19th-century translators, prominent members of the Russian Orthodox Church and language scholars. The translation had been generally unknown to the Russian public for more than a century.   (MILTON HENSCHEL)

Lutheran Communion. In a decision of historic proportions, the Lutheran World Federation (LWF) Council, meeting in Geneva in June 1998, unanimously approved the "Joint Declaration on the Doctrine of Justification" with the Roman Catholic Church. This approval came after a long study process in which 89 of the 124 LWF member churches expressed their opinion on the declaration. Of the churches responding, 91% voted "in favour of" the document, supporting its statement that divine forgiveness and salvation come only through God's grace and that good works flow from that. The declaration had raised considerable debate in some LWF churches, which questioned whether a sufficient consensus concerning the doctrine had been reached. The LWF Council vote indicated a

Lutheran understanding that there was agreement on justification to such a degree that condemnations made by both Lutherans and Roman Catholics regarding this doctrine during the Reformation period no longer applied to present-day churches. LWF General Secretary Ishmael Noko declared that the vote should be celebrated as a "historic moment for our two churches." Several days later the Vatican responded to the declaration by detailing a number of remaining differences while acknowledging a consensus in the basic truths. Many Lutherans questioned the degree of acceptance by the Roman Catholic Church. The LWF president, Bishop Christian Krause, called for careful study of the Vatican response.

The council also encouraged support by LWF churches for debt relief for the world's poor countries by 2000 and noted reports of human rights violations in Ethiopia. It requested that parties involved in the Middle East peace process resume negotiations and implement previously made commitments.

The Norwegian government appointed Gunnar Stålsett, a former LWF general secretary, as bishop of Oslo. Munib Younan was consecrated as the new Palestinian Lutheran bishop in Jerusalem.

The Evangelical Lutheran Church in America (ELCA), the second largest Lutheran body in the world, moved to implement full communion with three Reformed churches in the U.S. It continued its efforts to enter into full communion with the Episcopal Church in the U.S. after such a proposal was narrowly defeated in 1997. The ELCA also studied a proposal to enter into full communion with the Moravian Church in America in 1999.

The Evangelical Lutheran Church in Canada and the Anglican Church in Canada approved respectively in 1997 and 1998 statements of intention to take definitive action in 2001 on a proposal that they enter into full communion with each other. At its triennial convention in St. Louis, Mo., in July, the Lutheran Church—Missouri Synod elected Alvin Barry to his third term as president and pursued its plans for evangelization and closer ties with Lutheran churches in Eastern Europe.   (WILLIAM G. RUSCH)

Methodist Churches. The 1998 World Methodist Peace Award was awarded to Kofi Annan, secretary-general of the United Nations. The citation referred to Annan's "courage, creativity and consistency in the pursuit of human reconciliation and world peace."

The first-ever All-African Methodist Conference was held in Benoni, S.Af., in March and was attended by Methodist leaders from 16 African countries. A second conference was planned for Kenya in 2000. A nonjudicial body, the All-African Methodist Conference served as a forum for discussion, sharing, and learning, with the goal of promoting unity between churches and strengthening the African voice on relevant issues.

In 1998, for the first time, delegates from the Russia United Methodist Church were seated and participated with full rights in the Northern Europe Central Conference. The Russia Provisional Annual Conference was established and had its first meeting at Pushkin near St. Petersburg in May.

Representatives from about 200 Methodist schools and colleges around the world met in Bath, Eng., in July to celebrate the 250th anniversary of the opening of the old-

U.N. Secretary-General Kofi Annan gives a public address at Harvard University on September 17. In December Annan was named the winner of the 1998 World Methodist Peace Award. Frances Alguire, president of the World Methodist Council, said Annan was chosen for "his courage, creativity and consistency in the pursuit of human reconciliation and world peace."

est Methodist educational institution, the Kingswood School in England's Avon county. The event, organized by the International Association of Methodist-Related Schools, Colleges and Universities, preceded a conference on the theme "Methodism and Education: From Roots to Fulfillment."

World Methodism mourned the sudden death in August of the honorary president of the World Methodist Council, the Rev. Donald English. He had previously been elected twice as president of the British Methodist Conference and was chairperson of the World Methodist Council Executive from 1991 to 1996.

The 13th Lambeth Conference of the Anglican Communion gave its approval to the report of the Anglican/Methodist International Commission, "Sharing in the Apostolic Communion." The two communions agreed to establish a joint working party to develop mutual agreements acknowledging that each church belongs "to the one, holy, catholic apostolic Church," that in each "the word of God is authentically preached and the Sacraments are duly administered," and that "the two Churches share in the common confession and heritage of the apostolic faith."

The World Methodist Council announced that Brighton, Eng., would be the centre for the 18th World Methodist Conference, to be held in late July 2001. As many as 4,000 delegates were expected to attend.

(JOHN C.A. BARRETT)

Pentecostal Churches. In September 1998 more than 100,000 Pentecostals gathered in Seoul, South Korea, in Olympic Stadium to celebrate the 18th Pentecostal World Conference (PWC). Daily sessions met in Cho Yonggi's Yoido Full Gospel Church, the world's largest congregation, with more than 730,000 members. With the retirement of Chairman Ray Hughes, the Advisory Committee elected Thomas Trask of the American Assemblies of God to lead the PWC for the next three years. The number of Pentecostals and Charismatics in the world was reported to be 540 million, sec-

ond only to the membership of the Roman Catholic Church.

Korean Pentecostal churches continued to grow rapidly during the year. In May Cho dedicated a massive new office building in Seoul for his daily newspaper, the *Kook Min Daily News,* which had one million subscribers. Across town in Anyang, Cho's younger brother, Cho Yong Mok, served as pastor of the third largest church in the world, with 150,000 members.

The International Church of the Foursquare Gospel Annual Convention, meeting in Palm Springs, Calif., in April, elected Paul Risser to serve as the fifth president of the church. In August the Church of God (Cleveland, Tenn.) reelected Paul Walker of Atlanta, Ga., to serve a second term as general overseer. His assistant, Lamar Vest, was elected chairman of the National Association of Evangelicals. The Church of God reported five million members worldwide.

The General Conference of the Pentecostal Assemblies of Canada, which convened in Saskatoon, Sask., in August, voted for the first time to allow ordained women ministers to serve on the highest executive boards of the church. William Morrow was reelected to head the church for two more years.

In October the International Pentecostal Holiness Church celebrated its centennial year with special ceremonies in Oklahoma and North Carolina. Its sister church, the mostly African-American Fire-Baptized Holiness Church of God, celebrated its one hundred years of existence at its headquarters in Greenville, S.C., in June.

(VINSON SYNAN)

Reformed, Presbyterian, and Congregational Churches. At its 23rd General Council (Debrecen, Hung., 1997) the World Alliance of Reformed Churches (WARC) had approved the lifting of its suspension of the Dutch Reformed Church in South Africa, imposed in 1982 because of that church's support of apartheid, on condition that the General Synod of the church acknowledge that apartheid was wrong and

sinful "not simply in its effects and operations but also in its fundamental nature." In October 1998 the General Synod complied with the request. Unity negotiations between the Dutch Reformed churches in South Africa continued during the year.

The first meeting of the new WARC Executive Committee, elected at the 23rd General Council, took place in Geneva at the end of June. The main item on the agenda was the *processus confessionis*—a process of progressive recognition, education, and confession in all member churches regarding economic injustice and environmental destruction.

The *Handbook of Reformed Churches Worldwide* was one of the fruits of the Mission in Unity project, begun in the 1980s by the John Knox International Reform Centre in Geneva. This ambitious attempt to list and describe all the Reformed churches in the world and their relationships to one another was edited by Jean-Jacques Bauswein and Lukas Vischer and was scheduled for publication in January 1999.

In October a meeting to discuss future cooperation took place in The Netherlands between representatives of WARC and the Reformed Ecumenical Council (REC); this too was a result of the Mission in Unity project. REC had been established in 1946 on a stricter confessional basis than WARC, but subsequently the gap between the two organizations narrowed. In 1998 REC consisted of a council of 34 Reformed and Presbyterian churches from 23 countries; approximately half of these churches also belonged to WARC.

Four new churches were admitted to membership by WARC in 1998: the Africa Inland Church (The Sudan), the Congregational Church of India, the Christian Reformed Church of Honduras, and the United Evangelical Church of Ecuador. By the end of 1998, WARC linked more than 75 million Christians in 214 churches in 105 countries.

(PÁRAIC RÉAMONN)

The Religious Society of Friends. Work for peace was at the forefront of Friends' (Quakers') concerns in 1998. The Quaker UN offices in Geneva and New York City collaborated with others interested in limiting worldwide traffic in light weapons; worked with the International Campaign to Ban Landmines, which received the Nobel Peace Prize in 1997; and continued its action to prevent the enrollment of children in armed combat. In the Great Lakes region of Africa, Norwegian Quakers expanded their Change Agents development project beyond Uganda in order to involve peace work supported by African Quakers. In Rwanda Friends held peace and reconciliation seminars, and Australian Quakers offered a statement of apology for historic wrongs done to the Aboriginal people.

Mission work focused both on service and on evangelism. Education, health, rural development, and urban renewal received support in the Americas and in Africa, and evangelical Friends churches grew stronger in the Philippines, Taiwan, Nepal, Indonesia, and other Asian countries.

A Quaker Youth Pilgrimage in mid-1998 involved young people from Europe and North America in study and service in England and Sweden. Women and men from Kenya, Jamaica, and Cuba joined North American colleagues at the United Society of Friends Women and Quaker Men International Triennials in Iowa. The Committee of Latin American Friends launched a program of study publications and seminars for pastors. Growing interest in Quakerism in Eastern Europe contributed to gatherings in mid-1998 for inquirers in Brno, Czech Rep.; in Karpacz, Pol.; and in Zvenigorod, Russia. New executive secretaries took office in three Sections of Friends World Committee for Consultation—Joseph Andugu (Africa), Cilde Grover (Americas), and Tony Fitt (Europe and Middle East). Jack Patterson became the Quaker UN representative in New York City and Lori Heninger the associate representative.

(ELIZABETH DUKE)

Salvation Army. In March 1998 a group of 150 Protestants and Roman Catholics, including youth from the Salvation Army Ireland Divisional Youth Chorus, demonstrated their shared Christian ideals by traveling to Washington, D.C., where they were greeted by and sang for both U.S. Pres. Bill Clinton and Irish Prime Minister Bertie Ahern. In April the Salvation Army, as an international movement, was accepted as an associate member of the World Evangelical Fellowship.

The devastation in Central America caused by Hurricane Mitch in October and November prompted the deployment of relief teams to assist stricken families in Honduras, Nicaragua, Costa Rica, and

Braving snow and subzero temperatures, Moscow residents line up in November for free soup offered by the Salvation Army. Only a few nongovernment organizations in Russia had the means to offer relief to the country's rapidly growing homeless population. The Salvation Army provided soup, coffee, and clothing to homeless persons in a number of Russian cities throughout the year.

OLEG NIKISHIN—AP/WIDE WORLD

Guatemala. Salvation Army territories throughout the world contributed to this effort, providing financial support, food, blankets, and medicines.

In September the Army in the U.K. introduced its new uniform. Made available to all soldiers, it consisted of a navy blue blouson jacket and navy blue skirt or trousers. The uniform was designed to be more modern, economical, and practical for its wearers while remaining identifiable to the public. Also in September it was announced that a donation of $80 million, the largest-ever gift to the Army, had been made by Joan Kroc, widow of the founder of the McDonald's restaurants.   (SARAH MILLER)

Seventh-day Adventist Church. In 1998 the Seventh-day Adventist world membership increased to more than 10 million. The church continued to grow fastest in Central and South America, Africa, and Asia. Since 1994 Adventist membership had doubled to about 25,000 in Cuba, where the denomination constructed a new seminary and refurbished almost all of its churches. An Adventist gathering in Papua New Guinea drew a crowd of some 60,000 members; the governor-general of that nation, Sir Silas Atopare, was an Adventist.

Marking the largest single evangelistic thrust in its history, the church launched a five-week series of meetings during October and November. The nightly programs, which originated on the campus of Andrews University, Berrien Springs, Mich., were sent via satellite to viewers at about 4,000 sites on every continent and were translated into 40 languages. Earlier in the year an evangelistic campaign originating in Soweto, S.Af., had been transmitted to viewers throughout Africa.

Meeting in Foz do Iguaçu, Braz., delegates from around the world to the church Annual Council discussed the role of the central body (the General Conference) in the Adventist Church structure at the beginning of the new century. They also considered the strengths and limitations of congregationalism and the empowerment of parish leaders.

The four-year dialogue with the Lutheran World Federation concluded with conversations held at Cartigny, Switz. A joint report issued at the close of the dialogue recommended that Adventists and Lutherans recognize the basic Christian commitment of each other's faith communions. While pointing out areas of agreement and disagreement between the two bodies, the report urged Lutherans and Adventists to encourage and nurture consultative linkage for the good of the entire Christian community and the betterment of humanity. The scholarly papers used as the basis for the four-year conversation were to be edited and published jointly in a single volume.

(WILLIAM G. JOHNSSON)

Unitarian (Universalist) Churches. Important resolutions were passed at the 90th annual General Assembly of Unitarian and Free Christian Churches in Chester, Eng., in April 1998. One supported the "Jubilee 2000" initiative calling for cancellation of the debts of the world's poorest nations. Another sought to reform the proposed Multilateral Agreement on Investment so that it would establish binding responsibilities on multinational corporations rather than further extending their rights.

Examining the theme "Fulfilling the Promise," more than 4,000 registrants—the largest number ever achieved by the (North American) Unitarian Universalist Association (UUA)—met June 25–30, 1998, in Rochester, N.Y. Much progress was reported on the new denominationwide "Journey Toward Wholeness antiracism program," which also emphasized multiculturalism. The church sponsored special workshops under trained facilitators throughout the U.S.

Efforts to achieve an equitable gender balance in the North American denomination's ministry and headquarters' departments had by 1998 resulted in a shift from one extreme to another. In 1981, 12% of all ministers in churches were women; by 1998 the percentage had increased to approximately 50%. The personnel of UUA departments, once predominantly male, were now more than two-thirds female.

To provide a ministry and spiritual home for isolated religious liberals, the Church of the Larger Fellowship was founded in Boston in 1944. By 1998 two full-time ministers were providing a fluctuating but growing membership of about 2,700 adults and 800 children with religious education; sermon and worship materials; pastoral services by phone, E-mail, and correspondence; and a lending library.

Celebrations on March 29 honouring the centenary of the Unitarian Church in Auckland, N.Z., drew a large congregation from the area covered by the Australia and New Zealand Unitarian Association. The Rev. David Rankin left one of the largest parishes in the U.S., in Grand Rapids, Mich., to lead the Auckland church into its second century.

(JOHN NICHOLLS BOOTH)

United Church of Canada. The United Church of Canada, the nation's largest Protestant denomination, experienced a year of controversy in 1998. In October 1997 the Rev. William Phipps, the church moderator, generated much debate as a result of a newspaper interview in which he questioned certain, more orthodox views about Jesus such as his divinity. Many supported the moderator, but others did not. Conservative groups within the denomination called for his resignation. The controversy reflected the wide range of theological positions within the United Church and encouraged many church members to study and reflect anew about the role of Jesus Christ in the world today.

In 1997 the United Church was named as a defendant in connection with a case of sexual abuse. The incident took place in a now-closed Native American residential school at Port Alberni, B.C. In June 1998 the British Columbia Supreme Court found both the United Church and the federal government vicariously liable for sexual assaults committed by a former school employee. The church appealed the judgment.

Early in 1998 the church created a fund to help victims of the ice storm that beset areas of Ontario, Quebec, and the Maritime Provinces in January. It also went on record as opposing any military violence against the people of Iraq and called for a federal inquiry into gambling in Canada.

During the most recent fiscal year, the denomination's two million members and other adherents raised almost Can$320 million for all purposes. Congregations continued to focus most of their money and energy on local mission projects, and so contributions to the church's national mission fund increased only slightly. The church during the year established a committee to make plans for celebration of the denomination's 75th anniversary in the year 2000.   (DOUGLAS L. FLANDERS)

United Church of Christ. The commitment of the United Church of Christ (UCC) to becoming a fully inclusive "multiracial, multicultural church" permeated the life of the denomination in 1998. A number of events, including "Pentecost '98," a national gathering held in Chicago in May, helped energize that commitment. Subjects discussed at the meeting included recruitment and support of African-American, Hispanic/Latino, Asian-American/Pacific Islander, and Native American people and churches.

Ecumenical activities were high on the church's agenda. Efforts were undertaken to implement full communion, affirmed in 1997, with the Presbyterian Church (U.S.A.), the Reformed Church in America, and the Evangelical Lutheran Church in America. A rapidly accelerating number of partnerships with other denominations, both in the United States and around the world, were entered into by UCC congregations, conferences, and national bodies. The UCC remained an active participant in the Consultation on Church Union, the World Alliance of Reformed Churches, the National Council of Churches in the U.S., and the World Council of Churches.

A number of developments celebrating the church's historic commitment to issues of justice and freedom for all people centred on the so-called Amistad event in the 19th century, during which church members helped free African slaves transported to New England on the ship *La Amistad.* The committee organized to support the slaves eventually became the American Missionary Association, one of the national mission agencies of the UCC. In March the keel of a replica of the ship was laid at Mystic (Conn.) Seaport. The ship was to serve as a floating classroom on race relations.

Other activities throughout the year included the Scripture Project, which explored the nature and authority of scripture in the context of the church's theological diversity, and an invitation to churches to discuss whether the church should bless committed same-sex relationships. The church also completed the construction of a hotel on the site of the national offices in Cleveland, Ohio.   (PAUL H. SHERRY)

ROMAN CATHOLIC CHURCH

The weekly Angelus messages of Pope John Paul II, plus his addresses to visiting delegations, emphasized the concerns of the Roman Catholic Church during 1998. These included international peace and justice and issues involving human life. In October the pope celebrated the 20th anniversary of his reign as pontiff.

The Vatican's permanent observer to the UN, Suzanne Scorsone, addressed the UN Commission on the Status of Women. Speaking for the Vatican, she called for respect for the essential dignity of women and the full participation of women in public and professional life. The Vatican joined more than 120 nations in signing the convention to ban land mines. The pope called for a peaceful resolution to American-Iraqi ten-

sions and to the conflict between ethnic Albanians and Serbs in Kosovo. Indian bishops called for an end to caste prejudices in the church and also asked for land distribution among "Dalits" ("the oppressed"). The church unsuccessfully called upon several African governments to suspend violence against minorities.

The church promoted, with varying success, its agenda in defense of all human life. South African bishops continued to protest the 1997 law guaranteeing abortion on demand for up to 12 weeks. Efforts were made to oppose the widespread practice of forced teenage marriage in Kenya. German bishops were instructed by Rome to monitor more closely the 264 pregnancy counseling centres controlled by the church (15% of such centres in Germany). Women who visited such a centre and obtained a certificate testifying to having done so were eligible under German law for an abortion. Women's groups and the local church hierarchy pressed the government of Peru to halt programs of forced contraception and sterilization. Mexican bishops spoke out against the widespread practice of contraception, partly as a moral issue and partly because, according to current projections, the declining birthrate was causing the average age of the Mexican population to increase rapidly; those older than 60 were expected to constitute at least 50% of the total population in 15 years. In Britain Basil Cardinal Hume spoke out sharply against euthanasia.

Violence against Catholics continued in some parts of the world during the year. Islamic fundamentalism led to the closing of Catholic clubs in Khartoum, The Sudan, and to the rigorous implementation of antiblasphemy laws that targeted non-Muslims in Pakistan. In protest against the laws, Bishop John Joseph of Faisalabad committed suicide. Nationalist sentiment, sometimes augmented by militant Hinduism, provoked several incidents in India. A Catholic hospital was plundered by gangs of Hindu youths chanting anti-Christian slogans in Maharashtra state. Six missionaries and two lay workers were murdered in Rwanda. Three Chinese priests of the "underground" church were arrested. One was quickly released, and Bishop Thomas Zeng Jingmu of Yujiang was released early from his incarceration for political crimes. An American interfaith delegation explored religious repression in China but did not bring about any changes in government policy, which was that any punishment received by the Catholic Church was not for religious reasons but for polit-

ical offenses. Archbishop Juan José Gerardi Conedera of Guatemala City was murdered April 26. Prior to his murder, he had spoken out against abuses by Guatemala's former military government.

On February 21 the pope held his seventh consistory for naming new cardinals, elevating 22. Though there were no encyclicals during the year, the pope did issue two important pastoral letters. *Ad tuendam fidem* (May 28) demanded that all clergy and teachers subscribe to an oath of loyalty to basic Catholic doctrines. The Vatican insisted that the letter merely explained and enforced existing provisions of canon law. Critics, however, feared a crackdown on dissidents. *Dies Domini* (July 5) called for strict observance of the Sunday mass obligation while also insisting on the need for a weekly day of rest and renewal.

On March 16, after several years of preparatory work, the Vatican issued "We Remember: A Reflection on the Shoah." While arguing that the church "as such" was not responsible for anti-Semitism, the document accepted responsibility for many individual acts over the years that contributed to a climate of violence and hostility against Jews. The Shoah was attributed to Nazi ideology and secularism. The response of Jewish groups ranged from gratitude at the

A man prays during a mass given by Pope John Paul II in Kubwa, Nigeria. In March 1998 the pope made his second visit to Nigeria to encourage that nation's Catholic community, which made up about 15% of the population.

issuance of such a statement to deep disappointment that it did not go farther. A Catholic-Jewish commission began exploring the possibility of opening the relevant Vatican archives to scholars.

Ecumenism moved at differing paces on several fronts. Serious discussions began on how to adapt Catholicism to the cultures of Africa and Asia, where Catholics were rapidly growing minorities. Catholic, Orthodox, and Protestant clergies in Asia and Catholic and Evangelical groups in the U.S. sought common ground, mutual respect, and the avoidance of proselytism. Catholic and Orthodox relations in former Soviet republics and satellite nations remained tense. Russian Pres. Boris Yeltsin visited the Vatican to reassure the pope regarding Russia's freedom of conscience law, the original wording of which accorded freedom to Russia's "traditional faiths: Orthodoxy, Islam, Buddhism, and Judaism." Partly owing to Vatican pressure, the word *Orthodoxy* was changed to *Christianity.* Anglicans and Catholics made no further progress on intercommunion. Lutherans and Catholics could not agree completely on the Doctrine of Justification but found more common ground.

The pope made several trips, including his first-ever visit to Cuba in January. Whether the pope's efforts improved the lot of the church and of the Cuban people, as his similar efforts undeniably had for the church and people of Eastern Europe, remained to be seen. In March the pope made his second visit to Nigeria to encourage that nation's Catholic community, which made up about 15% of the population. In June the pope visited Austria in an attempt to reconcile that country's overwhelmingly Catholic population after a decade of clumsy administrative maneuvers and the sexual improprieties of its disgraced former archbishop. In October the pope visited Croatia.

(THOMAS F.X. NOBLE)

THE ORTHODOX CHURCH

During 1998 the Orthodox churches in the former communist countries continued to voice discontent with the World Council of Churches (WCC). The Russian Orthodox Church, for example, was concerned with the increasingly liberal and nontraditional stance of the WCC. Following the decision in May 1997 of the Orthodox Church of Georgia to withdraw from the WCC, representatives of the Russian and Georgian churches met on March 11, 1998, to discuss their grievances with the WCC. Proposals were made for presentation at a meeting of all Orthodox churches scheduled for late April in Thessaloniki, Greece. On April 9, however, the Bulgarian Orthodox Church announced that it was withdrawing from the WCC because of its nontraditional tendencies. The meeting in Thessaloniki, attended by 15 self-governing Orthodox churches, took place April 29–May 2. Although some of the churches wanted total withdrawal from the WCC, a compromise recommended that the Orthodox member churches of the WCC express their concerns at the Assembly, to be held in December at Harare, Zimbabwe, without voting or participating in the worship services.

Archbishop Seraphim, head of the Orthodox Church of Greece, died on April

10, 1998. He had held the post for 24 years, longer than any other Greek archbishop. (*See* OBITUARIES.) On April 28 Christodoulos of Dimitriada was elected the new archbishop of Athens and all Greece. Enthroned May 9, he immediately began challenging Greek society with a fresh program of outreach to young people that gained him popularity.

In Russia enforcement began of a law passed late in 1997 that required new religious groups to function for 15 years before registering permanently as national religious organizations. Western civil and religious leaders opposed the law. Also in Russia, public attention was focused on the burial of the remains of Tsar Nicholas II and his family, who were murdered by the Bolsheviks in 1918 in Yekaterinburg. The burial took place in St. Petersburg on July 17 with Russian Pres. Boris Yeltsin present, but Russian Orthodox Patriarch Aleksey II, who refused to acknowledge the remains as authentic, did not attend.

Metropolitan Jeremiah of France (ecumenical patriarchate) was elected president of the Conference of European Churches, the major ecumenical European church organization, on Nov. 12, 1997. In Estonia Semyon Kruzhkov was elected titular bishop of Abyssos on March 19 to assist Archbishop John of Karelia and all Finland, the administrator of the Autonomous Estonian Church. On August 2 the Albanian Orthodox Church celebrated the sixth anniversary of the restoration of the Orthodox Autocephalous Church of Albania with a newly constituted Holy Synod of three bishops under His Beatitude, Archbishop Anastasios.

On February 11 Metropolitan Vasily, head of the Polish Autocephalous Orthodox Church, died. Succeeding him, with the title metropolitan of Warsaw and all Poland, was Sawa, the archbishop of Bialystok and Gdansk. Sawa had served as the abbot of Jabloczino Monastery and as dean of the Orthodox department of the Academy of Christian Theology in Warsaw.

Notable among the recent rise of conversions to the Orthodox Church in the United States was theologian and historian Jaroslav Pelikan, Sterling professor of history emeritus at Yale University New Haven, Conn. The author of more than 30 books, Pelikan was received into the Orthodox Church on March 25 at the chapel of St. Vladimir's Orthodox Seminary in Crestwood, N.Y.

(STANLEY S. HARAKAS)

ORIENTAL ORTHODOX CHURCHES

Karekin II, the Armenian patriarch of Istanbul, died in Turkey on March 10, 1998. Subsequently, Archbishop Mesrob Mutafyan, who had served as the head of the patriarchal synod since 1990, was elected acting patriarch of the 65,000-member church body. On August 17, however, Turkish authorities refused to acknowledge the decision, appointing retired archbishop Shahan Sivaciyan in Mutafyan's place. Protests followed when the Armenian community refused to accept the Turkish decision. Consequently, on October 14 Mutafyan was elected as the 84th Armenian patriarch of Istanbul.

His Holiness Karekin I, catholicos of all Armenians, visited Egypt and Germany in January and February, and he traveled to the United States and Canada in June to celebrate the 100th anniversary of the founding of the diocese of the Armenian Church in America. Among the Eastern Orthodox leaders he visited was Archbishop Spyridon of the Greek Orthodox archdiocese.

A delegation from the New York City Council of Churches visited Egypt March 10–15 and declared that reports of the persecution of members of the Coptic Orthodox Church in that country had been overstated. In July, however, Egyptian military units closed and sealed a Coptic church in the vicinity of Maadi, a town near Cairo. Coptic Orthodox Pope Shenouda and other religious leaders protested the action. On August 14 police violence in the village of El-Kosheh killed two persons. International protests were lodged with the Egyptian government.

St. Mark's Coptic Cathedral in Cairo was the location for the consecration of the first patriarch of the Orthodox Church of Eritrea. The former archbishop of Eritrea was proclaimed Patriarch Philipos I at age 92.

(STANLEY S. HARAKAS)

JUDAISM

In February 1998 Susan Aranoff of Agunah Inc., on behalf of her organization, encouraged several leading rabbis in New York City to find an acceptable solution to the growing problem of agunahs. According to Jewish law, a woman whose husband is alive may not remarry until she receives from him "get," or religious divorce. Should the husband refuse his consent to this procedure, the wife may become agunah ("chained"), unable to remarry under Orthodox auspices.

Russian Pres. Boris Yeltsin attended the opening in the first week of September of a new $10 million synagogue in Moscow. Money for the building, situated in the city's huge war memorial complex, was raised by Russia's Jews. "The fact that President Yeltsin went there was extraordinary. This is the first time the President of Russia has ever been at a Jewish event," said Moscow's chief rabbi, Pinchas Goldschmidt, who helped organize the ceremony. This project should be seen in relation to the "grass roots" renaissance of Jewish religious life in former Soviet countries, which flowed from a variety of small activist groups of various denominations rather than from any central, official "establishment."

Serious questions about the relationship between church and state arose during the year as a result of activities of Orthodox and other religious groups. These ranged from comments both in favour and in condemnation of U.S. Pres. Bill Clinton in the Monica Lewinsky affair to demonstrations by Lubavich Hasidim in New York City urging the prime minister of Israel to oppose territorial compromise in his negotiations with the Palestinians to the controversy surrounding the voting directives given by the aged Iraqi-born Israeli mystic Rabbi Yitzhak Kadouri. In connection with the latter, both the Ashkenazi and Sephardi chief rabbis of Israel warned against the "exaggerated and improper use of rabbis," suggesting that though it is acceptable for rabbis to comment on specific political issues that have some religious dimension, it is not proper that rabbis be accorded cultic status to dictate who should govern and how.

Neither Reform nor Conservative Jews appeared to be looking forward to the rebuilding of the Temple in Jerusalem, and even among the Orthodox there was little enthusiasm for the restoration of a Temple with animal sacrifices. Many justified this attitude by arguing that, according to Jewish law, the Temple would be restored only under the direction of the Messiah. Even so, a fringe group, the Machon ha-Miqdash (Temple Institute) in Jerusalem, opened a museum and developed educational initiatives to make people aware of what they believed was the central place of the Temple in Jewish tradition and practice.

The International Catholic-Jewish Liaison Committee met at Vatican City on March 23–26 under the chairmanship of Edward Cardinal Cassidy. It endorsed, with some criticisms from the Jewish side, the recent Catholic document on the Holocaust and also approved a Common Declaration on the Environment, which not only spelled out how the common scripture and subsequent traditions of both Catholics and Jews placed responsibility on humans to safeguard the world and its threatened resources but also acknowledged the pressure of population growth as a significant factor in environmental degradation. Catholic-Jewish relations were, however, placed under strain by the continued erection of crosses at the Nazi death camp near Auschwitz and by the canonization of Edith Stein and the beatification of Alojzije Stepinac in October; both were regarded by the Catholic Church as martyrs to Nazism, but many Jews observed that Stein died because of her Jewish origins rather than her Catholic faith and that Stepinac allegedly cooperated during World War II with the Nazi-oriented regime in Croatia.

In February Rabbi Eliahu Bakshi-Doron, Sephardi chief rabbi of Israel, led an international Jewish delegation to a UNESCO-sponsored "day of reflection and dialogue" with Muslim leaders in Rabat, Mor. In light of the political tensions between the Arab world and Israel, Bakshi-Doron remarked, "Just being able to sit and talk about [the conflict] here in a Muslim country is a step in the right direction."

(NORMAN SOLOMON)

BUDDHISM

China in 1998 celebrated the 2,000th anniversary of the introduction of Buddhism into the country, inaugurating a Buddhist research centre in April and sponsoring an international festival in September. Also in April, Chinese officials denounced as fake a Buddha tooth that Tibetan monks in India had given to Taiwan. While in transit the tooth was worshipped by thousands of Thai Buddhists, and it then was ceremoniously received by 30,000 Taiwanese Buddhists.

After demonstrations in support of the Dalai Lama in March, Chinese authorities in April evicted 50 Tibetan nuns from Drag Yerpa, removing them forcibly from meditation caves, and in May arrested 15 Tibetan monks. In April China unsuccessfully petitioned Japan to block the Dalai Lama's participation at an international Buddhist conference in Tokyo. In November, the Dalai Lama met in the U.S. with Pres. Bill Clinton. They agreed that talks between China and the Dalai Lama were necessary; China denounced the meeting.

Buddhist leader Maha Ghosananada (centre) leads a procession through Takeo province, Cambodia. In July Ghosananada, the recipient of the 1998 Niwano Peace Prize, led 2,500 Buddhists in marches and religious services in support of peaceful national elections in Cambodia.

In July Maha Ghosananada, Cambodian supreme patriarch and the recipient of the 1998 Niwano Peace Prize, led 2,500 Buddhists in marches and religious services in support of peaceful national elections. Opposition parties denounced the victory of Hun Sen's Cambodian People's Party, charging intimidation that included forced oaths of party loyalty at Buddhist pagodas. Clashes between groups of monks who favoured Hun Sen and those who opposed him erupted during and after the election; some resulted in beatings and arrests.

A coordinated celebration of the Buddha's birthday in May was hailed as an important step toward the reunification of North and South Korea. In June, following two years of anti-Buddhist attacks that included vandalism, arson, and intimidation, South Korean Buddhist organizations strongly condemned religious discrimination and demanded a government apology for pro-Christian bias. In May Buddhists in Russia unsuccessfully protested the removal of a valuable Tibetan manuscript from Ulan-Ude for exhibition in the U.S.; 50 monks and laymen were beaten and detained, which sparked further protests.

Burmese exiles in January accused Myanmar of having executed three monks and arrested dozens more during late 1997 and also of restricting the ordination of pro-democracy monks. In April Amnesty International reported widespread human rights abuses against Burmese civilians, including Buddhist monks. During the same month, Burmese officials asked Thailand to execute members of the Democratic Karen Buddhist Army who entered Thai territory. In June Thailand's Supreme Sangha Council outlawed moneymaking Buddhist funerals and ordered temples to provide free funerals for those who were destitute. In July, after a suburban temple unveiled a statue of the Buddha standing on a globe with his arm raised in victory, the Sangha Council tight-ened control over religious imagery. In March Buddhist activist Sulak Sivaraksa was arrested for obstructing construction of a gas pipeline on the Thai-Burmese border.

In Sri Lanka the Sinhala Commission, a Buddhist group, in July accused Great Britain of colonial-era crimes against Buddhism, demanding an apology and restitution. Tamil separatists were suspected in the bombing of Kandy's Dalada Maligawa ("Temple of the Tooth," one of Sri Lanka's holiest Buddhist shrines) in January, which killed at least 11 but failed to damage the Buddha's tooth. Buddhist monks led thousands in June 1997 and February 1998 demonstrations and hunger strikes against government plans to sell the Eppawala phosphate deposit to an American corporation known for environmental abuses. The March 1998 bestowal of *upasampada* (higher ordination) on 22 Sri Lankan nuns at Dambulla, following the October 1996 *upasampada* of the first Sri Lankan nun, in Taiwan, formally ended a 1,500-year lapse in the Theravada nuns' order.

A fire in April destroyed Bhutan's famous Paro Taktsang monastery, killing one monk. In May fire gutted part of the Todai Temple in Nara, Japan. (JONATHAN S. WALTERS)

HINDUISM

From January to April 1998, millions of Hindus from around the world made the pilgrimage to the holy city of Haridwar, India, on the banks of the sacred Ganges River for the triennial Kumbh Mela, the great "Festival of the Pot." Because this Kumbh Mela was the last one of the 20th century, it was considered especially auspicious, and far greater numbers than usual made the pilgrimage to Haridwar, one of the four sites among which the festival rotates. On April 13–14 an estimated four million pilgrims ritually bathed in the Ganges to mark the most propitious day of the festival. Local govern-ment officials took special measures to prevent not only the sorts of mishaps, including crowd stampedes, that had marred several past celebrations of the mela but also possible terrorist activity arising from the Hindu-Muslim conflict in Kashmir.

Although the Kumbh Mela concluded without major incident, another pilgrimage was marked by tragedy. As many as 60 pilgrims were among the more than 200 who died in landslides in northern Uttar Pradesh, near the Tibetan border, in August. The pilgrims were members of various groups making their way to Lake Manasarovar and Mt. Kailasa in the Tibetan Himalayas, sites sacred to Hindus as, respectively, the mythic source of the Ganges and the paradisiacal abode of the god Siva. Torrential monsoon rains had loosened the sides of the hills flanking the perilous route to these sites, and little could be done to rescue many who were stranded in remote, inaccessible mountain areas. The Indian government ordered the cancellation of the pilgrimage, and the chief minister of Uttar Pradesh called for a study of an alternative, less-hazardous route for future pilgrims.

Another major pilgrimage was conducted during July and August to the sacred cave of Amarnath high in the mountains of Kashmir, where Siva was worshiped in the form of a large stalagmite. Kashmiri militant organizations, seeking the separation of the state from India, had imposed a ban on the pilgrimage and attempted to disrupt it with explosive devices, which Indian security forces discovered before injuries could be inflicted.

The installation in March of a new coalition central government led by the Hindu nationalist Bharatiya Janata Party (BJP) raised fears among moderate Hindu and Muslim political leaders that the BJP would advance a religious ideology inimical to communal harmony. The new prime minister, A.B. Vajpayee (*see* BIOGRAPHIES), quickly sought to allay any fears that his government would pursue a Hindu nationalism that would violate the principles of a secular state embodied in India's constitution. His critics, however, attacked the government's decision to undertake nuclear bomb tests that bore the project name of Shakti, a word denoting sacred power in Sanskrit. In April a prominent Hindu religious leader, the abbot of monasteries in West Bengal state, spoke out against a Hindu nationalism that might exacerbate communal divisions.

In August, on the occasion of the 51st anniversary of India's independence, the Orissa state government announced a major project to restore some 400 ancient monuments, including temples as old as 700 years. The state and central governments

Hindu pilgrims gather on the banks of the Ganges River in Haridwar, India. From January to April 1998, millions of Hindus from around the world made the pilgrimage to Haridwar for the triennial Kumbh Mela, the great "Festival of the Pot."

had long been concerned about the 3,500 monuments in Orissa, the largest number in any state in the country; only 500 were protected in any manner against the vandalism that had stripped ancient Indian temples of sacred images for illicit but highly profitable marketing.   (H. PATRICK SULLIVAN)

ISLAM

As in recent years, two trends concerning Islam were most evident during 1998: outbreaks of violence and increasing awareness of the growth and spread of the religion. Violence continued in many Muslim lands and in some cases reached beyond them. Terrorist activities received wide publicity. Their notoriety elicited reactions from Muslims, especially those in Europe and North America, who were concerned that media reports reinforced stereotypes held by many non-Muslims that portrayed Muslims as often violent and Islam as condoning violence. As Islam continued to expand and become more visible in Europe and North America, Muslims in those areas organized to try to counter those stereotypes and to educate their neighbours as well as the media. Their efforts were made more difficult, however, by local problems that had been generated by the expansion and increased visibility of Islam. They included the building of mosques in areas where there had previously been few or no Muslims, distinctive styles of dress, and Muslim holiday celebrations.

In Muslim countries, as always, disentangling specifically Islamic elements from other political and social developments was very difficult. Indeed, some could not be separated, and many actions by Muslims were

better understood as expressing political or social concerns having religious undertones rather than vice versa. Islamist movements were prominent in many places, but upon analysis most of these could not be simplistically categorized as only religious fundamentalism. For example, violence continued in Algeria, where armed groups attacked whole villages; an international commission visited the country in August, but its initial findings as to the causes of the violence were inconclusive. In Afghanistan the forces of the Islamist Taliban were able to extend their political control to almost the entire country by defeating the opposition forces in the north at the end of the summer. They also continued to move toward enforcing Islamist interpretations of social behaviour; in June they ordered the closing of 100 girls' schools, viewing them as not conducive to a proper society. The killing of Iranian diplomatic personnel after the fall of Mazar-e Sharif in the north led to considerable tension between Afghanistan and Iran and the massing of troops by both countries on their common border. U.S.–Afghanistan relations suffered severely because of a U.S. bombing attack in late August of an alleged terrorist base in Afghanistan operated by Saudi millionaire Osama bin Laden. (*See* BIOGRAPHIES.) That raid, and one on a presumed chemical munitions factory in The Sudan at the same time, was carried out by the U.S. as a retaliatory strike in response to terrorist attacks on American embassies in Tanzania and Kenya in early August.

Turkey continued to move toward limiting Islamist influence in its political and social life. In January the Islamist Welfare Party was outlawed, and pressure against

openly Islamic activities was increased. By midyear the army, which for more than half a century had seen itself as responsible for the preservation of a secular state and society, had taken control of the nation's political life. In Pakistan in August, Prime Minister Nawaz Sharif announced that the Shari'ah (Islamic law) would be Pakistan's supreme law. In September an Iranian official source announced that Iran no longer supported condemning to death Salman Rushdie, author of the controversial book *The Satanic Verses.* Other sources, however, disputed that reversal of policy almost immediately, declaring the condemnation still in effect.

Although acts of terrorism, violence, and the struggle between Islamist forces and moderates continued, so also did the growth and increasing visibility of the vitality of Islam, especially in Europe and North America. At the end of July, a £3.5 million mosque in Edinburgh, funded by Saudi Arabia, was formally opened; an estimated 8,000 Muslims lived in that city. In Culver City, Calif., the King Fahd mosque, also Saudi-funded, was dedicated; by the end of 1998, there were an estimated 75 mosques in southern California. Groundbreaking took place in late June in Houston, Texas, for a mosque built by the Ahmadiyya sect of Islam. Of the estimated 10 million Ahmadis, some 12,000 were said to be in the U.S. Pres. Saddam Hussein of Iraq went forward with plans to build the largest mosque in the world in Baghdad. Designed to accommodate tens of thousands of worshippers, it would be larger than the al-Haram Mosque at Mecca and would have four minarets.

(REUBEN W. SMITH)

Worldwide Adherents of All Religions by Six Continental Areas, Mid-1998

	Africa	Asia	Europe	Latin America	Northern America	Oceania	World	%	Number of Countries
Christians	**356,277,000**	**283,734,000**	**558,729,000**	**462,965,000**	**256,882,000**	**24,451,000**	**1,943,038,000**	**32.8**	**238**
Affiliated Christians	323,782,000	275,836,000	536,092,000	456,919,000	222,678,000	20,045,000	1,835,352,000	31.0	238
Roman Catholics	114,316,000	106,399,000	286,124,000	442,808,000	69,536,000	7,318,000	1,026,501,000	17.3	235
Protestants	87,190,000	43,998,000	85,924,000	45,295,000	95,063,000	6,503,000	316,445,000	5.3	230
Orthodox	33,660,000	15,232,000	158,775,000	549,000	4,852,000	675,000	213,743,000	3.6	138
Anglicans	20,551,000	856,000	25,632,000	853,000	3,260,000	5,190,000	63,748,000	1.1	168
Other Christians	74,853,000	143,080,000	5,645,000	44,331,000	47,585,000	826,000	373,832,000	6.3	223
Unaffiliated Christians	32,495,000	7,898,000	22,637,000	2,041,000	34,204,000	4,406,000	107,686,000	1.8	202
Non-Christians	**407,502,000**	**3,305,143,000**	**170,677,000**	**36,569,000**	**47,196,000**	**5,009,000**	**3,986,801,000**	**67.2**	**238**
Atheists	420,000	121,451,000	23,444,000	2,673,000	1,569,000	356,000	149,913,000	2.5	165
Baha'is	2,263,000	3,260,000	126,000	825,000	753,000	105,000	6,764,000	0.1	221
Buddhists	138,000	348,806,000	1,517,000	622,000	2,445,000	266,000	353,794,000	6.0	128
Chinese folk religionists	33,000	377,795,000	250,000	184,000	839,000	61,000	379,162,000	6.4	91
Confucianists	0	6,207,000	11,000	0	0	23,000	6,241,000	0.1	15
Ethnic religionists	97,200,000	148,189,000	1,262,000	1,231,000	424,000	259,000	248,565,000	4.2	144
Hindus	2,411,000	755,500,000	1,382,000	785,000	1,266,000	345,000	761,689,000	12.8	114
Jains	65,000	3,850,000	0	0	7,000	0	3,922,000	0.1	10
Jews	230,000	4,139,000	2,530,000	1,121,000	5,996,000	95,000	14,111,000	0.2	138
Mandeans	0	38,000	0	0	0	0	38,000	0.0	2
Muslims	315,000,000	812,000,000	31,401,000	1,624,000	4,349,000	248,000	1,164,622,000	19.6	208
New-Religionists	27,000	98,548,000	155,000	604,000	759,000	51,000	100,144,000	1.7	62
Nonreligious	4,863,000	600,822,000	108,000,000	15,300,000	27,500,000	3,170,000	759,655,000	12.8	237
Shintoists	0	2,727,000	0	7,000	55,000	0	2,789,000	0.0	8
Sikhs	53,000	21,531,000	236,000	0	498,000	14,000	22,332,000	0.4	34
Spiritists	3,000	2,000	129,000	11,498,000	148,000	7,000	11,785,000	0.2	55
Zoroastrians	1,000	269,000	0	0	3,000	0	274,000	0.0	17
Other religionists	68,000	11,000	233,000	95,000	585,000	9,000	1,001,000	0.0	79
Total population	**778,484,000**	**3,588,877,000**	**729,406,000**	**499,534,000**	**304,078,000**	**29,460,000**	**5,929,839,000**	**100.0**	**238**

Continents. These follow current UN demographic terminology, which now divides the world into the six major areas shown above. *See* United Nations, *World Population Prospects: The 1996 Revision* (New York: UN, 1998), with populations of all continents, regions, and countries covering the period 1950–2025. Note that "Asia" now includes the former Soviet Central Asian states and "Europe" includes all of Russia and extends eastward to Vladivostok, the Sea of Japan, and the Bering Strait.
Countries. The last column enumerates sovereign and nonsovereign countries in which each religion or religious grouping has a numerically significant following.
Adherents. As defined and enumerated for each of the world's countries in *World Christian Encyclopedia* (1982), projected to mid-1998, adjusted for recent data.
Christians. Followers of Jesus Christ affiliated with churches (church members, including children: 1,835,352,000) plus persons professing in censuses or polls to be Christians though not so affiliated. Figures for the subgroups of Christians do not add up to the totals in the first line because some Christians adhere to more than one denomination.
Other Christians. This term in the above table denotes Catholics (non-Roman), marginal Protestants, crypto-Christians, and adherents of African, Asian, Black, and Latin-American indigenous churches.
Atheists. Persons professing atheism, skepticism, disbelief, or irreligion, including antireligious (opposed to all religion).
Buddhists. 56% Mahayana, 38% Theravada (Hinayana), 6% Tantrayana (Lamaism).
Chinese folk religionists. Followers of traditional Chinese religion (local deities, ancestor veneration, Confucian ethics, Taoism, universism, divination, some Buddhist elements).
Confucianists. Non-Chinese followers of Confucius and Confucianism, mostly Koreans in Korea.
Ethnic religionists. Followers of local, tribal, animistic, or shamanistic religions.
Hindus. 70% Vaishnavites, 25% Shaivites, 2% neo-Hindus and reform Hindus.
Jews. Adherents of Judaism. For detailed data on "core" Jewish population, *see* the annual "World Jewish Populations" article in the American Jewish Committee's *American Jewish Year Book*.
Muslims. 83% Sunnites, 16% Shi'ites, 1% other schools. Until 1990 the ethnic Muslims in the former U.S.S.R. who had embraced communism were not included as Muslims in this table. After the collapse of communism in 1990–91, these ethnic Muslims were once again enumerated as Muslims if they had returned to Islamic profession and practice.
New-Religionists. Followers of Asian 20th-century New Religions, New Religious movements, radical new crisis religions, and non-Christian syncretistic mass religions, all founded since 1800 and most since 1945.
Nonreligious. Persons professing no religion, nonbelievers, agnostics, freethinkers, dereligionized secularists indifferent to all religion.
Other religionists. Including 70 minor world religions and more than 10,000 national or local religions and a large number of spiritist religions, New Age religions, quasi religions, pseudoreligions, parareligions, religious or mystic systems, religious and semireligious brotherhoods of numerous varieties.
Total population. UN medium variant figures for mid-1998, as given in *World Population Prospects: The 1996 Revision.*

Religious Adherents in the United States of America, AD 1900–2000

Adherents	Year 1900	%	mid-1970	%	mid-1990	%	Annual Change, 1990–1995 Natural	Conversion	Total	Rate (%)	mid-1995	%	mid-2000	%
Christians	**73,270,000**	**96.4**	**189,322,000**	**90.1**	**216,727,000**	**85.3**	**2,219,100**	**-19,900**	**2,173,400**	**0.98**	**227,594,000**	**85.2**	**236,002,000**	**84.9**
Affiliated Christians	54,425,000	71.6	153,201,000	72.9	184,876,000	72.8	1,893,000	157,200	2,057,000	1.08	192,181,000	71.9	205,090,000	71.4
Roman Catholics	10,775,000	14.2	48,391,000	23.0	56,650,000	22.3	580,000	-23,200	557,000	0.96	56,800,000	21.3	57,000,000	20.5
Protestants	35,000,000	46.1	70,653,000	33.6	82,072,000	32.3	840,300	-154,700	685,600	0.82	85,500,000	32.0	88,800,000	32.0
Evangelicals	26,598,000	35.0	50,689,000	24.1	67,743,000	26.7	693,600	273,800	967,400	1.39	72,580,000	27.2	76,815,000	27.6
Anglicans	1,600,000	2.1	3,234,000	1.5	2,450,000	1.0	25,100	-51,400	-26,000	-1.07	2,425,000	0.9	2,400,000	0.9
Orthodox	400,000	0.5	4,387,000	2.1	4,250,000	1.7	43,500	232,700	276,200	5.79	5,631,000	2.1	6,260,000	2.3
Black Christians	5,750,000	7.6	19,679,000	9.4	32,598,000	12.8	333,800	106,600	440,400	1.32	34,800,000	13.0	37,200,000	13.4
Black Evangelicals	5,320,000	7.0	13,551,000	6.4	17,248,000	6.8	176,600	57,800	234,400	1.32	18,420,000	6.9	19,548,000	7.0
Catholics (non-Roman)	100,000	0.1	473,000	0.2	646,000	0.3	6,600	6,200	12,800	1.91	710,000	0.3	800,000	0.3
Other Christians	800,000	1.1	6,384,000	3.0	9,050,000	3.6	92,700	104,900	204,000	2.02	9,620,000	3.6	10,100,000	3.6
Unaffiliated Christians	18,845,000	24.8	36,121,000	17.2	31,851,000	12.5	326,100	-177,100	712,400	0.46	35,413,000	13.3	31,678,000	13.5
Non-Christians	**2,724,800**	**3.6**	**20,789,000**	**9.9**	**37,379,000**	**14.7**	**382,700**	**19,900**	**428,400**	**1.12**	**39,521,000**	**14.8**	**41,823,000**	**15.1**
Atheists	1,000	0.0	200,000	0.1	770,000	0.3	7,900	12,900	20,800	2.57	874,000	0.3	925,000	0.3
Baha'is	2,800	0.0	138,000	0.1	600,000	0.2	6,100	10,500	16,600	2.63	683,000	0.3	750,000	0.3
Buddhists	30,000	0.0	200,000	0.1	1,880,000	0.7	19,200	19,600	48,000	2.43	2,120,000	0.8	2,318,000	0.8
Chinese folk religionists	70,000	0.1	90,000	0.0	76,000	0.0	800	-1,200	-400	-0.53	74,000	0.0	70,000	0.0
Hindus	1,000	0.0	100,000	0.0	750,000	0.3	7,700	28,300	36,000	4.40	930,000	0.3	1,030,000	0.4
Jews	1,500,000	2.0	6,700,000	3.2	5,535,000	2.2	56,700	-60,100	-3,400	-0.06	5,518,000	2.1	5,500,000	2.0
Muslims	10,000	0.0	800,000	0.4	3,600,000	1.4	36,900	-3,500	44,000	1.19	3,820,000	1.4	4,175,000	1.5
Black Muslims	0	0.0	200,000	0.1	1,250,000	0.5	12,800	17,200	30,000	2.29	1,400,000	0.5	1,650,000	0.6
New-Religionists	0	0.0	110,000	0.1	575,000	0.2	5,900	-300	5,600	0.96	603,000	0.2	675,000	0.2
Nonreligious	1,000,000	1.3	11,730,000	5.6	22,233,000	8.7	227,600	4,600	232,200	1.02	23,394,000	8.8	24,700,000	8.9
Sikhs	0	0.0	1,000	0.0	160,000	0.1	1,600	4,400	6,000	3.50	190,000	0.1	220,000	0.1
Tribal religionists	100,000	0.1	70,000	0.0	280,000	0.1	2,900	2,100	5,000	1.73	305,000	0.1	350,000	0.1
Other religionists	10,000	0.0	650,000	0.3	920,000	0.4	9,400	8,600	18,000	1.88	1,010,000	0.4	1,110,000	0.4
Total population	**75,994,800**	**100.0**	**210,111,000**	**100.0**	**254,106,000**	**100.0**	**2,601,800**	**0**	**2,601,800**	**1.00**	**267,115,000**	**100.0**	**277,825,000**	**100.0**

Methodology. This table extracts a microcosm of the world table above. It depicts the United States, the country with the largest number of adherents to Christianity, the world's largest religion. Statistics for five points in time across the 20th century are presented. Each religion's *Annual change* is also analyzed by: *Natural* increase (births minus deaths, plus immigrants minus emigrants) per year and *Conversion* (new converts minus new defectors) per year, which together constitute the *Total* increase per year. *Rate* increase is then computed as percentage per year.
Structure. Vertically the table lists 26 major religious categories. The 12 major religions (including nonreligion) in the U.S. are listed alphabetically with largest (Christians) first. Indented names of groups in the "Adherents" column are subcategories of the groups above them and are also counted in these unindented totals, so they should not be added twice into the column total. Figures for Christians in 1970 and 1990 are built upon detailed head counts by churches, usually to the last digit. Totals are then rounded to the nearest 1,000. Because of rounding, the corresponding percentage figures may sometimes not total exactly 100%. Figures for AD 2000 are projections based on current long-term trends.
Christians are all persons who profess publicly to follow Jesus Christ as Lord and Saviour. This category is subdivided into **Affiliated Christians** (church members) and **Unaffiliated** (nominal) **Christians** (professing Christians not affiliated with any church). *See also* the note on Christians to the Worldwide table, above.
Evangelicals. Churches, agencies, and individuals that call themselves by this term usually emphasize five or more of several fundamental doctrines (salvation by faith, personal acceptance, verbal inspiration of Scripture, depravity of man, Virgin Birth, miracles of Christ, atonement, evangelism, Second Advent).
Black Christians. Members of denominations initiated by Africans, Caribbean islanders, or African Americans.
Other Christians. This term denotes members of denominations and churches that regard themselves as outside mainline Protestant/Catholic/Orthodox/Anglican Christianity.
Jews. Core Jewish population relating to Judaism, excluding Jewish persons professing a different religion.

(DAVID B. BARRETT; TODD M. JOHNSON)

Social Protection

Industrialized, emerging, and less-developed countries all continued to be concerned about existing strains and potential burdens on their social protection programs and took measures in 1998 toward improving the financial stability of their systems. In order to provide relief to public coffers and social insurance institutions, access to benefits was restricted or cut and measures were taken to increase the ability of benefit recipients to provide for themselves.

North America. A booming economy and election-year sensitivities shifted the focus of social protection activity in the United States from legislation to debate in 1998. The chief issue was the financial stability of Social Security, which provided retirement, disability, and survivors' benefits to more than 44 million Americans. The system collected about $100 billion a year more in payroll taxes than it paid out in benefits, but concern had been growing about what would happen when 77 million baby boomers started to retire after 2010. The percentage of Americans 65 and older, about 12.7% of the population in 1998, was expected to rise to 20.7% by 2050, and the ratio of workers to retirees, now 3–1, would shrink to 2–1. Some thought that the system would start running a deficit beginning in 2029, but the Social Security trustees reported that, owing to the strong economy, the problem would be deferred until 2032.

In his state of the union message, U.S. Pres. Bill Clinton said that the U.S. had to "save Social Security first" and called on Congress to use budget surpluses to shore up the system's trust fund. The White House led a national dialogue, with a series of "town hall" forums across the country, to discuss ideas for rescuing the largest U.S. social welfare program. Plans centred on four strategies: (1) increasing payroll taxes,

which were 12.4%, split equally between workers and employers, on salaries up to a maximum of $72,600 annually; (2) raising the retirement age, which was already scheduled to increase gradually from 65 to 67; (3) cutting benefits; and (4) revising the structure of the system. The latter proposal stirred the greatest controversy. Money in the Social Security trust fund had always been invested in safe but low-yielding government bonds. Several ideas for reform called for moving a portion of the funds into private savings accounts, a move that would invest it in riskier but higher-paying stocks.

The bipartisan National Commission on Retirement Policy, a group of congressmen, business leaders, and academicians, recommended allowing individuals to invest 2% of their payroll taxes in government-selected funds. It also called for raising the retirement age to 70 and creating a minimum benefit for low-income retirees. Several other proposals were introduced in Congress by both Republicans and Democrats. Critics of privatized accounts raised questions concerning the percentage of trust money that should be shifted to equities, who would do the investing, what would happen if the stock market went down, and whether the change would be fair for women and low-income retirees. Wary of tinkering with a popular program in an election year, Congress did not act on any of the proposals, although it did decide to hold 90% of the budget surplus in reserve until Social Security was solvent.

Like Social Security, Medicare, which provided health insurance to about 38 million Americans over the age of 64, also faced financial problems. As medical costs soared and increasing numbers of elderly persons entered the program, the cost of Medicare was expected to grow from less than 3% of gross domestic product to about 6%. The Social Security trustees' report said that Medicare was financially secure until 2008 and that its financial outlook for the

next 75 years had improved because of cost-cutting measures and other changes in 1997. The job of dealing with Medicare's solvency was given to a 19-member National Bipartisan Commission on the Future of Medicare, which was scheduled to present a plan to Congress on or before March 1, 1999.

The most significant new initiative by Congress in the realm of social protection was passage of the first complete overhaul in 60 years of U.S. public-housing policy. The landmark legislation created 90,000 new vouchers, or federal rent subsidies, for fiscal 1999 and authorized another 100,000 vouchers in each of the following two years. Three million Americans received federal help in paying their rent or buying an apartment, but, according to the most recent government survey, in 1995 there was a shortage of 4.4 million affordable rental units for low-income households.

An innovative feature of the new law allowed officials to offer apartments in public housing projects to working families with incomes of up to $40,000 a year. The hope was to bring stable, higher-income working tenants into those projects in an effort to create greater diversity, reduce drug use and other crimes, and improve the image of public housing. At least 40% of public housing, however, would continue to be reserved for the very poor—and 75% would be reserved for families making 30% or less of the median income in the area in which they lived.

Congress extended the Special Supplemental Nutrition Program for Women, Infants, and Children (WIC) through 2003, with new provisions to weed out fraud. The renewal included after-school snacks for teenagers in low-income areas and a three-year pilot school-breakfast program. WIC provided federally funded vouchers for infant formula, cereal, and other nutritious products to supplement the diets of about 7.3 million low-income pregnant women, infants, and children up to age five.

In October the long-planned computerized national child-support clearinghouse began operations. It matched child-support case information sent in by states with information about wage earners across the country in an effort to track down absent parents who owed annually about $17 billion for support.

No action was taken on requests by President Clinton to increase the minimum wage and to open Medicare to some 55–64-year-old retirees who would pay monthly premiums. They were among the 44 million Americans, including 12 million children, who lacked health insurance because they could not obtain it through work, could not afford it, or were ineligible for Medicare or Medicaid, the government insurance program for the poor.

Meanwhile, the impact of the historic 1996 welfare-reform law continued to expand. The U.S. Department of Health and Human Services (HHS) reported that 3.8 million individuals had left welfare rolls since passage of the reform law, which had reduced the caseload to its lowest level since 1969, and that 1.7 million adults who had been on welfare in 1996 were working in March 1997. According to HHS, states were spending more per person on welfare-to-work efforts than they had spent before passage of the reform.

At the second meeting of the National Bipartisan Commission on the Future of Medicare, held on April 20 in Washington, D.C., Federal Reserve Board Chairman Alan Greenspan (seated at table, far right) became the first person to testify before the commission. He discussed a broad range of economic issues affecting Medicare.

A march on City Hall was staged in New York City on August 22 by members of an organization representing welfare recipients forced to go to work since the enactment of the federal welfare reform law in 1996. Protesters targeted Mayor Rudolph Giuliani, who had vowed to eliminate welfare by 2000, and President Clinton, who had signed the largely Republican-supported law.

Despite the positive results, welfare reform remained a work in progress, with real and potential problems. Moving welfare recipients into jobs was likely to slow when the U.S. economy cooled and the availability of low-wage jobs shrank. In addition, those who made the jump from welfare to work in the first two years were generally the "easiest" cases; many of the more difficult ones, the people with fewer skills and less education and training, had not yet been placed. Cracks appeared in the support system, especially in providing child care for mothers entering the workforce and transportation to help newcomers get to their jobs. In response to public outcries and prodding from Clinton, Congress continued to "reform" the reform. It restored Supplemental Security Income to elderly and disabled immigrants and food stamps to 250,000 legal immigrants who had been dropped from the rolls.

The early success of welfare reform was aided by a dramatic drop in poverty and an increase in incomes. Census Bureau figures showed that the overall U.S. poverty rate fell to 13.3% in 1997, from 13.7% in 1996, which left 35.6 million people living below the poverty line of $16,400 annually for a family of four. At the same time, the median household income of American families, adjusted for inflation, rose 1.9% to $37,005. Virtually all sectors of the population—all races, single mothers and married couples, and most geographic regions—registered improvement. African-Americans and Hispanics had especially strong gains, with the poverty rate for African-Americans

falling to an all-time low of 26.5% and the Hispanic rate declining to 27.1%. Strong economic growth and low unemployment were cited as two of the main reasons for the improvement.

One of the most contentious issues in Canada was the proposed Seniors Benefit, which had been announced by Finance Minister Paul Martin in his 1996 budget and in 2001 would replace the existing Old Age Security and Guaranteed Income Supplement programs with a single payment. The goal of the new plan was to increase payments to low-income seniors while decreasing the amounts given to financially better-off recipients. After further scrutiny of the plan, however, investment advisers found that benefits would be eliminated entirely at a much lower income threshold ($52,000 for a single senior and $78,000 for a couple). Critics argued that the scheme penalized middle-income Canadians who had saved for retirement. In the face of rising opposition, Martin dropped the plan.

In October provincial finance ministers met with Martin and asked for more funding for health care, citing a federal budget surplus of some $3.5 billion. They argued that the provinces should be given a free hand to allocate money for health care without interference from the federal government and voiced concerns about entering partnerships, especially in light of a past $6.2 billion federal cut to health care.

Europe. In Austria a reform of the pension insurance system was essentially intended to raise the retirement age. It was

made easier, beginning in January, for individuals to qualify for a "flexible pension," a move that was designed to allow more people to remain partially employed instead of taking full retirement. Sweden, too, introduced incentives for workers to remain employed longer. In June the Rikstag (parliament) adopted a pension-reform bill that had been under discussion since 1994; the pensionable age would become flexible, with later retirement resulting in higher pensions based on lifetime income. At the time of retirement, the yearly pension entitlement would be calculated and would reflect the average life expectancy. A reform of the German pension system, adopted in late 1997, was scrapped in October by the new government of Gerhard Schröder. (*See* BIOGRAPHIES.)

In The Netherlands significant changes were introduced in January for the protection of people with disabilities. Employers were given the option, at least in part, of insuring themselves outside the social security scheme against the risk of their employees' becoming incapacitated. A "general contribution" was still payable to the fund, however, essentially to ensure the funding of existing disability pensions.

Expenditures were increased in Ireland for measures to support employment and reentry into the workforce. Finland revised the rules governing the granting of unemployment benefits to encourage unemployed persons to begin job training or retraining. Previously, anyone deciding to seek further education or training suffered substantial losses in benefits.

A number of countries modernized their social protection systems to promote fairness and opportunity. New approaches, including new technology, were used to improve welfare delivery and to reach those who were entitled to benefits but were not receiving them. At the same time, recipients were reviewed for continued eligibility. In March the U.K. government published a Green Paper that advocated a reform of welfare based on a new contract between citizens and government. The Green Paper detailed a series of measures to be achieved over the next 10–20 years, including a reduction in the proportion of working-age people living in households without wage earners, a guaranteed adequate retirement income for all, more support from the tax and benefit systems to families with children, and clearer gateways for determining eligibility for all types of benefits. In France, where it is necessary to have contributed for at least 40 years and to have reached the official retirement age of 60 in order to be entitled to an old-age pension, a special preretirement allowance was created to guarantee a minimum monthly stipend for longtime contributors under the age of 60. The measure would address the situation in which a person who had started working early in life, had contributed for 40 years, and then became unemployed before the age of 60 was without an adequate income. In Belgium a social identity card was issued by mutual-benefit societies to all persons covered by social insurance to substantiate their rights to benefits. The introduction in Italy of a "social credit card" was discussed; the card would contain information such as the personal income and assets of the insured person and would make it possible to allocate benefits according to individual circumstances.

In June the European Union social affairs ministers agreed to adopt a directive that would protect the supplementary pension rights of those people who were employed and self-employed and were moving within the EU. Pension rights would be preserved rather than transferred from one scheme to another; the cross-border payment of pensions would be guaranteed; and workers temporarily posted in another member state would remain affiliated with the scheme to which they had initially belonged.

The Romanian government initiated a series of measures in response to economic restructuring and privatization programs, which had negative effects on social welfare. Counseling, job-placement, and occupational reclassification services were established in cases of mass firings. Special compensatory payments were granted in the form of a lump sum, the amount of which varied according to the level of unemployment in the region.

Concerns about fund deficits, poor investment returns, and allegations of corruption led the Hungarian government to place its pension and health funds under more direct control. The funds previously had been supervised by two independent bodies. In January Hungary began implementing its new multilevel pension system, which comprised the mandatory social insurance pension (pay-as-you-go) scheme, new privately funded, mandatory private pension funds, and voluntary pension funds. Estonia agreed to establish a similar system, which was likely to be implemented in January 2000.

The Polish government announced that the introduction of a reformed pension system would be postponed. The new multilevel system would commence operations beginning April 1, 1999, instead of Jan. 1, 1999. The delay was due to parliamentary disagreements about the split in the flow of contributions between the existing state pension and the new system.

Industrialized Asia and the Pacific. Governments and program administrators in these regions streamlined welfare delivery and, at the same time, required welfare beneficiaries to assume greater personal responsibility. Beginning in July a new, simplified income-support payment was available to young people in Australia who were studying or looking for work. The new Youth Allowance replaced a number of existing payments. Those wishing to receive this payment needed to meet certain work or study requirements or participate in job-training programs. In New Zealand unemployment and illness benefits were replaced by a new community wage. The name change was designed to emphasize the focus on work requirements under the new program. Under a parallel administrative reform, the Income Support Service was merged with the Employment Service to create a new, one-stop agency that would address income-support needs and training needs and provide assistance in job searches. A new back-to-work child-care scheme was introduced in Singapore. Eligible mothers received a payment intended for child-care expenses so that they could find paid employment.

"Double dipping" was brought to an end in Japan. Starting in April people aged 60 or older and out of the workforce were no longer able to receive both an unemployment benefit and an old-age pension. They were required, instead, to choose one or the other. South Korea strengthened its unemployment protection. Beginning in July the unemployment insurance program was extended to cover employers with at least 5 employees, whereas previously only companies with 10 or more employees had been covered. The minimum waiting period for payment of unemployment benefits was increased from 30 to 60 days, and the minimum benefit was increased from 50% to 70% of the minimum monthly wage.

Emerging and Less-Developed Countries. Emerging and less-developed countries facing problems of inadequate social security coverage and financial imbalances sought to use scarce resources in the most efficient ways. Tanzania's National Provident Fund was converted into a social insurance scheme in July. Owing to inflation, the fund had provided only meagre lump-sum benefits, which many people used up quickly and then were left without support. With benefits now being paid in the form of pensions, it was hoped that hardships could be avoided. Entitlements to Moroccan family allowances were checked thoroughly, and the issue of daily illness allowances was subjected to strict controls before any moneys were awarded. An identity booklet was issued in Equatorial Guinea to insured individuals and their families in order to facilitate access to services and social benefits and also to help prevent fraudulent benefit claims.

In July Iran introduced co-payments for medical expenses to ensure a more efficient utilization of resources. Self-employed and voluntarily insured persons had to pay 25% of expenses for outpatient care and 10% of hospitalization costs.

The Social Security System in the Philippines continued to be computerized. Menu-driven workstations were set up in shopping malls and other public places to give members easy access to information.

The Latin-American countries continued to experiment with totally or partially privatized old-age pensions. In Bolivia, for example, pensioners were given new options concerning the payment of their pensions from private pension-fund administrators (AFPs). Contributions made to the system could be invested in an AFP-managed account, with pension payments depending on the performance of the fund, or accumulated savings could be used to purchase a fixed-amount life annuity from an approved insurance company.

(CHRISTIANE KUPTSCH; DAVID M. MAZIE)

HUMAN RIGHTS

Major human rights issues that gained prominence during 1998 included the adoption of measures for more effective prevention and prosecution of war crimes, conflicts involving ethnic minorities pursuing greater autonomy and self-determination within their own countries, activities associated with the commemoration of the 50th anniversary of the adoption of the Universal Declaration of Human Rights, and rising concern about human rights violations involving women.

War Crimes and the Punishment of Human Rights Violations. The overriding human rights issue of 1998 was the punishment of war crimes and crimes against humanity, particularly as a result of the increasing number of internal ethnic conflicts endangering minority civilian populations and producing the forced relocations of refugees on a massive scale. In Kosovo (a province of Serbia), Bosnia and Herzegovina, the Democratic Republic of the Congo (Congo [Kinshasa]), and Rwanda, minority populations became primary military targets on a scale that suggested "ethnic cleansing" and genocide. Serbian military forces in Kosovo used martial law to maintain control of a region in which 90% of the inhabitants were ethnic Albanians, and conducted large-scale offensives against civilian towns and villages believed sympathetic to the Albanians' demand for greater autonomy. As a result, an estimated 700 civilians were killed and 250,000 others were forced to flee their homes, the majority of them civilian bystanders caught in the cross fire. In Congo (Kinshasa) a UN human rights team and independent observers accused the military forces of Pres. Laurent Kabila of having massacred scores of Hutu refugees who had fled Rwanda to avoid reprisals from their alleged 1994–95 participation in the genocide against the Tutsi.

In July at an international conference in Rome, a new treaty was approved authorizing the creation of an International Criminal Court in The Hague to serve as a permanent UN tribunal prosecuting war crimes worldwide. Previously, the UN Security Council had established separate war crimes tribunals for individual conflicts, such as those in former Yugoslavia and Rwanda. This ad hoc approach had been widely criticized as often difficult to initiate and subject to political

pressures. Rejecting the new measure were China, Israel, and the U.S., which objected to several of the treaty's core provisions, including the independent authority given to the tribunal's prosecutor.

The International Criminal Tribunal for Rwanda sentenced Jean Kambanda, former prime minister of that country, to life imprisonment (the harshest penalty available) for having committed genocide by supporting and promoting the massacre of some 500,000 Tutsi when the Hutu briefly held power in 1994. Kambanda, who pleaded guilty to six charges of genocide, was the first person sentenced for genocide since World War II. Additional arrests and trials of alleged war criminals in former Yugoslavia also took place. Although indicted, former Bosnian president Radovan Karadzic and his principal military commander, Gen. Ratko Mladic, remained free; several important arrests, however, did take place, including the apprehension of Milorad Krnojelac, former commander of the notorious Foca prison camp.

In December while in the U.K., Augusto Pinochet, former president of Chile, was made the subject of a criminal extradition request by the government of Spain for human rights abuses during his regime. Although this request was initially rejected by the British courts on the basis of Pinochet's diplomatic immunity and the principle that former heads of state cannot be prosecuted by other countries, this decision was overturned by the House of Lords appeals court. It found that immunity did not apply to perpetrators of massive human rights violations on the scale committed during the Pinochet regime, marking the first time that abuses other than those associated with wars or internal armed conflicts were found subject to criminal sanctions. Later in the month, however, the House of Lords voided the decision and scheduled a rehearing in January 1999.

The 50th Anniversary of the Universal Declaration of Human Rights. At UN headquarters in Geneva, where the 50th-anniversary celebration took place, representatives from a number of nations stressed universality—paying equal attention to the economic, social, and developmental side of the human rights equation—rather than focusing primarily on political and civil rights concerns.

Amnesty International designated U.S. human rights compliance its major annual campaign theme and identified a diverse range of problems requiring attention, including the broadening use of the death penalty and its discriminatory impact on the poor and people of colour, the continued application of the death penalty to juvenile offenders in violation of international standards, abusive treatment of prisoners in the criminal justice system, and failure to comply with provisions in the Refugee and Torture Conventions preventing the return of victims of torture and persecution to their countries of origin.

Human Rights Violations Involving Women. Considerable attention was given to the discriminatory treatment of females im-

As Commissioner of the European Union Emma Bonino (right) looks on, a female physician from Afghanistan describes the repression of women by the Muslim Taliban regime at a news conference in Brussels on February 3. Among other human rights violations, Afghan females were denied the right to go to school and work outside the home.

posed under the extremist Muslim Taliban regime in Afghanistan. A report by a UN monitoring team found a wide range of human rights violations, including pronouncements prohibiting women and girls from leaving their homes without accompaniment, requiring women to wear heavily veiled clothing, and denying females the right to attend school and to be employed outside the home. These edicts were enforced by armed members of the Ministry for the Propagation of Islamic Orders and the Discouragement of Islamic Prohibitions, informally referred to as the department of vice and virtue, which patrolled the streets and arrested and assaulted violators of the rules.

A number of initiatives were aimed at documenting and ending the practice of forced prostitution and sex trafficking, especially in Southeast Asia. Illegal sex trafficking had been found rampant among Myanmar (Burmese) women and girls, many of whom were forced into prostitution and sex slavery in Thailand and, as a result, had a high incidence of HIV infection and AIDS.

Other Developments. Nigeria, which had suffered under one of the most repressive regimes in recent years, made an initial movement toward a more democratic government following the death in June of Gen. Sani Abacha; a potential successor, opposition leader Moshood Abiola, who had been imprisoned by Abacha after winning a 1993 presidential election, also died prior to being released. (*See* OBITUARIES.) This left an aide to Abacha, Gen. Abdulsalam Abubakar (*see* BIOGRAPHIES), as president. Abubakar took some initial steps toward democratic reform by releasing some former political prisoners and promising to hold new elections in 1999.

With a series of new detentions of political dissidents, China continued to be the focus of human rights concerns. A nine-day visit to China by U.S. Pres. Bill Clinton produced a major debate over whether the promotion of economic and political ties with Chinese leaders was a more effective method of improving human rights conditions than the adoption of more direct forms of confrontation and public criticism. As a result of Clinton's visit, Wang Dan and other well-known political prisoners were released, but other dissidents were arrested.

Facing severe economic difficulties, Indonesia replaced the longest-serving leader in Asia, President Suharto (*see* BIOGRAPHIES), who had been accused of major human rights violations, including the invasion of the Portuguese dependent territory of East Timor and suppression of the independence movement there. Several senior military officers—notably Lieut. Gen. Praboewo Subianto, director of the special forces unit known as Kopassus, which was implicated in numerous political kidnappings and disappearances during Suharto's regime—were called before a specially constituted Military Honor Council, which sought to improve the military's image by looking into past human rights violations. The council court-martialed 10 soldiers for kidnappings, beatings, and torture of civilians.

In April former Cambodian leader Pol Pot died in captivity (*see* OBITUARIES); he had carried out a policy of widespread genocide against political opponents in an action widely known as "the killing fields." Hun Sen, who replaced him, was cited by a UN report as responsible for the murders of nearly 100 political opponents since his successful 1997 coup. The UN Security Council was asked to consider the possibility of establishing a third war crimes tribunal for Cambodia—similar to those established for former Yugoslavia and Rwanda—to investigate Pol Pot's genocide and prosecute those responsible.

Despite some signs of more effective action by its UN-created war crimes tribunal, including the issuance of 21 indictments and the beginning of several trials, Rwanda was widely condemned for carrying out public executions of 22 suspected war criminals among several thousands being held for their roles in the 1994 genocide. An additional 100 remained under death sentences imposed by Rwandan authorities without fair trials.

There was a marked increase in Mexico of reports of torture, disappearances, and violence committed against civilians in the state of Chiapas, where indigenous Zapatistas demanded greater autonomy and political power. Human rights observers were barred from the region by the government and expelled from the country following massive demonstrations and police crackdowns in the aftermath of a massacre by paramilitary death squads in the town of Acteal. A large number of civilians, mostly women and children, were killed with weapons that reportedly came from a local police commander, who claimed he was acting under government orders.

South Africa's Truth and Reconciliation Commission issued its final report documenting the massive violations that occurred during the apartheid era. The Commission was widely praised for conducting a thorough investigation of past abuses and for mandating full disclosure by violators before granting them immunity from criminal prosecution.   (MORTON SKLAR)

Senior Citizen Housing

by Willem van Vliet

Demographic trends in industrialized countries worldwide showed a strong increase among older people. In 1998 Sweden was at the forefront of this development, with about 17% of its population aged 65 or older. Japan's population was aging faster than that of any other country and was projected to reach a record level of about 24% by 2025. Less-developed countries, with relatively younger populations, will age more slowly. The United States occupied a middle position. In 1996, 12.7% of its population was at least 65 years old. This percentage was expected to grow to 18.5% by 2025. The growth in the number of senior households will be especially strong among the oldest age groups. Projections indicated that the increasing number of people aged 85 and older will have significant implications for the design, planning, and management of housing and community environments.

In the late 1990s, more people than ever before were living longer lives in good health. In response to market demands by more affluent older persons seeking "active" lifestyles, the private sector produced age-restricted communities with a country-club ambience and a choice of leisure amenities. For another segment of the older population, however, advancing age was associated with increasing physical frailty, cognitive impairment, and economic vulnerability, requiring environments that were appropriately supportive.

Nursing Homes. In the U.S. and in much of Europe, about 5% of the population 65 and older resided in a nursing home.

A vast majority of these over 17,000 facilities were federally certified in the U.S. for Medicaid or Medicare reimbursement. They provided care to more than 1.7 million older persons, of whom more than 45% were 85 or older. Many nursing home residents suffered from chronic disabilities and serious functional limitations, and more than 80% needed assistance with bathing, dressing, walking, or eating.

Expenditures for nursing homes in the U.S. rose dramatically, from $1 billion in 1960 to $20 billion in 1980 to about $75 billion in 1997. More than one-third of this cost came from out-of-pocket payments by the residents and their families. Not only were nursing homes expensive, but their institutional character also stood in stark contrast to the residents' prior homes. The average nursing home contained more than 100 beds. National surveys found that most older people preferred aging-in-place in homelike environments. These preferences and the high costs of nursing homes helped produce a greater range of housing options.

Special Housing Options. In the past, the options of many older households in need of more supportive housing were restricted to institutional environments. By the end of the 1990s, however, a broader array of alternatives had emerged. These provided different combinations of services, care, and adapted design. The spectrum of available choices can be arranged to show a transition from independent to more dependent living arrangements providing full-time skilled care.

Among the former were *accessory units*—created in the space of single-family homes, with their own kitchen and bath and usually a separate entrance—and *Elder Cottage Housing Opportunity (ECHO) housing*, small movable homes designed especially to accommodate frail and disabled people and placed temporarily in the yard of a family member's home. Both offered potential social and economic benefits—companionship, added income, reduced rent, security, and mutual help. Such units were often restricted by land use reg-

(Left) In a swimming pool at a retirement community in Arizona, a group of elderly women practices synchronized swimming. Meeting the needs of senior citizens—an increasing number of whom are living longer lives and maintaining active lifestyles—is one of many challenges facing providers of senior citizen housing. (Above) Octogenarian Frank Wekstein pursues his passion for plants at an assisted-living community home in Florida. (Right) Noted American actress and entertainer Debbie Reynolds, on a visit to a nursing home in New Jersey, offers a portrait of herself to a fan.

ulations and resistance from local homeowners worried about a decline in property values. *Shared housing* and *single-room occupancy (SRO) units* catered to low-income elderly and provided minimal levels of support. In *congregate housing*, living units often had special design features (e.g., no thresholds between rooms) and communal areas for social activities and meals. They housed older persons whose incomes precluded more costly options such as age-restricted *retirement communities, assisted living facilities (ALFs),* or *Continuing Care Retirement Communities (CCRCs),* where an array of services was available against user-cost or on a for-profit basis.

In the U.S. ALFs increased rapidly to about 25,000 nationwide in 1998, becoming a $15 billion a year industry. Their estimated 700,000 residents occupied independent living units, while being able to take advantage of help tailored to their specific and changing needs. ALFs were not generally appropriate for persons requiring 24-hour skilled nursing or ongoing medical monitoring. Costs averaged $2,200 per month in 1996. It was not, however, unusual for new ALFs to charge in the $4,000 to $7,000 range, including meals. Nursing homes received about 60% of their revenue from the government, but 90% of the cost of assisted living was borne by the residents and their families. Regulatory oversight was still minimal, although changes were underway. Out of concerns over quality control and profitability, the industry established the Assisted Living Quality Coalition, in which major national organizations joined to develop performance measures and guidelines for minimum standards.

Aging-in-place. Approaches to housing provision for senior citizens that facilitate aging-in-place were fast gaining in popularity. They were favoured for not causing disruption of long established local social support networks and for allowing people to grow older in a familiar environment.

Programs promoting aging-in-place tended to be of two types. The first focused on architectural adaptations, technological innovations, and home automation. For example, many countries developed guidelines for universal design and adaptable housing that could be easily modified in response to the changing needs of the occupants. Such guidelines, in the form of recommendations or enforceable by law, might specify minimum doorwidth to accommodate wheelchairs or provisions for attaching grab bars on a bathroom wall. The second type of program made available supportive services in or near the home, including help with shopping, housekeeping, personal and health care.

A basic assumption behind aging-in-place was that it presupposed that the place to stay put in was a good one. This was not always the case, however. Many older persons lived in housing that was substandard, vermin-infested, or costly. In the U.S. housing costs were excessive for 64% of all renters and 14% of all owners aged 65 or older. These percentages were higher yet among Hispanics and African-Americans. There were also elderly who lived in neighbourhoods that were crime-ridden or isolated, without easy access to grocery stores, medical care, and social services. In these communities older people who could afford it moved away to better places. Others who were not so fortunate remained behind. For them, aging-in-place was an oppressive experience.

Broader Context. The broader context for senior citizen housing was set by a nation's general system of housing provision and the wider political economy and culture of which it was a part. In the developing world and the Far East, for example, strong traditions of filial care were undergoing change as a result of urbanization and modernization processes. In the U.S. the wider context was a market-based system, propelled by a private profit motive. Access to housing and services was chiefly a function of ability to pay a price resulting from a situation where supply would only respond to demand if it resulted in financial gain. Research in several advanced industrial economies showed how, under these circumstances, socioeconomic inequality in society at large was perpetuated and accentuated by the intergenerational transfer of wealth in the form of housing. At the same time senior citizens who could not translate their housing and service needs into an effective market demand were dependent on assistance programs put in place by public and nonprofit agencies. Their reliance on low fixed incomes, the increasing cost of housing, the loss of SRO units, and the erosion of the safety net magnified the challenges of meeting the housing needs of senior citizens. Indeed, older men and women made up a growing segment of the homeless.

Willem van Vliet is a professor in the College of Architecture and Planning at the University of Colorado and editor of The Encyclopedia of Housing *(1998).*

Sports and Games

St. Louis Cardinals first baseman Mark McGwire (see BIOGRAPHIES), who set major league baseball's new single-season record by belting 70 home runs in 1998, pumped life into a sport suffering from waning popularity, but his exploits also fueled the debate over the use of performance-enhancing drugs. McGwire admitted he had been using androstenedione—a testosterone-boosting compound—for more than a year. Chicago Cubs right fielder Sammy Sosa (see BIOGRAPHIES), whose 66 home runs also broke the previous record, admitted to using creatine, a popular amino-acid powder used to build muscle. Although neither substance was prohibited and both were available for over-the-counter purchase since being deregulated by the U.S. Food and Drug Administration in 1994, questions abounded about their long-term effects on the human body. Androstenedione had been banned by the National Football League, the International Olympic Committee, and the National Collegiate Athletics Association. Additional concerns arose regarding the influence national heroes such as McGwire and Sosa had on young people, who could come to view such risky practices as acceptable or even necessary to succeed.

In cycling one Tour de France team, Festina, was expelled from the 1998 race following the discovery of drugs in its possession. Two American track-and-field athletes, Olympic gold medalists shotputter Randy Barnes and sprinter Dennis Mitchell, were suspended by the sport's governing body for suspected drug use. Irish swimmer Michelle Smith-de Bruin, a three-time Olympic gold medalist, and members of the Chinese national swim team were banned from competition on the basis of drug-related matters. The U.S., Canada, and Australia entered into an agreement that allowed for reciprocal drug testing of athletes from any of the three nations, along with cooperative research into banned substances.

Australia was the big winner at the Commonwealth Games, held September 11–21 in Kuala Lumpur, Malaysia. Led by its swimmers, who won 23 gold medals in their events, Australia won 198 medals, 62 more than the English, their closest competitors. New Zealand took the gold in the games' first-ever rugby competition, and South Africa prevailed in the inaugural cricket competition. At the made-for-television Goodwill Games, held in New York City July 19–August 2, tragedy overshadowed a field of big-name winners as Chinese gymnast Sang Lan was paralyzed when she suffered a neck injury during a practice vault.

American balloonist Steve Fossett broke his own distance record during a fourth failed attempt to circumnavigate the globe. Fossett had traveled two-thirds of the way around the world when a storm ripped his balloon and sent him plunging into the Coral Sea off the coast of Australia. He was rescued in good condition by a passing yacht. Fossett's 1996 attempt had failed after just 36 hours; his 1997 attempt set the previous long-distance record before a fuel shortage forced him to land in India; and his third attempt ended after five days and 9,337 km (5,802 mi). (ANTHONY G. CRAINE)

ARCHERY

The 1998 European championships, four days of competition in the Olympic and compound bow divisions, were held in Boe, France, in August. The qualifying rounds were shot at 90 m, 70 m, 50 m, and 30 m, and the championship one-on-one rounds were all shot at 70 m (1 m=3.28 ft). The men's Olympic bow winner was Baljinima Tsyrempilov of Russia, with Lionel Torres of France second and Igor Parkhomenko of Ukraine third. The women's champion was Lina Pavchuk of Ukraine, with Vladlena Priestman of the U.K. second and Natalia Valeeva of Italy third. The compound bow men's champion was Randall Thomas of France, with Dejan Sitar of Slovenia second and Peter Andersson of Sweden third. In the women's division Fabiola Palazzini of Italy finished first, with Fatima Agudo of Spain second and Maryann Richardson of the U.K. third.

The National Archery Association (NAA) of the U.S. held its outdoor national championships in August in Canton, Mich. They consisted of two internationally sanctioned rounds shot at 90 m, 70 m, 50 m, and 30 m over four days of competition. The compound men's winner was Matt Cleland with

a record score of 2,760 out of a possible 2,880; Roger Hoyle placed second and Pete Swanney third. The women's compound winner was Sally Wunderle; Tara Swanney placed second and Jamie Van Natta third. The Olympic bow men's winner was Victor Wunderle with a score of 2,634 out of a possible 2,880; Jason McKittrick placed second and Justin Huish third. In the women's Olympic bow division, Janet Dykman outshot Denise Parker (second) and Ruth Rowe (third) to win the title with a score of 2,615 out of 2,880.

The NAA held its 18-m indoor championships in March at three locations. Richard Johnson won the men's Olympic bow division, and Ruth Rowe was the women's champion. The senior compound winners were Dave Cousins and Tara Swanney.

(LARRY WISE)

AUTOMOBILE RACING

Grand Prix Racing. The 1998 season of Formula One Grand Prix competition featured a series of hotly contested races as widely dispersed as Australia, Brazil, Argentina, San Marino, Spain, Monaco (with the sole remaining true road course),

DAVID GRAY—REUTERS

Kim Jo Sun (left) watches intently as teammate Lee Mi Jeong prepares to release a shot during the women's archery competition at the 13th Asian Games, held in Bangkok in December. Kim and Lee were members of the South Korean team that captured first place with a score of 494 points, a new world record.

FITA Outdoor World Target Archery Championships*				
Year	Men's individual		Men's team	
	Winner	Points	Winner	Points
1989	S. Zabrodsky (U.S.S.R.)	332	U.S.S.R.	985
1991	S. Fairweather (Austl.)	334	South Korea	998
1993	Park Kyung Mo (S.Kor.)	113	France	249
1995	Lee Kyung Chul (S.Kor.)	109	South Korea	255
1997	Kim Kyung Ho (S.Kor.)	108	South Korea	254
Year	Women's individual		Women's team	
	Winner	Points	Winner	Points
1989	Kim Soo Nyung (S.Kor.)	338	South Korea	995
1991	Kim Soo Nyung (S.Kor.)	333	South Korea	1,030
1993	Kim Hyo Jung (S.Kor.)	104	South Korea	236
1995	N. Valeyeva (Moldova)	113	South Korea	247
1997	Kim Du Ri (S.Kor.)	105	South Korea	242

*Olympic (recurve) division.

JEROME DELAY—AP/WIDE WORLD; LIONEL CIRONNEAU—AP/WIDE WORLD

(Above) Finnish race-car driver Mika Hakkinen maneuvers his McLaren-Mercedes around a difficult hairpin turn en route to winning the Monaco Grand Prix on May 24. (Right) After capturing the pole position during a practice run the day before the race, an elated Hakkinen gives a thumbs-up—a familiar gesture for him in 1998. With eight victories during the year, Hakkinen became the new world champion of Grand Prix racing.

Canada, France, the U.K., Austria, Germany, Hungary, Belgium, Italy, Luxembourg, and Japan. The season boasted a variety of circuits, the most advanced high-tech cars, and an intense rivalry for the annual Drivers' World Championship and the Constructors' Championship between defending champion Michael Schumacher of Germany in a Ferrari and Finnish driver Mika Hakkinen for McLaren-Mercedes. With millions of television viewers, worldwide interest was maintained at a high level.

In each race, which was of approximately two hours duration and somewhat less than 322 km (200 mi), every aspect of each racing car's performance was monitored by means of telemetry in the pits. Thus, modern Grand Prix racing, though ultimately the task of a driver, was closely related to the engineers and technicians who were in con-tinual contact with him via his headphones. With many millions of dollars invested by sponsors, competition was acute.

Another rivalry on the track in 1998 was the tire war between the American supplier Goodyear and the newly competing Japanese tire maker Bridgestone. Tires used during a race were of great importance, as drivers and crews faced a choice of three types of tire depending on whether the track surface was really wet, only partially slippery, or dry. Race results sometimes depended on the timing of pit stops for refueling and tire changing, which could occupy anything from about six seconds to nine seconds or more. Goodyear decided not to make racing tires for Formula One in 1999, to the great regret of many teams.

Race regulations were revised before the 1998 season, requiring less wing area (thus

Formula One Grand Prix Race Results, 1998		
Race	**Driver**	**Winner's time (hr:min:sec)**
Australian GP	M. Hakkinen	1:31:45.996
Brazilian GP	M. Hakkinen	1:37:11.747
Argentine GP	M. Schumacher	1:48:36.175
San Marino GP	D. Coulthard	1:34:24.593
Spanish GP	M. Hakkinen	1:33:37.621
Monaco GP	M. Hakkinen	1:51:23.595
Canadian GP	M. Schumacher	1:40:57.355
French GP	M. Schumacher	1:34:45.026
British GP	M. Schumacher	1:47:12.450
Austrian GP	M. Hakkinen	1:30:44.086
German GP	M. Hakkinen	1:20:47.984
Hungarian GP	M. Schumacher	1:45:25.550
Belgian GP	D. Hill	1:43:14.407
Italian GP	M. Schumacher	1:17:09.672
Luxembourg GP	M. Hakkinen	1:32:14.789
Japanese GP	M. Hakkinen	1:27:22.535

WORLD DRIVERS' CHAMPIONSHIP: Hakkinen 100 points, Schumacher 86 points, Coulthard 56 points.
CONSTRUCTORS' CHAMPIONSHIP: McLaren-Mercedes 156 points, Ferrari 133 points, Williams-Mecachrome 38 points.

International Cup for Formula One Manufacturers			
Year	**Car**	**Year**	**Car**
1993	Williams/Renault	1996	Williams/Renault
1994	Williams/Renault	1997	Williams/Renault
1995	Benetton/Renault	**1998**	**McLaren/Mercedes**

World Championship of Drivers		
Year	**Winner**	**Car**
1994	M. Schumacher (Ger.)	Benetton/Ford
1995	M. Schumacher (Ger.)	Benetton/Renault
1996	D. Hill (U.K.)	Williams/Renault
1997	J. Villeneuve (Can.)	Williams/Renault
1998	**M. Hakkinen (Fin.)**	**McLaren/Mercedes**

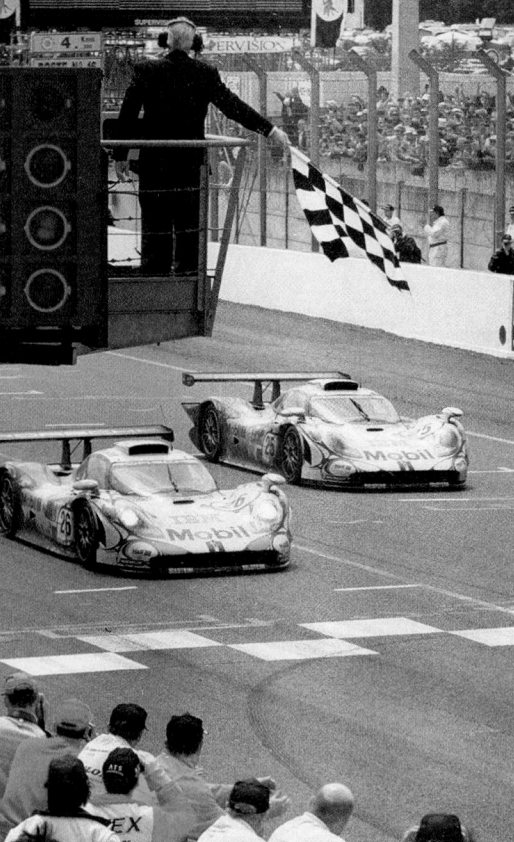

Driving the last leg of the Le Mans 24-hour race for the Porsche team, Stephane Ortelli (left) powers his car past the checkered flag in first place, giving Porsche its third consecutive victory in the grueling event.

Le Mans 24-Hour Grand Prix d'Endurance		
Year	Car	Drivers
1994	Dauer Porsche	Y. Dalmas, H. Haywood, M. Baldi
1995	McLaren	Y. Dalmas, J.J. Lehto, M. Sekiya
1996	Joest TWR Porsche	M. Reuter, D. Jones, A. Wurz
1997	Joest Porsche	M. Alboreto, S. Johansson, T. Kristensen
1998	**Porsche GT1**	**A. McNish, L. Aiello, S. Ortelli**

Monte-Carlo Rally		
Year	Car	Driver
1994	Ford Escort	Delecour
1995	Subaru Impreza	Sainz
1996	Ford Escort	Bernardini
1997	Subaru	Liatti
1998	**Toyota Corolla**	**Sainz**

reducing downforce on the wheels) and a narrower tire section, but these changes made very little difference to the speeds, which could exceed 322 km/h (200 mph) on long straight sections. Interest was increased by the entry of three-time world champion Jackie Stewart's team of Stewart-Fords, powered with the Zetc-R V10 engine and driven by Stewart's son Paul and Rubens Barrichello. Former world champion Alain Prost of France was running a new team of Peugeot-powered Prosts, but neither team made a significant showing.

Damon Hill, the 1996 British world champion, drove a Jordan Mugen-Honda after his defection from the Arrows team, but, although he occasionally showed some of his former skills and a few good results, he failed to repeat the success of his rides for Williams-Renault. At the beginning of the

season the McLaren-Mercedes cars with British-built Ilmor power units were dominant, but Ferrari staged a steady comeback, and so the question arose as to whether Schumacher in a Ferrari would take the title for the third time or would the Drivers' Championship go to his Finnish rival. Hakkinen drove his McLaren-Mercedes magnificently at Barcelona and on the difficult streets of Monaco. He was victorious at Melbourne, Australia, where his teammate, David Coulthard of Scotland, waved him to pass after a controversial agreement that whichever man got to the first corner first should lead. In the rain at Silverstone in England, Hakkinen held a fearful spin at some 258 km/h (160 mph), but it was Schumacher and Ferrari that took the finishing flag.

In the Luxembourg Grand Prix, over the testing Nürburgring track in Germany, Hakkinen outdrove Schumacher, and he won at Hockenheim, Ger., in spite of worries that not enough fuel was left in his car. It was apparent, however, that Schumacher was the best driver in Formula One, with thoughtful pre-race planning, extremely quick driving, and the ability to snap past slower cars. Under Jean Todt, Ferrari's racing manager, the Italian cars improved with each race in spite of such unfortunate incidents as a broken suspension at Monaco, a collision with Coulthard's McLaren at a corner in the Belgian Grand Prix, an engine breakdown at Melbourne, and racing on an unsuitable type of Goodyear tire at Nürburgring. Consequently, before the decisive final race at Japan's Suzuka circuit Hakkinen and Schumacher had an equal number of championship points.

After one false start, Schumacher stalled his engine on the starting line, and the race had to be stopped again. When it was restarted, Schumacher, from the required back of the grid, drove the race of his career, coming up through the field unbeliev-

ably quickly and cleanly, although Hill was difficult to overtake after the slower cars had been picked off. After the pit stops it might have been a race to the end, but debris on the road burst one of the Ferrari's back tires, which ended the race for Schumacher. Hakkinen, who achieved his eighth win of the season, was a delighted world champion. Schumacher, with six victories, finished second in the Drivers' Championship, and Coulthard, who won in San Marino, was third.   (WILLIAM C. BODDY)

Rallies and Other Races. Hakkinen was not the only Finnish auto racing champion in 1998, as Tommi Mäkinen (Mitsubishi) captured a record third consecutive world rally title. Two-time overall champion

Stock-car-racing king Jeff Gordon celebrates in the victory lane following his win at the AC Delco 400 in Rockingham, N.C., on November 1. He clinched his third NASCAR Winston Cup championship with the win and tied Richard Petty's record of 13 victories in one season.

In his ninth try at the Indianapolis 500, veteran driver Eddie Cheever, Jr., crosses the finish line in May to win the world's oldest auto race. He beat Buddy Lazier by 3.191 seconds after taking the lead for good on the 178th lap. Cheever took home $1.4 million for the victory, the most memorable triumph in his long racing career.

Carlos Sainz of Spain, who had returned to Toyota after five years of driving with other teams, started the season in January with his third Monte-Carlo rally victory and came within 300 m (984 ft) of defeating Mäkinen for the overall title. In the final event of the season, the Rally of Britain, with Mäkinen already out of the race and Sainz ensconced in fourth place, the Spanish driver needed only to finish to overtake his rival for the championship. Just 300 m short of the finish line, however, the engine of Sainz's Toyota caught fire, putting him out of the race. Toyota also came close to its first victory in the grueling Le Mans 24-hour endurance race, but gearbox problems forced the Toyota GT1 into the pits and allowed Porsche to win for the third straight time. The Porsche drivers—Alan McNish, Laurent Aiello, and Stephane Ortelli—covered some 4,789 km (2,974 mi) at an average 199.6 km/h (124 mph).

U.S. Auto Racing. Jeff Gordon and his Dupont Refinishes Chevrolet Monte Carlo team (headed by crew chief Ray Evernham) dominated the National Association for Stock Car Auto Racing (NASCAR) in 1998, the 50th year of competition for the U.S.'s largest and most diverse form of auto competition. Gordon, age 27, became the youngest driver to win three NASCAR Winston Cup championships and tied Richard Petty's record of 13 victories in one season (1975). He also amassed more than $6 million in race winnings, as he easily surpassed the Fords of Dale Jarrett ($3.3 million), Mark Martin ($3 million), and Rusty Wallace (approximately $2 million), who followed him in the final standings. Later he spurned feelers to switch to Formula One racing or any form of single-seat automobile competition. His multicoloured car was particularly potent in Winston Cup's classic races. After seven-time season titlist Dale Earnhardt (Chevrolet) won $1,059,105 in the Daytona 500, at an average speed of 172.712 mph, Gordon won the Brickyard 400 at Indianapolis Motor Speedway, the Pepsi Southern 500 at Darlington, S.C., and the longest event, the Coca-Cola 600 at Charlotte, N.C. Some 25 drivers earned $1 million or more from the 33-race Winston Cup series. Meanwhile, Dale Earnhardt, Jr., son of the Daytona victor, won the Busch Series season crown, and Ron Hornaday captured the Craftsman Truck title.

In open-wheel, single-seater racing, owner-driver Eddie Cheever, Jr., won the world's oldest race, the 82nd Indianapolis 500, and $1.4 million by 3.191 seconds over

Indy Car Champions*	
Year	Driver
1994	A. Unser, Jr.
1995	J. Villeneuve
1996	J. Vasser
1997	A. Zanardi
1998	**A. Zanardi**

*CART champion.

Indianapolis 500		
Year	Winner	Avg. speed in mph
1994	A. Unser, Jr.	160.872
1995	J. Villeneuve	153.616
1996	B. Lazier	147.956
1997	A. Luyendyk	145.827
1998	**E. Cheever, Jr.**	**145.155**

National Association for Stock Car Auto Racing (NASCAR) Winston Cup Champions	
Year	Winner
1994	D. Earnhardt
1995	J. Gordon
1996	T. Labonte
1997	J. Gordon
1998	**J. Gordon**

Buddy Lazier in a similar Dallara-chassied Aurora. It was the former Grand Prix driver's ninth try at Indy. Former Formula 2000 driver Steve Knapp in a G-Force–chassied Aurora was third, with Davey Hamilton (G-Force Aurora) and Cheever's teammate Robby Unser completing the top five. Average speed was 145.155 mph, well below pole-position winner Billy Boat's 223.503 mph. The race, which was part of an 11-event Pep Boys Indy Racing League (IRL) season, paid a total purse of $8.7 million. The increasing depth of driver talent showed in IRL's final standings, as Kenny Brack, a 32-year-old Swede driving for the A.J. Foyt team, finished first for the season, besting Hamilton and Tony Stewart. The three-year-old IRL displayed increasing strength against its rival Championship Auto Racing Teams (CART) with successful events on NASCAR super speedways.

The Target/Chip Ganassi Racing team Reynard-Honda dominated the 19-event CART FedEx U.S. Auto Racing series for the third season in a row: Alex Zanardi won the championship by 285–169 over teammate Jimmy Vasser. Dario Franchitti (also in a Reynard-Honda) was third, with Adrian Fernandez (Reynard-Ford) fourth and Greg Moore (Reynard-Mercedes) fifth. The series

was contested in Canada, Australia, and Brazil, as well as the U.S. Its season championship, however, was decided long before its richest race, the California Marlboro 500. By winning the million-dollar first prize there, Vasser out-earned his Formula One–bound champion teammate, Zanardi, $1,589,250 to $1,219,250. Franchitti was the only other CART star to accumulate a million dollars in prizewinnings. In one of the closest races of the season, Vasser finished 0.360 sec ahead of Moore at an average speed of 153.785 mph in the California 500. Zanardi was third, Fernandez fourth, and Mauricio Gugelmin (Reynard-Mercedes) fifth. The fastest qualifier was Scott Pruett (Ford) at 233.748 mph.

The Rolex 24 Hours of Daytona, sanctioned in 1998 by a new combination of the Sports Car Club of America (SCCA) and the U.S. Road Racing Club, remained the premier event of its kind in the U.S. Ferrari won its first Daytona overall victory in 31 years. The drivers of the Momo 333SP were owner Gianpiero Moretti plus Arie Luyendyk, Mauro Baldi, and Didier Theys. The margin of victory was eight laps of the 3.56-mi course over the GT-1 class winner, a Porsche 911 driven by Danny Sullivan, Allan McNish, Jorg Mueller, Dirk Mueller, and Uwe Alzen. Paul Gentilozzi's Rocketsports Corvette became champion of the SCCA's oldest pro series, the Trans-American. (ROBERT J. FENDELL)

BADMINTON

Many badminton experts were surprised when 20-year-old Peter Gade Christensen of Denmark finished 1997 on top of the men's singles world rankings. At the Japan Open in January 1998, however, Gade Christensen easily defeated Luo Yigang of China to win the sport's first major event of the year and proved his number-one status was no accident. Gong Zhichao of China rose to the top of the women's singles world rankings by way of her victory over compatriot and top seed Ye Zhaoying.

The All-England Championships in March were characterized by early defeats of the world's number-one singles players. Zhang Ning of China upset Gong Zhichao and reached the final, only to lose to Ye Zhaoying. In the men's event Ong Ewe Hock of Malaysia defeated Gade Christensen in the third round and advanced to the final, where Sun Jun of China prevailed. Chinese players claimed a third title when world women's doubles champions

All-England Championships—Singles		
Year	Men	Women
1994	H. Arbi (Indon.)	S. Susanti (Indon.)
1995	P.-E. Hoyer-Larsen (Den.)	Lim Xiao Qing (Swed.)
1996	P.-E. Hoyer-Larsen (Den.)	Bang Soo Hyun (S.Kor.)
1997	Dong Jiong (China)	Ye Zhaoying (China)
1998	**Sun Jun (China)**	**Ye Zhaoying (China)**

Uber Cup (women)		
Year	Winner	Runner-up
1989–90	China	S.Korea
1991–92	China	S.Korea
1993–94	Indonesia	China
1995–96	Indonesia	China
1997–98	**China**	**Indonesia**

Thomas Cup (men)		
Year	Winner	Runner-up
1989–90	China	Malaysia
1991–92	Malaysia	Indonesia
1993–94	Indonesia	Malaysia
1995–96	Indonesia	Denmark
1997–98	**Indonesia**	**Malaysia**

World Badminton Championships				
Year	Men's singles	Women's singles	Men's doubles	Women's doubles
1989	Yang Yang (China)	Li Lingwei (China)	Li Yongbo, Tian Bingyi (China)	Lin Ying, Guan Weizhen (China)
1991	Zhao Jianhua (China)	Tang Jiuhong (China)	Park Joo Bong, Kim Moon Soo (S.Kor.)	Guan Weizhen, Nong Qunhua (China)
1993	J. Suprianto (Indon.)	S. Susanti (Indon.)	R. Subagja, R. Gunawan (Indon.)	Nong Qunhua, Zhou Lei (China)
1995	H. Arbi (Indon.)	Ye Zhaoying (China)	R. Subagja, R. Mainaky (Indon.)	Gil Young Ah, Jang Hye Ock (S.Kor.)
1997	P. Rasmussen (Den.)	Ye Zhaoying (China)	B. Sigit, C. Wijaya (Indon.)	Ge Fei, Gu Jun (China)

Ge Fei and Gu Jun eliminated Ra Kyung Min and Jang Hye Ock of South Korea. South Korean players captured the men's doubles and mixed doubles titles.

The Uber Cup and Thomas Cup competitions—the women's and men's world team championships, respectively—were staged in Hong Kong in May. The Indonesian men's team emphasized its dominance by winning its third consecutive Thomas Cup, with a 3–2 victory over Malaysia. The superb singles play of Indonesia's Hendrawan—in his first Thomas Cup appearance—established him as a new international badminton star. Four months later Hendrawan gave another glimpse of his promising future by defeating Sun Jun and Gade Christensen in the Singapore Open. The Chinese women's team regained the Uber Cup title with a 4–1 win over defending champion Indonesia. Key matches were Ye Zhaoying's defeat of Indonesia's Susi Susanti and Gong Zhichao's triumph as she came back from three match points down in the second set to vanquish Mia Audina. As 1998 drew to a close, Susanti, one of the game's legendary competitors, announced her retirement.   (DONN GOBBIE)

BASEBALL

Energized by an unprecedented home-run barrage featuring sluggers Mark McGwire and Sammy Sosa (*see* BIOGRAPHIES), in 1998 major league baseball produced a season that was hailed as the "greatest ever" by some experts. With two expansion franchises—the Arizona Diamondbacks and Tampa Bay Devil Rays—attracting more than 6.1 million spectators, National League (NL) and American League (AL) teams combined for a record paid attendance in excess of 70 million fans.

World Series. The New York Yankees, baseball's most storied franchise, won their second World Series in three years and their 24th in 35 attempts by sweeping the San Diego Padres four games to none in the best-of-seven series. The Yankees kicked off the World Series in dramatic fashion, beating the Padres 9–6 at Yankee Stadium in the opener on October 17. The Padres built a 5–2 lead behind their best pitcher, Kevin Brown, but the Yankees roared back with seven runs in the seventh inning. Chuck Knoblauch stroked a three-run home run to create a 5–5 tie before Tino Martinez ripped a grand slam off Mark Langston to enliven the crowd of 56,712. The next night the Yankees eased to a 9–3 triumph behind pitcher Orlando Hernández, whose brother Livan starred in 1997 for the world champion Florida Marlins. Bernie Williams and Jorge Posada each hit a two-run homer before 56,692 spectators. In two games the Yankees had collected 18 runs and 25 hits.

Final Major League Standings, 1998											
AMERICAN LEAGUE											
East Division				**Central Division**				**West Division**			
Club	W.	L.	G.B.	Club	W.	L.	G.B.	Club	W.	L.	G.B.
New York*	114	48	—	Cleveland*	89	73	—	Texas*	88	74	—
Boston*	92	70	22	Chicago	80	82	9	Anaheim	85	77	3
Toronto	88	74	26	Kansas City	72	89	16½	Seattle	76	85	11½
Baltimore	79	83	35	Minnesota	70	92	19	Oakland	74	88	14
Tampa Bay	63	99	51	Detroit	65	97	24				
NATIONAL LEAGUE											
East Division				**Central Division**				**West Division**			
Club	W.	L.	G.B.	Club	W.	L.	G.B.	Club	W.	L.	G.B.
Atlanta*	106	56	—	Houston*	102	60	—	San Diego*	98	64	—
New York	88	74	18	Chicago*	89	73	13	San Francisco	89	73	9
Philadelphia	75	87	31	St. Louis	83	79	19	Los Angeles	83	79	15
Montreal	65	97	41	Cincinnati	77	85	25	Colorado	77	85	21
Florida	54	108	52	Milwaukee	74	88	28	Arizona	65	97	33
				Pittsburgh	69	93	33				

*Gained play-off berth.

World Series*			
Year	Winning team	Losing team	Results
1994	not held		
1995	Atlanta Braves (NL)	Cleveland Indians (AL)	4–2
1996	New York Yankees (AL)	Atlanta Braves (NL)	4–2
1997	Florida Marlins (NL)	Cleveland Indians (AL)	4–3
1998	**New York Yankees (AL)**	**San Diego Padres (NL)**	**4–0**

*AL—American League; NL—National League.

The Padres returned home for game three on October 20, but their fortunes did not change. The Yankees won 5–4, rallying from a 3–0 deficit. Scott Brosius hit two home runs, including a three-run blast in the eighth inning, to propel New York to victory before 64,667 fans. The Yankees completed their sweep one night later in San Diego, beating the Padres 3–0 behind the strong pitching of starter Andy Pettitte and Mariano Rivera, who closed for his third save of the series. The Yankees scored a single run in the sixth inning and two in the eighth against Brown before 65,427—the largest baseball crowd in Padres history.

The Yankees thus earned their first World Series sweep since 1950. Brosius, who batted only .203 for the Oakland A's in 1997 before being acquired in a trade, was voted Most Valuable Player (MVP) of the series. Combined with their regular-season record, the Yankees amassed 125 victories—the most of any team in history—and lost only 50.

Play-offs. The Yankees advanced to the World Series with relative ease. The AL East Division champions won three straight games in the best-of-five series over the Texas Rangers, who finished first in the West. In the other AL Division series, the Cleveland Indians of the Central Division defeated the Boston Red Sox in four games. The Red Sox qualified for the play-offs as a wild-card team (the best of the second-place teams in the league).

The Yankees beat the Indians 7–2 in the AL Championship Series opener

Scott Brosius jumps for joy as his New York Yankees complete their 4–0 sweep of the San Diego Padres in the World Series on October 21. His consistent play helped the Yankees to their second World Series title in three years and a place in baseball history as one of the greatest teams ever. Brosius was voted Most Valuable Player of the series.

ERIC DRAPER—AP/WIDE WORLD

Chicago Cubs star Sammy Sosa is hoisted into the air by teammates after smacking his 62nd home run to surpass Roger Maris's legendary home-run mark of 61. Although he went on to hit 66 homers for the season, Sosa was eclipsed by St. Louis Cardinals slugger Mark McGwire, who was the first to break Maris's record and who wound up with an amazing season total of 70 home runs.

at Yankee Stadium on October 6 but lost consecutive games to the Indians by 4–1 in New York and 6–1 in Cleveland. The Yankees drew even the next day, however, with a 4–0 conquest behind the strong pitching of Hernández. The Yankees won again 5–3 in Cleveland a day later, then clinched the pennant by vanquishing the Indians 9–5 in New York on October 13.

The Padres, who finished first in the NL West, began their postseason by defeating the Houston Astros, leaders in the Central Division, 2–1. Brown struck out a postseason record 16 batters in six innings. Houston won the next game at home 5–4 but lost by 2–1 and 6–1 in San Diego and was eliminated in four games. In the other NL Division series, the Atlanta Braves swept the wild-card entry, the Chicago Cubs, in three games.

The underdog Padres then stunned the Braves by winning the first three games of the NL Championship Series—by 3–2 and 3–0 in Atlanta and by 4–1 in San Diego. The Braves rallied to beat the Padres by 8–3 and 7–6, but upon returning to Atlanta, the Padres eliminated the Braves 5–0 on October 14.

Regular Season. The highlight of the regular season was the home-run chase waged by McGwire of the St. Louis Cardinals and Sosa of the Cubs. McGwire clubbed 70 home runs and Sosa 66. Thus, they both shattered the previous mark of Yankee Roger Maris, who hit 61 in 1961, and thereby broke the standard of 60 established by Yankee Babe Ruth in 1927.

Although Maris's record had lasted longer than Ruth's, baseball insiders thought 1998 might be a landmark season. The quality of pitching was deemed to have been thinned by the addition of the two new teams. McGwire had served warning by hitting 58 home runs in 1997. Sosa had never amassed more than 40 in any single season.

McGwire hit his first home run of the 1998 season in the Cardinals' opening game on March 31. Sosa waited until his fourth game to initiate his quest. After that, both men went off on their own, often hitting homers minutes apart. McGwire had a 27–13 advantage through May, but Sosa surged in June with 20, the most home runs by any major leaguer in any month. By August 31, tied at 55, both players were well ahead of Maris's pace and only one shy of the NL home-run record of 56 established by Chicago's Hack Wilson in 1930.

McGwire tied Maris on September 7 by hitting number 61 in St. Louis against Mike Morgan of the Cubs. The next night McGwire lined his shortest home run of the season—measured at 104 m (341 ft)—off Cub Steve Trachsel to reach the magical number 62. The game was interrupted for 11 minutes by spontaneous celebrations. McGwire entered the stands to share the moment with Maris's widow and family; Sosa jogged in from right field to hug the new home-run king.

On September 13 Sosa passed Maris by hitting his 61st and 62nd against the

Milwaukee Brewers at Chicago's Wrigley Field. McGwire tied Sosa at 66 on September 25, but in each of his last two home games, McGwire hit two home runs, the 70th coming on September 27 against Carl Pavano of the Montreal Expos with two out in the seventh inning. Throughout the odyssey McGwire and Sosa developed a long-distance friendship, and each credited the other for the double assault on baseball's most honoured achievement.

When Maris hit his 61st home run, it occurred in the last game of a 162-game schedule. Because Ruth had hit 60 in a 154-game schedule, Ford Frick, then the commissioner of baseball, required that Maris's accomplishment be accompanied by an appropriate explanation. The "asterisk" was subsequently removed. No such qualifiers were required for McGwire, who hit his 62nd homer in the Cardinals' 145th game, or Sosa, who reached 62 in his 150th game.

At the conclusion of the 162-game regular season, two teams vying for the NL wild-card spot were tied with identical records—the Cubs of the Central Division and the San Francisco Giants from the West. Thus, a one-game play-off was staged at Wrigley Field on September 28, and the Cubs won 5–3 to advance to their series against Atlanta.

Kerry Wood, a pitcher for the Cubs, tied the single-game record by striking out 20 Astros in a one-hit victory on May 6. In his next start Wood struck out 13

Diamondbacks, establishing a record for most strikeouts in consecutive games and earning him NL rookie of the year honours. Oakland outfielder Ben Grieve was named AL rookie of the year.

On May 17 David Wells of the Yankees pitched only the 15th perfect game in major league history. Cal Ripken, Jr., who broke Lou Gehrig's mark for most consecutive games played (2,130), voluntarily ended his streak on September 20 when he sat out after playing his 2,632nd game in a row.

Bernie Williams of the Yankees won the AL batting title with a .339 average. Ken Griffey, Jr., of the Seattle Mariners led the league in home runs with 56, and Juan Gonzalez of Texas led with 157 runs batted in. Gonzalez was later voted league MVP. Three pitchers won 20 games—Roger Clemens of the Toronto Blue Jays, who captured a record fifth AL Cy Young award, David Cone of the Yankees, and Rick Helling of Texas. Rickey Henderson of Oakland stole the most bases (66), and Boston's Tom Gordon recorded the most saves (46). With the output of Griffey and Greg Vaughn of San Diego, four players reached the 50-home-run mark for the first time in history. The Yankees' inspiring Joe Torre was named AL manager of the Year.

Larry Walker of the Colorado Rockies won the NL batting title with a .363 average. McGwire's 70 homers led the league, while Sosa, his season-long rival, paced the league in runs batted in (158) and was voted the league's MVP. Atlanta's Tom Glavine, who won his second NL Cy Young award, was the league's only 20-game winner. Tony Womack of the Pittsburgh Pirates had the most stolen bases (58), and Trevor Hoffman of San Diego the most saves (53). Larry Dierker of the Astros was voted the NL's top manager.

Barry Bonds of the Giants became the first player ever to hit 400 career home runs and steal 400 bases. Dennis Eckersley of the Red Sox made his 1,071st pitching appearance, surpassing Hoyt Wilhelm's record.

The Yankees, with 114 regular-season victories, broke the AL record of 111 established by Cleveland in 1954 but fell short of the Cubs' major league mark of 116. Atlanta posted the best record in the NL, 106–56. The Marlins, who had won the World Series in 1997, dispersed many of their best players for financial reasons and sagged to a record of 54–108, the poorest in either league.

Little League World Series. Toms River, N.J., defeated Kashima, Japan, by a score of 12–9 to win the Little League World Series

At the Little League World Series in Williamsport, Pa., on August 29, players from the Toms River, N.J., team mob outfielder Chris Cardonne (centre) following Cardonne's sixth-inning two-run homer. The home run gave Toms River a 10–8 lead over Kashima, Japan, and the team hung on for a 12–9 victory.

on August 29 in Williamsport, Pa. The championship was the first for a team from the U.S. since Long Beach, Calif., claimed the title in 1993.   (ROBERT WILLIAM VERDI)

Latin America. The 1998 Caribbean Series was held in Puerto La Cruz, Venez., February 3–8. The Northern Eagles (Águilas del Cibao), representing the Dominican Republic, went undefeated with a 6–0 record to win their second consecutive championship. Puerto Rico's entry, the Mayagüez Indians, finished second with a 4–2 record, and Mexico (Mazatlán) and Venezuela (Lara) tied for last place, both at 1–5.

Cuba posted a 9–0 record, including a 7–1 win over South Korea in the gold medal game to win the International Baseball Association's world championship in Italy in early August. Two weeks later the Cuban national team went undefeated in eight games, including a 13–3 win over Nicaragua, to win another gold medal at the Central American and Caribbean Games in Maracaibo, Venez.

The Oaxaca Warriors defeated the Monclova Steelers four games to none in the championship series of the Mexican League. It was the first title for Oaxaca, which was only in its third year of operation.

In major league baseball Atlanta Braves pitcher Dennis Martinez, from Nicaragua, posted his 245th win, surpassing the previous record of 243 for a pitcher from Latin America held by Juan Marichal from the Dominican Republic. Sammy Sosa (*see* BIOGRAPHIES), Chicago Cubs outfielder

from the Dominican Republic, hit 66 home runs during the 1998 season, topping the previous record of 47 for most homers by a player born in Latin America, which was held by George Bell (Dominican Republic), Andres Galarraga (Venezuela), and Juan Gonzalez (Puerto Rico). (MILTON JAMAIL)

Japan. The Yokohama BayStars of the Central League defeated the Seibu Lions of the Pacific League four games to two in the 1998 postseason best-of-seven Japan Series. It was the second time the BayStars, formerly the Taiyo Whales of Kawasaki and the only organization in Japanese baseball without the owning company's name in the team name, had advanced to the championship series. The last time was in 1960, when the Whales swept the series four games to none against the Daimai Orions of Tokyo.

Yokohama's manager, Hiroshi Gondo, who as a pitcher in the 1960s won 35 games and most of the pitching titles in his rookie year, won the championship in only his first year as manager. Gondo had revolutionized Japanese baseball in the 1970s when he introduced the notion of relief pitching. The BayStars of 1998 were close to the ideal for Gondo, with five solid starters, six long relievers, and a formidable short reliever, Kazuhiro Sasaki, whose record of 1 win, 1 loss, 45 saves, and an earned run average of 0.64 eventually earned him the vote as the Central League's Most Valuable Player.

All the season batting titles were won by left-handed batters: Hideki Matsui of the Yomiuri Giants, with 34 home runs and 100 runs batted in, and Takanori Suzuki of the BayStars, with a batting average of .337, in the Central League; Nigel Wilson (33 home runs and 124 runs batted in) of the Nippon Ham Fighters and Ichiro Suzuki (batting average .358) of the Orix BlueWave in the Pacific League. Especially noteworthy was Suzuki, who at the age of 24 had been the league's leading hitter for five straight years. (TOSHIHIKO SUZUKI)

Caribbean Series		
Year	Winning team	Country
1994	Licey Tigers	Dominican Republic
1995	San Juan Senators	Puerto Rico
1996	Culiacán Tomato Growers	Mexico
1997	Northern Eagles	Dominican Republic
1998	**Northern Eagles**	**Dominican Republic**

Japan Series*			
Year	Winning team	Losing team	Results
1994	Yomiuri Giants (CL)	Seibu Lions (PL)	4–2
1995	Yakult Swallows (CL)	Orix BlueWave (PL)	4–1
1996	Orix BlueWave (PL)	Yomiuri Giants (CL)	4–1
1997	Yakult Swallows (CL)	Seibu Lions (PL)	4–1
1998	**Yokohama BayStars (CL)**	**Seibu Lions (PL)**	**4–2**

*CL—Central League; PL—Pacific League.

BASKETBALL

United States. *Professional.* In 1998 the unsinkable Michael Jordan and the incomparable Chicago Bulls rolled to their sixth National Basketball Association (NBA) championship in eight years, capping a difficult 1997–98 season with their third straight crown. Along the way they left a trail of excitement and controversy throughout the country but especially in Chicago. Astonishingly, the long-playing feud between front-office boss Jerry Krause and Bulls coach Phil Jackson did not derail the title run. Neither did the animosity between Krause and Scottie Pippen (*see* BIOGRAPHIES), the second Bulls superstar. Incensed by the management's unwillingness to renegotiate his contract, Pippen repeatedly insisted he would finish his career elsewhere in the NBA.

Throughout the season, whenever the air got thick with charges and countercharges flying between Krause and his employees, "Air" Jordan would stage another of his routinely magnificent performances to put the spotlight back on basketball. His task was a little easier because Dennis Rodman's incentive-laden contract induced the flamboyant Bulls rebounding specialist to keep his customary attention-grabbing antics under wraps for most of the season.

In the play-offs Jordan, perhaps the world's most recognizable and respected athlete, saved his best for last. With the Bulls trailing in the last minute, he scored on a driving layup and a jump shot from the foul circle to beat the Utah Jazz 87–86 in the decisive sixth game of the finals. For the second straight year, Jordan frustrated Utah's Karl ("The Mailman") Malone and John Stockton in the title showdown, winning his sixth finals Most Valuable Player award (along with his fifth regular-season MVP) and proving he was still the NBA's best player.

When it all finally ended with another huge victory celebration in Chicago, Jackson kept his season-long promise to walk away from his coaching hot seat. "This was our last dance, and it was a wonderful waltz," Jackson said, casting a pall over the victory festivities. It was interpreted by many fearful Bulls fans as the first move toward breaking up this NBA dynasty. Immediately, the furor about Jordan's future reemerged. He repeatedly vowed to retire if Jackson and Pippen left the Bulls but then hedged during a summer of uncertainty.

The NBA owners added another complication—not just for Jordan but for the entire league—when they imposed a July 1 lockout over stalled negotiations for a new labour agreement with the NBA Players Association. The move put contract signings and player transfers between teams in limbo. It also gave Jordan, Pippen, and the Bulls some extra time to ponder the future of the franchise.

In women's basketball the Houston Comets, led by two-time MVP Cynthia Cooper, won its second consecutive Women's NBA title, beating the Phoenix Mercury 80–71 in the decisive final game in the best-of-three series. The Columbus Quest captured its second American Basketball League championship. On December 22 the ABL filed for bankruptcy and canceled the remainder of the season.

College. Those "Comeback Cats," the Kentucky Wildcats, continued an old tradition of success for a new keeper of their basketball flame in 1997–98. Coach Tubby Smith directed Kentucky to its seventh National Collegiate Athletic Association (NCAA) championship in his first season as head coach. It was a triumphal journey for the first African-American to hold that post, although far from an easy one. Utah opened a 10-point halftime lead on Smith's team in the San Antonio (Texas) Alamodome, a hole too deep to escape in any previous NCAA tournament final. Yet it was Kentucky pulling away at the end for a decisive 78–69 victory over the Runnin' Utes.

Few of Kentucky's rabid fans anticipated that Smith would so swiftly fill the shoes of departed coach Rick Pitino, whose popularity had reached near-cult status. After taking the Wildcats to the 1996 national championship and then losing 1997's title game to Arizona in overtime, Pitino had moved to the NBA, accepting a lucrative offer to coach the Boston Celtics. Despite having such a difficult act to follow, Smith won over the skeptics with his confident coaching style and sense of humour.

Kentucky needed all of that togetherness to reach the Final Four for the third straight year in the wide-open NCAA tournament. In early rounds the Wildcats had to come from behind in the second half to erase a 17-point deficit against Duke and wipe out Stanford's 10-point edge. Utah, however, coached by the popular Rick Majerus, provided the sternest test. Paced by centre Michael Doleac, the Runnin' Utes relied on their season-long staples, rebounding and defense, to take a 41–31 lead into the intermission. After that, Kentucky double-teamed Doleac, and fatigue

Chicago Bulls star forward Scottie Pippen (left) keeps the ball out of the reach of Utah Jazz guard Jeff Hornacek in Game 6 of the NBA championship finals. Stellar play by Pippen and teammate Michael Jordan helped Chicago win the game and clinch the best-of-seven series, giving the Bulls their sixth NBA title in eight years.

National Basketball Association (NBA) Championship			
Season	Winner	Runner-up	Results
1993–94	Houston Rockets	New York Knicks	4–3
1994–95	Houston Rockets	Orlando Magic	4–0
1995–96	Chicago Bulls	Seattle SuperSonics	4–2
1996–97	Chicago Bulls	Utah Jazz	4–2
1997–98	**Chicago Bulls**	**Utah Jazz**	**4–2**

NBA Final Standings, 1997–98											
EASTERN CONFERENCE						WESTERN CONFERENCE					
Team	Won	Lost	Team	Won	Lost	Team	Won	Lost	Team	Won	Lost
Atlantic Division			Central Division			Midwest Division			Pacific Division		
*Miami	55	27	*Chicago	62	20	*Utah	62	20	*Seattle	61	21
*New York	43	39	*Indiana	58	24	*San Antonio	56	26	*L.A. Lakers	61	21
*New Jersey	43	39	*Charlotte	51	31	*Minnesota	45	37	*Phoenix	56	26
Washington	42	40	*Atlanta	50	32	*Houston	41	41	*Portland	46	36
Orlando	41	41	*Cleveland	47	35	Dallas	20	62	Sacramento	27	55
Boston	36	46	Detroit	37	45	Vancouver	19	63	Golden State	19	63
Philadelphia	31	51	Milwaukee	36	46	Denver	11	71	L.A. Clippers	17	65
			Toronto	16	66						

*Gained play-off berth.

became a major factor in the turnaround. The Utes could not cope with Kentucky guard Jeff Sheppard, who added clutch defense to his 16 points. Sheppard was named Most Outstanding Player of the Final Four for having given the Wildcats the spark they needed to pull away in the closing minutes.

Just before the Final Four began, a chill went through the nation's collegiate basketball coaches, assembled in San Antonio for their annual meeting. Two Northwestern University basketball players were under federal indictment for allegedly having conspired to shave points in three games during the 1995 season, thereby creating the potential for large profits in betting on those games by gamblers in on the fix. The case renewed fears that gambling on sporting events was a major problem on college campuses throughout the U.S. The NCAA distributed a sports-wagering information packet at the Final Four, condemning the potential threat to the integrity of sports contests posed by gambling.

In women's basketball the Tennessee dynasty rolled on, capturing its third straight national championship with a convincing

Kentucky Wildcats center Nazr Mohammed (right) goes up against Utah Runnin' Utes forward Hanno Mottöla in the NCAA championship game. After trailing 41–31 at halftime, Kentucky wore down a tenacious Utah team to claim its second NCAA title in three years.

93–75 victory over Louisiana Tech in the NCAA tournament final at Kansas City, Mo. The Tennessee team, which boasted an awesome array of talent under coach Pat Summitt (*see* BIOGRAPHIES), was unbeaten in all 39 games during the 1997–98 season and extended its unprecedented winning streak to 45 over two years. The best—or perhaps the worst for frustrated opponents of the Lady Volunteers—might still be down the road. "I firmly believe [Tennessee] is the best women's team ever assembled," said Baylor coach Sonja Hogg. "People will expect them to win the national championship again, and for many more years." Freshman Tamika Catchings's 27 points led the way for the Lady Vols in the NCAA tournament final, and teammate Chamique Holdsclaw, voted the Most Outstanding Player for her

Final Four performance, was the nation's dominant woman athlete through the entire season.   (ROBERT G. LOGAN)

International. In 1998 basketball was the world's second largest sport in terms of participation, with more than 250 million players in over 203 countries, all of which were affiliated with the International Basketball Federation, the world governing body.

The final rounds of the world championships for men and women were the major international basketball events of the year. Yugoslavia was installed as the favourite for the men's gold medal once it was confirmed that U.S. Dream Team IV would not be participating owing to the NBA lockout. Yugoslavia let no one down, defeating Russia 64–62 in the final played in Athens. The U.S. overcame the host nation, Greece, to win the bronze. More than 332,000 spectators attended the entire championship tournament, with more than 1,830,000,000 people worldwide watching the event on

Houston Comets star Cynthia Cooper (right) drives past Phoenix Mercury forward Umeki Webb in Game 3 of the WNBA championship finals. Led by two-time MVP Cooper, the Comets beat the Mercury in the best-of-three series to claim its second consecutive WNBA title.

Division I National Collegiate Athletic Association (NCAA) Championship—Men			
Year	Winner	Runner-up	Score
1994	Arkansas	Duke	76–72
1995	UCLA	Arkansas	89–78
1996	Kentucky	Syracuse	76–67
1997	Arizona	Kentucky	84–79
1998	**Kentucky**	**Utah**	**78–69**

Division I National Collegiate Athletic Association (NCAA) Championship—Women			
Year	Winner	Runner-up	Score
1994	North Carolina	Louisiana Tech	60–59
1995	Connecticut	Tennessee	70–64
1996	Tennessee	Georgia	83–65
1997	Tennessee	Old Dominion	68–59
1998	**Tennessee**	**Louisiana Tech**	**93–75**

National Invitation Tournament (NIT) Championship			
Year	Winner	Runner-up	Score
1994	Villanova	Vanderbilt	80–73
1995	Virginia Tech	Marquette	65–64
1996	Nebraska	St. Joseph's	60–56
1997	Michigan	Florida State	82–73
1998	**Minnesota**	**Penn State**	**79–72**

television. In the women's championship in Berlin, the U.S. beat Russia 71–65 in the final, its sixth world basketball crown.

Brazil won the South American men's championship with a 96–72 victory over Paraguay in the final played in Santa Fe, Arg. The third Southeast Asia championship for men, played in Manila, was won by the host nation, the Philippines, which defeated Thailand in the final. The 15th African championship for women was played in Nairobi, Kenya, and was won by Senegal, which defeated the Democratic Republic of the Congo 73–59 in the final.

The major club competition during the 1997–98 European season, the European Championship for Men's Clubs, was won by Kinder Bologna (Italy), which defeated AEK Athens (Greece), runner-up the previous season, 58–44 in Barcelona, Spain. In other European competitions, BC Zalgiris (Lithuania) gained the European Cup by beating Stefanel Milan (Italy); Verona (Italy)

defeated Crvena Zvezda (Yugoslavia) to take the European Korac Cup; Bourges (France) retained the Women's European Champions Cup with a victory over Getafe Madrid (Spain); and the Ronchetti Cup went to Hungary with Sopron defeating ASPTT Cede (France).

In January in Remington, Ind., the Harlem Globetrotters, the world-famous American team of basketball entertainers, played their 20,000th game.

(MARK HANNEN)

BILLIARD GAMES

Carom Billiards. Dick Jaspers of The Netherlands won the 1997 Billiards Worldcup Association world three-cushion championship in a four-stop tournament series. Jaspers's two victories, the Turkish Open in Goynuk and the Belgian World Cup in Antwerp, earned him enough points for the overall title. Six-time world champion Torbjörn Blomdahl of Sweden won the tour's final stop, the International Dutch Open in Barendrecht, and finished the year in second place. Frédéric Caudron of Belgium was the champion at the Wetsteijn Dutch Open World Cup in Oosterhout, which earned him third place overall.

The 1997 United States Billiard Association (USBA) national three-cushion championship in New York City was won by Sang Chun Lee with a final points-per-inning (PPI) average of 1.492. The South Korean-born New Yorker shared high-run honours (12) and posted the event's best game (15 points in four innings, with a 3.75 PPI average). The 1998 USBA national championship also was won by Lee; it was his ninth consecutive U.S. championship. He averaged 1.478 PPI over the 13 games of the event. Carlos Hallon of Miami, Fla., finished second. The tournament PPI grand average was a record 1.002, the first time the 1.000 PPI level had ever been exceeded by the field as a whole.

Lee, who was the world champion in 1993, also was a key player in a new three-cushion billiards promotional enterprise launched in 1998. The Carom Corner Tour (CCT), a five-stop series of tournaments around the U.S., guaranteed both larger prize funds and the presence of the popular Lee at all locations. Despite sanctioning squabbles with the USBA and some financial strains, the CCT drew the world's top players to all five well-attended events. Lee won the tour kickoff in Miami, as well as the fourth and fifth stops; Hallon took the second, and Blomdahl won the third in his only CCT appearance. A highlight of the fifth CCT stop (in Chicago) was young Turkish star Semih Sayginer's breaking of the 20-year-old U.S. tournament high-run record (19) with a finished run of 20.

Pocket Billiards. "There's so much politics [sic] and animosity involved." Those words from veteran Buddy Hall of Kentucky spoke volumes about the status of men's professional pocket billiards in the U.S. in 1998. There seemed to be no end to the power struggles that had marked the past several years in the men's professional game. Indeed, by 1998 the two factions in the battle for control of the professional men's tournament circuit, the Professional Billiards Tour (PBT) and the Professional Cuesports Association (PCA), had apparently fought themselves into virtual extinc-

tion. The PBT had no sanctioned events in 1998; the PCA's calendar listed a few events, but none was dependent on PCA sanctioning. A veteran observer opined that "never have so many been led so far astray by so few in the quest of so little." That might prove to be a harsh assessment, but certainly neither group was a significant factor during the year.

Without PBT or PCA tours, the players scrambled to find whatever competition was available. The first and biggest was the Camel Pro Billiard Series, which had evolved after repeated efforts by R.J. Reynolds's Camel brand cigarettes to promote an event in concert with the PBT failed. Already sponsoring several successful amateur events, Camel decided to offer a professional tournament series without the PBT's blessing. An eight-stop tour was the result, each event worth $60,000–$75,000 in direct prize money, with $300,000 in bonus prize money (based on performance points) to be awarded at year's end. Additional events and prize money were promised for the future. Camel was prevented by law from being a television sponsor, however, and since TV was considered by many to be the critical promotional vehicle in pool's effort to reach big-time-sport status, some grave concerns remained for players and fans alike.

A few individual tournaments carried on bravely through it all, most notably the longest-running (and richest) such event in the country, the U.S. Nine-Ball Open. In the 23rd Open, in Norfolk, Va., Hall was the winner, pocketing $25,000. He also scored wins on the Camel tour (first stop), the Mali Florida tour, and the Mizerak Senior Tour (MST). The MST, in its second year, was a haven of peace amid the political tempest found at most other events.

The Women's Professional Billiard Association (WPBA), meanwhile, continued to conduct its annual 12-stop WPBA Classic

Tennessee forward Tamika Catchings (right) puts a move on Louisiana Tech forward Monica Maxwell during the NCAA women's tournament's final game. Led by Catchings's 27 points, Tennessee rolled to a 93–75 victory over Louisiana Tech to extend its winning streak to 45 games over two years.

World Amateur Basketball Championship—Men		
Year	Winner	Runner-up
1990	Yugoslavia	U.S.S.R.
1992	United States	Croatia
1994	United States	Russia
1996	United States	Yugoslavia
1998	**Yugoslavia**	**Russia**

World Amateur Basketball Championship—Women		
Year	Winner	Runner-up
1990	United States	Yugoslavia
1992	Unified Team	China
1994	Brazil	China
1996	United States	Brazil
1998	**United States**	**Russia**

World Three-Cushion Championship	
Year	Winner
1993	Sang Lee (U.S.)
1994	T. Blomdahl (Swed.)
1995	T. Blomdahl (Swed.)
1996	T. Blomdahl (Swed.)
1997	**D. Jaspers (Neth.)**

WPA World Nine-Ball Championships	
Year	Men's champion
1994	T. Okumura (Japan)
1995	O. Ortmann (Ger.)
1996	R. Souquet (Ger.)
1997	J. Archer (U.S.)
1998	**K. Takahashi (Japan)**
Year	Women's champion
1994	E. Mataya-Laurance (U.S.)
1995	G. Hofstatter (Austria)
1996	A. Fisher (U.K.)
1997	A. Fisher (U.K.)
1998	**A. Fisher (U.K.)**

World Professional Snooker Championship			
Year	Winner	Year	Winner
1993	S. Hendry	1996	S. Hendry
1994	S. Hendry	1997	K. Doherty
1995	S. Hendry	**1998**	**J. Higgins**

German luger Georg Hackl rushes past spectators during the men's luge competition at the 1998 Winter Olympics. Reaching speeds in excess of 129 km/h (80 mph), Hackl won his third consecutive singles luge gold medal to become only the sixth athlete in Winter Olympics history to win an event three straight times.

Tour with steadily increasing popularity, prize money, and television coverage. The primary beneficiary midway through the 1998 season was once again the transplanted English star Allison Fisher, who led the tour in both victories and earnings. In November she captured a record third consecutive World Pool–Billiard Association world nine-ball title. Kunihiko Takahashi of Japan won the men's championship. Fisher also won Player of the Year honours for the second straight year; the men's Player of the Year was veteran Philippines star José Parica.

(BRUCE H. VENZKE)

Snooker. Fourteen nations were represented at the Grand Prix snooker tournament in Preston, Eng., in October 1998, a record for the final stages of a major world tournament. Interest was expanded by a series of qualifying events in Asia, North America, Europe, Australia, Africa, and the Middle East.

Of a nucleus of rising young players, none made a greater impact than Marco Fu of Hong Kong; he reached the final of the Grand Prix, in which he was beaten 9–2 by Stephen Lee of England. Fu had disposed of two outstanding English players, Ronnie O'Sullivan and Peter Ebdon, in earlier rounds. At age 20, he was playing in only his fourth tournament since winning the world amateur title and turning professional. Shokat Ali of Pakistan and Quinten Hann of Australia also distinguished themselves. Hann defeated the new world professional (and, later, U.K) champion, John Higgins of Scotland, 5–1 in the first round, but Ali failed to reach the quarterfinals.

Lee's success in the Grand Prix, for which he received £60,000 ($99,000), pushed him from ninth position to fourth in the world rankings, behind Higgins, O'Sullivan, and six-time world champion Stephen Hendry of Scotland.   (SYDNEY E. FRISKIN)

BOBSLEDDING AND LUGE

After 34 years the U.S. finally captured its first Olympic medals in the luge competition, but the spotlight belonged to legendary German luger Georg Hackl. (*See* BIOGRAPHIES.) Reaching speeds in excess of 129 km/h (80 mph), Hackl won his third consecutive singles luge gold medal, becoming only the sixth athlete in Winter Olympics history to win an event three straight times. In so doing, Hackl once again foiled the gold medal aspirations of Austria's Markus Prock, the previous world champion. Hackl's time of 3:18.436 was more than half a second better than that of silver medalist Armin Zoeggeler of Italy. Prock finished a disappointing fourth and thereby marked the fourth Olympics in which Hackl had bested the eight-time world champ. American Wendel Suckow, the 1993 world champion, finished sixth. In doubles the German tandem of Jan Behrendt and Stefan Krause won the gold medal by 0.22 sec, the closest margin of victory in Olympic history. The Germans edged out Americans Gordy Sheer and Chris Thorpe, the 1997 World Cup champs, who took silver. Meanwhile, the U.S.'s reigning World Cup titlists, Mark Grimmette and Brian Martin, won the bronze.

In the women's luge Germany placed three competitors among the top four, winning gold and silver. Silke Kraushaar edged teammate Barbara Niedernhuber by 0.002 sec, the closest margin in Olympic history, whereas Susi Erdmann, one of the pre-event favourites, finished a disappointing fourth.

In terms of close races, the bobsledders managed to outdo the lugers by producing ties for medals in the two-man and four-man events. In the two-man event, the Italian team of Guenther Huber and Antonio Tartaglia led Pierre Lueders and David MacEachern of Canada by 0.03 sec heading into the fourth and decisive run. After the Italians produced a run of 54.27 sec, the Canadians turned the tables with a run of 54.24 sec, so that both teams finished with identical times of 3:37.24. This represented the first time Olympic bobsledding had produced cochampions.

In the four-man competition, the U.K. and France tied for the bronze, and Germany 2 blew away the competition for gold. German driver Christoph Langen, who also won bronze in the two-man, steered his sled to a 0.60-sec win over Swiss driver Marcel Rohner. Langen became the first German from former West Germany to win gold. The past four German winners had been from former East Germany.

French driver Bruno Mingeon moved up from sixth to third with a great final run to tie Britain's Sean Olsson for the bronze medal and the second tie in as many competitions. American driver Brian Shimer, a veteran of three previous Olympics, had toiled for more than 10 years in an attempt to end the U.S.'s 42-year medal drought in the bobsled competition, but his sled finished fifth in the four-man, just 0.02 sec out of medal contention. Shimer and brakeman Garrett Hines finished a disappointing 10th in the two-man event.   (GREG GUSS)

BOWLING

World Tenpins. To open the 1997–98 international calendar year, the AMF Bowling World Cup finals were held in Cairo in November 1997. Through national eliminations the female and male champions of nearly 100 countries qualified for the tournament. The grand finals took place under clear skies on temporary bowling lanes constructed near the great pyramids. In the women's competition Tseng Su-fen of Taiwan overcame South Korea's Lee Ji Soon 236–225. In the men's roll-off, Christian Nokel of Germany defeated Taiwan's Peng Yung-nein 210–200.

The world's best young (under-17) athletes gathered in Moscow in July to compete in the first World Youth Games, with bowling one of the 40 sports on the program. Tracy Ward and Chris Detmore of the U.S. won mixed doubles, Isao Yamamoto of Japan gained the boys' singles title, and Lisa John of the U.K. captured gold in the girls' singles competition. Guatemala was host to the FIQ (Fédération International des Quilleurs) American Zone youth bowling championships during the same month. As expected, the U.S. sent the strongest team, which prevailed in seven events. Other winners included Eduardo Soria of Mexico (boys' singles), Paola Gómez of Colombia (girls' singles), and Guatemalan Sofia Granda, who captured the all-events' crown in front of a home audience.

Taiwan welcomed bowlers from Asia, Australia, and Oceania to the 15th FIQ Asian Bowling Championships in July. Competitors from South Korea were victorious in four men's and three women's events. Cara Honeychurch of Australia was the biggest individual winner, with gold medals in women's singles and all-events. Bowlers from more than 25 countries competed in the fifth world youth championship, held in August in Inchon, S.Kor. Individual champions included Shalin Zulkifli of Malaysia (girls' singles and all-events), American Shawn Evans (boys' singles), and Petteri Salonen of Finland (boys' all-events).

The European team championships were held in Malmö, Swed., in June. For the first time, the usual favourites in the men's division, Finland and Sweden, were not among the top five teams and did not qualify for the World Tenpin Team Cup to be bowled in October in The Netherlands. In the European final The Netherlands defeated Spain 589–516. Sweden finished first in the men's competition for the World Tenpin Team Cup, and Finland repeated its Euroopean victory in the women's event.

(YRJÖ SARAHETE)

U.S. Tenpins. In 1998 the Professional Bowlers Association (PBA) emerged successfully from its first season affiliated with the CBS television network after 36 years with the ABC network. The men's organization matches appeared on CBS on Saturday afternoons April–June under a contract that provided for the PBA to purchase the one-hour slot from CBS, produce its own shows, and sell commercial time. The PBA and CBS reached an agreement during the year that would keep the bowling matches on the network through 2000 and would add a 10th tournament, the World Invitational, in 1999. During the nine PBA tournaments broadcast in a 10-week period in 1998, the audience averaged 2.5 million viewers, according to PBA Commissioner Mark Gerberich, despite the late-spring schedule that caused the tournaments to compete with outdoor activities. A new format for the final round was used. The second-, third-, and fourth-place finishers in the qualifying round bowled one game each, and the high scorer then met the qualifying leader for the championship.

For the third year in a row Walter Ray Williams, Jr., of Stockton, Calif., was named PBA Player of the Year. He won five tournaments including the U.S. Open and set a record for a single season average of 226.13. His prize money totaled $238,225. Runner-up Parker Bohn III of Jackson, N.J., won four tournaments and reached the title round of the prestigious American Bowling Congress (ABC) Masters Tournament at the National Bowling Stadium in Reno, Nev., by bowling a 300 game on television, good for a $10,000 bonus, but then lost to Mike Aulby of Indianapolis, Ind., 224–192. In November Pete Weber and Teata Semiz were inducted into the PBA Hall of Fame. Also in November Tony Roventini of Milwaukee, Wis., became the second person to bowl an ABC-approved 900 series.

(JOHN J. ARCHIBALD)

BOXING

The world heavyweight championship, reduced to an all-time low in 1997 when for-

MAX NASH—AP/WIDE WORLD

British heavyweight fighter Herbie Hide (right) pummels Damon Reed (U.S.) during a World Boxing Organization title match in April. Defending his lightly regarded championship belt, Hide needed just 52 seconds to knock out his severely overmatched challenger.

mer champion Mike Tyson (U.S.) bit the ear of Evander Holyfield (U.S.) in a World Boxing Association (WBA) title clash in Las Vegas, Nev., made little recovery in 1998. With Tyson's suspension by the Nevada State Athletic Commission not lifted until October, there was a lack of lucrative matches. The one exception would have been a bout between Holyfield, the WBA and International Boxing Federation (IBF) champion, and Lennox Lewis (U.K.), the World Boxing Council (WBC) titleholder. The stranglehold that promoter Don King had on competition for the title held up proceedings, however, because King had to spend months in court fighting allegations that he had been involved in an insurance fraud against Lloyd's of London. He eventually won the case and later flew to London to negotiate a Holyfield-Lewis clash for the WBA, IBF, and WBC titles, which was scheduled to take place in March 1999. Tyson applied for a license to box in New Jersey but suddenly withdrew and reapplied in Nevada, which demanded that he undergo an examination for mental stability. With his license restored, Tyson was scheduled to fight Francois Botha (S.Af.) in January 1999.

There were, therefore, no memorable heavyweight title bouts in 1998. Holyfield retained the WBA and IBF versions of the championship, outpointing Vaughan Bean (U.S.) over 12 rounds at Atlanta, Ga., in September. A week later Lewis retained the WBC crown against former European

Professional Bowlers Association (PBA) Tournament of Champions			
Year	Champion	Year	Champion
1993	G. Branham	1996	D. D'Entremont
1994	N. Duke	1997	J. Gant
1995	M. Aulby	1998	B. Goebel

ABC Bowling Championships—Regular Divisions				
Year	Singles	Score	All-events	Score
1994	J. Weltzien	810	T. Holt	2,190
1995	M. Surina	826	J. Kwiatkowski	2,191
1996	D. Scudder, Jr.	823	S. Kurtz	2,224
1997	J. Socha	847	J. Richgels	2,241
1998	J. Gaines	814	C. Barnes	2,151

WIBC Bowling Championships—Open Division				
Year	Singles	Score	All-events	Score
1994	V. Fifield	716	W. Macpherson-Papanos	1,940
1995	B. Owen	749	B. Owen	1,983
1996	C. Berlanga	723	L. Nichols	1,985
1997	J. Schmidt	765	K. Cameron	2,039
1998	N. Glandon	714	L. Johnson	1,989

FIQ World Bowling Championships—Men				
Year	Singles	Pairs	Triples	Team (fives)
1983	T. Cariello (U.S.)	Australia	Sweden	Finland
1987	P. Rolland (Fr.)	Sweden	United States	Sweden
1991	Ying Chieh Ma (Taiwan)	United States	United States	Taiwan
1995	M. Doi (Can.)	Sweden	Netherlands	Netherlands

FIQ World Bowling Championships—Women				
Year	Singles	Pairs	Triples	Team (fives)
1983	L. Sulkanen (Swed.)	Denmark	West Germany	Sweden
1987	E. Piccini (Mex.)	United States	United States	United States
1991	M. Beckel (Ger.)	Japan	Canada	South Korea
1995	D. Ship (Can.)	Thailand	Australia	Finland

champion Zeljko Malrovic (Croatia) after 12 punishing rounds in Uncasville, Conn. Previously, Lewis had successfully defended the title by stopping Shannon Briggs (U.S.) in five rounds at Atlantic City, N.J. He was then scheduled to face Henry Akinwande (U.K.) in New York City, but a blood test on Akinwande revealed hepatitis B and the match was called off.

The heavyweight situation sank even lower when the World Boxing Organization (WBO) sanctioned two title defenses by Herbie Hide (U.K.) against the almost unknown Damon Reed (U.S.) and Willi Fischer (Germany). Fischer was halted after 24 seconds of the second round, and Hide knocked out Reed in 52 seconds. The latter bout set a record for the fastest heavyweight championship knockout, the previous mark having been set when James J. Jeffries flattened Jack Finnegan in 55 seconds in 1900.

The outstanding champion of the year was again Oscar de la Hoya (U.S.). The 25-year-old, who had won titles ranging from featherweight to welterweight, remained undefeated after 29 contests. A crowd of 50,000 attended his successful defense of the WBC welterweight crown when he defeated Patrick Charpentier (France) in three rounds at El Paso, Texas, in June. In September at Las Vegas de la Hoya stopped the legendary Julio César Chávez (Mexico) after eight rounds, thereby repeating a four-round win he had gained over the Mexican in 1996. Chávez had taken part in 35 world title fights and had suffered only three defeats in 105 contests.

Roy Jones, Jr., (U.S.) established himself as one of the best light heavyweights in many years, knocking out Virgil Hill (U.S.) in a nontitle bout, but the WBC titleholder's ambitions to earn bigger purses among the heavyweights were dampened during a 12-round victory over WBA light heavyweight champion Lou Del Valle (U.S.). In the fight Jones suffered his first-ever count as a professional when knocked down in the eighth round.

Naseem Hamed (U.K.), the WBO featherweight champion, remained undefeated, knocking out Wilfredo Vazquez (P.R.) in seven rounds at Manchester, Eng. His audi-

World Heavyweight Champions No Weight Limit
WBA
Evander Holyfield (U.S.; 11/6/93)
Michael Moorer (U.S.; 4/22/94)
George Foreman (U.S.; 11/5/94) stripped of title in 1995
Bruce Seldon (U.S.; 4/8/95)
Mike Tyson (U.S.; 9/7/96)
Evander Holyfield (U.S.; 11/9/96)
WBC
Oliver McCall (U.S.; 9/24/94)
Frank Bruno (U.K.; 9/2/95)
Mike Tyson (U.S.; 3/16/96) gave up title in 1996
Lennox Lewis (U.K.; 2/7/97)
IBF
Evander Holyfield (U.S.; 11/6/93)
Michael Moorer (U.S.; 4/22/94)
George Foreman (U.S.; 11/5/94) gave up title in 1995
Francois Botha (S.Af.; 12/9/95) stripped of title in 1996
Michael Moorer (U.S.; 6/22/96)
Evander Holyfield (U.S.; 11/8/97)

World Cruiserweight Champions Top Weight 195 Pounds
WBA
Bobby Czyz (U.S.; 3/8/91) vacant
Orlin Norris (U.S.; 11/6/93)
Nate Miller (U.S.; 7/22/95)
Fabrice Tiozzo (Fr.; 11/8/97)
WBC
Massimiliano Duran (Italy; 7/27/90)
Anaclet Wamba (Fr.; 7/20/91)
Marcelo Dominguez (Arg.; 4/19/96)
Juan Carlos Gomez (Cuba; 2/21/98)
IBF
Adolpho Washington (U.S.; 8/31/96)
Uriah Grant (U.S.; 6/21/97)
Imamu Mayfield (U.S.; 11/8/97)
Arthur Williams (U.S.; 10/30/98)

Boxing's "Golden Boy," welterweight Oscar de la Hoya (U.S.), mixes it up with legendary Mexican fighter Julio César Chávez during the first round of their World Boxing Council title bout in September. Convincingly outboxed by his young adversary, the aging Chávez was unable to continue fighting after the eighth round. Having fought more than 100 bouts in his long career, Chávez pondered retirement after the loss.

World Light Heavyweight Champions Top Weight 175 Pounds			
WBA
Virgil Hill (U.S.; 9/29/92)
Dariusz Michalczewski (Ger.; 6/13/97) stripped of title in 1997
Lou Del Valle (U.S.; 9/20/97)
Roy Jones, Jr. (U.S.; 7/18/98)
WBC
Fabrice Tiozzo (Fr.; 6/16/95)
Roy Jones, Jr. (U.S.; 11/23/96)
Montell Griffin (U.S.; 3/21/97)
Roy Jones, Jr. (U.S.; 8/7/97)
IBF
Virgil Hill (U.S.; 11/23/96)
Dariusz Michalczewski (Ger.; 6/13/97) gave up title in 1997
William Guthrie (U.S.; 7/19/97)
Reggie Johnson (U.S.; 2/6/98)

World Middleweight Champions Top Weight 160 Pounds			
WBA
Jorge Castro (Arg.; 8/12/94)
Shinji Takehara (Japan; 12/19/95)
William Joppy (U.S.; 6/24/96)
Julio César Green (Dom.Rep.; 8/23/97)
William Joppy (U.S.; 1/31/98)
WBC
Julian Jackson (U.S.; 3/17/95)
Quincy Taylor (U.S.; 8/19/95)
Keith Holmes (U.S.; 3/16/96)
Hassine Cherifi (Fr.; 5/2/98)
IBF
James Toney (U.S.; 5/10/91) gave up title in 1993
Roy Jones, Jr. (U.S.; 5/22/93) gave up title in 1994
Bernard Hopkins (U.S.; 4/29/95)

World Welterweight Champions Top Weight 147 Pounds			
WBA
Crisanto España (Venez.; 10/31/92)
Ike Quartey (Ghana; 6/4/94) stripped of title in 1998
James Page (U.S.; 10/10/98)
WBC
Simon Brown (Jam.; 3/18/91)
James McGirt (U.S.; 11/29/91)
Pernell Whitaker (U.S.; 3/6/93)
Oscar de la Hoya (U.S.; 4/12/97)
IBF
Simon Brown (Jam.; 4/23/88) gave up title in 1991
Maurice Blocker (U.S.; 10/4/91)
Felix Trinidad (P.R.; 6/19/93)

World Super Middleweight Champions Top Weight 168 Pounds			
WBA
Victor Cordoba (Pan.; 4/5/91)
Michael Nunn (U.S.; 9/12/92)
Steve Little (U.S.; 2/26/94)
Frank Liles (U.S.; 8/12/94)
WBC
Thulane Malinga (S.Af.; 3/2/96)
Vincenzo Nardiello (Italy; 7/6/96)
Robin Reid (U.K.; 10/12/96)
Thulane Malinga (S.Af.; 12/19/97)
Richie Woodhall (U.K.; 3/27/98)
IBF
Iran Barkley (U.S.; 1/10/92)
James Toney (U.S.; 2/13/93)
Roy Jones, Jr. (U.S.; 11/18/94) gave up title in 1997
Charles Brewer (U.S.; 6/21/97)
Sven Ottke (Ger.; 10/24/98)

World Junior Middleweight Champions Top Weight 154 Pounds (also called super welterweight)			
WBA
Pernell Whitaker (U.S.; 3/4/95) gave up title in 1995
Carl Daniels (U.S.; 6/16/95)
Julio César Vásquez (Arg.; 12/16/95)
Laurent Boudouani (Fr.; 8/21/96)
WBC
Terry Norris (U.S.; 5/7/94)
Luis Santana (Dom.Rep.; 11/12/94)
Terry Norris (U.S.; 8/19/95)
Keith Mullings (U.S.; 12/6/97)
IBF
Terry Norris (U.S.; 12/16/95) gave up title in 1997
Raul Marquez (U.S.; 4/12/97)
Yory Boy Campas (Mex.; 12/6/97)
Fernando Vargas (U.S.; 12/12/98)

World Junior Welterweight Champions Top Weight 140 Pounds (also called super lightweight)			
WBA
Frankie Randall (U.S.; 9/17/94)
Juan Martin Coggi (Arg.; 1/13/96)
Frankie Randall (U.S.; 8/16/96)
Khalid Rahilou (Fr.; 1/11/97)
Sharmba Mitchell (U.S.; 10/10/98)
WBC
Julio César Chávez (Mex.; 5/13/89)
Frankie Randall (U.S.; 1/29/94)
Julio César Chávez (Mex.; 5/7/94)
Oscar de la Hoya (U.S.; 6/7/96) gave up title in 1997
IBF
Charles Murray (U.S.; 5/15/93)
Jake Rodriguez (P.R.; 2/13/94)
Kostya Tszyu (Austl.; 1/28/95)
Vince Phillips (U.S.; 5/31/97)

ence rating on the HBO cable network broke records in the U.S. He had earned $1.7 million when stopping Kevin Kelley (U.S.) in New York City's Madison Square Garden at the end of 1997. Though Hamed retained his title and unbeaten record by outpointing Wayne McCullough in Atlantic City at the end of October, his performance was criticized in light of his prefight boast of knocking out McCullough in three rounds.

The end of a long, long trail appeared to have arrived for Roberto Duran. The 47-year-old Panamanian, fighting for the 116th time in 31 years, was battered in three rounds when challenging William Joppy (U.S.) for the WBA middleweight crown. It was a mismatch against a champion 20 years younger. Azumah Nelson (Ghana), one of Africa's greatest champions, announced his retirement. During his career of almost 20 years he won WBC featherweight and super featherweight titles.

A bizarre end to a fight occurred when Bernard Hopkins (U.S.) defended the IBF middleweight crown against Robert Allen (U.S.). In the fourth round Hopkins was accidentally pushed from the ring by the referee, injuring his ankle so that he could not continue the fight, which was then declared "no contest."

Despite much opposition women began establishing themselves in the sport. Female boxers, judges, and managers operated regularly in Nevada and New Jersey. Among them Mia Rosales St. John, a 31-year-old

mother of two, commanded large purses. There was an outcry, however, when Maria Nieves-Garcia was found to be 21 weeks

pregnant during the medical test before her scheduled fight against Christy Martin (U.S.). The British Boxing Board of Control

In a World Boxing Organization featherweight championship fight in October, British titleholder "Prince" Naseem Hamed (left) nails his Irish opponent, Wayne McCullough, while the referee attempts to break their clinch. A rising star known for his unorthodox style of boxing, Hamed preserved his unbeaten record by outpointing McCullough.

DONNA CONNOR—AP/WIDE WORLD

World Lightweight Champions **Top Weight 135 Pounds**
WBA
Tony Lopez (U.S.; 10/24/92)
Dingaan Thobela (S.Af.; 6/26/93)
Olzubek Nazarov (Russia; 10/30/93)
Jean-Baptiste Mendy (Fr.; 5/16/98)
WBC
Miguel González (Mex.; 8/24/94) gave up title in 1996
Jean-Baptiste Mendy (Fr.; 4/20/96)
Steve Johnston (U.S.; 3/1/97)
Cesar Bazan (Mex.; 6/13/98)
IBF
Rafael Ruelas (U.S.; 2/19/94)
Oscar de la Hoya (U.S.; 5/6/95) gave up title in 1995
Philip Holiday (S.Af.; 8/19/95)
Shane Mosley (U.S.; 8/2/97)

World Junior Featherweight Champions **Top Weight 122 Pounds** (also called super bantamweight)
WBA
Raul Pérez (Mex.; 10/7/91)
Wilfredo Vásquez (P.R.; 3/27/92)
Antonio Cermeno (Venez.; 5/13/95) gave up title in 1997
Enrique Sanchez (Mex.; 2/8/98) vacant
Nestor Garza (Mex.; 12/12/98)
WBC
Tracy Patterson (U.S.; 6/23/92)
Hector Acero-Sánchez (U.S.; 8/26/94)
Daniel Zaragoza (Mex.; 11/6/95)
Erik Morales (Mex.; 9/6/97)
IBF
Welcome Ncita (S.Af.; 3/10/90)
Kennedy McKinney (U.S.; 12/2/92)
Vuyani Bungu (S.Af.; 8/20/94)

World Flyweight Champions **Top Weight 112 Pounds**
WBA
Aquiles Guzmán (Venez.; 9/26/92)
David Griman (Venez.; 12/92)
San Sow Ploenchit (Thai.; 2/13/94)
José Bonilla (Venez.; 11/14/96)
Hugo Soto (Arg.; 5/29/98)
WBC
Muangchai Kittlkasem (Thai.; 2/15/91)
Yury Arbachakov (Russia; 6/23/92)
Chatchai Dutchboygym (Sasakul) (Thai; 5/9/97)
Manny Pacquiao (Phil.; 12/4/98)
IBF
Francisco Tejedor (Colom.; 2/95)
Danny Romero (U.S.; 4/22/95) gave up title in 1996
Mark Johnson (U.S.; 5/4/96) **vacant**

World Junior Lightweight Champions **Top Weight 130 Pounds** (also called super featherweight)
WBA
Genaro Hernandez (U.S.; 11/22/91) gave up title in 1995
Choi Yong Soo (S.Kor.; 10/21/95)
Takanori Hatakeyama (Japan; 9/5/98)
WBC
Azumah Nelson (Ghana; 2/29/88)
Jesse James Leija (U.S.; 5/7/94)
Gabriel Ruelas (U.S.; 9/17/94)
Azumah Nelson (Ghana; 12/1/95)
Genaro Hernandez (U.S.; 3/22/97)
Floyd Mayweather (U.S.; 10/3/98)
IBF
Eddie Hopson (U.S.; 4/22/95)
Tracy Patterson (U.S.; 7/9/95)
Arturo Gatti (U.S.; 12/15/95) **gave up title in 1998**
Roberto Garcia (U.S.; 3/13/98)

World Bantamweight Champions **Top Weight 118 Pounds**
WBA
Veeraphol Sahaprom (Thai.; 9/17/95)
Nana Konadu (Ghana; 1/28/96)
Daorung Chuvatana Siriwat (Thai.; 10/26/96)
Nana Konadu (Ghana; 6/21/97)
Johnny Tapia (U.S.; 12/6/98)
WBC
Yasuei Yakushiji (Japan; 12/22/93)
Wayne McCullough (N.Ire.; 7/30/95)
Sirimongkol Singmanassuk (Thai.; 8/10/96)
Joichiro Tatsuyoshi (Japan; 11/22/97)
Veeraphol Nakonluang (Thai.; 12/29/98)
IBF
Orlando Canizales (U.S.; 7/9/88) gave up title in 1994
Harold Mestre (Colom.; 1/21/95)
Mbulelo Botile (S.Af.; 4/29/95)
Tim Austin (U.S.; 7/19/97)

World Junior Flyweight Champions **Top Weight 108 Pounds**
WBA
Choi Hi Yong (S.Kor.; 2/4/95)
Carlos Murillo (Pan.; 1/13/96)
Keiji Yamaguchi (Japan; 5/21/96)
Pichitnoi Siriwat (Thai.; 12/3/96)
WBC
Michael Carbajal (U.S.; 3/13/93)
Chiquita Gonzalez (Mex.; 2/19/94)
Saman Sorjaturong (Thai.; 7/15/95)
IBF
Chiquita Gonzalez (Mex.; 2/19/94)
Saman Sorjaturong (Thai.; 7/15/95) vacant
Michael Carbajal (U.S.; 3/16/96)
Mauricio Pastrana (Colom.; 1/18/97) stripped of title in 1997
Mauricio Pastrana (Colom.; 12/13/97) **stripped of title in 1998**
Will Grigsby (U.S.; 12/18/98)

World Featherweight Champions **Top Weight 126 Pounds**
WBA
Eloy Rojas (Venez.; 12/4/93)
Wilfredo Vasquez (P.R.; 5/18/96) **gave up title in 1998**
Freddie Norwood (U.S.; 4/3/98) stripped of title in 1998
Antonio Cermeno (Venez.; 10/3/98)
WBC
Alejandro González (Mex.; 1/7/95)
Manuel Medina (Mex.; 9/23/95)
Luisito Espinosa (Phil.; 12/11/95)
IBF
Manuel Medina (Mex.; 8/12/91)
Tom Johnson (U.S.; 2/26/93)
Naseem Hamed (U.K.; 2/8/97) gave up title in 1997
Hector Lizarraga (U.S.; 12/13/97)
Manuel Medina (Mex.; 4/24/98)

World Junior Bantamweight Champions **Top Weight 115 Pounds** (also called super flyweight)
WBA
Alima Goitia (Venez.; 7/22/95)
Yokthai Sithoar (Thai.; 8/24/96)
Satoshi Iida (Japan; 12/23/97)
Jesus Rojas (Venez.; 12/23/98)
WBC
Moon Sung Kil (S.Kor.; 1/20/90)
José Luis Bueno (Mex.; 11/13/93)
Hiroshi Kawashima (Japan; 5/4/94)
Gerry Peñalosa (Phil.; 2/20/97)
Cho In Joo (S. Kor.; 8/29/98)
IBF
Carlos Salazar (Arg.; 10/7/95)
Harold Grey (Colom.; 4/27/96)
Danny Romero (U.S.; 8/24/96)
Johnny Tapia (U.S.; 7/18/97) **gave up title in 1998**

World Mini-flyweight Champions **Top Weight 105 Pounds** (also called strawweight)
WBA
Choi Hi Yong (S.Kor.; 2/2/91)
Ohashi Hideyuki (Japan; 10/14/92)
Chana Porpaoin (Thai.; 2/10/93)
Rosendo Alvarez (Nic.; 12/2/95)
Ricardo López (Mex.; 11/13/98)
WBC
Napa Kiatwanchai (Thai.; 11/13/88)
Choi Jum Hwan (S.Kor.; 11/12/89)
Ohashi Hideyuki (Japan; 2/7/90)
Ricardo López (Mex.; 10/25/90)
IBF
Manny Melchor (Phil.; 9/6/92)
Ratanapol Vorapin (Thai.; 12/10/92) stripped of title in 1996
Ratanapol Vorapin (Thai.; 5/16/96)
Zolani Petelo (S.Af.; 12/27/97)

lost a legal battle when Jane Couch (Eng.) took it to court. Couch had boxed in the U.S. and claimed that she had had to turn down lucrative matches in the U.K. because women were not allowed to box professionally there. Two bouts between young women had taken place in amateur tournaments in England. Because of Couch's legal victory the British Board was required to grant professional licenses to women.

(FRANK BUTLER)

CHESS

In 1998 the chess world continued to be confused by the various rival claimants for the title of world champion. Viswanathan Anand of India, who won acclaim as the best player of the year after a series of convincing tournament victories, also won the British Chess Federation prize for Book of the Year when he produced an annotated collection of his best games. Paradoxically,

Anand had lost in the Fédération Internationale des Échecs (FIDE) world championship in January to the defending FIDE champion, Anatoly Karpov of Russia, in the new knockout system, in which a loss eliminates the losing player from the competition.

Anand emerged as the challenger to Karpov after an exhausting series of short, knockout matches played at Gröningen, Neth., in December 1997. In the final of this

Defending champion Anatoly Karpov of Russia (right) looks on as challenger Viswanathan Anand of India ponders a move during the opening match of the Fédération Internationale des Échecs world chess championship finals in Lausanne, Switz., on January 2. Karpov defended his title successfully, prevailing in a two-game tiebreaker with Anand after the two competitors had played to a 3–3 draw.

series he defeated the best English player, Michael Adams, in an event in which the Russians did not show their usual superiority. The knockout system was a break with over a century of tradition, and its perceived unfairness was underlined for Anand when he had to travel to Lausanne, Switz., to meet Karpov with little time for recuperation. The challenger held the basic six-game contest to a 3–3 draw but lost the two-game tiebreaker 0.5–1.5.

Meanwhile, Garry Kasparov, the undefeated former FIDE champion and the world's strongest player according to the international rating system, played very little. Kasparov had forfeited his title in 1993 over a dispute with FIDE concerning the location of the championship series with then-challenger Nigel Short of England. Kasparov and Short went on to found the rival Professional Chess Association, which Kasparov later left to form the "World Chess Coouncil." In 1998 Kasparov suffered another reverse when his planned title match with Aleksey Shirov of Spain failed to take place in October after the financing plans collapsed.

In the summer the controversial president of FIDE, Kirsan Ilyumzhinov of the Russian republic of Kalmykia, announced his candidacy for the Russian presidency. At the same time he was embroiled in turmoil over his plan to introduce an annual knockout FIDE world title system. The plan was resisted by Karpov on the grounds that his contract with

FIDE stipulated that the winner of the 1998 Karpov-Anand match would hold the title for two years. Karpov's successful advocacy of his rights led to the cancellation of a planned world title knockout series in Las Vegas, Nev., late in the year. Since Karpov had an unsuccessful year apart from the Anand match, he was unable to resist the plan that he would have to enter this knockout, whenever it came to be organized, at a far earlier stage.

Ilyumzhinov was involved in further controversy when human rights groups made attempts to persuade the 140 member countries of FIDE to boycott the main team event of the year, the World Chess Olympiad, scheduled to start in late September in Elista, the capital of Kalmykia. The event

started late due to the failure to complete the new venue in time, but it attracted 110 teams to the main event, a Swiss-system contest that was shortened to 13 rounds to allow for the delay.

The U.S. men led throughout but eventually lost to the Russian I team. The leading men's scores were Russia I (with 35.5 game points from a possible 52); the U.S. (34.5); Ukraine (32.5); Israel (32.5); China,

FIDE Olympiad—Men		
Year	Winner	Runner-up
1992	Russia	Uzbekistan
1994	Russia	Bosnia
1996	Russia	Ukraine
1998	**Russia**	**United States**

FIDE Olympiad—Women		
Year	Winner	Runner-up
1992	Georgia	Ukraine
1994	Georgia	Hungary
1996	Georgia	China
1998	**China**	**Russia**

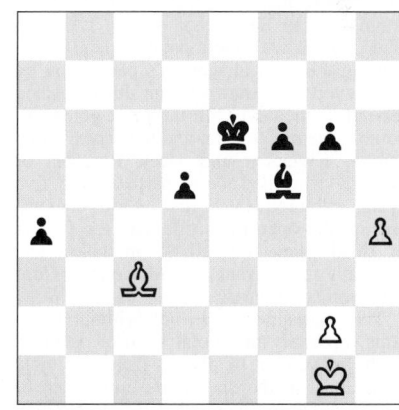

The 117-year-old monthly *British Chess* magazine ran a competition among 10 experts to see what they thought was the most amazing move of all time. Although such older examples as Levitsky–Marshall, Breslau, Pol., 1912, were supported, the winner was the endgame coup 47:Bf5-h3, played in the diagrammed position from Topolov–Shirov, Linares, Spain, 1998.

FIDE Chess Championship—Men		
Year	Winner	Runner-up
1990	G. Kasparov (U.S.S.R.)	A. Karpov (U.S.S.R.)
1993	A. Karpov (Russia)	J. Timman (Neth.)
1996	A. Karpov (Russia)	G. Kamsky (U.S.)
1998	**A. Karpov (Russia)**	**V. Anand (India)**

FIDE Chess Championship—Women		
Year	Winner	Runner-up
1988	M. Chiburdanidze (U.S.S.R.)	N. Ioseliani (U.S.S.R.)
1991	Xie Jun (China)	M. Chiburdanidze (U.S.S.R.)
1993	Xie Jun (China)	N. Ioseliani (Georgia)
1996	Z. Polgar (Hung.)	Xie Jun (China)

Germany, and Georgia (tied with 31.5); Russia II and Hungary (tied with 31). A notable failure was that of England, which had often been in the top six in recent years, but this time finished 11th (30.5). China scored a notable success in taking the gold medal in the women's section, followed by Russia and Georgia.

The two main individual tournaments of the year were the traditional events at Linares, Spain, in February and at Tilburg, Neth., beginning in late October, shortly after the end of the Olympiad. The former, a double-round contest for seven players, was won by Anand (7.5 points out of 12), followed by Shirov (7), Kasparov and Vladimir Kramnik of Russia (both 6.5), Peter Svidler of Russia (5.5), Vasily Ivanchuk of Ukraine (5), and Veselin Topalov of Bulgaria (4). The latter event, for 12 players, was also captured by Anand (7.5 points), with such favoured players as Kramnik and Adams finishing fifth and seventh, respectively. Nick de Firmian took the U.S. title at Denver, Colo., in November, while Short made a triumphant return to the U.K. championship in August to win the title after a tiebreaker with Matthew Sadler.

Notable deaths during the year included Laszlo Szabo, the leading Hungarian player of the two decades after World War II, and Yefim Geller of Ukraine, who was one of the most dynamic Soviet players of the same period. Young talents who drew attention were Peter Leko of Hungary, aged 19, who finished second to Anand at Tilburg, and 15-year-old Ruslan Ponomaryov, who won the Ukrainian zonal in November.

(BERNARD CAFFERTY)

CONTRACT BRIDGE

The 1998 world championships of contract bridge—with six open and women's (one invitational), two senior (over age 55), and four junior (under 26) world titles to be won—were held in Lille, France, from August 21 to September 4. The U.S. finished on top with the most medals (10), including the gold in women's pairs, won by Jill Meyers and Shawn Quinn. Italy finished second (7 medals) with the most golds (5), notably the men's team and the mixed pairs. Michal Kwiecien and Jacek Pszczola of Poland, who had been partners for five years, captured their first world championship, the open pairs title, and led Poland to third place overall (5 medals). The women's team event (the McConnell Cup) was won by Austria.

The tournament was not without problems. Probably the worst mistake occurred in the movement of players from one table to the next in the open pairs final. Each of the 72 qualifying pairs was supposed to play two boards against every other pair. The error affected 40 pairs, including the second-place finishers, David Berkowitz and Larry Cohen of the U.S., who did not play against five pairs. They had to be given an average of their results on the other 132 deals.

Arguably the most notable victory was by Boris Schapiro of the U.K., who captured the senior pairs with his partner, Irving Gordon. At 89 years old, Schapiro comfortably broke the record for the oldest contract bridge world champion. (The previous record was held by Waldemar von Zedtwitz, who was 74 when he won the world mixed

pairs title in 1970.) Schapiro had previously won two other world titles: the Bermuda Bowl in 1955 and the mixed teams in 1962.

Another event of interest happened during the invitational Par Contest, in which 12 difficult deals composed by Pietro Bernasconi of Switzerland were played by 30 men, 4 women, and GIB, a computer program written by Matt Ginsberg, a research professor of computer science at the University of Oregon. The contest was won by American Michael Rosenberg; GIB placed 12th.

Although the 13th worldwide pairs tournament, held on June 5–6, was once again the biggest contest in terms of the number of competitors, with some 60,000 players taking part, it was the lowest participation in the event's history. The top rankings were dominated by players from the U.S. The highest score of 1,865 (77.7%) was achieved by Ray Boehne of Monterey, Calif., and James Coventry of Salinas, Calif. They were playing together for the first time and spent only 10 minutes discussing their methods. The second highest score overall was 1,820 (75.8%) by Mark Hupert and Mark Lombard, both of Philadelphia.

The major news story was the dissolution of the world's most successful pair over the past three decades: Bob Hamman and Bobby Wolff of the U.S. Between 1972,

when they formed a partnership, and 1998, they won seven world championships together (five Bermuda Bowls, one Team Olympiad, and one open pairs) and numerous U.S. national titles, the most impressive streak being four consecutive Spingolds in 1993–97, a record unlikely to be equaled.

(PHILLIP ALDER)

CRICKET

The first Test of the 1998 series between the West Indies and England—held in Sabina Park in Kingston, Jam.—would forever be remembered as cricket's craziest hour. After 66 minutes and 61 balls, the match became the first in the history of Test cricket to be abandoned because of a dangerous pitch. In just over an hour England had lost three wickets for 17 runs and the England physiotherapist had been called onto the pitch six times to treat the batsmen for blows to the hand, elbow, and head. When another ball

Bermuda Bowl		
Year	Winner	Runner-up
1991	Iceland	Poland
1993	Netherlands	Norway
1995	United States	Canada
1997	France	United States

World Team Olympiad				
Year	Open winner	Open runner-up	Women's winner	Women's runner-up
1988	United States	Austria	Denmark	United Kingdom
1992	France	United States	Austria	United Kingdom
1996	France	Indonesia	United States	China

World Contract Bridge Pair Championship			
Year	Open winners	Women's winners	Mixed winners
1994	Marcin Lesniewski, Marek Szymanowski (Pol.)	Carla Arnolds, Bep Vriend (Neth.)	Danuta Hocheker, Apolinare Kowalski (Pol.)
1998	Michal Kwiecien, Jacek Pszczola (Pol.)	Jill Meyers, Shawn Quinn (U.S.)	Enza Rossano, Antonio Vivaldi (Italy)

In 1998 the International Bridge Press Association awarded two prizes for the best-played deal of the year: one for juniors and one for older players. The winner in the former category was Igor Grzejdziak, for his performance in this deal. He was playing for Poland against Norway in the European Junior Teams Championship.

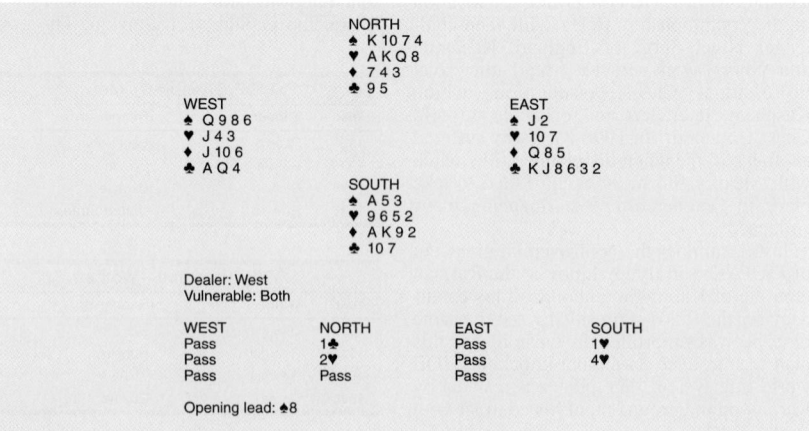

	NORTH	
	♠ K 10 7 4	
	♥ A K Q 8	
	♦ 7 4 3	
	♣ 9 5	
WEST		EAST
♠ Q 9 8 6		♠ J 2
♥ J 4 3		♥ 10 7
♦ J 10 6		♦ Q 8 5
♣ A Q 4		♣ K J 8 6 3 2
	SOUTH	
	♠ A 5 3	
	♥ 9 6 5 2	
	♦ A K 9 2	
	♣ 10 7	

Dealer: West
Vulnerable: Both

WEST	NORTH	EAST	SOUTH
Pass	1♣	Pass	1♥
Pass	2♥	Pass	4♥
Pass	Pass	Pass	

Opening lead: ♠8

North could not open one diamond, one heart, or one spade, because those bids promise at least five-card suits in his methods.

West led the ♠8, third-highest from four or six cards, or lowest from three. (This agreement is popular in the tournament world because it usually counts out the suit quicker than the traditional fourth-highest.)

Declarer looks destined to lose four tricks: one spade, one diamond, and two clubs. However, Grzejdziak found a beautiful deceptive play: He let West win trick one! Declarer called for the four from the dummy, and when East correctly played the two, Grzejdziak dropped the three.

Of course, West could have switched effectively to clubs, yet that looked dangerous. West, therefore, continued with the ♠6. Declarer took East's jack with his ace, drew trumps, returned to his hand with a diamond, and led his last spade, finessing dummy's ten when West played the nine. One of South's club losers disappeared on the ♠K, and Grzejdziak had only three losers: one spade, one diamond, and one club.

from C.A. Walsh leapt off a length and struck B.P. Thorpe on the fingers, the umpire gestured to the match referee and the two captains, B.C. Lara, in his first Test as West Indian captain, and M.A. Atherton of England, for talks on the field. After a lengthy discussion, the match was abandoned as a draw. There was little dissent from players, commentators, or even the crowd, many of whom had flown from England to watch the Test. The soil of the newly relaid pitch was cracked and uneven, totally unfit for Test cricket and an enormous embarrassment to the West Indies Cricket Board, the president of which was

Jamaican. The umpire was widely praised for his decision to call off the match, and an extra Test was hurriedly arranged for in Trinidad.

The West Indies went on to win the series but more narrowly than the 3–1 score suggested. England won the third Test in Trinidad and was favoured to square the series in Barbados when the first rain of the year spoiled its chances. Only in the final Test in Antigua did the West Indians, led by their two fast bowlers, C.E.L. Ambrose (who took 30 wickets in the series at an average of 14.27) and Walsh (22 wickets at 25.59), assert its traditional domination.

England's most prolific bowler for the series and the whole year was A.R.C. Fraser, who took 27 wickets at 18.22 and bowled with nagging accuracy and unbreakable will throughout. At the end of the series, after four years and 52 Tests, Atherton, England's longest-serving captain, stepped down to be replaced in the spring by A.J. Stewart.

Despite an unexpected defeat by India, for whom captain S.R. Tendulkar confirmed his reputation as the finest batsman of his generation, Australia justified its position as unofficial world champion with series victories over New Zealand and South Africa. Australia's superiority relied on solid batting

Test Series Results, October 1997–September 1998			
Host/Ground	Date	Scores	Result
Pak./Rawalpindi	Oct. 6–10	Pak. 456 and 182 for 6; S.Af. 403	Drawn
Pak./Sheikhupura	Oct. 17–21	S.Af. 402; Pak. 53 for 1	Drawn (rain)
Pak./Faisalabad	Oct. 24–27	S.Af. 239 and 214; Pak. 308 and 92	S.Af. won by 53 runs; S.Af. won series 1–0
Austl./Brisbane	Nov. 7–11	Austl. 373 and 294 for 6 dec; N.Z. 349 and 132	Austl. won by 186 runs
Austl./Perth	Nov. 20–23	N.Z. 217 and 174; Austl. 461	Austl. won by an innings and 70 runs
Austl./Hobart	Nov. 27–Dec. 1	Austl. 400 and 138 for 2 dec; N.Z. 251 for 6 dec and 223 for 9	Drawn; Austl. won series 2–0
Pak./Peshawar	Nov. 17–20	W.Ind. 151 and 211; Pak. 381	Pak. won by an innings and 19 runs
Pak./Rawalpindi	Nov. 29–Dec. 3	W.Ind. 303 and 139; Pak. 471	Pak. won by an innings and 29 runs
Pak./Karachi	Dec. 6–9	W.Ind. 216 and 212; Pak. 417 and 15 for 0	Pak. won by 10 wickets; Pak won series 3–0
India/Chandigarh	Nov. 19–23	SriL. 369 and 251 for 6 dec; India 515 for 9 dec	Drawn
India/Nagpur	Nov. 26–30	India 485	Drawn (rain)
India/Bombay	Dec. 3–7	India 512 and 181 for 9 dec; SriL. 361 and 166 for 7	Drawn; Series drawn 0–0
Austl./Melbourne	Dec. 26–30	Austl. 309 and 257; S.Af. 186 and 273 for 7	Drawn
Austl./Sydney	Jan. 2–5	S.Af. 287 and 113; Austl. 421	Austl. won by an innings and 21
Austl./Adelaide	Jan. 30–Feb. 3	S.Af. 517 and 193 for 6 dec; Austl. 350 and 227 for 7	Drawn; Austl. won series 1–0
SriL./Kandy	Jan. 7–11	SriL. 469 for 9 dec and 11 for 2; Zimb. 140 and 338	SriL. won by 8 wickets
SriL./Columbo	Jan. 14–18	Zimb. 251 and 299; SriL. 225 and 326 for 5	SriL. won by 5 wickets; SriL. won series 2–0
W.Ind./Kingston	Jan. 29	Eng. 17 for 3	Match abandoned
W.Ind./Port-of-Spain	Feb. 5–9	Eng. 214 and 258; W.Ind. 191 and 282 for 7	W.Ind. won by 3 wickets
W.Ind./Port-of-Spain	Feb. 13–16	W.Ind. 159 and 210; Eng. 145 and 225 for 7	Eng. won by 3 wickets
W.Ind./Georgetown	Feb. 27–March 2	W.Ind. 352 and 197; Eng. 170 and 137	W.Ind. won by 242 runs
W.Ind./Bridgetown	March 12–16	Eng. 403 and 233 for 3 dec; W.Ind. 262 and 112 for 2	Drawn
W.Ind./St. John's	March 20–24	Eng. 127 and 321; W.Ind. 500 for 7 dec	W.Ind. won by an innings and 52 runs; W.Ind. won series 3–1
S.Af./Johannesburg	Feb. 14–18	S.Af. 364 and 44 for 0; Pak. 329	Drawn
S.Af./Durban	Feb. 26–March 2	Pak. 259 and 226; S.Af. 231 and 225	Pak. won by 29 runs
S.Af./Port Elizabeth	March 6–10	S.Af. 293 and 206 for 7 dec; Pak. 106 and 134	S.Af. won by 259 runs; Series drawn 1–1
N.Z./Wellington	Feb. 19–22	Zimb. 180 and 250; N.Z. 411 and 20 for 0	N.Z. won by 10 wickets
N.Z./Auckland	Feb. 26–28	Zimb. 170 and 277; N.Z. 460	N.Z. won by an innings and 13 runs; N.Z. won series 2–0
India/Madras	March 6–10	India 257 and 418 for 4 dec; Austl. 328 and 168	India won by 179 runs
India/Calcutta	March 18–21	Austl. 233 and 181; India 633 for 5 dec	India won by an innings and 219 runs
India/Bangalore	March 25–28	India 424 and 169; Austl. 400 and 195 for 2	Austl. won by 8 wickets; India won series 2–1
S.Af./Cape Town	March 19–23	S.Af. 418 and 264; SriL. 306 and 306	S.Af. won by 70 runs
S.Af./Pretoria	March 27–30	SriL. 303 and 122; S.Af. 200 and 226 for 4	S.Af. won by 6 wickets; S.Af. won series 2–0
Zimb./Bulawayo	March 14–18	Zimb. 321 and 302 for 4 dec; Pak. 256 and 258 for 6	Drawn
Zimb./Harare	March 21–25	Zimb. 277 and 268; Pak. 354 and 192 for 7	Pak. won by 3 wickets; Pak. won series 1–0
SriL./Colombo	May 27–31	N.Z. 305 and 444 for 6 dec; SriL. 285 and 297	N.Z. won by 167 runs
SriL./Galle	June 3–7	N.Z. 193 and 114; SriL. 323	SriL. won by an innings and 16 runs
SriL./Colombo	June 10–13	SriL. 206 and 282; N.Z. 193 and 131	SriL. won by 164 runs; SriL. won series 2–1
Eng./Birmingham	June 4–8	Eng. 462 and 170 for 8; S.Af. 343	Drawn
Eng./London (Lord's)	June 18–21	S.Af. 360 and 15 for 0; Eng. 110 and 264	S.Af. won by 10 wickets
Eng./Manchester	July 2–6	S.Af. 552 for 5 dec; Eng. 183 and 369 for 9	Drawn
Eng./Nottingham	July 23–27	S.Af. 374 and 208; Eng. 336 and 247 for 2	Eng. won by 8 wickets
Eng./Leeds	Aug. 6–10	Eng. 230 and 240; S.Af. 252 and 195	Eng. won by 23 runs; Eng. won series 2–1
Eng./London (The Oval)	Aug. 27–31	Eng. 445 and 181; SriL. 591 and 37 for 0	SriL. won by 10 wickets

All-Time First-Class Test Cricket Standings (as of Sept. 30, 1998)															
	England			Australia			South Africa			West Indies			New Zealand		
	Wins	Draws	Losses	W	D	L	W	D	L	W	D	L	W	D	L
England v.	——	——	——	92	85	114	49	45	21	28	42*	57	36	38	4
Australia v.	114	85	92	——	——	——	34	17	14	35	22†	29	15	12	7
South Africa v.	21	45	49	14	17	34	——	——	——	0	0	1	12	6	3
West Indies v.	51	42	28	29	22†	35	1	0	0	——	——	——	10	14	4
New Zealand v.	4	38	36	7	12	15	3	6	12	4	14	10	——	——	——
India v.	14	38	32	11	18†	25	2	4	4	7	35	28	13	16	6
Pakistan v.	9	32	14	11	15	14	1	1	2	10	12	12	18	16	5
Sri Lanka v.	2	1	3	0	3	7	0	2	3	0	2	1	4	7	7
Zimbabwe v.	0	2	0	‡			0	0	1	‡			0	5	3

	India			Pakistan			Sri Lanka			Zimbabwe		
	W	D	L	W	D	L	W	D	L	W	D	L
England v.	32	36	14	14	32	9	3	1	2	0	2	0
Australia v.	25	18†	11	14	15	11	7	3	0	‡		
South Africa v.	4	4	2	2	1	1	3	2	0	1	0	0
West Indies v.	28	35	7	12	12	10	1	2	0	‡		
New Zealand v.	6	16	13	5	16	18	7	7	4	3	5	0
India v.	——	——	——	4	33	7	7	11	1	1	1	0
Pakistan v.	7	33	4	——	——	——	9	7	3	6	3	1
Sri Lanka v.	1	11	7	3	7	9	——	——	——	4	3	0
Zimbabwe v.	0	1	1	1	3	6	0	3	4	——	——	——

*Including one match abandoned. †Including one tie. ‡No matches.

Cricket World Cup				
Year	Result			
1979	West Indies	286–9	England	194
1983	India	183	West Indies	140
1987	Australia	253–5	England	246–8
1992	Pakistan	249–6	England	227
1996	Sri Lanka	245–3	Australia	241

and the leg-spin bowling of S.K. Warne, who took 20 wickets against South Africa, 11 of them in the second Test. South Africa came close to drawing the series in the final Test, but without A.A. Donald, its most effective fast bowler, who was injured, the team lacked the penetration to take the last three Australian wickets.

Donald featured in an enthralling personal duel with Atherton in the fourth Test at Nottingham, Eng. Furious that a legitimate appeal for a catch behind the wicket had been turned down, the South African bowled a series of short-pitched balls from round the wicket that tested Atherton's courage to the limit. He survived, and England won, squaring a series that had appeared to be lost. In the fifth Test at Headingley, England was victorious on the final morning. It was the first time in 12 years that England had won a full series against a major competitor and four decades since it had come from behind to win a series in the deciding Test. The one blemish in the series was the consistently poor standard of umpiring, which brought renewed calls for increased use of video cameras.

The euphoria was short-lived as England was comprehensively outplayed by Sri Lanka, for whom the off-spinner M. Muralitharan took 16 wickets for 220 runs in the one-off Test. The controversial Muralitharan had been no-balled for throwing earlier in his career, but his curious bent-arm action (caused by his physical inability to straighten his right arm) had been officially cleared by the International Cricket Council. Accusations surfaced once again during the Test, which soured Sri Lanka's victory. Sri Lanka also relied on S.T. Jayasuriya, who batted a faultless 213 off just 278 balls as the touring team won its first Test victory on English soil.

Despite continuing allegations about match-fixing and Wasim Akram's abrupt resignation as captain, Pakistan enjoyed a good year, with a victory over a demoralized West Indian side and a drawn series in South Africa. India, led by two centuries from Tendulkar and one from the former captain, M. Azharuddin, won a series against Australia for the first time in 18 years. Australia's women cricketers fared better in India, beating New Zealand in Calcutta to win the sixth women's World Cup.

In England the rights for televising home Tests from the summer of 1999 were taken away from the BBC after 60 years and given to the independent Channel 4 in a bid to attract wider audiences to Test cricket. Leicestershire secured the county championship, Essex captured the last Benson and Hedges one-day cup, and Lancashire won both the NatWest Trophy and the one-day AXA Sunday league. Western Australia beat Tasmania by seven wickets in the Sheffield Shield final, Orange Free State won South Africa's four-day Super Sport series, Karachi City took Pakistan's Quaid-i-Azam Trophy, Karnataka gained the Ranji Trophy in India, and the Leeward Islands and Guyana shared the President's Cup, the West Indies's domestic first-class trophy.

(ANDREW LONGMORE)

Australian cricketer Shane Warne bowls during the first Test between Australia and India in March. After the Indian tour Warne underwent surgery on his right shoulder and was out of action for the remainder of the season.

World Curling Championship—Men		
Year	Winner	Runner-up
1994	Canada	Sweden
1995	Canada	Scotland
1996	Canada	Scotland
1997	Sweden	Germany
1998	**Canada**	**Sweden**

World Curling Championship—Women		
Year	Winner	Runner-up
1994	Canada	Scotland
1995	Sweden	Canada
1996	Canada	United States
1997	Canada	Norway
1998	**Sweden**	**Denmark**

CURLING

Approximately 350 years after it became established as a recreational pastime in Scotland, curling in February 1998 joined the ranks of official Olympic sports at the Games in Nagano, Japan. There Swiss skip Patrick Huerlimann unexpectedly routed Canada's Mike Harris 9–3. Only three Swiss men's teams (in 1992, 1981, and 1975) and one women's team (1983) had previously claimed world titles. Norway's Eigil Ramsfjell finished third, defeating a U.S. foursome skipped by Tim Somerville in the bronze-medal match. Rounding out the Olympic men's card in order of finish were Japan, Sweden, Great Britain, and Germany.

Three-time world champion Sandra Schmirler of Canada added Olympic gold to her career winnings with a 7–5 victory over Denmark's Helena Blach Lavrsen in the women's final. Elisabet Gustafson skipped Sweden to the bronze medal, with Scotland's Kirsty Hay, representing Great Britain, falling to fourth place. The remain-

FRED CHARTRAND—AP/WIDE WORLD

Canadian skip Sandra Schmirler (centre) releases a rock and lead Marcia Gudereit (left) and second Joan McCusker sweep during the curling competition at the Winter Olympics in Nagano, Japan. In 1998 curling was included for the first time as an official Olympic sport.

ing four Olympic finishers were, in order, Japan, Norway, the U.S., and Germany.

Less than two months later at the world championships in Kamloops, B.C., Gustafson prevailed on the women's side, handing Blach Lavrsen her second disappointment of the winter with a 7–3 Swedish victory in the final. It was Gustafson's third world championship in seven years. Canada, with Schmirler's rink finally relegated to the sidelines in the highly competitive Canadian championship a week earlier, finished third under skip Cathy Borst. The remaining competitors were Norway, Germany, Switzerland, Scotland, Japan, the U.S., and Finland.

Skip Wayne Middaugh returned Canada, which had been shut out of the medals in 1997, to the men's world pinnacle, beating defending champion Peter Lindholm of Sweden 7–4 in the final. Markku Uusi-paavalniemi of Finland finished third, defeating 1991 world champion David Smith of Scotland. Rounding out the top 10 were Norway, the U.S., Denmark, Switzerland, Australia, and Germany.

(BRUCE CHEADLE)

CYCLING

The struggle to control doping—in particular the widespread use of the human growth hormone erythropoietin (EPO)—dominated cycling in 1998. The issue came to a head during the Tour de France, the premier event on the cycling calendar, after quantities of EPO, which stimulates the production of

Tour de France		
Year	Winner	Kilometres
1994	M. Indurain (Spain)	3,978
1995	M. Indurain (Spain)	3,635
1996	B. Riis (Den.)	3,764
1997	J. Ullrich (Ger.)	3,944
1998	**M. Pantani (Italy)**	**3,831**

Cycling Champions, 1998					
Event	Winner	Country	Event	Winner	Country
WORLD CHAMPIONS—TRACK			**WORLD CHAMPIONS—MOUNTAIN BIKES**		
Men			**Men**		
Sprint	F. Rousseau	France	Cross-country	C. Dupouey	France
Individual pursuit	P. Ermenault	France	Downhill	N. Vouilloz	France
Kilometre time trial	A. Tournant	France	**Women**		
40-km points	J. Llaneras	Spain	Cross-country	L. Leboucher	France
Team pursuit	A. Fedanko, S. Matveyev, R. Podgorny, A. Simonenko	Ukraine	Downhill	A.-C. Chausson	France
Keirin	J. Fiedler	Germany	**MAJOR ELITE ROAD-RACE WINNERS**		
Olympic sprint	V. Le Quellec, F. Rousseau, A. Tournant	France	Tour de France	M. Pantani	Italy
60-km Madison	E. De Wilde, M. Gilmore	Belgium	Tour of Italy	M. Pantini	Italy
Women			Tour of Spain	A. Olano	Spain
Sprint	F. Ballanger	France	Tour of Switzerland	S. Garzelli	Italy
Individual pursuit	L. Tyler-Sharman	Australia	Milan–San Remo	E. Zabel	Germany
500-m time trial	F. Ballanger	France	Tour of Flanders	J. Museeuw	Belgium
25-km points	T. Ruano	Spain	Paris–Roubaix	F. Ballerini	Italy
			Liège–Bastogne–Liège	M. Bartoli	Italy
			Amstel Gold	R. Jaermann	Switzerland
WORLD CHAMPIONS—ROAD			San Sebastian Classic	F. Casagrande	Italy
Men			HEW–Cyclassics Cup	L. van Bon	Netherlands
Individual road race	O. Camenzind	Switzerland	Grand Prix Suisse	M. Bartoli	Italy
Individual time trial	A. Olano	Spain	Paris–Tours	J. Durand	France
Women			Paris–Nice	F. Vandenbroucke	Belgium
Individual road race	D. Ziliute	Lithuania	Ghent–Wevelgem	F. Vandenbroucke	Belgium
Individual time trial	L. Zijlaard-van Moorsel	Netherlands	Flèche Wallonne	B. Hamburger	Denmark
			Tour of Romandie	L. Dufaux	Switzerland
			Dauphiné Libéré	A. De Las Cuevas	Spain
WORLD CHAMPION—CYCLO-CROSS			Midi-Libre	L. Dufaux	Switzerland
	M. DeClercq	Belgium	Dunkirk 4-Day	A. Vinkourov	Kazakstan
			Grand Prix of Frankfurt	F. Baldato	Italy

On the 19th stage of the Tour of Italy (Giro d'Italia) in June, Italian cyclist Marco Pantani crosses the finish line in first place. He went on to win the tour and later in the year also triumphed in the Tour de France.

medals in 12 events, accounted for two new world records, and surpassed its own world mark in the three-man Olympic sprint (44.338 sec over a distance of 750 m [2,460 ft]). Felicia Ballanger of France topped her own record (set at high altitude in 1995), with a time of 34.010 sec to win the women's 500-m time trial for the fourth successive year. In the team pursuit competition Ukraine won its first world title.

The world road championships took place at Valkenburg, Neth., in October. Oscar Camenzind gave Switzerland its first title in the elite (called professional until 1996) men's road race championship since 1951. For the second consecutive year, Michele Bartoli of Italy won the World Cup series, decided over 10 one-day road races.

(JOHN R. WILKINSON)

EQUESTRIAN SPORTS

Thoroughbred Racing. *United States.* Major developments in the business aspect of thoroughbred racing in the U.S., Real Quiet's failure to become America's 12th Triple Crown winner, and Skip Away's domination of the handicap division for most of the year generated a majority of the sport's headlines in 1998. In a collective effort by industry leaders to increase public awareness

of horse racing, the National Thoroughbred Racing Association (NTRA) was formed. Comprised of racetracks, owners, breeders, horsemen's associations, off-track betting organizations, and sales companies, among others, the NTRA's objective was to create a comprehensive marketing strategy for the sport, increase television exposure, and build a prosperous future for thoroughbred racing and breeding.

On March 12 it was announced that officials of Equibase Co. and *Daily Racing Form* had signed a licensing agreement to create a uniform database of information and standardized statistics for thoroughbred racing. Previously the two organizations collected their own information on races, including the compilation of charts and past performances. The 104-year-old *Daily Racing Form,* which chronicled the sport both editorially and statistically, was purchased in August by a group of private investors.

Following his victories in the Kentucky Derby and the Preakness Stakes, Real Quiet attempted to become America's 12th Triple Crown champion in the 130th running of the Belmont Stakes on June 6. During an epic stretch battle witnessed by a near-record on-track crowd of 80,162, jockey Kent Desormeaux was unable to prevent Real Quiet's four-length lead at the eighth pole from diminishing to a head-bob loss by a nose at the wire to Victory Gallop, the colt that had finished second to him in the first two jewels of the Triple Crown.

Skip Away, the Eclipse Award-winning older male of 1997, won seven straight graded stakes in 1998, including five Grade-I events, to make a strong case for himself

oxygen-rich red blood cells, and testosterone-based steroids were found in a Festina team car searched by customs officers on the French-Belgian border. The Festina team was subsequently expelled from the Tour, as the race continued against a backdrop of police raids, arrests, official questioning, and the discovery of other prohibited substances, including corticosteroids and masking agents. The police action led to the withdrawal of six other teams from the race, a two-hour riders' strike at the start of stage 12, and a slowdown on the 17th stage to Aix-les-Bains.

On July 23 seven of the nine Festina riders admitted to taking drugs administered by team doctors—with or without their knowledge. Swiss rider Alex Zülle, a two-time winner of the Tour of Spain, told police he had used EPO for four years under supervision. The sport's governing body, the Union Cycliste Internationale, was criticized for what many considered its failure to take decisive action as the extent of drug abuse became known and for its apparent reluctance to impose sanctions.

The doping scandal overshadowed an outstanding victory by Italian rider Marco Pantani, who became the seventh rider to win the Tour de France and Tour of Italy (Giro d'Italia) in the same year. Pantani finished 181st in the prologue time trial, raced in Ireland, where the Tour was based for the first three days, but he dominated in the mountains, winning stages in both the Pyrenees and Alps. He took the overall lead on the 15th of the 21 stages and had an advantage of 3 min 21 sec over 1997 winner Jan Ullrich of Germany when the race finished in Paris on August 2.

The world track championships were held in Bordeaux, France, in August. The host nation repeated its 1997 total of six gold

Veteran jockey Pat Day celebrates atop Awesome Again after winning the $4 million Breeders' Cup Classic at Churchill Downs on November 7. It was four-year-old Awesome Again's sixth victory of the year.

Major Thoroughbred Race Winners, 1998

Race	Won by	Jockey	Race	Won by	Jockey
United States			**England**		
Acorn	Jersey Girl	M. Smith	Two Thousand Guineas	King of Kings	M. Kinane
Alabama Stakes	Banshee Breeze	J. Bailey	One Thousand Guineas	Cape Verdi	L. Dettori
Apple Blossom	Escena	J. Bailey	Derby	High-Rise	O. Peslier
Ashland Stakes	Well Chosen	C.R. Woods, Jr.	Oaks	Shahtoush	M. Kinane
Beldame	Sharp Cat	C. Nakatani	St. Leger	Nedawi	J. Reid
Belmont	Victory Gallop	G. Stevens	Coronation Cup	Silver Patriarch	P. Eddery
Breeders' Cup Juvenile	Answer Lively	J. Bailey	Ascot Gold Cup	Kayf Tara	L. Dettori
Breeders' Cup Juvenile Fillies	Silverbulletday	G. Stevens	Eclipse Stakes	Daylami	L. Dettori
Breeders' Cup Sprint	Reraise	C. Nakatani	King George VI and Queen Elizabeth Diamond Stakes	Swain	L. Dettori
Breeders' Cup Mile	Da Hoss	J.R. Velazquez	Sussex Stakes	Among Men	M. Kinane
Breeders' Cup Distaff	Escena	G. Stevens	International Stakes	One So Wonderful	P. Eddery
Breeders' Cup Turf	Buck's Boy	S. Sellers	Dubayy Champion Stakes	Alborada	G. Duffield
Breeders' Cup Classic	Awesome Again	P. Day	**France**		
Champagne	The Groom Is Red	C. Nakatani	Poule d'Essai des Poulains	Victory Note	J. Reid
Cigar Mile Handicap	Sir Bear	J. Bailey	Poule d'Essai des Pouliches	Zalaiyka	G. Mosse
Coaching Club American Oaks	Banshee Breeze	J. Bailey	Prix du Jockey-Club	Dream Well	C. Asmussen
Donn Handicap	Skip Away	J. Bailey	Prix de Diane	Zainta	G. Mosse
Eddie Read	Subordination	D.R. Flores	Prix Ganay	Astarabad	G. Mosse
Florida Derby	Cape Town	S. Sellers	Prix Lupin	Croco Rouge	S. Guillot
Flower Bowl Invitational	Auntie Mame	J.R. Velazquez	Grand Prix de Paris	Limpid	O. Peslier
Futurity	Lemon Drop Kid	J.R. Velazquez	Grand Prix de Saint-Cloud	Fragrant Mix	O. Peslier
Gulfstream Park Handicap	Skip Away	J. Bailey	Prix Vermeille	Leggera	T. Quinn
Haskell Invitational	Coronado's Quest	M. Smith	Prix de l'Arc de Triomphe	Sagamix	O. Peslier
Hollywood Derby	Vergennes	J. Velazquez	Grand Criterium	Way of Light	C. Asmussen
Hollywood Futurity	Tactical Cat	L. Pincay, Jr.	**Ireland**		
Hollywood Gold Cup	Skip Away	J. Bailey	Irish Two Thousand Guineas	Desert Prince	O. Peslier
Hollywood Starlet	Excellent Meeting	K. Desormeaux	Irish One Thousand Guineas	Tarascon	J. Spencer
Hollywood Turf Cup	Lazy Lode	C. Nakatani	Irish Derby	Dream Well	C. Asmussen
Hollywood Turf Handicap	Storm Trooper	K. Desormeaux	Irish Oaks	Winona	J. Murtagh
Hopeful Stakes	Lucky Roberto	R. Davis	Irish St. Leger	Kayf Tara	J. Reid
Jockey Club Gold Cup	Wagon Limit	R. Davis	Irish Champion Stakes	Swain	L. Dettori
Kentucky Derby	Real Quiet	K. Desormeaux	**Italy**		
Kentucky Oaks	Keeper Hill	D.R. Flores	Derby Italiano	Central Park	D. O'Donohoe
Man o' War	Daylami	J. Bailey	Gran Premio del Jockey Club	Silver Patriarch	P. Eddery
Matriarch Stakes	Squeak	A. Solis	**Germany**		
Matron	Oh What A Windfall	S. Sellers	Deutsches Derby	Robertico	A. Starke
Meadowlands Cup	K.J.'s Appeal	J.R. Velazquez	Grosser Preis von Baden	Tiger Hill	A. Suborics
Metropolitan	Wild Rush	J. Bailey	Europa-Preis	Taipan	S. Guillot
Mother Goose	Jersey Girl	M. Smith	**Australia**		
Oaklawn Handicap	Precocity	C. Gonzalez	Caulfield Cup	Taufan's Melody	R. Cochrane
Oak Tree Turf Championship	Military	C. Nakatani	Cox Plate	Might and Power	J. Cassidy
Pacific Classic	Free House	C. McCarron	Melbourne Cup	Jezabeel	C. Munce
Pimlico Special	Skip Away	J. Bailey	**Dubayy**		
Preakness	Real Quiet	K. Desormeaux	Dubayy World Cup	Silver Charm	G. Stevens
Santa Anita Derby	Indian Charlie	G. Stevens	**Japan**		
Santa Anita Handicap	Malek	A.O. Solis	Japan Cup	El Condor Pasa	M. Ebina
Spinaway Stakes	Things Change	J. Santos			
Spinster	Banshee Breeze	R. Albarado			
Super Derby	Arch	C. Nakatani			
Travers	Coronado's Quest	M. Smith			
Turf Classic	Buck's Boy	S. Sellers			
Whitney	Awesome Again	P. Day			
Woodward	Skip Away	J. Bailey			

The Kentucky Derby

Year	Horse	Jockey
1994	Go For Gin	C. McCarron
1995	Thunder Gulch	G. Stevens
1996	Grindstone	J. Bailey
1997	Silver Charm	G. Stevens
1998	**Real Quiet**	**K. Desormeaux**

The Preakness Stakes

Year	Horse	Jockey
1994	Tabasco Cat	P. Day
1995	Timber Country	P. Day
1996	Louis Quatorze	P. Day
1997	Silver Charm	G. Stevens
1998	**Real Quiet**	**K. Desormeaux**

The Belmont Stakes

Year	Horse	Jockey
1994	Tabasco Cat	P. Day
1995	Thunder Gulch	G. Stevens
1996	Editor's Note	R. Douglas
1997	Touch Gold	C. McCarron
1998	**Victory Gallop**	**G. Stevens**

Triple Crown Champions—U.S.

Year	Horse
1946	Assault
1948	Citation
1973	Secretariat
1977	Seattle Slew
1978	Affirmed

as Horse of the Year. The streak was snapped when he finished third in the Jockey Club Gold Cup on October 10, a race he had won in 1996 and 1997.

Following a sixth-place finish in the $4 million Breeders' Cup Classic at Churchill Downs on November 7, a race in which he competed as the defending champion, Skip Away was retired to stud. He completed his career with earnings of $9,616,360, second in the history of the sport only to Cigar ($9,999,815), while finishing worse than third only twice in 38 lifetime starts.

The Breeders' Cup Classic matched one of the classiest fields of thoroughbreds ever assembled, including reigning champions Skip Away and Silver Charm and the most recent two Belmont Stake winners, Touch Gold and Victory Gallop. The 2-km (1¼-mi) event was captured by four-year-old Awesome Again, his sixth victory of an unblemished 1998 campaign. Nationwide wagering on the entire Breeders' Cup XV program established an all-time North American single-day record. The total handle amounted to $91,439,031, easily breaking the previous record of $82.6 million set in 1993.

Silver Charm, the 1997 Eclipse Award-winning three-year-old colt, became the first Kentucky Derby winner to race outside of the U.S. since Carry Back ran in the 1962 Prix

Wally Hennessey drives harness horse Moni Maker across the finish line to win the $500,000 Breeders' Crown final at the Meadowlands on August 1. The five-year-old Moni Maker was the most successful trotter in the world in 1998.

de l'Arc de Triomphe. Silver Charm captured the 1998 $4 million Dubayy World Cup on March 28, defeating Sheikh Muhammad al-Maktoum's Swain in a photo finish after the two horses engaged in a stirring stretch duel.

Arlington International Racecourse officials, citing an unfavourable economic and political environment in Illinois, chose not to hold a race meeting in 1998, which forced cancellation of the Arlington Million. The track would stay closed in 1999, and the future remained very much in doubt. The disturbing trend continued in 1998 with the November 8 closing of Detroit Race Course. Michigan's only one-mile thoroughbred racetrack, which opened in 1950, was sold for development after the owner, Ladbroke Racing, cited losses of more than $18 million since 1985. Nearly 20 racetracks across the U.S. had ceased operations during the past two decades. Meanwhile, Canadian industrialist Frank Stronach, owner of Awesome Again, signed a letter of intent in November to purchase Santa Anita Park in Arcadia, Calif. The historic track, which opened in 1934, had been acquired by Meditrust Cos. in November 1997.

Woodford Cefis "Woody" Stephens, one of the most successful trainers in thoroughbred racing history, died on August 22, at the age of 84 (*see* OBITUARIES).

(JOHN G. BROKOPP)

International. Sheikh Muhammad al-Maktoum of the United Arab Emirates (U.A.E.), the moving force behind most of his family's huge racing interests, threw the sport of thoroughbred racing in Great Britain into a panic at the end of 1997 with a speech written by him and his principal trainer, John Gosden, and delivered by the chief executive of the Emirates Racing Association, Michael Osborne. The sheikh made his intentions clear: either prize money must improve in 1998 or the family would transfer its horses elsewhere.

Statistics produced for the international conference held in Paris each October showed that in 1997 owners in Britain had recouped only 23% of their costs in prize money. This placed Britain 36th in a list of 41 countries. Although the top 10 included only 3 racing locations of international importance in the sport—Argentina (1st), Hong Kong (8th), and the U.A.E. (10th)—and

some of the figures appeared unreliable, that did not alter their significance. British racing could not compete with Japan (15th), where owners could expect to recover 79% of their costs, or even the U.S. (25th), where the return to owners had fallen from 47% in 1996 to 42% in 1997. The number of horses in training in Britain had increased during the past four years, and the competitiveness of racing, thanks in large part to foreign owners such as the Maktoums (the leading owners in Britain nearly every year since 1985), was much greater than the strength of the economy would justify. Any plan for radical change in 1998 met immediate resistance from the strongest group in British racing, the bookmaking industry. The government also was reluctant to become involved in the financial dispute between racing and bookmaking and in discussions over the level of the national betting tax, set at 6.75%.

Sheikh Muhammad had already broken an ancient custom—that it was the owner's part to pay the bills and enjoy whatever glory might come his way on the racecourse while everything else was the department of the trainer—when he withdrew all his horses from one of the leading British trainers, Henry Cecil, in late 1995. He also greatly reduced the number of horses he had with the leading trainer in France, Andre Fabre. Meanwhile, he extended the operations of Godolphin stable, over which he had absolute control.

The general direction of Godolphin policy was revealed when it was announced in April that the sheikh had taken a five-year lease, with an option of another five years, on the former racecourse at Evry, southeast of Paris, which had closed at the end of 1996. David Loder, who began training at Newmarket late in the 1992 season and saddled Desert Prince to claim victory in three Group 1 mile events in 1998, was expected

2,000 Guineas		
Year	Horse	Jockey
1994	Mister Baileys	J. Weaver
1995	Pennekamp	T. Jarnet
1996	Mark of Esteem	F. Dettori
1997	Entrepreneur	M. Kinane
1998	**King of Kings**	**M. Kinane**

The Derby		
Year	Horse	Jockey
1994	Erhaab	W. Carson
1995	Lammtarra	W.R. Swinburn
1996	Shaamit	M. Hills
1997	Benny The Dip	W. Ryan
1998	**High-Rise**	**O. Peslier**

The St. Leger		
Year	Horse	Jockey
1994	Moonax	P. Eddery
1995	Classic Cliche	L. Dettori
1996	Shantou	F. Dettori
1997	Silver Patriarch	P. Eddery
1998	**Nedawi**	**J. Reid**

Triple Crown Champions—British	
Year	Winner
1915	Pommern
1917	Gay Crusader
1918	Gainsborough
1935	Bahram
1970	Nijinsky

Melbourne Cup		
Year	Horse	Jockey
1994	Jeune	W. Harris
1995	Doriemus	D. Oliver
1996	Saintly	D. Beadman
1997	Might and Power	J. Cassidy
1998	**Jezabeel**	**C. Munce**

The Hambletonian Trot		
Year	Horse	Driver
1994	Victory Dream	M. Lachance
1995	Tagliabue	J. Campbell
1996	Continentalvictory	M. Lachance
1997	Malabar Man	M. Burroughs
1998	**Muscles Yankee**	**J. Campbell**

to train 100 Godolphin-owned two-year-olds there. The arrival of such a powerful stable was a welcome boost for racing in France, where the supremacy of the Fabre stable had been virtually unchallenged.

Sheikh Muhammad had enjoyed little success with horses trained in Australia and the U.S. He had much greater control over Godolphin, which was based in Britain April through October and for the rest of the year in the U.A.E., where Godolphin's Swain just barely lost the Dubayy World Cup to the American champion Silver Charm. In July the stable became the first to take the first three places in a Group 1 race, since the European pattern system was introduced in 1971, when Daylami, Faithful Son, and Central Park did so in the 1998 Eclipse Stakes.

Faithful Son was sent to Australia to contest the Caulfield and Melbourne cups, but he finished fourth at Caulfield behind another British visitor, the 66–1 Taufan's Melody, and seventh in Melbourne. In a thrilling finish, the five-year-old New Zealand-trained mare Jezabeel came from behind to defeat another New Zealand mare, Champagne, by a neck in the Melbourne Cup, with the British trio of Persian Punch, Taufan's Melody, and Yorkshire close behind. Australia provided only one of the first seven finishers in that nation's greatest thoroughbred race. Might and Power, Australia's 1997–98 Horse of the Year, was not in the field. Winner of the Caulfield and Melbourne cups in 1997, the five-year-old gelding added the Cox Plate in October 1998, cutting more than two seconds off the course record. Phar Lap, in 1930–31, was the only previous horse to win the Cox Plate after winning the Melbourne Cup.   (ROBERT W. CARTER)

Harness Racing. Certainly the most fittingly named harness horse in 1998 was Moni Maker. The five-year-old American mare raced on two continents and made money everywhere she went. Moni Maker towered over her foes in stature and in ability. Because of her size she did not reach top form until she was three years old, and then she never stopped improving. By 1998 she was unquestionably the best trotter in the world.

Moni Maker's Swedish-born trainer, Jimmy Takter, took her to Europe in early 1998 looking for worthy opponents. Takter knew she might not be in peak form at first, but the one race he coveted was the Elitlopp ("Elite race") in Stockholm in May. Moni Maker competed in races in Italy and Norway to prepare for the Elitlopp, and what she did to her foes in the Swedish race left Takter in awe. He said that it was perhaps the greatest racing performance ever, and certainly few of the 35,000 spectators would argue. Moni Maker and driver Wally Hennessey sat on the outside of rival Huxtable Hornline in the final heat, a tactic that often spells doom, but Hennessey had confidence in the big mare. When he asked her to trot, she astonished the crowd by leaving her pursuers in the dust to win in a record time of 1 min 53.3 sec. The bay mare later returned to the U.S. and humbled the best trotters there in some midsummer classics before returning to Europe in November.

While Moni Maker was making headlines with her accomplishments, two three-year-old colts were making headlines for what they almost did. The trotter Muscles Yankee and the pacer Shady Character won the first two legs of the Triple Crowns for their gaits, but each failed in the third leg.

When Muscles Yankee won the $1 million Hambletonian, the first leg of the Triple Crown for trotters, at the Meadowlands in early August, harness racing thought that a new star had arrived. He was so superior to his opponents that many of his pursuers in the Hambletonian opted not to race in the Yonkers Trot, the second leg of the Triple Crown. Muscles Yankee also won that race easily. Many then conceded the third leg of the Triple Crown, the Kentucky Futurity, to the two-time winner. The track even held a Triple Crown party on the eve of the race. No one, however, told the trotter Trade Balance and trainer-driver David Wade that Muscles Yankee could not be beaten. Wade launched an aggressive challenge in the opening heat, and Muscles Yankee surprisingly capitulated. Muscles Yankee had a chance to salvage the Triple Crown in the race's second heat, but once again Trade Balance outdueled the favourite to end his Triple Crown quest.

Among the three-year-old pacers Shady Character won the Cane Pace and the Little Brown Jug in close finishes to set up a try for the Triple Crown. In the Messenger Stakes, however, Fit for Life triumphed, as Shady Character finished sixth in the final heat.

France's greatest trotting classic, the Prix d'Amerique, was won by the seven-year-old mare Dryade des Bois, driven by Jos Verbeeck of Belgium, a driver with such an uncanny skill for getting the best from a horse that he was widely called "Magic Jos." In 1998 American driver Walter Case became the first person to win more than 1,000 races in a single season. Competing primarily at Yonkers Raceway in New York, he passed the former record of 853 wins in a single season.   (DEAN A. HOFFMAN)

Steeplechasing. Cool Dawn, a former point-to-pointer, was a 25–1 winner of the 1998 Cheltenham Gold Cup, but there were no shocks in the Champion Hurdle, in which the Irish-trained Istabraq scored by 12 lengths. Earth Summit won the Grand National, adding what was clearly the world's richest race over jumps to earlier successes in the Scottish (in 1994) and Welsh versions (1997). The Grand National again triggered controversy as three horses were killed during the race and only 6 of the 37 starters completed the course.

François Doumen trained the winner of the Grand Steeple-Chase de Paris for the fifth time since 1991 when First Gold (his fourth individual winner) was successful in May. Al Capone II, the 1997 winner, missed the Grand-Steeple but showed that he was still the top French jumper when he won the richest end-of-season chase, the Prix La Haye Jousselin, for the sixth consecutive year.

Show Jumping and Dressage. Rodrigo Pessoa from Brazil, winner of the World Cup at Helsinki, Fin., in April 1998, in October went on to become the youngest show jumping world champion. Pessoa, the 25-year-old son of Nelson Pessoa, rode his father's Baloubet du Rouet in Finland but switched to Gandini Lianos for the World Equestrian Games (WEG) in Rome. Franke Sloothaak, who was second in Rome on San Patrignano Joly, was also a member of the victorious German quartet in the WEG team competition.

Isabell Werth on Nissan Gigolo retained the world title in the four-day dressage competition at the WEG by the narrowest of margins from Anky van Grunsven on Gestion Bonfire. Germany's all-female quartet, led by Werth and including three of the top four individuals, won the team event. New Zealanders reigned supreme in horse trials and, with four riders in the top five, easily won the team competition at the WEG.   (ROBERT W. CARTER)

Rodrigo Pessoa of Brazil guides his horse over a jump en route to winning the show jumping World Cup final in Helsinki, Fin., in April. Pessoa is the 25-year-old son of Nelson Pessoa, winner of more than 150 Grand Prix show jumping events.

World Fencing Championships—Men						
Year	Individual			Team		
	Foil	Épée	Sabre	Foil	Épée	Sabre
1992	P. Omnès (Fr.)	E. Srecki (Fr.)	B. Szabo (Hung.)	Germany	Germany	Unified Team
1993	A. Koch (Ger.)	P. Kolobkov (Russia)	G. Kirienko (Russia)	Germany	Italy	Hungary
1994	R. Tucker (Cuba)	P. Kolobkov (Russia)	F. Becker (Ger.)	Germany	France	Russia
1995	D. Chevtchenko (Russia)	E. Srecki (Fr.)	G. Kirienko (Russia)	Cuba	Germany	Italy
1996	A. Puccini (Italy)	A. Beketov (Russia)	S. Pozdnyakov (Russia)	Russia	Italy	Russia
1997	S. Golubitsky (Ukr.)	E. Srecki (Fr.)	S. Pozdnyakov (Russia)	France	Cuba	France
1998	**S. Golubitsky (Ukr.)**	**H. Obry (Fr.)**	**L. Tarantino (Italy)**	**Poland**	**Hungary**	**Hungary**

World Fencing Championships—Women				
Year	Individual foil	Team foil	Individual épée	Team épée
1993	F. Bortolozzi (Italy)	Germany	O. Jermakova (Est.)	Hungary
1994	B. Szabo (Rom.)	Romania	L. Chiesa (Italy)	Spain
1995	L. Badea (Rom.)	Italy	J. Jakimiuk (Pol.)	Hungary
1996	L. Badea (Rom.)	Italy	L. Flessel (Fr.)	France
1997	G. Trillini (Italy)	Italy	M. Garcia-Soto (Cuba)	Hungary
1998	**S. Bau (Ger.)**	**Italy**	**L. Flessel (Fr.)**	**France**

Polo. From March to April 1998, 10 teams took part in the U.S. Open held at the Palm Beach (Fla.) Polo Club. Escue, led by brothers Sebastian and Pite Merlos, defeated Isla Carroll in the final. Fifteen-time Open winner Memo Gracida (*see* BIOGRAPHIES) and his younger brother Carlos headed the losing team, which previously had won the Gold Cup of the Americas and the Challenge and Sterling cups. In Boca Raton, Fla., White Birch, led by Mariano Aguerre of Argentina, downed Outback in the final of the United States Polo Association's Gold Cup.

Ellerston was by far the best team in the English high-handicap season. With an outstanding performance by Adolfo Cambiaso, helped by Gonzalo Pieres, the team outclassed Carlos Gracida's Labegoree and C.S. Brooks to win the Queen's and Gold (English Open) cups, respectively. Ellerston later defeated Lovelocks—which gained the Warwickshire Cup—for the Prince Philip Trophy, and Chile bested England 8–7 to secure the Coronation Cup.

Cambiaso also shone in Argentina, with a record 67 goals for his team, Ellerstina, which retained the championship of the most important tournament in the world, the Argentine Open. Indios Chapaleufú I, composed of the four Heguy brothers (Horacio, Jr., Gonzalo, Bautista, and Marcos), was the winner of the Hurlingham and Player's opens.

In Sotogrande, Spain, Geebung, led by Sebastian Merlos, won the Gold Cup, defeating John Smith in the final. Santa Maria, the local quartet, took the Silver Cup for the third straight year. Raffa and La Palmeraie were the best teams in the French season, winning the Paris Open and the Silver Cup, respectively. The International Polo Federation organized the fifth world championship for quartets with handicaps of 10–14 goals, at the Santa Barbara (Calif.) Polo and Racquet Club in August. The tournament was won by Argentina for the third time, overpowering defending champion Brazil 13–8 in the final, while England downed the U.S. 11–8 for third place.

One of the major figures in polo, Horacio Heguy, Sr., died during the year. The second generation of the family dynasty, he played on teams that won the English Gold Cup 20 times between 1958 and 1980.

(JORGE ADRIÁN ANDRADES)

FENCING

The 1997–98 season saw fencing's world senior championships moved from July to October as part of the Fédération Internationale d'Escrime's (FIE's) attempt to attract wider television interest. This inconvenienced some participants, especially those for whom the dates clashed with the academic calendar, but on balance it was considered a good move by FIE President René Roch, who had long recognized the difficulty faced by smaller sports competing for media attention with association football (soccer) and other major spectator sports. It was particularly significant in 1998 because of the domination of world media by the soccer World Cup in France.

When the championships took place in October in La Chaux-de-Fonds, Switz., 74 nations were represented. Twelve countries won at least one medal, with perennial favourites France and Italy each taking a total of six. Only Sergey Golubitsky of Ukraine, who captured his second consecutive individual foil, and the Italian women, who took the team foil, were repeat winners from 1997. Sabine Bau of Germany was victorious in the women's foil after a seven-year string of winners from Italy or Romania.

Technical changes were recommended at foil to make refereeing easier and more objective. Over recent years at world level, foil theory and practice had diverged to the point where referees were forced to judge the validity of an attack based on their perception of a fencer's intentions rather than on traditional movements. In addition the development of certain movements had, in the opinion of many, produced an inelegant spectacle. The FIE hoped that changes to timing in the electrical circuits, particularly the time the point remains on the target, would address these problems. The other significant technical change involved the sabre blade, which would be made less flexible to keep the point from flicking over an otherwise good defensive action by an opponent.

(GRAHAM MORRISON)

FIELD HOCKEY

In 1998 the Fédération Internationale de Hockey (FIH) introduced changes into field hockey, a 16-player game with 11 players on the field and 5 on the sideline ready to play at short notice as substitutes. The experimental no-offside rule was formally incorporated into the laws of the game, and substitutions by the attacking sides at penalty corners were forbidden. The decision to prohibit substitutions at penalty corners was made to eliminate specialist marksmen who scrambled onto the field to strike a corner and then rushed back to the bench. In the view of the FIH these specialists, who were not also all-around hockey players, were undesirable in the game.

An extensive study of the composition and manufacture of field hockey sticks was also conducted during the year. As a result the existing definition of a stick, which dictated that its head (but not necessarily other parts) must be made of wood, would continue to apply.

Other developments were announced in May in Utrecht, Neth., where the ninth World Cup tournaments for men and women were held concurrently for the first time. Cuba and Ghana were selected as the first two countries to receive funding through a pilot FIH development program supported by the International Olympic Committee (IOC). The IOC also guaranteed a permanent place for field hockey in the Olympics and increased the number of women's teams to 12 for the 2004 Olympic Games in Athens. At the 1996 Olympics in Atlanta, Ga., there were 8 women's teams. That number was increased to 10 for the 2000 Games in Sydney, Australia.

The Netherlands, which had won in Atlanta in 1996, became holders of both the Olympic and World Cup titles by winning the men's event at Utrecht. The same distinction was achieved by the women of Australia.

The Dutch men also won the Champions Trophy tournament at Lahore, Pak., in November. Field hockey was included in the Commonwealth Games for the first time in 1998. Australia triumphed in the women's event with an 8–1 victory in the final over England and in the men's competition with a 4–0 win in the final against Malaysia.

(SYDNEY E. FRISKIN)

World Cup Field Hockey Championship—Men		
Year	Winner	Runner-up
1990	Netherlands	Pakistan
1994	Pakistan	Netherlands
1998	**Netherlands**	**Spain**

World Cup Field Hockey Championship—Women		
Year	Winner	Runner-up
1990	Netherlands	Australia
1994	Australia	Argentina
1998	**Australia**	**Netherlands**

FOOTBALL

Association Football (Soccer). *Europe.* During the summer of 1998 all eyes were on France, where 32 national teams faced off in the 16th World Cup finals. In the final match, held on July 12 at the new Stade de France in Saint-Denis, near Paris, the host team, led by star midfielder Zinedine Zidane (*see* BIOGRAPHIES), routed defending champion Brazil 3–0. (*See* Sidebar.)

During the year all 51 members of the Union des Associations Européennes de Football (UEFA) entered the ninth European Football Championship. For the first time two countries, Belgium and The Netherlands, would share the staging of the final tournament in 2000. Newcomers to the competition were Andorra and Bosnia and Herzegovina.

On June 8 voting took place for a new president of the Fédération Internationale de Football Association (FIFA), the world governing body, to replace the retiring incumbent João Havelange of Brazil, who had been president since 1974. Joseph S. Blatter of Switzerland, previously the general secretary to FIFA, defeated the UEFA president, Lennart Johansson of Sweden.

Johansson was left with a crisis brought about by a group of investors anxious to approach the wealthiest clubs in Western Europe to form an independent European Super League. While the three major European cup competitions had undergone considerable structural change in recent years and would continue to be affected, the clamour for further financial rewards prompted the idea of a breakaway organization. The concept of a Super League dated back 60 years when, as air travel began to expand in the years before World War II, leading clubs in England and on the continent were expressing the desire to form a European League of Nations.

In September BSkyB, the satellite television company owned by multimillionaire media magnate Rupert Murdoch (*see* BIOGRAPHIES), made a bid of £623.4 million for the Manchester United club. The proposed sale, one of the biggest financial deals in sports, brought a feverish rush among other parties interested in buying into other English Premier League clubs.

Widespread interest in the current European tournaments was again revealed with the live television transmission to some 200 countries worldwide of the 43rd European Cup of Champion Clubs final in the new Amsterdam Arena on May 20. Real Madrid from Spain was hoping to win its seventh title at the expense of Italy's Juventus, which was trying for a third trophy. The venue represented the first UEFA final to be held in a stadium with a removable roof. The Italians had the better of the opening 20 minutes and continued to be wasteful with the greater scoring opportunities, Filippo Inzaghi being the chief culprit. As the match wore on, Real Madrid gained confidence and in the 67th minute achieved the breakthrough. A centre from Clarence Seedorf was cleared by the Juventus de-fense, but only to Roberto Carlos, who had his short kick blocked by the Italian goalkeeper, Angelo Peruzzi, only for the ball to run loose to Predrag Mijatovic. The Yugoslav rounded Peruzzi and clipped his shot in from a narrow angle. It was enough to win the game for the Spaniards. Real's German coach, Jupp Heynckes, was dismissed eight days after the final, more as a punishment for failing to lift the team higher than fourth in the Spanish League than as any reflection on his European triumph.

The 38th Cup-Winners' Cup final was held in the Rasunda Stadium in Stockholm on May 13. Chelsea (England) won its first European title since 1971, when it had beaten Real Madrid in the same competition. Stuttgart (Germany) conceded the match to Chelsea's only score, a goal in the 71st minute from substitute Gianfranco Zola, who had been on the field just 22 seconds. Chelsea had been the better team throughout the match but failed to capitalize on its overall superiority. Stuttgart had more opportunities to score in a first half marked by erratic play from both teams. The nearest Stuttgart came to scoring was in the 18th minute, when Bulgarian striker

FIFA World Cup				
Year	Result			
1990	West Germany	1	Argentina	0
1994	Brazil*	0	Italy	0
1998	France	3	Brazil	0

*Won on penalty kicks.

European Cup-Winners' Cup				
Season	Result			
1993–94	Arsenal (Eng.)	1	Parma (Italy)	0
1994–95	Real Zaragosa (Spain)	2	Arsenal (Eng.)	1
1995–96	Paris St.-Germain	1	Rapid Vienna	0
1996–97	Barcelona	1	Paris St.-Germain	0
1997–98	Chelsea (Eng.)	1	Stuttgart (Ger.)	0

European Cup of Champion Clubs				
Season	Result			
1993–94	AC Milan	4	Barcelona	0
1994–95	Ajax Amsterdam	1	AC Milan	0
1995–96	Juventus (Italy)*	1	Ajax Amsterdam	1
1996–97	Borussia Dortmund (Ger.)	3	Juventus (Italy)	1
1997–98	Real Madrid	1	Juventus (Italy)	0

*Won on penalty kicks.

Association Football National Champions					
Nation	League Winners	Cup Winners	Nation	League Winners	Cup Winners
Albania	Vllaznia	Apolonia	Italy	Juventus	Lazio
Andorra	Principat	Principat	Latvia	Skonto Riga	Skonto Riga
Argentina	River Plate		Liechtenstein	—	Vaduz
Armenia	VFC Erevan	Taument	Lithuania	Kareda	Ekranes
Austria	Sturm Graz	Ried	Luxembourg	Jeunesse Esch	Grevenmacher
Azerbaijan	Kopaz	Kopaz	Macedonia	Sileks	Vardar
Belarus	Dynamo Minsk	Lokomotiv 96	Malta	Valleta	Hibernians
Belgium	FC Brugge	Genk	Moldova	Zimbru Chisinau	Zimbru Chisinau
Bolivia	Bolivar		Netherlands	Ajax	Ajax
Brazil	Vasco da Gama	Gremio	Northern Ireland	Cliftonville	Glentoran
Bulgaria	Litets	Levski	Norway	Rosenborg	Valerengen
Chile	Colo Colo		Paraguay	Olimpia	
Colombia	America Cali		Peru	Alianza	
Croatia	Croatia Zagreb	Croatia Zagreb	Poland	LKS Lodz	Amica
Cyprus	Anorthosis	Anorthosis	Portugal	Porto	Porto
Czech Republic	Sparta Prague	Jablonec	Romania	Steaua	Rapid
Denmark	Brondby	Brondby	Russia	Spartak Moscow	Spartak Moscow
Ecuador	Barcelona		San Marino	Folgore	Faetano
England	Arsenal	Arsenal	Scotland	Celtic	Hearts
Estonia	Flora	Flora	Slovakia	Kosice	Spartak Trnava
Faroe Islands	B36 Torshavn	GI Gotu	Slovenia	Branik Maribor	Rudar
Finland	HJK Helsinki	Haka	Spain	Barcelona	Barcelona
France	Lens	Paris St.-Germain	Sweden	Halmstad	Helsingborg
Georgia	Dynamo Tbilisi	Dynamo Batumi	Switzerland	Grasshoppers	Lausanne
Germany	Kaiserslautern	Bayern Munich	Turkey	Galatasaray	Besiktas
Greece	Olympiakos	Panionios	Ukraine	Dynamo Kiev	Dynamo Kiev
Hungary	Ujpest	MTK Budapest	Uruguay	Penarol	
Iceland	IBV Vestmann	IBK Keflavik	Venezuela	Minerven	
Ireland	St. Patrick's	Cork City	Wales	Barry Town	Bangor City
Israel	Beitar Jerusalem	Maccabi Haifa	Yugoslavia	Obilic	Partizan Belgrade

World Cup

France easily won the 16th World Cup, beating Brazil 3–0 in the final at Saint-Denis, near Paris, on July 12, 1998. The tournament, which had 32 finalists for the first time, was largely disappointing, the overall standard of play being generally of a low-key nature. Although the Fédération Internationale de Football Association (FIFA) called France 98 a successful World Cup, most independent critics rated it as a tournament of quantity rather than quality. The delay of almost a week between teams' first and second matches unnecessarily prolonged the competition in its initial stage in sharp contrast to the knockout phase in the second round, when the first two matches provided the winners with a respite of another six days compared with only four days rest for those playing on the last day of the round.

Statistics revealed that 1,881 shots were taken in the 64 matches, 891 of them on target from which 171 goals were scored. There were 667 corners and 379 offside decisions, as well as 2,135 offenses of one kind or another. Considering that 64 matches were contested, it was not surprising that a record number of yellow (250) and red (22) cards were shown to players. There was an alarming increase in the unlawful use of hands and arms by players in tackling opponents and in attempting to gain unfair advantage at set-pieces.

One of the French trio shown red cards was Zinedine Zidane (see BIOGRAPHIES). After being suspended for two games, Zidane returned as the saviour of France in the final, in which he scored the first two goals with rare, headed corner shots—the first in the 27th minute and the second within seconds of the halftime interval. In the dying seconds of the match, Emmanuel Petit added a third goal for France. It was the 1,000th in the country's football history and the 1,755th overall in World Cup finals.

The real drama of the final match had occurred before the kickoff, when Brazil's Ronaldo, the FIFA Player of the Year, was rushed to the hospital for tests following a night in which he had suffered a seizure. He was named a late addition to the Brazilian team, but he was clearly not in either the right physical or mental condition for playing in a match of this magnitude. The episode seemed to affect the entire Brazilian team, which gave one of its poorest displays in a final tournament.

In a competition devoid of memorable individual accomplishment, outstanding scoring contributions were made by David Beckham with a free kick for England against Colombia, Michael Owen for a breathtaking solo effort for England against Argentina, and, in the finest effort of all, Dennis Bergkamp of The Netherlands. Against Argentina, Bergkamp controlled a lofted 46-m (50-yd) pass from Frank de Boer with one touch, beat his marker with the second, and finished clinically with the third to score the winning goal in the 89th minute. Bergkamp, however, had been fortunate to avoid a red card in the match against Yugoslavia, and Beckham was dismissed for a moment of stupidity against Argentina.

Croatia was the surprise team, deservedly finishing in third place, and Croatia's Davor Suker was the tournament's leading scorer with six goals. Fan violence was chiefly restricted to England's followers, though the German fans were involved in some unsavoury incidents. Lothar Matthaus of Germany set a World Cup record by appearing in his 25th match in a final tournament, increasing his overall total of games for his country to 129. Within two months of the final match, 22 of the 32 national coaches involved in the tournament had either been fired or had resigned.

(JACK ROLLIN)

Krassimir Balakov had a short kick saved by Chelsea's Dutch goalkeeper, Ed de Goey.

For the 27th UEFA Cup final, the match was staged at the Parc des Princes in Paris and not as home and away games as in previous years. In an all-Italian final Internazionale from Milan beat Lazio of Rome 3–0. South American players scored all the goals, with Ivan Zamorano of Chile outpacing the Lazio rearguard to score as early as the fifth minute for the first goal. Javier Zanetti of Argentina added a second goal after 60 minutes from 22.9 m (25 yd), and Ronaldo of Brazil strode in for number three 10 minutes later.

Such was the cosmopolitan nature of the European game in 1998 that the 82 players who appeared in the three regional finals represented 20 different nations: Europe (15), South America (4), and Africa (1). Italy, with three finalists, had 28 of those players as members of five of the six final teams, Germany had 8, while Spain and France had 6 each. Lazio had 10 Italian players, but Chelsea had only 4 Englishmen. Only 41 of the finalists played for a club from their own country. Zola's strike for Chelsea was the only goal by an Italian in any of the three European finals.

On the domestic front, there was mixed fortune in Italy. Juventus won its 25th League championship, five points ahead of Internazionale, while Lazio won the Italian Cup for the second time, beating AC Milan 3–2 on aggregate in the final. Barcelona had a convincing nine-point lead in Spain to record its 15th championship, while Ajax finished a massive 17 points in front of runners-up PSV Eindhoven in the Dutch

Youri Djorkaeff of France (right) and Rivaldo of Brazil chase after the ball during the World Cup final at Saint-Denis, near Paris, on July 12. France won the World Cup for the first time in its history, beating Brazil 3–0. The victory ignited the biggest party in Paris since the end of World War II.

CHARLES PLATIAU—REUTERS

Soccer fans celebrate on the Champs-Élysées in Paris after France defeated Brazil in the World Cup final. In the background, the message "Merci Zizou" appears in lights on the Arc de Triomphe, a thank-you note to Zinedine Zidane, star player for the French team.

The Americas. Brazil in 1998 was again the best team in the Americas, finishing second in the World Cup (*see* Sidebar). The nation's clubs also made a clean sweep of the international trophies open to them. Vasco da Gama, which was celebrating its 100th anniversary, won the South American club championship (Libertadores de América Cup), Palmeiras gained the new Mercosur Cup, Santos took the CONMEBOL trophy, and Atlético Nacional of Colombia won the new Merconorte Cup.

Corinthians won the Brazilian championship, and Palmeiras took the Brazil Cup. In Chile Colo Colo took the title for the third year in a row, and in Colombia the professional league's 50th championship was won by Deportivo Cali in the final round after Once Caldas had taken the long (50-game) regular championship. In Argentina Vélez Sarsfield won the 1997–98 season-closing championship, and Boca Juniors gained the 1998–99 season-opening championship. In Mexico Toluca won its first title in 23 years in the 1997–98 season summer championship final against Necaxa, which went on to win the 1998–99 winter championship.

In finals between two tournament winners Nacional took the Uruguayan title after five years of domination by Montevideo rival Peñarol, and Olimpia retained the championship in Paraguay. Universitario became Peru's champion, Blooming won in Bolivia, and Liga Deportiva Universitaria de Quito triumphed in Ecuador. In Venezuela Atlético Zulia gained the 1997–98 championship, and Union Atlético Tachira won the 1998–99 season-opening tournament.

Notably, both the CONCACAF Club Champions Cup and the Inter-American Cup left the region for the first time, both taken by defending U.S. champion D.C. United. In the Inter-American Cup the U.S. team defeated Vasco da Gama 2–1 on aggregate in the two-match final. A tired Vasco da Gama—having played more than 70

League and underlined its superiority by beating PSV 5–0 in the cup final. Ajax also scored 112 goals in its 34-match program. The honour as The Netherlands' leading marksman went to Nikos Machlas of Greece playing for another Dutch club, Vitesse. Machlas scored 34 goals during the 32 matches in which he appeared. Europe's foremost goal scorer was Rhinor Rauffman of the Cypriot club Omonia Nicosia, with 42 of that club's 90 League goals.

One of the best team performances occurred in Germany, where recently promoted Kaiserslautern won the Bundesliga against the favoured Bayern Munich. The

closest championship was in France, where Lens won on superior goal difference from Metz. In Scotland Celtic managed at last to stem the tide of success achieved by its Glasgow rivals, the Rangers, winning the title and preventing the Rangers from obtaining their 10th successive championship. Dynamo Tbilisi achieved its ninth successive Georgian League title, while in Latvia, Skonto Riga was unbeaten in 24 championship-winning games. In Poland a serious rift between the sports ministry and the football federation threatened to end in the suspension of all Polish teams from international competition.   (JACK ROLLIN)

Libertadores de América Cup			
Year	Winner (country)	Runner-up (country)	Scores
1994	Vélez Sarsfield (Arg.)	São Paulo (Braz.)	1–0, 0–1, 5–3*
1995	Grêmio (Braz.)	Atletico Nacional (Colom.)	3–1, 1–1
1996	River Plate (Arg.)	América (Colom.)	0–1, 2–0
1997	Cruzeiro (Braz.)	Sporting Cristal (Peru)	0–0, 1–0
1998	**Vasco da Gama (Braz.)**	**Barcelona (Ecua.)**	**2–0, 2–1**

*Winner determined in penalty shootout after tiebreaking game.

U.S. College Football National Champions	
Season	Champion
1993–94	Florida State
1994–95	Nebraska
1995–96	Nebraska
1996–97	Florida
1997–98	Michigan*/Nebraska*
1998–99	**Tennessee**

*Tied.

Rose Bowl				
Season	Result			
1993–94	Wisconsin	21	UCLA	16
1994–95	Penn State	38	Oregon	20
1995–96	Southern California	41	Northwestern	32
1996–97	Ohio State	20	Arizona State	17
1997–98	Michigan	21	Washington State	16
1998–99	**Wisconsin**	**38**	**UCLA**	**31**

Orange Bowl				
Season	Result			
1993–94	Florida State	18	Nebraska	16
1994–95	Nebraska	24	Miami	17
1995–96	Florida State	31	Notre Dame	26
1996–97	Nebraska	41	Virginia Tech	21
1997–98	Nebraska	42	Tennessee	17
1998–99	**Florida**	**31**	**Syracuse**	**10**

Sugar Bowl				
Season	Result			
1993–94	Florida	41	West Virginia	7
1994–95	Florida State	23	Florida	17
1995–96	Virginia Tech	28	Texas	10
1996–97	Florida	52	Florida State	20
1997–98	Florida State	31	Ohio State	14
1998–99	**Ohio State**	**24**	**Texas A&M**	**14**

Cotton Bowl				
Season	Result			
1993–94	Notre Dame	24	Texas A&M	21
1994–95	Southern California	55	Texas Tech	14
1995–96	Colorado	38	Oregon	6
1996–97	Brigham Young	19	Kansas State	15
1997–98	UCLA	29	Texas A&M	23
1998–99	**Texas**	**38**	**Mississippi State**	**11**

Tennessee defensive back Dwayne Goodrich (23) steps in front of Florida State wide receiver Peter Warrick to intercept a pass during the Fiesta Bowl on Jan. 4, 1999. Goodrich returned the interception for a touchdown, and Tennessee went on to beat Florida State 23–16 for the national championship.

games during the year—also lost 2–1 to European Cup holders Real Madrid for the Intercontinental Cup in Tokyo.

Back in the U.S., D.C. United failed to capture its third straight Major League Soccer (MLS) championship, as the Chicago Fire, an expansion franchise in its first season, vanquished a stunned United 2–0 in the MLS Cup final on October 25 before a crowd of 51,350 in Pasadena, Calif. Less than a week later Chicago defeated the Columbus Crew 2–1 in overtime to win the U.S. Open Cup.   (ERIC WEIL)

U.S. Football. *College.* The University of Tennessee won its first U.S. college football national championship since 1951 by defeating Florida State University 23–16 in the Fiesta Bowl at Tempe, Ariz., on Jan. 4, 1999. The game was the first ever to be designated before the season as the national championship game for the teams in Division I-A of the National Collegiate Athletic Association (NCAA), but it was not the culmination of a championship tournament, as used in the NCAA's three other divisions. Instead, the two finalists were determined by the last regular-season rankings in the Bowl Championship Series Poll, which applied a mathematical formula to each top team's won–lost record, its opponents' aggregate won–lost record, and its ranking in established news media polls. Florida State (11–2) finished third in the final writers' and coaches' polls, ranking behind Southeastern Conference champion Tennessee (13–0) and Big Ten cochampion Ohio State (11–1).

The regular season ended with Tennessee and Conference USA champion Tulane (12–0) both undefeated, but Tulane did not qualify for the Fiesta Bowl because its opponents were considered relatively weak. Two other teams entered the last weekend undefeated, but Pacific-10 champion UCLA and Kansas State lost their December 5 games, enabling Florida State to qualify for the championship game. Florida State, which tied Georgia Tech for the Atlantic

Coast Conference title, was the highest ranked of six teams that finished the regular season with one defeat.

Behind Florida State, the writers' poll ranked Arizona (12–1), Florida (10–2), Wisconsin (11–1), Tulane, UCLA, Georgia Tech, and Kansas State, which lost the Big Twelve championship game to Texas A&M (11–3). The coaches' poll reversed the order of Wisconsin and Florida and ranked Kansas State ninth, followed by Western Athletic Conference champion Air Force (12–1). Other Division I-A conference winners were Syracuse (8–4) in the Big East, Idaho (9–3) in the Big West, and Marshall (12–1) in the Mid-American, from which Miami (Ohio) was not invited to one of the 23 bowl games despite a 10–1 record.

Ricky Williams of Texas won the Heisman Trophy and Maxwell Award, both given to the most outstanding player, and the Doak Walker Award for the top running back, as he led Division I-A with 2,124 yd rushing and 27 touchdown runs. Dat Nguyen of Texas A&M was also a multiple winner with the top defensive player's Chuck Bednarik Award and the Vince Lombardi Trophy for the best lineman. The most prominent Coach of the Year awards went to Bill Snyder of Kansas State and Phillip Fulmer of Tennessee.

Florida State's defense allowed only 214.8 yd per game and a passing efficiency rating of 79.9, both best in Division I-A, and ranked second in rushing yards and points allowed. Ohio State's per-game yield of 67.4 yd rushing was the best, and it finished behind Florida State in the three other main defensive categories. Wisconsin allowed the fewest points, 10.2 per game. The offensive per-game leaders were Kansas State with 48.0 points, Louisville with 559.6 total yards, Army with 293.8 yd rushing, and Louisiana Tech with 432.1 yd passing behind a quarterback and receiver who swept most of the individual categories: Tim Rattay led all passers with 4,943 yd passing, 46 touchdown passes, and 4,840 yd total offense, while Troy Edwards was the leader with 140 catches, 1,996 yd on receptions, 31 touchdowns, 188 points, and 2,784 all-purpose yards. Other award winners were Sebastian Janikowski of Florida State, the Lou Groza winner as best kicker and field-goal leader with 27; Michael Bishop of Kansas State, the Davey O'Brien winner as best quarterback; Kris Farris of UCLA, the Outland Trophy winner as best interior lineman; Chris Claiborne of Southern California, the Dick Butkus winner as best linebacker; and Antoine Winfield of Ohio State, the Jim Thorpe winner as best defensive back.

Professional. The Denver Broncos capped a spectacular season with their second consecutive National Football League (NFL) championship, defeating the surprising Atlanta Falcons by a score of 34–19 in Super Bowl XXXIII on Jan. 31, 1999, in Miami, Fla. The Broncos' 38-year-old quarterback, John Elway (*see* BIOGRAPHIES), who was named the game's Most Valuable Player (MVP), passed for 336 yd, including an 80-yd touchdown pass to wide receiver Rod Smith, and ran for another touchdown.

Super Bowl					
	Season	**Result**			
XXVIII	1993–94	Dallas Cowboys (NFC)	30	Buffalo Bills (AFC)	13
XXIX	1994–95	San Francisco 49ers (NFC)	49	San Diego Chargers (AFC)	26
XXX	1995–96	Dallas Cowboys (NFC)	27	Pittsburgh Steelers (AFC)	17
XXXI	1996–97	Green Bay Packers (NFC)	35	New England Patriots (AFC)	21
XXXII	1997–98	Denver Broncos (AFC)	31	Green Bay Packers (NFC)	24
XXXIII	**1998–99**	**Denver Broncos (AFC)**	**34**	**Atlanta Falcons (NFC)**	**19**

NFL Final Standings, 1998

AMERICAN CONFERENCE

Eastern Division	W	L	T	Central Division	W	L	T	Western Division	W	L	T
*New York Jets	12	4	0	*Jacksonville	11	5	0	*Denver	14	2	0
*Miami	10	6	0	Tennessee	8	8	0	Oakland	8	8	0
*Buffalo	10	6	0	Pittsburgh	7	9	0	Seattle	8	8	0
*New England	9	7	0	Baltimore	6	10	0	Kansas City	7	9	0
Indianapolis	3	13	0	Cincinnati	3	13	0	San Diego	5	11	0

NATIONAL CONFERENCE

Eastern Division	W	L	T	Central Division	W	L	T	Western Division	W	L	T
*Dallas	10	6	0	*Minnesota	15	1	0	*Atlanta	14	2	0
*Arizona	9	7	0	*Green Bay	11	5	0	*San Francisco	12	4	0
New York Giants	8	8	0	Tampa Bay	8	8	0	New Orleans	6	10	0
Washington	6	10	0	Detroit	5	11	0	Carolina	4	12	0
Philadelphia	3	13	0	Chicago	4	12	0	St. Louis	4	12	0

*Qualified for play-offs.

Denver Broncos running back Terrell Davis (30) explodes through a gap in the New York Jets defensive line during Denver's convincing 23–10 victory in the AFC Championship game on January 17. Davis's rushing prowess was a major reason the Broncos made it to the Super Bowl for a second straight year.

To reach the Super Bowl Denver defeated Miami 38–3 and staged a second-half comeback to beat the New York Jets 23–10. Atlanta defeated San Francisco 20–18 and then upset Minnesota 30–27 in overtime.

All six divisions crowned new champions in 1998. Two of them, Atlanta and the Jets, joined the wild-card Arizona Cardinals in play-off seasons that ended years of frustration. Atlanta, the most improved team with a seven-game jump from 1997, won its first division title since 1980; the Jets won their first since 1969, and the Cardinals followed their first winning season in 14 years with their first play-off appearance since they played in St. Louis in 1982 and their first postseason victory since they played in Chicago in 1947. Pittsburgh missed the play-offs after qualifying for six consecutive years, leaving San Francisco alone with the longest streak at seven.

It was a big year for older quarterbacks, and especially big for three veterans whose best seasons had seemed to be behind them. The National Football League's (NFL's) top five passer ratings belonged, respectively, to Minnesota's 35-year-old Randall Cunningham, the Jets' Vinny Testaverde, 35; San Francisco's Steve Young, 37; Atlanta's Chris Chandler, 33; and Elway, 38; followed by four more passers over 30 in the top 10. Cunningham had been out of football in 1996, Testaverde had been re-

leased by Baltimore after losing his starting job in 1997, and Buffalo's 10th-ranked Doug Flutie, 36, had spent the previous eight seasons in the Canadian Football League, where he won its Most Outstanding Player Award six times but did not erase the memory of four previous unimpressive NFL seasons. In other passing categories the league leaders were Young, who passed for 36 touchdowns, Cunningham with touchdowns on 8.0% of his attempts, Chandler with 9.65 yd per attempt, and Green Bay's Brett Favre with 4,212 yd and a 63.0 completion percentage that beat Carolina's Steve Beuerlein on the fifth decimal point. Favre also set a record with at least 30 touchdown passes for the fifth consecutive season.

The veteran passers contributed to an offensive resurgence that was widely attributed to improved deciphering of complicated defenses. Minnesota and Denver became two of only six teams in history to score more than 500 points in a season. Minnesota, the third team ever to win 15 games, broke a 15-year-old league record with 556 points and led the league with 270.5 yd passing per game. San Francisco gained the second highest yardage

total in history with 425.0 yd per game and also led the league with 159.0 yd rushing per game. Denver led the American Football Conference (AFC) in total and rushing yardage and in points, with 501. Limiting opponents' yardage was less predictive of success, as league defensive leaders San Diego (263.0 total yards per game and 71.3 yd rushing) and Philadelphia (170.0 yd passing) had losing records.

Minnesota kicker Gary Anderson set NFL records with 164 kicking points and a 35-for-35 success on field goal attempts, which included a league-high 14 field goals from at least 40 yd and more than doubled the only previous perfect season of 17-for-17. Jason Elam's 63-yd field goal for Denver tied a 28-year-old record, Randy Moss of Minnesota led the league with a rookie record of 17 touchdowns on pass receptions, and Denver's Terrell Davis became the fourth 2,000-yd rusher with 2,008. Davis also led the league with 23 total touchdowns, 21 on runs, and 5.1 yd per carry with at least 100 attempts. Other offensive league leaders were O.J. McDuffie with 90 catches for Miami, Antonio Freeman with 1,424 yd receiving for Green Bay, and Marshall Faulk with 2,227 total yards from scrimmage for Indianapolis. Eric Moulds of Buffalo led the AFC with 1,368 yd receiving with an average of 20.4 yd per catch, Frank Sanders of Arizona was the leader in the National Football Conference (NFC) with 89 catches, and Jamal Anderson of Atlanta led the NFC with 1,846 yd rushing on 410 carries, a league record. The kick return leaders were Deion Sanders of Dallas, averaging 15.6 yd on punts, and Terry Fair of Detroit, 28.0 yd on kickoffs. Tennessee's Craig Hentrich led all punters with averages of 39.3 net yards and 47.2 gross yards.

A new $17.6 billion television contract for eight years helped the league sell the expansion Cleveland Browns franchise for a

Minnesota Vikings rookie wide receiver Randy Moss pitches the football to a fan after catching a 49-yd touchdown pass from quarterback Randall Cunningham during a 28–14 victory against the Green Bay Packers on November 22. In 1998 Moss emerged as one of the NFL's premier receivers.

Grey Cup				
Year	Result			
1994	British Columbia Lions (WFC)	26	Baltimore Stallions (EFC)	23
1995	Baltimore Stallions (SD)	37	Calgary Stampeders (ND)	20
1996	Toronto Argonauts (ED)	43	Edmonton Eskimos (WD)	37
1997	Toronto Argonauts (ED)	47	Saskatchewan Roughriders (WD)	23
1998	**Calgary Stampeders (WD)**	**26**	**Hamilton Tiger-Cats (ED)**	**24**

AFL Final Standings, 1998 (League ladder after round 22)				
Team*	W	L	D	Points
North Melbourne	16	6	0	64
Western Bulldogs	15	7	0	60
Sydney	14	8	0	56
Melbourne	14	8	0	56
Adelaide	13	9	0	52
St. Kilda	13	9	0	52
West Coast	12	10	0	48
Essendon	12	10	0	48

*Teams that qualified for play-offs.

record $530 million. The Browns would begin playing in 1999, three years after the original Browns moved to Baltimore as the Ravens. The Tennessee Oilers, two years removed from Houston, changed their nickname to the Titans for the 1999 season. In the Arena Football League's first network telecast on August 23, the Orlando Predators won the league's 12th championship game 62–31 over the Tampa Bay Storm.

(KEVIN M. LAMB)

Canadian Football. The Calgary Stampeders won the Canadian Football League (CFL) championship by defeating the Hamilton Tiger-Cats 26–24 in the Grey Cup on November 22, when Mark McLoughlin kicked a 35-yd field goal on the game's last play. Calgary quarterback Jeff Garcia was the game's Most Outstanding Player. Hamilton rebounded from a 2–16 record in 1997 to a record of 12 wins, 5 losses, and 1 tie and a share of the Eastern Division title with Montreal, which it eliminated from the play-offs on a game-ending field goal. Western Division winner Calgary (12–6) led the league in total offense and rushing defense, while Montreal was the leader in rushing offense, and Toronto led in passing offense and total and pass defense.

Mike Pringle of Montreal won the CFL's Most Outstanding Player award, set records with 2,065 yd rushing and 13 consecutive 100-yd games, and tied his own record with 2,414 yd from scrimmage. Hamilton slotback Mike Morreale was the Most Outstanding Canadian, Hamilton linebacker Joe Montford was the Most Outstanding Defensive Player and led the league with 21 sacks and six forced fumbles, British Columbia cornerback Steve Muhammad was the Most Outstanding Rookie and interception leader with 10, and Calgary tackle Fred Childress was the Most Outstanding Offensive Lineman. Toronto slotback Derrell Mitchell's 160 catches set a league record, and Lui Passaglia of British Columbia kicked a league-high 52 field goals in his record 23rd season.

(KEVIN M. LAMB)

Australian Football. The Adelaide Crows made it back-to-back premierships in 1998 and became the first club since Hawthorn in 1988–89 to win successive flags in the Australian Football League (AFL). They also became the first club to win the title from fifth place following the 22-round home and away series. Adelaide, the underdogs, stormed home in the second half against North Melbourne to win the grand final by 35 points in front of a crowd of 94,431 at the Melbourne Cricket Ground. The final score was Adelaide 15.15 (105) to North 8.22 (70). In the second half Adelaide kicked 11.12 to 2.7. Andrew McLeod of Adelaide was voted best on the ground, thus becoming the first player to win consecutive Norm Smith Medals.

While Adelaide took the premiership accolades, the Melbourne FC produced the

fairy-tale story of the season, coming from bottom place on the ladder (16th) in 1997 to fourth and a place in the preliminary finals in 1998. The AFL had a record attendance for the home and away series: 6,117,177, which beat the previous record of 5,842,591 established in 1997.

Robert Harvey, of St. Kilda, won the Brownlow Medal (for the best and fairest player) for the second straight year—the first player to do so since Keith Greig of North Melbourne in 1973–74. Other major honours went to North Melbourne for winning the preseason Ansett Australia Cup competition, Wayne Carey for winning the Michael Tuck Medal in the Ansett Cup series, and Tony Lockett for winning the Coleman Medal as the AFL top goalkicker (109) in the home and away series.

(GREG HOBBS)

Kicker Mark McLoughlin of the Calgary Stampeders follows through on his game-winning 35-yd field goal in the final seconds of the Grey Cup on November 22. The field goal gave the Stampeders a thrilling 26–24 victory over the Hamilton Tiger-Cats.

FRED GREENSLADE—REUTERS

Rugby Football. In 1998 Rugby Union was all about change and about one side in particular—South Africa—moving back into the world's number one spot. The resurgence of South Africa's Springboks resulted from the efforts of one man, coach Nick Mallett, who brought democracy back to the side and let the players express their undoubted talents. Before the 1998 Tri-Nations championship, which was held in July and August, Mallett's Springboks were rated second or third in the world, but four wins in four matches against Australia and New Zealand made the Springboks favourites for the 1999 World Cup. In the two previous Tri-Nations competitions the South Africans had never even won a match outside of their own country, but in 1998 they reigned supreme, scoring 80 points.

Australia finished a creditable second after wins against New Zealand. The summer saw the rebirth of the Australians, as they found a running outside half in Stephen Larkham. Before Larkham's arrival Australia had failed to replace Michael Lynagh, its star of the 1991 and 1995 World Cups. For New Zealand the picture was far more bleak, as it lost five consecutive matches for the first time in 50 years. Good news for the Kiwis came at the women's World Cup, however, where they swept to a convincing victory, beating the U.S. in the final 44–12.

The new type of expansive Rugby Union played in the Southern Hemisphere was starting to have an effect in the Northern Hemisphere, with more tries (55) scored than for more than 80 years. For the British teams, however, still racked with the move to professionalism, summer tours to the Southern Hemisphere were a disaster. Wales, Scotland, and England were decimated by withdrawals due to

injury and unavailability, and the results were an embarrassment. England lost 76–0 to Australia, and Wales conceded 96 points to South Africa. In the Five Nations France completed a hat trick of championship wins, and the tournament was all but decided in the first match when the French beat England 24–17. Meanwhile, in the Latin Cup Argentina showed that it expected to be a force to contend with in the World Cup by coming close (32–27) to toppling the French.

Bath won the club championship in Europe, while the Super 12 title was taken by New Zealand's Canterbury Crusaders, breaking the Southern Hemisphere stranglehold previously held by the Auckland Blues. Violence unfortunately marred the season in both hemispheres. Bath's Kevin Yates was suspended for allegedly biting London Scottish's Simon Fenn, and in South Africa Wickus Van Heerden was banned for a similar offense.

In Rugby League the newly formed Rugby League International Federation announced plans to stage Tri-Nations tournaments between England, New Zealand, and Australia in 1999 and 2001 as well as World Cups in 2000 and 2002. The Wigan Warriors won the European Super League competition but lost in the Challenge Cup final to the Sheffield Eagles 17–8. In the Southern Hemisphere the 20-team National Rugby League, formed by the reunification of the Super League and the Australian Rugby League agreed upon at the end of 1997, staged its first premiership. In the grand final the Brisbane Broncos, the 1997 Super League champions, came from behind in the second half to defeat the Canterbury Bulldogs 38–12. (PAUL MORGAN)

South African wing Pieter Rossouw (left) evades a tackle attempt by Australian centre Tim Horan during a Tri-Nations match in Johannesburg on August 22. The South Africans prevailed in the Rugby League match and went on to capture the 1998 Tri-Nations championship.

Five Nations Championship

Year	Result
1994	Wales
1995	England*
1996	England
1997	France*
1998	**France***

*Grand Slam winner.

Rugby Union World Cup

Year	Result			
1987	New Zealand	29	France	9
1991	Australia	12	England	6
1995	South Africa	15	New Zealand	12

Rugby League World Cup

Year	Result			
1975*	Australia[†]			
1977*	Australia	13	Great Britain	12
1988	Australia	25	New Zealand	12
1992	Australia	10	Great Britain	6
1995	Australia	16	England	8

*Called International Championship from 1975 to 1977.
[†]Championships played without a grand final match; England was the runner-up.

Record of International Test Matches 1871 to Aug. 31, 1998

	England Wins	Draws	Losses	Scotland Wins	Draws	Losses	Ireland Wins	Draws	Losses	Wales Wins	Draws	Losses	British Isles* Wins	Draws	Losses
England v.				59	17	39	65	8	38	44	12	48			
Scotland v.	39	17	59				59	1	45	44	2	56			
Ireland v.	38	8	65	45	1	59				37	6	59			
Wales v.	48	12	44	56	2	44	59	6	37						
British Isles* v.															
South Africa v.	10	1	4	7	0	3	10	1	1	10	1	0	19	4	10
New Zealand v.	17	1	4	18	2	0	13	1	0	14	0	3	23	2	6
Australia v.	14	1	7	11	0	7	11	0	6	11	0	8	2	0	8
France v.	28	7	40	35	3	32	42	5	25	31	3	38			

	South Africa Wins	Draws	Losses	New Zealand Wins	Draws	Losses	Australia Wins	Draws	Losses	France Wins	Draws	Losses
England v.	4	1	10	4	1	17	7	1	14	40	7	28
Scotland v.	3	0	7	0	2	18	7	0	11	32	3	35
Ireland v.	1	1	10	0	1	13	6	0	11	25	5	42
Wales v.	0	1	10	3	0	14	8	0	11	38	3	31
British Isles* v.	10	4	19	6	2	23	8	0	2			
South Africa v.				24	3	22	26	0	11	18	5	5
New Zealand v.	22	3	24				70	5	30	24	0	8
Australia v.	11	0	26	30	5	70				10	2	13
France v.	5	5	18	8	0	24	13	2	10			

*The British Isles ("British Lions") is a combined team from the four "Home Unions" (England, Ireland, Scotland, and Wales).

GOLF

Golf prides itself on being a sport for all ages, and around the world in 1998 the proof was there for everyone to see. American Mark O'Meara, age 41, became the oldest player ever to win two of the game's four major championships (the Masters, U.S. Open, British Open, and the U.S. Professional Golfers' Association of America [PGA] championship) in the same year; 58-year-old Jack Nicklaus shone again on the big stage; 53-year-old Hale Irwin set record winnings for a single tour; a 17-year-old amateur finished fourth in the British Open; and two 20-year-olds (a first-year professional and an amateur) fought out a play-off for the U.S. Women's Open championship.

Eldrick ("Tiger") Woods remained the leader of the younger generation, heading the world rankings for the majority of the season, but his second full season as a professional failed to reach the dizzying heights of the first. The Masters title he had won in record-breaking fashion at the Augusta (Ga.) National Club in 1997 was one of the two that passed into O'Meara's hands, and Woods was succeeded as leading money winner on the PGA tour by David Duval, who amassed winnings of $2,591,031. That would have been a record figure for any player in one season on a single tour but for the fact that Irwin retained his position atop the U.S. Senior tour with an incredible $2,861,945. In the past three seasons on the circuit, Irwin had won nearly $7 million in prize money—over $1 million more than in his 26-year PGA tour career.

No one could dethrone Colin Montgomerie on the PGA European tour; two late victories enabled the 35-year-old Scot to win the Order of Merit for a record sixth successive year with £993,077 (about $1,640,000). He also captured the $1 million first prize in the Andersen Consulting World Championship of Golf at Grayhawk in Scottsdale, Ariz.

O'Meara won the Masters in dramatic fashion, holing a 6.1-m (20-ft) birdie putt on the final green to defeat Fred Couples and Duval by a single shot with a nine-under-par total of 279—nine higher than Woods's winning score 12 months earlier. It ended O'Meara's 18-year wait for his first major championship. The performance of the week, however, came from Nicklaus, winner of the Masters title a record six times and battling a troublesome hip complaint, who turned back the clock to finish tied for sixth. Nicklaus was playing in the tournament for a record 40th time and had been honoured on the eve of the event.

Nicklaus finished tied for 43rd in the U.S. Open at the Olympic Club in San Francisco two months later, but then golf's "Golden Bear" announced that he would not be playing in either the British Open at Royal Birkdale Golf Club in Southport, Eng., or the PGA championship at Sahalee Country Club, near Seattle, Wash. That brought to an end an astonishing run, stretching back to 1957, of 154 successive major championships for which he was eligible. Nicklaus's 18 victories (plus 2 U.S. Amateurs) were accepted as a record that might stand for all time.

The U.S. Open was won for the second time in six years by Lee Janzen, who pushed fellow American Payne Stewart into second place just as he had in 1993. Seven strokes behind after three holes of the final round, Janzen recorded a two-under-par 68 to Stewart's 74 to win by one stroke with a level-par total of 280. It was the best final-round comeback in the championship in 25 years.

As at the Masters, the U.S. Open winner had to share the limelight. Casey Martin, who suffered from a degenerative circulatory disease in his right leg called Klippel-Trenauney-Weber Syndrome, had won a court case against the PGA tour for the right to ride in PGA tournaments. He came through a play-off in the qualifying event to become the first player ever to be allowed

Mark O'Meara putts for birdie on the final green to win the 1998 Masters in Augusta, Ga., on April 12.

to use a motorized golf cart while playing in a major championship and finished the U.S. Open in a highly creditable tie for 23rd, one shot behind his former college teammate Woods. Reigning U.S. Amateur champion Matt Kuchar, having already finished 21st at the Masters, was tied for fourth after two rounds and eventually, on his 20th birthday, finished joint 14th.

Good as that was, 17-year-old English amateur Justin Rose eclipsed it at the British Open. A qualifier like Martin, Rose achieved fourth place, the best by an amateur in the championship since American Frank Stranahan finished in a tie for second in 1953. After a windswept four days, Rose, who subsequently turned professional and failed to survive a single halfway cut in his first 10 starts, finished one stroke behind

British Open Tournament (men)	
Year	Winner
1994	N. Price (Zimb.)
1995	J. Daly (U.S.)
1996	T. Lehman (U.S.)
1997	J. Leonard (U.S.)
1998	**M. O'Meara (U.S.)**

United States Open Championship (men)	
Year	Winner
1994	E. Els (S.Af.)
1995	C. Pavin (U.S.)
1996	S. Jones (U.S.)
1997	E. Els (S.Af.)
1998	**L. Janzen (U.S.)**

Masters Tournament	
Year	Winner
1994	J. Olazábal (Spain)
1995	B. Crenshaw (U.S.)
1996	N. Faldo (U.K.)
1997	T. Woods (U.S.)
1998	**M. O'Meara (U.S.)**

U.S. Professional Golfers' Association (PGA) Championship	
Year	Winner
1994	N. Price (Zimb.)
1995	S. Elkington (Austl.)
1996	M. Brooks (U.S.)
1997	D. Love III (U.S.)
1998	**V. Singh (Fiji)**

British Amateur Championship (men)	
Year	Winner
1994	L. James (U.K.)
1995	G. Sherry (U.K.)
1996	W. Bladon (U.K.)
1997	C. Watson (U.K.)
1998	**S. Garcia (Spain)**

United States Amateur Championship (men)	
Year	Winner
1994	T. Woods (U.S.)
1995	T. Woods (U.S.)
1996	T. Woods (U.S.)
1997	M. Kuchar (U.S.)
1998	**H. Kuehne (U.S.)**

Women's British Open Championship	
Year	Winner
1994	L. Neumann (Swed.)
1995	K. Webb (Austl.)
1996	E. Klein (U.S.)
1997	K. Webb (Austl.)
1998	**S. Steinhauer (U.S.)**

Ladies' British Amateur Championship	
Year	Winner
1994	E. Duggleby (U.K.)
1995	J. Hall (U.K.)
1996	K. Kuehne (U.S.)
1997	A. Rose (U.K.)
1998	**K. Rostron (U.K.)**

United States Women's Open Championship	
Year	Winner
1994	P. Sheehan (U.S.)
1995	A. Sorenstam (Swed.)
1996	A. Sorenstam (Swed.)
1997	A. Nicholas (U.S.)
1998	**Pak Se Ri (S. Kor.)**

United States Women's Amateur Championship	
Year	Winner
1994	W. Ward (U.S.)
1995	K. Kuehne (U.S.)
1996	K. Kuehne (U.S.)
1997	S. Cavalleri (Italy)
1998	**G. Park (U.S.)**

Ladies' Professional Golf Association (LPGA) Championship	
Year	Winner
1994	L. Davies (U.K.)
1995	K. Robbins (U.S.)
1996	L. Davies (U.K.)
1997	C. Johnson (U.S.)
1998	**Pak Se Ri (S. Kor)**

Woods and two behind O'Meara and American Brian Watts. The tie on the level-par total of 280 resulted in a four-hole play-off for Watts and O'Meara, who began it with a birdie four, never lost the advantage, and thereby completed his double of the Masters and British Open.

O'Meara thus went into the PGA championship with a chance to become only the second player in golfing history to win three majors in a season (American Ben Hogan accomplished it in 1953). He threatened to do so into the final day but eventually finished tied for fourth, five strokes behind Fiji's Vijay Singh, winner by two over American Steve Stricker with a nine-under-par total of 271.

O'Meara, who also beat Woods in the final of the Cisco World Match Play Championship at Wentworth, Surrey, Eng., won the PGA tour's Player of the Year award despite finishing only seventh on the final money list. Duval's seven victories within 12 months enabled him to finish more than $350,000 ahead of second-place Singh in prize money, with Jim Furyk third and Woods fourth. Montgomerie had three European tour victories, and the final Order of Merit table showed him £90,000 (nearly $150,000) ahead of Northern Ireland's Darren Clarke and £178,000 (nearly $295,000) above England's Lee Westwood, who won seven tournaments and was named the tour's Player of the Year.

As a rookie on the Ladies Professional Golf Association (LPGA) tour, Pak Se Ri (*see* BIOGRAPHIES) of South Korea was a power in the women's game. Pak won the first two major championships in which she played—the McDonald's LPGA championship at DuPont Country Club in

Wilmington, Del., and the U.S. Women's Open at Blackwolf Run in Kohler, Wis., where she and American amateur Jenny Chuasiriporn tied on the six-over-par aggregate of 290, the latter after holing a 12.2-m (40-ft) putt on the final green. The play-off, in which both were trying to become the youngest-ever champion and Chuasiriporn only the second amateur winner (Catherine Lacoste of France won as an amateur in 1967), was still unresolved after 18 holes, but at the second extra hole Pak made a 5.5-m (18-ft) birdie putt. One week later Pak won the Jamie Farr Kroger Classic in Sylvania, Ohio, with a record-low 23-under-par 261 and a second-round 10-under-par 61, the lowest score in LPGA history.

Sweden's Annika Sörenstam was the leading money winner on the LPGA tour for the third time in four years, but she could not win back the Solheim Cup for Europe. At Muirfield Village Golf Course in Dublin, Ohio, the U.S. held on to the trophy by a 16–12 margin with a team that included Tammie Green, who was six months pregnant, and Sherri Steinhauer, winner of the Weetabix Women's British Open at Royal Lytham and St. Anne's in Lancashire, Eng. Sörenstam's compatriot Helen Alfredsson was the top earner on the European LPGA tour with £125,975 (about $208,000), but because of a loss of sponsors there were fewer tournaments and only eight players earned more than £40,000 ($66,000).

The U.S. regained the Curtis Cup women's amateur trophy from Great Britain

and Ireland, winning 10–8 at Minikahda Club in Minneapolis, Minn. Chuasiriporn was a member of the team but did not win a match and then, as she had done earlier at the U.S. Women's Open, came in second again at the U.S. Women's Amateur at Barton Hills Country Club near Ann Arbor, Mich. This time the player to beat her was 19-year-old South Korean-born American Grace Park.

The British Ladies' Amateur championship was won by England's Kim Rostron and the British men's title by Spain's 18-year-old Sergio Garcia, who also reached the semifinals of the U.S. Amateur Championships. The eventual champion there was American Hank Keuhne, whose sister, Kelli, was U.S. Women's Amateur champion in 1995 and 1996.

South Africa retained the Alfred Dunhill Cup at the Royal and Ancient Golf Club of St. Andrews in Fife, Scot., while the year ended with two firsts—a surprising victory for England (represented by Nick Faldo and David Carter) in the World Cup of Golf at Gulf Harbour, Auckland, N.Z., and a commanding win for the International Team over the U.S. in the Presidents Cup at Royal Melbourne, Australia. The final margin was a resounding 20½–11½ with the unbeaten Japanese player Shigeki Maruyama being named man of the match and Australian Greg Norman making a successful recovery from the shoulder surgery that had kept him out of the action for much of the season.

(MARK GARROD)

American golfer Lee Janzen shows off his U.S. Open championship trophy in June. Janzen came from behind in the final round to defeat Payne Stewart narrowly and claim his second U.S. Open title in six years.

Walker Cup (men; amateur)

Year	Result
1989	Britain and Ireland 12½, United States 11½
1991	United States 14, Britain and Ireland 10
1993	United States 19, Britain and Ireland 5
1995	Britain and Ireland 14, United States 10
1997	United States 18, Britain and Ireland 6

World Cup (men; professional)

Year	Winner
1994	United States (F. Couples and D. Love III)
1995	United States (F. Couples and D. Love III)
1996	South Africa (E. Els and W. Westner)
1997	Ireland (P. Harrington and P. McGinley)
1998	**England (N. Faldo and D. Carter)**

Curtis Cup (women; amateur)

Year	Result
1990	United States 14, Britain and Ireland 4
1992	Britain and Ireland 10, United States 8
1994	Britain and Ireland 9, United States 9
1996	Britain and Ireland 11½, United States 6½
1998	**United States 10, Britain and Ireland 8**

Ryder Cup (men; professional)

Year	Result
1989	Europe 14, United States 14
1991	United States 14½, Europe 13½
1993	United States 15, Europe 13
1995	Europe 14½, United States 13½
1997	Europe 14½, United States 13½

(LEFT) BLAKE SELL—REUTERS; (RIGHT) TIMOTHY A. CLARY—AFP; (BELOW) RON FREHM—AP/WIDE WORLD

(Top left) Alina Kabayeva of Russia performs her gold-medal-winning routine during the ribbon competition in the Goodwill Games rhythmic gymnastics finals. (Top right) American gymnast Dominique Moceanu displays her skill on the balance beam en route to becoming the first non-Russian woman to capture a Goodwill Games all-around title. (Below) During the Goodwill Games men's apparatus gymnastics finals, Ivan Ivankov of Belarus performs on the parallel bars. Ivankov won the men's all-around title.

GYMNASTICS

In May 1998 the Group Rhythmic Gymnastics World Championships took place in Seville, Spain. In a close contest Belarus won the overall title with a score of 39.366, followed by Spain (39.133) and Russia (39.132).

The Goodwill Games held in New York City in July provided the major international competition in artistic gymnastics. Dominique Moceanu of the U.S. reigned as the all-around champion in her first major competition since sharing the team gold at the 1996 Olympic Games. Moceanu, who scored a 38.662, also became the first non-Russian woman to win a Goodwill Games all-around gold medal. Romanian gymnasts Maria Olaru and Simona Amanar took second and third all-around with scores of 37.975 and 37.850, respectively. Vanessa Atler of the U.S. won two event finals, scoring a 9.662 on vault and 9.775 on floor exercise. Russia's Svetlana Khorkina won gold on the uneven bars with a 9.825, and American Kristen Maloney topped the competition on the balance beam with a score of 9.775.

On the men's side, reigning world champion Ivan Ivankov of Belarus won the all-around title with a score of 57.500, followed by Russia's Aleksey Bondarenko (56.700) and American Blaine Wilson (56.575). All six of the individual men's events were won by different gymnasts. Russia's Aleksey Nemov and Nikolay Krukov won floor exercise and pommel horse, scoring 9.725 and 9.650, respectively. The still rings title went to Chris LaMorte of the U.S. with a score of 9.70. Sergey Fedorchenko of Kazakstan finished first on vault with a 9.650, China's Xu Huang won parallel bars with a 9.725, and Ivankov scored 9.725 on the horizontal bar to win the title.

In rhythmic competition at the Goodwill Games, Russia's Alina Kabayeva earned the all-around title with a score of 39.781, followed by Yelena Vitrichenko of Ukraine

World Gymnastics Championships—Men

Year	All-around Team	All-around Individual	Horizontal bar	Parallel bars
1994	China	I. Ivankov (Bela.)	V. Sherbo (Bela.)	Liping Huang (China)
1995	China	Li Xiaoshuang (China)	A. Wecker (Ger.)	V. Sherbo (Bela.)
1996	not held	not held	J. Carballo (Spain)	R. Charipov (Ukr.)
1997	China	I. Ivankov (Bela.)	J. Tanskanen (Fin.)	Zhang Jinjing (China)

Year	Pommel horse	Rings	Vault	Floor exercise
1994	M. Urzica (Rom.)	Y. Chechi (Italy)	V. Sherbo (Bela.)	V. Sherbo (Bela.)
1995	Li Donghua (Switz.)	Y. Chechi (Italy)	A. Nemov (Russia)* G. Misutin (Ukr.)*	V. Sherbo (Bela.)
1996	Pae Gil Su (N.Kor.)	Y. Chechi (Italy)	A. Nemov (Russia)	V. Sherbo (Bela.)
1997	V. Belenki (Ger.)	Y. Chechi (Italy)	S. Fedorchenko (Kazak.)	A. Nemov (Russia)

*Tied.

World Gymnastics Championships—Women

Year	All-around Team	All-around Individual	Balance beam
1994	Romania	S. Miller (U.S.)	S. Miller (U.S.)
1995	Romania	L. Podkopayeva (Ukr.)	Mo Huilan (China)
1996	not held	not held	D. Kochetkova (Russia)
1997	Romania	S. Khorkina (Russia)	G. Gogean (Rom.)

Year	Uneven parallel bars	Vault	Floor exercise
1994	Li Luo (China)	G. Gogean (Rom.)	D. Kochetkova (Russia)
1995	S. Khorkina (Russia)	S. Amanar (Rom.)* L. Podkopayeva (Ukr.)*	G. Gogean (Rom.)
1996	S. Khorkina (Russia)* Ye. Piskun (Bela.)*	G. Gogean (Rom.)	G. Gogean (Rom.)* Kui Yuanyuan (China)*
1997	S. Khorkina (Russia)	S. Amanar (Rom.)	G. Gogean (Rom.)

*Tied.

with a 39.657 and Yevgeniya Pavlina of Belarus with a 39.640. Kabayeva won three of the four events, including hoop (9.983), clubs (9.958), and ribbon (9.941). Vitrichenko took the rope title with a 9.908.

It was announced that the International Trampoline Federation and the International Federation of Sports Acrobatics would be allowed to join the International Gymnastics Federation, provided they dissolved their respective federations by year's end.

(LUAN PESZEK)

ICE HOCKEY

North America. The National Hockey League (NHL) season of 1997–98 ended on a sentimental note when the Detroit Red Wings won their second-straight Stanley Cup, once again taking the final series in four consecutive games. The Red Wings became the first team in six seasons to win back-to-back Stanley Cups when they finished their sweep of the Washington Capitals with a 4–1 victory on June 16, 1998. It gave Scotty Bowman a record-equaling eighth Stanley Cup as a coach and wrote a fitting conclusion to the emotional season that followed the Red Wings' first championship in 42 years. The 1996–97 season saw the Red Wings sweep Philadelphia for the NHL title only to have their euphoria abruptly ended six days later by a limousine crash that severely injured defenseman Vladimir Konstantinov and team masseur Sergey Mnatsakanov. The Red Wings' 1998 celebration started after the final game ended at Washington, and Konstantinov came out on the ice in his wheelchair, wearing a Detroit jersey. He was presented the Stanley Cup by his teammates before they took him around the ice on a victory lap.

The Red Wings' success was equally sweet for Steve Yzerman, the 15-year vet-

eran and team captain whose leadership was obvious in his play-off statistics (6 goals, 18 assists) and defensive intensity. Once labeled a player who could not lead his team to victory in big games, Yzerman turned in an exceptional all-around performance that earned the Conn Smythe Trophy, awarded to the Most Valuable Player (MVP) in the play-offs.

From the NHL's 26 teams that battled through an 82-game season before the play-offs began, the Dallas Stars led the league in both victories (49) and points (109) to win their division, 10 points in front of the runner-up Red Wings (44 wins). New Jersey (107 points), Pittsburgh (98), and Colorado (95) were the other division winners who advanced into the 16-team play-offs.

The Capitals moved into the Stanley Cup final for the first time in the 24-year history of the Washington franchise by beating Boston 4 games to 2, Ottawa 4–1, and Buffalo 4–2. Three Washington victories in the hotly contested Buffalo series came in overtime against Sabres goalie Dominik Hasek (*see* BIOGRAPHIES), the Czech-born Winter Olympics hero. The Red Wings stormed back into the final series by beating Phoenix, St. Louis, and Dallas, all by the margin of 4 games to 2.

In their second title-clinching challenge, Detroit established a trend that kept pressure on the Capitals throughout the series. The Red Wings simply scored first in every game, taking no longer than the sixth shot to gain a 1–0 lead. In game three of the series the Red Wings scored on their very first shot, 35 seconds after the opening face-off. Detroit also got superb goaltending from

(continued on page 360)

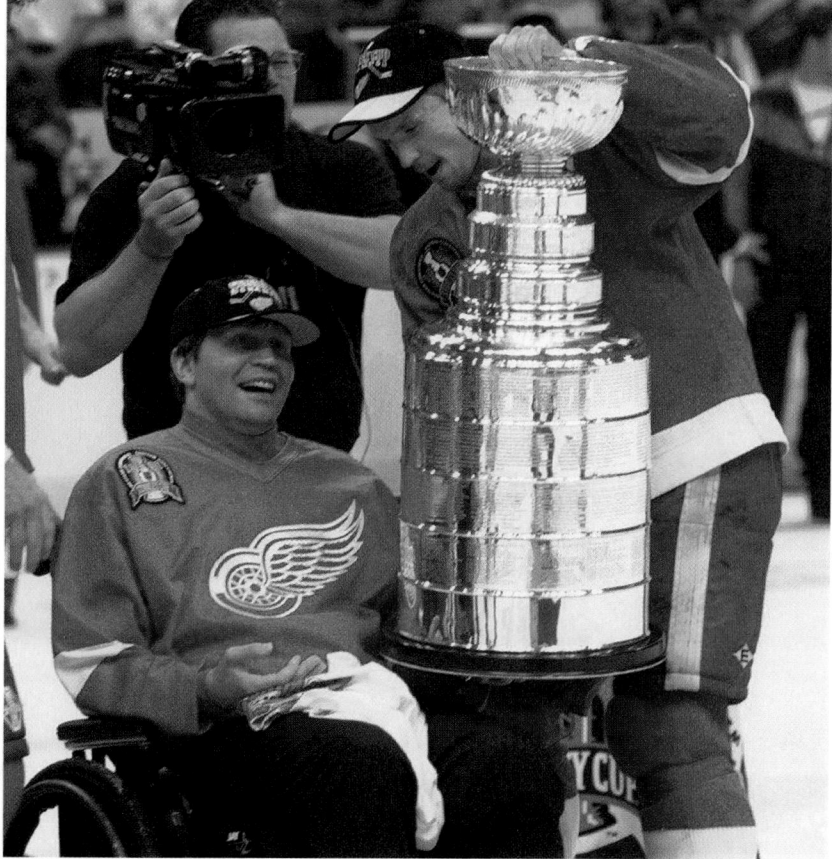

Detroit Red Wings captain Steve Yzerman (right) presents the Stanley Cup to teammate Vladimir Konstantinov after the Red Wings won their second-straight NHL title. Konstantinov was injured in a crash after helping the Red Wings win the Stanley Cup in 1997.

PAUL CHIASSON—AP/WIDE WORLD

The XVIII Olympic Winter Games

by Melinda C. Shepherd

On Feb. 6, 1998, the bell at the 1,350-year-old Buddhist temple Zenkoji in Nagano, Japan, welcomed the world to celebrate the XVIII Olympic Winter Games. For the next 16 days Nagano, located in the Japanese Alps 220 km (137 mi) northwest of Tokyo, played host to 2,450 athletes representing 72 national Olympic committees from every inhabited continent, including countries as far away as Israel, Kenya, and Chile. The opening ceremonies, which were broadcast around the world, featured 150 local children, a traditional Japanese purification ritual, and a ceremonial blessing by American-born sumo wrestler Akebono.

Medals were awarded in 68 events, including the recently added sports of curling, snowboarding, and women's ice hockey. In the end, 24 countries won at least one medal. Germany led the medal standings with a total of 29 (12 gold), followed by Norway (25 total), Russia (18), Austria (17), Canada (15), and the U.S. (13). Japan finished with 10 medals, 5 of them gold.

For the first time, the National Hockey League (NHL) suspended its regular season in order to allow professionals to participate in the Olympics, but the favoured Americans and Canadians were overshadowed by the gold-medal-winning Czech Republic, led by NHL star goalie Dominik Hasek. (See BIOGRAPHIES.) The Americans dominated women's ice hockey, however, winning that sport's first gold medal 3–1 over second-place Canada. In speed skating the introduction of the Dutch-designed clapskate into the Games caused a stir as the world or Olympic record fell in every event. Gunda Niemann-Stirnemann of Germany won three individual medals, raising her career total to eight. (See BIOGRAPHIES.)

In figure skating 15-year-old world champion Tara Lipinski (see BIOGRAPHIES) gave a sparkling performance in the free skate to come from behind after the short program and defeat fellow American Michelle Kwan.

On the slopes Hermann Maier of Austria recovered from a devastating crash in the Alpine downhill to capture two gold medals. (See BIOGRAPHIES.) Nordic skiing was dominated by Larissa Lazutina of Russia, who medaled in every women's race, and Bjørn Dæhlie of Norway (see BIOGRAPHIES), whose 4 medals (including 3 golds) raised his career total to 12 and made him the most medaled athlete in Winter Olympic history. Snowboarder Ross Rebagliati of Canada was temporarily stripped of his gold medal when he tested positive for marijuana, but the medal was reinstated after the Court for Arbitration of Sport ruled that the International Olympic Committee (IOC) had never specifically placed marijuana on its list of banned substances. The IOC later announced that in the future marijuana and other recreational drugs would be added to the list.

In other sports, Georg Hackl of Germany (see BIOGRAPHIES) won his third consecutive gold medal in singles luge. Masahiko ("Happy") Harada (see BIOGRAPHIES) made up for a poor showing at the 1994 Games in Lillehammer, Nor., and a disastrous first jump with a spectacular 137-m (450-ft) second jump to help Japan win the team gold in ski jumping.

Melinda C. Shepherd is associate editor of Encyclopædia Britannica Yearbooks.

(ABOVE) ERIC DRAPER—AP/WIDE WORLD; (LEFT) WOLFGANG RATTAY—REUTERS; (RIGHT) DOUG MILLS—AP/WIDE WORLD

(Above) Sumo wrestlers perform on centre stage; (Left) jets fly over the stadium at the conclusion of the opening ceremonies; (Right) the Olympic flame is lit by former Olympic figure skater Midori Ito.

Olympic Champions, XVIII Winter Games, Nagano

Alpine Skiing

Men

Event	Champion	Result
Downhill	J.-L. Cretier (France)	1 min 50.11 sec
Slalom	H.-P. Buraas (Nor.)	1 min 49.31 sec
Giant slalom	H. Maier (Austria)	2 min 38.51 sec
Super G	H. Maier (Austria)	1 min 35.82 sec
Combined event	M. Reito (Austria)	3 min 8.06 sec

Women

Event	Champion	Result
Downhill	K. Seizinger (Ger.)	1 min 28.89 sec
Slalom	H. Gerg (Ger.)	1 min 32.40 sec
Giant slalom	D. Compagnoni (Italy)	2 min 50.59 sec
Super G	P. Street (U.S.)	1 min 18.02 sec
Combined event	K. Seizinger (Ger.)	2 min 40.74 sec

Nordic Skiing

Men

Event	Champion	Result
10-km cross-country	B. Dæhlie (Nor.)	27 min 24.5 sec
15-km cross-country	T. Alsgaard (Nor.)	39 min 13.7 sec
30-km cross-country	M. Myllylae (Fin.)	1 hr 33 min 55.8 sec
50-km cross-country	B. Dæhlie (Nor.)	2 hr 5 min 8.2 sec
40-km relay	Norway	1 hr 40 min 55.7 sec
90-m ski jump	J. Soininen (Fin.)	234.5 pt
120-m ski jump	K. Funaki (Japan)	272.3 pt
120-m team ski jump	Japan	933.0 pt
Nordic combined	B.E. Vik (Nor.)	41 min 21.1 sec
Nordic team combined	Norway	54 min 11.5 sec

Women

Event	Champion	Result
5-km cross-country	L. Lazutina (Russia)	17 min 37.9 sec
10-km cross-country	L. Lazutina (Russia)	46 min 6.9 sec
15-km cross-country	O. Danilova (Russia)	44 min 55.4 sec
30-km cross-country	J. Tchepalova (Russia)	1 hr 22 min 1.5 sec
20-km relay	Russia	55 min 13.5 sec

Biathlon

Men

Event	Champion	Result
10 km	O.E. Bjoerndalen (Nor.)	27 min 16.2 sec
20 km	H. Hanevold (Nor.)	56 min 16.4 sec
30-km relay	Germany	1 hr 21 min 36.2 sec

Women

Event	Champion	Result
7.5 km	G. Koukleva (Russia)	23 min 8.0 sec
15 km	Ye. Dafovska (Bulg.)	54 min 52.0 sec
30-km relay	Germany	1 hr 40 min 13.6 sec

Freestyle Skiing

Men

Event	Champion	Result
Moguls	J. Moseley (U.S.)	26.93 pt
Aerials	E. Bergoust (U.S.)	255.64 pt

Women

Event	Champion	Result
Moguls	T. Satoya (Japan)	25.06 pt
Aerials	N. Stone (U.S.)	193.00 pt

Snowboarding

Men

Event	Champion	Result
Giant slalom	R. Rebagliatti (Can.)	2 min 3.96 sec
Halfpipe	G. Simmen (Switz.)	85.2 pt

Women

Event	Champion	Result
Giant slalom	K. Ruby (France)	2 min 17.34 sec
Halfpipe	N. Thost (Ger.)	74.6 pt

Figure Skating

Event	Champion	Result
Men	I. Kulik (Russia)	1.5 pt
Women	T. Lipinski (U.S.)	2.0 pt
Pairs	O. Kazakova and A. Dmitriyev (Russia)	1.5 pt
Ice dancing	P. Grishuk and Ye. Platov (Russia)	2.0 pt

Speed Skating

Men

Event	Champion	Result
500 m	H. Shimizu (Japan)	35.76 sec/35.59 sec*
1,000 m	I. Postma (Neth.)	1 min 10.71 sec*
1,500 m	A. Sondral (Nor.)	1 min 47.87 sec†
5,000 m	G. Romme (Neth.)	6 min 22.20 sec†
10,000 m	G. Romme (Neth.)	13 min 15.33 sec†

Women

Event	Champion	Result
500 m	C. Lemay-Doan (Can.)	38.39 sec/38.21 sec*
1,000 m	M. Timmer (Neth.)	1 min 16.51 sec*
1,500 m	M. Timmer (Neth.)	1 min 57.58 sec†
3,000 m	G. Niemann-Stirnemann (Ger.)	4 min 7.29 sec*
5,000 m	C. Pechstein (Ger.)	6 min 59.61 sec†

Short-Track Speed Skating

Men

Event	Champion	Result
500 m	T. Nishitani (Japan)	42.862 sec
1,000 m	Kim Dong Sung (S.Kor.)	1 min 32.428 sec
5,000-m relay	Canada	7 min 6.075 sec

Women

Event	Champion	Result
500 m	A. Perrault (Can.)	46.568 sec
1,000 m	Chun Lee Kyung (S.Kor.)	1 min 42.776 sec
3,000-m relay	South Korea	4 min 16.260 sec†

Ice Hockey

Event	Team	Result
Men (winning team)	Czech Republic	5–1–0
Women (winning team)	United States	6–0–0

Curling

Event	Team	Result
Men (winning team)	Switzerland	5–2–0
Women (winning team)	Canada	6–1–0

Bobsledding

Event	Team	Result
Two man	Italy	3 min 37.24 sec
Four man	Germany	2 min 39.41 sec

Luge

Event	Champion	Result
Men (singles)	G. Hackl (Ger.)	3 min 18.436 sec
Men (doubles)	S. Krausse and J. Berhendt (Ger.)	1 min 41.105 sec
Women (singles)	S. Kraushaar (Ger.)	3 min 23.779 sec

*Olympic record. †World record.

(continued from page 357)

Chris Osgood, who allowed only seven goals in 99 shots against him. He held the Caps to a single goal in three of the four games.

Heartening as the Red Wings' success was to fans in Michigan, the NHL suffered poor television ratings elsewhere in 1998. The league also was embarrassed by the unruly behavior of its North American representatives to the Winter Olympics and concerned over concussions suffered by several elite players, including Paul Kariya of Anaheim, Eric Lindros of Philadelphia, and Pat LaFontaine of the New York Rangers.

In the NHL All-Star Game on Jan. 18, 1998, North America overcame a hat trick (three goals) by right wing Teemu Selanne to beat the World team 8–7. Selanne, a Finn who played for Anaheim, became the first European to score an All-Star Game hat trick and win MVP honours.

On June 25 Hasek became the first goalie in NHL history to win the Hart and Vezina trophies in consecutive seasons. They are awarded to the league's MVP and best goalie, respectively. Jaromir Jagr of Pittsburgh, Hasek's teammate on the Czech team that captured the Winter Olympics gold medal, won the Art Ross Trophy as the league's highest scorer (102 points). Rob Blake of Los Angeles won the Norris Trophy as the league's outstanding defenseman, and Jere Lehtinen of Dallas gained the Selke Trophy as best defensive forward. Ron Francis of Pittsburgh won the Lady Byng Trophy for good sportsmanship, and Sergey Samsonov of Boston was awarded the Calder Trophy as the NHL's top rookie. The Jack Adams Award for Outstanding Coach went to Pat Burns of Boston, winning for the third time with his third team.

In late June the NHL board of governors adopted rule changes to increase scoring by reducing the area of the goalie crease and moving the net 0.6 m (2 ft) farther from the end boards, to 4 m (13 ft). The Nashville Predators, the league's 27th franchise, selected 26 players in the NHL expansion draft, while new expansion teams were announced for Minnesota; Atlanta, Ga.; and Columbus, Ohio.   (RON REID)

International. For the first time in the 74-year history of the Winter Olympics,

NHL Final Standings, 1998

EASTERN CONFERENCE	Won	Lost	Tied	Points	WESTERN CONFERENCE	Won	Lost	Tied	Points
Atlantic Division					**Central Division**				
*New Jersey	48	23	11	107	*Dallas	49	22	11	109
*Philadelphia	42	29	11	95	*Detroit	44	23	15	103
*Washington	40	30	12	92	*St. Louis	45	29	8	98
New York Islanders	30	41	11	71	*Phoenix	35	35	12	82
New York Rangers	25	39	18	68	Chicago	30	39	13	73
Florida	24	43	15	63	Toronto	30	43	9	69
Tampa Bay	17	55	10	44					
Northeast Division					**Pacific Division**				
*Pittsburgh	40	24	18	98	*Colorado	39	26	17	95
*Boston	39	30	13	91	*Los Angeles	38	33	11	87
*Buffalo	36	29	17	89	*Edmonton	35	37	10	80
*Montreal	37	32	13	87	*San Jose	34	38	10	78
*Ottawa	34	33	15	83	Calgary	26	41	15	67
Carolina	33	41	8	74	Anaheim	26	43	13	65
					Vancouver	25	43	14	64

*Qualified for play-offs.

The Stanley Cup

Season	Winner	Runner-up	Games
1993–94	New York Rangers	Vancouver Canucks	4–3
1994–95	New Jersey Devils	Detroit Red Wings	4–0
1995–96	Colorado Avalanche	Florida Panthers	4–0
1996–97	Detroit Red Wings	Philadelphia Flyers	4–0
1997–98	**Detroit Red Wings**	**Washington Capitals**	**4–0**

World Hockey Championship

Year	Winner
1994	Canada
1995	Finland
1996	Czech Republic
1997	Canada
1998	**Sweden**

NHL players were allowed to compete for medals in ice hockey at the Games in Nagano, Japan, in 1998. Six women's teams also competed in the Olympics for the first time. In both instances, the Americans and Canadians entered the tournament as co-favourites.

On the men's side, the U.S. had defeated Canada in the finals of the 1996 World Cup, establishing itself as the team to beat. With all the talk about Wayne Gretzky's first Olympics and the U.S.'s first legitimate chance at gold since the 1980 "Miracle on Ice," the pundits, however, largely ignored Czech Republic goaltender Dominik "The Dominator" Hasek. The NHL's two-time defending Most Valuable Player (MVP) and top goaltender, Hasek allowed only six goals in six Olympic games as he led the Czech Republic to its first ice hockey gold medal. After stirring performances in victories over

the U.S. (4–1) and Canada (2–1 in a semifinal shoot-out), he shut out arch rival Russia in the gold medal match (an amazing feat considering that Russian forward Pavel Bure almost single-handedly defeated Finland in the semifinals with a five-goal performance). When Petr Svoboda beat Russian goalie Mikhail Shtalenkov on a 15-m (50-ft) slapshot with 11:52 to play in the final period for a 1–0 lead, Czech fans around the world began to celebrate.

Meanwhile, in Canada the mood was less buoyant. After losing the semifinal shoot-out to Hasek and the Czechs, ending their dream of a first ice hockey gold medal since 1952, Canada lost the bronze medal match to Finland 3–2. Despite the absence of its top scoring threat, Teemu Selanne, Finland used opportunistic offense and solid defense to upset the flat Canadians, who outshot the Finns 34–15.

The U.S. and Sweden, both favoured to win a medal, failed even to reach the medal round. To make matters worse, after the U.S. was knocked out of medal contention by the Czechs, several unidentified U.S. players allegedly vandalized their dormitory rooms, bringing negative publicity off the ice to a team that had been a disappointment on the ice.

While the men's tournament was filled with surprises, the women's tournament played out exactly as expected—until the finals. The U.S. and Canada easily advanced to the gold medal match. In an early round the U.S. had defeated Canada 7–4 by scoring six unanswered goals after the Canadian women had taken a 4–1 lead. The final proved to be a much tighter contest. After a scoreless first period, American Gretchen Ulion beat Canadian goaltender Manon Rheaume at the 2:38 mark of the second period. Ulion's teammate Shelley Looney shoved in a rebound at the 10:57 mark of the third period to increase the U.S.'s lead to 2–0. Six minutes later, however, Canada's Danielle Goyette, the tournament's leading goal scorer, capitalized on a power

Canadian goalie Manon Rheaume blocks a shot by American Gretchen Ulion in the first period of the women's ice hockey final at the Winter Olympics. In an exciting game, the U.S. team prevailed to claim the first gold medal for women in the sport.

play opportunity and beat American goalie Sarah Tueting.

Tueting then snuffed out several potentially golden opportunities for Canada, and after Rheaume was pulled with less than a minute remaining and replaced by an extra attacker, American Sandra Whyte scored an empty-net goal to seal the victory. The U.S. finished the tournament with a perfect 6–0 record, while Canada dropped to 4–2. The win represented the first time the U.S. had defeated Canada in a championship setting, having lost the previous four world championships. Finland won the bronze medal, defeating China 4–1.

At the men's world championships in Zürich, Switz., in May, Sweden avenged its poor Olympic showing, defeating Finland, which had eliminated the Swedes in Nagano, 1–0 in the first game of a two-leg final that concluded with a scoreless second game. The Czech Republic, minus Hasek, crushed Switzerland 4–0 for the bronze medal. (GREG GUSS)

ICE SKATING

Figure Skating. After the sordid Tonya Harding–Nancy Kerrigan controversy that had focused added attention on the 1994 Winter Olympics in Lillehammer, Nor., the competition between two other Americans, 15-year-old Tara Lipinski (see BIOGRAPHIES) and 17-year-old Michelle Kwan, at the 1998 Games in Nagano, Japan, was as welcome a duel as it was splendid. At two recent previous meetings, including the 1998 U.S. championships just prior to the Olympics, Kwan had handily defeated Lipinski. In Nagano Kwan, the 1996 world champion, jumped out to an early lead over Lipinski, the 1997 world champion, after a nearly perfect short program. In the free skate Kwan landed seven triple jumps, in-

cluding a flawless opening triple lutz–double toe loop, but she held back on one of her most difficult jumps, earning just 5.7s and 5.8s in technical merit while garnering 5.9s for artistry. Lipinski capitalized on the opening left by Kwan, earning 5.8s and 5.9s for technical merit and similar scores for artistry. Six of the nine judges placed Lipinski in first place, which gave her the gold medal and a place in history. Lipinski surpassed Sonja Henie, Norway's 1928 Olympic gold medalist, by two months to become the youngest figure-skating champion in Olympic history. China's Chen Lu, the 1995 world champion, took the bronze.

On the men's side Ilia Kulik of Russia emerged from a trio of gold-medal hopefuls after the short program by turning in one of the most dominant long programs of the decade. Kulik's series of 5.9s separated the 20-year-old Russian from Todd Eldredge, the five-time U.S. champion and 1996 world champion, and three-time world champion Elvis Stojko of Canada. Stojko, who had won silver at Lillehammer, was hoping to earn Canada's first men's figure-skating gold medal. A pulled groin muscle prevented him from attempting his trademark quadruple toe–triple toe combination, but his eight triples were good enough for silver. Eldredge suffered a series of failed triple combinations and a crash, which left the door open for France's Philippe Candeloro, who captured the bronze.

Russia continued its dominance in the pairs competition, with Oksana Kazakova and Artur Dmitriyev holding off teammates Yelena Berezhnaya and Anton Sikharulidze for the gold. Since 1964 either a Soviet or a Russian pair had won gold in this event, a streak of 10 consecutive Olympics. The Russian team of Pasha (formerly Oksana) Grishuk and Yevgeny Platov won the ice-dancing competition, but not without some controversy. Grishuk and Platov, who had won the gold medal at Lillehammer, turned in a flawed performance in which Grishuk stumbled. Nevertheless, judges refused

to place the four-time world champions behind the other Russian pair, Anjelika Krylova and Oleg Ovsyannikov, and sparked a heated debate that could eventually lead to a retooling of the way ice dancing was judged at future international events.

Although Krylova and Ovsyannikov fell short at the Olympics, they managed to claim the title against a depleted field at the world championships the following month. In all, the Russians captured three more golds at the event, held in Minneapolis, Minn. Russia's Aleksey Yagudin won the men's title, and Berezhnaya and Sikharulidze prevailed in

AMY SANCETTA—AP/WIDE WORLD

American figure skater Tara Lipinski shows near-flawless technical form during her free skate at the Winter Olympics in February. She went on to win the gold medal, besting rival Michelle Kwan.

World Ice Speed-Skating Records Set in 1998 on Major Tracks			
Event	Name	Country	Time
MEN			
500 m	Hiroyasu Shimizu	Japan	34.82 sec
1,000 m	Sylvain Bouchard	Canada	1 min 9.60 sec
1,500 m	Adne Sondral	Norway	1 min 46.43 sec
3,000 m	Bart Veldkamp	Belgium	3 min 48.91 sec
5,000 m	Gianni Romme	Netherlands	6 min 21.49 sec
10,000 m	Gianni Romme	Netherlands	13 min 8.71 sec
WOMEN			
1,000 m	Christine Witty	Canada	1 min 14.96 sec
1,500 m	Anni Friesinger	Germany	1 min 56.95 sec
3,000 m	Gunda Niemann-Stirnemann	Germany	4 min 5.08 sec
	Gunda Niemann-Stirnemann	Germany	4 min 1.67 sec
5,000 m	Gunda Niemann-Stirnemann	Germany	6 min 58.63 sec

World Ice Speed-Skating Records Set in 1998 on Short Tracks			
Event	Name	Country	Time
MEN			
500 m	Nicola Franceschina	Italy	41.938 sec
	Li Jiajun	China	41.81 sec
3,000 m	Kim Dong Sung	S.Korea	4 min 46.727 sec
WOMEN			
500 m	Yevgenia Radanova	Bulgaria	44.690 sec
1,000 m	Yang Yang (A)	China	1 min 31.991 sec
1,500 m	Yevgenia Radanova	Bulgaria	2 min 25.14 sec
3,000-m relay	An Sang Mi	S.Korea	4 min 16.260 sec
	Chun Lee Kyung		
	Kim Yun Mi		
	Won Hye Kyung		

World All-Around Speed-Skating Champions—Men	
Year	Winner
1994	J.O. Koss (Nor.)
1995	R. Ritsma (Neth.)
1996	R. Ritsma (Neth.)
1997	I. Postma (Neth.)
1998	**I. Postma (Neth.)**

World All-Around Speed-Skating Champions—Women	
Year	Winner
1994	E. Hunyady (Austria)
1995	G. Niemann (Ger.)
1996	G. Niemann (Ger.)
1997	G. Niemann (Ger.)
1998	**G. Niemann-Stirnemann (Ger.)**

World Speed-Skating Sprint Championships		
Year	Men	Women
1994	D. Jansen (U.S.)	B. Blair (U.S.)
1995	Kim Yoon Man (S.Kor.)	B. Blair (U.S.)
1996	S. Klevchenya (Russia)	C. Witty (U.S.)
1997	S. Klevchenya (Russia)	F. Schenk (Ger.)
1998	**J. Bos (Neth.)**	**C. LeMay Doan (Can.)**

World Short-Track Speed-Skating Championships—Overall Winners		
Year	Men	Women
1994	M. Gagnon (Can.)	N. Lambert (Can.)
1995	Chae Ji Hoon (S.Kor.)	Chun Lee Kyung (S.Kor.)
1996	M. Gagnon (Can.)	Chun Lee Kyung (S.Kor.)
1997	Kim Dong Sung (S.Kor.)	Chun Lee Kyung (S.Kor.), Yang Yang (China)
1998	**M. Gagnon (Can.)**	**Yang Yang (China)**

World Figure Skating Champions—Men	
Year	Winner
1994	E. Stojko (Can.)
1995	E. Stojko (Can.)
1996	T. Eldredge (U.S.)
1997	E. Stojko (Can.)
1998	**A. Yagudin (Russia)**

World Figure Skating Champions—Women	
Year	Winner
1994	Y. Sato (Japan)
1995	Chen Lu (China)
1996	M. Kwan (U.S.)
1997	T. Lipinski (U.S.)
1998	**M. Kwan (U.S.)**

World Figure Skating Champions—Pairs	
Year	Winners
1994	Ye. Shishkova, V. Naumov (Russia)
1995	R. Kovarikova, R. Novotny (Cz.Rep.)
1996	M. Yeltsova, A. Bushkov (Russia)
1997	M. Wötzel, I. Steur (Ger.)
1998	**Ye. Berezhnaya, A. Sikharulidze (Russia)**

World Ice Dancing Champions	
Year	Winners
1994	O. Grichuk, Ye. Platov (Russia)
1995	O. Grichuk, Ye. Platov (Russia)
1996	O. Grichuk, Ye. Platov (Russia)
1997	O. Grichuk, Ye. Platov (Russia)
1998	**A. Krylova, O. Ovsyannikov (Russia)**

(ABOVE) AMY SANCETTA—AP/WIDE WORLD; (BELOW) BLAKE SELL—REUTERS

(Above) From left, Olympic figure skating bronze medalist Philippe Candeloro of France, gold medalist Ilia Kulik of Russia, and silver medalist Elvis Stojko of Canada acknowledge the cheers of the crowd. (Below) Artur Dmitriyev and Oksana Kazakova of Russia perform their gold-medal-winning routine in the Olympic figure-skating pairs competition.

the pairs. In the women's competition Kwan regained the world championship after Lipinski decided to turn professional and did not compete. Not a single Olympic champion competed in the world championships, and only 4 of the 12 medalists from Nagano were present.

Speed Skating. It was only fitting that The Netherlands should dominate the speed-skating events at Nagano, since it was Dutch scientists who developed the clapskate, which had turned the sport on its ear in 1997. The revolutionary design of the clapskate featured a hinged front toe with a retractable back heel that audibly clapped when it hit the base of the skate. The skate allowed the blade to stay on the ice longer and provided skaters with more power per stroke.

That increased power translated into five new world records in 11 events. Dutch skater Gianni Romme shattered the world record by more than 15 seconds in the 10,000 m shortly after breaking his own world record in the 5,000 m. Romme led a Dutch men's team that won 9 of 15 medals. Marianne Timmer of The Netherlands broke the 1,500-m women's world record and won two golds, but German women took home an Olympic-best six medals, led by Gunda Niemann-Stirnemann (*see* BIOGRAPHIES) with a gold and two silvers. American sprinter Chris Witty, the world-record holder in the women's 1,000 m, was upset in that event by Timmer, who established an Olympic record in edging Witty by 0.28 second. Nagano marked the first Olympics since 1984 in Sarajevo in which American speed skaters failed to win at least one gold medal.

A month later at the world championships in Heerenven, Neth., Niemann-Stirnemann set a world record in the 3,000-m event and just missed one in the 5,000 m on the way to capturing her seventh overall title. Ids Postma of The Netherlands retained the men's all-around championship.

Aside from four medals won by Canadians, short-track speed skating in Nagano was dominated by Asian nations. South Korea won six medals, including three golds. China also captured six medals, and Japan took home two. South Korea's Chun Lee Kyung turned in the top individual performance, with two golds and a bronze. Takafumi Nishitani won Japan's first-ever medal in Olympic short track. Canada's Annie Perreault triumphed in the 500-m event after teammate Isabelle Charest, the reigning world-record holder, crashed with just two laps to go in her race. At the world short-track championships in Vienna in March, Canadian, Chinese, and South Korean skaters continued to dominate, led by Marc Gagnon of Canada, who won his fourth overall title, and China's Yang Yang, who won her second.

(GREG GUSS)

JUDO

Competition in international judo in 1998 got underway January 10–11 in Japan with the Masutaro Shoriki Cup international tournament. Gold medalists included *judoka* from Japan, South Korea, and the U.S., with the host country winning five of the eight

World Judo Championships—Men

Year	Open weights	60 kg	65 kg	71 kg
1989	N. Ogawa (Japan)	A. Totikashvili (U.S.S.R.)	D. Becanovic (Yugos.)	T. Koga (Japan)
1991	N. Ogawa (Japan)	T. Koshino (Japan)	G. Quellmalz (Ger.)	T. Koga (Japan)
1993	R. Kubacki (Pol.)	R. Sonada (Japan)	Y. Nakamura (Japan)	Yung Chung Hoon (S.Kor.)
1995	D. Douillet (Fr.)	N. Ojeguine (Russia)	U. Quellmalz (Ger.)	D. Hideshima (Japan)
1997	R. Kubacki (Pol.)	T. Nomura (Japan)	Kim Hyuk (S.Kor.)	K. Nakamura (Japan)

Year	78 kg	86 kg	95 kg	+95 kg
1989	Kim Bying Ju (S.Kor.)	F. Canu (Fr.)	K. Kurtanidze (U.S.S.R.)	N. Ogawa (Japan)
1991	D. Lascau (Ger.)	H. Okada (Japan)	S. Traineau (Fr.)	S. Kosorotov (U.S.S.R.)
1993	Chun Ki Young (S.Kor.)	Y. Nakamura (Japan)	A. Kovacs (Hung.)	D. Douillet (Fr.)
1995	T. Koga (Japan)	Chun Ki Young (S.Kor.)	P. Nastula (Pol.)	D. Douillet (Fr.)
1997	Cho In Chul (S.Kor.)	Jeon Ki Young (S.Kor.)	P. Nastula (Pol.)	D. Douillet (Fr.)

World Judo Championships—Women

Year	Open weights	48 kg	52 kg	56 kg
1989	E. Rodríguez (Cuba)	K. Briggs (U.K.)	S. Rendle (U.K.)	C. Arnaud (Fr.)
1991	Zhuang Xiaoyan (China)	C. Nowak (Fr.)	A. Giungi (Italy)	M. Blasco (Spain)
1993	B. Maksymow (Poland)	R. Tamura (Japan)	R. Verdecia (Cuba)	N. Fairbrother (U.K.)
1995	M. van der Lee (Neth.)	R. Tamura (Japan)	M.-C. Restoux (Fr.)	D. González (Cuba)
1997	D. Beltran (Cuba)	R. Tamura (Japan)	M.-C. Restoux (Fr.)	I. Fernández (Spain)

Year	61 kg	66 kg	72 kg	+72 kg
1989	C. Fleury (Fr.)	E. Pierantozzi (Italy)	I. Berghmans (Belg.)	Fengliang Gao (China)
1991	F. Eickoff (Ger.)	E. Pierantozzi (Italy)	Kim Mi Jong (S.Kor.)	Moon Ji Yoon (S.Kor.)
1993	G. van de Cavaye (Belg.)	Cho Min Sun (S.Kor.)	Leng Chin Hui (China)	J. Hagn (Ger.)
1995	Jung Sung Sook (S.Kor.)	Cho Min Sun (S.Kor.)	C. Luna (Cuba)	A. Seriese (Neth.)
1997	S. Vandenhende (Fr.)	K. Howey (U.K.)	N. Anno (Japan)	C. Cicot (Fr.)

categories. In the All-Japan women's championships held in Tokyo on May 2–3, Ryoko Tamaura beat Tomoe Makabe by *yusei* decision for her eighth consecutive title. Shinichi Shinohara won the All-Japan championships for men on April 29 at the Nippon Budokan.

The International Judo Federation's (IJF's) executive board approved having North Korea and South Korea compete as a unified team at the world cup team competition in Minsk, Belarus, in September and authorized changing the men's over 95-kg class to an over 100-kg category and the women's over 72-kg class to an over 78-kg class. In the competition Japan won the men's title by beating Brazil 5–1. Defending champion France tied for third place with Russia. Cuba's women's team took the gold medal with a 4–2 victory over France, while Belgium and China tied for the bronze. In an attempt by the IJF to emphasize the importance of an *ippon* full-point victory, a special award was scheduled to be launched at the 1999 world championships for *judoka* who compiled the highest percentage of *ippon* wins at the world championships.

(ANDY ADAMS)

RODEO

After a three-year hiatus from championship contention brought about by a string of injuries, 29-year-old Ty Murray of Stephenville, Texas, returned to action in 1998 to win his seventh world champion all-around cowboy title in the Professional Rodeo Cowboys Association (PRCA). Murray clinched the title at the season-ending $4.2 million National Finals Rodeo, held December 4–13 at the Thomas & Mack Center in Las Vegas, Nev.

Ty Murray of Stephenville, Texas, finds the ride a little hard atop a bull named Hard Copy during the National Finals Rodeo in Las Vegas, Nev., in December. Murray stayed on long enough to win the event and claim his seventh world champion all-around cowboy title.

With the victory, Murray eclipsed the records of Larry Mahan and Tom Ferguson, each of whom gained six world all-around championships in his respective career. In addition to winning the all-around, Murray captured his second world title in bull riding with season earnings of $167,154. That, coupled with earnings of $20,688 in bareback riding and $76,820 in saddle bronc riding, brought the cowboy's aggregate earnings for the year to $264,672.

As in the past, the PRCA and Women's Professional Rodeo Association world titles were determined by season earnings and were awarded in eight standard rodeo disciplines: bareback riding, steer wrestling, calf roping, saddle bronc riding, team roping, women's barrel racing, bull riding, and steer roping. The all-around title was conferred on the cowboy who won the most money in at least two of the different disciplines.

Mark Gomes of Hutchinson, Kan., claimed his first world title in bareback riding with earnings of $142,530. After setting a regular-season record for arena earnings, calf roper Cody Ohl of Stephenville, Texas, snared 4 of 10 rounds at the National Finals to win his event handily. Ohl, who claimed his first world title in 1997, successfully defended it in 1998 with earnings of $222,794. Also defending their 1997 titles were team ropers Speed Williams of Jacksonville, Fla., and Rich Skelton of Llano, Texas, who earned $128,472 and $127,646, respectively.

Saddle bronc rider and defending all-around champion Dan Mortensen of Manhattan, Mont., added a fifth saddle bronc riding world championship to his accomplishments. He easily defeated the field in Las Vegas by winning 5 of 10 rounds and ended the season with $227,378. Another repeat winner was Kristie Peterson of Elbert, Colo., who gained her fourth women's barrel racing championship with $212,998, a new record for the event.

Mike Smith of Baton Rouge, La., claimed his first world championship in steer

Men's World All-Around Rodeo Championship			
Year	Winner	Year	Winner
1993	T. Murray	1996	J. Beaver
1994	T. Murray	1997	D. Mortensen
1995	J. Beaver	**1998**	**T. Murray**

wrestling with season earnings of $161,862. Earlier, 40-year-old Guy Allen of Hobbs, N.M., had stretched his record for steer roping world titles to 13 at the conclusion of the National Finals Steer Roping held in Guthrie, Okla., on October 30–31.

In August Steve Hatchell, formerly commissioner of the National Collegiate Athletic Association Big 12 Conference, took over as the new head of the PRCA. He replaced Lewis Cryer, who had served as PRCA commissioner since 1988. Hatchell planned to increase rodeo's popularity through televised events, advertising, and stepped-up public relations and marketing efforts.   (GAVIN FORBES EHRINGER)

ROWING

At the 1998 world rowing championships on their home waters in Cologne, Germany emerged as leader of the 52 nations participating in the 14 events for men and 10 for women. Italy and the U.K. finished second and third among the 14 nations sharing the titles, of which only 13 changed hands. The U.S., Australia, Canada, Switzerland, Russia, and Romania were also prominent in the final medal table. Six championships were won by no more than one second and another 10 by less than two seconds.

In men's heavyweight classes Germany successfully defended the double sculls and coxless pairs, and Australia also won twice in coxed fours and pairs. Rob Waddell of New Zealand became the new single sculls champion, and Italy retained the quadruple sculls with the biggest margin of the championships, 4.94 sec. Against determined opposition,

Steven Redgrave captured a record eighth career title as the U.K. retained the coxless fours by 1.38 sec, with only 0.19 sec covering the next three finishes. The American team faced an even tougher task against Germany to retain the eights by 0.68 sec, with the next three boats 0.81 sec behind.

Italy took the lightweight men's single sculls and narrowly retained the quadruple sculls. Though Denmark was pressed hard to retain the coxless fours title, Poland recaptured the double sculls more comfortably. The coxless pairs went to France, and, in the tightest finish of the championships, Germany defeated the U.S. by 0.28 sec, with Italy 0.50 sec behind, in eights.

Germany retained its women's titles in open and lightweight quadruple sculls. Two other successful defending champions were Canada in open coxless pairs and Romania in eights. The U.K. won twice in open double sculls and lightweight coxless pairs, the U.S. took lightweight double sculls, the singles went to Switzerland, Irina Fedotova of Russia became the new single sculls champion, and Ukraine triumphed in coxless fours.

In the World Cup competition held in Hazewinkel, Belg.; Munich, Ger.; and Lucerne, Switz.; the top nations were: Germany 137 points, the U.K. 112, Denmark 93, Australia 86, and Romania 77. Germany won medals in all 14 events of the world junior rowing championships in Ottensheim, Austria, including six gold and six silver. Romania took two titles, and the remaining gold medals went to Argentina, Australia, China, Estonia, Russia, and Yugoslavia. In the Under-23 International for the Nations

Lightweight quadruple scull gold medalists (from left) Paolo Pittino, Elia Luini, Lorenzo Bertini, and Franco Sancassani of Italy listen to the Italian national anthem at the conclusion of the World Rowing Championships in Cologne, Ger., in September.

Cup in Ioannina, Greece, Italy topped the medal table with three victories, Australia and France won twice, and Denmark and Germany each took one gold.

The Henley Royal Regatta in England attracted a record 552 entries from countries outside the U.K., which won seven of the trophies. For the U.S. the reigning world champion, Jamie Koven, won the Diamond Challenge Sculls, Harvard University triumphed in the Ladies' Challenge Plate (eights), and the Augusta (Ga.) Sculling Center took the Queen Mother Challenge Cup (quadruple sculls). The Silver Goblets (coxless pairs) and Double Sculls Challenge Cup went to France, which was defeated in the Grand Challenge Cup (eights) by Germany. Croatia won the Prince Philip Challenge Cup (coxed fours), and Maria Brandin (Sweden) won the women's single sculls for the fifth year.

In the 144th Boat Race, the rowers from Cambridge became the tallest, heaviest, and fastest winners in the series when they de-

World Rowing Championships—Men

Year	Single sculls	Min:s	Double sculls	Min:s	Coxed pairs	Min:s
1994	A. Willims (Ger.)	6:46.33	R. Thorsen, L. Bjoenness (Nor.)	6:08.33	T. Frankovic, I. Boraska (Croatia)	6:42.16
1995	I. Cop (Slov.)	6:52.93	L. Christensen, M. Haldbo-Hansen (Den.)	6:17.01	L. Sartori, G. DeStabile (Italy)	7:35.11
1996	X. Müller (Switz.)	6:44.85	D. Tizzano, A. Abbagnale (Italy)	6:16.90	Y. Schulte, L. Prevot (Fr.)	7:18.26
1997	J. Koven (U.S.)	6:44.86	S. Volkert, A. Hajek (Ger.)	6:13.35	S. Fentress, J. Irving (U.S.)	6:56.30
1998	**R. Waddell (N.Z.)**	**6:39.65**	**S. Volkert, A. Hajek (Ger.)**	**6:13.20**	**N. Green, J. Tomkins (Austl.)**	**6:45.01**

Year	Coxless pairs	Min:s	Coxed fours	Min:s	Coxless fours	Min:s	Eights	Min:s
1994	S. Redgrave, M. Pinsent (U.K.)	6:18.65	Romania	6:06.69	Italy	5:48.44	United States	5:24.50
1995	S. Redgrave, M. Pinsent (U.K.)	6:28.11	United States	6:37.50	Italy	5:58.28	Germany	5:53.40
1996	S. Redgrave, M. Pinsent (U.K.)	6:20.09	Romania	6:25.74	Australia	6:06.37	Netherlands	5:42.74
1997	M. Andrieux, J.-C. Rolland (Fr.)	6:27.69	France	6:04.17	United Kingdom	5:52.40	United States	5:27.20
1998	**R. Sens, D. Kirchhoff (Ger.)**	**6:22.32**	**Australia**	**6:09.43**	**United Kingdom**	**5:48.06**	**United States**	**5:38.78**

World Rowing Championships—Women

Year	Single sculls	Min:s	Double sculls	Min:s	Quadruple sculls	Min:s
1994	T. Hansen (Den.)	7:23.96	P. Baker, B. Lawson (N.Z.)	6:45.30	Germany	6:11.73
1995	M. Brandin (Swe.)	7:26.00	M. McBean, K. Heddle (Can.)	6:55.76	Germany	6:40.80
1996	Ye. Khodotovich (Bela.)	7:32.21	M. McBean, K. Heddle (Can.)	6:56.84	Germany	6:27.44
1997	Ye. Khodotovich (Bela.)	7:29.30	E. Meike, K. Boron (Ger.)	6:51.07	Germany	6:16.15
1998	**I. Fedotova (Russia)**	**7:25.09**	**United Kingdom**	**6:48.85**	**Germany**	**6:24.38**

Year	Coxless pairs	Min:s	Coxless fours	Min:s	Eights	Min:s
1994	C. Gosse, H. Cortin (Fr.)	7:01.77	Netherlands	6:30.76	Germany	6:07.42
1995	M. Still, K. Slatter (Austl.)	7:12.70	United States	7:03.53	United States	6:50.73
1996	M. Still, K. Slatter (Austl.)	7:01.39	United States	6:49.48	Romania	6:19.73
1997	E. Robinson, A. Korn (Can.)	7:08.09	United Kingdom	6:40.30	Romania	6:02.40
1998	**E. Robinson, A. Korn (Can.)**	**7:05.19**	**Ukraine**	**6:30.63**	**Romania**	**6:14.62**

The Diamond Challenge Sculls		
Year	Winner	Min:s
1994	X. Müller (Grasshopper, Switz.)	7:35
1995	J. Jaanson (Parnu, Est.)	7:24
1996	M.L.O. Vervoorn (Delft, Neth.)	7:42
1997	G.M.P. Searle (Molesey B.C.)	7:38
1998	**J. Koven (U.S.)**	**7:56**

Grand Challenge Cup		
Year	Winner	Min:s
1994	Charles River and San Diego	6:13
1995	San Diego Training Center	5:59
1996	Imperial College and Queens Tower	6:11
1997	Institutes of Sport, Australia	6:03
1998	**Hansa Dortmund and Berlin, Ger.**	**6:18**

feated Oxford by three lengths to widen Cambridge's lead to 75–68. The winning time of 16 min 19 sec broke the record of 16 min 45 sec set by Oxford in 1984.

(KEITH L. OSBORNE)

SAILING (YACHTING)

Sailing in 1998 was dominated by the Whitbread Round-the-World Race. It was contested in level-rated (no scoring adjustments) "Whitbread 60s," which featured a powerful water-ballasted design equipped with the latest technology in satellite communication that was linked to the Internet, allowing spectators from around the world to follow the race on a daily basis for the first time. The racing itself was exciting, as the small fleet remained bunched closely, chasing the weather patterns, predictions of which were provided by a shore-based professional weather service and made available to all boats. A win in the final transatlantic phase of the race by *EF Language,* skippered by Paul Cayard, assured victory on total points over *Merit Cup,* which edged *EF Language* by 15 minutes on the final leg from France to England but fell 138 points behind overall.

In the U.S. the Key West Race Week (257 entries from 17 countries) and the Southern Ocean Racing Conference (173 boats) continued to be the winter high points in offshore sailing, drawing the latest in new designs. The Australian Sydney–Hobart Race provided very tight racing for the boats but no new course records, as *Brindabella* crossed the line first and *Beau Geste* won on corrected time, a method of factoring a boat's handicap. The U.S. Newport–Bermuda Race was among the slowest on record, with *Alexia* (an ILC Maxi) taking some 90 hours to cross the line first, while *Kodiak* (cruiser-racer) and *Blue Yankee* (racer) earned victories with corrected times of more than 86 hours for the 1,022-km (635-mi) race. The Rolex Commodores Cup, sailed off England's southern coast, was dominated by the German Red Team, composed of *Hexe, Sequana,* and *Topas.*

The yacht *EF Language* leads the Whitbread fleet out of Sydney Harbour, Australia, at the start of the fourth leg of the Whitbread Round-the-World Race in January. Skippered by Paul Cayard, *EF Language* earned a total-points victory in the event.

STEPHEN MUNDAY—ALLSPORT

The Kenwood Cup in Hawaii was captured by the New Zealand team in the boats *Big Apple II, G'Net,* and *White Cloud.* The International Sailing Federation's (ISAF's) second quadrennial world championship regatta, staged in Dubayy, U.A.E., for some 1,100 sailors, featured sparkling racing under nearly ideal conditions. The largest-ever Kiel (Ger.) Week, however, provided competition for some 5,000 sailors and 2,000 boats from 50 countries.

On the political front, the Star class boat was back in the Olympic lineup after an International Olympic Committee decision allowing an 11th medal for sailing at the 2000 Games in Sydney, Australia. This reversal represented a major victory for the class, which had been caught off-guard when its elimination from the event was announced. The ISAF/Sperry Topsider World Sailor of the Year (male) was Peter Goss of the U.K., who was recognized for his rescue of Raphael Dinelli in the Vendee Globe Race. Female recipients were Ukrainians Ruslana Taran and Yelena Pakholchik, who were honoured for their consistently outstanding performance in 470 competitions.

Three more distance records fell in 1998: Roy Disney in *Pyewacket,* having set a new

Bermuda Race		
Year	Winning yacht	Owner
1990	Denali	L. Huntington
1992	Constellation	U.S. Naval Academy
1994	Gaylark	K. Smith
1996	Boomerang	G. Coumantaros
1998	**Kodiak**	**L. Ecclestone**

Transpacific Race		
Year	Winning yacht	Owner
1989	Silver Bullet	J. DeLaura
1991	Chance	R. McNulty
1993	Silver Bullet	J. DeLaura
1995	Merlin	D. Sinclair
1997	Ralphie	J. Montgomery

Admiral's Cup	
Year	Winning team
1989	United Kingdom
1991	France
1993	Germany
1995	Italy
1997	United States

America's Cup					
Year	Winning yacht	Owner	Skipper	Losing Yacht	Owner
1983	Australia II (Australia)	A. Bond and syndicate	J. Bertrand	Liberty (U.S.)	Maritime College at Fort Schuyler Foundation, Inc.
1987	Stars & Stripes (U.S.)	Sail America syndicate	D. Conner	Kookaburra III (Australia)	K. Parry and syndicate
1988	Stars & Stripes (U.S.)	Sail America syndicate	D. Conner	New Zealand (New Zealand)	M. Fay
1992	America³ (U.S.)	America³ Foundation	B. Koch	Il Moro di Venezia (Italy)	Compagnia della Vela di Venezia
1995	Black Magic (N.Z.)	P. Blake and Team New Zealand	R. Coutts	Young America	Pact 95 syndicate

World Class Boat Champions, 1998		
Class	Winner	Country
Etchells 22	D. Knuelman/P. Sustronk	Canada
Europe	S. Johnsen	Denmark
Finn	M. Kusznierewicz	Poland
2.4 Metre	B. Rikard	Finland
470 (men)	G. Philippe/T. Cariou	France
470 (women)	R. Taran/ Y. Paholchik	Ukraine
49er	C. Nicholson/ D. Phillips	Australia
505	N. Trotman/M. Mills	U.S.
J/24	T. Hutchinson	U.S.
Optimist	P. Mattia	Italy
Soling	G. Shaidouko	Russia
Star	C. Beashel/D. Giles	Australia
Tornado	D. Bundock/J. Forbes	Australia

record in the Transpacific Race in 1997, set a new time of 6 days 14 hr 23 min in the Pacific Cup (San Francisco–Honolulu). Christophe Auquin, who established the Vendée Globe record in 1997, shattered the transatlantic record with a run of 9 days 22 hr 59 min. Steve Fossett in *Lakota* set a new single-handed transpacific (California–Hawaii) mark of 7 days 22 hr 38 min.

America's Cup preparations continued around the world. By the end of January, 16 yacht clubs from 10 countries had registered and paid their earnest deposits of $250,000. Disaster struck the Sydney-to-Hobart race in December, when high winds and heavy seas caused the deaths of six sailors and forced more than half of the boats to seek shelter or be abandoned. The U.S. yacht *Sayonara* won the race.   (JOHN B. BONDS)

SKIING

Alpine Skiing. In 1998 Hermann "the Herminator" Maier (*see* BIOGRAPHIES) became the first Austrian to win the overall Alpine World Cup title since Karl Schranz in 1970. Maier won 10 World Cup events and two individual titles, sweeping the supergiant slalom (super G) races, winning the giant slalom title, and finishing second in the downhill standings.

In February, however, just three days before he captured gold in the super G at the Olympic Games in Nagano, Japan, Maier's career appeared to be in jeopardy after he suffered one of the most spectacular crashes in skiing history. Traveling at nearly 105 km/h (65 mph) near the top of the downhill course, Maier lost control and was propelled head-first into the frozen retaining walls. Plowing through two fences, the 26-year-old Austrian miraculously escaped unhurt.

Maier's downhill crash opened the gate for France's Jean-Luc Cretier, who edged Norway's Lasse Kjus to win France's first downhill gold since Jean-Claude Killy's 20 years earlier. Overall, the Austrian men captured 8 of a possible 15 Alpine medals.

Italy's Alberto Tomba failed in his bid to become the first skier to win medals in four different Olympics. He crashed in the giant slalom and finished a disappointing 17th on his first run down the slalom course before dropping out of the event. Tomba's teammate Deborah Compagnoni, by winning the women's giant slalom, became the first skier to win gold in three consecutive Olympics.

When the snow, fog, and rain relented after dogging skiers and schedule-makers at Nagano for nearly six days, Katja Seizinger of Germany stole the show. By winning the downhill gold, she became the first woman in Winter Olympics history to win consecutive golds in the same event. Seizinger went on to win the combined gold, with her teammates Martina Ertl and Hilde Gerg completing a German sweep of that event. Gerg also won gold in the women's slalom, erasing a 0.6-sec lead held by Compagnoni to win by just 0.06 sec. Zali Steggall captured Australia's first Alpine medal by placing third in the slalom. The German women took home six Alpine medals, and Seizinger's three medals tied a record for most in a single Winter Olympics. American downhiller Picabo Street overcame a serious

1996 knee injury to win the super G over the favoured Germans. Street skied cautiously, however, in her specialty, the downhill, and missed a medal by 0.17 sec. Later Street suffered a season-ending injury in a crash during a World Cup event in Switzerland. Seizinger capped the season with the women's overall World Cup title.

Nordic Skiing. Norway ended Japan's six-year reign as Nordic combined champions with a dominant Olympic performance on the ski-jumping half of the event. Bjarte Engen Vik, who won the individual gold, helped bring home the gold in the team event as well, while the host Japanese fell to fifth. The Japanese, however, led by Masahiko "Happy" Harada (*see* BIOGRAPHIES) pleased the home crowd by winning team gold in ski jumping.

Norway's cross-country legend Bjørn Dæhlie (*see* BIOGRAPHIES) established records for most Olympic gold medals (8) and most medals in the Winter Games (12) by winning three golds, but the baton may have been passed to his teammate Thomas Alsgaard, who edged Dæhlie for the 15-km pursuit gold medal at Nagano and then won his first World Cup title.

DIETHER ENDLICHER—AP/WIDE WORLD

Hermann Maier of Austria speeds downhill during the Olympic supergiant slalom competition en route to taking the gold medal.

World Alpine Skiing Championships—Slalom						
Year	Men's slalom	Men's giant slalom	Men's supergiant	Women's slalom	Women's giant slalom	Women's supergiant
1994	T. Stangassinger (Austria)	M. Wasmeier (Ger.)	M. Wasmeier (Ger.)	V. Schneider (Switz.)	D. Compagnoni (Italy)	D. Roffe-Steinrotter (U.S.)
1995	not held					
1996	A. Tomba (Italy)	A. Tomba (Italy)	A. Skaardal (Nor.)	P. Wiberg (Swed.)	D. Compagnoni (Italy)	I. Kostner (Italy)
1997	T. Stiansen (Nor.)	M. von Grünigen (Switz.)	A. Skaardal (Nor.)	D. Compagnoni (Italy)	D. Compagnoni (Italy)	I. Kostner (Italy)
1998	**H.-P. Buraas (Nor.)**	**H. Maier (Austria)**	**H. Maier (Austria)**	**H. Gerg (Ger.)**	**D. Compagnoni (Italy)**	**P. Street (U.S.)**

World Alpine Skiing Championships—Downhill		
Year	Men	Women
1994	T. Moe (U.S.)	K. Seizinger (Ger.)
1995	not held	
1996	P. Ortlieb (Austria)	P. Street (U.S.)
1997	B. Kernen (Switz.)	H. Lindh (U.S.)
1998	**J.-L. Cretier (Fr.)**	**K. Seizinger (Ger.)**

World Alpine Skiing Championships—Combined		
Year	Men	Women
1994	L. Kjus (Nor.)	P. Wiberg (Swed.)
1995	not held	
1996	M. Girardelli (Lux.)	P. Wiberg (Swed.)
1997	K.A. Aamodt (Nor.)	R. Götschl (Austria)
1998	**M. Reiter (Austria)**	**K. Seizinger (Ger.)**

(Above) From left, Olympic alpine combined skiing gold medalist Katja Seizinger, silver medalist Martina Ertl, and bronze medalist Hilde Gerg, all of Germany, wave during the awards ceremony in Nagano, Japan. (Right) Jonny Moseley of the U.S. executes his "360 Mute Grab" stunt during the freestyle skiing moguls competition at the Winter Olympics. Moseley's gold medal in the event helped the U.S. bring home three golds in the Olympic freestyle skiing competitions.

Russia's Larissa Lazutina medaled in all five women's Olympic cross-country races, capturing three golds. On the World Cup circuit, Lazutina rode the wave of her Olympic success by winning the last two events of the season to surpass Norway's Bente Martinsen for the overall title.

Freestyle Skiing. The U.S. captured three of a possible four gold medals in one of the most spectacular events of the Nagano Olympics. Jonny Moseley of the U.S. won gold with his signature "360 Mute Grab" at the end of a flawless moguls run. Moseley's golden stunt, which involved grabbing his inside ski while making a complete spin in the air, pushed him past Janne Lahtela and Sami Mustonen, respectively, for Finland. Americans Eric Bergoust and Nikki Stone won the top spots in the aerial finals. Stone, who nearly quit the sport after suffering a series of back injuries, avenged a disappointing finish at the 1994 Olympics in Lillehammer, Nor., in which she failed to qualify for the final.

Snowboarding. The youthfulness and exuberance that propelled snowboarding from a North American sideshow event to full-medal status for the first time at the 1998 Olympics also managed to give the sport a black eye. Canadian men's giant slalom gold medalist

Alpine World Cup		
Year	Men	Women
1994	K.A. Aamodt (Nor.)	V. Schneider (Switz.)
1995	A. Tomba (Italy)	V. Schneider (Switz.)
1996	L. Kjus (Nor.)	K. Seizinger (Ger.)
1997	L. Alphand (Fr.)	P. Wiberg (Swed.)
1998	**H. Maier (Austria)**	**K. Seizinger (Ger.)**

Nordic World Cup		
Year	Men	Women
1994	V. Smirnov (Kazak.)	M. Di Centa (Italy)
1995	B. Dæhlie (Nor.)	Ye. Vyalbe (Russia)
1996	B. Dæhlie (Nor.)	M. Di Centa (Italy)
1997	B. Dæhlie (Nor.)	Ye. Vyalbe (Russia)
1998	**T. Alsgaard (Nor.)**	**L. Lazutina (Russia)**

World Nordic Skiing Championships—Ski Jump					
Year	90-m hill	120-m hill	Team jump	Combined	Team combined
1994	E. Bredesen (Nor.)	J. Weissflog (Ger.)	Germany	F.-B. Lundberg (Nor.)	Japan
1995	T. Okabe (Japan)	T. Ingebrigtsen (Nor.)	Finland	F.-B. Lundberg (Nor.)	Japan
1996	not held				
1997	J. Ahonen (Fin.)	M. Harada (Japan)	Finland	K. Ogiwara (Japan)	Norway
1998	**J. Soininen (Fin.)**	**K. Funaki (Japan)**	**Japan**	**B.E. Vik (Nor.)**	**Norway**

World Nordic Skiing Championships—Men					
Year	10-km	15-km	30-km	50-km	Relay
1994	B. Dæhlie (Nor.)	B. Dæhlie (Nor.)	T. Alsgaard (Nor.)	V. Smirnov (Kazak.)	Italy
1995	V. Smirnov (Kazak.)	V. Smirnov (Kazak.)	V. Smirnov (Kazak.)	S. Fauner (Italy)	Norway
1996	not held				
1997	B. Dæhlie (Nor.)	B. Dæhlie (Nor.)	A. Prokurorov (Russia)	M. Myllyla (Fin.)	Norway
1998	**B. Dæhlie (Nor.)**	**T. Alsgaard (Nor.)**	**M. Myllyla (Fin.)**	**B. Dæhlie (Nor.)**	**Norway**

World Nordic Skiing Championships—Women					
Year	5-km	10-km	15-km	30-km	Relay
1994	L. Yegorova (Russia)	L. Yegorova (Russia)	M. Di Centa (Italy)	M. Di Centa (Italy)	Russia
1995	L. Lazutina (Russia)	L. Lazutina (Russia)	L. Lazutina (Russia)	Ye. Vyalbe (Russia)	Russia
1996	not held				
1997	Ye. Vyalbe (Russia)	Ye. Vyalbe (Russia)	Ye. Vyalbe (Russia)	Ye. Vyalbe (Russia)	Russia
1998	**L. Lazutina (Russia)**	**L. Lazutina (Russia)**	**O. Danilova (Russia)**	**J. Tchepalova (Russia)**	**Russia**

Ross Rebagliatti was temporarily stripped of his medal after testing positive for marijuana. Although his medal was later restored, Rebagliatti's brush with the law overshadowed some remarkable performances and stigmatized a sport composed mainly of teens and young adults. Switzerland's Gian Simmen captured the men's halfpipe gold by nearly three points over Daniel Franck of Norway and Ross Powers of the U.S., while Germany's Nicola Thost edged Norway's Stine Brun Kjeldaas by 0.4 point for the women's gold. As expected, Karine Ruby of France won gold in the women's giant slalom.

(GREG GUSS)

SQUASH

As squash continued to press its claims for inclusion in the 2004 Olympic Games, 1998 was notable for the sport's debut at the Commonwealth Games in September. Singles and doubles were on the program in Kuala Lumpur, Malaysia, and the historical strength of the Commonwealth countries meant that the majority of top-flight men and women players were included. The world's top-ranked player, Peter Nicol of Scotland, took the men's gold, beating Canadian Jonathon Power 3–9, 9–2, 9–1, 2–9, 9–2 in the final, while the Australian duo Michelle Martin and Sarah Fitz-Gerald contested the women's title. Martin, edged off the top-ranking spot by Fitz-Gerald since 1996, had carried all before her in early 1998 on her way back to world number one status, gaining her sixth straight British Open in April and overcoming her rival yet again at the Games 9–0, 9–6, 9–5.

The women's competitive year ended in stunning fashion in Stuttgart, Ger., in

Peter Nicol of Scotland (left) reaches for the ball as Jonathon Power of Canada looks on during the men's squash singles final at the Commonwealth Games in September. Nicol prevailed to take home the gold medal; Power later defeated Nicol in the World Open final.

November, when Fitz-Gerald captured her third consecutive World Open title by beating Martin 10–8 in the memorable deciding game after trailing 2–8 and needing to save no less than eight match balls. Immediately thereafter, the two paired up to lead Australia to the world team title, beating England 3–0 in the final.

The men's pattern for the year was set in the British Open when Jansher Khan of Pakistan, who had been ranked first in the world for six years but was some way short of fitness after surgery, was beaten by Nicol in the final. Khan finished the year by falling out of the top 10 after several months of injury. The men's World Open was played in December in Qatar, where Power avenged his Commonwealth Games result against Nicol to become the first North American world champion, winning the final 15–17, 15–7, 15–9, 15–10.   (ANDREW SHELLEY)

SWIMMING

The year 1998 began with a bang—and a bust—as more than 1,300 of the world's best swimmers, representing a record 119 countries, gathered in Perth, Australia, for the Fédération Internationale de Natation Amateur (FINA) world swimming and diving championships. Michael Klim of Australia and, from the U.S., Jenny Thompson were the outstanding swimmers at Perth, each taking home four gold medals. Although no world records were set—a first for this meet—a total of eight world championship records fell. The U.S. edged Australia in the overall medal count 24–20, with the Americans dominating the women's events and the Australians narrowly winning the majority of the men's.

Klim, who had been named as the 1997 male World Swimmer of the Year by *Swimming World* magazine, picked up where he left off by winning the 200-m freestyle (1 min 47.41 sec) and the 100-m butterfly in world championship record time (52.25 sec), just missing his own world record. He also swam on Australia's winning 4 × 200-m freestyle and 4 × 100-m medley relay teams. The Australian win in the medley relay marked the first time the U.S. had lost that event in international competition. Klim added silver medals in the 100-m freestyle, behind training partner Aleksandr Popov of Russia, and the 400-m freestyle relay and a bronze medal in the 50-m freestyle.

Thompson recorded individual wins in the 100-m butterfly (setting a world championship record of 58.46 sec) and the 100-m freestyle (54.95 sec). She picked up two additional golds as a member of both the U.S. 4 × 100-m freestyle and 4 × 100-m medley relay teams (which set a U.S. and world championship record of 4 min 1.93 sec) and a silver for the 4 × 200-m freestyle relay.

American Lenny Krayzelburg, the only man besides Klim to win more than one event, took gold in both the 100-m and 200-m backstroke races and then added a silver in the medley relay. Chen Yan of China was the only woman other than Thompson to win multiple events, as she touched the wall

Members of the U.S. women's 4 × 100-m medley team, (from left) Jenny Thompson, Lea Maurer, Kristy Kowal, and Amy Van Dyken, celebrate after winning the event at the FINA world swimming and diving championships.

World Open Championship—Men	
Year	Winner
1994	Jan. Khan (Pak.)
1995	Jan. Khan (Pak.)
1996	Jan. Khan (Pak.)
1997	R. Eyles (Austl.)
1998	**J. Power (Can.)**

World Open Championship—Women	
Year	Winner
1994	M. Martin (Austl.)
1995	M. Martin (Austl.)
1996	S. Fitz-Gerald (Austl.)
1997	S. Fitz-Gerald (Austl.)
1998	**S. Fitz-Gerald (Austl.)**

British Open Championship—Men	
Year	Winner
1993–94	Jan. Khan (Pak.)
1994–95	Jan. Khan (Pak.)
1995–96	Jan. Khan (Pak.)
1996–97	Jan. Khan (Pak.)
1997–98	**P. Nicol (Scot.)**

British Open Championship—Women	
Year	Winner
1993–94	M. Martin (Austl.)
1994–95	M. Martin (Austl.)
1995–96	M. Martin (Austl.)
1996–97	M. Martin (Austl.)
1997–98	**M. Martin (Austl.)**

World Swimming Records Set in 1998 in 50-m Pools			
Event	Name	Country	Time
MEN			
4 × 200-m freestyle relay	Australian National Team	Australia	7 min 11.86 sec
WOMEN			
50-m breaststroke	Penny Heyns	South Africa	30.95 sec

World Swimming Records Set in 1998 in 25-m Pools			
Event	Name	Country	Time
MEN			
50-m freestyle	Mark Foster	U.K.	21.48 sec
	Mark Foster	U.K.	21.31 sec
400-m freestyle	Ian Thorpe	Australia	3 min 39.82 sec
1,500-m freestyle	Grant Hackett	Australia	14 min 19.55 sec
50-m backstroke	Thomas Rupprath	Germany	24.13 sec
50-m breaststroke	Mark Warnecke	Germany	26.70 sec
100-m breaststroke	Frederik DeBurghgraeve	Belgium	58.79 sec
200-m breaststroke	Andrey Korneyev	Russia	2 min 07.79 sec
50-m butterfly	Milos Milosevic	Croatia	23.30 sec
100-m butterfly	Michael Klim	Australia	51.16 sec
	Michael Klim	Australia	51.07 sec
200-m butterfly	James Hickman	U.K.	1 min 51.76 sec
400-m individual medley	Matthew Dunn	Australia	4 min 04.24 sec
4 × 50-m freestyle relay	Netherlands national team	Netherlands	1 min 26.99 sec
WOMEN			
50-m butterfly	Jenny Thompson	U.S.	26.48 sec
100-m butterfly	Jenny Thompson	U.S.	56.90 sec
100-m individual medley	Hu Xiaowen	China	1 min 0.60 sec
	Martina Moracova	Slovakia	1 min 0.43 sec
4 × 50-m freestyle relay	German national team	Germany	1 min 39.56 sec

Irina Lashko of Russia performs a dive in the women's 1-m springboard competition at the FINA world swimming and diving championships. Lashko collected the gold medal, while her compatriot, Vera Ilyina, won the silver.

GREG WOOD—AFP

Swimmer Michael Klim of Australia races toward the finish and the gold medal in the men's 100-m butterfly at the Fédération Internationale de Natation Amateur world swimming and diving championships in January.

TORSTEN BLACKWOOD—AFP

first in both the 400-m freestyle and 400-m individual medley.

Popov, having recovered from a near-fatal stabbing he sustained after the 1996 Olympics, failed in his attempt to become the first swimmer ever to win the same two events in three successive world championships. He successfully defended one title with a championship record (48.93 sec) in the 100-m freestyle, swimming's glamour event, but the title of "world's fastest man in the water" went to Bill Pilczuk of the U.S., who upset Popov in the 50-m race.

Even before the meet began, it was mired in a controversy that had developed during the previous October. At their national games in Shanghai, Chen Yan and Wu Yanyan shattered two world records. Subsequently, four swimmers from China who were not ranked among the world's top 150 vaulted to the top of the world rankings, and Chinese swimmers completely dominated almost every women's event. Critics accused the Chinese of using performance-enhancing drugs—a charge that was vigorously denied by Chinese and FINA officials.

As the Chinese team arrived in Australia in January, customs agents seized bioengineered human growth hormone—reportedly enough for the entire Chinese team for two weeks—in the bag of swimmer Yuan Yuan. Her coach, Zhou Zhewen, said she was delivering the drug to an Australian friend, in itself a contravention of Australia's drug-trafficking laws. Both Yuan and Zhou were sent home in disgrace and later banned from the sport. During the championships four other Chinese swimmers tested positive for a diuretic drug, used solely as a masking agent for steroid use. All four were banned from competition for two years.

At the FINA congress held before the world championships, a bid to reduce the penalty for steroid use from four years to two was defeated. The reduction had been introduced by FINA's executive committee with the endorsement of the International Olympic Committee. In a related development, Michelle Smith-de Bruin of Ireland, who won three gold medals at the 1996 Olympic Games amid suspicions of drug use, was found to have adulterated her urine sample taken in an out-of-competition test in January. She was later suspended from competition for four years.

Swimming events at the Goodwill Games, held in New York City on July 28–August 2, featured a dual-meet format with four men's and four women's teams vying for cash prizes. The U.S. won the women's team title, and the World All-Stars took the men's. South African Penny Heyns, a double Olympic champion in 1996, set a world record for the 50-m breaststroke (30.95 sec), a newly sanctioned event. Australia won 23 of 32 events at the Commonwealth Games, held in Kuala Lumpur, Malaysia, in September. The Australian men's 800-m freestyle relay team—featuring 15-year-old Ian Thorpe, Daniel Kowalski, Matthew Dunn, and Michael Klim—broke the world record with a time of 7 min 11.86 sec. Meanwhile, Australia's Susie O'Neill continued her three-year unbeaten streak in the 200-m butterfly and won a record eight

World Swimming and Diving Championships—Men

Freestyle

Year	50 m	100 m	200 m	400 m	1,500 m	
1986	T. Jager (U.S.)	M. Biondi (U.S.)	M. Gross (W.Ger.)	R. Henkel (W.Ger.)	R. Henkel (W.Ger.)	
1991	T. Jager (U.S.)	M. Biondi (U.S.)	G. Lamberti (Italy)	J. Hoffmann (Ger.)	J. Hoffmann (Ger.)	
1994	A. Popov (Russia)	A. Popov (Russia)	A. Kasvio (Fin.)	K. Perkins (Austl.)	K. Perkins (Austl.)	
1998	**B. Pilczuk (U.S.)**	**A. Popov (Russia)**	**M. Klim (Austl.)**	**I. Thorpe (Austl.)**	**G. Hackett (Austl.)**	

Backstroke / Breaststroke / Butterfly

	Backstroke 100 m	Backstroke 200 m	Breaststroke 100 m	Breaststroke 200 m	Butterfly 100 m	Butterfly 200 m
1986	I. Polyansky (U.S.S.R.)	I. Polyansky (U.S.S.R.)	V. Davis (Can.)	J. Szabo (Hung.)	P. Morales (U.S.)	M. Gross (W.Ger.)
1991	J. Rouse (U.S.)	M. López Zubero (Spain)	N. Rozsa (Hung.)	M. Barrowman (U.S.)	A. Nesty (Suriname)	M. Stewart (U.S.)
1994	M. López Zubero (Spain)	V. Selkov (Russia)	N. Rozsa (Hung.)	N. Rozsa (Hung.)	R. Szukala (Pol.)	D. Pankratov (Russia)
1998	**L. Krayzelburg (U.S.)**	**L. Krayzelburg (U.S.)**	**F. De Burghgraeve (Belg.)**	**K. Grote (U.S.)**	**M. Klim (Austl.)**	**D. Silantiev (Ukr.)**

Individual medley / Team relays

	Individual medley 200 m	Individual medley 400 m	4 x 100-m freestyle	4 x 200-m freestyle	4 x 100-m medley
1986	T. Darnyi (Hung.)	T. Darnyi (Hung.)	United States	East Germany	United States
1991	T. Darnyi (Hung.)	T. Darnyi (Hung.)	United States	Germany	United States
1994	J. Sievinen (Fin.)	T. Dolan (U.S.)	United States	Sweden	United States
1998	**M. Wouda (Neth.)**	**T. Dolan (U.S.)**	**United States**	**Australia**	**Australia**

Diving

	1-m springboard	3-m springboard	Platform	3-m synchronized	10-m synchronized
1986		G. Louganis (U.S.)	G. Louganis (U.S.)		
1991	E. Jongejans (Neth.)	K. Ferguson (U.S.)	Sun Shuwei (China)		
1994	E. Stewart (Zimb.)	Yu Zhuocheng (China)	D. Saoutine (Russia)		
1998	**Yu Zhuocheng (China)**	**D. Sautin (Russia)**	**D. Sautin (Russia)**	**China**	**China**

World Swimming and Diving Championships—Women

Freestyle

Year	50 m	100 m	200 m	400 m	800 m
1986	T. Costache (Rom.)	K. Otto (E.Ger.)	H. Friedrich (E.Ger.)	H. Friedrich (E.Ger.)	A. Strauss (E.Ger.)
1991	Zhuang Yong (China)	N. Haislett (U.S.)	H. Lewis (Austl.)	J. Evans (U.S.)	J. Evans (U.S.)
1994	Le Jingyi (China)	Le Jingyi (China)	F. van Almsick (Ger.)	Yang Aihua (China)	J. Evans (U.S.)
1998	**A. Van Dyken (U.S.)**	**J. Thompson (U.S.)**	**C. Poll (C.Rica)**	**Chen Yan (China)**	**B. Bennett (U.S.)**

Backstroke / Breaststroke / Butterfly

	Backstroke 100 m	Backstroke 200 m	Breaststroke 100 m	Breaststroke 200 m	Butterfly 100 m	Butterfly 200 m
1986	B. Mitchell (U.S.)	C. Sirch (E.Ger.)	S. Gerasch (E.Ger.)	S. Hörner (E.Ger.)	K. Gressler (E.Ger.)	M. Meagher (U.S.)
1991	K. Egerszegi (Hung.)	K. Egerszegi (Hung.)	L. Frame (Austl.)	E. Volkova (U.S.S.R.)	Qian Hong (China)	S. Sanders (U.S.)
1994	He Cihong (China)	He Cihong (China)	S. Riley (Austl.)	S. Riley (Austl.)	Liu Limin (China)	Liu Limin (China)
1998	**L. Maurer (U.S.)**	**R. Maracineanu (Fr.)**	**K. Kowal (U.S.)**	**A. Kovacs (Hung.)**	**J. Thompson (U.S.)**	**S. O'Neill (Austl.)**

Individual medley / Team relays

	Individual medley 200 m	Individual medley 400 m	4 x 100-m freestyle	4 x 200-m freestyle	4 x 100-m medley
1986	K. Otto (E.Ger.)	K. Nord (E.Ger.)	East Germany	East Germany	East Germany
1991	Lin Li (China)	Lin Li (China)	United States	Germany	United States
1994	Lu Bin (China)	Dai Guohong (China)	China	China	China
1998	**Wu Yanyan (China)**	**Chen Yan (China)**	**United States**	**Germany**	**United States**

Diving

	1-m springboard	3-m springboard	Platform	3-m synchronized	10-m synchronized
1986		Gao Min (China)	Chen Lin (China)		
1991	Gao Min (China)	Gao Min (China)	Fu Mingxia (China)		
1994	Chen Lixia (China)	Tan Shuping (China)	Fu Mingxia (China)		
1998	**I. Lashko (Russia)**	**Y. Pakhalina (Russia)**	**O. Zhupina (Ukr.)**	**Russia**	**Ukraine**

medals in the competition: six gold and two silver.

Four men's short-course (25-m pool) world records fell during the nine rounds of World Cup competition, and three more short-course world marks fell at the Australian national championships in September. Eleven new records were set in December, seven by men and four by women.

At year's end *Swimming World* named Thorpe and Thompson male and female World Swimmer of the Year for 1998.

Diving. Dmitry Sautin of Russia reaffirmed his claim as the world's greatest male diver when he won both the 3-m springboard and the 10-m platform by more than 50 points at the world championships in Perth. Sautin, the 1996 Olympic champion on the platform, brushed aside a challenge from Tian Liang of China to win his signature event, then just as easily dismissed China's Zhou Yilin to win the 3-m. In the 1-m springboard competition China's Yu Zhuocheng, the 1996 Olympic silver medalist at 3-m, edged Troy Dumais of the U.S. by less than two points. Chinese duos won both the men's synchronized events. Yu teamed with Xu Hao to take the 3-m competition over a German team, while Tian and Sun Shuwei beat another German squad to take the 10-m event.

The women's competition was dominated by the Russians and Ukrainians. Irina Lashko of Russia, a 1996 Olympic silver medalist at 3-m, edged teammate Vera Ilyina to win the 1-m springboard. On the 3-m board Russia's Yuliya Pakhalina was an easy winner over China's Guo Jingjing. Olena Zhupina of Ukraine disposed of China's Cai Yuyan to take the 10-m platform. In women's synchronized diving Lashko and Pakhalina took the gold at 3-m ahead of a Chinese duo, while the Ukrainian team of Zhupina and Svetlana Serbina just edged another Chinese squad to emerge the victors on the platform.

Synchronized Swimming. Russia reconfirmed its dominance in synchronized swimming at the world championships in Perth, winning all of the available titles. Olga Sedakova took the solo title ahead of France's Virginie Dedieu, then teamed with Olga Brousnikina to win gold in the duet ahead of a Japanese duo. In team competi-

tion the Russians emerged the victors again, followed by Japan and the U.S.

At the Goodwill Games the Russians again took the team title, as the U.S. passed Japan for the silver. In the duet Brousnikina and Mariya Kiseleva defeated the U.S. team of Bill May and Kristina Lum. It marked the first appearance of a male synchronized swimmer in international competition. In August the U.S. synchronized swimming organization's request to have May compete at the 1999 Pan American Games was denied.

(PHILLIP WHITTEN)

TABLE TENNIS

Vladimir Samsonov of Belarus, the 1997 world men's singles runner-up, justified his ranking as the International Table Tennis Federation's (ITTF's) top male player in 1998, winning not only the climactic 1997 Pro Tour grand final but also all the most prestigious 1998 European tournaments, including the European championship, the Europe Top 12, and the European Masters. Other prominent players included Croatia's Zoran Primorac, the 1997 men's World Cup winner; Jörg Rosskopf of Germany, who won the 1998 World Cup; and Jean-Michel Saive of Belgium, the 1998 U.S. Open champion. Luxembourg's Ni Xia Lian, formerly the world mixed doubles champion for China, captured the 1998 European women's championship and her third straight Europe Top 12 title.

China's "old wave" stars Wang Tao and Deng Yaping won, respectively, the men's and women's singles and doubles in China's 1997 national games, while Kong Linghui (1998 Japan Open winner) and Liu Guoliang (1998 China Open winner) triumphed in the 1997 Pro Tour men's doubles final. Newer players were led by Wang Nan, winner of the women's World Cup in both

One of the world's top table tennis players, Ni Xia Lian of Luxembourg poses with her son and the trophy she collected after winning the 1998 European women's singles championship in Eindhoven, Neth., on May 3.

1997 and 1998, the 1997 Pro Tour doubles final, and the 1998 China Open.

In an effort to induce longer rallies for more spectator appeal, the ITTF took steps to make racket play more predictable and sought to restrict service and increase the ball size. An innovative Pro Tour move allowed a player to call for a single one-minute time-out during a match.

(TIM BOGGAN)

TENNIS

Adding lustre to an already prodigious record, Pete Sampras of the U.S. reached two more landmarks in an arduous yet rewarding 1998 season. Victorious at Wimbledon for the fifth time in a six-year stretch, he tied Björn Borg's modern men's record for championships won at that shrine of the sport. That triumph was the primary reason why Sampras concluded his sixth consecutive year as the world's top-ranked player on the official Association of Tennis Professionals (ATP) computer, breaking a record he had shared with Jimmy Connors (reigned 1974–78). Sampras captured only 4 of 22 tournaments he played in 1998, but his overall consistency separated him from his rivals.

Lindsay Davenport established herself as the best woman player in the world for the year, the first native-born American woman to realize that feat since Chris Evert in 1981.

For only the second time since the inception of "Open Tennis" in 1968, eight different men and women garnered Grand Slam titles in a year of sweeping change. Martina Hingis of Switzerland, Arantxa Sánchez Vicario of Spain, Jana Novotna of the Czech Republic, and Davenport captured the four major women's crowns, while Sampras, Petr Korda of the Czech Republic, Carlos Moya of Spain, and Patrick Rafter of Australia swept the major titles among the men. Sampras was the leading money winner in the men's game with earnings of $3,931,497. At the top of the list for the women was Hingis at $3,175,631.

In other essential developments, the singularly unpredictable American Andre Agassi made a substantial move from number 122 in the world at the end of 1997 up to number 6 for 1998, an unprecedented rise in the rankings. For the first time since the official rankings were introduced in 1973, two Spanish men were stationed in the world's top five for the year, with Moya fifth and ATP Tour world champion Alex Corretja

Table Tennis World Cup	
Year	Men
1994	J.-P. Gatien (Fr.)
1995	Kong Linghui (China)
1996	Liu Guoliang (China)
1997	Z. Primorac (Cro.)
1998	**J. Rosskopf (Ger.)**
Year	Women
1996	Deng Yaping (China)
1997	Wang Nan (China)
1998	**Wang Nan (China)**

1998 Table Tennis World Rankings*	
Men	Women
1. Vladimir Samsonov (Bela.)	1. Deng Yaping (China)
2. Kong Linghui (China)	2. Li Ju (China)
3. Zoran Primorac (Cro.)	3. Wang Nan (China)
4. Liu Guoliang (China)	4. Ni Xia Lian (Lux.)
5. Jan-Ove Waldner (Swed.)	5. Wang Chen (China)

* ITTF ranking as of October 1998.

World Table Tennis Championships—Mixed	
Year	Heydusek Prize
1989	Yoo Nam Kyu, Hyung Jung Hwa (S.Kor.)
1991	Wang Tao, Liu Wei (China)
1993	Wang Tao, Liu Wei (China)
1995	Wang Tao, Liu Wei (China)
1997	Liu Guoliang, Wu Na (China)

World Table Tennis Championships—Men			
Year	St. Bride's Vase (singles)	Iran Cup (doubles)	Swaythling Cup (team)
1991	J. Persson (Swed.)	P. Karlsson, T. Von Scheele (Swed.)	Sweden
1993	J.-P. Gatien (Fr.)	Wang Tao, Lu Lin (China)	Sweden
1995	Kong Linghui (China)	Wang Tao, Lu Lin (China)	China
1997	J.-O. Waldner (Swed.)	Kong Linghui, Liu Guoliang (China)	China

World Table Tennis Championships—Women			
Year	G. Geist Prize (singles)	W.J. Pope Trophy (doubles)	Corbillon Cup (team)
1991	Deng Yaping (China)	Gao Jun, Chen Zihe (China)	Korea
1993	Hyun Jung Hwa (S.Kor.)	Liu Wei, Qiao Yunping (China)	China
1995	Deng Yaping (China)	Deng Yaping, Qiao Hong (China)	China
1997	Deng Yaping (China)	Deng Yaping, Yang Ying (China)	China

third. The swift ascendancy of the gifted African-American Venus Williams continued, as she rose to fifth on the women's list. Germany's indefatigable Steffi Graf—eight times the world's best player between 1987 and 1996—recouped from knee surgery in 1997 and a series of injuries in 1998, rising to ninth in the women's rankings with a late-season surge. Two other American former

DAVE CAULKIN—AP/WIDE WORLD

champions, Jim Courier and Michael Chang, slipped in the men's listing.

Australian Open. Returning to Melbourne, where she had become the youngest Grand Slam singles titlist of the century in 1997, Hingis defended her crown admirably, halting Spain's tenacious Conchita Martínez 6–3, 6–3 in the final. Seeded second behind Hingis, Davenport won a stirring, three-set quarterfinal from Williams but was upended by Martínez in a three-set semifinal showdown.

Sampras seemed primed to secure a third championship "down under," moving into the quarterfinals without the loss of a set. He fell in four sets against one of the game's great counterattackers, however, losing to Slovakia's Karol Kucera. Kucera could not sustain the lofty standards he set against Sampras, bowing in four sets to Korda in the semifinal. Appearing in only his second major final, Korda secured his first Grand Slam championship with a powerful performance against Marcelo Rios, the enigmatic Chilean, and concluded the year ranked second behind Sampras. In this battle of left-handers, Korda prevailed 6–2, 6–2, 6–2, but the calibre of his tennis declined dramatically the rest of the year.

French Open. After a startling run to the Australian Open final the previous year, Moya had performed sporadically in subsequent tournaments. At Roland Garros, however, he put all of the pieces of his game together persuasively and was rewarded with

American Pete Sampras serves to Goran Ivanisevic of Croatia during the Wimbledon finals in July. Although Ivanisevic pushed him to five sets, Sampras held on to successfully defend his title.

his first major title. In an emotional final Moya's larger stroke arsenal was too much for master strategist Corretja as he marched confidently to a 6–3, 7–5, 6–3 victory. When it was over Corretja climbed over the net and embraced his exhilarated countryman. Top-seeded Sampras had departed in the second round against Paraguay's Ramón Delgado in straight sets.

Another Spanish stalwart competitor captured the women's crown. Taking the title for the third time in a 10-year period, Sánchez Vicario demonstrated her exemplary prowess as a match player. In the final she ousted sentimental favourite Monica Seles of the U.S. 7–6, 0–6, 6–2. A three-time winner who had stopped Sánchez Vicario in the 1991 final, Seles had contemplated skipping the event in 1998 when her father died less than two weeks before the tournament. She cut down the top-seeded Hingis 6–3, 6–2 in the semifinals before falling short in the hard-fought final. Sánchez Vicario had barely escaped defeat in the fourth round when she took on Serena Williams, the younger sister of Venus Williams, who was appearing in her first French Open. Williams took a 6–4, 5–2 lead but could not sustain her advantage, losing 11 of the last 14 games.

Wimbledon. Approaching the world's most prestigious tournament, Sampras was surrounded by skeptics. He had won only 2 of 10 tournaments during the year, struggling to reach the top of his game. Perhaps sensing he had arrived at a crucial moment, Sampras responded by stamping his authority on the grass courts of the All-England Club for the fifth time in six years and recorded his 11th victory in 13 career Grand Slam finals. Succeeding in his first-ever five-set final in a major event, Sampras

Australian Open Tennis Championships—Singles

Year	Men	Women
1994	P. Sampras (U.S.)	S. Graf (Ger.)
1995	A. Agassi (U.S.)	M. Pierce (Fr.)
1996	B. Becker (Ger.)	M. Seles (U.S.)
1997	P. Sampras (U.S.)	M. Hingis (Switz.)
1998	**P. Korda (Cz.Rep.)**	**M. Hingis (Switz.)**

Australian Open Tennis Championships—Doubles

Year	Men	Women
1994	P. Haarhuis, J. Eltingh	G. Fernandez, N. Zvereva
1995	J. Palmer, R. Reneberg	A. Sánchez Vicario, J. Novotna
1996	S. Edberg, P. Korda	A. Sánchez Vicario, C. Rubin
1997	T. Woodbridge, M. Woodforde	M. Hingis, N. Zvereva
1998	**J. Bjorkman, J. Eltingh**	**M. Hingis, M. Lucic**

French Open Tennis Championships—Singles

Year	Men	Women
1994	S. Bruguera (Spain)	A. Sánchez Vicario (Spain)
1995	T. Muster (Austria)	S. Graf (Ger.)
1996	Ye. Kafelnikov (Russia)	S. Graf (Ger.)
1997	G. Kuerten (Braz.)	I. Majoli (Cro.)
1998	**C. Moya (Spain)**	**A. Sánchez Vicario (Spain)**

French Open Tennis Championships—Doubles

Year	Men	Women
1994	B. Black, J. Stark	G. Fernandez, N. Zvereva
1995	P. Haarhuis, J. Eltingh	G. Fernandez, N. Zvereva
1996	Ye. Kafelnikov, D. Vacek	L. Davenport, M.J. Fernandez
1997	Ye. Kafelnikov, D. Vacek	G. Fernandez, N. Zvereva
1998	**J. Eltingh, P. Haarhuis**	**M. Hingis, J. Novotna**

All-England (Wimbledon) Tennis Championships—Singles

Year	Men	Women
1994	P. Sampras (U.S.)	C. Martínez (Spain)
1995	P. Sampras (U.S.)	S. Graf (Ger.)
1996	R. Krajicek (Neth.)	S. Graf (Ger.)
1997	P. Sampras (U.S.)	M. Hingis (Switz.)
1998	**P. Sampras (U.S.)**	**J. Novotna (Cz.Rep.)**

All-England (Wimbledon) Tennis Championships—Doubles

Year	Men	Women
1994	T. Woodbridge, M. Woodforde	G. Fernandez, N. Zvereva
1995	T. Woodbridge, M. Woodforde	A. Sánchez Vicario, J. Novotna
1996	T. Woodbridge, M. Woodforde	H. Sukova, M. Hingis
1997	T. Woodbridge, M. Woodforde	G. Fernandez, N. Zvereva
1998	**J. Eltingh, P. Haarhuis**	**M. Hingis, J. Novotna**

United States Open Tennis Championships—Singles

Year	Men	Women
1994	A. Agassi (U.S.)	A. Sánchez Vicario (Spain)
1995	P. Sampras (U.S.)	S. Graf (Ger.)
1996	P. Sampras (U.S.)	S. Graf (Ger.)
1997	P. Rafter (Austl.)	M. Hingis (Switz.)
1998	**P. Rafter (Austl.)**	**L. Davenport (U.S.)**

United States Open Tennis Championships—Doubles

Year	Men	Women
1994	P. Haarhuis, J. Eltingh	A. Sánchez Vicario, J. Novotna
1995	T. Woodbridge, M. Woodforde	G. Fernandez, N. Zvereva
1996	T. Woodbridge, M. Woodforde	G. Fernandez, N. Zvereva
1997	Ye. Kafelnikov, D. Vacek	L. Davenport, J. Novotna
1998	**S. Stolle, C. Suk**	**M. Hingis, J. Novotna**

Davis Cup (men)			
Year	Winner	Runner-up	Results
1994	Sweden	Russia	4–1
1995	United States	Russia	3–2
1996	France	Sweden	3–2
1997	Sweden	United States	5–0
1998	**Sweden**	**Italy**	**4–1**

Fed Cup (women)			
Year	Winner	Runner-up	Results
1994	Spain	United States	3–0
1995	Spain	United States	3–2
1996	United States	Spain	5–0
1997	France	Netherlands	4–1
1998	**Spain**	**Switzerland**	**3–2**

overcame a despondent Goran Ivanisevic of Croatia 6–7, 7–6, 6–4, 3–6, 6–2. Ivanisevic twice was one point away from a two sets-to-love lead, but he did not exploit those opportunities, and from 2–2 in the final set, Sampras took 16 of the last 19 points.

British hopes were raised by the stirring showing of 23-year-old Tim Henman, a quarterfinalist the previous two years. This time Henman eliminated Rafter and Korda to set up a semifinal meeting with Sampras. Henman stretched the champion to four sets but was outclassed 6–3, 4–6, 7–5, 6–3. Ivanisevic survived a strenuous skirmish with 1996 Wimbledon champion Richard Krajicek of The Netherlands but came through 15–13 in the fifth set after squandering two match points in the fourth.

The 29-year-old Novotna, who had twice before failed in the Wimbledon final, won her first Grand Slam title. She reversed the result of the 1997 final by taking apart her doubles partner, Hingis, 6–4, 6–4 in the semifinals. Having overcome that hurdle, the third-seeded Novotna then defeated Nathalie Tauziat of France 6–4, 7–6 in the final. Tauziat had upset second-seeded Davenport 6–3, 6–3 in the quarterfinals, while Natasha Zvereva of Belarus surprised Seles 7–6, 6–2 in the same round.

U.S. Open. Following his stirring triumph at the 1997 Open, Rafter had not competed on the same level for a long time, but in the weeks leading up to the defense of his U.S. title, he had played the best brand of tennis in his entire career. Over the summer on hard courts, he won three of his last four tournaments leading up to Flushing Meadows, and his self-assurance carried him convincingly to a second straight U.S. championship. In the final he collected the last 10 games in a row, committed a mere five unforced errors in the match, and cut down countryman Mark Philippoussis 6–3, 3–6, 6–2, 6–0.

In the semifinal round Rafter was in a precarious position against four-time titlist Sampras, who was in search of a record-tying 12th Grand Slam singles championship. Sampras built a lead of two sets to one over the agile Australian, but at the end of the third set the American strained his left quadruples muscle near the hip. His mobility hindered, Sampras battled on gamely, but Rafter won 6–7, 6–4, 2–6, 6–4, 6–3. In the opening round Rafter

had seemed on his way out of the tournament when he trailed two sets to love against the free-wheeling, smooth-stroking Hicham Arazi, a two-time French Open quarterfinalist from Morocco playing with unrestrained inspiration. Arazi soon lost all of his composure, however, disputing every close line call and releasing his anxiety on the umpire. Rafter rebounded commandingly to win 4–6, 4–6, 6–3, 6–3, 6–1.

The two best women players in the world clashed in the final, and Davenport emerged a slightly surprising 6–3, 7–5 winner over Hingis, taking her first major title in her first Grand Slam final appearance. Hingis, the defending champion, was not the same player who had swept three of the four major titles in 1997. She had a monumental opportunity to take control of the match when she served for the second set at 5–4, but when she did not convert the chance, Davenport's more penetrating groundstrokes enabled her to regain the upper hand and close out the contest.

Other Events. Spain stopped Switzerland 3–2 to take the Fed Cup final for women at Geneva in September. Although the redoubtable Hingis captured both points for her nation with singles wins over Sánchez-Vicario (who had altered the spelling of her name less than two weeks earlier) and Martínez, she could not carry Switzerland to victory in the final of the international team competition. Three months later Sweden confronted Italy in the men's Davis Cup final. As the curtain closed on the 1998 season, the Swedes retained their status as the champion nation with a 4–1 win over the

OSAMU HONDA—AP/WIDE WORLD

American Lindsay Davenport proudly displays her U.S. Open trophy after upsetting defending champion Martina Hingis of Switzerland in the women's final. It was Davenport's first Grand Slam tennis title.

Italians, who had surprised the U.S. in the penultimate round.   (STEVE FLINK)

TRACK AND FIELD SPORTS (ATHLETICS)

A revamping of the European summer circuit to include a distinct Golden League of super-elite competitions made news in track and field in 1998, as did a large number of world records in the long-distance runs.

Golden League. In 1998 the International Amateur Athletic Federation (IAAF) elevated six of the top invitational meetings (held at Oslo, Rome, Monte-Carlo, Zürich, Brussels, and Berlin) of its annual Grand Prix series into a new and elite circuit of competitions called the Golden League. In its first season the Golden League awarded shares of a $1 million jackpot to all athletes in 12 designated events who won their competitions at each of the six meets plus the Golden League/Grand Prix final, which was held in Moscow on September 5. Several top athletes signed contracts with the IAAF guaranteeing that they would contest all seven Golden League meets, but competitors outside this superstar group met a payment structure that rewarded competition performance rather than appearances. Each individual Golden League event at the six meets paid prize money ranging from $15,000 for first place down to $1,000 for eighth.

At the conclusion of the final, 1,500-m runner Hicham El Guerrouj of Morocco, distance runner Haile Gebrselassie of Ethiopia, and sprinter Marion Jones of the U.S. split the jackpot three ways for the biggest payday ever on the formerly amateur circuit. Each athlete augmented the take with additional prize money for Grand Prix leaderships and payouts based on winning at the final itself. Jones pocketed $633,333, El Guerrouj won $583,333, and Gebrselassie received $483,333.

American 400-m hurdler Bryan Bronson, who had won his six previous Golden League races, entered the final with a chance to share in the million dollars as well, but lost out when he finished sixth in his event. He had achieved his last victory just four days earlier in Berlin by the narrowest of margins when he defeated world champion Stéphane Diagana of France by just 0.01 sec. At the final it was Diagana who proved Bronson's undoing, winning in 48.30 sec to the American's 48.94 sec. Bronson earned $7,000 for the sixth-place race finish and $50,000 for his third-place finish in the overall men's Grand Prix standings, but the loss cost him well over $300,000.

A number of prominent athletes and their agents criticized the new emphasis on pay-for-play events and contended that the physical and mental demands of winning so many times in a two-month period were too high. At season's end, however, IAAF Pres. Primo Nebiolo announced plans to expand the Golden League in future years.

World Cup. At the World Cup, held in the thin high-altitude air of Johannesburg, S.Af., on September 11–13, Jones capped a phenomenal

(From left) Sprinter Marion Jones of the U.S., distance runner Haile Gebrselassie of Ethiopia, and 1,500-m runner Hicham El Guerrouj of Morocco share the podium and the prize money at the conclusion of the first year of an elite new circuit of races, the Golden League.

ALEXANDER ZEMLIANICHENKO—AP/WIDE WORLD

season by winning the 100 m in 10.65 sec and the 200 m in 21.62 sec. These were World Cup meet records and the fastest sprint times of 1998. Both marks had been bettered previously only by world-record holder Florence Griffith Joyner (*see* OBITUARIES) in her stunning Olympic season in 1988. Jones produced the 200-m time despite running into a head wind of 0.6 m (2 ft) per sec. On the meet's chilly, wet last day, she faced German star Heike Drechsler in the long jump. The 33-year-old Drechsler, who had won her first World Cup long jump title in 1985, leaped 7.07 m (23 ft 2¹/₂ in). Jones jumped 7.00 m (22 ft 11³/₄ in) and had to accept her only loss of the season. Jones, nonetheless, was the undisputed key performer as the U.S. women's squad defeated Europe 96–94 for its first World Cup win ever. She also picked up $120,000, as the meet awarded prize money along with medals for the first time.

In the men's competition the African squad won its third consecutive team crown, despite the fact that Europe led 107–105

when runners lined up for the final event, the 4 × 400-m relay. The African relay squad had to finish at least three places ahead of Europe to secure the overall win. While the U.S. won the event in 2 min 59.29 sec, Africa (at 3 min 1.08 sec) placed third to Europe's seventh (3 min 3.95 sec) and achieved a one-point victory, 110–109.

The outstanding men's individual performance came from Obadele Thompson of Barbados, who won the 100 m in 9.87 sec. As with Jones in the women's sprints, Thompson was helped by the lowered wind resistance resulting from Johannesburg's high altitude.

Men's International Competition. El Guerrouj and Gebrselassie put their stamp

IAAF World Cup—Men

	100 metre	200 metre	400 metre	800 metre	1,500 metre
1992	L. Christie (Gr.Brit.)	R. Caetano da Silva (Amer.)	S. Bada (Africa)	D. Sharpe (U.K.)	M. Suleiman (Asia)
1994	L. Christie (Gr.Brit.)	J. Regis (Gr.Brit.)	A. Pettigrew (U.S.)	M. Everett (U.S.)	N. Morceli (Africa)
1998	**O. Thompson (Amer.)**	**F. Fredericks (Africa)**	**I. Thomas (Gr.Brit.)**	**N. Schumann (Ger.)**	**L. Rotich (Africa)**

	3,000 metre	5,000 metre	10,000 metre	Steeplechase	110-m hurdles
1992	—	F. Bayesa (Africa)	A. Abebe (Africa)	P. Barkutwo (Africa)	C. Jackson (U.K.)
1994	—	B. Lahlafi (Africa)	K. Skah (Africa)	M. Kiptanui (Africa)	T. Jarrett (Gr.Brit.)
1998	**D. Baumann (Ger.)**	**D. Komen (Africa)**	**—**	**D. Kallabis (Ger.)**	**F. Balzer (Ger.)**

	400-m hurdles	4 × 100-m relays	4 × 400-m relays	Triple jump	High jump
1992	S. Matete (Africa)	United States	Africa	J. Edwards (U.K.)	Y. Sergeyenko (UT)
1994	S. Matete (Africa)	Great Britain	Great Britain	Y. Quesada (Amer.)	J. Sotomayor (Amer.)
1998	**S. Matete (Africa)**	**Great Britain**	**United States**	**C. Friedek (Ger.)**	**C. Austin (U.S.)**

	Pole vault	Long jump	Shot put	Discus throw	Hammer throw
1992	I. Potapovich (UT)	I. Pedroso (Amer.)	M. Stulce (U.S.)	T. Washington (U.S.)	T. Gécsek (Europe)
1994	O. Brits (Africa)	F. Salle (Gr.Brit.)	C.J. Hunter (U.S.)	V. Dubrovshchik (Europe)	A. Abduvaliyev (Asia)
1998	**M. Tarasov (Europe)**	**I. Pedroso (Amer.)**	**J. Godina (U.S.)**	**V. Alekna (Europe)**	**T. Gecsek (Europe)**

	Javelin throw	Team
1992	J. Zelezny (Europe)	Africa
1994	S. Backley (Gr.Brit.)	Africa
1998	**S. Backley (Gr.Brit.)**	**—**

IAAF World Cup—Women

	100 metre	200 metre	400 metre	800 metre	1,500 metre
1992	N. Voronova (UT)	M.-J. Pérec (Europe)	J. Miles (U.S.)	M. Mutola (Africa)	Y. Podkopayeva (UT)
1994	I. Privalova (Europe)	M. Ottey (Amer.)	I. Privalova (Europe)	M. Mutola (Africa)	H. Boulmerka (Africa)
1998	**M. Jones (U.S.)**	**M. Jones (U.S.)**	**F. Ogunkoya (Africa)**	**M. Mutola (Africa)**	**S. Masterkova (Russia)**

	3,000 metre	5,000 metre	10,000 metre	100-m hurdles	400-m hurdles
1992	D. Tulu (Africa)	—	D. Tulu (Africa)	A. López (Amer.)	S. Farmer-Patrick (U.S.)
1994	Y. Murray (Gr.Brit.)	—	E. Meyer (Africa)	A. López (Amer.)	S. Gunnell (Gr.Brit.)
1998	**G. Szabo (Europe)**	**S. O'Sullivan (Europe)**	**—**	**G. Alozie (Africa)**	**N. Bidouane (Africa)**

	4 × 100-m relays	4 × 400-m relays	Triple jump	High jump	Long jump
1992	Asia	Americas	—	I. Quintero (Amer.)	H. Drechsler (Ger.)
1994	Africa	Great Britain	A. Biryukova (Europe)	B. Bilac (Europe)	I. Kravets (Europe)
1998	**United States**	**Germany**	**O. Vasdeki (Europe)**	**M. Iagar-Dinescu (Europe)**	**H. Drechsler (Ger.)**

	Shot put	Discus throw	Javelin throw	Team
1992	B. Laza (Amer.)	M. Marten (Amer.)	T. Sanderson (U.K.)	Unified Team
1994	Zhihong Huang (Asia)	I. Wyludda (Europe)	T. Hattestad (Europe)	Europe
1998	**V. Pavlysh (Europe)**	**F. Dietzsch (Ger.)**	**J. Stone (Oceania)**	**—**

1998 World Outdoor Records—Men

Event	Competitor and country	Performance
1,500 m	Hicham El Guerrouj (Mor.)	3 min 26.00 sec
5,000 m	Haile Gebrselassie (Eth.)	12 min 39.36 sec
10,000 m	Haile Gebrselassie (Eth.)	26 min 22.75 sec
Marathon*	Ronaldo da Costa (Braz.)	2 hr 6 min 5 sec
4 × 400–m relay	United States (Jerome Young, Antonio Pettigrew, Tyree Washington, Michael Johnson)	2 min 54.20 sec

*Not an officially ratified event; best performance on record.

1998 World Indoor Records—Men

Event	Competitor and country	Performance
60 m	Maurice Green (U.S.)	6.39 sec
2,000 m*	Haile Gebrselassie (Eth.)	4 min 52.86 sec
3,000 m	Daniel Komen (Kenya)	7 min 24.90 sec
5,000 m	Daniel Komen (Kenya)	12 min 51.48 sec

*Not an officially ratified event; best performance on record.

World Track and Field Championships—Men

Event	1995	1997
100 m	D. Bailey (Can.)	M. Greene (U.S.)
200 m	M. Johnson (U.S.)	A. Boldon (Trin.)
400 m	M. Johnson (U.S.)	M. Johnson (U.S.)
800 m	W. Kipketer (Den.)	W. Kipketer (Den.)
1,500 m	N. Morceli (Alg.)	H. El Guerrouj (Mor.)
5,000 m	I. Kirui (Kenya)	D. Komen (Kenya)
10,000 m	H. Gebrselassie (Eth.)	H. Gebrselassie (Eth.)
steeplechase	M. Kiptanui (Kenya)	W.B. Kipketer (Kenya)
110-m hurdles	A. Johnson (U.S.)	A. Johnson (U.S.)
400-m hurdles	D. Adkins (U.S.)	S. Diagana (Fr.)
marathon	M. Fiz (Spain)	A. Anton (Spain)
20-km walk	M. Didoni (Italy)	D. García (Mex.)
50-km walk	V. Kononen (Fin.)	R. Korzeniowski (Pol.)
4 × 100-m relay	Canada (R. Esmie, G. Gilbert, B. Surin, D. Bailey)	Canada (R. Esmie, G. Gilbert, B. Surin, D. Bailey)
4 × 400-m relay	United States (M. Ramsey, D. Mills, B. Reynolds, M. Johnson)	United States (J. Young, A. Pettigrew, C. Jones, T. Washington)
high jump	T. Kemp (Bahamas)	J. Sotomayor (Cuba)
pole vault	S. Bubka (Ukr.)	S. Bubka (Ukr.)
long jump	I. Pedroso (Cuba)	I. Pedroso (Cuba)
triple jump	J. Edwards (U.K.)	Y. Quesada (Cuba)
shot put	J. Godina (U.S.)	J. Godina (U.S.)
discus throw	L. Riedel (Ger.)	L. Riedel (Ger.)
hammer throw	A. Abduvaliyev (Tajik.)	H. Weis (Ger.)
javelin throw	J. Zelezny (Cz.Rep.)	M. Corbett (S.Af.)
decathlon	D. O'Brien (U.S.)	T. Dvorak (Cz.Rep.)

1998 World Outdoor Records—Women

Event	Competitor and country	Performance
Steeplechase*	Svetlana Rogova (Russia)	9 min 57.62 sec
2 mi*	Sonia O'Sullivan (Ire.)	9 min 19.56 sec
Marathon*	Tegla Loroupe (Kenya)	2 hr 20 min 47 sec
Hour*	Tegla Loroupe (Kenya)	18.34 km (11.396 mi)
Pole vault	Emma George (Austl.)	4.57 m (15 ft 0 in)
	Emma George (Austl.)	4.58 m (15 ft 1/4 in)
	Emma George (Austl.)	4.59 m (15 ft 3/4 in)
Hammer throw	Mihaela Melinte (Rom.)	72.64 m (238 ft 4 in)

*Not an officially ratified event; best performance on record.

1998 World Indoor Records—Women

Event	Competitor and country	Performance
2,000 m*	Gabriela Szabo (Rom.)	5 min 30.53 sec
Pole vault	Emma George (Austl.)	4.55 m (14 ft 11 in)
Triple jump	Ashia Hansen (Gr.Brit.)	15.16 m (49 ft 9 in)

*Not an officially ratified event; best performance on record.

World Track and Field Championships—Women

Event	1995	1997
100 m	G. Torrence (U.S.)	M. Jones (U.S.)
200 m	M. Ottey (Jam.)	Z. Pintusevich (Ukr.)
400 m	M.-J. Pérec (Fr.)	C. Freeman (Austl.)
800 m	A. Quirot (Cuba)	A. Quirot (Cuba)
1,500 m	H. Boulmerka (Alg.)	C. Sacramento (Port.)
5,000 m	S. O'Sullivan (Ire.)	G. Szabo (Rom.)
10,000 m	F. Ribeiro (Port.)	S. Barsosio (Kenya)
100-m hurdles	G. Devers (U.S.)	L. Engquist (Swed.)
400-m hurdles	K. Batten (U.S.)	N. Bidouane (Mor.)
marathon	M. Machado (Port.)	H. Suzuki (Japan)
10-km walk	I. Stankina (Rus.)	A. Sidoti (Italy)
4 × 100-m relay	United States (C. Mondie-Milner, C. Guidry, C. Gaines, G. Torrence)	United States (C. Gaines, M. Jones, I. Miller, G. Devers)
4 × 400-m relay	United States (K. Graham, R. Stevens, C. Jones, J. Miles)	Germany (A. Feller, U. Rohlander, A. Rucker, G. Breuer)
high jump	S. Kostadinova (Bul.)	H. Haugland (Nor.)
long jump	F. May (Italy)	L. Galkina (Russia)
triple jump	I. Kravets (Ukr.)	S. Kasparkova (Cz.Rep.)
shot put	A. Kumbernuss (Ger.)	A. Kumbernuss (Ger.)
discus throw	E. Zvereva (Bel.)	B. Faumuina (N.Z.)
javelin throw	N. Shikolenko (Bel.)	T. Hattestad (Nor.)
heptathlon	G. Shouaa (Syria)	S. Braun (Ger.)

on the year with new world records. In January at Karlsruhe, Ger., Gebrselassie lowered the indoor 3,000-m record to 7 min 26.14 sec—an improvement of more than 4 sec on his own two-year-old world record. Gebrselassie's indoor campaign also included a 2,000-m world record of 4 min 52.86 sec. In the outdoor season Gebrselassie set a record in his first race—at Hengelo, Neth., on June 1—when he covered 10,000 m in 26 min 22.75 sec to regain the world record that Paul Tergat of Kenya had taken from him nine months earlier. Twelve days later in Helsinki, Fin., Gebrselassie took back the 5,000-m world record that he had lost to another Kenyan, Daniel Komen; he finished in 12 min 39.36 sec, chipping 0.38 sec from the mark set by Komen in 1997. With these records in his possession once more, Gebrselassie successfully concentrated on winning Golden League races.

Hampered by a groin injury early in the year, miler El Guerrouj made his second Golden League 1,500-m win—on July 14 in Rome—one to remember, with the first outdoor world record of his career. El Guerrouj knocked 1.37 sec from the standard Nouredine Morceli of Algeria had set in 1995, running virtually the whole race ahead of Morceli's pace and then sprinting his last lap in 53.10 sec to finish in 3 min 26.00 sec. Racing twice more in the next four days, El Guerrouj ran the mile in 3 min 44.60 sec to come within 0.21 sec of the record and the 2,000 m in 4 min 48.36 sec, just 0.48 sec short of the record.

A hypercompetitive sprint campaign featured no single commanding athlete, but a plethora of fast times. Maurice Greene of the U.S. set a world record of 6.39 sec for 60 m during the indoor season, ran 9.90 sec for 100 m outdoors, and won 11 of 16 races at 100 m and 200 m. Greene's training partner, Ato Boldon of Trinidad and Tobago, added to his own reputation with a blistering one-day double of 9.86 sec for 100 m and 19.88 sec for 200 m in Athens in June. Boldon also

Obadele Thompson (left) of the Americas team sprints across the finish line to win the 100-m final at the IAAF World Cup in Johannesburg in September. Dwain Chambers (right) of Great Britain edged out Tim Harden (centre) of the U.S. for third place.

AP/WIDE WORLD

ran the 100 m at the Commonwealth Games in 9.88 sec, the fifth sub-9.90-sec clocking of his career. This represented a record for consistency at that level of competition matched by no other sprinter in history. Bronson dominated in the 400-m hurdles, with victories in 17 of 18 races, losing only at the Golden League/Grand Prix final.

Boston Marathon		
Year	Men	h:min:s
1994	C. N'Deti (Kenya)	2:07:15
1995	C. N'Deti (Kenya)	2:09:22
1996	M. Tanui (Kenya)	2:09:16
1997	L. Aguta (Kenya)	2:10:34
1998	**M. Tanui (Kenya)**	**2:07:34**
Year	Women	h:min:s
1994	U. Pippig (Ger.)	2:21:45
1995	U. Pippig (Ger.)	2:25:11
1996	U. Pippig (Ger.)	2:27:12
1997	F. Roba (Eth.)	2:26:23
1998	**F. Roba (Eth.)**	**2:23:21**

New York City Marathon		
Year	Men	h:min:s
1994	G. Silva (Mex.)	2:11:21
1995	G. Silva (Mex.)	2:11:00
1996	G. Leone (Italy)	2:09:54
1997	J. Kagwe (Kenya)	2:08:12
1998	**J. Kagwe (Kenya)**	**2:08:45**
Year	Women	h:min:s
1994	T. Loroupe (Kenya)	2:27:37
1995	T. Loroupe (Kenya)	2:28:06
1996	A. Catuna (Rom.)	2:28:18
1997	F. Rochat-Moser (Switz.)	2:28:43
1998	**F. Fiacconi (Italy)**	**2:25:17**

World Cross Country Championships— Men		
Year	Individual	Team
1994	W. Sigei (Kenya)	Kenya
1995	P. Tergat (Kenya)	Kenya
1996	P. Tergat (Kenya)	Kenya
1997	P. Tergat (Kenya)	Kenya
1998	**P. Tergat (Kenya)**	**Kenya**

World Cross Country Championships— Women		
Year	Individual	Team
1994	H. Chepngeno (Kenya)	Portugal
1995	D. Tulu (Eth.)	Kenya
1996	G. Wami (Eth.)	Kenya
1997	D. Tulu (Eth.)	Ethiopia
1998	**S. O'Sullivan (Ire.)**	**Morocco**

World Marathon Cup*		
Year	Men	Women
1989	K. Metaferia (Eth.)	S. Marchiano (U.S.)
1991	Y. Tolstikov (U.S.S.R.)	R. Mota (Port.)
1993	R. Nerurkar (U.K.)	Wang Junxia (China)
1995	D. Wakiihuri (Kenya)	A. Catuna (Rom.)
1997	Spain	Japan

*Team event from 1997.

World Volleyball Championships		
Year	Men	Women
1990	Italy	U.S.S.R.
1992	Brazil	Cuba
1994	Italy	Cuba
1996	Netherlands	Cuba
1998	**Italy**	**Cuba**

On the field, shot-putter John Godina competed 17 times and never lost in 1998, winning the Grand Prix final and World Cup titles among other honours. In Salinas, Calif., in May, he put the shot 21.58 m (70 ft 9¾ in) and threw the discus 69.91 m (229 ft 4 in) for the longest one-day combination ever.

In July American Michael Johnson, who had run on world-record-setting 4 × 400-m relay teams in 1992 and 1993, turned his speed in that direction again at the Goodwill Games in New York City. The U.S. team of Jerome Young, Antonio Pettigrew, Tyree Washington, and Johnson reeled off a world record few expected, trimming 0.09 sec from the old 4 × 400-m mark with their time of 2 min 54.20 sec.

Women's International Competition. Jones continued as track and field's most distinguished woman athlete in 1998. The 22-year-old former basketball player contested 37 finals in 16 countries at 100 m, 200 m, 400 m, the long jump, and the indoor 60 m. She led the seasonal list in her technically weakest event, the long jump, spanning 7.31 m (23 ft 11¾ in) and losing only once—by less than 7.6 cm (3 in)—in her World Cup matchup with Drechsler. On the track Jones was untouchable. In 19 outings at 100 m, of which 17 were finals, she averaged faster than 10.80 sec. With a pair of 10.71-sec clockings and her altitude-aided World Cup victories in both dashes, Jones firmly established herself as history's second fastest woman, after Griffith Joyner. When rising French talent Christine Arron positioned herself to challenge Jones with a speedy European Championships 100 m in 10.73 sec, Jones raced her in Brussels and left Arron 1.5 m (5 ft) behind. Jones's total prize money and appearance fees for the year were estimated to total some $2,000,000.

Ireland's Sonia O'Sullivan set the standard for doubling in 1998. On consecutive days in March she won world cross country titles at 4 km and 8 km. At the European Championships, held in Budapest on August

18–23, O'Sullivan won gold at 10,000 m and 5,000 m. At the World Cup O'Sullivan held herself to just one race and won the 5,000 m.

Cross Country and Marathon Running. The tide of world-record setting that swept through distance running also reached the men's and women's marathon events. At Rotterdam, Neth., in April, Tegla Loroupe of Kenya dropped the women's record to 2 hr 20 min 47 sec. A 19-sec improvement on the standard set by Ingrid Kristiansen of Norway in 1985, Loroupe's run was not without controversy, as she was paced for the entire race by two male runners who blocked the wind for her.

The surprise destroyer of Ethiopian runner Belayneh Dinsamo's 10-year-old men's world record was Ronaldo da Costa, an unheralded Brazilian running just his second marathon. His 2 hr 6 min 5 sec clocking at the Berlin marathon in September improved the record by 45 sec. Da Costa, who became the first marathoner in history to average over 20 km/h (12.5 mph), ran the second half of his race in an awe-inspiring 1 hr 1 min 23 sec.

The world cross country championships, held in Marrakech, Mor., in March, included short- and long-course races for the first time, doubling the number of senior events. While O'Sullivan monopolized the women's individual titles, Tergat, a long-course specialist, won his fourth individual crown in a row.

(SIEG LINDSTROM)

VOLLEYBALL

In 1998 two significant rule changes were instituted by volleyball's international organization—the Fédération Internationale de Volley Ball (FIVB)—to speed up the sport, which often included matches on the elite level that lasted more than three hours. The creation of the "libero" position added more defense and specialization to the sport. The libero was a defensive specialist, who was allowed an unlimited number of substitutions to play in the back row. The libero

could not serve, block, or set the ball in front of the three-metre line. This new rule, which began as an experiment in 1996 and was used at each of the major international events in 1998, allowed smaller volleyball players to play on the international level. The experiment was to be fully adopted for the 1999 campaign.

The FIVB also announced changes to the scoring system for international volleyball matches. The scoring system for the best-three-of-five matches was altered so that the first team to register 25 points in rally scoring (and to lead by two points) would win the game. This rule was to be installed for the first four games of each match, while the fifth game would be played to 15 points. Teams would be allowed to score regardless of whether they served or started on defense. Previously, rally scoring was used in the fifth games, and only the serving team could score points during the first four games.

On the court in 1998, Cuba and Italy won the women's and men's titles, respectively, at the world championships in Japan. For the Cuban women, it marked the second consecutive world championship and sixth major title, while Italy, which had failed to win at the Olympic Games, captured its third successive world championship crown.

(RICHARD WANNINGER)

WEIGHT LIFTING

In 1998 the 69th men's world championships and the 12th women's world championships were held in Lahti, Fin. The events comprised eight new body-weight classes for men (down from 10) and seven body-weight classes for women (down from nine), as approved by the International Weightlifting Federation in 1997 and effective in 1998.

Greece and Bulgaria topped the tally in the men's event with the same number of medals (five) and points (566) and were separated only by the number of overall gold medals. Greece won three overall gold medals, one silver, and one bronze to place first. Bulgaria captured two overall gold medals, one silver, and two bronze and finished in second place. Super heavyweight Andrey Chemerkin of Russia earned his third overall title. Chinese weight lifters broke one world record, and Bulgaria and Greece each broke two.

China dominated the women's event, capturing 13 gold medals and 3 silver and scoring 508 points. Taiwan won 5 gold medals, and Finland took 2. China (19 medals) topped the final tally, followed by Taiwan (16), Bulgaria (5), Russia (4), and Finland, Colombia, and Hungary (3 each). Chinese athletes broke four world records.

(DRAGOMIR CIOROSLAN)

WRESTLING

Freestyle and Greco-Roman. In April 1998 Russia captured the 26th World Cup of freestyle wrestling when heavyweight

World Weight Lifting Champions, 1998

MEN

Weight class	Winner and country	Performance
56 kg (123 lb)	Halil Mutlu (Turkey)	295 kg (650.3 lb)
62 kg (136.5 lb)	Leonidas Sabanis (Greece)	320 kg (705.4 lb)
69 kg (152 lb)	Plamen Jeliazkov (Bulgaria)	350 kg (771.6 lb)
77 kg (169.5 lb)	Zlatan Vanev (Bulgaria)	365 kg (804.6 lb)
85 kg (187 lb)	Pyrros Dimas (Greece)	387.5 kg (854.2 lb)
94 kg (207 lb)	Akakios Kakiasvilis (Greece)	400 kg (881.8 lb)
105 kg (231 lb)	Igor Razoryonov (Ukraine)	422.5 kg (931.4 lb)
+105 kg (+231 lb)	Andrey Chemerkin (Russia)	437.5 kg (964.5 lb)

WOMEN

Weight class	Winner and country	Performance
48 kg (105.5 lb)	Li Yunli (China)	182.5 kg (402.3 lb)
53 kg (116.5 lb)	Wang Xiufen (China)	210 kg (462.9 lb)
58 kg (127.5 lb)	Kuo Ping-Chun (Taiwan)	207.5 kg (457.4 lb)
63 kg (138.5 lb)	Chen Jui-Lien (Taiwan)	225 kg (496 lb)
69 kg (152 lb)	Tang Weifang (China)	240 kg (529.1 lb)
75 kg (165 lb)	Karoliina Lundahl (Finland)	230 kg (507 lb)
+75 kg (+165 lb)	Tang Gonghong (China)	255 kg (562.1 lb)

Andrey Shumilin defeated Tom Erickson of the U.S. 1–0 in overtime, giving the Russians a 16–15 victory and the gold medal. The U.S. finished second, followed by Iran, Cuba, Germany, and Japan. The U.S. came back to defeat Russia 16–14 for the gold medal in the Goodwill Games held July 25–26 in New York City. The turning point for the Americans was Tony Purler's fall over Murad Ramazanov at 58 kg. The U.S. claimed three individual gold medals, the same number as Russia, while Iran took two.

In the freestyle world championships held in Tehran on September 8–11, host Iran won the team title with 63 points, including three champions and six medalists. Russia was second with 54 points, and the U.S. was third.

At the Greco-Roman world championships held in Gävle, Swed., on August 27–30, the Russians won the team title with four individual champions, and South Korea was second, followed by Turkey and Kazakstan. Russian superheavyweight Aleksandr Karelin won the title at 130 kg with a fall in the finals over Matt Ghaffari of the U.S., earning his 11th straight world or Olympic gold medal, the most of any wrestler in history. In 1998 Karelin, who had never lost an international wrestling match, was the only wrestler with eight career world gold medals and three Olympic golds.

(JOHN HOKE)

Sumo. In 1998 *ozeki* (champion) Musashimaru won the New Year's tournament (Hatsu *Basho*) with a 12–3 record for his third championship. Wakanohana captured both the Haru *Basho* in March and the Natsu *Basho* in May to gain promotion as the 66th *yokozuna* (grand champion). It marked the first time that sumo had two brothers designated as *yokozuna*. Takanohana, Wakanohana's younger brother, clinched the *yusho* (victory) of the Nagoya *Basho* in July and then triumphed again in September at the Aki *Basho* for his 20th title. Lowly ranked number 12 *maegashira* (senior wrestler) Kotonishiki stunned the sumo world by winning the Kyushu *Basho* in November with a 14–1 record.

In January the Sumo Association elected Tokitsukaze Oyakata, formerly the *ozeki* Yutakayama, as the new *rijicho* (chairman). Former *komusubi* (junior champion second class) Kenko died in March at the age of 30 from a pulmonary condition. Hawaiian-born *ozeki* Konishiki retired in September to embark on a new career in the world of entertainment.

(ANDY ADAMS)

1998 Sumo Tournament Champions

Tournament	Location	Winner	Winner's record
Hatsu *Basho* (New Year's tournament)	Tokyo	Musashimaru	12–3
Haru *Basho* (spring tournament)	Osaka	Wakanohana	14–1
Natsu *Basho* (summer tournament)	Tokyo	Wakanohana	12–3
Nagoya *Basho* (Nagoya tournament)	Nagoya	Takanohana	14–1
Aki *Basho* (autumn tournament)	Tokyo	Takanohana	13–2
Kyushu *Basho* (Kyushu tournament)	Fukuoka	Kotonishiki	14–1

World Wrestling Championships—Freestyle*

Year	48 kg	52 kg (54 kg)	57 kg (58 kg)	62 kg (63 kg)	68 kg (69 kg)
1993	A. Vila (Cuba)	V. Jordanov (Bulg.)	Terry Brands (U.S.)	Tom Brands (U.S.)	A.A. Fallah (Iran)
1994	A. Vila (Cuba)	V. Jordanov (Bulg.)	A. Puerto (Cuba)	M. Azizov (Russia)	A. Leipold (Ger.)
1995	V. Orudzhev (Russia)	V. Jordanov (Bulg.)	Terry Brands (U.S.)	E. Tedeev (Ukr.)	A. Gevorkian (Arm.)
1996	Kim Il (N.Kor.)	V. Jordanov (Bulg.)	K. Cross (U.S.)	Tom Brands (U.S.)	V. Bogiyev (Russia)
1997		W. Garcia (Cuba)	M. Talaee (Iran)	A. Kenari (Iran)	A. Gevorkian (Arm.)
1998		S. Henson (U.S.)	A.R. Dabier (Iran)	S. Barzakov (Bulg.)	A. Gevorkian (Arm.)

Year	74 kg (76 kg)	82 kg (85 kg)	90 kg	100 kg (97 kg)	130 kg (130 kg)
1993	Park Jang (S.Kor.)	S. Ozturk (Tur.)	A. Jadidi (Iran)	L. Khabelov (Russia)	B. Baumgartner (U.S.)
1994	T. Ceylan (Tur.)	L. Jabrailov (Moldova)	R. Khadem (Iran)	A. Sabejey (Ger.)	M. Demir (Tur.)
1995	B. Saytyev (Russia)	K. Jackson (U.S.)	R. Khadem (Iran)	K. Angle (U.S.)	B. Baumgartner (U.S.)
1996	B. Saytyev (Russia)	Kh. Magomedov (Russia)	R. Khadem (Iran)	K. Angle (U.S.)	M. Demir (Tur.)
1997	B. Saytyev (Russia)	L. Gutches (U.S.)		K. Kuramagomedov (Russia)	Z. Guclu (Tur.)
1998	B. Saytyev (Russia)	A.R. Heydari (Iran)		A. Jadidi (Iran)	A. Rodríguez (Cuba)

*Figures in parentheses represent new weight classes established in 1997.

World Wrestling Championships—Greco-Roman Style*

Year	48 kg	52 kg (54 kg)	57 kg (58 kg)	62 kg (63 kg)	68 kg (69 kg)
1993	W. Sánchez (Cuba)	R. Martínez (Cuba)	A. Manukjan (Arm.)	S. Martynov (Russia)	I. Duguchiyev (Russia)
1994	W. Sánchez (Cuba)	A. Mkrtchyan (Ger.)	J. Melnichenko (Kazak.)	S. Martynov (Russia)	I. Duguchiyev (Russia)
1995	Sim Kwon Ho (S.Kor.)	S. Danielane (Russia)	D. Hall (U.S.)	S. Martynov (Russia)	R. Adzhy (Ukr.)
1996	Sim Kwon Ho (S.Kor.)	A. Nazaryan (Arm.)	Y. Melnichenko (Kazak.)	W. Zawadzki (Pol.)	R. Wolny (Pol.)
1997		E. Yildiz (Tur.)	Y. Melnichenko (Kazak.)	S. Eroglu (Tur.)	Son Sang Pil (S.Kor.)
1998		Sim Kwon Ho (S.Kor)	Kim In Sub (S.Kor.)	M. Manukian (Kazak.)	A. Tretyakov (Russia)

Year	74 kg (76 kg)	82 kg (85 kg)	90 kg	100 kg (97 kg)	130 kg (130 kg)
1993	N. Alamanza (Cuba)	M. Yerlikaya (Tur.)	G. Koguashvili (Russia)	M. Ljungberg (Swed.)	A. Karelin (Russia)
1994	M. Iskandarian (Russia)	T. Zander (Ger.)	G. Koguashvili (Russia)	A. Wronski (Pol.)	A. Karelin (Russia)
1995	Y. Riemer (Fr.)	H. Yerlikaya (Tur.)	H. Baser (Tur.)	M. Ljungberg (Swed.)	A. Karelin (Russia)
1996	F. Ascuy (Cuba)	H. Yerlikaya (Tur.)	V. Oleynyk (Ukr.)	A. Wronski (Pol.)	A. Karelin (Russia)
1997	M. Yli-Hannuksela (Fin.)	S. Tsuir (Russia)		G. Koguashvili (Russia)	A. Karelin (Russia)
1998	B. Baiseitov (Kazak.)	A. Menshikov (Russia)		G. Koguashvili (Russia)	A. Karelin (Russia)

*Figures in parentheses represent new weight classes established in 1997.

Transportation

The upheaval in financial markets, together with currency failure in a number of countries, had a marked effect on transportation in 1998. Many infrastructure projects were canceled or deferred, and operations were placed under severe scrutiny.

Governments throughout the world were increasingly focused on issues of integration, attempting to achieve an effective, seamless system for both passengers and freight. The main thrust of development shifted to rehabilitation and extension of existing networks and to improvement of the vehicles and ancillary systems. The short-term goals of transportation authorities were to employ existing technology effectively so as to achieve acceptable safety and environmental standards.

With the growing reliance within transport on the integration of services, there was increasing concern about possible disruption caused by the year 2000 problem (Y2K) in computer systems. (*See* COMPUTERS AND INFORMATION SYSTEMS: *Sidebar.*) All sectors of transportation were planning for the significant amount of work needed to avoid the potentially severe adverse impacts of Y2K.   (JOHN H. EARP)

AVIATION

The world airline industry had a successful financial year in 1997, due mainly to continuing efforts to reduce costs, the advantages stemming from an increasing number of alliances, and low fuel prices. According to the UN's International Civil Aviation Organization (ICAO), scheduled carriers returned an operating profit of 5.7% of operating revenues, with income at $291 billion and expenses at $274 billion. This marked the fifth year in a row that the industry had shown a positive outcome.

Pierre Jeanniot, director general of the International Air Transport Association (IATA), the airlines' own trade body with more than 250 members, warned against too much optimism, however, pointing out that when the 1997 profit was added to those made in 1994–96, it still left the airlines $800 million short of recovering their losses from earlier in the decade. The figures also disguised a far from homogeneous regional profitability picture, he added. Preliminary 1998 figures, moreover, confirmed a substantial slowing.

Asia/Pacific airlines, traditionally among the best performers, began to suffer from the economic downturn in that part of the world. Their 1997 results were "collectively probably their worst-ever," according to Jeanniot, and a survey of the opinions of chief executive officers of carriers in the region caused IATA to revise downward its 1997–2001 growth forecasts from 7.7% per year to 4.4% for passengers and from 9% to 6.5% for cargo. Airlines operating to, from, and within the region were expected to make $2 billion less net profit and to carry 30 million fewer passengers and one million tons less freight in 2001 than had been previously forecast.

Airlines in Europe, Africa, and North America showed growth close to the world average. The performance of those in the Middle East was below average. Overall, IATA airlines carried 1,273,000,000 passengers and 26 million tons of cargo during 1997, up, respectively, 6.8% and 7.8% from 1996. Chicago's O'Hare International Airport was the world's busiest in 1997, with a throughput of 70.3 million passengers, while Memphis (Tenn.) Airport handled the most air freight, at 2.2 million tons, according to Airports Council International figures.

North American and European carriers owed much of their success to strong economic conditions, and in Europe the major airlines were able to shrug off the impact of a number of small newcomers whose start-up had been facilitated by European Union aviation liberalization. In both regions airlines continued to pursue with vigour "code-share" alliances, which enabled them to sell seats on one another's aircraft. IATA estimated that by the end of 1997 there were some 600 such alliances throughout the airline world. It was a trend that increasingly worried fair-trading and antimonopolistic bodies. The airlines' worries included the growing burden of taxation, charges rising for using navigation and airport facilities, growing pressure from environmental lobbies, and the year 2000 computer bug.

Carriers claimed that many governments were devising new ways of tapping the industry as a source of revenues for general treasuries. IATA gave examples—a tax equivalent to $17 per seat on departing international flights in Norway, with the intention, according to IATA, "of reducing demand for air transport," and a 7.5% tax in the U.S. on mileage awards for frequent flyers.

International airlines paid $7.3 billion in airport landing and related charges and $5.9

Hundreds of Palestinians crowd a tarmac runway to celebrate the opening of the Gaza International Airport on November 24. The new airport was located in Rafah, at the foot of the Gaza Strip.

ADEL HANA—AP/WIDE WORLD

billion in navigation charges in 1997, increases, respectively, of $800 million and $700 million over 1996. Together, these charges represented 9.6% of the airlines' international operating costs, compared with 8.9% the previous year.

In September 1997 an aircraft emissions surcharge went into effect at Zürich, Switz., the first time that emissions had been reflected in the structure for user charges. IATA director general Jeanniot commented, "Ultimately, no airline, whatever its region, will be able to stand aloof from environmental matters, as pressure for energy taxes mounts, and serious efforts to cut oil consumption begin to bite. The environmental debate has more to do with politics and public sympathy than with technology and scientific fact."

Massive users of computers, airlines, air traffic control organizations, and airports, backed by both ICAO and IATA, initiated a campaign to ensure that the advanced technology on which they rely would recognize the year 2000. IATA member airlines spent a total of $1.6 billion to ensure that their information technology would be up to date when the new century arrived.

From the safety point of view the year was an improvement over 1996, with a total of 864 fatalities in 23 accidents, compared with 1,418 in 25 accidents. There were 17,777 airliners on the world register (12,384 jets, 5,393 turboprops) compared with 17,019 (11,798 jets, 5,221 turboprops) in 1996. Both major civil aircraft manufacturers—the Boeing Co. of the U.S. and the European consortium, Airbus Industrie—stepped up production rates to meet rising airline industry orders, though late in the year the lack of orders from Asia caused Boeing to lay off several thousand workers.
(ARTHUR REED)

SHIPPING AND PORTS

According to figures released by Lloyd's Register of Shipping, during 1997 the world fleet of merchant ships grew by 2.8% to 522.2 million gt (gross tons), an increase of 14.3 million gt over the previous year. The tanker fleet grew by only 0.5%, and general cargo ships, under strong competition from containerships, increased by only 0.1%. In contrast, as the bulk carriers ordered in the strong freight market of 1995 were delivered, the bulk carrier fleet increased by 3.1%. The most startling gain was registered by the containership fleet, which grew by 13.5%.

July 1, 1998, was a key date for shipping because major International Maritime Organization (IMO) initiatives entered into force at that time. A new Chapter IX of the International Convention for Safety of Life at Sea (SOLAS) made the International Safety Management Code mandatory, and a new version of Chapter III of SOLAS dealing with lifesaving appliances and arrangements came into force. A proposal for a harmonized Code of Safety for Ships in Polar Waters was submitted to the IMO D41 meeting (subcommittee on design and machinery). This was an attempt to agree on a common approach by the major classification societies and national administrations, which had their own rules for ships operating in polar waters.

Closely allied to shipping industry trends was the enormous scale of investment in

The interior of the vast arrival hall at the new Hong Kong International Airport on Lantau Island is shown above. One of the world's largest civil engineering projects, the airport opened on July 6. It offered road and rail links to the city and featured a shopping centre.

world port and harbour projects. Optimism was clearly the dominant factor in 1997–98, a time when terminal operators were faced with a new challenge—an 8,000-TEU (20-ft equivalent units) containership of over 100,000 deadweight tons. China and India had huge port projects under way during the year, with Shanghai forecast to become the world's fifth largest container port by 2020. Even a medium-sized maritime country such as Spain planned to invest $472 million on its ports in 1999 through state-owned Puertos del Estado.

The world's largest independent port operator, Hutchison Port Holdings (HPH), was involved in the opening in The Bahamas of the $78 million Freeport Container Port, a joint venture between HPH and the Grand Bahama Development Co. Port Raysut, a new container terminal at Salalah in southern Oman, opened in November. The privately owned facility would cut Europe-Asia transit times by as much as three and a half days. Port Raysut was expected to rank among the world's top 20 container ports within a year. (EDWARD CROWLEY)

FREIGHT AND PIPELINES

Freight operators experienced a difficult year in 1998, especially in East Asia. The economic crisis in that region sapped busi-ness confidence in markets that already were reeling from the impact of globalization and consolidation. Among the less-developed countries investment in infrastructure concentrated on efficiencies within and access to ports. In the U.S. the $2 billion Alameda Corridor project to link the ports of Long Beach, Calif., and Los Angeles to transcontinental rail yards nearby the latter city—a project made necessary by the strong growth of the U.S. Pacific ports—was scheduled to begin construction shortly. Mexican ports, in the wake of their 1993 privatization, were emerging as profitable gateways.

Bright spots in Asia included a new port link to Colombo, Sri Lanka, and sustained growth of trade into China. Singapore and Hong Kong continued to vie for the title of busiest container port. Hong Kong planned to open a new container terminal in 2001 and two more on Lantau Island thereafter. The Port of Singapore Authority signed a long-term service agreement with China Ocean Shipping Co., which was expected to help maintain the Authority's volume throughput and underlined the importance of the Chinese market.

Driven by an unprecedented demand for energy, pipeline construction increased. In the U.S. construction was at the highest level since the early 1980s, and in the rest of the world construction was up 8% over 1997. One-third of all the new projects were in the U.S., a result of an increase in offshore drilling in the Gulf of Mexico. Onshore projects included the 3,055-km (1,900-mi) Alliance pipeline from western Canada to Chicago; the 730-km (455-mi) Lakehead pipeline from Superior, Wis., to Mokena, Ill.; and the 644-km (400-mi) pipeline from Lake Erie to White Plains, N.Y.

Russia and Turkey agreed to join in building a 1,200-km (745-mi) $3.3 billion pipeline across the Black Sea. In Central Asia new projects included a 1,509-km (940-mi) $1.6 billion pipeline from Turkmenistan through Iran to Turkey and a 3,200-km (2,000-mi) line from Kazakstan to Iran. Farther east, plans for a trans-Asian gas pipeline network linking India to Myanmar (Burma) were disrupted by terrorist bombs and technical difficulties. In South America the success of the Bolivia-Brazil pipeline, which took 20 years to come to fruition, generated the need for a second line. (JOHN H. EARP)

ROADS AND TRAFFIC

Notwithstanding the economic difficulties of 1998 and the increasing awareness of the detrimental effects of car emissions, the aspirations to own and use a car continued un-

abated. Roads and their traffic provided the backbone of transportation in both the developed and less-developed countries.

Although the scale of national road programs was being cut back, key links in strategic networks continued to be constructed. The Trans-Kalahari Highway was completed during the year (*see* Sidebar), as was the Tokyo Bay crossing that included a 4.4-km bridge and 9.4-km of tunnel (1 km=0.62 mi). Under construction were the 2.3-km Selatin twin tunnel as part of the Izmir-Aydin expressway in Turkey, and the 1.9-km Molldiete tunnel as part of the 3.2-km bypass to Ravensburg in Germany. In Australia projects included a 1.6-km long tunnel to ease congestion in Perth's city centre at a cost of $197 million and construction in Melbourne to provide a missing link between the city's four radial freeways at a cost of $82.5 million.

Traffic in urban areas was likely to become more controlled, as three projects that opened during the year demonstrated. In Milan, to encourage the use of public transportation, automobiles were almost completely banned from the city centre. Marseille, France, embarked on a traffic control scheme to divert cars around its urban area, and Paris planned to organize an annual clean transport day with restrictions on automobiles. During the year Paris and New York City forged an agreement to pool experiences regarding the control of motor vehicles. This extended to traffic management by intelligent systems, parking control, enhancement of facilities for pedestrians and cyclists, and priority for public transportation. The U.K. government was committed to changing the balance of car use in favour of more environmentally friendly systems of transportation.   (JOHN H. EARP)

INTERCITY RAIL

The dominant goals of intercity rail service during recent years, high-speed trains and privatization, expanded in 1998 to include objectives based on providing convenient, modernized, and value-for-the-money services. The high-speed network was being extended, but its rate of expansion in core European services slowed during the year. A rail crash at Eschede, Ger., in June that killed 98 passengers focused thoughts on safety issues.

Sweden began planning a high-speed rail line on its east coast, and Germany planned to link Hannover and Berlin. Japan an-

---

Trans-Kalahari Highway

In March 1998 the residents of Botswana and Namibia met at Buitepos on the border between the two countries to inaugurate formally the Trans-Kalahari Highway. The new road formed part of the strategic coast-to-coast route that linked Maputo, Mozambique, on the Indian Ocean to Walvis Bay on the Atlantic coastline of Namibia. It was designed to serve as the backbone of an economic corridor and was expected to usher in a new era of east-west economic integration while at the same time consolidating the Southern African Development Community's (SADC's) vision of a free-trade area. The highway was also intended to free the landlocked Botswana from dependence on South Africa for routes to a deep-water port.

The two-lane all-weather road through Botswana to Gobabis, Namibia, which took six years to complete, closed the gap in the cross-continental highway. The 600-km (1 km=0.62 mi) section from Lobatse to Buitepos inside Botswana cost $77 million, with major funding provided by the Arab Bank for Economic Development in Africa, the Japanese Overseas Economic Cooperation Fund, and the Nordic Investment Bank. The final 94-km section linking Gobabis and Buitepos cost $15 million, with funding assistance for equipment and materials provided by the African Development Bank.

In addition to providing a strategic and regional link, the highway reduced the distance from Namibia to the industrial hub of Gauteng province, S.Af., by about 400 km. At the year's end some links and spurs from the highway still needed to be built or improved, and an equitable cost-recovery plan that would ensure the financing of the highway's necessary maintenance and upkeep had to be established.

The underlying objective of the highway was to stimulate economic development in the heart of southern Africa. In recalling the founding dream of the SADC in 1980, Pres. Sir Ketumile Masire of Botswana noted that the original aim was to "focus on a unified market economy with strong regional links, where each country could add value according to its own abilities; to the benefit of the region."

The highway was part of an overall development plan for transport and communications intended to act as a catalyst for promoting social and economic integration and promote economic prosperity.   (JOHN H. EARP)

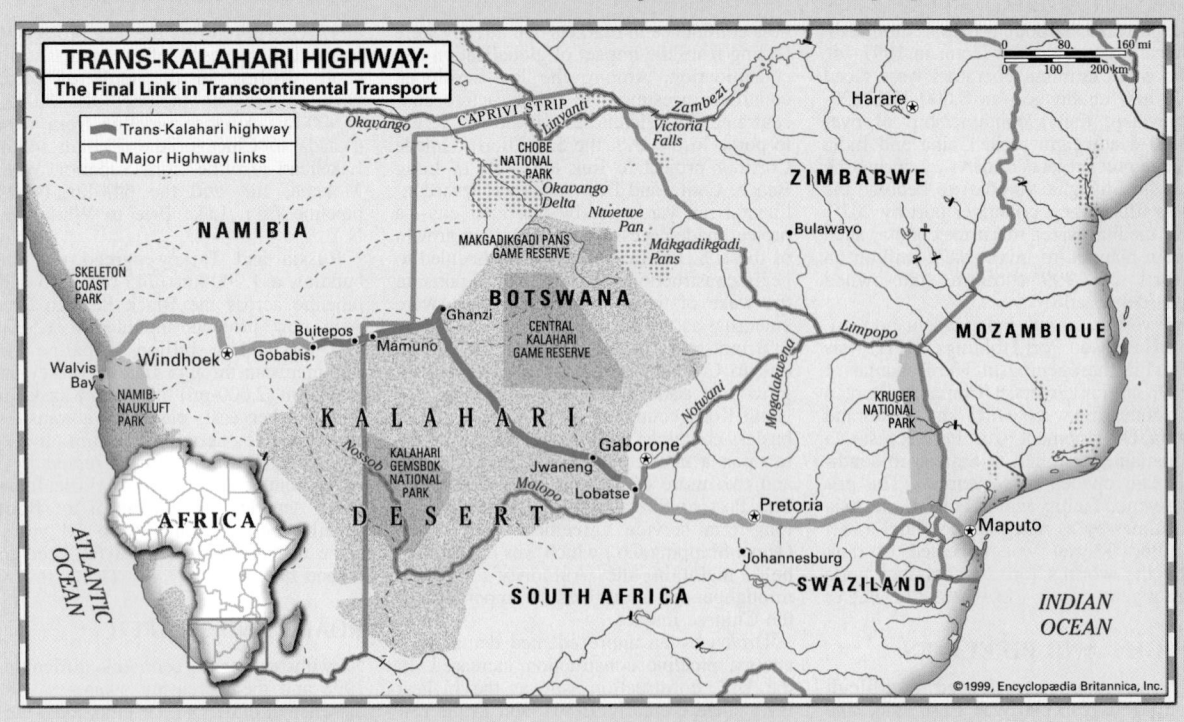

TRANS-KALAHARI HIGHWAY:
The Final Link in Transcontinental Transport

— Trans-Kalahari highway
— Major Highway links

Dancers perform on April 3 during the official presentation of German Railway's new high-speed ICT train. The first ICT train was scheduled to make its maiden trip in the summer of 1999 on the route between Stuttgart and Zürich.

nounced a $10 billion development plan to extend its Shinkansen high-speed network to link Kagoshima with Sapporo. In the U.S., where passengers accounted for only 1% of railroad traffic, Amtrak, the government-supported operator of almost all of the nation's intercity passenger trains, planned a $3.5 billion network radiating out from Chicago. The construction of the 517-km (1 km=0.62 mi) Boston–New York City line was scheduled to be completed in 1999. High-speed projects in Asia suffered a setback during the year because of the region's economic difficulties. The Milan-Genoa link in Italy was canceled because the train was likely to generate extremely loud noise in the narrow valleys through which it would pass.

The emphasis on improving rolling stock meant that during the next four years 10 or more major railways in Europe would rely on tilting trains for their main line services. In the Philippines the government sought BOT/BLT (build-operate-transfer/build-lease-transfer) arrangements in order to restore its railway to profitability. Kansas City/Southern expanded a 2,750-km regional network to a 16,000-km system, and Canadian National expanded its operations by a $2.4 billion merger in order to reach the Gulf of Mexico. In Peru there were plans to build three new railways totaling 1,300 km. A Brazilian iron ore company, Cia. Vale do Rio Doce, which was privatized in 1997, demonstrated that its two heavy-haul railways could be profitable.

The number of rail-airport links continued to grow with Brussels, Oslo, London Heathrow, and Hong Kong—all opening in 1998. An emphasis on interchange facilities and customer-oriented stations was exemplified by the new plans for the principal railway stations in Zürich, Switz., and Berlin. (JOHN H. EARP)

URBAN MASS TRANSIT

As cities in 1998 faced up to planning for the new millennium, there was a growing awareness that urban mass transit played a critical role in the quality of urban life. Policy statements from civic and public transportation authorities had a common theme: investment in their cities could be stimulated by mass transit networks. Developing such facilities generally demanded both public and private participation, although Rio de Janeiro; Montevideo, Uruguay; and São Paulo, Braz., privatized their urban transport during 1998.

New systems opened in Ankara, Turkey; Sofia, Bulg.; Warsaw; and Taegu, the third city in South Korea to have mass transit. Tehran opened its rehabilitated system, and Lisbon added a new line. The new Meteor Line in Paris was driverless. Other cities with newly opened links included Madrid; Munich, Ger.; Tokyo; and Los Angeles (the Red Line to Hollywood). Cities that were constructing and/or extending their metro systems included Cairo, Singapore, and St. Louis, Mo.; and Paris planned to build a second Meteor Line. Ottawa; Vienna; Casablanca, Mor.; Seattle, Wash.; and Novosibirsk, Russia, had well-advanced plans.

Equally impressive was the extent of commitment to light rail systems. Karachi, Pak.; Kuala Lumpur, Malaysia; and Munich opened new lines in 1998. Cities with projects under construction included Sacramento, Calif.; Sydney, Australia; and Stockholm (which was to be privately operated). Cities planning light rail systems included Abu Dhabi, U.A.E.; Brisbane, Australia; Krakow, Pol.; Málaga, Spain; and Salt Lake City, Utah. Much effort was being put into devising low-floor vehicles for both light rail and subway systems, and the industry was attempting to standardize its approach. New designs were introduced in Göteborg, Swed.; Vevey, Switz.; and Düsseldorf, Ger.; principally to enhance the passenger appeal of the vehicle.

Buses remained the backbone of urban systems. Advances during the year included new light vehicle designs; compressed natural gas engines in Sacramento, Calif.; and on-street priority that included reversible lanes in Adelaide, Australia. Ann Arbor, Mich., pioneered a new operating system that included AVL (automatic vehicle location), computerized dispatching, smart cards for ticketing, and automated vehicle component monitoring.

People-mover systems and monorails were becoming less expensive to develop but were more likely to be used for resorts or links to systems rather than as primary urban transportation. Boston opened a new $2.9 million shuttle to the MBTA Orange Line, and Las Vegas, Nev., linked its downtown hotels with a monorail. (JOHN H. EARP)

One of the oldest underground transport systems in the world, the Paris Métro received a long-overdue facelift in 1998. Driverless trains, renovated stations, and a new underground line were among the many features introduced.

HURRICANES AND GLOBAL WARMING

If you thought it felt warm in 1998, you were not mistaken. According to NASA, the World Meteorological Organization, and the National Oceanic and Atmospheric Administration, the year was the warmest in known history. These organizations, three of the world's most respected authorities in climatology, concurred that the average worldwide temperature for 1998 was the highest on record. How responsible humans were for the surge in global warming remained open to debate, but one thing was certain: rising temperatures increased the incidence of powerful hurricanes, which drew much of their strength from warm ocean waters. Two major hurricanes during the year provided deadly evidence of that.

The first, Hurricane Georges, struck in late September. With winds of up to 193 km/h (120 mph), Georges pummeled the Caribbean, leaving many islands in shambles and claiming the lives of at least 300 persons in the region. Georges then moved on to swamp the U.S. Gulf Coast, dumping heavy rain on parts of Louisiana, Mississippi, Alabama, and Florida and causing four deaths.

One month later an even stronger hurricane, Mitch, wreaked havoc in Central America. This hurricane was blocked by a front and remained off the coast for several days. Producing torrential rain, Mitch triggered numerous floods and mud slides. More than 1.5 million persons lost their homes, and thousands died, including some 5,657 confirmed deaths in Honduras and 1,845 in Nicaragua at year's end. Mitch finally weakened in early November. By then, authorities had recognized it as the worst Atlantic basin hurricane in 200 years.

Although record temperatures were not expected for 1999, many weather experts feared that devastating hurricanes like Georges and Mitch would continue to occur, as a 20-year trend of global temperatures above the long-term average showed little sign of abating.

(Left) Outside Guatemala City, people cross a temporary footbridge over a road washed away by Mitch. (Below) This Catholic church was among many buildings in the village of Fonds Verrettes, Haiti, destroyed or damaged by flooding from Georges. (Above left) Residents of Key West, Fla., seek shelter as Hurricane Georges approaches. (Above right) Flood victims recover in a hospital in Chinandega, Nicaragua.

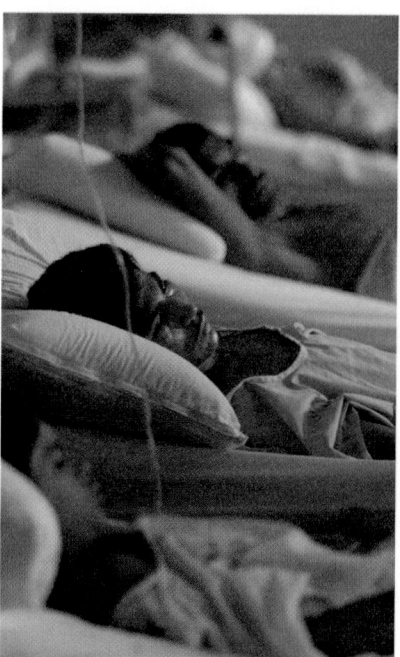

(Right) A Honduran man stands among banana trees destroyed by Hurricane Mitch. (Middle left) A policeman in the Dominican Republic wears a handkerchief for protection against the dust and odors caused by drying mud and human and animal remains. (Middle right) A Haitian girl sorts through what is left of her home in the aftermath of Hurricane Georges. (Bottom) People in Valle de Sula, Honduras, wait to be rescued from a roof.

World Affairs

The global recession that spread in 1998, the deepest since World War II in parts of the world, was bound to have far-ranging political consequences. All countries were affected by it, but some, by necessity, more than others. Most severely hit were the underfunded Asian economies and, as a result of declining commodity prices, countries heavily dependent on the export of raw materials such as oil. At the same time, it became abundantly clear that the international financial system that had served the world economy well since 1945 was in urgent need of reform. Consequently, international economics rather than political issues took pride of place in the deliberations of world leaders of the developed as well as the less-developed countries during the year under review.

The immediate crisis began in Thailand in July 1997 and subsequently spread to South Korea, one of the powerhouses of the world economy; the South Korean crisis necessitated the largest intervention ever made by the World Bank. By early 1998 Malaysia was affected; its government placed the responsibility on international currency speculators. At the same time, also in the wake of an economic crisis, student unrest in Indonesia led to widespread riots, often against the ethnic Chinese, and eventually, in late May, to the resignation of President Suharto (*see* BIOGRAPHIES), who had ruled the country for more than three decades. Finally, during the spring and summer of 1998, Japan, the leading force in Asia and the second largest economy in the world, had to face the full impact of the crisis, which also led to a change of government.

The reasons for the economic meltdown were somewhat different in each case. In Japan the banking system was heavily indebted, and the government's policy of dealing with the situation by cutting taxes and increasing spending to stimulate economic growth had only a limited effect. Elsewhere, the immediate problem was the overvaluation of the country's assets, which tempted speculators but eventually led to a sharp decline in the value of the national currencies. In most cases, however, these were not just currency crises. The basic reasons went deeper. They were structural in character and included weak banking systems; "crony capitalism," in which funds were diverted to those favoured by government leaders rather than to those most capable of using them; bad loans; investments in unproductive enterprises; and, in some countries, ineffective tax collection. These weaknesses helped to create a situation that made the economies of those nations particularly vulnerable to sudden movements of global capital such as the withdrawal of investments.

Much thought was given to finding a way out of the crisis—in the short run by establishing rescue funds and stabilizing the currencies and the stock exchanges of the countries most affected. At meetings of heads of government in Singapore, Washington, Moscow, and elsewhere, it became clear that the international organizations established after World War II (the World Bank and the International Monetary Fund) did not have sufficient means to cope with this assignment and that new initiatives were needed. What was originally known as the "Asian currency crisis" had ripple effects and by late 1998 had generated a general crisis of confidence that manifested itself notably on the world's stock markets. Among the Latin-American countries, Venezuela, Colombia, and, above all, Brazil were affected by the free-market upheaval. The opening up of the Brazilian market had brought that country $45 billion in investments in 1997, but it also caused high interest rates and lost jobs, a high social cost for large sections of the population. At the year's end the challenges facing Brazil to prevent a collapse were daunting. (*See* Spotlight: *The Troubled World Economy.*)

The political consequences of the economic crisis were only too clear in the case of Russia. The political and social equilibrium of the country had been tenuous for years, and the immediate crisis came to a head in March when Pres. Boris Yeltsin suddenly dismissed Prime Minister Viktor Chernomyrdin because (according to the official version) his government had been lacking in "initiative and dynamism." He was replaced by a young and not-very-well-known technocrat, Sergey Kiriyenko, whose government lasted only five months. The pressures on the ruble, reflecting the weakness of the economy, resulted in a disastrous fall in the value of the currency. Massive tax evasion also continued, and the government found itself unable to service the massive loans it had received or, worse yet, pay its employees. Yeltsin, who began to lose his hold as his health deteriorated, wanted Chernomyrdin back, but the legislature refused to give its approval, and as a compromise Yevgeny Primakov (*see* BIOGRAPHIES) was appointed prime minister.

The Russian crisis caused alarm in the West, both in view of its potential political repercussions and because there seemed to be no obvious solution. Pouring more money into the Russian economy would not be a long-term solution, but allowing the country to slide into chaos was equally unacceptable.

The economic crisis mostly overshadowed political and military tensions. One exception was the explosion of five nuclear devices by the new nationalist government in India (and six more by Pakistan just two weeks later). These events confirmed that nuclear proliferation was running its inexorable course. International investigations did not establish that Iraq and Iran had been building nuclear weapons, but the investigations did conclude that those countries had acquired long-distance missiles as well as nonconventional weapons. U.S. attempts to continue UN inspections of possible production of weapons of mass destruction in Iraq were successfully barred by the Iraqi government.

Major civil wars in Africa (Democratic Republic of the Congo and Sierra Leone) continued their course. The innovation in these wars was the intervention in the conflicts by neighbouring countries such as Nigeria, Zimbabwe, Angola, and South Africa. In addition, there were armed conflicts in Lesotho, The Sudan, and Burundi, and for a short time full-scale war broke out between Eritrea and Ethiopia, which had formerly been close allies.

In Europe the trend toward political success for left-of-centre parties continued with the victory in Germany of the Social Democrats over the Christian Democrats, who had been in power for 16 years. In Italy the left-of-centre government headed by Romano Prodi collapsed, but his successor was the former communist Massimo D'Alema. The military confrontations in former Yugoslavia continued, but the focus switched from Bosnia and Herzegovina to Kosovo, where the Serbian government at the end of February mounted a military offensive against Kosovo's ethnic Albanian majority, who were seeking greater autonomy. Repression and fighting increased during the subsequent months as a separatist Albanian army took form, and it was only owing to severe pressure and the issuing of

Pres. Luigi Scalfaro of Italy (left) joins the nation's new prime minister, former communist Massimo D'Alema, at a ceremony introducing Italy's 56th government since the end of World War II.

a NATO ultimatum that the Yugoslav government in Belgrade showed willingness to negotiate with the ethnic Albanians.

American peace initiatives were successful in Northern Ireland. A majority of the Irish electorate voted for new constitutional arrangements that seemed to satisfy the minimum demands of the two warring sides in a conflict that had lasted for centuries. American peacemaking faced greater difficulties in its attempts to bring Israelis and

breaking agreements that ended the Persian Gulf War in 1991 and an accord made with Secretary-General Kofi Annan in February, as well as defying a succession of Security Council resolutions. Barring access to all monitoring sites, Iraq went beyond the cat-and-mouse game it had played with the UN when it banned various inspections in January, February, and August. In October the Security Council twice unanimously condemned the Iraqi action, calling on the gov-

counted for material sufficient to make 200 tons of the chemical weapon. On October 26, American, French, and Swiss scientists agreed that Iraqis had loaded some of their missiles with VX and then used detergents to wash it off.

On April 27 the Security Council extended sanctions against Iraq because of inadequate cooperation. The International Atomic Energy Agency reported on July 27 that, though it had no evidence that Iraq had nuclear weapons, Baghdad's failure to account for key nuclear equipment and technical blueprints left open the possibility that it had hidden the necessary documents and material for future use.

On August 5, after Butler refused (because he lacked proof) to certify that Iraq had destroyed all its weapons of mass destruction, Iraq announced again that it would no longer cooperate with UNSCOM until it was "reformed" and moved from New York City to Geneva or Vienna to reduce alleged U.S. influence. The next day the Security Council called the Iraqi position "totally unacceptable" and urged Baghdad "not to implement its decision."

Butler reported to the Council on September 3 that Iraq not only was blocking surprise inspections but was also interfering with routine monitoring, and on September 9 the Council resolved unanimously not to review events in Iraq again until inspectors were allowed to resume their jobs. In November the U.S. with British support again began to build up forces to use against Iraq to enforce the UN resolutions, and all operational UNSCOM teams left the country.

On November 13, Annan appealed to Iraq to make a "wise decision" and resume cooperating with UNSCOM. Two days later, with their planes already en route to attack Iraq, the U.S. and U.K. accepted new Iraqi "unconditional" assurances that UNSCOM inspectors could resume their work, and the attack was called off. UNSCOM inspectors recommenced their work, but on November 20, Iraq refused to produce documents that UNSCOM requested, saying that they were irrelevant or no longer existed. Butler reported the matter to the Security Council on November 24, the same day that the Council approved the fifth six-month renewal of the "oil for food" program.

On December 8 UNSCOM launched intensive surprise searches for weapons, but was blocked the next day from inspecting the Baghdad headquarters of the ruling Ba'th Party. On December 15, the International Atomic Energy Agency announced that Iraq's cooperation after November 17 had been satisfactory, but Butler accused Iraq once again of failing to cooperate.

The United States and Britain, acting on warnings given in November that Iraqi obstruction would invite military action without further notice, began a 70-hour missile and bombing attack on Iraq on December 16. Annan called the bombing a "sad day for the world," adding that his thoughts were with the 307 UN humanitarian workers still in the country (93 were later withdrawn and then returned after the military action ended). China, France, and Russia criticized the attacks as violating the UN Charter. Iraq then announced that it would under no circumstances allow UNSCOM to return to Iraq.

On December 23, Iraq refused to allow UN observers monitoring its border with

Richard Butler, head of the UN Special Commission charged with finding and destroying Iraq's weapons of mass destruction, reports to the UN in September that Iraq is not cooperating with his inspectors.

Palestinians together. The accords achieved in a conference in Maryland in October helped to give fresh momentum to a peace process that had run out of steam. Given the widely differing long-term aspirations of the two sides, however, it was difficult to regard this as more than a stopgap measure in a conflict likely to endure for a long time.

(WALTER LAQUEUR)

UNITED NATIONS

Owing to the failure of the United States to pay its full dues to the UN since 1995, a virtually bankrupt UN limped through 1998 only because some members, including a few less-developed countries, provided interest-free loans, because a few nongovernmental organizations (NGOs) contributed funds, and because the UN did not reimburse European and Third World countries and Japan for providing peacekeeping troops. Enforced economies severely reduced the UN's peacekeeping capacity and impeded the work of the war crimes tribunals at The Hague. The most serious problem for the UN in 1998, however, came from Iraq, which put a complete end to the work of the UN Special Commission (UNSCOM) charged with destroying its weapons of mass destruction.

Iraq. Iraq's ultimate challenge came on October 31, when it announced that it would no longer cooperate with UNSCOM, thus

ernment to rescind its decision and "resume immediate, complete and unconditional cooperation" with UNSCOM.

On February 7 and 8, during the year's first major confrontation between the UN and Iraq, U.S. Pres. Bill Clinton and British Prime Minister Tony Blair warned that they would use force, if necessary, to press Iraqi Pres. Saddam Hussein to allow UNSCOM to fulfill its duties. Iraq then offered to open eight "presidential" sites to international inspection for 60 days. On February 22, Secretary-General Annan negotiated an agreement with Hussein in Baghdad granting UN weapons inspectors unrestricted access if some inspections were observed by senior diplomats. Inspections resumed on March 5, and by April 3 UNSCOM teams had inspected all the presidential sites without finding any prohibited materials.

All through the year UNSCOM head Richard Butler warned the Security Council that the commission found it increasingly difficult to determine whether Iraq had actually destroyed all of its weapons of mass destruction. His evidence showed that Iraq was hiding biological and chemical weapons and refusing to supply an honest and full accounting. Iraq asserted that its project to produce VX nerve gas had failed, but UNSCOM found that Iraqis had actually produced four tons of it, still could produce VX in industrial quantities, and had not ac-

Kuwait to fly into its territory, and three days later, it announced that it would fire on any aircraft flying in the "no flight" zones that the U.S., Britain, and France created over Iraq in 1991 and 1992 to protect Kurdish minorities and Shi'ite Muslims. Fire was exchanged between British and U.S. planes and Iraqi ground installations in late December.

Administration and Budget. The United States owed $1,180,000,000 to the UN at the year's end. The secretary-general said on March 9 that the only beneficiaries of a "cash-starved" UN were "aggressors . . . violators of human rights, drug dealers, and [illegal] arms merchants." He noted he had reduced the budget, engaged fewer personnel, tightened management, streamlined legislative processes, and introduced "sunset provisions" for programs as they expired.

The U.S. Congress included nearly $1 billion for the UN in the budget for fiscal 1998, but it barred the use of federal funds for international family-planning organizations. President Clinton vetoed the bill on October 21 because it tied UN dues to "unrelated and controversial social provisions, which endanger the health of women . . . even though . . . countries where women have access to strong family planning actually had fewer abortions." Instead, the U.S. paid $197 million before a two-year deadline on arrears set by the UN Charter would have deprived it of its vote in the General Assembly.

Former Yugoslavia. During the year UN and NATO troops captured several alleged war criminals and turned them over to the International Criminal Tribunal for the Former Yugoslavia at The Hague. The court rendered several judgments against prisoners charged with having committed war crimes and crimes against humanity between 1992 and 1995.

The Security Council, with China abstaining, imposed an arms embargo on Yugoslavia on March 31 to press Yugoslav Pres. Slobodan Milosevic to abandon the use of violence against ethnic Albanians in the Serbian province of Kosovo. On September 23 the Council threatened international intervention if the attacks continued. It called for an immediate cease-fire and the start of negotiations between the Serbian-dominated Yugoslav army and the ethnic Albanian Kosovo Liberation Army.

On October 1 the Security Council condemned atrocities against civilians in Kosovo and demanded that the guilty parties be caught and punished. Four days later the secretary-general told the Council that, despite its resolutions, Serbian security forces continued to carry out punitive operations against ethnic Albanians in Kosovo in a campaign of "terror and violence." On October 24 the Council (with China and Russia abstaining) called on Yugoslavia to implement fully and promptly its pledge to remove its troops from Kosovo and to allow ethnic Albanian refugees to return. Threats of military action by NATO troops led Milosevic to comply. On November 5, however, he insisted that Kosovo's problems were internal and barred investigators dispatched by the international tribunal from conducting a fact-finding mission in Kosovo. The Security Council on November 17 told Yugoslavia to let the investigators carry out their assignment, but they were not allowed to proceed.

Democratic Republic of the Congo. After weeks during which the government of Pres. Laurent Kabila harassed investigators and then detained a Canadian member of the UN team, the UN on April 9 suspended its investigation into alleged massacres of Rwandan refugees in the Democratic Republic of the Congo (Zaire until May 29, 1997) during 1996–97. On April 15 Secretary-General Annan withdrew the investigators. On November 28, leaders of the Congo and neighbouring countries supporting armed rebels in the Congo agreed, after talks with Annan in Paris, to sign a cease-fire agreement by mid-December. Rebel leader Ernest Wamba dia Wamba said, however, that fighting would continue until details of the cease-fire became clearer. Annan also proposed a peacekeeping force along the borders of the Congo to reduce interference from Rwanda and Uganda.

Rwanda. On April 30 the Security Council created a third judicial chamber for the International Criminal Tribunal for Rwanda in Arusha, Tanz., in order to speed its proceedings. Former Rwandan prime minister Jean Kambanda on May 1 pleaded guilty to charges of genocide, the first time that anyone had entered such a plea before an international tribunal, including proceedings at Nürnberg, Ger., after World War II. On September 4 the tribunal sentenced Kambanda to life in prison for his part in the 1994 genocide of the Tutsi and some allied Hutu in Rwanda, and he thus became the first person to be sentenced for the crime of genocide.

On September 2 the tribunal had handed down its first guilty verdict of genocide, against a former mayor, Jean-Paul Akayesu, convicted of responsibility for the deaths of more than 2,000 people and the rapes of dozens of Tutsi women. On October 2 he was sentenced to serve three life terms plus 80 years concurrently for nine counts of genocide, rape, and crimes against humanity.

Human Rights. On December 9, the 50th anniversary of the international convention against genocide, the General Assembly for the first time listed anti-Semitism as a form of racism. On December 10, at the headquarters of the UN Educational, Scientific, and Cultural Organization in Paris, the UN opened a one-week celebration of the 50th anniversary of the Universal Declaration on Human Rights.

China signed the International Covenant on Civil and Political Rights on October 5. A Chinese UN delegate said that a 10-day visit to China by Mary Robinson, UN high commissioner for human rights, in September had helped both sides understand each other better.

The Commission on Human Rights condemned Israel on March 27 for killing and torturing Palestinians and on April 3, for the second year in a row—after having heard criticisms of U.S. courts for unfair, arbitrary, and racist use of the death penalty—called for a worldwide moratorium on death penalty executions. The commission criticized Iran on April 22 for using torture, amputations, and stonings as punishments. A day earlier it had refused for the first time since 1992 to call on Cuba to release people detained for political activities, and on October 14 the General Assembly, by a vote of 157–2 (U.S. and Israel), urged the U.S. to end its economic embargo of Cuba.

Peacekeeping. The Security Council on March 27 unanimously approved a 1,350-member all-African peacekeeping mission for the Central African Republic to succeed a comparable French force that departed on April 15. In July the UN reported that more civilians (17) than soldiers (13) had been killed during the year in UN missions around the world. On October 29 the UN asked countries contributing to peacekeeping operations to send no civilian police officers or military observers under age 25 and to send troops preferably over age 21 and never under 18. The objective was to ensure that only "experienced, mature, and well trained" people served as peacekeepers. The UN also wished to avoid any apparent conflict with its campaign against children in combat. At the year's end the U.S. and Somalia were the only two countries that had not ratified the Convention on the Rights of the Child, and the U.S. was blocking efforts to amend the treaty to raise the age limit for combat from 15 to 18. The U.S. wanted a 17-year-old cutoff because Americans could take part in some military service at that age.

Arms Trade. On April 23, at meetings of the UN Commission on Crime Prevention and Criminal Justice in Vienna, the U.S., Canada, and Brazil sponsored a resolution aimed at curbing illicit trafficking in firearms. It marked the first time that the U.S. had endorsed a UN resolution regulating firearms.

Drugs. Just before the General Assembly met on June 8–9 to discuss narcotics, more than 500 prominent people from throughout the world wrote to Secretary-General Annan stating that the war on drugs was "causing more harm than drug abuse itself." They believed that the UN's antidrug efforts had not been effective because illicit drugs remained the world's most lucrative cash crop. They charged that the antidrug war "empowered organized criminals, corrupted governments, . . . eroded internal security, stimulated violence and distorted economic markets and moral values." The Assembly called on governments to establish effective drug-prevention, treatment, and rehabilitation programs by 2003 and to develop strategies for eliminating or significantly reducing illicit drug crop cultivation by 2008.

Treaties. On July 17 in Rome the UN completed the statute for a permanent international criminal court. A total of 120 nations endorsed the treaty, 21 abstained, and 7 (China, Iraq, Israel, Libya, Qatar, Yemen, and the U.S.) opposed it. Negotiators resumed talks on November 2 in Buenos Aires, Arg., over details in the Kyoto Protocol (1997) on global warming. Though the treaty had been signed by more than 150 countries—including the U.S. on November 12 over congressional opposition—little progress had been made in cutting emissions of greenhouse gases throughout the world. The Buenos Aires meetings ended on November 13, and negotiators accepted a two-year schedule for adopting operational rules for cutting emissions of waste industrial gases believed to cause global warming.

(RICHARD N. SWIFT)

COMMONWEALTH OF NATIONS

Politically, Commonwealth attention in 1998 focused again on West Africa, where progress toward democracy was made. In Sierra Leone, within weeks of the February overthrow of the rebel government and restoration of Pres. Ahmad Tejan Kabbah,

Commonwealth experts went to the nation to help rebuild its judiciary and police, restore the mining sector, and develop projects for youth employment. A new police training school was established. These gains were threatened at year's end, however, as the rebels again approached Freetown.

In June Nigeria's relationship with the Commonwealth was transformed with the death of Gen. Sani Abacha. (*See* OBITUARIES.) Whereas Abacha had refused dialogue for nearly two years, his successor as head of state, Gen. Abdulsalam Abubakar (*see* BIOGRAPHIES), was on the phone to the Commonwealth secretary-general, Chief Emeka Anyaoku, within days of taking office. Abubakar sought technical support to help restore civilian rule. The Commonwealth response, following Nigeria's speedy release of political prisoners, was positive. Anyaoku, himself a Nigerian, met with Abubakar in Nigeria in July and at the same time visited the imprisoned Chief Moshood Abiola, perceived winner of the aborted 1993 elections. Abiola died days later. (*See* OBITUARIES.)

The Commonwealth offered technical assistance to the new Independent National Electoral Commission of Nigeria and discussed help in planning and observing elections rescheduled to install civilian rule in May 1999. At the same time, Nigeria, suspended from the Commonwealth since 1995, was told it could not return to full membership until a democratically elected government was in place. The Commonwealth Ministerial Action Group (CMAG) of foreign ministers met a Nigerian delegation led by the new foreign minister, Ignatius Olisemeka, in London on October 9. CMAG recommended that Commonwealth members begin lifting sanctions against Nigeria. Membership suspension, a more decisive step than any taken by the UN or the Organization of African Unity, had helped to confer international pariah status on the nation.

Precedent was set in Seychelles when a joint Commonwealth–La Francophonie observer group was sent to the nation for its presidential and National Assembly election (March 20–22). A team led by Sir John Compton, former prime minister of St. Lucia, included two Canadians—one representing English-speaking and one French-speaking Canada. The team expressed concern about how the election was conducted but said that the end result "accurately reflected the will of the people." A Commonwealth observer group led by Sir Lynden Pindling, a former prime minister of The Bahamas, went to Lesotho for the National Assembly elections on May 23. The group recorded concerns about the polling and disappointment that voting had not produced a multiparty parliament. Some proportional system of parliamentary representation was suggested. Later the government was almost overthrown. South African and Botswanan troops moved in. Serious fighting ensued, but the elected government survived.

When Commonwealth finance ministers met in Ottawa (September 30–October 1), British Chancellor of the Exchequer Gordon Brown (*see* BIOGRAPHIES) led moves to press international financial institutions to speed help for the heavily indebted poor countries. Commonwealth countries put themselves in the forefront of international pressure for debt relief at the subsequent World Bank–International Monetary Fund meetings.

(DEREK INGRAM)

EUROPEAN UNION

During the closing months of 1998, final preparations were made for the most ambitious step yet toward achieving a more united Europe—the launch in January 1999 of European economic and monetary union (EMU), including eventually a single European currency. These last stages of the operation were, however, overshadowed by the worldwide financial and economic crisis. In spite of international currency and stock market turmoil, particularly during the second half of the year, there was growing confidence that EMU would begin on schedule and lead to the introduction of the new single currency, the euro, into full circulation by the middle of 2002.

Commonwealth finance ministers (left to right) Gordon Brown (U.K.), Owen Arthur (Barbados), Chief Emeka Anyaoku (Commonwealth secretary-general), and Paul Martin (Canada) relax during a meeting in Ottawa, Ont., in September.

Lingering doubts about the capacity of the 11 European Union (EU) countries to accomplish the single-currency project gradually disappeared during the year. In sharp contrast to much of the rest of the world economy, the EU countries, and the core 11 single-currency economies in particular, continued to experience strong growth. At the end of October, however, the European Commission in Brussels conceded that the global economic downturn would slow the pace of the EU's economic expansion. Some detected in this admission the beginnings of a possible conflict between the strict rules laid down for currency stability in the development of the single currency and those wanting a stronger policy emphasis on growth and employment.

During the year technical planning for the stage-by-stage introduction of the euro was matched by growing debate on the need for increased integration of the economies of the 11 single-currency countries. The governments of those nations began discussions in the spring in Brussels about closer coordination of national policies on a range of economic issues, including taxation of capital savings and energy, employment, and increased competitiveness. In spite of some objections from the British government, which decided to keep sterling out of the single-currency project for the present, the 11 finance ministries met separately and with increasing frequency to prepare for monetary union.

The most difficult and politically sensitive of the issues to be resolved before EMU could be finally launched was the selection of the future president of the new European Central Bank (ECB). This was the subject of a lengthy and acrimonious summit meeting of EU heads of government in Brussels on May 2 and 3. Finally, the EU leaders chose the former president of the Dutch central bank, Wim Duisenberg (*see* BIOGRAPHIES), over a rival French candidate, Jean-Claude Trichet. This was accomplished, however, only after a political deal in which Duisenberg would retire before the end of his eight-year term to make way for Trichet.

After the appointment of Duisenberg, the focus of attention switched to the prospects for EU economic growth in the aftermath of the launch of EMU. By October it had become clear that the world economic crisis would adversely affect the rate of economic growth in the EU countries during 1999. The European Commission conceded that overall EU economic growth in 1999 would be 2.4%, compared with earlier forecasts of 3.2%. The Commission and the ECB continued to insist that the single-currency countries would not face outright recession, unlike much of Asia, Russia, parts of Latin America, and, possibly, the U.S.

At the year-end EU summit, held in Vienna, progress in converting economic growth into improved levels of employment was critically scrutinized. At the end of September, the European Commission issued a progress report on the measures taken by all 15 member governments to introduce greater labour market flexibility, improved training and education, and other measures to stimulate employment. The Commission warned EU member nations that, in spite of a reduction in the numbers out of work in 1998, unemployment, at more than 15% of the labour force in the EU as a whole, remained unacceptably high.

The election of a Social Democratic–Greens coalition government in Germany during October was widely seen as marking a clear shift in the political balance of power between right and left in the EU. The new German government, headed by Gerhard Schröder (*see* BIOGRAPHIES), soon made it clear that it favoured a more interventionist economic policy than had the outgoing Christian Democratic administration led by Helmut Kohl.

By the autumn months a new political alliance of left-of-centre governments, led by France and Germany, was emerging within the EU. This was further reinforced by the arrival in October of a new left-of-centre coalition in Italy led by Massimo D'Alema. As a consequence, socialist or social democratic parties led or participated in 13 of the 15 EU member governments by the end of 1998.

During its six-month presidency of the EU, the United Kingdom had the responsibility for the launch of the other major EU project—its enlargement to include new member states from Central and Eastern Europe as well as from the Mediterranean region. At a heads of government conference in Cardiff, Wales, on June 15–16, the EU agreed that negotiations should begin with an initial group of six applicant member states: the Czech Republic, Poland, Hungary, Slovenia, Cyprus, and Estonia. It was also agreed that a number of other applicants, including Bulgaria, Romania, Latvia, Lithuania, and Slovakia, needed a longer period to achieve economic and political reforms before accession negotiations could begin. Those countries were assured, however, that if they made sufficient progress toward economic and political reform, they might be included in the first "fast-track" group of applicants. As a result of the general election in Malta in September, that nation's government reinstated the country's bid for EU membership, which had been withdrawn four years earlier by the Labour Party government.

The fact that Turkey was not chosen for formal membership negotiations caused a worsening in relations between that nation and the EU. The Turkish government declined to participate in a wider conference on European cooperation held in London in June, protesting that it was being discriminated against unfairly because it was predominantly Islamic. The EU governments strongly denied this charge and insisted that the main obstacles to Turkey's eventual EU membership were related to its poor human rights record.

At the Cardiff conference the EU leaders adopted an ambitious program of internal policy reform designed to allow the EU to undertake the heavy additional responsibilities that would accompany enlargement. These were set out in a major strategic document, Agenda 2000, which included measures to reform the EU budget and its major spending policies—most notably the Common Agricultural Policy and measures to help the economies of the less-developed member states.

At a special heads of government summit held at the end of October under the Austrian presidency, which took over from the U.K. for the second half of the year, a start was made on discussions about further institutional reform of the EU. The meeting, held in Austria near Klagenfurt, concen-

Chosen in May as the president of the European Central Bank, Wim Duisenberg of The Netherlands (right) shakes hands with his chief rival for the office, Jean-Claude Trichet of France.

trated on the issue of "subsidiarity," the doctrine under which the EU should decide only those matters that could not be dealt with effectively at the national or regional level.

EU leaders made it clear, however, that a range of other constitutional reforms would have to be settled during 1999 before the conclusion of negotiations with the "first-wave" accession countries. Among the issues that were not resolved during 1998 was a further extension of the principle of decisions by majority vote (rather than unanimity) in the EU Council of Ministers. Differences also remained about a proposed "reweighting" of the votes of member states in the Council in order to favour those countries with larger populations. Finally, the 15 EU governments had to agree on steps to streamline the European Commission in advance of expanding its membership to perhaps 30 or more members over the next decade or two.

Once again, in 1998 the challenges of foreign and security policy proved to be among the most daunting to face the EU. Although the new Treaty of European Union, agreed upon at Amsterdam in December 1997, included provisions to strengthen the so-called EU Common Foreign and Security Policy, these could not come into force until the treaty was ratified in all 15 member nations.

By the end of 1998, it was evident that this process would not be concluded before the middle of 1999.

The outbreak of conflict in the Serbian province of Kosovo highlighted the weakness and disunity of the EU in foreign and security affairs. Open conflict broke out during the summer when the Yugoslav government of Slobodan Milosevic used military force to repress the Albanian-speaking majority population of Kosovo. It became clear that military action by NATO might be necessary because of the inability of the EU countries to take joint military action on their own.

It had earlier been agreed that NATO's European member states should take more direct responsibility for handling purely European security crises. As 1998 drew to a close, however, there was still no formal agreement between NATO and the Western European Union, the security and defense organization of the EU, for NATO military resources to be made available for purely European peacekeeping or peacemaking missions.

The emergence of the global financial crisis, begun in Asia in the second half of 1997, led to new questions about the pace and direction of future world trade liberalization moves. In spite of proposals by the

European Commission, there was little enthusiasm in either the U.S. or the EU for a transatlantic free-trade area. Some concern was expressed on both sides of the Atlantic in the closing months of 1998 that with slower economic growth expected in 1999, there could be a slide into trade protectionism. The U.S. in particular pressed the EU to open up its markets to increased volumes of cheap Asian exports, partly to take the pressure off American markets.

During 1998 relations between the EU and Russia deteriorated, notably after the economic crisis during the summer led to a large devaluation of the ruble and to fears that Russia might reverse its policies of economic reform. Similar concerns surfaced at the end of the year about the future direction of reform in Ukraine lest that also affect relations with the EU. On the other hand, during the year closer links were forged between the EU and regional organizations in Latin America, a process that culminated in the decision to call an EU–Latin-American heads of government summit in 1999.   (JOHN PALMER)

COMMONWEALTH OF INDEPENDENT STATES

In its most crisis-ridden year since the fall of the Soviet Union, Russia careened from political shakeups to economic meltdown. The nation's severe problems weakened its position in the Commonwealth of Independent States (CIS) and in the world at large. On March 23 Russian Pres. Boris Yeltsin fired his entire Cabinet, including Prime Minister Viktor Chernomyrdin. Chernomyrdin's replacement, Sergey Kiriyenko, was unable to prevent Russia's descent to total financial collapse. On August 17, with state coffers empty, Moscow devalued the ruble and imposed a moratorium on repayment of foreign debts. Within days the country defaulted on

billions of dollars in treasury bills and bonds, banks lost liquidity, and millions of Russians lost savings and wages. Kiriyenko was sacked. Russia's drama, against the background of the Asian economic crisis, exacerbated an ongoing flight of Western capital from the less-developed nations. The effect on other CIS economies was widespread.

Ukraine held parliamentary elections in March. The Communist Party and its allies significantly increased their representation by capturing 40% of the seats in the 450-member parliament. Both the democrats in the centrist Ukrainian Popular Movement and the party of Pres. Leonid Kuchma fared poorly (32 and 17 seats, respectively). The results, coupled with an upcoming presidential election in 1999, left Ukrainian politics in a stalemate.

Armenian Pres. Levon Ter-Petrosyan resigned in February over disagreements with an international peace plan for Nagorno-Karabakh, a territory within Azerbaijan inhabited mostly by Armenians. Calls by his successor, Robert Kocharyan, to resume peace talks were rejected by Azerbaijan in this long-standing conflict. Nevertheless, except for a violent interlude in Georgia's Abkhazia republic, the Caucasus nations as a whole passed a year of relative calm.

Among the Central Asian nations, Uzbekistan and Tajikistan joined with Russia in calling for a united front against the militant Islamic Taliban rulers in Afghanistan. The idea foundered, however, because of a lack of interest in other Central Asian nations. The Central Asians did, however, continue to explore common action against such regional problems as drug trafficking. An evolving development at the year's end was moves against his political opposition by Pres. Nursultan Nazarbayev of Kazakstan, who was running for reelection in 1999.

Russia's post-August prime minister, Yevgeny Primakov (*see* BIOGRAPHIES), late

in the year appeared to be setting a lower priority on Moscow's relations with the West. Concurrently, his officials sought to restore Russia's standing in the CIS with promises of Commonwealth-wide reform. In December Yeltsin and Belarusian Pres. Alyaksandr Lukashenka signed an agreement to begin unification of the two countries' currencies and create a common citizenship.

(KATHLEEN MIHALISKO)

MULTINATIONAL AND REGIONAL ORGANIZATIONS

Severely challenged by the social and political unrest produced by the Asian economic crisis, foreign ministers of the Association of Southeast Asian Nations (ASEAN, whose members included Brunei, Indonesia, Laos, Malaysia, Myanmar [Burma], the Philippines, Singapore, Thailand, and Vietnam) held their annual meeting in Manila on July 24, 1998. ASEAN's reluctance to "interfere" in its members' internal affairs rendered the organization incapable, according to some observers, of providing a concerted response to the year's financial disasters. Thereafter, ASEAN had to face serious challenges to its effectiveness on economic, political, and environmental fronts. The foreign ministers hoped, nonetheless, to build on the 30 years of peace that the organization had maintained among its members and move forward to establish an ASEAN free-trade area by 2003 and to continue nurturing the Asia-Pacific regional institutions, especially the ASEAN Regional Forum on Security.

The ministers had hoped that free and fair elections on July 26 would pave the way for them to admit Cambodia into ASEAN at a meeting in Hanoi in December. Admitting Cambodia would complete the formal inclusion in ASEAN of all 10 countries of Southeast Asia, a long-standing objective. Cambodia had been scheduled to join early in 1998, but a violent internal power struggle forced a postponement. Irregularities during the election in July delayed its invitation to join the organization in 1998, but the decision was made to admit Cambodia soon.

U.S. Secretary of State Madeleine Albright told delegates to the annual ASEAN Regional Forum on July 27 that the political situation in Myanmar was worsening: "Arrests aimed at decimating the opposition continue. Members of legal political parties are being prevented from traveling in their own country. The Burmese economy is falling apart. A whole generation of young people is being lost as universities, and now even high schools, stay closed for fear of unrest." Her remarks were delivered out of concern for the health and safety of Myanmar opposition leader Daw Aung San Suu Kyi, who was at the time being held prisoner in her automobile 50 km (30 mi) west of Yangon (Rangoon) after she had tried to drive 109 km (68 mi) farther west to meet with members of her political party. Albright was in effect challenging ASEAN's contention that the way to improve the record of Myanmar on human rights was to "engage" the country in the international political process. On August 13 Myanmar rejected a request by UN Secretary-General Kofi Annan to receive a special emissary to discuss "current development" in the nation.

The Philippines and Thailand, two of the most democratic of the ASEAN members,

While hospitalized in Moscow in December, Russian Pres. Boris Yeltsin (left) is encouraged by his prime minister, Yevgeny Primakov, to recover fully from his bout with pneumonia before returning to work.

In San Juan, Puerto Rico, Mayor Sila Calderon (left) and Popular Democratic Party leader Anibal Acevedo Vila celebrate following a nationwide referendum, in which voters endorsed the status of Puerto Rico as a commonwealth.

also spoke out against the repressive policies of Myanmar. Myanmar had hoped to use ASEAN as a shield against criticism from the West and had not anticipated criticism from inside the organization. Myanmar officials called all the criticisms "presumptuous" and insisted that it would adhere to its own agenda.

Also during the year ASEAN "strongly deplored" the nuclear weapons tests conducted by India and Pakistan in May. The tests created regional tensions and struck a serious blow at efforts to halt the spread of nuclear weapons, according to ASEAN members.

Argentina and Brazil reported on July 24 to a regional economic summit meeting of the Southern Cone Common Market (Mercosur) in Ushuaia, Arg., that they had failed to complete a long-awaited agreement for common tariffs on automobiles. They did agree to drop all tariffs in 2000 for cars and parts produced in the Mercosur countries, which also included Uruguay and Paraguay.

Mercosur in 1998 reported with pride that since its creation in 1991, the total international trade of the member countries had doubled; by 1998 it had become the fourth largest trading bloc in the world. The organization continued to discuss standardizing its external tariffs and creating a common social security treaty. Argentina, which assumed the rotating presidency of Mercosur in June, raised the possibility of creating a common currency throughout the region during the decade beginning in 2010. The idea emulated the common currency plans in Europe, which were to take effect in 1999. In a book published in July, Jagdish Bhagwati, former adviser to the General

Agreement on Tariffs and Trade and an economist at Columbia University, New York City, discussed the possibility that Mercosur's high external tariffs had caused its members to import from one another even when it would have been more efficient to buy elsewhere. (RICHARD N. SWIFT)

DEPENDENT STATES

Europe and the Atlantic. In January 1998 the U.K. announced that its 13 remaining dependent territories would be recategorized as British overseas territories (BOTs). The question of British citizenship for 11 of the BOTs, which had been debated since before the handover of Hong Kong to China in 1997, remained under review. Residents of two BOTs, Gibraltar and the Falkland Islands/Islas Malvinas, already had British citizenship.

Spain appeared to reverse its long-held policy of refusing direct talks with Gibraltar when it issued an invitation in April to the territory's chief minister, Peter Caruana. Spanish Foreign Minister Abel Matutes later seemed to back away from the invitation, however, and at year's end no talks had been scheduled. In July the U.K. and Spain settled one bilateral dispute and agreed to allow NATO to expand its use of Gibraltar as a communications centre. Relations with Argentina improved somewhat in October, when Pres. Carlos Menem expressed regret over Argentina's participation in the 1982 war with the U.K. over the Falkland Islands and made his first visit to the U.K. Shortly before Menem's historic visit, however, the Argentine Senate reasserted the country's claim of sovereignty over the islands, passing

bills that would impose fines on firms drilling for offshore oil around the Falklands and on boats found fishing in the same waters.

Denmark faced new governments in both of its overseas territories in 1998. In Greenland Jonathan Motzfeldt, who had been prime minister during 1979–91, was returned to office in late 1997. He vowed to

Dependent States[1]	
Australia	**Portugal**
Christmas Island	Macau
Cocos (Keeling) Islands	**United Kingdom**
Norfolk Island	Anguilla
Denmark	Bermuda
Faroe Islands	British Virgin Islands
Greenland	Cayman Islands
France	Falkland Islands
French Guiana	Gibraltar
French Polynesia	Guernsey
Guadeloupe	Isle of Man
Martinique	Jersey
Mayotte	Montserrat
New Caledonia	Pitcairn Island
Réunion	Saint Helena
Saint Pierre and Miquelon	Tristan Da Cunha
Wallis and Futuna	Turks and Caicos Islands
Netherlands, The	**United States**
Aruba	American Samoa
Netherlands Antilles	Guam
New Zealand	Northern Mariana Islands
Cook Islands	Puerto Rico
Niue	Virgin Islands (of the U.S.)
Tokelau	

[1]Excludes territories (1) to which Antarctic Treaty is applicable in whole or in part, (2) without permanent civilian population, (3) without internationally recognized civilian government (Western Sahara), or (4) representing unadjudicated unilateral or multilateral territorial claims.

push for more local input in upcoming negotiations between the U.S. and Denmark concerning U.S. military bases on the island. Motzfeldt's government also approved a second permit for offshore oil drilling in June. Spiraling unemployment (mainly due to a slump in fisheries) and Danish involvement in a 1993 local banking scandal continued to stir anti-Copenhagen sentiment in the Faroe Islands. Parties seeking greater independence made gains in elections to the Faroes' 32-seat Loftingid (parliament) in May. The new three-party coalition comprised Prime Minister Anfinn Kallsberg's pro-autonomy People's Party (8 seats), the pro-independence Republican Party (8 seats), and the Home Rule Party (7 seats).

Caribbean and Bermuda. The opposition Progressive Labour Party (PLP) finally ended the United Bermuda Party's (UBP's) 30-year hold on power in Bermuda in November, when it won the general election by 26 seats to 14. Since its establishment in 1963, the PLP had primarily represented the interests of the majority black population, whereas the UBP was largely supported by the white electorate and the business community. The challenges facing Prime Minister Jennifer Smith's new administration included safeguarding privileges for offshore banks, which were under threat by the European Union (EU), and dealing with a nascent drug-transshipment problem.

The government of the British Virgin Islands (BVI) also reacted angrily to proposals from the EU on so-called unfair tax competition, which sought to deprive offshore banking havens of their tax-efficient status. Small, mainly colonial, territories like the BVI and Bermuda traditionally earned a substantial part of their revenue from registration fees paid by offshore banks and other financial institutions. With the U.K.'s remaining Caribbean colonies due to assume a new status as BOTs, BVI and other offshore havens insisted they would fight to preserve their tax privileges.

The Chances Peak volcano in the Soufrière Hills in Montserrat continued to rumble during the year. Eruptions of hot rocks and ash persisted into mid-November, and the central and southern portions of the island remained uninhabitable. Experts warned that those areas would continue to be threatened by the volcano for several years. The U.K., meanwhile, had drawn up a £75 million (about U.S. $125 million) development program for the north, to be undertaken during 1998–2001. The British government admitted having made mistakes in its handling of the volcano crisis. The island's resident population was estimated to be down to a mere 3,200, compared with 11,000 when the volcano came to life in 1995.

Anguilla began moves during 1998 to upgrade its constitution to one similar to that of Bermuda and hoped to have it in place by the time of the next general election, due in March 1999. Chief Minister Robert Hughes launched a public debate on the matter during the year. In 1998 the British-appointed governor had complete executive authority over the island.

The Netherlands Antilles acquired a new government in June, after months of uncertainty following the January 1998 elections. The new administration was headed by Prime Minister Susanne ("Suzy") Camelia-Römer of the National People's Party and contained representatives from six different parties.

On December 13 a slight majority (50.2%) of Puerto Ricans voted for "none of the above" in a plebiscite ballot and thus rejected full independence from the U.S., quasi-independence known as "free association," and statehood in favour of continuing as a commonwealth. It was the second time in a decade Puerto Rican voters had chosen to retain the status quo.

Pacific. In American Samoa the government faced a financial crisis, defaulting on payments on highway construction, harbour maintenance, and medical treatment in Hawaii. The situation was eased by a tem-

Hong Kong citizens walk under election posters through the rain to vote in May in the region's first election since it became a part of China.

ANAT GIVON—AP/WIDE WORLD

porary short workweek, a freeze on government hiring, increased taxes on alcohol and tobacco, and advance tax payments from the area's largest company. The budget for financial year 1998–99 was set at $216 million, including $33 million in U.S. federal grants. The economy was also hit by the planned closure (because of immigration difficulties and federal trade laws) of a garment factory employing 300 workers, mostly Chinese on short-term work permits. In September an attempt to impeach Gov. Tauese Sunia for abuse of office was initiated. In the November general elections U.S. Rep. Eni Faleomavaega was reelected with 86% of the vote, but in elections for the local House of Assembly, 7 of 13 sitting members were defeated. El Niño weather patterns brought problems to American Samoa and other Pacific islands throughout the year. (*See* Spotlight: *El Niño's Impact on Oceania.*)

Talks between the U.S. government and the Commonwealth of the Northern Mariana Islands over relative rights and powers made little progress. The federal government sought to control immigration and wages in the territory in light of concerns over the garment industry. With more than 30 factories

and 40,000 Asian migrant workers, the Northern Marianas' economy was seriously affected by the Asian economic crisis, which also caused a collapse in tourism. A budget of $249 million was approved for the 1999 financial year, with the government finding it difficult to raise the matching funds necessary to maximize opportunities for federal grants.

In November 1997 Manihiki in the northern Cook Islands had been struck by Cyclone Martin, which killed 19 people, destroyed most of the houses and crops, and led to about half of the island's population's being evacuated to Rarotonga. The government continued with its program of economic restructuring, which had seen the public service halved and more emphasis on private-sector development. One consequence was a sharp increase in out-migration, mostly to New Zealand, with a population decline from 19,000 to 16,500. The government's budget for 1998–99 projected revenue of $NZ 46 million (U.S. $23.2 million) and expenditure of $NZ 43 million (U.S. $21.7 million).

In July the French government announced the demolition and closure of the Mururoa nuclear-testing site, leaving only basic infrastructure facilities, including the harbour, airport, and protective sea walls. France, which had conducted 193 nuclear tests in Polynesia during 1966–96, mostly at Mururoa, would continue to monitor the health of those living around the former test zone. After the 1996 elections were annulled in 11 of the 41 seats for the Territorial Assembly, new elections were held in May 1998. Seven of the 11 seats went to the supporters of the territorial president, Gaston Flosse. The elections were followed by allegations of vote buying.

In a November 1998 referendum, New Caledonians voted overwhelmingly for continuing ties with France but having a greater degree of autonomy. The referendum (confined to those who had resided in the territory continuously since the signing of the Matignon Accords in 1988) was based on the Nouméa Accord negotiated in April, which recognized indigenous rights and cultures and provided for future governance through provincial and territorial assemblies. France would retain control over foreign affairs, defense, public order, security, and finance. New Caledonia was invited to join the South Pacific Forum from 1999 with observer status.

East Asia. Hong Kong marked its first full year as a special administrative region of China by holding the first free and open election under the Chinese flag on May 24. The election to the Legislative Council brought back into office most of Hong Kong's well-known democratic leaders, including Martin Lee, who had refused, as a matter of principle, to serve on the interim, appointed provisional legislature. Against all expectations, the voter turnout rose dramatically, 53% against 36% in the last election before the handover. The year's second landmark event was the opening on July 6 of a new $20 billion airport built on a reclaimed island off Chek Lap Kok Island.

The jobless rate in Hong Kong reached a 15-year high of 5% by mid-1998, and the year was marred by a deepening recession, worries over the stability of the local currency, and an unprecedented decision by the government to intervene massively in its local stock market. The government spent approximately $15 billion of its $96.5 billion in foreign currency reserves buying shares in top local companies. (See *China*, below.)

Negotiations continued during 1998 for the smooth transfer of Macau from Portuguese to Chinese sovereignty on Dec. 20, 1999. In March China established a Preparatory Committee of the Macau Special Administrative Region, which passed a motion in November that would allow Sino-Portuguese residents of mixed parentage to retain their Portuguese passports after the handover. Chinese triad gangs were blamed for the ongoing violence in Macau, which included gangland-style shootings and car bombs. The Portuguese governor general, Vasco Rocha Vieira, said local police (aided by reinforcements from Portugal) were making progress in the fight against organized crime in the colony, which boasted popular—and lucrative—gambling casinos. In September China triggered concerns when it announced plans to deploy troops in Macau to handle national security after the handover.

(TODD CROWELL; BARRIE MACDONALD; DAVID RENWICK; MELINDA C. SHEPHERD)

ANTARCTICA

Ice averaging 2,160 m (7,085 ft) in thickness covers about 98% of the continent of Antarctica, which has an area of 14 million sq km (5.4 million sq mi). There is no indigenous human population, and there is no land-based industry. Human activity consists mainly of scientific research. The 43-nation Antarctic Treaty is the managerial mechanism for the region south of latitude 60° S, which includes all of Antarctica. The treaty reserves the area for peaceful purposes, encourages cooperation in science, prescribes environmental protection, allows inspections to verify adherence, and defers the issue of territorial sovereignty.

A historic new agreement, the Protocol on Environmental Protection to the Antarctic Treaty, entered into force on Jan. 14, 1998, after its ratification by the 26 Antarctic Treaty consultative (voting) nations. The protocol, which had been drafted in 1991, strengthened the original (1959) Antarctic Treaty, which designated Antarctica as a natural reserve devoted to peace and science. A widely noted feature of the protocol was its prohibition of mining and other activities relating to mineral resources, except for scientific research. More generally, it committed researchers to environmental impact assessments for both governmental and private proposed activities. It increased protection of plants and animals and their ecosystems throughout the region, and it designated certain areas for even more stringent protection. It prohibited or limited disposal of waste and discharge of pollutants. The protocol gave priority to scientific research, acknowledging the unique opportunities that Antarctica offered for understanding regional and global processes. Research groups had to make joint plans to respond to environmental emergencies, and compliance provisions included compulsory dispute settlement between member nations.

Fisheries in Antarctic waters reported that during the 1997–98 year (July 1–June 30) they landed 92,456 metric tons, of which 87% was krill (*Euphasia superba*) and 12% was the Patagonian toothfish (*Dissostichus eleginoides*). The highly marketable toothfish is an extremely slow-growing species that can live for more than 50 years and reach 2 m (6 ft) in length. The catch was about the same as reported the previous year. Japan and Poland led in the krill catch, and Chile, Australia, France, and South Africa caught the most Patagonian toothfish.

A major concern in recent years had been the high catch of the Patagonian toothfish, over and above the official numbers, that had taken place without regard to fishing regulations. Scientists estimated that during the 1997–98 season this unregulated fishing landed five to six times more than the regulated fishery and would likely affect the sustainability of the toothfish stock. The concern also extended to the correspondingly higher incidental mortality of seabirds caused by longline fishing. Allegedly illegal fishing in Antarctic waters in 1998 resulted in the seizure (by France and Australia) of at least eight fishing ships. Member nations of the Convention on the Regulation of Antarctic Mineral Resource Activities in mid-1998 were considering methods to combat unregulated fishing, including use of satellite-linked vessel monitoring, a vessel registry, improved controls over national fishing vessels, improved controls on fish landings and sales, and sanctions to prevent trade in fish harvested in an unregulated way.

Tourism in Antarctica rose substantially. A total of 9,604 tourists visited in the 1997–98 summer, up from more than 7,300 the previous year. Nearly all were passengers on 13 commercial ships that made 92 trips. About 200, however, arrived on yachts or commercial aircraft. The U.S. was the country of origin of 43% of the year's shipborne tourists. Germany, Australia, the U.K., Japan, and Switzerland also contributed significant numbers. The Antarctic Peninsula (Antarctica's northernmost region) was the most popular destination, but two tour ship visits were made to McMurdo, a U.S. research station that, at latitude 78° S, was Antarctica's southernmost port.

The U.S. Navy in late 1998 began its last season of Antarctic operations. The withdrawal would close a 160-year history that began in the late 1830s with the navy's U.S. Exploring Expedition, which proved Antarctica a continent. The Air National Guard took over navy flying, and private firms were given other responsibilities that the navy had performed in recent decades to support research sponsored by the National Science Foundation.

Science continued as Antarctica's main endeavour in 1998. Much of the research was performed to understand the continent and its role in world processes, especially climate change. Because of the extremely cold and dry atmosphere over interior Antarctica, astronomy and astrophysics flourished, particularly at the geographic South Pole, where the U.S. operated a year-round station. In all, 18 nations operated 36 year-round research stations. They and nine others, all Antarctic Treaty members, operated numerous additional summer research sites on the continent.

On Vega Island off the Antarctic Peninsula, Argentine and U.S. scientists found a fossil tooth of the first duck-billed dinosaur, or hadrosaur, to be discovered outside the Americas. The tooth was in sands 65 million–70 million years old, from the Cretaceous Period. The find provided additional support for the existence of a land bridge between South America and Antarctica at that time. Scientists believed that dinosaurs and probably marsupial mammals used the bridge to disperse from the Americas to Australia via Antarctica. The hadrosaur discovery implied that Antarctica had a much different climate at that time, one that would support a robust ecosystem that provided vegetation to support these large plant eaters.

In another find nearby, an ancient type of marine community typical of 450 million years ago resurfaced in fossils of near-modern age—fossil communities only 40 million years old dominated by brittle stars and sea lilies (marine invertebrates similar to starfish). As Antarctica entered its current deep freeze, scientists believed, cooling ocean temperatures suppressed predation and increased nutrient upwelling in the ocean surrounding the continent, which allowed the ancient creatures to reestablish themselves. The discovery revealed the impact global climate change can have on marine life.

The Antarctic ozone hole was the largest ever in 1998, extending over an area nearly twice the size of the continent and extending higher above the Earth's surface than had previously been measured. A deep winter chill in the stratosphere, rather than increased manmade chlorofluorocarbons (CFCs), got the blame; the cold increased the amount of clouds on whose surfaces CFCs destroy ozone. Scientists revised their estimate of the beginning of ozone recovery to 2015 for lower latitudes, but they said that the effect of greenhouse gases, which ironically chill the high stratosphere even while warming the lower atmosphere, would keep the Antarctic ozone hole as extensive as ever.

The West Antarctic Ice Sheet, which if it melted would raise sea level some 5.5 m (18 ft), provided unsettling news in 1998. Researchers sifting through mud drilled from underneath it reported that it had disintegrated to next to nothing at least once in the last 1.3 million years. In addition, space radar images hinted that Pine Island Glacier, a major ice outlet, was retreating inland by more than 1 km (0.62 mi) a year, a rate that most models indicated would speed up if it continued. Collapse of the entire ice sheet could happen within two centuries, raising sea level at an alarming rate for the world's coastal areas. Other models suggested a slower collapse, in 4,000–7,000 years.

(GUY G. GUTHRIDGE)

ARCTIC REGIONS

Gov. Tony Knowles of Alaska in 1998 announced the first new North Slope oil field in 10 years. The Badami oil field, located about 55 km (1 km=0.62 mi) from Prudhoe Bay, was owned by BP Ltd. The field's recoverable reserves were estimated at 120 million bbl and were expected to produce up to 30,000 bbl of oil a day during its 25-year life. Construction of the site injected $200 million into the Alaskan economy, and the state was expected to receive $350 million in royalties during the life of the field.

Under a controversial plan announced in August, an area of almost two million

hectares (1 ha=2.47 ac) in the National Petroleum Reserve on Alaska's North Slope would be reopened to oil and gas leasing. U.S. Secretary of the Interior Bruce Babbitt indicated that the government was seeking to achieve in the reserve a balance between protecting sensitive environmental areas that provide habitat for caribou, grizzly bears, and birds and allowing drilling on land that industry believed was rich in oil. The nine million-hectare reserve was created in 1923 to ensure that the U.S. Navy had access to oil in a national emergency. According to industry estimates, it may hold between 400 million and one billion barrels of oil, far less than the Prudhoe Bay oil fields to the east.

The plan did not affect the Arctic National Wildlife Refuge, farther east along the Beaufort Sea coast. In May a U.S. Geological Survey report increased the mid-range estimate of oil under the refuge to 20.7 billion bbl, up from the 13.8 billion bbl previously reported in 1987. The increased estimates were based on data from drilling sites outside the refuge, new computer analyses of seismic data collected in 1987, and the impacts of improved oil-recovery technologies that reduced the cost of production and the adverse environmental effects.

In August it was reported that a Canadian company, Foothills Pipelines Ltd., had committed itself to a 22% interest in a new pipeline project—the Alaskan North Slope Project Sponsor Agreement. The multibillion-dollar project would involve the building of gas-conditioning facilities on the North Slope, a 1,300-km pipeline to Valdez, a gas-liquefaction facility, and tankers to transport the gas to markets. The agreement was seen as an encouragement for future northern natural gas development in the western Canadian Arctic. Governor Knowles pointed out that Alaska's North Slope was endowed with an estimated one trillion cubic metres of natural gas (1 cu m=35.3 cu ft). He indicated that the project would create an estimated 10,000 construction jobs as well as 600 permanent jobs operating the pipeline and other facilities.

In September the *Yukon News* reported on a meeting in Anchorage, Alaska, of the Northern Forum, a nongovernmental organization of 22 regional governments—territories, prefectures, provinces, and counties—from across the Arctic. Among the problems discussed were air pollution in the polar regions; reindeer herding in Norway, Sweden, Finland, and Russia; the management of fish stocks that were being depleted in Norway, Alaska, and Russia; forest-management issues in northern Sweden and the Yukon in Canada; tourist development; exchange programs for students; and the possible creation of an international Arctic development bank.

The government of the Northwest Territories (NWT) in Canada laid out its vision for administering the western portion of the NWT after the eastern portion became a separate political entity—called Nunavut—in April 1999. The controversial proposal was for a new kind of "partnership government" between native leaders and the territorial government to govern the western NWT as equal partners. The proposal also called on the Canadian government to transfer control of oil, gas, and minerals to the people who lived in the North. The fact that the NWT government might eventually become unrepresentative of all the people in its territory—split evenly between the native and nonnative population—went to the heart of one of the most sensitive issues in the North.

In a judgment known as the Delgamuukw case, the Supreme Court of Canada ruled in December 1997 that native people have a constitutional and historic right to their ancestral lands and that governments cannot override that right without appropriate consultation and compensation. The court also ruled that oral history—information and knowledge passed from generation to generation—must be regarded as serious evidence in determining native claims. One result of the Delgamuukw case was that the Inuit and other native people of Arctic Labrador and Quebec were able to challenge governments successfully concerning the development of several large projects, including the nickel mine at Voisey Bay being developed by Inco. Ltd. and the proposed $12 billion development of the hydroelectric potential of the lower Churchill River in Labrador.

The $19.5 million Project SHEBA—short for Surface Heat Budget of the Arctic Ocean—ended in mid-October, one year after the Canadian Coast Guard ship *Des Groseilliers* had rammed its way 200 km into the Arctic Ocean ice pack. The icebreaker was allowed to freeze there as a floating research station while as many as 15 crew and 45 scientists from Canada, Japan, The Netherlands, and the U.S. conducted experiments in temporary buildings set up on the ice surrounding the vessel. The study's main purpose was to look at the impact of global warming on the polar ice pack, half of which freezes and refreezes each year. Some scientists predicted that if the Earth heated up by means of global warming, the ice could vanish. Other SHEBA studies found that the Arctic Ocean was more productive than scientists had predicted and that mercury, one of the contaminants measured, was found in snow at 20 times the level found in southern Canada. During its year-long drift *Des Groseilliers* traveled 11–19 km a day.

New atmospheric and scientific data reported in September were consistent with computer models that predicted that higher latitudes would be disproportionately impacted by higher temperatures. For example, while summer temperatures were 4.86° C (2.7° F) above normal across Canada, they were more than 9° C (5° F) above normal in parts of the NWT. These higher temperatures matched other data recorded throughout the world. The *Yukon News* reported in August that global warming would likely prove detrimental to the native subsistence economy. Trapping, for example, would be affected because prime fur requires freezing temperatures, which were now occurring later in the winter, when there is little daylight.

Following an international agreement reached in Scotland in June, Greenland closed its commercial salmon fishery, cutting off an industry that caught a large number of fish as they headed home to Canadian rivers. This was the first time in history no commercial fishermen were allowed to catch Canadian salmon in the eastern Arctic. Canada had previously shut down the commercial fisheries on its east coast. The closing down of these fisheries was estimated to have saved approximately 25,000 salmon in 1998.

A British explorer, David Hempleman-Adams, achieved the last leg of what was called the "adventurers' grand slam" when he completed a 965.5-km journey on foot to reach the geographic North Pole at the end of April. He previously had climbed the highest peaks of all seven continents and had reached three of the four poles, magnetic and geographic, both north and south. He and his Norwegian trekking partner, Rune Gjeldnes, completed the journey on skis 54 days after leaving their starting point on Ward Hunt Island in Canada's Arctic.

(KENNETH DE LA BARRE)

By arriving at the geographic North Pole in April, David Hempleman-Adams of the U.K. (right, with daughter Camilla and Norwegian explorer Rune Gjeldnes) achieved the "adventurer's grand slam"—by climbing the highest mountain on each continent and reaching the two geographic and two magnetic poles.

WORLD LEGISLATIVE ELECTION RESULTS

The following table is a guide to the principal political parties and coalitions of the world. All countries that were independent on Dec. 31, 1998, are included, except the Vatican City State. In most instances parties are included only if represented in elected parliaments (in the lower house in bicameral legislatures). (Party names may be condensed or omitted for reasons of space or to more clearly indicate party groupings.) The first column under "Parliamentary representation" indicates the number of seats obtained in the most recent general election and excludes nonelective seats and seats still undecided. If only a portion of the seats were at stake, the figure given indicates the total number of seats held by each party after the election. The column in parentheses represents the number of seats won in the penultimate election. Single-party penultimate election results may be combined if a coalition was formed at the most recent election. The date of the most recent election follows the name of the country.

The capital letters in the column "Affiliation" show the relative positions of the parties within the political spectrum of each country. The key chosen is as follows: ER-extreme right; R-right; CR-centre right; C-centre; CL-centre left; SD-social democratic; S-strictly defined socialist; L-broadly defined left (may or may not be Marxist); K-strictly defined communist; and EL-extreme left. In addition, within some countries there are political organizations that exist chiefly to advance a special interest as distinct from a political orientation. These are represented by lowercase letters as follows: x-parties that have repudiated former communist affiliation; e-parties based on distinct regional, ethnic, or linguistic identity; r-parties based on religion, often fundamentalist; g-environmental, or Green; and p-parties based largely on personalities.

The number in the column "Voting strength" indicates proportions of the valid votes cast for the respective parties. (STEPHEN NEHER; MELINDA C. SHEPHERD)

World Legislative Election Results

Country Name of party	Affiliation	Voting strength (%)	Parliamentary representation	
Afghanistan				
Islamic emirate from October 1997				
Albania (June–July 1997)				
Democratic Party	CR	25.7	29	(122)
Social Democratic Party	S	2.5	8	—
Socialist Party of Albania	x	52.8	101	(10)
Greek minority party	e	2.8	4	(3)
Others	—	16.2	13	(5)
Algeria (June 1997)				
Islamic Salvation Front	ERr		*	
Islamic Renaissance Movement (Nahda)	r	9.9	34	
Movement of the Islamic Society (Hamas)	Cr	16.8	69	
National Democratic Rally	C	38.3	156	
National Liberation Front	S	16.1	62	
Pro-Berber parties	e	9.9	39	
Other parties	—	3.8	9	
Independents	—	5.2	11	
Andorra (February 1997)				
Liberal Union	CR	...	18	(5)
National Democratic Grouping	CR	...	6	(8)
New Democracy	CL	...	2	(5)
Others and independents	—	...	2	(10)
Angola (September 1992)				
Popular Liberation Movement of Angola–Labour Party (MPLA–PT)	x	53.7	129	(203)
National Union for the Total Independence of Angola (UNITA)	—	34.1	70†	—
Others	—	12.2	21	—
Antigua and Barbuda (March 1994)				
Antigua Labour Party	C	54.4	11	(15)
United Progressive Party	C	43.7	5	(1)
Barbuda People's Movement	e	1.4	1	(1)
Argentina (October 1997)				
Justicialist National Movement (Peronist)	CR–CL	36.1	118	(136)
Radical Civic Union }				(69)
Front for a Country in Solidarity (Frepaso coalition) }	CL	45.7	110	(26)
Others	—	18.2	29	(26)
Armenia (July 1995)				
Republic Bloc (coalition)	—	42.7	119	
National Democratic Union	—	7.5	5	
Shamiram Women's Movement	—	16.9	8	
Armenian Communist Party	K	12.1	7	
Others and independents	—	20.8	51	
Australia (October 1998)				
National Party of Australia	R	5.4	16	(18)
Liberal Party of Australia	C	34.0	64	(76)
Australian Labor Party	L	40.1	66	(49)
Others and independents	—	20.5	2	(5)
Austria (December 1995)				
Freedom Movement	R	21.9	40	(42)
Liberal Forum	—	5.5	10	(11)
Austrian People's Party	C	28.3	53	(52)
Austrian Social Democratic Party	SD	38.1	71	(65)
The Green Alternative	Lg	4.8	9	(13)
Azerbaijan (November 1995–February 1996)				
New Azerbaijan Party and allies	p	...	115	
Others	—	...	9	
Bahamas, The (March 1997)				
Free National Movement	CR	57.0	34	(34)
Progressive Liberal Party	C	42.0	6	(15)
Bahrain				
Consultative Council (advisory body)	—	—	—	
Bangladesh (June–September 1996)				
Bangladesh Nationalist Party	CR	...	113	(212)
National Party	CR	...	33	‡
Awami League	SD	...	176	‡
Bangladesh Islamic Assembly	r	...	3	‡
Others	—	...	5	(2)
Barbados (September 1994)				
Democratic Labour Party	C	38.8	8	(18)
National Democratic Party	—	12.1	1	(0)
Barbados Labour Party	SD	48.8	19	(10)
Belarus				
House of Representatives	—	—	110	
Belgium (May 1995)				
National Front (French)	ERe	2.3	2	(1)
Vlaams Blok (Flemish)	ERe	7.8	11	(12)
Volksunie (Flemish)	Re	4.7	5	(10)
Liberals { Flemish	CR	13.1	21	(26)
Liberals { French	CR	10.3	18	(20)
Social Christians { Flemish	C	17.2	29	(39)
Social Christians { French	C	7.7	12	(18)
Socialist { Flemish	SD	12.6	20	(28)
Socialist { French	SD	11.9	21	(35)
Greens { Flemish	g	4.4	5	(7)
Greens { French	g	4.0	6	(10)
Others	—	4.0	0	(6)
Belize (August 1998)				
United Democratic Party	R	39.2	3	(16)
People's United Party	C	59.3	26	(13)
Benin (March–May 1995)				
Government party and allies	—	...	32	
Opposition parties	—	...	50	
Bhutan				
National Assembly, nonparty	—	—	105	
Bolivia (June 1997)				
Civic Solidarity Union	R	15.9	21	(20)
Nationalist Revolutionary Movement	CR	17.7	26	(52)
Nationalist Democratic Action	p	22.3	33 }	(35)
Movement of the Revolutionary Left	SD	16.7	25 }	
Conscience of the Fatherland	CL	15.8	17	(13)
Free Bolivia Movement	L	2.5	4	(7)
United Left (coalition)	L–K	3.7	4	(0)
Others	—	5.4	0	(3)
Bosnia and Herzegovina (September 1998)				
Serb nationalists (xenophobic)	er	21	7 }	(9)
Less-extreme Serb nationalists	er	15	4 }	
Croat nationalists	er	16	7	(8)
Bosnian Muslim nationalists	er	32	18	(19)
Multiethnic parties	SD–L	13	6	(6)
Botswana (October 1994)				
Botswana Democratic Party	C	54.4	27	(31)
Botswana National Front	CL	37.1	13	(3)
Brazil (October 1998)				
Brazilian Progressive Party	CR	...	60	(89)
Liberal Front Party	C	...	105	(90)
Brazilian Democratic Movement	C	...	82	(107)
Brazilian Labour Party	C	...	31	(31)
Brazilian Social Democratic Party	CL	...	99	(62)
Democratic Labour Party	SD	...	26	(34)
Brazilian Socialist Party	S	...	19	(14)
Workers' Party	S	...	58	(49)
Others	—	...	33	(37)
Brunei				
Legislative Council (nonelected)	—	—	—	
Bulgaria (April 1997)				
Bulgarian Business Bloc	R	4.9	12	(13)
United Democratic Forces (coalition)	CR	52.3	137	(87)
Euro-Left (coalition)	SD	5.5	14	—
Democratic Left (coalition)	L	22.1	58	(125)
Movement for Rights and Freedoms (Turkish)	e	7.6	19	(15)
Burkina Faso (May–June 1997)				
Government party and allies	...	76.0	103	(84)
Opposition parties	...	16.6	8	(23)
Burundi (June 1993)				
Burundi Democratic Front	—	72.6	65	
Unity for National Progress	—	21.9	16	
Cambodia (July 1998)				
Funcinpec	CR	31.7	43	(58)
Sam Rangsi Party	p	14.3	15	—
Buddhist Liberal Democrats	—	...	0	(10)
Cambodian People's Party	L	41.4	64	(51)
Others	—	12.6	0	(1)
Cameroon (May–August 1997)				
Government party	R	...	116	(88)
Allied party	e	...	1	(6)
Cameroon People's Union	—	...	1	(18)
National Union for Democracy and Progress (Islamist)	Cr	...	13	(68)
Social Democratic Front	SD	...	43	†
Others	—	...	6	(0)
Canada (June 1997)				
Reform Party of Canada	R	19.4	60	(52)
Progressive Conservative Party	CR	18.9	20	(2)
Liberal Party of Canada	C	38.4	155	(177)
New Democratic Party	SD	11.0	21	(9)
Bloc Québécois	e	10.7	44	(54)
Others and independents	—	1.6	1	(1)
Cape Verde (December 1995)				
Movement for Democracy	—	61.3	50	(56)
African Party for the Independence of Cape Verde	—	29.8	21	(23)
Democratic Convergence Party	—	6.7	1	—
Central African Republic (November–December 1998)				
Central African People's Liberation Movement	—	...	49	(34)
Allies/independents	—	...	6	(40)
Others	—	...	54	(11)
Chad (January–February 1997)				
Patriotic Salvation Movement	p	...	63	
Allied party	—	...	15	
Union for Renewal and Democracy	p	...	29	
Others	—	...	16	
Chile (December 1997)				
Union for Chile	ER–R	36.2	47	(50)
Coalition of Parties for Democracy	C–L	50.6	70	(70)
Leftist alliance	L–EL	7.5	0	(0)
Others	—	5.7	3	(0)
China (October 1997–March 1998)				
Chinese Communist Party	K	...	2,130 }	2,978
Nonparty	—	...	849 }	
Columbia (March 1998)				
Social Conservative Party (traditional agrarian interests)	R	27	52	(56)
Liberal Party (traditional commercial/industrial interests)	C	54	98	(94)
Others and independents	—	19	11	(15)
Comoros				
Transitional government from September 1997	—	—	—	
Congo, Democratic Republic of the				
Military government from May 1997	—	—	—	
Congo, Republic of the				
Military-backed transitional government from November 1997	—	—	—	
Costa Rica (February 1998)				
Social Christian Unity Party	CR	44.9	27	(25)
Libertarian Movement Party	C	1.7	2	—
National Liberation Party	CL	42.6	23	(28)
Democratic Force	L	5.1	2	(2)
Others	—	5.7	3	(2)
Côte d'Ivoire (November 1995–December 1996)				
Democratic Party of Côte d'Ivoire	—	...	149	(147)
Rally of Republicans	C	...	13	(14)
Ivorian Popular Front	SD	...	13	(10)
Croatia (October 1995)				
Croatian Party of Rights	ERe	5.0	4	(5)
Croatian Democratic Union	Re	45.2	75	(85)
Moderate opposition coalition	R–C	18.3	20	(6)
Croatian Social-Liberal Party	CL	11.6	11	(14)
Social Democratic Party	x	8.9	9	(11)
Others and independents	—	11.0	8	(17)
Cuba (January 1998)				
Government (single) party	K	...	601	(589)
Cyprus				
Greek Zone (May 1996)				
Democratic Rally/Liberals	R	34.5	20	(20)
Democratic Party	CR	16.4	10	(11)
EDEK–SK (Socialists)	CL	8.1	5	(7)
Free Democrats Movement	CL	3.7	2	—
Progressive Party of the Working People	L	33.0	19	(18)
Turkish Zone (December 1998)				
National Unity Party	CR	40.3	24	(17)
Democratic Party	—	22.6	13	(15)
Republican Turkish Party	S	13.3	6	(13)
Others	—	13.8	7	(5)
Czech Republic (June 1998)				
Republicans	ER	3.9	0	(18)
Civic Democratic Party	R	27.7	63	(68)
Freedom Union	CR	8.6	19	—
Christian Democrats	CR	9.0	20	(18)

World Legislative Election Results

Country / Name of party	Affiliation	Voting strength (%)	Parliamentary representation	
Czech Social Democratic Party	SD	32.3	74	(61)
Communist Party of Bohemia and Moravia	K	11.0	24	(22)
Others	—	7.5	0	(13)
Denmark (March 1998)				
Danish People's Party	ER	7.4	13	(11)
Progress Party	ER	2.4	4	
Liberal Party	R	24.0	42	(42)
Conservative People's Party	R	8.9	16	(27)
Christian People's Party	CR	2.4	4	(0)
Centre Democrats	C	4.3	8	(5)
Radical Liberal Party	C	3.9	7	(8)
Social Democrats	CL	35.9	63	(62)
Socialist People's Party	L	7.6	13	(13)
Red-Green Unity List	Lg	2.7	5	(6)
Faroe Islands (seats allotted)	—	—	2	(2)
Greenland (seats allotted)	—	—	2	(2)
Independents	—	—	0	(1)
Djibouti (December 1997)				
Popular Rally for Progress and allies	—	78.6	65	(65)
Dominica (June 1995)				
Dominica Freedom Party	CR	35.8	5	(11)
Dominica United Workers' Party	CL	34.4	11	(6)
Labour Party	L	29.6	5	(4)
Independents/others	—	0.2	0	(1)
Dominican Republic (May 1998)				
Social Christian Reformist Party	R	...	16	(50)
Dominican Liberation Party	C	...	50	(13)
Dominican Revolutionary Party	CL	...	83	(57)
Ecuador (May 1998; % of national vote)				
Ecuadorian Conservative Party	R	5.5	2	(2)
Social Christian Party	CR	25.1	26	(27)
Popular Democracy	C	20.0	35	(12)
Ecuadorian Roldosist Party	C	18.8	25	(19)
Democratic Left	SD	16.3	17	(4)
Alfarist Radical Front	L	—	3	(3)
Democratic Popular Movement	EL	4.5	2	(2)
New Country Movement	g	9.8	6	(8)
Others	—	—	9	(5)
Egypt (November–December 1995)				
Muslim Brotherhood	r	—	*	*
New Wafd Party	R	...	6	‡
National Democratic Party	CR	...	317	(348)
National Progressive Unionist	L	...	5	(6)
Other parties	—	...	3	—
Independents	—	...	113	(83)
El Salvador (March 1997)				
National Conciliation Party	R	8.6	11	(4)
Nationalist Republican Alliance (Arena)	R	34.9	28	(39)
Liberal Democratic Party	p	3.1	2	—
Christian Democratic Party and ally	C	11.7	10	(18)
Other centrist parties	CR–CL	9.2	6	(2)
Farabundo Martí National Liberation Front	L	32.5	27	(21)
Equatorial Guinea (November 1993)				
Democratic Party	—	...	68	(41)
Principal opposition parties	—	—	‡	—
Others	—	...	12	—
Eritrea				
Transitional government from May 1993	—	—	—	
Estonia (March 1995)				
Republican and Conservative People's Party	R	5.0	5	—
Pro-Patria ("Fatherland") Coalition	CR	7.9	8	(29)
Estonian Reform Party	CR	16.2	19	—
Estonian Centre Party	CL	14.2	16	—
Coalition and Rural People's Union	CL/x	32.2	41	(17)
Moderates	SD	6.0	6	(12)
Our Home Is Estonia (pro-Russian alliance)	e	5.9	6	—
Others	—	12.6	0	(43)
Ethiopia (May–June 1995)				
Ethiopian People's Revolutionary Democratic Front	—	...	493	
Major opposition parties	—	—	‡	
Others and independents	—	...	54	
Fiji (February 1994)				
Ethnic Fijian seats	e	...	37	(37)
Ethnic Indian seats	e	...	27	(27)
Chinese/European seats	e	...	4	(4)
Multiracial seat	e	...	1	(1)
Rotuma Island	e	...	1	(1)
Finland (March 1995)				
Finnish Christian Union	R	3.0	7	(8)
National Coalition	CR	17.9	39	(40)
Swedish People's Party	e	5.1	12	(12)
Finnish Centre	C	19.9	44	(55)
Social Democratic Party	S	28.3	63	(48)
Left-Wing Alliance	L–K	11.2	22	(19)
Green Union	g	6.5	9	(10)
Others	—	8.1	4	(8)
France (May–June 1997; 1st round %s)				
National Front	ER	14.9	1	(0)
Rally for the Republic	R	15.7	139	(247)
Other right-wing parties	R	6.6	8	(24)
Union for French Democracy	CR	14.2	109	(213)
Socialist Party	S	23.5	246	(54)
Other left-wing parties	L	4.2	29	(16)
French Communist Party	K	9.9	37	(23)
The Greens	g	6.8	8	(0)
Gabon (December 1996–January 1997)				
Gabonese Democratic Party	p	...	82	(66)
National Rally of Woodcutters	C	...	12	(17)
Gabonese Progress Party	—	...	8	(19)
Others and independents	—	...	18	(18)
Gambia, The (January 1997)				
Alliance for Patriotic Reorientation and Construction	p	52.1	33	
Opposition parties	—	44.1	10	
Independents	—	3.8	2	
Georgia (November–December 1995)				
All-Georgian Union of Revival (Adzharian Muslim)	er	6.8	32	—
National Democratic Party	CR	8.0	34	(12)
Citizens' Union of Georgia	C	23.7	106	—
Others and independents	—	61.5	63	(228)
Germany (September 1998)				
Christian Social Union	R	6.7	47	(50)
Christian Democratic Union	CR	28.4	198	(244)
Free Democratic Party	CR–C	6.2	44	(47)
Social Democratic Party	SD	40.9	298	(252)
Party of Democratic Socialism	x	5.1	35	(30)
Alliance '90/The Greens	g	6.7	47	(49)
Ghana (December 1996)				
National Democratic Congress	p	...	134	(189)
New Patriotic Party	CR	...	60	(0)
Others	—	...	6	(11)
Greece (September 1996)				
Political Spring	CR	2.9	0	(10)
New Democracy	CR	38.1	108	(111)
Panhellenic Socialist Movement (Pasok)	S	41.5	162	(170)
Democratic Social Movement	L	4.4	9	
Progressive Left Coalition	L–K	5.1	10	(0)
Communist Party	K–EL	5.6	11	(9)
Grenada (June 1995)				
Grenada United Labour Party	R	26.8	2	(4)
National Democratic Congress	C	31.1	5	(7)
New National Party	C	32.7	8	(2)
Others	—	9.4	0	(2)
Guatemala (November 1995)				
National Advancement Party	Rp	34.7	43	(24)
Guatemalan Republican Front	Rp	19.5	21	(32)
Other rightist parties	R	8.7	3	(3)
National Alliance (coalition)	C	13.0	7	(21)
New Guatemala Democratic Front	CL	8.5	6	—
Guinea (June 1995)				
Presidential party and allies	—	...	76	
Opposition parties	—	...	38	
Guinea-Bissau (July 1994)				
African Party for the Independence of Guinea and Cape Verde	L	46.0	62	(150)
Guinea-Bissau Resistance	—	19.2	19	—
Other opposition parties	—	34.8	19	—
Guyana (December 1997)				
People's National Congress (black interests)	Le	40.6	26	(31)
People's Progressive Party (East Indian interests)	Le	55.3	36	(32)
Others	—	2.7	3	(2)
Haiti (June–September 1995)				
Lavalas movement	C–L	...	68	
Others and independents	—	...	15	
Honduras (November 1997)				
National Party	R	41.5	55	(55)
Liberal Party	CR	49.6	67	(71)
Christian Democratic Party	C	2.6	2	(0)
National Innovation and Unity Party–Social Democratic	SD	4.1	3	(2)
Democratic Unification Party	L–EL	2.1	1	—
Hungary (May 1998)				
Justice and Life Party	ER	5.5	14	(0)
Independent Smallholders'	R	13.8	48	(26)
Hungarian Democratic Forum	CR	3.1	17	(37)
Christian Democrats	CR	2.6	0	(22)
Young Democrats–Civic Party	CR	28.2	148	(20)
Free Democrats	CL	7.9	24	(70)
Hungarian Socialist Party	x	32.3	134	(209)
Others and independents	—	6.6	1	(2)
Iceland (April 1995)				
Independence Party	R	37.1	25	(26)
Progressive Party	C	23.3	15	(13)
Women's Alliance	CL	4.9	3	(5)
People's Movement	CL	7.2	4	(10)
Social Democratic Party	SD	11.4	7	
People's Alliance	L	14.3	9	(9)
India (February–June 1998)				
Bharatiya Janata Party (Hindu)	Rr	37.2	179	(161)
Allied parties	Rr		73	(34)
Congress (I)	C	29.7	141	(136)
Allied parties	C		24	(5)
United Front (coalition)	CL–K	21.9	97	(170)
Others (includes vacant seats)	—	11.2	29	(37)
Indonesia (May 1997)				
Governing coalition of groups	—	74.3	325	(282)
United Development Party (Muslim interests)	r	22.6	89	(62)
Party representing Christian and nationalist interests	—	3.1	11	(56)
Iran (March 1996–February 1997)				
Association of Combatant Clergy "group"	ERr	...	113	(155§)
Servants of Construction "group"	Rr	...	86	(115§)
Others	—	...	62	
Iraq (March 1996)				
Ba'th Party	—	...	160	(250)
Allied independents	—	...	60	
Ireland (June 1997)				
Progressive Democrats	R	4.7	4	(10)
Fianna Fail (Republican)	C	39.3	77	(68)
Fine Gael (United Ireland)	C	27.9	54	(45)
Labour Party	SD	10.4	17	(33)
Democratic Left	S	2.5	4	(4)
Sinn Fein ("Ourselves Alone")	EL	2.6	1	(0)
Green Alliance	g	2.8	2	(1)
Others and independents	—	9.8	7	(5)
Israel (May 1996)				
Moledet	ER	2.3	2	(3)
United Torah Judaism (orthodox)	r	3.2	4	(4)
Shas (orthodox)	r	8.5	10	(6)
National Religious Party	r	7.8	9	(6)
Likud and allies	R	25.1	32	(40)
Israel for Immigration (Russian)	Ce	5.7	7	—
The Third Way	C	3.1	4	—
Israel Labor Party	SD	26.8	34	(44)
Meretz	CL	7.4	9	(12)
United Arab List	e	2.9	4	(2)
Hadash	L	4.2	5	(3)
Italy (April 1996)				
Northern League	Re	10.1	59	(366)
Right-wing alliance	R	44.0	246	
National Alliance	R	15.7	107	(109)
Forza Italia	R	20.6	110	(112)
United Christian Democrats	CR	5.8	29	—
Centrist parties	C	43.4	319	(46)
Left-wing pact/alliance	L			(213)
Democratic Party of the Left	SD	21.1	163	(114)
Green Federation	g	2.5	...	(11)
Communist Refoundation Party	K	8.6	35	(41)
Others	—	2.5	6	(5)
Jamaica (December 1997)				
Jamaica Labour Party	CL	39.4	10	(8)
People's National Party	L	55.6	50	(52)
Japan (October 1996)				
Liberal-Democratic Party	R	38.6	239	(223)
Democratic Party	—	10.1	52	—
New Frontier Party (Shinshinto)	R–SD	28.0	156	(160)
Social Democratic Party	SD	2.2	15	(70)
Japan Communist Party	L	12.5	26	(15)
Others and independents	—	8.6	12	(43)
Jordan (November 1997)				
Islamic Action Front	r	—	‡	(16)
Tribal/traditional candidates	C	...	62	(49)
Independent Islamists	r	...	8	(10)
Leftists and Nationalists	L	...	10	
Kazakstan (December 1995–February 1996)				
Pro-presidential parties	—	...	53	
Opposition	—	...	14	
Kenya (December 1997)				
Kenya African National Union	—	...	107	(100)
Forum for Restoration of Democracy–Kenya	—	...	17	(31)
Democratic Party	—	...	39	(23)
National Development Party	—	...	21	—
Others	—	...	26	(34)
Kiribati (September 1998)				
Government grouping	p	...	14	(13)
Others and independents	—	—	26	(26)
Korea, North (July 1998)				
Korean Workers' Party and allies	K	...	687	(687)
Korea, South (April 1996)				
United Liberal Democrats	R	16.2	50	—
New Korea Party	R	34.5	139	(149)
National Congress for New Politics	C	25.3	79	—
Democratic Party	CL	11.2	15	(97)
Others and independents	—	12.8	16	(53)
Kuwait (October 1996)				
Islamic moderates and fundamentalists	r	...	14	(19)
Government supporters	—	...	19	(15)
Tribal candidates and independents	—	...	11	
Liberal opposition	—	...	4	(6)
Kyrgyzstan (February–April 1995)				
Pro-government independents	—	...	90	
Others	—	...	15	
Laos (December 1997)				
Government (single) party	K	...	98	(85)
Nonparty	—	...	1	(0)

World Legislative Election Results

Country / Name of party	Affiliation	Voting strength (%)	Parliamentary representation	
Latvia (October 1998)				
Popular Movement for Latvia	ERp	1.7	0	(16)
Fatherland and Freedom	ERe	14.7	17	(14)
People's Party (probusiness)	CR	21.2	24	—
Latvian Way Union	C	18.1	21	(17)
New Party	C	7.3	8	—
Master Democratic Party	—	1.6	0	(18)
Popular Harmony Party (pro-Russian)	CL	14.1	16	(6)
Latvian Social Democratic Union	SD	12.8	14	(0)
Others	—	8.5	0	(29)
Lebanon (August–September 1996)				
Christian	—	—	64	
Maronite	—	—	34	
Greek Orthodox	—	—	14	
Greek Catholic	—	—	8	
Armenian Orthodox	—	—	5	
Others	—	—	3	
Muslim/Druze	—	—	64	
Sunnite	—	—	27	
Shi'ite	—	—	27	
Druze	—	—	8	
'Alawite	—	—	2	
Lesotho (May 1998)				
Basotho Congress Party	—	…	0	(65)
Basotho National Party	—	24.5	1	(0)
Lesotho Congress for Democracy	—	60.7	78	—
Liberia (July 1997)				
National Patriotic Party	p	…	49	
Others	—	…	15	
Libya				
General People's Congress	—	—	760	
Liechtenstein (January–February 1997)				
Progressive Citizens' Party	CR	39.2	10	(11)
Fatherland Union	C	49.2	13	(13)
Free List	g	11.6	2	(1)
Lithuania (October 1996–March 1997)				
Christian Democrats	CR	12.2	16	(13)
Homeland Union	CR	29.8	70	—
Reform Movement (Sajudis)	CR	—	—	(29)
Centre Union	C	8.2	13	(2)
Social Democratic Party	SD	6.6	12	(8)
Democratic Labour Party	x	9.5	12	(74)
Others and independents	—	33.7	15	(15)
Luxembourg (June 1994)				
Christian Social People's Party	CR	29.3	21	(22)
Democratic Party	C	11.6	12	(11)
Socialist Workers' Party	S	33.5	17	(18)
Communist Party	K	2.8	0	(1)
Action Committee for Democracy and Justice	—	7.1	5	(4)
Green Alternative	g	10.2	5	(4)
Macedonia (October–November 1998)				
Liberal-Democratic Party	C	7.0	4	(30)
Pro-Macedonian alliance	Ce	38.8	59	(0)
Social Democratic Union	S	25.1	29	(58)
Pro-Albanian parties	e	19.3	25	(14)
Others	—	9.8	2	(18)
Madagascar (May 1998)				
Pro-Ratsiraka party	p	…	63 }	
Allied parties	—	…	31 }	(63)
Independents and others	—	…	31 }	
Anti-Ratsiraka parties	—	…	25	(75)
Malawi (May 1994)				
United Democratic Front	—	46.4	84	—
Malawi Congress Party	—	33.6	55	(136)
Alliance for Democracy	—	18.9	36	—
Malaysia (April 1995)				
Islamic parties	CR	17.4	13	(15)
National Front coalition	e	64.0	162	(127)
Democratic Action Party	SD	12.1	9	(20)
Others and independents	—	6.5	8	(18)
Maldives (December 1994)				
People's Council, nonparty	—	…	40	
Mali (July–August 1997)				
Alliance for Democracy in Mali	p	…	128	(74)
Principal opposition parties	—	—	‡	—
Others	—	…	19	(42)
Malta (September 1998)				
Nationalist Party	R	51.8	35	(34)
Malta Labour Party	SD	47.0	30	(35)
Marshall Islands (November 1995)				
House of Representatives, nonparty	—	—	33	
Mauritania (October 1996)				
Government party	R	…	70	(67)
Principal opposition parties	…	…	1	(†)
Others and independents	—	…	8	(12)
Mauritius (December 1995)				
Mauritian Socialist Movement and allied parties	—	19.7	0 }	(59)
Mauritian Militant Movement } Mauritian Labour Party and allied parties }	—	65.2	60	(3)
Others	—	15.1	2	—
Mexico (July 1997)				
National Action Party (PAN)	CR	26.9	122	(119)
Institutional Revolutionary Party (PRI)	C–CL	38.5	239	(300)
Democratic Revolutionary Party	SD	25.8	125	(71)
Labour Party	L	2.6	6	(10)
Mexican Green Ecologist Party	g	4.0	8	(0)
Micronesia, Federated States of (March–April 1997)				
Congress, nonparty	—	…	14	(14)
Moldova (March 1998)				
Party for Romanian integration	Re	…	0	(9)
Democratic Convention of Moldova	CR	19.2	26	—
Pro-Romanian alliance	CRe	8.8	11	(11)
Agrarian Democrats (pro-Moldovan)	C–x	3.7	0	(56)
Centrist alliance	C	18.2	24	—
Pro-Russian bloc	xe	…	0	(28)
Party of Moldovan Communists	K	30.1	40	—
Monaco (February 1998)				
Campora list	p	…	18	(15)
Others	p	…	0	(3)
Mongolia (June 1996)				
United Heritage Party	R	1.6	1	—
Democratic Alliance coalition	C–SD	47.0	50	(5)
People's Revolutionary Party	—	40.5	25	(71)
Morocco (November–December 1997)				
Justice and Welfare (Islamist)	r	—	*	*
National Entente (coalition)	CR	24.8	100	(129)
Popular Constitutional and Democratic Movement	Cr	4.1	9	(0)
Centre (coalition)	C	27.3	97	(66)
Democratic Bloc (coalition)	CL–L	34.3	102	(114)
Others	—	9.5	17	(24)
Mozambique (October 1994)				
Mozambique Liberation Front (Frelimo)	x	44.3	129	(250)
Mozambique National Resistance (Renamo)	—	37.8	112	
Democratic Union	—	5.2	9	
Myanmar				
Military government since September 1988	—	—	—	
Namibia (December 1994)				
Democratic Turnhalle Alliance	C	20.8	15	(21)
South West Africa People's Organization (SWAPO)	L	73.9	53	(41)
Others	—	5.3	4	(10)
Nauru (February 1997)				
Parliament, nonparty	p	—	18	(18)
Nepal (November 1994)				
National Democratic Party	R	17.9	20	(4)
Nepali Congress Party	C	33.4	83	(110)
Communist parties	K	30.9	88	(82)
Others and independents	—	17.8	14	(9)
Netherlands, The (May 1998)				
Calvinist parties	Rr	5.0	8	(7)
People's Party for Freedom and Democracy (Liberals)	CR	24.7	39	(31)
Christian Democratic Appeal	C	18.4	28	(34)
Democrats 66	CL	9.0	14	(24)
Labour Party	SD	29.0	45	(37)
Green Left	Lg	7.3	11	(5)
Socialist Party	L	3.5	5	(2)
Others	—	3.1	0	(10)
New Zealand (October 1996)				
New Zealand First	CR	13.1	17	(2)
National Party	CR	34.1	44	(50)
United New Zealand	C	0.9	1	—
ACT New Zealand (libertarian)	—	6.2	8	—
Labour Party	CL	28.3	37	(45)
The Alliance (coalition)	L	10.1	13	(2)
Nicaragua (October 1996)				
National Opposition Union	—	—	—	(51)
Right-wing parties	R	7.6	9	(1)
Liberal Alliance coalition	R–C	46.0	42	—
Sandinist National Liberation Front	CL–EL	36.5	36	(39)
Others	—	9.9	6	(1)
Niger (November 1996–January 1997)				
Government party	—	…	59	—
Major opposition parties	—	—	‡ }	(83)
Others and independents	—	…	24 }	
Nigeria				
Military or transitional governments since 1993	—	—	—	
Norway (September 1997)				
Progress Party (libertarian)	—	15.3	25	(10)
Conservative Party	R	14.3	23	(28)
Christian People's Party	CR	13.7	25	(13)
Centre Party	CR	7.9	11	(32)
Liberal Party	C	4.5	6	(1)
Norwegian Labour Party	SD	35.0	65	(67)
Socialist Left Party	S	6.0	9	(13)
Others	—	3.3	1	(1)
Oman				
Oman Council (advisory bodies)	—	—	—	
Pakistan (February 1997)				
Pakistan Muslim League (Nawaz)	—	…	134	(73)
Pakistan Muslim League (Junejo)	—	…	0	(6)
Pakistan People's Party	CL	…	18	(86)
Awami National Party	CL	…	9	(3)
Muhajir National Movement	e	…	12	(†)
Others and independents	—	…	31	(39)
Palau (November 1996)				
House of Delegates, nonparty	—	—	16	
Panama (May 1994)				
Democratic Revolutionary Party and allies	—	…	31	(12)
Others	—	…	41	(55)
Papua New Guinea (June 1997)				
People's Progress Party	Rp	…	16	(10)
People's Democratic Movement	Rp	…	10	(15)
United Party (Pangu Pati)	Cp	…	13	(22)
Others	p	…	30	(31)
Independents	—	…	40	(31)
Paraguay (May 1998)				
National Republican Association–Colorado Party	R	53.8	45	(38)
Authentic Radical Liberal Party	CL }	42.7	26	(33)
National Encounter	— }		9	(9)
Peru (April 1995)				
Popular Christian Party	R	3.1	3	(8)
Popular Action	CR	3.3	4	—
Change 90-New Majority (coalition of independents)	p	52.1	67	(44)
Union for Peru	p	14.0	17	—
Independent Moralizing Front	p	4.9	6	(7)
American Popular Revolutionary Alliance	CL	6.5	8	—
Others	—	16.1	15	(21)
Philippines (May 1998)				
National People's Coalition	R	4.3	15	(23)
Democratic Filipino Struggle	R	1.8	7	(21)
Liberal Party	CR	2.7	14	…
People Power–National Union of Christian Democrats and allies	CR	14.1	50	(141)
Struggle of the Filipino Masses	p	27.1	110	—
Others and independents	—	50.0‖	21	(16)
Poland (September 1997)				
Movement for the Reconstruction of Poland	R	5.6	6	—
Solidarity Electoral Alliance	R–CR	33.8	201	—
Other rightist parties/groups	R–CR	…	0	(38)
Freedom Union	C	13.4	60	(74)
Labour Union	L	4.4	0	(41)
Democratic Left Alliance	—	27.1	164	(171)
Polish Peasant Party	—	7.3	27	(132)
German minority	e	…	2	(4)
Portugal (October 1995)				
Popular Party	R	9.1	15	(5)
Social Democratic Party	CR	34.0	88	(135)
Portuguese Socialist Party	CL	43.9	112	(72)
Unified Democratic Coalition	L–K	8.6	15	(17)
Others	—	4.4	0	(1)
Qatar				
Consultative Council (advisory body)	—	—	—	
Romania (November 1996)				
Romanian National Unity Party	ERe	4.4	18	(30)
Greater Romania Party	ERe	4.5	19	(16)
Democratic Convention of Romania	CR	30.2	122	(82)
Social Democratic Union	SD	12.9	53	(43)
Social Democracy Party	x	21.5	91	(117)
Hungarian Democratic Union	e	6.6	25	(27)
Others	—	19.9	0	(13)
Russia (December 1995)				
Liberal Democratic Party	ERe	11.2	51	(64)
Power to the People (right–left nationalist)	e	1.8	9	—
Our Home Is Russia	CR	10.1	55	—
Russia's Democratic Choice	CR	3.9	9	(76)
Congress of Russian Communities	Ce	4.3	5	—
Forward Russia!	C	1.9	3	—
Yabloko (Bloc of Three)	CL	6.9	45	(28)
Women of Russia	CL	4.6	3	(24)
Communist Party	L	22.3	157	(45)
Agrarian Party	L	3.8	20	(55)
Workers' Russia	EL	4.5	1	(0)
Other parties	—	…	15	(137)
Independents	—	…	77	(21)
Rwanda				
Transitional government from July 1994	—	—	—	
Saint Kitts and Nevis (July 1995)				
People's Action Movement	CL	…	1	(4)
St. Kitts-Nevis Labour Party	L	…	7	(4)
Concerned Citizens' Movement	e	…	2	(2)
Nevis Reformation Party (pro-secessionist)	e	…	1	(1)
Saint Lucia (May 1997)				
United Workers' Party	C	36.6	1	(11)
St. Lucia Labour Party	CL	61.3	16	(6)
Saint Vincent and the Grenadines (June 1998)				
New Democratic Party	C	45.8	8	(12)
Unity Labour Party	CL	54.2	7	(3)

World Legislative Election Results

Country / Name of party	Affiliation	Voting strength (%)	Parliamentary representation
Samoa (April 1996)			
Human Rights Protection Party	—	43.5	24 (30)
National Development Party	—	26.1	11 (14)
Independents and other	—	30.4	14 (3)
San Marino (May 1998)			
Christian Democrats	CR	40.9	25 (26)
Popular Democratic Alliance	C	9.8	6 (4)
Socialist Party	S	23.2	14 (14)
Progressive Democratic Party	x	18.6	11 (11)
Other parties	—	7.5	4 (5)
São Tomé and Príncipe (November 1998)			
Party of Democratic Convergence	—	...	8 (17)
Independent Democratic Action	—	...	16 (14)
Movement for the Liberation of São Tomé and Príncipe	CL	...	31 (27)
Saudi Arabia			
Consultative Council (advisory body)	—	—	—
Senegal (May 1998)			
Senegalese Democratic Party	CL	19.1	23 (27)
Socialist Party	SD	50.2	93 (84)
Let Us Unite Senegal (coalition)	L	7.7	6 (3)
Democratic Renewal	p	13.2	11 —
Others	—	9.8	7 6
Seychelles (March 1998)			
People's Progressive Front	Sp	61.7	30 (28)
Democratic Party	p	12.1	1 (4)
United Opposition	—	26.1	3 (1)
Sierra Leone (February 1996)			
Government party and allies	pe	61.5	46
United National People's Party	pe	21.6	17
Others	—	16.9	5
Paramount chiefs (nonparty)	e	—	12
Singapore (January 1997)			
People's Action Party	p	65.0	81 (77)
Singapore People's Party	C	2.3	1 —
Singapore Democratic Party	CL	10.6	0 (3)
Workers' Party	L	14.2	1 (1)
Slovakia (September 1998)			
Slovak National Party	Re	9.1	14 (9)
Movement for a Democratic Slovakia	CRp	27.0	43 (61)
Slovak Democratic Coalition	CR–C	26.3	42 (36)
Party of Civic Understanding	CL	8.0	13 —
Party of the Democratic Left	x	14.7	23 (13)
Hungarian Coalition	e	9.1	15 (17)
Others	—	5.8	0 (14)
Slovenia (November 1996)			
Slovenian National Party	ER	3.2	4 (12)
Slovenian People's Party	R	19.4	19 (10)
Slovenian Christian Democrats	CR	9.6	10 (15)
Social Democratic Party	C–SD	16.1	16 (4)
Liberal Democracy of Slovenia	CL	27.0	25 —
Centre-left parties	CL	—	— (33)
United List of Social Democrats	x	9.0	9 } (14)
Pensioner's party		4.3	5
Hungarian/Italian minorities	e	—	2 (2)
Solomon Islands (August 1997)			
Mamaloni supporters	p	...	24 (21)
Alliance for Change (coalition)	—	...	26 (17)
Others and independents	—	...	0 (9)
Somalia			
No government since 1991	—	—	—
South Africa (April 1994)			
Freedom Front	ER	2.2	9
National Party	CR	20.4	82
Inkatha Freedom Party	e	10.5	43
Democratic Party	C	1.7	7
African National Congress	CL	62.7	252
Pan-Africanist Congress	EL	1.2	5
Others	—	1.3	2
Spain (March 1996)			
Popular Party	CR	38.7	156 (141)
Basque Nationalist Party	Ce	1.3	5 (5)
Canarian Coalition	Ce	0.9	4 (4)
Convergence and Union (Catalan)	CLe	4.6	16 (17)
Spanish Socialist Workers' Party	SD	37.6	141 (159)
United Left	L–K	10.5	21 (18)
Galician Nationalist Bloc	Le	0.9	2 (0)
Herri Batasuna (Basque radicals)	ELe	0.7	2 (2)
Other regional parties	e	1.6	3 (4)
Sri Lanka (August 1994)			
United National Party	CR	44.0	94 (125)
People's Alliance	CL	48.9	105 } (86)
Others and independents	—	3.6	14
Sri Lanka Muslim Congress	r	1.8	7 (4)
Tamil United Liberation Front	e	1.7	5 (10)

Country / Name of party	Affiliation	Voting strength (%)	Parliamentary representation
Sudan, The (March 1996)			
Government supporters	—	...	264
Principal opposition forces	—	—	‡
Suriname (May 1996)			
National Democratic Party	p	25.6	16 (12)
Democratic Alternative '91	SD	12.4	4 } (9)
Pendawa Lima (Javan party)	e	10.0	4
New Front coalition	CLe	41.4	24 (30)
Alliance	—	9.3	3 —
Swaziland (September–October 1998)			
House of Assembly, nonparty	—	—	55 (55)
Sweden (September 1998)			
Christian Democrats	R	11.8	42 (15)
Moderate Coalition Party	CR	22.7	82 (80)
Centre Party	CR	5.1	18 (27)
Liberal People's Party	C	4.7	17 (26)
Social Democrats	S	36.6	131 (161)
Left Party	x	12.0	43 (22)
Green Ecology Party	g	4.5	16 (18)
Switzerland (October 1995)			
Freedom Party	R	4.0	7 (8)
Swiss People's Party	R	14.9	29 (25)
Christian Democrats	CR	17.0	34 (36)
Liberal Party	CR	2.7	7 (10)
Radical Democrats	C	20.2	45 (44)
Social Democrats	SD	21.8	54 (42)
Green Party	g	5.0	9 (14)
Others	—	14.4	15 (21)
Syria (November–December 1998)			
Ba'th Party and allies	—	...	167 (167)
Independents	—	...	83 (83)
Taiwan (December 1998)			
New Party (prounification)	R	7.1	11 21
Nationalist (Kuomintang)	—	46.4	123 (85)
Democratic Progressive Party (proindependence)	—	29.6	70 (54)
Others and undetermined	—	16.9	21 (4)
Tajikistan (February–March 1995)			
Communist Party	K	...	60
Others and independents	—	...	119
Western/Islamic parties			*
Tanzania (October–November 1995)			
NCCR–Mageuzi	C	...	16 —
Government party	S	...	186 (216)
Civic United Front (pro-Zanzibar autonomy)	e	...	24 —
Others	—	...	6 —
Thailand (November 1996)			
Thai Nation	R	...	39 (92)
Thai Citizens	Rp	...	18 (18)
National Development Party	Rp	...	52 (53)
Social Action Party	CR	...	20 (22)
New Aspiration Party	p	...	125 (57)
Democrat Party	C	...	123 (86)
Others	—	...	16 (63)
Togo (February 1994–August 1996)			
Rally of the Togolese People	p	...	40
Allied party and independents	—	...	3
Action Committee for Renewal	—	...	33
Union for Democracy	—	...	5
Tonga (January 1996)			
Noble representatives	—	—	9 (9)
People's Party (pro-democracy commoners)	—	...	6 (6)
Other commoners	—	...	3 (3)
Trinidad and Tobago (November 1995)			
People's National Movement	C	48.8	17 (21)
National Alliance for Reconstruction	C	4.8	2 (2)
United National Congress	SD	45.7	17 (13)
Tunisia (March 1994)			
Government party	CL	97.7	144 (141)
Opposition parties	—	2.3	19 (0)
Turkey (December 1995)			
Nationalist Action Party	ER	8.2	0 } (62)
Welfare (Refah) Party	Rr	21.3	158
True Path Party	CR	19.2	135 (178)
Motherland Party	CR	19.7	132 (115)
Democratic Left Party	CL	14.7	76 (7)
Republican People's Party	CL	10.7	49 —
Other leftist	CL–L	...	0 (88)
Turkmenistan (December 1994)			
Government (single) party	x	...	50
Tuvalu (March 1998)			
Parliament, nonparty	—	—	12
Uganda (June 1996)			
National Assembly, nonparty	—	—	276

Country / Name of party	Affiliation	Voting strength (%)	Parliamentary representation
Ukraine (March 1998)			
Extreme nationalist parties	ERe	...	3 (5)
Less-extreme nationalist parties	Re	...	4 (15)
Ukrainian Popular Movement (Rukh; pro-Ukrainian)	Ce	9	45 (21)
Centrist parties	C–CL	24	96 (17)
Communist party and allies	K–EL	38	164 (132)
Independents and others	—	...	108 (230)
United Arab Emirates			
Federal National Council (advisory body)	—	—	—
United Kingdom (May 1997)			
U.K. Unionist Party	ERe	0.04	1 (1)
Democratic Unionist Party	ERe	0.3	2 (3)
Ulster Unionist Party	Re	0.8	10 (9)
Conservative Party	R–CR	30.7	165 (336)
Liberal Democrats	C–CL	16.8	46 (20)
Social Democratic and Labour Party (Northern Ireland)	CLe	0.6	3 (4)
Labour Party	CL–L	43.2	418 (271)
Sinn Fein (Northern Ireland)	ELe	0.4	2 (0)
Scottish National Party	e	2.0	6 (3)
Plaid Cymru (Welsh nationalists)	e	0.5	4 (4)
Other	—	4.6	2 (0)
United States (November 1998)			
Republican	R–CR	...	222 (227)
Democratic	C–L	...	212 (207)
Other	L	...	1 (1)
Uruguay (November 1994)			
National (Blanco) Party	C	31.4	31 (39)
Colorado Party	C	32.5	32 (30)
New Space	CL	5.1	5 (9)
Progressive Encounter	L	30.8	31 —
Broad Front	L	—	— (21)
Uzbekistan (December 1994–January 1995)			
People's Democratic Party and allies	x	100.0	250
Opposition parties			*
Vanuatu (March 1998)			
Union of Moderate Parties	—	...	12 (17)
National United Party	p	...	11 (9)
Unity Front coalition	—	...	— (20)
Party of Our Land	—	...	18 —
Others and independents	—	...	11 (4)
Venezuela (November 1998)			
Venezuela Project	CR	10.4	... —
Social Christian Party	CR	12.0	... (54)
Democratic Action	CL	24.1	... (55)
The Radical Cause	EL	3.0	... (40)
Political Pole coalition	p	32.2	... } (55)
Others and independents	—	18.3	...
Vietnam (July 1997)			
Vietnamese Communist Party	K	...	384 } (395)
Allies	—	...	63
Independents	—	...	3
Yemen (April 1997)			
Yemeni Alliance for Reform	Rr	18.5	54 (62)
General People's Congress	p	57.4	187 (123)
Yemeni Socialist Party	L	—	‡ (56)
Others and independents	—	24.1	60 (60)
Yugoslavia (November 1996)			
Serbian Radical Party	ERe	18.5	16 (34)
Zajedno (Together) (four-party coalition)	CR–CLe	23.9	22 }
Serbian Democratic Movement	Ce		(20)
Democratic Party	C		(5)
Socialist Party of Serbia and allies	xe	48.1	64 (47)
Democratic Party of Socialists of Montenegro	xe	...	20 (17)
People's Party (Montenegrin pro-Serbian)	e	...	8 (4)
Others	—	...	8 (11)
Zambia (November 1996)			
Movement for Multiparty Democracy	50	60.1	131 (125)
United National Independence Party	p	—	‡ (25)
Others and independents	—	39.9	19 (0)
Zimbabwe (April 1995)			
Zimbabwe African National Union-Patriotic Front	—	82.3	118 (117)
Others and independents	—	17.1	2 (3)

* Banned. † Expelled September 1998. ‡ Boycotted. § Approximate. ‖ Includes invalid votes.

AFGHANISTAN

Area: 652,225 sq km (251,825 sq mi)
Population (1998 est.): 24,792,000 (including Afghan refugees estimated to number more than 1,100,000 in Pakistan and about 1,400,000 in Iran)
Capital: Kabul
Chief of state: President Burhanuddin Rabbani; de facto Taliban Supreme Leader, Mullah Mohammad Omar
Head of government: de facto Taliban council leader, Mullah Mohammad Rabbani

Military successes by Afghanistan's Taliban government appeared to move the country closer to a unified political authority in 1998 than at any other time since the Soviet invasion of 1979. This consolidation of power, however, provoked international and regional tensions that threatened to destabilize the region and the Muslim world.

Official Taliban restrictions on the education and employment of women brought critical reaction from the UN and other aid workers. In June the Taliban closed Kabul's private schools for women, including vocational training programs. The European Commission, complaining of restrictions on education, health care, and employment for women, suspended millions of dollars of funding for aid projects in July. Ordered to move their activities to a compound outside the city, most international aid workers left Kabul rather than comply.

In August Mazar-e Sharif, the centre of anti-Taliban resistance in Afghanistan, fell to Taliban forces. This ended a stalemate in which Afghanistan had been divided between the Taliban, who controlled Kabul and the south of the country, and forces allied with the government of Burhanuddin Rabbani, confined mostly to an area north of the Hindu Kush. The Rabbani government had been driven from Kabul in September 1996 by the Taliban but had joined with Uzbek militia and troops of the Hezb-i Wahdat, a Shi'ite group of ethnic Hazara Afghans, in the Northern Alliance. After the fall of Mazar-e Sharif, Hazara fighters withdrew toward their central Afghan stronghold in Bamiyan, whereas forces led by Tajik commander Ahmad Shah Masoud continued to resist from mountainous areas north of Kabul. By mid-September Bamiyan too had fallen, and the Taliban controlled more than 90% of Afghanistan.

Only Pakistan, Saudi Arabia, and the United Arab Emirates recognized the Islamic Emirate of Afghanistan under Supreme Leader (Amir-ul-Momenin) Mullah Mohammad Omar and a Council of Ministers headed by Mullah Mohammad Rabbani. Most other countries and the UN continued to recognize the Islamic State of Afghanistan, led by Pres. Burhanuddin Rabbani.

The consolidation of authority by the predominantly Pashtun Taliban aggravated tensions between Pashtuns and Afghanistan's other ethnic groups. In addition, the circumstances of the Taliban victory exposed a profound split between the staunchly Sunni Taliban and Shi'ite Iran, which had supported Afghanistan's Shi'ite minority. Taliban forces had occupied Mazar-e Sharif for a few days in 1997. During their withdrawal several thousand Taliban fighters had been taken captive and, as mass graves later revealed, massacred. The Taliban held Hazara forces primarily responsible for these killings. At the same time, Iran, long seen as military backers of the Shi'ite Hazara, became a focus of Taliban hostility.

During the capture of Mazar-e Sharif in August, at least nine Iranians were killed when their consulate was stormed. Iran reacted by announcing a buildup of 200,000 troops along its border with Afghanistan, and Taliban officials proclaimed their readiness to attack Iranian cities with missiles.

On August 20 U.S. missiles fired from the Arabian Sea struck training camps near Khost, south of Kabul, reportedly killing more than 20. The U.S. said that the camps were terrorist training bases used by Saudi Arabian dissident Osama bin Laden (see BIOGRAPHIES), who was suspected of having financed the August 7 bombings of U.S. embassies in Kenya and Tanzania. The Taliban refused to hand over bin Laden, who had been living in exile in Afghanistan since 1996. In November the Taliban reported that, since they had received no evidence from the U.S. of bin Laden's culpability, he was a free man.

In February an earthquake struck the area near Rustaq in Takhar province, near the border with Tajikistan. Reports suggested that more than 4,000 may have died. In May a second earthquake shook the same location, and aid workers reported that 5,000 had died. (See DISASTERS.)

(STEVEN SEGO)

ALBANIA

Area: 28,748 sq km (11,100 sq mi)
Population (1998 est.): 3,331,000
Capital: Tiranë
Chief of state: President Rexhep Mejdani
Head of government: Prime Minister Fatos Nano and, from October 2, Pandeli Majko

Albania in 1998 continued to suffer from its harsh political polarization. The opposition Democratic Party (PDS) of former president Sali Berisha ended a parliamentary boycott that it had started the previous year, demanding the resignation of the Socialist-dominated coalition government. Ignoring calls by the Organization for Security and Cooperation in Europe and the Council of Europe, the PDS declined to participate in the parliamentary commission that was working on a draft constitution. Following widespread allegations of government inefficiency and corruption in his administration, Socialist Prime Minister Fatos Nano reshuffled his Cabinet in mid-April, reducing the number of ministers. Success in local by-elections in June confirmed continuing popular support for his coalition.

In late August police arrested former defense minister Safet Zhulali, former interior minister Halit Shamata, former chairman of state control Blerim Cela, and three other former officials of Berisha's government on charges of crimes against humanity in conjunction with their alleged roles in the suppression of unrest in 1997. The six were charged with having ordered the use of chemical weapons, airplanes, and helicopters against civilians. Subsequently, Berisha called on his supporters to bring down the government "with all means," saying that the

Young Afghan girls sit outside their home in a village near Kabul. In June Afghanistan's Taliban government closed more than 100 private schools that had been educating girls in defiance of a ban on women attending school. Official Taliban restrictions on the education and employment of women brought critical reaction from the UN.

ZAHEERUDDIN ABDULLAH—AP/WIDE WORLD

arrests were politically motivated. On September 14, after the killing of a Berisha aide, Berisha supporters seized government buildings in Tiranë. Government forces counterattacked and reoccupied the buildings, and on September 15 Berisha surrendered two tanks posted outside his headquarters after the government threatened to use force if his followers did not give up their weapons.

Intraparty squabbling led to Prime Minister Nano's resignation on September 28, and he was replaced by 30-year-old Socialist Pandeli Majko a few days later. Pres. Rexhep Mejdani signed into law Albania's first post-communist constitution on November 28.

More that 13,000 refugees fled into Albania after the eruption in February of civil war between the Serbian police and army and the ethnic Albanian separatist Kosovo Liberation Army (UCK) in the neighbouring province of Kosovo. The Albanian Foreign Ministry repeatedly charged Yugoslavia with border violations that included shelling and sniping and with conducting massacres of Kosovo's civilian population. It also called for NATO military intervention to stop the fighting.

(FABIAN SCHMIDT)

ALGERIA

Area: 2,381,741 sq km (919,595 sq mi)
Population (1998 est.): 30,045,000
Capital: Algiers
Chief of state: President Liamine Zeroual
Head of government: Prime Minister Ahmed Ouyahia and, from December 15, Smail Hamdani

Violence continued to plague Algeria in 1998. Massacres during and just after the Islamic holy month of Ramadan, which coincided with January, were initially blamed on the extremist clandestine opposition coalition, the Armed Islamic Group (GIA). Subsequent investigations, however, suggested that government security forces were involved, and in early April two mayors in Relizane province were arrested for complicity in the attacks and 120 policemen were accused of involvement in murder, extortion, and kidnapping. At least 10 extrajudicial executions by the security forces were also revealed, and in September Pres. Liamine Zeroual authorized official support to resolve the issue of Algeria's "disappeared."

Despite the ongoing violence, the security forces extended their activities against the GIA during the year. Security in major population centres improved, and the GIA

seemed to have been pushed away from the central Mitidja plain toward the west of the country. The army's truce with the other major armed Islamic group, the Army of Islamic Salvation (AIS), held, and there were AIS–GIA clashes in June in which 50 persons died. Despite official claims that only 26,000 persons had died since 1992, outside observers estimated the true figure to be more than 70,000.

The crisis in Algeria increasingly attracted external attention. Officials representing the European Union visited Algiers in early February, and a European parliamentary delegation followed later that month. Despite severe criticism over its human rights record at the UN Human Rights Conference in Geneva, the Algerian government invited a UN mission to visit in July. The mission concluded that the government was not involved in massacres and significant human rights abuses.

Political conflicts continued throughout the year. Thirty small political parties that failed to meet electoral law criteria were banned in May. Ethnic tensions increased in June and July after the murder of a leading Berber singer and the introduction of an Arabization law, which required the use of Arabic in public. The president's adviser, Muhammad Betchine, and the prime minister, Ahmed Ouyahia, were subjected to a sustained hostile media campaign in July and August and, to general surprise, President Zeroual resigned in early September. New presidential elections were called for spring 1999. Observers concluded that he had been forced out by the army command, despite Algeria's 1995 democratic constitution. His departure was followed in November by those of Betchine and the justice minister, Muhammad al-Adami. Prime Minister Ouyahia also resigned in December, to be replaced by Smail Hamdani, a former ambassador.

Despite the International Monetary Fund's enthusiastic endorsement of Algeria's economic reforms in September,

social tensions increased during the year, with unemployment at 28% and the national trade union threatening a general strike in April and October. The IMF standby facility, which expired in May, was not renewed, despite IMF prompting. The government agreed to speed up the privatization process, avoiding job losses as much as possible, and anxiety was expressed over the dominance of the oil and gas sector in the economy. The 21% increase in Algeria's oil quota granted by OPEC in January did not improve matters, and the budget had to be redrafted in June. Although Algeria's buoyant foreign exchange reserves would ensure that debt repayment would continue on schedule, the outlook for 1999 was bleak.

(GEORGE JOFFÉ)

ANDORRA

Area: 468 sq km (181 sq mi)
Population (1998 est.): 65,200
Capital: Andorra la Vella
Chiefs of state: Co-princes of Andorra, the president of France and the bishop of Urgell, Spain
Head of government: Prime Minister Marc Forné Molné

With the European Union's new border-free trade policy in place, there was in 1998 a huge increase in the export of British cigarettes to Andorra (amounting to three packs a day per capita). This set off alarms within Andorra, and in March the EU sent fraud investigators there to check on tobacco smuggling. They found that organized gangs from Ireland and Great Britain were buying cigarettes in Andorra and smuggling them to their own countries, where they were sold

Angry Algerian women, holding a picture of popular Berber folk singer Matoub Lounes, who was killed in June by a dozen armed men, demonstrate in the streets of Tizi-Ouzou against his assassination. Matoub was well-known for his pro-democracy, anti-Islamist positions. Ethnic tensions increased in Algeria after his murder.

THOMAS COEX—AFP PHOTO

on the black market and 70–80% tax levies were thereby avoided. The loss of tax revenues in the EU was estimated at $5 billion annually. The Andorran government pledged cooperation and raised retail taxes on cigarettes but did not make smuggling a penal offense.

In April Andorra's foreign minister, Albert Pintat, met for official talks with his counterpart in Cuba. They pledged that the two countries would continue to enjoy friendly relations. (ANNE ROBY)

ANGOLA

Area: 1,246,700 sq km (481,354 sq mi)
Population (1998 est.): 10,865,000
Capital: Luanda
Chief of State: President José Eduardo dos Santos
Head of government: Prime Minister Fernando José França van-Dúnem

In January 1998 the prospects for peace in Angola seemed better than they had for some time. At a meeting on January 9 between Pres. José dos Santos and delegates from the government and the rebel National Union for the Total Independence of Angola (UNITA), implementation of the terms of the Lusaka Protocol, the peace accord of 1994, was scheduled to be completed by February 28. Characteristically, however, a meeting between dos Santos and Jonas Savimbi, UNITA's leader, scheduled for the middle of February, was first postponed for two weeks and then lapsed completely; Savimbi maintained that it would be unsafe for him to travel to Luanda, whereas dos Santos was said to be too ill to leave the capital. Nevertheless, on March 6 UNITA claimed to have demobilized all its forces, and the government, though skeptical of the truth of the claim, responded by legalizing UNITA as a political party. Three members of UNITA were appointed as provincial governors on March 16, and four days later Savimbi was accorded special status. His privileges included armed bodyguards, residences, and trips abroad.

Behind these promising developments, however, recriminations rumbled on. The government was accused of having announced the demobilization of UNITA's forces prematurely, with a view to making the troops still under arms illegal. The government responded by claiming that, in spite of the demobilization claims, UNITA's soldiers were beginning to regain control of surrendered territory. A further meeting between the government and UNITA was held on April 16–17 against a background of renewed reports that the latter's troops were active in a number of provinces, but no agreement was reached regarding the resumption of control over those areas by the government.

The peace process received a severe setback when a UN special representative, Alioune Blondin Beye, was killed in an airplane crash on June 26. A successor, Issa Diallo, was appointed in August, but, in the meantime, dialogue between the opposing parties came virtually to a halt.

The resumption of full-scale civil war was presaged by the massacre of more than 200 people in the diamond-mining province of Lunda Norte in July, with the government and UNITA accusing each other of responsibility for the killings. Exasperated by UNITA's continued procrastination, the government opened an offensive against a rebel base in the north of the country, near the town of Milando, on August 5. The objective seemed to be to put pressure on UNITA to implement the Lusaka Protocol rather than to oust the rebels from their main stronghold in the central highlands. Soon afterward government forces became deeply involved in fighting in the Democratic Republic of the Congo in support of Pres. Laurent Kabila, their aim being to close the routes by which supplies of arms and other materials could reach UNITA. In September the government suspended all UNITA representatives in the parliament as well as the four UNITA members of the Cabinet. Later, military officials of the Southern African Development Community (SADC) agreed that UNITA should be crushed by the forces of the SADC in alliance with the Angolan Army. Intense fighting resumed in December with government attacks on the UNITA strongholds of Andulo and Bailundo.

(KENNETH INGHAM)

ANTIGUA AND BARBUDA

Area: 442 sq km (171 sq mi)
Population (1997 est.): 64,500 (excluding evacuees from Montserrat)
Capital: Saint John's
Chief of state: Queen Elizabeth II, represented by Governor-General James Carlisle
Head of government: Prime Minister Lester Bird

The problems facing Antigua and Barbuda's offshore banking sector continued in 1998. Three such banks were closed early in the year, following similar action against eight others in 1997. In May six men were arrested in the U.S. for allegedly using an Antiguan bank to launder money improperly obtained from U.S. investors. Antigua and Barbuda, in common with other Caribbean governments, stepped up the battle against money laundering.

Attorney and member of parliament Vere Bird, Jr., brother of Prime Minister Lester Bird, was recovering after having been shot in the jaw in late 1997 by one of his clients, Cyril Bufton. Bufton had apparently become incensed over Bird's failure to secure better terms from the government for the removal of himself and his wife from nearby Guiana Island. The government was permitting Asian investors to develop the site into a major resort complex. Various legal maneuvers by the opposition United Progressive Party failed to stop the move. Bufton was charged with attempted murder.

In September Hurricane Georges battered the Caribbean islands, killing two people and injuring several others on Antigua.

(DAVID RENWICK)

ARGENTINA

Area: 2,780,092 sq km (1,073,400 sq mi)
Population (1998 est.): 36,125,000
Capital: Buenos Aires
Head of state and government: President Carlos Saúl Menem, assisted by Ministerial Coordinator Jorge Rodríguez

The administration of Pres. Carlos Menem was in its next-to-last year in 1998, with Menem's term due to expire in early December 1999 and presidential elections (along with those for half of the Chamber of Deputies) due to be held during the previous two months (probably in October 1999). Despite the relatively long time remaining before the vote, 1998 from the outset was dominated in the political sphere by electoral considerations.

In January the list of presidential candidates was led by Graciela Fernández Meijide of the Frepaso coalition, with more than one-third of the votes in opinion surveys. Fernando de la Rúa, the mayor of Buenos Aires and Meijide's rival from within the electoral Alliance formed between Frepaso and the Radical Civic Union (UCR) in August 1997, was in second place. The tables turned, however, following a very strong showing by de la Rúa in the November 29 primary election. Leading candidates from the ruling Justicialist National Movement (Peronist Party) included Eduardo Duhalde (governor of Buenos Aires province), Ramón Ortega (former governor of Tucumán province), and Menem.

Efforts to secure changes in the electoral and constitutional rules to permit Menem to run for a third consecutive term were prominent during the first half of the year. On March 19 the national electoral tribunal voted to give the nation's Supreme Court the final decision on this issue. This ruling had not been delivered by July, and at a special convention of the Justicialists on July 17, Menem sought to win the party's endorsement for a third term.

Menem won the support of the convention, but, faced with the threat of a party split, he declared on July 21 that he would not press ahead with his reelection bid. This appeared to have staved off a major rift, although tensions between Duhalde and Menem remained high.

Despite Menem's diminished popularity in Argentina, which was underscored by a number of unsavoury developments during the year, including allegations of corruption affecting senior levels of government, his international prestige continued to grow. This was exemplified in the final quarter of the year when he received an invitation to address the International Monetary Fund (IMF)–World Bank annual meetings jointly with U.S. Pres. Bill Clinton. This was followed by important state visits in Europe, not least to the U.K. at the end of October.

Compared with growth officially estimated at 8.4% in 1997, the expansion of gross domestic product (GDP) proceeded at a slower rate in 1998 under the impact of the financial crisis in Asia. This was con-

firmed by first-quarter GDP figures published in June, indicating a growth rate of 6.9% over the year; this was revised in September to 7.2%. Toward the end of August, Finance Secretary Pablo Guidotti stated that the official projection for 1998 GDP growth had been revised to 4.8%. Unemployment remained high, at 13.2% in both May and August. A series of budget cuts was introduced by Economy Minister Roque Fernández in a bid to ensure that the country would meet the budget deficit targets agreed upon with the IMF and also to help underpin investor confidence. Inflation remained low, at about 1.1% in the year to the end of September, with monthly rates of 0 in both August and September.

On the trade front, export expansion was undermined by low commodity prices in the wake of the Asian crisis and reduced demand from Brazil, whereas import growth remained relatively strong. This increased the deficit to $3,390,000,000 in the eight months to the end of August; during the same period of 1997, the deficit had totaled $1,730,000,000. Despite the difficult international financial market conditions prevailing in late 1998, by October 5 Argentina was able to announce that it had secured some $5.7 billion in new financing from the World Bank ($2 billion), Inter-American Development Bank ($2 billion), and private foreign banks and a local bond issue ($1.7 billion), which was sufficient to cover financing needs through March 1999. The peso remained stable at parity with the U.S. dollar, underpinned by reserves in excess of $25 billion and by growing bank deposits.

(SUSAN M. CUNNINGHAM)

ARMENIA

Area: 29,743 sq km (11,484 sq mi). Some 12–15% of neighbouring Azerbaijan (including the 4,400-sq km [1,700-sq mi] disputed region of Nagorno-Karabakh [Armenian: Artsakh]) has been occupied by Armenian forces since 1993.
Population (1998 est.): officially 3,800,000; actually about 3,000,000 (plus 150,000 in Nagorno-Karabakh)
Capital: Yerevan
Chief of state: Presidents Levon Ter-Petrosyan and, from February 4 (acting until April 9), Robert Kocharyan
Head of government: Prime Ministers Robert Kocharyan and, from April 10, Armen Darbinyan

A fundamental disagreement surfaced in January 1998 between Pres. Levon Ter-Petrosyan and Prime Minister Robert Kocharyan over the best way to resolve the conflict with Azerbaijan over Nagorno-Karabakh. Ter-Petrosyan advocated the peace plan proposed by the Organization for Security and Cooperation in Europe in September 1997 as a basis for negotiating concessions, but Kocharyan rejected it. After the defense and security ministers made clear their support for Kocharyan, Ter-Petrosyan's authority rapidly crumbled. Ter-Petrosyan resigned as president on February 3. In accor-

dance with the constitution, the presidential powers devolved on Kocharyan pending elections for a new president on March 16. In that poll none of the 12 candidates gained the required 50% majority. In the second round on March 30, Kocharyan won with 59% of the vote; the election was, however, marred by charges of fraud.

Kocharyan proclaimed a policy of national reconciliation, lifting the ban imposed by his predecessor on the Dashnak (Armenian Revolutionary Federation) party and releasing its leading members from prison. He also offered one of the Dashnak leaders and three defeated presidential candidates posts as his advisers and created a presidential council intended to provide those political parties not represented in the National Assembly with a forum to discuss policy. Kocharyan appointed Economy and Finance Minister Armen Darbinyan prime minister. Neither those appointments nor encouraging economic trends succeeded, however, in dispelling public suspicion that the new leadership was as corrupt as its predecessor. The murder in August of respected Prosecutor-General Henrik Khachatryan in his office by a subordinate who then committed suicide marked the definitive end of Kocharyan's political honeymoon. Deputy Defense Minister Vakhram Khorkhoruni was shot dead outside his home on December 10.

In November, after months of debate, the National Assembly adopted a new election law drafted by the Yerkrapah, which had become the largest faction in the National Assembly, that allocated most of the seats in the next legislature to single-member districts. Ten opposition parties decried that provision as intended to facilitate vote-rigging and threatened to boycott the election scheduled for June 1999. The Yerkrapah merged with the Republican Party of Armenia in November to create a new centrist nationalist-oriented party, described by its leader, Defense Minister Vazgen Sargsyan, as Kocharyan's power base.

Kocharyan during the year initiated a reevaluation of Armenia's foreign-policy priorities, seeking to accelerate the nation's integration into Western organizations. He also sought to promote cooperation with neighbouring Georgia and Iran, especially in regard to energy and transportation.

(ELIZABETH FULLER)

AUSTRALIA

Area: 7,682,300 sq km (2,966,200 sq mi)
Population (1998 est.): 18,725,000
Capital: Canberra
Chief of state: Queen Elizabeth II, represented by Governor-General Sir William Deane
Head of government: Prime Minister John Howard

Domestic Affairs. Prime Minister John Howard began 1998 in an optimistic and overwhelmingly popular position. His initiative in calling and overseeing an independent constitutional convention was applauded by

public opinion. Most Australians regarded the constitutional convention as an opportunity to shape national identity by cutting Australia's links with the British monarchy and establishing a republican form of government. After two weeks of debate, the delegates voted in support of Australia's becoming a republic. Howard immediately announced that a referendum would be held in 1999 to ask Australians if they approved of a change to the constitution to replace the queen with a president chosen by two-thirds of a joint session of the federal parliament.

In the months following the convention, however, it was downhill all the way for the government, as Howard's popularity steadily declined in the months before the general election, scheduled for October 3. The Liberal Party and the National Party, members of Howard's coalition government, lost votes to Pauline Hanson's anti-immigrant One Nation Party in the Queensland state elections, and such was the apparent popularity of One Nation that it seemed likely to hold the balance of power in future federal parliaments. In the election, however, Howard and his coalition retained power, though it lost seats to the Australian Labor Party. Hanson lost her seat, as One Nation gained about 8% of the vote, down from 23% in the Queensland election, and won only a seat in the Senate. Also during the election, in a referendum in the Northern Territory, voters rejected statehood.

The Howard government experienced mixed fortunes in a battle it waged to reform Australia's waterfront. The workplace relations minister, Peter Reith, suffered a conspicuous reverse when his plans to replace trade union stevedores with nonunion labour failed. In April Chris Corrigan, the chairman of Patrick Stevedoring, one of the major employers of the waterfront labour, sacked his entire unionized workforce. Corrigan predicted that the company would move forward with a new workforce. His firm had been assisted by the National Farmers Federation to set up a nonunion stevedoring operation on Melbourne's Webb dock, action that led it into a head-on conflict with the Maritime Union of Australia. Reith endorsed the company's action, declaring that the firing of 1,400 workers was a decisive turning point in the history of reform on the Australian waterfront and gave Australia the opportunity to have a waterfront that would allow the country to compete against the best in the world. This did not turn out to be the case. After a protracted legal debate in the Federal Court and the High Court, the final judgment was in favour of the stevedores. The Australian wharfs remained unionized, but the workers accepted job losses and layoffs.

The Economy. Australia began 1988 in good economic shape. The federal treasurer, Peter Costello, delivered a budget surplus of $A 2,700,000,000 (U.S. $1,710,000,000), the first surplus in Australia in eight years. Costello predicted that Australia would have one of the highest growth rates in the developed world, 3%, and described economic fundamentals as being as good as they had been for 25 years, with low inflation, low interest rates, declining unemployment, and reduced debt. Later in the year, however, despite Costello's efforts to quarantine the Australian economy from the Asian financial crisis, Australia was hurt by the downturn in regional economic activity. The fall

in the value of the Japanese yen dragged the Australian dollar down with it. Overseas investors decided to pull their funds out of Australia, concluding that the major regional trading partners of Australia—Japan, Indonesia, China, Malaysia, and Thailand—would be unlikely to experience levels of growth sufficient to absorb the traditional Australian exports of minerals and primary produce. This blow from abroad put considerable strain on the government's low-interest-rate policy, which was seen by the prime minister as crucial to his chances of election victory. The slowdown in Australian growth also made it more difficult for Costello to convince public opinion that a new goods and services tax (GST) was the best way forward in the quest to reform Australia's taxation system. In July, however, a television campaign financed by business interests spelled out the potential benefits of reform to Australia's indirect taxation system. Featuring blood loss during a surgical operation as a metaphor for income loss through hidden indirect taxes, the campaign asked Australians to weigh the benefits of a 15% goods and services tax in return for personal tax cuts and the abolition of indirect taxes.

A setback for the government economic plan was the decision of Independent Sen. Mal Colston not to support the complete sale of Telstra, Australia's telecommunication company. Colston explained that he opposed the full sale of Telstra because it would reduce service delivery in rural areas and provincial towns and cause job losses. This left the government in trouble, as it had planned to use the funds it derived from the sale of the utility to provide income-tax cuts that would offset the effect of the GST. As it could no longer forge ahead with a full sale of Telstra, the government decided to sell only an additional 16% of Telstra shares until consumer safeguards were guaranteed by new legislation.

Foreign Affairs. The disastrous earthquake and tidal wave that struck northern Papua New Guinea, a potential war in the Persian Gulf, and civil unrest in Indonesia, one of Australia's most important trading partners and nearest neighbours, provided challenges for Australian foreign policy makers in 1998.

Australia was quick to swing into action following the devastation of Papua New Guinea villages in July. Field hospital and army and air force personnel flew to the devastated area to provide an immediate first response to the tragedy. Earlier in the year Australia had prepared once again for battle in the Middle East. Prime Minister Howard committed 250 Australian troops to join the U.S. in a coalition against Iraq, which was defying the UN over arms-inspection procedures. Howard contacted U.S. Pres. Bill Clinton to tell him that Australia would contribute a Special Air Services Squadron, two Royal Australian Air Force Boeing 707 refueling aircraft, and intelligence and medical personnel to back up the demand that the UN be allowed to visit installations. As it turned out, Australian military action was not required in the Gulf, although the troops were sent to the area.

The continuing economic crisis in Asia provided a major headache for Australian foreign policy makers, although Australia saw the economic storm in Asia as an opportunity to demonstrate "regional mateship" and to demonstrate to its neighbours that Australia was not a fair-weather friend. Australia and Japan were the only two countries to contribute to all three International Monetary Fund packages to Thailand, Indonesia, and South Korea. In addition, Australia pledged to provide $A 236 million in aid to Vietnam.

On May 15 Australia faced trouble in its relations with Indonesia when rioting and looting broke out in several Indonesian cities, including the capital, Jakarta. A total of 758 Australians traveled on charter flights back to Australia in May. Minister for Foreign Affairs Alexander Downer reassured Indonesia that Australia would continue to cooperate with the Indonesian government and people as they went about implementing economic, political, and legal reforms. Australia stood ready to assist where it could, said Downer, and welcomed Indonesian Pres. B.J. Habibie's new approach to human rights and to political, legal, and economic reforms.

Australia faced difficult foreign policy problems in its dealings with India and Pakistan. When the Indian government carried out nuclear tests in defiance of world public opinion, Australia recalled its High Commission from India, and also summoned the Indian High Commission in Canberra to the Foreign Ministry to rebuke them. Downer unreservedly condemned India's action and said that Australia expected India to desist from any more tests and to sign the Comprehensive Test Ban Treaty. Australia stopped all nonhumanitarian aid, canceled all planned ministerial visits, ended military and naval flights and visits, withdrew the Australian defense attaché from New Delhi, sent home Indians serving with the Australian defense forces, and recalled Australian military personnel working in India. All defense contracts with India were canceled.

Downer was equally outraged and even-handed in his sanctions when soon afterward Pakistan disregarded Australian advice and followed India's lead. He was deeply disappointed that Pakistan, in carrying out nuclear tests, had cast a major shadow over what had been a positive relationship. Pakistan's action, said Downer, was a flagrant defiance of international nonproliferation principles and had serious implications for global and regional security.

(A.R.G. GRIFFITHS)

Australian Prime Minister John Howard holds a newspaper announcing his narrow reelection victory in October. He managed to retain power despite seeing his popularity steadily decline in the months before the election. His coalition government lost seats to the Australian Labor Party.

AUSTRIA

Area: 83,859 sq km (32,378 sq mi)
Population (1998 est.): 8,070,000
Capital: Vienna
Chief of state: President Thomas Klestil
Head of government: Chancellor Viktor Klima

Austria's coalition government, led by Social-Democratic Party of Austria (SPÖ) leader Viktor Klima, consolidated its position in 1998, boosting its prospects in the federal elections that would have to be held before the end of 1999. The junior party in the government, the centre-right Austrian People's Party (ÖVP), partially reversed the decline it had suffered in previous years with good results in state elections in April and consistently high opinion poll ratings throughout the year. The ÖVP had been in danger of being squeezed between its coalition partner on the left and the radical Freedom Party of Austria (FPÖ) on the right. The ÖVP was helped by accelerating economic growth and the end-to-austerity measures after Austria met the criteria for participation in the European Union's (EU) single currency. The party also won back supporters from the FPÖ after a financial scandal badly dented the FPÖ's image as an anticorruption party free from SPÖ–ÖVP influences.

The prestige associated with Austria's tenure of the rotating EU presidency during the last half of the year strengthened the government and did much to cement the coalition. Ministers were obligated to work together on a tight schedule, and the parties cooperated to maintain a united front while Austria was in the European spotlight. Discord between the coalition parties lingered below the surface, however, notably over the issue of Austria's neutrality and, in particular, relations with NATO. In March 1996 a parliamentary committee had been established to assess alternative security options. The SPÖ, in line with public opinion, opposed joining NATO, whereas the ÖVP was strongly in favour. Agreement could not be reached, and the committee's report remained unpublished.

The sense of active participation in European affairs during Austria's EU presidency may have helped tilt public opinion in favour of membership, but there was still great concern that when the EU was enlarged, workers from the new member states would have the right to live and work in Austria. Opinion polls suggested that most Austrians opposed such a move, fearing a large influx of economic migrants. The FPÖ, a party that had built its reputation in recent years by scapegoating foreign residents, ably exploited these fears. Popular concern was also evident at the rising level of foreign, particularly German, acquisitions of Austrian businesses. The wave of takeovers that followed accession to the EU continued in 1998, most notably when food retail group Julius Meinl AG, a national institution, was absorbed by a large German concern.

The Austrian economy enjoyed strong growth with low inflation and low unemployment in 1998. Economic growth accelerated as the upturn in the wider European economy increased exports of goods and services. High levels of investment also boosted growth as both Austrian and foreign-owned firms geared up to meet expected higher demand in Europe and increase penetration into former communist bloc countries to the east. Unemployment remained under 5%—one of the lowest in the EU—without triggering any upward pressure on inflation. Another important factor in the improved economic performance was the resurgence of tourism, an industry that was proportionately more significant to the gross domestic product of Austria than to that of other tourism centres such as Spain and Greece. Following a decline in the mid-1990s and thanks to a strong schilling and proliferation of cheap airline fares from overseas, the number of tourist visits rose slightly. Equally important, growth was registered in the key German tourist market, and unfavourable exchange-rate adjustments were partially reversed.

(DAN O'BRIEN)

AZERBAIJAN

Area: 86,600 sq km (33,400 sq mi), including the 5,500-sq km (2,100-sq mi) exclave of Nakhichevan and the 4,400-sq km (1,700-sq mi) disputed region (with Armenia) of Nagorno-Karabakh
Population (1998 est.): 7,650,000
Capital: Baku
Head of state and government: President Heydar Aliyev, assisted by Prime Minister Artur Rasizade

Political developments in 1998 revolved around the presidential election in October. Fearful lest Pres. Heydar Aliyev mobilize all available state resources to engineer his reelection for a second five-year term, some 30 political parties and organizations joined to form the Movement for Democratic Elections, with the stated objective of ensuring equally fair conditions for all candidates. Neither that organization nor the tiny opposition minority within the legislature could prevent the National Assembly from adopting election-related laws that were viewed as favouring the incumbent. In June five of the country's most influential opposition figures—former president Abulfaz Elchibey (Azerbaijan Popular Front Party), Isa Gambar (Musavat Party), Ilyas Ismailov (Democratic Party of Azerbaijan), Lala Shovket Gajiyeva (Liberal Party), and exiled former National Assembly speaker Rasul Guliyev—issued a joint statement affirming their intention to boycott rather than participate in an undemocratic election.

Under pressure from the opposition and international organizations, Aliyev instructed the National Assembly to amend the election legislation and issued a decree abolishing media censorship, but he rejected opposition demands for broader political liberalization. The opposition then organized unsanctioned demonstrations and protest marches in Baku and other cities to demand that the election be postponed. On September 12 dozens of people were hurt in clashes between protesters and police, and dozens more were arrested.

Aliyev ultimately defeated five rival candidates, winning 76% of the vote in an election that international monitors said did not meet international standards. Three of the defeated candidates refused to accept the outcome as valid and organized demonstrations in Baku on November 7 and 8, in which participants, demanding that the election results be annulled, again clashed with police. Twenty independent newspaper editors launched a hunger strike in November to protest official reprisals against the press.

The forced resignation in early February of Pres. Levon Ter-Petrosyan of Armenia and the subsequent election of Robert Kocharyan, the former president of the unrecognized Republic of Nagorno-Karabakh, as his successor delayed the resumption of the ongoing international efforts to mediate a settlement of the conflict between Azerbaijan and Armenia over Nagorno-Karabakh, an area within Azerbaijan but with a population about 80% Armenian. Following Aliyev's reelection the mediators put forward a new peace proposal in November that provided for Azerbaijan and Nagorno-Karabakh to form a common state. Azerbaijan rejected that proposal but said it was prepared to resume talks based on the 1997 peace proposal that Nagorno-Karabakh had rejected.

Azerbaijan, Georgia, Turkey, and Kazakstan affirmed their support for routing the main export pipeline for Azerbaijan's Caspian Sea oil from Baku to Ceyhan on Turkey's Mediterranean coast. The largest Western oil consortium operating in Azerbaijan, however, postponed choosing between that route and an alternative to Georgia's Black Sea port of Supsa. (See Spotlight: *Central Asian Oil Conflicts.*)

(ELIZABETH FULLER)

BAHAMAS, THE

Area: 13,939 sq km (5,382 sq mi)
Population (1998 est.): 293,000
Capital: Nassau
Chief of state: Queen Elizabeth II, represented by Governor-General Orville Turnquest
Head of government: Prime Minister Hubert Ingraham

Hotel construction continued apace in The Bahamas during 1998. Among the new projects were the second phase of the Sandals Royal Bahamian Resort, a $20 million expansion of the Breezes Hotel to provide 210 new rooms and suites, and a new hotel, marina, and residential housing project called the Old Bahamas Bay Resort.

The government continued its privatization drive, agreeing in March to divest partially the assets of the Bahamas Telecommunications Corp. The Gulf Union Bank was liquidated when the central bank, which had earlier ordered Gulf Union to cease operations, could find no suitable buyer.

An outcry was raised during the year by a group of "concerned Christians" against the visit of cruise ships specifically organized for gay tourists. The government refused to ban such cruises, arguing that The Bahamas could not discriminate on the grounds of sexual orientation.

Repatriation of Cuban refugees from The Bahamas continued in 1998, with 126 being sent back in May, followed by an additional 68 in June. The U.S. government requested that The Bahamas adopt a "humanitarian" attitude to the question of Cuban refugees.

(DAVID RENWICK)

BAHRAIN

Area: 694 sq km (268 sq mi)
Population (1998 est.): 633,000
Capital: Manama
Chief of state: Emir Isa ibn Sulman al-Khalifah
Head of government: Prime Minister Khalifah ibn Sulman al-Khalifah

The political unrest that Bahrain had experienced since the end of 1994 declined noticeably at the street level in 1998, but the government continued to hold about 1,000 Muslim Shi'ite prisoners without trial on charges of antigovernment activity. The Shi'ites, who constituted 70% of the population, were calling for a full restitution of the 1975 constitution, jobs for the unemployed, and the return of political exiles from abroad. In early December Interior Minister Sheik Muhammad bin Khalifah al-Khalifah accused Lebanese living in the country of working with local citizens and Shi'ites outside Bahrain to destabilize the country.

Political stability was important for Bahrain, as the country was trying to compete with Dubayy as a centre for offshore banking in the region. At the beginning of 1998, deposits in Bahrain's banks totaled $71.4 billion, garnered from Arab countries, Europe, and other parts of the world.

Relations between Bahrain and Iran, which had begun to deteriorate in 1996, improved. On Nov. 11, 1997, Iran's minister of foreign affairs paid an official visit to Bahrain. In 1996 Iran had been accused of sponsoring an underground Shi'ite organization, Hezbollah Bahrain.

Bahrain's litigation with Qatar over the ownership of the Hawar Islands (now under Bahraini control) continued throughout the year, with Saudi Arabia and the United Arab Emirates attempting to mediate the dispute. Bahrain announced plans to build a hotel and other tourist facilities on the islands, which were believed to contain important natural gas resources. (LOUAY BAHRY)

BANGLADESH

Area: 147,570 sq km (56,977 sq mi)
Population (1998 est.): 127,567,000
Capital: Dhaka
Chief of state: President Shahabuddin Ahmed
Head of government: Prime Minister Sheikh Hasina Wazed

Bangladesh in 1998 was once again hit hard by the forces of nature, suffering the worst floods of the century in a two-month period ended in mid-September. About two-thirds of the country was left under water, more than 1,000 people were killed, and more than 30 million people were left homeless. Some 300,000 cases of diarrhea were reported, many of them among children. The situation was further compounded when the vital road between Dhaka and the port of Chittagong was flooded for more than a month, which adversely affected the country's ability to export. According to government officials, the country's rice crop was completely destroyed, and Bangladesh would need at least two million tons of grain to tide it over to the end of the year. The government sought $879 million in foreign aid for emergency

A girl in Bahrain walks along a wall scrawled with graffiti slogans urging the government to restore the parliament, which was abolished in 1975. Restoration of the parliament continued to be a main theme among Muslim Shi'ites, who constituted 70% of Bahrain's population. During the year Shi'ites also called for jobs for the unemployed and the return of political exiles from abroad.

relief and postflood rehabilitation, including $240 million worth of food. In the wake of the floods, Prime Minister Sheikh Hasina Wazed said that the government would build an approximately 50-km (30-mi)-long embankment to protect the capital from floods.

On February 10 the Shanti Bahini rebels, a guerrilla group that had been fighting a more than 20-year insurgency for greater regional autonomy for the indigenous population of the Chittagong Hill Tracts (CHT) in southeastern Bangladesh, surrendered their weapons under the terms laid down by an agreement between them and the government in December 1997. As part of the agreement,

the government declared a general amnesty for all armed rebels in the CHT and for individuals previously active in the political wing of the Shanti Bahini. The Bangladesh Nationalist Party (BNP), led by former prime minister Khaleda Zia, rejected this agreement and refused to return to Parliament unless the government rescinded the accord. Following the signing of a memorandum of understanding with the government on March 2, the BNP decided to end the six-month boycott and return to Parliament on March 9. The leadership of the BNP made this decision because of the party's inability to attract widespread popular support for its stance on

this issue and the increased division within the party over this matter. On April 15, however, the BNP walked out of Parliament in protest against the introduction of four bills concerning the December peace agreement with the Shanti Bahini. The BNP accused the government of acting unconstitutionally by attempting to push the bills quickly through Parliament without sufficient debate and of violating the March memorandum. Nevertheless, with its majority in Parliament, the government was able to pass the four bills at the beginning of May.

On June 9 the BNP organized a 25,000-strong "long march" from Dhaka to

A passenger train is stranded by flood waters near Dhaka, Bangladesh. During a two-month period in 1998, about two-thirds of Bangladesh was under water, more than 1,000 people were killed, and more than 30 million others were left homeless. According to government officials, the country's rice crop was completely destroyed.

German ambassador Horst Winkelmann prepares to leave Belarus in June. Winkelmann was among several diplomats ordered home for consultations after the Belarusian government locked them out of their residences at the Drazdy complex, near Minsk.

Chittagong in opposition to the peace agreement. This led to the country's largest popular uprising in two years, with demonstrators using the event as an opportunity to vent their general disapproval with the government's policies and with the increased level of corruption, political violence, and human rights abuses against opponents of the government.

On November 9 a civil court sentenced to death 15 of 19 people accused in the 1975 murder of Sheikh Mujibur Rahman, founder of Bangladesh and father of the prime minister. Five defendants were present at the trial, and the rest were tried in absentia. The sentences were to be carried out in public by firing squad. The verdict led to widespread violence at antigovernment rallies, resulting in two dead and more than 200 injured.

In June the Bangabandhu Bridge, the longest in South Asia and the 11th longest in the world, was opened. The $1 billion structure stretched 4.8 km (3 mi) across the Jamuna River.   (CLAUDE RAKISITS)

BARBADOS

Area: 430 sq km (166 sq mi)
Population (1998 est.): 265,000
Capital: Bridgetown
Chief of state: Queen Elizabeth II, represented by Governor-General Sir Clifford Husbands
Head of government: Prime Minister Owen Arthur

Barbados during 1998 continued working toward membership in the seven-nation Organization of Eastern Caribbean States (OECS), part of the larger Caribbean Community and Common Market (Caricom). A form of confederation was ultimately envisaged for the OECS members, and a joint task force was appointed to examine the matter. Barbados was larger than any other OECS member and viewed its association with the group as increasing its power base within Caricom.

The Barbados central bank forecast a 2.5% growth rate in 1998, down from previous years, primarily because of shortfalls in sugar production. The Barbados National Oil Co. in April launched a major new drilling program that was designed to increase production to 2,500 bbl per day within 12 months. The drilling was being partly funded and managed by Waggoner, an American independent oil company.

Late in the year Barbados moved to place more emphasis on trade and economic relations with Asian countries, despite that region's economic problems. It was particularly looking toward Japan for tourists.

(DAVID RENWICK)

BELARUS

Area: 207,595 sq km (80,153 sq mi)
Population (1998 est.): 10,235,000
Capital: Minsk
Head of state and government: President Alyaksandr G. Lukashenka, assisted by Prime Minister Syarhey Ling

Belarus in 1998 experienced a year of political tension and economic problems and became increasingly isolated from the West. Pres. Alyaksandr Lukashenka imposed new penalties on those who opposed him, including a possible four-year jail sentence for "insults" to the president. Consequently, the year was marked by court cases against those detained in demonstrations, particularly members of the Belarusian Popular Front, whose acting chairman, Lyavon Barcheusky, and deputy chairman, Yury Khadyka, were incarcerated briefly in April. In general, however, there were fewer antigovernment demonstrators than in the past; the 10,000 on March 22 to commemorate the declaration of independence in 1918 was by far the largest.

The president announced that parliamentary elections would be held in the year 2000 and presidential elections in 2001, according to the amended—but in violation of the former—constitution. Late in the year most leftist parties were united in a Popular Patriotic Union, one goal of which was to push for a referendum on confidence in the president in June 1999, in lieu of a presidential election in 1999 as warranted by the 1994 constitution.

During the year Belarus suffered its most severe economic and financial crisis to date. Though official figures provided a picture of impressive economic growth (a rise in gross domestic product of about 12%), the Ministry of Economy acknowledged that the nation was badly in need of foreign loans. Belarus continued to trade by barter rather than money, and the currency was in a free fall against the U.S. dollar. Though the official exchange rate was held at 50,400 rubels to the dollar, the Interbank currency exchange was offering 350,000 rubels to the dollar by early September. Banking came increasingly under governmental control as Lukashenka removed the chairman of the national bank, Hennady Aleynikov, and replaced him with a close ally, former first deputy prime minister Pyotr Prokopovich. Because its economy was closely tied to that of Russia, Belarus also suffered from the financial crisis in Russia that began in the summer of 1998.

The government in 1998 pursued a dual foreign policy: first to try to make clear the nature of the Russia-Belarus Union and to promote closer relations with other former Soviet republics, and second to expand ties and military cooperation with Iran, Syria, Egypt, India, and China. In the former category the main question was the resolution of the issue of dual citizenship and the powers designated to the Union Parliament.

Relations with the rest of the world were strained. During part of the year the Minsk office of the International Monetary Fund was closed, but by late November it had reopened. In June the Belarusian government tried to evict the ambassadors of 22 countries from their residences at the Drazdy

complex, near Minsk, ordering them to leave their homes by June 10. On June 18 the Drazdy complex was declared to be the property of the presidential administration, and on the following day the diplomats were locked out. On June 22 the ambassadors of the U.K., Greece, France, Germany, and Italy were ordered home for consultations, and the U.S. soon followed suit. Lukashenka subsequently declared that alternative accommodations would soon be found for the ambassadors.   (DAVID R. MARPLES)

BELGIUM

Area: 30,528 sq km (11,787 sq mi)
Population (1998 est.): 10,208,000
Capital: Brussels
Chief of state: King Albert II
Head of government: Prime Minister Jean-Luc Dehaene

Belgium's highest-profile trial in many years opened in Brussels on Sept. 2, 1998, when

Former Belgian deputy prime minister Willy Claes arrives at the Justice Palace in Brussels. Claes was among three former senior ministers and other officials convicted in December on charges of having awarded lucrative contracts in exchange for kickbacks given to Belgium's Socialist parties.

BENOIT DOPPAGNE—REUTERS

several senior politicians and their advisers faced charges of having awarded lucrative defense contracts in the late 1980s in exchange for kickbacks to funds of the country's French- and Dutch-speaking Socialist parties. The defendants included three former senior ministers—Willy Claes (a former deputy prime minister and former secretary-general of NATO), Guy Coëme (one-time defense minister), and Guy Spitaels (former minister-president of Wallonia)—and French businessman Serge Dassault. None of the accused was charged with having benefited personally from the payments, which were allegedly made when the Belgian government placed contracts with the Italian company Agusta to purchase 46 army helicopters and with the French company Dassault to supply advanced electronic equipment to Belgium's F-16 jets. Announcing its verdict on December 23, the Cour de Cassation gave suspended sentences of three years to Claes, two years to Coëme, Spitaels, and Dassault, and three months to two years to the eight other defendants.

The damaging allegations surfaced as a result of investigations into the 1991 murder of former deputy prime minister André Cools, who was shot as he left his Liège flat early on the morning of July 18. In June a court in Tunis, Tunisia, sentenced his two killers to 20 years in prison.

On April 23 the convicted pedophile and alleged child murderer Marc Dutroux briefly escaped from his police escort. Although he was recaptured within four hours, the incident was greeted by a mixture of anger and incredulity throughout the country and forced the resignations of Justice Minister Stefaan De Clerk, Interior Minister Johan Vande Lanotte, and the head of the national police force (gendarmerie), Willy Deridder. Lanotte's successor, Louis Tobback, resigned in September after a Nigerian woman collapsed and died when Belgian police tried to deport her forcibly.

A 17-month parliamentary investigation concluded in February that a combination of incompetence, professional jealousy, and structural weaknesses in the judicial and police systems—rather than any protection from senior politicians or magistrates—had enabled Dutroux and his accomplice, Michel Nihoul, to escape detection for so long. The report forced the government to reorganize the country's three different police forces—gendarmerie, judicial police, and communal police—and to create a federal prosecutor's office.

Despite the succession of political setbacks, Prime Minister Jean-Luc Dehaene was determined to lead his centre-left coalition government through to general elections in mid-1999. As a sign of its confidence, the government announced at the start of 1998 that the next elections would be held on June 13, 1999.

Belgium's corporate world began to restructure itself in 1998. In May Belgium's largest holding company, Société Générale de Belgique, which was created in 1822 and once controlled one-third of the country's economy, was fully taken over by its parent company, France's Suez Lyonnaise des Eaux. Also, the Belgo-Dutch insurance combine Fortis took over Generale Bank, creating Belgium's biggest and Europe's 15th largest banking and insurance firm. A break with the past took place at the start of the year when the world's oldest operating stock exchange, at Antwerp, which had been founded in 1531, closed its doors as its remaining business moved to Brussels.
                    (RORY WATSON)

BELIZE

Area: 22,965 sq km (8,867 sq mi)
Population (1998 est.): 235,000
Capital: Belmopan
Chief of state: Queen Elizabeth II, represented by Governor-General Colville Young
Head of government: Prime Ministers Manuel Esquivel and, from August 28, Said Musa

Sept. 10, 1998, marked the 200th anniversary of the Battle of St. George's Cay, during which the British defeated a Spanish fleet and thereby ended Spain's claim to Belize. The two-week celebration followed soon after the general elections. On August 27 some 90% of the eligible voters went to the polls to elect a government for the next five years. The People's United Party (PUP) won a landslide victory over the ruling United Democratic Party (UDP). Of the 29 available seats in the House of Representatives, the PUP won 26 and the UDP 3. Taking office on August 28, Prime Minister Said Musa stated that his government would be one of "national unity, national reconciliation, and national renewal."

After having served for 15 years as leader of the UDP, former prime minister Manuel Esquivel officially stepped down on August 31. In September he was replaced by Dean Barrow as the leader of the UDP in the House of Representatives.

Under the UDP government, the 1998–99 budget called for several tax changes, including the removal of the value-added tax from telephone bills, the abolition of income tax on yearly earnings below $20,000, and the introduction of a new business tax. Business leaders criticized the business tax because they believed it would further damage the already ailing tourism industry. The new government proposed a comprehensive review of the entire tax structure.
                    (INES PARKER)

BENIN

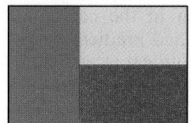

Area: 112,680 sq km (43,500 sq mi)
Population (1998 est.): 6,101,000
Capital: Porto-Novo (executive and ministerial offices remain in Cotonou)
Head of state and government: President Mathieu Kérékou, assisted by Prime Minister Adrien Houngbedji until May 8 and, from May 14, government spokesman Pierre Osho

Striking civil servants shut down the government of Benin on Feb. 16, 1998, when a four-day work stoppage was called by the nation's five main public-service unions. They were protesting the government's decision to accept the insistence by the International Monetary Fund (IMF) and the World Bank that a merit system for promotion and pay raises be adopted. On February 19 the post and telecommunications union joined the walkout after new talks with both the government and officials of the IMF and World Bank had broken down earlier in the week. The unions, representing 40,000 civil servants, demanded not only that the merit system be dropped but also that salary arrears of $39 million arising from the automatic promotion system be paid. Two weeks later an agreement was reached, and a pay increase for the civil service, amounting to between 5% and 8%, was announced. Insisting that the pact would have no impact on inflation, as it would be funded from budget reserves, the government committed itself to a partial payment of salary arrears. Officially, however, it remained committed to salary and promotion reforms.

Benin's ruling coalition was shattered on May 8, when Prime Minister Adrien Houngbedji, along with three other ministers from his opposition Party of Democratic Renewal, resigned from Pres. Mathieu Kérékou's Cabinet. Six days later Kérékou reshuffled his Cabinet and announced that the new 18-member government would no longer include a prime minister but would instead have a "government spokesman."
(NANCY ELLEN LAWLER)

BHUTAN

Area: 47,000 sq km (18,150 sq mi)
Population (1998 est.): 633,000 (excluding Bhutanese of Nepalese origin declared stateless by the Bhutanese government in late 1990, nearly 100,000 of whom are now refugees in Nepal)
Capital: Thimphu
Head of state and government: Druk Gyalpo (King) Jigme Singye Wangchuk

Bhutan took a major step toward constitutional government in 1998. The king, after dismissing the appointed Cabinet in June, agreed to the National Assembly's choice of new ministers, even though they differed from the nominees he had recommended. Furthermore, the king agreed to grant the National Assembly the right to test his rule in periodic votes of confidence and even demand his abdication.

Remaining unresolved was the issue of the repatriation to Bhutan of the nearly 100,000 Bhutanese of Nepalese origin who had lived in eight UN-monitored refugee camps in eastern Nepal since 1990, when Bhutan launched a national policy that everyone was to adhere to Bhutanese Buddhist traditions. Adding to the problem was the dismissal in early 1998 of 219 Nepalese-speaking civil servants, many of whom were related to pro-democracy activists or to refugees in the UN camps. Human rights activists attempted to use Prince Charles's visit to Bhutan in February as an opportunity to draw international attention to the plight of the Bhutanese refugees.
(CLAUDE RAKISITS)

BOLIVIA

Area: 1,098,581 sq km (424,164 sq mi)
Population (1998 est.): 7,957,000
Capitals: La Paz (administrative) and Sucre (judicial)
Head of state and government: President Hugo Bánzer Suárez

Interparty bickering and new corruption scandals marked the first year of Bolivia's new coalition government in 1998. The former mayor of La Paz, Gaby Candia (ousted in January and replaced by Germán Monroy), was accused of having spent $1.6 million of public funds on improper land dealings; the accusation was seen by many, however, as a move to undermine the opposition Nationalist Revolutionary Movement. Meanwhile, Conscience of the Fatherland, the junior member of the governing coalition, was unhappy with the government's commitment to privatization and reduced public spending. Its attempt to reconcile its populist principles with the policies of the new government caused ruptures within the party, with some members calling for a complete withdrawal from the coalition.

Bono Solidario, or Bonosol, the public pension system set up by the previous government, was scrapped during the year owing to lack of funds. A new scheme, Bolivida, was introduced in June. It would provide a minimum annual payment of $90 upon retirement to those who were aged 50 or older on Dec. 1, 1995. Funding would come from 30% of the Collective Capitalization Fund, which contained the proceeds of the previous government's capitalization program, estimated at $1.5 billion. The government planned to use the remaining two-thirds of the fund to finance a new scheme that would provide individual share funds, estimated at $400 apiece, for all those aged between 21 and 50 on Dec. 1, 1995. Beneficiaries would be able to cash in their shares when they reached 65.

The devastating effects of the previous year's El Niño on crops, land, homes, and health continued to leave their mark on the country. The most severely affected regions were Oruro, Potosí, and Chuquisaca. Government estimates revealed that more than 40% of the population of those provinces needed emergency help. El Niño caused agricultural output to fall by 3.9% during the first half of 1998. Crops farmed in the western highlands, among them corn, potatoes, cotton, and wheat, were the worst hit. Only soybeans, Bolivia's highest export earner, survived the adverse weather conditions, with just a 0.1% decline in the harvest.

The government continued to have difficulty persuading coca growers in the Chapare region to cooperate in its antinarcotics program. The growers claimed that

Union members march in protest against the Bolivian government's destruction of coca leaf plantations in the Chapare region. In 1998 the government continued to eradicate coca crops as part of its antinarcotics program, but coca growers maintained that the government's alternative crop-development programs provided insufficient compensation.

the government's alternative crop-development proposals were insufficient compensation for eradicating their coca crops. Protests came to a head in June; clashes between coca growers and security forces resulted in more than 10 deaths. The leader of the coca growers, Evo Morales, called for former president Gonzalo Sánchez de Lozada to be brought to trial for human rights abuses committed by the previous government in the Chapare region.   (ALAN MURPHY)

BOSNIA AND HERZEGOVINA

Area: 51,129 sq km (19,741 sq mi)
Population (1998 est.): 3,366,000, excluding about 850,000 refugees in adjacent countries and Western Europe
Capital: Sarajevo
Heads of state: Tripartite presidency headed by Alija Izetbegovic and from October 13, Zivko Radisic
Heads of government: Two cochairmen of the Council of Ministers

International efforts to rebuild and stabilize Bosnia and Herzegovina continued to show progress in 1998, but they fell short of achieving the goal of establishing the multinational country as a stable, functioning state, able to run its own affairs. During the year about 100,000 refugees returned, nearly twice as many as in the previous two years. Of those, 30,000 returned to their prewar municipalities as minorities—20,000 in the Federation of Bosnia and Herzegovina (the part of the nation populated predominantly by Croats and Muslims) and 10,000 in Republika Srpska (Serb Republic).

In an effort to increase international authority over the implementation of the Dayton Peace Agreement, signed in 1995, the powers of the Office of the High Representative (OHR) were expanded in December 1997. In 1998 High Representative Carlos Westendorp pushed through a series of measures aimed at speeding up that process. These included a common vehicle license plate, which made it possible for Bosnians to travel throughout the country with a reasonable degree of security, and a new Bosnian flag and passport. He appointed special envoys to supervise the implementation of the peace agreement in strategic parts of the country and dismissed local officials if they blocked such efforts. His office also instituted a systematic restructuring of the media by wresting control of the principal television stations from the ruling parties, placing international supervisors in the stations, and imposing new regulatory proce-

dures. In November Westendorp proposed a 30% increase in his office's 1999 budget, so that "critical tasks" of postwar reconstruction could move forward.

Domestic political institutions, however, failed to function properly and expeditiously. The NATO-led peacekeeping mission remained in the nation almost three years after the peace accord came into force, and, because of fears that if it withdrew, the country would quickly slide back into war, there seemed little prospect that it would do so in the near future. Five separate, internationally supervised elections, including a general election in September 1998, did not produce a situation in which the peace process could be judged as self-sustaining. Bosniac (Muslim) and Croat parallel institutions existed, but officials often behaved more as representatives of their ethnic groups and political parties than as public servants of the federation. Theoretically, a joint command for the federation army existed, but in practice separate Muslim and Croat military formations remained, along with the Republika Srpska armed forces, so Bosnia continued to have three military forces representing the three wartime (1992–95) protagonists.

In the September general election, federation Pres. Alija Izetbegovic's coalition placed first in the federation, winning some 52% of the votes; Serbian Radical Party (SRS) candidate Nikola Poplasen defeated the West-backed Biljana Plavsic of the moderate nationalist Serbian People's Alliance for the presidency of Republika Srpska; and Kresimir Zubak of the New Croatian Initiative lost to Ante Jelavic, candidate of the hard-line Croat Democratic Community (HDZ), for the Croat seat on the federation's three-member presidency. The election of the moderate Zivko Radisic over hard-liner Momcilo Krajisnik as the Serb representative on the presidency somewhat offset Poplasen's victory. As expected, Izetbegovic was reelected as the Bosniac representative.

The most crushing defeat for the international community came when the Social Democrats failed to win in the canton of Tuzla-Podrinje. Experts had predicted great changes for Bosnia's political scene emanating from Tuzla's Social Democrats.

Most of the other election results revealed a slight departure from hard-line nationalism. In the federation the Coalition for a United and Democratic Bosnia and Herzegovina won a majority in the legislature with 68 seats, and the HDZ dropped from 36 seats to 28. The Social Democratic Party gained 19 seats, and a group of small nonnationalist parties won 7. Also, for the first time, the Republika Srpska-based Socialist Party took two seats.

The economy of the federation continued to deteriorate. Although industrial production in 1997 increased by 35% in relation to 1996, the rate of growth slowed down. Many Bosnians worked in low-level jobs—as chauffeurs and secretaries, for example. Salaries were often paid after delays of several months, and workers' strikes were becoming more frequent. Enterprises accumulated debts exceeding $750 million, of which 88% was incurred by state enterprises.   (MILAN ANDREJEVICH)

BOTSWANA

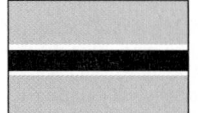

Area: 581,730 sq km (224,607 sq mi)
Population (1998 est.): 1,448,000
Capital: Gaborone
Head of state and government: Presidents Sir Ketumile Masire and, from April 1, Festus Mogae

A Bosnian mine-disposal specialist hunts for land mines at a Jewish cemetery in Sarajevo. A number of teams worked in Bosnia and Herzegovina throughout 1998 to rid the country of the estimated one million land mines that remained three years after the war ended with the signing of the Dayton peace accord in December 1995.

SAVA RADOVANOVIC—AP/WIDE WORLD

Botswana was an island of stability in southern Africa during 1998. The country enjoyed economic prosperity as its growth rate hovered around 7% and its vast diamond reserves generated fiscal surpluses. The nation also witnessed a successful changing of the guard when its president of 18 years, Ketumile Masire, stepped down on March 31 to make way for Festus Mogae, the former vice president and minister of finance and development and planning. Though Masire had overseen a period of rising prosperity, it was widely assumed that his ruling party, the Botswana Democratic Party (BDP), engineered his ouster in favour of Mogae.

It was uncertain during the year whether the BDP could remain in power, a position it had enjoyed since Botswana attained independence in 1966. The main opposition party, the Botswana National Front (BNF), gained popularity, especially in urban areas. As a result, many BDP politicians were seeking to replace Mogae with Lieut. Gen. Ian Khama, a charismatic former soldier and the son of Botswana's founding president, Seretse Khama.

Notwithstanding economic growth and a peaceful presidential transition, Botswana was confronted with several pressing issues. Poverty was rampant, affecting about half of the country's population, and unemployment was acute, especially among young people. The spread of sexually transmitted diseases also skyrocketed; reportedly, some 30% of sexually active Botswanans aged 15–49 were infected with the HIV virus. Finally, relations with its neighbour Namibia were strained owing to a conflict over scarce water resources. (MICHAEL TETELMAN)

BRAZIL

Area: 8,547,404 sq km (3,300,171 sq mi)
Population (1998 est.): 161,766,000
Capital: Brasília
Head of state and government: President Fernando Henrique Cardoso

During January and February 1998, Pres. Fernando Cardoso pressed ahead with his bid to push through constitutional reforms in the areas of social security (pensions) and government administration (civil service and state enterprises). In February the administrative reform won Senate approval (leaving regulatory matters to be dealt with), and the Chamber of Deputies approved the social security bill in the first-round vote (the bill having already been approved by the Senate). A favourable second-round vote was achieved at the beginning of June, but a number of opposition amendments were not completed prior to the elections, these going through only in early November.

By late March the prospect of a Cabinet reshuffle was evident, as ministers running for other offices had to resign by April 4, six months prior to the election date. On March 30 former planning minister José Serra, a close associate of the president and a cofounder of the Social Democratic Party (PSDB), was confirmed in the post of health minister. In early April the other main

Outside the Federal Income Tax building in São Paulo, unemployed Brazilians demonstrate in November against Pres. Fernando Cardoso's economic austerity plan. Protesters feared that Cardoso's efforts to avert a monetary collapse and reduce public deficits would mean higher taxes and drastic cuts in social spending.

changes were announced, with Edward Amadeo becoming labour minister (succeeding Paulo Paiva, who took the planning portfolio) and new incumbents at agriculture, justice, industry, social security, and institutional reform. There was no change to the key post of finance minister, held by Pedro Malan, which was to prove important as global economic difficulties intensified.

Late in April two of Cardoso's key political allies died: Communication Minister Sergio Motta and government Chief Whip Luís Eduardo Magalhaes. This unexpected development required Cardoso to take the lead in pushing through his reform agenda at a time close to the onset of his reelection campaign. The latter part of May and much of June registered some erosion of popular support for the president in the opinion polls, but by early July support for Cardoso was rebuilding. Through August and September he maintained the confidence of

the electorate by adopting a pragmatic stance and demonstrating a firm commitment to dealing with economic problem areas, particularly the deficits on the public sector and current accounts.

On October 4 Cardoso was reelected with 53.1% of the valid votes, comfortably ahead of Luiz Inácio ("Lula") da Silva (31.7%), while Ciro Gomes, a former PSDB member running for the small Popular Socialist Party (PPS), finished third with almost 11%. In the 513-member Chamber of Deputies, the seats won by the main pro-government parties were as follows: Liberal Front Party (PFL), 105; PSDB, 99; Brazilian Democratic Movement (PMDB), 82; Progressive Renewal Party (PPB), 60; and Labour Party (PTB), 31. The leading left-of-centre opposition parties, the Workers' Party (PT) and Democratic Labour Party (PDT), took 58 and 26 seats, respectively. In the 81-member Senate, the PMDB

(continued on page 414)

By 1998 the common market concept within Latin America, as exemplified by Mercosur (Argentina, Brazil, Paraguay, and Uruguay, with Chile and Bolivia joining as associate members), several bilateral trade agreements, and the rejuvenation of the Andean Community and the Central American Common Market, was contributing to a diminution of old geopolitical rivalries in favour of interdependence. These moves toward economic integration, however, highlighted the poor state of the region's infrastructure. The World Bank and Interamerican Development Bank estimated that if Latin America was to maintain and upgrade only modestly its transport sector alone, $14 billion would have to be spent annually. For such a sum government funding would be insufficient, and efforts were being made to involve the private sector and multilateral agencies. This was being achieved through privatization, new project financing, and innovative investment funds, but in 1998 it appeared that repercussions from the economic crises in Asia and Russia might force a reduction in spending by Latin-American governments and foreign investors.

Historically the main intercontinental roadway has been the 48,000-km (1 km=0.62 mi) Pan-American Highway, which extends from Alaska to Argentina and Chile. At only one place does it remain uncompleted, the 400-km Darién Gap in Panama and Colombia. Despite the difficulty of the terrain (jungle and swamp) and, more recently, environmental considerations, schemes to traverse the gap continue to be assessed. In 1995 Peru completed the rehabilitation of the 2,600-km highway in its territory, which has greatly reduced the driving time from Ecuador to Chile. The work was carried out by private firms. Ecuador has also looked to the pri-

SPOTLIGHT

LATIN AMERICA'S NEW TRANSPORTATION LINKS

by Ben Box

Illustration by Tom Curry

vate sector to help with the maintenance of its part of the highway, which costs about $45 million annually. Farther north, a new Caracas-Bogotá highway was under consideration, as well as a railway across the Venezuelan and Colombian plains to cope with growing cross-border trade.

The increased emphasis on regional trade encouraged the paving of the Pan-American Highway north of Manaus, Braz., to join with its paved counterpart in Venezuela. A branch is planned to extend east into Guyana to form part of the planned trans-Guiana highway, envisaged as a continuous road from Georgetown, Guyana, through that nation and Suriname into French Guiana and from there via the Saint-Georges–Oiapoque border crossing into the Brazilian state of Amapá. The resulting network will join Caracas and the Orinoco River in Venezuela with two Amazonian cities (Macapá and Manaus) and the three Guianas.

Two major projects are under way to meet the transport demand in the Mercosur region. The first is the expressway from São Paulo, Braz., to Buenos Aires, Arg., with a planned extension to Santiago, Chile. Estimated at $2.5 billion at its announcement in 1992, the 2,500-km superhighway was designed to improve and widen existing roads. It will also utilize a new 42-km toll bridge, to be built over the Río de la Plata from Colonia de Sacramento, Uruguay, to Buenos Aires at a cost of $1 billion. The Super Highway is to be developed in conjunction with the Hidrovía (waterway), an ambitious project in which the Paraná-Paraguay river system will open a trade corridor from the interior of the continent to the Atlantic Ocean. The rivers flow through Brazil, Bolivia, Paraguay, Uruguay, and Argentina, and since 1992 the five countries have been studying the transport po-

Workers at the Panama Canal (left) take measurements for the installation of a new railway. During the year the Panama Canal, which was scheduled to come under Panamanian jurisdiction on Jan. 1, 2000, was being upgraded in a $1 billion program to be completed in 2002. (Opposite, above) The Pan-American Highway stretches through the Andes Mountains in Ecuador. A portion of the highway, the 400-km Darién Gap, remains uncompleted.

tential that would result from widening and dredging those parts that have been difficult to navigate. At its fullest extent, the Hidrovía was envisioned as a 3,400-km artery from Cáceres, Mato Grosso, Braz., to Nueva Palmira on the Uruguayan bank of the Río de la Plata. One major difficulty is the necessity to take barges around the Itaipú hydroelectric dam on the Paraná.

In March 1998 Brazil withdrew from the Hidrovía but continued with other plans to make better use of its rivers for transportation; one example is the Tietê-Paraná river system. The Tietê River flows from São Paulo state to join the Paraná River at the state border with Mato Grosso do Sul. Argentina is also developing its river transport system. In May 1995 the Río de la Plata–Paraná corridor was transferred to the private sector, which then provided 24-hour navigation that will greatly reduce transport costs on the route. A major challenge that remains for Mercosur is that the rail networks of the two largest markets, Brazil and Argentina, use different gauges. Unless that can be resolved, trains will be unable to replace trucks in the expansion of traditional and nontraditional exports.

Planners in Bolivia regard the country as an ideal hub for commerce in South America, even though its transport infrastructure suffers from a lack of resources. Work progressed on the Cochabamba–Santa Cruz road and its extension to the Brazilian border to complete a paved route from west to east. The Bolivian railway network, Enfe, was taken over in 1996 by Chile's Cruz Blanca, which hopes to create a railway through Bolivia connecting São Paulo with Antofagasta, Chile, and thus link the Atlantic and Pacific coasts. Chile and Argentina are also facing the challenge of constructing a comprehensive road network between the Atlantic and Pacific coasts. Under preliminary study is a low-altitude tunnel across the Andes from Mendoza to Santiago.

In Central America the Panama Canal, which is to come under Panamanian jurisdiction on Jan. 1, 2000, is being upgraded in a $1 billion program due for completion in 2002. Any further expansion would involve new locks and perhaps even a parallel sea-level canal. The railway that runs beside the canal is in desperate need of rebuilding, which has been undertaken in a $60 million joint venture between Kansas City Southern Industries and Mi-Jack Products. Panama is facing competition, however: a shallow-draft canal for barges through Nicaragua; a new canal through Colombia; "dry canals" (railways carrying container traffic from port to port) through Nicaragua, Costa Rica (with an associated new port north of Puerto Limón), or the isthmus of Tehuantepec in Mexico; and a rail/road "dry canal" through Honduras and El Salvador.

Ben Box has written extensively on Latin American subjects and is editor of Footprint Handbooks.

RIC ERGENBRIGHT—CORBIS

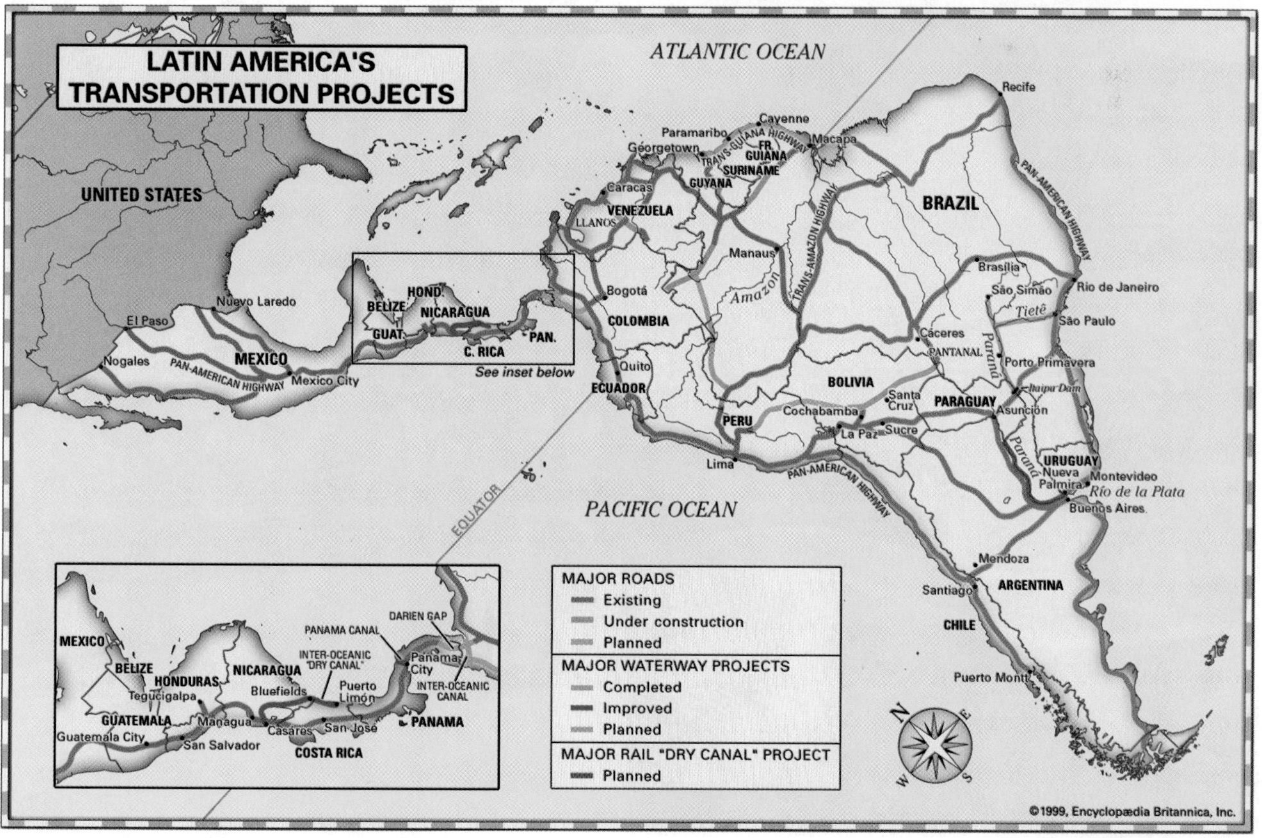

LATIN AMERICA'S TRANSPORTATION PROJECTS

ATLANTIC OCEAN

PACIFIC OCEAN

MAJOR ROADS
- Existing
- Under construction
- Planned

MAJOR WATERWAY PROJECTS
- Completed
- Improved
- Planned

MAJOR RAIL "DRY CANAL" PROJECT
- Planned

©1999, Encyclopædia Britannica, Inc.

(continued from page 411)
became the largest party, with 27 seats, followed by PFL with 20, PSDB with 16, and PT with 7. Most of the 27 contests for governor were won by candidates from parties in the pro-government alliance (including 7 for the PSDB), with the opposition taking 6 overall.

The favourable results for Cardoso, as well as for the loose coalition of parties backing him, ran counter to the crisis environment that had intensified since July and that had brought the government into negotiations with the International Monetary Fund (IMF) and creditors in an effort to avert a collapse of the real; this followed huge capital outflows in August and September that totaled approximately $30 billion, reducing reserves to about $52 billion and driving up interest rates to almost 50%. In order to obtain contingency financing from these sources, the government in late December enacted measures designed to raise $5.6 billion to help reduce the budget deficit.

It was agreed with the IMF that a budget surplus of 2.6% of gross domestic product (GDP) would be achieved in 1999, increasing to 2.8% in 2000 and 3% in 2001. For such targets to be viable, austerity measures totaling $84.5 billion over the three-year period were announced on October 28. While most of these were awaiting congressional approval, on November 13 the IMF and multilateral and bilateral creditors announced a standby loan totaling approximately $41.3 billion.

The economy showed only moderate growth of 1.22% in the first half of 1998 compared with the same period of 1997, and in the third quarter there was a decline of 0.14% from the corresponding period of the previous year as manufacturing industry contracted sharply (down 4.09%) and industry overall fell 2.06%. Annual GDP growth of about 0.5% appeared likely (after 3.7% in 1997).

(SUSAN M. CUNNINGHAM)

BRUNEI

Area: 5,765 sq km (2,226 sq mi)
Population (1998 est.): 315,000
Capital: Bandar Seri Begawan
Head of state and government: Sultan and Prime Minister Haji Hassanal Bolkiah Mu'izzaddin Waddaulah

The Asian financial crisis had an impact even on the rich sultanate of Brunei in 1998. The annual budget was halved by B$605 million (U.S. $357 million), but that caused such an outcry in the business community that B$352 million (U.S. $208 million) was reinjected to stimulate the economy. Construction suffered, especially after the collapse of Amedeo, a diversified conglom-

erate owned by Prince Jefri Bolkiah, the sultan's youngest brother. Thousands of foreign workers, especially those in the construction and tourism industries, were sent home because of the faltering economy. The sultan visited other countries in Southeast Asia and promised financial help in the crisis, but he was forced to rescind these offers when Brunei's own coffers were found to be depleted. With the Amedeo losses reportedly running into billions of dollars, Prince Jefri left Brunei in April and was removed from all government posts by July.

(ROGER MITTON)

BULGARIA

Area: 110,994 sq km (42,855 sq mi)
Population (1998 est.): 8,273,000
Capital: Sofia
Chief of state: President Petar Stoyanov
Head of government: Prime Minister Ivan Kostov

The major preoccupation of Bulgaria's government in 1998 was the consolidation of the economic stability achieved in 1997. This had to be done in order for the nation to secure loans from external sources, particularly the

Bulgarians pay their last respects to Todor Zhivkov, who led the Bulgarian Communist Party from 1954 to 1989, in Sofia on August 9. Zhivkov died on August 5. His coffin was placed at the stairs of the former Royal Palace, across the street from the mausoleum of Georgi Dimitrov, Zhivkov's predecessor.

International Monetary Fund (IMF); these loans were necessary for the country's economic viability. The external lenders demanded intensified economic reform, and the government delivered. On May 9 the National Assembly sanctioned the ending of subsidies to the agricultural sector and endorsed the principles of a market economy, including privatization. In July Prime Minister Ivan Kostov announced that by the end of the year one-half of the equity of the Bulgarian Telecommunications Co. would be in private hands. Future privatizations were to include arms-manufacturing plants, Balkan Airlines, a number of banks, and Bulgaria's largest oil refinery. Kostov also announced his intention to impose tighter fiscal policies.

These statements of intended reform made possible some progress with the IMF. In late July and early August, negotiations produced an agreement under which the IMF would lend Bulgaria $800 million, and a similar sum would be loaned from other sources. At the beginning of September, however, the IMF insisted that the loan was still dependent upon Bulgaria's taking an additional 15 "prior actions."

The party political front remained quiet. In February a new centre-left coalition, the Bulgarian Euroleft, was formed, and in July four liberal parties formed the Liberal Democratic Alliance, of which former president Zhelyu Zhelev was made honorary president.

There were signs of some tension between the political authorities and the military. In March Pres. Petar Stoyanov dismissed Maj. Gen. Angel Marin, the commander in chief of Missile Troops and Artillery Forces, who had criticized the government's decision to reduce spending on the army. In July the chief of the General Staff, Col. Gen. Miho Mihov, announced that more than 1,000 officers were to be removed from the active list; a number of senior officers were also moved or retired.

Bulgaria experienced some ethnic tensions as well. In June in the northern city of Lom, Roma (Gypsies) protested against discrimination in employment and the nonpayment of welfare benefits, and in September Bulgarian Turks complained about the removal of three plaques commemorating ethnic Turks executed in 1988 for their alleged involvement in a series of bombings that killed eight people in 1984–85. On the other hand, Bulgaria allowed broadcasts in Turkish and, for the first time in 50 years, permitted the circumcision of Muslim boys.

On August 5 Todor Zhivkov, who led the Bulgarian Communist Party from 1954 to 1989, died. (*See* OBITUARIES.)

(RICHARD J. CRAMPTON)

BURKINA FASO

Area: 274,400 sq km (105,946 sq mi)
Population (1998 est.): 11,266,000
Capital: Ouagadougou
Chief of state: President Blaise Compaoré
Head of government: Prime Minister Kadré Désiré Ouédraogo

Massacred bodies lie in a field near Bujumbura Airport in Burundi. Army barracks at the airport and a village nearby were the focus of an attack by Hutu rebels on January 1. At least 150 persons were killed, including 100 civilians, many of them women and children. The Tutsi-led government forces eventually repulsed the attack.

Burkina Faso was host to a number of major African events and conferences in 1998. The Africa Cup, the continent's top soccer tournament, was held in Ouagadougou in February, as was the 20th Franco-African Meeting, attended by foreign ministers from about 40 nations with ties to France. On June 8 the three-day annual summit of the Organization of African Unity, under the chairmanship of Pres. Blaise Compaoré, opened. In December African heads of state met in Ouagadougou to discuss concerns about regional conflicts, especially the war in the Democratic Republic of Congo.

In November Compaoré was reelected president with 88% of the vote. His closest rival was Ram Ouedraogo of the Green Party with 7%. Most opposition candidates boycotted the election, accusing Compaoré of rigging the voter registration process in his favour. Approximately 56% of the nation's eligible voters cast ballots, a gain of more than 30% over the last presidential election in 1991. (NANCY ELLEN LAWLER)

BURUNDI

Area: 27,816 sq km (10,740 sq mi)
Population (1998 est.): 5,537,000
Capital: Bujumbura
Head of state and government: President Pierre Buyoya, assisted by Prime Minister Pascal-Firmin Ndimira

In the early-morning hours of Jan. 1, 1998, approximately 2,000 Hutu rebels attacked the army barracks at Bujumbura Airport and a nearby village, killing at least 150 people before government forces repulsed them. Burundian Pres. Pierre Buyoya claimed that

Tanzania had supported the rebels, a charge Tanzanian Pres. Benjamin Mkapa denied. Both countries amassed troops on their common border. The Organization of African Unity (OAU) condemned the attack and dispatched a delegation to urge all parties to join talks mediated by former Tanzanian president Julius Nyerere. Buyoya's government refused to participate, charging that Nyerere favoured the Hutu.

On June 15, however, OAU-sponsored peace talks, mediated by Nyerere and with Burundi in attendance, opened in Arusha, Tanz. The participants agreed to begin a cease-fire on July 20, the beginning of a second round of talks. The second round began as scheduled, but procedural disputes hampered the talks, and no substantial progress was made; the participants, however, agreed to reconvene for a third round of negotiations on October 13. Insecurity returned to the north of the country when, shortly after the July talks ended, at least 6,000 refugees fled rebel attacks.

Regional leaders meeting in Kampala, Uganda, announced on February 21 that economic sanctions against Burundi would continue until the government negotiated with the rebels and moved toward civilian rule. The sanctions had begun after Buyoya's 1996 coup and included an arms embargo as well as bans on commercial flights and all exports. Citing hardship, the Burundian government repeatedly called for the lifting of sanctions. In March the World Food Programme began a humanitarian airlift to the country, the first since the sanctions started.

On June 11 Buyoya was sworn in as head of state under the Transitional Constitutional Act passed five days earlier. This resolved the impasse between the president, who favoured transitional legislation, and members of the National Assembly who preferred the 1992 constitution (suspended when Buyoya took power).

(MATTHEW A. CENZER)

Prince Norodom Ranariddh (second from right) and his wife offer food to Buddhist monks at a temple in Phnom Penh, Cambodia, prior to the July 26 election. After the party of Ranariddh's rival, Hun Sen, claimed the largest share of National Assembly seats in the election, Ranariddh and fellow opposition leader Sam Rangsi alleged widespread electoral fraud.

CAMBODIA

Area: 181,916 sq km (70,238 sq mi)
Population (1998 est.): 10,751,000
Capital: Phnom Penh
Chief of state: King Norodom Sihanouk
Head of government: First Prime
   Minister Ung Huot until September 16;
   Second Prime Minister and, from
   November 14, Prime Minister
   Hun Sen

In 1998 Cambodia held its second democratic election since a 1991 UN-brokered peace agreement brought a semblance of stability to the war-ravaged nation. Optimists had hoped the poll would settle the crippling rivalry between strongman Hun Sen and Prince Norodom Ranariddh, whom Hun Sen had driven from the co-premiership in a 1997 coup. The election re-

sults only intensified their personal feud, however, and prompted months of political paralysis and violence, an outcome of far more import to the nation than the death of notorious Khmer Rouge leader Pol Pot in April. (*See* OBITUARIES.)

Long before voters went to the polls on July 26, there was reason to believe that the election would not be credible. During the campaign the opposition accused Hun Sen's Cambodian People's Party (CPP) of intimidating voters and murdering political opponents, yet when the polling was done, scores of international observers pronounced the voting sufficiently free and fair. One even dubbed the exercise a "miracle on the Mekong."

The jubilation was short-lived. Even as early returns showed Hun Sen's party headed for the largest share of National Assembly seats, the opposition began to cry foul. Ranariddh, leader of the royalist Funcinpec Party (FP), and Sam Rangsi (also spelled Rainsy), a former finance minister and leader of the small Sam Rangsi Party (SRP), both alleged widespread electoral fraud and demanded a recount. Within days,

electoral officials announced a revised tally: the CPP won 64 seats, the FP claimed 43 seats, and the SRP managed to earn 15 seats in the 122-member assembly. As expected, the National Election Committee, which was effectively controlled by Hun Sen, subsequently upheld the new results.

The matter did not end there, however. The CPP had failed to win the two-thirds majority required for forming a government. Hun Sen had no choice but to form a coalition, but Rangsi and Ranariddh refused to join one until their charges of electoral fraud were adequately investigated. Hun Sen allowed a limited recount that confirmed his victory, and Ranariddh and Rangsi initiated mass protests in late August outside the National Assembly. At the same time, Rangsi went on a rhetorical offensive against Cambodia's Vietnamese minority— a move widely seen as a deliberate affront to Hun Sen, whose rise to power had come during Vietnam's occupation of Cambodia in the 1980s. Besides putting himself on a collision course with the strongman, Rangsi lost international credibility, especially when protesters killed ethnic Vietnamese

and defaced a monument heralding the two nations' friendship. For some two weeks Hun Sen allowed the opposition demonstrations to continue, but after a grenade was thrown at one of his residences, he ordered police to end the rallies.

Leaders of the international community called upon the warring parties to hammer out a coalition government. Cambodia's ailing King Norodom Sihanouk, Ranariddh's father, offered to mediate talks between Hun Sen and the opposition. The king managed to persuade his son and Rangsi to convene the assembly so as to head off a constitutional crisis. On September 24, the day of the convening ceremony, a bomb explosion narrowly missed a vehicle carrying Hun Sen. Dubbing the incident an assassination attempt, Hun Sen accused the opposition leaders of having instigated the attack and issued stern warnings to them. Rangsi and Ranariddh, fearing for their safety, fled to Thailand in October. In November, however, a coalition government was formed between Hun Sen and Prince Ranariddh.

In December the Association of Southeast Asian Nations decided to admit Cambodia as its 10th member.

(ROBIN PAUL AJELLO)

CAMEROON

Area: 475,442 sq km (183,569 sq mi)
Population (1998 est.): 15,029,000
Capital: Yaoundé
Chief of state: President Paul Biya
Head of government: Prime Minister
Peter Mafany Musonge

Economic prospects brightened in Cameroon in 1998; the inflation rate hovered around 2%, and real economic growth was expected to be 5%. In January, following the dismissal of the airline's managing director and chairman, Cameroon Airline pilots walked out for five days. The underlying cause of the strike, however, was the proposed privatization of the enterprise. In other areas the government sought private investors for several large state industries, among them cotton, sugar, telecommunications, and water. Germany agreed to reschedule $367 million of debt over a 25-year period. As a result of this and other debt-rescheduling agreements, 1998–99 budgetary expenditures were expected to be 2% lower than during the previous year. The World Bank granted Cameroon a $180 million credit on June 25, and in September the International Monetary Fund expressed its satisfaction with the country's progress in the first year of its new three-year structural-adjustment program.

Progress toward achieving a free press was less evident. In January Pius Njawe, editor of the leading opposition newspaper, *Le Messager,* was jailed for having printed a story suggesting that Pres. Paul Biya had suffered heart problems during a soccer match held on Dec. 21, 1997. On April 14 the Douala Appeals Court upheld the verdict but reduced Njawe's two-year sentence to 10 months.

The dispute between Cameroon and Nigeria over the oil-rich Bakassi peninsula came no closer to resolution. Four years after Cameroon had filed a complaint with the UN, the International Court of Justice finally opened hearings on the sovereignty over the area on March 2. Three days later Cameroon accused Nigeria of delay tactics. On May 7 Nigeria charged Cameroon with trying to provoke war by moving 2,000 troops to the border and launching a rocket attack on a Nigerian fishing village.

(NANCY ELLEN LAWLER)

CANADA

Area: 9,970,610 sq km (3,849,674 sq mi)
Population (1998 est.): 30,677,000
Capital: Ottawa
Chief of state: Queen Elizabeth II, represented by Governor-General Roméo LeBlanc
Head of government: Prime Minister Jean Chrétien

Domestic Affairs. The possibility of Quebec's secession remained a central theme in Canadian politics in 1998. Attention was focused on the internal politics of Quebec, which had been transformed by the emergence after April 30 of a charismatic figure, Jean Charest. (*See* BIOGRAPHIES.) On that date Charest took over the leadership of the provincial Liberal Party. This made him the chief spokesman

for federalism in the province. During the referendum on secession in 1995, Charest had been an energetic proponent of a united Canada. Lucien Bouchard, Quebec's separatist premier, decided that Charest's new role signaled the need for an election. His Parti Québécois (PQ) government had been in office for four years. If Bouchard won the election, a referendum on independence would likely follow. If Charest won, there would be no further vote on Quebec secession. A poll in late March revealed that 59% of all Quebeckers favoured the status quo, whereas 31% supported independence.

Charest made it plain that in his opinion the endless debate over separation had sapped the economic strength of the province. Quebec's unemployment rate stood 2% above the national average, and since 1978 some 400,000 people had left the province. It was in everyone's interest, he believed, to concentrate on measures, such as an easing of the tax burden, that would promote economic growth.

The PQ government, first under Premier Jacques Parizeau and then under Bouchard, had resolutely downsized government operations and reduced expenditures in an effort to balance the budget. Public servants had been dismissed and grants for hospitals, education, and social services curtailed. The objective was to put Quebec's financial house in order before the public was called upon again to vote on separation. Inevitably, the retrenchment resulted in some loss of popularity for the administration and its forceful leader. There were also signs of internal tensions within the separatist camp. Bouchard had never been a hard-line separatist, preferring to express his vision of the

(continued on page 420)

As other justices file in behind him, Canadian Supreme Court Chief Justice Antonio Lamer prepares to open hearings on whether Quebec could secede from Canada. On August 20 the court unanimously decided that any attempt by Quebec to secede would "violate the Canadian legal order." The separatist Parti Québécois government refused to participate in the hearings.

TOM HANSON—AP/WIDE WORLD/CP

New sites and new data from old sites are changing the understanding of the peopling of the Americas. For decades the consensus was that the first Americans were big-game hunters who traveled from Asia across the Bering Land Bridge near the end of the Ice Age, about 12,000 years ago. Named for an occupation site in Clovis, N.M., these earliest people, called Paleoindians, are known for their fluted spear points. The Clovis people were thought to have settled in the interior plains of North America between 11,500 and 11,000 years ago. From there, they colonized the Western Hemisphere, following the diminishing game through the upland plains of Central America and the Andes, avoiding the coasts and tropical forests and reaching the tip of South America by 10,000 years ago, the end of the glacial period.

The Clovis migration theory developed early in the history of radiocarbon dating, before much was known of regions outside the Clovis heartland. Abundant new data from several of those areas now cast doubt on the theory. According to these findings, Clovis was not settled early enough to be the ancestor of Central and South American Paleoindians. Several well-documented sites south of the U.S. border are as early as or earlier than Clovis. In addition, few Ice Age cultures on either side of the land bridge had fluted points or hunted big game.

In the interior and coasts of northeast Asia, known late glacial cultures do not include any big-game hunting groups with fluted points. For example, the people of Diuktai in interior Siberia had stemmed, often triangular points and lived by generalized foraging. People near lakes used stemmed projectile points and foraged for small game, fish, and edible plants. In Japan, then connected to the mainland, people also had stemmed points and fished, gathered nuts and roots, and hunted smaller game for their sustenance.

Located just across the Bering Strait in Alaska, the Nenana culture is considered the most likely ancestor of the Paleoindians. Its age, verified by 20 consistent radiocarbon dates from four sites, spans the years from about 11,800 to 10,700 years ago. With its triangular, nonfluted points and generalized collecting and hunting, the culture is similar to some in contemporary Asia. Site refuse from the earlier part of the occupation contains plant remains and abundant bones of bison, other large and small mammals, birds, fish, and snails. The only mammoth bones, however, were fossils scavenged from paleontological sites for tools. The environment appears to have been a woodlands dominated by birch and willow.

In the high plains the revised Paleoindian sequence now extends from about 11,100 to 8,500 years ago. It still begins with the Clovis culture, whose fluted points are found at mammoth and bison kill sites. Contrary to prior understanding, however, none of the seven definitively dated Clovis occupations is earlier than about 11,200 years ago. After about 10,900 years ago, there is a transition to the

SPOTLIGHT

THE PEOPLING OF THE AMERICAS

by Anna C. Roosevelt

Illustration by Tom Curry

Folsom people, who hunted bison with small, finely flaked points with long flutes.

Evidence of early migration had been missing from the Pacific coast, which was flooded after the Ice Age, but Daisy Cave on a hilly channel island near Santa Barbara, Calif., is the site of a newly dated occupation started before 10,500 years ago. The shellfish and carbonized plants that were dated indicate an adaptation to pine-clad coasts that were wetter and cooler than the area is today.

In Eastern North America, several fluted point sites have single dates as early as 11,000 but the Paleoindian sequence has not yet been filled out. (The few pre-Clovis dates are from levels without secure cultural association.) Southeastern points are often termed "Clovis," but their manufacture and shapes resemble those of Folsom, and in some areas the custom of fluting lasts into postglacial times. Eastern sites are often damaged by plowing or erosion, but some have yielded food remains such as fishbone, indicating broader subsistence than specialized big-game hunting.

Central America lacks unequivocal evidence for Paleoindians. There are no well-dated, published Central American sites that appear to have been stopping places on the Clovis migration. The few fluted points are undated surface finds and resemble the postglacial points of southeastern North America. Despite the lack of early human sites, however, charcoal in Panamanian pollen cores suggests that humans passed through the area's upland rain forests about 11,000 years ago.

In South America many late Pleistocene complexes have been discovered. Contrary to the Clovis theory, the oldest are as early as or earlier than Clovis and are distinct culturally. Triangular and/or stemmed points as in the Asian tradition were found at most of the sites. The food remains indicate collecting and small-game hunting in diverse habitats ranging from the desert coast of the Pacific and the Atlantic tropical rain forests to the pampas and the icy shores of Patagonia.

At Taima Taima, an oil field site in northern Venezuela, fragmentary tools were found with cut mastodon bones in a spring where cultural and natural materials had become mixed. One tool is a bipointed style point. The ancient habitat was swampy, wooded, and subtropical. The radiocarbon dates range too widely for comfort—from about 41,000 to 12,000 B.P. Late Pleistocene people may have killed mastodon there, but exactly when is not certain. In nearby Colombia the earliest securely dated sites are lowland camps from 10,400 to 8,000 years old. Some of these sites contain triangular points, while others have ground-stone tools. Food remains are tropical forest fruits and nuts. The only highland sites are disturbed and of uncertain age.

In the Andes highlands of Peru, early work had uncovered possible big-game kill sites dating to as early as 20,000 years ago, but these had no clear association with humans. Sites with triangular and sometimes stemmed points and diverse

modern fauna and flora date to between about 11,500 and 8,500 before the present. The first secure evidence of early Paleoindians on the Pacific coast was from two south Peruvian sites with beginning dates between 11,100 and 10,700 years ago. At Quebrada Tacajuay and Quebrada Jaguay, the ancient hearths contained carbonized fragments of stone tools and remains of shellfish, small fish, and birds, but no large game.

For more than 100 years, researchers have claimed that there were very early human sites in the tropical forests of eastern South America. By the end of 1998, 10 sites had produced beginning dates of 11,000 years ago or slightly earlier. A few produced dates as early as 50,000 years ago, and one was claimed to be hundreds of thousands of years old. Though the earliest dates lacked secure cultural context, extensive cross-dating of plant remains and human skeletons (by radiocarbon) and stone tools and sediments (by thermoluminescence and optically stimulated luminescence) at several sites confirmed initial dates of at least 11,000 years ago. Unlike Clovis sites, those in Brazil include painted caves and rock shelters. Food remains include nuts, legumes, fish, shellfish, and small game animals. Among the artifacts are triangular, sometimes stemmed points but no fluted points. The newly dated sites include Caverna da Pedra Pintada, Santana de Riacho, and Boquete in Brazil. Contrary to some climate theories, east Brazilian forests were denser than today, according to the patterns of ancient species and their carbon isotope ratios.

Monte Verde, Chile, is a boggy stream-bed site where mastodon bones, wet preserved plant remains, and a handful of stone tools—three bipoints and a crude biface—were found. Earlier researchers disagreed about the site's reliability, but when judged by the standards applied to other sites, Monte Verde remains questionable. Results of datings on

possibly worked bone and wood were not conclusive because fossil bone and wood occur naturally here. The only cultural remains were the four tools, most of which were found on the surface, and a few food remains from nonlocal plants, which were not dated. Dates obtained from the site range from 14,000 to 12,000 years—too wide a span for a single occupation. Since postglacial people lived nearby, the points and food remains could well be intrusions.

Two roughly contemporary early Paleoindian cultures have been identified in far southern South America. The Fell culture had long been known from Patagonian caves and rock shelters. Fishtail points are distinctive Fell artifacts that once were equated with Clovis points but now are known to have been made and shaped differently. Although extinct horse and sloth remains were found at a few sites, most animals hunted were smaller game, such as guanaco and local birds. The existing 12 radiocarbon dates range between about 11,000 and 10,000 years ago. Farther north and west was the Los Toldos culture, whose sites contain rock paintings; stemmed, triangular points; and evidence of foraging for many kinds of food.

All the new evidence, therefore, has revealed that the first Americans had settled in many different regions by 11,000 years ago. Not only the plains but also the coasts and tropical forests were occupied by the earliest-known people. Thus, Clovis was just one regional specialization among many. Although the new data suggest a different scenario for colonization of the hemisphere, the much earlier dates remain problematic. An initial entry at about 12,000 years ago remains the most viable conclusion.

Anna C. Roosevelt is a professor of anthropology at the University of Illinois at Chicago, and a curator of archaeology at the Field Museum of Natural History in Chicago.

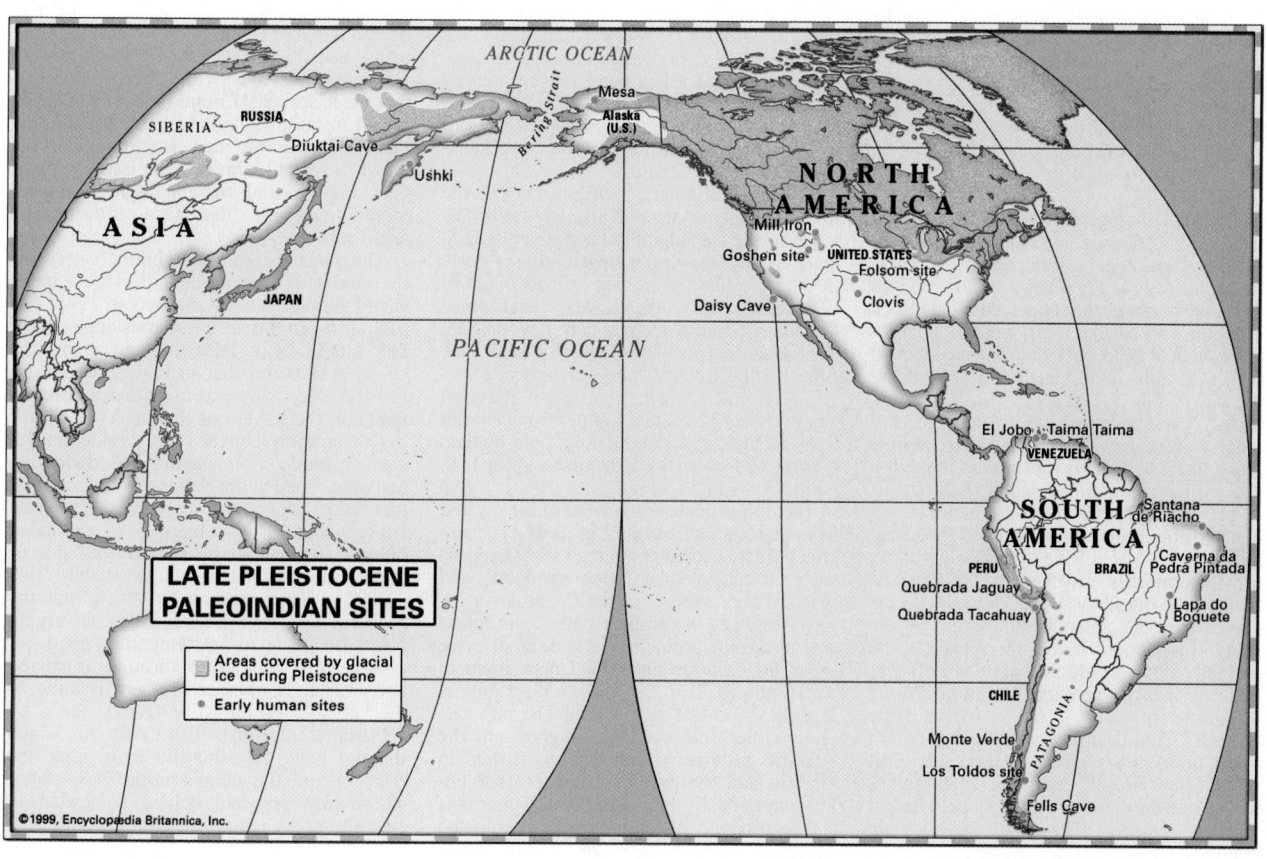

LATE PLEISTOCENE PALEOINDIAN SITES

Areas covered by glacial ice during Pleistocene
Early human sites

©1999, Encyclopædia Britannica, Inc.

(continued from page 417)
future in the form of a partnership between a sovereign Quebec and the rest of Canada. Wishing to give himself freedom to maneuver on the referendum issue, he sponsored a resolution at a party meeting on September 19–20 that authorized him to hold a vote on separation only if "winning conditions" existed. The action raised doubts about Bouchard's commitment to independence among militant separatists such as Parizeau.

The federal government's response to the issue of Quebec secession had become firmer since the Liberal Party's accession to power in 1993. A central feature of the stiffer approach was to plan to refer to the Supreme Court the question of whether Quebec could separate unilaterally from the rest of Canada. This proposal had been made in September 1996; hearings before the court were held over four days beginning Feb. 16, 1998. On August 20 the court issued a unanimous decision on the questions referred to it.

The first of the three questions referred to the court was basic: Does Quebec have the right to secede unilaterally? The court's response was direct. Any step on the part of Quebec to leave Canada had to be in accordance with Canada's constitution. Because the constitution does not mention separatism, such a step would "violate the Canadian legal order." The court, however, went on to say that Canadians in every part of the country could not be indifferent to a firm expression by the majority of Quebeckers if they decided that they wished to leave Canada.

The second question—Does international law provide any sanction for Quebec to secede?—was also disposed of in a firm manner. Looking for precedents, the court found them only in colonial situations or where individuals or groups suffered under extreme oppression. Quebec was not in these categories. It was not a colony but a free and equal member of a democratic federation. Its citizens enjoyed the same rights as other Canadians and so could in no legal sense be described as "oppressed."

Responding to the third question, the court ruled that there was no conflict between domestic and international law over Quebec secession. A referendum on secession might express Quebec's popular will on the subject, but it could have no legal effect. The court noted that there were other principles that had to be taken into account in regard to this issue, including federalism, the rule of law, the rights of individuals and minorities, and the democratic rights of other Canadians. The only way to resolve those interests, it concluded, was through a process of negotiation in good faith.

The court did not enter into a discussion of the difficult questions involved in negotiation. These would have to be dealt with by the governments involved in the process. Among the questions were: How should the constitution be amended to permit secession? How should a vote for separation be worded? What would constitute a sufficient majority in any vote over separation? Would a simple majority (50% plus one) be enough? Could border changes be brought about under a secession process? Very important, how would the rights of aborigines in Quebec be determined if Quebec desired to leave Canada? (They had made it plain that they did not favour their inclusion in an independent Quebec.) What were the interests of the other provinces in negotiations over secession? What would happen if negotiations failed?

Bouchard and his government accepted the court's conclusions calmly, even though they had refused to participate in the hearings. The court's decision had validated the referendum process, the PQ government claimed. Sovereignty, the PQ concluded, was a legitimate, democratically endorsed option for Quebec. The federal government also took the decision quietly. It returned to the argument that its main concern was to see the Canadian federal system revised in such a way that Quebec would be comfortable within it. No further steps could be taken until after the results of the next Quebec election were known. A federalist victory in the province would lay the question to rest.

The results of the election, in which more than 78% of the eligible voters participated, surprised most observers. The two parties finished with almost the same standing as in the previous election in 1994. The PQ won 75 seats and the Liberals 48. Bouchard was set back by the results, which denied him the sweeping majority he believed necessary for a successful referendum. In Charest, federalism had not found its saviour in Quebec.

The Progressive Conservatives needed a new national leader to replace Charest. They chose Joe Clark, who had been prime minister in a short-lived Conservative administration in 1979–80.

The Economy. As in other countries in the Western world, the Canadian economy faltered in the face of global turmoil in 1998. Strong growth in the early months of the year could not be sustained as the shock waves from the Asian collapse reached North America. British Columbia, as the Canadian region most dependent on the Asian market, experienced the most damaging impact, but other parts of the country were also affected. For the year a growth rate of about 3.2% in gross domestic product (GDP) was estimated. This was lower than earlier expectations.

The most dramatic consequence of the uncertainties in Asia was a steady fall in the value of the Canadian dollar against its U.S. counterpart. The dollar began sinking early in the year and by August 26 had fallen to U.S. 63.8 cents, the lowest level since Canada adopted a decimal currency in 1858. The Bank of Canada, which had held back from raising interest rates for fear of slowing economic growth, intervened the next day by raising its rate a full percentage point to 6%. This stabilized the dollar, but by then it had suffered an 11% decline against U.S. currency within a year.

The dollar's fall was related to the decline in commodity prices during 1998. The decline affected some of Canada's key exports, such as oil, metals, forest products, and wheat. Other aspects of the Canadian economy followed a familiar pattern. Inflation was not yet a problem, the consumer price index hovering around 1%. Unemployment was higher than in the U.S., with a jobless level of 8.3% late in the year. The rate varied across the country—higher in the Atlantic provinces and Quebec, lower in Ontario and the prairie provinces, and uncharacteristically high in British Columbia.

The prospect of bank mergers dominated financial circles in 1998. On January 23 two of the country's largest banks, The Royal Bank of Canada and the oldest Canadian bank, the Bank of Montreal, announced that they planned to combine if the government approved their plans. Three months later, on April 17, another merger project was revealed. The second largest bank in the country, the Canadian Imperial Bank of Commerce, declared that it would merge with the fifth largest, the Toronto-Dominion Bank. The federal government laid down a series of steps that the banks would have to follow to win approval for their unions, including public hearings by parliamentary committees and an examination by the Competition Bureau. A task force on banking, reporting on September 15, recommended that each merger be assessed on its merits, taking into account its effect on consumers, bank employment, and competition within Canada and abroad.

Finance Minister Paul Martin submitted his fifth budget on February 24. Its high point was Martin's announcement that in fiscal year 1997–98 the federal budget would be balanced for the first time since 1969–70. On October 14 Martin reported that the budget had actually recorded a surplus of $3.5 billion in fiscal 1997–98. It was a proud achievement for the finance minister, who, on taking office in 1993, had inherited a deficit of $45 billion. An improving economy had produced larger revenues, and the decline in interest rates had lowered payments on the national debt. The debt stood at about $583 billion in 1998. Martin promised tax cuts of $7.2 billion over the next three years, mostly to lower- and middle-class Canadians, in an effort to improve their after-tax incomes.

International Affairs. Canada won one of the 10 elected seats on the UN Security Council in a vote on October 8. Canada had been a member of the Security Council once every decade since the UN was founded. Foreign Minister Lloyd Axworthy declared that, as a Security Council member, Canada hoped to build up a constituency within the General Assembly that would support its views on global humanitarian issues such as checking the illicit trade in "light weapons," including assault rifles, hand grenades, and small mortars.

The northern Pacific salmon fishery off the coasts of Canada and the U.S. experienced another year of conflicts in 1998. The basic problem lay in the serious depletion of fish stocks, especially salmon, along the coast, a situation that increased the rivalry between the fishermen of both countries to maintain their share of the catch.

Cooperation between the two countries was desirable in managing this dwindling resource. The Pacific Salmon Treaty of 1985 had been intended to carry out this function, but constant disagreement between stakeholders (fishing interests) on either side of the border had made it unworkable. Two special envoys appointed to look into the problem had recommended that an urgent effort be made to set temporary goals for 1998. This was done through localized agreements, a number of them relating to the valuable Fraser River fishery, made by Canada (acting for British Columbia, which did not have the authority to regulate the fishery) and the neighbouring U.S. states. These arrangements helped somewhat to ease the pressures on the salmon runs.

(D.M.L. FARR)

CAPE VERDE

Area: 4,033 sq km (1,557 sq mi)
Population (1998 est.): 400,000
Capital: Praia
Chief of state: President Antonio Mascarenhas Monteiro
Head of government: Prime Minister Carlos Veiga

After disputes within the ruling Movement for Democracy, the party president and prime minister, Carlos Veiga, strengthened his position in 1998 when he reshuffled his Cabinet in April and May, bringing in a new minister of foreign affairs and appointing the former minister for economic coordination as deputy prime minister. As a member of an association of Portuguese-speaking African countries, Cape Verde played an important role in relation to conflicts elsewhere on the continent. After war broke out in Guinea-Bissau in June, the Community of Portuguese-Speaking Countries (Portugal, Brazil, Angola, Cape Verde, Guinea-Bissau, Mozambique, and São Tomé and Príncipe) held a summit in Praia, at which steps were taken to promote a cease-fire. Peace talks were later held in Praia between the government of Guinea-Bissau and the rebels, and an agreement was negotiated.

Cape Verde remained heavily dependent on the International Monetary Fund and the World Bank, which helped it reschedule some of its debt, and on transfers from an estimated 700,000 Cape Verdeans living abroad; these transfers represented 20% of gross domestic product. More than 25% of the population on the republic's nine inhabited islands remained unemployed.

(CHRISTOPHER SAUNDERS)

CENTRAL AFRICAN REPUBLIC

Area: 622,436 sq km (240,324 sq mi)
Population (1998 est.): 3,376,000
Capital: Bangui
Chief of state: President Ange-Félix Patassé
Head of government: Prime Minister Michel Gbezera-Bria

On April 15, 1998, the Inter-African Mission to Monitor the Implementation of the Bangui Agreements, charged with maintaining security in the Central African Republic following a series of 1996 army mutinies, was replaced by a UN-sponsored 1,350-strong peacekeeping force. France withdrew the last of its 1,400 troops from the nation on that same date. On May 11 Pres. Ange-Félix Patasse and Pres. Laurent Kabila of the Democratic Republic of the Congo signed a defense pact.

On August 15 the Independent Electoral Commission announced that parliamentary elections, originally scheduled for late September, would be postponed until November 22 in order to update and verify the voter rolls. In the election, held in two rounds, on November 22 and December 13, President Patassé's Central African People's Liberation Movement gained control of the 109-member parliament by winning 47 seats and then gaining the support of five independents and a defector from the opposition.

As part of its attempts to qualify for an International Monetary Fund loan, the government on May 22 announced that various tax and customs exemptions were being discontinued, an action designed to reduce the budget deficit for 1998 by about 25%. In July the IMF granted the nation a $66 million three-year loan to bolster its economic-reform program.

(NANCY ELLEN LAWLER)

CHAD

Area: 1,284,000 sq km (495,755 sq mi)
Population (1998 est.): 7,360,000
Capital: N'Djamena
Chief of state: President Lieut. Gen. Idriss Déby
Head of government: Prime Minister Nassour Ouaidou Guelendouksia

In May 1998 a peace agreement between the government of Chad and the main group of rebels, the Armed Forces for a Federal Republic (FARF), was signed; in succeeding months it proved to have been more effectively implemented than had a 1997 agreement. A border dispute with Nigeria remained unresolved; in May government forces clashed with Nigerian troops on Lake Chad. Refugees from the fighting in the Darfur region of western Sudan continued to enter the country. A visit by Libyan chief of state Col. Muammar al-Qaddafi proved highly successful and a diplomatic coup for Pres. Idriss Déby.

The main bone of contention within Chad in 1998 was the pipeline project, designed to carry high-quality crude oil from the oil fields 480 km (300 mi) south of N'Djamena to the Atlantic port of Kribi in Cameroon. Some critics of the project expressed concern about the environmental impact of the pipeline, which could endanger two national parks; others were concerned about its impact on the movement of people and livestock. FARF feared that those in power would not share the revenues that would accrue from the project with the people of the south. The estimated cost of the pipeline was about $3 billion, and though Exxon and Shell were to pay for most of it, with the French company Elf having a small share in the consortium, the project required World Bank approval, and that was delayed. If production began in 2001, as planned, and lasted 30 years, Chad would become Africa's fourth largest exporter of oil, and the project could double the nation's per capita income.

(CHRISTOPHER SAUNDERS)

CHILE

Area: 756,626 sq km (292,135 sq mi)
Population (1998 est.): 14,822,000
Capitals: Santiago (national) and Valparaíso (legislative)
Head of state and government: President Eduardo Frei Ruiz-Tagle

Although the attempt by Spain to extradite ex-Pres. Augusto Pinochet from London on charges of human rights abuses overshad-

In March Chilean lawmakers, protesting against Gen. Augusto Pinochet as he assumes a seat as senator for life, hold up pictures of persons who disappeared during Pinochet's rule from 1973–90. Later in the year Pinochet was arrested in London after Spain requested his extradition on charges of having had hundreds of Spanish citizens killed.

owed Chilean politics after October, most of the year was dominated by the impact of the Asian economic crisis and by preparations for the 1999 presidential elections. Pinochet's retirement in March as army commander to become a senator for life as laid down under his 1980 constitution aroused controversy, including a vote in January by the Chamber of Deputies opposing his entry to the Senate on the grounds that he had never been democratically elected president (his 1981 victory having been as the only candidate). While his membership of the Senate strengthened the right wing, preventing the government from achieving the two-thirds majority needed to alter the constitution and abolish non-elected senators, Pinochet's retirement led to an improvement in civil-military relations. His successor, Gen. Ricardo Izurieta, struck a different note in his first address to the troops, stressing his faith in the democratic institutions and the military's subordination to the civilian authorities.

Pinochet's detention provoked a vigorous debate about the human rights abuses of the 1973–90 dictatorship. While his supporters argued that Pinochet had diplomatic immunity, opinion polls suggested that two-thirds of Chileans considered him guilty and that most wanted him tried, in Chile. Although fears were expressed for political stability, the government, under extreme pressure from the military, pressed for his release and took measures to indicate extreme displeasure with the British and Spanish governments.

Earlier in the year there had been speculation that the governing Concertación coalition could split over the choice of a presidential candidate for 1999 and present two candidates, one each from the Christian Democrats and the Socialists, thus handing victory to the right-wing Union for the Progress of Chile. The midterm congressional elections of December 1997 indicated a shift of strength within the coalition: while the Socialist Party retained its support, the Christian Democrat vote fell, strengthening the claims of the Socialist Ricardo Lagos to the Concertación candidacy in 1999. Consistently shown by opinion polls to be the country's most popular politician, Lagos resigned as minister of public works in September to plan his campaign. The accompanying Cabinet reshuffle resulted in the departure of seven ministers and an increase in the power of Finance Minister Eduardo Aninat, an opponent of Lagos. The possibility of a split in the Concertación was averted by an agreement to hold a presidential primary early in 1999; the main candidates were to be Lagos and the Christian Democrat Andrés Zaldivar, president of the Senate.

The economy was badly affected by the Asian crisis and low international copper prices; one-third of Chilean exports were to Asia (16% to Japan) and 40% of export earnings were from copper. The Russian debt default in September caused the Santiago stock market to lose 50% of its value. The government responded by increasing interest rates (in September the Banco Central's interbank rate was raised to 14%), allowing the peso to depreciate more rapidly and reducing spending by $685 million. In April the Finance Ministry also attempted to stimulate domestic savings, introducing new saving incentives into a measure that increased pensions.

The fall in export earnings was reflected in an increase in the trade deficit, projected at $2.4 million compared with $1.3 million in 1997. Growth in per capita gross domestic product was estimated at 4.6% compared with 7.1% in 1997. Government projections for annual inflation were 4.7%, down from 6% in 1997. Unemployment at the year's end was estimated at 5.9%, up from 5.3% for 1997.   (CHARLIE NURSE)

CHINA

Area: 9,572,900 sq km (3,696,100 sq mi), including Tibet and excluding Taiwan (See *Taiwan*, below.)
Population (1998 est., excluding Taiwan): 1,242,980,000
Capital: Beijing
Chief of state: President Jiang Zemin
Head of government: Premiers Li Peng and, from March 17, Zhu Rongji

Two series of waves battered China in 1998, causing deep concern to China's leaders and the public alike. First were the waves of the Chang Jiang (Yangtze River) and the Nen and Songhua rivers, whose overflowing waters brought large-scale devastation and significant loss of life to central and northeastern China. Second were the waves of the Asian financial crisis, which threatened the stability of China's currency, eroded the rate of economic growth, and, by extension, posed a threat to the social and political order. Spurred by the latter danger, China's leaders finally tackled the monumental problem of reforming the country's state-owned enterprises and banking system, intensified the fight against official corruption, and attempted—with only partial success—to sustain a high rate of economic growth. The overthrow of President Suharto in Indonesia gave Chinese leaders an object lesson about the risks that soft authoritarian regimes face when times turn bad. In the international arena China basked in the glow of U.S. Pres. Bill Clinton's nine-day state visit at midyear. Meanwhile, relations with Taiwan came out of the deep freeze. Thus, compared with most of its Asian neighbours, China came through the year in remarkably good shape.

Domestic Affairs. An expected reshuffling of the government leadership took place at the meeting of the National People's Congress (NPC) in March. Li Peng, having completed his second and final term as premier, became the head of the NPC, replacing Qiao Shi. The latter, a rival of Pres. Jiang Zemin (*see* BIOGRAPHIES), had been ousted from the top leadership at the 15th Congress of the Communist Party of China (CPC) in October 1997. Li was replaced as premier on March 17 by Zhu Rongji, who, as deputy premier, had been in overall command of China's economy for several years. A career technocrat and protégé of the late paramount leader Deng Xiaoping, Zhu was a former mayor and party boss of Shanghai. Although noted for having persuaded Shanghai demonstrators to disperse peacefully during the nationwide pro-democracy

student protests in 1989, in contrast to the violent suppression of protests in Beijing, he had shown little interest in political reform.

Two other significant leadership changes occurred in 1998. Deputy Foreign Minister Tang Jiaxuan was promoted to the top spot in the Ministry of Foreign Affairs. He replaced Qian Qichen, who was elevated to deputy premier. Wu Yi, the top-ranking woman in the government, was promoted to state councillor, and her position as minister of foreign trade and economic development was assumed by her deputy, Shi Guangsheng. Jiang, who doubled as CPC general secretary, appeared secure at the top of the political hierarchy.

In a bold challenge to his erstwhile colleagues, Zhao Ziyang, under house arrest since his ouster from the premiership during the 1989 pro-democracy movement, sent an open letter to the CPC Central Committee in June calling upon the CPC to acknowledge its error in perpetrating the Tiananmen Square massacre and asking the party to accelerate the process of democratization. His appeal elicited no public response. Freed after nearly a decade of imprisonment and probation, Bao Tong, Zhao's former chief aide, echoed Zhao's call for democratization in interviews with foreign journalists. Ordered to hold his tongue, he declined. Meanwhile, Jiang quietly fostered a somewhat more open political climate in which intellectuals and researchers in official think tanks were allowed to explore alternative political forms and ideas. Organized opposition of any sort remained out of bounds, however. When, in conformance with existing state regulations, small groups of Chinese democrats in several cities tried to register their proposed China Democratic Party as a civic organization, their applications were rejected and they were harassed, detained, and threatened with further punishment if they persisted. Unlike Taiwan's ruling Kuomintang, which had allowed the formation of an opposition party in 1986, the CPC oligarchy remained unwilling to risk any challenge to its power. In a public relations gesture before President Clinton's visit to China, Beijing released imprisoned student leader Wang Dan on medical parole to the U.S., but it continued to crack down hard on numerous lower-profile dissenters as well as on ethnic nationalists in Tibet and Xinjiang.

Jiang surprised many observers by having Chen Xitong, former Beijing party boss and Political Bureau member, sentenced to a 16-year prison term for engaging in massive corruption and embezzlement of public funds. In so doing, Jiang signaled his willingness to hunt big tigers as well as small game. Jiang, who had spent much of the past decade cultivating military support, went after the largest game of all when he ordered the People's Liberation Army (PLA) to divest itself of its nondefense assets. Since the 1970s the PLA had acquired a parallel economic empire in fields such as electronics, real estate (including hotels and even brothels), pharmaceuticals, transportation, and foreign trade. Jiang ordered the military to concentrate on its national security objectives. Meanwhile, PLA Chief of Staff Fu Quanyou stressed the need for the PLA to acquire high-tech weapons. Savings from a proposed reduction in PLA force by 500,000 troops were expected to be used to upgrade military technology.

In his inaugural speech as premier, Zhu announced a radical restructuring of the government bureaucracy, targeting the elimination or merger of 15 ministries, including those of coal, labour, metallurgy, machine building, and chemicals, as well as the paring of 4 million of the 33 million government jobs. Expansion and contraction of the government bureaucracy had occurred periodically since the 1950s but never before when the state sector was diminishing as a share of the national economy and the government was actively promoting privatization. Zhu also announced a three-year timetable for the reform of state-owned enterprises (SOEs), a move foreshadowed in Jiang's report to the 15th Congress of the CPC. The government wanted to accelerate the transformation, merger, or elimination of debt-ridden and noncompetitive industrial behemoths of the old command economy days. Furloughs, reductions in force, and cutbacks in hours and pay had affected an estimated 20 million–30 million workers by 1998. State-run labour exchanges or reemployment centres had only begun to address the serious problems of unemployment and underemployment. Small-scale protests by laid-off workers increased in frequency and intensity but posed little threat to the authorities in the absence of independent trade union organizations, which were strictly prohibited.

The banking industry, too, was in serious straits as a result of many years during which government directives and personal connections rather than economic rationality dictated loan policy. Chinese banking authorities claimed that only 5–6% of outstanding loans were unrecoverable, but outside estimates ranged much higher. In February Beijing announced that it would recapitalize the four largest state banks, which accounted for 90% of all loans, via an infusion of $33 billion. Meanwhile, the head of the People's Bank of China floated a plan to reorganize China's central banking system along the lines of the U.S. Federal Reserve system. Zhu and other top officials earned the gratitude of world leaders by pledging not to devalue China's currency, the yuan. It was widely feared that devaluation of the Chinese currency would set off another round of devaluation in Asian countries—Thailand, Indonesia, and South Korea in particular—that were struggling to recover from the financial crisis. It was uncertain how long China could afford to maintain the yuan at its current rate of exchange, however. Meanwhile, plans to make the yuan a fully convertible currency were shelved.

After years of inflation in the early 1990s, China experienced a mild deflation in 1998 as the retail price index fell by 2.1% in the first half of the year. Despite an inflow of $27 billion in foreign investment and a foreign trade surplus of more than $30 billion, China's foreign exchange holdings held steady at $140 billion. This suggested an unauthorized capital outflow estimated in the tens of billions of dollars annually. In order to stem this tide, alarmed Chinese authorities tightened controls on foreign exchange transactions.

An even greater worry for the government was the slowdown in the rate of economic growth caused by shrinking Asian export markets, diminishing foreign investment, and slackened domestic consumer spending. In 1997 gross domestic product had grown at a rate of 8.8%. Chinese leaders set a 1998 growth target of 8%, an ambitious figure in light of the brewing global economic crisis. Toward this goal Beijing announced a three-year domestic economic stimulus package of $1.2 trillion focused on developing China's infrastructure. Highway and railroad construction, bridge building, electric power generation, and water conservancy projects were among those slated to receive significant infusions of capital. Another high-priority area was urban housing, where a great backlog of demand existed. In another radical departure from past practice, the government announced the phasing out of highly subsidized housing, which many Chinese had come to expect as a birthright. In its place, apartment and home ownership

Soldiers in Daqing, China, work furiously to move corn threatened by flood waters. Massive flooding occurred in July–August in the middle reaches of the Chang Jiang (Yangtze River) and along the Nen and Songhua rivers. Hundreds of thousands of flood victims were forced from their homes. The relief system proved inadequate and gave rise to widespread criticism.

was encouraged, and banks began to provide mortgage loans to China's expanding new middle class. With all these efforts, the economy grew 7.2% during the first nine months of 1998—short of the government's target but still much better than any of its Asian neighbours.

Massive flooding, which had been a major problem in China since ancient times, occurred in July–August in the middle reaches of the Chang Jiang in central China and, more unusually, along the Nen and Songhua rivers in northeastern China. More than 3,000 people died in the floods, millions of rural homes were destroyed, and hundreds of thousands of flood victims were forced to camp out for many weeks on the roofs of their houses or on the tops of levees. (*See* DISASTERS.) The relief system proved inadequate to the task and gave rise to widespread criticism. Chinese scientists and engineers also faulted the government for its long-term failure to allocate sufficient funds for strengthening dikes as well as for its having turned a blind eye to such practices as the clear-cutting of timber along the upper reaches of the rivers. In order to protect the imperiled metropolises of Wuhan on the Chang Jiang and Harbin on the Songhua, many small towns and rural communities were sacrificed to the floodwaters as their sheltering dikes were dynamited to divert the raging waters. Some 275,000 PLA troops were mobilized to fight the floods, the largest peacetime mobilization in China's history. Media images of valiant soldiers battling chest-high waters and rescuing civilians helped erase the stigma of corruption and smuggling that had become attached to the PLA. Ultimately, the impact of the flooding, which caused an estimated $20 billion in damages, was more local than national.

Hong Kong. Hong Kong, which had become a special administrative region of China on July 1, 1997, was much more severely hit by the Asian financial crisis than the rest of China. Both imports and exports declined, and the economy, in recession, shrank an estimated 7% in the third quarter. Unemployment rose to its highest level in 15 years, and the bellwether Hang Seng stock index declined sharply. In a departure from previous laissez-faire practice, Hong Kong authorities intervened in currency markets to defend the Hong Kong dollar, which was pegged to the U.S. dollar, against currency speculators.

In May elections for the Legislative Council, Hong Kong voters expressed overwhelming support for the democratic parties and political leaders whom Beijing had excluded from the interim Hong Kong legislature it appointed in 1996. The electoral system, constructed to deny a popular majority, nevertheless delivered an equal number of seats to Martin Lee's Democratic Party, which garnered about 42% of the vote, and to pro-Beijing parties, which gained 3%.

Taiwan and International Relations. Anxious about the growing strength of Taiwan's pro-independence Democratic Progressive Party, China ended its nearly three-year moratorium on contact with Taiwan, which had been instituted to protest Taiwan Pres. Lee Teng-hui's June 1995 visit to the U.S. In April China's quasi-official Association for Relations Across the Taiwan Strait welcomed a delegation from its Taiwanese counterpart, the Straits Exchange Foundation. Negotiations began for a high-level meeting between the heads of the two organizations.

The political turmoil in Indonesia that led to President Suharto's resignation resulted in mob violence against Chinese-Indonesians. Rioters attacked and destroyed countless Chinese-owned businesses and raped hundreds of ethnic Chinese women. After a diplomatic silence that incensed public opinion in China, Beijing lodged protests with Indonesia. University students in Beijing delivered a protest petition to the Indonesian embassy, and students and women activists conducted an unauthorized demonstration in front of the embassy as well.

China criticized India's series of nuclear tests in May and vigorously rejected the Indian government's claim that a nuclear-armed China posed a serious threat to India's security. Until this development, relations between the two had been slowly improving. Beijing issued only a pro forma expression of regret over the nuclear tests of its ally Pakistan, whose nuclear program had been greatly facilitated by infusions of Chinese technology and know-how.

Relations with the U.S. took centre stage in China's dealings with the outside world. In the face of contrary evidence, China continued to deny it had channeled illegal campaign contributions to the Democratic Party during the 1996 U.S. elections. Congressional Republicans also shined the spotlight on alleged improper dealings between China's aerospace industry, which was closely linked to China's military establishment, and American contractors. Human rights organizations had difficulty focusing attention on China's human rights problems in the face of the Clinton administration's apparent indifference to these concerns. As noted above, the release of imprisoned dissident Wang was timed to maximize the impression that China was making progress in the area of human rights, a perspective echoed by the U.S. government. An interfaith group of American religious leaders returned from a brief visit to China to offer a generally positive assessment of the state of religious freedom there.

Reciprocating Jiang's successful state visit to the U.S. in October 1997, President Clinton paid an extended state visit to China in late June–early July. The Clinton entourage first visited the ancient capital of Xian to view its cultural relics before proceeding to Beijing, Shanghai, Guilin, and Hong Kong. Many Chinese felt that the Clinton visit represented an affirmation of China's emergence as a global power. In a surprise move, Jiang allowed Clinton to talk directly to the Chinese public via television and radio, and he engaged Clinton in a debate of sorts on sensitive issues, including Tibet, the Tiananmen Square massacre, and the human rights situation in China. Clinton in turn praised Jiang as a wise statesman who was the right man to lead China toward a bright future. To a skeptical, hand-picked student audience at Beijing University, Clinton preached the virtues of American-style democracy. Clinton-Jiang pronouncements on regional and global affairs were not welcomed in India, among other places, where an emerging Sino-American axis of global leadership was deemed both presumptuous and dangerous. Nevertheless, China made real progress in 1998 toward its long-term goal of recognition as a global power. (STEVEN I. LEVINE)

FERNANDO LLANO—AP/WIDE WORLD

COLOMBIA

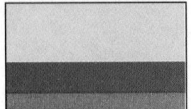

Area: 1,141,568 sq km (440,762 sq mi)
Population (1998 est.): 37,685,000
Capital: Santafé de Bogotá, D.C.
Head of state and government:
   Presidents Ernesto Samper Pizano and, from August 7, Andrés Pastrana Arango

Revolutionary Armed Forces of Colombia guerrillas keep watch over a roadblock aimed at disrupting the first round of Colombia's national elections in March. Despite roadblocks and shootings by guerrilla groups on polling day, voters turned out in impressive numbers. The ruling Liberal Party maintained its lead in the legislature.

Pres. Ernesto Samper Pizano completed his four-year term of office in 1998, personally discredited by what many considered his mismanagement of government affairs and thoroughly tainted by drug-money scandals. When the long-awaited national elections arrived, the two main guerrilla groups, the Revolutionary Armed Forces of Colombia (FARC) and the National Liberation Army (ELN), made considerable efforts to disrupt them. Voters, nevertheless, turned out in im-

pressive numbers to decide on the future members of the legislature (March) and the new president (May–June). With the slogan "Vote for peace," the ruling Liberal Party maintained its lead in the legislature but with reduced majorities in both the Senate and the House of Representatives. The turnout of 45% of the electorate was the highest in several years in spite of an "armed strike" by FARC and the ELN on polling day in many parts of the country.

The run-up to the presidential election was accompanied by initiatives to start peace negotiations between the government and the left-wing groups, including secret meetings with the ELN in Madrid and discussions with FARC's "diplomatic representative" in Mexico. At the same time, however, those groups stepped up terrorist operations in Colombia, especially in the south (Caquetá and Meta departments) and in the northwest near the Caribbean coast.

The first round of the presidential election on May 31 gave Horacio Serpa Uribe, the Liberal Party candidate, a wafer-thin margin over Andrés Pastrana Arango (*see* BIOGRAPHIES) of the Social Conservative Party. With each polling 35% of the vote, a runoff election was necessary. With the help of votes given in the first ballot to other candidates, notably to Noemí Sanín Posada, who led in Bogotá and other major cities, Pastrana on June 21 eventually won with six million votes, the largest number ever obtained by a presidential candidate.

The victory was widely acclaimed in Colombia as a break with the past and, especially, with Samper. Businesses reacted favourably, and Pastrana's promises to seek a peace formula with FARC and the ELN were welcomed. Meetings began under the auspices of the Roman Catholic Church in Mainz, Ger., and a civilian High Commissioner for Peace was appointed. There were, however, several setbacks, notably coordinated attacks on the military, the police, oil installations, and banks on the eve of Pastrana's inauguration on August 7.

Upon taking office, Pastrana also began to cope with the country's other problems. The growing fiscal deficit of about 3.5% of gross domestic product was a major threat to monetary stability and investor confidence. Changes to the tax system and tougher sanctions on tax evasion were presented to the legislature and were expected to be agreed upon in early 1999. Pressure on the peso led to a devaluation of 9% in August. The construction industry was in poor shape, a main cause of rising unemployment, which at nearly 16% in midyear was the highest on record.

The elements were not kind to Colombia in 1998. Severe droughts in the centre and north of the country reduced fruit and flower production. River levels were 40% of normal, and navigation all but ceased on the Rio Magdalena, affecting merchandise and oil exports. As reservoir levels dropped, some rationing of electric power became necessary. Weakening world prices affected coffee, oil, and coal export revenues.

(PETER POLLARD)

COMOROS

Area: 1,862 sq km (719 sq mi), excluding the 375-sq km (145-sq mi) island of Mayotte, a de facto dependency of France since 1976
Population (1998 est.): 546,000 (excluding 134,000 on Mayotte)
Capital: Moroni
Chief of state and head of government: President Mohamed Taki Abdoulkarim, and, from November 6, President Tadjiddine Ben Said Massounde (acting)

The year 1998 dawned with the secession crisis on the islands of Anjouan and Moheli unresolved. In February Anjouan voters approved a new constitution affirming their independence. An Organization of African Unity delegation arrived on Anjouan on March 18 in an unsuccessful attempt to persuade its leaders to return to the federation. On July 7, however, Anjouan Pres. Foundi Abdallah Ibrahim dismissed the government of Prime Minister Chamassi Said Omar, a strong supporter of secession and reunion with France, and announced that the new government would begin reconciliation negotiations with the Comoran government. After a failed assassination attempt against Foundi in December, violence broke out on Anjouan.

In May the capital, Moroni, witnessed several days of violent protests. Demonstrators clashed with police over the closing of an opposition radio station. On May 29 Pres. Mohamed Taki Abdoulkarim dissolved the government and formed a new one the next day without a prime minister. On November 6 Taki died of natural causes, and Tadjiddine Ben Said Massounde took over as acting president.   (MATTHEW A. CENZER)

CONGO, DEMOCRATIC REPUBLIC OF THE (ZAIRE)

Area: 2,344,858 sq km (905,354 sq mi)
Population (1998 est.): 46,674,000
Capital: Kinshasa
Head of state and government: President Laurent-Désiré Kabila

On May 25, 1998, Pres. Laurent Kabila promulgated a decree that established a national constituent and legislative assembly. This apparent move toward democracy was, however, belied by a series of arrests of people believed to be critical of the government, including, in January, two opposition leaders, Joseph Olenghankoy and Arthur Z'Ahidi Ngoma. Former prime minister Étienne Tshisekedi was banished to his home village in Kasai-Oriental province in February for continuing his political activities. He was released on July 1 and allowed to return to Kinshasa, where a week later he made a speech that resulted in the arrest of 40 of his followers.

Kabila's resistance to open government was further demonstrated in April, when the UN team that had arrived the previous August to investigate charges of large-scale human rights abuses by the forces that had brought Kabila to power was withdrawn because the government had put too many ob-

stacles in its way. On June 30 the team submitted a report that it acknowledged was incomplete but that nevertheless upheld many of the charges. To the dismay of human rights organizations, the UN Security Council decided to take no immediate action on the report.

Unrest that began in the eastern part of the country early in the year blossomed into open rebellion on August 2. The leading dissidents were the Banyamulenge, of Tutsi origin, who had supported Kabila's rise to power but who now felt rejected by the president in favour of members of his own ethnic group. They also feared reprisals from members of rival ethnic factions who had suffered at their hands during the power struggle in 1997 but were able to enlist the support of disaffected members of former president Mobutu's army and others who felt let down by Kabila.

The rebels made rapid conquests in the east, and, with the backing of the governments of Rwanda and Uganda, which had been angered by the failure of Kabila to prevent raiders from threatening their borders, rebel soldiers were flown to Kitona in southwestern Congo. Both Uganda and Rwanda, however, persisted in claiming that none of their troops were involved in the fighting. From Kitona the rebels advanced to capture the Atlantic port of Matadi and the Inga hydroelectric dam, which not only supplied electricity to Kinshasa but also provided power for the Shaba copper mines and even for Zimbabwe. They then moved against Kinshasa itself.

An attempt at mediation by the Southern African Development Community (SADC) on August 18–19 ended in disagreement.

Government troops at the People's Palace in Kinshasa, Democratic Republic of the Congo, herd prisoners of war onto a transport truck in September. In 1998 Pres. Laurent Kabila's forces claimed victory against an ethnic Tutsi-supported rebellion in western Congo.

DAVID GUTTENFELDER—AP/WIDE WORLD

South Africa persisted in trying to find a diplomatic solution, but Zimbabwe, Angola, and Namibia, fearing the effects of a destabilized Congo, offered armed intervention in support of Kabila. The arrival of troops, tanks, and aircraft from those southern neighbours, later reinforced by soldiers from Chad and The Sudan, quickly turned the tide against the rebels in the west. The latter were permitted to quit Matadi and the Inga dam without heavy fighting, and the threat to Kinshasa was also lifted.

Efforts by the SADC to engineer a cease-fire later in August and again in November made little progress, ostensibly because Kabila refused to meet the rebels face-to-face. Fighting continued in the east, with the rebels attempting to seize the diamond mines of Kasai-Oriental to help finance their campaign. On October 21 Zimbabwe, Angola, and Namibia responded by opening a second front in the east. Late in December Kabila and Pres. Denis Sassou-Nguesso of the Republic of the Congo signed a nonaggression pact. (KENNETH INGHAM)

CONGO, REPUBLIC OF THE

Area: 342,000 sq km (132,047 sq mi)
Population (1998 est.): 2,658,000
Capital: Brazzaville
Chief of state: President Denis Sassou-Nguesso

Despite several outbreaks of violence in Brazzaville by former militiamen loyal to ousted Pres. Pascal Lissouba, the Republic of the Congo managed in 1998 to return to a degree of normalcy after the previous year's civil war. Between 10,000 and 15,000 people died in that conflict, which culminated in the return to power of former military leader Denis Sassou-Nguesso in October 1997. In January 1998 the UN prepared to close down its refugee camp in neighbouring Kinshasa as thousands of Congolese began returning home. The airport reopened to commercial flights on February 18, and French businesses, a dominant presence in the private sector, returned to the country and resumed operations. Much of the capital had been destroyed in the shelling, and in April the government announced that a housing bank would be established to assist people in rebuilding homes. Although Sassou-Nguesso committed his government to a return to multiparty democracy by 2001, no new date was set for the elections that had been canceled as a result of the conflict. Sassou-Nguesso late in December signed a nonaggression pact with Pres. Laurent Kabila of the Democratic Republic of the Congo.

The economy struggled to overcome the effects of the war; its cost was estimated at CFAF 500 billion (about $890 million). Gross domestic product in the oil-rich nation fell by 16.7% in 1997 owing to a combination of the disruption of production internally and a drop in world oil prices. The African Development Bank announced a $500,000 grant on June 24 for emergency health aid. (NANCY ELLEN LAWLER)

COSTA RICA

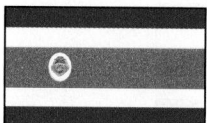

Area: 51,100 sq km (19,730 sq mi)
Population (1998 est.): 3,533,000
Capital: San José
Head of state and government:
Presidents José María Figueres Olsen and, from May 8, Miguel Angel Rodríguez Echeverría

Presidential elections held on Feb. 1, 1998, were won by economist Miguel Angel Rodríguez Echeverría of the Social Christian Unity Party (PUSC). Although he had consistently led in opinion polls, Rodríguez won by a smaller margin than expected, only two percentage points above the candidate for the ruling National Liberation Party (PLN). Some 30% of the eligible voters did not go to the polls. The PUSC won 27 seats in the Legislative Assembly, the PLN won 23, and smaller parties took 7. The new president took office on May 8 and pledged to focus his administration on helping women, young people, and the poor. In 1998 one in five people in Costa Rica lived in poverty. In August a budget was presented to the Assembly that aimed to cut the fiscal deficit from 3.7% of gross domestic product in 1998 to 1.7% by the end of 1999 by reducing government expenditures and internal debt. It was announced that the domestic electricity market would be opened up to competition, although there were no plans for a massive sale of state-owned utility companies.

Early in the year the multinational banana producer Del Monte reached an agreement with the trade union SITRAP, giving it the right to organize and move freely on Del Monte's plantations. Chiquita and Dole, two other large banana producers in Costa Rica, were also targets of pressure for improved labour rights by the action groups Banana Link and the World Development Movement. (SARAH CAMERON)

CÔTE D'IVOIRE

Area: 322,463 sq km (124,504 sq mi)
Population (1998 est.): 15,446,000
Seats of government: predominantly Abidjan; some ministries have relocated to Yamoussoukro
Chief of state: President Henri Konan Bédié
Head of government: Prime Minister Daniel Kablan Duncan

Opposition parties accused the ruling Democratic Party of Côte d'Ivoire (PDCI) of threatening the nation's democratic system of government by the passage on June 30, 1998, of a bill to reform the constitution. To take effect from the next presidential election in 2000, this bill would extend the presidential term from five to seven

years and would give the chief executive powers to postpone elections in the event of a major crisis.

On September 7 thousands of opposition supporters marched in Abidjan to protest the changes. Thousands more demonstrators took to the streets a week later in Abidjan again, Bouake, and other cities. Their demands were unlikely to be met, however, as the PDCI held 148 of the 175 seats in the National Assembly.

Having achieved a 7% growth rate in gross domestic product in 1997, the economy continued its strong performance. GDP was expected to grow by 6.8% in 1998. In February the government announced that its privatization program would conclude its work during the year with the sale of an additional 17 state-owned firms.

On February 22 the International Monetary Fund (IMF) praised the country's progress in controlling its budget deficit and inflation rates, and final agreement on a new structural adjustment program was reached on March 17. A joint Paris Club, IMF, and World Bank debt-relief plan was signed on March 31. The coffee industry, second in importance only to cocoa, would begin to be deregulated during the next growing season. On September 16 a new French-speaking West African regional stock exchange opened in Abidjan.

In other developments the World Islamic Congress convened in Abidjan on February 18. In April the Ministry of Defense announced that it would provide the largest contingent, 225 soldiers, to the new UN peacekeeping force in the Central African Republic. The government banned all school demonstrations following protests by students after police bullets killed a 16-year-old youth on May 14. Ministers from West African and Portuguese-speaking countries met in Abidjan in late September in an effort to end the rebellion in Guinea-Bissau. (NANCY ELLEN LAWLER)

CROATIA

Area: 56,610 sq km (21,857 sq mi)
Population (1998 est.): 4,672,000
Capital: Zagreb
Chief of state: President Franjo Tudjman
Head of government: Prime Minister Zlatko Matesa

The year 1998 began well for Croatia with the return of eastern Slavonia to full Croatian sovereignty on January 15, ending six years of Yugoslav military occupation and United Nations administration. UN forces were replaced by observers from the Organization for Security and Cooperation in Europe, who were mandated to oversee the return of Serbian and Croatian refugees. Though progress was indeed made on Serb refugee returns, Croatia was again denied entry into the European Union's aid program because of the government's failure to liberalize the state-controlled electronic media and to change electoral laws favouring the ruling Croatian Democratic Union (HDZ).

In January the government sold a controlling stake in the largest daily newspaper, *Vecernji list,* to a secret owner believed to be close to the ruling party. The appearance on April 6 of the country's first independent daily, *Jutarnji list,* however, promised to challenge the government's grip over the print media; the paper's circulation approached that of *Vecernji list* by the year's end.

Tensions between moderate and authoritarian elements within the ruling party came to the fore on September 25, when Pres. Franjo Tudjman's Chief of Cabinet, Hrvoje Saranic, publicly attacked presidential adviser Ivic Pasalic for using the intelligence services and the media to attack his political opponents. Saranic later resigned in protest against Tudjman's refusal to stop this practice.

The collapse in April of the state-controlled Dubravacka Banka, one of the nation's largest banks, exposed the corrupt relationship that existed between the banking sector and party officials and their business allies. The banking scandal brought down the local HDZ-run government in Dubrovnik and initiated a nationwide banking crisis that caused a number of banks to seek government assistance in order to avoid bankruptcy.

The liquidity problem afflicting the economy was blamed on the government's tight fiscal and monetary policies, highlighted by the introduction at the beginning of the year of a single-rate value-added tax (VAT) that replaced the complicated myriad of customs and other taxes placed on all goods and services. The VAT did succeed in taxing the large informal economy, estimated at between one-quarter and one-third of gross domestic product, and that led to an unexpectedly large government budget surplus that would help decrease by nearly half Croatia's 12.5% current account deficit for 1997.

In July the International Monetary Fund (IMF) warned Croatia to refrain from further wage hikes for government workers and suggested that the government place more restrictions on the surge of bank credits to household and corporate borrowers and hasten privatization of public enterprises. With unemployment stubbornly hovering at 17%, however, the government did not believe it could follow the IMF advice, particularly after February 20, when 10,000 people took to the streets in Zagreb demanding higher wages and condemning the government's authoritarian style.

Despite these problems, the nation's economic growth reached 4%, far below the string of four years of high growth but still respectable, considering the international financial turmoil and the uncertain banking sector. Inflation remained at under 4%, and the government was able to maintain the stability of the currency. Tourism revenues grew a modest 6% over the previous year. Starting in June, the government privatized through vouchers $2 billion in state assets to some 300,000 citizens.

An agreement signed between Croatia and Bosnia and Herzegovina provided the latter with port access to the sea at Ploce. Soon afterward Yugoslavia opened a consulate in Vukovar, a Croatian town bordering Serbia, further normalizing relations between these former enemies.

(MAX PRIMORAC)

CUBA

Area: 110,861 sq km (42,804 sq mi)
Population (1998 est.): 11,116,000
Capital: Havana
Head of state and government: President of the Council of State and President of the Council of Ministers Fidel Castro Ruz

In January 1998 Pope John Paul II visited Cuba for the first time. He celebrated open-air masses in Santa Clara, Camagüey, Santiago de Cuba, and in the Plaza de la Revolución in Havana; the latter was attended by some 300,000 people, including Pres. Fidel Castro Ruz. The pope preached in favour of freedom and social justice. He criticized the U.S. for its stance toward Cuba, describing the U.S. blockade as "unjust and ethically unacceptable," and also spoke out against abortion, contraception, and divorce, all available in Cuba. Following the pope's visit some 300 Cuban prisoners were pardoned and released from jail as a result of negotiations with the Vatican.

The pope also held discussions with the U.S. administration, following which Pres. Bill Clinton announced an end to the ban on humanitarian flights and cash remittances from the U.S. to Cuba. Cubans in the U.S. were allowed to send up to $300 per quarter to relatives in Cuba. The first direct flight from Miami, Fla., to Havana since March 1996 was made in July.

The *New York Times* in July published a long interview with Luis Posada Carriles, a Cuban-born, CIA-trained terrorist who had been convicted of bombing a Cuban airliner off Barbados in 1976 and had served nine years in a Venezuelan prison. In the interview he admitted to more recent attacks against Cuban property, claiming to have organized the 1997 bombings in Havana hotels and to have had his activities financed by the late Jorge Mas Canosa and other leaders of the Cuban-American National Foundation (CANF). A CANF director, José Antonio Llama, and six other men were indicted in August by a U.S. federal grand jury in San Juan, P.R., on charges of plotting to kill President Castro. The charges related to a four-year period, but they specifically mentioned a plot discovered in 1997 when Castro visited Margarita Island, Venezuela, for a summit meeting.

Although political repression was reported to have eased after the pope's visit, four Cuban political dissidents, held in prison since July 1997, were charged in September with acts against state security, specifically sedition. They were expected to be put on trial by the end of the year and faced jail sentences of five or six years.

Elections were held on January 11 for the National Assembly and 14 provincial assemblies. Only 1.7% of the 7.9 million electorate abstained, and of those who went to the polls 95% cast valid votes. President Castro and his brother, Raúl, the armed forces minister, received 99% of the vote. The large turnout and the result were interpreted as overwhelming support for the

Castro regime despite the hardships of the past few years.

Five eastern provinces—Holguín, Las Tunas, Santiago de Cuba, Granma, and Guantánamo—suffered severe drought in 1998, which resulted in a loss of food production, particularly in grains, beans, fruits, and vegetables, as well as in the forthcoming sugar and coffee harvests. The situation became so serious that emergency relief was granted, and on September 1 the UN World Food Programme announced an emergency food-aid appeal for food imports and distribution to those in need. Late in September eastern Cuba was hit by Hurricane Georges, which brought winds of more than 175 km/h (110 mph) and ripped through the forests of the region. Banana, cocoa, and coffee crops were wiped out in some areas, sugarcane fields were flattened and flooded, and six people were killed. Some 720,000 people were evacuated from the path of the storm. There was flood damage to some 40,000 homes, and many roads, bridges, railways, and power and communications lines were knocked out.

Economic growth was reported to have been 4% in the first half of the year despite a poor sugar harvest. The increase was led by tourism, fishing, and tobacco, with exports of cigars growing strongly. Foreign investment continued to rise, with Canadian investment forecast to increase from $200 million to $1 billion by the end of 2000.

(SARAH CAMERON)

CYPRUS

Area: 9,251 sq km (3,572 sq mi) for the entire island; the area of the Turkish Republic of Northern Cyprus (TRNC), proclaimed unilaterally (1983) in the occupied northern third of the island, 3,355 sq km (1,295 sq mi)
Population (1998 est.): island 861,000; TRNC only, 188,000 (including recent Turkish settlers and Turkish military)
Capital: Lefkosia/Lefkosa (also known as Nicosia)
Head(s) of state and government: President Glafcos Clerides; of the TRNC, President Rauf Denktash

Cyprus in 1998 remained divided into the mainly Greek Republic of Cyprus, the Turkish Republic of North Cyprus, and the British Sovereign Base Areas. Although intercommunal problems continued to dominate the island's life, the year held some promise. In September North Cyprus Pres. Rauf Denktash presented a new proposal for a confederated state, with both sides retaining sovereignty over their areas. Although the idea was initially criticized by the Greek Cypriot government, serious discussions were expected to be underway by early 1999.

In elections in February, Glafcos Clerides maintained leadership of Greek Cyprus by less than 1% of the vote. In March formal talks began for membership in the European Union. Greek Cyprus enacted legislative changes, including decriminalizing homosexuality, in order to meet EU standards.

An elderly woman leads a donkey across a dry riverbed in Gauntánamo province, Cuba, one of five eastern provinces that suffered severe drought in 1998. On September 1 the UN World Food Programme announced an emergency food-aid appeal for food imports and distribution to those Cubans in need.

The opening of a military air base and the continued plans for purchase of a Russian air defense missile system for Greek Cyprus caused the U.S. and the U.K. to express unease. The issue reflected the increasingly close ties between Cyprus and Russia.

The economy recovered from the slump of previous years, although the Greek sector continued to be much more prosperous than the Turkish side. Tourism increased significantly. Water troubles approached crisis levels, with water reserves down to a dangerous low. The completion of a pipeline for desalinized water solved the problem only partially.   (GEORGE H. KELLING)

CZECH REPUBLIC

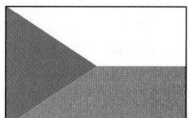

Area: 78,866 sq km (30,450 sq mi)
Population (1998 est.): 10,302,000
Capital: Prague
Chief of state: President Vaclav Havel
Head of government: Prime Ministers Josef Tosovsky and, from July 17, Milos Zeman

In the Czech Republic 1998 brought political change and continued economic difficulty. Parliamentary elections, held two years ahead of schedule on June 19–20, brought a left-wing government to power for the first time since communism's collapse in 1989. Before the elections the country was plagued by political uncertainty, with several major parties discredited by funding scandals. Josef Tosovsky's caretaker government, which took office in January, tried to address pressing economic problems, including the deregulation of rents and energy prices. Attention was also focused on firm restructuring and privatization, most notably with the sale in March of a 36% stake in IPB (Investicni a Postovni Banka) to the Japanese firm Nomura Securities. Meanwhile, political uncertainty was further aggravated by the poor health of Pres. Vaclav Havel. Although Havel was narrowly reelected on January 20 for a second five-year term, he underwent several serious operations and was bedridden much of the year. Christian Democratic Union (KDU–CSL) Chairman Josef Lux announced his departure from politics for medical reasons in September.

The centre-left Czech Social Democratic Party (CSSD) emerged the winner in the June elections with 32.3% of the vote and 74 of 200 parliamentary seats, followed by its long-term rival, the Civic Democratic Party (ODS), with 27.7% and 63 seats. In order to form a majority government, both the CSSD and the ODS would have required the cooperation of at least two of the three smaller parliamentary parties: the KDU–CSL, Freedom Union, and the Communists, with the latter not seen as a real option. After both parties' talks with the KDU–CSL and Freedom Union fell apart, CSSD Chairman Milos Zeman and his ODS counterpart, Vaclav Klaus, forged a controversial "opposition agreement" whereby the ODS agreed to tolerate a solidly CSSD minority government. In return Klaus was elected parliament chairman, and the two parties discussed instituting a majority electoral system.

With local and Senate elections scheduled for November 13–14, Freedom Union and the KDU–CSL formed a coalition with two nonparliamentary parties in an attempt to ensure sufficient representation to block absolute control by the two big parties. They were unable to accomplish this, however. ODS was the winner in the elections.

The new CSSD government announced that it would focus on such issues as fighting corruption and economic crime, speeding up economic growth, and improving capital market transparency. It also planned to raise the minimum wage and to halt church restitution, the return to the church of property that had been confiscated by the communist government. There was also talk of decreasing the independence of the Czech National Bank. Although the ODS attacked the CSSD program as "populist," ODS deputies ensured its passage by leaving the chamber during the vote. Still, the ODS set up a shadow Cabinet in late September to distinguish itself from the CSSD government.

Despite the CSSD's leftist rhetoric the new Cabinet had limited room to maneuver because of the troublesome economic situation, which was characterized by budgetary difficulties, a widening foreign-trade deficit, and growing unemployment. The state budget deficit reached 25 billion koruny in 1998 (31.68 koruny=U.S. $1). In the second quarter of 1998, gross domestic product dropped 2.4% compared with the same period the previous year, and it was expected to fall 1% for the year as a whole. Annual inflation rose 11.5% in August, whereas real wages grew at an annual rate of 1.7% and unemployment reached an all-time high of 6.4%. The foreign-trade deficit was expected to reach 85 billion koruny–100 billion koruny for the year as a whole.

Aside from economic difficulties, the government was also restrained by its reliance on right-wing opposition parties to approve legislation. The question of the 1999 budget draft was especially problematic. The government's initial budget draft was strongly criticized and failed to gain sufficient support in the parliament. A second draft, with a budget deficit totaling 31 billion koruny, won parliamentary approval in late November.

In its foreign policy the new government reaffirmed the Czech Republic's commitment to NATO and European Union integration as well as to strengthening ties with neighbouring countries. Zeman's first foreign visit was to neighbouring Austria, which at the time held the EU chairmanship. During the summer Zeman had a quarrel with German officials after he compared Sudeten Germans with Czech political extremists, but bilateral relations improved after the Social Democrats won the German elections in September. Czech-Slovak relations improved dramatically after a new government was formed in Slovakia.

(SHARON FISHER)

KELD NAVNTOFT—AP/WIDE WORLD/NORDFOTO

![Union workers demonstrate outside the Folketing (parliament) in Copenhagen.]

Union workers demonstrate outside the Folketing (parliament) in Copenhagen. In May the government passed legislation that put an end to Denmark's biggest strike since 1985. The 11-day action by some 500,000 private-sector workers crippled manufacturing industries, construction, and transportation across the country.

DENMARK

Area: 43,094 sq km (16,639 sq mi)
Population (1998 est.): 5,303,000
Capital: Copenhagen
Chief of state: Queen Margrethe II
Head of government: Prime Minister
Poul Nyrup Rasmussen

In Denmark 1998 was an eventful year, with parliamentary elections and an important referendum on Europe dominating the political scene. In a very close contest, the ruling centre-left Social Democratic–Radical Liberal minority government of Poul Nyrup Rasmussen, prime minister since 1993, proved the pollsters wrong by clinging to power in a general election in March. In the vote Rasmussen's centre-left government and its leftist allies held on to a total of 90 seats in the 179-seat Folketing (parliament),

including two members from the North Atlantic territories of the Faroe Islands and Greenland; the centre-right opposition bloc, headed by the Liberals, won 89 seats. The big winner at the polls was the far-right Danish People's Party; campaigning on an anti-immigration platform, it more than tripled its representation to 13 seats.

After the March elections the focus switched to Europe. In April, after a lengthy hearing, the nation's Supreme Court unanimously threw out a petition from a citizens' group questioning the constitutionality of Denmark's membership in the European Union (EU). This ruling paved the way for a nationwide referendum on May 28 on the country's adhesion to the Amsterdam Treaty, signed in 1997 at an EU summit in the Dutch capital. The Amsterdam Treaty made job creation a formal EU goal, supported increased cooperation in foreign affairs, and allowed for the EU to expand in order to take in countries in Eastern Europe. Much to the relief of the EU and Denmark's political establishment, the notoriously "Euroskeptical" Danes voted by a clear 55% to 45% in favour of the treaty.

In May the government intervened to pass legislation putting an end to the country's biggest strike since 1985—an 11-day action by about 500,000 private-sector workers—which crippled manufacturing industries, construction, and transportation and cost Denmark about a billion kroner a day in lost output. In June a major economic austerity package was imposed to prevent the economy from overheating, but late in the year the pace of the country's otherwise impressive economic upturn was clearly becoming dented by the global financial crisis, which caused a particularly severe drop in agricultural exports.

On a more bizarre level, Copenhagen made world headlines in January when the Little Mermaid statue, the Danish capital's tourist icon located on the city's waterfront, suffered its second decapitation in 35 years. The mermaid's severed head was quickly retrieved—in fairly good condition—after it was found in a box outside a local television station, and a Danish TV cameraman was later jailed for the act of vandalism on Denmark's 85-year-old landmark.

(CHRISTOPHER FOLLETT)

DJIBOUTI

Area: 23,200 sq km (8,950 sq mi)
Population (1998 est.): 652,000
Capital: Djibouti
Chief of state and head of government:
President Hassan Gouled Aptidon, assisted
by Prime Minister Barkat Gourad
Hamadou

Pro-government parties captured all 65 seats
in the national legislature in elections on
Dec. 19, 1997. Citing fraud and a lack of
international monitoring, opposition parties
called for a boycott of the polls. Pres.
Hassan Gouled Aptidon reappointed Barkat
Gourad Hamadou prime minister, a post he
had held since 1978.

In July high-level delegations from
Djibouti visited Iran to sign agreements on
economic cooperation. This effort resulted in
Iranian pledges of assistance with the construction of an oil refinery in the country.

In May President Aptidon, who was
the chairman of the Inter-Governmental
Authority on Development, an organization
of seven northeastern African nations, traveled to Addis Ababa, Eth., with the hope of
mediating the border dispute between
Ethiopia and Eritrea. His efforts failed to
end the crisis. By the middle of June,
Djibouti had increased army patrols on its
borders, and in November it closed its embassy in Asmara, Eritrea.

(MATTHEW A. CENZER)

DOMINICA

Area: 750 sq km (290 sq mi)
Population (1998 est.): 76,400
Capital: Roseau
Chief of state: President Crispin Anselm
Sorhaindo and, from October 6, Vernon
Shaw
Head of government: Prime Minister
Edison James

The government announced plans in January
1998 to make Dominica the "premier offshore jurisdiction not only in the Caribbean
but the world." The offshore sector comprised international business companies,
banks, gaming companies, and the economic
citizenship program, which allows foreigners to purchase Dominican passports. This
program was doing well for the economy,
earning some U.S. $3 million since 1996.

The European Union (EU) moved to help
Dominica lessen its dependence on bananas
during the year through an allocation of $2.2
million to assist with agricultural diversification. Like the other Windward Islands,
Dominica relied heavily on bananas as an
export earner, but the crop's future was uncertain owing to continuing challenges to
the EU's marketing regime from U.S. and
Latin-American growers.

The 1998–99 budget in July was set at
EC$433.9 million and included the intro-
duction of a value-added tax for the first
time in Dominica, though the tax had long
been used in other Caribbean territories.
Because 60% of world trade was likely to
become tariff-free during the next 10 years,
Dominica would receive much less income
from that source, and so the government decided to move away from taxes based on international trade and toward consumption-
type taxes on internal transactions.

(DAVID RENWICK)

DOMINICAN REPUBLIC

Area: 48,671 sq km (18,792 sq mi)
Population (1998 est.): 7,883,000
Capital: Santo Domingo
Head of state and government: President
Leonel Fernández Reyna

Congressional and municipal elections took
place on May 16, 1998, six days after the
death of José Peña Gómez (*see* OBITUARIES),
the founder and leader of the opposition
Dominican Revolutionary Party (PRD). The
PRD won a landslide victory with 83 seats
in the Chamber of Deputies (to 49 for the
governing Dominican Liberation Party and
an estimated 15 for the Social Christian
Reformist Party) and 24 in the Senate (4 and
2, respectively).

Pres. Leonel Fernández Reyna paid a historic three-day visit to Haiti in June, the first
by a Dominican head of state since 1936.
The two countries agreed to set up joint border patrols to limit the traffic of drugs, arms,
stolen goods, and contraband and to start a
direct postal service between the two countries, the first in 60 years. There was less
progress in talks on migration and tourism.

Two of Latin America's longtime leaders, Cuban
dictator Fidel Castro (left) and former president
of the Dominican Republic Joaquín Balaguer,
meet at Balaguer's home in Santo Domingo in
August. The meeting was viewed as a symbolic
closing chapter for Balaguer, who had been out
of office since 1996.

JOHN RILEY—AP/WIDE WORLD

The president announced emergency measures on July 1 to control public spending,
and the following day the peso was devalued by 8.5%. Government wages were
frozen, and public works construction projects were to be prioritized, in contrast to the
preelection rush to build that had resulted in
inflationary pressures and unpaid bills to
contractors. The economy was also struggling with exceptionally low nickel prices
and the lowest sugar harvest ever as a result
of Hurricane Georges, which struck the
country hard in September. The U.S.
Agency for International Development reported that the death toll from the storm was
likely to exceed 500. More than 300,000
people were given emergency accommodations, and more than 500,000 homes were
damaged. Roads and bridges collapsed under torrential rains and mud slides, and electricity and water supplies were wiped out.

(SARAH CAMERON)

ECUADOR

Area: 272,045 sq km (105,037 sq mi), in-
cluding the 8,010-sq km (3,093-sq mi)
Galápagos Islands
Population (1998 est.): 12,175,000
(Galápagos Islands, about 15,000)
Capital: Quito
Chief of state and head of government:
Presidents Fabián Alarcón Rivera and,
from August 10, Jamil Mahuad Witt

Elections to replace interim Pres. Fabián
Alarcón Rivera took place in 1998. The
country's largest political grouping, the
Social Christian Party (PSC), did not field a
candidate, and the two top finishers in the
first round on May 31 were Jamil Mahuad
Witt of the Popular Democracy Party (DP)
and Alvaro Noboa of the Ecuadorian
Roldosist Party. In the second-round runoff
between the two, on July 12, Mahuad,
mayor of Quito, won with 51% of the vote.
The PSC managed to maintain a strong base
in the National Congress, winning 26 seats,
compared with the DP's 36 in elections in
July.

Although Mahuad was vague on how he
proposed to fulfill his campaign pledges on
dealing with unemployment, housing, and
the health service, he was clear on his proposals for the national debt. This would be
renegotiated to seek longer repayment terms,
with a portion to be written off. Mahuad inherited a fiscal deficit of 7% of gross domestic product, aggravated by a drop in the
price of oil and a 15% decline in export earnings. Among the many major political reforms passed by the National Congress was
a ban preventing any government member
who had been indicted on corruption charges
from running for election to office unless he
or she had been formally acquitted in court.
This was aimed especially at preventing
Abdalá Bucaram Ortíz—the former president who had been removed from office in
February 1997 for mental incompetence and
then, faced with corruption charges, had fled
the country—from attempting a political
comeback. Also passed was a rule abolish-

HIERRO LEE—AP/WIDE WORLD

Students release doves at an outdoor Mass held in Guayaquil, Ecuador, after praying for a peaceful resolution to the border disputes between Ecuador and Peru. Following a first meeting between the presidents of the two countries on September 4, a peace treaty ending decades of strife over a few small, remote areas was signed in Brazil on October 26.

ing midterm elections and Congress's power to impeach ministers.

After a difficult year, border disputes between Ecuador and Peru that had been going on for decades were finally settled. At the end of August both sides withdrew their troops from the disputed spots and, following a face-to-face meeting in September, Mahuad and Peruvian Pres. Alberto Fujimori signed a peace treaty on October 26 in Brasília, Braz., with the U.S., Brazil, Chile, and Argentina mediating.

(ALAN MURPHY)

EGYPT

Area: 997,739 sq km (385,229 sq mi)
Population (1998 est.): 63,261,000
Capital: Cairo
Chief of state: President Hosni Mubarak
Head of government: Prime Minister Kamal al-Janzuri

One of the major problems that the Egyptian government had to face during 1998 was the uproar by human rights activists and expatriate Copts concerning the persecution of the Christian Coptic minority in Egypt. Maurice Sadiq, the head of the Egyptian Human Rights Centre for National Unity, called upon the Egyptian authorities to confront the issue of persecution, to which the Copts were subjected on both official and popular levels. To demonstrate this persecution Sadiq was quoted in April saying, "Building a cabaret in Egypt does not require a decision by the highest echelons nor a presidential decree, whereas building or renovating a church or even repairing its water

system required a decree by the president of the republic." Discrimination on the official level was revealed by the fact that Copts were barred from holding in the Egyptian Cabinet the powerful portfolios of foreign affairs, defense, and interior and from holding positions of governor, security chief, and president of a university. The Coptic language was not taught in any Egyptian university. Also, although Christian Coptic students were obliged to study and memorize Qur'anic verses, "all school curricula do not contain a single verse of the Bible." On the popular level, Sadiq said that Christians were cursed in a large number of mosques at every prayer and made a serious charge against the Egyptian authorities in the following statement: "I invite everyone to go to the Cairo Security Directorate every Saturday to see Christians, mostly underage girls or employees, who are threatened with dismissal from their jobs, declare their conversion to Islam."

Pres. Hosni Mubarak during the year tried to bolster his position in the Middle East by playing a role in the Arab-Israeli peace process but without any tangible success. On April 28 Israeli Prime Minister Benjamin Netanyahu visited Mubarak. In May during a visit to France, Mubarak and French Pres. Jacques Chirac proposed an international conference "to revive the stalled peace talks." Palestinian Authority leader Yasir Arafat consequently visited Mubarak in Cairo on May 24, and another meeting was held in Cairo, on July 5, that included Mubarak, Arafat, and King Hussein of Jordan to coordinate their efforts for the peace process. Nothing, however, came of these efforts.

President Mubarak was also involved in the Syrian and Lebanese aspects of the peace process. On January 14 he met with Syrian Pres. Hafez al-Assad in Damascus. When on April 1 the Israeli Cabinet accepted UN Resolution 425 of March 19, 1978, which called for Israel's unilateral

withdrawal from Lebanon, the Syrian president rushed to Cairo to elicit the support of Mubarak to prevent the Israeli withdrawal. Mubarak obliged and fully supported the Syrian position; the Israeli initiative could have ended the conflict perpetuated by Lebanon's Hezbollah organization, which was supported and armed by Syria. Assad made two more visits to Egypt, on April 24 and July 26, to coordinate his efforts with those of Mubarak.

On April 22 the Cairo Society for Peace, the first Arab organization that openly called for peace between the Arabs and Israel, was established. Its membership of 70 included prominent intellectuals and writers.

In successful shuttle diplomacy during October, President Mubarak was able to defuse the mounting tension between Turkey and Syria. Turkey had accused Syria of aiding the rebel Kurdistan Workers' Party and allowing its leader, Abdullah Ocalan, to operate against Turkey from Syria and Lebanon.

The Egyptian government continued its campaign against Islamic fundamentalists. Although incidents that involved militants decreased during 1998, attacks continued in Upper Egypt, south of Cairo. On March 23 police killed four supporters of Islamic militants in Manfalut and arrested two others, and on May 16 police killed four Islamic militants in Mallawi. The Ministry of the Interior had pursued a policy of releasing Islamic militants whose repentance had been confirmed or who had severed their relations with Islamic organizations that were involved in terrorism. Hundreds were released and handed over to their families in the presence of their representatives in the People's Assembly, who pledged to guarantee their good behaviour. The Ministry of Religious Endowments by the end of 1998 controlled only 35,000 mosques of the 65,000 that existed in Egypt. The ministry hoped to achieve its goal of controlling all the mosques by 2000.   (MARIUS K. DEEB)

EL SALVADOR

Area: 21,041 sq km (8,124 sq mi)
Population (1998 est.): 5,752,000
Capital: San Salvador
Head of state and government: President Armando Calderón Sol

On Jan. 19, 1998, Pres. Carlos Roberto Reina Idiaquez of Honduras and Pres. Armando Calderón of El Salvador signed a protocol to resolve the frontier problems that had arisen from the 1992 World Court ruling on the border disputes. Both countries agreed to proceed with demarcation of the border within a year. At the end of 1997, only 130 km (81 mi) of the 374-km (232-mi) border had been marked. Individuals affected by territorial allocations were to be guaranteed their civil and human rights.

In April, El Salvador became the first country in Central America to establish private pension funds. Pension fund administrators would manage customers' accounts and invest contributions. This strengthened

both the stock exchange and savings and investments and created thousands of jobs.

U.S. State Department documents released in June concerning the 1980 rape and murder of three U.S. Catholic nuns and a female churchworker revealed a cover-up by U.S. and El Salvadoran authorities. Four members of the National Guard and their immediate superior had been convicted of the murders and sentenced to 30 years in prison in 1984. The declassified documents showed that the defense minister of El Salvador had reported to the U.S. ambassador that he suspected the murders had been ordered by a member of the high command. Both governments subsequently denied any involvement of high-ranking military officials. In June three of the five national guardsmen were released under a law intended to decrease prison overcrowding.

Public security continued to be a matter of national concern. With 58,000 reported crimes, including 8,281 murders in 1997, El Salvador was one of the most violent countries in the world. In June the minister for public security called for more police resources and denied requests for a state of emergency and a suspension of constitutional rights. A month later President Calderón recommended that the death penalty be restored to stem the rising tide of violent crime. In September Calderón announced that the U.S. government had been asked to help investigate three murder cases dating from 1994, 1995, and 1997. Progress had stalled because government authorities had been implicated and accused of complicity.   (SARAH CAMERON)

EQUATORIAL GUINEA

Area: 28,051 sq km (10,831 sq mi)
Population (1998 est.): 454,000
Capital: Malabo
Chief of state: President Brig. Gen.
    Teodoro Obiang Nguema Mbasogo
Head of government: Prime Minister
    Angel Serafin Seriche Dougan

The economic fortunes of Equatorial Guinea were being transformed in 1998 by the continued exploitation of the oil and gas discovered about 10 years earlier off the island of Bioko. During the year production increased, to 80,000 bbl of oil per day, and construction of a plant to convert gas to methanol was begun. Much of the oil wealth, however, never reached the public treasury.

The country continued to be governed in a semidictatorial manner by Pres. Teodoro Obiang Nguema. His ruling Democratic Party was accused by the main opposition party, the Popular Union, of violating an agreement reached in March about the conduct of the elections scheduled for late in 1998. The government, meanwhile, was harshly criticized by Amnesty International and Spain for its treatment of separatists, who in January had attacked the military barracks on Bioko as part of their campaign

for self-determination. After the attack a number of Bubis, the original population of Bioko, were detained under inhumane conditions, tortured, and then tried for treason; one of their leaders, Martin Puye, died after several weeks in prison.

(CHRISTOPHER SAUNDERS)

ERITREA

Area: 121,144 sq km (46,774 sq mi)
Population (1998 est.): 3,842,000
    (including about 350,000 refugees in
    The Sudan)
Capital: Asmara
Head of state and government: President
    Isaias Afwerki

One of the most dramatic examples of Eritrea's assertion of independence and self-reliance occurred in late 1997 when it issued its own currency, the nakfa. This was particularly significant in that Eritrea's economy had historically been intricately intertwined with that of Ethiopia. More than two-thirds of the country's external trade at the beginning of 1998 was with Ethiopia. The nakfa was initially pegged to the Ethiopian birr at a rate of 1:1; the Ethiopians, however, were unhappy with this arrangement and insisted that future economic transactions between the two countries be in hard currency. By early 1998 the spirit of cooperation between Eritrea and Ethiopia had deteriorated to hostility.

Tensions between the two countries erupted into armed conflict on May 6 when an armed force entered Ethiopia's northwestern Tigre province from Eritrea. Initially, there was a skirmish between Ethiopian policemen and the intruders, but this was soon followed by a more significant military intervention from Eritrea, which resulted in the occupation of the border town of Badame and an air raid on the northern town of Mekele. The Ethiopians retaliated with an aerial bombardment of the airport at Eritrea's capital, Asmara. For the next five weeks, battles were fought in several places along the common border between the two countries.

Occupation of the Badame area had been disputed since the armed conflict against Ethiopia's Marxist regime in 1991. Once that regime had been overthrown, a joint commission was set up to attempt to devise a mutually agreeable resolution to the problem. Those negotiations failed, however. The government of Eritrea claimed that the territory in question was originally a part of the Italian colony of Eritrea, whereas the Ethiopians maintained that it was a historic part of Greater Tigre. In June a team of diplomats from the U.S. and Rwanda brokered an uneasy truce. The peace plan called for Eritrea to withdraw from the disputed territory, after which there would be international mediation. Although the Ethiopians accepted this plan, the Eritreans did not.

In preparation for a further escalation of the conflict, Eritrea, like Ethiopia, used the uneasy cease-fire period after July to increase its military strength. An attempt by

As part of a nationwide effort to reduce El Salvador's soaring crime rate, a policeman in San Salvador conducts a random weapons check of gang members. Other measures taken to fight crime in El Salvador in 1998 included calls for more police resources and a proposal to restore the death penalty.

LUIS ROMERO—AP/WIDE WORLD

A few of the 14,000 Eritreans expelled from Ethiopia in 1998 are welcomed home in June by a cheering crowd in the town of Om Hajer. Eritrea fiercely criticized the deportations, which Ethiopia carried out after armed conflict erupted between the two countries along their common border on May 6.
SAMI SALLINEN—AP/WIDE WORLD

the Organization of African Unity at mediation failed in November, and border incidents continued through the end of the year. At the same time the government had to cope with an influx of more than 14,000 deportees from Ethiopia.

(EDMOND J. KELLER)

ESTONIA

Area: 45,227 sq km (17,462 sq mi)
Population (1998 est.): 1,447,000
Capital: Tallinn
Chief of state: President Lennart Meri
Head of government: Prime Minister Mart Siimann

Political activity in Estonia in 1998 focused on the legislative elections scheduled for March 1999. There was much discussion of controlling the proliferation of parties by means of a law to ban election alliances. Such a measure was adopted on November 17 with the expectation that the number of parties with seats in the unicameral Riigikogu (parliament) would fall from 12 to 8. A few days later the opposition Moderate Party and the Republican and Conservative People's Party, partners in just such an election alliance, moved to merge.

Most indicators continued to show a robust performance by the economy, although Estonia was not immune to the financial turmoil in Russia. Hardest hit, perhaps, were the banks. The two largest, Hansapank and Hoiupank, merged in January. The new Hansapank was the only one of the three largest banks in the country to show a profit in 1998, however. Forekspank, the third largest, in October announced a merger with

the Estonian Investments Bank to form a new institution, Optiva.

In its foreign relations Estonia continued to concentrate its activities on Western Europe and in particular on the welcome decision made late in 1997 to include Estonia among the countries on the "fast track" for membership in the European Union. It was pointed out that 65% of Estonia's foreign trade was now with EU countries, and fully 50% with Finland and Sweden. A Baltic "Charter of Partnership" was signed in Washington, D.C., on January 16, and this may have helped smooth some ruffled feathers in Latvia and Lithuania, Estonia's neighbours not included on the EU fast track. Estonia's often strained relationship with Russia continued to be the focus of much attention during the year. Russia posted a high-level ambassador to Estonia, and the bilateral negotiations to revise the two nations' border proceeded well.   (EDITOR)

ETHIOPIA

Area: 1,133,882 sq km (437,794 sq mi)
Population (1998 est.): 58,390,000
Capital: Addis Ababa
Chief of state: President Negasso Gidada
Head of government: Prime Minister Meles Zenawi

In 1998 Ethiopia's economic growth appeared to be slowing. In part this was due to heavy rains that in 1997 had damaged crops, which thus led to food shortages. Because of unresolved tariff issues, fertilizers needed for the stimulation of agricultural production languished on ships docked at the Eritrean port of Assab. Economic prob-

lems were exacerbated by the escalating border tensions between Ethiopia and Eritrea in the middle of the year. It was, therefore, projected that the economy would grow by only about 3%, down from the more than 5% a year earlier. This trend, however, did not seem to have affected Ethiopia's primary export commodity, coffee, which accounted for more than 60% of the country's exports. In fact, the coffee sector was thriving under recently introduced free-market conditions.

Foreign private investors were slow to be drawn to Ethiopia, in part because of the government's cautious approach to economic liberalization. International donors continued to pressure the government, especially on the need for land reform. As of 1998, the nation's constitution stipulated that land was the sole property of the state and the people of Ethiopia.

Its deteriorating relations with Eritrea compounded Ethiopia's economic difficulties. In November 1997 Eritrea issued its own currency, the nakfa, which was initially pegged to the Ethiopian birr at a rate of 1:1. At that time almost 70% of Eritrea's trade was with Ethiopia, and Eritrea seemed to have assumed that the two countries would utilize their respective currencies to trade with each other. Ethiopia, however, countered by proposing that future trade between the two countries be in hard currency. This dispute wreaked havoc on both economies.

Relations between Eritrea and Ethiopia erupted in war in early May. The event that triggered the conflict was a skirmish between Ethiopian policemen and alleged armed invaders from Eritrea in the northwestern town of Badame, Tigre. This was a part of a border zone that had long been disputed between the two nations. Armed conflict continued in the region for more than a month, until negotiators from Rwanda and the United States issued a peace proposal. The proposal called for Eritrea to withdraw from the Badame region, to be followed by

international mediation. This initiative failed, however, and by late summer both countries were on a firm war footing. By that time more than 14,000 Eritrean residents of Ethiopia, accused of sedition, had been expelled, and about 6,000 residents of Eritrea had been similarly evicted.

Because of the problems with Eritrea, Ethiopia began to utilize the port of Djibouti for its imports. The government claimed that Djibouti was superior to Assab because it could handle a higher volume of traffic. In support of this expanded relationship, the road between Dire Dawa and Djibouti was upgraded, and there were plans to do the same with the rail system. Eritrea accused Djibouti of taking sides with Ethiopia and broke off diplomatic relations with Djibouti in November.   (EDMOND J. KELLER)

FIJI

Area: 18,272 sq km (7,055 sq mi)
Population (1998 est.): 793,000
Capital: Suva
Chief of state: President Ratu Sir Kamisese Mara
Head of government: Prime Minister Sitiveni Rabuka

After having conducted a commission of inquiry and extensive public consultations, Fiji introduced a new constitution in July 1998. The document, which protected the preeminent position of ethnic Fijians, also included a bill of rights and provision for a human rights commission. In recognition of these, India, which had severed relations with Fiji in 1987, reestablished diplomatic representa-

tion. In October the Christian Democratic Alliance Party was formed, declaring its intention to support the traditional political system, which is based on leadership by chiefs.

The economy contracted by 2.5% in 1997, with an additional 3% drop predicted for 1998. Because of global economic trends, the Asian economic crisis, and declining commodity prices, Fiji's currency was devalued by 20% in January. This adjustment helped boost employment in the garment industry and encouraged tourism, which had record receipts in the first six months of 1998 and the highest number of visitors ever (37,500) in August 1998.

By April Fiji was facing its worst drought in more than 50 years, with crops seriously affected and water shortages in many urban areas. The production of raw sugarcane was almost halved, and more than half of the country's 22,000 sugar farmers lost their entire crop. In May the government allocated F$38,000,000 ($19,460,000) for crop rehabilitation, and in September sugar farmers received interest-free loans totaling F$8,000,000.   (BARRIE MACDONALD)

FINLAND

Area: 338,145 sq km (130,559 sq mi)
Population (1998 est.): 5,154,000
Capital: Helsinki
Chief of state: President Martti Ahtisaari
Head of government: Prime Minister Paavo Lipponen

On June 2, 1998, the Finnish forest industry corporation Enso announced that it would merge with the Swedish corporation

Stora and thereby create Europe's largest forestry enterprise and the second largest in the world, after International Paper Co. of the United States. The government of Finland, with a 44% stake in Enso, would remain the biggest shareholder in the new firm. Enso and Stora posted aggregate sales of $11 billion in 1997.

A poll in September revealed that a slight majority of the nation had swung behind the government's decision that the country would enter the economic and monetary union of the European Union at the beginning of 1999. Unemployment declined during the year but remained high at a predicted 11%. Though the country ran a current-account surplus, government debt remained high.

In July a Finnish senior military commander was reprimanded for saying that the territory of Karelia, ceded to the Soviet Union after the conflict between the two countries in 1939–45, should be restored to Finland. The area had contained one-tenth of the territory of Finland and one-tenth of its population, but in 1998 it contained a quarter of a million Russians. These, Brig. Gen. Kari Hietanen told a Karelian association, could be resettled elsewhere in Russia. Restoration of the territory to Finland was "largely a question of the will to right historic wrongs," he said. Pres. Martti Ahtisaari said that Finland would not raise the issue of the return with Russia but that people were entitled to discuss it.

Late in September *Iltasanomat,* Finland's major newspaper, reported that Olli Mattila, an official at the Ministry of Foreign Affairs, was under investigation; it was suspected that he had passed confidential European Union documents to Russia. He was the son of Olavi J. Mattila, a former high state official close to Urho Kekkonen, president from 1956 to 1981, who maintained close ties to Kremlin leaders during his long tenure. The newspaper wrote that Nikolay Makarov, whom it identified as an alleged member of the Russian intelligence service KGB, was one of two officials at the Russian embassy told to leave Finland because of the incident. Foreign Minister Tarja Halonen, commenting at a news conference, admitted that the case was "sad" but said that the documents involved were not important ones. Nonetheless, an announcement by a state prosecutor on December 30 indicated that Mattila would be charged with spying. Espionage was considered an act of treason, and such charges were extremely unusual in Finland.

(EDWARD M. SUMMERHILL)

Ethiopian militia members prepare to leave for the front lines after war broke out in May between Ethiopia and Eritrea. After a month of fighting between the two countries, an international team of diplomats came up with a peace plan, which was accepted by the Ethiopians but not by the Eritreans.

SAYYID AZIM—AP/WIDE WORLD

FRANCE

Area: 543,965 sq km (210,026 sq mi)
Population (1998 est.): 58,841,000
Capital: Paris
Chief of state: President Jacques Chirac
Head of government: Prime Minister
Lionel Jospin

For the French generally, 1998 was a vintage year, above all because they won soccer's World Cup, the most watched sporting event on the planet and one for which they had the extra satisfaction of serving as host. This boost to French spirits was only slightly diminished by the subsequent doping scandals that afflicted the annual Tour de France bicycle race.

The fortunes of the Socialist-led government of Prime Minister Lionel Jospin also rose as unemployment, long the bugbear of the French economy, receded and as economic expansion allowed France to qualify for the European Monetary Union without squeezing public spending too hard. The main right-wing opposition parties fared less well and thereby indirectly weakened the standing of Pres. Jacques Chirac. They lost ground in the March regional elections, and this caused some of them to become more dependent on alliances with the far-right National Front.

In foreign policy France acted dismissively in regard to minor aspects of

GAEL CORNIER—AP/WIDE WORLD

Hundreds of thousands of soccer fans pack the Champs-Élysées in Paris during a parade for the French team that captured the World Cup with a 3–0 victory over Brazil on July 12. The victory was especially sweet for France, since it hosted the event in 1998.

European Union (EU) law by flouting wild bird protection laws but was decisive and, indeed, aggressive on the major issue of the new European Central Bank (ECB). Chirac took the EU summit meeting in May to the brink of breakdown before he succeeded in forcing the Dutch president of the ECB eventually to step down early in favour of Jean-Claude Trichet, governor of the Bank of France, who would serve a full eight-year term as head of the bank. This row led to a further cooling of relations with Germany. In contrast, France paid more care to its relations and consultations with the U.S., perhaps because the two countries disagreed on many issues.

Political Affairs. The year started unpromisingly for Jospin, whose ruling Socialist Party had its office occupied on January 22 by a wildcat movement of the unemployed demanding an increase in government welfare payments. The protesters also occupied 26 welfare offices throughout the country. The demonstrators received support from Jospin's coalition allies—the Communists, the small left-wing Citizens Movement (MDC) and the Greens.

Jospin, however, rode out these coalition tensions and refused protesters' demands that the welfare dole be brought close to the minimum wage level. Later, the threat of street unrest diminished as the unemployment rate fell below 12%. Airing more specific grievances, 150,000 hunters marched through Paris on February 15 to complain about EU restrictions on hunting migratory birds during their nesting period, and in early June, Air France pilots tried to exploit the government's desire to attract foreign fans to the World Cup by striking to maintain current pilot pay levels after the state-owned airline was partly privatized. Jospin stood firm, and the pilots caved in after 10 days.

The issue of European economic and monetary union continued to cut across party lines. The April 8 parliamentary vote adapting the Bank of France's statutes to the Maastricht Treaty on European Union divided both sides, as did the National Assembly vote on April 22 by 334 votes to 49 in favour of the euro, the single European currency. The government split, with the Socialists and Greens for and the Communists and MDC against the new currency. The centre-right Union for French Democracy (UDF) federation voted for the euro, whereas their Gaullist partners, the Rally for the Republic (RPR), walked out of the debate despite Chirac's plea to support the new currency.

The opposition parties had already been shaken by the consequences of the March 15 regional elections. These gave the government coalition 39.6%, the UDF-RPR coalition 35.6%, the National Front (FN) 15.5%, the far left 4.7%, and other minor parties 4.6%. As a result of the vote, the UDF and RPR held less than half the regions in their own right; in order to retain power in four regions—Rhône-Alpes, Picardie, Languedoc-Roussillon, and Bourgogne—UDF leaders resorted to support from the FN.

This caused an uproar within the UDF, which on April 8 expelled Jacques Blanc of Languedoc-Roussillon, Charles Baur of Picardie, and Charles Millon of Rhône-Alpes, whereas Jean-Pierre Soissons of Bourgogne quit of his own accord. Millon, a former defense minister and Chirac ally, announced on April 17 the creation of a new

party, the Right. With the apparently increasing power of the FN giving urgency to unity between the two mainstream centre-right formations, the RPR and UDF sought to close ranks by announcing on May 14 a new electoral pact, dubbed the Alliance. Two days later, however, a key UDF component, the Liberal Democracy (formerly the Republican) Party, said it would quit the UDF and merge directly into the Alliance.

The FN was also encountering problems. On April 2 a court condemned its founder-leader, Jean-Marie Le Pen, for his assault on a political opponent during the 1997 election and barred him from holding office for two years. While appealing the ruling, Le Pen decided to name his wife, Jany, to head his party list for the 1999 European Parliament elections. His number two man in the party, Bruno Mégret, whose softer style had helped the FN make inroads into the traditional right, criticized this nomination and was publicly lambasted by Le Pen. Their quarrel worsened. On December 23 Mégret and six key supporters were expelled from the FN, and they looked certain to found a new party. In addition, the FN lost its sole parliamentary deputy in a May 3 by-election at Toulon.

The racism issue was, indirectly, kept alive by the trial in Bordeaux of Maurice Papon, who had been an official of France's World War II Vichy government. On April 2 Papon was sentenced to 10 years in prison for having helped deport Jews to Nazi Germany. Corsican separatists on February 6 assassinated Claude Erignac, the central government prefect on the island, and on May 8 they exploded a bomb at the Provence regional executive offices in Marseilles. On February 18 a Paris court sentenced 36 Islamic militants to terms of up to 10 years in prison for their part in the 1995 bombings in France.

The Economy. The year was one of the best ever for the French economy. It expanded by 3–3.1% as a result of strong domestic household spending and corporate investment, which more than compensated for the fall in foreign demand for French goods associated with the economic decline in Asia and Russia. This reduced the budget deficit to 2.9% of national output, below the 3% guideline needed for France's qualification for European monetary union.

Strong growth helped create some 250,000 new jobs and brought down the unemployment rate to 11.5% in November. Honouring its major election pledge of 1997, the government also cut the standard workweek from 39 to 35 hours, to be applied to companies with more than 20 employees by the year 2000 and to those with smaller workforces by 2002. The aim was to oblige companies to open up new job slots in order to maintain production. Not surprisingly, the measure was opposed by business groups and championed by most labour unions.

With the left wing of his coalition largely placated by the 35-hour week, Jospin resumed the privatization and restructuring that his Gaullist predecessors had started. Some lame-duck enterprises had required substantial state aid to remain in business and to prepare them for sale. France was therefore relieved when on May 20 the European Commission gave final approval to the F 125 billion (about $21.9 billion) of French government aid and guarantees that had been ac-

corded to Crédit Lyonnais and upheld the F 20 billion ($3.5 billion) paid in 1994 to Air France. In return, the EC required the eventual privatization of both these state companies.

After a slow start, privatization moved forward. The government announced plans to sell or reduce its stake in France Telecom, GAN insurance, the CIC bank, and some smaller financial institutions. In the sensitive defense and aerospace sector, the government in June reduced its stake in Thomson-CSF electronics to 43% as a result of the latter's merger with Alcatel. The Lagardère group was allowed to take a one-third stake in state-owned Aerospatiale.

Foreign Policy. Obscured a bit by the popular euphoria over France's 3–0 victory over Brazil in the July 12 World Cup final was the serious blow to the French political and financial establishment's self-esteem dealt a few days earlier by the announcement of the linkup between the Frankfurt and London stock exchanges. This was seen in Paris as an omen that France was being outflanked by a new axis between the pro-European government of Great Britain's Tony Blair and a Germany grown tired of its special relationship across the Rhine. The concern was reinforced by warnings from Daimler-Benz Aerospace of Germany and British Aerospace that they might leave France behind in their quest to form a single large European aerospace company to rival the new giants in the U.S. The French and German governments also abandoned their plan to develop spy satellites.

By the year's end France's leaders had established some rapport with the new German government of Gerhard Schröder, but made more progress in improving relations with Britain and the U.S. During the summer Jospin paid successful visits to both countries. With the U.S., France agreed on April 8 to a new bilateral aviation treaty, which had taken two years of negotiation after the lapse of their previous 1992 airline pact. Generally, the more relaxed tone in Franco-American relations prevented disagreements, such as that over the Middle East, from degenerating into acrimony, as had happened previously.

France remained engaged in Middle East diplomacy. Chirac invited Hafez al-Assad to Paris on July 16, the Syrian president's first visit to the West in 22 years. Paris talked early in the year of supplementing U.S. diplomacy in the Arab-Israeli dispute, but was happy to take a back seat in the autumn as the U.S. made fresh efforts to break the impasse. On May 18 the U.S. and the EU came to terms over U.S. sanctions on companies doing business with Libya and Iran; the

dispute arose out of the move by Total of France to invest in Iranian gas.

During the 1998 UN-Iraq crisis over weapons inspection, France distanced itself from the confrontational tactics of the U.S. and in February tried to play a mediating role. In December, France disagreed with U.S. and British bombing of Baghdad but refrained from overt criticism and ended 1998 seeking a new UN consensus on Iraq.

(DAVID BUCHAN)

GABON

Area: 267,667 sq km (103,347 sq mi)
Population (1998 est.): 1,208,000
Capital: Libreville
Chief of state: President Omar Bongo
Head of government: Prime Minister Paulin Obame-Nguéma

The National Rally of Woodcutters, Gabon's largest opposition party, broke into two rival factions on July 20, 1998, after dissidents, led by the party's secretary-general, Pierre-André Kombila Koumba, challenged the leadership of party founder Father Paul Mba Abessole. Abessole, runner-up to Omar Bongo in the controversial 1993 presidential elections, met with his followers at the end of the month. The split assured Bongo an easy victory (66% of the vote) in the December election.

The fall in world oil prices and the economic weakness in Asia, Gabon's largest market for its timber products, contributed to the government's decision to increase

budgetary expenditures for 1999 by only 2%. Log exports were expected to drop by 30%, and little growth was projected in oil revenues. Overall economic growth was likely to be only 1%.

Privatization of Gabon's railway system was scheduled to be completed by the end of the year. This followed the successful sale of the state-owned water and power company in 1997. Also destined for privatization, Air Gabon was aiming to replace its fleet of six outdated aircraft in order to make the company more attractive to prospective buyers.

In February a new regional organization designed to promote economic integration and common political institutions, the Economic and Monetary Community of Central Africa (CEMAC), was created in Libreville. A favourite project of President Bongo, CEMAC comprised Cameroon, Central African Republic, Republic of the Congo, Chad, Equatorial Guinea, and Gabon.   (NANCY ELLEN LAWLER)

GAMBIA, THE

Area: 10,689 sq km (4,127 sq mi)
Population (1998 est.): 1,292,000
Capital: Banjul
Head of state and government: President Capt. Yahya Jammeh

Pres. Yahya Jammeh, who had come to power in a military coup in 1994 and been confirmed in power in a presidential elec-

Voters in Libreville, Gabon, wait outside the gate at a heavily guarded polling center to cast their ballots in the presidential elections in December. A split in the country's largest opposition party allowed Pres. Omar Bongo, who had been in office since 1967, to win another seven-year term.

tion in September 1996, governed The Gambia in 1998 through his Alliance for Patriotic Reorientation and Construction, which enjoyed a large majority in the National Assembly. Several actions during the year demonstrated that he ruled the nation in a highly authoritarian manner. In June four leading opposition politicians were arrested when they protested against corruption and a financial scandal. The main opposition party, the United Democratic Party, sued for damages when its former leader, Dadawa Jawara, was held under arrest. Opposition and human rights groups, along with the Commonwealth, accused Jammeh of violating human rights and abusing freedom of expression. He closed a radio station and a newspaper; the mysterious death of the former finance minister was not explained; and there was much corruption, despite promises that it would be rooted out. In March Jammeh visited Libya and rallied Libyan leader Col. Muammar al-Qaddafi to his support.

The Gambia's economy remained highly dependent on external funding. In 1998 the tourist industry had not yet fully recovered from its collapse following the military takeover. In June The Gambia sent 300 troops to Sierra Leone to help the West African peacekeeping force restore order there.   (CHRISTOPHER SAUNDERS)

GEORGIA

Area: 69,492 sq km (26,831 sq mi)
Population (1998 est.): 5,431,000
Capital: Tbilisi
Head of state and government: President Eduard A. Shevardnadze, assisted by Ministers of State Nikoloz Lekishvili until July 26 and, from August 7, Vazha Lortkipanidze

Georgia in 1998 was racked by renewed hostilities in Abkhazia and a series of political upheavals that the country's leadership blamed on supporters of the late president Zviad Gamsakhurdia. On February 9 Pres. Eduard Shevardnadze narrowly escaped assassination. Some of the perpetrators were arrested within days, which impelled their associates to take hostage four UN observers in western Georgia to demand their comrades' release. Georgian officials negotiated the UN observers' release. The kidnappers' leader escaped but was shot dead in late March trying to evade capture by Georgian security officials. In mid-October a Georgian army colonel led a mutiny in western Georgia that was quashed within 24 hours by army troops.

Shevardnadze fired Defense Minister Vardiko Nadibaidze in late April, appointing Davit Tevzadze in his place. In late July the entire Cabinet resigned after Nikoloz Lekishvili stepped down as minister of state, but most ministers retained their posts in the new government headed by former ambassador to Moscow Vazha Lortkipanidze. Finance Minister Mikhail Chkuaseli resigned on November 14, complaining that the failure to implement measures to eliminate tax eva-

sion had augmented a huge budget deficit; his successor, Davit Onoprishvili, pledged to reduce the deficit without endangering monetary stability.

Unhappy with endemic corruption and failure to implement reforms of local government and the judiciary, only some 35–40% of voters participated in local elections on November 15. Despite waning support, the ruling Citizens' Union of Georgia retained an overall majority in most districts. The All-Georgian Union of Revival, headed by Aslan Abashidze, a possible challenger to Shevardnadze in the presidential election in 2000, fared poorly outside Ajaria.

Sporadic clashes in southern Abkhazia in the spring between Georgian guerrillas and Abkhaz police erupted in May into full-scale fighting, which the Russian peacekeeping force stationed in the region did nothing to prevent. Up to 36,000 ethnic Georgians were compelled to flee their homes. Talks in Moscow in June between senior Georgian and Abkhaz representatives and UN-mediated negotiations in Geneva in July and in Greece in October resulted in the drafting of bilateral agreements abjuring the future use of force and stipulating conditions for the repatriation of Georgian displaced persons and Georgian economic aid for Abkhazia.

Shevardnadze's June meeting with South Ossetian leader Lyudvig Chibirov failed to expedite a political agreement between that breakaway region and the central Georgian government. A visit to Georgia in November by Pres. Robert Kocharyan of Armenia reflected the desire of both countries to expand economic cooperation and to neutralize growing nationalist sentiment among the 200,000-strong Armenian community in southern Georgia.   (ELIZABETH FULLER)

GERMANY

Area: 357,022 sq km (137,847 sq mi)
Population (1998 est.): 82,148,000
Capital: Bonn; capital designate: Berlin
Chief of state: President Roman Herzog
Head of government: Chancellor Helmut Kohl and, from October 27, Gerhard Schröder

Germany in 1998 was dominated by the national election in September. The election campaign engrossed the nation for much of the year. By far the most important electoral issue was the country's critical economic situation, unemployment having increased to 11.2% by the end of 1997. The centre-right coalition, consisting of the Christian Democratic Union (CDU), Christian Social Union (CSU), and the Free Democratic Party, claimed that an economic turnaround and upswing were in process, whereas the "Red-Green" (Social Democratic Party [SPD] and assorted ecologists) opposition asserted that any such phenomenon was merely seasonal if it existed at all.

The two facts that could not be denied in the nine-month campaign were that Helmut Kohl had been chancellor for 16 consecutive years, the longest tenure since that of Otto

von Bismarck, and that he was 63.5 kg (140 lb) overweight. In an age of round-the-clock television exposure, the chancellor's appearance was to many a constant reminder that he was set on overstaying his leave in public office. He commanded great respect even among his political opponents, yet his considerable stature as a statesman marshaled against his candidacy as a politician. Like Winston Churchill, Kohl was a wartime leader, albeit the Cold War. As with Churchill, once the war was over, he was dumped by the electorate.

Kohl's gift for the simplification of complex issues was eminently suited to the political culture that the confrontation with the Soviet Union had imposed on international affairs. The same gift enabled him to see through the myth of the Soviet state, providing the insight that the behemoth was little more than a political fiction whose credibility and credit had run out. This perception provided the basis for his decision to snatch German reunification from a disintegrating communist bloc and a crippled Soviet Union.

The irony of the situation was complex. Kohl's prodigious feat involved the introduction of free elections in eastern Germany, but this resulted in his removal from office because he could not possibly satisfy the soaring expectations born of the very act of enfranchisement. There had been no great need for money in East Germany, because there was little to buy, but after reunification there was more to buy and, thus, a greater need for money. Consequently, the gulf between those with and those without financial means became much wider.

An economy of scarcity marked by widespread equality with full employment was rapidly replaced by an economy of supply-side abundance and widespread individual want. Within a very short time, the eastern Germans felt themselves the victims of capitalistic exploitation, a second-class citizenry almost one-fifth of whom were unemployed. In this sense Helmut Kohl was the architect and engineer of his own political demise. His electoral defeat was the worst in his party's history. (*See* Sidebar.)

The underlying truth of the situation was that much of West Germany's and West Berlin's exemplary prosperity had been subsidized by the strategic prerequisite of financing the Cold War. The subsidies involved in this strategy were enormous, involving decades of deficit spending and the consequent accumulation of a huge national debt. The victory over communism was an economic victory. The bill covering the enormous expense involved in securing the victory was political. The Cold War beggared Eastern Europe and enriched Western Europe, but eight years after its end it cost Kohl his fifth term in office and the leadership of a party, the CDU, that he left in disarray and dejection.

Victory over communism had not, however, been the CDU's main concern. The main thrust of CDU policy under Kohl and Konrad Adenauer before him was the consummation of European union. Their common conviction was that Germany's only future lay in a united Europe. It was the Christian Democrats who saw to it that West Germany's financial contribution to the EU was larger than that of any other member nation, achieving under Kohl a whopping 30% of the EU's total budget. It was Kohl

Deutschland hat einen neuen Kanzler.

Workers in Bonn, Ger., add the slogan "Germany Has a New Chancellor" to an election poster for Gerhard Schröder in September. Schröder ousted Helmut Kohl as chancellor when his party, the left-of-centre Social Democratic Party, won a plurality of seats in the national election. Kohl had served as chancellor for 16 years.

who worked tirelessly to achieve the Maastricht Treaty and its stipulation of a maximum of deficit spending not to exceed 3.5% of gross domestic product as the prerequisite to membership in an economic and monetary union (EMU) to go into effect on January 1, 1999—proof that the Christian Democrats had learned something about deficit budgeting.

In 1998 Germany fairly exploded with entrepreneurial élan. In a scramble of international takeovers, BMW and Volkswagen bought Rolls-Royce Ltd. The publishing house of Bertelsmann bought out Random House and therewith became the U.S.'s largest book publisher and also acquired the prestigious Berlin Verlag, reinforcing its position as the world's largest publishing group. (*See* MEDIA AND PUBLISHING: *Sidebar.*) Other German publishers followed suit, Axel Springer Verlag AG acquiring the publishing group Econ and List and Holzbrinck, the third German publishing giant, forming a new group with Weltbild of Augsburg. The great concerns were positioning themselves for unbridled global competition in anticipation of the disappearance of Germany's price-control mechanism for books. Against this giantism, the smaller publishers were powerless.

In September the business coup of the year took place with the merger of Daimler-Benz and the Chrysler Corp.; DaimlerChrysler AG was born into fifth place among the automakers of the world. At DM 99 billion, the German automobile industry accounted for 20% in value of all German exports during the year (DM 1.78=$1). Meanwhile, other

German industrial giants were shaking off their classical designations by diversifying. Moving away from bulk steel production, Mannesmann switched to the manufacture of automobile components and spare parts. It had long since become the chief contributor to the telecommunications industry. Hoechst, a successor of I.G. Farben, refined its chemical production to include medicants and insecticides. Allianz, Germany's largest insurance conglomerate, took over the French insurance group AGF. Adidas bought out the French firm Salomon to become the second largest supplier of sports articles in the world.

The National Election

The most surprising result of the national election in Germany on Sept. 27, 1998, was the magnitude of the electoral shift. The left-of-centre Social Democratic Party (SPD), led by Gerhard Schröder (*see* BIOGRAPHIES) and campaigning on pledges to reduce unemployment and increase social justice for all Germans, received 40.9% of the vote, an increase of 4.5% over 1994. The centre-right Christian Democratic Union/Christian Social Union (CDU/CSU), led by longterm Chancellor Helmut Kohl, received 35.1%, a decrease of 6.2% from 1994.

The Greens, campaigning on environmental issues, won 6.7%, a decline of 0.06% from 1994. The centre Free Democratic Party (FDP) gained 6.2%, a loss of 0.07% from 1994, and the Party of Democratic Socialism (PDS) received 5.1%, a gain of 0.07%. Voter participation was 82.3%, a gain of 3.3%

over 1994. The apportionment of parliamentary seats was as follows: SPD 298 (+46), CDU/CSU 245 (–49), Greens 47 (–2), FDP 44 (–3), and PDS 35 (+5).

For the first time since 1972, the SPD formed the strongest group in the Bundestag. The CDU/CSU suffered its worst showing ever, losing 109 electoral districts, a full one-third of the country's total, to the SPD. The CDU/CSU also lost heavily in the state elections. Of the 16 state governments, the CDU/CSU won in only three: Bavaria, Baden-Württemberg, and Saxony. In Thuringia, Berlin, and Bremen, the CDU shared power in coalition with the SPD. Also for the first time since the early 1950s, there were five groups in the Bundestag. Insofar as candidates for coalition were concerned, the CDU/CSU was at a disadvantage, with only the FDP an acceptable partner. (GEORGE BAILEY)

As 1998 ended, it clearly had been a year of superlatives in German industry, the value of exports increasing from DM 117 billion in 1997 to some DM 141 billion.

Germany's largest firms were subject as such to the economy of scale, in which increases in per capita productivity were equated with proportionate decreases in the number of places of work. Increased automation and electronic innovation were further curtailing the need for human hands in the workplace. The result was that, despite concerted efforts of the government, unemployment in 1998 could be reduced only to 10.2%, a decrease of only 1% from 1997. At the same time, the number of bankruptcies remained roughly constant at an estimated 33,000.

The supreme irony of Germany's employment dilemma was the reversal of the alliance between workers and their unions. In the conditions of a global economy, labour unions demonstrably reduced the competitiveness of their members, which thus exposed the union movement as the chief formal cause of unemployment. The need for flexibility, as expressed in the willingness of the individual to assume more initiative and greater responsibility for his or her own welfare, was touted by the new Red-Green coalition as the panacea for the scourge of systemic unemployment.

Soon after the election it was announced by the Federal Institute for Labour in Nürnberg that there had been an upswing in the German economy. Unemployment declined in the first half of 1998 to 3,965,000, and eastern Germany's percentage of total exports doubled to 6%.

In more than one sense, the previous government, but with a healthier majority than four votes in the Bundestag (federal parliament) and at least a simple majority in the Bundesrat (federal council), would have been in a better position to plan and carry out the painful demolition of much of the German social welfare overhead. The Social Democrats would have to jump over their own shadows to do so. Their coalition partners the Greens, with their agenda of an immediate shutdown of nuclear power plants, would not be much help. (The Social Democrats reckoned that the effective withdrawal from atomic energy would take about 25 years.) The great bugaboo for any party or coalition, however, was the simple fact that there was no financial basis for any action. Federal, state, and city governments were all virtually bankrupt and in heavy debt. The national debt—DM 2.5 trillion by the end of 1998—required an allotment of 11% of the budget to make the necessary interest payments. The problem, consequently, was the raising of revenue.

The new government's first discussion on tax reform resulted in its resolve to reduce the "incidental costs" (for health care, unemployment insurance, payment for sick leave, 30 vacation days per annum) of German labour to less than 40% of their present total, a reduction that would render German labour globally competitive and decrease government expenditure proportion-

ately. Beyond that there was talk of the pet project of the Greens, an "ecological tax" formulated to reward observers and punish offenders of ecological strictures. There was also talk of a reduction of the income tax to a span of 20–40%, effective in three stages by 2002. These were, however, only tentative steps to address the problem and were also a reminder that SPD campaign strategy involved blocking the conservative coalition's attempts at meaningful tax reform. A more definite measure was brought into prospect by Chancellor Schröder on the first day of the talks. This was the decision to subsidize as a top priority the apprenticeship for employment of 100,000 young people. Schröder, a self-made man, was determined to dispel the apparition of a permanent underclass, a noncitizenry of dropouts unable to cope in today's world.

Much would depend on whether Schröder could exercise his flexibility politically within the policy constraints of his coalition. Any German government, however, was going to find itself harnessed by the rules and regulations of the EU. The economic sovereignty of the member nations would be curtailed by the introduction of the euro and monetary union. Schröder's coalition would also find itself subordinated to no small extent to a larger European unification, particularly in foreign policy, and one that favoured the German states rather than the federal government. For example, the collection of taxes would be the prerogative of the states.

The global economic crisis that began in Asia in 1997 complicated matters still further, but it highlighted the necessity to distinguish between the commercial movement of capital and financial speculation based on the purchase and sale of securities or foreign exchange in different markets and to regulate the distinction.

Traditionally, the SPD was a party dedicated to social justice through a political approach to economics. The CDU/CSU, by contrast, was dedicated to entrepreneurial freedom in the economic approach to politics. The final irony of 1998, ushering in a new era, was that the political fate of the SPD would be determined by the party's performance in the economic field of the open market.   (GEORGE BAILEY)

Pres. Jerry John Rawlings of Ghana (left) appears with U.S. Pres. Bill Clinton and First Lady Hillary Clinton at an outdoor rally in Accra on March 23. Attended by hundreds of thousands of Ghanaians eager to see Clinton on his 12-day tour of Africa, the rally boosted spirits in a country that faced economic problems and drought in 1998.

GHANA

Area: 238,533 sq km (92,098 sq mi)
Population (1998 est.): 18,497,000
Capital: Accra
Head of state and government: Chairman of the Provisional National Defense Council and President Jerry John Rawlings

Long considered one of the few success stories in West Africa, Ghana saw its star tarnished in 1998. Economic growth declined during the year, and the budgetary deficit and inflation grew. As a result, most Ghanaians still endured severe poverty; the country's per capita income remained less than $500 per year.

Some of these economic problems stemmed from factors outside of the government's control. Drought gripped the country, crippling hydroelectric plants and reducing power production by 40%. The fall of the worldwide gold price further hurt the Ghanaian economy, for gold was one of the country's main exports. The economy also suffered, however, from the nation's endemic corruption. The arrest of Ghana's police inspector rocked the public's confidence in police and law enforcement. There were several protests during the year expressing anger over corruption as well as over the rising water and electricity prices. Despite these problems, Ghana's president, Jerry Rawlings, maintained his popularity. The public did not associate him with corruption, and the main opposition party was weak.

Foreign policy was one of the country's few bright spots during 1998. Ghana was the first stop on Bill Clinton's 12-day tour of Africa, and the U.S. president promised aid to help build more power plants. (*See* Spotlight: *Clinton's Africa Trip.*) Ghana's government also worked to resolve some long-standing tensions with neighbours. In mid-May Pres. Gnassingbé Eyadéma of Togo made a visit to Ghana, his first in 31 years of power.   (MICHAEL TETELMAN)

On March 23, 1998, U.S. Pres. Bill Clinton arrived in Accra, Ghana, to begin a six-country, 12-day visit to Africa, the most extensive journey to that continent ever undertaken by a U.S. leader. He went with high hopes, hailing "the beginning of a new African renaissance." In retrospect, however, it seemed that the visit might instead have provided grounds for scrutinizing more carefully the premises upon which U.S. policy toward Africa was formulated.

The visit began on an upbeat note with enthusiastic crowds assembling to offer their greetings. The president, in turn, seemed genuinely eager to improve trading opportunities between the U.S. and Africa. The African growth and opportunity bill was being debated in the U.S. Congress with the object of promoting his aim, and his slogan "Trade Not Aid" underlined his determination to replace the discouraging feelings of dependency on the part of the Africans with a dynamic and mutually beneficial partnership.

To that end Clinton initially targeted a handful of countries deemed to have already demonstrated reformist tendencies—countries in which progress had been made toward a more democratic form of government, toward the establishment of internal security, and toward economic recovery and the elimination of corruption. These, henceforward, would be the criteria upon which further opportunities for profitable cooperation with the U.S. would depend. Eritrea, Ethiopia, Uganda, and Rwanda in particular were singled out as fulfilling these requirements and also because they were led, it was thought, by men of a younger, pragmatic generation with whom the U.S. could do business. Further, there was also South Africa, a nation that had set an example of magnanimity and renewal.

Yet even for the most optimistic observer, there were discernible obstacles to the fulfillment of this well-intentioned plan. In the first place, all the countries on which the president focused attention had been, and still were, heavily dependent upon foreign aid for whatever economic progress they had made. In addition, discussions that took place in a meeting with East African heads of state, held in Entebbe, Uganda, forced Clinton to revise fundamentally his interpretation of what constituted progress toward a democratic form of government. Multiparty democracy, which he had taken as his aim, was conspicuously absent from the countries singled out for approval. Nor, to the dispassionate observer, was there much evidence that a multiparty system had provided the best recipe for internal political stability elsewhere in the continent. In South Africa too, the highlight of his visit, Clinton had to review his plans when Pres. Nelson Mandela made it clear that trade was no substitute for aid in countries as poor and as lacking in natural resources as were those in Africa.

The outbreak of hostilities between Eritrea and Ethiopia on May 6 inscribed a powerful question mark against the president's faith in the good intentions of the pragmatic young leaders who were to bring in a new era of cooperation in the Great Lakes region of Africa. The rebellion that began shortly afterward, with the support of Uganda and Rwanda, in the eastern provinces of the Democratic Republic of the Congo raised yet further doubts.

The question then arose as to why President Clinton, whose intentions were patently sincere, assumed that the African leaders with whom he was dealing were at one with him in his aims. One explanation was the information that had been supplied to him. U.S. policy in Africa since the time of the Cold War had been bedeviled by the phenomenon immortalized by the novelist Rudyard Kipling as the "Great Game." In the late 19th century, British attitudes toward Russian intervention in Asia had been coloured by the reports of official, semiofficial, and private adventurers enjoying the thrill of clandestine operations beyond the frontiers of India and not infrequently embellishing, if not actually inventing, accounts of Russian machinations and the vacillating loyalties of local chieftains. These activities were repeated in Africa during the Cold War by Americans of a similar cast of mind.

SPOTLIGHT

PRESIDENT CLINTON'S AFRICA TRIP: SEEING THINGS AS THEY ARE

by Kenneth Ingham

Illustration by Tom Curry

As a result, an opportunistic power seeker such as Jonas Savimbi was regularly described as "pro-Western" and supplied with arms to conduct a profoundly damaging rebellion against the self-styled Marxist government of Angola. Similarly, the unscrupulous "pro-Western" Mobuto Sese Seko was helped to become president of Zaire and oppressor of his people as a "bulwark against the spread of Communism in Tropical Africa."

Even before the Cold War had ended, the exponents of the late-20th-century version of the Great Game had discovered the wellspring of a new series of plots against the interests of the West in the Muslim governments of Libya and The Sudan. Thus accused, the Muslim leaders' not-unnatural reaction had been to conform more closely to the character defined for them by their opponents. In this situation of heightened tension, the readiness of the presidents of Uganda, Eritrea, and Ethiopia to give assistance to the rebels against the Sudanese government may well, whatever their underlying reasons, have been represented to U.S. policy makers as reinforcing the reformist and pro-Western character currently attributed to them.

These considerations reveal the need for a reassessment of U.S. policy toward Africa. If, as President Clinton clearly intended to demonstrate by his visit, the U.S. is eager to help Africa overcome the constraints that poverty, corruption, and political instability have imposed on the continent's development, it is necessary to understand and give priority to the genuine needs and aspirations of individual African countries rather than using them as pawns in a geopolitical power struggle.

Kenneth Ingham is Emeritus Professor of History at the University of Bristol, England.

GREECE

Area: 131,957 sq km (50,949 sq mi)
Population (1998 est.): 10,543,000
Capital: Athens
Chief of state: President Konstantinos
Stephanopoulos
Head of government: Prime Minister
Konstantinos Simitis

The main issues in Greece in 1998 were local elections, economic reform, and relations
with Turkey and Cyprus. The elections on
October 11 and October 18 were the first to
be held after a recent administrative reform
greatly reduced the number of municipalities.
The main opposition party, New Democracy,
won the three biggest cities and carried 27 of
the country's 64 prefectures. The ruling
Panhellenic Socialist Movement (Pasok) lost
heavily but still prevailed in 433 of 900 municipalities. Probably because of Pasok's
weak showing Prime Minister Konstantinos
("Kostas") Simitis shuffled his Cabinet,
called a vote of confidence, and won it after
pressuring Pasok deputies to support him.

Simitis also aimed at restructuring
Greece's economic framework, especially
the oversized public sector. In January a new
tax bill was submitted to the legislature. On
June 24 the government submitted a new

draft bill on labour relations that would provide part-time work in the public sector and
generally promote flexibility in the labour
market. These attempts to overhaul the
economy met with numerous protests from,
among others, teachers, farmers, seamen,
and pilots.

On March 14 the Greek drachma was devalued by about 14%. This enabled the
Greek currency to join the European
Union's exchange-rate mechanism, helped
to improve the competitiveness of Greek
products, and put a temporary end to speculative attacks against the drachma.

The government's measures helped to improve the state of the economy, but the momentum of the past years was somewhat
lost. Gross domestic product and industrial
output continued to grow, and inflation fell
but at a lower rate than in previous years. In
August year-on-year inflation stood at 5%,
twice the government's year-end target of
2.5%. In mid-September the government
had to adjust its target for the 1999 budget
deficit, partly owing to the international financial crisis. The International Monetary
Fund, in its annual report on the Greek
economy, urged the government to adhere
strictly to its austerity program and radically
restructure the public sector.

High on the privatization agenda in 1998
were Olympic Airways and Ionian Bank.
Two top officials of Olympic resigned in
1998, and talks between the government,
Olympic's management, and staff proved
difficult. Repeated strikes and protests
added to the company's woes. A bill to re-

structure the carrier was passed on April 9,
but amid continued conflict Olympic's survival seemed far from certain as no prospective buyers came forward. The attempt to
privatize Ionian Bank also led to protests
and strikes, and an offer to sell the bank was
canceled on August 25 because all bids were
deemed unsatisfactory.

New Democracy, the main opposition
party, continued to be plagued by internal
strife. On February 3, after failing to vote
against a government-sponsored bill, three
of the party's legislators were expelled and
three had their membership suspended. By
contrast, Pasok managed to remain relatively disciplined, although a clash within
the party between "reformers" and "pop-
ulists" may have only been postponed until
a party congress set for March 1999.

Throughout the year Greece witnessed an
unprecedented number of terrorist attacks,
mostly on banks, businesses, and diplomats'
cars. In the summer disastrous forest fires
hit the country, some of which threatened
Athens and some of the country's most popular tourist areas.

Foreign relations were dominated by relations with Turkey. Greece's continued backing of Cyprus on all issues concerning that
nation's Turkish-speaking minority, including
Cyprus's plan to install Russian antiaircraft
missiles, did not help improve the situation.
Also, Greece complained about frequent violations of its airspace by Turkish military
planes. Renewed Turkish proposals to demil-
itarize the Greek Aegean Islands were rejected by Greece. Several high-level meetings

A man looks on helplessly as a forest fire rages outside an Athens suburb. Disastrous forest fires plagued Greece in 1998. Some of the fires
threatened Athens, Mt. Olympus, and the ancient sites of Olympia.

DIMITRI MESSINIS—AP/WIDE WORLD

Mourners line the streets of Guatemala City, Guat., to watch the funeral procession of Bishop Juan Gerardi Conedera, who was bludgeoned to death on April 26, two days after he co-presented a report that blamed the army for most of the estimated 150,000 deaths during Guatemala's years of civil unrest.
SCOTT SADY—AP/WIDE WORLD

failed to bring about any improvement in relations between the two countries, although in June both sides agreed to implement fully a 1988 agreement concerning rules of conduct related to military activities in the Aegean. Relations with Macedonia continued to improve, and Greece continued to be one of Macedonia's main trading partners. Relations with Albania and Bulgaria also improved. Greece largely followed the EU line in the Kosovo crisis.

In 1998 Greece lost two important personalities. On April 23 former prime minister and president Konstantinos Karamanlis died, and, after 24 years at the helm of the Greek Orthodox Church, Archbishop of Athens and All Greece Serphim died on April 10 (*see* OBITUARIES). Seraphim was succeeded by Metropolitan Christodoulos of Dimitriadas.

(STEFAN KRAUSE)

GRENADA

Area: 344 sq km (133 sq mi)
Population (1998 est.): 100,400
Capital: Saint George's
Chief of state: Queen Elizabeth II, represented by Governor-General Daniel Williams
Head of government: Prime Minister Keith Mitchell

Following the death in 1997 of its founder, Sir Eric Gairy, the opposition Grenada United Labour Party, the country's longest-existing political group, found itself a new president in April 1998. He was Herbert Preudhomme, a Gairy loyalist and former deputy prime minister. Gairy's death triggered a power struggle within the party, which by the end of 1998 had not yet been fully resolved.

Cuban Pres. Fidel Castro paid a well-received visit to Grenada in early August as part of a three-nation tour of the English-speaking Caribbean. His strong support of a previous regime that had espoused socialist causes and deprived Grenadans of many of their freedoms appeared to have been forgotten. Only the opposition Democratic Labour Party publicly opposed the visit, demanding changes in Cuba's human rights record. Prime Minister Keith Mitchell, however, seemed prepared to overlook the Castro regime's less-attractive features and insisted that most Caribbean governments were prepared to accept Cuba "without changes." Castro's willingness to provide aid to the English-speaking Caribbean was compared favourably with the continual whittling down of U.S. assistance. Grenada was offered 50 more scholarships to Cuban universities during the visit.   (DAVID RENWICK)

GUATEMALA

Area: 108,889 sq km (42,042 sq mi)
Population (1998 est.): 10,802,000
Capital: Guatemala City
Head of state and government: President Alvaro Arzú Irigoyen

On April 26, 1998, two days after he co-presented the "Guatemala: Never Again" report on the 36-year civil conflict, Bishop Juan Gerardi Conedera was bludgeoned to death in what was immediately interpreted as a political murder. International condemnation of the killing was swift, and Pres. Alvaro Arzú Irigoyen declared three days of national mourning and established a Cabinet-level investigative commission. The report blamed the army for some 80% of the approximately 150,000 deaths and 50,000 disappearances during the conflict, which

ended in December 1996. The bishop had spent three years researching the atrocities with the aim of achieving a reconciliation and future peace. The UN Human Rights Commission had recently voted to end its 19-year special scrutiny of Guatemala, a decision that was welcomed by all political parties. Human rights groups, however, opposed the decision and saw the assassination as proof that violations still existed. Otto Ardón, the government prosecutor investigating the affair, resigned on December 3, dogged by criticism that he had not seriously examined the role of the Guatemalan military in the killing.

In May Guatemala became the first sovereign state to file a lawsuit against the American tobacco industry in order to recover health care costs related to tobacco.

The government pushed ahead with its privatization policy. In September a consortium led by Iberdrola of Spain took control of the state electricity company after having successfully bid $520 million in July—the biggest transaction ever in Guatemala. At the beginning of October, the privatization of the state telecommunications company was completed. After several delays the sale went ahead even though there was only one offer received at the auction.

In view of the havoc wreaked by Hurricane Mitch in Honduras and Nicaragua in late October, Guatemala got off relatively lightly, although more than 250 deaths were reported.   (SARAH CAMERON)

GUINEA

Area: 245,857 sq km (94,926 sq mi)
Population (1998 est.): 7,477,000 (including about 500,000 refugees from Liberia and Sierra Leone)
Capital: Conakry
Head of state and government: President Gen. Lansana Conté, assisted by Prime Minister Sidya Touré

Throughout 1998 tens of thousands of refugees from the fighting in neighbouring Sierra Leone poured over the borders into UN refugee camps in Guinea. In June, citing security concerns about border fighting, Pres. Lansana Conté ordered a halt in aid deliveries to the camps. In response to an appeal from the UN High Commissioner for Refugees, he lifted the ban, but the onset of the rainy season seriously hindered access to the camps.

In addition to its participation in the West African peacekeeping force in Sierra Leone, Guinea sent troops and military equipment in June to aid the embattled Guinea-Bissau president, João Bernardo Vieira.

Repercussions from the February 1996 army mutiny continued to be felt as six senior military officers were arrested on February 13, accused of complicity in the uprising. On the same day, a military tribunal began the trial of 96 people charged with having fomented the mutiny. After a seven-month trial the court on September 25 found 45 defendants guilty, sentencing them to prison terms of up to 15 years.

Elections on December 14 returned President Conté to office with a comfortable 56% of the vote. At year's end the government was investigating alleged antigovernment activities of opposition leader Alpha Condé of the Guinean People's Rally, who had returned from exile to contest the election.

Signaling its satisfaction with Guinea's economic reforms, the International Monetary Fund approved a two-year, $31 million structural adjustment loan on April 3.
                    (NANCY ELLEN LAWLER)

GUINEA-BISSAU

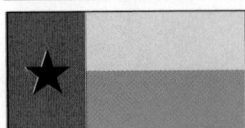

Area: 36,125 sq km (13,948 sq mi)
Population (1998 est.): 1,206,000
Capital: Bissau
Chief of state: President João Bernardo Vieira
Head of government: Prime Ministers Carlos Correia and, from December 8, Francisco José Fadul

The worst crisis in Guinea-Bissau since the end of the war of national liberation in 1974 erupted on June 7, 1998, the day after Pres. João Bernardo Vieira sacked Ansumane Mane as chief of staff of the armed forces, alleging that he had been involved in arms trafficking and support for separatists in the Senegalese province of Casamance. The bulk of the army mutinied and began shelling the capital, Bissau. Vieira asked the Economic Community of West Africa to send a peacekeeping force to repel the rebel attacks. Instead, however, only Senegal and Guinea sent troops to support his government. Fighting spread from the capital to other parts of the country, and some 250,000 people were displaced.

After mediation by the seven-nation Community of Portuguese-Speaking Countries, a cease-fire was signed in late July. An agreement reached in September provided for a buffer corridor between Guinea-Bissau and Senegal that would be monitored, but rebels insisted that Senegalese troops be withdrawn from that area. Francisco Fadul, an adviser of Vieira's who had sided with the rebels, was named prime minister in December amid calls to form a government of national reconciliation.
                    (CHRISTOPHER SAUNDERS)

GUYANA

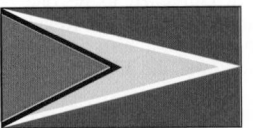

Area: 215,083 sq km (83,044 sq mi)
Population (1998 est.): 782,000
Capital: Georgetown
Chief of state: President Janet Jagan
Head of government: Prime Minister Sam Hinds

Mediation by Guyana's fellow Caribbean Community and Common Market (Caricom) member nations finally in 1998 brought an end to the sometimes violent and racially tinged demonstrations that had erupted after the general election on Dec. 15, 1997. The People's Progressive Party (PPP)/Civic coalition, headed by Cheddi Jagan's American-born widow, Janet, won about 55% of the valid votes under the country's proportional representation system, and Jagan became president. (*See* BIOGRAPHIES.) The opposition People's National Congress, led by Desmond Hoyte, vigorously disputed the result, however, and initiated the street protests in Georgetown.

A Caricom team devised a formula, acceptable to both sides, that provided for an audit of the election results, constitutional reform, and, perhaps most important from

On the outskirts of Bissau, Guinea-Bissau's capital city, troops loyal to rebel military leader Ansumane Mane fire guns and rocket-propelled grenades at a position held by forces sent from Senegal to support the government of Pres. João Bernardo Vieira. A cease-fire was signed in late July.

Hoyte's point of view, another general election within three years. The audit reported in June that, whatever minor inefficiencies and delays may have been associated with the election, the PPP/Civic had won fairly.

(DAVID RENWICK)

HAITI

Area: 27,700 sq km (10,695 sq mi)
Population (1998 est.): 6,781,000
Capital: Port-au-Prince
Chief of state: President René Préval

At the beginning of 1998, there was still no resolution over the appointment of a prime minister to succeed Rosny Smarth, who had resigned in June 1997. Pres. René Préval reported that Haiti had lost $162.5 million in foreign aid because of the deadlock in the Chamber of Deputies, and the World Bank reported that, because of Haiti's bureaucratic failures, only $800 million of the $2.8 billion allocated in foreign aid had been disbursed. In February the two main groups in the Chamber reached an agreement that they hoped would end the political breakdown, but the agreement collapsed at the beginning of March. In March the president nominated for the second time Hervé Denis, an economist, for the post of prime minister. His candidacy had been rejected previously in November 1997, and, although this time it was approved by 41 votes to 23 in the Chamber, it was rejected again in April by the Senate, one vote short of a majority. President Préval renewed negotiations with the leaders of the political parties to find a compromise prime ministerial candidate, but he was accused of delaying until the election for a new Chamber of Deputies. In July Education Minister Jacques Edouard Alexis was nominated as head of government, with the support of the main party, but he was opposed by other political factions. In November Parliament was recalled for a special session to debate the state auditing board's unfavourable report on Alexis's period in office, which further reduced his chances of becoming prime minister.

Amnesty International reported in midyear that torture, brutality, and extrajudicial killings were still prevalent in Haiti. It warned of the consequences of failing to prosecute human rights violators and the slowness of judicial reform. It was announced on August 4 that, following a two-month inquiry, 315 police officers had been dismissed for drug smuggling, corruption, and human rights abuses. A group of people, mostly former army officers, were arrested because of their links with a former paramilitary group and the discovery of arms and uniforms of the Tontons Macoutes, the militia of the former dictatorship.

The president of the Dominican Republic, Leonel Fernández, paid a three-day visit to Port-au-Prince in June, the first by a Dominican head of state since 1936. The two presidents agreed to operate joint border patrols to limit trafficking in drugs, arms, stolen goods, and contraband. Their meeting followed a session of the Dominican-Haitian Commission, which negotiated agreements on tourism, border duties, cultural exchanges, and a direct postal service. The issue of Haitian migration to the Dominican Republic remained unresolved, and deportations of thousands of Haitian labourers continued.

The UN estimated that forest cover in Haiti was only 1.5% of the total land area and that deforestation continued. During the rainy season some two hectares (five acres) of soil an hour was washed into the sea from the mountains because of the lack of trees and ground cover.

The devastation caused by Hurricane Georges in September was, therefore, intensified by erosion. On October 19 the death toll in Haiti was officially given as 213, expected to rise to 240, while 80 Haitians died in the Dominican Republic and more than 170,000 were homeless. Damage to the country's infrastructure and agriculture was severe; 75% of the first rice crop was washed away. Floods and the lack of drinking water were expected to bring disease to an already impoverished population.

(SARAH CAMERON)

HONDURAS

Area: 112,492 sq km (43,433 sq mi)
Population (1998 est.): 5,919,000
Capital: Tegucigalpa
Heads of state and government:
  Presidents Carlos Roberto Reina Idiaquez and, from January 27, Carlos Roberto Flores Facussé

Hurricane Mitch swept across the Caribbean and entered Honduran waters as a Category Five hurricane in the last week of October 1998. The 320-km/h (200-mph) winds dropped as the storm stalled over the mainland, but the subsequent tropical depression dumped unprecedented rainfall over the country. The Bay Islands were the first hit. The island of Guanaja lost all its trees and

Residents of Salifouret, Haiti, work to remove sand deposited on their village by Hurricane Georges, which caused devastating floods throughout the country in September. Crops almost ready for harvest were ruined by the storm, and more than 170,000 persons were forced from their homes.

DANIEL MOREL

A resident of Tegucigalpa, Honduras, sorts through what is left of his grocery store in December, more than a month after Hurricane Mitch pounded Central America. Mitch was considered the worst Atlantic basin hurricane in 200 years. The number of confirmed deaths in Honduras reached 6,500, and hundreds of others were missing and feared dead.

nearly all the houses. Those remaining were badly damaged, and the entire population was rendered homeless.

The scale of the damage on the mainland emerged gradually over the next two weeks. Whole communities disappeared completely. Year-end figures gave 5,657 dead, although the total number of those buried under a sea of mud may never be known. A half-million were left homeless. All the major rivers in the highlands burst their banks and unleashed a torrent on the villages below. Some 89 major bridges and countless minor ones were washed away. Even the capital, Tegucigalpa, was not spared when the Choluteca River rose 12 m (40 ft), swollen by the collapse of dams and flood barriers upstream. Severed communications and transport led to starvation. Aid workers battled against the threat of disease as Hondurans tried to cope with the flood waters and stinking mud containing rotting corpses.

Agricultural damage was extensive. The fruit companies predicted that no bananas, Honduras's main export crop, would be sold abroad until 2000. Joblessness faced 17,000 banana workers. Foreign aid arrived quickly as further assistance was sought from international agencies in the form of grants and debt relief.   (SARAH CAMERON)

HUNGARY

Area: 93,030 sq km (35,919 sq mi)
Population (1998 est.): 10,117,000
Capital: Budapest
Chief of state: President Arpad Goncz
Head of government: Prime Ministers Gyula Horn and, from July 6, Viktor Orban

In 1998 the Hungarian political landscape gradually turned into a bipolar system of two major political blocs: to the left and the right of centre. The general elections in May brought a surprise victory of the centre-right Federation of Young Democrats (Fidesz)–Hungarian Civic Party, which promised improvements in the welfare system as an antidote to the bitter austerity program of the outgoing Hungarian Socialist Party–Alliance of Free Democrats coalition. Fidesz won 42% of the parliamentary vote in alliance with the remnants of the Hungarian Democratic Forum, the backbone of Hungary's first democratically elected government (1990–94). The two parties later joined in coalition with the populist, right-wing Independent Smallholders' Party. These three parties controlled 55% of the seats in the legislature.

Voters turned on the previous coalition primarily for economic reasons. The Socialists and the Alliance had come to power on the promise of professionalism and moderation as well as greater economic sophistication, but in office their politicians often behaved with a degree of arrogance and even malfeasance. Several corruption scandals were revealed in the media, and the coalition's stabilization program, intended to improve macroeconomic balance, also failed to gain them much popularity.

The new government of 34-year-old Prime Minister Viktor Orban immediately launched a radical reform of state administration, rearranging ministries and creating a supraministry of the economy. In addition, the boards of the social security funds and centralized social security payments were fired. Following the German model, Orban strengthened the prime minister's office and placed a new minister to oversee the work of his Cabinet. After purging former officials, the ruling coalition appointed several of its own party faithful to independent

agencies such as the National Tax Office, a move that was severely criticized by the opposition. The new government created a government newspaper and purged the state-controlled media as well.

The dominance of the right-wing alliance in the central government was tempered by the results of municipal elections in October, when Hungarians voted more Socialist than Fidesz candidates into office. Free Democrat Gabor Demszky was re-elected mayor of Budapest, and independent candidates fared extremely well, netting a record 47% of municipal positions. Former prime minister Gyula Horn stepped down as president of the Socialist Party, which elected Laszlo Kovacs, a former foreign minister, to succeed him.

Orban's economic policy was aimed at cutting taxes and social insurance contributions over four years and reducing inflation and unemployment. Among its first measures the government abolished university tuition fees and reintroduced universal maternity benefits. The government announced its intention to continue the Socialist-Liberal stabilization program and pledged to narrow the budget deficit, which had widened to 5% of gross domestic product (GDP) during the year. The previous Cabinet had almost completed the privatization of government-run industries and had launched a comprehensive pension reform. The Socialists had avoided two major socioeconomic issues, however—reform of health care and the agricultural system—

New Hungarian Prime Minister Viktor Orban (foreground) speaks at the first parliamentary session following the May general elections, in which his party, the Federation of Young Democrats–Hungarian Civic Party, won a plurality of the vote. Orban promised tax cuts and swift economic improvements.

and these remained to be tackled by Orban's government.

The Asian and Russian economic crises prompted a major drop in the Hungarian stock exchange, but even so the national economy registered a 5% growth in GDP, up from 4% in 1997. The inflation rate dropped from 18% in 1997 to 16% in 1998, the lowest figure in postcommunist times. During the year Hungary moved closer to membership in the European Union; the general screening of the country's readiness to join began in March.

(ZSOFIA SZILAGYI)

ICELAND

Area: 102,819 sq km (39,699 sq mi)
Population (1998 est.): 276,000
Capital: Reykjavík
Chief of state: President Ólafur Ragnar Grímsson
Head of government: Prime Minister Davíd Oddsson

Iceland's economy continued to grow at a rapid pace in 1998. Gross domestic product (GDP) was estimated to have increased by more than 5% for the third year in succession. Much of this growth stemmed from an improving fish catch, following several years of conservation efforts, and from a spurt in plant and power investment. A sharp rise in domestic demand led to a large current account deficit, estimated at 6–7% of GDP.

Fish catch quotas became an increasing source of controversy. The government allotted an annual fish catch free of charge to individual boats, which they could then trade among themselves at a market price. Many, however, believed that the quota—a commonly owned resource—should be sold to the boats at a market price. On December 3 the Supreme Court declared unconstitutional a provision that limited the number of boats to those in existence in 1982–83 or their equivalent replacements.

Taking advantage of Iceland's homogeneous population and extensive genealogy records, a multinational company, deCODE genetics Inc., established operations in the nation with the purpose of conducting commercial-based research into the genetic tracing of diseases. The company persuaded the government to introduce a bill in the legislature that would allow all patient records to be merged into a common database at the company's expense in return for a 12-year exclusive user license. The bill, which passed on December 17, aroused much controversy, pitting doctor-patient confidentiality against advancing science.

The government during the year accelerated its campaign of privatizing financial institutions. It planned to sell shares in two state-owned commercial banks and an investment bank as quickly as the market would allow.

Two of Iceland's leftist political parties, the Social Democrats and the People's Alliance, planned to present a joint ticket in the 1999 parliamentary election. Together in 1998 they held 17 seats in the 63-member legislature.

(BJÖRN MATTHÍASSON)

INDIA

Area: 3,165,596 sq km (1,222,243 sq mi)
Population (1998 est.): 994,004,000
Capital: New Delhi
Chief of state: President Kocheril Raman Narayanan
Head of government: Prime Ministers Inder Kumar Gujral and, from March 19, Atal Bihari Vajpayee

India gained a new, rightist government in March, became a nuclear weapon state in May, and spent the rest of 1998 coping with the political and economic consequences of these developments. Frictions within the new ruling coalition were also of concern during the year.

Domestic Affairs. The nation's 12th general elections to the Lok Sabha (House of the People) were held in February–March, following the resignation of the United Front government led by I.K. Gujral in November 1997. Of the 605,880,000 eligible voters, 61.97% exercised their franchise. The vote was split three ways, among the coalitions led, respectively, by the ultranationalist Bharatiya Janata Party (BJP), the Congress (I) Party, and the United Front. The strength of the BJP rose from 161 to 179. The Congress gained 5 seats for a total of 141. The Janata Dal, the main component of the United Front, which had headed the two previous governments, lost heavily, winning only 6 seats against 45 previously.

The Congress, headed by Sonia Gandhi (widow of Rajiv Gandhi), and the United Front showed no interest in forming a government. The BJP, even with the support of the All-India Anna Dravida Munnetra Kazhagam (18 seats), the Samata Party (12), Biju Janata Dal (9), the Shiromani Akali Dal (8), Trinamul Congress (7), Shiv Sena (6), and an assortment of smaller parties, fell a dozen seats short of having 50% of the Lok Sabha. The BJP then made a deal with the Telugu Desam Party (12 seats), a constituent of the United Front, by electing a TDP member as speaker of the house, and also received support from the National Conference (2) and four independents. As a result the strength of the BJP-led alliance rose to about 265, and it was able to form the government.

Atal Bihari Vajpayee (*see* BIOGRAPHIES), elected leader of the BJP parliamentary party, was sworn in as prime minister on March 19. The government proved its majority in the Lok Sabha on March 28, securing 274 votes against 261. The Cabinet was expanded on December 5 with the addition of three new ministers, all from the BJP.

Elections were also held to the assemblies of five states. The BJP was victorious in Gujarat, the United Front retained power in Tripura, and the Congress won in Nagaland and Meghalaya. In Himachal Pradesh the Congress gained a majority but soon lost power because of a split, and a BJP-led coalition took office. BJP governments received a jolt in elections held in four states on November 25. The BJP lost Rajasthan and Delhi states to the Congress, which also retained Madhya Pradesh but lost Mizoram.

The Vajpayee government suffered a defeat in September when its recommendation, taken on the advice of the governor of the state of Bihar to dismiss the state's government and promulgate president's rule under Article 356 of the constitution, was not accepted by Pres. K.R. Narayanan. The state chief minister, Rabri Devi of the Rashtriya Janata Dal, meanwhile won a vote of confidence in the Bihar assembly. Earlier, in February, the governor of Uttar Pradesh had dismissed the BJP-led government of Kalyan Singh and appointed Jagdambika Pal as chief minister, but the state's High Court restored Singh and India's Supreme Court upheld the decision. In July Wilfred De Souza became the chief minister of Goa by forming his own party and bringing down the Congress government, but his government fell in November.

When it accepted office, the ruling coalition announced a "National Agenda for Governance," the main points of which were a review of the nation's nuclear policy, the formation of three new states (Uttaranchal, Vananchal, and Chattisgarh by splitting Uttar Pradesh, Bihar, and Madhya Pradesh, respectively), increased empowerment of women by means of reserving for them one-third of all seats in the national legislature and state assemblies, and the appointment of a commission to review the constitution.

The review of the nuclear policy was prompt and dramatic. Three nuclear devices (one believed to be thermonuclear) were exploded at Pokharan in Rajasthan on May 11. This was met with immediate disapproval on the part of the nuclear-weapons nations and their allies. The U.S. placed sanctions against technological cooperation with India and investment in its industries and demanded that India forthwith sign the Comprehensive Test Ban Treaty (CTBT). The International Monetary Fund, the World Bank, and Japan announced suspension of credits. Two more explosions were carried out on May 13.

Proclaiming itself to be a nuclear-weapon power, India offered to observe a voluntary moratorium on further tests and to engage in negotiations for signing the CTBT. Pressure on India became even greater when Pakistan responded by carrying out six nuclear explosions on May 28 and 30. The two countries were then urged to begin a serious dialogue to settle the issue of control of Kashmir. Vajpayee met Prime Minister Nawaz Sharif of Pakistan at the conference of the South Asian Association for Regional Co-operation in Sri Lanka in July and also in New York City in September. Speaking at the United Nations General Assembly in September, Vajpayee reiterated India's readiness to sign the CTBT to enable it to come into force in 1999.

Progress was halting on several other items of the National Agenda for Governance. Disagreement between parties prevented the passage of the bill for the reservation of legislative seats for women. The Bihar assembly rejected the central proposal to carve out a new Vananchal state, and the Shiromani Akali Dal objected to the plan to form Uttaranchal out of the mountain districts of Uttar Pradesh,

A hot-air balloon emblazoned with an anti-nuclear message flies over the Taj Mahal in India. Three nuclear devices were detonated in Rajasthan on May 11, prompting immediate disapproval on the part of nuclear-weapons nations and their allies. After India exploded two more nuclear devices, Pakistan responded by carrying out six nuclear explosions later in May.

JOHN MCCONNICO—AP/WIDE WORLD

although the state assembly endorsed the proposal. The government appointed a three-member Central Vigilance Commission, which would have the power to oversee the Central Bureau of Investigation and the Enforcement Directorate.

A furor was caused in August when Justice M.C. Jain, who conducted an inquiry into Rajiv Gandhi's assassination in 1991, said in his final report, to the legislature, that the role of the Tamil Nadu chief minister, M. Karunanidhi, needed further investigation. Earlier, in January, a special court had sentenced 26 persons to death for their part in the former prime minister's assassination. The verdict was stayed by the Supreme Court in March. In Mumbai (Bombay) a judge inquiring into the Hindu-Muslim riots in the city in 1992–93 blamed the Shiv Sena leader, Bal Thackeray, for inciting trouble. In October the Supreme Court asked the Maharashtra government to explain why it had not acted on the judge's report.

The Economy. The stock markets plunged to an 18-month low in early October, with the Bombay Stock Exchange's Sensitive Index declining to 2804 on December 3, the lowest point in two years. The rupee weakened further, quoting at 42.55 to the dollar on December 3, compared with 38.92 on Dec. 4, 1997. The inflation rate, which was 4.8% in 1997–98, rose to 8.54% during the week ending November 14. In dollar terms exports declined by 7.9%, compared with an increase of 5.3% in 1996–97.

Gross domestic product (GDP) rose 5.1% in 1997–98, compared with an average of 7.5% during the preceding three years. Agricultural production fell by 1.5%, compared with a growth of 7.9% in 1996–97. Overall industrial growth was 5.9%, compared with 5.6% in 1996–97.

The budget of the government for 1998–99, presented on June 1, promised the continuance of economic reforms with stress on *swadeshi* (economic nationalism). It permitted private investment up to 74% in non-strategic public-sector enterprises and also announced the launch of "Resurgent India Bonds." By August 25 these bonds had brought in $4,160,000,000 from nonresident Indians. Outlay on infrastructure was increased by 35% and for the atomic energy department by 68%. A provision of Rs 90,000,000,000 was made for food subsidies. Total receipts (revenue plus capital) were placed at Rs 2,679,270,000,000 and the fiscal deficit at Rs 910,250,000,000 (5.6% of GDP). The budget also announced increases in fuel and fertilizer prices, which were withdrawn almost immediately owing to public outcry.

Assam, West Bengal, and North Orissa were devastated by floods in July–August, believed to be the century's worst. A cyclone killed more than 1,100 persons in Gujarat and ruined the port of Kandla in June. A landslide in the Pithoragarh district of Uttar Pradesh wiped out the entire village of Malapa in August, causing 210 deaths. A train accident at Khanna in Punjab on November 26 killed 213 people. Severe drought affected Rajasthan and South Orissa.   (H.Y. SHARADA PRASAD)

INDONESIA

Area: 1,937,179 sq km (747,949 sq mi)
Population (1998 est.): 202,957,000
Capital: Jakarta
Head of state and government:
Presidents Suharto and, from May 21,
Bacharuddin Jusuf ("B.J.") Habibie

Indonesia's New Order came to an end in 1998. For 32 years the country's political system had served President Suharto (*see* BIOGRAPHIES), but then during 10 days in May it abandoned him. On May 12 security forces opened fire on unarmed students at Jakarta's Trisakti University. Angered over Suharto's handling of the Asian economic crisis, student demonstrators had been calling for him to step down. Four students were killed, and dozens of others were injured in the incident. Within 24 hours the killings had sparked massive riots and an anti-ethnic Chinese pogrom that turned Jakarta into a war zone. More than 1,000 persons died in the riots; dozens of women were believed to have been raped; and some 40 malls, 2,400 shops, and 1,100 cars were looted or destroyed. It took days for the military to quell the violence, but it flared up again later in the year.

By May 19 thousands of students occupied the parliament building, and soldiers guarded Jakarta's city centre. Many of Suharto's political allies threatened to unseat him, and his Cabinet ministers promised to quit. More important, however, public opposition had grown so strong that Suharto could no longer count on the military's support. On the morning of May 21, he announced his resignation. The man who had ruled Indonesia for nearly a third of a century ceded power to Bacharuddin Jusuf ("B.J.") Habibie, who had been his protégé for decades but had served as his vice president for only two months. After Suharto's address General Wiranto, commander of Indonesia's armed forces, promised that the military would back Habibie as the nation's new president.

Although protesters called Habibie merely a figurehead and expressed concern that Suharto would remain Indonesia's de facto leader, Habibie assumed office promising to heed the calls for substantial political reform. He appointed a new Cabinet that included members of Indonesia's two main opposition parties. He fired Suharto's eldest daughter as social affairs minister and Suharto's longtime friend Mohamad ("Bob") Hasan as trade and industry minister. He named a committee to draft less-restrictive political laws, allowed a free press, promised parliamentary elections in June 1999 and presidential elections by the end of the year, and agreed to presidential term limits (two five-year terms). Habibie also granted amnesty to 104 political prisoners, though not to East Timor independence leader José Alexandre ("Xanana") Gusmão. He promised East Timor greater autonomy but refused to discuss independence.

In addition, Habibie ordered an investigation into whether there was, as many suspected, a mastermind behind the May riots in Jakarta. According to the government's National Commission for Human Rights, witnesses confirmed that many of the attacks on residents and property had been carried out by organized groups of men, though reports that the military or other security forces were involved could not be conclusively confirmed. Habibie also launched an investigation into the source of Suharto's wealth, which was estimated in the billions of dollars. In early September Suharto appeared on television to deny allegations that he had diverted funds from charities that he headed and that his six children had made vast fortunes during his term. Habibie's government audited the charities, however, and said that preliminary investigations indicated there may have been some irregularities. The government subsequently canceled contracts that Suharto's children held with state companies. In December Suharto was suspected of corruption related to a tax-free car import scheme headed by one of his sons. After Habibie oversaw the successful renegotiation of repayment terms for $80 billion in private debt, the International Monetary Fund resumed making incremental payments.

Reforms undertaken by the military included reducing its presence in East Timor. In other provinces where secessionist movements still showed some signs of life, activists were able for the first time to discuss human rights violations openly. The military not only considered the possibility that the Jakarta riots had been organized by someone within its ranks but also conducted an investigation into the kidnappings of at least a dozen political activists between February and May. Several senior officers were questioned; Suharto's son-in-law, Lieut. Gen. Prabowo Subianto, head of an elite special forces unit, was discharged. Nevertheless, the credibility of the military was tarnished, and its dual political and security roles were challenged. The military relinquished 20 of the 75 seats reserved for it in the legislature.

Although Habibie at first called himself a transitional figure, by year's end he had indicated that he would run for another term as president. Hopes for democratic change in Indonesia received a boost in July when Golkar, the country's dominant political party, elected reformer Akbar Tanjung as its new chairman over Edi Sudradjat, a retired army general and a former defense minister who was backed by supporters of Suharto. Akbar, a close Habibie aide, was the president's personal choice for the party chairmanship, and his victory greatly improved Habibie's ability to set the political agenda and remain in office. The most prominent opposition parties included the National Mandate Party, headed by Suharto critic Amien Rais; the National Awakening Party, led by Muslim leader Abdurrahman Wahid; and the Indonesian Democratic Party, a faction of which was led by Megawati Sukarnoputri, the daughter of the country's founding president.

Indonesia's economic situation remained grim in 1998. At the end of the year, the rupiah was worth just 25% of its value 18 months earlier, and inflation had risen to at least 80%. The economy contracted by 13.6% in the first nine months of the year, and most observers expected that it would ultimately shrink by 15–20% by year's end. The government expected 22% of the workforce, or 20 million people, to be unemployed by the end of 1998. It was possible that as many as 100 million people—one-half of the country's population—would fall below the poverty line in 1998. Spurred by the economic troubles, Indonesia's crime rate rose significantly. General Wiranto acknowledged that much of the unrest stemmed from increasing poverty. There was an expected shortage of 3.1 million tons of rice; food that was available was priced beyond the reach of many Indonesians.

Business also slowed dramatically. After the May riots, many foreign investors and ethnic Chinese—traditional mainstays of the Indonesian economy—fled the country. Both groups were reluctant to return—the foreign investors because of political and economic uncertainties, the Chinese because of safety concerns.   (SUSAN BERFIELD)

Thousands of Indonesian students crowd the steps and roof of the parliament building in Jakarta during an antigovernment protest in May. The fierce defiance of student demonstrators was a major factor in the erosion of support for President Suharto, who announced on May 21 that he would step down after 32 years in office.

As 1998 drew to a close, the world was caught in the grips of the most serious financial crisis since the Great Depression of the 1930s. Starting in Thailand in July 1997, the crisis spread spasmodically to much of the rest of Asia, parts of Latin America, and Russia over the next 18 months. By the end of the year, it posed a direct threat to the U.S. economy, which was in the midst of the eighth year of an expansion that had sent the stock market to record levels. Somewhat less menaced was Europe, which was on the verge of adopting a single currency (the euro) in 1999 for 11 countries (Germany, France, Italy, Spain, Portugal, Belgium, The Netherlands, Austria, Finland, Ireland, and Luxembourg).

Some figures convey the magnitude of the collapse. In 1998 the economies of Indonesia, South Korea, and Thailand were expected to shrink by roughly 15%, 7%, and 8%, respectively, according to estimates by the International Monetary Fund (IMF). In 1996—the last year before the crisis broke—those economies, as measured by their gross domestic product (GDP), had grown 8% (Indonesia), 7.1% (South Korea), and 5.5% (Thailand). Meanwhile, Japan's economy had slipped into its worst post–World War II recession, with GDP expected to drop 2.8% in 1998. Economic growth in China and much of Latin America was also slowing, though it was unclear whether they would actually experience recessions (drops in output).

The economic crisis confounded the received wisdom of only a few years earlier that had celebrated the "Asian miracle." In this view Asian societies—led by Japan—had devised a distinctive formula for economic growth that promised to make them the envy of the world. The formula seemed unassailable—a strong work ethic, an emphasis on education, high savings and investment rates, and successful export industries. The shrewd combination of government direction and reliance on the market seemed to outperform purer market societies (the U.S.) or strict command-and-control economies (the former Soviet Union).

On one level the unraveling of the Asian miracle could be explained. It was always part myth. As economist Paul Krugman of the Massachusetts Institute of Technology and others pointed out, Asia's rapid growth depended heavily on those high savings and investment rates. (Between 1990 and 1996, investment as a share of GDP was 37% in South Korea, 32% in Indonesia, and 41% in Thailand. The comparable U.S. figure was 17%.) High investment enabled these countries to industrialize, but returns on the investments (their profitability and efficiency) were not particularly high by international standards. What this suggested was that once the most basic investments were exhausted, Asian countries would have trouble sustaining their high levels of economic growth.

Such a situation did not have to trigger a crisis, however. Two factors did so: first, belief in the Asian miracle was widespread bolstering confidence about the region's future; and second, this optimism—along with the relaxation of gov-

SPOTLIGHT

THE TROUBLED WORLD ECONOMY

by Robert J. Samuelson

Illustration by Tom Curry

ernment restrictions against foreign investment (usually referred to as "capital controls")—generated huge inflows of overseas funds as outside investors tried to profit from the miracle. These funds arrived as bank loans, portfolio investment (for example: mutual funds buying stocks of local companies), bond purchases, and direct investment (building factories or buying control of local firms). Between 1990 and 1996, five Asian countries (Indonesia, South Korea, Philippines, Malaysia, and Thailand) received almost $300 billion in foreign investment.

The result was boom—and bust. As foreign funds poured in, local economies flourished. Dollars and yen were converted into local currencies (the Thai baht, the Korean won, or the Indonesian rupiah) and spent. With their bulging foreign exchange reserves (those same dollars and yen), the countries imported more of everything, from industrial machinery to luxury cars. Once disenchantment occurred, however, the process reversed itself. Investors saw that much of the capital inflow had been wasted; too many office buildings or factories had been built to provide attractive profits or, on loans, to repay interest and principal. Consequently, those investors withdrew funds or, if that was impossible, decided against new commitments. In 1996 the same five Asian countries recorded capital inflows of about $73 billion; in 1997 they had capital outflows of about $11 billion.

The change pushed most of the five countries into recession (Philippines was least affected). As investors rushed to convert local currencies back into dollars, yen, or Deutsche Marks, the countries faced a dilemma: whether to raise interest rates sharply to persuade investors to keep funds in local currencies or to allow deep drops in their exchange rates. Both approaches hurt. High interest rates punished local companies and depressed spending, and lower exchange rates made imports more costly and also harmed local companies by making repayment of dollar loans more expensive.

At the year's end the outlook for the world economy remained unclear. Almost all the Asian countries in crisis had received large loans from the International Monetary Fund and other international agencies in return for commitments to improve bank regulation and curb unproductive investment projects. Unemployment in those countries had jumped sharply. Meanwhile, the U.S. and European economies continued to grow, but financial markets (for stocks, bonds, and foreign exchange) had grown more erratic as investors became more nervous. The danger remained that eroded confidence—which might hurt consumer spending and business investment—and lower exports might cause a business slump in either the U.S. or Europe. With much of the world already in recession, that was a chilling prospect.

Robert J. Samuelson writes a syndicated column for Newsweek *and The Washington Post Writers Group and is the author of* The Good Life and Its Discontents: The American Dream in the Age of Entitlement, 1945–1995.

header: "World Affairs: Iraq 451"

IRAN

Area: 1,645,258 sq km (635,238 sq mi)
Population (1998 est.): 61,531,000
(excluding about 1.4 million Afghan refugees and nearly 600,000 Iraqi refugees)
Capital: Tehran
Supreme political and religious authority: *Rahbar* (Spiritual Leader) Ayatollah Sayyed Ali Khamenei
Head of state and government: President Mohammad Khatami

Expectations that there might be rapid political change in Iran in 1998 following the consolidation of power under Pres. Mohammad Khatami were dashed. The president's conservative opponents inside the regime retained considerable political authority and an ability to block Khatami's reforms. On March 2 supporters of the Islamic hard-liners attacked a demonstration in Tehran in favour of the president and thereby signaled the beginning of a campaign of violent confrontation between the liberals and the conservatives. The liberal press was hounded by Islamist extremists, the worst incidents being the detention of dissident journalist Faraj Sarkuhi and the death sentence on Morteza Firoozi, former editor of *Iran News,* and the murders of six intellectuals in November and December.

On April 4 Gholamhossein Karbaschi, the mayor of Tehran and an ally of President Khatami, was detained on charges of corruption by the antireformist authorities in the judiciary. Karbaschi was found guilty on July 23 and was banned from public office for 10 years, sentenced to two years in prison, and fined $533,000. The Karbaschi affair led to a bitter debate between conservatives and hard-liners and to a polarization of national opinion. The judiciary came under attack in the liberal press, and popular sentiment in favour of reform became more openly articulated. On June 21 a majority of the Majlis (parliament) voted to impeach the interior minister, Abdullah Nouri, after he attempted to reassert his ministry's authority over management of the provinces against that of the Majlis. These cases underlined the undiminished strength of the hard-liners to gain their political ends at the national level.

The secular opposition made its voice heard through the press and the writings of dissidents such as Farj Sarkuhi, who denounced "the atmosphere of fear" in Iran. A riot against local government authorities took place in a suburb of Tehran on May 4, and further violence erupted in the capital on July 6, when banks and municipal buildings were attacked. Strikes in favour of Ayatollah Hossein Ali Montazeri, who had questioned whether Iran should continue under religious rule, occurred in Esfahan in April.

There were some domestic successes for President Khatami. In May a political party, Executives for Construction, was officially recognized, and the first female senior judge was appointed in June. Despite the rising level of hard-line violence, freedom of speech improved, as was indicated by open debate of formerly banned topics such as relations with the U.S. and the sanctity of personal rights.

The government achieved notable gains in normalizing its relations with other countries. The U.S. was a principal target in this process, with President Khatami calling on January 7 for a "thoughtful dialogue," to which both U.S. Pres. Bill Clinton and Secretary of State Madeleine Albright responded favourably in June. Participation of Iran and the U.S. in international sports events such as wrestling and the soccer World Cup in midyear gave the nation an opportunity to demonstrate additional signs of goodwill though this was later offset by an attack in Tehran on a bus carrying a U.S. business delegation. Iranian contacts with the European Union (EU) improved dramatically in September when the government officially disassociated itself from the death threat that had been imposed by Islamic extremists on Salman Rushdie, the British author of the novel *The Satanic Verses.* In the Middle East as a whole, Iran experienced improved relations, especially with Saudi Arabia. In September, however, an altercation with the Taliban government of Afghanistan over the killing of Iranian diplomats in that country led to full-scale military exercises in the frontier provinces adjacent to Afghanistan. The threat of war was averted only by Taliban promises of strong action against those involved in the death of the diplomats.

The Iranian economy deteriorated during the year as oil income fell by 25% against annual budget expectations of $14 billion and the decline of Asian markets resulted in a drop of 30% in carpet exports. By September

On trial for corruption, Gholamhossein Karbaschi, the mayor of Tehran, denies all charges against him during his final address to the court in July. Although Karbaschi was eventually found guilty, many observers viewed his arrest as part of an attempt by hard-liners in Iran to topple key moderate officials.

MOHAMMAD SAYYAD—AP/WIDE WORLD/CP

the value of the rial had plummeted on the free (black) market to 6,250 to the U.S. dollar, against an export rate of 3,000 to the dollar. Iran officially opened its oil sector to foreign participation following the waiving of U.S. sanctions on EU oil companies in May.   (KEITH S. MCLACHLAN)

IRAQ

Area: 435,052 sq km (167,975 sq mi)
Population (1998 est.): 21,722,000
Capital: Baghdad
Head of state and government: President and Prime Minister Saddam Hussein

In December 1998 relations between Iraq and the international community took a turn for the worse. On December 14 the UN chief weapons inspector, Richard Butler, submitted a report to the UN accusing Iraq of failing to cooperate with the UN inspectors. Three days later, on December 17, the United States and Great Britain began a four-day air attack on selected targets in Iraq, including key military installations, government buildings, and communications centres that were believed either to facilitate Iraq's capabilities for producing weapons of mass destruction or to pose a threat to its neighbours. Both countries also announced that they would support efforts of the Iraqi opposition to unseat the Iraqi president, Saddam Hussein.

Since the fall of 1997, Iraq had toughened its stand against sanctions and the international weapons monitors. These sanctions were to remain until the UN Security Council had been assured that Iraq had destroyed all its weapons of mass destruction and the means to produce them. In February there was a major crisis between Iraq and the UN Security Council over Iraq's refusal to allow weapons inspectors access to "presidential" and "sensitive areas." The UN Security Council denounced the Iraqi refusal, and the U.S., supported by Great Britain, mobilized military forces in the Persian Gulf and threatened Iraq with the use of force to guarantee the UN Special Commission (UNSCOM) inspectors access to all areas in Iraq as needed. A military confrontation was avoided when UN Secretary-General Kofi Annan reached an agreement with Iraq on February 22 in which Iraq withdrew its objections to UNSCOM's spot inspections. Cooperation broke down again on August 5, however, when Iraq suspended relations with the UNSCOM inspectors while allowing monitoring of known sites to continue. The UN Security Council rejected this action and on September 9 canceled the regular bimonthly review of the sanctions, a move that effectively continued them indefinitely.

Late in December after the bombing had stopped Iraq fired missiles at U.S. and British aircraft that were patrolling the "no-fly" zones (barred to Iraqi aircraft) in northern and southern Iraq. No planes were shot down, and they retaliated by bombing an Iraqi air defense battery.

On February 20 the UN Security Council passed a resolution increasing the amount of

David Trimble, leader of the Ulster Unionist Party, displays the Northern Ireland Peace Agreement in April after his party voted in favour of the deal. For their efforts to find a peaceful solution to the conflict in Northern Ireland, Trimble and Social and Democratic Labour Party leader John Hume were awarded the 1998 Nobel Prize for Peace.

oil Iraq would be allowed to export under the "oil for food" program. The decision was made after it became obvious that the income generated by current oil sales was insufficient for satisfying the population's basic needs. Now in their eighth year, sanctions had taken a heavy toll on the Iraqi people. The standard of living was drastically lowered, and the rate of inflation remained high. Hardest hit was the once-flourishing middle class, which suffered so much that its continued existence as a social force was threatened.

The two main Kurdish parties, the Kurdish Democratic Party (KDP) of Mas'ud al-Barzani and the Patriotic Union of Kurdistan (PUK) of Jalal at-Talabani, continued to control separate parts of northern Iraq. The two groups had been fighting since 1994, despite mediation by the U.S. and several past agreements to end their feuds. In September the U.S. brokered an agreement between the two leaders that included revenue and power sharing, a general election, and a security arrangement including a pledge to circumscribe the activities of the anti-Turkish Kurdistan Workers Party (PKK) in northern Iraq. The two sides also endorsed a form of "federalism," the details of which were not specified, for the Kurds in Iraq after Pres. Saddam Hussein left power. Turkey was alarmed by this agreement, which appeared to recognize a "Kurdish political entity" in northern Iraq. Mindful of the restiveness of its own Kurdish population, Turkey announced that it would restore full diplomatic relations with Iraq and sent a Turkish ambassador to Baghdad for the first time since 1992.

Iraq also improved relations with Syria and Iran. On July 14 an agreement to open the oil pipeline connecting Iraq's Kirkuk field to the Syrian port of Banias was announced. The pipeline was shut down by Syria in 1982 during the Iran-Iraq war. Iraq and Syria also met in the fall of 1998 to discuss distribution of waters from the Euphrates River, an important source of irrigation for both countries. The source of the Euphrates is in Turkey, and both Iraq and Syria accused Turkey of affecting downstream flow by building dikes and other irrigation works. Turkey declined

an invitation to attend these meetings. An overland border station between Iran and Iraq was opened, and on April 2, 1998, the two countries exchanged 862 prisoners captured during the Iran-Iraq war. It was also agreed that Iraq would allow Iranian pilgrims to visit the Shi'ite holy cities in Iraq, and in mid-August the first group of Iranian pilgrims crossed the border into Iraq.

(LOUAY BAHRY)

IRELAND

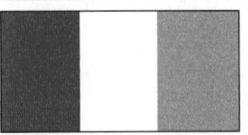

Area: 70,285 sq km (27,137 sq mi)
Population (1998 est.): 3,647,000
Capital: Dublin
Chief of state: President Mary McAleese
Head of government: Prime Minister Bertie Ahern

Political life in Ireland was dominated during 1998 by attempts to resolve the conflict in Northern Ireland. The resolution eventually took place on a global scale, with the direct involvement of three governments—Ireland, the United Kingdom, and the United States—and the indirect participation of other countries and blocs.

Within the republic there was support from all political parties for the proposed agreement, which would create a Northern Ireland Assembly, establish north-south political structures, and amend Ireland's 1937 constitution by removing from it the claim to Northern Ireland. The delicacy with which this was handled and the huge commitment made to the agreement by Prime Minister Bertie Ahern played a significant role in securing agreement on April 10. It changed, in a permanent way, the relationship between Northern Ireland and Ireland and also altered the relationships of both parts of Ireland with the U.K.

On May 22 the electorate went to the polls in a referendum that had a dual pur-

pose: first, to indicate support for the agreement and to sanction the proposed amendments to the constitution; and second, to vote on the Amsterdam Treaty, a series of commitments that governments of countries in the European Union (EU) agreed to in 1997 that covered such areas as human rights, a common European defense policy, and increased powers for the European Parliament. The voters indicated their support for the agreement by a resounding 94%. The response to the Amsterdam Treaty was different, however, with 62% of the people voting in favour of it and 38% against.

The signing of the agreement represented only the beginning of a long and difficult process of negotiation. Although the political parties in Ireland recognized the difficulties faced by the leader of the Northern Ireland Assembly, David Trimble (see NOBEL PRIZES), in maintaining Ulster Unionist Party support for the agreement, they placed considerable emphasis on bringing the Northern Ireland executive into existence at the expense of the need for the decommissioning of paramilitary arms. This was insufficiently recognized in Ireland as a major handicap facing Trimble in the implementation of the agreement, and it came as no surprise that the October 31 deadline for the appointment of a Northern Ireland executive was not achieved. On December 18, however, the Protestant majority and Roman Catholic minority finally agreed to establish a 10-minister Executive Cabinet for Northern Ireland that would include two members of Sinn Fein, the political wing of the Irish Republican Army. Resolution of the disarmament issue was postponed.

The first full year of Ahern's term of office as leader of the minority Fianna Fail government greatly enhanced his standing as both politician and statesman. He was helped not only by his role in negotiating the agreement but also by the remarkable performance of the Irish economy. Growth throughout the year was well ahead of the European average, and unemployment was reduced considerably. By October the inflation rate had slowed to 3%, which suggested that the rising trend in consumer prices evident in recent months had peaked. This cleared the way for the central bank to start cutting interest rates to the levels prevailing in the EU but still left Ireland with one of the highest inflation rates in the EU. Trade figures revealed that the economic boom continued unabated. In June, as exports surged by 16% to £4.3 billion (U.S. $6.1 billion), Ireland's external trade surplus rose to a record £1.7 billion (U.S. $2.4 billion). The benefits of the boom were not, however, equally distributed throughout the country. In October the Combat Poverty Agency reported that up to one-third of Irish children were living in poverty.

In April a Freedom of Information Act came into being. This affirmed the right of members of the public to obtain access to information in the possession of public bodies. This new legislative structure was responsible for the work of two investigative tribunals that laid bare evidence of financial corruption. The same laws, as well as the evidence presented to the tribunals, led to investigation by the media, which resulted in the discovery of widespread tax and banking irregularities. On November 26 Tony Blair addressed the Irish parliament, the first British prime minister to do so in the 76 years that Ireland had been independent.   (MAVIS ARNOLD)

ISRAEL

Area: 20,320 sq km (7,846 sq mi), not including territory occupied in the June 1967 war (Emerging Palestinian Autonomous Areas)
Population (1998 est.): 5,740,000
Capital: Jerusalem is the proclaimed capital of Israel (since Jan. 23, 1950) and the actual seat of government, but recognition has generally been withheld by the international community.
Chief of state: President Ezer Weizman
Head of government: Prime Minister Benjamin Netanyahu

The Emerging Palestinian Autonomous Areas (the West Bank and the Gaza Strip), mid-1998

Total area: West Bank 5,900 sq km (2,270 sq mi), of which about 180 sq km is under Palestinian administration, about 4,130 sq km under Israeli administration, and about 1,590 sq km under joint administration; Gaza Strip 363 sq km (140 sq mi), of which about 236 sq km is under Palestinian administration and about 127 sq km under Israeli administration
Population (1998 est.): West Bank 1,881,000, including 1,734,000 Arabs and 147,000 Jews; Gaza Strip 1,082,000, including 1,076,000 Arabs and 6,000 Jews
Principal administrative centres: Ram Allah and Gaza
Head of government: President Yasir Arafat

Israeli-Palestinian relations again dominated the political agenda in 1998 as growing mistrust between the parties threatened the Oslo peace process launched in 1993. Only determined U.S. mediation kept the ailing process alive, culminating toward the end of the year in a major diplomatic coup; on October 23, after an acrimonious 19-month-long deadlock, Israel and the Palestinians signed an agreement in the U.S. that stipulated further Israeli withdrawal from the West Bank and Palestinian efforts to clamp down on terrorist acts against Israel. The groundbreaking deal was hammered out during an intensive nine-day summit at the Wye Plantation in Maryland. U.S. Pres. Bill Clinton took the initiative to save the process after a breakdown of trust between Israeli Prime Minister Benjamin Netanyahu and Palestinian Authority (PA) Chairman Yasir Arafat had rendered further unmediated contacts between the parties futile.

Part of the problem was Arafat's insistence that he would unilaterally declare a Palestinian state on May 4, 1999, the date the Oslo peace process was to have been completed, and Netanyahu's threat to take strong retaliatory measures against such a move. To preempt a potentially dangerous escalation, Clinton summoned Arafat and Netanyahu to the Wye Plantation and exerted heavy pressure on both.

The result was the Wye Memorandum, which spelled out in precise detail steps to be taken by Israel and the Palestinians to complete the interim peace deal they had

been negotiating for five years and also laid the foundation for negotiations on a permanent settlement of the Israeli-Palestinian conflict. Israel would carry out two long-overdue redeployments of its troops in the West Bank in three phases over a 12-week period, and the scope of a third and final interim redeployment would be decided by a joint committee. The Palestinians promised to crack down on the Hamas and Islamic Jihad military infrastructure, arrest 30 wanted terrorists, reduce their police force, collect illegal weapons, prohibit incitement against Israel, and complete the formal annulment of clauses in the Palestinian Covenant calling for Israel's destruction.

Netanyahu had insisted on strict reciprocity, with Israeli commitments contingent on the Palestinians' carrying out their undertakings. The Wye Memorandum also provided for a beefed-up CIA presence to monitor implementation by both sides.

No sooner had the memorandum been signed than the familiar pattern of mutual recrimination resurfaced, calling the new agreement into question. On October 29 a Hamas suicide bomber failed in a bid to ram a bus full of schoolchildren in the Gaza area, and on November 6 two Islamic Jihad bombers were killed in an abortive car bombing outside Jerusalem's Mahane Yehuda market. Netanyahu took both incidents as evidence of Arafat's unwillingness to crack down on terrorism. The atmosphere was further soured by angry exchanges as to how the Palestinian Covenant was to be annulled.

After a reaffirmation by the Palestinian leader of his strategic commitment to peace, Israel released 250 Palestinian prisoners and went ahead with the first stage of the agreed withdrawal on November 20. In an operation code-named "calling card," 10 small towns and 18 villages between Nablus and Jenin were handed over to the Palestinians. The

International Airport in Gaza was inaugurated four days later with the arrival of a flight from Egypt.

Because it entailed putting the Palestinians in control of as much as 40% of the West Bank, the Wye Memorandum brought Netanyahu into conflict with right-wing groups in Israel. Ironically, approval of the memorandum in the Knesset (parliament) on November 17 by an overwhelming 75 votes to 19 with 9 abstentions was due to blanket support by the opposition parties. As for the governing coalition, two National Religious Party Cabinet ministers voted against the memorandum, and seven other ministers abstained. In January David Levy had resigned as foreign minister, pulling his five-person Gesher faction out of the coalition and reducing Netanyahu's majority to two. Consequently, the government's chances of survival in the aftermath of the Wye agreement seemed slim. Leading figures in Netanyahu's Likud Party advised him to form a national unity government with the main opposition Labor Party or to call early elections. When Netanyahu's efforts to achieve a unity government failed, he joined with a majority of legislators and voted to dissolve his government. Elections were scheduled for May 17, 1999. In the meantime further enactment of provisions of the Wye accord seemed uncertain at best.

The deadlock in the peace process until the Wye breakthrough affected Israel's relations with the United States, Europe, and the Arab world. In a January visit to the U.S., Netanyahu further strained his uneasy personal ties with Clinton by meeting with two of the president's most vehement critics, "moral majority" leaders Jerry Falwell and Pat Robertson. The extent to which the U.S. administration had become more receptive to Palestinian concerns during the long deadlock was underscored by President Clinton's unprecedented visit to Gaza in

Demonstrating in Tel Aviv on November 11, an Israeli right-wing supporter holds up a poster of Prime Minister Benjamin Netanyahu emblazoned with the message "Netanyahu Go Home." Steadfastly against turning over parts of the West Bank to the Palestinians, right-wingers were angered by the Israeli government's ratification of the Wye accord.

December during which the annulment of the Palestinian Covenant was finally reaffirmed.

Strains in Israel's relations with Europe came to the fore when British Foreign Secretary Robin Cook, representing the U.K. presidency of the European Union, visited the controversial Har Homa construction site in Jerusalem on March 17, and, contrary to a previous agreement with the Israelis, shook hands with a Palestinian leader there. It was the start of construction work on the site by the Israelis a year earlier that had led to the collapse of the Palestinian-Israeli peace talks and the ensuing stalemate.

To improve ties with the Arab world and counter domestic criticism of rising casualties in Israel's self-declared security zone in southern Lebanon, Defense Minister Yitzhak Mordechai launched an initiative in January for an Israeli pullback. It was based on UN Resolution 425, which called for Israeli withdrawal and Lebanese military control of the evacuated areas. Mordechai declared that Israel would withdraw if the Lebanese army guaranteed security in the south. His offer was rejected by the Lebanese, who insisted that the resolution called for Israeli withdrawal with no strings attached. Mediation efforts by France and the UN failed.

Despite the strains on ties with other nations in the region, Israel's strategic relationship with Turkey strengthened. In early January U.S., Turkish, and Israeli naval forces took part in "Operation Reliant Mermaid," a joint search-and-rescue operation off the Mediterranean coast. Israeli and Turkish military industries tightened cooperation on a wide range of issues, and Israel won a contract to upgrade 48 Turkish F-5 fighter planes at a cost of $75 million.

Israel won another foreign-policy success in August with its rescue mission to Nairobi after a terrorist bombing of the American embassy there. In a highly publicized five-day operation, the Israeli team rescued three people from under the rubble and located almost 100 bodies.

On the domestic front the government and the defense establishment suffered a number of setbacks. On February 24 Danny Yatom, the head of Israel's intelligence service, the Mossad, resigned after a series of organizational blunders. Although a "clarification committee" on the abortive assassination attempt five months earlier by Mossad agents on Hamas official Khaled Mish'al in Amman, Jordan, cleared the prime minister, it was sharply critical of Yatom. Revelation of another bungled operation in Switzerland only days after the committee's report was published forced Yatom's hand. He was replaced by Ephraim Halevy, who had played a leading role in peacemaking with Jordan, and his appointment gave a much-needed boost to Israel-Jordan ties, badly hurt by the Mish'al affair.

On March 4 Pres. Ezer Weizman, supported by the opposition Labor Party, was reelected, defeating the prime minister's candidate, Shaul Amor in the Knesset 63–49. Tensions between Weizman and Netanyahu were exacerbated as the outspoken president criticized the prime minister's failure to take the peace process forward.

In May Israel marked the 50th anniversary of its founding, but the jubilee celebrations failed to rouse public enthusiasm. Organizers were criticized for not giving ad-

equate weight to the labour movement's contribution. There was further controversy when a modern dance sequence was dropped from the main gala event because of opposition from orthodox Jews. The incident triggered bitter recrimination between secular and orthodox Israelis.

Late in the year the Israeli economy showed signs of stress. A sharp devaluation of the shekel against the dollar in October forced inflation up from an annual rate of about 4% to an estimated 9%. Other economic indicators pointed to a deepening slowdown—growth in the third quarter was 1.4%, the lowest in a decade; investments were down by 21.7%; and exports were down by 18.8%. The most worrying statistic for the government was an unemployment figure of more than 9%

(LESLIE D. SUSSER)

ITALY

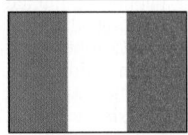

Area: 301,323 sq km (116,341 sq mi)
Population (1998 est.): 57,650,000
Capital: Rome
Chief of state: President Oscar Luigi Scalfaro
Head of government: Prime Minister Romano Prodi and, from October 21, Massimo D'Alema

A former communist became prime minister of Italy in 1998 for the first time in the country's history following the collapse of a centre-left government in power for more than two years, a duration exceeded only once in post-World War II Italy. The main achievement of the outgoing government was to have enabled Italy during the year to qualify as founder member of the European Monetary Union.

Massimo D'Alema, leader of the Democratic Party of the Left, heir to the Italian Communist Party, was sworn in as prime minister of Italy on October 21, 12 days after the government of Romano Prodi lost a confidence motion by a single vote. He took power after bringing together a heterogeneous coalition of seven parties ranging from the extreme left to the centre-right. D'Alema's 26-member Cabinet included, also for the first time, two Marxists as well as six women and three former prime ministers. It was voted into office by 333 votes to 281, with three abstentions.

The so-called "Olive Tree" coalition of Romano Prodi had come to grief following its desertion in parliament by deputies loyal to Fausto Bertinotti, leader of "Communist Refoundation," a mathematically vital segment of Prodi's majority. Bertinotti broke with the government over the 1999 draft budget which he said reflected the unwelcome "moderation" of a government that needed to turn more to the left. When Prodi then called for a vote of confidence, Armand Cossutta, a senior hard-line Marxist in the "Refoundation," expressed fears of a return to power by the right wing in case of a government defeat and pledged it the support of his supposed 22 followers in parliament. Prodi's survival seemed assured, albeit by a

narrow margin, but two deputies, including one of Cossutta's, experienced last-minute changes of mind, and the government was defeated by 313–312.

The Prodi government's most notable feat in 1998 was to have ensured, in May, the country's entry into Europe's economic and monetary union (EMU), a feat brought off against all its partners' expectations and one that qualified it to be included in the launch of the single European currency (the euro) in January 1999. For Italy this was no routine event. Prodi and many others had seen entry into the EMU as imperative to Italy's future competitiveness in Europe and to the modernization of its cumbersome economic system.

Entry into the EMU was achieved as the result of a spectacular economic turnaround aimed at, and brought about by, compliance with the entry criteria stipulated by the 1992 Maastricht Treaty. A series of tight budgets included rigorous measures that produced a drastic drop in both inflation and the general government deficit (to below 3% of gross domestic product), cuts in long-term interest rates, a strengthened currency, and a slowdown in the growth of Italy's enormous public debt, partly obtained by privatizations of state-owned concerns. Heavy taxation, spending cuts, and a onetime levy on the public known as the "Euro tax" were among the costs of the operation and of achieving fiscal rectitude. To align its rate with those of other euro countries, Italy in December cut its floor discount rate to 3%.

A major political setback took place in June when, after 18 months of negotiation, attempts to reform Italy's 1948 constitution, in keeping with the government's electoral mandate and acknowledged as essential to help limit political instability in the country, failed in the parliament. A draft report on reform had been presented to the Chamber of Deputies in January by a 70-member "Two-Chamber Commission" consisting of leaders of the main parties. It proposed a "tempered semipresidential system" as well as a new balloting procedure and changes in the structure of the judiciary. The process came to an abrupt halt without a vote, however, when Silvio Berlusconi, leader of the right-wing opposition, withdrew his party's support for reform in a dispute over the powers of a hypothetical future president to dissolve the parliament.

Berlusconi did not overtly explain his move, but political analysts unanimously suggested that in part it could be connected to his brushes with the law and his intolerance of a proposed reform that would fail to "draw the claws" of prosecutors that he accused anew in 1998 of being politically motivated against him. By July courts in Milan had three times handed down jail sentences against Berlusconi, one of them pardoned, for condoning the bribing of excise officials, for illicit funding of former Socialist Party leader Bettino Craxi, and for fraudulent accounting. Six additional cases were pending against him. Berlusconi commented, "It's the old communist practice of clapping the opposition in jail."

Throughout 1998 Italy was dogged with problems of illegal immigration as clandestine groups of many nationalities continued to attempt to land unintercepted on the country's long coastline. The majority were ferried across the narrow Adriatic Sea to the shores of Puglia and Calabria after paying

PLINIO LEPRI—AP/WIDE WORLD

Kurdish women in Rome march in support of Kurdistan Workers' Party (PKK) leader Abdullah Ocalan, who was arrested in Italy after stepping off a plane from Moscow, where he had been seeking political asylum. Regarded as a terrorist by Turkish authorities, Ocalan was revered by Turkish Kurds. His separatist PKK had been using Syria as a base for raids into Turkey.

exorbitant sums to racketeers. Eastern Europeans mainly used land routes. In January the arrival in Italy of some 1,200 Kurds from Turkey and Iraq led to a meeting in Rome of European police chiefs reportedly concerned that Italy might become a gateway into Europe for illegal immigrants. In March Italy tightened its border controls under a new law that provided for the immediate expulsion of those arriving without documentation or for their temporary detention for checks of documentation. The Interior Ministry reported late in the year that there had been some 43,000 expulsions. In August difficult talks produced a signed agreement with Tunisia on deportation back home for some 3,000 of its nationals, most of whom had landed in Sicily, and on future Tunisian curbs on illegal migration. For its part Italy pledged Tunisia $90 million, part of which was to be used to improve coastal surveillance to prevent illegal migration.

In May more than 160 people were killed and 1,665 left homeless when parts of Mt. Alvarno, north of Salerno in southern Italy, loosened by three days of incessant rain, turned into avalanches of mud that, with the speed of toboggans, submerged or invaded five townships. Alerted by explosions as the mud slides began, many inhabitants fled, but the victims were buried alive. Worst hit, with 137 killed, was Sarno, located beneath a flank of the mountain. One survivor said, "It was worse than an earthquake, because with mud you don't even have time to pray." During an ensuing controversy officials ascribed the catastrophe to denuding of the mountain through deforestation, arson, un-

curbed settlement, and neglect.

In February, 20 people crossing an Alpine valley in a ski-lift gondola plunged to their death when a U.S. Marine EA-6B Prowler jet sliced through the lift's cables as the skiers began a descent from Mt. Cermis near the town of Cavalese. The plane, with a crew of four, was based at the NATO station of Aviano in northern Italy. An attempt by Italian prosecutors to put on trial the crew of the plane and three of their superior officers at the base was quashed in July when a judge in Trento ruled prosecution in Italy juridically untenable under the Treaty of London, which provides for military personnel to be tried in their home country. The U.S. embassy in Rome said Richard Ashby and Joseph Schweitzer, respectively pilot and navigator of the Prowler, were to face a court-martial at Camp Lejeune, North Carolina, in February 1999 and that "administrative sanctions" had been taken against three officers at the Aviano base. In existence at the time of the accident was an Italian ban on flying lower than 600 m (1,970 ft).

There was shock in the art world in May when three armed men stole three masterpieces estimated to be worth at least $34 million—two paintings by Van Gogh and one by Cézanne—at night from the National Gallery of Modern Art in Rome, its three guards having been tied up. Police recovered the paintings undamaged in July and arrested eight Italians. Two of the paintings were found under a bed and on top of a wardrobe in an apartment in Rome, and the third was found in Turin.   (DEREK WILSON)

JAMAICA

Area: 10,991 sq km (4,244 sq mi)
Population (1998 est.): 2,554,000
Capital: Kingston
Chief of state: Queen Elizabeth II, represented by Governor-General Sir Howard Cooke
Head of government: Prime Minister Percival J. Patterson

The opposition Jamaica Labour Party (JLP) failed to make an impression on the voters in local government elections in 1998. The People's National Party, which already controlled the central government on the basis of its victory in the December 1997 general election, won all 13 of Jamaica's parishes in the September 10 poll, as well as the main municipal body, the Kingston and St. Andrew Corp.

The JLP, headed by Edward Seaga, had initially decided to boycott the local election because of Seaga's continuing dissatisfaction with the country's electoral system. The party changed its mind, however, after Prime Minister Percival Patterson agreed to speed up electoral reform, which had begun in the 1997 general election when voter identification cards with photographs were used for the first time.

At least eight more financial institutions had to be taken over by the government's

Financial Sector Adjustment Co. (Finsac) during 1998 as banks, insurance companies, and building societies collapsed owing to a decline in asset values. By late 1998 Finsac had spent about J$100,000,000,000 (U.S. $2,750,000,000) to support failed financial institutions.   (DAVID RENWICK)

JAPAN

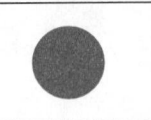

Area: 377,819 sq km (145,877 sq mi)
Population (1998 est.): 126,398,000
Capital: Tokyo
Chief of state: Emperor Akihito
Head of government: Prime Ministers Ryutaro Hashimoto and, from July 30, Keizo Obuchi

Throughout 1998 a stubborn recession dominated domestic politics in Japan, prompting a change in the prime ministership and stunning legislative losses for the ruling Liberal-Democratic Party (LDP). The nation's expected role as an engine of growth for Asia and the rest of the world remained in doubt. By June gross domestic product (GDP) had dropped for three consecutive quarters. Economists for the International Monetary Fund (IMF) noted that the financial problems faced by Japan's neighbours would in turn have an increasing effect on the world's second largest economy. In foreign affairs Japan's relations with the U.S. and China were generally positive, whereas its relations with Russia remained strained and those with North Korea deteriorated.

Domestic Affairs. On January 12 Prime Minister Ryutaro Hashimoto opened the new session of the Diet (parliament) with an address devoted entirely to the economy. He called for emergency measures to shore up the nation's ailing banking system. Shortly afterward, polls showed that his Cabinet's approval rate had fallen to about 31% and that the disapproval rate had risen to around 50%.

Hashimoto's difficulties increased on January 28 when Finance Minister Hiroshi Mitsuzuka resigned after Tokyo prosecutors raided the Finance Ministry and arrested two of its bank inspectors on charges of accepting bribes from Japanese banks. In a speech to the lower house of the Diet on February 16, Hashimoto attempted to turn attention away from the scandal by declaring that the nation's primary task was to find ways to solve problems inherited from Japan's speculative "bubble" economy of the 1980s.

Meanwhile, opposition parties began to reorganize in preparation for the upper house elections on July 12. A true opposition force to the LDP emerged when the Democratic Party of Japan (DPJ) absorbed a number of smaller parties. On March 31 the DPJ chose Naoto Kan, a popular former Cabinet member, to be its president. A poll in February had revealed that the public favoured Kan as

Japan's next prime minister. Leaders of the Japanese Trade Union Confederation promised to back the new DPJ.

On June 12 the lower house rejected a no-confidence motion against the Hashimoto Cabinet by a narrow margin, 273–207. Those who favoured dismissal of the administration blamed it for Japan's economic woes. After the Diet session ended on June 25, some 475 hopefuls filed to run in the upper house elections. Half of the 252 seats in the upper house were open. A vigorous campaign ensued, in which the economy was the focus of every agenda.

To gain a majority in the upper house, Japan's ruling LDP had to win 69 seats. The LDP suffered a staggering defeat, however, winning only 45 seats to bring its total to 103. The defeat amounted to a public no-confidence vote. The DPJ, led by Kan, won 27 to bring its total to 47 seats. The Japan Communist Party scored a minor victory, winning 15 seats to boost its total in the upper house to 23.

Although newspapers noted that Hashimoto was not solely to blame for the setback, he resigned as prime minister on July 13, taking full responsibility for the de-

Newly elected Japanese Prime Minister Keizo Obuchi delivers his first speech before the Diet (parliament) in Tokyo on August 7. He promised tax cuts and increased government spending as part of a plan for "economic reconstruction" of Japan's ailing economy.

feat. On July 21 three LDP leaders registered their candidacies to replace Hashimoto as LDP president. The favourite among the LDP's veteran power brokers was Foreign Minister Keizo Obuchi (*see* BIOGRAPHIES), who headed the largest of the five LDP factions. Opinion polls, however, revealed that Obuchi had less public support than did his two rivals, former chief Cabinet secretary Seiroku Kajiyama and Health and Welfare

Minister Junichiro Koizumi. Nevertheless, Obuchi was elected LDP president on July 24. The Diet convened in a special session on July 30. The lower house, which was dominated by the LDP, voted to appoint Obuchi prime minister. The upper house selected Kan, but the Japanese constitution provided that in such a split the vote of the lower house would prevail.

Upon being named prime minister, Obuchi immediately appointed a new Cabinet, which he said would be dedicated to economic reform. To the public's dismay, he distributed 16 of the 20 portfolios to LDP members. Obuchi's own faction took five posts. Without significant experience in handling financial issues, Obuchi recruited former prime minister Kiichi Miyazawa to be finance minister. Most observers agreed that Miyazawa was a recognized expert on international economics.

In November the LDP sought to increase its power in the parliament by forming a coalition with the Liberal Party. The new grouping, however, remained 11 seats short of a majority in the upper-house.

The Economy. On March 30 the Diet approved a $60.5 billion stopgap budget for the first 18 days of fiscal 1998. Arguments over fiscal policy delayed adoption of the regular budget, set at $599.5 billion, until April 8. The government also launched "Big Bang" policies (named after a British deregulation plan) that included easing restrictions on foreign exchange, granting more autonomy to the Bank of Japan, and allowing banks to sell over-the-counter investment trusts. These steps were intended to implement Hashimoto's 1986 pledge to make Japan's fiscal markets "more free, fair, and global."

On April 24 the government unveiled a comprehensive stimulus package worth $128 billion, the largest ever compiled. The plan offered no tax cuts and provided increased public expenditures for social infrastructure. The package also promised aid to ailing Asian economies through export-import funding. The Japan Research Institute, a private think tank, predicted that public-works spending would not lead to sustainable growth, however. The Bank of Japan noted that the expected boost might be weakened if the downturn in employment and income continued.

On July 2 the government formally announced a plan to establish "bridge banks" to take over failed banks and to extend loans to sound borrowers. The scheme called for new inspection procedures and the appointment of financial conservators and was to be organized through the Deposit Insurance Corporation with stabilization funds. On October 16, after months of political wrangling, the Diet finally appropriated some $500 billion to rescue the nation's top 19 banks. In November the banks began to dip into the funds.

In 1998 Japan was feeling the effects of becoming directly involved in the global economy. Chief Cabinet Secretary Nonaka expressed "strong concern" over the sharp decline in value of the yen against the dollar. The decline, he said, emphasized Japan's urgent need for monetary reform.

Other economic indicators gave the Japanese little more comfort. Returns filed on the Tokyo Stock Exchange for fiscal year 1997 showed that the pretax profits of corporations other than financial houses had declined 2.3% from a year earlier. This was the worst performance since the "oil shock" recession in the 1970s. Grim corporate sentiment, shrinkage of investment by small and medium firms, a decline in housing starts, and sluggish consumer demand all were factors in the stagnant economy. By midyear GDP was shrinking at an annualized rate of 3.3%, its weakest performance on record. Some experts were predicting it to decline another 1% by the end of fiscal year 1998.

In November the government approved a $195 billion economic stimulus package. It included $67.5 billion for public works projects and $50 billion for tax cuts.

Foreign Affairs. Despite the recession at home and fiscal problems in other parts of Asia, Japan as an economic power continued to attract attention. The Ministry of Finance announced that May was the 14th consecutive month in which the current account surplus rose. The surplus ballooned to $10 billion, up 62.2% from the previous year, owing to sluggish domestic demand and a sharp decline in imports. In 1997 the custom-cleared trade surplus had climbed for the first time in five years, up 48.5% to $77.7 billion, and it reached $88 billion in April 1998. This trend marked a return to early 1990s levels, which caused much friction abroad, especially with the U.S.

Japan remained the world's largest creditor nation for the seventh straight year. In 1997 net external assets—held by the government and business, less liabilities—totaled $9.9 billion, up 20.5%. For the seventh year Japan remained the top aid donor, at $9.4 billion, despite budget cuts and a depreciating yen. In May, while still foreign minister, Obuchi promised the Association of Southeast Asian Nations $20 million in assistance. In July Japan offered $300,000 in emergency aid to Papua New Guinea, which had been devastated by a tsunami.

The international community nevertheless remained critical of Japan's domestic policies. On August 13 the IMF made specific proposals, including that the nation reduce its consumption tax, adopt permanent income tax cuts, and reform its postal savings system. Soon afterward, the Ministry of Finance rejected the IMF's assessment and any cut in the consumption tax. Japan's foreign minister in the Obuchi administration, Masahiko Komura, had earlier assured U.S. Secretary of State Madeleine Albright that Japan would revive its economy and help end the Asian financial crisis.

Otherwise, relations with the U.S. revolved as usual around security concerns. On July 4 Albright arrived in Tokyo to brief the Japanese on U.S. Pres. Bill Clinton's recently completed nine-day visit to China. In a joint press conference with the foreign minister, she insisted that the president's failure to stop off in Japan did not constitute neglect. Bilateral relations with Japan remained the American "cornerstone" for security in Asia.

On April 27 Japan authorized two bills to implement noncombat support of U.S. forces in "areas surrounding Japan." Opposition blocs were critical of the vague wording, which, they claimed, violated Japan's no-war

constitution. Nevertheless, Albright and Obuchi drafted the Japan-U.S. Acquisitions and Cross-Servicing Agreement. This was the most expansive interpretation of Japan's defense responsibilities since the adoption of the constitution in 1947. On August 11 the naval warship USS *Kitty Hawk* arrived at the Yokosuka naval base to join Japan's Maritime Self-Defense Forces in maneuvers.

During the year Japan's relations with Russia remained strained by an argument over what the Japanese called the "Northern Territories." These were four small islands at the southern tip of the Kurils, historically Japanese-ruled but occupied by the Russians since 1945. The dispute had blocked a formal pact between the two nations to end World War II. In two informal summit meetings—one in November 1997 at Krasnoyarsk, Siberia, and one in April 1998 at Kawana, Shizuoka prefecture, Japan—Hashimoto and Russian Pres. Boris Yeltsin seemed to be looking for a break in the impasse. Hashimoto proposed a demarcation line to include the two islets in Japan's domain. Yeltsin advocated Russian administration of the islands until a formal pact was signed. On May 8 Obuchi met Russian Foreign Minister Yevgeny Primakov in London. They agreed to accelerate peace treaty negotiations toward a target date of 2000. After he became prime minister, Obuchi was the first Japanese leader to visit Russia since 1973. On November 13 he met with Yeltsin, and the two leaders agreed on the treaty target date.

Relations between Japan and China occurred on several levels. On an official level, Japan's defense agency chief, Fumio Kyuma, and Chinese Defense Minister Chi Haotian signed an agreement on February 4 in Tokyo to increase bilateral cooperation. On May 3 Chi warned that U.S.-Japan defense cooperation guidelines would violate China's sovereignty if they included the Taiwan Strait. On August 9 Foreign Minister Komura became the first Obuchi Cabinet minister to visit China. He was given a short lecture by Chinese Pres. Jiang Zemin, who urged that Japan assume "a correct understanding" of its aggression against China in World War II. Jiang had planned in September to become the first Chinese president to visit Tokyo, but massive flooding in China postponed his trip until late November.

The South Korean government announced on April 21 that it would abandon its efforts to elicit compensation from Japan for the South Korean women who were forced to serve as prostitutes ("comfort women") for Japanese troops during World War II, though it said it would continue to demand an official apology from Japan. The South Korean government decided to pay each of the 152 women who had claimed compensation some $23,000 from its own funds. On April 27 Japan's Yamaguchi district court ruled that the Japanese government owed compensation to three South Korean comfort women and awarded each of the women $2,300. It was the first such court ruling in a lawsuit by victims of Japan's military-run brothels.

During most of 1998, the Japanese government continued conversations with representatives of North Korea. On June 8 Tokyo promised Pyongyang $1 billion in aid to help build two light-water nuclear reactors. Japan, the U.S., South Korea, and the

European Union had been scheduled to sign a resolution on funding the reactors on August 31, but that day North Korea fired a two-stage ballistic missile over Japan. The missile's first stage fell in the Sea of Japan; its second stage flew over the nation, falling into the Pacific Ocean some 580 km (360 mi) northeast of Misawa. On September 1 Japan lodged a strong protest against North Korea by cutting food aid and the promised funds for the reactors.

More ominous clouds appeared on Japan's horizon in the direction of South Asia. On May 11–13 India set off five nuclear tests. Obuchi protested to India's ambassador to Japan, Siddharth Singh, and threatened sanctions. On May 14 Japan froze new loans to India. To Japan's dismay, Pakistan answered India by detonating five nuclear devices on May 28. Japan, Pakistan's biggest aid donor and trade partner, again protested by suspending loans. On June 2 Obuchi expressed a wish to hold a conference in Tokyo to help resolve the territorial dispute between India and Pakistan over Kashmir. In a speech to the UN General Assembly in New York City on September 21, he criticized India and Pakistan for threatening the campaign against nuclear proliferation and North Korea for disturbing security in Asia.

(ARDATH W. BURKS)

JORDAN

Area: 89,326 sq km (34,489 sq mi)
Population (1998 est.): 4,682,000 (including about 1,300,000 Palestinian refugees)
Capital: Amman
Head of state and government: King Hussein, assisted by Prime Ministers 'Abd as-Salam al-Majali and, from August 20, Fayez Tarawneh

King Hussein left Jordan in July 1998 for an extended stay in the United States to undergo treatment for B-cell (non-Hodgkin's) lymphoma. He turned over the daily affairs of the kingdom to his brother, Crown Prince Hassan, who won admiration for the way in which he discharged his duties. Despite his illness, King Hussein continued his efforts to help mediate an agreement between Israel and the Palestinian Authority. In June, at a meeting in Amman with Israeli Defense Minister Yitzhak Mordechai, Hussein supported a U.S. proposal for a withdrawal by Israel from an additional 13% of the West Bank, which was resisted by the Israeli government. Jordan meanwhile resisted efforts by Syria to halt the normalization of its relations with Israel. Numerous consultations were held with Israeli leaders to facilitate an agreement. Late in December Crown Prince Hassan announced that Hussein had been cured of his cancer and had left the hospital. The king had been treated with chemotherapy and had received a transplant from his own bone marrow.

In October King Hussein was invited by U.S. Pres. Bill Clinton to help break the deadlock in the Israeli-Palestinian talks at

the Wye Plantation in Maryland. The negotiations produced an agreement to which the king lent his personal prestige. In Jordan Hussein was widely praised for his efforts.

Military cooperation with the U.S. continued. Jordan received $100 million in military assistance in 1998, on top of the $30 million it had received the previous year, and it was to be given an additional $45 million in the 1998–99 fiscal year to help finance the purchase of 16 F-16 fighter jets. Jordan was also receiving $150 million in economic and development aid annually from the U.S. Joint military exercises with the U.S. were again held in 1998. Jordan and Turkey announced plans for increased military cooperation; Turkey was to help upgrade Jordanian weaponry. Relations between Jordan and Syria deteriorated because Syria had mounted a campaign in the spring to pressure Arab nations to halt normalization with Israel.

A new Cabinet was formed on August 20 under Prime Minister Fayez Tarawneh, former chief of the Royal Court and ambassador to the United States. The outgoing Cabinet under 'Abd as-Salam al-Majali was embarrassed in its final days by a scandal concerning polluted water supplies to the capital, which led to the legal prosecution of government officials, and also by inaccurate government figures that exaggerated estimates of economic growth; the real figure for 1997 was 2.7% rather than the 5% claimed by official accounts.

Jordan's relations with the European Union (EU) continued to improve. In November 1997 Jordan and the EU had signed an agreement that provided free access for Jordanian agricultural and industrial products to European markets and promoted direct investment in Jordan. The European Parliament was expected to ratify the agreement by the end of 1998. There was further progress in repairing relations with Kuwait, marked by the first visit by a Jordanian Cabinet member to the emirate since the Persian Gulf War in 1990–91. Jordan also was discussing a preliminary agreement for a $350 million, 750-km (470-mi) oil pipeline from Iraq to the kingdom. Political and economic cooperation with Egypt continued.

(JENAB TUTUNJI)

KAZAKSTAN

Area: 2,724,900 sq km (1,052,090 sq mi)
Population (1998 est.): 15,797,000
Capital: Astana
Head of state and government: President Nursultan Nazarbayev, assisted by Prime Minister Nurlan Balgimbayev

Kazakstan's new capital, Astana (formerly Aqmola), was formally dedicated on June 10, 1998. Parliament and most of the government had begun working there in the first half of the year. The move was unpopular with civil servants, who dreaded the severe weather in the north, and with opposition politicians and others who objected to the expense involved in refurbishing the shabby Soviet-era city.

At the end of February, several major opposition parties and political movements founded a coalition to contest parliamentary elections scheduled for 1999. The new People's Front of Kazakstan included the Communist and Socialist parties, the liberal Azamat Movement, the nationalist Azat Movement, and the Slavic interest group Lad. The legislature in October approved constitutional amendments that increased the president's term from five to seven years and moved the election up to January 1999.

Unpaid salaries and pensions fueled popular dissatisfaction in many parts of Kazakstan in 1998. Although some sectors of the economy grew, the benefits were not widely evident, and some cities reported unemployment levels near 100%. At the beginning of the year, inhabitants of the southern city of Zhanatas staged a hunger strike to protest unpaid wages. The purchase by a French firm of the phosphorite mine and mill on which the town depended seemed to defuse the tension, but by the end of the year, the city of Kostanay, a major agricultural and industrial centre in the north, was reported to be dying as its population left in search of jobs.

Government efforts to counter the country's economic problems included a much-publicized war on corruption, which was de-

Pictured below is the central square in Astana, the new capital of Kazakstan. Replacing the old capital of Almaty in the southeastern part of the country, Astana was formally dedicated in June. Extensive efforts went into refurbishing the new capital, located in northern Kazakstan, before the dedication.

clared a threat to national security, and a decision announced by Prime Minister Nurlan Balgimbayev in August to reduce state budget expenditures by 25% in 1998. The budget cut was blamed on the falling world prices for many of Kazakstan's exports such as oil and nonferrous metals and the Asian financial crisis. Balgimbayev promised that pensions, state salaries, education, and health care would not be affected by the cuts.

At the beginning of July, the former capital, Almaty, was the site of a summit on regional security at which the foreign ministers of Kazakstan, Kyrgyzstan, Tajikistan, Russia, and China confirmed their commitment to the confidence-building measures set forth in the Shanghai Agreement of 1996. During the summit Kazakstan's Pres. Nursultan Nazarbayev and Chinese Pres. Jiang Zemin signed an agreement ending a border dispute between the two countries. Under the agreement Kazakstan received slightly more than half of two disputed areas. Relations between these two countries, particularly in the sphere of trade and joint ventures, improved significantly in 1998.

Kazakstan's relations with Russia improved with the signing in July of an accord dividing the northern part of the Caspian Sea between the two countries and an agreement on fees for use of Kazakstan's Baykonur Space Centre by the Russian space program.   (BESS BROWN)

KENYA

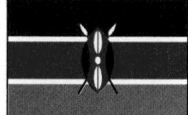

Area: 582,646 sq km (224,961 sq mi)
Population (1998 est.): 28,337,000
Capital: Nairobi
Head of state and government: President Daniel arap Moi

Pres. Daniel arap Moi's victory in the presidential elections at the end of 1997 once again owed more to the disunity of his opponents than to his own popularity. With 13 opposition candidates contesting the election, Moi's success in capturing a little more than 40% of the votes meant that his challengers were easily eliminated. A similar picture emerged in the legislative elections, held at the same time. Although not all the followers of Kenneth Matiba, leader of one of the strongest opposition parties, followed his call to abstain from voting, their disarray allowed the Kenya African National Union to

SAYYID AZIM—AP/WIDE WORLD

Kenyans attend a memorial and prayer service for victims of the terrorist bombing of the U.S. embassy in Nairobi on August 7. A bomb detonated outside the embassy claimed the lives of some 260 persons and injured more than 5,000. The incident overshadowed other problems in Kenya for a time.

have little difficulty in returning to office. Widespread criticism of the conduct of the elections appeared well-founded, but independent observers concluded that the irregularities did not seriously distort the result.

At his inauguration ceremony on January 5, Moi committed himself to the elimination of the corruption that in July 1997 had caused the International Monetary Fund (IMF) and other donors to decide to withhold financial assistance. Three days after the inauguration, however, the announcement that veteran politician Simeon Nyachae was to replace the widely respected Musalia Mudavadi as finance minister cast doubt on the president's dedication to change. This appeared particularly damaging because the country's finances had already suffered heavily as a result of violence in 1997 that had led to a decline in tourism, the source of 20% of foreign exchange income. Still worse were the effects of flooding early in the year in eastern Kenya, which created a desperate demand for food and medical aid while seriously disrupting the already-undermaintained transport system upon which that aid depended.

Although the IMF continued to stand firmly by its resolution to suspend aid, the World Bank offered in March to provide an emergency loan of $100 million to assist in the rehabilitation of the road system from Mombasa to Nairobi. This would help the flood-stricken areas and also facilitate the transport of goods between the Kenyan coast and Uganda and Rwanda. Shortly afterward, the U.S. provided two C-130 Hercules aircraft to assist the World Food Programme in supplying aid to the flooded areas.

Early in March Nyachae confounded his critics by announcing a series of strict measures to be implemented immediately and aimed at curbing the budget deficit, which was expected to rise to 3.9% of gross domestic product, as opposed to earlier estimates of 1.7%. These measures included a cut in government spending, higher taxes on fuel, an increase in value-added tax rates, and the collection of income tax arrears. The minister took his rigorous policy several steps farther in his budget on June 11. The government, he said, could no longer afford to implement the agreement made just before the elections to increase teachers' salaries by 200% over a five-year period. Salary increases for civil servants also were to be restricted to a maximum of 4% per year, and there would be cuts in some of their benefits.

In making these announcements, Nyachae was taking a grave risk, because the teachers' union was powerful and the civil servants could disrupt many public services. He won admiration in many other quarters, however, and even his political opponents were sympathetic to his aims.

A meeting in May, sponsored by the recently appointed Inter-Parties Parliamentary Committee to make plans for constitutional reform, was canceled because of disagreements between the participants. After a stormy start, however, a second forum, held in Nairobi in June, made useful progress, thanks to the efforts of church leaders who took part in the discussions and the willingness of political leaders to moderate their disagreements. It was agreed that a committee consisting of 10 members should be formed to redraft the Kenya Review Commission Act.

Other issues were temporarily submerged by the bombing by terrorists of the U.S. embassy in Nairobi on August 7; about 260 people, including 247 Kenyans, were killed in the embassy and adjacent streets and buildings, and more than 5,000 were injured. Two men were later arrested and charged with having planned the attack.

(KENNETH INGHAM)

SPOTLIGHT

CENTRAL ASIAN OIL CONFLICTS

by Robert Corzine

Illustration by Tom Curry

At the end of the 19th century, the Caspian Sea region in Asia was one of the biggest suppliers of oil to the world. Seven decades of Soviet rule in this century, however, effectively cut off the region—and its energy resources—from international markets. The big question in the late 1990s was whether the newly emerged Caspian and Central Asian republics of Azerbaijan, Kazakstan, Turkmenistan, and Uzbekistan would be able to overcome considerable political and economic barriers to become leading exporters of oil and natural gas in the 21st century.

The uncertainty about the region's potential for development stemmed from several sources, not least of which were differing opinions about its eventual oil and gas reserve base. According to the International Energy Agency (IEA), estimates of proven oil reserves in the area—the three Central Asian republics and Azerbaijan in Transcaucasia—vary between 15 billion and 40 billion bbl, with an additional 70 billion to 150 billion bbl considered possible.

Although some believed the region had the potential to rival the Middle East as an oil producer, the IEA was more circumspect. A more accurate comparison, it said, would be with the North Sea: "As such, it could be a significant alternative source of oil and gas supply, helping to increase world energy security." A combination of low oil prices and the complex politics of the area could, however, combine to delay or even stop the development of the region's energy reserves.

The geopolitical fault lines of Central Asia and the Caspian region were reflected in the bitter debates that accompanied various proposals to build pipelines from the region. Political and commercial agreements on pipeline routes are a prerequisite for the region to achieve its full potential. They have, however, proved to be especially difficult to achieve, given the conflicting strategic interests of the countries involved.

The most contentious issue in 1998 was a plan by the Azerbaijan International Operating Co. (AIOC)—the 11-member international consortium developing three offshore fields in Azerbaijan—to build a main export pipeline from the region. The U.S. regarded this pipeline as the foundation for an "energy corridor" across the Caspian Sea. It wanted the companies to support a plan to build a line from Baku, the Azerbaijani capital, to Ceyhan on Turkey's Mediterranean Sea coast. Additional oil and gas from Kazakstan and Turkmenistan could then be shipped across the Caspian through an undersea pipeline that would link up with the Baku-Ceyhan line.

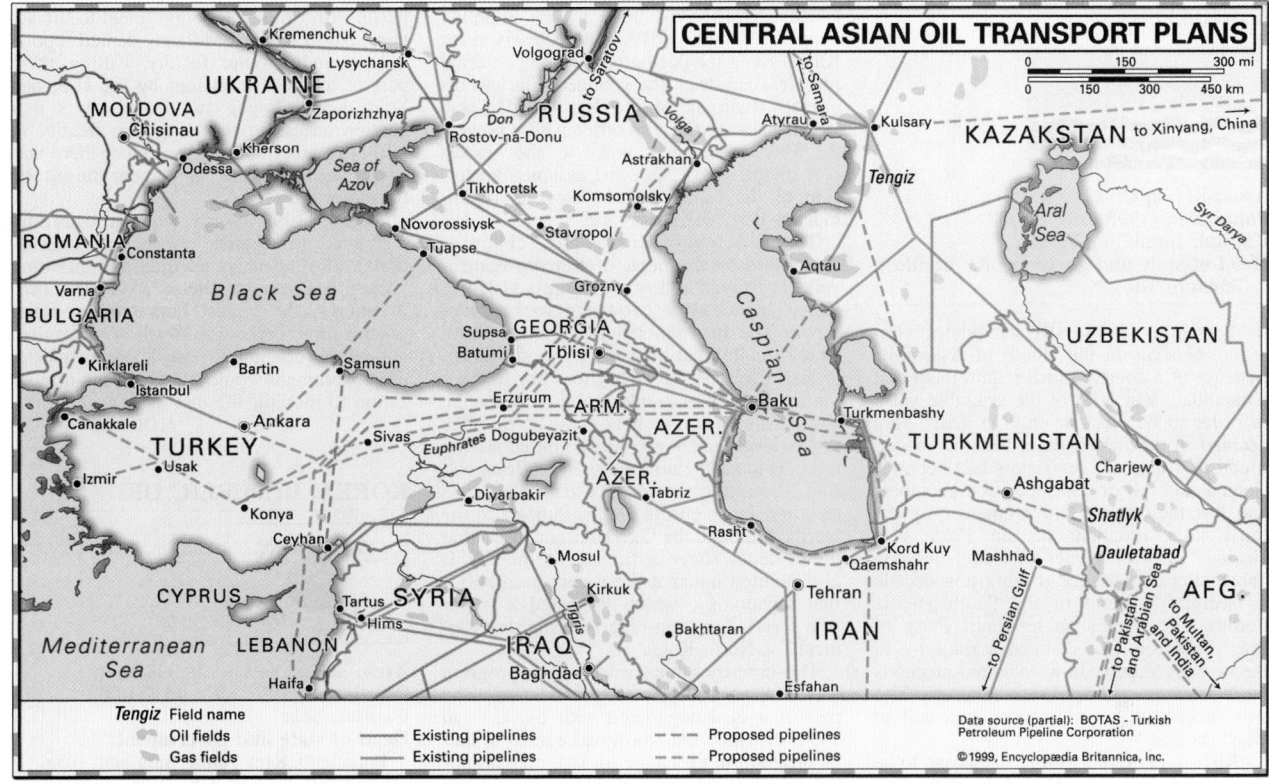

CENTRAL ASIAN OIL TRANSPORT PLANS

Tengiz Field name
▪ Oil fields — Existing pipelines - - - Proposed pipelines
▪ Gas fields — Existing pipelines - - - Proposed pipelines

Data source (partial): BOTAS - Turkish Petroleum Pipeline Corporation

©1999, Encyclopædia Britannica, Inc.

Advocates of the plan said it would secure the political and economic independence of the Caspian republics, as it would give them access to world markets without having to go through Russia or Iran, the two dominant powers in the region. The transit revenues would also underpin Turkey, the most important U.S. ally in the area.

With a projected cost of $3.7 billion, the Baku-Ceyhan line would be, however, the most expensive of three options that were being assessed by the AIOC and the Azerbaijani government, the two bodies that would make the final decision. The AIOC was thought to prefer a more modest pipeline to Supsa on the Black Sea coast of Georgia, from where tankers would then take the oil to world markets via the narrow Bosporus Strait in Turkey. The Turkish government opposed this idea, insisting that the environmental dangers were too great to allow more tankers through the Bosporus.

The pipeline debate was further complicated by the roles of Russia and Iran. Russia was wary of projects that might undermine its traditional political influence in the region, although it would probably not try to stop a Baku-Ceyhan project as long as significant volumes of Caspian crude continued to be exported via its territory.

A pipeline through Iran was not one of the AIOC's options, but the Tehran government was busy in 1998 promoting Iran's potential as a "land bridge" between Central Asia and the Caspian region and the oil-export terminals on the Persian Gulf. As a first step Iran wanted to "swap" oil with

Caspian and Central Asian producers. It would use the imported crude in its northern refineries and make available a similar amount of Iranian crude for export at Persian Gulf ports. Iran said that eventually it would be willing to switch all its inland refineries to Caspian and Central Asian crude and to reverse its oil pipelines in order to enable direct exports from the region. Iran was also eager to act as a conduit for gas exports from Turkmenistan to Turkey.

The other pipeline project with a history of political wrangling was the Caspian Pipeline Consortium's (CPC) plan to build a nearly $2.5 billion line from the giant Tengiz field in Kazakstan to a new export terminal at Novorossiysk on Russia's Black Sea coast. The consortium finally received the go-ahead in November and was expected to be a litmus test of Russia's intentions in the region. Although Moscow would benefit substantially from transit revenues, Russian support for the CPC had often been lukewarm, given that the main beneficiary would be Kazakstan.

It was not only pipeline routes that aroused strong passions in the region. The ownership of the Caspian Sea itself remained to be settled. Russia and Kazakstan solved their boundary dispute, but Turkmenistan and Azerbaijan continued to quarrel over the status of one offshore field, and Iran insisted that it be awarded one-fifth of the Caspian should the five nations that border the sea agree to split it into national sectors.

As of the end of 1998, the legal dispute had not stopped any foreign projects from going ahead. It looked increasingly likely, however, that low oil prices would do so in 1999. If crude prices, which ended 1998 at just over $10 per barrel, do not recover to the $15–$20-per-barrel range, oil executives say, it will be difficult to justify the tens of billions of dollars that will be needed to develop the region's reserves.

The national emblem of Azerbaijan is silhouetted in this view of a dock for oil rigs in Baku on the shore of the Caspian Sea. The Transcaucasian republic of Azerbaijan is reportedly sitting on a huge reserve of Caspian oil, but the absence of a major export pipeline from Baku remains a formidable obstacle to development.

Robert Corzine is the Energy Correspondent for the Financial Times.

KIRIBATI

Area: 811 sq km (313 sq mi)
Population (1998 est.): 84,000
Capital: Bairiki, on Tarawa
Head of state and government: President Teburoro Tito

In September 1998, 191 candidates contested 42 seats in the House of Assembly. Because of a constitutional requirement that a candidate win 50% of the available votes in order to be elected, only 15 seats were decided in the first ballot. After the second round of voting, 25 legislators had been reelected and 11 of 18 opposition members had lost their seats. One woman, only the third since independence in 1979, was elected, as was former president Ieremia Tabai after an absence of almost a decade as secretary-general of the South Pacific Forum. The Maneaban te Mauri Party of Pres. Teburoro Tito claimed a majority in the new legislature. In presidential elections in November, sitting Pres. Teburoro Tito was successful, securing more than half of all votes cast.

Kiribati persisted with its campaign to be recognized as the country that would first reach the new millennium, seeking international acceptance for the renaming of Caroline Island in the Phoenix group as Millennium Island. In adjusting the conventional International Date Line to ensure a single time zone for the entire country, Kiribati extended its boundaries to the east, which thus provided the basis for its millennium claims.

Japan's National Space Development Agency began preparing plans for a rocket-monitoring station and landing facilities for unmanned space shuttles on Kiritimati (Christmas Island). Also on Kiritimati the U.K. and Kiribati began a study of the long-term effects of the nuclear testing on the island in the 1950s. (BARRIE MACDONALD)

KOREA, DEMOCRATIC PEOPLE'S REPUBLIC OF

Area: 122,762 sq km (47,399 sq mi)
Population (1998 est.): 21,234,000
Capital: Pyongyang
Chief of state: Chairman of the National Defense Commission Kim Jong Il
Head of government: Chairman of the Council of Ministers (Premier) Hong Sang Nam

In September 1998, exactly 50 years after Kim Il Sung founded the Democratic People's Republic of Korea, his son Kim Jong Il formally assumed the nation's highest post, completing a transition that had begun with the elder Kim's death in July 1994. Kim Jong Il did not become president, however. That position was written out of

North Korea's constitution by the Supreme People's Assembly (SPA), which reserved for Kim Il Sung the posthumous title of "eternal president." Instead, the younger Kim was reelected chairman of the National Defense Commission (NDC), an office whose powers the SPA expanded to make it "the highest post of the state." Kim had assumed leadership of the ruling Korean Workers (Communist) Party in October 1997.

The reelection of Kim as NDC chairman came hard on the heels of a major controversy in foreign affairs. On August 31 North Korea launched a two-stage rocket over Japan. The international reaction to North Korea's claim that the rocket was not meant to test a missile but rather to carry a satellite into orbit was deeply skeptical, since the North was known to have ballistic missiles under development and had admitted selling missiles to such countries as Syria, Iran, and Iraq. Protesting the rocket's path across its territory, Japan cut its food shipments to the North. Although the U.S. later conceded that the evidence suggested a satellite launch, it also pointed out that the rocket used solid-fuel technology, which indicated a major step forward in long-range-missile development for North Korea.

The country's nuclear weapons program was supposed to have remained frozen as part of a deal negotiated with the U.S. in 1994, in which the North had agreed to halt its program in exchange for two civilian nuclear reactors and fuel oil. Photographs from U.S. spy satellites, however, purportedly showed work proceeding on an underground nuclear facility near Yongbyon. Reports of the facility persuaded the U.S. Congress to stop supplying fuel oil to North Korea. Pres. Bill Clinton, however, used his authority to divert $15 million from special funds in or-

der to fulfill the U.S. commitment to the accord. North Korea steadfastly denied reports of the underground facility, calling them part of a smear campaign by the U.S. and South Korea. Pyongyang denied a U.S. delegation access to the Yongbyon facility in mid-November, and by December there was fear that the entire agreement might be breaking down.

During 1998 North Korea's economy continued to stagnate. Numerous international relief agencies testified to continuing widespread hunger there. Médecins sans Frontières, the largest humanitarian relief organization working in North Korea, pulled out of the country in late September after the government would not allow the organization to monitor the distribution of food.
(TODD CROWELL)

KOREA, REPUBLIC OF

Area: 99,268 sq km (38,328 sq mi)
Population (1998 est.): 46,451,000
Capital: Seoul
Head of state and government: Presidents Kim Young Sam and, from February 25, Kim Dae Jung

On Feb. 25, 1998, Kim Dae Jung made history when he was sworn in as South Korea's first president from a party in opposition to the New Korea (later Grand National) Party. Soon after taking office, Kim, a former political prisoner, pardoned some 2,300 pris-

North Korean farmers work in February to remove topsoil in preparation for fertilizing their fields near Pyongyang. As the country's economy stagnated during the year, the population of North Korea continued to be devastated by famine. By 1998 most residents had come to depend on government rations.

Kim Dae Jung (center), the new president of South Korea, waves to the crowd at his inauguration ceremony in Seoul on February 25. A former political prisoner, Kim became the first South Korean president from a party other than the New Korea (later Grand National) Party. During 1998 he worked to broaden his appeal nationwide.

oners and waived the traffic fines of more than five million South Koreans. Some human rights groups, however, criticized Kim for releasing or reducing sentences for only 22 of the 41 inmates that Amnesty International considered prisoners of conscience and for not repealing South Korea's strict National Security Law, which forbade Southerners from expressing support for North Korea.

As he had promised during his campaign, Kim appointed Kim Jong Pil, the leader of a minority party in the National Assembly, as prime minister. To help broaden his appeal nationwide, the president had forged an alliance with Kim Jong Pil's United Liberal Democrats, ideologically at opposite ends of the political spectrum from the president's own party, the National Congress for New Politics (NCNP). For much of the year, Kim Jong Pil carried the prefix "acting" in front of his title, since the defeated Grand National Party (GNP) began the year with a majority of seats in the National Assembly and boycotted the vote for the president's nominee for prime minister. The rest of the new Cabinet largely comprised relatively little-known academics and legislators.

During the year Kim was gradually able to assemble a parliamentary majority for the NCNP, primarily through defections from the GNP and by the demise of the independent party that had formed in December 1997 to support the presidential aspirations of Rhee In Je. At midyear Kim launched an anticorruption drive, which the GNP insisted was meant to further weaken it. Eight GNP assemblymen were placed under investigation. GNP members expressed their complaints by boycotting the National Assembly and holding rallies across the country.

More than any other Korean politician in recent years, Kim was determined to change the nature of the South's relations with North Korea. His new "sunshine" policy emerged soon after he took office. The main elements of the policy included allowing South Koreans the opportunity to visit relatives in the North, permitting businessmen to travel there to discuss commercial deals, and relaxing rules governing South Korean investment in the North. Perhaps the most concrete result of Kim's new policy was Chung Ju Yung's personal mission to Pyongyang in June. The founder of the Hyundai conglomerate and a North Korean native, Chung delivered some 50 trucks loaded with cattle to help feed North Koreans, and he negotiated a deal whereby South Koreans would be allowed to visit Mt. Kumgang, a popular tourist spot on Korea's eastern coast just north of the demilitarized zone. The first such visit took place in mid-November.

On a diplomatic level, direct talks between North and South Korea resumed in Beijing after a hiatus of four years, though the negotiators failed to agree on main points of contention dealing with food aid and family visits. During an official visit to the U.S., Kim urged the U.S. to lift economic sanctions against North Korea, something considered very unlikely, given rising concern in Washington that North Korea was reneging on a deal negotiated in 1994 to curb its suspected nuclear weapons program. The same topic was discussed when U.S. Pres. Bill Clinton visited Seoul in November.

Kim's biggest challenge was to try to lead South Korea out of its worst economic slump since the end of the Korean War. As a presidential candidate he had hinted that he might seek to renegotiate an agreement with the International Monetary Fund (IMF) on the terms of a $57 billion bailout loan extended in December 1997. Once elected, however, he endorsed the agreement and

worked to implement the terms, which included a restructuring of financial institutions and business conglomerates burdened with bad debts. The IMF predicted that the economy would contract by 7% in 1998. Unemployment rose to about 10%.

Kim visited Europe, the U.S., and China during the year, but perhaps his most important foreign policy initiative came in October with his visit to Japan. During a four-day trip to Tokyo, he extended an invitation to Emperor Akihito to visit South Korea. Such a visit, if approved by the Japanese government, would be a first. In a surprising move, the Japanese government issued a written apology expressing "deep remorse" for Japan's occupation of Korea from 1910 to 1945. For his part, Kim let it be known that he wanted to phase out a ban on Japanese cultural products, such as movies and cartoons, that had been in effect since the end of the Korean War. The lifting of the ban would undoubtedly prove popular among South Korea's young people, but Kim intended to treat the matter cautiously so as not to injure South Korea's own entertainment industry, especially while the economy was still fragile. He hoped the ban would be removed by 2002.

(TODD CROWELL)

KUWAIT

Area: 17,818 sq km (6,880 sq mi)
Population (1998 est.): 1,866,000
Capital: Kuwait City
Head of state and government: Emir Sheikh Jabir al-Ahmad al-Jabir as-Sabah, assisted by Prime Minister Crown Prince Sheikh Saad al-Abdullah as-Salim as-Sabah

Low oil prices caused 1998 to be an extremely difficult year for all oil producers, and Kuwait was obliged to take a hard look at its industry and initiate some significant changes. In March Kuwait joined with other OPEC and non-OPEC producers in an accord to cut production. It was not until late summer that this attempt to counter the worst price collapse in the oil market since 1986 began to stabilize prices. In August industry observers learned that Kuwait's national oil company, the Kuwait Petroleum Corp., would undergo extensive restructuring. Under a proposal made by Kuwait's Supreme Petroleum Council, the body charged with devising national oil policy, the two largest affiliates in the domestic oil sector, the Kuwait Oil Co., which carried out exploration and production, and the Kuwait National Petroleum Co., which managed the country's three large refineries, were to be merged. Even more significant for the long-term structure of Kuwait's oil industry was a proposal to invite foreign participation in the industry.

The domestic economy was a major worry for Kuwaitis throughout 1998, with the stock market reaching a low of slightly less than 2000 in July. Privatization of some government holdings, which began under

Traders at the Kuwait Stock Exchange follow the exchange's tumbling price index in October. Hurt by low oil prices, the domestic economy was a major worry for Kuwaitis throughout 1998. By year's end the government was considering dropping certain free public services and introducing income taxes in an effort to raise money.

the auspices of the Kuwait Investment Authority in 1994, in the absence of a strategic plan, had by late 1998 earned $10 billion for the government.

The government that had been formed following the October 1996 election fell in March 1998 as the result of a successful no-confidence vote against the information minister, Saud Nasir as-Sabah, a member of the ruling family and former Kuwaiti ambassador to the United States. The reshuffled Cabinet, however, included most of the members of the old Cabinet.

(MARY ANN TÉTREAULT)

KYRGYZSTAN

Area: 199,900 sq km (77,200 sq mi)
Population (1998 est.): 4,691,000
Capital: Bishkek
Head of state and government: President Askar Akayev, assisted by Prime Ministers Apas Jumagulov, from March 24, Kubanychbek Jumaliyev, and, from December 25, Jumabek Ibraimov

In Kyrgyzstan months of vigorous controversy led up to the referendum on Oct. 17, 1998, on a series of constitutional amendments. Proposals to limit the immunity from arrest of parliamentary deputies as well as their control over the country's budgetary process were actively opposed by many legislators and political activists, who interpreted the proposals as a weakening of the legislative branch and a strengthening of the presidential administration. Another amendment prohibited the passage of laws restricting freedom of information.

An amendment introducing private ownership of land was a response to pressure from international lending agencies, which expected that private owners could then use their land as collateral to obtain loans for improvements. Many agriculturalists opposed private ownership, however, fearing that owners would be forced by economic necessity to sell to speculators and proponents of agribusiness. The creation of a private market in land was opposed in the southern part of the country on the grounds that it could stir up tensions between Kyrgyz and Uzbeks, which already had led to bloody riots over land and water in the summer of 1990.

There was a further shake-up at the end of the year, when the Cabinet was dismissed by Pres. Askar Akayev for failing to address the country's economic problems including, presumably, a corruption scandal that had led to the arrest of a dozen top government officials. Jumabek Ibraimov was confirmed as prime minister on December 25, and he announced the members of his new Cabinet on December 30.

Kyrgyzstan's economy slowly improved during 1998, but pensions and salaries of civil servants were frequently in arrears. There was a high level of popular resentment against those who were doing well in the new market economy. A spillage of poisonous wastes from a Kyrgyz-Canadian gold mine stirred up controversy over the exploitation of the country's natural resources for the benefit of the few.   (BESS BROWN)

LAOS

Area: 236,800 sq km (91,429 sq mi)
Population (1998 est.): 5,261,000
Capital: Vientiane (Viangchan)
Chief of state: Presidents Nouhak Phoumsavan and, from February 24, Gen. Khamtai Siphandon
Head of government: Prime Ministers Gen. Khamtai Siphandon and, from February 24, Sisavath Keobounphanh

During the first week of January 1998, results of the elections held on Dec. 21, 1997, became known. The communist Lao People's Revolutionary Party won all but one of the 99 seats in the National Assembly. Four noncommunist candidates

approved by the Lao Front for National Construction had been allowed to run. The first plenary session of the Assembly met at the end of February to elect the nation's leaders. As expected, Pres. Nouhak Phoumsavanh retired and was replaced by Khamtai Siphandon, prime minister since 1991. Khamtai retained his position as head of the Politburo and thus greatly consolidated his power. Vice Pres. Sisavath Keobounphanh, who had been sidelined in 1991 and rehabilitated in 1996, was promoted to prime minister.

The second session of the National Assembly met September 29 to consider the budget and economic development. Earlier, in what promised to be a change in foreign relations, President Khamtai had replaced the ambassadors to Thailand, Vietnam, Cambodia, Indonesia, Australia, Germany, and the U.S.

On May 25 a military plane normally used by President Khamtai crashed in northern Laos, killing Vietnam's visiting vice-defense minister, Gen. Dao Trong Lich. In June the European Union called for Laos's admission to the World Trade Organization within one year and offered further economic and humanitarian assistance while urging additional free-market reforms. In August, amid much controversy, Thailand began preparations to repatriate thousands of ethnic Hmong Laotian refugees, including anticommunist dissidents.

The East Asian financial crisis affected Laos badly. By October the kip had depreciated by more than 200%. Inflation, up from 8% in 1997, was approaching 100%, and no economic growth was anticipated. In June the International Monetary Fund severely criticized Laos's handling of its economy, but the IMF's rehabilitation measures met strong resistance from the nation's central bank and Finance Ministry. Compounding the problem was the economic slowdown in neighbouring Thailand, which resulted in the postponement of planned investments in industrial infrastructure and a railway link. In October the Asian Development Bank warned that the ambitious Mekong River Basin economic development plan was also adversely affected. Japan, however, pledged to proceed with financing the construction of a second Mekong River bridge at Savanakhet. (ROBERT WOODROW)

LATVIA

Area: 64,610 sq km (24,946 sq mi)
Population (1998 est.): 2,445,000
Capital: Riga
Chief of state: President Guntis Ulmanis
Head of government: Prime Ministers Guntars Krasts and, from November 3, Vilis Kristopans

Elections, a referendum, the problem of the Russian minority, and foreign affairs issues dominated the headlines in Latvia in 1998. A new, four-year Parliament consisting of 62 deputies from three right-wing parties and 38 from three left-wing parties was elected in October. Ranking first with 24

deputies was the right-wing People's Party of former prime minister Andris Skele. Aiming for a stable coalition government, Pres. Guntis Ulmanis passed over the controversial Skele and named Vilis Kristopans of the Latvian Way Union as the new prime minister to replace Guntars Krasts, who finished his term with a balanced budget and positive macroeconomic indicators, despite the negative impact of Russia's economic crisis on Latvia.

Responding to recommendations of the European Union and the Organization for Security and Cooperation in Europe to accelerate the integration of Russian-speaking residents, in June Parliament amended the citizenship law to ease the naturalization of noncitizens (about 26% of the population) and grant citizenship to children born in Latvia to stateless parents. The amendments were approved in a referendum. In October Parliament added to the constitution a section on human rights to replace a constitutional law of December 1991.

Relations with Russia declined after demonstrations in March by Russian-speaking retirees over the high cost of living in Riga, the Latvian capital. Russia accused Latvia of gross human rights violations. The commemoration held by Latvian World War II veterans conscripted by Nazi Germany prompted Moscow to conclude that Riga was condoning fascism. Russia's rhetoric and threats of sanctions drew meagre response abroad, however, and subsided as its economy deteriorated. The withdrawal of the Russian troops manning the Soviet-era antimissile radar at Skrunda and the facility's dismantling proceeded on schedule.

In January the U.S.-Baltic Charter was signed. Latvia joined the World Trade Organization in October. In December, however, there was disappointment when the European Union did not open accession negotiations with Latvia or the other candidate countries. (DZINTRA BUNGS)

LEBANON

Area: 10,400 sq km (4,016 sq mi)
Population (1998 est.): 3,506,000 (excluding Palestinian refugees estimated to number more than 350,000)
Capital: Beirut
Chief of state: Presidents Elias Hrawi and, from November 24, Gen. Emile Lahoud
Head of government: Prime Minister Rafiq al-Hariri and, from December 2, Salim al-Hoss

The National Assembly on October 15 elected Lebanon's first new president since the end of the civil war in 1990. Gen. Emile Lahoud's election was supported by the

Outgoing Lebanese Pres. Elias Hrawi (right) decorates new Pres. Emile Lahoud at an inauguration ceremony in Baabda on November 24. The ceremony marked the first smooth transition of power in Lebanon in nearly 30 years. The election of Lahoud, Lebanon's army chief, was supported by the army and the Syrians, with whom the new president hoped to build strong ties.

army and the Syrians. The first regional elections in 35 years for new municipal councils in 650 municipalities resulted in growing support for Shi'ite Muslim Hezbollah. Opponents of Prime Minister Rafiq al-Hariri did well in Tripoli and in the southern suburbs of Beirut, where Hezbollah won over Hariri's candidates and those of the Shi'ite Amal Party. In Baalbek, however, where Hezbollah began in 1982, the party lost to supporters of Sheikh Subhi at-Tufayli's "Hungry Revolution" party. In the south Hezbollah won the seats in its stronghold at Nabatiya but lost in other areas.

Despite their low voter turnout, Christians won 12 of the 24 seats in the Beirut council. Christian interest in redistricting the city into separate districts to guarantee Christian representation was refused, but at the last minute Hariri brokered an alliance between the Christian Phalangist Party, the formerly outlawed Lebanese Forces, Hezbollah, and

the Armenian Revolutionary Federation that resulted in the split in the council between Muslims and Christians. Although unexpected, the return of veteran politician Salim al-Hoss as prime minister in December did not seem to signal a change in course.

The government raised $1 billion through the sale of bonds, primarily to Lebanese banks and Middle Eastern interests, to be used to restructure Lebanon's debt and ease the pressure on the nation's currency. The lifting of the travel ban in August 1997 for Americans visiting Lebanon enabled the U.S. to join the Europeans in bidding for contracts for the rebuilding of Beirut and also led to an increase in tourism. Hotels, restaurants, museums, and airport facilities were rebuilt and refurbished, the summer festivals at Baalbek and Beiteddine reinstated, and the Casino du Liban in the Christian area of Jounieh reopened.

Israel's declaration in March that it would withdraw its forces from Lebanon if the latter could ensure border security in the south was rejected by Prime Minister Hariri, who insisted that Israel comply with UN resolution 425, calling for unconditional withdrawal. On April 1 the Israeli government endorsed the UN resolution on the condition that Lebanon ensure border security. This too was rejected by both Lebanon and Syria, which dismissed the offer of withdrawal as an attempt to negotiate separately with Lebanon and with Syria. In August fighting between Israel and Hezbollah resumed in south Lebanon after a hiatus of several months.   (REEVA S. SIMON)

LESOTHO

Area: 30,355 sq km (11,720 sq mi)
Population (1998 est.): 2,090,000
Capital: Maseru
Chief of state: King Letsie III
Head of government: Prime Ministers Ntsu Mokhehle and, from May 29, Bathuel Pakalitha Mosisili

Lesotho in late 1998 suffered its greatest crisis since achieving independence. Political tensions, which had run high for years, boiled over after the general election on May 23. In that election the opposition parties gained 40% of the vote, but the ruling Lesotho Congress for Democracy Party of Ntsu Mokhehle, the long-standing prime minister, won all but 2 of the 80 contested seats. The three main opposition parties then claimed widespread and systematic fraud and protested to the High Court that they were denied access to voters' rolls and other relevant documentation to prove their allegations. After the court in July authorized their access to the documentation, evidence of irregularities began to emerge, and protests began in early August in Maseru, where crowds besieged the royal palace and urged King Letsie III to use his powers to annul the elections and put in place a government of national unity. But Letsie had been crowned only after accepting a circumscribed role as king, and he refused to act.

As protests mounted in Maseru, the Southern African Development Community intervened, under South African leadership, and a commission was appointed under Judge Pius Langa, deputy president of South Africa's Constitutional Court, to investigate the allegations of electoral fraud. When the report was released, it found that irregularities had taken place but not on a sufficient scale to suggest that the election results should be annulled.

Part of the army had by then come out in support of the opposition parties, and senior officers fled into South Africa. In late September South African troops, followed by troops from Botswana, entered the country in response to a request from Prime Minister Pakalitha Mosisili, who had taken over in late May from the ailing Mokhehle. They claimed that law and order had broken down and that a military coup was imminent. The South African troops met much fiercer resistance than they had expected, as they tried to take control of Maseru and the Katse Dam in the interior. An orgy of looting of shops and businesses in the central business district of Maseru left much of the capital in ruins. After the SADC troops had restored order, negotiations led to an agreement that a multiparty interim authority would be established to hold a new election in 2000.
(CHRISTOPHER SAUNDERS)

LIBERIA

Area: 97,754 sq km (37,743 sq mi)
Population (1998 est.): 2,772,000 (excluding Liberian refugees temporarily residing in surrounding countries estimated to number about 325,000)
Capital: Monrovia
Head of state and government: President Charles Taylor

Despite 1997 elections and the presence of ECOMOG (Economic Community of West African States Cease-Fire Monitoring Group) peacekeepers, Liberia experienced continued insecurity throughout 1998. Seven years of civil war had left the country's economy and infrastructure in ruins. Nearly 80% of the government's 1998 budget of $41 million was allotted to defense.

The ECOMOG commander accused Pres. Charles Taylor of filling the restructured Liberian army with members of his former militia. This claim was echoed by former

DAVID GUTTENFELDER—AP/WIDE WORLD

A member of ECOMOG, the West African peacekeeping force, guards the vehicle of Liberian Pres. Charles Taylor in January. Although ECOMOG's mandate expired in February, some of its soldiers remained in Liberia and, according to opposition leaders, harassed and intimidated supporters of former faction leader Roosevelt Johnson.

faction leader Roosevelt Johnson, who charged that government troops had repeatedly tried to kill him. Opposition leaders continually complained of harassment and intimidation by security forces. The situation reached a climax in August when Taylor declared Johnson a security risk and accused Guinea and Sierra Leone of supporting plots to topple Taylor's government. Troops loyal to Taylor conducted extensive security operations in Monrovia, and Johnson took refuge in the U.S. embassy compound in late September. Monrovia became the scene of widespread looting and gun battles between soldiers and Johnson supporters. Johnson later fled to Nigeria.

Throughout the year the United Nations High Commissioner for Refugees and other humanitarian groups attempted to repatriate Liberian refugees from neighbouring countries. Citing insecurity in Liberia, many refugees refused to return. Nearly half a million Liberians were refugees, and approximately 750,000 were internally displaced.
(MATTHEW A. CENZER)

LIBYA

Area: 1,757,000 sq km (678,400 sq mi)
Population (1998 est.): 5,691,000
Capital: Tripoli (policy-making body meets in Surt)
Chief of state: (de facto) Col. Muammar al-Qaddafi; (nominal) Secretary of the General People's Congress Zanati Muhammad az-Zanati
Head of government: Secretary of the General People's Committee (Premier) 'Abd al-Majid al-Qa'ud

After almost eight years of a standoff between Libya and the U.S. and the U.K., there were moments in 1998 when it seemed that a trial of the two Libyans alleged to have been involved in the crash of Pan Am Flight 103 over Lockerbie, Scot., on Dec. 21, 1988, would be arranged. The location of the trial had been a source of conflict arising from different interpretations of the Montreal Convention. The convention states that in the event of a case such as the Lockerbie disaster, legal processes can be conducted in the place where the disaster occurred, in the nation from which any of the accused might come, or in a third neutral nation agreed upon by the parties involved.

Libya had agreed to a trial in a neutral country as early as 1992, but the U.S. and the U.K. insisted on a trial in Scotland or the U.S. Because Libya would not yield the alleged Libyan suspects for trial in Scotland, the U.S. and the U.K. prevailed on the UN General Assembly to impose a severe economic boycott on Libya. A total ban on air traffic was enforced in 1992.

In August 1998, however, the British government, with U.S. approval, shifted its position and communicated to Libya its willingness to see the case tried in The Netherlands before a Scottish judge according to Scottish law. The initial response from Libya was favourable. By October, however, the Libyan leader, Col. Muammar al-Qaddafi, had had second thoughts, and his legal advisers communicated that the security arrangements for the two Libyans during the proposed trial were unsatisfactory. He also rejected the condition of the British government that any sentence be served in Scotland. At year's end the positions were deadlocked, and the trial seemed to be as far off as ever.

The Libyan economy continued to be weakened by the 1992 UN trade embargo and especially by the decline in international oil prices. Libyan oil remained in demand, however, because of its high quality and Libya's location close to Western Europe. In regard to the embargo, Qaddafi became dissatisfied during the year with his Arab neighbours, stating that much stronger support for his position was coming from African governments south of the Sahara. He particularly welcomed the initiative of the heads of state of Uganda, Chad, Niger, and Eritrea, who ignored the UN air traffic embargo and flew to a meeting in Surt on September 30 to discuss the emergency in the Democratic Republic of the Congo.

(J.A. ALLAN)

LIECHTENSTEIN

Area: 160 sq km (62 sq mi)
Population (1998 est.): 31,400
Capital: Vaduz
Chief of state: Prince Hans Adam II
Head of government: Mario Frick

With the theme "Small Is Beautiful," Liechtenstein in 1998 began preparations to serve as host of the eighth Games of the Small States of Europe, scheduled for May 24–29, 1999, in Vaduz. A new stadium at Schaan opened in August for the track and field trials. Trials for judo took place in September and for squash and table tennis in October. Cycling, swimming, tennis, volleyball, and rifle competitions were also held in order to ensure that Olympic competition standards were satisfied. Some 700 athletes from Andorra, Iceland, Luxembourg, Malta, Monaco, San Marino, and Cyprus were expected to participate with Liechtenstein in these mini-Olympics.

The status and numbers of refugees in Liechtenstein posed problems during the year. In the case of 13 Tibetans who had lived in Liechtenstein for five years and been denied asylum, the administration and appellate court found that they could not be returned to their home country and had to be treated as refugees. By late in the year, the number of refugees from the Serbian province of Kosovo had overwhelmed the capacity of the receiving centre in Vaduz.

The economy continued to grow. With low price increases, low interest rates, and little unemployment, there were no problem areas.   (ANNE ROBY)

LITHUANIA

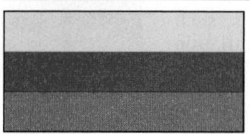

Area: 65,301 sq km (25,213 sq mi)
Population (1998 est.): 3,704,000
Capital: Vilnius
Chief of state: President Valdas Adamkus
Head of government: Prime Minister
   Gediminas Vagnorius

On Jan. 4, 1998, runoff elections for president were held. The émigré environmentalist Valdas Adamkus won by a narrow margin over his postcommunist opponent, Arturas Paulauskas.

Adapting his administrative experience in the U.S. Environmental Protection Agency, Adamkus quickly became the country's most popular figure, increasing both the power and the prestige of the presidency as an institution. The ruling coalition of the Homeland Union (Conservatives of Lithuania) and the Christian Democrats continued structural and legislative reforms aimed at deepening economic transformation and preparing the way for eventual European Union (EU) membership.

Foreign direct investment increased substantially (the annual rate of inflation was less than 5%), but trade and current account deficits increased. The economic crisis in Russia had only a limited effect on Lithuania because of Lithuania's success in disengaging from the economy of the former U.S.S.R.

The decision by the EU not to commence formal negotiations with Lithuania for EU membership in 1999 was a major disappointment because the government had made accession talks its primary goal. Lithuania continued to improve its ties with its neighbours, placing particular emphasis on fostering good relations with Poland.

(SAULIUS A. GIRNIUS)

LUXEMBOURG

Area: 2,586 sq km (999 sq mi)
Population (1998 est.): 425,000
Capital: Luxembourg
Chief of state: Grand Duke Jean
Head of government: Prime Minister
   Jean-Claude Juncker

In a letter to the legislature on March 4, 1998, Grand Duke Jean named his son, Prince Henri, "lieutenant-representative," which allowed him to represent his father in all official duties and thereby set the stage for Henri to succeed to the throne. Grand Duke Jean had taken office on Nov. 12, 1964.

Prime Minister Jean-Claude Juncker in his state of the nation address declared information technology the "fourth factor of production." With further investment in electronic infrastructure, accelerated intensive training for schoolchildren and the unemployed, and the legal framework in place, he aimed to develop Luxembourg as a center of electronic commerce.

Luxembourg's economy in 1998 continued its steady growth of the previous 15 years. Prime Minister Juncker attributed its success as follows: "As a small country we have the ability to make decisions quickly. As we say in Luxembourg: 'Schnellboot gegen Tank [the speedboat takes on the tank].' "   (ANNE ROBY)

MACEDONIA

Area: 25,713 sq km (9,928 sq mi)
Population (1998 est.): 2,023,000
Capital: Skopje
Chief of state: President Kiro Gligorov
Head of government: Prime Ministers
   Branko Crvenkovski and, from
   November 30, Ljubco Georgievski

Parliamentary elections were held in Macedonia on October 18 and November 1. Under a new election system, 35 deputies were elected on proportional lists and the remaining 85 under a single-mandate-constituency system. The nationalist Internal Macedonian Revolutionary Organization–Democratic Party for Macedonian National Unity won 49 seats, and its coalition partner, the newly formed Democratic Alternative, 13. The ruling Social Democratic Union of Macedonia garnered 27; their coalition partners, the Socialist Party, took 1; and the Liberal Democratic Party got 4. The two major Albanian parties had formed an electoral alliance; the Party for Democratic Prosperity (a government party for six years) won 14 seats and the Democratic Party of Albanians 10. One seat went to the Union of Roma.

IMRO-DPMNU and two other parties formed a coalition under Prime Minister

Ljubco Georgievski on November 30. Among his priorities Georgievski named economic reform, reduction of unemployment, the fight against corruption and organized crime, and integration into European and transatlantic structures.

Although relations between the Macedonian majority and the sizable ethnic Albanian minority remained problematic, there were no major incidents. The crisis in Kosovo bore on Macedonian Albanians, however, as they supported their brethren in the adjacent Serbian province. The government claimed that units of the Kosovo Liberation Front were also active in Macedonia.

Mindful of the Kosovo crisis, Pres. Kiro Gligorov and then-Prime Minister Branko Crvenkovski called for U.S. or NATO troops to be stationed in Macedonia after the mandate of the United Nations Preventive Deployment Force (UNPREDEP) expired. On July 21 UNPREDEP's mandate was extended to Feb. 28, 1999, and its strength was increased from 750 to more than 1,000 members. NATO's Partnership for Peace held large-scale maneuvers in September. Macedonia's small army was upgraded, with Germany supplying 60 armoured personnel carriers in October.

The economy experienced significant gross domestic product growth for the first time since independence. Inflation remained low, but unemployment and the very low rate of direct foreign investment were problems. In June seven people were sentenced for the collapse of a pyramid scheme in 1996 in which 23,000 people lost a total of about $65 million.   (STEFAN KRAUSE)

MADAGASCAR

Area: 587,041 sq km (226,658 sq mi)
Population (1998 est.): 14,463,000
Capital: Antananarivo
Chief of state and, from July 23, head of government: President Didier Ratsiraka
Head of government: Prime Ministers Pascal Rakotomavo and, from July 23, in a reduced role, Tantely Andrianarivo

In April 1998 the High Constitutional Court confirmed the results of a national referendum, held on March 15, in which 50.96% of the voters approved a set of amendments to the constitution. These not only shifted the country from a unitary to a federal system, involving the grant of a large measure of autonomy to the nation's six provinces, but also shifted power from the legislature to the executive branch, reducing the power of the National Assembly and creating a strong presidential regime.

In the election that followed in mid-May, the party of Pres. Didier Ratsiraka, the Vanguard of the Malagasy Revolution (AREMA), gained a more sweeping victory than expected over the main opposition party of former prime minister Norbert Ratsirahonana. Before the election AREMA had held a small minority of seats; afterward it had 63 seats in the 150-seat Assembly.

Mama Cecilia Kadzamila, partner of Hastings Banda, the former president of Malawi, sits at the foot of his coffin during his funeral on Dec. 3, 1997. Banda's death ended the rule of one of Africa's most brutal dictators.

The opposition spoke of fraud but accepted the result. In early July, 18 ministers left the government in an attempt to force Ratsiraka to replace the prime minister. When Prime Minister Pascal Rakotomavo resigned, Ratsiraka became head of government as well as chief of state, with a new prime minister, Tantely Andrianarivo, serving in a subsidiary capacity.

The country's economic crisis continued, with the International Monetary Fund threatening to withhold aid if the government did not pursue fiscal reforms, such as controlling inflation and improving tax collection. In addition, the World Bank continued to press for the privatization of state-owned enterprises such as Air Madagascar and Telecom Malagasy.
(CHRISTOPHER SAUNDERS)

MALAWI

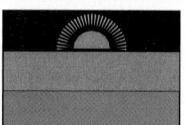

Area: 118,484 sq km (45,747 sq mi)
Population (1998 est.): 9,840,000
Capital: A capital is not designated in the 1994 constitution. Current government operations are divided between Lilongwe (ministerial and financial), Blantyre (executive and judicial), and Zomba (legislative)
Head of state and government: President Bakili Muluzi

The burial, on Dec. 3, 1997, of former president Hastings Banda in a new cemetery for presidents at Lilongwe was a significant event not only for his own country but for all of sub-Saharan Africa as yet another of the old-style single-minded figures who had led their countries to political independence was ushered from the scene. The visit to Malawi of U.K. Secretary for International Development Clare Short in early January 1998 was indicative of a less-flamboyant era. Her aim was to demonstrate Britain's commitment to assisting the world's least-developed countries through closer partnership.

On March 30 Pres. Bakili Muluzi reshuffled his Cabinet. One of the most significant changes was the transfer of responsibility for finance from Vice Pres. Justin Malawezi to Cassim Chilumpha, previously minister of justice and attorney general. Edda Chitalo, one of only two women in the 22-member Cabinet, assumed responsibility for the newly designated portfolio of human resources management and development. In preparation for the presidential and parliamentary elections scheduled to be held in 1999, the National Assembly passed a law on June 5 giving increased powers and a greater measure of independence to the electoral commission.   (KENNETH INGHAM)

MALAYSIA

Area: 329,733 sq km (127,311 sq mi)
Population (1998 est.): 22,083,000
Capital: Kuala Lumpur
Chief of state: *Yang di-Pertuan Agong* (Paramount Ruler) Tuanku Ja'afar ibni al-Marhum Tuanku Abdul Rahman
Head of government: Prime Minister Dato Seri Mahathir bin Mohamad

Malaysia had expected 1998 to be the year that it proudly showed off to the rest of the world the remarkable accomplishments of years of prosperity. The capital, Kuala Lumpur, played host to two high-profile international events, the Commonwealth Games (in which Malaysians won 10 gold medals and placed fourth in the competi-

tion) and the annual summit meeting of the Asia-Pacific Economic Cooperation (APEC) forum. As it turned out, however, both events were overshadowed by the biggest political convulsion in the country since the race riots of 1969.

The drama began on September 2, when Prime Minister Dato Seri Mahathir bin Mohamad fired Anwar Ibrahim from his posts as deputy premier and finance minister. One day later Anwar was expelled from the party, the dominant United Malays National Organization (UMNO). In the ensuing storm many Malaysians flocked to support him under the banner of *reformasi* ("reform" in Bahasa Malaysia), demanding an end to what they considered a corrupt political system. On September 20 Anwar was arrested under the Internal Security Act, a controversial law that allowed for detention without trial.

Anwar was soon released from detention but almost immediately was brought up on formal charges of corruption and sodomy. He appeared in court on September 29, pleading innocence to all charges. Photographs showing him with a black eye, suggesting that he had been beaten in custody, further inflamed the situation, sparking demonstrations well into October (although police managed to keep them from spinning out of control). Meanwhile, Anwar's wife, Wan Azizah, strongly defended her husband, describing charges of sexual misconduct as being a clumsy attempt to discredit him. The lurid trial was continuing at year's end.

At one time Anwar had been seen as the logical successor to Mahathir, who had been prime minister since 1981. In 1997 Mahathir seemed relaxed enough about the succession to take a two-month vacation from running the country's affairs, leaving it in Anwar's hands. The East Asian financial crisis and Malaysia's consequent deepening recession (once averaging 8% growth per annum, the country's economy contracted by an estimated 7% in 1998), however, helped precipitate the split between the two men. Anwar favoured maintaining open markets and international investment, whereas Mahathir was openly and often vocally suspicious of various international "plots" to undermine the Malaysian economy.

Their disagreement was presaged by the appointment of former finance minister Daim Zainuddin as a special economic adviser. Daim shared Mahathir's enthusiasm for low interest rates and increased public spending. Mahathir accompanied the firing of Anwar as finance minister (he took the portfolio for himself) by imposing controls on the Malaysian currency in order to remove it as an object of speculation and to permit the country to maintain lower interest rates than would be necessary to defend a free-floating currency.

Domestic politics impinged on foreign affairs when the presidents and prime ministers of 21 nations fronting the Pacific Ocean arrived in Kuala Lumpur for the annual APEC summit. Several, including Pres. Joseph Estrada of the Philippines (*see* BIOGRAPHIES) and U.S. Secretary of State Madeleine Albright, pointedly met with Wan Azizah to demonstrate their support for her husband. U.S. Vice Pres. Al Gore (substituting for Pres. Bill Clinton, who was distracted by the weapons-inspection crisis in Iraq) raised the stakes even higher when at

the annual banquet he likened *reformasi* to the People's Power Revolt in the Philippines and other democratic landmarks.

The year was also marked by spats with neighbouring Singapore, including the sovereignty over a railroad terminal in Singapore and Malaysia's refusal to allow the Singaporean air force to fly over its territory on training missions. Singapore's Senior Minister Lee Kuan Yew also ruffled some feathers with the publication of the first volume of his memoirs, which contained frank observations about some of Malaysia's founders.   (TODD CROWELL)

MALDIVES

Area: 298 sq km (115 sq mi)
Population (1998 est.): 270,000
Capital: Male
Head of state and government: President Maumoon Abdul Gayoom

Maldives began 1998 with a new constitution. Ratified on Nov. 27, 1997, it became law on January 1. The number of administrative atolls was increased from 19 to 20, and for the first time presidential elections with more than one candidate were held. Five candidates campaigned for the presidency, and in September the legislature voted for the incumbent, Maumoon Abdul Gayoom, who had won the nationwide referendum for a new five-year term with more than 90% of the vote. It was his fifth term as president.

In August Mohammed Nawaz Sharif, the prime minister of Pakistan, inaugurated the new parliament building in Male. It had been built by Pakistan as a gift for the people of Maldives.

On the tiny island of Kaashidhoo, President Gayoom on February 23 opened a climate observatory to gather data on climate changes and global warming. The low-lying Maldives, where the average altitude was only one metre (3.28 ft) above sea level, would be particularly vulnerable to the ef-

fects of global warming and subsequent rising sea levels. The multinational research project was led by the U.S. National Science Foundation.

Another project to keep Maldives above the waves was the creation of a new island near the capital island of Male. Work began in October 1997 to build Hulhumale 1.5 m (4.9 ft) above sea level. It was expected to be able to house some 125,000 people, about half the country's population.
(ANNE ROBY)

MALI

Area: 1,248,574 sq km (482,077 sq mi)
Population (1998 est.): 10,109,000
Capital: Bamako
Chief of state: President Alpha Oumar Konaré
Head of government: Prime Minister Ibrahima Boubacar Keita

Student unrest over inadequate grants forced the government to close all educational institutions on Jan. 8, 1998. Several student leaders were arrested. On January 22, after intense negotiations and the release of the jailed protesters, the Association of Schoolchildren and Students agreed to accept an initial increase of 5% on the understanding that a broad-based committee would be established to examine all aspects of the problem. On April 27 civil servants agreed to a 5% pay raise.

The ruling Alliance for Democracy in Mali won an easy victory on June 21 in the municipal elections for 19 existing communes, with opposition parties boycotting the repeatedly delayed poll. Elections for seats in 682 newly created communes were scheduled for November 29.

Rice production rose to record levels during the year owing to a large increase in acreage and the introduction of advanced technologies. On March 25 the government agreed to take the initial steps toward privatization of its water and power companies.

Wan Azizah, wife of Malaysian Deputy Premier and Finance Minister Anwar Ibrahim, speaks with reporters on November 13 as she leaves the court in Kuala Lumpur where her husband was being tried on charges of abuse of power and sexual misconduct. She described the charges as an attempt by Anwar's political enemies to discredit him.

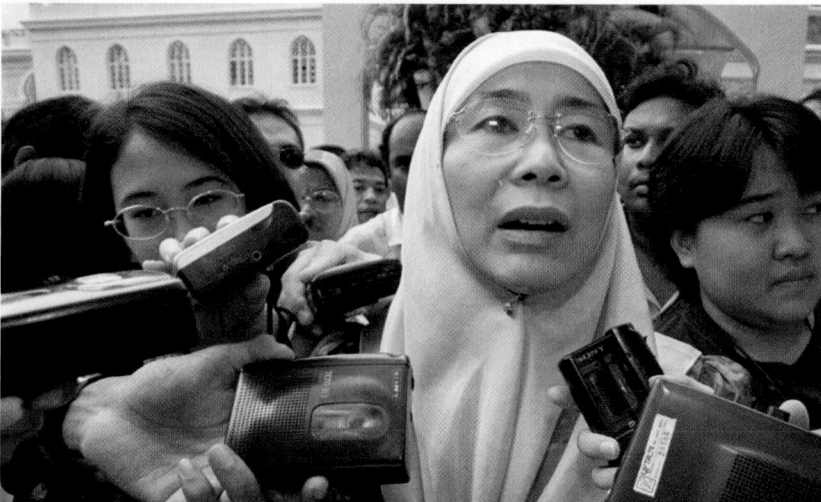

Cotton, the country's most important export crop, suffered from an unusually dry planting season in June. In July an agreement was signed between the government and a Japanese-Brazilian consortium to build a new cotton gin for the production of thread destined for the international market.

(NANCY ELLEN LAWLER)

MALTA

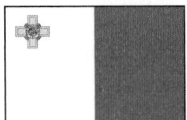

Area: 316 sq km (122 sq mi)
Population (1998 est.): 377,000
Capital: Valletta
Chief of state: President Ugo Mifsud Bonnici
Head of government: Prime Ministers Alfred Sant and, from September 6, Eddie Fenech Adami

The highlight of 1998 in Malta was the premature, unexpected change of government. Prime Minister Alfred Sant introduced into Parliament the Cottonera waterfront development project, in which local and American investments were involved. It was criticized by the opposition Nationalist Party and some from the Malta Labour Party. The prime minister declared that approval of the project was to be considered a vote of confidence in the government. On July 7 the motion to approve was defeated 35–34 as not only the Nationalist opposition but also former prime minister Dom Mintoff voted against it. Consequently, an early election was held on September 5, less than two years after the 1996 vote.

On a turnout of more than 95% of the eligible voters, the Nationalist Party returned to power with a five-seat majority, obtaining almost 52% of the votes, as against 47% polled by Labour. Immediately on taking office on September 6, the new prime minister, Eddie Fenech Adami, reactivated Malta's application of 1990 to join the European Union, which had been frozen by the Labour government in October 1996. The foreign ministers of the EU welcomed Malta's revived bid and ordered an assessment to establish whether the island qualified for membership and whether it would be part of the next EU enlargement.

(ALBERT GANADO)

MARSHALL ISLANDS

Area: 181 sq km (70 sq mi)
Population (1998 est.): 62,800
Capital: Majuro
Head of state and government: President Imata Kabua

In August 1998 Pres. Imata Kabua announced the formation of a new Cabinet; he recruited two former opposition senators and dismissed three ministers who had voted to ban gambling in the Marshall Islands. The new government was soon challenged in a vote of no confidence—the first in the nation's parliament in 19 years of constitutional government. The president and his supporters thwarted the move by withdrawing from the parliament for six weeks and thus denying it a quorum. When a vote was taken, the president survived by one vote in the 33-member assembly.

The nation continued to face serious economic difficulties, with inflation running at 10% and little investment because of the weak government and inadequate infrastructure. In June the government cut all state salaries by 12.5% but still faced a deficit at the end of the year.

Also contributing to the economic difficulties was a drought caused by the El Niño weather pattern. By April some islands were out of freshwater, and the U.S. provided assistance with desalination and water-purification equipment; water was also barged to some islands.   (BARRIE MACDONALD)

MAURITANIA

Area: 1,030,700 sq km (398,000 sq mi)
Population (1998 est.): 2,511,000
Capital: Nouakchott
Chief of state: President Col. Maaouya Ould Sidi Ahmad Taya
Head of government: Prime Ministers Mohamed Lemine Ould Guig and, from November 16, Cheikh Afia Ould Mohamed Khouna

The arrest of three human rights activists for participating in a French television program about slavery in Mauritania sparked protests by the country's lawyers, who went on a 24-hour strike in Nouakchott on Jan. 21, 1998. The Arab Regional Program for Human Rights Activists, based in Cairo, called on Arab governments and international human rights groups to pressure the government to free the three men. In February Morocco's Organization of Human Rights protested the arrest in Mauritania of a fourth person for antislavery activities. Sentences of 13 months each in prison were upheld by the appeals court in Nouakchott on March 24, but Pres. Maaouya Ould Sidi Ahmad Taya immediately pardoned the rights activists.

On April 12 clashes between Mauritanian refugees and Senegalese villagers in Kidira district, just south of the frontier, resulted in the death of seven persons, and three more

Maltese election officials count ballots a day after national elections were held on September 5. Claiming almost 52% of the votes, the Nationalist Party returned to power with a five-seat majority in Parliament. Nationalist Party leader Eddie Fenech Adami assumed the prime ministership on September 6.

died in additional incidents during the next week. On April 24 the Paris Club of creditor nations placed Mauritania on its list of heavily indebted nations expected to become eligible for special debt relief. President Taya reshuffled his government on July 12 and dismissed the ministers for foreign affairs and rural development.

The economy was expected to grow by about 5% in 1998, with inflation hovering around 4.7%. Work continued on a new investment code designed to increase private foreign participation in the economy, particularly in the mining and fishery sectors.

(NANCY ELLEN LAWLER)

MAURITIUS

Area: 2,040 sq km (788 sq mi)
Population (1998 est.): 1,157,000
Capital: Port Louis
Chief of state: President Cassam Uteem
Head of government: Prime Minister Navin Ramgoolam

Throughout 1998 Mauritius pursued bilateral economic agreements with southern African nations. In February Prime Minister Navin Ramgoolam visited South Africa, where he and Pres. Nelson Mandela signed a protection-of-investments agreement. In March Ramgoolam announced that Mauritius would join the proposed South Africa–Malaysia underwater cable and thus make Mauritius "a bridge between Asia and Africa." The Bank of Mauritius announced a joint venture with the South African Reserve Bank to implement an electronic payment system modeled on the South African Multiple Option Settlement system.

In August Mauritius refused to join other members of the Southern African Development Community (SADC) in sending troops to assist embattled Pres. Laurent Kabila of the Democratic Republic of the Congo. Mauritius was host of the September SADC summit, during which the agenda focused on economic integration and regional insecurity. Prime Minister Ramgoolam urged the adoption of a free-trade agreement. Late in the year the government revised its sales tax and debated reducing the public-sector payroll, measures prompted by fear of inflation and the Asian economic crisis. (MATTHEW A. CENZER)

MEXICO

Area: 1,958,201 sq km (756,066 sq mi)
Population (1998 est.): 95,830,000
Capital: Mexico City
Head of state and government: President Ernesto Zedillo Ponce de León

The year 1998 began on a sombre note for the administration of Pres. Ernesto Zedillo

Demonstrators calling for more action by the Mexican government to crack down on alleged money laundering protest outside a bank in Mexico City in May by hanging fake dollar bills on a clothesline. During the year officials from 12 of Mexico's largest banks were indicted on charges of laundering drug money.

Ponce de León. The country was still in a state of shock following the massacre of some 45 Indian peasants in the municipality of Chenalho within the impoverished southern state of Chiapas on Dec. 22, 1997. Those murdered and dozens more who were injured were alleged to be sympathizers of the Zapatista National Liberation Army (EZLN). It soon became apparent that government paramilitary groups may have been responsible for these acts of violence, and Attorney General Jorge Madrazo was sent to Chiapas to investigate this possibility. Meanwhile, the Interior Ministry, under the control of Emilio Chuayffet, responded to the episode by intensifying troop movements in Chiapas, drawing widespread criticism. Chuayffet's general approach to the massacre was viewed as flawed, and on Jan. 3, 1998, he resigned. He was quickly replaced by Agriculture Minister Francisco Labastida Ochoa.

Zedillo also took the opportunity to announce on January 5, that former foreign minister (and chief debt negotiator) Angel Gurria would become finance minister; that office had been vacated by Guillermo Ortiz when his appointment as governor of the central bank (Banco de Mexico) was confirmed in late December 1997. One of Gurria's first acts in his new post was to announce cuts in spending in an effort to help offset the low level of income from oil (which accounted for about 40% of budget revenues) and the less-favourable economic environment as the Asian financial crisis continued to unfold. Additional budget cuts were announced in late March and July.

Further Cabinet changes were made on May 13, with the appointment of former interior secretary Esteban Moctezuma Barragán as social development secretary and the replacement of Javier Bonilla as labour secretary by the head of the state workers' social security institute, José Antonio González. Moctezuma was a close associate of Zedillo, and so his appointment was viewed as a possible signal that he might be groomed as Zedillo's successor as the presidential nominee of the ruling

Institutional Revolutionary Party (PRI) in the elections scheduled for 2000. Zedillo, however, continued to emphasize that he did not intend to adhere to the PRI's long-standing tradition of the president choosing his successor and wished the party to make the choice.

On May 19 relations with the U.S. were undermined temporarily when U.S. authorities announced that officials from 12 of Mexico's largest 19 banks were being indicted on charges of laundering drug money. This followed a secret investigation known as Operation Casablanca and appeared to contradict the spirit of an alliance formed between the two countries a year earlier in which the U.S. undertook to observe Mexican sovereignty and work as a partner in the offensive against the drug cartels.

Developments for most of the year appeared to preclude significant progress toward a definitive peace settlement with the EZLN in Chiapas. Evidence of further militarization and the resignation in early June of mediator Bishop Samuel Ruiz as well as the collapse of the organization he chaired raised tensions and reinforced the Zapatistas' reluctance to return to the negotiations, which had been stalled since early 1997. Devastating floods in Chiapas in September and dissatisfaction with the conduct of state elections on October 4 did not help the situation, but progress again seemed possible when the EZLN on October 18 offered to restart talks with the congressional commission for peace and reconciliation. Negotiations collapsed again in late November.

Although the PRI appeared to have adjusted to some extent to having lost its majority control of the Chamber of Deputies following the July 1997 elections, a major problem arose in connection with banking reform proposals submitted in April. These included the incorporation into the domestic debt of some $65 billion of bad bank loans incurred in the wake of the 1994–95 financial crisis. This move was opposed by the two main opposition parties, the Democratic Revolutionary Party (PRD) and

the National Action Party (PAN), and they succeeded in early June in winning an audit of the scheme, which delayed further consideration of the matter until the final quarter of the year. By early November it appeared that compromise proposals (to convert two-thirds of the original total into public debt) might be close, with PAN likely to back the government. Both PAN and the PRI were, however, pressing for Ortiz to be called to account for the poor handling of the original scheme. On December 30, just 36 hours before the constitutional deadline, PAN and PRI deputies agreed on an unusually austere budget that would entail spending cuts well beyond the 10% or so planned by Zedillo's government.

In regard to other economic matters, growth was slowed by international conditions, especially the financial crisis in Asia. Continuing strong demand from the

GREG BAKER—AP/WIDE WORLD

Sanjaasurengiyn Oyun lights incense at a shrine to her murdered brother, Zorig, at her family's home in Ulaanbaatar, Mongolia. The October 2 murder of Zorig, the leader of the 1989 Mongolian democracy movement, shattered the peace that had marked the nine-year transition from communism to free-market democracy.

U.S., however, helped to ensure that the annual rise in gross domestic product would be over 4%, as compared with 7% in 1997. Inflation appeared likely to exceed the official target ceiling of 12%, with about 15% seeming probable for the year (after 15.7% in 1997). The weakening of the peso to about 10 per $1 from about 8 at the end of 1997, together with moves ending subsidies on staples such as tortillas, contributed to the upward pressure on prices.

Following years when the trade account was in surplus—more than $7 billion in 1995 and over $6 billion in 1996—the surplus declined in 1997 to $624 million as the nation's economic recovery continued. This development intensified during 1998, with a first-half deficit of more than $3 billion rising to more than $5 billion by the end of the year. The current account was also moving more sharply into deficit and was expected to total about $15 billion for the year, compared with $10.8 billion projected in the original budget forecast.

(SUSAN M. CUNNINGHAM)

The government of the Federated States of Micronesia continued with its restructuring program in 1998, though an audit during the year was critical of its planning, implementation, and financial controls. The program aimed to reduce the size of the public sector in anticipation of the expiration of the current Compact of Free Association with the United States and indications that the new agreement would not match the $1,355,000,000 that the U.S. granted under the current (1986–2001) compact.

Throughout the year Micronesia was affected by the drought associated with the El Niño weather phenomenon. In November 1997 legislation to cover water-conservation-and-distribution projects had been introduced, and in February a state of emergency was declared. Many atolls ran out of freshwater, crops were damaged, and public health suffered; there was a noticeable increase in the incidence of hepatitis, gastrointestinal diseases, and cholera. U.S. Pres. Bill Clinton approved $6.5 million in disaster relief.   (BARRIE MACDONALD)

Elections to the Moldovan Parliament held on March 22, 1998, were won by the Party of Moldovan Communists (PCM) with 30% of the vote. The PCM was forced into opposition, however, by a loose centre-right coalition known as the Alliance for Democracy and Reforms (ADR) and made up of the Democratic Convention of Moldova, the pro-presidential Movement for a Democratic and Prosperous Moldova (MMDP), and the Party of Democratic Forces. Through his proxies in the MMDP, Pres. Petru Lucinschi was able to steer the composition of the new Cabinet and ensure that Prime Minister Ion Ciubuc and the foreign affairs, defense, and security ministers retained their posts. This patched-together government was eventually approved by Parliament on May 21. Growing dissent within the ADR soon undermined the effectiveness of both the Cabinet and the legislature, however. On July 31 the PMDP joined forces with the communist opposition in Parliament to approve the transit of radioactive waste from the nuclear energy plant on the Danube River at Kozloduy, Bulg., through Moldova to Russia, much to the dismay of their ADR partners.

Relations with the breakaway Transdniester region remained tense despite a mediation summit held on March 20 in Odessa, Ukraine, with the good offices of Ukrainian Pres. Leonid D. Kuchma and Russian Prime Minister Viktor S. Chernomyrdin.

Moldova's economy was seriously affected by the Russian financial crisis. Russia formerly had received over 60% of the country's exports. Moldova's foreign debts reached some $1.3 billion, but the national currency remained relatively stable.

(DAN IONESCU)

MICRONESIA, FEDERATED STATES OF

Area: 701 sq km (271 sq mi)
Population (1998 est.): 108,000
Capital: Palikir, on Pohnpei
Head of state and government: President Jacob Nena

MOLDOVA

Area: 33,700 sq km (13,000 sq mi)
Population (1998 est.): 4,243,000
Capital: Chisinau
Chief of state: President Petru Lucinschi
Head of government: Prime Minister Ion Ciubuc

MONACO

Area: 1.95 sq km (0.75 sq mi)
Population (1998 est.): 32,000
Chief of state: Prince Rainier III
Head of government: Minister of State
Michel Leveque

In legislative elections held in February 1998 for the 18-member National Council, the National and Democratic Union Party won 15 seats in the first round of voting on February 1 and the 3 remaining seats on February 8. The two other political parties that fielded candidates failed to win a seat. On February 19 Michel Leveque was reappointed minister of state.

Prince Albert piloted Monaco's bobsled team in the Winter Olympic Games in February. Earlier that month he had traveled to Japan on an official visit to foster Japanese investment in his country. Speculation continued about when he might succeed his father, Prince Rainier III, as chief of state. (ANNE ROBY)

MONGOLIA

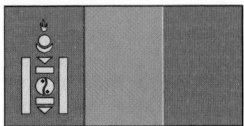

Area: 1,566,500 sq km (604,800 sq mi)
Population (1998 est.): 2,413,000
Capital: Ulaanbaatar
Chief of state: President Natsagiyn Bagabandi
Head of government: Prime Ministers Mendsaikhan Enkhsaikhan until April 20, Tsakhiagiyn Elbegdorj from April 23 until July 24, and, from December 9, Janlaviyn Narantstatsralt

In March 1998 the ruling Democratic Alliance (DA) coalition of National Democrats and Social Democrats decided to appoint the leader of the National Democrats, Tsakhiagiyn Elbegdorj, head of the parliamentary coalition. The government of Prime Minister Mendsaikhan Enkhsaikhan resigned on April 20, and on April 23 Elbegdorj was appointed prime minister. Soon afterward his government approved the merger of the bankrupt state-owned Reconstruction Bank with the private Golomt Bank. Alleging that ministers had obtained loans from the Reconstruction Bank just before it collapsed, the ex-communist People's Revolutionary Party (MPRP) boycotted the Great Hural (parliament). When the government modified the merger and then canceled it, the MPRP returned to the Great Hural to introduce a no-confidence motion, which was carried 42–33 on July 24. As a result, the Elbegdorj government resigned.

The DA decided to nominate Davaadorjiyn Ganbold, the chairman of the Great Hural's Economic Standing Committee, to be the next prime minister. Pres. Natsagiyn Bagabandi rejected him,

however, on the grounds that he had done nothing to resolve the bank-merger dispute. President Bagabandi proposed his own candidate, Dogsomyn Ganbold (not related), a National Democrat member of the Great Hural, but he was ignored by the DA leadership, which proposed Rinchinnyamyn Amarjargal, the acting minister of external relations. President Bagabandi accepted Amarjargal's nomination, but on September 2 it was rejected by the Great Hural by one vote. The murder on October 2 of the leader of the 1989 Mongolian democratic revolution, Sanjaasurengiyn Zorig, acting minister of infrastructure development, deprived the DA of another potential prime minister. Finally, on December 9, the political crisis was ended when Janlaviyn Narantsatsralt, the mayor of Ulaan Bataar, was approved as prime minister by the Great Hural.
(ALAN J.K. SANDERS)

MOROCCO

Area: 710,850 sq km (274,461 sq mi), including the 252,120-sq km (97,344-sq mi) area of the disputed Western Sahara annexation
Population (1998 est.): 28,060,000, of which Western Sahara 288,000.
Capital: Rabat
Head of state and government: King Hassan II, assisted by Prime Minister 'Abd al-Latif Filali and, from February 4, 'Abd ar-Rahman Youssoufi

The new parliamentary system in Morocco was introduced in January 1998 with the appointment of presidents for the upper and lower chambers. In February the veteran Socialist Union of Popular Forces leader, 'Abd ar-Rahman Youssoufi, was asked to form a government, and in March the new coalition government was announced, with the interior, defense, justice, foreign affairs, and religious portfolios remaining unchanged. Its policies were to be directed toward a resolution of the long-standing Western Sahara dispute, social issues, and bureaucratic reform. Economic policy would remain fundamentally unchanged, though, in a bid to maximize agricultural output, import taxes on grains were doubled to encourage domestic production.

The determination of the new government to break with the past soon became evident. The prime minister, during meetings with his North African counterparts, encouraged the revival of the regional Arab Maghreb Union and sought to reduce tensions with Algeria despite disagreements over Western Sahara. The remaining political prisoners were released, and the exiled Abraham Serfaty had his Moroccan passport restored as the justice system was overhauled. The draft budget in June sought to cut unemployment and reduce administrative costs while raising spending on health and housing without increases in taxation.

Progress on the Western Sahara issue was less encouraging. A dispute continued over the status of three tribes, totaling 65,000 persons, and, despite the registration of 147,000 persons as voters in the proposed referendum for self-determination, the referendum itself had to be delayed a year beyond its December 1998 deadline. The new government appeared as determined as its predecessors to ensure a Moroccan victory despite considerable external support for the opposition Polisario Front, particularly from Algeria.

The Asian and Russian crises had marginal direct effects on the Moroccan economy, although concern was expressed that cheap Asian exports might hurt Morocco's exports to Europe, and citrus exports to Russia were expected to be cut. The key to economic performance, as ever, was the agricultural sector. Good rains ensured an improved grain output, and gross domestic product grew by an estimated 7%, compared with a decline in 1997. (GEORGE JOFFÉ)

New Moroccan Prime Minister 'Abd ar-Rahman Youssoufi (left) pays his respects to King Hassan II (right) during a ceremony in Rabat on March 3 that marked the 37th anniversary of the king's ascension to the throne. Youssoufi's new coalition government was announced the same month.

MOZAMBIQUE

Area: 812,379 sq km (313,661 sq mi)
Population (1998 est.): 18,641,000
Capital: Maputo
Head of state and government: President
Joaquim Chissano, assisted by Prime
Minister Pascoal Mocumbi

In a speech on Jan. 1, 1998, Pres. Joaquim
Chissano expressed satisfaction with the
country's economic achievements in 1997.
Gross domestic product grew 6.6% during the
year, and inflation fell below 10% (a figure
later corrected to 5.8%). Looking forward to
1998, he said that the government hoped to
achieve economic growth of 9.5% and keep
inflation below 10%, but he did not conceal
his concern about the high rate of unemployment and the heavy burden of foreign debt.

Among the measures adopted by the government to improve the economic situation
was a joint initiative with South Africa and
Swaziland, announced in May, to attract investment in tourism and agriculture in the
border region of the three countries. This
initiative involved a commitment to build
and improve road communications. Steady
progress was also made in opening up the
Maputo "corridor" to facilitate the transport
of goods between the Mozambican port of
Maputo and Witbank, in the industrial heartland of South Africa, and eventually across
the continent. (*See* TRANSPORTATION:
Sidebar.)

A meeting of the International Monetary
Fund, World Bank, and other creditors in
April brought further hope with the promise
of a reduction in the country's foreign debt
by $1.4 billion in June 1999, subject to the
government's continuing to implement the
program of economic and social reform laid
down by the IMF. This was intended to reduce the overall debt to what the IMF
deemed to be a "sustainable level."
Satisfaction with the announcement was
quickly muted, however, when it appeared
that the IMF had based its proposals on figures that differed from those on which the
government had made its own forecast. The
IMF had foreseen increased revenue from
exports, which seemed unlikely in view of
the fall in world prices for cotton and the
decline in shipments of cashew nuts.
Meanwhile, workers taking part in the May
Day parade through Maputo protested that
the 13.5% rise in the statutory minimum
wage proposed by the government was
wholly inadequate. In addition, major industrial projects intended to boost the economy were still on the drawing board. During
a visit in October, Portuguese Prime
Minister António Guterres agreed to a
rescheduling of Mozambique's debt and a
loan to renovate the Cuamba-Lichinga railway in the north of the country.

On the political front, the Mozambique
National Resistance (Renamo) and other opposition parties boycotted the local elections
held in June. Renamo protested that the government had refused to include opposition
party officials in the independent bodies appointed to supervise the voting.

(KENNETH INGHAM)

MYANMAR (BURMA)

Area: 676,577 sq km (261,228 sq mi)
Population (1998 est.): 47,305,000
Capital: Yangon (Rangoon)
Head of state and government: Chairman
of the State Peace and Development
Council Gen. Than Shwe

Myanmar witnessed in 1998 increased confrontation between the State Peace and
Development Council (SPDC; a military
junta) and the opposition National League
for Democracy (NLD). Although the SPDC
attempted to present a less-authoritarian image than the preceding ruling junta, it nevertheless suppressed dissension as harshly
and swiftly as its predecessor. In April San
San, a prominent NLD member who was
elected to the parliament in 1990, was sentenced to 25 years in prison for having criticized the country's military government in
a radio interview.

On June 23 the NLD sent an ultimatum
to the SPDC calling on the government to
convene by August 21 the parliament, in
which the NLD had won a majority in the
1990 elections that were subsequently annulled by the government. The SPDC ignored the demand and instead clamped
down on opposition dissent. On July 17,
dozens of MPs were arrested for defying
the new government restrictions requiring
them to report twice a day to authorities in
their respective townships.

On July 24 the government prevented
NLD leader Daw Aung San Suu Kyi from
attending a meeting with other party colleagues, blocking her car approximately 50
km (30 mi) from the capital. Suu Kyi refused to back down and remained in the car
for six days until government forces forced
her to return to her home. On September 2
almost 4,000 students, demanding the convening of the parliament, staged the biggest
protest against the government in nearly two
years. In a move to preempt further opposition action, including the convening of the
parliament, the government arrested 110
NLD members on September 6.

By September 9 the number of party
members arrested had increased to 220, and,
according to sources in the NLD, by mid-
September more than 900 NLD members
had been detained since May, with 196 of
them MPs elected in 1990. This was the
biggest wave of arrests since the pro-democracy demonstrations of 1988. Undeterred by
the SPDC's arrests, a 10-member NLD committee, including Suu Kyi, declared that it
would act as the country's legitimate government until a formal parliamentary session
was called and that all laws issued by the
SPDC were null and void.

There were 54 more arrests in October
following street demonstrations at the university and near the Sule pagoda in downtown
Yangon. The UN human rights investigator
for Myanmar was again denied entry into
the country in November. Rumours circulated in late December that the SPDC might
be planning to deport Suu Kyi and close
down the NPD early in 1999.

(CLAUDE RAKISITS)

NAMIBIA

Area: 825,118 sq km (318,580 sq mi)
Population (1998 est.): 1,622,000
Capital: Windhoek
Chief of state and head of government:
President Sam Nujoma, assisted by
Prime Minister Hage Geingob

The ruling South West Africa People's
Organization (SWAPO) in August 1998
gave its backing to a third term for Pres.
Sam Nujoma, even though this required
amending the constitution. Though many
opposed a third term, SWAPO clearly did
not want a contest between contenders for
the post. Nujoma then showed his hand by
agreeing to send Namibian troops to the
Democratic Republic of the Congo (Congo
[Kinshasa]). Fighting alongside Angolan
forces, the Namibians helped the regime of
Laurent Kabila survive against rebel attacks.
In protest against SWAPO's support for a
third term and the sending of troops to the
Congo (Kinshasa), the Namibian ambassador in London, Ben Ulenga, resigned in
late August but appeared not to have a clear
strategy to challenge those in power.

A strongly authoritarian culture continued
to undermine Namibia's democratic preten-
sions. Annoyed at criticism of the dam and
hydroelectric project at Epupa on the
Kunene River and of his decision to send
troops to the Congo, Nujoma sometimes
chose to single out whites and threaten them
with possible expulsion. The country's dispute with Botswana over two islands on
their joint border remained unresolved, and
Namibia's declared intention to divert water
from the Kavango River caused further tension, for Botswana feared its Okavango
Delta would become a desert.

Namibia's currency, tied to the South
African rand, fell by 30% in the worldwide
financial crisis that began in May. Economic
problems elsewhere reduced demand for
Namibian minerals. One of the country's
largest mines, at Tsumeb, was forced to
close, with a loss of thousands of jobs.

(CHRISTOPHER SAUNDERS)

NAURU

Area: 21.2 sq km (8.2 sq mi)
Population (1998 est.): 10,500
Capital: Government offices in Yaren
district
Head of state and government:
Presidents Kinza Clodumar and, from
June 18, Bernard Dowiyogo

Nauru increased its world stature in 1998
when Pres. Kinza Clodumar announced in
January that the island republic would apply
for full membership in the United Nations.
Also during the year Clodumar's reputation
as a leading voice in the Pacific environ-

mental debate resulted in Nauru's becoming a full member of the Commonwealth. In the spring Clodumar told the Asian Development Bank board of governors, meeting in Geneva, that the current economic climate jeopardized many of the reforms being taken by Pacific Island governments at the urging of the bank.

Nevertheless, Clodumar lost a no-confidence vote in the parliament on June 18. Veteran politician Bernard Dowiyogo was subsequently re-elected president of Nauru by all 18 MPs. (A.R.G. GRIFFITHS)

NEPAL

Area: 147,181 sq km (56,827 sq mi)
Population (1998 est.): 21,959,000
Capital: Kathmandu
Chief of state: King Birendra Bir Bikram Shah Dev
Head of government: Prime Ministers Surya Bahadur Thapa and, from April 15, Girija Prasad Koirala

Prime Minister Surya Bahadur Thapa, leader of the National Democratic Party, incited political disorder on Jan. 8, 1998, when he asked King Birendra to dissolve the parliament and set a date for new elections. Thapa requested early elections following a threatened vote of no confidence by the opposition United Communist Party of Nepal–Marxist and Leninist. The king remained undecided about the issue and, after referring it to the Supreme Court for advice, decided to support the opposition's call for a special session of the parliament to discuss the no-confidence motion. On February 20 Thapa's government survived the vote and thus ended the constitutional crisis.

As agreed upon when the coalition government was formed in 1997, Prime Minister Thapa conceded the prime ministership to Girija Prasad Koirala, the leader of the Nepali Congress Party, the largest of the coalition partners. Thirteen NCP-UML ministers resigned en masse on December 15, but Koirala was able to strike an agreement with the communists and form a new coalition, with himself continuing as prime minister, on December 21.

Almost 250 people were killed in monsoon-induced floods and landslides between June and September, particularly in the lowlands of the central and southeastern Terai region. (CLAUDE RAKISITS)

NETHERLANDS, THE

Area: 41,526 sq km (16,033 sq mi)
Population (1998 est.): 15,691,000
Capital: Amsterdam; seat of government, The Hague
Chief of state: Queen Beatrix
Head of government: Prime Minister Wim Kok

At the Royal Palace in Kathmandu on April 15, Nepal's King Birendra (centre) administers the oath of office to newly appointed Prime Minister Girija Prasad Koirala (right) and Deputy Prime Minister Shailaja Acharya (left). Koirala, leader of the Nepali Congress Party, had served as prime minister from 1991–94. Acharya was Koirala's niece.

Local elections were held throughout The Netherlands on March 4, 1998. They were regarded as the final test for the administration of Prime Minister Wim Kok before the general elections in May. The coalition of the liberal parties—People's Party for Freedom and Democracy (VVD) and Democrats 66 (D66)—and the Labour Party as a whole withstood the challenge to their dominance. D66 lost half of its support, but this was balanced by a slight growth of the other parties. The radical right-wing Centre Democratic Party was defeated decisively, losing all of its seats in the large cities.

General elections for the 150-seat Second Chamber of the parliament took place on May 6. Substantial victories were achieved by the Labour Party of Prime Minister Wim Kok, which increased its representation in the Chamber from 37 to 45 seats; the VVD, up from 31 to 38; and the socialist-ecologist Green Left Party, up from 5 to 11. Though

The town of Hoogezand in The Netherlands is inundated by floodwater in late October. Days of relentless rain spelled trouble for many parts of The Netherlands beginning in September.

D66 suffered a loss of 10 seats, the coalition strengthened its position in the parliament. The largest opposition group, the centre-right Christian Democratic Appeal, lost five seats, down from 34 to 29. The party had dominated Dutch politics for many years until losing in the election of 1994.

Prime Minister Kok inaugurated his new Cabinet on August 3. The major change involved the resignation of Hans van Mierlo as minister of foreign affairs and his replacement by Jozias van Aartsen. Van Mierlo, a leading light of D66, retired from political life.

In September Queen Beatrix gave her traditional speech to open the new parliamentary year. She forecast that the nation's economic growth would slow down somewhat in the near future. Government budgets for the first time in years would be increased slightly. Growth in private consumption was expected. The Netherlands was one of the 11 nations whose participation in the EU's economic and monetary union was formally endorsed on May 3.

Beginning in September, continual rainfall caused serious trouble for The Netherlands. During September much of the nation's southwest was inundated. In October and November the northeast suffered comparable damage. Agricultural losses were extensive. The only positive aspect was that the project to strengthen the dikes along the major rivers was almost completed.   (KLAAS J. HOEKSEMA)

NEW ZEALAND

Area: 270,534 sq km (104,454 sq mi)
Population (1998 est.): 3,801,000
Capital: Wellington
Chief of state: Queen Elizabeth II, represented by Governor-General Sir Michael Hardie-Boys
Head of government: Prime Minister Jennifer Shipley

Throughout 1998 New Zealand political alliances continued to react to the resignation in November 1997 of Prime Minister Jim Bolger at the urging of his National Party members of Parliament. Dissatisfied with the influence of coalition partner New Zealand First, the legislators installed Transport Minister Jennifer Shipley as prime minister. She was given the responsibility of cutting the coalition partner down to size while maintaining legislative voting strength that would enable her minority government to stay in power. In August 1998 she sacked as treasurer the junior party's leader Winston Peters, divided that party by retaining some of its ministers, installed a National Party colleague as her deputy in place of Peters, and saw the coalition collapse a few days later.

With fast-moving parliamentary leaders negotiating sporadic support for the minority government on various issues, Shipley aimed for credible control over legislation, which included relaxed criteria for immigration. Some of the New Zealand First team she had retained in the Cabinet pro-

vided a basis for support in Parliament; they were assisted when it suited them by the right-wing ACT New Zealand and various independent legislators who could be courted at certain times. The situation was precarious, but the minority government managed to hold on.

Peters's sacking followed his walkout from a stalemated meeting of a coalition disputes committee; he was followed by the Cabinet ministers from his party. Subsequently, Peters's New Zealand First party fell apart, and he was left as leader of the remnants but with no government role. In a revamped Cabinet named at the end of August, Shipley promoted Education Minister Wyatt Creech as her deputy. Next in seniority were Bill Birch (finance), John Luxton (agriculture), Bill English (health), and Max Bradford (commerce), who rose from 19th to 6th.

New Zealand Prime Minister Jennifer Shipley (right) listens to Australian Prime Minister John Howard as he speaks at a press conference in Sydney on February 20. Among other topics, the two leaders discussed economic relations between New Zealand and Australia and the impact that the Asian financial crisis would have on their countries.

DAVID GRAY—REUTERS

As treasurer, Peters had left behind, with his mid-May budget, a "tough-love" welfare regime that would require some who were receiving unemployment benefits to prove an interest in working for their living or else have their benefits reduced. In budgeting for a healthy surplus, he began the process of abolishing tariffs on imported automobiles, increased spending on education by $197 million and on health by 6%, and increased the tax on gasoline by 2.1 cents per litre. The budget confirmed that the impact of the Asian financial crisis would delay the proposed tax cuts until at least 2000–01. New Zealand was technically in recession from about mid-September. Gross domestic product had declined for two consecutive quarters, and the economy was growing at its slowest rate since 1993.

In other developments the government in October completed a $170 million land grievance settlement with the major tribe of the South Island, Ngai Tahu. During February and March, Auckland suffered a five-week electrical blackout caused by the failure of power cables.

(JOHN A. KELLEHER)

NICARAGUA

Area: 131,812 sq km (50,893 sq mi)
Population (1998 est.): 4,763,000
Capital: Managua
Head of state and government: President Arnoldo Alemán

The weather was the most important topic in Nicaragua in 1998. Early in the year the El Niño phenomenon caused serious drought in the north, with some 50,000 families affected by hunger. The World Food Programme launched a U.S. $3.2 million emergency aid scheme in May. The drought also led to the loss through fire of large areas of tropical forest.

A greater disaster struck in late October, however, in the form of two weeks of heavy rains that accompanied Hurricane Mitch, which some called the worst storm in the Atlantic basin in 200 years. Mitch hit Honduras hardest, but Nicaragua reported more damage than it suffered in the 1972 Managua earthquake. There were 1,845 confirmed deaths by the end of the year, with perhaps half a million homeless. Some 250 mm (10 in) of rain fell, causing large-scale flooding and mud slides. The crater lake on Casita volcano was breached on October 30, covering several villages in deep mud. The infrastructure of the country was badly damaged. Early estimates were that 30% of the coffee crop was destroyed. International relief was quick in coming, although distribution locally was often sluggish.

Divisions within the opposition Sandinista National Liberation Front (FSLN) were sharpened by the accusations made in March 1998 by Zoilamérica Narváez Murillo, FSLN leader Daniel Ortega's stepdaughter, that she was sexually abused and raped by him in her youth. Reflecting support inside and outside the party, Ortega was overwhelmingly reelected secretary-general in May. His wife, Rosario Murillo, and Narváez's brother rejected the charges, which a criminal court dismissed on a technicality. Narváez, herself a Sandinista member, was backed by a dissident faction, led by Henry Petrie, which was expelled from the FSLN over the issue.

In March the International Monetary Fund (IMF) authorized a $136 million enhanced structural-adjustment facility for the country. The IMF, however, requested further reforms in the tax and social security systems and in public administration. Under IMF terms Nicaragua was to sell parts of the

state telecommunications company, Enitel, in 1999. The proceeds would be directed toward foreign reserves, infrastructure investment, and housing. (BEN BOX)

NIGER

Area: 1,267,000 sq km (489,000 sq mi)
Population (1998 est.): 9,672,000
Capital: Niamey
Head of state and government: President Gen. Ibrahim Baré Maïnassara, assisted by Prime Minister Ibrahim Assane Mayaki

The government's decision to concentrate on reducing its heavy external debt at the expense of public-sector salaries caused prolonged unrest during 1998. Teachers, unpaid for the previous seven months, walked out on January 19. On February 21 soldiers in Diffa mutinied, demanding four months of salary arrears. The mutiny quickly spread to Agadez and Zinder. On February 27 university students in Niamey demonstrated in support of the mutineers and also protested the nonpayment of their grants for 20 months, which prompted the government to close the university. Although soldiers returned to their barracks on March 1, after having been promised immediate payment of two months of salary, the political crisis deepened. The alliance of eight opposition parties, the Front for the Restoration and Defense of Democracy, organized protests throughout the country calling for the resignation of Pres. Ibrahim Baré Maïnassara. New battles between security forces and students in Niamey erupted on April 18 as students demanded the reopening of the university and payment of their grants. Disturbances lasted for more than a week before calm returned to the capital. At the end of May, members of the Republican Guard, who were responsible for state security, revolted. They had not been paid for several months. The government attempted to defuse the unrest throughout the country by various promises to meet wage demands, but even the amount owed to its 40,000 civil servants seemed unlikely to be paid without a fresh infusion of emergency aid.

On July 31 Niger's opposition parties reached an agreement with the government over reforms of the electoral system and consequently agreed to participate in the local elections scheduled for November but postponed until February 1999. A peace accord between the government and the Toubou rebels of the Democratic Renewal Front, the only Tuareg group not to have signed the 1997 general peace agreement, was reached in August.

Heavy rains fell in August and September, damaging roads and bridges and leaving 30,000 homeless.

(NANCY ELLEN LAWLER)

NIGERIA

Area: 923,768 sq km (356,669 sq mi)
Population (1998 est.): 110,532,000
Capital: Abuja; judiciary and some ministries remain in Lagos, the former capital
Head of state and government: Chairmen of the Provisional Ruling Council Gen. Sani Abacha and, from June 9, Gen. Abdulsalam Abubakar

At the beginning of 1998, Nigeria teetered on a precipice. Gen. Sani Abacha, the country's head of state, maintained his iron grip on the government. The regime continued to arrest potential rivals and activists calling for democratic reforms, including former chief of general staff Lieut. Gen. Oladipo Diya and more than 20 others for allegedly planning a coup.

To deflect growing opposition Abacha announced that democratic elections would be

AP/WIDE WORLD

Survivors of a flood triggered by Hurricane Mitch look over a washed-out portion of the Pan-American Highway near Posoltega, Nicaragua. In late October the powerful hurricane tore through Central America, producing torrential rain and creating winds as high as 241 km/h (150 mph). Mitch left at least 1,845 persons dead and hundreds of others missing in Nicaragua.

held on August 1. International observers and democracy activists in Nigeria denounced the proposal, noting that Abacha intended to remain in office by holding noncompetitive elections. The Nigerian government also tried to divert criticism by intervening in other West African countries. In February Nigerian troops routed a military-led rebel government in Sierra Leone and restored its exiled president, Ahmad Tejan Kabbah.

PETER OBE—AP/WIDE WORLD

A Nigerian man holds up spent bullets fired by riot police during a demonstration in Lagos following the sudden death of Gen. Sani Abacha, Nigeria's head of state, on June 8. Abacha was replaced by Gen. Abdulsalam Abubakar despite calls by opposition leaders to install the imprisoned Chief Moshood Abiola as president. Abiola's death on July 7 sparked further violence.

Economic woes reflected and contributed to political instability and repression. Nigeria's currency, the naira, plummeted, which required the government to intervene in foreign exchange markets. The country also suffered constant fuel, electricity, and water shortages. In response the government halted its public-investment program, which was intended to reduce unemployment and poverty as well as reverse the collapse of education and health systems. The government instead poured money into Abacha's upcoming presidential campaign.

With no real reform in sight, anti-Abacha opposition intensified. A new opposition party emerged, the United Action for Democracy (UAD), which comprised 26 human rights and pro-democracy groups. The UAD called for a popular democratic government, the immediate and unconditional release of political prisoners, and the immediate transfer of power from the military to a transitional government of national unity. The UAD insisted that the new government be headed by jailed leader Chief Moshood Abiola, the undeclared winner of the annulled presidential elections held in 1993. On March 3 the UAD organized a march in

Lagos that was broken up by police using tear gas and clubs.

At the end of April, Abacha took stronger measures to solidify his hold on power. General Diya and five others were sentenced to death, and the government stepped up its public relations campaign. Army officers were forced to wear Abacha lapel pins, and the presidential campaign handed out discounted television sets and sacks of rice.

Abacha also arranged for the country's five legal political parties to endorse him as the sole presidential candidate. This maneuver prompted the vast majority of Nigerians to boycott elections for a national assembly. In May violent antigovernment protests broke out in Ibadan, Nigeria's second largest city, and 38 activists were arrested.

On June 8 Abacha suddenly died of an apparent heart attack. (*See* OBITUARIES.) He was replaced by his chief of defense staff, Gen. Abdulsalam Abubakar. (*See* BIOGRAPHIES.) Opposition leaders called for the regime to install Abiola as president of a transitional government. Instead, Abubakar released nine prominent political prisoners, including former head of state Gen. Olusegun Obasanjo, but Abiola remained behind bars, and his health deteriorated rapidly. Several weeks later Abiola died, and violent demonstrations erupted in his native southwestern Nigeria. (*See* OBITUARIES.)

Abubakar implemented some important reforms. By the end of July, he had released scores of political prisoners and promised to disband the five parties set up by Abacha. He also announced that the military regime

would hand over power to an elected government in May 1999 in "free and fair" elections. The presidential elections were set for February 1999.

On October 17 a leaking state-owned gasoline pipeline exploded in the town of Jesse, and the resulting fireball killed at least 700 people. (*See* DISASTERS.)

(MICHAEL TETELMAN)

NORWAY

Area: 323,758 sq km (125,004 sq mi)
Population (1998 est.): 4,429,000
Capital: Oslo
Chief of state: King Harald V
Head of government: Prime Minister Kjell Magne Bondevik

Norway's economy in 1998 experienced another year of growth, though it was not as strong as the preceding five years. Compared with 1997 gross domestic product grew by 2.5%, public consumption by 2%, private consumption by 3.5%, the consumer price index by 2.3%, and wages by as much as 5%. Wage growth was especially high in the public sector. An increase of 2.5% in the number of jobs until midsummer indicated an unemployment rate for 1998 of 3.5%. Consequently, the employment rate of the population's total labour force reached 74%, a level never before attained. The major reason for this was the steady growth in the number of women who worked (68.8% by midsummer 1998).

Even with such comfortable percentages, Norwegians experienced a growing mistrust in the country's near future. A representative symptom was the falling value of the Norwegian krone as measured against the U.S. dollar ($1=about NKr 7.5) and the British pound sterling (£1=about NKr 13). Two international situations accounted for part of the decline; low prices for Norway's oil ($12–$13 per barrel, crude Brent) caused an immediate cut in public incomes, and the Asian financial crisis, expanding to Russia and Asia, reduced Norwegian exports to those markets. Consequently, with a view to foreign investors, the Bank of Norway from March to August raised the interest rate by as much as 4.5% but apparently with no immediate effect. A domestic reason for the decline was the instability in Parliament that was produced by the general elections in October 1997. Prime Minister Kjell Magne Bondevik's coalition government controlled only 45 seats of the 165 in the legislature. This government, therefore, was constantly required to compromise which resulted in declining confidence in the strength of the government and in the international value of the krone. With the support of two rightist parties the government managed to get its 1999 budget approved.

The fluctuations in the krone were, however, only surface troubles in the Norwegian economy in 1998. The government's draft budget, presented to the legislature on October 5, included a surplus of NKr 56 billion intended for transfer to the Government Petroleum Fund for investments abroad.

Without help from the petroleum sector, the budget of NKr 480 billion would have presented a deficit of NKr 5 billion. When oil prices fell below $10 a barrel (crude Brent) late in the year, the surplus intended for the Petroleum Fund was nullified with serious implications for growth.

(GUDMUND SANDVIK)

OMAN

Area: 309,500 sq km (119,500 sq mi)
Population (1998 est.): 2,364,000
Capital: Muscat
Head of state and government: Sultan and Prime Minister Qabus ibn Sa'id

Major domestic political events in Oman in late 1997 and early 1998 included the establishment of a new governmental body, the State Council, which was appointed by Sultan Qabus to prioritize the agenda of the government. At the same time, Qabus decreed that the Shura Council become an entirely elected body, removing his power to appoint one-third of its members. Qabus also reshuffled the Cabinet in January, appointing Yusuf ibn 'Alawi ibn 'Abdallah as foreign minister and Muhammad ar-Rumhi as oil minister.

On the economic front Oman continued to experience diminished revenues caused by falling oil prices. Oil Minister Rumhi on several occasions called for oil-producing countries to agree to reduce production levels.

In foreign affairs Oman continued its efforts to establish close economic, political, and military ties with Iran. Numerous high-level visits were exchanged between the two countries, and an Iranian firm won the competition to construct a power plant in Solaleh, Oman. Relations with Yemen were strained in March when Yemeni secessionist leader 'Ali al-Bid, who was exiled in Oman, publicly renewed calls for an independent South Yemen. Oman also accused Yemen of supporting Islamist rebels who sought to overthrow the Omani regime.

(DAVID COLVIN)

PAKISTAN

Area: 796,095 sq km (307,374 sq mi), excluding the 83,716-sq km Pakistani-administered portion of Jammu and Kashmir
Population (1998 est.): 141.9 million, excluding 4 million residents of Pakistani-administered Jammu and Kashmir and 1.1 million Afghan refugees
Capital: Islamabad
Chief of state: President Rafiq Tarar
Head of government: Prime Minister Mohammed Nawaz Sharif

The government of Prime Minister Mohammed Nawaz Sharif began 1998 by taking Sharif's predecessor and archfoe Benazir Bhutto to court on charges of corruption and illegally amassing wealth overseas, mainly in Swiss banks. While Bhutto herself remained free, her husband, Asif Ali Zardari, languished in prison awaiting trial throughout the year. Two years after Bhutto had been dismissed from the government for alleged corruption, the cases against her and her allies remained unproven, and the legal process against her moved at a snail's pace. Ironically, corruption investigations came to haunt Sharif in October, after it was revealed that he had stashed away far more undeclared wealth overseas than had Bhutto. That led for more calls for the beleaguered Sharif to be sacked by the president and for the charges against Bhutto to be dropped.

Sharif began 1998 seeing his closest ally, Rafiq Tarar, installed as president of Pakistan on January 1. Because of this relationship, Sharif appeared to be in no danger of being removed from office, even as criticism of the government for its failure to stem violence and prevent the economy from deteriorating mounted for much of the year.

Though Sharif had no reason to fear sacking by the president, his relationship with Pakistani military leaders remained tenuous. For much of the year, he took veiled criticism from the military leaders in his stride. In June the army chief of staff, Gen. Jehangir Karamat, warned that "economic resilience and internal stability were as important to national security as military and nuclear capability," hinting broadly that Sharif was ignoring the mounting economic problems and was using tests of missiles and nuclear devices to divert attention from them as well as from the increasing civil strife. On October 5 Karamat used even harsher words to criticize the prime minister and urged him to set up a National Security Council (of military and civilian

leaders) to deal with the problems facing the country. Sharif refused to set up the council, and Karamat, just a few months from his mandatory retirement age, resigned. He was replaced by the nation's fourth-ranked general, Pervez Musharraf, after which two more highly ranked generals resigned.

Relations with India were turbulent for much of the year. By May South Asia had become the focus of global attention, with nuclear devices exploded on both sides of the border. In early April Pakistan had fired the first shot by testing its Ghauri intermediate-range missile—capable of carrying a nuclear warhead—an event that infuriated the Indian government. On May 11 India conducted three underground nuclear tests, its first tests since 1974, and on May 13 it conducted two more. That led to demonstrations in Pakistan with protesters urging the government to conduct its own tests and restore the balance of power in the region or resign. As the days passed, the protests grew louder, and military leaders joined in calling for the government to carry out the tests promptly to "restore national honour and pride." As the pressure mounted, world leaders appealed to Sharif to end the nuclear tests. On May 28, however, Pakistan conducted five nuclear tests, and on May 30 it exploded another. Pakistan and India then spent the next several months facing international condemnation and economic sanctions from the U.S., Europe, and Japan. Indian and Pakistani officials met in September and October to discuss the tensions in the region and attempt to resolve long-standing issues; they promised to adhere to the Comprehensive Test Ban Treaty.

Sectarian violence continued unabated throughout the year. Clashes between Islamic fundamentalist groups and the minority Qadiani sect as well as with Christians claimed dozens of lives. In May Faisalabad City's Roman Catholic Bishop John Joseph committed suicide following

Pakistani Prime Minister Nawaz Sharif (front row, second from right) and other government officials visit a nuclear test site in Chagai on June 19. In May Pakistan detonated six nuclear devices in retaliation for nuclear weapons testing by India earlier in the month. The tests led to international condemnation and economic sanctions against both countries.

the death sentence imposed on a Christian man accused of blasphemy. The bishop's suicide led to violence in Lahore and Faisalabad between Christians and hard-line Islamic fundamentalists.

Pakistan's economy suffered from the sanctions that followed the nuclear tests. Consequently, economic growth was projected at under 4% for 1998, compared with earlier forecasts of 5.5%.

(ASSIF A. SHAMEEN)

PALAU

Area: 488 sq km (188 sq mi)
Population (1998 est.): 18,100
Provisional capital: Koror; a site on Babelthuap was designated to be the permanent capital
Head of state and government: President Kuniwo Nakamura

The leader of Palau, the newest member of the United Nations, testified at the UN in 1998 about his country's problem with drug trafficking. Pres. Kuniwo Nakamura told the UN General Assembly special session on drugs that an imported form of methamphetamine had been supplied to users as young as 13.

Nakamura visited Davao City, Phil., in May as part of a delegation that also included the speaker of the House of Delegates, Ignacio Anastacio, and the Senate leader, Isodoro Rudimch. As part of a strategy to develop Palau as an emerging market in the world economy, Nakamura concentrated his negotiations on such industries as tuna canning and fisheries. Palau Trade and Commerce Minister Okada Techitong later signed a partnership agreement for trade with the Philippines in June 1998 to build on existing export-import links in cement and roofing materials. The bilateral agreement was also expected to benefit the 5,000 Filipinos working on Palau. (A.R.G. GRIFFITHS)

PANAMA

Area: 75,517 sq km (29,157 sq mi)
Population (1998 est.): 2,767,000
Capital: Panama City
Head of state and government: President Ernesto Pérez Balladares

Almost two-thirds of those who voted in a referendum in August 1998 rejected the proposal to change the Panamanian constitution and permit Pres. Ernesto Pérez Balladares to run for reelection in May 1999. The president desired a second five-year term to continue economic reforms and to be in charge when the U.S. surrendered complete control of the Panama Canal on Dec. 31, 1999. The ruling Democratic Revolutionary Party

(PRD) was divided over the reelection issue, but the electorate's decision did not guarantee victory for the opposition parties in the 1999 elections. Pérez Balladares's harsh economic policies were cited as one of the reasons for his defeat and for further splits in the PRD.

In September the U.S. and Panama abandoned negotiations on the establishment of an international antinarcotics centre. Disagreements over the terms of the project led to an impasse that prompted the U.S. to announce in July that it was considering other locations for the centre. Opinion polls indicated that a majority of Panamanians were in favour of the centre, but some opposed any American presence on Panamanian soil after December 1999.

During the first half of the year, drought caused by El Niño lowered the Panama Canal's water reserves to such an extent that draft restrictions were introduced for shipping. Having been increased by 8.2% in January 1997, tolls were raised again, by 7.5%, in January 1998. The transit fee for small vessels was raised to $1,500 in May. These measures, designed to finance expansion of the canal as it approached maximum capacity and also to minimize delays, led to concern about the rising cost of using the canal. In addition, plans to reactivate the transisthmus railway and to establish other Central American trade corridors raised further doubts about the canal's future.

(BEN BOX)

PAPUA NEW GUINEA

Area: 462,840 sq km (178,704 sq mi)
Population (1998 est.): 4.6 million
Capital: Port Moresby
Chief of state: Queen Elizabeth II, represented by Governor-General Silas Atopare
Head of government: Prime Minister Bill Skate

Papua New Guinea faced complex difficulties in 1998, made worse by a disastrous tidal wave on July 17 at Vanimo and by the world economic crisis that was severely affecting Pacific nations in particular. U.S. Secretary of State Madeleine Albright visited the nation after the tidal wave and increased U.S. disaster aid to more than $1 million. Despite the unexpected disaster, Prime Minister Bill Skate managed the coalition ministry well, dislocated though it was by a split in the United Party during which party founder Sir Michael Somare, his son Arthur, and others moved over to the opposition.

On the positive side, another former party leader and ex-prime minister, Sir Rabbie Namaliu, joined the government to assist Skate in an attempt to solve the long-running problem of the secession movement on the island of Bougainville. A turning point in the conflict came when the UN Security Council approved the creation of a five-member UN political office in Bougainville to monitor the peace agreement between the Papua New Guinean government and the se-

cessionists. Skate also met the rebel leaders Joseph Kabui and Francis Ona and agreed to withdraw Papua New Guinean defense forces from Bougainville as part of the peace process.

An amendment to the constitution was passed by the legislature on October 2 that would establish a Bougainville Reconciliation Government as of Jan. 1, 1999. The BRG was charged with preparing the way for democratic elections to take place in June 1999. (A.R.G. GRIFFITHS)

PARAGUAY

Area: 406,752 sq km (157,048 sq mi)
Population (1998 est.): 5,223,000
Capital: Asunción
Head of state and government:
Presidents Juan Carlos Wasmosy and, from August 15, Raúl Cubas Grau

The 1998 presidential elections demonstrated the fragility of democracy in Paraguay and the divisions within the governing Colorado Party. In March the Supreme Military Tribunal imposed a 10-year sentence on former general Lino Oviedo, winner of the 1997 Colorado presidential primary, for having led an attempted coup in 1996. Though preelection polls indicated the race would be tightly contested, Oviedo's running mate, Raúl Cubas Grau, named Colorado candidate by the Supreme Court, won the May election with the slogan "Cubas in government, Oviedo in power."

In June the congressional opposition passed a bill limiting the president's powers of amnesty; prisoners would have to serve at least half their sentences, and restrictions on their civil and political rights would not be affected by amnesty. This would keep Oviedo locked up until 2003 and prevent his running for president until 2008. In August, however, three days after his inauguration, Cubas reduced Oviedo's sentence to three months (which he had already served). The Supreme Court questioned the constitutionality of the reduction, and impeachment procedures against Cubas were initiated in the legislature, where a new cross-party alliance, the National Democratic Front (FDN), including anti-Oviedo Colorados, was formed. The outcome was a stalemate, with the FDN not strong enough to force impeachment but able to block legislation. Congress asked for the Supreme Court to review the decision to free Oviedo, and on December 2 the judges annulled Prime Minister Cubas's decree and ordered the general back to prison.

Against this background Paraguay's economic problems multiplied. The Asian financial crisis and its impact on Brazil led to a decline in the exchange rate and a drop in central bank reserves. In the third banking crisis since 1995, the central bank closed eight domestic financial institutions. Growth of gross domestic product was expected to drop to 1.6% from 2.5% in 1997. Inflation was projected to leap from 6.2% in 1997 to 19% in 1998. (CHARLIE NURSE)

During 1997–98 the El Niño weather pattern wreaked more havoc and destruction on the Pacific Islands than it had since 1982–83. The adverse effects included severe drought in the western Pacific, an increased frequency of cyclonic storms in the eastern Pacific, and consequent impacts on subsistence agriculture, export production, public health, and housing.

El Niño ("The Child," in reference to the Christ Child) was the name given by South American fishermen to the warm current that sweeps the Pacific coast every few years, arriving at about Christmas and replacing the usually cold Humboldt current from the south for months at a time. Now recognized as part of a broader phenomenon (the El Niño Southern Oscillation), this variant on the usual weather pattern results in increased rainfall and more frequent cyclonic storms in the eastern Pacific. For the western Pacific, El Niño causes long periods of reduced rainfall—with resultant drought conditions in the worst-affected areas—and cooler ocean temperatures that reduce the risk but not the occurrence of cyclonic storms. (*See* EARTH SCIENCES: *Oceanography*.) The warmer sea temperatures (by 3°–4° C [5.4°–7.2° F]) increase sea levels by as much as 0.5 m (1.6 ft), which can threaten coastal settlements in much the same way as global warming is projected to do during the next century. There is already concern that the more frequent occurrence of El Niño since 1977 represents a trend.

La Niña ("The Girl Child") brings contrasting conditions, with cooler ocean temperatures, less rain, and less frequent cyclones in the east and an increased risk of cyclones in Fiji and the islands to the west. As early as July 1997 the Southern Oscillation Index suggested that a severe El Niño pattern could be expected. By December 1997 ocean temperatures were at their highest this century. Toward the end of 1998 the Index indicated that, rather than a return to "normality," a major La Niña could be expected, bringing drier conditions to French Polynesia, the Cook Islands, and Tokelau; an increased incidence of cyclonic storms in Fiji, Vanuatu, New Caledonia, and Solomon Islands; and an easing of drought conditions on the eastern coasts of Australia and New Zealand.

The 1997–98 El Niño followed a classic pattern. Early in 1997 warmer ocean temperatures were in evidence on the Pacific coast of South America; by midyear, reduced rainfall (sometimes as little as 10% of the usual precipitation) in the western Pacific had given way to serious drought conditions in Papua New Guinea, Solomon Islands, the Federated States of Micronesia, and the Marshall Islands. Similar conditions were experienced in eastern Australia and New Zealand. The season for strong cyclonic storms, usually defined as November to March, was particularly severe in the eastern Pacific in 1997–98, with French Polynesia experiencing four major cyclones during that period. In the adjacent Cook Islands, Cyclone Martin was the most severe in living memory. Although El Niño generally results in a reduced risk of severe storm activity in the western Pacific, Solomon Islands

SPOTLIGHT

EL NIÑO'S IMPACT ON OCEANIA

by Barrie Macdonald

Illustration by Tom Curry

and Vanuatu were both struck by cyclones in January 1998.

In Papua New Guinea some 750,000 people were affected by drought through 1997 and early 1998, resulting in crop failure and consequent malnutrition, with claims of up to 70 deaths attributable to starvation. Mining operations at Ok Tedi and Porgera were suspended because of the lack of water. With Australian assistance, relief measures, including the distribution of food, were implemented. In the smaller islands and atolls of Micronesia, drought conditions were particularly severe, continuing beyond mid-1998 and leading to the declaration of disaster-area status in the Federated States of Micronesia and the Marshall Islands. Measures taken to alleviate drought conditions included the importation of desalination plants and of equipment that treated groundwater to make it drinkable and also the shipment of water by barges to the worst-affected islands.

Further effects of El Niño included 50% reductions of sugar exports from Fiji, coffee exports from Papua New Guinea, and squash exports from Tonga. Fisheries were also affected. The warmer water temperatures on the South American coast caused a sharp reduction in the anchovy harvest. Tuna, a highly migratory species, usually congregate for some months of the year to the north of New Guinea; under El Niño conditions, stocks were more dispersed, and Solomon Islands had a catch that was one-third larger than usual. With some 70% of the world's tuna fishery in the Pacific Ocean, the implications of such shifts for nations that depended on the exploitation of an exclusive economic zone were obvious.

Aside from their direct costs, both droughts and storms adversely affected subsistence and cash crops for a significant number of Pacific Islanders, further depressing economic activity in much of the region. The drought also increased the incidence of bush fires in countries ranging from Papua New Guinea to Samoa, damaging health as well as forests. Compromised water supplies resulted in an increase of gastrointestinal diseases and in an increased vulnerability to cholera in some areas.

At a time when many of the smaller Pacific Islands countries faced global warming with some trepidation, perceiving rising sea levels as endangering their existence, the increasing frequency of El Niño posed a threat that was at least as damaging in its potential effects and was more immediate in its impact. The climatic extremes generated by this system and its cold-water-current opposite, La Niña, carry severe risks for those very small countries, with their fragile ecosystems, weak infrastructures, and narrow resource bases. Most were already heavily dependent on foreign aid for capital development and, in some cases, for recurrent expenditures. For certain, their economic struggles will only be accentuated by the continuing climatic challenge.

Barrie Macdonald is a professor of history at Massey University, Palmerston, N.Z.

A masked supporter of former Paraguayan general Lino Oviedo points a toy gun at police officers during a demonstration outside the Supreme Court building in Asunción in December. Protesters were calling for the resignation of Supreme Court members who had ordered Oviedo to finish serving a 10-year prison sentence for his 1996 attempt to topple former president Juan Carlos Wasmosy. Newly elected Pres. Raúl Cubas Grau in August had reduced Oviedo's sentence to three months already served.

DANIEL PIRIS—AP/WIDE WORLD

PERU

Area: 1,285,216 sq km (496,225 sq mi)
Population (1998 est.): 24,801,000
Capital: Lima
Head of state and government: President Alberto Fujimori

Following the disastrous effects of El Niño on Peru in 1997, Pres. Alberto Fujimori suffered another major crisis in July 1998 when the Shell Oil Co. and Mobil Corp. withdrew from the multimillion-dollar Camisea natural gas project. Signed in May 1996, the "contract of the century" was designed to alleviate Peru's energy shortage. Shell and Mobil,

however, had been unable to agree with the government on the pricing of gas in Lima and the export of gas to Brazil. Fujimori, keen to assuage a public that had given him a popularity rating of only 22% in opinion polls, quickly stated that another company would be found to take over the Camisea project.

Fujimori's unpopularity was further driven home by a more than 4,000-person protest march through Lima on July 16. A petition with 1.4 million signatures was presented to the National Electoral Authority, requesting a referendum on whether Fujimori should be allowed to run for a third term. In spite of the amendment to the constitution allowing presidents to run for only two successive terms, Fujimori had in 1996 pushed through Congress a law of "authentic interpretation" of the constitution, allowing him to run for election once more. The opposition grouping, Democratic Centre, submitted a draft bill repealing the "authen-

tic interpretation" law, but the bill was defeated in Congress. During the vote on the bill, there were public demonstrations outside the Congress building and a fracas inside, during which Daniel Espichán of progovernment Change 90–New Majority was punched in the face by Javier Díaz Canselo of the Union for Peru.

The opposition was further angered when, on September 15, the National Electoral Authority announced that the petition for a referendum contained only about 800,000 genuine names, many of them repeated dozens of times. The Democratic Centre denied that it had falsified the petition, complaining that rejection of the referendum was an infringement of Peruvians' human rights and claiming that the charges of falsification amounted to political persecution.

President Fujimori heightened pressure on Ecuador to resolve the continuing border dispute by refusing to attend the inauguration of the new Ecuadorian president, Jamil Mahuad, on August 10. This followed Fujimori's traditional patriotic speech on July 28, in which he said that Peru would not hesitate to defend its territorial sovereignty.

Tension was further heightened by Ecuador's movement of troops 20 km (12.5 mi) into Peruvian territory in early August. The resignation of Peru's armed forces chief, Nicolás Hermoza Ríos, was seen by many commentators as part of the process to end the border dispute quickly. Hermoza had been a staunch opponent of withdrawal of troops from the disputed areas, and his removal was seen as part of an agreement between Fujimori and Mahuad, who also replaced his top military commander. The two chiefs of state finally signed the historic peace accord at ceremonies in Brasília, Braz., on October 26.   (ALAN MURPHY)

PHILIPPINES

Area: 300,076 sq km (115,860 sq mi)
Population (1998 est.): 73,131,000
Capital: Quezon City (designated national government centre and the location of the lower house of the legislature and some ministries; many government offices are in Manila or suburbs
Head of state and government:
Presidents Fidel V. Ramos and, from June 30, Joseph Estrada

Joseph Estrada (*see* BIOGRAPHIES) became president of the Philippines on June 30, 1998, with Gloria Macapagal-Arroyo as vice president. In elections on May 11 for a six-year term, Estrada won 40% of the vote, against 15.9% for his nearest rival, José de Venecia, who was backed by the retiring president, Fidel V. Ramos. Macapagal-Arroyo won 47% of the vote to defeat the vice presidential candidate on Estrada's ticket. Estrada, who had been vice president under Ramos, assigned her responsibility for social welfare and development.

Estrada, a former star of B movies, campaigned on a law-and-order platform and said that fighting corruption would be a high

Newly elected Philippine Pres. Joseph Estrada (centre) takes the oath of office on June 30 in Malalos. Despite lacking the support of outgoing president Fidel Ramos, the country's business community, and the influential Roman Catholic Church, Estrada, a former star of B movies, captured 40% of the vote in the May 11 presidential election.

priority. He charged that under Ramos 40% of the Philippines' budget was lost through corruption. He gave his inaugural address in the national language, Pilipino, to emphasize ties to the common people in a nation run by an English-speaking elite. Many businessmen, fearing his populist appeals, worried that he would emphasize a redistribution of wealth rather than continue the economic reforms intended to raise production and living standards.

When Estrada seemed the likely winner, businessmen who had been accused of looting the country under former president Ferdinand Marcos started supporting and advising him. Chief among them was Eduardo Cojuangco, who had fled abroad when Marcos was overthrown in 1986 but returned to run, unsuccessfully, for president in 1992. With Estrada admitting limited knowledge of economics, the important role played by Marcos's friends caused widespread apprehension. Ramos warned that the return of "Marcos cronies" would frighten off badly needed foreign investment.

Economic output held steady during 1998, as the Philippines was less affected by the general East Asian recession than were most other countries in the region. Exports rose, led by electronic equipment. Drought as a result of El Niño devastated crop production, causing a 7.2% slump in agricultural output in the first half of 1998. With agriculture employing 40% of the workforce and providing 20% of total national output, the drought hurt the entire economy. Despite popular expectations that Estrada would raise living standards, the president's options were limited by a budget deficit. The government announced a 25% cut in all its spending. The International Monetary Fund said that the nation's tax-collection system was "seriously flawed."

Estrada during the year sought to deal with a continuing insurgency in the southern Philippines. A Muslim group, the Moro Islamic Liberation Front, fought sporadic battles on Mindanao Island and adjacent islands for a separate Muslim state. The group had rejected previous presidents' arrange-

ments for more autonomy as inadequate, and its demands for independence remained unchanged under Estrada.

The Supreme Court on October 6 overturned a corruption conviction in 1993 of Marcos's widow, Imelda. She had faced a possible 12 years in prison for fraud but never served any time.

One of the passenger ferryboats that provided the main link between the nation's islands sank near Manila during the early

morning hours of September 19. At least 43 people were killed. Typhoon Zeb killed 69 people and destroyed crops in mid-October. On December 3 a fire in an orphanage in the capital killed at least 30, most of them children.　　　(HENRY S. BRADSHER)

POLAND

Area: 312,685 sq km (120,728 sq mi)
Population (1998 est.): 38,665,000
Capital: Warsaw
Chief of state: President Aleksander Kwasniewski
Head of government: Prime Minister Jerzy Buzek

The right-wing government dominated by the Solidarity trade union that was formed after the September 1997 parliamentary elections devoted its first full year in power to an ambitious agenda of reforms. Many of these had been planned under the first wave of Solidarity governments in the early 1990s, but their adoption was interrupted by the victory of the former communists in the 1993 parliamentary elections.

A first reform priority for 1998 was local government. Poland had inherited from communism a highly centralized system of public administration. The first Solidarity government began devolving power to elected local bodies in 1990, creating the *gmina*, an elected local council at the level

Parliamentary lawmakers in Poland vote on an administrative reform plan proposed by the Solidarity government in June. Among other initiatives, the parliament endorsed a government plan to reduce the number of Polish voivodships, or provinces, from 49 to 16. Under the reform plan, Poland would shed the remains of its communist-era bureaucratic system to give local governments more power.

of the town or village. *Gminas* took financial responsibility for local schools, roads, and public order, but local government reform had stalled there. In their election campaigns both parties that took the reins of government in 1997, the Solidarity Electoral Action (AWS) and the Freedom Union (UW), had pledged further decentralization.

By the end of 1998, a hard-fought series of legislative changes had transformed the country's administrative structure. A new institution of elected local government, the *powiat,* had been created to exercise power at the level between the *gmina* and the existing voivodship (*województwo,* or province). The existing 49 voivodships had been con-

LUISA FERREIRA—AP/WIDE WORLD

A Portuguese woman passes by anti-abortion posters in Lisbon just prior to a national referendum on abortion in June. Despite a heated campaign waged by organizations on both sides of the issue, so few Portuguese citizens bothered to make it to the polls that the vote had to be discarded for not meeting a minimum turnout.

solidated into 16 larger units. The new voivodships, charged with setting regional development strategies, also gained assemblies elected in general ballots. The principle underlying the reforms was to place responsibility for public spending at the lowest level possible, with the aim of ensuring that money was spent in the most efficient and transparent manner possible. The reform was politically contested, but conflict centred on the number of new voivodships rather than any substantive issue. Mobilizing pockets of local resistance from cities slated for downgrading from voivodship capitals, the opposition and Pres. Aleksander Kwasniewski forced the government to compromise and raise the number of voivodships from 13 to 16.

Elections to all three levels of local government on October 11 provided the year's major test for Poland's political parties. The results underlined the domination of the two major parties, the AWS and the opposition Democratic Left Alliance. Each party took control of eight voivodship assemblies. The UW had a poor showing, in part owing to controversial proposals by its leader, Leszek Balcerowicz, the deputy prime minister and finance minister, to eliminate tax deductions. The Polish Peasant Party, which had suffered a humiliating defeat in the 1997 parliamentary elections, reemerged as a potential

"third force," in Polish local government if not nationally.

A revolutionary reform of the country's pension system was the year's other main legislative achievement. The reform package, scheduled for launching in April 1999, was designed to forestall a fiscal crisis in the new century by shifting pension funding from a governmental to a partially private basis. The reform, modeled on precedents in Chile and Argentina, required employees under 30 to contribute part of their social security taxes to one of two dozen private pension funds. Employees aged 30 to 50 could choose to join the new system or remain in the old one. The reform was revolutionary in the sense that, starting with the generation of Poles now joining the labour force, pension payments would depend on actual returns achieved by the investment funds rather than on a fixed percentage of final salaries.

A seventh straight year of buoyant economic growth helped provide a financial cushion to fund the government's reform plans. Poland's economy expanded by approximately 5% in 1998, although the rate of growth slowed dramatically during the year as the financial crisis that began in East Asia reduced demand for Polish exports. The zloty made a brief dip but quickly recovered; real appreciation was the stronger trend, as investors continued to pour money into the country, attracted by major privatizations such as the sale of 25% of TPSA, the country's monopoly fixed-line telephone operator. Poland's cumulative foreign direct investment totaled $30 billion in 1998. The rate of inflation fell to less than 9% at the end of the year.

In March the European Commission opened formal accession talks, confirming Poland's place on the "fast track" for membership in the European Union. Delays in downsizing the country's steel and coal industries threatened to complicate negotiations, although by the year's end the government had completed plans to cut employment in coal mining by some 100,000 and in steel by about 45,000.   (LOUISA VINTON)

PORTUGAL

Area: 92,135 sq km (35,574 sq mi)
Population (1998 est.): 9,964,000
Capital: Lisbon
Chief of state: President Jorge Sampaio
Head of government: Prime Minister
    António Guterres

Culminating five years of hard work, the EXPO '98 World Exposition opened in May 1998 in Lisbon. Though some 10 million saw the sprawling fair, which celebrated the 500th anniversary of Vasco da Gama's discovery of a sea route to India, attendance was far below the forecast of 15 million, and a deficit for the project estimated at $400 million was left.

Also in May, Portugal finally achieved a much-hoped-for national goal by being chosen to enter the European Monetary Union along with 10 other members of the European Union (EU). That decision gave the official seal of approval to the nation's decade-long campaign to control inflation, reduce the government's budget deficit, and lower interest rates. Those efforts resulted in above-average growth for an EU country in 1998.

The 1999 draft budget called for further reductions in the government deficit and once again included increased spending on items close to the Socialist government's heart, including health care, education, and the justice system. Cost reductions would be achieved mainly through the personnel cuts in some government ministries and by increased efforts to collect taxes efficiently. The budget was important because the Socialists faced a general election in late 1999, and although they did not want to provoke a spending spree, some popularist measures such as public works projects were expected to be enacted in order to woo votes. With the main opposition parties still fragmented, most analysts believed that the Socialist Party had a good chance of winning the 1999 election and perhaps even gaining an absolute majority in the parliament.

The year was marred by a shockingly low turnout at a much-publicized abortion referendum in June, at which just 32% of the country's 8.4 million eligible voters went to the polls. It was Portugal's first referendum, and a 50% turnout was required for the result to be binding. Consequently, the vote was thrown out. Political analysts considered the result particularly surprising because of the intense emotions stirred by the high-profile attention given to the campaigns of each side. Some 51% of voters turned out for another, less-emotional referendum on November 8, on whether the country should be broken up into eight mainland administrative regions. They rejected the proposal almost two to one.

Portugal suffered some setbacks on the international front, with renewed civil war in the former colonies of Angola and Guinea-Bissau damaging the nearly constant efforts of Portuguese officials to help broker a lasting peace. Also, many observers believed that Portugal did not take advantage of Indonesia's disorder to advance the process of autonomy for East Timor, a former Portuguese colony illegally annexed by Indonesia in 1976. Negotiations were broken off in late November. Honour was somewhat recouped, however, when Portugal was host to the eighth annual Ibero-American Summit in Oporto, which brought together 21 heads of state from Latin-American countries, Spain, and Portugal. Portuguese Prime Minister António Guterres presided over negotiations to achieve a lasting peace between Ecuador and Peru, and the leaders hammered out a strategy to try to protect their regional economies from global turmoil by

calling on the major industrial countries to get their houses in order.

The year ended on a strong positive note when Portuguese writer José Saramago won the Nobel Prize for Literature for his "parables sustained by imagination, compassion and irony." Saramago flew to Lisbon from his home on the Spanish island of Lanzarote after winning the prize and was cheered by crowds of well-wishers. (*See* NOBEL PRIZES.)   (ERIK T. BURNS)

QATAR

Area (including Hawar Islands, also claimed by Bahrain): 11,437 sq km (4,416 sq mi)
Population (1998 est.): 579,000
Capital: Doha
Head of state and government: Emir Sheikh Hamad ibn Khalifah ath-Thani, assisted by Prime Minister Sheikh Abdullah ibn Khalifah ath-Thani

Qatar continued in 1998 to take steps to raise gradually the level of public participation in government. The emir announced plans to establish a 29-member municipal council, which would be open to women, to be elected in February 1999. In May the sight of some 50 women contesting in a

public track and field meet before a crowd of more than 35,000 sparked debate over the participation of women in such events.

After the November 1997 Doha regional economic conference, which was boycotted by Egypt and other Arab states, Qatar placed a ban on employing Egyptian workers, but it lifted the ban in June 1998. In April military officials signed a defense and military cooperation agreement with Russia. Qatar's national oil-distribution company reached agreement in July with a consortium of German and South Korean firms to increase the capacity of two existing oil refineries and build two additional refineries in the Musay'id region.   (DAVID COLVIN)

ROMANIA

Area: 237,500 sq km (91,699 sq mi)
Population (1998 est.): 22,491,000
Capital: Bucharest
Chief of state: President Emil Constantinescu
Head of government: Prime Ministers Victor Ciorbea and, from April 12, Radu Vasile

The crisis at the end of 1997 in the ruling coalition in Romania—consisting of the centre-right Democratic Convention of

Romania, the centre-left Social Democratic Union (USD), and the ethnic-based Hungarian Democratic Union of Romania (UDMR)—carried over into 1998. Following the December 1997 resignation of two key ministers from the Democratic Party (PD; the leading force in the USD), on January 7 Prime Minister Victor Ciorbea rejected a call by the PD to reinstate one of them, so that party withdrew its support. The protracted government agony lasted until March 30, when, under pressure from his own National Peasant Party–Christian Democratic, the coalition's main constituent, Ciorbea eventually announced his resignation as both prime minister and Bucharest mayor. Radu Vasile was designated to replace Ciorbea, and the new Cabinet was sworn in by Pres. Emil Constantinescu on April 15. Vasile pledged to accelerate economic reforms, including privatization of major state firms, and sharply reduce state bureaucracy. Because of the government crisis, the 1998 budget cleared the parliament on May 26, and this delay had a negative impact on both foreign creditors and investors. Romania's credibility was also affected by revelations about widespread corruption within the government. A large-scale cigarette-smuggling scandal broke in April and led to the dismissal and arrest of several senior customs, army, and secret service officers.

By early June new government crises were looming. The UDMR threatened to leave the coalition if the education law was not changed to allow the operation of a state-run Hungarian-language university. Also in June, several senior officials, in-

Police cadets in Romania march in a military parade in Bucharest on December 1 to commemorate the 80th anniversary of the defeat of the Central Powers and the doubling of Romania's territory by the addition of Transylvania, Bukovina, and Bessarabia. The huge cost of the day's celebrations ignited criticism by some who were worried about the country's already impoverished budget.

cluding Health Minister Francisc Baranyi (UDMR), were forced to resign because of alleged links with the former communist secret service.

In mid-July Vasile admitted that little progress had been made in restructuring and privatizing industry, and Finance Minister Daniel Daianu warned that the annual deficit might be much higher than the 3.6% envisaged in the budget. Daianu also threatened to resign if the government followed through on a deal with Bell Helicopters Textron to purchase 96 helicopters in order to help modernize the armed forces. Daianu was abruptly dismissed on September 23. On October 19 Privatization Minister Sorin Dimitriu resigned under criticism for the slow pace of economic reforms.

On December 23, two days after the parliament had rejected a no-confidence motion presented by the leftist-nationalist opposition, the Cabinet decided to restructure itself, cutting the number of ministries from 24 to 17. Finally, on December 28, the government signaled that it was prepared to speed up economic reforms by allowing the State Property Fund to initiate legal action to close 30 loss-making state companies.

In March President Constantinescu attended the London conference of European Union member states and candidates, and in July he took advantage of a nine-day visit in the U.S. to argue before a joint session of Congress that his country played a key role in Balkan stability and should therefore be admitted to NATO. In October Romania agreed to allow limited access to its air space in the event of NATO military intervention in the Serbian province of Kosovo.

(DAN IONESCU)

RUSSIA

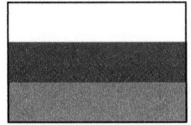

Area: 17,075,400 sq km (6,592,800 sq mi)
Population (1998 est.): 146,861,000
Capital: Moscow
Chief of state: President Boris Yeltsin
Head of government: Prime Ministers Viktor Chernomyrdin until March 23, Sergey Kiriyenko until August 23, and, from September 11, Yevgeny Primakov

Domestic Affairs. Pres. Boris Yeltsin's health deteriorated during 1998 until he was reportedly working no more than a few hours a day. On the increasingly rare occasions that he was seen in public, Yeltsin appeared weak and confused. On a state visit to Central Asia in October, he stumbled, spoke incoherently, and signed his name slowly. By late in the year, Yeltsin's popularity was at an all-time low, and calls for his resignation were increasing. The communist-dominated opposition launched impeachment proceedings. Yeltsin's aides insisted that he was suffering from nothing more serious than exhaustion and would serve out his term, due to expire in mid-2000. In October, however, they announced that the president was handing day-to-day management of state affairs over to Prime Minister Yevgeny Primakov (*see* BIOGRAPHIES) and would concentrate on ensuring a smooth succession.

Power remained a highly personalized commodity, and Yeltsin's incapacitation contributed to the vacuum of state power that was the country's most serious problem. Everyone agreed that the 1993 constitution, which had been tailor-made for Yeltsin, generated instability by failing to distribute power evenly between the legislature and the executive. Amending the constitution was so difficult, however, that there seemed little chance that the situation could be changed in that way. Yeltsin replaced the government twice during the year, acting each time on an apparent whim and provoking alarm about Russia's political and economic stability. On March 23 he fired the entire Cabinet of Viktor Chernomyrdin, his prime minister of five years, saying that economic reform was not dynamic enough. Instead, Yeltsin named virtually unknown Energy Minister Sergey Kiriyenko as acting prime minister. Many expressed doubts about Kiriyenko's youth and inexperience. The lower house of the Russian parliament, the State Duma, rejected his candidacy twice. Only after a month-long standoff, during which Yeltsin threatened to dissolve the legislature, did the Duma on April 24 confirm Kiriyenko on the third vote.

Kiriyenko appointed a new, heavily reformist Cabinet, but concerns about the financial crisis in Asia and the slump in world oil prices were already prompting investors to withdraw from Russia. Budget cuts did nothing to restore confidence, since the main problem was seen to be not the size of the budget deficit but the fact that it was larger than the government's ability to raise revenue. Investor confidence was further undermined by concern about the extent of Russia's foreign indebtedness. In an effort to defend the currency and stem the flight of capital, the central bank in May hiked interest rates to a dizzying 150%. Investors were not reassured, and markets continued to plunge. As the government dug itself deeper into a pit of indebtedness, wage arrears accumulated. Coal miners were hard hit; for several weeks in the summer, they blocked sections of the Trans-Siberian railroad, effectively cutting the country in two. As time wore on, they added calls for the resignation of Yeltsin and his government to their wage demands.

Kiriyenko's government struggled to put together a program of emergency measures to resolve the financial crisis. In July the International Monetary Fund agreed to Russia's request for new emergency credits to prop up the ruble, putting together a package of IMF, World Bank, and Japanese government money totaling $22.6 billion. The loan depended on Russia's fulfilling a series of measures to reduce the budget deficit by cutting expenditures and increasing tax receipts. The Duma rejected many of these measures when they were put forward by the government, approving measures that Kiriyenko said would provide only one-third of the targeted revenues. The IMF signaled its disquiet later in July by disbursing a first payment of only $4.8 billion instead of the $5.6 billion anticipated. The value of the ruble resumed its fall.

On August 17 Kiriyenko's government and the central bank announced an effective devaluation of the ruble by extending the exchange-rate band within which the ruble traded against the dollar by 34%. The ruble promptly fell below the new "floor," and the central bank soon gave up trying to keep the currency within even the new, widened band. The government imposed restrictions on foreign exchange operations, freezing trade in short-term government debt (Treasury bills, known as GKOs) and uni-

Russians display icons and portraits of Tsar Nicholas II and his wife, Alexandra, during a procession in St. Petersburg on the 80th anniversary of their execution by the Bolsheviks. The remains of the last Russian tsar and most of the imperial family were buried in St. Petersburg in July at a ceremony attended by Pres. Boris Yeltsin.

GRIGORY DUKOR—REUTERS

Avon Calling

During the 1990s the untapped direct-sales markets in Russia and China provided a prime opportunity for Avon Products Inc. and Mary Kay Corp., two leading American cosmetic companies, to expand their businesses overseas. Women in those countries had long been employed in jobs for which they were overqualified and/or received low wages. When the companies attracted these women to their sales forces, the relationship became mutually beneficial—a significant increase in revenue for the firms and increased financial opportunity, job satisfaction, and self-esteem for the women.

The Mary Kay vision, part of which was "to provide women with an unparalleled opportunity for financial independence, career, and personal fulfillment," found a ready reception in 1993 in Russia, where the company was greeted by a number of enthusiastic women eager to purchase and pitch its products door-to-door. Among the saleswomen's ranks were doctors and engi-

neers who discarded their previous jobs for better pay, more satisfying work conditions, and a more reliable source of income—the late payment of salaries was a continuing problem. Mary Kay's "women-only" policy also offered them a financial opportunity not available to their husbands, and some men soon saw their wives become the major breadwinners. In addition, Mary Kay's sales representatives were rewarded financially for recruiting others, an incentive that aided in the proliferation of the sales force, which by 1998 had swelled to some 65,000. Although many Russian Mary Kay customers earned meagre salaries, a great number of them would spend as much as two-thirds of their incomes on beauty products.

China also provided a welcome environment for direct selling after opening its doors in 1990 to a number of businesses, among them Avon. Just one year after Avon began operations there, some women reportedly had left their state jobs to sell full time for Avon and were

earning several times their state salaries. In 1992 sales posted in China were $8 million; by 1997 that figure had skyrocketed to some $75 million. In April 1998, however, the large investment made by Avon was threatened by a State Council edict that made all direct selling illegal. At least 20 million Chinese were involved in some form of direct marketing, and thousands rioted in opposition to the ban. The crackdown was largely intended to eliminate a number of unscrupulous organizations involved in pyramid schemes, but there were also reports that the large and enthusiastic sales meetings held by some companies had a cultlike air that made Chinese officials nervous. In June Avon announced that the company had received permission to operate in China at wholesale and retail levels only, which meant that changes were in store for many who had enjoyed the independence that Avon's direct-selling structure had offered.

(SANDRA LANGENECKERT)

A pensioner in a Moscow market examines a new banknote. Beginning in midyear, pressures on the Russian ruble began to drive its value down, and at the end of 1998 it was worth about 4½ cents. compared to nearly 17 cents in January.

laterally announcing a restructuring of that debt. It also declared a 90-day moratorium on commercial foreign debt servicing. The ruble went into free fall as Russians sought frantically to buy dollars. Western creditors lost heavily. A large part of Russia's fledgling banking sector was destroyed, since many banks had large GKO holdings and the larger banks had substantial dollar borrowings.

A week later, on August 23, Yeltsin fired Kiriyenko and declared his intention of returning Chernomyrdin to office. This time the Duma dug in its heels. After it twice re-

jected Chernomyrdin's candidacy, Yeltsin, his power clearly on the wane, backed down. Instead, he nominated Foreign Minister Primakov, who on September 11 was overwhelmingly approved by the Duma.

Primakov's appointment restored political stability because he was seen as a compromise candidate able to heal the rifts between Russia's quarreling interest groups. There was popular enthusiasm, too, when he promised to make the payment of wage and pension arrears his government's first priority. Primakov invited members of all the leading parliamentary factions into his Cabinet.

The appointment of Yury Maslyukov—a communist who had been the last head of the U.S.S.R. State Planning Agency—as first deputy premier in charge of the economy, however, prompted fears of a return to Soviet-era policies. Apprehension intensified with the appointment of Viktor Gerashchenko to head the central bank. Gerashchenko had held the same post in 1992–94, when he allowed a rapid growth of the money supply and thereby fueled high inflation.

Primakov's government acted with caution, and by year's end the feared printing of money had not begun. Primakov nonetheless had great difficulty in persuading his coalition government to agree on an economic rescue program. Maslyukov's first proposals for reviving the economy were sharply criticized by Finance Minister Mikhail Zadornov, and it was not until late October that a new draft was submitted to the IMF. This included plans to let the ruble float, introduce some price controls, and expand the role of the government in regulating the economy. Calling the program a significant step backward from market reforms, the IMF expressed concern about the lack of projected cuts in public spending and continued to withhold the second installment of its emergency loan, originally due in September. In late October the national and regional governments together took control of Kamaz, Russia's largest manufacturer of trucks, in return for assuming approximately one-third of its debts.

Inflation was 84.4% in 1998, up from 11% in 1997 and eating away at popular living standards. Gross domestic product fell 5% by comparison with the year before. Real (i.e., inflation-adjusted) incomes fell 15.6% by comparison with 1997. The ruble lost 71% of its value, ending 1998 at 20.65 to the U.S. dollar compared to 5.96 at the beginning of the year. Meanwhile, market reform was discredited in the eyes of much

of the population. Anatoly Chubais, one of those who oversaw the early phases of Russia's economic transformation, commented in September that he originally had expected Russia's transition to the market to be difficult and to last "three, five, seven years." Now, he said, "it is clear that it will take decades."

Alarmed by the nation's financial crisis and determined to protect their populations from hardship, many of Russia's regional leaders went their own ways without consulting the federal government. Tensions heightened as it became clear that the 1998 grain harvest would be the worst in more than 40 years. Many regions responded to the August crisis by imposing price controls on foodstuffs and trying to prevent the shipment of goods produced in their territories to neighbouring regions. The republics of Tatarstan and Kalmykia announced that they were halting the payment of taxes to the federal budget; Buryatia and the Samara region ordered local branches of Moscow banks not to transfer payments outside republic borders; and the Republic of Sakha declared that it was assuming control of its gold production and cutting back sales to the federal centre. Observers began to warn of a real danger that the Russian Federation might disintegrate—not by design but by default. With the exception of the breakaway Republic of Chechnya, which continued to maintain its independence, none of the regions wanted the federation to dissolve, but there was concern that the federal government was powerless to keep the country together.

As for war-ravaged Chechnya, the cash-strapped Russian government met none of its promises of financial aid. Russia, consequently, was unable to influence developments in the republic, where civil war seemed increasingly likely. Warlords resorted to kidnapping and gunrunning, and there were fears that lawlessness would spill over from Chechnya to neighbouring parts of the northern Caucasus. In October three British and one New Zealand engineers were kidnapped for ransom; their decapitated bodies were found in December.

Violent crime also continued in the rest of Russia. The nation was shocked by the assassination in St. Petersburg of Galina Starovoytova, one of Russia's leading democratic parliamentarians, in November.

In July Yeltsin unexpectedly attended the entombment in St. Petersburg of Russia's last tsar and his family. Yeltsin used the occasion to condemn the murders of the imperial family by the Bolsheviks as "one of the most shameful episodes" in Russian history. A commentator predicted that Yeltsin would be remembered for two things: "the overthrow of communism and the burial of the tsar."

Foreign Affairs. Russia's foreign relations in 1998 were characterized by continuity. In September Primakov was replaced as foreign minister by his former first deputy and close political associate, Igor Ivanov. Russia lacked the political, military, and economic power to reclaim the U.S.S.R.'s role as a great power, but the government worked hard to maintain relations with old allies such as India and Iraq and to improve relations with China, Iran, and Japan. In May a telephone hot line opened between the Kremlin and the Chinese president's office.

Tensions arose between Russia and the U.S. and its allies. In February Yeltsin warned that threatened U.S. military strikes against Iraq could spark a world war. Later in the year Moscow denounced NATO's threats to use force against Serbia over its policy toward the province of Kosovo and the U.S.-British air strikes against Iraq. Primakov continued to voice strong opposition to NATO's planned eastward enlargement, and Russia clashed with the U.S. over a lucrative Russian-Indian nuclear deal. During the summer the G-7 group of leading industrialized nations renamed itself the G-8 and welcomed Russian participation in its deliberations, but the innovation was quietly dropped after the August financial crisis revealed the full weakness of Russia's economy.

By fall Russia's foreign relations were becoming stymied by Yeltsin's failing health. Meanwhile, a number of Russia's republics pursued their own foreign relations with increasing vigour. This aroused resentment on the part of the federal government, which was, however, powerless to prevent it.

Planned reforms of the military were stalled, due partly to lack of funding and partly to Yeltsin's September firing of Security Council Secretary Andrey Kokoshin. The International Institute for Strategic Studies noted in its annual report that lack of money was undercutting Russia's ability to carry out military operations.

In May–July, for example, not one of Russia's 26 nuclear-powered ballistic missile submarines was at sea. There were reports of malnutrition among young conscripts and of hardship suffered by officers and their families as a result of wage arrears. In December the Russian and Belarusian presidents signed a series of accords aimed at unifying their two countries, perhaps as soon as mid-1999, with a common currency and a common citizenship but retaining separate armed forces and distinct foreign policies. The move was seen by some as an attempt to promote the reintegration of the former Soviet republics.

(ELIZABETH TEAGUE)

Jean Kambanda, who served as prime minister during the 1994 massacres of hundreds of thousands of Tutsi and moderate Hutu in Rwanda, receives his preliminary sentencing after being found guilty of genocide and related charges by the International Criminal Tribunal for Rwanda in Arusha, Tanz. Kambanda was the first person to be convicted of genocide by an international court.

RWANDA

Area: 26,338 sq km (10,169 sq mi)
Population (1998 est.): 7,956,000
Capital: Kigali
Head of state and government: President Pasteur Bizimungu, in conjunction with Vice President Paul Kagame and Prime Minister Pierre Celestin Rwigema

Rwanda experienced insecurity throughout 1998 as the predominantly Hutu Interahamwe militia clashed with the Tutsi-dominated army. Hardest hit were the central and northwestern regions, where the rebel forces were strongest. Rebel militias targeted Tutsi and those Hutu who sought the protection of the army. In response the army attacked those thought to be aiding the rebels. Although exact figures were difficult to establish, civilian casualties were undoubtedly high. In March, for example, military sources claimed that more than 120 suspected rebels had been killed in Gitarama, southwest of Kigali. The same region witnessed over 100 casualties from rebel attacks the following month. In several incidents rebels stormed prisons and freed some of the approximately 130,000 suspects awaiting trial on charges related to the 1994 genocide.

Rwandan courts continued to try those accused of committing crimes against humanity in 1994. Pleading guilty usually brought a life sentence, whereas conviction could bring the death penalty. The first death sentences were carried out on April 24, when 22 people convicted of genocide were publicly executed by police firing squads. They were among the first to be sentenced, and about 100 others awaited execution. After extensive administrative and logistic delays, the UN-sponsored International Criminal

Tribunal on Rwanda (ICTR) in Arusha, Tanz., completed its first cases. In May former Rwandan prime minister Jean Kambanda pleaded guilty to six charges of genocide and was sentenced to life imprisonment. He agreed to assist ICTR prosecutors and to testify against other defendants.

In August Pres. Laurent Kabila of the Democratic Republic of the Congo charged Rwanda and Uganda with supporting insurgents in the east of his country and of trying to establish a "Tutsi empire" in central Africa. Rwanda at first denied involvement, but on November 6, Vice Pres. Paul Kagame confirmed that Rwandan troops had been active in the Congo since August.

(MATTHEW A. CENZER)

SAINT KITTS AND NEVIS

Area: 269 sq km (104 sq mi)
Population (1998 est.): 42,300
Capital: Basseterre
Chief of state: Queen Elizabeth II, represented by Governor-General Cuthbert Sebastian
Head of government: Prime Minister Denzil Douglas

Nevis's threatened secession from the St. Kitts and Nevis federation dominated the political agenda in 1998. The possible breakup alarmed leaders of the Caribbean Community and Common Market (Caricom); even the U.S. government expressed concern.

Ultimately, the Concerned Citizens Movement (CCM) administration, led by Nevis Premier Vance Amory, failed to obtain the necessary two-thirds majority in the secession referendum held in August. The "yes" vote, however, was 61.7%—a clear indication of the unhappiness in Nevis with the policies of Denzil Douglas's government in St. Kitts. Caricom appointed a mission to visit St. Kitts and Nevis to restore the relationship between the two parts of the state.

In July the death penalty was reintroduced in St. Kitts and Nevis when David Wilson, convicted in 1996 of a 1994 murder, was executed.

Over 80% of the housing stock was estimated to have been destroyed by Hurricane Georges, which swept through St. Kitts and Nevis in September. Overall damage was assessed at close to $40 million.

(DAVID RENWICK)

SAINT LUCIA

Area: 617 sq km (238 sq mi)
Population (1998 est.): 151,000
Capital: Castries
Chief of state: Queen Elizabeth II, represented by Governor-General George Mallet
Head of government: Prime Minister Kenny Anthony

Poor prison conditions in St. Lucia were again highlighted in February 1998. Further unrest in the main penitentiary in Castries left one officer badly injured. An attempt was made to set fire to the building; weapons and drugs were also found. A new prison commissioner was appointed to reform the prison.

In June former prime minister Sir John Compton was restored as head of the opposition United Workers Party (UWP). His successor, Vaughan Lewis, had failed to attract voter support in the 1997 general election, and the party won only one of the 17 seats contested. Compton's return, however, was not immediately beneficial. The governing St. Lucia Labour Party (SLP) under Prime Minister Kenny Anthony easily retained the West Castries–Barbonneau seat in a by-election in July.

The inquiry into alleged corruption during Compton's last administration prior to 1997 continued throughout 1998. British Queen's Counsel Sir Louis Blom-Cooper led the inquiry, taking over from former judge Monica Joseph, who had been accused of bias by both Compton and Lewis.

Prime Minister Kenny Anthony made a visit to Tokyo in June, where he received an offer for a $7.3 million loan to construct a fisheries complex at the town of Vieux Fort. Plans to reconstruct and enlarge the cruise ship facility at Point Seraphin were also announced.

(DAVID RENWICK)

SAINT VINCENT AND THE GRENADINES

Area: 389 sq km (150 sq mi)
Population (1998 est.): 113,000
Capital: Kingstown
Chief of state: Queen Elizabeth II, represented by Governor-General Sir David Jack
Head of government: Prime Minister Sir James Fitz-Allen Mitchell

In June 1998 the New Democratic Party (NDP), headed by Sir James Mitchell, narrowly won a fourth straight term in the general election. The NDP obtained 8 of the 15 House of Assembly seats, whereas the Unity Labour Party (ULP), led by Vincent Beache, won the other 7.

The ULP, however, received 54.6% of the vote, compared with 45.3% for the NDP. The opposition objected to the election result, and Beache demanded that another poll be held within nine months. Opposition supporters scuffled with police and government ministers when the new House of Assembly first met in July.

The NDP promised to cut taxes and planned to develop agriculture and tourism. Newly appointed Finance Minister Arnhim Eustace was regarded as a possible successor to Fitz-Allen, who said he would not contest another election.

The premier of the island of Nevis, Vance Amory, gives an interview in his office in Charlestown, the capital. Citizens of the 93-sq-km (36-sq-mi) Caribbean island went to the polls on August 11 to vote whether to secede from its federation with the larger island of St. Kitts.

Voters line up at a polling station in Saint Vincent and the Grenadines to cast their ballots in the general election on June 15. With unemployment hovering around 45% and the country's banana industry on shaky ground, the opposition Unity Labour Party made a strong showing but fell one seat short of capturing a majority in the House of Assembly.

In September Fitz-Allen initiated talks with the opposition to reform the constitution. Although Beache welcomed the proposal, his conditions included publication of a previously unreleased report on constitutional change.   (DAVID RENWICK)

SAMOA

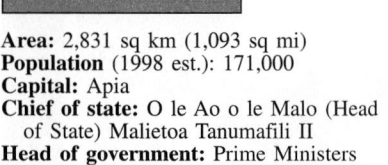

Area: 2,831 sq km (1,093 sq mi)
Population (1998 est.): 171,000
Capital: Apia
Chief of state: O le Ao o le Malo (Head of State) Malietoa Tanumafili II
Head of government: Prime Ministers Tofilau Eti Alesana and, from November 24, Tuila'epa Sa'ilele Malielegaoi

The government of Samoa in 1998 continued its policy of economic liberalization. Beginning in January central bank controls were eased, and commercial banks were allowed to set interest rates. In the 1998–99 budget, released in May, the government abolished most excise taxes and cut tariffs, import duties, and income tax. For 1998–99, revenue was estimated at SA$334 million and expenditure at SA$345 million (SA$3.09=U.S. $1).

Tension continued between the government and newspapers, with the prime minister successful in a legal action for libel. The government also declared that it would fund costs for ministers and senior civil servants to sue the news media for comments concerning them in their capacity as public officials. Tofilau Eti Alesana, prime minister since 1985, resigned in November for reasons of health.

Bush fires in Savai'i, started for the purpose of land clearance, burned out of control under dry conditions and destroyed nearly a quarter of the island's forests.
(BARRIE MACDONALD)

SAN MARINO

Area: 61.2 sq km (23.6 sq mi)
Population (1998 est.): 26,100
Capital: San Marino
Heads of state and government: The republic is governed by two *capitani reggenti,* or coregents, appointed every six months by a popularly elected Great and General Council.

Elections in May 1998 confirmed support for the Christian Democrat–Socialist alliance formed in 1992; it gained 64.1% of the vote, notwithstanding the claim by the opposition that the government was riddled with corruption. The government promised sweeping reforms during the next five years in order to streamline bureaucratic procedures and render the state more responsive to the needs of its citizens. Gabriele Gatti, the state secretary for foreign affairs, represented San Marino at a widely attended conference in Rome that sought to establish an international criminal court responsible for hearing war crimes and similar atrocities.

Victory by the incumbent alliance came as no surprise, considering the nation's sustained growth and prosperity, marked by a continual influx of new citizens. San Marino reported an unemployment rate of slightly over 3% and a minimal crime rate.
(GREGORY O. SMITH)

SÃO TOMÉ AND PRÍNCIPE

Area: 1,001 sq km (386 sq mi)
Population (1998 est.): 136,000
Capital: São Tomé
Chief of state: President Miguel Trovoada
Head of government: Prime Ministers Raul Bragança Neto and, from December 24, Guilherme Posser da Costa

Discontent with the government of Pres. Miguel Trovoada mounted in 1998. The army was dissatisfied with its pay, and other critics continued to be unhappy with the country's recognition of Taiwan, which had caused the loss of ties with China. Civil servants went on strike in March. Also during that month the Forum of Unity for National Reconstruction brought together the nation's various groups in an attempt to end the chronic political instability. In June Trovoada played a leading role in trying to defuse the crisis in Guinea-Bissau, serving as chair of a meeting of the five Portuguese-speaking African countries. Following general elections in November, Guilherme Posser da Costa took over as prime minister.

The two-island nation remained poor. Attempts to establish a customs-free zone on the west coast of the island of Príncipe were not successful, and the country remained heavily dependent on international aid. The main export commodity, cocoa, went mainly to Germany and The Netherlands, and most of the aid the country received came from the European Union.
(CHRISTOPHER SAUNDERS)

SAUDI ARABIA

Area: 2,248,000 sq km (868,000 sq mi)
Population (1998 est.): 20,786,000
Capital: Riyadh
Head of state and government: King
Fahd

Owing to the illness of King Fahd, Crown Prince 'Abdallah ibn 'Abd al-'Aziz, half brother of the king, ran the day-to-day affairs of Saudi Arabia in 1998. Under his tenure the rapprochement with Iran, which had begun in 1997 with the visit of Iranian Foreign Minister Ali Akbar Velayati, continued. In December 1997 a high-level Saudi delegation attended the Iranian-chaired Organization of the Islamic Conference summit, where 'Abdallah offered to mediate between Iran and the U.S. in order to reach a settlement of their differences. In February 1998 the former president of Iran, Ayatollah Ali Hashemi Rafsanjani, visited Saudi Arabia for almost two weeks, meeting with Saudi businessmen; and in March an Iranian warship docked at Jiddah. At the same time that they were moving toward closer relations with Iran, the Saudis did not support American efforts to pressure Iraq on the issue of weapons inspections.

In addition, although both the Saudis and the Americans had originally suspected that Iran was directly or indirectly responsible for the bombing at the Khobar housing complex in June 1996 that killed 19 U.S. soldiers, in March Saudi Minister of the Interior Nayif ibn 'Abd al-'Aziz announced that the investigation of the Khobar bombing had been completed, and in May he said that only Saudi nationals had been involved in the attack. The U.S. considered the investigation still open and accused the Saudis of a lack of cooperation, but by June the FBI had removed from the country all but one of its investigators, who had been acting as liaison with the Saudis. At the year's end, however, 4,500 American military personnel remained in Saudi Arabia. In July, however, the Saudi government stated that the investigation was continuing.

Lower oil prices resulted in projections of a budget deficit in fiscal 1998 of $10.7 billion at a time when the kingdom was spending more money for education in order to prepare increased numbers of Saudi nationals to replace foreign workers. According to its policy in regard to the private sector, the government began to expel illegal immigrants so that Saudis could fill their jobs. As of 1998, foreign workers composed 90% of the workforce in the private sector. Most public-sector jobs were already held by Saudi nationals.

The British nurses imprisoned for the murder of Australian nurse Yvonne Gilford were pardoned by King Fahd in May and returned to the U.K. During the annual pilgrimage to Mecca, 118 people were trampled to death when pilgrims fell from an overpass on the plains of Mena during the last day of the hajj. In October Crown Prince 'Abdallah traveled to the U.S. to confer with executives of U.S. oil companies. He sought their advice on ways for his nation to best develop its vast reserves of oil and natural gas.   (REEVA S. SIMON)

SENEGAL

Area: 196,712 sq km (75,951 sq mi)
Population (1998 est.): 9,723,000
Capital: Dakar
Chief of state: President Abdou Diouf
Head of government: Prime Minister
Habib Thiam and, from July 3,
Mamadou Lamine Loum

The 16-year-old conflict between the government of Senegal and the separatist Movement of Democratic Forces of

Muslims perform the sacred rite known as "stoning the devil" on the last day of the hajj, the annual pilgrimage to Mecca. On April 9, 118 persons died in a stampede that occurred as tens of thousands of worshipers made their way across a bridge to perform the rite. An estimated 2.3 million Muslims from some 100 countries made the journey to Mecca in 1998.

Casamance (MFDC) erupted in several violent clashes during 1998, despite a call on January 13 for peace by Father Diamacoune Senghor, secretary-general of the MFDC. Secessionists killed 6 civilians in February and another 7 on April 9, and they lost 10 men themselves in heavy fighting against the army on April 21.

In February the president of Guinea-Bissau ordered the arrest of several army officers who were accused of supplying arms to the MFDC. Senegal in June sent some 1,500 troops to Guinea-Bissau to aid its president in putting down an attempted military coup. The Senegalese government charged the MFDC with fighting alongside the Guinea-Bissau rebels. After capturing an important Guinea-Bissau army camp on June 14, Senegalese forces bombarded the northern town of Ingore. According to observers, approximately 100 people died in the shelling.

Claiming that the ruling Socialist Party (PS) was undemocratic, a dissident faction broke away on April 1 and vowed to join with the main opposition party, the Senegalese Democrats, in contesting the May 24 parliamentary elections. This had little effect, however, as the election gave the PS a comfortable majority of 93 of the 140 seats. Only in the Casamance, where 36 people were killed in the weeks preceding the elections, were there serious disturbances.   (NANCY ELLEN LAWLER)

SEYCHELLES

Area: 455 sq km (176 sq mi)
Population (1998 est.): 79,400
Capital: Victoria
Head of state and government: President France-Albert René

Seychelles held national elections in March 1998. Pres. France-Albert René won with 66% of the vote. His closest challenger, Wavel Ramkalawan of the United Opposition party, garnered 27% and led the parliamentary opposition. René's Seychelles People's Progressive Front dominated the parliamentary poll, capturing 61% of the vote and taking 30 of 34 seats in the national legislature.

The International Monetary Fund recommended decisive action to avert economic crisis caused primarily by a budget deficit of nearly $70 million. In response the government trimmed welfare benefits and considered reducing the country's free health care benefits. René announced plans to introduce school fees, ending a policy of universal free education. Other plans included higher taxes on alcohol, cigarettes, gasoline, and vehicles and a bond issue.

In May a 60% drop in fish harvests was blamed on increased water temperatures. Although the export fishing industry was not affected, the situation had wider economic implications. Seychelles depended heavily on tourist revenue, and continued warm water could threaten the archipelago's extensive coral reefs and pristine ecology.
                     (MATTHEW A. CENZER)

Pres. Ahmad Tejan Kabbah of Sierra Leone makes a gesture of thanks in March after returning from a 10-month exile. A multinational force composed largely of Nigerian soldiers wrested Freetown from the control of Sierra Leone's military junta, allowing Kabbah to return and form a new government.

SIERRA LEONE

Area: 71,740 sq km (27,699 sq mi)
Population (1998 est.): 4,577,000 (including more than 450,000 Sierra Leonean refugees temporarily residing in Guinea and Liberia)
Capital: Freetown
Head of state and government: Presidents Maj. Johnny Paul Koroma and, from March 20, Ahmad Tejan Kabbah

As 1998 began in Sierra Leone, the army battled militia forces loyal to ousted president Ahmad Tejan Kabbah in Bo, the country's second largest city. To aid the militia, ECOMOG (Economic Community of West African States Cease-Fire Monitoring Group) tripled the number of its troops in the country. This multinational force, composed largely of Nigerian soldiers, pledged to remove the military government and return Kabbah to power. Pro-Kabbah forces made significant gains in the diamond-rich eastern part of the country. Following aerial bombardments in mid-February, ECOMOG forces captured Freetown and forced Lieut. Col. Johnny Paul Koroma to flee along with other leaders of the military junta. On March 10 Kabbah returned to the capital, and 10 days later he named a new government. The UN lifted an oil embargo that had been enacted in response to the coup, and ECOMOG forces loosened their blockade of the country. Although Kabbah's government and ECOMOG troops controlled the capital, rebels loyal to the ousted military govern-

ment continued to fight in the east and south of the country. Throughout the year ECOMOG battled the rebels, with the city of Bo changing hands several times. Fighting later broke out in the north, and at the year's end rebels were threatening Freetown.

The ongoing fighting exacerbated an already critical humanitarian situation. More than 180,000 Sierra Leonean refugees in Guinea were threatened with starvation, and additional refugees fled the country as rebel activity intensified. The fighting, combined with blockades, contributed to widespread hunger and disease in rebel-controlled areas. According to the UN World Food Programme, half a million people inside the country were threatened with starvation.

In a step toward reconstruction, the UN organized a conference in July in Freetown to plan rebuilding efforts. The government continued to call on the international community for humanitarian assistance. President Kabbah also appealed for help in disarming rebel militias and reintegrating their members into society.
                     (MATTHEW A. CENZER)

SINGAPORE

Area: 646 sq km (249 sq mi)
Population (1998 est.): 3,164,000
Chief of state: President Ong Teng Cheong
Head of government: Prime Minister Goh Chok Tong

For Singapore, 1998 could be summed up as the year of the reality check. Despite the regional economic crisis that had been under way since July 1997, Singapore appeared to be in fairly good shape coming into 1998—at least compared with its neighbours. From the outset of the crisis, Singapore's leaders had repeatedly pronounced that the republic's "sound fundamentals" would protect it from the worst effects of the "Asian flu" that had ravaged other economies and currencies. Singapore had run budget surpluses for years (the last deficit was recorded in 1986 during the last recession) and had accumulated nearly $80 billion in reserves; its banks were well capitalized and its economy seemingly in good shape.

Such confidence was to prove premature, however, as Singapore belatedly succumbed to the economic contagion. The first major jolt came in January, in the wake of Indonesia's collapse, when the Singapore dollar plummeted from 1.67 to the U.S. dollar to 1.8. (It later recovered and ended the year at 1.64.) The stock and property markets then began a roller-coaster ride during which the benchmark Straits Times Index dropped as much as 47% in early September from the start of the year before rallying in the final quarter to close only 7.4% down. Likewise, the property market plunged some 40% in value from its peak in May 1996.

On the political front, predominantly Chinese Singapore watched in horror as its large Muslim neighbour Indonesia descended into economic and political chaos, which cul-

minated in longtime President Suharto's ouster during bloody riots in May that targeted Indonesia's ethnic Chinese population. Singapore's military went on heightened alert and stepped up border and naval patrols, fearful of a worst-case "meltdown scenario" in Indonesia that would send hundreds of thousands if not millions of Indonesian refugees fleeing to the small nation.

Meanwhile, perennially prickly relations with Malaysia, Singapore's other large mostly Muslim neighbour, took a sharp turn for the worse as long-simmering disputes over water and a railway line came to a head during the summer. Thus, Singapore faced the nightmarish scenario of being at odds with its two largest neighbours, with whom its economy was closely tied.

If this was not bad enough, Singapore slid into recession as it registered its first consecutive quarters of negative growth since 1986. From a high of 7.8% growth in 1997, the government estimated an increase of 1.3% in 1998.   (ANDREA HAMILTON)

SLOVAKIA

Area: 49,036 sq km (18,933 sq mi)
Population (1998 est.): 5,425,000
Capital: Bratislava
Chief of state: President Michal Kovac until March 2; some functions of chief of state assumed by the prime minister thereafter.
Head of government: Prime Ministers Vladimir Meciar and, from October 29, Mikulas Dzurinda

Slovakia's parliamentary elections on September 25–26 brought dramatic change and overshadowed other events of 1998. Four opposition parties won a constitutional majority and removed Prime Minister Vladimir Meciar's party, the Movement for a Democratic Slovakia (HZDS), from power. The HZDS defeat came despite its lavish campaign and government-sponsored changes in the election law approved by the parliament in May that were apparently aimed at hindering the opposition.

The HZDS won 27% of the vote, but the centre-right opposition Slovak Democratic Coalition (SDK) trailed closely with 26.33%. HZDS attempts to form a Cabinet were welcomed only by the Slovak National Party (SNS). A four-party coalition agreement was signed on October 28, with SDK Chairman Mikulas Dzurinda as prime minister and participation in the government from the SDK, Party of the Democratic Left, the centre-left Party of Civic Understanding, and the ethnically oriented Party of the Hungarian Coalition.

In its program statement, the Dzurinda government focused on freedom, equality, justice, democracy, and tolerance as its basic principles. It also sought to reduce the balance of payments deficit.

Slovakia was without a president for much of the year. Pres. Michal Kovac's term expired in March, but the parliament was unable to agree on a replacement. Meciar took over most presidential duties.

Slovakia's new Cabinet was faced with a troublesome economic situation, the legacy of the Meciar government. Gross domestic product growth continued to be strong, with an expected annual increase of approximately 5% in 1998, and annual inflation had risen just 5.9% as of September. Other economic figures, however, were far less promising. The growing foreign trade and state budget deficits were worrying, as was the rising state debt. Whereas privatization had moved quickly under Meciar's Cabinet, the restructuring necessary in many firms remained to be carried out, and special measures needed to rescue the banking sector awaited implementation. Despite several years of strong economic growth, unemployment remained at about 14%. On October 1 the National Bank of Slovakia was forced to float the national currency, the koruna (crown), and abolish the 7% fluctuation band within which it was fixed against a mark-dollar basket.

The top foreign relations objective of the Dzurinda government was putting Slovakia on track for early European Union membership. Just after the elections, Slovakia's neighbours were actively pushing for the country's speedy integration. The situation remained difficult for Slovakia's Roma (Gypsy) population, particularly after summer floods ravaged two villages. Because of an inflow of Roma from Slovakia applying for refugee status, Great Britain imposed a visa requirement for Slovak nationals on October 7.   (SHARON FISHER)

SLOVENIA

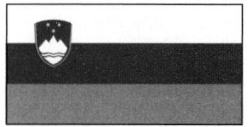

Area: 20,256 sq km (7,821 sq mi)
Population (1998 est.): 1,985,000
Capital: Ljubljana
Chief of state: President Milan Kucan
Head of government: Prime Minister Janez Drnovsek

On Jan. 1, 1998, Slovenia began a two-year term as a nonpermanent member of the United Nations Security Council. Slovenia's ambassador to the UN, Danilo Turk, served as Security Council president in August.

Slovenia joined five other countries invited to participate in negotiations intended to lead to full membership in the European Union. Membership would require Slovenia to change many laws and regulations to come into compliance with EU standards. The country's largest political parties were united in supporting EU membership, but many of the changes that would be required (in agricultural policy, for example) were certain to prove painful.

In November Prime Minister Janez Drnovsek made his first official visit to the U.S., and in meetings with U.S. Pres. Bill Clinton and other government officials, he reiterated Slovenia's strong desire for eventual full membership in NATO. Slovenia continued its participation in NATO's "Partnership for Peace" program, and the largest Partnership for Peace military exercise in 1998 took place in southern Slovenia in November. A small Slovene military unit continued its participation in the peacekeeping force in Bosnia and Herzegovina, and another small unit joined a similar entity on Cyprus.

A strong earthquake on April 12 caused considerable property damage in lightly populated northwestern Slovenia. Heavy rains on November 4–5 caused widespread flooding across much of the country. Damages were estimated to exceed $200 million.

Church-state relations remained unsettled. Matters of dispute included the role of the church in the country's educational system, the return to the church of all properties na-

Surrounded by jubilant supporters, Slovak Democratic Coalition (SDK) leader Mikulas Dzurinda (centre) points at a television screen showing results of Slovakia's parliamentary elections in September. The SDK made significant gains, and a four-party coalition agreement was signed on October 28, with Dzurinda as prime minister.

DAVID BRAUCHLI—NEWSMAKERS

tionalized by the previous communist government, and the financing of church activities. On June 3 the Vatican beatified the first bishop of the Maribor diocese, Anton M. Slomsek (1800–62), the first Slovene to attain this status.

Slovenia continued to sustain a moderate rate of economic growth, at 4%. The rate of inflation was 8%, and unemployment totaled 13%.   (RUDOLPH M. SUSEL)

SOLOMON ISLANDS

Area: 28,370 sq km (10,954 sq mi)
Population (1998 est.): 426,000
Capital: Honiara
Chief of state: Queen Elizabeth II, represented by Governor-General Moses Pitakaka
Head of government: Prime Minister Bartholomew Ulufa'alu

Prime Minister Bartholomew Ulufa'alu in 1998 faced political uncertainty that culminated in the dismissal of the minister of finance in July. In September the government survived a motion of no confidence in the National Parliament, after which Ulufa'alu reshuffled his Cabinet. In October former prime minister Solomon Mamaloni became leader of the opposition, replacing Job Duddley Tausinga.

The economy suffered from the Asian financial crisis and from the collapse of the log market. Forestry exports declined from 650,000 metric tons in 1997 to 360,000 metric tons in 1998, reducing export earnings from SI$309 million (U.S. $67 million) to SI$101 million (U.S. $22 million).

Continuing drought in the western Solomons and Cyclone Katrina in January made disaster relief measures necessary, especially on the islands of Rennell and Bellona. These developments were associated with the El Niño weather pattern, which also caused a rise in sea temperature that contributed to the largest tuna catch in the Solomon Islands since 1983.
                    (BARRIE MACDONALD)

SOMALIA

Area: 637,000 sq km (246,000 sq mi; including the 176,000-sq km [68,000-sq mi] area of the unilaterally declared [in 1991] and unrecognized Republic of Somaliland)
Population (1998 est.): 6,842,000 (including 4,300,000 residents of Somaliland; excluding 400,000 refugees in neighbouring countries)
Capital: Mogadishu; Hargeysa is the capital of Somaliland
Head of state and government: Somalia had no functioning government in 1998.

Moves to reunite Somalia, a country still divided between factions based on clans and subclans, made little progress in 1998. The factions were grouped into two loose alliances: the Somali Salvation Alliance headed by Ali Mahdi Muhammad and the Somali National Alliance, first formed by Gen. Muhammad Farah Aydid, who died in 1996, and in 1998 led by his son, Hussein Aydid. At the end of the year, a breakaway third alliance emerged.

In the Cairo declaration of December 1997, the Ali Mahdi and Hussein factions had agreed to a cease-fire and a national reconciliation conference. The conference was scheduled for February 1998 in the southern town of Baidoa after Hussein's forces had withdrawn from the town. It was, however, postponed three times during the year, as Hussein's forces continued to hold Baidoa against the Rahanwein Resistance Army, which represented the clans native to the area.

On the other hand, negotiations aimed at the reunification of Mogadishu and the reopening of the port and airport seemed to be progressing. In February free movement across the city began as checkpoints were dismantled. In August Ali Mahdi and Hussein met in Tripoli, Libya, and agreed to establish a new common administration in the Benaadir region around Mogadishu, and in September a joint administration and multiclan militia was established. Ali Mahdi and Hussein failed, however, to carry all the members of their two alliances with them, and those opposed to the pact formed a coalition.

In July part of the northeast declared itself an independent state under the name Puntland, with its capital at Garoowe and Col. Abdullahi Yusuf Ahmed as its president. This move represented a split within the Somali Salvation Democratic Front, which had previously maintained a comparatively stable regional government in the northeast. In the northwest the self-declared Republic of Somaliland continued to function in spite of its failure to gain international recogni-

tion. The political situation there remained largely stable, but the republic's economy suffered considerably from a Saudi Arabian ban on its livestock exports.

In August a peace deal was reached in the southwestern Gedo region after heavy fighting between the al-Itihad Islamic movement and a faction of the Somali National Front (Marehan clan). The latter was reportedly backed by Ethiopia, retaliating for attacks by al-Itihad within its own borders.

The impact of the floods that overwhelmed the valley of the Jubba River at the end of 1997 continued, and in April heavy rains hampered relief efforts. In July there were floods on the Shabelle River near the town of Balad.   (VIRGINIA R. LULING)

SOUTH AFRICA

Area: 1,219,090 sq km (470,693 sq mi)
Population (1998 est.): 42,835,000
Capitals (de facto): Pretoria (executive); Bloemfontein (judicial); Cape Town (legislative)
Head of state and government: President Nelson Mandela

In 1998 South Africa experienced bizarre allegations of conspiracies and also a political crisis in the national sport of rugby. In midyear the value of the rand plunged amid bitter controversy between the African National Congress (ANC) and its allies over economic policy. On his 80th birthday in July, Pres. Nelson Mandela married Graça Machel, widow of Samora Machel, former president of Mozambique.

Domestic Affairs. Opening Parliament on February 6, President Mandela highlighted the achievements of the ANC-led govern-

South African Pres. Nelson Mandela and his new wife, Graça Machel, celebrate their wedding and Mandela's 80th birthday at a reception outside Johannesburg on July 19. During the year Mandela was praised for reducing the crime rate, increasing exports, and attracting foreign investment, though he admitted that not all of his government's promises had been met.

WALTER DHDLADLA—AP/WIDE WORLD/POOL AFP

ment while admitting that not all promises had been met. In particular, the target of one million new houses by 1999 would not be achieved. Moreover, he stated, the economy continued to shed too many jobs. On the positive side he pointed to 1.3 million people who had obtained water supplies, 421,000 who now had telephones, and 400,000 whose homes were wired for electricity; in addition, more than 500 health clinics were opened. Most serious crimes, he claimed, had decreased. Exports had increased, and incentives had attracted foreign investment, particularly to initiatives such as the Maputo corridor (linking South Africa and Mozambique). Leaders of opposition parties claimed that the ANC had the right ideas but was not implementing them properly.

In March Mandela appointed a judicial inquiry into an intelligence report alleging a conspiracy to overthrow the government, involving army generals, the ANC, and other politicians. The inquiry found the allegations in the report to be "fraudulent and of no substance." It was widely believed that the report had been drawn up by white right-wing elements seeking to destabilize the government.

During the midyear economic crisis, with the rand plunging in value, both Mandela and Deputy Pres. Thabo Mbeki delivered unprecedentedly harsh rebukes to the Congress of South African Trade Unions (COSATU) and the South African Communist Party (SACP), partners with the ANC in the Triple Alliance, for their opposition to the government's Growth, Employment, and Redistribution (GEAR) macroeconomic policy. COSATU and the SACP regarded GEAR as pro-business and antilabour and opposed its goals of reduced budget deficits, privatization, and more flexible labour markets. They argued for more government spending, including large-scale public works programs to create jobs and provide housing. Also, during the crisis the government announced that the governor of the Reserve Bank, Chris Stals, would be replaced at the end of his term in August 1999 by Minister of Labour Tito Mboweni, who would become the first black South African to hold the position.

South African rugby experienced serious difficulties. Mandela appointed a commission of inquiry into allegations of racism and corruption in the South African Rugby Football Union (SARFU), which challenged in court his right to appoint such a commission. Unprecedentedly, the president was ordered by the court to appear as a witness. In the course of his testimony, Mandela called the SARFU president, Louis Luyt, "a pitiless dictator." In April the court overruled the appointment of the commission. Following this decision, the National Sports Council, claiming that Mandela's court appearance had humiliated him and the office of the presidency, called for the SARFU executive to resign or face an international rugby boycott. Luyt was eventually compelled to resign in May, and the new executive apologized to Mandela. In August the judge of the case caused an outcry when he presented reasons for his judgment, including that Mandela was a "less than satisfactory" witness who used the court as a "podium for political rhetoric."

The Truth and Reconciliation Commission (TRC), concerned with human rights violations under apartheid, completed its main work at the end of July and submitted a five-volume report to President Mandela in late October. Since the TRC's inception in 1995, some 20,000 people had been involved in hearings, as victims or perpetrators. The hearings in 1998 included revelations on the chemical and biological weapons program of the apartheid regime. Former president P.W. Botha was convicted and fined R 10,000 (R 1=about U.S. $0.18), with a one–year prison sentence suspended, for refusing to give evidence to the TRC about his government's policy toward human rights violations. Ferdi Barnard, a former agent of the apartheid regime's Civil Cooperation Bureau, was found guilty in June of the murder of antiapartheid activist David Webster in 1989 and 24 other crimes and received two life sentences.

The Heath Commission, investigating apartheid-era corruption in the amount of at least R 16 billion, reported that it had "taken root through the entire administration." Former Bophuthatswana president Lucas Mangope was convicted on 105 counts of theft totaling R 4,840,000. Several provincial ANC parliamentary officials were found guilty of corruption and mismanagement and were forced to resign their positions.

The National Party (NP) continued its decline. The Democratic Party (DP) won a number of former NP strongholds in municipal by-elections. Former and present NP leaders defected to the DP and the United Democratic Movement (UDM), formed by Roelf Meyer and Bantu Holomisa in 1997. Hernus Kriel was replaced as premier and NP provincial leader in the Western Cape by Gerald Morkel, the first Coloured person in the NP's history to hold such offices. Though rapprochement between Gatsha Buthelezi's Inkatha Freedom Party (IFP) and the ANC continued, Cabinet Minister Sipo Mzimela, who aired the idea of an IFP-ANC merger, was forced by the IFP to recant and subsequently was replaced as IFP deputy chairman and removed from his position in the Cabinet.

The Economy. Affected by the ripples flowing from the economic crisis in Asia, the rand (which had remained stable since 1996) plunged 30% against the dollar, mainly from late May to mid-July, which caused the prime lending rate to soar to 24% and seriously affected the country's economic growth prospects. Gross domestic product grew by 1.7% in 1997, and its growth in 1998 was estimated after the rand's crisis at 0.5%. The government's revised figure for unemployment (bringing it into line with international definitions) was an estimated 22.9% (37.6% according to old estimates).

Inflation, which averaged 8.6% in 1997, declined to 5% in April 1998 but had risen to 9.1% by September. The Reserve Bank replaced the bank rate with a more flexible "repo rate" system of monetary management in March. Initially set at 15% (equivalent to a 1% cut in the bank rate), it was raised sharply during the rand crisis, which caused a general increase in interest rates.

The budget in March projected 1998–99 spending at R 201.2 billion (a rise of 6.4%) and revenue at R 176.6 billion (up 9.3%). At 21% of the budget, interest payments continued to be the largest item, with education constituting 26% and health 14% of noninterest spending. The budget deficit was targeted at 3.9% (actual 1997–98 deficit was 4.3% against a targeted 4%).

Workdays lost to strikes in 1998 reached the highest figure since 1994. A conference on job creation involving government, labour, and business was held in late October. Mzi Khumalo resigned in January as chairman and from the board of Johannesburg Consolidated Investments in what was seen as a setback for black empowerment, though other advances were made by black business during the year.

Foreign Affairs. In September the ANC-led government undertook its first military foray, controversially sending troops into Lesotho at the request of its government to prevent a coup. In August there was schism in the South African Development Community (SADC) when Zimbabwe and Angola sent troops to support the government of the Democratic Republic of the Congo and South Africa did not.

South Africa took the chair of the 113-member Non-Aligned Movement, which met in Durban in September, and stressed the necessity for reform of the international economic order. In late March, U.S. Pres. Bill Clinton visited South Africa for 3 days as part of an 11-day, six-nation tour of Africa. He praised the ANC government and expressed wishes for a strong South Africa and a continued partnership between the two countries. President Mandela reaffirmed the government's intention of continuing relations with "pariah" states such as Cuba and Libya and expressed reservations concerning the Africa trade bill under discussion in the U.S. Congress (See Spotlight: *President Clinton's Africa Trip*).

In a bizarre episode Foreign Affairs Ministry official Robert McBride spent six months in detention in Mozambique after his arrest in March on charges of arms smuggling and spying. McBride, imprisoned during the apartheid regime for the bombing of a beachfront bar in Durban, said his intention was to trap a Mozambican arms dealer. It was widely believed that he had been framed by apartheid-era agents still serving in South African government intelligence.

(MARTIN LEGASSICK)

SPAIN

Area: 505,990 sq km (195,364 sq mi)
Population (1998 est.): 39,371,000
Capital: Madrid
Chief of state: King Juan Carlos I
Head of government: Prime Minister José María Aznar López

Spain experienced an eventful year in 1998, as significant developments took place at both international and national levels. One that had a far-reaching effect was the extradition request by the Spanish government of the former Chilean dictator, Gen. Augusto Pinochet, who was arrested in October in London on a warrant signed by Spanish and British judges. The case became a cause célèbre, prompting extradition requests from France, Switzerland, and Sweden. Pinochet stood accused of a host of crimes, ranging

from individual cases of citizens of the prosecuting countries being killed or "disappeared" to the widespread use of torture and kidnapping, crimes against humanity, and even genocide.

The Pinochet affair polarized Spain between those who approved of the extradition request (70%) and those who opposed it on the grounds that it would destabilize the fragile Chilean democracy. The case proved the maturity of the relatively young democratic regime in Spain; the right-wing government headed by Prime Minister José Aznar López decided not to interfere with the decisions of the judiciary (even though legally able to do so) and sanctioned the official extradition warrant with Cabinet approval.

Spanish foreign policy during 1998 concentrated on Latin America and Europe, but the traditional links with the Maghreb nations (Morocco, Algeria, and Tunisia) remained, exemplified by bilateral agreements and mutual cultural and economic visits. Prime Minister Aznar and a delegation of business leaders visited several Latin-

American countries, which allowed Spain to establish closer relations there, especially with Peru and Colombia. The visit by the foreign minister to Cuba ended a period of tension affecting relations between Madrid and Havana. This improved relationship had been in evidence when Pres. Fidel Castro of Cuba met Prime Minister Aznar at the Ibero-American conference in Portugal, a periodic major diplomatic and political event that all of the countries of Latin America, plus Portugal and Spain, attended.

The year marked a turning point in the internal politics of Spain. The October regional elections in the Basque country consolidated the influence and power of two major nationalist parties, the Basque Nationalist Party (PNV) and Herri Batasuna (HB). The former, the mainstream moderate nationalist organization, confirmed its position as the largest group in the Autonomous Parliament, and the latter (to the left within the nationalist spectrum) made important gains. A reinforced self-confidence resulting from these triumphs allowed the Euskadi Ta Askatasuna (ETA)

separatist group (generally regarded as the military wing of HB) to confirm a cease-fire that had been declared in September. The example of the cease-fire and the subsequent peace agreement in Northern Ireland played a substantial role in helping to ease the Basque-Spanish conflict. Spain, in turn, further facilitated this process by promising generous compensation for the victims of ETA terrorism and thereby helping to neutralize potential opposition to the ensuing negotiations. The open-minded attitude of the Aznar government on the issue seemed to be rewarded by an increased share of the vote for the centre-right Popular Party (in charge of the national government in Madrid) in the Basque elections. Nationalist fervour culminated in a "summit" of the major nationalist parties of Catalonia, the Basque country, and Galicia, which ended with the "Barcelona Declaration," stating common goals and strategies to achieve increased autonomy but within the Spanish state.

Ecological issues came to the fore in Spain during the year. A vigorous public debate created a new awareness of topics such as environmental pollution and deforestation, and a host of organizations competed to spread the ecological message. The government, conscious of the political implications of this new concern, was also party to the debate and promised active cooperation.

The economy suffered the effects of the global recession unleashed by the financial crisis in Asia, and the Ministry for the Economy reduced its estimate of economic growth for 1999 from 3.9% to 3.7%. The sharp decline of share prices on the Madrid and Barcelona stock exchanges (on average about 20%) created cause for concern among both business associations and trade unions. The latter voiced their concern at the risk of increased unemployment, which remained around 18%.

As a reaction against attempts to liberalize the current abortion laws, Roman Catholic groups renewed their antiabortion campaigns. In other developments former interior minister José Barrionuevo was imprisoned for his role in the 1983 kidnapping of a businessman; salaries increased an average of 2.3%; and illegal immigration from North Africa continued to be a problem that fed worries about racism and xenophobia. A study published during the year revealed deep-seated antagonism toward immigrants and foreigners in general in Spain as well as the existence of well-organized, though small, neo-Nazi groups.

(BENNY POLLACK)

DENIS DOYLE—AP/WIDE WORLD

Demonstrators against Gen. Augusto Pinochet celebrate in Madrid after the British government upheld his October arrest in London. Spain had accused the former Chilean dictator of ordering the murder of hundreds of Spanish citizens who disappeared in Chile during Pinochet's 1973–90 regime.

SRI LANKA

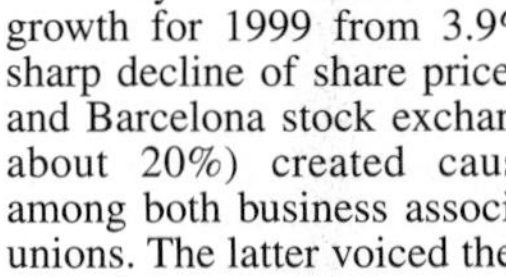

Area: 65,610 sq km (25,332 sq mi)
Population (1998 est.): 18,729,000
Capitals: Sri Jayawardenepura Kotte (legislative and judicial); Colombo (executive)
Head of state and government: President Chandrika Kumaratunga, assisted by Prime Minister Sirimavo Bandaranaike

The 15-year-old civil war in Sri Lanka continued unabated in 1998. On January 25, 10 days before the celebration of the 50th anniversary of the nation's independence, the Temple of the Tooth in Kandy was hit by a truck bomb, which killed at least 11 people, injured 23, and caused great damage to this holiest of Buddhist sites. Although responsibility for the attack was not claimed by the Liberation Tigers of Tamil Eelam (LTTE), the group that had been fighting the central government since 1983 in its quest for an independent homeland for Sri Lanka's two million Tamils, the government suspected it of having perpetrated the act. Accordingly, it outlawed the LTTE. Until then the government had refused to do so for fear of jeopardizing future negotiations with the group. Soon afterward, the LTTE struck again. A bus loaded with two shrapnel-packed bombs exploded near the main train station in Colombo, killing 37 people and wounding more than 250.

Soldiers in Colombo, Sri Lanka, look over the wreckage caused by a bomb suspected to have been set off by the Liberation Tigers of Tamil Eelam, the group that had been fighting the central government since 1983 in its quest for an independent homeland for Sri Lanka's two million Tamils. Some 28 persons were killed in the March explosion.

Throughout 1998 government forces continued their military campaign, Sure Victory, begun in May 1997 with the primary objective being the recapture of a 72.5-km (45-mi) strategic road linking the Jaffna Peninsula with the rest of the island. On September 11 the LTTE, with the aim of undermining the government's attempt to reinstate civil administration on the Jaffna Peninsula, killed the mayor of Jaffna City and the region's top army brigadier in a bomb attack. On September 28 the government admitted that at least 237 of its soldiers and Tamil Tiger rebels had been killed when the LTTE attacked the defense lines around Kilinochchi, at the northern end of the strategic road. After three days of intense fighting, the LTTE managed to recapture Kilinochchi, their former headquarters, which they had lost to the Sri Lankan army in 1996. According to government sources, close to 600 people had been killed, including 377 rebels and more than 200 Sri Lankan soldiers. The loss of Kilinochchi was a major blow to the morale of the Sri Lankan army. The government's capture of Manukalam at the southern end of the strategic road that same week was no substitute for the defeat in the north. On December 6 the government called off the Sure Victory campaign.

There were indications in late October that the government and the LTTE were looking for an opening to resume peace talks. Pres. Chandrika Kumaratunga insisted, however, that the government would reject LTTE calls for unconditional talks, stressing that the Tamil Tigers would have to first lay down their arms. (*See* Sidebar.)

(CLAUDE RAKISITS)

The Liberation Tigers

Formed in 1972, the Liberation Tigers of Tamil Eelam (LTTE), with an estimated strength in 1998 of about 9,000 guerrillas, had fought since 1983 to establish an independent Tamil state, Eelam, in the northern and eastern provinces of Sri Lanka, where most of the country's Tamil minority resided. One of the world's most sophisticated and tightly organized insurgent groups, the LTTE during the 1970s carried out a number of guerrilla attacks. Following large-scale violence that broke out in Sri Lanka in July 1983 in retaliation for the killing of 13 soldiers by Tamil guerrillas, the LTTE launched a full-scale "armed revolutionary struggle" against the government. By May 1985 the LTTE was in control of Jaffna and most of the Jaffna Peninsula in northern Sri Lanka, and by 1986 it had eliminated most of its rival Tamil groups.

The LTTE lost control of Jaffna in October 1987 to an Indian peacekeeping force (IPKF) that had been sent to Sri Lanka to assist in the implementation of a complete cease-fire. Following the withdrawal of the IPKF in March 1990, however, the Tigers grew in strength and conducted several successful guerrilla operations. These included an August 1992 land-mine explosion in Jaffna, which killed 10 senior military commanders; the May 1993 assassination of Sri Lankan Pres. Ranasinghe Premadasa; and a January 1996 suicide bomb attack on the central bank of Colombo, which killed 100 people.

Although the LTTE and the government resumed peace talks in January 1995, at which the LTTE indicated that it would be willing to accept some form of self-government instead of full independence, by April of that year the talks had broken down, and the Tigers unilaterally ended the truce. Fighting has not ceased since that time, and the Tigers have rejected government proposals. In 1998 the Tigers remained a credible force, as demonstrated by their ability to resist government attempts in 1997–98 to take control of the strategic road linking the Jaffna Peninsula with the rest of the island. Although the LTTE had recently indicated an interest in resuming negotiations with the government, Tiger activity seemed likely to continue.

(CLAUDE RAKISITIS)

SUDAN, THE

Area: 2,503,890 sq km (966,757 sq mi)
Population (1998 est.): 33,551,000
Capitals: Khartoum (executive and ministerial) and Omdurman (legislative)
Head of state and government: President and Prime Minister Lieut. Gen. Omar Hassan Ahmad al-Bashir

In January 1998 the Sudan People's Liberation Army (SPLA), based in southern Sudan, launched a new campaign in its long-running civil war against the government.

Both sides claimed victories, but little progress appeared to have been made by either combatant. The main outcome was that food shortages in the south became increasingly severe, and external aid agencies claimed that in order to avert famine in the region, they had to be permitted to fly in more food and other forms of relief.

On May 3 the government responded by permitting additional flights to be made to the Bahr al-Ghazal province, the most seriously affected area, but the SPLA claimed that this was a token gesture to win sympathy immediately prior to new negotiations, which opened in Nairobi, Kenya, the following day. Although neither side appeared to be in a mood for compromise, the meeting did result in an agreement that there should be a referendum on self-determination for the south, though no date was fixed for it to take place and there was a dispute as to the area covered by "the south." The SPLA wanted to extend the definition to include an oil-bearing region that the government, in conjunction with Chinese contractors and other financial backers, was just beginning to develop and had no intention of relinquishing. The government, for its part, gave no indication that it was prepared to waive its insistence upon Islamic law, even in the predominantly non-Muslim south.

An apparently more promising development took place on June 30 when Pres. Omar Hassan al-Bashir signed into law a new constitution. Significantly, it canceled the former ban on political parties, though strict control of criticism of the government remained in force until the day the law was promulgated. On July 15 the SPLA called a unilateral three-month humanitarian cease-fire in Bahr al-Ghazal, and in August the government called a cease-fire throughout the whole southern Sudan to permit relief organizations to send in supplies.

All these hopeful signs were jeopardized when the U.S. destroyed a pharmaceutical factory in Khartoum with long-range missiles on August 20 in retaliation for the bombing of U.S. embassies in Nairobi and Dar es Salaam, Tanz., by terrorists. The U.S. claimed to have convincing evidence that the factory had played a key role in the bombings. (KENNETH INGHAM)

SURINAME

Area: 163,820 sq km (63,251 sq mi)
Population (1998 est.): 418,000
Capital: Paramaribo
Head of state and government: President Jules Wijdenbosch

On May 5, 1998, details from a report by the International Monetary Fund, previously kept secret by the Suriname government, were leaked. In the report Suriname was declared to be "practically bankrupt."

Legal proceedings began on May 5 against the suspects in the unsuccessful attempt to overthrow the government on Oct. 25, 1997. The defendants were mainly low-ranking soldiers who felt they had been un-

A woman in search of seeds to boil into gruel sifts through soil and leaves in Bahr al-Ghazal province, the area of The Sudan most seriously affected by famine. On May 3 the Sudanese government permitted external aid agencies to make additional flights to Bahr al-Ghazal to deliver food and other forms of relief.

derpaid throughout the civil war, but motives for the coup attempt remained unclear. The soldiers were found guilty and on August 14 received prison sentences.

Protest marches against the government of Pres. Jules Wijdenbosch took place on June 24. The protesters were reacting to a government decision to privatize the state-owned oil companies. Workers at the oil companies also staged strikes.

In June Suriname announced plans to establish a nature reserve carved out of its vast Amazonian rain forest. The reserve covered 16,000 sq km (4,000,000 ac), roughly 12% of Suriname's territory. A Washington, D.C.-based environmental group, Conservation International, worked in conjunction with Suriname to develop the preserve. The group also raised $1 million for management costs. Suriname hoped that industries such as ecotourism and sales of forest products would boost its ailing economy and improve its image abroad.

(KLAAS J. HOEKSEMA)

SWAZILAND

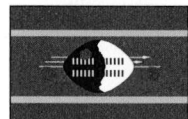

Area: 17,364 sq km (6,704 sq mi)
Population (1998 est.): 966,000
Capitals: Mbabane (administrative and judicial), Lozitha and Ludzidzini (royal), and Lobamba (legislative)
Chief of state and head of government: King Mswati III, assisted by Prime Minister Sibusiso Barnabas Dlamini

Although Swaziland remained peaceful during 1998, it was becoming more unstable. In October elections for the parliament were held, despite the fact that all political parties were banned. Opposition groups and labour unions, particularly the powerful Swaziland Federation of Trade Unions, called for a general boycott of the election. Few voters reportedly registered, and in response the government raided the homes of several opposition leaders.

Like those of other southern African countries, Swaziland's economy faltered

during the year. The global downturn weakened the country's currency, and exports remained stagnant. As the downturn continued, crime surged. The country also was rocked by corruption. Several prominent lawyers and politicians, including the former minister of justice and one of the king's advisers, were accused of defrauding the government.

The government did make some positive strides, however. Construction began on the Maguga Dam, which would reduce the country's dependency on South African electricity. In March Swaziland signed an agreement with Mozambique and South Africa to create a regional tourist and agricultural zone linked by highways and railroads. (MICHAEL TETELMAN)

SWEDEN

Area: 449,964 sq km (173,732 sq mi)
Population (1998 est.): 8,860,000
Capital: Stockholm
Chief of state: King Carl XVI Gustaf
Head of government: Prime Minister Göran Persson

The highlight of a busy political year in 1998 was the general election in September, in which the ruling Social Democrats slumped to their worst result in 70 years—but still clung to power. Prime Minister Göran Persson's parliamentary minority was sharply reduced by voters angry at persistently high unemployment and cuts in Sweden's cherished welfare system. The

Social Democrats saw their number of seats fall from 161 to 131 in the 349-member Riksdag (parliament).

Elsewhere, this might have precipitated a change of government. Persson, however, was able to stay in office for two reasons. First, the Social Democrats, though weakened, remained unchallenged as the largest party. This was chiefly due to the failure of the main opposition Moderate Coalition Party to capitalize on the government's unpopularity. Led by Carl Bildt, the former peace envoy to Bosnia and Herzegovina, the Moderates added just two seats to their tally of 80 from the previous election in 1994. Also, Persson shored up his power base by agreeing immediately after the election to an informal alliance with two left-wing parties, the former communist Left Party and the Greens. The Social Democrats had spent the previous four years in an ad hoc alliance with the rurally based Centre Party, which also fared poorly in the election.

Fears of a possible leftward lurch in government policy caused brief jitters on financial markets. Investors were subsequently mollified by assurances from Persson and his finance minister, Erik Asbrink, that the government would not be pressured into loosening fiscal policy.

Two weeks after the election, Persson unveiled one of the most sweeping Cabinet reshuffles in Swedish history, with eight ministers leaving their posts. Among the newcomers was Mona Sahlin, the former deputy prime minister, who in 1995 had been poised to become the party's new leader before she was forced to resign over her private use of a government credit card. Sahlin's political rehabilitation was ensured by her appointment as a junior minister in a new "superministry" responsible for promoting economic growth.

Outside the political arena, the year got off to a bright start with Stockholm starting a 12-month stint as Cultural Capital of Europe. In February the business world came under the microscope after controversy arose over high pay awards to top corporate executives. The issue was ignited when Stora, a leading forestry company, sacked its chief executive but not before granting him a SKr 64 million severance package (SKr 1=about U.S. $0.13). The size of the payment, initially concealed from company stockholders, prompted the resignation of Stora's chairman and government demands for companies to regulate executive pay more rigorously.

In October attention shifted to the announcement of proposals for far-reaching cutbacks in Sweden's military spending. Defense department officials, facing intense political pressure to curb expenditures, presented a policy document aimed at effectively freezing defense spending at its year-2000 level for the first 10 years of the next millennium. Among a host of other measures was a reduction in the universal conscription service and the mothballing of aging military hardware. Reflecting significant changes in northern European security requirements following the collapse of the Soviet Union, the measures were aimed at achieving a government savings of SKr 2 billion a year over the next five years. They were to be debated by the Riksdag during the first few months of 1999.

For many Swedes the year drew to an end on a distressing note. Two tragedies—a fire in Göteborg that killed 63 youths at a discotheque and the murder of a four-year-old child by two young boys, aged five and seven—prompted outpourings of national grief and soul-searching. The fire, in late October, was the worst in Sweden during peacetime. Most of the dead were immigrant teenagers unable to escape from an overfull dance hall. The killing of the four-year-old boy occurred in August, but the culprits—who were below the age of criminal responsibility and would not be tried—were not discovered until November.

(GREG MCIVOR)

SWITZERLAND

Area: 41,285 sq km (15,940 sq mi)
Population (1998 est.): 7,118,000
Capitals: Bern (administrative) and Lausanne (judicial)
Head of state and government: President Flavio Cotti

After four years of arduous bilateral negotiations, Switzerland and the European Union signed an agreement on Dec. 10, 1998, for the country's entry into the European Economic Area, commonly regarded as a halfway house to full EU membership. Intended to come into force in 2001, following parliamentary approval, the accord covered such subjects as transportation, reciprocal rights on employment and residence, research cooperation, public procurement (government contract bids), and mutual acceptance of trade documentation. The ink was hardly dry on the agreement when the extreme-right Swiss Democrats announced they would collect signatures for a national referendum they hoped would reject it.

Although a referendum on full EU membership would take place in the future, it was not expected to happen soon. Likely to be dealt with much earlier was the issue of joining the United Nations.

Although Switzerland had long been a member of the UN specialized agencies, such as the World Health Organization, a vote in 1986 on joining the UN resulted in an astonishing 75% "no"; considerations of traditional neutrality, as in the EU vote, were a major factor in the decision. An opinion poll in May 1998, however, showed 57.2% favouring UN membership and 69% supporting proposals for a Swiss solidarity corps able to help throughout the world in any catastrophe.

Once again, refugees were a problem, prosperous Switzerland acting for them like a magnet. Though thousands were being refused entry each month, the nation's frontiers were not difficult to slip across illegally for those—particularly "economic refugees"—able to enlist the services of a "passeur." Once into the country they could "lose" their identity papers and seek political asylum. Unless one's application was altogether unconvincing, that person was then assured of a bed and food while his or her case was considered. The Kosovo conflict led to a fresh influx of an estimated 40,000, including many families with young children. With air-raid shelters already full, the authorities were obliged to open up barracks and detail 5,600 soldiers on compulsory military service to help.

The threat of a boycott of Swiss banks by U.S. investors, as called for by the World

Relatives and friends of victims of a fire at a discotheque in Göteborg, Swed., gather to mourn the day after the disaster occurred in late October. The fire—the worst in Sweden during peacetime—killed 63 youths who were among hundreds of young people crowded into the dance hall when the blaze started.

Jewish Congress, led to an agreement by the banks to pay $1,250,000,000 as compensation for assets, mainly Jewish, held by them since before World War II. Several banks and insurance companies in other countries followed suit.

The Swiss banks' image was further damaged by the disclosure that the United Bank of Switzerland (UBS), which had been formed recently by the merger of two of the three leading banks and thereby having become what was described as "the world's second largest bank," had lost some $704 million. This had gone into a U.S. high-risk investment fund apparently in hope of realizing up to 40% profit.

Inflation for the year was officially estimated at 0% (0.5% in 1997). By September unemployment was down to 3.2%, the lowest level in six years. Young people, however, continued to experience difficulties in finding jobs, as did women. In April the national debt exceeded Sw F 100 billion (U.S. $69 billion) for the first time.   (ALAN MCGREGOR)

SYRIA

Area: 185,180 sq km (71,498 sq mi)
Population (1998 est.): 15,335,000
Capital: Damascus
Head of state and government: President Gen. Hafez al-Assad, assisted by Prime Minister Mahmud Zubi

Syria reacted to the blossoming strategic partnership between Israel and Turkey during 1998 by cultivating closer ties with Iraq and strengthening its own military establishment. The minister of health traveled to Baghdad at the end of March in the first official visit to Iraq by a Syrian Cabinet minister in two decades. A month later the two governments inaugurated a duty-free zone along their common border to encourage bilateral trade. July witnessed the signing of an agreement to reopen the pipeline linking the oil fields of northern Iraq to the Syrian terminus at Baniyas on the Mediterranean Sea; the line had been shut down since 1982. In the wake of a visit to Damascus by the Iraqi minister of commerce, Syrian officials announced plans to increase exports of sugar, medicine, soap, and other staples to Iraq. The two governments also began rehabilitating the trade centres located in one another's capitals that had stood abandoned since the late 1970s.

Meanwhile, Syrian commanders took steps to build up the armed forces. In May the government signed a deal with Russia worth some $400 million to supply the air force with sophisticated S-300 missile defense batteries, the same weapons that Moscow had agreed to sell the Greek government in Cyprus in January 1997. The deal complemented an earlier agreement to equip the Syrian army with some 1,000 Russian-made laser-guided antitank missiles. Russia's ambassador in Damascus called such contracts a way to "help maintain stability in the Middle East" and told reporters that Syrian units had taken part in military exercises inside Russia at the end of 1997.

In early July Syria's long-serving chief of staff, Gen. Hikmat Shihabi, announced his retirement. He was immediately succeeded by the former deputy chief of staff, Gen. 'Ali Aslan, a hero of the 1973 war with Israel. At the same time, the head of intelligence, Maj. Gen. Bashir an-Najjar, was dismissed and replaced by Maj. Gen. Mahmud ash-Shaqqa, the commander of Syria's expeditionary force in the Persian Gulf during the 1990–91 war. Knowledgeable observers speculated that these changes in command reflected the leadership's intention to reinvigorate the armed forces in the face of persistent Israeli operations in southern Lebanon and sporadic attacks against Syrian workers by dissident Lebanese militias.

It was under these circumstances that Pres. Hafez al-Assad flew to Paris on July 16 for three days of talks with French Pres. Jacques Chirac. The Syrian leader carefully avoided endorsing a proposal championed by Chirac to convene a new Middle East peace conference under European auspices, although the two presidents did sign protocols that rescheduled Syria's outstanding debts to France and set up procedures governing French investment in Syria.

In elections for the national legislature in December President al-Assad's National Progressive Front coalition won all of the 167 seats it contested. The remaining 83 seats were taken by nominally independent candidates.

On July 24 Turkish Prime Minister Mesut Yilmaz told a rally commemorating the 1939 transfer to Turkey of the former Syrian district surrounding the port of Iskandarun that "those who have their eyes fixed on Turkish territory" should harbour no illusions that they might ever gain control over "even a square centimetre of the territory of this country." He went on to charge that Syria had stepped up its support for the Kurdistan Workers' Party in an attempt to seize the province.   (FRED H. LAWSON)

TAIWAN

Area: 36,179 sq km (13,969 sq mi)
Population (1998 est.): 21,843,000
Capital: Taipei
Chief of state: President Lee Teng-hui
Head of government: President of the Executive Yuan (Premier) Vincent Siew

The Kuomintang (KMT), the ruling party of the Republic of China (ROC) on Taiwan, increased its previous razor-thin majority in the legislature to 123 of 225 seats in elections on Dec. 5, 1998. The KMT's charismatic candidate for mayor, Ma Ying-jeou, upset incumbent Chen Shui-bian, a leading figure in the main opposition Democratic Progressive Party (DPP), which had championed the cause of an independent Taiwan. Ma's victory also dealt a serious blow to Chen's presidential aspirations. Although the DPP won the mayoralty in Kaohsiung, Taiwan's second largest city, it garnered only 70 seats in the legislature, a disappointing performance that raised doubts about the leadership of DPP Chairman Lin

Yi-hsiung, who had assumed that post in June. The New Party, which favoured Taiwan's reintegration with mainland China, won 11 seats, and the remaining 21 were split among smaller parties and independent candidates.

The surprising KMT victory strengthened the hand of Premier Vincent Siew as well as that of Pres. Lee Teng-hui, whose term was to expire in 2000. More important, it eased fears of a truculent reaction from China that might have been expected in the event of a DPP victory. Although China disliked President Lee, whom it often accused of being a covert supporter of independence for Taiwan, Chinese leaders were even less enamoured of the DPP. The DPP's position, hammered out earlier in the year, was that "Taiwan enjoys independent sovereignty and that Taiwan's sovereignty must not be treated as a subject for negotiations," according to DPP Secretary-General Chiou I-jen. This was totally at variance with Beijing's position that Taiwan was a province of China that had to be reunited with the motherland.

After three years of first acting out and then sulking over President Lee's 1995 visit to the United States, China agreed to resume the cross-straits dialogue with Taiwan that it had unilaterally suspended. In mid-October Koo Chen-fu, chairman of Taiwan's quasi-official Straits Exchange Foundation, met in Beijing with his counterpart, Wang Daohan, chairman of China's Association for Relations Across the Taiwan Straits. Although the dialogue was resumed, Taiwan made it clear that discussion of core political issues would not be on the agenda anytime soon.

China continued to squeeze Taiwan diplomatically in the international arena, enticing four of Taiwan's erstwhile diplomatic partners to switch their recognition from Taiwan to China. Of these, South Africa was by far the most important, the others being the Central African Republic, Guinea-Bissau, and Tonga. Taiwan picked up one new partner when it established relations with the Marshall Islands. Throughout the year Taiwan continued to resist China's efforts to isolate it. In March Vice Pres. Lien Chan paid visits to Jordan, the United Arab Emirates, Bahrain, and Malaysia. U.S. Secretary of Energy Bill Richardson attended a U.S.-Taiwan business conference in November.

On the domestic front, the legislature finally passed a controversial measure to downsize the Taiwan provincial government, a measure that Taiwan provincial governor James Soong had bitterly opposed. In July Cheng Chung-mo, a grand justice of Taiwan's highest court, replaced Liao Cheng-hao as minister of justice following an embarrassing internal feud in the ministry that forced Liao to resign.

The KMT's good fortunes in the December legislative elections were grounded in the satisfactory performance of Taiwan's economy, an island of prosperity and stability in an Asia-Pacific region battered by the Asian economic crisis. Taiwan's economy grew at an annual rate of 5.2%. The value of its currency, which had declined in 1997, stabilized in 1998, and international reserves dipped only slightly. Consumer prices rose a modest 2.6%, although the stock market declined 13% during the year. The modest decline in Taiwan's

(continued on page 502)

Whereas the Western world regarded the creation of Israel in May 1948 as a triumph for humanity—the righting for Jews of the terrible wrong of the Holocaust—Israel's Arab neighbours saw the event as a catastrophe. The argument of the early Zionist leaders that the Jews, through their enterprise and skill, would bring the benefits of modernization to the Palestinian Arabs was not accepted by the latter. They did not think they needed such help, and they feared the usurpation of their ancestral homeland by foreigners who were supported by the major powers—the United States and the Soviet Union in particular.

The 1947 UN partition resolution proposed to divide the territory of Mandatory Palestine—the area between the Jordan River Valley and the Mediterranean Sea—into a Jewish state and an Arab state in economic union, with Jerusalem established as an international enclave. Although the 650,000 Jews in Palestine owned only 7% of the land, 55% of it was to go to the Jewish state, whereas the 1.2 million Palestinian Arabs would receive 45%. The Arab governments and the Palestinian Arabs rejected both the concept of partition and the terms of the resolution and decided to oppose it by force. In the armed struggle that followed, the Arabs, in spite of the intervention of Arab armies, were defeated by the better organized and equipped Jews, who ended up with 77% of the land.

For the Arabs the most immediate result was the creation of a refugee problem. Some 725,000 Arab Palestinians left the area that became Israel. Such direct testimony as exists indicated that many refugees left in fear as the fighting intensified. Others were "encouraged" to leave by Israeli psychological warfare, and a substantial number were expelled by the Israeli army, sometimes brutally. Despite a number of UN resolutions calling for repatriation of the refugees after the fighting stopped, the Israelis refused to permit it. The Israelis tended to emphasize the security problem that the return of the refugees would create, but the political problem was perhaps greater. Approximately 42% of the population of the area allocated to the Jewish state by the partition resolution was Arab, and, given differences in population-growth rates, the Arabs would soon have outnumbered the Jews. As it is, the 150,000 Arabs allowed to remain in the area controlled by Israel, plus their descendants, now number nearly one million.

The Arab states reacted by refusing to accept or recognize Israel and imposed an economic boycott on that country. Although this limited Israel's economic potential, it also imposed limitations on the Arabs. Aside from the loss of well-established markets for their produce and labour, Syria and Jordan could no longer use the oil refinery and port of Haifa, and the Iraq Petroleum Co.'s oil pipeline across the desert from Baghdad had to be rerouted. Jordan had no access to the sea except through the port of Aqaba, to which there was no paved road. Land communication between Egypt and the Arab states east of the Jordan became impossible.

SPOTLIGHT

ISRAEL'S IMPACT ON THE MIDDLE EAST, 1948–98

by Richard B. Parker

Illustration by Tom Curry

To avoid overflying Israel, air routes had to be changed, often at considerable expense, and the transit trade through Haifa, which had been important to Jordan and Palestine, shifted to Beirut.

These obstacles were overcome in time, but it required wrenching adjustments in trade patterns and the severe loss of income to towns like Jerusalem, which had benefited from the flow of goods and tourists between the Mediterranean and the Arab hinterland to the East. Ironically, Israel, forced by the boycott to leapfrog over its neighbours to find markets, became a major exporter of technology throughout the world and in 1998 had a per capita income and physical quality of life far superior to other nations in the region.

The Palestine problem also became an overriding issue in Arab politics and a source of much tension and instability. In both Syria and Egypt, and eventually in Iraq, the incompetence of the old regime in the 1948 war was a major justification for seizure of power by the military, and Jordan's King Abdullah was assassinated in 1951 because he had dealt directly with the Israelis on a division of the spoils in Palestine.

A desire to avenge the 1948 defeat and fears of Israeli expansionism became an obsession with the Arabs. Enormous amounts of money that could have gone to social and economic programs were spent on armaments and military preparations. Israel responded in kind, and the "Near East" (the Arab states and Israel plus Iran) became the less-developed world's largest importer of weapons. Three major Arab-Israeli wars causing tens of thousands of casualties were fought—in 1956, 1967, and 1973—before any movement toward a meaningful peace began.

Today Israel is at peace with Egypt and Jordan but not with Syria, Lebanon, Iraq, or Saudi Arabia. It has the substance, if not the form, of diplomatic relations with Morocco, Tunisia, Oman, and Qatar. Its 1994 treaty with Jordan, as well as regional economic conferences in which it has participated, has raised hope for meaningful economic cooperation with the Arab world, but results to date have been limited, in part because Israel is no longer as interested in Arab markets as it once was but also because of Arab dissatisfaction with the lack of progress in implementation of the Oslo accords between Israel and the Palestinians signed in the U.S. on Aug. 13, 1993. These accords set forth a six-year program for arrival at a final Israeli settlement with the Palestinians. Significant progress has been made, but major differences remain regarding such issues as territory, creation of a Palestinian state, the status of Jerusalem, and the refugees. In the absence of agreement on those problems, and in the absence of peace with Syria, Israel has remained a *nakba*, or disaster, as far as most Arabs are concerned.

Richard B. Parker is a scholar in residence at the Middle East Institute, Washington, D.C.

(continued from page 500)
economy affected female workers more than men, and the rate of women's participation in the economy dropped slightly. Compared with its counterparts in Thailand, Indonesia, and South Korea, however, Taiwan's female labour force was still doing well.

(STEVEN I. LEVINE)

TAJIKISTAN

Area: 143,100 sq km (55,300 sq mi)
Population (1998 est.): 6,112,000
Capital: Dushanbe
Chief of state: President Imomali Rakhmonov
Head of government: Prime Minister Yahyo Azimov

In Tajikistan during 1998 it seemed to many that the process of implementing the 1997 peace agreement was grinding to a halt. The accord, which ended five years of civil war, had been signed by the two major combatants, the government of Tajikistan and the United Tajik Opposition (UTO), a coalition of Islamic and secular democratic forces. Many smaller groups were excluded, and in 1998 they made their presence felt through military assaults and a series of killings that undermined the peace process. Also less than constructive were some actions of the Tajik government, which was reluctant to accept opposition members in the coalition government as required by the terms of the peace agreement or to prepare for constitutional changes and elections that were specified in the agreement.

In January the opposition briefly suspended its participation in the National Reconciliation Commission, created to oversee implementation of the peace agreement. Shortly afterward Pres. Imomali Rakhmonov agreed to appoint five UTO members to posts in a coalition government being slowly assembled under the terms of the peace agreement. At the end of February, the peace process received a boost when Akbar Turajonzoda, deputy head of the UTO, returned from exile in Iran to take up the post of first deputy prime minister. Turajonzoda's appeal for the Islamic Rebirth Party to be given an equal chance to contest planned elections was rejected by the parliament, which adopted a law prohibiting religious-based political parties. President Rakhmonov vetoed the law but asserted publicly that he would not tolerate an Islamic government in Tajikistan.

Among the groups excluded from the peace process was the National Revival Bloc of a former prime minister, Abdumalik Abdullojonov, which represented the interests of the Leninabad region in northern Tajikistan. Political antagonism between the north and Dushanbe worsened in March with the sentencing to death of six northerners, including Abdullojonov's brother, on charges of having attempted to assassinate Rakhmonov in 1997.

Violence undermined the peace process in late March and early April when government and opposition forces engaged in major military clashes near Dushanbe. The government accused the UTO of inability to restrain its own forces. In June an important UTO military leader was killed in Dushanbe. The following month four members of the UN Military Observers mission (UNMOT) were killed. Though the killings were sharply condemned by both the government and the UTO, they resulted in a drastic reduction in the international presence in Tajikistan. Most UNMOT observers were removed, and the U.S. embassy was closed in September for security reasons. On July 31 the head of Tajikistan's customs service was assassinated; a prominent Muslim clergyman was killed in August; and UTO official Otakhon Latifi, the most prominent opposition figure to be assassinated to date, died in September.

(BESS BROWN)

A funeral is held in Dushanbe, Tajikistan, for four members of the UN Military Observers mission who were shot dead in July, apparently by a renegade opposition group. In 1998 many small opposition groups in Tajikistan made their presence felt through military assaults and killings that undermined the peace process in the country.

TANZANIA

Area: 945,090 sq km (364,901 sq mi)
Population (1998 est.): 30,609,000
De facto capital: Dar es Salaam; the legislature meets in Dodoma, the capital designate
Chief of state and head of government: President Benjamin William Mkapa, assisted by Prime Minister Frederick Tulway Sumaye

Zanzibar was the main focus of attention in Tanzania as 1998 began. On January 12 Chief Emeka Anyaoku, the Commonwealth secretary-general, visited the island in an attempt to settle the long-running dispute between the government and the main opposition party, the Civic United Front (CUF). The controversy had begun when the CUF accused the authorities of having mismanaged the 1995 elections to the presidency and the National Asssembly. In December 1997 police had arrested about 15 members of the opposition, accusing them of plotting to overthrow the government, and on January 3 two more arrests were made. Anyaoku presented the contending parties with a set of proposals that called upon each to take positive steps to calm the atmosphere and to achieve a functioning legislature with full representation by all elected members.

On the mainland both the general public and foreign observers waited to see how Pres. Benjamin Mkapa would pursue the anticorruption campaign that he had said was under way when he reported to the national congress of the ruling Revolutionary Party of Tanzania (Chama Cha Mapinduzi) in October 1997 that 1,500 civil servants had already been dismissed. An indicator of a change in the climate of public morality could be seen in the resignation of Hassy Kitine, minister of state in the office of the president, on August 9 after widespread criticism of his wife's receiving medical treatment abroad.

In April, having failed to renegotiate a contract with the Malaysian company Independent Power Tanzania (IPTL) to construct a 100-MW diesel power plant, the government decided to default on the contract and, if necessary, to take the issue to international arbitration. This was the result of prolonged pressure from the World Bank and International Monetary Fund, which had insisted that the government either renegotiate the terms of the contract or cancel it altogether. The IPTL plan, it was maintained, was uneconomical because it committed the government to buying the total output of the plant at two and a half times the cost of power expected to be produced from the offshore Songo Songo gas project financed by the World Bank and a number of bilateral donors. Answering charges that it had entered into the agreement with IPTL in 1995 with undue haste and secrecy, the government pleaded that it had been an emergency measure taken in response to an acute shortage of power due to prolonged drought.

On August 7 terrorists detonated a bomb at the U.S. embassy in Dar es Salaam, killing 11 people and injuring more than 80.

Authorities walk outside the U.S. embassy in Dar es Salaam, Tanz., on August 8, one day after a terrorist bomb severely damaged the building and claimed the lives of 11 persons. The incident occurred on the same day that the U.S. embassy was bombed in Nairobi, Kenya.

On December 16 the U.S. government indicted five men, all still at large, for their involment; two other men were in custody in Tanzania.   (KENNETH INGHAM)

THAILAND

Area: 513,115 sq km (198,115 sq mi)
Population (1998 est.): 61,201,000
Capital: Bangkok
Chief of state: King Bhumibol Adulyadej
Head of government: Prime Minister Chuan Leekpai

Inevitably, political activity in Thailand in 1998 was overshadowed by the tough strictures imposed by the International Monetary Fund (IMF). Compliance with fiscal and administrative reforms in return for disbursements from the IMF's $17.2 billion rescue package won the government of Prime Minister Chuan Leekpai considerable international praise. The determination of Finance Minister Tarrin Nimmanhaeminda to implement these measures in the face of hardship for business and labour bore fruit by the end of the year, with the widespread belief that Thailand would emerge from the financial crisis fairly quickly. Amendments to laws on bank capitalization, credit, and bankruptcy competed for legislative attention with new laws on electoral reform mandated by the 1997 constitution.

In March the government easily survived a no-confidence motion, but Chuan nevertheless strengthened his six-party coalition in September by bringing in Chart Pattana, adding 51 seats for a total of 255 in the 393-seat House of Representatives. Chart Pattana's leader Korn Dabbaransi took over the scandal-plagued Health Ministry, where

revelations of kickbacks in the purchase of medical supplies had forced high-level resignations. Other scandals emerged in the Ministries of Agriculture, Education, Forestry, and Transport. Many Thais, knowing that such misdeeds would usually go unreported, saw the revelations as progress in the fight against corruption.

Chuan unexpectedly appointed Gen. Surayud Chulanont as army commander in late September. Surayud, vowing that the era of military interference in politics was gone for good, promptly resigned from the Senate. His predecessor, Gen. Chettha Thanajaro, meanwhile, accepted a position as adviser to Interior Minister Sanan Kajornprasart. An order for eight F-18 fighters from the U.S. was canceled, but, with a $250 million penalty charge in addition to a $74.5 million deposit at stake, U.S. Pres. Bill Clinton agreed in March to buy the aircraft for American forces. Efforts to get the deposit refunded failed, however.

Unemployment created by the recession rose to 1,800,000, or 6% of the workforce. In May the government announced that 200,000 of the 1,500,000 state jobs would be eliminated. Work permits for half a million foreign workers were not renewed, but, following protests by rice millers, exceptions were made for 95,000 low-paid jobs that Thais were unwilling to perform. Bangkok's once-huge construction industry evaporated. Staff at Thai embassies was reduced, and government-funded students abroad were told to return home. Transportation infrastructure projects, however, were not much affected, and in October test runs for Bangkok's first mass-transit system began. Deputy Prime Minister Bhichai Rattakul admitted, however, that not all the facilities for the Asian Games, due to begin in Bangkok on December 6, would be

ready. All was well, however, and the Games were a huge success.

Prodded by the IMF, the Cabinet in September resolved to begin privatizing 59 state enterprises engaged in telecommunications, electricity, oil refining, finance, ground transportation, tobacco, and air transportation. The IMF's initial stipulation of a 1% budget surplus was relaxed, and the year ended with a 2% deficit. Six insolvent banks and 12 finance companies were taken over by the Bank of Thailand as remaining institutions struggled to recapitalize. On August 14 the government set aside $7.2 billion for new equity in the banking sector, and in October debate began on a new bankruptcy law to restore investor confidence. The gross national product for the year was expected to decline by 8%, and inflation was falling toward an anticipated 7%. The Financial Restructuring Authority, set up to oversee the disposal of nonperforming financial assets, unsuccessfully auctioned some $12 billion worth of business loans in December. The unsold debt was bought by U.S. firm Goldman-Sachs Group L.P. (ROBERT WOODROW)

TOGO

Area: 56,785 sq km (21,925 sq mi)
Population (1998 est.): 4,906,000
Capital: Lomé
Chief of state: President Gen. Gnassingbé Eyadema
Head of government: Prime Minister Kwassi Klutse

Pres. Gnassingbé Eyadema, Africa's longest-serving head of state (31 years), was returned to office in the presidential election on June 21, 1998. Defeating five opposition candidates, including Gilchrist Olympio, son of Togo's assassinated first president, Eyadema took 52% of the vote. Hundreds of demonstrators took to the streets on election day to protest being left off the electoral rolls, and international observers expressed serious doubts about the conduct of the election. On June 24 five members of the independent National Election Commission, including its head, resigned in protest against being intimidated and persecuted following the election. Security forces killed one man and injured three in a violent confrontation with opposition supporters on June 26 in Afagnan. Despite a government ban on street demonstrations, opposition parties began a new series of protests on July 4.

Eyadema took the oath of office on July 24 for what would be, under the new constitution, his final term. On September 2 Prime Minister Kwassi Klutse named a new 27-member Cabinet. Opposition parties refused to accept all offers of portfolios in the new government.

The economy was buoyed by a 33% increase in phosphate exports and a record cotton crop. In April Nigeria agreed to alleviate Togo's perennial energy shortage by providing half of the country's daily electricity needs. (NANCY ELLEN LAWLER)

TONGA

Area: 750 sq km (290 sq mi)
Population (1998 est.): 97,900
Capital: Nuku'alofa
Head of state and government: King Taufa'ahau Tupou IV, assisted by Prime Minister of Privy Council Baron Vaea

The midyear celebrations for the 80th birthday of King Taufa'ahau Tupou IV provided a sense of national unity in an otherwise controversial year. The Supreme Court ruled that a statement in the *Wall Street Journal* by 'Akilisi Pohiva, leader of Tonga's pro-democracy movement, that the king was an authoritarian ruler appeared true and not defamatory. There was also political controversy over revenue from Earth-orbiting satellite slots claimed by Tonga and managed by a company 60% owned by the king's daughter, Princess Pilolevu. In November Tonga broke diplomatic relations with Taiwan and established them with China.

Economic growth on the island nation slowed as the Asian financial crisis caused a decline in tourists from that region and lower remittance income from Tongans working overseas. Government expenditure approved for 1998–99 totaled T$129 million ($80.4 million).

Climatic conditions caused a further decline in economic activity. In January Cyclone Ron caused widespread damage that particularly affected the northern islands. Heavy rain in February caused serious losses in food crops.

(BARRIE MACDONALD)

These workers at a rice mill in Bangkok were among thousands of workers affected when rice mills throughout Thailand shut down in July to protest the government's decision not to renew the work permits of foreigners, many of whom held jobs that paid below the minimum wage. The shutdown ended when exceptions were made for 95,000 foreigners.

TRINIDAD AND TOBAGO

Area: 5,128 sq km (1,980 sq mi)
Population (1998 est.): 1,275,000
Capital: Port of Spain
Chief of state: President Arthur Napoleon Raymond Robinson
Head of government: Prime Minister Basdeo Panday

Major developments in the all-important energy sector dominated events in Trinidad and Tobago during 1998. In January Amoco Trinidad announced the discovery of 40 million–70 million bbl of oil in one of its offshore fields; the estimate was later upgraded to 50 million–100 million bbl. In February the government signed production-sharing contracts with several international oil companies for exploration in the deep waters off the eastern coast of Trinidad, where billions of barrels of oil were believed to be located. In July Enron Oil and Gas Co. of the U.S. said that it had discovered the largest gas field in its history, estimated to contain 17 billion–28 billion cu m (600 billion–1 trillion cu ft), off Trinidad's southeast coast.

The nation's eighth ammonia plant, Farmland Ammonia, owned by two U.S. companies, was officially inaugurated in July. Its production capacity of 600,000 tons a year made Trinidad and Tobago the world's largest exporter of ammonia.

(DAVID RENWICK)

TUNISIA

Area: 164,150 sq km (63,378 sq mi)
Population (1998 est.): 9,380,000
Capital: Tunis
Chief of state: President Gen. Zine al-Abidine Ben Ali
Head of government: Prime Minister Hamed Karoui

On March 1, 1998, Tunisia's new association agreement with the European Union, ushering in a new industrial free-trade area between the two partners, came into effect. The 1998 budget, submitted in January, had included proposals to increase value-added-tax rates to compensate for customs revenue losses as a result of the agreement. By July, 713 of the 2,000 companies targeted by the agreement for structural-adjustment aid up to the year 2001 had applied for such aid, and 282 had been approved, receiving D 744.6 million of the estimated D 2.2 billion in modernization costs for the private sector (D 1=$0.92). European aid was agreed upon in May in return for a Tunisian promise to speed up the nation's privatization program. As a result, 50 state-owned companies were to be privatized in the next two years.

In July the International Monetary Fund indicated its satisfaction with Tunisia's eco-

On their way to St. Patrick's Anglican Church in Mt. Pleasant, Tobago, on Palm Sunday are (from left) U.S. Ambassador to Trinidad and Tobago Edward Shumaker, Secretary of State Madeleine Albright, and the Rev. Phillip Isaac. During her visit to Trinidad and Tobago, Albright met with leaders to discuss trade and environment issues.

nomic progress, projecting future growth of gross domestic product at 6% per year, although it warned that further attention would have to be given to reducing unemployment and ensuring that the current account remained under control. In October details of the proposed 1999 budget became public; a 6% increase in expenditure was expected, despite worries over Tunisia's competitiveness in foreign markets as a result of the Asian crisis.

Tunisia also sought to increase its economic links with neighbouring nations, having already established free-trade-area agreements with Egypt (signed in August), Morocco, and Libya. In June a visit by Turkey's Pres. Suleyman Demirel resulted in expanded trade ties. Pres. Gen. Zine al-Abidine Ben Ali visited Libya in September in an effort to strengthen energy links. Tunisian and Italian olive-oil producers planned to set up joint marketing facilities, even though tension between the two countries continued because of illegal immigration from Tunisia.

Despite accusations of corruption against members of his family and six other major families in April, President Ben Ali reasserted his control of the political arena in August when he was reelected chairman of the Rassemblement Constitutionelle Démocratique and thus became the movement's presidential candidate for a third term in 1999.

Tunisia's human rights record was again criticized in February when veteran human rights activist Khemais Ksila was sentenced to five years in prison for "offending public order and spreading antigovernment propaganda." At the European Parliament in October, the American group Human Rights Watch renewed the criticism despite Tunisian objections. (GEORGE JOFFÉ)

TURKEY

Area: 779,452 sq km (300,948 sq mi)
Population (1998 est.): 64,567,000
Capital: Ankara
Chief of state: President Suleyman Demirel
Head of government: Prime Minister Mesut Yilmaz

The celebration of the 75th anniversary of the republic on October 29 and the commemoration of the 60th anniversary of the death of its founder, Kemal Ataturk, on November 10 helped counteract the depressing effect of continued political instability and social division in Turkey in 1998.

The campaign against the influence of Islam in politics intensified. On January 16 the Constitutional Court decreed that the Islamist Welfare Party (RP) should be dissolved, its assets confiscated, and its leader, Necmettin Erbakan, and six of his followers banned from politics for five years. When the decision took effect on February 22, a successor, the Virtue Party (FP), was formed, and almost all the deputies of RP transferred to it. On May 14 the FP elected as leader Recai Kutan, a former minister in the Erbakan administration. On September 23 the Appeals Court confirmed a 10-month prison sentence, with consequent loss of political rights, for Recep Tayyip Erdogan, the Islamist mayor of Istanbul.

A decision of the Constitutional Court depriving university rectors of any latitude in applying the ban on the wearing of head

Relatives of veterans of the Turkish War of Independence (1919–23) pose in front of the mausoleum of Kemal Atatürk, founder of the modern Republic of Turkey, during the celebration of the 75th anniversary of the republic on October 29.

scarves by women students led to Islamist demonstrations when the academic year opened in the autumn. A Turkish Airlines domestic flight was diverted by a hijacker on September 14 in an act of protest against the ban.

The minority secular coalition government formed by Mesut Yilmaz, leader of the centre-right Motherland Party, resigned on November 25 when Parliament censured it over irregularities in the privatization of state assets. Following this, two attempts were made to form a government, but both proved unsuccessful. In an unusual move, President Demirel first asked Bulent Ecevit, a former prime minister and leader of the Democratic Left Party, which had minority status with only 61 members in the 550-member Parliament. Ecevit approached Yilmaz, but was ultimately defeated by the opposition of the conservative True Path Party led by Tansu Ciller, also a former prime minister, as well as other leftist parties.

For the second attempt Demirel chose Yalim Erez, the former minister of industry and commerce under Prime Minister Yilmaz. He was equally frustrated, however, when he was also derailed by the opposition of Ciller, determined not to yield an iota to her rivals. Yilmaz remained as caretaker as the year ended. According to law, on January 10 Demirel could appoint a prime minister who would then form a government based on the various parties' representation in the legislature.

Throughout the year the government was shaken by successive revelations about links between prominent politicians and criminal gangs. A supporter of the prime minister, Minister of State Eyup Asik, resigned from the legislature on September 24 when a recording of conversations he had held with a Turkish fugitive, subsequently imprisoned in France, was made public.

On July 22 Prime Minister Yilmaz obtained the approval of the legislature for a wide-ranging tax-reform law. It was a key measure in the government's program that aimed to reduce inflation to 50% by the end of 1998 and 20% a year later. An agreement was reached to have the program monitored by the staff of the International Monetary Fund. In September, however, as the world financial crisis began to threaten Turkey, the government was forced to reduce the tax burden, first on banks and then on shareholders. This did not stop the Istanbul Stock Exchange from losing more than half its capitalization between July and October. Nevertheless, inflation dropped substantially. During the first nine months of the year, wholesale prices rose by 40% (against 61% the previous year) and consumer prices by 49% (64% in 1997).

There was no letup in the guerrilla campaign waged by the radical Kurdistan Workers Party (PKK). On October 1 President Demirel told the legislature that Turkey reserved the right to retaliate if Syria continued to afford facilities to the PKK. Following mediation by Egyptian Pres. Hosni Mubarak, who visited Ankara on October 6, Syria agreed to desist from any action threatening public order in Turkey. A protocol to this effect was signed by Turkish and Syrian officials on October 20. Abdullah Ocalan, who had led the PKK armed campaign from Syria since 1984, moved to Moscow and later to Rome. When Italy refused to extradite him, Turkey retaliated with a boycott of Italian goods. Cooperation with Israel increased, and joint U.S.-Turkish-Israeli naval exercises were held to test procedures for rescues at sea.

Turkey's determination to stand by the Turkish Republic of Northern Cyprus (which Turkey was alone in recognizing) was reaffirmed by Yilmaz in July and

Demirel in August. The lack of progress in solving the conflict with Greece in Cyprus contributed to Turkey's continued failure to be accepted into the European Union; economic relations, however, continued to develop within the framework of customs unions begun in 1996. (ANDREW MANGO)

TURKMENISTAN

Area: 488,100 sq km (188,500 sq mi)
Population (1998 est.): 4,731,000
Capital: Ashgabat
Head of state and government: President Saparmurad Niyazov

The authoritarianism of Turkmenistan's Pres. Saparmurad Niyazov appeared to weaken somewhat in 1998 with his promise that greater power would be transferred from the presidential administration to the country's professional parliament. The president's interest in promoting democratization was encouraged by his official visit to the U.S. in April. A few nongovernmental organizations were allowed to register with the government, but potential political opposition was sharply discouraged, although several political prisoners were released prior to the trip to Washington.

Niyazov's efforts to forge a Turkmen national consciousness from a disparate group of tribes appeared to receive a setback when a group of soldiers killed several people and took several hostages in western Turkmenistan in September. A number of high-ranking military officials, including the

minister of defense and the chief of staff, were dismissed because of the incident, which the president said had resulted from putting tribal loyalties ahead of the national interest.

Turkmenistan's economy received a boost with the opening of a gas pipeline to northern Iran, a project seen as the first stage in the creation of an alternate route for the export of the country's gas and oil that would end its dependence on using Russian pipelines. Turkmen officials actively promoted plans to construct a pipeline through Afghanistan to ports in Pakistan; with this objective, contacts were developed with the Afghan Taliban, a move that angered some of Turkmenistan's Central Asian neighbours. (*See* Spotlight: *Central Asian Oil Disputes.*)

The necessity for Turkmenistan to develop its gas and oil export capability without delay was illustrated by the country's desperate financial situation that resulted from the inability of its customers from the former Soviet Union, particularly Ukraine, to pay gas bills that had accumulated over several years.

(BESS BROWN)

TUVALU

Area: 25.6 sq km (9.9 sq mi)
Population (1998 est.): 10,400
Capital: Government offices in Vaiaku, Fongafale islet, of Funafuti atoll
Chief of state: Queen Elizabeth II, represented by Governor-General Tulaga Manuella
Head of government: Prime Minister Bikenibeu Paeniu

Elections for Parliament took place in March 1998. To select 12 legislators, the country's 4,000 voters were faced with 36 candidates, all male. In the election former prime minister Kamuta Latasi lost his seat, and Prime Minister Bikenibeu Paeniu was easily returned along with 10 supporting MPs.

The 1998 budget of $A 13,600,000 was allocated as follows: $A 3,720,000 for development, $A 3,550,000 for reinvestment in the country's trust fund, and the balance for operational expenses ($A 1=U.S. $0.61). Tuvalu continued its attempts to seek innovative sources of revenue, such as the practice of selling passports (U.S. $11,000 per person and $22,000 per family), despite the possibility that some countries would not recognize the passports for entry purposes. The government also sold the licensing of its Internet domain name, ".tv," to a Canadian company for U.S. $50 million plus a share of future profits.

(BARRIE MACDONALD)

UGANDA

Area: 241,038 sq km (93,065 sq mi)
Population (1998 est.): 22,167,000
Capital: Kampala
Head of state and government: President Yoweri Museveni, assisted by Prime Minister Kintu Musoke

In 1998 Uganda and Pres. Yoweri Museveni, in particular, enjoyed widespread international attention and approval. In January Museveni was host of a World Bank meeting attended by the heads of a number of other African nations, and later in the month Pres. Nelson Mandela of South Africa was a guest at the 12th-anniversary celebrations of the ruling National Resistance Movement. On March 24–25 U.S. Pres. Bill Clinton paid a visit to Uganda, during which he lavished praise on Museveni.

Uganda's record continued to be impressive in many respects. Inflation was down, and the budget deficit was reduced in 1996–97 to 1.9% of gross domestic product. The privatization program was also making progress, the most striking development being an agreement with MTN Uganda, a consortium combining South African, Swedish, Ugandan, and Rwandan interests, to buy a license covering the full range of telecommunications services. The government hoped that this arrangement would lead to a rapid expansion in the service. It also planned to improve feeder roads and to reform the land laws in order to provide greater security of tenure and thereby reduce poverty. In response to these efforts, donors continued to give generous support, and on April 8, as part of the Initiative for Heavily Indebted Poor Countries program, the World Bank and International Monetary Fund agreed that Uganda was eligible to receive debt relief from external donors equivalent to 20% of its external debt.

Despite this progress, the country remained dependent upon external aid for 80% of its development capital and 45% of its recurrent expenditures. Two-thirds of the population remained below the absolute poverty level, defined as having an income less than $1 a day.

Torrential rains in late 1997 and early 1998 severely damaged the cotton and coffee crops and also the country's main export routes, the roads to the coast at Mombasa, Kenya. An additional drain on Uganda's resources resulted from the continued problem of rebels in parts of the north and west. So effective were the incursions of the Lords Resistance Army into the Acholi region of northern Uganda that the government decided that it was necessary to confine virtually the whole population of that area to protected villages. This not only inhibited farming but also proved increasingly ineffective as the rebels grew bolder while the Acholi themselves grew steadily more discontented with the government's intervention. The cost of military action also increased the cost of defense well beyond the government's budgeted figure.

Uganda's involvement in the warfare in Rwanda and the Democratic Republic of the Congo led to reprisals in the shape of attacks in June and again in August by another group of rebels, calling themselves the Allied Democratic Forces. Although these raids, in the Kabarole district in the west, were on a limited scale, they posed further unwelcome problems for the nation's security forces. (KENNETH INGHAM)

UKRAINE

Area: 603,700 sq km (233,100 sq mi)
Population (1998 est.): 50,302,000
Capital: Kiev
Chief of state: President Leonid Kuchma
Head of government: Prime Minister Valery Pustovoytenko

The year 1998 was a particularly difficult one for Ukraine, which suffered from the financial crisis in Russia and also proved unable to overcome a political impasse be-

South African Pres. Nelson Mandela (left) is welcomed by Ugandan Pres. Yoweri Museveni upon his arrival at the Kampala airport in January. Mandela was invited to Uganda to participate in celebrating the 12th anniversary of the ruling National Resistance Movement, the Museveni-led party that came to power in 1986.

ALEXANDER JOE—AFP PHOTO

In Kiev, Ukraine, two servicemen cast their ballots in the March 29 parliamentary elections. With dozens of political parties to choose from, Ukrainian voters struggled to decide which one could best lead the country out of its economic decline.

tween the government and the legislature. On March 29 Ukraine held parliamentary elections. Almost a quarter of the electorate voted for the Communist Party (24.68%), with the Ukrainian Popular Movement (Rukh) a distant second at 9.4%. Left-wing parties (Communists, the Socialist/Agrarian coalition, and Progressive Socialists) won 180 of the 450 seats. Electing a chairman of the parliament proved a protracted affair. After 19 attempts, Oleksandr Tkachenko of the Peasants' Party of Ukraine was voted into office with the support of 232 deputies (six more than the minimum required).

From the perspective of Pres. Leonid Kuchma and his administration, the new parliament proved as difficult to work with as had been its predecessor. In October Prime Minister Valery Pustovoytenko survived a no-confidence vote (203–108) as the Left faction continued to criticize what it perceived as the government's excessive dependence on the International Monetary Fund and compliance with IMF "dictates."

Politics in Ukraine during the year were oriented toward the presidential elections of 1999. According to a poll in November, former parliamentary chairman and leader of the Socialist Party Oleksandr Moroz was the leading candidate, with 20% of the vote. He was followed by Communist Party leader Petro Symonenko at 18%, with President Kuchma (a declared candidate) trailing well behind with only 11%.

Kuchma and his government were blamed for Ukraine's continuing economic ills and increasing corruption. Gross domestic product (GDP) fell by 3.2% in 1997. The first nine months of 1998 appeared to herald an improvement, however, as GDP rose by 0.2% compared with the same period in

1997, industrial output was up by 0.3%, and production of consumer goods increased 4.1%. With inflation at a low 2.3%, Ukraine seemed to have achieved a breakthrough in halting an economic decline that had begun in 1991. In the wake of the financial collapse in Russia, however, this rejuvenation proved to be illusory. In September there were large declines in the output of steel (a fall of 22% compared with September 1997) and metalworking products. End-of-year figures indicated that industrial output fell 1.5% in 1998.

The Ukrainian government made little progress in the fight against corruption. On April 28 the president signed an edict that anticipated taking this battle into the parliament and courts by stripping immunity from parliamentary deputies and judges. This move followed the assassination of Vadym Hetman, chairman of Ukraine's Interbank Currency Exchange and the leader of the Group of Independent Deputies in the parliament. In September Berlin-based Transparency International, whose mission was to oppose corruption in international business, conducted a detailed survey of 85 countries to adjudge the degree of corruption in each one. Of the 85, Ukraine tied for 69th. Corruption reached the highest levels of the administration and was believed to have played a major part in the gradual leftward political shift on the part of much of the population, which equated corruption with privatization and market forces.

Ukraine's industry continued to struggle with current and past problems. On April 4 a methane gas explosion at the Skochinsky coal mine in Donetsk resulted in 63 fatalities and 71 injuries. The mine had long been known to be dangerous, but adequate maintenance had been ignored because of the shortage of funds.

As Ukraine restarted its third reactor at the Chernobyl station on May 16, the effects of the 1986 accident there continued to be reported. Health Minister Andriy Serdyuk stated on April 22 that more than 12,500 of those who were involved in the cleanup campaign had died from radiation sickness, and many of the 350,000 who took part in decontamination and repair work at the plant were suffering from thyroid cancer, leukemia, and other ailments. Those figures were not supported by all sources, however, and there was some speculation that they were related to requests for additional aid for the nation's nuclear power industry. Though Ukraine continued to work with the Group of Seven industrial countries, the European Bank for Reconstruction and Development, and other agencies for the development of new reactors at the Rivne and Khmelnytskyy stations (the total cost was said to be about $1.6 billion), it recently turned to Russia to help finance the new plants, frustrated at delays in funding from the West.

In foreign affairs Ukraine moved closer to Russia but continued to maintain good relations with the United States and Europe. On January 14 the Ukrainian parliament ratified the Treaty of Friendship, Cooperation, and Partnership with Russia that had been signed in May 1997. In February President Kuchma traveled to Moscow, where he assured Russia that Ukraine had no intention of joining NATO. Kuchma and Russian Pres. Boris Yeltsin signed an agreement on economic cooperation for the period 1998–2007.

On September 18–19, following the Russian crisis, Yeltsin and Kuchma met in Moscow and agreed to a joint approach to financial problems and to a free-trade zone between the two countries.   (DAVID R. MARPLES)

UNITED ARAB EMIRATES

Area: 83,600 sq km (32,280 sq mi)
Population (1998 est.): 2,744,000
Capital: Abu Dhabi
Chief of state: President Sheikh Zaid ibn Sultan an-Nahayan
Head of government: Prime Minister Sheikh Maktum ibn Rashid al-Maktum

Because of the substantial dependence on petroleum exports by the United Arab Emirates (UAE), its economy in 1998 felt the impact of declining world oil prices. The UAE reduced oil production in 1998 by nearly 10%, joining other producers in an effort to boost prices, but oil revenues were 25% lower than in 1997. The country's trade surplus was the lowest in a decade, and growth of gross domestic product (GDP) slowed. The federal budget issued in July 1998 projected a deficit much larger than in the previous year.

The UAE, however, proved to be less affected by the oil market and the Asian economic slump than were many other countries. A major reason was that the nation's nonoil

UN Secretary-General Kofi Annan speaks at the opening of the Gulf Cooperation Council summit meeting in Abu Dhabi, UAE. The December summit focused on the impact of declining world oil prices on Arab states.

sector continued to expand, reaching 70% of GDP. The UAE's GDP per capita was highest in the region and ranked 14th in the world, higher than that of Sweden, Belgium, and The Netherlands.

In May the crown prince of Abu Dhabi met in Washington, D.C., with government leaders and announced his country's decision to purchase 80 American fighter aircraft. This was the UAE's largest military purchase, worth more than $6 billion. Earlier in the year the UAE had completed another aircraft purchase, worth more than $2 billion, from France.   (WILLIAM A. RUGH)

UNITED KINGDOM

Area: 244,100 sq km (94,251 sq mi)
Population (1998 est.): 59,126,000
Capital: London
Chief of State: Queen Elizabeth II
Head of Government: Prime Minister
  Tony Blair

Domestic Affairs. The Labour Party government, which had been elected in May 1997, continued in 1998 its program of reforming the United Kingdom's constitution. On May 7 Londoners voted to accept government plans for a new assembly and a directly elected mayor for the nation's capital. On a low turnout (34%), 72% voted in favour of the plans. This decision meant that London would have an elected citywide administration for the first time since the abolition of the Greater London Council in 1986.

In November the government announced it would start legislating immediately to remove hereditary peers from the House of Lords. At the beginning of the 1998–99 parliamentary session, the Lords contained 1,298 members, of whom 750 had inherited their title (usually from their father). Of the 339 hereditary peers who belonged to one of the three main parties, 298 were Conservative, 24 Liberal Democrat, and 17 Labour. In a radio interview in July, Blair made it clear that his long-term ambition was to undertake a more fundamental reform of the Lords: "There are two stages of reform: one is getting rid of the hereditary peers, and secondly there is the longer term reform for a more democratically elected second chamber. I think it is important that we do both things."

In a Lords debate on October 14, Baroness Jay, the leader of the House of Lords (a Cabinet position), responded to charges that the prime minister would have excessive powers of patronage during the interim period, when the House of Lords would consist almost exclusively of life peers. She announced the establishment of an "Appointments Commission" to oversee the appointment of future life peers and to prevent improper use of political patronage. She also announced the establishment of a royal commission to consider options for long-term reform of the House of Lords.

On December 2 William Hague, the leader of the Conservative Party, sacked Lord Cranborne, the party's leader in the House of Lords, after it emerged that Cranborne had

negotiated a secret deal with Blair under which 91 hereditary peers would keep their speaking and voting rights until the long-term future of the House of Lords had been settled. Despite Cranborne's dismissal, Blair announced that he would stick to the deal, hoping that enough Conservative peers would tolerate the bill abolishing the rest of Britain's hereditary peerages to ensure its smooth passage through Parliament in 1999.

One unexpected jolt to the government's constitutional program occurred on October 27, when Ron Davies resigned as secretary of state for Wales and, two days later, as Labour's candidate to be first secretary of the new assembly for Wales. Davies admitted to a "moment of madness" the previous night on Clapham Common, an area in south London often used by men seeking casual gay sex. Davies's encounters resulted in the theft of his car and wallet and an attempt to blackmail him. Rather than succumb to blackmail, he gave a statement to the police and resigned from the Cabinet. In the media coverage that followed this resignation, two members of Blair's Cabinet were publicly identified as homosexuals. (A third gay minister had openly acknowledged his sexuality more than a decade earlier.) Although considerable controversy surrounded the media's actions, none attached to the ministers themselves, who continued as Cabinet members with Blair's full support.

Davies was the first person to resign from Blair's Cabinet; Blair had, however, dismissed four Cabinet ministers in July. As part of his reshuffle, he promoted one of his closest allies, Peter Mandelson, to secretary for trade and industry. A former Labour Party official, Mandelson had masterminded Labour's successful election campaign in 1997 but was distrusted by many Labour MPs, who regarded him as devious and manipulative. He had played a crucial behind-the-scenes role in securing Blair's election as Labour Party leader in 1994, and his widely acknowledged closeness to, and influence on, Blair caused him to be named in October 1998 as fourth in a list of people who wielded the greatest influence on men and women in Britain. On December 23, however, Mandelson was forced to resign from the government following newspaper reports that he had secretly borrowed £373,000 ($620,000) two years earlier from a fellow minister, Geoffrey Robinson, who was under investigation by Mandelson's own department for alleged breaches of company law.

Despite the prime minister's commanding majority in the House of Commons, which meant that he had no need to rely on any other party to pass legislation, the prime minister established a close working relationship with Paddy Ashdown, the leader of the Liberal Democrats. On

November 11 they issued a joint statement in which they agreed that their two parties would widen the scope of their cooperation in a joint Cabinet committee from constitutional reform (on which the committee had worked since soon after the 1997 election) to other policy areas.

Although Blair's government was slow to deliver on a number of its election promises (for example, hospital waiting lists continued to rise until mid-1998 before starting to fall), Labour remained substantially more popular than the opposition Conservatives. According to a Gallup poll published in November 1998, 18 months after Labour came to office, Labour was favoured by 56% of those surveyed (up 12 percentage points since the 1997 general election), the Conservatives by 25% (down 6), and the Liberal Democrats by 13% (down 4). Labour's 31-point lead comfortably exceeded that achieved by any previous governing party in the 60-year history of opinion polls in the U.K.

Charles, prince of Wales, who celebrated his 50th birthday on November 14, also enjoyed high opinion-poll ratings. Following the death of Diana, princess of Wales, in August 1997, the prince managed to establish a fresh image as both a caring father and a future king. He continued, however, to be dogged by controversy over his relationship with Camilla Parker Bowles, a divorcée. Although polls detected widespread public tolerance of the relationship, they also showed that the prince would place his reputation at risk were he to marry her and

(continued on page 512)

Seated next to her husband, Prince Philip, Queen Elizabeth II faces the House of Lords during the opening of Parliament in November. At the opening she announced a government bill to strip hereditary peers of their right to vote in the House of Lords, Britain's unelected upper chamber.

AP/WIDE WORLD

Before World War I every nation in Europe except France, Portugal, and Switzerland was a monarchy. In 1998, by contrast, only eight monarchies remained, if very small states such as Liechtenstein and Monaco were excluded. The eight were Belgium, Denmark, Luxembourg, The Netherlands, Norway, Spain, Sweden, and the United Kingdom. The British monarchy differed from the others in that the queen was an international monarch, the sovereign not only of Britain but also of 15 Commonwealth countries outside Europe.

There are two reasons for the demise of monarchy in much of Europe. The first is defeat in war. The collapse of Austria-Hungary, Germany, and Russia during World War I resulted in the end of the Habsburg, Hohenzollern, and Romanov dynasties, respectively. In World War II collaboration with fascism ended the Italian monarchy, and after the war the new communist regimes rapidly removed the sovereigns of Bulgaria and Romania.

The second reason is the process of democratic change. Monarchies have survived in Europe only where they have accommodated themselves to democracy rather than resisting it. In Europe monarchy exists in limited, constitutional form.

SPOTLIGHT

WHITHER EUROPE'S MONARCHIES?

by Vernon Bogdanor

Illustration by Tom Curry

A democracy whose head of state is a sovereign links two conflicting, some would say contradictory, notions. A democracy is a form of government in which political authority derives from popular election. A sovereign, by contrast, does not rule because of election but instead by inheritance and for life. This conflict has been resolved by means of the concept of a constitutional monarchy, one that operates in accord with constitutional rules. These rules, which may be either legal or nonlegal, limit the power of the sovereign and ensure that he or she acts in accordance with democratic norms.

Monarchs in modern Europe have three major kinds of functions. Constitutional functions include appointing a prime minister and dissolving the parliament. In Britain these duties are generally of a formal nature. Because Britain's electoral system generally yields a clear winner, there is rarely any dispute as to who ought to be appointed prime minister after a general election. Since 1918 there have been only three occasions when that has not been the case—the general elections of 1923, 1929, and February 1974.

In the other European monarchies, however, elections are held under various systems of proportional representation. These rarely yield clear majorities for a single party. Coalition or minority government thus becomes the norm. This gives the sovereign some leeway because it may be unclear as to who ought to be appointed prime minister after a general election. It may also be unclear as to whether a prime minister is entitled to a dissolution of the parliament, for there might well be an alternative majority within the legislature capable of sustaining an alternative government.

In the Scandinavian monarchies the sovereign generally plays a comparatively passive constitutional role. In Belgium, The Netherlands, and Luxembourg, however, the sovereign tends to be more active. Sometimes, indeed, the views of the sovereign in those countries influence the outcome of the government-formation process. This influence is generally used to secure national unity. In both Belgium and The Netherlands, the sovereign has played a unifying role in societies divided by language and religion, respectively.

The second set of functions undertaken by the sovereign is ceremonial in kind. Sovereigns carry out a wide range of public engagements and duties. These engagements—once dismissed by French Pres. Charles de Gaulle as opening exhibitions of chrysanthemums—are means by which the sovereign can be seen as fulfilling the third and most important function, that of representation. In the modern world the central role of a constitutional monarch is a symbolic or representational one, in which he or she represents and symbolizes not just the government but the nation. The ceremonial functions are an important means of fulfilling this function, since, to be an effective symbol, a sovereign must be seen. The great advantage of monarchy is that it is a system in which the head of state is free from party ties. It is generally easier for a hereditary monarch to represent the nation

It was all smiles for this princely trio in London on August 4. Prince Charles (centre) enjoys a moment with his sons, Prince Harry (left) and Prince William, as they get ready to pose for pictures with the Queen Mother on her 98th birthday.

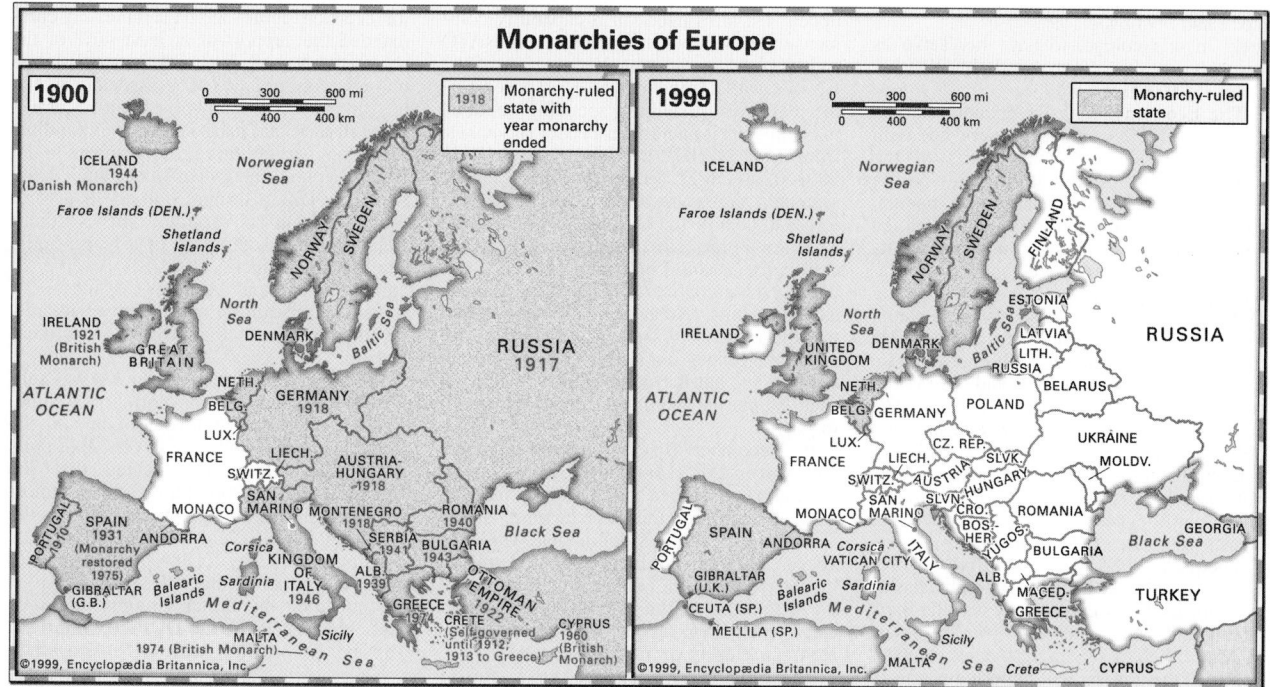

Monarchies of Europe

1900

0 300 600 mi
0 400 400 km

1918 — Monarchy-ruled state with year monarchy ended

ICELAND 1944 (Danish Monarch)
Norwegian Sea
Faroe Islands (DEN.)
Shetland Islands
NORWAY
SWEDEN
North Sea
IRELAND 1921 (British Monarch)
GREAT BRITAIN
DENMARK
Baltic Sea
RUSSIA 1917
NETH.
BELG.
GERMANY 1918
ATLANTIC OCEAN
LUX.
FRANCE
LIECH.
SWITZ.
AUSTRIA-HUNGARY 1918
PORTUGAL 1910
SPAIN 1931 (Monarchy restored 1975)
ANDORRA
MONACO
SAN MARINO
MONTENEGRO 1918
SERBIA 1941
ROMANIA 1940
Black Sea
Corsica
KINGDOM OF ITALY 1946
ALB. 1939
BULGARIA 1943
OTTOMAN EMPIRE 1922
GIBRALTAR (G.B.)
Balearic Islands
Sardinia
Sicily
GREECE 1974
CRETE (Self-governed until 1912; 1913 to Greece)
CYPRUS 1960 (British Monarch)
MALTA 1974 (British Monarch)
Mediterranean Sea
©1999, Encyclopædia Britannica, Inc.

1999

0 300 600 mi
0 400 400 km

Monarchy-ruled state

ICELAND
Norwegian Sea
Faroe Islands (DEN.)
Shetland Islands
NORWAY
SWEDEN
FINLAND
IRELAND
UNITED KINGDOM
North Sea
DENMARK
Baltic Sea
ESTONIA
LATVIA
LITH.
RUSSIA
BELARUS
RUSSIA
NETH.
BELG.
GERMANY
POLAND
UKRAINE
ATLANTIC OCEAN
LUX.
FRANCE
LIECH.
SWITZ.
CZ. REP.
SLVK.
AUSTRIA
HUNGARY
MOLDV.
SLVN.
CRO.
BOS.-HER.
YUGO.
ROMANIA
GEORGIA
MONACO
SAN MARINO
ITALY
PORTUGAL
SPAIN
ANDORRA
VATICAN CITY
BULGARIA
Black Sea
GIBRALTAR (U.K.)
CEUTA (SP.)
Corsica
Balearic Islands
Sardinia
ALB.
MACED.
GREECE
TURKEY
MELLILA (SP.)
Sicily
MALTA
Mediterranean Sea
Crete
CYPRUS
©1999, Encyclopædia Britannica, Inc.

than it is for a president, who will often be a politician, chosen through an election that might have been divisive.

In 1998 the European constitutional monarchies seemed securely based, and, although there were republican movements in a number of European countries, they appeared to pose no real threat to the sovereigns. Nevertheless, monarchs faced new challenges in the modern world, a world in which deference and respect for authority were in decline and in which institutions were required to justify themselves in utilitarian terms. In Britain the archbishop of Canterbury declared after the coronation of Elizabeth II in 1953 that the nation had been close to God on that occasion; in 1956 an opinion survey showed that 34% of the population believed that the queen had actually been chosen by God. Sentiments of that kind are now rare, and the European monarchies have been compelled to modernize themselves, becoming more open and more involved in welfare and charitable activities. The mystical monarchy has thus become transmuted into the welfare monarchy.

Constitutional monarchy survives in a small number of nations in Western Europe, where it depends on popular support. In 1969 the duke of Edinburgh, husband of Queen Elizabeth II, declared that "it is a complete misconception to imag-

ine that monarchy exists in the interests of the monarch. It doesn't. It exists in the interests of the people." In the contemporary world monarchy has become dependent upon the people, and yet at its best it serves not to limit the democratic principle of rule by the people but to underpin and sustain it.

Vernon Bogdanor is a professor of government at the University of Oxford.

In order to survive in the modern world, monarchies in Europe have had to accommodate themselves to democracy. At right, Argentine Pres. Carlos Menem (foreground, left) reviews an honour guard with King Carl XVI Gustaf of Sweden (foreground, right) outside the Royal Palace in Stockholm on May 26.

(continued from page 509)
seek, in due course, to have her serve as queen beside him. (*See* Spotlight: *Whither Europe's Monarchies?*)

The Economy. With the economic boom of the mid-1990s coming to an end and with serious problems in many parts of the world—notably Asia and Russia—posing problems for British banks and exporters, 1998 provided a test of the ability of the new Labour government to demonstrate its claim to be able to replace "boom and bust" with greater stability. Conditions during 1998 seemed initially to support this claim. Unemployment continued to fall—to 1.3 million according to the traditional measure (the welfare claimant count) and 1.8 million according to international definitions. The economy grew by almost 3%, and inflation did not exceed the government's 2.5% target. By the end of the year, however, global pressures had caused a sharp loss of business confidence. Gordon Brown (*see* BIOGRAPHIES), the chancellor of the Exchequer, acknowledged that growth would slow markedly in the months ahead.

At the centre of controversy was the Bank of England, which had been given the power in May 1997 to set interest rates independently of the government. Ignoring warnings of an impending slowdown, the bank raised its base interest rate from 7.25% to 7.5% in June. This helped the pound rise to a value equivalent to more than DM 3.10, which attracted criticism from many industrialists and trade unions, who feared that jobs and exports would be lost. Later in the year, however, the bank reversed its policy and started reducing interest rates. By the end of the year, the base rate was down to 6.25%, and sterling had fallen to DM 2.77.

Foreign Affairs. The U.K. held the presidency of the European Union (EU) for the first six months of 1998. Few concrete changes emerged, but an atmosphere of businesslike cooperation was enhanced by the fact that Blair's government was more supportive of the EU than had been the previous Conservative administration. The U.K.'s main contribution was to win acceptance in principle for the need to reform the EU's budget, Common Agricultural Policy, and structural funds.

During the early months of 1998, U.K. ministers were embroiled in a controversy—the "Arms to Africa affair"—over the supply of weapons, in defiance of United Nations sanctions, to help Pres. Ahmad Tejan Kabbah return to power in Sierra Leone and replace the military junta that had seized power in May 1997. Before Kabbah's return, in February 1998 it emerged that his forces had received arms from a British company, Sandline International. Sandline was run by two former Special Air Service officers, who claimed to have been acting with the support of the Foreign Office. Robin Cook, the foreign secretary, denied these claims and established an independent inquiry to examine the allegations that the sanctions had been defied. The report, published in July, concluded that Britain's high commissioner in Sierra Leone had exceeded his authority in supporting Sandline and that Foreign Office officials should have known more and acted sooner to uphold the UN embargo; the report, however, exonerated ministers from knowledge or blame.

On July 8 the government published the results of its Strategic Defence Review. It upheld Britain's need for a capability commensurate with its membership in NATO and its place as a permanent member of the UN Security Council. It also proposed that the real level of defense spending continue to decline, as it had under the Conservatives, from 2.8% of GDP in 1996–97 to 2.4% in 2001–02. George Robertson, the defense secretary, emphasized the need for British forces to be able to contribute to Joint Rapid Reaction Forces; to this end two new aircraft carriers would be commissioned, capable of carrying twice as many aircraft as the existing ships. Robertson also announced that the U.K. would retain a "minimum nuclear deterrence," consisting of three Trident submarines, but the number of warheads on each submarine would be reduced from 96 to 48.

In December British Tornado bombers took part in Desert Fox, the four-day bombing campaign against Iraq's military installations. Britain was the only member of the EU to join in the U.S.-led action. This provoked criticism from France and undermined the intended effect of an agreement signed at the beginning of the month between Blair and French Pres. Jacques Chirac to cooperate more closely on military matters.

Toward the end of the year, strains emerged in the U.K.'s relations with Chile. On October 16 Gen. Augusto Pinochet, Chile's former dictator, was arrested in London following a request from Spain to extradite him on charges of murder, torture, and kidnapping. Pinochet, who had come to the U.K. for medical treatment, was forced to remain in the London area while Spain's request was considered. Pinochet's lawyers and the Chilean government argued that Pinochet enjoyed diplomatic immunity and should therefore be allowed to fly home to Santiago.

On November 25, by a 3–2 majority, a panel of U.K. Law Lords ruled that Pinochet no longer enjoyed diplomatic immunity and that the extradition proceedings should therefore go ahead. On December 11 Pinochet appeared before magistrates in south London, and he faced the start of the formal extradition process. On December 17, however, a new panel of Law Lords ruled that there had been procedural defects in the November 25 decision and that new hearings should be heard early in 1999 to reconsider whether Pinochet enjoyed diplomatic immunity.

Northern Ireland. On April 10 Blair announced that a peace agreement had been reached between all but one of the main political groups in Northern Ireland, ranging from Sinn Fein and the Social Democratic and Labour Party (SDLP), representing Irish nationalists, to the Ulster Unionists and Ulster Democratic Party, representing the unionist community. The one significant party that opposed the agreement was the Democratic Unionist Party (DUP), led by Ian Paisley. The agreement—which had been brokered by former U.S. senator George Mitchell; Mo Mowlam, the U.K.'s Northern Ireland secretary; and, during the final, tense 72 hours, Tony Blair—provided for a series of linked procedures for moving toward partial self-government for the province.

The agreement established a 108-member Northern Ireland Assembly, to be elected by proportional representation and governed by a set of rules that would ensure that no major decision could be made unless it commanded the support of at least 40% of the representatives of both the nationalist and unionist communities. The assembly would be run by a 12-member executive drawn from all the main parties. Sinn Fein (and the Protestant paramilitary groups) agreed to decommission all their weapons by June 2000; the Ulster Unionists agreed to accept a voice for the Irish government in Northern Ireland's future by means of a North-South Ministerial Council. The Irish government agreed to amend Articles 2 and 3 of Ireland's constitution and thereby withdrew its historic claim to the territory of Northern Ireland.

On May 22 the peace agreement was subjected to referenda in Northern Ireland, where 71% voted in favour of it, and the Republic, where 94% voted "yes." Exit polls in Northern Ireland indicated that the Roman Catholic community voted almost unanimously for the agreement, whereas the Protestants were evenly divided. The referenda paved the way for the first elections to the new Northern Ireland Assembly on June 25, in which the Ulster Unionists won 28 seats, the SDLP 24, the DUP 20, Sinn Fein 18, and six smaller parties 18. Altogether, pro-agreement parties won 80 seats and antiagreement parties 28. Following the election David Trimble, leader of the Ulster Unionists, was elected first minister of the new assembly (*see* NOBEL PRIZES), and Seamus Mallon of the SDLP was elected deputy first minister.

The prevailing mood of optimism was punctured by a car bomb in the centre of the market town of Omagh in Northern Ireland on August 15. The death toll, about 28, was the highest of any single incident since the eruption of violence in the late 1960s. A small splinter group calling itself the "Real IRA" claimed responsibility. Under pressure from Sinn Fein, the Real IRA announced a cease-fire on August 18. Four days later another splinter group, the Irish National Liberation Army also called a cease-fire. This left only one tiny group, Continuity IRA, committed to armed struggle.

The Omagh bombing caused the U.K. government to recall Parliament from its summer recess for a special two-day session on September 2–3 to pass the Criminal Justice (Terrorism and Conspiracy) Act. The act, which was similar to legislation being passed by the Irish Parliament at the same time, reduced the burden of proof needed to convict a suspect of membership in an unlawful organization. It also made it a criminal offense to conspire in the U.K. to commit terrorist acts outside the U.K. By the end of 1998, however, nobody had been charged under the new legislation.

Toward the end of the year, tensions emerged among the parties involved in the peace process as the IRA announced that it would take no early steps to decommission any of its weapons. Hague joined with the Ulster Unionists in calling for a suspension of the program of releasing prisoners convicted of terrorist offenses. Mowlam, however, insisted on maintaining the prisoner-release program, arguing in a newspaper article on December 31 that the Good Friday agreement "did not make [decommissioning] a precondition for progress in other areas, and the Government is not about to start unraveling what the parties agreed."

(PETER KELLNER)

UNITED STATES

Area: 9,363,364 sq km (3,615,215 sq mi),
including 204,446 sq km of inland water
but excluding the 155,534 sq km of
the Great Lakes that lie within U.S.
boundaries
Population (1998 est.): 270,262,000
Capital: Washington, D.C.
Head of state and government: President
Bill Clinton

In 1998 the United States experienced the
best of times and the worst of times. On one
level the national economy moved steadily
forward through its eighth consecutive year
of vigorous expansion, accompanied by remarkably low and declining inflation, interest rates, and unemployment. On an individual basis it was a great time to be an
American, with the economy producing
record real personal income, hundreds of
thousands of new jobs, and lofty financial
market prices for a prosperous and satisfied
public. On another level, however, the national body politic was in turmoil. Years of
investigations into various charges against
Pres. Bill Clinton coalesced during 1998
into a focused probe of his efforts to evade
a sexual harassment lawsuit, which led to
his impeachment at the year's end by a
partisan and divided U.S. House of
Representatives. The disconnection between
the sunny economic conditions and the
stormy wrangling in the capital split the
country into two camps, a larger one happy
with their lot under Clinton and bored by
Washington's seeming obsession with scandal and a smaller group outraged by
Clinton's conduct and determined to see him
removed.

The fragmented national mood confounded public opinion pollsters and helped
produce an inconclusive national midterm
election in November. With his personal
popularity incongruously bolstered by the
assaults on his character, President Clinton
won almost every important battle with the
Republican Congress when final tax and
spending measures were enacted in October.
The setbacks seemed to demoralize Republicans and energize the president's core supporters. Although most commentators predicted that Republicans would add to their
majorities among governors and in the U.S.
House and Senate, the election produced no
change in the Senate and a reduction in the
slim Republican advantage in the House.
That result in turn prompted another major
surprise: Clinton's chief Republican nemesis, controversial Speaker of the House
Newt Gingrich, resigned his post and
thereby effectively became the first major
victim of the Clinton scandal.

The Economy. Although Clinton's problems captured more headlines, the most significant news of 1998 was the continuing
awesome and enduring strength of the
American economy, which loomed like a
colossus over a troubled world. Nearly three
million new American jobs were created,
many of them high-paying positions in
technology, pharmaceuticals, finance, and
health care. The national economy shook off

a spate of bad external news and grew at a
3.5% rate for a third consecutive year,
nearly double the rate at which economists
begin to fear overheating. Yet inflation remained well below 2%, even while unemployment sank to a 29-year low of 4.3%,
real incomes rose at near-historic rates,
housing construction was booming, and
consumer confidence reached a record high.

If the U.S. had merely been leading
worldwide economic growth, its business
performance would have been impressive
enough. More remarkably, the muscular
American economic engine surged forward
even as trouble enveloped much of the
world, refusing to slow significantly as other
major economies faltered and stalled. When
the year started, Japan was mired in a long-
term economic malaise, and other vibrant
Asia economies, especially Thailand, South
Korea, Indonesia, and Malaysia, were still
reeling from a 1997 currency crisis. By
midyear the small but emerging Russian
economy had begun to unravel as the ruble
began to lose value, and rumours of trouble
in Brazil and Argentina had reached Wall
Street.

In July the U.S. stock market seemed to
lose heart under the accumulated weight of
world adversity and began a long, steady
price drop, erasing in two short months a
20% gain posted early in the year. The Dow
Jones industrial average fell from 9338 to
7539 by September, and a major New York
hedge fund, Long-Term Capital Management,
heavily invested in Russia, was threatened
with bankruptcy. Once again, as it had
through much of the record American peacetime expansion, the U.S. Federal Reserve
System rode to the rescue. Under Chairman
Alan Greenspan's supervision, a consortium
of private lenders poured liquidity into the
fund, effectively taking it over. Greenspan
also orchestrated three small but rapid reductions in short-term interest rates over a seven-
week period from September to November.
The cuts in the federal funds rate—from
5.5% to 5.25% to 5% to 4.75%—helped Wall
Street recover its footing and reverse the
downturn. By year's end the Dow had made
its most spectacular comeback in history,
eliminating the entire summer decline and
again threatening record territory, even as the
country's political leadership seemed to be
disintegrating.

The hearty American economic performance produced a political side benefit:
elimination of the federal government's
chronic budget deficit. The red ink had hit
a high of $290 billion in 1992, and admin-
istration economists had projected permanent $200 billion deficits as recently as
1996. The relentless surge of the national
economy, however, reduced social expenditures (especially as the 1996 national
welfare-reform law took full effect) and
increased tax revenues far more rapidly
than any economist could predict. When
President Clinton and Congress agreed on a
balanced-budget deal in August 1997, the
1998 deficit was estimated at $90 billion.
By January 1998 the projected deficit
had shrunk to $22 billion, but when the fis-
cal year ended in October, authorities announced a surplus of $70 billion and
forecast future black ink as far as the eye
could see.

Domestic Affairs. In Washington, D.C.,
the vibrant economy did little to pacify an
increasing partisanship that infected the na-

tion's capital. Lawmakers were distracted
during the year by the Clinton inquiry and
worried about upcoming elections. For his
part, the president was unable to provide effective and consistent leadership throughout
the year. As a result, the year was more notable for legislation defeated than for initiatives approved. Congress did approve a massive $216 billion highway and transit
reauthorization that provided many new
public works projects in every congressional
district during the next six years. Also, when
polls showed overwhelming public support,
Clinton signed a Republican-backed reform
bill ordering the Internal Revenue Service to
become more responsive to the concerns of
American taxpayers.

Most other major legislative initiatives
died in partisan crossfire. Going down to defeat were plans to fund a massive national
missile defense effort, to cap punitive damages in product-liability cases, to overturn
the president's partial-birth-abortion veto,
and to reform bankruptcy laws (all opposed
by Democrats), and efforts to hike the minimum wage and to expand patient's rights in
their dealings with health care providers and
employers (both blocked by Republicans).

An effort to reform the nation's easily
evaded campaign finance laws also died on
the U.S. Senate floor. In August the House
approved a measure limiting both "soft
money" and "independent expenditures,"
two major loopholes in campaign laws.
Unlimited soft money dollars flowed from
corporations, labour unions, and other interested groups directly to major political party
coffers; independent expenditures allowed
groups to spend without limit as long as they
purported to advocate issue positions rather
than individual candidates. Republicans
feared the plan would not curb Democratic-
oriented donors such as labour unions and
environmental activists as much as it would
inhibit GOP-leaning contributors such as
businesses. Consequently, a month later a
substantial minority of 48 Republican senators talked the Senate version to death via
filibuster, refusing to stop talking until the
measure was abandoned.

An attempt to fashion a comprehensive
national settlement with tobacco companies
over costs of smoking-related health problems met a similar fate. A bill implementing a $368 billion proposed settlement in
1997 was shepherded easily through the
Senate Commerce Committee by Chairman
John McCain. It would have raised federal
cigarette taxes by $1.10 per pack, restricted
tobacco advertising, ordered Federal Drug
Administration regulation of tobacco, and
established fines if the incidence of teenage
smoking failed to drop. Antismoking senators then raised the industry cost to $516 bil-
lion and dropped company protections
against future litigation. At that time the
four major tobacco firms ceased negotiations and started a $40 million advertising
campaign, attacking the Senate bill as a
large tax increase to fund new government
spending programs. Even though a majority
of senators continued to favour the bill, they
could not break another filibuster, and the
measure died.

Incidence of crime, particularly violent
offenses, dropped in the U.S. for the sixth
consecutive year, but several high-profile
acts nonetheless raised fears about trends in
American society. In July a deranged gun-
man attempting to enter the U.S. Capitol

building in Washington killed two policemen, the first deaths ever recorded at the
Capitol. The offender was critically
wounded and was later found mentally in-
competent to stand trial. Young students
with firearms were involved in two highly
publicized tragedies. In Jonesboro, Ark., two
boys, 11 and 13, killed 4 students and a
teacher and wounded 10 others in a shooting spree at their junior high school in
March. Two months later a 15-year-old
Springfield, Ore., boy shot and killed his
parents and then took their guns to his high-
school cafeteria, where he shot 24 students,
2 of them fatally. Three white men, two
wearing tattoos identifying them as members of a white racist prison gang, were
charged with murder after an African-
American man was dragged to death behind
a pickup truck near Jasper, Texas, in June.
In Laramie, Wyo., an openly gay University
of Wyoming student was kidnapped from a
bar, tied to a fence in a rural area, and
beaten to death by two men. The incidents
prompted renewed calls for new laws to
combat so-called hate crimes and illegal
possession of firearms.

Investigating the President. Throughout
his long political career, President Clinton
had benefited from his extraordinary communication skills, a talent that enabled him
to demonstrate empathy with his audience
and to turn close arguments decisively in his
favour. This skill often infuriated his rivals,
who complained that his verbal adroitness
hid a lack of character and appreciation for
the truth. For years Clinton sailed serenely
over those criticisms. In 1998, however,
through a series of wildly improbable and
unexpected events, he became enmeshed in
a quagmire over credibility that culminated
at the year's end with his becoming only the
second president in history to be impeached
by the U.S. House of Representatives.

Clinton was compelled to give a sworn
deposition as defendant in a sexual harass-
ment civil rights lawsuit filed by Paula
Jones, a former Arkansas state employee.
Jones, having alleged that then governor
Clinton had improperly propositioned her in
a Little Rock hotel room in 1991, sought ev-
idence of other extramarital adventures by
Clinton. At the January 17 deposition,
Clinton generally denied all but one such af-

fair (he belatedly acknowledged a previously denied liaison with Gennifer Flowers),
but he specifically rejected suggestions he
had dallied with a former White House intern named Monica Lewinsky. An Arkansas
federal judge, relying in part on Clinton's
denials, subsequently dismissed Jones's case
against him.

Unknown to Clinton, however, Linda
Tripp, a former White House employee, had
secretly recorded some 20 hours of conversations with her friend Lewinsky in which
the young woman detailed an intimate relationship with the president. Tripp took her
evidence to Kenneth Starr (see BIOGRA-
PHIES), the court-appointed independent
counsel who had been investigating Clinton
and associates for three years. Starr received
court approval to expand his investigation to
the Lewinsky matter.

Through the spring, as Starr's grand ju-
ries gathered evidence on Lewinsky, the administration attempted to block testimony of
various Clinton aides and security officers
by asserting privilege claims, but most were

(TOP LEFT AND BOTTOM RIGHT) GREG GIBSON—AP/WIDE WORLD; (TOP
RIGHT AND OPPOSITE PAGE) KHUE BUI—AP/WIDE WORLD; (BOTTOM LEFT)
MICHAEL S. GREEN—AP/WIDE WORLD

(Clockwise from top left) Paula Jones, whose
sexual harassment suit against Pres. Bill
Clinton led to an investigation into his
relationship with former White House intern
Monica Lewinsky, arrives with her husband
at Clinton's attorney's office; Linda Tripp
faces questions about her taped telephone
conversations with Lewinsky from reporters
outside the federal court house; on August 17
Clinton prepares for a television appearance
in which he admitted to an "inappropriate
relationship" with Lewinsky; newspapers
heralding the president's impeachment hit
the street on December 19. (Opposite) House
Democrats walk out in protest against the
impeachment proceedings. They returned in
time to complete the historic vote.

rejected by the courts. After months of delay Lewinsky hired new lawyers and eventually began cooperating with Starr. Clinton on August 17 gave an extraordinary interview via video to the Starr grand jury, now admitting an "inappropriate relationship" with Lewinsky but invoking precise word definitions to deny that he had lied or committed perjury in his previous sworn statements. Far from indicating damage, Clinton's high public-approval ratings actually rose following these concessions.

In the fall a series of unexpected and virtually unprecedented events rocked Washington. Starr sent the U.S. House two truckloads of documents with a message alleging that Clinton may have committed at least five impeachable offenses in his handling of the Jones suit and subsequent investigation. Most commentators predicted the charges would aid Republicans in November elections, but the GOP actually lost five House seats. House Speaker Gingrich, a severe Clinton critic, then announced his resignation. At that point pundits declared any impeachment inquiry dead, killed in effect by will of the voters. Instead, however, the House Judiciary Committee under Chairman Henry Hyde conducted a hearing and voted along strict party lines to recommend impeachment of the president on four counts.

In December the matter moved to the full Republican-controlled House, with Democrats continuing to complain that Clinton was being charged with personal offenses in his private life that had nothing to do with public conduct of his office. Only a few minutes before the actual voting, Gingrich's designated successor as speaker of the House, Louisiana Rep. Robert Livingston, announced that he would resign from the House after acknowledging he had engaged in extramarital affairs. The House then impeached Clinton on two counts, perjury and obstruction of justice, again largely along partisan lines, with only a half dozen representatives from each party straying from the party-line vote.

Foreign Affairs. The treaty ending the 1991 Persian Gulf War specified that international sanctions against Iraq should remain in place until United Nations inspectors could verify that Saddam Hussein's missile, biological, chemical, and nuclear weapons programs had been completely dismantled. As the year began, the U.S. and Great Britain sent a major military task force to the Persian Gulf to force compliance with inspection demands. In February UN Secretary-General Kofi Annan flew to Baghdad and hammered out an 11th-hour agreement calling for "unconditional and unrestricted" access for inspections. That pact began to fray almost immediately, as Iraq demanded a certain date for the con-

clusion of weapons monitoring. In August Saddam Hussein suspended cooperation with inspectors, which precipitated yet another slowly evolving crisis. Meanwhile, the top American inspector, Scott Ritter, resigned his post, accusing the Clinton administration of deliberately canceling aggressive inspections to avoid provoking Hussein. On November 13, following another allied military buildup in the region, President Clinton ordered U.S. forces to attack Iraq. After B-52 bombers were airborne, however, Clinton announced that Iraq had "backed down" and had promised full cooperation with inspectors.

That agreement lasted little more than a month. UN inspectors, whom the Iraqis

---

The Limits of Power of the Independent Counsel

On Sept. 9, 1998, the report of the Office of the Independent Counsel (OIC) was presented to the U.S. Congress. The culmination of a four-year, $40 million investigation by Independent Counsel Kenneth Starr (*see* BIOGRAPHIES) into the conduct of U.S. Pres. Bill Clinton (*see* BIOGRAPHIES), the report concluded that "substantial and credible information" existed that Clinton had committed acts that constituted possible grounds for impeachment. As the American public absorbed the salacious details of Clinton's sexual relationship with Monica Lewinsky, a White House intern half his age, some questioned the broad powers granted to Starr to unearth such information.

The OIC (also known as a special prosecutor) was established under federal statute to conduct politically sensitive investigations. Special prosecutors played prominent roles in both the Watergate and the Iran-Contra affairs. In

both these earlier cases, however, the purpose of the investigation was clearly defined from the outset. Starr's investigation, on the other hand, changed focus several times, which led some observers to suggest that its goal was not to expose the truth but to disable the president politically. The administration pointed out that in 445 pages the report referred only twice to the Whitewater land deal, the original target of the investigation, whereas it referred to the issue of sex more than 500 times.

More significant concerns, however, arose from the OIC's ever-expanding jurisdiction. Under the terms of the independent counsel statute, if the OIC uncovers criminal conduct not within its jurisdiction, it may ask the Department of Justice to conduct its own preliminary investigation to determine whether to expand the OIC's jurisdiction. In January 1998 the OIC requested such additional jurisdiction, claiming that evidence ex-

isted that Clinton and Lewinsky were planning to commit perjury in the Paula Jones sexual harassment suit. The additional jurisdiction was granted on the basis of audiotapes made by Linda Tripp, a friend of Lewinsky, of conversations between the two. The Clinton administration cried foul, claiming that Starr's use of Tripp to obtain the information was an unlawful expansion of the investigation. Starr for his part said that Tripp had come forward with the allegations herself and that the OIC had a duty to conduct its own preliminary investigation prior to seeking increased jurisdiction.

Despite misgivings about the broad scope of the OIC probe, the Starr report was submitted to the House Judiciary Committee. Starr had used his statutory powers to the fullest extent allowed by law. On December 19, based on his findings, the House voted articles of impeachment against President Clinton.

(JOHN H. MATHEWS)

A floral tribute marks the spot where Matthew Shepard, an openly gay University of Wyoming student, was beaten to death near Laramie, Wyoming. The murder prompted nationwide calls for harsher laws against hate crimes.

called deliberately provocative, were turned away from political and military sites. In mid-December, just one day before the House was to vote on his impeachment, Clinton again issued orders for joint U.S.-British air strikes on Iraq. The resulting 70-hour bombardment produced uncertain damage to Iraqi installations but an apparently decisive political result; at year's end Hussein declared he would no longer allow UN inspectors to operate within his country.

Within minutes on August 7, U.S. embassies in Nairobi, Kenya, and Dar es Salaam, Tanz., were hit by terrorist bombs that killed about 270, including 12 American citizens. Authorities in a dozen countries quickly developed information linking the attacks to Al-Qaeda, a militant Islamic Army offshoot run by Saudi-born millionaire Osama bin Laden. (*See* BIOGRAPHIES.) On August 20 the U.S. military fired 75 Tomahawk cruise missiles at a bin Laden military training compound in eastern Afghanistan and at a pharmaceuticals factory in Khartoum, Sudan, that U.S. authorities claimed manufactured the "precursors" of chemical weapons.

The U.S. policy of stopping nuclear weapons proliferation suffered several setbacks during the year. Catching U.S. intelligence largely unaware, India conducted a series of underground nuclear tests on May 11 and 13. President Clinton announced economic sanctions against India and dispatched a high-level delegation to dissuade rival Pakistan from duplicating the feat. Pakistan, however, performed six of its own weapons tests on May 28 and 30, again prompting U.S.-led world economic sanctions. Both countries declared a moratorium on future tests, and by early November Clinton had canceled the short-lived sanctions.

Clinton achieved a number of unqualified foreign policy successes during 1998. He was universally credited with a vital role in the brokering of a historic agreement to end 80 years of religious-based strife in Northern Ireland. He achieved a similar apparent breakthrough in the Middle East peace process in late October when Israeli Prime Minister Benjamin Netanyahu and Palestinian leader Yasir Arafat signed an interim agreement for Israeli withdrawal from part of the occupied West Bank. Clinton brought the two sides together and laid plans for what turned out to be an intense nine-day series of closed meetings at the Wye River Conference Center on Maryland's Eastern Shore.

As the Asia currency crisis appeared to bottom out during the year, the U.S. Congress reluctantly endorsed International Monetary Fund efforts to shore up foundering world economies. Republican congressmen faulted the IMF's secrecy and claimed that the organization's stringent lending requirements helped compound troubles faced by some countries. The U.S.'s regular $3.5 billion dues were eventually authorized, however, and another $17.9 billion special contribution was approved as part of the year-end budget deal in October.

(DAVID C. BECKWITH)

DEVELOPMENTS IN THE STATES, 1998

Riding a tailwind from a strong national economy, state and local governments in the United States again enjoyed the luxury of surplus revenues during 1998 and gained more power in developing national policies. For the fifth consecutive year, states enacted multibillion-dollar tax cuts. Their financial outlook was further brightened at the year's end when tobacco companies finalized a settlement exceeding $200 billion overall to compensate states for the costs of tobacco-related health care.

Highly charged social policy issues—including affirmative action, bilingual education, homosexual marriage, late-term abortion, and legal gambling—dominated election campaigns and legislative deliberations during the year. As the U.S. Congress continued to cede some powers back to states, authorities grappled with problems concerning the proper relationship between federal and state governments. Forty-four states held regular legislative sessions during 1998, and 13 staged special sessions.

Party Strengths. Democrats scored modest gains in national elections in November, winning 37 state legislative seats from Republican control. Before the elections Democrats were in charge of both houses in 20 state legislatures, Republicans had 19, and 10 were split (Nebraska has a nonpartisan unicameral legislature). For 1999, 20 states were in Democratic control, 17 in Republican, and 12 split between the parties.

In 36 governorships contested nationwide, there were nine changes of party control. Democratic governors were replaced by Republicans in Colorado, Florida, Nebraska, and Nevada, but Democrats took over for Republican governors in Alabama, California, Iowa, and South Carolina. One of the most publicized races occurred in Minnesota, where a former professional wrestler running on the Reform Party ticket, Jesse ("The Body") Ventura, prevailed in a high-turnout election. For 1999 the gubernatorial lineup nationwide was 31 Republicans, 17 Democrats, and 2 independents, compared with a 32–17–1 tally in 1998. Arizona made history by electing women to the state's top five constitutional offices.

Government Structures and Powers. Courts wrestled with the legality of laws approved in the early 1990s that had mandated term limits for state officials. Washington's Supreme Court ruled unconstitutional a 1992 term-limits initiative, stating that any change must be accomplished through a state constitutional amendment. In Michigan and California federal judges ruled that state term-limit laws did not violate the U.S. Constitution.

Voters in Arizona and Massachusetts approved campaign finance overhaul initiatives that provided public funding for candidates and lower permissible limits on political contributions. New York City voters also established a voluntary campaign finance system banning corporate donations and requiring disclosure of contributions by those doing business with the city.

Voters in Oregon approved a measure allowing virtually all elections to be conducted exclusively by mail, making the state the first to retire precinct voting. Backers claimed mail-in ballots, already used in Oregon local elections, were cheaper to administer, were more convenient, and encouraged higher turnout.

In a referendum approved by a divided U.S. Congress, Puerto Rico on December 13 voted on four choices: statehood, independence, independence with a "free association" with the U.S., or continuation of its status as a U.S. commonwealth. None of these options won a majority, but anti-statehood forces claimed victory.

Government Relations. Federalism, the proper relationship between the national and state governments, continued to generate controversy during the year. The federal

government published, and later revoked, an executive order effectively repealing previous federalism accords with states. State and local officials claimed that the disputed order eliminated an agreement that federal authorities would consider federalism principles before taking action and also reneged on promises to cut unfunded federal mandates on states.

Although the 1996 federal welfare-reform law continued to generate praise, wrangling continued over details. States reported that welfare rolls had been trimmed by nearly 3.5 million since enactment of the law but objected to federal demands for 178 items of background information on welfare recipients and their families.

Politics continued to infect preparations for the 2000 census that would help determine legislative reapportionment and state eligibility for federal aid. The Clinton administration pressed for the use of statistical sampling procedures to combat alleged undercounting of poor and minorities, whereas Republicans insisted on a "hard" or actual count. The administration at the year's end appealed to the U.S. Supreme Court a federal court decision that ruled sampling to be unconstitutional, and the GOP-controlled Congress guaranteed census funding only through mid-1999.

Finances. A humming national economy kept state treasuries in robust shape during 1998, with states projecting a record $34 billion total surplus at the year's end. Although many states spent part of their excess revenue on government programs and others stashed a portion away in "rainy day" funds, 35 states cut taxes by a record $6.8 billion during the year. The reductions amounted to 1.5% of the 1997 tax collections, but eight states—Colorado, Connecticut, Kansas, Maine, Massachusetts, Minnesota, Nebraska, and Ohio—reduced their taxes by 4% or more.

Thirty states lowered personal income taxes. Corporate income rates were reduced in 25 states. Sales and use taxes dropped in 21 states, led by sales tax reductions of 0.5% in Nebraska and Maine. As states pursued a settlement with tobacco companies, cigarette and tobacco taxes remained unchanged by legislatures, although California voters approved a 50-cent-per-pack increase to fund early-childhood education and other antismoking programs. Wyoming was the only other state to approve a notable tax boost, a hike in the motor-fuel tax, to combat sluggish resource-based revenues and increased education-spending needs.

Montana voters narrowly approved a state constitutional amendment requiring voter approval of any new or increased taxes, effectively taking taxing authority away from the state legislature. A New Mexico constitutional amendment gave the legislature power to limit property tax increases. Nebraska voters, however, by a two-to-one margin, rejected a proposal to cap state and local taxes; opponents said that the measure could hurt school funding.

Health and Welfare. Bulging state treasuries received even more good news on November 20 when states reached a sweeping $206 billion resolution of health claims against four tobacco manufacturers. The money was to be paid over 25 years for states to use as they saw fit, but most announced plans to use part of the proceeds on antismoking education programs. As part of the deal, cigarette makers agreed to im-

JIM MONE—AP/WIDE WORLD

Former professional wrestler Jesse Ventura takes a break during his campaign for governor of Minnesota. Ventura, the Reform Party candidate, won on a high voter turnout.

pose severe limits on cigarette brand advertising and to initiate antismoking campaigns of their own.

Earlier in the year Texas had announced a $15.3 billion tobacco settlement, and Minnesota settled a lawsuit with a more than $6 billion accord. The deals were technically repayment of state Medicaid costs to treat sick smokers. A more comprehensive $368.5 billion settlement with the federal government fell apart in June when antitobacco activists made additional claims, including denial of company immunity against private lawsuits and tax-increase demands that would have raised cigarette prices close to $5 per pack.

Numerous courts ruled on state laws attempting to ban late-term abortions. By the year's end 19 states had approved such laws, but courts had blocked enforcement in 10 and the remainder were under legal challenge. The U.S. Supreme Court refused to settle the controversy in 1998, declining to hear an appeal from lower court judgments that an Ohio late-term abortion law was unconstitutional. Washington and Colorado voters turned down initiatives outlawing late-term abortions as "infanticide," but the same Colorado voters also approved a measure requiring parental notification and a 48-hour waiting period for minors seeking an abortion.

States split on the question as to whether medical prescriptions for Viagra, a new drug improving potency in males, should be reimbursed with state Medicaid funds. (See HEALTH AND DISEASE: Sidebar.) Even after the federal government advised that such claims should be paid when based on medical necessity, a majority of states refused to comply.

Education. States continued to struggle with school-financing issues, including proposals to balance public-school funding between wealthy and poor districts. Even greater controversy swirled around voucher pilot programs and other plans challenging historic public-school funding.

The U.S. Supreme Court rejected a lawsuit against Wisconsin's model school-voucher program. That left in place a 1998 Wisconsin Supreme Court ruling that tax-

payer-paid vouchers to religious schools did not violate the Constitution's prohibition on government policies that promote religion. High courts in Arizona, Maine, Ohio, and Vermont were considering similar challenges to state pilot voucher programs at the year's end.

Colorado voters turned down a school-choice referendum that would have provided up to $2,500 per pupil in state-tax credits for sending children to private schools, including those affiliated with a religion. President Clinton vetoed a congressional bill that would have provided $3,200 "opportunity scholarships" to private or parochial schools for 2,000 District of Columbia students.

In a closely watched election with national implications, California voters abolished bilingual education in the state public-school system. Opponents noted that about 1.4 million of the state's 5.6 million students did not understand English well enough to keep up in school, but Proposition 227 mandated that the problem be addressed by more intensive instruction in English.

Massachusetts, the 44th state to test new teacher applicants, made national headlines in April when only 41% of prospective teachers passed a basic accreditation exam. Repeat testing in July and October produced only slightly better pass rates of 53% and 55%. The testing was opposed by teachers unions, which were fighting a proposal by Gov. Paul Cellucci that current teachers be forced to take the tests as well.

Law and Justice. Statistics released during the year revealed that serious crime had dropped by 2% during 1997, the sixth consecutive annual decrease in reported crime. The totals included a 3% decrease in violent crime, including 7% reductions in murder and robbery, and a 2% decrease in the more numerous property crimes. Early figures for 1998 were sharply down again. Authorities again attributed the trend to an aging national population, tougher sentencing, increased prison capacity, and a crackdown on minor offenses.

States executed 68 men and women during 1998, the vast majority by lethal injection, a reduction from the 74 recorded a year earlier. In one highly publicized case, Christian activists unsuccessfully appealed to Texas Gov. George W. Bush for clemency for Karla Faye Tucker, who had undergone a religious conversion following her conviction for two brutal murders in 1983.

The pace of executions again failed to keep up with court imposition of death sentences. At the year's end, the Death Penalty Information Center counted 3,517 prisoners on death row in 37 state and federal prisons.

In a clear trend voters in five western states—Alaska, Arizona, Nevada, Oregon, and Washington—approved initiatives allowing doctors to prescribe marijuana for patients with serious or terminal illnesses. Arizona's proposition permitted the legal use of other drugs, including LSD and heroin, if a physician prescribed them. Additionally, Oregon voters turned down a measure that would have required jail time for small-time marijuana users.

The U.S. Supreme Court rejected a constitutional challenge to New Jersey's "Megan's law," which required authorities to notify residents when convicted sex offenders moved into their neighbourhoods. Louisiana and Tennessee voters approved

crime victims' rights initiatives, including the right to be heard and the right to be notified when the accused left custody.

Attempting to model legal action after tobacco litigation, the cities of New Orleans, Chicago, and Boston announced plans to sue 15 handgun manufacturers for obstructing regulations, ignoring safety measures, and foregoing safety warnings on their products. Wisconsin voters added a right to bear arms for security, defense, and hunting to the state constitution.

Voters in Michigan, home state of Jack Kevorkian, soundly defeated a ballot initiative to legalize doctor-assisted suicide. A criminal statute banning the practice had been approved by the state legislature earlier in 1998. The action left Oregon as the only state with a "Death with Dignity" law allowing physicians to aid voluntary suicide.

Ethics. Maryland state Sen. Larry Young (Dem.) was expelled by his colleagues in January over allegations that he misused his position to collect fees from health care companies and a state college that were seeking good government relations. Michigan state Sen. Henry Stallings (Dem.) resigned just before the full Senate was about to vote on expelling him over charges that he used more than $5,000 in public funds to pay a staff member to run his Detroit art gallery.

Former Arizona governor Fife Symington (Rep.) was sentenced to two and a half years in prison, five years of probation, and a fine of $60,000 after his conviction on charges that he lied to get millions in loans to save

Multiple sclerosis patient Jeanelle Bluhm of Portland, Oregon, admits to using marijuana to relieve pain. Voters in five western states approved the medicinal use of marijuana.

his failing real-estate empire. A leader in Maine's initiatives to cap state taxes, Carol Palesky, was sentenced to five years in prison for aggravated forgery. She was accused of having submitted altered documents and having forged names of dead persons to petitions.

Former Louisiana governor Edwin Edwards (Dem.) was indicted with five others on November 6 on 28 felony counts, including racketeering conspiracy to extort millions from businesses seeking lucrative riverboat casino licenses. Two previous indictments of Edwards on other corruption charges had led to a hung jury and an acquittal. Edward diPrete, the Republican former governor of Rhode Island, was convicted and sent to prison late in the year for irregularities in the granting of state contracts.

President Clinton agreed to pay a former state employee, Paula Jones, $850,000 to settle a long-running sexual-harassment lawsuit stemming from his tenure as Arkansas governor. In the settlement Clinton did not apologize or admit responsibility.

Prisons. Even while the nation's crime rate was in a sustained decline, both prison-construction expenditures and inmate populations continued to rise. State expenditures for penal buildings, however, rose 2.6%, well below the average increase of the past decade.

Statistics released at midyear showed that the number of prisoners housed in state and federal facilities had grown by 5.2% over the previous 12 months to a record 1,244,544, which included 1,131,581 inmates in state and 112,973 in federal institutions. On a typical day an additional 567,079 men and women were being held in the nation's jails. The figures showed that the nation's prison population had grown by more than 60% since 1990, which caused 32 states to report inmate populations over 100% of prison capacity. Although women (6.4% of all prisoners) and older prisoners remained a distinct minority, their numbers grew faster than did those of other prisoners. More than 3 of every 100 adult black males were imprisoned on a given day, compared with 1.3 of every 100 Hispanic males and 0.37 of every 100 white males.

Gambling. After three years of relative inactivity, proponents of legalized games of chance scored several advances in 1998. Voters showed an increased tolerance for gaming outside traditional areas, particularly when added state revenue for high-priority programs such as education appeared to be at stake.

California voters easily approved a measure requiring the governor to ne-

gotiate gaming compacts on Native American reservations. The initiative campaign attracted a record $100 million in funding, including a reported $25 million in opposition from Nevada gaming interests.

Environment. Citing pollution problems, opponents of major hog-farming operations gained support during 1998. South Dakota voters restricted corporations from buying or farming new land or otherwise investing in new farm or livestock production. The measure was aimed at stopping corporate hog farming. Colorado also enacted tight new regulations on hog farming.

Oklahoma eliminated property taxes for pollution-control equipment. Montana voters approved a proposition banning the use of cyanide in open-pit mining for gold and silver. Bond issues to finance environmental projects were approved by voters in Arkansas, Maine, Michigan, and North Carolina.

Equal Rights. By nearly two to one, Washington voters approved an initiative banning race and gender preferences in local and state government programs. The measure tracked an identically worded initiative approved by California voters in 1996. The University of Washington immediately announced it would suspend its race-conscious admissions policies.

In an early 1998 election, Maine voters by a 52–48 margin removed sexual orientation from the state's 1997 antidiscrimination law. Gay rights supporters attributed their defeat to low voter turnout and urged the state legislature to reenact the stricken law. Voters in Alaska and Hawaii overwhelmingly approved amendments to state constitutions banning homosexual marriages.

Alabama voters decisively backed a state constitutional amendment to "prohibit the burdening of the free exercise of religion" by government. By a 62–38 margin, South Carolina voters removed a state constitutional clause banning interracial marriage.

Consumer Protection. California voters narrowly turned down an initiative prohibiting the use of union dues money for political purposes without direct permission from the union members. After ironing out differences with state interests, Congress approved the Internet Tax Freedom Act, effectively barring new or special state taxes on Internet commercial transactions. Proponents said fast-growing "electronic commerce" should not be saddled with any tax burden beyond levies on ordinary transactions.

Washington became the first state to ban "spamming," the sending of unwanted E-mail advertisements over computers. The new law prohibited sending such messages from a computer in the state or to an E-mail address held by a Washington resident. Iowa and Connecticut became the first states to forbid banks to impose surcharges, or "convenience fees," on non-account holders who used the banks' automated teller machines.

Attorneys general for 25 states reached an agreement with American Family Publishers in early 1998 over allegations that the firm used deceptive practices targeting the elderly in their magazine sales mailings. The states received a total of $1,250,000 and a promise that future mailings would no longer claim the recipient had won a nonexistent or valueless prize and would make it clear that buying magazines was not necessary.

(DAVID C. BECKWITH)

URUGUAY

Area: 176,215 sq km (68,037 sq mi)
Population (1998 est.): 3,216,000
Capital: Montevideo
Head of state and government: President
Julio María Sanguinetti

The location of the secretariat of the Southern Cone Common Market (Mercosur)—the customs union of Brazil, Argentina, Uruguay, and Paraguay—in Montevideo helped Uruguay in 1998 to consolidate its position within the group. Physical links were strengthened with the signing of the contract to construct an estimated $120 million gas pipeline from Buenos Aires, Arg., to Montevideo. There was concern, however, that the negative effects of the world financial crisis on Brazil and Argentina would limit economic development. The Colorado/Blanco coalition government predicted gross domestic product growth of 3–4% in 1998, compared with around 6% in 1997. Manufacturing performed strongly in late 1997, and a good 1997–98 tourist season boosted the hotel and restaurant sector. This was accompanied by vigorous domestic consumption. Inflation, which fell to about 15% in 1997, continued its downward trend, registering 9.9% in the 12 months prior to October 1998.

The government continued to reduce the state's role in selected areas of the economy.

A plebiscite in June on private participation in power generation approved the ending of the state monopoly. This was a blow to the left-wing Broad Front coalition, especially to its leader, Tabaré Vásquez, who was firmly opposed to this liberalization.

With party primaries due in April 1999, prior to general elections in October, a dispute emerged within the Broad Front as to whether the coalition should field a candidate for president agreed upon by all the member parties. Meanwhile, leaders of the National (Blanco) Party feared that internal divisions would ruin its chance for an outright victory in 1999. The Colorado Party by the end of 1998 had not chosen its candidate.   (BEN BOX)

UZBEKISTAN

Area: 447,400 sq km (172,700 sq mi)
Population (1998 est.): 24,091,000
Capital: Tashkent
Chief of state and head of government:
President Islam Karimov, assisted by
Prime Minister Otkir Sultonov

The democratization process in Uzbekistan suffered setbacks in 1998 with the adoption of revisions in the legislation on elections that restricted the possibility of multiple candidates and limited active participation of political parties in the election process. In a speech to the Supreme Assembly in August, however, Pres. Islam Karimov called for the development of a civil society and a strong middle class as the best guarantees against economic and social instability and the spread of Islamic fundamentalism.

Deeply frightened by the successes of the extreme fundamentalist Islamic Taliban movement in northern Afghanistan, Uzbekistan's leadership actively promoted a negotiated settlement, under UN auspices, of the fighting in the neighbouring country. In September the Uzbek foreign minister took part in a UN-sponsored meeting of the Contact Group of Afghanistan's neighbour states, plus the U.S. and Russia, to devise ways to restore peace in Afghanistan. At the same time, Uzbekistan sought to strengthen its security ties as well as its readiness to counter a military assault.

Pressure on Islam was sharply intensified in 1998 with the adoption of a revised law on religion in April and with a wave of arrests in Namangan, a city in the Fergana Valley famous for its social conservatism and Muslim piety. Three groups were tried before Uzbekistan's Supreme Court on charges of seeking to overthrow the constitutional order by force and set up an Islamic state. Some of the defendants were also accused of having received training in terrorism at Islamic fundamentalist camps in Afghanistan, Tajikistan, and Pakistan. The government of Pakistan angrily denied the existence on its territory of camps training Uzbek terrorists.

Plans for expansion of Uzbekistan's industry were thwarted by another cotton harvest below expectation and also by a slowdown in foreign investment due to the nonconvertibility of the national currency, rampant corruption and bureaucratic intransigence, and continuing problems in repatriating profits. The government had little success in countering these drawbacks with tax breaks and other inducements. In connection with an important conference on energy in Tashkent, the Uzbek capital, it was announced that six new oil and gas fields in the western part of the country would be open to foreign investment. (*See* Spotlight: *Central Asian Oil Disputes.*)

In March the Uzbek government announced that the Zoroastrian new year, Navruz, would be celebrated as a national holiday and the occasion for a spring cultural festival.   (BESS BROWN)

Uzbek Pres. Islam Karimov (right) supports ailing Russian Pres. Boris Yeltsin during an official ceremony in the Uzbek capital of Tashkent on October 11. Yeltsin's illness, described as a respiratory infection, caused him to cut short his visit to Uzbekistan, which, like Russia, faced economic and social problems during the year.

VANUATU

Area: 12,190 sq km (4,707 sq mi)
Population (1998 est.): 182,000
Capital: Vila
Chief of state: President Jean-Marie Leye
Head of government: Prime Ministers
Serge Vohor and, from March 30,
Donald Kalpokas

In a national election in March 1998 for 52 seats in Parliament, the Vanua'aku Party won 18, the Union of Moderate Parties 12, the National United Party 11, and others 11. Donald Kalpokas, leader of the Vanua'aku

Among those who gathered in St. Peter's Square on October 16 for an outdoor mass were some 20,000 Poles, who had traveled to the Vatican City from their homeland to help Pope John Paul II celebrate the 20th anniversary of his papacy. The first non-Italian pope in more than four centuries, Pope John Paul II was a native of Wadowice, Pol.

Party and former vice president, formed a coalition government with the National United Party on March 30. The coalition collapsed within a few months, after which Kalpokas formed a new coalition with the Union of Moderate Parties.

Despite the previous government's repeal of enabling legislation, Kalpokas's government maintained the office of ombudsman. Ombudsman Marie-Noelle Ferrieux-Patterson had been criticized because of a series of damning reports on ministerial behaviour and corruption in government—most recently over the illegal issue of passports, misuse of cyclone-relief funds by the prime minister, and the misappropriation of retirement funds; the latter led to riots and a state of emergency when subscribers tried to withdraw their savings. During the year the government announced the privatization of airports and in August introduced a 12.5% value-added tax.   (BARRIE MACDONALD)

VATICAN CITY STATE

Area: 44 ha (109 ac)
Population (1998 est.): 850
Chief of state: (sovereign pontiff) Pope John Paul II
Head of administration: Secretary of State Angelo Cardinal Sodano, who heads a pontifical commission of five cardinals

In 1998 Karol Wojtyla celebrated the 20th anniversary of his papacy. It was an eventful year in terms of the pope's aim to es-

tablish the Vatican as a key player in international affairs, as evidenced by his epochal journey to Cuba. This five-day sojourn was perhaps as influential as the pope's 1979 pastoral visit to then-communist Poland or his more recent visits to Lebanon and Bosnia and Herzegovina.

Asia and most of the Middle East, however, continued to resist the 78-year-old pontiff's new evangelizing efforts. Important steps were taken to open the way to a more active role for the Vatican in these parts of the world; audiences were granted to Russian Pres. Boris Yeltsin and to Palestinian leader Yasir Arafat. The Vatican also held its fourth continental synod. Devoted to Asia, the synod brought together bishops from all over the Orient with the exception of China. The status of Jerusalem was also discussed during the synod.

Pope John Paul II created 22 new cardinals; since his 1978 rise to office, he had appointed 106 of the current 123 cardinals.
                (GREGORY O. SMITH)

See also RELIGION: *Roman Catholic Church.*

VENEZUELA

Area: 912,050 sq km (352,144 sq mi)
Population (1998 est.): 23,242,000
Capital: Caracas
Head of state and government: President Rafael Caldera

After a period of recovery in 1997, the economy of Venezuela contracted during most of

1998. Gross domestic product grew by 5.1% in 1997, but it was expected to decline by 2.5% by the end of 1998. One of the main reasons for the economy's troubles was the drop in international oil prices. As part of an agreement with Saudi Arabia and Mexico to curb oil production, Venezuela reduced its output by 200,000 bbl per day, which resulted in a projected $600 million decline in revenue for the year. Venezuela's 1998 budget, 40% of which was accounted for by oil, was originally based on a crude-oil price of $15.50 per barrel, but by late 1998 the price had fallen to less than $12 per barrel.

Another major area of the economy adversely affected by oil prices was the currency, which depreciated by 1.5% per month before stabilizing in October. Devaluation was a subject of great controversy throughout the year. In August Coordination and Planning Minister Teodoro Petkoff accused the banks of being involved in a financial conspiracy. Disip, the secret police, was instructed to investigate an alleged forged statement in a news agency wire saying that the government was about to decree a 17–20% devaluation of currency. The rumours proved false, however.

Pressure on the government to devalue the currency came from the risk-rating agency Moody's, which lowered the country's rating by one notch in 1998. The government immediately prepared a package aimed at reducing the $1,560,000,000 of debt-servicing obligations without borrowing from abroad. This would include $325 million in proceeds from privatizing Sidor, the state-owned steel company; $194 million from the sale of shares in the Corporación Andina de Fomento; increased contributions from Petróleos de Venezuela, the state oil company; and the reprogramming of future debt-servicing obligations, which averaged $4 billion–$5 billion per year.

The financial crisis set the scene for the legislative elections on November 8. The most popular candidate in the opinion polls was Hugo Chávez of the Patriotic Pole coalition. Chávez, a retired lieutenant colonel, was well known as the leader of an abortive military uprising in 1992. He backpedaled on his earlier nationalist and populist stance and promised "Tony Blair-style Third Way policies," which would include privatization measures. To improve his image with wealthy Venezuelans, he swapped casual clothes for a suit and necktie, and in October he invited bankers and investors to a conference to hear his ideas on reforming the constitution by means of a referendum.

This approach paid off for Chávez. In the November election his left-wing coalition won 34% of the seats in the legislature. The centre-left Democratic Action Party won 22%, and the conservative Social Christian Party won 11%.

In the election for president in December Chávez won decisively over businessman Henrique Salas Romer. The margin of victory, 56.5%–39.5%, was the largest in a Venezuelan presidential election in 40 years. Approximately 65% of the eligible voters went to the polls, a high figure for Venezuela. Moreover, Chávez became the first president in 40 years who was not a member of one of the country's dominant political parties.   (ALAN MURPHY)

VIETNAM

Area: 331,041 sq km (127,816 sq mi)
Population (1998 est.): 76,236,000
Capital: Hanoi
Chief of state: President Tran Duc Luong
Head of government: Prime Minister
    Phan Van Khai

Vietnam began 1998 with a new political leader. Hard-liner Gen. Le Kha Phieu became chief of the Communist Party on Dec. 29, 1997. During his first months as the country's most powerful figure, he showed little enthusiasm for reform. Soon after his elevation he shuffled the ruling Politburo, dropping pragmatist Nguyen Tan Dung in favour of conservative soulmate Pham The Duyet. Phieu also expanded the Politburo by adding four new members.

The East Asian financial crisis began to affect Vietnam during 1998, but the nation was spared the worst of it and turned in one of the best performances of any East Asian economy. Early in the year it became clear that Vietnam would not be able to meet its 9% growth target. Output was expected to expand by 6.1%, down from 8.8% in 1997, and was forecast to fall to a gain of about 5% in 1999. In the first nine months of 1998, exports rose by less than 5%, after having averaged 25–30% annually the previous five years. Vietnam devalued the dong twice to maintain export competitiveness.

Bad weather, including a major typhoon in the central part of the country in November, disrupted agricultural production. Inflation, meanwhile, crept up to 8.2% during the first 10 months of the year. Saddled with an estimated $11 billion in foreign debt, Vietnam faced a serious balance of payments problem. In December international donors pledged additional loans and aid totaling $2.7 billion. Foreign direct investment—already slowing when the financial crisis broke—declined to about 60% of the 1997 total. Investors continued to complain about bureaucratic interference and also about the limited implementation and lax enforcement of laws and regulations. The National Assembly in November approved new mechanisms to deal with the growing number of public complaints.

In September Vietnam allowed jailed dissident Doan Viet Hoat to leave for the U.S. 5 years into his 15-year sentence for publishing a pro-democracy newsletter. Former top military leader and party ideologue Gen. Tran Do continued to rile Communist bosses. In a letter from him addressed to Phieu, Tran Do denounced the lack of democracy in the country and the concentration of power in the ruling party.

On the diplomatic front, Vietnam took significant steps during the year. Pres. Tran Duc Luong visited Moscow in August. Russia pledged to expand arms sales to Vietnam and help the nation build an oil refinery and electric power plants. In October Phan Van Khai made the first visit to China by a prime minister since ties with Beijing were normalized in 1991. Both sides agreed to accelerate negotiations over lingering territorial disputes, aiming for a resolution by 2000. The following month Vietnam joined the Asia-Pacific Economic Cooperation organization at APEC's annual meeting in Kuala Lumpur, Malaysia. In December Vietnam was host of the sixth summit of the Association of Southeast Asian Nations, a regional organization that it joined in 1995.

A military plane crash in Laos in May killed 14 senior officers, including 5 generals. During the year two former senior officials died: Nguyen Van Linh, who served as Communist Party general secretary from 1986 to 1991 (*see* OBITUARIES), and Nguyen Co Thach, who was foreign minister from 1980 to 1991. In August Roman Catholics celebrated the 200th anniversary of an apparition of the Virgin Mary in the village of La Vang. The gathering was the

Residents of the central Vietnamese village of Hoi An evacuate their homes in November in order to escape flooding caused by Typhoon Dawn. The typhoon, the worst to hit the region in 30 years, claimed the lives of more than a hundred persons. In addition, devastating floods knocked out a main highway and damaged hundreds of thousands of homes.

largest-ever Catholic event to take place in Vietnam.   (ALEJANDRO REYES)

YEMEN

Area: 555,000 sq km (214,300 sq mi)
Population (1998 est.): 16,496,000
Capital: San'a'
Chief of state: President Maj. Gen. Ali Abdallah Salih
Head of government: Prime Ministers Faraj Said ibn Ghanem until April 29 and, from May 14, 'Abd-al Karim al-Iryani

In May 1998 'Abd-al Karim al-Iryani became Yemen's prime minister, a post he had held in Yemen (San'a') in 1980–83. Iryani had most recently been serving as foreign minister and had also at various times held other ministerial posts, including planning and education.

The long-standing Yemeni-Saudi negotiations to delineate their common border made little progress in 1998. Yemeni-Saudi relations, in fact, suffered a brief setback in July when Saudi forces attacked a small Yemeni contingent on Duwaima Island in the Red Sea. Peace was restored quickly, but the island continued to be claimed by each country. Another foreign-policy problem was resolved in October, however, when an international arbitration tribunal in The Hague decided in Yemen's favour in a territorial dispute with Eritrea over the Hanish Islands.

On December 28 a group calling itself the Aden-Abyan Islamic Army kidnapped 16 tourists in southern Yemen, 12 from the U.K. and 2 each from the U.S. and Australia. They were taken to a remote mountain retreat, where on December 29 Yemeni security forces attacked the kidnappers. In the ensuing gun battle four tourists, two kidnappers, and one policeman were killed. The other 12 tourists were freed.
                              (WILLIAM A. RUGH)

YUGOSLAVIA

Area: 102,173 sq km (39,449 sq mi)
Population (1998 est.): 10,664,000
Capital: Belgrade
Chief of state: President Slobodan Milosevic
Head of government: Prime Ministers Radoje Kontic and, from May 19, Momir Bulatovic

Yugoslavia's descent into poverty, ethnic violence, and authoritarianism continued unabated in 1998. Armed conflict between Serbs and ethnic Albanians in Kosovo, an underdeveloped province of Serbia, the population of which was about 90% ethnic Albanian, made the process of democratization especially difficult. The UN-imposed economic embargo of Serbia and Montenegro, which had been lifted at the end of the Bosnian war, was reimposed because of the violence in Kosovo. The sanctions that cut the country off from normal flows of capital remained in place in order to pressure Yugoslavia into living up to the commitments it made in the 1995 Dayton Peace Agreement and also to work toward a resolution in Kosovo.

Throughout the year the inability of international negotiators to completely halt the fighting in Kosovo led to threats of NATO air strikes. In October Pres. Slobodan Milosevic agreed to a truce that ended eight months of combat between Yugoslavia's security forces and the ethnic Albanian Kosovo Liberation Army. The truce was arranged by U.S. envoy Richard Holbrooke. (*See* BIOGRAPHIES.) Under the deal, Milosevic would allow the Organization for Security and Cooperation in Europe to provide up to 2,000 civilians to monitor a cease-fire in Kosovo and to promote a political settlement that would give Kosovo greater autonomy. Late in December, however, the cease-fire was broken when government forces attacked an ethnic Albanian stronghold.

As the violence increased dramatically in Kosovo, Milosevic's Socialist Party of Serbia and its coalition partners took the opportunity as an excuse to further intensify its clampdown on any form of dissension. New regulations at the University of Belgrade forced the closing of departments and the reassigning of faculty to nonexistent posts or into forced retirement or dismissal. The independent media faced a new wave of fines and confiscation of property, and nongovernmenal organizations were harassed or had their missions impeded. Foreign radio broadcasts were also banned, and locals working for or interviewed by such broadcasters were labeled "spies" and "enemies of the state."

In the face of severe economic crisis, the country's democratic-oriented opposition virtually disintegrated, and, as a result, the Serbian Radical Party under Vojislav Seselj strengthened its power base. Late in the year Milosevic dismissed the head of the secret security service, Jovica Stanisic, who had been regarded by some as the number two man in the regime, and Yugoslav Army Chief of Staff Gen. Momcilo Perisic, who quickly called the move "inappropriate and illegal." Before his dismissal Perisic had criticized Milosevic for having allowed Yugoslavia to become a "pariah state," opposed the use of his soldiers against ethnic Albanian civilians in Kosovo, and had told Milosevic that he would play no part in any armed move against a Montenegrin bid for independence.

During the year Montenegro, Serbia's smaller partner in the Yugoslav federation, was another major concern for Milosevic. Milo Djukanovic's victory in the 1997 presidential elections in Montenegro (he assumed office in January 1998) over Milosevic's protégé Momir Bulatovic and Djukanovic's party's triumph in parliamentary balloting in May were seen as the severest blow to Milosevic's regime since his coming to power in 1986. Montenegro halted its transfer of tax revenue to the federal government, which it claimed was not legally constituted, and Montenegrin officials publicly discouraged men from reporting for Yugoslav military service. Montenegro announced plans to open its own liaison offices in five foreign capitals and considered establishing a separate Montenegrin currency. Djukanovic denounced Milosevic's refusal to grant autonomy to Kosovo and accused him of stifling freedom and economic reform.

The Yugoslav economy continued its rapid downward decline, with no signs of hope or improvement. After having endured years of mismanagement, institutionalized corruption, and resistance to full-fledged market-oriented reforms and with the situation exacerbated by six years of international sanctions and the current Kosovo crisis, much of the population had become focused on how to survive in poverty. Unemployment was close to 50%, and the strength of the Yugoslav economy was about half its 1989 level. Milosevic bought himself some economic breathing space by selling 49% of the state telephone company in 1997 to Stet of Italy and OTE of Greece for about $1 billion. The reimposition of more stringent sanctions in 1998 in response to the violent conflict in Kosovo blocked further sales of state assets, however. In addition, the expense of Belgrade's Kosovo operations was estimated by officials at $1 million per day, and this alone appeared to be pushing Yugoslavia closer to total economic collapse.   (MILAN ANDREJEVICH)

ZAMBIA

Area: 752,614 sq km (290,586 sq mi)
Population (1998 est.): 9,461,000
Capital: Lusaka
Head of state and government: President Frederick Chiluba

In spite of protests by several donor countries against the three-month state of emergency imposed by Pres. Frederick Chiluba after the abortive army coup in October 1997, the National Assembly overwhelmingly voted in favour of extending it in 1998 for an additional three months beginning on February 3. On March 17, however, the president recognized the damage done to prospects of external aid by the prolongation of the state of emergency and put an end to it. On June 1 former president Kenneth Kaunda was released from house arrest, and all charges against him of concealing knowledge of the attempted coup were withdrawn. Kaunda then announced his wish to give up his 40-year leadership of the United National Independence Party when arrangements could be made for a suitable successor to be elected.

The optimistic budget introduced by Finance Minister Ronald Penza on January 30 could not conceal the extent of Zambia's economic problems and, not least, its difficulty in achieving the level of privatization called for by potential aid donors. As an example of the latter problem, the sharp decline in the world price for copper from $2,600 per metric ton in 1997 to $1,700 in 1998 resulted in the failure to sell the Nkana and Nchanga mines; on April 2 negotiations between the government and the Kafue Consortium were called off, the consortium failing to make what the government be-

One of a group of Serbian policemen beats on a pair of ethnic Albanian civilians during a March 2 riot in Pristina, the capital of the province of Kosovo. Tens of thousands of ethnic Albanians had come out to protest Serbian violence, which intensified in 1998. Slobodan Milosevic, president of the Federal Republic of Yugoslavia, refused to grant autonomy to the province, whose population was about 90% ethnic Albanian.

lieved to be a reasonable offer. The decline in aid also contributed to Penza's replacement as minister of finance by Edith Nawakwi, formerly minister of agriculture. On November 6 Penza was murdered.

The fall in earnings from cobalt and copper continued to have an adverse effect on Zambia, but there was some relief when a meeting of donors in Paris on May 13 pledged $530 million in aid; they insisted, however, that continued support would be dependent upon economic reform and better government. Floods in parts of the country coupled with drought in others forced the government to plan to import 400,000 metric tons of corn. To help with this problem, the UN World Food Programme offered K 38 billion (U.S. $17.3 million) in emergency relief.   (KENNETH INGHAM)

ZIMBABWE

Area: 390,757 sq km (150,872 sq mi)
Population (1998 est.): 11,044,000
Capital: Harare
Head of state and government: President Robert Mugabe

Opposition to Pres. Robert Mugabe and the ruling Zimbabwe African National Union–Patriotic Front party took a variety of forms in 1998 and led to numerous reversals of policy on the part of the government. On January 16 it was reported that, in response to a loan agreement with the European Union, the government had decided to shelve its plan, announced only six weeks earlier, to confiscate some 1,500, mainly white-owned, farms. Less than a month later, Mugabe reversed this decision and said the plan would be put into action, but in early March, when the International Monetary Fund threatened to withdraw a loan worth $174 million unless the situation was clarified, the plan was significantly modified.

The issue was revived in June when a number of squatters moved onto six farms east of Harare in what was said to be a protest against the government's failure to find land for them. Others believed the move had been inspired by the government, which on July 1 announced a new plan to settle 100,000 families on 5.1 million ha (12.5 million ac) to be bought from white farmers. It was hoped that the money to fund this undertaking would be provided by external donors. Although they recognized the need for land reform, the donors rejected Mugabe's plan as too ambitious and agreed only to support a two-year pilot project. In November Mugabe again changed course by ordering the immediate seizure of 841 white-owned farms.

A 21% increase in the cost of corn flour, the staple food of the country, introduced in January led to riots in Harare and the immediate cancellation of the increase; it was, however, reintroduced later in the year. There was dismay, too, at the announcement on February 2 of lavish pensions and other retirement benefits for the president and his family as well as the two vice presidents and their families—dismay that turned to anger when a peaceful demonstration on February 24 in favour of increased pensions for other government employees was dispersed by police using batons and tear gas. Subsequently, a two-day general strike to protest tax increases and higher food prices met with widespread support when labour unions urged people to stay at home rather than confront the police on the streets. There was further rioting in November after Mugabe awarded himself and the 55 members of the Cabinet 20% pay raises. This was followed by an increase in import duties on a number of goods and a 75% increase in the cost of petroleum.

Throughout the year the uncertainty engendered by the government's vacillating land policy, a 21% increase in civil servants' pay, and the fall in world demand for tobacco combined to force down the exchange value of the currency. In this situation Mugabe's costly decision in August to send troops to assist Pres. Laurent Kabila of the Democratic Republic of the Congo in his fight against rebels met with little popular enthusiasm.   (KENNETH INGHAM)

CONTRIBUTORS

Adams, Andy. Editor and Publisher, *Sumo World.* Author of *Sumo; Sumo World Record Book.* •SPORTS AND GAMES: *Judo; Wrestling:* Sumo

Adams, Rebecca Knapp. Managing Editor, *Art & Antiques.* •ART, ANTIQUES, AND COLLECTIONS: *Introduction*

Ajello, Robin Paul. Senior Editor, *Asiaweek* magazine. •WORLD AFFAIRS: *Cambodia*

Alder, Phillip. Syndicated Bridge Columnist and Teacher. Author of *Get Smarter at Bridge.* •SPORTS AND GAMES: *Contract Bridge*

Alexander, Steve. Freelance Writer. •COMPUTERS AND INFORMATION SYSTEMS: *Sidebar*

Allaby, Michael. Writer and Lecturer. Author of *Basic Environmental Science; Facing the Future.* •THE ENVIRONMENT: *Environmental Issues; International Environmental Activities*

Allan, J.A. Professor of Geography, School of Oriental and African Studies, University of London. Author of *Water and Peace in the Middle East.* •WORLD AFFAIRS: *Libya*

Andrades, Jorge Adrián. •SPORTS AND GAMES: *Equestrian Sports:* Polo

Andrejevich, Milan. Associate Editor, Encyclopædia Britannica. •WORLD AFFAIRS: *Bosnia and Herzegovina; Yugoslavia*

Archibald, John J. Retired Feature Writer, St. Louis (Mo.) *Post-Dispatch;* Adjunct Professor, Washington University, St. Louis. Member of the American Bowling Congress Hall of Fame. •SPORTS AND GAMES: *Bowling:* U.S. Tenpins

Arnold, Mavis. Freelance Journalist, Dublin. •WORLD AFFAIRS: *Ireland*

Arrington, Leonard J. Formerly Church Historian, Church of Jesus Christ of Latter-day Saints. Coauthor of *The Mormon Experience* and others. •RELIGION: *Church of Jesus Christ of Latter-day Saints*

Aurora, Vincent. Adjunct Professor, Fordham University, New York City. •LITERATURE: *French:* France

Baber, Bonnie. Senior Editor, *Footwear News* magazine. •BUSINESS AND INDUSTRY REVIEW: *Apparel:* Footwear

Backe, Everett E. Senior Scientist and Professor, Institute of Textile Technology, Charlottesville, Va. Author of *Cotton Ginners Handbook.* •BUSINESS AND INDUSTRY REVIEW: *Textiles:* Cotton; Silk; Wool

Bahry, Louay. Adjunct Professor of Political Science, Washington, D.C. Author of *The Baghdad Bahn.* •WORLD AFFAIRS: *Bahrain; Iraq*

Bailey, George. Author of *Galileo's Children; Germans.* •WORLD AFFAIRS: *Germany; Germany:* Sidebar

Balaban, Avraham. Professor of Modern Hebrew Literature, University of Florida. Author of *A Different Wave of Hebrew Fiction: Postmodernist Israel.* •LITERATURE: *Jewish:* Hebrew

Bamia, Aida A. Associate Professor of Arabic Language and Literature; Editor, *Al-'Arabiyya,* University of Florida. •LITERATURE: *Arabic*

Barrett, David B. Research Professor of Missiometrics, Regent University, Virginia Beach, Va. Author of *World Christian Encyclopedia; Schism and Renewal in Africa.* •RELIGION: *Tables (in part)*

Barrett, George. Editor, *Hardwood Publishing Co.* •BUSINESS AND INDUSTRY REVIEW: *Wood Products:* Wood

Barrett, John C.A. Headmaster, The Leys School, Cambridge, Eng.; Chairman of Education Committee, World Methodist Council. Author of *Family Worship in Theory and Practice.* •RELIGION: *Methodist Churches*

Beckwith, David C. Director of Government Relations, Electronic Data Systems, Inc., Washington, D.C. •WORLD AFFAIRS: *United States; United States:* State and Local Affairs

Bell, Tom. Classifier, Encyclopædia Britannica •OBITUARIES *(in part)*

Berfield, Susan. Senior Writer, *Asiaweek* magazine. •WORLD AFFAIRS: *Indonesia*

Bickelhaupt, David L. Professor Emeritus, Fisher College of Business, Ohio State University. •BUSINESS AND INDUSTRY REVIEW: *Insurance*

Binczewski, George J. Principal Technical Adviser, S.C. Systems, Moraga, Calif. •BUSINESS AND INDUSTRY REVIEW: *Materials and Metals:* Light Metals

Bird, Thomas E. The Jewish Studies Program, Queens College, City University of New York. •LITERATURE: *Jewish:* Yiddish

Blackmore, Heather A. Editorial Assistant, Encyclopædia Britannica •BIOGRAPHIES *(in part)*

Boddy, William C. Founder and Editor, *Motor Sport,* London. Author of *Aero-Engined Racing Cars, etc.,* and M.B.E. •SPORTS AND GAMES: *Automobile Racing:* Grand Prix Racing

Boden, Edward. Editor, *Black's Veterinary Dictionary.* •HEALTH AND DISEASE: *Veterinary Medicine*

Bogdanor, Vernon. Professor of Government, Oxford University. •WORLD AFFAIRS: *Spotlight:* Whither Europe's Monarchies?

Boggan, Tim. Historian, U.S.A. Table Tennis Association (USATT). Author of *Winning Table Tennis.* •SPORTS AND GAMES: *Table Tennis*

Bonds, John B. Adjunct Professor, The Citadel, Charleston, S.C. •SPORTS AND GAMES: *Sailing (Yachting)*

Booth, John Nicholls. Lecturer and Writer. Author of *The Quest for Preaching Power; Psychic Paradoxes;* and others. •RELIGION: *Unitarian (Universalist) Churches*

Boswall, Jeffery. Freelance Lecturer on Wildlife Television. •LIFE SCIENCES: *Ornithology*

Box, Ben. Editor, Footprint Handbooks. •WORLD AFFAIRS: *Nicaragua; Panama; Uruguay; Spotlight:* Latin America's New Transportation Links

Boye, Roger. Formerly Coin Columnist, *Chicago Tribune.* •ART, ANTIQUES, AND COLLECTIONS: *Numismatics*

Bradsher, Henry S. Foreign Affairs Writer. •WORLD AFFAIRS: *Philippines*

Brazee, Rutlage J. Geophysical Consultant. •EARTH SCIENCES: *Geophysics*

Brecher, Kenneth. Professor of Astronomy and Physics, Boston University. •MATHEMATICS AND PHYSICAL SCIENCES: *Astronomy*

Brockmann, Stephen. Associate Professor of German Studies, Carnegie Mellon University, Pittsburgh, Pa. •LITERATURE: *German*

Brokopp, John G. Specialist and writer on equestrian racing. •SPORTS AND GAMES: *Equestrian Sports:* Thoroughbred Racing: United States

Brown, Bess. Human Dimension Specialist, OSCE Liaison Office for Central Asia. Author of *Authoritarianism in the New States of Central Asia.* •WORLD AFFAIRS: *Kazakhstan; Kyrgyzstan; Tajikistan; Turkmenistan; Uzbekistan*

Buchan, David. Diplomatic Editor, *Financial Times;* Correspondent, *Financial Times,* Paris. •WORLD AFFAIRS: *France*

Bungs, Dzintra. Guest Analyst, Stiftung Wissenschaft und Politik, Ebenhausen, Ger. •WORLD AFFAIRS: *Latvia*

Burks, Ardath W. Professor Emeritus of Asian Studies, Rutgers University, New Brunswick, N.J. Author of *Japan: A Postindustrial Power.* •WORLD AFFAIRS: *Japan*

Burns, Erik T. Bureau Chief, Dow Jones Newswires, Lisbon. •WORLD AFFAIRS: *Portugal*

Butler, Frank. Formerly Sports Editor, *News of the World.* Author of *The Good, the Bad and the Ugly: A Story of Boxing.* •SPORTS AND GAMES: *Boxing*

Cafferty, Bernard. Associate Editor, *British Chess Magazine.* •SPORTS AND GAMES: *Chess*

Call, Christopher. Editor, Encyclopædia Britannica; Adjunct Faculty, Elmhurst College, Elmhurst, Ill. •BIOGRAPHIES *(in part)*

Cameron, Sarah. Freelance Writer and Editor, Footprint Handbooks. •WORLD AFFAIRS: *Costa Rica; Cuba; Dominican Republic; El Salvador; Guatemala; Haiti; Honduras*

Campbell, Paul J. Professor of Mathematics and Computer Science, Beloit College, Beloit, Wis. •MATHEMATICS AND PHYSICAL SCIENCES: *Mathematics*

Campbell, Robert. Architect and Architecture Critic. Author of *Cityscapes of Boston;* Coauthor of *American Architecture of the 1980s.* •ARCHITECTURE AND CIVIL ENGINEERING: *Architecture*

Cantwell, Bruce. Senior Developer, My Envoy. •PERFORMING ARTS: *Theatre:* Sidebar

Cardinale, Diane P. Assistant Communications Director, Toy Manufacturers of America, Inc. •BUSINESS AND INDUSTRY REVIEW: *Games and Toys*

Carter, Robert W. Journalist, London. •SPORTS AND GAMES: *Equestrian Sports:* Show Jumping and Dressage; Steeplechasing; Thoroughbred Racing: *International*

Cenzer, Matthew A. Lecturer in History, Northwestern University, Evanston, Ill. •WORLD AFFAIRS: *Burundi; Comoros; Djibouti; Liberia; Mauritius; Rwanda; Seychelles; Sierra Leone*

Chappell, Duncan. Deputy President, Federal Administrative Appeals Tribunal, Sydney, Australia. •LAW, CRIME, AND LAW ENFORCEMENT: *Crime; Law Enforcement*

Chapple, Abby. President, Consumer Communications, Largent, W.Va. •BUSINESS AND INDUSTRY REVIEW: *Home Furnishings:* Furniture

Cheadle, Bruce. Reporter, The Canadian Press. •SPORTS AND GAMES: *Curling*

Cheuse, Alan. Writing Faculty, English Department, George Mason University, Fairfax, Va.; Book Commentator, National Public Radio. Author of *The Light Possessed* and others. •LITERATURE: *English:* United States

Cho, Joohee. Special Correspondent, Contributor, CNBC Asia, MSNBC.com, Television Asia. •BIOGRAPHIES *(in part)*

Cioroslan, Dragomir. National Coach for U.S.A. Weightlifting, Inc. •SPORTS AND GAMES: *Weight Lifting*

Clark, David D. Managing Editor, *World Literature Today.* •LITERATURE: *English:* Other Literature in English

Clarke, Douglas L. Captain, U.S. Navy (ret.); Military Analyst. Author of *The Missing Man: Politics and the MIA.* •MILITARY AFFAIRS

Clarke, R.O. Lecturer and Consultant on Industrial Relations, London. •ECONOMIC AFFAIRS: *Labour-Management Relations*

Cogle, T.C.J. Consultant, *Electrical Review.* •BUSINESS AND INDUSTRY REVIEW: *Electrical*

Colvin, David. Managing Editor, *The Middle East Journal.* •WORLD AFFAIRS: *Oman; Qatar*

Corzine, Robert. Energy Correspondent, *Financial Times.* •BUSINESS AND INDUSTRY REVIEW: *Energy:* Alternative Energy; Natural Gas; Petroleum; WORLD AFFAIRS: *Spotlight:* Central Asian Oil Conflicts

Cosgrave, Bronwyn. Commissioning Editor, British *Vogue.* •BIOGRAPHIES *(in part);* FASHIONS

Coveney, Michael. Theatre Critic, *The Daily Mail.* Author of *The World According to Mike Leigh* and others. •PERFORMING ARTS: *Theatre:* Great Britain and Ireland

Craine, Anthony G. Freelance Writer. •BIOGRAPHIES *(in part);* SPORTS AND GAMES: *Introduction*

Crampton, Richard J. Professor of East European History and Fellow of St. Edmund Hall, University of Oxford, Oxford, Eng. Author of *Eastern Europe in the Twentieth Century* and others. •WORLD AFFAIRS: *Bulgaria*

Crowell, Todd. Senior Writer, *Asiaweek* magazine. •WORLD AFFAIRS: *Dependent States:* East Asia; *Korea, Democratic People's Republic of; Korea, Republic of; Malaysia*

Crowley, Edward. Freelance Marine and Offshore Journalist; Director, Technical Writing Services. •BUSINESS AND INDUSTRY REVIEW: *Shipbuilding;* TRANSPORTATION: *Shipping and Ports*

Cunningham, Susan M. Economic and Political Analyst; Freelance Writer. Author of *Latin America Since 1945.* •WORLD AFFAIRS: *Argentina; Brazil; Mexico*

Currie, Elliott. Criminologist, Center for Study of Law and Society, University of California, Berkeley; Author of *Crime and Punishment in America* and others. •LAW, CRIME, AND LAW ENFORCEMENT: *Special Report:* Children Killing Children

Curwen, Peter J. Professor of Business, Sheffield (Eng.) Business School. Author of *The U.K. Publishing Industry* and others. •MEDIA AND PUBLISHING: *Book Publishing* (international); *Book Publishing:* Sidebar

Czerwinski, Edward J. Professor Emeritus, State University of New York, Stony Brook. •LITERATURE: *Eastern European*

Dailey, Meghan. Art Historian/Critic, based in New York. •ART, ANTIQUES, AND COLLECTIONS: *Art Exhibitions; Painting and Sculpture*

Davis, Stephen P. Assistant Editor, Encyclopædia Britannica. •OBITUARIES *(in part)*

Deam, John B. Retired Technical Director, AMT—The Association for Manufacturing Technology, McLean, Va. •BUSINESS AND INDUSTRY REVIEW: *Machinery and Machine Tools*

Deanin, Rudolph D. Professor, Department of Plastics Engineering, University of Massachusetts at Lowell. Author of *Plastics Additives.* •BUSINESS AND INDUSTRY REVIEW: *Materials and Metals:* Plastics

Deeb, Marius K. Professor, SAIS, Johns Hopkins University, Washington, D.C. Author of *Political Parties and Democracy in Egypt.* •WORLD AFFAIRS: *Egypt*

de la Barre, Kenneth. Director, the Bridge Group. •WORLD AFFAIRS: *Arctic Regions*

Denselow, Robin. Rock Music Critic, *The Guardian;* Current Affairs Reporter, BBC Television. Author of *When the Music's Over: The Politics of Pop.* •PERFORMING ARTS: *Music:* Popular (international)

de Puy, Norman R. Minister, American Baptist Churches; Editor and Publisher, *Cabbages and Kings* newsletter. •RELIGION: *Baptist Churches*

Dicks, Geoffrey R. U.K. Economist, Greenwich NatWest. Author of *Sources of World Financial and Banking Information.* •BUSINESS AND INDUSTRY REVIEW: *Introduction*

Dixon, Bernard. Science Writer; Consultant; Editor, *Medical Science Research.* Author of *Power Unseen: How Microbes Rule the World* and others. •HEALTH AND DISEASE *Medicine* (international); *Mental Health*

Doll, Susan. Freelance Writer, Instructor of Film History, School of the Art Institute of Chicago and Oakton Community College. Author of *Best of Elvis* and others. •BUSINESS AND INDUSTRY REVIEW: *Home Furnishings:* Housewares

Dooling, Dave. Freelance Aerospace Writer, D² Associates. •MATHEMATICS AND PHYSICAL SCIENCES: *Space Exploration*

Dowd, Siobhan. Columnist, *Literary Review* (London); *Glimmer Train* (U.S.). Author of *This Prison Where I Live.* •LITERATURE: *English:* United Kingdom

Driscoll, Peter. Senior Partner, PCI—Fibres and Raw Materials. •BUSINESS AND INDUSTRY REVIEW: *Textiles:* Introduction; Man-Made Fibres

Duke, Elizabeth. General Secretary, Friends World Committee for Consultation. •RELIGION: *Religious Society of Friends*

Eadington, William R. Professor of Economics, Director, Institute for Study of Gambling and Commercial Gaming, University of Nevada, Reno. •BUSINESS AND INDUSTRY REVIEW: *Gambling*

Earp, John H. Director, Halcrow Fox and Associates. •TRANSPORTATION: *Introduction; Freight and Pipelines; Intercity Rail; Roads and Traffic;* Sidebar; *Urban Mass Transit*

Ehringer, Gavin Forbes. Rodeo Columnist, *Western Horseman.* •SPORTS AND GAMES: *Rodeo*

Ellis, Roger. Editor, *Mining Journal,* London. •BUSINESS AND INDUSTRY REVIEW: *Mining*

Fagan, Brian. Professor of Anthropology, University of California, Santa Barbara. Author of *Time Detectives.* •ANTHROPOLOGY AND ARCHAEOLOGY: *Archaeology:* Western Hemisphere; *Archaeology:* Sidebar

Farr, D.M.L. Professor Emeritus of History, Carleton University, Ottawa. •WORLD AFFAIRS: *Canada*

Fendell, Robert J. Board Member, Amelia Island Concours d'Elegance. Columnist, *Sport Scene Florida.* Author of *Encyclopedia of Motor Racing Greats.* •SPORTS AND GAMES: *Automobile Racing:* U.S. Auto Racing

Fenwick, M.J. Associate Professor of Latin American and Caribbean Literature, University of Memphis, Tenn. •LITERATURE: *Spanish:* Latin America

Finch, Andrew. Assistant Director, Government and Public Affairs, American Association of Museums. •LIBRARIES AND MUSEUMS: *Museums* (United States)

Finkin, Jordan. Copy Editor, Encyclopædia Britannica. •OBITUARIES *(in part)*

Fischer, Adelheid. Freelance Writer. •OBITUARIES *(in part)*

Fisher, Sharon. Central European Specialist, London. •WORLD AFFAIRS: *Czech Republic; Slovakia*

Flagg, Gordon. Managing Editor, *American Libraries.* •LIBRARIES AND MUSEUMS: *Libraries* (United States)

Flanders, Douglas L. Development Officer, *The United Church Observer.* •RELIGION: *The United Church of Canada*

Flink, Steve. Senior Correspondent, *Tennis Week* magazine; Freelance Journalist. •SPORTS AND GAMES: *Tennis*

Flores, Ramona Monette S. Professor, University of the Philippines; Editorial Consultant, *Masks and Voices, Hit the Podium;* Editor-in-Chief, *Pahinungód Annual Journal.* •MEDIA AND PUBLISHING: *Radio* (international); *Television* (international)

Follett, Christopher. Denmark Correspondent, *The Times;* Danish Correspondent, Radio Sweden; Newscaster, Radio Denmark; Local Correspondent for Reuters News Agency, Copenhagen. Author of *Fodspor paa Cypern.* •WORLD AFFAIRS: *Denmark*

Freeman, Laurie. Freelance Writer and Editor. •BUSINESS AND INDUSTRY REVIEW: *Advertising*

Fridovich, Irwin. James B. Duke Professor of Biochemistry, Duke University Medical Center, Durham, N.C. •LIFE SCIENCES: *Molecular Biology (in part)*

Fridovich-Keil, Judith L. Assistant Professor, Department of Genetics, Emory University School of Medicine, Atlanta, Ga. •LIFE SCIENCES: *Molecular Biology (in part)*

Friedrich, Mary Jane. Freelance Editor. •BIOGRAPHIES *(in part);* NOBEL PRIZES *(in part);* OBITUARIES *(in part)*

Friskin, Sydney E. Hockey Correspondent, *The Times.* •SPORTS AND GAMES: *Billiard Games:* Snooker; *Field Hockey*

Fuller, Elizabeth. Editor, *Newsline,* Radio Free Europe, Radio Liberty, Prague. •WORLD AFFAIRS: *Armenia; Azerbaijan; Georgia*

Ganado, Albert. Lawyer. Coauthor of *A Study in Depth of 143 Maps Representing the Great Siege of Malta of 1565* and others. •WORLD AFFAIRS: *Malta*

Garrod, Mark. Golf Correspondent, PA Sport, U.K. Contributor to *Golf World* and *Amateur Golf* magazines. Secretary of the Association of Golf Writers. •SPORTS AND GAMES: *Golf*

Gaughan, Thomas. Associate Director of Libraries, Illinois Institute of Technology, Chicago. •LIBRARIES AND MUSEUMS: *Libraries* (international)

Gibbons, Anne R. Freelance Writer. •LIFE SCIENCES: *Entomology*

Gibbons, J. Whitfield. Professor of Ecology, Savannah River Ecology Laboratory, University of Georgia. Author of *Keeping All the Pieces* and others. •LIFE SCIENCES: *Zoology*

Gill, Martin J. Information and Computer Expert, F.A.O. EASTFISH. •AGRICULTURE AND FOOD SUPPLIES: *Fisheries*

Girnius, Saulius A. State Consultant, Republic of Lithuania Government. •WORLD AFFAIRS: *Lithuania*

Glasgall, William. Senior Editor, *Business Week* magazine. •ECONOMIC AFFAIRS: *Special Report:* The IMF's Changing Role

Gobbie, Donn. Director of Publicity and Media Relations, U.S. Badminton Association. •SPORTS AND GAMES: *Badminton*

Goldsmith, Arthur. Freelance Writer. Author of *The Camera and Its Images.* •ART, ANTIQUES, AND COLLECTIONS: *Photography;* BUSINESS AND INDUSTRY REVIEW: *Photography*

Gould, Stephen Jay. Professor of Geology; Curator of Invertebrate Paleontology, Harvard University; Museum of Comparative Zoology, Cambridge, Mass. •COMMENTARY: *Tragic Optimism for a Millennium Dawning*

Greeman, Adrian Lee. Editor, *Civil Engineer International.* •ARCHITECTURE AND CIVIL ENGINEERING: *Bridges*

Green, Anthony L. Copy Supervisor, Encyclopædia Britannica. •BIOGRAPHIES *(in part)*

Green, Theresa. Information Officer, British Glass. •BUSINESS AND INDUSTRY REVIEW: *Materials and Metals:* Glass

Greskovic, Robert. Freelance Writer. Author of *Ballet 101.* •PERFORMING ARTS: *Dance:* North America

Griffiths, A.R.G. Associate Professor in History, Flinders University of South Australia. Author of *Contemporary Australia; Beautiful Lies.* •WORLD AFFAIRS: *Australia; Nauru; Palau; Papua New Guinea*

Grumet, Robert S. Anthropologist, New Hope, Pa. Author of *Historic Contact* and others. •ANTHROPOLOGY AND ARCHAEOLOGY: *Anthropology:* Cultural

Guss, Greg. Freelance Writer, *Sport Magazine.* •SPORTS AND GAMES: *Bobsledding and Luge; Ice Hockey* (International); *Ice Skating; Skiing*

Guthridge, Guy G. Manager, Antarctic Information Program, U.S. National Science Foundation. •WORLD AFFAIRS: *Antarctica*

Halman, Talat S. Distinguished Visiting Professor, Bilkent University, Ankara, Turkey. Author of *Poetry of Ancient Anatolia and Near East.* •LITERATURE: *Turkish*

Hamilton, Andrea. Staff Correspondent, *Asiaweek* magazine. •WORLD AFFAIRS: *Singapore*

Hammer, William R. Professor and Chair, Department of Geology, Augustana College, Rock Island, Ill. Author of contributions to Dinofest II International Proceedings, National Academy of Sciences, Philadelphia; *Antarctic Paleobiology.* •LIFE SCIENCES: *Paleontology;* LIFE SCIENCES: Sidebar

Hannen, Mark. Competitions Manager, English Basket Ball Association. •SPORTS AND GAMES: *Basketball:* International

Harakas, Stanley S. Emeritus Archbishop Iakovos Professor of Orthodox Theology, Holy Cross Greek Orthodox School of Theology. Author of *Health and Medicine in the Eastern Orthodox Tradition* and others. •RELIGION: *Oriental Orthodox Church; The Orthodox Church*

Haub, Carl V. Demographer, Population Reference Bureau. Author of *Population Change in the Former Soviet Union* and others. •POPULATION TRENDS: *Demography*

Hawkland, William D. Chancellor Emeritus of Law and Boyd Professor, Louisiana State University, Baton Rouge, La. •LAW, CRIME, AND LAW ENFORCEMENT: *Court Decisions*

Heinzl, John. Business Reporter, *Toronto Globe and Mail.* •BUSINESS AND INDUSTRY REVIEW: *Retailing; Retailing:* Sidebar

Hendershott, Myrl C. Professor of Oceanography, Scripps Institution of Oceanography, La Jolla, Calif. •EARTH SCIENCES: *Oceanography*

Henschel, Milton. President, Watchtower Bible and Tract Society. •RELIGION: *Jehovah's Witnesses*

Hering, Howard. Administrative Manager, Frederick Wildman and Sons. •BUSINESS AND INDUSTRY REVIEW: *Beverages:* Wine

Higgs, Kimball. Assistant Vice President, Sotheby's Book Department. •ART, ANTIQUES, AND COLLECTIONS: *Antiquarian Books*

Hobbs, Greg. Chief Writer, Australian Football League. Author of books on Australian Football. •SPORTS AND GAMES: *Football: Australian*

Hoeksema, Klaas J. Staff Member, Institute for Polytechnics, Amsterdam. •WORLD AFFAIRS: *Netherlands, The; Suriname*

Hoffman, Dean A. Executive Editor, *Hoof Beats* magazine. •SPORTS AND GAMES: *Equestrian Sports:* Harness Racing

Hoke, John. Publisher, *Amateur Wrestling News.* •SPORTS AND GAMES: *Wrestling*

Hollar, Sherman. Assistant Editor, Encyclopædia Britannica. •BIOGRAPHIES *(in part)*; DISASTERS

Homel, David. Author of *Rat Palms* and others. •LITERATURE: *French:* Canada

Hope, Thomas W. Chairman/Editor, Hope Reports, Inc. Author of *America's Top 100 Contract Producers.* •PERFORMING ARTS: *Motion Pictures:* Nontheatrical Films

Hunt, Carla. Freelance Journalist. •BUSINESS AND INDUSTRY REVIEW: *Special Report:* Ecotourism: The New Face of Travel

IEIS. International Economic Information Services. •ECONOMIC AFFAIRS: *World Economy; Stock Exchanges* (international)

Ingham, Kenneth. Emeritus Professor of History, University of Bristol, Eng. Author of *Politics in Modern Africa: The Uneven Tribal Dimension* and others. •WORLD AFFAIRS: *Angola; Congo, Democratic Republic of the (Zaire); Kenya; Malawi; Mozambique; Spotlight:* Clinton's Trip to Africa; *Sudan, The; Tanzania; Uganda; Zambia; Zimbabwe*

Ingram, Derek. Consultant Editor, Gemini News Service. Author of *Commonwealth for a Colour-Blind World; The Imperfect Commonwealth.* •WORLD AFFAIRS: *Commonwealth of Nations*

Ionescu, Dan. Journalist, Radio Free Europe, Romanian/Moldovan Desk. Former Senior Research Analyst with Open Media Research Institute, Prague. •WORLD AFFAIRS: *Moldova; Romania*

Jackson, Peter S. Wyse. Secretary-General, Botanic Gardens Conservation International, U.K. •THE ENVIRONMENT: *Botanical Gardens*

Jamail, Milton. Lecturer, Department of Government, University of Texas at Austin. •SPORTS AND GAMES: *Baseball:* Latin America

Jessell, Harry A. Editor, *Broadcasting & Cable.* •MEDIA AND PUBLISHING: *Radio* (U.S., *in part*); *Radio:* Amateur Radio *(in part)*; *Television* (U.S., *in part*)

Joffé, George. Journalist and Writer on North African and Middle Eastern Affairs. Deputy Director, RIIA, London. •WORLD AFFAIRS: *Algeria; Morocco; Tunisia*

Johnson, Todd M. Director, World Evangelization Research Center. Coauthor of *World Christian Encyclopedia.* •RELIGION: *Tables (in part)*

Johnsson, William G. Editor, *Adventist Review.* Author of *Behold His Glory* and others. •RELIGION: *Seventh-day Adventist Church*

Jones, David G.C. Honorary Lecturer in Physics, University of Sussex, Brighton, Eng. Author of *Atomic Physics.* •MATHEMATICS AND PHYSICAL SCIENCES: *Physics*

Jones, Gary A. Manager of Committees on Publication, the First Church of Christ, Scientist, Boston. •RELIGION: *Church of Christ, Scientist*

Jones, W. Glyn. Professor Emeritus of Scandinavian Studies, University of East Anglia, Norwich, Eng. Author of *Colloquial Danish* and others. •LITERATURE: *Danish*

Jotischky, Helma. Head of Business Intelligence, Paint Research Association. Author of *The Americas* and others. •BUSINESS AND INDUSTRY REVIEW: *Paints and Varnishes*

Karimi-Hakkak, Ahmad. Professor of Persian Languages and Literature, University of Washington. •LITERATURE: *Persian*

Kazamaru, Yoshihiko. Literary Critic. •LITERATURE: *Japanese*

Keich, Catherine. Index Editor, Encyclopædia Britannica. •BIOGRAPHIES *(in part)*

Kelleher, John A. Journalist, New Zealand. Formerly Editor, *Dominion* and *Dominion Sunday Times* (Wellington). •WORLD AFFAIRS: *New Zealand*

Keller, Edmond J. Professor, Political Science, University of California, Los Angeles. •WORLD AFFAIRS: *Eritrea; Ethiopia*

Kelling, George H. Historian, Wilford Hall Air Force Medical Center, Lackland AFB, Texas. Author of *Countdown to Rebellion: British Policy in Cyprus 1939–1955.* •WORLD AFFAIRS: *Cyprus*

Kellner, Peter. Political Commentator, BBC Television; Columnist, *The Observer,* London. Author of *The Civil Servants: An Inquiry into Britain's Ruling Class* and others. •BIOGRAPHIES *(in part)*; WORLD AFFAIRS: *United Kingdom*

Kelly, John J., Jr. Assistant Administrator for Weather Services, National Oceanic and Atmospheric Administration. •EARTH SCIENCES: *Meteorology and Climate*

Kessler, Beth. Assistant Editor, Encyclopædia Britannica. •BIOGRAPHIES *(in part)*; OBITUARIES *(in part)*

Knox, Richard A. Specialist Energy Writer, Technical Press Services. •BUSINESS AND INDUSTRY REVIEW: *Energy:* Nuclear

Koberstein, Wayne. Editor in Chief, *Pharmaceutical Executive* magazine. •BUSINESS AND INDUSTRY REVIEW: *Pharmaceuticals*

Koelsch, James R. Freelance Journalist, Discrete Parts Manufacturing Industry. •BUSINESS AND INDUSTRY REVIEW: *Materials and Metals:* Metalworking

Kovel, Ralph and Terry. Authors; Publishers. Authors of *Kovels' Antiques & Collectibles Price List 1998.* •ART, ANTIQUES, AND COLLECTIONS: *Antiques and Collectibles*

Kowalski, Lawrence. Copy Supervisor, Encyclopædia Britannica. •BIOGRAPHIES *(in part)*

Krause, Stefan. Historian and Balkan Specialist, London. •WORLD AFFAIRS: *Greece; Macedonia*

Kroll, Thomas E. Lecturer, Roosevelt University and Northwestern University, Chicago; President, Thomas Kroll Associates. Author of *Introduction to Data Processing; C Language Programming.* •BUSINESS AND INDUSTRY REVIEW: *Microelectronics; Telecommunications*

Kuiper, Kathleen. Senior Editor, Encyclopædia Britannica. Editor, *Merriam-Webster's Encyclopedia of Literature.* •BIOGRAPHIES *(in part)*; OBITUARIES *(in part)*

Kummerfeld, Donald D. President, Magazine Publishers of America. •MEDIA AND PUBLISHING: *Magazines:* United States

Kuptsch, Christiane. Research Officer, ISSA. •SOCIAL PROTECTION (international)

Lamb, Kevin M. Special Projects Writer, *Dayton* (Ohio) *Daily News.* Author of *Quarterbacks, Nickelbacks & Other Loose Change.* •SPORTS AND GAMES: *Football:* Canadian; U.S.

Lamb, Robert E. Executive Director, American Philatelic Society. •ART, ANTIQUES, AND COLLECTIONS: *Philately*

Langeneckert, Sandra. Copy Editor, Encyclopædia Britannica. •BIOGRAPHIES *(in part)*; OBITUARIES *(in part)*; WORLD AFFAIRS: *Russia:* Sidebar

Laqueur, Walter. Chairman, International Research Council, Center for Strategic and International Studies, Washington, D.C. Author of *Europe in Our Time* and others. •WORLD AFFAIRS: *Introduction*

Laskey, Elizabeth. Freelance Writer. •BIOGRAPHIES *(in part)*; OBITUARIES *(in part)*

Lavallée, H.-Claude. Professor, Pulp and Paper Research Centre, University of Quebec at Trois-Rivières. •BUSINESS AND INDUSTRY REVIEW: *Wood Products:* Paper and Pulp

Lawler, Nancy Ellen. Professor Emeritus, Oakton Community College, Des Plaines, Ill. Author of *Soldiers of Misfortune* and others. •WORLD AFFAIRS: *Benin; Burkina Faso; Cameroon; Central African Republic; Congo, Republic of the; Côte d'Ivoire; Gabon; Guinea; Mali; Mauritania; Niger; Senegal; Togo*

Lawson, Fred H. James Irvine Professor of Government, Mills College, Oakland, Calif. •WORLD AFFAIRS: *Syria*

Lawson, Richard L. General, USAF (retired). President and Chief Executive Officer, National Mining Association. •BUSINESS AND INDUSTRY REVIEW: *Energy:* Coal

Legassick, Martin. Professor, History Department, University of Western Cape, Bellville, S.Af. •WORLD AFFAIRS: *South Africa*

Lehman, Richard L. Professor, College of Engineering, Rutgers University, New Brunswick, N.J. Author of *Handbook on Continuous Fiber Reinforced Ceramic Composites.* •BUSINESS AND INDUSTRY REVIEW: *Materials and Metals:* Ceramics

Levine, Beth. Freelance Writer. Author of *Divorce: Young People Caught in the Middle* and others. •MEDIA AND PUBLISHING: *Book Publishing* (United States)

Levine, Steven I. Mansfield Professor of Asia Pacific Affairs, The Mansfield Center, University of Montana. •WORLD AFFAIRS: *China; Taiwan*

Lindstrom, Sieg. Managing Editor, *Track & Field News.* •SPORTS AND GAMES: *Track and Field Sports (Athletics)*

Litweiler, John. Jazz Critic. Author of *The Freedom Principle: Jazz After 1958; Ornette Coleman: A Harmolodic Life.* •OBITUARIES *(in part)*; PERFORMING ARTS: *Music:* Jazz

Logan, Robert G. Sportswriter, *Daily Herald* (Arlington Heights, Ill.). Author of *Cubs Win* and others. •SPORTS AND GAMES: *Basketball:* United States

Longmore, Andrew. Chief Sports Feature Writer, *The Independent;* formerly Assistant Editor, *The Cricketer.* •SPORTS AND GAMES: *Cricket*

Luling, Virginia R. Independent Researcher, Africa Campaigns Officer, Survival International. •WORLD AFFAIRS: *Somalia*

Macdonald, Barrie. Professor of History, Massey University, Palmerston, N.Z. •WORLD AFFAIRS: *Dependent States:* Pacific; *Fiji; Kiribati; Marshall Islands; Micronesia, Federated States of; Samoa; Solomon Islands; Spotlight:* El Niño's Impact on Oceania; *Tonga; Tuvalu; Vanuatu*

McElroy, John. Editorial Director, *Automotive Industries.* •BUSINESS AND INDUSTRY REVIEW: *Automobiles*

McGinn, Anne Platt. Research Associate, Worldwatch Institute. •AGRICULTURE AND FOOD SUPPLIES: *Special Report:* Aquaculture: Fulfilling Its Promise

McGregor, Alan. Freelance Contributor, *The Times; The Lancet;* Swiss Radio International; CBS Radio. •WORLD AFFAIRS: *Switzerland*

McIvor, Greg. Stockholm Correspondent, *Financial Times.* •WORLD AFFAIRS: *Sweden*

McLachlan, Keith S. Professor Emeritus, School of Oriental and African Studies, University of London. Author of *Boundaries of Modern Iran.* •WORLD AFFAIRS: *Iran*

McLellan, Joseph. Music Critic Emeritus, *The Washington Post.* •PERFORMING ARTS: *Music:* Classical; *Music:* Sidebar

McMillan, Anne. Co-Chairman, Committee 6 (Surveys and Publications) of the International Bar Association's Human Rights Institute. •LAW, CRIME, AND LAW ENFORCEMENT: *International Law*

Mango, Andrew. Foreign Affairs Analyst. Author of *Turkey: The Challenge of a New Role.* •WORLD AFFAIRS: *Turkey*

Mantzavrakos, Afrodite. Editorial Production Coordinator, Encyclopædia Britannica. •BIOGRAPHIES *(in part);* OBITUARIES *(in part)*

Marples, David R. Professor of History, University of Alberta. Author of *Belarus: From Soviet Rule to Nuclear Catastrophe* and others. •WORLD AFFAIRS: *Belarus; Ukraine*

Mathews, John H. Attorney/Investigator, City of Chicago Board of Ethics. •BIOGRAPHIES *(in part);* OBITUARIES *(in part);* WORLD AFFAIRS: *United States:* Sidebar

Matthíasson, Björn. Economist, Ministry of Finance, Iceland. •WORLD AFFAIRS: *Iceland*

Mazie, David M. Staff Writer, *Reader's Digest;* Freelance Journalist. •SOCIAL PROTECTION (U.S.)

Meisner, Nadine. Freelance Dance Critic. •PERFORMING ARTS: *Dance:* European

Mermel, T.W. Consulting Engineer; formerly Chairman, Committee on World Register of Dams, International Commission on Large Dams. •ARCHITECTURE AND CIVIL ENGINEERING: *Dams*

Michael, Tom. Associate Editor, Encyclopædia Britannica. •BIOGRAPHIES *(in part);* NOBEL PRIZES *(in part);* OBITUARIES *(in part)*

Mihalisko, Kathleen. Senior Systems Engineer, J.G. Van Dyke, Inc. •WORLD AFFAIRS: *Commonwealth of Independent States*

Miller, Sarah. Press Officer, The Salvation Army. •RELIGION: *Salvation Army*

Mills, Stephanie. Author of *In Service of the Wild: Restoring and Reinhabiting Damaged Land.* •THE ENVIRONMENT: *Special Report: Ecological Restoration*

Mitton, Roger. Senior Correspondent, *Asiaweek* magazine. •WORLD AFFAIRS: *Brunei*

Morgan, Paul. Deputy Editor, *Rugby World.* •SPORTS AND GAMES: *Football:* Rugby Football

Morris, Jacqui M. Editor, *Oryx.* •THE ENVIRONMENT: *Wildlife Conservation*

Morrison, Graham. Press Officer, British Fencing Federation; Correspondent, *Daily Telegraph; Country Life;* Déléqué de Presse, Fédération Internationale d'Escrime. •SPORTS AND GAMES: *Fencing*

Munns, Thomas E. Senior Program Officer, National Materials Advisory Board, National Research Council. •BUSINESS AND INDUSTRY REVIEW: *Materials and Metals:* Advanced Composites

Murphy, Alan. Associate Editor, Footprint Handbooks. •WORLD AFFAIRS: *Bolivia; Ecuador; Peru; Venezuela*

Naylor, Ernest. Professor Emeritus, University of Wales, Bangor. •LIFE SCIENCES: *Marine Biology*

Neher, Stephen. Associate Editor, Encyclopædia Britannica. •WORLD AFFAIRS: *World Legislative Election Results (in part)*

Noble, Thomas F.X. Professor of History, University of Virginia. Author of *Soldiers of Christ: Saints and Saints' Lives.* •RELIGION: *Roman Catholic Church*

Nurse, Charlie. Lecturer, Politics Department, Anglia Polytechnic University, England. •WORLD AFFAIRS: *Chile; Paraguay*

O'Brien, Dan. Editor/Economist (Europe), Economist Intelligence Unit. •WORLD AFFAIRS: *Austria*

O'Donoghue, Michael. Lecturer in Gemology, London Guildhall University. •BUSINESS AND INDUSTRY REVIEW: *Gemstones*

Ogden, Shepherd. President, The Cook's Garden. Author of *Step by Step Organic Flower Gardening* and others. •THE ENVIRONMENT: *Gardening*

O'Leary, Margaret Hayford. Associate Professor of Norwegian, St. Olaf College, Northfield, Minn. •LITERATURE: *Norwegian*

O'Quinn, Jim. Editor in Chief, *American Theatre* magazine. •PERFORMING ARTS: *Theatre:* U.S. and Canada

Orr, Jay. Music Writer, *The Tennessean.* •PERFORMING ARTS: *Music:* Popular (U.S.)

Osborne, K.L. Editor, *British Rowing Almanack.* Author of *Boat Racing in Britain, 1715–1975* and *One Man Went to Row.* •SPORTS AND GAMES: *Rowing*

Oster, Rose-Marie G. Professor, Department of Germanic Studies, University of Maryland. •LITERATURE: *Swedish*

Paarlberg, Philip L. Associate Professor of Agricultural Economics, Purdue University, West Lafayette, Ind. •AGRICULTURE AND FOOD SUPPLIES: *Agricultural Commodities; International Issues*

Palmer, John. Director, European Policy Centre; Former European Editor, *The Guardian.* Author of *Europe Without America: The Crisis in Atlantic Relations.* •WORLD AFFAIRS: *European Union*

Parker, Ines. Freelance Writer. •WORLD AFFAIRS: *Belize*

Parker, Richard B. Scholar-in-Residence, Middle East Institute, Washington, D.C. •WORLD AFFAIRS: *Spotlight:* Israel's Impact on the Middle East, 1948-1998

Parker, Sandy. Publisher, fur industry newsletter; Contributing Editor, *Fur World.* •BUSINESS AND INDUSTRY REVIEW: *Apparel: Furs*

Pertile, Lino. Professor of Romance Languages and Literature, Harvard University. Editor of *Cambridge History of Italian Literature.* •LITERATURE: *Italian*

Peszek, Luan. Publications Director, U.S.A. Gymnastics; Editor, *U.S.A. Gymnastics* magazine; *Technique* magazine. •SPORTS AND GAMES: *Gymnastics*

Peterseim, Locke. Copy Editor, Encyclopædia Britannica. •BIOGRAPHIES *(in part);* OBITUARIES *(in part)*

Pfeffer, Irving. Attorney. Author of *The Financing of Small Business.* •ECONOMIC AFFAIRS: *Stock Exchanges* (North America)

Pollack, Benny. Professor of Iberian and Latin American Politics, University of Liverpool. •WORLD AFFAIRS: *Spain*

Pollard, Peter. Associate Editor, Footprint Handbooks. •WORLD AFFAIRS: *Colombia*

Prasad, H.Y. Sharada. Formerly Information Adviser to the Prime Minister of India. •WORLD AFFAIRS: *India*

Primorac, Max. President, Center for Civil Society in Southeastern Europe, Washington, D.C. •WORLD AFFAIRS: *Croatia*

Prince, Greg W. Executive Editor, *Beverage World.* •BUSINESS AND INDUSTRY REVIEW: *Beverages:* Beer; Soft Drinks; Spirits

Qian Zhongwen. Senior Research Fellow, Literature Institute, Chinese Academy of Social Sciences. •LITERATURE: *Chinese*

Rakisits, Claude. International Affairs Consultant. •WORLD AFFAIRS: *Bangladesh; Bhutan; Myanmar (Burma); Nepal; Sri Lanka; Sri Lanka:* Sidebar

Rauch, Robert. Freelance Editor and Writer. •BIOGRAPHIES *(in part)*

Réamonn, Páraic. Communications Director, World Alliance of Reformed Churches. •RELIGION: *Reformed, Presbyterian, and Congregational Churches*

Rebelo, L.S. Reader Emeritus; Visiting Professor, Department of Portuguese Studies, King's College, University of London. •LITERATURE: *Portuguese:* Portugal

Reed, Arthur. Senior Editor, Europe, *Air Transport World.* Author of *Britain's Aircraft Industry;* Coauthor of *RAE Farnborough.* •TRANSPORTATION: *Aviation*

Reid, Ron. Staff Sportswriter, *Philadelphia Inquirer.* •SPORTS AND GAMES: *Ice Hockey* (North America)

Renwick, David. Freelance Journalist. •WORLD AFFAIRS: *Antigua and Barbuda; Bahamas, The; Barbados; Dependent States:* Caribbean and Bermuda; *Dominica; Grenada; Guyana; Jamaica; Saint Kitts and Nevis; Saint Lucia; Saint Vincent and the Grenadines; Trinidad and Tobago*

Reyes, Alejandro. Senior Correspondent, *Asiaweek* magazine. •WORLD AFFAIRS: *Vietnam*

Richards, Amanda E. Freelance Writer. •LITERATURE: Sidebar

Ridgway, Laurence. Consultant, Contributor, and Producer of Symposia, *World Tobacco* magazine. •BUSINESS AND INDUSTRY REVIEW: *Tobacco*

Riggan, William. Editor, *World Literature Today,* University of Oklahoma. •LITERATURE: *Introduction*

Robinson, David. Film Critic and Historian. Author of *A History of World Cinema; Chaplin: His Life and Art.* •PERFORMING ARTS: *Motion Pictures*

Roby, Anne. Freelance Writer and Editor. •MEDIA AND PUBLISHING: *Magazines* (international); *Newspapers;* WORLD AFFAIRS: *Andorra; Liechtenstein; Luxembourg; Maldives; Monaco*

Rodnitzky, Laura. Freelance Writer. •BIOGRAPHIES *(in part);* OBITUARIES *(in part)*

Rollin, Jack. Executive Editor, *Rothmans Football Yearbook.* Compiler of Playfair Football *Who's Who.* Author of *World Cup 1930–1990* and others. •BIOGRAPHIES *(in part);* SPORTS AND GAMES: *Football:* Association Football (Soccer): *Europe; Football:* Sidebar

Romano, Frank J. Professor of Graphic Arts, School of Printing Management and Sciences, Rochester (N.Y.) Institute of Technology. •BUSINESS AND INDUSTRY REVIEW: *Printing*

Roosevelt, Anna C. Professor, University of Illinois at Chicago; Curator of Archaeology, Field Museum of Natural History, Chicago. •WORLD AFFAIRS: *Spotlight:* The Peopling of the Americas

Rugh, William A. President, AMIDEAST. •WORLD AFFAIRS: *United Arab Emirates; Yemen*

Rundall, Rebecca. Freelance Writer. •BIOGRAPHIES *(in part);* OBITUARIES *(in part)*

Rusch, William G. Director, Commission on Faith and Order, National Council of Churches of Christ. •RELIGION: *Lutheran Communion*

Russell, Cristine. Freelance Science Writer and Special Health Correspondent, *Washington Post.* •HEALTH AND DISEASE: *Medicine* (U.S.); Sidebar

Russell, James S. Editor-at-Large, *Architectural Record* magazine; Architecture Critic, *Philadelphia Inquirer.* •ARCHITECTURE AND CIVIL ENGINEERING: *Buildings*

Rutherford, Andrew. Professor, University of Southampton, Eng. Author of *Transforming Criminal Policy* and others. •LAW, CRIME, AND LAW ENFORCEMENT: *Prisons and Penology*

Samuelson, Robert J. Columnist, *Newsweek* magazine; The Washington Post Writer's Group. •WORLD AFFAIRS: *Spotlight:* The Troubled World Economy

Sanders, Alan J.K. Lecturer in Mongolian Studies, School of Oriental and African Studies, University of London. Author of *The Historical Dictionary of Mongolia* and others. •WORLD AFFAIRS: *Mongolia*

Sandvik, Gudmund. Professor Emeritus of Legal History, Faculty of Law, University of Oslo. •WORLD AFFAIRS: *Norway*

Sarahete, Yrjö. Secretary Emeritus, Fédération Internationale des Quilleurs. •SPORTS AND GAMES: *Bowling:* World Tenpins

Saunders, Christopher. Associate Professor, History Department, University of Cape Town, S.Af. Author of *The Making of the South African Past.* •WORLD AFFAIRS: *Cape Verde; Chad; Equatorial Guinea; Gambia, The; Guinea-Bissau; Lesotho; Madagascar; Namibia; São Tomé and Príncipe*

Schalet, Benjamin. Classifier, Encyclopædia Britannica. •BIOGRAPHIES *(in part)*; OBITUARIES *(in part)*

Schmidt, Fabian. Project Director, Albanian Media Monitoring Project by the Institute of Journalism in Transition. •WORLD AFFAIRS: *Albania*

Sego, Stephen. Freelance Journalist; formerly Director, Radio Free Afghanistan. •WORLD AFFAIRS: *Afghanistan*

Shackleford, Peter. Regional Representative for Europe, World Tourism Organization. •BUSINESS AND INDUSTRY REVIEW: *Tourism*

Shameen, Assif A. Regional Correspondent for *Asiaweek* magazine. •WORLD AFFAIRS: *Pakistan*

Shelley, Andrew. Chairman, JSM, London. •SPORTS AND GAMES: *Squash*

Shepherd, Melinda C. Associate Editor, Encyclopædia Britannica. •SPORTS AND GAMES: *Special Report:* The XVIII Olympic Winter Games; WORLD AFFAIRS: *Dependent States:* Europe and the Atlantic; *World Legislative Election Results (in part)*

Sherry, Paul H. President, United Church of Christ. •RELIGION: *United Church of Christ*

Shimizu, Teiji. Freelance Reporter. •BIOGRAPHIES *(in part)*

Shipp, Glover. Managing Editor, *The Christian Chronicle.* Adjunct Professor, Oklahoma Christian University, Oklahoma City, Okla. •RELIGION: *Churches of Christ*

Shoemaker, Alan H. Collection Manager, Riverbanks Zoological Park, Columbia, S.C. •THE ENVIRONMENT: *Zoos*

Shubinsky, Valery. Literary Columnist, *Vecherny Peterburg.* •LITERATURE: *Russian*

Simon, Reeva S. Assistant Director, Middle East Institute, Columbia University, New York City. •WORLD AFFAIRS: *Lebanon; Saudi Arabia*

Simons, Paul. Writer; Television Producer. Author of *Weird Weather.* •LIFE SCIENCES: *Botany*

Sklar, Morton. Director, World Organization Against Torture; Judge, Administrative Tribunal for OAS. Editor, *The Status of Human Rights in the United States* and *Torture in the U.S.* Author of *The Right to Travel* and others. •SOCIAL PROTECTION: *Human Rights*

Slayman, Andrew. Senior Editor, *Archaeology* magazine. •ANTHROPOLOGY AND ARCHAEOLOGY: *Archaeology:* Eastern Hemisphere

Smith, Donald. Editor, *Rubber World.* •BUSINESS AND INDUSTRY REVIEW: *Materials and Metals:* Rubber

Smith, Gregory O. Dean of Academic Affairs, Rome International University. •WORLD AFFAIRS: *San Marino; Vatican City State*

Smith, Patrick. Journalist, Deputy Editor, *World Highways.* •ARCHITECTURE AND CIVIL ENGINEERING: *Roads*

Smith, Reuben W. Emeritus Professor of History, University of the Pacific, Stockton, Calif. •RELIGION: *Islam*

Solomon, Norman. Fellow, Oxford Centre for Hebrew and Jewish Studies, Oxford, Eng. Author of *The Analytic Movement.* •RELIGION: *Judaism*

Sparks, Karen J. Managing Editor, Encyclopædia Britannica. •OBITUARIES *(in part)*

Spencer, Peter L. Editor, *Consumers' Research* magazine. •ECONOMIC AFFAIRS: *Consumer Affairs* (U.S.)

Stern, Irwin. Former Senior Lecturer in Portuguese, Columbia University, New York City. •LITERATURE: *Portuguese:* Brazil

Sullivan, H. Patrick. Dean and Professor Emeritus of Religion, Vassar College, Poughkeepsie, N.Y. •RELIGION: *Hinduism*

Summerhill, Edward M. Part-Time Staff Member, Reuters; Freelance Writer, Finnish News Agency. •WORLD AFFAIRS: *Finland*

Sumner, David E. Journalism Professor; Contributor to Episcopal Church periodicals. Author of *The Episcopal Church's History: 1945–1985* and others. •RELIGION: *Anglican Communion*

Susel, Rudolph M. Editor, *American Home; Our Voice.* •WORLD AFFAIRS: *Slovenia*

Susser, Leslie D. Diplomatic Correspondent, *The Jerusalem Report.* Coauthor of *Shalom Friend: The Life and Legacy of Yitzhak Rabin.* •WORLD AFFAIRS: *Israel*

Suzuki, Toshihiko. Communication Officer, the Delegation of the European Commission, Japan. •SPORTS AND GAMES: *Baseball:* Japan

Swift, Richard N. Professor Emeritus of Politics, New York University. •WORLD AFFAIRS: *Multinational and Regional Organizations; United Nations*

Synan, Vinson. Dean, School of Divinity, Regent University, Virginia Beach, Va. Author of *Holiness-Pentecostal Tradition; Pentecostal Churches.* •RELIGION: *Pentecostal Churches*

Szilagyi, Zsofia. Freelance Writer. •WORLD AFFAIRS: *Hungary*

Taishoff, Lawrence B. Chairman Emeritus, *Broadcasting & Cable.* •MEDIA AND PUBLISHING: *Radio* (U.S., *in part*); *Radio:* Amateur Radio *(in part); Television* (U.S., *in part*)

Taylor, Jolanda Vanderwal. Associate Professor, Department of German/Dutch, University of Wisconsin, Madison. •LITERATURE: *Netherlandic*

Teague, Elizabeth. Senior Analyst, Jamestown Foundation, United Kingdom. •WORLD AFFAIRS: *Russia*

Tetelman, Michael. Visiting Assistant Professor, Department of History, Northwestern University, Evanston, Ill. •WORLD AFFAIRS: *Botswana; Ghana; Nigeria; Swaziland*

Tétreault, Mary Ann. Professor of Political Science, Iowa State University, Ames, Iowa. Author of *The Kuwait Petroleum Corporation and the Economics of the New World Order* and others. •WORLD AFFAIRS: *Kuwait*

Thomas, Robert Murray. Professor Emeritus of Education and Head, Program in International Education, University of California, Santa Barbara. •EDUCATION

Tikkanen, Amy. Freelance Writer. •BIOGRAPHIES *(in part)*; OBITUARIES *(in part)*

Todd, Amy. Manager, Sotheby's; Freelance Journalist. •ART, ANTIQUES, AND COLLECTIONS: *Art Auctions and Sales*

Tomchuck, Linda. Freelance Writer. •OBITUARIES *(in part)*

Trickett, Anthony. General Manager, Economic Affairs, International Iron and Steel Institute. •BUSINESS AND INDUSTRY REVIEW: *Materials and Metals:* Iron and Steel

Tugend, Alina. Press and Publications Officer, Consumers International. •ECONOMIC AFFAIRS: *Consumer Affairs* (international)

Turner, Darrell J. Religion Writer, *Journal Gazette* (Fort Wayne, Ind.). •RELIGION: *Introduction*

Tutunji, Jenab. Assistant Professorial Lecturer, Political Science, George Washington University, Washington, D.C. •WORLD AFFAIRS: *Jordan*

Uhlick, Lawrence R. Executive Director and General Counsel, Institute of International Bankers. •ECONOMIC AFFAIRS: *Banking*

UNHCR. The Office of the United Nations High Commissioner for Refugees. •POPULATION TRENDS: *Refugees and International Migration*

Utt, Roger L. Editor, *Puerta del Sol;* formerly Assistant Professor of Spanish, Department of Romance Languages and Literatures, University of Chicago. •LITERATURE: *Spanish:* Spain

Van Vliet, Willem. Professor, University of Colorado; Editor, *The Encyclopedia of Housing.* •SOCIAL PROTECTION: *Special Report:* Senior Citizen Housing

Venzke, Bruce H. Associate Editor, *Pool & Billiard Magazine;* Past President, Billiard Congress of America. •SPORTS AND GAMES: *Billiard Games:* Carom Billiards; Pocket Billiards

Verdi, Robert William. Sports Columnist, *Chicago Tribune.* Coauthor of *Once a Bum, Always a Dodger; Holy Cow!;* and others. •SPORTS AND GAMES: *Baseball* (U.S.)

Vinton, Louisa. Editor-in-Chief, Economist Intelligence Unit, Vienna. •WORLD AFFAIRS: *Poland*

Wallenfeldt, Jeff. Associate Editor, Encyclopædia Britannica. •BIOGRAPHIES *(in part)*

Wallis, Shani. Independent Technical Journalist. •ARCHITECTURE AND CIVIL ENGINEERING: *Tunnels*

Walters, Jonathan S. Associate Professor of Religion and Asian Studies, Whitman College, Walla Walla, Wash. Author of *History of Kelaniya.* •RELIGION: *Buddhism*

Wang Hee Soo. Sports Journalist, *Joongangilbo.* •BIOGRAPHIES *(in part)*

Wanninger, Richard S. •SPORTS AND GAMES: *Volleyball*

Warren, J. Robert. Retired Editor, Asia-Pacific Report, *Chemical Market Reporter.* •BUSINESS AND INDUSTRY REVIEW: *Chemicals*

Watson, Rory. European Correspondent, *The Herald.* Coauthor of *American Express Guide to Brussels.* •WORLD AFFAIRS: *Belgium*

Way, Diane Lois. Lawyer; Historical Researcher. •BIOGRAPHIES *(in part)*

Wechsler, Helen J. Senior Manager, International Programs, American Association of Museums. •LIBRARIES AND MUSEUMS: *Museums* (international)

Weil, Eric. Sports Editor, *Buenos Aires Herald;* South American Correspondent for *World Soccer* magazine. •SPORTS AND GAMES: *Football:* Association Football (Soccer): Latin America

Whitney, Barbara. Copy Supervisor, Encyclopædia Britannica. •BIOGRAPHIES *(in part)*; OBITUARIES *(in part)*

Whitten, Phillip. Editor-in-Chief, *Swimming World* magazine. •SPORTS AND GAMES: *Swimming*

Wilkinson, John R. Sportswriter, Coventry Newspapers. •SPORTS AND GAMES: *Cycling*

Willis, Clifford L. Director of News and Information, Office of Communication, Christian Church (Disciples of Christ). •RELIGION: *Christian Church (Disciples of Christ)*

Wilson, Derek. Correspondent, BBC, Rome. Author of *Rome, Umbria and Tuscany.* •WORLD AFFAIRS: *Italy*

Wilson, Michael. Freelance Aviation Writer and Consultant. •BUSINESS AND INDUSTRY REVIEW: *Aerospace*

Wise, Larry. Golden Eagle Archery Staff. Author of *Tuning Your Compound Bow* and others. •SPORTS AND GAMES: *Archery*

Wolf, Allison Wheeler. Freelance Writer. Formerly Director of Communications, American Apparel Manufacturers Association. •BUSINESS AND INDUSTRY REVIEW: *Apparel:* Clothing

Woodrow, Robert. Formerly Assistant Managing Editor, *Asiaweek* magazine. •WORLD AFFAIRS: *Laos; Thailand*

Woods, Elizabeth. Writer. Author of *If Only Things Were Different (I): A Model for a Sustainable Society; Bird Salad;* and others. •LITERATURE: *English:* Canada

Woods, Michael. Science Editor, Block News Alliance. Author of *Science on Ice: Research in Antarctica.* •MATHEMATICS AND PHYSICAL SCIENCES: *Chemistry;* NOBEL PRIZES *(in part)*

Woollen, Anthony. Former Editor, *Food Manufacture.* Former Editor, *Food Industries Manual.* •AGRICULTURE AND FOOD SUPPLIES: *Food Processing*

Wright, Andrew G. Senior Editor, *Engineering News-Record.* •BUSINESS AND INDUSTRY REVIEW: *Building and Construction*

Wyllie, Peter John. Professor, Division of Geological and Planetary Sciences, California Institute of Technology, Pasadena, Calif. Author of *The Dynamic Earth; The Way the Earth Works.* •EARTH SCIENCES: *Geology and Geochemistry*

Zegura, Stephen L. Professor of Anthropology, University of Arizona. •ANTHROPOLOGY AND ARCHAEOLOGY: *Anthropology:* Physical

1999
Britannica
World Data

Encyclopædia Britannica, Inc.
Chicago
London/New Delhi/Paris/Rome
Seoul/Sydney/Tokyo

CONTENTS

INTRODUCTION

Britannica World Data provides a statistical portrait of some 217 countries and dependencies of the world, at a level appropriate to the significance of each. It contains 194 country statements (the "Nations of the World" section), ranging in length from one to four pages, and permits, in the 24 major thematic tables (the "Comparative National Statistics" [CNS] section), comparisons among these larger countries and 23 smaller states.

Updated annually, *Britannica World Data* is particularly intended as direct, structured support for many of Britannica's other reference works—encyclopaedias, yearbooks, atlases—at a level of detail that their editorial style or design do not permit.

Like the textual, graphic, or cartographic modes of expression of these other products, statistics possess their own inherent editorial virtues and weaknesses. Two principal goals in the creation of *Britannica World Data* were up-to-dateness and comparability, each possible to maximize separately, but not always possible to combine. If, for example, research on some subject is completed during a particular year (x), figures may be available for 100 countries for the preceding year ($x - 1$), for 140 countries for the year before that ($x - 2$), and for 180 countries for the year before that ($x - 3$).

Which year should be the basis of a thematic compilation for 217 countries so as to give the best combination of up-to-dateness and comparability? And, should $x - 1$ be adopted for the thematic table, ought up-to-dateness in the country table (for which year x is already available) be sacrificed for agreement with the thematic table? In general, the editors have opted for maximum up-to-dateness in the country statistical boxes and maximum comparability in the thematic tables.

Comparability, however, also resides in the meaning of the numbers compiled, which may differ greatly from country to country. The headnotes to the thematic tables explain many of these methodological problems; the Glossary serves the same purpose for the country statistical pages. Published data do not always provide the researcher or editor with a neat, unambiguous choice between a datum compiled on two different bases (say, railroad track length, or route length), one of which is wanted and the other not. More often a choice must be made among a variety of official, private, and external intergovernmental (UN, FAO, IMF) sources, each reporting its best data but each representing a set of problems: (1) of methodological variance from (or among) international conventions; (2) of analytical completeness (data for a single year may, successively, be projected [based on 10 years' data], preliminary [for 12 months], final, revised or adjusted, etc.); (3) of time frame, or accounting interval (data may represent a full Gregorian calendar year [preferred], a fiscal year, an Islamic or other national or religious year, a multiyear period or average [when a one-year statement would contain unrepresentative results]); (4) of continuity with previous data; and the like. Finally, published data on a particular subject may be complete and final but impossible to summarize in a simple manner. The education system of a single country may include, for example, public and private sectors; local, state, or national systems; varying grades, tracks, or forms within a single system; or opportunities for double-counting or fractional counting of a student, teacher, or institution. When no recent official data exist, or they exist, but may be suspect, the tables may show unofficial estimates, a range (of published opinion), analogous data, or no data at all.

The published basis of the information compiled is the statistical collections of Encyclopædia Britannica, Inc., some of the principal elements of which are enumerated in the Bibliography. Holdings for a given country may include any of the following: the national statistical abstract; the constitution; the most recent censuses of population; periodic or occasional reports on vital statistics, social indicators, agriculture, mining, labour, manufacturing, domestic and foreign trade, finance and banking, transportation, and communications. Further information is received in a variety of formats—telephone, letter, fax, microfilm and microfiche, and most recently, in electronic formats such as computer disks, CD-ROMs, and the Internet. So substantial had the resources of the Internet become by the previous research year that it was thought possible, for the first time, to add uniform resource locators (URLs) to the great majority of country pages and a number of the CNS tables (summary world sites with data on all countries still being somewhat of a rarity) so as to apprise the reader of the possibility and means to access current information on these subjects year-round.

The recommendations offered are usually to official sites (national statistical offices, general national governments, central banks, embassies, intergovernmental organizations [especially the UN Development Programme], and the like). Though often dissimilar in content, they will usually be updated year-round, expanded as opportunity permits, and lead on to related sites, such as parliamentary offices, information offices, diplomatic and consular sites, news agencies and newspapers, and, beyond, to the myriad academic, commercial, and private sites now accessible from the personal computer. While these URLs were correct and current at the time of writing, they may be subject to change.

The great majority of the social, economic, and financial data contained in this work should not be interpreted in isolation. Interpretive text of long perspective, such as that of the *Encyclopædia Britannica* itself; political, geographic, and topical maps, such as those in the *Britannica Atlas;* and recent analysis of political events and economic trends, such as that contained in the articles of the *Book of the Year,* will all help to supply analytic focus that numbers alone cannot. By the same token, study of those sources will be made more concrete by use of *Britannica World Data* to supply up-to-date geographic, demographic, and economic detail.

GLOSSARY

A number of terms that are used to classify and report data in the "Nations of the World" section require some explanation.

Those italicized terms that are used regularly in the country compilations to introduce specific categories of information (*e.g., birth rate, budget*) appear in this glossary in italic boldface type, followed by a description of the precise kind of information being offered and how it has been edited and presented.

All other terms are printed here in roman boldface type. Many terms have quite specific meanings in statistical reporting, and they are so defined here. Other terms have less specific application as they are used by different countries or organizations. Data in the country compilations based on definitions markedly different from those below will usually be footnoted.

Terms that appear in small capitals in certain definitions are themselves defined at their respective alphabetical locations.

Terms whose definitions are marked by an asterisk (*) refer to data supplied only in the larger two- to four-page country compilations.

access to services, a group of measures indicating a population's level of access to public services, including electrical power, treated public drinking water, sewage removal, and fire protection.*

activity rate, *see* participation/activity rates.

age breakdown, the distribution of a given population by age, usually reported here as percentages of total population in 15-year age brackets. When substantial numbers of persons do not know, or state, their exact age, distributions may not total 100.0%.

area, the total surface area of a country or its administrative subdivisions, including both land and inland (nontidal) water area. Land area is usually calculated from "mean low water" on a "plane table," or flat, basis.

area and population, a tabulation usually including the first-order administrative subdivisions of the country (such as the states of the United States), with capital (headquarters, or administrative seat), area, and population. When these subdivisions are especially numerous or, occasionally, nonexistent, a planning, electoral, census, or other nonadministrative scheme of regional subdivisions has been substituted.

associated state, *see* state.

atheist, in statements of religious affiliation, one who professes active opposition to religion; "nonreligious" refers to those professing only no religion, nonbelief, or doubt.

balance of payments, a financial statement for a country for a given period showing the balance among: (1) transactions in goods, services, and income between that country and the rest of the world, (2) changes in ownership or valuation of that country's monetary gold, SPECIAL DRAWING RIGHTS, and claims on and liabilities to the rest of the world, and (3) unrequited transfers and counterpart entries needed (in an accounting sense) to balance transactions and changes among any of the foregoing types of exchange that are not mutually offsetting. Detail of national law as to what constitutes a transaction, the basis of its valuation, and the size of a transaction visible to fiscal authorities

all result in differences in the meaning of a particular national statement.*

balance of trade, the net value of all international goods trade of a country, usually excluding reexports (goods received only for transshipment), and the percentage that this net represents of total trade.

Balance of trade refers only to the "visible" international trade of goods as recorded by customs authorities and is thus a segment of a country's BALANCE OF PAYMENTS, which takes all visible and invisible trade with other countries into account. (Invisible trade refers to imports and exports of money, financial instruments, and services such as transport, tourism, and insurance.) A country has a fav-ourable, or positive (+), balance of trade when the

value of exports exceeds that of imports and negative (–) when imports exceed exports.

barrel (bbl), a unit of liquid measure. The barrel conventionally used for reporting crude petroleum and petroleum products is equal to 42 U.S. gallons, or 159 litres. The number of barrels of crude petroleum per metric ton, ranging typically from 6.20 to 8.13, depends upon the specific gravity of the petroleum. The world average is roughly 7.33 barrels per ton.

birth rate, the number of live births annually per 1,000 of midyear population. Birth rates for individual countries may be compared with the estimated world annual average of 25.0 births per 1,000 population between 1990 and 1995.

budget, the annual receipts and expenditures— of a central government for its activities only;

Abbreviations

Measurements

cu m	cubic metre(s)
kg	kilograms(s)
km	kilometre(s)
kW	kilowatt(s)
kW-hr	kilowatt-hour(s)
metric ton-km	metric ton-kilometre(s)
mi	mile(s)
passenger-km	passenger-kilometre(s)
passenger-mi	passenger-mile(s)
short ton-mi	short ton-mile(s)
sq km	square kilometre(s)
sq m	square metre(s)
sq mi	square mile(s)
troy oz	troy ounce(s)
yr	year(s)

Political Units and International Organizations

CACM	Central American Common Market
Caricom	Caribbean Community and Common Market
CFA	Communauté Financière Africaine
CFP	Comptoirs Françaises du Pacifique
CIS	Commonwealth of Independent States
CUSA	Customs Union of Southern Africa
E.Ger.	East Germany
EC	European Communities
EU	European Union
FAO	United Nations Food and Agriculture Organization
IMF	International Monetary Fund
OECD	Organization for Economic Cooperation and Development
OECS	Organization of Eastern Caribbean States
U.A.E.	United Arab Emirates
U.K.	United Kingdom
UNDP	United Nations Development Programme
U.S.	United States
U.S.S.R.	Union of Soviet Socialist Republics
W.Ger.	West Germany

Months

Jan.	January	Oct.	October
Feb.	February	Nov.	November
Aug.	August	Dec.	December
Sept.	September		

Miscellaneous

AIDS	Acquired Immune Deficiency Syndrome
avg.	average
c.i.f.	cost, insurance, and freight
commun.	communications
CPI	consumer price index
est.	estimate(d)
excl.	excluding
f.o.b.	free on board
GDP	gross domestic product
GNP	gross national product
govt.	government
incl.	including
mo.	month(s)
n.a.	not available (in text)
n.e.s.	not elsewhere specified
no.	number
pl.	plural
pos.	position
pub. admin.	public administration
PVC	Polyvinyl Chloride
SDR	Special Drawing Right
SITC	Standard International Trade Classification
svcs.	services
teacher tr.	teacher training
transp.	transportation
voc.	vocational
$	dollar (of any currency area)
£	pound (of any currency area)
...	not available (in tables)
—	none, less than half the smallest unit shown, or not applicable (in tables)

does not include state, provincial, or local governments or semipublic (parastatal, quasi-nongovernmental) corporations unless otherwise specified. Figures for budgets are limited to ordinary (recurrent) receipts and expenditures, wherever possible, and exclude capital expenditures—*i.e.,* funds for development and other special projects originating as foreign-aid grants or loans.

When both a recurrent and a capital budget exist for a single country, the former is the budget funded entirely from national resources (taxes, duties, excises, etc.) that would recur (be generated by economic activity) every year. It funds the most basic governmental services, those least able to suffer interruption. The capital budget is usually funded by external aid and may change its size considerably from year to year.

capital, usually, the actual seat of government and administration of a state. When more than one capital exists, each is identified by kind; when interim arrangements exist during the creation or movement of a national capital, the de facto situation is described.

Anomalous cases are annotated, such as those in which (1) the de jure designation under the country's laws differs from actual local practice (*e.g.,* Benin's designation of one capital in constitutional law, but another in actual practice), (2) international recognition does not validate a country's claim (as with the proclamation by Israel of a capital on territory not internationally recognized as part of Israel), or (3) both a state and a capital have been proclaimed on territory recognized as part of another state (as with the Turkish Republic of Northern Cyprus).

capital budget, see budget.

causes of death, as defined by the World Health Organization (WHO), "the disease or injury which initiated the train of morbid events leading directly to death, or the circumstances of accident or violence which produced the fatal injury." This principle, the "underlying cause of death," is the basis of the medical judgment as to cause; the statistical classification system according to which these causes are grouped and named is the *International List of Causes of Death,* the latest revision of which is the Tenth. Reporting is usually in terms of events per 100,000 population. When data on actual causes of death are unavailable, information on morbidity, or illness rate, usually given as reported cases per 100,000 of infectious diseases (notifiable to WHO as a matter of international agreement), may be substituted.

chief of state/head of government, paramount national governmental officer(s) exercising the highest executive and/or ceremonial roles of a country's government. In general usage, the chief of state is the formal head of a national state. The primary responsibilities of the chief of state may range from the purely ceremonial—convening legislatures and greeting foreign officials—to the exercise of complete national executive authority. The head of government, when this function exists separately, is the officer nominally charged (by the constitution) with the majority of actual executive powers, though they may not in practice be exercised, especially in military or single-party regimes in which effective power may reside entirely outside the executive governmental machinery provided by the constitution. A prime minister, for example, usually the actual head of government, may in practice exercise only Cabinet-level authority.

In communist countries an official identified as the chief of state may be the chairman of the policy-making organ, and the official given as the head of government the chairman of the nominal administrative/executive organ.

c.i.f. (trade valuation): *see* imports.

colony, an area annexed to, or controlled by, an independent state but not an integral part of it; a non-self-governing territory. A colony has a charter and may have a degree of self-government. A crown colony is a colony originally chartered by the British government.

commonwealth (U.K. and U.S.), a self-governing political entity that has regard to the common weal, or good; usually associated with the United Kingdom or United States. Examples include the Commonwealth of Nations (composed of independent states [from 1931 onward]), Puerto Rico since 1952, and the Northern Marianas since 1979.

communications, collectively, the means available for the public transmission of information within a country. Data are tabulated for: daily newspapers and their total circulation; radio and television as total numbers of receivers; telephone data as "main lines," or the number of subscriber lines (not receivers) having access to the public switched network; cellular telephones as number of subscribers; and facsimile machines and personal computers as number of units. For each, a rate per 1,000 persons is given.

constant prices, an adjustment to the members of a financial time series to eliminate the effect of inflation year by year. It consists of referring all data in the series to a single year so that "real" change may be seen.

constitutional monarchy, see monarchy.

consumer price index (CPI), also known as the retail price index, or the cost-of-living index, a series of index numbers assigned to the price of a selected "basket," or assortment, of basic consumer goods and services in a country, region, city, or type of household in order to measure changes over time in prices paid by a typical household for those goods and services. Items included in the CPI are ordinarily determined by governmental surveys of typical household expenditures and are assigned weights relative to their proportion of those expenditures. Index values are period averages unless otherwise noted.

coprincipality, see monarchy.

current prices, the valuation of a financial aggregate as of the year reported.

daily per capita caloric intake (supply), the calories equivalent to the known average daily supply of foodstuffs for human consumption in a given country divided by the population of the country (and the proportion of that supply provided, respectively, by vegetable and animal sources). The daily per capita caloric intake of a country may be compared with the corresponding recommended minimum daily requirement. The latter is calculated by the Food and Agriculture Organization of the United Nations from the age and sex distributions, average body weights, and environmental temperatures in a given region to determine the calories needed to sustain a person there at normal levels of activity and health. The daily per capita caloric requirement ranges from 2,200 to 2,500.

de facto population, for a given area, the population composed of those actually present at a particular time, including temporary residents and visitors (such as immigrants not yet granted permanent status, "guest" or expatriate workers, refugees, or tourists), but excluding legal residents temporarily absent.

de jure population, for a given area, the population composed only of those legally resident at a particular time, excluding temporary residents and visitors (such as "guest" or expatriate workers, refugees, or tourists), but including legal residents temporarily absent.

deadweight tonnage, the maximum weight of cargo, fuel, fresh water, stores, and persons that may safely by carried by a ship. It is customarily measured in long tons of 2,240 pounds each, equivalent to 1.016 metric tons. Deadweight tonnage is the difference between the tonnage of a fully loaded ship and the fully unloaded tonnage of that ship.

See also gross ton.

death rate, the number of deaths annually per 1,000 of midyear population. Death rates for individual countries may be compared with the estimated world annual average of 9.3 deaths per 1,000 population between 1990 and 1995.

density (of population), usually, the DE FACTO POPULATION of a country divided by its total area. Special adjustment is made for large areas of inland water, desert, or other uninhabitable areas—*e.g.,* excluding the ice cap of Greenland.

dependent state, constitutionally or statutorily organized political entity outside of and under the jurisdiction of an independent state (or a federal element of such a state) but not formally annexed to it (*see* Table).

Dependent states[1]

Australia	**Norway**
Christmas Island	Jan Mayen
Cocos (Keeling) Islands	Svalbard
Norfolk Island	**Portugal**
China	Macau
Hong Kong	**United Kingdom**
Denmark	Anguilla
Faroe Islands	Bermuda
Greenland	British Virgin Islands
France	Cayman Islands
French Guiana	Falkland Islands
French Polynesia	Gibraltar
Guadeloupe	Guernsey
Martinique	Isle of Man
Mayotte	Jersey
New Caledonia	Montserrat
Réunion	Pitcairn Island
Saint Pierre and Miquelon	Saint Helena and Dependencies
Wallis and Futuna	Turks and Caicos Islands
Netherlands, The	**United States**
Aruba	American Samoa
Netherlands Antilles	Guam
New Zealand	Northern Mariana Islands
Cook Islands	Puerto Rico
Niue	Virgin Islands (of the U.S.)
Tokelau	

[1]Excludes territories (1) to which Antarctic Treaty is applicable in whole or in part, (2) without permanent civilian population, (3) without internationally recognized civilian government (Western Sahara, Gaza Strip), or (4) representing unadjudicated unilateral or multilateral territorial claims.

direct taxes, taxes levied directly on firms and individuals, such as taxes on income, profits, and capital gains. The *immediate* incidence, or burden, of direct taxes is on the firms and individuals thus taxed; direct taxes on firms may, however, be passed on to consumers and other economic units in the form of higher prices for goods and services, blurring the distinction between direct and indirect taxation.

distribution of income/wealth, the portion of personal income or wealth accruing to households or individuals constituting each respective decile (tenth) or quintile (fifth) of a country's households or individuals.*

divorce rate, the number of legal, civilly recognized divorces annually per 1,000 population.

doubling time, the number of complete years required for a country to double its population at its current rate of natural increase.

earnings index, a series of index numbers comparing average wages in a collective industrial sample for a country or region with the same industries at a previous period to measure changes over time in those wages. It is most commonly reported for wages paid on a daily, weekly, or monthly basis; annual figures may represent total income or averages of these shorter periods. The scope of the earnings index varies from country to country; The index is often limited to earnings in manufacturing industries. The index for each country applies to all wage earners in a designated group and ordinarily takes into account basic wages (overtime is normally distinguished), bonuses, cost-of-living allowances, and contributions toward social security. Some countries include payments in kind. Contributions toward social security by employers are usually excluded, as are social security benefits received by wage earners.

economically active population, *see* population economically active.

education, tabulation of the principal elements of a country's educational establishment, classified as far as possible according to the country's own system of primary, secondary, and higher levels (the usual age limits for these levels being identified in parentheses), with total number of schools (physical facilities) and of teachers and students (whether full- or part-time). The student-teacher ratio is calculated whenever available data permit.

educational attainment, the distribution of the population age 25 and over with completed educations by the highest level of formal education attained or completed; it must sometimes be reported, however, for age groups still in school or for the economically active only.

emirate, *see* monarchy.

enterprise, a legal entity formed to conduct a business, which it may do from more than one establishment (place of business or service point).

ethnic/linguistic composition, ethnic, racial, or linguistic composition of a national population, reported here according to the most reliable breakdown available, whether published in official sources (such as a census) or in external analysis (when the subject is not addressed in national sources).

exchange rate, the value of one currency compared with another, or with a standardized unit of account such as the SPECIAL DRAWING RIGHT, or as mandated by local statute when one currency is "tied" by a par value to another. Rates given usually refer to free market values when the currency has no, or very limited, restrictions on its convertibility into other currencies.

exports, material goods legally leaving a country (or customs area) and subject to customs regulations. The total value and distribution by percentage of the major items (in preference to groups of goods) exported are given, together with the distribution of trade among major

trading partners (usually single countries or trading blocs). Valuation of goods exported is free on board (f.o.b.) unless otherwise specified. The value of goods exported and imported f.o.b. is calculated from the cost of production and excludes the cost of transport.

external debt, public and publicly guaranteed debt with a maturity of more than one year owed to nonnationals of a country and repayable in foreign currency, goods, or services. The debt may be an obligation of a national or subnational governmental body (or an agency of either), of an autonomous public body, or of a private debtor that is guaranteed by a public entity. The debt is usually either outstanding (contracted) or disbursed (drawn).

external territory (Australia), *see* territory.

federal, consisting of first-order political subdivisions that are prior to and independent of the central government in certain functions.

federal republic, *see* republic.

federation, union of coequal, preexisting political entities that retain some degree of autonomy and (usually) right of secession within the union.

fertility rate, *see* total fertility rate.

financial aggregates, tabulation of seven-year time series, providing principal measures of the financial condition of a country, including: (1) the exchange rate of the national crurency against the U.S. dollar, the pound sterling, and the International Monetary Fund's SPECIAL DRAWING RIGHT (SDR), (2) the amount and kind of international reserves (holdings of SDRs, gold, and foreign currencies) and reserve position of the country in the IMF, and (3) principal economic rates and prices (central bank discount rate, government bond yields, and industrial stock [share] prices). For BALANCE OF PAYMENTS, the origin in terms of component balance of trade items and balance of invisibles (net) is given.*

fish catch, the live-weight equivalent of the aquatic animals (including fish, crustaceans, mollusks, etc., but excluding whales, seals, and other aquatic mammals) caught in freshwater or marine areas by national fleets and landed in domestic or foreign harbours for commercial, industrial, or subsistence purposes.

f.o.b. (trade valuation): *see* exports.

food, see daily per capita caloric intake.

form of government/political status, the type of administration provided for by a country's constitution—whether or not suspended by extralegal military or civil action, although such de facto administrations are identified—together with the number of members (elected, appointed, and ex officio) for each legislative house, named according to its English rendering. Dependent states (*see* Table) are classified according to the status of their political association with the administering country.

gross domestic product (GDP), the total value of the final goods and services produced by residents and nonresidents within a given country during a given accounting period, usually a year. Unless otherwise noted, the value is given in current prices of the year indicated. The *System of National Accounts* (SNA, published under the joint auspices of the UN, IMF, OECD, EC, and World Bank) provides a framework for international comparability in classifying domestic accounting aggregates and international transactions comprising "net factor income from abroad," the measure that distinguishes GDP and GNP.

gross national product (GNP), the total value of final goods and services produced both from within a given country *and* from external (foreign) transactions in a given accounting period, usually a year. Unless otherwise noted, the value is given in current prices of the year indicated. GNP is equal to GROSS DOMESTIC PRODUCT (*q.v.*) adjusted by net factor income from abroad, which is the income residents

receive from abroad for factor services (labour, investment, and interest) less similar payments made to nonresidents who contribute to the domestic economy.

gross ton, volumetric unit of measure (equaling 100 cubic feet [2.83 cu m]) of the permanently enclosed volume of a ship, above and below decks available for cargo, stores, or passenger accommodation. Net, or register, tonnage exempts certain nonrevenue spaces—such as those devoted to machinery, bunkers, crew accommodations, and ballast—from the gross tonnage. *See also* deadweight tonnage.

head of government, see chief of state/head of government.

health, a group of measures including number of accredited physicians currently practicing or employed and their ratio to the total population; total hospital beds and their ratio; and INFANT MORTALITY RATE.

household, economically autonomous individual or group of individuals living in a single dwelling unit. A family household is one composed principally of individuals related by blood or marriage.

household income and expenditure, data for average size of a HOUSEHOLD (by number of individuals) and median household income. Sources of income and expenditures for major items of consumption are given as percentages.

In general, household income is the amount of funds, usually measured in monetary units, received by the members (generally those 14 years old and over) of a household in a given time period. The income can be derived from (1) wages or salaries, (2) nonfarm or farm SELF–EMPLOYMENT, (3) transfer payments, such as pensions, public assistance, unemployment benefits, etc., and (4) other income, including interest and dividends, rent, royalties, etc. The income of a household is expressed as a gross amount before deductions for taxes. Data on expenditure refer to consumption of personal or household goods and services; they normally exclude savings, taxes, and insurance; practice with regard to inclusion of credit purchases differs markedly.

immigration, usually, the number and origin of those immigrants admitted to a nation in a legal status that would eventually permit the granting of the right to settle permanently or to acquire citizenship.*

imports, material goods legally entering a country (or customs area) and subject to customs regulations; excludes financial movements. The total value and distribution by percentage of the major items (in preference to groups of goods) imported are given, together with the direction of trade among major trading partners (usually single countries), trading blocs (such as the European Union), or customs areas (such as Belgium-Luxembourg). The value of goods imported is given free on board (f.o.b.) unless otherwise specified; f.o.b. is defined above under EXPORTS.

The principal alternate basis for valuation of goods in international trade is that of cost, insurance, and freight (c.i.f.); its use is restricted to imports, as it comprises the principal charges needed to bring the goods to the customs house in the country of destination. Because it inflates the value of imports relative to exports, more countries have, latterly, been estimating imports on an f.o.b. basis as well.

incorporated territory (U.S.), *see* territory.

independent, of a state, autonomous and controlling both its internal and external affairs. Its date usually refers to the date from which the country was in effective control of these affairs within its present boundaries, rather than the date independence was proclaimed or the date recognized as a de jure act by the former administering power.

indirect taxes, taxes levied on sales or transfers of selected intermediate goods and services, in-

cluding excises, value-added taxes, and tariffs, that are ordinarily passed on to the ultimate consumers of the goods and services. Figures given for individual countries are limited to indirect taxes levied by their respective central governments unless otherwise specified.

infant mortality rate, the number of children per 1,000 live births who die before their first birthday. Total infant mortality includes neonatal mortality, which is deaths of children within one month of birth.

invisibles (invisible trade), see balance of trade.

kingdom, see monarchy.

labour force, portion of the POPULATION ECONOMICALLY ACTIVE (PEA) comprising those most fully employed or attached to the labour market (the unemployed are considered to be "attached" in that they usually represent persons previously employed seeking to be reemployed), particularly as viewed from a short-term perspective. It normally includes those who are self-employed, employed by others (whether full-time, part-time, seasonally, or on some other less than full-time, basis), and, as noted above, the unemployed (both those previously employed and those seeking work for the first time). In the "gross domestic product and labour force" table, the majority of the labour data provided refer to population economically active, since PEA represents the longer-term view of working population and, thus, subsumes more of the marginal workers who are often missed by shorter-term surveys.

land use, distribution by classes of vegetational cover or economic use of the land area only (excluding inland water, for example, but not marshland), reported as percentages. The principal categories utilized include: (1) forest, which includes natural and planted tracts, (2) meadows and pastures, which includes land in temporary or permanent use whose principal purpose is the growing of animal fodder, (3) agricultural and under permanent cultivation, which includes temporary and permanent cropland, as well as land left fallow less than five years, but capable of being returned to production without special preparation, and (4) other, which includes built-up, wasteland, watercourses, and the like.

leisure, the principal monetary expenditures, uses, or reported preferences in the use of the individual's free time for recreation, rest, or self-improvement.*

life expectancy, the number of years a person born within a particular population group (age cohort) would be expected to live, based on actuarial calculations.

literacy, the ability to read and write a language with some degree of competence; the precise degree constituting the basis of a particular national statement is usually defined by the national census and is often tested by the census enumerator. Elsewhere, particularly where much adult literacy may be the result of literacy campaigns rather than passage through a formal educational system, definition and testing of literacy may be better standardized.

major cities, usually the five largest cities proper (national capitals are always given, regardless of size); fewer cities may be listed if there are fewer urban localities in the country. For multi-page tables, 10 or more may be listed.* Populations for cities will usually refer to the city proper—*i.e.,* the legally bounded corporate entity, or the most compact, contiguous, demographically urban portion of the entity defined by the local authorities. Occasionally figures for METROPOLITAN AREAS are cited when the relevant civil entity at the core of a major agglomeration had an unrepresentatively small population.

manufacturing, mining, and construction enterprises/retail sales and service enterprises, a detailed tabulation of the principal industries in these sectors, showing for each industry the number of enterprises and employees, wages in that industry as a percentage of the general average wage, and the value of that industry's output in terms of value added or turnover.*

marriage rate, the number of legal, civilly recognized marriages annually per 1,000 population.

material well-being, a group of measures indicating the percentage of households or dwellings possessing certain goods or appliances, including automobiles, telephones, television receivers, refrigerators, air conditioners, and washing machines.*

merchant marine, the privately or publicly owned ships registered with the maritime authority of a nation (limited to those in Lloyd's of London statistical reporting of 100 or more GROSS TONS) that are employed in commerce, whether or not owned or operated by nationals of the country.

metropolitan area, a city and the region of dense, predominantly urban, settlement around the city; the population of the whole usually has strong economic and cultural affinities with the central city.

military expenditure, the apparent value of all identifiable military expenditure by the central government on hardware, personnel, pensions, research and development, etc., reported here both as a percentage of the GNP, and a comparison to the world average, and as a per capita value in U.S. dollars.

military personnel, see total active duty personnel.

mobility, the rate at which individuals or households change dwellings, usually measured between censuses and including international as well as domestic migration.*

monarchy, a government in which the CHIEF OF STATE holds office, usually hereditarily and for life, but sometimes electively for a term. The state may be a coprincipality, emirate, kingdom, principality, sheikhdom, or sultanate. The powers of the monarch may range from absolute (*i.e.,* the monarch both reigns and rules) through various degrees of limitation of authority to nominal, as in a constitutional monarchy, in which the titular monarch reigns but others, as elected officials, effectively rule.

monetary unit, currency of issue, or that in official use in a given country; name, spelling, and abbreviation in English according to International Monetary Fund recommendations or local practice; name of the lesser, usually decimal, monetary unit constituting the main currency; and valuation in U.S. dollars and U.K. pounds sterling, usually according to free-market or commercial rates.

See also exchange rate.

natural increase, also called natural growth, or the balance of births and deaths, the excess of births over deaths in a population; the rate of natural increase is the difference between the BIRTH RATE and the DEATH RATE of a given population. The estimated world average during 1990–95 was 15.7 per 1,000 population, or 1.57% annually. Natural increase is added to the balance of migration to calculate the total growth of that population.

net material product, see material product.

nonreligious, see atheist.

official language(s), that (or those) prescribed by the national constitution for day-to-day conduct and publication of a country's official business or, when no explicit constitutional provision exists, that of the constitution itself, the national gazette (record of legislative activity), or like official documents. Other languages may have local protection, may be permitted in parliamentary debate or legal action (such as a trial), or may be "national languages," for the protection of which special provisions have been made, but these are not deemed official. The United States, for example, does not yet formally identify English as "official," though it uses it for virtually all official purposes.

official name, the local official form(s), short or long, of a country's legal name(s) taken from the country's constitution or from other official documents. The English-language form is usually the protocol form in use by the country, the U.S. Department of State, and the United Nations.

official religion, generally, any religion prescribed or given special status or protection by the constitution or legal system of a country. Identification as such is not confined to constitutional documents utilizing the term explicitly.

organized territory (U.S.), see territory.

overseas department (France), see department.

overseas territory (France), see territory.

parliamentary state, see state.

part of a realm, a dependent Dutch political entity with some degree of self-government and having a special status above that of a colony (*e.g.,* the prerogative of rejecting for local application any law enacted by The Netherlands).

participation/activity rates, measures defining differential rates of economic activity within a population. Participation rate refers to the percentage of those employed or economically active who possess a particular characteristic (sex, age, etc.); activity rate refers to the fraction of the total population who *are* economically active.

passenger-miles, or **passenger-kilometres,** aggregate measure of passenger carriage by a specified means of transportation, equal to the number of passengers carried multiplied by the number of miles (or kilometres) each is transported. Figures given for countries are often calculated from ticket sales and ordinarily exclude passengers carried free of charge.

people's republic, see republic.

place of birth/national origin, if the former, numbers of native- and foreign-born population of a country by actual place of birth; if the latter, any of several classifications, including those based on origin of passport at original admission to country, on cultural heritage of family name, on self-designated (often multiple) origin of (some) ancestors, and on other systems for assigning national origin.*

political status, see form of government/political status.

population, the number of persons present within a country, city, or other civil entity at the date of a census of population, survey, cumulation of a civil register, or other enumeration. Unless otherwise specified, populations given are DE FACTO, referring to those actually present, rather than DE JURE, those legally resident but not necessarily present on the referent date. If a time series, noncensus year, or per capita ratio referring to a country's total population is cited, it will usually refer to midyear of the calendar year indicated.

population economically active, the total number of persons (above a set age for economic labour, usually 10–15 years) in all employment statuses—self-employed, wage- or salary-earning, part-time, seasonal, unemployed, etc. The International Labour Organisation defines the economically active as "all persons of either sex who furnish the supply of labour for the production of economic goods and services." National practices vary as regards the treatment of such groups as armed forces, inmates of institutions, persons seeking their first job, unpaid family workers, seasonal workers and persons engaged in part-time economic activities. In some countries, all or part of these groups may be included among the economically active, while in other countries the same groups may be treated as inactive. In general, however, the data on economically active population do not include students, persons occupied solely in family or household work, retired persons, persons living entirely on

their own means, and persons wholly dependent upon others.

See also labour force.

population projection, the expected population in the years 2000 and 2010, embodying the country's own projections wherever possible. Estimates of the future size of a population are usually based on assumed levels of fertility, mortality, and migration. Projections in the tables, unless otherwise specified, are medium (*i.e.,* most likely) variants, whether based on external estimates by the United Nations, World Bank, or U.S. Department of Commerce or on those of the country itself.

price and earnings indexes, tabulation comparing the change in the CONSUMER PRICE INDEX over a period of seven years with the change in the general labour force's EARNINGS INDEX for the same period.

principality, *see* monarchy.

production, the physical quantity or monetary value of the output of an industry, usually tabulated here as the most important items or groups of items (depending on the available detail) of primary (extractive) and secondary (manufactured) production, including construction. When a single consistent measure of value, such as VALUE ADDED, can be obtained, this is given, ranked by value; otherwise, and more usually, quantity of production is given.

public debt, the current outstanding debt of all periods of maturity for which the central government and its organs are obligated. Publicly guaranteed private debt is excluded. For countries that report debt under the World Bank Debtor Reporting System (DRS), figures for outstanding, long-term EXTERNAL DEBT are given.

quality of working life, a group of measures including weekly hours of work (including overtime); rates per 100,000 for job-connected injury, illness, and mortality; coverage of labour force by insurance for injury, permanent disability, and death; workdays lost to labour strikes and stoppages; and commuting patterns (length of journey to work in minutes and usual method of transportation).*

railroads, mode of transportation by self-driven or locomotive-drawn cars over fixed rails. Length-of-track figures include all mainline and spurline running track but exclude switching sidings and yard track. Route length, when given, does not compound multiple running tracks laid on the same trackbed.

recurrent budget, *see* budget.

religious affiliation, distribution of nominal religionists, whether practicing or not, as a percentage of total population. This usually assigns to children the religion of their parents.

republic, a state with elected leaders and a centralized presidential form of government, local subdivisions being subordinate to the national government. A *federal republic* (as distinguished from a unitary republic) is a republic in which power is divided between the central government and the constituent subnational administrative divisions (*e.g.,* states, provinces, or cantons) in whom the central government itself is held to originate, the division of power being defined in a written constitution and jurisdictional disputes usually being settled in a court; sovereignty usually rests with the authority that has the power to amend the constitution. A *unitary republic* (as distinguished from a federal republic) is a republic in which power originates in a central authority and is not derived from constituent subdivisions. A *people's republic,* in the dialectics of Communism, is the first stage of development toward a communist state, the second stage being a *socialist republic.* An *Islamic republic* is structured around social, ethical, legal, and religious precepts central to the Islamic faith.

retail price index, *see* consumer price index.

retail sales and service enterprises, *see* manufacturing, mining, and construction enterprises/retail sales and service enterprises.

roundwood, wood obtained from removals from forests, felled or harvested (with or without bark), in all forms.

rural, see urban-rural.

self-employment, work in which income derives from direct employment in one's own business, trade, or profession, as opposed to work in which salary or wages are earned from an employer.

self-governing, of a state, in control of its internal affairs in degrees ranging from control of most internal affairs (though perhaps not of public order or of internal security) to complete control of all internal affairs (*i.e.,* the state is autonomous) but having no control of external affairs or defense. In this work the term self-governing refers to the final stage in the successive stages of increasing self-government that generally precede independence.

service/trade enterprises, see manufacturing, mining, and construction enterprises/retail sales and service enterprises.

sex distribution, ratios, calculated as percentages, of male and female population to total population.

sheikhdom, *see* monarchy.

social deviance, a group of measures, usually reported as rates per 100,000 for principal categories of socially deviant behaviour, including specified crimes, alcoholism, drug abuse, and suicide.*

social participation, a group of measures indicative of the degree of social engagement displayed by a particular population, including rates of participation in such activities as elections, voluntary work or memberships, trade unions, and religion.*

social security, public programs designed to protect individuals and families from loss of income owing to unemployment, old age, sickness or disability, or death and to provide other services such as medical care, health and welfare programs, or income maintenance.

socialist republic, *see* republic.

sources of income, *see* household income and expenditure.

Special Drawing Right (SDR), a unit of account utilized by the International Monetary Fund (IMF) to denominate monetary reserves available under a quota system to IMF members to maintain the value of their national currency unit in international transactions.*

state, in international law, a political entity possessing the attributes of: territory, permanent civilian population, government, and the capacity to conduct relations with other states. Though the term is sometimes limited in meaning to fully independent and internationally recognized states, the more general sense of an entity possessing a *preponderance* of these characteristics is intended here. It is, thus, also a first-order civil administrative subdivision, especially of a federated union. An associated state is an autonomous state in free association with another that conducts its external affairs and defense; the association may be terminated in full independence at the instance of the autonomous state in consultation with the administering power. A *parliamentary state* is an independent state of the Commonwealth that is governed by a parliament and that may recognize the British monarch as its titular head.

structure of gross domestic product and labour force, tabulation of the principal elements of the national economy, according to standard industrial categories, together with the corresponding distribution of the labour force (when possible POPULATION ECONOMICALLY ACTIVE) that generates the GROSS DOMESTIC PRODUCT.

sultanate, *see* monarchy.

territory, a noncategorized political dependency; a first-order administrative subdivision; a dependent political entity with some degree of self-government, but with fewer rights and less autonomy than a colony because there is no charter. An *external territory* (Australia) is a territory situated outside the area of the country. An *organized territory* (U.S.) is a territory for which a system of laws and a settled government have been provided by an act of the United States Congress. An *overseas territory* (France) is an overseas subdivision of the French Republic with elected representation in the French Parliament, having individual statutes, laws, and internal organization adapted to local conditions.

ton-miles, or **ton-kilometres,** aggregate measure of freight hauled by a specified means of transportation, equal to tons of freight multiplied by the miles (or kilometres) each ton is transported. Figures are compiled from waybills (nationally) and ordinarily exclude mail, specie, passengers' baggage, the fuel and stores of the conveyance, and goods carried free.

total active duty personnel, full-time active duty military personnel (excluding militias and part-time, informal, or other paramilitary elements), with their distribution by percentages among the major services.

total fertility rate, the sum of the current age-specific birth rates for each of the child-bearing years (usually 15–49). It is the probable number of births, given present fertility data, that would occur during the lifetime of each woman should she live to the end of her child-bearing years.

tourism, service industry comprising activities connected with domestic and international travel for pleasure or recreation; confined here to international travel and reported as expenditures in U.S. dollars by tourists of all nationalities visiting a particular country and, conversely, the estimated expenditures of that country's nationals in all countries of destination.

transfer payments, see household income and expenditure.

transport, all mechanical methods of moving persons or goods. Data reported for national establishments include: for railroads, length of track and volume of traffic for passengers and cargo (but excluding mail, etc.); for roads, length of network and numbers of passenger cars and of commercial vehicles (*i.e.,* trucks and buses); for merchant marine, the number of vessels of more than 100 gross tons and their total deadweight tonnage; for air transport, traffic data for passengers and cargo and the number of airports with scheduled flights.

unincorporated territory (U.S.), *see* territory.

unitary republic, see republic.

urban-rural, social characteristic of local or national populations, defined by predominant economic activities, "urban" referring to a group of largely nonagricultural pursuits, "rural" to agriculturally oriented employment patterns. The distinction is usually based on the country's own definition of urban, which may depend only upon the size (population) of a place or upon factors like employment, administrative status, density of housing, etc.

value added, also called value added by manufacture, the gross output value of a firm or industry minus the cost of inputs—raw materials, supplies, and payments to other firms—required to produce it. Value added is the portion of the sales value or gross output value that is actually created by the firm or industry. Value added generally includes labour costs, administrative costs, and operating profits.

The Nations of the World

Afghanistan

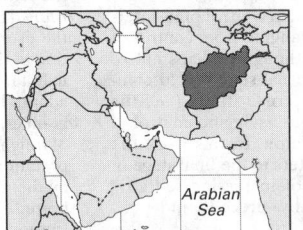

Official name[1]: Islamic Emirate of Afghanistan (Persian and Pashtu long-form names, n.a.).
Form of government: Islamic emirate.
Head of state and government: Leader of the faithful[2].
Capital: Kabul.
Official languages: Pashto; Dari (Persian).
Official religion: Islam.
Monetary unit: 1 afghani (Af) = 100 puls (puli); valuation (Sept. 25, 1998) 1 U.S.\$ = Af 4,750; 1 £ = Af 8,087.

Area and population[3]

Regions	area sq mi	area sq km	population 1993 estimate
Central	11,657	30,192	3,481,400
East	9,802	25,386	1,567,500
East-central	21,739	56,304	685,600
North	29,520	76,457	2,421,900
North-east	30,233	78,304	2,518,300
South	19,525	50,569	1,659,600
South-west	77,000	199,430	2,188,700
West	46,187	119,624	1,497,500
TOTAL	251,825[4]	625,225[4]	16,020,500

Demography

Population (1998): 24,792,000[5].
Density (1998): persons per sq mi 98.4, persons per sq km 38.0.
Urban-rural (1995): urban 20.0%; rural 80.0%.
Sex distribution (1997): male 51.50%; female 48.50%.
Age breakdown (1997): under 15, 43.0%; 15–29, 27.4%; 30–44, 16.2%; 45–59, 8.9%; 60–74, 3.8%; 75 and over, 0.7%.
Population projection: (2000) 26,668,000; (2010) 34,098,000.
Doubling time: 24 years.
Ethnic composition (early 1990[5]): Pashtun 38%; Tajik 25%; Ḥazāra 19%; Uzbek 6%; Chahar Aimak, Turkmen, Balochi, and other 12%.
Religious affiliation (1990): Sunnī Muslim 84%; Shī'ī Muslim 15%; other 1%.
Major cities (1988): Kabul 700,000[6]; Kandahār (Qandahār) 225,500; Herāt 177,300; Mazār-e Sharīf 130,600.

Vital statistics

Birth rate per 1,000 population (1997): 43.0 (world avg. 25.0).
Death rate per 1,000 population (1997): 18.0 (world avg. 9.3).
Natural increase rate per 1,000 population (1997): 25.0 (world avg. 15.7).
Total fertility rate (avg. births per childbearing woman; 1997): 6.1.
Life expectancy at birth (1996): male 46.4 years; female 45.2 years.

National economy

Budget (1987–88). Revenue: Af 79,800,000,000. Expend.: Af 105,800,000,000.
Gross national product (1996): U.S.\$5,666,000,000 (U.S.\$250 per capita).

Structure of gross domestic product and labour force

	1992–93 in value Af '000,000[7]	% of total value	labour force	% of labour force
Agriculture	61,400	48.5	4,276,100	67.2
Manufacturing	32,800	25.9	298,900	4.7
Mining and public utilities				
Construction	12,400	9.8	81,400	1.3
Transp. and commun.	5,300	4.2	139,900	2.2
Trade	12,400	9.8	420,600	6.6
Pub. admin., services	2,400	1.9	929,300	14.6
Other			214,300	3.4
TOTAL	126,700	100.0[8]	6,360,500	100.0

Public debt (external, outstanding; 1993): U.S.\$5,381,000,000.
Production (metric tons except as noted). Agriculture, forestry, fishing (1997): wheat 1,700,000, corn (maize) 360,000, grapes 330,000, rice 300,000, potatoes 235,000, barley 180,000, almonds 9,000, opium poppy 600–3,000; livestock (number of live animals) 14,300,000 sheep, 2,200,000 goats, 1,500,000 cattle, 300,000 horses, 265,000 camels; roundwood (1995) 7,680,000 cu m; fish catch (1994) 1,300. Mining and quarrying (1995): salt 13,000; copper 5,000; gypsum 3,000; barite 2,000. Manufacturing (by production value in Af '000,000; 1988–89): food products 4,019; leather and fur products 2,678; textiles 1,760; printing and publishing 1,070; industrial chemicals (including fertilizers) 1,053; footwear 999. Construction (Af '000,000; 1985): 1,094. Energy production (consumption): electricity (kW-hr; 1994) 687,000,000 (815,000,000); coal

(metric tons; 1994) 6,000 (6,000); petroleum products (metric tons; 1994) none (280,000); natural gas (cu m; 1994) 175,032,000 (175,032,000).
Population economically active (1994)[9]: total 5,557,000; activity rate of total population 29.4% (participation rates: female 9.0%; unemployed 3.4%).

Consumer price index (1990 = 100)

	1988	1989	1990	1991	1992	1993	1994
Consumer price index	64.3	83.1	100.0	266.0	420.8	563.9	676.7

Tourism: receipts (1993) U.S.\$1,000,000; expenditures (1987) U.S.\$1,000,000.
Land use (1994): forested 2.9%; meadows and pastures 46.0%; agricultural and under permanent cultivation 12.4%; other 38.7%.

Foreign trade[10]

Balance of trade (current prices)

	1989	1990	1991	1992	1993	1994
U.S.\$'000,000	−249	−351	−265	−236	+234	−306
% of total	29.1%	38.7%	27.4%	24.7%	15.5%	34.1%

Imports (1994): U.S.\$602,000,000 (1989–90; machinery 37.7%, basic manufactures 18.3%, minerals and fuels 10.9%). *Major import sources* (1994): Japan 14.4%; Singapore 7.1%; China 5.2%; India 5.0%; Pakistan 4.6%.
Exports (1994): U.S.\$296,000,000 (1992; dried fruits and nuts 51.3%, carpets and rugs 13.1%, karakul wool and hides 4.9%, cotton 1.4%). *Major export destinations* (1994): Belgium-Luxembourg 3.8%; Pakistan 3.7%.

Transport and communications

Transport. Railroads (1995): length 25 km. Roads (1995): total length 21,000 km (paved 13%). Vehicles (1995): passenger cars 34,000; trucks and buses 31,000. Merchant marine: none. Air transport (1993): passenger-km 197,000,000; metric ton-km cargo 11,000,000[11]; airports (1996) 3.

Communications

Medium	date	unit	number	units per 1,000 persons
Daily newspapers	1994	circulation	216,000	11.0
Radio	1996	receivers	1,670,000	73.7
Television	1995	receivers	180,000	10.0
Telephones	1995	main lines	29,000	1.4

Education and health

Educational attainment (1980). Population age 25 and over having: no formal schooling 88.5%; some primary education 6.8%; complete primary 0.3%; some secondary 1.2%; postsecondary 3.2%. *Literacy* (1995): Total population age 15 and over literate 31.5%; males 47.2%; females 15.0%.

Education (1994–95)

	schools	teachers	students	student/ teacher ratio
Primary	1,753[12]	20,055[13]	1,312,197	...
Secondary	819[12]	17,548[13]	512,851	...
Voc., teacher tr.	33[12]			...
Higher[14]	5[15]	444[16]	9,367[16]	21.1[16]

Health (1988–93): physicians 2,347 (1 per 6,690 persons); hospital beds 5,331 (1 per 2,945 persons); infant mortality rate (1997) 147.0.
Food (1992): daily per capita caloric intake 1,523 (vegetable products 89%, animal products 11%); 62% of FAO recommended minimum requirement.

Military

Total active duty personnel (1996): no identifiable military units appear to represent the central government. *Military expenditure as percentage of GNP* (1990): 15.0% (world 4.4%); per capita expenditure U.S.\$29.

[1]Taleban gained effective control of nearly the entire country in August 1998. [2]Title of the supreme leader of the Taleban. [3]In 1993 an administrative reorganization created 32 provinces (*wilayah*), but detailed breakdown of area and population is unavailable. [4]Detailed breakdown does not account for 6,162 sq mi (15,960 sq km), which is included in the total. [5]Including Afghan refugees estimated to number about 1.1 million in Pakistan and about 1.4 million in Iran. [6]1993 estimate. [7]At prices of 1978–79. [8]Detail does not add to total given because of rounding. [9]Based on settled population only; unemployment data is 1990. [10]Exports are f.o.b. and imports are c.i.f. [11]1992. [12]1992–93. [13]1993–94. [14]Includes universities only. [15]1988–89. [16]1989–90.

Internet resources for further information:
- Afghanistan Today http://frankenstein.worldweb.net/afghan
- Arthur Paul Afghanistan Collection http://www.unomaha.edu/~world/cas/collection.html

Albania

Official name: Republika e Shqipërisë
(Republic of Albania).
Form of government: unitary multiparty
republic with one legislative house
(People's Assembly [155])[1].
Chief of state: President.
Head of government: Prime Minister.
Capital: Tirana (Tiranë).
Official language: Albanian.
Official religion: none.
Monetary unit: 1 lek = 100 qindars;
valuation (Sept. 25, 1998)
1 U.S.$ = 147.15 leks;
1 £ = 250.52 leks.

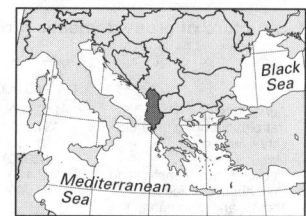

Area and population

Provinces	Capitals	area sq mi	area sq km	population 1990 estimate
Berat	Berat	396	1,027	180,489
Dibër	Peshkopi	605	1,568	153,775
Durrës	Durrës	327	848	251,029
Elbasan	Elbasan	572	1,481	248,676
Fier	Fier	454	1,175	251,115
Gjirokastër	Gjirokastër	439	1,137	67,392
Gramsh	Gramsh	268	695	44,791
Kolonjë	Ersekë	311	805	25,291
Korçë	Korçë	842	2,181	218,219
Krujë	Krujë	234	607	109,876
Kukës	Kukës	514	1,330	104,731
Lezhë	Lezhë	185	479	63,505
Librazhd	Librazhd	391	1,013	73,871
Lushnjë	Lushnjë	275	712	137,830
Mat	Burrel	397	1,028	78,754
Mirditë	Rrëshen	335	867	51,701
Përmet	Përmet	359	929	40,419
Pogradec	Pogradec	280	725	73,333
Pukë	Pukë	399	1,034	50,286
Sarandë	Sarandë	424	1,097	89,459
Shkodër	Shkodër	976	2,528	241,549
Skrapar	Çorovoda	299	775	47,605
Tepelenë	Tepelenë	315	817	51,022
Tiranë	Tirana (Tiranë)	478	1,238	374,483
Tropojë	Bajram	403	1,043	45,965
Vlorë	Vlorë	621	1,609	180,725
TOTAL		11,100[2]	28,748	3,255,891

Demography

Population (1998): 3,331,000.
Density (1998): persons per sq mi 300.1, persons per sq km 115.9.
Urban-rural (1995): urban 42.4%; rural 57.6%.
Sex distribution (1995): male 49.50%; female 50.50%.
Age breakdown (1996): under 15, 34.1%; 15–29, 24.2%; 30–44, 20.1%; 45–59, 12.4%; 60–74, 7.5%; 75 and over, 1.7%.
Population projection: (2000) 3,401,000; (2010) 3,784,000.
Doubling time: 47 years.
Ethnic composition (1989): Albanian 98.0%; Greek 1.8%; Macedonian 0.2%.
Religious affiliation (1995): Muslim 70.0%; Albanian Orthodox 7.3%; other Orthodox 4.0%; Roman Catholic 5.2%; other 13.5%.
Major cities (1990): Tirana 243,000; Durrës 85,400; Elbasan 83,300.

Vital statistics

Birth rate per 1,000 population (1996): 22.6 (world avg. 25.0).
Death rate per 1,000 population (1996): 7.7 (world avg. 9.3).
Natural increase rate per 1,000 population (1996): 14.9 (world avg. 15.7).
Total fertility rate (avg. births per childbearing woman; 1996): 2.7.
Marriage rate per 1,000 population (1990): 8.9.
Divorce rate per 1,000 population (1990): 0.8.
Life expectancy at birth (1995): male 68.5 years; female 74.3 years.
Major causes of death per 100,000 population: n.a.; however, principal health problems in the mid-1990s included malnutrition (especially of children).

National economy

Budget (1995). Revenue: 54,024,000,000 leks (taxes 73.6%, of which excise taxes 19.3%, social security contributions 17.1%, import duties and export taxes 11.5%, value-added tax 10.3%; nontax revenue 26.4%). Expenditures: 77,134,000,000 leks (current expenditure 76.1%, of which personnel costs 23.9%, social security 18.2%, government operations and maintenance 15.9%, service of public debt 6.5%; capital expenditure 23.9%).
Public debt (1996): U.S.$672,500,000.
Production (metric tons except as noted). Agriculture, forestry, fishing (1996): cereals 537,600; vegetables and melons 459,500 (mainly beans, peas, onions, tomatoes, cabbage, eggplants, and carrots), potatoes 137,000; livestock (number of live animals) 2,500,000 sheep, 1,900,000 goats, 850,000 cattle, 4,300,000 poultry; roundwood (1994) 409,000 cu m; fish catch (1995) 3,488. Mining and quarrying (1995): copper ore 258,000; chromite 243,000. Manufacturing (value of production in '000 leks; 1993)[3]: food products 824,000; textiles 263,000; clothing 139,000. Construction (1990): 12,428 units. Energy production (consumption): electricity (kW-hr; 1994) 3,903,000,000 (3,903,000,000); coal (metric tons; 1994) 179,000 (179,000); crude petroleum (barrels; 1994) 3,527,800 (2,703,500); petroleum products (metric tons; 1994) 261,000 (261,000); natural gas (cu m; 1994) 77,000,000 (77,000,000).
Gross national product (1996): U.S.$2,705,000,000 (U.S.$820 per capita).

Structure of gross domestic product and labour force

	1994 in value '000,000 leks	1994 % of total value	1995 labour force	1995 % of labour force
Agriculture	92,254	55.5	778,000	58.7
Manufacturing, mining, public utilities	20,966	12.6	95,000	7.2
Construction	15,732	9.5	21,000	1.6
Transp. and commun.	5,546	3.3	30,000	2.3
Trade			62,000	4.7
Pub. admin., defense	31,799	19.1	...	...
Services			79,000	6.0
Other	—	—	260,000[4]	19.6
TOTAL	166,297	100.0	1,325,000	100.0[2]

Population economically active (1995): total 1,325,000; activity rate of total population 63.0% (1993; participation rates: ages 15–64, 90.2%; female 49.0%; unemployed 12.9%).

Price and earnings indexes (December 1993 = 100)

	1993	1994	1995	1996	1997
Consumer price index	90.9	111.4	120.0	135.3	180.2
Earnings index	...	...	...	...	...

Household income and expenditure. Average household size (1989) 4.7; annual income per rural household 80,835 leks (U.S.$ value, n.a.); sources of income: wages 53.0%, transfers from relatives abroad 21.5%, social insurance 11.4%; expenditure: n.a.

Foreign trade

Balance of trade (current prices)

	1991	1992	1993	1994	1995	1996	1997
'000,000 leks	−208	−470	−490	−460	−475	−678	−535
% of total	58.8%	77.1%	68.7%	62.0%	53.7%	58.2%	62.8%

Imports (1995): U.S.$679,000,000 (food, beverages, live animals, and tobacco 22.3%; manufactured goods 21.2%; machinery and transport equipment 20.3%; mineral fuels 9.7%; chemicals 6.8%). *Major import sources:* Italy 37.9%; Greece 26.8%; Bulgaria 8.0%; Germany 4.6%; Turkey 4.1%.
Exports (1995): U.S.$205,000,000 (miscellaneous manufactured articles 45.6%; crude materials 24.7%; manufactured goods 14.1%). *Major export destinations:* Italy 51.5%; Greece 9.9%; Turkey 6.2%; Belgium-Luxembourg 5.4%.

Transport and communications

Transport. Railroads: length (1996) 670 km; passenger-km 197,000,000; metric ton-km cargo 428,000. Roads (1995): total length 15,500 km (paved 30%). Vehicles (1995): passenger cars 58,682; trucks and buses 34,441. Merchant marine (1992): vessels (100 gross tons and over) 24; total deadweight tonnage 80,954. Air transport (1995): passenger-km 3,519,000; short ton-mi 223,000, metric ton-km 325,000; airports (1997) with scheduled flights 1.

Communications

Medium	date	unit	number	units per 1,000 persons
Daily newspapers	1995	circulation	185,000	54
Radio	1996	receivers	550,000	157
Television	1995	receivers	300,000	89
Telephones	1995	main lines	42,000	12
Facsimile machines	1995	units	600	0.2

Education and health

Educational attainment (1989). Population age 10 and over having: primary education 65.3%; secondary 29.1%; higher 5.6%. *Literacy* (1989): total population age 10 and over literate 91.8%; males 95.5%; females 88.0%.

Education (1993)

	schools	teachers	students	student/ teacher ratio
Primary (age 6–13)	1,777	32,098	535,713	16.7
Secondary (age 14–17)	47[5]	4,149	73,259	17.7
Voc., teacher tr.[5]	466	7,390	138,000	18.7
Higher	8[5]	1,774	30,185	17.0

Health (1994): physicians 6,154 (1 per 552 persons); hospital beds 10,200 (1 per 333 persons); infant mortality rate per 1,000 live births (1996) 49.2.
Food (1995): daily per capita caloric intake 2,324 (vegetable products 64%, animal products 36%); 96% of FAO recommended minimum requirement.

Military

Total active duty personnel (1996): 54,000 (army 83.3%, navy 4.6%, air force 12.1%). *Military expenditure as percentage of GNP* (1995): 1.1% (world 2.8%); per capita expenditure U.S.$14.

[1]A transitional constitution was adopted on April 29, 1991. The proposed text of a permanent constitution was rejected in a referendum on Nov. 6, 1994. [2]Detail does not add to total given because of rounding. [3]Value of production in constant prices of 1990. [4]Includes 171,000 undistributed unemployed. [5]1990.

Internet resources for further information:
• UNDP Human Development Report—Albania 1996
  http://www.undp.org/undp/rbec/nhdr/1996/albania
• Albanian Ministry of Foreign Affairs
  http://www.tirana.al/minjash/

Algeria

Official name: Al-Jumhūrīyah al-Jazā'irīyah ad-Dīmuqrāṭīyah ash-Sha'bīyah (Arabic) (Democratic and Popular Republic of Algeria).
Form of government: multiparty republic with two legislative bodies (Council of Nation [144][1]; National People's Assembly [380]).
Chief of state: President.
Head of government: Prime Minister.
Capital: Algiers.
Official language: Arabic.
Official religion: Islam.
Monetary unit: 1 Algerian dinar (DA) = 100 centimes; valuation (Sept. 25, 1998) 1 U.S.$ = DA 57.33; 1 £ = DA 97.60.

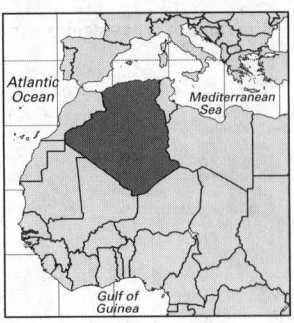

Population (1987 census)

Provinces	population	Provinces	population	Provinces	population
Adrar	217,678	Djelfa	494,494	Oum el-Bouaghi	403,936
Aïn Defla	537,256	Ghardaïa	216,140	Relizane	544,877
Aïn Temouchent	274,990	Guelma	353,309	Saïda	235,494
Alger	1,690,191	Illizi	18,930	Sétif	1,000,694
Annaba	455,888	Jijel	472,312	Sidi bel-Abbès	446,277
Batna	752,617	Khenchela	246,541	Skikda	622,510
El-Bayadh	153,254	Laghouat	212,388	Souk Ahras	296,077
Béchar	185,346	Mascara	566,901	Tamanrasset	95,822
Bejaïa	700,952	Médéa	652,863	Et-Tarf	275,315
Biskra	430,202	Mila	511,605	Tébessa	410,233
Blida	702,188	Mostaganem	505,932	Tiaret	575,794
Bordj Bou Arreridj	424,828	M'Sila	604,693	Tindouf	16,428
Bouira	526,900	Naâma	113,700	Tipaza	620,151
Boumerdes	650,975	Oran	932,473	Tissemsilt	228,120
Ech-Chleff	684,192	Ouargla	284,454	Tizi Ouzou	936,948
Constantine	664,303	El-Oued	376,909	Tlemcen	714,862
				TOTAL	23,038,942[2]

Demography

Area: 919,595 sq mi, 2,381,741 sq km.
Population (1998): 30,045,000.
Density (1998): persons per sq mi 32.7, persons per sq km 12.6.
Urban-rural (1995): urban 55.8%; rural 44.2%.
Sex distribution (1995): male 50.60%; female 49.40%.
Age breakdown (1995): under 15, 39.0%; 15–29, 29.6%; 30–44, 17.3%; 45–59, 8.2%; 60–74, 4.6%; 75 and over, 1.3%.
Population projection: (2000) 31,345,000; (2010) 37,943,000.
Doubling time: 31 years.
Ethnic composition (1992): Arab c. 80%; Berber c. 20%, of which Kabyle c. 13%, Shawia c. 6%.
Religious affiliation (1990): Muslim 99.9%, of which Sunnī 99.5%, Ibāḍīyah 0.4%; Roman Catholic 0.1%.
Major cities (1987): Algiers (1995) 2,168,000 (metro area; 3,702,000); Oran 609,823; Constantine 440,842; Annaba 222,518; Batna 181,601.

Vital statistics

Birth rate per 1,000 population (1996): 28.5 (world avg. 25.0).
Death rate per 1,000 population (1996): 5.9 (world avg. 9.3).
Natural increase rate per 1,000 population (1996): 22.6 (world avg. 15.7).
Total fertility rate (avg. births per childbearing woman; 1996): 3.6.
Marriage rate per 1,000 population (1996): 5.7.
Life expectancy at birth (1996): male 67.2 years; female 69.5 years.
Notified cases of infectious diseases per 100,000 population (1990): hepatitis 15.1; typhoid fever 11.3; measles 7.2; cholera 5.2; tuberculosis 4.8.

National economy

Budget (1995). Revenue: DA 600,900,000,000 (export taxes on hydrocarbons 50.8%; value-added taxes 16.1%). Expenditures: DA 627,700,000,000 (current expenditure 70.8%; development expenditure 23.1%; other 6.1%).
Land use (1994): forested 1.6%; meadows and pastures 13.3%; agricultural and under permanent cultivation 3.4%; other (mostly desert) 81.7%.
Production (metric tons except as noted). Agriculture, forestry, fishing (1996): wheat 2,800,000, barley 1,690,000, potatoes 1,150,000, tomatoes 718,000, dates 360,600, olives 313,300, onions 312,900, oranges 236,700, grapes 132,300; livestock (number of live animals) 17,565,000 sheep, 2,895,000 goats; roundwood (1995) 2,517,000 cu m; fish catch (1995) 106,246. Mining and quarrying (1996): iron ore (gross weight) 2,245,000; phosphate rock (gross weight) 1,051,000; mercury 10,669 flasks. Manufacturing (value added in U.S.$'000,000; 1994): food products 686; iron and steel 594; fabricated metal products 489; cement, bricks, and tiles 358; transport equipment 333; electrical machinery 227. Construction (dwellings completed; 1995): 166,900. Energy production (consumption): electricity (kW-hr; 1994) 19,888,000,000 (18,764,000,000); coal (metric tons; 1994) 20,000 (1,280,000); crude petroleum (barrels; 1995) 278,860,000 ([1994] 160,307,000); petroleum products (metric tons; 1994) 39,543,000 (10,862,000); natural gas (cu m; 1995) 60,600,000,000 ([1994] 19,209,000,000).
Household income and expenditure. Average household size (1992) 6.9; income per household: n.a.; sources of income (1995): wages and salaries 43.1%, self-employment 38.3%, transfers 18.6%; expenditure (1988): food and beverages 52.3%, transportation and communications 12.0%, clothing and footwear 8.6%, housing and energy 6.7%, other 20.4%.
Gross national product (1996): U.S.$43,726,000,000 (U.S.$1,520 per capita).

Structure of gross domestic product and labour force

| | 1994 | | 1990 | |
	in value DA '000,000	% of total value	labour force	% of labour force
Agriculture	140,500	9.5	907,490	15.9
Petroleum and natural gas	334,200[3]	22.7[3]	55,000	1.0
Other mining	2,200	0.2	...	...
Manufacturing	137,000[3]	9.3[3]	646,390	11.3
Public utilities, construction	182,100	12.4	651,370	11.4
Pub. admin., defense	187,000	12.7	1,318,370	23.1
Transp. and commun.			252,230	4.4
Trade	488,400[4]	33.2[4]	444,970	7.8
Other			1,435,180[5]	25.1[5]
TOTAL	1,471,400	100.0	5,711,000	100.0

Population economically active (1994): total 6,814,000; activity rate of population 24.8% (participation rates [1987] ages 15–64, 44.3%; female 9.2%; unemployed [1995] more than 28%).

Price and earnings indexes (1990 = 100)

	1991	1992	1993	1994	1995	1996	1997
Consumer price index	125.9	165.8	199.8	257.8	340.8	414.6	435.0[6]
Earnings index[7]	131.1	170.2	199.1	203.8	224.2	246.6	...

Public debt (external, outstanding; 1996): U.S.$30,808,000.
Tourism: (1995) receipts from visitors U.S.$27,000,000; expenditures by nationals abroad U.S.$135,000,000.

Foreign trade[8]

Balance of trade (current prices)

	1991	1992	1993	1994	1995	1996
U.S.$'000,000	+4,107	+2,489	+1,337	−1,005	+308	+3,740
% of total	21.1%	12.6%	7.1%	5.5%	1.5%	18.0%

Imports (1994): U.S.$9,599,000,000 (food 29.4%, of which cereals and preparations 13.8%; nonelectrical machinery 14.7%, iron and steel 9.5%). *Major import sources* (1995): France 29.6%; Spain 10.5%; Italy 8.2%; U.S. 8.0%; Germany 5.6%.
Exports (1994): U.S.$8,594,000,000 (crude petroleum 45.7%, natural gas 31.2%, refined petroleum 18.8%). *Major export destinations* (1995): Italy 18.8%; U.S. 14.8%; France 11.8%; Spain 8.0%; Germany 7.9%.

Transport and communications

Transport. Railroads (1995): route length 2,965 mi, 4,772 km; (1994) passenger-km 2,524,000,000; metric ton-km cargo 2,400,000,000. Roads (1995): total length 102,424 km (paved 69%). Vehicles (1995): passenger cars 871,000; trucks and buses 566,000. Air transport (1996)[9]: passenger-km 2,644,000,000; metric ton-km cargo 14,826,000; airports (1996) 28.

Communications

Medium	date	unit	number	units per 1,000 persons
Daily newspapers	1994	circulation	1,440,000	52
Radio	1996	receivers	3,500,000	122
Television	1995	receivers	2,000,000	71
Telephones	1995	main lines	1,176,300	42
Cellular telephones	1995	subscribers	4,700	0.2
Facsimile machines	1995	units	5,200	0.2
Personal computers	1995	units	85,000	3.0

Education and health

Educational attainment (1989). Percentage of economically active population age 16 and over having: no formal schooling 38.2%; Qur'ānic education 0.9%; primary 20.8%; secondary 11.1%; vocational 19.7%; higher 9.3%.
Literacy (1995): total population age 15 and over literate 10,531,000 (61.6%); males literate 6,368,000 (73.9%); females literate 4,163,000 (49.0%).

Education (1995–96)

	schools	teachers	students	student/ teacher ratio
Primary (age 6–11)	17,186	169,010	4,617,000	27.3
Secondary (age 12–17)	3,954	150,397	2,544,864	16.9
Higher[10]	...	14,475	233,019	16.1

Health (1994): physicians 25,796 (1 per 1,066 persons); hospital beds 53,612 (1 per 513 persons); infant mortality rate per 1,000 live births (1996) 48.7.
Food (1995): daily per capita caloric intake 3,042 (vegetable products 90%, animal products 10%); 127% of FAO recommended minimum requirement.

Military

Total active duty personnel (1996): 123,700 (army 86.5%, navy 5.4%, air force 8.1%). *Military expenditure as percentage of GNP* (1995): 3.2% (world 2.8%); per capita expenditure U.S.$43.

[1]Includes 48 nonelected seats appointed by the president. [2]De facto population. [3]Petroleum and natural gas includes (and Manufacturing excludes) refined petroleum and manufacture of hydrocarbons. [4]Includes import duties of DA 119,100,000,000. [5]Includes 1,141,278 unemployed. [6]Average of 2nd quarter. [7]Public workers only; all data based on January averages of gross income. [8]Imports c.i.f.; exports f.o.b. [9]Air Algérie. [10]1994–95.

Internet resources for further information:
• **Office National des Statistiques (French)**
  http://www.ons.dz/
• **Permanent Mission of Algeria to the UN**
  http://www.algeria-un.org/nspage.html

Andorra

Official name: Principat d'Andorra;
(Principality of Andorra).
Form of government: parliamentary
coprincipality with one legislative
house (General Council [28]).
Chiefs of state: President of France;
Bishop of Urgell, Spain.
Head of government: Head of
Government.
Capital: Andorra la Vella.
Official language: Catalan.
Official religion: none[1].
Monetary unit: There is no local
currency of issue; the French franc
and Spanish peseta are both in
circulation. 1 franc (F) = 100 centimes;
1 peseta (Pta) = 100 céntimos.
Valuation (Sept. 25, 1998)
1 U.S.$ = F 5.60, 1 £ = F 9.53;
1 U.S.$ = Ptas 141.88,
1 £ = Ptas 241.55.

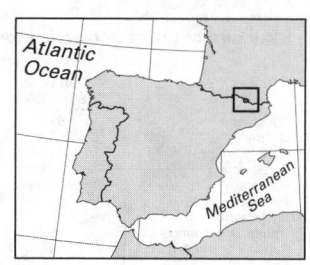

Area and population

Parishes	Capitals	area sq mi	area sq km	population 1997[2] estimate
Andorra la Vella	Andorra la Vella	49[3]	127[3]	21,721
Canillo	Canillo	74	191	2,518
Encamp	Encamp			9,800
La Massana	La Massana	25	65	5,785
Les Escaldes–Engordany	—	3	3	15,182
Ordino	Ordino	33	85	1,931
Sant Julià de Lòria	Sant Julià de Lòria	3	3	7,542
TOTAL		181	468	64,479

Demography

Population (1998): 65,200.
Density (1998): persons per sq mi 360.2, persons per sq km 139.3.
Urban-rural (1995): urban 62.5%; rural 37.5%.
Sex distribution (1996): male 52.71%; female 47.29%.
Age breakdown (1993): under 15, 16.3%; 15–29, 27.7%; 30–44, 27.2%; 45–59, 15.1%; 60–74, 9.9%; 75 and over, 3.8%.
Population projection: (2000) 66,000; (2010) 72,000.
Doubling time: 92 years.
Ethnic composition (by nationality; 1997): Spanish 44.4%; Andorran 20.2%; Portuguese 10.7%; French 6.8%; other nationality 6.6%; undeclared nationality 11.3%.
Religious affiliation (1992): Roman Catholic 92.0%; Protestant 0.5%; Jewish 0.4%; other 7.1%.
Major cities (1997): Andorra la Vella 21,984[4]; Les Escaldes 15,182; Encamp 9,800.

Vital statistics

Birth rate per 1,000 population (1996): 10.9[5] (world avg. 25.0).
Death rate per 1,000 population (1996): 3.1[5] (world avg. 9.3).
Natural increase rate per 1,000 population (1996): 7.8[5] (world avg. 15.7).
Total fertility rate (avg. births per childbearing woman; 1996): 1.1.
Marriage rate per 1,000 population (1995): 2.2.
Life expectancy at birth (1995): male 75.6 years; female 81.7 years.
Major causes of death per 100,000 population: n.a.; however, health problems are those of a developed country—cardiovascular disease, hypertension, malignant neoplasms (cancers).

National economy

Budget (1996). Revenue: Ptas 25,449,000,000 (indirect taxes on commodities 76.6%, property income 11.4%). Expenditures: Ptas 25,795,000,000 (administrative costs 26.2%, capital expenditures 24.0%, education and recreation 15.9%, general public services 8.7%, social welfare 5.1%, health 3.3%).
Public debt (1994): about U.S.$125,000,000.
Production. Agriculture (1996): tobacco 1,023 metric tons; other traditional crops include hay, potatoes, and grapes; livestock (number of live animals; 1996) 1,965 sheep[6], 1,141 cattle, 682 horses. Quarrying: small amounts of marble are quarried. Manufacturing (value of recorded exports in Ptas '000; 1996): motor vehicles and parts 1,190,000; electrical machinery and apparatus 779,000; clothing 778,000; newspapers and periodicals 613,000; furniture 276,000; other products include cigars and cigarettes and liqueurs. Construction (approved new building construction; 1996): 175,000 sq m. Energy production (consumption): electricity (kW-hr; 1996) 109,000,000 (335,000,000); coal, none (n.a.); crude petroleum, none (n.a.); petroleum products, none (n.a.); natural gas, none (n.a.).
Tourism (1997): about 6,000,000 visitors; number of hotels (1996) 222.
Population economically active (1996)[7]: total 28,071; activity rate of total population 43.5% (participation rates: ages 15–64, 59.4%; female, n.a.; unemployed, unofficially, none[8]).

Price and earnings indexes (1991 = 100)

	1992	1993	1994	1995	1996	1997	1998[9]
Consumer price index[10]	105.9	110.8	116.1	121.4	125.8	128.2	130.2
Annual earnings index[11]	107.6	114.4	117.1	121.2	127.3	...	...

Gross domestic product (1996): U.S.$1,206,000,000 (U.S.$18,790 per capita)[12].

Structure of labour force[7]

	1996 labour force	1996 % of labour force
Agriculture } Mining	192	0.7
Manufacturing	1,233	4.4
Construction	4,598	16.4
Public utilities	...	...
Transp. and commun.	...	...
Trade	5,438	19.4
Restaurants, hotels	5,367	19.1
Finance, real estate, insurance	1,254	4.5
Pub. admin., defense	3,452	12.3
Services	5,005	17.8
Other	1,532	5.4
TOTAL	28,071	100.0

Land use (1994): forested 22.0%; meadows and pastures 56.0%; agricultural and under permanent cultivation 2.0%; other 20.0%.
Household income and expenditure. n.a.

Foreign trade

Balance of trade (current prices)

	1991	1992	1993	1994	1995	1996
Ptas '000,000	...	−112,179	−113,282	−117,786	−125,507	−129,579
% of total	...	93.0%	91.1%	89.7%	91.1%	91.7%

Imports (1996): Ptas 135,460,000,000 (food, beverages, and tobacco 29.0%; machinery and apparatus 14.1%; chemicals and chemical products 9.1%; transport equipment 7.6%; textiles and wearing apparel 7.6%; photographic and optical goods and watches and clocks 4.6%). *Major import sources:* Spain 40.9%; France 30.8%; Germany 4.3%; U.S. 4.0%; U.K. 3.9%.
Exports (1996): Ptas 5,881,000,000 (motor vehicles and parts 20.2%; electrical machinery and apparatus 13.2%; clothing 13.2%; newspapers and periodicals 10.4%; food and beverages 5.9%). *Major export destinations:* Spain 49.9%; France 39.4%; Germany 1.3%; Switzerland 1.3%.

Transport and communications

Transport. Railroads: none; however, both French and Spanish railways stop near the border. Roads (1994): total length 167 mi, 269 km (paved 74%). Vehicles (1996): passenger cars 35,358; trucks and buses 4,238. Merchant marine: vessels (100 gross tons and over) none. Airports (1997) with scheduled flights: none.

Communications

Medium	date	unit	number	units per 1,000 persons
Daily newspapers	1994	circulation	4,000	62
Radio	1996	receivers	10,000	156
Television	1993	receivers	20,000	315
Telephones	1996	main lines	30,964	480
Cellular telephones	1996	subscribers	5,343	83
Facsimile machines	1995	units	1,300	20

Education and health

Educational attainment (mid-1980s). Percentage of population age 15 and over having: no formal schooling 5.5%; primary education 47.3%; secondary education 21.6%; postsecondary education 24.9%; unknown 0.7%. *Literacy:* resident population is virtually 100% literate.

Education (1996–97)

	schools	teachers	students	student/ teacher ratio
Primary/Lower secondary (age 7–15)	12	...	5,424	...
Upper secondary	6	...	2,655	...
Higher	—	—	—	—

Health: physicians (1994) 132 (1 per 491 persons); hospital beds (1993) 114 (1 per 556 persons); infant mortality rate per 1,000 live births (1995) 7.7.
Food (1995)[13]: daily per capita caloric intake 3,463 (vegetable products 67%, animal products 33%); 139% of FAO recommended minimum requirement.

Military

Total active duty personnel (1996): none. France and Spain are responsible for Andorra's external security; a 32-person police force is assisted in alternate years by either French gendarmerie or Barcelona police.

---

[1]Roman Catholicism enjoys special recognition in accordance with Andorran tradition. [2]January 1. [3]Andorra la Vella includes Les Escaldes–Engordany and Sant Julià de Lòria. [4]1995. [5]Official government figures. [6]Large herds of sheep and goats from Spain and France feed in Andorra in the summer. [7]Labour force receiving wages only; total population economically active equals 31,775. [8]The restricted size of the indigenous labour force necessitated high levels of immigration in the late 1980s and early 1990s to serve the tourist trade; emigration exceeded immigration in 1994 and 1995 because of a labour force surplus. [9]May. [10]Consumer price index of Spain. [11]Per Andorran Office of Social Security. [12]Tourism (including winter-season sports, fairs, festivals, and income earned from low-duty imported manufactured items) and the banking system (of some importance as a tax haven for foreign financial investment and transactions) are the primary sources of GDP. [13]Composite values derived from Spanish and French food data.

Internet resources for further information:
• Andorra National Information Centre
  http://www.andorra.ad/cniauk.html
• The Principality of Andorra
  http://www.xmission.com/~dderhak/andorra.htm

Angola

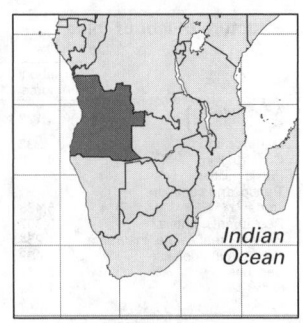

Official name: República de Angola (Republic of Angola).
Form of government: unitary multiparty republic with one legislative house (National Assembly [220])[1].
Head of state and government: President[2].
Capital: Luanda.
Official language: Portuguese.
Official religion: none.
Monetary unit: 1 readjusted Kwanza[3] = 100 lwei; valuation (Sept. 25, 1998) 1 U.S.$ = readjusted Kwanza 257,100; 1 £ = readjusted Kwanza 437,800.

Area and population

Provinces	Capitals	area sq mi	area sq km	population 1997 estimate[4]
Bengo	Caxito	12,112	31,371	...
Benguela	Benguela	12,273	31,788	...
Bié	Kuito	27,148	70,314	...
Cabinda	Cabinda	2,807	7,270	...
Cunene	N'Giva	34,495	89,342	...
Huambo	Huambo	13,233	34,274	...
Huíla	Lubango	28,958	75,002	...
Kuando Kubango	Menongue	76,853	199,049	...
Kuanza Norte	N'Dalatando	9,340	24,190	...
Kuanza Sul	Sumbe	21,490	55,660	...
Luanda	Luanda	934	2,418	...
Lunda Norte	Lucapa	39,685	102,783	...
Lunda Sul	Saurimo	17,625	45,649	...
Malanje	Malanje	37,684	97,602	...
Moxico	Lwena	86,110	223,023	...
Namibe	Namibe	22,447	58,137	...
Uíge	Uíge	22,663	58,698	...
Zaire	M'Banza Kongo	15,494	40,130	...
TOTAL		481,354[5]	1,246,700	10,624,000

Demography

Population (1998): 10,865,000.
Density (1997): persons per sq mi 22.6, persons per sq km 8.7.
Urban-rural (1996): urban 31.6%; rural 68.4%.
Sex distribution (1997): male 50.41%; female 49.59%.
Age breakdown (1997): under 15, 44.7%; 15–29, 25.8%; 30–44, 15.8%; 45–59, 8.9%; 60 and over, 4.8%.
Population projection: (2000) 11,487,000; (2010) 14,932,000.
Doubling time: 26 years.
Ethnic composition (1983): Ovimbundu 37.2%; Mbundu 21.6%; Kongo 13.2%; Luimbe-Nganguela 5.4%; Nyaneka-Humbe 5.4%; Chokwe 4.2%; Luvale (Luena) 3.6%; Luchazi 2.4%; Ambo (Ovambo) 2.4%; Lunda 1.2%; Mbunda 1.2%; other 2.2%.
Religious affiliation (1995): Christian 70.1%, of which Roman Catholic 50.7%, Protestant 14.6%; traditional beliefs 29.9%.
Major cities (1995): Luanda 2,081,000; Huambo 203,000[6]; Benguela 155,000[6]; Lobito 150,000[6]; Lubango 105,000[7].

Vital statistics

Birth rate per 1,000 population (1996): 44.6 (world avg. 25.0).
Death rate per 1,000 population (1996): 17.7 (world avg. 9.3).
Natural increase rate per 1,000 population (1996): 26.9 (world avg. 15.7).
Total fertility rate (avg. births per childbearing woman; 1996): 6.3.
Marriage rate per 1,000 population (1972): 4.5.
Life expectancy at birth (1996): male 44.7 years; female 49.1 years.
Major causes of death (percentage of total deaths; 1990): diarrheal diseases 25.8%; malaria 19.4%; cholera 7.3%; acute respiratory infections 6.8%.

National economy

Budget (1997). Revenue: NKz 694,600,000,000[3] (1994; tax revenue 98.4%, of which income taxes 71.8%, petroleum taxes 19.0%, import duties 4.3%; non-tax revenue 1.6%). Expenditures: NKz 521,300,000,000[3] (1994; defense and internal security 56.5%; administration 29.0%; health 3.4%; education 2.6%; other 8.5%).
Public debt (external, outstanding; 1996): U.S.$9,400,000,000.
Tourism: receipts (1994) U.S.$13,000,000; expenditures (1993) U.S.$66,000,000.
Household income and expenditure. Average household size (1980) 4.8; annual income per household: n.a.; sources of income: n.a.; expenditure: n.a.
Production (metric tons except as noted). Agriculture, forestry, fishing (1996): cassava 2,500,000, corn (maize) 398,000, sugarcane 330,000, bananas 295,000, sweet potatoes 190,000, dry beans 175,000, millet 102,000, palm oil 52,000, peanuts (groundnuts) 23,000, coffee 5,000; livestock (number of live animals) 3,309,000 cattle, 1,470,000 goats, 810,000 pigs, 245,000 sheep, 6,500,000 chickens; roundwood (1995) 7,005,000 cu m; fish catch (1995) 93,847. Mining and quarrying (1994): diamonds 1,350,000 carats. Manufacturing (1994): bread 15,082; wheat flour 4,496; sugar 3,190[8]; pasta 3,190[8]; corn flour 2,513; laundry soap 530; leather shoes 132,000 pairs[8]; beer 123,300 hectolitres; soft drinks 69,050 hectolitres[7]; fabric 3,038,000 sq m; matches 6,357,000 boxes[7]. Construction (value in NKz '000,000[3]; 1986): residential 608; nonresidential 1,977. Energy production (consumption): electricity (kW-hr; 1992) 1,855,000,000 (1,855,000,000); coal, none (none); crude petroleum (barrels; 1992) 192,634,000 (10,373,000); petroleum products (metric tons; 1992) 1,317,000 (346,000); natural gas (cu m; 1992) 166,576,000 (166,576,000).
Gross national product (1996): U.S.$2,972,000,000 (U.S.$270 per capita).

Structure of gross domestic product and labour force

	1994 in value NKz '000,000,000[3]	1994 % of total value	1991 labour force	1991 % of labour force
Agriculture	85,567	11.9	2,892,000	69.4
Mining	367,436	51.1		
Manufacturing	24,448	3.4		
Construction	11,505	1.6		
Finance	3,595	0.5	438,000	10.5
Trade	72,624	10.1		
Public utilities	—	—		
Transp. and commun.	15,100	2.1		
Pub. admin., defense	138,778	19.3		
Services			836,000	20.1
Other	...	...		
TOTAL	719,053	100.0	4,166,000	100.0

Population economically active (1991): total 4,166,000; activity rate of total population 40.3% (participation rates over age 10, 60.1%; female 38.4%).

Price and earnings indexes (1991 = 100)

	1991	1992	1993	1994
Consumer price index	100.0	595.0	11,534.0	123,639.0
Monthly earnings index	100.0	150.0	1,000.0	8,800.0

Land use (1995): forested 18.5%; meadows and pastures 43.3%; agricultural and under permanent cultivation 2.8%; other 35.4%.

Foreign trade

Balance of trade (current prices)

	1992	1993	1994	1995	1996
U.S.$'000,000	+1,845	+1,437	+1,563	+1,863	+2,879
% of total	31.6%	32.9%	35.0%	33.4%	39.6%

Imports (1995): U.S.$1,700,000,000 (1991; current consumption goods 50.2%, capital goods 20.2%, intermediate consumption goods 18.9%, transport equipment 6.8%). *Major import sources* (1991): Portugal 29.8%; U.S. 10.5%; France 9.7%; Japan 7.8%; Brazil 7.3%.
Exports (1995): U.S.$3,880,000,000 (mineral fuels 74.6%, diamonds 2.5%). *Major export destinations* (1991): U.S. 56.6%; Germany 5.6%; Brazil 4.9%; The Netherlands 4.2%; U.K. 3.4%; Belgium 3.3%.

Transport and communications

Transport. Railroads (1988): route length 1,739 mi, 2,798 km; passenger-mi 203,000,000, passenger-km 326,000,000; short ton-mi cargo 1,178,000,000, metric ton-km cargo 1,720,000,000. Roads (1995): total length 45,128 mi, 72,626 km (paved 25%). Vehicles (1995): passenger cars 197,000; trucks and buses 26,000. Merchant marine (1992): vessels (100 gross tons and over) 113; total deadweight tonnage 123,479. Air transport (1993)[9]: passenger-mi 589,000,000, passenger-km 948,000,000; short ton-mi cargo 77,000,000, metric ton-km cargo 113,000,000; airports (1997) with scheduled flights 17.

Communications

Medium	date	unit	number	units per 1,000 persons
Daily newspapers	1995	circulation	121,500[10]	11[10]
Radio	1995	receivers	450,000	39
Television	1995	receivers	550,000	48
Telephones	1995	main lines	60,000	5.2
Cellular telephones	1995	subscribers	2,000	0.2

Education and health

Educational attainment: n.a. *Literacy* (1990): percentage of population age 15 and over literate 41.7%; males literate 55.6%; females literate 28.5%.

Education (1990–91)

	schools	teachers	students	student/ teacher ratio
Primary (age 7–10)	6,308[11]	31,062	990,155	31.9
Secondary (age 11–16)	5,276[11]	5,138[12]	166,812	...
Voc., teacher tr.	...	566[12]	19,687	...
Higher	1[11]	439	6,534	14.9

Health (1990): physicians 662 (1 per 15,136 persons); hospital beds 11,857 (1 per 845 persons); infant mortality rate per 1,000 live births (1995) 142.1.
Food (1995): daily per capita caloric intake 1,927 (vegetable products 93%, animal products 7%); 82% of FAO recommended minimum requirement.

Military

Total active duty personnel (1997): 98,000 (army 89.5%, navy 1.4%, air force 9.1%). *Military expenditure as percentage of GNP* (1995): 3.1% (world 2.8%); per capita expenditure U.S.$22.

[1]National unity government of the two major political parties sworn in April 11, 1997, became ineffective on Aug. 31, 1998, when 70 UNITA members were expelled from the National Assembly. [2]President assisted by Prime Minister. [3]In July 1995 a readjusted Kwanza, equivalent to 1,000 New Kwanza (NKz) was introduced; previously in September 1990 the Kwanza (Kz) was replaced at par, by the New Kwanza (NKz). [4]Unified national estimates and projections based on sample surveys, partial censuses, and analysis of provincial vital statistics. [5]Detail does not add to total given because of rounding. [6]1983. [7]1984. [8]1989. [9]TAAG Airline only. [10]Circulation for four newspapers only. [11]1985–86. [12]1989–90.

Internet resources for further information:
• Official Home Page of the Republic of Angola http://www.angola.org/

Antigua and Barbuda

Official name: Antigua and Barbuda.
Form of government: constitutional
monarchy with two legislative
houses (Senate [17]; House of
Representatives [17[1]]).
Chief of state: British Monarch
represented by Governor-General.
Head of government: Prime Minister.
Capital: Saint John's.
Official language: English.
Official religion: none.
Monetary unit: 1 Eastern Caribbean
dollar (EC$) = 100 cents; valuation
(Sept. 25, 1998) 1 U.S.$ = EC$2.70;
1 £ = EC$4.60.

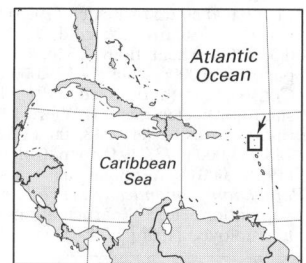

Area and population	area		population
	sq mi	sq km	1991 census
Parishes[2]			
Saint George	9.3	24.1	4,473
Saint John's	28.5	73.8	35,635
Saint Mary	22.0	57.0	5,303
Saint Paul	18.5	47.9	6,117
Saint Peter	12.7	32.9	3,622
Saint Phillip	17.0	44.0	2,964
Islands[2]			
Barbuda	62.0	160.6	1,241
Redonda	0.5	1.3	[3]
TOTAL	170.5	441.6	59,355[4]

Demography

Population (1998): 69,100[5].
Density (1998): persons per sq mi 405.3, persons per sq km 156.5.
Urban-rural (1995): urban 36.5%; rural 63.5%.
Sex distribution (1991): male 48.20%; female 51.80%.
Age breakdown (1991): under 15, 30.4%; 15–29, 27.8%; 30–44, 20.5%; 45–59, 10.2%; 60–74, 7.7%; 75 and over, 3.4%.
Population projection: (2000) 70,000; (2010) 71,000.
Doubling time: 50 years.
Ethnic composition (1994): black 91.3%; mixed 3.7%; white 2.4%; Syrian/Lebanese 0.6%; Indo-Pakistani 0.4%; Amerindian 0.3%; other 1.3%.
Religious affiliation (1991): Protestant 73.7%, of which Anglican 32.1%, Moravian 12.0%, Methodist 9.1%, Seventh-day Adventist 8.8%; Roman Catholic 10.8%; Jehovah's Witness 1.2%; Rastafarian 0.8%; other religion/no religion/not stated 13.5%.
Major cities (1991): Saint John's 22,342.[6]

Vital statistics

Birth rate per 1,000 population (1995): 20.9 (world avg. 25.0); (1988) legitimate 23.4%; illegitimate 76.6%.
Death rate per 1,000 population (1995): 6.7 (world avg. 9.3).
Natural increase rate per 1,000 population (1995): 14.2 (world avg. 15.7).
Total fertility rate (avg. births per childbearing woman; 1996): 1.7.
Marriage rate per 1,000 population (1988): 4.9.
Divorce rate per 1,000 population (1988): 0.2.
Life expectancy at birth (1996): male 71.5 years; female 75.8 years.
Major causes of death per 100,000 population (1988): diseases of the circulatory system 237.5; malignant neoplasms (cancers) 44.5; diseases of the respiratory system 44.5; endocrine and metabolic disorders 25.4; ill-defined conditions 68.6.

National economy

Budget (1995). Revenue: EC$289,600,000 (taxes on international transactions 35.2%, of which import duties 15.8%; consumption taxes 26.6%; nontax revenue 13.4%; income taxes 9.8%). Expenditures: EC$355,400,000 (current expenditures 86.1%; development expenditures 13.9%).
Public debt (external, outstanding; end of 1995): U.S.$235,500,000.
Production (metric tons except as noted). Agriculture, forestry, fishing (1996): tropical fruit (including papayas, guavas, soursops, and oranges) 5,500, mangoes 1,300, eggplants 250, lemons and limes 220, carrots 210, "Antiguan Black" pineapples 150; livestock (number of live animals) 15,700 cattle, 12,200 sheep; roundwood, n.a.; fish catch (1995) 470. Mining and quarrying: crushed stone for local use. Manufacturing (1994): beer and malt 166,000 cases; T-shirts 179,000 units; other manufactures include cement, handicrafts, small appliances, and electronic components. Construction (1995): gross value of building applications EC$154,000,000. Energy production (consumption): electricity (kW-hr; 1994) 117,500,000 (105,700,000); coal, none (none); crude petroleum, none (none); petroleum products (metric tons; 1994) negligible (101,000); natural gas, none (none).
Population economically active (1991): total 26,753; activity rate of total population 45.1% (participation rates: ages 15–64, 69.7%; female 45.6%; unemployed [1994] 6.7%).

Price and earnings indexes (1990 = 100)						
	1991	1992	1993	1994	1995	1996
Consumer price index	105.7	108.9	112.2	116.2	119.5	124.3
Weekly earnings index[7]	100.0	112.7	...	...	...	...

Household income and expenditure. Average household size (1991) 3.2; income per household: n.a.; sources of income: n.a.; expenditure (1974)[8]: food

and nonalcoholic beverages 42.9%, housing 23.3%, transportation 10.0%, clothing and footwear 7.5%, energy 5.5%, alcoholic beverages and tobacco 3.6%, other 7.2%.
Gross national product (at current market prices; 1996): U.S.$482,000,000 (U.S.$7,330 per capita).

Structure of gross domestic product and labour force				
	1995		1991	
	in value EC$'000,000	% of total value	labour force	% of labour force
Agriculture, fishing	43.5	3.2	1,040	3.9
Quarrying	20.6	1.5	64	0.2
Manufacturing	22.7	1.7	1,444	5.4
Construction	119.3	8.8	3,109	11.6
Public utilities	52.9	3.9	435	1.6
Transp. and commun.	215.8	15.9	2,395	9.0
Trade, restaurants, and hotels	255.8	18.9	8,524	31.9
Finance, real estate	171.5	12.6	1,454	5.4
Pub. admin., defense	217.9	16.1	2,572	9.6
Services	81.2	6.0	5,207	19.5
Other	154.0[9]	11.4[9]	509	1.9
TOTAL	1,355.2	100.0	26,753	100.0

Land use (1994): forested 11.0%; meadows and pastures 9.0%; agricultural and under permanent cultivation 18.0%; other 62.0%.
Tourism: receipts from visitors (1995) U.S.$328,500,000; expenditures by nationals abroad (1994) U.S.$25,000,000.

Foreign trade[10]

Balance of trade (current prices)						
	1989	1990	1991	1992	1993	1994
U.S.$'000,000	–316	–325	–326	–347	–375	–403
% of total	83.4%	83.0%	76.7%	71.4%	78.6%	83.1%

Imports (1992): U.S.$417,000,000 ([11]agricultural products 9.0%, other [including petroleum products for reexport] 91.0%). *Major import sources* (1989)[11]: United States 27.0%; United Kingdom 16.0%; Canada 4.0%; OECS 3.0%; Italy 3.0%.
Exports (1992): U.S.$70,000,000 ([11]reexports [significantly, petroleum products reexported to neighbouring islands] 78.0%, domestic exports 22.0%). *Major export destinations* (1989)[11]: United States 41.0%; United Kingdom 19.0%; Germany 19.0%.

Transport and communications

Transport. Railroads[12]. Roads (1995): total length 152 mi, 245 km (paved 56%). Vehicles (1995): passenger cars 13,588; trucks and buses 1,342. Merchant marine (1992): vessels (100 gross tons and over) 292; total deadweight tonnage 997,381. Air transport (1993): passenger-km 140,000,000, passenger-km 225,000,000; (1991) short ton-mi cargo 137,000, metric ton-km cargo 200,000; airports (1996) with scheduled flights 2.

Communications				units per 1,000
Medium	date	unit	number	persons
Daily newspapers	1994	circulation	—	—
Radio	1996	receivers	50,000	776
Television	1995	receivers	28,000	435
Telephones	1995	main lines	20,000	311

Education and health

Educational attainment (1991). Percentage of population age 25 and over having: no formal schooling 1.1%; primary education 50.5%; secondary 33.4%; higher (not university) 5.4%; university 6.2%; other/unknown 3.4%. *Literacy* (1990): total population age 15 and over literate 40,000 (90.0%).

Education (1994–95)				student/
	schools	teachers	students	teacher ratio
Primary (age 5–11)	43[13]	439	11,506	26.2
Secondary (age 12–16)	12[12]	277	4,294	15.5
Higher	1	16	46	2.9

Health (1992): physicians 59 (1 per 1,083 persons); hospital beds 369 (1 per 173 persons); infant mortality rate per 1,000 live births (1996) 17.2.
Food (1995): daily per capita caloric intake 2,406 (vegetable products 65%, animal products 35%); 102% of FAO recommended minimum requirement.

Military

Total active duty personnel (1995): a 100-member defense force is part of the Eastern Caribbean regional security system.

[1]Directly elected seats only; attorney general and speaker may serve ex officio if they are not elected to House of Representatives. [2]Community councils on Antigua and the local government council on Barbuda are the organs of local government. [3]Uninhabited. [4]Unadjusted de jure population excluding institutionalized population; de jure population adjusted for undercount (including institutionalized population) is 63,896. [5]Includes evacuees from Montserrat. [6]Large settlements include (1991): All Saints 2,230; Liberta 1,473; Codrington 814. [7]Construction sector. [8]Weights of consumer price index components. [9]Net indirect taxes less imputed bank service charges. [10]Exports f.o.b.; imports c.i.f. [11]Estimated percentages. [12]Privately owned tracks are mostly nonoperative. [13]1991–92.

Internet resources for further information:
•**Antigua and Barbuda High Commission (London)**
 http://antigua-barbuda.com/

Argentina

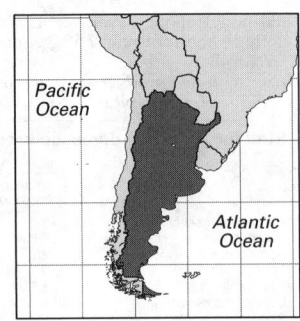

Official name: República Argentina (Argentina Republic).
Form of government: federal republic with two legislative houses (Senate [72]; Chamber of Deputies [257]).
Head of state and government: President[1].
Capital: Buenos Aires.
Official language: Spanish.
Official religion: Roman Catholicism.
Monetary unit: 1 peso (pl. pesos)[2] (Arg$) = 100 centavos; valuation (Sept. 25, 1998) 1 U.S.$ = Arg$1.00; 1 £ = Arg$1.70.

Area and population

Provinces	Capitals	area sq mi	area sq km	population 1995 estimate
Buenos Aires	La Plata	118,754	307,571	13,333,670
Catamarca	Catamarca	39,615	102,602	287,567
Chaco	Resistencia	38,469	99,633	890,548
Chubut	Rawson	86,752	224,686	396,800
Córdoba	Córdoba	63,831	165,321	2,914,972
Corrientes	Corrientes	34,054	88,199	852,685
Entre Ríos	Paraná	30,418	78,781	1,063,416
Formosa	Formosa	27,825	72,066	444,367
Jujuy	San Salvador de Jujuy	20,548	53,219	551,804
La Pampa	Santa Rosa	55,382	143,440	280,876
La Rioja	La Rioja	34,626	89,680	246,158
Mendoza	Mendoza	57,462	148,827	1,500,818
Misiones	Posadas	11,506	29,801	877,904
Neuquén	Neuquén	36,324	94,078	460,395
Río Negro	Viedma	78,384	203,013	556,674
Salta	Salta	60,034	155,488	952,174
San Juan	San Juan	34,614	89,651	550,641
San Luis	San Luis	29,633	76,748	320,109
Santa Cruz	Río Gallegos	94,187	243,943	180,115
Santa Fe	Santa Fe	51,354	133,007	2,934,220
Santiago del Estero	Santiago del Estero	52,645	136,351	696,092
Tierra del Fuego[3]	Ushuaia	8,210	21,263	96,917
Tucumán	San Miguel de Tucumán	8,697	22,524	1,209,716
Other federal entity				
Distrito Federal	Buenos Aires	77	200	2,988,006
TOTAL		1,073,399[4]	2,780,092	34,586,635[4]

Demography

Population (1998): 36,125,000[5].
Density (1998): persons per sq mi 33.6, persons per sq km 13.0.
Urban-rural (1991): urban 86.9%; rural 13.1%.
Sex distribution (1995): male 49.06%; female 50.94%.
Age breakdown (1995): under 15, 28.9%; 15–29, 24.8%; 30–44, 19.0%; 45–59, 14.1%; 60–74, 9.8%; 75 and over, 3.4%.
Population projection: (2000) 37,032,000; (2010) 41,474,000.
Ethnic composition (1986): European 85%; mestizo and Amerindian 15%.
Religious affiliation (1995): Roman Catholic 87.7%; other 12.3%.
Major cities (1991)[6]: Buenos Aires (1995) 2,988,006 (Greater Buenos Aires 11,295,555); Greater Córdoba 1,208,713; Greater Rosario 1,118,984.

Vital statistics

Birth rate per 1,000 population (1995–2000): 19.9 (world avg. 25.0).
Death rate per 1,000 population (1995–2000): 7.9 (world avg. 9.3).
Natural increase rate per 1,000 population (1995–2000): 12.0 (world avg. 15.7).
Total fertility rate (avg. births per childbearing woman; 1995–2000): 2.6.
Life expectancy at birth (1995–2000): male 69.6 years; female 76.8 years.
Major causes of death per 100,000 population (1993): heart disease 247.1; neoplasma (cancers) 143.5; diseases of the brain 75.8; accidents 32.8.

National economy

Budget (1995). Revenue: U.S.$55,650,600,000 (current revenue 96.9%, of which tax revenue 90.0%, nontax revenue 6.5%, other 0.4%; capital revenue 3.1%). Expenditure: U.S.$55,560,600,000 (1989; social security 35.3%; economic services 16.0%; education 9.9%; defense 9.9%; debt service 7.4%).
Public debt (external, outstanding; 1996): U.S.$62,392,000,000.
Gross national product (1996): U.S.$295,131,000,000 (U.S.$8,380 per capita).

Structure of gross domestic product and labour force

	1994 in value Arg$'000,000[2]	1994 % of total value	1980 labour force	1980 % of labour force
Agriculture	13,665.7	4.8	1,200,992	12.0
Mining	4,672.7	1.7	47,171	0.5
Manufacturing	56,443.3	20.0	1,985,995	19.9
Construction	18,858.5	6.7	1,003,175	10.1
Public utilities	4,735.5	1.7	103,256	1.0
Transp. and commun.	15,234.5	5.4	460,476	4.6
Trade	41,132.0	14.6	1,702,080	17.0
Finance	50,267.0	17.8	395,704	4.0
Pub. admin., defense, Services	71,970.8	25.6	2,399,039	24.0
Other	4,665.0[7]	1.7[7]	691,302	6.9
TOTAL	281,645.0[4]	100.0	9,989,190	100.0

Production (metric tons except as noted). Agriculture, forestry, fishing (1996): sugarcane 17,600,000, wheat 15,200,000, soybeans 12,654,000, corn (maize) 10,466,000, sunflower seeds 5,300,000, grapes 2,728,000; livestock (number of live animals) 54,000,000 cattle, 17,000,000 sheep; roundwood (1995)

11,450,000 cu m; fish catch (1995) 930,592. Mining and quarrying (1995): silver 1,536,386 troy oz; gold 26,910 troy oz. Manufacturing (1994): cement 6,306,000; wheat flour 3,346,000; vegetable oil 3,027,000; sugar 1,110,000; paper 966,000; wine 14,179,000 hectolitres; beer 11,293,000 hectolitres. Construction (authorized; 1994): 15,081,456 sq m. Energy production (consumption): electricity (kW-hr; 1994) 66,196,000,000 (67,162,000,000); coal (metric tons; 1994) 348,000 (1,596,000); crude petroleum (barrels; 1994) 245,053,000 (173,749,000); petroleum products (metric tons; 1994) 21,499,000 (19,743,000); natural gas (cu m; 1994) 28,675,000,000 (31,293,000,000).
Population economically active (1995): total 14,345,171; activity rate of total population 41.5% (participation rates; ages 15–64, 64.5%; female 36.9%; unemployed [1996] 17.0%).

Price and earning indexes (1990 = 100)[2]

	1992	1993	1994	1995	1996	1997
Consumer price index	339.0	375.0	391.0	404.0	405.0	407.0
Monthly earnings index[8]	324.0	365.0	390.0	384.0	386.0	...

Household size and expenditure. Average household size (1991) 3.8; expenditure (1985–86): food 38.2%, transportation 11.6%, housing 9.3%, energy 9.0%, clothing 8.0%, health 7.9%, recreation 7.5%, other 8.5%.
Tourism (1995): receipts U.S.$4,306,000,000; expenditures U.S.$2,067,000,000.
Land use (1994): forest 18.6%; pasture 51.9%; agriculture 9.9%; other 19.6%.

Foreign trade[9]

Balance of trade (current prices)

	1991	1992	1993	1994	1995	1996
U.S.$'000,000	+4,572	−1,388	−1,576	−4,002	+2,985	+1,621
% of total	23.6%	5.4%	5.7%	11.3%	7.7%	3.5%

Imports (1994): U.S.$21,590,000,000 (machinery and transport equipment 52.0%, chemical products 14.0%, manufactured products 12.9%, food products and live animals 4.6%). *Major import sources:* U.S. 22.8%; Brazil 19.9%; Italy 6.6%; Germany 6.4%; France 5.0%; Chile 3.9%; Uruguay 3.7%.
Exports (1994): U.S.$15,839,000,000 (food products and live animals 35.2%, manufactured products 12.5%, machinery and transport equipment 11.2%, petroleum and petroleum products 10.4%, vegetable and animal oils 9.6%, chemical products 5.9%). *Major export destinations:* Brazil 23.1%, U.S. 11.0%; The Netherlands 7.5%; Chile 6.3%; Italy 4.1%; Uruguay 4.1%.

Transport and communications

Transport. Railroads (1995): route length 33,821 km; passenger-km (1994) 6,460,159,000; metric ton-km cargo 7,613,000,000. Roads (1995): total length 134,278 mi, 216,100 km (paved 29%). Vehicles (1995): passenger cars 4,665,329; commercial vehicles and buses 1,181,569. Air transport (1995): passenger-km 11,785,000,000; metric ton-km cargo 1,330,000,000; airports (1997) with scheduled flights 39.

Communications

Medium	date	unit	number	units per 1,000 persons
Daily newspapers	1992	circulation	4,780,000	137
Radio	1996	receivers	21,500,000	614
Television	1995	receivers	12,000,000	347
Telephones	1995	main lines	5,531,700	160
Cellular telephones	1995	subscribers	340,700	9.9
Facsimile machines	1995	units	50,000	1.4
Personal computers	1995	units	850,000	25

Education and health

Educational attainment (1991). Percentage of population age 25 and over having: no formal schooling 5.7%; less than primary education 22.3%; primary 34.6%; incomplete secondary 12.5%; complete secondary 12.8%; higher 12.0%. *Literacy* (1995): percentage of total population age 15 and over literate 96.2%; males literate 96.2%; females literate 96.2%.

Education (1994–95)

	schools	teachers	students	student/teacher ratio
Primary (age 6–12)	25,448	286,885	5,126,307	17.9
Secondary (age 13–17)[10]	7,239	233,564	2,238,091	9.6
Higher	1,705	118,695	926,793	7.8

Health (1992): physicians 88,800 (1 per 376 persons); hospital beds 147,200 (1 per 227 persons); infant mortality rate (1995–2000) 22.0.
Food (1995): daily per capita caloric intake 3,110 (vegetable products 70%, animal products 30%); 131% of FAO recommended minimum requirement.

Military

Total active duty personnel (1997): 73,000 (army 56.2%, navy 27.4%, air force 16.4%). *Military expenditure as percentage of GNP* (1995): 1.7% (world 2.8%); per capita expenditure U.S.$137.

---

[1]Assisted by a ministerial coordinator who exercises general administration of the country. [2]On Jan. 1, 1992, the austral was replaced by the peso at a ratio of 10,000 to 1. [3]Area of Tierra del Fuego (province since 1991) excludes claims to British-held islands in the South Atlantic Ocean. [4]Detail does not add to total given because of rounding. [5]Includes 2 million illegal immigrants from Bolivia and Paraguay. [6]*Municipios.* [7]Import duties. [8]Manufacturing sector only. [9]Import figures are f.o.b. in balance of trade and c.i.f. in commodities and trading partners. [10]Secondary includes vocational and teacher training.

Internet resources for further information:
• **National Institute of Statistics and Censuses (Spanish only)** http://www.indec.mecon.ar/default.htm

Armenia

Official name: Hayastani Hanrape-tut'yun (Republic of Armenia).
Form of government: unitary multiparty republic with a single legislative body (National Assembly [190]).
Head of state: President.
Head of government: Prime Minister.
Capital: Yerevan.
Official language: Armenian.
Official religion: none[1].
Monetary unit[2]: 1 dram = 100 lumas; valuation (Sept. 25, 1998) official, 1 U.S.$ = 502.38 drams; 1 £ = 855.30 drams.

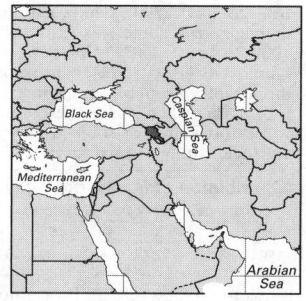

Area and population	area		population
Regions	sq mi	sq km	1995 estimate
Aragatsotn	1,064	2,755	161,700
Ararat	812	2,104	302,100
Armavir	479	1,241	314,000
Gegharkunik	1,573	4,073	255,800
Lori	1,464	3,791	391,700
Kotayk	811	2,100	327,100
Shirak	1,034	2,679	357,600
Syunik	1,739	4,505	161,400
Vayots-Dzor	891	2,308	69,700
Tavush	1,043	2,702	170,000
Cities			
Yerevan	81	210	1,248,700
Other	493[3]	1,278[3]	
TOTAL	11,484[4]	29,743[4, 5]	3,759,800[5]

Demography

Population (1998): 3,800,000 (de jure); *c.* 3,000,000 (de facto)[6].
Density (1998): persons per sq mi 330.9, persons per sq km 127.8.
Urban-rural (1995): urban 67.6%; rural 32.4%.
Sex distribution (1994): male 48.42%; female 51.58%.
Age breakdown (1993): under 15, 30.1%; 15–29, 24.4%; 30–44, 22.4%; 45–59, 12.3%; 60–74, 8.6%; 75 and over, 2.2%.
Population projection: (2000) 3,827,000; (2010) 3,796,000.
Doubling time: n.a.; doubling time exceeds 100 years.
Ethnic composition (1989): Armenian 93.3%; Azerbaijani 2.6%; other 4.1%.
Religious affiliation (1995): Armenian Apostolic 64.5%; other Christian 1.3%; other (mostly nonreligious) 34.2%.
Major cities (1991): Yerevan 1,283,000; Gyumri 163,000[7]; Kirovakan 76,000[7].

Vital statistics

Birth rate per 1,000 population (1995): 13.3 (world avg. 25.0); (1993) legitimate 86.0%; illegitimate 14.0%.
Death rate per 1,000 population (1995): 6.5 (world avg. 9.3).
Natural increase rate per 1,000 population (1995): 6.8 (world avg. 15.7).
Total fertility rate (avg. births per childbearing woman; 1994): 2.0.
Marriage rate per 1,000 population (1995): 4.2.
Divorce rate per 1,000 population (1995): 0.8.
Life expectancy at birth (1994): male 67.0 years; female 73.7 years.
Major causes of death per 100,000 population (1993): circulatory diseases 395.6; cancers 78.6; respiratory diseases 38.3; accidents and violence 24.2.

National economy

Budget (1995). Revenue: 103,834,000,000 drams (tax revenue 64.0%, of which enterprise profits tax 23.0%, value-added tax 16.4%, payroll tax 10.3%, income tax 6.6%, other taxes 7.7%; grants 18.3%; nontax 17.7%). Expenditures: 155,492,000,000 drams (current expenditures 75.6%, of which pensions and social welfare 16.0%, interest 10.4%, wages 8.7%, health and education 8.3%, other 32.3%[8]; capital expenditure and net lending 24.4%).
Public debt (external, outstanding; 1996): U.S.$434,100,000.
Land use (1994): forest 13.4%; pasture 23.1%; agriculture 20.1%; other 43.4%.
Gross national product (1996): U.S.$2,387,000,000 (U.S.$630 per capita).

Structure of net material product and labour force				
	1995			
	in value '000,000 drams	% of total value	labour force	% of labour force
Agriculture	167,475	32.7	492,000	31.5
Manufacturing, mining } Public utilities	164,834	31.6	352,000	22.5
Construction	48,368	9.3	96,000	6.2
Transp. and commun.	17,687	3.4	27,000	1.7
Trade	42,927	8.2	63,000	4.0
Pub. admin., defense	—	—	29,000	1.9
Services	—	—	341,000	21.8
Other	80,994	14.8	162,000[9]	10.4[9]
TOTAL	522,285	100.0	1,562,000	100.0

Production (metric tons except as noted). Agriculture, forestry, fishing (1996): potatoes 423,163, tomatoes 180,361, wheat 168,000, grapes 158,200, apples 118,000, barley 105,000; livestock (number of live animals) 561,000 sheep and goats, 496,500 cattle, 79,000 pigs, 2,700,000 poultry; roundwood (1991) 44,100 cu m; fish catch (1995) 4,500. Mining and quarrying (1995): copper 10,000,000; perlite 200,000; molybdenum 5,000. Manufacturing (value in '000,000 drams; 1994): machine-building and metalworking equipment 18,436; food products

13,842; chemicals 5,330; metals 5,259; construction materials 3,154; textiles 2,500; leather products 2,335. Construction (1995): 284,000 sq m. Energy production (consumption): electricity (kW-hr; 1995) 5,560,000,000 (5,674,000,000); coal (metric tons; 1994) none (36,000); crude petroleum (barrels; 1994) none (1,195,000); petroleum products (metric tons; 1994) none (356,000); natural gas (cu m; 1994) none (883,773,000).
Population economically active (1995): total 1,562,000; activity rate of total population 41.5% (1994; participation rates: ages 16–59 [male], 16–54 [female] 75.4%; female [1994] 45.0%; unemployed 4.3%).

Price and earnings indexes (1995 = 100)					
	1993	1994	1995	1996	1997
Consumer price index	1	36	100	119	135
Earnings index	...	...	...	...	...

Household income and expenditure. Average household size (1989) 4.7; income per household (1994) 47,352 drams (U.S.$153); sources of income (1994): wages and salaries 52.3%, agricultural income 7.7%, other 40.0%; expenditure (1994): goods and services 78.0%, taxes and payments to government 22.0%.

Foreign trade

Balance of trade (current prices)				
	1993	1994	1995	1996
U.S.$'000,000	−98.0	−180.8	−402.0	−469.2
% of total	23.9%	43.2%	42.5%	44.7%

Imports (1995): U.S.$672,900,000 (food products 33.4%, mineral products 33.1%, jewelry 4.3%, other 29.2%). *Major import sources:* former Soviet Union (FSU) 49.6%, of which Russia 19.9%, Turkmenistan 19.2%, other FSU 10.6%; non-FSU 50.4%, of which U.S., Iran, France, and Belgium are the biggest sources.
Exports (1995): U.S.$270,900,000 (jewelry 33.1%, machinery and equipment 14.7%, mineral products 10.6%). *Major export destinations:* FSU 61.7%, of which Russia 32.6%, Turkmenistan 25.3%, other FSU 3.8%; non-FSU 38.3%, of which Iran 13.0%, Belgium 11.3%, Germany 3.7%.

Transport and communications

Transport. Railroads (1996): length 515 mi, 829 km; (1995) passenger-mi 196,000,000, passenger-km 316,000,000; short ton-mi cargo 3,345,000,000, metric ton-km cargo 4,884,000,000. Roads (1996): length 4,600 mi, 7,500 km (paved 98%). Vehicles (1991): passenger cars 2,782, trucks and buses 12,034. Air transport (1990): passenger-mi 3,453,000,000, passenger-km 5,556,-900,000; short ton-mi cargo 34,000,000, metric ton-km cargo 49,000,000; airports (1997) 1.

Communications				units per 1,000 persons
Medium	date	unit	number	
Daily newspapers	1995	circulation	80,000	23
Television	1995	receivers	900,000	241
Telephones	1995	main lines	583,000	155
Facsimile machines	1995	units	300	0.1

Education and health

Educational attainment (1989). Percentage of population age 25 and over having: primary education or no formal schooling 7.4%; some secondary 18.6%; completed secondary and some postsecondary 57.7%; higher 13.8%. *Literacy* (1989): total population age 15 and over literate 98.8%; males literate 99.4%; females literate 98.1%.

Education (1994–95)	schools	teachers	students	student/ teacher ratio
Primary (age 6–13) } Secondary (age 14–17)	1,400	54,000[8]	574,500	11.0[8]
Voc., teacher tr.	69[8]	...	25,200[8]	...
Higher	14	...	36,500	...

Health (1994): physicians 13,000 (1 per 288 persons); hospital beds 30,000 (1 per   rsons); infant mortality rate 14.7.

Military

Total active duty personnel (1997): *c.* 58,600 (army 100%). *Military expenditure as percentage of GNP* (1995): 0.9% (world 2.8%); per capita expenditure U.S.$23.

[1]The constitution provides for the right to practice the religion of one's choice. In practice, the law imposes restrictions on religious freedom. The 1991 Law on Religious Organizations establishes the separation of church and state, but recognizes the Armenian Apostolic Church (the Armenian Orthodox Church) as having special status. The law requires all nonapostolic religious denominations to register with the Ministry of Justice and prohibits proselytizing. [2]The Armenian dram was introduced on Nov. 22, 1993, to replace the Russian ruble, at a rate of 200 Russian rubles to 1 dram. [3]Area of Lake Sevan. [4]In addition, nearly 20% of neighbouring Azerbaijan (including the 4,400-sq km geographic region of Nagorno-Karabakh [Armenian: Artsakh] has been occupied by Armenian forces since 1993. [5]Detail does not add to total given because of rounding. [6]About 1/5 of Armenia's population has left the country since 1993 because of an energy crisis. [7]1989; reduced in population by evacuation following Dec. 7, 1988, earthquake. [8]1993–94. [9]Includes 106,000 unemployed and 56,000 undistributed employed.

Internet resources for further information:
• **Armenia Human Development Report 1996**
http://www.undp.org/undp/rbec/nhdr/1996/armenia/
• **Trade Point Armenia Home Page** http://tpa-gw1.amilink.net/

Australia

Official name: Commonwealth of Australia.
Form of government: federal parliamentary state (formally a constitutional monarchy) with two legislative houses (Senate [76]; House of Representatives [148]).
Chief of state: British Monarch represented by Governor-General.
Head of government: Prime Minister.
Capital: Canberra.
Official language: English.
Official religion: none.
Monetary unit: 1 Australian dollar ($A) = 100 cents; valuation (Sept. 25, 1998) 1 U.S.$ = $A 1.70; 1 £ = $A 2.89.

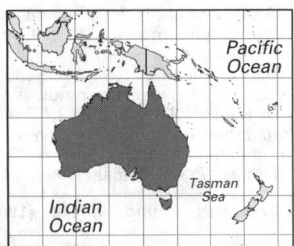

Area and population

States	Capitals	area sq mi	area sq km	population 1996 census
New South Wales	Sydney	309,500	801,600	6,038,696
Queensland	Brisbane	666,900	1,727,200	3,368,850
South Australia	Adelaide	379,900	984,000	1,427,936
Tasmania	Hobart	26,200	67,800	459,659
Victoria	Melbourne	87,900	227,600	4,373,520
Western Australia	Perth	975,100	2,525,500	1,726,095
Territories				
Australian Capital Territory	Canberra	900	2,400	299,243
Northern Territory	Darwin	519,800	1,346,200	195,101
TOTAL		2,966,200	7,682,300	17,892,423[1]

Demography

Population (1998): 18,725,000.
Density (1998): persons per sq mi 6.3, persons per sq km 2.4.
Urban-rural (1996): urban 85.0%; rural 15.0%.
Sex distribution (1996): male 49.46%; female 50.54%.
Age breakdown (1996): under 15, 21.6%; 15–24, 14.5%; 25–44, 30.8%; 45–64, 21.0%; 65 and over, 12.1%.
Population projection: (2000) 19,117,000; (2010) 21,018,000.
Doubling time: 99 years.
Ethnic composition (1996): white 95.2%; aboriginal 2.0%; Asian 1.3%; other 1.5%.
Religious affiliation (1991): Christian 74.0%, of which Roman Catholic 27.3%, Anglican Church of Australia 23.9%, other Protestant 19.2% (Uniting Church and Methodist 8.2%, Presbyterian 4.3%), Orthodox 2.8%, other Christian 0.8%; Muslim 0.9%; Buddhist 0.8%; Jewish 0.4%; no religion 12.9%; other 11.0%.
Major cities (1995): Sydney 3,772,700; Melbourne 3,218,100; Brisbane 1,489,100; Perth 1,262,600; Adelaide 1,081,000; Newcastle 466,000; Canberra-Queanbeyan 331,800; Gold Coast–Tweed 326,900; Wollongong 253,600; Hobart 194,700.
Place of birth (1996): 73.9% native-born; 26.1% foreign-born, of which Europe 12.4% (United Kingdom 6.3%[2], Italy 1.3%, Greece 0.7%, Germany 0.6%, The Netherlands 0.5%, other Europe 3.0%), Asia and Middle East 5.6%, New Zealand 1.6%, Africa, the Americas, and other 6.5%.
Mobility (1995–96). Population age 15 and over living in the same residence as in 1994: 81.6%; different residence between states, regions, and neighbourhoods 18.4%.
Households (1993–94). Total number of households 6,616,800. Average household size 2.6; 1 person 21.8%, couples only 25.8%, couples with dependent children only 23.7%, nonfamily members 12.4%, single parent with children 6.6%, other 9.7%.
Immigration (1996): permanent immigrants admitted 96,970, from United Kingdom and Ireland 12.8%, New Zealand 11.8%, China 7.6%, Vietnam 4.8%, Hong Kong 4.6%, India 4.4%, Philippines 3.9%, South Africa 3.2%, Bosnia and Herzegovina 3.2%, Yugoslavia 3.1%, Sri Lanka 2.2%, Refugee arrivals (1994–95): 13,600.

Vital statistics

Birth rate per 1,000 population (1996): 14.1 (world avg. 25.0); (1993) legitimate 75.0%; illegitimate 25.0%.
Death rate per 1,000 population (1996): 6.9 (world avg. 9.3).
Natural increase rate per 1,000 population (1996): 7.2 (world avg. 15.7).
Total fertility rate (avg. births per childbearing woman; 1996): 1.82.
Marriage rate per 1,000 population (1996): 6.0.
Divorce rate per 1,000 population (1996): 2.7.
Life expectancy at birth (1996): male 75.4 years; female 81.1 years.
Major causes of death per 100,000 population (1995): diseases of the circulatory system 296.0; cancers 190.0; respiratory diseases 52.0; accidents, poisoning, and violence 41.0; endocrine, nutritional, and metabolic diseases 23.0; digestive system diseases 21.0; nervous system diseases 17.0.

Social indicators

Educational attainment (1995). Percentage of population age 15 to 64 having: no formal schooling 0.3%; incomplete secondary education 36.3%; completed secondary 17.8%[3, 4]; postsecondary, technical, or other certificate/ diploma 33.7%; university 11.9%.
Quality of working life (1995–96). Average workweek: 40.5 hours (16.8%[4] overtime). Annual rate per 100,000 workers for: accidental injury and indus-

trial disease, 3,200[5]; death, n.a. Proportion of employed persons insured for damages or income loss resulting from: injury 100%[5]; permanent disability 100%[5]; death 100%[5]. Working days lost to industrial disputes per 1,000 employees (1995): 79. Means of transportation to work (1986): private automobile 69.4%; public transportation 10.1%; motorcycle and bicycle 3.2%; foot 6.6%; other 10.7%. Discouraged job seekers (considered by employers to be too young or too old, having language or training limitations, or no vacancies in line of work; 1995): 1.3% of labour force.

Distribution of family income (1990[6])

percentage of family income by decile

1	2	3	4	5	6	7	8	9	10 (highest)
1.4%	3.1%	4.2%	5.5%	6.9%	8.6%	10.6%	13.3%	17.2%	29.2%

Access to services (1976). Proportion of dwellings having access to: electricity 99.5%; bathroom 96.0%; flush toilet 92.2%; kitchen 97.9%; public sewer 73.4%.
Social participation. Eligible voters participating in last national election (1996): 95.8%; voting is compulsory. Population age 16 and over participating in voluntary work: n.a. Trade union membership in total workforce (1996): 31%.
Social deviance (1996). Offense rate per 100,000 population for: murder 3.8; sexual assault 78.7; assault 620.8; auto theft 672.2; unarmed robbery, burglary, and housebreaking 4,608.2; armed robbery 34.0. Incidence per 100,000 in general population of: alcoholism, n.a.; prisoners with drug offenses (1994) 8.8; suicide (1995) 13.1.
Material well-being (1995). Households possessing: automobile 85%; telephone 95%; refrigerator 99.7%; air conditioner 32.3%[7]; personal computers 23.0%[4]; washing machine 90.0%; central heating 3.9%[7]; swimming pool 10.1%[7].

National economy

Gross national product (1996): U.S.$367,802,000,000 (U.S.$20,090 per capita).

Structure of gross domestic product and labour force

	1994–95[8] in value $A '000,000	1994–95[8] % of total value	1995–96 labour force	1995–96 % of labour force
Agriculture	13,592	3.3	421,900	4.7
Mining	17,983	4.4	85,300	0.9
Manufacturing	64,623	15.7	1,111,400	12.3
Construction	27,031	6.5	600,300	6.6
Public utilities	13,449	3.3	80,800	0.9
Transp. and commun.	36,978	9.0	546,700	6.0
Trade[9]	78,442	19.0	2,106,500	23.2
Finance, real estate	91,176	22.1	1,111,400	12.3
Pub. admin., defense	15,226	3.7	378,700	4.2
Services	56,324	13.6	1,844,200	20.3
Other	–2,231[10]	–0.6[10]	779,200[11]	8.6[11]
TOTAL	412,593	100.0	9,066,400	100.0

Budget (1996–97). Revenue: $A 130,160,000,000 (income tax 71.2%, of which individual 50.7%, corporate 15.1%; excise duties and sales tax 21.0%). Expenditures: $A 129,686,000,000 (social security and welfare 37.7%; health 15.0%; economic and public services 12.7%; transfers to state governments 12.9%; interest on public debt 7.5%).
Public debt (1996–97): $A 96,453,000,000.
Tourism (1996): receipts from visitors U.S.$8,127,500,000; expenditures by nationals abroad U.S.$5,038,800,000.

Manufacturing, mining, and construction enterprises (1994–95)[12]

	no. of establishments[13]	no. of employees	Turnover per person employed ($A '000)[13]	annual turnover ($A '000,000)
Manufacturing				
Food, beverages, and tobacco	3,514	163,100	243.4	41,010
Metal products	7,522	147,400	229.6	34,691
Machinery and equipment	8,988	202,800	178.0	38,189
Chemical, petroleum, and coal products	3,009	91,100	330.0	30,462
Printing and publishing	5,265	94,200	139.0	13,621
Miscellaneous manufacturing	5,973	54,000	102.1	5,754
Wood and paper products	3,973	63,800	174.1	11,360
Nonmetallic mineral products	1,909	39,000	225.4	8,951
Textile, clothing, footwear, and leather	4,456	76,600	124.6	9,786
Mining				
Coal, oil, and gas	254	29,600	...	17,023
Metallic minerals	261	25,700	...	11,913
Nonmetallic minerals[14]	699	8,799	...	2,240
Construction[15]	98,100	518,200	...	34,407

Production (gross value in $A '000 except as noted). Agriculture, forestry, fishing (1995–96): livestock slaughtered 6,066,400 (cattle 3,474,300, sheep and lambs 1,005,000, poultry 964,600, pigs 589,200); wheat 4,602,000, wool 2,686,800, barley 1,347,000, sugarcane 1,319,700, cotton 851,000[16], grapes 680,600, potatoes 378,000[16], oats 311,000[16], apples 269,800[16], bananas 254,700[16], sorghum 242,000[16], oranges 214,800[16], rice 216,000[16], tomatoes 166,000[16], carrots 133,000[16], pears 73,400[16], onions 54,100, peaches 50,000[16], pineapples 43,300[16], corn (maize) 41,000, tobacco 40,000[16], cauliflower 33,700[5]; livestock (number of live animals; 1997) 121,900,000 sheep, 26,250,000 cattle, 2,410,000 pigs, 73,509,000 poultry; roundwood (1995) 22,458,000 cu m; fish catch (1995) 219,499 metric tons. Mining and quarrying (metric tons [tons of contained metal]; 1995–96): iron ore 142,936,000; bauxite 42,655,000; zinc 930,000; lead 455,000; copper 437,000; tin 8,175; gold 253,504 kg; diamonds 40,693,000 carats. Manufacturing (value added in U.S.$'000,000 except as noted: 1994): food products 10,043; transport equipment 5,860; metal products 5,234; printing and publishing 4,946: non-ferrous

metals 4,624; woven woolen cloth 8,624,000 sq m[16]. Construction (buildings completed, by value in $A '000; 1995–96): new dwellings 12,105,700; alterations and additions to dwellings 2,283,500; nonresidential 10,728,400.

Retail and service enterprises (1991–92)

	no. of establishments	no. of employees	total wages and salaries ($A '000,000)	annual turnover ($A '000,000)
Retail				
Motor vehicle dealers, gasoline and tire dealers	37,305	220,661	2,572[17]	44,954
Food stores	53,166	406,299	2,461[17]	43,963[16]
Department and general stores	459	87,148	1,175[17]	11,209[16]
Clothing, fabrics, and furniture stores	21,688	91,138	965[17]	7,957[16]
Household appliances and hardware stores	14,268	75,355	629	12,588[16]
Recreational goods	...	...	...	6,299[16]
Services[5]				
Real estate agents	7,265	51,922	...	2,798.7
Architectural services	4,409	16,204	...	945.2
Surveying services	1,175	6,964	...	481.2
Consulting engineering services	5,454	28,208	...	2,325.2
Legal services	8,850	63,108	...	5,105.2
Accounting services	8,699	60,000	...	4,051.2
Computing services	4,894	30,062	...	3,928.8
Advertising services	858	9,083	...	842.1
Market research services	174	8,064	...	251.7
Business management services	686	4,933	...	506.6

Energy production (consumption): electricity (kW-hr; 1994) 167,151,000,000 (167,151,000,000); coal (metric tons; 1994) 176,078,000 (52,678,000); crude petroleum (barrels; 1994) 159,160,000 (202,490,000); petroleum products (metric tons; 1994) 33,086,000 (33,707,000); natural gas (cu m; 1994) 25,185,000,000 (17,438,000,000).

Population economically active (1995–96): total 9,066,400; activity rate of total population 49.9% (participation rates: over age 15, 63.7%; female 42.9%; unemployed 8.5%).

Price and earnings indexes (1990 = 100)

	1992	1993	1994	1995	1996	1997	1998[18]
Consumer price index	104.2	106.1	108.1	113.2	116.1	116.4	116.6
Weekly earnings index	109.3	111.3	115.0	120.8	125.7	130.8	134.2

Household income and expenditure (1993–94). Average household size 2.6; average annual income per household $A 37,700 (U.S.$27,585); sources of income: wages and salaries 72.7%, transfer payments 13.0%, self-employment 7.5%, other 6.8%; expenditure: food and beverages 18.7%, transportation and communications 15.3%, housing 13.9%, recreation 13.3%, household durable goods 6.6%, clothing and footwear 5.7%, health 4.6%, energy 2.8%, other 19.1%.

Financial aggregates

	1991	1992	1993	1994	1995	1996	1997[19]
Exchange rate, $A 1.00 per:							
U.S. dollar	0.78	0.74	0.68	0.73	0.74	0.80	0.73
£	0.44	0.42	0.45	0.48	0.47	0.51	0.46
SDR	0.53	0.50	0.49	0.53	0.50	0.55	0.54
International reserves (U.S.$)							
Total (excl. gold; '000,000)	16,535	11,208	11,102	11,285	11,896	14,534	16,189
SDRs ('000,000)	290	96	82	73	55	37	23
Reserve pos. In IMF ('000,000)	351	577	550	506	502	482	491
Foreign exchange ('000,000)	15,894	10,536	10,470	10,076	11,340	14,016	15,676
Gold ('000,000 fine troy oz)	7.93	7.93	7.90	7.90	7.9	7.9	3.16[20]
% world reserves	0.8	0.8	0.9	0.9	0.9	0.9	...
Interest and prices							
Central bank discount (%)	10.99	6.96	5.83	5.75	5.75	5.75[18]	...
Govt. bond yield (short-term; %)	9.94	7.25	5.63	7.65	7.60[20]	7.53	5.58[21]
Industrial share prices (1990 = 100)	96.4	100.3	104.7	112.9	114.2	152.0	180.3[21]
Balance of payments (U.S.$'000,000)							
Balance of visible trade	+3,529	+1,640	−29	−3,280	−4,166	−891	...
Imports, f.o.b.	38,833	41,173	42,666	50,661	57,311	60,955	15,562[18]
Exports, f.o.b.	42,362	42,183	42,637	47,331	53,145	60,064	17,599[18]
Balance of invisibles	−11,036	−10,971	−9,666	−16,364	−19,040	−15,977	−2,010[18]
Balance of payments, current account	−11,131	−11,076	−9,876	−16,717	−19,107	−15,870	−2,043[18]

Land use (1995): agricultural and under permanent cultivation 6.3%; other 93.7% (of which, meadows and pastures [1994] 54.2%).

Foreign trade

Balance of trade (current prices)

	1993	1994	1995	1996	1997	1998[21]
$A '000,000	454	−3,183	−5,810	−1,424	−1,383	−704
% of total	0.4%	2.4%	3.9%	0.9%	0.8%	1.5%

Imports (1995–96): $A 77,819,000,000 (machinery 33.4%, of which office machines and automatic data-processing equipment 7.7%; basic manufactures 14.2%, of which textile yarn and fabrics 3.0%, paper and paper products 2.5%, iron and steel 1.8%; transport equipment 13.5%, of which road motor vehicles 10.2%; chemicals and related products 11.4%; mineral fuels and lubricants 5.5%; food and live animals 3.7%; crude materials [inedible] excluding fuels 2.0%; beverages and tobacco 0.6%). *Major import sources*: U.S. 22.6%; Japan 13.9%; U.K. 6.3%; Germany 6.2%; China 5.1%.

Exports (1995–96): $A 75,999,000,000 (food and live animals 20.1%, of which cereals and cereal preparations 6.5%, meat and meat preparations 4.3%, sugar, sugar preparations, and honey 2.3%, dairy products 2.2%, crude materials excluding fuels 19.4%, of which metalliferous ores and metal scrap 11.4%, textile fibres and their waste 5.3%; mineral fuels and lubricants 16.6%,

of which coal, coke, and briquettes 10.3%, petroleum, petroleum products, and natural gas 4.2%; basic manufactures 12.9%). *Major export destinations*: Japan 21.6%; South Korea 8.7%; New Zealand 7.4%; U.S. 6.0%; China 5.0%; Singapore 4.7%; Taiwan 4.5%; Hong Kong 4.0%.

Trade by commodity group (1995–96)

		imports		exports	
SITC Group		U.S.$'000,000	%	U.S.$'000,000	%
00	Food and live animals	2,159	3.8	9,671	18.3
01	Beverages and tobacco	374	0.6	431	0.8
02	Crude materials, excluding fuels	1,297	2.3	10,127	19.1
03	Mineral fuels, lubricants, and related materials	2,916	5.1	8,882	16.8
04	Animal and vegetable oils, fat, and waxes	193	0.3	190	0.4
05	Chemicals and related products, n.e.s.	6,112	10.6	2,090	3.9
06	Basic manufactures	8,495	14.8	7,647	14.4
07	Machinery and transport equipment	26,939	46.9	6,764	12.8
08	Miscellaneous manufactured articles	8,096	14.1	1,877	3.5
09	Goods not classified by kind	842	1.5	5,295	10.0
TOTAL		57,423	100.0	52,974	100.0

Direction of trade (1995–96)

	imports		exports	
	U.S.$'000,000	%	U.S.$'000,000	%
Africa	361	0.6	763	1.6
Asia	21,463	37.7	28,651	58.4
Japan	8,869	15.6	11,369	23.2
South America	641	1.1	553	1.1
North and Central America	13,720	24.1	4,351	8.9
United States	12,577	22.1	3,423	7.0
Europe	15,414	27.1	6,152	12.5
EEC	14,405	25.3	5,795	11.8
Russia	27	0.05	108	0.2
Other Europe	982	1.7	249	0.5
Oceania	3,262	5.7	5,364	10.9
New Zealand	2,491	4.4	3,921	8.0
Other	2,020	3.6	3,239	6.6
TOTAL	56,881	100.0[22]	49,073	100.0

Transport and communications

Transport. Railroads[23]: route length (1995) 22,385 mi, 36,026 km; passenger journeys 407,170,000[4]; short ton-mi cargo 67,716,000,000[24, 25], metric ton-km cargo 98,864,000[24, 25]. Roads (1995): total length 556,145 mi, 895,030 km (paved 38.6%). Vehicles (1995): passenger cars 8,370,000; trucks and buses 2,640,300. Merchant marine (1994): vessels (150 gross tons and over) 90; total deadweight tonnage 3,499,527. Air transport (1996)[26]: passenger-mi 44,687,000,000, passenger-km 71,917,000,000; short ton-mi cargo 1,257,000,000, metric ton-km cargo 1,836,000,000; airports (1996) with scheduled flights 400.

Communications

Medium	date	unit	number	units per 1,000 persons
Daily newspapers	1994	circulation	4,600,000	258
Radio	1996	receivers	21,000,000	1,148
Television	1995	receivers	11,565,000	641
Telephones	1996	main lines	9,500,000	519
Cellular telephones	1996	subscribers	3,815,000	209
Facsimile machines	1995	units	475,000	26
Personal computers	1996	units	5,700,000	312

Education and health

Literacy (1996): total population literate, virtually 100%[27].

Education (1995)

	schools	teachers	students	student/teacher ratio
Primary (age 6–12)	9,865	202,401	1,833,681	...
Secondary (age 13–17)			1,275,656	...
Vocational[28]	234[29]	19,210[30]	917,801	47.8
Higher	95[31]	25,916[31]	604,177	...

Health: physicians (1995–96) 45,800 (1 per 400 persons); hospital beds (1994–95) 77,494 (1 per 226 persons); infant mortality rate (1996) 5.7.
Food (1995): daily per capita caloric intake 3,068 (vegetable products 66%, animal products 34%); 115% of FAO recommended minimum requirement.

Military

Total active duty personnel (1997): 57,400 (army 44.3%, navy 24.9%, air force 30.8%). *Military expenditure as percentage of GNP* (1995): 2.5% (world 2.8%); per capita expenditure U.S.$465.

[1]Total includes 3,323 persons in nondelimited areas. [2]Includes both Northern Ireland and Republic of Ireland. [3]Completed highest level of secondary school available. [4]1994. [5]1992–93. [6]December. [7]1983. [8]At 1989–90 prices. [9]Trade includes hotels and restaurants. [10]Less imputed bank service charges. [11]Mostly unemployed. [12]Excludes operations of single-establishment enterprises employing fewer than four persons. [13]1993–94. [14]1990–91. [15]1991–92. [16]1994–95. [17]1985–86. [18]First quarter. [19]August. [20]Fourth quarter. [21]Second quarter. [22]Detail does not add to total given because of rounding. [23]Government railways only. [24]1995–96. [25]Includes government and private freight. [26]Includes Qantas and Ansett Australia. [27]A national survey conducted in 1996 put the number of persons who had very poor literacy and numeracy skills at about 17% of the total population (age 15 to 64). [28]Includes special education. [29]1986. [30]Full-time staff. [31]1989.

Internet resources for further information:
• **Australian Bureau of Statistics http://www.abs.gov.au**

Austria

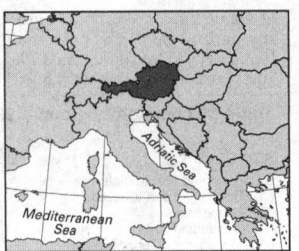

Official name: Republik Österreich (Republic of Austria).
Form of government: federal state with two legislative houses (Federal Council [64]; National Council [183]).
Chief of state: President.
Head of government: Chancellor.
Capital: Vienna.
Official language: German.
Official religion: none.
Monetary unit: 1 Austrian Schilling (S) = 100 Groschen; valuation (Sept. 25, 1998) 1 U.S.$ = S 11.76; 1 £ = S 20.02.

Area and population

States	Capitals	area sq mi	area sq km	population 1995 estimate
Burgenland	Eisenstadt	1,531	3,966	274,000
Kärnten	Klagenfurt	3,681	9,533	561,000
Niederösterreich	Sankt Pölten	7,403	19,174	1,518,000
Oberösterreich	Linz	4,625	11,979	1,386,000
Salzburg	Salzburg	2,763	7,155	507,000
Steiermark	Graz	6,327	16,388	1,206,000
Tirol	Innsbruck	4,883	12,648	658,000
Vorarlberg	Bregenz	1,004	2,601	343,000
Wien (Vienna)	—	160	415	1,593,000
TOTAL		32,378[1]	83,859	8,047,000[1]

Demography

Population (1998): 8,070,000.
Density (1998): persons per sq mi 249.2, persons per sq km 96.2.
Urban-rural (1991): urban 64.5%; rural 35.5%.
Sex distribution (1995): male 48.50%; female 51.50%.
Age breakdown (1995): under 15, 17.5%; 15–29, 21.4%; 30–44, 23.2%; 45–59, 18.1%; 60–74, 13.6%; 75 and over, 6.2%.
Population projection: (2000) 8,080,000; (2010) 8,115,000.
Doubling time: not applicable; population is stable.
Ethnic composition (national origin; 1991): Austrian 93.4%; citizens of former Yugoslavia 2.5%; Turkish 1.5%; German 0.7%; other 1.9%.
Religious affiliation (1995): Roman Catholic 75.1%; nonreligious and atheist 8.6%; Protestant (mostly Lutheran) 5.4%; Muslim 2.1%; Eastern Orthodox 0.7%; Jewish 0.1%; other 1.9%; unknown 6.1%.
Major cities (1991): Vienna 1,539,848; Graz 237,810; Linz 203,044; Salzburg 143,978; Innsbruck 118,112.

Vital statistics

Birth rate per 1,000 population (1996): 10.8 (world avg. 25.0); (1995) legitimate 72.6%; illegitimate 27.4%.
Death rate per 1,000 population (1996): 9.9 (world avg. 9.3).
Natural increase rate per 1,000 population (1996): 0.9 (world avg. 15.7).
Total fertility rate (avg. births per childbearing woman; 1996): 1.5.
Marriage rate per 1,000 population (1995): 5.3.
Divorce rate per 1,000 population (1995): 2.3.
Life expectancy at birth (1995): male 73.5 years; female 80.1 years.
Major causes of death per 100,000 population (1995): diseases of the circulatory system 539.9; malignant neoplasms (cancers) 243.5.

National economy

Budget (1994). Revenue: S 819,990,000,000 (tax revenue 90.8%, of which social security contributions 38.8%, individual income taxes 17.2%, value-added taxes 14.9%). Expenditures: S 915,900,000,000 (social security and welfare 46.4%; health 13.5%; education 9.6%; defense 2.2%).
National debt (end of year 1996): U.S.$127,440,000,000.
Production (metric tons except as noted). Agriculture, forestry, fishing (1995): sugar beets 2,886,000, corn (maize) 1,474,000, barley 1,065,000, wheat 1,301,000, potatoes 724,000, apples 324,000, rye 314,000, grapes 290,000, rapeseed 263,000, pears 124,000; livestock (number of live animals) 3,706,000 pigs, 2,326,000 cattle, 13,157,000 chickens; roundwood (1995) 14,405,000 cu m; fish catch (1995) 4,458. Mining and quarrying (1995): iron ore 2,107,000; magnesite 783,000; high-grade graphite 12,000. Manufacturing (value added in S '000,000,000; 1994): electrical machinery and apparatus 47.1; nonelectrical machinery and apparatus 37.3; beverages and tobacco products 31.0; chemicals and chemical products 26.8; fabricated metals 24.9; transport equipment 23.9. Construction (completed in S '000,000,000; 1994): residential 31.1; nonresidential; 28.9. Energy production (consumption): electricity (kW-hr; 1995) 56,587,000,000 (54,077,000,000); coal (metric tons; 1994) 1,391,000 ([1995] 4,651,000); crude petroleum (barrels; 1995) 7,309,000 ([1994] 65,465,000); petroleum products (metric tons; 1994) 8,460,000 (10,330,000); natural gas (cu m; 1995) 1,482,000,000 (7,193,000,000).
Tourism (U.S.$'000,000; 1996): receipts U.S.$13,821; expenditures U.S.$12,105.
Population economically active (1995): total 3,808,000; activity rate of total population 47.3% (participation rates: ages 15–64 [1993] 69.3%; female 41.8%; unemployed [1996] 7.0%).

Price and earnings indexes (1990 = 100)

	1991	1992	1993	1994	1995	1996	1997
Consumer price index	103.3	107.5	111.4	114.7	117.3	119.4	121.0
Monthly earnings index	105.2	110.3	116.1	120.7	126.0	...	...

Gross national product (at current market prices; 1996): U.S.$226,510,000,000 (U.S.$28,110 per capita).

Structure of gross domestic product and labour force

	1995 in value S '000,000	1995 % of total value	1995 labour force	1995 % of labour force
Agriculture	35,500	1.6	243,800	6.4
Mining	8,250	0.4	11,000	0.3
Manufacturing	466,800	20.5	806,900	21.2
Construction	169,210	7.4	330,800	8.7
Public utilities	64,450	2.8	37,000	1.0
Transp. and commun.	141,820	6.2	233,900	6.1
Trade, restaurants	375,560	16.5	756,500	19.9
Finance, real estate	464,800	20.5	338,400	8.9
Pub. admin., defense	360,030	15.8 }	861,400	22.6
Services	105,750	4.7 }		
Other	80,180[2]	3.5[2]	188,300[3]	4.9[3]
TOTAL	2,272,280[1]	100.0[1]	3,808,000	100.0

Household income and expenditure. Average household size (1995) 2.5; net median income per household (1993) S 291,930 (U.S.$25,110); expenditure (1993): food and beverages 17.4%, transportation 16.3%, housing 14.5%, cafe and hotel expenditures 10.7%.
Land use (1994): forested 39.2%; meadows and pastures 24.3%; agricultural and under permanent cultivation 18.3%; other 18.2%.

Foreign trade[4]

Balance of trade (current prices)

S '000,000,000	1991	1992	1993	1994	1995	1996
	−112.9	−106.4	−97.7	−116.4	−88.0	−100.6
% of total	10.5%	9.8%	9.5%	10.2%	7.1%	7.6%

Imports (1995): S 668,000,000,000 (machinery and transport equipment 36.9%, of which road vehicles 11.4%, electrical machinery and apparatus 6.6%; chemicals and related products 10.7%; food products 5.3%; clothing 4.7%).
Major import sources: Germany 43.6%; Italy 8.8%; France 4.9%; United States 4.2%; Switzerland 3.8%; The Netherlands 3.4%.
Exports (1995): S 580,000,000,000 (machinery and transport equipment 39.0%, of which electrical machinery and apparatus 7.5%; road vehicles 7.3%; chemical products 9.2%; paper and paper products 6.3%; iron and steel 5.7%).
Major export destinations: Germany 38.4%; Italy 8.8%; Switzerland 5.4%; France 4.4%; Hungary 3.6%; United Kingdom 3.3%.

Transport and communications

Transport. Railroads (1995)[5]: length 5,672 km; passenger-km 10,476,000,000; (1996) metric ton-km cargo 13,908,000,000. Roads (1995): total length 130,023 km (paved 100%). Vehicles (1995): passenger cars 3,593,588; trucks and buses 300,042. Air transport[6] (1995): passenger-km 7,566,000,000; metric ton-km cargo 175,595,000; airports (1996) with scheduled flights 6.

Communications

Medium	date	unit	number	units per 1,000 persons
Daily newspapers	1994	circulation	3,736,000	465
Radio	1996	receivers	4,170,000	584
Television	1995	receivers	2,706,000	336
Telephones	1995	main lines	3,749,000	466
Cellular telephones	1995	subscribers	383,500	48
Facsimile machines	1995	units	284,700	35
Personal computers	1995	units	124,200	15

Education and health

Educational attainment (1993). Percentage of population age 25 and over having: lower-secondary education 37.5%; vocational education ending at secondary level 44.6%; completed upper secondary 6.1%; higher vocational 5.5%; higher 6.3%. *Literacy:* virtually 100%.

Education (1995–96)

	schools	teachers	students	student/teacher ratio
Primary/lower secondary (age 6–13)	4,557	65,977	649,994	9.9
Upper secondary/voc. (age 14–17)	693	39,553	295,473	7.5
Higher	447[7]	14,322[7]	222,095	15.9[7]

Health (1996): physicians 27,869[8] (1 per 289 persons); hospital beds 68,641 (1 per 117 persons); infant mortality rate per 1,000 live births 5.0.
Food (1995): daily per capita caloric intake 3,417 (vegetable products 65%, animal products 35%); 130% of FAO recommended minimum requirement.

Military

Total active duty personnel (1996): 55,800 (army 92.3%; navy, none; air force 7.7%). *Military expenditure as percentage of GNP* (1994): 1.0% (world 3.0%); per capita expenditure U.S.$232.

---

[1]Detail does not add total given because of rounding. [2]Value-added tax plus import duties (S 196,990,000,000) less imputed bank service charges (S 116,810,000,000). [3]Includes 173,000 unemployed. [4]Imports c.i.f., exports f.o.b. [5]Federal railways only. [6]Austrian Airlines, Lauda Air, and Tyrolean Airways. [7]1994–95. [8]Includes 6,506 doctors in training.

Internet resources for further information:
• Austrian Central Office of Statistics http://www.oestat.gv.at
• Austrian Press and Information Service (Washington, D.C.) http://www.austria.org/index.html

Azerbaijan

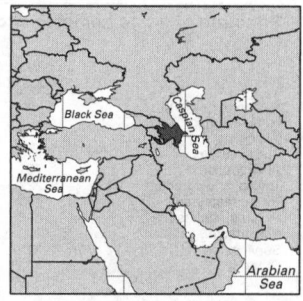

Official name: Azärbayean Respublikasi (Azerbaijani Republic).
Form of government: federal multiparty republic with a single legislative body (National Assembly [125[1]]).
Head of state and government: President assisted by Prime Minister.
Capital: Baku (Azerbaijani: Bakı).
Official language: Azerbaijani.
Official religion: none.
Monetary unit: 1 manat (A.M.) = 100 gopik; valuation (Sept. 25, 1998) free rate, 1 U.S.$ = A.M. 3,950; 1 £ = A.M. 6,725.

Area and population

Administative/ geographic units	Capitals	area		population
		sq mi	sq km	1991 estimate
Autonomous Republic				
Naxçivan	Naxçivan	2,100	5,500	305,700
Geographic region				
Nagorno-Karabakh[2]	Xankändi (Stepanakert)	1,700	4,400	193,300
Capital city				
Baku (Bakı)	—	...	...	1,713,300
Others[3]	—	29,600	76,700	4,924,300
TOTAL		33,400	86,600	7,136,600

Demography

Population (1998): 7,650,000.
Density (1998): persons per sq mi 229.0, persons per sq km 88.3.
Urban-rural (1995): urban 53.0%; rural 47.0%.
Sex distribution (1995): male 49.20%; female 50.80%.
Age breakdown (1995): under 15, 33.2%; 15–29, 26.1%; 30–44, 18.1%; 45–59, 10.1%; 60–69, 5.8%; 70 and over, 6.7%.
Population projection: (2000) 7,749,000; (2010) 8,202,000.
Doubling time: 50 years.
Ethnic composition (1995): Azerbaijani 89.0%; Russian 3.0%; Lezgian 2.2%; Armenian 2.0%; other 3.8%.
Religious affiliation (1995): Muslim (mostly Shī'ī) 93.4%; Russian Orthodox 1.1%; Armenian Apostolic (Orthodox) 1.1%; other 4.4%.
Major cities (1995): Baku (metro area) 2,500,000; Gäncä (formerly Kirovabad) 291,000; Sumqayıt (Sumgait) 268,000; Mingäçevir (Mingechaur) 96,000.

Vital statistics

Birth rate per 1,000 population (1996): 16.9 (world avg. 25.0); (1994) legitimate 94.8%; (1994) illegitimate 5.2%.
Death rate per 1,000 population (1996): 6.5 (world avg. 9.3).
Natural increase rate per 1,000 population (1996): 10.4 (world avg. 15.7).
Total fertility rate (avg. births per childbearing woman; 1993): 2.8.
Marriage rate per 1,000 population (1994): 6.3.
Divorce rate per 1,000 population (1994): 0.8.
Life expectancy at birth (1994): male 65.2 years; female 73.9 years.
Major causes of death per 100,000 population (1994): diseases of the circulatory system 336.3; accidents, poisoning, and violence 99.1; diseases of the respiratory system 98.6; malignant neoplasms (cancers) 67.6; diseases of the digestive system 31.7; infectious and parasitic diseases 29.0; endocrine and metabolic disorders 14.2; diseases of the nervous system 12.1.

National economy

Budget (1995). Revenue: A.M. 1,872,500,000,000 (tax revenue 52.2%, of which enterprise profits tax 21.8%, value-added tax 9.4%, individual income tax 6.2%, excise tax 4.7%, other 10.1%; nontax revenue 34.0%, of which foreign exchange revenue 16.9%, customs 3.7%; other 13.8%). Expenditures: A.M. 2,395,300,000,000 (goods and services 30.5%; social protection 22.3%; wages and salaries 16.3%; subsidies 9.7%; capital expenditure 3.3%; other 17.9%).
Public debt (external, outstanding; 1996): U.S.$244,900,000.
Production (metric tons except as noted). Agriculture, forestry, fishing (1996): cereals 1,032,000, fruit 957,000, vegetables (except potatoes) 377,000, cotton 274,000, potatoes 209,000, tobacco 68,000, tea 4,000; livestock (number of live animals) 4,574,000 sheep and goats, 1,658,000 cattle, 32,000 horses, 31,000 pigs, 16,000,000 poultry; roundwood (1993) 17,000 cu m; fish catch (1995) 38,000. Mining and quarrying (1995): iron ore 1,000,000; alunite 600,000. Manufacturing (value of production in A.M. '000,000; 1994): textiles 110,265; processed foods 107,943; machine-building and metalworking equipment 82,939; chemical products 60,977; construction materials 34,164; ferrous and nonferrous metals 23,184; meat and dairy products 22,540; clothing 11,847. Construction (1994): completed residential 779,000 sq m. Energy production (consumption): electricity (kW-hr; 1994) 17,600,000,000 (17,800,000,000); coal (metric tons; 1994) none (8,000); crude petroleum (barrels; 1994) 70,393,000 (76,672,000); petroleum products (metric tons; 1994) 6,259,000 (6,208,000); natural gas (cu m; 1994) 5,549,000,000 (7,706,000,000).
Household income and expenditure. Average household size (1989) 4.8; income per household: n.a.; sources of income (1993): wages and salaries 50.9%, agricultural income 24.0%, social benefits 10.2%; expenditure: food 61.2%, clothing 11.1%, services 3.0%.
Gross national product (at current market prices; 1996): U.S.$3,642,000,000 (U.S.$480 per capita).

Structure of gross domestic product and labour force

	1993		1994	
	in value A.M. '000,000	% of total value	labour force	% of labour force
Agriculture	42,653	26.8	899,000	34.4
Mining	}			
Manufacturing	39,035	24.5	374,000	14.3
Public utilities	}			
Construction	11,438	7.2	192,000	7.4
Transp. and commun.	12,532	7.9	176,000	6.7
Trade	8,452	5.3	141,000	5.4
Finance	11,278	7.1	13,000	0.5
Pub. admin., defense	9,415	5.9	49,000	1.9
Services	24,016	15.1	698,000	26.7
Other	626	0.4	72,000[4]	2.8
TOTAL	159,445[5]	100.0[5]	2,614,000	100.0[5]

Population economically active (1994): total 2,614,000, activity rate of total population 35.1% (participation rates: ages 16–59 [male], 16–54 [female] 71.5%; female 45.0%; unemployed [1995] 1.0%).

Price and earnings indexes (1993 = 100)

	1993	1994	1995	1996
Consumer price index	100	1,764	9,025	10,817
Monthly earnings index	100	742	2,994	2,963

Tourism (1995): receipts from visitors U.S.$2,000,000; expenditures by nationals abroad U.S.$4,000,000.
Land use (1994): forest 11.0%; pasture 25.4%; agriculture 48.5%; other 15.1%.

Foreign trade

Balance of trade (current prices)

	1992	1993	1994	1995	1996	1997
U.S.$'000,000	+573.3	+357.6	−140.4	−122.0	−329.4	−13.0
% of total	22.3%	22.0%	9.9%	10.1%	20.7%	0.8%

Imports (1995): U.S.$666,400,000 (food products 41.5%, machinery and equipment 18.4%, chemical products 10.9%, metals 6.3%). *Major import sources:* Turkey 21.1%; Russia 13.2%; Iran 12.0%; Turkmenistan 7.6%; Ukraine 5.1%; Kazakstan 2.7%.
Exports (1995): U.S.$544,400,000 (petroleum products 57.8%, cotton 21.4%, machinery and equipment 8.4%, food products 7.1%, metals 3.3%). *Major export destinations:* Iran 29.8%; Russia 18.1%; United Kingdom 9.0%.

Transport and communications

Transport. Railroads (1994): length 2,120 km; passenger-km 1,081,000,000; metric ton-km cargo 4,416,000,000. Roads (1995): total length 57,770 km (paved 93.8%). Vehicles (1995): passenger cars 289,000; trucks and buses 88,800. Merchant marine: vessels (100 gross tons and over) n.a.; total deadweight tonnage, n.a. Air transport (1994): passenger-km 2,026,000,000; metric ton-km cargo 49,000,000; airports (1997) with scheduled flights 3.

Communications

Medium	date	unit	number	units per 1,000 persons
Daily newspapers	1995	circulation	210,000	28
Television	1995	receivers	1,600,000	212
Telephones	1995	main lines	640,000	86
Cellular telephones	1995	subscribers	6,000	0.8
Facsimile machines	1995	units	2,500	0.1

Education and health

Educational attainment (1995). Percentage of population age 15 and over having: primary education or no formal schooling 12.1%, some secondary 9.1%; completed secondary and some postsecondary 27.5%; higher 7.6%. *Literacy* (1989): percentage of total population 15 and over literate 97.3%; males literate 98.9%; females 95.9%.

Education (1994–95)

	schools	teachers	students	student/ teacher ratio
Primary (age 6–13)	} 4,502	156,000	1,486,000	9.5
Secondary (age 14–17)				
Voc., teacher tr.	78	...	73,000	...
Higher	23	...	89,100	...

Health (1994): physicians 29,000 (1 per 256 persons); hospital beds 74,000 (1 per 100 persons); (1996) infant mortality rate per 1,000 live births 20.3.

Military

Total active duty personnel (1997): 66,700 (army 80.0%, navy[6] 3.3%, air force 16.7%). *Military expenditure as percentage of GNP* (1995): c. 2.8% (world 2.8%); per capita expenditure (1995) U.S.$40.

---

[1]Includes one vacant seat reserved for Nagorno-Karabakh representative. [2]Controlled by Armenian forces from mid-1993. [3]Includes 59 districts and 10 cities with limited self-government in 1998; some districts and cities have been controlled by Armenian forces from mid-1993. [4]Includes 24,000 undistributed unemployed and 48,000 undistributed employed. [5]Detail does not add to total given because of rounding. [6]Azerbaijan shares a portion of the Caspian flotilla.

Internet resources for further information:
• Azerbaijan Republic http://www.president.az/azerbaijan/azerbaijan.htm

Bahamas, The

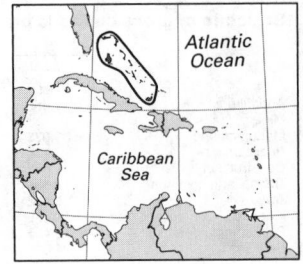

Official name: The Commonwealth of The Bahamas.
Form of government: constitutional monarchy with two legislative houses (Senate [16]; House of Assembly [40]).
Chief of state: British Monarch represented by Governor-General.
Head of government: Prime Minister.
Capital: Nassau.
Official language: English.
Official religion: none.
Monetary unit: 1 Bahamian dollar (B$) = 100 cents; valuation (Sept. 25, 1998) 1 U.S.$ = B$1.00; 1 £ = B$1.70.

Area and population	area[1]		population
Islands and Island Groups[2]	sq mi	sq km	1990 census
Abaco, Great and Little	649	1,681	10,034
Acklins	192	497	405
Andros	2,300	5,957	8,187
Berry Islands	12	31	628
Bimini Islands	9	23	1,639
Cat Island	150	388	1,698
Crooked and Long Cay	93	241	412
Eleuthera	187	484	7,993
Exuma, Great, and Exuma Cays	112	290	3,556
Grand Bahama	530	1,373	40,898
Harbour Island	3	8	1,219
Inagua, Great and Little	599	1,551	985
Long Island	230	596	2,954
Mayaguana	110	285	312
New Providence	80	207	172,196
Ragged Island	14	36	89
Rum Cay	30	78	53
San Salvador	63	163	465
Spanish Wells	10	26	1,372
Other uninhabited cays and rocks	9	23	—
TOTAL	5,382	13,939[3]	255,095

Demography

Population (1998): 293,000.
Density (1998)[4]: persons per sq mi 75.3, persons per sq km 29.1.
Urban-rural (1995): urban 86.0%; rural 14.0%.
Sex distribution (1995): male 48.91%; female 51.09%.
Age breakdown (1995): under 15, 29.3%; 15–29, 28.6%; 30–44, 23.2%; 45–59, 11.6%; 60–74, 5.1%; 75 and over, 2.2%.
Population projection: (2000) 302,000; (2010) 343,000.
Doubling time: 42 years.
Ethnic composition (1993): black 85.0%; white 12.0%; Asian or Hispanic 3.0%.
Religious affiliation (1995): non-Anglican Protestant 45.4% of which Baptist 17.5%; Roman Catholic 16.8%; Anglican 10.8%; other/nonreligious 27.0%.
Major cities (1990): Nassau 172,196[5]; Freeport/Lucaya 26,574; Marsh Harbour 3,611; Bailey Town 1,490; Dunmore Town (Harbour Island) 1,219.

Vital statistics

Birth rate per 1,000 population (1995): 22.5 (world avg. 25.0); (1994) legitimate 44.7%; illegitimate 55.3%.
Death rate per 1,000 population (1995): 5.9 (world avg. 9.3).
Natural increase rate per 1,000 population (1995): 16.6 (world avg. 15.7).
Total fertility rate (avg. births per childbearing woman; 1996): 2.0.
Marriage rate per 1,000 population (1994): 9.2.
Divorce rate per 1,000 population (1994): 1.7.
Life expectancy at birth (1996): male 68.0 years; female 77.2 years.
Major causes of death per 100,000 population (1994): circulatory diseases 137.8; infectious diseases 99.1, of which AIDS 88.1; cancers 86.6.

National economy

Budget (1996–97). Revenue: B$714,900,000 (import taxes 47.2%, stamp taxes 17.8%, departure taxes 8.3%, fines and forfeits 6.3%, business and professional licenses 5.1%). Expenditures: B$765,800,000 (education 17.4%, health 13.8%, general administration 13.8%, public works and water supply 12.4%, interest on public debt 11.7%, public order 10.4%, defense 2.8%).
National debt (March 1997): U.S.$1,556,000,000.
Production (value of export production in B$'000 except as noted). Agriculture, forestry, fishing (1996): crayfish 54,000, poultry products 26,300, citrus (particularly grapefruits and limes) 12,000, sponges 1,100, other marine products 2,500; roundwood (1995) 117,000 cu m. Mining and quarrying (value of export production; 1996): salt 18,100, aragonite 4,900. Manufacturing (value of export production; 1996): pharmaceuticals and other chemical products (1995) 74,200; rum 5,200. Construction (value of construction completed in B$'000,000; 1996): residential 92; nonresidential 65. Energy production (consumption): electricity (kW-hr; 1995) 1,254,000,000 (1,085,000,000); coal, none (none); crude petroleum, none (none); petroleum products (metric tons; 1994) negligible (555,000); natural gas, none (none).
Tourism (1996): receipts U.S.$1,458,000,000; expenditures U.S.$240,000,000.
Household income and expenditure. Average household size (1994) 3.9; income per household (1994) B$27,000 (U.S.$27,000); sources of income: n.a.; expenditure (1995)[6]: housing 32.8%, transportation and communications 14.8% food and beverages 13.8%, household furnishings 8.9%.
Gross national product (1996): U.S.$3,391,000,000 (U.S.$11,940 per capita).

Structure of gross domestic product and labour force

	1992		1994	
	in value B$'000,000	% of total value	labour force[7]	% of labour force
Agriculture, fishing	89	2.9	6,614	4.7
Manufacturing	105	3.4	5,060	3.6
Mining			2,010	1.4
Public utilities	88	2.9		
Construction	91	3.0	8,651	6.1
Transp. and commun.	227	7.4	10,821	7.7
Trade, restaurants	705	23.0	36,507	25.9
Finance, real estate	610	19.9	11,940	8.5
Pub. admin., defense	179	5.8	40,063	28.4
Services	523	17.1		
Other	443[8]	14.5[8]	19,348[9]	13.7[9]
TOTAL	3,059[3]	100.0[3]	141,014	100.0

Population economically active (1994)[10]: total 138,700; activity rate of total population 50.7% (participation rates: ages 15–64, 77.8%; female 46.8%; unemployed [1996] 13%).

Price and earnings indexes (1991 = 100)						
	1992	1993	1994	1995	1996	1997	1998
Consumer price index	105.8	108.6	110.2	112.4	114.0	114.6	116.0[11]
Annual earnings index[12]	112.8	116.8[13]	...	...	...	...	...

Land use (1994): forest 32.4%; pasture 0.2%; agriculture 1.0%; other 66.4%.

Foreign trade[14, 15]

Balance of trade (current prices)						
	1991	1992	1993	1994	1995	1996
B$'000,000	−866	−845	−792	−904	−1,067	−1,060
% of total	65.8%	68.7%	70.9%	73.0%	75.2%	72.4%

Imports (1995): B$1,243,000,000 (machinery and transport equipment 24.8%; food products 16.8%; petroleum for domestic use 12.6%; chemicals and chemical products 8.1%). *Major import sources*[16]: U.S. 92.8%; EC 2.8%.
Exports (1995): B$176,000,000 (domestic exports 52.6%, of which crayfish 31.9%, salt 7.7%; reexports 47.4%, of which machinery and transport equipment 26.1%). *Major export destinations:* U.S. 81.1%; EC 9.2%; Canada 1.9%.

Transport and communications

Transport. Railroads: none. Roads (1995): total length 1,522 mi, 2,450 km (paved 57%). Vehicles (1994): passenger cars 46,089; trucks and buses 11,858. Merchant marine (1992): vessels (100 gross tons and over) 1,061; total deadweight tonnage 33,081,652. Air transport (1994): passenger-mi 119,000,000, passenger-km 191,000,000; short ton-mi cargo 12,300, metric ton-km cargo 18,000; airports (1997) with scheduled flights 22.

Communications				units per 1,000 persons
Medium	date	unit	number	
Daily newspapers	1994	circulation	35,000	126
Radio	1996	receivers	80,000	282
Television	1995	receivers	50,000	179
Telephones	1995	main lines	77,000	277
Cellular telephones	1995	subscribers	2,400	8.6
Facsimile machines	1995	units	500	1.8

Education and health

Educational attainment (1990). Percentage of population age 25 and over having: no formal schooling 3.5%; incomplete primary education 25.4%; complete primary/incomplete secondary 57.6%; complete secondary/higher 13.5%. *Literacy* (1995): total percentage age 15 and over literate 98.2%.

Education (1993–94)	schools	teachers	students	student/ teacher ratio
Primary (age 5–10)	115	1,581	33,343	21.1
Secondary (age 11–16)	...	1,775	28,363	16.0
Higher[17]	1	300	3,201	10.7

Health: physicians (1992) 373 (1 per 709 persons); hospital beds (1993) 1,081 (1 per 249 persons); infant mortality rate per 1,000 live births (1995) 19.0.
Food (1995): daily per capita caloric intake 2,498 (vegetable products 68%, animal products 32%); 103% of FAO recommended minimum requirement.

Military

Total active duty personnel (1996): 860 (coast guard 100%). *Military expenditure as percentage of GNP* (1996)[18]: 0.6% (world, n.a.); per capita expenditure U.S.$74.

[1]Includes areas of lakes and ponds, as well as lagoons and sounds almost entirely surrounded by land; area of land only is about 3,890 sq mi (10,070 sq km). [2]Family (Out) Islands (all islands other than New Providence) are administered by commissioners assigned by the central government. [3]Detail does not add to total given because of rounding. [4]Land area only. [5]Population cited is for New Providence Island. [6]Weights of retail price index components. [7]Survey date of official figures is unknown. [8]Includes net indirect taxes (B$430,000,000) and statistical discrepancy (B$13,000,000). [9]Includes 594 not adequately defined and 18,754 unemployed. [10]As of May. [11]April. [12]Annual mean household income. [13]May. [14]Imports c.i.f.; exports f.o.b. [15]Official Bahamian statistics exclude trade data for crude petroleum imported for storage by foreign companies, hormones, and inorganic and organic chemicals. [16]Excludes all petroleum imports. [17]College of The Bahamas only. [18]Includes police.

Internet resources for further information:
• The Government of The Bahamas http://www.bahamas.net.bs/government

Bahrain

Official name: Dawlat al-Baḥrayn
(State of Bahrain).
Form of government: monarchy
(emirate)[1].
Chief of state: Emir.
Head of government: Prime Minister.
Capital: Manama.
Official language: Arabic.
Official religion: Islam.
Monetary unit: 1 Bahrain dinar
(BD) = 1,000 fils; valuation (Sept. 25,
1998) 1 BD = U.S.$2.65 = £1.54.

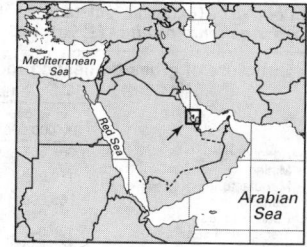

Area and population

Regions[2]	area		population
			1991
	sq mi	sq km	census
Al-Gharbīyah (Western)	60.3	156.1	22,034
Al-Ḥadd	2.3	6.0	8,610
Jidd (Judd) Ḥafṣ	8.3	21.6	44,769
Al-Manāmah (Manama)	10.0	25.8	136,999
Al-Muḥarraq	6.2	16.0	74,245
Ar-Rifāʿ	112.6	291.6	49,752
Ash-Shamālīyah (Northern)	14.2	36.8	33,763
Ash-Sharqīyah (Eastern)	...	...	3,242[3]
Sitrah	11.1	28.8	36,755
Al-Wusṭā (Central)	13.6	35.2	34,304
Towns with special status			
Ḥammād	5.1	13.1	29,055
Madīnat ʿĪsā	4.8	12.4	34,509
Islands			
Ḥawār[4] and other	19.5	50.6	2
TOTAL	268.0	694.2[5]	508,037

Demography

Population (1998): 633,000.
Density (1998): persons per sq mi 2,361.9, persons per sq km 911.8.
Urban-rural (1995): urban 90.3%; rural 9.7%.
Sex distribution (1994): male 57.78%; female 42.22%.
Age breakdown (1994): under 15, 31.5%; 15–29, 25.5%; 30–44, 30.8%; 45–59, 8.5%; 60–74, 3.0%; 75 and over, 0.6%.
Population projection: (2000) 660,000; (2010) 780,000.
Doubling time: 32 years.
Ethnic composition (1991): Bahraini Arab 63.6%; Persian, Indian, Pakistani, and other Asians 30.3%; other Arab 3.5%; European 1.2%; other 1.4%.
Religious affiliation (1991): Muslim 81.8%, of which Shīʿī 61.3%, Sunnī 20.5%; Christian 8.5%; other 9.7%.
Major cities (1991): Manama (1992) 140,401; Ar-Rifāʿ 45,956; Al-Muḥarraq 45,337; Madīnat ʿĪsā 34,509.

Vital statistics

Birth rate per 1,000 population (1994): 27.4 (world avg. 25.0); legitimate 100%.
Death rate per 1,000 population (1994): 5.4 (world avg. 9.3).
Natural increase rate per 1,000 population (1994): 22.0 (world avg. 15.7).
Total fertility rate (avg. births per childbearing woman; 1994): 3.6.
Marriage rate per 1,000 population (1993): 6.4.
Divorce rate per 1,000 population (1993): 1.3.
Life expectancy at birth (1994): male 69.0 years; female 72.4 years.
Major causes of death per 100,000 population (1991): diseases of the circulatory system 100.4; malignant neoplasms (cancers) 34.1; diseases of the respiratory system 29.7; accidents and violence 28.5; endocrine, nutritional, and metabolic diseases 17.4; congenital anomalies 13.8.

National economy

Budget (1996). Revenue: BD 633,300,000 ([1995] entrepreneurial and property income 57.7%, import duties 8.4%, foreign grants 6.7%). Expenditures: BD 627,300,000 ([1995] general administration and public order 28.5%, defense 17.3%, education 13.4%, fuel and energy 9.6%, health 9.3%, transportation and communications 9.0%).
Public debt (external, outstanding; 1991): U.S.$1,810,000,000[6].
Population economically active (1991): total 226,448; activity rate of total population 44.6% (participation rates: ages 15–64, 66.1%; female 17.5%; unemployed [1997] c. 30%).

Price and earnings indexes (1990 = 100)

	1990	1991	1992	1993	1994	1995	1996
Consumer price index	100.0	100.8	100.6	103.1	104.0	106.8	106.6
Earnings index	...	...	...	...	...	...	...

Production (metric tons except as noted). Agriculture, forestry, fishing (1997): fruit (excluding melons) 25,095, cow's milk 20,000, dates 20,000, tomatoes 5,000, hen's eggs 3,050; livestock (number of live animals) 29,400 sheep, 18,000 goats, 16,500 cattle; fish catch (1994) 9,031. Manufacturing (barrels; 1994): gas oil 28,900,000; fuel oil 20,900,000; kerosene 10,400,000; gasoline 7,700,000; jet fuel 7,100,000; naphtha 1,860,000; propane 1,500,000; butane 1,190,000; aluminum (1996) 461,200 metric tons. Construction (permits issued; 1991): residential 5,931; nonresidential 718. Energy production (consumption): electricity (kW-hr; 1994) 4,550,000,000 (4,550,000,000); crude petroleum (barrels; 1996) 14,124,000 ([1994] 89,516,000); petroleum products (metric tons; 1996) 13,100,000 (538,000); natural gas (cu m; 1996) 10,210,000,000 (10,210,000,000).

Gross national product (1996): U.S.$4,693,000,000 (U.S.$7,840 per capita).

Structure of gross domestic product and labour force

	1996		1991	
	value in BD '000,000[7]	% of total value	labour force	% of labour force
Agriculture	22.0	1.1	5,108	2.3
Mining	396.0	19.7	3,638	1.6
Manufacturing	393.5	19.5	26,618	11.8
Construction	98.8	4.9	26,738	11.6
Public utilities	35.6	1.8	2,898	1.3
Transp. and commun.	184.5	9.2	13,789	6.1
Trade	207.4	10.3	29,961	13.2
Finance	371.7	18.4	17,256	7.6
Pub. admin., defense	373.7	18.5 }		
Services	105.1	5.2 }	83,944	37.1
Other	−172.6	−8.6	16,498	7.3
TOTAL	2,015.7	100.0	226,448	100.0[5]

Household income and expenditure. Average household size (1991) 5.8; income per household: n.a.; sources of income: n.a.; expenditure (1984): food and tobacco 33.3%, housing 21.2%, household durable goods 9.8%, transportation and communications 8.5%, recreation 6.4%, clothing and footwear 5.9%, education 2.7%, health 2.3%, energy and water 2.2%.
Land use (1994): meadows and pastures 5.8%; agricultural and under permanent cultivation 2.9%; built-on and wasteland 91.3%.
Tourism (1995): receipts from visitors U.S.$288,000,000; expenditures by nationals abroad U.S.$163,000,000.

Foreign trade

Balance of trade (current prices)

	1992	1993	1994	1995	1996	1997
BD '000,000	−300.3	−50.6	−49.3	+149.3	+191.7	+170.5
% of total	10.3%	1.8%	1.8%	5.1%	5.9%	5.5%

Imports (1995): BD 1,397,100,000 (crude petroleum products 35.8%, transport equipment and machines 16.0%, food and live animals 9.3%, chemicals 8.9%). *Major import sources:* United States 8.3%; United Kingdom 5.9%; Saudi Arabia 4.9%; Australia 4.8%; Japan 4.1%; Germany 4.0%.
Exports (1995): BD 1,546,400,000 (petroleum products 59.7%, basic manufactured goods 27.3%). *Major export destinations:* Saudi Arabia 6.1%; South Korea 3.8%; Japan 3.5%; United States 3.2; India 2.5%.

Transport and communications

Transport. Railroads: none. Roads (1995): total length 2,835 km (paved 74.6%). Vehicles (1995): passenger cars 141,901; trucks and buses 29,584. Merchant marine (1992): vessels (100 gross tons and over) 87; total deadweight tonnage 192,487. Air transport (1996)[8]: passenger-km 2,758,800,000; metric ton-km cargo 105,754,000; airports (1997) with scheduled flights 1.

Communications

Medium	date	unit	number	units per 1,000 persons
Daily newspapers	1994	circulation	70,000	128
Radio	1995	receivers	320,000	555
Television	1995	receivers	255,000	442
Telephones	1995	main lines	140,900	244
Cellular telephones	1995	subscribers	27,600	48
Facsimile machines	1995	units	5,700	9.9
Personal computers	1995	units	29,000	50

Education and health

Educational attainment (1991). Percentage of population age 25 and over having: no formal education 38.4%; primary education 26.2%; secondary 25.1%; higher 10.3%. *Literacy* (1995): percentage of population age 15 and over literate 85.2%; males literate 89.1%; females literate 79.4%.

Education (1994–95)

	schools	teachers	students	student/ teacher ratio[9]
Primary (age 6–11)	124	3,536[10]	72,329	20.8
Secondary (age 12–17)	35[11]	2,305[10]	48,944	20.2
Voc., teacher tr.	9[11]	820[10]	7,113	8.2
Higher	4[11]	655[12]	7,676[12]	11.7

Health (1993): physicians 482 (1 per 1,115 persons); hospital beds 1,529 (1 per 352 persons); infant mortality rate per 1,000 live births (1994) 23.8.

Military

Total active duty personnel (1997): 11,000 (army 77.3%, navy 9.1%, air force 13.6%). *Military expenditure as percentage of GNP* (1995): 5.4% (world 2.8%); per capita expenditure U.S.$473.

---

[1]Appointed 40-member Consultative Council is an advisory body only. [2]Regions have no administrative function; the creation of four actual administrative units was begun in 1997. [3]Ash-Sharqīyah includes population of Ḥawār and other islands. [4]Also claimed by Qatar. [5]Detail does not add to total given because of rounding. [6]Includes long-term private debt not guaranteed by the government. [7]In purchasers' value at current prices. [8]One-fourth apportionment of international flights of Gulf Air (jointly administered by the governments of Bahrain, Oman, Qatar, and the United Arab Emirates). [9]1993–94. [10]Teachers in public education only. [11]1987–88. [12]1993–94.

Internet resources for further information:
• **University of Bahrain** http://www.uob.bh/
• **Bahrain Telephone Company**
  http://www.batelco.com.bh/dbahrain/intro.htm

Bangladesh

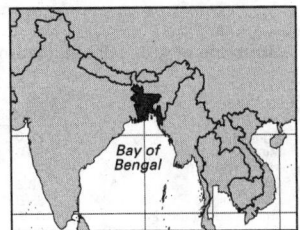

Official name: Gana Prajātantrī Bangladesh (People's Republic of Bangladesh).
Form of government: unitary multiparty republic with one legislative house (Parliament [330[1]]).
Chief of state: President.
Head of government: Prime Minister.
Capital: Dhākā.
Official language: Bengali.
Official religion: Islam.
Monetary unit: 1 Bangladesh taka (Tk) = 100 paisa; valuation (Sept. 25, 1998) 1 U.S.$ = Tk 47.10; 1 £ = Tk 80.19.

Area and population		area		population
				1991
Divisions[2]	Administrative centres	sq mi	sq km	census[3]
Barisal	Barisal	5,134	13,297	7,757,334
Chittagong	Chittagong	13,039	33,771	21,865,850
Dhākā	Dhākā	12,015	31,119	33,939,848
Khulna	Khulna	8,600	22,274	13,243,054
Rājshāhi	Rājshāhi	13,326	34,513	27,499,727
Sylhet	Sylhet	4,863	12,596	7,149,372
TOTAL		56,977	147,570	111,455,185

Demography

Population (1998): 127,567,000.
Density (1998): persons per sq mi 2,239, persons per sq km 864.5.
Urban-rural (1997): urban 20.0%; rural 80.0%.
Sex distribution (1996): male 51.72%; female 48.28%.
Age breakdown (1996): under 15, 42.0%; 15–29, 26.4%; 30–44, 17.8%; 45–59, 8.9%; 60–74, 3.8%; 75 and over, 1.1%.
Population projection: (2000) 131,999,000; (2010) 153,084,000.
Doubling time: 48 years.
Ethnic composition (1997): Bengali 97.7%; tribal 1.9%, of which Chakmā 0.4%, Saontāl 0.2%, Marma 0.1%; other 0.4%.
Religious affiliation (1991): Muslim 88.3%; Hindu 10.5%; Buddhist 0.6%; Christian 0.3%; other 0.3%.
Major cities (1991)[4]: Dhākā 6,105,160; Chittagong 2,040,663; Khulna 877,388; Rājshāhi 517,136; Mymensingh 185,517[5].

Vital statistics

Birth rate per 1,000 population (1997): 26.8 (world avg. 25.0).
Death rate per 1,000 population (1997): 12.2 (world avg. 9.3).
Natural increase rate per 1,000 population (1997): 14.6 (world avg. 15.7).
Total fertility rate (avg. births per childbearing woman; 1997): 3.2.
Marriage rate per 1,000 population (1995): 10.2.
Divorce rate per 1,000 population (1981): 3.6.
Life expectancy at birth (1997): male 58.0 years; female 58.0 years.
Major causes of death (1990; percentage of recorded deaths): typhoid fever 19.8%; old age 14.8%; tetanus 10.1%; tuberculosis and other respiratory diseases 8.7%; diarrhea 6.4%; suicide, accidents, and poisoning 5.1%; high blood pressure and heart diseases 5.0%.

National economy

Budget (1994–95). Revenue: Tk 216,940,000,000 (revenue receipts 62.9%, of which sales tax 20.2%, customs duties 14.8%, income taxes 9.7%, dividends and profits from public enterprises 7.2%; development receipts 37.1%). Expenditures: Tk 196,084,000,000 (development expenditure 49.0%; employee compensation 22.0%; goods and services 13.8%; transfer payments 12.9%).
Production (metric tons except as noted). Agriculture, forestry, fishing (1996): paddy rice 27,000,000, sugarcane 7,446,000, wheat 1,320,000, jute 770,000, bananas 630,000, pulses 545,000, oilseeds 520,000, mangoes 189,000, pineapples 150,000, tea 51,000; livestock (number of live animals) 30,330,000 goats, 24,340,000 cattle, 1,155,000 sheep, 882,000 buffalo, 123,000,000 chickens, 16,200,000 ducks; roundwood (1995) 32,044,000 cu m; fish catch (1995) 1,170,365. Mining and quarrying (1995): marine salt 350,000; industrial limestone 23,500. Manufacturing (value added in U.S.$'000,000; 1994): textiles 617; chemicals 473; food products 359; wearing apparel 225; tobacco products 225; electrical machinery 88; paper and paper products 86. Construction: n.a. Energy production (consumption): electricity (kW-hr; 1994) 10,010,000,000 (10,010,000,000); coal (metric tons; 1994) none (198,000); crude petroleum (barrels; 1994) 134,000 (8,966,000); petroleum products (metric tons; 1994) 1,104,000 (2,006,000); natural gas (cu m; 1994) 6,635,000,000 (6,635,000,000).
Household income. Average household size (1991) 5.6; average annual income per household (1991–92) Tk 40,092 (U.S.$1,061); sources of income (1991–92): self-employment 51.6%, wages and salaries 23.1%, transfer payments 10.3%, other 15.0%; expenditure (1991–92): food and drink 66.6%, housing and rent 10.4%, energy 5.6%, clothing and footwear 4.7%, other 12.7%.
Population economically active (1990): total 51,200,000; activity rate of total population 46.9% (participation rates: over age 10, 69.7%; female 39.3%; unemployed 1.0%[6]).

Price and earnings indexes (1990 = 100)							
	1991	1992	1993	1994	1995	1996	1997
Consumer price index	107.2	111.8	111.8	115.8	122.5	125.8	133.0
Earnings index[7]	104.9	109.3	114.8	121.7	...	...	...

Public debt (external, outstanding; 1996): U.S.$15,403,000,000.
Gross national product (1996): U.S.$31,217,000,000 (U.S.$260 per capita).

Structure of gross domestic product and labour force				
	1994–95		1990	
	in value Tk '000,000	% of total value	labour force	% of labour force
Agriculture	361,367	30.9	33,303,000	65.0
Mining			15,000	—
Manufacturing }	112,948	9.7	5,925,000	11.6
Construction	69,209	5.9	525,000	1.0
Public utilities	23,646	2.0	40,000	0.1
Transp. and commun.	139,049	11.9	1,611,000	3.1
Trade	100,548	8.6	4,285,000	8.4
Finance	23,127	2.0	296,000	0.6
Public admin., defense	62,308	5.3 }	5,200,000	10.2
Services and other	278,059	23.8 }		
TOTAL	1,170,261	100.0[8]	51,200,000	100.0

Land use (1994): forest 14.6%; pasture 4.6%; agriculture 74.5%; other 6.3%.
Tourism (1995): receipts U.S.$23,000,000; expenditures U.S.$229,000,000.

Foreign trade

Balance of trade (current prices)						
	1991	1992	1993	1994	1995	1996
Tk '000,000	−48,564	−55,276	−52,113	−59,665	−107,719	−110,988
% of total	28.2%	25.3%	22.5%	21.9%	29.7%	28.7%

Imports (1994–95): Tk 234,530,000,000 (textile yarn, fabrics, and made-up articles 22.6%; machinery and transport equipment 12.4%; petroleum and products 6.1%; chemicals 5.9%; cereals and preparations 4.2%; iron and steel 3.5%). *Major import sources* (1993): Japan 12.5%; India 9.5%; Hong Kong 8.0%; South Korea 6.9%; China 5.1%; Singapore 4.6%; U.S. 4.3%.
Exports (1994–95): Tk 131,310,000,000 (ready-made garments 56.6%; jute manufactures 10.4%; fish and prawns 10.1%; hides, skins, and leather 6.7%; fertilizers 2.4%; raw jute 2.0%; tea 1.0%). *Major export destinations* (1993): Western Europe 40.2%; U.S. 33.6%; Association of Southeast Asian Nations (ASEAN) 4.0%; Hong Kong 2.7%; Japan 2.5%.

Transport and communications

Transport. Railroads (1994–95): route length 1,681 mi, 2,706 km; passenger-mi 2,508,000,000, passenger-km 4,037,000,000; short ton-mi cargo 521,000,000, metric ton-km cargo 760,000,000. Roads (1995): total length 104,709 mi, 168,513 km (paved 9%). Vehicles (1994): passenger cars 82,198; trucks and buses 104,860. Merchant marine (1994): vessels (100 gross tons and over) 301; total deadweight tonnage 566,775. Air transport (1993–94)[9]: passenger-mi 1,763,000,000, passenger-km 2,838,000,000; short ton-mi cargo 82,000,000, metric ton-km cargo 121,000,000; airports with scheduled flights (1997) 8.

Communications				units per 1,000
Medium	date	unit	number	persons
Daily newspapers	1994	circulation	51,000	0.4
Radio	1996	receivers	8,000,000	65
Television	1995	receivers	600,000	5.0
Telephones	1995	main lines	286,600	2.4
Cellular telephones	1995	subscribers	2,500	—
Facsimile machines	1995	units	4,000	—

Education and health

Educational attainment (1991). Percentage of population age 25 and over having: no formal schooling 65.4%; primary education 17.1%; secondary 13.8%; postsecondary 3.7%. *Literacy* (1995): total population age 15 and over literate 38.1%; males literate 49.4%; females literate 26.1%.

Education (1993–94)				student/
	schools	teachers	students	teacher ratio
Primary (age 6–10)	66,168	242,252	15,185,000	62.7
Secondary (age 11–17)	11,019	135,217	4,884,000	36.1
Voc., teacher tr.	152	1,857	29,923	16.1
Higher	1,268	36,000	1,032,635	28.7

Health (1994): physicians 24,911 (1 per 4,759 persons); hospital beds 35,800 (1 per 3,312 persons); infant mortality rate (1997) 79.
Food (1995): daily per capita caloric intake 2,017 (vegetable products 97%, animal products 3%); 87% of FAO recommended minimum requirement.

Military

Total active duty personnel (1997): 121,000 (army 83.5%, navy 8.7%, air force 7.8%). *Military expenditure as percentage of GNP* (1995): 1.7% (world 2.8%); per capita expenditure U.S.$4.

---

[1]Includes 30 seats reserved for women. [2]Geographic reorganization at the district level took place in 1993; each division is now divided into the following number of new districts: Barisal 6, Chittagong 11, Dhākā 17, Khulna 10, Rājshāhi 16, and Sylhet 4. [3]Adjusted for underenumeration. [4]Metropolitan population. [5]Municipal population. [6]Excluding underemployment. [7]Wage earnings in manufacturing. [8]Detail does not add to total given because of rounding. [9]Bangladesh Biman only.

Internet resources for further information:
• **Permanent Mission to the United Nations**
  http://www.undp.org:81/missions/bangladesh/
• **Asian Development Bank: Statistics of DMCs: Bangladesh**
  http://internotes.asiandevbank.org/notes/ban1/BANNACT.htm

Barbados

Official name: Barbados.
Form of government: constitutional monarchy with two legislative houses (Senate [21]; House of Assembly [28]).
Chief of state: British Monarch represented by Governor-General.
Head of government: Prime Minister.
Capital: Bridgetown.
Official language: English.
Official religion: none.
Monetary unit: 1 Barbados dollar (BDS$) = 100 cents; valuation (Sept. 25, 1998) 1 U.S.$ = BDS$2.01; 1 £ = BDS$3.42.

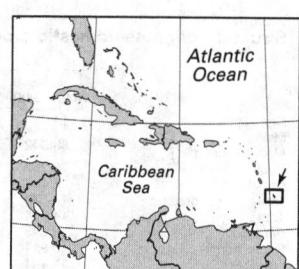

Area and population

Parishes[1]	area		population 1990 census
	sq mi	sq km	
Christ Church	22	57	47,050
St. Andrew	14	36	6,346
St. George	17	44	17,905
St. James	12	31	21,001
St. John	13	34	10,206
St. Joseph	10	26	7,619
St. Lucy	14	36	9,455
St. Michael[2]	15	39	97,516
St. Peter	13	34	11,263
St. Philip	23	60	20,540
St. Thomas	13	34	11,590
TOTAL	166	430[3]	260,491

Demography

Population (1998): 265,000.
Density (1998): persons per sq mi 1,597, persons per sq km 617.
Urban-rural (1990): urban 37.9%; rural 62.1%.
Sex distribution (1996): male 47.86%; female 52.14%.
Age breakdown (1996): under 15, 23.8%; 15–29, 25.8%; 30–44, 24.8%; 45–59, 12.8%; 60–74, 7.9%; 75 and over, 4.9%.
Population projection: (2000) 266,000; (2010) 270,000.
Doubling time: n.a.; doubling time exceeds 100 years.
Ethnic composition (1990): black 92.5%; white 3.2%; mixed 2.8%; other 1.5%.
Religious affiliation (1990): Anglican 33.0%; other Protestant 29.8%, of which Pentecostal 12.7%, Methodist 5.9%; nonreligious 20.2%; Roman Catholic 4.4%; not stated 2.7%; other 9.9%.
Major cities (1990): Bridgetown 6,070 (urban area 85,000); Speightstown, c. 3,500.

Vital statistics

Birth rate per 1,000 population (1996): 13.3 (world avg. 25.0); (1979) legitimate 26.9%; illegitimate 73.1%.
Death rate per 1,000 population (1996): 9.1 (world avg. 9.3).
Natural increase rate per 1,000 population (1996): 4.2 (world avg. 15.7).
Total fertility rate (avg. births per childbearing woman; 1996): 1.8.
Marriage rate per 1,000 population (1993): 8.5.
Divorce rate per 1,000 population (1993): 16.7.
Life expectancy at birth (1996): male 71.6 years; female 77.2 years.
Major causes of death per 100,000 population (1992): diseases of the circulatory system 366.8; malignant neoplasms (cancers) 178.5; endocrine and metabolic disorders 120.2; accidents, poisonings, and violence 40.3; diseases of the respiratory system 40.0; diseases of the digestive system 28.9; infectious and parasitic diseases 19.0; diseases of the nervous system 17.1.

National economy

Budget (1996–97). Revenue: BDS$1,231,064,000[4] (tax revenue 91.9%, of which goods and services taxes 39.1%, personal income and company taxes 32.3%, import duties 7.4%; nontax revenue 8.1%). Expenditures: BDS$1,359,104,000 (current expenditure 83.5%, of which education 18.1%, health 11.8%, economic services 10.4%, social security and welfare 8.2%).
Production (metric tons except as noted). Agriculture, forestry, fishing (1995): raw sugar 38,500, sweet potatoes 5,202, yams 2,570, lettuce 1,909, cabbage 1,823, onions 1,804, cucumbers 1,428, carrots 1,305, tomatoes 1,153, pumpkins 1,080, cassava 818; livestock (number of live animals; 1993) 66,000 sheep, 45,000 pigs, 38,000 goats, 33,000 cattle; roundwood, n.a.; fish catch 3,286. Manufacturing (value added in BDS$'000; 1995): food, beverages, and tobacco (mostly sugar, molasses, rum, beer, and cigarettes) 108,000; paper products, printing, and publishing 33,400; metal products and assembly-type goods (mostly electronic components) 28,000; textiles and wearing apparel 11,700. Construction (value added in BDS$; 1996): 151,400,000. Energy production (consumption): electricity (kW-hr; 1994) 571,000,000 (571,000,000); coal, none (none); crude petroleum (barrels; 1994) 452,000 (1,909,000); petroleum products (metric tons; 1996) 255,000 (314,000); natural gas (cu m; 1994) 22,065,000 (22,065,000).
Household income and expenditure. Average household size (1990) 3.5; income per household (1988) BDS$13,455 (U.S.$6,690); sources of income: n.a.; expenditure (1994): food 39.4%, housing 16.8%, transportation 10.5%, household operations 8.1%, alcohol and tobacco 6.4%, fuel and light 5.2%, clothing and footwear 5.0%, other 8.6%.
Population economically active (1996): total 135,800; activity rate of total population 51.5% (participation rates: ages 15 and over, 67.6%; female 61.9%; unemployed 15.8%).

Price and earnings indexes (1990 = 100)

	1991	1992	1993	1994	1995	1996	1997
Consumer price index	106.3	112.7	114.0	114.1	116.2	119.0	128.2
Hourly earnings index	...	...	...	...	...	...	...

Gross national product (1996): U.S.$295,131,000,000 (U.S.$8,380 per capita).

Structure of gross domestic product and labour force

	1996			
	in value BDS$'000,000	% of total value	labour force	% of labour force
Agriculture, fishing	205.6	5.2	6,000	4.4
Mining	18.7[5]	0.5[5]	...	...
Manufacturing	206.7	5.2	9,700	7.1
Construction	151.4	3.8	9,900	7.3
Public utilities	115.8[5]	2.9[5]	1,800	1.3
Transp. and commun.	315.5	7.9	4,400	3.2
Trade, restaurants	1,054.7	26.5	28,200	20.8
Finance, real estate	563.6	14.1	8,300	6.1
Pub. admin., defense	598.9	15.0 }	46,100	34.0
Services	146.1	3.6 }		
Other	610.8[6]	15.3[6]	21,400[7]	15.8[7]
TOTAL	3,987.8	100.0	135,800	100.0

Public debt (external, outstanding; 1996): U.S.$381,600,000.
Tourism: receipts from visitors (1995) U.S.$680,000,000; expenditures by nationals abroad (1993) U.S.$52,000,000.

Foreign trade[8]

Balance of trade (current prices)

	1992	1993	1994	1995	1996	1997
BDS$'000,000	−568.8	−689.3	−753.8	−917.0	−1,106	−1,411
% of total	42.6%	48.9%	50.9%	49.3%	49.6%	55.6%

Imports (1996): BDS$1,667,287,000 (retained imports 92.0%, of which machinery 17.8%, food and beverages 15.6%, construction materials 6.8%, chemicals 6.4%, fuels 5.4%; reexported imports 8.0%). *Major import sources* (1996): U.S. 40.5%; Trinidad and Tobago 10.8%; U.K. 8.4%; Canada 5.1%; Jamaica 1.6%.
Exports (1996): BDS$556,690,000 (domestic exports 76.3%, of which sugar 12.8%, chemicals 9.8%, electrical components 9.7%, rum 2.1%, margarine and lard 2.1%, clothing 1.4%; reexports 23.7%). *Major export destinations* (1996): U.K. 16.8%; U.S. 13.5%; Jamaica 7.5%; Trinidad and Tobago 6.3%; Canada 4.4%; St. Lucia 3.8%; Guyana 2.9%.

Transport and communications

Transport. Railroads: none. Roads (1995): total length 1,000 mi, 1,610 km (paved 95%). Vehicles (1995): passenger cars 43,711; trucks and buses 10,583[9]. Merchant marine (1992): vessels (100 gross tons and over) 37; total deadweight tonnage 84,000. Air transport (1995): passenger arrivals 699,000, passenger departures 707,400; cargo unloaded 8,382 metric tons, cargo loaded 4,717 metric tons; airports (1997) with scheduled flights 1.

Communications

Medium	date	unit	number	units per 1,000 persons
Daily newspapers	1994	circulation	41,405	157
Radio	1996	receivers	300,000	1,134
Television	1995	receivers	75,000	287
Telephones	1995	main lines	90,100	345
Cellular telephones	1995	subscribers	4,600	17.7
Facsimile machines	1995	units	1,800	6.8
Personal computers	1995	units	15,000	57.5

Education and health

Educational attainment (1990). Percentage of population age 25 and over having: no formal schooling 0.4%; primary education 23.7%; secondary 60.3%[10]; higher 11.2%; other 4.4%. *Literacy* (1995): total population age 15 and over literate 97.4%; males literate 98.0%; females literate 96.8%.

Education (1989–90)

	schools	teachers	students	student/ teacher ratio
Primary (age 3–11)[11]	106	1,553	26,662	17.2
Secondary (age 12–16)	33	1,406	21,259	15.1
Vocational[12]	8	79	996	12.6
Higher[13]	1	153	1,314	8.6

Health (1992): physicians 312 (1 per 842 persons); hospital beds 1,966 (1 per 134 persons); infant mortality rate per 1,000 live births (1996) 14.2.
Food (1995): daily per capita caloric intake 3,207 (vegetable products 74%, animal products 26%); 133% of FAO recommended minimum requirement.

Military

Total active duty personnel (1997): 610 (army 82.0%, navy 18.0%). *Military expenditure as percentage of GNP* (1995): 0.8% (world 2.8%); per capita expenditure U.S.$50.

---

[1]Parishes and city of Bridgetown have no local administrative function. [2]Includes city of Bridgetown. [3]Detail does not add to total given because of rounding. [4]Current revenue only. [5]Mining excludes natural gas; Public utilities includes natural gas. [6]Net indirect taxes. [7]Unemployed. [8]Import figures are f.o.b. in balance of trade and c.i.f. in commodities and trading partners. [9]Includes taxis. [10]Includes composite senior. [11]1991–92. [12]1987–88. [13]University of the West Indies, Cave Hill campus.

Internet resources for further information:
• Central Bank of Barbados http://www.bajan.com/cenbnet/welcome.html

Belarus

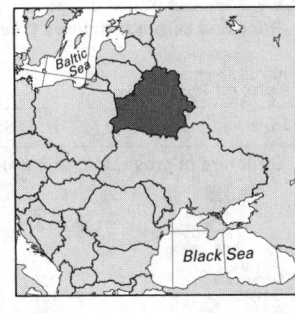

Official name: Respublika Belarus (Republic of Belarus).
Form of government[1]: unitary multiparty republic with two legislative bodies (Council of the Republic [64]; House of Representatives [110]).
Head of state and government: President assisted by Prime Minister.
Capital: Minsk.
Official languages: Belarusian; Russian.
Official religion: none.
Monetary unit[2]: rubel (Rbl; plural rubli) valuation (Sept. 25, 1998) free rate, 1 U.S.$ = Rbl 177,500; 1 £ = Rbl 302,200.

Area and population

Provinces	Capitals	area		population
		sq mi	sq km	1995 estimate
Brest	Brest	12,700	32,800	1,508,000
Homel (Gomel)	Homel	15,600	40,400	1,594,000
Hrodno (Grodno)	Hrodno	9,700	25,000	1,209,000
Mahilyoŭ (Mogilyov)	Mahilyoŭ	11,200	29,100	1,259,000
Minsk (Mensk)	Minsk	15,500	40,200	3,288,000
Vitebsk	Vitebsk	15,500	40,100	1,439,000
TOTAL		80,200[3]	207,600[3]	10,297,000

Demography

Population (1998): 10,235,000.
Density (1998): persons per sq mi 127.7, persons per sq km 49.3.
Urban-rural (1996): urban 68.9%; rural 31.1%.
Sex distribution (1995): male 47.00%; female 53.00%.
Age breakdown (1995): under 15, 22.0%; 15–29, 20.8%; 30–44, 23.6%; 45–59, 16.1%; 60–69, 10.4%; 70 and over, 7.1%.
Population projection: (2000) 10,178,000; (2010) 10,227,000.
Doubling time: not applicable; population is declining.
Linguistic composition (1989): Belarusian 65.6%; Russian 31.9%; Ukrainian 1.3%; other 1.2%.
Religious affiliation (1995): Belarusian Orthodox 31.6%; Roman Catholic 17.7%; other (mostly nonreligious) 50.7%.
Major cities (1995): Minsk 1,695,000,000; Homel 514,000; Mahilyoŭ 366,000.

Vital statistics

Birth rate per 1,000 population (1996): 9.3 (world avg. 25.0); (1994) legitimate 87.9%; illegitimate 12.1%.
Death rate per 1,000 population (1996): 13.0 (world avg. 9.3).
Natural increase rate per 1,000 population (1996): –3.7 (world avg. 15.7).
Total fertility rate (avg. births per childbearing woman; 1993): 1.9.
Marriage rate per 1,000 population (1994): 7.3.
Divorce rate per 1,000 population (1994): 4.3.
Life expectancy at birth (1994): male 63.5 years; female 74.3 years.
Major causes of death per 100,000 population (1994): diseases of the circulatory system 621.4; malignant neoplasms (cancers) 181.4; accidents and violence 138.5; diseases of the respiratory system 65.2.

National economy

Budget (1995). Revenue: Rbl 35,018,000,000,000[2] (value-added tax 28.4%, taxes on profits 23.8%, taxes on income 9.4%, excise taxes 8.0%, Chernobyl surcharges 7.9%, taxes on international trade 5.7%, other 16.8%). Expenditures: Rbl 37,888,000,000,000[2] (education 17.5%, health 15.2%, subsidies 10.8%, transfers 9.4%, Chernobyl expenditures 7.9%, lending minus repayments 5.1%, capital expenditure 4.1%, other 30.0%[4]).
Public debt (external, outstanding; 1996): U.S.$665,000,000.
Household income and expenditure. Average household size (1989) 3.2; income per household (1995) Rbl 2,400,000[2]; sources of income (1994): wages and salaries 47.1%, transfers 45.6%, agricultural income 7.3%; expenditure (1994): retail goods 70.6%, taxes 4.6%, health services 3.8%.
Production (metric tons except as noted). Agriculture, forestry, fishing (1996): potatoes 10,881,000, cereal 5,318,000, other vegetables 1,176,000, sugar beets 1,011,000, fruit 377,000; livestock (number of live animals) 5,054,000 cattle, 3,895,000 pigs, 262,000 sheep and goats, 229,000 horses, 39,000,000 poultry; roundwood (1996) 10,015,000 cu m; fish catch (1995) 15,000. Mining and quarrying (1995): peat 4,000,000; potash 3,200,000. Manufacturing (value of production in Rbl '000,000[2]; 1994): machine-building equipment 1,086,650; chemical products 659,438; food products 562,438; construction materials 142,555. Construction (1991): 5,395,000 sq m. Energy production (consumption): electricity (kW-hr; 1995) 24,918,000,000 (32,113,000,000); coal (1994) none (1,199,000); crude petroleum (barrels; 1995) 14,162,000 (94,463,000); petroleum products (1994) 10,735,000 (10,002,000); natural gas (cu m; 1995) 266,000,000 (13,840,000,000).
Population economically active (1995): 4,636,000; activity rate of total population 45.2% (participation rate: ages 16–59 [male], 16–54 [female] 83.5%; female [1991] 53.3%; unemployed 2.4%).

Price and earnings indexes (1992 = 100)

	1992	1993	1994	1995	1996
Consumer price index	100	1,290	29,946	242,349	370,043
Monthly earnings index	100	1,207	1,936	14,888	23,899

Gross national product (1996)[5]: U.S.$22,452,000,000 (U.S.$2,070 per capita).

Structure of gross domestic product and labour force

	1995			
	in value Rbl '000,000[2, 6]	% of total value	labour force	% of labour force
Agriculture	14,223	12.0	804,000	17.3
Mining } Manufacturing	30,342	25.6	1,161,000	25.0
Public utilities	6,282	5.3	...	...
Construction	6,637	5.6	279,000	6.0
Transp. and commun.	14,578	12.3	279,000	6.0
Trade	14,934	12.6	222,000	4.8
Finance	9,245	7.8	44,000	0.9
Public admin., defense	3,911	3.3	63,000	1.4
Services	11,141	9.4	827,000	17.8
Other	7,230[7]	6.1	957,000[8]	20.6
TOTAL	118,523	100.0	4,636,000	100.0[9]

Tourism: receipts from visitors, n.a.; expenditures by nationals abroad, n.a.
Land use (1994)[10]: forested 33.7%; meadows and pastures 14.1%; agricultural and under permanent cultivation 30.5%; other 21.7%.

Foreign trade

Balance of trade (current prices)

	1993	1994	1995	1996	1997
U.S.$'000,000	–569	–556	–856	–1,655	–1,388
% of total	12.6%	10.0%	8.3%	13.6%	8.7%

Imports (1996): U.S.$6,919,000,000 (1995; Commonwealth of Independent States [CIS] 93.8%, mainly petroleum, natural gas, rolled metal, coal; non-CIS 6.2%, mainly intermediate inputs [rubber, paint, rolled metal] and consumer goods [cars, shoes, cotton textiles]). *Major import sources:* Russia 46.2%; Ukraine 14.3%; Germany 9.3%; Lithuania 4.3%; Poland 3.9%.
Exports (1996): U.S.$5,264,000,000 (1995; CIS 88.9%, mainly trucks, diesel fuel, synthetic fibres, refrigerators, tires, potassium fertilizer, milk and milk products, tractors; non-CIS commodities 11.1%, potassium and nitric fertilizers, trucks, refrigerators, tires, tractors, consumer durables). *Major export destinations:* Russia 47.0%; Ukraine 16.7%; Poland 4.8%; Germany 4.5%.

Transport and communications

Transport. Railroads (1995): length 5,488 km; passenger-km 16,000,000,000; (1994) metric ton-km cargo 27,963,000,000. Roads (1995): total length 51,547 km (paved 98.6%). Vehicles (1995): passenger cars 955,256; trucks and buses 9,289. Merchant marine (1992): vessels (100 gross tons and over) n.a.; total deadweight tonnage 18,373,000,000. Air transport (1994): passenger-km 1,390,000,000; metric ton-km cargo 10,000,000; airports (1997) 1.

Communications

Medium	date	unit	number	units per 1,000 persons
Daily newspapers	1995	circulation	1,899,000	187
Radio	1996	receivers	3,200,000	311
Television	1995	receivers	2,700,000	265
Telephones	1995	main lines	1,968,000	190
Cellular telephones	1995	subscribers	5,900	600
Facsimile machines	1995	units	8,900	900

Education and health

Educational attainment (1989). Percentage of population age 25 and over having: no formal schooling or primary education only 23.0%; some secondary 16.8%; completed secondary and some postsecondary 49.4%; higher 10.8%.

Education (1995–96)

	schools	teachers	students	student/ teacher ratio
Primary (age 6–13) } Secondary (age 14–17)	4,900	127,000	1,561,000	12.3
Voc., teacher tr.	149	...	122,400	...
Higher	59	16,900[11]	197,400	10.5[11]

Literacy (1989): total population age 15 and over literate 7,690,000 (97.9%); males literate 3,661,000 (99.4%); females literate 4,029,000 (96.6%).
Health (1995): physicians 46,000 (1 per 224 persons); hospital beds 127,000 (1 per 81 persons); infant mortality rate per 1,000 live births 12.6.

Military

Total active duty personnel (1997): 81,800 (army 61.7%, air force and air defense 26.9%, other 11.4%). *Military expenditure as percentage of GNP* (1995): 0.8% (word 2.8%); per capita expenditure U.S.$32.

[1]Legal status of new constitution approved by referendum on Nov. 27, 1996, and legislative bodies established per this constitution are controversial. Council of the Republic contains 8 unelected seats. [2]On Aug. 20, 1994, the rubel became the unit of account replacing the Belarusian ruble, which was formally recognized as the sole legal tender on May 18, 1994. The conversion took place at the rate of 10 Belarusian rubles per 1 rubel. [3]Rounded area figures; exact area figures are 80,153 sq mi (207,595 sq km). [4]Includes expenditure arrears and statistical discrepancy. [5]Ruble-area GNP and exchange rate data very speculative. [6]Provisional estimates. [7]Includes Rbl 1,256,000,000,000 and Rbl 5,884,000,000,000 of imputed payments to financial intermediaries. [8]Includes 131,000 unemployed and 692,000 undistributed employed. [9]Detail does not add to total given because of rounding. [10]25% of Belarusian territory severely affected by radioactive fallout from Chernobyl. [11]1993–94.

Internet resources for further information:
• The Native Byelorussian WWW-server for Businessmen
  http://www.belarus.net/
• United Nations Office in Belarus
  http://www.un.minsk.by

Belgium

Official name: Koninkrijk België
(Dutch); Royaume de Belgique
(French) (Kingdom of Belgium).
Form of government: federal
constitutional monarchy with
a Parliament composed of two
legislative chambers (Senate [71[1]];
House of Representatives [150]).
Chief of state: Monarch.
Head of government: Prime Minister.
Capital: Brussels.
Official languages: Dutch; French;
German.
Official religion: none.
Monetary unit: 1 Belgian franc
(BF) = 100 centimes; valuation (Sept.
25, 1998) 1 U.S.$ = BF 34.47;
1£ = BF 58.69.

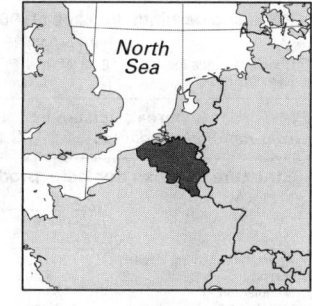

Area and population		area		population
Regions[3] **Provinces**	**Capitals**	sq mi	sq km	1996[2] estimate
Brussels-Capital	—	62	161	948,122
Flanders	—	5,221[4]	13,522	5,880,357
Antwerp	Antwerp	1,107	2,867	1,631,243
East Flanders	Ghent	1,151	2,982	1,351,777
Flemish Brabant[5]	Leuven	813	2,106	999,186
Limburg	Hasselt	935	2,422	775,302
West Flanders	Brugge	1,214	3,145	1,122,849
Wallonia	—	6,504[4]	16,844	3,314,568
Hainaut	Mons	1,462	3,786	1,284,761
Liège	Liège	1,491	3,862	1,013,729
Luxembourg	Arlon	1,714	4,440	241,339
Namur	Namur	1,415	3,666	435,677
Walloon Brabant[5]	Wavre	421	1,091	339,062
TOTAL		11,787	30,528[4]	10,143,047

Demography

Population (1998): 10,208,000.
Density (1997): persons per sq mi 866.0, persons per sq km 334.4.
Urban-rural (1996[6]): urban 96.8%; rural 3.2%.
Sex distribution (1996[6]): male 49.02%; female 50.98%.
Age breakdown (1994[2]): under 15, 18.1%; 15–29, 20.7%; 30–44, 22.7%; 45–59, 17.3%; 60–74, 15.1%; 75 and over, 6.1%.
Population projection: (2000) 10,260,000; (2010) 10,149,000.
Doubling time: not applicable; doubling time exceeds 100 years.
Nationality (1992): Belgian 91.0%; Italian 2.4%; Moroccan 1.4%; French 0.9%; Turkish 0.8%; Dutch 0.6%; other 2.9%.
Religious affiliation (1995): Roman Catholic 87.9%; Muslim 2.5%; other Christian 2.4%, of which Protestant 1.0%; Jewish 0.3%; other 6.9%.
Major cities (1996[2]): Brussels 136,424[7] (948,122[8]); Antwerp 455,852; Ghent 226,464; Charleroi 205,591; Liège 190,525.

Vital statistics

Birth rate per 1,000 population (1996): 11.4 (world avg. 25.0); (1989) legitimate 88.7%; illegitimate 11.3%.
Death rate per 1,000 population (1996): 10.4 (world avg. 9.3).
Natural increase rate per 1,000 population (1996): 1.0 (world avg. 15.7).
Total fertility rate (avg. births per childbearing woman; 1990–95): 1.6.
Marriage rate per 1,000 population (1994): 5.1.
Divorce rate per 1,000 population (1994): 2.2.
Life expectancy at birth (1991–93): male 73.0 years; female 79.8 years.
Major causes of death per 100,000 population (1989): diseases of the circulatory system 412.8; malignant neoplasms (cancers) 274.6; accidents and violence 64.6; diseases of the respiratory system 50.1.

National economy

Budget (1994). Revenue: BF 2,292,500,000,000 (direct taxes 52.3%, indirect taxes 40.8%). Expenditures: BF 2,668,700,000,000 (government departments 27.9%, debt service 27.7%, domestic transfers 16.3%).
Public debt (1998[2]): U.S.$265,600,000,000.
Production (metric tons except as noted). Agriculture, forestry, fishing (1997[6]): sugar beets 5,245,000, potatoes 2,490,000, wheat 1,910,000, barley 435,500, apples 302,400, tomatoes 300,000; livestock (number of live animals) 7,050,000 pigs, 3,000,000 cattle, 161,000 sheep, 24,000 horses; roundwood (1995[6]) 4,185,000 cu m; fish catch (1995) 36,445. Mining and quarrying (1994): quartz 500,000; barite 30,000; granite (Belgium bluestone) 2,105,000 cu m; marble 330 cu m. Manufacturing (value added in U.S.$'000,000; 1994): chemicals 4,771; transport equipment 3,632; textiles 2,056; plastics 2,045; printing 1,968; furniture 1,632. Construction (1993): residential 33,063,000 cu m; nonresidential 42,864,000 cu m. Energy production (consumption): electricity (kW-hr; 1994) 72,236,000,000 (76,219,000,000); coal (metric tons; 1994) 753,000 (13,050,000); crude petroleum (barrels; 1994) none (206,706,000); petroleum products (metric tons; 1994) 25,373,000 (17,036,000); natural gas (cu m; 1994) 1,351,000 (11,531,000,000).
Tourism (1995[6]): receipts U.S.$5,593,700,000; expenditures U.S.$9,038,100,000.
Household income and expenditure. Avg. household size (1991) 2.7; sources of income (1992): wages 49.6%, transfer payments 20.7%, property income 18.8%, self-employment 10.9%; expenditure (1992): food 18.0%, housing 17.0%, transp. 13.3%, health 11.8%, durable goods 10.7%, clothing 7.7%.
Gross national product (1996): U.S.$268,633,000,000 (U.S.$26,440 per capita).

Structure of gross domestic product and labour force				
	1996		1996	
	in value BF '000,000	% of total value	labour force	% of labour force
Agriculture	101,900	1.2	104,100	2.5
Mining	20,600	0.2	10,000	0.2
Manufacturing	1,761,900	21.2	754,400	18.0
Construction	391,700	4.7	254,100	6.1
Public utilities	204,300	2.5	29,400	0.7
Transp. and commun.	634,500	7.6	286,200	6.8
Trade	2,213,000	26.6	682,500	16.3
Finance			401,400	9.6
Pub. admin., defense	2,612,600	31.5	1,244,700	29.7
Services				
Other	364,300[9]	4.4[9]	429,300[10]	10.2[10]
TOTAL	8,305,000[4]	100.0[4]	4,196,000[4]	100.0[4]

Population economically active (1996): total 4,196,000; activity rate 41.3% (participation rates: ages 14–64, 61.1%; female 41.6%; unemployed 9.6%).

Price and earnings indexes (1990 = 100)							
	1991	1992	1993	1994	1995	1996	1997
Consumer price index	103.2	105.7	108.6	111.2	112.8	115.2	117.0
Hourly earnings index	105.1	110.1	112.4	114.7	...	...	...

Land use (1994[6]): forest 21.3%; pasture 21.0%; agriculture 24.2%; other 33.5%.

Foreign trade[6]

Balance of trade (current prices)						
	1992	1993	1994	1995	1996	1997
BF '000,000	+67,500	+370,500	+513,000	+427,700	+402,000	+404,000
% of total	0.9%	4.7%	5.9%	4.4%	4.5%	3.5%

Imports (1994): BF 4,206,413,900,000 (machinery 25.6%; chemicals 13.0%; food 8.9%; diamonds 7.2%; mineral fuels 6.9%; petroleum products 4.8%). *Major import sources:* Germany 20.2%; The Netherlands 17.7%; France 16.1%; U.K. 9.4%.
Exports (1994): BF 4,588,184,500,000 (machinery 28.1%; chemicals 16.7%, of which plastics 5.1%; food 9.1%; diamonds 6.8%; iron and steel 6.0%; textiles 5.0%; petroleum products 2.8%). *Major export destinations:* Germany 21.0%; France 19.0%; The Netherlands 13.2%; U.K. 8.5%.

Transport and communications

Transport. Railroads (1995): route length 3,368 km; passenger-km 6,757,000,-000; metric ton-km cargo 7,787,000,000. Roads (1995): total length 142,555 km (paved 97%). Vehicles (1996): passenger cars 4,339,231; trucks and buses 431,376. Merchant marine (1992): vessels (100 gross tons and over) 232; total deadweight tonnage 218,506. Air transport (1994): passenger-km 7,496,412,000; metric ton-km cargo 422,249,000; airports (1997) 2.

Communications				units per 1,000 persons
Medium	date	unit	number	
Daily newspapers	1995	circulation	3,089,000	304
Radio	1994	receivers	7,690,000	757
Television	1995	receivers	4,700,000	464
Telephones	1995	main lines	4,632,100	457
Cellular telephones	1995	subscribers	235,000	23.2
Facsimile machines	1995	units	165,000	16.3
Personal computers	1995	units	1,400,000	138

Education and health

Educational attainment (1981). Percentage of population age 15 and over having: less than secondary education 44.4%; lower secondary 26.5%; upper secondary 17.0%; vocational 2.9%; teacher's college 0.6%; university 3.5%.
Literacy (1995): virtually 99% literate.

Education (1993–94)				student/ teacher ratio
	schools	teachers	students	
Primary (age 6–12)	4,453	72,589[11, 12]	731,527	...
Secondary (age 12–18)	1,950	110,599[13]	796,914	...
Voc., teacher tr.[13]	304	14,548[14]	155,192	...
Higher[13]	21	10,517[14]	123,320	...

Health: physicians (1996[2]) 38,363 (1 per 264 persons); hospital beds (1994) 77,181 (1 per 131 persons); infant mortality rate (1996) 5.6.
Food (1995): daily per capita caloric intake 3,530 (vegetable products 68%, animal products 32%); 134% of FAO recommended minimum requirement.

Military

Total active duty personnel (1997): 44,450 (army 64.1%, navy 6.1%, air force 27.0%, medical service 2.8%). *Military expenditure as percentage of GNP* (1996): 1.7% (world 2.8%); per capita expenditure U.S.$439.

[1]Excludes children of the monarch serving ex officio from age 18. [2]January 1. [3]Corresponding to three language-based federal community councils: Dutch (Flanders), French (Wallonia), and bilingual (Brussels-Capital) having authority in cultural affairs; a fourth (German) community council lacks expression as an administrative region. [4]Detail does not add to total given because of rounding. [5]Former Brabant province divided on Jan. 1, 1995. [6]Includes Luxembourg. [7]1991. [8]Région Bruxelloise. [9]Represents a statistical correction. [10]Includes 404,200 unemployed. [11]Includes preschool teachers. [12]1992–93. [13]1991–92. [14]1987–88.

Internet resources for further information:
• Belgian Federal Government On Line http://belgium.fgov.be/

Belize

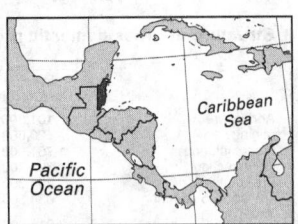

Official name: Belize.
Form of government: constitutional monarchy with two legislative houses (Senate [8[1]]; House of Representatives [29[2]]).
Chief of state: British Monarch represented by Governor-General.
Head of government: Prime Minister.
Capital: Belmopan.
Official language: English.
Official religion: none.
Monetary unit: 1 Belize dollar (BZ$) = 100 cents; valuation (Sept. 25, 1998) 1 U.S.$ = BZ$2.00[3]; 1 £ = BZ$3.41.

Area and population

Districts	Capitals	area sq mi	area sq km	population 1994 estimate
Belize	Belize City	1,663	4,307	62,939
Cayo	San Ignacio	2,006	5,196	41,594
Corozal	Corozal	718	1,860	31,412
Orange Walk	Orange Walk	1,790	4,636	33,855
Stann Creek	Dangriga	986	2,554	19,957
Toledo	Punta Gorda	1,704	4,413	19,243
TOTAL		8,867[4]	22,965[4, 5]	209,000

Demography

Population (1998): 235,000.
Density (1998): persons per sq mi 26.5, persons per sq km 10.2.
Urban-rural (1994): urban 47.5%; rural 52.5%.
Sex distribution (1996): male 50.02%; female 49.98%.
Age breakdown (1996): under 15, 41.6%; 15–29, 26.4%; 30–44, 16.3%; 45–59, 8.6%; 60 and over, 7.1%.
Population projection: (2000) 248,000; (2010) 307,000.
Doubling time: 26 years.
Ethnic composition (1991): mestizo (Spanish-Indian) 43.6%; Creole (predominantly black) 29.8%; Mayan Indian 11.0%; Garifuna (black-Carib Indian) 6.7%; white 3.9%; East Indian 3.5%; other or not stated 1.5%.
Religious affiliation (1991): Roman Catholic 57.7%; Protestant 34.3%, of which Anglican 7.0%, Pentecostal 6.3%, Methodist 4.2%, Seventh-day Adventist 4.1%, Mennonite 4.0%; other Christian 1.7%; other 0.3%; none or not stated 6.0%.
Major cities (1996): Belize City 52,670; Orange Walk 14,960; San Ignacio/ Santa Elena 11,315; Corozal 8,020; Belmopan 6,490.

Vital statistics

Birth rate per 1,000 population (1996): 32.8 (world avg. 25.0); (1992) legitimate 41.6%; illegitimate 58.4%.
Death rate per 1,000 population (1996): 5.7 (world avg. 9.3).
Natural increase rate per 1,000 population (1996): 27.1 (world avg. 15.7).
Total fertility rate (avg. births per childbearing woman; 1996): 4.1.
Marriage rate per 1,000 population (1994): 6.3.
Divorce rate per 1,000 population (1993): 0.6.
Life expectancy at birth (1996): male 66.6 years; female 70.6 years.
Major causes of death per 100,000 population (1990): accidents 92.6; heart diseases 84.7; diseases of the respiratory system 57.1; malignant neoplasms (cancers) 52.4; cerebrovascular disease 47.6; diabetes mellitus 37.0.

National economy

Budget (1996–97). Revenue: BZ$302,800,000 (current revenue 88.3%; development revenue 11.7%). Expenditures: BZ$375,000,000 (current expenditures 71.2%; development expenditures 28.8%, of which foreign grants and loans 27.0%).
Tourism (1995): receipts from visitors U.S.$78,000,000; expenditures by nationals abroad U.S.$21,000,000.
Production (metric tons except as noted). Agriculture, forestry, fishing (1996): sugarcane 1,091,000, oranges 127,900, bananas 67,000, grapefruits 44,000, corn (maize) 28,200, rice 9,600, coconuts 3,200, red kidney beans 3,100, cacao 182, honey (1994) 72; livestock (number of live animals) 60,000 cattle, 22,000 pigs, 1,300,000 chickens; roundwood (1994) 187,600 cu m; fish catch (1995) 1,366, of which shrimp 635, lobsters 392, conchs 184, freshwater and marine fish 155. Mining and quarrying (1995): sand and gravel 320,000; limestone 310,000. Manufacturing (1995): sugar (1996) 110,500; molasses 46,500; fertilizer 26,600; flour 11,500; orange concentrate (1996) 113,000 hectolitres; beer 41,100 hectolitres; grapefruit concentrate (1996) 34,000 hectolitres; cigarettes 94,000,000 units; garments (1996) 2,100,000 units. Construction (publicly financed buildings under construction; 1991): residential 180 units; nonresidential, n.a. Energy production (consumption): electricity (kW-hr; 1994) 110,000,000 (110,000,000); coal, none (none); crude petroleum, none (none); petroleum products (metric tons; 1994) none (81,000); natural gas, none (none).
Household income and expenditure. Average household size (1991) 4.9; average annual income of employed head of household (1993) BZ$6,450[6] (U.S.$3,225[6]); sources of income; n.a.; expenditure (1990): food, beverages, and tobacco 34.0%, transportation 13.7%, energy and water 9.1%, housing 9.0%, clothing and footwear 8.8%, household furnishings 8.0%.
Population economically active (1996): total 75,450; activity rate of total population 34.1% (participation rates: ages 14–64, 58.5%; female 30.8%; unemployed 13.8%).

Price and earnings indexes (1990 = 100)

	1991	1992	1993	1994	1995	1996	1997
Consumer price index	102.3	104.7	106.2	109.0	112.1	119.3	120.6
Earnings index	...	...	...	...	...	...	...

Public debt (external, outstanding; 1996): U.S.$252,300,000.
Gross national product (1996): U.S.$600,000,000 (U.S.$2,700 per capita).

Structure of gross domestic product and labour force

	1995 in value BZ$'000[7]	1995 % of total value	1996 labour force	1996 % of labour force
Agriculture, fishing, forestry	205,800	20.9	18,650	24.7
Mining	6,200	0.6	85	0.1
Manufacturing	135,600	13.7	6,770	9.0
Construction	65,400	6.6	3,250	4.3
Public utilities	36,400	3.7	925	1.2
Transp. and commun.	100,700	10.2	3,845	5.1
Trade, restaurants	170,400	17.3	13,815	18.3
Finance, real estate, insurance	121,300	12.3	1,760	2.3
Pub. admin., defense	123,900	12.6	} 15,015	19.9
Services	59,800	6.1		
Other	−39,500[8]	−4.0[8]	11,335[9]	15.0[9]
TOTAL	986,000	100.0	75,450	100.0[5]

Land use (1994): forested 92.1%; meadows and pastures 2.2%; agricultural and under permanent cultivation 3.6%; other 2.1%.

Foreign trade[10]

Balance of trade (current prices)

	1991	1992	1993	1994	1995	1996
BZ$'000,000	−222.5	−217.2	−237.8	−170.6	−144.4	−129.4
% of total	31.4%	27.9%	30.3%	22.0%	18.3%	16.2%

Imports (1995): BZ$517,000,000 (machinery and transport equipment 25.8%; food and beverages 18.3%; mineral fuels and lubricants 11.5%; chemicals and chemical products 10.7%). *Major import sources:* U.S. 54.0%; Mexico 11.0%; U.K. 6.3%; Netherlands Antilles 5.0%; Canada 3.0%.
Exports (1995): BZ$323,400,000 (domestic exports 88.4%, of which raw sugar 29.5%, orange concentrate 13.9%, bananas 13.6%, marine products 9.6%, garments 9.0%; reexports 11.6%). *Major export destinations:* U.K. 42.0%; U.S. 36.0%; Germany 5.0%; Canada 4.0%.

Transport and communications

Transport. Railroads: none. Roads (1995): total length 1,721 mi, 2,770 km (paved 19%). Vehicles (1993): passenger cars 10,667; trucks and buses 6,108. Merchant marine (1992): vessels (100 gross tons and over) 32; total deadweight tonnage 45,706. Air transport (1995)[11]: passenger arrivals 174,824, passenger departures 191,409; cargo loaded 299 metric tons, cargo unloaded 1,176 metric tons. Airports (1997) with scheduled flights 9.

Communications

Medium	date	unit	number	units per 1,000 persons
Radio	1996	receivers	29,620	133
Television	1995	receivers	23,547	109
Telephones	1995	main lines	28,900	134
Cellular telephones	1995	subscribers	1,200	5.6
Facsimile machines	1995	units	500	2.3
Personal computers	1995	units	6,000	28

Education and health

Educational attainment (1991). Percentage of population age 25 and over having: no formal schooling 13.0%; primary education 64.3%; secondary 14.9%; higher 6.6%; other 1.2%. *Literacy* (1991): total population age 14 and over literate 75,500 (70.3%).

Education (1996–97)

	schools	teachers	students	student/ teacher ratio
Primary (age 5–12)	245	1,976[12]	52,994	25.9[12]
Secondary (age 13–16)	30	740[12]	10,648	13.7[12]
Higher	11	...	2,469	...

Health: physicians (1995) 139 (1 per 1,546 persons); hospital beds (1993) 585 (1 per 350 persons); infant mortality rate per 1,000 live births (1996) 33.9.
Food (1992): daily per capita caloric intake 2,662 (vegetable products 75%, animal products 25%); 118% of FAO recommended minimum requirement.

Military

Total active duty personnel (1996): 1,050 (army 95.2%, maritime wing 4.8%). *Military expenditure as percentage of GNP* (1995): 1.6% (world 2.8%); per capita expenditure U.S.$41.

---

[1]Excludes president of the Senate, who may be elected by the Senate from outside its appointed membership. [2]Excludes speaker of the House of Representatives, who may be elected by the House from outside its elected membership. [3]The Belize dollar is officially pegged to the U.S. dollar. [4]Includes offshore cays totaling 266 sq mi (689 sq km). [5]Detail does not add to total given because of rounding. [6]Estimated figure for about 33,000 employed heads of household. [7]At factor cost. [8]Less imputed bank service charges. [9]Includes 910 not adequately defined and 10,425 unemployed. [10]Import figures are f.o.b. in balance of trade and c.i.f. in commodities and trading partners. [11]Belize international airport only. [12]1994–95.

Internet resources for further information:
• Belize Information Service Home Page http://www.belize.gov.bz/bis.htm

Benin

Official name: République du Bénin (Republic of Benin).
Form of government: multiparty republic with one legislative house (National Assembly [83[1]]).
Head of state and government: President, assisted by Prime Minister[2].
Capital[3]: Porto-Novo.
Official language: French.
Official religion: none.
Monetary unit: 1 CFA franc (CFAF) = 100 centimes; valuation (Sept. 25, 1998) 1 U.S.$ = CFAF 560.38; 1 £ = CFAF 954.05.

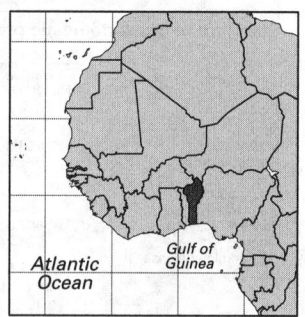

Area and population		area		population
				1992
Provinces[4]	Capitals	sq mi	sq km	census
Atacora	Natitingou	12,050	31,200	648,330
Atlantique	Cotonou	1,250	3,200	1,060,310
Borgou	Parakou	19,700	51,000	816,278
Mono	Lokossa	1,500	3,880	646,954
Ouémé	Porto-Novo	1,800	4,700	869,492
Zou	Abomey	7,200	18,700	813,985
TOTAL		43,500	112,680	4,855,349

Demography

Population (1998): 6,101,000.
Density (1998): persons per sq mi 140.3, persons per sq km 54.1.
Urban-rural (1994): urban 41.0%; rural 59.0%.
Sex distribution (1997): male 48.83%; female 51.17%.
Age breakdown (1997): under 15, 48.0%; 15–29, 27.5%; 30–44, 13.5%; 45–59, 7.2%; 60–74, 3.1%; 75 and over, 0.7%.
Population projection: (2000) 6,517,000; (2010) 8,955,000.
Doubling time: 21 years.
Ethnic composition (1992): Fon 39.7%; Yoruba (Nago) 12.1%; Adjara 11.1%; Bariba 8.6%; Aizo 8.6%; Somba (Otomary) 6.6%; Fulani 5.6%; other 7.7%.
Religious affiliation (1991): traditional beliefs, including voodoo 62.0%; Christian 23.3%, of which Roman Catholic 21.0%, Protestant 2.3%; Muslim 12.0%; other 2.7%.
Major cities (1992): Cotonou 533,212; Porto-Novo 177,600; Djougou 132,192; Abomey-Calavi 125,565; Parakou 106,708.

Vital statistics

Birth rate per 1,000 population (1997): 46.0 (world avg. 25.0).
Death rate per 1,000 population (1997): 13.0 (world avg. 9.3).
Natural increase rate per 1,000 population (1997): 33.0 (world avg. 15.7).
Total fertility rate (avg. births per childbearing woman; 1997): 6.6.
Marriage rate per 1,000 population (1980–85): 12.8.
Divorce rate per 1,000 population (1980–85): 0.8.
Life expectancy at birth (1996): male 50.7 years; female 54.7 years.
Major causes of death per 100,000 population (1995): n.a.; however, of the 13,680 reported cases of selected infectious diseases (notifiable to the World Health Organization), measles 77%, tuberculosis 18%, leprosy 4%, acquired immune deficiency syndrome (AIDS) 2%, neonatal tetanus 0.2%.

National economy

Budget (1997). Revenue: CFAF 183,984,000,000 (1996; current receipts 68.2%, of which nonpetroleum fiscal receipts and customs duties 56.3%, other nonfiscal receipts 11.9%). Expenditures: CFAF 295,547,000,000 (1996; current expenditures 63.9%, of which salaries 24.9%, debt service 12.2%).
Production (metric tons except as noted). Agriculture, forestry, fishing (1997): cassava 1,451,628, yams 1,346,040, corn (maize) 503,818, seed cotton 444,124, sorghum 111,843, tomatoes 71,714, peanuts (groundnuts) 84,206, dry beans 58,966, sweet potatoes 67,732, millet 28,758, coconuts 20,000, sugarcane 29,594, karité nuts (shea nuts) 15,000, paddy rice 21,788, palm kernels 13,300[5], bananas 13,000, mangoes 12,000, oranges 12,000, pineapples 3,000, tobacco 325; livestock (number of live an¹ ¹als; 1997) 1,350,000 cattle, 1,012,960 goats, 601,183 sheep, 584,000 pigs, 25,000,000 chickens; roundwood (1995) 5,899,000 cu m; fish catch (1995) 37,000. Mining and quarrying (1993): limestone 500,000, marine salt 100. Manufacturing (1995): cement 380,000[6]; cotton fibre 103,000; meat 68,000; wheat flour 11,515; palm oil 9,432. Construction: n.a. Energy production (consumption): electricity (kW-hr; 1994) 6,000,000 (248,000,000); coal, none (none); crude petroleum (barrels; 1994) 2,130,000 (41,000); petroleum products (metric tons; 1994) none (144,000); natural gas, none (none).
Land use (1995): agricultural and under permanent cultivation 17.0%; other 83.0% (of which [1994] forested 30.7%, meadows and pastures 4.0%).
Tourism (1995): receipts from visitors U.S.$27,000,000; expenditures by nationals abroad U.S.$19,000,000[7].
Population economically active (1992): total 2,085,400; activity rate of total population 43.0% (participation rates: ages 15–64, 73.4%; female 42.6%; unemployed, n.a.).

Price and earnings indexes (1990 = 100)						
	1991	1992	1993	1994	1995	1996	1997
Consumer price index	100.0	104.0	104.5	144.7	165.7	173.8	179.8
Hourly earnings index[8]	100.0	100.0	100.0	144.1	...	...	...

Gross national product (1996): U.S.$1,998,000,000 (U.S.$350 per capita).

Structure of gross domestic product and labour force				
	1995		1992	
	in value CFAF '000,000,000	% of total value	labour force	% of labour force[9]
Agriculture	351.5	33.9	1,147,746	55.0
Mining	7.2	0.7	661	0.0
Manufacturing	83.7	8.1	160,406	7.7
Public utilities	6.8	0.7	1,176	0.1
Construction	49.6	4.8	51,655	2.5
Transp. and communications	78.0	7.5	52,837	2.5
Trade	215.6	20.8	432,501	20.7
Finance			3,106	0.1
Pub. admin., defense	79.8	7.7	164,544	7.9
Services	103.6	10.0		
Other	60.0	5.8	70,814	3.4
TOTAL	1,035.8	100.0	2,085,446	100.0[10]

Public debt (external, outstanding; 1996): U.S.$1,449,000,000.
Household income and expenditure. Average household size (1992) 5.9; income per household (1983) U.S.$240; sources of income; self-employement 73.7%, wages and salaries 26.3%; expenditure: n.a.

Foreign trade

Balance of trade (current prices)						
	1992	1993	1994	1995	1996	1997
CFAF '000,000,000	−64.2	−53.2	−22.2	−138.8	−123.3	−150.7
% of total	26.6%	19.7%	4.9%	25.2%	22.1%	24.4%

Imports (1996): CFAF 280,200,000,000 (1990; manufactured goods 28.8%, of which cotton yarn and fabric 10.7%; food products 24.7%, of which cereals 17.6%; machinery and transport equipment 10.9%; chemical products 10.0%; refined petroleum products 8.5%; beverages and tobacco 7.3%). *Major import sources* (1995): France 27.1%; United Kingdom 9.6%; China 9.3%; Thailand 9.1%; Hong Kong 8.8%; The Netherlands 5.6%; United States 4.8%; Germany 4.3%.
Exports (1996): CFAF 216,200,000,000 (cotton yarn 49.6%, crude petroleum 2.9%, seed cotton 2.3%). *Major export destinations* (1995): Brazil 18.2%; Portugal 13.5%; Morocco 10.3%; Libya 7.5%; India 6.5%; Italy 4.5%; United States 4.5%.

Transport and communications

Transport. Railroads (1994): length 359 mi, 578 km; passenger-mi 66,500,000, passenger-km 107,000,000; short ton-mi cargo 173,000,000 metric ton-km cargo 253,000,000. Roads (1995): total length 5,257 mi, 8,460 km (paved 31.4%). Vehicles (1995): passenger cars 22,200; trucks and buses 12,400. Merchant marine (1992): vessels (100 gross tons and over) 12; total deadweight tonnage 210. Air transport (1996)[11]: passenger-mi 139,644,000, passenger-km 224,736,000; short ton-mi cargo 11,247,000, metric ton-km cargo 16,420,000; airports (1997) with scheduled flights 1.

Communications				units per 1,000
Medium	date	unit	number	persons
Daily newspapers	1994	circulation	12,000	2
Radio	1995	receivers	400,000	73
Television	1995	receivers	20,000	4
Telephones	1995	main lines	27,500	5
Cellular telephones	1995	subscribers	1,100	0.2
Facsimile machines	1995	units	500	0.1

Education and health

Educational attainment (1992). Percentage of population age 25 and over having: no formal schooling 78.5%; primary education 10.8%; some secondary 8.2%; secondary 1.2%; postsecondary 1.3%. *Literacy* (1995): total percentage of population age 15 and over literate 37.0%; males literate 48.7%; females literate 25.8%.

Education (1993–94)				student/
	schools	teachers	students	teacher ratio
Primary	2,889	12,343	602,069	48.8
Secondary	145	2,384	97,480	40.9
Voc., teacher tr.	14	283	4,873	17.2
Higher	16	602	9,964	16.5

Health: physicians (1993) 363 (1 per 14,216 persons); hospital beds (1993) 1,235 (1 per 4,182 persons); infant mortality rate (1997) 103.0.
Food (1995): daily per capita caloric intake 2,405 (vegetable products 96%, animal products 4%); 105% of FAO recommended minimum requirement.

Military

Total active duty personnel (1997): 4,800 (army 93.8%, navy 3.1%, air force 3.1%). *Military expenditure as percentage of GNP* (1995): 1.2% (world 2.8%); per capita expenditure U.S.$4.

[1]Includes one seat that was to remain vacant per the electoral code. [2]Office of Prime Minister occupied by Government Spokesman from May 1998. [3]Porto-Novo, the official capital established under the constitution, is the seat of the legislature, but the president and most government ministers reside in Cotonou. [4]In 1997 an administrative reorganization was announced consisting of 12 *départements*, but detailed breakdown of area and population is unavailable. [5]1996. [6]1993. [7]1994. [8]Minimum hourly industrial wage; January 1. [9]Age 10 years and over. [10]Detail does not add to total given because of rounding. [11]Represents ¹/11 of the traffic of Air Afrique, which is operated by 11 West African states.

Internet resources for further information:
• Découvrez la République du Bénin http://planben.intnet.bj/

Bhutan

Official name: Druk-Yul (Kingdom of Bhutan).
Form of government: constitutional[1] monarchy with one legislative house (National Assembly [150[2]]).
Head of state and government: Monarch assisted by the Council of Ministers[1].
Capital: Thimphu.
Official language: Dzongkha (a Tibetan dialect).
Official religion: Mahāyāna Buddhism.
Monetary unit: 1 ngultrum[3] (Nu) = 100 chetrum; valuation (Sept. 25, 1998) 1 U.S.$ = Nu 42.51; 1 £ = Nu 72.37.

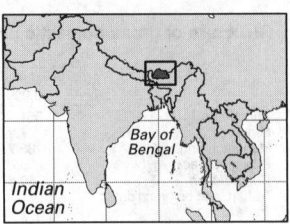

Area and population

Districts	Capitals	area sq mi	area sq km	population 1998 estimate
Bumthang	Jakar	1,150	2,990	...
Chhukha	Chhukha	...	...	...
Chirang	Damphu	310	800	...
Dagana	Dagana	540	1,400	...
Gaylegphug	Gaylegphug	1,020	2,640	...
Ha	Ha	830	2,140	...
Lhuntshi	Lhuntshi	1,120	2,910	...
Mongar	Mongar	710	1,830	...
Paro	Paro	580	1,500	...
Pema Gatsel	Pema Gatsel	150	380	...
Punakha	Punakha	2,330	6,040	...
Samchi	Samchi	830	2,140	...
Samdrup Jongkhar	Samdrup Jongkhar	900	2,340	...
Shemgang	Shemgang	980	2,540	...
Tashigang	Tashigang	1,640	4,260	...
Thimphu	Thimphu	630	1,620	...
Tongsa	Tongsa	570	1,470	...
Wangdi Phodrang	Wangdi Phodrang	1,160	3,000	...
TOTAL		18,150[4, 5]	47,000[4, 5]	633,000[6]

Demography

Population (1998): 633,000[6].
Density (1998): persons per sq mi 34.9, persons per sq km 13.5.
Urban-rural (1997): urban 7.0%; rural 93.0%.
Sex distribution (1988): male 50.97%; female 49.03%.
Age breakdown (1988): under 15, 40.3%; 15–29, 26.4%; 30–44, 16.5%; 45–59, 10.5%; 60–74, 5.2%; 75 and over, 1.1%.
Population projection: (2000) 662,000; (2010) 821,000.
Doubling time: 26 years.
Ethnic composition (1993): Bhutiā (Ngalops) 50.0%; Nepalese (Gurung) 35.0%; Sharchops 15.0%.
Religious affiliation (1998): Buddhist 75.0%; Hindu 25.0%.
Major cities (1993): Thimphu 30,340; Phuntsholing 10,000[7].

Vital statistics

Birth rate per 1,000 population (1997): 41.3 (world avg. 25.0); legitimate, n.a.; illegitimate, n.a.
Death rate per 1,000 population (1997): 13.9 (world avg. 9.3).
Natural increase rate per 1,000 population (1997): 27.4 (world avg. 15.7).
Total fertility rate (avg. births per childbearing woman; 1997): 5.9.
Marital status of population 15 years and over (1985): married 71.2%; single 19.7%; widowed 7.5%; divorced 1.6%.
Divorce rate per 1,000 population: n.a.
Life expectancy at birth (1997): male 51.0 years; female 53.0 years.
Major causes of death (percentage distribution; 1989): respiratory tract infections 19.5%; diarrhea/dysentery 15.2%; skin infections 12.2%; parasitic worm infestations 10.0%; malaria 9.4%.

National economy

Budget (1996–97). Revenue: Nu 5,107,000,000 (internal revenue 38.8%, grants from UN and other international agencies 33.5%, grants from government of India 27.7%). Expenditures: Nu 5,663,000,000 (capital expenditures 61.2%, current expenditures 38.8%).
Public debt (external, outstanding; 1996): U.S.$86,300,000.
Production (metric tons except as noted). Agriculture, forestry, fishing (1996): oranges 58,000, rice 50,000, corn (maize) 39,000, potatoes 34,000, sugarcane 13,000, green peppers and chilies 8,500, millet 7,000, apples 5,500, wheat 5,000, barley 4,000, pulses 1,600; livestock (number of live animals) 435,000 cattle, 75,000 pigs, 59,000 sheep, 42,000 goats, 30,000 horses; roundwood (1995) 1,399,000 cu m; fish catch (1995) 340. Mining and quarrying (1995): limestone 267,000; dolomite 249,000; gypsum 52,000. Manufacturing (value in Nu '000,000; 1994): chemical products 419.0; cement 255.1; wood board products 230.6; distillery products 178.3; processed fruits 103.0. Construction (number of buildings completed; 1977–78): residential 10; nonresidential (guest house) 1. Energy production (consumption): electricity (kW-hr; 1994) 1,682,000,000 (230,000,000); coal (metric tons; 1994) 2,000 (20,000); crude petroleum, none (n.a.); petroleum products (metric tons; 1994) none (31,000); natural gas, none (n.a.).
Household income and expenditure. Average household size (1980) 5.46[6]; income per household: n.a.; sources of income: n.a.; expenditure (1979): food 72.3%, clothing 21.2%, energy 3.7%, household durable goods 0.7%, personal effects and other 2.1%.
Gross national product (at current market prices; 1996): U.S.$282,000,000 (U.S.$390 per capita).

Structure of gross domestic product and labour force

	1995 in value Nu '000,000	1995 % of total value	1984 labour force	1984 % of labour force
Agriculture	3,912.8	41.6	303,000[8]	87.2
Mining	193.1	2.0		
Manufacturing	1,088.8	11.6		
Construction	921.9	9.8		
Trade	730.7	7.8		
Public utilities	826.1	8.8	3,000[8]	0.9
Transportation and communications	687.6	7.3		
Finance	525.2	5.6		
Pub. admin., defense	751.4	8.0	12,000[8]	3.4
Services			30,000[8]	8.5[9]
Other	−231.0[10]	−2.5[10]	...	...
TOTAL	9,406.6	100.0	348,000	100.0

Population economically active (1984)[6]: total 348,000; activity rate of total population 53.4% (participation rates: ages 15–64, 94.8%; female 55.0%; unemployed 6.5%).

Price and earnings indexes (1990 = 100)

	1990	1991	1992	1993	1994	1995	1996
Consumer price index	100.0	112.3	130.2	144.8	154.9	169.6	184.6
Earnings index	...	...	...	...	...	...	...

Land use (1994): forested 66.0%; meadows and pastures 5.8%; agricultural and under permanent cultivation 2.8%; other 25.4%.
Tourism (1995): receipts from visitors U.S.$5,830,000; expenditures by nationals abroad, n.a.

Foreign trade[11]

Balance of trade (current prices)

	1989–90	1990–91	1991–92	1992–93	1993–94	1994–95
Nu '000,000	−481.6	−583.5	−687.9	−1,633.6	−966.2	−1,337.4
% of total	17.5%	18.3%	17.4%	30.8%	18.7%	23.1%

Imports (1994–95): Nu 3,562,400,000 ([12]petroleum products 7.4%, rice 6.9%, motor vehicles and parts 5.1%, iron and steel products 2.0%, fabrics 1.2%, machinery parts 0.4%). *Major import source:* India 77.2%.
Exports (1994–95): Nu 2,225,000,000 ([12]electricity 24.9%, cement 12.8%, timber and wood manufactures 11.5%, fruit and vegetables 9.5%). *Major export destination:* India 93.8%.

Transport and communications

Transport. Railroads: none. Roads (1995): total length 1,998 mi, 3,216 km (paved [1991] 79%). Vehicles (1988): passenger cars 2,590; trucks and buses 1,367. Merchant marine: none. Air transport (1996): passenger-mi 29,000,000, passenger-km 46,000,000; metric ton-km cargo, n.a.; airports (1997) with scheduled flights 1.

Communications

Medium	date	unit	number	units per 1,000 persons
Radio	1996	receivers	23,000	27
Television	...	receivers	...	...
Telephones	1995	main lines	5,200	6.3
Facsimile machines	1995	units	300	0.4

Education and health

Educational attainment: n.a. *Literacy* (1995 est.): total population age 15 and over literate 42.2%; males literate 56.2%; females literate 28.1%

Education (1990)

	schools	teachers	students	student/ teacher ratio
Primary (age 7–11)[13]	235	1,859	56,773	30.5
Secondary (age 12–16)	31	662	15,984	24.1
Voc., teacher tr.	8	149	1,822	12.2
Higher	2	57	519	9.1

Health: physicians (1994) 100 (1 per 8,000 persons); hospital beds 970 (1 per 825 persons); infant mortality rate per 1,000 live births (1997) 105.
Food (1975–77): daily per capita caloric intake 2,058 (vegetable products 98%, animal products 2%); 89% of FAO recommended minimum requirement.

Military

Total active duty personnel (1993): about 7,000 (army 100%).

---

[1]There is no formal constitution, but a form of constitutional monarchy is in place; reforms in July 1998 curtailed the powers of the monarchy. [2]Includes 45 nonelective seats occupied by representatives of the King and religious groups. [3]Indian currency is also accepted legal tender; the ngultrum is at par with the Indian rupee. [4]2,700 sq mi (7,000 sq km) are not included in the district area totals. [5]Includes Chhukha area. [6]Excludes nearly 100,000 Bhutanese of Nepalese origin declared stateless by the Bhutanese government in late 1990. [7]1982. [8]Derived value. [9]Includes 6.5% with no occupation. [10]Imputed bank service charges. [11]Import figures are c.i.f. in balance of trade, commodities, and trading partners. [12]Trade data with India only. [13]1993.

Bolivia

Official name: República de Bolivia (Republic of Bolivia).
Form of government: unitary multiparty republic with two legislative houses (Chamber of Senators [27]; Chamber of Deputies [130]).
Head of state and government: President.
Capitals: La Paz (administrative); Sucre (judicial).
Official languages: Spanish, Aymara, Quechua.
Official religion: Roman Catholicism.
Monetary unit: 1 boliviano (Bs) = 100 centavos; valuation (Sept. 25, 1998) 1 U.S.$ = Bs 5.57; 1 £ = Bs 9.48.

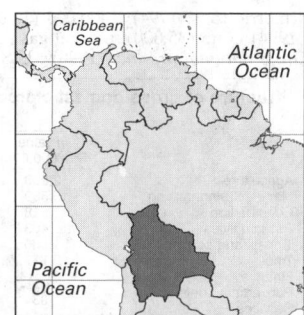

Area and population

Departments	Capitals	area sq mi	area sq km	population 1997 estimate
Beni	Trinidad	82,458	213,564	336,633
Chuquisaca	Sucre	19,893	51,524	549,835
Cochabamba	Cochabamba	21,479	55,631	1,408,071
La Paz	La Paz	51,732	133,985	2,268,824
Oruro	Oruro	20,690	53,588	383,498
Pando	Cobija	24,644	63,827	53,124
Potosí	Potosí	45,644	118,218	746,618
Santa Cruz	Santa Cruz	143,098	370,621	1,651,950
Tarija	Tarija	14,526	37,623	368,506
TOTAL		424,164	1,098,581	7,767,059

Demography

Population (1998): 7,957,000.
Density (1998): persons per sq mi 18.8, persons per sq km 7.2.
Urban-rural (1997): urban 61.2%; rural 38.8%.
Sex distribution (1997): male 49.68%; female 50.32%.
Age breakdown (1995): under 15, 40.6%; 15–29, 27.5%; 30–44, 16.3%; 45–59, 9.6%; 60–74, 5.0%; 75 and over, 1.0%.
Population projection: (2000) 8,329,000; (2010) 10,229,000.
Doubling time: 29 years.
Ethnic composition (1996): Indian 55.0%; mestizo 30.0%; white 15.0%.
Religious affiliation (1995): Roman Catholic 88.5%; Protestant 9.0%; other 2.5%.
Major cities (1993): La Paz 784,976; Santa Cruz 767,260; Cochabamba 448,756; El Alto 446,189; Oruro 201,831; Sucre 144,994.

Vital statistics

Birth rate per 1,000 population (1997): 33.5 (world avg. 25.0).
Death rate per 1,000 population (1997): 9.2 (world avg. 9.3).
Natural increase rate per 1,000 population (1997): 24.3 (world avg. 15.7).
Total fertility rate (avg. births per childbearing woman; 1997): 4.4.
Marriage rate per 1,000 population (1980): 4.8.
Life expectancy at birth (1997): male 59.6 years; female 62.9 years.
Major causes of death (percentage of total registered deaths; 1980–81): infectious and parasitic diseases 23.9%; diseases of the circulatory system 19.5%; diseases of the respiratory system 14.0%; accidents, homicides, and violence 9.8%; diseases of the digestive system 8.6%.

National economy

Budget (1995). Revenue: Bs 5,256,100,000 (taxes on goods and services 39.5%, income of government enterprises 24.6%, property taxes 10.2%, taxes on international trade 6.7%, social security contributions 6.5%, income taxes 2.5%). Expenditures: Bs 6,801,600,000 (education 19.3%, social security 16.0%, public services 14.0%, transportation and communications 12.3%, defense 8.4%, public order and safety 8.1%, health 6.2%).
Production (metric tons except as noted). Agriculture, forestry, fishing (1996): sugarcane 4,120,000, soybeans 862,000, potatoes 715,000, corn (maize) 613,000, bananas and plantains 495,000, rice 344,000, cassava 311,000, wheat 99,000, coffee 22,000; livestock (number of live animals) 8,039,000 sheep, 6,118,000 cattle, 2,482,000 pigs, 1,496,000 goats, 631,000 asses, 322,000 horses; roundwood (1995) 2,208,000 cu m; fish catch (1995) 6,308. Mining and quarrying (metric tons of pure metal; 1996): zinc 144,764; lead 16,538; tin 14,778; silver 384; gold 14.9. Manufacturing (value added in U.S.$'000; 1994): petroleum products 375; food products 169; beverages 99; nonmetal mineral products 36; textiles 23; printing and publishing 19; nonferrous metals 18. Construction (1985)[1]: residential dwellings 226. Energy production (consumption): electricity (kW-hr; 1994) 2,876,000,000 (2,892,000,000); coal, none (none); crude petroleum (barrels; 1994) 8,937,000 (9,268,000); petroleum products (metric tons; 1994) 1,183,000 (1,257,000); natural gas (cu m; 1994) 3,425,000,000 (1,159,000,000).
Population economically active (1992): total 2,530,409; activity rate of total population 33.6% (participation rates: ages 15–64, 63.6%; female 39.0%; unemployed 2.5%).

Price and earnings indexes (1992 = 100)

	1992	1993	1994	1995	1996	1997
Consumer price index	100.0	108.5	117.1	129.0	145.0	151.9
Monthly earnings index[2]	100.0	116.0	135.0	151.3	171.2	...

Gross national product (at current market prices; 1996): U.S.$6,302,000,000 (U.S.$830 per capita).

Structure of gross domestic product and labour force

	1996 in value Bs '000[3]	1996 % of total value[3]	1992 labour force[4]	1992 % of labour force[4]
Agriculture	2,906,264	14.9	984,407	38.9
Mining	1,923,665	9.9	52,623	2.1
Manufacturing	3,264,962	16.8	222,485	8.8
Construction	705,764	3.6	129,409	5.1
Public utilities	418,125	2.2	6,086	0.2
Transp. and commun.	1,944,309	10.0	116,800	4.6
Trade	2,359,237	12.1	232,429	9.2
Finance	2,221,079	11.4	54,711	2.2
Pub. admin., defense	1,796,796	9.3 }	406,928	16.1
Services	839,871	4.3 }		
Other	1,066,142[5]	5.5[5]	324,531	12.8
TOTAL	19,446,214	100.0	2,530,409	100.0

Public debt (external, outstanding; 1996): U.S.$4,238,000,000.
Household income and expenditure. Average household size (1992): 3.8; average annual income per household: n.a.; sources of income: n.a.; expenditure (1988): food 35.5%, transportation and communications 17.7%, housing 14.8%, household durable goods 7.3%, clothing and footwear 5.1%, beverages and tobacco 4.5%, recreation 2.7%, health 2.1%, education 0.3%.
Tourism (1995): receipts from visitors U.S.$146,000,000; expenditures by nationals abroad U.S.$148,000,000.
Land use (1994): forested 53.5%; meadows and pastures 24.4%; agricultural and under permanent cultivation 2.2%; other 19.9%.

Foreign trade[6]

Balance of trade (current prices)

	1991	1992	1993	1994	1995	1996
U.S.$'000,000	−45.1	−294.9	−384.1	−89.3	−162.5	−313.4
% of total	2.6%	17.2%	20.9%	4.1%	6.9%	12.1%

Imports (1996): U.S.$1,635,023,000 (capital goods 39.1%, of which capital goods for industry 22.0%, transport equipment 15.9%; raw materials 36.8%, of which raw materials for industry 26.5%; consumer goods 21.2%, of which durable consumer goods 10.7%, nondurable consumer goods 10.5%). *Major import sources* (1995): United States 18.2%; Brazil 14.5%; Japan 13.8%; Argentina 10.4%; Chile 7.5%; Peru 5.0%; Germany 4.7%.
Exports (1996): U.S.$1,295,308,000 (soybeans 15.5%; zinc 11.7%; petroleum 10.9%; gold 9.7%; natural gas 7.3%; tin 6.4%; timber 6.4%; silver 4.9%). *Major export destinations* (1995): U.S. 23.3%; U.K. 15.1%; Peru 14.2%; Argentina 12.0%; Germany 5.4%; The Netherlands 4.3%; France 3.6%.

Transport and communications

Transport. Railroads (1993): route length 2,295 mi, 3,694 km; passenger-mi 216,800,000, passenger-km 348,900,000; short ton-mi cargo 521,900,000, metric ton-km cargo 761,900,000. Roads (1995): total length 34,478 mi, 55,487 km (paved 5%). Vehicles (1995): passenger cars 213,666; trucks and buses 133,984. Merchant marine (1992): vessels (100 gross tons and over) 1; total deadweight tonnage 15,765. Air transport (1996): passenger-mi 912,000,000, passenger-km 1,468,000,000; short ton-mi cargo 31,655,000, metric ton-km cargo 46,216,000; airports (1997) with scheduled flights 14.

Communications

Medium	date	unit	number	units per 1,000 persons
Daily newspapers	1994	circulation	500,000	69
Radio	1996	receivers	4,250,000	560
Television	1995	receivers	1,500,000	202
Telephones	1995	main lines	347,800	47
Cellular telephones	1995	subscribers	7,200	1.0

Education and health

Educational attainment (1992). Percentage of population age 25 and over having: no formal schooling 23.3%; some primary 20.3%; primary education 21.7%; some secondary 9.0%; secondary 6.5%; some higher 5.0%; higher 4.8%; not specified 9.4%. *Literacy* (1992): total population age 15 and over literate 79.5%; males literate 87.7%; females literate 71.8%.

Education (1990–91)

	schools[7]	teachers	students	student/ teacher ratio
Primary (age 6–13)	9,758	51,763	1,278,775	24.7
Secondary (age 14–17)	724 }	12,434	219,232	17.6
Voc., teacher tr.	47 }			
Higher[8]	10	4,261	109,503	25.7

Health (1994): physicians 1,976 (1 per 3,663 persons); hospital beds 7,203 (1 per 1,005 persons); infant mortality rate per 1,000 live births (1997) 67.
Food (1995): daily per capita caloric intake 2,192 (vegetable products 83%, animal products 17%); 92% of FAO recommended minimum requirement.

Military

Total active duty personnel (1997): 33,500 (army 74.6%, navy 13.4%, air force 12.0%). *Military expenditure as percentage of GNP* (1995): 2.3% (world 2.8%); per capita expenditure U.S.$18.

[1]National government sponsored only. [2]Private-sector earnings in La Paz. [3]In 1990 prices. [4]Population 7 years of age and over. [5]Net import duties. [6]Import figures are f.o.b. in balance of trade and c.i.f. for commodities and trading partners. [7]1986–87. [8]1991–92.

Internet resources for further information:
• Instituto Nacional de Estadística http://www.ine.gov.bo/
• UNDP Bolivia http://guf.pnud.bo/bolbrief.htm

Bosnia and Herzegovina[1]

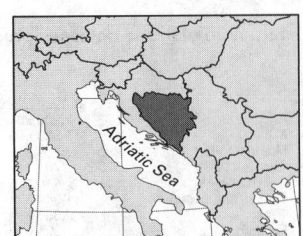

Official name: Bosna i Hercegovina (Bosnia and Herzegovina).
Form of government: federal multiparty republic with bicameral legislature (Senate [15[2]]; House of Representatives [42]).
Chiefs of state: Tripartite presidency.
Heads of government: Two cochairmen assisted by the Council of Ministers.
Capital: Sarajevo.
Official language: Bosnian.
Official religion: none.
Monetary unit: 1 marka[3] (KM) = 100 pfenning; valuation (Sept. 25, 1998) 1 U.S.$ = KM 1.67; 1 £ = KM 2.84.

Area and population (1991 census)[4]

Districts	population	Districts	population	Districts	population
Banja Luka	195,139	Grude	15,976	Pucarevo	30,624
Banovići	26,507	Han Pijesak	6,346	Rogatica	21,812
Bihać	70,896	Jablanica	12,664	Rudo	11,572
Bijeljina	96,796	Jajce	44,903	Sanski Most	60,119
Bileća	13,269	Kakanj	55,857	Sarajevo	525,980
Bosanska Dubica	31,577	Kalesija	41,795	Šekovići	9,639
Bosanska Gradiška	60,062	Kalinovik	4,657	Šipovo	15,553
Bosanska Krupa	58,212	Kiseljak	24,081	Skender Vakuf	19,416
Bosanski Brod	33,962	Kladanj	16,028	Sokolac	14,833
Bosanski Novi	41,541	Ključ	37,233	Srbac	21,660
Bosanski Petrovac	15,552	Konjic	43,636	Srebrenica	37,211
Bosanski Šamac	32,835	Kotor Varoš	36,670	Srebrenik	40,769
Bosansko Grahovo	8,303	Kreševo	6,699	Stolac	18,845
Bratunac	33,575	Kupres	10,728	Tešanj	48,390
Brčko	87,332	Laktaši	29,910	Teslić	59,632
Breza	17,266	Lištica	26,437	Titov Drvar	17,079
Bugojno	46,843	Livno	39,526	Tomislavgrad	29,261
Busovaća	18,883	Ljubinje	4,162	Travnik	70,402
Čajniće	8,919	Ljubuški	27,182	Trebinje	30,879
Capljina	27,852	Lopare	32,400	Tuzla	131,861
Cazin	63,406	Lukavac	56,830	Ugljevik	25,641
Čelinac	18,666	Maglaj	43,294	Vareš	22,114
Čitluk	14,709	Modriča	35,413	Velika Kladuša	52,921
Derventa	56,328	Mostar	126,067	Višegrad	21,202
Doboj	102,546	Mrkonjić Grad	27,379	Visoko	46,130
Donji Vakuf	24,232	Neum	4,268	Vitez	27,728
Foča	40,513	Nevesinje	14,421	Vlasenica	33,817
Fojnica	16,227	Odžak	30,651	Zavidovići	57,153
Gacko	10,844	Olovo	16,901	Zenica	145,577
Glamoč	12,421	Orašje	28,201	Žepče	22,840
Goražde	37,505	Posušje	16,659	Živinice	54,653
Gornji Vakuf	25,130	Prijedor	112,470	Zvornik	81,111
Gracanica	59,050	Prnjavor	46,894	TOTAL	4,365,639
Gradačac	56,378	Prozor	19,601		

Demography

Area: 19,741 sq mi, 51,129 sq km.
Population (1998)[5]: 3,366,000.
Density (1998)[5]: persons per sq mi 170.5, persons per sq km 65.8.
Urban-rural (1981): urban 36.2%; rural 63.8%.
Sex distribution (1991): male 49.79%; female 50.21%.
Age breakdown (1991): under 15, 23.4%; 15–29, 26.5%; 30–44, 22.8%; 45–64, 16.0%; 65 and over, 11.3%.
Population projection: (2000) 3,592,000; (2010) 3,737,000.
Ethnic composition (1991): Bosniak 49.2%; Serb 31.3%; Croat 17.3%.
Religious affiliation (1995): Muslim 40.0%; Serbian Orthodox 28.4%; Roman Catholic 13.5%; other (mostly nonreligious) 18.0%.
Major cities (1991): Sarajevo (1997) 360,000; Banja Luka 143,079; Zenica 96,027; Tuzla 83,770; Mostar 75,865.

Vital statistics

Birth rate per 1,000 population (1996): 7.9 (world avg. 25.0); (1993) legitimate 92.6%; illegitimate 7.4%.
Death rate per 1,000 population (1996): 15.4 (world avg. 9.3).
Natural increase rate per 1,000 population (1996): –8.5 (world avg. 15.7).
Total fertility rate (avg. births per childbearing woman; 1996): 1.0.
Marriage rate per 1,000 population (1991): 6.0.
Divorce rate per 1,000 population (1991): 0.3.
Life expectancy at birth (1996): male 51.2 years; female 61.4 years.
Major causes of death per 100,000 population (1989): circulatory diseases 344.1; malignant neoplasms (cancers) 122.6; accidents, violence, and poisoning 47.1; digestive system diseases 29.2; respiratory diseases 29.0.

National economy

Budget (1997). Revenue: DM 618,000,000 (primarily customs duties). Expenditures: DM 598,500,000 (defense 41.0%, disability benefits 29.3%).
Production (metric tons except as noted). Agriculture, forestry, fishing (1996): corn (maize) 589,000, potatoes 347,000, wheat 166,000, barley 47,000; livestock (head) 314,000 cattle, 276,000 sheep, 165,000 pigs; roundwood (1995) 40,000 cu m; fish catch (1995) 2,500. Mining (1995): iron ore (gross weight) 150,000; bauxite 75,000; barite (concentrate) 2,000. Manufacturing (1995): cement 150,000; crude steel 115,000; pig iron 100,000; coke 100,000. Construction (residential units constructed; 1990) 26,568. Energy production (consumption): electricity (kW-hr; 1994) 1,921,000,000 (2,081,000,000); coal

(metric tons; 1994) 1,400,000 (1,400,000); petroleum products (metric tons; 1994) none (35,000); natural gas (cu m; 1994) none (378,000,000).
Gross national product (1996)[6]: U.S.$1,867,000,000 (U.S.$600 per capita).

Structure of gross domestic product and labour force

	1989		1990	
	in value Din '000,000[7]	% of total value	labour force[8]	% of labour force[8]
Agriculture	2,963	10.9	39,053	3.8
Manufacturing, mining	15,589	57.6	496,190	48.3
Construction	1,918	7.1	74,861	7.3
Public utilities	403	1.5	22,345	2.2
Transp. and commun.	1,600	5.9	68,798	6.7
Trade	3,777	13.9	130,914	12.8
Finance			38,686	3.8
Pub. admin., defense Services Other	834	3.1	155,411	15.1
TOTAL	27,084	100.0	1,026,258	100.0

Population economically active (1991): total 992,000; activity rate of total population 22.7% (participation rates: ages 15–64, 35.6%; female [1990] 37.7%; unemployed [1996] 75.0%).

Price and earnings indexes (1985 = 100)

	1984	1985	1986	1987	1988	1989	1990
Consumer price index	58	100	188	400	1,188	16,169	109,000
Monthly earnings index	...	...	...	...	...	...	...

Household income and expenditure. Average household size (1991) 3.4; income per household (1990) Din 72,850[6] (U.S.$6,437); sources of income (1990): wages 53.2%, transfers 18.2%, self-employment 12.0%, other 16.6%; expenditure (1988): food 41.3%, clothing 8.3%, fuel and lighting 7.8%, housing 7.8%, transportation 6.0%, beverages and tobacco 5.7%.

Foreign trade[6]

Balance of trade (current prices)

	1991	1992	1993	1994	1995	1996
U.S.$'000,000	...	...	–339	–614	–891	–1,708
% of total	...	...	66.6%	89.5%	89.7%	83.3%

Imports (1996)[6]: U.S.$1,879,000,000. *Major import sources:* Croatia 32%; Slovenia 15%; Germany 13%; Italy 13%; Hungary 6%.
Exports (1996)[6]: U.S.$171,000,000. *Major export destinations:* Croatia 34%; Italy 26%; Germany 16%; Slovenia 8%; United States 5%.

Transport and communications

Transport. Railroads (1991): route length 1,021 km; passenger-km 554,000,000; metric ton-km cargo 1,946,000,000. Roads (1991): total length 21,168 km (paved 54%). Vehicles (1990): passenger cars 438,080; trucks and buses 50,578. Airports (1997) with scheduled flights 1[9].

Communications

Medium	date	unit	number	units per 1,000 persons
Daily newspapers	1995	circulation	520,000	150
Television	1995	receivers	325,000	94
Telephones	1995	main lines	237,800	69

Education and health

Educational attainment (1981). Percentage of population age 15 and over having: less than full primary education 49.5%; primary 24.2%; secondary 21.7%; postsecondary and higher 4.3%. *Literacy* (1981): total population age 10 and over literate 2,962,400 (85.5%); males 96.5%; females 76.6%.

Education (1990–91)

	schools	teachers	students	student/ teacher ratio
Primary (age 7–14)	2,205	23,369	539,875	23.1
Secondary (age 15–18)	238	9,030	172,063	19.1
Higher	44	2,802	37,541	13.4

Health: physicians (1996) 4,500[6] (1 per 703 persons); hospital beds (1990) 19,858 (1 per 217 persons); infant mortality rate (1996) 43.2.

Military

Total active duty personnel (1997): 40,000 (army 100%).

[1]Government structure provided for by Dayton accords and constitutions of 1993 and 1994 is being implemented in stages since formal signing of peace accord on Dec. 14, 1995. [2]All seats are nonelective. [3]An interim currency pegged to the German Deutsche Mark (DM) at a 1 to 1 ratio, the marka (or Konvertibilna marka, "convertible mark"; KM) was introduced on June 22, 1998, to replace the Bosnian dinar (BD) at a rate of 100 BD to 1 KM. [4]First-order subdivisions as of late 1996 comprised two autonomous regions: the *c.* 26,100 sq km Federation of Bosnia and Herzegovina (which is further divided into 10 cantons) and the *c.* 25,000 sq km Republika Srpska. [5]Excludes about 1,000,000 refugees in adjacent countries and Western Europe. [6]Estimated figures. [7]Yugoslav new dinar (Din). [8]Excludes 28,000 workers in the private sector. [9]Sarajevo Airport reopened in August 1996.

Internet resources for further information:
• **Embassy of Bosnia and Herzegovina** (Washington, D.C.)
  http://www.bosnianembassy.org/
• **Office of the High Representative** in Bosnia and Herzegovina
  http://www.ohr.int/

Botswana

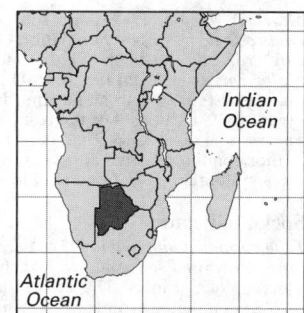

Official name: Republic of Botswana.
Form of government: multiparty republic with one legislative body[1] (National Assembly [46[2]]).
Head of state and government: President.
Capital: Gaborone.
Official language: English[3].
Official religion: none.
Monetary unit: 1 pula (P) = 100 thebe; valuation (Sept. 25, 1998) 1 U.S.$ = P 4.48; 1 £ = P 7.63.

Area and population		area		population
				1991
Districts	Capitals	sq mi	sq km	census
Barolong	...	773	2,003	18,400
Central	Serowe	57,039	147,730	412,970
Ghanzi	Ghanzi	45,525	117,910	24,719
Kgalagadi	Tsabong	41,290	106,940	31,134
Kgatleng	Mochudi	3,073	7,960	57,770
Kweneng	Molepolole	13,857	35,890	170,437
Ngwaketse	Kanye	10,219	26,467	128,989
North East	Masunga	1,977	5,120	43,354
North West				
Chobe	Kasane	8,031	20,800	14,126
Ngamiland	Maun	33,359	86,400	57,811
Okavango	Orapa	8,776	22,730	36,723
South East	Ramotswa	687	1,780	43,584
Towns[4]				
Francistown	—	31	79	65,244
Gaborone	—	65	169	133,468
Jwaneng	—	39	100	11,188
Lobatse	—	16	42	26,052
Orapa	—	7	17	8,827
Selebi-Pikwe	—	19	50	39,772
Sowa	—	61	159	2,228
TOTAL		224,607[5]	581,730	1,326,796

Demography

Population (1998): 1,448,000.
Density (1997): persons per sq mi 6.4, persons per sq km 2.5.
Urban-rural (1996): urban 29.2%; rural 70.8%.
Sex distribution (1996): male 49.02%; female 50.98%.
Age breakdown (1995): under 15, 43.2%; 15–29, 28.5%; 30–44, 16.5%; 45–59, 7.9%; 60–74, 3.2%; 75 and over, 0.7%.
Population projection: (2000) 1,479,000; (2010) 1,570,000.
Doubling time: 23 years.
Ethnic composition (1983): Tswana 75.5%; Shona 12.4%; San (Bushman) 3.4%; Khoikhoin (Hottentot) 2.5%; Ndebele 1.3%; other 4.9%.
Religious affiliation (1997): traditional beliefs 55.0%; African Christian 27.5%; Protestant 13.5%; Roman Catholic 4.0%.
Major cities (1993): Gaborone 156,803; Francistown 75,678; Selebi-Pikwe 42,350; Molepolole 41,730; Kanye 34,233.

Vital statistics

Birth rate per 1,000 population (1991–95): 37.1 (world avg. 25.0); (1986) legitimate 28.8%[6]; illegitimate 71.2%[6].
Death rate per 1,000 population (1991–95): 6.6 (world avg. 9.3).
Natural increase rate per 1,000 population (1991–95): 30.5 (world avg. 15.7).
Total fertility rate (avg. births per childbearing woman; 1996): 4.3.
Marriage rate per 1,000 population (1987): 1.6.
Life expectancy at birth (1993): male 59.5 years; female 65.6 years.
Major causes of death (as percentage of total of inpatient deaths[7]; 1992): respiratory diseases 14.3%; pneumonia 10.0%; digestive diseases 8.9%; cerebrovascular disease 4.2%; AIDS 3.9%; kidney disease 3.0%.

National economy

Budget (1996–97). Revenue: P 5,421,300,000 (mineral royalties 47.4%, customs and excise taxes 20.1%, property income 17.8%, interest income 4.6%). Expenditures: P 6,057,000,000 (1995–96; economic services 40.4%, education 20.8%, public order and safety 3.5%, social welfare 3.0%, health 2.5%).
Population economically active (1991): total 441,203; activity rate of total population 33.2% (participation rates: ages 15–64, 59.6%; female 38.4%, unemployed 13.9%).

Price and earnings indexes (1990 = 100)							
	1991	1992	1993	1994	1995	1996	1997
Consumer price index	111.8	129.8	148.4	164.1	181.3	199.6	218.2
Monthly earnings index	113.6	133.5	162.0	169.8	181.6	...	...

Public debt (external, outstanding; 1996): U.S.$606,500,000.
Tourism (1995): receipts U.S.$162,000,000; expenditures U.S.$145,000,000.
Production (metric tons except as noted). Agriculture, forestry, fishing (1996): cereals 82,900 (of which sorghum 55,100, corn [maize] 23,000, millet 4,000), vegetables and melons 16,000, pulses 14,000, fruits 10,500, tubers 9,000; livestock (number of live animals) 1,950,000 cattle, 1,900,000 goats, 250,000 sheep, 237,500 mules and asses, 31,500 horses; roundwood (1995) 1,584,000 cu m; fish catch (1993) 2,000. Mining and quarrying (1996): copper 20,979; nickel 17,461; cobalt 405; diamonds 17,707,062 carats. Manufacturing (value adder in P '000,000; 1994): food products 164.3; wearing apparel 78.9; paper and paper products 28.0; industrial chemicals 18.7; wood products 17.5.

Construction (value added in P '000,000; 1995–96): 877,900. Energy production (consumption): electricity (kW-hr; 1993) 970,000,000 (970,000,000); coal (metric tons; 1992) 901,452 (n.a.); crude petroleum, none (n.a.).
Gross national product (1994): U.S.$4,037,000,000 (U.S.$2,800 per capita).

Structure of gross domestic product and labour force				
	1995–96		1991	
	in value P '000,000	% of total value	labour force	% of labour force
Agriculture	546,200	3.7	97,626	22.1
Mining	5,084,800	34.2	13,264	3.0
Manufacturing	686,200	4.6	26,470	6.0
Construction	877,900	5.9	57,510	13.0
Public utilities	312,500	2.1	6,388	1.4
Transp. and commun.	507,200	3.4	11,398	2.6
Trade	2,474,000	16.6	35,194	8.0
Finance	1,231,300	8.3	13,286	3.0
Pub. admin., defense	2,517,700	16.9	34,002	7.7
Services	638,800	4.3	72,064	16.3
Other	...	...	74,001[8]	16.8[8]
TOTAL	14,876,600	100.0	441,203	100.0[5]

Household income and expenditure (1991). Average household size 4.8; average annual income per household (1985–86) P 3,910 (U.S.$2,080); sources of income (1987): wages and salaries 73.3%, self-employment 15.9%, transfers 10.8%; expenditure: food 39.4%, household durable goods 14.0%, rent and services 13.3%, transportation 13.1%, clothing 5.6%, health 2.3%.
Land use (1994): forest 46.8%; pasture 45.2%; agriculture 0.7%; other 7.3%.

Foreign trade[9]

Balance of trade (current prices)						
	1990	1991	1992	1993	1994	1995
P '000,000	241.3	398.1	299.1	668.4	1,216.3	1,623.6
% of total	3.8%	5.6%	4.2%	8.4%	14.0%	15.6%

Imports (1995): P 5,304,800,000 (1994; machinery and transport equipment 29.6%, of which transport equipment 12.0%, food, beverages, and tobacco 17.6%; chemical and rubber products 9.7%; metal and metal products 9.4%; textiles and footwear 8.9%; wood and paper 5.8%; mineral fuels 5.7%). *Major import sources:* Customs Union of Southern Africa (CUSA) 73.9%; South Korea 7.1%; Zimbabwe 5.5%; U.K. 2.5%; U.S. 2.0%.
Exports (1995): P 5,931,600,000 (1994; diamonds 79.9%; copper-nickel matte 5.6%; textiles 3.8%; meat products 3.7%). *Major export destinations:* U.K. 37.5%; CUSA 21.5%; Zimbabwe 3.0%; U.S. 0.9%.

Transport and communications

Transport. Railroads (1995): length 603 mi, 971 km; passenger-km 86,000,000; metric ton-km cargo 1,710,000[10]. Roads (1995): total length 11,388 mi, 18,327 km (paved 25%). Vehicles (1994): passenger cars 27,058; trucks and buses 42,696. Merchant marine: none. Air transport (1994)[11]: passenger-km 58,370,000; metric ton-km cargo 540,000; airports (1997) 4.

Communications				units per 1,000
Medium	date	unit	number	persons
Daily newspapers	1995	circulation	42,100	29.0
Radio	1995	receivers	1,190,000	821
Television	1995	receivers	35,000	24.0
Telephones	1995	main lines	59,700	41.1
Facsimile machines	1995	units	3,100	2.1

Education and health

Educational attainment (1991). Percentage of population age 25 and over having: no formal schooling 42.9%; primary education 17.3%; some secondary 32.3%; complete secondary 3.9%; postsecondary 3.7%. *Literacy* (1995): total population over age 15 literate 591,700 (69.8%); males literate 324,900 (80.5%); females literate 266,800 (59.9%).

Education (1994)				student/
	schools	teachers	students	teacher ratio
Primary (age 6–13)	669	11,726	310,050	26.4
Secondary (age 14–18)	188	4,712	86,684	18.4
Voc., teacher tr.	45	966	6,373	6.6
Higher	1	507	5,062	10.0

Health (1994): physicians 339 (1 per 4,395 persons); hospital beds (1993) 3,299 (1 per 434 persons); infant mortality rate 39.0.
Food (1995): daily per capita caloric intake 2,153 (vegetable products 83%, animal products 17%); 93% of FAO recommended minimum requirement.

Military

Total active duty personnel (1997): 7,500 (army 93.3%, navy, none [land locked], air force 6.7%). *Military expenditure as percentage of GNP* (1995): 5.3% (world 2.8%); per capita expenditure U.S.$155.

---

[1]In addition, the House of Chiefs, a 15-member body consisting of chiefs, subchiefs, and associated members, serves in an advisory capacity to the government. [2]Including four specially elected members and two nonelective seats. [3]Tswana is the national language. [4]Areas are included with respective district totals; population figures are not included with district totals. [5]Detail does not add to total given because of rounding. [6]Registered births only. [7]Represents nearly 30% of all deaths. [8]Includes 61,265 unemployed. [9]Import figures are f.o.b. in balance of trade and c.i.f. in commodities and trading partners. [10]1994. [11]Air Botswana only.

Brazil

Official name: República Federativa
do Brasil (Federative Republic
of Brazil).
Form of government: multiparty
federal republic with 2 legislative
houses (Senate [81]; Chamber of
Deputies [513]).
Chief of state and government:
President.
Capital: Brasília.
Official language: Portuguese.
Official religion: none.
Monetary unit: 1 real[1] = 100 centavos;
valuation (Sept. 25, 1998)
1 U.S.$ = 1.18 reais; 1 £ = 2.01 reais.

Marriage rate per 1,000 population (1994): 5.0.
Divorce rate per 1,000 population (1994): 0.6.
Life expectancy at birth (1996): male 56.7 years; female 66.8 years.
Major causes of death per 100,000 population (1994)[14]: diseases of the circulatory system 238; accidents, murder, and violence 104; malignant neoplasms
(cancers) 94; diseases of the respiratory system 79; endocrine, metabolic, and
nutritional disorders 45; infectious and parasitic diseases 41; birth trauma and
other conditions originating in the perinatal period 37; diseases of the digestive system 36; ill-defined conditions 147.

Social indicators

Educational attainment (1995)[6]. Percentage of population age 10 and over having: no formal schooling or less than one year of primary education 16.2%;
incomplete primary 55.9%; complete primary 7.6%; incomplete secondary
4.6%; complete secondary 9.1%; incomplete undergraduate 2.4%; complete
undergraduate 3.9%; unknown 0.3%.

Distribution of income (1988)[6, 15]

percentage of national income by decile

1	2	3	4	5	6	7	8	9	10 (highest)
0.7	1.7	2.2	3.4	3.9	5.0	6.8	9.9	15.9	50.5

Quality of working life. Annual estimated rate per 100,000 insured workers
(1990) for: on-the-job injury 2,032; industrial illness 17; death 4. Proportion
of labour force participating in national social insurance system (1990):
50.1%. Proportion of formally employed population receiving minimum
wage (1993): 25.0%.
Access to services (1995)[6]. Proportion of households having access to: electricity 91.7%, of which urban households having access 98.6%, rural households having access 62.9%; safe public (piped) water supply 71.3%, of which
urban households having access 85.4%, rural households having access
11.6%; public (piped) sewage system 39.5%, of which urban household having access 48.2%, rural households having access 3.2%; no sewage disposal
11.4%, of which urban households having no disposal 3.5%, rural households
having no disposal 40.9%.
Social participation. Voting is mandatory for national elections; in the October
1994 elections blank or otherwise invalid ballots accounted for as many as
15% of all votes cast. Trade union membership in total workforce (1991):
16,748,155. Practicing Roman Catholic population in total affiliated Roman
Catholic population (1990): 25%.
Social deviance (1990). The incidence of crime is not accurately reported.
Crimes resulting in imprisonment: 159,071, of which murder 7.3%, assault
11.0%, theft, burglary, and housebreaking 26.6%, robbery and extortion
12.2%, narcotics trafficking 6.3%, narcotics usage 4.5%. Suicide: 5,142.
Leisure. Favourite leisure activities include: playing soccer, dancing, rehearsing all year in neighbourhood samba groups for celebrations of Carnival, and
competing in water sports, volleyball, and basketball.
Material well-being (1995)[6]. Households possessing: telephone 22.3%, of which
urban 26.7%, rural 3.5%; colour television receiver 60.9%, of which urban
69.8%, rural 23.3%; refrigerator 74.8%, of which urban 83.4%, rural 38.7%;
washing machine 26.6%, of which urban 31.2%, rural 7.3%.

National economy

Gross national product (1996): U.S.$709,591,000,000 (U.S.$4,400 per capita).

Area and population

States	Capitals	area sq mi	area sq km	population 1995 estimate[2]
Acre	Rio Branco	59,132	153,150	455,200
Alagoas	Maceió	10,785	27,933	2,685,400
Amapá	Macapá	55,388	143,454	326,200
Amazonas	Manaus	609,200	1,577,820	2,320,200
Bahia	Salvador	219,034	567,295	12,646,000
Ceará	Fortaleza	56,505	146,348	6,714,200
Espírito Santo	Vitória	17,836	46,194	2,786,700
Goiás	Goiânia	131,772	341,289	4,308,400
Maranhão	São Luís	128,713	333,366	5,231,300
Mato Grosso	Cuiabá	350,120	906,807	2,313,600
Mato Grosso do Sul	Campo Grande	138,286	358,159	1,912,800
Minas Gerais	Belo Horizonte	227,176	588,384	16,505,300
Pará	Belém	483,850	1,253,165	5,448,600
Paraíba	João Pessoa	21,848	56,585	3,340,000
Paraná	Curitiba	77,108	199,709	8,712,800
Pernambuco	Recife	38,200	98,938	7,445,200
Piauí	Teresina	97,444	252,379	2,725,000
Rio de Janeiro	Rio de Janeiro	16,954	43,910	13,296,400
Rio Grande do Norte	Natal	20,582	53,307	2,582,300
Rio Grande do Sul	Porto Alegre	108,905	282,062	9,578,600
Rondônia	Porto Velho	92,090	238,513	1,339,500
Roraima	Boa Vista	86,918	225,116	262,200
Santa Catarina	Florianópolis	36,851	95,443	4,836,600
São Paulo	São Paulo	96,066	248,809	33,699,600
Sergipe	Aracaju	8,514	22,050	1,605,300
Tocantins	Palmas	107,499	278,421	1,007,000
Federal District				
Distrito Federal	Brasília	2,248	5,822	1,737,800
Disputed areas[3]		1,149	2,977	—
TOTAL		3,300,171[4, 5]	8,547,404[4, 5]	155,822,400[4]

Demography

Population (1998): 161,766,000.
Density (1998): persons per sq mi 49.0, persons per sq km 18.9.
Urban-rural (1995)[6]: urban 79.0%; rural 21.0%.
Sex distribution (1995)[6]: male 48.99%; female 51.01%.
Age breakdown (1995)[6]: under 15, 32.2%; 15–29, 26.9%; 30–44, 20.6%; 45–59,
11.9%; 60 and over, 8.4%.
Population projection: (2000) 165,561,000; (2010) 181,918,000.
Doubling time: 60 years.
Racial composition (1995)[6]: white 54.4%; mulatto and mestizo 40.1%; black
and black/Amerindian 4.9%; Asian 0.5%, Amerindian 0.1%.
Religious affiliation (1995)[6]: Catholic 74.3%[7], of which Roman Catholic 72.3%[7];
Protestant 23.2%, of which Pentecostal 19.1%; other Christian 0.9%; other
1.6%.
Major cities (1991)[8] *and metropolitan areas/urban agglomerations* (1995): São
Paulo 9,393,753 (16,417,000[9]); Rio de Janeiro 5,473,909 (9,888,000[9]); Salvador
2,070,296 (2,819,000[9]); Belo Horizonte 1,529,566 (3,899,000[9]); Brasília
1,492,542 (1,778,000[10]); Recife 1,296,995 (3,168,000[9]); Porto Alegre 1,237,223
(3,349,000[9]); Manaus 1,005,634 (1,189,000[10]); Goiânia 912,136 (1,033,000[10]);
Curitiba 841,882 (2,270,000[9]); Belém 765,476 (1,574,000[9]); Campinas 748,076
(1,607,000[10]); Fortaleza 743,335 (2,660,000[9]).

Other principal cities (1991)[8]

	population		population		population
Aracaju	401,676	Natal	459,827	São Bernardo	
Campo Grande	516,403	Niterói	400,586[11]	do Campo	550,030[12]
Guarulhos	544,698[12]	Nova Iguaçu	562,062[11]	São Jose dos	
João Pessoa	497,306	Osasco	566,949[12]	Campos	385,879
Juiz de Fora	377,538	Ribeirão Preto	416,186	Sorocaba	348,952
Londrina	355,062	Santo André	518,272[12]	Teresina	556,073
Maceió	554,727	Santos	415,554[13]	Uberlândia	354,710

Place of birth/national origin (1991): native-born Brazilians 99.47%; natural-
ized citizens 0.11%; foreigners 0.42%.
Families (1990)[6]. Average family size 3.9; 1–2 persons 26.2%, 3 persons 21.3%,
4 persons 21.5%, 5–6 persons 22.3%, 7 or more persons 8.7%.
Emigration: Emigration for economic opportunity accelerated in the 1980s. By
1995 it was officially estimated that 1–2.5 million Brazilians lived outside of
Brazil. Emigrants' most popular destinations in order of preference are the
United States, Japan, and the United Kingdom.

Vital statistics

Birth rate per 1,000 population (1996): 20.8 (world avg. 25.0).
Death rate per 1,000 population (1996): 9.2 (world avg. 9.3).
Natural increase rate per 1,000 population (1996): 11.6 (world avg. 15.7).
Total fertility rate (avg. births per childbearing woman; 1996): 2.3.

Structure of gross domestic product and labour force

	1995 in value R$ '000,000[1, 16]	1995 % of total value	1993 labour force[6]	1993 % of labour force
Agriculture	68,290	12.2	18,253,856	25.7
Mining	5,867	1.0	...	...
Public utilities	14,198	2.5	...	...
Manufacturing	123,821	22.0	9,486,435	13.4
Construction	45,124	8.0	4,289,159	6.0
Transportation and communications	30,702	5.5	2,283,978	3.2
Trade	38,037	6.8	8,474,935	11.9
Finance, real estate	42,824	7.6	1,929,077	2.7
Pub. admin., defense	70,154	12.5	3,044,332	4.3
Services	162,097	28.9	17,418,896	24.5
Other	–39,333[17]	–7.0[17]	5,784,710[18]	8.2[18]
TOTAL	561,781	100.0	70,965,378	100.0[4]

Budget. Revenue (1995): R$320,178,000,000 (development receipts 62.6%, of
which credits 58.4%; current receipts 37.4%, of which social contributions
19.3% [including social security 9.2%], taxes 13.3%). Expenditures:
R$320,178,000,000 (administration and planning 59.5%; social welfare 13.9%;
regional development 6.0%; health and sanitation 4.9%; agriculture 3.1%;
education 2.7%; defense and public order 2.6%).
Public debt (external, outstanding; 1996): U.S.$94,587,000,000.
Production ('000 metric tons except as noted). Agriculture, forestry, fishing
(1996): sugarcane 324,414, corn (maize) 32,011, cassava 24,569, soybeans
23,171, oranges 21,848, rice 10,039, bananas 5,738, wheat 3,277, dry beans
2,776, potatoes 2,656, tomatoes 2,650, papayas 2,200, coffee 1,264, cashew
apples 1,250, pineapples 1,052, seed cotton 1,032, coconuts 984, onions 944,
tangerines 760[19], grapes 731, sweet potatoes 655, apples 653, cottonseed 650,
lemons and limes 495, tobacco 476, mangoes 435, cotton lint 360, sorghum
310, cacao beans 313, cashews 187, peanuts (groundnuts) 154, maté 150, sisal
133, palm oil 76, garlic 57, castor beans 48, natural rubber 30, brazil nuts
25; livestock (number of live animals) 165,000,000 cattle, 36,600,000 pigs,
18,000,000 sheep, 6,300,000 horses; roundwood (1995) 220,263,000 cu m, of
which fuelwood 114,052,000 cu m, sawlogs and veneer logs 47,779,000 cu m,
pulpwood 30,701,000 cu m; fish catch (1995) 800, of which freshwater fishes 202. Mining and quarrying (value of export production in U.S.$'000,000;
1996): iron ore 2,668; semifinished copper 165; ferroniobium 153; bauxite

115; granite 97; semifinished tin 68; kaolin (clay) 65; manganese 55; asbestos 35; gemstones (1994) 27; gold production for both domestic use and export 1,833,000 troy oz; Brazil is also a world-leading producer of high-quality grade quartz and tantalum. Manufacturing (value added in U.S.$'000,000; 1994): food products 19,450; transport equipment 16,050; paints, soaps, drugs, and medicines 15,600; electrical machinery 12,350; nonelectrical machinery 11,600; industrial chemicals 11,000; iron and steel 8,800; textiles 7,100; fabricated metals 6,000; cement, bricks, and tiles 5,700; paper and paper products 5,250. Construction (authorized[20]; 1987): residential 20,090,000 sq m; nonresidential 8,180,000 sq m.

Land use (1994): forested 57.7%; meadows and pastures 21.9%; agricultural and under permanent cultivation 6.0%; other 14.4%.

Manufacturing enterprises (1992)

	no. of enter- prises	number of labourers	wages of labourers as a % of avg. of all mfg. wages	value added in producer's prices (in CR$'000,000,000[1])[21]
Chemical products (incl. pharmaceuticals)	2,795	360,800	170.4	1,351
Food products	5,241	548,400	63.8	1,040
Nonelectrical machinery	2,086	297,000	120.7	994
Fabricated metals, iron and steel, and nonferrous metals	2,325	377,200	123.9	923
Transport equipment	830	282,000	162.1	784
Electrical machinery	1,366	215,900	135.5	591
Textiles	1,439	242,600	64.4	379
Nonmetallic mineral products	1,638	145,200	91.5	369
Paper and paper products	824	116,900	103.6	296
Clothing and footwear	2,480	459,200	37.6	272
Publishing and printing	920	103,000	121.7	226
Plastics	828	106,500	83.5	193
Beverages	508	84,900	93.0	178
Rubber products	439	54,500	97.9	91
Wood and wood products (excl. furniture)	860	79,500	45.4	91
Furniture	845	72,100	48.9	86

Population economically active (1993)[6]: total 70,965,378; activity rate of total population 47.9% (participation rates: ages 15–59, 72.7%; female 39.6%; unemployed [May 1996] 5.9%[22, 23]).

Price and earnings indexes (1993 = 100)

	1993	1994	1995	1996	1997	1998[24]
Consumer price index	100	2,176	3,613	4,182	4,472	4,612
Monthly earnings index[25]	100	...	...	...	...	...

Tourism (1995): receipts U.S.$2,171,000,000; expenditures U.S.$4,245,000,000.

Retail trade enterprises (1993)

	no. of enterprises	total no. of employees	annual wage as a % of all trade wages	annual values of sales in Cr$'000,000,000
Vehicles, new and used; parts	5,239	241,299	133.8	1,939
General merchandise stores (including food products)	3,260	328,303	93.0	1,432
Gas stations	11,302	139,348	94.5	942
Clothing, footwear, and apparel	4,654	189,980	90.2	479
Electronics, furniture, kitchenware, and antiques	2,476	101,439	100.1	446
Metal products, lumber, glass, and construction materials	6,192	126,136	85.7	395
Food, beverages, and tobacco	3,423	64,432	73.2	246
Pharmaceutical and cosmetic products	1,816	55,069	94.4	241
Agricultural and industrial equipment and machinery	1,980	43,171	115.3	189

Family income and expenditure (1993). Average family size 3.7[6]; annual income per family Cr$608,364 (U.S.$2,178[6, 26]); sources of income (1987–88)[27]; wages and salaries 62.4%, self-employed 14.7%, transfers 10.9%, other 12.0%; expenditure (1987–88)[27]; food and beverages 25.3%, housing, energy, and household furnishings 21.3%, transportation and communications 15.0%, clothing and footwear 12.9%, health care 9.1%.

Financial aggregates[28]

	1992	1993	1994	1995	1996	1997[29]
Exchange rate, reais[1] per:						
U.S. dollar	.002	.049	.846	.973	1.039	1.064
£	.003	.073	1.322	1.508	1.506	1.734
SDR	.006	.163	1.235	1.446	1.495	1.453
International reserves (U.S.$)						
Total (excl. gold; '000,000)	22,521	30,604	37,070	49,708	58,323	54,117
SDRs ('000,000)	1	2	—	1	1	—
Reserve pos. in IMF ('000,000)	—	—	—	—	—	—
Foreign exchange ('000,000)	22,520	30,602	37,069	49,707	58,322	54,117
Gold ('000,000 fine troy oz)	2.23	2.93	3.71	4.58	3.69	4.75
% world reserves	0.24	0.32	0.37	0.50	0.41	0.53
Interest and prices						
Central bank discount (%)	1,489	5,757	56	39	24	22
Govt. bond yield (%)	...	...	...	...	...	...
Industrial share prices	...	...	...	...	...	...
Balance of payments (U.S.$'000,000)						
Balance of visible trade	+15,239	+14,329	+10,861	–3,157	...	...
Imports, f.o.b.	20,554	25,711	33,241	49,663	...	...
Exports, f.o.b.	35,793	39,630	44,102	46,506	...	...
Balance of invisibles	–9,150	–14,309	–12,014	–14,979	...	...
Balance of payments current account	+6,089	+20	–1,153	–18,136	...	...

Energy production (consumption): electricity (kW-hr; 1996) 273,827,000,000 ([1995] 243,836,000,000); coal (metric tons; 1996) 5,400,000 ([1994] 16,434,-

000); crude petroleum (barrels; 1996) 293,997,000 ([1994] 469,227,000); petroleum products (metric tons; 1994) 55,111,000 (57,042,000); natural gas (cu m; 1996) 9,181,000,000[30] ([1994] 4,103,000,000); carburant alcohol (cu m; 1995) 9,946,000 (9,946,000).

Foreign trade

Balance of trade (current prices)

	1992	1993	1994	1995	1996	1997
U.S.$'000,000	+15,239	+13,299	+10,466	–3,115	–5,554	–8,372
% of total	27.4%	20.8%	13.7%	3.3%	5.5%	7.3%

Imports (1995): U.S.$49,621,000,000 (nonelectrical and electrical machinery and apparatus 27.7%, chemicals and chemical products 12.7%, mineral fuels 12.5%, transport equipment 11.9%). *Major import sources:* United States 23.9%; Argentina 10.4%; Germany 10.0%; Italy 5.5%; Japan 5.1%; France 2.7%; South Korea 2.4%; Saudi Arabia 2.3%; Canada 2.2%; Chile 2.2%.
Exports (1995): U.S.$46,506,000,000 (iron and steel 8.7%, nonelectrical machinery and apparatus 8.5%, mineral ores 5.9%, motor vehicles 5.9%, wood pulp, paper, and paper products 5.9%, coffee 4.4%, refined sugar and confectionery 4.3%, aluminum and related products 3.3%, electrical machinery and apparatus 3.2%, footwear and other leather products 3.2%). *Major export destinations:* United States 18.7%; Argentina 8.7%; Japan 6.7%; The Netherlands 6.3%; Germany 4.6%; Italy 3.7%; Belgium 3.4%; United Kingdom 2.9%; Paraguay 2.8%; Chile 2.6%.

Transport and communications

Transport. Railroads: route length (1995) 18,578 mi, 29,899 km; passenger-mi 9,009,000,000, passenger-km 14,498,000,000; short ton-mi cargo 93,455,-000,000, metric ton-km cargo 136,442,000,000. Roads (1995): total length 1,205,000 mi, 1,939,000 km (paved 9%). Vehicles (1995): passenger cars 12,000,000; trucks and buses 3,160,689. Air transport (1996)[31]: passenger-mi 22,471,000,000, passenger-km 36,164,000,000; short ton-mi cargo 1,118,-000,000, metric ton-km cargo 1,632,000,000; airports (1995) with scheduled flights 139.

Communications

Medium	date	unit	number	units per 1,000 persons
Daily newspapers	1994	circulation	7,200,000	47
Radio	1996	receivers	55,000,000	348
Television	1995	receivers	30,000,000	193
Telephones	1995	main lines	12,082,600	78
Cellular telephones	1995	subscribers	1,285,500	8.2
Facsimile machines	1995	units	200,000	1.3
Personal computers	1995	units	2,000,000	13

Education and health

Literacy (1995)[32]: total population age 15 and over literate 91,100,000 (83.3%); males literate 45,200,000 (83.3%); females literate 45,900,000 (83.2%).

Education (1994)

	schools	teachers	students	student/ teacher ratio
Primary (age 7–14)	195,545	1,335,270	31,101,662	23.3
Secondary (age 15–17)	13,449	295,542	4,510,199	15.3
Higher	851	155,776	1,661,034	10.7

Health: physicians (1993) 222,658 (1 per 681 persons); hospital beds (1993) 509,270 (1 per 298 persons); infant mortality rate per 1,000 live births (1996) 55.3.
Food (1995): daily per capita caloric intake 2,834 (vegetable products 81%, animal products 19%); 119% of recommended minimum requirement.

Military

Total active duty personnel (1996): 295,000 (army 66.0%, navy 17.0%, air force 17.0%). *Military expenditure as percentage of GNP* (1995): 1.7% (world 2.8%); per capita expenditure U.S.$68.

[1]The real (R$) replaced the cruzeiro real (CR$) on July 1, 1994, at a rate of 2,750 cruzeiros reais to 1 real (a rate par to the U.S.$ on that date). Previously, the cruzeiro real replaced the cruzeiro (Cr$) at a rate of 1,000 cruzeiros to 1 cruzeiro real on Aug. 2, 1993; the cruzeiro replaced the new cruzado (NCz$) at a rate of 1 to 1 on March 16, 1990; and the new cruzado replaced the (old) cruzado (Cz$) at a rate of 1,000 (old) to 1 new on Jan. 15, 1989. [2]Projection based on 1991 census. [3]Area in dispute between Ceará and Piauí. [4]Detail does not add to total given because of rounding. [5]Land area excluding inland water is 3,265,076 sq mi (8,456,508 sq km). [6]Excludes rural population of Acre, Amapá, Amazonas, Pará, Rondônia, and Roraima. [7]Includes syncretic Afro-Catholic cults having Spiritist beliefs and rituals. [8]Revised preliminary census. [9]Officially defined metropolitan area. [10]Officially defined urban agglomeration. [11]Within Rio de Janeiro metropolitan area. [12]Within São Paulo metropolitan area. [13]1991 population estimate of urban agglomeration is 1,173,000. [14]Projected rates based on about 67% of total deaths. [15]As of 1992, 33,000,000 Brazilians lived in extreme poverty (more than half of whom lived in the nine states of the northeast). [16]At factor cost. [17]Less imputed bank service charges. [18]Includes 1,389,089 not adequately defined and 4,395,621 unemployed. [19]Includes mandarin oranges, satsuma oranges, and clementines. [20]Urban construction only for 74 cities. [21]1993. [22]Six largest metropolitan regions only. [23]Excludes workers in the extremely large informal sector. [24]March. [25]Minimum wages. [26]Based on end-of-year exchange rate. [27]Based on 10,408,833 families in Brazil's nine largest metropolitan regions. [28]End-of-period figures. [29]April. [30]Includes wasted gas. [31]TAM, Transbrasil, VARIG, and VASP airlines only. [32]By official estimate; functional literacy, however, may be as low as 42% of total population over age 15.

Internet resources for further information:
- IBGE: Instituto Brasileiro de Geografia e Estatística (Portuguese version) http://www.ibge.gov.br/
- IBGE: Instituto Brasileiro de Geografia e Estatística (English version) http://www.ibge.gov.br/english/e-home.htm

Brunei

Official name: Negara Brunei
 Darussalam (State of Brunei, Abode
 of Peace).
Form of government: monarchy
 (sultanate)[1].
Head of state and government: Sultan.
Capital: Bandar Seri Begawan.
Official language: Malay[2].
Official religion: Islam.
Monetary unit: 1 Brunei dollar
 (B$) = 100 cents; valuation (Sept. 25,
 1998) 1 U.S.$ = B$1.69;
 1 £ = B$2.88.

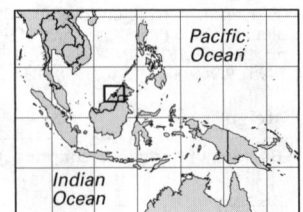

Area and population

Districts	Capitals	area sq mi	area sq km	population 1995 estimate
Belait	Kuala Belait	1,052	2,724	60,000
Brunei and Muara	Bandar Seri Begawan	220	571	195,000
Temburong	Bangar	504	1,304	8,500
Tutong	Tutong	450	1,166	32,500
TOTAL		2,226	5,765	296,000

Demography

Population (1998): 315,000.
Density (1998): persons per sq mi 141.5, persons per sq km 54.6.
Urban-rural (1997): urban 58.0%; rural 42.0%.
Sex distribution (1995): male 52.91%; female 47.09%.
Age breakdown (1993): under 15, 34.0%; 15–29, 28.0%; 30–44, 24.9%; 45–59,
 8.7%; 60 and over, 4.4%.
Population projection: (2000) 331,000; (2010) 410,000.
Doubling time: 35 years.
Ethnic composition (1992): Malay 67.1%; Chinese 15.4%; other indigenous
 6.0%; Indian and other 11.5%.
Religious affiliation (1991): Muslim 67.2%; Buddhist 12.8%; Christian 10.0%;
 other religions and nonreligious 10.0%.
Major cities (1991): Bandar Seri Begawan 45,867[3]; Kuala Belait 21,163; Seria
 21,082; Tutong 13,049.

Vital statistics

Birth rate per 1,000 population (1997): 23.3 (world avg. 25.0); (1982) legitimate
 99.6%; illegitimate 0.4%.
Death rate per 1,000 population (1997): 3.0 (world avg. 9.3).
Natural increase rate per 1,000 population (1997): 20.3 (world avg. 15.7).
Total fertility rate (avg. births per childbearing woman; 1997): 2.9.
Marriage rate per 1,000 population (1993): 7.1.
Divorce rate per 1,000 population (1992): 1.1.
Life expectancy at birth (1997): male 73.0 years; female 78.0 years.
Major causes of death per 100,000 population (1992): cardiovascular disease
 55.3; malignant neoplasms (cancers) 37.3; accidents, poisoning, and violence
 30.6; cerebrovascular diseases 19.0; pneumonia 12.3; hypertensive diseases
 9.7; congenital anomalies 9.7.

National economy

Budget (1995). Revenue: B$3,538,000,000 (nontax revenue 68.4%, of which
 property income 19.4%, commercial receipts 7.7%; tax revenue 31.6%, of
 which corporate income tax 22.8%, import duty 2.8%). Expenditures:
 B$3,649,000,000 (current expenditure 62.1%; development expenditure
 19.8%; charged expenditure 12.6%).
Public debt (external, outstanding): none.
Tourism (1990): receipts from visitors U.S.$35,000,000; expenditures by nation-
 als abroad, n.a.
Production (metric tons except as noted). Agriculture, forestry, fishing (1996):
 vegetables and melons 8,500, cassava 4,890, cassava 1,500,
 rice 1,000, pineapples 650; livestock (number of live animals) 5,000 goats,
 4,000 pigs, 3,500 buffalo, 1,800 cattle, 2,500,000 chickens; roundwood (1995)
 295,000 cu m; fish catch (1995) 4,812. Mining and quarrying (1992): other
 than petroleum and natural gas, none except sand and gravel for construction. Manufacturing (1994): gasoline 172,000; diesel oils 122,000; jet fuels
 59,000; fuel oil 55,000; kerosene 4,000. Construction (value in B$'000,000;
 1989): residential 26.2; nonresidential 5.1. Energy production (consumption):
 electricity (kW-hr; 1994) 1,315,000,000 (1,315,000,000); coal, none (none);
 crude petroleum (barrels; 1994) 59,087,000 (1,930,000); petroleum products
 (metric tons; 1994) 856,000 (852,000); natural gas (cu m; 1994) 8,794,000,000
 (1,938,000,000).
Population economically active (1991): total 111,955; activity rate of total population 43.0% (participation rates: ages 15–64, 67.6%; female 32.9%; unemployed 4.7%).

Price and earnings indexes (1990 = 100)

	1989	1990	1991	1992	1993	1994	1995
Consumer price index	98.0	100.0	101.6	102.9	107.3	109.9	116.5
Monthly earnings index[4]	...	...	76.9	87.5	...	...	...

Household income and expenditure. Average household size (1991) 5.8; income
 per household: n.a.; sources of income: n.a.; expenditure (1990): food 38.7%,
 transportation and communications 19.9%, housing 18.6%, clothing 6.4%,
 other 16.4%.

Gross national product (at current market prices; 1996): U.S.$7,546,000,000
 (U.S.$25,160 per capita).

Structure of gross domestic product and labour force

	1995 in value B$'000,000	1995 % of total value	1991 labour force	1991 % of labour force
Agriculture	188	2.7	2,162	1.9
Mining				
Manufacturing }	2,756	39.0	9,397	8.4
Construction	405	5.7	14,145	12.6
Public utilities	74	1.1	2,223	2.0
Transportation and communications	299	4.2	5,392	4.8
Trade	596	8.4	15,404	13.8
Finance	549	7.8	5,807	5.2
Services	2,390	33.8	52,121	46.6
Other	−188	−2.7	5,304[5]	4.7[5]
TOTAL	7,069	100.0	111,955	100.0

Land use (1994): forested 85.4%; meadows and pastures 1.1%; agricultural
 and under permanent cultivation 1.3%; other 12.2%.

Foreign trade

Balance of trade (current prices)

	1989	1990	1991	1992	1993	1994
B$'000,000	+1,998	+2,197	+2,417	+1,946	+1,672	+866
% of total	37.4%	37.7%	39.2%	33.7%	29.3%	14.7%

Imports (1994): B$2,517,000,000 (machinery and transport equipment 40.0%,
 manufactured goods 21.5%, miscellaneous manufactured articles 17.2%,
 food and live animals 11.2%, chemicals 4.9%, crude materials 2.3%, beverages and tobacco 2.1%). *Major import sources:* ASEAN 47.0%, of which
 Singapore 28.9%, Malaysia 11.9%; EEC 17.3%; United States 11.3%; Japan
 9.2%.
Exports (1994): B$3,383,200,000 (crude petroleum 45.8%, natural gas 41.8%,
 petroleum products 3.1%). *Major export destinations:* Japan 54.6%; ASEAN
 26.1%, of which Thailand 11.0%, Singapore 10.6%; South Korea 13.7%;
 Taiwan 2.7%.

Transport and communications

Transport. Railroads (1993)[6]: length 12 mi, 19 km. Roads (1994): total length
 1,527 mi, 2,457 km (paved 59%). Vehicles (1995): passenger cars 141,371;
 trucks and buses 16,557. Merchant marine (1992): vessels (100 gross tons
 and over) 51; total deadweight tonnage 349,718. Marine transport (1992):
 cargo loaded 20,411,000 metric tons, cargo unloaded 1,377,000 metric tons.
 Air transport (1996): passenger-mi 1,685,000,000, passenger-km 2,712,000,-
 000; short ton-mi cargo 74,028,000, metric ton-km cargo 108,079,000; airports
 (1996) with scheduled flights 1.

Communications

Medium	date	unit	number	units per 1,000 persons
Daily newspapers	1994	circulation	20,000	70
Radio	1996	receivers	125,000	417
Television	1995	receivers	90,000	308
Telephones	1995	main lines	68,100	233
Cellular telephones	1995	subscribers	35,900	123
Facsimile machines	1995	units	2,000	6.8
Personal computers	1995	units	8,000	27

Education and health

Educational attainment (1991). Percentage of population age 25 and over having: no formal schooling 17.0%; primary education 43.3%; secondary 26.3%;
 postsecondary and higher 12.9%; not stated 0.5%. *Literacy* (1991): total population age 15 and over literate 149,901 (87.8%); males literate 84,425
 (92.5%); females literate 65,476 (82.5%).

Education (1995)

	schools	teachers	students	student/ teacher ratio
Primary (age 5–11)[7]	170	3,380	55,241	15.5
Secondary (age 12–20)	37	2,157	27,801	13.4
Voc., teacher tr.	6	370	1,966	5.2
Higher	4	325	1,606	4.7

Health (1993): physicians 197 (1 per 1,398 persons); hospital beds 967 (1 per
 285 persons); infant mortality rate per 1,000 live births (1997) 9.0.
Food (1995): daily per capita caloric intake 2,849 (vegetable products 78%,
 animal products 22%); 127% of FAO recommended minimum requirement.

Military

Total active duty personnel (1996): 5,000[8] (army 78.0%, navy 14.0%, air force
 8.0%). *Military expenditure as percentage of GNP* (1995): 6.0% (world 2.8%);
 per capita expenditure U.S.$920.

---

[1]A nonelective 21-member body advises the sultan on legislative matters. [2]All official
 documents that must be published by law in Malay are, however, also required to be
 issued in an official English version as well. [3]1988 metropolitan area population estimate. [4]Nonagricultural sectors only; 1985 = 100. [5]Mostly unemployed. [6]Privately owned.
 [7]Includes preprimary. [8]All services form part of the army.

Internet resources for further information:
• **Brunei Darussalam http://www.brunet.bn/**

Bulgaria

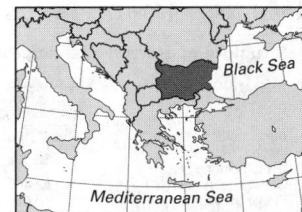

Official name: Republika Bŭlgaria (Republic of Bulgaria).
Form of government: unitary multiparty republic with one legislative body (National Assembly [240]).
Chief of state: President.
Head of government: Prime Minister.
Capital: Sofia.
Official language: Bulgarian.
Official religion: none[1].
Monetary unit: 1 lev (leva) = 100 stotinki; valuation (Sept. 25, 1998) 1 U.S.$ = 1,673 leva; 1 £ = 2,848 leva.

Area and population		area		population
Regions	**Capitals**	sq mi	sq km	1996 estimate
Burgas	Burgas	5,685	14,724	846,524
Khaskovo	Khaskovo	5,338	13,824	897,863
Lovech	Lovech	5,849	15,150	990,307
Montana	Mikhaylovgrad	4,095	10,607	615,629
Plovdiv	Plovdiv	5,245	13,585	1,213,966
Ruse	Ruse	4,187	10,843	760,029
Sofiya	Sofia (Sofiya)	7,344	19,021	966,502
Varna	Varna	4,606	11,929	901,160
City Commune				
Sofiya	Sofia (Sofiya)	506	1,311	1,192,735
TOTAL		42,855	110,994	8,384,715

Demography

Population (1998): 8,273,000.
Density (1998): persons per sq mi 193.0, persons per sq km 74.5.
Urban-rural (1996): urban 52.6%; rural 47.4%.
Sex distribution (1996): male 47.80%; female 52.20%.
Age breakdown (1995): under 15, 16.9%; 15–29, 20.5%; 30–44, 20.0%; 45–59, 19.4%; 60–74, 17.6%; 75 and over, 5.6%.
Population projection: (2000) 8,179,000; (2010) 7,926,000.
Doubling time: not applicable; population is declining.
Ethnic composition (1992): Bulgarian 83.2%; Turkish 9.4%; Gypsy 3.6%; other 1.3%.
Religious affiliation (1995): Bulgarian Orthodox 36.5%, Protestant 1.4%, Roman Catholic 0.8%; Sunnī Muslim 13.1%; other (mostly nonreligious) 47.8%.
Major cities (1996): Sofia 1,116,823; Plovdiv 344,326; Varna 301,421; Burgas 199,470; Ruse 168,051.

Vital statistics

Birth rate per 1,000 population (1996): 8.6 (world avg. 25.0); (1995) legitimate 74.3%; illegitimate 25.7%.
Death rate per 1,000 population (1996): 14.0 (world avg. 9.3).
Natural increase rate per 1,000 population (1996): −5.4 (world avg. 15.7).
Total fertility rate (avg. births per childbearing woman; 1995): 1.2.
Marriage rate per 1,000 population (1996): 4.3.
Divorce rate per 1,000 population (1995): 1.3.
Life expectancy at birth (1995): male 67.1 years; female 74.9 years.
Major causes of death per 100,000 population (1995): diseases of the circulatory system 869.8; malignant neoplasms (cancers) 192.4; accidents, poisoning, and violence 66.0; diseases of the respiratory system 63.0.

National economy

Budget (1995). Revenue: 328,328,900,000 leva (tax revenue 79.8%, of which social insurance 22.4%, value-added tax 18.1%, income tax 11.1%, profit tax 10.1%, excises 7.1%, customs and duties 6.5%, other 4.5%; nontax revenue 15.2%; other 5.0%). Expenditures: 377,923,300,000 leva (debt service 32.9%, social insurance 24.6%, defense 9.4%, education 9.4%, economic services 4.7%).
Tourism (1995): receipts from visitors U.S.$473,000,000; expenditures by nationals abroad U.S.$195,000,000.
Production (metric tons except as noted). Agriculture, forestry, fishing (1996): wheat 1,788,000, corn (maize), 1,198,000, sunflower seeds 530,000, barley 459,000, grapes 350,000, tomatoes 330,000 potatoes 302,000; livestock (number of live animals) 3,383,000 sheep, 2,140,000 pigs, 757,000 goats, 632,000 cattle; roundwood (1995) 1,970,000 cu m; fish catch (1995) 23,400. Mining and quarrying (1995): zinc 75,000. Manufacturing (value of production in '000,000 leva; 1995): chemical and oil processing 186,592; food, beverages, and tobacco 162,596; metallurgy and ore mining 96,394; machine and metalworking 81,156; electronic and electrical equipment 37,871; other goods 220,947. Construction (1995): residential 429,972 sq m; nonresidential 156,890. Energy production: electricity (kW-hr; 1994) 39,306,000,000; coal (metric tons; 1994) 30,833,000; crude petroleum (barrels; 1995) 343,100; petroleum products (metric tons; 1993) 4,010; natural gas (cu m; 1995) 60,094,000.
Household income and expenditure. Average household size (1995) 3.0; income per household (1995) 189,523 leva (U.S.$2,824); sources of income (1995): wages and salaries 37.5%, self-employment in agriculture 25.2%, transfer payments 15.7%; expenditure (1995): food 42.8%, housing and energy 7.5%, clothing 7.2%, transportation 6.6%, household durable goods 4.0%, health care 3.5%, education and culture 2.9%.
Land use (1995): forested 30.2%; meadows and pastures 16.2%; agricultural and under permanent cultivation 38.0%; other 15.6%.

Gross national product (1996): U.S.$9,924,000,000 (U.S.$1,190 per capita).

Structure of gross domestic product and labour force				
	1995			
	in value '000,000 leva	% of total value	labour force	% of labour force
Agriculture	239,451	12.9	783,000	21.1
Manufacturing, mining	767,083	41.2	956,000	25.8
Construction	99,454	5.3	188,000	5.1
Transp. and commun.	136,480	7.3	251,000	6.8
Trade	196,845	10.6	357,000	9.6
Public utilities, housing	142,059	7.6	81,000	2.2
Finance	73,883	4.0	51,000	1.4
Pub. admin., defense	67,530	3.6	76,000	2.1
Services	135,804	7.3	532,000	14.4
Other	2,414	0.1	430,000[2]	11.6[2]
TOTAL	1,861,003	100.0[3]	3,705,000	100.0[3]

Population economically active (1995): total 3,705,000; activity rate of total population 44.2% (1992; participation rates: age 16–59 [male], 16–54 [female] 70.2%; female 48.4%; unemployed 11.4%).

Price and earnings indexes (1990 = 100)							
	1990	1991	1992	1993	1994	1995	1996
Consumer price index	100.0	438.5	786.6	1,228	2,296	3,722	8,300
Monthly earnings index	100.0	267.3	622.1	965.0	1,485	2,170	3,793

Public debt (external, outstanding; 1996): U.S.$8,138,000,000.

Foreign trade

Balance of trade (current prices)						
	1992	1993	1994	1995	1996	1997
'000,000,000 leva	−12.8	−28.6	+10.8	+20.3	+32.3	+47.2
% of total	6.5%	12.2%	2.4%	2.8%	1.8%	0.3%

Imports (1996): 827,500,000,000 leva (1995; machine-building and metalworking equipment 13.8%; electrical and electronic equipment 7.6%; food, beverages, and tobacco 7.1%; textiles and knitwear 4.5%). *Major import sources:* C.I.S. 40.5%; Germany 10.9%; Italy 5.9%; Greece 3.4%; France 3.0%.
Exports (1996): 859,800,000,000 leva (1995; chemicals and plastics 25.9%; food, beverages, and tobacco 16.9%; machine-building and metalworking equipment 16.9%; textiles and knitwear 3.3%). *Major export destinations:* C.I.S. 19.4%; Italy 9.7%; Germany 9.1%; Turkey 8.2%.

Transport and communications

Transport[4]. Railroads (1995): track length 6,507 km; (1996) passenger-km 5,065,000,000; metric ton-km cargo 7,549,000,000. Roads (1995): length 37,320 km (paved 92%). Vehicles (1995): cars 1,647,571; trucks and buses 20,495. Merchant marine (1995): vessels (100 gross tons and over) 61; deadweight tonnage 391,000. Air transport (1995): passenger-mi 1,765,000,000, passenger-km 2,840,000,000; short ton-mi cargo 24,100,000, metric ton-km cargo 35,200,000; airports (1996) with scheduled flights 3.

Communications				units per 1,000 persons
Medium	date	unit	number	
Daily newspapers	1995	circulation	1,179,000	141
Television	1995	receivers	3,011,000	359
Telephones	1995	main lines	2,563,000	306
Cellular telephones	1995	subscribers	20,900	2.5
Facsimile machines	1995	units	15,000	1.8
Personal computers	1995	units	180,000	21.5

Education and health

Educational attainment (1992). Percentage of population age 25 and over having: no formal schooling 4.7%; incomplete primary education 12.5%; primary 31.9%; secondary 35.7%; higher 15.0%. *Literacy* (1992): total population age 15 and over literate 97.9%; males literate 98.7%; females literate 97.1%.

Education (1995–96)	schools	teachers	students	student/teacher ratio
Primary (age 6–14) } Secondary (age 15–17) }	3,325	70,763	963,582	13.6
Voc., teacher tr.	535	19,141	213,337	11.1
Higher	88	25,339	248,571	9.8

Health (1995): physicians 29,069 (1 per 288 persons); hospital beds 89,190 (1 per 94 persons); (1996) infant mortality rate per 1,000 live births 15.6.
Food (1995): daily per capita caloric intake 2,907 (vegetable products 78%, animal products 22%); 116% of FAO recommended minimum requirement.

Military

Total active duty personnel (1995): 101,900 (army 75.9%, navy 2.9%, air force 21.2%). *Military expenditure as percentage of GNP* (1995): 2.8% (world 2.8%); per capita expenditure U.S.$125.

[1]Bulgaria has no official religion; the 1991 constitution, however, refers to Eastern Orthodoxy as the "traditional" religion. [2]Includes 6,455 undistributable employed and 423,773 unemployed. [3]Detail does not add to total given because of rounding. [4]Public sector.

Internet resources for further information:
• **National Statistical Institute of the Republic of Bulgaria**
  http://www.acad.bg/BulRTD/nsi/index.htm

Burkina Faso

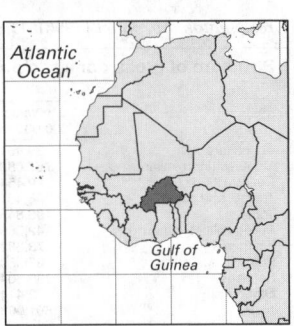

Atlantic Ocean

Gulf of Guinea

Official name: Burkina Faso (Burkina Faso).
Form of government: multiparty republic with one advisory body (Chamber of Representatives [178]) and one legislative body (National Assembly [111]).
Chief of state: President.
Head of government: Prime Minister.
Capital: Ouagadougou.
Official language: French.
Official religion: none.
Monetary unit: 1 CFA franc (CFAF) = 100 centimes; valuation (Sept. 25, 1998) 1 U.S.$ = CFAF 560.38; 1 £ = CFAF 954.05.

Area and population

Territorial collectivities	Capitals	area sq mi	area sq km	population 1991 estimate
Bam	Kongoussi	1,551	4,017	173,516
Bazéga	Kombissiri	2,051	5,313	352,104
Bougouriba	Diébougou	2,736	7,087	242,986
Boulgou	Tenkodogo	3,488	9,033	465,845
Boulkiemde	Koudougou	1,598	4,138	393,900
Comoé	Banfora	7,102	18,393	296,083
Ganzourgou	Zorgho	1,578	4,087	223,555
Gnagna	Bogandé	3,320	8,600	272,203
Gourma	Fada N'Gourma	10,275	26,613	350,336
Houé	Bobo-Dioulasso	6,438	16,672	724,803
Kadiogo	Ouagadougou	451	1,169	652,377
Kénédougou	Orodara	3,207	8,307	162,010
Kossi	Nouna	5,088	13,177	389,360
Kouritenga	Koupéla	628	1,627	227,060
Mouhoun	Dédougou	4,032	10,442	329,115
Nahouri	Pô	1,484	3,843	119,144
Namentenga	Boulsa	2,994	7,755	214,564
Oubritenga	Ziniaré	1,812	4,693	328,682
Oudalan	Gorom Gorom	3,879	10,046	123,495
Passoré	Yako	1,575	4,078	232,278
Poni	Gaoua	4,000	10,361	258,647
Sanguie	Réo	1,994	5,165	234,079
Sanmatenga	Kaya	3,557	9,213	404,563
Sèno	Dori	5,202	13,473	269,892
Sissili	Léo	5,303	13,736	297,598
Soum	Djibo	5,154	13,350	217,972
Sourou	Tougan	3,663	9,487	313,355
Tapoa	Diapaga	5,707	14,780	187,785
Yatenga	Ouahigouya	4,746	12,292	558,318
Zoundwéogo	Manga	1,333	3,453	175,166
TOTAL		105,946	274,400	9,190,791

Demography

Population (1998): 11,266,000.
Density (1998): persons per sq mi 106.3, persons per sq km 41.1.
Urban-rural (1991): urban 14.0%; rural 86.0%.
Sex distribution (1997): male 48.65%; female 51.35%.
Age breakdown (1997): under 15, 48.1%; 15–29, 27.0%; 30–44, 12.6%; 45–59, 7.5%; 60–74, 3.9%; 75 and over, 0.9%.
Population projection: (2000) 11,892,000; (2010) 15,371,000.
Ethnic composition (1983): Mossi 47.9%; Mande 8.8%; Fulani 8.3%; Lobi 6.9%; Bobo 6.8%; Senufo 5.3%; Grosi 5.1%; Gurma 4.8%; Tuareg 3.3%.
Religious affiliation (1994): Muslim 50%; traditional beliefs 40%; Christian (mostly Roman Catholic) 10%.
Major cities (1993): Ouagadougou 690,000; Bobo-Dioulasso 300,000; Koudougou 105,000; Ouahigouya 38,902[1]; Banfora 35,319[1].

Vital statistics

Birth rate per 1,000 population (1996): 47.0 (world avg. 25.0).
Death rate per 1,000 population (1996): 20.0 (world avg. 9.3).
Natural increase rate per 1,000 population (1996): 27.0 (world avg. 15.7).
Total fertility rate (avg. births per childbearing woman; 1996): 6.8.
Life expectancy at birth (1996): male 43.5 years; female 42.9 years.
Major causes of death (ages 15 and under; 1991): malaria, respiratory diseases, intestinal infectious diseases, meningitis.

National economy

Budget (1995). Revenue: CFAF 224,800,000,000 (1993; import duties 23.4%, personal income taxes 18.8%, sales taxes 14.7%). Expenditures: CFAF 244,800,000,000 (wages and salaries 25.2%, debt service 6.2%).
Public debt (external, outstanding; 1996): U.S.$1,160,000,000.
Tourism: receipts (1995) U.S.$22,000,000; expenditures (1994) U.S.$23,000,000.
Production (metric tons except as noted). Agriculture, forestry, fishing (1996): sorghum 1,314,000, millet 785,000, sugarcane 400,000, corn (maize) 222,000, peanuts (groundnuts) 213,300, seed cotton 170,000, rice 124,000, pulses 22,000, sweet potatoes 20,000, sesame 6,000, cassava 2,000; livestock (number of live animals) 7,300,000 goats, 5,800,000 sheep, 4,350,000 cattle, 19,000,000 chickens; roundwood (1995) 10,033,000 cu m; fish catch (1995) 8,000. Mining and quarrying (1995): gold 672 kg[2]; silver 100 kg[3]. Manufacturing (1995): sugar 47,107; flour 31,046; soap 5,787; edible oils 4,286; soft drinks and beer 287,000 hectolitres; printed fabric 5,297,000 sq m; bicycles 11,150 units; mopeds 8,673 units; cigarettes 47,000,000 packets. Construction (value added in CFAF; 1995): 62,400,000,000. Energy production (consumption): electricity (kW-hr; 1994) 216,000,000 (216,000,000); crude petroleum, none (n.a.); petroleum products (metric tons; 1994) none (309,000).

Gross national product (1996): U.S.$2,410,000,000 (U.S.$230 per capita).

Structure of gross domestic product and labour force

	1995 in value CFAF '000,000	1995 % of total value	1991 labour force	1991 % of labour force
Agriculture	367,100	31.6	4,293,784	91.8
Mining	} 232,300	} 20.0	2,590	0.1
Manufacturing			51,694	1.1
Construction	62,400	5.4	11,016	0.2
Public utilities	10,600	0.9	3,844	0.1
Transp. and commun.	44,700	3.8	15,041	0.3
Trade	140,400	12.1	120,314	2.6
Finance	...	...	2,075	—
Pub. admin., defense	} 248,200	} 21.3	111,556	2.4
Services				
Other	57,200[4]	4.9[4]	67,279[5]	1.4[5]
TOTAL	1,163,000[6]	100.0	4,679,193	100.0

Population economically active (1991): total 4,679,193; activity rate 50.9% (participation rates: over age [1988] 10, 78.1%; female 48.7%; unemployed 1.1%).

Price and earnings indexes (1990 = 100)

	1991	1992	1993	1994	1995	1996	1997
Consumer price index	102.5	100.5	101.1	126.5	135.8	144.2	147.3
Hourly earnings index[7]	100.0	100.0	...	...	...	...	...

Household income and expenditure. Average household size (1985) 6.2; average annual income per household CFAF 303,000 (U.S.$640); sources of income: n.a.; expenditure (1985)[8]: food 38.7%, transportation 18.6%, electricity and fuel 13.7%, beverages 9.0%, health 5.2%, housing 5.1%.
Land use (1994): forest 50.5%; pasture 21.9%; agriculture 13.0%; other 14.6%.

Foreign trade[9]

Balance of trade (current prices)

	1991	1992	1993	1994	1995	1996
CFAF '000,000	+99.80	+93.10	+69.30	−22.90	+1.96	−122.85
% of total	22.8%	24.4%	18.1%	5.6%	0.3%	28.3%

Imports (1995): CFAF 242,100,000,000 (capital equipment 31.1%, food products 14.4%, petroleum products 10.6%, raw materials 8.7%). *Major import sources* (1993): France 24.5%; Côte d'Ivoire 17.9%; Nigeria 6.6%; Japan 6.4%; China 5.6%; United States 4.3%; The Netherlands 4.3%.
Exports (1995): CFAF 164,400,000,000 (raw cotton 42.2%, live animals 18.9%, gold 12.1%, hides and skins 8.9%). *Major export destinations* (1993): Côte d'Ivoire 34.9%; France 21.1%; Mali 5.4%; Taiwan 3.5%; Japan 3.5%.

Transport and communications

Transport. Railroads (1995)[10]: route length 386 mi, 622 km; passenger-km 202,000,000; metric ton-km cargo 45,000,000. Roads (1995): total length 7,771 mi, 12,506 km (paved 16%). Vehicles (1995): passenger cars 16,800; trucks and buses 17,222. Merchant marine: none. Air transport (1993): pasenger-km 217,154,000; metric ton-km cargo 34,204,000; airports (1997) 2.

Communications

Medium	date	unit	number	units per 1,000 persons
Daily newspapers	1995	circulation	17,000[11]	1.6[11]
Radio	1996	receivers	512,500	48.3
Television	1995	receivers	45,500	4.4
Telephones	1995	main lines	30,000	2.9

Education and health

Educational attainment (1985). Percentage of population age 10 and over having: no formal schooling 86.1%; some primary 7.3%; general secondary 2.2%; specialized secondary and postsecondary 3.8%; other 0.6%. *Literacy* (1995): percentage of total population age 15 and over literate 19.2%; males literate 29.5%; females literate 9.2%.

Education (1993–94)

	schools	teachers	students	student/ teacher ratio
Primary	2,971	10,300	600,032	58.2
Secondary	173[12]	3,346	116,033	34.7
Vocational	22[12]	639	8,808	13.8
Higher	9[12]	571	8,815	15.4

Health (1991): physicians 341 (1 per 27,158 persons); hospital beds 5,041 (1 per 1,837 persons); infant mortality rate (1996) 117.8.
Food (1995): daily per capita caloric intake 2,155 (vegetable products 96%, animal products 4%); 91% of FAO recommended minimum requirement.

Military

Total active duty personnel (1997): 5,800 (army 96.6%, air force 3.4%). *Military expenditure as percentage of GNP* (1995): 2.9% (world 2.8%); per capita expenditure U.S.$7.

[1]1985. [2]Officially marketed gold only; does not include substantial illegal production. [3]1992. [4]Includes indirect taxes less imputed bank service charges and subsidies. [5]Includes 49,819 unemployed. [6]Detail does not add to total given because of rounding. [7]January 1; index refers to the *S.M.I.G.* (*salaire minimum interprofessionnel guaranti*), a form of minimum professional wage. [8]Weights of consumer price index components; Ouagadougou only. [9]Imports figures are c.i.f. in balance of trade and f.o.b. in commodities and trading partners. [10]Passenger-km and metric ton-km cargo figures are based on traffic between Abidjan, Côte d'Ivoire, and Ouagadougou. [11]Circulation for 3 newspapers only. [12]1991–92.

Burundi

Official name: Republika y'u Burundi
(Rundi); République du Burundi
(French) (Republic of Burundi).
Form of government: transitional
regime with one legislative house
(Transitional National Assembly [121[1]]).
Head of state and government:
President, assisted by Prime Minister.
Capital: Bujumbura.
Official languages: Rundi; French.
Official religion: none.
Monetary unit: 1 Burundi franc
(FBu) = 100 centimes; valuation (Sept.
25, 1998) 1 U.S.$ = FBu 457.70;
1 £ = FBu 779.23.

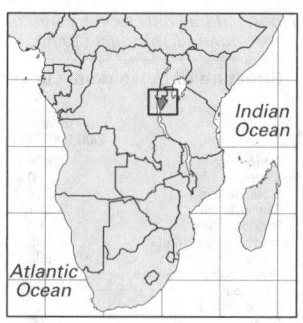

Area and population

Provinces	Capitals	area		population
		sq mi	sq km	1990 census
Bubanza	Bubanza	420	1,089	222,953
Bujumbura	Bujumbura	509	1,319	608,931
Bururi	Bururi	952	2,465	385,490
Cankuzo	Cankuzo	759	1,965	142,707
Cibitoke	Cibitoke	631	1,636	279,843
Gitega	Gitega	764	1,979	565,174
Karuzi	Karuzi	563	1,457	287,905
Kayanza	Kayanza	476	1,233	443,116
Kirundo	Kirundo	658	1,703	401,103
Makamba	Makamba	757	1,960	223,799
Muramvya	Muramvya	593	1,535	441,653
Muyinga	Muyinga	709	1,836	373,382
Ngozi	Ngozi	569	1,474	482,246
Rutana	Rutana	756	1,959	195,834
Ruyigi	Ruyigi	903	2,339	238,567
TOTAL LAND AREA		10,019	25,949	
INLAND WATER		721	1,867	
TOTAL		10,740	27,816	5,292,793[2]

Demography

Population (1998): 5,537,000.
Density (1998)[3]: persons per sq mi 552.7, persons per sq km 213.4.
Urban-rural (1990): urban 6.3%; rural 93.7%.
Sex distribution (1995): male 48.94%; female 51.06%.
Age breakdown (1995): under 15, 46.2%; 15–29, 25.9%; 30–44, 16.4%; 45–59, 7.0%; 60–74, 3.5%; 75 and over, 1.0%.
Population projection: (2000) 5,931,000; (2010) 7,539,000.
Doubling time: 28 years.
Ethnic composition (1983): Rundi 97.4%, of which Hutu 82.8%, Tutsi 13.6%; Twa Pygmy 1.0%; other 2.6%.
Religious affiliation (1990): Roman Catholic 65.1%; Protestant 13.8%; Muslim 1.6%; nonreligious 18.6%; traditional beliefs 0.3%; other 0.6%.
Major cities (1990): Bujumbura (1994) 300,000; Gitega 101,827; Bururi 15,816; Ngozi 14,511; Cibitoke 8,280.

Vital statistics

Birth rate per 1,000 population (1996): 42.7 (world avg. 25.0).
Death rate per 1,000 population (1996): 17.8 (world avg. 9.3).
Natural increase rate per 1,000 population (1996): 24.9 (world avg. 15.7).
Total fertility rate (avg. births per childbearing woman; 1996): 6.5.
Marriage rate per 1,000 population: n.a.
Divorce rate per 1,000 population: n.a.
Life expectancy at birth (1996): male 44.3 years; female 47.3 years.
Major causes of death: n.a.; however, major health problems include malaria, influenza, diarrheal diseases, measles, and AIDS.

National economy

Budget (1995). Revenue: FBu 59,600,000,000 (customs duties 37.1%, excise duties 22.6%, income tax 19.2%, taxes on goods and services 14.6%, administrative receipts 2.4%). Expenditures: FBu 69,100,000,000 (wages and salaries 27.5%, goods and services 18.4%, subsidies and transfers 9.8%, public debt 6.3%).
Tourism (1995): receipts from visitors U.S.$1,000,000; expenditures by nationals abroad U.S.$25,000,000.
Production (metric tons except as noted). Agriculture, forestry, fishing (1996): bananas 1,544,000, sweet potatoes 670,000, cassavas 549,000, dry beans 288,000, sugarcane 148,000, corn (maize) 144,000, yams and taros 103,000, sorghum 66,000, potatoes 42,000, rice 42,000, coffee 25,000, millet 11,000, peanuts (groundnuts) 10,000, wheat 9,000; livestock (number of live animals) 900,000 goats, 390,000 cattle, 320,000 sheep, 4,000,000 chickens; roundwood (1995) 4,969,000 cu m; fish catch (1995) 21,100. Mining and quarrying (1991): peat 10,026; kaolin clay 6,682; lime 86; gold 804 troy oz. Manufacturing (1994): beer 1,382,670 hectolitres; carbonated beverages 201,400 hectolitres; cigarettes 584,580,000 units; blankets 248,438 units; footwear 74,890 pairs. Construction: n.a. Energy production (consumption): electricity (kW-hr; 1994): 147,000,000 (192,000,000); coal, none (n.a.); crude petroleum, none (n.a.); petroleum products (metric tons; 1994) none (71,000); natural gas, none (n.a.); peat (metric tons; 1994) 12,000 (12,000).
Land use (1994): forested 12.7%; meadows and pastures 38.6%; agricultural and under permanent cultivation 45.9%; other 2.8%.
Gross national product (at current market prices; 1996): U.S.$1,066,000,000 (U.S.$170 per capita).

Structure of gross domestic product and labour force

	1995		1990	
	in value FBu '000,000	% of total value	labour force	% of labour force
Agriculture	126,664	47.8	2,574,443	93.1
Mining			1,419	—
Public utilities }	1,296	0.5	1,672	0.1
Manufacturing	27,855	10.5	33,867	1.2
Construction	11,436	4.3	19,737	0.7
Transportation and communications	8,892	3.4	8,504	0.3
Trade	8,709	3.3	25,822	0.9
Finance	...	...	2,005	0.1
Pub. admin., defense	37,866	14.3 }	85,191	3.1
Services	4,648	1.7		
Other	37,623[4]	14.2[4]	13,270	0.5
TOTAL	264,990[2]	100.0	2,765,945[2]	100.0

Public debt (external, outstanding; 1996): U.S.$1,081,000,000.
Population economically active (1991): total 2,779,777; activity rate of total population 52.9% (participation rates: ages 15–64, 91.4%; female 52.6%; unemployed, n.a.).

Price and earnings indexes (1990 = 100)

	1991	1992	1993	1994	1995	1996	1997
Consumer price index	109.0	111.0	121.7	139.8	166.7	210.8	276.5
Earnings index	...	...	...	...	...	...	...

Household income and expenditure. Average household size (1990) 4.6; income per household: n.a.; sources of income: n.a.; expenditure[5]: food 59.6%, clothing and footwear 11.1%, furniture and household goods 6.0%, energy and water 5.8%, housing 4.4%, other 13.1%.

Foreign trade

Balance of trade (current prices)

	1992	1993	1994	1995	1996	1997
FBu '000,000	−30,751	−26,417	−22,603	−24,018	−24,039	−13,438
% of total	50.0%	44.0%	29.9%	31.1%	53.5%	18.4%

Imports (1995): FBu 52,082,000,000 (1994; machinery and transport equipment 21.3%, food and food products 17.9%, petroleum products 8.2%, pharmaceutical products 6.4%). *Major import sources:* Belgium-Luxembourg 14.8%; France 9.2%; Germany 8.8%; Japan 6.1%; United States 5.7%; The Netherlands 4.5%; Kenya 4.3%.
Exports (1995): FBu 28,872,000,000 (coffee 80.7%, tea 7.8%, cotton 1.6%, animal hides and skins 1.2%). *Major export destinations:* Germany 21.6%; Belgium-Luxembourg 17.6%; France 10.9%; United States 6.7%; Rwanda 3.6%; United Kingdom 3.6%; The Netherlands 2.3%; Zaire 1.6%.

Transport and communications

Transport. Railroads: none. Roads (1995): total length 8,997 mi, 14,480 km (paved 7%). Vehicles (1995): passenger cars 16,800; trucks and other vehicles 15,000. Merchant marine (1979): vessels (100 gross tons and over) 1; total gross tonnage 385. Air transport (1994)[6]: passenger arrivals 28,762, departures 33,750; cargo loaded 1,760 short tons (1,597 metric tons), unloaded 14,841 short tons (13,463 metric tons); airports (1997) with scheduled flights 1.

Communications

Medium	date	unit	number	units per 1,000 persons
Daily newspapers	1996	circulation	20,000	3.4
Radio	1996	receivers	300,000	50
Television	1995	receivers	40,000	7.0
Telephones	1995	main lines	17,200	2.7
Cellular telephones	1995	subscribers	300	0.1
Facsimile machines	1995	units	100	—

Education and health

Educational attainment: n.a. *Literacy* (1995): percentage of total population age 15 and over literate 35.3%; males literate 49.7%; females literate 22.5%.

Education (1992–93)

	schools	teachers	students	student/ teacher ratio
Primary (age 6–11)	1,418	10,400	651,086	62.6
Secondary (age 12–18)	113[7]	2,562	55,713	21.7
Higher	8	556	4,256	7.6

Health (1990): physicians 168 (1 per 31,777 persons); hospital beds 10,370 (1 per 515 persons); infant mortality rate per 1,000 live births (1996) 104.8.
Food (1995): daily per capita caloric intake 1,749 (vegetable products 97%, animal products 3%); 75% of FAO recommended minimum requirement.

Military

Total active duty personnel (1996): 18,500 (army 100%). *Military expenditure as percentage of GNP* (1995): 4.4% (world 2.8%); per capita expenditure U.S.$6.

---

[1]Includes 40 additional nominated seats per Transitional Constitutional Act of June 6, 1998. [2]Detail does not add to total given because of rounding. [3]Based on land area. [4]Indirect taxes less subsidies. [5]Weights of consumer price index components. [6]Figures for Bujumbura airport only. [7]1990–91.

Cambodia

Official name: Preah Reach Ana Pak Kampuchea (Kingdom of Cambodia)[1].
Form of government: constitutional monarchy with one legislative house (National Assembly [122]).
Chief of state: King.
Head of government: Prime minister[2].
Capital: Phnom Penh.
Official language: Khmer.
Official religion: Buddhism.
Monetary unit: 1 riel = 100 sen; valuation (Sept. 25, 1998)
1 U.S.$ = 3,800.00 riels;
1 £ = 6,469.50 riels.

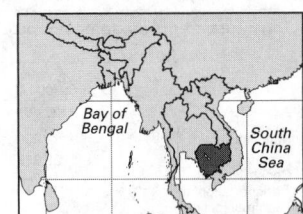

Area and population		area		population
				1987
Provinces	Capitals	sq mi	sq km	estimate
Bântéay Méan Cheăy	...	3	3	3
Bătdâmbâng	Bătdâmbâng	7,353[3]	19,044[3]	837,000[3]
Kâmpóng Cham	Kâmpóng Cham	4,053	10,498	1,244,000
Kâmpóng Chhnăng	Kâmpóng Chhnăng	2,131	5,520	257,000
Kâmpóng Spœ	Kâmpóng Spœ	2,709	7,016	396,000
Kâmpóng Thum	Kâmpóng Thum	4,730	12,251	441,000
Kâmpôt	Kâmpôt	3,808	9,862	412,000
Kândal		1,472	3,813	838,000
Kaôh Kŏng	Krŏng Kaôh Kŏng	4,301	11,140	30,000
Krâchéh	Krâchéh	4,283	11,094	182,000
Môndôl Kiri	Senmonorom	5,517	14,288	18,000
Ôtdâr Méan Cheăy[4]	...	...	...	...
Poŭthĭsăt	Poŭthĭsăt	4,900	12,692	204,000
Preăh Vihéar	Phnum Tbéng Méan Cheăy	5,541	14,350	80,000
Prey Vêng	Prey Vêng	1,885	4,883	782,000
Rôtânăh Kiri	Lumphăt	4,163	10,782	52,000
Siĕmréab[4]	Siĕmréab	4,237	10,897	555,000
Stœng Trêng	Stœng Trêng	4,328	11,209	46,000
Svay Riĕng	Svay Riĕng	1,145	2,966	340,000
Takêv	Takêv	1,474	3,818	618,000
Municipalities				
TOTAL LAND AREA		68,045	176,238	
Phnom Penh		18	46	564,000
Preăh Seihânŭ		27	69	61,000
Kêb		...	...	...
INLAND WATER		2,192	5,678	
TOTAL		70,238[5]	181,916	7,957,000

Demography

Population (1998): 10,751,000.
Density (1998)[6]: persons per sq mi 158.0, persons per sq km 61.0.
Urban-rural (1995): urban 21%; rural 79%.
Sex distribution (1997): male 48.24%; female 51.76%.
Age breakdown (1997): under 15, 45.4%; 15–29, 25.3%; 30–44, 17.1%; 45–59, 7.6%; 60–74, 3.8%; 75 and over, 0.8%.
Population projection: (2000) 11,207,000; (2010) 13,433,000.
Ethnic composition (1994): Khmer 88.6%; Vietnamese 5.5%; Chinese 3.1%; Cham 2.3%; other (Thai, Lao, and Kola) 0.5%.
Religious affiliation (1994): Buddhist 95%; Muslim 2%; other 3%.
Major cities (1987): Phnom Penh 920,000[7]; Bătdâmbâng 45,000; Kâmpóng Cham 33,000; Pursat 16,000; Kâmpóng Chhnăng 15,000.

Vital statistics

Birth rate per 1,000 population (1997): 43.0 (world avg. 25.0).
Death rate per 1,000 population (1997): 15.0 (world avg. 9.3).
Natural increase rate per 1,000 population (1997): 28.0 (world avg. 15.7).
Total fertility rate (avg. births per childbearing woman; 1997): 5.8.
Life expectancy at birth (1997): male 52 years; female 55 years.
Major causes of death per 100,000 population: n.a.; however, major health problems include tuberculosis, malaria, and pneumonia. Violence, acts of war, and military ordnance (especially unexploded mines) remain hazards.

National economy

Budget (1996). Revenue: 797,500,000,000 riels (taxes on international trade 46.9%; indirect taxes 22.3%, of which consumption taxes 8.3%; nontax revenue 27.6%). Expenditures: 1,395,100,000,000 riels (current expenditure 61.2%, of which economic and financial affairs 26.8%, defense 21.4%, education 12.3%, public health 8.7%; development expenditure 38.8%).
Public debt (external, outstanding; 1996): U.S.$2,032,000,000.
Tourism (1995): receipts U.S.$100,000,000; expenditures U.S.$8,000,000.
Production (metric tons except as noted). Agriculture, forestry, fishing (1996): rice 3,500,000, sugarcane 205,000, bananas 140,000, roots and tubers 138,000 (of which cassava 90,000, sweet potatoes 30,000), corn (maize) 60,000, oranges 60,000, rubber 40,000, mangoes 30,000, soybeans 18,000, tobacco leaves 10,000; livestock (number of live animals; 1997) 2,800,000 cattle, 2,050,000 pigs, 770,000 buffalo, 14,300,000 chickens and ducks; roundwood (1995) 7,765,000 cu m; fish catch (1995) 112,510. Mining and quarrying (1995): legal mining is confined to fertilizers, salt, and construction materials. Manufacturing (value of production in '000,000 riels; 1988): cigarettes 1,064.5; food 116.9; chemical products (including rubber) 83.5; light industries (including textiles) 63.2; mechanical equipment and parts 46.8; building materials 4.5. Construction: n.a. Energy production (consumption): electricity (kW-hr; 1994) 187,000,000 (187,000,000); petroleum products (metric tons; 1994) none (159,000).

Household income and expenditure. Average household size (1980) 5.6.
Gross domestic product (1996): U.S.$3,088,000,000 (U.S.$300 per capita).

Structure of gross domestic product and labour force				
	1995		1996	
	in value '000,000,000 riels	% of total value	labour force	% of labour force
Agriculture	3,826	53.1	3,732,000	72.6
Mining	20	0.3		
Manufacturing	367	5.1		
Construction	561	7.8		
Public utilities	50	0.7		
Transp. and commun.	248	3.4	1,406,000	27.4
Trade	983	13.7		
Public admin., defense	283	3.9		
Services	862	12.0		
Other				
TOTAL	7,200	100.0	5,138,000	100.0

Population economically active (1993): total 4,010,000; activity rate of total population 43.1% (participation rates: ages 15–64, 86.2%; female 55.8%).

Price and earnings indexes (1994 = 100)							
	1991	1992	1993	1994	1995	1996	1997
Consumer price index	31.8	64.7	119.7	100.0	105.3	115.9	119.6
Earnings index	...	...	...	...	...	...	...

Land use (1994): forested 69.1%; meadows and pastures 8.5%; agricultural and under permanent cultivation 21.7%; other 0.7%.

Foreign trade[8]

Balance of trade (current prices)						
	1991	1992	1993	1994	1995	1996
U.S.$'000,000	−33.0	−86.0	−203.0	−275.0	−382.0	−395.0
% of total	7.1%	14.0%	31.7%	22.9%	19.1%	24.3%

Imports (1996): U.S.$1,010,000,000 (1995; gold 32.8%; cigarettes 20.7%; gasoline and diesel oil 11.7%; motorcycles 3.9%; motor vehicles 2.4%). *Major import sources* (1995): Singapore 35.7%; Thailand 23.8%; Vietnam 6.8%.
Exports (1996): U.S.$615,000,000 (1995; reexports 50.4%; domestic exports 49.6%, of which sawn timber 16.5%, logs 11.8%, rubber 5.6%). *Major export destinations* (1995): Thailand 42.7%; Singapore 11.1%; India 7.6%.

Transport and communications

Transport. Railroads (1995): length 380 mi, 612 km; passengers transported (1994) 500,000; cargo transported (1994) 100,000 metric tons. Roads (1995): total length 7,643 mi, 12,300 km (paved 34%). Vehicles (1996): passenger cars 42,210; trucks and buses 9,005. Merchant marine (1992): vessels (100 gross tons and over) 3; total deadweight tonnage 3,839. Air transport (1977): passenger-mi 26,098,800, passenger-km 42,000,000; short ton-mi cargo 274,000, metric ton-km cargo 400,000; airports (1997) with scheduled flights 8.

Communications				units per 1,000
Medium	date	unit	number	persons
Radio	1995	receivers	1,192,000	124.0
Television	1995	receivers	76,900	8.0
Telephones	1996	main lines	10,100	1.0
Cellular telephones	1995	subscribers	14,400	1.5
Facsimile machines	1995	units	960	0.1

Education and health

Educational attainment: n.a. *Literacy* (1993): total population age 15 and over literate 3,895,000 (65.3%); males literate 79.7%; females literate 53.4%.

Education (1994–95)				student/
	schools	teachers	students	teacher ratio
Primary (age 6–10)	4,539[9]	37,827	1,703,316	45.0
Secondary (age 11–16)	440[9]	16,349	297,555	18.2
Voc., teacher tr.	65[9]	2,618[9]	16,350	...
Higher	9[9]	784	11,652	14.9

Health: physicians (1994) 1,200 (1 per 7,900 persons); hospital beds (1994) 12,098[10] (1 per 791 persons); infant mortality rate (1997) 106.
Food (1995): daily per capita caloric intake 2,012 (vegetable products 94%, animal products 6%); 91% of FAO recommended minimum requirement.

Military

Total active duty personnel (1997)[11]: 140,500 (army 59.8%, navy 3.6%, air force 1.0%, provincial 35.6%). *Military expenditure as percentage of GNP* (1995): 3.1% (world 2.8%); per capita expenditure U.S.$9.

[1]The United Nations Transitional Authority in Cambodia (UNTAC) assumed administrative responsibility for Cambodia in March 1992. Cambodian sovereignty, however, was retained by a Supreme National Council (SNC) until UN-supervised elections were held May 23–29, 1993. The Kingdom of Cambodia was proclaimed from Sept. 24, 1993. [2]A single prime minister was head of government from November 1998 per the king's forced moral persuasion. [3]Bântéay Méan Cheăy included in Bătdâmbâng. [4]The area and population of Ôtdâr Méan Cheăy is included with Siĕmréab. [5]Detail does not add to total given because of rounding. [6]Based on land area. [7]1994 estimate. [8]Trade statistics do not indicate whether imports are c.i.f. or f.o.b.; illegal or undeclared trade is not accounted for in the foreign-trade figures shown here. [9]1992–93. [10]Public hospitals only. [11]Figures include provincial and exclude paramilitary forces.

Internet resources for further information:
• Cambodian Information Center http://www.cambodia.org

Cameroon

Official name: République du
  Cameroun (French); Republic of
  Cameroon (English).
Form of government: unitary multiparty
  republic with one legislative house
  (National Assembly [180]).
Chief of state: President.
Head of government: Prime Minister.
Capital: Yaoundé.
Official languages: French; English.
Official religion: none.
Monetary unit: 1 CFA franc
  (CFAF) = 100 centimes; valuation
  (Sept. 25, 1998) 1 U.S.$ = CFAF 560.38;
  1 £ = CFAF 954.05.

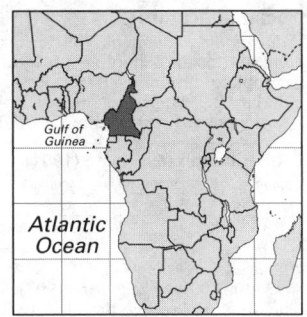

Gulf of
Guinea

Atlantic
Ocean

Area and population

Provinces	Capitals	area sq mi	area sq km	population 1987 census
Adamoua	Ngaoundéré	24,591	63,691	495,200
Centre	Yaoundé	26,613	68,926	1,651,600
Est	Bertoua	42,089	109,011	517,200
Extrême-Nord	Maroua	13,223	34,246	1,855,700
Littoral	Douala	7,814	20,239	1,354,800
Nord	Garoua	25,319	65,576	832,200
Nord-Ouest	Bamenda	6,877	17,810	1,237,400
Ouest	Bafoussam	5,356	13,872	1,339,800
Sud	Ebolowa	18,189	47,110	373,800
Sud-Ouest	Buea	9,448	24,471	838,000
LAND AREA		179,519	464,952	
INLAND WATER		4,051	10,492	
TOTAL		183,569[1]	475,442[1]	10,495,700

Demography

Population (1998): 15,029,000.
Density (1998)[2]: persons per sq mi 81.9, persons per sq km 31.6.
Urban-rural (1991): urban 41.2%; rural 58.8%.
Sex distribution (1991): male 49.88%; female 50.12%.
Age breakdown (1991): under 15, 46.4%; 15–29, 24.4%; 30–44, 15.1%; 45–59, 8.6%; 60 and over 5.5%.
Population projection: (2000) 15,892,000; (2010) 20,632,000.
Doubling time: 25 years.
Ethnic composition (1983): Fang 19.6%; Bamileke and Bamum 18.5%; Duala, Luanda, and Basa 14.7%; Fulani 9.6%; Tikar 7.4%; Mandara 5.7%; Maka 4.9%; Chamba 2.4%; Mbum 1.3%; Hausa 1.2%; French 0.2%; other 14.5%.
Religious affiliation (1990): Roman Catholic 34.7%; animist 26.0%; Muslim 21.8%; Protestant 17.5%.
Major cities (1991): Douala 1,200,000; Yaoundé 1,000,000; Bafoussam 200,000; Garoua 120,000; Maroua 80,000.

Vital statistics

Birth rate per 1,000 population (1995–2000): 39.3 (world avg. 25.0).
Death rate per 1,000 population (1995–2000): 11.9 (world avg. 9.3).
Natural increase rate per 1,000 population (1995–2000): 27.4 (world avg. 15.7).
Total fertility rate (avg. births per childbearing woman; 1995–2000): 5.3.
Life expectancy at birth (1995–2000): male 54.5 years; female 57.2 years.
Major causes of death per 100,000 population: n.a.; however, major health problems include measles, malaria, tuberculosis of respiratory system, anemias, meningitis, and intestinal obstruction and hernia.

National economy

Budget (1995–96). Revenue: CFAF 654,900,000,000 (petroleum royalties 21.8%; taxes on goods and services 19.7%; customs duties 18.0%). Expenditures: CFAF 775,200,000,000 (current expenditure 94.4%, of which debt services 45.1%, wages and salaries 24.3%, goods and services 15.1%).
Public debt (external, outstanding; 1996): U.S.$8,356,000,000.
Gross national product (1996): U.S.$8,356,000,000 (U.S.$610 per capita).

Structure of gross domestic product and labour force

	1995–96 in value CFAF '000,000,000	1995–96 % of total value	1985 labour force	1985 % of labour force
Agriculture	1,836	40.2	2,900,871	74.0
Mining	334	7.3	1,793	0.1
Manufacturing	453	9.9	174,498	4.5
Construction	220	4.8	66,684	1.7
Public utilities			3,522	0.1
Transp. and commun.			51,688	1.3
Trade	1,230	26.9	154,014	3.9
Finance			8,009	0.2
Services			292,922	7.5
Public admin., defense	370	8.1		
Other	128	2.8	263,634	6.7
TOTAL	4,571	100.0	3,917,635	100.0

Household income and expenditure. Average household size (1980) 5.2; average annual income per household (1983)[3] U.S.$420; sources of income: n.a.; expenditure (1993)[3]: food 49.1%, housing 18.0%, transportation and communications 13.0%, health 8.6%, clothing 7.6%, recreation 2.4%.
Tourism (1993): receipts U.S.$47,000,000; expenditures U.S.$225,000,000.
Population economically active (1991): total 4,740,000; activity rate of total population 40.0% (participation rates [1985]: ages 15–69, 66.3%; female 38.5%; unemployed, n.a.).

Price and earnings indexes (1992 = 100)

	1991	1992	1993	1994	1995	1996
Consumer price index	100.1	100.0	96.8	130.8	149.0	156.0
Earnings index	...	...	...	...	...	...

Production (metric tons except as noted). Agriculture, forestry, fishing (1996): sugarcane 1,350,000, cassava 1,300,000, bananas 980,000, plantains 970,000, corn (maize) 654,000, vegetables and melons 385,000, sweet potatoes 180,000, palm oil 130,000, cacao 120,000, yams 110,000, peanuts (groundnuts) 100,000, millet 100,000, rice 80,000, palm kernels 56,000; livestock (number of live animals) 4,900,000 cattle, 3,800,000 sheep, 3,800,000 goats, 1,410,000 pigs; roundwood (1994) 13,948,000 cu m; fish catch (1995) 63,947. Mining and quarrying (1994): marble 200,000; pozzolana 130,000; aluminum 85,000; limestone 57,000; tin ore and concentrate 4. Manufacturing (value added in CFAF '000,000; 1994): beverages 49,314; wood and wood products 42,756; rubber and plastic products 38,928; food products 30,030; iron and steel products 29,424; textiles 20,113; refined petroleum products 17,888; industrial chemicals 8,559; pottery, china, and earthenware 6,773; paper products 3,652. Construction (1983): residential 230,400 sq m; nonresidential 51,100 sq m. Energy production (consumption): electricity (kW-hr; 1994) 2,740,000,000 (2,740,000,000); coal (metric tons; 1994) 1,000 (1,000); crude petroleum (barrels; 1993) 39,462,000 (7,889,000); petroleum products (metric tons; 1994) 1,023,000 (1,014,000); natural gas, none (n.a.).
Land use (1994): forested 77.1%; meadows and pastures 4.3%; agricultural and under permanent cultivation 15.1%; other 3.5%.

Foreign trade

Balance of trade (current prices)

	1990	1991	1992	1993	1994	1995
CFAF '000,000,000	+164.0	+186.5	+179.3	+221.3	+223.7	+398.8
% of total	17.7%	18.0%	22.6%	26.2%	15.7%	24.4%

Imports (1994–95): CFAF 464,700,000,000 (semifinished goods 18.8%; food, beverages, and tobacco 14.2%; industrial equipment 12.4%; transport equipment 11.0%). *Major import sources* (1995): France 39.2%; United States 9.7%; Germany 9.1%; Japan 6.9%; Belgium-Luxembourg 6.8%; Italy 4.5%; The Netherlands 4.3%; United Kingdom 3.9%.
Exports (1994–95): CFAF 811,000,000,000 (crude petroleum 38.1%; lumber 11.0%; cocoa 8.4%; coffee 7.3%; aluminum 6.7%; cotton 3.7%). *Major export destinations* (1995): France 29.7%; Italy 16.6%; Spain 14.3%; The Netherlands 13.0%; South Korea 2.8%; Germany 2.3%.

Transport and communications

Transport. Railroads (1995): route length 625 mi, 1,006 km; passenger-mi 197,000,000, passenger-km 317,000,000; short ton-mi cargo 556,000,000, metric ton-km cargo 812,000,000. Roads (1991): total length 30,074 mi, 48,400 km (paved 8%). Vehicles (1995): passenger cars 92,200; trucks and buses 60,000. Merchant marine (1992): vessels (100 gross tons and over) 47; total deadweight tonnage 39,797. Air transport (1992): passenger-mi 196,000,000, passenger-km 315,000,000; short ton-mi cargo 26,712,000, metric ton-km cargo 39,000,000; airports (1997) with scheduled flights 5.

Communications

Medium	date	unit	number	units per 1,000 persons
Daily newspapers	1995	circulation	66,000	5.0
Radio	1995	receivers	4,100,000	325
Television	1995	receivers	960,000	72.1
Telephones	1995	main lines	59,700	4.5
Cellular telephones	1995	subscribers	2,800	0.2

Education and health

Educational attainment (1976). Percentage of population age 15 and over having: no schooling 51.1%; primary education 41.7%; some postprimary 0.2%; secondary 5.7%; some postsecondary 0.3%; higher 0.2%; other 0.8%.
Literacy (1995): percentage of total population age 15 and over literate 63.4%; males literate 75.0%; females literate 52.1%.

Education (1994–95)

	schools	teachers	students	student/ teacher ratio
Primary (age 6–14)	6,801	40,970	1,896,722	46.3
Secondary (age 15–24)	388[4]	14,917	459,068	30.8
Vocational	220[4]	5,885	91,779	15.6
Higher[5]	5[4]	1,086	33,177	30.5

Health: physicians (1989) 945 (1 per 11,848 persons); hospital beds (1988) 29,285 (1 per 371 persons); infant mortality rate (1995–2000) 58.0.
Food (1995): daily per capita caloric intake 2,214 (vegetable products 94%, animal products 6%); 95% of FAO recommended minimum requirement.

Military

Total active duty personnel (1997): 13,100 (army 87.8%, navy 9.9%, air force 2.3%). *Military expenditure as percentage of GNP* (1994): 1.9% (world 3.0%); per capita expenditure U.S.$8.

---

[1]Detail does not add to total given because of rounding. [2]Based on land area. [3]Weights of consumer price index components. [4]1986–87. [5]1990–91.

Internet resources for further information:
• **Presidency of the Republic of Cameroon**
  http://www.camnet.cm/celcom/anglais/homepr.htm

Canada

Official name: Canada.
Form of government: federal multiparty parliamentary state with two legislative houses (Senate [104]; House of Commons [301]).
Chief of state: Queen of Canada (British Monarch).
Representative of chief of state: Governor-General.
Head of government: Prime Minister.
Capital: Ottawa.
Official languages: English; French.
Official religion: none.
Monetary unit: 1 Canadian dollar (Can$) = 100 cents; valuation (Sept. 25, 1998) 1 U.S.$ = Can$1.51; 1 £ = Can$2.57.

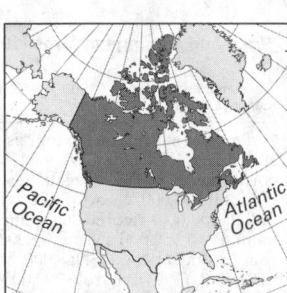

Area and population

Provinces	Capitals	area sq mi	area sq km	population 1997 estimate
Alberta	Edmonton	255,287	661,190	2,847,000
British Columbia	Victoria	365,948	947,800	3,933,300
Manitoba	Winnipeg	250,947	649,950	1,145,200
New Brunswick	Fredericton	28,355	73,440	762,000
Newfoundland	St. John's	156,649	405,720	563,600
Nova Scotia	Halifax	21,425	55,490	947,900
Ontario	Toronto	412,581	1,068,580	11,407,700
Prince Edward Island	Charlottetown	2,185	5,660	137,200
Quebec	Quebec	594,860	1,540,680	7,419,900
Saskatchewan	Regina	251,866	652,330	1,023,500
Territories				
Northwest Territories[1]	Yellowknife	1,322,910	3,426,320	67,500
Yukon Territory	Whitehorse	186,661	483,450	31,600
TOTAL		3,849,674	9,970,610	30,286,600[2]

Demography

Population (1998): 30,677,000.
Density (1998)[3]: persons per sq mi 8.6, persons per sq km 3.3.
Urban-rural (1996): urban 77.9%; rural 22.1%.
Sex distribution (1997): male 49.53%; female 50.47%.
Age breakdown (1997): under 15, 19.8%; 15–29, 20.7%; 30–44, 25.5%; 45–59, 17.7%; 60–74, 11.0%; 75 and over, 5.3%.
Population projection: (2000) 31,472,000; (2010) 35,065,000.
Doubling time: not applicable; doubling time exceeds 100 years.
Ethnic origin (1991): French 22.8%; British 20.8%; German 3.4%; Italian 2.8%; Chinese 2.2%; Amerindian and Inuktitut (Eskimo) 1.7%; Ukrainian 1.5%; Dutch 1.3%; multiple origin and other 43.5%[4].
Religious affiliation (1991): Roman Catholic 45.2%; Protestant 36.4%; Eastern Orthodox 1.9%; Jewish 1.2%; Muslim 0.9%; Buddhist 0.6%; Hindu 0.6%; nonreligious 12.5%; other 0.7%.
Major metropolitan areas (1996): Toronto 4,263,757; Montreal 3,326,510; Vancouver 1,831,665; Ottawa-Hull 1,010,498; Edmonton 862,597; Calgary 821,628; Quebec 671,889; Winnipeg 667,209; Hamilton 624,360; London 398,616.

Other metropolitan areas (1996)

	population		population		population
Chicoutimi-Jonquière	160,454	Regina	193,652	Sherbrooke	147,384
Halifax	332,518	St. Catharines–Niagara	372,406	Sudbury	160,488
Kitchener	382,940	St. John's	174,051	Trois Rivières	139,956
Oshawa	268,773	Saskatoon	219,056	Victoria	304,287
				Windsor	278,685

Place of birth (1991): 84.6% native-born; 15.4% foreign-born, of which United Kingdom 2.6%, other European 5.9%, Asian countries 3.8%, United States 0.9%, other 2.2%.
Mobility (1991). Population living in the same residence as in 1986: 53.3%; different residence, same municipality 23.2%; same province, different municipality 15.9%; different province 3.9%; different country 3.7%.
Households (1995). Total number of households 11,243,000. Average household size 2.6; 1 person 24.9%, 2 persons 32.9%, 3 persons 16.5%, 4 persons 16.8%, 5 or more persons 8.9%. Family households (1995): 7,879,700 (70.1%), nonfamily 3,363,300 (29.1%, of which 1 person 83.3%).
Immigration (1994): permanent immigrants admitted 223,875, from Hong Kong 19.7%, Philippines 8.5%, India 7.7%, China 5.6%, Taiwan 3.3%, Sri Lanka 3.0%, United States 2.8%, Vietnam 2.8%, United Kingdom 2.7%; refugee arrivals 19,089.

Vital statistics

Birth rate per 1,000 population (1996): 12.5 (world avg. 25.0); (1985) legitimate 83.8%; illegitimate 16.2%.
Death rate per 1,000 population (1996): 7.2 (world avg. 9.3).
Natural increase rate per 1,000 population (1996): 5.3 (world avg. 15.7).
Total fertility rate (avg. births per childbearing woman; 1993): 1.9.
Marriage rate per 1,000 population (1995): 5.4.
Divorce rate per 1,000 population (1995): 2.7.
Life expectancy at birth (1996): male 74.9 years; female 81.2 years.
Major causes of death per 100,000 population (1994): diseases of the circulatory system 247.1; malignant neoplasms (cancers) 196.0; diseases of the respiratory system 55.4; accidents and violence 42.5 (including suicide 12.8).

Social indicators

Educational attainment (1991). Percentage of population age 25 and over having: no formal schooling 1.0%; less than complete primary education 4.0%; complete primary 11.7%; lower-level secondary 34.3%; upper-level secondary 27.7%; postsecondary 21.4%; graduates by level (1987): 4-year higher degree 101,960, master's 15,790, doctorate 2,385.

Distribution of income (1991)

percentage of national income by quintile

1	2	3	4	5 (highest)
5.3%	13.6%	19.7%	25.9%	35.5%

Quality of working life (1995). Average workweek: 38.4 hours. Annual rate per 100,000 workers for (1990): injury, accident, or industrial illness 3,320; death 5.1[5]. Average days lost to labour stoppages per 1,000 employee-workdays (1995): 0.5. Average duration of journey to work (1983): 23 minutes[6] (automobile 72.8%, public transportation 17.3%, other 9.9%). Rate per 1,000 workers of discouraged (unemployed no longer seeking work; 1983): 10.5.
Access to services (1990). Proportion of households having access to: electricity 100.0%; public water supply 99.8%; public sewage collection 99.3%.
Social participation. Eligible voters participating in last national election (June 1997): c. 70%. Population over 18 years of age participating in voluntary work (1987): 27.0%. Union membership in total workforce (1992): 29.7%. Practicing religious population in total affiliated population (1991): 87.6%.
Social deviance (1994). Offense rate per 100,000 population for: violent crime 1,037, of which assault 8.8[7], sexual assault 111.0[7], homicide 1.8; property crime 5,212, of which auto theft 546, burglary 1,326. Incidence per 100,000 in general population of: alcoholism 2,285; drug abuse 258.
Leisure (1992). Favourite leisure activities (hours weekly): television 15.3; social time 12.7; reading 3.5; sports and entertainment 0.9.
Material well-being (1995). Households possessing: automobile 74.5%, of which two or more 21.7%; telephone 98.5%; radio 98.9%; colour television 98.5%; refrigerator 99.7%; central air conditioner 24.6%[8]; cable television 73.4%; video recorder 82.1%; microwave oven 83.4%.

National economy

Gross national product (1996): U.S.$569,899,000,000 (U.S.$19,020 per capita).

Structure of gross domestic product and labour force

	1995 in value Can$'000,000[9]	1995 % of total value	1996 labour force	1996 % of labour force
Agriculture	15,421	2.8	453,300	3.0
Mining	23,678	4.4	279,900	1.8
Manufacturing	102,384	18.9	2,082,500	13.8
Construction	27,221	5.0	718,600	4.7
Public utilities	17,632	3.2	147,000	1.0
Transp. and commun.	48,605	9.0	872,600	5.8
Trade	65,494	12.1	2,361,200	15.6
Finance	86,772	16.0	799,900	5.3
Pub. admin., defense	32,690	6.0	820,100	5.4
Services	122,110	22.5	5,141,200	33.9
Other	—	—	1,469,200[10]	9.7[10]
TOTAL	542,007[11]	100.0[2]	15,145,400[2]	100.0

Budget (1995–96). Revenue: Can$145,453,000,000 (individual income taxes 45.1%, value-added tax 15.2%, corporate income tax 9.9%, import duties 2.6%). Expenditures: Can$177,703,000,000 (1995–96; social services 32.5%, public debt interest 26.9%, defense 8.2%, health 4.7%, education 2.9%).
National debt (1996): Can$569,691,000,000.
Tourism (1996): receipts U.S.$8,811,500,000; expenditures U.S.$11,168,000,000.

Manufacturing, mining, and construction enterprises (1993)

	no. of establishments	no. of employees	weekly wages as a % of avg. of all mfg. wages	annual value added (Can$'000,000)
Manufacturing				
Food and beverages	3,202	216,000	100.7	20,110
Transport equipment	1,224	187,000	144.3	19,430
Chemicals and related products	1,396	97,000	142.0	12,860
Machinery	4,000	129,000	125.0	9,130
Electrical and electronic products	1,176	104,000	133.6	8,520
Printing, publishing, and related products	4,655	125,000	111.1	8,500
Paper and related products	651	101,000	152.1	7,890
Wood	2,201	100,000	109.3	7,880
Primary metals	417	85,000	155.2	7,790
Metal fabricating	3,287	106,000	113.6	6,290
Rubber and plastic	1,394	85,000	112.3	5,900
Textiles	1,057	60,000	88.4	3,600
Nonmetallic mineral products	1,519	44,000	125.4	3,440
Wearing apparel	1,923	85,000	67.4	3,220
Petroleum and coal products	170	16,000	189.5	2,560
Furniture and fixtures	1,965	50,000	91.5	2,310
Tobacco products industries	17	5,000	184.5	1,220
Mining[12]	1,232	113,000	...	29,650
Construction[13]	...	800,000	121.7	28,182

Production (metric tons except as noted). Agriculture, forestry, fishing (1996): wheat 23,024,000, barley 13,590,000, corn (maize) 7,000,000, rapeseed 6,089,000, potatoes 3,800,000, oats 3,475,000, soybeans 2,820,000, vegetables 2,098,883 (of which tomatoes 500,590, carrots 330,920, onions 174,051, cabbage 143,000), dry peas 1,690,000, linseed 1,115,000, sugar beets 1,030,000, apples 560,000; livestock (number of live animals) 12,767,300 cattle, 12,223,700 pigs, 622,300 sheep, 350,000 horses; roundwood (1996) 188,432,000 cu m; fish catch (1995) 1,010,582. Mining and quarrying (1996): iron ore 36,030,000; zinc 1,187,829; copper 655,891; lead 246,083; nickel 184,548; uranium 11,448; molybdenum 8,845; silver 1,228 kg; gold 164.1 kg. Manufacturing (value-added

in Can$'000,000[9]; 1996): transportation equipment 16,181.7; electrical products 12,570.7; food 10,556.6; chemical products 8,159.1; paper products 7,755.9; metal products 6,467.8; wood products 5,371.4; printing and publishing 4,288.8; rubber and plastic products 3,890.4; machinery 3,797.0; wearing apparel 2,079.0; textile 2,008.3; furniture 1,774.7. Construction (value-added in Can$'000,000[9]; 1996): residential 6,683.8; nonresidential 20,001.7.

Service enterprises (1988)

	no. of enterprises	no. of employees[14]	weekly wages as a % of all wages	annual sales (Can$'000,000)
Retail trade				
Motor vehicle dealers	...	79,800	...	35,917
Food stores	...	213,400	...	35,187
Service stations	...	63,700	...	14,612
Department stores	...	[15]	...	13,271
Clothing stores	...	50,200	...	7,486
Pharmacies	...	52,400	...	7,459
Furniture and appliance stores	...	62,100	...	4,447
Automotive stores	...	31,500	...	3,767
General merchandise	...	231,700[15]	...	3,109
Sporting goods	...		...	2,669
General stores	...	[15]	...	2,415
Hardware stores	...	17,300	...	1,824
Shoe stores	...	18,400	...	1,599
Jewelry stores	...	14,000	...	1,215
Variety stores	...	45,100	...	1,057

Energy production (consumption): electricity (kW-hr; 1994) 554,186,000,000 (510,272,000,000); coal (metric tons; 1994) 72,824,000 (52,229,000); crude petroleum (barrels; 1994) 638,633,000 (507,557,000); petroleum products (metric tons; 1994) 87,161,000 (77,264,000); natural gas (cu m; 1994) 148,129,000,000 (78,223,000,000).

Population economically active (1996): total 15,145,400; activity rate of total population 50.5% (participation rates: ages 15–64, 64.8%; female 45.2%[16]; unemployed 9.7%).

Price and earnings indexes (1990 = 100)

	1991	1992	1993	1994	1995	1996	1997
Consumer price index	105.6	107.2	109.2	109.4	111.8	113.5	115.4
Hourly earnings index[17]	105.5	108.2	110.5	111.5	113.1	116.7	117.8

Household income and expenditure (1995). Average household size 2.6; average annual income per family (1994) Can$54,153 (U.S.$39,655); sources of income (1995): wages and salaries 57.0%, transfer payments 20.7%, property and entrepreneurial income 13.7%, profits 8.6%; expenditure (1992): housing 24.7%[18], food 15.5%, transp. and commun. 15.3%, household durable goods 9.1%, recreation 8.4%, clothing 5.1%, health 4.3%, education 3.0%.

Financial aggregates

	1992	1993	1994	1995	1996	1997[19]
Exchange rate, Can$ per:						
U.S .dollar	1.21	1.29	1.36	1.37	1.36	1.39
£	2.14	1.94	2.09	2.17	2.13	2.26
SDR	1.75	1.82	2.05	2.03	1.97	1.95
International reserves (U.S.$)						
Total (excl. gold; '000,000)	11,431	12,481	12,286	15,049	20,422	21,818
SDRs ('000,000)	1,039	1,062	1,148	1,177	1,168	1,146
Reserve pos. in IMF ('000,000)	1,011	948	919	1,243	1,226	1,135
Foreign exchange ('000,000)	9,382	10,471	10,219	12,629	18,028	19,536
Gold ('000,000 fine troy oz)	9.94	6.05	3.89	3.41	3.09	3.09
% world reserves	1.07	0.65	0.43	0.38	0.34	0.35
Interest and prices						
Central bank discount (%)	7.36	4.11	7.43	5.79	3.25	3.50[20]
Govt. bond yield (%)	8.77	7.85	8.63	8.28	7.50	5.99[20]
Industrial share prices (1990 = 100)	99.5	114.1	125.2	129.6	154.0	205.8[20]
Balance of payments (U.S.$'000,000)						
Balance of visible trade,	5,981	7,612	12,202	22,341	30,062	...
of which:						
Imports, f.o.b.	−126,370	−136,418	−151,290	−167,513	−175,737	...
Exports, f.o.b.	132,351	144,030	163,492	189,854	205,799	...
Balance of invisibles	−27,951	−31,481	−29,590	−31,034	−27,254	...
Balance of payments, current account	−22,060	−23,869	−17,388	−8,693	−2,808	...

Land use (1994): forested 53.6%; meadows and pastures 3.0%; agricultural and under permanent cultivation 4.9%; built-on, wasteland, and other 38.5%.

Foreign trade

Balance of trade (current prices)

	1992	1993	1994	1995	1996	1997
Can$'000,000,000	8.2	12.1	19.3	38.7	36.4	25.5
% of total	3.2%	3.4%	4.5%	7.9%	7.1%	4.5%

Imports (1996): Can$239,576,900,000 (machinery and transport equipment 53.4%, of which motor vehicles 21.4%; food, feed, beverages, and tobacco 11.8%; petroleum and energy products 4.0%; forestry products 0.8%). *Major import sources*: U.S. 67.4%; Japan 4.5%; Mexico 2.5%; U.K. 2.5%; Germany 2.1%; China 2.1%; France 1.5%; Italy 1.2%; South Korea 1.2%.

Exports (1996): Can$280,566,300,000 (machinery and transport equipment 44.8%, of which motor vehicles 22.6%; mineral fuels 9.1%, of which crude petroleum 3.5%; food 8.7%, of which wheat 2.0%; lumber 5.6%; newsprint and paper products 4.4%; wood pulp 2.2%). *Major export destinations*: U.S. 82.3%; Japan 3.7%; U.K. 1.4%; Germany 1.2%; China 1.0%; South Korea 1.0%; France 0.6%; The Netherlands 0.6%.

Trade by commodities (1995)

	imports		exports	
SITC Group	U.S.$'000,000	%	U.S.$'000,000	%
00 Food and live animals	8,228.8	5.0	11,472.2	6.0
01 Beverages and tobacco	750.6	0.5	869.7	0.4
02 Crude materials, excluding fuels	5,856.7	3.6	23,684.2	12.3
03 Mineral fuels, lubricants, and related materials	6,004.4	3.6	16,108.8	8.4
04 Animal and vegetable oils, fats, and waxes	...	...	...	...
05 Chemicals and related products, n.e.s.	12,858.5	7.8	10,900.3	5.7
06 Basic manufactures	21,761.6	13.2	32,268.3	16.8
07 Machinery and transport equipment	84,554.2	51.4	75,069.9	39.1
08 Miscellaneous manufactured articles	19,051.6	11.6	9,613.2	5.0
09 Goods not classified by kind	5,034.9	3.1	10,495.1	5.5
TOTAL	164,333.6[21]	100.0[21]	192,132.1[21]	100.0[21]

Direction of trade (1996)

	imports		exports	
	U.S.$'000,000	%	U.S.$'000,000	%
Africa	1,516	0.9	907	0.4
Asia	21,683	12.8[2]	17,081	8.5
China	3,610	2.1	2,067	1.0
Japan	7,664	4.5	7,471	3.7
Taiwan	2,099	1.2	1,020	0.5
Other	8,310	4.9	6,523	3.3
Americas	122,129	71.8	168,437	84.2[2]
United States	114,626	67.4	164,761	82.3
Mexico	4,281	2.5	855	0.4
Other Americas	3,222	1.9	2,821	1.4
Europe	20,412	12.0	12,661	6.3
EU	16,704	9.8	10,783	5.4
Other Europe	3,708	2.2	1,878	0.9
Oceania	1,189	0.7	859	0.4
TOTAL	170,038[21, 22]	100.0[21, 22]	200,146[21]	100.0[21]

Transport and communications

Transport. Railroads (1995): length 71,592 km; passenger-km 1,430,000,000; metric ton-km cargo 271,032,000,000. Roads (1995): total length 1,021,000 km (paved 35%). Vehicles (1995): passenger cars 14,280,000; trucks and buses 3,895,600. Merchant marine (1993): vessels (100 gross tons and over) 1,049; total deadweight tonnage 1,910,000. Air transport (1996): passenger-km 56,016,000,000; metric ton-km cargo 1,780,980,000; airports (1997) with scheduled flights 269.

Communications

Medium	date	unit	number	units per 1,000 persons
Daily newspapers	1995	circulation	6,330,000	215
Radio	1994	receivers	26,878,000	919
Television	1995	receivers	18,917,000	647
Telephones	1995	main lines	17,457,300	590
Cellular telephones	1995	subscribers	2,589,800	87.5
Facsimile machines	1995	units	525,000	18.1
Personal computers	1995	units	5,700,000	192

Education and health

Literacy (1986): total population age 15 and over literate 18,745,000 (96.6%); males literate (1975) 8,003,000 (95.6%); females literate (1975) 8,182,000 (95.7%).

Education (1994–95)

	schools	teachers	students	student/teacher ratio
Primary (age 6–14)	12,700	148,724	2,413,126	17.8
Secondary (age 14–18)	3,324	133,358	2,469,552	...
Postsecondary and higher[23]	265	64,100[24]	1,209,386[25]	14.4[24]

Health: physicians (1994) 54,786 (1 per 534 persons); hospital beds (1993) 163,399 (1 per 177 persons); infant mortality rate (1995) 6.1.

Food (1995): daily per capita caloric intake 3,093 (vegetable products 71%, animal products 29%); 116% of FAO recommended minimum requirement.

Military

Total active duty personnel (1997): 61,600 (army 35.6%, navy 15.3%, air force 23.7%, not identified by service 25.4%). *Military expenditure as percentage of GNP* (1995): 1.7% (world 2.8%); per capita expenditure U.S.$318.

[1]On May 25, 1993, the Prime Minister and Inuit representatives signed an agreement (following a number of territory-wide referendums), officially establishing Nunavut as a territory in 1999. It would comprise 2,201,400 sq km (844,960 sq mi) of the eastern part of Northwest Territories, with a population of 22,000 (17,500 Inuit). [2]Detail does not add to total given because of rounding. [3]Based on land area of 3,558,096 sq mi (9,215,430 sq km). [4]Includes 4.0% who are of both French and British origin. [5]1992. [6]Urban areas. [7]1991. [8]1989. [9]At prices of 1986. [10]GDP at current values in 1995 is Can$776,299,000,000. [11]1990. [12]1988. [13]1984. [14]Department and General stores included with General merchandise. [15]1995. [16]Manufacturing only. [17]Includes energy and utilities. [18]October. [19]September. [20]Detail does not add to total because of discrepancies in estimates. [21]Total for imports includes U.S.$3,220,000,000 (1.9% of total imports; mostly special transactions) not distributable by region. [22]1996–97. [23]1993–94. [24]Includes 248,231 part-time university students.

Internet resources for further information:
• Statistics Canada http://www.statcan.ca

Cape Verde

Official name: República de Cabo Verde (Republic of Cape Verde).
Form of government: multiparty republic with one legislative house (National People's Assembly [72]).
Chief of state: President.
Head of government: Prime Minister.
Capital: Praia.
Official language: Portuguese.
Official religion: none.
Monetary unit: 1 escudo (C.V.Esc.)[1] = 100 centavos; valuation (Sept. 25, 1998) 1 U.S.$ = C.V.Esc. 99.69; 1 £ = C.V.Esc. 169.72.

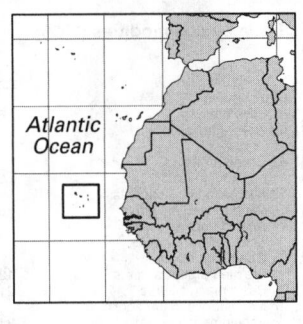

Area and population

Island Groups Islands/Counties[2] Counties	Capitals	area sq mi	area sq km	population 1990 census
Leeward Islands		696[3]	1,803	221,537
Brava	Nova Sintra	26	67	6,975
Fogo				
Mosteiros[4]	São Filipe }	184	476	33,902
São Filipe				
Maio	Porto Inglês	104	269	4,969
Santiago		383	991	175,691
Praia	Praia	153	396	82,802
Santa Catarina	Assomada	94	243	41,584
Santa Cruz	Pedra Badejo	58	149	25,892
São Domingos[4]		...	...	....
Tarrafal	Tarrafal	78	203	25,413
Windward Islands		861[3]	2,230	119,954
Boa Vista	Sal Rei	239	620	3,452
Sal	Santa Maria	83	216	7,715
Santo Antão		300	779	43,845
Paúl	Pombas	21	54	8,121
Porto Novo	Porto Novo	215	558	14,873
Ribeira Grande	Ponta do Sol	64	167	20,851
São Nicolau	Ribeira Brava	150	388	13,665
São Vicente[5]	Mindelo	88	227	51,277
TOTAL		1,557	4,033	341,491

Demography

Population (1998): 400,000.
Density (1998): persons per sq mi 256.8, persons per sq km 99.2.
Urban-rural (1990): urban 29.7%; rural 70.3%.
Sex distribution (1990): male 47.29%; female 52.71%.
Age breakdown (1990): under 15, 45.1%; 15–29, 27.2%; 30–44, 11.4%; 45–59, 7.9%; 60 and over, 8.4%.
Population projection: (2000) 411,000; (2010) 464,000.
Doubling time: 25 years.
Ethnic composition (1986): mixed 71.0%; black 28.0%; white 1.0%.
Religious affiliation (1995): Roman Catholic 95.9%; Protestant and other 4.1%.
Major cities (1990): Praia 61,644; Mindelo 47,109; São Filipe 5,616.

Vital statistics

Birth rate per 1,000 population (1997): 35.5 (world avg. 25.0); (1989) legitimate 28.9%; illegitimate 71.1%.
Death rate per 1,000 population (1997): 7.8 (world avg. 9.3).
Natural increase rate per 1,000 population (1997): 27.7 (world avg. 15.7).
Total fertility rate (avg. births per childbearing woman; 1997): 5.2.
Marriage rate per 1,000 population (1990): 4.5.
Divorce rate per 1,000 population: n.a.
Life expectancy at birth (1997): male 66.8 years; female 73.4 years.
Major causes of death per 100,000 population (1987): enteritis and other diarrheal diseases 97.4; heart disease 77.9; malignant neoplasms (cancers) 47.9; pneumonia 46.4; accidents, poisoning, and violence 44.0.

National economy

Budget (1995). Revenue: C.V.Esc. 8,404,000,000 (import duties 44.7%; income taxes 25.4%; property income taxes 5.8%; transfers 5.1%; municipal taxes 1.2%). Expenditures: C.V.Esc. 19,128,000,000 (capital expenditure 51.5%; current expenditure 48.5%, of which wages and salaries 20.6%, transfers 8.7%, public debt 6.3%, goods and services 1.5%).
Public debt (external, outstanding; 1996): U.S.$202,400,000.
Tourism (1995): receipts from visitors U.S.$10,000,000; expenditures by nationals abroad U.S.$12,000,000.
Production (metric tons except as noted). Agriculture, forestry, fishing (1996): sugarcane 12,500, bananas 6,000, coconuts 5,000, vegetables (including melons) 4,200, fruits (except melons) 4,000, cassava 3,000, potatoes 2,090, sweet potatoes 1,150; livestock (number of live animals) 460,000 pigs, 109,000 goats, 21,000 cattle; roundwood, n.a.; fish catch (1995) 7,081. Mining and quarrying (1992): salt 4,000. Manufacturing (1994): bread 3,926[6]; paint 492; canned tuna 273; cigarettes 94; beer 4,162,033 litres; soft drinks 932,154 litres; other items also manufactured are rum and flour. Construction (1982): residential C.V.Esc. 365,800,000; nonresidential C.V.Esc. 1,700,000. Energy production (consumption): electricity (kW-hr; 1994) 59,527,000 (46,570,000); coal, none (none); crude petroleum, none (none); petroleum products (metric tons; 1995) none (70,329); natural gas, none (none).
Gross national product (1996): U.S.$393,000,000 (U.S.$1,010 per capita).

Structure of gross domestic product and labour force

	1993 in value C.V.Esc. '000,000	1993 % of total value	1990 labour force	1990 % of labour force
Agriculture	4,878	20.7	29,876	24.7
Manufacturing	1,515	6.4	5,520	4.6
Public utilities	698	3.0	883	0.7
Mining	67	0.2	410	0.3
Construction	4,814	20.4	22,722	18.9
Transp. and commun.	2,898	12.3	6,138	5.1
Trade	5,634	23.9	12,747	10.6
Finance	939	4.0	821	0.7
Pub. admin., defense	1,936	8.2 }	17,358	14.4
Services	221	0.9 }		
Other			24,090	20.0
TOTAL	23,600[3]	100.0[3]	120,565	100.0

Population economically active (1990): total 120,565; activity rate of total population 35.3% (participation rates: ages 15–64, 64.3%; female 38.0%; unemployed, 25.8%).

Price and earnings indexes (1990 = 100)

	1991	1992	1993	1994	1995	1996
Consumer price index	110.0	113.0	125.0	128.0	137.0	146.0
Monthly earnings index	117.0	140.0	121.0	124.0	141.0	...

Land use (1994): forest 0.2%; pasture 6.2%; agriculture 11.2%; other 82.4%.
Household income and expenditure. Average household size (1990) 5.1; income per household: n.a.; sources of income: n.a.; expenditure (1988): food 51.1%, housing, fuel, and power 13.5%, beverages and tobacco 11.8%, transportation and communications 8.8%, household durable goods 6.9%, other 7.9%.

Foreign trade[7]

Balance of trade (current prices)

	1990	1991	1992	1993	1994	1995
C.V.Esc. '000,000	−9,097	−10,031	−11,907	−12,075	−13,678	−18,708
% of total	92.0%	92.0%	94.8%	95.1%	95.1%	93.2%

Imports (1994): C.V.Esc. 14,012,000,000 (1993; food 34.6%, transport equipment 13.3%, machinery and apparatus 11.4%, nonmetallic mineral products 10.3%, metal products 7.3%). *Major import sources* (1993): Portugal 33.6%; The Netherlands 8.5%; Germany 4.9%; France 4.4%; U.S. 3.5%.
Exports (1994): C.V.Esc. 333,300,000 (1993; fish and fish preparations 62.6%, bananas 11.7%). *Major export destinations* (1993): Portugal 48.8%; Angola 16.0%; The Netherlands 3.4%.

Transport and communications

Transport. Railroads: none. Roads (1995): total length 680 mi, 1,095 km (paved 78%). Vehicles (1993): passenger cars 6,479; trucks and buses 2,099. Merchant marine (1992): vessels (100 gross tons and over) 42: total deadweight tonnage 30,921. Air transport (1994)[8]: passenger-mi 106,000,000, passenger-km 171,000,000; short ton-mi cargo 13,156,000, metric ton-km cargo 19,207,000; airports (1997) with scheduled flights 9.

Communications

Medium	date	unit	number	units per 1,000 persons
Radio	1995	receivers	57,000	146
Television	1995	receivers	1,000	2.6
Telephones	1995	main lines	21,500	55
Facsimile machines	1995	units	1,000	2.6

Education and health

Educational attainment (1990). Percentage of population age 25 and over having: no formal schooling 47.9%; primary 40.9%; incomplete secondary 3.9%; complete secondary 1.4%; higher 1.5%; unknown 4.4%. *Literacy* (1995): total population age 15 and over literate 71.6%; males literate 81.4%; females literate 63.8%.

Education (1993–94)

	schools	teachers	students	student/teacher ratio
Primary (age 7–12)	370[6]	2,657	78,173	29.4
Secondary (age 13–17)	16[9]	438	11,808	27.0
Voc., teacher tr.	3[9]	94[10]	2,289	...
Higher	...	...	...	...

Health (1987): physicians 77 (1 per 4,208 persons); hospital beds 625 (1 per 550 persons); infant mortality rate per 1,000 live births (1995) 55.9.
Food (1994): daily per capita caloric intake 3,031 (vegetable products 83%, animal products 17%); 129% of FAO recommended minimum requirement.

Military

Total active duty personnel (1997): 1,100 (army 90.9%, air force 9.1%). *Military expenditure as percentage of GNP* (1995): 1.0% (world 3.0%); per capita expenditure U.S.$10.

---

[1]Fixed par value rate, announced March 13, 1998, between the Cape Verde escudo and Portuguese escudo not in effect as of September 1998. [2]Island/county areas are coterminous except Fogo, Santiago, and Santo Antão islands. [3]Details does not add to total given because of rounding. [4]Created after the 1990 census; adjusted areas and populations not available. [5]Includes Santa Luzia Island, which is uninhabited. [6]1991. [7]Imports are c.i.f. [8]TACV airline only. [9]1986–87. [10]Vocational teachers only.

Central African Republic

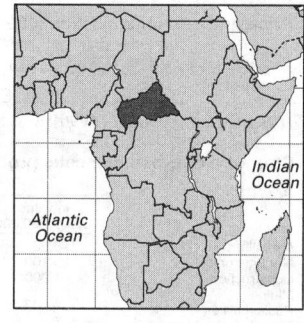

Official name: République Centrafricaine (Central African Republic).
Form of government: multiparty republic with one legislative body (National Assembly [85[1]]).
Chief of state: President.
Head of government: Prime Minister.
Capital: Bangui.
Official languages: French; Sango.
Official religion: none.
Monetary unit: 1 CFA franc (CFAF) = 100 centimes; valuation (Sept. 25, 1998) 1 U.S.$ = CFAF 560.38; 1 £ = CFAF 954.05.

Area and population

Prefectures	Capitals	area sq mi	area sq km	population 1988 census
Bamingui-Bangoran	Ndélé	22,471	58,200	28,643
Basse-Kotto	Mobaye	6,797	17,604	194,750
Haut-Mbomou	Obo	21,440	55,530	27,113
Haute-Kotto	Bria	33,456	86,650	58,838
Kemo	Sibut	6,642	17,204	82,884
Lobaye	Mbaïki	7,427	19,235	169,554
Mambéré-Kadéï	Berbérati	11,661	30,203	230,364
Mbomou	Bangassou	23,610	61,150	119,252
Nana-Gribizi	Kaga-Bandoro	7,721	19,996	95,497
Nana-Mambéré	Bouar	10,270	26,600	191,970
Ombella-M'poko	Boali	12,292	31,835	180,857
Ouaka	Bambari	19,266	49,900	208,332
Ouham	Bossangoa	19,402	50,250	262,950
Ouham-Pendé	Bozoum	12,394	32,100	287,653
Sangha-Mbaéré	Nola	7,495	19,412	65,961
Vakaga	Birao	17,954	46,500	32,118
Autonomous commune				
Bangui	Bangui	26	67	451,690
TOTAL		240,324	622,436	2,688,426

Demography

Population (1998): 3,376,000.
Density (1998): persons per sq mi 14.0, persons per sq km 5.4.
Urban-rural (1996): urban 39.0%; rural 61.0%.
Sex distribution (1997): male 49.30%; female 50.70%.
Age breakdown (1997): under 15, 44.1%; 15–29, 27.3%; 30–44, 15.1%; 45–59, 8.2%; 60–74, 4.2%; 75 and over, 1.1%.
Population projection: (2000) 3,516,000; (2010) 4,314,000.
Doubling time: 30 years.
Ethnolinguistic composition (1988): Baya (Gbaya) 23.7%; Banda 23.4%; Mandjia 14.7%; Ngbaka 7.6%; Sara 6.5%; Mbum 6.3%; Kare 2.4%; French 0.1%; other 15.3%.
Religious affiliation (1995): Christian 42.7%, of which Protestant 25.6% (Baptist 19.6%, other Protestant 5.9%), Roman Catholic 16.9%, other Christian 0.2%; traditional beliefs 24.0%; Muslim 15.0%; other 18.3%.
Major cities (1994): Bangui 524,000; Berbérati 47,000; Bouar 43,000; Bambari 41,000; Carnot 41,000; Bossangoa 33,000.

Vital statistics

Birth rate per 1,000 population (1997): 39.0 (world avg. 25.0).
Death rate per 1,000 population (1997): 17.0 (world avg. 9.3).
Natural increase rate per 1,000 population (1997): 22.0 (world avg. 15.7).
Total fertility rate (avg. births per childbearing woman; 1997): 5.2.
Life expectancy at birth (1996): male 47.0 years; female 52.0 years.
Mortality: n.a.; however, principal causes of death in the mid-1990s included respiratory infections (especially tuberculosis and pneumonia), diseases of the digestive system, meningitis, diarrheal diseases, malnutrition, cardiovascular diseases, malaria, viral hepatitis, and AIDS.

National economy

Budget (1996). Revenue: CFAF 45,800,000,000 (taxes 96.1%, nontax receipts 3.9%). Expenditures: CFAF 114,400,000,000 (capital expenditure 50.5%, current expenditure 49.5%).
Public debt (external, outstanding; 1996): U.S.$844,300,000.
Land use (1994): forest 75.0%; meadows 4.8%; agriculture 3.2%; other 17.0%.
Tourism (1993): receipts U.S.$3,000,000; expenditures U.S.$43,000,000[2].
Production (metric tons except as noted). Agriculture, forestry, fishing (1997): cassava 578,700, yams 320,000, bananas 100,000, peanuts (groundnuts) 97,800, plantains 78,000, corn (maize) 65,000, seed cotton 50,000, sesame seeds 32,000, pulses 26,000, sorghum 25,000, oranges 20,000, coffee 18,000, cottonseed 10,000[2], paddy rice 9,000, cotton lint 7,000[2]; livestock (number of live animals) 2,926,000 cattle, 1,350,000 goats, 596,000 pigs, 3,600,000 chickens; roundwood (1995) 3,864,000 cu m; fish catch (1995) 13,300. Mining and quarrying (1996): gold 98 kg[3], diamonds 487,300 carats[4]. Manufacturing (value added in U.S.$'000; 1994): food, beverages, and tobacco 19,000; chemical products 3,000; wood products 2,000; textiles, wearing apparel, and leather products 1,000; transport equipment 1,000. Construction (1992)[5]: residential 10,052 sq m; nonresidential 82,411 sq m. Energy production (consumption): electricity (kW-hr; 1994) 101,000,000 (101,000,000); coal, none (none); crude petroleum, none (none); petroleum products (metric tons; 1994) none (79,000); natural gas, none (none).
Gross national product (1996): U.S.$1,024,000,000 (U.S.$310 per capita).

Structure of gross domestic product and labour force

	1995 in value CFAF '000,000[6]	1995 % of total value	1988 labour force	1988 % of labour force
Agriculture	282,800	53.4	1,113,900	80.4
Mining	32,700	6.2	15,400	1.1
Manufacturing	46,600	8.8	22,400	1.6
Construction	25,000	4.7	7,000	0.5
Public utilities	4,300	0.8	1,500	0.1
Transp. and commun.	15,600	2.9	1,500	0.1
Trade	56,600	10.7	118,000	8.5
Other services	25,200	4.8	15,600	1.1
Pub. admin., defense	41,000	7.7	91,700	6.6
TOTAL	529,800	100.0	1,387,000	100.0

Population economically active (1988): total 1,186,972; activity rate of total population 48.2% (participation rates: ages 15–64, 78.3%; female 46.8%; unemployed 7.5%).

Price and earnings indexes (1990 = 100)

	1991	1992	1993	1994	1995	1996	1997
Consumer price index[5]	97.8	96.5	93.7	116.7	139.1	144.3	145.9
Earnings index	...	...	...	...	...	...	...

Household income and expenditure. Average household size (1988) 4.7; average annual income per household CFAF 91,985 (U.S.$435); sources of income: n.a.; expenditure (1991)[7]: food 70.5%, clothing 8.5%, other manufactured products 7.6%, energy 7.3%, services (including transportation and communications, recreation, and health) 6.1%.

Foreign trade

Balance of trade (current prices)

	1990	1991	1992	1993	1994	1995
CFAF '000,000,000	−9.3	−13.0	−10.1	−4.5	+4.3	−0.7
% of total	12.4%	32.9%	15.2%	6.7%	2.7%	0.4%

Imports (1995): CFAF 94,203,000,000 (1992; food products 22.2%, transportation equipment 16.6%, chemical products 13.7%, energy products 11.0%). *Major import sources:* France 37.0%; Japan 24.3%; Cameroon 6.3%; Germany 3.7%; Belgium-Luxembourg 3.2%; United States 2.6%.
Exports (1995): CFAF 93,524,000,000 (diamonds 49.7%, coffee 15.7%, wood products 15.0%, cotton 12.1%). *Major export destinations:* Belgium-Luxembourg 40.1%; France 16.0%; Democratic Republic of the Congo 2.1%; Republic of the Congo 1.1%; United Kingdom 1.1%.

Transport and communications

Transport. Railroads: none. Roads (1996): total length 14,900 mi, 24,000 km (paved 2%). Vehicles (1995): passenger cars 9,500; trucks and buses 7,000. Merchant marine: vessels (100 gross tons and over) none. Air transport (1996)[8]: passenger-mi 139,644,000, passenger-km 224,736,000; short ton-mi cargo 11,247,000, metric ton-km cargo 16,420,000; airports[9] (1997) 1.

Communications

Medium	date	unit	number	units per 1,000 persons
Daily newspapers	1995	circulation	2,000	1.0
Radio	1995	receivers	245,000	75.0
Television	1995	receivers	16,000	5.0
Telephones	1995	main lines	7,800	2.4
Cellular telephones	1995	subscribers	100	0.03
Facsimile machines	1995	units	200	0.06

Education and health

Educational attainment (1988). Percentage of population age 10 and over having: no formal schooling 59.3%; primary education 29.6%; lower secondary 7.5%; upper secondary 2.3%; higher 1.3%. *Literacy* (1995): total population age 15 and over literate 60.0%; males literate 68.5%; females literate 52.4%.

Education (1991–92)

	schools	teachers	students	student/ teacher ratio
Primary (age 6–11)	930[10]	4,004[10]	277,961	...
Secondary (age 12–18)	46[10]	845[10]	42,263	...
Vocational	11	11	1,477	...
Higher[12]	1	139	2,923	21.0

Health (1992): physicians 157 (1 per 18,660 persons); hospital beds (1991) 4,258 (1 per 672 persons); infant mortality rate (1997) 108.0.
Food (1995): daily per capita caloric intake 1,885 (vegetable products 91%, animal products 9%); 83% of FAO recommended minimum requirement.

Military

Total active duty personnel (1997): 2,650[13] (army 94.3%; navy, none; air force 5.7%). *Military expenditure as percentage of GNP* (1994): 3.2% (world 3.0%); per capita expenditure U.S.$10.

[1]To be increased to 109 as of November 1998 elections. [2]1994. [3]1995. [4]An unknown but substantial amount is believed to be smuggled out of the country annually. [5]Bangui only. [6]At factor cast. [7]Weights of consumer price index components. [8]Represents 1/11 of the traffic of Air Afrique, which is operated by 11 West African states. [9]International air service only. [10]1990–91. [11]Included with secondary. [12]University of Bangui only. [13]Excludes 2,300 gendarmerie, who are part of the armed forces.

Internet resources for further information:
• Central African Republic http://www.africa.co.uk/country/cenafrep.htm

Chad

Official name: Jumhūrīyah Tshad (Arabic); République du Tchad (French) (Republic of Chad).
Form of government: unitary republic with one legislative body (National Assembly [125]).
Chief of state: President.
Head of government: Prime Minister.
Capital: N'Djamena.
Official languages: Arabic; French.
Official religion: none.
Monetary unit: 1 CFA franc (CFAF) = 100 centimes; valuation (Sept. 25, 1998) 1 U.S.\$ = CFAF 560.38; 1 £ = CFAF 954.05.

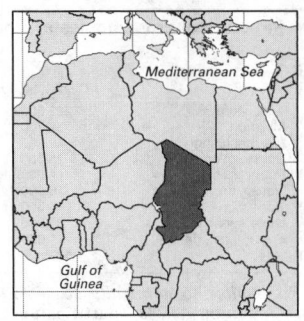

Area and population		area		population
				1993
Préfectures	**Capitals**	sq mi	sq km	census
Batha	Ati	34,285	88,800	288,458
Biltine	Biltine	18,090	46,850	184,807
Borkou-Ennedi-Tibesti	Faya Largeau	231,795	600,350	73,185
Chari-Baguirmi	N'Djamena	32,010	82,910	1,251,906
Guéra	Mongo	22,760	58,950	306,253
Kanem	Mao	44,215	114,520	279,927
Lac	Bol	8,620	22,320	252,932
Logone Occidental	Moundou	3,357	8,695	455,489
Logone Oriental	Doba	10,825	28,035	441,064
Mayo-Kebbi	Bongor	11,625	30,105	825,158
Moyen-Chari	Sarh	17,445	45,180	738,595
Ouaddaï	Abéché	29,436	76,240	543,900
Salamat	Am Timan	24,325	63,000	184,403
Tandjilé	Laï	6,965	18,045	453,854
TOTAL		495,755[1]	1,284,000	6,279,931

Demography

Population (1998): 7,360,000.
Density (1998): persons per sq mi 14.8, persons per sq km 5.7.
Urban-rural (1995): urban 21.4%; rural 78.6%.
Sex distribution (1993): male 48.46%; female 51.54%.
Age breakdown (1993): under 15, 47.9%; 15–29, 24.5%; 30–44, 14.6%; 45–59, 7.1%; 60–74, 4.2%; 75 and over, 1.3%.
Population projection: (2000) 7,760,000; (2010) 10,055,000.
Doubling time: 27 years.
Ethnolinguistic composition (1993): Sara 27.7%; Sudanic Arab 12.3%; Mayo-Kebbi peoples 11.5%; Kanem-Bornu peoples 9.0%; Ouaddaï peoples 8.7%; Hadjeray (Hadjaraï) 6.7%; Tangale (Tandjilé) peoples 6.5%; Gorane peoples 6.3%; Fitri-Batha peoples 4.7%; Fulani (Peul) 2.4%; other 4.2%.
Religious affiliation (1993): Muslim 53.9%; Christian 34.7%, of which Roman Catholic 20.3%, Protestant 14.4%; traditional beliefs 7.4%; other 4.0%.
Major cities (1993): N'Djamena 530,965; Moundou 282,103; Bongor 196,713; Sarh 193,753; Abéché 187,936; Doba 185,461.

Vital statistics

Birth rate per 1,000 population (1995): 44.6 (world avg. 25.0).
Death rate per 1,000 population (1995): 17.7 (world avg. 9.3).
Natural increase rate per 1,000 population (1995): 26.9 (world avg. 15.7).
Total fertility rate (avg. births per childbearing woman; 1995): 5.9.
Life expectancy at birth (1995): male 44.9 years; female 49.6 years.

National economy

Budget (1996). Revenue: CFAF 110,170,000,000 (taxes 89.1%, of which taxes on income and profits 36.1%, taxes on international trade 31.2%, taxes on goods and services 18.6%; nontax revenue 10.9%). Expenditures: CFAF 151,794,000,000 (current expenditure 50.9%, of which government salaries 20.3%, government matériel 11.2%, defense 8.4%, debt service 5.5%, transfer payments 2.5%; capital expenditure 49.1%).
Tourism: receipts from visitors (1994) U.S.\$36,000,000; expenditures by nationals abroad U.S.\$26,000,000.
Production (metric tons except as noted). Agriculture, forestry, fishing (1996): sorghum 444,146[2], sugarcane 330,000[2], millet 257,631[2], yams 240,000, seed cotton 213,000[2], cassava 195,000, rice 97,728[2], corn (maize) 74,631[2], peanuts (groundnuts) 64,400, sweet potatoes 58,000, pulses 34,000, mangoes 32,000, dates 18,000, onions 14,000, sesame seeds 13,088, potatoes 8,000; livestock (number of live animals) 4,959,000 cattle, 3,271,000 goats, 2,219,000 sheep, 656,946 camels, 4,400,000 chickens; roundwood (1995) 4,512,000 cu m; fish catch (1995) 60,000. Mining and quarrying (1996): aggregate (gravel) 170,000; limited commercial production of natron (10,000) and salt; artisanal gold production. Manufacturing (1996): cotton fibre 61,700; refined sugar 27,455; soap 2,958; woven cotton fabrics 881,000 metres; edible oil 125,491 hectolitres; beer 117,100 hectolitres; cigarettes 35,000,000 packs; bicycles 3,444 units. Construction: n.a. Energy production (consumption): electricity (kW-hr; 1996) 92,066,000 (68,638,000); petroleum products (metric tons; 1994) none (31,000).
Household income and expenditure (1993). Average household size 5.0; average annual income per household CFAF 96,806 (U.S.\$458); sources of income (1995–96; urban) "informal"[3]-sector employment and entrepreneurship 36.7%, transfers 24.8%, wages 23.6%, ownership of real estate 8.6%; expenditure (1983)[4]: food 45.3%, health 11.9%, energy 5.8%, clothing 3.3%.
Population economically active (1993): total 2,719,497; activity rate of total population 43.9% (participation rates: over age 15, 72.0%; female 47.9%; unemployed 0.6%).

Price and earnings indexes (1990 = 100)							
	1991	1992	1993	1994	1995	1996	1997
Consumer price index	104.2	100.9	93.8	131.7	143.6	161.4	170.6
Earnings index	...	...	...	...	...	...	...

Gross national product (1996): U.S.\$1,035,000,000 (U.S.\$160 per capita).

Structure of gross domestic product and labour force				
	1996		1993	
	in value CFAF '000,000	% of total value	labour force	% of labour force
Agriculture	98,931	43.2	1,903,492	83.0
Manufacturing	29,109	12.7	33,670	1.5
Construction	1,909	0.8	10,885	0.5
Mining			756	—
Public utilities }	1,833	0.8	2,026	0.1
Transp. and commun.			13,252	0.6
Trade and finance }	63,176	27.6	179,169	7.8
Pub. admin., defense			61,875	2.7
Services }	22,257	9.7	79,167	3.4
Other	11,843	5.2	9,311	0.4
TOTAL	229,058	100.0	2,293,603	100.0

Public debt (external, outstanding; 1995): U.S.\$913,700,000.
Land use (1994): forested 25.7%; meadows and pastures 35.7%; agricultural and under permanent cultivation 2.6%; other 36.0%.

Foreign trade

Balance of trade (current prices)					
	1992	1993	1994	1995	1996
CFAF '000,000,000	−16.6	−15.1	−42.6	−13.9	−21.2
% of total	14.8%	14.9%	22.1%	5.3%	7.4%

Imports (1996): CFAF 153,900,000,000 (1983; petroleum products 16.8%; cereal products 16.8%; pharmaceutical products and chemicals 11.5%; machinery and transport equipment 8.5%, of which transport equipment 7.3%; electrical equipment 5.7%; textiles 2.9%; raw and refined sugar 2.3%). *Major import sources* (1996[5]): France 34.7%; Cameroon 24.1%; Belgium-Luxembourg 7.4%; Nigeria 6.5%; Portugal 5.6%.
Exports (1996[5]): CFAF 132,700,000,000 (1995; cotton lint 59.4%; live cattle 10.9%; live sheep and goats 4.9%). *Major export destinations* (1996): Portugal 34.7%; Germany 11.3%; Costa Rica 6.5%; United States 5.6%; France 5.6%.

Transport and communications

Transport. Railroads: none. Roads (1995): total length 32,700 km (paved 1%). Vehicles (1995): passenger cars 9,630; trucks and buses 14,360. Air transport (1996)[6]: passenger-km 224,736,000; metric ton-km cargo 16,420,000; airports (1997) with scheduled flights 1.

Communications				units per 1,000 persons
Medium	date	unit	number	
Daily newspapers	1995	circulation	1,500	0.2
Radio	1995	receivers	1,310,000	205.9
Television	1995	receivers	50,000	7.9
Telephones	1995	main lines	5,300	0.8
Facsimile machines	1995	units	200	0.03

Education and health

Educational attainment (1993). Percentage of economically active population age 15 and over having: no formal schooling 81.1%; Qur'ānic education 4.2%; primary education 11.2%; secondary education 2.7%; higher education 0.3%; professional education 0.5%. *Literacy* (1995): percentage of total population age 15 and over literate 48.1%; males literate 62.1%; females literate 34.7%.

Education (1994–95)				student/
	schools	teachers	students	teacher ratio
Primary (age 6–12)	2,447	9,404[7]	591,784[7]	62.9[7]
Secondary (age 13–19)	66[8]	2,046	82,559	40.4
Voc., teacher tr.	25[9]	157	3,277	20.9
Higher[10]	4	311	3,049	9.8

Health (1993): physicians 217 (1 per 27,765 persons); hospital beds 3,962 (1 per 1,521 persons); infant mortality rate per 1,000 live births (1995) 122.
Food (1995): daily per capita caloric intake 1,913 (vegetable products 94%, animal products 6%); 80% of FAO recommended minimum requirement.

Military

Total active duty personnel (1997): 30,350 (army 82.4%; navy, none; air force 1.2%; paramilitary 16.4%). *Military expenditure as percentage of GNP* (1995): 3.1% (world 2.8%); per capita expenditure U.S.\$5.

[1]Detail does not add to total given because of rounding. [2]1996–97. [3]Not reported to fiscal authorities. [4]Capital city only. [5]Based on direction of trade data (analysis of reports of trading partners, rather than country's own customs data). [6]One-eleventh portion of total traffic of Air Afrique, which is operated by 11 West African states. [7]1995–96. [8]1988–89. [9]1987. [10]Universities and equivalent institutions only.

Internet resources for further information:
• CIA World Factbook—Chad
  http://www.odci.gov/cia/publications/factbook/index.html
• Chad—A Country Study
  http://lcweb2.loc.gov/frd/cs/tdtoc.html

Chile

Official name: República de Chile (Republic of Chile).
Form of government: multiparty republic with two legislative houses (Senate [48[1]]; Chamber of Deputies [120]).
Head of state and government: President.
Capital: Santiago[2].
Official language: Spanish.
Official religion: none.
Monetary unit: 1 peso (Ch$) = 100 centavos; valuation (Sept. 25, 1998) 1 U.S.$ = Ch$469.55; 1 £ = Ch$799.41.

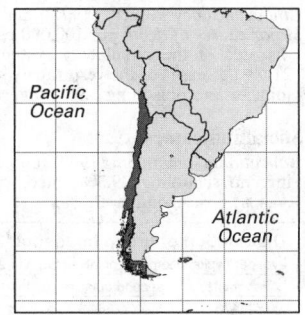

Area and population[3]

Regions	Capitals	area sq mi	area sq km	population 1995 census
Aisén del General Carlos Ibáñez del Campo	Coihaique	42,095	109,025	88,782
Antofagasta	Antofagasta	48,820	126,444	415,481
Araucanía	Temuco	12,300	31,858	853,187
Atacama	Copiapó	29,179	75,573	202,810
Bío-Bío	Concepción	14,258	36,929	1,753,662
Coquimbo	La Serena	15,697	40,656	525,432
Libertador General Bernardo O'Higgins	Rancagua	6,319	16,365	684,179
Los Lagos	Puerto Montt	25,868	66,997	957,212
Magallanes y la Antártica Chilena	Punta Arenas	50,979	132,034	181,551
Maule	Talca	11,700	30,302	902,646
Santiago, Región Metropolitana de	Santiago	5,926	15,349	5,783,703
Tarapacá	Iquique	22,663	58,698	410,343
Valparaíso	Valparaíso	6,331	16,396	1,478,281
TOTAL		292,135[4]	756,626[4]	14,237,275[5]

Demography

Population (1998): 14,822,000.
Density (1998): persons per sq mi 50.7, persons per sq km 19.6.
Urban-rural (1995): urban 85.8%; rural 14.2%.
Sex distribution (1995): male 49.40%; female 50.60%.
Age breakdown (1994): under 15, 30.5%; 15–29, 25.5%; 30–44, 22.1%; 45–59, 12.7%; 60–74, 6.9%; 75 and over, 2.3%.
Population projection: (2000) 15,211,000; (2010) 17,010,000.
Doubling time: 50 years.
Ethnic composition (1992): European and mestizo 89.7%; Araucanian (Mapuche) 9.6%; Aymara 0.5%; Rapa Nui Polynesian 0.2%.
Religious affiliation (1992): Roman Catholic 76.7%; Protestant 13.2%; atheist and nonreligious 5.8%; other 4.3%.
Major cities (1995): Greater Santiago 5,076,808; Concepción 350,268; Viña del Mar 322,220; Valparaíso 282,168; Talcahuano 260,915; Temuco 239,340.

Vital statistics

Birth rate per 1,000 population (1995): 19.7 (world avg. 25.0).
Death rate per 1,000 population (1995): 5.5 (world avg. 9.3).
Natural increase rate per 1,000 population (1994): 14.2 (world avg. 15.7).
Total fertility rate (avg. births per childbearing woman; 1994): 2.3.
Life expectancy at birth (1995): male 71.8 years; female 77.8 years.
Major causes of death per 100,000 population (1993): diseases of the circulatory system 157.4; malignant neoplasms (cancers) 111.5; accidents and adverse effects 66.1; diseases of the respiratory system 64.9.

National economy

Budget (1994). Revenue: Ch$4,843,100,000,000 (income from taxes 84.3%, nontax revenue 15.7%). Expenditures: Ch$4,481,980,000,000 (social security and welfare 33.3%, economic affairs and services 15.4%, education 13.9%).
Public debt (external, outstanding; 1996): U.S.$4,890,000.
Population economically active (1995): total 5,274,200; activity rate of total population 37.8% (participation rates: ages 15–64, 58.6%; female 32.4%; unemployed 4.7%).

Price and earnings indexes (1993 = 100)

	1991	1992	1993	1994	1995	1996	1997
Consumer price index	77.2	89.2	100.0	112.0	120.9	129.7	138.0
Monthly earnings index	...	...	100.0	105.0	118.4	135.4	147.6

Production (metric tons except as noted). Agriculture, forestry, fishing (1996): sugar beets 2,804,000, grapes 1,527,000, tomatoes 1,370,000, wheat 1,227,000, corn (maize) 932,000, apples 910,000, potatoes 828,000, onions (dry) 390,000, oats 200,000, rice 154,000, barley 64,000; livestock (number of live animals) 4,516,000 sheep, 3,858,000 cattle, 1,486,000 pigs; roundwood (1995) 31,365,000 cu m; fish catch (1995) 7,590,900. Mining (1995): iron 8,174,000; copper 2,488,000; zinc 30,000; molybdenum 17,889; silver 1,032,000 kg; gold 39,180 kg. Manufacturing (value added in U.S.$'000; 1994): food products 2,725,000; metal and metal products 2,123,000; petroleum and petroleum products 1,042,000; paper and paper products 782,000; beverages 671,000; nonmetallic mineral products 535,000. Construction (1994)[6]: residential 7,049,369 sq m; nonresidential 2,875,935 sq m. Energy production (consumption): electricity (kW-hr; 1994) 25,250,000,000 (25,250,000,000); coal (metric tons; 1994) 1,182,000 (3,145,000); crude petroleum (barrels; 1994) 4,459,000 (54,141,000);

petroleum products (metric tons; 1994) 7,136,000 (8,399,000); natural gas (cu m; 1994) 1,954,000,000 (1,865,000,000).
Gross national product (1996): U.S.$70,060,000,000 (U.S.$4,860 per capita).

Structure of gross domestic product and labour force

	1994 in value Ch$'000,000[7]	1994 % of total value	1995 labour force	1995 % of labour force
Agriculture	486,595	8.3	809,700	15.4
Mining	470,974	8.0	93,200	1.8
Manufacturing	1,003,765	17.1	861,500	16.3
Construction	322,992	5.5	410,700	7.8
Public utilities	160,600	2.8	28,100	0.5
Transp. and commun.	454,329	7.8	400,500	7.6
Trade	993,408	17.0	974,100	18.5
Finance	972,559	16.6	340,100	6.4
Pub. admin., defense	159,952	2.7	1,322,800	25.1
Services	397,881	6.8		
Other	431,956[8]	7.4[8]	33,500[9]	0.6[9]
TOTAL	5,855,011	100.0	5,274,200	100.0

Household income and expenditure. Average household size (1994) 3.8; average annual income per household (1994) Ch$5,981,706 at November prices (U.S.$12,552); sources of income (1990): wages and salaries 75.1%, transfer payments 12.0%, other 12.9%; expenditure (1989): food 27.9%, clothing 22.5%, housing 15.2%, transportation 6.4%.
Tourism (1995): receipts U.S.$900,000,000; expenditures U.S.$774,000,000.

Foreign trade[10]

Balance of trade (current prices)

	1992	1993	1994	1995	1996	1997
U.S.$'000,000	+749	−979	+660	+1,384	−1,147	−1,343
% of total	3.9%	5.1%	2.9%	4.5%	3.6%	3.8%

Imports (1994): U.S.$11,359,400,000 (intermediate goods 51.8%; capital goods 28.7%; consumer goods 17.5%). *Major import sources:* U.S. 23.2%; Japan 8.9%; Brazil 8.8%; Argentina 8.4%; Germany 4.9%; France 3.2%.
Exports (1994): U.S.$11,645,100,000 (industrial products 44.9%, of which foodstuffs 18.6%, paper and paper products 7.9%, chemical and petroleum products 6.3%; mining 43.8%). *Major export destinations:* U.S. 17.3%; Japan 17.0%; Argentina 5.5%; Brazil 5.2%; Germany 5.0%; Taiwan 4.6%.

Transport and communications

Transport. Railroads (1995): length 4,084 mi, 6,572 km; passenger-km 689,000,000; metric ton-km cargo 2,329,246,000[11]. Roads (1995): total length 49,550 mi, 79,750 km (paved 14%). Vehicles (1995): passenger cars 888,645; trucks and buses 469,142. Air transport (1995): passenger-km 6,332,843,000; metric ton-km cargo 1,348,083,000; airports (1997) with scheduled flights 23.

Communications

Medium	date	unit	number	units per 1,000 persons
Daily newspapers	1994	circulation	1,411,000	101
Radio	1996	receivers	4,400,000	305
Television	1995	receivers	4,000,000	280
Telephones	1995	main lines	1,884,800	132
Cellular telephones	1995	subscribers	197,300	13.8
Facsimile machines	1995	units	15,000	1.0
Personal computers	1995	units	540,000	37.8

Education and health

Educational attainment (1992). Percentage of population age 25 and over having: no formal schooling 5.7%; primary education 44.2%; secondary 42.2%; higher 7.9%. *Literacy* (1995): total population age 15 and over literate 95.2%; males 95.4%; females 95.0%.

Education (1994)

	schools	teachers	students	student/ teacher ratio
Primary (age 6–13)	8,323	78,813	2,119,737	26.9
Secondary (age 14–17)[12]	2,956[13]	50,187	664,498	13.2
Higher	201[13]	18,084[14]	315,653[15]	...

Health (1994): physicians 16,000 (1 per 875 persons); hospital beds 43,076 (1 per 326 persons); infant mortality rate per 1,000 live births (1995) 11.1.
Food (1995): daily per capita caloric intake 2,769 (vegetable products 78%, animal products 22%); 113% of FAO recommended minimum requirement.

Military

Total active duty personnel (1997): 94,300 (army 54.1%; navy 31.6%; air force 14.3%). *Military expenditure as percentage of GNP* (1995): 3.8% (world 2.8%); per capita expenditure U.S.$158.

---

[1]Includes 10 nonelective seats. [2]Legislative bodies meet in Valparaíso. [3]Excludes the 480,000-sq mi (1,250,000-sq km) section of Antarctica claimed by Chile (and administered as part of Magallanes y la Antártica Chilean region) and "inland" (actually tidal) water areas. The 1992 census population of Chilean-claimed Antarctica was 126. [4]Includes 205 sq mi (530 sq km) of waters, known as Laguna del Desierto, lost in a border dispute with Argentina, resolved on Oct. 21, 1994. [5]Population projection based on 1992 census. [6]Construction approved and already begun only. [7]In constant prices of 1986. [8]Less imputed bank service charges. [9]Includes unemployed not previously employed. [10]Import figures are f.o.b. in balance of trade and c.i.f. for commodities and trading partners. [11]1994. [12]Includes vocational. [13]1988. [14]Universities only. [15]1993.

Internet resources for further information:
• Ministry General Secretariat of the Government; Communication and Culture Secretariat http://www.segegob.cl/seg-ingl/index2i.html

China

Official name: Chung-hua Jen-min
Kung-ho-kuo (People's Republic
of China).
Form of government: single-party
people's republic with one legislative
house (National People's Congress
[2,979]).
Chief of state: President.
Head of government: Premier.
Capital: Peking (Beijing).
Official language: Mandarin Chinese.
Official religion: none.
Monetary unit: 1 Renminbi (yuan)
(Y) = 10 jiao = 100 fen; valuation Sept.
25, 1998) 1 U.S.$ = Y 8.28;
1 £ = Y 14.10.

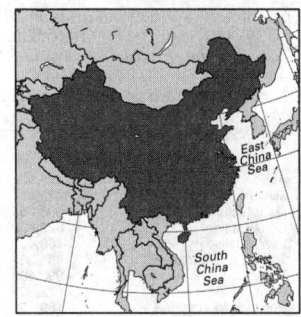

Area and population[1, 2]

Provinces	Capitals	area sq mi	area sq km	population 1996[3] estimate
Anhwei (Anhui)	Ho-fei (Hefei)	54,000	139,900	60,130,000
Chekiang (Zhejiang)	Hang-chou (Hangzhou)	39,300	101,800	43,190,000
Fukien (Fujian)	Fu-chou (Fuzhou)	47,500	123,100	32,370,000
Hainan (Hainan)	Hai-k'ou (Haikou)	13,200	34,300	7,240,000
Heilungkiang (Heilongjiang)	Harbin	179,000	463,600	37,010,000
Honan (Henan)	Cheng-chou (Zhengzhou)	64,500	167,000	91,000,000
Hopeh (Hebei)	Shih-chia-chuang (Shijiazhuang)	78,200	202,700	64,370,000
Hunan (Hunan)	Ch'ang-sha (Changsha)	81,300	210,500	63,920,000
Hupeh (Hubei)	Wu-han (Wuhan)	72,400	187,500	57,720,000
Kansu (Gansu)	Lan-chou (Lanzhou)	141,500	366,500	24,380,000
Kiangsi (Jiangxi)	Nan-ch'ang (Nanchang)	63,600	164,800	40,630,000
Kiangsu (Jiangsu)	Nanking (Nanjing)	39,600	102,600	70,660,000
Kirin (Jilin)	Ch'ang-ch'un (Changchun)	72,200	187,000	25,920,000
Kwangtung (Guangdong)	Canton (Guangzhou)	76,100	197,100	68,680,000
Kweichow (Guizhou)	Kuei-yang (Guiyang)	67,200	174,000	35,080,000
Liaoning (Liaoning)	Shen-yang (Shenyang)	58,300	151,000	40,920,000
Shansi (Shanxi)	T'ai-yüan (Taiyuan)	60,700	157,100	30,770,000
Shantung (Shandong)	Chi-nan (Jinan)	59,200	153,300	87,050,000
Shensi (Shaanxi)	Sian (Xi'an)	75,600	195,800	35,140,000
Szechwan (Sichuan)	Ch'eng-tu (Chengdu)	210,800	546,000	98,650,000
Tsinghai (Qinghai)	Hsi-ning (Xining)	278,400	721,000	4,810,000
Yunnan (Yunnan)	K'un-ming (Kunming)	168,400	436,200	39,900,000
Autonomous regions				
Inner Mongolia (Nei Monggol)	Hu-ho-hao-t'e (Hohhot)	454,600	1,177,500	22,840,000
Kwangsi Chuang (Guangxi Zhuang)	Nan-ning (Nanning)	85,100	220,400	45,430,000
Ningsia Hui (Ningxia Hui)	Yin-ch'uan (Yinchuan)	25,600	66,400	5,130,000
Sinkiang Uighur (Xinjiang Uygur)	Wu-lu-mu-ch'i (Urumqi)	635,900	1,646,900	16,610,000
Tibet (Xizang)	Lhasa	471,700	1,221,600	2,400,000
Municipalities				
Chungking (Chongqing)	—	8,900	23,000	14,600,000
Peking (Beijing)	—	6,500	16,800	12,510,000
Shanghai (Shanghai)	—	2,400	6,200	14,150,000
Tientsin (Tianjin)	—	4,400	11,300	9,420,000
TOTAL		3,696,100[4]	9,572,900[4]	1,211,210,000[5]

Demography

Population (1998): 1,242,980,000.
Density (1998): persons per sq mi 336.3, persons per sq km 129.8.
Urban-rural (1997): urban 32.0%; rural 68.0%.
Sex distribution (1995): male 51.03%; female 48.97%.
Age breakdown (1990): under 15, 27.7%; 15–29, 31.0%; 30–44, 20.7%; 45–59, 12.0%; 60–74, 6.9%; 75 and over, 1.7%.
Population projection: (2000) 1,263,098,000; (2010) 1,341,848,000.
Doubling time: 77 years.
Ethnic composition (1990): Han (Chinese) 91.96%; Chuang 1.37%; Manchu 0.87%; Hui 0.76%; Miao 0.65%; Uighur 0.64%; Yi 0.58%; Tuchia 0.50%; Mongolian 0.42%; Tibetan 0.41%; Puyi 0.23%; Tung 0.22%; Yao 0.18%; Korean 0.17%; Pai 0.14%; Hani 0.11%; Kazak 0.10%; Tai 0.09%; Li 0.09%; other 0.51%.
Religious affiliation (1980): nonreligious 51.9%; Chinese folk-religionist 20.1%; atheist 12.0%; Buddhist 8.5%; Christian 6.0%; Muslim 1.4%; other 0.1%.
Major cities (1990): Shanghai 7,496,509; Peking 5,769,607; Tientsin 4,574,689; Shen-yang 3,603,712; Wu-han 3,284,229; Canton 2,914,281; Harbin 2,443,398; Chungking (Chongqing) 2,266,772; Nanking 2,090,204; Sian 1,959,044; Talien (Dalian) 1,723,302; Ch'eng-tu 1,713,255; Ch'ang-ch'un 1,679,270; T'ai-yüan 1,533,884; Tsinan 1,480,915; Ch'ing-tao (Qingdao) 1,459,195; An-shan (Anshan) 1,203,986; Fu-shun 1,202,388; Lan-chou 1,194,640; Cheng-chou 1,159,679; Tzu-po (Zibo) 1,138,074; K'un-ming 1,127,411.
Households (1995). Average rural household size 4.5; urban household size 3.2. Family households (1990): 277,390,000 (99.4%); collective 1,671,000 (0.6%).

Vital statistics

Birth rate per 1,000 population (1997): 16.4 (world avg. 25.0).
Death rate per 1,000 population (1997): 7.1 (world avg. 9.3).
Natural increase rate per 1,000 population (1997): 9.3 (world avg. 15.7).
Total fertility rate (avg. births per childbearing woman; 1997): 1.8.
Marriage rate per 1,000 population (1995): 7.7.
Divorce rate per 1,000 population (1995): 0.9.

Life expectancy at birth (1997): male 68.0 years; female 72.0 years.
Major causes of death per 100,000 population (percentage distribution; 1995)[6]: diseases of the circulatory system 22.2%; malignant neoplasms (cancers) 21.9%; diseases of the respiratory system 15.7%; diseases of the heart 15.3%; injuries and poisoning 6.9%; digestive diseases 3.3%.

Social indicators

Educational attainment (1990). Percentage of population age 25 and over having: no schooling 29.3%; incomplete primary 34.3%; completed primary 34.4%; postsecondary 2.0%.

Distribution of urban household income (1995)

avg. per capita income by quintile (avg. Y 4,288)

first quintile	second quintile	third quintile	fourth quintile	fifth quintile
Y 2,478	Y 3,364	Y 4,074	Y 4,958	Y 7,134

Quality of working life (1991). Average workweek: 48 hours. Annual rate per 100,000 workers for: injury or accident, n.a.; industrial illness, n.a.; death, n.a. Funds for pensions and social welfare relief (1995): Y 154,180,000,000. Average days lost to labour stoppages per 1,000 workdays: n.a. Average duration of journey to work: n.a. Method of transport: n.a. Rate per 1,000 workers of discouraged (unemployed no longer seeking work): n.a.
Access to services. Proportion of communes having access to electricity (1979) 87.1%. Percentage of urban population with: safe public water supply (1995) 93.0%; public sewage collection. n.a.; public fire protection, n.a.
Social participation. Eligible voters participating in last national election: n.a. Population participating in voluntary work: n.a. Trade union membership in total labour force (1991): 17.9%. Practicing religious population in total affiliated population: n.a.
Social deviance. Annual reported arrest rate per 100,000 population (1986) for: property violation 20.7; infringing personal rights 7.2; disruption of social administration 3.3; endangering public security 1.0[7].
Leisure. Favourite leisure activities: n.a.
Material well-being (1995). Urban families possessing (number per family): bicycles 1.9; televisions 1.2; washing machines 0.9; refrigerators 0.7; sewing machines 0.6; cameras 0.3. Rural families possessing (number per family): bicycles 1.5; televisions 0.8; sewing machines 0.7; washing machines 0.2.

National economy

Gross national product (at current market prices; 1996): U.S.$906,079,000,000 (U.S.$750 per capita).

Structure of gross national product and labour force

	1995 in value Y '000,000,000	1995 % of total value	1995 labour force ('000)[8]	1995 % of labour force[8]
Agriculture	1,199.30	20.6	330,180	52.9
Mining	}		10,670	1.7
Manufacturing	} 2,435.37	41.8	98,030	15.7
Construction	381.96	6.6	33,220	5.3
Public utilities	...	...	2,580	0.4
Transp. and commun.	323.65	5.6	19,420	3.1
Trade	509.44	8.7	42,920	6.9
Finance	...	...	3,560	0.6
Pub. admin.	...	...	10,420	1.7
Services	976.33	16.7	28,050	4.5
Other	...	...	44,830	7.2
TOTAL	5,826.05	100.0	623,880	100.0

Budget (1995). Revenue: Y 736,661,000,000 (taxes 93.7%; funds collected for energy and transport projects and others 6.3%). Expenditures: Y 791,438,000,000 (culture, education, and public health 21.5%; capital construction 11.2%; government administration 8.1%; enterprise development 6.7%; agricultural development 6.6%; defense 4.7%; urban public works 3.7%).
Public debt (external, outstanding; 1996): U.S.$102,260,000,000.
Tourism: receipts from visitors (1995) U.S.$8,733,000,000; expenditures by nationals abroad U.S.$3,688,000,000.

Retail and service enterprises (1992)

	no. of enterprises	no. of employees	annual wage as a % of all wages	annual gross output value (Y '000,000)
Retail trade	10,063,000	24,345,000	...	...
Grocery stores	171,000	1,213,000	...	...
Department stores	174,000	2,120,000	...	...
Other food shops	120,000	824,000	...	...
Agricultural supplies stores	100,000	508,000	...	...
Electrical appliances stores	96,000	930,000	...	...
Household supplies stores	71,000	377,000	...	...
Grain and oil shops	81,000	783,000	...	...
Textile stores	40,000	288,000	...	...
Drugstores	32,000	251,000	...	...
Bookstores	28,000	151,000	...	...
Coal stores	16,000	200,000	...	...
Service trade	1,842,000	4,522,000	...	...
Repair shops	742,000	1,110,000	...	...
Barbershops	508,000	779,000	...	...
Hotels	189,000	1,427,000	...	...
Photo studios	98,000	225,000	...	...

Production (metric tons except as noted). Agriculture, forestry, fishing (1996): grains—rice 197,200,000, corn (maize) 127,810,000, wheat 110,315,000, sorghum 4,098,000, barley 3,500,000, millet 2,701,000; oilseeds—soybeans 13,010,000, peanuts (groundnuts) 10,230,000, rapeseed 9,166,000, sunflower seeds 1,290,000; fruits and nuts—watermelons 21,708,000, apples 17,058,000, oranges 8,050,000, cantaloupes 5,962,000, pears 5,921,000; other—sweet potatoes 100,196,000, sugarcane 70,840,000, potatoes 36,769,000, sugar beets 16,726,000, cabbage 16,214,000, tomatoes 15,532,000, cucumbers 13,351,000,

seed cotton 12,609,000, onions 9,630,000, eggplants 9,325,000, garlic 8,574,000, tobacco leaves 3,210,000, tea 614,000; livestock (number of live animals) 452,199,000 pigs, 149,908,000 goats, 127,261,000 sheep, 108,910,000 cattle, 23,315,000 water buffalo, 10,745,000 asses, 10,071,000 horses, 2,902,000,000 chickens, 483,000,000 ducks; roundwood (1995) 297,653,000 cu m; fish catch (1995) 24,433,321. Mining and quarrying (1996): metal concentrates—zinc 1,119,000, copper 906,000, lead 530,000, antimony 99,000, tin 56,000, tungsten 24,000; metal ores—iron ore 250,000,000, bauxite 5,500,000, manganese ore 5,000,000[9], silver 250[9], gold 140[9]; nonmetals—salt 28,990,000, gypsum 7,500,000, phosphates 7,000,000[9], talc 2,500,000, fluorspar 2,000,000, barite 1,500,000, graphite 350,000[9], asbestos 250,000. Manufacturing (1996): cement 490,000,000; rolled steel 86,110,000; chemical fertilizer 26,600,000; paper and paperboard 24,000,000[9]; sulfuric acid 18,890,000; sugar 6,500,000; cotton yarn 4,900,000; cotton fabrics 22,120,000,000 m; cigarettes 34,420,000 cases; colour television sets 21,090,000 units; household washing machines 9,448,000 units[9]; household refrigerators 9,280,000 units; motor vehicles 1,490,000 units. Construction (1995): residential 1,074,330,000 sq m; nonresidential 381,670,000 sq m. Distribution of industrial production (percentage of total value of output by sector; 1978 [1995]): state-operated enterprises 80.6% (34.0%); collectives 19.2% (36.6%); privately operated enterprises 0.2% (29.4%). Retail sales (percentage of total sales by sector; 1978 [1995]): state-operated enterprises 90.5% (29.8%); collectives 7.4% (19.3%); privately operated enterprises 2.1% (50.9%).

Manufacturing and mining enterprises (1995)

	no. of enterprises	no. of employees[10]	annual wages as a % of avg. of all wages[11]	annual gross output value (Y '000,000)
Manufacturing				
Machinery, transport equipment, and metal manufactures,	131,810	17,740,000	96.7	1,462,671
of which,				
Metal products	30,728	1,930,000	...	165,072
Industrial equipment	29,631	4,050,000	...	236,569
Transport equipment	19,445	3,700,000	...	330,328
Electronic goods	7,997	1,720,000	...	253,048
Measuring equipment	5,637	860,000	...	42,570
Textiles	25,686	6,730,000	95.5	460,400
Garments	20,007	1,750,000	...	147,015
Foodstuffs,	61,983	4,760,000	87.5	620,008
of which,				
Food processing	30,711	1,980,000	...	304,510
Beverages	14,719	1,210,000	...	115,568
Tobacco manufactures	423	330,000	...	100,423
Chemicals,	59,010	7,470,000	92.1	733,852
of which,				
Pharmaceuticals	5,388	1,020,000	...	96,126
Plastics	19,255	1,090,000	...	112,765
Secondary forest products (including paper and stationery)	38,130	2,410,000	96.1	164,602
Primary forest products	1,237	1,160,000	114.3	16,493
Mining				
Nonferrous and ferrous metals	5,915	840,000	107.6	43,410
Crude petroleum	134	1,280,000	...	142,846
Coal	11,953	5,210,000	119.8	115,516

Energy production (consumption): electricity (kW-hr; 1994) 928,083,000,000 (926,037,000,000); coal (metric tons; 1994) 1,239,902,000 (1,231,928,000); crude petroleum (barrels; 1994) 1,069,320,000 (1,024,375,000); petroleum products (metric tons; 1994) 106,629,000 (114,972,000); natural gas (cu m; 1994) 17,540,000,000 (17,540,000,000).

Financial aggregates[12]

	1990	1991	1992	1993	1994	1995	1996
Exchange rate, Y per:							
U.S. dollar	5.22	5.43	5.75	5.80	8.45	8.32	8.31
£	10.06	10.16	8.70	8.59	13.18	12.90	12.96
SDR	7.43	7.77	7.91	7.97	12.33	12.36	11.93
International reserves (U.S.$)							
Total (excl. gold; '000,000)	29,586	43,674	20,620	22,387	52,914	75,377	107,039
SDRs ('000,000)	562	577	419	484	539	582	614
Reserve pos. in IMF ('000,000)	430	433	758	704	755	1,216	1,396
Foreign exchange ('000,000)	28,594	42,664	19,443	21,199	51,620	73,579	105,029
Gold ('000,000 fine troy oz)	12.7	12.7	12.7	12.7	12.7	12.7	12.7
% world reserves	1.4	1.4	1.4	1.4	1.4	1.4	1.4
Interest and prices							
Central bank discount (%)	...	...	...	...	...	...	...
Govt. bond yield (%)	...	...	...	...	...	...	...
Industrial share prices	...	...	...	...	...	...	...
Balance of payments (U.S.$'000,000)							
Balance of visible trade,	+9,165	+8,743	+5,183	−10,654	+7,290	+18,050	+19,535
of which:							
Imports, f.o.b.	−42,354	−50,176	−64,385	−86,313	−95,271	−110,060	−131,542
Exports, f.o.b.	51,519	58,919	69,568	75,659	102,561	128,110	151,077
Balance of invisibles	+2,833	+5,022	+1,218	−955	−758	−11,774	−12,437
Balance of payments, current account	+11,998	+13,765	+6,401	−11,609	+6,532	+6,276	+7,098

Household income and expenditure. Average household size (1995) 3.7; rural household 4.5, urban household 3.2. Average annual income per household Y 11,555; rural household Y 10,474, urban household Y 13,851. Sources of income: rural household (1995)—income from household businesses 80.3%, wages 15.2%, other 4.5%; urban household (1995)—wages 80.6%, business income 5.7%, other 13.7%. Expenditure (1995): rural household—food 58.6%, housing 13.9%, cultural activities 7.8%, clothing 6.9%, household materials 5.2%, health 3.2%, transportation 2.6%; urban household—food 49.9%, clothing 13.5%, cultural activities 8.8%, household materials 8.4%, housing 7.1%, transportation 4.8%, health 3.1%.

Population economically active (1995): total 696,600,000; activity rate of total population 57.8% (participation rates: over ages 15, 76.8%[13]; female 49.7%[13]; unemployed 10.4%). Urban workforce by sector 1978 (1995): state enterprises 74,500,000 (109,550,000); collectives 20,000,000 (30,760,000); self-employment or privately run enterprises 150,000 (8,770,000).

Price and earnings indexes (1990 = 100)

	1991	1992	1993	1994	1995	1996	1997
Consumer price index	105.1	114.1	133.5	165.9	193.9	210.0	215.9
Annual earnings index[14]	109.3	126.7	157.5	212.1	257.0	...	...

Land use (1994): forested 14.0%; meadows and pastures 42.9%; agricultural and under permanent cultivation 10.3%; other 32.8%.

Foreign trade[15]

Balance of trade (current prices)

	1991	1992	1993	1994	1995	1996
U.S.$'000,000	+8,743	+5,183	−10,654	+7,290	+18,050	+19,535
% of total	8.0%	3.9%	6.6%	3.7%	7.6%	6.9%

Imports (1995): U.S.$132,078,000,000 (machinery and transport equipment 39.9%; products of textile industries, rubber and metal products 21.8%; chemical and related products 13.1%; inedible raw materials 7.7%; food and live animals 4.6%; mineral fuel and lubricants 3.9%). *Major import sources:* Japan 22.0%; United States 12.2%; Taiwan 11.2%; South Korea 7.8%; Hong Kong 6.5%; Germany 6.1%; Russia 2.9%; Singapore 2.6%; Italy 2.4%; France 2.0%; Australia 2.0%.

Exports (1995): U.S.$148,770,000,000 (products of textile industries, rubber and metal products 21.7%; machinery and transport equipment 21.1%; food and live animals 6.7%; chemicals and allied products 6.1%; mineral fuels and lubricants 3.6%; inedible raw materials 2.9%). *Major export destinations:* Hong Kong 24.2%; Japan 19.1%; United States 16.6%; South Korea 4.5%; Germany 3.8%; Singapore 2.4%; The Netherlands 2.2%; Taiwan 2.1%.

Transport and communications

Transport. Railroads (1995): length 45,319 mi, 72,934 km; passenger-mi 220,319,000,000, passenger-km 354,570,000,000; short ton-mi cargo 881,539,-000,000, metric ton-km cargo 1,287,000,000,000. Roads (1995): total length 718,931 mi, 1,157,009 km (paved 90%). Vehicles (1995): passenger cars 4,179,000; trucks and buses 5,213,270. Merchant marine (1992): vessels (100 gross tons and over) 2,390: total deadweight tonnage 20,657,996. Air transport (1995): passenger-mi 42,334,000,000, passenger-km 68,130,000,000; short ton-mi cargo 1,527,000,000, metric ton-km cargo 2,230,000,000; airports (1996) with scheduled flights 113.

Communications

Medium	date	unit	number	units per 1,000 persons
Daily newspapers	1994	circulation	27,790,000	23
Radio	1996	receivers	215,950,000	177
Television	1995	receivers	227,880,000	189
Telephones	1995	main lines	40,706,000	34
Cellular telephones	1995	subscribers	3,629,000	3.0
Facsimile machines	1995	units	270,000	0.2
Personal computers	1995	units	2,600,000	2.2

Education and health

Literacy (1995): total population age 15 and over literate 81.5%; males literate 89.9%; females literate 72.7%.

Education (1995)

	schools	teachers	students	student/teacher ratio
Primary (age 7–13)	849,123	6,539,000	159,064,000	24.3
Secondary (age 13–17)	81,020	3,334,000	53,710,000	16.1
Secondary specialized	14,196	549,000	8,205,000	14.9
Higher	1,054	401,000	2,906,000	7.2

Health (1995): physicians 1,918,000 (1 per 628 persons); hospital beds 3,141,000 (1 per 384 persons); infant mortality rate per 1,000 live births (1997) 39.

Food (1995): daily per capita caloric intake 2,741 (vegetable products 82%, animal products 18%); 116% of FAO recommended minimum requirement.

Military

Total active duty personnel (1997): 2,840,000 (army 73.6%, navy 9.9%, air force 16.5%). *Military expenditure as percentage of GNP* (1995): 2.3% (world 2.8%); per capita expenditure U.S.$53.

---

[1]Names of the provinces, autonomous regions, and municipalities are stated in conventional form, followed by Pinyin transliteration; names of capitals are stated in conventional form or Wade-Giles transliteration, followed by Pinyin transliteration. [2]Data for Taiwan, Quemoy and Matsu (parts of Fukien province occupied by Taiwan), and Hong Kong (which reverted to China from British administration July 1, 1997) are excluded. [3]January 1. [4]Includes 4,600 sq mi (11,900 sq km) not shown separately. [5]Total includes servicemen not assigned to any political division and discrepancies between provincial and national estimates. [6]Based on urban sample population. [7]Excludes arrests for anti-Communist activities. [8]Employed only. [9]1995. [10]In state-owned and collective-owned industries only. [11]1979. [12]Exchange rates and international reserves are end-of-year figures. [13]1987. [14]Average annual wage in industrial establishments in urban areas. [15]Imports and exports f.o.b.

Internet resource for further information:
• Embassy of The People's Republic of China http://www.china-embassy.org/

Colombia

Official name: República de Colombia (Republic of Colombia).
Form of government: unitary, multiparty republic with two legislative houses (Senate [102]; House of Representatives [161]).
Head of state and government: President.
Capital: Santafé de Bogotá, D.C.
Official language: Spanish.
Official religion: none.
Monetary unit: 1 peso (Col$) = 100 centavos; valuation (Sept. 25, 1998) 1 U.S.$ = Col$1,547; 1 £ = Col$2,633.

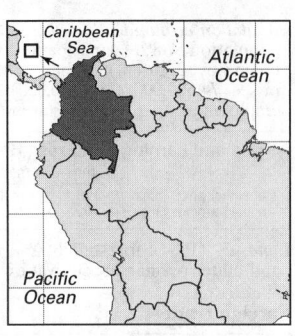

Area and population		area		population
Departments	**Capitals**	sq mi	sq km	1993 census[1]
Antioquia	Medellín	24,445	63,912	4,919,619
Atlántico	Barranquilla	1,308	3,388	1,837,468
Bolívar	Cartagena	10,030	25,978	1,702,188
Boyacá	Tunja	8,953	23,189	1,315,579
Caldas	Manizales	3,046	7,888	1,030,062
Caquetá	Florencia	34,349	88,965	367,898
Cauca	Popayán	11,316	29,308	1,127,678
Cesar	Valledupar	8,844	22,905	827,219
Chocó	Quibdó	17,965	46,530	406,199
Córdoba	Montería	9,660	25,020	1,275,623
Cundinamarca	Santafé de Bogotá, D.C.	8,735	22,623	1,875,337
Huila	Neiva	7,680	19,890	843,798
La Guajira	Riohacha	8,049	20,848	433,361
Magdalena	Santa Marta	8,953	23,188	1,127,691
Meta	Villavicencio	33,064	85,635	618,427
Nariño	Pasto	12,845	33,268	1,443,671
Norte de Santander	Cúcuta	8,362	21,658	1,162,474
Orinoquía-Amazonía	...	186,519	483,083	688,805
Quindío	Armenia	712	1,845	495,212
Risaralda	Pereira	1,598	4,140	844,184
San Andrés y Providencia	San Andrés	17	44	61,040
Santander	Bucaramanga	11,790	30,537	1,811,741
Sucre	Sincelejo	4,215	10,917	701,105
Tolima	Ibagué	9,097	23,562	1,286,078
Valle	Cali	8,548	22,140	3,736,090
Capital District				
Santaté de Bogotá, D.C.		613[2]	1,587[2]	5,484,244
TOTAL		440,762[2]	1,141,568[2]	37,422,791

Demography

Population (1998): 37,685,000.
Density (1998): persons per sq mi 85.5, persons per sq km 33.0.
Urban-rural (1990): urban 70.3%; rural 29.7%.
Sex distribution (1996): male 49.24%; female 50.76%.
Age breakdown (1996): under 15, 33.5%; 15–29, 28.1%; 30–44, 21.5%; 45–59, 10.4%; 60–74, 5.3%; 75 and over, 1.2%.
Population projection: (2000) 38,905,000; (2010) 44,771,000.
Doubling time: 35 years.
Ethnic composition (1985): mestizo 58.0%; white 20.0%; mulatto 14.0%; black 4.0%; mixed black-Indian 3.0%; Amerindian 1.0%.
Religious affiliation (1995): Roman Catholic 91.9%; other 8.1%.
Major cities (1993): Santafé de Bogotá, D.C. 5,484,244; Cali 1,847,176; Medellín 1,834,881; Barranquilla 1,090,916.

Vital statistics

Birth rate per 1,000 population (1996): 25.9 (world avg. 25.0).
Death rate per 1,000 population (1996): 5.9 (world avg. 9.3).
Natural increase rate per 1,000 population (1996): 20.0 (world avg. 15.7).
Total fertility rate (avg. births per childbearing woman; 1996): 2.9.
Life expectancy at birth (1996): male 65.4 years; female 73.3 years.
Major causes of death per 100,000 population (1990)[3]: homicide with firearms 101.0; malignant neoplasms (cancers) 82.6; ischemic heart disease 70.4; accidents 49.0; infectious and parasitic diseases 25.5.

National economy

Budget (1995). Revenue: Col$13,405,350,000,000 (indirect taxes 36.9%, direct taxes 26.8%, credit resources 22.3%). Expenditures: Col$9,510,848,000,000 (education 20.2%, finance and public credit 16.9%, defense 12.4%).
Public debt (external, outstanding; 1996): U.S.$14,814,000,000.
Tourism (1995): receipts U.S.$851,000,000; expenditures U.S.$822,000,000.
Production (metric tons except as noted). Agriculture, forestry, fishing (1996): sugarcane 32,500,000, plantains 3,212,000, potatoes 2,594,000, bananas 2,100,000, rice 1,787,000, corn 1,058,000, coffee 821,800; livestock (no. of live animals) 26,088,000 cattle, 3,708,000 vicuña[4], 2,540,000 sheep, 2,431,000 pigs; roundwood (1995) 20,491,000 cu m; fish catch (1995) 167,080. Mining and quarrying (1996): iron ore 605,716; salt 560,252; gold 710,013 troy oz[5]; silver 169,252 troy oz[5]; emeralds 6,305,903 carats[5]. Manufacturing (value added in Col$'000,000; 1992): processed food 1,160,600; beverages 953,400; textiles and clothing 631,700; machinery and electrical apparatus 351,200; paper products 266,500. Construction (no. of permits; 1996)[6]: residential 6,118; nonresidential 3,138. Energy production (consumption): electricity (kW-hr; 1994) 43,474,000,000 (43,617,000,000); coal (metric tons; 1994) 22,527,000 (6,476,000); petroleum (barrels; 1994) 168,202,000 (97,085,000); petroleum products (metric tons; 1994) 12,510,000 (11,682,000); natural gas (cu m; 1994) 5,111,119,000 (5,111,119,000).
Gross national product (1996): U.S.$80,174,000,000 (U.S.$2,140 per capita).

Structure of gross domestic product and labour force				
	1995		1980	
	in value Col$'000,000	% of total value	labour force	% of labour force
Agriculture	9,513,515	13.1	2,412,413	28.5
Mining	3,973,366	5.5	49,740	0.6
Manufacturing	13,573,048	18.8	1,136,735	13.4
Construction	4,628,555	6.4	242,191	2.9
Public utilities	2,344,821	3.2	44,233	0.5
Transp. and commun.	6,897,403	9.5	352,623	4.2
Trade	7,184,183	9.9	1,261,633	14.9
Finance			278,210	3.2
Pub. admin., defense	24,292,123	33.6	1,998,460	23.6
Services				
Other			690,762[7]	8.2[7]
TOTAL	72,407,014	100.0	8,467,000	100.0

Population economically active (1985): total 9,558,000; activity rate 34.3% (participation rates: over age 12, 49.4%; female 32.8%; unemployed 4.3%).

Price and earnings indexes (1990 = 100)							
	1991	1992	1993	1994	1995	1996	1997
Consumer price index	130.4	165.6	203.1	251.5	304.2	365.8	433.6
Monthly earnings index[8]	126.1	158.9	198.7	...	...	...	...

Household income and expenditure. Average household size (1985) 4.7; sources of income (1992): wages 45.1%, self-employment 35.4%, transfer payments 14.2%; expenditure (1992): food 34.2%, transportation 18.5%, housing 7.8%, health care 6.4%, household durable goods 5.7%, clothing 4.5%.
Land use (1994): forest 22.0%; pasture 18.2%; agriculture 5.7%; other 54.1%.

Foreign trade[9]

Balance of trade (current prices)						
	1992	1993	1994	1995	1996	1997
U.S.$'000,000	+936.3	−1,969.8	−2,620.8	−2,795.7	−2,206.7	−2,886.5
% of total	7.3%	12.2%	13.5%	12.1%	9.4%	11.1%

Imports (1996): U.S.$13,676,000,000 (machinery and transport equipment 45.3%, chemicals 24.7%, vegetable products 7.5%, metals 6.6%, food and tobacco 6.1%, paper and paper products 3.5%). *Major import sources* (1995): U.S. 39.1%; Venezuela 9.8%; Japan 7.6%; Germany 5.8%.
Exports (1996): U.S.$10,574,000,000 (petroleum products 27.4%, coffee 14.9%, chemicals 10.2%, forestry and fisheries 10.0%, textiles and apparel 8.1%, coal 8.0%, food 7.1%). *Major export destinations* (1995): U.S. 34.9%; Germany 7.3%; Peru 6.1%; Venezuela 5.5%; Ecuador 4.1%; Japan 3.6%.

Transport and communications

Transport. Railroads (1992): route length (1994) 3,230 km; passenger-km 15,524,000; metric ton-km cargo 242,917,000. Roads (1995): total length 106,600 km (paved 12%). Vehicles (1995): cars 1,150,000; trucks 550,000. Merchant marine (1992): vessels (100 gross tons and over) 101; deadweight tonnage 403,047. Air transport (1995): passenger-km 4,565,477,000; metric ton-km cargo 965,828,000; airports (1997) 43.

Communications				units per 1,000
Medium	date	unit	number	persons
Daily newspapers	1994	circulation	1,910,020[10]	55[10]
Radio	1996	receivers	5,400,000	151
Television	1995	receivers	7,314,000	188
Telephones	1995	main lines	3,872,800	100
Cellular telephones	1995	subscribers	274,600	7.1
Personal computers	1995	units	630,000	16

Education and health

Educational attainment (1985). Percentage of population age 25 and over having: no schooling 15.3%; primary education 50.1%; secondary 25.4%; higher 6.8%; not stated 2.4%. *Literacy* (1995): population age 15 and over literate 91.3%; males literate 91.2%; females literate 91.4%.

Education (1994)				student/
	schools	teachers	students	teacher ratio
Primary (6–10)	46,707	170,526	4,327,507	25.4
Secondary (11–16)	8,161	141,484	2,879,681	20.3
Higher[11]	235[12]	54,164	510,649	9.4

Health: physicians (1992) 33,498 (1 per 1,078 persons); hospital beds (1989) 45,888 (1 per 693 persons); infant mortality rate (1995) 26.9.
Food (1995): daily per capita caloric intake 2,758 (vegetable products 84%, animal products 16%); 119% of FAO recommended minimum requirement.

Military

Total active duty personnel (1997): 146,300 (army 82.7%, navy 12.3%, air force 5.0%). *Military expenditure as percentage of GNP* (1995): 2.6% (world 2.8%); per capita expenditure U.S.$55.

[1]Adjusted figures. [2]Detail does not add to total given because of rounding. [3]Estimates based on about 75% of total deaths. [4]1991. [5]1995. [6]Construction permits for 7 metropolitan areas and 10 cities. [7]Includes unemployed. [8]Minimum legal wages revised annually January 2. [9]Import figures are f.o.b. in balance of trade and c.i.f. in commodities and trading partners. [10]Circulation for 26 newspapers only. [11]1992. [12]1987.

Internet resource for further information:
• **National Administration Department of Statistics**
  http://www.dane.gov.co

Comoros[1]

Official name: Jumhurīyat al-Qumur al-Ittihādīyah al-Islāmīyah (Arabic); République Fédérale Islamique des Comores (French) (Federal Islamic Republic of the Comoros).
Form of government: transitional regime[2].
Head of state and government[2]: Interim President assisted by Prime Minister.
Capital: Moroni.
Official languages: Comorian; Arabic; French.
Official religion: Islam.
Monetary unit: 1 Comorian franc (CF) = 100 centimes; valuation (Sept. 25, 1998) 1 U.S.\$ = CF 418.73; 1 £ = CF 712.89.

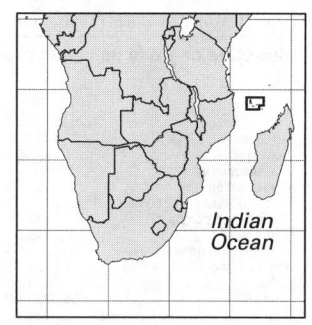

Indian Ocean

Area and population

Islands[3]	Capitals	area		population
		sq mi	sq km	1995 estimate
Mwali (Mohéli)	Fomboni	112	290	27,600
Nzwani (Anjouan)[4, 5]	Mutsamudu	164	424	211,900
Ngazidja (Grande-Comore)	Moroni	443	1,148	250,500
TOTAL		719	1,862	490,000

Demography

Population (1998): 546,000.
Density (1998): persons per sq mi 759.4, persons per sq km 293.2.
Urban-rural (1995)[6]: urban 30.8%; rural 69.2%.
Sex distribution (1991): male 49.49%; female 50.51%.
Age breakdown (1995)[6]: under 15, 48.5%; 15–29, 26.4%; 30–44, 13.8%; 45–59, 7.3%; 60–74, 3.4%; 75 and over, 0.6%.
Population projection: (2000) 581,000; (2010) 782,000.
Doubling time: 20 years.
Ethnic composition (1995): nearly all Comorian (a mixture of Bantu, Arab, Malay, and Malagasy peoples).
Religious affiliation (1995): Sunnī Muslim 99.3%; other 0.7%.
Major cities (1991): Moroni 30,000; Mutsamudu 20,000; Domoni (1990) 8,000; Fomboni (1990) 5,600.

Vital statistics

Birth rate per 1,000 population (1996): 45.8 (world avg. 25.0).
Death rate per 1,000 population (1996): 10.3 (world avg. 9.3).
Natural increase rate per 1,000 population (1996): 35.5 (world avg. 15.7).
Total fertility rate (avg. births per childbearing woman; 1996): 6.7.
Marriage rate per 1,000 population: n.a.[7]
Divorce rate per 1,000 population: n.a.
Life expectancy at birth (1996): male 56.4 years; female 61.0 years.
Major causes of death per 100,000 population: n.a.; however, major diseases include malaria (afflicts 80–90% of the adult population), tuberculosis, leprosy, and kwashiorkor (a nutritional deficiency disease).

National economy

Budget (1996). Revenue: CF 22,873,000,000 (tax revenue 43.5%, grants 36.0%, loans 14.6%, nontax revenue 5.9%). Expenditures: CF 29,513,000,000 (current expenditures 61.8%, development expenditures 38.2%).
Production (metric tons except as noted). Agriculture, forestry, fishing (1996): coconuts 60,000[6], bananas 57,000, cassava 49,700, pulses 8,760, taro 8,300, corn (maize) 3,700, cloves 2,000, vanilla 150, ylang-ylang essence 40, other export crops grown in small quantities include coffee, cinnamon, and tuberoses; livestock (number of live animals[6]) 128,000 goats, 50,000 cattle, 14,500 sheep; roundwood, n.a.; fish catch (1995) 13,200. Mining and quarrying: sand, gravel, and crushed stone from coral mining for local construction. Manufacturing: products of small-scale industries include processed vanilla and ylang-ylang, cement, handicrafts, soaps, soft drinks, woodwork, and clothing. Construction: n.a. Energy production (consumption): electricity (kW-hr; 1996) 30,900,000 ([1994] 17,742,000); coal, none (none); crude petroleum, none (none); petroleum products (metric tons; 1994) none (22,000); natural gas, none (none).
Population economically active (1991): total 215,000; activity rate of total population 44.4% (participation rates: ages 10 years and over, 57.8%; female 40.0%; unemployed 20%).

Price and earnings indexes (1993 = 100)

	1992	1993	1994	1995	1996
Consumer price index	98.2	100.0	125.0	133.9	138.7
Monthly earnings index	...	100.0	121.0	137.0	...

Tourism (1996): receipts from visitors U.S.\$20,300,000; expenditures by nationals abroad U.S.\$5,100,000.
Public debt (external, outstanding; 1996): U.S.\$192,900,000.
Household income and expenditure. Average household size (1985) 5.6; income per household: n.a.; sources of income: n.a.; expenditure (1993)[10]: food and beverages 67.3%, clothing and footwear 11.6%, tobacco and cigarettes 4.1%, energy 3.8%, health care 3.2%, household furnishings 3.0%, other 7.0%.
Gross national product (at current market prices; 1996): U.S.\$228,000,000 (U.S.\$450 per capita).

Structure of gross domestic product and labour force

	1996		1980	
	in value CF '000,000	% of total value	labour force[11]	% of labour force
Agriculture, fishing	31,636	38.6	53,063	53.3
Mining	...	...	62	0.1
Manufacturing	4,361	5.3	3,946	4.0
Construction	5,054	6.2	3,267	3.3
Public utilities	1,068	1.3	129	0.1
Transportation and communications	3,093	3.8	2,118	2.1
Trade, restaurants, hotels	22,832	27.9	1,873	1.9
Finance, insurance	3,115	3.8	237	0.2
Public admin., defense	12,114	14.8	2,435	2.5
Services	401	0.5	4,646	4.7
Other	−1,827[12]	−2.2	27,687[12]	27.8[12]
TOTAL	81,847	100.0	99,463	100.0

Land use (1994)[6]: forested 17.9%; meadows and pastures 6.7%; agricultural and under permanent cultivation 44.9%; other 30.5%.

Foreign trade[13]

Balance of trade (current prices)

	1993	1994	1995	1996
CF '000,000,000	−7.9	−14.2	−15.8	−17.1
% of total	39.3%	61.2%	65.1%	77.1%

Imports (1996): CF 24,659,000,000 (rice 13.5%, petroleum products 13.5%, vehicles 7.6%, meat and fish 6.0%, iron and steel 3.7%, other 40.4%). *Major import sources:* France 39.4%; Pakistan 7.7%; South Africa 6.6%; United Arab Emirates 6.3%.
Exports (1996): CF 2,436,000,000 (vanilla 42.5%, ylang-ylang 26.5%, cloves 8.6%). *Major export destinations:* France 48.9%; Germany 13.6%; United States 11.8%; Réunion and Madagascar 11.8%.

Transport and communications

Transport. Railroads: none. Roads (1995): total length 544 mi, 875 km (paved 76%). Vehicles (1995): passenger cars 7,080; trucks and buses 4,870. Merchant marine (1992): vessels (100 gross tons and over) 6; total deadweight tonnage 3,579. Air transport (1994): passenger-mi 1,900,000, passenger-km 3,000,000; short ton-mi cargo, n.a., metric ton-mi cargo, n.a.; airports (1997) with scheduled flights 2.

Communications

Medium	date	unit	number	units per 1,000 persons
Radio	1996	receivers	61,000	122
Television	1993	receivers	200	0.4
Telephones	1996	main lines	4,980	9.9
Facsimile machines	1995	units	100	0.2

Education and health

Educational attainment (1980). Percentage of population age 25 and over having: no formal schooling 56.7%; Qur'anic school education 8.3%; primary 3.6%; secondary 2.0%; higher 0.2%; not specified 29.2%. *Literacy* (1995)[6]: total population age 15 and over literate 192,000 (57.0%); males literate 108,000 (64.0%); females literate 84,000 (50.0%).

Education (1993–94)

	schools	teachers	students	student/ teacher ratio
Primary (age 7–12)	275	1,737[14]	77,837	43.0[14]
Secondary (age 13–19)	...	613[15]	17,474	25.5[15]
Teacher training	...	...	163	...
Higher	...	...	400	...

Health: physicians (1993) 77[16] (1 per 6,600[16] persons); hospital beds (1990) 649 (1 per 715 persons); infant mortality rate per 1,000 live births (1996) 75.3.
Food (1995): daily per capita caloric intake 1,850 (vegetable products 94%, animal products 6%); 79% of FAO recommended minimum requirement.

Military

Total active duty personnel (1995): 800[17]. *Military expenditure as percentage of GNP: n.a.*

[1]Excludes Mayotte, a *collectivité territoriale* ("territorial collectivity") of France, unless otherwise indicated. [2]From Sept. 13, 1997. [3]Island names in Comorian (French), respectively. [4]Unilateral independence declared in early August 1997. [5]Formal secession as of approved referendum of Oct. 26, 1997, was not internationally recognized. [6]Includes Mayotte. [7]In the early 1990s, 20% of adult men had more than one wife. [8]Moroni only. [9]July average for government employees only. [10]Weights of consumer price index components for Moroni. [11]The wage labour force was very small in 1995; total of less than 7,000 including government employees, and less than 2,000 excluding them. [12]Not adequately defined. [13]Imports are f.o.b. in balance of trade and c.i.f. in commodities and trading partners. [14]Public education only. [15]1991–92. [16]Estimated figure. [17]Permanent presence of French military personnel in the Comoros to be expected per agreement ratified in December 1996.

Internet resource for further information:
• **Welcome to the World Wide Web site of the Comoro Islands (unofficial)**
http://www.ksu.edu/sasw/comoros/comoros.html

Congo, Democratic Republic of the

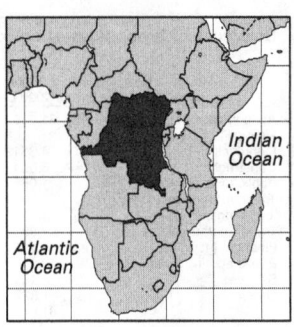

Official name: République Democratique du Congo (Democratic Republic of the Congo).
Form of government: transitional military regime[1].
Chief of state: President.
Capital: Kinshasa.
Official languages: French; English.
Official religion: none.
Monetary unit: Congolese franc (FC)[2]; valuation (June 17, 1998)
1 U.S.$ = FC 1.4;
1 £ = FC 0.8.

Area and population

Provinces	Capitals	area sq mi	area sq km	population 1994 estimate
Bandundu	Bandundu	114,154	295,658	4,907,000
Bas-Congo	Matadi	20,819	53,920	2,578,000
Equateur	Mbandaka	155,712	403,292	4,789,000
Kasai-Occidental	Kananga	59,746	154,742	3,117,000
Kasai-Oriental	Mbuji-Mayi	65,754	170,302	3,778,000
Katanga	Lubumbashi	191,845	496,877	5,602,000
Maniema	Kindu	51,062	132,250	1,048,000[3]
Nord-Kivu	Goma	22,967	59,483	3,546,000[3]
Orientale	Kisangani	194,302	503,239	5,432,000
Sud-Kivu	Bukavu	25,147	65,130	3,093,000[3]
City				
Kinshasa	—	3,848	9,965	4,655,000
TOTAL		905,354[4]	2,344,858	42,545,000[3]

Demography

Population (1998): 49,001,000.
Density (1998): persons per sq mi 54.1, persons per sq km 20.9.
Urban-rural (1995): urban 29.1%; rural 70.9%.
Sex distribution (1995): male 49.41%; female 50.59%.
Age breakdown (1995): under 15, 47.3%; 15–29, 25.9%; 30–44, 14.1%; 45–59, 8.1%; 60–74, 3.8%; 75 and over, 0.8%.
Population projection: (2000) 51,988,000; (2010) 70,276,000.
Ethnic composition (1983): Luba 18.0%; Kongo 16.1%; Mongo 13.5%; Rwanda 10.3%; Azande 6.1%; Bangi and Ngale 5.8%; Rundi 3.8%; Teke 2.7%; Boa 2.3%; Chokwe 1.8%; Lugbara 1.6%; Banda 1.4%; other 16.6%.
Religious affiliation (1995): Roman Catholic 41.0%; Protestant 32.0%; indigenous Christian 13.4%, of which Kimbanguist 13.0%; other Christian 0.8%; Muslim 1.4%; traditional beliefs and other 11.4%.
Major cities (1994): Kinshasa 4,655,313; Lubumbashi 851,381; Mbuji-Mayi 806,475; Kisangani 417,517; Kananga 393,030.

Vital statistics

Birth rate per 1,000 population (1990–95): 47.5 (world avg. 25.0).
Death rate per 1,000 population (1990–95): 14.5 (world avg. 9.3).
Natural increase rate per 1,000 population (1990–95): 33.0 (world avg. 15.7).
Total fertility rate (avg. births per childbearing woman; 1990–95): 6.7.
Life expectancy at birth (1990–95): male 50.4 years; female 53.7 years.
Major causes of death per 100,000 population: n.a.; however, major causes in the early 1990s included malaria, measles, diarrhea, acute respiratory infections, and AIDS.

National economy

Budget (1996). Revenue: U.S.$374,000,000 (customs duties and taxes on international trade 33.4%; taxes on mining production 11.2%; other revenues 55.3%). Expenditures: U.S.$1,163,000,000 (debt service 71.5%, of which external 62.7%, domestic 8.8%; wages and salaries 6.4%; foreign-financed capital expenditure 5.2%).
Public debt (external, outstanding; 1996): U.S.$9,262,000,000.
Land use (1994): forested 76.7%; meadows and pastures 6.6%; agricultural and under permanent cultivation 3.5%; other 13.2%.
Production (metric tons except as noted). Agriculture, forestry, fishing (1996): cassava 18,000,000, plantains 2,270,000, sugarcane 1,300,000, corn (maize) 1,100,000, peanuts (groundnuts) 580,000, rice 430,000, bananas 412,000, sweet potatoes 410,000, yams 315,000, mangoes 212,000, papayas 210,000, palm oil 181,000, oranges 156,000, pineapples 145,000, dry beans 125,000, seed cotton 77,000, palm kernels 72,000, coffee 60,000, natural rubber 11,000[5]; livestock (number of live animals) 4,172,000 goats, 1,480,000 cattle, 1,157,000 pigs, 1,043,000 sheep, 34,000,000 chickens; roundwood (1995) 48,747,000 cu m; fish catch (1995) 158,627. Mining and quarrying (1996): copper (metal content) 39,647; cobalt (metal content) 4,041; zinc (metal content) 3,162; gold 1,252 kg; diamonds 22,240,000 carats. Manufacturing (1995): iron and steel 965,000; cement 194,000; sugar 82,461; soap 46,773; tires 50,000 units; printed fabrics 15,728,000 sq m; matches 3,305,000 packs; shoes 1,600,000 pairs; beer 1,781,000 hectolitres; soft drinks 807,000 hectolitres. Energy production (consumption): electricity (kW-hr; 1994) 5,545,000,000 (4,523,000,000); coal (metric tons; 1995) 14,400 ([1994] 136,000); crude petroleum (barrels; 1995) 10,087,000 ([1994] 2,782,000); petroleum products (metric tons; 1994) 350,000 (1,024,000); natural gas, none (none).
Household income and expenditure. Average household size (1982) 6.0; average annual income per household Z 1,200[2] (U.S.$209); sources of income: n.a.; expenditure (1985): food 61.7%, housing and energy 11.5%, clothing and footwear 9.7%, transportation 5.9%, furniture and utensils 4.9%.

Gross national product (1996): US$5,727,000,000 (U.S.$130 per capita).

Structure of gross domestic product and labour force

	1995 in value Z '000,000[2]	1995 % of total value	1991 labour force	1991 % of labour force
Agriculture	21,248,000	58.0	9,021,000	65.1
Mining	1,591,000	4.3		
Manufacturing	2,365,000	6.5		
Construction	845,000	2.3	2,200,000	15.9
Public utilities	604,000	1.6		
Transp. and commun.	1,023,000	2.8		
Trade	6,114,000	16.7		
Pub. admin., defense	483,000	1.3		
Finance and services	2,038,000	5.6	2,627,000	19.0
Other	313,000	0.9		
TOTAL	36,622,000[4]	100.0	13,848,000	100.0

Population economically active (1991): total 13,848,000; activity rate 35.9% (participation rates: [1987]: over age 10, 57.4%; female 40.8%).

Price and earnings indexes (1992 = 10)

	1993	1994	1995	1996	1997
Consumer price index	199	47,501	304,915	2,313,781	6,374,748
Earnings index	...	...	...	...	...

Tourism (1993): receipts U.S.$6,000,000; expenditures U.S.$16,000,000.

Foreign trade[6]

Balance of trade (current prices)

	1991	1992	1993	1994	1995	1996
U.S.$'000,000	+108	+403	+477	+643	+581	+708
% of total	3.4%	18.5%	26.3%	33.8%	25.0%	27.8%

Imports (1995): U.S.$870,200,000 (non-oil 94.0%; oil 6.0%). *Major import sources*[7, 8] (1995): Belgium-Luxembourg 15.0%; U.S. 6.7%; Germany 6.0%; France 4.2%; The Netherlands 4.0%; China 3.6%; Italy 3.3%.
Exports (1995): U.S.$1,451,500,000 (diamonds 17.2%, crude petroleum 11.4%, coffee 8.8%, copper 7.9%). *Major export destinations*[7] (1995): Belgium-Luxembourg 36.3%; U.S. 16.9%; Italy 9.7%; Japan 5.0%.

Transport and communications

Transport. Railroads (1994)[9]: length (1996) 5,138 km; passenger-km 29,000,000; metric ton-km cargo 176,000,000. Roads (1995): total length 154,027 km (paved 2%). Vehicles (1995): passenger cars 762,000; trucks and buses 55,000. Air transport (1991)[10]: passenger-km 144,242,000; metric ton-km cargo 21,046,000; airports (1997) with scheduled flights 22.

Communications

Medium	date	unit	number	units per 1,000 persons
Daily newpapers	1995	circulation	120,000	2.7
Radio	1995	receivers	3,480,000	79.3
Television	1995	receivers	22,000	0.5
Telephones	1995	main lines	36,000	0.8
Cellular telephones	1995	subscribers	10,000	0.2
Facsimile machines	1995	units	5,000	0.1

Education and health

Educational attainment: n.a. *Literacy* (1995): percentage of total population age 15 and over literate 77.3%; males literate 86.6%; females literate 67.7%.

Education (1994–95)

	schools	teachers	students	student/teacher ratio
Primary (age 6–11)	14,885	121,054	5,417,506	44.8
Secondary (age 12–17)	4,276[11]	59,325[11]	640,298[12]	22.6[11]
Voc., teacher tr.	11	11	701,148[12]	11
Higher	...	3,873[13]	93,266	15.9[13]

Health: physicians (1990) 2,469 (1 per 15,584 persons); hospital beds (1986) 68,508 (1 per 487 persons); infant mortality rate (1990–95) 93.
Food (1995): daily per capita caloric intake 1,879 (vegetable products 97%, animal products 3%); 85% of FAO recommended minimum requirement.

Military

Total active duty personnel (1997): Former Zairean armed forces disbanded 1997; some 20,000–40,000 personnel of the Congo Liberation Army subsequently constituted the national armed forces. *Military expenditure as percentage of GNP* (1995): 0.3% (world 2.8%); per capita expenditure U.S.$0.

---

[1]From May 1997; new draft constitution was under review in 1998. [2]The new zaïre (NZ) replaced the (old) zaïre (Z) at a rate of 3,000,000 (old) zaïres to 1 NZ on Oct. 22, 1993; the Congolese franc (FC) replaced the new zaïre (NZ) at a rate of FC 1 to NZ 100,000 on July 1, 1998. [3]Estimated to account for division of former Kivu province. [4]Detail does not add to total given because of rounding. [5]1995. [6]Imports c.i.f.; exports f.o.b. [7]DOT (Direction of Trade) valuation; the valuation as the sum of all known trading partners, by external analysis, rather than as the reported sum of the country's own trade data. [8]The DOT valuation is approximately 45% higher than values shown. [9]Traffic statistics are for services operated by the Zaire National Railways (SNCZ), which controls more than 90% of the country's total rail facility. [10]Air Zaire only; declared bankrupt 1995. [11]Secondary includes Voc., teacher tr. [12]1993–94. [13]1989.

Internet resource for further information:
• Zaire—A Country Study
   http://lcweb2.loc.gov/frd/cs/zrtoc.html

Congo, Republic of the

Official name: République du Congo (Republic of the Congo).
Form of government: transitional[1] regime with one legislative house (National Transitional Council [75]).
Chief of state: President.
Capital: Brazzaville.
Official language: French[2].
Official religion: none.
Monetary unit: 1 CFA franc (CFAF) = 100 centimes; valuation (Sept. 25, 1998) 1 U.S.$ = CFAF 560.38; 1 £ = CFAF 954.05.

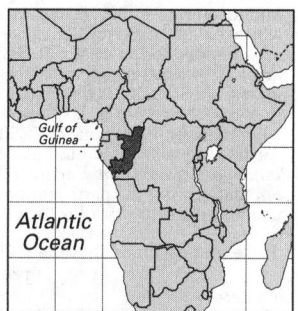

Area and population

Regions	Capitals	area sq mi	area sq km	population 1992 estimate
Bouenza	Madingou	4,733	12,258	177,357
Cuvette Est	Owando	} 28,900	74,850	151,839
Cuvette Ouest	Ewo			
Kouilou	Pointe-Noire	5,270	13,650	89,296
Lékoumou	Sibiti	8,089	20,950	74,420
Likouala	impfondo	25,500	66,044	70,675
Niari	Loubomo	10,007	25,918	120,077
Plateaux	Djambala	14,826	38,400	119,722
Pool	Kinkala	13,110	33,955	182,671
Sangha	Ouesso	21,542	55,795	35,961
Communes				
Brazzaville	—	39	100	937,579
Loubomo	—	7	18	83,605
Mossendjo	—	2	5	16,405
Nkayi	—	3	8	42,465
Ouesso	—	2	5	16,171
Pointe-Noire	—	17	44	576,206
TOTAL		132,047	342,000	2,694,449

Demography

Population (1998): 2,658,000.
Density (1998): persons per sq mi 20.1, persons per sq km 7.8.
Urban-rural (1991): urban 41.1%; rural 58.9%.
Sex distribution (1995): male 48.92%; female 51.08%.
Age breakdown (1995): under 15, 45.6%; 15–29, 26.4%; 30–44, 14.6%; 45–59, 8.1%; 60–74, 4.2%; 75 and over, 1.0%.
Population projection: (2000) 2,776,000; (2010) 3,368,000.
Doubling time: 23 years.
Ethnic composition (1983): Kongo 51.5%; Teke 17.3%; Mboshi 11.5%; Mbete 4.9%; Punu 3.0%; Sango 2.7%; Maka 1.8%; Pygmy 1.5%; other 5.8%.
Religious affiliation (1995): Roman Catholic 40.9%; traditional beliefs 32.9%; Protestant 24.2%; Muslim 2.0%.
Major cities (1992): Brazzaville 937,579; Pointe-Noire 576,206; Loubomo 83,605; Nkayi 42,465; Mossendjo 16,405.

Vital statistics

Birth rate per 1,000 population (1990–95): 44.7 (world avg. 25.0).
Death rate per 1,000 population (1990–95): 14.9 (world avg. 9.3).
Natural increase rate per 1,000 population (1990–95): 29.8 (world avg. 15.7).
Total fertility rate (avg. births per childbearing woman; 1990–95): 6.3.
Life expectancy at birth (1990–95): male 48.9 years; female 53.8 years.
Major causes of morbidity and mortality in the early 1990s included malaria, acute respiratory infections, diarrhea, trauma, helminthiasis[3], and sexually transmitted diseases.

National economy

Budget (1996). Revenue: CFAF 353,750,000,000 (petroleum revenue 59.6%; nonpetroleum receipts 40.4%, of which [1995] customs duties 19.2%, income tax 12.6%). Expenditures: CFAF 380,500,000,000 (debt service 39.6%; salaries 27.9%; transfers and subsidies 8.7%, goods and services 7.1%).
Public debt (external, outstanding; 1996): U.S.$4,665,000,000.
Production (metric tons except as noted). Agriculture, forestry, fishing (1996): cassava 720,000, sugarcane 460,000, plantains 99,000, bananas 46,000, peanuts (groundnuts) 28,000, corn (maize) 26,000, avocados 26,000, yams 17,000, palm oil 17,000, pineapples 13,000, cacao beans 2,000, coffee 1,000; livestock (number of live animals) 312,000 goats, 114,000 sheep, 70,000 cattle; roundwood (1995) 3,834,000 cu m; fish catch (1995) 35,024. Mining and quarrying (1997): artisanal extraction of gold only. Manufacturing (1994): residual fuel oil 288,000; cement 87,400; distillate fuel oils 95,000; aviation gas 58,000; gasoline 58,000; kerosene 52,000; refined sugar 27,000; wheat flour 15,131[4]; dried, cured, or salted fish 4,000[5]; cigarettes 655,000,000 cartons; mechanical cultivators 294,404 units[5]; beer 507,000 hectolitres; soft drinks 220,000 hectolitres; cotton textiles 1,800,000 m[4]; veneer sheets 35,000 cu m[4]; footwear 300,000 pairs[6]. Energy production (consumption): electricity (kW-hr; 1994) 435,000,000 (547,000,000); crude petroleum (barrels; 1996) 80,300,000 ([1994] 8,040,000); petroleum products (metric tons; 1994) 570,000 (540,000); natural gas (cu m; 1994) 5,125,000 (5,125,000).
Household income and expenditure. Average household size (1984) 5.2; income per household: n.a.; sources of income: n.a.; expenditure (1977)[7, 8]: food, beverages, and tobacco 62.0%, housing 10.1%, transportation and recreation 8.6%, clothing and footwear 6.9%, fuel, energy, and water 5.7%, health and medical care 3.8%.
Gross national product (1996): U.S.$1,813,000,000 (U.S.$670 per capita).

Structure of gross domestic product and labour force

	1996 in value CFAF '000,000[9]	1996 % of total value	1991 labour force	1991 % of labour force
Agriculture, forestry, fishing	119,600	9.7	471,000	59.1
Petroleum	500,700	40.6		
Manufacturing, mining	94,300	7.6 }	101,000	12.7
Construction	18,000	1.5		
Public utilities	15,800	1.3		
Trade	137,700	11.2 }		
Transp. and commun.	90,800	7.4	225,000	28.2
Pub. admin., defense	124,000	10.0		
Services	80,200	6.5		
Other	53,600	4.3	—	—
TOTAL	1,234,700	100.0[10]	797,000	100.0

Population economically active (1992): total 886,000; activity rate of total population 37.4% (participation rates: [1984]: ages 15–64, 54.0%; female 45.6%; unemployed[11] 2.3%).

Price and earnings indexes (1990 = 100)

	1991	1992	1993	1994	1995	1996
Consumer price index[7]	109.2	111.3	113.6	170.1	206.5	206.0
Earnings index	...	...	...	...	...	...

Land use (1994): forested 58.3%; meadows and pastures 29.3%; agricultural and under permanent cultivation 0.5%; other 11.9%.
Tourism (1995): receipts U.S.$4,000,000; expenditures U.S.$39,000,000.

Foreign trade

Balance of trade (current prices)

	1991	1992	1993	1994	1995	1996
CFAF '000,000,000	+154.1	+214.8	+168.6	+247.3	+313.4	+42.6
% of total	36.1%	52.5%	38.6%	30.2%	36.6%	3.2%

Imports (1995): CFAF 271,910,000,000 (1991[12]; machinery and transport equipment 38.0%, basic manufactures 27.4%, food and live animals 11.2%, chemicals and chemical products 8.4%, mineral fuels 3.2%, beverages and tobacco 2.3%). *Major import sources:* France 32.0%; U.S. 9.6%; The Netherlands 6.6%; Italy 4.4%; Belgium-Luxembourg 3.8%; Germany 3.3%.
Exports (1995): CFAF 585,300,000,000 (petroleum and petroleum products 84.6%, wood and wood products 8.4%, other 7.0%). *Major export destinations:* U.S. 22.6%; Italy 15.4%; The Netherlands 12.5%; France 9.2%.

Transport and communications

Transport. Railroads: (1995) length 795 km; passenger-km 302,000,000; metric ton-km cargo 267,000,000. Roads (1995): total length 12,760 km (paved 10%). Vehicles (1995): passenger cars 36,100; trucks and buses 15,600. Air transport (1996)[13]: passenger-km 224,736,000; metric ton-km cargo 16,420,000; airports (1997) with scheduled flights 10.

Communications

Medium	date	unit	number	units per 1,000 persons
Daily newspapers	1992	circulation	19,000	8.0
Radio	1995	receivers	808,000	312
Television	1995	receivers	44,000	17.0
Telephones	1995	main lines	21,400	8.1
Facsimile machines	1995	units	100	0.4

Education and health

Educational attainment (1984). Percentage of population age 25 and over having: no formal schooling 58.7%; primary education 21.4%; secondary education 16.9%; postsecondary 3.0%. *Literacy* (1995): total population age 15 and over literate 74.9%; males literate 83.1%; females literate 67.2%.

Education (1995–96)

	schools	teachers	students	student/ teacher ratio
Primary (age 6–13)	1,612	7,060	497,305	70.4
Secondary (age 14–18)	238[14]	5,710	189,381	33.2
Voc., teacher tr.	60[14]	1,463	25,269	17.3
Higher	12[14]	656[15]	13,806[15]	21.0[15]

Health: physicians (1990) 613 (1 per 3,595 persons); hospital beds (1989) 4,817 (1 per 446 persons); infant mortality rate per 1,000 live births (1990–95) 84.
Food (1995): daily per capita caloric intake 2,141 (vegetable products 93%, animal products 7%); 96% of FAO recommended minimum requirement.

Military

Total active duty personnel (1997): 10,000 (army 80.0%, navy 8.0%, air force 12.0%). *Military expenditure as percentage of GNP* (1995): 2.5% (world 2.8%); per capita expenditure U.S.$19.

[1]From February 1998 until November 2000. [2]"Functional" national languages are Lingala and Monokutuba. [3]Parasitic infestation by helminthic worms. [4]1993. [5]1992. [6]1990. [7]European households only; Brazzaville. [8]Cost-of-living components. [9]At current factor cost. [10]Detail does not add to total given because of rounding. [11]Previously employed only. [12]Based on c.i.f. valuation. [13]Represents 1/11 of the traffic of Air Afrique, which is operated by 11 African states. [14]1989. [15]1992.

Costa Rica

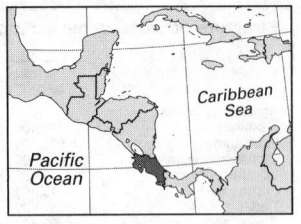

Official name: República de Costa Rica (Republic of Costa Rica).
Form of government: unitary multiparty republic with one legislative house (Legislative Assembly [57]).
Head of state and government: President.
Capital: San José.
Official language: Spanish.
Official religion: Roman Catholicism.
Monetary unit: 1 Costa Rican colón (₡) = 100 céntimos; valuation (Sept. 25, 1998) 1 U.S.$ = ₡263.10; 1 £ = ₡447.93.

Area and population

Provinces	Capitals	area sq mi	area sq km	population 1996[1] estimate
Alajuela	Alajuela	3,766	9,753	601,674
Cartago	Cartago	1,207	3,125	378,188
Guanacaste	Liberia	3,915	10,141	266,198
Heredia	Heredia	1,026	2,657	270,096
Limón	Limón	3,548	9,188	255,248
Puntarenas	Puntarenas	4,354	11,277	375,639
San José	San José	1,915	4,959	1,220,412
TOTAL		19,730[2]	51,100	3,367,455

Demography

Population (1998): 3,533,000.
Density (1998): persons per sq mi 179.1, persons per sq km 69.1.
Urban-rural (1995): urban 44.0%; rural 56.0%.
Sex distribution (1995): male 50.50%; female 49.50%.
Age breakdown (1996): under 15, 34.5%; 15–29, 27.0%; 30–44, 21.2%; 45–59, 10.4%; 60–74, 5.4%; 75 and over, 1.5%.
Population projection: (2000) 3,673,000; (2010) 4,333,000.
Doubling time: 36 years.
Ethnic composition (1993): white 87.0%; mestizo 7.0%; black/mulatto 3.0%; East Asian (mostly Chinese) 2.0%; Amerindian 1.0%.
Religious affiliation (1995): Roman Catholic 86.0%; Protestant 9.3%, of which Pentecostal 4.9%; other Christian 2.4%; other 2.3%.
Major cities (1996): San José 324,011[3] (metropolitan area 968,367); Limón 57,216; Alajuela 49,568; San Isidro de El General 41,912; Desamparados 39,221[4].

Vital statistics

Birth rate per 1,000 population (1995): 23.8 (world avg. 25.0); legitimate 53.4%; illegitimate 46.6%.
Death rate per 1,000 population (1995): 4.2 (world avg. 9.3).
Natural increase rate per 1,000 population (1995): 19.6 (world avg. 15.7).
Total fertility rate (avg. births per childbearing woman; 1995): 2.8.
Marriage rate per 1,000 population (1995): 7.1.
Divorce rate per 1,000 population (1992): 1.1.
Life expectancy at birth (1990–95): male 71.9 years; female 77.5 years.
Major causes of death per 100,000 population (1994): diseases of the circulatory system 126.6, of which ischemic heart disease 59.8, cerebrovascular disease 29.6; malignant neoplasms (cancers) 80.0; diseases of the respiratory system 40.6; accidents 36.1; diseases of the digestive system 24.6.

National economy

Budget (1995). Revenue: ₡427,400,000,000 (tax revenue 85.5%, of which social security contributions 25.9%, sales tax 20.2%, import duties 11.5%, income taxes 11.0%; nontax revenue 14.1%). Expenditures: ₡472,200,000,000 (health 20.7%, social security and welfare 19.9%, interest payments 19.3%, education 16.8%, general public services 6.7%, public order 6.2%).
Public debt (external, outstanding; 1996): U.S.$2,889,000,000.
Gross national product (1996): U.S.$9,081,000,000 (U.S.$2,640 per capita).

Structure of gross domestic product and labour force

	1995 in value ₡'000,000,000	1995 % of total value	labour force	% of labour force
Agriculture, forestry, fishing	289	17.4	252,500	20.5
Mining	308	18.6	2,500	0.2
Manufacturing			192,100	15.6
Construction	38	2.3	73,900	6.0
Public utilities	56	3.4	12,300	1.0
Transp. and commun.	88	5.3	61,600	5.0
Trade, restaurants	335	20.2	225,400	18.3
Finance, real estate	202	12.2	50,500	4.1
Public administration	232	14.0	287,000	23.3
Services	109	6.6		
Other			73,900[5]	6.0
TOTAL	1,659[2]	100.0	1,231,600[2]	100.0

Production (metric tons except as noted). Agriculture, forestry, fishing (1996): sugarcane 3,620,000, bananas 2,100,000, pineapples 260,000, rice 186,400, oranges 165,000, coffee 142,600, cassava 125,000, plantains 105,000, palm oil 96,800, potatoes 63,900, other products include other tropical fruits, cut flowers, and ornamental plants grown for export; livestock (number of live animals) 1,585,000 cattle, 300,000 pigs, 16,500,000 chickens; roundwood (1995) 4,806,000 cu m; fish catch (1994) 20,849, of which shrimp 5,468. Mining and quarrying (1995): limestone (1994) 1,700,000; gold 16,000 troy oz.

Manufacturing (value added in ₡'000,000; 1993): food products 51,902, of which bakery products 11,651; soft drinks and carbonated waters 11,044; malt liquors and malt 10,561; radio, television, and communications equipment 7,494; wearing apparel 6,943; plastic products 6,800. Construction (completed; 1995): 1,515,000 sq m. Energy production (consumption): electricity (kW-hr; 1995) 4,843,000,000 (4,342,000,000); coal, none (none); crude petroleum (barrels; 1994) none (4,757,000); petroleum products (metric tons; 1994) 538,000 (1,396,000); natural gas, none (none).
Population economically active (1994): total 1,187,005; activity rate of total population 38.7% (participation rates: ages 15–69, 59.7%; female 30.1%; unemployed [July 1996] 6.2%).

Price and earnings indexes (1990 = 100)

	1991	1992	1993	1994	1995	1996	1997
Consumer price index	128.7	156.8	172.1	195.4	240.7	282.9	320.3
Monthly earnings index[6]	120.3	144.5	176.2	207.6	250.0	...	...

Tourism (1995): receipts U.S.$661,000,000; expenditures U.S.$332,000,000.
Household income and expenditure. Average household size (1996) 4.1[7]; average annual household income (1996) ₡1,247,867 (U.S.$5,980)[7]; sources of income (1987–88): wages and salaries 61.0%, self-employment 22.6%, transfers 9.6%, other 6.8%; expenditure (1987–88): food and beverages 39.1%, housing and energy 12.1%, transportation 11.6%, household furnishings 10.9%, other 26.3%.
Land use (1994): forested 30.8%; meadows and pastures 45.8%; agricultural and under permanent cultivation 10.4%; other 13.0%.

Foreign trade[8]

Balance of trade (current prices)

	1992	1993	1994	1995	1996	1997
U.S.$'000,000	−697.6	−890.5	−782.6	−400.7	−465.6	−807.7
% of total	14.0%	18.2%	14.9%	7.1%	7.2%	11.0%

Imports (1995): U.S.$3,024,800,000 (raw materials for industry 37.2%; nondurable consumer goods 18.7%; capital goods for industry 14.4%; durable consumer goods 10.9%). *Major import sources:* U.S. 44.2%; Japan 5.5%; Venezuela 5.5%; Mexico 4.5%; other Central American countries 7.6%.
Exports (1995): U.S.$2,624,100,000 (bananas 23.7%; coffee 15.5%; textiles, clothing, and footwear 5.7%[9], fish and shrimp 4.6%[10]; ornamental plants, leaves, and flowers 4.3%). *Major export destinations*[11]: U.S. 50%; Germany 8%; Nicaragua 3%; Canada 3%; United Kingdom 3%.

Transport and communications

Transport. Railroads (1995): route length 590 mi, 950 km[12]. Roads (1995): total length 22,121 mi, 35,600 km (paved 17%). Vehicles (1995): passenger cars 259,000; trucks and buses 132,940. Merchant marine (1992): vessels (100 gross tons and over) 24; total deadweight tonnage 8,368. Air transport (1995)[13]: passenger-mi 1,135,000,000, passenger-km 1,827,000,000; short-ton mi cargo 29,982,000, metric ton-km cargo 43,773,000; airports (1996) 14.

Communications

Medium	date	unit	number	units per 1,000 persons
Daily newspapers	1994	circulation	333,000	102
Radio	1996	receivers	760,000	224
Television	1995	receivers	340,000	102
Telephones	1995	main lines	557,200	167
Cellular telephones	1995	subscribers	18,700	5.6
Facsimile machines	1995	units	2,200	0.1

Education and health

Educational attainment (1996)[7]: Percentage of population age 5 and over having: no formal schooling 11.7%; incomplete pirmary education 28.5%; complete primary 25.8%; incomplete secondary 16.0%; complete secondary 9.0%; higher 8.5%; other/unknown 0.5%. *Literacy* (1995): total population age 15 and over literate 2,118,000 (94.8%); males literate 1,054,000 (94.7%); females literate 1,064,000 (95.0%).

Education (1995)

	schools	teachers	students	student/ teacher ratio
Primary (age 7–12)	3,544	15,806[14]	508,923	31.4[14]
Secondary (age 13–17)	285	...	207,231	...
Higher	29	...	79,959	...

Health (1996): physicians 4,422 (1 per 763 persons); hospital beds 5,961 (1 per 566 persons); infant mortality rate per 1,000 live births (1995) 13.3.
Food (1992): daily per capita caloric intake 2,883 (vegetable products 83%, animal products 17%); 129% of FAO recommended minimum requirement.

Military

Paramilitary expenditure as percentage of GNP (1995): 0.3% (world, n.a.); per capita expenditure U.S.$8. The army was officially abolished in 1948. Paramilitary (police) forces had 7,000 members in 1996.

[1]January 1. [2]Detail does not add to total given because of rounding. [3]Population of San José canton. [4]Within San José metropolitan area. [5]Includes 63,500 unemployed. [6]Data for July average of each year. [7]Based on a July 1996 survey. [8]Imports c.i.f.; exports f.o.b. [9]Based on 1993 data. [10]Based on 1994 data. [11]Estimated figures. [12]Rail service suspended in June 1995 because of a lack of funds. [13]Lacsa (Costa Rican Airlines) only. [14]1994.

Internet resources for further information:
• **Bienvenido a las paginas del Gobierno de Costa Rica**
http://www.casapres.go.cr/

Côte d'Ivoire

Official name: République de Côte d'Ivoire (Republic of Côte d'Ivoire [Ivory Coast][1]).
Form of government: multiparty republic with one legislative house (National Assembly [175]).
Chief of state: President.
Head of government: Prime Minister.
Capital: Abidjan (de facto; legislative).
Capital designate: Yamoussoukro (de jure; administrative).
Official language: French.
Official religion: none.
Monetary unit: 1 CFA franc (CFAF) = 100 centimes; valuation (Sept. 25, 1998) 1 U.S.$ = CFAF 560.38; 1 £ = CFAF 954.05.

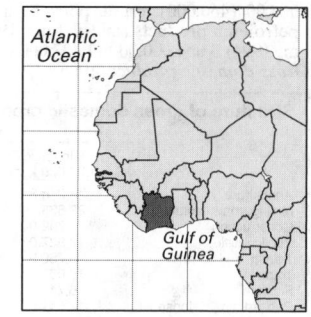

Area and population (1988 census)

Department	area sq km	population	Department	area sq km	population
Abengourou	5,200	216,058	Guiglo	11,220	170,321
Abidjan	8,550	2,485,847	Issia	3,590	195,663
Aboisso	6,250	225,895	Katiola	9,420	130,635
Adzopé	5,230	237,870	Korhogo	12,500	390,229
Agboville	3,850	203,493	Lakota	2,730	116,771
Agnibilékrou	1,700	84,349	Man	4,990	294,724
Bangolo	2,060	79,979	Mankono	10,660	123,362
Béoumi	2,820	90,327	M'bahiakro	5,460	102,531
Biankouma	4,950	98,236	Odiénné	20,600	169,764
Bondoukou	10,040	174,251	Oumé	2,400	141,268
Bongouanou	5,570	224,958	Sakassou	1,880	59,362
Bouaflé	3,980	165,822	San-Pédro	6,900	170,669
Bouaké	4,700	450,594	Sassandra	5,190	108,090
Bouna	21,470	135,813	Séguéla	11,240	121,235
Boundiali	7,895	127,847	Sinfra	1,690	121,903
Dabakala	9,670	81,820	Soubré	8,270	310,790
Daloa	5,450	359,753	Tabou	5,440	58,147
Danané	4,600	222,839	Tanda	6,490	204,070
Daoukro	3,610	86,494	Tengréla	2,200	54,847
Dimbokro	4,920	141,968	Tiassalé	3,370	133,708
Divo	7,920	387,106	Touba	8,720	107,886
Duékoué	2,930	102,168	Toumodi	2,780	80,802
Ferkessedougou	17,728	172,893	Vavoua	6,160	168,292
Gagnoa	4,500	276,217	Yamoussoukro	6,160	281,442
Grand-Lahou	2,280	52,559	Zuénoula	2,830	114,027
			TOTAL	320,763[2]	10,815,694

Demography

Population (1998): 15,446,000.
Density (1998): persons per sq mi 124.1, persons per sq km 47.9.
Urban-rural (1995): urban 43.6%; rural 56.4%.
Sex distribution (1993): male 50.77%; female 49.23%.
Age breakdown (1993): under 15, 48.8%; 15–29, 24.7%; 30–44, 14.1%; 45–59, 8.1%; 60–64, 1.7%; 65 and over, 2.6%.
Population projection: (2000) 16,190,000; (2010) 20,565,000.
Ethnolinguistic composition (1988)[3]: Akan 41.8%; Voltaic 16.3%; Malinke 15.9%; Kru 14.6%; Southern Mande 10.7%; other 0.7%.
Religious affiliation (1988): Muslim 38.7%; Catholic 20.8%; animist 17.0%; atheist 13.4%; Protestant 5.3%, excluding Harrism (1.4%); other 3.4%.
Major cities (1988): Abidjan (1990) 2,168,000; Bouaké 329,850; Daloa 121,842.

Vital statistics

Birth rate per 1,000 population (1990–95): 49.9 (world avg. 25.0).
Death rate per 1,000 population (1990–95): 15.1 (world avg. 9.3).
Natural increase rate per 1,000 population (1990–95): 34.8 (world avg. 15.7).
Total fertility rate (avg. births per childbearing woman; 1990–95): 7.4.
Life expectancy at birth (1990–95): male 49.7 years; female 52.4 years.
Major causes of death per 100,000 population: n.a.; however, AIDS was a major cause of both morbidity and mortality among adults in the mid-1990s.

National economy

Budget (1996). Revenue: CFAF 1,272,400,000 (current revenues 81.8%, principally (1995) import taxes and duties 22.8%, taxes on income, goods, and services 18.3%, export taxes 16.1%). Expenditures: CFAF 1,062,900,000,000 (wages and salaries 36.7%, debt service 30.1%; other 28.6%).
Production (metric tons except as noted). Agriculture, forestry, fishing (1996): yams 2,824,000[4], cassava 1,564,000[4], plantains 1,300,000[4], sugarcane 1,236,000[4], paddy rice 1,223,000[4], cacao beans 1,254,480, corn (maize) 552,000, palm oil 265,693, bananas 258,026, cotton seed 217,216; coconuts 213,000, coffee 195,981, rubber 79,299; livestock (number of live animals) 1,314,000 sheep, 1,277,000 cattle, 1,027,000 goats; roundwood (1995) 14,290,000 cu m; fish catch (1995) 70,526. Mining and quarrying (1994): gold 1,500 kg; diamonds 15,000 carats. Manufacturing (value added in CFAF '000,000,000; 1993): meat products 717, chemicals 357, cocoa and chocolate 275, leather products 275, fabricated metal products 191, photographic and optical goods 129, Energy production (consumption): electricity (kW-hr; 1995) 2,915,000,000 (2,140,000,000); crude petroleum (barrels; 1994) 2,441,000 (24,623,000); petroleum products (metric tons; 1994) 2,320,000 (2,306,000).
Household income and expenditure. Average household size (1988) 5.4; average annual income per household n.a.; sources of income: n.a.; expenditure (1992–93)[5]: food 48.0%, transportation 12.2%, clothing 10.1%, energy and water 8.5%, housing 7.8%, household equipment 3.4%.
Gross national product (1996): U.S.$9,434,000,000 (U.S.$660 per capita).

Structure of gross domestic product and labour force

	1995		1994	
	in value CFAF '000,000,000	% of total value	labour force	% of labour force
Agriculture	1,572.9	31.3	2,886,000	51.1
Manufacturing and mining	876.8	17.4		
Construction and public utilities	99.1	2.0	650,000	11.5
Transp. and commun.	362.9	7.2		
Trade	1,024.6	20.4		
Public admin., defense	442.2	8.8	2,112,000	37.4
Services	395.9	7.9		
Other (customs receipts)	257.0	5.1		
TOTAL	5,031.4	100.0[6]	5,648,000	100.0

Public debt (external, outstanding; 1996): U.S.$11,367,000,000.
Population economically active (1994): total 5,648,000; activity rate of total population 41.1% (participation rates: over ages 10, 64.3%; female 33.8%).

Price and earnings indexes (1990 = 100)

	1991	1992	1993	1994	1995	1996	1997
Consumer price index	101.7	106.0	108.3	136.5	156.0	159.9	168.9
Hourly earnings index[7]	100.0	100.0	100.0	100.0	110.0	110.0	...

Tourism (1995): receipts U.S.$72,000,000; expenditures U.S.$159,000,000.

Foreign trade

Balance of trade (current prices)

	1992	1993	1994	1995	1996	1997
CFAF '000,000,000	+138.53	+114.2	+457.9	+552.6	+711.8	+672.7
% of total	10.1%	8.7%	17.7%	16.7%	18.9%	16.5%

Imports (1995): CFAF 1,379,200,000,000 (food and food products 18.9%, crude and refined petroleum 17.0%, transport equipment 9.0%, plastics 4.7%, paper and paper products 4.7%, pharmaceuticals 4.5%, electrical equipment 4.1%). *Major import sources:* France 32.0%; Nigeria 19.6%; U.S. 5.9%; Ghana 4.0%; Germany 3.9%; Italy 3.8%.
Exports (1995): CFAF 1,931,800,000,000 (cocoa beans and products 33.5%, coffee and coffee products 11.0%, wood and wood products 9.3%, petroleum products 9.2%, fish products 6.5%, cotton and cotton cloth 4.4%). *Major export destinations:* France 18.1%; The Netherlands 8.3%; Germany 7.8%; Italy 7.6%; Mali 5.9%; Burkina Faso 5.0%.

Transport and communications

Transport. Railroads (1995): route length 639 km; passenger-km 129,000,000; metric ton-km cargo 58,000,000. Roads (1995): total length 50,160 km (paved 9.6%). Vehicles (1995): passenger cars 271,000; trucks and buses 150,000. Air transport (1996)[8]: passenger-km 224,736,000; metric ton-km cargo 16,420,000; airports (1997) 5.

Communications

Medium	date	unit	number	units per 1,000 persons
Daily newspapers	1995	circulation	198,000	13.9
Radio	1995	receivers	1,600,000	112
Television	1995	receivers	810,000	56.8
Telephones	1995	main lines	115,800	8.1

Education and health

Educational attainment (1988). Percentage of population age 6 and over having: no formal schooling 60.0%; Koranic school 3.6%; primary education 24.8%; secondary 10.7%; higher 0.9%. *Literacy* (1995): percentage of population age 15 and over literate 40.1%; males 49.9%; females 30.0%.

Education (1994–95)

	schools	teachers	students	student/teacher ratio
Primary (age 7–12)	7,185	36,058	1,609,929	44.6
Secondary (age 13–19)[9]	147	9,505	463,810	48.8
Vocational	...	1,424	11,037	7.8
Higher[10]	...		51,215	...

Health: physicians (1990) 1,020 (1 per 11,745 persons); hospital beds (1993) 7,928 (1 per 1,698 persons); infant mortality rate (1990–95) 92.0.
Food (1995): daily per capita caloric intake 2,517 (vegetable products 96%, animal products 4%); 109% of FAO recommended minimum requirement.

Military

Total active duty personnel (1997): 8,400 (army 81.0%, navy 10.7%, air force 8.3%). *Military expenditure as percentage of GNP* (1995): 1.1% (world avg. 2.8%); per capita expenditure U.S.$7.

[1]Since 1986, Côte d'Ivoire has requested that the French form of the country's name be used as the official protocol version in all languages. [2]Total area per more recent survey is 322,463 sq km; breakdown of that area by department is not available. [3]"Ivoirian" nationals only, representing about 65% of the de facto population. [4]1996. [5]Weights of consumer price index components for a worker's family living in the capital city. [6]Detail does not add to total given because of rounding. [7]January 1; index refers to the S.M.I.G. (*salaire minimum interprofessionel garanti*), a form of minimum professional wage. [8]Represents 1/11 share of traffic of Air Afrique, which is operated by 11 West African states. [9]Data exclude 208 private schools, with (1992) 107,096 students. [10]1993–94.

Internet resources for further information:
• Côte d'Ivoire—A Country Study
http://lcweb2.loc.gov/frd/cs/citoc.html

Croatia

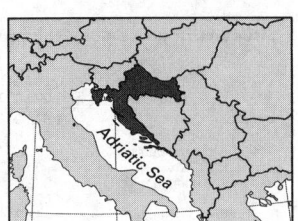

Official name: Republika Hrvatska (Republic of Croatia).
Form of government: multiparty republic with a two-chambered legislature (House of Zupanije[1] [68[2]]; House of Representatives [127[3]]).
Head of state: President.
Head of government: Prime Minister.
Capital: Zagreb.
Official language: Croatian (Serbo-Croatian).
Official religion: none.
Monetary unit: 1 kuna (plural kune)[4] = 100 lipa; valuation (Sept. 25, 1998) 1 U.S.$ = 6.13 kune; 1 £ = 10.44 kune.

Area and population (1991 census)		area		population
				1991
City	Capitals	sq mi	sq km	census
Zagreb	—	497	1,288	867,717
County				
Bjelovar-Bilogora	Bjelovar	1,019	2,640	144,042
Dubrovnik-Neretva	Dubrovnikvn	689	1,784	126,329
Istria	Pazin	1,087	2,815	204,346
Karlovac	Karlovac	1,278	3,311	174,105
Koprivnica-Križevci	Koprimica	688	1,783	129,907
Krapina-Zagorje	Krapina	477	1,235	149,534
Lika-Senj	Gospić	1,447	3,748	71,215
Medimurje	Čakovec	282	730	119,866
Osijek-Baranja	Osijek	1,397	3,619	331,979
Požega-Slavonija	Požega	917	2,374	134,548
Primorje-Gorski Kotar	Rijeka	1,381	3,578	323,130
Šibenik	Šibenik	722	1,871	109,171
Sisak-Moslavina	Sisak	1,976	5,117	287,002
Slavonski Brod-Posavina	Slavonski Brod	782	2,026	174,998
Split-Dalmatia	Split	1,745	4,520	474,019
Varaždin	Varaždin	478	1,238	187,343
Virovitica-Podravina	Virovitica	798	2,068	104,625
Vukovar-Srijem	Vukovar	943	2,442	231,241
Zadar-Knin	Zadar	2,453	6,352	272,003
Zagreb	Zagreb	800	2,071	167,145
TOTAL		**21,856**	**56,610**	**4,784,265**

Demography

Population (1998): 4,672,000.
Density (1997): persons per sq mi 213.8, persons per sq km 82.5.
Urban-rural (1991): urban 54.2%; rural 45.8%.
Sex distribution (1991): male 48.50%; female 51.50%.
Age breakdown (1991): under 15, 19.4%; 15–29, 20.7%; 30–44, 22.7%; 45–59, 18.3%; 60–74, 12.9%; 75 and over, 4.5%; not stated 1.5%.
Population projection: (2000) 4,681,000; (2010) 4,634,000.
Ethnic composition (1991): Croat 78.1%; Serb 12.1%; Muslims 0.9%; Hungarians 0.5%; Slovene 0.5%; other 7.9%.
Religious affiliation (1997): Roman Catholic 72.1%; Eastern Orthodox 14.1%; Muslim 1.3%; other 12.5%.
Major cities (1991): Zagreb 867,717; Split 200,459; Rijeka 167,964.

Vital statistics

Birth rate per 1,000 population (1995): 10.5 (world avg. 25.0); (1994) legitimate 92.4%; illegitimate 7.6%.
Death rate per 1,000 population (1995): 10.6 (world avg. 9.3).
Natural increase rate per 1,000 population (1995): –0.1 (world avg. 15.7).
Total fertility rate (avg. births per childbearing woman; 1993): 1.5.
Marriage rate per 1,000 population (1994): 5.3.
Divorce rate per 1,000 population (1994): 1.0.
Life expectancy at birth (1991): male 68.6 years; female 76.0 years.
Major causes of death per 100,000 population (1993): diseases of the circulatory system 533.2; cancers 218.0; accidents, violence, and poisoning 95.0; diseases of the digestive system 49.7; diseases of the respiratory system 45.3.

National economy

Budget (1996). Revenue: 31,085,318,000 kune[4] (sales tax 63.2%, customs and import fees 15.6%, income tax 14.2%). Expenditures: 31,621,691,000 kune[4] (defense 36.6%, social insurance 13.8%, education 11.7%).
Land use (1994): forest 37.1%; pasture 19.3%; agriculture 21.6%; other 22.0%.
Population economically active (1991): total 2,040,000; activity rate 42.6% (participation rates: ages 15–64, 57.2%; female 42.8%; unemployed 11.2%).

Price and earnings indexes (1992 = 100)						
	1992	1993	1994	1995	1996	1997
Consumer price index	100.0	1,583.3	3,284.4	3,413.6	3,561.2	3,708.4
Annual earnings index	100.0	1,605.2	3,734.2	5,453.2	6,092.3	7,124.3

Production (metric tons except as noted). Agriculture, forestry, fishing (1996): corn (maize) 1,883,000, sugar beets 906,000, wheat 741,000, potatoes 665,000, grapes 373,000, barley 88,000, plums 38,215; livestock (number of live animals) 1,196,000 pigs, 462,000 cattle, 427,000 sheep; roundwood 2,912,000 cu m; fish catch (1995) 31,533. Mining and quarrying (1995): lime 150,000; gypsum 50,000. Manufacturing (value added in U.S.$'000,000; 1996): food products 895; transport equipment 425; electrical machinery 362; textiles 285; wearing apparel 260. Construction (value in kune; 1994): residential 1,966,315; nonresidential 4,590,289. Energy production (consumption): electricity (kW-hr; 1994) 8,275,000,000 (11,840,000,000); coal (metric tons; 1994

96,000 (460,000); crude petroleum (barrels; 1994) 11,559,000 (37,280,000); petroleum products (metric tons; 1994) 4,462,000 (3,148,000); natural gas (cu m; 1994) 3,054,000,000 (1,427,000,000).
Gross domestic product (1996): U.S.$18,130,000,000 (U.S.$3,800 per capita).

Structure of gross domestic product and labour force				
	1994		1991	
	in value '000,000 kune[4]	% of total value	labour force	% of labour force
Agriculture	9,248.8	11.0	265,000	13.0
Mining, manufacturing	23,538.1	28.0	613,000	30.0
Construction	1,792.0	2.1	98,000	4.8
Public utilities	12,927.0	15.4	32,700	1.6
Transp. and commun.	3,750.9	4.5	120,000	5.9
Trade	10,057.3	12.0	163,000	8.0
Finance	6,741.0	8.0	60,400	3.0
Pub. admin., defense	12,541.6	15.0	315,000	15.4
Services	3,327.8	4.0	80,700	4.0
Other			292,200[5]	14.3[5]
TOTAL	83,924.5	100.0	2,040,000	100.0

Household income and expenditure. Average household size (1991) 3.1; income per household (1990) Din 165,813[4] (U.S.$14,650); sources (1990): self-employment 40.8%, wages 40.2%, transfers 12.1%, other 6.9%; expenditure (1988): food 34.2%, transportation 9.3%, clothing 8.6%, housing 8.3%, energy 7.6%, drink and tobacco 5.1%, durable goods 4.5%, health care 4.3%.

Foreign trade[6]

Balance of trade (current prices)[7]						
	1991	1992	1993	1994	1995	1996
'000,000 kune[4]	–7,160	–3,877	–1,636	–3,604	–5,962	–3,276
% of total	7.8%	2.2%	5.5%	10.0%	18.7%	26.6%

Imports (1996): U.S.$7,787,000,000 (1994; machinery and transport equipment 25.9%; products classified by constituent material 15.2%; miscellaneous ready-made products 14.6%; mineral fuels, lubricants, and similar products 11.8%; chemical products 10.4%; food and live animals 9.5%; raw materials except fuel 2.9%; beverages and tobacco 1.2%). *Major import sources:* Germany 20.6%; Italy 18.3%; Slovenia 9.9%; Austria 7.7%.
Exports (1996): U.S.$4,512,000,000 (1994; miscellaneous ready-made products 29.0%; machinery and transport equipment 17.5%; products classified according to constituent material 15.2%; chemical products 12.9%; mineral fuels, lubricants, and similar products 9.3%; food and live animals 9.3%; raw materials except fuel 5.0%; beverages and tobacco 1.6%). *Major export destinations:* Italy 21.0%; Germany 18.6%; Slovenia 13.5%; Bosnia 12.2%.

Transport and communications

Transport. Railroads (1994): length 2,699 km; passenger-km 962,000,000; metric ton-km cargo 1,563,000,000. Roads (1995): total length 26,929 km (paved 82%). Vehicles (1994): passenger cars 698,391; trucks and buses 53,860. Merchant marine (1994): cargo ships 155. Air transport (1997): passenger-km 563,000,000; metric ton-km cargo 2,268,000; airports (1997) 4.

Communications				units per 1,000
Medium	date	unit	number	persons
Daily newspapers	1995	circulation	2,600,000	575
Radio	1996	receivers	1,100,000	230
Television	1995	receivers	1,100,000	230
Telephones	1995	main lines	1,287,000	269
Cellular telephones	1995	subscribers	34,000	7.1
Facsimile machines	1995	units	38,000	8.0
Personal computers	1995	units	100,000	21

Education and health

Educational attainment (1991). Percentage of population age 15 and over having: no schooling or unknown 10.1%; less than full primary education 21.2%; primary 23.4%; secondary 36.0%; postsecondary and higher 9.3%. *Literacy* (1991): population age 15 and over literate 96.7%; males 98.8%; females 94.8%.

Education (1994–95)				student/
	schools	teachers	students	teacher ratio
Primary (age 7–14)	1,928	24,194	431,795	17.8
Secondary (age 15–18)	482	15,269	196,740	12.9
Voc., teacher tr.	3	79	2,660	33.7
Higher	61	5,814	77,525	13.3

Health (1994): physicians 9,138 (1 per 524 persons); hospital beds 28,230 (1 per 169 persons); (1995) infant mortality rate per 1,000 live births 8.9.

Military

Total active duty personnel (1997): 58,000 (army 86.2%, navy 5.2%, air force and air defense 8.6%). *Military expenditure as percentage of GNP* (1995): 5.0% (world 2.8%).

[1]Translated as communes or municipalities. [2]Includes 5 nonelective seats. [3]Includes 12 seats reserved for Croatians abroad. [4]On Jan. 1, 1990, the Yugoslav new dinar (Din), equal to 10,000 Yugoslav old dinars (Din), was introduced. On Dec. 23, 1991, the Croatian dinar (HrD) was introduced at parity with the Yugoslav new dinar, which it replaced as Croatia's official currency. On May 30, 1994, the kuna, equal to 1,000 Croatian dinars, was introduced. [5]Includes unemployed and private sector. [6]Import figures are f.o.b. in balance of trade and c.i.f. for commodities and trading partners. [7]Balance of trade recalculated to reflect currency changes.

Internet resources for further information:
• **Central Bureau of Statistics** http://www.dzs.hr/Eng/Default.htm

Cuba

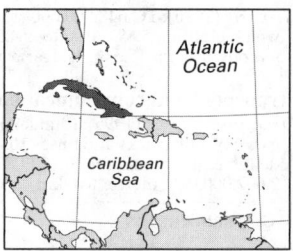

Official name: República de Cuba (Republic of Cuba).
Form of government: unitary socialist republic with one legislative house (National Assembly of the People's Power [601]).
Head of state and government: President.
Capital: Havana.
Official language: Spanish.
Official religion: none.
Monetary unit: 1 Cuban peso (CUP) = 100 centavos; valuation (Sept. 25, 1998) 1 U.S.$ = 23.00 CUP[1]; 1 £ = 39.16 CUP.

Area and population

Provinces	Capitals	area sq mi	area sq km	population 1990[2] estimate
Camagüey	Camagüey	6,174	15,990	744,744
Ciego de Avila	Ciego de Avila	2,668	6,910	367,489
Cienfuegos	Cienfuegos	1,613	4,178	366,531
Ciudad de la Habana[3]	—	281	727	2,107,557
Granma	Bayamo	3,232	8,372	793,868
Guantánamo	Guantánamo	2,388	6,186	499,182
Holguín	Holguín	3,591	9,301	997,735
La Habana[4]	Havana	2,213	5,731	647,280
Las Tunas	Las Tunas	2,544	6,589	495,133
Matanzas	Matanzas	4,625	11,978	612,268
Pinar del Río	Pinar del Río	4,218	10,925	694,306
Sancti Spíritus	Sancti Spíritus	2,604	6,744	430,662
Santiago de Cuba	Santiago de Cuba	2,382	6,170	995,370
Villa Clara	Santa Clara	3,345	8,662	810,249
Special municipality				
Isla de la Juventud	Nueva Gerona	926	2,398	73,319
TOTAL		42,804	110,861	10,635,693[5]

Demography

Population (1998): 11,116,000.
Density (1998): persons per sq mi 259.7, persons per sq km 100.3.
Urban-rural (1995): urban 76.0%; rural 24.0%.
Sex distribution (1994): male 50.20%; female 49.80%.
Age breakdown (1994): under 15, 22.8%; 15–29, 28.0%; 30–44, 21.8%; 45–59, 15.2%; 60–74, 8.4%; 75 and over, 3.8%.
Population projection: (2000) 11,201,000; (2010) 11,516,000.
Ethnic composition (1994): mixed 51.0%; white 37.0%; black 11.0%; other 1.0%.
Religious affiliation (1995): nonreligious 57.9%; Roman Catholic 39.5%; Protestant 2.4%; other 0.2%.
Major cities (1993): Havana 2,175,995; Santiago de Cuba 440,084; Camagüey 293,961; Holguín 242,085; Guantánamo 207,796.

Vital statistics

Birth rate per 1,000 population (1997): 13.2 (world avg. 25.0).
Death rate per 1,000 population (1997): 7.4 (world avg. 9.3).
Natural increase rate per 1,000 population (1997): 5.8 (world avg. 15.7).
Total fertility rate (avg. births per childbearing woman; 1997): 1.5.
Marriage rate per 1,000 population (1992): 17.7.
Divorce rate per 1,000 population (1993): 6.0.
Life expectancy at birth (1997): male 72.8 years; female 77.7 years.
Major causes of death per 100,000 population (1992): heart disease 173.4; malignant neoplasms (cancers) 115.5; cerebrovascular disease 60.9; accidents 45.8; diseases of the blood vessels 23.5; influenza and pneumonia 22.7.

National economy

Budget (1990). Revenue: CUP 12,463,200,000. Expenditures: CUP 14,448,400,000 (capital investment 37.7%; education and public health 20.4%; social, cultural, and scientific activities 17.3%; defense, internal security 9.5%).
Production (metric tons except as noted). Agriculture, forestry, fishing (1996): sugarcane 40,000,000, potatoes 364,000, oranges and tangerines 291,000, grapefruit 261,000, bananas and plantains 260,000, cassava 250,000, rice 223,000; livestock (number of live animals) 4,650,000 cattle, 1,500,000 pigs, 19,000,000 chickens; roundwood (1995) 3,152,000 cu m; fish catch (1995) 93,435. Mining and quarrying (1996): nickel 50,000; chromite 30,000. Manufacturing (value added in U.S.$'000,000; 1990): tobacco products 2,629; food products 1,033; beverages 358; chemical products 354; transport equipment 225; nonelectrical machinery 176. Construction (gross value of construction in CUP '000,000; 1989): residential 227; nonresidential 872. Energy production (consumption): electricity (kW-hr; 1996) 8,654,000,000 (8,654,000,000); coal (metric tons; 1994) none (153,000); crude petroleum (barrels; 1994) 6,552,000 (38,326,000); petroleum products (metric tons; 1994) 4,456,000 (7,905,000); natural gas (cu m; 1994) 39,004,000 (39,004,000).
Public debt (external, outstanding; 1996): U.S.$12,000,000,000.
Household income and expenditure. Average household size (1990) 3.7; average annual income per household (1982) CUP 3,680 (U.S.$4,330); sources of income (1982): wages and salaries 57.3%, bonuses and other payments 42.7%; personal consumption (1989): food 26.7%, other retail purchases 60.5%, transportation services 5.4%, energy 2.7%, value of self-produced and consumed food 1.5%, household repairs 1.3%, other 1.9%.
Population economically active (1988): total 4,570,236; activity rate of total population 43.7% (participation rates: over age 15, 56.9%; female 36.1%; unemployed 60.%).

Price and earnings indexes (1985 = 100)

	1983	1984	1985	1986	1987	1988	1989
Implicit consumer price deflator index	94.9	98.0	100.0	101.4	102.8	103.1	...
Monthly earnings index[6]	95.9	99.0	100.0	100.1	98.1	99.6	100.0

Tourism: receipts from visitors (1995) U.S.$1,100,000,000; expenditures by nationals abroad (1990) U.S.$48,000,000.
Gross national product (1996): U.S.$12,892,000,000 (U.S.$1,170 per capita).

Structure of gross domestic product and labour force

	1994 in value[7] CUP '000,000	1994 % of total value	1989 labour force[6]	1989 % of labour force
Agriculture	879.4	6.8	721,100	20.4
Mining	97.5	0.8		
Manufacturing	3,340.6	26.0	767,500	21.8
Public utilities	350.0	2.7		
Construction	383.9	3.0	344,300	9.8
Transp. and commun.	708.7	5.5	235,900	6.7
Finance, insurance	492.4	3.8	21,700	0.6
Trade	2,935.2	22.8	395,300	11.2
Public administration	—	—	151,700	4.3
Services	3,680.6	28.6	835,700	23.7
Other	—	—	53,400	1.5
TOTAL	12,868.3[8]	100.0	3,526,600	100.0

Land use (1994): forested 23.7%; meadows and pastures 27.0%; agricultural and under permanent cultivation 30.7%; other 18.6%.

Foreign trade[9]

Balance of trade (current prices)

	1991	1992	1993	1994	1995	1996
U.S.$'000,000	−1,332	−412	−551	−797	−1,166	−1,179
% of total	38.4%	15.1%	19.2%	24.4%	28.3%	24.4%

Imports (1996): U.S.$3,010,000,000 (1992; mineral fuels and lubricants 39.4%, food and live animals 25.4%, machinery and transport equipment 15.8%, chemicals 6.9%, basic manufactures 6.6%, inedible crude materials 3.2%). *Major import sources:* Spain 17.0%; Russia 16.9%; Mexico 11.6%; France 7.2%; Canada 6.2%; Argentina 4.5%.
Exports (1996): U.S.$1,831,000,000 (1992; sugar 63.4%, minerals and concentrates 10.6%, fish products 5.9%, raw tobacco and tobacco products 4.6%, citrus and other agricultural products 3.4%). *Major export destinations:* Russia 20.2%; Canada 16.1%; The Netherlands 11.1%; China 6.8%.

Transport and communications

Transport. Railroads (1994): length 2,987 mi, 4,807 km; passenger-km 2,347,000,000; metric ton-km cargo 645,000,000. Roads (1986): total length 28,928 mi, 46,555 km (paved 27%). Vehicles (1988): passenger cars 241,300; trucks and buses 208,400. Air transport (1996): passenger-km 3,450,000,000; metric ton-km cargo 56,300,000; airports with scheduled flights (1997) 14.

Communications

Medium	date	unit	number	units per 1,000 persons
Daily newspapers	1995	circulation	1,315,000	122
Radio	1995	receivers	3,608,000	327
Television	1995	receivers	2,200,000	200
Telephones	1995	main lines	353,200	32
Cellular telephones	1995	subscribers	1,900	0.2
Facsimile machines	1995	units	400	0.1

Education and health

Educational attainment (1981). Percentage of population age 25 and over having: no formal schooling or some primary education 39.6%; completed primary 26.6%; secondary 29.6%; higher 4.2%. *Literacy* (1995 est.): total population age 15 and over literate 95.7%; males literate 96.2%; females literate 95.3%.

Education (1995–96)

	schools	teachers	students	student/ teacher ratio
Primary (age 6–11)	9,862	90,565	1,074,153	11.9
Secondary (age 12–17)	2,175[10]	46,772	460,348	9.8
Voc., teacher tr.	618[10]	27,267	244,253	9.0
Higher	35[10]	22,967	122,346	5.3

Health (1992): physicians 46,860 (1 per 231 persons); hospital beds 80,684 (1 per 134 persons); infant mortality rate per 1,000 live births (1997) 7.3.
Food (1995): daily per capita caloric intake 2,291 (vegetable products 84%, animal products 16%); 99% of FAO recommended minimum requirement.

Military

Total active duty personnel (1997): 60,000 (army 75.0%, navy 8.3%, air force 16.7%). *Military expenditure as percentage of GDP* (1995): 1.6% (world 2.8%); per capita expenditure: U.S.$32.

---

[1]Exchange house rate. [2]January 1. [3]Province coextensive with the city of Havana. [4]Province bordering the city of Havana on the east, south, and west. [5]The 1993 census total was 10,900,000; detail, n.a. [6]State sector only; excludes military and unemployed. [7]At constant 1981 prices. [8]At factor cost. [9]Imports c.i.f.; exports f.o.b. [10]1989–90.

Internet resources for further information:
• CubaNet http://www.cubanet.org/

Cyprus

Island of Cyprus

Area: 3,572 sq mi, 9,251 sq km.
Population (1998): 861,000[1].

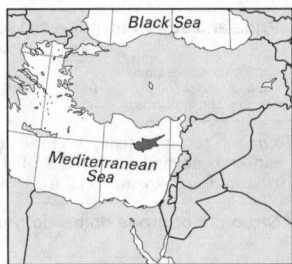

Two de facto states currently exist on the island of Cyprus: the Republic of Cyprus (ROC), predominantly Greek in character, occupying the southern two-thirds of the island, which is the original and still the internationally recognized de jure government of the whole island; and the Turkish Republic of Northern Cyprus (TRNC), proclaimed unilaterally Nov. 15, 1983, on territory originally secured for the Turkish Cypriot population by the July 20, 1974, intervention of Turkey. Only Turkey recognizes the TRNC, and the two ethnic communities have failed to reestablish a single state. Provision of separate data below does not imply recognition of either state's claims but is necessitated by the continuing lack of unified data.

Republic of Cyprus

Official name: Kipriakí Dimokratía (Greek); Kıbrıs Cumhuriyeti (Turkish) (Republic of Cyprus).
Form of government: unitary multiparty republic with a unicameral legislature (House of Representatives [80[2]]).
Head of state and government: President.
Capital: Lefkosia (Nicosia).
Official languages: Greek; Turkish.
Monetary unit: 1 Cyprus pound (£C) = 100 cents; valuation (Sept. 25, 1998) 1 £C = U.S.$2.04 = £1.20.

Demography

Area[3]: 2,276 sq mi, 5,896 sq km.
Population (1998): 673,000[4].
Urban-rural (1996[5]): urban 68.5%; rural 31.5%.
Age breakdown (1994[5]): under 15, 25.3%; 15–29, 21.8%; 30–44, 22.4%; 45–59, 15.6%; 60–74, 10.2%; 75 and over, 4.7%.
Ethnic composition (1992): Greek Cypriot 95.1%; British 0.8%; other 4.1%.
Religious affiliation (1995): Cypriot Orthodox 92.0%; Maronite 1.3%; other 6.7%.
Urban areas (1994[5]): Lefkosia 186,400[6]; Limassol 143,400; Larnaca 64,000.

Vital statistics

Birth rate per 1,000 population (1995): 15.4 (world avg. 25.0).
Death rate per 1,000 population (1995): 7.7 (world avg. 9.3).
Natural increase rate per 1,000 population (1995): 7.7 (world avg. 15.7).
Life expectancy at birth (1994–95): male 75.3 years; female 79.8 years.

National economy

Budget (1995). Revenue: £C 1,270,800,000 (indirect taxes 39.2%, direct taxes 25.4%, social security contributions 20.1%). Expenditures: £C 1,310,700,000 (current expenditures 87.9%, development expenditures 11.7%).
Tourism (1996): receipts U.S.$1,679,000,000; expenditures U.S.$340,000,000.
Household expenditure (1992): food and beverages 22.7%, transportation and communications 15.6%, expenditures in cafes and hotels 13.6%.
Gross national product (1996): U.S.$8,926,000,000 (U.S.$13,720 per capita).

Structure of gross domestic product and labour force

| | 1996 | | | |
	in value £C '000,000	% of total value	labour force	% of labour force
Agriculture	179.5	4.4	30,000	9.8
Mining	12.4	0.3	800	0.3
Manufacturing	464.0	11.3	43,300	14.1
Construction	354.0	8.6	25,200	8.2
Public utilities	89.8	2.2	1,500	0.5
Transp. and commun.	337.0	8.2	19,200	6.2
Trade	781.6	19.1	76,900	25.0
Finance, insurance	702.9	17.1	23,300	7.6
Pub. admin., defense	537.3	13.1	} 64,400	21.0
Services	341.6	8.3 }		
Other	301.2	7.4	22,400[7]	7.3[7]
TOTAL	4,101.3	100.0	307,000	100.0

Production. Agriculture (value of production in £C '000,000; 1993): milk 27.9, potatoes 24.1, poultry 24.1, barley 21.8, pork 20.0, grapes 15.6. Manufacturing (value added in £C '000,000; 1994): food 66.8; wearing apparel 44.4; cement, bricks, and tiles 41.7; beverages 41.3; cigarettes and cigars 30.8. Energy production: electricity (kW-hr; 1995) 2,473,000,000.

Foreign trade[8]

Imports (1996): £C 1,857,500,000 (consumer goods 33.1%; transport equipment 10.2%; capital goods 9.2%; mineral fuels 8.4%). *Major import sources:* U.S. 16.8%; U.K. 11.2%; Italy 9.2%; Greece 7.2%; Germany 7.1%.

Exports (1996): £C 648,900,000 (reexports 57.9%[9]; domestic exports 34.1%, of which clothing 5.8%, potatoes 4.3%; ships' stores 8.0%). *Major export destinations:* Russia 17.5%, Bulgaria 15.1%; U.K. 10.4%; Greece 5.8%.

Transport and communications

Transport. Roads (1995): total length 10,150 km (paved 57%). Vehicles (1995): cars 219,749; trucks and buses 103,852. Merchant marine (1992): vessels 1,416; deadweight tonnage 36,198,083. Air transport (1995)[10]: passenger-km 2,667,000,000; metric ton-km cargo 36,187,000; airports (1996) 2.

Communications

Medium	date	unit	number	units per 1,000 persons
Daily newspapers	1995	circulation	86,700	135
Radio	1995	receivers	184,000	287
Television	1995	receivers	102,500	160
Telephones	1995	main lines	347,300	541
Cellular telephones	1995	subscribers	44,500	69
Facsimile machines	1995	units	7,000	11

Education and health

Educational attainment (1992). Percentage of population age 25 and over having: no formal schooling 5.1%; higher education 17.0%. *Literacy* (1992): population age 15 and over literate 95.2%; male 97.8%; female 92.8%.

Education (1994–95)

	schools	teachers	students	student/ teacher ratio
Primary (age 6–11)	383	3,498	64,884	18.5
Secondary (age 12–17)	107	3,832	53,738	14.0
Vocational	11	509	4,066	8.0
Higher	32	648	7,765	12.0

Health (1993): physicians 1,455 (1 per 433 persons); hospital beds 3,297 (1 per 191 persons); infant mortality rate per 1,000 live births (1995) 9.0.

Internet resources for further information:
• **The Cyprus Government** http://www.pio.gov.cy/
• **Central Bank of Cyprus** http://www.centralbank.gov.cy/cyprus/index.html

Turkish Republic of Northern Cyprus

Official name: Kuzey Kıbrıs Türk Cumhuriyeti (Turkish) (Turkish Republic of Northern Cyprus).
Capital: Lefkoşa (Nicosia).
Official language: Turkish.
Monetary unit: 1 Turkish lira (LT) = 100 kurush; valuation (Sept. 25, 1998) 1 U.S.$ = LT 276,485; 1 £ = LT 470,716.
Population (1998): 188,000[1] (Lefkoşa 39,973[11, 12]; Gazimağusa 27,742[11, 12]).
Ethnic composition (1993): Turkish 98.6%; other 1.4%.

Structure of gross domestic product and labour force

| | 1995 | | 1994 | |
	in value LT '000,000,000	% of total value	labour force	% of labour force
Agriculture and fishing	3,530	10.2	17,738	23.2
Mining and manufacturing	3,168	9.1	8,207	10.7
Construction	1,291	3.7 }	9,584	12.5
Public utilities	1,353	3.9 }		
Transp. and commun.	3,006	8.7	6,228	8.1
Trade, restaurants	6,455	18.6	8,004	10.5
Pub. admin.	7,156	20.6	16,589	21.7
Finance, real estate }				
Services }	6,398	18.4	9,460	12.4
Other	2,361[13]	6.8[13]	704[14]	0.9[14]
TOTAL	34,718	100.0	76,514	100.0

Budget (1995). Revenue: U.S.$293,300,000 (domestic sources 62.0%, loans 28.5%, aid from Turkey 9.5%). Expenditures: U.S.$293,300,000 (current expenditures 88.3%).
Imports (1995): U.S.$366,100,000 (machinery and transport equipment 16.5%, food 10.9%). *Major import sources:* Turkey 53.2%; U.K. 13.5%.
Exports (1995): U.S.$67,300,000 (ready-made garments 35.4%, citrus fruits 32.8%). *Major export destinations:* U.K. 35.4%; Turkey 30.0%.

Education (1995–96)

	schools	teachers	students	student/ teacher ratio
Primary (age 7–11)	92	1,055	15,524	14.7
Secondary (age 12–17)	41	816	11,511	14.1
Vocational	10	342	1,969	5.8
Higher	7	...	17,375	...

Health (1995): physicians 272 (1 per 667 persons); hospital beds 902 (1 per 201 persons); infant mortality rate per 1,000 live births 4.9.

Internet resources for further information:
• **Turkish Republic of Northern Cyprus** http://www.cypnet.com/.ncyprus/root.html

[1]Includes 50,000 "settlers" from Turkey and 35,000 Turkish military in the TRNC; excludes 3,900 British military in the Sovereign Base Areas (SBA) in the ROC and 1,100 UN peacekeeping forces. [2]Twenty-four seats reserved for Turkish Cypriots are not occupied. [3]Area includes 99 sq mi (256 sq km) of British military SBA and c. 107 sq mi (c. 278 sq km) of the UN Buffer Zone. [4]Excludes British and UN military forces. [5]January 1. [6]ROC only. [7]Includes 9,400 unemployed. [8]Imports c.i.f.; exports f.o.b. [9]Mainly cigarettes and consumer electronics. [10]Cyprus Airways. [11]Preliminary figures. [12]1996. [13]Customs duties. [14]Unemployed.

Czech Republic

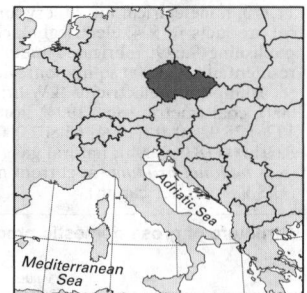

Official name: Česká Republika.
Form of government: unitary multiparty republic with two legislative houses (Senate [81[1]]; Chamber of Deputies [200]).
Chief of state: President.
Head of government: Prime Minister.
Capital: Prague.
Official language: Czech.
Official religion: none.
Monetary unit[2]: 1 koruna (Kč) = 100 halura; valuation (Sept. 25, 1998) 1 U.S.$ = 29.97 Kč 1 £ = 51.02 Kč

Area and population

Regions	Capitals	area sq mi	area sq km	population 1996[3] estimate
Jižny Čechy	České Budějovice	4,381	11,346	700,831
Jižní Morava	Brno	5,802	15,028	2,057,239
Severní Čechy	Ústí nad Labem	3,011	7,799	1,178,208
Severní Morava	Ostrava	4,273	11,068	1,972,336
Střední Čechy	Prague	4,253	11,014	1,106,738
Východní Čechy	Hradec Králové	4,340	11,240	1,235,641
Zapadní Čechy	Plzeň	4,199	10,875	860,496
Capital city				
Prague	—	192	496	1,209,855
TOTAL		30,450[4]	78,866	10,321,344

Demography

Population (1998): 10,302,000.
Density (1998): persons per sq mi 338.3, persons per sq km 130.6.
Urban-rural: n.a.
Sex distribution (1995): male 48.60%; female 51.40%.
Age breakdown (1995): under 15, 18.3%; 15–29, 23.3%; 30–44, 21.1%; 45–59, 19.3%; 60–74, 13.4%; 75 and over, 4.6%.
Population projection: (2000) 10,290,000; (2010) 10,464,000.
Doubling time: not applicable; population is declining.
Ethnic composition (1991): Czech 81.2%; Moravian 13.2%; Slovak 3.1%; Polish 0.6%; German 0.5%; Silesian 0.4%; Gypsy 0.3%; Hungarian 0.2%; Ukrainian 0.1%; other 0.4%.
Religious affiliation (1991): Roman Catholic 39.0%; Protestant 4.3%, of which Czechoslovak Brethren Reformed 2.0%, Czechoslovak Hussite 1.7%, Silesian Evangelical 0.3%; Eastern Orthodox 0.2%; Greek Catholic 0.1%; other Christian 0.3%; undenominational 39.9%; other 16.2%.
Major cities (1996): Prague 1,210,000; Brno 388,900; Ostrava 324,800; Plzeň 171,200; Olomouc 104,800.

Vital statistics

Birth rate per 1,000 population (1996): 8.8 (world avg. 25.0); (1995) legitimate 84.4%; illegitimate 15.6%.
Death rate per 1,000 population (1996): 10.9 (world avg. 9.3).
Natural increase rate per 1,000 population (1996): –2.1 (world avg. 15.7).
Total fertility rate (avg. births per childbearing woman; 1995): 1.4.
Marriage rate per 1,000 population (1996): 5.2.
Divorce rate per 1,000 population (1996): 3.2.
Life expectancy at birth (1995): male 70.0 years; female 76.9 years.
Major causes of death per 100,000 population (1995): diseases of the circulatory system 638.4; malignant neoplasms (cancers) 277.1; accidents, poisoning, and violence 82.3; diseases of the respiratory system 49.1; diseases of the digestive system 41.9; diseases of the genitourinary system 15.3.

National economy

Budget (1996). Revenue: Kč 482,800,000,000[2] (taxes 55.6%, of which value-added tax 22.6%, consumer tax 12.7%, income tax 10.1%, external trade tax 4.1%, other taxes 6.1%; social security 36.1%; other revenue 8.3%). Expenditures: Kč 484,400,000,000[2] (current expenditures 83.2%, of which social security 31.2%, subsidies to organizations 26.1%, defense 9.7%, enterprise subsidies 5.6%, health care 3.6%, education 3.5%, transfers to local budgets 3.5%; capital expenditures 11.8%; other 5.0%).
Public debt (external, outstanding; 1996): U.S.$12,017,000,000.
Production (metric tons except as noted). Agriculture, forestry, fishing (1996): cereals 6,683,000 (of which wheat 3,732,000, barley 2,305,000, rye 220,000, corn [maize] 143,000), sugar beets 4,317,000, potatoes 1,758,000; livestock (number of live animals) 4,016,000 pigs, 1,989,000 cattle, 26,600,000 poultry; roundwood (1995) 12,060,000 cu m; fish catch (1995) 22,579. Mining and quarrying (1996): limestone 13,100; kaolin 3,320. Manufacturing (value of production in Kč '000,000[2]; 1995): machinery and transport equipment 71,885; metal products 49,076; food products 36,568; chemical products 17,786; textiles 16,262. Construction (value in Kč '000,000[2]; 1994): residential 6,889; nonresidential 26,416. Energy production (consumption): electricity (kW-hr; 1994) 58,705,000,000 (58,260,000,000); coal (metric tons; 1994) 10,886,000 (6,907,000); crude petroleum (barrels; 1994) 938,000 (48,312,000); petroleum products (metric tons; 1994) 4,384,000 (5,514,000); natural gas (cu m; 1994) 242,000,000 (7,339,000,000).
Household income and expenditure. Average household size (1996) 2.9; income per household (1996) Kč 243,043[2] (U.S.$8,942); sources of income (1996[3]): wages and salaries 66.7%, transfer payments 27.6%, other 5.7%; expenditure (1996): food and beverages 25.6%, housing and utilities 11.3%, household durable goods 7.3%, clothing and footwear 7.2%, other 48.6%.

Population economically active (1997): total 5,469,500; activity rate of total population 53.0% (participation rates: [1996] ages 15–59 [male], 15–54 [female] 96.6%; female 44.0%; [1996] unemployed 3.1%).

Price and earnings indexes (1991 = 100)

	1991	1992	1993	1994	1995	1996	1997
Consumer price index	100.0	102.4	123.8	136.2	148.6	161.7	175.4
Annual earnings index	100.0	109.2	151.8	180.0	213.3	252.0	279.2

Gross national product (1996): U.S.$48,861,000,000 (U.S.$4,740 per capita).

Structure of gross domestic product and labour force

	1995 in value Kč '000,000[2]	1995 % of total value	1997 labour force	1997 % of labour force
Agriculture	60,500	5.0	284,000	5.2
Mining and manufacturing	340,000	28.1	1,471,900	26.9
Construction	71,600	5.9	470,600	8.6
Public utilities	63,700	5.3	94,900	1.7
Transportation and communications	72,600	6.0	384,700	7.0
Trade	133,700	11.0	822,500	15.0
Finance	116,100	9.6	345,500	6.3
Pub. admin., defense	118,100	9.7	317,500	5.8
Services	183,900	15.2	743,200	13.6
Other	51,800	4.3	534,700[4]	9.8[4]
TOTAL	1,212,000	100.0[5]	5,469,500	100.0[5]

Land use (1994): forested 33.3%; meadows and pastures 11.3%; agricultural and under permanent cultivation 43.0%; other 12.4%.

Foreign trade

Balance of trade (current prices)

	1991	1992	1993	1994	1995	1996
Kč '000,000[2]	+41,680	–45,300	+10,100	–20,600	–93,892	–157,715
% of total	5.9%	8.4%	1.3%	2.4%	7.6%	11.7%

Imports (1996): Kč 755,278,000,000[2] (machinery and transport equipment 38.2%, manufactured goods 19.3%, chemicals 11.8%, fuels and lubricants 8.7%). *Major import sources:* Germany 29.8%; Slovakia 9.6%; Russia 7.4%; Italy 5.9%; Austria 5.8%.
Exports (1996): Kč 594,952,000,000[2] (manufactured goods 28.8%, machinery and transport equipment 32.7%, miscellaneous manufactured articles 14.8%, chemicals 9.1%, inedible crude materials, except fuel 4.7%, mineral fuels and lubricants 4.7%). *Major export destinations:* Germany 36.0%; Slovakia 14.2%; Austria 6.4%; Italy 3.3%; Russia 3.2%.

Transport and communications

Transport. Railroads (1995): length 9,430 km; passenger-km 8,023,000,000; metric ton-km cargo 25,468,000,000. Roads (1995): total length 124,770 km (paved 13%). Vehicles (1995): passenger cars 3,113,476; trucks and buses 204,238. Merchant marine (1993): vessels (oceangoing) 18; total deadweight tonnage 514,126. Air transport (1995): passenger-km 2,555,062,000; metric ton-km 33,473,000; airports (1996) with scheduled flights 2.

Communications

Medium	date	unit	number	units per 1,000 persons
Daily newspapers	1994	circulation	2,259,000	219
Television	1995	receivers	4,200,000	407
Telephones	1995	main lines	2,444,200	237
Cellular telephones	1995	subscribers	48,900	4.7
Facsimile machines	1995	units	73,600	7.1
Personal computers	1995	units	550,000	53.2

Education and health

Educational attainment (1991). Percentage of adult population having: no schooling and incomplete primary 31.7%; complete secondary 58.6%; higher 8.5%. *Literacy* (1990): total population age 15 and over literate 8,170,442 (100%); males literate 3,914,080 (100%); females literate 4,256,362 (100%).

Education (1995–96)

	schools	teachers	students	student/ teacher ratio
Primary (age 6–14)	4,212	63,019	1,004,565	15.9
Secondary (age 15–18)	361	10,903	133,093	12.2
Voc., teacher tr.	832	18,458	229,909	12.5
Higher	23	12,892	139,774	9.4

Health (1995): physicians 38,462 (1 per 268 persons); hospital beds 74,510 (1 per 138 persons; (1996) infant mortality rate per 1,000 live births 6.0.
Food (1995): daily per capita caloric intake 3,175 (vegetable products 71%, animal products 29%); 128% of FAO recommended minimum requirement.

Military

Total active duty personnel (1996): 44,000 (army 63.6%, air force 36.4%). *Military expenditure as percentage of GNP* (1995): 2.3% (world 2.8%); per capita expenditure (1995): U.S.$229.

[1]First Czech Senate elected November 1996. [2]The koruna (Kč) was introduced Feb. 8, 1993, at par with the former Czechoslovak koruna (Kčs), which it replaced. [3]January 1. [4]Includes 204,000 employed with second job, 188,300 people with disabilities, and 16,400 nondistributable. [5]Detail does not add to total given because of rounding.

Internet resources for further information:
• Czech Statistical Office http://infox.eunet.cz/csu/csu_e.html

Denmark

Official name: Kongeriget Danmark (Kingdom of Denmark).
Form of government: parliamentary state and constitutional monarchy with one legislative house (Folketing [179]).
Chief of state: Danish Monarch.
Head of government: Prime Minister.
Capital: Copenhagen.
Official language: Danish.
Official religion: Evangelical Lutheran.
Monetary unit: 1 Danish krone (Dkr; plural kroner) = 100 øre; valuation (Sept. 25, 1998) 1 U.S.$ = Dkr 6.36; 1 £ = Dkr 10.83.

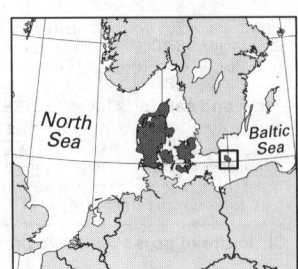

Area and population[1]		area		population
				1996[2]
Counties	Capitals	sq mi	sq km	estimate
Århus	Århus	1,761	4,561	625,224
Bornholm	Rønne	227	588	45,186
Frederiksborg	Hillerød	520	1,347	353,674
Fyn	Odense	1,346	3,486	470,528
København	—	203	526	607,344
Nordjylland	Ålborg	2,383	6,173	490,836
Ribe	Ribe	1,209	3,132	223,097
Ringkøbing	Ringkøbing	1,874	4,853	271,730
Roskilde	Roskilde	344	891	225,520
Sønderjylland	Åbenrå	1,520	3,938	252,929
Storstrøm	Nykøbing Falster	1,312	3,398	257,495
Vejle	Vejle	1,157	2,997	339,818
Vestsjælland	Sorø	1,152	2,984	289,852
Viborg	Viborg	1,592	4,122	232,254
Municipalities				
Copenhagen (København)	—	34	88	476,751
Frederiksberg	—	3	9	88,789
TOTAL		16,639[3]	43,094[3]	5,251,027

Demography

Population (1998): 5,303,000.
Density (1998): persons per sq mi 318.7, persons per sq km 123.1.
Urban-rural (1995): urban 85.2%; rural 14.8%.
Sex distribution (1996[2]): male 49.37%; female 50.63%.
Age breakdown (1996[2]): under 15, 17.5%; 15–29, 20.8%; 30–44, 22.1%; 45–59, 19.9%; 60–74, 12.7%; 75 and over, 7.0%.
Population projection: (2000) 5,340,000; (2010) 5,506,000.
Doubling time: not applicable; population is stable.
Ethnic composition (1996[2])[4]: Danish 95.8%; Asian 1.6%, of which Turkish 0.7%; residents of former Yugoslavia 0.5%; other Scandinavian 0.4%; African 0.3%; other 1.4%.
Religious affiliation (1995): Evangelical Lutheran 87.0%; other Christian 1.7%; Muslim 1.5%; other/nonreligious 9.8%.
Major urban areas (1994): Greater Copenhagen 1,346,289; Århus 209,404; Odense 143,029; Ålborg 116,567; Frederiksberg 88,789[5, 6].

Vital statistics

Birth rate per 1,000 population (1996): 12.9 (world avg. 25.0); (1995) legitimate 53.5%; illegitimate 46.5%.
Death rate per 1,000 population (1996): 11.6 (world avg. 9.3).
Natural increase rate per 1,000 population (1996): 1.3 (world avg. 15.7).
Total fertility rate (avg. births per childbearing woman; 1995): 1.8.
Marriage rate per 1,000 population (1995): 6.7.
Divorce rate per 1,000 population (1995): 2.5.
Life expectancy at birth (1994–95): male 72.6 years; female 77.8 years.
Major causes of death per 100,000 population (1995): malignant neoplasms (cancers) 296.6; ischemic heart disease 242.3; cerebrovascular disease 105.9.

National economy

Budget (1995)[7]. Revenue: Dkr 589,933,000,000 (direct taxes 52.3%, indirect taxes 29.7%). Expenditures: Dkr 604,806,000,000 (social security assistance 32.6%, education 11.7%, welfare services 9.8%, health 8.4%, defense 2.9%).
National debt (end of year; 1995): Dkr 663,653,000,000.
Tourism (1996): receipts U.S.$3,425,000; expenditures U.S.$4,142,000,000.
Population economically active (1996): total 2,796,501; activity rate of total population 52.7% (participation rates: ages 15–64, 79.1%; female 45.3%; unemployed [April 1996–March 1997] 8.4%).

Price and earnings indexes (1990 = 100)							
	1992	1993	1994	1995	1996	1997	1998
Consumer price index	104.5	105.9	108.0	110.2	112.6	115.0	117.3[8]
Hourly earnings index	106.2	108.6	113.3	117.2	...	...	...

Household income and expenditure. Average household size (1996) 2.2; income per household (1988) Dkr 199,354 (U.S.$29,613); expenditure (1993): housing 22.9%, food and beverages 17.9%, transportation and communications 15.5%, recreation 8.3%, household furnishings 6.1%, energy 6.1%.
Production (in Dkr '000,000 except as noted). Agriculture, forestry, fishing (value added; 1995): pork 16,005, milk 11,152, beef 3,554, wheat 3,411, barley 2,731, flowers and plants 2,541, mink furs 1,991; roundwood (1995) 2,288,000 cu m; fish catch (1995) 2,041,133 metric tons. Mining and quarrying (1994): sand and gravel 24,829,000 cu m; chalk 3,522,000 cu m. Manufacturing (value added; 1994): food products 38,325, of which meat

11,170; nonelectrical machinery and apparatus 23,331; chemicals and chemical products 18,504; electrical machinery and apparatus 14,428; printing and publishing 9,649; fabricated metals 9,479. Construction (completed; 1995): residential 1,375,000 sq m; nonresidential 3,573,000 sq m. Energy production (consumption): electricity (kW-hr; 1995) 34,332,000,000 ([1994] 36,252,000,-000); coal (metric tons; 1994) none (13,087,000); crude petroleum (barrels; 1996) 75,920,000 ([1994] 65,802,000); petroleum products (metric tons; 1994) 8,691,000 (8,069,000); natural gas (cu m; 1994) 4,902,000,000 (2,992,000,000).
Gross national product (at current market prices; 1996): U.S.$168,917,000,000 (U.S.$32,100 per capita).

Structure of gross domestic product and labour force				
	1995			
	in value Dkr '000,000[9]	% of total value	labour force	% of labour force
Agriculture, fishing	34,999	4.2	115,000	4.1
Mining	7,225	0.9	4,000	0.1
Manufacturing	167,943	20.2	521,200	18.6
Construction	47,015	5.7	164,100	5.9
Public utilities	16,172	1.9	16,500	0.6
Transp. and commun.	79,261	9.5	188,800	6.7
Trade, restaurants	108,604	13.1	435,500	15.5
Finance, real estate	158,299	19.0	261,500	9.3
Pub. admin., defense	183,466	22.1	156,800	5.6
Services	52,935	6.4	739,300	26.4
Other	−24,185[10]	−2.9[10]	199,500[11]	7.1[11]
TOTAL	831,733[3]	100.0[3]	2,802,400[3]	100.0[3]

Land use (1994): forested 10.5%; meadows and pastures 7.5%; agricultural and under permanent cultivation 55.9%; other 26.1%.

Foreign trade[12]

Balance of trade (current prices)						
	1992	1993	1994	1995	1996	1997
Dkr '000,000	+35,166	+43,077	+41,596	+29,500	+31,206	+25,293
% of total	7.7%	9.1%	8.6%	5.9%	5.8%	4.2%

Imports (1995): Dkr 236,587,000,000 (goods for household consumption 25.8%, transport equipment and parts 11.1%, machinery and apparatus 8.7%). *Major import sources:* Germany 22.8%; Sweden 12.2%; The Netherlands 7.3%; United Kingdom 7.0%; France 5.4%; Norway 5.0%.
Exports (1995): Dkr 266,087,000,000 (nonelectrical and electrical machinery 25.1%, fresh or frozen swine meat 6.0%, pharmaceuticals 4.7%, furniture 4.6%, textiles and clothing 4.5%). *Major export destinations:* Germany 23.2%; Sweden 10.0%; United Kingdom 8.1%; Norway 6.1%; France 5.5%.

Transport and communications

Transport. Railroads (1995): route length 2,865 km; passenger-km 4,834,000,-000; metric ton-km cargo 1,985,000,000. Roads (1995): total length 71,420 km (paved 100%). Vehicles (1995): passenger cars 1,729,405; trucks and buses 288,464. Air transport (1996)[13]: passenger-km 5,376,000,000; metric ton-km cargo 170,768,000; airports (1996) with scheduled flights 13.

Communications				units per 1,000
Medium	date	unit	number	persons
Daily newspapers	1995	circulation	1,610,000	308
Radio	1996	receivers	5,200,000	988
Television	1995	receivers	2,700,200	516
Telephones	1995	main lines	3,202,500	612
Cellular telephones	1995	subscribers	822,300	157
Facsimile machines	1995	units	250,000	48
Personal computers	1995	units	1,416,000	270

Education and health

Educational attainment (1995). Percentage of population age 25–69 having: completed lower secondary or not stated 40.0%; completed upper secondary or vocational 40.3%; advanced vocational 6.0%; undergraduate 8.9%; graduate 4.8%. *Literacy:* virtually 100%.

Education (1994–95)				student/
	schools	teachers	students	teacher ratio
Primary/lower secondary (age 7–15)	2,536	58,500[14]	605,798	10.4[14]
Upper secondary (age 16–18)	153	11,000[14]	75,793	6.8[14]
Vocational	237	12,000[14]	168,417	13.6[14]
Higher	158	8,000[14]	155,661	19.5[14]

Health (1994): physicians 14,497 (1 per 358 persons); hospital beds 26,170 (1 per 199 persons); infant mortality rate per 1,000 live births (1996) 5.7.
Food (1995): daily per capita caloric intake 3,704 (vegetable products 54%, animal products 46%); 138% of FAO recommended minimum requirement.

Military

Total active duty personnel (1996): 32,900 (army 57.8%, navy 18.2%, air force 24.0%). *Military expenditure as percentage of GNP* (1994): 1.9% (world 3.0%); per capita expenditure U.S.$522.

[1]Excludes the Faroe Islands and Greenland. [2]January 1. [3]Detail does not add to total given because of rounding. [4]Based on nationality. [5]Within Greater Copenhagen. [6]1996. [7]Includes both central and local governments. [8]June. [9]At factor cost. [10]Imputed bank service charges. [11]Includes 4,000 not adequately defined and 195,500 with previous employment. [12]Imports c.i.f., exports f.o.b. [13]Danish share of Scandinavian Airlines System (scheduled air service only) and Maersk Air. [14]1993–94.

Internet resources for further information:
• Statistics Denmark http://www.dst.dk/internet/startuk.htm

Djibouti

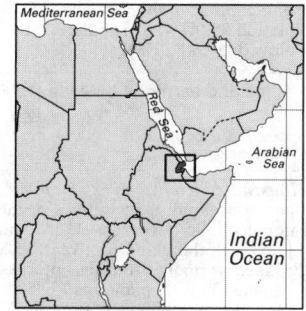

Official name: Jumhūrīyah Jībūtī
(Arabic); République de Djibouti
(French) (Republic of Djibouti).
Form of government: multiparty
republic with one legislative house
(National Assembly [65]).
Head of state and government:
President.
Capital: Djibouti.
Official languages: Arabic; French.
Official religion: none.
Monetary unit: 1 Djibouti franc
(DF) = 100 centimes; valuation (Sept.
25, 1998) 1 U.S.$ = DF 177.72;
1 £ = DF 302.57.

Area and population		area[1]		population
				1982
Districts	**Capitals**	sq mi	sq km	estimate
'Alī Sabīh (Ali-Sabieh)	'Alī Sabīh	925	2,400	15,000
Dikhil	Dikhil	2,775	7,200	30,000
Djibouti	Djibouti	225	600	200,000
Obock	Obock	2,200	5,700	15,000
Tadjoura (Tadjourah)	Tadjoura	2,825	7,300	30,000
TOTAL		8,950	23,200	335,000[2]

Demography

Population (1998): 652,000[3].
Density (1998): persons per sq mi 72.8, persons per sq km 28.1.
Urban-rural (1995): urban 82.8%; rural 17.2%.
Sex distribution (1997): male 51.62%; female 48.38%.
Age breakdown (1997): under 15, 42.7%; 15–29, 25.9%; 30–44, 15.1%; 45–59,
11.7%; 60–74, 4.0%; 75 and over, 0.6%.
Population projection: (2000) 687,000; (2010) 866,000.
Doubling time: 32 years.
Ethnic composition (1983): Somali 61.7%, of which Issa 33.4%, Gadaboursi
15.0%, Issaq 13.3%; Afar 20.0%; Arab (mostly Yemeni) 6.0%; European
4.0%; other (refugees) 8.3%.
Religious affiliation (1995): Sunnī Muslim 97.2%; Christian 2.8%, of which
Roman Catholic 2.2%, Orthodox 0.5%, Protestant 0.1%.
Major city and towns (1989): Djibouti 383,000[4]; 'Alī Sabīh 4,000; Tadjoura
3,500; Dikhil 3,000.

Vital statistics

Birth rate per 1,000 population (1997): 42.0 (world avg. 25.0).
Death rate per 1,000 population (1997): 15.0 (world avg. 9.3).
Natural increase rate per 1,000 population (1997): 27.0 (world avg. 15.7).
Total fertility rate (avg. births per childbearing woman; 1997): 6.0.
Marriage rate per 1,000 population (1982): 6.7.
Divorce rate per 1,000 population (1982): 1.9.
Life expectancy at birth (1997): male 48.6 years; female 52.6 years.
Major causes of death (percentage of total deaths [infants and children to age
10, district of Djibouti only]; 1984): diarrhea and acute dehydration 16.0%;
malnutrition 16.0%; poisoning 11.0%; tuberculosis 6.0%; acute respiratory
disease 6.0%; malaria 6.0%; anemia 6.0%; heart disease 2.0%; kidney disease 1.0%; other ailments 19.0%; no diagnosis 11.0%.

National economy

Budget (1996)[5]. Revenue: DF 25,395,000,000 (tax revenue 92.5%, of which
domestic taxes [construction, gambling, market fees, licenses] 33.5%, wages
and salary tax 14.5%, surcharge on khat 8.8%, income and profit tax 6.4%;
nontax revenue 7.5%). Expenditures: DF 30,430,000,000 (current expenditures 88.7%, of which defense and mobilization 23.2%, education 9.8%,
health 4.9%; capital expenditures 11.3%).
Tourism (1993): receipts from visitors U.S.$13,000,000; expenditures by nation-
als abroad U.S.$15,000,000.
Production (metric tons except as noted). Agriculture, forestry, fishing (1997):
vegetables and melons 22,390, of which tomatoes 1,000, eggplant 45; livestock
(number of live animals) 507,000 goats, 470,000 sheep, 190,000 cattle, 62,000
camels, 8,200 asses; roundwood, n.a.; fish catch (1995) 350. Mining and quarrying: mineral production limited to locally used construction materials and
evaporated salt. Manufacturing (1991): structural detail, n.a.; main products
include furniture, nonalcoholic beverages, meat and hides, light electro-
mechanical goods, and mineral water. Construction (1994): 53,900 sq m.
Energy production (consumption): electricity (kW-hr; 1994) 185,000,000
(185,000,000); firewood and charcoal, n.a. (n.a.)[6]; coal, none (n.a.); crude
petroleum, none (n.a.); petroleum products (metric tons; 1994) none
(127,000); natural gas, none (n.a.); geothermal, wind, and solar resources are
substantial but largely undeveloped.
Population economically active (1991): total 282,000; activity rate of total population 61.5% (participation rates: over age 10, 70.4%; female 40.8%; unemployed [1987] *c.* 40–50%).

Price and earnings indexes (1990 = 100)							
	1990	1991	1992	1993	1994	1995	1996
Consumer price index[7]	100.0	106.8	110.4	115.3	122.8	128.8	134.2
Earnings index	...	...	...	...	...	...	...

Household income and expenditure. Average household size (1985)[8] 7.2; income per household: n.a.; sources of income (1976): wages and salaries

51.6%, self-employment 36.0%, transfer payments 10.5%, other 1.9%; expenditure (expatriate households; 1984): food 50.3%, energy 13.1%, recreation
10.4%, housing 6.4%, clothing 1.7%, personal effects 1.4%, health care 1.0%,
household goods 0.3%, other 15.4%.
Public debt (external, outstanding; 1996): U.S.$226,000,000.
Gross national product (1996): U.S.$485,000,000 (U.S.$790 per capita).

Structure of gross domestic product and labour force				
	1996		1991	
	in value DF '000,000	% of total value	labour force	% of labour force
Agriculture	2,623	3.0	212,000	75.2
Mining	—	—		
Manufacturing	4,331	5.0	31,000	11.0
Construction	4,708	5.5		
Public utilities	6,300	7.3		
Transp. and commun.	13,231	15.3		
Trade	13,378	15.5		
Finance	8,261	9.6	39,000	13.8
Pub. admin., defense	18,368	21.3		
Services	4,023	4.7		
Other	10,992	12.7	...	...
TOTAL	86,215	100.0[9]	282,000	100.0

Land use (1994): forested 0.9%; meadows and pastures 56.1%; agricultural and
under permanent cultivation[10]; built-on, wasteland, and other 43.0%.

Foreign trade

Balance of trade (current prices)					
	1992	1993	1994	1995	1996
U.S.$'000,000	−205.9	−183.9	−180.7	−167.4	−160.9
% of total	65.9%	56.4%	61.6%	69.0%	67.0%

Imports (1996): U.S.$200,500,000 (food, beverages, khat, and tobacco 41.3%;
machinery and electric appliances 19.0%; petroleum products 8.0%; clothing
and footwear 7.6%; chemical products 4.8%; base metals and base metal
products 4.8%; transport equipment 3.4%). *Major import sources:* France
15.0%; Ethiopia 10.9%; Italy 7.8%; Saudi Arabia 7.5%; U.K. 6.0%.
Exports (1996): U.S.$39,600,000 (1991; unspecified special transactions 71.7%;
live animals [including camels] 15.5%; food and food products 12.8%). *Major
export destinations:* Ethiopia 44.8%; Somalia 38.2%; Yemen 8.2%; Saudi
Arabia 3.3%.

Transport and communications

Transport. Railroads (1995): length (1989) 66 mi, 106 km; passenger-mi
173,000,000, passenger-km 279,000,000; short ton-mile cargo 187,000,000[11],
metric ton-km cargo 273,000,000[11]. Roads (1995): total length 1,796 mi, 2,890
km (paved 13%). Vehicles (1994): passenger cars 13,500; trucks and buses
3,000. Merchant marine (1992): vessels (100 gross tons and over) 10; total
deadweight tonnage 4,090. Air transport (1995)[12]: passengers handled
120,145; metric tons of freight handled 12,291; airports (1997) with scheduled
flights 1.

Communications				units per 1,000
Medium	date	unit	number	persons
Daily newspapers	1990	circulation	4,000	7.6
Radio	1995	receivers	48,000	80.0
Television	1995	receivers	26,000	43.0
Telephones	1996	main lines[13]	8,169	13.5
Facsimile machines	1996	units[13]	142	0.2

Education and health

Educational attainment: n.a. Literacy (1995): percentage of population age 15
and over literate 46.2%; males literate 60.3%; females literate 32.7%.

Education (1996–97)				student/
	schools	teachers	students	teacher ratio
Primary (age 6–11)	81[14]	1,005[14]	33,960	...
Secondary (age 12–18)	26[15]	628[14]	11,628	...
Voc., teacher tr.				
Higher	1[15]	13[15]	130[16]	...

Health (1989): physicians 97 (1 per 5,258 persons); hospital beds[17] 1,383 (1 per
369 persons); infant mortality rate per 1,000 live births (1997) 105.
Food (1995) daily per capita caloric intake 1,831 (vegetable products 88%, animal products 12%); 79% of FAO recommended minimum requirement.

Military

Total active duty personnel (1997): 9,600[18] (army 83.3%, navy 2.1%, air force
2.1%, paramilitary 12.5%). *Military expenditure as percentage of GNP* (1995):
4.5% (world 2.8%); per capita expenditure U.S.$52.

---

[1]Original figures are those given in sq km; sq mi equivalent is rounded to appropriate
level of generality. [2]Includes 45,000 persons not distributed by district. [3]Includes
70,000–100,000 refugees and illegal immigrants. [4]1995 estimate. [5]Preliminary.
[6]Represents about 15% of total energy consumption. [7]Based on expatriates' expenditures. [8]City of Djibouti only. [9]Detail does not add to total given because of rounding.
[10]In 1988–89 only 1,005 acres (407 hectares) of land were cultivated. [11]Based on total
weight of Ethiopian exports and imports transported to and from the port of Djibouti.
[12]Djibouti International Airport only. [13]Number of users. [14]1994–95. [15]1991. [16]1995–96.
[17]Public health facilities only. [18]Excludes 3,900 French troops.

Internet resources for further information:
• **Bienvenue à Djibouti http://www.intnet.dj/djibouti.html**

Dominica

Official name: Commonwealth of
Dominica.
Form of government: multiparty
republic with one legislative house
(House of Assembly [32[1]]).
Chief of state: President.
Head of government: Prime Minister.
Capital: Roseau.
Official language: English.
Official religion: none.
Monetary unit: 1 East Caribbean
dollar (EC$) = 100 cents; valuation
(Sept. 25, 1998) 1 U.S.$ = EC$2.70;
1 £ = EC$4.60.

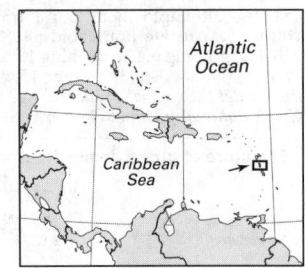

Area and population	area		population
Parishes	sq mi	sq km	1991 census
St. Andrew	69.3	179.6	11,106
St. David	49.0	126.8	6,977
St. George	20.7	53.5	20,365
St. John	22.5	58.5	4,990
St. Joseph	46.4	120.1	6,183
St. Luke	4.3	11.1	1,552
St. Mark	3.8	9.9	1,943
St. Patrick	32.6	84.4	8,929
St. Paul	26.0	67.4	7,495
St. Peter	10.7	27.7	1,643
TOTAL	285.3[2]	739.0[2]	71,183[3]

Demography

Population (1998): 76,400.
Density (1998): persons per sq mi 267.8; persons per sq km 103.4.
Urban-rural: n.a.
Sex distribution (1991): male 49.78%; female 50.22%.
Age breakdown (1991): under 15, 33.3%; 15–29, 28.3%; 30–44, 16.3%; 45–59, 9.7%; 60 and over, 11.8%; unknown, 0.6%.
Population projection: (2000) 78,000; (2010) 86,000.
Doubling time: 54 years.
Ethnic composition (1991): black 89.1%; mixed race 7.2%; Amerindian/Carib 2.4%; white 0.4%; other 0.7%; not stated 0.2%.
Religious affiliation (1991): Roman Catholic 70.1%; six largest Protestant groups 17.2%, of which Seventh-day Adventist 4.6%, Pentecostal 4.3%, Methodist 4.2%; other 8.9%; nonreligious 2.9%; unknown 0.9%.
Major towns (1991): Roseau 15,853; Portsmouth 3,621; Marigot 2,919; Atkinson 2,518; Mahaut 2,372.

Vital statistics

Birth rate per 1,000 population (1996): 18.4 (world avg. 25.0); (1991) legitimate 24.1%; illegitimate 75.9%.
Death rate per 1,000 population (1996): 5.3 (world avg. 9.3).
Natural increase rate per 1,000 population (1996): 13.1 (world avg. 15.7).
Total fertility rate (avg. births per childbearing woman; 1996): 1.9.
Marriage rate per 1,000 population (1990): 3.3.
Divorce rate per 1,000 population (1990): 0.4.
Life expectancy at birth (1996): male 74.5 years; female 80.4 years.
Major causes of death per 100,000 population (1990): diseases of the circulatory system 273.5, of which ischemic heart diseases 120.8, hypertensive disease 88.8; malignant neoplasms (cancers) 116.6; endocrine, metabolic, and nutritional disorders 51.4; diseases of the respiratory system 43.0; infectious and parasitic diseases 37.5.

National economy

Budget (1995–96). Revenue: EC$194,100,000 (tax revenue 67.9%, of which consumption taxes 25.1%, taxes on income and profits 18.3%; grants 15.7%; nontax revenue 14.1%; other 2.3%). Expenditures: EC$219,100,000 (current expenditures 70.4%; development expenditures 29.6%).
Public debt (external, outstanding; 1996): U.S.$94,000,000.
Land use (1994): forested 66.0%; meadows and pastures 3.0%; agricultural and under permanent cultivation 23.0%; other 8.0%.
Tourism (1995): receipts from visitors U.S.$35,700,000; expenditures by nationals abroad U.S.$4,300,000.
Gross national product (at current market prices; 1996): U.S.$228,000,000 (U.S.$3,090 per capita).

Structure of gross domestic product and labour force				
	1995		1991	
	in value EC$'000,000	% of total value	labour force[4]	% of labour force[4]
Agriculture	100.9	19.8	7,344	30.8
Mining	4.4	0.9	65	0.3
Manufacturing	35.8	7.0	1,947	8.2
Construction	44.4	8.7	2,819	11.8
Public utilities	21.0	4.1	304	1.3
Transportation and communications	88.4	17.3	1,202	5.0
Trade, hotels, restaurants	76.7	15.0	3,658	15.4
Finance, real estate	} 82.7	} 16.2	810	3.4
Services			3,446	14.5
Pub. admin., defense	92.9	18.2	1,520	6.4
Other	−36.8[5]	−7.2[5]	699	2.9
TOTAL	510.3[6]	100.0	23,814	100.0

Population economically active (1991): total 26,364; activity rate of total population 38.0% (participation rates: ages 15–64, 62.4%; female 34.5%; unemployed [1994] 23%).

Price and earnings indexes (1990 = 100)							
	1992	1993	1994	1995	1996	1997	1998[7]
Consumer price index	111.4	113.1	113.1	114.6	116.5	119.3	119.7
Earnings index	...	...	...	...	...	...	...

Household income and expenditure. Average household size (1991) 3.6; income per household: n.a.; sources of income: n.a.; expenditure (1984)[8]: food and nonalcoholic beverages 43.1%, housing and utilities 16.1%, transportation 11.6%, clothing and footwear 6.5%, household furnishings 6.0%.
Production (metric tons except as noted). Agriculture, forestry, fishing (1995): bananas 39,928[9], plantains 15,358, root crops 14,818 (of which dasheens 6,710, yams 4,479, tanias 3,326), grapefruit 10,682, coconuts 8,853, oranges 4,340, limes 3,314, mangoes 1,633, pepper 144, bay oil 16; livestock (number of live animals: 1996) 13,400 cattle, 9,700 goats, 7,600 sheep; roundwood, n,a,; fish catch 842 metric tons. Mining and quarrying: pumice, limestone, and sand and gravel are quarried primarily for local consumption. Manufacturing (value of production in EC$'000; 1996): toilet soap 19,633; laundry soap 17,240; crude coconut oil 1,615; bottled spring water 323,000 cases[10]; other products include fruit juices, beer, garments, furniture, paint, and cardboard boxes. Construction (value of starts; 1993): U.S.$12,100,000. Energy production (consumption): electricity (kW-hr; 1994) 52,400,000 (43,500,000); coal, none (none); crude petroleum, none (none); petroleum products (metric tons; 1994) none (23,000); natural gas, none (none).

Foreign trade[11]

Balance of trade (current prices)						
	1991	1992	1993	1994	1995	1996
EC$'000,000	−110.5	−140.3	−123.6	−137.3	−199.3	−216.1
% of total	26.9%	32.7%	32.3%	35.8%	46.4%	44.5%

Imports (1995): EC$314,300,000 ([12]machinery and transport equipment 28.5%; basic manufactures 25.1%; food 18.4%; chemicals and chemical products 12.8%). *Major import sources:* Caricom countries 25.8%; U.S. (including Puerto Rico) 23.4%; U.K. 13.7%; France 8.2%; Japan 7.6%.
Exports (1995): EC$115,000,000 (manufactured exports 49.3%, of which coconut-based laundry and toilet soaps 32.9%; agricultural exports 47.7%, of which bananas 38.5%; reexports 3.0%). *Major export destinations*[13]: U.K. 53.5%; Caricom countries 24.2%; U.S. (including Puerto Rico) 15.7%.

Transport and communications

Transport. Railroads: none. Roads (1995): total length 475 mi, 765 km (paved 50%). Vehicles (1995): passenger cars 2,770; trucks and buses 2,839. Merchant marine (1992): vessels (100 gross tons and over) 7; total deadweight tonnage 3,153. Air transport (1991): passenger arrivals 43,312, passenger departures, n.a.; cargo unloaded 259 metric tons, cargo loaded 415 metric tons; airports (1996) with scheduled flights 2.

Communications				units per 1,000
Medium	date	unit	number	persons
Radio	1996	receivers	65,000	875
Television	1995	receivers	5,200	70
Telephones	1995	main lines	17,800	240
Facsimile machines	1995	units	300	4.0

Education and health

Educational attainment (1991). Percentage of population age 25 and over having: no formal schooling 4.2%; primary education 78.4%; secondary 11.0%; higher vocational 2.3%; university 2.8%; other/unknown 1.3%. *Literacy* (1990): total population age 15 and over literate, c. 42,000 (90.0%).

Education (1994–95)				student/
	schools	teachers	students	teacher ratio
Primary	64	641	12,627	29.8
Secondary	13[14] }		6,493 }	
Higher[14]	2	34	484	14.2

Health: physicians (1993) 24 (1 per 2,952 persons); hospital beds (1992) 241 (1 per 298 persons); infant mortality rate per 1,000 live births (1996) 9.6.
Food (1995): daily per capita caloric intake 3,032 (vegetable products 79%, animal products 21%); 125% of FAO recommended minimum requirement.

Military

Total active duty personnel (1996): none[15].

---

[1]Includes 22 seats that are elective (including speaker if elected from outside of the House of Assembly) and 10 seats that are nonelective (including 9 appointees of the president and the attorney general serving ex officio). [2]Area breakdown by parish is based on 1961 survey. Total area of Dominica per more recent survey is 290 sq mi (750 sq km). [3]Includes institutionalized population of 1,717. [4]Employed persons only. [5]Net of indirect taxes less imputed banking service charge. [6]Detail does not add to total given because of rounding. [7]February. [8]Weights of consumer price index components. [9]1996. [10]1990. [11]Imports c.i.f.; exports f.o.b. [12]Breakdown based on 1992 imports valued at EC$299,200,000. [13]Excludes reexports. [14]1992–93. [15]300-member police force includes a coast guard unit.

Internet resources for further information:
• Dominica (official web site) http://www.dominica.dm/contents.htm

Dominican Republic

Official name: República Dominicana (Dominican Republic).
Form of government: multiparty republic with two legislative houses (Senate [30]; Chamber of Deputies [149]).
Head of state and government: President.
Capital: Santo Domingo.
Official language: Spanish.
Official religion: none[1].
Monetary unit: 1 Dominican peso (RD$) = 100 centavos; valuation (Sept. 25, 1998) 1 U.S.$ = RD$15.80; 1 £ = RD$26.90.

Area and population

Provinces	area sq km	population 1993 preliminary census	Provinces	area sq km	population 1993 preliminary census
Azua	2,532	194,209	Monte Cristi	1,925	94,429
Baoruco	1,283	101,742	Monte Plata	2,633	162,630
Barahona	1,739	157,772	Pedernales	2,077	16,975
Dajabón	1,021	63,995	Peravia	1,648	199,661
Duarte	1,605	272,277	Puerto Plata	1,857	255,061
El Seíbo	1,786	94,244	Salcedo	440	99,965
Espaillat	838	197,617	Samaná	854	73,094
Hato Mayor	1,329	76,761	San Cristóbal	1,265	409,381
Independencia	2,008	38,185	San Juan	3,571	247,029
La Altagracia	3,010	112,396	San Pedro de Macorís	1,255	212,886
Elías Piña	1,424	59,321	Sánchez Ramírez	1,196	158,218
La Romana	654	158,132	Santiago	2,836	690,548
La Vega	2,286	335,140	Santiago Rodríguez	1,112	60,015
María Trinidad Sánchez	1,271	122,165	Santo Domingo[2]	1,401	2,134,779
Monseñor Nouel	992	144,327	Valverde	823	146,087
			TOTAL	48,671	7,089,041[3]

Demography

Population (1998): 7,883,000.
Density (1998): persons per sq mi 419.5, persons per sq km 162.0.
Urban-rural (1993): urban 55.5%; rural 44.5%.
Sex distribution (1993): male 49.90%; female 50.10%.
Age breakdown (1995): under 15, 35.1%; 15–29, 29.0%; 30–44, 19.8%; 45–59, 9.9%; 60–74, 4.9%; 75 and over, 1.3%.
Population projection: (2000) 8,142,000; (2010) 9,503,000.
Doubling time: 38 years.
Ethnic composition (1993): mixed 73%; white 16%; black 11%.
Religious affiliation (1995): Roman Catholic 81.8%; Protestant 6.4%; other Christian 0.6%; other 11.2%.
Major urban centres (1993): Santo Domingo 1,555,656[4]; Santiago 364,859; La Romana 132,834; San Francisco de Macorís 129,943; San Pedro de Macorís 123,987.

Vital statistics

Birth rate per 1,000 population (1996): 23.5 (world avg. 25.0).
Death rate per 1,000 population (1996): 5.7 (world avg. 9.3).
Natural increase rate per 1,000 population (1996): 17.8 (world avg. 15.7).
Total fertility rate (avg. births per childbearing woman; 1996): 2.7
Marriage rate per 1,000 population (1992): 3.6.
Life expectancy at birth (1996): male 66.9 years; female 71.3 years.
Major causes of death per 100,000 population (1985)[5]: diseases of the circulatory system 165; infectious and parasitic diseases 85; malignant neoplasms (cancers) 45; diseases of the respiratory system 41.

National economy

Budget (1995–96). Revenue: RD$26,494,000,000 (tax revenue 87.8%, of which taxes on goods and services 45.5%, import duties 24.7%, income taxes 16.7%; nontax revenue 6.3%; grants and loans 5.9%). Expenditures: RD$26,846,-000,000 (development expenditure 53.9%; current expenditure 46.1%).
Public debt (external, outstanding; 1996): U.S.$3,515,000,000.
Gross national product (1996): U.S.$12,765,000,000 (U.S.$1,600 per capita).

Structure of gross domestic product and labour force

	1995 in value RD$'000,000	% of total value	labour force	% of labour force[6]
Agriculture	20,322	12.7	...	12.9
Mining	4,390	2.8	...	0.4
Manufacturing	28,152	17.5	...	17.5
Construction	15,282	9.5	...	4.6
Public utilities	3,051	1.9	...	0.6
Transp. and commun.	16,429	10.2	...	6.5
Trade, restaurants	29,697	18.5	...	21.2
Finance, real estate	16,194	10.1	...	3.4
Pub. admin., defense	13,626	8.5	}	24.6
Services	13,314	8.3		
Other	—	—	...	8.3[7]
TOTAL	160,456[8]	100.0	...	100.0

Production (metric tons except as noted). Agriculture, forestry, fishing (value of production in RD$'000,000; 1995): coffee 2,067, rice 1,781, chicken meat 1,692, sugarcane 1,586, milk 1,524, plantains 1,238, beef 1,077, beans 1,043, cacao beans 535, eggs 507, bananas 495, fish 110; roundwood (1995) 982,300

cu m. Mining (1996): nickel 30,400; gold 122,501 troy oz. Manufacturing (1995–96)[9]: cement 1,551,000; refined sugar 109,900; beer 2,010,000 hectolitres; rum 395,600 hectolitres; cigarettes 201,800,000 20-units packs. Construction (value of authorized private construction in RD$'000,000; 1992): 2,519. Energy production (consumption): electricity (kW-hr; 1995) 6,044,000,000 (3,292,000,000); coal (metric tons; 1994) none (104,000); crude petroleum (barrels; 1994) none (14,594,000); petroleum products (metric tons; 1994) 1,782,000 (3,199,000); natural gas, none (none).
Tourism (1995): receipts U.S.$1,604,000,000; expenditures U.S.$85,000,000.
Population economically active (1991)[10]: total 2,758,000; activity rate of total population 37.6% (participation rates: age 10 and over, 50.3%; female 29.0%; unemployed [1994] 28.0%).

Price and earnings indexes (1990 = 100)

	1992	1993	1994	1995	1996	1997	1998[11]
Consumer price index	153.3	161.4	174.7	196.6	207.2	224.4	230.2
Annual earnings index[12]	130.0	150.0	150.0	180.0	...	...	...

Household income and expenditure. Average household size (1993) 3.9; average income: n.a.; sources of income: n.a.; expenditure (1980–85): food and beverages 46.0%, housing 10.0%, household goods 8.0%.
Land use (1994): forested 12.4%; meadows and pastures 43.4%; agricultural and under permanent cultivation 30.6%; other 13.6%.

Foreign trade[13]

Balance of trade (current prices)

	1992	1993	1994	1995	1996	1997
U.S.$'000,000	−1,613	−1,607	−1,620	−2,020	−2,390	−2,701
% of total	58.9%	61.1%	56.0%	56.9%	59.5%	60.5%

Imports (1995): U.S.$2,786,000,000 (crude petroleum and petroleum products 21.7%; agricultural products 17.2%, of which cereals 5.3%). *Major import sources*[10]: U.S. 44%; Venezuela 11%; Mexico 6%; Japan 5%.
Exports (1995): U.S.$766,000,000[14] (ferronickel 31.6%; raw sugar 13.3%; raw coffee 10.6%; cacao 7.1%; gold 5.4%). *Major export destinations:* U.S. 47.6%; The Netherlands 14.1%; Puerto Rico 6.5; South Korea 4.6%; Canada 4.4%.

Transport and communications

Transport. Railroads (1995)[15]: route length 1,083 mi, 1,743km. Roads (1995): total length 7,643 mi, 12,300 km (paved 49%). Vehicles (1995): passenger cars 209,000; trucks and buses 141,400. Air transport (1994)[16]: passenger-mi 145,396,000, passenger-km, 233,992,000; short ton-mi cargo 1,738,000, metric ton-km cargo 2,537,000: airports (1997) 7.

Communications

Medium	date	unit	number	units per 1,000 persons
Daily newspapers	1994	circulation	264,000	35
Radio	1996	receivers	1,180,000	154
Television	1995	receivers	728,000	97
Telephones	1995	main lines	569,000	76
Cellular telephones	1995	subscribers	33,000	4.4
Facsimile machines	1995	units	2,500	0.3

Education and health

Educational attainment (1981). Percentage of population age 25 and over having: no formal schooling 48.0%; incomplete primary education 31.7%; complete primary 4.0%; secondary 14.0%; higher 2.3%. *Literacy* (1995): total population age 15 and over literate, *c.* 4,164,000 (82.1%); males literate, *c.* 2,118,000 (82.0%); females literate, *c.* 2,046,000 (82.2%).

Education (1994–95)

	schools	teachers	students	student/ teacher ratio
Primary (age 6–13)	4,001	42,135	1,462,722	34.7
Secondary (age 14–17)	...	10,757	240,441	22.4
Voc. teacher tr.	...	1,297	22,795	17.6
Higher[17]	7	5,091	73,461	14.4

Health (1994): physicians[18] 6,869 (1 per 1,076 persons); hospital beds[18] 8,621 (1 per 858 persons); infant mortality rate per 1,000 live births (1996) 47.7.
Food (1995): daily per capita caloric intake 2,323 (vegetable products 84%, animal products 16%); 103% of FAO recommended minimum.

Military

Total active duty personnel (1996): 24,500 (army 61.2%, navy 16.3%, air force 22.5%). *Military expenditure as percentage of GNP* (1994): 1.1% (world 3.0%); per capita expenditure U.S.$16.

[1]Roman Catholicism is the state religion per concordat with Vatican City. [2]National district. [3]Final census figure is 7,293,390. [4]Urban population of national district. [5]Projected rates based on about 60% of total deaths. [6]Official central bank estimates. [7]Not adequately defined. [8]Detail does not add to total given because of rounding. [9]Excludes free-zone sector for reexport (mostly ready-made garments) employing (1995) 184,000. [10]Estimated figures. [11]March. [12]Minimum wage in private sector. [13]Excludes free zones. [14]Excludes 1995 reexports of free zones equaling U.S.$1,764,000,000. [15]Most track is privately owned and serves the sugar industry only. [16]Dominicana and Dominair airlines. [17]Universities only. [18]Public sector only.

Internet resources for further information:
• **Banco Central de la Republica Dominicana**
  http://www.bancentral.gov.do/

Ecuador

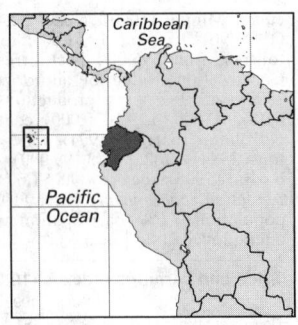

Official name: República del Ecuador (Republic of Ecuador).
Form of government: unitary multiparty republic with one legislative house (National Congress [125]).
Head of state and government: President.
Capital: Quito.
Official language: Spanish.
Official religion: none.
Monetary unit: 1 Sucre (S/.) = 100 centavos; valuation (Sept. 25, 1998) 1 U.S.$ = S/. 6,310.00; 1 £ = S/. 10,742.78.

Area and population

Regions Provinces	Capitals	area sq mi	area sq km	population 1997 estimate
Amazonica				
Morona-Santiago	Macas	13,100	33,930	131,845
Napo	Tena	9,918	25,690	146,319
Pastaza	Puyo	11,496	29,774	57,339
Sucumbíos	Nueva Loja	7,076	18,327	128,512
Zamora-Chinchipe	Zamora	8,923	23,111	94,339
Costa				
El Oro	Machala	2,259	5,850	524,466
Esmeraldas	Esmeraldas	5,884	15,239	389,967
Guayas	Guayaquil	7,916	20,503	3,201,672
Los Ríos	Babahoyo	2,770	7,175	630,303
Manabí	Portoviejo	7,289	18,879	1,211,064
Insular				
Galápagos	Puerto Baquerizo Moreno	3,093	8,010	14,713
Sierra				
Azuay	Cuenca	3,137	8,125	597,798
Bolívar	Guaranda	1,521	3,940	178,706
Cañar	Azogues	1,205	3,122	210,340
Carchi	Tulcán	1,392	3,605	160,983
Chimborazo	Riobamba	2,536	6,569	412,836
Cotopaxi	Latacunga	2,344	6,072	299,443
Imbabura	Ibarra	1,760	4,559	316,793
Loja	Loja	4,257	11,026	418,292
Pichincha	Quito	4,987	12,915	2,295,739
Tungurahua	Ambato	1,288	3,335	428,116
TOTAL		105,037[1, 2]	272,045[2]	11,936,858[3]

Demography

Population (1998): 12,175,000.
Density (1998): persons per sq mi 115.9, persons per sq km 44.8.
Urban-rural (1997): urban 62.0%; rural 38.0%.
Sex distribution (1997): male 50.23%; female 49.77%.
Age breakdown (1997): under 15, 35.4%; 15–29, 29.1%; 30–59, 28.9%; 60 and over, 6.6%.
Population projection: (2000) 12,646,000; (2010) 14,899,000.
Ethnic composition (1989): Amerindian 40.0%; mestizo 40.0%; white 15.0%; black 5.0%.
Religious affiliation (1995): Roman Catholic 93.4%; other 6.6%.
Major cities (1997): Guayaquil 1,973,880; Quito 1,487,513; Cuenca 255,028.

Vital statistics

Birth rate per 1,000 population (1995): 15.8[4] (world avg. 25.0); (1982) legitimate 67.9%; illegitimate 32.1%.
Death rate per 1,000 population (1995): 4.4[4] (world avg. 9.3).
Natural increase rate per 1,000 population (1995): 11.4[4] (world avg. 15.7).
Total fertility rate (avg. births per childbearing woman; 1994): 3.1.
Marriage rate per 1,000 population (1992): 6.4[4, 5].
Divorce rate per 1,000 population (1992): 0.6[4, 5].
Life expectancy at birth (1994): male 67.5 years; female 72.6 years.
Major causes of death per 100,000 population (1995): circulatory diseases 55.1; accidents, poisoning, and violence 29.2; pneumonia 27.2; diabetes mellitus 15.4; neoplasms (cancers) 12.7; parasitic diseases 12.2.

National economy

Budget (1995). Revenue: S/. 4,972,654,000,000 (income from petroleum 42.8%, indirect taxes 40.1%, direct taxes 17.1%). Expenditures: S/. 4,972,654,000,000 (general administration 48.7%, debt service 16.2%, subsidies 14.5%).
Production (metric tons except as noted). Agriculture, forestry, fishing (1996): sugarcane 6,750,000, bananas 5,309,000, rice 1,346,000, corn (maize) 855,000; livestock (live animals) 5,105,000 cattle, 2,621,000 pigs, 1,709,000 sheep, 63,105,000 chickens; roundwood (1995) 10,361,000 cu m; fish catch (1994) 339,915. Mining and quarrying (1994): limestone 1,900,000; gold 7,000 kg. Manufacturing (value added in S/. '000,000; 1994): chemical products 2,115,314; food products 803,936; nonmetallic mineral products 256,750; textiles 226,901. Construction (in S/.; 1992)[6]: residential 93,166,704,000; nonresidential 58,102,274,000. Energy production (consumption): electricity (kW-hr; 1994) 8,163,000,000 (8,163,000,000); crude petroleum (barrels; 1994) 123,998,000 (35,436,000); petroleum products (metric tons; 1994) 6,499,000 (5,135,000); natural gas (cu m; 1994) 204,000,000 (204,000,000).
Household income and expenditure. Average household size (1990) 4.1; average annual income per household (1995) S/. 9,825,610 (U.S.$3,830); sources of income (1995): self-employment 70.9%, wages 16.0%, transfer payments 6.7%, other 6.4%; expenditure (1995): food and tobacco 37.9%, transportation and communications 15.0%, clothing 9.2%, household furnishings 6.5%, housing and utilities 5.3%, health care 4.6%.

Population economically active (1990): total 3,359,767; activity rate of total population 34.8% (participation rates: ages 8 and over, 44.0%; female 26.4%; unemployed [1994] 7.1%).

Price and earnings indexes (1990 = 100)

	1991	1992	1993	1994	1995	1996	1997
Consumer price index	148.7	229.9	333.3	424.3	521.6	648.3	847.4
Hourly earnings index[7]	125.0	187.5	206.3	218.8	...	...	...

Public debt (external, outstanding; 1996): U.S.$12,435,000,000.
Gross national product (1996): U.S.$17,531,000,000 (U.S.$1,500 per capita).

Structure of gross domestic product and labour force

	1995 in value S/. '000,000[8]	1995 % of total value	1990 labour force	1990 % of labour force
Agriculture	37,033	17.2	1,035,712	30.8
Mining	31,348	14.6	20,870	0.6
Manufacturing	32,794	15.3	370,338	11.0
Construction	5,225	2.4	196,716	5.9
Public utilities	2,956	1.4	12,660	0.4
Transp. and commun.	19,313	9.0	131,084	3.9
Trade	31,679	14.7	476,730	14.2
Finance	25,467	11.8	81,357	2.4
Pub. admin., defense	15,579	7.2	838,129	24.9
Services	12,683	5.9		
Other	997[9]	0.5[9]	196,171[10]	5.8[10]
TOTAL	215,074	100.0	3,359,767	100.0[1]

Tourism (1995): receipts U.S.$255,000,000; expenditures U.S.$235,000,000.

Foreign trade[11]

Balance of trade (current prices)

	1992	1993	1994	1995	1996	1997
U.S.$'000,000	+1,031.9	+680.7	+508.0	+532.4	+1,510.5	+709.5
% of total	20.7%	13.3%	7.3%	6.6%	18.3%	7.3%

Imports (1995): U.S.$4,195,159,000 (machines and transport equipment 40.0%, basic manufactures 18.8%, chemicals 17.4%, food and live animals 6.3%, mineral fuels 5.9%). *Major import sources:* U.S. 31.2%; Colombia 9.6%; Japan 7.9%; Venezuela 6.1%; Germany 4.7%; Brazil 4.5%.
Exports (1995): U.S.$4,321,900,000 (food and live animals 47.6%, mineral fuels 30.2%, basic manufactures 2.7%, crude materials 2.3%). *Major export destinations:* U.S. 42.7%; Colombia 5.7%; Chile 4.5%; Italy 4.0%.

Transport and communications

Transport. Railroads (1994): route length 966 km; passenger-km 27,000,000; metric ton-km cargo 9,000,000. Roads (1995): total length 43,106 km (paved 18%). Vehicles (1995): passenger cars 395,000; trucks and buses 58,650. Air transport (1994): passenger-km 1,410,000,000; metric ton-km cargo 162,000,000; airports (1996) 14.

Communications

Medium	date	unit	number	units per 1,000 persons
Daily newspapers	1994	circulation	808,000	72
Radio	1996	receivers	3,240,000	277
Television	1995	receivers	900,000	79
Telephones	1995	main lines	748,200	65
Cellular telephones	1995	subscribers	49,800	4.3
Facsimile machines	1995	units	30,000	2.6
Personal computers	1995	units	45,000	3.9

Education and health

Educational attainment (1990). Percentage of population age 25 and over having: no formal schooling 2.2%; incomplete primary 54.3%; primary 28.0%; postsecondary 15.5%. *Literacy* (1995): total population age 15 and over literate 90.1%; males 92.0%; females 88.2%.

Education (1992–93)

	schools[12]	teachers	students	student/ teacher ratio
Primary (age 4–12)	16,146	63,347	1,986,753	31.4
Secondary (age 12–18) Vocational	2,207	62,630	813,557	13.0
Higher	21	12,856[13]	206,541[13]	16.1[13]

Health: physicians (1993) 12,149 (1 per 904 persons); hospital beds (1992) 17,253 (1 per 623 persons); infant mortality rate (1995) 30.5.
Food (1992): daily per capita caloric intake 2,583 (vegetable products 86%, animal products 14%); 113% of FAO recommended minimum requirement.

Military

Total active duty personnel (1996): 57,100 (army 87.6%, navy 7.2%, air force 5.2%). *Military expenditure as percentage of GNP* (1994): 3.5% (world 3.0%); per capita expenditure U.S.$49.

[1]Detail does not add to total given because of rounding. [2]Includes 884 sq mi (2,289 sq km) in nondelimited areas. [3]Total includes 87,273 persons in nondelimited areas. [4]Excluding nomadic Indian tribes. [5]Based on incomplete registration. [6]Authorized construction in Cuenca, Guayaquil, and Quito only. [7]General minimum wage. [8]At constant 1975 prices. [9]Minus imputed bank services plus gross import duties. [10]Includes unemployed persons not previously employed. [11]Import figures are f.o.b. in balance of trade and c.i.f. for commodities and trading partners. [12]1986–87. [13]1989–90.

Internet resources for further information:
• Instituto Nacional de Estadística y Censos (in Spanish)
  http://www4.inec.gov.ec/

Egypt

Official name: Jumhūrīyah Miṣr al-'Arabīyah (Arab Republic of Egypt).
Form of government: republic with one legislative house (People's Assembly [454[1]]).
Chief of state: President.
Head of government: Prime Minister.
Capital: Cairo.
Official language: Arabic.
Official religion: Islam.
Monetary unit: 1 Egyptian pound (£E) = 100 piastres; valuation (Sept. 25, 1998) 1 U.S.\$ = £E 3.41; 1 £ = £E 5.81.

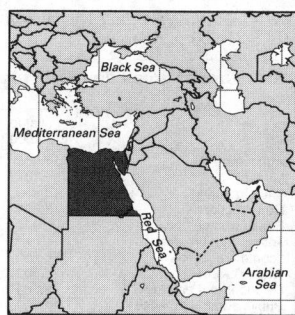

(192,342); petroleum products ('000 metric tons; 1994) 26,424 (16,630); natural gas ('000,000 cu m; 1994) 10,544 (10,544).
Gross national product (1996): U.S.\$64,275,000,000 (U.S.\$1,080 per capita).

Structure of gross domestic product and labour force

	1995–96[10]		1992	
	in value £E '000,000	% of total value	labour force	% of labour force
Agriculture	24,470	16.0	5,535,000	35.0
Mining (petroleum) }			44,900	0.3
Manufacturing }	41,335	26.9	2,014,600	12.7
Construction	7,898	5.1	884,200	5.6
Public utilities	3,190	2.1	147,300	0.9
Transp. and commun.	16,116[11]	10.5[11]	777,700	4.9
Trade	28,545[12]	18.6[12]	1,332,100	8.4
Finance	8,832	5.8	237,100	1.5
Pub. admin., defense, services	11,150	7.3	3,420,200	21.6
Other	11,833	7.7	1,416,000[13]	8.9[13]
TOTAL	153,369	100.0	15,814,800[14]	100.0[14, 15]

Household income and expenditure. Average household size (1986) 4.9; expenditure (1986–87)[16]: food 55.7%, clothing 10.9%, housing 10.5%.
Tourism (1995): receipts U.S.\$2,800,000,000; expenditures U.S.\$1,278,000,000.

Area and population

Regions Governorates	Capitals	area sq mi	area sq km	population 1995 estimate
Frontier				
Al-Bahr al-Aḥmar	Al-Ghurdaqah	78,643	203,685	115,000
Janūb Sīnā'	Aṭ-Ṭūr	12,796	33,140	35,000
Maṭrūḥ	Marsā Maṭrūḥ	81,897	212,112	186,000
Shamāl Sīnā'	Al-'Arīsh	10,646	27,574	219,000
Al-Wādī al-Jadīd	Al-Khārijah	145,369	376,505	136,000
Lower Egypt				
Al-Buḥayrah	Damanhūr	3,911	10,130	3,973,000
Ad-Daqahlīyah	Al-Manṣūrah	1,340	3,471	4,226,000
Dumyāṭ	Dumyāṭ	227	589	898,000
Al-Gharbīyah	Ṭanṭā	750	1,942	3,437,000
Al-Ismā'īlīyah (Ismailia)	—	557	1,442	681,000
Kafr ash-Shaykh	Kafr ash-Shaykh	1,327	3,437	2,266,000
Al-Minūfīyah	Shibīn al-Kawm	592	1,532	2,672,000
Al-Qalyūbīyah	Banhā	387	1,001	3,045,000
Ash-Sharqīyah	Az-Zaqāzīq	1,614	4,180	4,220,000
Upper Egypt				
Aswān	Aswān	262	679	1,042,000
Asyūṭ	Asyūṭ	600	1,553	2,843,000
Banī Suwayf	Banī Suwayf	510	1,322	1,836,000
Al-Fayyūm	Al-Fayyūm	705	1,827	1,995,000
Al-Jīzah	Al-Jīzah	32,878	85,153	4,525,000
Al-Minyā	Al-Minyā	873	2,262	3,372,000
Qinā	Qinā	715[2]	1,851[2]	2,607,000
Sawhāj	Sawhāj	597	1,547	3,067,000
Urban				
Būr Sa'īd (Port Said)	—	28	72	467,000
Al-Iskandarīyah (Alexandria)	—	1,034	2,679	3,431,000
Al-Qāhirah (Cairo)	—	83	214	6,955,000
Al-Uqṣur (Luxor)	—	...[2]	...[2]	159,000
As-Suways (Suez)	—	6,888	17,840	411,000
TOTAL		385,229	997,739	58,819,000

Demography

Population (1998): 63,261,000.
Density (1998): persons per sq mi 164.2, persons per sq km 63.4.
Urban-rural (1996): urban 43.0%; rural 57.0%.
Sex distribution (1997): male 50.52%; female 49.48%.
Age breakdown (1997): under 15, 36.5%; 15–29, 28.4%; 30–44, 18.5%; 45–59, 10.8%; 60–74, 4.9%; 75 and over, 0.9%.
Population projection: (2000) 65,627,000; (2010) 77,345,000.
Ethnic composition (1986): Egyptian 99.9%; other 0.1%.
Religious affiliation (1990): Sunnī Muslim c. 90%; Christian c. 10%[3].
Major cities ('000; 1996): Cairo 9,900[4]; Alexandria 3,700[4]; Al-Jīzah 2,144[5].

Vital statistics

Birth rate per 1,000 population (1997): 28.0 (world avg. 25.0).
Death rate per 1,000 population (1997): 9.0 (world avg. 9.3).
Natural increase rate per 1,000 population (1997): 19.0 (world avg. 15.7).
Total fertility rate (avg. births per childbearing woman; 1997): 3.5.
Life expectancy at birth (1994): male 65.4 years; female 69.5 years.

National economy

Budget (1995–96). Revenue: £E 60,893,000,000 (general taxes 62.8%, of which income tax 22.5%, sales taxes 17.2%, customs duties 13.0%; oil revenue 7.7%; Suez Canal fees 4.9%). Expenditures: £E 63,889,000,000 (current expenditure 81.3%, of which debt servicing 25.1%, wages and salaries 22.0%).
Public debt (external, outstanding; 1996): U.S.\$28,918,000,000.
Population economically active (1995–96): total 16,925,000; activity rate 28.1% (participation rates: ages 15–64, 49.0%; unemployed 9.4%).

Price and earnings indexes (1990 = 100)

	1992	1993	1994	1995	1996	1997	1998[6]
Consumer price index	136.1	152.5	165.0	190.9	204.7	214.1	218.3
Annual earnings index[7]	133.9	155.4	...	...	...	...	...

Production ('000; metric tons except as noted). Agriculture, forestry, fishing (1997): sugarcane 14,105, wheat 5,600, corn (maize) 5,180, tomatoes 5,038, rice 4,900, oranges 1,608, cotton 890, sorghum 650; livestock ('000; number of live animals) 3,491 sheep, 3,250 goats, 2,800 buffalo, 2,700 cattle, 42,000 chickens, 10,380 pigeons[8]; roundwood (1995) 2,698,000 cu m; fish catch (1995) 310. Mining and quarrying (1995): kaolin 293,381; iron ore 2,430; salt 1,900. Manufacturing (1995–96): cement 17,200; nitrate fertilizers 7,354; sugar 1,131; cotton yarn 275; refrigerators 373,000 units[9]; automobiles 6,800 units[9]. Construction (1992–93): urban residential units 123,098. Energy production (consumption): electricity ('000,000 kW-hr; 1994) 47,920 (47,920); coal ('000 metric tons; 1994) n.a. (1,852); crude petroleum ('000 barrels; 1994) 323,676

Foreign trade[17]

Balance of trade (current prices)

	1992	1993	1994	1995	1996	1997
U.S.\$'000,000	−5,242	−5,959	−6,271	−8,314	−9,505	−9,293
% of total	46.2%	56.9%	49.2%	54.6%	57.3%	54.2%

Imports (1995–96): U.S.\$13,826,400,000 (machinery and transport equipment 29.7%; foodstuffs 20.9%; iron and steel products 9.5%; chemical products 3.9%). *Major import sources:* U.S. 18.9%; Germany 9.6%; Italy 7.6%.
Exports (1995–96): U.S.\$4,592,800,000 (petroleum and petroleum products 48.5%; cotton yarn, textiles, and clothing 12.5%; basic metals and manufactures 5.4%). *Major export destinations:* Italy 18.6%; U.S. 11.1%.

Transport and communications

Transport. Railroads (1995): length 4,810 km; passenger-km 47,992,000,000[18]; metric ton-km cargo 2,336,000,000[18]. Roads (1995): length 58,000 km (paved 78%). Vehicles (1995): passenger cars 1,280,000; trucks and buses 423,300. Inland water (1996–97): Suez Canal, number of transits 14,704; metric ton cargo 354,591,000. Air transport (1996)[19]: passenger-km 8,742,200,000; metric ton-km cargo 197,974,000; airports (1997) 11.

Communications

Medium	date	unit	number	units per 1,000 persons
Daily newspapers	1995	circulation	2,600,000	43.0
Radio	1995	receivers	19,400,000	312.0
Television	1995	receivers	6,850,000	110.0
Telephones	1995	main lines	2,716,200	46.3
Cellular telephones	1995	subscribers	7,400	0.1
Facsimile machines	1995	units	21,600	0.4
Personal computers	1995	units	235	0.004

Education and health

Literacy (1995): total population age 15 and over literate 51.4%; males 63.6%; females 38.8%.

Education (1995–96)

	schools	teachers	students	student/teacher ratio
Primary (age 6–11)[20]	16,188	302,916	7,470,437	24.7
Secondary (age 12–17)[20]	7,307[18]	235,313	4,242,245	18.0
Vocational	1,351[18]	133,794	1,900,406	14.2
Teacher training	56[18]	650[7]	2,664[7]	4.1
Higher	12[21]	38,828[18, 22]	696,988[23]	...

Health: physicians (1996) 129,000 (1 per 472 persons); hospital beds (1994) 113,020 (1 per 515 persons); infant mortality rate (1997) 71.0.
Food (1995): daily per capita caloric intake 3,327 (vegetable products 94%, animal products 6%); 132% of FAO recommended minimum requirement.

Military

Total active duty personnel (1997): 450,000 (army 71.1%, navy 4.4%, air force [including air defense] 24.5%). *Military expenditure as percentage of GNP* (1995): 5.7% (world 2.8%); per capita expenditure U.S.\$43.

[1]Includes 10 nonelective seats. [2]The area of Al-Uqṣur (Luxor) is included with Qinā governorate. [3]According to the 1986 census, the Christian population of Egypt was 5.9% of the total; this figure is considered by some external authorities to understate the Christian population by as much as 60%. [4]Population of urban agglomeration. [5]1992. [6]First quarter. [7]Average nominal wages for each fiscal year (e.g., 1990–91). [8]1991. [9]1992–93. [10]At 1991–92 constant prices. [11]Transportation includes earnings from traffic on the Suez Canal. [12]Trade includes restaurants and hotels. [13]Unemployed and those seeking work for the first time. [14]Total includes 5,700 persons not classifiable by sector. [15]Detail does not add to total given because of rounding. [16]Weight of consumer price components; urban households only. [17]Import figures are c.i.f.; export figures are f.o.b. [18]1993–94. [19]Egypt Air only. [20]Data exclude 1,770 primary and 1,449 secondary schools in the Al-Azhar education system. [21]Universities only. [22]Excludes Al-Azhar University. [23]1994–95.

Internet resources for further information:
• Egypt State Information Service http://www.sis.gov.eg/
• Egypt's Information Highway http://www.idsc.gov.eg/
• Arab Net http://www.arab.net

El Salvador

Official name: República de El Salvador (Republic of El Salvador).
Form of government: republic with one legislative house (Legislative Assembly [84]).
Chief of state and government: President.
Capital: San Salvador.
Official language: Spanish.
Official religion: none[1].
Monetary unit: 1 colón (₡) = 100 centavos; valuation (Sept. 25, 1998)
1 U.S.$ = ₡8.76; 1 £ = ₡14.91.

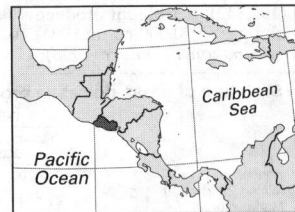

Area and population		area		population
				1992 census
Departments	Capitals	sq mi	sq km	
Ahuachapán	Ahuachapán	479	1,240	261,188
Cabañas	Sensuntepeque	426	1,104	138,426
Chalatenango	Chalatenango	779	2,017	177,320
Cuscatlán	Cojutepeque	292	756	178,502
La Libertad	Nueva San Salvador	638	1,653	513,866
La Paz	Zacatecoluca	473	1,224	245,915
La Unión	La Unión	801	2,074	255,565
Morazán	San Francisco	559	1,447	160,146
San Miguel	San Miguel	802	2,077	403,411
San Salvador	San Salvador	342	886	1,512,125
San Vicente	San Vicente	457	1,184	143,003
Santa Ana	Santa Ana	781	2,023	458,587
Sonsonate	Sonsonate	473	1,225	360,183
Usulután	Usulután	822	2,130	310,362
TOTAL		8,124	21,041[2]	5,118,599

Demography

Population (1998): 5,752,000.
Density (1998): persons per sq mi 708.0, persons per sq km 273.4.
Urban-rural (1994): urban 54.8%; rural 45.2%.
Sex distribution (1993): male 47.53%; female 52.47%.
Age breakdown (1993): under 15, 39.9%; 15–29, 27.1%; 30–44, 15.4%; 45–59, 9.7%; 60 and over, 7.9%.
Population projection: (2000) 5,925,000; (2010) 6,850,000.
Doubling time: 33 years.
Ethnic composition (1993): mestizo (white and Indian) 89.0%; Amerindian 10.0%; white 1.0%.
Religious affiliation (1995): Roman Catholic 78.2%; Protestant 17.1%, of which Pentecostal 13.3%; other Christian 1.9%; other 2.8%.
Major cities (1992)[3]: San Salvador 422,570 (metro area 1,522,126); Soyapango 251,811[4]; Santa Ana 202,337; San Miguel 182,817; Mejicanos 145,000[4].

Vital statistics

Birth rate per 1,000 population (1996): 27.7 (world avg. 25.0).
Death rate per 1,000 population (1996): 6.6 (world avg. 9.3).
Natural increase rate per 1,000 population (1996): 21.1 (world avg. 15.7).
Total fertility rate (avg. births per childbearing woman; 1996): 3.2.
Marriage rate per 1,000 population (1992): 4.3.
Divorce rate per 1,000 population (1992): 0.5.
Life expectancy at birth (1996): male 65.5 years; female 72.4 years.
Major causes of death per 100,000 population (1991)[5]: diseases of the circulatory system 109; violence 66; accidents 62; malignant neoplasms (cancers) 44; infectious and parasitic diseases 39; ill-defined conditions 74.

National economy

Budget. Revenue (1995): ₡10,535,000,000 (sales taxes 43.5%, income taxes 26.6%, import duties 16.9%, nontax revenue 5.5%). Expenditures (1994): ₡10,264,300,000 (general public services 13.2%, education 13.2%, police 9.8%, fuel and energy 9.1%, health 8.3%, defense 8.1%).
Production (metric tons except as noted). Agriculture, forestry, fishing (1996): sugarcane 3,900,000, corn (maize) 639,600, sorghum 198,600, coffee 126,000, bananas 62,700, rice 50,500, dry beans 50,500, oranges 41,500, tobacco 1,240; livestock (number of live animals) 1,286,000 cattle, 400,000 pigs, roundwood (1994) 6,504,000 cu m; fish catch (1995) 15,812, of which crustaceans (1994) 4,844. Mining and quarrying (1993): limestone 2,600,000 metric tons. Manufacturing (value added in ₡'000,000[6]; 1995): food products 2,807; chemical products 854; beverages 837; textiles 738; petroleum products 668; nonmetallic mineral products 493; metallic products 471. Construction (buildings completed; 1993): residential 650,000 sq m; nonresidential 296,000 sq m. Energy production (consumption): electricity (kW-hr; 1994) 3,324,000,000 (3,415,000,000); coal, none (none); crude petroleum (barrels; 1994) none (7,469,000); petroleum products (metric tons; 1994) 985,000 (1,343,000).
Household income and expenditure. Average household size (1992–93): 4.8; average income per household (1992–93): ₡22,930 (U.S.$2,562); expenditure (1990–91)[7]: food and beverages 37.0%, housing 12.1%, transportation and communications 10.2%, clothing and footwear 6.7%.
Population economically active (1995): total 2,136,400; activity rate of total population 39.1% (participation rates: ages 15–64, 62.9%; female 37.1%; unemployed 7.6%).

Price and earnings indexes (1991 = 100)							
	1992	1993	1994	1995	1996	1997	1998[8]
Consumer price index	111.2	131.8	145.8	160.4	176.0	184.0	190.1
Monthly earnings index[9]	110.1	127.5	143.4	...	...	...	...

Gross national product (at current market prices; 1996): U.S.$9,868,000,000 (U.S.$1,700 per capita).

Structure of gross domestic product and labour force				
	1995			
	in value ₡'000,000	% of total value	labour force	% of labour force
Agriculture	11,683	13.8	584,900	27.4
Mining	389	0.5	1,100	0.1
Manufacturing	18,598	21.9	402,900	18.9
Construction	3,851	4.5	146,900	6.9
Public utilities	920	1.1	8,300	0.4
Transportation and communications	6,258	7.4	86,400	4.0
Trade	16,592	19.5	413,800	19.4
Finance, real estate	9,384	11.0	27,800	1.3
Public admin., defense	4,721	5.6	432,600	20.2
Services	12,568	14.8		
Other	—	—	31,600	1.5
TOTAL	84,962[2]	100.0[2]	2,136,400[2]	100.0[2]

Public debt (external, outstanding; 1996): U.S.$2,297,000,000.
Tourism (1995): receipts U.S.$75,000,000; expenditures U.S.$72,000,000.
Land use (1994): forested 5.0%; meadows and pastures 29.5%; agricultural and under permanent cultivation 35.2%; other 30.3%.

Foreign trade[10]

Balance of trade (current prices)						
	1992	1993	1994	1995	1996	1997
U.S.$'000,000	−1,101.0	−1,180.5	−1,448.9	−1,855.3	−1,646.5	−1,614.3
% of total	48.0%	44.6%	47.1%	48.2%	44.6%	37.3%

Imports (1994): U.S.$2,261,600,000 (chemicals and chemical products 16.5%, transport equipment 12.4%, food and beverages 11.7%, nonelectrical machinery and equipment 11.6%). *Major import sources:* U.S. 41.5%; Guatemala 10.7%; Japan 6.3%; Venezuela 6.1%; Mexico 4.7%.
Exports (1994): U.S.$812,700,000 (coffee 32.5%, paper and paper products 7.0%, clothing 4.6%, pharmaceuticals 4.2%, raw sugar 4.2%). *Major export destinations:* U.S. 22.6%; Guatemala 21.9%; Germany 14.9%; Costa Rica 8.9%.

Transport and communications

Transport. Railroads (1995): route length 562 km; (1994) passenger-km 5,540,000; (1994) metric ton-km cargo 29,640,000. Roads (1995): total length 12,320 km (paved 14%). Vehicles (1995): passenger cars 102,000; trucks and buses 159,700. Air transport (1994)[11]: passenger-km 1,978,000,000; metric ton-km cargo 14,333,000; airports (1997) with scheduled flights 1.

Communications				units per 1,000 persons
Medium	date	unit	number	
Daily newspapers	1994	circulation	284,000	53
Radio	1996	receivers	2,080,000	373
Television	1995	receivers	500,700	91
Telephones	1995	main lines	284,800	52
Cellular telephones	1995	subscribers	13,500	2.5
Facsimile machines	1990	units	3,500	0.7

Education and health

Educational attainment (1992): Percentage of population over age 25 having: no formal schooling 34.7%; incomplete primary education 37.6%; complete primary[12] 10.8%; secondary 9.4%; higher technical 2.4%; incomplete undergraduate 1.1%; complete undergraduate 2.9%; other/unknown 1.1%.
Literacy (1992): total population age 15 and over literate, 2,326,800 (74.1%); males literate, 1,141,007 (77.4%); females literate, 1,185,793 (71.3%).

Education (1993)	schools	teachers	students	student/ teacher ratio
Primary (age 7–15)	3,961	26,259[13]	1,042,256	39.7[13]
Secondary (age 16–18)	...	...	29,527	...
Voc. teacher tr.	...	...	88,588	...
Higher[14]	...	4,643	77,359	16.7

Health (1993): physicians 4,525 (1 per 1,219 persons); hospital beds 9,379 (1 per 588 persons); infant mortality rate per 1,000 live births (1996) 31.5.
Food (1995): daily per capita caloric intake 2,577 (vegetable products 89%, animal products 11%); 113% of FAO recommended minimum requirement.

Military

Total active duty personnel (1996): 28,400 (army 90.5%, navy 3.9%, air force 5.6%). *Military expenditure as percentage of GNP* (1995): 1.1% (world 2.8%); per capita expenditure U.S.$18.

---

[1]Roman Catholicism, although not official, enjoys special recognition in the constitution. [2]Detail does not add to total given because of rounding. [3]Population of *municipios* (second-order administrative units). [4]Within San Salvador metropolitan area. [5]Projected rates based on about 80% of total deaths. [6]At constant price of 1990. [7]536,628 urban households only. [8]May. [9]Private sector only. [10]Imports c.i.f., exports f.o.b. [11]Taca airlines only. [12]Education completed through ninth grade. [13]Public schools only. [14]Universities and equivalent institutions only.

Internet resources for further information:
• **Banco Central de Reserva de El Salvador**
  http://www.bcr.gob.sv/

Equatorial Guinea

Official name: República de Guinea Ecuatorial (Republic of Equatorial Guinea).
Form of government: republic with one legislative house (Chamber of People's Representatives [80[1]]).
Chief of state: President.
Head of government: Prime Minister.
Capital: Malabo.
Official languages: Spanish; French.
Official religion: none.
Monetary unit[2]: 1 CFA franc (CFAF) = 100 centimes; valuation (Sept. 25, 1998) 1 U.S.$ = CFAF 560.38; 1 £ = CFAF 954.05.

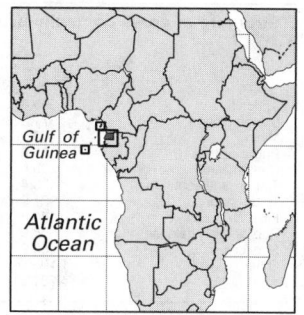

Area and population

Regions Provinces	Capitals	area sq mi	area sq km	population 1987 estimate
Insular		785[3]	2,034	70,280
Annobón	Palé	7	17	2,360
Bioko Norte	Malabo	300	776	56,600
Bioko Sur	Luba	479	1,241	11,320
Continental		10,045[3]	26,017	259,950
Centro-Sur	Evinayong	3,834	9,931	55,970
Kie-Ntem	Ebebiyin	1,522	3,943	74,050
Litoral[4]	Bata	2,573	6,665	75,640
Wele-Nzas	Mongomo	2,115	5,478	54,290
TOTAL		10,831[3]	28,051	330,230

Demography

Population (1998): 454,000.
Density (1998): persons per sq mi 41.9, persons per sq km 16.2.
Urban-rural (1992): urban 29.4%; rural 70.6%.
Sex distribution (1995): male 49.25%; female 50.75%.
Age breakdown (1995): under 15, 43.2%; 15–29, 25.5%; 30–44, 15.6%; 45–59, 9.3%; 60–74, 5.3%; 75 and over, 1.1%.
Population projection: (2000) 478,000; (2010) 615,000.
Doubling time: 27 years.
Ethnic composition (1995): Fang 82.9%; Bubi 9.6%; other 7.5%.
Religious affiliation (1995): Roman Catholic 93.1%; other 6.9%.
Major cities (1983): Malabo 30,418; Bata 24,308; Ela-Nguema 6,179; Campo Yaunde 5,199; Los Angeles 4,079.

Vital statistics

Birth rate per 1,000 population (1994): 40.7 (world avg. 25.0); legitimate, n.a.; illegitimate, n.a.
Death rate per 1,000 population (1994): 14.7 (world avg. 9.3).
Natural increase rate per 1,000 population (1994): 26.0 (world avg. 15.7).
Total fertility rate (avg. births per childbearing woman; 1994): 5.3.
Marriage rate per 1,000 population: n.a.
Divorce rate per 1,000 population: n.a.
Life expectancy at birth (1994): male 50.0 years; female 54.3 years.
Major causes of death per 100,000 population: n.a.; however, major diseases include malaria (about 24% of total mortality), respiratory infections (12% of mortality), cholera, leprosy, trypanosomiasis (sleeping sickness), and waterborne (especially gastrointestinal) diseases.

National economy

Budget (1995). Revenue: CFAF 27,468,000,000 (domestic revenue 49.3%, of which tax revenue 32.1%, nontax revenue 9.9%, oil revenue 7.3%; foreign grants 50.7%). Expenditures: CFAF 29,452,000,000 (capital expenditure 64.2%; current expenditure 34.7%, of which interest 12.0%, salaries 9.0%).
Public debt (external, outstanding; 1995): U.S.$222,200,000.
Gross national product (at current market prices; 1996): U.S.$217,000,000 (U.S.$530 per capita).

Structure of gross domestic product and labour force

	1995 in value CFAF '000,000	1995 % of total value	1983 labour force	1983 % of labour force
Agriculture, forestry	41,479	46.2	59,390	57.9
Manufacturing, mining	23,494	26.2	1,616	1.6
Construction	3,724	4.1	1,929	1.9
Public utilities	2,680	3.0	224	0.2
Transportation and communications	1,606	1.8	1,752	1.7
Trade	7,404	8.2	3,059	3.0
Finance	1,669	1.9	409	0.4
Pub. admin., defense	4,080	4.5 }	8,377	8.2
Services	2,270	2.5 }		
Other	1,409	1.6	25,809	25.2
TOTAL	89,815	100.0	102,565	100.0[3]

Production (metric tons except as noted). Agriculture, forestry, fishing (1996): roots and tubers 86,000 (of which cassava 49,000, sweet potatoes 37,000), bananas 17,000, coconuts 8,000, coffee 7,000, palm oil 5,000, cacao beans 4,500, palm kernels 3,000; livestock (number of live animals) 36,000 sheep, 8,100 goats, 5,300 pigs, 4,800 cattle; roundwood (1995) 714,000 cu m; fish catch (1995) 3,800. Mining and quarrying: details, n.a.; however, in addition to quarrying for construction materials, unexploited deposits of iron ore, lead, zinc, manganese, and molybdenum are present; the offshore Alba gas-condensate

field, opened in 1992, achieved commercial production of 7,000 barrels of condensate per day in 1994 (11 months). Manufacturing (1995): veneer sheets 9,300. Construction: n.a. Energy production (consumption): electricity (kW-hr; 1994) 20,000,000 (20,000,000); coal, none (n.a.); crude petroleum[5], none (n.a.); petroleum products (metric tons; 1994) none (41,000); natural gas, none (n.a.).
Population economically active (1991): total 148,000; activity rate of total population 41.0% (participation rates [1983]: ages 15–64, 66.7%; female 35.7%; unemployed 24.2%).

Price and earnings indexes (1990 = 100)

	1987	1988	1989	1990	1991	1992	1993
Consumer price index	92.3	93.4	98.9	100.0	96.8	89.9	93.5
Earnings index	...	...	...	...	...	...	...

Household income and expenditure. Average household size (1980) 4.5; income per household: n.a.; sources of income (1988): wages and salaries 57.0%, business income 42.0%, other 1.0%; expenditure (1988): food and beverages 62.0%, clothing and footwear 10.0%; medical care 6.0%.
Tourism: tourism is a government priority but remains undeveloped.
Land use (1994): forested 65.2%; meadows and pastures 3.7%; agricultural and under permanent cultivation 8.2%; built-on, wasteland, and other 22.9%.

Foreign trade

Balance of trade (current prices)

	1990	1991	1992	1993	1994	1995
CFAF '000,000,000	−8.5	−15.5	−2.8	0.0	+17.1	+5.2
% of total	29.7%	43.7%	9.3%	0.0%	31.0%	6.4%

Imports (1995): CFAF 37,900,000,000 (capital equipment 52.7%; petroleum products 4.5%; other 42.8%). *Major import sources:* Cameroon 40.6%; Spain 18.2%; France 14.3%; United States 7.8%; Belgium 6.5%; The Netherlands 5.2%; Italy 3.9%.
Exports (1995): CFAF 43,100,000,000 (petroleum products 44.6%; wood 41.6%; food products 5.9%, of which cocoa 5.8%). *Major export destinations:* United States 34.0%; Japan 17.4%; China 12.7%; Spain 12.7%; Portugal 4.6%; The Netherlands 4.6%; France 4.6%; Nigeria 3.5%.

Transport and communications

Transport. Railroads: none. Roads (1993): total length 1,667 mi, 2,682 km (paved 19%). Vehicles (1994): passenger cars 6,500; trucks and buses 4,000. Merchant marine (1992): vessels (100 gross tons and over) 3; total deadweight tonnage 6,699. Air transport (1990): passenger-mi 4,000,000, passenger-km 7,000,000; short ton-mi cargo (1985) 700,000, metric ton-km cargo (1985) 1,000,000; airports (1997) with scheduled flights 1.

Communications

Medium	date	unit	number	units per 1,000 persons
Daily newspapers	1994	circulation	1,000	2.4
Radio	1996	receivers	200,000	464
Television	1995	receivers	37,000	88
Telephones	1995	main lines	2,500	5.9
Facsimile machines	1995	units	100	0.2

Education and health

Educational attainment (1983). Percentage of population age 15 and over having: no schooling 35.4%; some primary education 46.6%; primary 13.0%; secondary 2.3%; postsecondary 1.1%; not specified 1.6%. *Literacy* (1983): percentage of total population age 15 and over literate 62.2%; males literate 77.8%; females literate 48.6%.

Education (1993–94)

	schools	teachers	students	student/ teacher ratio
Primary (age 6–11)	781	1,381	75,751	54.9
Secondary (age 12–17)	9[6]	466	14,511	31.1
Voc., teacher tr.[7]	1[6]	122	2,105	17.3
Higher	4[6]	58	578	10.0

Health: physicians (1990) 99 (1 per 3,532 persons); hospital beds (1990) 992 (1 per 350 persons); infant mortality rate per 1,000 live births (1994) 102.6.
Food (latest): daily per capita caloric intake 2,230; 68% of FAO recommended minimum requirement.

Military

Total active duty personnel (1997): 1,320 (army 83.3%, navy 9.1%, air force 7.6%). *Military expenditure as percentage of GNP* (1995): 1.6% (world 2.8%); per capita expenditure U.S.$5.

[1]Conduct of November 1993 legislative elections was unacceptable to international observers. [2]As of Jan. 1, 1985, Equatorial Guinea became a member of the franc zone, substituting the CFA franc for the previous monetary unit, the ekwele; the CFA franc has a par value of 100 CFA francs to the French franc. [3]Detail does not add to total given because of rounding. [4]Includes three islets in Corisco Bay. [5]Equatorial Guinea announced an oil strike off Bioko in 1995 having an estimated production capacity of 10,000 barrels per day. [6]1987–88. [7]Efforts are being undertaken to provide the training necessary to qualify nondegree teachers for service. Also, teacher-training schools are to be expanded in order to increase the number of primary-school teachers.

Eritrea

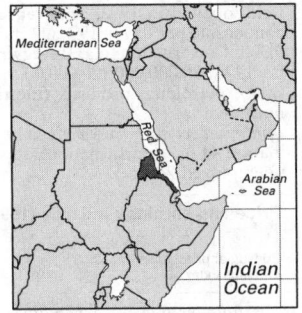

Official name: State of Eritrea.
Form of government: transitional
regime with one interim
legislative body
(Transitional National Assembly [150][1]).
Head of state and government:
President.
Capital: Asmara.
Official language: none.
Official religion: none.
Monetary unit: Nafka[2] = 100 cents;
valuation (Dec. 31, 1997)
1 U.S.$ = Br 7.28; 1 £ = Br 12.39.

Area and population

Regions[4]	Capitals	area[3] sq mi	area[3] sq km	population 1997 estimate
Debub-Keih-Bahri	Asseb (Aseb)	10,660	27,600	...
Semien-Keih-Bahri	Massawa (Mitsiwa)	10,730	27,800	...
Anseba	Keren	8,960	23,200	...
Gash-Barka	Barentu	12,820	33,200	...
Debub	Mendefera	3,090	8,000	...
Maekel	Asmara (Asmera)	500	1,300	...
TOTAL		46,770[5]	121,100	3,590,000

Demography

Population (1998): 3,842,000.
Density (1998): persons per sq mi 82.1, persons per sq km 31.7.
Urban-rural (1992): urban 16.3%; rural 83.7%.
Sex distribution (1997): male 50.00%; female 50.00%.
Age breakdown (1997): under 15, 42.8%; 15–29, 29.3%; 30–44, 13.6%; 45–59, 9.1%; 60–74, 4.2%; 75 and over, 1.0%.
Population projection: (2000) 4,142,000; (2010) 5,737,000.
Doubling time: 28 years.
Linguistic composition (1976): Tigrinya 49.0%; Tigré 31.7%; Afar 4.3%; Hedareb 3.9%; Bilen 3.1%; Saho 3.0%; Kunama 2.7%; Nara 2.1%; Rashaida 0.3%.
Religious affiliation (1995): Muslim 69.3%; Christian 30.7% (almost all Eritrean Orthodox).
Major cities (1992): Asmara 400,000; Asseb 50,000; Keren 40,000; Massawa 40,000; Mendefera 14,833[6].

Vital statistics

Birth rate per 1,000 population (1995–2000): 39.8 (world avg. 25.0).
Death rate per 1,000 population (1995–2000): 14.7 (world avg. 9.3).
Natural increase rate per 1,000 population (1995–2000): 25.1 (world avg. 15.7).
Total fertility rate (avg. births per childbearing woman; 1995–2000): 5.3.
Marriage rate per 1,000 population (1992): 6.8.
Divorce rate per 1,000 population: n.a.
Life expectancy at birth (1995–2000): male 49.1 years; female 52.1 years.
Major causes of death per 100,000 population: n.a.; morbidity (principal causes of illness) arises mainly in malaria and other infectious diseases, parasitic infections, malnutrition, diarrheal diseases, and dysenteries.

National economy

Budget (1995). Revenue: Br 1,345,200,000 (taxes 53.2%, of which direct taxes 25.3%, import duties 16.7%, indirect taxes 11.2%; nontax revenue 46.8%). Expenditures: Br 2,657,100,000 (current expenditure 80.2%, of which materials 32.0%, wages and salaries 24.3%; capital 19.8%).
Public debt (external, outstanding; 1996): U.S.$45,900,000.
Production (metric tons except as noted). Agriculture, forestry, fishing (1996): cereals 124,000, roots and tubers 110,000, sorghum 80,000, millet 35,000, barley 35,000, pulses 33,000, vegetables and melons 30,000, wheat 12,000, corn (maize) 10,000, sesame seeds 7,000, dry beans 4,000, chickpeas 4,000; livestock (number of live animals) 1,530,000 sheep, 1,400,000 goats, 1,320,000 cattle, 69,000 camels; fish catch (1995) 3,773, of which artisanal fisheries 746. Mining and quarrying (1995): salt 305,120; marble and granite are quarried, as are sand and aggregate (gravel) for construction; deposits of copper, zinc, mica, gold, iron, manganese, nickel, and lead exist but remain unexploited. Manufacturing (gross value in Br '000; 1995): beverages 163,400; food products 122,000; chemical products 101,900; leather products and shoes 57,900; textile products 54,300; metal products 47,000; nonmetallic products 31,300; paper and printing products 19,100; tobacco and matches 13,400. Construction: reconstruction, after some 30 years of civil war, is a principal concern of the government. Energy production: energy resources include hydroelectricity, fossil fuels, geothermal power, coal, biogas, solar power, and wind; commercial electricity production for 1986–87 was 148,664,000 kW-hr.
Household income and expenditure. Average household size (1984) 4.5; average annual income per household: n.a.; sources of income: n.a.; expenditure: n.a.
Persons economically active: n.a.

Price and earnings indexes (December 1992 = 100)

	1991	1992	1993	1994	1995
Consumer price index[7]	91.9	100.0	119.2	127.4	141.3
Earnings index	...	...	...	...	...

Gross national product (at current market prices; 1996): U.S.$807,000,000 (U.S.$220 per capita).

Structure of gross domestic product and labour force

	1995 in value Br '000,000	1995 % of total value	1992 labour force	1992 % of labour force
Agriculture	390.8	8.4	647	2.6
Manufacturing	571.3	12.2	11,894	48.3
Mining	2.1	0.1	292	1.2
Public utilities	59.8	1.3	2,284	9.3
Construction	235.6	5.0	298	1.2
Transp. and commun.	453.4	9.7	3,126	12.7
Trade	921.9	19.7	597	2.4
Finance	136.8	2.9	382	1.6
Pub. admin., defense	558.0	11.9	} 5,001	} 20.3
Services	156.2	3.3		
Other	1,195.7[8]	25.5[8]		
TOTAL	4,681.5[5]	100.0	24,621[5]	100.0[5]

Tourism (1993): 12 major hotels.
Land use (1994): forested 7.3%; agricultural and under permanent cultivation 5.1%; meadows and pastures 69.0%; other (predominantly barren land) 18.6%.

Foreign trade

Balance of trade (current prices)

	1992	1993	1994	1995
U.S.$'000,000	–263.0	–239.0	–331.0	–323.0
% of total	89.8%	76.8%	71.9%	66.6%

Imports (1995): Br 2,608,500,000 (machinery and transport equipment 45.2%, manufactured goods 19.1%, food products 17.1%, chemical products 6.0%, raw materials 2.5%, petroleum and petroleum products 1.9%, animal and vegetable oils 1.2%). *Major import sources:* Saudi Arabia 19.6%[9]; Italy 17.5%; United Arab Emirates 9.2%; Germany 5.9%; United States 5.9%; Ethiopia 5.5%; United Kingdom 3.8%; The Sudan 3.0%.
Exports (1995): Br 529,500,000 (raw materials 29.8%, food products 26.2%, manufactured goods 19.3%, beverages and tobacco 3.8%, machinery and transport equipment 3.8%, chemical products 2.5%). *Major export destinations:* Ethiopia 63.3%; The Sudan 16.4%; Yemen 4.9%; Saudi Arabia 3.7%; Italy 2.2%; Germany 0.5%.

Transport and communications

Transport. Railroads (1997): a 190-mi (306-km) rail line that formerly connected Massawa and Agordat is currently under reconstruction. A 24-mi (38-km) section between Amatere and Demas townships was reopened on Jan. 4, 1997. Roads (1995): total length 2,442 mi, 3,930 km (paved 21%). Vehicles (1995): automobiles 5,350, trucks and buses, n.a. Merchant marine: vessels (100 gross tons and over) n.a. Air transport (1993)[10]: passenger arrivals 47,645[11], passenger departures 42,548[11]; short ton cargo handled 25,907[12], metric ton cargo handled 28,557[12]; airports (1997) with scheduled flights 2.

Communications

Medium	date	unit	number	units per 1,000 persons
Television	1995	receivers	22,000	6.0
Telephones	1995	main lines	17,200	4.8
Facsimile machines	1995	units	800	0.2

Education and health

Literacy (1993): total population literate c. 20%.

Education (1995–96)

	schools	teachers	students	student/ teacher ratio
Primary (age 7–12)	537	5,828	241,725	41.5
Secondary (age 13–18)	86[13]	2,031	78,902	38.8
Voc., teacher tr. [14]	4[13]	133	1,246	9.4
Higher[15]	1	144	2,032	14.1

Health (1993): physicians 69 (1 per 36,000 persons); hospital beds (1986–87): 2,449 (1 per 1,100 persons); infant mortality rate per 1,000 live births (1995–2000) 98.0.
Food (1993): daily per capita caloric intake 1,750 (vegetable and animal products, n.a.): 93% of FAO recommended minimum requirement.

Military

Total active duty personnel (1997): estimated strength of Eritrean armed forces (predominantly former guerrillas) is some 45,000 to be reduced to 35,000.

[1]New constitution adopted on May 23, 1997; future scheduled election date for permanent legislature not set in September 1998. [2]The Nakfa was introduced in July 1997 as the new national currency; the Ethiopian birr (Br) will eventually be phased out. [3]Approximate figures. The published total area is 46,774 sq mi (121,144 sq km); water area is 7,776 sq mi (20,140 sq km). [4]On May 20, 1995, a resolution was approved dividing the country into six administrative regions, which would then be divided into region, subregion, and village categories. [5]Detail does not add to total given because of rounding. [6]1989. [7]Asmara only; year-end. [8]Including indirect taxes less subsidies. [9]Saudi Arabia is a transshipment point; not all goods included here are of Saudi Arabian origin. [10]Asmara airport only. [11]January to June only. [12]1987–88. [13]1992–93. [14]1994–95. [15]1993–94; full-time students only.

Internet resource for further information:
• Government of Eritrea http://www.NetAfrica.org/eritrea/

Estonia

Official name: Eesti Vabariik (Republic of Estonia).
Form of government: unitary multiparty republic with a single legislative body (Riigikogu[1] [101]).
Chief of state: President.
Head of government: Prime Minister.
Capital: Tallinn.
Official language: Estonian.
Official religion: none.
Monetary unit: 1 kroon (EEK) = 100 sents; valuation (Sept. 25, 1998)
1 U.S.$ = EEK 13.36;
1 £ = EEK 22.75.

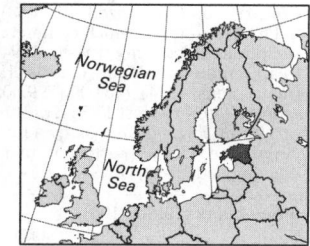

Area and population		area		population
				1995[2]
Counties	Capitals	sq mi	sq km	estimate
Harju	Tallinn	1,673	4,333	559,106
Hiiu	Kärdla	395	1,023	11,953
Ida-Viru	Jõhvi	1,299	3,364	206,418
Järva	Paide	1,013	2,623	43,639
Jõgeva	Jõgeva	1,005	2,604	42,146
Lääne	Haapsalu	920	2,383	32,586
Lääne-Viru	Rakvere	1,337	3,464	75,533
Pärnu	Pärnu	1,856	4,806	99,563
Põlva	Põlva	836	2,165	36,315
Rapla	Rapla	1,151	2,980	40,058
Saare	Kuressaare	1,128	2,922	40,759
Tartu	Tartu	1,193	3,090	154,483
Valga	Valga	790	2,047	40,014
Viljandi	Viljandi	1,386	3,589	64,377
Võru	Võru	890	2,305	44,633
TOTAL		17,462[3, 4]	45,227[3, 4]	1,491,583

Demography

Population (1998): 1,447,000.
Density (1998)[5]: persons per sq mi 88.4, persons per sq km 34.1.
Urban-rural (1996): urban 69.4%; rural 30.6%.
Sex distribution (1996): male 47.23%; female 52.77%.
Age breakdown (1995): under 15, 20.7%; 15–29, 21.0%; 30–44, 21.7%; 45–59, 18.1%; 60–74, 13.8%; 75 and over, 4.7%.
Population projection: (2000) 1,421,000; (2010) 1,351,000.
Ethnic composition (1994): Estonian 63.9%; Russian 29.0%; Ukrainian 2.7%; Belarusian 1.6%; Finnish 1.0%; other 1.8%.
Religious affiliation (1995): Christian 38.1%, of which Estonian Orthodox 19.6%, Evangelical Lutheran 13.7%; other (mostly nonreligious) 61.9%.
Major cities (1996): Tallinn 434,763; Tartu 101,901; Narva 75,211; Kohtla-Järve 68,533; Pärnu 51,807.

Vital statistics

Birth rate per 1,000 population (1996): 9.0 (world avg. 25.0); (1994) legitimate 59.1%; illegitimate 40.9%.
Death rate per 1,000 population (1996): 12.9 (world avg. 9.3).
Natural increase rate per 1,000 population (1996): –3.9 (world avg. 15.7).
Total fertility rate (avg. births per childbearing woman; 1995): 1.3.
Marriage rate per 1,000 population (1994): 4.9.
Divorce rate per 1,000 population (1994): 3.7.
Life expectancy at birth (1993): male 62.4 years; female 73.8 years.
Major causes of death per 100,000 population (1993): diseases of the circulatory system 792.9, of which ischemic heart diseases 485.6, cerebrovascular disease 255.6; malignant neoplasms (cancers) 225.3; accidents 110.5.

National economy

Budget (1995). Revenue: EEK 15,952,000,000 (payments for social security and welfare 31.7%, value-added taxes 27.0%, personal income taxes 24.5%, corporate taxes 7.3%). Expenditures: EEK 15,498,000,000 (current expenditure 94.8%, capital expenditure 5.2%).
Public debt (external, outstanding; 1996): U.S.$216,500,000.
Production (metric tons except as noted). Agriculture, forestry, fishing (1996): potatoes 500,000, barley 273,000, oats 100,000, wheat 100,000, rye 70,000, apples 17,000; livestock (number of live animals) 449,000 pigs, 370,400 cattle; roundwood (1996) 3,901,000 cu m; (1995) fish catch 212,000. Mining and quarrying (value of production in EEK '000,000; 1994): oil shale 781; peat 121. Manufacturing (value of production in EEK '000,000; 1994): meat and meat products 1,502; chemicals and chemical products 1,502; dairy products 1,368; fish and fish products 1,156; beverages 1,091; cement, bricks, and tiles 923; wood and wood products (excluding furniture) 922; textiles 908. Construction (value of construction in EEK '000,000; 1994): residential 295; nonresidential 1,836. Energy production (consumption): electricity (kW-hr; 1994) 9,152,000,000 (5,288,000,000); oil shale (metric tons; 1994) 16,000,000[6] (16,299,000); coal and coke (metric tons; 1994) none (97,000); crude petroleum, none (n.a.); natural gas (cu m; 1994) none (645,000,000).
Population economically active (1995): total 726,700; activity rate of total population 48.7% (participation rates [1989]: ages 15–64, 68.5%; female 52.5%; unemployed [1995] 3.6%).

Price and earnings indexes (1994 = 100)					
	1994	1995	1996	1997	1998[7]
Consumer price index	100.0	128.8	158.4	176.2	194.1
Monthly earnings index	100.0	139.1	176.3	203.7[7]	...

Household income and expenditure. Average household size (1994) 3.1[8]; average net income per household (1994) EEK 46,303 (U.S.$3,681)[8]; sources of income (1994)[9]: wages and salaries 53.0%, transfers 12.8%, self-employment 5.7%, other 28.5%; expenditure (1994)[9]: food and beverages 41.0%, housing 9.6%, transportation 9.2%, clothing and footwear 8.4%.
Gross national product (1996): U.S.$4,509,000,000 (U.S.$3,080 per capita).

Structure of gross domestic product and labour force				
	1994		1995	
	in value EEK '000,000	% of total value	labour force	% of labour force
Agriculture, fishing	2,787	9.2	85,900	11.8
Mining	540	1.8	10,300	1.4
Manufacturing	5,059	16.7	137,400	18.9
Public utilities	883	2.9	19,600	2.7
Construction	1,666	5.5	47,900	6.6
Trade, restaurants	5,615	18.6	109,300	15.0
Transp. and commun.	2,734	9.1	55,400	7.6
Finance, real estate	2,452	8.1	36,800	5.1
Pub. admin., defense	1,216	4.0	36,500	5.0
Services	2,418	8.0	123,900	17.0
Other	4,858[10]	16.1	63,700	8.8
TOTAL	30,228	100.0	726,700	100.0[11]

Tourism (1995): receipts U.S.$353,000,000; expenditures U.S.$90,000,000.
Land use (1994): forest 44.7%; pasture 7.2%; agriculture 32.2%; other 15.9%.

Foreign trade[12]

Balance of trade (current prices)					
	1992	1993	1994	1995	1996
EEK '000,000	+813	–302	–2,942	–5,841	–10,854
% of total	7.9%	1.4%	8.0%	12.2%	18.1%

Imports (1996): EEK 38,366,000,000 (mineral fuels and chemical products 23.4%, electrical and nonelectrical machinery 21.9%, foodstuffs 15.6%). *Major import sources:* Finland 36.2%; Russia 12.9%; Germany 8.9%.
Exports (1996): EEK 24,618,000,000 (mineral fuels and chemical products 18.1%, foodstuffs 16.1%, textiles and clothing 14.4%, wood and paper products 12.6%). *Major export destinations:* Finland 18.3%; Russia 16.7%; Sweden 11.4%; Latvia 8.4%; Germany 7.0%.

Transport and communications

Transport. Railroads (1996): route length 1,018 km; (1995) passenger-km 421,000,000; metric ton-km cargo 3,612,000,000. Roads (1995): total length 14,992 km (paved 54%). Vehicles (1995): passenger cars 383,000; trucks and buses 96,700. Merchant marine (1992): vessels (100 gross tons and over) 234; (1994) total deadweight tonnage 695,000. Air transport (1996)[13]: passenger-km 120,000,000; metric ton-km cargo 762,000; airports (1997) 1.

Communications				units per 1,000
Medium	date	unit	number	persons
Daily newspapers	1995	circulation	373,000	242
Television	1995	receivers	610,000	411
Telephones	1995	main lines	412,000	277
Cellular telephones	1995	subscribers	31,000	21
Facsimile machines	1995	units	13,000	8.7
Personal computers	1995	units	10,000	6.7

Education and health

Educational attainment (1989). Percentage of persons age 25 and over having: no formal schooling 2.2%; primary education 39.0%; secondary 45.1%; higher 13.7%. *Literacy* (1989): percentage of population age 15 and over literate 99.7%; males literate 99.9%; females literate 99.6%.

Education (1994–95)	schools	teachers	students	student/ teacher ratio
Primary } Secondary }	741	15,453	218,600	14.1
Vocational	84	1,585	27,806	17.5
Higher	22	...	23,169	...

Health (1994): physicians 4,680 (1 per 319 persons); hospital beds 12,521 (1 per 119 persons); (1996) infant mortality rate per 1,000 live births 12.1.
Food (1995): daily per capita caloric intake 2,836 (vegetable products 65%, animal products 35%); 111% of FAO recommended minimum requirement.

Military

Total active duty personnel (1997): 3,510 (army 95.4%, navy 4.6%). *Military expenditure as a percentage of GNP* (1995): 1.1% (world 2.8%); per capita expenditure U.S.$80.

[1]Official legislation bans translation of parliament's name. [2]January 1. [3]Total includes 1,092 sq mi (2,827 sq km) of inland water, of which the Estonian portion of Lake Peipus (590 sq mi [1,529 sq km]) is not distributed by county. [4]Total includes 1,596 sq mi (4,133 sq km) of Baltic Sea islands. [5]Based on land area only. [6]Estimated figure. [7]April. [8]Monthly average for December. [9]Annual average. [10]Includes taxes (EEK 4,076,000,000) less subsidies (EEK 675,000,000). [11]Detail does not add to total given because of rounding. [12]Imports f.o.b. in balance of trade and c.i.f. in commodities and trading partners. [13] Estonian Air.

Internet resource for further information:
• **Statistical Office of Estonia**
   http://www.stat.ee/wwwstat/eng_stat/

Ethiopia

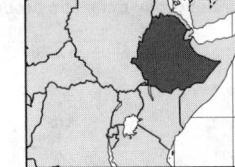

Official name: Federal Democratic
Republic of Ethiopia.
Form of government: federal republic[1]
with two legislative houses (Federal
Council [117]; Council of People's
Representatives [548]).
Chief of state: President.
Head of government: Prime Minister.
Capital: Addis Ababa.
Official language: none[2].
Official religion: none.
Monetary unit: 1 birr (Br) = 100 cents;
valuation (Sept. 25, 1998) 1 U.S.$ =
Br 6.99; 1 £ = Br 11.90.

Area and population		area		population
Regions[3]	Capital	sq mi	sq km	1994 census
Addis Ababa	...	...	...	2,112,737
Affar	...	...	...	1,106,383
Amhara	...	...	...	13,834,297
Benishangul-Gumuz	...	...	...	460,459
Dire Dawa	...	...	...	251,864
Gambela	...	...	...	181,862
Hariai	...	...	...	131,139
Oromiya	...	...	...	18,732,525
Southern Nations, Nationalities and Peoples	...	...	...	10,377,028
Tigray	...	...	...	3,136,267
TOTAL		437,794	1,133,882	...

Demography

Population (1998): 58,390,000.
Density (1998): persons per sq mi 133.4, persons per sq km 51.5.
Urban-rural (1995): urban 11.5%; rural 88.5%.
Sex distribution (1996): male 50.07%; female 49.93%.
Age breakdown (1996): under 15, 45.9%; 15–29, 26.6%; 30–44, 14.8%; 45–59,
8.2%; 60–74, 3.7%; 75 and over, 0.8%.
Population projection: (2000) 60,967,000; (2010) 74,832,000.
Ethnolinguistic composition (1983)[4]: Amhara 37.7%; Galla (Oromo) 35.3%;
Tigrinya 8.6%; Gurage 3.3%; Ometo (Omotic) 2.7%; Sidamo 2.4%.
Religious affiliation (1995): Ethiopian Orthodox 34.1%; Muslim 30.1%; tradi-
tional beliefs 12.2%; other Christian 8.3%; other 15.3%.
Major cities (1994): Addis Ababa 2,112,737; Dire Dawa 164,851; Harar 131,139;
Nazret 127,842; Gonder 112,249.

Vital statistics

Birth rate per 1,000 population (1995–2000): 48.2 (world avg. 25.0).
Death rate per 1,000 population (1995–2000): 16.2 (world avg. 9.3).
Natural increase rate per 1,000 population (1995–2000): 32.0 (world avg 15.7).
Total fertility rate (avg. births per childbearing woman; 1995–2000): 7.0
Life expectancy at birth (1995–2000): male 48.4 years; female 51.6 years.
Major causes of death (1987–88)[4,5]: infectious and parasitic diseases 33.1%;
respiratory diseases 15.7%; digestive system diseases 10.7%.

National economy

Budget (1995–96). Revenue: Br 6,817,300,000 (taxes 69.3%, of which import
duties 25.3%, income and profit tax 23.9%, sales tax 14.0%, export duties
1.7%; nontax revenue 30.7%). Expenditures: Br 8,573,200,000 (general services 20.4%; social services 15.9%, of which education 10.6%, public health
3.6%; debt payment 9.8%).
Public debt (external, outstanding; 1996): U.S.$9,483,000,000.
Tourism (1995): receipts U.S.$36,000,000; expenditures U.S.$25,000,000.
Gross national product (1996): U.S.$6,042,000,000 (U.S.$100 per capita).

Structure of gross domestic product and labour force[4]				
	1993–94		1995[6]	
	in value Br '000,000	% of total value	labour force	% of labour force
Agriculture	13,754.1	54.4	21,605,317	88.6
Manufacturing, mining	1,932.3	7.6	401,535	1.6
Construction	736.0	2.9	61,232	0.3
Public utilities	254.8	1.0	17,066	0.1
Transp. and commun.	1,163.5	4.6	103,154	0.4
Trade	2,551.3	10.1	935,937	3.8
Finance	2,035.2	8.0	19,451	0.1
Pub. admin., defense	1,792.7	7.1	}	
Services	1,008.2	4.0	1,252,224	5.1
Other	66.6[7]	0.3[7]	}	
TOTAL	25,294.7	100.0	24,395,916	100.0

Production (metric tons except as noted). Agriculture, forestry, fishing (1996):
corn (maize) 3,250,000, sorghum 1,980,000, wheat 1,970,000, sugarcane
1,600,000, barley 1,570,000, millet 360,000, potatoes 350,000, yams 263,000,
coffee 230,000, seed cotton 45,500; livestock (number of live animals)
29,900,000 cattle, 21,700,000 sheep, 16,700,000 goats, 8,580,000 horses, mules,
and asses, 1,000,000 camels; roundwood (1995) 48,454,000 cu m; fish catch
(1995) 6,400. Mining and quarrying (1994)[4]: cement 400,000; limestone
200,000; salt 165,000; gold 128,603 troy oz; platinum 48 troy oz. Manufacturing
(gross value in Br '000[8]; 1991–92)[4]: food and beverages 555,800; textiles
251,400; leather and shoes 162,300; cigarettes 106,000; chemicals 53,400.

Construction (authorized; 1987–88)[4,9]: residential 260,251 sq m; nonresidential 63,346 sq m, of which commercial 16,994 sq m. Energy production (consumption)[4]: electricity (kW-hr; 1994) 1,284,000,000 (1,284,000,000); coal, none
(n.a.); crude petroleum (barrels; 1994) n.a. (5,637,000); petroleum products
(metric tons; 1994) 746,000 (899,000); natural gas, n.a. (n.a.).
Land use (1994): forest 13.3%; pasture 20.0%; agriculture 11.0%; other 55.7%.
Population economically active (1995): total 24,606,100; activity rate of total
population 43.4% (participation rates: ages 15–64, 72.2%; female 41.5%;
unemployed [1993][4] 62.9%).

Price index (1990 = 100)[4]							
	1991	1992	1993	1994	1995	1996	1997
Consumer price index	135.7	150.0	155.3	167.1	183.9	174.6	168.1

Household income and expenditure. Average household size (1984)[4] 4.5; income per household (1981–82)[4] Br 1,728 (U.S.$835); sources of income
(1981–82): self-employment 79.5%, wages and salaries 0.2%, other 20.3%;
expenditure (1988)[4]: food 66.7%, fuel and power 15.9%, clothing and
footwear 6.8%, health care 3.1%, education 2.5%, household goods 2.1%.

Foreign trade

Balance of trade (current prices)[4]					
	1990	1991	1992	1993	1994	1995
Br '000,000	–1,271.6	–433.1	–1,360.5	–2,325.1	–2,708.3	–4,449.6
% of total	50.8%	55.5%	60.3%	53.9%	39.6%	46.1%

Imports (1994–95): Br 6,546,274,000 (motor vehicles 15.5%, petroleum products 15.2%, food and live animals 13.9%, machinery [including aircraft]
10.9%, metal wares 8.6%, fertilizers 5.3%, textiles 3.5%, pharmaceuticals
3.0%, chemicals 2.7%). *Major import sources:* Saudi Arabia 15.1%; U.S.
13.0%; Italy 11.1%; Germany 9.6%; Japan 6.1%; U.K. 4.9%.
Exports (1994–95): Br 2,834,844,000 (coffee 63.5%, hides 13.2%, pulses 3.6%,
petroleum products 3.4%). *Major export destinations:* Germany 30.8%; Japan
13.0%; Italy 7.6%; Djibouti 6.8%; U.S. 6.0%; France 5.8%.

Transport and communications

Transport. Railroads (1994–95)[10]: length 782 km; passenger-km 151,000,000;
metric ton-km cargo 93,000,000. Roads (1995): total length 19,400 km (paved
15%). Vehicles (1995): passenger cars 45,559; trucks and buses 20,462. Air
transport (1996)[11]: passenger-km 1,889,029,000; metric ton-km cargo
118,093,000; airports (1997) 31.

Communications				units per 1,000 persons
Medium	date	unit	number	
Daily newspapers	1996	circulation	77,000	1.3
Radio	1996	receivers	9,000,000	153
Television	1995	receivers	230,000	4.0
Telephones	1995	main lines	142,500	2.5
Facsimile machines	1995	units	1,400	—

Education and health

Educational attainment: n.a. *Literacy* (1995): total population age 15 and over
literate 35.5%; males 45.5%; females 25.3%.

Education (1994–95)	schools	teachers	students	student/ teacher ratio
Primary (age 7–12)	9,276	83,113	2,722,192	32.8
Secondary (age 13–18)	1,209[12]	22,779	747,142	32.8
Voc., teacher tr.	...	826	9,103	11.0
Higher	11[13]	1,937	32,671	16.9

Health: physicians (1988)[4] 1,466 (1 per 30,195 persons); hospital beds (1986–87)[4]
11,745 (1 per 3,873 persons); infant mortality rate (1995–2000) 107.0.
Food (1992)[4]: daily per capita caloric intake 1,610 (vegetable products 93%,
animal products 7%); 69% of FAO recommended minimum.

Military

Total active duty personnel (1997): the estimated strength of Ethiopian armed
forces was some 120,000. *Military expenditure as percentage of GNP* (1995):
2.2% (world 2.8%); per capita expenditure U.S.$2.

[1]New republic formally established on Aug. 22, 1995. [2]Amharic is the "working" language of the Federal Democratic Republic of Ethiopia. [3]Ethiopia now has 10 administrative regions as of the 1995 reorganization; area and capital detail were unavailable in
late 1998. [4]Includes Eritrea. [5]Percentage of illnesses in a sample population of hospital
outpatients. [6]For age 10 and up. [7]Less imputed bank service charges. [8]At constant prices
of 1978–79. [9]Addis Ababa only. [10]Includes 62 mi (100 km) of the Chemin de Fer
Djibouti-Ethiopiën (CDE) in Djibouti; excludes 190 mi (306 km) of Northern Ethiopia
Railway, not in use since 1978. [11]Ethiopian Airlines only. [12]1985–86. [13]1983–84.

Fiji

Official name: Sovereign Democratic Republic of Fiji.
Form of government[1]: republic with two legislative houses (Senate [34[2]]; House of Representatives [70]).
Chief of state: President.
Head of government: Prime Minister.
Capital: Suva.
Official language: English.
Official religion: none
Monetary unit: 1 Fiji dollar (F$) = 100 cents; valuation (Sept. 25, 1998) 1 U.S.$ = F$2.06; 1 £ = F$3.51.

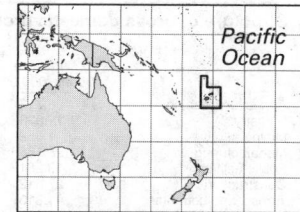

Area and population

Divisions		area		population
Provinces	Capitals	sq mi	sq km	1996 census
Central	Suva			
Naitasiri	—	643	1,666	126,641
Namosi	—	220	570	5,742
Rewa	—	105	272	101,547
Serua	—	320	830	15,461
Tailevu	—	369	955	48,216
Eastern	Levuka			
Kadavu	—	185	478	9,535
Lau	—	188	487	12,211
Lomaiviti	—	159	411	16,214
Rotuma	—	18	46	2,810
Northern	Labasa			
Bua	—	532	1,379	14,988
Cakaudrove	—	1,087	2,816	44,321
Macuata	—	774	2,004	80,207
Western	Lautoka			
Ba	—	1,017	2,634	212,197
Nadroga-Navosa	—	921	2,385	54,083
Ra	—	518	1,341	30,904
TOTAL	—	7,055[3]	18,272[3]	775,077

Demography

Population (1998): 793,000.
Density (1998): persons per sq mi 112.4, persons per sq km 43.4.
Urban-rural (1996): urban 46.4%; rural 53.6%.
Sex distribution (1996): male 50.82%; female 49.18%.
Age breakdown (1996): under 15, 35.4%; 15–29, 27.4%; 30–44, 20.7%; 45–59, 11.4%; 60–74, 4.2%; 75 and over, 0.9%.
Population projection: (2000) 811,000; (2010) 912,000.
Doubling time: 38 years.
Ethnic composition (1996): Fijian 50.8%; Indian 43.7%[4]; other 5.5%.
Religious affiliation (1986): Christian 52.9%; Hindu 38.1%; Muslim 7.8%; Sikh 0.7%; other 0.5%.
Major cities (1996; "urban centres"): Suva 167,421; Lautoka 42,917; Nadi 30,791; Labasa 24,187; Nausori 21,645.

Vital statistics

Birth rate per 1,000 population (1997): 22.7 (world avg. 25.0); (1978) legitimate 82.7%; illegitimate 17.3%.
Death rate per 1,000 population (1997): 4.6 (world avg. 9.3).
Natural increase rate per 1,000 population (1997): 18.1 (world avg. 15.7).
Total fertility rate (avg. births per childbearing woman; 1997): 2.8.
Marriage rate per 1,000 population (1988): 9.6.
Life expectancy at birth (1997): male 70.0 years; female 75.0 years.
Major causes of death per 100,000 population (1987): diseases of the circulatory system 153.4; malignant neoplasms (cancers) 35.5; accidents, poisoning, and violence 32.2; diseases of the respiratory system 31.7; diabetes mellitus 27.3; infectious and parasitic diseases 18.2; birth trauma 16.5.

National economy

Budget (1995). Revenue: F$702,429,000 (income taxes, estate taxes, and gift duties 56.0%; customs duties and port dues 29.6%; fees, royalties, and sales 6.4%). Expenditures: F$681,048,000 (departmental expenditure 72.0%; public-debt charges 23.7%; pensions and gratuities 4.3%).
Public debt (external, outstanding; 1996): U.S.$146,500,000.
Production (metric tons except as noted). Agriculture, forestry, fishing (1996): sugarcane 4,110,000, coconuts 210,000, cassava 25,600, taro 21,900, paddy rice 18,500, bananas 6,300, sweet potatoes 4,000, tomatoes 3,000, yams 2,700, pineapples 2,500; livestock (number of live animals) 354,000 cattle, 211,000 goats, 121,000 pigs; roundwood (1995) 598,200 cu m; fish catch (1995) 34,577. Mining and quarrying (1995): gold 3,477 kg; silver 1,572 kg. Manufacturing (U.S.$'000,000; 1994): food products 84; wearing apparel 28; wood and wood products 16; beverages 15; chemical products 13. Construction (1995): residential 97,000 sq m; nonresidential 64,000 sq m. Energy production (consumption): electricity (kW-hr; 1994) 520,000,000 (520,000,000); coal (metric tons; 1994) none (20,000); crude petroleum, none (n.a.); petroleum products (metric tons; 1994) none (201,000); natural gas, none (n.a.).
Population economically active (1986): total 241,160; activity rate of total population 33.7% (participation rates: ages 15–64, 56.0%; female 21.2%; unemployed [1990] 6.4%).

Price and earnings indexes (1990 = 100)

	1991	1992	1993	1994	1995	1996	1997
Consumer price index	106.5	111.7	117.5	118.2	120.8	124.5	128.7
Earnings index	...	...	...	...	...	...	...

Gross national product (1996): U.S.$1,983,000,000 (U.S.$2,470 per capita).

Structure of gross domestic product and labour force

	1995		1986	
	in value F$'000[5]	% of total value	labour force	% of labour force
Agriculture	198,235	20.5	106,305	44.1
Mining	1,544	0.2	1,345	0.5
Manufacturing	116,148	12.0	18,106	7.5
Construction	45,782	4.7	11,786	4.9
Public utilities	13,924	1.4	2,154	0.9
Transp. and commun.	156,688	16.2	13,151	5.4
Trade	211,696	21.8	26,010	10.8
Finance	119,595	12.3	6,016	2.5
Pub. admin., defense } Services	138,699	14.3	36,619	15.2
Other	−33,540[6]	−3.4[6]	19,668[7]	8.2[7]
TOTAL	968,771	100.0	241,160	100.0

Household income and expenditure. Average household size (1986) 5.7; income per household (1980) F$2,837 (U.S.$3,546); sources of income (1973): wages and salaries 81.5%, self-employment 9.1%, other 9.4%; expenditure (1991[8]): food, beverages, and tobacco 41.5%, housing and energy 21.4%, transportation and communications 12.9%, household durable goods 6.5%.
Tourism (1995): receipts from visitors U.S.$312,000,000; expenditures by nationals abroad U.S.$55,000,000.
Land use (1994): forested 64.9%; agricultural and under permanent cultivation 14.2%; meadows and pastures 9.5%; other 11.4%.

Foreign trade

Balance of trade (current prices)

	1991	1992	1993	1994	1995	1996
F$'000,000	−279.57	−275.23	−521.42	−409.36	−454.45	−225.26
% of total	20.1%	20.9%	30.7%	20.4%	22.9%	10.9%

Imports (1996): F$1,380,071,000 (durable manufactures 25.9%; machinery and transport equipment 23.8%; food, beverages, and tobacco 15.1%; mineral fuels 13.4%; miscellaneous manufactured consumer articles 11.6%; chemicals 7.4%). *Major import sources:* Australia 44.4%; New Zealand 14.8%; United States 9.3%; Japan 5.2%; Singapore 5.0%; Taiwan 2.6%; China 2.5%; Thailand 1.8%; United Kingdom 1.8%; Hong Kong 1.7%.
Exports (1996)[9]: F$790,960,000 (sugar 34.5%; clothing 23.7%; gold 10.3%; fish 7.6%; timber 5.8%; molasses 2.8%; coconut oil 0.7%). *Major export destinations*[10]: Australia 33.4%; United Kingdom 18.1%; United States 10.0%; Japan 8.6%; New Zealand 4.5%; Portugal 4.4%; Malaysia 3.8%.

Transport and communications

Transport. Railroads (1995)[11]: length 370 mi, 595 km. Roads (1995): total length 3,200 mi, 5,100 km (paved 20%). Vehicles (1995): passenger cars 49,712; trucks and buses 33,928. Merchant marine (1992): vessels (100 gross tons and over) 64; total deadweight tonnage 60,444. Air transport (1996)[12]: passenger-km 1,194,652,000; metric ton-km cargo 75,367,000; airports(1997) with scheduled flights 13.

Communications

Medium	date	unit	number	units per 1,000 persons
Daily newspapers	1995	circulation	54,000	68
Radio	1996	receivers	450,000	561
Television	1995	receivers	70,000	89
Telephones	1995	main lines	64,800	83
Cellular telephones	1995	subscribers	2,200	2.8
Facsimile machines	1995	units	3,000	3.8

Education and health

Educational attainment (1986). Percentage of population age 25 and over having: no formal schooling 28.3%; primary only 19.1%; some secondary 44.1%; secondary 4.1%; postsecondary 3.3%; other 1.1%. *Literacy* (1995): total population age 15 and over literate 91.6%; males literate 93.8%; females literate 89.3%.

Education (1992)

	schools	teachers	students	student/teacher ratio
Primary (age 5–15)	693	4,644	145,630	31.4
Secondary (age 16–19)	142	3,045	60,237	19.8
Voc., teacher tr.	45	625	7,283	11.6
Higher[13]	5[14]	277	7,908	28.5

Health: (1994) physicians 295 (1 per 2,576 persons); hospital beds (1993) 1,747 (1 per 438 persons); infant mortality rate per 1,000 live births (1997) 20.0.
Food (1995): daily per capita caloric intake 3,078 (vegetable products 81%, animals products 19%); 135% of FAO recommended minimum requirement.

Military

Total active duty personnel (1997): 3,600 (army 91.7%, navy 8.3%, air force, none). *Military expenditure as percentage of GNP* (1995): 1.7% (world 2.8%); per capita expenditure U.S.$42.

---

[1]A new constitution became effective on July 27, 1998. [2]All seats are appointed. [3]Detail does not add to total given because of rounding. [4]The emigration of Indian population after the coup in 1987 has resulted in the reemergence of a Fijian majority. [5]Constant 1977 prices. [6]Less imputed bank service charges. [7]Not stated and unemployed. [8]Weights of consumer price index components based on 3,000 urban households. [9]Excludes reexports valued at F$226,438,000. [10]Based on exports of local products only. [11]Owned by the Fiji Sugar Corporation. [12]Air Pacific only. [13]1991. [14]1983.

Finland

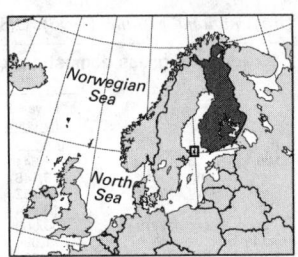

Official name: Suomen Tasavalta (Finnish); Republiken Finland (Swedish) (Republic of Finland).
Form of government: multiparty republic with one legislative house (Parliament [200]).
Chief of state: President.
Head of government: Prime Minister.
Capital: Helsinki.
Official languages: none[1].
Official religion: none[2].
Monetary unit: 1 markka (Fmk) = 100 penniä, valuation (Sept. 25, 1998) 1 U.S.$ = Fmk 5.09; 1 £ = Fmk 8.67.

Area and population

Provinces	Capitals	area sq mi	area sq km	population 1998 estimate[3]
Åland (Ahvenamaa)	Mariehamn (Maarianhamina)	599	1,552	25,392
Etelä-Suomi	Hämeenlinna	13,273	34,378	2,037,147
Itä-Suomi	Mikkeli	23,444	60,720	603,724
Länsi-Suomi	Turku	31,264	80,975	1,829,093
Lappi	Rovaniemi	38,203	98,946	199,051
Oulu	Oulu	23,773	61,572	452,942
TOTAL		130,559[4, 5]	338,145[4, 5]	5,147,349

Demography

Population (1998): 5,154,000.
Density (1998)[6]: persons per sq mi 43.8, persons per sq km 16.9.
Urban-rural (1997): urban 65.1%; rural 34.9%.
Sex distribution (1997): male 48.72%; female 51.28%.
Age breakdown (1997): under 15, 18.9%; 15–29, 18.9%; 30–44, 22.6%; 45–59, 20.4%; 60–74, 13.2%; 75 and over, 6.0%.
Population projection: (2000) 5,189,000; (2010) 5,194,000.
Doubling time: not applicable; population is stable.
Linguistic composition (1997): Finnish 92.9%; Swedish 5.7%; other 1.4%.
Religious affiliation (1998): Evangelical Lutheran 85.6%; Finnish (Greek) Orthodox 1.1%; nonreligious 12.3%; other 1.0%.
Major cities (1997): Helsinki 532,053 (metro area [1995] 874,953); Espoo 196,260[7]; Tampere 186,026; Vantaa 168,778[7]; Turku 166,929; Oulu 111,556.

Vital statistics

Birth rate per 1,000 population (1996): 11.8 (world avg. 25.0); (1995) legitimate 66.9%; illegitimate 33.1%.
Death rate per 1,000 population (1996): 9.6 (world avg. 9.3).
Natural increase rate per 1,000 population (1996): 2.2 (world avg. 15.7).
Total fertility rate (avg. births per childbearing woman; 1996): 1.7.
Marriage rate per 1,000 population (1995): 4.6.
Divorce rate per 1,000 population (1995): 2.7.
Life expectancy at birth (1995): male 72.8 years; female 80.2 years.
Major causes of death per 100,000 population (1994): ischemic heart diseases 262.5; malignant neoplasms (cancers) 192.3; cerebrovascular disease 112.4; diseases of the respiratory system 71.8; accidents 50.8.

National economy

Budget (1996). Revenue: Fmk 192,989,000,000 (value-added taxes 23.6%, loans 20.4%, income and property taxes 20.1%, excise duties 12.7%). Expenditures: Fmk 192,985,000,000 (social security and health 25.0%; state debt 15.2%; education 12.2%; agriculture 5.9%; defense 4.6%).
National debt (September 1996): U.S.$88,873,000,000.
Tourism (in U.S.$'000,000; 1996): receipts 1,674; expenditures 2,366.
Production (metric tons except as noted). Agriculture, forestry, fishing (1995): silage 5,633,000, barley 1,763,000, sugar beets 1,110,000, oats 1,097,000, potatoes 798,000, turnips 125,000; livestock (number of live animals) 1,295,000 pigs, 1,185,000 cattle, 208,000 reindeer; roundwood 50,217,000 cu m; fish catch 184,829. Mining and quarrying (1995): chromite (gross weight) 598,000. Manufacturing (value added in Fmk '000,000; 1994): wood pulp, paper, and paperboard 19,818; nonelectrical machinery 12,091; electrical machinery 9,390; food products 9,193; printing and publishing 7,129; iron and steel 4,806; industrial and basic chemicals 4,611. Construction (completed; 1995): residential 8,700,000 cu m; nonresidential 14,830,000 cu m. Energy production (consumption): electricity (kW-hr; 1996) 66,756,000,000 ([1994] 65,420,000,000); coal (metric tons; 1994) none (7,501,000); crude petroleum (barrels; 1994) none (66,747,000); petroleum products (metric tons; 1994) 10,898,000 (9,734,000); natural gas (cu m; 1994) none (3,390,000,000).
Population economically active (1995): total 2,521,000; activity rate of total population 49.4% (participation rates: ages 15–64, 73.5%; female 47.0%; unemployed [May 1996–April 1997] 15.5%).

Price and earnings indexes (1990 = 100)

	1992	1993	1994	1995	1996	1997	1998[8]
Consumer price index	107.4	109.7	110.9	112.0	112.6	113.4	115.0
Annual earnings index	108.4	109.2	111.4	116.6	121.1	123.5[9]	...

Household income and expenditure (1994). Average household size 2.2; disposable income per household Fmk 129,000 (U.S.$24,700); sources of disposable income: wages and salaries 70.1%, transfer payments 8.7%, self-employment 8.7%, other 12.5%; expenditure (1994): housing and energy 28.7%, food and beverages 22.9%, transportation and communications 20.0%.
Gross national product (1996): U.S.$119,086,000,000 (U.S.$23,240 per capita).

Structure of gross domestic product and labour force

	1995 in value Fmk '000,000	% of total value	labour force	% of labour force
Agriculture, fishing	8,713	1.8 }	176,000	7.0
Forestry	12,933	2.7 }		
Mining	1,852	0.4	5,000	0.2
Manufacturing	128,186	26.8	486,000	19.3
Public utilities	13,261	2.8	26,000	1.0
Construction	27,812	5.8	174,000	6.9
Transp. and commun.	41,813	8.8	177,000	7.0
Trade, restaurants	52,590	11.0	353,000	14.0
Finance, real estate	90,157	18.9	198,000	7.8
Pub. admin., defense	91,437	19.1 }	832,000	33.0
Services	13,187	2.8 }		
Other	−4,429	−0.9	96,000[10]	3.9[10]
TOTAL	477,512	100.0	2,521,000[4]	100.0[4]

Land use (1994): forested 76.1%; meadows and pastures 0.4%; agricultural and under permanent cultivation 8.5%; other 15.0%.

Foreign trade[11]

Balance of trade (current prices)

	1992	1993	1994	1995	1996	1997
Fmk '000,000	+12,516	+30,949	+33,552	+47,465	+44,802	+52,506
% of total	6.2%	12.4%	12.2%	15.6%	13.7%	14.2%

Imports (1996): Fmk 140,996,000,000 (raw materials 50.2%; consumer goods 21.2%; mineral fuels 8.9%). *Major import sources:* Germany 15.1%; Sweden 11.9%; U.K. 8.8%; U.S. 7.4%; Russia 7.3%; Japan 5.2%; France 4.5%.
Exports (1996): Fmk 185,798,000,000 (metal products and machinery 40.3%; paper, paper products, and publishing 23.4%; chemicals and chemical products 9.7%). *Major export destinations:* Germany 12.1%; Sweden 10.7%; U.K. 10.2%; U.S. 7.9%; Russia 6.1%; France 4.2%; The Netherlands 4.0%.

Transport and communications

Transport. Railroads: route length (1995) 5,859 km; passenger-km 2,616,000,000; metric ton-km cargo 9,564,000,000. Roads (1996): total length[12] 77,722 km (paved 63%). Vehicles (1996): passenger cars 1,900,855; trucks and buses 260,115. Air transport (1996)[13]: passenger-km 10,709,000,000; metric ton-km cargo 241,302,000; airports (1996) 24.

Communications

Medium	date	unit	number	units per 1,000 persons
Daily newspapers	1995	circulation	2,368,000	464
Radio	1996	receivers	4,950,000	966
Television	1995	receivers	1,900,000	372
Telephones	1995	main lines	2,796,000	547
Cellular telephones	1995	subscribers	1,017,600	199
Facsimile machines	1995	units	132,000	26
Personal computers	1995	units	930,000	182

Education and health

Educational attainment (1995). Percentage of population age 25 and over having: incomplete upper-secondary education 45.1%; complete upper secondary or vocational 41.5%; higher 13.4%. *Literacy:* virtually 100%.

Education (1995–96)

	schools	teachers	students	student/ teacher ratio
Primary/Lower Secondary (age 7–15)	4,474	...	588,162	...
Upper Secondary (age 16–18)	477	...	134,851	...
Voc. (incl. higher)	520	21,245[14]	199,200	9.5[14]
Higher	21	7,790[14]	133,359	16.4[14]

Health (1995): physicians 13,771[15] (1 per 371 persons); hospital beds (1994) 49,877[16] (1 per 102 persons); infant mortality rate per 1,000 live births (1996) 3.9.
Food (1995): daily per capita caloric intake 3,022 (vegetable products 59%, animal products 41%); 112% of FAO recommended minimum requirement.

Military

Total active duty personnel (1996): 32,500 (army 80.0%, navy 7.7%, air force 12.3%). *Military expenditure as percentage of GNP* (1994): 2.1% (world 3.0%); per capita expenditure U.S.$386.

[1]Finnish and Swedish were official languages until mid-1995 and national languages thereafter. [2]The Evangelical Lutheran and Finnish (Greek) Orthodox churches have special recognition. [3]January 1st. [4]Detail does not add to total given because of rounding. [5]Total includes land area of 117,580 sq mi (304,529 sq km) and inland water area of 12,979 sq mi (33,616 sq km). [6]Based on land area only. [7]Within Helsinki urban area. [8]April. [9]Average of 2nd and 3rd quarters. [10]Includes 85,000 unemployed persons not previously employed and 11,000 not adequately defined. [11]Imports c.i.f., exports f.o.b. [12]Excludes Åland Islands. [13]Finnair only. [14]1994–95. [15]Registered professionals of working age. [16]Excludes beds in hospitals operated by specialized institutions.

Internet resources for further information:
• Embassy of Finland (Washington, D.C.) http://www.finland.org/facts.html
• Statistics Finland http://www.stat.fi/sf/tilsivue.html

France

Official name: République Française (French Republic).
Form of government: republic with two legislative houses (Parliament; Senate [321], National Assembly [577]).
Chief of state: President.
Head of government: Prime Minister
Capital: Paris
Official language: French.
Official religion: none.
Monetary unit: 1 franc (F) = 100 centimes; valuation (Sept. 25, 1998) 1 U.S.$ = F 5.60; 1 £ = F 9.53

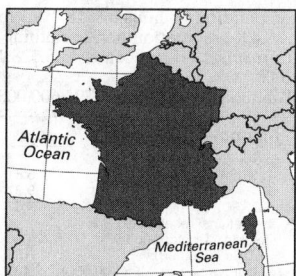

Atlantic Ocean / Mediterranean Sea

Area and population

Regions Departments	Capitals	area sq mi	area sq km	population 1995[1] census
Alsace				
Bas-Rhin	Strasbourg	1,836	4,755	994,100
Haut-Rhin	Colmar	1,361	3,525	695,700
Aquitaine				
Dordogne	Périgueux	3,498	9,060	388,700
Gironde	Bordeaux	3,861	10,000	1,263,500
Landes	Mont-de-Marsan	3,569	9,243	318,300
Lot-et-Garonne	Agen	2,070	5,361	303,600
Pyrénées-Atlantiques	Pau	2,952	7,645	592,200
Auvergne				
Allier	Moulins	2,834	7,340	352,500
Cantal	Aurillac	2,211	5,726	155,200
Haute-Loire	Le Puy	1,922	4,977	206,600
Puy-de-Dôme	Clermont-Ferrand	3,077	7,970	601,100
Basse-Normandie				
Calvados	Caen	2,142	5,548	633,800
Manche	Saint-Lô	2,293	5,938	484,100
Orne	Alençon	2,356	6,103	294,700
Bourgogne				
Côte-d'Or	Dijon	3,383	8,763	507,300
Nièvre	Nevers	2,632	6,817	230,400
Saône-et-Loire	Mâcon	3,311	8,575	554,800
Yonne	Auxerre	2,868	7,427	331,400
Bretagne				
Côtes-d'Armor	Saint-Brieuc	2,656	6,878	536,600
Finistère	Quimper	2,600	6,733	840,600
Ille-et-Vilaine	Rennes	2,616	6,775	836,700
Morbihan	Vannes	2,634	6,823	633,000
Centre				
Cher	Bourges	2,793	7,235	321,100
Eure-et-Loir	Chartres	2,270	5,880	410,100
Indre	Châteauroux	2,622	6,791	234,400
Indre-et-Loire	Tours	2,366	6,127	545,800
Loir-et-Cher	Blois	2,449	6,343	312,500
Loiret	Orléans	2,616	6,775	609,300
Champagne-Ardenne				
Ardennes	Charleville-Mézières	2,019	5,229	292,000
Aube	Troyes	2,318	6,004	293,100
Haute-Marne	Chaumont	2,398	6,211	200,100
Marne	Châlons-sur-Marne	3,151	8,162	567,300
Corse[2]				
Corse-du-Sud	Ajaccio	1,550	4,014	124,400
Haute-Corse	Bastia	1,802	4,666	135,300
Franche-Comté				
Doubs	Besançon	2,021	5,234	494,100
Haute-Saône	Vesoul	2,070	5,360	229,900
Jura	Lons-le-Saunier	1,930	4,999	252,100
Territoire de Belfort	Belfort	235	609	137,100
Haute-Normandie				
Eure	Évreux	2,332	6,040	535,400
Seine-Maritime	Rouen	2,424	6,278	1,241,500
Île-de-France				
Essonne	Évry	696	1,804	1,145,900
Hauts-de-Seine	Nanterre	68	176	1,405,300
Paris	Paris	40	105	2,130,900
Seine-et-Marne	Melun	2,284	5,915	1,179,300
Seine-Saint-Denis	Bobigny	91	236	1,405,500
Val-de-Marne	Créteil	95	245	1,234,700
Val-d'Oise	Pontoise	481	1,246	1,108,400
Yvelines	Versailles	882	2,284	1,367,700
Languedoc-Roussillon				
Aude	Carcassonne	2,370	6,139	305,300
Gard	Nîmes	2,260	5,853	607,100
Hérault	Montpellier	2,356	6,101	859,900
Lozère	Mende	1,995	5,167	72,800
Pyrénées-Orientales	Perpignan	1,589	4,116	376,200
Limousin				
Corrèze	Tulle	2,261	5,857	236,300
Creuse	Guéret	2,149	5,565	127,100
Haute-Vienne	Limoges	2,131	5,520	355,500
Lorraine				
Meurthe-et-Moselle	Nancy	2,024	5,241	716,200
Meuse	Bar-le-Duc	2,400	6,216	194,000
Moselle	Metz	2,400	6,216	1,015,900
Vosges	Épinal	2,268	5,874	385,400
Midi-Pyrénées				
Ariège	Foix	1,888	4,890	136,600
Aveyron	Rodez	3,373	8,736	266,700
Gers	Auch	2,416	6,257	172,300
Haute-Garonne	Toulouse	2,436	6,309	990,700
Hautes-Pyrénées	Tarbes	1,724	4,464	224,000
Lot	Cahors	2,014	5,217	157,000
Tarn	Albi	2,223	5,758	341,700
Tarn-et-Garonne	Montauban	1,435	3,718	205,200
Nord-Pas-de-Calais				
Nord	Lille	2,217	5,742	2,556,800
Pas-de-Calais	Arras	2,576	6,671	1,438,000

Area and population (continued)

	Capitals	sq mi	sq km	1995[1] census
Pays de la Loire				
Loire-Atlantique	Nantes	2,631	6,815	1,089,400
Maine-et-Loire	Angers	2,767	7,166	721,200
Mayenne	Laval	1,998	5,175	281,900
Sarthe	Le Mans	2,396	6,206	521,600
Vendée	La Roche-sur-Yon	2,595	6,720	525,700
Picardie				
Aisne	Laon	2,845	7,369	539,500
Oise	Beauvais	2,263	5,860	762,700
Somme	Amiens	2,382	6,170	553,100
Poitou-Charentes				
Charente	Angoulême	2,300	5,956	341,200
Charente-Maritime	La Rochelle	2,650	6,864	540,700
Deux-Sèvres	Niort	2,316	6,004	346,800
Vienne	Poitiers	2,699	6,990	390,400
Provence-Alpes–Côte d'Azur				
Alpes-de-Haute-Provence	Digne	2,674	6,925	138,800
Alpes-Maritimes	Nice	1,660	4,299	1,011,100
Bouches-du-Rhône	Marseille	1,964	5,087	1,797,000
Hautes-Alpes	Gap	2,142	5,549	118,800
Var	Toulon	2,306	5,973	872,900
Vaucluse	Avignon	1,377	3,567	489,600
Rhône-Alpes				
Ain	Bourg-en-Bresse	2,225	5,762	500,400
Ardèche	Privas	2,135	5,529	282,900
Drôme	Valence	2,521	6,530	426,800
Haute-Savoie	Annecy	1,694	4,388	617,300
Isère	Grenoble	2,869	7,431	1,064,600
Loire	Saint-Étienne	1,846	4,781	748,500
Rhône	Lyon	1,254	3,249	1,561,900
Savoie	Chambéry	2,327	6,028	366,800
TOTAL		210,026	543,965	58,010,100[3]

Demography

Population (1998): 58,841,000.
Density (1998): persons per sq mi 280.2, persons per sq km 108.2.
Urban-rural (1996): urban 72.9%; rural 27.1%.
Sex distribution (1996): male 48.71%; female 51.29%.
Age breakdown (1995): under 15, 19.7%; 15–29, 21.4%; 30–44, 22.2%; 45–59, 16.9%; 60–74, 13.6%; 75 and over, 6.2%.
Population projection: (2000) 59,317,000; (2010) 61,757,000.
Doubling time: not applicable; doubling time exceeds 100 years.
Ethnolinguistic composition (1990): French (mother tongue) 93.6%, of which fully or substantially bilingual in Occitan 2.7%, German (mostly Alsatian) 2.6%, Breton 1.0%, Catalan 0.4%; Arabic 2.5%; other 3.9%.
Religious affiliation (1997): Roman Catholic 76.3%; Muslim 5.5%; Protestants 2.4%; other 15.8%.
Major cities (1990): Paris 2,152,423 (metropolitan area 9,060,257); Marseille 800,550 (1,231,082); Lyon 415,487 (1,262,223); Toulouse 358,658 (608,430); Nice 342,439 (475,507); Strasbourg 252,338 (338,483); Nantes 244,995 (492,255); Bordeaux 210,336 (685,456); Montpellier 207,996 (236,788).
National origin (1990): French 93.6%, of which Martiniquais 0.2%, Guadeloupian 0.2%, Réunionese 0.2%; Portuguese 1.1%; Algerian 1.1%; Moroccan 1.0%; Italian 0.4%; Spanish 0.4%; Turkish 0.3%; other 2.1%.
Mobility (1990). Population living in same residence as in 1982: 51.4%; same region 89.0%; different region 8.8%; different country 2.2%.
Households (1993). Average household size 2.6; 1 person 27.7%, 2 persons 32.0%, 3 persons 17.4%, 4 persons 14.7%, 5 persons or more 8.2%. Family households (1990): 14,118,940 (72.1%); nonfamily 5,471,460 (27.9%, of which 1-person 24.6%).
Immigration (1994): immigrants admitted 64,102 (Algeria 13.6%, Morocco 12.3%, Turkey 7.3%, Tunisia 3.4%, Sri Lanka 2.7%, Lebanon 1.3%).

Vital statistics

Birth rate per 1,000 population (1996): 12.6 (world avg. 25.0); (1994) legitimate 63.9%; illegitimate 36.1%.
Death rate per 1,000 population (1996): 9.2 (world avg. 9.3).
Natural increase rate per 1,000 population (1996): 3.4 (world avg. 15.7).
Total fertility rate (avg. births per childbearing woman; 1995): 1.7.
Marriage rate per 1,000 population (1996): 4.8.
Divorce rate per 1,000 population (1993): 1.9.
Life expectancy at birth (1994): male 73.7 years; female 81.8 years.
Major causes of death per 100,000 population (1994): heart disease and other circulatory diseases 286.7; malignant neoplasms (cancers) 247.6; accidents and violence 76.9; respiratory diseases 63.7; digestive tract diseases 43.7.

Social indicators

Educational attainment (1990). Percentage of population age 25 and over having: primary 22.1%; lower secondary 7.8%; higher secondary and vocational 29.4%; postsecondary 11.6%; undeclared attainment 29.1%.

Distribution of income (1984)

percentage of household income by quintile				
1	2	3	4	5 (highest)
7.1%	12.3%	17.1%	23.2%	40.3%

Quality of working life. Average workweek (1994): 38.9 hours. Annual rate per 100,000 workers for: injury or accident 5,322 (deaths 0.8%); accidents in transit to work 708 (deaths 68.3); industrial illness 16.6[4]; death 4.8[4]. Average days lost to labour stoppages per 1,000 workers (1993): 23.0. Average length of journey to work (1990): 8.7 mi (14 km).
Access to services (1992). Proportion of dwellings having: central heating 86.0%; piped water 97.0%; indoor plumbing 95.8%.
Social participation. Eligible voters participating in last (May and June 1997) national election: *c.* 78%. Population over 15 years of age participating in voluntary associations: 28.0%.

Social deviance. Offense rate per 100,000 population (1994) for; murder 0.8; rape 11.3; other assault 290.8; theft (including burglary and housebreaking) 5,204.2. Incidence per 100,000 in general population of: alcoholism, n.a. (deaths related to alcoholism; 1991) 5.0; suicide (1993) 21.1.

Leisure (1987–88). Participation rate for favourite leisure activities: watching television 82%; reading magazines 79%; listening to radio 75%; entertaining relatives 64%; visiting relatives 61%; attending fairs/expositions 56%.

Material well-being (1994). Households possessing: automobile 79.5%; colour television 92.4%; VCR 52.8%; refrigerator 99.0%, washing machine 89.4%.

National economy

Gross national product (1996): U.S.$1,533,619,000,000 (U.S.$26,270 per capita).

Structure of gross domestic product and labour force

	1995 in value F '000,000	% of total value	labour force	% of labour force
Agriculture	183,444	2.6	1,026,000	4.1
Mining	57,507	0.8	118,900	0.5
Manufacturing	1,542,442	21.8	3,992,700	15.8
Construction	342,836	4.8	1,466,600	5.8
Public utilities	178,069	2.5	162,900	0.6
Transp. and commun.	433,518	6.1	1,272,800	5.0
Trade[5]	1,012,441	14.3	3,482,000	13.8
Finance	320,501	4.5	601,900	2.4
Pub. admin., defense	1,323,570	18.7	6,248,100	24.7
Services	1,290,922	18.2	3,953,800	15.7
Other	403,238[6]	5.7[6]	2,934,600[7]	11.6[7]
TOTAL	7,088,488	100.0	25,260,300	100.0

Budget (1996). Revenue: F 1,552,100,000,000 (value-added taxes 49.1%; direct taxes 38.2%; customs taxes 10.2%). Expenditure: F 1,541,300,000,000 (education 22.5%, defense 15.6%, debt service 14.7%, social welfare 10.8%).

Manufacturing enterprises (1995)

	no. of enter-prises[8]	no. of employees	annual salaries as a % of avg. of all salaries[8]	annual value added (F '000,000)
Food products	55,197	545,900	87	208,065
Transport equipment	4,293	508,700	108	167,357
Electrical machinery	15,620	433,600	118	156,221
Iron and steel	27,847	403,800	96	131,376
Mechanical equipment	32,134	390,300	104	127,637
Petroleum refineries	180	46,200	174	117,041
Printing, publishing	30,359	231,900	125	83,083
Textiles and wearing apparel	29,701	281,500	78	63,633
Rubber products	5,875	204,200	94	57,758
Chemical products	1,442	102,100	128	51,146
Paper and paper products	1,916	101,500	102	38,585
Metal products	442	43,700	103	28,115
Glass products	1,536	52,400	104	16,638
Footwear	4,236	55,400	75	12,970

Production (metric tons except as noted). Agriculture, forestry, fishing (1997): wheat 34,070,000, sugar beets 32,171,000, corn (maize) 15,110,000, barley 10,161,000, grapes 7,000,000, potatoes 6,500,000, rapeseed 3,512,000, dry peas 3,087,000, sunflower seeds 2,193,000, apples 2,192,000, tomatoes 785,000, carrots 644,000, green peas 575,000, oats 563,000, cauliflower 530,000, lettuce 528,000, peaches 474,000, sorghum 426,000, string beans 325,000, onions 324,000; livestock (number of live animals) 20,300,000 cattle, 14,968,000 pigs, 10,126,000 sheep, 1,114,000 goats; roundwood (1995) 46,345,000 cu m; fish catch (1995) 793,413. Mining and quarrying (1995): iron ore 1,500,000; potash salts 800,000; bauxite 130,800; uranium 840; gold 151,124 troy oz; silver 48,231 troy oz. Manufacturing (1995): cement 19,896,000; crude steel 18,132,000; pig iron 12,876,000; paper products 8,700,000; rubber products 619,400, of which tires 59,268,000 units; aluminum 586,000; automobiles 3,200,000 units. Construction (dwelling units completed; 1993) 299,000.

Retail trade enterprises (1995[1])

	no. of enter-prises	no. of employees	weekly wages as a % of all wages	annual turnover (F '000,000)
Large food stores	4,373	385,402	...	617,222
Clothing stores	51,873	195,535	...	126,504
Pharmacies	22,301	126,508	...	121,980
Small food stores	64,565	163,474	...	110,928
butcher shops	21,548	59,962	...	36,732
Furniture stores	7,179	53,080	...	54,390
Electrical and electronics stores	10,990	55,560	...	43,995
Department stores	736	35,074	...	27,741
Publishing and paper	15,083	40,375	...	24,591
Gas, coal, and other energy products	6,042	25,375	...	19,204

Energy production (consumption)[9]: electricity (kW-hr; 1994) 475,622,000,000 (412,454,000,000); coal (metric tons; 1994) 8,039,000 (21,809,900); crude petroleum (barrels; 1994) 20,297,000 (562,907,000); petroleum products (metric tons; 1994) 69,078,000 (66,994,000); natural gas (cu m; 1994) 2,517,200,000 (33,449,900,000).

Population economically active (1995): total 25,260,300; activity rate of total population 43.4% (participation rates: ages 15–64, 67.6% [10]; female 45.0%; unemployed 11.7%).

Price and earnings indexes (1990 = 100)

	1991	1992	1993	1994	1995	1996	1997
Consumer price index	103.2	105.7	107.9	109.7	111.6	113.9	115.2
Earnings index	104.4	108.4	111.7	115.0	116.0	118.2	121.4

Household income and expenditure (1995). Average household size 2.6; average annual income per household F 302,560 (U.S.$60,610); sources of income: wages and salaries 70.0%, self-employment 24.4%, social security 5.6%,

expenditure: housing 18.2%, food 16.8%, transportation 14.5%, health 10.4%, recreation 6.9%, clothing 5.4%.

Tourism (1996): receipts U.S.$28,181,700,000; expenditures U.S.$17,505,400,000.

Public debt (1997): F 3,794,600,000,000 (U.S.$657,840,000,000).

Financial aggregates

	1992	1993	1994	1995	1996	1997[10]
Exchange rate, F per:						
U.S. dollar	5.51	5.90	5.35	4.90	5.24	6.05
£	9.37	8.73	8.35	7.60	8.90	9.81
SDR	7.57	8.10	7.80	7.28	7.53	8.25
International reserves (U.S.$)						
Total (excl. gold; '000,000)	27,028	22,649	26,257	26,853	26,796	29,011
SDRs ('000,000)	163	331	362	955	981	968
Reserve pos. in IMF ('000,000)	2,482	2,310	2,375	2,756	2,695	2,400
Foreign exchange	24,384	20,008	23,520	23,142	23,120	25,643
Gold ('000,000 fine troy oz)	81.85	81.85	81.85	81.85	81.85	81.85
% world reserves	8.7	8.7	8.7	9.1	9.0	9.2
Interest and prices						
Central bank discount (%)	9.50	9.50	9.50	...	...	...
Govt. bond yield (%)	8.60	6.91	8.52	7.59	6.39	5.58
Industrial share prices (1990 = 100)	102.3	112.6	112.5	102.5	115.9	152.4
Balance of payments (U.S.$'000,000)						
Balance of visible trade	1,661	8,418	7,868	11,175	15,099	...
Imports, f.o.b.	223,561	187,873	215,593	259,225	258,963	...
Exports, f.o.b.	225,222	196,291	223,461	270,400	274,062	...
Balance of invisibles	1,819	3,503	263	5,268	5,412	...
Balance of payments, current account	3,480	11,921	8,128	16,443	20,511	...

Land use (1994): forest 27.3%; pasture 19.3%; agriculture 35.4%; other 18.0%.

Foreign trade

Balance of trade (current prices)

	1992	1993	1994	1995	1996	1997
F '000,000,000	+31.0	+89.5	+50.7	+62.7	+85.7	+170.4
% of total	1.3%	3.9%	2.0%	2.2%	3.0%	5.3%

Imports (1995): F 1,380,400,000,000 (machinery and transport equipment 38.5%, of which transport equipment 14.6%; agricultural products 11.0%; chemicals 8.4%; fuels 6.9%). *Major import sources:* Germany 18.3%; Italy 9.9%, U.K. 9.5%; Belgium-Luxembourg 8.8%; Spain 6.1%; U.S. 6.1%.

Exports (1995): F 1,428,800,000,000 (machinery and transport equipment 42.6%, of which transport equipment 19.5%; agricultural products 15.1%; chemical products 8.4%; plastics 3.2%). *Major export destinations:* Germany 17.7%; Italy 9.5%; Belgium-Luxembourg 8.6%; U.K. 7.6%; U.S. 7.4%.

Transport and communications

Transport. Railroads (1995): route length 31,940 km; passenger-km 55,470,000,000; metric ton-km cargo 47,400,000,000. Roads (1995): total length 812,700 km (paved [1985] 92%). Vehicles (1995): passenger cars 25,100,000; trucks and buses 5,005,000. Merchant marine (1992): vessels (100 gross tons and over) 729; total deadweight tonnage 4,981,027. Air transport (1994): passenger-km 67,500,000,000; metric ton-km cargo 11,300,000,000; airports (1996) with scheduled flights 61.

Communications

Medium	date	unit	number	units per 1,000 persons
Daily newspapers	1994	circulation	13,685,000	235
Radio	1995	receivers	50,000,000	860
Television	1995	receivers	33,600,000	579
Telephones	1995	main lines	32,400,000	558
Cellular telephones	1995	subscribers	1,379,000	23.8
Facsimile machines	1995	units	96,200	1.6
Personal computers	1995	units	7,800,000	134

Education and health

Literacy (1980): total population literate 41,112,000 (98.8%); males literate 19,933,000 (98.9%); females literate 21,179,000 (98.7%).

Education (1994–95)

	schools	teachers	students	student/ teacher ratio
Primary (age 6–10)	41.244	301,699[11]	4,012,600	...
Secondary (age 11–18)	11,212	454,000[12]	4,486,063 1,251,295 }	12.6[12]
Voc., teacher tr. }				
Higher	1,062[13]	52,663[12]	2,107,600	...

Health: physicians (1994) 160,235 (1 per 361 persons); hospital beds (1995) 679,731 (1 per 86 persons); infant mortality rate (1996) 4.9.

Food (1995): daily per capita caloric intake 3,588 (vegetable products 62%, animal products 38%); 142% of FAO recommended minimum requirement.

Military

Total active duty personnel (1996): 398,900 (army 59.3%, navy 15.9%, air force 22.2%, other 2.6%). *Military expenditure as percentage of GNP* (1995): 3.1% (world 2.8%); per capita expenditure U.S.$826.

[1]January 1. [2]In May 1992, Corse was granted local autonomy (with its own directly elected assembly), changing its regional status to "territorial collective." [3]Detail does not add to total given because of rounding. [4]1989. [5]Includes hotels. [6]Imputed rents and imputed bank service charges. [7]Unemployed. [8]1991. [9]All energy statistics include Monaco. [10]August. [11]Includes preprimary teachers. [12]1993–94. [13]1988–89.

Internet resources for further information:
• **Economie et Statistique**
  http://www.insee.fr/vf/produits/pub/ecostat/index.htm

Gabon

Official name: République Gabonaise (Gabonese Republic).
Form of government: unitary multiparty republic with a Parliament comprising two legislative houses (Senate [91]; National Assembly [120]).
Chief of state: President.
Head of government: Prime Minister.
Capital: Libreville.
Official language: French.
Official religion: none.
Monetary unit: 1 CFA franc (CFAF) = 100 centimes; valuation (Sept. 25, 1998) 1 U.S.$ = CFAF 560.38; 1 £ = CFAF 954.05.

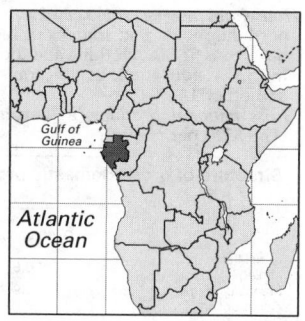

Area and population

| | | area | | population |
| | | | | 1983 |
Provinces	Capitals	sq mi	sq km	census[1]
Estuaire	Libreville	8,008	20,740	463,187
Haut-Ogooué	Franceville	14,111	36,547	104,301
Moyen-Ogooué	Lambaréné	7,156	18,535	42,316
Ngounié	Mouila	14,575	37,750	77,781
Nyanga	Tchibanga	8,218	21,285	39,430
Ogooué-Ivindo	Makokou	17,790	46,075	48,862
Ogooué-Lolo	Koulamoutou	9,799	25,380	43,915
Ogooué-Maritime	Port-Gentil	8,838	22,890	97,913
Woleu-Ntem	Oyem	14,851	38,465	97,271
TOTAL		103,347[2]	267,667	1,014,976

Demography

Population (1998): 1,208,000.
Density (1998): persons per sq mi 11.7, persons per sq km 4.5.
Urban-rural (1993): urban 73.1%; rural 26.9%.
Sex distribution (1995): male 49.32%; female 50.68%.
Age breakdown (1995): under 15, 39.1%; 15–29, 22.3%; 30–44, 17.2%; 45–59, 12.4%; 60–74, 7.2%; 75 and over, 1.7%.
Population projection: (2000) 1,244,000; (2010) 1,445,000.
Doubling time: 32 years.
Ethnic composition (1983): Fang 35.5%; Punu, Sira, and Nzebi 16.9%; Mpongwe 15.1%; Mbete 14.2%; other 18.3%.
Religious affiliation (1995): Christian 79.9%, of which Roman Catholic 50.1%, Protestant 18.0%; traditional beliefs 19.1%; Muslim 1.0%.
Major cities (1993): Libreville 362,386; Port-Gentil 80,841; Franceville 30,246; Oyem 22,669; Moanda 21,921.

Vital statistics

Birth rate per 1,000 population (1990–95): 37.2 (world avg. 25.0).
Death rate per 1,000 population (1990–95): 15.5 (world avg. 9.3).
Natural increase rate per 1,000 population (1990–95): 21.8 (world avg. 15.7).
Total fertility rate (avg. births per childbearing woman; 1990–95): 5.3.
Life expectancy at birth (1990–95): male 51.9 years; females 55.2 years.
Major causes of death per 100,000 population: n.a.; however, in the early 1990s major causes of morbidity and mortality included malaria, shigellosis (infection with dysentery), tetanus, cardiovascular diseases, trypanosomiasis, and tuberculosis.

National economy

Budget (1996). Revenue: CFAF 755,100,000,000 (oil revenues 59.5%; customs duties 16.6%; other current revenues 23.9%). Expenditures: CFAF 676,500,000,000 (current expenditure 75.7%, of which wages and salaries 27.3%, service on public debt 25.6%; capital expenditure 22.8%).
Public debt (external, outstanding; 1996): U.S.$3,874,000,000.
Tourism (1995): receipts from visitors U.S.$4,000,000; expenditures by nationals abroad U.S.$112,000,000.
Production (metric tons except as noted). Agriculture, forestry, fishing (1996): roots and tubers 408,000 (of which cassava 220,000, yams 120,000, taro 65,000), plantains 250,000, sugarcane 220,000, corn (maize) 27,000, peanuts (groundnuts) 15,000, bananas 9,000, palm oil 3,000, cacao beans 1,000; livestock (number of live animals) 172,000 sheep, 165,000 pigs, 84,000 goats, 39,000 cattle, 3,000,000 chickens; roundwood (1995) 4,347,000 cu m; fish catch (1995) 27,978. Mining and quarrying (1996): manganese ore 1,983,000; uranium ore 623,000. Manufacturing (1994): fuel oil 289,000; diesel and gas oil 240,000; cement 147,789; kerosene 100,000; wheat flour 31,000[3]; refined sugar 13,687; beer 816,419[4] hectolitres; soft drinks 415,613[4] hectolitres; cigarettes 399,000,000 units[3]; plywood 47,100,000 cu m; textiles are also significant. Energy production (consumption): electricity (kW-hr; 1995) 1,024,000,000 (794,000,000); crude petroleum (barrels; 1995) 132,500,000 ([1994] 11,600,000); petroleum products (metric tons; 1994) 776,000 (633,000); natural gas (cu m; 1994) 129,000,000 (129,000,000); fuelwood (cu m; 1994) 2,812,000 (2,812,000).
Population economically active (1993): total 375,944; activity rate of total population 37.0% (participation rates [1985]: ages 15–64, 68.2%; female 38.4%; unemployed [1996] 20%).
Household income and expenditure. Average household size (1993) 5.2; income per household: n.a.; sources of income (1983): private sector 73.4%, public sector 26.6%; expenditure (1969)[5]: food and tobacco 54.7%, clothing and footwear 17.5%, housing 13.0%, recreation 6.6%, transportation and communications 6.3%, health care 1.9%.

Price and earnings indexes (1990 = 100)

	1990	1991	1992	1993	1994	1995	1996
Consumer price index	100.0	105.4	100.2	91.3	124.3	136.7	141.8
Earnings index	...	...	...	...	...	...	...

Land use (1994): forested 77.2%; meadows and pastures 18.2%; agricultural and under permanent cultivation 1.8%; other 2.8%.
Gross national product (1996): U.S.$4,444,000,000 (U.S.$3,950 per capita).

Structure of gross domestic product and labour force

| | 1996 | | 1993 | |
	in value CFAF '000,000	% of total value	labour force	% of labour force
Agriculture, forestry, fishing	198,700	7.1	156,000[6]	41.6
Mining	1,190,500	42.6		
Manufacturing	166,300	6.0	43,000[6]	11.5
Construction	98,900	3.5		
Public utilities	40,300	1.4		
Transportation and communications	147,600	5.3		
Trade	424,300	15.2	115,000[6]	30.7
Finance	14,900	0.5		
Services	265,900	9.5		
Pub. admin., defense	245,300	8.8	61,000[6]	16.2
TOTAL	2,792,800[2]	100.0[2]	376,000[2]	100.0

Foreign trade

Balance of trade (current prices)

	1991	1992	1993	1994	1995	1996
CFAF '000,000	+386,100	+362,800	+419,400	+882,000	+870,800	+1,095,800
% of total	44.3%	43.6%	46.7%	50.6%	49.3%	52.5%

Imports (1996): CFAF 495,900,000,000 ([1994] machinery and mechanical equipment 32.1%, food and agricultural products 17.5%, transport equipment 15.1%, construction materials 14.0%, chemical products 13.1%). *Major import sources* (1996): France 35.2%; Africa 28.0%; other EEC 20.9%; United States 4.8%; Japan 3.9%.
Exports (1996): CFAF 1,591,700,000 (crude petroleum and petroleum products 81.4%, wood 12.3%, manganese ore and concentrate 4.9%, uranium ore and concentrate 0.8%). *Major export destinations* (1996): United States 50.0%; France 16.3%; other EU 11.9%; Japan 8.3%; Africa 2.3%.

Transport and communications

Transport. Railroads (1995): length 424 mi, 683 km; passenger-km 77,000,000; metric ton-km cargo carried 503,000,000. Roads (1995): total length 4,850 mi, 7,800 km (paved 10%). Vehicles (1992): passenger cars 23,000; trucks and buses 17,000. Merchant marine (1992): vessels (100 gross tons and over) 29; total deadweight tonnage 30,186. Air transport (1996)[7]: passenger-mi 452,000,000, passenger-km 728,000,000; short ton-mi cargo 23,700,000, metric ton-km cargo 34,600,000; airports (1997) with scheduled flights 17.

Communications

Medium	date	unit	number	units per 1,000 persons
Daily newspapers	1996	circulation	40,000	34.1
Radio	1995	receivers	200,000	173
Television	1995	receivers	40,000	34.6
Telephones	1995	main lines	32,000	27.7
Cellular telephones	1995	subscribers	4,000	3.5
Facsimile machines	1995	units	400	0.3
Personal computers	1995	units	6,000	5.2

Education and health

Educational attainment of economically active population (1993): none, or incomplete primary 37.7%; complete primary 32.1%; complete secondary 16.4%; postsecondary certificate or degree 13.8%. *Literacy* (1995): total population age 15 and over literate 63.2%; males literate 73.7%; females literate 53.3%.

Education (1994–95)

	schools	teachers	students	student/ teacher ratio
Primary	1,105	4,709	247,018	52.5
Secondary	51[8]	1,897	56,457	29.8
Voc., teacher tr.	29[8]	485	9,261	19.1
Higher[9, 10]	2	299	3,000	10.0

Health: physicians (1989) 448 (1 per 2,377 persons); hospital beds (1985) 5,156 (1 per 197 persons); infant mortality rate per 1,000 live births (1990–95) 94.
Food (1995): daily per capita caloric intake 2,511 (vegetable products 86%, animal products 14%); 107% of FAO recommended minimum requirement.

Military

Total active duty personnel (1997): 4,700 (army 68.1%, navy 10.6%, air force 21.3%), excluding 600 French troops. *Military expenditure as percentage of GNP* (1995): 2.6% (world 2.8%); per capita expenditure U.S.$90.

[1]De jure; excludes nonnationals numbering 100,000 to 150,000 (mainly West African) prior to their large-scale expulsion in February 1995. [2]Detail does not add to total given because of rounding. [3]1992. [4]1995. [5]Libreville only. [6]Derived values. [7]Air Garbon only. [8]1984–85. [9]Universities only. [10]1991–92.

Internet resources for further information:
• **Welcome to Gabon (official site: Presidency of Gabon) http://presidence-gabon.com/index-a.html**

Gambia, The

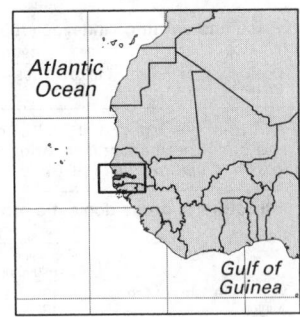

Official name: The Republic of the Gambia.
Form of government: multiparty republic[1] with one legislative house (National Assembly [49])[2].
Head of state and government: President[1].
Capital: Banjul.
Official language: English.
Official religion: none.
Monetary unit: 1 dalasi (D) = 100 butut; valuation (Sept. 25, 1998) 1 U.S.$ = D 10.22; 1 £ = D 17.40.

Area and population

| | | area | | population |
| | | | | 1993 |
Divisions	Capitals	sq mi	sq km	census[3]
Kombo St. Mary[4, 5]	Kanifing	29	76	228,214
Lower River	Mansakonko	625	1,618	65,146
MacCarthy Island	Kuntaur/Georgetown	1,117	2,894	156,021
North Bank	Kerewan	871	2,256	156,462
Upper River	Basse	799	2,069	155,059
Western	Brikama	681	1,764	234,917
City				
Banjul[5]	—	5	12	42,326
TOTAL		4,127[6]	10,689[6]	1,038,145

Demography

Population (1998): 1,292,000.
Density (1998)[7]: persons per sq mi 388.5, persons per sq km 150.0.
Urban-rural (1993): urban 36.7%; rural 63.3%.
Sex distribution (1993): male 50.08%; female 49.92%.
Age breakdown (1993): under 15, 43.8%; 15–29, 27.7%; 30–44, 15.1%; 45–59, 6.8%, 60–74, 3.5%; 75 and over, 1.4%; not stated 1.7%.
Population projection: (2000) 1,381,000; (2010) 1,864,000.
Doubling time: 23 years.
Ethnic composition (1993): Malinke 34.1%; Fulani 16.2%; Wolof 12.6%; Dyola 9.2%; Soninke 7.7%; other 20.2%.
Religious affiliation (1993); Muslim 95.0%; Christian 4.0%; traditional beliefs and other 1.0%.
Major cities/urban areas (1986): Serekunda 102,600[4]; Banjul 42,326 (Greater Banjul 270,540[5, 8]); Brikama 24,300; Bakau 23,600[4]; Farafenni 10,168[9].

Vital statistics

Birth rate per 1,000 population (1997): 43.9 (world avg. 25.0); legitimate, n.a.; illegitimate, n.a.
Death rate per 1,000 population (1997): 13.3 (world avg. 9.3).
Natural increase rate per 1,000 population (1997): 30.6 (world avg. 15.7).
Total fertility rate (avg. births per childbearing woman; 1997): 5.8.
Marriage rate per 1,000 population: n.a.
Divorce rate per 1,000 population: n.a.
Life expectancy at birth (1997): male 51.2 years; female 55.8 years.
Major causes of death per 100,000 population: n.a.; however, major infectious diseases include malaria, gastroenteritis and dysentery, pneumonia and bronchitis, measles, schistosomiasis, and whooping cough.

National economy

Budget (1995–96). Revenue: D 861,700,000 (tax revenue 79.9%, of which import duties and excises 31.8%, income taxes 15.8%, sales tax 7.6%; nontax revenue and grants 20.1%). Expenditures: D 877,700,000 (administrative expenses 24.9%; goods and services 17.4%; interest payments 15.8%; agriculture 11.2%; education and culture 9.2%; transportation and communications 6.9%; public services 2.2%).
Production (metric tons except as noted). Agriculture, forestry fishing (1996): millet 61,500, peanuts (groundnuts) 46,000, paddy rice 19,600, corn (maize) 10,000, cassava 6,000, seed cotton 4,500, pulses (mostly beans) 4,000, palm oil 2,500, palm kernels 2,000; livestock (number of live animals) 323,000 cattle, 224,000 goats, 159,000 sheep; roundwood (1995) 1,220,700 cu m; fish catch (1993) 20,479, of which Atlantic Ocean 18,079, inland water 2,400. Mining and quarrying: sand and gravel are excavated for local use. Manufacturing (value of production in D '000; 1982): processed food, including peanut and palm-kernel oil 62,878; beverage 10,546; textiles 3,253; chemicals and related products 1,031; nonmetals 922; printing and publishing 358; leather 150. Construction: n.a. Energy production (consumption): electricity (kW-hr; 1994) 75,000,000 (75,000,000); coal, none (none); crude petroleum, none (none); petroleum products (metric tons; 1994) none (75,000); natural gas, none (none).
Public debt (external, outstanding; 1996): U.S.$412,000,000.
Population economically active (1992); total 412,000; activity rate of total population 47.2% (participation rates: [1983] ages 15–64, 78.2%; female 46.3%; unemployed, n.a.).

Price and earnings indexes (1990 = 100)

	1991	1992	1993	1994	1995	1996	1997
Consumer price index	108.6	118.9	126.6	128.7	137.7	139.3	143.2
Earnings index	...	...	...	...	...	...	...

Tourism (1995): receipts from visitors U.S.$23,000,000; expenditures by nationals abroad U.S.$16,000,000.

Household income and expenditure. Average household size (1983) 8.3; income per household: n.a.; sources of income: n.a.; expenditure (1991)[10]: food and beverages 58.0%, clothing and footwear 17.5%, energy and water 5.4%, housing 5.1%, education, health, transportation and communications, recreation, and other 14.0%.
Gross national product (at current market prices; 1996): U.S.$386,000,000 (U.S.$320 per capita).

Structure of gross domestic product and labour force

| | 1995–96 | | 1983 | |
	in value D '000,000[11]	% of total value	labour force	% of labour force
Agriculture	120.9	21.3	239,940	73.7
Mining			66	0.0
Manufacturing	32.9	5.7	8,144	2.5
Construction	28.2	5.0	4,373	1.3
Public utilities	3.2	0.6	1,233	0.4
Transp. and commun.	112.1	19.8	8,014	2.5
Trade	91.2	16.1	16,551	5.1
Finance	36.3	6.4	4,577	1.4
Public administration	60.7	10.6	8,295	2.5
Services	22.3	4.0	9,381	2.9
Other	59.7[12]	10.5[12]	25,049[13]	7.7[13]
TOTAL	567.5	100.0	325,623	100.0

Land use (1994): forested 10.0%; meadows and pastures 19.0%; agricultural and under permanent cultivation 17.2%; built-on area, wasteland, and other 53.8%.

Foreign trade

Balance of trade (current prices)

	1993	1994	1995	1996	1997
D '000,000	−1,767.5	−1,665.1	−1,184.6	−2,160.5	−2,687.3
% of total	59.4%	70.7%	79.2%	85.7%	90.2%

Imports (1995–96): D 2,062,900,000 (1993–94: basic manufactures 25.4%; food 24.7%; machinery and transport equipment 23.5%; mineral fuels and lubricants 6.0%; chemicals and related products 5.1%). Major import sources: China 24.7%; Belgium-Luxembourg 10.1%; United Kingdom 8.5%; Hong Kong 7.7%; Senegal 5.4%; Thailand 4.9%.
Exports (1995–96): D 1,318,900,000 (1993–94; domestic exports 15.7%, of which groundnuts 8.5%; reexports 84.3%[14]). Major export destinations: Belgium-Luxembourg 50.4%; Japan 21.5%; Guinea 6.2%; Hong Kong 4.3%; United Kingdom 3.6%; France 2.6%; Spain 2.2%.

Transport and communications

Transport. Railroads: none. Roads (1995): total length 1,483 mi, 2,640 km (paved 35%). Vehicles (1995): passenger cars 7,950; trucks and buses 8,240. Merchant marine (1992): vessels (100 gross tons and over) 11; total deadweight tonnage 2,029. Air transport (1992): passenger arrivals and departures 275,000; cargo 3,000 metric tons; airports (1997) with scheduled flights 1.

Communications

Medium	date	unit	number	units per 1,000 persons
Daily newspapers	1994	circulation	2,000	2.0
Radio	1995	receivers	140,000	126
Television	1995	receivers	6,000	6.1
Telephones	1995	main lines	19,200	17
Cellular telephones	1995	subscribers	1,400	1.3
Facsimile machines	1995	units	1,000	0.9

Education and health

Educational attainment (1973). Percentage of population age 20 and over having: no formal schooling 90.8%; primary education 6.2%; secondary 2.6%; higher 0.4%. Literacy (1995): total population age 15 and over literate 38.6%; males literate 52.8%; females literate 24.9%.

Education (1994)

	schools	teachers	students	student/ teacher ratio
Primary (age 8–14)	250	3,158	105,471	33.4
Secondary (age 15–21)[15]	32	1,126	27,120	24.1
Postsecondary	9[16]	155	1,591	10.3

Health (1990–91): physicians 61 (1 per 14,536 persons); hospital beds 601 (1 per 1,475 persons); infant mortality rate per 1,000 live births (1997) 79.
Food (1994): daily per capita caloric intake 2,157 (vegetable products 95%, animal products 5%); 91% of FAO recommended minimum requirement.

Military

Total active duty personnel (1997): 875. Military expenditure as percentage of GNP (1995): 4.8% (world 2.8%); per capita expenditure U.S.$13.

[1]Established by new constitution effective Jan. 16, 1997. Presidential elections of September 1996 did not meet international standards. [2]Includes 4 nonelective seats. [3]Preliminary. [4]Kombo St. Mary includes the urban areas of Serekunda and Bakau. [5]Kombo St. Mary and Banjul city make up Greater Banjul. [6]Includes inland water area of 2,077 sq km (802 sq mi). [7]Based on land area only. [8]1993. [9]1983. [10]Low-income population in Banjul and Kombo St, Mary only; weights of consumer price index components. [11]At constant prices of 1976–77. [12]Indirect taxes. [13]Not adequately defined. [14]Mostly unofficial trade with Senegal. [15]Includes teacher training and vocational. [16]1984–85.

Internet resources for further information:
• Official WWW Site of The Republic of The Gambia
  http://www.Gambia.com/

Georgia

Official name: Sak'art'velo (Georgia)[1].
Form of government: unitary multiparty republic with a single legislative body (Parliament [235]).
Head of state and government: President.
Capital: T'bilisi.
Official language: Georgian.
Official religion: none[2].
Monetary unit: 1 Georgian lari[3] = 100 tetri; valuation (Sept. 25, 1998) 1 U.S.$ = 1.36 lari; 1 £ = 2.32 lari.

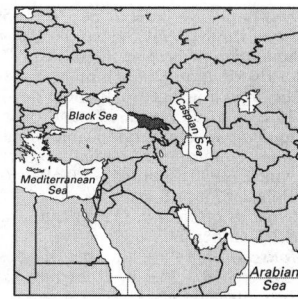

Area and population

Autonomous republics	Capitals	area sq mi	area sq km	population 1993[4] estimate
Abkhazia[5]	Sokhumi (Sukhumi)	3,343	8,660	516,600
Ajaria	Bat'umi	1,120	2,900	386,700
Districts				
Guria	...	785	2,033	160,800
Imereti	...	2,452	6,349	788,900
Kakheti	...	4,717	12,217	464,000
Kvemo Kartli	...	2,615	6,772	601,500
Racha-Lechkumi	...	1,245	3,224	45,400
Samegrelo	...	1,697	4,395	418,100
Samtskhe-Javakheti	...	2,017	5,224	198,800
Shida Kartli[6]	...	3,043	7,882	485,900
Svaneti	...	1,694	4,389	23,200
Tianeti	...	1,569	4,063	43,800
City				
T'bilisi	...	534	1,384	1,271,800
TOTAL		26,831	69,493[7]	5,405,400[7]

Demography

Population (1998): 5,431,000.
Density (1998): persons per sq mi 202.4, persons per sq km 78.2.
Urban-rural (1995): urban 55.6%; rural 44.4%.
Sex distribution (1994): male 47.60%; female 52.40%.
Age breakdown (1989): under 15, 24.8%; 15–29, 24.1%; 30–44, 19.2%; 45–59, 17.5%; 60–74, 10.8%; 75 and over, 3.6%.
Population projection: (2000) 5,432,000; (2010) 5,234,000.
Doubling time: n.a.
Ethnic composition (1989): Georgian 70.1%; Armenian 8.1%; Russian 6.3%; Azerbaijani 5.7%; Ossetian 3.0%; Greek 1.9%; Abkhazian 1.8%; other 3.1%.
Religious affiliation (1995): Christian 46.2%, of which Georgian Orthodox 36.7%, Armenian Apostolic 5.6%, Russian Orthodox 2.7%, other Christian 1.2%; Sunni Muslim 11.0%; other (mostly nonreligious) 42.8%.
Major cities (1997): T'bilisi 1,253,100; K'ut'aisi 240,000; Rust'avi 158,000.

Vital statistics

Birth rate per 1,000 population (1995): 10.9 (world avg. 25.0); (1989) legitimate 82.3%; illegitimate 17.7%.
Death rate per 1,000 population (1995): 8.1 (world avg. 9.3).
Natural increase rate per 1,000 population (1995): 2.8 (world avg. 15.7).
Total fertility rate (avg. births per childbearing woman; 1995): 2.1.
Marriage rate per 1,000 population (1995): 4.0.
Divorce rate per 1,000 population (1995): 0.5.
Life expectancy at birth (1994): male 69.0 years; female 76.0 years.
Major causes of death per 100,000 population (1995): diseases of the circulatory system 569.6; malignant neoplasms (cancers) 63.4; accidents, poisoning, and violence 44.7; diseases of the digestive system 30.3.

National economy

Budget (1997). Revenue: 639,900,000 lari[3] (tax revenue 65.5%, of which value-added tax 41.3%, excise tax 8.1%, customers duties 6.7%, individual income tax 5.4%, company profit tax 3.8%, other taxes 0.2%; grants 9.3%; other revenue 25.2%). Expenditures: 839,900,000 lari[3] (social protection 24.2%; defense and public order 20.9%; housing and services 11.9%; education 6.1%; health care 5.7%; other expenditures 31.2%).
Population economically active (1995): total 1,730,000; activity rate of total population 32.2% (participation rates [1992]: ages 16–59 [male], 16–54 [female] 72.9%; female [1989] 45.9%; unemployed [1996] 6.0%).

Price and earnings indexes (1992 = 100)

	1992	1993	1994	1995	1996
Consumer price index	100	1,500	236,000	621,000	704,000
Monthly earnings index	100	1,400	310,000	785,000	...

Production (metric tons except as noted). Agriculture, forestry, fishing (1996): watermelons 750,000, corn (maize) 395,000, potatoes 360,000, grapes 350,000, tomatoes 220,000, apples 140,000, cabbages 90,000, oranges 66,000; livestock (number of live animals) 980,000 cattle, 725,000 sheep and goats, 353,000 pigs, 12,000,000 poultry; roundwood, n.a.; fish catch (1995) 46,000. Mining and quarrying (1996): manganese ore 97,000. Manufacturing (1995): metallurgy 239; chemical and timber 109; machinery 58. Construction (1994): 12,100 sq m. Energy production (consumption): electricity (kW-hr; 1994) 6,803,000,000 (7,603,000,000); coal (metric tons; 1994) 34,000 (274,000); crude petroleum (barrels; 1994) 542,000 (2,008,000); petroleum products (metric tons; 1994) none (n.a.); natural gas (cu m; 1994) 8,969,000 (2,797,000,000).

Gross national product (1996): U.S.$4,590,000,000 (U.S.$850 per capita).

Structure of net material product and labour force

	1995 in value '000,000 lari[3]	% of total value	labour force[8]	% of labour force
Agriculture	432	31.5	90,000	8.6
Mining				
Manufacturing	401	13.5	251,700	24.0
Public utilities				
Construction	67	4.9		
Transp. and commun.	78	5.7	78,100	7.4
Trade	325	23.7	41,100	3.9
Finance	...	...		
Public administration, defense			44,100	4.2
Services	...	...	211,100	20.1
Other	284	20.7	334,700[9]	31.9
TOTAL	1,587	100.0	1,050,800	100.0[7]

Public debt (external, outstanding; 1996): U.S.$1,100,000,000.
Household income and expenditure. Average household size (1989) 4.1; income per household: n.a.; sources of income (1993): wages and salaries 34.5%, benefits 21.9%, agricultural income 21.6%, other 22.0%; expenditure (1993): taxes 42.5%, retail goods 32.3%, savings 16.4%, transportation 4.2%.

Foreign trade

Balance of trade (current prices)

	1992	1993	1994	1995	1996
U.S.$'000,000	+19	−133	−279	−339	−555
% of total	14.1%	31.7%	53.6%	32.8%	45.3%

Imports (1995): U.S.$686,100,000 (oil and gas 47.0%; textiles, clothing, shoes 28.5%; food products 16.1%; electricity 3.0%; petroleum products 2.9%). *Major import sources* (1996): Turkey 13.3%; Russia 12.3%; United States 10.3%; Bulgaria 9.5%; Germany 8.1%.
Exports (1995): U.S.$347,200,000 (food products 30.0%; ferrous metals 29.7%; textiles 7.0%; chemicals 5.0%). *Major export destinations* (1996): Armenia 29.8%; Russia 18.6%; Turkey 12.1%; Azerbaijan 9.0%.

Transport and communications

Transport. Railroads (1996): 1,583 km; (1989) passenger-km 17,000,000; cargo traffic, n.a. Roads (1995): 21,000 km (paved 93.5%). Vehicles (1995): passenger cars 441,828; trucks and buses 50,220. Merchant marine: vessels (1,000 gross tons and over) 54; total deadweight tonnage 1,108,068. Air transport (1989): passenger-km 5,295,600,000; metric ton-km cargo, n.a.; airports (1997) with scheduled flights 1.

Communications

Medium	date	unit	number	units per 1,000 persons
Television	1995	receivers	1,200,000	220
Telephones	1995	main lines	554,000	103
Cellular telephones	1995	subscribers	200	0.04
Facsimile machines	1995	units	500	0.1

Education and health

Educational attainment (1989). Percentage of population age 25 and over having: primary education or no formal schooling 12.3%; some secondary 15.2%; completed secondary and some postsecondary 57.4%; higher 15.1%.

Education (1993–94)

	schools	teachers	students	student/ teacher ratio
Primary (age 6–13)	3,788	...	815,000	...
Secondary (age 14–17)				
Voc., teacher tr.	...	...	29,300	...
Higher	19	...	93,000	...

Health (1993): physicians 29,900 (1 per 182 persons); hospital beds 57,100 (1 per 95 persons); infant mortality rate per 1,000 live births (1995) 17.8.

Military

Total active duty personnel (1997): 17,600 (army 71.6%, air force 17.0%, navy 11.4%). About 8,500 Russian troops remained in Georgia in late 1997. *Military expenditure as percentage of GNP* (1995): 2.4% (world 2.8%); per capita expenditure U.S.$37.

[1]No long-form name per 1995 constitution. [2]Special recognition is given to Georgian Orthodox Church. [3]The Georgian lari, introduced Sept. 25, 1995, replaced the Georgian coupon, at a rate of 1,000,000 coupons to 1 lari; on the same date, the Georgian lari became the sole legal tender. The Georgian coupon had been introduced April 5, 1993, at par with the Russian ruble. [4]January 1. [5]Abkhazia adopted a constitution declaring it an independent state on Nov. 26, 1994; on Feb. 9, 1995, it was granted wider autonomy within Georgia; attainment of full national autonomy remains in dispute. [6]The northern half of Shida Kartli is roughly equivalent to South Ossetia. In March 1997 the separatist of South Ossetia was given autonomous region status by the Georgian government, but its final status was unresolved in September 1998. [7]Detail does not add to total given because of rounding. [8]State sector only. [9]Includes 65,450 unemployed and 269,250 undistributed employed.

Internet resources for further information:
• **UNDP Human Development Report Georgia 1996**
  http://www.undp.org/undp/rbec/nhdr/1996/georgia/
• **Embassy of Georgia in the United States of America**
  http://www.steele.com/embgeorgia/embassy.htm
• **Parliament of Georgia** http://www.parliament.ge

Germany

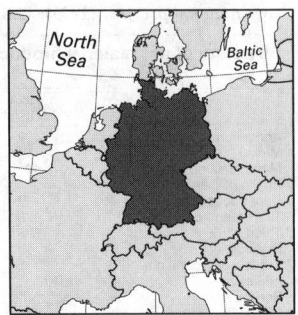

Official name: Bundesrepublik Deutschland (Federal Republic of Germany).
Form of government: federal multiparty republic with two legislative houses (Federal Council [69]; Federal Diet [672]).
Chief of state: President.
Head of government: Chancellor.
Seat of government: Bonn (Berlin is capital designate).
Official language: German.
Official religion: none.
Monetary unit: 1 Deutsche Mark (DM) = 100 Pfennige; valuation (Sept. 25, 1998) 1 U.S.$ = DM 1.67; 1 £ = DM 2.84.

Density (1998): persons per sq mi 595.9, persons per sq km 230.1.
Urban-rural (1996[1]): urban 86.1%; rural 13.9%.
Population projection: (2000) 82,510,000; (2010) 84,346,000.
Sex distribution (1996[1]): male 48.68%; female 51.32%.
Age breakdown (1996[1]): under 15, 16.2%; 15–19, 19.4%; 30–44, 23.8%; 45–59, 19.6%; 60–74, 14.6%; 75 and over, 6.4%.
Doubling time: not applicable; doubling time exceeds 100 years.
Ethnic composition (by nationality; 1997[1]): German 91.1%; Turkish 2.5%, of which (1990) Kurdish *c.* 0.5%, Yugoslav 1.7%; Italian 0.7%; Greek 0.4%; Polish 0.3%; other 3.3%.
Religious affiliation: (1995) Lutheran 40.8%, Roman Catholic 33.9%, Muslim 2.1%, other 23.2%.
Households (1996). Number of households 37,281,000; average household size 2.2; 1 person 35.4%, 2 persons 32.3%, 3 persons 15.5%, 4 persons 12.2%, 5 or more persons 4.6%.

Vital statistics

Birth rate per 1,000 population (1995): 9.4 (world avg. 25.0); legitimate 83.9%; illegitimate 16.1%.
Death rate per 1,000 population (1995): 10.8 (world avg. 9.3).
Natural increase rate per 1,000 population (1995): –1.4 (world avg. 15.7).
Total fertility rate (avg. births per childbearing woman; 1994): 1.5.
Marriage rate per 1,000 population (1995): 5.3.
Divorce rate per 1,000 population (1994): 2.0.
Life expectancy at birth (1995): male 73.0 years; female 79.5 years.
Major causes of death per 100,000 population (1995): diseases of the circulatory system 525.8; malignant neoplasms (cancers) 260.7, of which bronchial, lung, and tracheal 45.5; diseases of the respiratory system 66.0, of which pneumonia 21.6, chronic bronchitis 14.2; suicide 15.8.

Social indicators

Educational attainment (1995). Percentage of population age 25 and over having: primary and lower secondary 57.1%; intermediate secondary 18.4%; vocational secondary 7.3%; post-secondary and higher (all levels) 17.2%.
Quality of working life. Average workweek (1995): 39.6 hours. Annual rate per 100,000 workers (1993) for: injuries or accidents at work 4,808; deaths, including commuting accidents, 6.7. Proportion of labour force insured for damages of income loss resulting from: injury, virtually 100%; permanent disability, virtually 100%; death, virtually 100%. Average days lost to labour stoppages per 1,000 workers (1996): 4.1.

Distribution of income (1993)[3]
percentage of household income by quintile

1	2	3	4	5 (highest)
6.5	1.8	17.3	27.2	37.2

Access to services. Proportion of dwellings (1996) having: electricity, virtually 100%; piped water supply, virtually 100%; flush sewage disposal (1993) 98.4%; public fire protection, virtually 100%.
Social participation. Eligible voters participating in last (October 1994) national election 79.1%. Trade union membership in total workforce (1994): *c.* 27%. Practicing religious population (1994): 5% of Protestants and 25% of Roman Catholics "regularly" attend religious services.
Social deviance (1995). Offense rate per 100,000 population for: murder and manslaughter 4.8; sexual abuse 58, of which child molestation 20, rape and forcible sexual assault 14; robbery 78; assault and battery 117; theft 4,712. Incidence per 100,000 in general population (late 1970s) of: alcoholism 2,500–3,000; drug and substance abuse 650; suicide (1995) 15.8.
Material well-being (1996; median income)[3]. Households possessing: automobile 96.1%; telephone 99.5%; colour television receiver 95.9%; refrigerator 79.3%; washing machine 97.7%; home freezer 72.1%; personal computer 48.8%; video recorder 80.1%.

Recreational and leisure activities[3]
(Monthly household expenditures, 1996; median income)

Activity	DM	percentage
Vacations	201	25.0
Expenditures for motor vehicles	115	14.3
Sporting and camping equipment and sporting events	115	14.3
Televisions, radios, and their fees	79	9.8
Books, newspapers, and magazines	66	8.2
Gardening and pets	50	6.2
Games and toys	40	5.0
Visits to theatre and cinema	22	2.7
Photographic and moviemaking equipment and film	18	2.2
Tools	6	0.7
Other activities	92	11.5
TOTAL	803[2]	100.0[2]

National economy

Budget (1996). Revenue: DM 1,753,518,000,000 (taxes 83.9%). Expenditures: DM 1,864,196,000,000 (pensions and other social security payments 33.8%, purchase of current goods and services 22.3%, personnel costs 20.9%).
Total national debt (1996): DM 1,372,400,000,000.
Production (value of production in DM except as noted; 1995–96). Agriculture, forestry, fishing: cereal grains 5,713,000,000, fruits 3,031,000,000, flowers and ornamental plants 2,655,000,000, sugar beets 2,453,000 ,000, grapes for wine 2,336,000,000, vegetables 2,055,000,000, potatoes 1,862,000,000, tree nurseries 1,710,000,000, oilseed crops 1,018,000,000; livestock (number of live animals; 1995) 24,377,900 pigs, 15,760,600 cattle, 3,148,000 sheep, 87,695,200 poultry; roundwood (1996) 38,970,000 cu m, of which industrial roundwood 35,175,000 cu m; fish catch (metric tons; 1995) 298,017. Mining and quarrying (metric

Area and population

States Administrative districts	Capitals	area sq mi	area sq km	population 1996[1] estimate
Baden-Württemberg	Stuttgart	13,804	35,752	10,319,400
Freiburg	Freiburg	3,613	9,357	2,087,000
Karlsruhe	Karlsruhe	2,671	6,919	2,644,400
Stuttgart	Stuttgart	4,076	10,558	3,862,300
Tübingen	Tübingen	3,443	8,918	1,725,600
Bayern	Munich	27,240	70,551	11,993,500
Mittelfranken	Ansbach	2,798	7,246	1,667,300
Niederbayern	Landshut	3,988	10,330	1,143,400
Oberbayern	Munich	6,768	17,530	3,978,100
Oberfranken	Bayreuth	2,792	7,230	1,110,500
Oberpfalz	Regensburg	3,741	9,690	1,054,500
Schwaben	Augsburg	3,859	9,994	1,722,100
Unterfranken	Würzburg	3,294	8,532	1,317,700
Berlin	—	344	891	3,471,400
Brandenburg	Potsdam	11,382	29,479	2,542,000
Bremen	Bremen	156	404	679,800
Hamburg	Hamburg	292	755	1,707,900
Hessen	Wiesbaden	8,152	21,114	6,009,900
Darmstadt	Darmstadt	2,874	7,445	3,684,600
Giessen	Giessen	2,078	5,381	1,055,900
Kassel	Kassel	3,200	8,289	1,269,400
Mecklenburg-Vorpommern	Schwerin	8,946	23,170	1,823,100
Niedersachsen	Hannover	18,382	47,610	7,780,400
Braunschweig	Braunschweig	3,126	8,097	1,679,600
Hannover	Hannover	3,493	9,046	2,139,000
Lüneburg	Lüneburg	5,986	15,504	1,602,100
Weser-Ems	Oldenburg	5,777	14,963	2,359,700
Nordrhein-Westfalen	Düsseldorf	13,158	34,078	17,893,000
Arnsberg	Arnsberg	3,090	8,002	3,827,500
Detmold	Detmold	2,517	6,518	2,012,900
Düsseldorf	Düsseldorf	2,042	5,289	5,290,600
Köln	Köln	2,844	7,365	4,188,600
Münster	Münster	2,665	6,903	2,573,500
Rheinland-Pfalz	Mainz	7,662	19,846	3,977,900
Koblenz	Koblenz	3,117	8,072	1,489,900
Rheinhessen-Pfalz	Mainz	2,646	6,852	1,982,600
Trier	Trier	1,901	4,923	505,400
Saarland	Saarbrücken	992	2,570	1,084,400
Sachsen	Dresden	7,109	18,413	4,566,600
Sachsen-Anhalt	Magdeburg	7,894	20,446	2,738,900
Dessau	Dessau	1,652	4,280	573,100
Halle	Halle/Saale	1,710	4,428	909,400
Magdeburg	Magdeburg	4,532	11,738	1,256,400
Schleswig-Holstein	Kiel	6,089	15,770	2,725,500
Thüringen	Erfurt	6,244	16,171	2,503,800
TOTAL		137,847[2]	357,022[2]	81,817,500

Demography

Population (1998): 82,148,000.
Major cities (1995): Berlin 3,470,200; Hamburg 1,706,800; Munich 1,240,600; Cologne 964,200; Frankfurt am Main 651,200; Essen 616,400; Dortmund 600,000; Stuttgart 587,000; Düsseldorf 571,900; Bremen 549,000; Duisburg 535,200; Hannover 524,600; Nürnberg 494,100.

Other principal cities (1995)

city	population	city	population	city	population
Aachen	247,400	Heilbronn	121,700	Neuss	148,600
Augsburg	261,000	Herne	179,900	Oberhausen	224,900
Bergisch Gladbach	105,200	Hildesheim	106,000	Offenbach am Main	116,600
Bielefeld	324,000	Ingolstadt	111,900	Oldenburg	150,500
Bochum	400,500	Jena	101,800	Osnabrück	167,900
Bonn	291,700	Kaiserslautern	102,000	Paderborn	132,100
Bottrop	119,900	Karlsruhe	276,600	Pforzheim	118,400
Braunschweig	253,600	Kassel	201,400	Potsdam	137,600
Bremerhaven	130,800	Kiel	247,300	Recklinghausen	127,200
Chemnitz	271,400	Koblenz	109,300	Regensburg	126,000
Cottbus	124,600	Krefeld	249,900	Remscheid	122,700
Darmstadt	139,100	Leipzig	478,200	Reutlingen	108,400
Dresden	472,900	Leverkusen	161,900	Rostock	231,300
Erfurt	212,600	Lübeck	216,900	Saarbrücken	187,800
Erlangen	101,500	Ludwigshafen am Rhein	168,000	Salzgitter	117,700
Freiburg im Breisgau	198,300	Magdeburg	263,000	Schwerin	117,200
Fürth	108,100	Mainz	184,500	Siegen	111,300
Gelsenkirchen	291,800	Mannheim	315,100	Solingen	165,700
Gera	125,000	Moers	107,000	Ulm	115,400
Göttingen	127,200	Mönchengladbach	266,000	Wiesbaden	266,400
Hagen	212,700			Witten	105,000
Halle an der Saale	287,400	Mülheim an der Ruhr	176,700	Wolfsburg	126,800
Hamm	183,700			Wuppertal	382,400
Heidelberg	138,400	Münster	264,500	Würzburg	127,700
				Zwickau	103,900

tons; 1996): potash 34,600,000. Manufacturing (value added at factor cost in DM '000,000; 1994): capital equipment 250,212, of which machinery 88,631, transport equipment 70,647; electrical equipment 64,067; chemicals (including pharmaceuticals) 62,401, food and beverages 39,578; plastics and other synthetic products 28,108; glass and ceramic products 24,094; furniture and other wood products 17,024; paper products 12,608; textiles 8,743; clothing 5,847. Construction (newly completed buildings, sq m; 1995): residential 47,263,000; nonresidential 47,229,000.

Manufacturing, mining, and construction enterprises (1995)

	no. of enter- prises[4]	no. of employees	wages as a % of avg. of all wages[3, 5]	annual gross production value (DM '000,000)
Manufacturing	39,316	6,644,000	100.0	2,059,072
of which				
Road and motor vehicles	827	694,000	112.6	260,587
Machinery (nonelectric)	5,803	1,039,000	99.6	248,037
Machinery and appliances (electric)	2,427	795,000	106.0	226,297
Chemical	1,292	551,000	102.7	224,693
Food and beverages	4,421	546,000	90.0	218,037
Petroleum and natural gas	54	25,000	124.1	113,716
Rubber and plastic products	2,560	358,000	...	88,127
Glass and ceramics	2,398	282,000	...	74,286
Wood and wood products	2,039	127,000	83.8	31,726
Textiles	1,296	149,000	81.8	31,641
Mining and quarrying	782	188,000	105.3	40,084
Construction	24,738	1,486,000	100.0	259,416

Energy production (consumption): electricity (kW-hr; 1994) 528,221,000,000 (530,558,000,000); hard coal (metric tons; 1994) 57,623,000 (66,255,000); lignite (metric tons; 1994) 207,077,000 (209,308,000); crude petroleum (barrels; 1994) 21,535,000 (793,500,000); petroleum products (metric tons; 1994) 99,578,000 (113,839,000); natural gas (cu m; 1994) 20,904,000,000 (92,770,000,000).

Gross national product (at current market prices; 1996): U.S.$2,364,632,000,000 (U.S.$28,870 per capita).

Structure of gross domestic product and labour force

	1996			
	in value DM '000,000	% of total value	labour force	% of labour force
Agriculture	37,150	1.0	942,000	2.4
Public utilities, mining	82,420	2.3	454,000	1.1
Manufacturing	843,810	23.8	8,356,000	20.9
Construction	217,270	6.1	2,881,000	7.2
Transportation and communications	176,680	5.0	1,923,000	4.8
Trade	294,820	8.3	4,696,000	11.7
Finance, real estate	497,570	14.0	1,182,000	3.0
Services	809,670	22.9	9,728,000	24.3
Pub. admin., defense	387,040	10.9	3,320,000	8.3
Other	194,570	5.5	6,503,000[6]	16.3[6]
TOTAL	3,541,000	100.0[2]	39,985,000	100.0

Population economically active (1996): total 39,985,000; activity rate of total population 48.8% (participation rates: ages 15–64, 71.0%; female 42.9%; unemployed 10.0%).

Price and earnings indexes (1991 = 100)

	1992	1993	1994	1995	1996	1997
Consumer price index	105.1	109.7	112.7	114.8	116.5	118.6
Hourly earnings index	107.1	113.5	115.3	...	...	...

Household income and expenditure. Average annual income per household (1996[3]) DM 82,488 (U.S.$54,816); sources of take-home income: wages 78.8%, self-employment 11.6%, transfer payments 9.6%; expenditure: rent 23.9%, food and beverages 21.2%, transportation 18.0%, entertainment, education, and leisure 11.4%, household operations, durables, and maintenance 7.2%, clothing and footwear 6.4%.

Tourism (1996): receipts U.S.$15,787,500,000; expenditures U.S.$49,557,600,000.

Financial aggregates[7]

	1991	1992	1993	1994	1995	1996	1997
Exchange rate, DM per:							
U.S. dollar	1.5160	1.6140	1.7263	1.5488	1.4335	1.5548	1.7341
£	2.8360	2.4404	2.1988	2.4207	2.2219	2.6285	2.8399
SDR	2.1685	2.2193	2.3712	2.2610	2.1309	2.2357	2.4180
International reserves (U.S.$)							
Total (excl. gold; '000,000)	63,001	90,967	77,640	77,363	85,005	83,178	77,587
SDRs ('000,000)	1,917	841	962	1,114	2,001	1,907	1,788
Reserve pos. in IMF ('000,000)	3,567	4,239	3,951	4,030	5,210	5,468	5,946
Foreign exchange	57,517	85,877	72,727	72,219	77,794	75,083	69,853
Gold ('000,000 fine troy oz)	95.18	95.18	95.18	95.18	95.18	95.18	95.18
% world reserves	10.13	10.24	10.43	10.46	10.48	10.52	10.69
Interest and prices							
Central bank discount (%)	8.0	8.3	4.8	4.5	3.0	2.5	2.5
Govt. bond yield (%)	8.6	8.0	6.3	6.7	6.5	5.6	5.1
Industrial share prices (1990 = 100)[8]	91.5	87.3	93.6	106.1	103.3	117.9	161.5
Balance of payments (U.S.$'000,000,000)							
Balance of visible trade	19.92	28.72	41.75	51.68	66.12	71.21	71.75
Imports, f.o.b.	383.48	401.51	340.73	378.59	457.10	488.22	439.3
Exports, f.o.b.	403.37	430.23	382.49	430.27	523.22	519.44	511.08
Balance of invisibles	−37.11	−47.34	−55.06	−71.86	−87.67	−84.99	−74.52
Balance of payments, current account	−17.67	−19.14	−13.87	−20.94	−22.56	−13.78	−2.77

Service enterprises (1991)

	no. of enter- prises	no. of employees	weekly wages as a % of all wages	annual turnover (DM '000,000)
Gas	151	37,000	...	42,228
Water	183	40,000	...	3,443
Electrical power	462	296,000	...	147,076
Transport				
air	133	57,390	...	20,270
buses	6,054	192,869	...	12,586
rail	1	416,199	...	14,697
shipping	1,449	9,076	...	...
Communications				
press	2,452	240,075	...	31,096
film[9]	615	3,000	...	836
Postal services	17,616[10]	652,573	...	68,346
Hotels and restaurants	135,141	652,251	...	60,257
Wholesale trade	36,605[10]	1,214,000	...	1,015,984
Retail trade	152,629	2,241,000	...	605,755

Land use (1994): forest 30.6%; pasture 15.1%; agriculture 19.9%; other 34.4%

Foreign trade

Balance of trade (current prices)

	1992	1993	1994	1995	1996
DM '000,000,000	+45.91	+75.81	+88.73	+103.40	+117.35
% of total	3.6%	6.4%	6.8%	7.4%	8.0%

Imports (1996): DM 669,060,500,000 (machinery and transport equipment 33.4%, of which road transport equipment 9.9%, electrical machinery other than office equipment 6.7%, office equipment and computers 4.4%; chemicals and chemical products 8.6%, of which organic chemical products 2.0%, unfabricated plastics 1.6%; food and beverages 7.8%, of which fruits and vegetables 2.7%, meat and meat products 1.2%, coffee, tea, and cocoa 0.9%; mineral fuels 7.7%, of which crude petroleum and petroleum products 5.3%, natural gas 1.9%; clothing 6.4%; iron and steel 2.6%; furniture 1.5%). *Major import sources:* France 10.3%; The Netherlands 8.3%; Italy 8.0%; U.S. 7.1%; U.K. 6.6%; Belgium 6.1%; Japan 4.9%; Switzerland 3.8%; Austria 3.7%.

Exports (1996): DM 771,913,400,000 (machinery and transport equipment 49.6%, of which road transport equipment 16.4%, electrical machinery other than office equipment 7.9%, office equipment 2.4%; chemicals and chemical products 13.1%, of which organic chemical products 2.6%, unfabricated plastics 2.3%). *Major export destinations:* France 10.9%; U.K. 8.0%; U.S. 7.8%; The Netherlands 7.4%; Italy 7.4%; Belgium-Luxembourg 6.2%; Austria 5.6%; Switzerland 4.9%; Spain 3.6%; Japan 2.7%; Sweden 2.4%.

Transport and communications

Transport. Railroads (1995): length 49,094 mi, 80,297 km; passengers carried 1,656,000,000; passenger-mi 39,507,000,000, passenger-km 63,581,000,000; short ton-mi cargo 48,537,000,000, metric ton-km cargo 70,863,000,000. Roads (1996): total length 142,207 mi, 228,860 km (paved 99%). Vehicles (1997[1]): passenger cars 41,045,200; trucks and buses 2,381,500. Merchant marine (1995): vessels (100 gross tons and over) 1,476; total deadweight tonnage 5,721,000. Air transport (1995): passengers carried 34,584,000; passenger-mi 39,883,016,000, passenger-km 64,185,615,000; short ton-mi cargo 3,997,192,000, metric ton-km cargo 5,835,802,000; airports (1997) 35.

Communications

Medium	date	unit	number	units per 1,000 persons
Daily newspapers	1994	circulation	30,641,000	375
Radio	1995	receivers	150,000,000	1,836
Television	1995	receivers	45,000,000	551
Telephones	1995	main lines	40,400,000	495
Cellular telephones	1995	subscribers	3,750,000	45.9
Facsimile machines	1995	units	1,446,600	17.7
Personal computers	1995	units	13,500,000	165

Education and health

Health (1996): physicians 279,335 (1 per 293 persons); dentists 61,404 (1 per 1,334 persons); hospital beds (1995) 628,658 (1 per 130 persons); infant mortality rate per 1,000 live births 5.3.

Education (1995–96)

	schools	teachers	students	student/ teacher ratio
Primary (age 6–10)	17,910	199,623	3,634,342	18.2
Secondary (age 10–19)	17,711	402,472	5,822,242	14.5
Voc., teacher tr.	9,245	107,548	2,435,753	22.6
Higher	335	152,401	1,838,456	12.1

Food (1995): daily per capita caloric intake 3,265 (vegetable products 68%, animal products 32%); 123% of FAO recommended minimum requirement.

Military

Total active duty personnel (1997): 347,100 (army 69.6%, navy 8.1%, air force 22.3%). *Military expenditure as percentage of GNP* (1995): 1.9% (world 2.8%); per capita expenditure U.S.$496.

[1]January 1. [2]Detail does not add to total given because of rounding. [3]Former West Germany only. [4]Establishments with 20 or more workers only. [5]1994. [6]Includes 4,003,000 unemployed. [7]End-of-period figures unless footnoted otherwise. [8]Period averages. [9]1984. [10]1990.

Internet resources for further information:
• **Federal Statistical Office of Germany**
  http://www.statistik-bund.de/e_home.htm

Ghana

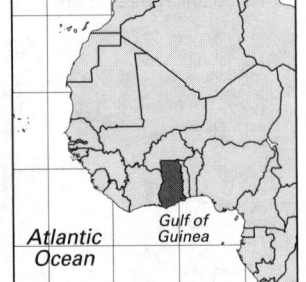

Official name: Republic of Ghana.
Form of government: unitary multiparty
republic with one legislative house
(House of Parliament [200]).
Head of state and government:
President.
Capital: Accra.
Official language: English.
Official religion: none.
Monetary unit: 1 cedi (₵) = 100
pesewas; valuation (Sept. 25, 1998)
1 U.S.$ = ₵2,325; 1 £ = ₵3,958.

Atlantic Ocean

Gulf of Guinea

Area and population

Regions[2]	Capitals	area sq mi	area sq km	population 1991[1] estimate
Ashanti	Kumasi	9,417	24,389	2,485,766
Brong-Ahafo	Sunyani	15,273	39,557	1,432,971
Central	Cape Coast	3,794	9,826	1,359,861
Eastern	Koforidua	7,461	19,323	2,003,235
Greater Accra	Accra	1,253	3,245	1,696,170
Northern	Tamale	27,175	70,384	1,389,105
Upper East	Bolgatanga	3,414	8,842	921,196
Upper West	Wa	7,134	18,476	526,398
Volta	Ho	7,942	20,570	1,432,971
Western	Sekondi-Takoradi	9,236	23,921	1,374,483
TOTAL		92,098[3]	238,533	14,622,156

Demography

Population (1998): 18,497,000.
Density (1998): persons per sq mi 200.8, persons per sq km 77.5.
Urban-rural (1996): urban 36.8%; rural 63.2%.
Sex distribution (1996): male 49.66%; female 50.34%.
Age breakdown (1990): under 15, 46.8%; 15–29, 26.2%; 30–44, 14.4%; 45–59,
8.0%; 60–74, 3.8%; 75 and over, 0.8%.
Population projection: (2000) 19,272,000; (2010) 22,929,000.
Doubling time: 23 years.
Ethnolinguistic composition (1983): Akan 52.4%, Mossi 15.8%; Ewe 11.9%;
Ga-Adangme 7.8%; Gurma 3.3%; Yoruba 1.3%; other 7.5%.
Religious affiliation (1991–92): Christian 64.1%, of which African Christian
29.3%, Protestant 20.1%, Roman Catholic 14.7%; traditional beliefs 17.6%;
Muslim 14.4%; other 3.9%.
Major cities (1988[1]): Accra 949,100; Kumasi 385,200; Tamale 151,100; Tema
110,000; Sekondi-Takoradi 103,600.

Vital statistics

Birth rate per 1,000 population (1990–95): 41.7 (world avg. 25.0); legitimate,
n.a.; illegitimate, n.a.
Death rate per 1,000 population (1990–95): 11.7 (world avg. 9.3).
Natural increase rate per 1,000 population (1990–95): 30.0 (world avg. 15.7).
Total fertility rate (avg. births per childbearing woman; 1993): 5.9.
Life expectancy at birth (1993): male 53.3 years; females 57.2 years.
Major causes of death per 100,000 population: n.a.; however, principal infec-
tious diseases as a percentage of outpatients (1989): malaria 43.8%, respira-
tory infections (including tuberculosis) 8.0%, diarrheal diseases 6.7%, intesti-
nal worms 3.1%.

National economy

Budget (1995). Revenue: ₵1,690,791,000,000 (import-export duties 29.6%, of
which cocoa export duty 11.5%[4]; excise and value-added taxes 21.5%, of
which petroleum tax 13.2%; income taxes 16.3%; divestiture of government
assets 6.6%). Expenditures: ₵1,697,893,000,000 (1994; education 22.3%; debt
service 20.1%; health 6.9%; transportation and communications 5.3%; social
security and welfare 3.6%; defense 2.9%).
Public debt (external, outstanding; 1994): U.S.$4,684,000,000.
Production (metric tons except as noted). Agriculture, forestry, fishing (1997):
roots and tubers 10,500,000 (of which cassava 6,800,000, yams 2,250,000, taro
1,450,000), cereals 1,770,000 (of which corn [maize] 1,000,000, sorghum
350,000, rice 220,000, millet 200,000), bananas and plantains 1,804,000, cacao
350,000, coconuts 240,000, tomatoes 160,000, peanuts (groundnuts) 135,000,
sugarcane 110,000, oranges 50,000, palm kernels 34,000, lemons and limes
30,000, pulses 20,000; livestock (number of live animals) 2,200,000 goats,
2,100,000 sheep, 1,150,000 cattle, 395,000 pigs, 13,300,000 chickens; roundwood (1996) 26,473,000 cu m; fish catch (1995) 344,460 (of which anchovies
65,497). Mining and quarrying (1996): bauxite 383,370; manganese ore
266,420; gold 50,079 kg; diamonds 773,126 carats. Manufacturing (value
added in ₵; 1993): tobacco 71,474,700,000; footwear 60,350,600,000; chemical
products 40,347,600,000; beverages 36,167,000,000; metal products
35,121,700,000; petroleum products 32,143,500,000; textiles 18,278,600,000;
machinery and transport equipment 9,525,700,000. Construction (value added
in ₵; 1994) 171,129,000,000. Energy production (consumption): electricity
(kW-hr; 1994) 6,167,000,000 (5,857,000,000); coal (metric tons; 1994) none
(3,000); crude petroleum (barrels; 1994) none (7,498,000); petroleum products (metric tons; 1994) 921,000 (1,100,000); natural gas, none (n.a.).
Tourism (1994): receipts U.S.$228,000,000; expenditures U.S.$20,000,000.
Household income and expenditure. Average household size (1984) 4.9; average annual income per household (1978) ₵9,600 (U.S.$[5]); sources of income:
n.a.; expenditure (1978): food 57.4%, clothing 14.3%, housing 11.5%, transportation and communications 3.3%, health care 1.3%.
Gross national product (1996): U.S.$6,223,000,000 (U.S.$360 per capita).

Structure of gross domestic product and labour force

	1995 in value ₵'000,000	1995 % of total value	1984 labour force	1984 % of labour force
Agriculture	3,325,912	44.0	3,310,967	59.4
Mining	131,809	1.7	26,828	0.5
Manufacturing	712,467	9.4	588,418	10.5
Construction	255,422	3.4	64,686	1.2
Public utilities	146,288	1.9	15,437	0.3
Transp. and commun.	474,803	6.3	122,806	2.2
Trade	1,152,750	15.2	792,147	14.2
Finance	292,073	3.9	27,475	0.5
Pub. admin., defense	705,312	9.3	97,548	1.7
Services			376,168	6.7
Other	360,331[6]	4.8[6]	157,624[7]	2.8[7]
TOTAL	7,557,167	100.0[3]	5,580,104	100.0

Population economically active (1984): total 5,580,104; activity rate of total
population 45.4% (participation rates: over age 15, 82.5%; female 51.2%;
unemployed 2.8%).

Price and earnings indexes (1990 = 100)

	1991	1992	1993	1994	1995	1996	1997
Consumer price index	118.0	129.9	162.3	202.7	354.4	473.7	605.8
Monthly earnings index	117.2	...	...	...	...	...	...

Land use (1994): forest 42.2%; pasture 36.9%; agriculture 19.0%; other 1.9%.

Foreign trade

Balance of trade (current prices)

	1991	1992	1993	1994	1995	1996
U.S.$'000,000	−320.7	−470.2	−664.3	−353.1	−256.6	−366.0
% of total	13.8%	19.2%	23.8%	12.6%	4.6%	10.4%

Imports (1994): U.S.$1,579,900,000 (1987; machinery 28.1%; mineral fuels
14.0%; chemicals 12.0%; food 5.2%). *Major import sources:* Germany 13.7%;
U.K. 12.1%; U.S. 11.7%; France 5.4%; Italy 4.8%.
Exports (1994): U.S.$1,226,800,000 (gold 44.7%; food 26.3%, of which cocoa
26.1%; logs and sawn timber 13.5%; electricity 4.6%; diamonds 1.7%). *Major
export destinations:* U.K. 15.5%; Italy 7.9%; Japan 6.7%; U.S. 6.6%; Germany
5.5%; France 4.0%.

Transport and communications

Transport. Railroads (1993): route length 592 mi, 953 km; passenger-mi
731,400,000, passenger-km 1,177,000,000; short ton-mi cargo 93,906,000, metric ton-km cargo 137,100,000. Roads (1994): total length 24,000 mi, 38,700 km
(paved 40%). Vehicles (1994): passenger cars 86,200; trucks and buses
130,000. Merchant marine (1992): vessels (100 gross tons and over) 155; total
deadweight tonnage 130,977. Air transport (1996)[8]: passenger-mi 407,
073,000, passenger-km 655,122,000; short ton-mi cargo 20,239,000, metric
ton-km cargo 29,549,000; airports (1996) with scheduled flights 1.

Communications

Medium	date	unit	number	units per 1,000 persons
Daily newspapers	1993	circulation	1,060,000	64.4
Radio	1995	receivers	4,300,000	249
Television	1995	receivers	265,000	15.3
Telephones	1995	main lines	60,000	3.5
Cellular telephones	1995	subscribers	6,200	0.4
Facsimile machines	1995	units	4,500	0.3
Personal computers	1995	units	20,000	1.2

Education and health

Educational attainment (1984). Percentage of population age 25 and over having: no formal schooling 60.4%; primary education 7.1%; middle school
25.4%; secondary 3.5%; vocational and other postsecondary 2.9%; higher
0.6%. *Literacy* (1995): total population age 15 and over literate 6,160,000
(64.5%); males literate 3,570,000 (75.9%); females literate 1,850,000 (53.5%).

Education (1991–92)

	schools	teachers	students	student/ teacher ratio
Primary (6–12)	11,056	66,068	1,796,490	27.2
Secondary (13–20)	5,540	43,367	816,528	18.8
Voc., teacher tr.[9]	957	422	13,232	31.4
Higher[9]	16	700	9,274	13.2

Health: physicians (1994) 735 (1 per 22,970 persons); hospital beds (1994) 26,455
(1 per 638 persons); infant mortality rate per 1,000 live births (1994) 83.
Food (1996): daily per capita caloric intake 2,622 (vegetable products 96%,
animal products 4%): 114% of FAO minimum recommended requirement.

Military

Total active duty personnel (1997): 7,000 (army 71.4%, navy 14.3%, air force
14.3%). *Military expenditure as percentage of GNP* (1995): 1.4% (world
2.8%); per capita expenditure U.S.$5.

[1]January 1. [2]Government administration has been decentralized to the local level of 103
district assemblies, 4 municipal assemblies, and 3 metropolitan assemblies. [3]Detail does
not add to total given because of rounding. [4]1994. [5]Unofficial 1978 exchange rate (7.5
to 9.9 times the official rate) does not permit meaningful conversion into other currencies. [6]Import duties and statistical adjustments less imputed bank service charges.
[7]Unemployed only. [8]Ghana Airways only. [9]1989–90.

Internet resources for further information:
• **Ghana Fact Sheet http://www.macroint.com/dhs/press/gh-fac.html**

Greece

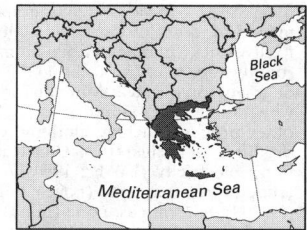

Official name: Ellinikí Dhimokratía (Hellenic Republic).
Form of government: unitary multiparty republic with one legislative house (Greek Chamber of Deputies [300]).
Chief of state: President.
Head of government: Prime Minister.
Capital: Athens.
Official language: Greek.
Official religion: Eastern Orthodox.
Monetary unit: 1 drachma (Dr) = 100 lepta; valuation (Sept. 25, 1998)
1 U.S.$ = Dr 290.03; 1 £ = Dr 493.78.

Area and population		area		population
Regions		sq mi	sq km	1991 census
Anatolikí Makedhonía kaí Thráki	(Eastern Macedonia and Thrace)	5,466	14,157	570,496
Attikí	(Attica)	1,470	3,808	3,523,407
Dhytikí Ellás	(Western Greece)	4,382	11,350	707,687
Dhytikí Makedhonía	(Western Macedonia)	3,649	9,451	293,015
Iónioi Nísoi	(Ionian Islands)	891	2,307	193,734
Ípiros	(Epirus)	3,553	9,203	339,728
Kedrikí Makedhonía[1]	(Central Macedonia)	7,393	19,147	1,710,513
Kríti	(Crete)	3,218	8,336	540,054
Nótion Aiyaíon	(Southern Aegean)	2,041	5,286	257,481
Pelopónnisos	(Peloponnesos)	5,981	15,490	607,428
Stereá Ellás	(Central Greece)	6,004	15,549	582,280
Thessalía	(Thessaly)	5,420	14,037	734,846
Vóreion Aiyaíon	(Northern Aegean)	1,481	3,836	199,231
TOTAL		50,949	131,957	10,259,900

Demography

Population (1998): 10,542,000.
Density (1998): persons per sq mi 206.9, persons per sq km 79.9.
Urban-rural (1996): urban 65.7%; rural 34.3%.
Sex distribution (1996): male 49.23%; female 50.77%.
Age breakdown (1995): under 15, 17.1%; 15–29, 22.6%; 30–44, 20.8%; 45–59, 18.1%; 60–74, 15.4%; 75 and over, 6.0%.
Population projection: (2000) 10,566,000; (2010) 10,869,000.
Doubling time: not applicable; doubling time exceeds 100 years.
Ethnic composition (1995[2]): Greek 98.5%; Turkish 0.9%; other 0.6%.
Religious affiliation (1995): Christian 95.2%, of which Eastern Orthodox 94.0, Protestant 0.6%, Roman Catholic 0.5%; Muslim 1.3%; other 3.5%.
Major cities (1991): Athens 772,072; Thessaloníki 383,967; Piraeus (Piraiévs) 182,671; Pátrai 152,570; Peristérion 137,288.

Vital statistics

Birth rate per 1,000 population (1996): 9.7 (world avg. 25.0); (1995) legitimate 97.0%; illegitimate 3.0%.
Death rate per 1,000 population (1996): 9.6 (world avg. 9.3).
Natural increase rate per 1,000 population (1996): 0.1 (world avg. 15.7).
Total fertility rate (avg. births per childbearing woman; 1993): 1.4.
Marriage rate per 1,000 population (1995): 6.1.
Divorce rate per 1,000 population (1994): 0.7.
Life expectancy at birth (1990): male 74.6 years; female 79.4 years.
Major causes of death per 100,000 population (1995): diseases of the circulatory system 491.3, of which cerebrovascular disease 181.9, ischemic heart disease 121.3; malignant neoplasms (cancers) 210.6; respiratory disease 55.1, of which pneumonia 33.7, bronchitis, emphysema, and asthma 16.5.

National economy

Budget (1996). Revenue: Dr 14,578,000,000,000[3] (indirect and excise taxes 30.2%, direct taxes 16.6%, European Community 5.3%). Expenditures: Dr 14,590,553,000,000 (1994: health and social insurance 5.5%, defense 4.0%, education and culture 3.4%, police and justice systems 1.5%).
Public debt (1996): U.S.$27,180,000,000.
Tourism (1996): receipts U.S.$3,684,100,000; expenditures U.S.$1,176,800,000.
Production (metric tons except as noted). Agriculture, forestry, fishing (1997): sugar beets 3,500,000, corn (maize) 2,045,000, wheat 2,016,000, tomatoes 1,903,500, olives 1,600,000, grapes 1,226,800, potatoes 1,050,000, oranges 950,000, peaches and nectarines 530,000, barley 357,000, apples 280,000, cabbages 280,000, rice 230,000, cucumbers 170,000; livestock (number of live animals) 9,606,000 sheep, 5,847,000 goats, 951,000 pigs, 600,000 cattle, 28,500,000 chickens; roundwood (1996) 2,006,000 cu m; fish catch (1995) 198,217. Mining and quarrying (1996): bauxite 1,881,000; zinc 13,000[4]; lead 11,000[4]; chromium ore 5,650[4, 5]. Manufacturing (value added in Dr '000,000; 1995): food, beverages, and tobacco 694,431; chemicals 402,133; textiles 257,555; paper and printing 208,696; transport equipment 148,767; clothing and footwear 137,524. Construction (value of completed buildings in Dr; 1994): residential 801,300,000; nonresidential 31,004,400,000. Energy production (consumption): electricity (kW-hr; 1994) 40,623,000,000 (41,005,000,000); coal (metric tons; 1994) 56,741,000 (59,569,000); crude petroleum (barrels; 1994) 3,589,000 (102,721,000); petroleum products (metric tons; 1994) 15,078,000 (14,311,000); natural gas (cu m; 1994) 55,047,000 (55,047,000).
Household income and expenditure. Average household size (1993–94) 2.9; income per household Dr 3,900,000 (U.S.$15,660); sources of income (1994): property and entrepreneurial income 54.5%, wages and salaries 27.9%, transfer payments 17.6%; expenditure: food 35.7%, transportation 14.7%, clothing and footwear 13.0%, housing 8.6%, education 6.5%, other 21.5%.
Gross national product (1996): U.S.$120,021,000,000 (U.S.$8,210 per capita).

Structure of gross domestic product and labour force				
	1995			
	in value Dr '000,000	% of total value	labour force	% of labour force
Agriculture	2,538,766	14.2	781,900	18.4
Mining	213,615	1.2	15,600	0.4
Manufacturing	2,483,098	13.9	577,700	13.6
Construction	1,102,673	6.2	252,300	5.9
Public utilities	433,992	2.4	41,500	1.0
Transp. and commun.	1,309,314	7.4	248,000	5.8
Trade	2,455,455	13.8	848,700	20.0
Finance	568,044	3.2	241,000	5.7
Pub. admin., defense	3,347,139	18.8	817,200	19.2
Services	1,932,091	10.8		
Other	1,432,478[6]	8.0[6]	424,700[7]	10.0[7]
TOTAL	17,816,664[8]	100.0[8]	4,248,500[8]	100.0

Population economically active (1995): total 4,248,500; activity rate of total population 40.6% (participation rates: ages 15–64, 60.7%; female 38.1%; unemployed 10.0%).

Price and earnings indexes (1990 = 100)						
	1991	1992	1993	1994	1995	1996	1997
Consumer price index	119.5	138.4	158.4	175.7	191.4	207.1	218.5
Hourly earnings index	116.7	132.8	146.7	165.9	187.9	204.1	222.3

Land use (1994): forest 20.3%; pasture 40.7%; agriculture 27.2%; other 11.8%.

Foreign trade[9]

Balance of trade (current prices)						
	1992	1993	1994	1995	1996	1997
Dr '000,000,000	−2,561.5	−3,117.4	−2,931.0	−3,471.0	−4,311.8	−5,235.2
% of total	40.5%	44.6%	39.2%	40.6%	48.6%	52.6%

Imports (1995): Dr 5,908,368,000,000 (machinery and transport equipment 32.5%; food 14.0%, of which meat products 4.0%, dairy products 2.2%; chemical products 8.9%; crude petroleum 5.1%). *Major import sources:* Germany 17.9%; Italy 15.7%; U.S. 9.0%; France 8.2%; U.K. 6.9%; The Netherlands 6.6%.
Exports (1995): Dr 2,540,891,000,000 (textiles 25.8%; food 25.6%; petroleum products 8.5%; minerals 3.7%; cotton 3.7%). *Major export destinations:* Germany 27.7%; U.S. 17.7%; Italy 8.4%; U.K. 6.6%; France 6.6%.

Transport and communications

Transport. Railroads (1994): route length 1,537 mi, 2,474 km; passenger-mi 869,300,000, passenger-km 1,399,000,000; short ton-mi cargo 210,000,000, metric ton-km cargo 307,000,000. Roads (1995): total length 72,350 mi, 116,440 km (paved 92%). Vehicles (1995): passenger cars 2,204,761; trucks and buses 908,423. Merchant marine (1995): vessels (100 gross tons and over) 2,128; total deadweight tonnage 29,863,000. Air transport (1995): passenger-mi 4,936,800,000, passenger-km 7,945,008,000; short ton-mi cargo 80,370,000, metric ton-km cargo 117,338,000; airports (1997) with scheduled flights 36.

Communications				units per 1,000 persons
Medium	date	unit	number	
Daily newspapers	1992	circulation	1,400,000	135
Radio	1995	receivers	4,200,000	402
Television	1995	receivers	4,630,000	442
Telephones	1995	main lines	5,162,800	493
Cellular telephones	1995	subscribers	273,000	26.1
Facsimile machines	1995	units	15,300	1.5
Personal computers	1995	units	350,000	3.3

Education and health

Educational attainment (1991). Percentage of population age 25 and over having: no formal schooling (illiterate) 6.8%; some primary education 10.6%; completed primary 39.7%; lower secondary 10.8%; higher secondary 20.6%; some postsecondary 4.9%; a degree from institution of higher education 6.6%. *Literacy* (1991): total population age 15 and over literate 7,870,000 (95.2%); males literate 3,900,000 (97.7%); females literate 3,970,000 (93.0%).

Education (1992–93)				student/ teacher ratio
	schools	teachers	students	
Primary (age 6–12)	7,634	37,549	745,666	19.9
Secondary (age 12–18)	2,988	45,794	700,488	15.3
Voc., teacher tr.	695	14,319	190,443	13.3
Higher[10]	17	9,124	115,464	12.6

Health: physicians (1994) 40,487 (1 per 258 persons); hospital beds (1993) 52,144 (1 per 199 persons); infant mortality rate per 1,000 live births (1996) 8.1.
Food (1995): daily per capita caloric intake 3,815 (vegetable products 78%, animal products 22%); 142% of FAO recommended minimum requirement.

Military

Total active duty personnel (1997): 162,300 (army 71.5%, navy 12.0%, air force 16.5%). *Military expenditure as percentage of GNP* (1995): 5.5% (world 2.8%); per capita expenditure U.S.$482.

[1]Includes Mount Athos (Ávion Óros), an autonomous, self-governing monastic region; 1991 population 1,557. [2]Greek government states there are no ethnic divisions in Greece. [3]Includes Dr 5,633,000,000,000 of domestic borrowing. [4]Metal content of ore. [5]1994. [6]Income from ownership of buildings. [7]Unemployed. [8]Detail does not add to total given because of rounding. [9]Imports c.i.f.; exports f.o.b. [10]1991–92.

Internet resources for further information:
• Greek Indexer http://www.hiway.gr/gi

Grenada

Official name: Grenada.
Form of government: constitutional
monarchy with two legislative
houses (Senate [13]; House of
Representatives [15[1]]).
Chief of state: British Monarch
represented by Governor-General.
Head of government: Prime Minister.
Capital: St. George's.
Official language: English.
Official religion: none.
Monetary unit: 1 East Caribbean dollar
(EC$) = 100 cents; valuation (Sept. 25,
1998) 1 U.S.$ = EC$2.70;
1 £ = EC$4.60.

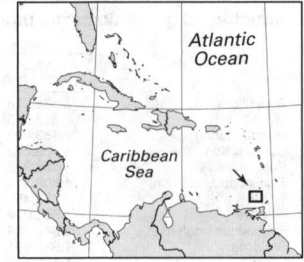

Area and population

Local Councils	Principal towns	area sq mi	area sq km	population 1991 census
Carriacou	Hillsborough	10	26	} 5,726
Petite Martinique	...	3	8	
St. Andrew	Grenville	38	99	24,135
St. David	...	17	44	11,011
St. George	...	25[2]	65[2]	27,373
St. John	Gouyave	14	35	8,752
St. Mark	Victoria	10	25	3,861
St. Patrick	Sauteurs	16	42	10,118
Town				
St. George's	—	2	2	4,621
TOTAL		133	344	95,597

Demography

Population (1998): 100,000.
Density (1998): persons per sq mi 751.9, persons per sq km 290.7.
Urban-rural (1991)[3]: urban 33.5%; rural 66.5%.
Sex distribution (1991): male 49.20%; female 50.80%.
Age breakdown (1991): under 15, 38.4%; 15–29, 25.8%; 30–44, 16.1%; 45–59, 8.9%; 60–74, 7.6%; 75 and over, 3.2%.
Population projection: (2000) 102,000; (2010) 120,000.
Doubling time: 52 years.
Ethnic composition (1991): black 84.9%; mixed 11.0%; Indo-Pakistani 3.0%; white 0.7%; other 0.4%.
Religious affiliation (1995): Roman Catholic 57.8%; Protestant 37.6%, of which Anglican 14.4%, Pentecostal 8.3%, Seventh-day Adventist 7.0%; other 4.6%, of which Rastafarian c. 3.0%.
Major localities (1991): St. George's 4,621; Gouyave 3,000[4]; Grenville 2,000[4].

Vital statistics

Birth rate per 1,000 population (1996): 21.35 (world avg. 25.0); (1987) legitimate 18.1%; illegitimate 81.9%.
Death rate per 1,000 population (1996): 7.95 (world avg. 9.3).
Natural increase rate per 1,000 population (1996): 13.45 (world avg. 15.7).
Total fertility rate (avg. births per childbearing woman; 1996): 3.8.
Marriage rate per 1,000 population (1991): 4.3.
Divorce rate per 1,000 population (1991): 0.8.
Life expectancy at birth (1996): male 68.4 years; female 73.4 years.
Major causes of death per 100,000 population (1987): diseases of the circulatory system 264.3; malignant neoplasms (cancers) 82.8; endocrine and metabolic diseases 57.3; diseases of the respiratory system 45.6; diseases of the digestive system 38.2; ill-defined conditions 209.1.

National economy

Budget (1995). Revenue: EC$226,480,000 (general sales taxes 31.7%, income taxes 19.0%, import duties 15.2%, grants from abroad 9.5%). Expenditures: EC$209,690,000 (education 16.8%, transportation and communications 14.1%, general administration 12.3%, health 10.4%).
Public debt (external, outstanding; 1996): U.S.$99,600,000.
Tourism (1995): receipts from visitors U.S.$58,000,000; expenditures by nationals abroad U.S.$4,000,000.
Gross national product (at current market prices; 1996): U.S.$285,000,000 (U.S.$2,880 per capita).

Structure of gross domestic product and labour force

	1995 in value EC$'000,000[6]	1995 % of total value	1991 labour force[7]	1991 % of labour force
Agriculture	61.7	11.9	4,223	17.1
Quarrying	2.6	0.5	126	0.5
Manufacturing	30.7	5.9	1,881	7.6
Construction	36.5	7.0	3,168	12.9
Public utilities	22.4	4.3	350	1.4
Transportation and communications	117.4	22.6	1,614	6.5
Trade, restaurants	109.5	21.1	5,149	20.9
Finance, real estate	67.6	13.0	866	3.5
Pub. admin., defense	89.1	17.1	1,738	7.1
Services	15.1	2.9	3,372	13.7
Other	-32.7[8]	-6.3[8]	2,163	8.8
TOTAL	519.9[9]	100.0	24,650	100.0

Production (metric tons except as noted). Agriculture, forestry, fishing (1996): bananas 8,600, coconuts 6,800, sugarcane 6,500, roots and tubers 3,000, nut-

meg, 1,920, avocados, 1,900, grapefruit 1,900, mangoes 1,700, cacao 1,567, mace 124, other crops include cotton, limes, cinnamon, cloves, and pimiento; livestock (number of live animals) 13,052 sheep, 7,000 goats, 5,300 pigs; roundwood, n.a.; fish catch (1995) 1,486. Mining and quarrying: excavation of gravel for local use. Manufacturing (value of production in EC$'000; 1995): wheat flour 10,174; soft drinks 8,558; beer 7,172; animal feed 4,698; rum 4,520; other products include clothing, edible coconut oil, paints, pharmaceutical products, and cigarettes. Construction: n.a. Energy production (consumption): electricity (kW-hr; 1994) 70,000,000 (70,000,000); coal, none (none); crude petroleum, none (none); petroleum products (metric tons; 1994) none (52,000); natural gas, none (none).
Household income and expenditure. Average household size (1991) 3.7; income per household (1988) EC$7,097 (U.S.$2,629); sources of income: n.a.; expenditure (1987): food, beverages, and tobacco 40.7%, household furnishings and operations 13.7%, housing 11.9%, transportation 9.1%, personal effects and medical care 8.6%.
Population economically active (1988): total 38,920; activity rate of total population 39.9% (participation rate: ages 15–65, 72.7%; female 48.6%; unemployed [1996] 17.5%).

Price and earnings indexes (1990 = 100)

	1991	1992	1993	1994	1995	1996	1997
Consumer price index	102.6	106.5	109.5	113.6	115.8	118.1	119.6
Annual earnings index[10]	108.0	118.8	124.1	131.5	138.3	144.8	...

Land use (1994): forested 9.0%; meadows and pastures 3.0%; agricultural and under permanent cultivation 35.0%; other 53.0%.

Foreign trade[11]

Balance of trade (current prices)

	1992	1993	1994	1995	1996
U.S.$'000,000	−94.5	−111.7	−105.3	−117.7	−144.7
% of total	68.7%	72.4%	68.2%	71.7%	77.5%

Imports (1995): U.S.$134,300,000 (food 23.8%; machinery and transport equipment 19.7%; basic manufactures 17.3%; chemicals and chemical products 7.9%). *Major import sources*[12]: United States 32%; United Kingdom 14%; Barbados 5%; Japan 4%; St. Vincent and the Grenadines 4%.
Exports (1995): U.S.$21,600,000 (domestic exports 89.4%, of which fish 15.7%, cocoa beans 15.3%, nutmeg 14.4%, bananas 8.8%, clothing 6.0%; reexports 10.6%). *Major export destinations*[12]: United States 18%; Germany 18%; United Kingdom 18%; St. Lucia 7%; Barbados 7%.

Transport and communications

Transport. Railroads: none. Roads (1995): total length 700 mi, 1,127 km (paved 51%). Vehicles (1991)[13]: passenger cars 4,739; trucks and buses 3,068. Merchant marine (1992): vessels (100 gross tons and over) 3; total deadweight tonnage 484. Air transport (1995)[14]: passenger arrivals 158,646, departures 161,232; cargo loaded 1,680 metric tons, cargo unloaded 555 metric tons; airports (1997) with scheduled flights 2.

Communications

Medium	date	unit	number	units per 1,000 persons
Radio	1996	receivers	45,000	460
Television	1995	receivers	15,000	154
Telephones	1995	main lines	23,200	238
Cellular telephones	1995	subscribers	400	4.1
Facsimile machines	1995	units	300	3.1

Education and health

Educational attainment (1991). Percentage of population age 25 and over having: no formal schooling 1.8%; primary education 74.9%; secondary 15.5%; higher 4.7%, of which university 2.8%; other/unknown 3.1%. *Literacy* (1992): total population age 15 and over literate 50,000 (85.0%).

Education (1994–95)

	schools	teachers	students	student/ teacher ratio
Primary (age 5–11)[15]	57	849	23,256	27.4
Secondary (age 12–6)[15]	19	381	7,260	19.1
Vocational	...	...	...	...
Higher[16]	1	66	651	9.9

Health (1996): physicians (1992) 47 (1 per 2,045 persons); hospital beds 439 (1 per 223 persons); infant mortality rate per 1,000 live births 14.3.
Food (1995): daily per capita caloric intake 2,713 (vegetable products 77%, animal products 23%); 112% of FAO recommended minimum requirement.

Military

Total active duty personnel (1993): [17]. *Military expenditure as percentage of GNP:* n.a.; per capita expenditure, n.a.

---

[1]Excludes the speaker, who may be elected from outside its elected membership. [2]St. George local council includes St. George's town. [3]Urban defined as St. George's town and St. George local council. [4]1987. [5]Based on year of registration. [6]At factor cost in 1990 prices. [7]Employed persons only. [8]Less imputed bank service charges. [9]Detail does not add to total given because of rounding. [10]Private sector only. [11]Imports c.i.f.; exports f.o.b. [12]Estimated figure(s). [13]Registered vehicles only. [14]Point Salines airport. [15]Excludes private schools. [16]1993–94; excludes Grenada Teachers' College. [17]The 750-member police force includes a paramilitary unit and a coast guard unit.

Guadeloupe

Official name: Département de la Guadeloupe (Department of Guadeloupe).
Political status: overseas department (France[1]) with two legislative houses (General Council [43]; Regional Council [41]).
Chief of state: President of France.
Heads of government: Commissioner of the Republic (for France); President of the General Council (for Guadeloupe); President of the Regional Council (for Guadeloupe).
Capital: Basse-Terre.
Official language: French.
Official religion: none.
Monetary unit: 1 French franc (F) = 100 centimes; valuation (Sept. 25, 1998) 1 U.S.$ = F 5.60; 1 £ = F 9.53.

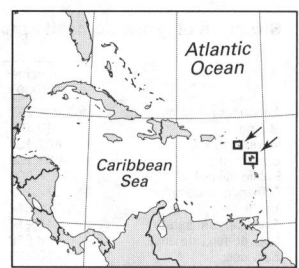

Area and population

Arrondissements	Capitals	area sq mi	area sq km	population 1990 census
Basse-Terre[2]	Basse-Terre	332	861	151,979
Pointe-à-Pitre[3]	Pointe-à-Pitre	297	769	192,643
Saint-Martin-Saint-Barthélemy[4]	Marigot	29	75	33,556
TOTAL		687[5]	1,780[5]	378,178[6]

Demography

Population (1998): 434,000.
Density (1998): persons per sq mi 631.7, persons per sq km 243.8.
Urban-rural (1995)[7]: urban 99.4%; rural 0.6%.
Sex distribution (1995): male 48.83%; female 51.17%.
Age breakdown (1995): under 15, 26.1%; 15–29, 27.5%; 30–44, 22.3%; 45–59, 13.1%; 60–74, 7.7%; 75 and over, 3.3%.
Population projection: (2000) 443,000; (2010) 482,000.
Doubling time: 58 years.
Ethnic composition (1991): Creole (mulatto) 77.0%; black 10.0%; Guadeloupe mestizo (French-East Asian) 10.0%; white 2.0%; other 1.0%
Religious affiliation (1995): Roman Catholic 81.1%; Jehovah's Witness 4.8%; Protestant 4.7%; other 9.4%.
Major communes (1990): Les Abymes 62,605; Saint-Martin 28,518; Pointe-à-Pitre 26,029 (141,000[8, 9]); Le Gosier 20,688; Basse-Terre 14,003 (53,000[8]).

Vital statistics

Birth rate per 1,000 population (1995): 16.3 (world avg. 25.0); (1994) legitimate 38.7%; illegitimate 61.3%.
Death rate per 1,000 population (1995): 5.7 (world avg. 9.3).
Natural increase rate per 1,000 population (1994): 10.6 (world avg. 15.7).
Total fertility rate (avg. births per childbearing woman; 1990–95): 2.2.
Marriage rate per 1,000 population (1995): 4.3.
Divorce rate per 1,000 population (1995): 1.3.
Life expectancy at birth (1990–95): male 71.1 years; female 78.0 years.
Major causes of death per 100,000 population (1992): diseases of the circulatory system 189.0; malignant neoplasms (cancers) 110.3; accidents, violence, and poisoning 66.3; diseases of the digestive system 33.3; infectious and parasitic diseases 29.3; endocrine and metabolic diseases 27.5.

National economy

Budget (1994). Revenue: F 2,971,000,000 (tax revenues 64.8%, of which direct taxes 33.7%; advances, loans, and transfers 29.8%; nontax revenues 4.6%). Expenditures: F 6,199,000,000 (current expenditures 65.6%, capital [development] expenditures 17.2%; advances and loans 17.1%).
Public debt (external, outstanding; 1990[10]): U.S.$58,000,000.
Tourism (1995): receipts from visitors U.S.$458,000,000; expenditures by nationals abroad, n.a.
Production (metric tons except as noted). Agriculture, forestry, fishing (1996): sugarcane 376,000, bananas 116,000, yams 7,000, plantains 6,000, sweet potatoes 5,000, pineapples 4,000, cucumbers and gherkins 4,000, tomatoes 3,000, melons 3,000, and flowers are also produced for export; livestock (number of live animals) 63,000 goats, 60,000 cattle, 14,000 pigs; roundwood (1995) 15,300 cu m; fish catch (1995) 9,530. Mining and quarrying (1993): pumice 210,000. Manufacturing (1996): cement 282,571; raw sugar 48,896; rum 66,483 hectolitres; other products include clothing, wooden furniture and posts, and metalware. Construction (buildings authorized; 1992): residential 358,474 sq m; nonresidential 160,084 sq m. Energy production (consumption): electricity (kW-hr; 1996) 1,098,000,000 (987,600,000); coal, none (none); crude petroleum, none (none); petroleum products (metric tons; 1994) none (446,000); natural gas, none (none).
Population economically active (1993): total 175,500; activity rate of total population 42.0% (participation rates: ages 15–64, 73.2%; [1990] female 45.5%; unemployed [1996] 27.8%).

Price and earnings indexes (1990 = 100)[11]

	1990	1991	1992	1993	1994	1995	1996[12]
Consumer price index	100.0	102.0	104.5	106.7	110.8	114.3	113.5
Monthly earnings index[13]	100.0	102.0	104.7	105.0	106.5	108.7[14]	109.6

Household income and expenditure. Average household size (1990) 3.4; income per household (1988) F 105,400 (U.S.$17,700); sources of income (1988): wages and salaries 78.9%, self-employment 12.7%, transfer payments 8.4%; expenditure (1990): food and beverages 30.9%, transportation and communications 20.5%, housing and lighting 11.3%, household durables 9.3%, clothing and footwear 9.3%, energy and fuel 7.7%.
Gross national product (1990): U.S.$1,160,000,000 (U.S.$2,970 per capita).

Structure of gross domestic product and labour force

	1989 in value F '000,000	1989 % of total value	1993 labour force	1993 % of labour force
Agriculture	1,177.4	9.2	9,079	5.2
Mining, manufacturing	758.4	5.9	10,376	5.9
Construction	949.3	7.4	15,564	8.9
Public utilities	38.7	0.3	...	...
Transp. and commun.	773.3	6.1	}	
Trade	2,499.6	19.6	54,474	31.0
Finance, real estate	848.8	6.6		
Pub. admin., defense	4,242.4	33.2	}	
Services	2,056.6	16.1	40,207	22.9
Other	−563.3[15]	−4.4[15]	45,800[16]	26.1[16]
TOTAL	12,781.2	100.0	175,500	100.0

Land use (1994): forest 39.1%; pasture 14.2%; agriculture 16.0%; other 30.7%.

Foreign trade

Balance of trade (current prices)

	1990	1991	1992	1993	1994	1995
F '000,000	−8,439	−8,209	−7,505	−7,309	−7,693	−8,655
% of total	86.3%	79.8%	83.8%	83.2%	82.0%	84.3%

Imports (1995): F 9,459,415,000 (consumer goods 26.5%, food and agriculture products 17.3%, machinery and equipment 15.7%, transport vehicles and parts 11.2%). *Major import sources* (1995): France 63.8%; other EEC 13.5%; United States 3.3%; Martinique 2.4%; Japan 2.2%.
Exports (1995): F 804,096,000 (bananas 25.4%, sugar 11.4%, rum 4.4%, melons 2.9%). *Major export destinations* (1995): France 65.8%; Martinique 10.5%; other EEC 10.3%; French Guiana 2.1%.

Transport and communications

Transport. Railroads: none. Roads (1996): total length 1,988 mi, 3,200 km (paved [1986] 80%). Vehicles (1993): passenger cars 101,600; trucks and buses 37,500. Merchant marine (1992): vessels (100 gross tons and over) 20; deadweight tonnage 4,430. Air transport (1996): passenger arrivals and departures 1,854,971; cargo handled 13,473 metric tons, cargo unloaded 4,823 metric tons; airports (1997) with scheduled flights 7.

Communications

Medium	date	unit	number	units per 1,000 persons
Daily newspapers	1995	circulation	35,000	81
Radio	1995	receivers	98,000	226
Television	1995	receivers	114,000	263
Telephones	1995	main lines	158,800	366
Facsimile machines	1995	units	3,400	7.8

Education and health

Educational attainment (1990). Percentage of population age 25 and over having: incomplete primary, or no declaration 59.8%; primary education 14.5%; secondary 19.0%; higher 6.7%. *Literacy* (1982): total population age 15 and over literate 225,400 (90.1%); males literate 108,700 (89.7%); females literate 116,700 (90.5%).

Education (1993–94)

	schools	teachers	students	student/teacher ratio
Primary (age 6–10)	334	3,167	38,092	12.0
Secondary (age 11–17) }	84	3,834	51,366	13.4
Vocational				
Higher[17]	1	121	4,673	38.6

Health (1991): physicians 590 (1 per 680 persons); hospital beds 3,230 (1 per 122 persons); infant mortality rate per 1,000 live births (1994) 7.9.
Food (1995): daily per capita caloric intake 2,732 (vegetable products 75%, animal products 25%); 129% of FAO recommended minimum requirement.

Military

Total active duty personnel (1994): 535 French troops.

[1]Guadeloupe elects 4 deputies and 2 senators to French parliament. [2]Comprises Basse-Terre 327 sq mi (848 sq km), pop. 149,943, and Îles des Saintes 5 sq mi (13 sq km), pop. 2,036. [3]Comprises Grande-Terre 228 sq mi (590 sq km), pop 177,570; Marie-Galante 61 sq mi (158 sq km), pop. 13,463; La Désirade 8 sq mi (20 sq km), pop. 1,610; and the uninhabited Îles de la Petite-Terre. [4]Comprises the French part of Saint-Martin 20 sq mi (52 sq km), pop. 28,518; Saint-Barthélemy 8 sq mi (21 sq km), pop. 5,038; and the small, uninhabited island of Tintamarre. [5]Total area includes 29 sq mi (75 sq km) not allocated by arrondissement. [6]Preliminary; final 1990 census total was 386,987. [7]Urban defined as locality with 2,000 or more inhabitants. [8]Urban agglomeration. [9]Includes Les Abymes. [10]Includes external long-term private debt not guaranteed by the government. [11]Base and indexes are end of year unless footnoted. [12]March. [13]Based on minimum-level wage of public employees. [14]June. [15]Less imputed bank service charges. [16]Unemployed. [17]University of Antilles-French Guiana, Guadeloupe campus.

Internet resources for further information:
• Guadeloupe: Présentation générale (in French)
http://www.outre-mer.gouv.fr/domtom/gua.htm

Guatemala

Official name: República de Guatemala (Republic of Guatemala).
Form of government: republic with one legislative house (Congress of the Republic [80]).
Head of state and government: President.
Capital: Guatemala City.
Official language: Spanish.
Official religion: none
Monetary unit: 1 quetzal (Q) = 100 centavos; valuation (Sept. 25, 1998)
1 U.S.$ = Q 6.51; 1 £ = Q 11.08.

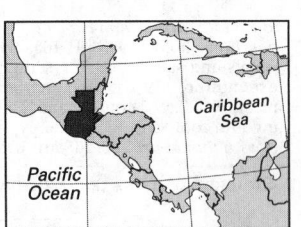

Area and population

Departments	Capitals	area sq mi	area sq km	population 1995 estimate[1]
Alta Verapaz	Cobán	3,354	8,686	670,815
Baja Verapaz	Salamá	1,206	3,124	205,481
Chimaltenango	Chimaltenango	764	1,979	385,856
Chiquimula	Chiquimula	917	2,376	274,091
El Progreso	Guastatoya (Progreso)	742	1,922	117,943
Escuintla	Escuintla	1,693	4,384	610,322
Guatemala	Guatemala City	821	2,126	2,246,170
Huehuetenango	Huehuetenango	2,857	7,400	816,376
Izabal	Puerto Barrios	3,490	9,038	370,538
Jalapa	Jalapa	797	2,063	211,830
Jutiapa	Jutiapa	1,243	3,219	387,177
Petén	Flores	13,843	35,854	310,008
Quetzaltenango	Quetzaltenango	753	1,951	623,571
Quiché	Santa Cruz del Quiché	3,235	8,378	652,022
Retalhuleu	Retalhuleu	717	1,856	268,996
Sacatepéquez	Antigua Guatemala	180	465	202,243
San Marcos	San Marcos	1,464	3,791	790,118
Santa Rosa	Cuilapa	1,141	2,955	291,611
Sololá	Sololá	410	1,061	274,356
Suchitepéquez	Mazatenango	969	2,510	403,618
Totonicapán	Totonicapán	410	1,061	333,634
Zacapa	Zacapa	1,039	2,690	174,450
TOTAL		42,042[2]	108,889	10,621,226

Demography

Population (1998): 10,802,000.
Density (1998): persons per sq mi 256.9, persons per sq km 99.2.
Urban-rural (1995): urban 38.7%; rural 61.3%.
Sex distribution (1995): male 50.49%; female 49.51%.
Age breakdown (1994): under 15, 44.0%; 15–29, 26.1%; 30–44, 15.8%; 45–59, 8.3%; 60 and over, 5.8%.
Population projection: (2000) 11,385,000; (2010) 14,631,000.
Doubling time: 24 years.
Ethnic composition (1994): Amerindian 42.8%; non-Amerindian 57.2%.
Religious affiliation (1995): Roman Catholic 75.9%, of which Catholic/traditional syncretist 25.0%; Protestant 21.8%; other Christian 1.3%; other 1.0%.
Major cities (1995): Guatemala City 1,167,495; Mixco 436,668; Villa Nueva 165,567; Chinautla 61,335; Amatitlan 40,229.

Vital statistics

Birth rate per 1,000 population (1994): 35.4 (world avg. 25.0).
Death rate per 1,000 population (1994): 7.5 (world avg. 9.3).
Natural increase rate per 1,000 population (1994): 27.9 (world avg. 15.7).
Total fertility rate (avg. births per childbearing woman; 1994): 4.8.
Marriage rate per 1,000 population (1993): 4.7.
Life expectancy at birth (1994): male 61.9 years; female 67.1 years.
Major causes of death per 100,000 population (1988): infectious and parasitic diseases 121.6; diseases of the respiratory system 110.8; perinatal causes 58.7; malnutrition 50.2; dehydration 18.5.

National economy

Budget (1996). Revenue: Q 8,605,100,000 (tax revenue 94.5%, of which taxes on goods and services 50.9%, income taxes 23.3%, customs duties 18.0%, nontax revenue 5.5%). Expenditures: Q 8,378,500,000 (current expenditures 73.6%, of which disbursements for goods and services 38.7%, transfer payments 23.3%; capital expenditures 26.4%).
Public debt (external, outstanding; 1996): U.S.$2,766,000,000.
Tourism (1995): receipts U.S.$277,000,000; expenditures U.S.$174,000,000.
Production (metric tons except as noted). Agriculture, forestry, fishing (1996): sugarcane 14,380,000, corn (maize) 1,135,896, bananas 676,692, coffee 207,000, tomatoes 129,168, oil palm fruit 126,000; livestock (number of live animals) 2,291,440 cattle, 950,408 pigs, 21,000,000 chickens; roundwood (1995) 14,123,400 cu m; fish catch (1995) 11,927. Mining and quarrying (1994): gypsum (1993) 60,000; iron ore 3,498; antimony ore 494. Manufacturing (value added in Q '000,000; 1995[3]): food and beverage products 273; clothing and textiles 111; machinery and metal products 51. Construction (value of buildings authorized in Q '000,000; 1991)[4]: residential 170.2; nonresidential 127.5. Energy production (consumption): electricity (kW-hr; 1994) 3,161,000,000 (3,161,000,000); crude petroleum (barrels; 1994) 2,632,000 (6,958,000); petroleum products (metric tons; 1994) 750,000 (1,805,000).
Household income and expenditure. Average household size (1994) 5.2; income per household (1989) Q 4,306 (U.S.$1,529); sources of income: n.a.; expenditure (1981): food 64.4%, housing and energy 16.0%, transportation and communications 7.0%, household furnishings 5.0%, clothing 3.1%.
Gross national product (1996): U.S.$16,018,000,000 (U.S.$1,470 per capita).

Structure of gross domestic product and labour force

	1996 in value Q '000[3]	1996 % of total value	1995 labour force	1995 % of labour force
Agriculture	1,035,227	24.0	1,798,227	58.1
Mining	19,429	0.4	3,095	0.1
Manufacturing	601,138	14.0	420,928	13.6
Construction	91,198	2.1	126,898	4.1
Public utilities	137,008	3.2	9,285	0.3
Transp. and commun.	377,172	8.8	77,377	2.5
Trade	1,060,614	24.6	225,940	7.3
Finance, real estate	418,214	9.7	} 371,407	} 12.0
Pub. admin., defense	316,818	7.4		
Services	250,729	5.8		
Other	—	—	61,901[5]	2.0[5]
TOTAL	4,307,547	100.0	3,095,058	100.0

Population economically active (1996): total 3,183,173; activity rate of total population 29.1% (participation rates [1994] ages 15–64, 51.0%; female 19.5%; unemployed 0.5%[6]).

Price and earnings indexes (1990 = 100)

	1991	1992	1993	1994	1995	1996	1997
Consumer price index	133.2	146.5	163.9	181.7	196.9	218.7	238.9
Annual earnings index[7]	126.6	162.3	203.8	232.7	291.1	349.9	...

Land use (1994): forested 53.6%; meadows and pastures 24.0%; agricultural and under permanent cultivation 17.6%; other 4.8%.

Foreign trade[8]

Balance of trade (current prices)

	1992	1993	1994	1995	1996	1997
U.S.$'000,000	−1,190.8	−1,096.2	−755.3	−692.0	−849.7	−1,198.7
% of total	35.7%	29.0%	19.9%	13.8%	17.3%	20.4%

Imports (1996): U.S.$3,146,223,700 (machinery 17.1%, mineral products 15.6%, chemical products 14.1%, transport equipment 12.3%, food products 7.7%, metal products 7.4%, plastic products 5.8%). *Major import sources:* United States 43.9%; Mexico 10.3%; Venezuela 5.3%; El Salvador 4.1%.
Exports (1995): U.S.$1,935,516,600 (coffee 23.3%, sugar 9.9%, bananas 7.6%, vegetable seeds 3.6%, legumes 3.3%). *Major export destinations:* United States 36.6%; El Salvador 12.7%; Honduras 6.9%; Germany 5.1%.

Transport and communications

Transport. Railroads (1996): route length 884 km; passenger-km (1991) 12,531,000; metric ton-km cargo 47,233,000. Roads (1995): total length 12,795 km (paved 28%). Vehicles (1994): passenger cars 102,000; trucks and buses 96,800. Air transport (1993)[9]: passenger-km 384,000,000; metric ton-km cargo 21,000,000; airports (1996) 2.

Communications

Medium	date	unit	number	units per 1,000 persons
Daily newspapers	1994	circulation	240,000	29
Radio	1996	receivers	570,000	52
Television	1995	receivers	475,000	45
Telephones	1995	main lines	289,500	27
Cellular telephones	1995	subscribers	30,000	2.8
Facsimile machines	1995	units	10,000	0.9
Personal computers	1995	units	30,000	2.8

Education and health

Educational attainment (1994). Percentage of population age 25 and over having: no formal schooling 45.2%; incomplete primary education 20.8%; complete primary 18.0%; some secondary 4.8%; secondary 7.2%; higher 4.0%. *Literacy* (1995): total population age 15 and over literate 55.6%; males literate 62.5%; females literate 48.6%.

Education (1993)

	schools	teachers	students	student/ teacher ratio
Primary (age 7–12)	10,770	44,220	1,393,921	31.5
Secondary (age 13–18)	1,274[10]	} 20,942	334,883	16.0
Voc., teacher tr.	626[10]			
Higher[11]	5	4,346	69,532	16.0

Health (1988): physicians 2,171 (1 per 3,999 persons); hospital beds (1987) 13,667 (1 per 602 persons); infant mortality rate (1994) 53.9.
Food (1995): daily per capita caloric intake 2,300 (vegetable products 92%, animal products 8%); 105% of FAO recommended minimum requirement.

Military

Total active duty personnel (1996): 44,200 (army 95.0%, navy 3.4%, air force 1.6%). *Military expenditure as percentage of GNP* (1995): 1.3% (world 2.8%); per capita expenditure U.S.$18.

[1]Adjusted for underenumeration in 1994 census. [2]Detail does not add to total given because of rounding. [3]At prices of 1958. [4]Private construction in Guatemala City metropolitan area only. [5]Persons in activities not adequately defined. [6]Officially unemployed; majority of economically active population is estimated to be underemployed. [7]Based on employees entitled to social security. [8]Import figures are f.o.b. in balance of trade and c.i.f. for commodities and trading partners. [9]Aviateca Airlines only. [10]1991. [11]1989.

Internet resources for further information:
• Banco de Guatemala (Spanish only) http://www.banguat.gob.gt/

Guinea

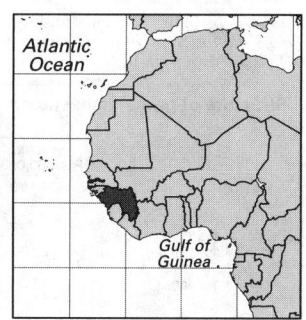

Official name: République de Guinée (Republic of Guinea).
Form of government: unitary multiparty republic with one legislative house (National Assembly [114 seats]).
Head of state and government: President assisted by Prime Minister[1].
Capital: Conakry.
Official language: French.
Official religion: none.
Monetary unit: 1 Guinean franc (GF) = 100 cauris; valuation (Sept. 25, 1998) 1 U.S.$ = GF 1,243; 1 £ = GF 2,116.

Area and population

Regions	Capitals	area sq mi	sq km	population 1983 census
Beyla	Beyla	6,738	17,452	161,347
Boffa	Boffa	1,932	5,003	141,719
Boké	Boké	3,881	10,053	225,207
Conakry	Conakry	119	308	705,280
Coyah (Dubréka)	Coyah	2,153	5,576	134,190
Dabola	Dabola	2,317	6,000	97,986
Dalaba	Dalaba	1,313	3,400	132,802
Dinguiraye	Dinguiraye	4,247	11,000	133,502
Faranah	Faranah	4,788	12,400	142,923
Forécariah	Forécariah	1,647	4,265	116,464
Fria	Fria	840	2,175	70,413
Gaoual	Gaoual	4,440	11,500	135,657
Guéckédou	Guéckédou	1,605	4,157	204,757
Kankan	Kankan	7,104	18,400	229,861
Kérouané	Kérouané	3,070	7,950	106,872
Kindia	Kindia	3,409	8,828	216,052
Kissidougou	Kissidougou	3,425	8,872	183,236
Koubia	Koubia	571	1,480	98,053
Koundara	Koundara	2,124	5,500	94,216
Kouroussa	Kouroussa	4,647	12,035	136,926
Labé	Labé	973	2,520	253,214
Lélouma	Lélouma	830	2,150	138,467
Lola	Lola	1,629	4,219	106,654
Macenta	Macenta	3,363	8,710	193,109
Mali	Mali	3,398	8,800	210,889
Mamou	Mamou	2,378	6,160	190,525
Mandiana	Mandiana	5,000	12,950	136,317
Nzérékoré	Nzérékoré	1,460	3,781	216,355
Pita	Pita	1,544	4,000	227,912
Siguiri	Siguiri	7,626	19,750	209,164
Télimélé	Télimélé	3,119	8,080	243,256
Tougué	Tougué	2,394	6,200	113,272
Yomou	Yomou	843	2,183	74,417
TOTAL		94,926[2]	245,857	5,781,014

Demography

Population (1998): 7,477,000.
Density (1998): persons per sq mi 78.8, persons per sq km 30.4.
Urban-rural (1990): urban 25.6%; rural 74.4%.
Sex distribution (1996): male 48.80%; female 51.20%.
Age breakdown (1995): under 15, 47.1%; 15–29, 25.9%; 30–44, 15.0%; 45–59, 7.8%; 60–74, 3.6%; 75 and over, 0.6%.
Population projection: (2000) 7,611,000; (2010) 9,440,000.
Doubling time: 29 years.
Ethnic composition (1990): Fulani 40.3%; Malinke 25.8%; Susu 11.0%; Kissi 6.5%; Kpelle 4.8%; other 11.6%.
Religious affiliation (1983): Muslim 86.9%; traditional beliefs 4.6%; other 8.5%.
Major cities (1983): Conakry (1993) 1,090,610; Kankan 55,010; Nzérékoré 44,598; Kindia 39,121; Kissidougou 30,724.

Vital statistics

Birth rate per 1,000 population (1996): 42.6 (world avg. 25.0).
Death rate per 1,000 population (1996): 18.7 (world avg. 9.3).
Total fertility rate (avg. births per childbearing woman; 1996): 5.7.
Life expectancy at birth (1996): male 42.7 years; female 47.5 years.
Major causes of death per 100,000 population: n.a.; however, in the mid-1990s, the major causes of illness were (in order): malaria, acute respiratory infections, intestinal parasitic diseases, gastroenteritis, and malnutrition.

National economy

Budget (1997). Revenue: GF 628,600,000,000 (current revenues 78.6%, of which mining sector 18.8%, other 59.8%; foreign aid 21.4%). Expenditures: GF 754,700,000,000 (current expenditure 50.8%, of which wages and salaries 23.6%, other goods and services 7.9%; capital spending 49.2%).
Public debt (external, outstanding; 1996): U.S. $2,981,000,000.
Tourism (1995): receipts U.S.$1,000,000; expenditures U.S.$21,000,000.
Production (metric tons except as noted). Agriculture, forestry, fishing (1996): fruits 990,000 (of which plantains 429,000, bananas 150,000, pineapples 67,000), roots and tubers 691,000 (of which cassava 440,000, sweet potatoes 130,000, yams 95,000), paddy rice 668,000, vegetables and melons 420,000, sugarcane 220,000, peanuts (groundnuts) 139,000, corn (maize) 90,000; livestock (number of live animals) 2,212,000 cattle, 760,000 goats, 618,000 sheep, 45,000 pigs, 7,000,000 chickens; roundwood (1995) 5,223,000 cu m; fish catch (1995) 68,766. Mining and quarrying (1996): bauxite 15,888,600; alumina 564,237; gold 7,863 kg[3]. Manufacturing (value of production in GF '000; 1985): corrugated and sheet iron 571,081; plastics 462,242; tobacco products

375,154; cement 326,138; printed matter 216,511. Energy production (consumption): electricity (kW-hr; 1995) 700,000,000 (700,000,000); petroleum products (metric tons; 1994) none (355,000).
Gross national product (1996): U.S.$3,804,000,000 (U.S.$560 per capita).

Structure of gross domestic product and labour force

	1994 in value GF '000,000,000	% of total value	1983 labour force	% of labour force
Agriculture, forestry, fishing	415.7	24.1	1,423,615	78.2
Mining	328.6	19.1	12,241	0.7
Manufacturing	79.6	4.6	11,215	0.6
Construction	119.5	6.9	9,115	0.5
Public utilities	3.7	0.2	3,205	0.2
Trans. and commun.	88.4	5.1	29,496	1.6
Trade, finance	448.7	26.0	40,865	2.0
Pub. admin., defense	91.3	5.3 }	137,600	7.5
Services	102.6	6.0 }		
Other	45.7	2.7	155,679	8.5
TOTAL	1,723.6[2]	100.0	1,823,031	100.0

Population economically active (1992); total 2,590,000; activity rate of total population 42.3% (participation rates [1983]: ages 15–64, 63.5%; female 39.4%; unemployed, n.a.).

Price and earnings indexes (1990 = 100)

	1990	1991	1992	1993	1994	1995	1996
Consumer price index	100.0	119.3	139.5	149.4	155.6	164.4	169.3
Annual salary index[4]	100.0	200.0	262.4	272.6	275.2	...	...

Household income and expenditure. Average household size (1983) 6.7; average annual income per capita (1984) GS 7,660 (U.S.$305); expenditure (1985): food 61.5%, health 11.2%, clothing 7.9%, housing 7.3%.
Land use (1994): forest 27.3%; pasture 43.5%; agriculture 3.3%; other 25.9%.

Foreign trade[5]

Balance of trade (current prices)

	1991	1992	1993	1994	1995	1996
U.S.$'000,000	−7.8	−91.2	−21.6	−169.7	−39.0	+111.2
% of total	0.6%	8.1%	1.9%	14.1%	3.2%	9.6%

Imports (1994): U.S.$687,000,000 (goods for mining companies 22.2%; goods for public sector 20.1%; other private sector 57.7%). *Major import sources:* France 19.5%; Côte d'Ivoire 16.0%; U.S. 7.1%; Belgium 6.9%.
Exports (1994): U.S.$625,900,000 (bauxite 43.4%; alumina 16.5%; gold 13.3%; coffee 9.1%; diamonds 6.4%; fish 3.1%). *Major export destinations:* Belgium 26.7%; U.S. 15.1%; Ireland 10.0%; Spain 9.6%; France 4.6%.

Transport and communications

Transport. Railroads (1997): route length 662 km; (latest) passenger-km 41,500,000; metric ton-km cargo 7,300,000. Roads (1997): total length 19,215 km (paved 10%). Vehicles (1992): passenger cars 23,155; trucks and buses 13,000. Air transport (1994): passenger-km 32,842,000; metric ton-km cargo 1,241,000; airports (1997) 1.

Communications

Medium	date	unit	number	units per 1,000 persons
Daily newspapers	1988	circulation	13,000	2.0
Radio	1995	receivers	230,000	34.3
Television	1995	receivers	65,000	9.7
Telephones	1995	main lines	10,900	1.6
Cellular telephones	1995	subscribers	1,000	0.15
Facsimile machines	1995	units	200	0.03
Personal computers	1995	units	1,000	0.15

Education and health

Educational attainment of those age 6 and over having attended school (1983): primary 55.2%; secondary 32.7%; vocational 3.4%; higher 8.7%. *Literacy* (1995): percentage of total population age 15 and over literate 35.9%; males 49.9%; females 21.9%.

Education (1995–96)

	schools	teachers	students	student/ teacher ratio
Primary (age 7–12)	3,237	11,875	584,161	49.2
Secondary (age 13–18)	225[6]	4,690	127,517	27.2
Voc., teacher tr.[8]	35[6]	1,302	9,278	7.1
Higher	10[6]	805[7, 8]	6,245[7, 8]	7.8[7, 8]

Health: physicians (1990) 773 (1 per 7,680 persons); hospital beds (1988) 3,382 (1 per 1,652 persons); infant mortality rate (1996) 134.
Food (1995): daily per capita caloric intake 2,161 (vegetable products 97%, animal products 3%); 94% of FAO recommended minimum requirement.

Military

Total active duty personnel (1997): 9,700 (army 87.6%, navy 4.1%, air force 8.2%) *Military expenditure as percentage of GNP* (1995): 1.5% (world 2.8%).

[1]President created extraconstitutional post of Prime Minister July 1996. [2]Detail does not add to total given because of rounding. [3]1995 reported figure to government of artisanal production; excludes artisanal production smuggled out of country. [4]Nonmilitary civil service employees. [5]Imports c.i.f.; exports f.o.b. in commodities and direction of trade. [6]1987–88. [7]1993. [8]Universities only.

Internet resources for further information:
• Welcome to Guinea http://www.guinee.net

Guinea-Bissau

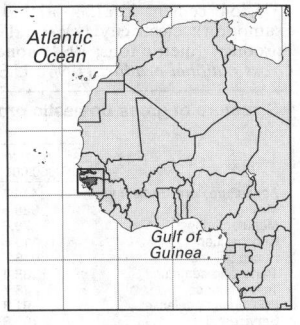

Official name: República da
  Guiné-Bissau (Republic of
  Guinea-Bissau).
Form of government: multiparty
  republic with one legislative house
  (National People's Assembly [100]).
Chief of state: President.
Head of government: Prime Minister.
Capital: Bissau.
Official language: Portuguese.
Official religion: none.
Monetary unit[1]: 1 CFA franc
  (CFAF) = 100 centimes; valuation
  (Sept. 25, 1998) 1 U.S.$ = CFAF 560.38;
  1 £ = CFAF 954.05.

Area and population

Regions	Capitals	area sq mi	area sq km	population 1991 census[2]
Bafatá	Bafatá	2,309	5,981	143,377
Biombo[3]	Bissau	324	840	60,420
Bolama	Bolama	1,013	2,624	26,691
Cacheu	Cacheu	1,998	5,175	146,980
Gabú	Gabú	3,533	9,150	134,971
Oio	Farim	2,086	5,403	156,084
Quinara	Fulacunda	1,212	3,138	44,793
Tombali	Catió	1,443	3,736	72,441
Autonomous Sector				
Bissau[3]	—	30	78	197,610
TOTAL		13,948[4]	36,125[4]	983,367

Demography

Population (1998): 1,206,000.
Density (1998)[5]: persons per sq mi 111.1, persons per sq km 42.9.
Urban-rural (1996): urban 22.0%; rural 78.0%.
Sex distribution (1997): male 48.52%; female 51.48%.
Age breakdown (1997): under 15, 42.7%; 15–29, 28.1%; 30–44, 15.4%; 45–59,
  9.2%; 60–74, 3.8%; 75 and over, 0.8%.
Population projection: (2000) 1,263,000; (2010) 1,579,000.
Doubling time: 33 years.
Ethnic composition (1979): Balante 27.2%; Fulani 22.9%; Malinke 12.2%;
  Mandyako 10.6%; Pepel 10.0%; other 17.1%.
Religious affiliation (1994): traditional beliefs 65%; Muslim 30%; Christian 5%.
Major cities (1979): Bissau 223,000[6]; Bafatá 13,429; Gabú 7,803; Mansôa 5,390;
  Catió 5,179.

Vital statistics

Birth rate per 1,000 population (1997): 39.0 (world avg. 25.0); legitimate, n.a.;
  illegitimate, n.a.
Death rate per 1,000 population (1997): 16.0 (world avg. 9.3).
Natural increase rate per 1,000 population (1997): 23.0 (world avg. 15.7).
Total fertility rate (avg. births per childbearing woman; 1997): 5.3.
Marriage rate per 1,000 population (1981): 0.1.
Divorce rate per 1,000 population: n.a.
Life expectancy at birth (1997): male 47.1 years; female 50.4 years.
Major causes of death per 100,000 population: n.a.; however, major diseases
  include tuberculosis of the respiratory system, whooping cough, typhoid
  fever, cholera, bacillary dysentery and amebiasis, malaria, pneumonia, and
  meningococcal infections; malnutrition is widespread.

National economy

Budget (1996). Revenue: PG 899,500,000,000 (1995; tax revenue 54.7%, of
  which customs 27.4%, tax on consumption 16.9%; nontax revenue 45.3%, of
  which fishing licenses 37.7%). Expenditures: PG 2,188,200,000,000 (1995; current expenditures 50.3%, of which goods and services 7.4%, wages and
  salaries 9.2%; capital expenditures 49.7%).
Production (metric tons except as noted). Agriculture, forestry, fishing (1997):
  rice 135,000, fruits 65,400[7], roots and tubers (sweet potatoes and cassava)
  60,000, cashews 35,000, plantains 29,000, millet 25,000, coconuts 25,000, vegetables 20,000, sorghum 19,000, peanuts (groundnuts) 18,000, corn (maize)
  14,000, palm kernels 8,000[7], sugarcane 5,500, bananas 4,000, palm oil 4,500[7],
  seed cotton 3,400; livestock (number of live animals) 475,000 cattle, 310,000
  pigs, 270,000 goats, 255,000 sheep, 850,000 chickens; roundwood (1995)
  579,000 cu m; fish catch (1995) 5,595. Mining and quarrying: extraction of
  construction materials only. Manufacturing (1997): fresh pork 9,720; palm oil
  5,000[8]; copra 5,000[7]; fresh beef 3,850; soap 2,900[6]; dried and smoked fish
  1,900[6]; animal hides 1,277[8], of which cattle 875[8], goat 194[8], sheep 158[8];
  sawlogs 40,000 cu m[8]; distilled liquor 13,000 hectolitres[6]. Construction: n.a.
  Energy production (consumption): electricity (kW-hr; 1994) 45,000,000
  (45,000,000); coal, none (none); crude petroleum, none (none); petroleum
  products (metric tons; 1994) none (75,000); natural gas, none (none).
Population economically active (1992): total 471,000; activity rate of total population 46.9% (participation rates (1991): over age 10, 67.1%; female 40.5%;
  unemployed, n.a.).

Price and earnings indexes (1990 = 100)

	1993	1994	1995	1996	1997	1998[9]
Consumer price index	395.8	455.9	662.7	998.9	1,489.4	1,499.9
Earnings index	...	...	...	...	...	...

Public debt (external, outstanding; 1996): U.S.$856,200,000.
Gross national product (at current market prices; 1996): U.S.$270,000,000
  (U.S.$250 per capita).

Structure of gross domestic product and labour force

	1996 in value PG '000,000[10]	1996 % of total value	1994 labour force	1994 % of labour force
Agriculture	35,100	53.0	365,000	77.2
Mining				
Manufacturing	7,500	11.3	21,000	4.5
Public utilities				
Construction	2,100	3.2		
Transportation and communications	1,600	2.4		
Trade	14,900	22.5	87,000	18.3
Finance, services	400	0.6		
Pub. admin., defense	4,600	6.9		
TOTAL	66,300[11]	100.0[11]	473,000	100.0

Tourism: n.a.
Land use (1994): forested 38.1%; meadows and pastures 38.4%; agricultural
  and under permanent cultivation 12.1%; other 11.4%.
Household income and expenditure. Average household size (1981) 4.1; income
  per household: n.a; sources of income: n.a.; expenditure: n.a.

Foreign trade[12]

Balance of trade (current prices)

	1991	1992	1993	1994	1995	1996
CFAF '000,000	–3,122	–9,491	–5,181	–15,950	–13,346	–24,210
% of total	57.6%	87.3%	37.3%	32.5%	50.1%	52.3%

Imports (1995): U.S.$71,900,000 (foodstuffs 35.6%, transport equipment
  11.7%, fuel and lubricants 11.5%, machinery 10.7%, building materials
  10.2%). *Major import sources:* Portugal 36.9%; The Netherlands 13.6%;
  China 8.3%; Japan 8.0%; Spain 4.3%; U.K. 3.8%; France 3.4%; U.S. 3.2%.
Exports (1995): U.S.$23,900,000 (cashews 85.8%, lumber 6.3%, cotton 5.4%).
  Major export destinations: India 87.8%; Portugal 10.2%; France 1.0%; Spain
  0.8%.

Transport and communications

Transport. Railroads: none. Roads (1995): total length 2,703 mi, 4,350 km
  (paved 10%). Vehicles (1995): passenger cars 6,300; trucks and buses 4,900.
  Merchant marine (1992): vessels (100 gross tons and over) 19; total deadweight tonnage 1,846. Air transport (1994): passenger-mi 3,700,000, passenger-km 6,000,000; short ton-mi cargo 700,000, metric ton-km cargo 1,000,000;
  airports (1997) with scheduled flights 2.

Communications

Medium	date	unit	number	units per 1,000 persons
Daily newspapers	1995	circulation	6,000	6.0
Radio	1995	receivers	47,200	42.0
Television	1995	receivers	...	...
Telephones	1995	main lines	9,900	8.8
Facsimile machines	1995	units	563	0.5

Education and health

Educational attainment (1979). Percentage of population age 7 and over having: no formal schooling or knowledge of reading and writing 90.4%; primary education 7.9%; secondary 1.0%; technical 0.5%; higher 0.2%. *Literacy*
  (1995): total population age 15 and over literate 54.9%; males literate 68.0%;
  females literate 42.5%.

Education (1988)

	schools	teachers	students	student/ teacher ratio
Primary (age 7–13)	632[13]	3,065[13]	100,369[14]	...
Secondary (age 13–18)	121[5]	824[15]	5,505	...
Voc., teacher tr.	4[13]	107	825	7.7

Health: physicians (1986) 274 (1 per 3,245 persons); hospital beds (1993) 1,300
  (1 per 797 persons); infant mortality rate per 1,000 live births (1997) 114.
Food (1995): daily per capita caloric intake 2,433 (vegetable products 93%,
  animal products 7%); 105% of FAO recommended minimum requirement.

Military

Total active duty personnel (1997): 7,250[16] (army 93.8%, navy 4.8%, air force
  1.4%). *Military expenditure as percentage of GNP* (1995): 2.8% (world 2.8%);
  per capita expenditure U.S.$6.

[1]Since Guinea-Bissau became a member of the French Franc Zone, the Guinea-
Bissau peso (PG) was replaced by the CFA franc in May 1997. [2]Preliminary. [3]Biombo
region excludes Bissau city. [4]Includes water area of about 3,089 sq mi (8,000 sq km).
[5]Based on land area of 10,859 sq mi (28,125 sq km). [6]1995. [7]1996. [8]1993. [9]March.
[10]Factor cost at constant 1986 prices. [11]Detail does not add to total given because
of rounding. [12]Import figures are c.i.f.; export figures are f.o.b. [13]1987. [14]1994–95.
[15]1986. [16]Excludes 2,000 gendarmes, who are part of the armed forces.

Internet resources for further information:
• Guinea-Bissau http://www.hmnet.com/africa/guineabis/guineabis.html
• Guiné-Bissau http://www.portugalnet.pt/encontro/guine/guine.html

Guyana

Official name: Co-operative Republic of Guyana.
Form of government: unitary multiparty republic with one legislative house (National Assembly [65[1]]).
Head of state and government: President.
Capital: Georgetown.
Official language: English.
Official religion: none.
Monetary unit: 1 Guyana dollar (G$) = 100 cents; valuation (Sept. 25, 1998) 1 U.S.$ = G$147.30; 1 £ = G$250.78.

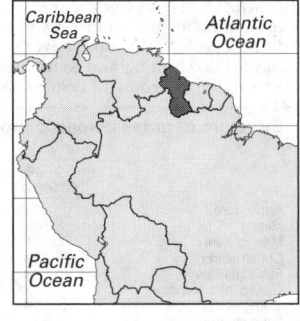

Area and population

Administrative Regions		Capitals	area sq mi	area sq km	population 1986 estimate
Region 1	(Barima–Waini)	Mabaruma	7,853	20,339	18,516
Region 2	(Pomeroon–Supenaam)	Anna Regina	2,392	6,195	41,966
Region 3	(Essequibo Islands–West Demerara)	Vreed en Hoop	1,450	3,755	102,760
Region 4	(Demerara–Mahaica)	Paradise	862	2,233	310,758
Region 5	(Mahaica–Berbice)	Fort Wellington	1,610	4,170	55,556
Region 6	(East Berbice–Corentyne)	New Amsterdam	13,998	36,255	148,967
Region 7	(Cuyuni–Mazaruni)	Bartica	18,229	47,213	17,941
Region 8	(Potaro–Siparuni)	Mahdia	7,742	20,052	5,672
Region 9	(Upper Takutu–Upper Essequibo)	Lethem	22,313	57,790	15,338
Region 10	(Upper Demerara–Berbice)	Linden	6,595	17,081	38,598
TOTAL			83,044[2]	215,083[2]	756,072

Demography

Population (1998): 782,000.
Density (1998)[3]: persons per sq mi 10.3, persons per sq km 4.0.
Urban-rural (1995): urban 36.2%; rural 63.8%.
Sex distribution (1995): male 49.46%; female 50.54%.
Age breakdown (1995): under 15, 32.2%; 15–29, 30.1%; 30–44, 22.2%; 45–59, 9.5%; 60–74, 4.8%; 75 and over, 1.2%.
Population projection: (2000) 787,000; (2010) 803,000.
Doubling time: 73 years.
Ethnic composition (1992–93): East Indian 49.4%; black (African Negro and Bush Negro) 35.6%; mixed 7.1%; Amerindian 6.8%; Portuguese 0.7%; Chinese 0.4%.
Religious affiliation (1995): Christian 40.9%, of which Protestant 27.5% (including Anglican 8.6%), Roman Catholic 11.5%, Ethiopian Orthodox 1.1%; Hindu 34.0%; Muslim 9.0%; other 16.1%.
Major cities (1992): Georgetown 248,500; Linden 27,200; New Amsterdam 17,700.

Vital statistics

Birth rate per 1,000 population (1996): 19.0 (world avg. 25.0).
Death rate per 1,000 population (1996): 9.5 (world avg. 9.3).
Natural increase rate per 1,000 population (1996): 9.5 (world avg. 15.7).
Total fertility rate (avg. births per childbearing woman; 1996): 2.2.
Marriage rate per 1,000 population: n.a.
Divorce rate per 1,000 population: n.a.
Life expectancy at birth (1996): male 57.5 years; female 62.8 years.
Major causes of death per 100,000 population (1990)[4]: diseases of the circulatory system 244.6, of which cerebrovascular disease 103.7, ischemic heart disease 56.8, diseases of pulmonary circulation and other forms of heart disease 49.3%; diseases of the digestive system 39.0; endocrine and metabolic disorders 37.3; diseases of the respiratory system 37.3.

National economy

Budget (1996–97): Revenue: G$36,293,000,000 (current revenue 94.3%, of which consumption taxes 29.5%, income taxes on companies 20.9%, personal income taxes 12.7%, import duties 10.2%; development revenue 5.7%, of which external grants 5.3%). Expenditures: G$42,305,000,000 (current expenditure 61.3%, of which debt charges 18.9%, personal emoluments 17.4%; development expenditure 38.7%).
Production (metric tons except as noted). Agriculture, forestry, fishing (1996): rice 334,515, raw sugar 280,066, coconuts 72,800, cassava (manioc) 35,100, plantains 21,000, bananas 17,000, pineapples 10,400; livestock (number of live animals) 190,000 cattle, 130,000 sheep[5], 7,500,000 chickens; roundwood 526,725 cu m; fish catch 58,446, of which shrimps and prawns 17,792. Mining and quarrying (1996): bauxite 2,470,567; gold 386,031 troy oz; diamonds 46,730 carats. Manufacturing (1996): flour 36,600; rum 237,200 hectolitres; cigarettes 400,000,000 units; soft drinks 4,253,000 cases; pharmaceuticals 20,300,000 tablets; other products include cotton cloth and dyed and printed fabrics. Construction: n.a. Energy production (consumption): electricity (kW-hr; 1996) 348,200,000 ([1995] 217,200,000); coal, none (none); crude petroleum, none (none); petroleum products (metric tons; 1994) none (343,000); natural gas, none (none).
Tourism: receipts from visitors (1995) U.S.$32,600,000; expenditures by nationals abroad U.S.$21,100,000.
Land use (1994): forested 83.8%; meadows and pastures 6.3%; agricultural and under permanent cultivation 2.5%; other 7.4%.
Household income and expenditure. Average household size (1980) 5.1; income per household, n.a.; sources of income, n.a.; expenditure, n.a.
Gross national product (1996): U.S.$582,000,000 (U.S.$690 per capita).

Structure of gross domestic product and labour force

	1996 in value G$'000,000[6]	1996 % of total value	1980 labour force	1980 % of labour force
Sugar	16,277[7]	19.4[7]	50,316	20.4
Other agriculture	15,530[8]	18.5[8]		
Fishing, forestry	7,429	8.8		
Mining	15,567	18.5	9,669	3.9
Manufacturing	3,078[9, 10]	3.7[9, 10]	28,980	11.8
Construction	3,747	4.4	7,024	2.8
Public utilities	[10]	[10]	2,850	1.2
Transp. and commun.	4,486	5.3	9,412	3.8
Trade	3,534	4.2	15,231	6.2
Finance, real estate	5,854	7.0	2,944	1.2
Pub. admin., defense	7,393	8.8	29,948	12.1
Services	1,193	1.4	29,295	11.9
Other	—	—	61,002[11]	24.7[11]
TOTAL	84,088	100.0	246,671	100.0

Population economically active (1987); total 270,074; activity rate of total population 35.7% (participation rates: ages 15–64, 60.4%; female 29.9%; unemployed, n.a.).

Price and earnings indexes (1990 = 100)

	1991	1992	1993	1994	1995	1996	1997
Consumer price index[12]	189.6	239.4	262.7	298.6	329.5	352.9	365.4
Earnings index	...	...	...	...	...	...	...

Public debt (external, outstanding; 1996): U.S.$1,370,000,000.

Foreign trade[13]

Balance of trade (current prices)

	1992	1993	1994	1995	1996	1997
U.S.$'000,000	−61.0	−68.3	−40.6	−40.8	−20.2	−34.2
% of total	7.4%	7.6%	4.2%	4.0%	1.7%	2.8%

Imports (1995): U.S.$536,800,000 (capital goods 35.0%; consumer goods 21.2%; fuels and lubricants 16.7%). *Major import sources*[14]: U.S. 29%; Italy 18%; Netherlands Antilles 17%; U.K. 11%; Japan 4%.
Exports (1996): U.S.$574,800,000 (domestic exports 96.2%, of which sugar 26.2%, gold 18.1%, rice 16.3%, bauxite 15.0%, timber 8.9%; reexports 3.8%).
Major export destinations (1995)[14]: Canada 26%; U.S. 25%; U.K. 22%.

Transport and communications

Transport. Railroads: [15]. Roads (1995): total length 4,859 mi, 7,820 km (paved 7%). Vehicles (1995): passenger cars 24,000; trucks and buses 9,000. Merchant marine (1992): vessels (100 gross tons and over) 82; total deadweight tonnage 13,509. Air transport (1994): passenger-mi 139,000,000, passenger-km 224,000,000; short ton-mi cargo 16,000,000, metric ton-km cargo 23,000,000; airports (1996) with scheduled flights 1[16].

Communications

Medium	date	unit	number	units per 1,000 persons
Daily newspapers	1995	circulation	44,500	585
Radio	1996	receivers	350,000	454
Television	1995	receivers	15,000	197
Telephones	1995	main lines	44,600	587
Cellular telephones	1995	subscribers	1,200	1.6

Education and health

Educational attainment (1980). Percentage of population age 25 and over having: no formal schooling 8.1%; primary education 72.8%; secondary 17.3%; higher 1.8%. *Literacy* (1995): total population age 15 and over literate, c. 511,000 (98.1%); males literate, c. 254,000 (98.6%); females literate, c. 257,000 (97.5%).

Education (1994–95)

	schools	teachers	students	student/ teacher ratio
Primary (age 6–11)	423[17]	3,453	100,806	29.2
Secondary (age 12–17)	93[17]	1,828	67,039	36.7
Voc., teacher tr.[17]	8	176	5,388	30.6
Higher[18]	...	492	8,257	16.8

Health: physicians (1993) 244 (1 per 3,148 persons); hospital beds (1989) 2,488 (1 per 305 persons); infant mortality rate per 1,000 live births (1996) 51.4.
Food (1995): daily per capita caloric intake 2,460 (vegetable products 88%, animal products 12%); 108% of FAO recommended minimum requirement.

Military

Total active duty personnel (1996): 1,717 (army 93.2%, navy 1.0%, air force 5.8%) *Military expenditure as percentage of GNP* (1994): 1.5% (world 3.0%); per capita expenditure U.S.$9.

[1]Includes 12 indirectly elected seats. [2]Includes inland water area equaling c. 7,000 sq mi (c. 18,000 sq km). [3]Based on land area only. [4]Based on incomplete data. [5]1995. [6]At factor cost. [7]Includes sugar manufacturing. [8]Includes rice manufacturing. [9]Excludes sugar and rice manufacturing. [10]Manufacturing includes Public utilities. [11]Represents "not stated." [12]Weights of consumer price index components for Georgetown, Linden, and New Amsterdam only. [13]Imports c.i.f.; exports f.o.b. [14]Estimated figure. [15]No public railways. [16]International only; domestic air service is provided on a charter basis. [17]1989–90. [18]1993–94.

Internet resources for further information:
• Basic Information on Guyana (unofficial)
  http://www.lasalle.edu/-daniels/guyexp/gy1001.htm

Haiti

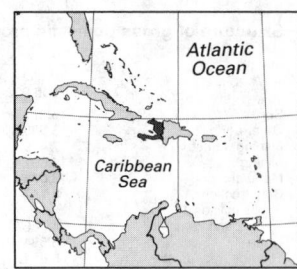

Official name: Repiblik Dayti (Haitian Creole); République d'Haïti (French) (Republic of Haiti).
Form of government: multiparty republic with two legislative houses (Senate [27]; Chamber of Deputies [83]).
Chief of state: President.
Head of government: Prime Minister.
Capital: Port-au-Prince.
Official languages: Haitian Creole; French.
Official religion: none[1].
Monetary unit: 1 gourde (G) = 100 centimes; valuation (Sept. 25, 1998) 1 U.S.$ = G 16.72; 1 £ = G 28.47.

Area and population

		area[2]		population
Departements	Capitals	sq mi	sq km	1995 estimate
Artibonite	Gonaïves	1,924	4,984	1,013,779
Centre	Hinche	1,419	3,675	490,790
Grand'Anse	Jérémie	1,278	3,310	641,399
Nord	Cap-Haïtien	813	2,106	759,318
Nord-Est	Fort-Liberté	697	1,805	248,764
Nord-Ouest	Port-de-Paix	840	2,176	420,971
Ouest	Port-au-Prince	1,864	4,827	2,494,862
Sud	Les Cayes	1,079	2,794	653,398
Sud-Est	Jacmel	781	2,023	457,013
TOTAL		10,695	27,700	7,180,294[3]

Demography

Population (1998): 6,781,000.
Density (1998): persons per sq mi 634.0, persons per sq km 244.8.
Urban-rural (1995): urban 32.6%; rural 67.4%.
Sex distribution (1995): male 49.09%; female 50.91%.
Age breakdown (1995): under 15, 40.2%; 15–29, 27.3%; 30–44, 17.0%; 45–59, 9.5%; 60–74, 4.8%; 75 and over, 1.2%.
Population projection: (2000) 6,992,000; (2010) 8,266,000.
Doubling time: 39 years.
Ethnic composition (1993): black 95.0%; mulatto/other 5.0%.
Religious affiliation (1995): Roman Catholic 68.5%[4]; Protestant 24.1%, of which Baptist 5.9%, Pentecostal 5.3%, Seventh-day Adventist 4.6%; other 7.4%.
Major cities (1995): Port-au-Prince 846,247 (metropolitan area 1,425,594); Carrefour 277,662[5]; Delmas 232,142[5]; Cap-Haïtien 100,638; Pétionville 69,543[5].

Vital statistics

Birth rate per 1,000 population (1996): 33.5 (world avg. 25.0).
Death rate per 1,000 population (1996): 15.5 (world avg. 9.3).
Natural increase rate per 1,000 population (1996): 18.0 (world avg. 15.7).
Total fertility rate (avg. births per childbearing woman; 1996): 4.8.
Life expectancy at birth (1996): male 47.3 years; female 51.3 years.
Major causes of death per 100,000 population (1982)[6]: infectious and parasitic diseases 46.0; diseases of the circulatory system 11.9; diseases associated with malnutrition 8.5; ill-defined conditions 115.2.

National economy

Budget (1996)[7]. Revenue: G 3,790,000,000 (customs duties 13.2%, grants 9.3%, other taxes 71.0%). Expenditures: G 4,120,000,000 (current expenditure 83.6%, subsidies 7.2%, interest on public debt 5.8%, development expenditure 3.4%).
Public debt (external, outstanding; 1996): U.S.$836,100,000.
Production (metric tons except as noted). Agriculture, forestry, fishing (1996): sugarcane 1,200,000, cassava (manioc) 350,000, plantains 270,000, bananas 239,200, mangoes 210,000, corn (maize) 204,100, yams 190,000, sweet potatoes 183,300, rice 95,900, sorghum 88,100, dry beans 49,200, avocados 45,000, coffee 27,000, sisal 5,600, cacao 4,200; livestock (number of live animals) 1,657,000 goats, 1,246,000 cattle, 500,000 pigs, 490,000 horses; roundwood (1995) 6,417,000 cu m; fish catch (1995) 5,500. Mining and quarrying: small amounts of limestone, calcareous clay, salt, and marble. Manufacturing (1995–96): cement 84,000[8]; essential oils (mostly amyris, neroli, and vetiver) 227[8]; cigarettes 837,900,000 units; malt liquor 13,800,000 bottles; beer 4,200,000 bottles; articles assembled for reexport (gross export value in U.S.$'000,000) 104.3, of which garments 95.0, sports equipment and toys 5.9, electronic components 2.7. Construction: n.a. Energy production (consumption): electricity (kW-hr; 1995–96) 575,000,000 (257,300,000); coal (metric tons; 1994) none (n.a.); crude petroleum, none (none); petroleum products (metric tons; 1994) none (166,000); natural gas, none (none).
Land use (1994): forested 5.1%; meadows and pastures 18.0%; agricultural and under permanent cultivation 33.0%; other 43.9%.
Population economically active (1990): total 2,679,140; activity rate of total population 41.1% (participation rates: ages 15–64, 64.8%; female 40.0%; unemployed [1996] unofficially more than 50.0%).

Price and earnings indexes (1990 = 100)

	1991	1992	1993	1994	1995	1996	1997
Consumer price index	115.4	137.8	178.7	249.0	317.7	383.1	461.9
Annual earnings index[9, 10]	100.0	100.0	100.0	100.0	240.0	...	...

Household income and expenditure. Average household size (1982) 4.4; average annual income of urban wage earners (1984): G 1,545 (U.S.$309); expenditure (1986–87)[11]: food, beverages, and tobacco 51.1%, household furnishings 9.2%, clothing and footwear 8.7%, transportation 7.6%.
Gross national product (1996): U.S.$2,282,000,000 (U.S.$310 per capita).

Structure of gross domestic product and labour force

	1995		1990	
	in value G '000,000[12]	% of total value	labour force	% of labour force
Agriculture	1,395	32.2	1,535,444	57.3
Mining	7	0.2	24,012	0.9
Manufacturing	314	7.3	151,387	5.6
Construction	398	9.2	28,001	1.0
Public utilities	39	0.9	2,577	0.1
Transp. and commun.	93	2.1	20,691	0.8
Trade, restaurants	598	13.8	352,970	13.2
Finance, real estate	} 1,360	} 31.4	5,057	0.2
Services			155,347	5.8
Pub. admin., defense				
Other	127[13]	2.9[13]	403,654[14]	15.1[14]
TOTAL	4,331	100.0	2,679,140	100.0

Tourism (in U.S.$'000,000; 1995): receipts 81; expenditures 35.

Foreign trade[15, 16]

Balance of trade (current prices)

	1992	1993	1994	1995	1996	1997
G '000,000	−2,009	−3,526	−2,547	−8,200	−9,034	−8,797
% of total	58.3%	63.1%	50.7%	71.1%	76.2%	68.8%

Imports (1995–96)[17]: U.S.$663,100,000 (food and live animals 33.1%, petroleum and derivatives 10.7%, animal and vegetable oils 9.2%, chemicals and chemical products 8.1%). *Major import sources* (1995)[18]: United States 65%; Japan 5%; France 4%; Germany 3%.
Exports (1995–96)[17]: U.S.$85,900,000 (domestic value added of reexport assembly plants [mostly clothing] 47.6%, handicrafts [includes wood carvings, paintings, and woven sisal products] 15.4%, coffee 7.9%, essential oils 6.6%). *Major export destinations* (1995)[18]: United States 76%; France 7%; Germany 5%; Italy 5%.

Transport and communications

Transport. Railroad (1995):[19]. Roads (1995): total length 2,535 mi, 4,080 km (paved 24%). Vehicles (1995): passenger cars 32,000; trucks and buses 21,000. Air transport (1994)[20]: passenger arrivals 167,882, passenger departures 177,072; cargo unloaded 11,967 metric tons, cargo loaded 10,087 metric tons; airports (1997) with scheduled flights 2.

Communications

Medium	date	unit	number	units per 1,000 persons
Daily newspapers	1994	circulation	45,000	7.1
Radio	1996	receivers	270,000	41
Television	1995	receivers	25,000	3.9
Telephones	1995	main lines	55,302	8.6

Education and health

Educational attainment (1986–87). Percentage of population age 25 and over having: no formal schooling 59.5%; primary education 30.5%; secondary 8.6%; vocational and teacher training 0.7%; higher 0.7%. *Literacy* (1995): total population age 15 and over literate 1,930,000 (45.0%); males literate 992,000 (48.0%); females literate 938,000 (42.2%).

Education (1992–93)

	schools	teachers	students	student/ teacher ratio
Primary (age 6–12)	6,111[21]	27,607	787,553	28.5
Secondary (age 13–18)	} 630[21]	10,174	193,624	19.0
Voc., teacher tr.				
Higher[22, 23]	2	777	11,546	14.9

Health (1993–94): physicians 641[24] (1 per 9,846 persons); hospital beds 6,473 (1 per 975 persons); infant mortality rate per 1,000 live births (1996) 103.8.
Food (1992): daily per capita caloric intake 1,706 (vegetable products 95%, animal products 5%); 75% of FAO recommended minimum requirement.

Military

Total active duty personnel:[25].

[1]Roman Catholicism has special recognition. [2]Estimated. [3]Official population projection based on 1982 census. [4]About 80% of all Roman Catholics also practice voodoo. [5]Within Port-au-Prince metropolitan area. [6]Public health facilities only. [7]Excludes G 6,900,000,000 in foreign aid. [8]1992–93. [9]Standard minimum wage. [10]The majority of Haitians work in subsistence agriculture, a sector where minimum wage legislation does not apply. [11]Based on nationwide sample survey of 3,120 households. [12]At prices of 1975–76. [13]Import duties. [14]Includes 63,975 not adequately defined and 339,679 officially unemployed. [15]Includes domestic value added only of reexport assembly plants. [16]Import figures c.i.f., export figures f.o.b. [17]For fiscal year ending September 30. [18]Estimated figures for calendar year. [19]A 50-mi (80-km) railway is privately owned. [20]Port-au-Prince Airport only. [21]1991–92. [22]Port-au-Prince universities only. [23]1995–96. [24]Public health services only. [25]The Haitian army was disbanded in 1995. A UN force provided security between April 1995 and December 1997 and supervised the creation of a national police force.

Internet resources for further information:
• **Embassy of Haiti (Washington, D.C.) (mostly French language)**
  http://www.haiti.org/embassy/

Honduras

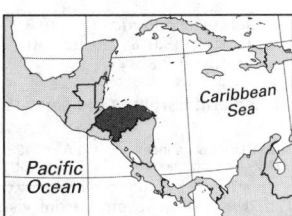

Official name: República de Honduras (Republic of Honduras).
Form of government: multiparty republic with one legislative house (National Assembly [128]).
Head of state and government: President.
Capital: Tegucigalpa[1].
Official language: Spanish.
Official religion: none.
Monetary unit: 1 Honduran lempira (L) = 100 centavos; valuation (Sept. 25, 1998) 1 U.S.\$ = L 13.62; 1 £ = L 23.19.

Area and population

Departments	Administrative centres	area sq mi	area sq km	population 1991 estimate
Atlántida	La Ceiba	1,641	4,251	255,000
Choluteca	Choluteca	1,626	4,211	309,000
Colón	Trujillo	3,427	8,875	164,000
Comayagua	Comayagua	2,006	5,196	257,000
Copán	Santa Rosa de Copán	1,237	3,203	226,000
Cortés	San Pedro Sula	1,527	3,954	706,000
El Paraíso	Yuscarán	2,787	7,218	277,000
Francisco Morazán	Tegucigalpa	3,068	7,946	878,000
Gracias a Dios	Puerto Lempira	6,421	16,630	37,000
Intibucá	La Esperanza	1,186	3,072	130,000
Islas de la Bahía	Roatán	100	261	24,000
La Paz	La Paz	900	2,331	112,000
Lempira	Gracias	1,656	4,290	180,000
Ocotepeque	Nueva Ocotepeque	649	1,680	77,000
Olancho	Juticalpa	9,402	24,351	309,000
Santa Bárbara	Santa Bárbara	1,975	5,115	291,000
Valle	Nacaome	604	1,565	121,000
Yoro	Yoro	3,065	7,939	355,000
TOTAL		43,277[2]	112,088[2]	4,708,000

Demography

Population (1998): 5,919,000.
Density (1998)[3]: persons per sq mi 136.3, persons per sq km 52.6.
Urban-rural (1994): urban 42.9%; rural 57.1%.
Sex distribution (1990): male 50.07%; female 49.93%.
Age breakdown (1990): under 15, 44.6%; 15–29, 28.3%; 30–44, 14.4%; 45–59, 7.8%; 60–74, 3.9%; 75 and over, 1.0%.
Population projection: (2000) 6,206,000; (2010) 7,370,000.
Doubling time: 24 years.
Ethnic composition (1987): mestizo 89.9%; Amerindian 6.7%; black (including Black Carib) 2.1%; white 1.3%.
Religious affiliation (1995): Roman Catholic 86.7%; Protestant 10.4%, of which Pentecostal 5.7%; other 2.9%.
Major cities (1995): Tegucigalpa 813,900[4]; San Pedro Sula 383,900; La Ceiba 89,200; El Progreso 85,400; Choluteca 76,400.

Vital statistics

Birth rate per 1,000 population (1993): 35.8 (world avg. 25.0); legitimate, n.a.; illegitimate, n.a.
Death rate per 1,000 population (1993): 6.4 (world avg. 9.3).
Natural increase rate per 1,000 population (1993): 29.4 (world avg. 15.7).
Total fertility rate (avg. births per childbearing woman; 1993): 4.9.
Marriage rate per 1,000 population (1983): 4.9.
Divorce rate per 1,000 population (1983): 0.4.
Life expectancy at birth (1993): male 64.8 years; female 69.2 years.
Major causes of death per 100,000 population (1983): diseases of the circulatory system 48.4; infectious and parasitic diseases 46.6; accidents and violence 42.2; diseases of the respiratory system 26.3.

National economy

Budget (1995). Revenue: L 9,900,900,000 (current revenue 68.8%, of which excise and sales taxes 23.3%, income taxes 19.6%, import duties 14.4%; capital revenue 31.2%). Expenditures: L 10,502,800,000 (current expenditure 53.6%; capital expenditure 17.9%; public-debt service 16.2%).
Public debt (external, outstanding; 1996): U.S.\$3,855,000,000.
Production (metric tons except as noted). Agriculture, forestry, fishing (1996): sugarcane 3,237,000, bananas 927,000, corn (maize) 580,000, pineapples 269,000, plantains 190,000, coffee 131,000, palm oil 76,600, sorghum 68,000, dry beans 55,000, rice 41,000; livestock (number of live animals) 2,182,000 cattle, 600,000 pigs, 14,000,0000 chickens; roundwood (1995) 6,362,000 cu m; fish catch (1995) 24,333. Mining and quarrying (1995): gypsum 26,000; salt 25,000; zinc 14,500; lead 2,000; copper 390. Manufacturing (1995): cement 995,100; raw sugar 406,000; wheat flour 216,000; beer 7,989,000 hectolitres; milk 672,260 hectolitres; cigarettes 2,388,500,000 units. Construction (value of private construction in L '000,000; 1995)[5]: residential 340.6; nonresidential 533.5. Energy production (consumption): electricity (kW-hr; 1994) 2,655,000,000 (2,672,000,000); coal, none (none); crude petroleum (barrels; 1992) none (3,064,000); petroleum products (metric tons; 1994) none (950,000).
Household income and expenditure. Average household size (1988) 5.4; income per household: n.a.; sources of income (1985): wages and salaries 58.8%, transfer payments 1.8%, other 39.4%; expenditure (1986): food 44.4%, utilities and housing 22.4%, clothing and footwear 9.0%, household furnishings 8.3%, health care 7.0%, transportation 3.0%, other 5.9%.
Tourism (1995): receipts U.S.\$80,000,000; expenditures U.S.\$57,000,000.
Gross national product (1996): U.S.\$4,012,000,000 (U.S.\$660 per capita).

Structure of gross domestic product and labour force

	1995 in value L '000,000[6]	1995 % of total value	1995 labour force	1995 % of labour force
Agriculture	7,973	24.5	766,000	42.7
Mining	655	2.0	4,200	0.2
Manufacturing	5,440	16.7	211,500	11.8
Construction	1,853	5.7	118,500	6.6
Public utilities	1,481	4.6	14,400	0.8
Transp. and commun.	1,715	5.3	50,100	2.8
Trade	3,453	10.6	194,000	10.8
Finance, real estate	4,759	14.6	36,700	2.0
Public admin., defense	1,793	5.5	400,800	22.3
Services	3,423	10.5		
TOTAL	32,545	100.0	1,796,200	100.0

Population economically active (1995): total 1,796,200; activity rate of total population 32.6% (participation rates: over age 15 [1992] 58.3%; female 31.7%; unemployed [1990] 40.0%).

Price and earnings indexes (1990 = 100)

	1991	1992	1993	1994	1995	1996	1997
Consumer price index	134.0	145.7	161.4	196.4	254.3	314.9	378.5
Weekly earnings index[7]	132.9	151.1	170.3	180.3	232.0	...	...

Land use (1994): forested 53.6%; meadows and pastures 13.8%; agricultural and under permanent cultivation 18.1%; other 14.5%.

Foreign trade[8]

Balance of trade (current prices)

	1991	1992	1993	1994	1995	1996
L '000,000	+11.9	−129.3	−208.6	−113.1	−42.1	−348.5
% of total	0.7%	7.5%	11.4%	6.3%	1.9%	11.7%

Imports (1995): U.S.\$1,587,600,000 (machinery and electrical equipment 17.1%, industrial chemicals 14.8%, mineral fuels 14.0%, metal products 8.7%, transport equipment 8.4%, plastics and resins 7.3%). *Major import sources:* United States 42.8%; Japan 4.7%; Germany 3.6%; Mexico 3.0%; Brazil 1.8%; Spain 1.8%; The Netherlands 1.5%.
Exports (1995): U.S.\$1,092,900,000 (coffee 32.0%, bananas 19.6%, shrimp and lobsters 14.5%, zinc 2.5%, frozen meats 1.2%). *Major export destinations:* United States 54.2%; Germany 6.9%; Belgium 4.8%; Japan 3.6%; Spain 3.6%; The Netherlands 2.1%; Italy 1.9%.

Transport and communications

Transport. Railroads (1989): length (1993) 614 mi, 988 km; passenger-km 7,700,000; metric ton-km cargo 30,200,000. Roads (1995): total length 9,383 mi, 15,100 km (paved 20%). Vehicles (1995): passenger cars 81,439; trucks and buses 170,006. Merchant marine (1992): vessels (100 gross tons and over) 966; total deadweight tonnage 1,437,321. Air transport (1994): passenger-mi 180,000,000, passenger-km 289,000,000; short ton-mi cargo 26,000,000, metric ton-km cargo 38,000,000; airports (1996) with scheduled flights 8.

Communications

Medium	date	unit	number	units per 1,000 persons
Daily newspapers	1995	circulation	240,000	45
Radio	1996	receivers	1,910,000	337
Television	1995	receivers	160,000	29
Telephones	1995	main lines	160,800	29

Education and health

Educational attainment (1988). Percentage of population age 10 and over having: no formal schooling 33.4%; primary education 50.1%; secondary education 13.4%; higher 3.1%. *Literacy* (1995): total population age 15 and over literate 72.7%; males literate 72.6%; females literate 72.7%.

Education (1995)

	schools	teachers	students	student/ teacher ratio
Primary (age 7–13)	8,168	28,978	1,008,092	34.8
Secondary (age 14–19) Voc., teacher tr.	661	12,480	184,589	14.8
Higher	8	3,676	54,293	14.8

Health: physicians (1990) 2,900 (1 per 1,586 persons); hospital beds (1994) 4,737 (1 per 1,126 persons); infant mortality rate (1993) 47.2.
Food (1995): daily per capita caloric intake 2,359 (vegetable products 88%, animal products 12%); 104% of FAO recommended minimum.

Military

Total active duty personnel (1996): 18,800 (army 85.1%, navy 5.3%, air force 9.6%). *Military expenditure as percentage of GNP* (1995): 1.4% (world 2.8%); per capita expenditure U.S.\$8.

---

[1]Tegucigalpa and adjacent city of Comayagüela jointly form the capital according to the constitution. [2]The 1993 area is 43,433 sq mi (112,492 sq km); breakdown by department is not available. [3]Based on the revised area. [4]Population cited is for Central District (Tegucigalpa and Comayagüela). [5]Tegucigalpa, San Pedro Sula, and 10 other urban centres. [6]At factor cost. [7]Official minimum wages in all sectors. Minimum wages were fixed from June 1981 to Jan. 1, 1990, when new minimum wages were introduced. [8]Import figures are f.o.b. in balance of trade and c.i.f. for commodities and trading partners.

Hong Kong

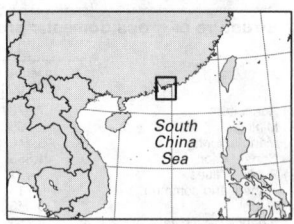

Official name: Hsiang Kang (Chinese); Hong Kong (English)[1].
Political status: Special Administrative Region[2] (People's Republic of China) with one legislative house (Legislative Council [60[3]]).
Head of state and government: Chief Executive.
Capital: None[4].
Official languages: Chinese; English[1].
Official religion: none.
Monetary unit: 1 Hong Kong dollar (HK$) = 100 cents; valuation (Sept. 25, 1998) 1 U.S.$ = HK$7.75; 1 £ = HK$13.19.

Area and population		area		population
				1996
Area		sq mi	sq km	census
Hong Kong Island		30.9	80.1	1,312,637
Kowloon and New Kowloon		18.0	46.5	1,987,996
New Territories		372.7	965.3	2,906,733
Marine		—	—	10,190
TOTAL		421.6	1,091.9	6,217,556

Demography

Population (1998): 6,660,000.
Density (1998): persons per sq mi 15,796.3, persons per sq km 6,099.2.
Urban-rural (1997): urban 100.0%.
Sex distribution (1996): male 50.06%; female 49.94%.
Age breakdown (1996)[5]: under 15, 18.9%; 15–29, 22.4%; 30–44, 29.4%; 45–59, 15.1%; 60–74, 10.5%; 75 and over, 3.7%.
Population projection: (2000) 6,833,000; (2010) 7,701,000.
Doubling time: not applicable; doubling time exceeds 100 years.
Linguistic composition (1991)[6]: Chinese 96.8%, of which Cantonese 88.7%; English 2.2%; other 1.0%.
Religious affiliation (1997): predominantly Buddhist and Taoist; however, there are about 260,000 Protestants (1994), 254,100 Roman Catholics, 50,000 Muslims, and 12,000 Hindus.

Vital statistics

Birth rate per 1,000 population (1996): 10.0 (world avg. 25.0); (1985) legitimate 94.5%; illegitimate 5.5%.
Death rate per 1,000 population (1996): 4.9 (world avg. 9.3).
Natural increase rate per 1,000 population (1996): 5.1 (world avg. 15.7).
Total fertility rate (avg. births per childbearing woman; 1995): 1.1.
Marriage rate per 1,000 population (1996): 5.9.
Life expectancy at birth (1996): male 75.9 years; female 81.5 years.
Major causes of death per 100,000 population (1996): malignant neoplasms (cancers) 156.1; diseases of the circulatory system 131.3; diseases of the respiratory system 96.6; accidents and poisoning 26.2; diseases of the digestive system 21.6; diseases of the genitourinary system 18.6.

National economy

Budget (1996–97). Revenue: HK$202,276,000,000 (earning and profit taxes 40.6%; indirect taxes 24.8%, of which entertainment and stamp duties 15.1%, duties 4.1%; capital revenue 18.4%). Expenditures: HK$217,194,000,000 (education 18.0%; housing 11.9%; health 11.5%; transportation and public works 11.1%; law and order 9.2%; social welfare 8.3%; culture and recreation 5.1%).
Gross domestic product (1996): U.S.$153,288,000,000 (U.S.$24,290 per capita).

Structure of gross domestic product and labour force				
	1995			
	in value HK$'000,000	% of total value	labour force	% of labour force
Agriculture	1,453	0.1		
Mining	268	—	534,600	17.8
Manufacturing	89,719	8.4		
Construction	49,753	4.6	229,300	7.7
Public utilities	23,562	2.2	[7]	[7]
Transp. and commun.	100,129	9.4	327,700	10.9
Trade	278,581	26.0	824,900	27.5
Finance, insurance, and real estate	253,492	23.7	341,700	11.4
Pub. admin., defense, and services	174,448	16.3	609,800	20.3
Other	99,969[8]	9.3[8]	132,700[7, 9]	4.4[7, 9]
TOTAL	1,071,374	100.0	3,000,700	100.0

Production (metric tons except as noted). Agriculture, forestry, fishing (1996): vegetables 76,000, fruits and nuts 5,230, field crops 660, milk 439, eggs 30,600,000 units; livestock (number of live animals) 288,000 pigs[10], 270 cattle, 3,290,000 chickens; roundwood (1995) 200,000 cu m; fish catch 175,130. Manufacturing (value added in HK$; 1994): wearing apparel 13,515,000,000; electrical and electronic products 12,621,000,000; textiles 11,595,000,000; publishing and printed material 9,949,000,000; basic metals and fabricated metal products 5,547,000,000; plastic products 2,495,000,000. Construction (1996): residential 819,000 sq m; nonresidential 1,067,000 sq m. Energy production (consumption): electricity (kW-hr; 1994) 26,741,000,000 (33,236,000,000); coal (metric tons; 1994) none (8,450,000); petroleum products (metric tons; 1994) none (4,472,000).

Population economically active (1996): total 3,093,800; activity rate of total population 49.0% (participation rates: over age 15, 61.8%; female 47.8%; unemployed 2.8%).

Price and earnings indexes (1990 = 100)							
	1991	1992	1993	1994	1995	1996	1997
Consumer price index	111.6	122.0	132.5	143.2	155.7	164.9	174.5
Daily earnings index[11]	110.4	121.4	133.2	143.6	160.4	167.6	...

Tourism (1995): receipts from visitors U.S.$9,314,000,000.
Household income and expenditure. Average household size (1996) 3.2; monthly income per household (1996) HK$17,500 (U.S.$2,300); sources of income: n.a.; expenditure (1994–95): food 29.5%, housing 28.8%, transportation and vehicles 7.8%, clothing and footwear 6.7%, durable goods 5.5%.
Land use (1995): forested 20.1%; agricultural and under permanent cultivation 5.8%; fishponds 1.5%; built-on, scrublands, and other 72.6%.

Foreign trade

Balance of trade (current prices)						
	1992	1993	1994	1995	1996	1997
HK$'000,000	−30,342	−26,347	−80,695	−146,994	−137,664	−159,141
% of total	1.6%	1.2%	3.3%	5.2%	4.7%	5.8%

Imports (1996): HK$1,537,013,000,000 (machinery and transport equipment 37.0%, of which electrical machinery 12.7%, telecommunications equipment 9.2%; textile yarn and fabrics 8.3%; chemicals and other related products 6.9%; apparel and accessories 6.9%). *Major import sources:* China 37.1%; Japan 13.6%; Taiwan 8.0%; U.S. 7.9%; Singapore 5.3%; South Korea 4.8%.
Exports (1996): HK$212,160,000,000[12] (clothing accessories and apparel 32.7%; electrical machinery 14.3%; watches and clocks 7.1%; textile fabrics 6.5%; office and automatic data-processing machines 6.2%; telecommunications equipment 4.0%; articles of artificial resins and plastics 2.7%; metal products 2.7%; paper and paper products 1.4%). *Major export destinations:* China 29.0%; U.S. 25.4%; Germany 5.4%; Japan 5.3%; U.K. 5.0%.

Transport and communications

Transport. Railroads (1995): route length 21 mi, 34 km; passenger-mi 2,231,000,000, passenger-km 3,591,000,000; short ton-mi cargo 68,000,000[13], metric ton-km cargo 99,000,000[13]. Roads (1996): total length 1,083 mi, 1,743 km (paved 100%). Vehicles (1996): passenger cars 325,131; trucks and buses 142,446. Air transport (1996): passenger arrivals 11,692,404, passenger departures 11,785,771; airports (1997) with scheduled flights 1.

Communications				units
				per 1,000
Medium	date	unit	number	persons
Daily newspapers	1995	circulation	2,951,000[14]	479[14]
Radio	1996	receivers	3,700,000	586
Television	1995	receivers	2,092,000	340
Telephones	1996	main lines	3,508,000	556
Cellular telephones	1995	subscribers	798,400	129
Facsimile machines	1995	units	284,900	46
Personal computers	1995	units	720,000	116

Education and health

Educational attainment (1996). Percentage of population age 15 and over having: no formal schooling 9.5%; primary education 22.6%; secondary 46.6%; matriculation 6.1%; nondegree higher 4.8%; higher degree 10.4%.
Literacy (1995): total population age 15 and over literate 92.2%; males literate 96.0%; females literate 88.2%.

Education (1996–97)				student/
	schools	teachers	students	teacher ratio
Primary (age 6–11)	856	19,710[15]	466,507	23.7[15]
Secondary (age 12–18)	498	22,777[15]	477,708	21.2[15]
Vocational	9	2,488[16]	48,837	18.5[16]
Higher	17	1,422[16]	87,411	32.4[16]

Health (1996): physicians 9,196[17] (1 per 686 persons); hospital beds 29,956 (1 per 211 persons); infant mortality rate per 1,000 live births 4.1.
Food (1995): daily per capita caloric intake 3,285 (vegetable products 68%, animal products 32%); 143% of FAO recommended minimum requirement.

Military

Total active duty personnel (1996): 850[18] (army 53.0%, navy 23.5%, air force 23.5%).

[1]English may also be used as an official language by executive authorities, legislature, and judiciary of Hong Kong. [2]On July 1, 1997, Hong Kong reverted to China as a Special Administrative Region in which the existing socioeconomic system would remain unchanged for a period of 50 years. [3]Includes 30 nonelective seats. The 60-seat provisional legislative body will be replaced with a permanent legislature by June 30, 1998. [4]Victoria, for some time, had been regarded as the capital because it had been the seat of the British administration of the Crown Colony. [5]Excludes transients and Vietnamese refugees. [6]Excludes about 59,000 Vietnamese refugees, about 1% of the population. [7]Other includes Public utilities. [8]Indirect taxes less subsidies. [9]Includes 95,600 unemployed. [10]Excludes local pigs not slaughtered in abattoirs. [11]September. [12]Excludes reexports valued at HK$1,1,85,758,000,000. [13]1994. [14]Thirty-two newspapers only. [15]1995–96. [16]1987–88. [17]Registered personnel; all may not be present and working in the country. [18]British forces with a few locally enlisted personnel.

Internet resources for further information:
• Census and Statistics Department http://www.info.gov/censtatd

Hungary

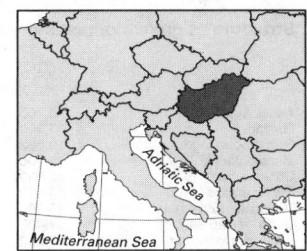

Official name: Magyar Köztársaság
(Republic of Hungary).
Form of government: unitary multi-party republic with one legislative
house (National Assembly [386[1]]).
Chief of state: President.
Head of government: Prime Minister.
Capital: Budapest.
Official language: Hungarian.
Official religion: none.
Monetary unit: 1 forint (Ft) = 100
filler; valuation (Sept. 25, 1998)
1 U.S.$ = Ft 218.38; 1 £ = Ft 371.79.

Area and population

Counties	Capitals	area sq mi	area sq km	population 1997[2] estimate
Bács-Kiskun	Kecskemét	3,251	8,420	538,000
Baranya	Pécs	1,710	4,430	407,000
Békés	Békéscsaba	2,174	5,631	400,000
Borsod-Abaúj-Zemplén	Miskolc	2,798	7,247	742,000
Csongrád	Szeged	1,646	4,263	425,000
Fejér	Székesfehérvár	1,688	4,373	425,000
Györ-Moson-Sopron	Györ	1,568	4,062	425,000
Hajdú-Bihar	Debrecen	2,398	6,211	549,000
Heves	Eger	1,404	3,637	327,000
Jász-Nagykun-Szolnok	Szolnok	2,165	5,607	419,000
Komárom-Esztergom	Tatabánya	869	2,251	311,000
Nógrád	Salgótarján	982	2,544	221,000
Pest	Budapest[3]	2,468	6,393	996,000
Somogy	Kaposvár	2,331	6,036	336,000
Szabolcs-Szatmár-Bereg	Nyíregyháza	2,292	5,937	572,000
Tolna	Szekszárd	1,430	3,704	248,000
Vas	Szombathely	1,288	3,337	271,000
Veszprém	Veszprém	1,791	4,639	378,000
Zala	Zalaegerszeg	1,461	3,784	299,000
Capital City				
Budapest[3]		203	525	1,885,000
TOTAL		35,919[4]	93,030[4]	10,174,000

Demography

Population (1998): 10,117,000.
Density (1998): persons per sq mi 281.7, persons per sq km 108.7.
Urban-rural (1996): urban 62.6%; rural 37.4%.
Sex distribution (1997): male 47.79%; female 52.21%.
Age breakdown (1997): under 15, 17.7%; 15–29, 22.8%; 30–44, 20.9%; 45–59, 19.1%; 60–74, 14.3%; 75 and over, 5.2%.
Population projection: (2000) 10,047,000; (2010) 9,845,000.
Ethnic composition (1993): Magyar 92%; Gypsy 3%; German 1%; Slovak 1%; Jewish 1%; Southern Slav 1%; other 1%.
Religious affiliation (1995): Christian 89.1%, of which Roman Catholic 63.1%, Protestant 25.5% (of which Reformed 19.8%, Lutheran 4.5%); Jewish 0.8%; other 10.1%.
Major cities (1997[2]): Budapest 1,885,000; Debrecen 210,000; Miskolc 178,000.

Vital statistics

Birth rate per 1,000 population (1996): 10.4 (world avg. 25.0); legitimate 77.6%; illegitimate 22.4%.
Death rate per 1,000 population (1996): 14.1 (world avg. 9.3).
Natural increase rate per 1,000 population (1996): –3.7 (world avg. 15.7).
Total fertility rate (avg. births per childbearing woman; 1996): 1.5.
Marriage rate per 1,000 population (1996): 4.9.
Divorce rate per 1,000 population (1996): 2.2.
Life expectancy at birth (1995): male 65.3 years; female 74.5 years.
Major causes of death per 100,000 population (1996): diseases of the circulatory system 680.4; malignant neoplasms (cancers) 320.0.

National economy

Budget (1997). Revenue: Ft 2,251,896,000,000 (value-added tax 27.8%, income tax 17.8%, payments by enterprises 16.5%, excise duties 11.8%). Expenditures: Ft 2,561,608,000,000 (debt service 32.3%, health 15.9%[5], education 15.7%[5], defense 11.3%[6], social security 8.1%).
Production (metric tons except as noted). Agriculture, forestry, fishing (1996): corn (maize) 5,917,000, sugar beets 4,687,000, wheat 3,924,000, potatoes 1,093,000, barely 930,000; livestock (number of live animals) 5,032,000 pigs, 977,000 sheep; roundwood (1996) 4,415,000 cu m; fish catch (1995) 27,406. Mining and quarrying (1996): bauxite 1,044,000; glass sand 325,000. Manufacturing (value of production in Ft '000,000; 1996): food, beverage, and tobacco products 986,000; machinery and equipment 981,000; chemicals and chemical products 821,000; basic metals and fabricated metal products 419,000. Construction (value of production in Ft '000,000; 1995): residential 23,689[7]; office buildings 21,213. Energy production (consumption): electricity (kW-hr; 1994) 33,486,000,000 (35,520,000,000); coal (metric tons; 1994) 14,111,000 (15,369,000); crude petroleum (barrels; 1994) 10,537,000 (47,138,000); petroleum products (metric tons; 1994) 6,356,000 (7,044,000); natural gas (cu m; 1994) 4,334,000,000 (9,350,000,000).
Land use (1994): forested 19.1%; meadows and pastures 12.4%; agricultural and under permanent cultivation 53.9%; other 14.6%.
Public debt (external, outstanding; 1996): U.S.$18,423,000,000.
Population economically active (1997[8]): total 4,284,200; activity rate of total population 42.2% (participation rates: ages 15–74, 54.9%; female [1996] 49.8%; unemployed 8.6%).

Price and earnings indexes (1990 = 100)

	1991	1992	1993	1994	1995	1996	1997
Consumer price index	134.2	165.0	202.1	240.2	308.2	380.6	450.2
Monthly earnings index	133.4	165.8	202.1	252.4	289.3	348.3	...

Gross national product (1996): U.S.$44,274,000,000 (U.S.$4,340 per capita).

Structure of gross domestic product and labour force

	1995 in value Ft '000,000[9]	1995 % of total value	1996 labour force	1996 % of labour force
Agriculture	351,100	6.4	326,500	7.3
Mining and manufacturing	1,125,500	20.5	943,400	21.1
Construction	238,700	4.3	218,300	4.9
Public utilities	166,900	3.0	100,200	2.2
Transp. and commun.	480,700	8.8	334,000	7.5
Trade	522,900	9.5	559,400	12.5
Finance, real estate	904,700	16.5	279,300	6.3
Public administration, defense	340,200	6.2	277,600	6.2
Services	731,100	13.3	767,600	17.2
Other	632,000[10]	11.5[10]	663,900[11]	14.9[11]
TOTAL	5,493,800	100.0	4,470,200	100.0[4]

Household income and expenditure. Average household size (1991) 2.8; income per household (1990) Ft 376,195 (U.S.$5,900); sources of income (1995): wages 59.4%, social security benefits (cash) 15.0%, real estate 6.0%; expenditure (1995): food and beverages 40.3%; transportation, communications, and automobile maintenance 19.9%; housing 16.3%; household durable goods 7.1%; culture and recreation 6.2%; clothing 6.1%.

Foreign trade

Balance of trade (current prices)

	1992	1993	1994	1995	1996
Ft '000,000,000	–19.5	–317.7	–362.8	–284.8	–466.4
% of total	1.1%	16.2%	13.8%	8.3%	10.4%

Imports (1996): Ft 2,468,100,000,000 (manufactured goods 46.9%, machinery and transport equipment 30.5%, fuels and electrical energy 13.6%, food and live animals 5.0%). *Major import sources:* Germany 23.6%; Russia 12.5%; Austria 9.5%; Italy 8.1%; France 4.2%; U.S. 3.5%; U.K. 3.3%.
Exports (1996): Ft 2,001,700,000,000 (manufactured goods 46.8%, machinery and transport equipment 25.5%, food and live animals 18.4%, fuels and electrical energy 4.1%). *Major export destinations:* Germany 29.0%; Austria 10.6%; Italy 8.0%; Russia 6.0%; France 3.7%; U.S. 3.5%.

Transport and communications

Transport. Railroads (1995): 13,181 km; (1996) passenger-km 9,358,000,000; metric ton-km cargo 7,600,000,000. Roads (1996): total length 29,999 km (paved 93%). Vehicles (1996): passenger cars 2,264,165; trucks and buses 322,000. Merchant marine (1992): vessels (100 gross tons and over) 15; total deadweight tonnage 93,204. Air transport (1996)[12]: passenger-km 2,762,000,-000; metric ton-km cargo 32,950,000; airports (1997) with scheduled flights 1.

Communications

Medium	date	unit	number	units per 1,000 persons
Daily newspapers	1995	circulation	2,321,000	228
Radio	1996	receivers	6,250,000	590
Television	1995	receivers	4,530,000	444
Telephones	1995	main lines	1,893,000	185
Cellular telephones	1995	subscribers	265,000	26
Facsimile machines	1995	units	45,000	4.4
Personal computers	1995	units	400,000	39

Education and health

Educational attainment (1990). Population age 25 and over having: no formal schooling 1.3%; primary education 57.9%; secondary 30.7%; higher 10.1%.
Literacy (1984): population age 15 and over literate 8,269,850 (98.9%); males literate 3,934,250 (99.2%); females literate 4,335,600 (98.6%).

Education (1996–97)

	schools	teachers	students	student/ teacher ratio
Primary (age 6–13)	3,765	83,658	966,000	11.5
Secondary (age 14–17)	980	29,462	361,400	12.3
Vocational	363	5,292	143,800	27.2
Higher	89	19,426	141,900	7.3

Health (1995): physicians 42,489 (1 per 240 persons); hospital beds 92,603 (1 per 110 persons); infant mortality rate per 1,000 live births (1996) 10.9.

Military

Total active duty personnel (1997): 49,100 (army 64.4%, air force 35.6%).
Military expenditure as percentage of GNP (1995): 1.5% (world 2.8%); per capita expenditures U.S.$95.

[1]Excludes 13 seats set aside for ethnic minorities. [2]January 1. [3]Budapest has separate county status. The area and population of the city are excluded from the large county (Pest), which it administers. [4]Detail does not add to total given because of rounding. [5]1993. [6]1994. [7]Includes hotel construction. [8]Second quarter. [9]At purchaser's prices. [10]Taxes on products. [11]Includes 168,000 undistributed employed and 495,900 unemployed. [12]Malév airlines only.

Internet resources for further information:
• **Embassy of the Republic of Hungary http://www.hungaryemb.org/**
• **Hungarian Central Statistical Office http://www.ksh.hu/eng/homeng.html**

Iceland

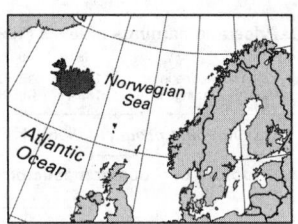

Official name: Lýdhveldidh Ísland (Republic of Iceland).
Form of government: unitary multiparty republic with one legislative house (Althing [63]).
Chief of state: President.
Head of government: Prime Minister.
Capital: Reykjavík.
Official language: Icelandic.
Official religion: Evangelical Lutheran.
Monetary unit: 1 króna (ISK) = 100 aurar; valuation (Sept. 25, 1998)
1 U.S.$ = ISK 69.06; 1 £ = ISK 117.57.

Area and population

| | | area | | population |
| | | | | 1996[1] |
Constituencies[2]	Principal centres	sq mi	sq km	estimate
Austurland	Egilsstadhir	8,491	21,991	12,684
Nordhurland eystra	Akureyri	8,636	22,368	26,652
Nordhurland vestra	Saudhárkrókur	5,055	13,093	9,989
Reykjanes	...	765[3]	1,982[3]	71,446
Reykjavík	Reykjavík	3	3	105,487
Sudhurland	Selfoss	9,735	25,214	20,626
Vestfirdhir	Ísafjördhur	3,657	9,470	8,856
Vesturland	Borgarnes	3,360	8,701	13,995
TOTAL		39,699	102,819	269,735

Demography

Population (1998): 276,000.
Density (1997)[4]: persons per sq mi 30.0, persons per sq km 11.6.
Urban-rural (1996): urban 91.9%; rural 8.1%.
Sex distribution (1997): male 50.11%; female 49.89%.
Age breakdown (1997): under 15, 24.0%; 15–29, 22.9%; 30–44, 22.8%; 45–59, 15.2%; 60–74, 10.2%; 75 and over, 4.9%.
Population projection: (2000) 281,000; (2010) 309,000.
Doubling time: 79 years.
Ethnic composition (1995)[5]: Icelandic 95.9%; Danish 0.8%; Swedish 0.5%; persons born in the United States 0.5%; German 0.3%; other 2.0%.
Religious affiliation (1996): Protestant 95.0%, of which Evangelical Lutheran 90.5%, other Lutheran 3.5%; Roman Catholic 1.0%; nonreligious 1.9%; other 2.1%.
Major cities (1996): Reykjavík 105,487 (urban area 160,629); Kópavogur 18,553[6]; Hafnarfjördhur 17,938[6]; Akureyri 15,009; Gardhabær 7,830[6].

Vital statistics

Birth rate per 1,000 population (1995): 16.0 (world avg. 25.0); legitimate 39.1%; illegitimate 60.9%.
Death rate per 1,000 population (1995): 7.2 (world avg. 9.3).
Natural increase rate per 1,000 population (1995): 8.8 (world avg. 15.7).
Total fertility rate (avg. births per childbearing woman; 1995): 2.1.
Marriage rate per 1,000 population (1995): 4.6.
Divorce rate per 1,000 population (1995): 1.8.
Life expectancy at birth (1994–95): male 76.5 years; female 80.6 years.
Major causes of death per 100,000 population (1994): diseases of the circulatory system 300.4, of which ischemic heart diseases 175.6, cerebrovascular disease 69.2; malignant neoplasms (cancers) 166.5; diseases of the respiratory system 80.1.

National economy

Budget (1995). Revenue: ISK 162,757,000,000 (indirect taxes 50.6%, of which value-added taxes 26.4%; direct taxes 41.8%; nontax revenue 7.6%). Expenditures: ISK 178,997,000,000 (health and welfare 40.2%, education 12.3%, communications 7.6%, general administration 4.9%, agriculture 4.1%).
Production (metric tons except as noted). Agriculture, forestry, fishing (1996): potatoes 11,200, silage 1,554,000 cu m, hay 1,338,000 cu m; livestock (number of live animals) 463,900 sheep, 80,500 horses, 74,800 cattle; fish catch (value in ISK '000,000; 1995) cod 14,390, shrimp 10,489, redfish 6,494, Greenland halibut 4,976, haddock 4,412. Mining and quarrying (1995): diatomite 28,100. Manufacturing (value added in ISK '000,000; 1993): preserved and processed fish 17,534; printing and publishing 5,020; fabricated metal products 3,996; meat 2,569; wood furniture 2,275. Construction (completed): residential (1995) 600,000 cu m; nonresidential (1994) 944,000 cu m. Energy production (consumption): electricity (kW-hr; 1996) 5,118,000,000 ([1995] 4,653,000,000); coal (metric tons; 1994) none (71,000); crude petroleum, none (none); petroleum products (metric tons; 1994) none (558,000); natural gas, none (none).
Land use (1994): forested 1.2%; meadows and pastures 22.7%; agricultural and under permanent cultivation 0.1%; other 76.0%.
Population economically active (April 1997): total 145,200; activity rate of total population 53.7% (participation rates: ages 16–74, 77.2%; female 46.3%; unemployed 3.9%).

Price and earnings indexes (1990 = 100)

	1992	1993	1994	1995	1996	1997	1998
Consumer price index	111.0	115.6	117.4	119.3	122.0	124.2	127.1[7]
Annual earnings index	111.5	113.1	114.5	119.6	127.3	136.0[7]	...

Tourism (1996): receipts from visitors U.S.$153,700,000; expenditures by nationals abroad U.S.$309,700,000.
Gross national product (1995): U.S.$6,686,000,000 (U.S.$24,950 per capita).

Structure of gross domestic product and labour force

| | 1995 | | 1997 | |
	in value ISK '000,000[8]	% of total value[8]	labour force[9]	% of labour force[9]
Agriculture	8,700	1.9	6,000	4.1
Fishing	33,700	7.4	6,600	3.4
Fish processing	19,600	4.3	7,700	5.3
Manufacturing	41,900	9.2	16,300	11.2
Construction	26,900	5.9	9,500	6.5
Public utilities	14,600	3.2	1,000	0.7
Transp. and commun.	26,900	5.9	9,900	6.8
Trade, restaurants	47,400	10.4	23,600	16.3
Finance, real estate	67,900	14.9	12,700	8.8
Public administration	62,500	13.7	5,900	4.1
Health, education, other services	21,900	4.8	40,200	27.7
Other	83,900[10]	18.4[10]	5,700[11]	3.9[11]
TOTAL	455,900	100.0	145,200[12]	100.0[12]

Public debt (December 1996): U.S.$3,416,200,000.
Household income and expenditure. Average household size (1990)[13] 3.6; annual income per household (1990)[13] ISK 2,605,563 (U.S.$44,712); sources of income (1995): wages and salaries 74.1%, pension 10.5%, self-employment 2.7%, other 12.7%; expenditure (1993): food and beverages 23.9%, housing 16.0%, transportation and communications 14.5%, recreation 9.6%, household furnishings 7.6%, clothing and footwear 7.5%, expenditures in restaurants and hotels 7.4%.

Foreign trade[14]

Balance of trade (current prices)

	1991	1992	1993	1994	1995	1996
ISK '000,000	–3,253	–392	+12,188	+20,098	+13,068	+1,467
% of total	1.7%	0.2%	6.9%	9.7%	5.9%	0.6%

Imports (1996): ISK 135,995,000,000 (nonelectrical machinery and apparatus 14.4%; electrical machinery and apparatus 8.7%; food products 8.7%; road vehicles 7.7%; crude petroleum and petroleum products 7.4%). *Major import sources:* Norway 13.5%; Germany 10.9%; United Kingdom 10.2%; United States 9.4%; Denmark 8.4%; Sweden 6.7%; The Netherlands 6.0%.
Exports (1996): ISK 126,304,000,000 (marine products 73.3%, of which frozen fish 28.7%, frozen shrimp 12.6%, salted fish 12.4%, fish meal 7.0%; aluminum 9.6%). *Major export destinations:* United Kingdom 19.0%; Germany 12.8%; United States 12.1%; Japan 9.8%; Denmark 7.2%; France 6.7%.

Transport and communications

Transport. Railroads: none. Roads (1996): total length 7,691 mi, 12,378 km (paved 25%). Vehicles (1996): passenger cars 124,909; trucks and buses 16,623. Merchant marine (1992): vessels (100 gross tons and over) 394; total deadweight tonnage 114,851. Air transport (1996)[15]: passenger-mi 1,850,000,-000, passenger-km 2,977,000,000; short ton-mi cargo 36,268,000, metric ton-km cargo 52,950,000; airports (1996) with scheduled flights 24.

Communications

Medium	date	unit	number	units per 1,000 persons
Daily newspapers	1994	circulation	137,000	515
Radio	1996	receivers	197,000	733
Television	1995	receivers	76,250	285
Telephones	1995	main lines	148,675	556
Cellular telephones	1995	subscribers	30,900	116
Facsimile machines	1995	units	4,100	15
Personal computers	1995	units	55,000	206

Education and health

Educational attainment: n.a. *Literacy:* virtually 100%.

Education (1996–97)

	schools	teachers	students	student/ teacher ratio
Primary/lower secondary (age 7–15)	205	3,549	42,212	11.9
Upper Secondary (age 16–19)	35	1,454	17,970	12.4
Higher	14	508	7,972	15.7

Health: physicians (1995) 797 (1 per 335 persons); hospital beds (1993) 2,798[16] (1 per 95 persons); infant mortality rate (1993–95 avg.) 4.6.
Food (1995): daily per capita caloric intake 3,159 (vegetable products 60%, animal products 40%); 119% of FAO recommended minimum requirement.

Military

Total active duty personnel (1996): 120 coast guard personnel; NATO-sponsored U.S.-manned Iceland Defense Force (1996): 2,200. *Military expenditure as percentage of GNP* (1995): none (world average 2.8%).

[1]December 1. [2]Constituencies are electoral districts. Actual local administration is based on towns or rural districts. [3]Reykjanes includes Reykjavík. [4]Population density calculated with reference to 9,191 sq mi (23,805 sq km) area free of glaciers, lava fields, and lakes. [5]By country of birth. [6]Within Reykjavík urban area. [7]July. [8]Breakdown by sector is estimated. [9]April. [10]Indirect taxes, statistical discrepancy, and production of private nonprofit institution less imputed bank service charges and subsidies. [11]Unemployed. [12]Detail does not add to total given because of rounding. [13]Based on sample survey. [14]Imports f.o.b. in balance of trade and c.i.f. for commodities and trading partners. [15]Icelandair only. [16]Excludes nursing wards in old-age homes.

Internet resources for further information:
• **The Icelandic Government (some Icelandic only)**
  http://www.stjr.is/en/stjren01.htm
• **Embassy of Iceland (Washington, D.C.) http://www.iceland.org/**

India

Official name: Bhārat (Hindī);
Republic of India (English).
Form of government: multiparty federal
republic with two legislative houses
(Council of States [245[1]], House of
the People [545[2]]).
Chief of state: President.
Head of government: Prime Minister.
Capital: New Delhi.
Official languages: Hindī; English.
Official religion: none.
Monetary unit: 1 Indian rupee
(Re, plural Rs) = 100 paise; valuation
(Sept. 25, 1998) 1 U.S.$ = Rs 42.51;
1 £ = Rs 72.37.

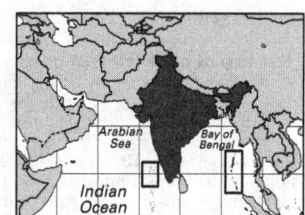

Religious affiliation (1995): Hindu 81.3%; Muslim 12.0%, of which Sunnī 9.0%,
Shī'ī 3.0%; Christian 2.3%, of which Protestant 1.1%, Roman Catholic 1.0%;
Sikh 1.9%; Buddhist 0.8%; Jain 0.4%; Zoroastrian 0.01%; other 1.3%.
Households (1991)[14]. Total households 151,032,898. Average household size
5.6; 1–2 persons 12.1%, 3–5 persons 44.4%, 6–8 persons 30.5%, 9 or more
persons 13.0%. Average number of rooms per household 2.2; 1 room 40.5%,
2 rooms 30.6%, 3 rooms 13.8%, 4 rooms 7.1%, 5 rooms 3.2%, 6 or more
rooms 3.9%, unspecified number of rooms 0.9%. Average number of persons per room 2.6. Shelterless (homeless) population estimated (1987) at
more than 100,000,000.

Vital statistics

Birth rate per 1,000 population (1996): 25.9 (world avg. 25.0).
Death rate per 1,000 population (1996): 9.6 (world avg. 9.3).
Natural increase rate per 1,000 population (1996): 16.3 (world avg. 15.7).
Total fertility rate (avg. births per childbearing woman; 1996): 3.2.
Marital status of male (female) population age 6 and over (1992–93): single
48.3% (37.1%); married 47.5% (55.2%); widowed 3.6% (7.2%); divorced or
separated 0.6% (0.5%).
Life expectancy at birth (1996): male 59.1 years; female 60.3 years.
Major causes of death per 100,000 population (1987)[15]: diseases of the circulatory system 227; infectious and parasitic diseases 215; diseases of the respiratory system 108; certain conditions originating in the perinatal period
108; accidents, homicide, and other violence 102; diseases of the digestive
system 48; diseases of the nervous system 43; malignant neoplasms (cancers)
41; endocrine, metabolic, and nutritional disorders 30; diseases of the blood
and blood-forming organs 25; ill-defined conditions 129.

Social indicators

Educational attainment (1981)[16]. Percentage of population age 25 and over
having: no formal schooling (illiterate) 64.8%; no formal schooling (literate)
1.0%; some primary education 7.1%; completed primary 10.9%; some secondary 6.2%; completed secondary 7.1%; higher vocational 0.4%; completed undergraduate degree 2.5%.

Distribution of expenditure (1992)

percentage of household expenditure by quintile

1	2	3	4	5 (highest)
8.5%	12.1%	15.8%	21.1%	42.5%

Quality of working life. Average workweek (1989): 42 hours[17]. Rate of fatal
(nonfatal) injuries per 100,000 industrial workers (1989) 17 (3,625)[17].
Employees covered under Employee's State Insurance Scheme (1991)
6,070,000; number of beneficiaries 26,749,000[17]. Agricultural workers in
servitude to creditors (early 1990s) 10–20%.
Access to services (1991). Percentage of total (urban, rural) households having access to: electricity for lighting purposes 42.4% (75.8%, 30.5%); attached
toilet or nearby latrine 23.7% (63.9%, 9.5%). Source of drinking water: piped
water 32.3%, well 32.2%, hand pump or tube well 30.0%, river or canal
2.0%, public tank 1.3%, other 2.2%.
Social participation. Eligible voters participating in last (April/May 1996)
national election: 57.9%. Trade union membership (early 1990s): c. 9,000,000.
Social deviance (1990)[18]. Offense rate per 100,000 population for: murder 4.1;
dacoity (gang robbery) 1.3; theft and housebreaking 56.6; riots 12.0. Rate of
suicide per 100,000 population (1991): 9.0.
Material well-being (1994). Households possessing: black and white television
receivers 18.8%, colour television receivers 6.3%, videocassette recorders
1.3%, refrigerators 6.9%, washing machines 2.3%.

National economy

Gross national product (1996): U.S.$357,759,000,000 (U.S.$380 per capita).

Area and population

States[3]	Capitals	area sq mi	area sq km	population 1994 estimate
Andhra Pradesh	Hyderābād	106,195	275,045	71,800,000
Arunāchal Pradesh	Itānagar	32,333	83,743	965,000
Assam	Dispur	30,285	78,438	24,200,000
Bihār	Patna	67,134	173,877	93,080,000
Goa	Panaji	1,429	3,702	1,235,000
Gujarāt	Gāndhīnagar	75,685	196,024	44,235,000
Haryāna	Chandīgarh	17,070	44,212	17,925,000
Himāchal Pradesh	Shimla	21,495	55,673	5,530,000
Jammu and Kashmir	Srīnagar	38,830	100,569	8,435,000
Karnātaka	Bangalore	74,051	191,791	48,150,000
Kerala	Trivandrum	15,005	38,863	30,555,000
Madhya Pradesh	Bhopāl	171,215	443,446	71,950,000
Mahārāshtra	Mumbai (Bombay)	118,809	307,713	85,565,000
Manipur	Imphāl	8,621	22,327	2,010,000
Meghālaya	Shillong	8,660	22,429	1,960,000
Mizoram	Āīzawl	8,140	21,081	775,000
Nāgāland	Kohīma	6,401	16,579	1,410,000
Orissa	Bhubaneshwar	60,119	155,707	33,795,000
Punjab	Chandīgarh	19,445	50,362	21,695,000
Rājasthān	Jaipur	132,140	342,239	48,040,000
Sikkim	Gangtok	2,740	7,096	444,000
Tamil Nādu	Chennai (Madras)	50,216	130,058	58,840,000
Tripura	Agartala	4,049	10,486	3,065,000
Uttar Pradesh	Lucknow	113,673	294,411	150,695,000
West Bengal	Calcutta	34,267	88,752	73,600,000
Union Territories				
Andaman and Nicobar Islands	Port Blair	3,185	8,249	322,000
Chandīgarh	Chandīgarh	44	114	725,000
Dādra and Nagar Haveli	Silvassa	190	491	153,000
Damān and Diu	Damān	43	112	111,000
Lakshadweep	Kavaratti	12	32	56,000
Pondicherry	Pondicherry	190	492	894,000
National Capital Territory[4]				
Delhi	Delhi	572	1,483	10,865,000
TOTAL		1,222,243[5]	3,165,596[5]	913,070,000[6]

Demography

Population (1998): 984,004,000.
Density (1998)[5]: persons per sq mi 805.1, persons per sq km 310.8.
Urban-rural (1995): urban 26.8%; rural 73.2%.
Sex distribution (1995): male 51.64%; female 48.36%.
Age breakdown (1995): under 15, 35.2%; 15–29, 27.2%; 30–44, 19.1%; 45–59,
11.2%; 60–74, 5.9%; 75 and over, 1.4%.
Population projection: (2000) 1,017,645,000; (2010) 1,182,000,000.
Doubling time: 43 years.
Linguistic composition (1991)[7]: Hindī 27.58% (including associated languages
and dialects, 39.85%); Bengalī 8.22%; Telugu 7.80%; Marāthī 7.38%; Tamil
6.26%; Urdū 5.13%; Gujarātī 4.81%; Kannada 3.87%; Malayālam 3.59%;
Oriyā 3.32%; Punjābī 2.76%; Assamese 1.55%; Bhīlī/Bhilodī 0.66%; Santhālī
0.62%; Kashmīrī 0.47%[8]; Gondī 0.25%; Sindhī 0.25%; Nepālī 0.25%;
Konkanī 0.21%; Tulu 0.18%; Kurukh 0.17%; Manipurī 0.15%; Bodo 0.14%;
Khandeshī 0.12%; other 3.26%. Hindī (66.00%) and English (19.00%) are
also spoken as lingua francas (second languages).
Major cities (1991): (*urban agglomerations;* 1995) Greater Mumbai (Greater
Bombay) 9,925,891 (15,093,000); Delhi 7,206,704 (9,882,000); Calcutta
4,399,819 (11,673,000); Chennai (Madras) 3,841,396 (5,906,000); Bangalore
3,302,296 (4,749,000); Hyderābād 3,145,939 (5,343,000); Ahmadābād 2,954,526
(3,688,000); Kānpur 1,879,420 (2,356,000); Nāgpur 1,624,752 (1,847,000);
Lucknow 1,619,115 (2,029,000); Pune 1,566,651 (2,940,000); New Delhi[9]
301,297.

Other principal cities (1991)

	population		population		population
Āgra	891,790	Indore	1,091,674	Rājkot	612,458
Allahābād	806,486	Jabalpur	764,586	Rānchi	599,306
Amritsar	708,835	Jaipur	1,458,183	Sholāpur	
Aurangābād	573,272	Jalandhar(Jullundur)	509,510	(Solāpur)	604,215
Bareilly	590,661	Jodhpur	666,279	Srīnagar	850,000[13]
Bhopāl	1,062,771	Kalyān[11]	1,014,557	Sūrat	1,505,872
Chandīgarh	510,565	Kota	537,371	Thāne (Thāna)[11]	803,389
Cochin (Kochi)	582,588	Ludhiāna	1,042,740	Trivandrum	699,872
Coimbatore	816,321	Madurai	940,989	Vadodara	
Farīdābād	617,717	Meerut	753,778	(Baroda)	1,061,598
Guwāhāti	584,342	Mysore	606,755	Vārānasi	
Gwalior	690,765	Nāshik (Nāsik)	656,925	(Benares)	932,399
Howrah (Hāora)[10]	950,435	Patna	917,243	Vijayawāda	701,827
Hubli-Dhārwād	648,298	Pimpri-Chinchwad[12]	517,083	Vishākhapatnam	752,037

Structure of gross domestic product and labour force

	1995–96 in value Rs '000,000,000[19]	1995–96 % of total value	1991 labour force[20]	1991 % of labour force[20]
Agriculture, forestry	2,748	27.9	191,340,829	60.9
Mining	197	2.0	1,751,275	0.6
Manufacturing	1,560	15.8	28,671,479	9.1
Construction	566	5.7	5,543,205	1.8
Public utilities	263	2.7	...	...
Transp. and commun.	764	7.8	8,017,746	2.5
Trade, restaurants	1,405	14.3	21,296,337	6.8
Finance, real estate	861	8.7	...	...
Pub. admin., defense	524	5.3	} 29,311,622	9.3
Services	594	6.0		
Other	376	3.8	28,198,877[21]	9.0[21]
TOTAL	9,858	100.0	314,131,370	100.0

Budget (1996–97). Revenue: Rs 1,982,500,000,000 (tax revenue 59.9%, of which
excise taxes 23.5%, customs duties 22.4%, corporation taxes 9.9%; nontax
revenue 40.1%, of which economic services 23.5%, interest receipts 10.8%).
Expenditures: Rs 2,297,300,000,000 (interest payments and debt servicing
26.1%; transportation 11.5%; grants to state governments 10.1%; defense
8.6%, communications 6.1%; agriculture 4.9%; social services 4.3%).
Public debt (external, outstanding; 1996): U.S.$74,406,000,000.
Production (in '000 metric tons except as noted). Agriculture, forestry, fishing (1996): sugarcane 255,000, cereals 214,082 (of which rice 120,012, wheat
62,620, sorghum 10,500, corn [maize] 8,660, pearl millet 7,000[22], finger millet 2,850[22]; fruits 40,197 (of which mangoes 10,000, bananas 9,935, oranges
2,000, lemons and limes 1,700, apples 1,200), oilseeds 27,361 (of which
peanuts [groundnuts] 8,000, rapeseed 6,000, cottonseed 5,101, soybeans 4,200,
sunflower seeds 1,450, castor beans 1,000); pulses 15,414 (of which chickpeas 6,000, pigeon peas 3,000), coconuts 8,700, seed cotton 7,651, cotton lint

2,550, jute 1,500, tea 715, tobacco 512, natural rubber 435, betel 248, ginger 210, pepper 46; livestock (number of live animals; 1996) 196,003,000 cattle, 120,270,000 goats, 80,102,000 water buffalo, 45,390,000 sheep, 14,855,000 pigs, 1,600,000 asses, 1,520,000 camels; roundwood (1995) 299,163,000 cu m, of which fuelwood 259,503,000 cu m, industrial roundwood 24,852,000; fish catch (metric tons; 1995) 4,905,921, of which marine fish 2,225,875, freshwater fish 2,207,318, crustaceans 364,237, cephalopods 103,739. Mining and quarrying (1995–96): limestone 94,032; iron ore 66,576; bauxite 5,448; manganese 720[23]; chromium 500[23]; zinc 171[23]; copper 57[23]; lead 42[23]; gold 65,600 troy oz; diamonds 29,900 carats. Manufacturing (in '000 metric tons except as noted; 1995–96): cement 69,032; finished steel 14,533; steel ingots 14,700[24]; refined sugar 14,788; nitrogenous fertilizers 7,950[24]; paper and paperboard 3,100[24]; soda ash 1,465; jute textiles 1,364[24]; aluminum 527; nylon and polyester yarns 357[24]; bicycles 9,426,000 units; motorcycles and scooters 2,035,000 units; power-driven pumps 513,000 units[24]; passenger cars and jeeps 414,200 units; passenger buses and trucks 259,100 units; cotton cloth 17,033,000,000 metres[24]; other important manufactured products include drugs and pharmaceuticals, computer software, gold jewelry, and silk goods. Construction (value of new construction in Rs; 1989-90): 563,670,000,000.

Manufacturing enterprises (1992–93)[25]

	no. of factories	no. of persons engaged	avg. wages as a % of avg. of all wages	annual value added (Rs '000,000)
Chemicals and chemical products,	7,886	640,400	155.6	107,519
of which fertilizers/pesticides	633	100,300	204.6	25,712
drugs and medicine	2,112	167,300	150.5	22,066
synthetic fibres	268	54,400	232.9	19,070
paints, soaps, and cosmetics	1,878	99,600	128.8	16,114
Textiles	14,789	1,397,300	86.7	59,140
Transport equipment,	5,552	718,300	137.9	50,284
of which motor vehicles	3,379	340,700	149.4	29,028
Nonelectrical machinery/apparatus	8,554	505,000	135.2	50,040
Electrical machinery/apparatus,	5,120	402,600	145.6	49,161
of which industrial machinery	1,924	162,600	173.7	21,066
communications equipment/TVs	1,194	124,100	131.3	16,050
Food products,	21,397	1,240,200	60.3	48,462
of which sugar	1,306	351,500	93.4	15,398
Iron and steel	3,388	490,200	147.0	48,123
Refined petroleum	79	24,400	247.1	27,972
Nonferrous basic metals	2,859	176,500	109.1	16,219
Fabricated metal products	7,038	239,900	96.1	13,468
Bricks, cement, plaster products	687	94,300	125.5	12,568
Rubber products	2,172	121,900	105.2	12,541
Tobacco products	7,786	493,700	28.4	12,513

Energy production (consumption): electricity (kW-hr; 1995–96) 380,100,000,000 ([1994] 385,902,000,000); coal (metric tons; 1995) 287,676,000 ([1994] 284,497,000); crude petroleum (barrels; 1995–96) 264,845,000 ([1994] 434,149,000); petroleum products (metric tons; 1994) 43,575,000 (56,722,000); natural gas (cu m; 1995) 17,022,000,000 ([1995–96] 20,388,000,000).

Financial aggregates[26]

	1991	1992	1993	1994	1995	1996	1997[27]
Exchange rate, Rs per:							
U.S. dollar	25.83	26.20	31.38	31.38	35.18	35.93	35.91
£	48.33	39.61	46.48	49.03	54.53	61.01	58.51
SDR	36.95	36.02	43.10	45.81	52.30	51.67	49.80
International reserves (U.S.$)							
Total (excl. gold; '000,000)	3,627	5,757	10,199	19,698	17,922	20,170	22,664
SDRs ('000,000)	46	4	100	2	139	122	2
Reserve pos. in IMF ('000,000)	—	292	292	310	316	306	295
Foreign exchange ('000,000)	3,580	5,461	9,807	19,386	17,467	19,742	22,367
Gold ('000,000 fine troy oz)	11.282	11.348	11.457	11.800	12.780	12.781	12.781
% world reserves	1.2	1.2	1.3	1.3	1.4	1.4	1.4
Interest and prices							
Central bank discount (%)	12.0	12.0	12.0	12.0	12.0	12.0	12.0
Advance (prime) rate (%)	17.9	18.9	16.3	...	...	...	...
Industrial share prices (1990 = 100)[28]	134.8	247.3	202.9	322.1	270.0	246.6	...
Balance of payments (U.S.$'000,000)							
Balance of visible trade	–2,992	–2,107	–522	...	...	...	...
Imports, f.o.b.	21,087	22,126	22,538	...	...	...	...
Exports, f.o.b.	18,095	20,019	22,016	...	...	...	...
Balance of invisibles	–1,300	–2,378	–1,354	...	...	...	...
Balance of payments, current account	–4,292	–4,495	–1,876	...	...	...	...

Land use (1994): forested 23.0%; meadows and pastures 3.8%; agricultural and under permanent cultivation 57.1%; other 16.1%.

Population economically active (1991): total 314,131,370; activity rate of total population 37.5% (participation rates: over age 15 [1981] 60.7%; female 28.6%; unemployed[29]).

Price and earnings indexes (1990 = 100)

	1992	1993	1994	1995	1996	1997	1998[30]
Consumer price index	127.3	135.4	149.2	164.5	179.2	192.1	206.2
Earnings index	...	...	...	...	...	...	...

Household income and expenditure. Average household size (1991)[14] 5.6; sources of income (1984–85): salaries and wages 42.2%, self-employed 39.7%, interest 8.6%, profits and dividends 6.0%, rent 3.5%; expenditure (1993–94): food and beverages 50.9%, transportation and communications 13.0%, clothing and footwear 9.8%, housing 5.7%, energy 4.2%.

Service enterprises (net value added at factor cost in Rs '000,000; 1992–93): wholesale and retail trade 766,500; transport and storage 420,610; community and social services 368,850; construction 358,330; finance 242,380; real estate and business services 215,840; electricity, gas, and steam 137,080.

Tourism: receipts from visitors (1995) U.S.$2,754,000,000; expenditures by nationals abroad (1994) U.S.$408,000,000.

Foreign trade[31, 32]

Balance of trade (current prices)

	1991–92	1992–93	1993–94	1994–95	1995–96	1996–97
Rs '000,000	–38,100	–96,870	–33,500	–72,970	–151,820	–193,000
% of total	4.1%	8.3%	2.3%	4.2%	6.7%	7.6%

Imports (1995–96): Rs 1,216,470,000,000 (mineral fuels and lubricants 20.7%; nonelectrical machinery 18.1%; precious and semiprecious stones 5.7%; electronic goods 5.1%; organic chemicals 4.7%). *Major import sources:* U.S. 10.5%; Germany 8.6%; Japan 6.6%; Saudi Arabia 5.5%; Kuwait 5.4%; U.K. 5.3%; Belgium 4.7%; United Arab Emirates 4.4%; Russia 3.3%.

Exports (1995–96): Rs 1,064,650,000,000 (agricultural and allied products 19.1%; cut and polished diamonds and jewelry 16.6%; ready-made garments 11.6%; machinery, transport equipment, metal products, iron and steel, and electronic components 11.4%; cotton yarn, fabrics, and thread 8.1%; chemicals and chemical products 7.4%; leather and leather manufactures 5.4%). *Major export destinations:* U.S. 17.4%; Japan 7.0%; U.K. 6.3%; Germany 6.2%; Hong Kong 5.7%; United Arab Emirates 4.5%; Belgium 3.5%; Russia 3.3%; Bangladesh 3.3%; Italy 3.2%.

Transport and communications

Transport. Railroads (1994–95): route length 38,935 mi, 62,660 km; passenger-mi 198,500,000,000, passenger-km 319,400,000,000; short ton-mi cargo 173,268,000,000, metric ton-km cargo 252,967,000,000. Roads (1995): total length 1,248,700 mi, 2,009,600 km (paved 50%). Vehicles (1995): passenger cars 2,720,000; trucks and buses 2,207,000,000. Air transport (1995)[33]: passenger-mi 12,563,000,000, passenger-km 20,219,000,000; short ton-mi cargo 437,871,000, metric ton-km cargo 639,280,000; airports (1996) with scheduled flights 66.

Communications

Medium	date	unit	number	units per 1,000 persons
Daily newspapers	1993	circulation	18,800,000	21
Radio	1996	receivers	111,000,000	117
Television	1995	receivers	20,000,000	21
Telephones	1995	main lines	10,600,000	11
Cellular telephones	1995	subscribers	135,600	0.14
Facsimile machines	1995	units	50,000	0.05
Personal computers	1995	units	1,200,000	1.3

Education and health

Literacy (1995): total population age 15 and over literate 315,600,000 (52.0%); males literate 205,100,000 (65.5%); females literate 110,500,000 (37.7%).

Education (1995–96)

	schools	teachers	students	student/ teacher ratio
Primary (age 6–10)	590,421	1,740,736	109,734,292	63.0
Secondary (age 11–17)	265,869	2,657,985	63,521,637	23.9
Higher[34]	8,407	286,000	5,007,000	17.5

Health (1992): physicians 410,875 (1 per 2,173 persons); hospital beds 642,103 (1 per 1,357 persons); infant mortality rate (1996) 71.1

Food (1995): daily per capita caloric intake 2,388 (vegetable products 93%, animal products 7%); 108% of FAO recommended minimum requirement.

Military

Total active duty personnel (1996): 1,145,000 (army 85.6%, navy 4.8%, air force 9.6%); personnel in paramilitary forces for border security 282,000. *Military expenditure as percentage of GNP* (1995): 2.4% (world 2.8%); per capita expenditure U.S.$8.

[1]Council of States can have a maximum of 250 members; a maximum of 12 of these members may be nominated by the president. [2]Includes 2 nonelective seats. [3]Government committed from April 1998 to creation of 3 new states from parts of Uttar Pradesh, Bihār, and Madhya Pradesh, respectively. [4]Effective government of new national capital territory in place from December 1993. [5]Excludes 46,976 sq mi (121,667 sq km) of territory claimed by India as part of Jammu and Kashmir but occupied by Pakistan or China; inland water constitutes 9.0% of total area of India (including all of Indian-claimed Jammu and Kashmir). [6]Detail does not add to total given because of rounding. [7]Mother tongue unless otherwise noted. [8]1981. [9]Within Delhi urban agglomeration. [10]Within Calcutta urban agglomeration. [11]Within Greater Mumbai urban agglomeration. [12]Within Pune urban agglomeration. [13]1990 estimate. [14]Excludes Jammu and Kashmir. [15]Projected rates based on about 3.5% of total deaths (317,392 registered deaths out of an estimated total of nearly 9,000,000 deaths). [16]Excludes Assam. [17]Data apply to the workers employed in the "organized sector" only (28 million in 1994, of which 20 million are employed in the public sector and 8 million are employed in the private sector); few legal protections exist for the other 348 million workers in the "unorganized sector." [18]Crimes reported to National Crime Records Bureau by police authorities of state governments. [19]At factor cost. [20]All persons aged 5 years or older designated "workers" per 1991 census. [21]Not adequately defined. [22]1995–96. [23]Approximate metal content of ore. [24]1994–95. [25]Establishments with 10 or more workers using electrical power and all establishments employing 20 or more workers. [26]End-of-period unless otherwise noted. [27]March. [28]Annual average. [29]Average number of registered unemployed during the first quarter of 1996 was 36,882,000. [30]January. [31]Imports c.i.f.; exports f.o.b. [32]Fiscal year beginning April 1. [33]Air-India, Indian Airlines, and Jet Airways only. [34]1993–94.

Internet resources for further information:

- **National Informatics Centre: Union Government**
  http://www.nic.in/htm/ug.htm
- **Ministry of External Affairs**
  http://www.meadev.gov.in/
- **Ministry of Finance: Budget and Economic Survey**
  http://www.nic.in/indiabudget/
- **Press Information Bureau (Government of India)**
  http://www.nic.in/India-Image/PIB/

Indonesia

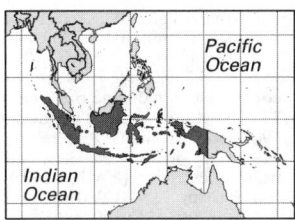

Official name: Republik Indonesia (Republic of Indonesia).
Form of government: unitary multiparty republic with two legislative houses (House of People's Representatives [480[1]]; People's Consultative Assembly [980[2]]).
Head of state and government: President.
Capital: Jakarta.
Official language: Indonesian (Bahasa Indonesia).
Official religion: monotheism.
Monetary unit: 1 Indonesian rupiah (Rp) = 100 sen; valuation (Sept. 25, 1998) 1 U.S.$ = Rp 10,850; 1 £ = Rp 18,472.

Area and population

Metropolitan district	Capitals	area sq mi	area sq km	population 1995 estimate
Jakarta Raya	Jakarta	228	590	9,160,500
Provinces				
Bali	Denpasar	2,147	5,561	2,902,200
Bengkulu	Bengkulu	8,173	21,168	1,415,000
Irian Jaya	Jayapura	162,928	421,981	1,956,300
Jambi	Jambi	17,297	44,800	2,383,400
Jawa Barat	Bandung	17,874	46,300	39,336,500
Jawa Tengah	Semarang	13,207	34,206	29,688,100
Jawa Timur	Surabaya	18,502	47,921	33,885,900
Kalimantan Barat	Pontianak	56,664	146,760	3,651,800
Kalimantan Selatan	Banjarmasin	14,541	37,660	2,900,400
Kalimantan Tengah	Palangkaraya	58,919	152,600	1,637,300
Kalimantan Timur	Samarinda	78,162	202,440	2,331,000
Lampung	Tanjung Karang	12,860	33,307	6,680,300
Maluku	Ambon	28,767	74,505	2,094,700
Nusa Tenggara Barat	Mataram	7,790	20,177	3,654,800
Nusa Tenggara Timur	Kupang	18,485	47,876	3,582,800
Riau	Pakanbaru	36,510	94,561	3,924,600
Sulawesi Selatan	Ujung Pandang	28,101	72,781	7,577,800
Sulawesi Tengah	Palu	26,921	69,726	1,947,500
Sulawesi Tenggara	Kendari	10,690	27,686	1,594,000
Sulawesi Utara	Menado	7,345	19,023	2,652,300
Sumatera Barat	Padang	19,219	49,778	4,328,200
Sumatera Selatan	Palembang	40,034	103,688	7,232,700
Sumatera Utara	Medan	27,331	70,787	11,145,300
Timor Timur[3]	Dili	5,743	14,874	843,100
Special autonomous districts				
Aceh	Banda Aceh	21,387	55,392	3,860,000
Yogyakarta	Yogyakarta	1,224	3,169	2,916,700
TOTAL		741,052	1,919,317	195,283,200

Demography

Population (1998): 202,957,000.
Density (1998): persons per sq mi 273.9, persons per sq km 105.7.
Urban-rural (1997): urban 37.0%; rural 63.0%.
Sex distribution (1990): male 49.88%; female 50.12%.
Age breakdown (1990): under 15, 36.5%; 15–29, 28.3%; 30–44, 18.1%; 45–59, 10.7%; 60–74, 5.3%; 75 and over, 1.1%.
Population projection: (2000) 209,342,000; (2010) 237,973,000.
Ethnolinguistic composition (1990): Javanese 39.4%; Sundanese 15.8%; Indonesian (Malay) 12.1%; Madurese 4.3%; Minang 2.4%; other 26.0%.
Religious affiliation (1990): Muslim 87.2%; Christian 9.6%, of which Roman Catholic 3.6%; Hindu 1.8%; Buddhist 1.0%; other 0.4%.
Major cities (1990): Jakarta 8,259,266; Surabaya 2,421,016; Bandung 2,026,893.

Vital statistics

Birth rate per 1,000 population (1997): 22.4 (world avg. 25.0).
Death rate per 1,000 population (1997): 7.9 (world avg. 9.3).
Natural increase rate per 1,000 population (1997): 14.5 (world avg. 15.7).
Total fertility rate (avg. births per childbearing woman; 1997): 2.6.
Marriage rate per 1,000 population (1993–94): 7.8[4].
Life expectancy at birth (1997): male 63.0 years; female 66.0 years.
Major causes of death (percent distribution, 1986): infectious and parasitic diseases 43.5%; diseases of the respiratory system 21.9%; cardiovascular diseases 9.7%; diseases of the nervous system 6.0%.

National economy

Budget (1997–98). Revenue: RP 88,061,000,000,000 (income tax 33.1%, value-added tax 27.9%, oil and gas revenues 16.9%, nontax revenue 9.6%, excise taxes 5.0%). Expenditures: RP 89,391,000,000,000 (general public services 33.7%, transfers and subsidies 13.1%, debt repayment 8.4%).
Public debt (external, outstanding; 1996): U.S.$60,108,000,000.
Tourism (1995): receipts U.S.$5,228,000,000; expenditures U.S.$2,172,000,000.
Production (metric tons except as noted). Agriculture, forestry, fishing (1996): rice 51,165,000, sugarcane 32,053,000, cassava 16,000,000, maize 8,925,000, palm oil 4,998,000, natural rubber 1,578,000; livestock (number of live animals) 14,323,000 goats, 11,930,000 cattle, 7,684,000 sheep, 3,140,000 buffalo; roundwood (1995) 185,895,000 cu m; fish catch (1995) 4,118,000. Mining and quarrying (1996): nickel ore 3,400,000; copper concentrate 1,760,000; bauxite 820,000; gold 83,660 kg. Manufacturing (value added in RP '000,000,000; 1994)[5]: textiles 8,055.4; transport equipment 6,796.7; tobacco products 6,194.6; food products 5,293.3; wood products 5,240.0. Energy production (consumption): electricity (kW-hr; 1994) 61,370,000,000 (61,370,000,000); coal (metric tons; 1994) 28,549,000 (3,461,000); crude petroleum (barrels; 1994) 561,265,000 (308,820,000); petroleum products (metric tons; 1994) 44,888,000 (36,428,000); natural gas (cu m; 1994) 59,532,000,000 (23,191,000,000).
Gross national product (1996): U.S.$213,384,000,000 (U.S.$1,080 per capita).

Structure of gross domestic product and labour force

	1996 in value Rp '000,000,000	1996 % of total value	1995 labour force[6]	1995 % of labour force[6]
Agriculture	86,212.1	16.3	35,233,270	44.0
Mining	43,893.2	8.3	643,332	0.8
Manufacturing	133,088.5	25.2	10,127,047	12.7
Construction	42,279.2	8.0	3,768,080	4.7
Public utilities	6,561.0	1.2	216,128	0.3
Transp. and commun.	35,553.7	6.7	3,458,155	4.3
Trade	88,451.2	16.7	13,883,682	17.3
Finance, real estate	46,839.6	8.9	658,497	0.8
Pub. admin., defense	29,531.4	5.6 }	} 12,121,869	} 15.1
Services	16,546.5	3.1 }		
Other	...	...	...	...
TOTAL	528,956.4	100.0	80,110,060	100.0

Population economically active: total (1995): 86,361,300; activity rate 44.3% (participation rates: over age 10, 56.6%; unemployed 7.2%).

Price and earnings indexes (1990 = 100)

	1991	1992	1993	1994	1995	1996	1997
Consumer price index	109.4	117.7	132.4	145.2	158.2	168.7	188.3
Earnings index[7]	114.6	127.1	150.0	195.8	233.3	...	...

Household income and expenditure. Average household size (1995) 4.3; income per household: n.a.; sources of income: n.a.

Foreign trade[8]

Balance of trade (current prices)

	1991	1992	1993	1994	1995	1996
U.S.$'000,000	+6,075	+4,937	+8,872	+11,496	+8,883	+5,285
% of total	11.6%	9.2%	13.4%	16.8%	10.8%	5.6%

Imports (1996): U.S.$42,929,000,000 (machinery and transport equipment 40.8%, basic manufactures 15.4%, chemicals 14.0%, mineral fuels 8.5%, crude materials 8.1%). *Major import sources:* Japan 19.8%; U.S. 11.8%; Germany 7.0%; Singapore 6.7%.
Exports (1996): U.S.$49,814,000,000 (crude petroleum 11.5%, natural gas 9.0%, plywood 7.2%, garments 7.2%, processed rubber 4.5%). *Major export destinations:* Japan 25.9%; U.S. 13.6%; Singapore 9.2%; Netherlands 3.3%.

Transport and communications

Transport. Railroads (1994): route length 6,583 km; passenger-km (1996) 15,924,000,000; metric ton-km cargo (1996) 3,912,000,000. Roads (1995): length 372,414 km (paved 47%). Vehicles (1995): passenger cars 2,107,299; trucks and buses 2,024,702. Air transport (1995): passenger-km 14,330,000,000; metric ton-km cargo 606,848,000; airports (1996) 81.

Communications

Medium	date	unit	number	units per 1,000 persons
Daily newspapers	1994	circulation	3,800,000	20
Radio	1996	receivers	26,000,000	132
Television	1995	receivers	28,000,000	145
Telephones	1995	main lines	3,290,900	17
Cellular telephones	1995	subscribers	218,600	1.1
Facsimile machines	1995	units	85,000	0.4
Personal computers	1995	units	730,000	3.8

Education and health

Educational attainment (1990). Percentage of population age 25 and over having: no schooling 34.6%; less than complete primary 28.2%; primary 23.3%; secondary 12.5%; higher 1.4%. *Literacy* (1995 est.): total population age 15 and over literate 83.8%; males literate 89.6%; females literate 78.0%.

Education (1994–95)

	schools	teachers	students	student/ teacher ratio
Primary (age 7–12)	149,464	1,172,640	26,200,023	22.3
Secondary (age 13–18)	27,117	595,962	8,864,001	14.9
Voc., teacher tr.[9]	3,502	102,114	1,405,220	13.8
Higher	1,236	150,607	2,229,796	14.8

Health (1994): physicians 28,989 (1 per 6,570 persons); hospital beds 116,847 (1 per 1,630 persons); infant mortality rate (1997) 51.
Food (1995): daily per capita caloric intake 2,732 (vegetable products 95%, animal products 5%); 126% of FAO recommended minimum.

Military

Total active duty personnel (1997): 284,000 (army 77.5%, navy 15.1%, air force 7.4%). *Military expenditure as percentage of GNP* (1995): 1.8% (world 2.8%); per capita expenditure U.S.$18.

[1]Includes 55 nonelective seats reserved for the military. [2]Includes the 480 members of the House of People's Representatives plus 500 other delegates. [3]The legality of Indonesian administration of this province is disputed by the United Nations. [4]Muslim population only. [5]Medium and large manufacturing establishments only. [6]Employed people only. [7]Based on minimum monthly wages. [8]Imports and exports are f.o.b. in balance of trade. [9]1993–94.

Internet resources for further information:
• **Central Bureau of Statistics http://www.bps.go.id/**

Iran

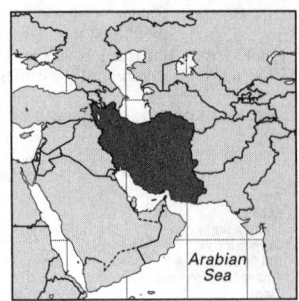

Official name: Jomhūrī-ye Eslāmī-ye Īrān (Islamic Republic of Iran).
Form of government: unitary Islamic republic with one legislative house (Islamic Consultative Assembly [270]).
Supreme political/religious authority: Leader[1].
Head of state and government: President.
Capital: Tehrān.
Official language: Farsī (Persian).
Official religion: Islam.
Monetary unit: 1 rial (Rls); valuation (Sept. 25, 1998) 1 U.S.$ = Rls 3,000[2]; 1 £ = Rls 5,108[2].

Area and population

Provinces	area sq km	1991 census population	Provinces	area sq km	population
Ardabīl	17,814	1,141,625	Khūzestān	67,132	3,175,852
Āzārbāyjān-e Gharbī	37,588	2,284,208	Kohkīlūyeh va		
Āzārbāyjān-e Sharqī	49,287	3,278,718	Būyer Ahmadī	14,261	496,739
Būshehr	25,357	694,252	Kordestān	27,855	1,233,480
Chahār Mahāll va			Lorestān	28,803	1,501,778
Bakhtīārī	14,820	747,297	Markazi	29,530	1,182,611
Esfahān	104,650	3,682,444	Māzandarān	46,456[3]	3,793,149[3]
Fārs	126,489	3,543,828	Qazvīn	4	4
Gilan	14,811	2,204,047	Qom	10,930	757,147
Golestān	3	3	Semnān	91,538	458,125
Hamadān	19,445	1,651,320	Sīstān va		
Hormozgān	68,476	924,433	Balūchestān	181,471	1,455,102
Īlām	19,086	440,693	Tehrān	53,693[4]	11,001,295[4]
Kermān	186,422	1,862,542	Yazd	72,342	691,119
Kermānshāhān	23,667	1,622,159	Zanjān	4	4
Khorāsān	313,335	6,013,200	TOTAL	1,645,258	55,837,163

Demography

Population (1998): 61,531,000[5].
Density (1998): persons per sq mi 96.9, persons per sq km 37.4.
Urban-rural (1995–96): urban 58.3%; rural 41.7%.
Sex distribution (1991): male 51.52%; female 48.48%.
Age breakdown (1991): under 15, 44.3%; 15–29, 26.6%; 30–44, 15.1%; 45–59, 8.2%; 60–74, 4.8%; 75 and over, 1.0%.
Population projection: (2000) 63,328,000; (2010) 73,130,000.
Doubling time: 26 years.
Ethnic composition (1995): Persian 51%; Azerbaijani 24%; Gīlaki/Māzāndarānī 8%; Kurd 7%; Arab 3%; Lurī 2%; Balochi 2%; other 3%.
Religious affiliation (1995): Muslim 99.0% (Shī'ī 93.4%, Sunnī 5.6%); Bahā'ī 0.6%; Christian 0.3%; Zoroastrian 0.05%; Jewish 0.05%.
Major cities (1994): Tehrān 6,750,043; Mashhad 1,964,489; Esfahān 1,220,595; Tabriz 1,166,203; Shīrāz 1,042,801; Ahvāz 828,380; Qom 780,453.

Vital statistics

Birth rate per 1,000 population (1996): 33.7 (world avg. 25.0).
Death rate per 1,000 population (1996): 6.6 (world avg. 9.3).
Total fertility rate (avg. births per childbearing woman; 1996): 4.7.
Marriage rate per 1,000 population (1993): 7.9.
Divorce rate per 1,000 population (1993): 0.5.
Life expectancy at birth (1996): male 66.1 years; female 68.7 years.
Major causes of death per 100,000 population (1990)[6]: diseases of the circulatory system 304; accidents and violence 108; malignant neoplasms (cancers) 61; diseases of the respiratory system 48; infectious diseases 34.

National economy

Budget (1996–97). Revenue: Rls 54,369,000,000,000 (oil revenue 51.5%, taxes 19.6%, other 28.9%). Expenditures: Rls 54,619,000,000,000 (current expenditure 58.5%, development expenditure 41.5%).
Public debt (external, outstanding; 1996): U.S.$15,917,000,000.
Tourism (1995–96): receipts U.S.$67,000,000; expenditures U.S.$241,000,000.
Gross national product (1995–96): U.S.$60,792,000,000 (U.S.$1,000 per capita).

Structure of gross domestic product and labour force

	1995–96 in value Rls '000,000,000[7]	1995–96 % of total value[7]	1991 labour force	1991 % of labour force
Agriculture	46,892	25.2	3,205,430	21.7
Petroleum, natural gas	29,069	15.6		
Other mining	884	0.5	} 100,545	0.7
Manufacturing	25,877	13.9	2,013,724	13.7
Construction	6,346	3.4	1,372,437	9.3
Public utilities	1,854	1.0	129,000	0.9
Transp. and commun.	11,435	6.2	762,178	5.2
Trade, restaurants	27,981	15.0	1,238,305	8.4
Finance, real estate	16,331	8.8	194,686	1.3
Pub. admin., defense	16,832	9.0		
Services	3,283	1.8	} 3,517,897	23.9
Other	−659[8]	−0.4[8]	2,202,502[9]	14.9[9]
TOTAL	186,125	100.0	14,736,704	100.0

Production (metric tons except as noted). Agriculture, forestry, fishing (1996): wheat 11,200,000, sugar beets 4,000,000, barley 3,000,000, rice 2,300,000, tomatoes 2,150,000, apples 2,000,000, grapes 1,900,000, sugarcane 1,900,000, oranges 1,600,000, onions 1,200,000, dates 795,000, lemons and limes 655,000,

corn (maize) 600,000, seed cotton 512,000, pistachios 282,000; livestock (number of live animals) 51,499,000 sheep, 8,492,000 cattle; roundwood (1995) 7,463,000 cu m; fish catch (1995) 368,300. Mining and quarrying (1994–95): gypsum 8,230,000[10]; iron ore (metal content) 4,300,000[11]; copper ore (metal content) 117,900; zinc ore (metal content) 72,900; chromite (metal content) 39,000. Manufacturing (value added in U.S.$'000,000; 1994): iron and steel 890; food products 755; textiles 635; transport equipment 473; electrical machinery 461; bricks, tiles. and cement 451. Energy production (consumption): electricity (kW-hr; 1995–96) 84,969,000,000 (79,128,000,000[11]); coal (metric tons; 1994) 980,000 (1,280,000); crude petroleum(barrels; 1995–96) 1,318,000,000 (343,300,000[11]); petroleum products (metric tons; 1994) 45,500,000 (47,180,000); natural gas (cu m; 1995–96) 39,100,000,000 (39,000,000,000).
Population economically active (1991): total 14,736,704; activity rate 26.4% (participation rates: ages 15–64, 46.8%; female 11.1%).

Price and earnings indexes (1990–91 = 100)

	1992–93	1993–94	1994–95	1995–96	1996–97	1997–98
Consumer price index	150.2	184.5	245.2	361.7	457.2	528.5
Daily earnings index[12]	136.9	161.4	200.4	278.2	...	...

Household income and expenditure. Average household size (1991): 5.1; income per urban household (1988) Rls 1,339,970 (U.S.$19,536); sources of urban income (1988): wages 37.4%, self-employment 30.5%, other 32.1%; expenditure (1990–91): food, beverages, and tobacco 42.6%[13], housing and energy 24.9%, clothing 11.8%.
Land use (1994): forest 7.0%; pasture 26.9%; agriculture 11.1%; other 55.0%.

Foreign trade

Balance of trade (current prices)

	1992–93	1993–94	1994–95	1995–96	1996–97	1997–98
U.S.$'000,000	−3,406	−1,207	+7,633	+5,586	+7,523	+3,511
% of total	7.9%	3.2%	24.4%	17.9%	20.1%	4.3%

Imports (1994–95): U.S.$11,795,000,000 (nonelectrical machinery 34.4%, electrical machinery 7.1%, iron and steel 5.9%, grains 5.8%, transportation equipment 5.4%). *Major import sources:* Germany 18.7%; Italy 8.5%; Japan 7.6%; Belgium 5.5%; U.A.E. 5.5%.
Exports (1994–95): U.S.$19,428,000,000 (petroleum and natural gas 75.2%, carpets 11.0%, pistachios 2.0%, iron and steel 1.8%). *Major export destinations:* Japan 15.1%; U.S. 13.9%; U.K. 9.2%; Germany 6.2%; S. Korea 4.8%.

Transport and communications

Transport. Railroads (1995): route length 4,527 mi, 7,286 km; (1993) passenger-km 6,422,000,000; metric ton-km cargo 9,124,000,000. Roads (1995): length 98,200 mi, 158,000 km (paved 59%). Vehicles (1994): passenger cars 1,630,000; trucks and buses 609,000. Merchant marine (1992): vessels (100 gross tons and over) 403; total deadweight tonnage 8,345,269. Air transport (1996)[14]: passenger-km 6,128,000,000; metric ton-km cargo 109,600,000; airports (1996) with scheduled flights 19.

Communications

Medium	date	unit	number	units per 1,000 persons
Daily newspapers	1994	circulation	1,200,000	20
Radio	1996	receivers	13,000,000	213
Television	1995	receivers	7,000,000	117
Telephones	1995	main lines	5,090,400	85
Cellular telephones	1995	subscribers	9,200	0.2
Facsimile machines	1995	units	30,000	0.5

Education and health

Educational attainment (1986). Percentage of population age 25 and over having: no formal schooling 12.8%; secondary education 38.0%; higher 7.8%.
Literacy (1994): total population age 15 and over literate 25,300,000 (72.1%); males literate 14,200,000 (78.4%); females literate 11,100,000 (65.8%).

Education (1994–95)

	schools	teachers	students	student/ teacher ratio
Primary (age 7–11)	61,889	311,531[15]	9,745,600	31.7[15]
Secondary (age 12–18)		228,869	7,284,611	31.8
Voc., teacher tr.	} 30,389[15]	20,418	368,218	18.0
Higher		36,366	478,455	13.2

Health (1995): physicians (1994) 37,000 (1 per 1,600 persons); hospital beds 93,000 (1 per 650 persons); infant mortality rate (1996) 52.7.
Food (1995): daily per capita caloric intake 2,955 (vegetable products 91%, animal products 9%); 123% of FAO recommended minimum requirement.

Military

Total active duty personnel (1996): 513,000 (revolutionary guard corps 23.4%, army 67.3%, navy 3.5%, air force 5.8%). *Military expenditure as percentage of GNP* (1995): 2.6% (world 2.8%); per capita expenditure U.S.$65.

[1]Not required to be a supreme theological authority. [2]Export rate. [3]Golestān province was created in December 1997 from part of Māzandarān province. [4]Tehrān province includes Qazvīn and Zanjān provinces. Qazvīn province was created in January 1997 from part of Zanjān province. [5]De jure estimate excluding refugees. [6]Projected rates based on about 20% of total deaths. [7]At factor cost. [8]Less imputed bank service charge. [9]Includes 1,640,092 unemployed. [10]1995. [11]1994. [12]Construction sector only. [13]Includes café and hotel expenditures. [14]Iran Air. [15]1993–94.

Internet resources for further information:
• Islamic Republic News Agency http://www.irna.co.uk/

Iraq

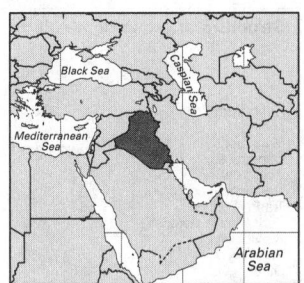

Official name: Al-Jumhūrīyah al-'Irāqīyah (Republic of Iraq).
Form of government: unitary multiparty[1] republic with one legislative house (National Assembly [220[2]]).
Head of state and government: President.
Capital: Baghdad.
Official language: Arabic[3].
Official religion: Islam.
Monetary unit: 1 Iraqi dinar (ID) = 20 dirhams = 1,000 fils; valuation (Sept. 25, 1998) 1 U.S.$ = 1,500 ID[4]; 1 £ = 2,550 ID[4].

Area and population

Governorates	Capitals	area[5] sq mi	sq km	population 1991 estimate
Al-Anbār	Ar-Ramādī	53,208	137,808	865,500
Bābil	Al-Ḥillah	2,163	5,603	1,221,100
Baghdād	Baghdad	1,572	4,071	3,910,900
Al-Baṣrah[5]	Basra	7,363	19,070	1,168,800
Dhī Qār	An-Nāṣirīyah	4,981	12,900	1,030,900
Diyālā	Ba'qūbah	6,828	17,685	1,037,600
Karbalā'	Karbalā'	1,944	5,034	567,600
Maysān	Al-'Amārah	6,205	16,072	524,200
Al-Muthannā	As-Samāwah	19,977	51,740	350,000
An-Najaf	An-Najaf	11,129	28,824	666,400
Nīnawā	Mosul	14,410	37,323	1,618,700
Al-Qādisiyah	Ad-Dīwānīyah	3,148	8,153	595,600
Ṣalāḥ ad-Dīn	Tikrīt	9,407	24,363	772,200
At-Ta'mīm	Karkūk (Kirkūk)	3,737	9,679	605,900
Wāsiṭ	Al-kūt	6,623	17,153	605,700
Kurdish Autonomous Region[6]				
Dahūk	Dahūk	2,530	6,553	309,300
Irbīl	Irbīl	5,820	15,074	928,400
As-Sulaymānīyah	As-Sulaymānīyah	6,573	17,023	1,124,200
LAND AREA		167,618	434,128	
OTHER[7]		357	924	
TOTAL		167,975	435,052	17,903,000

Demography

Population (1998): 21,722,000[8].
Density (1998): persons per sq mi 129.3, persons per sq km 49.9.
Urban-rural (1997): urban 68.1%; rural 31.9%.
Sex distribution (1996): male 51.23%; female 48.77%.
Age breakdown (1994): under 15, 41.1%; 15–29, 30.5%; 30–44, 16.0%; 45–59, 7.6%; 60–74, 3.7%; 75 and over, 1.1%.
Population projection: (2000) 23,151,000; (2010) 31,152,000.
Doubling time: 29 years.
Ethnic composition (1983): Arab 77.1%; Kurd 19.0%; Azerbaijani 1.7%; Assyrian 0.8%; other 1.4%.
Religious affiliation (1994): Shī'ī Muslim 62.5%; Sunnī Muslim 34.5%; Christian (primarily Chaldean rite and Syrian rite Roman Catholic and Nestorian) 2.7%; other (primarily Yazīdī syncretist) 0.3%.
Major cities (1987): Baghdad (1995; urban agglomeration) 4,478,000; Mosul 664,221; Irbīl 485,968; Karkūk (Kirkūk) 418,624; Al-Baṣrah 406,296.

Vital statistics

Birth rate per 1,000 population (1994): 34.1 (world avg. 26.0).
Death rate per 1,000 population (1994): 9.8 (world avg. 9.2).
Natural increase rate per 1,000 population (1994): 24.3 (world avg. 16.8).
Total fertility rate (avg. births per childbearing woman; 1996): 4.9.
Marriage rate per 1,000 population (1992): 7.8.
Life expectancy at birth (1994): male 57.3 years; female 60.4 years.
Major causes of death. Prior to the Gulf War (1990) the leading causes (in descending order) were: circulatory diseases, injury and poisoning, cancer, and congenital anomalies; since 1990, additional mortality has been attributed to deprivation of medical care and malnutrition consequent upon the imposition of UN sanctions, especially among children and other vulnerable populations.

National economy

Budget (1992). Revenue: ID 13,935,000,000. Expenditures: ID 13,935,000,000. Details of more recent budgets are not available.
Public debt (external, outstanding; 1994): U.S.$20,000,000,000.
Production (metric tons except as noted). Agriculture, forestry, fishing (1996): wheat 1,000,000, clover 820,000, tomatoes 800,000, dates 550,000, barley 500,000, potatoes 380,000, oranges 310,000, grapes 300,000, rice 270,000; livestock (number of live animals) 5,000,000 sheep, 1,000,000 cattle; roundwood (1995) 161,000 cu m; fish catch (1995) 22,550. Mining and quarrying (1995): sulfur 475,000; phosphate rock 440,000. Manufacturing (value added in U.S.$'000,000; 1994): refined petroleum 127; bricks, tiles, and cement 100; industrial chemicals 79; food products 59; metal products 28. Construction (authorized; 1991): residential 4,558,000 sq m; nonresidential 410,000 sq m. Energy production (consumption): electricity (kW-hr; 1994) 27,060,000,000 (27,060,000,000); coal, none (none); crude petroleum (barrels; 1996) 255,500,000 ([1994] 207,200,000); petroleum products (metric tons; 1994) 22,180,000 (21,215,000); natural gas (cu m; 1994) 3,170,000,000 (3,170,000,000).
Household income and expenditure (1988). Average household size 8.9; sources of income: self-employment 33.9%, wages and salaries 23.9%, transfers

23.0%, rent 18.6%; expenditure: food and beverages 50.2%, housing and energy 19.9%, clothing and footwear 10.6%.
Gross domestic product (1996): U.S.$11,500,000,000 (U.S.$540 per capita).

Structure of gross domestic product and labour force

	1992 in value ID '000,000[9]	1992 % of total value	1988 labour force	1988 % of labour force
Agriculture	20,844	35.1	477,264	11.6
Mining	230	0.4	60,701	1.5
Manufacturing	5,620	9.5	337,293	8.2
Construction	2,259	3.8	460,788	11.2
Public utilities	181	0.3	41,200	1.0
Transp. and commun.	5,947	10.0	266,233	6.4
Trade	15,190	25.6	281,877	6.8
Finance, real estate	4,692	7.9	41,532	1.0
Pub. admin., defense, and services	7,209	12.2	2,160,406	52.3
Other	−2,824	−4.8		
TOTAL	59,348	100.0	4,127,294	100.0

Population economically active (1988): total 4,127,294; activity rate of total population 24.7% (participation rates: ages 15–64, 45.3%; female 12.0%).

Price index (1990 = 100)

	1990	1991	1992	1993	1994	1995	1996
Consumer price index	100.0	287	860[10]	2,600[10]	10,000[10]	50,000[10]	275,000[10]

Tourism (1994): receipts U.S.$12,000,000; expenditures, n.a.
Land use (1994): forest 0.4%; pasture 9.1%; agriculture 13.1%; other 77.4%.

Foreign trade[11, 12]

Balance of trade (current prices)

	1990[10]	1991[10]	1992[10]	1993[10]	1994[10]	1995[10]
U.S.$'000,000	+5,587	−1,633	−2,199	−1,956	−1,518	−2,081
% of total	36.6%	66.3%	73.3%	68.8%	66.5%	71.3%

Imports (1995): U.S.$2,500,000,000[10] (agricultural products 42.7%, of which cereals 9.9%; unspecified 57.3%). *Major import sources*[13]: Jordan 49.0%; Turkey 17.0%; Hungary 15.0%; Switzerland 8.0%.
Exports (1995): U.S.$419,000,000[10] (mostly crude petroleum and petroleum products). *Major export destinations:* Jordan 98.0%.

Transport and communications

Transport. Railroads (1995): route length 2,032 km; (1993) passenger-km 1,566,000,000; (1993) metric ton-km cargo 1,649,000,000. Roads (1995): total length 46,500 km (paved 86%). Vehicles (1995): passenger cars 672,000; trucks and buses 368,000. Air transport: [14].

Communications

Medium	date	unit	number	units per 1,000 persons
Daily newspapers	1994	circulation	532,000	27
Radio	1996	receivers	3,700,000	167
Television	1995	receivers	1,000,000	48
Telephones	1995	main lines	675,000	33

Education and health

Educational attainment (1987). Percentage of population age 10 and over having: no formal schooling 52.8%; primary education 21.5%; secondary 11.6%; higher 4.1%; unknown 10.0%. *Literacy* (1995): total population age 15 and over literate 58.0%; males 70.7%; females 45.0%.

Education (1994–95)

	schools	teachers	students	student/ teacher ratio
Primary (age 6–11)	8,035	132,030	2,977,800	22.6
Secondary (age 12–17)	2,635	48,961	1,062,204	21.7
Voc., teacher tr.	310	9,903	135,711	13.7
Higher	12	11,847	201,984	17.0

Health (1993): physicians 8,787 (1 per 2,181 persons); hospital beds 27,202 (1 per 704 persons); infant mortality rate per 1,000 live births (1994) 91.9.
Food (1995): daily per capita caloric intake 2,268 (vegetable products 96%, animal products 4%); 94% of FAO recommended minimum requirement.

Military

Total active duty personnel (1997): 387,500 (army 90.3%, navy 0.7%, air force 9.0%). *Military expenditure as percentage of GDP* (1994): 18.0%[10] (world, n.a.); per capita expenditure U.S.$136.

[1]Multipartyism is officially authorized, but political power is in fact concentrated in a single-party apparatus. [2]Elective seats as of March 1996 elections; 30 additional seats allotted to the Kurdish Autonomous Region were filled by presidential appointment. [3]Kurdish is official in the Kurdish Autonomous Region only. [4]Exchange bureau (semi-official) rate. [5]Includes territory ceded to Kuwait as of Jan. 15, 1993. [6]De facto self-government between 1992 and 1996. Iraqi sovereignty over some of the area was reasserted in late 1996. [7]Territorial water at the mouth of the Shaṭṭ al-'Arab. [8]Census population of Oct. 16, 1997, equaled 22,017,983; 1998 estimate is from the current U.S. Census Bureau time series estimations. [9]At factor cost. [10]Estimated figure(s). [11]Imports c.i.f.; exports f.o.b. [12]UN-imposed trade sanctions in place from August 1990 through October 1997. [13]Based on estimated imports equaling U.S.$608,000,000. [14]No scheduled air service since June 1992.

Internet resources for further information:
- **Permanent Mission of Iraq to the United Nations (official site)** http://www.undp.org/missions/iraq
- **Iraq Foundation (unofficial)** http://www.iraqfoundation.org/

Ireland

Official name: Éire (Irish); Ireland[1] (English).
Form of government: unitary multi-party republic with two legislative houses (Senate [60[2]]; House of Representatives [166]).
Chief of state: President.
Head of government: Prime Minister.
Capital: Dublin.
Official languages: Irish; English.
Official religion: none.
Monetary unit: 1 Irish pound (£Ir) = 100 new pence; valuation (Sept. 25, 1998) 1 £Ir = U.S.$1.49 = £0.88.

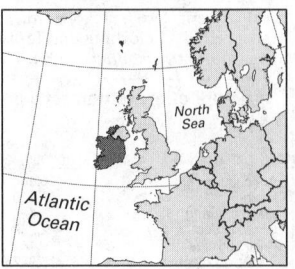

Area and population

Provinces Counties	area sq mi	area sq km	population 1996 census
Connacht	6,611	17,122	433,000
Galway[3]	2,293	5,940	189,000
Leitrim	581	1,525	25,000
Mayo	2,084	5,398	111,000
Roscommon	951	2,463	52,000
Sligo	693	1,796	56,000
Leinster	7,580	19,633	1,922,000[4]
Carlow	346	896	42,000
Dublin[5]	356	922	1,057,000
Kildare	654	1,694	135,000
Kilkenny	796	2,062	75,000
Laoighis	664	1,719	53,000
Longford	403	1,044	30,000
Louth	318	823	92,000
Meath	902	2,336	109,000
Offaly	771	1,998	59,000
Westmeath	681	1,763	63,000
Wexford	908	2,351	104,000
Wicklow	782	2,025	102,000
Munster	9,315	24,127	1,033,000
Clare	1,231	3,188	94,000
Cork[3]	2,880	7,460	420,000
Kerry	1,815	4,701	126,000
Limerick[3]	1,037	2,686	165,000
Tipperary North Riding	771	1,996	58,000
Tipperary South Riding	872	2,258	75,000
Waterford[3]	710	1,838	95,000
Ulster (part of)	3,093	8,012	234,000[4]
Cavan	730	1,891	53,000
Donegal	1,865	4,830	129,000
Monaghan	498	1,291	51,000
TOTAL LAND AREA	26,600	68,895[4]	
INLAND WATER	537	1,390	
TOTAL	27,137	70,285	3,622,000

Demography

Population (1998): 3,647,000.
Density (1997): persons per sq mi 134.4, persons per sq km 51.9.
Urban-rural (1996): urban 58.0%; rural 42.0%.
Sex distribution (1996): male 49.64%; female 50.36%.
Age breakdown (1996): under 15, 23.7%; 15–24, 17.5%, 25–44, 28.0%; 45–59, 15.6%; 60–74, 12.3%; 75 and over, 2.9%.
Population projection: (2000) 3,673,000; (2010) 3,837,000.
Religious affiliation (1991): Roman Catholic 91.6%; Church of Ireland (Anglican) 2.5%; Presbyterian 0.4%; other 5.5%.
Major cities (1996)[6]: Dublin 480,996; Cork 127,092; Galway 57,095.

Vital statistics

Birth rate per 1,000 population (1996): 13.9 (world avg. 25.0).
Death rate per 1,000 population (1996): 8.7 (world avg. 9.3).
Natural increase rate per 1,000 population (1996): 5.2 (world avg. 15.7).
Total fertility rate (avg. births per childbearing woman; 1994): 1.8.
Life expectancy at birth (1990–92): male 72.3 years; female 77.9 years.
Major causes of death per 100,000 population (1996): heart and circulatory diseases 385.2, of which ischemic heart diseases 210.0; malignant neoplasms (cancers) 201.8; respiratory disease 131.6, of which pneumonia 62.7.

National economy

Budget (1997). Revenue: £Ir 13,584,100,000 (income taxes 36.3%, value-added tax 25.5%, excise taxes 18.2%). Expenditures: £Ir 14,996,000,000 (social welfare 30.6%, health 16.5%, debt service 15.2%, education 14.7%).
Public debt (1995): U.S.$48,449,000,000.
Tourism (1995): receipts U.S.$2,688,000,000; expenditures U.S.$2,030,000,000.
Production (metric tons except as noted). Agriculture, forestry, fishing (1996): sugar beets 1,485,000, barley 1,225,000, wheat 771,000, potatoes 733,000, oats 146,000, milk 51,900,000[7] hectolitres; livestock (number of live animals)[8] 7,934,000 sheep, 7,423,000 cattle, 1,620,000 pigs; roundwood (1995) 2,204,000 cu m; fish catch (1995) 412,722. Mining and quarrying (1994): gypsum 367,300; zinc ore 194,000[9]; lead ore 53,700[9]. Manufacturing (value added in £Ir; 1990): metals and engineering goods 3,237,500,000; food products 1,828,300,000; chemical products 1,492,600,000. Construction (1996): residential 4,167,000 sq m; nonresidential 3,531,000 sq m. Energy production (consumption): electricity (kW-hr; 1994) 17,105,000,000 (17,105,000,000); coal (metric tons; 1994) 1,000 (2,695,000); crude petroleum (barrels; 1994) none (16,764,000); petroleum products (metric tons; 1994) 2,213,000 (4,879,000); natural gas (cu m; 1994) 2,565,000,000 (2,565,000,000).
Gross national product (1996): U.S.$62,040,000,000 (U.S.$17,110 per capita).

Structure of gross domestic product and labour force

1996	in value £Ir '000,000[10]	% of total value	labour force	% of labour force
Agriculture	2,858	7.5	136,000	9.2
Mining			5,000	0.3
Manufacturing	14,480	38.4	246,000	16.7
Construction			86,000	5.8
Public utilities			14,000	0.9
Transp. and commun.	6,749	17.9	80,000	5.4
Trade			273,000[11]	18.5[11]
Pub. admin., defense	1,931	5.1	76,000	5.2
Services	11,729	31.1	369,000	25.0
Finance			[11]	[11]
Other			191,000[12]	13.0[12]
TOTAL	37,747	100.0	1,475,000	100.0

Population economically active (1996): total 1,475,000; activity rate 40.7% (participation rates: ages 15–64, 59.2%[13]; unemployed 11.9%[14]).

Price and earnings indexes (1990 = 100)

	1991	1992	1993	1994	1995	1996	1997
Consumer price index	103.2	106.4	107.9	110.4	113.2	115.1	116.8
Weekly earnings index	104.4	108.6	114.4	117.8	120.5	123.4	126.6[15]

Household income and expenditure. Average household size (1996) 3.3; income per household (1994–95): £Ir 16,224 (U.S.$25,100); expenditure (1996)[16]: food and beverages 35.4%, transportation 13.9%, rent/household goods 11.6%.

Foreign trade[17]

Balance of trade (current prices)

	1992	1993	1994	1995	1996	1997
£Ir '000,000	3,549	4,945	5,470	7,206	7,750	10,360
% of total	11.8%	14.2%	13.7%	14.9%	14.8%	17.0%

Imports (1995): £Ir 20,347,300,000 (machinery and transport equipment 42.4%, chemicals 12.9%, manufactured goods 11.5%, food 7.2%, petroleum and petroleum products 3.3%, crude materials [inedible] 2.0%, beverages and tobacco 1.0%). *Major import sources:* U.K. 35.5% U.S. 17.5%; Germany 7.1%; Japan 5.2%; Singapore 4.0%; France 3.8%; The Netherlands 2.7%.
Exports (1995): £Ir 27,680,900,000 (machinery and transport equipment 34.6%, chemical products 18.8%, food 17.5%, manufactured goods 4.8%). *Major export destinations:* U.K. 25.7%; Germany 14.4%; France 9.4%; U.S. 8.2%.

Transport and communications

Transport. Railroads (1995): route length 1,947 km; passenger-km 1,331,900,-000; metric ton-km cargo 573,000,000. Roads (1995): length 92,340 km (paved 94%). Vehicles (1995): passenger cars 990,384; trucks and buses 155,153. Air transport (1996)[18]: passenger-km 5,126,177,000; metric ton-km cargo 102,055,000; airports (1996) 9.

Communications

Medium	date	unit	number	units per 1,000 persons
Daily newspapers	1996	circulation	542,000	151
Radio	1996	receivers	2,150,000	597
Television	1995	receivers	1,000,000	279
Telephones	1996	main lines	1,341,719	373
Cellular telephones	1995	subscribers	158,000	44
Facsimile machines	1995	units	80,000	22
Personal computers	1995	units	520,000	145

Education and health

Educational attainment (1991). Percentage of population age 15 and over having: primary education or no schooling 33.7%; secondary 42.7%; some postsecondary 12.6%; university or like institution 11.0%.

Education (1994–95)

	schools	teachers	students	student/teacher ratio
Primary (age 6–11)[19]	3,319	20,901	491,256	23.5
Secondary (age 12–18)	452	12,635	225,490	17.8
Voc., teacher tr.	327	8,019	146,050	18.2
Higher	29	4,889	88,925	18.2

Health: physicians (1984) 5,180 (1 per 681 persons); hospital beds (1994) 11,853[20] (1 per 301 persons); infant mortality rate (1994) 5.9.
Food (1995): daily per capita caloric intake 3,638 (vegetable products 69%, animal products 39%); 145% of FAO recommended minimum requirement.

Military

Total active duty personnel (1995): 12,900 (army 84.5%, navy 7.7%, air force 7.8%). *Military expenditure as percentage of GNP* (1995): 1.3% (world 2.8%); per capita expenditure U.S.$193.

[1]As provided by the constitution; the 1948 Republic of Ireland Act provides precedent for this longer formulation of the official name but, per official sources, "has not changed the usage *Ireland* as the name of the state in the English language." [2]Includes 11 nonelective seats. [3]Includes county borough(s). [5]Includes the three county councils of Dun Laoghaire–Rathdown, Fingal, and South Dublin. Established Jan. 1, 1994. [6]County boroughs. [7]1995. [8]June. [9]Metal content of ores. [10]At factor cost. [11]Trade includes Finance. [12]Unemployed. [13]1988. [14]April. [15]2nd quarter. [16]November. [17]Import figures are c.i.f. in balance of trade. [18]Aer Lingus only. [19]National schools only. [20]Acute-care public hospitals only.

Internet resources for further information:
• **Central Statistics Office (Ireland) http://www.cso.ie/index.html**

Israel

Official name: Medinat Yisra'el
(Hebrew); Isrā'īl (Arabic) (State
of Israel).
Form of government: multiparty
republic with one legislative house
(Knesset [120]).
Chief of state: President.
Head of government: Prime Minister.
Capital: Jerusalem is the proclaimed
capital of Israel and the actual seat
of government, but recognition of its
status as capital by the international
community has largely been withheld
pending final settlement of territorial
and other issues through peace talks
between Israel and the Arab parties
concerned.
Official languages: Hebrew; Arabic.
Official religion: none.
Monetary unit: 1 New (Israeli) sheqel
(NIS) = 100 agorot; valuation (Sept. 25,
1998) 1 U.S.$ = NIS 3.85;
1 £ = NIS 6.55.

Area and population		area[1]		population
				1996[2]
Districts	Capitals	sq mi	sq km	estimate
Central (Ha Merkaz)	Ramla	479	1,242	1,213,200
Haifa (Ḥefa)	Haifa	330	854	740,300
Jerusalem (Yerushalayim)	Jerusalem	240	622	662,700
Northern (Ha Ẓafon)	Tiberias	1,284	3,325	952,100
Southern (Ha Darom)	Beersheba	5,447	14,107	770,200
Tel Aviv	Tel Aviv–Yafo	66	170	1,141,900
TOTAL		7,846	20,320	5,480,400[3, 4]

Demography

Population (1998): 5,740,000[3, 4].
Density (1998)[3, 4]: persons per sq mi 731.6, persons per sq km 282.5.
Urban-rural (1996)[2]: urban 91.0%; rural 9.0%.
Sex distribution (1997): male 49.68%; female 50.32%.
Age breakdown (1997): under 15, 28.4%; 15–29, 25.2%; 30–44, 19.7%; 45–59, 13.7%; 60–74, 8.8%; 75 and over, 4.2%.
Population projection: (2000) 5,911,000; (2010) 6,847,000.
Ethnic composition (1997): Jewish 80.5%; Arab and other 19.5%.
Religious affiliation (1997): Jewish 80.5%; Muslim (mostly Sunnī) 14.6%; Christian 3.2%; Druze 1.7%.
Major cities (1997): Jerusalem 602,100; Tel Aviv–Yafo 353,100; Haifa 255,300; Rishon LeẒiyyon 171,100; Ḥolon 163,900; Petaḥ Tiqwa 154,500.

Vital statistics

Birth rate per 1,000 population (1997): 20.0 (world avg. 25.0); (1994)[5] legitimate 98.2%; illegitimate 1.8%.
Death rate per 1,000 population (1997): 6.0 (world avg. 9.3).
Natural increase rate per 1,000 population (1997): 14.0 (world avg. 15.7).
Total fertility rate (avg. births per childbearing woman; 1997): 2.7.
Marriage rate per 1,000 population (1996): 6.7.
Divorce rate per 1,000 population (1996): 1.7.
Life expectancy at birth (1997): male 76.3 years; female 80.2 years.
Major causes of death per 100,000 population (1994): heart diseases 211.3; cancers 140.5; cerebrovascular diseases 59.5; accidents 25.5.

National economy

Budget (1998). Revenue: NIS 156,800,000,000 (1996; income tax, property tax, and land improvement tax 39.0%, value-added tax 28.0%, sales tax and fuel tax 9.5%, royalties and interest 2.7%). Expenditures: NIS 164,400,000,000 (1996; defense 22.3%, labour and social welfare 16.8%, education and culture 16.2%, interest on loans 16.2%).
Public debt (1995): U.S.$23,950,000,000.
Gross national product (1996): U.S.$90,310,000,000 (U.S.$15,870 per capita).

Structure of gross domestic product and labour force	1993		1996	
	in value NIS '000,000	% of total value	labour force	% of labour force
Agriculture	3,197	2.4	51,000	2.4
Manufacturing, mining	29,007	21.5	405,100	18.8
Construction	9,678	7.2	150,000	6.9
Public utilities	2,263	1.7	18,500	0.9
Transp. and commun.	10,238	7.6	124,300	5.8
Trade	15,581	11.6	331,200	15.3
Finance	34,906	25.9	261,200[6]	12.1[6]
Public and community services	5,683	4.2	625,800[7]	29.0[7]
Services	30,482	22.6	33,800[8]	1.6[8]
Other	−6,368[9]	−4.7[9]	156,100[10]	7.2[10]
TOTAL	134,667	100.0	2,157,000	100.0

Production (metric tons except as noted). Agriculture, forestry, fishing (1997): watermelons 450,000, tomatoes 440,000, grapefruit 390,000, potatoes 260,000, wheat 140,000, seed cotton 131,000; livestock (number of live animals) 410,000 cattle, 340,000 sheep, 94,000 goats, 23,000,000 chickens; roundwood (1995) 113,000 cu m; fish catch (1995) 20,564. Mining and quarrying (1996): phosphate rock 2,450,000, potash 2,500,000. Manufacturing (1996): cement

6,723,000; polyethylene 144,147[11]; sulfuric acid 130,000[11]; cardboard 113,278; paper 114,403; chlorine 34,630; wine 12,733,000 litres[11]. Construction (1996): residential 7,010,000 sq m; nonresidential 2,380,000 sq m. Energy production (consumption): electricity (kW-hr; 1994) 28,315,000 (27,985,000); coal (metric tons; 1994) none (6,026,000); crude petroleum (barrels; 1994) 29,000 (88,682,000); petroleum products (metric tons; 1994) 10,589,000 (8,122,000); natural gas (cu m; 1994) 22,025,000 (22,025,000).
Population economically active (1996)[12]: total 2,157,000; activity rate 38.9% (participation rates: over ages 15, 53.7%; female 43.5%; unemployed 6.7%).

Price and earnings indexes (1990 = 100)							
	1992	1993	1994	1995	1996	1997	1998[13]
Consumer price index	133.2	147.8	166.0	182.7	203.3	221.6	226.4
Daily earnings index	125.9	140.6	155.6	178.5	203.3	233.5	250.5

Household income and expenditure (1996). Average household size 3.6; monthly income per household[14, 15] NIS 6,125 (U.S.$2,034); sources of income (1993)[14]: salaries and wages 63.4%, allowances and assistance 18.9%, self-employment 14.6%, other 3.1%; expenditure (1996): housing 22.6%, food, beverages, and tobacco 21.8%, household durable goods 7.3%, clothing, footwear, and personal goods 5.9%, transportation 4.1%, energy 4.0%.
Tourism (1995): receipts U.S.$2,784,000,000; expenditures U.S.$3,148,000,000.

Foreign trade[16]

Balance of trade (current prices)						
	1992	1993	1994	1995	1996	1997
U.S.$'000,000	−5,516	−7,798	−8,353	−10,533	−11,010	−8,278
% of total	21.6%	20.8%	19.8%	21.7%	21.1%	15.5%

Imports (1996): U.S.$29,949,000,000 (investment goods 17.7%; diamonds 14.1%; consumer goods 13.2%; fuel and lubricants 7.1%). *Major import sources:* U.S. 20.0%; Belgium 12.1%; Germany 9.4%; U.K. 8.8%; Italy 7.6%.
Exports (1996): U.S.$20,510,200,000 (machinery and transport equipment 29.5%; diamonds 25.6%; chemicals 11.8%; apparel 4.9%; food, beverages, and tobacco 3.9%; rubber and plastic 3.9%). *Major export destinations:* U.S. 30.6%; U.K. 6.7%; Japan 5.9%; Belgium 5.4%; Hong Kong 5.2%.

Transport and communications

Transport. Railroads (1996): route length 610 km; passenger-km 267,000,000[13]; metric ton-km cargo 1,176,000,000[13]. Roads (1995): total length 14,700 km (paved 100%). Vehicles (1997): passenger cars 1,174,000: trucks and buses 272,000. Merchant marine (1992): vessels (100 gross tons and over) 58; total deadweight tonnage 723,418. Air transport (1996)[17]: passenger-km 11,511,000,000; metric ton-km cargo 1,113,000,000; airports (1997) with scheduled flights 7.

Communications				units per 1,000
Medium	date	unit	number	persons
Daily newspapers	1995	circulation	1,500,000	271.0
Radio	1995	receivers	2,700,000	489.0
Television	1995	receivers	1,600,000	290.0
Telephones	1995	main lines	2,342,600	417.7
Cellular telephones	1995	subscribers	300,000	53.5
Facsimile machines	1995	units	140,000	25.0
Personal computers	1995	units	560,000	99.8

Education and health

Educational attainment (1991). Percentage of population age 25 and over having: no formal schooling 6.7%; primary 22.5%; secondary 39.6%; postsecondary, vocational, and higher 31.2%. *Literacy* (1995): total population age 15 and over literate 95.6%; males literate 97.7%; females literate 93.6%.

Education (1996–97)	schools[18]	teachers	students	student/ teacher ratio
Primary (age 6–13)	1,937	57,618[18]	691,800	...
Secondary (age 14–17)[19]	797	39,093[20]	478,900	...
Vocational, teacher tr.	435	17,141[20]	142,900	...
Higher	7	7,829[21]	101,700[22]	...

Health (1997): physicians (1996) 27,000 (1 per 206 persons); hospital beds 34,200 (1 per 165 persons); infant mortality rate per 1,000 live births 8.0.
Food (1995): daily per capita caloric intake 3,271 (vegetable products 81%, animal products 19%); 127% of FAO recommended minimum.

Military

Total active duty personnel (1997): 175,000 (army 76.6%, navy 5.1%, air force 18.3%). *Military expenditure as percentage of GNP* (1995): 9.6% (world 2.8%); per capita expenditure U.S.$1,646.

[1]Excluding West Bank (2,270 sq mi [5,879 sq km]), Gaza Strip (146 sq mi [378 sq km]), Golan Heights (454 sq mi [1,176 sq km]), and East Jerusalem (27 sq mi [70 sq km]). [2]January 1. [3]Includes population of Golan Heights (31,500) and East Jerusalem. [4]Excludes Israelis in Jewish localities (pop. [1996] 138,600) in the West Bank and Gaza Strip. [5]Jewish population only. [6]Finance includes other business activities. [7]Public and community services includes education, health, social, and personal services. [8]Services includes private households with domestic personnel. [9]Includes statistical discrepancies less imputed bank service charges. [10]Includes 144,200 unemployed. [11]1993. [12]Excludes armed forces; includes Israelis in occupied territories. [13]March. [14]Urban population only. [15]1995. [16]Import figures are c.i.f. in balance of trade; import and export figures are net gross for commodities and trading partners. [17]El Al only. [18]1995–96. [19]Includes intermediate schools. [20]1992–93. [21]1994–95. [22]1995–96.

Internet resources for further information:
• **Central Bureau of Statistics (Israel)** http://www.cbs.gov.il
• **Facts about Israel** http://www.israel-mfa.gov.il/facts/index.html

Italy

Official name: Repubblica Italiana (Italian Republic).
Form of government: republic with two legislative houses (Senate [326[1]]; Chamber of Deputies [630]).
Chief of state: President.
Head of government: Prime Minister.
Capital: Rome.
Official language: Italian.
Official religion: none.
Monetary unit: 1 lira (Lit, plural lire) = 100 centesimi; valuation (Sept. 25, 1998) 1 U.S.$ = Lit 1,652; 1 £ = Lit 2,813.

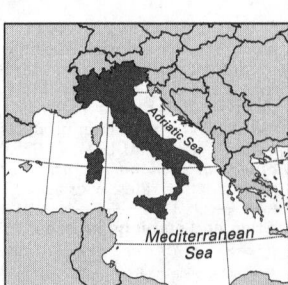

Adriatic Sea

Mediterranean Sea

Area and population		area		population
Regions Provinces[3]	Capitals	sq mi	sq km	1996[2] estimate[4]
Abruzzi	L'Aquila	4,168	10,794	1,270,591
Chieti	Chieti	999	2,587	388,276
L'Aquila	L'Aquila	1,944	5,034	303,879
Pescara	Pescara	473	1,225	292,202
Teramo	Teramo	752	1,948	286,234
Basilicata	Potenza	3,858	9,992	609,238
Matera	Matera	1,331	3,447	208,154
Potenza	Potenza	2,527	6,545	401,084
Calabria	Catanzaro	5,823	15,080	2,075,842
Catanzaro	Catanzaro	924	2,392	384,496
Cosenza	Cosenza	2,568	6,650	753,815
Crotone	Crotone	662	1,716	179,336
Reggio di Calabria	Reggio di Calabria	1,229	3,183	579,009
Vibo Valentia	Vibo Valentia	440	1,139	179,186
Campania	Naples	5,249	13,595	5,762,518
Avellino	Avellino	1,078	2,792	441,675
Benevento	Benevento	800	2,071	295,803
Caserta	Caserta	1,019	2,639	840,737
Napoli	Naples	452	1,171	3,098,397
Salerno	Salerno	1,900	4,922	1,085,906
Emilia-Romagna	Bologna	8,542	22,123	3,924,456
Bologna	Bologna	1,429	3,702	905,838
Ferrara	Ferrara	1,016	2,632	355,341
Forlì-Cesena	Forlì	969	2,510	350,158
Modena	Modena	1,039	2,690	609,723
Parma	Parma	1,332	3,449	392,018
Piacenza	Piacenza	1,000	2,589	266,363
Ravenna	Ravenna	718	1,859	349,992
Reggio nell'Emilia	Reggio nell'Emilia	885	2,292	429,865
Rimini	Rimini	154	400	265,158
Friuli-Venezia Giulia	Trieste	3,029	7,845	1,188,897
Gorizia	Gorizia	180	467	138,041
Pordenone	Pordenone	878	2,273	276,010
Trieste	Trieste	82	212	254,746
Udine	Udine	1,889	4,893	520,100
Lazio	Rome	6,642	17,203	5,202,098
Frosinone	Frosinone	1,251	3,239	489,923
Latina	Latina	869	2,251	497,632
Rieti	Rieti	1,061	2,749	150,305
Roma	Rome	2,066	5,352	3,774,987
Viterbo	Viterbo	1,395	3,612	289,251
Liguria	Genoa	2,092	5,418	1,658,513
Genova	Genoa	709	1,836	933,127
Imperia	Imperia	446	1,155	216,996
La Spezia	La Spezia	341	882	225,285
Savona	Savona	596	1,545	283,105
Lombardia	Milan	9,211	23,857	8,924,870
Bergamo	Bergamo	1,051	2,722	936,667
Brescia	Brescia	1,846	4,782	1,065,172
Como	Como	497	1,288	531,160
Cremona	Cremona	684	1,771	330,946
Lecco	Lecco	315	816	302,575
Lodi	Lodi	302	783	190,196
Mantova	Mantova	903	2,339	368,725
Milano	Milan	765	1,980	3,720,534
Pavia	Pavia	1,145	2,965	494,640
Sondrio	Sondrio	1,240	3,212	177,079
Varese	Varese	463	1,199	807,176
Marche	Ancona	3,743	9,693	1,443,172
Ancona	Ancona	749	1,940	440,239
Ascoli Piceno	Ascoli Piceno	806	2,087	365,826
Macerata	Macerata	1,071	2,774	298,295
Pesaro e Urbino	Pesaro	1,117	2,892	338,812
Molise	Campobasso	1,713	4,438	331,446
Campobasso	Campobasso	1,123	2,909	239,227
Isernia	Isernia	590	1,529	92,219
Piemonte	Turin	9,807[5]	25,399	4,288,866
Alessandria	Alessandria	1,375	3,560	433,300
Asti	Asti	583	1,511	209,798
Biella	Biella	352	913	190,728
Cuneo	Cuneo	2,665	6,903	551,373
Novara	Novara	530	1,373	339,375
Torino	Turin	2,637	6,830	2,220,724
Verbano-Cusio- Ossola	Verbania	858	2,221	161,248
Vercelli	Vercelli	806	2,088	182,320
Puglia	Bari	7,470	19,348	4,082,953
Bari	Bari	1,980	5,129	1,560,347
Brindisi	Brindisi	710	1,838	413,334
Foggia	Foggia	2,774	7,185	699,214
Lecce	Lecce	1,065	2,759	817,524
Taranto	Taranto	941	2,437	592,534
Sardegna	Cagliari	9,301	24,090	1,660,701
Cagliari	Cagliari	2,662	6,895	769,993
Nuoro	Nuoro	2,720	7,044	272,985
Oristano	Oristano	1,016	2,631	158,131
Sassari	Sassari	2,903	7,520	459,592
Sicilia (Sicily)	Palermo	9,926	25,709	5,094,735
Agrigento	Agrigento	1,175	3,042	475,669
Caltanissetta	Caltanissetta	822	2,128	282,999

Area and population (continued)				
Catania	Catania	1,371	3,552	1,088,323
Enna	Enna	989	2,562	186,145
Messina	Messina	1,254	3,248	683,315
Palermo	Palermo	1,927	4,992	1,240,252
Ragusa	Ragusa	623	1,614	297,378
Siracusa	Siracusa	814	2,109	406,566
Trapani	Trapani	951	2,462	434,088
Toscana	Florence	8,877	22,992[5]	3,523,238
Arezzo	Arezzo	1,248	3,232	316,735
Firenze	Florence	1,365	3,536	952,908
Grosseto	Grosseto	1,739	4,504	216,713
Livorno	Livorno	468	1,213	336,759
Lucca	Lucca	684	1,773	375,591
Massa-Carrara	Massa-Carrara	447	1,157	201,242
Pisa	Pisa	945	2,448	384,550
Pistoia	Pistoia	373	965	265,995
Prato	Prato	133	344	221,528
Siena	Siena	1,475	3,821	251,217
Trentino-Alto Adige	Bolzano	5,258	13,618	913,169
Bolzano-Bozen	Bolzano	2,857	7,400	451,563
Trento	Trento	2,401	6,218	461,606
Umbria	Perugia	3,265	8,456	825,910
Perugia	Perugia	2,446	6,334	602,276
Terni	Terni	819	2,122	223,634
Valle d'Aosta	Aosta	1,259	3,262	118,723
Veneto	Venice	7,090	18,364	4,433,060
Belluno	Belluno	1,420	3,678	211,996
Padova	Padova	827	2,142	835,029
Rovigo	Rovigo	691	1,789	245,314
Treviso	Treviso	956	2,477	757,864
Venezia	Venice	950	2,460	817,597
Verona	Verona	1,195	3,096	801,363
Vicenza	Vicenza	1,051	2,722	763,897
TOTAL		116,324[6]	301,277[6]	57,332,996

Demography

Population (1998): 57,650,000.
Density (1998): persons per sq mi 495.6, persons per sq km 191.4.
Urban-rural (1996[2]): urban 67.0%; rural 33.0%.
Sex distribution (1996): male 48.62%; female 51.38%.
Age breakdown (1996[2]): under 15, 14.9%; 15–29, 21.9%; 30–44, 21.7%; 45–59, 19.0%; 60–74, 15.8%; 75 and over, 6.7%.
Population projection: (2000) 57,903,000; (2010) 56,484,000.
Doubling time: not applicable; population stable.
Ethnolinguistic composition (1983): Italian 94.1%; Sardinian 2.7%; Rhaetian 1.3%; other 1.9%.
Religious affiliation (1996): Roman Catholic 81.7%; nonreligious 13.6%; Muslim 1.2%; other 3.5%.
Major cities (1996[2, 4]): Rome 2,654,187; Milan 1,306,494; Naples 1,050,234; Turin 923,106; Palermo 689,301; Genoa 659,116; Bologna 386,491; Florence 383,594; Catania 341,623; Bari 336,560; Venice 298,915.
National origin (1991): Italian 99.3%; foreign-born 0.7%, of which European 0.3%, African 0.2%, Asian 0.1%, other 0.1%.
Mobility (1991). Population living in the same commune as in 1986: 93.3%; another commune, same province 3.4%; different province 2.5%; abroad 0.8%.
Households. Average household size (1991) 2.7; composition of households: 1 person 19.5%, 2 persons 21.9%, 3 persons 25.2%, 4 persons 21.4%, 5 or more persons 12.0%. Family households (1991): 15,538,335 (73.8%); non-family 5,527,105 (26.2%), of which one-person 19.5%.
Immigration (1993): immigrants 100,401, from Europe 54.2%, of which EC countries 17.6%; Asia 16.4%; Africa 15.3%; Western Hemisphere 13.4%.

Vital statistics

Birth rate per 1,000 population (1996): 9.2 (world avg. 25.0); (1994) legitimate 90.2%; illegitimate 9.8%.
Death rate per 1,000 population (1996): 9.5 (world avg. 9.3).
Natural increase rate per 1,000 population (1996): –0.3 (world avg. 15.7).
Total fertility rate (avg. births per childbearing woman; 1996): 1.2.
Marriage rate per 1,000 population (1996): 4.7.
Divorce rate per 1,000 population (1994): 0.5.
Life expectancy at birth (1993): male 74.1 years; female 80.5 years.
Major causes of death per 100,000 population (1993): diseases of the circulatory system 423.7; malignant neoplasms (cancers) 270.5; diseases of the respiratory system 56.2; accidents and violence 49.8; diseases of the digestive system 49.8.

Social indicators

Educational attainment (1995). Percentage of labour force age 15 and over having: basic literacy or primary education 40.4%; secondary 30.5%; post-secondary technical training 5.1%; some college 19.2%; college degree 4.3%.
Quality of working life. Average workweek (1995): 37.0 hours. Annual rate per 100,000 workers (1988) for: injury or accident 3,697; death 5.7. Percentage of labour force insured for damages or income loss (1992) resulting from: injury 100%; permanent disability 100%; death 100%. Number of working days lost to labour stoppages per 1,000 workers (1995): 35. Average duration of journey to work: n.a. Rate per 1,000 workers of discouraged (unemployed no longer seeking work; 1990): 1.1.
Material well-being. Rate per 1,000 of population possessing (1995): telephone 434; automobile 550; television 436.
Social participation. Eligible voters participating in last national election (April 21, 1996): 91.0%. Trade union membership in total workforce (1990): c. 28%.
Social deviance (1995). Offense rate per 100,000 population for: murder 2.5; rape 3.2; assault 210.4; theft, including burglary and housebreaking 3,274.
Access to services (1991). Nearly 100% of dwellings have access to electricity, a safe water supply, and toilet facilities.

Leisure (1992). Favourite leisure activities (as percentage of household spending on culture): sporting events 17.8%; cinema 16.3%; theatre 14.0%.

National economy

Gross national product (1996): U.S.$1,140,484,000,000 (U.S.$19,880 per capita).

Structure of gross domestic product and labour force

	1996		1995	
	in value (Lit '000,000,000)	% of total value	labour force	% of labour force
Agriculture	53,302	2.9	1,490,000	6.6
Mining	80,154	4.3 }		
Manufacturing	302,074	16.4	4,622,000	20.3
Construction	92,943	5.0	1,615,000	7.1
Public utilities	107,653	5.8	257,000	1.1
Transp. and commun.	118,754	6.4	1,061,000	4.7
Trade	345,357	18.7	4,221,000	18.6
Finance	90,051	4.9	733,000	3.2
Pub. admin., defense	411,507[7]	22.3[7]	4,138,000	18.2
Services	244,895	13.3	1,873,000	8.2
Other	[7]	[7]	2,724,000[8]	12.0[8]
TOTAL	1,846,690	100.0	22,734,000	100.0

Budget (1995). Revenue: Lit 472,066,000,000,000 (income taxes 41.0%, of which individual 35.1%, corporate 5.9%; value-added and excise taxes 30.6%). Expenditures: Lit 696,860,000,000,000 (debt service 27.5%; social security 18.4%; education 9.1%; transportation 4.7%; defense 2.8%).
Public debt (1996): U.S.$1,440,200,000,000.
Tourism (1996): receipts U.S.$28,245,200,000; expenditures U.S.$12,681,500,000.

Manufacturing, mining, and construction enterprises (1993)

	no. of enterprises	no. of employees[9]	hourly wages as a % of avg. of all wages	annual value added (Lit '000,000,000)
Manufacturing				
Machinery (nonelectrical)	4,560	367,990	...	28,774
Electrical machinery	3,089	316,727	...	23,639
Food products	2,734	219,970	...	22,116
Industrial chemicals	1,215	199,279	...	21,444
Transport equipment	1,180	301,859	...	16,007
Textiles	3,514	215,387	...	14,335
Pottery, ceramics, and glass	2,312	159,138	...	13,322
Rubber and plastic products	1,677	112,839	...	9,271
Wearing apparel	4,063	185,072	...	8,592
Printing, publishing	1,383	90,998	...	8,588
Metal products	993	114,301	...	8,548
Paper and paper products	793	63,347	...	5,494
Petroleum and gas	23	9,478	...	3,898
Mining and quarrying	384	24,952	...	4,998
Construction	7,659	1,642,000	...	86,824

Production (metric tons except as noted). Agriculture, forestry, fishing (1997): sugar beets 13,000,000, grapes 9,459,000, corn (maize) 8,500,000, wheat 7,610,000, tomatoes 4,000,000, olives 2,452,000, potatoes 2,120,000, apples 2,071,000, oranges 1,973,000, peaches and nectarines 1,742,000, rice 1,424,000, barley 1,170,000; livestock (number of live animals) 10,531,000 sheep, 7,964,000 pigs, 7,018,000 cattle, 130,000,000 chickens; roundwood (1995) 9,802,000 cu m; fish catch (1995) 609,768. Mining and quarrying (1995): rock salt 3,430,374; feldspar 2,199,315; potash 1,438,850[10]; barite 85,661; zinc 43,669; lead 22,658. Manufacturing (1995): cement 33,714,914; crude steel 27,635,287; pig iron 11,677,789; glass 3,981,104; sulfuric acid 2,161,796; textiles 1,172,916; wine 62,618,000 hectolitres[10]; beer 10,616,173 hectolitres; olive oil 6,290,000 hectolitres[10]; 6,995,818 washing machines; 5,908,224 refrigerators; 2,913,468 motorized road vehicles, of which 1,372,034 automobiles, 824,597 motorcycles 245,527 trucks and buses; 2,779,827 colour televisions. Construction (1995): residential 77,162,182 cu m; commercial 64,729,419 cu m.

Service enterprises (1995)

	no. of enterprises[11]	no. of employees	hourly wage as a % of all wages	annual value added (Lit '000,000,000)
Public utilities	379	257,000	...	102,495
Transportation Communications }	2,508	1,061,000	...	115,512
Finance	...	733,000	...	88,363
Wholesale and retail trade	9,173	4,221,000	...	327,636
Pub. admin., services	...	4,138,000	...	208,888

Energy production (consumption): electricity (kW-hr; 1994) 231,783,000,000 (269,382,000,000); coal (metric tons; 1994) 267,000 (16,672,000); crude petroleum (barrels; 1994) 33,422,000 (582,644,000); petroleum products (metric tons; 1994) 83,049,000 (89,500,000); natural gas (cu m; 1994) 20,209,000,000 (48,326,000,000).
Population economically active (1995): total 22,734,000; activity rate of total population 39.7% (participation rates: ages 15–64, 57.3% female 37.3%; unemployed 11.3%).

Price and earnings indexes (1990 = 100)

	1991	1992	1993	1994	1995	1996	1997
Consumer price index	106.3	111.8	116.8	121.5	127.8	132.8	135.5
Earnings index	109.8	115.4	119.8	124.0	127.8	131.9	136.6

Household income and expenditure (1995). Average household size 2.7; average annual income per household (1984) Lit 19,692,000 (U.S.$11,208); sources of income (1991): salaries and wages 41.7%, property income and sel-employment 38.0%, transfer payments 20.3%; expenditure (1994): food and beverages 21.7%, housing 19.5%, transportation and communications 16.8%, recreation and education 6.4%.

Financial aggregates

	1992	1993	1994	1995	1996	1997[12]
Exchange rate, Lit per:						
U.S. dollar	1,232.4	1,573.7	1,612.4	1,628.9	1,530.6	1,759.5
£	2,175.8	2,363.7	2,469.6	2,571.2	2,690.8	2,864.5
SDR	2,022.4	2,340.5	2,379.2	2,355.7	2,200.9	2,399.2
International reserves (U.S.$)						
Total (excl. gold; '000,000)	27,643	27,545	32,265	34,905	45,948	51,096
SDRs ('000,000)	238	241	125	531[13]	29	55
Reserve pos. in IMF ('000,000)	2,439	2,164	2,033	1,963	1,855	1,728
Foreign exchange ('000,000)	24,966	25,140	30,107	32,942	44,064	49,318
Gold ('000,000 fine troy oz)	66.67	66.67	66.67	66.67	66.67	66.67
% world reserves	7.1	7.3	7.3	7.3	7.3	7.5
Interest and prices						
Central bank discount (%)	12.00	8.00	7.50	9.00	7.50	6.25[14]
Govt. bond yield (%)	13.67	11.21	10.57	11.98	8.93	6.19[14]
Industrial share prices (1990 = 100)	70.5	83.5	104.1	95.4	96.0	138.3[14]
Balance of payments (U.S.$'000,000)						
Balance of visible trade	3,088	32,825	35,497	44,082	60,822	...
Imports, f.o.b.	−175,067	−136,328	−154,308	−187,254	−190,021	...
Exports, f.o.b.	178,155	169,153	189,805	231,336	250,843	...
Balance of invisibles	−31,082	−21,763	−19,875	−18,378	−19,782	...
Balance of payments, current account	−27,994	11,062	15,622	25,704	−41,040	...

Land use (1994): forest 23.0%; pasture 15.4%; agriculture 37.9%; other 23.7%.

Foreign trade

Balance of trade (current prices)

	1992	1993	1994	1995	1996	1997
Lit '000,000,000	2,229	50,789	50,957	65,841	67,775	51,609
% of total	0.5%	10.6%	9.1%	9.6%	9.6%	6.8%

Imports (1994): Lit 332,409,083,000,000 (machinery and transport equipment 30.7%, of which transport equipment 11.3%, precision machinery 5.7%; chemicals 16.2%; metal 9.9%; food 6.4%; petroleum 4.5%; textiles 4.0%). *Major import sources:* Germany 19.2%; France 13.9%; U.K. 6.1%; The Netherlands 5.5%; Belgium-Luxembourg 4.8%; U.S. 4.8%.
Exports (1995): Lit 376,785,707,000,000 (machinery and transport equipment 42.0%, of which transport equipment 11.2%, electrical machinery 5.2%, precision machinery 3.7%; chemicals 10.3%; textiles 7.8%; wearing apparel 7.3%, of which shoes 2.6%; metal and processed metal 6.7%). *Major export destinations:* Germany 18.9%; France 13.1%; U.S. 7.2%; U.K. 6.2%.

Transport and communications

Transport. Railroads (1995): length 9,944 mi, 16,003 km; passenger-mi 30,882,000,000, passenger-km 49,700,000,000; short ton-mi cargo 28,499,000,000, metric ton-km cargo 41,608,000,000. Roads (1995): total length 195,334 mi, 314,360 km (paved 100%). Vehicles (1995): passenger cars 31,700,000; trucks and buses 5,127,000. Merchant marine (1994): vessels (100 gross tons and over) 1,966; total deadweight tonnage 7,149,453. Air transport (1993): passenger-mi 18,429,000,000, passenger-km 29,658,600,000; short ton-mi cargo 914,300,000, metric ton-km cargo 1,334,900,000; airports (1997) 34.

Communications

Medium	date	unit	number	units per 1,000 persons
Daily newspapers	1995	circulation	7,237,000	126
Radio	1994	receivers	45,350,000	790
Television	1995	receivers	25,000,000	436
Telephones	1995	main lines	24,854,000	434
Cellular telephones	1995	subscribers	3,864,000	67.4
Facsimile machines	1995	units	202,000	3.5
Personal computers	1995	units	4,800,000	83.4

Education and health

Literacy (1991): total population age 14 and over literate 47,376,663 (97.7%); males literate 22,897,907 (98.8%); females literate 24,478,756 (97.1%).

Education (1995–96)

	schools	teachers	students	student/ teacher ratio
Primary (age 6–10)	20,442	289,055	2,825,838	9.8
Secondary (age 11–18)	9,278	214,861	1,907,024	8.9
Voc., teacher tr.	7,888	313,001	2,661,760	8.5
Higher[15, 16]	48	58,874	1,601,873	27.2

Health (1993): physicians 207,319 (1 per 193 persons); hospital beds 380,423 (1 per 147 persons); infant mortality rate per 1,000 live births (1996) 6.0.
Food (1995): daily per capita caloric intake 3,458 (vegetable products 74%, animal products 26%); 137% of FAO recommended minimum requirement.

Military

Total active duty personnel (1997): 325,150 (army 57.9%, navy 13.5%, air force 19.6%, central staff 9.0%). *Military expenditure as percentage of GNP* (1995): 1.8% (world 2.8%); per capita expenditure U.S.$338.

[1]Includes 11 nonelective seats. [2]January 1. [3]Six provinces were created in 1992. [4]Resident population only. [5]Detail does not add to total given because of rounding. [6]The total area for Italy, per the latest survey, is 301,323 sq km (116,341 sq mi). [7]Pub. admin., defense includes other. [8]Unemployed. [9]Total number of persons engaged. [10]1993. [11]Enterprises with 20 or more persons engaged. [12]August. [13]November. [14]July. [15]Universities only. [16]1994–95.

Internet resources for further information:
• Tavole statistiche http://www.istat.it

Jamaica

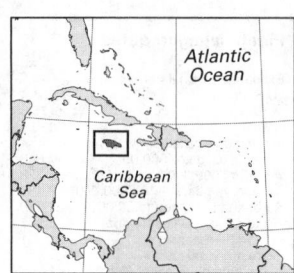

Official name: Jamaica.
Form of government: constitutional monarchy with two legislative houses (Senate [21]; House of Representatives [60]).
Chief of state: British Monarch represented by Governor-General.
Head of government: Prime Minister.
Capital: Kingston.
Official language: English.
Monetary unit: 1 Jamaica dollar (J$) = 100 cents; valuation (Sept. 25, 1998) 1 U.S.$ = J$35.80; 1 £ = J$60.95.

Area and population		area		population
				1994[1]
Parishes	Capitals	sq mi	sq km	estimate
Clarendon	May Pen	462	1,196	222,500
Hanover	Lucea	174	450	66,600
Kingston	[2]	8	22	[3]
Manchester	Mandeville	321	830	173,100
Portland	Port Antonio	314	814	78,500
Saint Andrew	[2]	166	431	697,000
Saint Ann	Saint Ann's Bay	468	1,213	154,500
Saint Catherine	Spanish Town	460	1,192	370,600
Saint Elizabeth	Black River	468	1,212	146,600
Saint James	Montego Bay	230	595	166,000
Saint Mary	Port Maria	236	611	113,700
Saint Thomas	Morant Bay	287	743	88,900
Trelawny	Falmouth	338	875	74,100
Westmoreland	Savanna-la-Mar	312	807	130,500
TOTAL		4,244	10,991	2,482,600

Demography

Population (1998): 2,554,000.
Density (1998): persons per sq mi 601.8, persons per sq km 232.4.
Urban-rural (1991): urban 50.2%; rural 49.8%.
Sex distribution (1995): male 49.74%; female 50.26%.
Age breakdown (1995): under 15, 32.3%; 15–29, 28.7%; 30–44, 19.7%; 45–59, 9.8%; 60 and over, 9.5%.
Population projection: (2000) 2,589,000; (2010) 2,814,000.
Doubling time: 39 years.
Ethnic composition (1982): black 74.7%; mixed black 12.8%; East Indian 1.3%; other 11.2%, of which not stated 9.5%.
Religious affiliation (1995): Protestant 39.0%, of which Pentecostal 10.5%, Seventh-day Adventist 6.1%, Baptist 5.3%; Roman Catholic 10.4%; Anglican 3.7%; other (including nonreligious) 46.9%[4].
Major cities (1991): Kingston 103,771[5] (metropolitan area 587,798); Spanish Town 92,383; Portmore 90,138; Montego Bay 83,446; May Pen 46,785.

Vital statistics

Birth rate per 1,000 population (1995): 23.2 (world avg. 25.0).
Death rate per 1,000 population (1995): 5.0 (world avg. 9.3).
Natural increase rate per 1,000 population (1995): 18.2 (world avg. 15.7).
Total fertility rate (avg. births per childbearing woman; 1995): 3.0.
Marriage rate per 1,000 population (1994): 6.1.
Life expectancy at birth (1990–95): male 71.4 years; female 75.8 years.
Major causes of death per 100,000 population (1991): diseases of the circulatory system 189.4; malignant neoplasms (cancers) 84.1; endocrine and metabolic disorders 51.3; diseases of the respiratory system 30.1.

National economy

Budget (1995–96). Revenue J$39,642,300,000 (tax revenue 85.6%, of which consumption taxes 32.3%, income taxes 30.6%, stamp duties 3.9%; nontax revenue 14.4%). Expenditures: J$48,334,200,000 (current expenditure 62.8%, of which debt interest 22.4%).
Public debt (external, outstanding; 1996): U.S.$3,183,000,000.
Production (metric tons except as noted). Agriculture, forestry, fishing (1996): sugarcane 2,624,000, yams 240,371, vegetables 218,200, citrus fruits 130,000, bananas 130,000, coconuts 115,000, pumpkins, squash, and gourds 42,000, plantains 34,769, sweet potatoes 33,000, cabbages 33,000, carrots 26,000, tomatoes 24,000; livestock (number of live animals) 440,000 goats, 420,000 cattle, 180,000 pigs; roundwood 354,700 cu m; fish catch (1995) 13,617. Mining and quarrying (1996): crude bauxite 3,924,800; alumina 3,199,500; (1995) gypsum 208,000. Manufacturing (value added in constant 1991–95 prices, J$'000,000; 1995): machinery and equipment 593.6; food processing 580.3; petroleum products 351.3; rubber and plastic products 324.1; textiles and clothing 257.0; tobacco and tobacco products 255.2; metal and nonmetallic products 223.6. Construction (1995): residential units completed 7,067[6]; factory space completed 6,989 sq m[7]. Energy production (consumption): electricity (kW-hr; 1994) 3,927,000,000 (3,927,000,000); coal, none (none); crude petroleum (barrels; 1994) none (5,893,000); petroleum products (metric tons; 1994) 825,000 (2,748,000); natural gas, none (none).
Population economically active (1995): total 1,150,000; activity rate of total population 46.0% (participation rates: ages 14 and over 58.7%; female 46.3%; unemployed 16.2%).

Price and earnings indexes (1990 = 100)							
	1991	1992	1993	1994	1995	1996	1997
Consumer price index	151.1	267.8	327.0	441.6	529.5	669.3	734.0
Earnings index	...	...	...	...	...	...	...

Gross national product (1996): U.S.$4,066,000,000 (U.S.$1,600 per capita).

Structure of gross domestic product and labour force				
	1995			
	in value J$'000,000	% of total value	labour force	% of labour force
Agriculture	15,323.1	9.4	223,200	19.4
Mining	11,711.7	7.2	7,000	0.6
Manufacturing	28,774.6	17.7	104,700	9.1
Construction	20,880.6	12.8	76,000	6.6
Public utilities	3,633.7	2.2	6,800	0.6
Transp. and commun.	13,918.9	8.6	44,500	3.9
Trade	38,505.0	23.7	201,400	17.5
Pub. admin., defense	13,960.2	8.6	}	
Finance, real estate	21,501.3	13.2	298,700	26.0
Services	6,454.5	4.0	}	
Other	−12,094.8[8]	−7.4[8]	187,800[9]	16.3[9]
TOTAL	162,568.8	100.0	1,150,000[10]	100.0

Household income and expenditure. Average household size (1991) 4.2; average annual income per household (1988) J$8,356 (U.S.$1,525); sources of income (1989): wages and salaries 66.1%, self-employment 19.3%, transfers 14.6%; expenditure (1988)[11]: food and beverages 55.6%, housing 7.9%, fuel and other household supplies 7.4%, health care 7.0%, transportation 6.4%.
Tourism (1995): receipts U.S.$1,069,000,000; expenditures U.S.$148,000,000.

Foreign trade[12]

Balance of trade (current prices)						
	1991	1992	1993	1994	1995	1996
U.S.$'000,000	−654	−636	−1,121	−957.7	−1,342.6	−1,527.3
% of total	22.2%	23.2%	34.9%	28.7%	31.9%	35.6%

Imports (1996): U.S.$2,906,679,000 (raw materials 55.7%, of which fuels 15.4%; consumer goods 25.7%, of which food 7.6%; capital goods 18.6%, of which machinery and apparatus 9.5%). *Major import sources:* U.S. 60.2%; U.K. 4.3%; Japan 4.1%; Venezuela 3.2%; Mexico 3.1%; France 2.8%.
Exports (1996): U.S.$1,379,421,000 (crude materials 49.7%; food 20.2%; beverages and tobacco 3.5%; chemicals 3.3%; machinery and transport equipment 2.3%; manufactured goods 1.4%). *Major export destinations:* U.S. 42.4%; U.K. 11.1%; Canada 9.2%; Norway 5.9%; France 4.6%; Germany 4.2%.

Transport and communications

Transport. Railroads (1991): route length 129 mi; 208 km; passenger-mi 12,127,000[7], passenger-km 19,516,000[7]; short ton-mi cargo 1,700,000, metric ton-km cargo 2,482,000. Roads (1995): total length 11,600 mi, 18,600 km (paved 71%). Vehicles (1994–95): passenger cars 86,791; trucks and buses 41,312. Air transport (1996)[13]: passenger-mi 1,204,001,000, passenger-km 1,937,655,000; short ton-mi cargo 136,014,000, metric ton-km cargo 198,577,000; airports (1997) with scheduled flights 4.

Communications				units
				per 1,000
Medium	date	unit	number	persons
Daily newspapers	1995	circulation	160,000	65
Radio	1996	receivers	1,859,000	739
Television	1995	receivers	773,000	306
Telephones	1995	main lines	291,800	116
Cellular telephones	1995	subscribers	45,200	18
Facsimile machines	1995	units	1,600	0.6

Education and health

Educational attainment (1982). Percentage of population age 25 and over having: no formal schooling 3.2%; some primary education 79.8%; some secondary 15.0%; complete secondary and higher 2.0%. *Literacy* (1995): total population age 15 and over literate 85%; males literate 80.8%; females literate 89.1%.

Education (1994–95)				student/
	schools	teachers	students	teacher ratio
Primary (age 6–11)[14]	788[15]	11,283	319,298	28.3
Secondary (age 12–16)	126	8,377	207,035	24.7
Voc., teacher tr.	18	950	15,898	16.7
Higher	15[16]	1,047[17]	24,200	17.9[17]

Health (1995): physicians 417[18] (1 per 6,043 persons); hospital beds (1993) 5,023 (1 per 492 persons); infant mortality rate per 1,000 live births 28.6.
Food (1995): daily per capita caloric intake 2,647 (vegetable products 84%, animal products 16%); 118% of FAO recommended minimum requirement.

Military

Total active duty personnel (1997): 3,320 (army 90.4%; coast guard 4.5%; air force 5.1%). Military expenditure as percentage of GNP (1995): 0.8% (world 2.8%); per capita expenditure U.S.$11.

[1]January 1. [2]The parishes of Kingston and Saint Andrew are jointly administered from the Half Way Tree section of Saint Andrew. [3]Kingston included with Saint Andrew. [4]Includes c. 0.7% Rastafarian. [5]City of Kingston is coextensive with Kingston parish. [6]51% public sector. [7]1990. [8]Less imputed service charges. [9]Includes 186,700 unemployed. [10]Detail does not add to total given because of rounding. [11]Weights of consumer price index components. [12]Import figures are c.i.f. [13]Air Jamaica only. [14]Includes lower-secondary students at all-age schools. [15]1991–92. [16]1988–89. [17]1987–88. [18]Public health only.

Internet resources for further information:
• Embassy of Jamaica
  http://www.caribbean-online.com/jamaica/embassy/washdc/

Japan

Official name: Nihon (Japan).
Form of government: constitutional monarchy with a national Diet consisting of two legislative houses (House of Councillors [252]; House of Representatives [500]).
Chief of state: Emperor.
Head of government: Prime Minister.
Capital: Tokyo.
Official language: Japanese.
Official religion: none.
Monetary unit: 1 yen (¥) = 100 sen; valuation (Sept. 25, 1998) 1 U.S.$ = ¥135.37; 1 £ = ¥230.47.

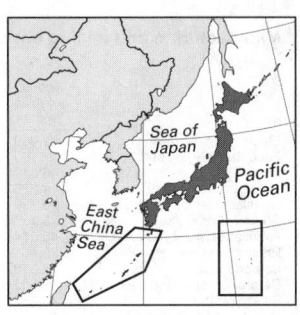

Area and population

Regions Prefectures	Capitals	area sq mi	area sq km	population 1996 estimate
Chūbu				
Aichi	Nagoya	1,984	5,139	6,897,481
Fukui	Fukui	1,619	4,192	828,971
Gifu	Gifu	4,091	10,596	2,106,718
Ishikawa	Kanazawa	1,621	4,198	1,182,300
Nagano	Nagano	5,245	13,585	2,206,290
Niigata	Niigata	4,857	12,579	2,492,352
Shizuoka	Shizuoka	3,001	7,773	3,749,247
Toyama	Toyama	1,642	4,252	1,125,618
Yamanashi	Kōfu	1,723	4,463	886,010
Chūgoku				
Hiroshima	Hiroshima	3,269	8,467	2,882,074
Okayama	Okayama	2,738	7,092	1,952,610
Shimane	Matsue	2,559[1]	6,629[1]	769,941
Tottori	Tottori	1,349[1]	3,494[1]	614,469
Yamaguchi	Yamaguchi	2,358	6,107	1,550,982
Hokkaidō				
Hokkaidō (Territory)	Sapporo	32,247	83,520	5,698,946
Kantō				
Chiba	Chiba	1,989	5,151	5,823,934
Gumma	Maebashi	2,454	6,356	2,011,046
Ibaraki	Mito	2,353	6,094	2,971,524
Kanagawa	Yokohama	928	2,403	8,281,848
Saitama	Urawa	1,467	3,799	6,809,303
Tochigi	Utsunomiya	2,476	6,414	1,992,807
Kinki				
Hyōgo	Kōbe	3,236	8,381	5,410,170
Mie	Tsu	2,231	5,778	1,848,617
Nara	Nara	1,425	3,692	1,438,618
Shiga	Ōtsu	1,551	4,016	1,298,444
Wakayama	Wakayama	1,824	4,725	1,079,579
Kyūshū				
Fukuoka	Fukuoka	1,916	4,963	4,951,909
Kagoshima	Kagoshima	3,539	9,167	1,793,350
Kumamoto	Kumamoto	2,860	7,408	1,861,916
Miyazaki	Miyazaki	2,986	7,735	1,177,436
Nagasaki	Nagasaki	1,588	4,113	1,541,327
Ōita	Ōita	2,447	6,338	1,230,268
Saga	Saga	942	2,440	885,566
Ryukyu				
Okinawa	Naha	871	2,255	1,282,705
Shikoku				
Ehime	Matsuyama	2,190	5,672	1,505,129
Kagawa	Takamatsu	727	1,883	1,027,839
Kōchi	Kōchi	2,744	7,107	815,003
Tokushima	Tokushima	1,601	4,146	831,922
Tohoku				
Akita	Akita	4,484[2]	11,613[2]	1,209,970
Aomori	Aomori	3,714[2]	9,619[2]	1,482,657
Fukushima	Fukushima	5,322	13,784	2,136,181
Iwate	Morioka	5,898	15,277	1,419,595
Miyagi	Sendai	2,815	7,292	2,338,370
Yamagata	Yamagata	3,601	9,327	1,255,863
Metropolis				
Tōkyō[3]	Tokyo	836	2,166	11,771,951
Urban prefectures				
Kyōto[4]	Kyōto	1,781	4,613	2,631,374
Ōsaka[4]	Ōsaka	722	1,869	8,803,792
TOTAL		145,883[5,6]	377,835[5,6]	125,864,022

Demography

Population (1998): 126,398,000.
Density (1998): persons per sq mi 866.4, persons per sq km 334.5.
Urban-rural (1995): urban 77.6%; rural 22.4%.
Sex distribution (1996[7]): male 49.03%; female 50.97%.
Age breakdown (1996[7]): under 15, 15.8%; 15–29, 21.8%; 30–44, 19.6%; 45–59, 21.9%; 60–74, 15.0%; 75 and over, 5.9%.
Population projection: (2000) 126,926,000; (2010) 127,657,000.
Doubling time: not applicable; doubling time exceeds 100 years.
Composition by nationality (1997[8]): Japanese 99.1%; Korean 0.5%; Chinese 0.2%; other 0.2%.
Place of birth (1995): 99.3% native-born; 0.7% foreign-born (mainly Korean).
Immigration (1995[8]): permanent immigrants/registered aliens admitted 1,354,011, from North and South Korea 50.0%, Taiwan, Hong Kong, and China 16.1%, Brazil 11.8%, Philippines 6.3%, United States 3.2%, Peru 2.6%, Thailand 1.0%, United Kingdom 0.9%, Vietnam 0.6%, Iran 0.6%, Canada 0.5%, Indonesia 0.5%, other 5.9%.
Major cities (1995): Tokyo 11,771,819; Yokohama 3,307,408; Ōsaka 2,602,352; Nagoya 2,152,258; Sapporo 1,756,968; Kyōto 1,463,601; Kōbe 1,423,830; Fukuoka 1,284,741; Kawasaki 1,202,811; Hiroshima 1,108,868; Kita-Kyūshū 1,019,522.

Other principal cities (1995)

	population		population		population
Akashi	287,613	Kakogawa	260,588	Okayama	616,056
Akita	312,035	Kanazawa	453,977	Okazaki	322,615
Amagasaki	488,574	Kashiwa	317,752	Ōmiya	433,768
Aomori	294,165	Kasugai	277,579	Ōtsu	276,331
Asahikawa	360,569	Kawagoe	323,345	Sagamihara	570,594
Chiba	856,882	Kawaguchi	448,801	Sakai	802,965
Fujisawa	368,636	Kōchi	322,077	Sendai	971,263
Fukui	255,601	Koriyama	324,831	Shimonoseki	259,791
Fukushima	285,745	Koshigaya	298,285	Shizuoka	474,089
Fukuyama	374,510	Kumamoto	650,322	Suita	342,794
Funabashi	540,814	Kurashiki	422,824	Takamatsu	330,997
Gifu	407,145	Machida	360,418	Takatsuki	362,259
Hachiōji	503,320	Maebashi	284,780	Tokorozawa	320,448
Hakodate	298,868	Matsudo	461,489	Tokushima	268,712
Hamamatsu	561,568	Matsuyama	460,870	Toyama	325,303
Higashi-Ōsaka	517,228	Miyazaki	300,054	Toyohashi	352,913
Himeji	470,986	Morioka	286,478	Toyonaka	398,912
Hirakata	400,130	Nagano	358,512	Toyota	341,038
Hiratsuka	253,818	Nagasaki	438,724	Urawa	453,300
Ibaraki	258,237	Naha	301,928	Utsunomiya	435,446
Ichihara	277,080	Nara	359,234	Wakayama	393,951
Ichikawa	440,527	Neyagawa	258,440	Yamagata	254,485
Ichinomiya	267,359	Niigata	494,785	Yao	276,658
Iwaki	360,497	Nishinomiya	390,388	Yokkaichi	285,777
Kagoshima	546,294	Ōita	426,981	Yokosuka	432,202

Religious affiliation (1995): Shintō and related religions 93.1%[9]; Buddhism 69.6%[9]; Christian 1.2%; other 8.1%.
Households (1995). Total households 43,447,100; average household size 2.9; composition of households 1 person 24.7%, 2 persons 23.1%, 3 persons 18.6%, 4 persons 19.0%, 5 persons 8.2%, 6 or more persons 6.4%. Family households 32,545,700 (74.9%); nonfamily 10,901,400 (25.1%), of which 1 person 10,768,000 (24.7%).

Type of household (1993)

Total number of occupied dwelling units: 40,835,000

	number of dwellings	percentage of total
by kind of dwelling		
exclusively for living	38,518,000	94.3
mixed use	169,000	0.4
combined with nondwelling	2,148,000	5.3
detached house	24,183,000	59.2
apartment building	14,253,000	34.9
tenement (substandard or overcrowded building)	2,205,000	5.4
other	194,000	0.5
by legal tenure of householder		
owned	24,410,000	59.8
rented	15,721,000	38.5
other	704,000	1.7
by kind of amenities		
flush toilet	30,524,000	74.7
bathroom	38,196,000	93.5
by year of construction		
prior to 1945	2,146,000	5.4
1945–70	9,700,000	24.3
1971–80	12,548,000	31.5
1981–87	9,258,000	23.2
1988–93	6,224,000	15.6

Mobility (October 1990). Population living in same residence as in October 1985, 74.7%; different residence, same town 9.5%; same prefecture 7.9%; different prefecture 7.6%; different country 0.3%.

Vital statistics

Birth rate per 1,000 population (1995): 9.5 (world avg. 25.0); (1985) legitimate 99.0%; illegitimate 1.0%.
Death rate per 1,000 population (1995): 7.4 (world avg. 9.3).
Natural increase rate per 1,000 population (1995): 2.1 (world avg. 15.7).
Total fertility rate (avg. births per childbearing woman; 1995): 1.4.
Marriage rate per 1,000 population (1995): 6.4; median age at first marriage men 28.5 years, women 26.2 years.
Divorce rate per 1,000 population (1995): 1.6.
Life expectancy at birth (1995): male 76.4 years; female 82.8 years.
Major causes of death per 100,000 population (1994): circulatory diseases 239.1, of which cerebrovascular disease 96.9; malignant neoplasms (cancers) 196.4; pneumonia and bronchitis 68.4; accidents and adverse effects 29.1, of which suicide 16.9; nephritis, nephrotic syndrome, and nephrosis 15.1; cirrhosis of the liver 13.3; diabetes mellitus 8.8.

Social indicators

Educational attainment (1990). Percentage of population age 25 years and over having: primary education 34.3%; secondary 44.5%; postsecondary 21.2%.

Distribution of income (1995)

percentage of average household income by quintile				
1	2	3	4	5 (highest)
11.5	15.5	19.1	22.7	31.2

Quality of working life. Average workweek (1995): 38.2 hours. Annual rate of industrial deaths per 100,000 workers (1994): 2.6. Proportion of labour force insured for damages or income loss resulting from injury, permanent disability, and death (1991): 50.1%. Average man-days lost to labour stoppages per 1,000,000 workdays (1995): 1.2. Average duration of journey to work (1988)[10]: 26.8 minutes (1983; 26.7% private automobile. 67.4% public

transportation, 5.5% taxi, 0.4% other). Rate per 1,000 workers of discouraged (unemployed no longer seeking work: 1993): 87.8.

Access to services (1989). Proportion of households having access to: gas supply 64.6%; safe public water supply 94.0%; public sewage collection 89.4%.

Social participation. Eligible voters participating in last national election (October 1996): 59.6%. Population 15 years and over participating in social-service activities on a voluntary basis (1991): 26.3%. Trade union membership in total workforce (1995): 18.9%.

Social deviance (1994). Offense rate per 100,000 population for: homicide 1.0; rape 1.3; robbery 2.2; larceny and theft 1,246.6. Incidence in general population of: alcoholism, n.a.; drug and substance abuse, n.a. Rate of suicide per 100,000 population: 16.7.

Leisure/use of personal time

Discretionary daily activities (1991)
(Population age 15 years and over)

	weekly average hrs./min.
Total discretionary daily time	5:56[7]
of which	
Hobbies and amusements	0:36
Sports	0:11
Learning (except schoolwork)	0:12
Social activities	0:05
Associations	0:29
Radio, television, newspapers, and magazines	2:23
Rest and relaxation	1:21
Other activities	0:21

Major leisure activities (1991)
(Population age 15 years and over)

	percentage of participation		
	male	female	total
Hobbies and amusements	93.0	90.8	91.9
Sports	84.2	72.1	78.0
Light exercises	30.8	34.1	32.0
Swimming	27.1	20.8	23.8
Bowling	33.0	23.1	27.9
Learning (except schoolwork)	36.3	37.0	36.7
Travel			
Domestic	72.7	68.3	70.4
Foreign	10.4	7.6	9.0

Material well-being (1994). Households possessing: automobile 79.7%; telephone, virtually 100%; colour television receiver 99.3%; refrigerator 98.9%; air conditioner 72.3%; washing machine 99.4%; vacuum cleaner 98.7%; videocassette recorder 82.8%; camera 86.8%; microwave oven 84.3%; compact disc player 53.8%.

National economy

Gross national product (1996): U.S.$5,149,185,000,000 (U.S.$40,940 per capita).

Structure of gross domestic product and labour force

	1995		1996	
	in value ¥'000,000,000	% of total value	labour force	% of labour force
Agriculture, fishing	9,325.0	1.9	3,560,000	5.3
Mining	1,019.9	0.2	60,000	0.1
Manufacturing	119,294.3	24.7	14,450,000	21.5
Construction	49,692.9	10.3	6,700,000	10.0
Public utilities	13,649.7	2.8	370,000	0.6
Transportation and communications	31,468.9	6.5	4,110,000	6.1
Trade	61,199.6	12.7	14,630,000	21.8
Finance	85,712.0	17.7	}	
Pub. admin., defense	38,967.6	8.1	20,680,000	30.8
Services	92,977.9	19.2	}	
Other	−20,377.8[11]	−4.2[11]	2,540,000[12]	3.8[12]
TOTAL	482,930.0	100.0[6]	67,110,000[6]	100.0

Budget (1996). Revenue: ¥54,076,000,000,000 (1995; income tax 34.9%; corporation tax 22.7%; value-added tax 10.3%; liquor and tobacco tax 5.7%; fuel taxes 4.4%; stamp duties 3.1%; customs duties 1.6%; carried-over surplus 1.1%). Expenditures: ¥75,104,924,000,000 (social security 19.0%; debt service 21.8%; public works 12.8%; culture, education, and science 8.3%; national defense 6.4%; pensions 2.2%).

Public debt (1997): U.S.$1,394,100,000,000 (¥259,642,100,000,000).

Population economically active (1996): total 67,110,000; activity rate of total population 53.3% (participation rates: age 15 and over, 63.4%[13]; female 40.5%; unemployed 3.4%).

Price and earnings indexes (1990 = 100)

	1991	1992	1993	1994	1995	1996	1997
Consumer price index	103.3	105.1	106.4	107.1	107.0	107.2	109.0
Monthly earnings index	103.4	105.6	107.7	110.2	112.5	114.6	116.3

Household income and expenditure (1995). Average household size 2.8; average annual income per household ¥6,849,800 (U.S.$72,824); sources of income (1992): wages and salaries 59.3%, transfer payments 19.5%, self-employment 10.1%, other 11.1%; expenditure: food 22.6%, transportation and communications 11.0%, recreation 9.5%, housing 6.7%, clothing and footwear 6.0%, fuel, light, and water charges 5.6%, education 5.3%, furniture and household utensils 3.7%, medical care 2.7%.

Tourism (1996): receipts from visitors U.S.$4,281,000,000; expenditures by nationals abroad U.S.$37,977,400,000.

Land use (1994): forested 66.4%; meadows and pastures 1.8%; agricultural and under permanent cultivation 11.7%; other 20.1%.

Manufacturing and mining enterprises (1994)

	no. of establishments	avg. no. of persons engaged	annual wages as a % of avg. of all mfg. wages	annual value added (¥'000,000,000)
Electrical machinery	31,389	1,773,000	100.1	18,382
Food, beverages, and tobacco	46,549	1,237,000	72.9	11,995
Transport equipment	14,226	937,000	122.5	11,626
Nonelectrical machinery	40,320	1,074,000	116.6	11,090
Chemical products	5,160	398,000	136.4	11,379
Fabricated metal products	46,214	813,000	100.6	7,748
Printing and publishing	26,461	536,000	121.2	6,467
Iron and steel	5,830	308,000	141.6	4,647
Ceramic, stone, and clay	19,326	433,000	100.5	5,031
Plastic products	18,862	443,000	92.8	4,134
Paper and paper products	10,410	271,000	100.1	3,062
Textiles	16,745	283,000	81.7	1,883
Apparel products	34,230	634,000	51.9	2,538
Nonferrous metal products	3,709	161,000	120.1	1,756
Precision instruments	5,928	206,000	100.8	1,657
Lumber and wood products	16,532	217,000	78.9	1,550
Furniture and fixtures	15,435	209,000	83.6	1,553
Rubber products	4,334	148,000	104.0	1,472
Petroleum and coal products	1,093	34,000	163.5	1,697
Leather products	4,810	64,000	69.0	378
Mining and quarrying	611	12,000	112.7	100

Energy production (consumption): electricity (kW-hr; 1994) 964,328,000,000 (964,382,000,000); coal (metric tons; 1994) 6,949,000 (123,099,000); crude petroleum (barrels; 1994) 3,958,000 (1,647,000,000); petroleum products (metric tons; 1994) 185,612,000, of which (by volume) diesel 32.8%, heavy fuel oil 25.5%, gasoline 19.8%, kerosene and jet fuel 15.0% (193,545,000); natural gas (cu m; 1994) 2,276,600,000 (61,101,700,000). Composition of energy supply by source (1994): crude oil and petroleum products 55.8%, coal 17.2%, natural gas 11.3%, nuclear power 11.9%, hydroelectric power 3.0%, other 0.8%. Domestic energy demand by end use (1994): mining and manufacturing 42.6%, residential and commercial 25.9%, transportation 24.1%, other 7.4%.

Financial aggregates

	1991	1992	1993	1994	1995	1996	1997
Exchange rate[14], ¥ per:							
U.S. dollar	125.20	124.75	111.85	99.74	102.30	116.00	129.95
£	234.21	188.62	172.27	157.59	158.56	196.97	214.11
SDR	179.09	171.53	153.63	145.61	152.86	166.80	175.34
International reserves (U.S.$)							
Total (excl. gold; '000,000)	72,059	71,623	98,524	125,860	183,250	216,648	219,648
SDRs ('000,000)	2,579	1,094	1,543	2,083	2,707	2,648	2,638
Reserve pos. in IMF ('000,000)	7,722	8,641	8,261	8,100	8,100	6,671	9,144
Foreign exchange ('000,000)	61,758	61,888	88,720	115,146	172,443	207,335	207,866
Gold ('000,000 fine troy oz)	24.23	24.23	24.23	24.23	24.23	24.23	24.23
% world reserves	2.6	2.6	2.6	2.6	2.7	2.7	2.7
Interest and prices							
Central bank discount (%)[14]	4.50	3.25	1.75	1.75	0.50	0.50	0.50
Govt. bond yield (%)	6.53	4.94	3.69	3.71	2.27	2.23	1.69
Industrial share prices							
(1990 = 100)	84.5	62.6	76.5	73.3	63.3	73.6	64.0
Balance of payments							
(U.S.$'000,000,000)							
Balance of visible trade	103.1	132.4	141.6	145.9	132.1	83.56	101.60
Imports, f.o.b.	203.5	198.5	209.7	238.2	297.2	316.72	409.24
Exports, f.o.b.	306.6	330.9	351.3	384.2	429.3	400.28	307.64
Balance of invisibles	−17.7	−14.8	−10.1	−16.7	−20.9	−17.68	−7.25
Balance of payments, current account	35.9	72.9	131.5	129.2	111.2	65.88	94.35

Retail and wholesale trade and services (1994)

	no. of establishments	avg. no. of employees	annual sales (¥'000,000,000)
Retail trade	1,499,948	7,384,143	143,325
Food and beverages	569,403	2,740,000	43,021
Grocery	65,174	715,000	16,986
Liquors	92,436	278,000	5,966
General merchandise	4,839	494,000	20,391
Department stores	2,267	478,000	19,976
Motor vehicles and bicycles	89,345	569,000	17,539
Apparel and accessories	225,714	789,000	14,269
Gasoline service stations	72,177	441,000	11,818
Furniture and home furnishings	144,368	563,000	11,557
Books and stationery	72,007	679,000	5,158
Wholesale trade	429,302	4,581,000	514,317
Machinery and equipment	97,691	1,165,000	110,808
General machinery except electrical	41,618	425,000	30,991
Motor vehicles and parts	17,942	225,000	29,308
General merchandise	1,159	61,000	91,717
Farm, livestock, and fishery products	42,537	445,000	56,954
Food and beverages	53,687	573,000	47,381
Minerals and metals	19,809	242,000	47,281
Building materials	50,152	406,000	32,641
Textiles, apparel, and accessories	40,970	407,000	30,461
Chemicals	17,011	172,000	21,486
Drugs and toilet goods	19,710	288,000	21,048

Production (metric tons except as noted). Agriculture, forestry, fishing (1997): rice 13,000,000, sugar beets 3,800,000, potatoes 3,365,000, cabbages 2,702,000, sugarcane 1,610,000, onions 1,278,000, sweet potatoes 1,181,000, apples 963,000, cucumbers 826,400, tomatoes 752,900, carrots 724,000, watermelons 616,500, wheat 550,000, lettuce 536,400, eggplants 478,400, pears 426,000, cantaloupes 400,000, grapes 255,000, pumpkins 242,000, barley 220,000, strawberries 201,500, peaches 156,000, oranges 136,000, soybeans 120,000, tea 90,000, green beans 75,000, tobacco 69,700, green peas 44,700; livestock (number of live animals) 9,809,000 pigs, 4,749,000 cattle,

31,000 goats, 30,000 horses, 25,000 sheep, 309,000,000 chickens; roundwood (1994) 18,887,000 cu m; fish catch (1995) 6,757,570, of which mackerel 794,580, sardines 661,390, Alaska pollack 338,507, squid 358,574, oysters 227,319, crabs 57,179, river eels 30,030, carp 19,217. Mining and quarrying (1996): limestone 202,897,000; silica stone 19,015,000; dolomite 3,905,000; pyrophyllite 618,000; zinc 79,700; lead 7,753; copper 1,145; tungsten 578[15]; silver 85,000 kg; gold 8,627 kg. Manufacturing (1994): semifinished steel 102,727,000[16]; crude steel 98,295,000; cement 91,624,000; hot-rolled steel products 87,982,000[16]; pig iron 73,776,000; sulfuric acid 6,594,000; fertilizers 6,047,000; plastic products 5,055,000; newsprint 2,971,800; spun yarn 656,000; synthetic fabrics 2,048,000,000 sq m; cotton fabrics 1,180,000,000 sq m; finished products (in number of units) 442,352,000 watches and clocks, 25,550,000 air conditioners, 20,171,000 electronic desk calculators, 19,202,000 videocassette recorders, 11,842,000 cameras, 9,445,000 colour television receivers, 7,997,000 video cameras, 7,801,000 passenger cars, 6,702,000 bicycles, 5,288,000 facsimile machines, 5,042,000 automatic washing machines, 4,952,000 electric refrigerators, 3,960,000 computers, 3,167,000 microwave ovens, 2,725,000 motorcycles, 2,144,000 photocopy machines. Construction (value in ¥'000,000; 1994): residential 26,870,000; nonresidential 54,559,000.

Foreign trade

Balance of trade (current prices)

	1992	1993	1994	1995	1996	1997
¥'000,000,000	+13,484	+13,376	+12,419	+9,998	+6,737	+9,982
% of total	18.6%	20.0%	18.1%	13.7%	8.1%	10.9%

Imports (1995): ¥31,534,000,000,000 (machinery and transport equipment 25.3%, food products 15.2%, petroleum and petroleum products 8.9%, textiles 7.3%, chemicals and chemical products 7.3%). *Major import sources:* United States 22.4%; China 10.7%; South Korea 5.1%; Australia 4.3%; Taiwan 4.3%; Indonesia 4.2%; Germany 4.1%; Canada 3.2%; Malaysia 3.1%; Thailand 3.0%.
Exports (1995): ¥41,532,000,000,000 (electrical machinery 25.6%, motor vehicles 12.0%, chemicals 6.8%, scientific and optical equipment 4.7%, iron and steel products 4.0%, textiles and allied products 2.0%). *Major export destinations:* United States 27.3%; South Korea 7.1%; Taiwan 6.5%; Hong Kong 6.3%; Singapore 5.2%; China 5.0%; Germany 4.6%; Thailand 4.5%; Malaysia 3.8%; United Kingdom 3.2%.

Trade by commodity group (1995)

	imports		exports	
SITC group	U.S.$'000,000	%	U.S.$'000,000	%
00 Food and live animals 01 Beverages and tobacco	45,748	13.6	1,612	0.4
02 Crude materials, excluding fuels	34,268[17]	10.2[17]	3,086[17]	0.7[17]
03 Mineral fuels, lubricants, and related materials	53,976	16.1	2,736	0.6
04 Animal and vegetable oils, fats, and waxes	17	17	17	17
05 Chemicals and related products, n.e.s.	23,862	7.1	29,254	6.6
06 Basic manufactures	39,847	11.8	49,848	11.2
07 Machinery and transport equipment	75,722	22.5	310,708	70.1
08 Miscellaneous manufactured articles	49,365	14.7	35,661	8.0
09 Goods not classified by kind	13,306	3.9	10,032	2.3
TOTAL	336,094	100.0[6]	442,937	100.0[6]

Direction of trade (1994)

	imports		exports	
	U.S.$'000,000	%	U.S.$'000,000	%
Africa	4,015	1.5	6,652	1.7
Asia	124,955	45.6	167,986	42.5
South America	7,055	2.6	5,598	1.4
North America and Central America	74,053	27.0	136,597	34.5
United States	63,067	23.0	118,693	30.0
other North and Central Am.	10,986	4.0	17,904	4.5
Europe	48,469	17.7	68,256	17.3
EU	36,168	13.2	60,056	15.2
Russia	3,481	1.3	1,167	0.3
other Europe	8,820	3.2	7,033	1.8
Oceania	16,771	6.1	10,676	2.7
TOTAL	274,123[6]	100.0[6]	395,201[6]	100.0[6]

Transport and communications

Transport. Railroads (1995): length 12,511 mi, 20,134 km; rolling stock—locomotives 1,787, passenger cars 25,973, freight cars 12,688; passengers carried 22,598,000,000[18]; passenger-mi 248,584,000,000, passenger-km 400,058,000,000; short ton-mi cargo 17,193,000,000, metric ton-km cargo 25,101,000,000. Roads (1994): total length 706,091 mi, 1,136,346 km (paved 73%). Vehicles (1995): passenger cars 44,680,000; trucks 21,934,000; buses 243,000. Merchant marine (1994): vessels (100 gross tons and over) 7,165; total deadweight tonnage 22,000,000. Air transport (1995): passengers carried 90,780,000; passenger-mi 80,959,200,000, passenger-km 130,291,500,000; short ton-mi cargo 4,486,800,000, metric ton-km cargo 6,550,600,000; airports (1996) with scheduled flights 73.

Distribution of traffic (1994)

	cargo carried ('000,000 tons)	% of national total	passengers carried ('000,000)	% of national total
Road	5,810.0	90.1	59,935.0	72.4
Rail (intercity)	79.0	1.2	22,598.0	27.3
Urban transport	—	—	17,445.0[15]	…
road	—	—	8,445.0[15]	…
rail	—	—	9,000.0[15]	…
Inland water	556.0	8.6	151.0	0.2
Air	0.9	0.0	74.0	0.1
TOTAL	6,445.9	100.0[6]	82,758.0[18]	100.0[18]

Communications

Medium	date	unit	number	units per 1,000 persons
Daily newspapers	1995	circulation	72,518,000	578
Radio	1995	receivers	100,000,000	799
Television	1995	receivers	77,500,000	619
Telephones	1995	main lines	61,106,000	488
Cellular telephones	1995	subscribers	10,204,000	82
Facsimile machines	1995	units	8,000,000	64
Personal computers	1995	units	19,100,000	152

Radio and television broadcasting (1994): total radio stations 1,340, of which commercial 481; total television stations 14,625, of which commercial 7,736. Commercial broadcasting hours (by percentage of programs; 1994): reports—radio 13.0%, television 21.0%; education—radio 3.4%, television 12.0%; culture—radio 14.9%, television 24.7%; entertainment—radio 67.6%, television 40.0%. Advertisements (daily average; 1994): radio 148, television 295.

Other communications media (1995)

Print	titles	Electronic[19]	traffic ('000)
Books (new)	58,310	Telegram	43,288
of which		Domestic	43,288
Social sciences	12,578	International	270
Fiction	11,427	Fax service	678[20]
Arts	7,540		
Natural sciences	4,460		
Engineering	4,774		
History	3,917	Post[22]	
Philosophy	2,731	Mail	23,887,000
Magazines/journals[21]	4,178	Domestic	23,534,000
Weekly	112	International	353,000
Monthly	2,848	Parcels	384,000
		Domestic	378,000
Cinema		International	6,000
Feature films	610		
Domestic	289		
Foreign	321		

Education and health

Literacy: total population age 15 and over literate, virtually 100%.

Education (1995)

	schools	teachers	students	student/ teacher ratio
Primary (age 6–11)	24,548	431,000	8,371,000	19.4
Secondary (age 12–17)	16,775	552,000	9,296,000	16.8
Higher	1,223	162,000	3,101,000	19.1

Health (1994): physicians 228,643 (1 per 546 persons); dentists 79,896 (1 per 1,564 persons); nurses 862,013 (1 per 145 persons); pharmacists 157,719 (1 per 792 persons); midwives 22,690[15] (1 per 5,476 persons); hospital beds (1992) 1,686,696 (1 per 74 persons), of which general 75.0%, mental 21.5%, tuberculosis 2.3%, other 1.2%; infant mortality rate per 1,000 live births 4.2.
Food (1995): daily per capita caloric intake 2,887 (vegetable products 79%, animal products 21%); 123% of FAO recommended minimum.

Military

Total active duty personnel (1996): 235,500 (army 62.9%, navy 18.2%, air force 18.9%). *Military expenditure as percentage of GNP* (1994): 1.0% (world 3.0%); per capita expenditure U.S.$366.

[1]Excludes Lake Naka (38 sq mi [98 sq km]), which is part of both Shimane and Tottori prefectures. [2]Excludes Lake Towada (23 sq mi [60 sq km]), which is part of both Akita and Aomori prefectures. [3]Part of Kantō geographic region, [4]Part of Kinki geographic region. [5]1987 survey (includes Lake Naka and Lake Towada); total area per 1994 survey equals 145,877 sq mi (377,819 sq km). [6]Detail does not add to total given because of rounding. [7]April 1. [8]January 1. [9]Many Japanese practice both Shintōism and Buddhism. [10]Applies to passengers carried within metropolitan areas only. [11]Import duties and statistical discrepancy less imputed bank service charge. [12]Includes 2,250,000 unemployed. [13]1995. [14]End of period. [15]1992. [16]1991. [17]Crude materials includes Animal and vegetable oils, fats, and waxes. [18]Totals do not include Urban transport. [19]1994. [20]Number of subscribers. [21]1996.

Internet resources for further information:
- **Bank of Japan: http://www.boj.or.jp/en/index.htm**
- **Economic Planning Agency of Japan: http://www.epa.go.jp/e-e/menu.html**
- **Statistics Bureau and Statistics Center (Japan): http://www.stat.go.jp/1.htm**

Jordan

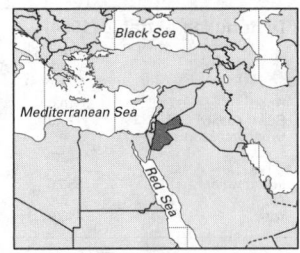

Official name: Al-Mamlakah al-Urdunnīyah al-Hāshimīyah (Al-Urdun) (Hashemite Kingdom of Jordan).
Form of government: constitutional monarchy with a National Assembly comprising two legislative houses (Senate [40[1]]; House of Deputies [80]).
Head of state and government: King assisted by Prime Minister.
Capital: Amman.
Official language: Arabic.
Official religion: Islam.
Monetary unit: 1 Jordan dinar (JD) = 1,000 fils; valuation (Sept. 25, 1998) JD 1.00 = U.S.$1.41 = £0.83.

Area and population		area		population
Governorates	Capitals	sq mi	sq km	1994 census[2]
'Ajlūn	'Ajlun	...[3]	...[3]	94,205
'Amman	Amman	4,097[4]	10,612[4]	1,567,908
Al-'Aqabah	Al-'Aqabah	...[5]	...[5]	79,745
Al-Balqā'	As-Salt	425	1,100	273,489
Irbid	Irbid	985[3]	2,551[3]	745,774
Jarash	Jarash	...[3]	...[3]	123,195
Al-Karak	Al-Karak	1,548	4,010	169,552
Ma'ān	Ma'ān	13,954[5]	36,141[5]	79,401
Mādabā	Mādabā	...[4]	...[4]	106,308
Al-Mafraq	Al-Mafraq	10,475	27,129	170,903
Aṭ-Ṭafīlah	Aṭ-Ṭafīlah	850	2,202	61,156
Az-Zarqā'	Az-Zarqā'	2,008	5,201	623,943
TOTAL		34,342[6]	88,946[6]	4,095,579

Demography

Population (1998): 4,682,000.
Density (1998): persons per sq mi 135.8, persons per sq km 52.4.
Urban-rural (1994): urban 78.6%; rural 21.4%.
Sex distribution (1994): male 52.15%; female 47.85%.
Age breakdown (1994): under 15, 41.4%; 15–29, 31.6%; 30–44, 14.8%; 45–59, 8.0%; 60–74, 3.5%; 75 and over, 0.7%.
Population projection: (2000) 5,025,000; (2010) 6,715,000.
Doubling time: 23 years.
Ethnic composition (1995): Arab 98%, of which Palestinian *c.* 50%; Circassian 1%; Armenian 1%.
Religious affiliation (1995): Sunnī Muslim 96.5%; Christian 3.5%.
Major cities (1994): Amman 963,490; Az-Zarqā' 344,524; Irbid 208,201; Aṣ-Ṣalt 187,014; Ar-Ruṣayfah 131,130; Al-Mafraq 109,841.

Vital statistics

Birth rate per 1,000 population (1994): 34.3 (world avg. 25.0).
Death rate per 1,000 population (1994): 3.0 (world avg. 9.3).
Natural increase rate per 1,000 population (1994): 31.3 (world avg. 15.7).
Total fertility rate (avg. births per childbearing woman; 1995): 5.9.
Life expectancy at birth (1995): male 64.4 years; female 69.9 years.
Major causes of death per 100,000 population: n.a.

National economy

Budget (1996 est.). Revenue: JD 1,777,600,000 (taxes 49.3%, of which sales tax 22.2%, custom duties 12.7%, income and profits taxes 9.8%; nontax 37.7%, of which licenses and fees 13.4%, postal, telegraph, and telephone 10.5%; external aid 12.9%). Expenditures: JD 1,801,100,000 (current 80.5%, of which defense 23.2%, wages and salaries 19.4%; capital construction 19.5%).
Public debt (external, outstanding; 1996): U.S.$7,137,000,000.
Production (metric tons except as noted). Agriculture, forestry, fishing (1997): tomatoes 474,000, grapes 84,267, olives 82,117, oranges and tangerines 81,-204, eggplants 73,500, cucumbers 68,000, cauliflower and cabbage 54,388, wheat 51,000, barley 44,730, lemons and limes 44,259, bananas 38,889; livestock (number of live animals) 2,100,000 sheep, 555,000 goats, 43,000 cattle, 18,000 camels, 78,000 chickens; roundwood (1995) 11,000 cu m; fish catch (1993) 62. Mining and quarrying (1996): phosphate ore 5,360,000; potash 1,800,000. Manufacturing (value added in JD '000; 1994): nonmetallic mineral products, pottery, and china 118,035; chemicals 99,411; food products 78,075; fabricated metal products, except machinery 31,755; refined petroleum 30,458; plastic products 27,181. Construction (1996): 5,471,000 sq m. Energy production (consumption): electricity (kW-hr; 1994) 5,075,-000,000 (5,075,000,000); crude petroleum (barrels; 1994) 14,400 (22,056,000); petroleum products (metric tons; 1994) 2,856,000 (3,641,000).
Land use (1994): forest 0.8%; pasture 8.9%; agriculture 4.6%; other 85.7%.
Tourism (1995): Receipts U.S.$696,000,000; expenditures U.S.$420,000,000.
Population economically active (1993): total 859,300; activity rate of total population 22.2% (participation rates: over age 15, 43.6%; female 14.0%; unemployed [1996] 13.0%).

Price and earnings indexes (1990 = 100)							
	1991	1992	1993	1994	1995	1996	1997
Consumer price index	108.2	112.5	116.2	120.3	123.1	131.1	135.1
Daily earnings index	100.0	...	...	...	...	...	...

Gross national product (1996): U.S.$7,088,000,000 (U.S.$1,650 per capita).

Structure of gross domestic product and labour force				
	1996		1993	
	in value JD '000,000[7]	% of total value	labour force	% of labour force
Agriculture	232.9	5.5	54,995	6.4
Mining	153.6	3.6		
Manufacturing	688.6	16.2	91,086	10.6
Construction	341.1	8.0	60,151	7.0
Public utilities	98.2	2.3	6,015	0.7
Transp. and commun.	591.8	13.9	57,573	6.7
Trade	480.1	11.3	129,754	15.1
Finance	766.8	18.0	24,920	2.9
Pub. admin., defense	792.7	18.6		
Services[8]	201.9	4.7	434,806	50.6
Other	−87.3[9]	−2.1[9]		
TOTAL	4,260.4	100.0	859,300	100.0

Household income and expenditure. Average household size (1995) 6.1; income per household (1995) JD 4,010 (U.S.$5,725); sources of income (1995): wages and salaries 51.4%, rent and property income 23.8%, transfer payments 13.7%, self-employment 11.1%; expenditure (1992): food and beverages 40.6%, housing and energy 26.9%, transportation 11.2%, clothing and footwear 8.2%, education 3.5%, health care 2.2%.

Foreign trade

Balance of trade (current prices)						
	1992	1993	1994	1995	1996	1997
JD '000,000	−1,384.7	−1,588.9	−1,367.4	−1,349.3	−1,851.0	−1,609.0
% of total	45.5%	47.9%	40.7%	35.2%	41.8%	38.2%

Imports (1996): JD 3,043,556,000 (machinery and transport equipment 26.0%; food and live animals 22.5%; mineral fuels 12.2%; chemicals and chemical products 10.8%; iron and steel 5.2%). *Major import sources:* Iraq 11.8%; United States 9.7%; Germany 8.0%; Italy 5.9%; France 4.9%.
Exports (1996): JD 1,288,171,000 (domestic goods 80.7%, of which chemicals and chemical products 25.7%, phosphate fertilizers 9.9%, potash 9.8%, fruits, vegetables, and nuts 6.4%, machinery and transport equipment 1.9%; reexports 19.3%). *Major export destinations*[10]: Saudi Arabia 12.5%: Iraq 9.2%; India 7.9%; United Arab Emirates 5.7%: Syria 3.9%.

Transport and communications

Transport. Railroads (1995): route length 677 km; passenger traffic was negligible; metric ton-km cargo 1,336,000,000[11]. roads (1995): total length 6,750 km (paved 100%). Vehicles (1995): passenger cars 167,828; trucks and buses 82,516. Merchant marine (1995): vessels (1,000 gross tons and over) 1; total deadweight tonnage 15,794. Air transport (1995)[12]: passenger-km 4,394,518,000; metric ton-km cargo 265,226,000; airports (1997) 2.

Communications				units per 1,000
Medium	date	unit	number	persons
Daily newspapers	1994	circulation	250,000	62
Radio	1996	receivers	980,000	224
Television	1995	receivers	740,000	176
Telephones	1995	main lines	317,400	75
Cellular telephones	1995	subscribers	11,500	2.7
Facsimile machines	1995	units	32,000	7.6
Personal computers	1995	units	35,000	8.3

Education and health

Educational attainment (1995). Percentage of population age 25 and over having: no formal schooling 31.8%; primary education 34.5%; secondary 13.9%; postsecondary and vocational 8.4%; higher 11.4%. *Literacy* (1995): percentage of population age 15 and over literate 86.6%; males literate 93.4%; females literate 79.4%.

Education (1993–94)				student/
	schools	teachers	students	teacher ratio
Primary (age 6–14)	2,482	48,158	1,036,079	21.5
Secondary (age 15–17)	741	4,597	93,773	20.4
Voc., teacher tr.	54	2,553	30,052	11.8
Higher	55[13]	4,280[14]	85,934[14]	20.1

Health (1995): physicians 6,839 (1 per 616 persons); hospital beds 7,440 (1 per 567 persons); (1994) infant mortality rate per 1,000 live births 34.0.
Food (1995): daily per capita caloric intake 2,734 (vegetable products 89%, animal products 11%); 111% of FAO recommended minimum requirement.

Military

Total active duty personnel (1997): 104,050 (army 86.5%, navy 0.6%, air force 12.9%). *Military expenditure as percentage of GDP* (1995): 7.7% (world 2.8%); per capita expenditure U.S.$117.

---

[1]Appointed by king. [2]Preliminary. [3]Irbid includes area of 'Ajlūn and Jarash governorates. [4]'Amman includes area of Mādabā governorate. [5]Ma'ān includes area of Al-'Aqabah governorate. [6]Excludes 147 sq mi (380 sq km) of territory per Israel-Jordan treaty of October 1994. [7]At factor cost. [8]Includes domestic help employed in households. [9]Less imputed bank service charges. [10]Domestic exports only. [11]For Aqaba Railway Corporation only. [12]Royal Jordanian airlines only. [13]1988–89. [14]Includes community colleges.

Internet resources for further information:
• The Hashemite Kingdom of Jordan http://www.iconnect.com/jordan/
• Jordan National Information System http://www.nic.gov.jo/

Kazakstan

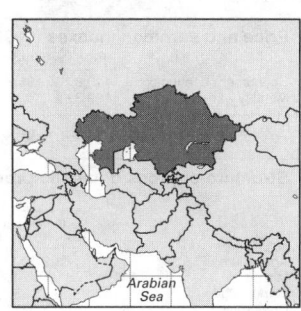

Official name: Qazaqstan Respüblīkasy (Republic of Kazakstan).
Form of government: unitary republic with a Parliament consisting of two chambers (Senate [47[1]] and Assembly [67]).
Head of state and government: President assisted by Prime Minister.
Capital: Astana[2].
Official language: Kazak[3].
Official religion: none.
Monetary unit[4]: 1 tenge (T) = 100 tiyn; valuation (Sept. 25, 1998) free rate, 1 U.S.$ = 80.48 tenge; 1 £ = 137.02 tenge.

Area and population

Provinces	Capitals	area sq mi	area sq km	population 1995 estimate
Almaty (Alma-Ata)	Almaty (Alma-Ata)	86,500[5]	224,200[5]	1,684,600
Aqmola[6]	Aqmola[2]	35,500	92,000	845,700
Aqtöbe	Aqtöbe	116,050	300,600	752,800
Atyraü	Atyraü	45,800	118,600	459,600
Batys Qazaqstan	Oral	58,400	151,300	669,800
Mangghystaü	Aqtaü	63,950	165,600	324,400
Ongtüstik Qazaqstan	Shymkent	45,300	117,300	1,987,800
Pavlodar	Pavlodar	48,200	124,800	943,600
Qaraghandy	Qaraghandy	165,250	428,000	1,754,500
Qostanay[6]	Qostanay	44,000	113,900	1,055,300
Qyzylorda	Qyzylorda	87,250[7]	226,000[7]	606,100
Shyghys Qazaqstan	Shyghys Qazaqstan	109,400	283,300	1,750,500
Soltüstik Qazaqstan	Petropavl	47,500	123,200	1,257,900
Torghay[6]	*Arqalyq*	*43,150*	*111,800*	*305,900*
Zhambyl	Zhambyl (Aullye-Ata)	55,700	144,300	1,039,600
Cities				
Almaty (Alma-Ata)	—	5	5	1,172,400
Baykonur (Leninsk)[8]	—	7	7	68,600
TOTAL		1,052,100[9]	2,724,900	16,679,100

Demography

Population (1998): 15,797,000.
Density (1998): persons per sq mi 15.0, persons per sq km 5.8.
Urban-rural (1996): urban 56.0%; rural 44.0%.
Sex distribution (1994): male 49.00%; female 51.00%.
Age breakdown (1991): under 15, 31.4%; 15–29, 25.1%; 30–44, 21.3%; 45–59, 12.2%; 60–69, 6.1%; 70 and over, 3.9%.
Population projection: (2000) 15,768,000; (2010) 16,158,000.
Ethnic composition (1996): Russian 47.4%; Kazak 39.3%; German 3.2%; Ukrainian 2.0%; Uzbek 1.9%; Tatar 1.4%; other 7.0%.
Religious affiliation (1995): Muslim (mostly Sunnī) 47.0%; Russian Orthodox 8.2%; Protestant 2.1%; other (mostly nonreligious) 42.7%.
Major cities (1995): Almaty (Alma-Ata) 1,172,400; Qaraghandy (Karaganda) 573,700; Shymkent (Chimkent) 397,600; Pavlodar 340,700.

Vital statistics

Birth rate per 1,000 population (1995): 16.7 (world avg. 25.0); (1994) legitimate 86.6%; illegitimate 13.4%.
Death rate per 1,000 population (1995): 10.2 (world avg. 9.2).
Natural increase rate per 1,000 population (1995): 6.5 (world avg. 15.7).
Total fertility rate (avg. births per childbearing woman; 1994): 3.1.
Marriage rate per 1,000 population (1994): 7.3.
Divorce rate per 1,000 population (1994): 2.5.
Life expectancy at birth (1994): male 64.0 years; female 73.0 years.
Major causes of death per 100,00 population (1994): diseases of the circulatory system 459.0; malignant neoplasms (cancers) 134.3; accidents, poisoning, and violence 125.6; diseases of the respiratory system 87.9.

National economy

Budget (1997). Revenue: 270,492,000 tenge (taxes on goods and services 32,6%, income, profits and capital gains taxes 31.7%, taxes on international trade 3.1%, nontax revenue 19.4%). Expenditures: 325,469,000,000 tenge (education 18.3%, health 14.5%, defense 5.9%, social security 5.4%).
Public debt (external, outstanding; 1996): U.S.$1,932,000,000.
Population economically active (1995): total 6,976,000; activity rate of total population 41.8% (participation rates: ages 16–59 [male], 16–54 [female] 80.1%; female [1994] 48.0%; unemployed 2.3%).

Price and earnings indexes (1994 = 100)

	1995	1996	1997
Consumer price index	286.6	389.5	384.4
Monthly earnings index	276.2	384.4	488.6

Production (metric tons except as noted). Agriculture, forestry, fishing (1996): wheat 7,678,000, barley 2,696,000, potatoes 1,656,000, oats 359,000, sugar beets 341,000; livestock (number of live animals) 19,953,000 sheep and goats, 6,860,000 cattle, 1,700,000 horses, 1,622,700 pigs; roundwood (1991) 1,974,000 cu m; fish catch (1995) 69,716. Mining and quarrying (1995): iron ore 15,-000,000; chrome 2,400,000; lead 190,000; zinc 40,000. Manufacturing (value of production in '000,000 tenge; 1996): food products 107,397; nonferrous metallurgy 89,052; ferrous metallurgy 81,026; machinery 52,168; chemical products 28,974; construction materials 23,239. Construction (1994): residential 2,300,000 sq m. Energy production (consumption): electricity (kW-hr;

1996) 58,657,000,000 (1994; 78,277,000,000); coal (metric tons; 1996) 76,597,-000 (1994; 76,357,000); crude petroleum (barrels; 1996) 166,800,000 (1994; 87,004,000); petroleum products (metric tons; 1994) 13,372,000 (14,306,000); natural gas (cu m; 1996) 6,397,000 (1994; 9,588,000,000).
Gross national product (1996): U.S.$22,213,000 (U.S.$1,350 per capita).

Structure of gross domestic product and labour force

	1995 in value '000,000 tenge	% of total value	labour force	% of labour force
Agriculture	123,830	12.1	1,442,000	20.7
Manufacturing, mining, public utilities	238,733	23.4	1,372,000	19.7
Construction	62.459	6.1	364,000	5.2
Transp. and commun.	108,203	10.6	507,000	7.3
Trade	164,481	16.1	1,035,000	14.8
Finance			334,000	4.8
Pub. admin., defense	322,016	31.6	1,664,000	23.9
Services				
Other	...	...	258,000[10]	3.7[10]
TOTAL	1,019,122	100.0[9]	6,976,000	100.0[9]

Household income and expenditure. Average household size (1989) 4.0; income per household (1991) 5,290 Russian rubles[4]: U.S.$ equivalent: n.a.[11]; sources of income (1994): salaries and wages 67.7%, social benefits 16.9%, agricultural income 5.8%, other 9.6%; expenditure (1994): retail goods 60.6%, taxes 16.8, services 11.7%, other 10.9%.

Foreign trade

Balance of trade (current prices)

	1992	1993	1994	1995	1996
U.S.$'000,000	−1,121	−414	−920	−222	−400
% of total	13.6%	4.2%	12.3%	2.1%	3.4%

Imports (1996): U.S.$6,017,000,000 (equipment and mechanical tools 8.7%, chemical industry products 8.3%, foodstuffs 7.4%, vehicles 6.0%). *Major import sources* (1995): Russia 64.7%; Germany 7.0%; Ukraine 5.3%.
Exports (1996): U.S.$5,617,000,000 (oil and gas condensate 23.9%, rolled ferrous metal 9.6%, refined copper 9.5%, grain 8.0%, coal 5.1%). *Major export destinations* (1995): Russia 64.1%; China 7.4%; Ukraine 6.8%.

Transport and communications

Transport. Railroads (1994): length 21,600 km; (1995) passenger-km 13,200,000,000; metric ton-km cargo 124,500,000,000. Roads (1995): total length 158,655 km (paved 68.4%). Vehicles (1995): passenger cars 1,030,000; trucks and buses 516,000. Air transport (1994): passenger-km 4,600,000,000; metric ton-km cargo 100,000,000; airports (1997) with scheduled flights 20.

Communications

Medium	date	unit	number	units per 1,000 persons
Television	1995	receivers	4,578,000	275
Telephones	1995	main lines	1,963,000	118
Cellular telephones	1995	subscribers	4,600	0.3
Facsimile machines	1995	units	2,900	0.2

Education and health

Educational attainment (1989). Population age 25 and over having: primary education or no formal schooling 16.2%; some secondary 19.8%; completed secondary and some postsecondary 54.1%; higher 9.9%. *Literacy* (1989): population age 15 and over literate 97.5%; males 99.1%; females 96.1%.

Education (1995–96)

	schools	teachers	students	student/teacher ratio
Primary (age 7–13)	8,700	262,000	3,060,000	11.7
Secondary (age 14–17)				
Voc., teacher tr.	3,504[12]	...	984,300[12]	...
Higher	69[12]	...	267,000[12]	...

Health (1995): physicians 62,000 (1 per 267 persons); hospital beds 193,000 (1 per 86 persons); infant mortality rate per 1,000 live births 27.9.

Military

Total active duty personnel (1997): 35,100 (army 57.0%, air force 43.0%). *Military expenditure as percentage of GNP* (1995): 0.9% (world avg. 2.8%); per capita expenditure U.S.$25.

[1]Includes 7 nonelective seats. [2]Akmola (Kazak: Aqmola; new capital replacing Almaty on Nov. 8, 1997) was renamed Astana on May 6, 1998. [3]Russian commands equal status with Kazak at state-owned organizations and bodies of local government per a law effective July 16, 1997. [4]The Kazak tenge was introduced Nov. 18, 1993, to replace the Russian ruble, at a rate of 500 Russian rubles to 1 tenge; on Nov. 25, 1993, the Kazak tenge became the sole legal tender. [5]Area of Almaty city included with Almaty province. [6]Torghay province abolished April 23, 1997; its area and population were divided between Aqmola and Qostanay provinces, but adjusted figures are not yet available. [7]Area of Baykonur city included with Qyzylorda province. [8]City serves Baykonur space centre and is to be under Russian jurisdiction between 1995 and 2015. [9]Detail does not add to total given because of rounding. [10]Includes 139,600 undistributed unemployed and 118,400 undistributed employed. [11]Ruble-area exchange rate for this period very speculative. [12]1994–95.

Internet resources for further information:
• **Kazakstan Human Development Report 1995**
  http://www.undp.org/undp/rbec/nhdr/kazakstan/

Kenya

Official name: Jamhuri ya Kenya
(Swahili); Republic of Kenya
(English).
Form of government: unitary multiparty
republic with one legislative house
(National Assembly [224[1]]).
Head of state and government:
President.
Capital: Nairobi.
Official languages: Swahili; English.
Official religion: none.
Monetary unit: 1 Kenya shilling[2]
(K Sh) = 100 cents; valuation (Sept. 25,
1998) 1 U.S.$ = K Sh 60.23;
1 £ = K Sh 102.54.

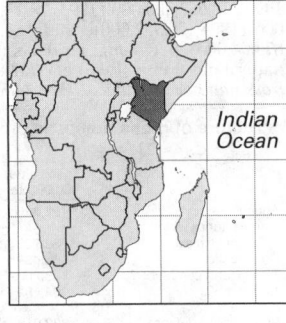

Indian
Ocean

Area and population

Provinces	Provincial headquarters	area sq mi	area sq km	population 1993 estimate
Central	Nyeri	5,087	13,176	3,626,000
Coast	Mombasa	32,279	83,603	2,155,000
Eastern	Embu	61,734	159,891	4,334,000
North Eastern	Garissa	48,997	126,902	408,000
Nyanza	Kisumu	6,240	16,162	4,041,000
Rift Valley	Nakuru	67,131	173,868	5,690,000
Western	Kakamega	3,228	8,360	3,035,000
Special area				
Nairobi	—	264	684	1,678,000
TOTAL		224,961[3]	582,646	24,967,000

Demography

Population (1998): 28,337,000.
Density (1998): persons per sq mi 126.0, persons per sq km 48.6.
Urban-rural (1995): urban 20.4%; rural 79.6%.
Sex distribution (1997): male 49.99%; female 50.01%.
Age breakdown (1997): under 15, 51.3%; 15–29, 26.5%; 30–44, 12.7%; 45–59,
6.3%; 60–74, 2.7%; 75 and over, 0.5%.
Population projection: (2000) 29,251,000; (2010) 32,443,000.
Doubling time: 33 years.
Ethnic composition (1989): Kikuyu 17.7%; Luhya 12.4%; Luo 10.6%; Kalenjin
9.8%; Kamba 9.8%; other 39.7%.
Religious affiliation (1995): Christian 63.7%, of which Protestant 28.2%,
Roman Catholic 19.5%, other Christian (mostly African Indigenous,
Anglican, Eastern Orthodox) 16.0%; Muslim 6.0%; other 30.3%.
Major cities (1989): Nairobi 1,504,900[4]; Mombasa 465,000; Kisumu 185,100;
Nakuru 162,800; Machakos 92,300[5].

Vital statistics

Birth rate per 1,000 population (1996): 32.4 (world avg. 25.0).
Death rate per 1,000 population (1996): 10.8 (world avg. 9.3).
Natural increase rate per 1,000 population (1996): 21.6 (world avg. 15.7).
Total fertility rate (avg. births per childbearing woman; 1996): 4.3.
Life expectancy at birth (1996): male 54.2 years; female 54.6 years.
Major causes of death per 100,000 population: n.a.; however, major infectious
diseases include AIDS, malaria, gastroenteritis, venereal diseases, diarrhea
and dysentery, trachoma, amebiasis, and schistosomiasis.

National economy

Budget (1995–96). Revenue: K Sh 151,316,000,000 (goods and services 34.5%,
income tax 31.7%, custom and excise duties 14.0%). Expenditures: K Sh
152,555,000,000 (recurrent expenditure 79.6%, development expenditure
20.4%).
Production (metric tons except as noted). Agriculture, forestry, fishing (1996):
sugarcane 4,810,000, corn (maize) 2,223,000, cassava 860,000, sweet potatoes
635,000, plantains 370,000, wheat 350,000, pineapples 270,000, pulses 270,000,
tea 255,000, bananas 220,000, potatoes 205,000, sorghum 140,000, coffee
98,000, barley 65,000, millet 59,000, coconuts 43,000, sisal 34,000, tomatoes
32,000, cashew nuts 15,000, sunflower seeds 15,000, seed cotton 12,000, tobacco 10,000, cotton seeds 8,000; livestock (number of live animals) 13,800,000
cattle, 7,400,000 goats, 5,600,000 sheep; roundwood (1995) 41,696,000 cu m;
fish catch (1995) 241,064, of which freshwater fish 95.3%. Mining and quarrying (1995): soda ash 218,450; fluorite 80,230; salt 71,400. Manufacturing
(value added in K£'000[2]; 1994): food products 639,000; machinery and transport equipment 233,000; beverages and tobacco 190,000; chemical products
168,000; metal products 125,000; paper and paper products 87,000; plastic
products 65,000; clothing and footwear 55,000. Construction (1990): residential 411,000 sq m; nonresidential 182,000 sq m. Energy production (consumption): electricity (kW-hr; 1994) 3,538,000,000 (3,802,000,000); coal (metric tons; 1994) none (109,000); crude petroleum (barrels; 1994) none
(15,928,000); petroleum products (metric tons; 1994) 1,949,000 (1,680,000).
Public debt (external, outstanding; 1996): U.S.$5,647,000,000.
Household income and expenditure. Average household size (1980) 6.2; average annual income per household: n.a.; sources of income: n.a.; expenditure
(1980): food 46.5%, housing 10.0%, furniture and utensils 9.4%, transportation 8.4%, clothing and footwear 7.7%, energy 2.6%, health 2.2%.
Tourism (1995): receipts from visitors U.S.$454,000,000; expenditures by
nationals abroad U.S.$135,000,000.
Population economically active (1992): total 10,633,000; activity rate of total
population 41.1% (participation rates [1985]: ages 15–64, 76.2%; female
40.9%; unemployed, n.a.).

Price and earnings indexes (1990 = 100)

	1991	1992	1993	1994	1995	1996	1997
Consumer price index	119.8	155.2	226.3	292.0	294.3	320.2	358.7
Monthly earnings index	109.3	...	...	...	...	...	...

Gross national product (1996): U.S.$8,661,000,000 (U.S.$320 per capita).

Structure of gross domestic product and labour force

	1995 in value K Sh '000,000	1995 % of total value	1995 labour force[6]	1995 % of labour force[6]
Agriculture	122,697	31.0	294,000	18.9
Mining	724	0.2	5,000	0.3
Manufacturing	43,185	10.9	205,000	13.1
Construction	18,353	4.6	76,000	4.9
Public utilities	5,441	1.4	23,000	1.5
Transp. and commun.	30,407	7.8	79,000	5.1
Trade	60,501	15.3	135,000	8.7
Finance	72,335	18.2	78,000	5.0
Pub. admin., defense	42,514	10.7	663,000	42.6
Services }				
Other				
TOTAL	396,157	100.0[3]	1,558,000	100.0

Land use (1994): forest 29.5%; pasture 37.4%; agriculture 8.0%; other 25.1%.

Foreign trade[7]

Balance of trade (current prices)

	1992	1993	1994	1995	1996	1997
K Sh '000,000	−5,923	−5,938	−16,738	−36,082	−44,762	−70,396
% of total	6.2%	3.7%	8.8%	15.6%	15.9%	22.7%

Imports (1995): U.S.$3,065,000 (machinery and transport equipment 35.4%,
chemical products 17.6%, petroleum and petroleum products 13.4%, food
and beverages 4.4%). *Major import sources:* United Kingdom 12.4%; United
Arab Emirates 8.9%; Japan 8.6%; India 7.5%; South Africa 7.4%; Germany
6.0%; Italy 5.2%; United States 3.6%; Saudi Arabia 2.0%.
Exports (1995): U.S.$1,873,100,000 (tea 17.6%, coffee [not roasted] 15.1%,
fruits and vegetables 5.0%, petroleum products 5.0%, cement 1.8%, hides
and skins 1.1%, soda ash 1.1%). *Major export destinations:* United Kingdom
11.9%; Germany 9.3%; Uganda 8.7%; Tanzania 7.1%; Pakistan 5.7%; The
Netherlands 5.2%; United States 5.1%.

Transport and communications

Transport. Railroads (1993): route length 1,885 mi, 3,034 km; passenger-mi
288,000,000, passenger-km 464,000,000; short ton-mi cargo 898,600,000, metric ton-km cargo 1,312,000,000. Roads (1995): total length 39,558 mi, 63,663
km (paved 14%). Vehicles (1995): passenger cars 271,000; trucks and buses
75,900. Merchant marine (1992): vessels (100 gross tons and over) 29; total
deadweight tonnage 11,649. Air transport (1996)[8]: passenger-mi 1,141,-
800,000, passenger-km 1,837,553,000; short ton-mi cargo 32,746,000, metric
ton-km cargo 47,809,000; airports (1997) with scheduled flights 11.

Communications

Medium	date	unit	number	units per 1,000 persons
Daily newspapers	1995	circulation	402,000[9]	14[9]
Radio	1996	receivers	3,000,000	103
Television	1995	receivers	462,000	18
Telephones	1995	main lines	239,600	9.0
Cellular telephones	1995	subscribers	2,300	0.1
Facsimile machines	1995	units	3,800	0.1
Personal computers	1995	units	18,000	0.7

Education and health

Educational attainment (1979). Percentage of population age 25 and over having: no formal schooling 58.6%; primary education 32.2%; some secondary
7.9%; complete secondary and higher 1.3%. *Literacy* (1995): total population over age 15 literate 78.1%; males literate 86.3%; females literate 70.0%.

Education (1993)

	schools	teachers	students	student/ teacher ratio
Primary (age 5–11)	15,804	173,002	5,428,600	31.4
Secondary (age 12–17)	2,639	31,657	517,577	16.3
Voc., teacher tr.	63	1,332[10]	29,593	13.4[10]
Higher	14	4,392[11]	88,180	8.1[11]

Health (1994): physicians 4,558 (1 per 5,999 persons); hospital beds 37,271 (1
per 734 persons); infant mortality rate per 1,000 live births (1996): 55.2.
Food (1995): daily per capita caloric intake 1,991 (vegetable products 88%,
animal products 12%); 86% of FAO recommended minimum requirement.

Military

Total active duty personnel (1996): 24,200 (army 84.7%, navy 5.0%, air force
10.3%). *Military expenditure as percentage of GNP* (1995): 2.3% (world
2.8%); per capita expenditure U.S.$6.

[1]Includes 14 nonelective seats. [2]Kenya pound (K£) as a unit of account equals 20 K
Sh. [3]Detail does not add to total given because of rounding. [4]1990. [5]1983. [6]Employed
persons only. [7]Import figures are f.o.b. in balance of trade and c.i.f. in commodities
and trading partners. [8]Kenya Airways only. [9]Circulation for four newspapers only.
[10]1987–88; teacher training only. [11]1990–91; universities only.

Internet resources for further information:
• Embassy of the Republic of Kenya http://www.embassyofkenya.com/

Kiribati

Official name: Republic of Kiribati.
Form of government: unitary republic with a unicameral legislature (House of Assembly [42[1]]).
Head of state and government: President.
Capital: Bairiki, on Tarawa Atoll.
Official language: English.
Official religion: none.
Monetary unit: 1 Australian Dollar ($A) = 100 cents; valuation (Sept. 25, 1998) 1 U.S.$ = $A 1.70; 1 £ = $A 2.89.

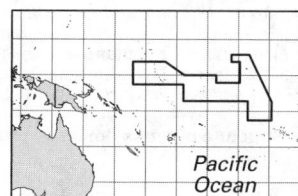

Pacific Ocean

Area and population

Island Groups Islands	Capitals	area[2] sq mi	sq km	population 1990 census
Gilberts Group	Bairiki Islet	110	286[3]	67,508
Abaiang	Tuarabu	7	18	5,233
Abemama	Kariatebike	11	27	3,218
Aranuka	Takaeang	5	12	1,002
Arorae	Roreti	3	9	1,440
Banaba	Anteeren	2	6	284
Beru	Taubukinberu	7	18	2,909
Butaritari	Butaritari	5	13	3,774
Kuria	Tabontebike	6	16	990
Maiana	Tebangetua	6	17	2,180
Makin	Makin	3	8	1,762
Marakei	Rawannawi	5	14	2,863
Nikunau	Rungata	7	19	1,994
Nonouti	Teuabu	8	20	2,814
Onotoa	Buariki	6	16	2,100
Tabiteuea North	Utiroa	10	26	3,201
Tabiteuea South	Buariki	5	12	1,331
Tamana	Bakaka	2	5	1,385
Tarawa North	Abaokoro	6	15	3,648
Tarawa South	Bairiki	6	16	25,380
Line Group	Kiritimati	192	496	4,782
Northern		167	432	—
Kiritimati (Christmas)	London	150	388	2,537
Tabuaeran (Fanning)	Paelau	13	34	1,309
Teraina (Washington)	Washington	4	10	936
Southern (Caroline [Millennium], Flint, Malden, Starbuck, Vostok)		25	64	—
Phoenix Group (Birnie, Enderbury, Kanton [Canton], McKean, Manra [Sydney], Nikumaroro [Gardner], Orona [Hull], Rawaki [Phoenix])	Kanton	11	29	45
TOTAL		313	811	72,335

Demography

Population (1998): 84,000.
Density (1998)[4]: persons per sq mi 300.0, persons per sq km 115.7.
Urban-rural (1997): urban 36.0%; rural 64.0%.
Sex distribution (1990): male 49.45%; female 50.55%.
Age breakdown (1990): under 15, 40.3%; 15–29, 27.5%; 30–44, 17.3%; 45–59, 9.2%; 60–74, 4.8%; 75 and over, 0.9%.
Population projection: (2000) 87,000; (2010) 94,700.
Doubling time: 35 years.
Ethnic composition (1990): I-Kiribati 97.4%; mixed (part I-Kiribati and other) 1.5%; Tuvaluan 0.5%; European 0.2%; other 0.4%.
Religious affiliation (1990): Roman Catholic 53.5%; Kiribati Protestant (Congregational) 39.2%; Bahā'ī 2.4%; Seventh-day Adventist 1.9%; Mormon 1.7%; other 1.3%.
Major cities (1990): urban Tarawa 25,154.

Vital statistics

Birth rate per 1,000 population (1994): 31.0 (world avg. 25.0); legitimate, n.a.; illegitimate, n.a.
Death rate per 1,000 population (1994): 11.0 (world avg. 9.3).
Natural increase rate per 1,000 population (1994): 20.0 (world avg. 15.7).
Total fertility rate (avg. births per childbearing woman; 1997): 3.3.
Marriage rate per 1,000 population (1988): 5.2.
Life expectancy at birth (1997): male 62.0 years; female 67.0 years.
Major causes of death per 100,000 population (1993): senility without mention of psychosis 61.2; stroke 39.1; diarrhea 37.8; hepatitis 32.5; diabetes mellitus 28.6; malnutrition 23.4; meningitis 18.2.

National economy

Budget (1995). Revenue: $A 42,200,000 (nontax revenue 71.1%, tax revenue 28.9%). Expenditures: $A 70,600,000 (current expenditure 68.1%, capital expenditure 31.9%).
Public debt (external, outstanding; 1993): U.S.$18,000,000.
Tourism (1995): receipts from visitors U.S.$1,000,000; expenditures by nationals abroad (1994) U.S.$3,000,000.
Production (metric tons except as noted). Agriculture, forestry, fishing (1996): coconuts 68,000, roots and tubers 8,100 (of which taro 1,600), copra (1994) 8,000, vegetables and melons 5,000, bananas 4,500, seaweed (1994) 1,200; livestock (number of live animals) 9,500 pigs, 300,000 chickens; fish catch (1995) 24,685. Mining and quarrying: none. Manufacturing (1991): processed copra 8,661; other important products are processed fish, baked goods,

clothing, and handicrafts. Energy production (consumption): electricity (kW-hr; 1993) 7,000,000 (7,000,000); coal, none (n.a.); crude petroleum, none (n.a.); petroleum products (metric tons; 1993) none (7,000).
Gross national product (1996): U.S.$75,000,000 (U.S.$920 per capita).

Structure of gross domestic product and labour force

	1994		1990	
	in value $A '000	% of total value	labour force	% of labour force
Agriculture, fishing	11,460	22.5	23,137[5]	71.0[5]
Mining	—	—	—	—
Manufacturing	379	0.7	622	1.9
Construction	1,100	2.2	339	1.0
Public utilities	860	1.7	301	0.9
Transp. and commun.	5,917	11.6	921	2.8
Trade	8,195	16.1	1,341	4.1
Finance	2,040	4.0	441	1.4
Pub. admin., defense	14,775	29.0	2,123	6.5
Services			2,286	7.0
Other	6,200	12.2	1,099[6]	3.4[6]
TOTAL	50,926	100.0	32,610	100.0

Population economically active (1990): total 32,610; activity rate of total population 45.1% (participation rates: over age 15, 75.6%; female 46.4%; unemployed 2.8%).

Price and earnings indexes (1985 = 100)

	1989	1990	1991	1992	1993	1994	1995
Consumer price index	120.8	126.9	131.7	138.3	146.7	154.2	164.2
Earnings index	...	...	...	...	...	...	...

Household income and expenditure. Average household size (1990) 6.6; income per household: n.a.; sources of income (1978): wages 69.7%, self-employment 21.4%, transfer payments 6.0%, other 2.9%; expenditure (1982): food 50.0%, tobacco and alcohol 14.0%, clothing 8.0%, transportation 8.0%, housing, energy, and household operation 7.5%.
Land use (1994): forest 2.7%; agricultural and under permanent cultivation 50.7%; other 46.6%.

Foreign trade

Balance of trade[7] (current prices)

	1992	1993	1994	1995	1996
$A '000	−44,882	−36,443	−29,303	−38,826	−41,000
% of total	88.8%	80.7%	68.1%	69.0%	75.0%

Imports (1994): $A 36,115,000 (food and live animals 31.6%; machinery and transport equipment 17.4%; basic manufactures 13.4%; mineral fuels 9.3%; beverages and tobacco 8.7%; chemicals 6.4%; crude materials 2.1%). *Major import sources:* France 27.6%; United States 26.2%; Australia 16.3%; Fiji 8.3%; Japan 7.5%; New Zealand 2.5%.
Exports (1994): $A 7,110,000 (domestic exports 73.4%, of which copra 63.0%, fish and fish preparations 6.2%, seaweed 4.2%; reexports 26.6%). *Major export destinations:* Japan 32.9%; United States 17.1%; Hong Kong 12.9%; Bangladesh 8.6%; Germany 8.6%; Malaysia 7.1%.

Transport and communications

Transport. Roads (1995): total length 407 mi, 655 km (paved [1991] 5%). Vehicles (1982): passenger cars 307; trucks and buses 130. Merchant marine (1992): vessels (100 gross tons and over) 7; total deadweight tonnage 2,685. Air transport (1993): passenger-mi 6,000,000, passenger-km 10,000,000; short ton-mi cargo 514,000[8], metric ton-km cargo 750,000[8]; airports (1996) with scheduled flights 17.

Communications

Medium	date	unit	number	units per 1,000 persons
Radio	1996	receivers	6,050	75
Television	1995	receivers	685	8.6
Telephones	1995	main lines	2,000	25
Facsimile machines	1995	units	200	2.5

Education and health

Educational attainment (1990)[9]. Percentage of population age 15 and over having: no schooling 6.9%; primary 67.8%; secondary 24.5%; higher 0.6%; not stated 0.2%. Literacy (1985): total population age 15 and over literate 90%.

Education (1993)

	schools	teachers	students	student/ teacher ratio
Primary (age 6–13)	92	537	16,316	30.4
Secondary (age 14–18)	9[7]	179	3,152	17.6
Voc., teacher tr.	6[7]	40	297	7.4
Higher[10]	—	—	—	—

Health: physicians (1993) 10 (1 per 7,687 persons); hospital beds (1990) 283 (1 per 253 persons); infant mortality rate per 1,000 live births (1996) 54.
Food (1995): daily per capita caloric intake 2,772 (vegetable products 88%, animal products 12%); 122% of FAO recommended minimum requirement.

[1]Includes two nonelective members. [2]Includes uninhabited islands. [3]Detail does not add to total given because of rounding. [4]Based on inhabited island areas (280 sq mi, [726 sq km]) only. [5]Includes 20,568 persons engaged in "village work" (subsistence agriculture or fishing). [6]Includes 900 unemployed. [7]Exports do not include reexports. [8]1990. [9]For indigenous population. [10]54 students overseas.

Korea, North

Official name: Chosŏn Minjujuŭi
In'min Konghwaguk (Democratic
People's Republic of Korea).
Form of government: unitary
single-party republic with one
legislative house (Supreme People's
Assembly [687]).
Chief of state: Head of State[1].
Head of state and government: Premier.
Capital: P'yŏngyang.
Official language: Korean.
Official religion: none.
Monetary unit: 1 won = 100
chŏn; valuation (Sept. 25, 1998)
1 U.S.$ = 2.20 won[2]; 1 £ = 3.75 won.

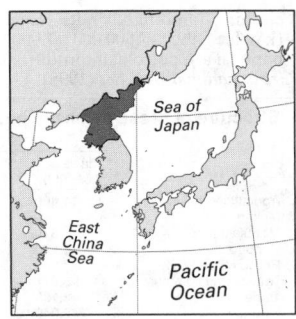

Area and population

Provinces	Capitals	area sq mi	area sq km	population[3] 1987 estimate
Chagang-do	Kanggye	6,551	16,968	1,156,000
Kangwŏn-do	Wŏnsan	4,306	11,152	1,227,000
North Hamgyŏng (Hamgyŏng-pukto)	Ch'ŏngjin	6,784	17,570	2,003,000
North Hwanghae (Hwanghae-pukto)	Sariwŏn	3,091	8,007	1,409,000
North Pyŏngan (P'yŏngan-pukto)	Sinŭiju	4,707[4]	12,191[4]	2,380,000
South Hamgyŏng (Hamgyŏng-namdo)	Hamhŭng	7,324	18,970	2,547,000
South Hwanghae (Hwanghae-namdo)	Haeju	3,090	8,002	1,914,000
South Pyŏngan (P'yŏngan-namdo)	P'yŏngsan	4,470	11,577	2,653,000
Yanggang-do	Hyesan	5,528	14,317	628,000
Special cities				
Kaesŏng	—	485	1,255	331,000
Namp'o	—	291	753	715,000
P'yŏngyang	—	772	2,000	2,355,000
Special district				
Hyangsan-chigu	—	4	4	28,000
TOTAL		47,399	122,762	19,346,000

Demography

Population (1998): 21,234,000.
Density (1998): persons per sq mi 448.0, persons per sq km 173.0.
Urban-rural (1995): urban 61.3%; rural 38.7%.
Sex distribution (1997): male 48.83%; female 51.17%.
Age breakdown (1997): under 15, 26.5%; 15–29, 26.0%; 30–44, 21.9%; 45–59, 15.2%; 60–74, 8.7%; 75 and over, 1.7%.
Population projection: (2000) 21,688,000; (2010) 23,505,000.
Ethnic composition (1989): Korean 99.8%; Chinese 0.2%.
Religious affiliation (1980): atheist or nonreligious 68.3%; traditional beliefs 15.6%; Ch'ŏndogyo 13.9%; Buddhist 1.7%; Christian 0.5%.
Major cities (1987): P'yŏngyang 2,500,000[5]; Hamhŭng 701,000; Ch'ŏngjin 520,000; Namp'o 370,000; Sunch'ŏn 356,000.

Vital statistics

Birth rate per 1,000 population (1996): 22.5 (world avg. 25.0).
Death rate per 1,000 population (1996): 5.3 (world avg. 9.3).
Natural increase rate per 1,000 population (1996): 17.2 (world avg. 15.7).
Total fertility rate (avg. births per childbearing woman; 1996): 2.3.
Marriage rate per 1,000 population (1987): 9.3.
Divorce rate per 1,000 population (1987): 0.2.
Life expectancy at birth (1997): male 69.0 years; female 75.0 years.
Major causes of death per 100,000 population (1986): diseases of the circulatory system 224.9; malignant neoplasms (cancers) 69.0; diseases of the digestive system 51.6; diseases of the respiratory system 46.7; injuries and poisoning 38.2; infectious and parasitic diseases 19.4.

National economy

Budget (1994). Revenue: 41,525,200,000 won (1984; turnover tax 55.0%, payments by state enterprises 30.0%). Expenditures: 41,525,200,000 won (national economy 67.8%, social and cultural affairs 19.8%, defense 11.6%).
Public debt (external, outstanding; 1993): U.S.$10,300,000,000.
Population economically active (1994)[6]: total 12,486,000; activity rate of total population 53.2% (participation rates [1988–93]: ages 15–64, 49.5%; female 46.0%; unemployed, n.a.).
Production (metric tons except as noted). Agriculture, forestry, fishing (1997): rice 2,300,000, potatoes 1,550,000, corn (maize) 1,500,000, cabbages 700,000, apples 650,000, sweet potatoes 455,000, soybeans 420,000, pears 120,000, peaches and nectarines 110,000, watermelons 105,000, wheat 100,000, cucumbers and gherkins 65,000, tomatoes 65,000, tobacco leaves 63,000, barley 55,000, millet 10,000, oats 10,000; livestock (number of live animals) 3,100,000 pigs, 1,150,000 cattle, 355,000 sheep, 265,000 goats, 14,000,000 chickens; roundwood (1995) 4,923,000 cu m; fish catch (1995) 1,850,000. Mining and quarrying (1995): iron ore 11,000,000; magnesite (metal content) 1,600,000; phosphate rock 520,000; sulfur 250,000; zinc 200,000; lead (metal content) 80,000; fluorspar 40,000; graphite 40,000; copper 16,000; silver 50; gold 5,000 kg. Manufacturing (1995): cement 17,000,000; crude steel 8,100,000; pig iron 6,600,000; coke 3,000,000; steel semimanufactures 2,700,000[7]; chemical fertilizers 2,500,000[7]; meat 259,200[5]; gasoline 8,600,000 barrels; textile fabrics 350,000,000 sq m[7]. Construction: n.a. Energy production (consumption): electricity (kW-hr; 1994) 37,000,000 (37,000,000); coal (metric tons; 1994) 71,500,000 (73,425,000); crude petroleum (barrels; 1994) none (16,492,500); petroleum products (metric tons; 1994) 2,835,000 (4,346,000).

Household income and expenditure. Average household size (1987) 4.8; average annual income per household (1980) 3,677 won (U.S.$4,275); sources of income: n.a.; expenditure (1984)[8]: food 46.5%, clothing 29.9%, furniture 3.8%, energy 3.3%, housing 0.6%.
Gross national product (1996): U.S.$20,867,000,000 (U.S.$970 per capita).

Structure of gross domestic product and labour force

	1982 in value '000,000 won	1982 % of total value	1990–92 labour force	1990–92 % of labour force
Agriculture	...	...	4,987,000	43.0
Mining and manufacturing	...	...	} 3,479,000	30.0
Construction	...	...		
Public utilities	...	...		
Transp. and commun.	...	...		
Trade	...	...		
Finance	...	...	} 3,131,000	27.0
Pub. admin., defense	...	...		
Services	...	...		
Other	...	...		
TOTAL	11,800	100.0	11,597,000	100.0

Land use (1994): forested 61.2%; meadows and pastures 0.4%; agricultural and under permanent cultivation 16.6%; other 21.8%.

Foreign trade[9]

Balance of trade (current prices)

	1990	1991	1992	1993	1994	1995
U.S.$ '000,000	−420.5	−764.7	−600.0	−600.0	−429.5	−880.0
% of total	21.0%	35.6%	18.8%	22.7%	20.4%	42.7%

Imports (1995): U.S.$1,470,000,000 (crude petroleum, coal and coke, industrial machinery and transport equipment [including trucks], industrial chemicals, textile yarn and fabrics, and grain are among the major imports). *Major import sources:* China 30.0%; Japan 15.8%; Austria 9.3%; Ukraine 5.9%.
Exports (1995): U.S.$590,000,000 (minerals [including lead, magnesite, zinc], metallurgical products [iron and steel, nonferrous metals], cement, agricultural products [including fish, grain, fruit and vegetables, tobacco], and manufactured goods [textile fabrics, clothing] are among the major exports). *Major export destinations:* Japan 31.4%; Austria 17.3%; India 6.9%.

Transport and communications

Transport. Railroads (1990): length 8,533 km. Roads (1992): total length 18,600 mi, 30,000 km (paved 6.2%). Vehicles (1990): passenger cars 248,000. Merchant marine (1992): vessels (100 gross tons and over) 100; total deadweight tonnage 951,222. Air transport (1994): passenger-mi 52,200,000, passenger-km 84,000,000; short ton-mi cargo 1,370,000, metric ton-km cargo 2,000,000; airports (1997) with scheduled flights 1.

Communications

Medium	date	unit	number	units per 1,000 persons
Daily newspapers	1994	circulation	5,000,000	213.0
Radio	1995	receivers	4,700,000	200.0
Television	1995	receivers	2,000,000	85.1
Telephones	1995	main lines	1,104,000	47.0

Education and health

Educational attainment (1987–88). Percentage of population age 16 and over having attended or graduated from postsecondary-level school: 13.7%. *Literacy* (1992): 95%.

Education (1987)

	schools	teachers	students	student/ teacher ratio
Primary (age 6–9)	6,122	138,945	1,543,000	11.1
Secondary (age 10–15)	...	111,000	2,468,000	22.2
Voc., teacher tr.	473[10]		220,000	...
Higher	281	27,000	390,000	14.4

Health (1989): physicians 57,690 (1 per 370 persons); hospital beds 290,590 (1 per 74 persons); infant mortality rate per 1,000 live births (1997) 52.0.
Food (1995)[11]: daily per capita caloric intake 2,360 (vegetable products 91%, animal products 9%); 109% of FAO recommended minimum requirement.

Military

Total active duty personnel (1997): 1,055,000 (army 87.5%, navy 4.4%, air force 8.1%). *Military expenditure as percentage of GNP* (1995): 28.6% (world 2.8%); per capita expenditure U.S.$255.

---

[1]Position in effect from Sept. 5, 1998. It is defined as an enhanced military post with revised constitutional powers. [2]Transfer rate; the black market rate (June 1997) was about 200 won to 1 U.S.$. [3]Civilian population only; UN cites a 1993 census total of 21,123,376, but details are not available. [4]North P'yŏngan includes special district of Hyangsan-chigu. [5]1996 estimate. [6]The Democratic People's Republic of Korea categorizes economically active as including students in higher education, retirees, and heads of households, as well as those in the civilian labour force. [7]1994. [8]Workers and clerical workers only. [9]Imports are f.o.b. [10]1986. [11]Owing to famine in 1996 and 1997, daily per capita caloric intake was reduced to less than 1,000 calories.

Internet resources for further information:
• Korean News http://www.kcna.co.jp
• United States Department of Energy http://www.eia.doe.gov/emeu/cabs/nkorea.html

Korea, South

Official name: Taehan Min'guk (Republic of Korea).
Form of government: unitary multiparty republic with one legislative house (National Assembly [299]).
Head of state and government: President, assisted by Prime Minister.
Capital: Seoul.
Official language: Korean.
Official religion: none.
Monetary unit: 1 won (W) = 100 chon; valuation (Sept. 25, 1998) 1 U.S.$ = W 1,386; 1 £ = W 2,360.

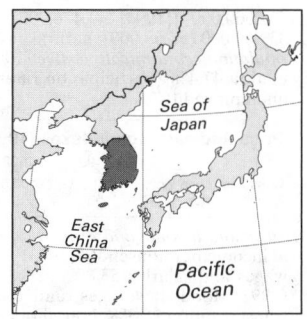

Area and population

Provinces	Capitals	area sq mi	area sq km	population 1995 census
Cheju-do	Cheju	712	1,845	505,442
Chŏlla-namdo	Kwangju	4,599	11,911	2,066,865
Chŏlla-pukto	Chŏnju	3,111	8,059	1,902,205
Ch'ungch'ŏng-namdo	Taejŏn	3,300	8,547	1,767,105
Ch'ungch'ŏng-pukto	Ch'ŏngju	2,870	7,433	1,396,481
Kangwŏn-do	Ch'unch'ŏn'	6,384	16,534	1,466,794
Kyŏnggi-do	Suwŏn	3,905	10,115	7,649,914
Kyŏngsang-namdo	Masan	4,466	11,566	3,845,569
Kyŏngsang-pukto	Taegu	7,345	19,022	2,676,344
Special cities				
Inch'ŏn-si	Inch'ŏn	369	955	2,307,618
Kwangju-si	Kwangju	193	501	1,257,504
Pusan-si	Pusan	289	749	3,813,814
Sŏul-t'ŭkpyŏlsi	Seoul	234	606	10,229,262
Taegu-si	Taegu	342	886	2,449,139
Taejŏn-si	Taejŏn	209	540	1,272,143
TOTAL		38,328	99,268	44,606,199

Demography

Population (1998): 46,451,000.
Density (1998): persons per sq mi 1,212, persons per sq km 467.9.
Urban-rural (1995): urban 81.0%; rural 19.0%.
Sex distribution (1996): male 50.34%; female 49.66%.
Age breakdown (1996): under 15, 22.6%; 15–29, 28.0%; 30–44, 25.5%; 45–59, 14.6%; 60–74, 7.5%; 75 and over, 1.8%.
Population projection: (2000) 47,386,000; (2010) 50,317,000.
Doubling time: 78 years.
Ethnic composition (1990): Korean 99.9%; other 0.1%.
Religious affiliation (1995): religious[1] 51.1%, of which Buddhist 23.3%, Protestant 19.8%, Roman Catholic 6.7%, Confucian 0.4%, Wonbulgyo 0.2%, Ch'ŏndogyo 0.1%, other 0.6%; nonreligious 48.9%.
Major cities (1995): Seoul 10,229,262; Pusan 3,813,814; Taegu 2,449,139; Inch'ŏn 2,307,618; Taejŏn 1,272,143.

Vital statistics

Birth rate per 1,000 population (1997): 15.1 (world avg. 25.0).
Death rate per 1,000 population (1997): 6.4 (world avg. 9.3).
Natural increase rate per 1,000 population (1997): 8.7 (world avg. 15.7).
Total fertility rate (avg. births per childbearing woman; 1997): 1.7.
Marriage rate per 1,000 population (1994): 6.8.
Divorce rate per 1,000 population (1994): 1.1
Life expectancy at birth (1997): male 69.0 years; female 76.0 years.
Major causes of death per 100,000 population (1994): diseases of the circulatory system 155.0; malignant neoplasms (cancers) 111.3; accidents, poisoning, and violence 72.0; diseases of the digestive system 39.6.

National economy

Budget (1996). Revenue: W 81,581,000,000,000 (taxes on goods and services 32.8%, income taxes 29.1%, nontax revenue 11.9%, social security contributions 7.7%, taxes on international trade 6.2%). Expenditures: W 73,582,000,000,000 (education 21.1%, defense 16.8%, social security and welfare 10.5%, agriculture 8.9%, transportation and communications 9.0%, agriculture 8.2%, public order 5.9%, general public services 4.5%).
Public debt (external, outstanding; 1995): U.S.$24,095,000,000.
Production (metric tons except as noted). Agriculture, forestry, fishing (1996): rice 6,284,000, cabbages 3,200,000, apples 630,000, tangerines 600,000, dry onions 570,000; livestock (number of live animals) 6,950,000 pigs, 3,463,000 cattle, 88,000,000 chickens; roundwood (1995) 6,485,000 cu m; fish catch (1993) 2,648,977. Mining and quarrying (1995): copper ore 233,000; iron ore 184,443; zinc concentrate 15,494. Manufacturing (1995): cement 56,101,000; pig iron 22,344,000; newsprint 956,864; polyvinyl chloride resin 914,201; woolen fabrics 17,773,134 sq m; colour television receivers 18,555,000 units; passenger cars 1,999,000 units. Construction (permits authorized; 1996): residential 71,404,000 sq m; nonresidential 73,226,000 sq m. Energy production (consumption): electricity (kW-hr; 1995) 163,270,000,000 (163,270,000,000); coal (metric tons; 1994) 7,438,000 (42,660,000); crude petroleum (barrels; 1994) none (544,639,000); petroleum products (metric tons; 1994) 103,580,000 (84,788,000); natural gas (cu m; 1994) none (3,864,000,000).
Household income and expenditure (1995)[2]. Average household size 3.7; income per household W 39,390,000 (U.S.$51,070); sources of income: wages 50.0%, other 50.0%; expenditure: food and beverages 25.5%, education and recreation 13.4%, transportation and communications 9.8%, clothing and footwear 7.0%, health care 4.4%, household durable goods 4.3%, utilities 3.7%, housing 3.4%, other 28.5%.

Gross national product (1996): U.S.$483,130,000,000 (U.S.$10,610 per capita).

Structure of gross domestic product and labour force

	1996 in value W '000,000,000[3]	% of total value	labour force	% of labour force
Agriculture	17,582.9	6.4	2,405,000	11.3
Mining	825.0	0.3	24,000	0.1
Manufacturing	82,849.0	30.0	4,677,000	22.1
Construction	31,128.2	11.3	1,968,000	9.3
Public utilities	6,881.9	2.5		
Transp. and commun.	22,976.6	8.3		
Trade	34,282.2	12.4		
Finance	47,366.8	17.2	11,689,000	55.2
Pub. admin., defense	15,274.0	5.5		
Services	15,593.1	5.7		
Other	1,089.8[4]	0.4[4]	425,000[5]	2.0[5]
TOTAL	275,849.5	100.0	21,188,000	100.0

Population economically active (1996): total 21,188,000; activity rate 46.5% (participation rates: ages 15 and over, 62.0%; female [1994] 40.1%; unemployed 2.0%).

Price and earnings indexes (1990 = 100)

	1991	1992	1993	1994	1995	1996	1997
Consumer price index	109.3	116.1	121.7	129.2	135.0	141.7	148.0
Monthly earnings index	116.9	135.2	149.9	173.1	190.2	213.5	224.6

Tourism (1995): receipts from visitors U.S.$5,587,000,000; expenditures by nationals abroad U.S.$5,903,000,000.

Foreign trade

Balance of trade (current prices)

	1991	1992	1993	1994	1995	1996
U.S.$'000,000	−3,968	−588	+2,880	−729	−2,896	−12,411
% of total	3.6%	0.4%	1.8%	0.5%	1.1%	4.6%

Imports (1996): U.S.$150,339,100,000 (machinery and transport equipment 36.3%, mineral fuels and lubricants 16.2%, manufactured goods 13.9%, chemicals 8.8%, inedible crude materials 7.3%). *Major import sources:* U.S. 22.2%; Japan 20.9%; Germany 4.8%; Saudi Arabia 4.4%; Australia 4.2%.
Exports (1996): U.S.$129,715,100,000 (machinery and transport equipment 52.1%, manufactured goods 20.8%, chemicals 7.1%, mineral fuels 3.0%). *Major export destinations:* United States 16.7%; Japan 12.2%; Hong Kong 8.6%; Singapore 5.0%; Germany 3.6%.

Transport and communications

Transport. Railroads (1995): length 6,554 km; passenger-km 29,292,000,000; metric ton-km cargo 13,838,000,000. Roads (1995): total length 74,235 km (paved 76%). Vehicles (1995): passenger cars 6,006,290; trucks and buses 2,462,611. Air transport (1995): passenger-km 48,504,000,000; metric ton-km cargo 5,729,328,000; airports (1996) with scheduled flights 14.

Communications

Medium	date	unit	number	units per 1,000 persons
Daily newspapers	1994	circulation	18,000,000	405
Radio	1996	receivers	42,000,000	928
Television	1995	receivers	10,430,000	233
Telephones	1995	main lines	18,600,200	415
Cellular telephones	1995	subscribers	1,641,000	37
Facsimile machines	1995	units	375,000	8.4
Personal computers	1995	units	5,420,000	121

Education and health

Educational attainment (1995). Percentage of population age 25 and over having: no formal schooling 8.5%; primary education or less 17.7%; some secondary and secondary 53.1%; postsecondary 20.6%. *Literacy* (1990): total population age 15 and over literate 98.0%; males 99.3%; females 96.7%.

Education (1996)

	schools	teachers	students	student/ teacher ratio
Primary (age 6–13)	5,732	137,912	3,800,540	27.6
Secondary (age 14–19)	3,790	157,731	3,683,857	23.4
Vocational	797	44,163	950,173	21.5
Higher	802	60,883	2,056,370	33.8

Health (1995): physicians 57,188 (1 per 784 persons); hospital beds 196,232 (1 per 229 persons); infant mortality rate per 1,000 live births (1996) 10.0.
Food (1995): daily per capita caloric intake 3,268 (vegetable products 84%, animal products 16%); 139% of FAO recommended minimum requirement.

Military

Total active duty personnel (1996): 660,000 (army 83.0%, navy 9.1%, air force 7.9%). *Military expenditure as percentage of GNP* (1994): 3.7% (world 3.0%); per capita expenditure U.S.$293.

[1]Refers to persons who have received commandments, accepted baptism, or entered a faith and who participate in a religious function regularly or put the religious idea into practice. [2]Excludes farm households. [3]At 1990 constant prices. [4]Import duties less imputed bank service charges. [5]Unemployed.

Internet resources for further information:
• **Korean Statistical Information System http://www.nso.go.kr/eindex.html**
• **KoreaNet http://www.iworld.net/Korea/**

Kuwait

Official name: Dawlat al-Kuwayt (State of Kuwait).
Form of government: Constitutional monarchy with one legislative body (National Assembly [64[1]]).
Head of state and government: Emir[2].
Capital: Kuwait City.
Official language: Arabic.
Official religion: Islam.
Monetary unit: 1 Kuwaiti dinar (KD) = 1,000 fils; valuation (Sept. 25, 1998) 1 KD = U.S.$3.30 = £1.94.

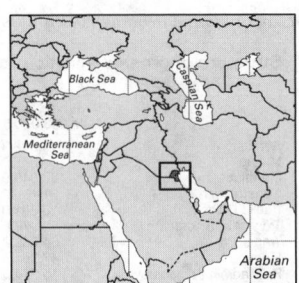

Area and population[3]		area		population[4]
Governorates[5]	Capitals	sq mi	sq km	1997 estimate
Al-Aḥmadī	Al-Aḥmadī	1,984	5,138	303,769
Al-Farwānīyah	Al-Farwānīyah	...	...	483,501
Al-Jahrā'	Al-Jahrā'	4,372	11,324	244,552
Capital	Kuwait City	38	98	296,327
Ḥawallī	Ḥawallī	138	358	481,121
Islands[6]	—	347	900	...
TOTAL		6,880[7]	17,818	1,809,270[4]

Demography

Population (1998): 1,866,000.
Density (1998): persons per sq mi 271.2, persons per sq km 104.7.
Urban-rural (1995): urban 97.0%; rural 3.0%.
Sex distribution (1995): male 61.45%; female 38.55%.
Age breakdown (1994): under 15, 29.4%; 15–29, 28.3%; 30–44, 30.5%; 45–59, 9.5%; 60–74, 2.0%; 75 and over, 0.3%.
Population projection: (2000) 2,017,000; (2010) 2,712,000.
Doubling time: 22 years.
Ethno-linguistic composition (1995): Arabic 78%; other 22%.
Religious affiliation (1995): Muslim 85%, of which Sunnī 45%, Shī'ī 30%; other Muslim 10%; other (mostly Christian and Hindu) 15.0%.
Major cities (1995): As-Sālimīyah 130,215; Qalīb ash-Shuyūkh 102,178; Ḥawallī 82,238; Abraq Khīṭān 63,628; Kuwait City 28,859.

Vital statistics

Birth rate per 1,000 population (1995): 24.3 (world avg. 25.0).
Death rate per 1,000 population (1995): 2.2 (world avg. 9.3).
Natural increase rate per 1,000 population (1995): 22.1 (world avg. 15.7).
Total fertility rate (avg. births per childbearing woman; 1994): 3.7.
Marriage rate per 1,000 population (1993): 8.0[8].
Divorce rate per 1,000 population (1993): 1.9[8].
Life expectancy at birth (1994): male 74.4 years; female 79.0 years.
Major causes of death per 100,000 population (1995): circulatory diseases 87.5; accidents, poisoning, and violence 35.8; cancers 24.9; respiratory diseases 12.3; congenital anomalies 11.3; endocrine, nutritional, and metabolic diseases 8.2; infectious and parasitic diseases 6.7; genitourinary diseases 6.0.

National economy

Budget[9] (1996–97). Revenue: KD 3,000,000,000 (oil revenue 85.3%). Expenditures: KD 4,210,000,000 (current expenditures 67.7%, of which transfers 21.1%, defense 20.2%, education 7.6%, health 6.3%; development expenditure 10.5%).
Public debt: n.a.
Tourism (1995): receipts from visitors U.S.$107,000,000; expenditures by nationals abroad U.S.$2,322,000,000.
Gross national product (1996): U.S.$35,901,000,000 (U.S.$20,470 per capita).

Structure of gross domestic product and labour force				
	1996			
	in value KD '000,000[10]	% of total value	labour force[11]	% of labour force[11]
Agriculture	37.9	0.4	23,400	1.9
Mining (oil sector)	4,127.4	44.5	8,600	0.7
Manufacturing	1,036.0	11.2	83,600	6.8
Construction	243.7	2.6	136,500	11.1
Public utilities	2.0	0.0	8,600	0.7
Transp. and commun.	397.1	4.3	44,300	3.6
Trade[12]	627.0	6.8	206,600	16.8
Finance and business services	950.6	10.3	43,100	3.5
Pub. admin., defense Services	} 1,953.1	21.1	597,800	48.6
Other	−97.7[13]	−1.1[13]	77,500	6.3
TOTAL	9,277.1	100.0[7]	1,230,000	100.0

Production (metric tons except as noted). Agriculture, forestry, fishing (1997): cucumber and gherkins 26,500, onions 20,500, tomatoes 20,500, eggplants 3,250, garlic 1,450; livestock (number of live animals) 320,000 sheep, 75,000 goats, 22,000 cattle, 8,600 camels; fish catch (1995) 8,706. Mining and quarrying (1994): sulfur 175,000; lime 35,000. Manufacturing (value added in KD '000; 1993): refined petroleum products 383,525; clothing and apparel 35,722; food products 35,610; fabricated metal products 33,343; cement, bricks, and tile 31,302; furniture and fixtures 15,103. Construction (floor area of new construction; 1995): residential 2,018,600 sq m; nonresidential 141,200 sq m. Energy production (consumption): electricity (kW-hr; 1994) 23,152,-000,000 (23,152,000,000); coal, none (none): crude petroleum (barrels; 1995)

657,000,000 ([1994] 44,426,000); petroleum products (metric tons; 1994) 33,869,000 (5,268,000); natural gas (cu m; 1994) 5,970,000,000 (5,970,000,000).
Population economically active (1995): total 746,408; activity rate of total population 47.4% (participation rates: ages 15–59, 70.7%; female [1988] 18.8%; unemployed 0.7%).

Price and earnings indexes (1990 = 100)							
	1991	1992	1993	1994	1995	1996	1997
Consumer price index	109.1	108.5	108.9	111.6	114.6	118.7	119.4
Earnings index	...	...	...	...	...	...	...

Household income and expenditure. Average household size (1986) 7.4; annual income per household (1973)[14] KD 4,246 (U.S.$12,907); sources of income: wages and salaries 53.8%, self-employment 20.8%, other 25.4; expenditure (1992): food, beverages, and tobacco 37.0%, housing and energy 18.7%, transportation 15.3%, household appliances and services 11.1%, clothing and footwear 10.0%, education and health 2.5%.
Land use (1994): forest 0.1%; pasture 7.7%; agriculture 0.3%; other 91.9%.

Foreign trade

Balance of trade (current prices)							
	1991	1992	1993	1994	1995	1996	1997
KD '000,000	−1,043	−198	+967	+1,354	+1,491	+1,951	+1,813
% of total	62.8%	4.9%	18.6%	25.4%	24.3%	28.0%	26.6%

Imports (1996): KD 2,507,170,000 (machinery and transport equipment 41.6%, manufactured goods 19.8%, food and live animals 14.0%, miscellaneous manufactured articles 12.9%, chemical products 7.2%, beverages and tobacco 1.1%). *Major import sources:* U.S. 16.7%; Japan 12.1%; Germany 7.0%; Italy 6.9%; Saudi Arabia 6.7%; U.K. 6.1%; France 4.0%; India 3.2%.
Exports (1996)[15]: KD 4,458,000,000 (crude petroleum and petroleum products 94.9%). *Major export destinations:* India 18.6%; Saudi Arabia 16.9%; U.A.E. 15.0%; U.S. 5.7%; China 4.9%; Philippines 2.6%; Bahrain 2.3%; Egypt 2.3%.

Transport and communications

Transport. Railroads: none. Roads (1995): total length 2,709 mi, 4,360 km (paved 81%). Vehicles (1995): passenger cars 545,000; trucks and buses 155,000. Merchant marine (1992): vessels (100 gross tons and over) 209; total deadweight tonnage 3,188,526. Air transport (1995)[16]: passenger-mi 3,184,038,000, passenger-km 5,124,223,000; short ton-mi cargo 225,837,000, metric ton-km cargo 329,717,000; airports (1997) with scheduled flights 1.

Communications				units per 1,000
Medium	date	unit	number	persons
Daily newspapers	1995	circulation	671,672	397
Radio	1995	receivers	1,000,000	592
Television	1996	receivers	800,000	456
Telephones	1994	main lines	373,000	230
Cellular telephones	1995	subscribers	119,520	70.7
Facsimile machines	1995	units	35,500	21.0
Personal computers	1995	units	96,530	57.1

Education and health

Educational attainment (1988). Percentage of population age 25 and over having: no formal schooling 44.8%; primary education 8.6%; some secondary 15.1%; complete secondary 15.1%; higher 16.4%. *Literacy* (1995 est.): total population age 15 and over literate 78.6%; males literate 82.2%; females literate 74.9%.

Education (1995–1996)				student/
	schools	teachers	students	teacher ratio
Primary (age 6–9)	251	9,414	140,979	15.0
Secondary (age 10–17)	409	18,700	204,194	10.9
Voc., teacher tr.	36	717	3,604	5.0
Higher[17]	1	960	16,767	17.5

Health (1995): physicians 3,642 (1 per 464 persons); hospital beds 4,093[18] (1 per 357 persons); infant mortality rate per 1,000 live births 11.1.
Food (1995): daily per capita caloric intake 3,160 (vegetable products 75%, animal products 25%); 131% of FAO recommended minimum requirement.

Military

Total active duty personnel (1997): 15,300 (army [including central staff] 71.9%, navy 11.8%, air force 16.3%). *Military expenditure as percentage of GNP* (1995): 11.6% (world 2.8%); per capita expenditure U.S.$1,919.

[1]50 elected seats include 4 elected Cabinet ministers; nonelected Cabinet ministers serving ex officio occupy the other 14 seats. [2]Assisted by prime minister. [3]Area of governorates reflects situation prior to Amiri Decree No. 156 of 1988, which established Al-Farwānīyah governorate; but population figures account for the reorganization. [4]Estimates based on census taken on April 23, 1995. [5]Governorates have no administrative function. [6]Bubian Island 333 sq mi (863 sq km) and Warba Island 14 sq mi (37 sq km). [7]Detail does not add to total given because of rounding. [8]Provisional. [9]Approved budget for 1996–97. [10]At purchaser's value. [11]Size of labour force and subtotal figures derived from percentages. [12]Trade includes restaurants and hotels. [13]Includes import duties and imputed bank service charges. [14]Kuwaiti households only. [15]Total exports and reexports include oil and non-oil, but breakdown by destination is derived from non-oil exports. [16]Kuwait Airways only. [17]1994–95. [18]1993; public hospitals only.

Internet resources for further information:
• **Central Bank of Kuwait** http://www.cbk.gov.kw
• **Kuwait Information Office (Washington, D.C.)**
  http://www.kuwait.info.nw.dc.us/main.htm

Kyrgyzstan

Official name: Kyrgyz Respublikasy (Kyrgyz Republic).
Form of government: unitary multiparty republic with two legislative houses (Assembly of People's Representatives [70]; Legislative Assembly [35]).
Head of state and government: President assisted by Prime Minister.
Capital: Bishkek (formerly Frunze).
Official language: Kyrgyz[1].
Official religion: none.
Monetary unit: 1 som = 100 tiyin; valuation (Sept. 25, 1998) free rate, 1 U.S.$ = 21.60 som; 1 £ = 36.77 som.

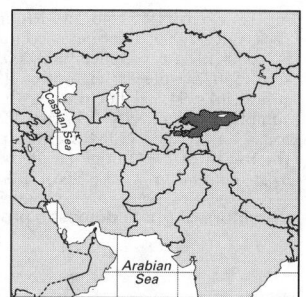

Area and population

Provinces	Capitals	area sq mi	area sq km	population 1993[2] estimate
Chüy (Chu)	Kara-Balta	7,200	18,700	774,000
Jalal-Abad (Dzhalal-Abad)	Jalal-Abad (Dzhalal-Abad)	15,200	39,500	812,800
Naryn	Naryn	18,300	47,300	267,900
Osh	Osh	14,700	38,100	1,360,900
Talas	Talas	4,400	11,400	203,000
Ysyk-Köl (Issyk-Kul)	Ysyk-Köl (Issyk-Kul)	16,800	43,500	429,300
City of republic subordination				
Bishkek (Frunze)	—	...	...	634,100
TOTAL		76,600[3]	198,500[3]	4,482,000

Demography

Population (1998): 4,691,000.
Density (1998): persons per sq mi 60.8, persons per sq km 23.5.
Urban-rural (1996): urban 34.7%; rural 65.3%.
Sex distribution (1996): male 49.35%; female 50.65%.
Age breakdown (1989): under 15, 37.5%; 15–29, 27.0%; 30–44, 16.3%; 45–59, 10.9%; 60–74, 6.2%; 75 and over, 2.1%.
Population projection: (2000) 4,797,000; (2010) 5,356,000.
Doubling time: 47 years.
Ethnic composition (1996[2]): Kyrgyz 59.7%; Russian 16.2%; Uzbek 14.1%; Ukrainian 1.7%; Tatar 1.2%; Kazak 0.9%; other 6.2%.
Religious affiliation (1997): Muslim (mostly Sunnī) 70.0%; Russian Orthodox 5.7%; other 24.3%.
Major cities (1991): Bishkek (Frunze) 631,300; Osh 218,700; Jalal-Abad 74,200; Tokmok 71,200; Kara-Köl 64,300.

Vital statistics

Birth rate per 1,000 population (1995): 25.9 (world avg. 25.0); (1994) legitimate 83.2%; illegitimate 16.8%.
Death rate per 1,000 population (1995): 8.1 (world avg. 9.3).
Natural increase rate per 1,000 population (1995): 17.8 (world avg. 15.7).
Total fertility rate (avg. births per childbearing woman; 1993): 3.3.
Marriage rate per 1,000 population (1994): 5.8.
Divorce rate per 1,000 population (1994): 1.2.
Life expectancy at birth (1994): male 64.0 years; female 72.0 years.
Major causes of death per 100,000 population (1993): diseases of the circulatory system 290.0; diseases of the respiratory system 125.0; accidents, poisoning, and violence 91.2; malignant neoplasms (cancers) 67.3; infectious and parasitic diseases 30.1; diseases of the digestive system 29.7.

National economy

Budget (1995). Revenue: 2,671,000,000 som (tax revenue 93.4%, of which value-added tax 27.7%, enterprise profits tax 15.5%, excise taxes 11.5%, personal income tax 10.8%, other 27.9%; nontax revenue 6.6%). Expenditures: 4,579,800,000 som (education 19.4%; social security 18.4%; health 10.9%; government services 7.4%; industrial expenditure 7.2%; public safety 6.8%; defense 4.9%).
Public debt (external, outstanding; 1996): U.S.$640,300,000.
Population economically active (1995): total 1,692,000; activity rate of total population 37.2% (1993; participation rates: ages 16–59 [male], 16–54 [female] 81.1%; female 49.0%; (1995) unemployed 1.1%).

Price and earnings indexes (1990 = 100)

	1988	1989	1990	1991	1992	1993	1994
Consumer price index	95.2	97.1	100.0	185.0	1,766	23,122	89,534
Monthly earnings index	84.5	90.9	100.0	166.9	1,179	12,559	...

Production (metric tons except as noted). Agriculture, forestry, fishing (1996): grain 1,419,000, potatoes 562,000, vegetables (other than potatoes) 369,000, fruit (other than grapes) 81,000, seed cotton 73,000, grapes 21,000; livestock (number of live animals) 4,279,000 sheep and goats, 869,000 cattle, 250,000 horses, 114,000 pigs; roundwood (1990) 6,000 cu m; fish catch (1995) 797. Mining and quarrying (1995): antimony 1,400; mercury 300; gold 850 kg. Manufacturing (value of production in '000,000 som; 1994): textiles 1,112; processed foods 729; ferrous and nonferrous metals 678; machinery and metalwork 650; construction materials 258; footwear and leather goods 89. Construction (1992): residential 1,232,000 sq m. Energy production (consumption): electricity (kW-hr; 1994) 12,932,000,000 (10,427,000,000); coal (metric tons; 1994) 298,000 (595,000); crude petroleum (barrels; 1994)

645,000 (154,000); petroleum products (metric tons; 1994) none (256,000); natural gas (cu m; 1994) 33,930,000 (1,008,000,000).
Household income and expenditure (1990). Average household size 4.7; income per household (1994) 4,359 som (U.S.$325.30); sources of income: wages and salaries 49.7%, pensions and stipends 11.1%, income from sale of agricultural products 3.5%, other 35.7%; expenditure: food and clothing 48.0%, health care 13.1%, housing 5.9%, cultural affairs 5.2%, appliances 4.4%.
Gross national product (at current market prices; 1996): U.S.$2,486,000,000 (U.S.$550 per capita)[4].

Structure of gross domestic product and labour force

	1994 in value '000,000 som	1994 % of total value	1995 labour force	1995 % of labour force
Agriculture	4,611	38.4	776,000	45.9
Mining Manufacturing Public utilities	2,462	20.5	205,000	12.1
Construction	409	3.4	66,000	3.9
Transp. and commun.	547	4.6	88,000	5.2
Trade	1,210	10.1	152,000	9.0
Finance	577	4.8	7,000	0.4
Public admin., defense	...	...	65,000	3.8
Services	1,443	12.0	278,000	16.4
Other	760	6.3	50,000	3.0
TOTAL	12,019	100.0[5]	1,692,000[5]	100.0[5]

Land use (1994): forest 3.7%; pasture 45.4%; agriculture 7.2%; other 43.7%.
Tourism (1995): receipts from visitors, U.S.$5,000,000; expenditures by nationals abroad, U.S.$6,000,000.

Foreign trade

Balance of trade (current prices)

	1993	1994	1995	1996
U.S.$'000,000	−166.3	−118.9	−263.4	−383.4
% of total	19.9%	14.9%	24.4%	27.4%

Imports (1996): U.S.$889,800,000 (1995; oil and gas 24.2%, machine-building equipment 15.4%, food products 14.4%, chemical products 4.5%, light industrial products 3.5%). *Major import sources:* Russian Federation 21.9%; Kazakstan 21.5%; Uzbekistan 17.0%; Turkey 7.3%; Cuba 4.3%.
Exports (1995): U.S.$506,400,000 (1995; food products 20.2%, light industrial products 20.1%, metals 17.7%, machinery 10.8%, oil and gas 9.9%). *Major export destinations:* Russian Federation 25.6%; Uzbekistan 17.1%; China 16.8%; Kazakstan 16.3%; U.K. 6.7%.

Transport and communications

Transport. Railroads (1995): length 249 mi, 400 km; (1992) passenger-mi 81,500,000, passenger-km 131,200,000; short ton-mi cargo 987,000,000, metric ton-km cargo 1,588,900,000. Roads (1995): total length 11,533 mi, 18,560 km (paved 91%). Vehicles (1995): passenger cars 164,000; trucks and buses, n.a. Air transport (1996): passenger-mi 2,738,000,000, passenger-km 4,408,000,000; short ton-mi cargo 40,512,000, metric ton-km cargo 65,199,000; airports (1997) with scheduled flights 2.

Communications

Medium	date	unit	number	units per 1,000 persons
Daily newspapers	1994	circulation	53,000	11
Television	1995	receivers	1,110,000	238
Telephones	1995	main lines	357,000	77

Education and health

Educational attainment (1989). Percentage of population age 19 and over having: primary education 4.7%; some secondary 20.9%; completed secondary 44.4%; some postsecondary 19.3%; higher 10.7%. *Literacy* (1989): total population age 15 and over literate 4,130,562 (97.0%); males literate 2,048,536 (98.6%); females literate 2,082,026 (95.5%).

Education (1995–96)

	schools	teachers	students	student/ teacher ratio
Primary (age 6–13)	1,885	24,086	473,077	19.7
Secondary (age 14–17)	1,474[6]	38,915	498,849	12.8
Voc., teacher tr.	53[6]	3,371	32,005	9.5
Higher	23[6]	3,691	49,744	13.5

Health (1995): physicians 15,000 (1 per 303 persons); hospital beds 41,000 (1 per 111 persons); (1996) infant mortality rate per 1,000 live births 31.5.
Food (1995): daily per capita caloric intake 2,183 (vegetable products 76%, animal products 24%); 85% of FAO recommended minimum requirement.

Military

Total active duty personnel (1997): 12,200 (army 80%, air force 20%). *Military expenditure as percentage of GNP* (1994): 0.7% (world 3.0%); per capita expenditure U.S.$12.

[1]Russian has special recognition without being official. [2]January. [3]Total area per more recent survey is 77,200 sq mi (199,900 sq km). [4]Ruble-area GNP and exchange-rate data are very speculative. [5]Detail does not add to total given because of rounding. [6]1993–94.

Internet resources for further information:
• National Human Development Report of the Kyrgyz Republic 1997 http://www.undp.bishkek.su/
• Welcome to the Kyrgyz Republic http://www.kyrgyzstan.org/

Laos

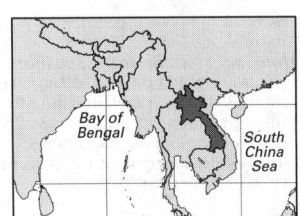

Official name: Sathalanalat
Paxathipatai Paxaxôn Lao (Lao
People's Democratic Republic).
Form of government: unitary
single-party people's republic with
one legislative house (National
Assembly[1] [99]).
Chief of state: President.
Head of government: Prime Minister.
Capital: Vientiane (Viangchan).
Official language: Lao.
Official religion: none.
Monetary unit: 1 kip (KN) = 100 at;
valuation (Sept. 25, 1998)
1 U.S.$ = KN 3,408; 1 £ = KN 5,802.

Area and population

Provinces	Capitals	area sq mi	area sq km	population 1995 estimate
Attapu	Attapu	3,985	10,320	87,700
Bokèo	Houayxay	2,392	6,196	114,900
Bolikhamxai	Pakxan	5,739	14,863	164,900
Champasak	Pakxé	5,952	15,415	503,300
Houaphan	Xam Nua	6,371	16,500	247,300
Khammouan	Thakhek	6,299	16,315	275,400
Louangnamtha	Louangnamtha	3,600	9,325	115,200
Louangphrabang	Louangphrabang	6,515	16,875	367,200
Oudomxay	Xay	5,934	15,370	211,300
Phôngsali	Phôngsali	6,282	16,270	153,400
Salavan	Salavan	4,128	10,691	258,300
Savannakhét	Savannakhét	8,407	21,774	674,900
Special Region	...	2,743	7,105	54,200
Viangchan	Muang Phôn-Hông	6,149	15,927	286,800
Xaignabouli	Xaignabouli	6,328	16,389	293,300
Xékong	Thong	2,959	7,665	64,200
Xiangkhoang	Phônsavan	6,131	15,880	201,200
Municipalities				
Viangchan	Vientiane (Viangchan)	1,514	3,920	531,800
TOTAL		91,429[2]	236,800	4,605,300

Demography

Population (1998): 5,261,000.
Density (1998): persons per sq mi 57.5, persons per sq km 22.2.
Urban-rural (1997): urban 23.0%; rural 77.0%.
Sex distribution (1995): male 49.46%; female 50.54%.
Age breakdown (1990): under 15, 43.7%; 15–29, 26.0%; 30–44, 16.2%; 45–59, 9.2%; 60–74, 4.2%; 75 and over, 0.7%.
Population projection: (2000) 5,557,000; (2010) 7,168,000.
Doubling time: 23 years.
Ethnic composition (1983): Lao-Lum (Lao) 67.0%; Lao-Theung (Mon-Khmer) 16.5%; Lao-Tai (Tai) 7.8%; Lao-Soung (Miao [Hmong] and Man [Yao]) 5.2%; other 3.5%.
Religious affiliation (1980): Buddhist 57.8%; tribal religionist 33.6%; Christian 1.8%, of which Roman Catholic 0.8%, Protestant 0.2%; Muslim 1.0%; atheist 1.0%; Chinese folk religionist 0.9%; none 3.8%; other 0.1%.
Major cities (1985): Vientiane (Viangchan) 178,203; Savannakhét 96,652; Louangphrabang 68,399; Pakxé 47,323.

Vital statistics

Birth rate per 1,000 population (1997): 44.3 (world avg. 25.0).
Death rate per 1,000 population (1997): 13.7 (world avg. 9.3).
Natural increase rate per 1,000 population (1997): 30.6 (world avg. 15.7).
Total fertility rate (avg. births per childbearing woman; 1997): 6.2.
Marriage rate per 1,000 population: n.a.
Divorce rate per 1,000 population: n.a.
Life expectancy at birth (1997): male 51.0 years; female 54.0 years.
Major causes of death per 100,000 population (incomplete, 1990): malaria 7.6; pneumonia 3.0; meningitis 1.5; diarrhea 1.2; tuberculosis 0.8.

National economy

Budget (1996–97). Revenue: KN 321,200,000,000 (taxes 66.2%, foreign grants 21.2%, nontax revenue 12.6%). Expenditures: KN 404,100,000,000 (current expenditure 47.9%, capital expenditure 52.1%).
Public debt (external, outstanding; 1996): U.S.$2,186,000,000.
Tourism (1995): receipts from visitors U.S.$51,000,000; expenditures by nationals abroad U.S.$30,000,000.
Population economically active (1989): total 1,888,000; activity rate of total population 49.0% (participation rates [1985]: ages 15–64, 84.2%; female 45.3%; unemployed [1994] 2.6%).

Price and earnings indexes (1990 = 100)

	1990	1991	1992	1993	1994	1995	1996
Consumer price index	100.0	113.4	124.6	132.4	141.4	169.1	191.2
Earnings index	...	...	...	...	...	...	...

Production (metric tons except as noted). Agriculture, forestry, fishing (1996): rice 1,414,000, sweet potatoes 111,000, sugarcane 87,000, corn (maize) 72,000, cassava 69,000, pineapples 35,000, melons 35,000, potatoes 31,000, oranges 25,000, bananas 22,000, seed cotton 20,000, coffee 10,000; livestock (number of live animals) 1,772,000 pigs, 1,212,000 water buffalo, 1,186,000 cattle, 159,000 goats, 26,000 horses, 11,656,000 chickens; roundwood (1995) 5,508,000 cu

m; fish catch (1995) 40,250. Mining and quarrying (1995): gypsum 110,000; rock salt 12,000; tin (metal content) 687. Manufacturing (1995): detergent 800,000; plastic products 500,000; nails 58,000; clothing 11,495,000 pieces; soap 550,000 pieces; cigarettes 45,000,000 packs; beer 126,300 hectolitres; soft drinks 94,800 hectolitres. Construction: n.a. Energy production (consumption): electricity (kW-hr; 1994) 905,000,000 (294,000,000); coal (metric tons; 1994) 1,000 (1,000); crude petroleum, n.a. (n.a.); petroleum products (metric tons; 1994) none (95,000); natural gas, n.a. (n.a.).
Gross national product (1996): U.S.$1,895,000,000 (U.S.$400 per capita).

Structure of gross domestic product and labour force

	1996 in value KN '000,000[3]	1996 % of total value	1989 labour force	1989 % of labour force
Agriculture	463,900	52.0	1,359,000	72.0
Manufacturing	138,300	15.5		
Mining	2,400	0.3		
Construction	30,100	3.4		
Public utilities	12,900	1.4		
Transp. and commun.	50,200	5.6	58,533	8.1
Trade	90,100	10.1		
Finance	41,500	4.7		
Pub. admin., defense	40,200	4.5		
Services				
Other	22,600	2.5		
TOTAL	892,200	100.0	1,888,000	100.0

Household income and expenditure. Average household size (1985) 6.0%; average annual income per household KN 3,710 (U.S.$371); sources of income: n.a.; expenditure: n.a.
Land use (1994): forested 54.4%; meadows and pastures 3.5%; agricultural and under permanent cultivation 3.9%; other 38.2%.

Foreign trade[4]

Balance of trade (current prices)

	1991	1992	1993	1994	1995	1996
U.S.$'000,000	−131.7	−133.0	−179.0	−263.7	−239.3	−366.8
% of total	45.8%	33.3%	27.8%	30.5%	25.6%	36.2%

Imports (1996): U.S.$689,600,000 (consumption goods 44.7%; investment goods 40.2%, of which construction and electrical equipment 14.7%, motor vehicles 10.4%; machinery and equipment 10.3%, materials for garment assembly 10.2%). *Major import sources:* Thailand 45.0%; Japan 7.6%; Vietnam 3.7%; China 3.4%; Singapore 2.5%; Hong Kong 1.2%.
Exports (1996): U.S.$320,700,000 (wood products 38.9%; garments 20.0%; electricity 9.3%; coffee 7.8%). *Major export destinations:* Vietnam 49.1%; Thailand 30.2%; France 2.6%; United Kingdom 2.1%; Germany 1.5%.

Transport and communications

Transport. Railroads: none. Roads (1995): total length 11,280 mi, 18,153 km (paved 14%). Vehicles (1995): passenger cars 17,200; trucks and buses 6,020. Merchant marine (1992): vessels (100 gross tons and over) 1; total deadweight tonnage 1,469. Air transport (1993): passenger-mi 29,000,000, passenger-km 46,000,000; short ton-mi cargo 3,000,000, metric ton-km cargo 4,000,000; airports (1996) with scheduled flights 11.

Communications

Medium	date	unit	number	units per 1,000 persons
Daily newspapers	1994	circulation	14,000	3.0
Radio	1996	receivers	575,000	116
Television	1995	receivers	80,000	17
Telephones	1995	main lines	20,400	4.2
Cellular telephones	1995	subscribers	1,500	0.3
Facsimile machines	1995	units	500	0.1

Education and health

Educational attainment (1985). Percentage of population age 6 and over having: no schooling 49.3%; primary 41.2%; secondary 9.1%; higher 0.4%.
Literacy (1995): total population age 15 and over literate 56.6%; males literate 69.4%; females literate 44.4%.

Education (1995–96)

	schools	teachers	students	student/ teacher ratio
Primary (age 6–10)	7,591	24,600	724,100	29.4
Secondary (age 11–16)	750[5]	35,100	886,500	25.3
Voc., teacher tr.	139[5]	1,600	9,400	5.9
Higher	9[5]	1,300	7,800	6.0

Health (1990): physicians 1,173 (1 per 3,555 persons); hospital beds 10,364 (1 per 402 persons); infant mortality rate per 1,000 live births (1997) 87.
Food (1995): daily per capita caloric intake 2,117 (vegetable products 94%, animal products 6%); 95% of FAO recommended minimum requirement.

Military

Total active duty personnel (1996): 37,000 (army 89.2%, navy 1.4%, air force 9.4%). *Military expenditure as percentage of GNP* (1995): 4.2% (world 2.8%); per capita expenditure U.S.$15.

---

[1]Formerly known as the Supreme People's Assembly. [2]Detail does not add to total given because of rounding. [3]At constant 1990 prices. [4]Import figures are c.i.f. in balance of trade and commodities. [5]1989–90. [6]1988–89.

Internet resources for further information:
• **Discovering Laos** http://www.laoembassy.com/discover/index.htm

Latvia

Official name: Latvijas Republika (Republic of Latvia).
Form of government: unitary multiparty republic with a single legislative body (Parliament, or Saeima [100]).
Chief of state: President.
Head of government: Prime Minister.
Capital: Riga.
Official language: Latvian.
Official religion: none.
Monetary unit: 1 lats (Ls; plural lati) = 100 santimi; valuation (Sept. 25, 1998) 1 U.S.$ = 0.59 lats; 1 £ = 1.00 lats.

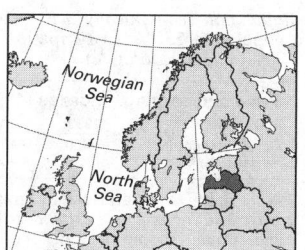

Area and population

	area	population		area	population
Cities	sq km	1995 estimate[1]	**Districts**	sq km	1995 estimate[1]
Daugavpils	72	120,152	Jelgava	1,613	37,473
Jelgava	60	71,129	Krāslava	2,288	39,438
Jūrmala	100	59,247	Kuldīga	2,503	41,047
Liepāja	60	100,271	Liepāja	3,589	51,677
Rēzekne	17	42,081	Limbaži	2,602	41,258
Riga	295	839,670	Ludza	2,566	40,128
Ventspils	46	47,005	Madona	3,348	48,725
			Ogre	1,816	63,870
Districts			Preiļi	2,042	43,656
Aizkraukle	2,558	44,046	Rēzekne	2,654	42,485
Alūksne	2,246	27,670	Rīga (Riga)	3,094	145,499
Balvi	2,384	32,715	Saldus	2,134	39,831
Bauska	1,884	53,890	Talsi	2,748	50,406
Cēsis	3,062	62,043	Tukums	2,457	56,748
Daugavpils	2,526	45,125	Valka	2,444	36,215
Dobele	1,680	41,513	Valmiera	2,377	61,901
Gulbene	1,876	29,797	Ventspils	2,471	14,363
Jēkabpils	2,998	58,469	TOTAL	64,610	2,529,543

Demography

Population (1998): 2,445,000.
Density (1998): persons per sq mi 98.0, persons per sq km 37.8.
Urban-rural (1996[1]): urban 69.0%; rural 31.0%.
Sex distribution (1996[1]): male 46.3%; female 53.7%.
Age breakdown (1996[1]): under 15, 20.4%; 15–29, 20.3%; 30–44, 21.5%; 45–59, 18.5%; 60–74, 14.3%; 75 and over, 5.0%.
Population projection: (2000) 2,394,000; (2010) 2,214,000.
Ethnic composition (1996): Latvian 55.1%; Russian 32.6%; Belarusian 4.0%; Ukrainian 2.9%; Polish 2.2%; Lithuanian 1.3%; other 1.9%.
Religious affiliation (1995): Christian 39.6%, of which Protestant 16.7% (of which Lutheran 14.6%), Roman Catholic 14.9%, Orthodox 8.0%; Jewish 0.6%; other (mostly nonreligious) 59.8%.
Major cities (1996[1]): Riga 826,508; Daugavpils 118,530; Liepāja 98,490; Jelgava 70,957; Jūrmala 59,002.

Vital statistics

Birth rate per 1,000 population (1996): 7.9 (world avg. 25.0); (1994) legitimate 73.6%; illegitimate 26.4%.
Death rate per 1,000 population (1996): 13.8 (world avg. 9.3).
Natural increase rate per 1,000 population (1996): –5.9 (world avg. 15.7).
Total fertility rate (avg. births per childbearing woman; 1996): 1.2.
Marriage rate per 1,000 population (1995): 4.4.
Divorce rate per 1,000 population (1995): 3.2.
Life expectancy at birth (1996): male 60.8 years; female 73.2 years.
Major causes of death per 100,000 population (1994): diseases of the circulatory system 917.0; accidents, poisoning, and violence 235.9; malignant neoplasms (cancers) 219.6; diseases of the respiratory system 52.8.

National economy

Budget (1995). Revenue: Ls 686,500,000 (social security contributions 34.1%, value-added taxes 32.0%, nontax revenue 13.0%, excises 7.5%, corporate income taxes 6.9%). Expenditures: Ls 756,390,000 (social security and welfare 41.3%, education 13.0%, health 6.8%, police 6.2%, defense 2.6%).
Production (metric tons except as noted). Agriculture, forestry, fishing (1996): potatoes 900,000, barley 384,000, wheat 306,000, sugar beets 245,000, vegetables and melons 232,000, fruits and berries 91,000; livestock (number of live animals) 553,000 pigs, 537,000 cattle, 72,100 sheep, 3,500,000 poultry; roundwood (1995) 6,907,000 cu m; fish catch (1995) 149,719. Mining and quarrying (1996): peat 462,700; gypsum 77,226. Manufacturing (value added in U.S.$'000,000; 1994): food products 193; beverages 76; transport equipment 59; wood and wood products 56; electrical machinery 42; textiles 41; nonelectrical machinery 39. Construction (1995): new residential 219,000,000 sq m. Energy production (consumption): electricity (kW-hr; 1995) 3,984,000,000 ([1994] 6,258,000,000); coal (1994) none (425,000); crude petroleum, n.a. (n.a.); petroleum products (1994) none (2,516,000); natural gas (cu m; 1994) none (886,000,000).
Household income and expenditure. Average household size (1989) 3.1; sources of income (1994): wages and salaries 67.0%, pensions and transfers 17.4%, self-employment 5.4%, other 10.2%; expenditure (1995): food and beverages 44.2%, housing and energy 14.1%, clothing and footwear 8.1%, transport and communications 7.8%, recreation and education 6.3%.
Public debt (external, outstanding; 1996): U.S.$298,000,000.
Gross national product (1996): U.S.$5,730,000,000 (U.S.$2,300 per capita).

Structure of gross domestic product and labour force

	1996		1995	
	in value Ls '000,000	% of total value	labour force[2]	% of labour force
Agriculture, forestry	218.9	7.9	220,000	17.2
Mining and quarrying	5.6	0.2	3,000	0.2
Manufacturing	529.9	19.1	208,000	16.3
Construction	117.0	4.2	71,000	5.6
Public utilities	134.5	4.9	17,000	1.3
Transp. and commun.	}		105,000	8.3
Trade			191,000	15.0
Finance	1,403.5	50.7	77,000	6.0
Pub. admin., defense	}		56,000	4.4
Services			241,000	18.9
Other	359.1[3]	13.0	87,000[4]	6.8
TOTAL	2,768.4[5]	100.0	1,276,000	100.0

Population economically active (1995): total 1,276,000; activity rate of total population 50.8% (participation rates: ages 15–64, n.a.; female 49.1%; unemployed [1997[6]] 7.5%).

Price and earnings indexes (1992 = 100)

	1993	1994	1995	1996	1997	1998
Consumer price index	208.8	283.8	354.7	417.1	452.3	478.0[6]
Annual earnings index	211.7	338.6	420.3	482.7	587.1	...

Land use (1994): forested 44.4%; meadows and pastures 12.4; agricultural and under permanent cultivation 27.0%; other 16.2%.

Foreign trade[7]

Balance of trade (current prices)

	1993	1994	1995	1996	1997
Ls '000,000	+37	–142	–235	–428	–541
% of total	2.8%	11.4%	14.6%	21.2%	21.8%

Imports (1996): Ls 1,278,000,000 (mineral products 22.2%, machinery and equipment 16.8%, chemicals and chemical products 11.0%, textiles 8.0%, base metals 6.4%). *Major import sources:* Russia 20.2%; Germany 13.8%; Finland 9.2%; Sweden 7.9%; Lithuania 6.3%.
Exports (1996): Ls 795,000,000 (forestry products 24.4%, textiles 16.9%, food and agricultural products 16.4%, machinery and apparatus 9.7%). *Major export destinations:* Russia 22.8%; Germany 13.8%; U.K. 11.1%; Lithuania 7.4%; Sweden 6.6%.

Transport and communications

Transport. Railroads (1996): length 2,413 km; passenger-km 1,182,000,000; metric-km cargo (1996) 12,412,000,000. Roads (1993): total length 64,693 km (paved 18.2%). Vehicles (1996): passenger cars 379,895; trucks and buses 90,184. Merchant marine (1992): cargo vessels 261; total deadweight tonnage 1,436,899. Air transport (1996): passenger-km 301,500,000; metric ton-km cargo 5,201,000; airports with scheduled flights (1996) 1.

Communications				units per 1,000 persons
Medium	date	unit	number	
Daily newspapers	1995	circulation	590,000	235
Radio	1996	receivers	1,396,000	560
Television	1996	receivers	1,126,000	452
Telephones	1995	main lines	704,500	280
Cellular telephones	1995	subscribers	15,000	6.0
Facsimile machines	1995	units	900	0.4
Personal computers	1995	units	20,000	8.0

Education and health

Educational attainment (1988). Percentage of population age 25 and over having: no formal schooling 0.6%; incomplete primary education 18.5%; complete primary 21.2%; secondary 46.3%; higher 13.4%. *Literacy* (1989): percentage of total population age 15 and over literate 99.5%.

Education (1996–97)				
	schools	teachers	students	student/ teacher ratio
Primary	643	23,779[8]	98,694	...
Secondary	376	41,029[8]	235,952	...
Vocational[9]	128	9,576[8]	43,170	...
Higher	28	...	55,434	...

Health (1995): physicians 8,400[10] (1 per 298 persons); hospital beds 27,800 (1 per 90 persons); infant mortality rate per 1,000 live births (1996) 15.9.
Food (1995): daily per capita caloric intake 2,967 (vegetable products 73%, animal products 27%); 116% of FAO recommended minimum requirement.

Military

Total active duty personnel (1997): 8,100 (border guard 44.4%, army 42.0%, navy 12.1%, air force 1.5%). *Military expenditure as percentage of GNP* (1995): 0.9% (world 2.8%); per capita expenditure U.S.$29.

[1]January 1. [2]Annual average official estimate. [3]Indirect taxes less subsidies. [4]Includes 6,000 not adequately defined and 81,000 unemployed. [5]Detail does not add to total given because of rounding. [6]June. [7]Imports are f.o.b. in balance of trade and c.i.f. for commodities and trading partners. [8]1995–96. [9]Includes special secondary institutions. [10]Includes dentists.

Internet resources for further information:
• **Embassy of Latvia (Washington, D.C.)** http://www.virtualglobe.com/latvia/
• **Central Statistical Bureau of Latvia** http://www.csb.lv/

Lebanon

Official name: Al-Jumhūrīyah al-Lubnānīyah (Republic of Lebanon).
Form of government: unitary multiparty republic with one legislative house (National Assembly [128])[1].
Chief of state: President.
Head of government: Prime Minister.
Capital: Beirut.
Official language: Arabic.
Official religion: none.
Monetary unit: 1 Lebanese pound (£L) = 100 piastres; valuation (Sept. 25, 1998) 1 U.S.$ = £L 1,512; 1 £ = £L 2,574.

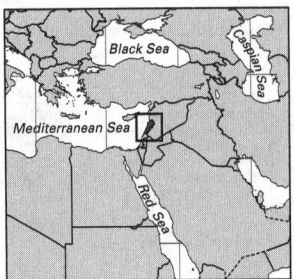

Area and population		area		population
				1970
Governorates	**Capitals**	sq mi	sq km	estimate
Bayrūt	Beirut (Bayrūt)	7	18	474,870
Al-Biqā'	Zaḥlah	1,653	4,280	203,520
Jabal Lubnān	B'abdā	753	1,950	833,055
Al-Janūb[2]	Sidon (Ṣaydā)	772	2,001	249,945
An-Nabaṭīyah[2]	An-Nabaṭīyah	...	...	...
Ash-Shamāl	Tripoli (Ṭarābulus)	765	1,981	364,935
TOTAL		4,016[3]	10,400[3]	2,126,325

Demography

Population (1998): 3,506,000.
Density (1998): persons per sq mi 873.0, persons per sq km 337.1.
Urban-rural (1995): urban 87.2%; rural 12.8%.
Sex distribution (1995): male 48.74%; female 51.26%.
Age breakdown (1994): under 15, 33.2%; 15–29, 29.3%; 30–44, 18.6%; 45–59, 11.1%; 60–74, 6.3%; 75 and over, 1.5%.
Population projection: (2000) 3,620,000; (2010) 4,164,000.
Doubling time: 35 years.
Ethnic composition (1996): Arab *c.* 93%, of which Lebanese *c.* 84%, Palestinian *c.* 9%; Armenian *c.* 6%; Kurd and other *c.* 1%.
Religious affiliation (1995): Muslim 55.3%, of which Shī'ī 34.0%, Sunnī 21.3%; Christian 37.6%, of which Catholic 25.1% (Maronite 19.0%, Greek Catholic or Melchite 4.6%), Orthodox 11.7% (Greek Orthodox 6.0%, Armenian Apostolic 5.2%), Protestant 0.5%; Druze 7.1%.
Major cities (1991): Beirut 1,100,000; Tripoli 240,000; Jūniyah 100,000; Zaḥlah 45,000[4]; Sidon (Ṣaydā) 38,000[4]; Tyre 14,000[4].

Vital statistics

Birth rate per 1,000 population (1990–95): 26.9 (world avg. 25.0).
Death rate per 1,000 population (1990–95): 7.1 (world avg. 9.3).
Natural increase rate per 1,000 population (1990–95): 19.8 (world avg. 15.7).
Total fertility rate (avg. births per childbearing woman; 1990–95): 3.1.
Life expectancy at birth (1990–95): male 66.6 years; female 70.5 years.
Major causes of death: n.a.

National economy

Budget (1996). Revenue: £L 4,022,000,000,000 (indirect taxes 46.7%, of which customs revenues 44.7%; direct taxes 14.3%, of which income tax 8.7%, property tax 3.1%; real estate fees 6.8%; miscellaneous taxes and fees 32.2%). Expenditures: £L 6,458,000,000,000 (current expenditures 86.0%, of which debt service 40.3%, salaries and wages 34.7%; capital expenditures 14.0%).
Production (metric tons except as noted). Agriculture, forestry, fishing (1997): grapes 350,000, potatoes 320,000, tomatoes 240,000, oranges 185,000, cucumbers and gherkins 162,000, apples 136,000, lemons and limes 99,500, olives 85,000, onions 72,000; livestock (number of live animals) 425,000 goats, 246,000 sheep, 80,000 cattle, 29,000,000 chickens; roundwood (1995) 515,000 cu m; fish catch (1995) 4,385. Mining and quarrying (1994): lime 15,000; salt 3,000; gypsum 2,000. Manufacturing (1993): cement 3,422,411[5]; distillate fuel 85,000; gasoline 70,000. Construction (1996): 13,499,868 sq m[6]. Energy production (consumption): electricity (kW-hr; 1995) 5,281,000,000 (5,005,000,000); coal, n.a. (none); crude petroleum (barrels; 1993) none (2,602,000); petroleum products (metric tons; 1993) 323,000 ([1994] 3,493,000).
Land use (1994): forested 7.8%; meadows and pastures 1.0%; agricultural and under permanent cultivation 29.9%; wasteland and other areas 61.3%.
Gross national product (1996): U.S.$12,118,000,000 (U.S.$2,970 per capita).

Structure of gross domestic product and labour force				
	1995			
	in value U.S.$'000,000[7]	% of total value	labour force	% of labour force
Agriculture	380	4.0	143,900	14.0%
Mining	—	—		
Manufacturing	1,235	13.0	277,600	27.0%
Construction	950	10.0		
Public utilities	2,375[8]	25.0[8]		
Transp. and commun.				
Trade	2,660	28.0		
Finance				
Real estate and business services	1,900	20.0	606,500	59.0%
Services				
Pub. admin., defense	8	8		
TOTAL	9,500	100.0	1,028,000	100.0%

Population economically active (1995): total 1,028,000; activity rate of total population 25.4% (participation rates: over age 15 [1988] 44%; female *c.* 30%; unemployed n.a.).

Price and earnings indexes (1990 = 100)							
	1990	1991	1992	1993	1994	1995	1996
Consumer price index	100.0	151.5	333.3	430.3	466.0	494.0	524.1
Wages index[9]	100.0	104.2	85.4	78.3	118.5	134.7	...

Public debt (external, outstanding; 1996): U.S.$1,933,000,000.
Household income and expenditure. Average household size (1987) 5.0; average annual income per household (1994) £L 2,400,000 (U.S.$1,430); sources of income (1974): wages 27.9%, transfers 3.0%, other 69.1%; expenditure (1966)[10]: food 42.8%, housing 16.8%, clothing 8.6%, health care 7.2%.
Tourism (1995): receipts from visitors U.S.$710,000,000.

Foreign trade[11]

Balance of trade (current prices)						
	1992	1993	1994	1995	1996	1997
U.S.$'000,000	–3,185	–4,222	–4,798	–5,770	–6,643	–6,880
% of total	72.6%	75.5%	76.4%	74.5%	76.4%	84.1%

Imports (1995): U.S.$7,295,000,000 (machinery and transport equipment 27.0%, metals and metal products 9.8%, mineral products 8.8%, processed food 7.8%, chemicals 6.7%). *Major import sources:* Italy 13.0%; U.S. 10.6%; Germany 8.4%; France 7.6%; Switzerland 4.6%.
Exports (1995): U.S.$985,000,000 (reexports 27.7%, paper products 21.8%, food and live animals 14.5%, machinery and transport equipment 9.5%, fibres and fibre products 8.2%, pearls and semiprecious stones and metals 7.0%, metals and metal products 6.7%). *Major export destinations*[12]: U.A.E. 28.8%; Saudi Arabia 11.2%; Syria 8.5%; France 6.1%; Jordan 3.5%.

Transport and communications

Transport. Railroads (1996)[13]: length 222 km. Roads (1996): total length 6,359 km (paved 95%). Vehicles (1995): passenger cars 1,197,521; trucks and buses 84,736. Merchant marine (1992): vessels(100 gross tons and over) 163; total deadweight tonnage 438,165. Air transport (1996)[14]: passenger-km 1,889,000,000; metric ton-km cargo 46,274,000; airports (1997) with scheduled flights 1.

Communications				units per 1,000
Medium	date	unit	number	**persons**
Daily newspapers	1994	circulation	500,000	172
Radio	1995	receivers	2,247,000	608
Television	1995	receivers	1,075,000	291
Telephones	1995	main lines	330,000	89
Cellular telephones	1995	subscribers	120,000	32
Facsimile machines	1995	units	3,000	0.8
Personal computers	1995	units	50,000	14

Education and health

Educational attainment: n.a. Literacy (1995): total population age 15 and over literate 1,829,000 (92.4%); males literate 94.7%; females literate 90.3%.

Education (1994–95)				student/
	schools	teachers	students	teacher ratio
Primary (age 5–9)	2,100[15]	22,810[16]	365,174	...
Secondary (age 10–16)	1,405[16]	21,344[16]	277,646	...
Voc., teacher tr.	275	6,065	45,776	7.5
Higher	20	7,173	79,029	11.0

Health (1995): physicians 6,987 (1 per 529 persons); hospital beds 11,596 (1 per 319 persons); infant mortality rate per 1,000 live births (1990–95) 34.0.
Food (1995): daily per capita caloric intake 3,270 (vegetable products 85.6%, animal products 14.4%); 132% of FAO recommended minimum.

Military

Total active duty personnel (1997): Lebanese national armed forces 55,100 (army 96.7%, navy 1.8%, air force 1.5%). External regular military forces include: UN peacekeeping force in Lebanon 4,488; Syrian army 30,000. Two civilian militias remained active in 1997, though on a much-reduced scale[17]: Shī'ī Muslim (pro-Iran Hezbollah [Party of God]) 3,000; predominantly Maronite Christian and some Shī'ī and Druze (South Lebanese Army) 2,500. *Military expenditure as percentage of GDP* (1995): 3.7% (world 2.8%); per capita expenditure: U.S.$111.

[1]The current legislature was elected between August and October 1996; one-half of its membership is Christian and one-half Muslim/Druze. [2]Al-Janūb includes An-Nabaṭīyah. [3]Includes water area of 66 sq mi (170 sq km) not distributed by governorate. [4]1988 estimate. [5]1995. [6]Permits authorized. [7]Although the Lebanese pound continues to be the official currency, most financial transactions are done in U.S. dollars. By 1993, however, the pound had once again stabilized against the dollar. [8]Public utilities and transportation and communications includes public administration and defense. [9]Based on minimum wage, in real terms. [10]Weights based on consumer price index components. For capital city only. [11]Imports are f.o.b. in balance of trade and c.i.f. in commodities and trading partners. [12]Domestic exports only; reexports not included. [13]Apart from a 14-mi (23-km) section delivering oil from the Zahrani refinery to a thermal power station serving Beirut, no passenger or general cargo track is currently in use. [14]MEA-Airliban international flights only. [15]1991–92. [16]1981–82. [17]Active personnel.

Internet resources for further information:
• **U.S. Embassy of Lebanon** http://www.erols.com/lebanon/stat.htm
• **Bank of Lebanon** http://www.bdl.gov.lb/
• **United Nations Development Programme—Lebanon** http://www.undp.org.lb

Lesotho

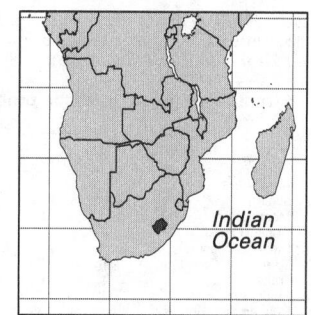

Official name: Lesotho (Sotho); Kingdom of Lesotho (English).
Form of government: multiparty republic[1] with 2 legislative houses (Senate [33[2]]; National Assembly [80]).
Chief of state: King.
Head of government: Prime Minister.
Capital: Maseru.
Official languages: Sotho; English.
Official religion: Christianity.
Monetary unit: 1 loti (plural maloti [M]) = 100 lisente; valuation (Sept. 25, 1998) 1 U.S.$ = M 5.83; 1 £ = M 9.93.

Area and population

Districts	Capitals	area sq mi	area sq km	population 1995 estimate[3]
Berea	Teyateyaneng	858	2,222	206,200
Butha-Buthe	Butha-Buthe	682	1,767	135,400
Leribe	Hlotse	1,092	2,828	349,500
Mafeteng	Mafeteng	818	2,119	259,000
Maseru	Maseru	1,652	4,279	400,200
Mohale's Hoek	Mohale's Hoek	1,363	3,530	231,300
Mokhotlong	Mokhotlong	1,573	4,075	100,300
Qacha's Nek	Qacha's Nek	907	2,349	86,800
Quthing	Quthing	1,126	2,916	151,900
Thaba-Tseka	Thaba-Tseka	1,649	4,270	136,200
TOTAL		11,720	30,355	2,056,800

Demography

Population (1998): 2,090,000[4].
Density (1998)[4]: persons per sq mi 178.3, persons per sq km 68.9.
Urban-rural (1992): urban 20.9%; rural 79.1%.
Sex distribution (1995): male 49.23%; female 50.77%.
Age breakdown (1995): under 15, 41.3%; 15–29, 27.0%; 30–44, 16.0%; 45–59, 9.1%; 60–74, 5.0%; 75 and over, 1.6%.
Population projection[4]: (2000) 2,167,000; (2010) 2,445,000.
Doubling time: 28 years.
Ethnic composition (1986): Sotho 85.0%; Zulu 15.0%.
Religious affiliation (1995): Christian 70.1%, of which Roman Catholic 39.0%, Protestant (mostly Presbyterian) 14.1%, African Christian 11.4%; other (mostly traditional beliefs) 29.9%.
Major urban centres (1986): Maseru 109,382; Maputsoe 20,000; Teyateyaneng 14,251; Mafeteng 12,667; Hlotse 9,595.

Vital statistics

Birth rate per 1,000 population (1995–2000): 35.4 (world avg. 25.0); legitimate, n.a; illegitimate, n.a.
Death rate per 1,000 population (1995–2000): 10.6 (world avg. 9.3).
Natural increase rate per 1,000 population (1995–2000): 24.8 (world avg. 15.7).
Total fertility rate (avg. births per childbearing woman; 1995–2000): 4.9.
Marriage rate per 1,000 population: n.a.
Divorce rate per 1,000 population: n.a.
Life expectancy at birth (1990–95): male 58.0 years; female 63.0 years.
Major causes of death per 100,000 population: n.a.; however, major diseases include malaria, typhoid fever, and infectious and parasitic diseases.

National economy

Budget (1995–96). Revenue: M 1,790,300,000 (1993–94; tax revenue 78.8%, of which customs receipts 53.5%, sales tax 10.1%, income tax 7.3%, company tax 4.6%; grants and nontax revenue 21.2%). Expenditures: M 1,608,800,000 (recurrent expenditure 67.5%, of which education 20.9%, public works [1994–95] 12.8%, health 6.7%, defense 6.4%; capital expenditure 32.5%).
Production (metric tons except as noted). Agriculture, forestry, fishing (1996): corn (maize) 199,000, roots and tubers 63,000, sorghum 31,000, wheat 20,000, vegetables 20,000, fruit 16,000, dry beans 4,500, dry peas 1,075; livestock (number of live animals) 1,200,000 sheep, 750,000 goats, 590,000 cattle, 152,000 asses, 120,000 horses, 70,000 pigs, 1,500,000 chickens; roundwood (1995) 709,000 cu m; fish catch (1994) 35. Mining and quarrying (1988): sand and gravel 50,000 cu m. Manufacturing (value added in U.S.$'000,000; 1994): food products 51; beverages 38; textiles 12; chemical products 8; metal products 4; wearing apparel 3. Construction (permits issued in M '000,000; 1996): residential 11.17; nonresidential 165.97. Energy production (consumption): electricity (kW-hr; 1988) 1,000,000 (n.a.); coal, none (n.a); petroleum, none (n.a.); natural gas, none (n.a.).
Public debt (external, outstanding; 1996): U.S.$611,600,000.
Tourism (1994): receipts from visitors U.S.$17,000,000; expenditures by nationals abroad U.S.$7,000,000.
Population economically active (1993): total 617,871; activity rate of total population 45.1% (participation rates: ages 15–64 [1986] 79.8%; female 23.7%; unemployed [1992] 35.0%).

Price and earnings indexes (1990 = 100)

	1990	1991	1992	1993	1994	1995	1996
Consumer price index	100.0	117.7	137.9	156.0	168.9	184.5	201.7
Annual earnings index[5]	100.0	112.7	123.5	132.7	144.6	166.9	...

Household income and expenditure. Average household size (1986) 4.8; average annual income per household (1986–87) M 2,832 (U.S.$1,297); sources

of income (1986–87): transfer payments 44.7%, self-employment 27.8%, wages and salaries 22.4%, other 5.1%; expenditure (1989): food 48.0%, clothing 16.4%, household durable goods 11.9%, housing and energy 10.1%, transportation 4.7%.
Gross national product (at current market prices; 1996): U.S.$1,331,000,000 (U.S.$660 per capita).

Structure of gross domestic product and labour force

	1995 in value M '000,000	1995 % of total value	1986 labour force	1986 % of labour force
Agriculture	395.5	10.5	474,171	66.2
Mining	2.7	0.1	6,446	0.9
Manufacturing	556.5	14.8	19,339	2.7
Construction	889.5	23.6	31,516	4.4
Public utilities	90.3	2.4	1,433	0.2
Transp. and commun.	122.8	3.3	5,014	0.7
Trade	332.9	8.9	22,204	3.1
Finance	440.9	11.7	3,581	0.5
Pub. admin., defense	467.4	12.4	17,907	2.5
Services	99.2	2.6	126,780	17.7
Other	366.4[6]	9.7[6]	7,879	1.1
TOTAL	3,764.1	100.0	716,270[7]	100.0[7]

Land use (1994): meadows and pastures 65.9%; agricultural and under permanent cultivation 10.5%; other 23.6%.

Foreign trade[8]

Balance of trade (current prices)

	1990	1991	1992	1993	1994	1995
M '000,000	−1,523.0	−1,976.0	−2,374.7	−2,435.9	−2,384.0	−2,867.4
% of total	83.3%	84.2%	79.3%	73.8%	70.1%	71.2%

Imports (1995): M 2,880,930,000 (1990; manufactured goods [excluding chemicals, machinery, and transport equipment] 42.5%; food and live animals 19.1%; machinery and transport equipment 15.3%; petroleum products 8.6%). *Major import sources:* Customs Union of Southern Africa 90.0%; Asia 5.9%; Europe 3.3%, of which European Economic Community 2.3%; the Americas 0.8%.
Exports (1995): M 395,110,000 (1994; manufactured goods 87.5%, of which clothing 54.8%, furniture 8.0%, footwear 6.9%, machinery and transport equipment 2.0%; crude materials 6.3%, of which wool 4.5%, mohair 1.7%; food and live animals 5.5%, of which cereals 1.5%, cattle 1.2%, vegetables 0.7%; chemicals 0.5%; diamonds 0.2%). *Major export destinations:* Customs Union of Southern Africa 51.6%; the Americas 37.6%; Europe 9.4%, of which European Economic Community 9.3%; Asia 0.2%.

Transport and communications

Transport. Railroads (1996): length 1.6 mi, 2.6 km. Roads (1995): total length 3,079 mi, 4,955 km (paved 18%). Vehicles (1995): passenger cars 11,100; trucks and buses 22,200. Merchant marine: vessels (100 gross tons and over) none. Air transport (1996): passenger-mi 3,900,000, passenger-km 6,200,000; short ton-mi cargo 395,000, metric ton-km cargo 577,000; airports (1997) with scheduled flights 1.

Communications

Medium	date	unit	number	units per 1,000 persons
Daily newspapers	1994	circulation	14,000	7.4
Radio	1996	receivers	1,100,000	558
Television	1995	receivers	13,000	6.7
Telephones	1995	main lines	17,800	9.2
Facsimile machines	1995	units	600	0.3

Education and health

Educational attainment (1986–87). Percentage of population age 10 and over having: no formal education 22.9%; primary 52.8%; secondary 23.2%; higher 0.6%. *Literacy* (1995): total population age 15 and over literate 849,700 (71.3%); males literate 468,000 (81.1%); females literate 381,700 (62.3%).

Education (1994–95)

	schools	teachers	students	student/ teacher ratio
Primary (age 6–12)	1,234	7,433	366,935	49.4
Secondary (age 13–17)	187[9]	2,597	61,615	23.7
Voc., teacher tr.[9]	9	225	2,326	10.3
Higher[9]	1	492	4,001	8.1

Health (1993): physicians 136 (1 per 14,306 persons); hospital beds (1992) 2,400 (1 per 765 persons); infant mortality rate per 1,000 live births 71.5.
Food (1995): daily per capita caloric intake 1,972 (vegetable products 93%, animal products 7%); 86% of FAO recommended minimum requirement.

Military

Total active duty personnel (1997): 2,000[10]. *Military expenditure as percentage of GNP* (1995): 1.9% (world 2.8%); per capita expenditure U.S.$14.

[1]New constitution, effective April 1993, ended seven years of military rule. [2]Composed of 22 chiefs and 11 nominated members. [3]De jure population. [4]Excludes absentee miners working in South Africa. [5]Based on average annual wages, including overtime, of mine workers. [6]Indirect taxes less imputed bank service charges. [7]Approximately 117,600 persons (c. 40% of Lesotho's adult male labour force) were employed as mine workers in South Africa in 1993. [8]Import figures are f.o.b. in balance of trade and c.i.f. in commodities and trading partners. [9]1993–94. [10]Royal Lesotho Defence Force.

Liberia

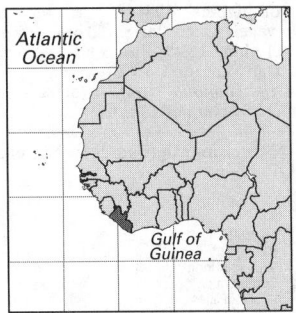

Official name: Republic of Liberia.
Form of government: multiparty
 republic with two legislative
 houses (Senate [26]; House of
 Representatives [64]).
Head of state and government:
 President.
Capital: Monrovia.
Official language: English.
Official religion: none.
Monetary unit: 1 Liberian dollar
 (L$) = 100 cents; valuation Sept. 25,
 1998) 1 U.S.$ = L$1.00[1]; 1 £ = L$1.70.

Area and population		area		population
Counties	Capitals	sq mi	sq km	1986 estimate
Bomi	Tubmanburg	755	1,955	67,300
Bong	Gbarnga	3,127	8,099	268,100
Grand Bassa	Buchanan	3,382	8,759	166,900
Grand Cape Mount	Robertsport	2,250	5,827	83,900
Grand Gedeh	Zwedru	6,575	17,029	109,000
Grand Kru	Barclayville	[2]	[2]	[2]
Lofa	Voinjama	7,475	19,360	261,000
Margibi	Kakata	1,260	3,263	104,000
Maryland	Harper	2,066[2]	5,351[2]	137,700[2]
Montserrado	Bensonville	1,058	2,740	582,400
Nimba	Sanniquellie	4,650	12,043	325,700
Rivercess	Rivercess City	1,693	4,385	39,900
Sinoe	Greenville	3,959	10,254	65,400
TOTAL		38,250[3]	99,067[3, 4]	2,221,300[5]

Demography

Population (1998): 2,772,000[6].
Density (1997): persons per sq mi 73.4[6], persons per sq km 28.4[6].
Urban-rural (1995): urban 44.9%; rural 55.1%.
Sex distribution (1995): male 50.69%; female 49.31%.
Age breakdown (1995): under 15, 44.5%; 15–29, 25.6%; 30–44, 15.6%; 45–59, 9.0%; 60–74, 3.9%; 75 and over, 1.4%.
Population projection: (2000) 3,090,000; (2010) 4,342,000.
Doubling time: 23 years.
Ethnic composition (1984): Kpelle 19.4%: Bassa 13.9%; Grebo 9.0%; Gio 7.8%; Kru 7.3%; Mano 7.1%; other 35.5%.
Religious affiliation (1995): traditional beliefs 63.0%[7]; Christian 21.0%, of which Protestant 13.5%, African Christian 5.1%, Roman Catholic 2.4%; Muslim 16.0%[7].
Major cities (1985): Monrovia 668,000[8]; Harbel 60,000; Gbarnga 30,000[9]; Buchanan 25,000; Yekepa 16,000.

Vital statistics

Birth rate per 1,000 population (1996): 42.8 (world avg. 25.0).
Death rate per 1,000 population (1996): 11.9 (world avg. 9.3).
Natural increase rate per 1,000 population (1996): 30.9 (world avg. 15.7).
Total fertility rate (avg. births per childbearing woman; 1996): 6.2.
Marriage rate per 1,000 population: n.a.
Divorce rate per 1,000 population: n.a.
Life expectancy at birth (1995): male 56.0 years; female 61.2 years.
Major causes of death per 100,000 population (1985)[10]: complications during pregnancy 632.6[11]; malaria 79.8; pneumonia 64.2; anemia 50.2; malnutrition 23.4; measles 12.7. Violence and acts of war were major causes of both morbidity and mortality from 1990 onward.

National economy

Budget (1993). Revenue: L$249,825,000 (1989; income and profits taxes 33.9%; import duties and consular fees 29.6%; excise tax 12.7%; property taxes 1.9%). Expenditures: L$273,930,000 (1988; current expenditure 91.1%, of which wages and salaries 34.1%, interest on public debt 13.1%, goods and services 7.8%, subsidies and grants 5.1%; development expenditure 8.9%).
Tourism: receipts from visitors (1986) U.S.$6,000,000; expenditures by nationals abroad, n.a.
Population economically active (1994): total 993,000; activity rate 43.5% (participation rates: ages 10–64, 64.0%; female 28.5%; unemployed [1996] 95%).

Price and earnings indexes (1990 = 100)							
	1989	1990	1991	1992	1993	1994	1995
Consumer price index	79.8	100.0	110.0	121.0	133.1	146.4	161.0
Earnings index	...	...	...	...	...	...	...

Production (metric tons except as noted). Agriculture, forestry, fishing (1996): sugarcane 235,000, cassava 213,000, oil palm fruit 155,000, rice 94,000, bananas 85,000, plantains 35,000, natural rubber 25,000, yams 20,000, coffee 3,000, cacao beans 500; livestock (number of live animals) 220,000 goats, 210,000 sheep, 120,000 pigs, 36,000 cattle, 3,500,000 chickens; roundwood (1995) 5,436,000 cu m; fish catch (1995) 7,782. Mining and quarrying: iron ore[12]; diamonds 150,000 carats[13]; gold 16,000 troy oz[14]. Manufacturing (1996): palm oil 45,000; cement 8,300[13]; cigarettes 22,000,000 units[15]; soft drinks 171,000 hectolitres[16]; beer 158,000 hectolitres[16]. Construction: n.a. Energy production (consumption): electricity (kW-hr; 1994) 485,000,000 (485,000,-000); coal, none (none); crude petroleum, none (none); petroleum products (metric tons; 1994) none (101,000); natural gas, none (none).
Public debt (external, outstanding; 1996): U.S.$1,111,000,000.

Household income and expenditure. Average household size (1983) 4.3; income per household: n.a.; sources of income: n.a.; expenditure: n.a.
Gross national product (1996): U.S.$1,174,000,000 (U.S.$490 per capita).

Structure of gross domestic product and labour force				
	1989		1994	
	in value L$'000,000	% of total value	labour force	% of labour force
Agriculture	410.7	34.4	676,000	68.1
Mining	122.3	10.2		
Manufacturing	81.6	6.8		
Construction	26.3	2.2		
Public utilities	19.0	1.6	77,000	7.7
Transp. and commun.	79.1	6.6		
Trade	63.3	5.3		
Finance	141.8	11.9		
Pub. admin., defense	139.4	11.7		
Services	35.5	3.0	240,000	24.2
Other	74.8[17]	6.3[17]		
TOTAL	1,193.6[4]	100.0	993,000	100.0

Land use (1994): forested 47.8%; meadows and pastures 20.8%; agricultural and under permanent cultivation 3.8%; other 27.6%.

Foreign trade[18]

Balance of trade (current prices)						
	1991	1992	1993	1994	1995	1996
U.S.$'000,000	−4,548	−4,987	−4,807	−5,393	−4,829	−2,718
% of total	82.3%	76.2%	86.9%	81.7%	71.7%	54.5%

Imports (1996): U.S.$3,854,000,000 (1990; machinery and transport equipment 26.9%, petroleum and petroleum products 23.5%, food and live animals 21.1%, basic manufactures 13.9%, chemicals 5.8%). *Major import sources* (1996): South Korea 25%; Japan 24%; France 9%; Singapore 9%; Croatia 8%.
Exports (1996): U.S.$1,136,000,000 (1988; iron ore 55.1%, rubber 28.0%, logs and timber 8.4%, diamonds 2.1%, gold 1.8%, coffee 1.5%). *Major export destinations* (1996): Belgium-Luxembourg 48%; Singapore 12%; Ukraine 11%; Norway 6%; Malaysia 5%.

Transport and communications

Transport. Railroads (1993)[12, 19]: route length 306 mi, 493 km; short ton-mi cargo 137,000,000, metric ton-km cargo 200,000,000. Roads (1995): total length 6,400 mi, 10,300 km (paved 6%). Vehicles (1995): passenger cars 10,300; trucks and buses 28,300. Merchant marine (1992): vessels (100 gross tons and over) 1,672; total deadweight tonnage 97,373,965. Air transport (1992): passenger-mi 4,300,000, passenger-km 7,000,000; short ton-mi cargo 68,000, metric ton-km cargo 100,000; airports (1997) with scheduled flights 1.

Communications				units per 1,000
Medium	date	unit	number	persons
Daily newspapers	1994	circulation	35,000	15
Radio	1995	receivers	600,000	263
Television	1995	receivers	45,000	20
Telephones	1995	main lines	4,500	2.0

Education and health

Educational attainment, n.a. Literacy (1995): total population age 15 and over literate 705,000 (38.3%); males literate 523,000 (53.9%); females literate 182,000 (22.4%).

Education (1980)				student/
	schools	teachers	students	teacher ratio
Primary (age 6–12)	1,651	9,099	167,000[13]	...
Secondary (age 13–18)	419	1,129	51,666	45.8
Voc., teacher tr.	6	63	2,322	36.9
Higher	3	472[20]	5,716[13]	...

Health: physicians (1992) 257 (1 per 8,333 persons); hospital beds, n.a.; infant mortality rate (1996) 108.1.
Food (1992): daily per capita caloric intake 1,640 (vegetable products 96%, animal products 4%); 71% of FAO recommended minimum requirement.

Military

Total active duty personnel: All militias were formally disarmed by February 1997. The 10,000-member West African (ECOMOG) peacekeeping force was expected to depart Liberia in February 1998. *Military expenditure as percentage of GNP* (1995): 2.2% (world 2.8%); per capita expenditure U.S.$21.

[1]Officially at par with the U.S.$; the unofficial free/black market exchange rate (a truer value of the L$) was roughly L$40 = U.S.$1 in August 1998. [2]Figures for Grand Kru included in Maryland. [3]Total area per more recent survey is 37,743 sq mi (97,754 sq km). [4]Detail does not add to total given because of rounding. [5]Includes 10,000 persons not allocated by county. [6]Excludes about 325,000 Liberian refugees in surrounding countries. [7]Rough estimate. [8]1990 estimate; the 1996 population is estimated to be 850,000 (including many persons displaced because of war). [9]1986. [10]Hospital inpatient morbidity rates. [11]1984. [12]Mining ceased in late 1992. [13]1993. [14]1995 gold production taxed for export (including gold imported from Sierra Leone and Guinea). [15]1992. [16]1988. [17]Import duties less imputed bank service charges. [18]All balance of trade and trading partner data are based on estimates. [19]For iron-ore transport only. [20]1987.

Internet resources for further information:
• **Liberian Daily News Bulletin** (link) http://www.africanews.org/west/liberia/

Libya

Official name: Al-Jamāhīrīyah al-ʿArabīyah al-Lībīyah ash-Shaʿbīyah al-Ishtirākīyah (Socialist People's Libyan Arab Jamahiria).
Form of government: socialist state with one policy-making body (General People's Congress [760]).
Chief of state: Muammar al-Qaddafi (de facto)[1]; Secretary of General People's Congress (de jure).
Head of government: Secretary of the General People's Committee (prime minister).
Capital: Tripoli[2].
Official language: Arabic.
Official religion: Islam.
Monetary unit: 1 Libyan dinar (LD) = 1,000 dirhams; valuation[3] (Sept. 25, 1998) 1 Libyan dinar = U.S.$2.59 = £1.52.

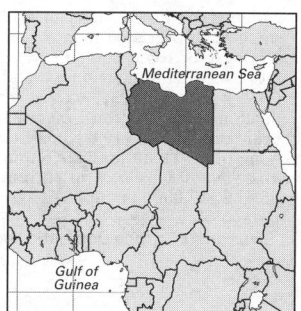

Area and population

Baladīyāt	Capitals	area sq mi	area sq km	population 1988 estimate
Banghāzī	Banghāzī	5,800	15,000	512,200
Al-Jabal al-Akhḍar	Al-Baydāʾ	14,300	37,000	308,300
Al-Jabal al-Gharbī	Gharyān	33,600	87,000	204,300
Khalīj Surt	Surt	145,200	376,000	382,100
Al-Kufrah	Al-Kufrah	186,900	484,000	23,800
Margib	Al-Khums	11,200	29,000	408,900
Marzūq	Marzūq	135,100	350,000	45,200
Nikāt al-Khums	Zuwārah	39,000	101,000	196,000
Sabhā	Sabhā	31,700	82,000	121,700
Ṭarābulus	Tripolic (Ṭarābulus)	1,200	3,000	1,083,100
Ṭubruq	Ṭubruq	32,400	84,000	110,900
Wādī al-Ḥaʾiṭ	Awbārī	40,500	105,000	49,600
Az-Zāwiyah	Az-Zāwiyah	1,500	4,000	326,500
TOTAL		678,400	1,757,000	3,772,600

Demography

Population (1998): 5,691,000.
Density (1998): persons per sq mi 8.4, persons per sq km 3.2.
Urban-rural (1995): urban 86.0%; rural 14.0%.
Sex distribution (1996): male 50.98%; female 49.02%.
Age breakdown (1995): under 15, 45.4%; 15–29, 26.4%; 30–44, 14.7%; 45–59, 9.1%; 60–74, 3.7%; 75 and over, 0.6%.
Population projection: (2000) 6,122,000; (2010) 8,708,000.
Doubling time: 19 years.
Ethnic composition (1995): Libyan Arab and Berber 79%; other 21% (mostly Egyptians, Sudanese, and Chadians).
Religious affiliation (1995): Sunnī Muslim 97.0%; other 3.0%.
Major cities (1995): Tripoli 1,682,000[4]; Banghāzī 804,000[4]; Miṣrātah 121,700[5]; Az-Zāwiyah 89,338[5].

Vital statistics

Birth rate per 1,000 population (1996): 44.4 (world avg. 25.0).
Death rate per 1,000 population (1996): 7.7 (world avg. 9.3).
Natural increase rate per 1,000 population (1996): 36.7 (world avg. 15.7).
Total fertility rate (avg. births per childbearing woman; 1996): 6.3.
Marriage rate per 1,000 population (1991): 5.1[6].
Divorce rate per 1,000 population (1988): 0.6[6].
Life expectancy at birth (1995): male 62.1 years; female 66.6 years.
Major causes of death per 100,000 population: n.a.; however, the main causes of hospital mortality in 1987 were injuries and poisoning 15.5%, diseases of the circulatory system 11.6%, conditions originating in the perinatal period 11.4%, diseases of the respiratory system 7.0%, neoplasms (cancers) 4.4%.

National economy

Budget (1991–92). Revenue: LD 2,655,000,000 (1990–91; current revenue 55.7%, of which oil revenues 17.7%, income taxes 13.7%, customs duties 9.7%, stamp duties 2.4%; capital revenue 44.3%). Expenditures: LD 2,846,-000,000 (1990–91; current expenditures 55.7%, of which municipalities 39.4%, education and scientific research 4.3%, health 2.7%; capital expenditures 44.3%, of which agriculture and land reclamation 13.6%, industry 5.3%).
Production (metric tons except as noted). Agriculture, forestry, fishing (1997): watermelons 179,000, wheat 168,000, barley 150,000, tomatoes 134,000, potatoes 130,000, oranges 79,000, onions 74,500, dates 67,000, olives 55,000, almonds 29,000; livestock (number of live animals) 4,400,000 sheep, 800,000 goats, 129,000 camels, 100,000 cattle, 16,600,000 chickens; roundwood (1995) 660,000 cu m; fish catch (1994) 8,800. Mining and quarrying (1996): lime 260,000[7]; salt 30,000; gypsum 4,000. Manufacturing (1993): distillate fuel 4,470,000; cement 2,300,000[7]; gasoline 1,995,000; jet fuel 1,160,000; crude steel 920,000; fertilizer 347,000[7]. Construction (gross value in LD; 1982): residential 127,051,000; nonresidential 200,877,000. Energy production (consumption): electricity (kW-hr; 1994) 17,800,000,000 (17,800,000,000); coal (metric tons; 1994) none (5,000); crude petroleum (barrels; 1996) 525,600,000 ([1994] 112,725,000); petroleum products (metric tons; 1994) 13,260,000 (7,480,000); natural gas (cu m; 1996) 6,200,000,000 ([1994] 4,910,000,000).
Population economically active (1993): total 1,192,000; activity rate of total population 23.6% (participation rates: ages 10 and over, 35.2%; female 9.8%; unemployed, n.a.).

Price index (1990 = 100)

	1989	1990	1991	1992	1993	1994	1995
Consumer price index	88.5	100.0	111.7	128.5	154.1	200.4	260.5

Public debt (long-term debt; 1992): U.S.$2,592,000,000.
Gross domestic product (1994): U.S.$32,900,000,000 (U.S.$6,510 per capita).

Structure of gross domestic product and labour force

	1992 in value[8] LD '000,000	1992 % of total value	1993 labour force	1993 % of labour force
Agriculture	638	7.5	119,000	10.0
Mining and quarrying	2,173	25.4		
Manufacturing	720	8.4	381,000	32.0
Construction	1,070	12.5		
Public utilities	193	2.3		
Transp. and commun.	539	6.3		
Trade	770	9.0		
Finance, insurance	986	11.5	692,000	58.0
Pub. admin., defense	885	10.4		
Services	574	6.7		
TOTAL	8,548	100.0	1,192,000	100.0

Household income and expenditure. Average household size (1980) 5.1; income per household: n.a.; sources of income: n.a.; expenditure (1977): food 37.2%, housing and energy 32.2%, transportation 9.4%, education and recreation 8.5%, clothing 6.9%, health care 3.3%.
Land use (1994): forested 0.5%; meadows and pastures 7.6%; agricultural and under permanent cultivation 1.2%; desert and built-up areas 90.7%.
Tourism (1994): receipts U.S.$7,000,000; expenditures U.S.$210,000,000.

Foreign trade[9, 10]

Balance of trade (current prices)

	1991	1992	1993	1994	1995	1996
U.S.$'000,000	+5,873	+4,778	+2,165	+3,637	+3,615	+4,896
% of total	35.5%	31.6%	16.8%	30.5%	27.1%	32.3%

Imports (1996): U.S.$5,137,000,000 (1991; manufactured goods 78.3%, agricultural goods 20.3%). *Major import sources:* Italy 21.7%; Germany 13.9%; U.K. 8.4%; France 6.8%; Turkey 5.6%; Tunisia 4.2%; Spain 3.7%.
Exports (1996): U.S.$10,033,000,000 (1991; crude petroleum 99.8%). *Major export destinations:* Italy 41.0%; Germany 18.0%; Spain 10.0%; Turkey 4.1%; France 4.1%; Switzerland 3.0%; The Sudan 2.3%.

Transport and communications

Transport. Railroads: none. Roads (1995): total length 81,600 km (paved 56%). Vehicles (1995): passenger cars 904,000; trucks and buses 322,000. Merchant marine (1992): vessels (100 gross tons and over) 150; total deadweight tonnage 1,223,589. Air transport (1996)[11]: passenger-km 412,353,000; metric ton-km cargo 284,000; airports with scheduled flights: n.a.

Communications

Medium	date	unit	number	units per 1,000 persons
Daily newspapers	1992	circulation	71,000	15
Radio	1995	receivers	1,000,000	191
Television	1995	receivers	550,000	105
Telephones	1995	main lines	318,000	61

Education and health

Educational attainment (1984). Percentage of population age 25 and over having: no formal schooling (illiterate) 59.7%; incomplete primary education 15.4%; complete primary 8.5%; some secondary 5.2%; secondary 8.5%; higher 2.7%. *Literacy (1995):* percentage of total population age 15 and over literate 76.2%; males literate 87.9%; females literate 63.0%.

Education (1992–93)

	schools	teachers	students	student/ teacher ratio
Primary (age 6–12)	2,744[12]	103,791	1,254,242	12.1
Secondary (age 13–18)	1,555[12]	14,941[13]	181,368[13]	12.1[13]
Voc., teacher tr.	195[12]	7,072[13]	94,961	10.8[13]
Higher	10[14]	...	72,899[13]	...

Health: physicians (1989–91) 4,749 (1 per 948 persons); hospital beds (1990) 18,503[15] (1 per 246 persons); infant mortality rate (1995) 61.4.
Food (1995): daily per capita caloric intake 3,126 (vegetable products 90%, animal products 10%); 132% of FAO recommended minimum requirement.

Military

Total active duty personnel (1997): 65,000 (army 53.8%, navy 12.3%, air force 33.9%). *Military expenditure as percentage of GNP (1995):* 6.0% (world 2.8%); per capita expenditure U.S.$381.

[1]No formal titled office exists. [2]Policy-making body (General People's Congress) meets in Surt. [3]Official exchange rate. [4]1988. [5]1988. [6]Registered events; incomplete to some degree. [7]1994. [8]At factor cost. [9]Dollar values based on IMF Direction of Trade Statistics (DOTS), which are compiled from available reports of trading partners (not the subject country's reports) and may, thus, be substantially incomplete. [10]Import figures are f.o.b. [11]Jamahiriya Libyan Arab Airlines. [12]1982–83. [13]1991–92. [14]1988–89. [15]Includes beds in clinics.

Internet resources for further information:
* CIA World Factbook—Libya
  http://www.odci.gov/cia/publications/

Liechtenstein

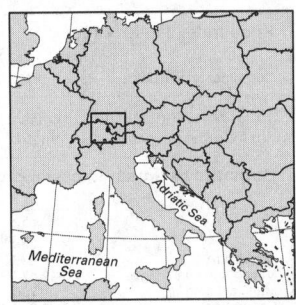

Official name: Fürstentum
Liechtenstein (Principality
of Liechtenstein).
Form of government: constitutional
monarchy with one legislative house
(Diet [25]).
Chief of state: Prince.
Head of government: Prime Minister.
Capital: Vaduz.
Official language: German.
Official religion: none.
Monetary unit: 1 Swiss franc
(Sw F) = 100 centimes; valuation
(Sept. 25, 1998) 1 U.S.$ = Sw F 1.38;
1 £ = Sw F 2.35.

Area and population

Regions Communes	area		population 1997[1] estimate
	sq mi	sq km	
Oberland	48.3	125.2	20,907
Balzers	7.6	19.6	3,972
Planken	2.0	5.3	333
Schaan	10.3	26.8	5,130
Triesen	10.2	26.4	3,988
Triesenberg	11.5	29.8	2,467
Vaduz	6.7	17.3	5,017
Unterland	13.4[2]	34.8	10,236
Eschen	4.0	10.3	3,459
Gamprin	2.4	6.1	1,138
Mauren	2.9	7.5	3,088
Ruggell	2.9	7.4	1,642
Schellenberg	1.4	3.5	909
TOTAL	61.8[2]	160.0	31,143

Demography

Population (1998): 31,400.
Density (1998): persons per sq mi 508.1, persons per sq km 196.3.
Urban-rural: n.a.
Sex distribution (1997[1]): male 48.73%; female 51.27%.
Age breakdown (1997[1]): under 15, 18.8%; 15–29, 22.3%; 30–44, 25.4%; 45–59, 19.4%; 60–74, 9.6%; 75 and over, 4.5%.
Population projection: (2000) 32,000; (2010) 34,700.
Doubling time: n.a.; doubling time exceeds 100 years.
Ethnic composition (1997[1]): Liechtensteiner 62.4%; Swiss 14.8%; Austrian 6.9%; German 3.4%; Italian 2.8%; other 9.7%.
Religious affiliation (1997[1]): Roman Catholic 80.0%; Protestant 7.5%; Muslim 3.3%; Eastern Orthodox 0.7%; atheist 0.6%; other 7.9%.
Major cities (1997[1]): Schaan 5,130; Vaduz 5,017.

Vital statistics

Birth rate per 1,000 population (1996): 13.0 (world avg. 25.0); (1995) legitimate 89.9%; illegitimate 10.1%.
Death rate per 1,000 population (1996): 7.4 (world avg. 9.3).
Natural increase rate per 1,000 population (1996): 5.6 (world avg. 15.7).
Total fertility rate (avg. births per childbearing woman; 1994): 1.5.
Marriage rate per 1,000 population (1996): 14.1.
Divorce rate per 1,000 population (1994): 1.4.
Life expectancy at birth (1996): male 66.5 years; female 77.8 years.
Major causes of death per 100,000 population (1996): diseases of the circulatory system 283.6; malignant neoplasms (cancers) 183.7; accidents, poisoning, and acts of violence 51.6%; diseases of the respiratory system 51.6.

National economy

Budget (1996). Revenue: Sw F 579,500,000 (taxes and interest 71.3%, customs duties and repayments 17.9%, investment income 8.9%; other revenue sources include real estate capital-gains taxes and death and estate taxes). Expenditures: Sw F 530,900,000 (financial affairs 36.2%, education 15.3%, social affairs 14.9%, transportation 12.9%, general administration 7.9%).
Public debt: none.
Tourism (1996): 119,264 tourist overnight stays; receipts from visitors, n.a.; expenditures by nationals abroad, n.a.
Population economically active (1997[1]): total 16,181; activity rate of total population 52.0% (participation rates: ages 15–64, 71.3%; female 40.3%; unemployed 2.7%).

Price and earnings indexes (1990 = 100)

	1990	1991	1992	1993	1994	1995	1996
Consumer price index[3]	100.0	105.8	110.2	113.7	114.7	116.8	117.8
Earnings index	...	...	...	...	...	...	...

Household income and expenditure. Average household size (1990) 2.7; income per household: n.a.; sources of earned income (1987): wages and salaries 92.9%, self-employment 7.1%; expenditure (1990)[4]: rent 20.9%, food 17.7%, transportation 11.0%, education and self-improvement 9.7%, clothing 7.0%, health 4.7%.
Production (metric tons except as noted). Agriculture, forestry, fishing (1996): silo corn (maize) 27,880[5], milk 12,801, potatoes 1,040[5], wheat 460[5], barley 416[5], grapes 150; livestock (number of live animals) 5,905 cattle, 3,352 sheep, 2,392 pigs; commercial timber (1996) 18,087 cu m; fish catch, n.a. Mining and quarrying: n.a. Manufacturing (1995): processed milk 12,801; milk for

whipped cream 2,654; yogurt 122; cheese 4; wine (1993) 635.2 hectolitres; small-scale precision manufacturing includes optical lenses, electron microscopes, electronic equipment, and high-vacuum pumps; metal manufacturing, construction machinery, and ceramics are also important. Construction (1995): residential 329,057 cu m; nonresidential 318,284 cu m. Energy production (consumption): electricity (kW-hr; 1996) 75,096,000 (259,303,000); coal (metric tons; 1995) none (26); petroleum products (metric tons; 1995) none (49,291); natural gas (cu m; 1994) none (19,350,000).
Gross national product (at current market prices; 1994): c. U.S.$1,130,000,000 (c. U.S.$37,000 per capita).

Structure of gross domestic product and labour force

	1988		1997[1]	
	in value Sw F '000	% of total value	labour force	% of labour force
Agriculture	...	...	316	2.0
Manufacturing	...	...	4,724	29.2
Construction	...	...	1,134	7.0
Public utilities	...	...	164	1.0
Transportation and communications	...	...	514	3.2
Trade, public accommodation	...	...	2,064	12.8
Finance, insurance, real estate	...	...	1,233	7.6
Pub. admin., defense	...	...	1,029	6.4
Services	...	...	4,563	28.2
Other	...	...	440[6]	2.7[6]
TOTAL	1,700,000	100.0	16,181	100.0[2]

Land use (latest): forested 34.8%; meadows and pastures 15.7%; agricultural and under permanent cultivation 24.3%; other 25.2%.

Foreign trade

Balance of trade (current prices)

	1990	1991	1992	1993	1994	1995
Sw F '000,000	+757.1	+822.8	+947.1	+1,024.2	+1,043.3	+1,078.0
% of total	27.8%	31.4%	30.6%	33.8%	33.1%	33.5%

Imports (1995): Sw F 1,071,796,000 (machinery and transport equipment 33.9%; other finished goods 24.4%; metal products 14.1%; limestone, cement, and other building materials 11.9%; unrefined and semifabricated metal 5.8%; chemical products 4.6%). *Major import sources:* n.a.
Exports (1995): Sw F 2,149,796,000 (machinery and transport equipment 46.9%; metal products 16.9%; other finished goods 12.1%; limestone, cement, and other building materials 10.3%; chemical products 8.1%). *Major export destinations* (1994): European Economic Community countries 39.6%; Switzerland 14.0%; other European Free Trade Association countries 6.0%; other 40.4%.

Transport and communications

Transport. Railroads (1996): length 11.5 mi, 18.5 km; passenger and cargo traffic, n.a. Roads (1995): total length 201 mi, 323 km. Vehicles (1997): passenger cars 19,926; trucks and buses 2,684. Merchant marine: none. Air transport: none.

Communications

Medium	date	unit	number	units per 1,000 persons
Daily newspapers	1995	circulation	17,355	564
Radio	1995	receivers	11,808	384
Television	1995	receivers	11,421	371
Telephones	1995	main lines	19,632	638

Education and health

Educational attainment (1990). Percentage of population not of preschool age or in compulsory education having: no formal schooling 0.3%; primary and lower secondary education 39.3%; higher secondary and vocational 47.6%; some postsecondary 7.4%; university 4.2%; other and unknown 1.1%.
Literacy: virtually 100%.

Education (1996–97)

	schools	teachers[7]	students	student/ teacher ratio
Primary (age 7–12)	14	144	1,998	13.9
Secondary (age 13–19)	8	164	1,887	11.5
Vocational[8]	2	247	2,515	10.2

Health: physicians (1995) 32 (1 per 962 persons); hospital beds[9] (1985) 100 (1 per 269 persons); infant mortality rate per 1,000 live births (1996) 7.4.
Food (1996)[10]: daily per capita caloric intake 3,440 (vegetable products 69%, animal products 31%); 129% of FAO recommended minimum requirement.

Military

Total active duty personnel: none. *Military expenditure as percentage of GNP:* none.

[1]January 1. [2]Detail does not add to total given because of rounding. [3]The index is for Switzerland, which is united with Liechtenstein in a customs and monetary union. [4]Household expenditures are taken from a 1986 Swiss sample survey; a similarity of consumption patterns is assumed. [5]1987. [6]Unemployed. [7]Full-time teachers only. [8]1994–95. [9]Liechtenstein has one hospital. Agreements with the Swiss cantons of St. Gallen and Graubünden and the Austrian Federal State of Vorarlberg allow use of certain hospitals. [10]Figures are derived from statistics for Switzerland and Austria.

Internet resources for further information:
• **Principality of Liechtenstein http://hkreuzer.phys.dal.ca/fl.htm**

Lithuania

Official name: Lietuvos Respublika (Republic of Lithuania).
Form of government: unitary multiparty republic with a single legislative body, the Seimas (141).
Head of state: President.
Head of government: Prime Minister.
Capital: Vilnius.
Official language: Lithuanian.
Official religion: none.
Monetary unit: 1 litas (plural litai) = 100 centai; valuation (Sept. 25, 1998) 1 U.S.$ = 4.00 litai; 1 £ = 6.81 litai.

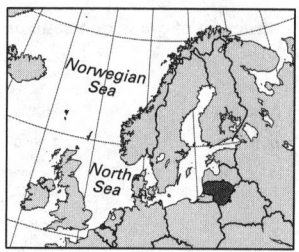

Area and population		area		population
Provinces	Capitals	sq mi	sq km	1996 estimate
Alytus	Alytus	2,095	5,425	202,600
Kaunas	Kaunas	3,154	8,170	756,300
Klaipėda	Klaipėda	2,219	5,746	415,800
Marijampolė	Marijampolė	1,723	4,463	198,500
Panevėžys	Panevėžys	3,042	7,880	323,6600
Šiauliai	Šiauliai	3,379	8,751	401,700
Tauragė	Tauragė	1,496	3,874	130,100
Telšiai	Telšiai	4,598	4,139	182,800
Utena	Utena	2,780	7,201	202,600
Vilnius	Vilnius	3,726	9,651	897,900
TOTAL		25,213[1, 2]	65,301[1, 2]	3,711,900

Demography

Population (1998): 3,704,000.
Density (1998): persons per sq mi 146.9, persons per sq km 56.7.
Urban-rural (1996): urban 67.8%; rural 32.2%.
Sex distribution (1996): male 47.22%; female 52.78%.
Age breakdown (1996): under 15, 21.6%; 15–29, 22.0%; 30–44, 22.1%; 45–59, 16.9%; 60–69, 9.7%; 70 and over, 7.7%.
Population projection: (2000) 3,702,000; (2010) 3,639,000.
Doubling time: not applicable.
Ethnic composition (1996): Lithuanian 81.6%; Russian 8.2%; Polish 6.9%; Belorusian 1.5%; Ukrainian 1.0%; other 0.8%.
Religious affiliation (1995): Roman Catholic 72.2%; Russian Orthodox 2.5%; Protestant 1.3%; other (mostly nonreligious) 24.0%.
Major cities (1996): Vilnius 573,200; Kaunas 410,800; Klaipėda 201,500; Šiauliai 146,500; Panevezys 132,300; Alytus 77,400.

Vital statistics

Birth rate per 1,000 population (1996): 10.6 (world avg. 25.0); (1995) legitimate 87.4%; illegitimate 12.6%.
Death rate per 1,000 population (1996): 11.6 (world avg. 9.3).
Natural increase rate per 1,000 population (1996): –1.0 (world avg. 15.7).
Total fertility rate (avg. births per childbearing woman; 1995): 1.5.
Marriage rate per 1,000 population (1995): 6.0.
Divorce rate per 1,000 population (1995): 2.8.
Life expectancy at birth (1995): male 63.6 years; female 75.2 years.
Major causes of death per 100,000 population (1995): circulatory diseases 654; malignant neoplasms (cancers) 203; accidents 176; respiratory diseases 49; digestive diseases 32.

National economy

Budget (1995). Revenue: 5,758,000,000 litai (value-added tax 34.3%, individual income tax 29.3%, excise taxes 10.7%, property tax 2.8%). Expenditures: 6,197,000,000 litai (economy 27.9%, education 21.8%, health 14.3%, social insurance 8.3%).
Production (metric tons except as noted). Agriculture, forestry, fishing (1996): potatoes 1,594,000, barley 1,000,000, wheat 550,000, sugar beets 650,000; livestock (number of live animals) 1,150,000 pigs, 1,100,000 cattle, 8,530,000 poultry; roundwood (1995) 4,495,000 cu m; fish catch (1993) 120,078. Mining and quarrying (1995): limestone 3,000,000; peat 214,000. Manufacturing (value of production in '000 litai; 1995): processed foods 4,781,421; textile and knitwear 1,748,812; chemicals 1,066,200; wood and wood products 630,334. Construction (1996): residential 2,000,900,000 litai. Energy production (consumption): electricity (kW-hr; 1994) 10,055,000,000 (11,199,000,000); coal (metric tons; 1994) none (482,000); crude petroleum (barrels; 1994) 682,000 (27,000,000); petroleum products (metric tons; 1994) 3,819,000 (3,606,000); natural gas (cu m; 1994) none (1,871,000,000).
Gross national product (1996): U.S.$8,455,000,000[3] (U.S.$2,280 per capita).

Structure of gross national product and labour force				
	1995			
	in value '000,000 litai	% of total value	labour force	% of labour force
Agriculture, forestry	2,222.5	9.3	391,800	22.4
Manufacturing, mining	6,180.9	25.9	306,200	17.5
Construction	1,590.5	6.7	114,700	6.5
Public utilities	723.3	3.0	42,300	2.4
Transp. and commun.	1,813.8	7.6	95,100	5.4
Trade	5,698.0	23.9	229,600	13.1
Finance	751.9	3.2	57,400	3.3
Pub. admin., defense	...	...	67,600	3.9
Services	...	...	244,900	14.0
Other	4,848.2	20.4	203,000[4]	11.6
TOTAL	23,829.0	100.0	1,752,600	100.0[2]

Population economically active (1995): total 1,753,000; activity rate of total population 47.2% (participation rates: ages 16–60/55[5], 83.0%; female [1993] 48.5%; unemployed 6.2%).

Price and earnings indexes (1994 = 100)							
	1991	1992	1993	1994	1995	1996	1997
Consumer price index	1.65	11.4	58.1	100	139.7	174.0	189.5
Monthly earnings index	6.84	15.8	52.5	100	143.4	195.0	242.4

Household income and expenditure (1995). Average household size (1989) 3.2; sources of income: wages 71.4%, pensions and grants 14.0%, self-employment in agriculture 6.6%, other 7.0%; expenditure: food 45.1%, nonfood goods 17.6%, services 15.6%, taxes 14.4%, agricultural expenses 4.3%.
Land use (1994): forested 30.4%; meadows and pastures 7.6%; agricultural and under permanent cultivation 53.9%; other 8.1%.
Tourism (1995): receipts from visitors U.S.$124,000,000; expenditures by nationals abroad U.S.$138,000,000.

Foreign trade

Balance of trade (current prices)					
	1993	1994	1995	1996	1997
LTL '000,000	–1,091	–1,278	–3,774	–4,815	–7,136
% of total	5.9%	7.3%	14.8%	12.7%	18.8%

Imports (1995): U.S.$3,083,000,000 (petroleum and gas 26.7%, machinery 16.5%, textiles 9.3%, chemicals 9.0%, transport equipment 7.5%, base metals 6.7%, prepared foods 4.5%). *Major import sources:* Russia 31.1%; Germany 15.2%; United Kingdom 4.3%; Poland 4.1%; Denmark 3.9%; Finland 3.6%.
Exports (1995): U.S.$2,707,000,000 (textiles 14.7%, chemicals 12.2%, mineral products 11.9%, machinery 10.8%, base metals 8.7%, live animals 8.4%, prepared foods 5.6%). *Major export destinations:* Russia 20.4%; Germany 14.4%; Belarus 10.7%; Ukraine 7.5%; Latvia 7.1%; The Netherlands 4.9%; Poland 3.9%.

Transport and communications

Transport. Railroads (1995): length 1,802 mi, 2,900 km; passenger-mi 702,000,000, passenger-km 1,130,000,000; short ton-mi cargo 5,264,000,000, metric ton-km cargo 7,685,000,000. Roads (1995): total length 38,178 mi, 61,442 km (paved 86%). Vehicles (1995): passenger cars 718,469; trucks and buses 110,696. Merchant marine (1995): vessels (100 gross tons and over) 95; total deadweight tonnage 569,288. Air transport (1996): passenger-mi 226,000,000, passenger-km 363,000,000; short ton-mi cargo 1,566,000, metric ton-km cargo 2,287,000; airports with scheduled flights (1996) 3.

Communications				units per 1,000 persons
Medium	date	unit	number	
Daily newspapers	1994	circulation	506,000	136
Radio	1995	receivers	1,500,000	404
Television	1995	receivers	1,350,000	364
Telephones	1995	main lines	941,000	254
Cellular telephones	1995	subscribers	14,800	4.0
Facsimile machines	1995	units	500	0.13
Personal computers	1995	units	24,000	6.5

Education and health

Educational attainment (1989). Percentage of population age 25 and over having: no schooling 9.1%; complete primary 21.3%; incomplete secondary 57.0%; postsecondary 12.6%. *Literacy* (1995[6]): total population age 15 and over literate 99.5%; males literate 99.6%; females literate 99.3%.

Education (1995–96)				student/ teacher ratio
	schools	teachers	students	
Primary and secondary	2,361	47,000	562,000	12.0
Voc., teacher tr.	106	4,671	49,000	10.5
Higher	15	9,003[7]	54,000	7.3[7]

Health (1995): physicians 14,737 (1 per 252 persons); hospital beds 40,262 (1 per 92 persons); infant mortality rate per 1,000 live births (1995) 12.4.

Military

Total active duty personnel (1996): 5,100 (army 82.3%, navy 6.9%, air force 10.8%). *Military expenditure as percentage of GNP* (1995): 0.5% (world 2.8%); per capita expenditure U.S.$21.

[1]Total includes 12 sq mi (30 sq km) not distributed by administrative subdivision. [2]Detail does not add to total given because of rounding. [3]GNP estimate is preliminary. [4]Includes 109,000 undistributable unemployed and 94,000 undistributable employed. [5]Males retire at age 60, females at 55. [6]Estimate. [7]1987–88.

Internet resources for further information:
• Lithuanian Department of Statistics http://www.std.lt

Luxembourg

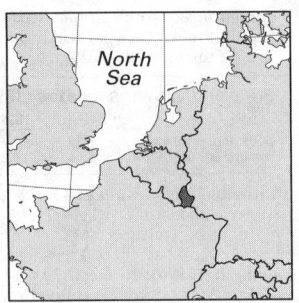

Official name: Groussherzogtum Lëtzebuerg (Luxemburgian); Grand-Duché de Luxembourg (French); Grossherzogtum Luxemburg (German) (Grand Duchy of Luxembourg).
Form of government: constitutional monarchy with two legislative houses (Council of State [21][1]; Chamber of Deputies [60]).
Chief of state: Grand Duke.
Head of government: Prime Minister.
Capital: Luxembourg.
Official language: none: Luxemburgian (national); French (used for most official purposes); German (lingua franca).
Official religion: none.
Monetary unit: 1 Luxembourg franc (Lux F) = 100 centimes; valuation (Sept. 25, 1998) 1 U.S.$ = Lux F 34.47; 1 £ = Lux F 58.69.

Area and population		area		population
Districts				1995[2]
Cantons		sq mi	sq km	estimate
Diekirch		447	1,157	60,900
Clervaux		128	332	11,300
Diekirch		92	239	24,600
Redange		103	267	12,000
Vianden		21	54	2,900
Wiltz		102	265	10,100
Grevenmacher		203	525	46,700
Echternach		72	186	13,000
Grevenmacher		82	211	19,400
Remich		49	128	14,300
Luxembourg		349	904	298,000
Capellen		77	199	34,200
Esch		94	243	122,700
Luxembourg				
(Ville et Campagne)		92	238	120,500
Mersch		86	224	20,600
TOTAL		999	2,586	406,600[3]

Demography

Population (1998): 425,000.
Density (1998): persons per sq mi 425.4, persons per sq km 164.3.
Urban-rural (1993): urban 88.0%; rural 12.0%.
Sex distribution (1996[2]): male 49.08%; female 50.92%.
Age breakdown (1996): under 15, 18.5%; 15–29, 19.6%; 30–44, 24.8%; 45–59, 18.0%; 60–74, 13.5%; 75 and over, 5.6%.
Population projection: (2000) 433,000; (2010) 462,000.
Doubling time: not applicable; population stable.
Ethnic composition (nationality; 1996[2]): Luxembourger 66.6%; Portuguese 12.5%; Italian 4.8%; French 3.6%; Belgian 2.6%; German 2.3%; other 7.6%.
Religious affiliation (1996): Roman Catholic 95.1%; other 4.9%.
Major cities (1995[2]): Luxembourg 76,446; Esch-sur-Alzette 24,255; Differdange 16,196; Dudelange 15,833; Petage 13,066.

Vital statistics

Birth rate per 1,000 population (1996): 13.7 (world avg. 25.0); (1995) legitimate 86.9%; illegitimate 13.1%.
Death rate per 1,000 population (1996): 9.4 (world avg. 9.3).
Natural increase rate per 1,000 population (1996): 4.3 (world avg. 15.7).
Total fertility rate (avg. births per childbearing woman; 1995): 1.7.
Marriage rate per 1,000 population (1995): 5.1.
Divorce rate per 1,000 population (1995): 1.8.
Life expectancy at birth (1990–92): male 72.6 years; female 79.1 years.
Major causes of death per 100,000 population (1995): circulatory diseases 392.1, of which ischemic heart disease and myocardial infarction 125.8, cerebrovascular disease 119.4; malignant neoplasms (cancers) 253.1.

National economy

Budget (1996). Revenue: Lux F 155,837,400,000 (income and excise taxes 57.9%, customs taxes 15.9%). Expenditures: Lux F 156,604,200,000 (social security 20.5%, education 12.0%, transportation 9.1%, administration 7.3%, defense 2.4%, debt service 1.1%).
Public debt (1996): U.S.$679,780,000.
Tourism (1989): receipts from visitors U.S.$286,000,000.
Production (metric tons except as noted). Agriculture, forestry, fishing (1995): barley 63,300, wheat 52,800, potatoes 22,800, rye 16,800, oats 11,800, sugar beets 10,400, apples 5,595; livestock (number of live animals) 213,887 cattle, 76,640 pigs; roundwood (1993) 305,200 cu m. Mining and quarrying (1987): sand and gravel 956,810; gypsum 420,000; crushed stone 344,841. Manufacturing (1994): steel 3,073,268; pig iron 1,926,890; milk 261,600; beef and pork 23,120; wine 179,998 hectolitres. Construction (1995): residential 514,616 sq m; nonresidential 320,184 sq m. Energy production (consumption): electricity (kW-hr; 1994) 1,190,000,000 (5,645,000,000); coal (metric tons; 1994) none (323,000); crude petroleum, none (n.a.); petroleum products (metric tons; 1994) none (1,721,000); natural gas (cu m; 1994) none (582,040,000).
Gross national product (1996): U.S.$18,850,000,000 (U.S.$45,360 per capita).

Structure of gross domestic product and labour force

	1995			
	in value Lux F '000,000	% of total value	labour force	% of labour force
Agriculture	5,174	1.1	5,800	2.7
Mining	4	4	4	4
Manufacturing	78,920[4]	17.4[4]	32,800[4]	15.4[4]
Construction	35,875	7.9	23,900	11.2
Public utilities	8,099	1.8	1,400	0.6
Transp. and commun.	27,505	6.1	14,500	6.8
Trade	65,419	14.4	44,700	20.9
Finance	91,922	20.2	20,100	9.4
Pub. admin., defense	63,644	14.0	29,900	14.0
Services	142,200	31.3	40,300	18.9
Other	−64,572[5]	−14.2[5]	...	...
TOTAL	454,193	100.0	213,500[3]	100.0[3]

Population economically active (1995): total 213,500; activity rate of total population 52.2% (participation rates: ages 15–64, 61.6%[6]; female 35.9%[6]; unemployed 3.0%).

Price and earnings indexes (1990 = 100)						
	1992	1993	1994	1995	1996	1997
Consumer price index	106.4	110.2	112.6	114.8	116.4	118.0
Hourly earnings index	112.0	116.5	121.8	127.7	...	...

Household income and expenditure. Average household size (1991) 2.6; income per household (1992) Lux F 1,438,000 (U.S.$44,700); sources of income (1992): wages and salaries 67.1%, transfer payments 28.1%, self-employment 4.8%; expenditure (1994): food, beverages, and tobacco 19.7%, housing 17.3%, transportation and communications 16.2%, household goods and furniture 9.9%, clothing and footwear 8.2%, health 7.9%.
Land use (1992): forested 34.2%; meadows and pastures 25.6%; agricultural and under permanent cultivation 23.2%; other 17.0%.

Foreign trade

Balance of trade (current prices)						
	1992	1993	1994	1995	1996	1997
Lux F '000,000	−56,300	−62,300	−61,500	−62,400	−71,100	−82,800
% of total	11.9%	13.3%	12.3%	12.0%	13.9%	14.4%

Imports (1995): Lux F 290,717,000,000 (machinery and transport equipment 46.9%; food 11.4%; mineral products 9.5%; chemicals 8.3%). *Major import sources:* Belgium 38.1%; Germany 29.8%; France 12.0%; The Netherlands 4.7%; U.S. 3.3%; Italy 2.1%.
Exports (1995): Lux F 228,263,000,000 (machinery and transport equipment 55.1%; plastics and rubber products 14.1%; textiles 6.6%; food 6.6%; chemicals 4.6%). *Major export destinations:* Germany 28.3%; France 19.7%; Belgium 13.3%; U.K. 6.3%; The Netherlands 5.3%; Italy 5.0%; U.S. 3.1%.

Transport and communications

Transport. Railroads (1995): route length 171 mi, 275 km; passenger-mi 176,000,000[7], passenger-km 284,000,000[7]; short ton-mi cargo 387,687,000, metric ton-km cargo 566,013,000. Roads (1996[2]): total length 3,206 mi, 5,160 km (paved 99%). Vehicles (1996[2]): passenger cars 231,666; trucks and buses 25,529. Merchant marine (1992): vessels (100 gross tons and over) 54; total deadweight tonnage 2,603,611. Air transport (1995): passenger arrivals 617,809, departures 624,088; airports (1997) with scheduled flights 1.

Communications				units per 1,000
Medium	date	unit	number	persons
Daily newspapers	1994	circulation	154,000	381
Radio	1995	receivers	240,000	586
Television	1991	receivers	134,845	384
Telephones	1994	main lines	221,898	550

Education and health

Educational attainment: n.a. Literacy (1995): virtually 100% literate.

Education (1994–95)				student/
	schools	teachers	students	teacher ratio
Primary (age 6–11)[8]	...	1,732	26,867	15.5
Secondary (age 12–18)	...	1,686	9,012	5.3
Voc., teacher tr.	...	2,904[9]	16,909	5.7[9]
Higher	1	200	1,100	5.5

Health (1996[2]): physicians 908 (1 per 454 persons); hospital beds (1995[2]) 4,443 (1 per 92 persons); infant mortality rate per 1,000 live births 4.9.
Food (1995): daily per capita caloric intake 3,530 (vegetable products 68%, animal products 32%); 134% of FAO recommended minimum.

Military

Total active duty personnel (1996): 800 (army 100.0%). *Military expenditure as percentage of GNP* (1994): 0.8% (world 3.0%); per capita expenditure U.S.$313.

[1]Has limited legislative authority. [2]January 1. [3]Detail does not add to total given because of rounding. [4]Manufacturing includes mining. [5]Imputed bank service charges. [6]1991. [7]1992. [8]Public schools only. [9]Vocational schools only.

Internet resources for further information:
• **STATEC: Luxembourg in Figures**
http://statec.gouvernement.lu/

Macedonia

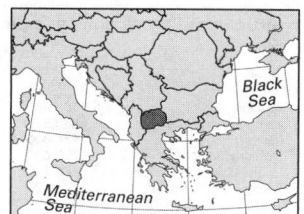

Official name[1]: Republika Makedonija (Republic of Macedonia).
Form of government: unitary multiparty republic with a unicameral legislative (Assembly [120]).
Head of state: President.
Head of government: Prime Minister.
Capital: Skopje.
Official language: Macedonian.
Official religion: none.
Monetary unit[2]: denar; valuation (Sept. 25, 1998) 1 U.S.$ = 52.13 denar; 1 £ = 88.75 denar.

Area and population (1994 census)

Administrative districts[3]	area sq km	population	Administrative districts[3]	area sq km	population
Berovo	806	19,737	Negotino	734	23,094
Bitola	1,798	106,012	Ohrid	1,069	60,841
Brod	924	10,912	Prilep	1,675	93,248
Debar	274	26,449	Probištip	326	16,373
Delčevo	589	25,052	Radoviš	735	30,378
Demir Hisar	443	10,321	Resen	739	17,467
Gevgelija	757	34,767	Skopje[4]	1,818	541,280
Gostivar	1,341	108,189	Štip	815	50,531
Kavadarci	1,132	41,801	Struga	507	62,305
Kičevo	854	53,044	Strumica	952	89,759
Kočani	570	48,105	Sveti Nikole	649	21,391
Kratovo	376	10,855	Tetovo	1,080	174,748
Kriva Palanka	720	25,112	Titov Veles	1,536	65,523
Kruševo	239	11,981	Valandovo	331	12,049
Kumanovo	1,212	126,543	Vinica	432	19,010
			TOTAL	25,713[5]	1,936,877

Demography

Population (1998): 2,023,000.
Density (1998): persons per sq mi 203.8, persons per sq km 78.7.
Urban-rural (1994): urban 58.7%; rural 41.3%.
Sex distribution (1994): male 50.39%; female 49.61%.
Age breakdown (1994): under 15, 24.8%; 15–29, 24.1%; 30–44, 22.3%; 45–59, 15.8%; 60–74, 10.6%; 75 and over, 2.4%.
Population projection: (2000) 2,064,000; (2010) 2,157,000.
Ethnic composition (1994): Macedonian 66.5%; Albanian 22.9%; Turkish 4.0%; Gypsy 2.0%; Serb 2.0%; other 2.6%.
Religious affiliation (1995): Serbian (Macedonian) Orthodox 54.2%; Sunnī Muslim 30.0%; other 15.8%.
Major cities (1994): Skopje 440,577; Bitola 75,386; Prilep 67,371; Kumanovo 66,237; Tetovo 50,376.

Vital statistics

Birth rate per 1,000 population (1995): 14.9. (world avg. 25.0); legitimate 91.5%; illegitimate 8.5%.
Death rate per 1,000 population (1995): 7.6 (world avg. 9.3).
Natural increase rate per 1,000 population (1995): 7.3 (world avg. 15.7).
Total fertility rate (avg. births per childbearing woman; 1995): 2.0.
Marriage rate per 1,000 population (1994): 7.6.
Life expectancy at birth (1995): male 68.8 years; female 75.0 years.
Major causes of death per 100,000 population (1993): diseases of the circulatory system 385.8; accidents, violence, and poisoning 35.3; diseases of the respiratory system 34.5; diseases of the digestive system 14.8.

National economy

Budget (1995). Revenue: 64,254,000,000 denar[2] (social security contributions 32.6%, excises taxes 19.1%, income and profits tax 17.3%, sales tax 12.3%). Expenditure: 66,032,000,000 denar[2] (pensions 24.1%, wages and salaries 22.7%, health 13.3%).
Tourism (1994): receipts from visitors U.S.$21,000,000; expenditures by nationals abroad U.S.$23,000,000.
Production (metric tons except as noted). Agriculture, forestry, fishing (1996): wheat 269,000, grapes 215,000, potatoes 157,000, corn (maize) 143,000; livestock (number of live animals) 2,320,000 sheep, 283,000 cattle, 175,000 pigs, 5,000,000 poultry; roundwood (1996) 774,000 cu m; fish catch (1995) 1,570 (all freshwater). Mining and quarrying (1995): copper ore 2,000,000; lead-zinc ore 430,000; refined silver 10,000 kilograms. Manufacturing (1995): cement 523,499; steel sheets 40,878; wool yarn 3,863; refrigerators 56,148 units; leather footwear 1,120,000 pairs; cotton fabric 15,525,000 sq m; cigarettes 10,615,000 units. Construction (residential, 1994): 348,004 sq m. Energy production (consumption): electricity (kW-hr; 1994) 5,924,000,000 (5,359,000,000); coal (metric tons; 1994) 6,900,000 (6,959,000); crude petroleum (barrels; 1993) none (8,063,000); petroleum products (metric tons; 1992) 556,000 (823,000); natural gas (cu m; 1993) none (269,100,000).
Population economically active (1995): total 596,600; activity rate 30.8% (participation rates: ages 15–64 [1991] 98.1%; [1994] female 25.5%; [1994] unemployed 32.0%).

Price and earnings indexes (1992 = 100)

	1992	1993	1994	1995	1996
Consumer price index	100.0	461.9	1,054	1,153	1,155
Earnings index[6]	100.0	595.7	1,221	1,352	1,388

Gross national product (1996): U.S.$1,956,000,000 (U.S.$990 per capita).

Structure of gross domestic product and labour force

	1993		1995	
	in value '000,000 denar[2]	% of total value	labour force	% of labour force
Agriculture	5,795	10.0	53,700	9.0
Mining and manufacturing	15,019	25.8	136,600	22.9
Construction	2,977	5.1	31,400	5.3
Public utilities	1,195	2.1	8,100	1.4
Transp. and commun.	3,433	5.9	21,000	3.5
Trade	3,959	6.8	34,100	5.7
Finance	3,201	5.5	10,900	1.8
Pub. admin., defense	11,330	19.5	15,300	2.6
Services	1,871	3.2	69,300	11.6
Other	9,363[7]	16.1[7]	216,200[8]	36.2
TOTAL	58,143	100.0	596,600	100.0

External debt (1996): U.S.$863,000,000.
Land use (1994): forested 38.9%; meadows and pastures 24.7%; agricultural and under permanent cultivation 25.7%; other 10.7%.
Household income and expenditure (1994). Average household size 3.8; income per household Din 49,635[2] (U.S.$1,223); sources of income: wages and salaries 59.9%, transfers payments 17.0%, transfers from abroad 13.4%, other 9.7%; expenditure: food 42.2%, fuel and lighting 7.5%, clothing and footwear 7.4%, transportation and communications 7.2%, drink and tobacco 7.0%, health care 4.7%, education and entertainment 3.2%.

Foreign trade

Balance of trade (current prices)

	1991	1992	1993	1994	1995
U.S.$'000,000	−225	−7	−172	−398	−232
% of total	8.9%	0.3%	7.5%	15.5%	8.7%

Imports (1995): U.S.$1,439,000,000 (machinery and transport equipment 19.0%, food products 17.0%, manufactured products 16.0%, chemical products 12.0%, petroleum products 12.0%). *Major import sources:* Germany 15.0%; Russia 8.0%; Bulgaria 7.0%; Italy 7.0%; U.K. 5.0%; Albania 4.0%.
Exports (1995): U.S.$1,204,000,000 (manufactured products 35.0%, machinery and transport equipment 13.0%, food products 11.0%, raw materials 8.0%, chemical products 6.0%). *Major export destinations:* Germany 13.0%; U.K. 7.0%; Italy 5.0%; Russia 4.0%.

Transport and communications

Transport. Railroads (1994): length 573 mi, 922 km; passenger-mi 41,642,000, passenger-km 67,000,000; short ton-mi cargo 103,426,000, metric ton-km cargo 151,000,000. Roads (1994): length 5,233 mi, 8,422 km (paved 62%). Vehicles (1994): passenger cars 263,181; trucks and buses 22,825. Merchant marine: n.a. Air transport (1993)[9]: passenger-mi 181,671,190, passenger-km 292,372,000; metric tons cargo transported 625; airports (1997) with scheduled flights 2.

Communications

Medium	date	unit	number	units per 1,000 persons
Daily newspapers	1995	circulation	44,000	21
Radio	1995	receivers	350,000	179
Television	1995	receivers	350,000	179
Telephones	1995	main lines	349,000	179

Education and health

Educational attainment (1981). Percentage of population age 15 and over having: less than full primary education 45.3%; primary 28.1%; secondary 21.2%; postsecondary and higher 5.1%; unknown 0.3%. *Literacy* (1981): total population age 10 and over literate 1,365,000 (89.1%); males literate 729,000 (94.2%); females literate 636,000 (83.8%).

Education (1994–95)

	schools	teachers	students	student/ teacher ratio
Primary (age 7–14)	1,050	13,102	258,955	19.9
Secondary (age 15–18)	95	4,520	77,754	16.5
Higher	27	1,122	26,959	24.0

Health (1994): physicians 4,505 (1 per 437 persons); hospital beds 10,644 (1 per 195 persons); (1995) infant mortality rate per 1,000 live births 27.3.

Military

Total active duty personnel (1997): 15,400 (army 100%). *Military expenditure as percentage of GNP* (1995): 3.3% (world 2.8%); per capita expenditure U.S.$30.

---

[1]Member of the United Nations under the name The Former Yugoslav Republic of Macedonia. [2]Macedonia left the Yugoslav currency area in September 1991, utilizing a local coupon alone until May 1992, when a transitional local currency, the denar, was introduced. The denar (valued initially at denar 255 = 1 U.S.$) circulated in parallel with the coupon until May 1993, when a differently defined denar was introduced, replacing both the transitional denar and the coupon. [3]Local government to be reorganized per September 1996 official announcement from 34 administrative districts into 123 municipalities. [4]The city of Skopje comprised five administrative districts. [5]Total includes 280 sq km of inland water not distributed by district. [6]Based on nominal net wages per worker. [7]Includes import duties, customs imputed rents, and statistical discrepancy. [8]Registered unemployed. [9]Palair Macedonian airline only.

Internet resources for further information:
• Secretariat of Information http://www.sinf.gov.mk/

Madagascar

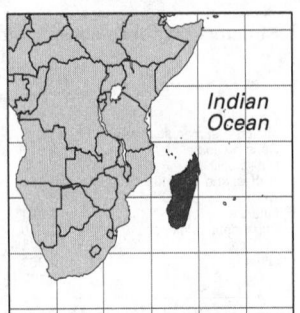

Official name: Repoblikan'i Madagasikara (Malagasy); République de Madagascar (French) (Republic of Madagascar).
Form of government: federal multiparty republic with one legislative house (National Assembly [150]).
Heads of state and government: President assisted by Prime Minister.
Capital: Antananarivo.
Official languages: [1].
Official religion: none.
Monetary unit: 1 Malagasy franc (FMG) = 100 centimes; valuation (Sept. 25, 1998) 1 U.S.$ = FMG 5,300; 1 £ = FMG 9,023.

Area and population

Provinces	Capitals	area sq mi	area sq km	population 1993 census[2]
Antananarivo	Antananarivo	22,503	58,283	3,483,236
Antsiranana	Antsiranana	16,620	43,046	942,410
Fianarantsoa	Fianarantsoa	39,526	102,373	2,671,150
Mahajanga	Mahajanga	57,924	150,023	1,330,612
Toamasina	Toamasina	27,765	71,911	1,935,330
Toliary	Toliary	62,319	161,405	1,729,419
TOTAL		226,658	587,041	12,092,157

Demography

Population (1998): 14,463,000.
Density (1998): persons per sq mi 63.8, persons per sq km 24.6.
Urban-rural (1991): urban 24.4%; rural 75.6%.
Sex distribution (1993): male 49.55%; female 50.45%.
Age breakdown (1995): under 15, 46.1%; 15–29, 26.2%; 30–44, 15.2%; 45–59, 8.0%; 60–74, 3.8%; 75 and over, 0.7%.
Population projection: (2000) 15,295,000; (2010) 20,096,000.
Doubling time: 25 years.
Ethnic composition (1983): Malagasy 98.9%, of which Merina 26.6%, Betsimisaraka 14.9%, Betsileo 11.7%, Tsimihety 7.4%, Sakalava 6.4%, Antandroy 5.3%; Comorian 0.3%; Indian and Pakistani 0.2%; French 0.2%; Chinese 0.1%; other 0.3%.
Religious affiliation (1997): traditional beliefs 52.0%; Christian 41.0%, of which Roman Catholic 21.3%, Protestant 19.7%; Muslim 7.0%.
Major cities (1993): Antananarivo 1,052,835; Toamasina 127,441; Antsirabe 120,239; Mahajanga 100,807; Fianarantsoa 99,005.

Vital statistics

Birth rate per 1,000 population (1996): 42.6 (world avg. 25.0).
Death rate per 1,000 population (1996): 14.4 (world avg. 9.3).
Natural increase rate per 1,000 population (1996): 28.2 (world avg. 15.7).
Total fertility rate (avg. births per childbearing woman; 1996): 5.9.
Marriage rate per 1,000 population: n.a.
Divorce rate per 1,000 population: n.a.
Life expectancy at birth (1996): male 51.1 years; female 53.3 years.
Major causes of death per 100,000 population: n.a.; however, major causes of death in the early 1990s included maternal and perinatal diseases, malaria, infectious and parasitic diseases, malnutrition, diarrhea, and respiratory diseases.

National economy

Budget (1995). Revenue: FMG 1,138,300,000,000 (taxes 97.6%, of which duties on trade 55.7%, value-added tax 20.4%, income tax 14.4%; nontax receipts 2.4%). Expenditures: FMG 1,888,700,000,000 (current expenditure 79.7%, of which debt service 31.6%, education 10.0%, general administration 7.7%, defense 6.1%, health 3.9%, agriculture 0.7%; capital expenditure 20.3%).
Production (metric tons except as noted). Agriculture, forestry, fishing (1996): paddy rice 2,600,000, cassava 2,450,000, sugarcane 2,200,000, sweet potatoes 500,000, potatoes 280,000, bananas 230,000, mangoes 202,000, corn (maize) 180,000, taro 140,000, oranges 83,000, coconuts 83,000, coffee 72,000, dry beans 70,000, pineapples 50,000, peanuts (groundnuts) 37,000, seed cotton 30,000, livestock (number of live animals) 10,320,000 cattle, 1,629,000 pigs, 1,329,000 goats, 756,000 sheep, 16,000,000 chickens; roundwood (1994) 9,151,000 cu m; fish catch (1995) 120,140. Mining and quarrying (1995): salt 80,000; chromite ore 74,000; graphite 13,900; mica 387; gold 200 kg[3]; in addition, a wide variety of semiprecious stones and gemstones are produced. Manufacturing (1995): cotton cloth 25,000,000, refined sugar 89,474, cement 45,009, soap 15,000, tobacco products 1,936, beer 318,842 hectolitres, fuel oil 177,329 cu m, gas oil 129,227 cu m, kerosene 110,764 cu m, gasoline 87,905 cu m, shoes 972,000 pairs. Construction (1986)[4]: residential 19,700 sq m; nonresidential 5,700 sq m. Energy production (consumption): electricity (kW-hr; 1994) 600,000,000 (605,000,000); coal (metric tons; 1994) none (14,000); crude petroleum (barrels; 1994) none (1,450,000); petroleum products (metric tons; 1994) 185,000 (348,000); natural gas, none (n.a.).
Household income and expenditure. Average household size (1993) 4.6[4]; average annual income per household: n.a.; sources of income (1975)[5]: wages and salaries 58.8%, self-employment 14.1%, other 27.1%; expenditure (1983)[4, 6]: food 60.4%, fuel and light 9.1%, clothing and footwear 8.6%, household goods and utensils 2.4%.
Gross national product (1996): U.S.$3,428,000,000 (U.S.$250 per capita).

Structure of gross domestic product and labour force

	1991 in value FMG '000,000[7]	1991 % of total value	1993 labour force	1993 % of labour force
Agriculture	1,488,350	32.6	5,100,000	86.2
Manufacturing	530,560	11.6	86,000	1.5
Mining	14,800	0.3		
Construction	52,600	1.2	46,000	0.8
Public utilities	86,950	1.9		
Transp. and commun.	747,920	16.4	42,000	0.7
Trade	497,990	10.9	149,000	2.5
Finance	70,020	1.5		
Services[8]	791,890	17.4	243,000	4.1
Pub. admin., defense	284,430	6.2	208,000	3.5
Other	...	...	40,000	0.7
TOTAL	4,565,510	100.0	5,914,000	100.0

Population economically active (1993): total 5,914,000; activity rate of total population 48.9% (participation rates [1985]: ages 15–64, 74.9%; female 39.3%; unemployed [1982] 0.6%).

Price and earnings indexes (1990 = 100)

	1991	1992	1993	1994	1995	1996	1997
Consumer price index	108.5	124.4	136.8	190.1	283.3	339.3	354.6
Annual earnings index[9]	127.1	134.5	146.1	189.0	264.6	...	...

Public debt (external, outstanding; 1996): U.S.$3,589,000,000.
Land use (1994): forest 39.9%; pasture 41.3%; agriculture 5.3%; other 13.5%.
Tourism (1995): visitors U.S.$60,000,000; U.S.$59,000,000.

Foreign trade

Balance of trade

	1992	1993	1994	1995	1996	1997
FMG '000,000,000	−316.9	−396.7	−161.9	−764.5	−840.4	−799.3
% of total	23.5%	28.4%	6.1%	19.6%	25.7%	31.5%

Imports (1994): FMG 1,150,780,000,000 (capital equipment 20.2%; food 16.8%, of which rice 6.9%; raw materials and spare parts 15.8%; nonfood consumer goods 15.3%; crude petroleum 11.4%). *Major import sources* (1995): France 30.5%; Germany 10.3%; Iran 10.3%; South Africa 6.5%; Japan 6.1%.
Exports (1994): FMG 849,960,000,000 (coffee 18.0%; vanilla 16.7%; shrimp 13.2%; cotton fabrics 2.9%; cloves and clove oil 2.6%; sugar 2.2%). *Major export destinations* (1995): France 29.2%; U.S. 6.7%; Japan 6.4%; Réunion 6.1%; Italy 5.6%; Belgium-Luxembourg 5.0%.

Transport and communications

Transport. Railroads (1991): route length 640 mi, 1,030 km; passenger-mi 152,000,000, passenger-km 245,000,000; short ton-mi cargo 90,000,000, metric ton-km cargo 132,000,000. Roads (1995): total length 30,968 mi, 49,837 km (paved 15%). Vehicles (1992): passenger cars 47,711; trucks and buses 34,341. Merchant marine (1992): vessels (100 gross tons and over) 85; total deadweight tonnage 82,077. Air transport (1996): passenger-mi 409,440,000, passenger-km 658,913,000; short ton-mi cargo 12,122,000, metric ton-km cargo 17,697,000; airports (1994) with scheduled flights 44.

Communications

Medium	date	unit	number	units per 1,000 persons
Daily newspapers	1995	circulation	59,000	4.0
Radio	1995	receivers	2,850,000	193
Television	1995	receivers	295,000	20.0
Telephones	1995	main lines	32,600	2.2

Education and health

Educational attainment: n.a. *Literacy* (1995): percentage of total population age 15 and over literate 45.7%; males literate 59.8%; females literate 32.0%.

Education (1993–94)

	schools	teachers	students	student/ teacher ratio
Primary (age 6–13)	13,624	37,676	1,504,668	39.9
Secondary (age 14–18)	1,142[10]	15,118	298,241	19.7
Voc., teacher tr.	611[11]	1,484[12]	17,419[12]	11.7[12]
Higher	5[10]	855[13]	42,681[13]	49.9[13]

Health: physicians (1990) 1,392 (1 per 8,279 persons); hospital beds (1989) 10,900 (1 per 1,029 persons); infant mortality rate (1996) 93.3.
Food (1995): daily per capita caloric intake 2,009 (vegetable products 91%, animal products 9%); 89% of FAO recommended minimum requirement.

Military

Total active duty personnel (1997): 21,000 (army 95.2%, navy 2.4%, air force 2.4%). *Military expenditure as percentage of GNP* (1995): 0.9% (world 2.8%); per capita expenditure U.S.$2.

---

[1]The 1992 constitution identifies Malagasy as the "national" language, although neither Malagasy nor French, the languages of the two official texts of the constitution, is itself "official." [2]Preliminary. [3]1994. [4]Antananarivo only. [5]Malagasy households only. [6]Weights of consumer price index components; excludes housing. [7]At factor cost. [8]Includes artisans and servants. [9]Average salary, all public employees, including military. [10]1988–89. [11]1987–88. [12]1990–91. [13]1992.

Internet resources for further information:
• Mission of Madagascar to the United Nations (Geneva; French, summary only in English) http://www3.itu.ch/MISSIONS/Madagascar

Malaŵi

Official name: Republic of Malaŵi.
Form of government: multiparty
republic with one legislative house
(National Assembly [177]).
Head of state and government:
President.
Capital: [1].
Official language: none.
Official religion: none.
Monetary unit: 1 Malaŵi kwacha
(MK) = 100 tambala; valuation
(Sept. 25, 1998) 1 U.S.$ = MK 40.05;
1 £ = MK 68.19.

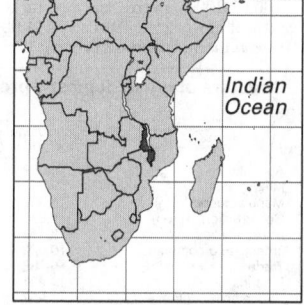

Indian
Ocean

Area and population

Regions Districts	Capitals	area sq mi	area sq km	population 1987 census
Central	Lilongwe	13,742	35,592	3,110,986
Dedza	Dedza	1,399	3,624	411,787
Dowa	Dowa	1,174	3,041	322,432
Kasungu	Kasungu	3,042	7,878	323,453
Lilongwe	Lilongwe	2,378	6,159	976,627
Mchinji	Mchinji	1,296	3,356	249,843
Nkhotakota	Nkhotakota	1,644	4,259	158,044
Ntcheu	Ntcheu	1,322	3,424	358,767
Ntchisi	Ntchisi	639	1,655	120,860
Salima	Salima	848	2,196	189,173
Northern	Mzuzu	10,398	26,931	911,787
Chitipa	Chitipa	1,353	3,504	96,794
Karonga	Karonga	1,141	2,955	148,014
Mzimba	Mzimba	4,027	10,430	433,696
Nkhata Bay	Nkhata Bay	1,579	4,090	138,381
Rumphi	Rumphi	2,298	5,952	94,902
Southern	Blantyre	12,260	31,753	3,965,734
Blantyre	Blantyre	777	2,012	589,525
Chikwawa	Chikwawa	1,836	4,755	316,733
Chiradzulu	Chiradzulu	296	767	210,912
Machinga	Machinga	2,303	5,964	515,265
Mangochi	Mangochi	2,422	6,272	496,578
Mulanje	Mulanje	1,332	3,450	638,062
Mwanza	Mwanza	886	2,295	121,513
Nsanje	Nsanje	750	1,942	204,374
Thyolo	Thyolo	662	1,715	431,157
Zomba	Zomba	996	2,580	441,615
TOTAL LAND AREA		36,400	94,276[2]	
INLAND WATER		9,347	24,208	
TOTAL		45,747	118,484	7,988,507

Demography

Population (1998): 9,840,000.
Density (1998)[3]: persons per sq mi 270.3, persons per sq km 104.4.
Urban-rural (1987): urban 10.7%; rural 89.3%.
Sex distribution (1987): male 48.40%; female 51.60%.
Age breakdown (1987): under 15, 46.0%; 15–29, 25.4%; 30–44, 14.5%; 45–59, 8.1%; 60 and over, 6.0%.
Population projection: (2000) 10,154,000; (2010) 11,330,000.
Doubling time: 41 years.
Ethnic composition (1983): Maravi (including Nyanja, Chewa, Tonga, and Tumbuka) 58.3%; Lomwe 18.4%; Yao 13.2%; Ngoni 6.7%; other 3.4%.
Religious affiliation (1995): Christian 50.3%, of which Protestant 20.5%, Roman Catholic 18.0%; Muslim 20.0%; traditional beliefs 10.0%; other 19.7%.
Major cities (1994): Blantyre 446,800; Lilongwe 395,500[4]; Mzuzu 62,700.

Vital statistics

Birth rate per 1,000 population (1996): 41.6 (world avg. 25.0).
Death rate per 1,000 population (1996): 24.5 (world avg. 9.3).
Natural increase rate per 1,000 population (1996): 17.1 (world avg. 15.7).
Total fertility rate (avg. births per childbearing woman; 1996): 5.9.
Life expectancy at birth (1996): male 35.9 years; female 36.5 years.
Major causes of death per 100,000 population (1986)[5]: infectious and parasitic diseases 711, of which malaria 270, diarrheal diseases 148, measles 128; malnutrition 267; diseases of the respiratory system 265.

National economy

Budget (1995–96). Revenue: MK 4,436,000,000 (tax revenue 86.9%, nontax revenue 10.9%, other 2.2%). Expenditures: MK 7,738,000,000 (wages and salaries 21.5%, debt service 20.9%).
Public debt (external, outstanding; 1996): U.S.$2,092,000,000.
Production (metric tons except as noted). Agriculture (1996): sugarcane 1,860,000, corn (maize) 1,793,000, potatoes 380,000, cassava 220,000, plantains 200,000, tobacco 142,000, bananas 91,000, dry beans 80,000, sorghum 55,000, peanuts (groundnuts) 40,000, tea 37,000; livestock (number of live animals) 1,257,000 goats, 700,000 cattle, 220,000 pigs, 101,000 sheep; roundwood (1995) 10,475,000 cu m; fish catch (1995) 45,427. Mining and quarrying (1995): limestone 173,800[6]; rubies, sapphires, and aquamarines 550 kg. Manufacturing (value added in MK '000; 1986): chemicals 30,805; textiles 19,630; food products 11,988; beverages 11,988; tobacco 9,480. Construction (value in MK; 1994): 41,700,000[7]. Energy production (consumption): electricity (kW-hr; 1994) 802,000,000 (802,000,000); coal (metric tons; 1994) none (15,000); petroleum products (metric tons; 1994) none (190,000).
Tourism: receipts (1995) U.S.$6,000,000; expenditures (1994) U.S.$15,000,000.
Land use (1994): forested 39.3%; meadows and pastures 19.6%; agricultural and under permanent cultivation 18.1%; other 23.0%.
Gross national product (1996): U.S.$1,832,000,000 (U.S.$180 per capita).

Structure of gross domestic product and labour force

	1996 in value MK '000,000[8]	1996 % of total value	1987 labour force	1987 % of labour force
Agriculture	493.3	43.4	2,967,933	85.8
Mining	...	...	7,164	0.2
Manufacturing	131.3	11.5	97,776	2.8
Construction	46.1	4.1	46,875	1.4
Public utilities	29.8	2.6	8,833	0.2
Transp. and commun.	57.2	5.0	24,863	0.7
Trade	128.8	11.3	94,445	2.7
Finance	119.5	10.5	5,590	0.3
Public administration	146.5	12.9 }	147,039	4.3
Services	48.4	4.3 }		
Other	−64.0[9]	−5.6[9]	57,235	1.6
TOTAL	1,136.8[2]	100.0	3,457,753	100.0

Population economically active (1987): total 3,457,753; activity rate 43.3% (participation rates: age 15–64, 84.6%; female 51.5%; unemployed 5.4%).

Price and earnings indexes (1990 = 100)

	1990	1991	1992	1993	1994	1995	1996
Consumer price index	100.0	112.6	138.2	163.7	222.6	408.2	561.6
Monthly earnings index	100.0	106.4	102.8	...	...	...	...

Household income and expenditure (1979–80). Average household size (1987) 4.3; income per household MK 1,934 (U.S.$2,419); sources of income: wages 83.3%, household enterprise 6.0%; expenditure (1990)[10]: food 55.5%, clothing and footwear 11.7%, housing 9.6%, household durable goods 8.4%.

Foreign trade[11]

Balance of trade (current prices)

	1989	1990	1991	1992	1993	1994
MK '000,000	−96.1	+180.1	+140.9	−103.4	−29.0	+247.3
% of total	6.1%	8.7%	5.6%	3.4%	1.0%	4.6%

Imports (1995): MK 7,254,949,000 (1990; transport equipment 9.2%, petroleum products 8.3%, clothing 3.8%, pharmaceutical products 2.2%). *Major import sources:* South Africa 44.4%; Germany 4.5%; U.K. 4.3%; United States 3.7%.
Exports (1995): MK 6,192,563,000 (tobacco 63.2%, tea 6.7%, sugar 6.5%, cotton 0.9%). *Major export destinations:* South Africa 16.2%; Germany 14.7%; Japan 11.1%; U.S. 10.9%; Mozambique 7.6%.

Transport and communications

Transport. Railroads (1994): route length 490 mi, 789 km; passenger-km 18,995,000; metric ton-km cargo 56,778,000. Roads (1995): total length 17,324 mi, 27,880 km (paved 18%). Vehicles (1995): passenger cars 25,400; trucks and buses 28,900. Air transport (1994)[12]: passenger-km 289,000,000; metric ton-km cargo 28,000,000; airports (1997) 5.

Communications

Medium	date	unit	number	units per 1,000 persons
Daily newspapers	1996	circulation	22,000[13]	2.3[13]
Radio	1996	receivers	1,060,000	112
Telephones	1995	main lines	34,300	3.5
Cellular telephones	1995	subscribers	400	—
Facsimile machines	1995	units	1,100	0.1

Education and health

Educational attainment (1987). Percentage of population age 25 and over having: no formal education 55.0%; primary education 39.8%; secondary and higher 5.2%. *Literacy* (1995): total population age 15 and over literate 56.4%; males literate 71.9%; females literate 41.8%.

Education (1989–90)

	schools	teachers	students	student/teacher ratio
Primary (age 6–13)[14]	3,425	45,775	2,860,819	62.5
Secondary (age 14–18)	94	1,096	48,332[14]	26.8
Teacher tr., voc.	13	250	1,080[14]	14.7
Higher	4	235	7,308[15]	11.4

Health: physicians (1989) 186 (1 per 47,634 persons); hospital beds (1987) 12,617 (1 per 627 persons); infant mortality rate per 1,000 live births (1996) 139.9.
Food (1995): daily per capita caloric intake 2,038 (vegetable products 97%, animal products 3%); 88% of FAO recommended minimum requirement.

Military

Total active duty personnel (1997): 5,000 (army 100%; marines, none; air force, none). *Military expenditure as percentage of GNP* (1995): 1.6% (world 2.8%); per capita expenditure U.S.$2.

---

[1]A capital is not designated in the 1994 constitution. Current government operations are divided among Lilongwe (ministerial and financial); Blantyre (executive and judicial); and Zomba (legislative). [2]Detail does not add to total given because of rounding. [3]Based on land area. [4]Includes Limbe. [5]Estimates based on reported inpatient deaths in hospitals, constituting an estimated 8% of total deaths. [6]1994. [7]Cities of Blantyre, Lilongwe, and Mzuzu only. [8]At constant prices of 1978. [9]Less imputed bank service charges. [10]Weights of consumer price index components, cities of Blantyre and Lilongwe only. [11]Import figures are f.o.b. in balance of trade and c.i.f. in commodities and trading partners. Reexports included in balance of trade, excluded from commodities and trading partners. [12]Air Malaŵi only. [13]Circulation for one newspaper only. [14]1994–95. [15]1993–94.

Malaysia

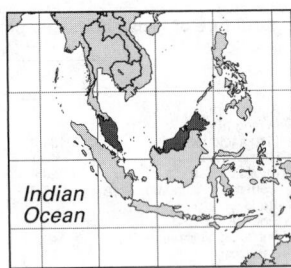

Indian Ocean

Official name: Malaysia.
Form of government: federal constitutional monarchy with two legislative houses (Senate [70[1]]; House of Representatives [192]).
Chief of state: Yang di-Pertuan Agong (Paramount Ruler).
Head of government: Prime Minister.
Capital: Kuala Lumpur[2].
Official language: Malay.
Official religion: Islam.
Monetary unit: 1 ringgit, or Malaysian dollar (RM) = 100 cents; valuation[3] (Sept. 25, 1998) 1 U.S.$ = RM 3.80; 1 £ = RM 6.47.

Area and population

Regions States	Capitals	area sq mi	area sq km	population 1991 census
East Malaysia				
Sabah	Kota Kinabalu	28,424	73,619	1,734,685
Sarawak	Kuching	48,050	124,449	1,642,771
West Malaysia				
Johor	Johor Baharu	7,331	18,986	2,069,740
Kedah	Alor Setar	3,639	9,426	1,302,241
Kelantan	Kota Baharu	5,761	14,920	1,181,315
Melaka	Melaka	637	1,651	506,321
Negeri Sembilan	Seremban	2,565	6,643	692,897
Pahang	Kuantan	13,886	35,964	1,045,003
Perak	Ipoh	8,110	21,005	1,877,471
Perlis	Kangar	307	795	183,824
Pulau Pinang	George Town	398	1,030	1,064,166
Selangor	Shah Alam	3,071	7,955	2,297,159
Terengganu	Kuala Terengganu	5,002	12,955	766,244
Federal Territories				
Kuala Lumpur	—	94	243	1,145,342
Labuan	—	36	92	54,241
TOTAL		**127,311**	**329,733**	**17,563,420**

Demography

Population (1998): 22,083,000.
Density (1998): persons per sq mi 173.5, persons per sq km 67.0.
Urban-rural (1997): urban 55.0%; rural 45.0%.
Sex distribution (1996): male 51.13%; female 48.87%.
Age breakdown (1996): under 15, 34.9%; 15–29, 28.0%; 30–44, 20.7%; 45–59, 10.6%; 60 and over, 5.8%.
Population projection: (2000) 23,036,000; (2010) 27,940,000.
Doubling time: 34 years.
Ethnic composition (1996): Malay and other indigenous 57.7%; Chinese 25.4%; Indian 7.2%; other nonindigenous 3.2%; noncitizen 6.5%.
Religious affiliation (1980): Muslim 52.9%; Buddhist 17.3%; Chinese folkreligionist 11.6%; Hindu 7.0%; Christian 6.4%; other 4.8%.
Major cities (1991): Kuala Lumpur 1,145,342; Ipoh 382,853; Johor Baharu 328,436; Melaka 296,897; Petaling Jaya 254,350.

Vital statistics

Birth rate per 1,000 population (1997); 25.6 (world avg. 25.0).
Death rate per 1,000 population (1997); 4.8 (world avg. 9.3).
Natural increase rate per 1,000 population (1997); 20.8 (world avg. 15.7).
Total fertility rate (avg. births per childbearing woman; 1997): 3.3.
Life expectancy at birth (1997): male 70.0 years; female 74.0 years.
Major causes of death per 100,000 population (1994): diseases of the circulatory system 54.0; accidents, homicide, and other violence 29.0; malignant neoplasms 20.4; birth injuries 18.5; infectious and parasitic diseases 15.4.

National economy

Budget (1997). Revenue: RM 60,778,000,000 (income tax 38.7%, taxes on goods and services 22.0%, nontax revenue 18.0%, taxes on international trade 12.6%). Expenditures: RM 41,413,000,000 (education 24.6%, defense and internal security 15.3%, general administration 12.3%, health 7.0%, trade and industry 3.0%, agriculture 3.0%).
Tourism (1995): receipts from visitors U.S.$3,910,000,000; expenditures by nationals abroad (1994) U.S.$1,737,000,000.
Population economically active (1996): total 8,398,200; activity rate 40.9% (participation rates: ages 15–64 66.9%; female [1990] 35.5%; unemployed 2.6%).

Price index (1990 = 100)

	1991	1992	1993	1994	1995	1996	1997
Consumer price index	104.4	109.3	113.2	117.4	123.6	128.0	131.4

Production (metric tons except as noted). Agriculture, forestry, fishing (1996): palm oil 8,386,000, rice 2,065,000, sugarcane 1,600,000, rubber 1,089,000, bananas 530,000, pineapples 200,000; livestock (number of live animals) 3,282,000 pigs, 720,000 cattle, 100,000,000 chickens; roundwood (1995) 45,573,000 cu m; fish catch (1995) 1,240,000. Mining and quarrying (1996): iron ore 325,114; bauxite 218,680; copper concentrates 87,580; tin concentrates 5,174. Manufacturing (1995): cement 10,713,000; refined sugar 1,052,000; fertilizer 269,000; plywood 3,506,000 cu m; radio receivers 38,767,000 units; automotive tires 11,368,000 units. Construction (completed; 1986)[4]: residential 8,809,100 sq m; nonresidential 959,900 sq m. Energy production (consumption): electricity (kW-hr; 1994) 39,975,000,000 (40,027,000,000); coal (metric tons; 1994) 174,000 (1,876,000); crude petroleum (barrels; 1994) 237,742,000

(100,021,000); petroleum products (metric tons; 1994) 11,406,000 (17,007,000); natural gas (cu m; 1994) 24,411,000,000 (13,166,000,000).
Gross national product (1996): U.S.$89,800,000,000 (U.S.$4,370 per capita).

Structure of gross domestic product and labour force

	1996 in value RM '000,000[5]	% of total value	labour force	% of labour force
Agriculture	16,489	12.7	1,375,900	16.4
Mining	9,257	7.1	41,800	0.5
Manufacturing	44,922	34.5	2,209,000	26.3
Construction	5,870	4.5	705,100	8.4
Public utilities	3,135	2.4	72,700	0.9
Transp. and commun.	10,022	7.7	420,400	5.0
Trade	16,185	12.4	1,353,700	16.1
Finance	14,231	10.9	394,500	4.7
Pub. admin., defense	11,907	9.2	876,600	10.4
Services	2,589	2.0	731,100	8.7
Other	−4,420[6]	−3.4[6]	217,400	2.6
TOTAL	130,187	100.0	8,398,200	100.0

Public debt (external, outstanding; 1996): U.S.$15,701,000,000.
Household income and expenditure. Average household size (1991) 4.9; annual income per household (1995) RM 24,080 (U.S.$9,620); sources of income: n.a.; expenditure (1983): food 28.7%, transportation 20.9%, recreation and education 11.0%, housing 10.2%, household durable goods 7.7%.

Foreign trade[7]

Balance of trade (current prices)

	1990	1991	1992	1993	1994	1995
RM '000,000	+7,947	+3,165	+11,446	+15,095	+12,628	+8,794
% of total	5.3%	1.7%	5.9%	6.6%	4.3%	2.4%

Imports (1995): RM 194,517,000,000 (machinery and transport equipment 60.6%, chemicals 6.9%, food 4.1%, inedible crude materials 2.4%, mineral fuels 2.3%). *Major import sources:* Japan 28.1%; U.S. 16.6%; Singapore 12.4%; Taiwan 5.1%; Germany 4.6%; South Korea 4.0%; Thailand 2.7%.
Exports (1995): RM 184,827,000,000 (machinery and transport equipment 55.1%, basic manufactures 8.9%, mineral fuels 7.0%, animal and vegetable oils 6.8%, inedible crude materials 6.4%, food 2.4%). *Major export destinations:* U.S. 20.7%; Singapore 20.3%; Japan 12.7%; Hong Kong 5.3%; U.K. 4.0%; Thailand 3.9%; Germany 3.2%.

Transport and communications

Transport. Railroads (1995): track length 1,791 km; passenger-km 1,284,000,000[8]; metric ton-km cargo 1,416,000,000[6]. Roads (1995); total length 93,975 km (paved 75%). Vehicles (1995): passenger cars 2,588,641; trucks and buses 465,940. Air transport (1995): passenger-km 22,558,000,000; metric ton-km cargo 1,160,036,000; airports (1997) 39.

Communications

Medium	date	unit	number	units per 1,000 persons
Daily newspapers	1994	circulation	2,800,000	139
Radio	1996	receivers	9,500,000	449
Television	1995	receivers	9,400,000	454
Telephones	1995	main lines	3,332,400	161
Cellular telephones	1995	subscribers	872,800	42
Facsimile machines	1995	units	58,100	2.8
Personal computers	1995	units	800,000	39

Education and health

Educational attainment (1980). Percentage of population age 25 and over having: no formal schooling 36.6%; primary education 42.1%; secondary 19.4%; higher 1.9%. *Literacy* (1995): total population age 15 and over literate 83.5%; males literate 89.1%; females literate 78.1%.

Education (1996)

	schools	teachers	students	student/ teacher ratio
Primary (age 7–12)	7,049	144,937	2,843,663	19.6
Secondary (age 13–19)	1,427	86,891	1,694,243	19.5
Voc., teacher tr.	101	6,044	47,770	7.9
Higher	48	12,247	191,290	15.6

Health (1995): physicians 9,608 (1 per 2,153 persons); hospital beds 40,780 (1 per 507 persons); infant mortality rate per 1,000 live births (1997) 11.
Food (1995): daily per capita caloric intake 2,807 (vegetable products 82%, animal products 18%); 126% of FAO recommended minimum.

Military

Total active duty personnel (1997): 111,500 (army 76.2%, navy 12.6%, air force 11.2%). *Military expenditure as percentage of GDP* (1995): 3.0% (world 2.8%); per capita expenditure U.S.$122.

[1]Includes 40 appointees of the Paramount Ruler; the remaining 30 are indirectly elected at different times. [2]The government plans to transfer to the new federal administrative centre at Putrajaya in 2000. [3]Pegged to the U.S. dollar at RM 3.80 = 1 U.S.$ on Sept. 2, 1998. [4]Results of the Central Bank Survey of four major towns: Kuala Lumpur, Shah Alam, Kelang, and Seberang Prai. [5]At constant prices of 1978. [6]Net bank service charges. [7]Import figures f.o.b. in balance of trade. [8]Peninsular Malaysia and Singapore.

Internet resources for further information:
• Department of Statistics http://spl.pnm.my/~stat/
• Malaysia http://www.jaring.my/
• Malaysian Information Services (English) http://penerangan.gov.my/

Maldives

Official name: Divehi Jumhuriyya
(Republic of Maldives).
Form of government: republic with one
legislative house (Majlis[1] [48[2, 3]]).
Head of state and government:
President.
Capital: Male'.
Official language: Divehi.
Official religion: Islam.
Monetary unit: 1 Maldivian rufiyaa
(Rf) = 100 laari; valuation (Sept. 25,
1998) 1 U.S.$ = Rf 11.77;
1 £ = Rf 20.04.

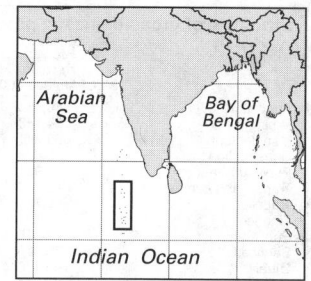

Area and population[4]

Administrative atolls	Capitals	area sq mi	area sq km	population 1995 census[5]
North Thiladhunmathi (Haa-Alifu)	Dhidhdhoo	...	...	13,657
South Thiladhunmathi (Haa-Dhaalu)	Nolhivaranfaru	...	...	14,769
North Miladhunmadulu (Shaviyani)	Farukolhu-funadhoo	...	...	10,462
South Miladhunmadulu (Noonu)	Manadhoo	...	...	10,096
North Maalhosmadulu (Raa)	Ugoofaaru	...	...	12,528
South Maalhosmadulu (Baa)	Eydhafushi	...	...	8,727
Faadhippolhu (Lhaviyani)	Naifaru	...	...	8,847
Male'(Kaafu)	Thulusdhoo	...	...	11,650
Ari Atoll Uthuru Gofi (Alifu)	Rasdhoo	...	...	5,340
Ari Atoll Dhekunu Gofi (Alifu)	Mahibadhoo	...	...	6,404
Felidhu Atoll (Vaavu)	Felidhoo	...	...	1,779
Mulakatholhu (Meemu)	Muli	...	...	4,810
North Nilandhe Atoll (Faafu)	Magoodhoo	...	...	3,167
South Nilandhe Atoll (Dhaalu)	Kudahuvadhoo	...	...	4,825
Kolhumadulu (Thaa)	Veymandoo	...	...	9,651
Hadhdhunmathi (Laamu)	Hithadhoo	...	...	10,192
North Huvadhu Atoll (Gaafu-Alifu)	Viligili	...	...	8,164
South Huvadhu Atoll (Gaafu-Dhaalu)	Thinadhoo	...	...	11,984
Foammulah (Gnyaviyani)	Foahmulah	...	...	6,971
Addu Atoll (Seenu)	Hithadhoo	...	...	17,648
Male'		...	...	62,973
TOTAL		115	298	244,644

Demography

Population (1998): 270,000.
Density (1998): persons per sq mi 2,348, persons per sq km 906.0.
Urban-rural (1997): urban 27.0%; rural 73.0%.
Sex distribution (1997): male 51.17%; female 48.83%.
Age breakdown (1997): under 15, 44.8%; 15–29, 27.7%; 30–44, 15.0%; 45–59, 7.3%; 60–74, 4.4%; 75 and over, 0.8%.
Population projection: (2000) 285,000; (2010) 364,000.
Doubling time: 21 years.
Ethnic composition: the majority is principally of Sinhalese and Dravidian extraction; Arab, African, and Negrito influences are also present.
Religious affiliation: virtually 100% Sunnī Muslim.
Major cities (1995): Male' 62,973.

Vital statistics

Birth rate per 1,000 population (1997): 41.8 (world avg. 25.0); legitimate, n.a.; illegitimate, n.a.
Death rate per 1,000 population (1997): 7.6 (world avg. 9.3).
Natural increase rate per 1,000 population (1997): 34.2 (world avg. 15.7).
Total fertility rate (avg. births per childbearing woman; 1997): 6.8.
Marriage rate per 1,000 population (1996): 9.6.
Divorce rate per 1,000 population (1996): 2.8.
Life expectancy at birth (1997): male 65.0 years; female 63.0 years.
Major causes of death per 100,000 population (1988): rheumatic fever 106.0; ischemic heart diseases 65.0; bronchitis, emphysema, and asthma 61.0; tetanus 23.5; tuberculosis 13.0; accidents and suicide 10.0.

National economy

Budget (1996). Revenue: Rf 1,968,900,000 (taxation 36.3%, nontax revenue 31.8%, loans for development 20.2%, foreign aid 11.1%). Expenditures: Rf 1,968,900,000 (social services 34.8%, social development 31.6%, economic development 23.9%).
Production (metric tons except as noted). Agriculture, forestry, fishing (1996): vegetables and melons 24,300, coconuts 13,000, fruits (excluding melons) 8,622, roots and tubers (including cassava, sweet potatoes, and yams) 7,731, copra (1994) 2,000; fish catch 105,413. Mining and quarrying: coral for construction materials. Manufacturing: details, n.a.; however, major industries include boat building and repairing, coir yarn and mat weaving, coconut and fish processing, lacquerwork, garment manufacturing, and handicrafts. Construction: n.a. Energy production (consumption): electricity (kW-hr; 1994) 46,000,000 (46,000,000); coal, none (n.a.); petroleum products (metric tons; 1994) none (35,000); natural gas, none (n.a.).
Tourism (1995): receipts from visitors U.S.$210,000,000; expenditures by nationals abroad (1994) U.S.$32,000,000.
Population economically active (1990): total 56,435; activity rate of total population 26.5% (participation rates: ages 15–64, 50.2%; female 19.9%; unemployed 0.9%).
Household income and expenditure (1990). Average household size 7.2; annual income per household Rf 2,616 (U.S.$274), sources of income: n.a.; expenditure (1981)[6]: food and beverages 61.8%, housing equipment 17.0%, clothing 8.0%, recreation and education 5.9%, transportation 2.6%, health 2.5%, rent 1.6%.

Public debt (external, outstanding; 1996): U.S.$162,600,000.
Gross national product (at current market prices; 1996): U.S.$277,000,000 (U.S.$1,080 per capita).

Structure of gross domestic product and labour force

	1996 in value Rf '000[7]	1996 % of total value	1990 labour force	1990 % of labour force
Agriculture[8]	263,300	18.2	14,117	25.0
Mining	24,400	1.7	496	0.9
Manufacturing	89,400	6.2	8,441	15.0
Public utilities			445	0.8
Construction	140,600	9.7	3,151	5.6
Transportation and communications	99,400	6.9	5,321	9.4
Trade	280,400	19.4	8,884	15.7
Finance	48,600	3.3	1,058	1.9
Public administration, defense	128,000	8.8	11,848	21.0
Services	97,000	6.7		
Other	276,900	19.1	2,674	4.7
TOTAL	1,448,000	100.0	56,435	100.0

Land use (1994): forested 3.3%; meadows and pastures 3.3%; agricultural and under permanent cultivation 10.0%; built-on, wasteland, and other 83.4%.

Foreign trade[9]

Balance of trade (current prices)

	1992	1993	1994	1995	1996	1997
U.S.$'000,000	−126.6	−133.7	−149.2	−186.1	−206.3	−233.8
% of total	61.3%	65.9%	61.9%	65.3%	63.5%	61.5%

Imports (1996): Rf 3,551,289,000 (machinery and transport equipment 27.9%, basic manufactures 23.7%, food and live animals 21.4%, petroleum products 9.1%). *Major import sources:* Singapore 32.0%; India 12.0%; Malaysia 8.5%; Sri Lanka 7.6%; United Kingdom 3.6%; Japan 3.5%.
Exports (1996): Rf 699,190,000 (canned fish 28.0%, yellowfin tuna 20.5%, apparel and clothing 17.4%, dried skipjack tuna 11.0%). *Major export destinations:* Sri Lanka 18.3%; United Kingdom 21.7%; United States 10.2%; Germany 10.8%; Japan 10.6%; Thailand 9.5%.

Transport and communications

Transport. Railroads: none. Roads: total length, n.a. Vehicles (1996): passenger cars 1,058; trucks and buses 1,244. Merchant marine (1992): vessels (100 gross tons and over) 44; total deadweight tonnage 78,994. Air transport (1994): passengers carried 38,000; passenger-km 7,000,000; airports (1997) with scheduled flights 5.

Communications

Medium	date	unit	number	units per 1,000 persons
Daily newspapers	1994	circulation	3,000	12
Radio	1996	receivers	25,000	96
Television	1995	receivers	4,750	19
Telephones	1995	main lines	13,900	55
Facsimile machines	1995	units	3,500	14
Personal computers	1995	units	3,000	12

Education and health

Educational attainment (1990). Percentage of population age 15 and over having: no standard passed 25.6%; primary standard 37.2%; middle standard 25.9%; secondary standard 6.3%; preuniversity 3.4%; higher 0.4%; not stated 1.2%. *Literacy* (1995): total population age 15 and over literate 93.2%; males literate 93.0%; females literate 93.3%.

Education (1992)

	schools	teachers	students	student/teacher ratio
Primary (age 6–11)	134	1,138[10]	45,333	36.7[10]
Secondary (age 11–18)	9[10]	291[10]	15,933	12.3[10]
Voc., teacher tr.	10[10]	52[10]	452	8.9[10]
Higher				

Health: physicians (1996) 99 (1 per 2,587 persons); hospital beds (1995) 305 (1 per 1,192 persons); infant mortality rate per 1,000 live births (1997) 50.
Food (1995): daily per capita caloric intake 2,485 (vegetable products 82%, animal products 18%); 112% of FAO recommended minimum requirement.

Military

Total active duty personnel: Maldives maintains a single security force numbering about 700–1,000; it performs both army and police functions.

[1]Also known or translated as Citizens' Majlis, Citizens' Council, or Citizens' Assembly. [2]Includes 8 nonelective seats. [3]The new constitution went into effect Jan. 1, 1998. [4]Maldives is divided into 20 administrative districts corresponding to atoll groups; arrangement shown here is from north to south. Total area excludes 34,634 sq mi (89,702 sq km) of tidal waters. [5]Preliminary results. [6]Weights of consumer price index components. [7]At 1985 prices. [8]Primarily fishing. [9]Import figures are f.o.b. in balance of trade and c.i.f. for commodities and trading partners. [10]1986.

Internet resources for further information:
• **Maldives Mission to the United Nations**
  http://www.undp.org:81/missions/maldives/maldives.htm

Mali

Official name: République du Mali (Republic of Mali).
Form of government: multiparty republic with one legislative house (National Assembly [147])[1].
Chief of state: President.
Head of government: Prime Minister.
Capital: Bamako.
Official language: French.
Official religion: none.
Monetary unit: 1 CFA franc (CFAF) = 100 centimes; valuation (Sept. 25, 1998) 1 U.S.$ = CFAF 560.38; 1 £ = CFAF 954.05.

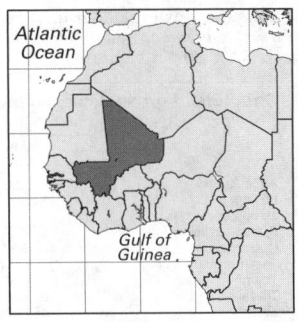

Area and population		area		population
Regions	**Capitals**	sq mi	sq km	1995 estimate
Gao	Gao	65,858	170,572	408,000[2]
Kayes	Kayes	46,233	119,743	1,245,000
Kidal	Kidal	58,467	151,430	[2]
Koulikoro	Koulikoro	37,007	95,848	1,462,000
Mopti	Mopti	30,509	79,017	1,423,000
Ségou	Ségou	25,028	64,821	1,579,000
Sikasso	Sikasso	27,135	70,280	1,521,000
Tombouctou	Timbuktu (Tombouctou)	191,743	496,611	462,000
District				
Bamako	Bamako	97	252	913,000
TOTAL		482,077	1,248,574	9,013,000

Demography

Population (1998): 10,109,000.
Density (1998): persons per sq mi 21.0, persons per sq km 8.1.
Urban-rural (1995): urban 26.1%; rural 73.9%.
Sex distribution (1997): male 48.71%; female 51.29%.
Age breakdown (1997): under 15, 47.3%; 15–29, 26.1%; 30–44, 13.3%; 45–59, 8.2%; 60–74, 4.2%; 75 and over, 0.9%.
Population projection: (2000) 10,751,000; (2010) 14,611,000.
Doubling time: 23 years.
Linguistic composition (1987): Bambara-Malinké-Dyula (-Dioula) 50.3%; Fulani (Peulh-Foulfoulbe) 10.7%; Dogon-Kado 6.9%; Songhaï-Djerma 6.3%; Soninké-Marka 6.3%; Tamashek-Bella (Berber) 4.2%; Minianka 3.9%; Senufo 2.4%; Bwa- (Bobo-) Dafing 2.3%; Bozo-Somono 2.0%; other 4.7%.
Religious affiliation (1995): Muslim 90%; traditional beliefs 9%; Christian 1%.
Major cities (1987): Bamako 800,000[3]; Ségou 88,877; Mopti 73,979; Sikasso 73,050; Gao 54,874.

Vital statistics

Birth rate per 1,000 population (1997): 50.0 (world avg. 25.0).
Death rate per 1,000 population (1997): 20.0 (world avg. 9.3).
Natural increase rate per 1,000 population (1997): 30.0 (world avg. 15.7).
Total fertility rate (avg. births per childbearing woman; 1997): 7.1.
Life expectancy at birth (1995): male 44.7 years; female 48.1 years.
Major causes of death per 100,000 population: n.a.; morbidity ([notified cases of illness] by cause as a percentage of all reported infectious disease; 1985): malaria 62.1%; measles 10.3%; amebiasis 10.3%; syphilis and gonococcal infections 6.0%; influenza 4.9%.

National economy

Budget (1996). Revenue: CFAF 313,300,000,000 (fiscal receipts 55.2%, nonfiscal receipts 14.0%). Expenditures: CFAF 324,700,000,000 (current expenditure 50.2%, of which wages and salaries 15.6%, interest on public debt 4.5%; capital expenditure 49.8%).
Public debt (external, outstanding; 1996): U.S.$2,776,000,000.
Tourism (1995): receipts from visitors U.S.$17,000,000; expenditures by nationals abroad U.S.$56,000,000.
Population economically active (1987): total 3,437,489; activity rate of total population 44.7% (participation rates: ages 15–64, 67.4%; female 37.4%; unemployed 0.8%).

Price and earnings indexes (1990 = 100)							
	1991	1992	1993	1994	1995	1996	1997
Consumer price index	101.8	95.4	95.2	117.3	133.0	142.1	141.6
Hourly earnings index[4]	100.0	100.0	100.0	100.0	...	...	...

Production (metric tons except as noted). Agriculture, forestry, fishing (1997): millet 1,030,000, sorghum 955,000, rice 623,000, seed cotton 500,000, corn (maize) 335,000, peanuts (groundnuts) 155,000, sweet potatoes 16,000; livestock (number of live animals) 14,500,000 goats and sheep, 5,725,000 cattle, 650,000 asses, 365,000 camels, 135,000 horses, 63,500 pigs; roundwood (1995) 6,539,800 cu m; fish catch (1994) 64,352. Mining and quarrying (1995): limestone 20,000; phosphate 3,000; iron oxide 708; gypsum 700[5]; gold 7,500 kg; silver 200 kg[5]. Manufacturing (1995): sugar 34,213; cement 11,197; soap 10,097; soft drinks 68,609 hectolitres; beer 41,690 hectolitres; shoes 111,000 pairs; cigarettes 114,928 cartons. Construction: n.a. Energy production (consumption): electricity (kW-hr; 1994) 289,000,000 (289,000,000); coal, none (n.a.); crude petroleum, none (n.a.); petroleum products (metric tons; 1994) none (149,000); natural gas, none (n.a.).
Gross national product (1996): U.S.$2,422,000,000 (U.S.$240 per capita).

Structure of gross domestic product and labour force

	1995		1987	
	in value CFAF '000,000	% of total value	labour force	% of labour force
Agriculture	440,950	40.5	2,802,722	82.2
Mining	34,143	3.1	1,524	—
Manufacturing	69,791	6.4	186,243	5.5
Construction	58,678	5.4	13,065	0.4
Public utilities	11,951	1.1	3,157	0.1
Transp. and commun.	45,742	4.2	6,174	0.2
Trade	209,765	19.3	158,892	4.7
Finance	9,222	0.9	320	—
Pub. admin., defense	62,515	5.8	158,704	4.6
Services	78,829	7.2	...	...
Other	66,378[6]	6.1[6]	78,470	2.3
TOTAL	1,087,964	100.0	3,409,271	100.0

Household income and expenditure. Average household size (1987) 5.6; average annual income per household: n.a.; sources of income: n.a.; expenditure (1986–87)[3, 7]: food 54.6%, clothing 14.2%, transportation and communications 11.9%, housing and energy 8.7%, household durable goods 4.2%.
Land use (1993): forested 5.7%; meadows and pastures 24.6%; agricultural and under permanent cultivation 2.0%; other 67.7%.

Foreign trade

Balance of trade (current prices)						
	1992	1993	1994	1995	1996	1997
CFAF '000,000,000	−70.1	−80.5	−170.0	−164.9	−167.9	−171.1
% of total	27.9%	28.9%	35.1%	27.2%	27.2%	22.0%

Imports (1995): CFAF 386,400,000,000 (machinery, appliances, and transport equipment 33.1%; food products 13.4%; construction products 10.2%; chemicals 9.2%; petroleum products 8.5%). *Major import sources:* Côte d'Ivoire 22.6%; France 17.3%; United Kingdom 3.8%; Belgium-Luxembourg 3.2%; China 2.5%; Germany 1.5%; Spain 1.1%.
Exports (1995): CFAF 234,700,000,000 (raw cotton and cotton products 55.5%; live animals 19.8%; gold 14.7%). *Major export destinations:* China 12.6%; Belgium-Luxembourg 8.7%; Spain 3.3%; France 2.9%; Côte d'Ivoire 2.1%; Germany 1.6%.

Transport and communications

Transport. Railroads (1994): route length 398 mi[8], 641 km[8]; passenger-mi 304,155,000, passenger-km 489,491,000; short ton-mi cargo 187,176,000, metric ton-km cargo 273,273,000. Roads (1995): total length 9,181 mi, 14,776 km (paved 12%). Vehicles (1995): passenger cars 24,700; trucks and buses 17,100. Merchant marine: vessels (100 gross tons and over) none. Air transport (1993)[9]: passenger-mi 139,675,000, passenger-km 224,736,000; short ton-mi cargo 11,247,000, metric ton-km cargo 16,420,000; airports (1997) with scheduled flights 9.

Communications				units per 1,000 persons
Medium	date	unit	number	
Daily newspapers	1994	circulation	40,000	4.4
Radio	1995	receivers	1,575,000	168
Television	1995	receivers	110,000	12
Telephones	1995	main lines	17,000	1.8

Education and health

Educational attainment (1987). Percentage of population age 6 and over having: no formal schooling 86.0%; primary education 12.5%; secondary 1.2%; postsecondary and higher 0.3%. *Literacy* (1995): Percentage of total population age 15 and over literate 1,760,000 (31.0%); males literate 1,084,000 (39.4%); females literate 676,000 (23.1%).

Education (1995–96)	schools	teachers	students	student/ teacher ratio
Primary (age 6–14)	1,996	8,738	608,444	69.6
Secondary (age 15–17)[10]	307[11]	4,549	112,670	24.8
Higher[12]	7	701	6,703	9.6

Health: physicians (1993) 483 (1 per 18,376 persons); hospital beds (1987) 3,430 (1 per 2,253 persons); infant mortality rate (1997) 124.
Food (1995): daily per capita caloric intake 2,149 (vegetable products 91%, animal products 9%); 91% of FAO recommended minimum requirement.

Military

Total active duty personnel (1996): 7,350 (army 93.9%, navy 0.7%, air force 5.4%). *Military expenditure as percentage of GNP* (1995): 1.8% (world 2.8%); per capita expenditure U.S.$5.

[1]Multiparty legislative elections held in March 1997 were annulled by the constitutional court; new elections were held in July and August. [2]Kidal region was created in May 1991 from the northern half of Gao region as a concession to Tuareg separatists. Separate data not available. [3]1995 estimate. [4]Minimum hourly wages of industrial workers. [5]1994. [6]Less imputed bank service charges. [7]Weights of consumer price index components. [8]1995. [9]Represents 1/11 of the traffic of Air Afrique, which is operated by 11 West African states. [10]Excludes vocational. [11]1991–92. [12]1990–91.

Internet resources for further information:
- **United Nations Development Program—Mali**
  http://www.undp.org/undp/fomli/
- **MaliNet** http://www.malinet.ml/index2.html
- **Embassy of Mali (Washington, D.C.)**
  http://www.maliembassy-usa.org/

Malta

Official name: Malta (Maltese); Malta (English).
Form of government: unitary multiparty republic with one legislative house (House of Representatives [65[1]]).
Chief of state: President.
Head of government: Prime Minister.
Capital: Valletta.
Official languages: Maltese; English.
Official religion: Roman Catholicism.
Monetary unit: 1 Maltese lira (Lm) = 100 cents = 1,000 mils; valuation[2] (Sept. 25, 1998) 1 U.S.$ = Lm 0.38; 1 £ = Lm 0.65.

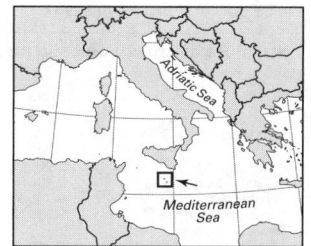

Area and population	area		population
Census regions[4]	sq mi	sq km	1996[3] estimate
Gozo and Comino	27	70	27,760
Inner Harbour	6	15	102,663
Northern	30	78	37,045
Outer Harbour	12	32	108,032
South Eastern	20	53	47,876
Western	27	69	48,754
TOTAL	122	316[5]	372,130

Demography

Population (1998): 377,000.
Density (1998): persons per sq mi 3,090, persons per sq km 1,193.
Urban-rural (1996): urban 89.7%; rural 10.3%.
Sex distribution (1996[3]): male 49.53%; female 50.47%.
Age breakdown (1996[3]): under 15, 21.6%; 15–29, 21.3%; 30–44, 22.7%; 45–59, 18.8%; 60–74, 11.5%; 75 and over, 4.1%.
Population projection: (2000) 382,000; (2010) 393,000.
Doubling time: 136 years.
Ethnic composition (by nationality; 1990): Maltese 95.7%; British 2.1%; other 2.2%.
Religious affiliation (1996): Roman Catholic 93.4%; other 6.6%.
Major cities (1996[3]): Birkirkara 22,055; Qormi 20,173; Hamrun 13,624; Sliema 13,470; Valletta 9,128.

Vital statistics

Birth rate per 1,000 population (1996): 12.2 (world avg. 25.0); (1995) legitimate 95.8%; illegitimate 4.2%.
Death rate per 1,000 population (1996): 7.5 (world avg. 9.3).
Natural increase rate per 1,000 population (1996): 4.7 (world avg. 15.7).
Total fertility rate (avg. births per childbearing woman; 1995): 1.8.
Marriage rate per 1,000 population (1995): 6.2.
Divorce rate per 1,000 population: n.a.
Life expectancy at birth (1995): male 74.9 years; female 79.5 years.
Major causes of death per 100,000 population (1995): diseases of the circulatory system 313.0; malignant neoplasms 197.1; diseases of the respiratory system 61.5; endocrine and metabolic diseases of the blood 28.3; diseases of the digestive system 26.4; accidents, poisoning, and violence 25.6.

National economy

Budget (1997). Revenue: Lm 476,945,000 (direct taxes 44.2%; indirect taxes 39.9%; nontax revenue 13.7%; foreign grants 2.2%). Expenditures: Lm 567,645,000 (recurrent expenditures 84.7%, of which social security 27.2%, education 10.4%, health 10.0%, debt service 4.9%, defense 4.2%; capital expenditure 15.3%).
Public debt (1997): U.S.$1,698,700,000.
Production (wholesale value in Lm except where noted). Agriculture, forestry, fishing (1995): vegetables 5,715,997 (of which tomatoes 845,855, melons 755,394, cauliflower 407,062, onions 422,676), fruits 758,040 (of which peaches 192,540, strawberries 188,281, grapes 71,124), potatoes 599,931; livestock (number of live animals; 1996) 69,000 pigs, 21,000 cattle, 16,000 sheep, 9,050 goats; fish catch 1,089,188. Quarrying (1993): 4,520,000. Manufacturing (value of sales in Lm; 1994–95): machinery and transport equipment 402,993,000; food 103,733,000; textiles and wearing apparel 80,813,000; paper and printing 40,610,000; chemicals 35,151,000. Construction (buildings completed; 1996): residential 3,360[6]; nonresidential 1,859. Energy production (consumption): electricity (kW-hr; 1994) 1,500,000,000 (1,500,000,000); coal (metric tons; 1994) none (300,000); crude petroleum, none (n.a.); petroleum products (metric tons; 1994) none (320,000).
Population economically active (1996): total 145,984; activity rate of total population 39.1% (participation rates: ages 15–64 [1985] 45.9%; female 27.5%; unemployed 3.6%).

Price and earnings indexes (1990 = 100)							
	1991	1992	1993	1994	1995	1996	1997
Consumer price index	102.5	104.2	108.5	113.0	117.5	120.5	124.4
Average weekly earnings	109.8	114.6	120.5	125.8	129.9	135.5	...

Household income and expenditure. Average household size (1985) 3.3; average annual income per household (1982) Lm 4,736 (U.S.$11,399); sources of income (1993): wages and salaries 63.8%, professional and unincorporated enterprises 19.3%, rents, dividends, and interest 16.9%; expenditure (1993): food and beverages 27.9%, transportation and communications 15.7%, household furnishings and operations 9.5%, recreation, entertainment, and

education 7.2%, clothing and footwear 6.9%, housing 5.5%, health 3.3%, tobacco 2.6%.
Tourism (1995): receipts from visitors U.S.$606,000,000; expenditures by nationals abroad U.S.$184,000,000.
Gross domestic product (1995): U.S.$3,241,600,000 (U.S.$8,712 per capita).

Structure of gross domestic product and labour force				
	1995		1996	
	in value Lm '000	% of total value	labour force	% of labour force
Agriculture	28,600	2.9	2,846	1.9
Manufacturing	236,800	24.0	33,788	23.1
Mining	} 37,400	3.8	} 6,938	4.8
Construction				
Public utilities	60,800	6.2	...	...
Transp. and commun.	67,700	6.8	11,828	8.1
Trade	129,000	13.1	25,819[7]	17.7[7]
Finance	73,800	7.5	3,725	2.6
Pub. admin., defense	162,000	16.4	32,419	22.2
Services	101,700	10.3	18,779	12.9
Other	89,400	9.0	9,839[8]	6.7[8]
TOTAL	987,200	100.0	145,983[5]	100.0

Land use (1994): agricultural and under permanent cultivation 40.6%; other (infertile clay soil with underlying limestone) 59.4%.

Foreign trade[9]

Balance of trade (current prices)							
	1991	1992	1993	1994	1995	1996	1997
Lm '000,000	−278.5	−256.9	−312.6	−326.4	−362.8	−383.7	−352.5
% of total	25.6%	20.7%	23.2%	21.6%	21.2%	23.5%	21.8%

Imports (1996): Lm 1,010,254,000 (machinery and transport equipment 48.2%, manufactured and semimanufactured goods 25.9%, food 9.2%, chemicals 7.4%, mineral fuels 5.4%, beverages and tobacco 1.3%). *Major import sources:* Italy 19.6%; France 15.8%; U.K. 14.2%; Germany 9.4%; U.S. 6.9%.
Exports (1996): Lm 570,344,000 (machinery and transport equipment 62.1%, manufactured 32.6%, chemicals 2.5%, food and live animals 1.9%, beverages and tobacco 0.5%). *Major export destinations:* France 16.1%; Germany 15.1%; U.S. 14.7%; Italy 12.5%; U.K. 8.4%.

Transport and communications

Transport. Railroads: none. Roads (1994): total length 997 mi, 1,604 km (paved 94%). Vehicles (1995): passenger cars 173,259; trucks and buses 41,849. Merchant marine (1992): vessels (100 gross tons and over) 889; total deadweight tonnage 17,073,207. Air transport (1995): passenger-mi 1,070,479,000, passenger-km 1,722,772,000; short ton-mi cargo 9,404,000, metric ton-km cargo 13,729,000; airports (1996) with scheduled flights 1.

Communications				units per 1,000
Medium	date	unit	number	persons
Daily newspapers	1996	circulation	54,000	145
Radio	1994	receivers	193,000	525
Television	1994	receivers	272,000	739
Telephones	1995	main lines	170,700	459
Cellular telephones	1995	subscribers	10,800	29
Facsimile machines	1995	units	3,200	300
Personal computers	1995	units	30,000	81

Education and health

Educational attainment (1967). Percentage of economically active population having: no formal schooling 10.8%; primary education 60.4%; lower secondary 3.4%; upper secondary 17.6%; technical secondary 3.9%; postsecondary and higher 3.9%. *Literacy* (1985): total population age 15 and over literate 250,419 (96.0%); males literate 121,899 (96.2%); females literate 128,520 (95.9%).

Education (1995–96)	schools	teachers	students	student/ teacher ratio
Primary (age 5–10)	111	1,990	35,479	17.8
Secondary (age 11–17)	59	2,679	29,907	20.9
Voc., teacher tr.	22	541	4,539	8.4
Higher[10]	1	284	3,679	13.0

Health (1996): physicians 925 (1 per 403 persons); hospital beds 2,140 (1 per 174 persons); infant mortality rate per 1,000 live births (1996) 10.5.
Food (1995): daily per capita caloric intake 3,387 (vegetable products 73%, animal products 27%); 136% of FAO recommended minimum requirement.

Military

Total active duty personnel (1996): 1,950 (army 100%). *Military expenditure as percentage of GNP* (1993): 0.9% (world 3.2%); per capita expenditure U.S.$63.

[1]As of September 1998 elections. [2]The Maltese lira is tied to the currencies of several principal trading partners. [3]January 1. [4]Data are reported according to census regions as of January 1993 rather than the 67 new "local administrative districts" (local councils) created between 1993 and 1998. [5]Detail does not add to total given because of rounding. [6]Dwellings completed. [7]Includes hotels and catering. [8]Includes 5,328 unemployed. [9]Import figures are f.o.b. in balance of trade and c.i.f. for commodities and trading partners. [10]1992–93.

Internet resources for further information:
• **Central Office of Statistics http://www.magnet.mt/home/cos/**

Marshall Islands

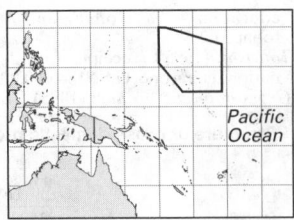

Official name: Majōl (Marshallese);
Republic of the Marshall Islands
(English).
Form of government: unitary republic
with two legislative houses (Council
of Iroij [12][1]; Nitijela [33]).
Head of state and government:
President.
Capital: Majuro (Dalap-Uliga-Darrit).
Official languages: Marshallese
(Kajin-Majōl); English.
Official religion: none.
Monetary unit: 1 U.S. dollar
(U.S.$) = 100 cents; valuation
(Sept. 25, 1998) 1 £ = U.S.$1.70.

Area and population	area		population
Election districts	sq mi	sq km	1988 census
Ailinglaplap	5.67	14.68	1,715
Ailuk	2.07	5.36	488
Arno	5.00	12.95	1,656
Aur	2.17	5.62	438
Bikini	2.32	6.01	10
Ebon	2.22	5.75	741
Enewetak	2.26	5.85	715
Jabat	0.22	0.57	112
Jaluit	4.38	11.34	1,709
Kili	0.36	0.93	602
Kwajalein	6.33	16.39	9,311
Lae	0.56	1.45	319
Lib	0.36	0.93	115
Likiep	3.96	10.26	482
Majuro	3.75	9.71	19,664
Maloelap	3.75	9.71	796
Mejit	0.72	1.86	445
Mili	6.15	15.93	854
Namorik	1.07	2.77	814
Namu	2.42	6.27	801
Rongelap	3.07	7.95	0
Ujae	0.72	1.86	448
Ujelang	0.67	1.74	0
Utrik	0.94	2.43	409
Wotho	1.67	4.32	90
Wotje	3.16	8.18	646
Other atolls	4.10	10.62	0
TOTAL	70.07	181.48[2]	43,380

Demography

Population (1998): 62,800.
Density (1998): persons per sq mi 897.1, persons per sq km 347.0.
Urban-rural (1988): urban 64.5%; rural 35.5%.
Sex distribution (1997): male 51.02%; female 48.98%.
Age breakdown (1997): under 15, 50.2%; 15–29, 26.0%; 30–44, 13.9%; 45–59, 6.5%; 60–74, 2.6%; 75 and over, 0.8%.
Population projection: (2000) 68,100; (2010) 91,400.
Doubling time: 18 years.
Ethnic composition (nationality; 1988): Marshallese 96.9%; other Pacific islanders 1.7%; Filipino 0.5%; all other 0.9%.
Religious affiliation (1995): Protestant 62.8%; Roman Catholic 7.1%; Mormon 3.1%; Jehovah's Witness 1.0%; other (mostly nonreligious) 26.0%.
Major cities (1995): Majuro (Dalap-Uliga-Darrit) 28,000; Ebeye 8,324[3].

Vital statistics

Birth rate per 1,000 population (1997): 46.0 (world avg. 25.0).
Death rate per 1,000 population (1997): 7.0 (world avg. 9.3).
Natural increase rate per 1,000 population (1997): 39.0 (world avg. 15.7).
Total fertility rate (avg. births per childbearing woman; 1997): 6.8.
Life expectancy at birth (1997): male 62.6 years; female 65.8 years.
Major causes of death per 100,000 population (1990–93)[4]: infectious and parasitic diseases 169.9; circulatory diseases 155.1; respiratory diseases 105.1; malignant neoplasms (cancers) 68.4; digestive diseases 63.3; accidents, injuries, and violence 36.7.

National economy

Budget (1995–96). Revenue: U.S.$80,100,000 (U.S. government grants 59.7%, income tax 9.4%, import tax 8.5%, value-added and excise taxes 6.1%, fishing rights 3.0%, interest income 2.7%). Expenditures: U.S.$77,400,000 (debt service 10.2%, education 9.9%, health services 8.8%, public works and social programs 4.9%, internal security 2.1%).
Production (metric tons except as noted). Agriculture, forestry, fishing (1991): copra 5,545, fruits 1,809 (of which pandanus 836, breadfruit 645, bananas 264, papaya 64), tubers 1,500 (of which taro 1,300, sweet potatoes 182), vegetables 136 (of which cabbage 36, pumpkins 36); livestock (number of live animals; 1994) 12,352 pigs, 59,086 chickens; roundwood, n.a.; fish catch (1995) 260. Mining and quarrying: high-grade phosphate mining on Ailinglaplap Atoll, quarrying of sand and aggregate for local construction only. Manufacturing (1995): copra 7,728 coconut oil and processed (chilled or frozen) fish are important products; the manufacture of handicrafts and personal items (clothing, mats, boats, etc.) by individuals is also significant. Construction (1994): value added U.S.$9,300,000. Energy production (consumption): electricity (kW-hr; 1994) 57,891,000 (57,891,000); coal, none (n.a.); gasoline, oil, and lubricants (barrels; 1988)[5] n.a. (84,588).
Public debt (external, outstanding; 1994–95): U.S.$141,200,000.

Gross national product (1996): U.S.$96,000,000 (U.S.$1,600 per capita).

Structure of gross domestic product and labour force	1995		1988	
	in value U.S.$'000	% of total value	labour force	% of labour force
Agriculture	15,700	14.9	2,150	18.7
Mining	300	0.3	2	—
Manufacturing	2,700	2.6	945	8.2
Public utilities	2,100	2.0	82	0.7
Construction	10,700	10.2	1,076	9.4
Transp. and commun.	6,500	6.2	537	4.7
Trade, restaurants, hotels	17,900	17.0	1,394	12.1
Finance, insurance, real estate	17,200	16.3	833	7.3
Public administration } Services	32,000	30.4	3,035	26.4
Other	200[6]	0.2[6]	1,434[7]	12.5[7]
TOTAL	105,300	100.0[2]	11,488	100.0

Land use (1989)[8]: forested 22.5%; meadows and pastures 13.5%; agricultural and under permanent cultivation 33.1%; other 30.9%.
Household income and expenditure. Average household size (1988) 8.7; income per household (1979) U.S.$3,366; sources of income: n.a.; expenditure (1982): food 57.7%, housing 15.6%, clothing 12.0%, personal effects and other 14.7%.
Population economically active (1988): total 11,488; activity rate of total population 26.5% (participation rates: over age 14, 54.1%; female 30.1%; unemployed 12.5%).

Price and earnings indexes (1990 = 100)	1989	1990	1991	1992	1993	1994	1995
Consumer price index	99.4	100.0	103.4	116.8	119.5	125.6	134.4
Earnings index	...	...	...	...	...	...	...

Tourism (1994): receipts from visitors U.S.$2,000,000; expenditures by nationals abroad, n.a.

Foreign trade

Balance of trade (current prices)	1990	1991	1992	1993	1994	1995
U.S.$'000,000	−53.9	−53.5	−52.6	−53.4	−49.3	−58.1
% of total	94.0%	90.3%	74.1%	77.7%	52.6%	27.2%

Imports (1995): U.S.$75,100,000 (food, beverages, and tobacco 28.2%, machinery and transport equipment 24.6%, mineral fuels and lubricants 24.0%, manufactured goods 8.9%, chemical products 2.5%). *Major import sources:* U.S. 51.0%; Guam 14.5%; Japan 7.5%; Australia 1.9%; Hong Kong 1.7%.
Exports (1995): U.S.$17,000,000 (chilled fish 38.8%, crude coconut oil 18.2%, pet fish 2.4%). *Major export destinations:* U.S. *c.* 80.0%; other *c.* 20.0%.

Transport and communications

Transport. Vehicles (1994): passenger cars 1,418; trucks and buses 193. Merchant marine (1992): vessels (100 gross tons and over) 35; total deadweight tonnage 4,182,356. Air transport (1994): passenger-km 49,000,000[9]; metric ton-km cargo 30,433; airports (1997) with scheduled flights 25.

Communications				units per 1,000 persons
Medium	date	unit	number	
Telephones	1993	main lines	2,300	44.2

Education and health

Educational attainment (1988). Percentage of population age 25 and over having: no grade completed 5.1%; elementary education 43.2%; secondary 39.7%; higher 11.4%; not stated 0.6%. *Literacy* (latest): total population age 15 and over literate 19,377 (91.2%); males literate 9,993 (92.4%); females literate 9,384 (90.0%).

Education (1994–95)	schools	teachers	students	student/ teacher ratio
Primary (age 6–14)	103	669	13,355	20.0
Secondary (age 15–18)	12	144	2,400	16.7
Voc., teacher tr.	...	...	...	...
Higher	...	...	...	...

Health (1995): physicians 17 (1 per 3,269 persons); hospital beds 108 (1 per 515 persons); infant mortality rate per 1,000 live births (1997) 45.7.

Military

Under the 1984 Compact of Free Association, the United States provides for the defense of the Republic of the Marshall Islands.

[1]Council of Iroij is an advisory body only. [2]Detail does not add to total given because of rounding. [3]1988. [4]Registered deaths only. [5]Import only. [6]Import duties less imputed bank service charges. [7]Includes 1,432 unemployed. [8]Data are for the former Trust Territory of the Pacific Islands. [9]1993.

Internet resources for further information:
• **RMI Online, Internet Guide to the Republic of the Marshall Islands**
  http://www.rmiembassyus.org/
• **Bank of Hawaii-Republic of the Marshall Islands Economic Report**
  http://www.boh.com/econ/frameset.asp?name=pacific

Martinique

Official name: Département de la Martinique (Department of Martinique).
Political status: overseas department (France) with two legislative houses (General Council [45]; Regional Council [41]).
Chief of state: President of France.
Heads of government: Prefect (for France); President of the General Council (for Martinique); President of the Regional Council (for Martinique).
Capital: Fort-de-France.
Official language: French.
Official religion: none.
Monetary unit: 1 French franc (F) = 100 centimes; valuation (Sept. 25, 1998) 1 U.S.$ = F 5.60; 1 £ = F 9.53.

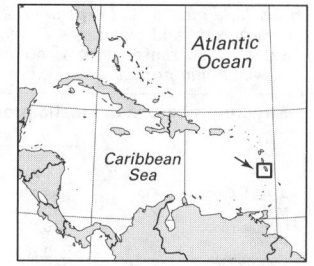

Area and population

Arrondissements	Capitals	area sq mi	area sq km	population 1990 census
Fort-de-France	Fort-de-France	147	381	187,275
Le Marin	Le Marin	158	409	93,411
La Trinité	La Trinité	131	338	78,893
TOTAL		436	1,128	359,579

Demography

Population (1998): 398,000.
Density (1998): persons per sq mi 912.8, persons per sq km 352.8.
Urban-rural (1995): urban 93.4%; rural 6.6%.
Sex distribution (1995): male 48.55%; female 51.45%.
Age breakdown (1995): under 15, 24.0%; 15–29, 25.8%; 30–44, 22.2%; 45–59, 14.0%; 60–74, 9.8%; 75 and over, 4.2%.
Population projection: (2000) 407,000; (2010) 440,000.
Doubling time: 77 years.
Ethnic composition (1983): mulatto 93.7%; French (metropolitan and Martinique white) 2.6%; East Indian 1.7%; other 2.0%.
Religious affiliation (1995): Roman Catholic 86.5%; Protestant 8.0% (mostly Seventh-day Adventist); Jehovah's Witness 1.6%; other 3.9%, including Hindu, syncretist, and nonreligious.
Major urban areas (1990): Fort-de-France 100,080; Le Lamentin 30,028; Schoelcher 19,825; Sainte-Marie 19,682; Le Robert 17,713.

Vital statistics

Birth rate per 1,000 population (1994): 14.9 (world avg. 25.0); (1992) legitimate 34.1%; illegitimate 65.9%.
Death rate per 1,000 population (1994): 5.8 (world avg. 9.3).
Natural increase rate per 1,000 population (1994): 9.1 (world avg. 15.7).
Total fertility rate (avg. births per childbearing woman; 1993): 1.9.
Marriage rate per 1,000 population (1994): 3.9.
Divorce rate per 1,000 population (1993): 0.9.
Life expectancy at birth (1993): male 74.7 years; female 81.0 years.
Major causes of death per 100,000 population (1992): diseases of the circulatory system 192.7; malignant neoplasms (cancers) 137.7; accidents, poisoning, and violence 48.2; diseases of the digestive system 32.2; diseases of the respiratory system 30.1; endocrine and metabolic disorders 29.3.

National economy

Budget (1994). Revenue: F 1,816,000,000 (general receipts from French central government and local administrative bodies 45.0%; tax receipts 34.0%, of which indirect taxes 19.5%, direct taxes 14.5%). Expenditures: F 1,816,000,000 (health and social assistance 42.0%; wages and salaries 16.7%; other administrative services 7.2%; debt amortization 5.0%).
Public debt (1994): U.S.$186,700,000.
Production (metric tons except as noted). Agriculture, forestry, fishing (1996): sugarcane 212,000, bananas 210,000, pineapples 30,000, plantains 14,000, yams 7,000, tomatoes 4,000, cucumbers and gherkins 3,000, melons 3,000, sweet potatoes 1,000; livestock (number of live animals) 42,000 sheep, 33,000 pigs, 30,000 cattle, 22,000 goats; roundwood (1994) 12,000 cu m; fish catch (1995) 5,377. Mining and quarrying (1992): pumice 140,000; sand and gravel for local construction. Manufacturing (1996): cement 214,807; processed pineapples 15,715; sugar 7,722; rum 45,326 hectolitres; other products include clothing, fabricated metals, and yawls and sails. Construction (buildings authorized; 1994): residential permits 6,893; nonresidential 113,279 sq m. Energy production (consumption): electricity (kW-hr; 1996) 977,000,000 (856,000,000); coal, none (none); crude petroleum (barrels; 1994) none (5,805,000); petroleum products (metric tons; 1994) 718,000 (554,000); natural gas, none (none).
Household income and expenditure. Average household size (1990) 3.3; income per household (1989) F 147,150 (U.S.$24,525); sources of income (1989): wages and salaries 80%, other 20%; expenditure (1993): food and beverages 32.1%, transportation and communications 20.7%, housing and energy 10.6%, household durable goods 9.4%, clothing and footwear 8.0%, education and recreation 5.4%, health care 5.2%, other 8.6%.
Tourism (1995): receipts from visitors U.S.$384,000,000; expenditures by nationals abroad, n.a.

Gross domestic product (1995): U.S.$3,942,000,000 (U.S.$10,000 per capita).

Structure of gross domestic product and labour force

	1991 in value F '000,000	1991 % of total value	1990 labour force	1990 % of labour force
Agriculture, fishing	1,152.2	5.5	8,445	5.2
Mining, manufacturing	1,592.0	7.7	9,706	6.0
Construction	1,078.6	5.2	9,298	5.7
Public utilities	493.7	2.4		
Transp. and commun.	1,282.3	6.2	6,673	4.1
Trade, restaurants, hotels	4,556.1	21.9	13,965	8.6
Finance, real estate, insurance	1,017.6	4.9	26,489	16.2
Pub. admin., defense	305.8	1.5	35,541	21.8
Services	3,424.5	16.4		
Other	5,883.2[1]	28.3[1]	52,900[2]	32.4[2]
TOTAL	20,786.0	100.0	163,017	100.0

Population economically active (1993): total 162,100[3]; activity rate of total population 43.0% (participation rates: ages 15–64, 73.8%; [1990] female 47.5%; unemployed [1996] 27.0%).

Price and earnings indexes (1990 = 100)

	1991	1992	1993	1994	1995	1996	1997
Consumer price index[4]	104.3	108.4	109.6	114.0	115.9	118.1	119.2
Monthly earnings index[5]	103.0	105.7	107.5	109.1	111.3	112.3	116.8

Land use (1994): forested 45.3%; meadows and pastures 13.2%; agricultural and under permanent cultivation 17.0%; other 24.5%.

Foreign trade[6]

Balance of trade (current prices)

	1992	1993	1994	1995	1996	1997
F '000,000	−7,982	−7,744	−7,877	−8,604	−8,987	−8,676
% of total	75.6%	78.0%	76.4%	78.2%	80.5%	78.6%

Imports (1996): F 10,072,400,000 (consumer goods 23.9%, goods for intermediate consumption [inputs to the manufacturing process changed or destroyed in the final product] 15.9%, automobiles 15.0%, professional equipment 15.2%, energy products 8.3%). *Major import sources* (1994): France 61.6%; United States 2.7%; Guadeloupe 1.1%; Venezuela 0.7%; other Caribbean 1.9%.
Exports (1996): F 1,086,000,000 ([1995] bananas 40.4%, refined petroleum 17.8%, rum 9.8%, melons 1.7%). *Major export destinations* (1994): France 47.5%; Guadeloupe 37.4%; French Guiana 3.3%.

Transport and communications

Transport. Railroads: none. Roads (1994): total length 1,299 mi, 2,091 km (paved [1988] 75%). Vehicles (1985): passenger cars 135,269; trucks and buses 7,328. Merchant marine (1992): vessels (100 gross tons and over) 6; total deadweight tonnage 1,121. Air transport (1996): passenger arrivals and departures 1,505,970; cargo handled 13,459 metric tons; airports (1997) with scheduled flights 1.

Communications

Medium	date	unit	number	units per 1,000 persons
Daily newspapers	1995	circulation	32,000	82.5
Radio	1995	receivers	77,000	198
Television	1995	receivers	65,000	168
Telephones	1995	main lines	155,200	400
Facsimile machines	1995	units	3,400	8.8

Education and health

Educational attainment (1990). Percentage of population age 25 and over having: incomplete primary, or no declaration 54.3%; primary education 18.0%; secondary 20.0%; higher 7.7%. *Literacy* (1982): total population age 15 and over literate 206,807 (92.5%); males literate 97,538 (91.8%); females literate 109,269 (93.2%).

Education (1993–94)

	schools	teachers	students	student/ teacher ratio
Primary (age 6–11)	276	3,251	33,532	10.3
Secondary (age 12–18) Vocational	76	3,736	47,172	12.6
Higher	1	99	4,486	45.3

Health (1991): physicians 625 (1 per 584 persons); hospital beds 3,747 (1 per 97 persons); infant mortality rate per 1,000 live births (1993) 4.0.
Food (1995): daily per capita caloric intake 2,865 (vegetable products 75%, animal products 25%); 118% of FAO recommended minimum requirement.

Military

Total active duty personnel (1994): 1,542 French troops.

[1]Includes an estimated F 5,474,000,000 produced in the nonmoney economy. [2]Unemployed. [3]Includes military reserve personnel. [4]Figures are end-of-year unless otherwise footnoted. [5]Based on minimum-level wage of public employees. [6]Imports c.i.f.; exports f.o.b.

Internet resources for further information:
• **Martinique: Présentation générale (in French)**
  http://www.outre-mer.gouv.fr/domtom/mar.htm

Mauritania

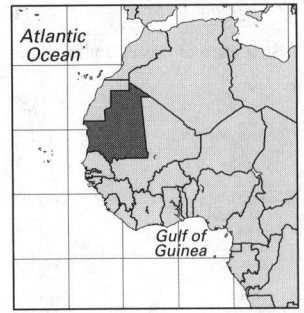

Official name: Al-Jumhūrīyah al-Islāmīyah al-Mūrītānīyah (Arabic) (Islamic Republic of Mauritania).
Form of government: unitary multiparty republic with two legislative houses (Senate [56]; National Assembly [79]).
Head of state and government: President assisted by the Prime Minister.
Capital: Nouakchott.
Official language: Arabic[1].
Official religion: Islam.
Monetary unit: 1 ouguiya (UM) = 5 khoums; valuation (Sept. 25, 1998)
1 U.S.$ = UM 208.83;
1 £ = UM 355.53.

Area and population		area		population
				1992
Regions	Capitals	sq mi	sq km	estimate
El-'Açâba	Kiffa	14,100	36,600	185,574
Adrar	Atar	83,100	215,300	62,906
Brakna	Aleg	13,000	33,800	207,590
Dakhlet Nouadhibou	Nouadhibou	8,600	22,300	83,246
Gorgol	Kaédi	5,300	13,600	201,301
Guidimaka	Sélibaby	4,000	10,300	129,797
Hodh ech-Chargui	Néma	70,600	182,700	234,011
Hodh el-Gharbi	'Ayoûn el-'Atroûs	20,600	53,400	175,089
Inchiri	Akjoujt	18,100	46,800	13,630
Tagant	Tidjikdja	36,800	95,200	67,939
Tiris Zemmour	Zouérate	97,600	252,900	37,534
Trarza	Rosso	26,200	67,800	217,867
Capital District				
Nouakchott	Nouakchott	400	1,000	480,395
TOTAL		398,000[2]	1,030,700	2,096,879[3]

Demography

Population (1998): 2,511,000.
Density (1998): persons per sq mi 6.3, persons per sq km 2.4.
Urban-rural (1995): urban 53.8%; rural 46.2%.
Sex distribution (1995): male 49.52%; female 50.48%.
Age breakdown (1995): under 15, 43.1%; 15–29, 27.3%; 30–44, 16.1%; 45–59, 8.3%; 60–74, 4.3%; 75 and over, 0.9%.
Population projection: (2000) 2,660,000; (2010) 3,582,000.
Doubling time: 22 years.
Ethnic composition (1993)[4]: Moor 70% (of which about 40% "black" Moor [Harātīn, or African Sudanic] and about 30% "white" Moor [Bidan, or Arab-Berber]); other black African 30% (mostly Wolof, Tukulor, Soninke, and Fulani).
Religious affiliation (1994): Sunnī Muslim 99.5%; Roman Catholic 0.2%; other 0.3%.
Major cities (1992): Nouakchott 735,000[5]; Nouadhibou 72,305; Kaédi 35,241; Kiffa 29,292[6]; Rosso 27,783[6].

Vital statistics

Birth rate per 1,000 population (1996): 46.9 (world avg. 25.0).
Death rate per 1,000 population (1996): 15.2 (world avg. 9.3).
Natural increase rate per 1,000 population (1996): 31.7 (world avg. 15.7).
Total fertility rate (avg. births per childbearing woman; 1996): 6.8.
Life expectancy at birth (1996): male 46.1 years; female 52.1 years.

National economy

Budget (1996). Revenue: UM 44,720,000,000 (tax revenue 59.0%, of which import taxes 12.6%, value-added taxes 10.8%, taxes on wages 8.4%; nontax revenue 39.1%, of which fishing royalties and penalties 31.6%). Expenditures: UM 36,740,000,000 (current expenditures 71.3%, of which interest on public debt 13.4%, defense 10.0%; development expenditures 22.5%; other 6.2%).
Land use (1994): forested 4.3%; meadows and pastures 38.3%; agricultural and under permanent cultivation 0.2%; desert 57.2%.
Production (metric tons except as noted). Agriculture, forestry, fishing (1996): sorghum 144,900, rice 52,800, dates 35,900, pulses 12,000, millet 7,500; livestock (number of live animals) 6,199,000 sheep, 4,133,000 goats, 1,312,000 cattle, 1,087,000 camels; roundwood (1995) 14,000 cu m; fish catch (metric tons; 1995) 90,000, of which octopuses 31,700[7]. Mining and quarrying (gross weight; 1996): iron ore 11,363,000; gold 57,900 troy oz[5]. Manufacturing (1994): cow's milk 91,000; goat's milk 77,000; meat 61,000, of which fresh beef and veal 18,000; hides and skins 4,318; cement, tiles, and bricks 5.9[8]; fabricated metal products 5.4[8]; paper and paper products 2.1[8]. Construction: n.a. Energy production (consumption): electricity (kW-hr; 1994) 148,000,000 (148,000,000); coal (metric tons; 1994) none (6,000); crude petroleum (barrels; 1994) none (6,905,000); petroleum products (metric tons; 1994) 835,000 (918,000); natural gas, none (none).
Population economically active (1994): total 687,000; activity rate of total population 31.3% (participation rates: over age 10 [1991] 45.5%; female 22.9%).

Price and earnings indexes (1990 = 100)							
	1991	1992	1993	1994	1995	1996	1997[9]
Consumer price index[10]	105.6	116.3	127.2	132.4	140.9	147.6	154.0
Monthly earnings index[11]	100.0	114.6	129.2	129.2	129.2	129.2	...

Household income and expenditure. Average household size, n.a.; expenditure (1990): food and beverages 73.1%, clothing and footwear 8.1%, energy and water 7.7%, transportation and communications 2.0%.
Gross national product (1996): U.S.$1,089,000,000 (U.S.$470 per capita).

Structure of gross domestic product and labour force				
	1996		1988	
	in value UM '000,000	% of total value	labour force	% of labour force
Agriculture, livestock	33,232	22.1	225,238	38.5
Mining	13,440	9.0	6,322	1.1
Manufacturing	16,117	10.7	5,630	1.0
Public utilities }			1,326	0.2
Construction	12,766	8.5	12,291	2.1
Transp. and commun.	10,282	6.9	8,378	1.4
Trade and finance	22,287	14.8	73,451	12.5
Services	10,210	6.8	86,807	14.8
Pub. admin., defense	15,684	10.5 }		
Other	16,124[12]	10.7[12]	166,366[13]	28.4[13]
TOTAL	150,142	100.0	585,809	100.0

Public debt (external, outstanding; 1996): U.S.$2,073,000,000.
Tourism (1996): receipts U.S.$2,000,000; expenditures U.S.$13,600,000.

Foreign trade

Balance of trade (current prices)						
	1991	1992	1993	1994	1995	1996
U.S.$'000,000	+36.7	−54.5	+2.6	+41.7	+75.8	+49.8
% of total	4.4%	6.3%	0.3%	5.6%	8.3%	5.4%

Imports (1996): U.S.$435,400,000 (petroleum products 30.5%, private sector foodstuffs 22.4%, imports for National Industrial and Mining Company 20.8%, public sector food aid 12.7%). *Major import sources* (1995)[14]: France 24%; Spain 8%, United States 7%, Belgium 6%, China 5%.
Exports (1996): U.S.$485,200,000 (fish 57.0%, of which cephalopods 28.8%; iron ore 42.7%). *Major export destinations* (1995)[14]: Japan 27%; Italy 18%; France 12%; Spain 11%; Côte d'Ivoire 6%.

Transport and communications

Transport. Railroads (1995): route length 437 mi, 704 km; passenger-km, negligible; (1993) metric ton-km cargo 6,890,000,000. Roads (1995): total length 4,700 mi, 7,600 km (paved 11%). Vehicles (1995): passenger cars 17,300; trucks and buses 9,210. Merchant marine (1992): vessels (100 gross tons and over) 126; total deadweight tonnage 23,875. Air transport (1996)[15]: passenger-km 224,736,000; metric ton-km cargo 16,420,000; airports (1997) with scheduled flights 9.

Communications				units per 1,000 persons
Medium	date	unit	number	
Daily newspapers	1994	circulation	1,000	0.05
Radio	1996	receivers	1,000,000	428
Television	1995	receivers	1,100	0.05
Telephones	1995	main lines	9,200	4.1
Facsimile machines	1995	units	300	0.01

Education and health

Educational attainment (1988). Percentage of population age 25 and over having: no formal schooling 60.8%; primary and incomplete secondary 34.1%; secondary 3.8%; higher 1.3%. *Literacy* (1995): percentage of total population age 15 and over literate 37.7%; males literate 49.6%; females literate 26.3%.

Education (1993–94)	schools	teachers	students	student/ teacher ratio
Primary (age 6–11)	1,635	5,181[16]	268,216[16]	51.8[16]
Secondary (age 12–17)	56[17]	1,776	43,861	24.7
Voc., teacher tr.	5[17]	162	1,949	12.0
Higher	4	72[16, 18]	2,850[16, 18]	39.6[16, 18]

Health: physicians (1994) c. 200 (1 per 11,085 persons); hospital beds (1988) 1,556 (1 per 1,217 persons); infant mortality rate per 1,000 live births (1996) 81.7.
Food (1995): daily per capita caloric intake 2,592 (vegetable products 83%, animal products 17%); 112% of FAO recommended minimum requirement.

Military

Total active duty personnel (1996): 15,650 (army 95.8%, navy 3.2%, air force 1.0%). *Military expenditure as percentage of GNP* (1995): 3.2% (world 2.8%); per capita expenditure U.S.$15.

[1]The 1991 constitution names Arabic as the official language and the following as national languages: Arabic, Fulani, Soninke, and Wolof. [2]Detail does not add to total given because of rounding. [3]Official population projection based on 1988 census. [4]Estimated figures; 1988 census data for ethnicity/race not released by the government. [5]1995. [6]1988. [7]Fish catch (1995) including foreign fishing vessels equals 424,500 metric tons. [8]1993 value added of production in U.S.$'000,000. [9]Average of second and third quarters. [10]Nouakchott only. [11]Statutory minimum wage rate of civil servants. [12]Indirect taxes. [13]Mostly unemployed. [14]Estimated figures. [15]Data represent 1/11 of the total scheduled traffic of Air Afrique. [16]1994–95. [17]1991–92. [18]University of Nouakchott only.

Internet resources for further information:
• **Embassy of Mauritania (Washington, D.C.)**
  http://www.embassy.org/mauritania/

Mauritius

Official name: Republic of Mauritius.
Form of government: republic with
  one legislative house (National
  Assembly [661]).
Chief of state: President.
Head of government: Prime Minister.
Capital: Port Louis.
Official language: English.
Official religion: none.
Monetary unit: 1 Mauritian rupee
  (Mau Re; plural Mau Rs) = 100 cents;
  valuation (Sept. 25, 1998) 1 U.S.$ =
  Mau Rs 24.26; 1 £ = Mau Rs 41.30.

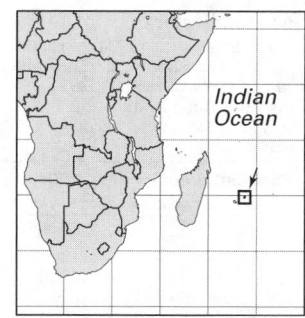

Indian
Ocean

Area and population

Islands Districts/Dependencies	area sq mi	area sq km	population 1996[2] estimate
Mauritius	720	1,865	1,094,430
Black River	100	259	49,819
Flacq	115	298	119,845
Grand Port	100	260	103,068
Moka	89	231	70,801
Pamplemousses	69	179	111,328
Plaines Wilhems	78	203	344,958
Port Louis	17	43	136,638
Rivière du Rempart	57	148	93,850
Savanne	95	245	64,123
Mauritian dependencies			
Agalega[3]			
Cargados Carajos Shoals (Saint Brandon)[3]	27	71	170
Rodrigues[4]	40	104	34,828
TOTAL	788[5]	2,040[5]	1,129,428

Demography

Population (1998): 1,157,000.
Density (1998): persons per sq mi 1,468.3, persons per sq km 567.1.
Urban-rural (1994): urban 43.6%; rural 56.4%.
Sex distribution (1995): male 50.02%; female 49.98%.
Age breakdown (1995)[6]: under 15, 27.3%; 15–29, 27.2%; 30–44, 24.6%; 45–59, 12.3%; 60–74, 6.8%; 75 and over, 1.8%.
Population projection: (2000) 1,169,000; (2010) 1,298,000.
Doubling time: 54 years.
Ethnic composition (1992): Indo-Pakistani 68.0%; Creole (mixed Caucasian, Indo-Pakistani, and African) 27.0%; Chinese 3.0%; white 2.0%.
Religious affiliation (1990): Hindu 50.6%; Roman Catholic 27.2%; Muslim 16.3%; Protestant 5.2%; Buddhist 0.3%; other 0.4%.
Major cities (1995): Port Louis 145,584; Beau Bassin-Rose Hill 98,014; Vacoas-Phoenix 95,600; Curepipe 77,765; Quatre Bornes 74,636.

Vital statistics

Birth rate per 1,000 population (1995): 18.3[6] (world avg. 25.0).
Death rate per 1,000 population (1995): 6.7[6] (world avg. 9.3).
Natural increase rate per 1,000 population (1995): 11.6[6] (world avg. 15.7).
Total fertility rate (avg. births per childbearing woman; 1995): 2.1[6].
Marriage rate per 1,000 population (1995): 9.5[6].
Life expectancy at birth (1993–95): male 66.5 years; female 74.0 years.
Major causes of death per 100,000 population (1995): diseases of the circulatory system 288.6; diseases of the respiratory system 63.4%; malignant neoplasms (cancers) 60.2; homicide, suicide, and accidents 49.9.

National economy

Budget (1995–96). Revenue: Mau Rs 14,250,100,000 (tax revenue 86.3%, of which import duties 39.3%, income tax 14.3%, sales tax 10.2%, excise tax 8.0%). Expenditures: Mau Rs 15,900,000,000 (social services 36.1%, of which education, art, and culture 14.6%, and social security 12.1%, health 8.0%).
Tourism (1995): receipts from visitors U.S.$430,000,000; expenditures by nationals abroad U.S.$159,000,000.
Public debt (external, outstanding; 1996): U.S.$1,153,000,000.
Gross national product (at current market prices; 1996): U.S.$4,205,000,000 (U.S.$3,710 per capita).

Structure of gross domestic product and labour force

	1996 in value Mau Rs '000,000	1996 % of total value	1995 labour force[7, 8]	1995 % of labour force[7, 8]
Agriculture	6,410	8.6	39,700	13.7
Mining	110	0.1	200	0.1
Manufacturing	15,490	20.8	103,800	35.8
Construction	4,300	5.8	10,800	3.7
Public utilities	1,550	2.1	3,500	1.2
Transp. and commun.	8,040	10.8	14,500	5.0
Trade	11,090	14.9	24,500	8.5
Finance	10,870	14.5	...	...
Pub. admin., defense	6,865	9.2	77,500	26.8
Services	4,250	5.7		
Other	5,625[9]	7.5[9]	15,100	5.2
TOTAL	74,600	100.0	289,600	100.0

Production (metric tons except as noted). Agriculture, forestry, fishing (1995): sugarcane 5,159,000, green tea 19,512, potatoes 15,718, tomatoes 13,486,

bananas 9,437, cabbages 5,200, black tea 5,000, pineapples 4,199, onions 3,600, peanuts (groundnuts) 1,049; livestock (number of live animals) 98,000 goats, 34,000 cattle, 17,000 pigs, 7,000 sheep; roundwood 12,400 cu m; fish catch (1995) 16,023. Manufacturing (value added in Mau Rs '000; 1994): apparel 5,065,000; beverages and tobacco 1,995,800; food products 1,580,400; metal and metal products 882,900; textile yarn and fabrics 676,400; chemical products 505,600. Construction (1994): residential 1,097,858 sq m; nonresidential 210,755 sq m. Energy production (consumption): electricity (kW-hr; 1995) 922,100,000 (904,000,000); coal (metric tons; 1994) none (65,000); petroleum products (metric tons; 1994) none (476,000).
Population economically active (1994)[10]: total 503,346; activity rate of total population 46.5% (participation rates: ages 15–64, 67.0%; female 34.5%; unemployed 7.1%).

Price and earnings indexes (1990 = 100)

	1991	1992	1993	1994	1995	1996	1997
Consumer price index	107.0	112.0	123.7	132.8	140.8	150.0	160.3
Monthly earnings index[8]	115.8	128.5	135.6	164.2	...	...	...

Household income and expenditure. Average household size (1990) 4.5[10]; income per household (1979) Mau Rs 15,540 (U.S.$2,430); sources of income (1990): salaries and wages 48.4%, entrepreneurial income 41.2%, transfer payments 10.4%; expenditure (1986–87)[11]: food, beverages, and tobacco 49.1%, housing 13.5%, transportation 9.3%, clothing and footwear 8.4%, recreation, entertainment, education, and cultural services 6.0%.
Land use (1994): forested 21.7%; meadows and pastures 3.4%; agricultural and under permanent cultivation 52.2%; other 22.7%.

Foreign trade

Balance of trade (current prices)

	1991	1992	1993	1994	1995	1996
Mau Rs '000,000	−5,667	−5,036	−7,327	−10,451	−7,607	−9,501
% of total	13.2%	11.1%	13.7%	17.8%	12.4%	13.1%

Imports (1995): Mau Rs 34,363,000,000 (manufactured goods classified chiefly by material 34.4%, machinery and transport equipment 25.8%, food 13.6%, chemicals 7.8%, mineral fuels and lubricants 7.0%, inedible crude materials excluding fuels 3.5%, animal and vegetable oils and fats 1.3%). *Major import sources:* France 12.9%; South Africa 11.1%; India 8.4%; United Kingdom 6.6%; Japan 4.8%; Hong Kong 4.8%; Germany 4.5%; Malaysia 2.9%.
Exports (1995): Mau Rs 27,326,000,000 (clothing 54.2%, sugar 23.1%, yarn 3.8%, pearls and precious stones 1.7%). *Major export destinations:* United Kingdom 33.6%; France 20.7%; United States 14.5%; Germany 5.7%.

Transport and communications

Transport. Railroads: none. Roads (1991): total length 1,138 mi, 1,831 km (paved 93%). Vehicles (1995): passenger cars 37,766; trucks and buses 10,625. Air transport (1996)[12]: passenger-km 3,403,889,000; metric ton-km cargo 136,344,000; airports (1997) with scheduled flights 1.

Communications

Medium	date	unit	number	units per 1,000 persons
Daily newspapers	1995	circulation	55,000[13]	49[13]
Radio	1996	receivers	400,000	353
Television	1995	receivers	168,300	150
Telephones	1995	main lines	148,228	132
Cellular telephones	1995	subscribers	11,700	10
Facsimile machines	1995	units	20,000	18
Personal computers	1995	units	36,000	32

Education and health

Educational attainment (1990). Percentage of population age 25 and over having: no formal education 18.3%; incomplete primary 42.6%; primary 6.1%; incomplete secondary 18.0%; secondary 13.1%; higher 1.9%. *Literacy* (1995): percentage of total population age 15 and over literate 82.9%; males literate 87.1%; females literate 78.8%.

Education (1995)

	schools	teachers	students	student/teacher ratio
Primary (age 5–12)	279	6,381	122,895	19.3
Secondary (age 12–20)	123	4,375	91,104	20.8
Voc., teacher tr.	19[14]	69[15]	2,052[16]	...
Higher	2	526[17]	2,344	7.7[17]

Health (1995): physicians 960 (1 per 1,182 persons); hospital beds (1993) 3,330 (1 per 351 persons); infant mortality rate per 1,000 live births 19.7[6].
Food (1995): daily per capita caloric intake 2,943 (vegetable products 84%, animal products 16%); 130% of FAO recommended minimum requirement.

Military

Total active duty personnel: none; however, a special 1,300-person paramilitary force ensures internal security. *Military expenditure as percentage of GNP* (1994): 0.3% (world 3.0%); per capita expenditure U.S.$10.

---

[1]Includes 4 nonelective seats. [2]January 1. [3]Administered directly from Port Louis. [4]Administered by resident commissioner assisted by local council. [5]Detail does not add to total given because of rounding. [6]Excludes Agalega and Cargados Carajos Shoals. [7]Employed persons in establishments employing 10 or more persons. [8]March. [9]Indirect taxes less imputed bank service charges. [10]Island of Mauritius only. [11]Current weights of CPI components; Island of Mauritius only. [12]Air Mauritius only. [13]Circulation for 5 newspapers only. [14]1992. [15]1982. [16]1993. [17]1991.

Mexico

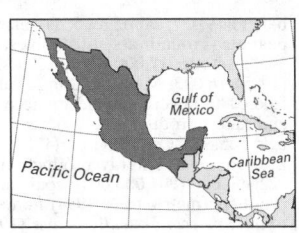

Official name: Estados Unidos
Mexicanos (United Mexican States).
Form of government: federal republic
with two legislative houses (Senate
[128]; Chamber of Deputies [500]).
Head of state and government:
President.
Capital: Mexico City.
Official language: Spanish.
Official religion: none.
Monetary unit: 1 Mexican
peso[1] (Mex$) = 100 centavos;
valuation (Sept. 25, 1998)
1 U.S.$ = Mex$10.25;
1 £ = Mex$17.45.

Area and population

States	Capitals	area sq mi	area sq km	population 1995 estimate
Aguascalientes	Aguascalientes	2,112	5,471	862,720
Baja California Norte	Mexicali	26,997	69,921	2,112,140
Baja California Sur	La Paz	28,369	73,475	375,494
Campeche	Campeche	19,619	50,812	642,516
Chiapas	Tuxtla Gutiérrez	28,653	74,211	3,584,786
Chihuahua	Chihuahua	94,571	244,938	2,793,537
Coahuila	Saltillo	57,908	149,982	2,173,775
Colima	Colima	2,004	5,191	488,028
Durango	Durango	47,560	123,181	1,431,748
Guanajuato	Guanajuato	11,773	30,491	4,406,568
Guerrero	Chilpancingo	24,819	64,281	2,916,567
Hidalgo	Pachuca	8,036	20,813	2,112,473
Jalisco	Guadalajara	31,211	80,836	5,991,176
México	Toluca	8,245	21,355	11,707,964
Michoacán	Morelia	23,138	59,928	3,870,604
Morelos	Cuernavaca	1,911	4,950	1,442,662
Nayarit	Tepic	10,417	26,979	896,702
Nuevo León	Monterrey	25,067	64,924	3,550,114
Oaxaca	Oaxaca	36,275	93,952	3,228,895
Puebla	Puebla	13,090	33,902	4,624,365
Querétaro	Querétaro	4,420	11,449	1,250,476
Quintana Roo	Chetumal	19,387	50,212	703,536
San Luis Potosí	San Luis Potosí	24,351	63,068	2,200,763
Sinaloa	Culiacán	22,521	58,328	2,425,675
Sonora	Hermosillo	70,291	182,052	2,085,536
Tabasco	Villahermosa	9,756	25,267	1,748,769
Tamaulipas	Ciudad Victoria	30,650	79,384	2,527,328
Tlaxcala	Tlaxcala	1,551	4,016	883,924
Veracruz	Xalapa (Jalapa)	27,683	71,699	6,737,324
Yucatán	Mérida	14,827	38,402	1,556,622
Zacatecas	Zacatecas	28,283	73,252	1,336,496
Federal District				
Distrito Federal	—	571	1,479	8,489,007
TOTAL		756,066	1,958,201	91,158,290

Demography

Population (1998): 95,830,000.
Density (1998): persons per sq mi 126.8, persons per sq km 48.9.
Urban-rural (1990): urban 71.3%; rural 28.7%.
Sex distribution (1995): male 49.88%; female 50.12%.
Age breakdown (1995): under 15, 35.9%; 15–29, 30.1%; 30–44, 18.2%; 45–59,
9.5%; 60–74, 4.8%; 75 and over, 1.5%.
Population projection: (2000) 98,881,000; (2010) 112,891,000.
Doubling time: 27 years.
Ethnic composition (1990): mestizo 60.0%; Amerindian 30.0%; Caucasian
9.0%; other 1.0%.
Religious affiliation (1995): Roman Catholic 90.4%; Protestant (including
Evangelical) 3.8%; other 5.8%.
Major cities (1990): Mexico City 9,815,795; Guadalajara 1,650,042; Ciudad
Netzahualcóyotl 1,255,456; Monterrey 1,068,996; Puebla 1,007,170; Juarez
789,522; León 758,279; Tijuana 698,752; Mérida 523,422; Chihuahua 516,153.
Place of birth (1990): 93.1% native-born; 6.9% foreign-born and unknown.
Mobility (1990). Population 5 years and older living in the same state as in
1985: 94.3%; different state 4.9%; unspecified 0.8%.
Households. Total households (1992) 17,152,000; distribution by size (1990): 1
person 1.0%, 2 persons 4.3%, 3 persons 8.9%, 4 persons 14.9%, 5 persons
17.4%, 6 persons 15.3%, 7 or more persons 38.2%. Family households (1990):
17,064,507 (98.4%); nonfamily 1,039,738 (1.3%); unspecified 256,554 (0.3%).
Immigration (1987): permanent immigrants admitted 72,649.
Emigration (1995): legal immigrants into the United States 89,900.

Vital statistics

Birth rate per 1,000 population (1995): 30.4 (world avg. 25.0); (1983) legitimate
72.5%; illegitimate 27.5%.
Death rate per 1,000 population (1995): 4.8 (world avg. 9.3).
Natural increase rate per 1,000 population (1995): 25.6 (world avg. 15.7).
Total fertility rate (avg. births per childbearing woman; 1995): 3.1.
Marriage rate per 1,000 population (1994): 7.2.
Divorce rate per 1,000 population (1995): 0.4.
Life expectancy at birth (1994): male 66.5 years; female 73.1 years.
Major causes of death per 100,000 population (1995): heart diseases 69.8;
malignant neoplasms (cancers) 52.9; accidents 39.0; diabetes mellitus 36.6;
cerebrovascular diseases 25.7; cirrhosis of the liver 23.3; conditions origi-
nating in the perinatal period 22.5; pneumonia and influenza 21.6; homicide
17.1.

Social indicators

Access to services (1994). Proportion of dwellings having: electricity 91.1%;
piped water supply 82.0%; drained sewage 67.7%.
Educational attainment (1992). Percentage of population age 15 and over having: no primary education 14.1%; some primary 22.3%; completed primary
20.7%; incomplete secondary 10.4%; complete secondary 24.2%; higher
8.3%.

Distribution of income (1994)

percentage of household income by quintile

1	2	3	4	5 (highest)
4.8	8.6	12.8	19.5	54.3

Quality of working life. Average workweek (1995): 43.4 hours[2]. Annual rate
(1992) per 100,000 insured workers for: temporary disability 6,426; indemni-
fication for permanent injury 239; death 18. Labour stoppages (1995): 96,
involving 12,249 workers. Average duration of journey to work: n.a. Method
of transport: n.a. Rate per 1,000 workers of discouraged (unemployed no
longer seeking work): n.a.
Social participation. Eligible voters participating in last national election
(1991): c. 60%. Population participating in voluntary work: n.a. Trade union
membership in total workforce: n.a. Practicing religious population in total
affiliated population: national average of weekly attendance (1993) 11%;
(1970) weekly attendance 10% of urban dwellers, 25% of rural dwellers; yearly attendance 55% of urban dwellers, 73% of rural dwellers.
Social deviance (1991). Criminal cases tried by local authorities per 100,000
population for: murder 60.3; rape 22.4; other assault 301.0; theft 703.8.
Incidence per 100,000 in general population of: alcoholism, n.a.; drug and
substance abuse, n.a.[3]; suicide (1994) 2.47.
Leisure (1985). Favourite leisure activities (average daily paid attendance): cinema 582,416; sporting events 31,518; live theatre 16,400; museums and archaeological sites 12,169; bullfights 3,049.
Material well-being (1985). Households possessing: radio 96%; television 73%;
washing machine 33%; automobile 29%; telephone 27%; refrigerator 23%.

National economy

Gross national product (1996): U.S.$314,718,000,000 (U.S.$3,670 per capita).

Structure of gross domestic product and labour force

	1996 in value Mex$'000,000[1]	1996 % of total value	1995[4] labour force	1995[4] % of labour force
Agriculture	74,959.1	5.8	8,378,000	23.6
Mining	17,575.3	1.3	147,000	0.4
Manufacturing	241,487.3	18.7	5,168,000	14.5
Construction	51,196.9	4.0	1,819,000	5.1
Public utilities	20,492.1	1.6	80,000	0.2
Transp. and commun.	120,768.1	9.3	1,461,000	4.1
Trade	236,186.9	18.2	7,799,000	21.9
Finance	195,310.4	15.1	1,104,000	3.1
Pub. admin., defense } Services	263,675.3	20.4	7,765,000	21.8
Other	71,966.2[5]	5.6[5]	1,836,400[6]	5.2[6]
TOTAL	1,293,617.6	100.0	35,558,400[7]	100.0[7]

Budget (1994). Revenue: Mex$213,467,00,000[1] (petroleum revenues 24.8%).
Expenditures: Mex$221,202,000,000[1] (transfers 53.7%, wages and salaries
19.1%, interest on public debt 12.2%).
Public debt (external, outstanding; 1996); U.S.$93,438,000,000.
Tourism (1995): receipts from visitors U.S.$6,164,000,000; expenditures by
nationals abroad U.S.$3,153,000,000.

Manufacturing, mining, and construction enterprises (1993)

	no. of enterprises	no. of employees ('000)	yearly wages as a % of avg. of all wages[8]	value added (Mex$'000,000[1, 8])
Manufacturing	266,033	3,174.4	97.5	20,950,900
Metal products	46,667[9]	955.6[9]	114.2[9]	6,605,300[9]
Chemicals	7,321	371.2	152.3	4,228,000
Food, beverages, and tobacco	91,894	679.3	86.4	3,378,700
Textiles and apparel	44,071	530.6	80.0	2,414,800
Iron and steel	401	57.4	128.2	1,332,400
Nonmetallic mineral products	24,397	181.8	98.6	1,177,700
Paper and printing	15,022	193.2	100.0	1,127,900
Wood and wood products	31,549	162.6	62.8	497,000
Nonelectrical machinery and transport equipment	9	9	...9	9
Electrical machinery	9	9	...9	9
Other manufactures	4,711	42.7	...	189,200
Mining	2,845	95.6	161.0	1,643,800
Construction	5,308[8]	342.4[8]	62.1	1,414,800

Production (metric tons except as noted). Agriculture, forestry, fishing (1996):
sugarcane 46,980,000, corn (maize) 17,300,000, sorghum 4,817,000, wheat
3,563,000, oranges 3,556,000, bananas 2,158,000, tomatoes 2,145,000, dry
beans 1,495,000, mangoes 1,420,000, lemons and limes 1,001,000, apples
645,000, barley 616,000, cottonseed 596,000, grapes 535,000, rice 455,000, soybeans 350,000, pineapples 181,000, strawberries 85,000, walnuts 18,000; livestock (number of live animals) 28,141,000 cattle, 15,405,000 pigs, 10,500,000
goats, 6,250,000 horses, 5,987,000 sheep, 3,550,000 turkeys, 3,270,000 mules,
3,250,000 asses, 386,000,000 chickens; roundwood (1995) 22,034,000 cu m; fish
catch (1995) 1,358,000. Mining and quarrying (value of production [metal
content] in Mex$'000[1]; 1993): copper 2,236,437; silver 1,339,057; zinc
1,321,759; gold 605,850; iron 530,658; lead 457,307; sulfur 219,833; gypsum
160,139; dolomite 119,728; fluorite 110,838; molybdenum 88,043; manganese
77,918; silica 68,956; bismuth 25,166; celestite 25,045. Manufacturing (gross
value of production in Mex$'000[1]; 1994): machinery and equipment
82,169,495; food, beverages, and tobacco products 64,399,498; chemical prod-

ucts 50,455,651; metal products 25,363,292; mineral products 17,074,973; paper and paper products 9,209,617; textiles 8,555,146. Construction (gross value of new construction, in Mex$'000,000[1]; 1985): residential 154,835; nonresidential 168,096.

Trade and service enterprises (1993)

	no. of establishments	no. of employees	yearly wage as a % of avg. of all wages[10]	annual income (Mex$'000,000[1])
Trade	1,208,779	2,969,786	...	565,728,373
Wholesale	68,919	631,802	...	249,597,035
Retail	1,139,860	2,337,984	...	316,131,338
Boutiques (excluding food products)	422,299	922,890	...	108,507,889
Food and tobacco speciality stores	671,050	991,911	...	65,305,180
Automobile, tire, and auto parts dealers	32,138	152,821	...	47,888,576
Small supermarkets and grocery stores	8,719	168,752	...	48,769,283
Gasoline stations	3,042	35,340	...	32,517,091
Other	2,612	66,270	...	13,143,319
Services	711,843	2,766,750	85.2	200,001,682
Professional services	130,475	652,148	77.9	53,533,318
Food and beverage services	677	11,258	...	1,012,369
Transp. and travel agencies	9,967	62,767	133.4	11,858,406
Lodging	9,913	151,445	...	8,960,922
Automotive repair	112,293	252,950	...	7,263,560
Educational services (private)	20,622	247,086	134.3	10,815,238
Medical and social assistance	79,748	203,348	206.4	7,497,794
Amusement services (cinemas and theatres)	4,855	65,608	148.9	9,845,129
Recreation	20,973	65,936	...	3,065,672
Other repair	72,129	104,478	...	2,625,370
Commercial and professional organizations	1,946	11,946	77.9	264,770
Other	248,245	937,780	49.9	83,259,134

Energy production (consumption): electricity (kW-hr; 1994) 144,276,000,000 (143,447,000,000); coal (metric tons; 1994) 8,898,000 (9,188,000); crude petroleum (barrels; 1994) 972,000,000 (500,000,000); petroleum products (metric tons; 1994) 83,618,000 (89,164,000); natural gas (cu m; 1994) 26,378,000,000 (27,206,000,000).
Population economically active (1995): total 35,558,484; activity rate of total population 39.4% (participation rates: ages 15–64, 61.8%; female 32.6%; unemployed 4.7%[4]).

Price and earnings indexes (1990 = 100)

	1991	1992	1993	1994	1995	1996	1997
Consumer price index	122.7	141.7	155.5	166.3	224.5	301.7	364.0
Monthly earnings index	129.1	292.9	164.7	174.6	192.1	279.2[11]	300.9

Household income and expenditure. Average household size (1992) 4.8; income per household (1989) Mex$3,461[1] (U.S.$1,384); sources of income (1992): wages and salaries 61.5%, property and entrepreneurship 29.1%, transfer payments 7.8%, other 1.6%; expenditure (1992): food, beverages, and tobacco 36.9%, housing (includes household furnishings) 25.2%, transportation and communications 10.1%, clothing and footwear 8.5%, recreation and entertainment 5.5%, health and medical services 3.5%.

Financial aggregates[1, 12]

	1991	1992	1993	1994	1995	1996	1997 (7 mo.)
Exchange rate, Mex$ per:							
U.S. dollar	3.018	3.095	3.116	3.375	6.419	7.599	7.886
£	5.114	5.464	4.680	5.164	10.132	11.867	13.180
SDR	4.393	4.284	4.266	7.774	11.361	11.289	10.609
International reserves (U.S.$)							
Total (excl. gold; '000,000)	17,726	18,942	25,110	6,278	16,847	19,433	24,566
SDRs ('000,000)	586	548	223	177	1,597	257	568
Reserve pos. in IMF ('000,000)	—	—	—	—	—	—	—
Foreign exchange	17,140	18,394	24,886	6,101	15,250	17,217	19,176
Gold ('000,000 fine troy oz)	0.92	0.69	0.48	0.43	0.51	0.26	0.22
% world reserves	0.10	0.07	0.05	0.05	0.06	0.03	0.02
Interest and prices							
Treasury bill rate	19.28	15.62	15.03	14.10	48.44	31.39	18.80
Balance of payments (U.S.$'000,000)							
Balance of visible trade, of which:	−7,279	−15,934	−13,481	−18,464	+7,089	+6,531	...
Imports, f.o.b.	−49,966	−62,130	−65,366	−79,347	−72,454	−89,469	...
Exports, f.o.b.	42,687	46,196	51,885	60,882	79,543	96,000	...
Balance of invisibles	−7,609	−8,508	−9,919	−11,198	−8,665	−8,454	...
Balance of payments, current account	−14,888	−24,442	−23,400	−29,662	−1,576	−1,923	...

Land use (1994): forest 25.5%; pasture 39.0%; agriculture 13.0%; other 22.5%.

Foreign trade

Balance of trade (current prices)

	1990	1991	1992	1993	1994	1995
Mex$'000,000,000	−7,494.0	−27,746	−57,138	−53,615	−80,166	+19,923
% of total	4.7%	14.4%	25.1%	22.2%	25.6%	3.4%

Imports (1996): U.S.$89,468,800,000 (intermediate goods 80.4%; capital goods 12.2%; consumer goods 7.4%). *Major import sources:* U.S. 75.6%; Japan 4.4%; Germany 3.5%; Canada 1.9%; South Korea 1.3%; France 1.1%.
Exports (1996): U.S.$97,922,700,000 (manufacturing goods 82.1%; crude petroleum 10.9%; agricultural goods 3.7%). *Major export destinations:* U.S. 84.0%; Japan 1.4%; Canada 1.2%; Italy 1.2%; Spain 1.0%; Germany 0.7%.

Trade by commodity group (1995)

	imports		exports	
SITC group	U.S.$'000,000	%	U.S.$'000,000	%
00 Food and live animals	3,225	4.4	5,434	6.8
01 Beverages and tobacco	144	0.2	585	0.7
02 Crude materials, excluding fuels	3,213	4.4	2,007	2.5
03 Mineral fuels, lubricants, and related materials	1,585	2.1	8,186	10.3
04 Animal and vegetable oils, fats, and waxes	581	0.8	—	—
05 Chemicals and related products, n.e.s.	6,899	9.3	3,876	4.9
06 Basic manufactures	12,377	16.7	8,982	11.3
07 Machinery and transport equipment	31,693	42.8	41,634	52.4
08 Miscellaneous manufactured articles	9,318	12.6	8,507	10.7
09 Goods not classified by kind	4,958	6.7	218	0.3
TOTAL[13]	73,993	100.0	79,489[7]	100.0[7]

Direction of trade (1996)

	imports		exports	
	U.S.$'000,000	%	U.S.$'000,000	%
Western Hemisphere	71,590	80.0	87,742	91.4
United States	67,629	75.6	80,663	84.0
Latin America and the Caribbean	2,217	2.5	5,898	6.2
Canada	1,744	1.9	1,181	1.2
Europe	8,423	9.4	4,798	5.0
EU	7,733	8.7	4,190	4.4
EFTA	484	0.5	398	0.4
Russia	—	—	—	—
Other Europe	206	0.2	210	0.2
Asia	8,587	9.6	2,457	2.5
Japan	3,901	4.4	1,363	1.4
Africa	219	0.3	65	0.1
Other	645	0.7	929	1.0
TOTAL	89,464	100.0	95,991	100.0

Transport and communications

Transport. Railroads (1995): route length (1996) 16,543 mi, 26,623 km; passenger-mi 1,118,000,000, passenger-km 1,800,000,000; short ton-mi cargo 24,509,000,000, metric ton-km cargo 37,243,000,000. Roads (1996): total length 194,054 mi, 312,301 km (paved 36%[14]). Vehicles (1995): passenger cars 8,330,000; trucks and buses 4,221,000. Merchant marine (1992): vessels (100 gross tons and over) 635; total deadweight tonnage 1,495,311. Air transport (1996): passenger-mi 12,901,853,000, passenger-km 20,763,559,000; short ton-mi cargo 1,348,141,000, metric ton-km cargo 1,968,250,000; airports (1996) 83.

Communications

Medium	date	unit	number	units per 1,000 persons
Daily newspapers	1995	circulation	10,500,000	115
Radio	1996	receivers	21,000,000	227
Television	1995	receivers	17,600,000	192
Telephones	1995	main lines	8,736,000	96
Cellular telephones	1995	subscribers	642,000	7.0
Facsimile machines	1995	units	180,000	2.0
Personal computers	1995	units	2,400,000	26

Education and health

Literacy (1995): total population age 15 and over literate 89.6%; males literate 91.8%; females literate 87.4%.

Education (1994–95)

	schools	teachers	students	student/teacher ratio
Primary (age 6–12)	91,857	507,669	14,572,202	28.7
Secondary (age 12–18)	22,255	256,831	4,493,173	17.5
Voc., teacher tr.[15]	6,571	77,347	1,076,700	13.9
Higher	10,341	319,561	3,763,938	11.8

Health (1994): physicians 146,021 (1 per 613 persons); hospital beds 74,891 (1 per 1,196 persons); infant mortality rate per 1,000 live births (1995) 17.5.
Food (1995): daily per capita caloric intake 3,136 (vegetable products 84%, animal products 16%); 131% of FAO recommended minimum requirement.

Military

Total active duty personnel (1997): 175,000 (army 74.3%, navy 21.1%, air force 4.6%). *Military expenditure as percentage of GNP* (1995): 1.0% (world 2.8%); per capita expenditure U.S.$25.

[1]The Mexican new peso, equivalent to 1,000 old Mexican pesos, was introduced on Jan. 1, 1993. On Jan. 1, 1996, the name of the currency was changed to Mexican peso. [2]Manufacturing only. [3]Through 1982, cannabis remained the most abused drug. [4]2nd quarter. [5]Imputed bank service charge. [6]Includes 1,677,400 unemployed persons. [7]Detail does not add to total given because of rounding. [8]1988. [9]Metal products includes Nonelectrical machinery and transport equipment and Electrical machinery. [10]1984. [11]4th quarter. [12]Exchange rates and treasury bill rates are period averages; international reserves are expressed in end-of-period rates. [13]Totals include adjustments of unspecified nature. [14]1993. [15]1992–93.

Internet resources for further information:
• **National Institute of Statistics, Geography, and Informatics**
  http://www.inegi.gob.mx/homeing/homeinegi/homeing.html

Micronesia, Federated States of

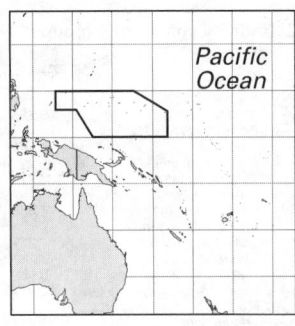

Pacific Ocean

Official name: Federated States of Micronesia.
Political status: federal republic in free association with the United States with one legislative house (Congress [14])[1].
Head of state and government: President.
Capital: Palikir, on Pohnpei.
Official language: none.
Official religion: none.
Monetary unit: 1 U.S. dollar (U.S.$) = 100 cents; valuation (Sept. 25, 1998) 1 £ = U.S.$1.70.

Area and population

States Major Islands	area		population
	sq mi	sq km	1994 census
Chuuk(Truk)	49.1	127.2	53,319
Weno (Moen) Islands	7.0	18.1	16,121
Kosrae	42.3	109.6	7,317
Kosrae Island	42.3	109.6	7,317
Pohnpei	133.3	345.2	33,692
Pohnpei Island	129.0	334.1	31,540
Yap	45.9	118.9	11,178
Yap Island	38.7	100.2	6,919
TOTAL	270.8[2]	701.4[2]	105,506

Demography

Population (1998): 108,000.
Density (1998): persons per sq mi 398.8, persons per sq km 154.0.
Urban-rural (1992): urban 26.0%; rural 74.0%.
Sex distribution (1994): male 51.11%; female 48.89%.
Age breakdown (1994): under 15, 43.5%; 15–29, 26.7%; 30–44, 16.8%; 45–59, 7.5%; 60–74, 4.4%; 75 and over, 4.4%.
Population projection: (2000) 110,000; (2010) 120,000.
Doubling time: 36 years.
Ethnic composition (1994): Chuukese 46.7%; Pohnpeian 24.3%; Kosraean 6.8%; Yapese 5.4%; Mortlockese 4.9%; Filipino 0.8%; other 11.1%.
Religious affiliation (1996): Christianity is the predominant religious tradition; Catholic 52.9%, Protestant 47.1%; the Kosraeans, Pohnpeians, and Trukese are mostly Protestant and the Yapese mostly Roman Catholic.
Major cities (1994): Weno (Moen) 16,121; Tol 4,816; Kolonia 6,660.

Vital statistics

Birth rate per 1,000 population (1995): 23.7 (world avg. 25.0); legitimate, n.a.; illegitimate, n.a.
Death rate per 1,000 population (1995): 4.0 (world avg. 9.3).
Natural increase rate per 1,000 population (1995): 19.7 (world avg. 15.7).
Total fertility rate (avg. births per childbearing woman; 1994): 2.5.
Marriage rate per 1,000 population: n.a.
Divorce rate per 1,000 population: n.a.
Life expectancy at birth (1994): male 65.7 years; female 69.6 years.
Major causes of death per 100,000 population (1991)[3]: diseases of the cerebrovascular system 89.6; diseases of the respiratory system 42.8, of which tuberculosis 8.9; malignant neoplasms (cancers) 38.8; homicide, suicide, and accidents 30.8; infectious and parasitic diseases 22.9 (with especially high morbidity rates for tuberculosis and leprosy).

National economy

Budget (1994–95). Revenue: U.S.$172,500,000 (external grants 65.1%; tax revenue 12.2%; fishing rights fees 12.1%). Expenditures: U.S.$169,100,000 (current expenditures 82.6%, of which government services 74.4%, transfer payments 7.0%, debt services 3.0%; capital expenditure 17.4%).
Public debt (external, outstanding; 1994–95): U.S.$119,500,000.
Production (metric tons except as noted). Agriculture, forestry, fishing: n.a.; however, Micronesia's major crops include coconuts (which provide annually more than 4,000 tons of copra), breadfruit, cassava, sweet potatoes, peppers, and a variety of tropical fruits (including bananas); livestock comprises mostly pigs and poultry; fish catch (1995) 21,150, of which skipjack tuna 15,000, yellowfin tuna 5,000. Mining and quarrying: quarrying of sand and aggregate for local construction only. Manufacturing: n.a.; however, copra and coconut oil, traditionally important products, are being displaced by garment production; the manufacture of handicrafts and personal items (clothing, mats, boats, etc.) by individuals is also important. Construction: n.a. Energy production (consumption): electricity (kW-hr; 1990) 40,000,000 (40,000,000); coal, none (n.a.); crude petroleum, none (n.a.); petroleum products (metric tons; 1992) none (77,000); natural gas, none (n.a.).
Household income and expenditure. Average household size (1994) 6.8; annual income per household (1994) U.S.$8,645; sources of income (1994): wages and salaries 51.8%, operating surplus 23.0%, social security 2.1%; expenditure (1985): food and beverages 73.5%.
Land use (1984)[4]: forested 22.5%; meadows and pastures 13.5%; agricultural and under permanent cultivation 33.5%; other 30.5%.
Gross national product (at current market prices; 1995): U.S.$215,000,000 (U.S.$2,040 per capita).

Structure of gross domestic product and labour force

	1983		1994	
	in value U.S.$'000,000	% of total value	labour force	% of labour force
Agriculture and fishing	44.9	42.2	7,375[5]	26.7[5]
Mining			42	0.2
Manufacturing			656	2.4
Construction			1,171	4.2
Public utilities	17.4	16.3	279	1.0
Transp. and commun.			727	2.6
Finance			632	2.3
Services			2,125	7.7
Trade	12.7	11.9	2,258	8.2
Public administration	31.5	29.6	8,092	29.3
Other			4,216[6]	15.2[6]
TOTAL	106.5	100.0	27,573	100.0[2]

Population economically active (1994): total 27,573; activity rate of total population 26.3% (participation rates: ages 15–64, 60.6%[7]; female 33.8%; unemployed 15.3%).

Price and earnings indexes (1992 = 100)

	1990	1991	1992	1993	1994	1995
Price index	91.6	95.2	100.0	106.0	110.2	114.6
Annual wage index[8]	...	...	100.0	109.4	110.3	115.8

Tourism (1990): number of visitors 23,171.

Foreign trade

Balance of trade (current prices)

	1989	1990	1991	1992	1993	1994
U.S.$'000,000	−55.4	−62.2	−59.9	−57.3	−80.3	−50.5
% of total	61.6%	58.9%	51.0%	40.8%	57.9%	24.3%

Imports (1994): U.S.$129,060,000 (manufactured goods 32.0%; food, beverages, and tobacco 24.3%; machinery and transport equipment 23.5%; mineral fuels 14.3%; chemicals 4.4%). *Major import sources:* United States (including Guam) 56.1%; Japan 32.0%; Australia 3.5%.
Exports (1994): U.S.$78,570,000 (marine products 94.3%; clothing and textiles 2.8%; agricultural products 2.1%, of which bananas 0.6%, copra 0.5%). *Major export destinations* (1992): Japan 80.0%; United States 9.3%; Guam 8.3%; South Pacific Region 2.4%.

Transport and communications

Transport. Railroads: none. Roads (1990): total length 140 mi, 226 km (paved 17%). Vehicles: passenger cars, trucks, and buses, n.a. Merchant marine (1997[9]): vessels (100 gross tons and over) 19; deadweight tonnage 9,200. Air transport: n.a.; airports (1997) with scheduled flights 4.

Communications				units per 1,000 persons
Medium	date	unit	number	
Radio	1995	receivers	70,000	664
Television	1995	receivers	2,000	19.0
Telephones	1995	main lines	7,900	74.9
Facsimile machines	1995	units	300	2.8

Education and health

Educational attainment (1994). Percentage of population age 25 and over having: no formal schooling 22.8%; some primary education 30.3%; some secondary 15.1%; secondary 13.6%; some college 13.6%; bachelors degree 3.1%; higher 1.6%. *Literacy* (1994): total population age 10 and over literate 69,779 (93.9%); males literate 35,688 (94.7%); females literate 34,091 (93.0%).

Education (1994)	schools[10]	teachers	students	student/ teacher ratio
Elementary (age 6–12)	177	1,051[11]	22,420	22.2[11]
Secondary (age 13–18)	16	314[11]	8,701	13.2[11]
College	1	...	1,461	...

Health (1993): physicians 50 (1 per 2,069 persons); hospital beds 325 (1 per 318 persons); infant mortality rate per 1,000 live births (1995) 20.4.
Food: daily per capita caloric intake, n.a.

Military

External security is provided by the United States.

[1]On Nov. 3, 1986, the United States unilaterally terminated the UN trusteeship it held over the Federated States of Micronesia (FSM), thus formally initiating their free-association political status. On Dec. 22, 1990, the United Nations Security Council joined the Trusteeship Council, which had endorsed the termination of the trusteeship in May 1986. [2]Detail does not add to total given because of rounding. [3]Based on registered deaths only. [4]Includes all areas formerly constituting the U.S. Trust Territory of the Pacific Islands. [5]Includes subsistence farming and fishing. [6]Unemployed. [7]1990. [8]Public sector only. [9]January 1. [10]1987–88. [11]1984–85.

Internet resources for further information:
• General Information on The FSM http://fsmgov.org/fsmgov

Moldova

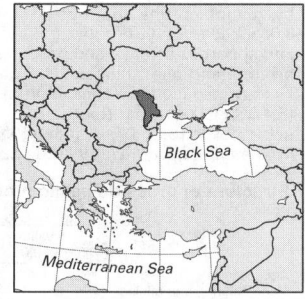

Official name: Republica Moldova (Republic of Moldova).
Form of government: unitary multiparty republic with a single legislative body (Parliament [101]).
Head of state: President.
Head of government: Prime Minister.
Capital: Chişinău.
Official language: Romanian[1].
Official religion: none.
Monetary unit: 1 Moldovan leu (plural lei) = 100 bani; valuation (Sept. 25, 1998) free rate, 1 U.S.$ = 4.95 Moldovan lei; 1 £ = 8.43 Moldovan lei.

Area and population
Administrative subdivisions[2]

Cities	area sq km	population 1993	Rural districts	area sq km	population 1993
Bălţi	...	159,420	Drochia	780	80,828
Cahul	...	43,259	Dubăsari	670	53,962
Chişinău	160	735,229	Edineţ	860	90,948
Dubăsari	...	24,243	Fălești	1,070	95,025
Orhei	...	37,887	Floreşti	830	76,987
Râbniţa	...	61,824	Glodeni	760	65,781
Soroca	...	41,461	Grigoriopol	820	52,326
Tighina (Bendery)	...	137,423	Hânceşti	1,350	118,255
Tiraspol	...	203,865	Ialoveni	930	87,749
Ungheni	...	38,462	Leova	720	51,987
			Nisporeni	760	81,626
Rural districts			Ocniţa	660	63,073
Anenii Noi	830	77,468	Orhei	1,100	95,523
Basarabeasca	660	43,765	Râbniţa	850	32,793
Brinceni	810	83,340	Rezina	670	55,494
Cahul	800	44,489	Rişcani	1,000	83,456
Cainari	...	42,755	Sângerei	1,020	91,684
Călăraş	760	84,442	Slobozia	960	113,823
Camenca	820	59,356	Şoldăneşti	560	46,696
Cantemir	860	61,126	Soroca	870	58,097
Căuşeni	1,120	72,999	Ştefan-Vodă	1,030	76,702
Ciadâr-Lunga	720	68,698	Străşeni	760	96,107
Cimişlia	1,170	61,089	Taraclia	620	45,912
Comrat	840	71,273	Teleneşti	860	76,886
Criuleni	850	91,783	Ungheni	1,070	79,525
Donduşeni	890	66,483	Vulcăneşti	930	62,193
			TOTAL	33,700[3]	4,345,577

Demography
Population (1998): 4,243,000.
Density (1998): persons per sq mi 326.4, persons per sq km 125.9.
Urban-rural (1995): urban 46.8%; rural 53.2%.
Sex distribution (1995): male 47.76%; female 52.24%.
Age breakdown (1989): under 15, 27.9%; 15–29, 22.9%; 30–44, 21.0%; 45–59, 15.6%; 60–74, 9.7%; 75 and over, 2.9%.
Population projection: (2000) 4,252,000; (2010) 4,397,000.
Doubling time: not applicable; doubling time exceeds 100 years.
Ethnic composition (1989): Moldovan 62.0%; Ukrainian 8.5%; Russian 23.1%; Gagauz 3.2%; Bulgarian 1.6%; other 1.6%.
Religious affiliation (1995): Orthodox 46.0%, of which Romanian Orthodox 35.0%, Russian Orthodox 9.5%; Catholic 1.8%, of which Roman Catholic 0.6%; Protestant 1.7%; Jewish 0.9%; other (mostly nonreligious) 49.6%.
Major cities (1993): Chişinău 657,775; Tiraspol 184,852; Bălţi 156,081.

Vital statistics
Birth rate per 1,000 population (1997): 14.3 (world avg. 25.0); (1995) legitimate 87.7%; illegitimate 12.3%.
Death rate per 1,000 population (1997): 12.3 (world avg. 9.3).
Natural increase rate per 1,000 population (1997): 2.0 (world avg. 15.7).
Total fertility rate (avg. births per childbearing woman; 1997): 1.9.
Marriage rate per 1,000 population(1994): 7.8.
Life expectancy at birth (1994): male 64.0 years; female 71.0 years.
Major causes of death per 100,000 population (1994): circulatory diseases 500.7; cancers 136.1; accidents and violence 113.3; digestive system diseases 110.4; respiratory diseases 75.1.

National economy
Budget (1995). Revenue: 1,916,000,000,000 lei (value-added tax 29.7%, enterprise profits tax 20.5%, income tax 10.5%, excise duties 9.7%, property tax 5.4%). Expenditures: 2,354,000,000,000 lei (education 24.1%, health care 15.6% interest payments 11.3%).
Public debt (external, outstanding; 1996): U.S.$559,500,000.
Land use (1994): forest 10.6%; pasture 10.9%; agriculture 75.9%; other 2.6%.
Production (metric tons except as noted). Agriculture, forestry, fishing (1996): sugar beets 1,807,000, grapes 850,000, corn (maize) 750,000, wheat 614,000, potatoes 331,000, apples 330,000; livestock (number of live animals) 1,302,000 sheep, 1,015,000 pigs, 726,000 cattle, 14,000,000 poultry; roundwood (1991) 125,000 cu m; fish catch (1995) 4,700. Mining and quarrying (1995): sand and gravel 376,000; gypsum 13,600. Manufacturing ('000,000 lei; 1995): food processing 1,446,824; machinery and metalworking 383,153; construction materials 164,198; textiles 57,283. Construction (1994): 127,200,000 lei. Energy production (consumption): electricity (kW-hr; 1994): 8,228,000,000 (8,579,000,000); coal (metric tons; 1994) none (2,141,000); crude petroleum (barrels; 1990) none (51,625,000); petroleum products (metric tons; 1994) none (1,085,000); natural gas (cu m; 1994) none (2,611,000,000).

Gross national product (1996): U.S.$2,542,000,000 (U.S.$590 per capita).

Structure of gross domestic product and labour force

	1994			
	in value '000 lei	% of total value	labour force	% of labour force
Agriculture	1,877,607	43.3	767,000	45.1
Manufacturing, mining	1,402,883	32.3	232,000	13.7
Public utilities	...	...	39,000	2.2
Construction	429,551	9.9	91,000	5.4
Transp. and commun.	350,028	8.1	73,000	4.3
Trade	253,969	5.8	107,000	6.3
Finance	...	...	20,000	1.2
Pub. admin., defense	...	...	32,000	1.9
Services	8,176	0.2	305,000	18.0
Other	15,879	0.4	33,000	1.9
TOTAL	4,339,079[4]	100.0	1,699,000	100.0

Population economically active (1994): total (1995) 1,693,000; activity rate of total population 44.8% (participation rates: ages 16–59 [male], 16–54 [female] 85.2%; female 53.0%; unemployed 1.4%).

Price and earnings indexes (1990 = 100)

	1990	1991	1992	1993	1994	1995
Consumer price index	100.0	262.0	3,605	33,780	71,310	88,420
Earnings index	100.0	183.0	402.0	353.0	192.0	244.0

Household income and expenditure. Average household size (1989) 3.4; income per household: n.a.; sources of income (1994): wages and salaries 41.2%, social benefits 15.3%, agricultural income 10.4%, other 33.1%; expenditure (1995): food and drink 49.1%, clothing 9.7%, health 4.1%.

Foreign trade

Balance of trade (current prices)

	1993	1994	1995	1996
U.S.$'000,000	−180	−54	−32	−274
% of total	16.6%	4.2%	2.1%	14.5%

Imports (1995): U.S.$773,000,000 (mineral products 46.0%, machinery 16.0%, agricultural goods and foodstuffs 9.0%, chemical products 8.0%, textiles and textile products 5.0%, metal and metal products 4.0%, other 12.0%). *Major import sources* (1995): Russia 32.0%; Ukraine 26.0%; Romania 7.0%.
Exports (1995): U.S.$741,000,000 (food and agricultural goods 72.0%, machinery 8.0%, textile products 5.0%, metals and metal products 4.0%, chemical products 1.0%, mineral products 1.0%, other 9.0%). *Major export destinations* (1995): Russia 47.0%; Romania 14.0%; Ukraine 8.0%; Belarus 4.0%.

Transport and communications
Transport. Railroads (1995): length 1,200 km; passenger-km 1,019,000,000; metric ton-km cargo 3,133,600,000. Roads (1995): total length 12,259 km (paved 87.2%). Vehicles (1995): passenger cars 169,941; trucks, and buses 69,069. Air transport (1994): passenger-km 225,000; metric ton-km cargo 1,000,000; airports (1997) 1.

Communications

Medium	date	unit	number	units per 1,000 persons
Daily newspapers	1994	circulation	106,000	24
Radio	1996	receivers	1,550,000	209
Television	1995	receivers	1,300	30
Telephones	1995	main lines	566,500	131
Facsimile machines	1995	units	600	0.1
Personal computers	1995	units	9,000	2.1

Education and health
Educational attainment (1989). Percentage of population age 15 and over having: no formal schooling or some primary education 24.5%; some secondary 20.4%; secondary or some postsecondary 46.4%; higher 8.7%. *Literacy* (1989): total population age 15 and over literate 96.4%.

Education (1995–96)

	schools	teachers	students	student/ teacher ratio
Primary (age 7–13) } Secondary (age 14–17) }	1,700	48,000	733,000	15.3
Voc., teacher tr.	64		27,943	
Higher	20	8,846	87,700	9.9

Health (1995): physicians 17,200 (1 per 250 persons); hospital beds 53,000 (1 per 82 persons); infant mortality rate per 1,000 live births 22.6.
Food (1995): daily per capita caloric intake 2,525 (vegetable products 81%, animal products 19%); 99% of FAO recommended minimum requirement.

Military
Total active duty personnel (1997): 11,030 (army 84.3%, air force 15.7%). *Military expenditure as percentage of GNP* (1995): 0.1% (world 2.8%); per capita expenditure U.S.$3.

[1]Officially designated Moldovan per constitution. [2]Area and population figures include the Gagauz autonomous region (1,800 sq km; pop. c. 200,000), recognized by the Moldovan government, and the separatist Transdniestrian republic (5,000 sq km; pop. c. 800,000), not recognized by the Moldovan government. [3]Total includes approximately 320 sq km (125 sq mi) not distributed by administrative subdivision. [4]Detail does not add to total given because of rounding.

Internet resources for further information:
• Moldova.Net http://www.moldova.net/

Mongolia

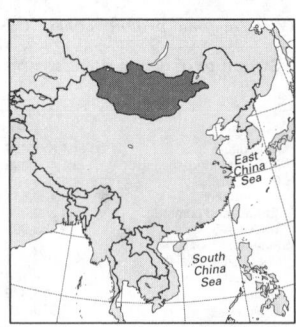

Official name: Mongol Uls
　(Mongolia).
Form of government: unitary multiparty
　republic with one legislative house
　(State Great Hural [76]).
Chief of state: President.
Head of govenment: Prime Minister.
Capital: Ulaanbaatar (Ulan Bator).
Official language: Khalkha Mongolian.
Official religion: none.
Monetary unit: 1 tugrik (Tug) = 100
　möngö; valuation (Sept. 25, 1998) 1
　U.S.\$ = Tug 840.56; 1 £ = Tug 1,431.05.

Area and population

Provinces	Capitals	area sq mi	area sq km	population 1997[1] estimate
Arhangay	Tsetserleg	21,000	55,000	105,000
Bayan-Ölgiy	Ölgiy	18,000	46,000	92,300
Bayanhongor	Bayanhongor	45,000	116,000	91,200
Bulgan	Bulgan	19,000	49,000	64,300
Darhan-Uul	Darhan	100	200	91,000
Dornod	Choybalsan	47,700	123,500	86,800
Dornogovi	Saynshand	43,000	111,000	48,900
Dundgovi	Manalgovi	30,000[2]	78,000[2]	53,700
Dzavhan	Uliastay	32,000	82,000	107,600
Govi-Altay	Altay	55,000	142,000	75,400
Govi-Sümber	Choyr	2	2	12,600
Hentiy	Öndörhaan	32,000	82,000	76,500
Hovd	Hovd	29,000	76,000	92,700
Hövsgöl	Mörön	39,000	101,000	122,000
Ömnögovi	Dalandzadgad	64,000	165,000	45,800
Orhon	Erdenet	300	800	66,700
Övörhangay	Arvayheer	24,000	63,000	115,100
Selenge	Sühbaatar	16,000	42,000	104,400
Sühbaatar	Baruun-Urt	32,000	82,000	60,200
Töv	Dzüünmod	31,000	81,000	112,200
Uvs	Ulaangom	27,000	69,000	104,300
Autonomous municipality				
Ulaanbaatar	—	800	2,000	627,300
TOTAL		**604,800[3]**	**1,566,500**	**2,356,000**

Demography

Population (1998): 2,413,000.
Density (1998): persons per sq mi 4.0, persons per sq km 1.5.
Urban-rural (1995): urban 62.0%; rural 38.0%.
Sex distribution (1997): male 50.04%; female 49.96%.
Age breakdown (1997): under 15, 37.7%; 15–29, 29.7%; 30–44, 19.1%; 45–59, 7.9%; 60–69, 4.3%; 70 and over, 1.3%.
Population projection: (2000) 2,496,000; (2010) 2,952,000.
Doubling time: 47 years.
Ethnic composition (1989): Khalkha Mongol 78.8%; Kazak 5.9%; Dörbed Mongol 2.7%; Bayad 1.9%; Buryat Mongol 1.7%; Dariganga Mongol 1.4%; other 7.6%.
Religious affiliation (1995): Tantric Buddhist (Lamaism) 96.0%; Muslim 4.0%.
Major cities (1996): Ulaanbaatar (Ulan Bator) 627,300[4]; Darhan 87,100; Choybalsan 79,900; Erdenet 59,100; Ölgiy (1991) 29,400.

Vital statistics

Birth rate per 1,000 population (1997): 25.0 (world avg. 25.0).
Death rate per 1,000 population (1997): 8.0 (world avg. 9.3).
Natural increase rate per 1,000 population (1997): 17.0 (world avg. 15.7).
Total fertility rate (avg. births per childbearing woman; 1997): 2.9.
Marriage rate per 1,000 population (1989): 7.8.
Divorce rate per 1,000 population (1989): 0.5.
Life expectancy at birth (1996): male 64.0 years; female 67.0 years.
Major causes of death per 100,000 population: n.a.; however, in the early 1990s, major causes of mortality included diseases of the cardiovascular system, diseases of the respiratory system, and diseases of the cerebrovascular system.

National economy

Budget (1997). Revenue: Tug 157,802,100,000 (taxes 69.7%, of which income tax 18.9%, social security contribution 14.5%, customs duties 13.2%, sales tax 13.1%; nontax revenue 30.3%). Expenditures: Tug 184,105,800,000 (social and cultural services, education, and health 58.6%; capital investment 11.0%; defense 8.1%; salaries in state-run enterprises 7.3%).
Public debt (external; 1996): U.S.\$474,000,000.
Population economically active (1995): total 868,200; activity rate of total population 37.7% (participation rates: ages 16–59 [1989] 77.9%; female [1992] 46.0%; unemployed 7.6%).

Price and earnings indexes (1990 = 100)

	1991	1992	1993	1994	1995	1996	1997
Consumer price index	...	363.7	1,340	2,513	4,033	5,882	8,506
Monthly earnings index	184.0	260.1	991.4	2,071.8	2,781.3	...	...

Production (metric tons except as noted). Agriculture, forestry, fishing (1997): wheat 198,060, potatoes 47,047, vegetables and melons 25,000; livestock (number of live animals) 13,606,000 sheep, 9,134,000 goats, 3,476,300 cattle, 2,400,000 horses, 390,000 camels, 19,085 pigs; roundwood (1995) 883,500 cu m; fish catch (1995) 130. Mining and quarrying (1996): fluorspar 565,100; copper 351,500; molybdenum 4,684; gold 5,242 kg. Manufacturing (value added

by manufacturing in Tug '000,000; 1994): textiles 8,899.7; food products 8,055.2; leather and footwear 2,415.5; construction materials 1,863.0; clothing and apparel 1,259.8; wood products 1,209.4; beverages 944.5; chemicals 413.4; printing and publishing 339.9. Construction (1994): residential 120,400 sq m. Energy production (consumption): electricity (kW-hr; 1994) 3,265,000,000 (3,472,000,000); coal (metric tons; 1994) 635,000 (635,000); petroleum products (metric tons; 1994) none (595,000).
Gross national product (1996): U.S.\$902,000,000 (U.S.\$360 per capita).

Structure of gross domestic product and labour force

	1995 in value Tug '000,005	1995 % of total value	1995 labour force	1995 % of labour force
Agriculture	1,430	16.1	345,300	39.8
Manufacturing and mining	2,404	27.0	101,300	11.7
Construction	208	2.3	27,700	3.2
Transp. and commun.	366	4.1	32,000	3.7
Trade	1,569	17.6	85,800	9.9
Services[6]	2,931[7]	32.9[7]	110,800	12.8
Other			165,300[8]	19.0[8]
TOTAL	**8,908**	**100.0**	**868,200**	**100.0[3]**

Household income and expenditure. Average family size (1993) 4.4; income per household (1992)[9] Tug 5,500 (U.S.\$140); sources of income (1993): wages and salaries 72.1%, transfer payments 9.7%, self-employment 9.5%[10], other 8.7%; expenditure (1991): food 48.6%, clothing 21.9%, housing 10.5%, transportation and communications 6.8%, household goods 4.1%.
Land use (1994): forest 8.8%; pasture 74.8%; agriculture 0.8%; other 15.6%.

Foreign trade

Balance of trade (current prices)

	1991	1992	1993	1994	1995	1996
U.S.\$'000,000	−12.9	−29.8	+19.4	+101.5	+58.0	−15.5
% of total	1.8%	3.7%	2.6%	18.6%	6.5%	1.8%

Imports (1996): U.S.\$438,283,000 (machinery and electronics 22.4%, mineral products 20.0%, motor vehicles and transport equipment 17.2%, food, beverages, and tobacco 13.1%, metals and finished products 7.3%). *Major import sources:* Russia 34.2%; Japan 17.5%; Germany 4.7%; South Korea 4.0%; Singapore 2.9%; U.S. 2.5%.
Exports (1996): U.S.\$422,897,000 (mineral products 59.2%, textile products 23.5%, metals and finished products 3.5%, live animals 3.2%). *Major export destinations:* Switzerland 25.4%; Russia 20.6%; China 17.7%; Japan 8.5%; U.K. 4.4%.

Transport and communications

Transport. Railroads (1994): length 2,083 km; passenger-km 789,600,000; metric ton-km cargo 2,131,700. Roads (1996): total length 50,000 km (paved 3%). Vehicles (1996): passenger cars 28,000; trucks and buses 28,000. Air transport (1994): passenger-km 115,000,000; metric ton-km cargo 12,000,000; airports (1997) with scheduled flights 1.

Communications

Medium	date	unit	number	units per 1,000 persons
Daily newspapers	1995	circulation	211,830	92.0
Radio	1995	receivers	170,460	74.0
Television	1997	receivers	148,983	60.7
Telephones	1997	main lines	91,971	37.5
Cellular telephones	1997	subscribers	900	0.4
Facsimile machines	1995	units	2,072	0.9
Personal computers	1995	units	460	0.2

Education and health

Educational attainment (1989). Percentage of population age 10 and over having: primary education 33.7%; some secondary 31.9%; complete secondary 16.9%; vocational secondary 9.4%; some higher and complete higher 8.1%.
Literacy (1995): percentage of total population age 15 and over literate 82.9%; males literate 88.6%; females literate 77.2%.

Education (1995–96)

	schools	teachers	students	student/ teacher ratio
Primary (age 6–12)	650	7,088	176,036	24.8
Secondary (age 13–16)		12,323	227,811	18.5
Vocational (age 16–18)	...	495	7,987	16.1
Higher	12[11]	1,341[12]	13,800[11]	...

Health (1993): physicians 5,911 (1 per 401 persons) hospital beds 23,400 (1 per 101 persons); infant mortality rate per 1,000 live births (1997) 68.0.
Food (1995): daily per capita caloric intake 1,897 (vegetable products 60%, animal products 40%); 78% of FAO recommended minimum requirement.

Military

Total active duty personnel (1997): 14,900[13] (army 94%, air force 6%). *Military expenditure as percentage of GNP* (1995): 24.% (world 2.8%); per capita expenditure U.S.\$8.

[1]January. [2]Dundgovi includes Govi-Sümber. [3]Detail does not add to total given because of rounding. [4]1997 estimate. [5]At constant prices of 1986. [6]Services includes finance, public administration, and defense. [7]Includes depreciation of fixed capital. [8]Includes 66,000 unemployed. [9]Urban households. [10]Includes income from agricultural cooperatives. [11]1994–95. [12]1991–92. [13]Includes 5,900 paramilitary forces.

Internet resources for further information:
• Mongolia Online http://www.MongoliaOnline.mn/english/

Morocco

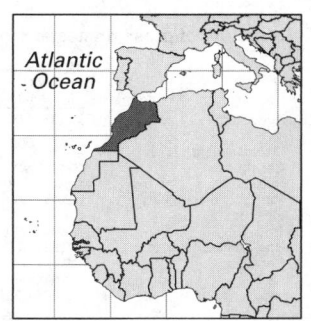

Official name: Al-Mamlakah al-Maghribīyah (Kingdom of Morocco).
Form of government: constitutional monarchy with two legislative houses (House of Councillors [270]; House of Representatives [325]).
Chief of state and head of government: King assisted by Prime Minister.
Capital: Rabat.
Official language: Arabic.
Official religion: Islam.
Monetary unit: 1 Moroccan dirham (DH) = 100 Moroccan francs; valuation (Sept. 25, 1998) 1 U.S.$ = DH 9.28; 1 £ = DH 15.80.

Population (1994 census)[1]

Regions	Principal urban centres	Population
Oued Eddahab-Lagouira	Dakhla	36,751
Laâyoune-Bojador-Sakia El-Hamra	Laâyoune	175,669
Guelmim-Es Semara	Guelmim	386,075
Sous-Massa-Drâa	Agadir-Idda ou Tanane	2,622,947[2]
Gharb-Chrarda-Beni Hsen	Kénitra	1,625,082
Chaouia-Ourdigha	Settat	1,554,241
Marrakech-Tensift-El Haouz	Marrakech-Ménara	2,724,204
Oriental	Oujda-Angad	1,768,691
Casablanca	Casa-Anfa	3,094,203
Rabat-Salé-Zemmour-Zaër	Rabat	1,985,602
Doukkala-Abda	Safi	1,793,458
Tadla-Azilal	Béni Mellal	1,324,662
Meknès-Tafilalt	Meknès-El Menzeh	1,903,790
Fès-Boulemane	Fès Jedid-Dar Dbibegh	1,322,473
Taza-Al Hoceïma-Taounate	Al-Hoceïma	1,719,837
Tangier-Tetouan	Tangier-Assilah	2,036,032
TOTAL		26,073,717

Demography

Area[1]: 274,460 sq mi, 710,850 sq km.
Population (1998): 28,060,000[1].
Density (1998): persons per sq mi 102.2, persons per sq km 39.5.
Urban-rural (1996): urban 48.9%; rural 51.1%.
Sex distribution (1996): male 50.06%; female 49.94%.
Age breakdown (1995): under 15, 36.1%; 15–29, 29.8%, 30–44, 18.9%; 45–59, 9.0%; 60–74, 5.0%; 75 and over, 1.2%.
Population projection[1]: (2000) 29,157,000; (2010) 34,426,000.
Ethnolinguistic composition (1995): Arabic 65%; Berber 33%; other 2%.
Religious affiliation (1995): Muslim (mostly Sunnī) 99.8%; Christian 0.1%; other (mostly Jewish) 0.1%.
Major urban areas (1994): Casablanca 2,941,000; Rabat-Salé 1,386,000; Fès 510,000.

Vital statistics

Birth rate per 1,000 population (1995): 27.9 (world avg. 25.0).
Death rate per 1,000 population (1995): 6.0 (world avg. 9.3).
Natural increase rate per 1,000 population (1995): 21.9 (world avg. 15.7).
Life expectancy at birth (1995): male 67.0 years; female 71.0 years.
Major causes of death (1989)[3]: childhood diseases 22.9%; circulatory diseases 15.4%; accidents 7.3%; infectious and parasitic diseases 6.3%; cancers 5.6%.

National economy

Budget. Revenue (1995): DH 87,172,000,000 (current account taxes 69.8%, of which value-added taxes 5.5%; capital revenue 22.6%; customs and stamp duties 7.5%). Expenditures (1995): DH 82,015,000,000 (current expenditure 76.0%, of which administrative expenses 52.2%, debt payment 20.5%; capital expenditure 24.0%).
Public debt (external, outstanding; 1996): U.S.$20,774,000,000.
Tourism (1995): receipts U.S.$1,163,000,000; expenditures U.S.$302,000,000.
Production (metric tons except as noted). Agriculture, forestry, fishing (1997): sugar beets 2,595,000, wheat 2,316,500, barley 1,324,000, potatoes 1,145,000, sugar cane 900,000, tomatoes 895,000, oranges 794,800; livestock (number of live animals) 16,500,000 sheep, 5,500,000 goats, 2,550,000 cattle, 115,000,000 chickens; roundwood (1996) 2,371,000 cu m; fish catch (1995) 846,201. Mining and quarrying (value of production in DH '000,000; 1994): phosphate rock 3,600.0; zinc 276.9; lead 234.1; copper 140.6. Manufacturing (value added in DH '000,000; 1994) food 10,159; chemical products 5,951; textiles 4,108. Construction (authorized, urban areas; 1994): residential 7,069,557 sq m, nonresidential 998,424 sq m. Energy production (consumption): electricity (kW-hr; 1994) 10,773,000,000 (11,693,000,000); coal (metric tons; 1994) 650,000 (2,200,000); crude petroleum (barrels; 1994) 60,800 (50,030,800); petroleum products (metric tons; 1994) 5,659,000 (6,792,000); natural gas (cu m; 1994) 25,100,000 (25,100,000).
Population economically active (1994): total 8,694,000; activity rate 32.8% (participation rates [1993]: over age 15, 52.4%; unemployed 16.0%).

Price index (1990 = 100)

	1991	1992	1993	1994	1995	1996	1997
Consumer price index	108.0	114.2	120.1	126.3	134.0	138.0	139.2
Monthly earnings index[4]	110.0	130.0	130.0	140.0[5]	...	...	...

Gross national product (1996): U.S.$34,936,000,000 (U.S.$1,290 per capita).

Structure of gross domestic product and labour force

	1995		1993	
	in value DH '000,000	% of total value	labour force	% of labour force
Agriculture	39,723	14.4	2,906,000	34.0
Mining	4,904	1.8		
Manufacturing	51,629	18.6	2,650,000	31.0
Construction	12,199	4.4		
Public utilities	22,370	8.1		
Transp. and commun.	17,306	6.2		
Trade	54,934	19.8		
Finance	...	...	2,991,000	35.0
Pub. admin., defense	37,382	13.5		
Services				
Other	36,431	13.2		
TOTAL	276,878	100.0	8,547,000	100.0

Household income and expenditure. Average household size (1994) 5.9; expenditure (1994)[6]: food 45.2%, housing 12.5%, transportation 7.6%.

Foreign trade[7]

Balance of trade (current prices)

	1992	1993	1994	1995	1996	1997
DH '000,000	–23,192	–28,740	–23,353	–26,071	–16,984	–15,508
% of total	25.5%	31.1%	24.1%	24.5%	12.4%	10.4%

Imports (1995): DH 72,869,000,000 (capital goods 22.3%; food, beverages, and tobacco 16.0%; energy products 13.8%; consumer goods 11.0%). *Major import sources:* France 21.8%; Spain 8.5%; U.S. 6.5%; Germany 6.3%.
Exports (1995): DH 40,240,000,000 (food 30.8%; consumer goods 23.7%; minerals 10.0%). *Major export destinations:* France 29.7%; Spain 9.4%; Japan 7.7%; India 5.4%; Italy 5.2%.

Transport and communications

Transport. Railroads (1994): route length 1,768 km; passenger-km 1,884,000,000; metric ton-km cargo 4,740,000,000. Roads (1995): total length 60,513 km (paved 50%). Vehicles (1995): passenger cars 1,030,000; trucks and buses 273,100. Air transport (1996)[8]: passenger-km 4,665,440,000; metric ton-km cargo 57,030,000; airports (1997) 11.

Communications

Medium	date	unit	number	units per 1,000 persons
Daily newspapers	1995	circulation	390,000	14.5
Radio	1995	receivers	6,000,000	222
Television	1995	receivers	2,500,000	92.7
Telephones	1995	main lines	1,158,000	42.9
Cellular telephones	1995	subscribers	29,500	1.1
Facsimile machines	1995	units	7,500	0.3
Personal computers	1995	units	45,000	1.7

Education and health

Educational attainment (1982). Percentage of population age 25 and over having: no formal education 47.8%; some primary education 47.8%; some secondary 3.8%; higher 0.6%. *Literacy* (1995): total population over age 15 literate 43.7%; males literate 56.6%; females literate 31.0%.

Education (1994–95)

	schools	teachers	students	student/teacher ratio
Primary (age 7–12)	6,205	154,650	3,914,282	25.3
Secondary (age 13–17)	451	29,364	391,639	13.3
Vocational[9]	562[10]	2,951	17,585	6.0
Higher	13[11]	9,038	266,032	29.4

Health (1994): physicians 8,838 (1 per 2,923 persons); hospital beds 26,407 (1 per 978 persons); infant mortality rate (1995) 45.8.
Food (1995): daily per capita caloric intake 3,157 (vegetable products 93%, animal products 7%); 130% of FAO recommended minimum requirement.

Military

Total active duty personnel (1997): 196,300 (army 89.1%, navy 4.0%, air force 6.9%). *Military expenditure as percentage of GDP* (1995): 4.3% (world 2.8%); per capita expenditure U.S.$47.

[1]Includes Western Sahara, annexure of Morocco whose future political status will be decided by a UN-sponsored referendum scheduled for 1999; Western Sahara area: 97,344 sq mi, 252,120 sq km; Western Sahara population (1998 est.) 288,000. [2]Difference between national total and sum of all other region totals, which were known. [3]Registered deaths of urban population only. [4]Minimum wage. [5]July 1. [6]Weights of consumer price index components. [7]Import figures are f.o.b. in balance of trade and c.i.f. for commodities and trading partners. [8]Royal Air Maroc only. [9]Excludes teacher training. [10]1991–92. [11]Universities only.

Internet resources for further information:
• Morocco Ministry of Communication http://www.mincom.gov.ma/

Mozambique

Official name: República de Moçambique (Republic of Mozambique).
Form of government: multiparty republic[1] with a single legislative house (Assembly of the Republic [250]).
Head of state and government: President assisted by the Prime Minister.
Capital: Maputo.
Official language: Portuguese.
Official religion: none.
Monetary unit: 1 metical (Mt; plural meticais) = 100 centavos; valuation (Sept. 25, 1998) 1 U.S.\$ = Mt 11,495; 1 £ = Mt 19,570.

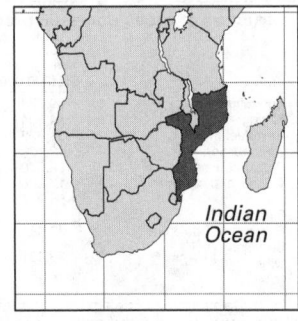

Area and population		area		population
				1991
Provinces	Capitals	sq mi	sq km	estimate
Cabo Delgado	Pemba	31,902	82,625	1,202,221
Gaza	Xai-Xai	29,231	75,709	1,401,485
Inhambane	Inhambane	26,492	68,615	1,156,958
Manica	Chimoio	23,807	61,661	609,512
Maputo	Maputo	9,944	25,756	840,757
Nampula	Nampula	31,508	81,606	2,841,416
Niassa	Lichinga	49,828	129,055	686,650
Sofala	Beira	26,262	68,018	1,427,493
Tete	Tete	38,890	100,724	734,561
Zambézia	Quelimane	40,544	105,008	2,619,281
City				
Maputo	—	232	602	931,591
TOTAL LAND AREA		308,642[2]	799,379	
INLAND WATER		5,019	13,000	
TOTAL		313,661	812,379	14,451,925[3]

Demography

Population (1998): 18,641,000.
Density (1998)[4]: persons per sq mi 60.4, persons per sq km 23.3.
Urban-rural (1990–94): urban 32.7%; rural 67.3%.
Sex distribution (1997): male 48.85%; female 51.15%.
Age breakdown (1997): under 15, 44.9%; 15–29, 27.9%, 30–44, 15.1%; 45–59, 8.2%; 60–74, 3.3%; 75 and over, 0.6%.
Population projection: (2000) 19,614,000; (2010) 24,809,000.
Ethnolinguistic composition (1983): Makua 47.3%; Tsonga 23.3%; Malawi 12.0%; Shona 11.3%; Yao 3.8%; Swahili 0.8%; Makonde 0.6%; Portuguese 0.2%; other 0.7%.
Religious affiliation (1995): traditional beliefs 47.0%; Muslim 28.2%; Christian 24.8%, of which Roman Catholic 11.6%, Protestant 9.2%.
Major cities (1991): Maputo 931,591; Beira 298,847; Nampula 250,473.

Vital statistics

Birth rate per 1,000 population (1997): 44.0 (world avg. 25.0).
Death rate per 1,000 population (1997): 18.0 (world avg. 9.3).
Natural increase rate per 1,000 population (1997): 26.0 (world avg. 15.7).
Total fertility rate (avg. births per childbearing woman; 1997): 6.1.
Marriage rate per 1,000 population (1974): 0.7.
Divorce rate per 1,000 population (1974): 0.01.
Life expectancy at birth (1995): male 46.8 years; female 49.5 years.

National economy

Budget (1995). Revenue: Mt 4,522,000,000 (1995; sales tax 47.8%, customs taxes 24.0%, individual income tax 16.6%). Expenditures: Mt 8,196,000,000 (current expenditure 52.2%, of which goods and services 23.6%, administrative salaries 22.3%, defense and security 19.4%; capital expenditure 47.8%).
Public debt (external, outstanding; 1996): U.S.\$5,433,000,000.
Production (metric tons except as noted). Agriculture, forestry, fishing (1997): cassava 5,342,000, corn (maize) 1,153,000, sugarcane 500,000, coconuts 440,000, sorghum 263,000, peanuts (groundnuts) 127,000, bananas 86,000; livestock (number of live animals) 1,290,000 cattle, 386,000 goats, 175,000 pigs, 122,000 sheep, 23,000,000 chickens; roundwood (1995) 18,390,000 cu m; fish catch (1995) 26,870. Mining and quarrying (1994): marine salt 40,000; bauxite 9,620; copper 1335,6; garnet 3,000 kg; gemstones 6,865 carats. Manufacturing (value in Mt '000,000; 1995): food processing 696,611; beverages and tobacco 395,871; textiles 207,378; nonmetallic mineral products 140,193; wood and cork products 134,951; chemical products 116,335; rubber products 87,827; clothing 82,123; machinery and transport equipment 72,507. Construction (value in Mt; 1994) 157,700,000. Energy production (consumption): electricity (kW-hr; 1994) 340,000,000 (728,000,000); coal (metric tons; 1994) 40,000 (60,000); crude petroleum (1993) none (none[7]); petroleum products (metric tons; 1994) none[7] (251,000); natural gas, none (none).
Population economically active (1980): total 5,671,290; activity rate 48.6% (participation rates: over age 15, 87.3%; female 52.4%; unemployed 1.7%).

Price and earnings indexes (1990 = 100)							
	1991	1992	1993	1994	1995	1996	1997
Consumer price index	132.9	193.4	275.0	448.8	693.1	1,005.0	1,060.6
Monthly earning index[8]	152.3	223.9	269.0	446.7	636.5	913.7	...

Gross national product (1996): U.S.\$1,472,000,000 (U.S.\$80 per capita).

Structure of gross domestic product and labour force				
	1995		1980	
	in value Mt '000,000	% of total value	labour force	% of labour force
Agriculture	5,018,000	25.5	4,754,831	83.8
Mining	3,395,000[9]	17.2[9]	73,425	1.3
Manufacturing			273,369	4.8
Construction	2,405,000	12.2	42,121	0.7
Public utilities	10	10	10	10
Transp. and commun.	2,454,000	12.5	77,025	1.4
Finance	...	...		
Trade	2,049,000	10.4	112,244	2.0
Pub. admin., defense	1,657,000	8.4	243,449[10]	4.3[10]
Services	2,191,000[10]	11.1[10]		
Other	514,000	2.6	94,826[11]	1.7[11]
TOTAL	19,685,000[2, 12]	100.0[2]	5,671,290	100.0

Household income and expenditure. Average family size (1992–93) 6.7[13]; income per household: n.a.; source of income (1992–93)[13]: wages and salaries 51.6%, self-employment 12.5%, barter 11.5%, private farming 7.7%; expenditure (1992–93)[13]: food, beverages, and tobacco 74.6%; housing and energy 11.7%; transportation and communications 4.7%; clothing and footwear 3.7%; education and recreation 1.4%; health 0.8%.
Land use (1994): forested 22.1%; meadows and pastures 56.1%; agricultural and under permanent cultivation 4.0%; other 17.8%.

Foreign trade[14]

Balance of trade (current prices)						
	1990	1991	1992	1993	1994	1995
U.S.\$'000,000	−648	−737	−716	−823	−868	−615
% of total	71.8%	69.5%	72.0%	75.7%	74.4%	64.5%

Imports (1995): U.S.\$783,600,000 (1990; foodstuffs 28.9%, capital equipment 22.9%, crude petroleum and derivatives 10.9%, machinery and spare parts 9.5%). *Major import sources* (1995): South Africa 37.6%; U.S. 6.7%; Japan 6.2%; Portugal 6.0%; U.K. 5.7%; France 5.6%.
Exports (1995): U.S.\$168,900,000 (shrimp 43.3%, cotton 11.7%, cashew nuts 5.6%, sugar 4.3%, copra 3.6%, petroleum 1.9%). *Major export destinations:* South Africa 21.6%; Spain 21.6%; Japan 13.0%; Portugal 10.4%.

Transport and communications

Transport. Railroads (1995): route length 1,940 mi, 3,123 km; passenger-mi 194,000,000, passenger-km 312,000,000; short ton-mi cargo 612,000,000, metric ton-km cargo 893,000,000. Roads (1995): total length 18,523 mi, 29,810 km (paved 18.6%). Vehicles (1995): passengers cars 84,000; trucks and buses 26,800. Air transport (1995): passenger-mi 239,000,000, passenger-km 384,000,000; short ton-mi cargo 6,000,000, metric ton-km cargo 9,000,000; airports (1997) with scheduled flights 7.

Communications				units per 1,000 persons
Medium	date	unit	number	
Daily newspapers	1995	circulation	130,000	8.0
Radio	1995	receivers	660.000	38.0
Television	1995	receivers	60,000	3.5
Telephones	1995	main lines	59,800	3.4
Facsimile machines	1995	units	...	0.4

Education and health

Literacy (1995): percentage of total population age 15 and over literate 40.1%; males literate 57.7%; females literate 23.3%.

Education (1995)				student/ teacher ratio
	schools	teachers	students	
Primary (age 5–19)	4,167	24,575	1,415,428	57.6
Secondary (age 10–16)[15]	239[16]	4,376	165,868	37.9
Voc., teacher tr.	31[16]	1,239	19,313	15.6
Higher	3[16]	833[16]	7,000	...

Health (1993): physicians 114[17] (1 per 131,991 persons); hospital beds 13,280 (1 per 1,133 persons); infant mortality rate per 1,000 live births (1997) 123.0.
Food (1995): daily per capita caloric intake 1,678 (vegetable products 97%, animal products 3%); 72% of FAO recommended minimum requirement.

Military

Total active duty personnel (1997): 5,100–6,100[18]. *Military expenditure as percentage of GNP* (1995): 5.4% (world 2.8%); per capita expenditure U.S.\$4.

[1]Mozambique adopted a new multiparty constitution that became effective on Nov. 30, 1990, but was amended on Oct. 29, 1996, to create autonomous local governments. The first multiparty elections took place on Oct. 27–29, 1994. [2]Detail does not add to total given because of rounding. [3]Excludes refugees in neighbouring countries estimated at about 1,200,000 in 1991; most of these refugees were repatriated between June 1993 and the fall of 1994. [4]Based on land area. [5]1990. [6]Metal content only. [7]Internal disorder and a lack of foreign exchange have brought importation of crude petroleum and the production of refined petroleum products practically to a halt. [8]Agricultural workers only. [9]Manufacturing includes fishing. [10]Services includes Public utilities. [11]Unemployed. [12]Reported as gross output. [13]City of Maputo only. [14]Import figures are c.i.f. [15]Includes the two stages of secondary education and the upper-level primary stage. [16]1994. [17]Government personnel only. [18]Estimate; approximately 80% are in the army.

Internet resources for further information:
- Mozambique http://www.hmnet.com/africa/mozambique/mz_tbl.html
- Mozambique Country Profile http://www.mbendi.co.za/cymzcy.htm

Myanmar (Burma)

Official name: Pyidaungzu Myanma Naingngandaw (Union of Myanmar).
Form of government: military regime.
Head of state and government: Chairman of the State Peace and Development Council.
Capital: Yangôn (Rangoon).
Official language: Burmese.
Official religion: none.
Monetary unit: 1 Myanmar kyat (K) = 100 pyas; valuation (Sept. 25, 1998) 1 U.S.$ = K 6.25; 1 £ = K 10.64[1].

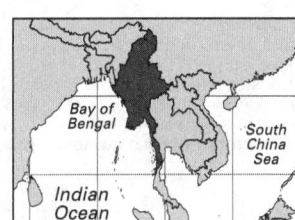

Area and population		area		population
				1994
Divisions	**Capitals**	sq mi	sq km	estimate
Irrawaddy (Ayeyarwady)	Bassein (Pathein)	13,567	35,138	6,107,000
Magwe (Magway)	Magwe (Magway)	17,305	44,820	4,067,000
Mandalay	Mandalay	14,295	37,024	5,823,000
Pegu (Bago)	Pegu (Bago)	15,214	39,404	4,607,000
Sagaing	Sagaing	36,535	94,625	4,889,000
Tenasserim (Tanintharyi)	Tavoy (Dawei)	16,735	43,343	1,187,000
Yangôn	Yangôn (Rangoon)	3,927	10,171	5,037,000
States				
Chin	Hakha	13,907	36,019	438,000
Kachin	Myitkyinä	34,379	89,041	1,135,000
Karen	Pa-an (Hpa-an)	11,731	30,383	1,323,000
Kayah	Loi-kaw	4,530	11,733	228,000
Mon	Moulmein (Mawlamyine)	4,748	12,297	2,183,000
Rakhine (Arakan)	Sittwe (Akyab)	14,200	36,778	2,482,000
Shan	Taunggyi	60,155	155,801	4,416,000
TOTAL		261,228	676,577	43,922,000

Demography

Population (1998): 47,305,000.
Density (1998): persons per sq mi 181.1, persons per sq km 69.9.
Urban-rural (1997): urban 27.0%; rural 73.0%.
Sex distribution (1993): male 49.72%; female 50.28%.
Age breakdown (1990): under 15, 36.0%; 15–29, 29.7%; 30–44, 17.8%; 45–59, 10.1%; 60–74, 5.3%; 75 and over, 1.1%.
Population projection: (2000) 48,852,000; (2010) 56,573,000.
Doubling time: 40 years.
Ethnic composition (1983): Burman 69.0%; Shan 8.5%; Karen 6.2%; Rakhine 4.5%; Mon 2.4%; Chin 2.2%; Kachin 1.4%; other 5.8%.
Religious affiliation (1990): Buddhist 89.1%; Christian 4.9%; Muslim 3.8%; other 2.2%.
Major cities (1983): Yangôn (Rangoon) 2,513,023; Mandalay 532,949; Moulmein (Mawlamyine) 219,961; Pegu (Bago) 150,528; Bassein (Pathein) 144,096.

Vital statistics

Birth rate per 1,000 population (1997): 27.4 (world avg. 25.0).
Death rate per 1,000 population (1997): 9.9 (world avg. 9.3).
Natural increase rate per 1,000 population (1997): 17.5 (world avg. 15.7).
Total fertility rate (avg. births per childbearing woman; 1997): 3.3.
Marriage rate per 1,000 population: n.a.
Divorce rate per 1,000 population: n.a.
Life expectancy at birth (1997): male 58.0 years; female 62.0 years.
Major causes of death per 100,000 population (1987): infectious and parasitic diseases 29.5; respiratory diseases 14.8; circulatory diseases 10.0; malignant neoplasms (cancers) 7.9; malnutrition 2.2.

National economy

Budget (1994–95). Revenue: K 32,029,000,000 (revenue from taxes 62.7%, of which taxes on goods and services 28.5%, taxes on international trade 13.2%; nontax revenue 35.4%; capital revenue 1.9%). Expenditures: K 48,021,000,000 (defense 36.8%; transportation 13.5%; education 11.7%; agriculture 10.3%; health 4.0%; social security and welfare 3.6%).
Public debt (external, outstanding; 1996): U.S.$4,804,000,000.
Tourism: receipts from visitors (1995) U.S.$38,000,000; expenditures by nationals abroad (1992) U.S.$16,000,000.
Production (metric tons except as noted). Agriculture, forestry, fishing (1996): rice 20,865,000, sugarcane 3,132,000, pulses 1,289,000, peanuts (groundnuts) 568,000, sesame seeds 351,000, plantains 285,000, corn (maize) 247,000, seed cotton 214,000; livestock (number of live animals) 10,121,000 cattle, 4,710,000 ducks, 3,229,000 pigs, 2,266,000 buffalo, 1,492,000 sheep and goats, 27,600,000 chickens; roundwood (1995) 23,281,000 cu m; fish catch (1994) 824,468. Mining and quarrying (1995–96): gypsum 35,481; copper concentrates 19,060; refined lead 1,512; tin concentrates 473; jade 261; refined silver 112,270 troy oz. Manufacturing (1994): cement 469,582; urea 149,000; sugar 47,600; washing soap 36,431; noodles 25,065; stationery paper 14,315; cotton fabrics 10,804,000 metres; cigarettes 440,000,000 units; gunny-bags 26,769,000 units; glass bottles 16,268,000 units. Construction (units; 1987–88)[2]: residential 1,193; nonresidential 1,483. Energy production (consumption): electricity (kW-hr; 1994) 3,500,000,000 (3,500,000,000); coal (metric tons; 1994) 76,000 (78,000); crude petroleum (barrels; 1994) 4,817,000 (6,893,000); petroleum products (metric tons; 1994) 757,000 (921,000); natural gas (cu m; 1994) 1,359,000,000 (1,359,000,000).
Household income and expenditure. Average household size (1994) 5.6; average annual income per household: n.a.; sources of income: n.a.; expenditure (1994)[3]: food and beverages 67.1%, fuel and lighting 6.6%, transportation 4.0%, charitable contributions 3.1%, medical care 3.1%.

Gross national product (1996): U.S.$119,334,000,000 (U.S.$2,610 per capita).

Structure of gross domestic product and labour force				
	1995–96			
	in value K '000,000	% of total value	labour force[4]	% of labour force[4]
Agriculture	295,200	62.2	11,848,000	67.4
Mining	2,784	0.6	116,000	0.7
Manufacturing	34,325	7.2	1,481,000	8.4
Construction	8,026	1.7	354,000	2.0
Public utilities	1,680	0.4	19,000	0.1
Transp. and commun.	8,238	1.7	441,000	2.5
Trade	106,595	22.4	1,715,000	9.7
Finance	788	0.2	1,339,000	7.6
Public admin., services	9,995	2.1		
Other	7,255	1.5	274,000	1.6
TOTAL	474,886	100.0	17,587,000	100.0

Population economically active (1995–96): total 18,766,000; activity rate of total population 41.2% (participation rates: ages 15–64 [1983] 64.2%; female [1987–88] 35.3%; unemployed 6.2%).

Price and earnings indexes (1990 = 100)							
	1991	1992	1993	1994	1995	1996	1997
Consumer price index	132.3	161.3	212.6	263.8	330.3	384.0	498.1
Monthly earning index[5]	92.8	129.4	144.8	...	...	...	...

Land use (1994): forested 49.3%; meadows and pastures 0.5%; agricultural and under permanent cultivation 15.3%; other 34.9%.

Foreign trade[6]

Balance of trade (current prices)						
	1991	1992	1993	1994	1995	1996
K '000,000	−1,055.4	−338.1	−948.4	−195.8	−2,050.7	−3,231.5
% of total	16.7%	4.9%	11.6%	2.1%	17.5%	28.3%

Imports (1994–95): K 8,332,000,000 (machinery and transport equipment 31.8%; basic manufactures 17.5%; chemicals 7.3%; animal and vegetable oils 9.7%; food and live animals 5.6%). *Major import sources:* Japan 23.6%; Singapore 14.6%; China 12.2%; Thailand 10.0%; Malaysia 9.4%; South Korea 4.7%; Indonesia 3.9%.
Exports (1994–95): K 5,405,000,000 (food and live animals 50.6%; inedible crude materials 28.2%; basic manufactures 4.6%). *Major export destinations:* Singapore 16.4%; Indonesia 15.6%; India 12.9%; Thailand 10.0%; China 5.1%; Hong Kong 5.0%.

Transport and communications

Transport. Railroads (1995–96): track length (1994) 5,060 km; passenger-km 4,894,000,000; metric ton-km cargo 880,000,000. Roads (1995): total length 27,600 km (paved 12%). Vehicles (1995): passenger cars 44,000; trucks and buses 42,000. Air transport (1995–96): passenger-km 438,000,000; metric ton-km cargo 3,212,000; airports (1996) 19.

Communications				units per 1,000 persons
Medium	date	unit	number	
Daily newspapers	1994	circulation	1,032,000	23
Radio	1996	receivers	3,300,000	72
Television	1995	receivers	1,000,000	22
Telephones	1995	main lines	146,700	3.3
Cellular telephones	1995	subscribers	2,100	0.05
Facsimile machines	1995	units	1,400	0.03

Education and health

Educational attainment (1983). Percentage of population age 25 and over having: no formal schooling 55.8%; primary education 39.4%; secondary 4.6%; religious 0.1%; postsecondary 0.1%. *Literacy* (1995): total population age 15 and over literate 83.1%; males literate 88.7%; females literate 77.7%.

Education (1994–95)				student/
	schools	teachers	students	teacher ratio
Primary (age 5–9)	35,856	169,748	5,711,202	33.6
Secondary (age 10–15)	2,916	71,904	1,779,503	24.7
Voc., teacher tr.	103	2,462	25,374	10.3
Higher	51	9,147	309,446	33.8

Health: physicians (1993–94) 12,245 (1 per 3,554 persons); hospital beds (1992–93) 27,830 (1 per 1,586 persons); infant mortality rate per 1,000 live births (1997) 79.
Food (1995): daily per capita caloric intake 2,752 (vegetable products 96%, animal products 4%); 127% of FAO recommended minimum requirement.

Military

Total active duty personnel (1996): 321,000 (army 93.5%, navy 3.7%, air force 2.8%). *Military expenditure as percentage of GNP* (1992): 4.0% (world 3.6%); per capita expenditure (1994) U.S.$57.

---

[1]Official exchange rate; black market exchange rate (July 15, 1998): 1 U.S.$ = K 350; 1 £ = K 575. [2]Construction Corporation activity only. [3]Yangôn only. [4]Employed only. [5]Wages in manufacturing. [6]Import figures are f.o.b. in balance of trade and c.i.f. in commodities and trading partners.

Internet resources for further information:
• Myanmar Home Page http://www.myanmar.com/e-index.html

Namibia

Official name: Republic of Namibia.
Form of government: republic with two
legislative houses (National Council[1]
[26]; National Assembly [72[2]]).
Head of state and government:
President.
Capital: Windhoek.
Official language: English.
Official religion: none.
Monetary unit: 1 Namibian dollar
(N$) = 100 cents; valuation (Sept. 25,
1998) 1 U.S.$ = N$5.83;
1 £ = N$ 9.93.

Area and population[3]

		area		population
Regions	Chief towns	sq mi	sq km	1992 estimate
Erongo[3]	Omaruru	24,602	63,719	98,500
Hardap	Mariental	42,428	109,888	80,000
Karas	Keetmanshoop	62,288	161,324	73,000
Khomas	Windhoek	14,210	36,804	161,000
Kunene	Opuwo	55,697	144,254	58,500
Liambezi	Katima Mulilo	7,541	19,532	92,000
Ohangwena	Oshikango	4,086	10,582	178,000
Okavango	Rundu	16,763	43,417	136,000
Omaheke	Gobabis	32,715	84,731	55,600
Omusati	Ongandjera	5,265	13,637	158,000
Oshana	Oshakati	2,042	5,290	159,000
Oshikoto	Tsumeb	10,273	26,607	176,000
Otjozondjupa	Grootfontein	40,667	105,327	85,000
Other		2	6	1,000
TOTAL		318,580[4]	825,118	1,511,600

Demography

Population (1998): 1,622,000.
Density (1998): persons per sq mi 5.1, persons per sq km 2.0.
Urban-rural (1996): urban 38.5%; rural 61.5%.
Sex distribution (1996): male 49.75%; female 50.25%.
Age breakdown (1991): under 15, 41.7%; 15–29, 28.8%; 30–44, 14.7%; 45–59,
7.8%; 60–74, 5.3%; 75 and over, 1.7%.
Population projection: (2000) 1,674,000; (2010) 1,915,000.
Doubling time: 27 years.
Ethnic composition (1991): Ovambo 50.7%; Nama 12.5%; Kavango 9.7%;
Herero 8.0%; San (Bushman) 1.9%; Tswana 0.4%; ohter 16.8%.
Religious affiliation (1995): Lutheran 51.4%; Roman Catholic 16.6%; African
Christian 7.0%; Anglican 5.6%; other 19.4%.
Major cities (1990): Windhoek 125,000; Swakopmund 15,500; Rundu 15,000;
Rehoboth 15,000; Keetmanshoop 14,000.

Vital statistics

Birth rate per 1,000 population (1990–95): 37.5 (world avg. 25.0).
Death rate per 1,000 population (1990–95): 11.9 (world avg. 9.3).
Natural increase rate per 1,000 population (1990–95): 25.6 (world avg. 15.7).
Total fertility rate (avg. births per childbearing woman; 1990–95): 5.7.
Life expectancy at birth (1990–95): male 57.5 years; female 60.0 years.
Major causes of death per 100,000 population: n.a.; however, in the early 1990s,
tuberculosis had become a serious problem (especially in the southern
regions); AIDS cases, while few, were increasing exponentially.

National economy

Budget (1996–97). Revenue: N$4,459,400,000 (customs taxes 30.2%, individ-
ual income taxes 16.5%, general sales tax 14.3%, nontax revenues 10.5%,
mining taxes 3.1%). Expenditures: N$5,072,600,000 (education 23.2%, health
and welfare 10.3%, transportation 6.1%, defense 5.8%, social security 5.4%).
Tourism (1995): receipts from visitors U.S.$263,000,000; expenditures by
nationals abroad U.S.$82,000,000.
Public debt (1997): U.S.$697,000,000.
Production (metric tons except as noted). Agriculture, forestry, fishing (1997):
roots and tubers 230,000, cereals 168,000 (of which millet 107,000, corn
[maize] 47,000, sorghum 10,000, wheat 4,100), fruits 10,000, vegetables and
melons 9,000, pulses 8,000, wool 3,026[5], karakul pelts 770,627 units[6]; livestock
(number of live animals; 1996) 2,136,545 sheep, 2,084,396 cattle, 1,670,822
goats; fish catch (1995) 285,980. Mining and quarrying (1996): diamonds
1,420,000 carats (mostly gem quality); zinc 69,689; copper 20,705; lead 18,845;
uranium 2,886; silver 1,350,500 troy oz; gold 70,417 troy oz. Manufacturing:
n.a.; products include cut gems (primarily diamonds), fur products (karakul),
processed foods (fish, meats, and dairy products), textiles, carved wood products, refined metals (copper and lead). Construction (value of buildings completed in N$'000,000; 1994): residential 347.7; nonresidential 160.4. Energy
production (consumption): electricity (kW-hr; 1992) 1,714,000,000 (1,714,-
000,000); coal, none (n.a.); crude petroleum, none (n.a.).
Population economically active: total (1991) 493,580; activity rate of total population, 34.9% (participation rates: ages 15–64, 61.3%; female 43.5%; unemployed 20.1%).

Price and earnings indexes (1990 = 100)

	1991	1992	1993	1994	1995	1996	1997[7]
Consumer price index	111.9	131.7	143.0	158.4	174.2	188.2	205.7
Earnings index	...	...	...	...	...	...	...

Household income and expenditure. Average household size (1991) 5.2; average annual income per household (1980) R 3,223 (U.S.$4,143); sources of
income (1992): wages and salaries 69.0%, income from property 25.6%,
transfer payments 5.4%; expenditure: n.a.
Gross national product (1996): US$3,569,000,000 (U.S.$2,250 per capita).

Structure of gross domestic product and labour force

	1995		1991	
	in value N$'000,000	% of total value	labour force[8]	% of labour force
Agriculture	1,502	15.4	189,929	38.5
Mining	1,097	11.2	14,686	3.0
Manufacturing	872	8.9	22,884	4.6
Construction	347	3.6	18,638	3.8
Public utilities	187	1.9	2,974	0.6
Transp. and commun.	566	5.8	9,322	1.9
Trade[9]	1,043	10.7	37,820	7.7
Finance	1,037	10.6	8,547	1.7
Services	135	1.4	} 89,541	18.1
Public administration and defense	2,697	27.7		
Other	267	2.7	99,239[10]	20.1[10]
TOTAL	9,750	100.0[4]	493,580	100.0

Land use (1994): forested 15.2%; meadows and pastures 46.2%; agricultural
and under permanent cultivation 0.8%; other 37.8%.

Foreign trade

Balance of trade (current prices)

	1991	1992	1993	1994	1995	1996
U.S.$'000,000	+102	+79	+122	+165	−98	−25
% of total	4.3%	3.0%	5.0%	6.6%	3.5%	0.9%

Imports (1994): N$4,467,700,000 (machinery and transport equipment 27.1%,
of which transport equipment 16.2%; food and live animals 22.3%; minerals
and fuels 11.4%; chemical products 8.1%). *Major import sources* (1993):
South Africa 87.0%[11]; Germany 3.0%; France 2.0%; Japan 2.0%.
Exports (1994): N$4,692,000,000 (minerals 50.1%, of which diamonds 31.4%;
food and live animals 47.0%, of which fish and fish products 28.6%, cattle
and meat products 12.6%; karakul pelts 0.2%). *Major export destinations*
(1993): United Kingdom 34.0%; South Africa 27.0%; Japan 10.0%; Spain
6.0%.

Transport and communications

Transport. Railroads: length (1995) 1,480 mi, 2,382 km; passenger-km 34,700,-
000; metric ton-km 1,077,000,000. Roads (1995): total length 25,130 mi,
40,450 km (paved 12%). Vehicles (1995): passenger cars 62,500; trucks and
buses 66,500. Merchant marine (1992): vessels (100 gross tons and over) 30;
total deadweight tonnage 5,874. Air transport (1996)[12]: passenger-km
756,000,000; metric ton-km cargo 23,000,000; airports (1997) with scheduled
flights 11.

Communications

Medium	date	unit	number	units per 1,000 persons
Daily newspapers	1994	circulation	43,300	27.4
Radio	1995	receivers	240,000	152
Television	1995	receivers	45,000	27.6
Telephones	1995	main lines	78,500	48.2
Cellular telephones	1995	subscribers	3,500	2.5

Education and health

Educational attainment (1991). percentage of population age 25 and over having: no formal schooling 35.1%; primary education 31.9%; secondary 28.5%;
higher 4.5%. *Literacy* (1991): total population age 15 and over literate
622,436 (75.8%); males literate 305,926 (77.7%); females literate 316,510
(73.9%).

Education (1994)

	schools	teachers	students	student/ teacher ratio
Primary (age 6–12)	933	10,912[13]	366,666	32.0[13]
Secondary (age 13–19)	114	2,534[14]	101,838	29.3[14]
Voc. teacher tr.	17	140[15]	1,503	11.9[15]
Higher	7	213[16]	6,523	11.8[16]

Health: physicians (1992) 324 (1 per 4,594 persons); hospital beds (1989) 6,997
(1 per 216 persons); infant mortality rate per 1,000 live birth (1993) 63.8.
Food (1995): daily per capita caloric intake 2,107 (vegetable products 88%,
animal products 12%); 92% of FAO recommended minimum requirement.

Military

Total active duty personnel (1997): 5,800 (army 98.3%, navy 1.7%[17]). *Military
expenditure as percentage of GNP* (1995): 1.6% (world 2.8%); per capita
expenditure U.S.$39.

[1]Mostly an advisory body. [2]72 elected and up to 6 appointed members. [3]Includes the
434 sq mi (1,124 sq km) district of Walvis Bay (1992 population estimate, 23,000) that
was jointly administered with South Africa from November 1992 to March 1994. [4]Detail
does not add to total given because of rounding. [5]1994. [6]1987. [7]July. [8]Includes more
than 140,000 nonwage (informal) workers. [9]Includes hotels. [10]Unemployed. [11]Includes
goods from other countries shipped via South Africa. [12]Namib Air only. [13]1992. [14]1990.
[15]1989. [16]1991. [17]Coast Guard for fishery protection.

Internet resources for further information:
• **Namibia Fact Sheet** http://www.emulateme.com/namibia.htm

Nepal

Official name: Nepāl Adhirājya (Kingdom of Nepal).
Form of government: constitutional monarchy with a bicameral parliament consisting of two legislative houses (National Council [60[1]]; House of Representatives [205]).
Chief of state: King.
Head of government: Prime Minister.
Capital: Kāthmāndu.
Official language: Nepālī.
Official religion: Hinduism.
Monetary unit: 1 Nepalese rupee (NRs) = 100 paisa (pice); valuation (Sept. 25, 1998) 1 U.S.$ = NRs 67.93; 1 £ = NRs 115.65.

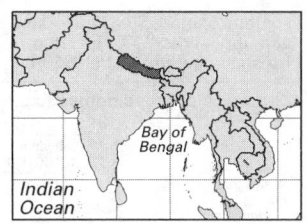

Area and population

Development regions Zones	Capitals	area sq mi	area sq km	population 1991 census
Eastern	Dhankūtā	10,987	28,456	4,446,749
Koshī	Dharān	3,733	9,669	1,728,247
Mechī	Ilam	3,165	8,196	1,118,210
Sāgarmāthā	Rājbiraj	4,089	10,591	1,600,292
Central	Kāthmāndu	10,583	27,410	6,183,955
Bāgmatī	Bhaktapur	3,640	9,428	2,250,805
Janakpur	Sindhulimādī	3,733	9,669	2,061,816
Nārāyanī	Hetaudā	3,210	8,313	1,871,334
Western	Pokharā	11,351	29,398	3,770,678
Dhawalāgiri	Bagluri	3,146	8,148	490,877
Gandakī	Chāme	4,740	12,275	1,266,128
Lumbinī	Butawal	3,465	8,975	2,013,673
Mid-western	Surkhet	16,362	42,378	2,410,414
Bherī	Nepālganj	4,071	10,545	1,103,043
Karnālī	Mānma	8,244	21,351	260,529
Rāptī	Tulsipur	4,047	10,482	1,046,842
Far-western	Dipāyal	7,544	19,539	1,679,301
Mahākālī	Dadeldhurā	2,698	6,989	664,952
Setī	Silgadhī	4,846	12,550	1,014,349
TOTAL		56,827	147,181	18,491,097

Demography

Population (1998): 21,959,000.
Density (1998): persons per sq mi 386.4, persons per sq km 149.2.
Urban-rural (1997): urban 15.0%; rural 85.0%.
Sex distribution (1997): male 50.20%; female 49.80%.
Age breakdown (1991): under 15, 42.3%; 15–29, 25.7%; 30–44, 16.7%; 45–59, 9.7%; 60–74, 4.7%; 75 and over, 0.9%.
Population projection: (2000) 23,042,000; (2010) 28,698,000.
Doubling time: 25 years.
Ethnic composition (1991): Nepalese 53.2%; Bihārī (including Maithilī and Bhojpurī) 18.4%; Tharu 4.8%; Tamang 4.7%; Newār 3.4%; Magar 2.2%; Abadhi 1.7%; other 11.6%.
Religious affiliation (1991): Hindu 86.5%; Buddhist 7.8%; Muslim 3.5%; Kirat 1.7%; Christian 0.2%; other 0.3%.
Major cities (1993 est.): Kāthmāndu 535,000; Lalitpur 190,000; Birātnagar 132,000; Bhaktapur 130,000.

Vital statistics

Birth rate per 1,000 population (1997): 36.6 (world avg. 25.0).
Death rate per 1,000 population (1997): 11.2 (world avg. 9.3).
Natural increase rate per 1,000 population (1997): 25.4 (world avg. 15.7).
Total fertility rate (avg. births per childbearing woman; 1996): 5.0.
Life expectancy at birth (1991): male 57.0 years; female 57.0 years.
Major causes of death per 100,000 population: n.a.; however, the leading causes of mortality are infectious and parasitic diseases, diseases of the respiratory system, and diseases of the nervous system.

National economy

Budget (1996). Revenue: NRs 30,303,000,000 (taxes on goods and services 39.7%, taxes on international trade 27.9%, income taxes 12.9%, state property revenues 7.9%, taxes on property 3.6%). Expenditures: NRs 49,485,-000,000 (education 13.9%, transport and communications 11.9%, agriculture 7.7%, housing 6.2%, health 5.0%, defense 4.4%, public order 4.4%, general public services 3.2%).
Public debt (external, outstanding; 1996): U.S.$2,349,000,000.
Land use (1994): forested 42.0%; meadows and pastures 14.6%; agricultural and under permanent cultivation 17.2%; other 26.2%.
Tourism (1995): receipts from visitors U.S.$117,000,000; expenditures by nationals abroad U.S.$136,000,000.
Production (metric tons except as noted). Agriculture, forestry, fishing (1996): rice 3,578,830, sugarcane 1,568,700, corn (maize) 1,331,060, wheat 1,012,930, potatoes 898,350, millet 282,440, pulses 185,640; livestock (number of live animals) 7,008,420 cattle, 5,783,140 goats, 3,302,200 buffalo, 859,000 sheep, 670,340 pigs; roundwood (1995) 20,822,000 cu m; fish catch (1995) 21,148. Mining and quarrying (1995): limestone 350,000; salt 7,000; talc 1,500. Manufacturing (value added in U.S.$'000; 1994): food products 70; textiles 70; wearing apparel 50; tobacco products 37; nonmetal mineral products 32. Construction: n.a. Energy production (consumption): electricity (kW-hr; 1994) 908,000,000 (940,000,000); coal (metric tons; 1994) none (115,000); petroleum products (metric tons; 1994) none (343,000).
Gross national product (1996): U.S.$4,710,000,000 (U.S.$210 per capita).

Structure of gross domestic product and labour force

	1994–95 in value NRs '000,000[2]	1994–95 % of total value	1991 labour force	1991 % of labour force
Agriculture	87,072	41.9	5,961,788	81.2
Mining	1,268	0.6	2,367	—
Manufacturing	19,559	9.4	150,051	2.0
Construction	23,560	11.3	35,658	0.5
Public utilities	1,923	0.9	11,734	0.2
Transp. and commun.	15,252	7.3	50,808	0.7
Trade	9,735	4.7	256,012	3.5
Finance	20,673	10.0	20,847	0.3
Services	19,563	9.4	752,019	10.3
Other	9,265[3]	4.5[3]	98,302	1.3
TOTAL	207,870	100.0	7,339,586	100.0

Population economically active (1991): total 7,339,586; activity rate of total population 39.7% (participation rates: ages 10 years and over, 57.0%; female 45.5%; unemployed [1980] 5.5%).

Price and earnings indexes (1990 = 100)

	1991	1992	1993	1994	1995	1996	1997
Consumer price index	115.6	135.4	145.5	157.7	169.7	185.6	191.0
Monthly earnings index[4]	136.7	113.2	123.3	...	...	...	...

Household income and expenditure (1984–85). Average household size (1991) 5.6; income per household NRs 14,796 (U.S.$853); sources of income: self-employment 63.4%, wages and salaries 25.1%, rent 7.5%, other 4.0%; expenditure: food and beverages 61.2%, housing 17.3%, clothing 11.7%, health care 3.7%, education and recreation 2.9%, transportation and communications 1.2%, other 2.0%.

Foreign trade[5]

Balance of trade (current prices)

	1990	1991	1992	1993	1994	1995
NRs '000,000	−13,037	−17,059	−16,255	−21,781	−37,402	−49,843
% of total	51.4%	46.5%	33.7%	36.5%	51.0%	58.0%

Imports (1994–95): NRs 65,587,000,000 (basic manufactured goods 38.7%; machinery and transport equipment 19.7%; chemicals 11.6%; food and live animals, chiefly for food 7.9%; mineral fuels and lubricants 7.2%; crude materials except fuels 6.0%). *Major import sources:* other Asia 70.3%; European Economic Community 15.3%[6]; Oceania 5.3%.
Exports (1994–95): NRs 17,940,000,000 (basic manufactures 51.6%; miscellaneous manufactures 32.7%; food and live animals, chiefly for food 9.1%; crude materials except fuels 2.9%; chemicals and drugs 1.7%). *Major export destinations:* Germany 45.8%; U.S. 36.0%; India 13.3%[6]; Switzerland 3.3%.

Transport and communications

Transport. Railroads (1993–94): route length (1996) 101 km; passengers carried 653,000; freight handled 9,151 metric tons. Roads (1995): total length 7,550 km (paved 41%). Vehicles (1990–91): passenger cars 4,949; trucks and buses 3,363. Air transport (1993–94): passenger-km 769,000,000; metric ton-km cargo 93,126,000; airports (1996) with scheduled flights 24.

Communications

Medium	date	unit	number	units per 1,000 persons
Daily newspapers	1994	circulation	162,000	8.2
Radio	1996	receivers	625,000	30
Television	1995	receivers	250,000	12
Telephones	1995	main lines	77,300	3.8
Facsimile machines	1995	units	600	0.03

Education and health

Educational attainment (1981). Percentage of population age 25 and over having: no formal schooling 41.2%; primary education 29.4%; secondary 22.7%; higher 6.8%. *Literacy* (1995): total population age 15 and over literate 27.5%; males literate 40.9%; females literate 14.0%.

Education (1995)

	schools	teachers	students	student/ teacher ratio
Primary (age 6–10)	22,157	85,621	3,191,600	37.3
Secondary (age 11–15) } Vocational	7,582	30,637	944,500	30.8
Higher	37[7]	4,925[8]	99,300	22.4[8]

Health (1995): physicians 1,478 (1 per 13,777 persons); hospital beds 3,188 (1 per 6,387 persons); infant mortality rate per 1,000 live births (1997) 83.
Food (1995): daily per capita caloric intake 2,367 (vegetable products 94%, animal products 6%); 108% of FAO recommended minimum requirement.

Military

Total active duty personnel (1996): 43,000 (army 99.5%, air force 0.5%). *Military expenditure as percentage of GNP* (1995): 0.9% (world 2.8%); per capita expenditure U.S.$2.

---

[1]Includes 10 members nominated by the king. [2]Tentative estimate. [3]Includes indirect taxes. [4]Real wage rates for unskilled industrial workers in Kāthmāndu. [5]Import figures are f.o.b. in balance of trade and c.i.f. for commodities and trading partners. [6]1993–94. [7]1993. [8]1991.

Internet resources for further information:
• Nepal Home Page http://www.info-nepal.com/

Netherlands, The

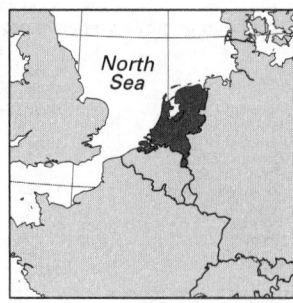

North
Sea

Official name: Koninkrijk der Nederlanden (Kingdom of The Netherlands).
Form of government: constitutional monarchy with a parliament (States General) comprising two legislative houses (First Chamber [75]; Second Chamber [150]).
Chief of state: Monarch.
Head of government: Prime Minister.
Seat of government: The Hague.
Capital: Amsterdam.
Official language: Dutch.
Official religion: none.
Monetary unit: 1 Netherlands guilder (f.) = 100 cents; valuation (Sept. 25, 1998) 1 U.S.$ = f. 1.88; 1 £ = f. 3.20.

Area and population

		area		population
				1996[1]
Provinces	Capitals	sq mi	sq km	estimate
Drenthe	Assen	1,024	2,652	457,300
Flevoland	Lelystad	551	1,426	272,800
Friesland	Leeuwarden	1,298	3,361	612,000
Gelderland	Arnhem	1,929	4,995	1,876,300
Groningen	Groningen	905	2,344	558,100
Limburg	Maastricht	837	2,167	1,133,700
Noord-Brabant	's-Hertogenbosch	1,907	4,938	2,290,400
Noord-Holland	Haarlem	1,027	2,660	2,468,400
Overijssel	Zwolle	1,288	3,337	1,054,000
Utrecht	Utrecht	524	1,356	1,070,600
Zeeland	Middelburg	692	1,792	367,400
Zuid-Holland	The Hague	1,104	2,860	3,332,900
TOTAL LAND AREA		13,085[2]	33,889[2]	
INLAND WATER		2,949	7,637	
TOTAL		16,033[2]	41,526[2]	15,493,900

Demography

Population (1998): 15,691,000.
Density (1998)[3]: persons per sq mi 1,199.2, persons per sq km 463.0.
Urban-rural (1996[1]): urban 91.0%; rural 9.0%.
Sex distribution (1996[1]): male 49.45%; female 50.55%.
Age breakdown (1996[1]): under 15, 18.4%; 15–29, 21.3%; 30–44, 23.9%; 45–59, 18.6%; 60–74, 12.1%; 75 and over, 5.7%.
Population projection: (2000) 15,835,000; (2010) 16,504,000.
Doubling time: not applicable; vital rates and net migration in near balance.
Ethnic composition (by nationality; 1997[1]): Netherlander 95.6%; Moroccan 0.9%; Turkish 0.8%; German 0.3%; other 2.4%.
Religious affiliation (1997[1]): Roman Catholic 32.0%; Dutch Reformed Church 15.0%; Calvinist 8.0%; Muslim 4.3%; Hindu 0.5%; other 2.2%; no religion 38.0%.
Major cities (1996[1]): Amsterdam 718,119; Rotterdam 592,745; The Hague 442,503; Utrecht 234,254; Eindhoven 197,374.

Vital statistics

Birth rate per 1,000 population (1995): 12.3 (world avg. 25.0); legitimate 84.5%; illegitimate 15.5%.
Death rate per 1,000 population (1995): 8.8 (world avg. 9.3).
Natural increase rate per 1,000 population (1995): 3.5 (world avg. 15.7).
Total fertility rate (avg. births per childbearing woman; 1995): 1.5.
Marriage rate per 1,000 population (1995): 5.3.
Divorce rate per 1,000 population (1995): 2.2.
Life expectancy at birth (1995): male 74.6 years; female 80.4 years.
Major causes of death per 100,000 population (1995): malignant neoplasms (cancers) 233.1, of which lung cancer 55.3; ischemic heart diseases 132.5; cerebrovascular diseases 79.7; accidents, poisoning, and violence 31.8.

National economy

Budget (1995). Revenue: f. 168,474,000,000 (income and corporate taxes 42.3%; value-added and excise taxes 36.8%; property taxes 0.9%). Expenditures: f. 225,262,000,000 (social security and public health 18.3%; education, scientific research, and culture 15.7%; defense 5.9%; transportation 4.9%).
Public debt (1997): U.S.$206,594,000,000.
Tourism (1996): receipts U.S.$6,144,300,000; expenditures U.S.$11,112,000,000.
Production (metric tons except as noted). Agriculture, forestry, fishing (1996): sugar beets 7,600,000, potatoes 7,363,000, wheat 1,213,000, apples 570,000, tomatoes 525,000, cucumbers 500,000, onions 453,000, barley 218,000; livestock (number of live animals; 1995) 13,958,000 pigs, 4,557,000 cattle, 1,674,000 sheep; roundwood (1995) 1,103,000 cu m; fish catch (1995) 521,377. Manufacturing (value added in f. '000,000; 1994): foodstuffs 15,771; chemicals 14,968; machinery 10,284; electrical machinery 9,172; publishing 7,513. Construction (buildings completed by value in f. '000,000; 1995): residential 14,300; nonresidential 9,800. Energy production (consumption): electricity (kW-hr; 1994) 79,677,000,000 (90,239,000,000); coal (metric tons; 1994) none (14,240,000); crude petroleum (barrels; 1994) 23,554,000 (403,458,000); petroleum products (metric tons; 1994) 59,758,000 (29,130,000); natural gas (cu m; 1994) 87,810,000,000 (48,841,000,000).
Household income and expenditure (1994). Average household size 2.4; income per household f. 59,739 (U.S.$32,824); sources of income: wages 81.6%, profits 12.8%, property income 5.6%; expenditure: rent 26.2%; food, beverages, and tobacco 18.0%; education and recreation 16.2%; transportation and communications 13.4%; clothing and footwear 7.1%; household furnishings and appliances 6.6%; health care 5.7%; other 6.8%.
Gross national product (1996): U.S.$402,565,000,000 (U.S.$25,940 per capita).

Structure of gross domestic product and labour force

	1995			
	in value f. '000,000	% of total value	labour force	% of labour force
Agriculture	19,988	3.5	244,000	3.3
Mining	15,447	2.7	12,000	0.2
Manufacturing	102,849	18.0	1,079,000	14.8
Construction	31,459	5.5	406,000	5.6
Public utilities	10,738	1.9	43,000	0.6
Transp. and commun.	45,902	8.0	406,000	5.6
Trade	90,071	15.8	1,342,000	18.4
Finance	[4]	[4]	880,000	12.1
Pub. admin., defense	[4]	[4]	2,418,000	33.1
Services	277,437[4]	48.7[4]		
Other	−23,991[5]	−4.2[5]	467,000[6]	6.4[6]
TOTAL	569,910[2]	100.0[2]	7,297,000	100.0[2]

Population economically active (1995): total 7,297,000; activity rate of total population 47.2% (participation rates: ages 15–64, 70.1%; female 41.9%; unemployed 6.3%).

Price and earnings indexes (1990 = 100)

	1991	1992	1993	1994	1995	1996	1997
Consumer price index	103.1	106.4	109.2	112.2	114.4	116.8	119.3
Hourly earnings index	103.7	108.2	111.7	113.8	115.0	117.0	120.5

Land use (1994): forested 10.3%; meadows and pastures 31.0%; agricultural and under permanent cultivation 28.0%; other 30.7%.

Foreign trade

Balance of trade (current prices)

	1992	1993	1994	1995	1996	1997
f. '000,000	+9,944	+26,706	+25,767	+29,554	+28,363	+32,461
% of total	2.1%	5.5%	4.8%	4.9%	4.4%	4.5%

Imports (1995): f. 285,139,000,000 (machinery and transport equipment 29.5%, chemicals 11.9%, food 10.7%, petroleum 4.3%, clothing 2.8%). *Major import sources:* Germany 23.4%; Belgium-Luxembourg 11.8%; U.K. 10.1%; U.S. 8.0%.
Exports (1995): f. 314,693,000,000 (machinery and transport equipment 24.2%, food 17.2%, chemicals and chemical products 16.6%, petroleum products 4.1%, iron and steel 2.2%, clothing 1.4%). *Major export destinations:* Germany 28.6%; Belgium-Luxembourg 12.9%; France 11.1%.

Transport and communications

Transport. Railroads (1995): length 2,739 km; passenger-km 13,977,000,000; metric ton-km cargo 3,097,000,000. Roads (1996): total length 124,064 km (paved 91%). Vehicles (1996): passenger cars 5,740,000; trucks and buses 680,000. Merchant marine (1993): vessels (100 gross tons and over) 399; total deadweight tonnage 2,874,000. Air transport (1995–96): passenger-km 45,531,000,000; metric ton-km cargo 3,635,218,000; airports (1996) 6.

Communications

Medium	date	unit	number	units per 1,000 persons
Daily newspapers	1994	circulation	4,600,000	299
Radio	1993	receivers	13,400,000	877
Television	1995	receivers	7,660,000	495
Telephones	1995	main lines	8,120,000	525
Cellular telephones	1995	subscribers	513,000	33.2
Facsimile machines	1995	units	500,000	32.3
Personal computers	1995	units	3,100,000	200.5

Education and health

Educational attainment (1995). Percentage of population ages 15–64 having: primary education 14.9%; secondary 65.7%; higher 19.4%. *Literacy:* virtually 100% literate.

Education (1995–96)

	schools	teachers[7]	students	student/ teacher ratio[7]
Primary (age 6–12)	7,411	99,031	1,477,000	15.7
Secondary (age 12–18)	1,124	89,370	868,000	7.7
Voc., teacher tr.	218	18,613	519,000	28.0
Higher	20	...	408,000	10.2

Health (1995[1]): physicians 37,493 (1 per 412 persons); hospital beds 85,579 (1 per 181 persons); infant mortality rate per 1,000 live births (1996) 5.1.
Food (1995): daily per capita caloric intake 3,230 (vegetable products 66%, animal products 34%); 120% of FAO recommended minimum requirement.

Military

Total active duty personnel (1996): 63,100 (army 51.3%, navy 22.2%, air force 19.6%, other[8] 6.9%). *Military expenditure as percentage of GNP* (1994): 2.2% (world 3.0%); per capita expenditure U.S.$464.

---

[1]January 1. [2]Detail does not add to total given because of rounding. [3]Based on land area only. [4]Services includes Finance and Pub. admin., defense. [5]Imputed bank service charge. [6]Includes 462,000 unemployed. [7]1990–91. [8]Includes 3,600 military police and 800 interservice personnel.

Internet resources for further information:
• **Statistics Netherlands** http://www.cbs.nl/indexeng.htm

New Zealand

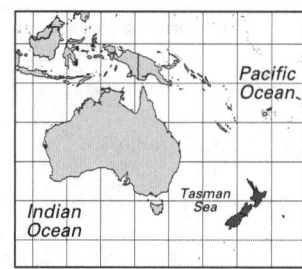

Official name: New Zealand (English); Aotearoa (Māori).
Form of government: constitutional monarchy with one legislative house (House of Representatives [120[1]]).
Chief of state: British Monarch, represented by Governor-General.
Head of government: Prime Minister.
Capital: Wellington.
Official languages: English; Māori.
Official religion: none.
Monetary unit: 1 New Zealand dollar ($NZ) = 100 cents; valuation (Sept. 25, 1998) 1 U.S.$ = $NZ 2.02; 1 £ = $NZ 3.44.

Area and population	area		population
Islands			1996
Regional Councils	sq mi	sq km	census
North Island	44,702	115,777	2,749,788
Auckland	...	...	1,077,205
Bay of Plenty	...	...	230,465
Gisborne[2]	...	...	46,089
Hawkes Bay	...	...	144,292
Manawatu-Wanganui	...	...	229,989
Northland	...	...	141,865
Taranaki	...	...	106,570
Waikato	...	...	357,294
Wellington	...	...	416,019
South Island	58,384	151,215	930,824
Canterbury	...	...	478,912
Marlborough[2]	...	...	40,242
Nelson[2]	...	...	42,073
Otago	...	...	193,132
Southland	...	...	100,758
Tasman[2]	...	...	40,036
West Coast	...	...	35,671
Offshore islands[3]	1,368	3,542	934
TOTAL	104,454	270,534	3,681,546

Demography

Population (1998): 3,801,000.
Density (1998): persons per sq mi 36.4, persons per sq km 14.0.
Urban-rural (1996): urban 85.0%; rural 15.0%.
Sex distribution (1996): male 49.15%; female 50.85%.
Age breakdown (1996): under 15, 23.0%; 15–29, 22.7%; 30–44, 23.1%; 45–59, 15.9%; 60–74, 10.6%; 75 and over, 4.7%.
Population projection: (2000) 3,878,000; (2010) 4,225,000.
Ethnic composition (1996)[4]: European 88.6%; Māori 15.1%; other Polynesian 5.8%; Asian 5.0%; other 0.5%.
Religious affiliation (1996): Christian 60.8%, of which Protestant 39.4% (including Anglican 17.5%), Roman Catholic 13.1%; nonreligious 24.7%; other religions/not specified 14.5%.
Major cities (1996): Auckland 353,670; Christchurch 313,969; Manukau 254,577; North Shore 170,913; Wellington 158,275.

Vital statistics

Birth rate per 1,000 population (1997): 15.4 (world avg. 25.0); (1996) legitimate 58.0%; illegitimate 42.0%.
Death rate per 1,000 population (1997): 7.6 (world avg. 9.3).
Natural increase rate per 1,000 population (1997): 7.8 (world avg. 15.7).
Total fertility rate (avg. births per childbearing woman; 1996): 2.0.
Life expectancy at birth (1996): male 74.0 years; female 80.0 years.
Major causes of death per 100,000 population (1994): diseases of the circulatory system 328.4, of which ischemic heart disease 188.7; malignant neoplasms (cancers) 204.3; diseases of the respiratory system 78.2.

National economy

Budget (1995–96). Revenue: $NZ 35,059,000,000 (income taxes 60.4%, taxes on goods and services 32.9%, nontax revenue 6.7%). Expenditures: $NZ 31,743,000,000 (social services 38.6%, health 16.5%, education 15.6%).
Public debt (year ending June 30, 1996): $NZ 31,747,000,000.
Tourism (1995): receipts U.S.$2,163,000,000; expenditures U.S.$1,283,000,000.
Production (metric tons except as noted). Agriculture, forestry, fishing (1997): apples 546,000, barley 377,998, wheat 255,316, corn (maize) 229,185; livestock (number of live animals) 47,394,000 sheep, 8,950,000 cattle, 400,000 pigs; roundwood (1995) 17,155,000 cu m; fish catch (1995) 612,243. Mining and quarrying (1995): limestone 3,930,000[5]; iron ore and sand concentrate 2,362,236; silver 27,800 kg; gold 12,100 kg. Manufacturing (1996–97): wood pulp 1,405,300; chemical fertilizers 1,365,000; yarn 21,302; beer 343,457,000 litres; footwear 2,840,000 pairs[6]; carpets 9,980,000 sq m. Energy production (consumption): electricity (kW-hr; 1994) 32,416,000,000 (32,416,000,000); coal (metric tons; 1994) 2,991,000 (2,191,000); crude petroleum (barrels; 1994) 14,401,000 (36,823,000); petroleum products (metric tons; 1994) 5,029,000 (4,504,000); natural gas (cu m; 1994) 4,442,300,000 (4,442,300,000).
Population economically active (1997[7]): total 1,806,000; activity rate 49.4% (participation rates: over age 15, 65.7%; female 44.6%; unemployed 6.4%).

Price and earnings indexes (1990 = 100)							
	1992	1993	1994	1995	1996	1997	1998
Consumer price index	103.6	105.0	106.8	110.8	113.4	114.7	116.2[8]
Weekly earnings index	104.8	105.5	108.5	111.8[9]	...	...	...

Gross national product (1996): U.S.$57,135,000,000 (U.S.$15,720 per capita).

Structure of gross domestic product and labour force				
	1993–94		1997[7]	
	in value $NZ '000,000	% of total value	labour force	% of labour force
Agriculture	6,673	8.3	149,900	8.3
Mining	1,121	1.4	4,500	0.2
Manufacturing	15,486	19.3	285,200	15.8
Construction	2,289	2.8	111,200	6.2
Public utilities	2,228	2.8	11,700	0.6
Transp. and commun.	6,433	8.0	101,600	5.6
Trade	12,675	15.8	355,200	19.7
Finance	17,791	22.2	205,400	11.4
Pub. admin., defense	8,716	10.8 }	458,600	25.4
Services	4,656	5.8 }		
Other	2,229[10]	2.8[10]	122,700[11]	6.8[11]
TOTAL	80,297	100.0	1,806,000	100.0

Household income and expenditure. Average household size (1995–96) 2.7; annual income per household[12] (1995–96) $NZ 46,282 (U.S.$32,140); sources of income (1994–95): wages and salaries 65.8%, transfer payments 15.2%, self-employment 9.8%, other 9.2%; expenditure (1996–97): housing 20.2%, transportation 18.2%, food 16.4%, household goods 13.7%, clothing 3.8%.
Land use (1994): forest 27.9%; pasture 50.4%; agriculture 14.2%; other 7.5%.

Foreign trade[13]

Balance of trade (current prices)						
	1992	1993	1994	1995	1996	1997
$NZ '000,000	+2,404.0	+3,120.0	+2,028.0	+1,068.9	+1,028.0	+798.0
% of total	7.1%	8.7%	5.2%	2.6%	2.5%	1.9%

Imports (1996): $NZ 21,352,500,000 (machinery 26.0%; minerals, chemicals, and plastics 21.7%; transport equipment 13.6%; basic manufactures 7.5%; food, beverages, and tobacco 7.1%; metals and metal products 6.1%; textiles, clothing, and footwear 5.2%). Major import sources: Australia 21.8%; U.S. 16.0%; Japan 12.3%; U.K. 5.0%; Germany 4.6%.
Exports (1996): $NZ 20,543,000,000 (food and live animals 45.9%; basic manufactures 25.4%; minerals, chemicals, and plastics 10.2%; metals and metal products 7.0%). Major export destinations: Australia 20.5%; Japan 16.1%; U.S. 9.0%; U.K. 6.1%; South Korea 5.0%; Hong Kong 3.3%.

Transport and communications

Transport. Railroads (1996): length 3,915 km; passenger journeys 10,953,000; metric ton-km cargo 3,324,000,000. Roads (1996): total length 91,864 km (paved 73%). Vehicles (1996): passenger cars 1,650,112; trucks and buses 351,494. Merchant marine (1992): vessels (100 gross tons and over) 139; total deadweight tonnage 279,805. Air transport[14] (1996): passenger-km 17,848,000,000; metric ton-km cargo 648,092,000; airports (1997) 36.

Communications				units per 1,000
Medium	date	unit	number	persons
Daily newspapers	1995	circulation	850,000	239.0
Radio	1995	receivers	3,550,000	997.0
Television	1995	receivers	1,830,000	514.0
Telephones	1996	main lines	1,719,000	477.0
Cellular telephones	1995	subscribers	386,600	108.0
Facsimile machines	1995	units	64,800	18.1
Personal computers	1995	units	797,300	222.7

Education and health

Educational attainment (1991). Percentage of population age 25 and over having: primary and some secondary education 54.9%; secondary 31.1%; higher 6.9%; not specified 6.1%[6]. Literacy: virtually 100.0%.

Education (1996)	schools	teachers	students	student/teacher ratio
Primary (age 5–12)[15]	2,397	23,379	455,671	19.5
Secondary (age 13–17)	339	15,246	227,934	14.9
Voc., teacher tr.	30	5,314	107,736	20.3
Higher[16]	7	5,982	105,690	17.7

Health (1996): physicians 11,557 (1 per 318 persons); hospital beds 22,488 (1 per 164 persons); infant mortality rate per 1,000 live births 6.7.
Food (1995): daily per capita caloric intake 3,379 (vegetable products 64%, animal products 36%); 128% of FAO recommended minimum requirement.

Military

Total active duty personnel (1997): 9,550 (army 46.1%, air force 31.9%, navy 22.0%). Military expenditure as percentage of GNP (1995): 1.3% (world 2.8%); per capita expenditure U.S.$211.

[1]Includes five elected seats allocated to Māoris. [2]Reorganized as a unitary authority that is administered by a district council with regional powers. [3]Includes Stewart, Chatham, Campbell, and Kermadec islands and persons on oil rigs. [4]Percentages add up to more than 100.0 as people specified more than one ethnic group on the 1996 census form. [5]1994. [6]1994–95. [7]March. [8]Second quarter. [9]May. [10]Includes import duties less imputed bank service charges. [11]Includes 116,000 unemployed. [12]Gross income. [13]Import figures are f.o.b. in balance of trade and c.i.f. in commodities and trading partners. [14]Air New Zealand only. [15]Includes 96 composite schools that provide both primary and secondary education. [16]Universities only.

Internet resources for further information:
• Statistics New Zealand Te Tari Tatau http://www.stats.govt.nz/statsweb.nsf
• The Press On-Line New Zealand News http://www.press.co.nz/

Nicaragua

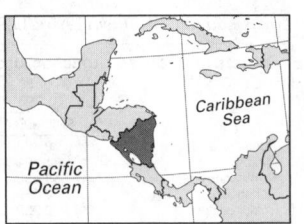

Official name: República de Nicaragua (Republic of Nicaragua).
Form of government: unitary multiparty republic with one legislative house (National Assembly [93[1]]).
Head of state and government: President.
Capital: Managua.
Official language: Spanish.
Official religion: none.
Monetary unit: 1 córdoba oro (C$)[2] = 100 centavos; valuation (Sept. 25, 1998) 1 U.S.$ = C$10.86; 1 £ = C$18.49.

Area and population

Departments	Capitals	area[3] sq mi	area[3] sq km	population 1995 census[4]
Boaco	Boaco	1,639	4,244	136,949
Carazo	Jinotepe	405	1,050	149,407
Chinandega	Chinandega	1,902	4,926	350,212
Chontales	Juigalpa	2,463	6,378	144,635
Estelí	Estelí	902	2,335	174,894
Granada	Granada	359	929	155,683
Jinotega	Jinotega	3,766	9,755	257,933
León	León	1,972	5,107	336,894
Madriz	Somoto	619	1,602	107,567
Managua	Managua	1,418	3,672	1,093,760
Masaya	Masaya	228	590	241,354
Matagalpa	Matagalpa	3,291	8,523	383,776
Nueva Segovia	Ocotal	1,206	3,123	148,492
Río San Juan	San Carlos	2,885	7,473	70,143
Rivas	Rivas	832	2,155	140,432
Autonomous regions				
North Atlantic	...	12,417	32,159	192,716
South Atlantic	Bluefields	10,582	27,407	272,252
TOTAL LAND AREA		46,884[5]	121,428	
INLAND WATER		4,009	10,384	
TOTAL		50,893	131,812	4,357,099

Demography

Population (1998): 4,763,000.
Density (1998)[6]: persons per sq mi 101.6, persons per sq km 39.2.
Urban-rural (1995): urban 54.4%; rural 45.6%.
Sex distribution (1995): male 49.28%; female 50.72%.
Age breakdown (1994): under 15, 44.2%; 15–29, 28.7%; 30–44, 15.5%; 45–59, 7.2%; 60–74, 3.6%; 75 and over, 0.8%.
Population projection: (2000) 5,045,000; (2010) 6,429,000.
Doubling time: 26 years.
Ethnic composition (1991): mestizo (Spanish/Indian) 69.0%; white 17.0%; black 9.0%; Amerindian 5.0%.
Religious affiliation (1995): Roman Catholic 73.0%; Protestant 16.5%, of which Evangelical 15.0%; nonreligious 8.4%; other 2.1%.
Major cities (1995)[4]: Managua 864,201; León 123,865; Chinandega 97,387; Masaya 88,971; Granada 71,783; Estelí 71,550.

Vital statistics

Birth rate per 1,000 population (1996): 33.8 (world avg. 25.0).
Death rate per 1,000 population (1996): 6.0 (world avg. 9.3).
Natural increase rate per 1,000 population (1996): 27.8 (world avg. 15.7).
Total fertility rate (avg. births per childbearing woman; 1996): 4.0.
Marriage rate per 1,000 population (1991): 3.3.
Divorce rate per 1,000 population (1991): 0.4.
Life expectancy at birth (1996): male 63.4 years; female 68.1 years.
Major causes of death per 100,000 population (1991)[7]: diseases of the circulatory system 142.0; infectious and parasitic diseases 100.0; accidents and violence 93.0; diseases of the respiratory system 73.0; malignant neoplasms (cancers) 56.0.

National economy

Budget (1995). Revenue: C$3,929,000,000 (tax revenue 74.6%, of which import duties 17.3%, excise taxes on petroleum products 14.6%; grants 20.2%). Expenditures: C$4,526,000,000 (current expenditure 62.8%, development expenditure 33.6%; net lending 3.6%).
Public debt (external, outstanding; 1996): U.S.$5,122,000,000.
Production (metric tons except as noted). Agriculture, forestry, fishing (1996): sugar cane 2,948,000, corn (maize) 332,640, rice 219,100, sorghum 127,300, dry beans 102,900, bananas 88,000, oranges 72,000, coffee 55,000, soybeans 24,100, sesame 14,800; livestock (number of live animals) 1,807,000 cattle, 410,000 pigs; roundwood (1995) 3,809,000 cu m; fish catch (1995) 13,503, of which shrimp 5,425. Mining and quarrying (1995): gold 42,300 troy oz. Manufacturing (value added in C$'000,000; 1995[8]): food, beverages, and tobacco 3,129; machinery and metal products 319; refined petroleum and rubber products 231; chemicals and chemical products 124. Construction (completed; 1991): 569 cu m. Energy production (consumption): electricity (kW-hr; 1995) 1,726,000,000 (1,130,000,000); coal, none (none); crude petroleum (barrels; 1994) none (4,178,000); petroleum products (metric tons; 1994) 540,000 (582,000); natural gas, none (none).
Tourism (in U.S.$'000,000; 1995): receipts 54.6; expenditures 40.
Population economically active (1994): total 1,407,700; activity rate of total population 34.8% (participation rates: over age 15 [1991] 62.0%; female [1991] 33.2%; unemployed [1996] 16.6%).

Price and earnings indexes (1992 = 100)

	1992	1993	1994	1995	1996	1997
Consumer price index	100.0	120.4	129.7	143.9	160.6	171.2[9]
Monthly earnings index[10]	100.0	111.8	126.7	142.9	...	...

Household income and expenditure. Average household size (1995) 5.8; income per household: n.a.; sources of income: n.a.; expenditure: n.a.
Gross national product (1996): U.S.$1,705,000,000 (U.S.$380 per capita).

Structure of gross domestic product and labour force

	1996 in value C$'000,000	1996 % of total value	1994 labour force	1994 % of labour force
Agriculture, forestry	5,981	34.9	415,400	29.5
Mining	133	0.8	7,300	0.5
Manufacturing	2,677	15.6	155,500	11.0
Construction	614	3.6	28,600	2.0
Public utilities	186	1.1	10,600	0.8
Transp. and commun.	612	3.6	30,000	2.1
Trade	4,184	24.4	189,000	13.4
Finance, real estate	859	5.0	16,200	1.2
Pub. admin., defense	928	5.4	81,900	5.8
Services	952	5.6	181,300	12.9
Other	—	—	291,900[11]	20.7[11]
TOTAL	17,126	100.0	1,407,700	100.0[5]

Land use (1994): forested 26.3%; meadows and pastures 45.3%; agricultural and under permanent cultivation 10.5%; other 17.9%.

Foreign trade[12]

Balance of trade (current prices)

	1992	1993	1994	1995	1996	1997
U.S.$'000,000	−547.8	−402.8	−433.5	−263.8	−381.5	−489.8
% of total	55.1%	43.0%	38.2%	20.0%	22.1%	28.0%

Imports (1996): U.S.$1,119,900,000 (capital goods 24.9%, consumer goods 24.7%, petroleum 14.1%). *Major import sources* (1995): U.S. 31.2%; CACM 23.9%; Venezuela 11.6%; Japan 5.2%.
Exports (1996): U.S.$634,800,000 (industrial products 24.4%, coffee 17.5%, crustaceans 10.9%, beef 6.9%, raw sugar 6.0%). *Major export destinations:* U.S. 38.1%; CACM 15.1%; Germany 10.4%; Spain 7.2%; The Netherlands 5.9%.

Transport and communications

Transport. Railroads: [13]. Roads (1995): total length 17,146 km (paved 10%). Vehicles (1995): passenger cars 72,413; trucks and buses 68,090. Air transport (1994)[14]: passenger-km 72,172,000; metric ton-km cargo 6,964,000; airports (1997) with scheduled flights 10.

Communications

Medium	date	unit	number	units per 1,000 persons
Daily newspapers	1994	circulation	130,000	31
Radio	1996	receivers	925,000	206
Television	1995	receivers	210,000	48
Telephones	1995	main lines	96,600	22
Cellular telephones	1995	subscribers	4,400	1.0

Education and health

Educational attainment: n.a. *Literacy* (1995): total population age 15 and over literate 1,574,000 (65.7%); males literate 727,000 (64.6%); females literate 847,000 (66.6%).

Education (1994)

	schools	teachers	students	student/ teacher ratio
Primary (age 7–12)	4,993	20,626	765,972	37.1
Secondary (age 13–18) Voc., teacher tr.	451	5,356	211,606	39.5
Higher	10	2,005	22,120	11.0

Health (1994): physicians 2,577 (1 per 1,566 persons); hospital beds 4,413 (1 per 914 persons); infant mortality rate per 1,000 live births (1996) 45.8.
Food (1995): daily per capita caloric intake 2,311 (vegetable products 92%, animal products 8%); 103% of FAO recommended minimum requirement.

Military

Total active duty personnel (1996): 17,000 (army 88.2%, navy 4.7%, air force 7.1%). *Military expenditure as percentage of GNP* (1995): 2.2% (world 2.8%); per capita expenditure U.S.$8.

[1]Includes three unsuccessful 1996 presidential condidates meeting special conditions. [2]The córdoba oro (gold cordoba), introduced in August 1990, circulated simultaneously with the new córdoba until April 30, 1991, when the new córdoba ceased to be legal tender; on April 30, 1 córdoba oro equaled 5,000,000 new córdobas. The new córdoba had been introduced in February 1988 at the rate of 1 new córdoba to 1,000 (old) córdobas. [3]Lakes and lagoons are excluded from the areas of departments and autonomous regions. [4]Final figures. [5]Detail does not add to total given because of rounding. [6]Based on land area. [7]Projected rates based on about 45% of total deaths. [8]At prices of 1980. [9]April. [10]Base and all indexes are for December only. [11]Unemployed persons previously employed. [12]Imports f.o.b. in balance of trade and c.i.f. in commodities and trading partners. [13]Railroad service ended in January 1994. [14]Nica only.

Internet resources for further information:
• Banco Central de Nicaragua: Informe Anual (Spanish language only) http://www.bcn.gob.ni/infanu/informes.html

Niger

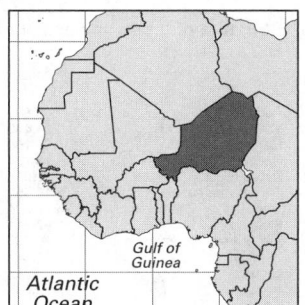

Official name: République du Niger (Republic of Niger).
Form of government: republic[1] with a single legislative body (National Assembly[2] [83[3]]).
Head of state and government: President assisted by Prime Minister.
Capital: Niamey.
Official language: French.
Official religion: none.
Monetary unit: 1 CFA franc (CFAF) = 100 centimes; valuation (Sept. 25, 1998) 1 U.S.$ = CFAF 560.38; 1 £ = CFAF 954.05.

Area and population

Departments	Capitals	area[4] sq mi	area[4] sq km	population 1990 estimate
Agadez[5]	Agadez	244,869	634,209	189,000
Diffa	Diffa	54,138	140,216	227,000
Dosso	Dosso	11,970	31,002	982,000
Maradi	Maradi	14,896	38,581	1,415,000
Tahoua	Tahoua	41,188	106,677	1,373,000
Tillabéri[6]	Tillabéri	34,863[7]	90,293[7]	1,818,000[7]
Zinder	Zinder	56,151	145,430	1,467,000
City				
Niamey	Niamey	[7]	[7]	[7]
TOTAL		458,075	1,186,408	7,471,000

Demography

Population (1998): 9,672,000.
Density (1998)[4]: persons per sq mi 19.8, persons per sq km 7.6.
Urban-rural (1995): urban 17.0%; rural 83.0%.
Sex distribution (1995): male 49.40%; female 50.60%.
Age breakdown (1995): under 15, 48.4%; 15–29, 25.7%; 30–44, 14.4%; 45–59, 7.5%; 60–74, 3.4%; 75 and over, 0.6%.
Population projection: (2000) 10,260,000; (2010) 13,678,000.
Doubling time: 23 years.
Ethnic composition (1988): Hausa 53.0%; Zerma- (Djerma-) Songhai 21.2%; Tuareg 10.4%; Fulani (Peul) 9.8%; Kanuri-Nanga 4.4%; Teda 0.4%; Arab 0.3%; Gurma 0.3%; other 0.2%.
Religious affiliation (1995): Muslim, primarily Sunnī, 88.7%; traditional beliefs 11.0%; Christian 0.3%.
Major cities (1988): Niamey 391,876; Zinder 119,827; Maradi 110,005; Tahoua 49,948; Agadez 32,272.

Vital statistics

Birth rate per 1,000 population (1996): 54.5 (world avg. 25.0).
Death rate per 1,000 population (1996): 24.6 (world avg. 9.3).
Natural increase rate per 1,000 population (1996): 29.9 (world avg. 15.7).
Total fertility rate (avg. births per childbearing woman; 1996): 7.4.
Marriage rate per 1,000 population: n.a.
Divorce rate per 1,000 population: n.a.
Life expectancy at birth (1996): male 41.1 years; female 40.2 years.
Major causes of death: n.a.; however, among selected major causes of infectious disease registered at medical facilities were malaria, measles, diarrhea, meningitis, pneumonia, diphtheria, tetanus, viral hepatitis, and poliomyelitis; malnutrition and shortages of trained medical personnel are widespread.

National economy

Budget (1996). Revenue: CFAF 123,500,000,000 (taxes 54.2%, external aid and gifts 38.8%, nontax revenue 7.0%). Expenditures: CFAF 120,200,000,000 (current expenditures 73.0%, development expenditures 27.0%).
Public debt (external, outstanding; 1996): U.S.$1,350,000,000.
Tourism (1995): receipts from visitors U.S.$15,000,000; expenditures by nationals abroad U.S.$21,000,000.
Gross national product (1996): U.S.$1,879,000,000 (U.S.$200 per capita).

Structure of gross domestic product and labour force

	1994 in value CFAF '000,000	1994 % of total value	1988 labour force[8]	1988 % of labour force
Agriculture	372,200	42.9	1,764,049	76.2
Mining	34,700	4.0	5,295	0.2
Manufacturing	56,900	6.6	65,793	2.8
Construction	16,100	1.9	13,742	0.6
Public utilities	18,400	2.1	1,778	0.1
Transp. and commun.	47,200	5.4	14,764	0.6
Trade and finance	130,000	15.0	210,354	9.1
Pub. admin., defense	94,700	10.9	59,271	2.6
Services	87,400	10.1	63,991	2.8
Other	10,300	1.2	116,657	5.0
TOTAL	867,800[9]	100.0[9]	2,315,694	100.0

Production (metric tons except as noted). Agriculture, forestry, fishing (1996): millet 1,832,000, cowpeas 430,000, sorghum 425,000, cassava (manioc) 225,000, onions 178,000, sugarcane 145,000, rice 70,000, peanuts (groundnuts) 57,000, tomatoes 47,000, tobacco leaf 930; livestock (number of live animals) 5,869,000 goats, 3,849,000 sheep, 1,987,000 cattle, 450,000 asses, 380,000 camels, 82,000 horses; roundwood (1995) 5,866,000 cu m; fish catch (1994) 2,200. Mining and quarrying (1996): salt 3,000[10]; uranium 3,326. Manufac-

turing (value added in CFAF '000,000; 1993): traditional-sector handicrafts 36,900; food and beverages 2,900; soaps and other chemical products 2,100; construction materials 600. Construction (value added in CFAF; 1994): 16,100,000,000. Energy production (consumption): electricity (kW-hr; 1994) 178,000,000 (375,000,000); coal (metric tons; 1994) 133,500 (174,000); crude petroleum, none (none); petroleum products (metric tons; 1994) none (211,000); natural gas, none (none).
Population economically active (1988)[8]: total 2,315,694; activity rate of total population 31.9% (participation rates: ages 15–64, 55.2%; female 20.4%).

Price and earnings indexes (1990 = 100)

	1991	1992	1993	1994	1995	1996	1997
Consumer price index	92.2	88.1	87.0	118.4	130.9	137.8	141.8
Annual earnings index[11]	101.2	103.5	108.0	123.6	...	...	...

Household income and expenditure. Average household size (1988) 6.4; income per household: n.a.; expenditure (1987): food and beverages 43.1%, housing 22.8%, clothing 10.0%.
Land use (1994): forested 2.0%; meadows and pastures 8.2%; agricultural and under permanent cultivation 2.9%; other (largely desert) 86.9%.

Foreign trade[12]

Balance of trade (current prices)

	1992	1993	1994	1995	1996	1997
CFAF '000,000	−38,487	−24,923	−56,997	−43,477	−31,800	−91,200
% of total	17.9%	13.3%	18.6%	13.2%	10.0%	22.5%

Imports (1994): CFAF 135,600,000,000 (consumer goods 72.3%, of which cereals 10.8%, petroleum products 7.7%; intermediate and capital goods 27.7%). *Major import sources*[13]: France 20%; Côte d'Ivoire 11%; China 4%; Belgium 4%; unspecified countries 14%.
Exports (1995): CFAF 143,000,000,000 (uranium 52.9%; livestock [mostly live cattle, sheep, and goats] 13.9%; cowpeas 5.2%). *Major export destinations* (1994)[13]: France 66%; Côte d'Ivoire 8%; United Kingdom 5%.

Transport and communications

Transport. Railroads: none. Roads (1995): total length 6,129 mi, 9,863 km (paved 9%). Vehicles (1995): passenger cars 37,500, trucks and buses 14,100. Air transport (1996)[14]: passenger-mi 139,644,000, passenger-km 224,736,000; short ton-mi cargo 11,247,000, metric ton-km cargo 16,420,000; airports (1996) with scheduled flights 6.

Communications

Medium	date	unit	number	units per 1,000 persons
Daily newspapers	1994	circulation	11,000	1.3
Radio	1996	receivers	440,000	48
Television	1995	receivers	25,000	2.8
Telephones	1995	main lines	13,300	1.5
Facsimile machines	1995	units	300	—

Education and health

Educational attainment (1988). Percentage of population age 25 and over having: no formal schooling 85.0%; Koranic education 11.2%; primary education 2.5%; secondary 1.1%; higher 0.2%. *Literacy* (1995): total population age 15 and over literate 641,000 (13.6%); males literate 482,000 (20.9%); females literate 159,000 (6.6%).

Education (1993–94)

	schools	teachers	students	student/ teacher ratio
Primary (age 7–12)	2,656	12,216	414,296	33.9
Secondary (age 13–19)	105[15]	2,219[16]	88,810	35.1[16]
Voc., teacher tr.	7[15]	175[16]	2,110	12.1[16]
Higher[17]	2	315	4,060	12.9

Health: physicians (1993) 242 (1 per 35,141 persons); hospital beds (1987) c. 3,500 (1 per 2,000 persons); infant mortality rate per 1,000 live births (1996) 117.6.
Food (1995): daily per capita caloric intake 2,136 (vegetable products 94%, animal products 6%); 91% of FAO recommended minimum requirement.

Military

Total active duty personnel (1996): 5,300 (army 98.1%, air force 1.9%). *Military expenditure as percentage of GNP* (1995): 1.2% (world 2.8%); per capita expenditure U.S.$2.

---

[1]Leader of military coup of January 1996 (now president) promulgated a new constitution on May 22, 1996; president approved dissolution of military ruling council in December 1996. [2]November 1996 elections to National Assembly were boycotted by major opposition parties. [3]Occupied seats only. [4]The departmental areas and total shown are obsolete. The total area, according to recent official estimates, is 489,000 sq mi (1,267,000 sq km); but subtotals distributing this total among the departments remain unpublished. [5]The peace accord signed in October 1994 provided for an eventual limited autonomy for the Tuaregs (a Berber-speaking people), who inhabit Agadez department. [6]Created 1992. [7]Tillabéri includes Niamey. [8]Excluding nomadic population. [9]Detail does not add to total given because of rounding. [10]1994. [11]Public sector only. [12]Imports c.i.f. in balance of trade and f.o.b. in commodities and trading partners. [13]Estimated figures. [14]Represents 1/11 of the traffic of Air Afrique, which is operated by 11 West African states. [15]1989–90. [16]1992–93. [17]Université de Niamey and École Nationale d'Administration du Niger only.

Internet resources for further information:
• Welcome to the Delegation of Niger at UNESCO
  http://www.unesco.org/delegates/niger/welcome.htm

Nigeria

Official name: Federal Republic of Nigeria.
Form of government: military regime[1].
Head of state and government: Chairman assisted by Provisional Ruling Council.
Capital: Abuja (Federal Capital Territory)[2, 3].
Official language: English.
Official religion: none.
Monetary unit: 1 Nigerian naira (₦) = 100 kobo; valuation (Sept. 25, 1998) 1 U.S.$ = ₦90.00; 1 £ = ₦153.23.

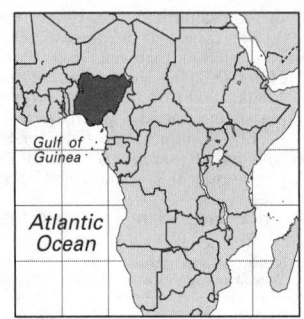

Gulf of Guinea
Atlantic Ocean

Area and population

States[3]	area sq km2	population 1995 estimate	States[4]	area sq km2	population 1995 estimate
Abia	6,320[5]	2,569,362[5]	Kebbi	36,800	2,305,768
Adamawa	36,917	2,374,892	Kogi	29,833	2,346,936
Akwa Ibom	7,081	2,638,413	Kwara	36,825	1,751,464
Anambra	4,844	3,094,783	Lagos	3,345	6,357,253
Bauchi	64,605[6]	4,801,569[6]	Niger	76,363	2,775,526
Bayelsa	7		Nassarawa	9	
Benue	34,059	3,108,754	Ogun	16,762	2,614,747
Borno	70,898	2,903,238	Ondo	20,959[8]	4,343,230[8]
Cross River	20,156	2,085,926	Osun	9,251	2,463,185
Delta	17,698	2,873,711	Oyo	28,454	3,900,803
Ebonyi	5	5	Plateau	58,030[9]	3,671,498[9]
Edo	17,802	2,414,919	Rivers	21,850[7]	4,454,337[7]
Ekiti	8	8	Sokoto	65,735[10]	4,911,118[10]
Enugu	12,831[5]	3,534,635[5]	Taraba	54,473	1,655,443
Gombe	6	6	Yobe	45,502	1,578,172
Imo	5,530	2,779,028	Zamfara	10	10
Jigawa	23,154	3,164,134			
Kaduna	46,053	4,438,007	**Federal Capital Territory**		
Kano	20,131	6,297,165	Abuja	7,315	423,391
Katsina	24,192	4,336,363	TOTAL	923,768	98,967,768

Demography

Population (1998): 110,532,000.
Density (1998): persons per sq mi 309.8, persons per sq km 119.6.
Urban-rural (1996): urban 40.1%; rural 59.9%.
Sex distribution (1996): male 49.57%; female 50.43%.
Age breakdown (1995): under 15, 45.6%; 15–29, 25.7%; 30–44, 15.7%; 45–59, 8.5%; 60–74, 3.8%; 75 and over, 0.7%.
Population projection: (2000) 117,171,000; (2010) 150,274,000.
Doubling time: 23 years.
Ethnic composition (1983): Hausa 21.3%; Yoruba 21.3%; Igbo (Ibo) 18.0%; Fulani 11.2%; Ibibio 5.6%; Kanuri 4.2%; Edo 3.4%; Tiv 2.2%; Ijaw 1.8%; Bura 1.7%; Nupe 1.2%; other 8.1%.
Religious affiliation (1995): Muslim 43.0%; Christian 35.3%, of which Protestant 20.0%, Roman Catholic 8.2%; African indigenous 19.0%; other 2.7%.
Major cities (1992): Lagos 1,347,000; Ibadan 1,295,000; Kano 699,900; Ogbomosho 660,600; Oshogbo 441,600; Ilorin 430,600.

Vital statistics

Birth rate per 1,000 population (1990–95): 45.4 (world avg. 25.0).
Death rate per 1,000 population (1990–95): 15.4 (world avg. 9.3).
Natural increase rate per 1,000 population (1990–95): 30.0 (world avg. 15.7).
Total fertility rate (avg. births per childbearing woman; 1990–95): 6.4.
Life expectancy at birth (1993): male 53.5 years; female 55.9 years.

National economy

Budget (1995). Revenue: ₦459,987,300,000 (petroleum royalties and rents 60.8%; import duties 8.1%; company income tax 4.8%; value-added tax 4.4%). Expenditures: ₦256,520,700,000 (recurrent expenditure 52.8%, of which debt service 19.9%, education 4.7%, health 1.8%, defense 0.5%; capital expenditure 47.2%).
Public debt (external, outstanding; 1996): U.S.$25,431,000,000.
Production (metric tons except as noted). Agriculture, forestry, fishing (1996): cassava 31,500,000, yams 23,264,000, sorghum 7,084,000, millet 5,681,000, corn (maize) 5,667,000, rice 3,122,000, peanuts (groundnuts) 1,723,000, plantains 1,712,000, taro 1,182,000, green peppers 970,000, palm oil 776,000; livestock (number of live animals) 24,500,000 goats, 18,115,000 cattle, 14,000,000 sheep; roundwood (1995) 111,049,000 cu m; fish catch (1995) 302,831. Mining and quarrying (1995): limestone 3,660,000; marble 22,460; tin 300[11, 12]. Manufacturing (value added in ₦'000,000; 1995): food and beverages 25,415; textiles 16,193; chemical products 11,181; machinery and transport equipment 5,639; paper products 2,828; wood products 996. Construction: n.a. Energy production (consumption): electricity (kW-hr; 1994) 14,790,000,000 (14,790,000,000); coal (metric tons; 1994) 50,000 (50,000); crude petroleum (barrels; 1994) 665,994,000 (84,452,000); petroleum products (metric tons; 1994) 5,234,000 (5,974,000); natural gas (cu m; 1994) 9,798,000,000 (9,798,000,000).
Tourism (1995): receipts U.S.$54,000,000; expenditures U.S.$144,000,000[13].
Household income and expenditure. Avg. household size (1995) 4.7; annual income per household (1992–93) ₦15,000 (U.S.$760); sources of income (1979): self-employment 49.4%, wages 30.2%, interest 5.4%, rent 4.7%, transfer payments 4.3%; expenditures (1979): food 53.0%, fuel and light 11.4%, clothing 6.0%, transportation 4.7%, household goods 3.8%, other 21.1%.
Gross national product (1996): U.S.$27,599,000,000 (U.S.$240 per capita).

Structure of gross domestic product and labour force

	1995 in value ₦'000,000	1995 % of total value	1986 labour force	1986 % of labour force
Agriculture	619,807	31.6	13,259,000	43.1
Mining[14]	794,450	40.5	6,800	0.1
Manufacturing	105,154	5.4	1,263,700	4.1
Construction	13,784	0.7	545,600	1.8
Public utilities	1,915	0.1	130,400	0.4
Transp. and commun.	48,855	2.5	1,111,900	3.6
Trade[15]	276,624	14.1	7,417,400	24.1
Finance	67,714	3.4	120,100	0.4
Pub. admin., defense	20,835	1.1 }	4,902,100	15.9
Services	11,547	0.6 }		
Other	...	...	2,008,500[16]	6.5[16]
TOTAL	1,960,686[17]	100.0	30,765,500	100.0

Population economically active (1993–94): total 29,000,000; activity rate 31.0% (participation rates: ages 15–59, 64.4%; female 44.0%; unemployed [1992] 4.0%).

Price and earnings indexes (1990 = 100)

	1991	1992	1993	1994	1995	1996	1997
Consumer price index	113.0	163.4	256.8	403.3	696.9	901.1	975.0
Earnings index	...	...	...	...	...	...	...

Land use (1994): forest 15.7%; pasture 43.9%; agriculture 35.9%; other 4.5%.

Foreign trade

Balance of trade (current prices)

	1991	1992	1993	1994	1995	1996
₦'000,000	+40,696	+76,298	+69,145	+76,677	+91,796	+746,996
% of total	20.2%	22.8%	18.8%	22.8%	6.5%	39.9%

Imports (1995): ₦111,728,000,000 (machinery and transport equipment 42.0%; manufactured goods [mostly iron and steel products, textiles, and paper products] 24.0%; chemicals 17.0%; food 8.4%). *Major import sources* (1992): Germany 18.9%; U.K. 17.8%; Belgium-Luxembourg 9.5%; U.S. 9.2%; France 7.4%.
Exports (1995): ₦220,408,900,000 (crude petroleum 94.8%; cocoa beans 0.7%; rubber 0.3%; other exports include cocoa products, textiles, and cashew nuts). *Major export destinations* (1992): U.S. 48.1%; Spain 16.6%; Italy 7.4%; Germany 7.2%; France 3.8%.

Transport and communications

Transport. Railroads (1993): length[18] 3,505 km; passenger-km 555,000,000; metric ton-km cargo 2,185,000. Roads (1995): total length 32,810 km (paved 83%). Vehicles (1995): passenger cars 663,000; trucks and buses 68,300. Merchant marine (1992): vessels (100 gross tons and over) 271; total deadweight tonnage 733,329. Air transport (1994): passenger-km 985,000,000; metric ton-km cargo 11,484,000[19]; airports (1996) 12.

Communications

Medium	date	unit	number	units per 1,000 persons
Daily newspapers	1995	circulation	1,760,000	18.0
Radio	1995	receivers	17,200,000	170.0
Television	1995	receivers	4,000,000	38.0
Telephones	1995	main lines	405,100	3.6
Cellular telephones	1995	subscribers	13,000	0.1
Personal computers	1995	units	440,000	4.1

Education and health

Literacy (1995): total population age 15 and over literate 34,969,000 (57.1%); males literate 20,027,000 (67.3%); females literate 14,669,000 (47.3%).

Education (1994–95)

	schools	teachers	students	student/ teacher ratio
Primary (age 6–12)	38,649	435,210	16,191,000	37.2
Secondary (age 12–17)	6,074	152,596	4,451,000	29.2
Voc., teacher tr.	376[20]	15,738[21]	391,583[21]	24.9[21]
Higher	31	12,103	228,000	18.8

Health (1994): physicians 21,739 (1 per 4,496 persons); hospital beds 91,346 (1 per 1,070 persons); infant mortality rate (1990–95) 84.2.
Food (1995): daily per capita caloric intake 2,508 (vegetable products 97%, animal products 3%); 106% of FAO recommended minimum requirement.

Military

Total active duty personnel (1996): 77,100 (army 80.4%, navy 7.3%, air force 12.3%). *Military expenditure as percentage of GNP* (1994): 0.8% (world 3.0%); per capita expenditure U.S.$3.

[1]New transitional military regime from June 1998 to be replaced by elected civilian government in May 1999. [2]Statutory transfer of capital from Lagos to Abuja took place in December 1991. [3]Judiciary and some ministries remain in Lagos, the former capital. [4]In October 1996 six new states were created: Bayelsa, Ebonyi, Ekiti, Gombe, Nassarawa, and Zamfara. [5]Ebonyi is included partly in Abia and partly in Enugu. [6]Bauchi includes Gombe. [7]Rivers includes Bayelsa. [8]Ondo includes Ekiti. [9]Plateau includes Nassarawa. [10]Sokoto includes Zamfara. [11]Metal content. [12]1996. [13]1994. [14]Includes ₦792,372,000,000 from petroleum and natural gas. [15]Includes hotels. [16]Includes 1,263,000 unemployed. [17]Detail does not add to total given because of rounding. [18]1995. [19]1992. [20]1987–88. [21]1988–89.

Internet resources for further information:
• **Embassy of Nigeria (Washington, D.C.)** http://tribeca.ios.com/~n123

Norway

Official name: Kongeriket Norge (Kingdom of Norway).
Form of government: constitutional monarchy with one legislative house (Parliament [165]).
Chief of state: King.
Head of government: Prime Minister.
Capital: Oslo.
Official language: Norwegian.
Official religion: Evangelical Lutheran.
Monetary unit: 1 Norwegian krone (NKr) = 100 øre; valuation (Sept. 25, 1998) 1 U.S.$ = NKr 7.40; 1 £ = NKr 12.60.

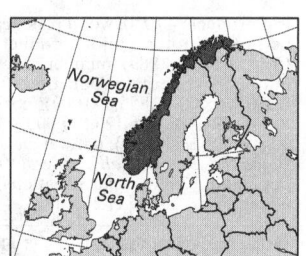

Area and population

Counties	Capitals	area[1] sq mi	sq km	population 1997[2] estimate
Akershus	—	1,898	4,917	446,385
Aust-Agder	Arendal	3,557	9,212	100,602
Buskerud	Drammen	5,763	14,927	230,763
Finnmark	Vadsø	18,779	48,637	75,643
Hedmark	Hamar	10,575	27,388	186,021
Hordaland	Bergen	6,036	15,634	426,896
Møre og Romsdal	Molde	5,832	15,104	241,493
Nordland	Bodø	14,798	38,327	240,304
Nord-Trøndelag	Steinkjer	8,647	22,396	127,236
Oppland	Lillehammer	9,726	25,191	182,443
Oslo	Oslo	175	454	493,973
Østfold	Moss	1,615	4,183	241,206
Rogaland	Stavanger	3,529	9,141	360,380
Sogn og Fjordane	Leikanger	7,189	18,620	108,032
Sør-Trøndelag	Trondheim	7,271	18,838	258,246
Telemark	Skien	5,913	15,315	163,467
Troms	Tromsø	10,032	25,984	151,191
Vest-Agder	Kristiansand	2,811	7,281	151,577
Vestfold	Tønsberg	856	2,216	206,108
TOTAL		125,004[3]	323,758[3]	4,391,966[4]

Demography

Population (1998): 4,429,000.
Density (1998): persons per sq mi 35.4, persons per sq km 13.7.
Urban-rural (1990): urban 75.0%; rural 25.0%.
Sex distribution (1996): male 49.45%; female 50.55%.
Age breakdown (1996): under 15, 19.4%; 15–29, 21.6%; 30–44, 21.8%; 45–59, 17.0%; 60–74, 12.8%; 75 and over, 7.4%.
Population projection: (2000) 4,468,000; (2010) 4,658,000.
Ethnic composition (by country of citizenship; 1995): Norway 96.3%; Denmark 0.4%; Sweden 0.3%; United Kingdom 0.3%; Pakistan 0.2%; United States 0.2%; Yugoslavia 0.2%; Iran 0.1%; other 2.0%.
Major cities (1997)[5]: Oslo 493,973; Bergen 224,130; Trondheim 144,599.

Vital statistics

Birth rate per 1,000 population (1996): 13.9 (world avg. 25.0); (1995) legitimate 52.4%; illegitimate 47.6%.
Death rate per 1,000 population (1996): 10.1 (world avg. 9.3).
Natural increase rate per 1,000 population (1996): 3.8 (world avg. 15.7).
Total fertility rate (avg. births per childbearing woman; 1995): 1.9.
Marriage rate per 1,000 population (1994): 4.8.
Divorce rate per 1,000 population (1994): 2.5.
Life expectancy at birth (1994): male 74.9 years; female 80.6 years.
Major causes of death per 100,000 population (1993): ischemic heart disease 237.7; malignant neoplasms (cancers) 227.8; cerebrovascular disease 128.5.

National economy

Budget (1995). Revenue: NKr 339,237,000,000 (social security taxes 24.6%, value-added taxes 24.2%, taxes on interest and dividends 9.2%, taxes on petroleum income and activity 3.1%). Expenditures: NKr 339,144,000,000 (social security and welfare 25.2%, health 7.9%, debt service 6.0%).
Land use (1994): forested 27.2%; meadows and pastures 0.4%; agricultural and under permanent cultivation 2.9%; built-up and other 69.5%.
Tourism (1995): receipts from visitors U.S.$2,386,000,000.
Production (metric tons except as noted). Agriculture, forestry, fishing (1996): barley 645,000, potatoes 400,000, oats 380,000, wheat 295,000; livestock (number of live animals) 2,400,000 sheep, 1,326,700 cattle, 768,400 pigs; roundwood (1995) 9,035,000 cu m; fish catch 2,630,664, of which herring 758,210, cod 360,328, saithe 222,044, redfish 160,701. Mining and quarrying (1996)[6]: iron ore 1,554,599, ilmenite-titanium 758,711, copper 31,736, zinc 8,619. Manufacturing (value added in NKr '000,000; 1994): machinery and equipment 37,194; paper and paper products 19,748; food products 17,375; wood products 8,133; chemical products 6,851. Construction (1996): residential 2,907,000 sq m; nonresidential 3,545,000 sq m. Energy production (consumption): electricity (kW-hr; 1994) 113,389,000,000 (113,256,000,000); coal (metric tons; 1994) 301,000 (914,000); crude petroleum (barrels; 1994) 977,367,000,000 (110,386,000,000); petroleum products (metric tons; 1994) 14,512,000 (7,703,000); natural gas (cu m; 1994) 31,347,000,000 (4,051,000,000).
Household income and expenditure. Average household size (1994) 2.3; consumption expenditure per household (1994) NKr 269,620 (U.S.$38,203); expenditure (1994): housing 25.3%, transportation 20.1%, food 13.9%, recreation and education 11.0%, household furniture and equipment 8.4%, clothing and footwear 6.5%.
Gross national product (1996): U.S.$151,198,000,000 (U.S.$34,510 per capita).

Structure of gross domestic product and labour force

	1995 in value NKr '000,000	% of total value	labour force	% of labour force
Agriculture	22,029	2.4	106,000	4.8
Mining	1,532	0.2	23,000	1.1
Crude petroleum and natural gas	102,660	11.1	...	...
Manufacturing	116,608	12.6	308,000	14.1
Construction	33,897	3.7	126,000	5.8
Public utilities	23,938	2.6	22,000	1.0
Transp. and commun.	90,257	9.7	170,000	7.8
Trade	100,419[7]	10.8[7]	357,000	16.3
Finance	147,983	16.0	160,000	7.3
Pub. admin., defense	144,418	15.6 }	803,000	36.7
Services	45,442	4.9 }		
Other	96,682	10.4	107,000[8]	4.9[8]
TOTAL	925,866[3]	100.0	2,186,000[3]	100.0[3]

Population economically active (1995): total 2,186,000; activity rate of total population 50.0% (participation rates: ages 16–64 [1994] 79.6%; female 43.6%; unemployed 4.9%).

Price and earnings indexes (1990 = 100)

	1991	1992	1993	1994	1995	1996	1997
Consumer price index	103.4	105.8	108.2	109.8	112.5	113.9	116.8
Hourly earnings index	105.1	108.5	111.6	114.8	118.8	123.5	128.6[9]

Public debt (1995): U.S.$41,157,000,000.

Foreign trade

Balance of trade (current prices)

	1992	1993	1994	1995	1996	1997
NKr '000,000	+61,730	+55,635	+51,512	+62,656	+85,980	+86,370
% of total	16.4%	14.0%	11.8%	11.9%	15.8%	14.7%

Imports (1996): NKr 229,720,000,000 (machinery and transport equipment 37.8%, of which road vehicles 10.0%, ships 2.6%; metals and metal products 10.8%, of which iron and steel 4.4%; food products 6.1%, of which fruits and vegetables 1.4%; petroleum products 4.5%). *Major import sources* (1995): Sweden 15.5%; Germany 14.0%; U.K. 9.8%; Denmark 7.6%.
Exports (1996): NKr 320,128,000,000 (fuels and fuel products 54.4%; machinery and transport equipment 11.1%; metals and metal products 10.7%; food products 7.6%, of which fish 6.7%). *Major export destinations* (1995): U.K. 20.3%; Germany 12.2%; Sweden 9.9%; The Netherlands 9.6%.

Transport and communications

Transport. Railroads (1995): route length 3,999 km; passenger-km 2,381,000,-000; metric ton-km cargo 2,715,000,000. Roads (1996): total length 90,262 km (paved 74%). Vehicles (1995): passenger cars 1,684,664; trucks and buses 382,017. Merchant marine (1995): vessels (100 gross tons and over) 1,597; total deadweight tonnage 20,834,000. Air transport (1995): passenger-km 8,753,444,000; metric ton-km cargo 933,439,000; airports (1996) 50.

Communications

Medium	date	unit	number	units per 1,000 persons
Daily newspapers	1995	circulation	2,170,000	498
Radio	1996	receivers	3,342,000	763
Television	1995	receivers	2,000,000	459
Telephones	1995	main lines	2,431,271	558
Cellular telephones	1995	subscribers	1,013,358	232
Facsimile machines	1995	units	130,000	30
Personal computers	1995	units	1,193,000	273

Education and health

Educational attainment (1994). Percentage of population age 16 and over having: lower secondary education 28.7%; higher secondary 51.9%; higher 19.4%. *Literacy* (1995): virtually 100% literate.

Education (1994–95)

	schools	teachers	students	student/ teacher ratio
Primary (age 7–12)	3,308	37,640	470,936	12.5
Secondary (age 13–18) and vocational	746	21,197	226,983	10.7
Higher	86[10]	10,366	169,306	16.3

Health: physicians (1996) 15,368 (1 per 285 persons); hospital beds (1994) 21,-967 (1 per 197 persons); infant mortality rate per 1,000 live births (1995) 4.1.
Food (1995): daily per capita caloric intake 3,274 (vegetable products 65%, animal products 35%); 122% of FAO recommended minimum requirement.

Military

Total active duty personnel (1996): 29,000 (army 50.7%, navy 22.1%, air force 27.2%). *Military expenditure as percentage of GNP* (1995): 2.7% (world avg. 2.8%); per capita expenditure U.S.$804.

---

[1]Excludes Svalbard and Jan Mayen (24,360 sq mi [63,080 sq km]). [2]January 1. [3]Detail does not add to total given because of rounding. [4]Includes the Norwegian population of Svalbard and Jan Mayen, registered as residents in municipalities on the mainland. [5]Population of municipalities. [6]Metal content of ore. [7]Includes hotels. [8]Unemployed. [9]2nd quarter. [10]The number of colleges is lower than in recent years because of reorganization.

Internet resources for further information:
• **Statistics Norway http://www.ssb.no/www-open/english**

Oman

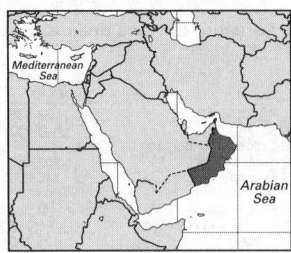

Official name: Salṭanat ‘Umān
(Sultanate of Oman).
Form of government: monarchy[1].
Head of state and government: Sultan.
Capital: Muscat.
Official language: Arabic.
Official religion: Islam.
Monetary unit: 1 rial Omani
(RO) = 1,000 baizas; valuation (Sept. 25,
1998) 1 RO = U.S.$2.60 = £1.53.

Area and population		area[2]		population
				1993
Regions	Capitals	sq mi	sq km	census
Al-Bāṭinah	Ar-Rustāq; Suḥār	4,850	12,500	564,677
Ad-Dākhilīyah	Nizwā; Samā,il	12,300	31,900	229,791
Ash-Sharqīyah	Ibrā; Şūr	14,200	36,800	258,344
Al-Wusṭa	Haymā’	30,750	79,700	17,067
Az-Ẓāhirah	Al-Buraymī; ‘Ibri	17,000	44,000	181,224
Governorates				
Masqaṭ	Muscat (masqaṭ)	1,350	3,500	549,150
Musandam	Khaṣab	700	1,800	28,727
Zufār (Dhofar)	Salālah	38,350	99,300	189,094
TOTAL		119,500	309,500	2,018,074

Demography

Population (1998): 2,364,000.
Density (1998): persons per sq mi 19.8, persons per sq km 7.6.
Urban-rural (1993): urban 71.7%; rural 28.3%.
Sex distribution (1993): male 58.37%; female 41.63%.
Age breakdown (1993): under 15, 41.0%; 15–29, 25.5%; 30–44, 21.9%; 45–59, 7.8%, 60–74, 2.9%; 75 and over, 0.9%.
Population projection: (2000) 2,533,000; (2010) 3,520,000.
Doubling time: 20 years.
Ethnic composition (1993): Omani Arab 73.5%; Indian 13.3%; Bangladeshi 4.3%; Pakistani (mostly Balochī) 3.1%; Egyptian 1.6%; other 4.2%.
Religious affiliation (1993): Muslim 87.7%, of which Ibāḍiyah Muslim c. 75% (principal minorities are Sunnī Muslim and Shī‘ī Muslim); Hindu 7.4%; Christian 3.9%; Buddhist 0.5%; other 0.5%.
Major cities (1990): Muscat 51,969[3]; Nizwā 62,880; Samā’il 44,721; Salālah 10,000[4].

Vital statistics

Birth rate per 1,000 population (1990–95): 43.7 (world avg. 25.0).
Death rate per 1,000 population (1990–95): 4.8 (world avg. 9.3).
Natural increase rate per 1,000 population (1990–95): 38.9 (world avg. 15.7).
Total fertility rate (avg. births per childbearing woman; 1996): 6.9.
Life expectancy at birth (1990–95): male 67.7 years; female 71.8 years.
Major causes of death per 100,000 population: n.a.; however, the main causes of hospital deaths in 1989 were diseases of the circulatory system 25.7%, perinatal problems 11.4%, malignant neoplasms (cancers) 7.6%, diseases of the respiratory system 7.1%, and infectious and parasitic diseases 7.1%.

National economy

Budget (1997). Revenue: RO 2,003,000,000 (oil revenue 75.0%; other 25.0%). Expenditures: RO 2,266,000,000 (current expenditure 80.1%, of which civil ministries 39.6%, defense 30.8%, interest paid on loans 5.3%; capital development projects and subsidies 17.6%).
Public debt (external, outstanding; 1996): U.S.$2,646,000,000.
Gross national product (1996): U.S.$13,135,000,000 (U.S.$5,950 per capita).

Structure of gross domestic product and labour force				
	1996		1993	
	in value RO ’000,000[5]	% of total value	labour force	% of labour force
Agriculture[6]	133.9	2.3	64,161	9.1
Mining	2,496.6	42.7	14,393	2.0
Manufacturing	253.7	4.3	60,433	8.6
Construction	130.1	2.2	108,154	15.3
Public utilities	50.3	0.9	4,465	0.6
Transp. and commun.	359.1	6.1	24,770	3.5
Trade	767.3[7]	13.1[7]	104,066	14.8
Finance	448.6[8]	7.7[8]	17,372	2.5
Pub. admin., defense	714.3	12.2	165,602	23.5
Services	457.9[9]	7.8[9]	111,268	15.8
Other	43.1[10]	0.7[10]	30,114	4.3
TOTAL	5,854.4	100.0	704,798	100.0[11]

Tourism (1995): receipts U.S.$92,000,000; expenditures U.S.$47,000,000.
Household income and expenditure. Average household size (1993) 8.0; income per household: n.a.; sources of income: n.a.; expenditure (1990): housing and utilities 27.8%, food, beverage, and tobacco 26.4%, transportation 19.8%, clothing and shoes 7.8%, household goods and furniture 6.1%, education, health services, entertainment, and other 12.1%.
Production (metric tons except as noted). Agriculture, forestry, fishing (1996): vegetables and melons 167,000 (of which watermelons 30,000), dates 133,000, bananas 26,000, mangoes 11,000, onions 9,000, potatoes 6,000, papayas 5,000, tobacco leaf 2,000, wheat 1,000; livestock (number of live animals) 735,000 goats, 148,000 sheep, 142,000 cattle, 94,000 camels, 3,000,000 chickens; fish catch (1995) 139,864. Mining and quarrying (1994): copper 6,500; silver 3,300 kg; gold 75 kg. Manufacturing (value of production in RO ’000,000; 1993): textiles and apparel 78,200; food products and beverages 72,930; chem-

ical products 40,950; wood products 5,950; metal products 4,200; paper products 360; other major products include refined petroleum products. Construction (1989): number of residential permits 3,408; nonresidential permits 353. Energy production (consumption): electricity (kW-hr; 1994) 7,856,000,000 (7,856,000,000); coal, none (none); crude petroleum (barrels; 1994) 294,380,000 (26,615,000); petroleum products (metric tons; 1994) 3,884,000 (1,589,000); natural gas (cu m; 1994) 6,665,890,000 (6,665,890,000).
Population economically active (1993)[11]: total 704,798; activity rate of total population 34.9% (participation rates: over age 15, 60.9%; female 9.7%; unemployed [1996] c. 20%).

Price and earnings indexes (1990 = 100)							
	1990	1991	1992	1993	1994	1995	1996
Consumer price index	100.0	104.6	105.6	106.9	106.1	104.7	105.0
Earnings index	...	...	...	...	...	...	...

Land use (1994): meadows and pastures 4.7%; agricultural and under permanent cultivation 0.3%; other (mostly desert and developed area) 95.0%.

Foreign trade[12]

Balance of trade (current prices)						
	1992	1993	1994	1995	1996	1997
RO ’000,000	+686	+483	+627	+700	+1,064	+1,001
% of total	19.1%	13.2%	17.2%	17.6%	23.2%	20.6%

Imports (1996): RO 1,760,100,000 (machinery and transport equipment 41.5%, basic manufactured goods 17.3%, food and live animals 12.9%, miscellaneous manufactured articles 9.0%, beverages and tobacco 4.2%). *Major import sources:* United Arab Emirates 23.7%; Japan 17.2%; United Kingdom 8.8%; United States 7.5%; Germany 5.2%; India 4.0%.
Exports (1996): RO 2,824,500,000 (domestic exports 86.3%, of which petroleum 80.2%, manufactured goods 2.7% [of which copper and copper products 0.9%], food and live animals 1.9%, mineral fuels and lubricants 0.5%; reexports 13.7%, of which machinery and transport equipment 8.9%). *Major export destinations*[13]: United Arab Emirates 41.6%; Iran 9.3%; Hong Kong 7.8%; United States 5.1%; Saudi Arabia 4.5%; Tanzania 4.4%.

Transport and communications

Transport. Railroads: none. Roads (1995): total length 19,160 mi, 30,830 km (paved c. 20%). Vehicles: automobiles (1995) 202,741, trucks and buses (1993) 108,600. Merchant marine (1992): vessels (100 gross tons and over) 26; total deadweight tonnage 11,727. Air transport (1996)[14]: passenger-mi 1,714,204,000, passenger-km 2,758,750,000; short ton-mi cargo 72,435,000, metric ton-km cargo 105,753,500; airports (1997) with scheduled flights 6.

Communications				units per 1,000
Medium	date	unit	number	persons
Daily newspapers	1994	circulation	63,000	31
Radio	1995	receivers	900,000	426
Television	1995	receivers	1,500,000	711
Telephones	1995	main lines	169,900	81
Cellular telephones	1995	subscribers	8,100	3.8
Facsimile machines	1995	units	1,600	0.8
Personal computers	1995	units	28,000	13.3

Education and health

Educational attainment (1993). Percentage of population age 15 and over having: no formal schooling (illiterate) 41.2%; no formal schooling (literate) 14.9%; primary 18.9%; secondary 21.1%; higher technical 2.0%; higher undergraduate 1.5%; higher graduate 0.1%; other 0.3%. *Literacy* (1993): total population age 15 and over literate 422,417 (58.8%); males literate 260,006 (71.1%); females literate 163,421 (46.2%).

Education (1993–94)				student/
	schools	teachers	students	teacher ratio
Primary (age 6–14)	415	11,158	297,209	26.6
Secondary (age 15–17)	128[15]	9,188	160,654	17.5
Voc., teacher tr.	25[15]	342	2,350	6.9
Higher	5[15]	732[16]	7,322[17]	...

Health (1995): physicians 2,476 (1 per 852 persons); hospital beds 4,411 (1 per 478 persons); infant mortality rate per 1,000 live births (1996) 28.2.
Food: daily per capita caloric intake, n.a.

Military

Total active duty personnel (1996): 43,500 (army 72.4%[18], navy 9.7%, air force 9.4%); foreign troops 3,700. *Military expenditure as percentage of GDP* (1995): 16.7% (world 2.8%); per capita expenditure U.S.$822.

[1]The Oman Council is an appointed advisory body consisting of a Council of State and a Consultative Council. [2]Approximate; no comprehensive survey of surface area has ever been carried out in Oman. [3]1993 census. [4]1982. [5]In purchasers’ values at current prices. [6]Agriculture includes fishing. [7]Trade includes restaurants and hotels. [8]Finance includes business services and real estate. [9]Services include education and health. [10]Other includes import taxes. [11]Non-Omani workers constitute 61.3% of the labour force. [12]Imports c.i.f.; exports f.o.b. [13]Non-oil exports only; includes reexports. [14]One-fourth apportionment of international flights of Gulf Air. [15]1989–90. [16]1990. [17]1991–92. [18]Including personnel of Royal Household units not formally part of army table of organization.

Internet resources for further information:
• **Oman 95 Yearbook**
  http://www.brunet.bn/php/kharti/book95.htm

Pakistan

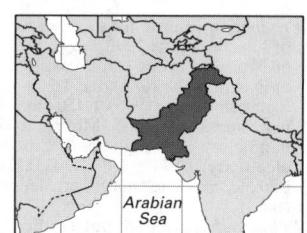

Official name: Islām-ī Jamhūrīya-e Pākistān (Islamic Republic of Pakistan).
Form of government: multiparty, federal Islamic republic with two legislative houses (Senate [87]; National Assembly [217]).
Chief of state: President.
Chief of government: Prime Minister.
Capital: Islāmābād.
Official language: Urdū.
Official religion: Islam.
Monetary unit: 1 Pakistan rupee (PRs) = 100 paisa, valuation (Sept. 25, 1998) 1 U.S.$ = PRs 50.07; 1 £ = PRs 85.24.

Area and population		area[1]		population
				1983
Provinces	Capitals	sq mi	sq km	estimate[2]
Balochistān	Quetta	134,051	347,190	4,611,000
North-West Frontier	Peshāwar	28,773	74,521	11,658,000
Punjab	Lahore	79,284	205,344	50,460,000
Sindh	Karāchi	54,407	140,914	20,312,000
Federally Administered Tribal Areas	...	10,509	27,220	2,329,000
Federal Capital Area				
Islāmābād	...	350	906	359,000
TOTAL		307,374	796,095	89,729,000

Demography

Population (1998)[3]: 141,900,000.
Density (1998)[4]: persons per sq mi 461.7, persons per sq km 178.2.
Urban-rural (1996): urban 32.4%; rural 67.6%.
Sex distribution (1996): male 52.50%; female 47.50%.
Age breakdown (1995): under 15, 41.3%; 15–29, 25.1%; 30–44, 17.1%; 45–59, 10.5%; 60–74, 4.9%; 75 and over, 1.1%.
Population projection: (2000) 147,140,000; (2010) 176,400,000.
Doubling time: 25 years.
Linguistic composition (1981): Punjābī 48.2%; Pashto 13.1%; Sindhī 11.8%; Saraiki 9.8%; Urdū 7.6%; other 9.5%.
Religious affiliation (1993): Muslim 95.0%[5]; Christian 2.0%; Hindu 1.8%; others (including Ahmadiyah) 1.2%.
Major cities (1981): Larāchi 5,208,132; Lahore 2,952,689; Faisalābād 1,104,209; Rāwalpindi 794,843; Islāmābād 204,364.

Vital statistics

Birth rate per 1,000 population (1997): 36.4 (world avg. 25.0).
Death rate per 1,000 population (1997): 7.9 (world avg. 9.3).
Natural increase rate per 1,000 population (1997): 28.5 (world avg. 15.7).
Total fertility rate (avg. births per childbearing woman; 1997): 5.1.
Marriage rate per 1,000 population (1975–80): 10.7.
Divorce rate per 1,000 population (1975–80): 0.3.
Life expectancy at birth (1997): male 63.0 years; female 65.0 years.
Major cause of death (percentage of total deaths; 1987): malaria 18.2%; childhood diseases 12.1%; diseases of digestive system 9.8%; diseases of respiratory system 9.2%; infection of intestinal tract 7.7%.

National economy

Budget (1995–96). Revenue: PRs 378,030,000,000 (customs duties 24.4%, nontax receipts 23.8%, income taxes 20.2%, excise taxes 13.6%, sales tax 13.4%). Expenditures: PRs 434,690,000,000 (public-debt service 36.2%, defense 26.5%, development 22.2%, general administration 3.9%).
Public debt (external, outstanding; 1996): U.S.$23,694,000,000.
Production (metric tons except as noted). Agriculture, forestry, fishing (1996): sugarcane 45,230,000, wheat 16,907,000, rice 5,551,000, seed cotton 4,597,000, cottonseed 3,065,000, corn (maize) 1,300,000, potatoes 1,064,000, chickpeas 638,000, rapeseed 246,000; livestock (number of live animals) 45,600,000 goats, 29,800,000 sheep, 20,200,000 buffalo, 17,900,000 cattle, 110,000,000 chickens; roundwood (1995) 29,665,000 cu m; fish catch (1994) 551,899. Mining and quarrying (1994–95): limestone 9,682,000; rock salt 890,000; gypsum 624,000; silica sand 152,000; chromite 13,513. Manufacturing (1994–95): cement 7,913,000; chemical fertilizers 3,826,000 of which urea 3,000,000; refined sugar 3,001,000; cotton yarn 1,370,000; vegetable products 678,000; industrial chemicals 377,000; paper and paperboard 215,000; jute textiles 67,300; cotton textiles 321,841,000 sq m; cigarettes 32,747,000,000 units; motor-vehicle tires 912,000 units; bicycles 475,000 units. Energy production (consumption): electricity (kW-hr; 1994) 57,147,000,000 (57,147,000,000); coal (metric tons; 1994) 3,534,000 (4,628,000); crude petroleum (barrels; 1994) 20,805,000 (50,063,000); petroleum products (metric tons; 1994) 5,778,000 (13,511,000); natural gas (cu m; 1994) 16,668,000,000 (16,668,000,000).
Population economically active (1995–96): total 36,700,000; activity rate of total population 27.9% (participation rates: ages 15–64 [1992–93] 50.4%; female [1992–93] 14.2%; unemployed 4.9%).

Price index (1990 = 100)							
	1991	1992	1993	1994	1995	1996	1997
Consumer price index	111.8	122.4	134.6	151.3	170.0	187.6	208.9

Gross national product (1996): U.S.$63,567,000,000 (U.S.$480 per capita).

Structure of gross domestic product and labour force				
		1995–96		
	in value PRs '000,000	% of total value	labour force	% of labour force
Agriculture	510,775	23.5	17,470,000	47.6
Mining	11,348	0.5		
Manufacturing	325,420	15.0	3,530,000	9.6
Construction	69,271	3.2	2,260,000	6.2
Public utilities	64,022	2.9	...	...
Transp. and commun.	190,409	8.8	1,730,000	4.7
Trade	324,364	14.9	4,460,000	12.1
Finance	144,007	6.6		
Pub. admin., defense	156,607	7.2	5,130,000	14.0
Services	155,407	7.1		
Other	223,277	10.3	2,120,000[6]	5.8[6]
TOTAL	2,174,907	100.0	36,700,000	100.0

Household income and expenditure (1988). Average household size 6.3; income per household PRs 25,572 (U.S.$1,420); sources of income: self-employment 56.0%, wages and salaries 22.0%, other 22.0%; expenditure: food 47.0%, housing 12.0%, clothing and footwear 8.0%, other 33.0%.
Tourism (1995): receipts U.S.$114,000,000; expenditures U.S.$449,000,000.
Land use (1994): forest 4.5%; pasture 6.5%; agriculture 27.7%; other 61.3%.

Foreign trade[7]

Balance of trade (current prices)						
	1991	1992	1993	1994	1995	1996
PRs '000,000	−28,537	−31,283	−54,352	−22,968	−78,506	−64,476
% of total	8.4%	7.9%	12.6%	4.9%	13.4%	8.8%

Imports (1994–95): PRs 332,835,000,000 (petroleum products 15.3%, vegetable oil and fats 9.8%, specialized machinery 9.1%, power-generating machinery 4.9%, road vehicles 4.2%, organic chemicals 4.2%, wheat 4.0%, iron and steel manufactures 3.6%, industrial machinery 3.4%). *Major import sources:* Japan 9.2%; U.S. 9.0%; Malaysia 8.5%; Germany 6.5%; Kuwait 5.6%; Italy 5.0%; U.K. 4.9%; Saudi Arabia 4.8%; China 4.2%; South Korea 3.1%.
Exports (1994–95): PRs 260,522,000,000 (textile fabrics 52.8%, ready-made garments 20.5%, rice 5.6%, leather goods 3.5%, fresh fish 1.9%, cotton 1.8%). *Major export destinations:* U.S. 16.6%; Germany 6.8%; U.K. 6.8%; Japan 6.4%; Dubayy 3.9%; France 3.2%; S. Korea 3.2%; Netherlands 3.1%.

Transport and communications

Transport. Railroads (1994–95): route length 8,775 km; passenger-km 17,555,000,000, metric ton-km cargo 5,661,000,000. Roads (1994–95): total length 123,585 mi, 198,891 km (paved 55%). Vehicles (1994): passenger cars 955,098; trucks and buses 225,829. Merchant marine (1992): vessels (100 gross tons and over) 73; total deadweight tonnage 513,823. Air transport (1996): passenger-km 11,123,000,000; metric ton-km cargo 423,424,000; airports (1997) 35.

Communications				units
				per 1,000
Medium	date	unit	number	persons
Daily newspapers	1994	circulation	2,840,000	22
Radio	1996	receivers	10,200,000	76
Television	1995	receivers	2,080,000	16
Telephones	1995	main lines	2,127,000	16
Cellular telephones	1995	subscribers	43,000	0.3
Facsimile machines	1995	units	159,000	1.2
Personal computers	1995	units	155,000	1.2

Education and health

Educational attainment (1981). Percentage of population age 25 and over having: no formal schooling 78.9%; some primary education 8.7%; some secondary 10.5%; postsecondary 1.9%. *Literacy* (1995): total population age 15 and over literate 37.8%; males literate 50.0%; females literate 24.4%.

Education (1995–96)				student/
	schools	teachers	students	teacher ratio
Primary (age 5–9)	115,744	337,400	11,484,000	34.0
Secondary (age 10–14)	20,243	281,700	4,819,000	17.1
Voc., teacher tr.	687	7,459	94,000	12.6
Higher	888	33,654	953,659	28.3

Health (1995): physicians 69,694 (1 per 1,863 persons); hospital beds 85,552 (1 per 1,517 persons); infant mortality rate per 1,000 live births (1997) 75.
Food (1995): daily per capita caloric intake 2,475 (vegetable products 86%, animal products 14%); 107% of FAO recommended minimum requirement.

Military

Total active duty personnel (1996): 587,000 (army 88.6%, navy 3.7%, air force 7.7%). *Military expenditure as percentage of GNP* (1994): 6.0% (world 3.0%); per capita expenditure U.S.$24.

[1]Excludes 32,323 sq mi (83,716 sq km) area of Pakistani-administered Jammu and Kashmir (comprising both Azad Kashmir [AK] and the Northern Areas [NA]). [2]Excludes Afghan refugees and population (1981; 2,542,000) of AK/NA. [3]Excludes 1,200,000 Afghan refugees and the population (3,900,000) of AK/NA. [4]Excludes area and population of AK/NA. [5]Mostly Sunnī, with Shī'ī comprising about 20% of total population. [6]Includes unemployed. [7]Import figures are f.o.b. in balance of trade and c.i.f for commodities and trading partners.

Internet resources for further information:
• **Government of Pakistan: http://www.pak.gov.pk/**

Palau

Official name: Belu'u er a Belau
(Palauan); Republic of Palau
(English).
Form of government: unitary republic
with a national congress composed of
two legislative houses (Senate [14];
House of Delegates [16]).
Head of state and government:
President.
Capital: Koror[1].
Official languages[2]: Palauan; English.
Official religion: none.
Monetary unit: 1 U.S. dollar
(U.S.$) = 100 cents; valuation (Sept. 25,
1998) 1 £ = U.S.$1.70.

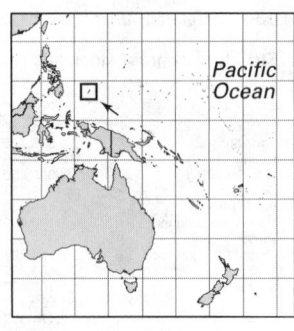

Pacific
Ocean

Area and population

States	area sq mi	area sq km	population 1995 census
Aimeliik	20	52	419
Airai	17	44	1,481
Angaur	3	8	193
Hatobohel	1	3	51
Kayangel	1	3	124
Koror	7	18	12,299
Melekeok	11	28	261
Ngaraard	14	36	421
Ngarchelong	4	10	253
Ngardmau	18	47	162
Ngatpang	18	47	221
Ngchesar	16	41	228
Ngeremlengui	25	65	281
Ngiwal	10	26	176
Peleliu	5	13	575
Sonsorol	1	3	80
Other			
Rock Islands	18	47	—
TOTAL	188[3]	488	17,225

Demography

Population (1998): 18,100.
Density (1998): Persons per sq mi 96.3, persons per sq km 37.1.
Urban-rural (1990): urban 59.6%; rural 40.4%.
Sex distribution (1995): male 53.49%; female 46.51%.
Age breakdown (1990): under 15, 30.3%; 15–29, 27.8%; 30–44, 22.8%; 45–59,
10.5%; 60–74, 6.4%; 75 and over 2.2%.
Population projection: (2000) 18,800; (2010) 21,700.
Doubling time: 35 years.
Ethnic composition (1995): Palauan 74.5%; Filipino 16.0%; Chinese 3.2%;
other Micronesian and other 6.3%.
Religious affiliation (1995): Roman Catholic 38.4%; Protestant 24.7%;
Modekne 26.5%; other 10.4%.
Major cities (1995): Koror 12,000.

Vital statistics

Birth rate per 1,000 population (1997): 21.0 (world avg. 25.0); legitimate, n.a.;
illegitimate, n.a.
Death rate per 1,000 population (1997): 7.0 (world avg. 9.3).
Natural increase rate per 1,000 population (1997): 14.0 (world avg. 15.7).
Total fertility rate (avg. births per childbearing woman; 1997): 2.7.
Marriage rate per 1,000 population: n.a.
Divorce rate per 1,000 population: n.a.
Life expectancy at birth (1997): male 69.1 years; female 73.0 years.
Major causes of death per 100,000 population (1993): diseases of the cir-
culatory system 192.9; malignant and benign neoplasms (cancers) 136.9;
accidents, poisoning, and violence 112.0; diseases of the respiratory system
43.6; infectious and parasitic diseases 43.6.

National economy

Budget (1997). Revenue: U.S.$52,869,000 (grants from the U.S. 59.6%, tax rev-
enue 33.7%). Expenditures: U.S.$59,867,000 (current expenditure 87.0%, of
which wages and salaries 44.0%; capital expenditure 13.0%).
Gross national product (at current market prices; 1997)[4]: U.S.$159,800,000
(U.S.$8,806 per capita).

Structure of gross domestic product and labour force

	1996 in value U.S.$'000	1996 % of total value	1995 labour force	1995 % of labour force
Agriculture, fisheries	9,890	6.8	724	8.7
Mining	2,908	2.0	1,165[5]	14.0[5]
Manufacturing				
Public utilities	1,998	1.4	[6]	[6]
Construction	13,102	9.0	[5]	[5]
Transportation and communications	21,608	14.9	435[6]	5.2[6]
Trade	58,663	40.4	1,448	17.3
Finance	4,425	3.0	122	1.5
Public administration, defense	24,984	17.2	2,292	27.5
Services	6,430	4.4	1,573	18.8
Other	1,262[7]	0.9[7]	588[8]	7.0[8]
TOTAL	145,270	100.0	8,347	100.0

Production (metric tons except as noted). Agriculture, forestry, fishing (value
of sales in U.S.$; 1993): eggs 262,701, fruit and vegetables 126,325, betel nuts
60,376, root crops (taro, cassava, sweet potatoes) 43,718; livestock (number
of live animals; 1984) pigs 1,343, cows 82, goats 52, poultry 9,500; roundwood,
n.a.; fish catch (1995) 1,450 (major species are parrot fish, snapper, unicorn
fish, and rabbitfish). Mining and quarrying: n.a. Manufacturing: includes
handicrafts and small items. Construction: Energy production (consumption):
electricity (kW-hr; 1994) 203,000,000 (203,000,000); coal, none (n.a.); crude
petroleum, none (n.a.); petroleum products, none (75,000); natural gas, none
(n.a.).
Public debt (external, outstanding; 1993): U.S.$100,000,000.
Tourism (1996): receipts from visitors U.S.$67,900,000.
Population economically active (1995): total 8,347; activity rate of total population 48.5% (participation rates: over age 15, 66.2%; female (1990) 36.9%;
unemployed 7.0%.
Land use: n. a.
Household income and expenditure. Average household size (1995) 4.9; income
per household (1989) U.S.$8,882; sources of income (1989): wages 63.7%,
social security 12.0%, self-employment 7.4%, retirement 5.5%, interest, div-
idend, or net rental 4.3%, remittance 4.1%, public assistance 1.0%, other
2.0%; expenditure: n.a.

Foreign trade[9]

Imports (1996): U.S.$72,400,000 (1984; food and agricultural raw materials
28.9%, machinery and transport equipment 24.5%, chemicals and related
products 4.0%). *Major import sources* (1984): United States 41.8%; Japan
38.2%.
Exports (1996): U.S.$14,300,000 (1984; food and agricultural raw materials
69.1%, manufactured goods 30.9%). *Major export destinations* (1984): Japan
58.8%; United States 8.0%.

Transport and communications

Transport. Railroads: none. Roads (1993): total length 40 mi, 64 km (paved
59%). Vehicles (1994): passenger cars and trucks 4,271. Merchant marine
(1991): vessels (100 gross tons and over) 4; total deadweight tonnage, n.a.
Air transport (1993): passenger arrivals 50,366, passenger departures 49,376;
airports (1997) with scheduled flights 1.

Communications

Medium	date	unit	number	units per 1,000 persons
Radio	1994	receivers	9,000	550.0
Television	1994	receivers	1,600	98.0
Telephones	1994	main lines	2,615	160.0

Education and health

Educational attainment (1990). Percentage of population age 25 and over having: no formal schooling 1.8%; some primary education 21.8%; completed
primary 5.5%; some secondary 13.3%; completed secondary 26.6%; some
postsecondary 11.1%; higher 19.9%. *Literacy* (1990): total population age 15
and over literate 10,288 (97.6%); males literate 5,677 (98.3%); females literate 4,611 (96.6%).

Education (1993)

	schools[10]	teachers[10]	students	student/teacher ratio
Primary (age 6–13)	26	289	2,635	...
Secondary (age 14–18)	6	[11]	1,021	...
Higher[12]	1	...	509	

Health (1990): physicians[13] 10 (1 per 1,518 persons); hospital beds 70 (1 per
200 persons); infant mortality rate per 1,000 live births (1997) 25.1.
Food: daily per capita caloric intake, n.a.

Military

The United States is responsible for the external security of Palau, as specified in the Compact of Free Association of Oct. 1, 1994.

[1]A site on Babelthuap is to be the eventual permanent capital. [2]Sonsorolese-Tobian is
also, according to official sources, considered an official language. [3]Detail does not add
to total given because of rounding. [4]Gross national product comprises U.S. government spending only. [5]Manufacturing includes Construction. [6]Transportation and communications includes Public utilities. [7]Includes import duties and imputed bank service
charge. [8]Includes unemployed. [9]Export and import figures are f.o.b. [10]1987. [11]Included
with primary. [12]Palau Community College. [13]Government-employed health personnel
only.

Internet resources for further information:
• **Republic of Palau Economic Report (Bank of Hawaii)**
　http://www.boh.com/econ/index.asp
• **U.S. Department of the Interior Office of Insular Affairs**
　http://www.doi.gov.oia/index.html
• **Palau Visitors Authority http://www.visit-palau.com**

Panama

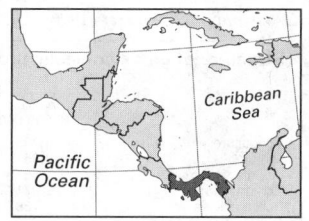

Official name: República de Panamá
  (Republic of Panama).
Form of government: multiparty
  republic with one legislative house
  (Legislative Assembly [72]).
Head of state and government:
  President assisted by Vice Presidents.
Capital: Panama City.
Official language: Spanish.
Official religion: none.
Monetary unit: 1 balboa (B) = 100 cents;
  valuation (Sept. 25, 1998)
  1 U.S.$ = B 1.00; 1 £ = B 1.70.

Area and population

Provinces	Capitals	area sq mi	area sq km	population 1996 estimate
Bocas del Toro	Bancas del Toro	3,376[1]	8,745[1]	123,655[1]
Chiriquí	David	3,341[1]	8,653[1]	412,981[1]
Coclé	Penonomé	1,902	4,927	191,677
Colón	Colón	1,888	4,890	190,697
Derién	La Palma	4,823[2]	12,491[2]	47,055[2]
Herrera	Chitré	904	2,341	101,775
Los Santos	Las Tablas	1,470	3,806	79,849
Panamá	Panama City	4,590	11,887	1,257,964
Veraguas	Santiago	4,339[1]	11,239[1]	220,110[1]
Indigenous districts				
Emberá		1,614[2]	4,180[2]	10,459[2]
Guaymí (Ngobe-Buglé)		[1]	[1]	[1]
Kuna Yala (San Blas)	El Provenir	910	2,357	38,268
TOTAL		29,157	75,517[3]	2,674,490

Demography

Population (1998): 2,767,000.
Density (1998): persons per sq mi 94.9, persons per sq km 36.6.
Urban-rural (1995): urban 53.3%; rural 46.7%.
Sex distribution (1995): male 50.56%; female 49.44%.
Age breakdown (1995): under 15, 33.4%; 15–29, 28.4%; 30–44, 19.7%; 45–59,
  11.0%; 60–74, 5.6%; 75 and over, 1.9%.
Population projection: (2000) 2,856,000; (2010) 3,266,000.
Doubling time: 40 years.
Ethnic composition (1992): mestizo 64.0%; black and mulatto 14.0%; white
  10.0%; Amerindian 8.0%; Asian 4.0%.
Religious affiliation (1995): Roman Catholic 80.2%; Protestant 15.0%, of
  which Pentecostal 8.4%; other Christian 1.6%; other 3.2%.
Major cities (1990): Panama City 445,902[4], San Miguelito 299,075[5, 6]; David
  65,763[7]; Colón 54,654; Barú 46,093[7].

Vital statistics

Birth rate per 1,000 population (1996): 22.5 (world avg. 25.0).
Death rate per 1,000 population (1996): 5.2 (world avg. 9.3).
Natural increase rate per 1,000 population (1996): 17.3 (world avg. 15.7).
Total fertility rate (avg. births per childbearing woman; 1996): 2.6.
Marriage rate per 1,000 population (1996): 5.6[8].
Divorce rate per 1,000 population (1994): 0.9[8].
Life expectancy at birth (1996): male 71.4 years; female 76.9 years.
Major causes of death per 100,000 population (1994): diseases of the circula-
  tory system 118.4; malignant neoplasms (cancers) 57.3; accidents 35.3; dis-
  eases of the respiratory system 24.0; homicide, suicide, and violence 22.7.

National economy

Budget (1996). Revenue: B 2,264,200,000 (current revenue 73.6%, of which
  nontax revenue 24.0%; development revenue 26.4%, of which foreign loans
  17.9%). Expenditures: B 2,264,200,000 (current expenditure 79.1%, of which
  debt services 30.8%, education 10.4%, health 5.9%; development expenditure 20.9%).
Public debt (external, outstanding; 1996): U.S.$5,136,000,000.
Production (metric tons except as noted). Agriculture, forestry, fishing (1996):
  sugarcane 1,669,000, bananas 910,000, rice 230,000, plantains 106,000, corn
  (maize) 108,000, oranges 26,900, pineapples 14,300, coffee 12,400, tobacco
  2,200; livestock (number of live animals; 1996) 1,456,000 cattle, 261,000 pigs;
  roundwood (1995) 1,069,800 cu m; fish catch (value of production in B
  '000,000; 1995): shrimps 38, fish 29. Mining and quarrying (1994): limestone
  757,000; gold 7,900 troy oz. Manufacturing (value of production in B '000,000;
  1995): food products 1,076, of which meat 276; refined petroleum 217; paper
  and paper products 145; beverages 139; plastic products 94. Construction
  (value of construction in B '000,000; 1995): residential 237; nonresidential
  102. Energy production (consumption): electricity (kW-hr; 1995) 3,519,000,-
  000 (2,870,000,000); coal (metric tons; 1994) none (52,000); crude petroleum
  (barrels; 1994) none (8,554,000); petroleum products (metric tons; 1994)
  1,480,000 (1,842,000); natural gas (cu m; 1994) none (59,967,000).
Tourism (1996): receipts from visitors U.S.$343,100,000; expenditures by na-
  tionals abroad U.S.$135,800,000.
Household income and expenditure. Average household size (1990) 4.4; average annual income per household (1990) B 5,450 (U.S.$5,450); expenditure
  (1983–84)[9]: food and beverages 34.9%, transportation and communications
  15.1%, housing and energy 12.6%, education and recreation 11.7%.
Population economically active (1995)[8]: total 1,006,147; activity rate of total
  population 42.0%[10] (participation rates: ages 15–69 [1993] 62.8%[10], female
  [1993] 34.0%[10], unemployed 13.7%).

Price and earnings indexes (1990 = 100)

	1992	1993	1994	1995	1996	1997	1998[11]
Consumer price index	103.1	103.6	104.9	105.9	107.3	108.6	108.7
Monthly earnings index[12]	101.6	105.8	108.9	111.7	...	...	...

Gross national product (1996): U.S.$8,249,000,000 (U.S.$3,080 per capita).

Structure of gross domestic product and labour force

	1996[13] in value B '000,000	1996[13] % of total value	1995[8] labour force	1995[8] % of labour force
Agriculture, fishing	515.6	8.5	185,231	18.4
Mining	8.1	0.1	2,618	0.3
Manufacturing	620.3	10.2	105,821	10.5
Construction	240.7	3.9	66,015	6.6
Public utilities	310.5	5.1	10,514	1.0
Transp. and commun.	782.2	12.8	68,210	6.8
Trade, restaurants	1,276.1	20.9	208,598	20.7
Finance, real estate	1,573.8	25.8	52,039	5.2
Pub. admin.	665.3	10.9	70,826	7.0
Services	357.6	5.9	197,479	19.6
Other	−251.8	−4.1	38,796	3.9
TOTAL	6,098.4	100.0	1,006,147	100.0

Land use (1994): forested 43.8%; meadows and pastures 19.8%; agricultural
  and under permanent cultivation 8.9%; other 27.5%.

Foreign trade[14, 15]

Balance of trade (current prices)

	1991	1992	1993	1994	1995	1996
B '000,000	−1,337	−1,537	−1,693	−1,862	−1,940	−2,211
% of total	65.1%	61.5%	62.5%	63.3%	62.9%	66.0%

Imports (1995): B 2,511,000,000 (machinery and apparatus 17.4%, mineral
  fuels 14.1%, transport equipment 11.6%, chemicals and chemical products
  11.5%). *Major import sources:* U.S. 39.1%; Colón Free Zone 14.5%; Ecuador
  5.3%; Japan 5.1%; Mexico 3.4%.
Exports (1995): B 571,000,000 (bananas 33.3%, shrimps 14.2%, coffee 5.7%,
  clothing 3.8%, fish products 3.4%). *Major export destinations:* U.S. 41.8%;
  Germany 12.5%; Costa Rica 7.2%; Sweden 4.9%; Belgium 4.8%.

Transport and communications

Transport. Railroads (1994): route length 220 mi, 354 km. Roads (1995): total
  length 6,706 mi, 10,792 km (paved 34%). Vehicles: passenger cars (1995)
  140,900; trucks and buses 79,000. Panama Canal traffic (1994–95): oceangoing transits 13,459; cargo 193,357,000 metric tons. Air transport[16]: passenger-km (1996) 871,500,000; metric ton-km cargo 9,338,000; airports (1996)
  with scheduled flights 10.

Communications

Medium	date	unit	number	units per 1,000 persons
Daily newspapers	1994	circulation	160,000	62
Radio	1996	receivers	527,000	5.1
Television	1995	receivers	204,539	13
Telephones	1995	main lines	304,000	8.8

Education and health

Educational attainment (1990). Percentage of population age 25 and over having: no formal schooling 11.6%; incomplete primary education 20.0%; complete primary 21.6%; secondary 28.7%; incomplete undergraduate 5.4%;
  complete undergraduate 7.0%; graduate 0.7%; other/unknown 5.0%.
Literacy (1995): total population age 15 and over literate 1,590,000 (90.8%).

Education (1995)

	schools	teachers	students	student/ teacher ratio
Primary (age 6–11)	2,845	14,998	362,142	24.1
Secondary (age 12–17) } Voc., teacher tr. }	399	11,627	216,217	18.6
Higher	9	4,689	76,839	16.4

Health (1995): physicians 3,074 (1 per 856 persons); hospital beds 7,138 (1 per
  369 persons); infant mortality rate per 1,000 live births (1996) 25.3.
Food (1995): daily per capita caloric intake 2,490 (vegetable products 79%,
  animal products 21%); 108% of FAO recommended minimum requirement.

Military

Total active duty personnel (1996): military abolished in 1991 was replaced by
  an 11,000-member national police force; U.S. forces in former Canal Zone
  number 7,000.

---

[1]The 2,700 sq mi- (7,000 sq km-) Guaymí indigenous district (*comarca*) was created in
December 1996 from parts of Bocas del Toro, Chiriquí, and Veraguas provinces. [2]Figures
subject to change with announcement of official demarcation of Emberá boundaries.
[3]Detail does not add to total given because of rounding. [4]1994. [5]1996. [6]Urban district
adjacent to Panama City. [7]Population of the *cabecera* (county seat) of the municipality. [8]Excludes indigenous population. [9]Panama City only. [10]Estimated figure. [11]April.
[12]Public sector only. [13]At prices of 1982. [14]Imports c.i.f.; exports f.o.b. [15]Excludes Colón
Free Zone (1994 imports f.o.b. B 4,990,000,000; 1994 reexports f.o.b. B 5,735,000,000,
of which textiles and clothing 25.8%, machinery and apparatus 22.3%). [16]COPA only.

Internet resources for further information:
• **Ministry of Planning and Economic Policy**
  http://www.mippe.gob.pa/menu.html

Papua New Guinea

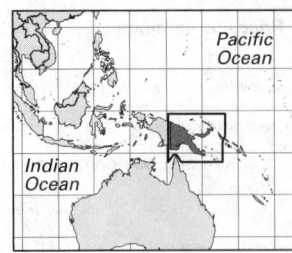

Official name: Independent State of Papua New Guinea.
Form of government: constitutional monarchy with one legislative house (National Parliament [109]).
Chief of state: British Monarch represented by Governor-General.
Head of government: Prime Minister.
Capital: Port Moresby.
Official language: English[1].
Official religion: none.
Monetary unit: 1 Papua New Guinea kina (K) = 100 toea; valuation (Sept. 25, 1998) 1 U.S.$ = K 2.28; 1 £ = K 3.88.

Area and population

Provinces	Administrative centres	area sq mi	area sq km	population 1990 census[2]
Bougainville	Arawa (Buka)	3,600	9,300	[3]
Central	Port Moresby (Central)	11,400	29,500	140,584
East New Britain	Rabaul	6,000	15,500	184,408
East Sepik	Wewak	16,550	42,800	248,308
Eastern Highlands	Goroka	4,300	11,200	299,619
Enga	Wabag	4,950	12,800	238,357
Gulf	Kerema	13,300	34,500	68,060
Madang	Madang	11,200	29,000	270,299
Manus	Lorengau	800	2,100	32,830
Milne Bay	Alotau (Samarai)	5,400	14,000	157,288
Morobe	Lae	13,300	34,500	363,535
National Capital District	Port Moresby	100	240	193,242
New Ireland	Kavieng	3,700	9,600	87,194
Oro (Northern)	Popondetta	8,800	22,800	96,762
Sandaun (West Sepik)	Vanimo	14,000	36,300	135,185
Simbu (Chimbu)	Kundiawa	2,350	6,100	183,801
Southern Highlands	Mendi	9,200	23,800	302,724
West New Britain	Kimbe	8,100	21,000	127,547
Western	Daru	38,350	99,300	108,705
Western Highlands	Mount Hagen	3,300	8,500	291,090
TOTAL		178,704[4]	462,840	3,529,538[5]

Demography

Population (1998): 4,600,000.
Density (1998): persons per sq mi 25.7, persons per sq km 9.9.
Urban-rural (1997): urban 17.0%; rural 83.0%.
Sex distribution (1990)[2]: male 52.09%; female 47.91%.
Age breakdown (1990): under 15, 40.4%; 15–29, 28.8%; 30–44, 16.9%; 45–59, 9.3%; 60–74, 4.3%; 75 and over, 0.3%.
Population projection: (2000) 4,812,000; (2010) 5,925,000.
Ethnic composition (1983): New Guinea Papuan 84.0%; New Guinea Melanesian 15.0%; other 1.0%.
Religious affiliation (1990): non-Anglican Protestant c. 64.0%, of which Evangelical Lutheran 23.2%, Seventh-day Adventist 8.1%, Pentecostal 7.1%; Roman Catholic 28.3%; Anglican 3.9%; other (mostly traditional beliefs) c. 3.8%.
Major cities (1990)[2]: Port Moresby 193,242; Lae 80,655; Madang 27,057; Wewak 23,224; Goroka 17,855.

Vital statistics

Birth rate per 1,000 population (1997): 32.4 (world avg. 25.0).
Death rate per 1,000 population (1997): 10.0 (world avg. 9.3).
Natural increase rate per 1,000 population (1997): 22.4 (world avg. 15.7).
Total fertility rate (avg. births per childbearing woman; 1997): 4.7.
Life expectancy at birth (1997): male 57.0 years; female 59.0 years.
Major causes of death per 100,000 population (1993): acute respiratory infections 34.6; pneumonia 27.8; meningitis 7.6; conditions originating from perinatal period 6.2; malaria 3.8.

National economy

Budget (1997). Revenue: K 1,882,000,000 (direct taxes 46.4%, indirect taxes 36.3%, nontax revenue 10.6%, foreign grants 6.7%). Expenditures: K 2,001,-000,000 (current expenditure 57.7%, transfer to provincial governments 28.4%, economic and infrastructure 13.9%).
Public debt (external, outstanding; 1996): U.S.$1,522,000,000.
Production (metric tons except as noted). Agriculture, forestry, fishing (1996): coconuts 700,000, bananas 650,000, sweet potatoes 450,000, sugarcane 300,000, palm oil 250,000, yams 222,000, taro 220,000, cassava 115,000, copra (1994) 100,000, palm kernels 62,000, coffee 60,000, cacao 30,000, pineapples 14,000, tea 9,000; livestock (number of live animals) 1,030,000 pigs, 110,000 cattle, 3,250,000 chickens; roundwood (1995) 8,772,000 cu m; fish catch (1995) 26,000. Mining and quarrying (1996): copper 186,715; silver 59,037 kg; gold 51,573 kg. Manufacturing (value added, in K; 1985): food, beverages, and tobacco 162,558,000; metals, metal products, machinery, and equipment 47,493,000; wood products 29,807,000. Construction (value in K; 1994)[6]: total 95,600,000. Energy production (consumption): electricity (kW-hr; 1994) 1,790,000,000 (1,790,000,000); coal (metric tons; 1994) none (1,000); petroleum products (metric tons; 1994) none (720,000).
Household income and expenditure. Average household size (1980) 4.6; income per household (1975–76) K 2,771 (U.S.$3,483); sources of income (1970): wages and salaries 57.3%, transfer payments 1.1%, self-employment and other 41.6%; expenditure (1987)[7]: food and beverages 40.9%, transportation and communications 13.0%, housing 12.5%, clothing and footwear 6.2%, heating and lighting 4.9%, services and other 22.5%.

Gross national product (1996): U.S.$5,049,000,000 (U.S.$1,150 per capita).

Structure of gross domestic product and labour force

	1996 in value K '000,000	1996 % of total value	1980 labour force[8]	1980 % of labour force[8]
Agriculture	1,785	26.5	564,500	77.0
Mining	1,851	27.5	4,300	0.6
Manufacturing	551	8.2	14,000	1.9
Construction	271	4.0	21,600	2.9
Public utilities	88	1.3	2,800	0.4
Transp. and commun.	348	5.2	17,400	2.4
Trade	576	8.6	25,100	3.4
Finance	64	0.9	4,500	0.6
Pub. admin., defense Services	} 888	13.2	77,100	10.5
Other	310	4.6	1,500	0.2
TOTAL	6,732[9]	100.0	732,800	100.0[4]

Land use (1994): forested 92.8%; agricultural and under permanent cultivation 0.9%; meadows and pastures 0.2%; other 6.1%.
Population economically active (1980)[8]: total 732,800; activity rate 24.6% (participation rates: over age 10, 35.2%; female 39.8%; unemployed 12.8%[10]).

Price and earnings indexes (1990 = 100)

	1991	1992	1993	1994	1995	1996	1997
Consumer price index	107.0	111.6	117.1	120.5	141.3	157.7	163.9
Weekly earnings index[11]	106.1	110.9	110.9	110.9	110.9	110.9	110.9

Tourism (1995): receipts U.S.$60,000,000; expenditures U.S.$75,000,000.

Foreign trade[12]

Balance of trade (current prices)

	1992	1993	1994	1995	1996	1997
K '000,000	+587.6	+1,416.9	+1,326.0	+1,780.0	+1,318.0	+937.5
% of total	18.7%	39.0%	33.2%	35.5%	24.8%	18.2%

Imports (1996): K 1,996,000,000 (1990; machinery and transport equipment 38.7%; basic manufactures 20.4%; food and live animals 17.9%; chemicals 7.5%; mineral fuels, lubricants, and related materials 2.7%). *Major import sources* (1995): Australia 52.2%; U.S. 14.8%; Singapore 7.4%; Japan 5.6%; New Zealand 3.6%; Hong kong 3.2%; U.K. 3.0%.
Exports (1996): K 3,313,900,000 (crude oil 32.4%; gold 23.3%; copper ore and timber 14.0%; concentrates 11.7%; coffee 5.7%; palm oil 5.5%; cocoa beans 1.4%). *Major export destinations* (1995): Australia 30.0%; Japan 24.3%; Germany 10.0%; U.K. 8.2%; South Korea 7.1%; U.S. 4.0%.

Transport and communications

Transport. Railroads: none. Roads (1986): total length 19,736 km (paved 6%). Vehicles (1994): passenger cars 13,000; trucks and buses 32,000. Merchant marine (1992): vessels (100 gross tons and over) 87; total deadweight tonnage 40,855. Air transport (1993): passenger-km 738,366,000; metric ton-km cargo 82,369,000; airports (1996) with scheduled flights 129.

Communications

Medium	date	unit	number	units per 1,000 persons
Daily newspapers	1994	circulation	65,000	15
Radio	1996	receivers	300,000	68
Television	1995	receivers	100,000	23
Telephones	1995	main lines	43,600	10
Facsimile machines	1995	units	800	0.2

Education and health

Educational attainment (1990). Percentage of population age 25 and over having: no formal schooling 82.6%; some primary education 8.2%; completed primary 5.0%; some secondary 4.2%. *Literacy* (1995 est.): total population age 15 and over literate 72.2%; males literate 81.0%; females literate 62.7%.

Education (1995)

	schools	teachers	students	student/ teacher ratio
Primary (age 7–12)	2,790	13,652	525,995	38.5
Secondary (age 13–16)	135[13]	2,415[14]	68,818	24.1[14]
Voc., teacher tr.	117[13]	878[14]	9,941	12.9[14]
Higher	2[13]	902[15]	13,663	7.1[15]

Health: physicians (1993) 736 (1 per 5,584 persons); hospital beds (1989) 15,335 (1 per 234 persons); infant mortality rate (1997) 62.0.
Food (1992): daily per capita caloric intake 2,613 (vegetable products 91%, animal products 9%); 115% of FAO minimum.

Military

Total active duty personnel (1997): 4,300 (army 88.4%, navy 9.3%, air force 2.3%). *Military expenditure as percentage of GNP* (1995): 1.4% (world 2.8%); per capita expenditure U.S.$25.

[1]The national languages are English, Tok Pisin (English Creole), and Motu. [2]Preliminary results. [3]Data unavailable because of civil insurrection. [4]Detail does not add to total given because of rounding. [5]Excludes an estimated population of 160,000 in the North Solomons, 4,500 people in remote areas, and an estimated foreign population of about 20,000–30,000. [6]Construction starts. [7]Weights of retail price index components. [8]Citizens of Papua New Guinea over age 10 involved in "money-raising activities" only. [9]International Monetary Fund estimate. [10]1997; in six urban centres. [11]Minimum wage of urban labourers; starting 1993, for whole country. [12]Import figures are f.o.b. in balance of trade and c.i.f. for commodities and trading partners. [13]1990. [14]1992. [15]1986.

Paraguay

Official name: República del Paraguay (Spanish); Tetä Paraguáype (Guaraní)(Republic of Paraguay).
Form of government: multiparty republic with two legislative houses (Senate [46[1]]; Chamber of Deputies [80]).
Head of state and government: President.
Capital: Asunción.
Official languages: Spanish; Guaraní.
Official religion: none[2].
Monetary unit: 1 Paraguayan Guaraní (G) = 100 céntimos; valuation (Sept. 25, 1998) 1 U.S.$ = G2,810; 1 £ = G4,784.

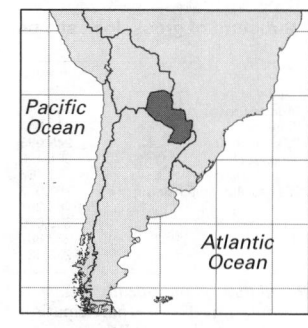

Area and population

Regions Departments	Capitals	area sq mi	area sq km	population 1992 census
Occidental		95,338	246,925	105,633
Alto Paraguay	Fuerte Olimpo	31,795	82,349	12,156
Boquerón	Filadelfia	35,393	91,669	29,060
Presidente Hayes	Pozo Colorado	28,150	72,907	64,417
Oriental		61,710	159,827	4,046,955
Alto Paraná	Ciudad del Este	5,751	14,895	406,584
Amambay	Pedro Juan Caballero	4,994	12,933	99,860
Asunción[3]	—	45	117	500,938
Caaguazú	Coronel Oviedo	4,430	11,474	386,412
Caazapá	Caazapá	3,666	9,496	129,352
Canindiyú	Salto del Guairá	5,663	14,667	103,785
Central	Asunción	952	2,465	866,856
Concepción	Concepción	6,970	18,051	167,289
Cordillera	Caacupé	1,910	4,948	198,701
Guairá	Villarrica	1,485	3,846	161,991
Itapúa	Encarnación	6,380	16,525	377,536
Misiones	San Juan Bautista	3,690	9,556	89,018
Ñeembucú	Pilar	4,690	12,147	69,770
Paraguarí	Paraguarí	3,361	8,705	208,527
San Pedro	San Pedro	7,723	20,002	280,336
TOTAL		157,048	406,752	4,152,588[4]

Demography

Population (1998): 5,223,000[4].
Density (1998): persons per sq mi 33.3, persons per sq km 12.8.
Urban-rural (1992): urban 50.3%; rural 49.7%.
Sex distribution (1992): male 50.23%; female 49.77%.
Age breakdown (1992): under 15, 40.1%; 15–29, 27.6%; 30–44, 18.7%; 45–59, 8.3%, 60–74, 4.2%; 75 and over, 1.1%.
Population projection: (2000) 5,496,000; (2010) 6,980,000.
Religious affiliation (1995): Roman Catholic 88.5%; Protestant 5.0%; other 6.5%.
Major cities (1992): Asunción 502,426; Ciudad del Este 133,893; San Lorenzo 133,311; Lambaré 99,681; Fernando de la Mora 95,287.

Vital statistics

Birth rate per 1,000 population (1995–2000): 31.3 (world avg. 25.0).
Death rate per 1,000 population (1995–2000): 5.4 (world avg. 9.3).
Natural increase rate per 1,000 population (1995–2000): 25.9 (world avg. 15.7).
Total fertility rate (avg. births per childbearing woman; 1995–2000): 4.2.
Marriage rate per 1,000 population (1992): 3.9[5].
Life expectancy at birth (1995–2000): male 67.5 years; female 72.0 years.
Major causes of death per 100,000 population (1993)[6]: diseases of the circulatory system 162.7; malignant neoplasms (cancers) 52.8: diseases of the respiratory system 38.1; infectious and parasitic diseases 32.7.

National economy

Budget (1996). Revenue: G2,937,992,000,000 (taxes on goods and services 46.5%, customs duties 15.1%, income on fixed assets 14.3%, royalty payments 12.6%, pension funds 7.2%, documentary tax 2.3%). Expenditures: G3,335,481,000,000 (education 21.3%; public works 11.4%, defense 8.1%, agriculture 8.2%, interior 7.2%, public health 7.2%, housing 5.2%).
Public debt (external, outstanding; 1996): U.S.$1,377,000,000.
Population economically active (1996): total 1,747,488; activity rate 35.3% (participation rates; 1992: ages 12 and over, 51.0%; female 23.8%; unemployed [1996] 9.8%).

Price and earnings indexes (1990 = 100)

	1991	1992	1993	1994	1995	1996	1997
Consumer price index	124.2	143.1	169.2	203.9	231.3	254.0	271.6
Earnings index	115.1	131.8	158.0	...	...	...	...

Production (metric tons except as noted). Agriculture, forestry, fishing (1996): cassava 2,770,000, sugarcane 2,736,000, soybeans 2,394,000, corn (maize) 654,000, seed cotton 330,000, oranges 175,000, lint cotton 115,000, bananas 67,000, sweet potatoes 67,000; livestock (number of live animals) 9,788,000 cattle, 2,525,000 pigs, 14,152,000 chickens; roundwood (1995) 10,401,000 cu m; fish catch (1995) 16,000. Mining and quarrying (1995): limestone 600,000; kaolin 74,000; gypsum 4,500. Manufacturing (value added in constant prices of 1982, G'000,000; 1995): food products 70,600; wood products and furniture 24,500; handicrafts 11,400; textiles 10,200; printing and publishing 7,800; non-metal products 6,900; petroleum products 6,400; leather and hides 5,700.

Energy production (consumption): electricity (kW-hr; 1994) 35,862,000,000 (3,090,000,000); crude petroleum (barrels; 1994) none (1,986,000): petroleum products (metric tons; 1994) 293,000 (1,011,000).
Gross national product (1996): U.S.$9,179,000,000 (U.S.$1,850 per capita).

Structure of gross domestic product and labour force

	1996 in value G'000,000[6]	1996 % of total value	1996 labour force	1996 % of labour force
Agriculture	291,745	26.5	559,042	32.0
Mining	5,133	0.5	2,568	0.1
Manufacturing	157,778	14.3	181,983	10.4
Construction	59,764	5.4	142,678	8.2
Public utilities	60,697	5.5	13,150	0.8
Transp. and commun.	52,180	4.8	55,972	3.2
Trade	279,758	25.4	224,210	12.8
Finance				
Pub. admin., defense	60,671	5.5	330,697	18.9
Services				
Other	133,432	12.1	237,188[8]	13.6[8]
TOTAL	1,101,158	100.0	1,747,488	100.0

Household income and expenditure. Average household size (1992) 4.7; sources of income (1989): wages and salaries 33.9%, transfer payments 2.5%.
Tourism (1995): receipts U.S.$213,000,000; expenditures U.S.$181,000,000.

Foreign trade[9]

Balance of trade (current prices)

U.S.$'000,000	1991	1992	1993	1994	1995	1996
	−538.3	−580.6	−752.3	−1,323.6	−1,887.6	−1,807.0
% of total	26.7%	30.7%	34.2%	44.8%	50.5%	46.4%

Imports (1996): U.S.$2,850,477,000[10] (machinery and transport equipment 33.5%, of which transport equipment 11.6%; fuels and lubricants 8.3%; chemicals and pharmaceuticals 4.6%). *Major import sources* (1996): Brazil 32.7%; Argentina 19.5%; U.S. 10.7%; Japan 6.2%; South Korea 3.4%.
Exports (1996): U.S.$1,043,446,000[10] (soybean flour 31.1%; cotton fibres 20.7%; timber 9.0%; oilseed cakes 8.2%; vegetable oil 7.4%, of which soybean oil 5.6%; processed meats 4.5%; hides and skins 4.2%). *Major export destinations* (1996): Brazil 49.9%; The Netherlands 16.5%; Argentina 9.2%; Uruguay 4.2%; United States 3.5%; Chile 2.4%; Italy 1.9%.

Transport and communications

Transport. Railroads (1994): route length 441 km; passenger-km 3,000,000; metric ton-km cargo 5,500,000. Roads (1995): total length 28,900 km (paved 9%). Vehicles (1993): passenger cars 174,212; trucks 76,565. Air transport (1994): passenger-km 1,235,000,000; metric ton-km cargo 11,700,000; airports (1997) 5.

Communications

Medium	date	unit	number	units per 1,000 persons
Daily newspapers	1995	circulation	194,000	40
Radio	1996	receivers	700,000	141
Television	1995	receivers	710,000	144
Telephones	1995	main lines	166,900	34
Cellular telephones	1995	subscribers	15,800	3.2
Facsimile machines	1995	units	1,700	0.4

Education and health

Educational attainment (1992). Percentage of population age 15 and over having: no formal schooling 7.0%; primary education 61.2%; secondary 23.2%; higher 6.6%; not stated 2.0%. *Literacy* (1995): percentage of total population age 15 and over literate 92.1%; males literate 93%; female literate 90.6%.

Education (1994–95)

	schools	teachers	students	student/ teacher ratio
Primary (age 7–12)	5,318	34,580	835,089	24.1
Secondary (age 13–18)[11]	1,102	20,793[12]	235,914	10.3[12]
Higher	2	742[12]	39,694	40.9[13]

Health (1993): physicians 3,341 (1 per 1,406 persons); hospital beds 5,435 (1 per 864 persons); infant mortality rate per 1,000 live births (1995–2000) 39.0.
Food (1995): daily per capita caloric intake 2,560 (vegetable products 77%, animals products 23%); 111% of FAO recommended minimum requirement.

Military

Total active duty personnel (1997): 20,200 (army 73.8%, navy 17.8%, air force 8.4%). *Military expenditure as percentage of GNP* (1995): 1.4% (world 2.8%), per capita expenditure U.S.$23.

---

[1]Includes one nonelective seat. Former President Wasmosy became senator-for-life in August 1998. [2]Roman Catholicism, although not official, enjoys special recognition in the 1992 constitution. [3]Asunción is the capital city, not a department. [4]The 1992 census figure is not adjusted for undercount. The 1998 population figure is adjusted for estimated undercount. [5]Civil Registry records only. [6]Reporting areas only (constituting about 75 percent of the total population). [7]1982 prices. [8]Includes 171,312 unemployed. [9]Imports are f.o.b. [10]Preliminary. [11]Includes vocational and teacher training. [12]1993–94. [13]1992–93.

Internet resources for further information:
• **Presidency of the Republic (Spanish only)**
  http://www.presidencia.gov.py/home
• **Dirección de Censos y Estadísticas Agropecuarias (Spanish only)**
  http://www.una.py/sitios/dcea/

Peru

Official name: República del Perú
(Spanish) (Republic of Peru).
Form of government[1]: unitary
multiparty republic with one
legislative house (Congress [120]).
Head of state and government:
President.
Capital: Lima.
Official languages: Spanish; Quechua;
Aymara.
Official religion: Roman Catholicism.
Monetary unit[2]: 1 nuevo sol (S/.) =
100 céntimos; valuation (Sept. 25, 1998)
1 U.$. = S/. 3.04; 1 £ = S/. 5.18.

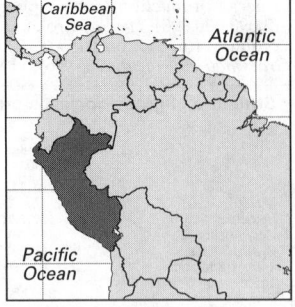

Area and population		area		population
				1997
Regions[3]	Capitals	sq mi	sq km	estimate
Andrés Avelino Cáceres	...	40,707	105,430	2,124,366
Arequipa	...	24,458	63,345	1,017,491
Chavín	...	15,686	40,627	1,035,321
Grau	...	15,661	40,562	1,665,555
Inca	...	66,696	172,741	1,607,279
José Carlos Mariátegui	...	40,081	103,809	1,551,264
La Libertad	...	9,873	25,570	1,390,568
Loreto	...	142,414	368,852	819,037
Los Libertadores-Wari	...	34,340	88,939	1,554,476
Nor Oriental del Marañón	...	33,486	86,728	2,773,098
San Martín	...	19,789	51,253	667,414
Ucayali	...	39,541	102,411	380,620
Department				
Lima	...	13,437	34,802	7,066,641
Constitutional Province				
Callao	Callao	57	147	717,913
TOTAL		496,225[4]	1,285,216	24,371,043

Demography

Population (1998): 24,801,000.
Density (1998) persons per sq mi 50.0, persons per sq km 19.3.
Urban-rural (1995): urban 71.2%; rural 28.8%.
Sex distribution (1995): male 49.67%; female 50.33%.
Age breakdown (1995): under 15, 35.9%; 15–29, 29.0%; 30–44, 18.2%; 45–59, 10.2%; 60–74, 5.3%; 75 and over, 1.4%.
Population projection: (2000) 25,662,000; (2010) 30,506,000.
Ethnic composition (1981): Quechua 47.1%; mestizo 32.0%; white 12.0%; Aymara 5.4%; other Amerindian 1.7%; other 1.8%.
Religious affiliation (1995) Roman Catholic 88.8%; Protestant 6.7%; other Christian 1.5%; other 3.0%.
Major cities (1993): metropolitan Lima 5,706,127; Arequipa 619,156; Callao 615,046; Trujillo 509,312; Chiclayo 411,536.

Vital statistics

Birth rate per 1,000 population (1995–2000): 24.9 (world avg. 25.0); (1977) legitimate 57.8%; illegitimate 42.2%.
Death rate per 1,000 population (1995–2000): 6.4 (world avg. 9.3).
Natural increase rate per 1,000 population (1995–2000): 18.5 (world avg. 15.7).
Total fertility rate (avg. births per childbearing woman; 1995–2000): 3.0.
Marriage rate per 1,000 population (1993): 4.1[5].
Live expectancy at birth (1995–2000): male 65.9 years; female 70.9 years.
Major causes of death per 100,000 population (1989): diseases of the circulatory system 115.3; respiratory diseases 100.2; infectious diseases 84.5; malignant neoplasms 72.9; accidents, poisoning, and violence 53.6.

National economy

Budget (1995). Revenue: S/. 21,048,000,000 (taxes on goods and services 45.9%; income taxes 15.9%; nontax revenue 11.2%; social security contributions 10.1%; import duties 9.4%). Expenditures: S/. 24,649,000,000 (current expenditure 82.7%, of which transfer payments 35.7%, interest payments 15.4%, wages and salaries 15.0%; capital expenditure 17.3%).
Public debt (external, outstanding; 1996): U.S.$20,415,000,000.
Tourism (1995): receipts U.S.$520,000,000; expenditures U.S.$302,000,000.
Production (metric tons except as noted). Agriculture, forestry, fishing (1996): sugarcane 6,600,000, potatoes 2,265,000, rice 1,203,000, plantains 1,060,000, corn (maize) 1,054,000, cassava 547,000, seed cotton 269,000; livestock (number of live animals) 12,502,000 sheep, 4,629,000 cattle, 2,490,000 pigs, 79,089,000 chickens; roundwood (1995) 12,580,000 cu m; fish catch (1994) 11,587,339. Mining and quarrying (1995): iron ore 3,835,000; zinc 689,000; copper 405,000; lead 233,000; silver 1,908. Manufacturing (value in S/. '000,000[6]; 1995): processed foods 214.6; base metal products 164.6; industrial chemicals 114.2; wood products 77.6; textiles 71.8. Construction (value in S/.'000,000[6]; 1992): residential 22.4; nonresidential 14.6. Energy production (consumption): electricity (kW-hr; 1994) 15,163,000,000 (15,163,000,000); coal (metric tons; 1994) 109,000 (406,000); crude petroleum (barrels; 1994) 47,000,000 (54,000,000); petroleum products (metric tons; 1994) 7,227,000 (5,798,000); natural gas (cu m; 1994) 191,000,000 (191,000,000).
Household income and expenditure. Average household size (1993) 5.1; income per household (1988) I/. 1,086,620[2] (U.S.$2,173); sources of income (1988): business income 65.1%, wages 31.2%, transfers 3.7%; expenditure (1990): food 29.4%, recreation and education 13.2%, household durables 10.1%, clothing and footwear 8.5%, transportation 7.5%, health 7.0%, other 24.3%.
Gross national product (1996): U.S.$58,671,000,000 (U.S.$2,420 per capita).

Structure of gross domestic product and labour force

	1995		1992	
	in value S/. [2]	% of total value	labour force	% of labour force
Agriculture	608,488	14.4	2,658,000	33.0
Mining	355,344	8.4	198,000	2.4
Manufacturing	943,088	22.3	840,000	10.4
Construction	361,496	8.5	300,000	3.7
Public utilities	71,463	1.7	25,000	0.3
Transp. and commun.	291,992	6.9	355,000	4.4
Trade	762,261	18.0	1,297,000	16.1
Finance	608,070	14.4	192,000	2.4
Services	230,867[7]	5.4[7]	2,199,000[7]	27.3[7]
TOTAL	4,233,069	100.0	8,064,000	100.0

Population economically active (1995): total 8,906,009; activity rate of total population 37.8% (participation rates: over age 15, 59.1%; female 34.7%; unemployed [1993] 7.1%).

Price and earnings indexes (1990 = 100)

	1991	1992	1993	1994	1995	1996	1997
Consumer price index	510	884	1,314	1,626	1,806	2,015	2,187
Monthly earnings index[8]	706	1,163	2,059	...	...	...	...

Land use (1994): forest 66.3%; pasture 21.2%; agricultural 3.2%; other 9.3%.

Foreign trade

Balance of trade (current prices)

	1992	1993	1994	1995	1996	1997
U.S.$'000,000	−566.7	−623.9	−1,095.2	−2,111.6	−1,996.5	−1,738.3
% of total	7.5%	8.2%	10.8%	15.9%	14.5%	11.3%

Imports (1995): U.S.$7,583,860,000 (raw and intermediate materials 31.2%, machinery 22.7%, transport equipment 14.8%, consumer goods 12.1%). *Major import sources:* U.S. 25.2%; Colombia 8.1%; Japan 7.0%; Brazil 5.6%.
Exports (1995): U.S.$4,976,782,000 (copper and copper products 23.0%, fish meal fodder 13.3%, zinc products 6.9%, coffee 5.3%, petroleum and derivatives 4.9%, lead products 4.2%, clothing and accessories 3.7%, textile yarn and fabric 3.2%). *Major export destinations:* U.S. 18.7%; Japan 9.2%; China 7.0%; Germany 6.4%; The Netherlands 5.6%; Italy 5.0%; Brazil 4.0%.

Transport and communications

Transport. Railroads (1993): route length 2,121 km; passenger-km 165,304,000; metric ton-km cargo 884,352,000. Roads (1995): total length 71,400 km (paved 11%). Vehicles (1995): passenger cars 505,766; trucks and buses 338,871. Air transport (1995): passenger-km 2,470,000,000; metric ton-km cargo 259,000,000; airports (1996) 27.

Communications

Medium	date	unit	number	units per 1,000 persons
Daily newspapers	1994	circulation	2,000,000	87
Radio	1996	receivers	5,300,000	221
Television	1995	receivers	2,000,000	85
Telephones	1995	main lines	1,109,200	47
Cellular telephones	1995	subscribers	73,500	3.1
Facsimile machines	1995	units	15,000	0.6
Personal computers	1995	units	140,000	5.9

Education and health

Educational attainment (1993). Percentage of population age 15 and over having: no formal schooling 12.3%; less than primary education 0.3%; primary 31.5%; secondary 35.5%; higher 20.4%. *Literacy* (1993): total population age 15 and over literate 12,108,699 (87.2%); males 6,330,056 (92.9%); females 5,778,643 (81.7%).

Education (1994–95)

	schools	teachers	students	student/ teacher ratio
Primary (age 6–11)	46,652	176,173	4,822,423	27.4
Secondary (age 12–16)	8,085	104,476	2,023,830	19.4
Voc., teacher tr.	2,425	12,293	270,576	22.0
Higher	886	49,249	714,512	14.5

Health (1992): physicians 20,124 (1 per 1,116 persons); hospital beds 44,100 (1 per 509 persons); infant mortality rate per 1,000 live births (1995–2000) 50.1.
Food (1995): daily per capita caloric intake 2,277 (vegetable products 83%, animal products 17%); 97% of FAO recommended minimum requirement.

Military

Total active duty personnel (1996): 125,000 (army 68.0%, navy 20.0%, air force 12.0%). *Military expenditure as percentage of GNP* (1995): 1.7% (world 2.8%); per capita expenditure U.S.$42.

[1]A new constitution promulgated in December 1993 replaced the 1980 constitution, which was suspended in April 1992. [2]A new currency, the nuevo sol, was introduced in January 1991, replacing the inti (abbrev.: I/.) at the rate of one million intis for one nuevo sol. [3]The regional administrative structure established in 1987 has been made functional only very slowly because of financing problems. [4]Detail does not add to total given because of rounding. [5]Excludes Indian jungle population; based on incomplete information. [6]At 1979 prices. [7]Includes public administration and other. [8]Estimate for Lima metropolitan area only.

Internet resources for further information:
• **Instituto Nacional de Estadística e Informática (Spanish)**
  http://www.inei.gob.pe/

Philippines

Official name: Republika ng Pilipinas (Pilipino); Republic of the Philippines (English).
Form of government: unitary republic with two legislative houses (Senate [24]; House of Representatives [260[1]]).
Chief of state and head of government: President.
Capital: Quezon City/Manila[2].
Official languages: Pilipino; English.
Official religion: none.
Monetary unit: 1 Philippine peso (P) = 100 centavos; valuation (Sept. 25, 1998) 1 U.S.$ = P43.78; 1 £ = P 74.54.

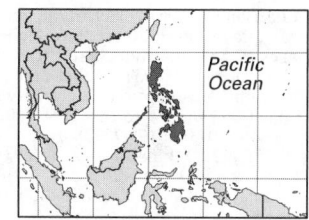

Pacific Ocean

Area and population	area		population
Regions	sq mi	sq km	1995 census
Bicol	6,808	17,633	4,325,307
Cagayan Valley	10,362	26,838	2,536,035
Caraga	7,277	18,847	1,942,687
Central Luzon	7,039	18,231	6,932,570
Central Mindanao	5,549	14,373	2,359,808
Central Visayas	5,773	14,951	5,014,588
Eastern Visayas	8,275	21,432	3,366,917
Ilocos	4,958	12,840	3,803,890
National Capital	246	636	9,454,040
Nothern Mindanao	5,418	14,033	2,483,272
Southern Mindanao	10,479	27,141	4,604,158
Southern Tagalog	18,117	46,924	9,940,722
Western Mindanao	6,194	16,042	2,794,659
Western Visayas	7,808	20,223	5,776,938
Autonomous Regions			
Cordillera	7,063	18,294	1,254,838
Muslim Mindanao	4,493	11,638	2,020,903
TOTAL	115,860[3]	300,076	68,614,162[4]

Demography

Population (1998): 73,131,000.
Density (1998): persons per sq mi 631.2, persons per sq km 243.7.
Urban-rural (1997): urban 56.0%; rural 44.0%.
Sex distribution (1996): male 50.29%; female 49.71%.
Age breakdown (1996): under 15, 35.9%; 15–29, 28.8%; 30–44, 19.4%; 45–59, 10.2%; 60–74, 4.6%; 75 and over, 1.1%.
Population projection: (2000) 76,320,000; (2010) 91,851,000.
Doubling time: 30 years.
Ethnic composition (by mother tongue of households; 1995): Pilipino (Tagalog) 29.3%; Cebuano 23.3%; Ilocano 9.3%; Hiligaynon Ilongo 9.1%; Bicol 5.7%; Waray 3.8%; Pampango 3.0%; Pangasinan 1.8%; other 14.7%.
Religious affiliation (1990): Roman Catholic 82.9%; Protestant 5.4%; Muslim 4.6%; Aglipayan (Philippine Independent Church) 2.6%; other 4.5%.
Major cities (1995): Quezon City 1,989,419; Manila 1,654,761; Caloocan 1,023,159; Davao 960,910[5]; Cebu 688,196[5]; Zamboanga 464,466[5].

Vital statistics

Birth rate per 1,000 population (1997): 28.7 (world avg. 25.0); (1982) legitimate 93.9%; illegitimate 6.1%.
Death rate per 1,000 population (1997): 5.8 (world avg. 9.3).
Natural increase rate per 1,000 population (1997): 22.9 (world avg. 15.7).
Total fertility rate (avg. births per childbearing woman; 1997): 3.7.
Life expectancy at birth (1997): male 66.0 years; female 70.0 years.
Major causes of death per 100,000 population (1992): heart disease 64.3; pneumonia 57.9; tuberculosis 25.0; accidents 19.6.

National economy

Budget (1996). Revenue: P 417,216,000,000 (taxes on goods and services 31.4%, income taxes 31.2%, international duties 24.7%, nontax revenues 12.7%). Expenditures: P 415,557,000,000 (education 18.3%, general public administration 17.2%, debt service 16.7%, utilities and infrastructure 10.9%).
Public debt (external, outstanding; 1996): U.S.$27,937,000.
Production (metric tons except as noted). Agriculture, forestry, fishing (1996): sugarcane 26,000,000, rice 11,283,570, coconuts 10,000,000, corn (maize) 4,151,332, bananas 3,292,387, pineapples 1,476,879; livestock (number of live animals) 9,025,950 pigs, 6,400,000, goats, 2,841,277 buffalo, 115,782,000 chickens; roundwood (1995) 39,857,000 cu m; fish catch (1995) 2,259,234. Mining and quarrying (1996): coal 1,047,336; nickel ore 378,921; copper concentrate 188,442; silver 19,202 kg; gold 10,605 kg. Manufacturing (gross value added in P '000,000; 1995)[6]: food products 176,200; petroleum and coal products 36,900; chemicals 35,700; footwear and clothing 30,400. Construction (private, authorized; 1996): residential P 31,162,071,000; nonresidential P 63,128,-161,000. Energy production (consumption): electricity (kW-hr; 1994) 26,425,-000,000 (26,425,000,000); coal (metric tons; 1994) 1,733,000 (2,503,000); crude petroleum (barrels; 1994) 2,186,000 (90,808,000); petroleum products (metric tons; 1994) 11,350,000 (12,559,000).
Household income and expenditure (1992). Average household size (1995) 5.1; income per family (1994) P 83,160 (U.S.$3,150); sources of income: wages 45.7%, business profits 42.5%, self-employment 8.4%, transfers 3.4%; expenditure: food, beverage, and tobacco 57.7%, household furnishings and operations 13.5%, transportation 5.0%, fuel and power 4.1%, clothing 3.7%.
Gross national product (1996): U.S.$83,298,000,000 (U.S.$1,160 per capita).

Structure of gross domestic product and labour force

	1995			
	in value P '000,000	% of total value	labour force	% of labour force
Agriculture	413,000	21.7	11,147,000	39.3
Mining	18,000	0.9	107,000	0.4
Manufacturing	438,000	23.0	2,617,000	9.2
Construction	107,000	5.6	1,302,000	4.6
Public utilities	49,000	2.6	114,000	0.4
Transp. and commun.	89,000	4.7	1,477,000	5.2
Trade	262,000	13.7	3,767,000	13.3
Finances	209,000	11.0	535,000	1.9
Services	321,000	16.8	4,600,000	16.2
Others			2,716,000[7]	9.5[7]
TOTAL	1,906,000	100.0	28,382,000	100.0

Population economically active (1995): total 28,382,000; activity rate 40.4% (participation rates: ages 15–64, 65.6%; female 37.4%; unemployed 9.5%).

Price and earnings indexes (1990 = 100)							
	1991	1992	1993	1994	1995	1996	1997
Consumer price index	118.7	129.3	139.1	151.7	164.0	177.8	186.7
Daily earnings index[8]	128.5	128.5	147.0	155.2	157.9	...	...

Tourism (1995): receipts U.S.$2,450,000,000; expenditures U.S.$422,000,000.

Foreign trade[9]

Balance of trade (current prices)						
	1992	1993	1994	1995	1996	1997
P '000,000	–121,250	–76,298	–212,086	–229,214	–311,291	–316,285
% of total	19.6%	22.5%	23.2%	20.3%	22.5%	17.5%

Imports (1996): U.S.$32,426,930,000 (machinery and transport equipment 29.8%, electronic materials and components 19.8, mineral fuels and lubricants 9.3%, iron and steel 4.4%, textile yarns and fabrics 3.6%). *Major import sources:* Japan 22.0%; United States 19.6%; Singapore 5.4%; Saudi Arabia 5.2%; South Korea 5.2%.
Exports (1996): U.S.$20,542,550,000 (electronics 39.9%, garments 11.8%, coconut oil 2.8%, ignition wiring sets 2.3%, computer peripherals 2.3%, woodcraft and furniture 2.2%). *Major export destinations:* United States 33.9%; Japan 17.9%; Singapore 6.0%; The Netherlands 5.4%; Hong Kong 4.2%.

Transport and communications

Transport. Railroads (1996): route length 897 km; passenger-km 70,000,000; metric ton-km cargo 1,476,000. Roads (1994): total length 161,035 km (paved 17%). Vehicles (1995): passenger cars 609,000; trucks and buses 221,900. Air transport (1996)[10]: passenger-km 12,854,000,000; metric ton-km cargo 328,817,000; airports (1996) with scheduled flights 21.

Communications				units per 1,000 persons
Medium	date	unit	number	
Daily newspapers	1994	circulation	4,286,000	65
Radio	1996	receivers	8,300,000	116
Television	1996	receivers	9,000,000	125
Telephones	1996	main lines	1,787,000	25
Cellular telephones	1995	subscribers	492,700	6.9
Facsimile machines	1995	units	35,000	0.5
Personal computers	1995	units	770,000	11

Education and health

Education attainment (1990). Percentage of population age 25 and over having: no grade completed 6.7%; elementary education 46.9%; secondary 24.3%; postsecondary 11.0%; college 10.6%; not stated 0.5%. *Literacy* (1995): total population age 15 and over literate 94.6%; males literate 95.0%; females literate 94.3%.

Education (1994–95)	schools	teachers	students	student/ teacher ratio
Primary (age 7–12)	35,671	324,418	10,903,529	33.6
Secondary (age 13–16)	5,880[11]	131,831	4,762,877	36.1
Voc., teacher tr.	1,261[12]			
Higher	975[11]	56,880[13]	1,582,820[11]	23.7[13]

Health: physicians (1993) 78,445 (1 per 849 persons); hospital beds (1993) 77,434 (1 per 860 persons); infant mortality rate per 1,000 live births (1997) 36.
Food (1995): daily per capita caloric intake 2,395 (vegetable products 85%, animal products 15%): 106% of FAO recommended minimum requirement.

Military

Total active duty personnel (1996): 107,500 (army 63.3%, navy 21.4%, air force 15.3%). *Military expenditure as percentage of GNP* (1994): 1.9% (world 3.0%); per capita expenditure U.S.$19.

[1]Includes 43 vacant seats. [2]And other Manila suburbs of the National Capital Region. [3]Detail does not add to total given because of rounding. [4]Includes 2,830 embassy employees abroad. [5]1994. [6]Manufacturing firms with 10 or more workers. [7]Mostly unemployed. [8]Wages in nonagricultural activities in the National Capital Region. [9]Import figures are f.o.b. in balance of trade and c.i.f. for commodities and trading partners. [10]Philippines Airlines only. [11]1993–94. [12]1991–92. [13]1990–91.

Internet resources for further information:
• **National Statistics Office http://www.census.gov.ph/**
• **Government Website http://www.neda.gov.ph/LINKS/gov_site.htm**

Poland

Official name: Rzeczpospolita Polska (Republic of Poland).
Form of government: unitary multiparty republic with two legislative houses (Senate [100]; Diet [460]).
Chief of state: President.
Head of government: Prime Minister.
Capital: Warsaw.
Official language: Polish.
Official religion: none[1].
Monetary unit: 1 zloty (Zł)[2] = 100 groszy; valuation (Sept. 25, 1998) 1 U.S.$ = Zł 3.55; 1 £ = Zł 6.04.

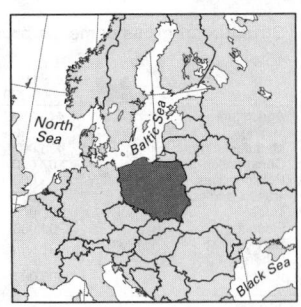

Area and population[3] (1996 estimate)

Provinces	area sq km	population	Provinces	area sq km	population[4]
Biała Podlaska	5,348	309,500	Opole	8,535	1,025,200
Białystok	10,055	700,700	Ostrołęka	6,498	408,400
Bielsko-Biała	3,704	918,600	Piła	8,205	494,000
Bydgoszcz	10,349	1,131,800	Piotrków	6,266	644,200
Chełm	3,866	249,900	Płock	5,117	522,000
Ciechanów	6,362	436,400	Poznań	8,151	1,353,700
Częstochowa	6,182	782,300	Przemyśl	4,437	414,600
Elbląg	6,103	491,400	Radom	7,294	763,800
Gdańsk	7,394	1,455,900	Rzeszów	4,397	746,300
Gorzów	8,484	510,800	Siedlce	8,499	661,700
Jelenia Góra	4,379	524,500	Sieradz	4,869	412,900
Kalisz	6,512	722,000	Skierniewice	3,960	424,000
Katowice	6,650	3,924,800	Słupsk	7,453	425,900
Kielce	9,211	1,136,600	Suwałki	10,490	485,500
Konin	5,139	479,700	Szczecin	9,982	990,500
Koszalin	8,470	521,900	Tarnobrzeg	6,283	609,300
Kraków	3,254	1,241,400	Tarnów	4,151	693,500
Krosno	5,702	506,600	Toruń	5,348	671,100
Legnica	4,037	523,600	Wałbrzych	4,168	739,400
Leszno	4,154	397,200	Warszawa	3,788	2,416,600
Łódź	1,523	1,116,200	Włocławek	4,402	435,000
Łomża	6,684	353,800	Wrocław	6,287	1,137,700
Lublin	6,792	1,026,800	Zamość	6,980	492,800
Nowy Sącz	5,576	733,100	Zielona Góra	8,868	674,100
Olsztyn	12,327	771,700	TOTAL	312,685	38,609,400

Demography

Population (1998): 38,665,000.
Density (1998): persons per sq mi 320.3, persons per sq km 123.7.
Urban-rural (1996): urban 61.8; rural 38.2%.
Sex distribution (1997): male 48.63%; female 51.37%.
Age breakdown (1997): under 15, 21.4%; 15–29, 22.9%; 30–44, 22.6%; 45–59, 17.0%; 60–74, 12.2%; 75 and over, 3.9%.
Population projection: (2000) 38,684,000; (2010) 39,969,000.
Ethnic composition (1995): Polish 97.6%; Ukrainian 0.6%; other 1.8%.
Religious affiliation (1995): Roman Catholic 90.7%; Orthodox and other 9.3%.
Major cities (1996[4]): Warsaw 1,638,300; Łódź 825,600; Kraków 745,400.

Vital statistics

Birth rate per 1,000 population (1997): 10.0 (world avg. 25.0); (1985) legitimate 95.0%; illegitimate 5.0%.
Death rate per 1,000 population (1997): 10.0 (world avg. 9.3).
Natural increase rate per 1,000 population (1997): 0.0 (world avg. 15.7).
Total fertility rate (avg. births per childbearing woman; 1997): 1.4.
Marriage rate per 1,000 population (1996): 5.3.
Divorce rate per 1,000 population (1995): 1.0.
Life expectancy at birth (1997): male 68.3 years; female 76.9 years,
Major causes of death per 100,000 population (1994): diseases of the circulatory system 512.7; malignant neoplasms (cancers) 201.0; accidents, poisoning, and violence 75.4; diabetes mellitus 14.2; infectious and parasitic diseases 6.8.

National economy

Budget (1996). Revenue: Zł 100,171,200,000 (income tax 37.8%, value-added tax 25.7%, excise tax 18.1%). Expenditures: Zł 109,671,200,000 (current expenditure 50.6%, interest on debts 16.4%, social benefits 15.8%).
Public debt (external, outstanding; 1996): U.S.$39,217,000,000.
Gross national product (1996): U.S.$124,682,000,000 (U.S.$3,230 per capita).

Structure of gross domestic product and labour force

	1995 in value Zł '000,000[5]	% of total value	labour force	% of labour force
Agriculture	18,965.9	6.6	4,045,900	23.8
Mining and manufacturing	72,003.0	25.2	3,728,800	21.9
Public utilities	10,570.9	3.7		
Construction	14,806.5	5.2	827,400	4.9
Transp. and commun.	17,260.8	6.0	838,100	4.9
Trade	39,003.0	13.6	2,089,000	12.3
Finance	22,743.1	8.0	268,200	1.6
Public administration	13,875.9	4.8	381,300	2.2
Services	38,806.5	13.6	2,234,900	13.1
Other	37,990.0[6]	13.3[6]	2,590,400[7]	15.2[7]
TOTAL	286,025.6	100.0	17,004,000	100.0[8]

Production (metric tons except at noted). Agriculture, forestry, fishing (1995): (value of production in Zł '000,000) potatoes 6,606, wheat 3,055, rye 1,421, sugar beets 1,075; livestock (number of live animals; 1997) 18,152,000 pigs, 7,306,000 cattle; roundwood 19,334,000 cu m; fish catch 451,346. Mining and

quarrying (1996): electrolytic cooper 425,000; zinc 165,000; lead 66,000. Manufacturing (value of production in Zł '000,000; 1995): food and beverages 52,558; machinery and transport equipment 33,372; chemicals 16,360. Construction (1995): 61,000 units, of which residential 31,100. Energy production (consumption): electricity ('000,000 kW-hr; 1994) 135,347 (132,668); coal ('000 metric tons; 1994) 200,700 (171,000); crude petroleum (barrels; 1994) 2,107,000 (99,757,000); petroleum products ('000 metric tons; 1994) 12,625 (13,807); natural gas ('000,000 cu m; 1994) 4,079 (10,908).
Population economically active (1995): total 17,004,000; activity rate of total population 44.0% (participation rates: over age 15, 66.9%; female 45.9%; unemployed [1996] 14.3%).

Price and earnings indexes (1990 = 100)

	1992	1993	1994	1995	1996	1997	1998[9]
Consumer price index	256.8	351.5	468.4	593.9	713.5	827.1	926.1
Monthly earnings index	228.5	320.0	421.4	595.9	752.7	903.4	1,035.3

Household income and expenditure (1995). Average household size 3.1; average annual income Zł 8,431 (U.S.$2,990); sources of income: wages 55.7%, social security benefits 32.5% (of which pensions 26.6%), self-employment 6.9%, other 4.9%; expenditure: food 39.7%, housing 20.6%, clothing 7.0%.
Tourism (1995): receipts U.S.$6,700,000,000; expenditures U.S.$5,500,000,000.
Land use (1994): forest 28.8%; meadow 13.3%; agricultural and under permanent cultivation 47.0%; other 10.9%.

Foreign trade

Balance of trade (current prices)

	1992	1993	1994	1995	1996	1997
Zł '000,000	−4,026	−8,262	−9,826	−14,987	−34,412	−54,418
% of total	10.1%	13.8%	11.1%	11.9%	20.7%	24.3%

Imports (1996): Zł 100,231,000,000 (1995; machinery and transport equipment 29.9%, manufactured goods 21.6%, chemicals 15.0%, miscellaneous manufactured articles 9.3%, mineral fuels and lubricants 9.1%, food 8.0%). Major import sources (1995): Germany 26.6%; Italy 8.5%; Russia 6.7%; U.K. 5.2%.
Exports (1996): Zł 65,819,000,000 (1995; manufactured goods 27.6%, machinery and transport equipment 21.1%, miscellaneous manufactured articles 20.9%, food 9.2%, mineral fuels and lubricants 8.2%, chemicals 7.7%). Major export destinations (1995): Germany 38.3%; The Netherlands 5.6%.

Transport and communications

Transport. Railroads (1996): length 23,986 km; passenger-km 26,635,000,000; metric ton-km cargo 69,116,000,000. Roads (1995): total length 372,479 km (paved 65%). Vehicles (1995): passenger cars 7,517,300; trucks and buses 1,472,300. Merchant marine (1992): vessels (100 gross tons and over) 644; total deadweight tonnage 4,314,308. Air transport (1996): passenger-km 4,633,000,000; metric ton-km cargo 74,000,000; airports (1997) 8.

Communications

Medium	date	unit	number	units per 1,000 persons
Daily newspapers	1995	circulation	5,400,000	140.0
Radio	1996	receivers[10]	10,193,000	263.3
Television	1996	receivers[10]	9,677,000	249.9
Telephones	1996	main lines	5,728,000	147.9
Cellular telephones	1995	subscribers	73,400	1.9
Facsimile machines	1995	units	30,900	0.8
Personal computers	1995	units	1,101,000	28.5

Education and health

Educational attainment (1988). Percentage of population age 15 and over having: no formal schooling or less that full primary education 6.4%; primary 38.8%; secondary 48.3%; higher 6.5%. Literacy (1988): 98.7%.

Education (1995–96)

	schools	teachers	students	student/ teacher ratio
Primary (age 7–14)	19,823	323,500	5,104,200	15.8
Secondary (age 15–18)	1,705	34,700	683,000	19.7
Voc., teacher tr.	8,887	88,700	1,729,300	19.5
Higher	179	71,300	794,600	11.1

Health (1996): physicians 88,523 (1 per 436 persons); hospital beds 213,969 (1 per 180 persons); infant mortality rate per 1,000 live births (1997) 14.0.
Food (1995): daily per capita caloric intake 3,307 (vegetable products 72%, animal products 28%); 126% of FAO recommended minimum.

Military

Total active duty personnel (1997): 241,750 (army 70%, navy 7%, air force 23%). Military expenditure as percentage of GNP (1995): 2.3% (world 2.8%); per capita expenditure U.S.$127.

[1]The 1997 Constitution of Poland specifies freedom of religion; the 1997 concordat with Vatican City (signed unilaterally by the Polish prime minister in May 1997), however, provides special recognition to Roman Catholicism. [2]On Jan. 1, 1995, the złoty was redenominated at a rate of 10,000 old złoty to 1 new złoty. [3]In July 1998 a bill was signed into law that reorganizes Poland into 16 new provinces; the reorganization was scheduled to take effect on Jan. 1, 1999. [4]January 1. [5]In purchasers' values. [6]Includes import duties and value-added tax. [7]Includes 2,233,000 unemployed. [8]Detail does not add to total given because of rounding. [9]July. [10]Number of licenses issued.

Internet resources for further information:
• Głównego Urzędu Statystycznego (Central Statistical Office)
  http://saturn.ci.uw.edu.pl/up/eng/00.html
• Polish World http://www.polishworld.com

Portugal

Official name: República Portuguesa (Portuguese Republic).
Form of government: republic with one legislative house (Assembly of the Republic [230]).
Chief of state: President.
Head of government: Prime Minister.
Capital: Lisbon.
Official language: Portuguese.
Official religion: none.
Monetary unit: 1 escudo (Esc) = 100 centavos; valuation (Sept. 25, 1998) 1 U.S.$ = Esc 171.31; 1 £ = Esc 291.66.

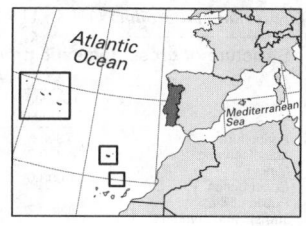

Area and population

Continental Portugal Districts	Capitals	area sq mi	area sq km	population 1993[1] estimate
Aveiro	Aveiro	1,081	2,800	658,400
Beja	Beja	3,947	10,223	166,500
Braga	Braga	1,041	2,695	754,700
Bragança	Bragança	2,547	6,597	154,700
Castelo Branco	Castelo Branco	2,555	6,616	211,800
Coimbra	Coimbra	1,533	3,971	425,400
Évora	Évora	2,856	7,396	172,400
Faro	Faro	1,925	4,986	342,000
Guarda	Guarda	2,139	5,540	185,400
Leiria	Leiria	1,354	3,508	426,200
Lisboa	Lisbon (Lisboa)	1,065	2,758	2,048,000
Portalegre	Portalegre	2,341	6,064	132,400
Porto	Porto	904	2,341	1,652,000
Santarém	Santarém	2,590	6,707	441,900
Setúbal	Setúbal	1,955	5,064	716,200
Viana do Castelo	Viana do Castelo	853	2,210	248,300
Vila Real	Vila Real	1,662	4,305	233,100
Viseu	Viseu	1,934	5,009	398,800
Azores (Açores) Autonomous Region	Ponta Delgada	868	2,247	237,800
Madeira Autonomous Region	Funchal	306	794	253,800
TOTAL		35,456[2]	91,831[2]	9,859,600[3]

Demography

Population (1998): 9,964,000.
Density (1998): persons per sq mi 281.0, persons per sq km 108.5.
Urban-rural (1996): urban 36.0%; rural 64.0%.
Sex distribution (1996): male 48.16%; female 51.84%.
Age breakdown (1995): under 15, 18.9%; 15–29, 23.6%; 30–44, 21.6%; 45–59, 16.6%; 60–74, 13.9%; 75 and over, 5.4%.
Population projection: (2000) 9,998,000; (2010) 10,170,000.
Nationality (1996): Portuguese 98.2%; Cape Verdean 0.4%; other 1.4%.
Religious affiliation (1995): Christian 94.8%, of which Roman Catholic 92.2%, Protestant 1.5%, other Christian (Jehovah's Witness 0.7%; Mormon 0.4%) 1.1%; Muslim 0.1%; other and nonreligious 5.1%.
Major cities (1991): Lisbon 663,394; Porto 302,467; Amadora 181,774.

Vital statistics

Birth rate per 1,000 population (1996): 11.1 (world avg. 25.0); (1990) legitimate 85.5%; illegitimate 14.5%.
Death rate per 1,000 population (1996): 10.8 (world avg. 9.3).
Natural increase rate per 1,000 population (1996): 0.3 (world avg. 15.7).
Total fertility rate (avg. births per childbearing woman; 1995): 1.4.
Life expectancy at birth (1995–96): male 71.3 years; females 78.6 years.
Major causes of death per 100,000 population (1994): circulatory diseases 431.2, of which cerebrovascular diseases 231.0, ischemic heart disease 91.4; malignant neoplasms (cancers) 193.6; respiratory diseases 71.5.

National economy

Budget (1995). Revenue: Esc 6,110,600,000,000 (import duties and excise taxes 36.7%, social security taxes 290.0%, income and inheritance taxes 24.2%). Expenditures: Esc 6,332,900,000,000 (1988; education 12.4%, health 9.8%, defense 6.6%, adminstration 5.3%, public works 2.8%).
Production (metric tons except as noted). Agriculture, forestry, fishing (1977): potatoes 1,400,000, grapes 1,240,000, tomatoes 1,020,000, corn (maize) 867,000, olives 300,000, wheat 289,000, apples 200,000, oranges 160,000, cabbages 140,000, rice 140,000, cork 91,870[4], carrots 83,000; livestock (number of live animals) 6,200,000 sheep, 2,344,000 pigs, 1,311,000 cattle; roundwood (1996) 9,447,800 cu m; fish catch (1995) 265,508. Mining and quarrying (1996): salt 609,639; copper 111,459; kaolin 95,900[4]; tin 8,304; zinc 5,675[5]; tungsten 1,343. Manufacturing (value added in Esc '000,000; 1994): petroleum refining 361,511; machinery and transport equipment 356,941; wearing apparel and footwear 301,942; textiles 273,161; food and beverages 232,161; tobacco 132,614; printing and publishing 114,839. Construction (1993): residential 4,793,000 sq m; nonresidential 2,045,167 sq m[6]. Energy production (consumption): electricity (kW-hr; 1994) 31,380,000,000 (32,268,000,000); coal (metric tons; 1994) 147,000 (5,225,000); crude petroleum (barrels; 1994) none (99,069,000); petroleum products (metric tons; 1994) 12,251,000 (10,159,000).
Household income and expenditure. Average household size (1991) 3.1; income per household: n.a.; sources of income (1994–95): wages and salaries 45.8%, property and entrepreneurial income 32.4%, transfer payments 21.5%; expenditure (1994–95): food 23.9%, housing 20.6%, transportation and communications 18.9%, clothing and footwear 6.3%, health 4.6%, other 25.7%.
Gross national product (1996): U.S.$100,934,000,000 (U.S.$10,160 per capita).

Structure of gross domestic product and labour force

	1993 in value Esc '000,000	1993 % of total value	1994 labour force	1994 % of labour force
Agriculture	489,476	3.7	490,200	10.8
Mining	113,243	0.8		
Manufacturing	3,417,963	25.8	1,025,800	22.5
Construction	699,267	5.3	330,800	7.2
Public utilities	551,164	4.2	36,700	0.8
Trade	2,474,801	18.6		
Finance	1,246,248	9.4		
Transp. and commun.	825,319	6.2	1,442,300	31.6
Services	2,477,083	18.7		
Pub. admin., defense	976,901	7.4	925,600	20.3
Other	...	...	310,000[7]	6.8[7]
TOTAL	13,271,465	100.0[3]	4,561,400	100.0

Public debt (1996): U.S.$40,504,000,000.
Population economically active (1994): total 4,561,400; activity rate of total population 46.1% (participation rates: ages 15–64, 69.0%[5]; female 44.5%; unemployed 6.8%).

Price and earnings indexes (1990 = 100)

	1991	1992	1993	1994	1995	1996	1997
Consumer price index	111.4	121.3	129.6	135.9	141.5	146.0	149.1
Annual earnings index[8]	114.2	129.8	140.1	146.7	...	...	...

Tourism (1996): receipts U.S.$4,325,200,000; expenditures U.S.$2,321,500,000.
Land use (1994): forest 35.9%; pasture 10.9%; agriculture 31.5%; other 21.7%.

Foreign trade

Balance of trade (current prices)

	1991	1992	1993	1994	1995	1996
Esc '000,000	−1,067,800	−1,144.6	−1,051.8	−1,099.9	−1,011.4	−1,096.8
% of total	18.5%	18.8%	17.5%	15.9%	14.7%	13.0%

Imports (1994): Esc 4,595,200,000,000 (machinery and transport equipment 34.2%, of which road vehicles and parts 15.1%; food and live animals 11.6%; chemicals and chemical products 9.8%; mineral fuels 8.8%; textiles 6.1%; office machines 3.2%). *Major import sources:* Spain 19.8%; Germany 13.8%; France 12.8%; Italy 8.5%; United Kingdom 6.6%; The Netherlands 4.3%.
Exports (1994): Esc 3,057,600,000,000 (textiles and wearing apparel 25.9%; machinery and transport equipment 21.2%, of which transport equipment 6.0%; footwear 8.7%; cork and wood products 6.2%; chemicals and chemical products 4.7%). *Major export destinations:* Germany 18.7%; France 14.7%; Spain 14.4%; United Kingdom 11.7%; United States 5.2%.

Transport and communications

Transport. Railroads (1995): route length 3,072 km; passenger-km 4,869,-000,000; metric ton-km cargo 2,018,000,000. Roads (1995): total length 68,732 km (paved 88%). Vehicles (1995): passenger cars 2,560,000; trucks and buses 219,696[9]. Merchant marine (1992): vessels (100 gross tons and over) 332; total deadweight tonnage 1,129,382. Air transport (1996): passenger-km 7,977,817,000; metric ton-km cargo 209,674,000; airports (1997) 16.

Communications

Medium	date	unit	number	units per 1,000 persons
Daily newspapers	1995	circulation	465,000	47
Radio	1995	receivers	2,776,000	280
Television	1995	receivers	3,300,000	333
Telephones	1995	main lines	3,586,000	362
Cellular telephones	1995	subscribers	340,800	34.4
Facsimile machines	1995	units	35,300	3.6
Personal computers	1995	units	600,000	60.5

Education and health

Educational attainment (1991). Percentage of population age 25 and over having: no formal schooling 16.1%; some primary education 61.5%; some secondary 10.6%; postsecondary 3.5%. *Literacy* (1995): total population age 15 and over literate 89.6%; males 92.5%; females 87.0%.

Education (1993–94)

	schools	teachers	students	student/ teacher ratio
Primary (age 5–11)	12,069	73,221	910,650	12.4
Secondary (age 12–19)	663	69,095[10]	749,838	11.3[10]
Vocational	214	[10]	28,627	[10]
Higher[11]	273	30,998[12]	236,537	6.9[12]

Health (1996): physicians 29,902 (1 per 332 persons); hospital beds 39,210 (1 per 253 persons); infant mortality rate per 1,000 live births (1996) 6.9.
Food (1996): daily per capita caloric intake 3,639 (vegetable products 74%, animal products 26%); 148% of FAO recommended minimum requirement.

Military

Total active duty personnel (1997): 59,300 (army 54.1%, navy 25.0%, air force 13.0%, paramilitary national guard 7.9%). *Military expenditure as percentage of GNP* (1995): 2.6% (world 2.8%); per capita expenditure U.S.$273.

[1]January 1. [2]Does not include 117 sq mi (304 sq km) of water areas comprising the Tagus and Sado estuaries and the Aveiro Lagoon. [3]Detail does not add to total given because of rounding. [4]1992. [5]1993. [6]1990. [7]Unemployed. [8]Based on average annual wage. [9]1994. [10]Secondary includes Vocational. [11]Includes teacher colleges. [12]1992–93.

Internet resources for further information:
• Instituto Nacional de Estatística http://www.ine.pt/

Puerto Rico

Official name: Estado Libre Asociado de Puerto Rico; Commonwealth of Puerto Rico.
Political status: self-governing commonwealth in association with the United States, having two legislative houses (Senate [29[1]]; House of Representatives [53[1]]).
Chief of state: President of the United States.
Head of government: Governor.
Capital: San Juan.
Official languages: Spanish; English.
Monetary unit: 1 U.S. dollar (U.S.$) = 100 cents; valuation (Sept. 25, 1998) 1 £ = U.S.$1.70.

Population (1995 estimate)

Municipio	population	Municipio	population	Municipio	population
Adjuntas	19,592	Fajardo	38,383	Naguabo	24,517
Aguada	37,651	Florida	8,434	Naranjito	29,016
Aguadilla	65,207	Guánica	21,596	Orocovis	24,075
Aguas Buenas	30,062	Guayama	41,994	Patillas	21,259
Aibonito	27,863	Guayanilla	27,316	Peñuelas	26,595
Añasco	27,007	Guaynabo	104,927	Ponce	189,988
Arecibo	100,755	Gurabo	32,003	Quebradillas	26,008
Arroyo	19,549	Hatillo	40,149	Rincón	13,589
Barceloneta	26,480	Hormigueros	16,121	Río Grande	48,997
Barranquitas	28,702	Humacao	57,643	Sabana Grande	23,244
Bayamón	231,845	Isabela	41,156	Salinas	29,962
Cabo Rojo	47,365	Jayuya	16,791	San Germán	36,925
Caguas	140,114	Juana Díaz	49,693	San Juan	433,705
Camuy	32,438	Juncos	41,424	San Lorenzo	36,435
Canóvanas	50,666	Lajas	26,704	San Sebastián	42,573
Carolina	188,427	Lares	32,282	Santa Isabel	19,546
Cataño	32,391	Las Marías	9,923	Toa Alta	58,240
Cayey	50,728	Las Piedras	30,111	Toa Baja	92,702
Ceiba	17,715	Loíza	27,904	Trujillo Alto	74,644
Ciales	19,447	Luquillo	18,407	Utuado	35,212
Cidra	49,326	Manatí	38,781	Vega Alta	35,828
Coamo	35,673	Maricao	5,979	Vega Baja	61,401
Comerío	20,914	Maunabo	13,503	Vieques	9,503
Corozal	36,304	Mayagüez	100,937	Villalba	22,695
Culebra	1,632	Moca	37,154	Yabucoa	40,602
Dorado	32,166	Morovis	33,388	Yauco	42,879
				TOTAL	3,782,862

Demography

Area: 3,515 sq mi, 9,104 sq km.
Population (1998): 3,786,000.
Density (1998): persons per sq mi 1,077.2, persons per sq km 415.9.
Urban-rural (1990): urban 71.2%; rural 28.8%.
Sex distribution (1992): male 48.43%; female 51.57%.
Age breakdown (1992): under 15, 27.2%; 15–29, 25.1%; 30–44, 20.4%; 45–59, 14.1%; 60–74, 9.2%; 75 and over, 4.0%.
Population projection: (2000) 3,836,000; (2010) 4,120,000.
Doubling time: 77 years.
Major cities (1990): San Juan 426,832; Ponce 159,151; Caguas 92,429; Mayagüez 83,010; Arecibo 49,545.

Vital statistics

Birth rate per 1,000 population (1996): 17.2 (world avg. 25.0).
Death rate per 1,000 population (1996): 7.9 (world avg. 9.3).
Natural increase rate per 1,000 population (1996): 9.3 (world avg. 15.7).
Total fertility rate (avg. births per childbearing woman; 1991): 2.2.
Marriage rate per 1,000 population (1992): 9.6.
Life expectancy at birth (1991): male 69.6 years; female 78.5 years.
Major causes of death per 100,000 population (1993): heart disease 142.6; cancers 95.4; diabetes 55.1; cerebrovascular disease 38.0; pneumonia and influenza 29.2.

National economy

Budget. Revenue (1995–96): U.S.$7,852,000,000 (income taxes 43.1%, excise taxes 17.3%, nontax revenue 5.0%, property taxes 1.0%, other receipts 33.6%). Expenditures (1992): U.S.$5,607,000,000 (education 30.3%, public safety and protection 11.4%, welfare 10.8%, health 10.7%).
Public debt (outstanding; 1995): U.S.$15,993,600,000.
Tourism (1995): receipts from visitors (1995) U.S.$1,826,100,000; expenditures by nationals abroad U.S.$833,000,000.
Production (in metric tons except as noted). Agriculture, forestry, fishing (1996): sugarcane 404,500; plantains 76,100; bananas 47,700; pineapples 18,500; oranges 16,700; pumpkins, squash, and gourds 16,300; coffee 12,800; mangoes 11,100; livestock (number of live animals) 326,000 cattle, 200,000 pigs; roundwood, n.a.; fish catch (1995) 2,629 metric tons. Mining (value of production in U.S.$'000; 1993): stone 50. Manufacturing (value added in U.S.$'000,000; 1995): chemicals, pharmaceuticals, and allied products 9,164; machinery and metal products 3,393; food products 2,269; clothing 510; printing and publishing 179; stone, clay, and glass products 171. Construction (authorized; 1985): residential 1,798,000 sq m; nonresidential 41,000 sq m.
Energy production (consumption): electricity (kW-hr; 1994) 17,880,000,000 (17,880,000,000); coal (metric tons; 1994) none (172,000); crude petroleum (barrels; 1994) none (43,980,000); petroleum products (metric tons; 1994) 6,256,000 (7,540,000); natural gas, none (none).

Gross national product (1996): U.S.$31,600,000,000 (U.S.$8,200 per capita).

Structure of gross domestic product and labour force

	1995–96		1995	
	in value U.S.$'000,000	% of total value	labour force	% of labour force
Agriculture	306.5	0.7	42,000	3.4
Manufacturing	18,860.7	41.4	205,000	16.7
Mining	} 1,003.0	} 2.2	1,000	0.1
Construction			84,000	6.8
Public utilities	} 3,486.7	} 7.7	14,000	1.1
Transp. and commun.			42,000	3.4
Trade	6,224.4	13.7	250,000	20.4
Finance, real estate	5,877.8	12.9	34,000	2.8
Pub. admin., defense	4,871.4	10.7	} 550,000	} 44.8
Services	4,991.0	11.0		
Other	−116.5[2]	−0.3[2]	7,000	0.6
TOTAL	45,505.0	100.0	1,228,000[3]	100.0[3]

Population economically active (1995): total 1,228,000; activity rate 32.2% (participation rates: ages 16–64, 52.9%; female 39.4%; unemployed 13.8%).

Price and earnings indexes (1990 = 100)

	1989	1990	1991	1992	1993	1994	1995
Consumer price index	96.1	100.0	105.3	108.1	111.3	114.5	119.1
Hourly earnings index[4]	95.4	100.0	104.1	...	...	...	...

Household income and expenditure (1995). Average family size 3.6; income per family U.S.$27,017; sources of income: wages and salaries 56.3%, transfers 29.5%, self-employment 6.4%, rent 5.2%, other 2.6%; expenditure (1995): food and beverages 20.4%, transportation 13.6%, health care 13.4%, housing and energy 12.2%, household furnishings 12.0%, recreation 8.9%.

Foreign trade

Balance of trade (current prices)

	1990	1991	1992	1993	1994	1995
U.S.$'000,000	+3,584	+5,419	+5,857	+3,405	+5,098	+4,995
% of total	10.2%	14.6%	16.2%	9.4%	13.3%	11.7%

Imports (1995–96): U.S.$19,060,900,000 (chemicals [all forms] 21.8%, electrical machinery 12.8%, food 11.3%, transport equipment 9.3%, nonelectrical machinery 7.3%, petroleum and petroleum products 6.1%, professional and scientific instruments 4.5%, clothing and textiles 4.4%). *Major import sources:* U.S. 62.5%; Japan 6.4%; Dominican Republic 4.0%; U.K. 2.9%.
Exports (1995–96): U.S.$22,944,400,000 (chemicals and chemical products 43.3%, food 14.5%, nonelectrical machinery 14.2%, electrical machinery 9.6%). *Major export destinations:* U.S. 87.8%; Dominican Republic 2.9%; Germany 1.0%; Belgium 0.9%; Japan 0.8%; U.K. 0.7%.

Transport and communications

Transport. Railroads (1988)[5]: length 59 mi, 96 km. Roads (1994): total length 14,379 mi, 23,140 km (paved 87%). Vehicles (1994): passenger cars 1,432,000; trucks and buses 229,000. Merchant marine: n.a. Air transport (1990–91): passenger arrivals 4,245,137, passenger departures 4,262,164; cargo loaded and unloaded 222,172 metric tons[6]; airports (1997) with scheduled flights 7.

Communications

Medium	date	unit	number	units per 1,000 persons
Daily newspapers	1994	circulation	670,000	182
Radio	1996	receivers	2,480,000	659
Television	1995	receivers	1,160,000	322
Telephones	1995	main lines	1,195,900	329
Cellular telephones	1995	subscribers	171,200	48
Facsimile machines	1995	units	543,300	146

Education and health

Educational attainment (1990): Percentage of population age 25 and over having: primary education 26.8%; some secondary 23.5%; complete secondary 21.0%; higher 28.7%. *Literacy (1990):* total population age 18 and over literate 2,122,860 (89.7%); males literate 1,001,878 (89.6%); females literate 1,120,982 (89.7%).

Education (1985–86)

	schools	teachers	students	student/teacher ratio
Primary (age 5–12)	1,542	18,359	427,582	23.3
Secondary (age 13–18)	395	13,612	334,661	24.6
Voc., teacher tr.	52	...	149,191	...
Higher	45	9,045	156,818	17.3

Health: physicians (1988) 9,422 (1 per 349 persons); hospital beds (1993–94) 9,598 (1 per 381 persons); infant mortality rate (1994) 11.5.

Military

Total active duty personnel (1992): 3,518 U.S. personnel.

[1]Includes (each house) 2 special at-large seats above usual legally mandated membership of body that were created under a constitutional provision to limit majority party's control of either house to two-thirds. [2]Statistical discrepancy. [3]Detail does not add to total given because of rounding. [4]Manufacturing sector only. [5]Privately owned railway for sugarcane transport only. [6]Handled by the Luis Muñoz Marín International Airport only.

Internet resources for further information:
• Puerto Rico, U.S.A. http://www.pr-eda.com/index.html

Qatar

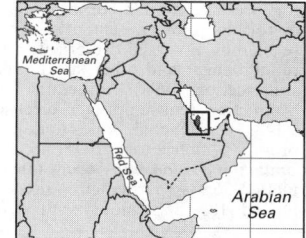

Official name: Dawlat Qaṭar (State of Qatar).
Form of government: monarchy (emirate)[1]; Islamic law is the basis of legislation in the state.
Heads of state and government: Emir assisted by Prime Minister.
Capital: Doha.
Official language: Arabic.
Official religion: Islam.
Monetary unit: 1 riyal (QR) = 100 dirhams; valuation (Sept. 25, 1998) 1 U.S.$ = QR 3.64; 1 £ = QR 6.20.

Area and population

Municipalities	Capitals	area sq mi	area sq km	population 1992 estimate
Ad-Dawḥah (Doha)	—	51	132	313,639
Al-Ghuwayrīyah	Al-Ghuwayrīyah	241	622	2,349
Jarayān al-Bāṭinah	Jarayān al-Bāṭinah	1,434	3,715	3,932
Al-Jumaylīyah	Al-Jumaylīyah	990[2]	2,565[2]	10,414
Al-Khawr	Al-Khawr	385	996	12,982
Ar-Rayyān	Ar-Rayyān	343	889	132,785
Ash-Shamāl	Madinat ash-Shamāl	348	901	6,323
Umm Salāl	Umm Salāl Muḥammad	190	493	16,110
Al-Wakrah	Al-Wakrah	430	1,114	34,185
TOTAL		4,416[3]	11,437[3]	532,719

Demography

Population (1998): 579,000.
Density (1998): persons per sq mi 131.2, persons per sq km 50.7.
Urban-rural (1995): urban 91.4%; rural 8.5%.
Sex distribution (1995): male 66.41%; female 33.59%.
Age breakdown (1994): under 15, 26.2%; 15–29, 21.5%; 30–44, 38.5%; 45–59, 11.7%; 60–74, 1.7%; 75 and over, 0.3%.
Population projection: (2000) 599,000; (2010) 693,000.
Doubling time: 42 years.
Ethnic composition (1995): Arab 40%; other (mostly Pakistanis, Indians, and Iranians) 60%.
Religious affiliation (1995): Muslim (mostly Sunnī) 95%; other 5%.
Major cities (1993): Doha 339,471; Ar-Rayyān 143,046; Al-Wakrah 30,976; Umm Salal 16,785.

Vital statistics

Birth rate per 1,000 population (1990–95): 19.9 (world avg. 25.0).
Death rate per 1,000 population (1990–95): 3.4 (world avg. 9.3).
Natural increase rate per 1,000 population (1990–95): 16.5 (world avg. 15.7).
Total fertility rate (avg. births per childbearing woman; 1990–95): 4.1.
Marriage rate per 1,000 population (1994): 2.8.
Divorce rate per 1,000 population (1994): 1.0.
Life expectancy at birth (1990–95): male 68.8 years; female 74.2 years.
Major causes of death per 100,000 population (1992): diseases of the circulatory system 56.9; injuries and poisoning 36.0; neoplasms (including benign neoplasms) 21.4; certain conditions originating in the perinatal period 11.1; diseases of the respiratory system 7.5; endocrine, metabolic, and nutritional diseases and immunity disorders 7.3; diseases of the digestive system 3.4; signs, symptoms, and ill-defined conditions 10.9.

National economy

Budget (1996–97)[4]. Revenue: QR 10,797,000,000 (crude oil about 90%). Expenditures: QR 13,747,000,000 (1994–95; wages and salaries 44.4%, state capital-development projects 41.7%, social and health services 8.1%, education 2.7%).
Production (metric tons except as noted). Agriculture, forestry, fishing (value of production in QR '000; 1994): milk and dairy products 142,898, forage 93,293, vegetables and other crops (except cereals) 73,172, beef 47,854, fruits and dates 29,413, poultry meat 28,036, eggs 12,345, cereals 1,748; livestock (number of live animals; 1997) 199,682 sheep, 172,071 goats, 47,000 camels, 13,651 cattle; roundwood, n.a.; fish catch (1995) 4,271. Mining and quarrying (1993): limestone 900,000; sulfur 60,000; gypsum, sand and gravel, and clay are also produced. Manufacturing (value added in QR '000,000; 1994): refined petroleum 919; chemical products 887; iron and steel 319; pottery, china, and earthenware 219; textiles and apparel 193; food, beverages, and tobacco 99; metal products 89; wood products and furniture 79. Construction (1992): residential 12,420 units; nonresidential 1,416 units. Energy production (consumption): electricity (kW-hr; 1994) 5,850,000,000 (5,850,000,000); coal, none (n.a.); crude petroleum (barrels; 1996) 173,380,000 (1994; 21,450,000); petroleum products (metric tons; 1994) 5,219,000 (701,000); natural gas (cu m; 1996) 13,500,000,000 ([1994] 13,500,000,000).
Tourism (1994): receipts and expenditures, n.a.; total number of tourists staying in hotels 241,000.
Population economically active (1988): total 292,568; activity rate of total population 53.7% (participation rates: ages 15–64, 80.8%; female 11.2%; unemployed [1986] 0.5%).

Price and earnings indexes (1990 = 100)

	1990	1991	1992	1993	1994	1995	1996
Consumer price index	100.0	104.4	107.6	106.7	108.1	111.3	119.5
Earnings index	...	...	...	...	...	...	...

Gross national product (1995): U.S.$7,448,000,000 (U.S.$11,600 per capita).

Structure of gross domestic product and labour force

	1995[4] in value QR '000,000	1995[4] % of total value	1988 labour force	1988 % of labour force
Agriculture	290	1.1	4,544	1.6
Oil sector	8,900	32.5	7,657	2.6
Manufacturing	3,120	11.4	10,627	3.6
Construction	1,850	6.8	64,213	21.9
Public utilities	403	1.5	3,672	1.3
Transportation	1,045	3.8	11,877	4.1
Trade	2,050	7.5	34,246	11.7
Finance	3,070	11.2	6,172	2.1
Pub. admin., defense	} 6,627	24.2	149,560	51.1
Services				
Other				
TOTAL	27,355	100.0	292,568	100.0

Household income and expenditure. Average household size (1986) 6.4; income per household: n.a.; sources of income (1988): wages and salaries 80.8%, rents and royalties 10.6%, self-employment 5.6%, other 3.0%; expenditure (1993): food 28.7%, transportation 19.3%, housing 12.4%, clothing 10.6%, education 7.6%, health 1.2%.
Land use (1994): meadows and pastures 4.5%; agricultural and under permanent cultivation 0.7%; built-up, desert, and other 94.7%.

Foreign trade

Balance of trade (current prices)[5]

	1990	1991	1992	1993	1994	1995
QR '000,000	+7,992	+5,423	+6,644	+5,154	+4,729	+1,714
% of total	39.3%	30.2%	31.2%	29.6%	27.9%	8.1%

Imports (1994): QR 7,015,600,000 (machinery and transport equipment 39.7%, manufactured goods 21.8%, food and live animals 13.2%, chemicals and chemical products 7.0%, raw materials 3.4%). *Major import sources:* Japan 13.4%; United States 10.6%; United Kingdom 10.3%; United Arab Emirates 6.9%; Germany 6.6%; Saudi Arabia 5.0%; Italy 4.3%.
Exports (1994): QR 11,453,000,000 (mineral fuels and lubricants 81.2%, chemicals and chemical products 10.4%, manufactured goods 5.9%). *Major export destinations* (1989): Japan 54.4%; Thailand 5.0%; Singapore 4.0%; South Korea 3.6%; United Arab Emirates 3.4%; Italy 2.7%; India 2.7%.

Transport and communications

Transport. Railroads: none. Roads (1995): total length 752 mi, 1,210 km (paved 90%). Vehicles (1994): passenger cars 125,700; trucks and buses 63,800. Merchant marine (1992): vessels (100 gross tons and over) 65; total deadweight tonnage 635,580. Air transport (1995)[6]: passenger-mi 1,719,000,000, passenger-km 2,766,000,000; short ton-mi cargo 77,400,000, metric ton-km cargo 113,000,000; airports (1997) with scheduled flights 1.

Communications

Medium	date	unit	number	units per 1,000 persons
Daily newspapers	1994	circulation	80,000	143
Radio	1995	receivers	180,000	322
Television	1995	receivers	252,000	451
Telephones	1995	main lines	122,700	219
Cellular telephones	1995	subscribers	18,500	33
Facsimile machines	1995	units	9,400	17
Personal computers	1995	units	30,000	54

Education and health

Educational attainment (1986). Percentage of population age 25 and over having: no formal education 53.3%, of which illiterate 24.3%; primary 9.8%; preparatory (lower secondary) 10.1%; secondary 13.3%; postsecondary 13.3%; other 0.2%. *Literacy* (1995): total population age 15 and over literate 460,000 (79.4%); males literate 298,000 (79.2%); females literate 122,000 (79.9%).

Education (1994–95)[7]

	schools	teachers	students	student/ teacher ratio
Primary (age 6–11)	169	5,853	52,130	8.9
Secondary (age 12–17)	123[8]	3,738	36,964	9.9
Vocational	3[8]	120	671	5.6
Higher	1[8]	637	7,794	12.2

Health: (1994) physicians 718 (1 per 793 persons); hospital beds 1,118 (1 per 509 persons); (1990–95) infant mortality rate per 1,000 live births 20.0.
Food: daily per capita caloric intake, n.a.

Military

Total active duty personnel (1997): 11,800 (army 72.0%, navy 15.3%, air force 12.7%). *Military expenditure as percentage of GNP* (1995): 4.4% (world 2.8%); per capita expenditure U.S.$617.

[1]Provisional constitution of 1970 provided limited constitutional forms but has not been fully implemented. [2]Includes area of unpopulated Hawar Islands (also claimed by Bahrain). [3]Includes approximately 4 sq mi (10 sq km) of area not distributed by municipalities. [4]Preliminary estimates. [5]After 1992, balance based on f.o.b. valuation of imports. [6]One-fourth apportionment of international flights of Gulf Air. [7]Public schools only; available detail for private schools (1991–92) included 17,728 primary students, 1,695 secondary students, and 1,465 teachers. [8]1993–94.

Internet resources for further information:
• Qatar Ministry of Foreign Affairs http://www.mofa.gov.qa/

Réunion

Official name: Département de la Réunion (Department of Réunion).
Political status: overseas department (France) with two legislative houses (General Council [47]; Regional Council [45]).
Chief of state: President of France.
Heads of government: Prefect (for France); President of General Council (for Réunion); President of Regional Council (for Réunion).
Capital: Saint-Denis.
Official language: French.
Official religion: none.
Monetary unit: 1 French franc (F) = 100 centimes; valuation (Sept. 25, 1998) 1 U.S.$ = F 5.60; 1 £ = F 9.53.

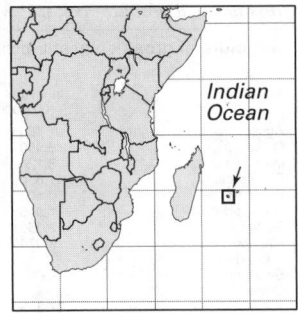

Area and population

Arrondissements	Capitals	area sq mi	area sq km	population 1990 census
Saint-Benoît	Saint-Benoît	285	737	85,132
Saint-Denis	Saint-Denis	163	421	207,158
Saint-Paul	Saint-Paul	180	467	113,071
Saint-Pierre	Saint-Pierre	341	883	192,462
TOTAL		968[1, 2]	2,507[1, 2]	597,823

Demography

Population (1998): 692,000.
Density (1998): persons per sq mi 714.9, persons per sq km 276.0.
Urban-rural (1995): urban 67.8%; rural 32.2%.
Sex distribution (1995): male 49.00%; female 51.00%.
Age breakdown (1995): under 15, 29.4%; 15–29, 27.7%; 30–44, 21.7%; 45–59, 12.2%; 60–74, 6.9%; 75 and over, 2.1%.
Population projection: (2000) 716,000; (2010) 847,000.
Doubling time: 49 years.
Ethnic composition (1983): mixed race 63.5%; East Indian 28.2%; Chinese 2.2%; white 1.9%; East African 1.1%; other 3.1%.
Religious affiliation (1995): Roman Catholic 89.4%; Pentecostal 2.7%; other Christian 1.8%; other (mostly Muslim) 6.1%.
Major cities (1990): Saint-Denis (1994) 104,454[3]; Le Port 29,190; Le Tampon 27,300; Saint-André 25,237; Saint-Pierre 23,899.

Vital statistics

Birth rate per 1,000 population (1996): 19.6 (world avg. 25.0); (1994) legitimate 44.1%; illegitimate 55.9%.
Death rate per 1,000 population (1996): 5.4 (world avg. 9.3).
Natural increase rate per 1,000 population (1996): 14.2 (world avg. 15.7).
Total fertility rate (avg. births per childbearing woman; 1996): 2.3.
Marriage rate per 1,000 population (1996): 4.9.
Divorce rate per 1,000 population (1995): 1.4.
Life expectancy at birth (1996): male 71.7 years; female 78.0 years.
Major causes of death per 100,000 population (1993): diseases of the circulatory system 170.1; malignant neoplasms (cancers) 99.7; accidents, suicide, and violence 65.3; diseases of the digestive system (including all deaths associated with alcoholism) 59.5; diseases of the respiratory system 41.5.

National economy

Budget (1995). Revenue: F 4,067,000,000 (receipts from the French central government and local administrative bodies 49.8%, subsidies and related receipts 12.8%, new loans 8.6%). Expenditures: F 4,066,000,000 (current expenditures 69.0%, development expenditures 31.0%).
Public debt (external, outstanding): n.a.
Tourism (1995): receipts U.S.$224,000,000; expenditures, n.a.
Gross national product (at current market prices; 1995): U.S.$5,850,000,000 (U.S.$8,880 per capita).

Structure of gross domestic product and labour force

	1992 in value F '000,000	1992 % of total value	1994 labour force	1994 % of labour force
Agriculture, fishing	1,200	3.6	12,015	5.0
Manufacturing	3,100	9.2	9,854	4.1
Construction	2,100	6.2	16,711	7.0
Public utilities	1,300	3.9	...	...
Transp. and commun.	2,000[4]	6.0[4]	5,495	2.3
Trade, restaurants	6,000[4]	17.9[4]	22,587	9.4
Finance, real estate, business services	7,200	21.4	11,148	4.7
Pub. admin., defense	10,700	31.8	23,678	9.9
Services			50,986	21.3
Other	—	—	86,905[5]	36.3[5]
TOTAL	33,600	100.0	239,379	100.0

Production (metric tons except as noted). Agriculture, forestry, fishing (1996): sugarcane 1,806,000 corn (maize) 18,000, cabbages 16,000, potatoes 15,000, pineapples 6,500, bananas 4,000, green onions and shallots 5,800, tomatoes 4,000, eggplants 3,200, pimento 430, ginger 95, tobacco 20, vanilla 6, geranium essence (1995) 5.2; livestock (number of live animals) 95,000 pigs, 32,000 goats, 26,500 cattle; roundwood (1995) 36,100 cu m; fish (value of catch in F '000,000; 1994) lobster 45[6], other 47. Mining and quarrying: gravel and sand

---

for local use. Manufacturing (value added in F '000,000; 1994): construction materials (mostly cement) 345; alcoholic and nonalcoholic beverages (excluding milk) 253; fabricated metals 252; printing and publishing 129; refined sugar and other sugar products 123. Construction (value of public construction; 1994): residential F 741,600,000; nonresidential, n.a. Energy production (consumption): electricity (kW-hr; 1996) 1,386,000,000 ([1995] 1,143,000,000); coal, none (none); crude petroleum, none (none); petroleum products (metric tons; 1995) none (507,000); natural gas, none (none).
Population economically active (1993): total 234,576; activity rate of total population 36.9% (participation rates: ages 15–64, 56.7%; female 41.7%; unemployed [July–September 1996] 39.7%).

Price and earnings indexes (December 1992 = 100)[7]

	1992	1993	1994	1995	1996	1997	1998[8]
Consumer price index	100.0	102.4	105.0	107.1	109.2	110.8	113.6
Monthly earnings index[9]	100.0	101.7	104.1	106.8	106.8	...	...

Household income and expenditure. Average household size (1994) 3.5; income per household (1994) F 114,900 (U.S.$20,695); sources of income (1994): wages and salaries and self-employment 68.9%, transfer payments 16.0%, interest, dividends, and self-employment 15.1%; expenditure (1994–95): food and beverages 22.0%, transportation and communications 19.0%, housing and energy 10.0%, household furnishings 8.0%, recreation 6.0%.
Land use (1994): forested 35.2%; meadows and pastures 4.8%; agricultural and under permanent cultivation 19.6%; other 40.4%.

Foreign trade

Balance of trade (current prices)

	1991	1992	1993	1994	1995	1996
F '000,000	−11,975	−11,542	−10,859	−12,109	−12,458	−13,143
% of total	87.6%	83.9%	84.5%	86.4%	85.7%	86.0%

Imports (1995): F 13,494,000,000 (consumer goods 25.3%, food and agricultural products 20.1%, transport equipment 14.2%, fabricated metals 7.0%, mineral fuels 4.7%). *Major import sources:* France 66.3%; Italy 3.5%; Bahrain 3.1%.
Exports (1995): F 1,036,000,000 (sugar 63.0%, machinery and apparatus 9.9%, transport equipment 4.5%, lobster 4.2%, rum 2.4%). *Major export destinations:* France 71.4%; Japan 6.1%; Belgium 5.0%.

Transport and communications

Transport. Railroads:[10]. Roads (1994): total length 1,711 mi, 2,754 km (paved [1991] 79%). Vehicles (1995): passenger cars 157,700; trucks and buses 38,600. Merchant marine (1992): vessels (100 gross tons and over) 7; total deadweight tonnage 33,476. Air transport (1996): passenger arrivals 629,034, passenger departures 624,733; cargo unloaded 13,678 metric tons, cargo loaded 4,396 metric tons; airports (1996) with scheduled flights 1.

Communications

Medium	date	unit	number	units per 1,000 persons
Daily newspapers	1994	circulation	55,000	85
Radio	1996	receivers	170,000	254
Television	1995	receivers	90,500	137
Telephones	1995	main lines	218,723	332
Facsimile machines	1995	units	1,900	2.9

Education and health

Educational attainment (1986–87). Percentage of population age 25 and over having: no formal schooling 18.8%; primary education 44.3%; lower secondary 21.6%; upper secondary 11.0%; higher 4.3%. *Literacy* (1996): total population age 16–66 literate 373,487 (91.3%); males literate 179,154 (89.9%); females literate 194,333 (92.7%).

Education (1994–95)

	schools	teachers	students	student/ teacher ratio
Primary (age 6–10)	345	...	73,702[11]	...
Secondary (age 11–17)	104	4,591[12]	71,694[11]	16.3[12]
Voc., teacher tr.		1,108[12]	15,055	12.4[12]
Higher[13]	1	242	8,058	33.3

Health (1995): physicians (1996) 1,164 (1 per 571 persons); hospital beds 2,902 (1 per 225 persons); infant mortality rate per 1,000 live births 7.3.
Food (1995): daily per capita caloric intake 3,308 (vegetable products 79%, animals products 21%); 146% of FAO recommended minimum requirement.

Military

Total active duty personnel (1996): 4,000 French troops[14].

---

[1]Detail does not add to total given because of rounding. [2]Indian Ocean islets administered by France from Réunion are excluded from total. Areas of these islets, which have no permanent population, are: Îles Glorieuses 1.9 sq mi (5.0 sq km), Île Juan de Nova 1.7 sq mi (4.4 sq km), Île Tromelin 0.4 sq mi (1.0 sq km), Bassas da India 0.1 sq mi (0.2 sq km), Île Europa 7.8 sq mi (20.2 sq km). [3]Urban population. [4]Transportation and communications includes hotels and restaurants. [5]Includes 2,621 not adequately defined and 84,284 unemployed. [6]Lobster are trapped around the islands of Saint-Paul and Nouvelle Amsterdam in the overseas territory of French Southern and Antarctic Lands. [7]Indexes refer to December. [8]March. [9]Minimum monthly wage in public administration. [10]No public railways; railways in use are for sugar industry. [11]1995–96. [12]1993–94. [13]University only. [14]Includes troops stationed on Mayotte.

Internet resources for further information:
• Ministère de l'Outre-mer (Paris) http://www.outre-mer.gouv.fr/domtom/reu.htm

Romania

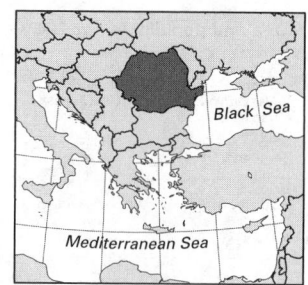

Official name: România (Romania).
Form of government: unitary republic with two legislative houses (Senate [143]; Assembly of Deputies [343[1]]).
Chief of state: President.
Head of government: Prime Minister.
Capital: Bucharest.
Official language: Romanian.
Official religion: none.
Monetary unit: 1 Romanian leu (plural lei) = 100 bani; valuation (Sept. 25, 1998) 1 U.S.$ = 9,098 lei; 1 £ = 15,488 lei.

Area and population

Counties	Capitals	area sq mi	area sq km	population 1994 estimate
Alba	Alba Iulia	2,406	6,231	408,457
Arad	Arad	2,954	7,652	482,144
Argeş	Piteşti	2,626	6,801	679,868
Bacău	Bacău	2,551	6,606	742,901
Bihor	Oradea	2,909	7,535	633,629
Bistriţa-Năsăud	Bistriţa	2,048	5,305	328,786
Botoşani	Botoşani	1,917	4,965	462,370
Brăila	Brăila	1,824	4,724	391,923
Braşov	Braşov	2,066	5,351	642,764
Buzău	Buzău	2,344	6,072	515,202
Călăraşi	Călăraşi	1,959	5,074	336,657
Caraş-Severin	Reşiţa	3,283	8,503	370,058
Cluj	Cluj-Napoca	2,568	6,650	727,033
Constanţa	Constanţa	2,724	7,055	747,441
Covasna	Sfântu Gheorghe	1,431	3,705	232,951
Dâmboviţa	Târgovişte	1,558	4,036	558,518
Dolj	Craiova	2,862	7,413	758,895
Galaţi	Galaţi	1,709	4,425	642,983
Giurgiu	Giurgiu	1,356	3,511	305,661
Gorj	Târgu Jiu	2,178	5,641	397,927
Harghita	Miercurea-Ciuc	2,552	6,610	347,145
Hunedoara	Deva	2,709	7,016	547,180
Ialomiţa	Slobozia	1,718	4,449	305,454
Iaşi	Iaşi	2,112	5,469	815,368
Maramureş	Baia Mare	2,400	6,215	539,718
Mehedinţi	Drobeta-Turnu Severin	1,892	4,900	330,017
Mureş	Târgu Mureş	2,585	6,696	607,355
Neamţ	Piatra Neamţ	2,274	5,890	584,364
Olt	Slatina	2,126	5,507	520,871
Prahova	Ploieşti	1,812	4,694	874,219
Sălaj	Zalău	1,486	3,850	264,448
Satu Mare	Satu Mare	1,701	4,405	398,401
Sibiu	Sibiu	2,093	5,422	448,474
Suceava	Suceava	3,303	8,555	708,571
Teleorman	Alexandria	2,224	5,760	477,527
Timiş	Timişoara	3,356	8,692	691,797
Tulcea	Tulcea	3,255	8,430	269,311
Vâlcea	Râmnicu Vâlcea	2,203	5,705	436,989
Vaslui	Vaslui	2,045	5,297	463,832
Vrancea	Focşani	1,878	4,863	394,257
Municipality				
Bucharest	Bucharest	703	1,820	2,339,156
TOTAL		91,699[2]	237,500	22,730,622

Demography

Population (1998): 22,491,000.
Density (1998): persons per sq mi 245.3, persons per sq km 94.7.
Urban-rural (1995): urban 55.4%; rural 44.6%.
Sex distribution (1995): male 49.27%; female 50.73%.
Age breakdown (1995): under 15, 20.4%; 15–29, 25.0%; 30–44, 20.5%; 45–59, 16.9%; 60–74, 13.6%; 75 and over, 3.6%.
Population projection: (2000) 22,374,000; (2010) 22,371,000.
Ethnic composition (1992): Romanian 90.7%; Hungarian 7.2%; other 2.1%.
Religious affiliation (1992): Romanian Orthodox 86.8%; Roman Catholic 5.1%; Greek Orthodox 1.0%; Pentecostal 1.0%; Muslim 0.2%; other 5.9%.
Major cities (1994): Bucharest 2,080,363; Constanţa 348,575; Iaşi 339,889; Timişoara 327,830; Galaţi 326,728.

Vital statistics

Birth rate per 1,000 population (1995): 10.4 (world avg. 25.0).
Death rate per 1,000 population (1995): 12.0 (world avg. 9.3).
Natural increase rate per 1,000 population (1995): –1.6 (world avg. 15.7).
Total fertility rate (avg. births per childbearing woman; 1993): 1.5.
Marriage rate per 1,000 population (1994): 6.8.
Divorce rate per 1,000 population (1990): 1.4.
Life expectancy at birth (1995): male 69.3 years; female 75.4 years.
Major causes of death per 100,000 population (1992): circulatory disease 707.7; cancers 163.4; respiratory disease 94.0; diseases of the digestive system 57.9.

National economy

Budget ('000,000,000,000 lei; 1996). Revenue: 32.5 (social security 25.0%, personal income tax 20.5%, value-added tax 16.5%). Expenditures: 36.8 (social security 27.3%, education 10.5%, health 8.2%, housing 5.6%).
Tourism (1995): receipts U.S.$574,000,000; expenditures U.S.$695,000,000.
Production (metric tons). Agriculture (1997): corn (maize) 11,500,000, wheat 7,100,000, potatoes 2,800,000, sugar beets 2,800,000, barley 1,500,000; livestock (number of live animals) 9,663,000 sheep, 8,235,000 pigs, 3,435,000 cattle; roundwood (1996) 12,616,000 cu m; fish catch (1995) 85,101. Mining (1995): iron 184,000; bauxite 174,000; zinc 35,000; copper 24,000. Manufacturing (value in U.S.$'000,000; 1994): food products 1,415; beverages 499; textiles 472; iron and steel 387; pottery 370; metal products 366; electrical machinery 358. Construction (1995): 9,300 dwelling units. Energy production (consumption): electricity (kW-hr; 1994) 55,136,000,000 (55,861,000,000); coal (metric tons; 1994) 40,547,000 (44,893,000); crude petroleum (barrels; 1994) 50,568,000 (109,995,000); pertroleum products (metric tons; 1994) 13,066,000 (10,291,000); natural gas (cu m; 1994) 15,868,000,000 (20,214,000,000).
Public debt (external, outstanding; 1996): U.S.$6,456,000,000.
Gross national product (1996): U.S.$36,191,000,000 (U.S.$1,600 per capita).

Structure of gross domestic product and labour force

	1994 in value '000,000,000 lei	% of total value	labour force	% of labour force
Agriculture	10,001	20.1	3,653,000	32.5
Industry[3]	16,091	32.3	2,881,700	25.6
Construction	3,010	6.0	562,700	5.0
Transp. and commun.	4,934	9.9	556,000	4.9
Trade	5,806	11.7	772,300	6.9
Finance	} 8,263	} 16.6	59,100	0.5
Pub. admin. Services			1,526,800	13.6
Other	1,690	3.4	1,237,400[3]	11.0[4]
TOTAL	49,795	100.0	11,249,000	100.0

Population economically active (1995): total 10,491,000; activity rate 46.2% (participation rates: ages 15–64, 67.2%[4]; female 44.2%[5]; unemployed 7.4%).

Price and earnings indexes (1990 = 100)

	1991	1992	1993	1994	1995	1996	1997
Consumer price index	274.4	854.0	3,033.1	7,181.2	9,496.6	13,184.1	33,588.2
Annual earnings index	221.3	597.4	1,804.8	4,142.0	...	9,513.3	18,829.5

Household income and expenditure. Average household size (1992) 3.1; income per household (1989) 73,500 lei (U.S.$4,940); sources of income (1982): wages 62.6%; expenditure (1989): food 51.1%; housing 16.4%.

Foreign trade

Balance of trade (current prices)

	1992	1993	1994	1995	1996	1997
U.S.$'000,000	–1,420.5	–1,127.8	–411.1	–1,576.7	–2,470.5	–1,980.3
% of total	14.0%	10.3%	3.2%	9.1%	13.2%	10.5%

Imports (1996): 10,368,000,000,000 lei (mineral fuels 25.4%, machinery and transport equipment 24.1%, textiles 12.0%, chemicals 8.4%). *Major import sources:* Germany 16.5%; Italy 15.6%; Russia 13.1%; France 4.8%.
Exports (1996): 10,272,827,000,000 lei (textiles 20.8%, mineral products 9.2%, chemicals 9.0%, machinery 8.0%, footwear 6.1%). *Major export destinations:* Germany 18.2%; Italy 16.6%; France 5.6%; U.K. 2.9%; U.S. 2.2%.

Transport and communications

Transport. Railroads (1995): length 11,365 km[6]; passenger-km 18,880,000,000; metric ton-km cargo 27,180,000,000. Roads (1992): length 153,014 km (paved 51%). Vehicles (1995): cars 2,197,777; trucks and buses 385,111. Merchant marine (1992): vessels (100 gross tons and over) 439; total deadweight tonnage 4,845,539. Air transport (1994): passenger-km 2,580,000,000; metric ton-km cargo 19,404,000; airports (1997) 8.

Communications

Medium	date	unit	number	units per 1,000 persons
Daily newspapers	1995	circulation	6,800,000	297
Radio	1996	receivers	4,500,000	198
Television	1995	receivers	4,580,000	201
Telephones	1995	main lines	2,968,000	131
Personal computers	1995	units	120,000	5.3

Education and health

Educational attainment (1992). Percentage of population age 25 and over having: no schooling 5.4%; some primary education 24.4%; some secondary 63.2%; postsecondary 6.9%. *Literacy* (1992): total population age 15 and over literate 96.7%; males 98.5%; females 95.0%.

Education (1994–95)

	schools	teachers	students	student/teacher ratio
Primary (age 6–9)[7]	13,963	168,702	2,532,169	15.0
Secondary (age 10–17)[8]	1,276	60,514	757,673	12.5
Voc., teacher tr.	1,530	9,360	345,394	36.9
Higher	63	20,452	255,162	12.5

Health: physicians (1993) 40,265 (1 per 565 persons); hospital beds (1992) 215,629 (1 per 105 persons); infant mortality rate (1995) 21.2.
Food (1995): daily per capita caloric intake 3,166 (vegetable products 78%, animal products 22%); 128% of FAO recommended minimum requirement.

Military

Total active duty personnel (1997): 227,000 (army 57.0%, navy 7.7%, air force 21.0%, other 14.3%). *Military expenditure as percentage of GNP* (1995): 2.5% (world 2.8%); per capita expenditure U.S.$115.

[1]Includes 15 nonelective seats. [2]Detail does not add to total given because of rounding. [3]Mining, manufacturing, and public utilities. [4]Unemployed. [5]1992. [6]1994. [7]Includes lower secondary. [8]Upper secondary only.

Internet resources for further information:
• Embassy of Romania (Washington, D.C.) http://www.embassy.org/romania

Russia

Official name: Rossiyskaya Federatsiya (Russian Federation).
Form of government: federal multiparty republic with a bicameral legislative body (Federal Assembly comprising a Federation Council [178] and a State Duma [450]).
Head of state: President.
Head of government: Prime Minister.
Capital: Moscow.
Official language: Russian.
Official religion: none.
Monetary unit: 1 ruble[1] (Rub) = 100 kopecks; valuation (Sept. 25, 1998) market rate, 1 U.S.$ = Rub 16.12; 1 £ = Rub 27.44.

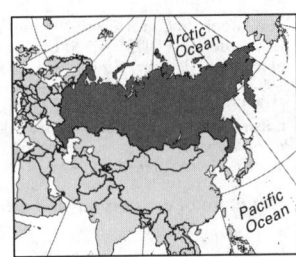

Area and population (continued)

	Capitals	area sq mi	area sq km	population
Koryak	Palana	116,400	301,500	33,000
Nenets	Naryan-Mar	68,100	176,400	48,000
Taymyr	Dudinka	332,900	862,100	47,000
Ust-Ordyn Buryat	Ust-Ordynsky	8,600	22,400	143,000
Yamalo-Nenets	Salekhard	289,700	750,300	488,000
Sakha (Yakutia)	Yakutsk	1,198,200	3,103,200	1,023,000
Severnaya Osetiya-Alaniya	Vladikavkaz	3,100	8,000	663,000
Tatarstan	Kazan	26,300	68,000	3,760,000
Tuva (Tyva)	Kyzyl-Orda	65,800	170,500	309,000
Udmurtia	Izhevsk	16,300	42,100	1,639,000
TOTAL		6,592,800	17,075,400	147,976,000

Demography

Population (1998): 146,861,000.
Density (1998): persons per sq mi 22.3, persons per sq km 8.6.
Urban-rural (1996): urban 73.2%; rural 26.8%.
Sex distribution (1996): male 46.94%; female 53.06%.
Age breakdown (1996): under 15, 21.0%; 15–29, 20.8%; 30–44, 24.5%; 45–59, 17.0%; 60–74, 12.9%; 75 and over, 3.8%.
Population projection: (2000) 145,905,000; (2010) 143,918,000.
Ethnic composition (1997): Russian 86.6%; Tatar 3.2%; Ukrainian 1.3%; Chuvash 0.9%; Bashkir 0.7%; Chechen 0.6%; Mordovian 0.5%; Belorussian 0.3%; other 5.9%.
Religious affiliation (1995): Russian Orthodox 16.3%; Muslim 10.0%; Protestant 0.9%; Jewish 0.4%; other (mostly nonreligious) 72.4%.
Major cities (1996): Moscow 8,400,000; St. Petersburg 4,200,000; Nizhny Novgorod 1,400,000; Novosibirsk 1,400,000; Yekaterinburg 1,300,000; Samara 1,200,000; Omsk 1,200,000; Chelyabinsk 1,100,000; Kazan 1,100,000; Ufa 1,100,000; Perm 1,000,000; Rostov-na-Donu 1,000,000.

Area and population

Federal Republics Other entities	Capitals	area sq mi	area sq km	population 1996[2] estimate
Adygeya	Maykop	2,900	7,600	450,000
Altay	Gorno-Altaisk	35,700	92,600	202,000
Bashkortostan	Ufa	55,400	143,600	4,097,000
Buryatiya	Ulan-Ude	135,600	351,300	1,053,000
Chechnia (Chechnya)[3, 4]	Grozny (Dzhokhar Ghala)	5	5	5
Chuvashiya	Cheboksary	7,100	18,300	1,361,000
Dagestan	Makhachkala	19,400	50,300	2,098,000
Ingushetiya[3]	Nazran	7,400[5]	19,300[5]	1,165,000[5]
Kabardino-Balkariya	Nalchik	4,800	12,500	790,000
Kalmykiya	Elista	29,400	76,100	319,000
Karachayevo-Cherkesiya	Cherkessk	5,400	14,100	436,000
Kareliya	Petrozavodsk	66,600	172,400	785,000
Khakasiya	Abakan	23,900	61,900	586,000
Komi	Syktyvkar	160,600	415,900	1,185,000
Mari-El	Yoshkar-Ola	9,000	23,200	766,000
Mordoviya	Saransk	10,100	26,200	956,000
Russia	Moscow	4,709,800[6]	12,198,300	124,333,000
Regions (Oblasts)				
Amur[7]	Blagoveshchensk	140,400	363,700	1,038,000
Arkhangelsk	Arkhangelsk	226,800	587,400	1,521,000
Astrakhan	Astrakhan	17,000	44,100	1,029,000
Belgorod	Belgorod	10,500	27,100	1,469,000
Bryansk	Bryansk	13,500	34,900	1,480,000
Chelyabinsk	Chelyabinsk	33,900	87,900	3,689,000
Chita	Chita	166,600	431,500	1,295,000
Irkutsk	Irkutsk	296,500	767,900	2,795,000
Ivanovo	Ivanovo	9,200	23,900	1,266,000
Kaliningrad[7]	Kaliningrad	5,800	15,100	932,000
Kaluga	Kaluga	11,500	29,900	1,097,000
Kamchatka	Petropavlovsk-Kamchatsky	182,400	472,300	411,000
Kemerovo	Kemerovo	36,900	95,500	3,063,000
Kirov	Kirov	46,600	120,800	1,634,000
Kostroma	Kostroma	23,200	60,100	806,000
Kurgan	Kurgan	27,400	71,000	1,112,000
Kursk	Kursk	11,500	29,800	1,347,000
Leningrad	St. Petersburg	33,200[8]	85,900[8]	1,676,000
Lipetsk	Lipetsk	9,300	24,100	1,250,000
Magadan	Magadan	178,100	461,400	258,000
Moskva (Moscow)	Moscow	18,100[9]	47,000[9]	6,597,000
Murmansk	Murmansk	55,900	144,900	1,048,000
Nizhny Novgorod	Nizhny Novgorod	28,900	74,800	3,727,000
Novgorod	Novgorod	21,400	55,300	743,000
Novosibirsk	Novosibirsk	68,800	178,200	2,749,000
Omsk	Omsk	53,900	139,700	2,176,000
Orenburg	Orenburg	47,900	124,000	2,229,000
Oryol (Orel)	Oryol	9,500	24,700	914,000
Penza	Penza	16,700	43,200	1,562,000
Perm	Perm	62,000	160,600	3,009,000
Pskov	Pskov	21,400	55,300	832,000
Rostov	Rostov-na-Donu	38,900	100,800	4,425,000
Ryazan	Ryazan	15,300	39,600	1,325,000
Sakhalin	Yuzhno-Sakhalinsk	33,600	87,100	648,000
Samara	Samara	20,700	53,600	3,312,000
Saratov	Saratov	38,700	100,200	2,739,000
Smolensk	Smolensk	19,200	49,800	1,172,000
Sverdlovsk[7]	Yekaterinburg	75,200	194,800	4,686,000
Tambov	Tambov	13,200	34,300	1,310,000
Tomsk	Tomsk	122,400	316,900	1,078,000
Tula	Tula	9,900	25,700	1,815,000
Tver	Tver	32,500	84,100	1,651,000
Tyumen	Tyumen	554,100	1,435,200	3,170,000
Ulyanovsk (Simbirsk)	Simbirsk	14,400	37,300	1,495,000
Vladimir	Vladimir	11,200	29,000	1,645,000
Volgograd	Volgograd	44,000	113,900	2,704,000
Vologda[7]	Vologda	56,300	145,700	1,350,000
Voronezh	Voronezh	20,200	52,400	2,504,000
Yaroslavl	Yaroslavl	14,100	36,400	1,451,000
Autonomous Region				
Yevreyskaya (Jewish)	Birobidzhan	13,900	36,000	210,000
Territories (Krays)				
Altay	Barnaul	65,300	169,100	2,690,000
Khabarovsk	Khabarovsk	304,500	788,600	1,571,000
Krasnodar	Krasnodar	29,300	76,000	5,044,000
Krasnoyarsk	Krasnoyarsk	903,400	2,339,700	3,106,000
Primorye (Maritime)[7]	Vladivostok	64,100	165,900	2,255,000
Stavropol	Stavropol	25,700	66,500	2,667,000
Federal cities				
Moscow	—	9	9	8,664,000
St. Petersburg[7]	—	8	8	4,801,000
Autonomous districts (Okrugs)[10]				
Agin Buryat	Aginskoye	7,300	19,000	79,000
Chukot	Anadyr	284,800	737,700	91,000
Evenk	Tura	296,400	767,600	20,000
Khanty-Mansi	Khanty-Mansiysk	202,000	523,100	1,331,000
Komi-Permyak	Kudymkar	12,700	32,900	157,000

Other principal cities (1995)

	population		population		population
Astrakhan	486,000	Krasnoyarsk	868,800	Tolyatti	702,300
Barnaul	658,200	Naberezhnye Chelny	529,300	Tula	532,300
Irkutsk	585,000	Novokuznetsk	586,000	Ulyanovsk (Simbirsk)	699,300
Izhevsk	654,400	Orenburg	532,100	Vladivostok	631,800
Kemerovo	502,500	Penza	533,900	Volgograd	1,002,800
Khabarovsk	617,800	Ryazan	539,800	Voronezh	907,800
Krasnodar	645,700	Saratov	902,200	Yaroslavl	629,000

Mobility (1989). Population living in the same residence as in 1988: 78.8%; different residence, same oblast 11.5%; different republic 9.7%.
Households (1994). Total family households 52,930,000; average household size 2.8; 2 persons 26.2%; 3 persons 22.6%; 4 persons 20.5%; 5 persons or more 11.5%. Population in family households (1989): 128,787,000 (87.0%), nonfamily population 19,254,000 (13.0%).

Vital statistics

Birth rate per 1,000 population (1995): 9.3 (world avg. 25.0); (1994) legitimate 80.4%; illegitimate 19.6%.
Death rate per 1,000 population (1995): 15.0 (world avg. 9.3).
Natural increase rate per 1,000 population (1995): –5.7 (world avg. 15.7).
Total fertility rate (avg. births per childbearing woman; 1995): 1.3.
Marriage rate per 1,000 population (1995): 7.3.
Divorce rate per 1,000 population (1995): 4.5.
Life expectancy at birth (1996): male 58.3 years; female 71.7 years.
Major causes of death per 100,000 population (1995): circulatory diseases 790.1; accidents, poisoning, and violence 236.6, of which suicide 41.4, murder 30.7; malignant neoplasms (cancers) 200.8; respiratory diseases 73.9; digestive diseases 46.1; infectious and parasitic diseases 20.7.

Social indicators

Educational attainment (1994). Percentage of population age 15 and over having: primary or no formal education 10.0%; some secondary 20.2%; secondary and some postsecondary 77.8%; higher and postgraduate 15.1%.
Quality of working life (1990). Average workweek: 40 hours. Annual rate per 100,000 workers of: injury or accident 569; industrial illness 5.3; death 11.2. Proportion of labour force insured for damages or income loss resulting from: injury 100%; permanent disability 100%; death 100%. Average days lost to labour stoppages per 1,000 workdays (1992): 1.1.
Access to services (1990). Proportion of dwellings having access to: electricity, virtually 100%; safe public water supply 94%; public sewage collection 92%; central heating 92%; bathroom 87%; gas 72%; hot water 79%.
Social participation. Eligible voters participating in last national election (1996): 68.8%. Trade union membership in total workforce (1989): 100%. Practicing religious population in total affiliated population (1991): 32%.
Social deviance. Offense rate per 100,000 population (1995) for: murder 21.4; rape 8.5; serious injury 41.7; larceny-theft 1,020.0. Incidence per 100,000 population (1992) of; alcoholism 1,727.5; substance abuse 25.1; suicide 26.5.
Material well-being (1994). Durable goods possessed per 100 family households: automobile 25; radio receiver 103; television receiver 116; refrigerator or freezer 95; washing machine 81; camera 37; motorcycle 23; bicycle 54.

National economy

Budget (1996). Revenue: Rub 329,000,000,000,000 (tax revenue 84.5%, of which profit tax 19.5%, value-added tax 18.4%, individual income tax 15.7%, property tax 11.2%, other taxes 19.7%; nontax revenue 15.5%). Expenditures: Rub 410,800,000,000,000 (current expenditure 74.3%, of which economy 23.3%, defense 20.9%, education 5.8%, health 3.0%, interest on foreign debt 2.4%; development expenditure 25.7%).
Public debt (external, outstanding: 1997)[11]: U.S.$100,463,000,000.
Gross national product (1996): U.S.$356,030,000,000 (U.S.$2,410 per capita).

Structure of gross domestic product and labour force

	1995			
	in value Rub '000,000	% of total value	labour force	% of labour force
Agriculture	143,282,300	8.8	10,500,000	14.4
Mining	} 511,393,000	} 31.4	} 17,200,000	} 23.5
Manufacturing				
Public utilities	64,266,500	3.9		
Construction	107,525,800	6.6	6,500,000	8.9
Transp. and commun.	170,936,800	10.5	5,300,000	7.2
Trade	310,086,500	19.0	6,500,000	8.9
Finance	145,000,900	8.9	900,000	1.2
Services	122,601,300	7.5	17,100,000	23.4
Pub. admin., defense	55,863,300	3.4	1,700,000	2.3
Other	...	...	7,440,000	10.2
TOTAL	1,630,956,400	100.0	73,140,000	100.0

Production (metric tons except as noted). Agriculture, forestry, fishing (1996): potatoes 38,529,000, wheat 34,900,000, sugar beets 16,132,000, barley 15,900,000, vegetables (other than potatoes) 11,099,000, oats 8,570,000, rye 5,900,000, sunflower seeds 2,764,900, corn (maize) 1,700,000, peas 1,000,000, buckwheat 620,000, millet 500,000, rice 500,000; livestock (number of live animals) 39,696,000 cattle, 25,800,000 sheep, 22,631,000 pigs; roundwood 96,250,000 cu m; fish catch 4,374,000. Mining and quarrying (1995): nickel 251,000,000; chrome ore 107,700,000; iron ore 78,300,000; tin 10,000,000; molybdenum 8,800,000; antimony 7,000,000; gold 4,249,000 troy oz. Manufacturing (1995): crude steel 51,600,000; pig iron 39,800,000; rolled steel 39,000,000; cement 36,400,000; mineral fertilizers 9,600,000; sulfuric acid 6,900,000; cellulose 4,193,000; synthetic resins and plastics 1,794,000; cardboard 1,298,000; caustic soda 1,156,000; detergents 296,000; synthetic fibres 216,000; cotton fabrics 1,235,000,000 sq m; silk fabrics 197,000,000 sq m; linen fabrics 131,000,000 sq m; wool fabrics 72,000,000 sq m; cigarettes 141,000,-000,000 units; watches 29,800,000 units; television receivers 1,888,000 units; refrigerators 1,766,000 units; washing machines 1,303,000 units; vacuum cleaners 911,000 units; passenger cars 835,000 units; bicycles 759,000 units; tape recorders 671,000 units; cameras 296,000 units; sewing machines 165,400 units; motorcycles 82,100 units; video recorders 20,900 units; leather footwear 67,300,000 pairs; beer 19,800,000 hectolitres; vodka and liquors 12,200,000 hectolitres; champagne 8,200,000 hectolitres; grape wine 1,460,000 hectolitres; brandy 171,400 hectolitres. Construction (1995): residential 14,600,000 sq m; nonresidential 26,400,000 sq m.

Manufacturing, mining, and construction enterprises (1995)

	no. of enterprises	no. of employees	monthly wages as a % of avg. of all wages[12]	value added (Rub '000,000,000)
Manufacturing				
Machinery and metal products	48,905	4,842,000	98.2	27,234
Fuel and energy	1,758	1,554,000	133.3	44,211
Metallurgy	2,158	1,248,000	124.3	26,437
Chemicals	23,027	2,432,000	94.1	17,934
Light industry	23,007	1,368,000	80.0	2,931
Food	14,713	1,514,000	100.1	12,886
Other industries	19,073	2,085,000	...	4,685
Building materials	8,359	994,000	108.2	3,761

Energy production (consumption): electricity (kW-hr; 1994) 875,914,000,000 (855,418,000,000); coal (metric tons; 1994) 176,754,000 (180,988,000); crude petroleum (barrels; 1994) 2,265,000,000 (1,375,000,000); Petroleum products (metric tons; 1994) 162,085,000 (126,758,000); natural gas (cu m; 1994) 498,-995,000,000 (327,275,000,000); peat (metric tons; 1994) 2,928,000 (4,007,000); oil shale (metric tons; 1994) 2,000,000 (1993; 3,300,000).
Population economically active (1995): total 73,140,000; activity rate of total population 49.5% (participation rates: ages 16–59 [male], 16–54 [female] 72.6%; female 46.7%; unemployed [1996] 9.1%).

Price and earnings indexes (1990 = 100)

	1991	1992	1993	1994	1995	1996
Consumer price index	192.7	2,800	27,900	112,100	221,300	269,500
Monthly earnings index	180.9	1,978	19,361	71,494	101,700	264,000

Land use (1994): forest 44.9%; pasture 5.2%; agriculture 7.7%; other 42.2%.
Household income and expenditure. Average household size (1995) 2.8; income per household: Rub 6,395,000 (U.S.$1,176); sources of income (1995): wages 77.8%, pensions and stipends 12.0%, other 10.2%; expenditure (1994): food 46.8%, clothing 13.6%, taxes and other financial payments 10.1%, furniture and household appliances 8.7%, transportation 6.1%, culture 5.1%.

Foreign trade

Balance of trade (current prices; non-CIS)

	1992	1993	1994	1995	1996	1997
U.S.$'000,000	+4,986	+17,490	+21,800	+32,879	+37,368	+19,749
% of total	6.7%	24.6%	27.9%	33.2%	37.3%	12.7%

Imports (1996): U.S.$45,438,000,000 (machinery and transport equipment 27.0%, food 24.3%, chemicals 13.5%, ferrous and nonferrous metals 8.2%, textiles and clothing 4.3%, fuels and lubricants 3.7%). *Major import sources*[13]: Germany 11.8%; Italy 5.3%; U.S. 5.2%; Finland 3.8%; France 2.9%; U.K. 2.6%.
Exports (1996): U.S.$84,387,000,000 (fuels and lubricants 45.5%, ferrous and nonferrous metals 19.1%, machinery and transport equipment 8.9%, chemicals 8.2%, precious metals 4.3%, forestry products 4.1%). *Major export destinations*[13]: Germany 8.2%; China 5.7%; U.S. 5.6%; Italy 5.0%; Switzerland 4.8%; The Netherlands 4.1%; U.K. 3.8%.

Trade by commodity group (1996)

	imports		exports	
SITC group	U.S.$'000,000	%	U.S.$'000,000	%
00 Food and live animals	11,028	24.3	1,654	1.9
02 Raw materials. excl. fuels	5,614	12.4	20,843	24.7
03 Mineral fuels, lubricants	1,703	3.6	38,365	45.5
05 Chemicals	6,140	13.5	6,899	8.2
65 Textile yarn, fabrics	894	2.0	555	0.7
07 Machinery and transport equip.	11,859	26.1	7,477	8.8
08 Misc. manufactured articles	8,200	18.1	8,594	10.2
TOTAL	45,438	100.0	84,387	100.0

Direction of trade (1994)

	imports		exports	
	U.S.$'000,000	%	U.S.$'000,000	%
Africa	217	0.8	512	1.0
Asia	4,650	16.5	9,985	20.4
Japan	1,114	3.9	2,245	4.6
South America	791	2.8	1,021	2.1
North and Central America	2,263	8.0	3,619	7.4
United States	2,069	7.3	3,373	6.9
Europe	20,020	70.9	33,872	69.1
EU	15,278	54.1	22,211	45.3
EFTA	3,154	11.2	9,373	19.1
other Europe	1,588	5.6	2,288	4.7
Oceania	300	1.1	42	0.1
TOTAL	28,241	100.0[6]	49,051	100.0[6]

Transport and communications

Transport. Railroads (1995): length 151,000 km; passenger-km 192,200,000,000; metric ton-km cargo 1,213,000,000. Roads (1995): total length 949,000 km (paved 79%). Vehicles (1993): passenger cars 10,499,000; trucks and buses 407,000. Air transport (1995): passenger-km 71,700,000,000; metric ton-km cargo 1,800,000,000; airports (1996) 75.

Distribution of traffic (1995)

	cargo carried ('000,000 tons)	% of national total	passengers carried ('000,000)	% of national total
Intercity transport			26,549	56.2
Road	1,441	41.7	22,817	48.3
Rail	1,028	29.7	1,833	3.9
Sea and river	203	5.9	32	0.1
Air	1	...	34	0.1
Pipeline	783	22.7	—	—
Urban transport			20,684	43.8
Road	—	—	86	0.2
Rail	—	—	20,598	43.6
TOTAL	3,456	100.0	47,233	100.0

Communications

Medium	date	unit	number	units per 1,000 persons
Daily newspapers	1994	circulation	39,301,000	267
Radio	1995	receivers	50,600,000	341
Television	1995	receivers	56,244,000	379
Telephones	1995	main lines	25,019,000	170
Cellular telephones	1995	subscribers	88,500	0.6
Facsimile machines	1995	units	30,600	0.2
Personal computers	1995	units	2,600,000	18

Education and health

Health (1995): physicians 630,000 (1 per 235 persons); hospital beds 1,860,000 (1 per 80 persons); infant mortality rate per 1,000 live births (1995) 18.0.

Education (1995–96)

	schools	teachers	students	student/ teacher ratio
Primary (age 6–13)	} 70,200	1,705,000	22,000,000	12.9
Secondary (age 14–17)				
Voc., teacher tr.	2,612	...	1,923,000	...
Higher	569	...	2,655,000	...

Food (1995): daily per capita caloric intake 2,926 (vegetable products 74%; animal products 26%); 114% of FAO recommended minimum.

Military

Total active duty personnel (1997): 1,240,000 (army 71.8%, navy 17.7%, air force 10.5%). *Military expenditure as percentage of GNP* (1995): 11.4% (world 3.0%); per capita expenditure U.S.$513.

[1]On Jan. 1, 1998, a (new) ruble was introduced; 1 (new) ruble is equivalent to 1,000 (old) rubles, data given in (old) rubles. [2]January 1995. [3]The former Chechen-Ingush republic was split into two separate republics June 4, 1992; the final status of Chechnia was unresolved in December 1998. [4]Republic is not signatory to the March 31, 1992, treaty establishing the Russian Federation. [5]Ingushetia's area and population include Chechnia. [6]Detail does not add to total given because of rounding. [7]Entity has formally proclaimed itself a federal republic; final status remains undetermined. [8]Leningrad region includes area of federal city of St. Petersburg. [9]Moskva region includes area of federal city of Moscow. [10]With the exception of the Chukot autonomous district (identified in Roman type), which has formally separated from Magadan region, all autonomous districts are administratively part of another national administrative subdivision, within which their area and population are included. [11]Total as of March 31, 1995; Russia has also assumed responsibility for the governmental and commercial debts of the former U.S.S.R., estimated to constitute a further U.S.$88,000,000,000. [12]1990. [13]Based on IMF Direction of Trade Statistics (DOTS), which values total trade with all known trading partners, rather than the customs statement of the subject country. Total DOTS valuation: imports U.S.$43,318,000,000, exports U.S.$81,438,000,000.

Internet resources for further information:
• **Permanent Mission of the Russian Federation to the United Nations**
http://www.undp.org/missions/russianfed

Rwanda

Official name: Repubulika y'u Rwanda (Rwanda); République Rwandaise (French); Republic of Rwanda (English).
Form of government: transitional regime with one legislative body (Transitional National Assembly[1] [70]).
Head of state and government: President in conjunction with Prime Minister and Vice President (Minister of Defense).
Capital: Kigali.
Official languages: Rwanda; French; English.
Official religion: none.
Monetary unit: 1 Rwanda franc (RF); valuation (Sept. 25, 1998) 1 U.S.$ = RF 311.03; 1 £ = RF 529.53.

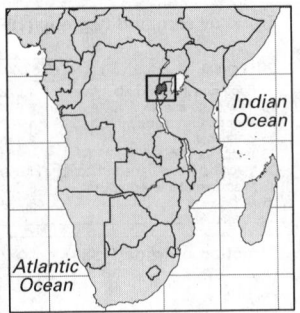

Area and population		area		population
Prefectures	**Capitals**	sq mi	sq km	1991 census
Butare	Butare	709	1,837	766,839
Byumba	Byumba	1,838	4,761	783,350
Cyangugu	Cyangugu	712	1,845	515,129
Gikongoro	Gikongoro	794	2,057	464,585
Gisenyi	Gisenyi	791	2,050	734,697
Gitarama	Gitarama	845	2,189	851,516
Kibungo	Kibungo	1,562	4,046	655,368
Kibuye	Kibuye	658	1,705	470,747
Kigali	Kigali (city)	1,159	3,002	918,869
Kigali (city)	—	45	116	237,782
Ruhengeri	Ruhengeri	642	1,663	766,112
TOTAL LAND AREA		9,757[2]	25,271	
TOTAL		10,169	26,338	7,164,994[3]

Demography

Population (1998): 7,956,000[4].
Density (1998): persons per sq mi 782.4, persons per sq km 302.1.
Urban-rural (1991): urban 5.4%; rural 94.6%.
Sex distribution (1996): male 49.56%; female 50.44%.
Age breakdown (1996): under 15, 46.1%; 15–29, 27.9%; 30–44, 15.1%; 45–59, 6.6%; 60–74, 3.5%; 75 and over, 0.8%.
Population projection: (2000) 8,337,000; (2010) 9,881,000.
Doubling time: 33 years.
Ethnic composition (1996): Hutu 80.0%; Tutsi 19.0%; Twa 1.0%.
Religious affiliation (1996): Roman Catholic 65%; Protestant 9.0%; Muslim 1.0%; indigenous beliefs and other 25.0%.
Major cities (1991): Kigali 237,782[3]; Ruhengeri 29,578[5]; Butare 28,645[5]; Gisenyi 21,918[5].

Vital statistics

Birth rate per 1,000 population (1996): 39.1 (world avg. 25.0); (1978) legitimate 94.9%; illegitimate 5.1%.
Death rate per 1,000 population (1996): 18.0 (world avg. 9.3).
Natural increase rate per 1,000 population (1996): 21.1 (world avg. 15.7).
Total fertility rate (avg. births per childbearing woman; 1996): 6.0.
Marriage rate per 1,000 population (1984)[6]: 2.5.
Life expectancy at birth (1996): male 42.9 years; female 43.6 years.
Major causes of death per 100,000 population: n.a.; however, principal causes in 1991 were malaria, bronchopneumonia, diarrhea, AIDS, pulmonary diseases, cerebrospinal meningitis, kwashiorkor, and road accidents.

National economy

Budget (1995). Revenue: RF 61,500,000,000 (grants 62.4%, taxes on goods and services 16.1%, import and export duties 14.5%, income tax 4.6%). Expenditures: RF 69,400,000,000 (capital expenditures 39.3%, goods and services 25.1%, wages 19.6%, debt payment 11.2%, transfers 4.8%).
Production (metric tons except as noted). Agriculture, forestry, fishing (1996): plantains 2,105,000, sweet potatoes 1,100,000, cassava 250,000, potatoes 150,000, sorghum 85,000, corn [maize] 71,000, coffee 21,000; livestock (number of live animals) 920,000 goats, 465,000 cattle, 250,000 sheep, 80,000 pigs; roundwood (1995) 5,660,000 cu m; fish catch (1995) 3,349. Mining and quarrying (1993): cassiterite (tin ore) 400; wolframite (tungsten ore) 175; gold 1,000 kg. Manufacturing (1994): cement 21,000; lye soap 2,200; sugar 600; beer 45,800,000 bottles; nonalcoholic beverages 21,900,000 bottles; textiles 2,800,000 metres. Energy production (consumption): electricity (kW-hr; 1994) 166,000,000 (177,000,000); petroleum products (metric tons; 1994) none (155,000); natural gas (cu m; 1994) 179,389 (179,389).
Population economically active (1991): total 3,649,000; activity rate of total population 50.2% (participation rates: ages 14–74 [1989] 46.3%; female 53.5%; unemployed, n.a.).

Price and earnings indexes (1990 = 100)							
	1990	1991	1992	1993	1994	1995	1996
Consumer price index	100.0	119.6	131.1	147.3	...	293.0	314.7
Earnings index	100.0	100.0	100.0	100.0	100.0	100.0	120.0[7]

Public debt (external, outstanding; 1996): U.S.$977,000,000.
Gross national product (1996): U.S.$1,268,000,000 (U.S.$190 per capita).

Structure of gross domestic product and labour force				
	1995		1989	
	in value RF '000,000	% of total value	labour force	% of labour force
Agriculture	114,622	35.0	2,832,557	90.1
Mining	81	—	4,691	0.2
Manufacturing	46,841	14.3	45,089	1.4
Construction	5,034	1.5	38,237	1.2
Public utilities	1,382	0.4	2,562	0.1
Transp. and commun.	17,055	5.2	7,333	0.2
Trade	58,251	17.8	80,026	2.6
Pub. admin., defense	16,508	5.0 }	123,147	3.9
Services	48,882	14.9 }		
Other	18,831[8]	5.8[8]	9,414	0.3
TOTAL	327,485[2]	100.0[2]	3,143,056	100.0

Tourism: receipts (1993) U.S.$2,000,000; expenditures (1992) U.S.$17,000,000.
Land use (1994): forested 10.1%; meadows and pastures 28.4%; agricultural and under permanent cultivation 47.4%; other 14.1%.
Household income and expenditure. Average household size (1991) 4.7; average annual income per household (1983) RF 122,870 (U.S.$1,300); sources of income (1977): self-employment 71.0%, salaries and wages 16.5%, transfers 9.5%; expenditure (1982)[9]: food 44.2%, housing 13.2%, clothing and footwear 11.4%, transportation 10.3%, household equipment 8.4%.

Foreign trade

Balance of trade (current prices)						
	1992	1993	1994	1995	1996	1997
RF '000,000	−29,346	−38,480	−13,214	−47,462	−60,268	−63,504
% of total	62.2%	80.3%	62.0%	61.7%	61.9%	54.8%

Imports (1995): U.S.$291,500,000 (food 35.2%, capital goods 17.6%, intermediate goods 11.1%, energy products 7.3%). *Major import sources* (1991): Belgium-Luxembourg 17.1%; Kenya 13.4%; France 6.8%; Germany 6.0%; Italy 2.8%; The Netherlands 2.7%; U.K. 2.1%; U.S. 1.0%; Zaire 0.7%.
Exports (1995): U.S.$51,200,000 (coffee 74.4%, tea 10.0%, hides and skins 4.9%). *Major export destinations* (1991): Germany 21.3%; The Netherlands 18.8%; Belgium-Luxembourg 11.8%; U.K. 6.4%; U.S. 5.8%; Italy 1.7%.

Transport and communications

Transport. Railroads: none. Roads (1995): total length 14,565 km (paved 10%). Vehicles (1995): passenger cars 11,900; trucks 15,900. Air transport: (1993) passenger-km 2,000,000; (1991) metric ton cargo loaded 2,674, metric ton cargo unloaded 4,794; airports (1997) with scheduled flights 2.

Communications				units per 1,000
Medium	date	unit	number	persons
Daily newspapers	1995	circulation	500	0.07
Radio	1995	receivers	525,000	78.4
Telephones	1995	main lines	15,000	2.2
Facsimile machines	1995	units	500	0.07

Education and health

Educational attainment (1978). Percentage of population age 25 and over having: no formal schooling 76.9%; some primary education 16.8%; complete primary education 4.0%; some secondary and complete secondary education 2.0%; some postsecondary vocational and higher education 0.3%. *Literacy* (1995): percentage of total population age 15 and over literate 60.5%; males literate 69.8%; females literate 51.6%.

Education (1991–92)				student/
	schools	teachers	students	teacher ratio
Primary (age 7–15)	1,710	18,937	1,104,902	58.3
Secondary (age 16–19)[10]	...	3,413	94,586	27.7
Higher[11]	3[12]	646	3,389	5.2

Health: physicians (1992) 150 (1 per 50,000 persons); hospital beds (1990) 12,152 (1 per 588 persons); infant mortality rate (1996) 114.2.
Food (1992): daily per capita caloric intake 1,821 (vegetable products 97%, animal products 3%); 78% of FAO recommended minimum requirement.

Military

Total active duty personnel (1997): 62,000 (army 100%). *Military expenditure as percentage of GNP* (1995): 5.2% (world 2.8%); per capita expenditure U.S.$20.

[1]Transitional National Assembly was appointed on Nov. 25, 1994, for an interim period of five years. [2]Detail does not add to total given because of rounding. [3]The population of Kigali decreased to about 100,000–120,000 because of the 1994 civil war. [4]Includes adjustments for (1) the death of an estimated 500,000 Tutsi killed during the events of 1994; (2) the return of 400,000–600,000 Tutsi herdsmen from surrounding countries who had been in exile since 1959; and (3) the loss of more than 2 million Hutu refugees in 1994 and the return of all but 150,000 of them by 1998. [5]De jure population only. [6]Excludes marriages not registered in court. [7]Minimum wage unchanged 1980–95; a 20% increase was made in 1996. [8]Indirect taxes plus statistical adjustments. [9]Weights of consumer price index components. [10]Includes vocational and teacher training. [11]1989–90. [12]1985.

Internet resources for further information:
• CIA World Factbook—Rwanda
   http://www.odci.gov/cia/publications/nsolo/factbook/rw.htm

Saint Kitts and Nevis

Official name: Federation of Saint Kitts and Nevis[1].
Form of government: constitutional monarchy with one legislative house (National Assembly [15[2]]).
Chief of state: British Monarch represented by Governor-General.
Head of government: Prime Minister.
Capital: Basseterre.
Official language: English.
Official religion: none.
Monetary unit: 1 Eastern Caribbean dollar (EC$) = 100 cents; valuation (Sept. 25, 1998) 1 U.S.$ = EC$2.70; 1 £ = EC$4.60.

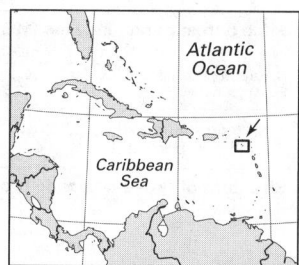

Area and population		area		population
				1995
Islands	Capitals	sq mi	sq km	estimate
Nevis[3]	Charlestown	36.0	93.2	8,010
St. Kitts	Basseterre	68.0	176.2	35,340
TOTAL		104.0	269.4	43,350

Demography

Population (1998): 42,300.
Density (1998): persons per sq mi 406.7, persons per sq km 157.0.
Urban-rural (1995): urban 42.9%; rural 57.1%.
Sex distribution (1990): male 51.56%; female 48.44%.
Age breakdown (1990): under 15, 32.5%; 15–29, 25.6%; 30–44, 18.9%; 45–59, 10.1%; 60–74, 8.9%; 75 and over, 4.0%.
Population projection: (2000) 43,000; (2010) 50,000.
Doubling time: 67 years.
Ethnic composition (1991): black 94.9%; mixed/white/Indo-Pakistani 5.1%.
Religious affiliation (1995): Protestant 84.6%, of which Anglican 25.2%, Methodist 25.2%, Pentecostal 8.4%, Moravian 7.6%; Roman Catholic 6.7%; other 8.7%.
Major towns (1994): Basseterre 12,605; Charlestown 1,411.

Vital statistics

Birth rate per 1,000 population (1995): 20.2[4] (world avg. 25.0); (1983) legitimate 19.2%; illegitimate 80.8%.
Death rate per 1,000 population (1995): 9.8[4] (world avg. 9.3).
Natural increase rate per 1,000 population (1995): 10.4[4] (world avg. 15.7).
Total fertility rate (avg. births per childbearing woman; 1996): 2.5.
Marriage rate per 1,000 population: n.a.
Divorce rate per 1,000 population: n.a.
Life expectancy at birth (1996): male 63.8 years; female 70.1 years.
Major causes of death per 100,000 population (1985): diseases of the circulatory system 443.2, of which cerebrovascular disease 220.5, diseases of pulmonary circulation and other heart disease 122.7; malignant neoplasms (cancers) 95.5.

National economy

Budget (1996). Revenue: EC$208,300,000 (tax revenue 68.9% of which taxes on international transactions 37.4%, income taxes 15.7%, consumption taxes 14.4%; nontax revenue 26.7%). Expenditures: EC$231,700,000 (current expenditure 85.9%; development expenditure 14.1%).
Production (metric tons except as noted). Agriculture, forestry, fishing (1996): sugarcane 203,740, coconuts 1,700, tropical fruit 1,500, sweet potatoes 250, onions 141; sea island cotton is grown on Nevis; livestock (number of live animals; 1996) 17,000 sheep, 13,000 goats, 3,000 pigs; roundwood, n.a.; fish catch (1995) 220. Mining and quarrying: excavation of sand for local use. Manufacturing (1996): raw sugar 20,249; molasses 6,000[5]; carbonated beverages 47,000 hectolitres[6]; beer 17,200 hectolitres[6]; other manufactures include electronic components, garments, footwear, and batik. Construction (value added; 1994): EC$57,000,000. Energy production (consumption): electricity (kW-hr; 1994) 86,000,000 (86,000,000); coal, none (none); crude petroleum, none (none); petroleum products (metric tons; 1994) none (32,000); natural gas, none (none).
Gross national product (1996): U.S.$240,000,000 (U.S.$5,870 per capita).

Structure of gross domestic product and labour force				
	1995		1994	
	in value EC$'000,000	% of total value	labour force[7]	% of labour force[7]
Sugarcane	13.4	2.0	1,525[8]	9.2[8]
Other agriculture, forestry, fisheries	18.0	2.7	914	5.5
Mining	1.9	0.3	29	0.2
Manufacturing	59.7	8.9	1,290[9]	7.8[9]
Construction	67.0	10.0	1,745	10.5
Public utilities	9.3	1.4	416	2.5
Transportation and communications	87.4	13.1	534	3.2
Trade, restaurants	131.2	19.6	3,367	20.3
Finance, real estate	87.7	13.1	3,708[10]	22.3[10]
Pub. admin., defense	101.9	15.3	2,738	16.5
Services	24.1	3.6	10	10
Other	66.1[11]	9.9[11]	342	2.1
TOTAL	667.7	100.0[12]	16,608	100.0[12]

Household income and expenditure. Average household size (1980) 3.7; average annual income per wage earner (1994) EC$9,940 (US$3,681); sources of income: n.a.; expenditure (1978)[13]: food, beverages, and tobacco 55.6%, household furnishings 9.4%, housing 7.6%, clothing and footwear 7.5%, fuel and light 6.6%, transportation 4.3%, other 9.0%.
Public debt (external, outstanding; 1995): U.S.$54,000,000.
Population economically active (1980): total 17,125; activity rate of total population 39.5% (participation rates: ages 15–64, 69.5%; female 41.0%; unemployed [1996] 4.5%).

Price and earnings indexes (1990 = 100)							
	1991	1992	1993	1994	1995	1996	1997
Consumer price index	104.2	107.2	109.1	112.0	115.0	117.9	128.0
Earnings index	...	...	...	...	...	...	...

Land use (1994): forested 17%; meadows and pastures 3%; agricultural and under permanent cultivation 39%; other 41%.
Tourism (1995): receipts from visitors U.S.$63,000,000; expenditures by nationals abroad U.S.$5,100,000.

Foreign trade[14]

Balance of trade (current prices)					
	1992	1993	1994	1995	1996
EC$'000,000	−120	−177	−211	−217	−242
% of total	36.1%	46.2%	53.3%	52.4%	55.8%

Imports (1995): EC$359,000,000 (basic and miscellaneous manufactures 35.3%, machinery 27.7%, food 17.1%, chemicals and chemical products 8.3%). *Major import sources:* United States 42.4%; Caricom countries 17.2%, of which Trinidad and Tobago 9.8%; United Kingdom 11.3%.
Exports (1995): EC$99,000,000 (machinery and transport equipment [mostly electronic good] 47.1%, sugar 39.3%). *Major export destinations* (1994): United States 46.6%; United Kingdom 26.4%; Caricom countries 9.3%, of which Antigua and Barbuda 2.6%.

Transport and communications

Transport. Railroads (1995)[15]: length 22 mi, 36 km. Roads (1995): total length 193 mi, 310 km (paved 43%). Vehicles (1991): passenger cars 3,700; trucks and buses 2,200. Merchant marine (1992): vessels (100 gross tons and over) 1; total deadweight tonnage 550. Air transport: passenger arrivals (1992) 123,195[16]; passenger departures, n.a.; cargo handled, n.a.; airports (1997) with scheduled flights 2.

Communications				units
				per 1,000
Medium	date	unit	number	persons
Radio	1995	receivers	26,000	659
Television	1995	receivers	9,500	241
Telephones	1994	main lines	14,000	355

Education and health

Educational attainment (1980). Percentage of population age 25 and over having: no formal schooling 1.1%; primary education 29.6%; secondary 67.2%; higher 2.1%. *Literacy* (1990): total population age 15 and over literate 25,500 (90.0%); males literate 13,100 (90.0%); females literate 12,400 (90.0%).

Education (1994–95)				student/
	schools	teachers	students	teacher ratio
Primary (age 5–12)[17]	31	366	7,101	19.4
Secondary (age 13–17)	7	326	4,541	13.9
Higher[18]	1	51	394	7.7

Health (1995): physicians (1992) 39 (1 per 1,057 persons); hospital beds 276 (1 per 142 persons); infant mortality rate per 1,000 live births 25.1[5].
Food (1995): daily per capita caloric intake 2,234 (vegetable products 76%, animal products 24%); 92% of FAO recommended minimum requirement.

Military

Total active duty personnel: in July 1997 the National Assembly approved a bill creating a 50-member army.

[1]Both Saint Christopher and Nevis and the Federation of Saint Christopher and Nevis are officially acceptable, variant, short- and long-form names of the country. [2]Includes 4 nonelective seats. [3]Nevis has full internal self-government. The Nevis legislature is subordinate to the National Assembly only with regard to external affairs and defense. [4]Based on year of registration rather than year of occurrence. [5]1994. [6]1991. [7]Employed persons only. [8]Includes sugar manufacturing. [9]Excludes sugar manufacturing. [10]Finance, real estate includes Services. [11]Net of indirect taxes less imputed service charge. [12]Detail does not add to total given because of rounding. [13]Weights of consumer price index components. [14]Imports f.o.b. in balance of trade and c.i.f. in commodities and trading partners. [15]Light railway serving the sugar industry on Saint Kitts. [16]Saint Kitts airport only. [17]1993–94. [18]1992–93.

Internet resources for further information:
• **Official web-site of the Government of St. Kitts & Nevis**
 http://www.stkittsnevis.net/

Saint Lucia

Official name: Saint Lucia.
Form of government: constitutional
monarchy with a Parliament
consisting of two legislative
chambers (Senate [11]; House of
Assembly [17[1]]).
Chief of state: British Monarch
represented by Governor-General.
Head of government: Prime Minister.
Capital: Castries.
Official language: English.
Official religion: none.
Monetary unit: 1 Eastern Caribbean
dollar (EC$) = 100 cents; valuation
(Sept. 25, 1998) 1 U.S.$ = EC$2.70;
1 £ = EC$4.60.

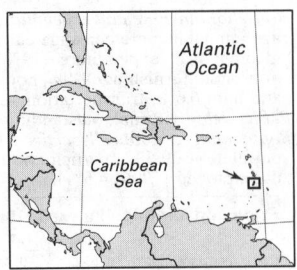

Atlantic
Ocean

Caribbean
Sea

Area and population

Districts	Capitals	area sq mi	area sq km	population 1992 estimate
Anse-la-Raye	Anse-la-Raye	18	47	5,218
Canaries	Canaries			1,864
Castries	Castries	31	79	53,883
Choiseul	Choiseul	12	31	6,638
Dennery	Dennery	27	70	11,574
Gros Islet	Gros Islet	39	101	13,996
Laborie	Laborie	15	38	7,763
Micoud	Micoud	30	78	15,636
Soufrière	Soufrière	19	51	7,962
Vieux Fort	Vieux Fort	17	44	13,617
TOTAL		238[2]	617[2]	138,151

Demography

Population (1998): 151,000.
Density (1998): persons per sq mi 634.5, persons per sq km 244.7.
Urban-rural (1995): urban 48.1%; rural 51.9%.
Sex distribution (1992): male 48.49%; female 51.51%.
Age breakdown (1992): under 15, 36.7%; 15–29, 29.4%; 30–44, 16.3%; 45–59, 8.8%; 60–74, 6.3%; 75 and over, 2.5%.
Population projection: (2000) 154,000; (2010) 172,000.
Doubling time: 37 years.
Ethnic composition (1990): black 90.5%; mixed 5.5%; East Indian 3.2%; white 0.8%.
Religious affiliation (1995): Roman Catholic 79.2%; Protestant 19.4%, of which Pentecostal 5.4%, Seventh-day Adventist 5.2%; other 1.4%.
Major city (1992): Castries city proper 2,063 (urban area 13,615).

Vital statistics

Birth rate per 1,000 population (1995): 25.2 (world avg. 25.0); legitimate 14.2%; illegitimate 85.8%.
Death rate per 1,000 population (1995): 5.9 (world avg. 9.3).
Natural increase rate per 1,000 population (1995): 19.3 (world avg. 15.7).
Total fertility rate (avg. births per childbearing woman; 1996): 2.5.
Marriage rate per 1,000 population (1995): 3.4.
Divorce rate per 1,000 population (1995): 0.2.
Life expectancy at birth (1996): male 67.5 years; female 75.0 years.
Major causes of death per 100,000 population (1992): diseases of the circulatory system 205.6, of which ischemic heart diseases 133.2; malignant neoplasms (cancers) 64.4; diseases of the respiratory system 48.5; infectious and parasitic diseases 31.1; ill-defined conditions 130.3.

National economy

Budget (1996–97). Revenue: EC$418,600,000 (consumption duties on imported goods 24.3%; taxes on income and profits 23.3%; import duties 15.9%; nontax revenue 10.2%; grants 6.5%). Expenditures: EC$456,900,000 (current expenditures 69.7%; development expenditures and net lending 30.3%).
Public debt (external, outstanding; 1996): U.S.$122,000,000.
Tourism (1995): receipts from visitors (1994) U.S.$229,500,000; expenditures by nationals abroad U.S.$25,100,000.
Production (metric tons except as noted). Agriculture, forestry, fishing (1996): bananas 135,000, mangoes 27,000, coconuts 18,000, yams 4,300, pepper 160, ginger 60; livestock (number of live animals; 1996) 14,700 pigs, 12,500 sheep, 12,450 cattle; roundwood, n.a.; fish catch (1995) 1,023. Mining and quarrying: excavation of sand for local construction and pumice. Manufacturing (value of production in EC$'000; 1995): paper products and cardboard boxes 50,173; alcoholic beverages and tobacco 30,893; electrical and electronic components 14,125; garments 8,903; refined coconut oil 6,335; food products 4,165. Construction (buildings approved; 1992): residential 91,900 sq m; non-residential 43,300 sq m. Energy production (consumption): electricity (kW-hr; 1994) 112,000,000 (112,000,000); coal, none (none); crude petroleum, none (none); petroleum products (metric tons; 1994) none (61,000); natural gas, none (none).
Household income and expenditure. Average household size (1991) 4.0; income per household: n.a.; sources of income: n.a.; expenditure (1982)[3]: food 46.8%, housing 13.5%, clothing and footwear 6.5%, transportation and communications 6.3%, household furnishings 5.8%, other 21.1%.
Population economically active (1992): total 57,797; activity rate of total population 41.8% (participation rates: ages 15–64, 72.7%; female 46.5%; unemployed [1995] 15%).

Price and earnings indexes (1990 = 100)

	1990	1991	1992	1993	1994	1995	1996
Consumer price index	100.0	105.7	111.1	112.0	115.0	121.6	114.1
Earnings index[4]	100.0	103.0	...	...	...	...	...

Gross national product (at current market prices; 1996): U.S.$553,000,000 (U.S.$3,500 per capita).

Structure of gross domestic product and labour force

	1995 in value EC$'000,000[5]	1995 % of total value[5]	1992 labour force[6]	1992 % of labour force[6]
Agriculture	135	10.5	2,824	8.9
Mining	7	0.5	...	...
Manufacturing	88	6.8	4,360	13.8
Construction	99	7.7	2,197	6.9
Public utilities	56	4.3	832	2.6
Transportation and communications	218	16.9	2,551	8.0
Trade, restaurants	334	25.9	8,714	27.5
Finance, real estate	212	16.5	3,488	11.0
Pub. admin., defense	180	14.0	6,758	21.3
Services	45	3.5	...	...
Other	−86[7]	−6.7[7]	—	—
TOTAL	1,288	100.0[8]	31,724	100.0

Land use (1994): forested 13%; meadows and pastures 5%; agricultural and under permanent cultivation 30%; other 52%.

Foreign trade[9]

Balance of trade (current prices)

	1991	1992	1993	1994	1995
U.S.$'000,000	−182	−179	−180	−202	−191
% of total	44.6%	41.0%	42.9%	50.2%	44.8%

Imports (1995): U.S.$306,000,000 (food 22.5%; machinery and transportation equipment 19.0%; chemicals and chemical products 9.5%; crude petroleum and petroleum products 7.5%). *Major import sources:* United States 36.2%; Caricom countries 22.3%, of which Trinidad and Tobago 12.4%; United Kingdom 11.1%; Japan 4.6%; Canada 3.9%.
Exports (1995): U.S.$115,000,000 (bananas 40.8%; clothing 12.1%; primarily paper and paperboard 6.2%; beer 3.8%). *Major export destinations:* United Kingdom 50.4%; United States 24.2%; Caricom countries 15.8%.

Transport and communications

Transport. Railroads: none. Roads (1994): total length 510 mi, 820 km (paved 88%). Vehicles (1993): passenger cars 10,000; trucks and buses 9,200. Merchant marine (1992): vessels (100 gross tons and over) 7; total deadweight tonnage 2,070. Air transport (1994)[10]: passenger arrivals 573,000, passenger departures 581,000; cargo unloaded 2,002 metric tons, cargo loaded 3,918 metric tons; airports (1997) with scheduled flights 2.

Communications

Medium	date	unit	number	units per 1,000 persons
Radio	1995	receivers	90,000	619
Television	1995	receivers	25,000	172
Telephones	1995	main lines	30,600	211
Cellular telephones	1995	subscribers	1,000	6.9

Education and health

Educational attainment (1980). Percentage of population age 25 and over having: no formal schooling 17.5%; primary education 74.4%; secondary 6.8%; higher 1.3%. *Literacy* (1995): about 82%.

Education (1992–93)

	schools	teachers	students	student/ teacher ratio
Primary (age 5–11)	88	1,204	32,545	27.0
Secondary (age 12–16)	14	524	9,550	18.2
Vocational	1	34	806	23.7
Higher	1	389	870	2.4

Health (1995): physicians (1992) 64 (1 per 2,159 persons); hospital beds 541 (1 per 269 persons); infant mortality rate per 1,000 live births 18.0.
Food (1995): daily per capita caloric intake 2,801 (vegetable products 73%, animal products 27%); 116% of FAO recommended minimum requirement.

Military

Total active duty personnel (1994): [11].

[1]Attorney general serves ex officio in House of Assembly if not elected (House of Assembly total 18). [2]Total includes the uninhabited 30 sq mi (78 sq km) Central Forest Reserve. [3]Castries area only. [4]Public sector only. [5]At factor cost in current prices. [6]Data exclude workers (all self-employed and many agricultural workers) not making contributions to the national insurance plan and all unemployed. [7]Less imputed bank service charges. [8]Detail does not add to total given because of rounding. [9]Imports c.i.f.; exports f.o.b. [10]Combined data for both Castries and Vieux Fort airports. [11]The more than 500-member police force includes a specially trained paramilitary unit and a coast guard unit.

Internet resources for further information:
• St. Lucia One Stop http://www.stluonestop.com/

Saint Vincent and the Grenadines

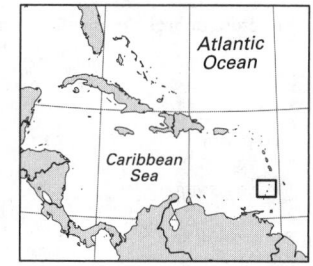

Official name: Saint Vincent and the Grenadines.
Form of government: constitutional monarchy with one legislative house (House of Assembly [211]).
Chief of state: British Monarch represented by Governor-General.
Head of government: Prime Minister.
Capital: Kingstown.
Official language: English.
Official religion: none.
Monetary unit: 1 Eastern Caribbean dollar (EC$) = 100 cents; valuation (Sept. 25, 1998) 1 U.S.$ = EC$2.70; 1 £ = EC$4.60.

Area and population

Constituencies[2]	area		population
	sq mi	sq km	1995 estimate[3]
Island of Saint Vincent			
Barrouallie	14.2	36.8	5,346
Bridgetown	7.2	18.6	7,746
Calliaqua	11.8	30.6	20,868
Chateaubelair	30.9	80.0	6,217
Colonarie	13.4	34.7	8,115
Georgetown	22.2	57.5	7,511
Kingstown (city)	1.9	4.9	15,908
Kingstown (suburbs)	6.4	16.6	11,063
Layou	11.1	28.7	6,164
Marriaqua	9.4	24.3	9,117
Sandy Bay	5.3	13.7	2,873
Saint Vincent Grenadines			
Nothern Grenadines	9.0	23.3	5,672
Southern Grenadines	7.5	19.4	2,934
TOTAL	150.3	389.3[4]	109,534

Demography

Population (1998): 113,000.
Density (1998): persons per sq mi 751.8, persons per sq km 290.3.
Urban-rural (1995)[5]: urban 24.6%; rural 75.4%.
Sex distribution (1995): male 49.90%; female 50.10%.
Age breakdown (1991): under 15, 37.2%; 15–29, 29.5%; 30–44, 16.1%; 45–59, 8.3%; 60–74, 6.4%; 75 and over, 2.5%.
Population projection: (2000) 114,000; (2010) 124,000.
Doubling time: 44 years.
Ethnic composition (1995): black 82.0%; mixed 13.9%; other 4.1%.
Religious affiliation (1995): Protestant 57.0%, of which Anglican 17.9%, Pentecostal 14.9%, Methodist 10.5%; Roman Catholic 10.7%; other/nonreligious 32.3%.
Major city (1995): Kingstown 15,908.

Vital statistics

Birth rate per 1,000 population (1995)[6]: 22.4 (world avg. 25.0); legitimate, n.a.; illegitimate, n.a.
Death rate per 1,000 population (1995)[6]: 6.6 (world avg. 9.3).
Natural increase rate per 1,000 population (1995)[6]: 15.9 (world avg. 15.7).
Total fertility rate (avg. births per childbearing woman; 1996): 2.0.
Marriage rate per 1,000 population (1994): 4.2.
Divorce rate per 1,000 population (1994): 0.8.
Life expectancy at birth (1996): male 71.4 years; female 74.5 years.
Major causes of death per 100,000 population (1994): diseases of the circulatory system 237.2, of which cerebrovascular diseases 55.7, ischemic heart disease 72.1; malignant neoplasms (cancers) 94.0; endocrine and metabolic disorders 68.4; infectious and parasitic diseases 44.7.

National economy

Budget (1995). Revenue: EC$194,800,000 (consumption duties on imports 28.9%, income taxes 24.6%, nontax revenue 12.4%, taxes on goods and services 11.7%, import duties 11.4%). Expenditures: EC$191,300,000 (current expenditure 87.0%; development expenditure 13.0%).
Public debt (external, outstanding; 1996): U.S.$86,200,000.
Land use (1994): forested 36%; meadows and pastures 5%; agricultural and under permanent cultivation 28%; other 31%.
Tourism (1995): receipts from visitors U.S.$47,200,000; expenditures by nationals abroad U.S.$5,600,000.
Production (metric tons except as noted). Agriculture, forestry, fishing (1996): bananas 55,000, coconuts 23,000, eddoes and dasheens[7] 6,252[8], sweet potatoes 1,700, mangoes 1,400, yams 1,100, oranges 960, lemons and limes 870, ginger 799[8], arrowroot starch 635[9], soursops, guavas, and papaws are other important fruits; livestock (number of live animals) 13,000 sheep, 9,400 pigs, 6,200 cattle; roundwood, n.a.; fish catch (1995) 1,480. Mining and quarrying: sand and gravel for local use. Manufacturing (export value of manufactures in U.S.$'000,000; 1995): packaged flour 8.7; packaged rice 6.4; other goods (mostly garments, sporting goods, and electronic goods) 8.1. Construction (gross floor area planned; 1994): 104,878 sq m. Energy production (consumption): electricity (kW-hr; 1995) 73,200,000 (64,100,000); coal, none (none); crude petroleum, none (none); petroleum products (metric tons; 1994) none (39,000); natural gas, none (none).
Gross national product (1996): U.S.$264,000,000 (U.S.$2,370 per capita).

Structure of gross domestic product and labour force

	1995		1991	
	in value EC$'000,000	% of total value	labour force	% of labour force
Agriculture, forestry, fishing	80.1	11.4	8,377	20.1
Mining	2.0	0.3	98	0.2
Manufacturing	50.5	7.2	2,822	6.8
Construction	67.9	9.7	3,535	8.5
Public utilities	29.7	4.2	586	1.4
Transportation and communications	120.9	17.2	2,279	5.5
Trade, restaurants	105.5	15.0	6,544	15.7
Finance, real estate	61.2	8.7	1,418	3.4
Pub. admin., defense	102.6	14.6 }	7,696	18.5
Services	10.3	1.5 }		
Other	71.0[10]	10.2[10]	8,327[11]	20.0[11]
TOTAL	702.0[4]	100.0	41,682	100.0[4]

Population economically active (1991): total 41,682; activity rate of total population 39.1% (participation rates: ages 15–64, 67.5%; female 35.9%; unemployed [1996] more than 30%).

Price and earnings indexes (1990 = 100)

	1991	1992	1993	1994	1995	1996	1997
Consumer price index	105.5	109.1	113.8	115.0	117.0	122.1	122.7
Daily earnings index[12]	100.0	100.0	100.0	100.0	100.0	...	...

Household income and expenditure. Average household size (1991) 3.9; income per household (1988) EC$4,579 (U.S.$1,696); sources of income: n.a.; expenditure (1975–76); food and beverages 59.8%, clothing 7.7%, household furnishings 6.6%, housing 6.3%, energy 6.2%, other 13.4%.

Foreign trade

Balance of trade (current prices)

	1990	1991	1992	1993	1994	1995	1996
U.S.$'000,000	−35.0	−52.9	−37.9	−61.0	−66.5	−57.4	−75.2
% of total	17.1%	22.8%	19.3%	34.8%	40.5%	31.7%	46.8%

Imports (1995): U.S.$119,400,000 (basic manufactures 44.8%; food products 21.1%; machinery and transport equipment 21.1%; chemical products 15.3%). *Major import sources:* United States 36.6%; Caricom countries 26.9%, of which Trinidad and Tobago 17.0%; United Kingdom 12.9%.
Exports (1995): U.S.$62,000,000 (domestic exports 93.8%, of which bananas 35.3%, packaged flour 14.0%, packaged rice 10.4%, eddoes and dasheens[7] 2.3%; reexports 6.2%). *Major export destinations:* Caricom countries 44.8%, of which St. Lucia 11.0%, Trinidad and Tobago 8.4%; United Kingdom 39.0%; United States 9.0%.

Transport and communications

Transport. Railroads: none. Roads (1995): total length 634 mi, 1,020 km (paved 31%). Vehicles (1994): passenger cars 5,753; trucks and buses 3,042. Merchant marine (1992): vessels (100 gross tons and over) 881; total deadweight tonnage 7,044,189. Air transport (1994): passenger arrivals 111,234, passenger departures 116,536; airports (1997) with scheduled flights 5.

Communications

Medium	date	unit	number	units per 1,000 persons
Radio	1995	receivers	65,000	591
Television	1995	receivers	17,700	161
Telephones	1995	main lines	18,200	165
Cellular telephones	1995	subscribers	100	0.9
Facsimile machines	1995	units	700	6.4

Education and health

Educational attainment (1980). Percentage of population age 25 and over having: no formal schooling 2.4%; primary education 88.0%; secondary 8.2%; higher 1.4%. *Literacy* (1991): total population age 15 and over literate 64,000 (96.0%).

Education (1993–94)

	schools	teachers	students	student/ teacher ratio
Primary (age 5–11)	65	1,080	21,386	19.8
Secondary (age 12–18)	21[13]	395	9,870	25.0
Voc., teacher tr.	2[13]	49	414	8.4

Health (1995): physicians (1992) 55 (1 per 2,000 persons); hospital beds 444 (1 per 248 persons); infant mortality rate per 1,000 live births 19.0[6].
Food (1995): daily per capita caloric intake 2,427 (vegetable products 83%, animal products 17%); 100% of FAO recommended minimum requirement.

Military

Total active duty personnel (1992): 634-member police force includes a coast guard and paramilitary unit.

[1]Includes 6 nonelective seats occupied by senators (rater than representatives); excludes speaker who may be elected from within or from outside of the House of Assembly membership. [2]For statistical purposes and the election of legislative representatives only. [3]January 1. [4]Detail does not add to total given because of rounding. [5]Urban defined as Kingstown and suburbs. [6]Based on year of registration rather than year of occurrence. [7]Varieties of taro roots. [8]1993. [9]1992–93. [10]Net of indirect taxes less imputed bank service charges. [11]Unemployed. [12]Minimum wage in private sector. [13]1991–92.

Internet resources for further information:
• **The Herald (unofficial daily newspaper) http://www.heraldsvg.com/**

Samoa[1]

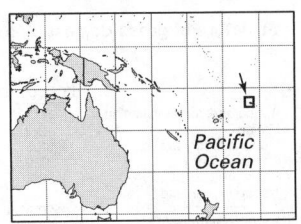

Official name: Malo Sa'oloto Tuto'atasi o Samoa (Samoan); Independent State of Samoa (English).
Form of government: constitutional monarchy[2] with one legislative house (Legislative Assembly [49]).
Chief of state: Head of State.
Head of government: Prime Minister.
Capital: Apia.
Official languages: Samoan; English.
Official religion: none.
Monetary unit: 1 tala (SA$[3], plural tala) = 100 sene; valuation (Sept. 25, 1998) 1 U.S.$ = SA$3.09; 1 £ = SA$5.27.

Area and population

Islands	area		population
			1991
Political Districts	sq mi	sq km	census
Savaii	659	1,707	45,050
Fa'aseleleaga			...
Gaga'emauga			...
Gaga'ifomauga			...
Palauli			...
Satupa'itea			...
Vaisigano			...
Upolu	432	1,119	116,248
A'ana			...
Aiga-i-le-Tai			...
Atua			...
Tuamasaga			...
Vaa-o-Fonoti			...
TOTAL	1,093[4]	2,831[4]	161,298

Demography

Population (1998): 171,100.
Density (1998): persons per sq mi 156.5, persons per sq km 60.4.
Urban-rural (1997): urban 21.0%; rural 79.0%.
Sex distribution (1991): male 52.45%; female 47.55%.
Age breakdown (1991): under 15, 40.6%; 15–29, 29.9%; 30–44, 14.6%; 45–59, 8.8%; 60–74, 5.0%; 75 and over, 1.1%.
Population projection: (2000) 174,000; (2010) 192,000.
Doubling time: 34 years.
Ethnic composition (1982): Samoan (Polynesian) c. 88%; Euronesian c. 10%; European c. 2%.
Religious affiliation (1995): Mormon 25.8%; Congregational 24.6%; Roman Catholic 21.3%; Methodist 12.2%; Pentecostal 8.0%; Seventh-day Adventist 3.9%; other Christian 1.7%; other 2.5%.
Major city (1991): Apia 34,126.

Vital statistics

Birth rate per 1,000 population (1997): 26.7 (world avg. 25.0); (1978) legitimate 43.5%; illegitimate 56.5%.
Death rate per 1,000 population (1997): 6.0 (world avg. 9.3).
Natural increase rate per 1,000 population (1997): 20.7 (world avg. 15.7).
Total fertility rate (avg. births per childbearing woman; 1997): 3.8.
Marriage rate per 1,000 population (1989)[5]: 5.3.
Divorce rate per 1,000 population (1989)[5]: 0.2.
Life expectancy at birth (1997): male 67.0 years; female 71.0 years.
Major causes of death (percent distribution; 1992)[5]: congestive heart failure 14.0%; malignant neoplasms (cancers) 11.0%; cerebrovascular diseases 8.0%; injury and poisoning 8.0%; pneumonia 6.0%; septicemia 6.0%; diabetes mellitus 4.0%; intestinal infectious diseases 2.0%.

National economy

Budget (1996–97). Revenue: WS$230,700,000 (tax revenue 55.4%; grants 30.3%; nontax revenue 14.3%). Expenditures: WS$243,800,000 (current expenditure 62.2%, of which net lending 2.3%; development expenditure 37.8%).
Production (metric tons except as noted). Agriculture, forestry, fishing (1996): coconuts 130,000, taro 36,900, bananas 10,000, papayas 10,000, pineapples 5,700, mangoes 4,900, avocados 1,700, cacao beans 400; livestock (number of live animals) 178,800 pigs, 26,000 cattle, 350,000 chickens; roundwood (1995) 131,000 cu m; fish catch (1994) 1,500. Mining and quarrying: n.a. Manufacturing (in WS$'000): beer 8,708; cigarettes 6,551; coconut cream 5,576; sawn wood 3,662; coconut oil 3,442; corned meat 2,905; soap 1,487; paints 1,457. Construction (permits issued in WS$; 1995): residential 7,749,000; commercial, industrial, and other 30,867,000. Energy production (consumption): electricity (kW-hr; 1994) 64,000,000 (64,000,000); coal, none (n.a.); crude petroleum, none (n.a.); petroleum products (metric tons; 1994) none (40,000).
Household income and expenditure. Average household size (1981) 5.1; income per household (1972) WS$1,518 (U.S.$2,200); sources of income (1972): wages 49.4%, self-employment 22.8%, remittances, gifts, and other assistance 18.0%, land rent 8.7%, other 1.1%; expenditure (1987)[6]: food 58.8%, transportation 9.0%, housing and furnishings 5.1%, fuel and lighting 5.0%, clothing 4.2%, other goods and services 1.9%, other 16.0%.
Public debt (external, outstanding; 1996): U.S.$162,800,000.
Gross national product (at current market prices; 1996): U.S.$200,000,000 (U.S.$1,170 per capita).

Structure of gross domestic product and labour force

	1996		1986	
	in value WS$'000,000	% of total value	labour force	% of labour force
Agriculture	172,000	39.9	29,023	63.6
Mining	...	...	1,587	3.5
Manufacturing	77,300	17.9 }		
Construction	8,300	1.9	62	0.1
Public utilities	27,500	6.4	855	1.9
Transp. and commun.	11,800	2.7	1,491	3.3
Trade	45,000	10.4	1,710	3.7
Finance	...	...	842	1.8
Pub. admin., defense	48,100	11.2 }	9,436	20.7
Services	41,500	9.6 }		
Other	...	...	629	1.4
TOTAL	431,500	100.0	45,635	100.0

Population economically active (1994): total 47,207; activity rate of total population 28.7% (participation rates: ages 15–64 [1981] 48.6%; female [1986] 18.8%).

Price and earnings indexes (1990 = 100)

	1991	1992	1993	1994	1995	1996	1997
Consumer price index	98.2	107.0	108.9	128.9	130.2	140.0	154.7
Earnings index	...	...	...	...	...	...	...

Tourism (1993): receipts from visitors U.S.$21,000,000; expenditures by nationals abroad U.S.$2,000,000.
Land use (1994): forested 47.3%; meadows and pastures 0.4%; agricultural and under permanent cultivation 43.1%; other 9.2%.

Foreign trade[7]

Balance of trade (current prices)

	1991	1992	1993	1994	1995	1996
WS$'000	–196,994	–238,965	–228,318	–178,638	–192,293	–199,996
% of total	83.9%	89.3%	87.4%	90.7%	81.5%	80.1%

Imports (1995): WS$235,353,000 (food 29.5%, industrial supplies 26.4%, machinery 21.6%, consumer goods 11.7%, petroleum products 10.1%). *Major import sources:* New Zealand 36.6%; Australia 20.9%; Fiji 12.0%; United States 11.9%; Japan 10.7%; Singapore 1.5%; Hong Kong 1.4%; Germany 1.0%.
Exports (1995): WS$21,859,000 (coconut oil 37.5%, coconut cream 22.6%, copra 10.2%, kava 6.7%, beer 5.3%, cigarettes 3.2%). *Major export destinations:* New Zealand 44.2%; Australia 22.2%; American Samoa 9.8%; Germany 4.3%; United States 1.7%.

Transport and communications

Transport. Railroads: none. Roads (1995): total length 485 mi, 781 km (paved 42%). Vehicles (1995): passenger cars 1,068; trucks and buses 1,169. Merchant marine (1997): vessels (100 gross tons and over) 7; total deadweight tonnage 6,501. Air transport: passenger, n.a.; cargo, n.a.; airports (1997) with scheduled flights 3.

Communications

Medium	date	unit	number	units per 1,000 persons
Radio	1996	receivers	75,000	448
Television	1995	receivers	5,000	30
Telephones	1995	main lines	7,800	47
Facsimile machines	1995	units	400	2.4

Education and health

Educational attainment (1981). Percentage of population age 25 and over having: some primary education 16.5%; complete primary 24.5%; some secondary 52.1%; complete secondary 3.1%; higher 2.0%; unknown 1.8%.
Literacy (1981): virtually 100%.

Education (1986–87)

	schools	teachers	students	student/ teacher ratio
Primary (age 5–11)	164[8]	1,511[9]	40,755	27.0
Secondary (age 12–18)	38[10]	492	11,395	23.2
Voc., teacher tr.	4[8]	37	228	6.2
Higher[8]	6	25	271	10.8

Health: physicians (1992) 60 (1 per 2,682 persons); hospital beds (1991) 863 (1 per 255 persons); infant mortality rate per 1,000 live births (1997) 59.
Food (1992): daily per capita caloric intake 2,828 (vegetable products 74%, animal products 26%); 124% of FAO recommended minimum requirement.

Military

No military forces are maintained; New Zealand is responsible for defense.

---

[1]In July 1997 the short form name of the country was officially changed from Western Samoa to Samoa. [2]According to the constitution, the current Head of State, paramount chief HH Malietoa Tanumafili II, will hold office for life. Upon his death, the monarchy will functionally cease, and future Heads of State will be elected by the Legislative Assembly. [3]Symbol of the monetary unit changed from WS$ to SA$ as of July 1997. [4]Total includes 2 sq mi (5 sq km) of uninhabited islands. [5]Registered only. [6]Consumer price index components. [7]Import figures are f.o.b. in balance of trade and c.i.f. in commodities and trading partners. [8]1983. [9]Includes some secondary teachers. [10]1982.

San Marino

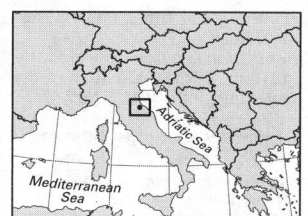

Official name: Serenissima Repubblica di San Marino (Most Serene Republic of San Marino).
Form of government: unitary multiparty republic with one legislative house (Great and General Council [60]).
Head of state and government: Captains-Regent (2).
Capital: San Marino.
Official language: Italian.
Official religion: none.
Monetary unit: 1 Italian lira (Lit; plural lire) = 100 centesimi; valuation (Sept. 25, 1998) 1 U.S.$ = Lit 1,652; 1 £ = Lit 2,813.

Area and population

Castles	Capitals	area sq mi	area sq km	population 1997[1] estimate
Acquaviva	Acquaviva	1.88	4.86	1,264
Borgo Maggiore	Borgo	3.48	9.01	5,358
Chiesanuova	Chiesanuova	2.11	5.46	866
Città	San Marino	2.74	7.09	4,350
Domagnano	Domagnano	2.56	6.62	2,207
Faetano	Faetano	2.99	7.75	870
Fiorentino	Fiorentino	2.53	6.56	1,798
Montegiardino	Montegiardino	1.28	3.31	717
Serravalle/Dogano	Serravalle	4.07	10.53	8,085
TOTAL		23.63[2]	61.19	25,515

Demography

Population (1998): 26,100.
Density (1998): persons per sq mi 1,104.5, persons per sq km 426.5.
Urban-rural (1997[1]): urban 89.3%; rural 10.7%.
Sex distribution (1997[1]): male 48.70%; female 51.30%.
Age breakdown (1997[1]): under 15, 14.9%; 15–29, 20.9%; 30–44, 25.0%; 45–59, 18.8%; 60–74, 14.0%; 75 and over, 6.4%.
Population projection: (2000) 26,900; (2010) 31,600.
Doubling time: not applicable; natural population growth is negligible.
Ethnic composition (1997[1]): Sammarinesi 83.1%; Italian 12.0%; other 4.8%.
Religious affiliation (1995): Roman Catholic 89.2%; Jehovah's Witness 1.2%; other 9.6%.
Major cities (1997[1]): Serravalle/Dogano 4,802; Borgo Maggiore 2,394; San Marino 2,294; Murata 1,549; Domagnano 1,048.

Vital statistics

Birth rate per 1,000 population (1992–96): 10.5 (world avg. 25.0); (1985) legitimate 95.2%; illegitimate 4.8%.
Death rate per 1,000 population (1992–96): 7.1 (world avg. 9.3).
Natural increase rate per 1,000 population (1992–96): 3.4 (world avg. 15.7).
Total fertility rate (avg. births per childbearing woman; 1996): 1.2.
Marriage rate per 1,000 population (1992–96): 8.1.
Divorce rate per 1,000 population (1991–95): 1.0.
Life expectancy at birth (1995): male 77.2 years; female 85.3 years.
Major causes of death per 100,000 population (1991–95): disease of the circulatory system 324.8; malignant neoplasms (cancers) 229.4; accidents, violence, and suicide 45.2; diseases of the respiratory system 10.7.

National economy

Budget (1995). Revenue: Lit 374,900,000,000 (indirect taxes 44.9%; direct taxes 28.9%; social security 17.8%). Expenditures: Lit 377,300,000,000 (current expenditures 46.8%, of which social security 39.9%, wages and salaries 30.8%; capital expenditures 6.7%; other 46.5%).
Public debt: n.a.
Tourism: number of tourist arrivals (1996) 3,345,381; receipts from visitors (1994) U.S.$252,500,000; expenditures by nationals abroad, n.a.
Population economically active (1996[1]): total 16,073; activity rate of total population 63.5% (participation rates: ages 15–64, 88.4%; female 40.2%; unemployed 3.1%).

Price and earnings indexes (1990 = 100)

	1989	1990	1991	1992	1993	1994	1995
Consumer price index	94.0	100.0	108.0	115.7	121.9	128.0	134.3
Earnings index	...	...	...	...	...	...	...

Household income and expenditure. Total number of households (1997[1]) 10,093; average household size 2.5; income per household: n.a.; sources of income: n.a.; expenditure (1991)[3]: food, beverages, and tobacco 22.1%, housing, fuel, and electrical energy 20.9%, transportation and communications 17.6%, clothing and footwear 8.0%, furniture, appliances, and goods and services for the home 7.2%, education 7.1%, health and sanitary services 2.6%, other goods and services 14.5%.
Production (metric tons except as noted). Agriculture, forestry, fishing[4]: wheat c. 4,400, grapes c. 700, barley c. 500; livestock (number of live animals; 1995) 954 cattle, 694 pigs. Manufacturing (1995): processed meats 366,177 kg, of which beef 273,515 kg, pork 85,688 kg, veal 6,902 kg; cheese 78,803 kg; butter 13,739 kg; milk 1,097,890 litres; yogurt 5,722 litres; other major products include electrical appliances, musical instruments, printing ink, paint, cosmetics, furniture, floor tiles, gold and silver jewelry, clothing,

and postage stamps. Construction (new units completed; 1995): residential 145; nonresidential 123. Energy production (consumption): all electrical power is imported via electrical grid from Italy (consumption, n.a.); coal, none (n.a.); crude petroleum, none (n.a.); petroleum products, none (n.a.); natural gas, none (n.a.).
Gross national product (at current market prices; 1994): U.S.$408,000,000 (U.S.$16,900 per capita).

Structure of labour force (1996[1])

	labour force	% of labour force
Agriculture	249	1.6
Manufacturing	5,256	32.7
Construction and public utilities	1,440	9.0
Transportation and communications	311	1.9
Trade	2,641	16.4
Finance and insurance	417	2.6
Services	1,432	8.9
Public administration and defense	3,832	23.8
Other	495[5]	3.1[5]
TOTAL	16,073	100.0

Land use (1985): agricultural and under permanent cultivation 74%; meadows and pastures 22%; forested, built-on, wasteland, and other 4%.

Foreign trade

Balance of trade: n.a. San Marino and Italy form a single customs area; separate figures for San Marino are not available.
Imports (1995): manufactured goods of all kinds, oil, and gold. *Major import source:* Italy.
Exports (1995): wine, wheat, woolen goods, furniture, wood, ceramics, building stone, dairy products, meat, and postage stamps. *Major export destination:* Italy.

Transport and communications

Transport. Railroads: none. (nearest rail terminal is at Rimini, Italy, 17 mi [27 km] northeast). Roads (1987): total length 147 mi, 237 km. Vehicles (1996[1]): passenger cars 23,561; trucks and buses 4,013. Merchant marine: vessels (100 gross tons and over) none. Air transport: airports with scheduled flights, none; there is, however, a heliport that provides passenger and cargo service between San Marino and Rimini, Italy, during the summer months.

Communications

Medium	date	unit	number	units per 1,000 persons
Daily newspapers	1995	circulation	2,000	82
Radio	1994	receivers	12,600	514
Television	1994	receivers	9,000	367
Telephones	1994	main lines	14,000	571

Education and health

Educational attainment (1997[1]). Percentage of population age 14 and over having: basic literacy[6] or primary education 35.6%; secondary 30.7%; some postsecondary 27.9%; higher degree 5.8%. *Literacy* (1997[1]): total population age 15 and over literate 21,885 (99.1%); males literate 10,546 (99.4%); females literate 11,339 (98.8%).

Education (1995–96)

	schools	teachers	students	student/teacher ratio
Primary (age 6–10)	14	217	1,134	5.2
Secondary (age 11–18)	3	134	771	5.8
Voc., teacher tr.	...	44[7]	428	6.2[7]
Higher	...	...	...	...

Health (1987): physicians 60 (1 per 375 persons); hospital beds 149 (1 per 151 persons); infant mortality rate per 1,000 live births (1990–94) 7.1.
Food (1995)[8]: daily per capita caloric intake 3,458 (vegetable products 74%, animal products 26%); 137% of FAO recommended minimum requirement.

Military

Total active duty personnel (1995): none[9]. *Military expenditure as percentage of national budget* (1992): 1.0% (world 3.6%); per capita expenditure (1987) U.S.$155.

[1]January 1. [2]Detail does not add to total given because of rounding. [3]Weighting coefficients for component expenditures are those of the 1991 official Italian consumer price index for the North-Central region of Italy. [4]Early 1980s. [5]Unemployed. [6]Includes 0.9 percent illiterate population. [7]1993–94. [8]Figures are for Italy. [9]Defense is provided by a public security force of about 50; all fit males ages 16–55 constitute a militia.

Internet resources for further information:
• San Marino http://www.emulateme.com/sanmarino.htm.

São Tomé and Príncipe

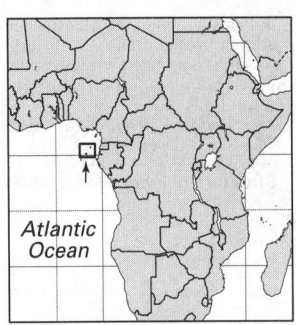

Official name: República democrática de São Tomé e Príncipe (Democratic Republic of São Tomé and Príncipe).
Form of government: Multiparty republic with one legislative house (National Assembly [55]).
Chief of state: President.
Head of government: Prime Minister.
Capital: São Tomé.
Official language: Portuguese.
Official religion: none.
Monetary unit: 1 dobra (Db) = 100 cêntimos; valuation (Sept. 25, 1998) 1 U.S.$ = Db 2,390; 1 £ = Db 4,069.

Area and population

Islands Districts	Capitals	area sq mi	area sq km	population 1991 census[1]
São Tomé		332	859	114,507
Aqua Grande	São Tomé	7	17	43,420
Cantagalo	Santana	46	119	11,421
Caué	São João Angolares	103	267	5,541
Lemba	Neves	88	229	9,448
Lobata	Guadalupe	41	105	13,101
Mé-Zóchi	Trindade	47	122	31,576
Autonomous Island		55	142	5,639
Príncipe	Santo António	55	142	5,639
TOTAL		386	1,001	120,146

Demography

Population (1998): 136,000.
Density (1998): persons per sq km 352.3, persons per sq km 135.9.
Urban-rural (1994): urban 44.1%; rural 55.9%.
Sex distribution (1997): male 49.24%, female 50.76%.
Age breakdown (1997): under 15, 47.5%; 15–29, 27.1%; 30–44, 12.5%; 45–59, 6.7%; 60–74, 4.9%; 75 and over, 1.3%.
Population projection: (2000) 141,000; (2010) 169,000.
Doubling time: 23 years.
Ethnolinguistic composition: mestiços, angolares (descendants of Angolan slaves), forros (descendants of freed slaves), serviçais (alien contract labourers), and tongas (children of serviçais) speak Portuguese; non-Portuguese-speaking Europeans speak French and Spanish.
Religious affiliation (1995): Roman Catholic, about 89.5%; remainder mostly Protestant, predominantly Seventh-day Adventist and an indigenous Evangelical Church.
Major cities (1991): São Tomé 43,420; Trindade 11,388[2]; Santana 6,190[2]; Neves 5,919[2]; Santo Amaro 5,878[2].

Vital statistics

Birth rate per 1,000 population (1995): 34.9 (world avg. 25.0); (1977) legitimate 9.8%; illegitimate 90.2%.
Death rate per 1,000 population (1995): 8.7 (world avg. 9.3).
Natural increase rate per 1,000 population (1995): 26.2 (world avg. 15.7).
Total fertility rate (avg. births per childbearing woman; 1995): 4.4.
Marriage rate per 1,000 population: n.a.
Divorce rate per 1,000 population: n.a.
Life expectancy at birth (1995): male 61.8 years; females 65.6 years.
Major causes of death per 100,000 population (1987): malaria 160.6; direct obstetric causes 76.7; pneumonia 74.0; influenza 61.5; anemias 47.3; hypertensive disease 32.1.

National economy

Budget (1996). Revenue: Db 36,547,000,000 (grants 63.6%; indirect taxes 16.7%, of which import taxes 7.0%, sales taxes 6.0%; nontax revenue 12.0%; direct taxes 7.7%). Expenditures: Db 68,387,000,000 (capital 60.8%; recurrent expenditure 39.2%, of which debt service 14.3%, personnel costs 6.1%, goods and services 5.0%).
Public debt (external, outstanding; 1996): U.S.$229,500,000.
Tourism (1990): receipts from visitors U.S.$2,000,000; expenditures by nationals abroad U.S.$2,000,000.
Production (metric tons except as noted). Agriculture, forestry, fishing (1996): coconuts 26,000, bananas 14,000, taro 7,000, vegetables and melons 3,300, corn (maize) 3,200, cacao 3,000, cereals 3,000, palm kernels 3,000, palmetto 3,000[3], cassava 2,600, fruits (other than melon) 1,900, copra 1,000[4]; livestock (number of live animals) 4,600 goats, 3,900 cattle, 2,400 sheep, 2,000 pigs; roundwood (1995) 9,000 cu m; fish catch (1995) 2,200, principally marine fish and shellfish. Mining and quarrying: some quarrying to support local construction industry. Manufacturing (value in Db; 1995): beer 880,000; clothing 679,000; lumber 369,000; bakery products 350,000; palm oil 228,000; soap 133,000; ceramics 87,000. Construction (1972): buildings authorized 44 (5,561 sq m, of which residential 3,698, mixed residential-commercial 1,361, commercial 502). Energy production (consumption): electricity (kW-hr; 1995) 18,664,000 (11,931,000); coal, none (n.a.); crude petroleum, none (n.a.); petroleum products (metric tons; 1994) none (25,000); natural gas, none (n.a.).
Household income and expenditure. Average household size (1981): 4.0; income per household: n.a.; sources of income: n.a.; expenditure (1995)[5]: food 71.9%, housing and energy 10.2%, transportation and communications 6.4%,

clothing and other items 5.3%, household durable goods 2.8%, education and health 1.7%.
Population economically active (1991): total 49,216; activity rate of total population 41.0% (participation rates [1981]: ages 15–64, 61.1%; female 32.4%; unemployed [1994[6]] 22.0%).

Price and earnings indexes (1990 = 100)

	1990	1991	1992	1993	1994	1995
Consumer price index	100.0	152.7	194.4	236.8	326.2	406.3
Earnings index	...	...	...	...	...	...

Gross national product (at current market prices; 1996): U.S.$45,000,000 (U.S.$330 per capita).

Structure of gross domestic product and labour force

	1996 in value Db '000,000	1996 % of total value	1991 labour force	1991 % of labour force
Agriculture	24,583	24.9	13,592	27.6
Mining	...	...	1,510	3.1
Manufacturing	5,250	5.3	1,510	3.1
Public utilities			269	0.6
Construction	12,487	12.6	2,866	5.8
Transportation and communications	18,754	19.0	2,186	4.4
Trade			4,451	9.0
Finance	7,484	7.6	176	0.4
Pub. admin., defense	21,788	22.0	5,592	11.4
Services	8,554	8.6	2,369	4.8
Other	...	...	16,205[7]	32.9[7]
TOTAL	98,900	100.0	49,216	100.0

Land use (1994): meadows and pastures 1.3%; agricultural and under permanent cultivation 54.0%, forest, built-on, wasteland, and other 44.7%.

Foreign trade[8]

Balance of trade (current prices)

	1991	1992	1993	1994	1995	1996
U.S.$'000,000	−24.6	−22.7	−25.4	−23.9	−24.2	−19.9
% of total	67.2%	67.8%	65.8%	64.8%	70.3%	67.0%

Imports (1995): U.S.$24,800,000 (capital goods 29.8%), food and other agricultural products 23.8%, petroleum products 15.4%). *Major import sources* (1996): Portugal 29.0%; Angola 13.3%; Belgium 10.1%; Japan 10.1%; France 8.1%; United Kingdom 4.4%; Italy 2.8%; Germany 1.2%; The Netherlands 0.8%; Gabon 0.4%.
Exports (1996): U.S.$4,900,000 (cocoa 96.4%). *Major export destinations* (1996): The Netherlands 63.9%; Germany 20.9%; Portugal 2.0%.

Transport and communications

Transport. Railroads: none. Roads (1994): total length 236 mi, 380 km (paved 66%). Vehicles (1994): passenger cars 4,581; trucks and buses 561. Merchant marine (1992): vessels (100 gross tons and over) 4; total deadweight tonnage 2,277. Air transport (1994): passenger-mi 5,000,000, passenger-km 8,000,000; short ton-mi cargo 700,000, short ton-km cargo 1,000,000; airports (1997) with scheduled flights 2.

Communications

Medium	date	unit	number	units per 1,000 persons
Radio	1996	receivers	31,000	232
Television	1995	receivers	21,000	154
Telephones	1995	main lines	2,500	19
Facsimile machines	1995	units	200	1.5

Education and health

Educational attainment (1981). Percentage of population age 25 and over having: no formal schooling 56.6%; incomplete primary education 18.0%; primary 19.2%; incomplete secondary 4.6%; complete secondary 1.3%; postsecondary 0.3%. *Literacy* (1981): total population age 15 and over literate 28,114 (54.2%); males literate 17,689 (70.2%); females literate 10,425 (39.1%).

Education (1989)

	schools	teachers	students	student/teacher ratio
Primary (age 6–13)	64	559	19,822	35.5
Secondary (age 14–18)	11[9]	318	7,446	23.4
Voc., teacher tr.	2[9]	18[10]	289	...
Higher	...	...	700[11]	...

Health: physicians (1989) 61 (1 per 1,881 persons); hospital beds (1983) 640 (1 per 158 persons); infant mortality rate per 1,000 live births (1995) 62.1.
Food (1995): daily per capita caloric intake 2,156 (vegetable products 96%, animal products 4%); 92% of FAO recommended minimum requirement.

Military

Total active duty personnel: a gendarmerie of about 900 men was to be established in the early 1900s. *Military expenditure as percentage of GNP* (1980): 1.6% (world 5.4%); per capita expenditure U.S.$6.

[1]Preliminary. [2]1981. [3]1988. [4]1994. [5]Weights based on CPI components. [6]First 10 months. [7]Includes 15,148 unemployed. [8]Import figures are c.i.f. [9]1984–85. [10]Vocational teachers only. [11]Students abroad, 1982–83.

Saudi Arabia

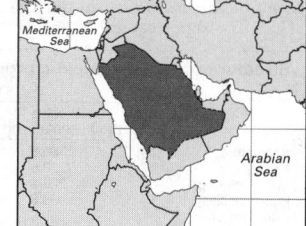

Official name: Al-Mamlakah
al-ʿArabīyah as-Saʿūdīyah (Kingdom
of Saudi Arabia).
Form of government: monarchy[1].
Head of state and government: King.
Capital: Riyadh.
Official language: Arabic.
Official religion: Islam.
Monetary unit: 1 Saudi riyal
(SRls) = 100 halalah; valuation (Sept.
25, 1998) 1 U.S.$ = SRls 3.75;
1 £ = SRls 6.38.

Area and population

Geographic Regions Administrative Regions[3]	Capitals	area[2] sq mi	sq km	population 1985 estimate
Al-Gharbīyah (Western)		—		3,043,189
Al-Bāḥah	Al-Bāḥah	6,000	15,000	...
Al-Madīnah al-Munawwarah	Medina (Al-Madīnah)	67,000	173,000	...
Makkah al-Mukarramah	Mecca (Makkah)	63,000	164,000	...
Al-Janūbīyah (Southern)		—		625,017
ʿAsīr	Abha	31,000	81,000	...
Jīzān	Jīzān	7,000	17,000	...
Najrān	Najrān	46,000	119,000	...
Ash-Shamālīyah (Northern)		—		679,476
Al-Ḥudūd ash-Shamālīyah (Northern Borders)	ʿArʿar	46,000	120,000	...
Al-Jawf	Sakākah	54,000	139,000	...
Tabūk	Tabūk	42,000	108,000	...
Ash-Sharqīyah (Eastern)		—		3,030,765
Ash-Sharqīyah (Eastern)	Ad-Dammām	274,000	710,000	...
Al-Wūsṭā (Central)		—		3,632,092
Hāʾil	Hāʾil	48,000	125,000	...
Al-Qaṣīm	Buraydah	25,000	65,000	...
Ar-Riyāḍ	Riyadh (Ar-Riyāḍ)	159,000	412,000	...
TOTAL		868,000	2,248,000	11,010,539[4]

Demography

Population (1998): 20,786,000.
Density (1998): persons per sq mi 23.9, persons per sq km 9.2.
Urban-rural (1995): urban 80.2%; rural 19.8%.
Sex distribution (1995): male 55.72%; female 44.28%.
Age breakdown (1995): under 15, 41.9%; 15–29, 24.5%; 30–44, 19.7%; 45–59, 9.5%; 60–74, 3.6%; 75 and over, 0.8%.
Population projection: (2000) 22,246,000; (2010) 31,198,000.
Doubling time: 23 years.
Ethnic composition (1995): Arab 90%; Afro-Asian 10%.
Religious affiliation (1992): Sunnī Muslim 93.3%; Shīʿī Muslim 3.3%; Christian 3.0%; other 0.4%.
Major cities (1991): Riyadh (Ar-Riyāḍ) 1,800,000; Jiddah 1,500,000; Mecca (Makkah) 630,000; Aṭ-Ṭāʾif 410,000; Medina 400,000.

Vital statistics

Birth rate per 1,000 population (1990–95): 35.1 (world avg. 25.0).
Death rate per 1,000 population (1990–95): 4.7 (world avg. 9.3).
Natural increase rate per 1,000 population (1990–95): 30.4 (world avg. 15.7).
Total fertility rate (avg. births per childbearing woman; 1990–95): 6.4.
Life expectancy at birth (1990–95): male 68.4 years; female 71.4 years.
Major causes of death per 100,000 population: n.a.

National economy

Budget (1997). Revenue: SRls 164,000,000,000 (oil revenues [1996] 76.0%).
Expenditures: SRls 181,000,000,000 (defense and security 37.6%, education 23.0%, health and social development 7.9%, transportation and communications 3.8%, municipal services 3.0%).
Public debt: n.a.
Production (metric tons except as noted). Agriculture, forestry, fishing (1997): wheat 1,500,000; barley 800,000; dates 597,000; tomatoes 500,000; potatoes 435,000; watermelons 410,000; grapes 135,000; cucumbers and gherkins 135,000; eggplants 70,000; pumpkins, squash, and gourds 70,000; carrots 30,000; millet 13,700; livestock (number of live animals) 7,800,000 sheep, 4,400,000 goats, 422,000 camels; fish catch (1994) 49,920. Mining and quarrying (1995): gypsum (1994) 337,573; gold 8,080 kg. Manufacturing (value added in U.S.$'000,000; 1994): industrial chemicals 2,663; cement, glass, and other nonmetal mineral products 875; refined petroleum 818; iron and steel 516; food, beverages, and tobacco 457; metal products 358; plastic products 206. Construction (1991): residential 16,077,677 sq m; nonresidential 2,204,894 sq m. Energy production (consumption): electricity (kW-hr; 1994) 66,760,000,000 (66,760,000,000); coal, n.a. (n.a.); crude petroleum (barrels; 1996) 2,993,000,000 ([1994] 588,700,000); petroleum products (metric tons; 1994) 87,769,000 (34,482,000); natural gas (cu m; 1994) 37,701,000,000 (37,701,000,000).
Land use (1994): forested 0.8%; meadows and pastures 55.8%; agricultural and under permanent cultivation 1.8%; built-on, waste, and other 41.6%.
Population economically active (1994): total 5,614,000; activity rate of total population 32.2% (participation rates [1988] ages 15–64, 59.1%, female 3.5%; unemployed [1997] c. 25%).

Price and earnings indexes (1990 = 100)

	1991	1992	1993	1994	1995	1996	1997
Consumer price index	104.9	104.8	105.9	106.5	111.7	113.0	113.1
Earnings index	...	...	...	...	...	...	...

Gross national product (1996): U.S.$136,640,000,0000 (U.S.$7,040 per capita).

Structure of gross domestic product and labour force

	1996		1990	
	in value[5] SRls '000,000	% of total value	labour force	% of labour force
Agriculture	32,162	6.3	569,200	9.9
Mining			3,500	0.1
Oil sector }	185,190	36.4	46,800	0.8
Manufacturing	47,652	9.4	374,900	6.5
Construction	44,447	8.7	944,100	16.4
Public utilities	853	0.2	126,900	2.2
Transp. and commun.	31,507	6.2	262,300	4.5
Trade	34,258	6.7	898,300	15.6
Finance	28,002[6]	5.5[6]	99,000	1.7
Pub. admin., defense	88,873	17.5	624,800	10.8
Services	13,800	2.7 }	1,822,000	31.6
Other	2,542[7]	0.5[7]		
TOTAL	509,286	100.0[8]	5,771,800	100.0[8]

Household income and expenditure. Average household size (1992) 6.1; income per household: n.a.; sources of income: n.a.; expenditure (1988)[9]: food 37%, housing 21%, transportation and communications 15%, clothing 8%, household furnishings 7%, education and entertainment 2%.
Tourism (in U.S.$'000,000): receipts (1989) 2,050; expenditures (1988) 2,000.
Pilgrims to Mecca from abroad (1996): more than 2,000,000.

Foreign trade[10]

Balance of trade (current prices)

	1992	1993	1994	1995	1996	1997
U.S.$'000,000	+20,039	+16,522	+21,289	+24,390	+35,370	+33,530
% of total	24.9%	24.2%	33.3%	32.2%	41.1%	39.1%

Imports (1996): SRls 103,979,000,000 (machinery and appliances 21.0%, transport equipment 15.3%, metals and metal articles 10.0%, chemicals and chemical products 8.1%, vegetables 7.4%, textiles and clothing 7.3%, live animals and animal products 4.9%). *Major import sources:* U.S. 21.9%; U.K. 9.0%; Germany 7.5%; Japan 7.0%; Italy 4.7%; Switzerland 4.7%.
Exports (1996): SRls 212,353,000,000[11] (petroleum 88.6%, of which crude 72.3%; petrochemicals 4.9%). *Major export destinations*[12]: Japan 16.9%; U.S. 15.0%; S. Korea 10.6%; Singapore 7.9%; France 4.5%; India 3.3%.

Transport and communications

Transport. Railroads (1995): route length 1,390 km; (1993–94) passenger-km 139,000,000; (1993–94) metric ton-km cargo 816,000,000. Roads (1995): total length 159,000 km (paved 42.7%). Vehicles (1995): passenger cars 1,710,000; trucks and buses 1,172,600. Merchant marine (1992): vessels (100 gross tons and over) 301; total deadweight tonnage 1,381,651. Air transport (1995)[13]: passenger-km 18,501,400,000; metric ton-km cargo 894,900,000; airports (1997) with scheduled flights 25.

Communications

Medium	date	unit	number	units per 1,000 persons
Daily newspapers	1994	circulation	950,000	54
Radio	1995	receivers	3,800,000	213
Television	1995	receivers	4,600,000	257
Telephones	1995	main lines	1,719,400	96
Cellular telephones	1995	subscribers	16,000	0.9
Facsimile machines	1995	units	78,700	4.4
Personal computers	1995	units	600,000	34

Education and health

Educational attainment (1986). Percentage of population age 25 and over having: no formal schooling 31.8%; primary, secondary, or higher education 68.2%. *Literacy* (1995): percentage of population age 15 and over literate 62.8%; males literate 71.5%; females literate 50.2%.

Education (1995–96)

	schools	teachers	students	student/ teacher ratio
Primary (age 6–12)	11,217	169,321	2,248,122	13.3
Secondary (age 13–18)	6,346[14]	105,056	1,375,753	13.1
Voc., teacher tr.	293[14, 15]	4,473	49,032	11.0
Higher[14]	77	18,039	233,710	13.0

Health (1995): physicians 30,306 (1 per 590 persons); hospital beds 41,916 (1 per 427 persons); infant mortality rate per 1,000 live births (1990–95) 29.0.
Food (1995): daily per capita caloric intake 2,746 (vegetable products 88%, animal products 12%); 113% of FAO recommended minimum requirement.

Military

Total active duty personnel (1997): 105,500 (army 66.4%, navy 12.8%, air force 20.9%). *Military expenditure as percentage of GDP* (1995): 13.5% (world 2.8%); per capita expenditure U.S.$919.

[1]Assisted by the Consultative Council consisting of 90 appointed members. [2]Estimated. [3]13 administrative regions created September 1993. [4]Preliminary 1992 census total 16,929,294; detail, n.a. [5]In producers' values at current prices. [6]Finance includes real estate and business services. [7]Other equals import duties less imputed bank services charge. [8]Detail does not add to total given because of rounding. [9]Urban middle-income households only. [10]Import figures are f.o.b. in balance of trade and c.i.f. in commodities and trading partners. [11]Includes re-exports. [12]Based on direction of trade statistics. [13]Domestic and international operation of Saudi Arabian Airlines. [14]1994–95. [15]Includes intermediate colleges.

Senegal

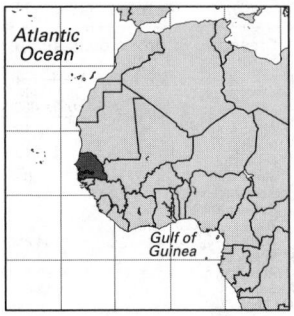

Official name: République du Sénégal (Republic of Senegal).
Form of government: multiparty republic with one legislative house (National Assembly [140]).
Chief of state: President.
Head of government: Prime Minister.
Capital: Dakar.
Official language: French.
Official religion: none.
Monetary unit: 1 CFA franc (CFAF) = 100 centimes; valuation (Sept. 25, 1998) 1 U.S.$ = CFAF 560.38; 1 £ = CFAF 954.05.

Area and population

Regions	Capitals	area sq mi	area sq km	population 1994 estimate
Dakar	Dakar	212	550	1,869,000
Diourbel	Diourbel	1,683	4,359	750,000
Fatick	Fatick	3,064	7,935	569,000
Kaolack	Kaolack	6,181	16,010	948,000
Kolda	Kolda	8,112	21,011	689,000
Louga	Louga	11,270	29,188	525,000
Saint-Louis	Saint-Louis	17,034	44,117	749,000
Tambacounda	Tambacounda	23,012	59,602	449,000
Thiès	Thiès	2,549	6,601	1,115,000
Ziguinchor	Ziguinchor	2,834	7,339	467,000
TOTAL		75,951	196,712	8,127,000[1]

Demography

Population (1998): 9,723,000.
Density (1998): persons per sq mi 128.0, persons per sq km 49.4.
Urban-rural (1995): urban 42.3%; rural 57.7%.
Sex distribution (1996): male 50.05%; female 49.95%.
Age breakdown (1995): under 15, 44.6%; 15–29, 26.9%; 30–44, 15.5%; 45–59, 8.3%; 60–74, 3.9%; 75 and over, 0.8%.
Population projection: (2000) 10,390,000; (2010) 14,362,000.
Doubling time: 21 years.
Ethnic composition (1988): Wolof 48.1%; Serer 12.6%; Peul (Fulani) and Tukulor 21.7%; Diola 5.0%; Malinke (Mandingo) 3.7%; other 8.9%.
Religious affiliation (1988): Sunnī Muslim 92.0%; traditional beliefs and other 6.0%; Christian (predominantly Roman Catholic) 2.0%.
Major cities (1994): Dakar 785,071 (urban agglomeration 1,869,323[2]); Thiès 216,381; Kaolack 193,115; Ziguinchor 161,680; Rufisque 138,837[3]; Saint-Louis 132,444.

Vital statistics

Birth rate per 1,000 population (1996): 45.5 (world avg. 25.0).
Death rate per 1,000 population (1996): 11.8 (world avg. 9.3).
Natural increase rate per 1,000 population (1996): 33.7 (world avg. 15.7).
Total fertility rate (avg. births per childbearing woman; 1996): 6.3.
Marriage rate per 1,000 population: n.a.[4].
Divorce rate per 1,000 population: n.a.
Life expectancy at birth (1996): male 53.7 years; female 59.3 years.
Major causes of death (percentage of officially confirmed deaths from infectious diseases only; 1988): malaria 44.8%; tetanus 17.8%; meningitis 15.3%; tuberculosis of respiratory system 10.4%.

National economy

Budget (1996). Revenue: CFAF 452,600,000,000 (tax revenue 80.7%, grants 11.1%, nontax revenue 8.2%). Expenditures: CFAF 452,000,000,000 (current expenditures 71.8%, development expenditure 28.2%).
Production (metric tons except as noted). Agriculture, forestry, fishing (1996): sugarcane 883,000, peanuts (groundnuts) 816,000, millet 650,000, paddy rice 160,000, sorghum 125,000, corn (maize) 110,000, oil palm fruit 70,000, cassava 56,000, seed cotton 37,000; livestock (number of live animals) 4,800,000 sheep, 3,250,000 goats, 2,900,000 cattle, 502,000 horses; roundwood (1995) 5,220,000 cu m; fish catch (1995) 261,000. Mining and quarrying (1996): phosphate 1,376,000; salt (1994) 87,600. Manufacturing (1993): cement (1994) 590,000; phosphoric acid (1996) 258,000; fertilizers 147,900; wheat flour (1995) 110,000; sugar 46,100; soap 35,700; canned fish 22,476; cigarettes (1992) 3,350,000,000 units; plastic footwear 507,500 pairs. Construction (authorized; 1993)[5]: residential 357,000 sq m; nonresidential 235,000 sq m. Energy production (consumption): electricity (kW-hr; 1994) 769,000,000 (408,000,000); coal, none (none); crude petroleum (barrels; 1994) none (6,392,000); petroleum products (metric tons; 1994) 856,000,000 (903,000,000); natural gas, none (none).
Population economically active (1988): total 2,347,556; activity rate of total population 34.0% (participation rates: ages 15–60, 53.1%; female 25.6%; unemployed [1992] 24.4%).

Price and earnings indexes (1990 = 100)

	1991	1992	1993	1994	1995	1996	1997
Consumer price index[5]	98.2	98.1	97.6	129.1	139.2	143.1	145.6
Hourly earnings index	...	...	...	...	...	...	...

Household income and expenditure. Average household size (1991) 8.7; average annual income per household: n.a.; sources of income: n.a.; expenditure (early 1980s): food 49%, clothing and footwear 11%, housing 7%, education 6%.

Public debt (external, outstanding; 1996): U.S.$3,891,000,000.
Gross national product (at current market prices; 1996): U.S.$18,206,000,000 (U.S.$3,410 per capita).

Structure of gross domestic product and labour force

	1996 in value CFAF '000,000,000[6]	1996 % of total value	1991 labour force	1991 % of labour force
Agriculture	360.8	21.4	1,789,467	65.3
Mining	2.6	0.2	1,998	0.1
Manufacturing	228.3	13.6	161,124	5.9
Public utilities	36.8	2.2	...	...
Construction	66.5	4.0	60,935	2.2
Transp. and commun.	159.0	9.4	58,081	2.1
Trade	355.4	21.1	378,241	13.8
Finance	...	...	4,623	0.2
Services	190.6	11.3	...	...
Pub. admin., defense	281.9	16.8	268,721	9.8
Other	—	—	16,286	0.6
TOTAL	1,681.9	100.0	2,739,476	100.0

Tourism (1995): receipts from visitors U.S.$130,000,000; expenditures by nationals abroad U.S.$75,000,000.
Land use (1994): forested 39.5%; meadows and pastures 29.6%; agricultural and under permanent cultivation 12.2%; other 18.7%.

Foreign trade[7]

Balance of trade (current prices)

	1991	1992	1993	1994	1995	1996	1997
CFAF '000,000,000	−133.2	−95.6	−151.8	−215.7	−219.8	−143.9	−154.7
% of total	25.2%	21.2%	29.6%	21.4%	20.3%	12.5%	12.5%

Imports (1995): U.S.$1,344,000,000 (agricultural products 34.5%, of which rice 7.1%, fixed vegetable oils 5.2%; capital goods 15.0%[9]; refined petroleum 11.0%[8]). *Major import sources:* France 37.8%; Cameroon 7.9%; Nigeria 6.9%; Italy 5.4%; Thailand 4.6%.
Exports (1995): U.S.$680,000,000 ([8]fish and crustaceans 28.0%; chemical products 12.0%; peanut [groundnut] oil 11.0%; phosphates 3.0%). *Major export destinations*[8]: France 30.0%; Italy 13.0%; Mali 7.0%; Spain 5.0%; India 4.0%.

Transport and communications

Transport. Railroads: (1995) route length 562 mi, 904 km; (1993) passenger-mi 128,000,000, passenger-km 206,000,000; short ton-mi cargo 476,000,000, metric ton-km cargo 695,000,000. Roads (1995): total length 9,060 mi, 14,580 km (paved 29%). Vehicles (1995): passenger cars 80,600, trucks and buses 32,410. Merchant marine (1992): vessels (100 gross tons and over) 183; total deadweight tonnage 27,473. Air transport (1996)[9]: passenger-mi 139,644,000, passenger-km 224,736,000; short ton-mi cargo 11,247,000, metric ton-km cargo 16,420,000; airports (1996) with scheduled flights 7.

Communications

Medium	date	unit	number	units per 1,000 persons
Daily newspapers	1994	circulation	50,000	5.9
Radio	1996	receivers	850,000	93
Television	1995	receivers	61,000	6.9
Telephones	1995	main lines	82,000	9.3
Cellular telephones	1995	subscribers	100	0.01
Personal computers	1995	units	60,000	6.8

Education and health

Educational attainment (1988). Percentage of population age 6–34 having: no formal schooling 62.6%; primary education 25.7%; secondary 8.4%; higher 0.8%; other 2.5%. *Literacy* (1995): percentage of total population age 15 and over literate 1,523,000 (33.1%); males literate 985,000 (43.0%); females literate 538,000 (23.2%).

Education (1992–93)

	schools	teachers	students	student/ teacher ratio
Primary (age 6–12)	2,454	12,711	738,550	58.1
Secondary (age 13–18)	359	5,509	182,140	33.1
Vocational	19	182	7,301	40.1
Higher[10]	2	784	16,733	21.3

Health (1992); physicians 520 (1 per 14,825 persons); hospital beds 7,408 (1 per 1,041 persons); infant mortality rate per 1,000 live births (1996): 64.0.
Food (1995): daily per capita caloric intake 2,416 (vegetable products 91%, animal products 9%); 102% of FAO recommended minimum requirement.

Military

Total active duty personnel (1996): 13,400[11] (army 89.9%, navy 5.2%, air force 4.9%). *Military expenditure as percentage of GNP* (1995): 1.6% (world 2.8%); per capita expenditure U.S.$9.

---

[1]Detail does not add to total given because of rounding. [2]Urbanized area of Pikine (1994 population estimate 855,287) is within Dakar urban agglomeration. [3]Within Dakar urban agglomeration. [4]In 1996 about half of all women lived in polygymous unions. [5]Capital region only. [6]At constant 1987 prices. [7]Imports f.o.b.; exports c.i.f. [8]Estimated figure(s). [9]Represents 1/11 of total international scheduled traffic of Air Afrique (government-supported airline of 11 West African countries). [10]Universities only; 1994–95. [11]Excludes 1,500 French troops.

Internet resources for further information:
• **République du Sénégal (French language only)**
  http://www.primature.sn/

Seychelles

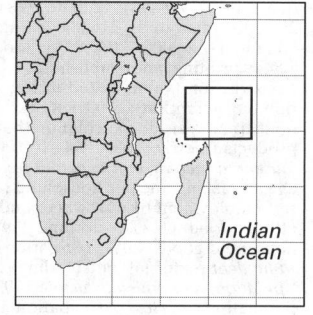

Official name: Repiblik Sesel (Creole);
Republic of Seychelles (English);
République des Seychelles (French).
Form of government: multiparty
republic with one legislative house
(National Assembly [34]).
Head of state and government:
President.
Capital: Victoria.
Official languages: none[1].
Official religion: none.
Monetary unit: 1 Seychelles rupee
(SR) = 100 cents; valuation (Sept. 25,
1998) 1 U.S.$ = SR 5.27;
1 £ = SR 8.97.

*Indian
Ocean*

Area and population		area		population
				1987
Island Groups	Capital	sq mi	sq km	census
Central (Granitic) group				
La Digue and satellites	—	6	15	1,926
Mahé and satellites	Victoria	61	158	61,183
Praslin and satellites	—	16	42	5,002
Silhouette	—	8	20	191
Other islands	—	2	4	0
Outer (Coralline) islands	—	83	214	296
TOTAL		176	455[2]	68,598

Demography

Population (1998): 79,400.
Density (1998): persons per sq mi 451.1, persons per sq km 174.5.
Urban-rural (1990): urban 59.3%; rural 40.7%.
Sex distribution (1997): male 48.37%; female 51.63%.
Age breakdown (1997): under 15, 30.2%; 15–29, 31.1%; 30–44, 21.9%; 45–59,
8.2%; 60–74, 6.0%; 75 and over, 2.6%.
Population projection: (2000) 82,000; (2010) 94,400.
Doubling time: 47 years.
Ethnic composition (1983): Seychellois Creole (mixture of Asian, African, and
European) 89.1%; Indian 4.7%; Malagasy 3.1%; Chinese 1.6%; English
1.5%.
Religious affiliation (1996): Roman Catholic 86.6%; other Christian (mostly
Anglican) 9.3%; Hindu 1.3%; other 2.8%.
Major city (1993): Victoria 25,000.

Vital statistics

Birth rate per 1,000 population (1997): 20.0 (world avg. 25.0); (1993) legitimate
21.6%; illegitimate 78.4%.
Death rate per 1,000 population (1997): 7.0 (world avg. 9.3).
Natural increase rate per 1,000 population (1997): 13.0 (world avg. 15.7).
Total fertility rate (avg. births per childbearing woman; 1997): 2.0.
Marriage rate per 1,000 population (1993): 11.3.
Divorce rate per 1,000 population (1993): 1.1.
Life expectancy at birth (1997): male 65.7 years; female 75.6 years.
Major causes of death per 100,000 population (1993): diseases of the cir-
culatory system 239.4, of which cerebrovascular disease 72.0; malignant
neoplasms (cancers) 141.2; diseases of the respiratory system 87.2, of which
pneumonia 23.5; infectious and parasitic diseases 49.8; diseases of the
digestive system 47.1; accidents and adverse effects 45.7.

National economy

Budget (1997). Revenue: SR 1,377,900,000 (customs taxes and duties 40.9%,
dividends and interest 10.8%, business taxes 10.6%, transfers from Social
Security Fund 7.3%, administrative fees 7.0%, fees and fines 4.1%, grants
2.9%). Expenditures: SR 1,363,100,000 (debt service 18.6%, capital projects
11.0%, education 10.6%, health 8.6%, social security 7.3%, tourism and
transport 6.7%, defense 3.7%).
Tourism (1996): receipts from visitors SR 531,400,000; expenditures by nationals abroad U.S.$24,000,000[3].
Land use (1994): forested 11.1%; agricultural and under permanent cultivation 15.6%; built-on, wasteland, and other 73.3%.
Gross national product (1996): U.S.$526,000,000 (U.S.$6,850 per capita).

Structure of gross domestic product and labour force				
	1996			
	in value SR '000,000	% of total value	labour force[4]	% of labour force
Agriculture	104.0	4.1	1,717	6.5
Mining, manufacturing, and construction	571.0	22.5	5,153	19.6
Tourism	240.0	9.4	4,846	18.4
Transportation and communications	726.5	28.6	4,076	15.5
Finance	255.0	10.0 }		
Pub. admin., defense	351.9	13.8 }	10,484	39.9
Other	293.3	11.5 }		
TOTAL	2,541.7	100.0[2]	26,276	100.0[2]

Production (metric tons except as noted). Agriculture, forestry, fishing (1997):
coconuts 3,600, bananas 1,850, copra 1,000[5], cinnamon 650, tea 250; livestock (number of live animals) 18,200 pigs, 4,900 goats, 2,100 cattle, 540,000
chickens; fish catch (1996) 4,508, of which (1989) jack 36.9%, snapper 20.8%,
mackerel 6.7%, kawakawa 5.3%. Mining and quarrying (1994): guano 5,000.

Manufacturing (1996): canned tuna 12,708; soft drinks 78,520 hectolitres;
beer and stout 63,650 hectolitres; cigarettes 62,000,000 units. Energy production (consumption): electricity (kW-hr; 1994) 126,000,000 (126,000,000);
coal, none (n.a.); crude petroleum, none (n.a.); petroleum products (metric
tons; 1994) none (55,000); natural gas, none (n.a.).
Population economically active (1993): total 28,100; activity rate of total population 38.9% (participation rates: ages 15–64 [1989] 74.3%; female [1989]
42.5%; unemployed 11.5%).

Price and earnings indexes (1990 = 100)							
	1992	1993	1994	1995	1996	1997	1998[6]
Consumer price index	105.3	106.7	108.7	108.4	107.2	107.9	109.3
Monthly earnings index	117.3	115.0	115.4	120.2	...	...	...

Public debt (external, outstanding; 1996): U.S.$138,100,000.
Household income and expenditure. Average household size (1987) 4.5; average annual income per household (1978) SR 18,480 (U.S.$2,658); sources of
income: wages and salaries 77.2%, self-employment 3.8%, transfer payments
3.2%; expenditure (1991–92): food and beverages 47.6%, housing 15.1%,
clothing and footwear 8.6%, transportation 8.0%, energy and water 7.4%,
recreation 6.7%, household and personal goods 6.6%.

Foreign trade

Balance of trade (current prices)						
	1992	1993	1994	1995	1996	1997
SR '000,000	−735.2	−969.8	−786.7	−855.7	−1,188.7	−1,131.4
% of total	59.9%	64.7%	60.6%	62.8%	46.1%	49.4%

Imports (1996): SR 1,882,419,000 (machinery and transport equipment 44.7%,
of which aircraft and spare parts 24.6%, electrical machinery 7.9%, nuclear
reactors, boilers, and other heavy machinery 6.9%; manufactured goods
18.7%, of which metal manufactures 5.0%, paper and wood products 3.6%;
food, beverages, and tobacco 18.3%; mineral fuels [including petroleum],
lubricants, and related materials 11.2%; chemicals 4.8%). *Major import
sources:* United States 26.5%; United Kingdom 11.3%; Yemen 10.6%; South
Africa 10.4%; Singapore 9.2%; France 7.0%; Italy 3.6%; India 2.4%; Japan
2.2%; Germany 2.1%; Spain 1.8%; Thailand 1.8%; The Netherlands 1.3%.
Exports (1996): SR 693,744,000[7] (canned tuna 24.5%; petroleum products
21.8%[8]; other fish, including dried shark fins 2.1%; frozen prawns 1.6%; cinnamon bark 0.7%). *Major export destinations* (1995)[9]: China 15.0%; United
Kingdom 12.4%; Thailand 11.5%; India 3.5%; Germany 2.6%; United States
1.8%; Japan 1.8%.

Transport and communications

Transport. Railroads: none. Roads (1996): total length 214 mi, 345 km (paved
80%). Vehicles (1995): passenger cars 5,100; trucks and buses 2,000. Merchant
marine (1992): vessels (100 gross tons and over) 9; total deadweight tonnage
3,337. Air transport (1996): passenger arrivals 151,000, passenger departures
151,000; metric ton cargo unloaded 3,390, metric ton cargo loaded 1,112; airports (1997) with scheduled flights 2.

Communications				units
				per 1,000
Medium	date	unit	number	persons
Daily newspapers	1995	circulation	3,000	41.0
Radio	1995	receivers	50,000	666.9
Television	1995	receivers	13,000	173.4
Telephones	1996	main lines	15,712	206.4
Cellular telephones	1996	subscribers	1,043	13.7
Facsimile machines	1996	units	650[10]	8.5

Education and health

Educational attainment (1987). Percentage of population age 12 and over having: no formal schooling 7.8%; primary education 51.5%; some secondary
12.2%; complete secondary 13.4%; vocational 9.9%; postsecondary 3.1%;
unspecified 2.1%. *Literacy* (1987): total population age 15 and over literate
37,984 (84.2%); males literate 18,427 (82.9%); females literate 19,557
(85.7%).

Education (1997)				student/
	schools	teachers	students	teacher ratio
Primary (age 6–15)	27[3]	633	9,825	15.5
Secondary (age 16–18)	20[11]	440	6,548	14.9
Voc., teacher tr.	1[11]	134	1,338	10.0

Health[12] (1996): physicians 84 (1 per 906 persons); hospital beds 414 (1 per
184 persons); infant mortality rate per 1,000 live births (1997) 17.0.
Food (1995): daily per capita caloric intake 2,428 (vegetable products 83%,
animal products 17%); 104% of FAO recommended minimum requirement.

Military

Total active duty personnel (1997): 400[13]. *Military expenditure as percentage of
GNP* (1995): 3.9% (world 2.8%); per capita expenditure U.S.$192.

---

[1]Creole, English, and French are all national languages per 1993 constitution. [2]Detail
does not add to total given because of rounding. [3]1995. [4]Excludes unemployed, self-
employed, and domestic workers. [5]1993. [6]March. [7]Includes SR 488,711,000 of reexports. [8]Items reexported. [9]Domestic export only. [10]Number of subscribers. [11]1994.
[12]Physicians and hospital beds in government hospitals only. [13]All services form part
of the army.

Internet resources for further information:
• **UN in Mauritius and Seychelles http://pub.intnet.mu/un**

Sierra Leone

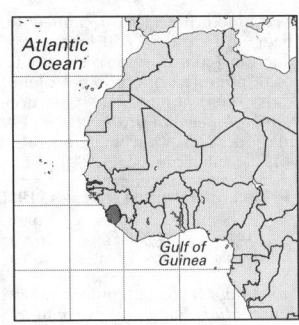

Official name: Republic of Sierra Leone.
Form of government: republic with one legislative body (Parliament [80[1]][2]).
Head of state and government: President.
Capital: Freetown.
Official language: English.
Official religion: none.
Monetary unit: 1 leone (Le) = 100 cents; valuation (Sept. 25, 1998) 1 U.S.$ = Le 1,550; 1 £ = Le 2,639.

Area and population		area		population
Provinces				1985
Districts	Capitals	sq mi	sq km	census[3]
Eastern Province	Kenema	6,005	15,553	960,551
Kailahun	Kailahun	1,490	3,859	233,839
Kenema	Kenema	2,337	6,053	337,055
Kono	Sefadu	2,178	5,641	389,657
Northern Province	Makeni	13,875	35,936	1,259,641
Bombali	Makeni	3,083	7,985	317,729
Kambia	Kambia	1,200	3,108	186,231
Koinaduga	Kabala	4,680	12,121	183,286
Port Loko	Port Loko	2,208	5,719	329,344
Tonkolili	Magburaka	2,704	7,003	243,051
Southern Province	Bo	7,604	19,694	741,377
Bo	Bo	2,015	5,219	268,671
Bonthe (incl. Sherbro)	Bonthe	1,339	3,468	105,007
Moyamba	Moyamba	2,665	6,902	250,514
Pujehun	Pujehun	1,585	4,105	117,185
Western Area[4]	Freetown	215	557	554,243
TOTAL		27,699	71,740	3,515,812

Demography

Population (1998): 4,577,000[5].
Density (1998): persons per sq mi 165.2, persons per sq km 63.8.
Urban-rural (1996): urban 37.0%; rural 63.0%.
Sex distribution (1996): male 49.02%; female 50.98%.
Age breakdown (1995): under 15, 44.2%; 15–29, 26.2%; 30–44, 15.7%; 45–59, 9.0%; 60–74, 4.2%; 75 and over, 0.7%.
Population projection: (2000) 4,866,000; (2010) 6,056,000.
Doubling time: 29 years.
Ethnic composition (1983): Mende 34.6%; Temne 31.7%; Limba 8.4%; Kono 5.2%; Bullom-Sherbro 3.7%; Fulani 3.7%; Kuranko 3.5%; Yalunka 3.5%; Kissi 2.3%; other 3.4%.
Religious affiliation (1993): Muslim 60.0%; traditional 30.0%; Christian 10.0%.
Major cities (1985): Freetown 469,776; Koidu–New Sembehun 80,000; Bo 26,000; Kenema 13,000; Makeni 12,000.

Vital statistics

Birth rate per 1,000 population (1990–95): 49.1 (world avg. 25.0); legitimate n.a.; illegitimate n.a.
Death rate per 1,000 population (1990–95): 25.1 (world avg. 9.3).
Natural increase rate per 1,000 population (1990–95): 24.0 (world avg. 15.7).
Total fertility rate (avg. births per childbearing woman; 1990–95): 6.5.
Marriage rate per 1,000 population: n.a.
Divorce rate per 1,000 population: n.a.
Life expectancy at birth (1990–95): male 41.4 years; female 44.6 years.
Major causes of death per 100,000 population: n.a.; however, the major diseases are malaria, tuberculosis, leprosy, measles, tetanus, and diarrhea.

National economy

Budget (1995–96). Revenue: Le 69,700,000,000 (customs duties 49.0%; excise taxes 20.2%; personal income tax 7.7%; corporate income tax 6.8%). Expenditures: Le 141,941,000,000 (recurrent expenditures 81.5%, of which defense 34.0%, debt service 11.3%, education 8.0%, health 4.3%, social security 1.6%; capital expenditures 18.5%).
Gross national product (1996): U.S.$925,000,000 (U.S.$200 per capita).

Structure of gross domestic product and labour force				
	1994–95		1991	
	in value Le '000,000	% of total value	labour force	% of labour force
Agriculture	275,327.5	38.8	945,000	61.7
Mining	119,229.2	16.8		
Manufacturing	61,475.3	8.6	275,000	18.0
Construction	15,788.2	2.2		
Public utilities	2,816.8	0.4		
Transp. and commun.	61,267.5	8.6		
Trade[8]	98,270.1	13.8		
Finance	14,732.2	2.1	312,000	20.3
Pub. admin., defense	19,844.9	2.8		
Services	12,308.9	1.7		
Other	29,329.7[9]	4.2[9]		
TOTAL	710,389.3[10]	100.0	1,532,000	100.0

Production (metric tons except as noted). Agriculture, forestry, fishing (1996): rice 391,700, cassava 281,400, sweet potatoes 46,400, peanuts (groundnuts) 35,800, tomatoes 32,000, palm kernels 29,160, plantains 26,000, coffee 25,000, sugarcane 21,000, millet 20,700, sorghum 20,500, cacao beans 10,000; livestock (number of live animals) 360,200 cattle, 301,900 sheep, 165,800 goats, 50,000 pigs; roundwood (1995) 3,327,600 cu m; fish catch (1995) 62,568. Mining and

quarrying (1995–96): bauxite 728,000[6]; rutile and ilmenite (titanium ores) 203,000[6]; diamonds 216,000 carats; gold 3,949 oz[7]. Manufacturing (value added in Le '000,000; 1993): food 36,117; chemicals 10,560; earthenware 1,844; printing and publishing 1,171; metal products 1,073; furniture 647. Construction (value added in Le; 1994–95): 15,788,200,000. Energy production (consumption): electricity (kW-hr; 1994) 237,000,000 (237,000,000); coal, none (n.a.); crude petroleum (barrels; 1994) none (2,148,000); petroleum products (metric tons; 1994) 168,000 (138,000); natural gas, none (n.a.).
Household income and expenditure. Average household size (1985) 6.6; average annual income per household (1984): U.S.$320; sources of income (1984): self-employment 61.6%, wages and salaries 27.9%, other 10.5%; expenditure (1989): food 66.2%, clothing 9.9%, housing 5.8%, transportation 4.4%, household goods 4.0%, recreation and education 3.8%, health 3.5%.
Public debt (external, outstanding; 1996): U.S.$892,000,000.
Population economically active (1991): total 1,532,000; activity rate of total population 35.9% (participation rates: ages 10–64, 53.3%; female 32.4%; unemployed [registered] 1992) 10.6%).

Price index (1990 = 100)							
	1991	1992	1993	1994	1995	1996	1997
Consumer price index	202.7	335.7	409.9	509.1	641.5	789.9	908.0

Tourism (1995): receipts U.S.$6,000,000; expenditures U.S.$2,000,000.
Land use (1994): forest 28.5%; pasture 30.7%; agriculture 7.5%; other 33.3%.

Foreign trade[11]

Balance of trade (current prices)						
	1991	1992	1993	1994	1995	1996
Le '000,000	−1,542	+2,142	−16,553	−20,742	−84,480	−150,622
% of total	1.7%	1.4%	11.0%	13.3%	70.1%	63.6%

Imports (1995–96): Le 144,896,500,000 (food and live animals 51.6%; fuels and lubricants 11.6%; chemicals 10.2%; machinery and transport equipment 8.9%; beverages and tobacco 2.7%; crude minerals 2.5%). *Major import sources* (1994–95): U.S. 42.7%; The Netherlands 14.2%; U.K. 5.7%; Indonesia 3.7%; Germany 3.0%.
Exports (1995–96): Le 39,935,100,000 (mineral exports 56.4%, of which diamonds 50.6%, rutile [titanium ore] 5.7%; cocoa 5.0%; coffee 3.7%; reexports 4.8%). *Major export destinations* (1994–95): U.S. 44.8%; U.K. 17.3%; Belgium 16.8%; The Netherlands 4.1%; Germany 2.0%.

Transport and communications

Transport. Railroads (1990): length 52 mi, 84 km. Roads (1995): total length 7,254 mi, 11,674 km (paved 11%). Vehicles (1995): passenger cars 20,860; trucks and buses 11,014. Merchant marine (1992): vessels (100 gross tons and over) 62; total deadweight tonnage 18,384. Air transport (1985)[12]: passenger-mi 68,290,000, passenger-km 109,903,000; short ton-mi cargo 1,400,000, metric ton-km cargo 2,044,000; airports (1997) with scheduled flight 1.

Communications				units per 1,000
Medium	date	unit	number	persons
Daily newspapers	1995	circulation	9,200	2
Radio	1995	receivers	330,000	72
Television	1995	receivers	1,600	0.3
Telephones	1995	main lines	16,600	4

Education and health

Educational attainment (1985). Percentage of population age 5 and over having: no formal schooling 64.1%; primary education 18.7%; secondary 9.7%; higher 1.5%. *Literacy* (1995): total population age 15 and over literate 791,000 (31.4%); males literate 555,000 (45.4%); females 236,000 (18.2%).

Education (1992–93)				student/
	schools	teachers	students	teacher ratio
Primary (age 5–11)	1,643	10,595	267,425	25.2
Secondary (age 12–18)	167	4,313	70,900	16.4
Voc., teacher tr.	44	709	7,756	10.9
Higher[13]	2	257	2,571	10.0

Health: physicians (1992) 404 (1 per 10,832 persons); hospital beds (1988) 4,025 (1 per 980 persons); infant mortality rate (1990–95) 166.
Food (1995): daily per capita caloric intake 2,029 (vegetable products 96%, animal products 4%); 88% of FAO recommended minimum requirement.

Military

Total active duty personnel (1996): 14,200 (army 98.6%, navy 1.4%, air force, none). *Military expenditure as percentage of GNP* (1995): 4.6% (world 2.8%); per capita expenditure U.S.$9.

[1]Includes 12 paramount chiefs elected to represent each of the provincial districts. [2]The popularly elected government overthrown in May 1997 was restored to power in February 1998 by ECOMOG, a Nigerian-led West African military force. [3]Preliminary figures exclude adjustment for underenumeration; adjusted total is 3,760,000. [4]Not officially a province; the administration of the Western Area is split among Greater Freetown (the city and its suburbs) and other administrative bodies. [5]Including more than 450,000 Sierra Leonean refugees temporarily residing in Guinea and Liberia. [6]1994–95; production ceased January 1995 with seizure of mines by rebel forces. [7]1994–95. [8]Includes hotels. [9]Import duties less imputed bank service charges. [10]Detail does not add to total given because of rounding. [11]Import c.i.f.; exports f.o.b. [12]International flights only. [13]1990–91.

Internet resources for further information:
• **Sierra Leone** http://www.Sierra-Leone.org

Singapore

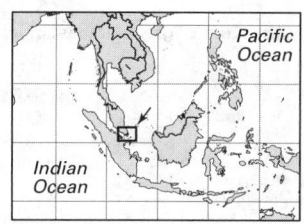

Official name: Hsin-chia-p'o
 Kung-ho-kuo (Mandarin Chinese);
 Republik Singapura (Malay);
 Singapore Kudiyarasu (Tamil);
 Republic of Singapore (English).
Form of government: unitary multiparty
 republic with one legislative house
 (Parliament [90[1]]).
Chief of state: President.
Head of state government: Prime Minister.
Capital: Singapore.
Official languages: Chinese; Malay;
 Tamil; English.
Official religion: none.
Monetary unit: 1 Singapore dollar
 (S$) = 100 cents; valuation (Sept. 25,
 1998) 1 U.S.$ = S$1.69; 1 £ = S$2.88.

Population (1990 census)

Census division[2]	population	Census division[2]	population	Census division[2]	population
Alexandra	27,245	Henderson	18,445	Nee Soon East	58,651
Aljunied	51,669	Hong Kah Central	48,379	Nee Soon South	49,771
Ang Mo Kio	35,814	Hong Kah North	33,265	Pasir Panjang	35,824
Ayer Rajah	44,977	Hong Kah South	37,900	Paya Lebar	41,903
Bedok	22,032	Hougang	36,774	Potong Pasir	32,992
Boon Lay	39,249	Jalan Besar	28,298	Punggol	68,270
Boon Teck	22,652	Jalan Kayu	34,907	Queenstown	19,676
Braddell Heights	47,738	Joo Chiat	35,777	Radin Mas	35,730
Brickworks	10,593	Jurong	74,696	Sembawang	28,039
Bukit Batok	44,918	Kaki Bukit	32,782	Serangoon Gardens	44,702
Bukit Gombak	46,149	Kallang	34,178	Siglap	36,022
Bukit Merah	18,666	Kampong Chai Chee	33,928	Tampines East	41,474
Bukit Panjang	95,827	Kampong Glam	29,481	Tampines North	73,634
Bukit Timah	47,056	Kampong Kembangan	33,510	Tampines West	38,833
Buona Vista	23,873	Kampong Ubi	40,682	Tanah Merah	32,314
Cairnhill	48,445	Kebun Baru	36,878	Tanglin	43,544
Changi	50,003	Kim Keat	28,538	Tanjong Paper	29,217
Changkat	41,995	Kim Seng	23,683	Teck Ghee	26,622
Cheng San	27,821	Kolam Ayer	22,420	Telok Blangah	29,157
Chong Boon	32,174	Kreta Ayer	29,631	Thomson	71,345
Chong Pang	38,613	Kuo Chuan	26,968	Tiong Bahru	27,468
Chua Chu Kang	43,465	Leng Kee	28,886	Toa Payoh	22,811
Clementi	37,635	Macpherson	23,764	Ulu Pandan	42,923
Eunos	52,976	Marine Parade	31,003	West Coast	46,052
Fengshan	27,285	Moulmein	33,872	Whampoa	18,285
Geylang Serai	36,800	Mountbatten	23,891	Yio Chu Kang	28,589
Geyang West	34,560	Nee Soon Central	47,032	Yuhua	32,733
				TOTAL	3,016,379

Demography

Area: 249.5 sq mi, 646.1 sq km.
Population (1998)[3]: 3,164,000.
Density (1998): persons per sq mi 12,681, persons per sq km 4,897.
Urban-rural: urban 100.0%.
Sex distribution (1996): male 50.29%; female 49.71%.
Age breakdown (1996): under 15, 22.8%; 15–29, 22.8%; 30–44, 28.9%; 45–59, 15.5%; 60–74, 7.4%; 75 and over, 2.6%.
Population projection: (2000) 3,288,000; (2010) 3,985,000.
Doubling time: 64 years.
Ethnic composition (1996): Chinese 77.3%; Malay 14.1%; Indian 7.3%.
Religious affiliation (1995)[4]: Buddhist 31.9%; Taoist 22.0%; Muslim 14.9%; Christian 12.9%; Hindu 3.3%; traditional beliefs 0.5%; nonreligious 14.5%.

Vital statistics

Birth rate per 1,000 population (1996): 16.0 (world avg. 25.0).
Death rate per 1,000 population (1996): 5.1 (world avg. 9.3).
Natural increase rate per 1,000 population (1996): 10.9 (world avg. 15.7).
Total fertility rate (avg. births per childbearing woman; 1996): 1.7.
Marriage rate per 1,000 population (1996): 7.9.
Divorce rate per 1,000 population (1994): 1.3.
Life expectancy at birth (1996): male 74.4 years; female 78.9 years.
Major causes of death per 100,000 population (1994): diseases of the circulatory system 185.3; malignant neoplasms (cancers) 128.9; diseases of the respiratory system 87.0; accidents, poisoning, and violence 32.5.

National economy

Budget (1996). Revenue: S$28,038,000,000 (income tax 34.0%, nontax revenue 21.8%, motor vehicle taxes 8.7%, goods and services tax 6.4%, customs and excise duties 5.9%). Expenditures: S$19,175,000,000 (security 36.5%, education 18.2%, general services 9.1%, communications 5.6%, health 5.5%).
Production (metric tons except as noted). Agriculture, forestry, fishing (1996): vegetables and fruits 5,310; livestock (number of live animals) 2,000,000 chickens; fish catch 9,665. Mining and quarrying (value of output in S$; 1994): granite 75,800,000. Manufacturing (value added in S$'000,000; 1995): machinery and appliances 18,752.6; chemical products 3,113.2; fabricated metal products 2,355.4; transport equipment 2,322.4; paper products 2,064.1. Construction (completed; 1994): residential 3,999,000 sq m; nonresidential 2,213,000 sq m. Energy production (consumption): electricity (kW-hr; 1994) 20,676,000,000 (20,585,000,000); crude petroleum (barrels; 1994) none (408,-800,000); petroleum products (metric tons; 1994) 47,760,000 (18,989,000).
Household income and expenditure. Average household size (1990) 4.2; income per household (1993) S$45,948 (U.S.$28,437); sources of income (1987–88): wages 81.2%, self-employment 16.8%, transfer payments and other 2.0%;

expenditure (1992–93): food 30.0%, housing costs and furnishings 23.4%, transportation and communications 15.8%, recreation and education 9.0%, clothing and footwear 6.1%, health 2.8%, others 12.9%.
Gross national product (1996): U.S.$92,987,000,000 (U.S.$30,550 per capita).

Structure of gross domestic product and labour force

	1996			
	in value S$'000,000[5]	% of total value[5]	labour force[6]	% of labour force[6]
Agriculture	192.2	0.2	} 3,700	0.2
Quarrying	28.0	...		
Manufacturing	29,485.5	26.9	406,300	23.2
Construction	8,982.8	8.2	115,000	6.6
Public utilities	1,868.6	1.7	7,200	0.4
Transp. and commun.	14,500.7	13.2	195,300	11.2
Trade	19,834.9	18.1	405,900	23.2
Finance	29,905.2	27.2	246,000	14.1
Services	11,454.6	10.4	367,700	21.0
Other	−6,465.4[7]	−5.9[7]	1,000[8]	0.1[8]
TOTAL	109,787.1	100.0	1,748,100	100.0

Population economically active (1995): total 1,748,200; activity rate of total population 58.5% (participation rates: ages 15 and over, 64.3%; female 38.7%; unemployed 2.7%).

Price and earnings indexes (1990 = 100)

	1991	1992	1993	1994	1995	1996	1997
Consumer price index	103.4	105.8	108.2	111.5	113.5	115.0	117.3
Monthly earnings index	109.2	118.1	125.5	136.5	144.8	153.6	162.3

Tourism (1995): receipts U.S.$8,212,000,000; expenditures U.S.$5,134,000,000.

Foreign trade[9]

Balance of trade (current prices)

	1991	1992	1993	1994	1995	1996
S$'000,000	−5,770	−7,490	−10,338	−216	+1,178	+1,631
% of total	2.7%	3.5%	4.1%	0.1%	0.4%	0.5%

Imports (1996): S$185,183,400,000 (office machines 11.7%, crude petroleum 6.1%, telecommunications apparatus 5.5%, electric power machinery 3.7%, petroleum products 3.3%, scientific instruments 3.0%, industrial machinery 2.5%). *Major import sources:* Japan 18.2%; U.S. 16.3%; Malaysia 15.0%; Thailand 5.5%; Taiwan 4.0%; Saudi Arabia 3.8%; Germany 3.7%.
Exports (1996): S$176,271,900,000 (office machines 26.5%, telecommunications apparatus 8.0%, petroleum products 7.7%, optical instruments 2.1%, electrical circuit apparatus 2.0%, industrial machinery 1.6%, clothing 1.1%). *Major export destinations:* U.S. 18.4%; Malaysia 18.0%; Hong Kong 8.9%; Japan 8.2%; Thailand 5.7%; Taiwan 4.0%; Germany 3.1%.

Transport and communications

Transport. Railroads (1996): length 83 km. Roads (1995): total length 3,035 km (paved [1994] 97%). Vehicles (1996): passenger cars 384,450; trucks and buses 139,113. Air transport (1996): passenger-km 53,640,000,000; metric ton-km cargo 4,191,000,000; airports (1997) 1.

Communications

Medium	date	unit	number	units per 1,000 persons
Daily newspapers	1995	circulation	1,015,100	340
Radio	1996	receivers	822,000	270
Television	1995	receivers	650,000	218
Telephones	1995	main lines	1,429,000	478
Cellular telephones	1995	subscribers	291,900	98
Facsimile machines	1995	units	55,600	19
Personal computers	1995	units	515,000	172

Education and health

Educational attainment (1990). Percentage of population age 25 and over having: no schooling 64.0%; primary education 31.3%; postsecondary 4.7%. *Literacy* (1990): total population age 10 and over literate 89.1%; males literate 95.1%; females literate 83.0%.

Education (1995)

	schools	teachers	students	student/ teacher ratio
Primary (age 6–11)	199	10,356	261,648	25.3
Secondary (age 12–18)	178	9,777	203,662	20.8
Voc., teacher tr.	11	1,382	9,476	6.9
Higher	7	6,902	83,914	12.2

Health (1996): physicians 4,566 (1 per 667 persons); hospital beds 10,668 (1 per 285 persons); infant mortality rate per 1,000 live births 3.8.
Food (1988–90): daily per capita caloric intake 3,121 (vegetable products 76%, animal products 24%); 136% of FAO recommended minimum requirement.

Military

Total active duty personnel (1996): 53,900 (army 83.5%, navy 5.4%, air force 11.1%). *Military expenditure as percentage of GNP* (1995): 4.7% (world 2.8%); per capita expenditure U.S.$1,329.

---

[1]Includes 7 nonelective seats. [2]The census divisions have no administrative function. [3]De jure population. [4]De jure population aged 10 years and over. [5]At prices of 1990. [6]Employed only. [7]Imputed bank service charges. [8]Activities not adequately defined. [9]Import figures are f.o.b. in balance of trade.

Internet resources for further information:
 • **Statistics Singapore http://www.singstat.gov.sg/**

Slovakia

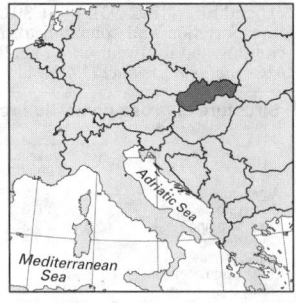

Official name: Slovenská Republika (Slovak Republic).
Form of government: unitary multiparty republic with one legislative house (National Council [150]).
Chief of state: President.
Head of government: Prime Minister.
Capital: Bratislava.
Official language: Slovak.
Official religion: none.
Monetary unit: 1 Slovak koruna (Sk) = 100 halura; valuation (Sept. 25, 1998) 1 U.S.$ = Sk 34.84; 1 £ = Sk 59.32.

Area and population

Regions[1]	Capitals	area sq mi	area sq km	population 1997[2] estimate
Banská Bystrica	Banská Bystrica	3,651	9,455	664,024
Bratislava	Bratislava	793	2,053	618,904
Košice	Košice	2,607	6,753	758,494
Nitra	Nitra	2,449	6,343	717,585
Prešov	Prešov	3,472	8,993	773,121
Trenčín	Trenčín	1,738	4,501	610,135
Trnava	Trnava	1,602	4,148	548,898
Žilina	Žilina	2,621	6,788	687,771
TOTAL		18,933	49,035[3]	5,378,932

Demography

Population (1998): 5,425,000.
Density (1998): persons per sq mi 286.5, persons per sq km 110.6.
Urban-rural (1991): urban 56.8%; rural 43.2%.
Sex distribution (1995): male 48.69%; female 51.31%.
Age breakdown (1995): under 15, 22.3%; 15–29, 23.8%; 30–44, 22.9%; 45–59, 15.9%; 60–74, 11.5%; 75 and over, 3.6%.
Population projection: (2000) 5,466,000; (2010) 5,676,000.
Doubling time: not applicable; population growth is negligible.
Ethnic composition (1995): Slovak 85.7%; Hungarian 10.6%; Gypsy 1.6%; Czech 1.1%; Ruthenian 0.3%; Ukrainian 0.3%; German 0.1%; other 0.3%.
Religious affiliation (1991): Roman Catholic 60.3%; nonreligious and atheist 9.7%; Protestant 7.9%, of which Slovak Evangelical 6.2%, Reformed Christian 1.6%; Greek Catholic 3.4%; Eastern Orthodox 0.7%; other 18.0%.
Major cities (1996): Bratislava 452,053; Košice 240,915; Prešov 92,687.

Vital statistics

Birth rate per 1,000 population (1996): 11.2 (world avg. 25.0); legitimate 86.0%; illegitimate 14.0%.
Death rate per 1,000 population (1996): 9.5 (world avg. 9.3).
Natural increase rate per 1,000 population (1995): 1.6 (world avg. 15.7).
Total fertility rate (avg. births per childbearing woman; 1996): 1.5.
Marriage rate per 1,000 population (1996): 5.1.
Divorce rate per 1,000 population (1996): 1.8.
Life expectancy at birth (1996): male 68.8 years; female 76.7 years.
Major causes of death per 100,000 population (1995): diseases of the circulatory system 541.1; malignant neoplasms (cancers) 206.5.

National economy

Budget (1995). Revenue: Sk 163,138,000,000 (tax revenue 80.3%; nontax revenue 16.3%; customs 3.3%; insurance 0.1%). Expenditures: Sk 171,437,000,000 (education, health, and social welfare 39.7%; debt service 6.8%).
Public debt (external, outstanding; 1996): U.S.$3,891,000,000.
Production (metric tons except as noted). Agriculture, forestry, fishing (1996): cereals 3,941,000 (of which wheat 2,112,000, barley 960,000, corn [maize] 650,000, rye 105,600); livestock (number of live animals) 2,076,000 pigs, 929,000 cattle, 430,000 sheep; roundwood (1995) 4,887,000 cu m; fish catch (1993) 2,773. Mining and quarrying (1995): iron ore 820,000; lead-zinc ore 300,000; copper ore 280,000. Manufacturing (1995): crude steel 3,958,000; pig iron 3,207,000[4]; cement 2,981,000; plastic and resins 449,900; flour 375,000; nitrogenous fertilizers 229,300; cotton yarn 11,655; beer 4,369,000 hectolitres; refrigerators and freezers 330,200 units. Construction (1991): residential 1,147,000 sq m. Energy production (consumption): electricity (kW-hr; 1994) 24,740,000,000 (25,898,000,000[5]); coal (metric tons; 1995) 3,725,000 (14,390,000[5]); crude petroleum (barrels; 1994) 492,850 (32,866,000); petroleum products (metric tons; 1993) 3,603,000 (2,323,000); natural gas (cu m; 1994) 288,000,000 (5,037,986,000[5]).
Household income and expenditure. Average household size (1995) 4.0; income per household (1994) Sk 48,190[7] (U.S.$1,545[7]); sources of income (1995): wages and salaries 78.9%, transfer payments 8.1%, other 13.0%; expenditure (1995): food and beverages 26.4%, taxes 18.7%, clothing and footwear 8.7%, housing 7.7%, household durable goods 3.5%, other 35.0%.
Population economically active (1995): total 2,586,300; activity rate of total population 48.2% (participation rates: ages 15–64, 76.4%; female 66.0%; unemployed 6.1%).

Price and earnings indexes (1990 = 100)

	1991	1992	1993	1994	1995	1996	1997
Consumer price index	100.1	109.9	139.9	158.6	174.4	184.5	195.8
Annual earnings index	100.0	118.7	140.1	166.0	198.5	227.6	238.4

Gross national product (1996): U.S.$18,206,000,000 (U.S.$3,410 per capita).

Structure of gross domestic product and labour force

	1995 in value Sk '000,000	1995 % of total value	1995 labour force[6]	1995 % of labour force
Agriculture	32,634	6.3	208,000	9.7
Mining and manufacturing	140,378	27.1	582,000	27.2
Construction	26,418	5.1	158,000	7.4
Public utilities	24,346	4.7	51,000	2.4
Transp. and commun.	48,174	9.3	158,000	7.4
Trade	116,550	22.5	303,000	14.2
Finance	29,526	5.7	33,000	1.5
Pub. admin., defense	34,188	6.6	381,000	17.8
Services	65,786	12.7	184,000	8.6
Other	—	—	80,000	3.7
TOTAL	518,000	100.0	2,138,000	100.0[3]

Land use (1994): forested 40.6%; meadows and pastures 17.0%; agricultural and under permanent cultivation 32.9%; other 9.5%.

Foreign trade

Balance of trade (current prices)

	1993	1994	1995	1996	1997
Sk '000,000	−26,920	+2,564	−5,695	−70,260	−49,475
% of total	7.4%	0.6%	1.1%	11.5%	7.7%

Imports (1995): Sk 260,791,000,000 (machinery and transport equipment 28.9%; semimanufactured products 17.8%; petroleum and petroleum products 17.5%; chemical products 13.6%; manufactured products 8.0%). *Major import sources:* Czech Republic 27.8%; Russian Federation 16.6%; Germany 14.3%; Austria 5.1%; Italy 4.6%; Poland 2.8%.
Exports (1995): Sk 255,096,000,000 (semimanufactured products 40.4%; machinery and transport equipment 18.8%; chemical products 13.2%; manufactured goods 12.2%; food, beverages, and tobacco 5.9%). *Major export destinations:* Czech Republic 35.3%; Germany 18.8%; Austria 5.0%.

Transport and communications

Transport. Railroads (1995): length 3,665 km; passenger-km 4,202,000,000; metric ton-km cargo 13,674,000,000. Roads (1995): total length 17,869 km (paved, n.a.). Vehicles (1995): passenger cars 1,015,794; trucks and buses 97,516. Merchant marine: n.a. Air transport (1994): passenger-km 60,283,000,000; metric ton-km cargo 5,557,000; airports (1996) with scheduled flights 2.

Communications

Medium	date	unit	number	units per 1,000 persons
Daily newspapers	1994	circulation	1,363,000	256[4]
Television	1995	receivers	1,157,000	216
Telephones	1995	main lines	1,119,000	208
Cellular telephones	1995	subscribers	12,300	2.3
Facsimile machines	1995	units	44,700	5.3

Education and health

Educational attainment (1991). Percentage of adult population having: incomplete primary education 0.5%; primary and incomplete secondary 30.6%; complete secondary 58.6%; higher 9.4%; unknown 0.9%. *Literacy* (1990): total population age 15 and over literate 3,980,202 (100%); males literate 1,916,410 (100%); females literate 2,063,792 (100%).

Education (1995–96)

	schools	teachers	students	student/ teacher ratio
Primary (age 6–14)	2,485	39,224	661,082	16.7
Secondary (age 15–18)	190	5,457	76,380	14.0
Voc., teacher tr.	364	9,558	119,853	12.5
Higher	14	8,014	74,322	9.3

Health (1995): physicians 14,081 (1 per 381.2 persons); hospital beds 62,634 (1 per 86 persons); infant mortality rate per 1,000 live births (1996) 10.2.

Military

Total active duty personnel (1996): 47,000 (army 70.2%, air force 29.8%). *Military expenditure as percentage of GNP* (1994): 2.4% (world 3.0%); per capita expenditure U.S.$160.

---

[1]Based on administrative reorganization effective from July 1996. [2]January 1. [3]Detail does not add to total given because of rounding. [4]1995. [5]1993. [6]Excluding women on regular and additional maternity leave and including employees with a second job. [7]Households of employees with two children and wife not economically active.

Internet resources for further information:
• **Slovak Information Agency** http://www.sia.gov.sk

Slovenia

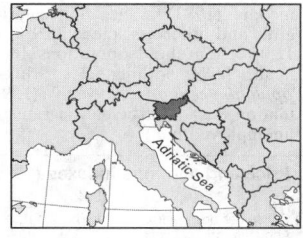

Official name: Republika Slovenija (Republic of Slovenia).
Form of government: unitary multiparty republic with two legislative houses (National Council [40]; National Assembly [90]).
Head of state: President.
Head of government: Prime Minister.
Capital: Ljubljana.
Official language[1]: Slovene.
Official religion: none.
Monetary unit: 1 Slovene tolar (SIT; plural tolarji) = 100 stotin; valuation (Sept. 25, 1998) 1 U.S.$ = 158.77 tolarji; 1 £ = 270.31 tolarji.

Area and population		area		population
Statistical regions	Capital	sq mi	sq km	1995 estimate
Dolenjska	—	642	1,663	101,917
Gorenjska	—	824	2,135	192,523
Goriška	—	897	2,322	118,627
Koroška	—	401	1,041	73,715
Notranjsko-kraška	—	562	1,456	49,214
Obalno Kraško	—	403	1,043	100,193
Osrednjeslovenska	—	1,369	3,546	507,486
Podravska	—	837	2,168	324,156
Pomurska	—	516	1,336	128,923
Savinjska	—	919	2,380	256,076
Spodnjeposavska	—	349	905	73,750
Zasavska	—	102	263	45,820
TOTAL	—	7,821	20,256[2]	1,972,400

Demography

Population (1998): 1,985,000.
Density (1998): persons per sq mi 253.8, persons per sq km 98.0.
Urban-rural (1991): urban 50.5%; rural 49.5%.
Sex distribution (1995): male 48.59%; female 51.41%.
Age breakdown (1995): under 15, 18.1%; 15–29, 22.3%; 30–44, 23.8%; 45–59, 17.9%; 60–74, 13.6%; 75 and over, 4.3%.
Population projection: (2000) 1,982,000; (2010) 2,004,000.
Doubling time: not applicable; population is static.
Ethnic composition (1991): Slovene 87.8%; Croat 2.8%; Serb 2.4%; Bosnian Muslim 1.4%; Hungarian (Magyar) 0.4%; other 5.2%.
Religious affiliation (1995): Christian 86.2%, of which Roman Catholic 82.7%, Orthodox 2.0%, Protestant 1.3%; Muslim 1.0%; other 12.8%.
Major cities (1995): Ljubljana 269,621; Maribor 134,289; Novo Mesto 50,862; Kranj 50,791; Celje 49,459.

Vital statistics

Birth rate per 1,000 population (1996): 9.3 (world avg. 25.0); legitimate 70.2%; illegitimate 29.8%.
Death rate per 1,000 population (1996): 4.8 (world avg. 9.3).
Natural increase rate per 1,000 population (1996): 4.5 (world avg. 15.7).
Total fertility rate (avg. births per childbearing woman; 1995): 1.3.
Marriage rate per 1,000 population (1995): 4.2.
Divorce rate per 1,000 population (1995): 0.8.
Life expectancy at birth (1994–95): male 70.3 years; female 77.8 years.
Major causes of death per 100,000 population (1995): circulatory diseases 408.1; cancers 235.6; accidents 87.6; respiratory diseases 74.7; digestive diseases 56.7; endocrine and metabolic disorders 28.8.

National economy

Budget (1995). Revenue: SIT 1,006,794,900,000 (taxes 52.3%, of which value-added tax 28.1%, income tax 14.5%, duties 7.7%, social security 40.2%; non-tax revenue 5.9%; privatization 1.6%). Expenditures; SIT 1,016,005,400,000 (pensions 26.9%; work of provider organizations 15.6%; health services 12.9%; social transfers 7.4%; capital expenditure 5.8%; defense 3.1%).
Public debt (external, outstanding; 1996): U.S.$2,038,000,000.
Production (metric tons except as noted). Agriculture, forestry, fishing (1996): potatoes 407,000, corn (maize) 322,000, sugar beets 295,000, wheat 167,000, grapes 105,000; livestock (number of live animals) 592,000 pigs, 496,000 cattle, 9,320,000 poultry; roundwood (1995) 1,709,000 cu m; fish catch (1995) 2,929. Mining and quarrying (1995): glass sand 200,000; pumice 40,000; ferrosilico calcium 12,000. Manufacturing (1995): cement 991,000; crude steel 407,000; paper 278,000; glue 85,632; welded tubular steel 61,575; refrigerators 863,000 units; telephones 749,000 units; washing machines and dryers 242,000 units; motorcycles 56,198 units. Construction (in '000 sq m; 1996): residential 581; nonresidential 4,596. Energy production (consumption): electricity (kW-hr; 1994) 12,616,000,000 (9,376,000,000); coal (metric tons; 1994) 4,854,000 (4,915,000); crude petroleum (barrels; 1994) 12,578 (1993; 3,540,000); petroleum products (metric tons; 1993) 452,000 (1,966,000); natural gas (cu m; 1994) 12,595,000 (396,000,000).
Household income and expenditure. Average household size (1994) 3.1; income per household (1995) SIT 1,805,135 (1994; U.S.$10,191); sources of income (1995): wages 53.2%, transfers 24.6%, self-employment 9.7%, other 12.5%; expenditure (1995): food 23.1%, transportation 16.2%, clothing 7.3%, health care 6.7%, education and entertainment 6.7%, energy 5.8%, household durable goods 4.8%, housing 4.3%.
Gross national product (1996): U.S.$18,390,000,000 (U.S.$9,240 per capita).

Structure of gross domestic product and labour force

	1995			
	in value SIT '000,000	% of total value	labour force	% of labour force
Agriculture	95,674	4.3	8,840	1.0
Mining	23,119	1.1		
Manufacturing	538,351	24.5	235,457	24.7
Construction	97,368	4.4	29,725	3.1
Public utilities	52,803	2.4	8,427	1.0
Transp. and commun.	140,221	6.4	29,893	3.1
Trade	225,478	10.2	55,855	5.9
Finance	305,324	13.9	36,509	3.8
Pub. admin., defense	101,747	4.6	40,146	4.2
Services	269,929	12.3	146,694	15.4
Other	352,007[3]	15.9[3]	360,454[4]	37.8[4]
TOTAL	2,202,021	100.0	952,000	100.0

Population economically active (1995): total 952,000; activity rate 58.7% (participation rates: ages 15–64, 83.0%; female 45.2%; unemployed 7.4%).

Price and earnings indexes (1990 = 100)							
	1992	1993	1994	1995	1996	1997	1998
Consumer price index	659	867	1,040	1,172	1,285	1,402	1,529[5]
Monthly earnings index	546	826	1,059	1,256	1,442	1,606	...

Land use (1994): forest 53.2%; pasture 24.8%; agricultural 11.6%; other 10.4%.
Tourism (1995): receipts U.S.$1,079,000,000; expenditures U.S.$413,000,000.

Foreign trade[6]

Balance of trade (current prices)						
	1992	1993	1994	1995	1996	1997
U.S.$'000,000	+789	−154	−338	−771	−882	−772
% of total	6.3%	1.2%	2.4%	4.4%	5.0%	4.4%

Imports (1995): U.S.$9,492,000,000 (machinery and transport equipment 33.8%, chemicals 12.1%, basic manufactures 10.6%, food 6.7%, mineral fuels 6.6%). *Major import sources:* Germany 23.2%; Italy 17.0%; Austria 9.7%; France 8.4%; Croatia 6.1%.
Exports (1995): U.S.$8,316,000,000 (machinery and transport equipment 31.4%, basic manufactures 28.5%, chemicals 10.5%, food 3.2%, mineral fuels 1.2%). *Major export destinations:* Germany 30.2%; Italy 14.6%; Croatia 10.7%; France 8.2%; Austria 6.4%.

Transport and communications

Transport. Railroads (1995): length 746 mi, 1,201 km; passenger-km 595,-000,000; metric ton-km cargo 2,881,000,000. Roads (1994): total length 9,158 mi, 14,739 km (paved 79%). Vehicles (1995): passenger cars 698,211; trucks and buses 40,206. Merchant marine (1995): vessels (100 gross tons and over) 13; total deadweight tonnage 346,466. Air transport (1995): passenger-mi 382,000,000, passenger-km 614,000,000; short ton-mi cargo 2,271,000, metric ton-km cargo 3,655,000; airports (1996) 1.

Communications				units per 1,000
Medium	date	unit	number	persons
Daily newspapers	1994	circulation	360,000	181
Radio	1997	receivers	630,000	317
Television	1995	receivers	745,000	374
Telephones	1995	main lines	614,800	309
Cellular telephones	1995	subscribers	27,000	13.6
Facsimile machines	1995	units	15,500	7.8
Personal computers	1995	units	95,000	47.7

Education and health

Educational attainment (1991). Percentage of population age 15 and over having: less than full primary education 17.1%; primary 29.9%; secondary 42.8%; postsecondary and higher 8.8%. *Literacy* (1991): virtually 100%.

Education (1994–95)				student/
	schools	teachers	students	teacher ratio
Primary (age 7–14)	850	15,471	210,989	13.6
Secondary (age 15–18)	224	9,748	102,117	10.5
Higher[7]	28	2,783	45,951[8]	14.5

Health (1995): physicians 2,298[9] (1 per 858 persons); hospital beds 11,411 (1 per 173 persons); infant mortality rate per 1,000 live births 5.5.

Military

Total active duty personnel (1997): 9,550 (army 100%). *Military expenditure as percentage of GNP* (1995): 1.5% (world 2.8%); per capita expenditure U.S.$175.

[1]Hungarian and Italian are official in autochthonous Hungarian and Italian communities. [2]Detail does not add to total given because of rounding. [3]Includes taxes on production, imports, and subsidies. [4]Includes 70,000 unemployed and 290,454 nondistributable employed. [5]July. [6]Imports f.o.b. in balance of trade and c.i.f. in commodities and trading partners. [7]1993–94. [8]1995–96. [9]Physicians and dental physicians in hospitals only.

Internet resources for further information:
• **Statistical Office of the Republic of Slovenia**
 http://www.sigov.si/zrs/eng/index.html

Solomon Islands

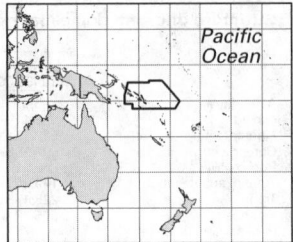

Official name: Solomon Islands.
Form of government: constitutional monarchy with one legislative house (National Parliament [50]).
Chief of state: British Monarch represented by Governor-General.
Head of government: Prime Minister.
Capital: Honiara.
Official language: English.
Official religion: none.
Monetary unit: 1 Solomon Islands dollar (SI$) = 100 cents; valuation (Sept. 25, 1998) 1 U.S.$ = SI$4.99; 1 £ = SI$8.50.

Area and population

Provinces	Capitals	area sq mi	area sq km	population 1997 estimate
Central Islands	Tulagi	237	615	30,071[1]
Choiseul	Taro	1,481	3,837	[2]
Guadalcanal	Honiara	2,060	5,336	61,243
Isabel	Buala	1,597	4,136	22,653
Makira	Kira Kira	1,231	3,188	29,110
Malaita	Auki	1,631	4,225	105,882
Rennell and Bellona	Tigoa	259	671	1
Temotu	Santa Cruz	334	865	21,159
Western	Gizo	2,114	5,475	95,193[2]
Capital Territory				
Honiara	—	8	22	45,610
TOTAL		10,954[3]	28,370	410,921

Demography

Population (1998): 426,000.
Density (1998): persons per sq mi 38.9, persons per sq km 15.0.
Urban-rural (1997): urban 18.0%; rural 82.0%.
Sex distribution (1996): male 51.65%; female 48.35%.
Age breakdown (1996): under 15, 43.7%; 15–29, 28.7%; 30–44, 15.2%; 45–59, 8.1%; 60–74, 3.6%; 75 and over, 0.7%.
Population projection: (2000) 459,000; (2010) 600,000.
Doubling time: 22 years.
Ethnic composition (1986): Melanesian 94.2%; Polynesian 3.7%; other Pacific Islander 1.4%; European 0.4%; Asian 0.2%; other 0.1%.
Religious affiliation (1986): Christian 96.6%; of which Protestant 75.7% (including Church of Melanesia [Anglican] 33.9%), Roman Catholic 19.2%; traditional beliefs 2.1%; other 1.3%.
Major cities (1986)[4]: Honiara 43,643[5]; Gizo 3,727; Auki 3,262; Kira Kira 2,585; Buala 1,913.

Vital statistics

Birth rate per 1,000 population (1997): 36.2 (world avg. 25.0).
Death rate per 1,000 population (1997): 4.1 (world avg. 9.3).
Natural increase rate per 1,000 population (1997): 32.1 (world avg. 15.7).
Total fertility rate (avg. births per childbearing woman; 1997): 5.0.
Marriage rate per 1,000 population: n.a.
Divorce rate per 1,000 population: n.a.
Life expectancy at birth (1997): male 69.0 years; female 74.0 years.
Major causes of death per 100,000 population (1990): respiratory diseases 22.4; diarrheal diseases 13.6; malaria 10.0.

National economy

Budget (1996). Revenue: SI$484,900,000 (foreign grants 30.6%, taxes on goods and services 25.1%, taxes on foreign trade 20.5%, nontax revenue 15.1%, income taxes 8.7%). Expenditures: SI$540,100,000 (administrative 40.8%, capital expenditure 38.1%, interest payments 11.3%, subsidies and transfers 9.8%).
Tourism: receipts from visitors (1993) U.S.$6,000,000; expenditures by nationals abroad (1992) U.S.$11,000,000.
Land use (1994): forested 87.5%; meadows and pastures 1.4%; agricultural and under permanent cultivation 2.0%; other 9.1%.
Gross national product (at current market prices; 1996): U.S.$349,000,000 (U.S.$900 per capita).

Structure of gross domestic product and labour force

	1995 in value SI$ '000[6]	1995 % of total value	1993 labour force[7]	1993 % of labour force
Agriculture	115,600	35.6	8,106	27.4
Mining	200	0.1		
Manufacturing	12,200	3.7	2,844	9.6
Construction	7,600	2.3	977	3.3
Public utilities	4,800	1.5	245	0.8
Transportation and communications	18,800	5.8	1,723	5.8
Trade	27,200	8.4	3,390	11.5
Finance	13,500	4.1	1,144	3.9
Pub. admin., defense			4,303	14.6
Services	72,300	22.2	6,845	23.1
Other	52,900	16.3	...	...
TOTAL	325,100	100.0	29,577	100.0

Household income and expenditure. Average household size (1996) 5.8; average annual income per household[8] (1983) SI$1,010 (U.S.$1,160); sources of income (1983): wages and salaries 74.1%, self-employment, remittances, gifts, and other assistance 25.9%; expenditure (1992)[9]: food 46.8%, housing 11.0%, household operations 10.9%, transportation 9.9%, recreation and health 7.9%, clothing 5.7%, drinks and tobacco 5.0%.
Population economically active (1993): total 29,577[7]; activity rate of total population 8.3% (participation rates: ages 15–60 [1986] 98.6%; female 22.6%; unemployed n.a.).

Price and earnings indexes (1990 = 100)

	1991	1992	1993	1994	1995	1996	1997
Consumer price index	115.1	118.3	138.7	157.6	172.7	193.0	208.7
Annual earnings index[7]	121.2	140.5	142.8	...	...	...	...

Production (metric tons except as noted). Agriculture, forestry, fishing (1996): coconuts 225,000, sweet potatoes 63,000, palm oil and kernels 33,000, taro 27,000, yams 20,500, vegetables and melons 5,900, cacao beans 2,700; livestock (number of live animals) 55,000 pigs, 10,000 cattle, 145,000 chickens; roundwood (1995) 872,000 cu m; fish catch (1995) 46,462. Mining and quarrying (1994): gold 997 troy oz. Manufacturing (1993): processed fish 34,700; sawnwood 16,000 cu m; other major industries include beer brewing, soap and tobacco manufacturing, garment manufacturing, weaving, wood carving, fiberglass products, boatbuilding, and leatherworking. Construction (gross value in SI$ in Honiara; 1994): residential 9,508,000; nonresidential 11,151,000. Energy production (consumption): electricity (kW-hr; 1994) 30,000,000 (30,000,000); coal none (n.a.); petroleum products (metric tons; 1994) none (50,000); natural gas, none (n.a.).
Public debt (external, outstanding; 1996): U.S.$97,900,000.

Foreign trade[10]

Balance of trade (current prices)

	1989	1990	1991	1992	1993	1994
SI$'000	−47,300	−21,030	−23,770	+59,150	+33,520	−246
% of total	12.1%	5.6%	5.0%	11.0%	5.9%	0.0%

Imports (1994): SI$468,121,000 (machinery and transport equipment 38.0%, manufactured goods 19.9%, food 13.1%, mineral fuels and lubricants 8.2%). *Major import sources:* Australia 37.2%; Japan 17.1%; New Zealand 9.6%; Singapore 8.4%; United States 2.8%; Thailand 2.7%.
Exports (1994): SI$467,875,000 (timber products 59.2%, fish products 21.2%, palm oil products 9.5%, copra 4.2%, cacao beans 2.7%). *Major export destinations:* Japan 41.1%; South Korea 14.1%; United Kingdom 13.1%; The Netherlands 8.5%; Thailand 4.5%; Singapore 3.4%; Australia 1.5%.

Transport and communications

Transport. Railroads: none. Roads (1995): total length 826 mi, 1,330 km (paved 2%). Vehicles (1993): passenger cars 2,052; trucks and buses 2,574. Merchant marine (1992): vessels (100 gross tons and over) 33; total deadweight tonnage 4,985. Air transport (1994): passenger-mi 40,000,000, passenger-km 65,000,000; short ton-mi cargo 3,000,000, metric ton-km cargo 5,000,000; airports (1997) with scheduled flights 21.

Communications

Medium	date	unit	number	units per 1,000 persons
Radio	1996	receivers	38,000	96
Television	1995	receivers	6,000	16
Telephones	1995	main lines	6,500	17
Cellular telephones	1995	subscribers	200	0.5
Facsimile machines	1995	units	800	2.1

Education and health

Educational attainment (1986)[11]. Percentage of population age 25 and over having: no schooling 44.4%; primary education 46.2%; secondary 6.8%; higher 2.6%. *Literacy* (1976): total population age 15 and over literate 55,500 (54.1%); males 33,600 (62.4%); females 21,900 (44.9%).

Education (1994)

	schools	teachers	students	student/ teacher ratio
Primary (age 7–12)	520	2,510	73,120	29.1
Secondary (age 13–18)	23	618	7,981	12.9
Voc., teacher tr.[12]	1	...	...	...
Higher[12]	1	...	...	...

Health (1990): physicians 52 (1 per 6,154 persons); hospital beds 265 (1 per 1,208 persons); infant mortality rate per 1,000 live births (1997) 23.
Food (1995): daily per capita caloric intake 2,131 (vegetable products 93%, animal products 7%); 93% of FAO recommended minimum requirement.

Military

Total active duty personnel: no military forces are maintained, but a police force of 475 provides internal security.

---

[1]Central Islands includes Rennell and Bellona. [2]Western includes Choiseul. [3]Detail does not add to total given because of rounding. [4]Ward populations. [5]1996. [6]At 1985 factor cost. [7]Persons employed in the monetary sector only. [8]Public-service earnings. [9]Retail price index components. [10]Import figures are f.o.b. [11]Indigenous population only. [12]Vocational and teacher training are carried out at the College of Higher Education.

Somalia[1]

Official name: Soomaaliya (Somali)(Somalia).
Form of government: republic[2].
Head of state and government: [2].
Capital: Mogadishu.
Official languages: Somali; Arabic.
Official religion: Islam.
Monetary unit: 1 Somali shilling (So.Sh.) = 100 cents; valuation (Sept. 25, 1998) 1 U.S.$ = So.Sh. 2,620[3]; 1 £ = So.Sh. 4,461.

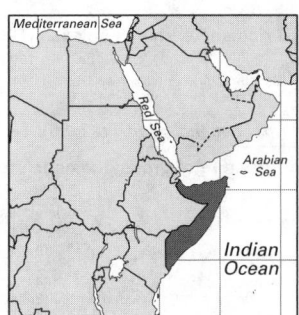

Area and population

Regions	Capitals	area sq mi	area sq km	population 1980 estimate
Bakool	Xuddur	10,000	27,000	148,700
Banaadir	Mogadishu (Muqdisho)	400	1,000	520,100
Bari	Boosaaso	27,000	70,000	222,300
Bay	Baydhabo	15,000	39,000	451,000
Galguduud	Dhuusamarreeb	17,000	43,000	255,900
Gedo	Garbahaarrey	12,000	32,000	235,000
Hiiraan	Beledweyne	13,000	34,000	219,300
Jubbada Dhexe	Bu'aale	9,000	23,000	147,800
Jubbada Hoose	Kismaayo	24,000	61,000	272,400
Mudug	Gaalkacyo	27,000	70,000	311,200
Nugaal	Garoowe	19,000	50,000	112,200
Sanaag	Ceerigaabo	21,000	54,000	216,500
Shabeellaha Dhexe	Jawhar	8,000	22,000	352,000
Shabeellaha Hoose	Marka	10,000	25,000	570,700
Togdheer	Burao	16,000	41,000	383,900
Woqooyi Galbeed	Hargeysa	17,000	45,000	655,000
TOTAL		246,000[3]	637,000	5,074,000

Demography

Population (1998): 6,842,000[4].
Density (1998): persons per sq mi 27.8, persons per sq km 10.7.
Urban-rural (1991): urban 37.2%; rural 62.8%.
Sex distribution (1996): male 51.21%; female 48.79%.
Age breakdown (1996): under 15, 44.4%; 15–29, 27.1%; 30–44, 16.1%; 45–59, 6.9%; 60–74, 4.0%; 75 and over, 1.5%.
Population projection: (2000) 7,434,000; (2010) 10,132,000.
Doubling time: 27 years.
Ethnic composition (1983): Somali 98.3%[5]; Arab 1.2%; Bantu 0.4%; other 0.1%.
Religious affiliation (1995): Sunnī Muslim 99.9%; other 0.1%.
Major cities (1990): Mogadishu 900,000; Hargeysa 90,000; Kismaayo 90,000; Berbera 70,000; Marka 62,000.

Vital statistics

Birth rate per 1,000 population (1996): 44.3 (world avg. 25.0); legitimate, n.a.; illegitimate, n.a.
Death rate per 1,000 population (1996): 18.2 (world avg. 9.3).
Natural increase rate per 1,000 population (1996): 26.1 (world avg. 15.7).
Total fertility rate (avg. births per childbearing woman; 1996): 6.5.
Marriage rate per 1,000 population: n.a.
Divorce rate per 1,000 population: n.a.
Life expectancy at birth (1996): male 44.6 years; female 47.8 years.
Major causes of death per 100,000 population: n.a.; however, major diseases include leprosy, malaria, tetanus, and tuberculosis; civil violence, malnutrition, and poor health services remained epidemic in the mid-1990s.

National economy

Budget (1991). Revenue: So.Sh. 151,453,000,000 (domestic revenue sources, principally indirect taxes and import duties 60.4%; external grants and transfers 39.6%). Expenditures: So.Sh. 141,141,000,000 (general services 46.9%; economic and social services 31.2%; debt service 7.0%).
Public debt (external, outstanding; 1996): U.S.$1,918,000,000.
Production (metric tons except as noted). Agriculture, forestry, fishing (1996): fruits (excluding melons) 210,000, sugarcane 210,000, sorghum 145,000, corn (maize) 142,000, bananas 47,000, cassava 40,000, sesame seed 25,000, beans 14,000, dates 9,500, seed cotton 6,000, other forest products include khat, frankincense, and myrrh; livestock (number of live animals) 13,500,000 sheep, 12,500,000 goats, 6,100,000 camels, 5,200,000 cattle; roundwood (1995) 9,025,000 cu m; fish catch (1995) 14,850. Mining and quarrying (1992): sepiolite 2,000 kilograms. Manufacturing (value added in So.Sh.; 1988): food 794; cigarettes and matches 562; hides and skins 420; paper and printing 328; plastics 320; chemicals 202; beverages 144. Construction (value added in So.Sh.; 1991): 51,100,000,000. Energy production (consumption): electricity (kW-hr; 1994) 259,000,000 (259,000,000); coal, none (n.a.); crude petroleum (barrels; 1991) n.a. (806,000); petroleum products (metric tons; 1991) none (59,000); natural gas, none (n.a.).
Household income and expenditure. Average household size (1980) 4.9; income per household: n.a.; sources of income: n.a.; expenditure (1983)[6]: food and tobacco 62.3%, housing 15.3%, clothing 5.6%, energy 4.3%, other 12.5%.
Tourism: receipts from visitors (1986) U.S.$8,000,000; expenditures by nationals abroad (1983) U.S.$13,000,000.
Population economically active (1991): total 3,215,000; activity rate of total population 40.9% (participation rates [1987] over age 10, 63.1%; female 48.7%; unemployed n.a.).

Price and earnings indexes (1990 = 100)

	1989	1990	1991	1992	1993	1994	1995
Consumer price index[7]	100.0	240.0	372.2	507.4	630.7	749.8	872.1
Earnings index	...	...	...	...	...	...	...

Gross national product (1996): U.S.$706,000,000 (U.S.$110 per capita).

Structure of gross domestic product and labour force

	1991 in value So.Sh. '000,000	% of total value	labour force	% of labour force
Agriculture	867,500	64.5	2,275,000	70.8
Mining	2,700	0.2		
Manufacturing	59,200	4.4	336,000	10.4
Construction	51,100	3.8		
Public utilities	9,400	0.7		
Transp. and commun.	80,700	6.0		
Trade	125,000	9.3		
Finance	45,700	3.4	604,000	18.8
Pub. admin., defense	80,700	6.0		
Services	30,900	2.3		
Other	−8,100	−0.6		
TOTAL	1,344,900[3]	100.0	3,215,000	100.0

Land use (1994): forest 25.5%; pasture 68.6%; agriculture 1.6%; other 4.3%.

Foreign trade[8]

Balance of trade (current prices)

	1991	1992	1993	1994	1995	1996
U.S.$'000,000	−69	−99	−146	−133	−48	−95
% of total	27.5%	29.6%	38.4%	32.8%	14.2%	21.0%

Imports (1995): U.S.$193,000,000 (agricultural products 38.0%, of which raw sugar 16.1%, rice 7.8%, wheat 5.0%; unspecified 62.0%). *Major import sources* (1996)[9]: Kenya 28%; Djibouti 21%; Saudi Arabia 6%; Brazil 6%.
Exports (1995): U.S.$145,000,000 (agricultural products 51.4%, of which live sheep and goats 40.0%, bananas 6.9%, live camels and cattle 4.3%; other 48.6%). *Major export destinations* (1996)[9]: Saudi Arabia 55%; Yemen 19%; Italy 11%; United Arab Emirates 9%.

Transport and communications

Transport. Railroads: none. Roads (1995): total length 14,300 mi, 23,000 km (paved 12%). Vehicles (1995): passenger cars 11,800; trucks and buses 12,200. Merchant marine (1992): vessels (100 gross tons and over) 28; total deadweight tonnage 18,496. Air transport (1991): passenger-mi 81,000,000, passenger-km 131,000,000; short ton-mi cargo 3,000,000, metric ton-km cargo 5,000,000; airports (1997) with scheduled flights 1.

Communications

Medium	date	unit	number	units per 1,000 persons
Radio	1995	receivers	300,000	45
Television	1995	receivers	118,000	18
Telephones	1995	main lines	15,000	2.2

Education and health

Educational attainment: n.a. *Literacy* (1995): percentage of total population age 15 and over literate 24%; males literate 36%; females literate 14%.

Education (1986–87)

	schools	teachers	students	student/ teacher ratio
Primary (age 6–14)	1,125	8,208	171,830	20.9
Secondary (age 15–18)	82	2,109	42,764	20.3
Voc., teacher tr.	21	498	4,809	9.7
Higher	1	...	1,692	...

Health: physicians (1987) 323 (1 per 19,973 persons); hospital beds (1985) 5,536 (1 per 1,130 persons); infant mortality rate (1996) 126.
Food (1993–94 avg.): daily per capita caloric intake 1,545; 67% of FAO recommended minimum requirement.

Military

Total active duty personnel (1997): clan warfare since 1991. *Military expenditure as percentage of GNP* (1990): 0.9% (world 4.3%); per capita expenditure U.S.$1.

---

[1]Proclamation of a "Republic of Somaliland" by the Somali National Movement in May 1991 on territory corresponding to the former British Somaliland (which unified with the former Italian Trust Territory of Somalia to form Somalia in 1960) had received no international recognition by October 1998. This entity represented about a quarter of Somalia's territory and about two-thirds of its population. [2]No effective central government exists in October 1998. [3]In January 1998 6,400 So.Sh. equaled 1 U.S.$ on the black market. [4]Detail does not add to total given because of rounding. [5]Includes 4.3 million residents of the "Republic of Somaliland"; excludes 400,000 refugees in neighbouring countries. [6]The Somali are divided into six major clans, of which four are predominantly pastoral (representing c. 70% of the population) and two are predominantly agricultural (representing c. 20% of the population); the remainder are urban dwellers with less clan identification. [7]Mogadishu only. [8]Reported inflation rate. [9]Imports c.i.f.; exports f.o.b. [10]Estimated figures.

Internet resources for further information:
• **USAID: Greater Horn Information Exchange: Somalia**
  http://gaia.info.usaid.gov/horn/somalia/somalia.html
• **CIA World Factbook: Somalia**
  http://www.odci.gov/cia/publications/factbook/index.html

South Africa

Official name: Republic of South Africa (English).
Form of government: multiparty republic with two legislative houses (National Council of Provinces [90]; National Assembly [400])[1].
Head of state and government: President[1].
Capitals (de facto): Pretoria (executive); Bloemfontein (judicial); Cape Town (legislative).
Official languages: [2].
Official religion: none.
Monetary unit: 1 rand (R) = 100 cents; valuation (Sept. 25, 1998) 1 U.S.$ = R 5.83; 1 £ = R 9.93.

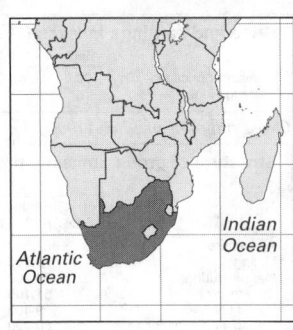

Area and population

Provinces	Capitals	area sq mi	area sq km	population 1996 census[3]
Eastern Cape	Bisho	65,475	169,580	5,865,000
Free State	Bloemfontein	49,993	129,480	2,470,000
Gauteng	Johannesburg	6,568	17,010	7,171,000
KwaZulu–Natal	Ulundi	35,560	92,100	7,672,000
Mpumalanga	Nelspruit	30,691	79,490	2,646,000
Northern Province	Pietersburg	47,842	123,910	4,128,000
Northern Cape	Kimberley	139,703	361,830	746,000
North West	Mafikeng (Mmabatho)	44,911	116,320	3,043,000
Western Cape	Cape Town	49,950	129,370	4,118,000
TOTAL		470,693	1,219,090	37,859,000

Demography

Population (1998)[4]: 42,835,000.
Density (1998): persons per sq mi 91.0, persons per sq km 35.1.
Urban-rural (1996): urban 55.4%; rural 44.6%.
Sex distribution (1996): male 47.98%; female 52.02%.
Age breakdown (1995): under 15, 37.3%; 15–29, 27.1%; 30–44, 18.5%; 45–59, 10.4%; 60–74, 5.2%; 75 and over, 1.5%.
Population projection[4]: (2000) 43,982,000; (2010) 47,503,000.
Doubling time: 43 years.
Ethnic composition (1995): black 76.3%, of which Zulu *c.* 22.0%, Xhosa *c.* 18.0%, Pedi *c.* 9.0%, Sotho *c.* 7.0%, Tswana *c.* 7.0%, Tsonga *c.* 3.5%, Swazi *c.* 3.0%; white 12.7%; Coloured 8.5%; Asian 2.5%.
Religious affiliation (1991)[5]: Christian 66.4%, of which Protestant 36.6%, black independent churches 22.2%, Roman Catholic 7.6%; Hindu 1.3%; Muslim 1.1%; nonreligious 1.2%; other/traditional beliefs 30.0%.
Major cities (1991)[6]: Cape Town 2,350,157; Johannesburg 1,916,063[7]; Durban 1,137,378; Pretoria 1,080,187; Port Elizabeth 853,204.

Vital statistics

Birth rate per 1,000 population (1996): 27.4 (world avg. 25.0).
Death rate per 1,000 population (1996): 11.1 (world avg. 9.3).
Natural increase rate per 1,000 population (1996): 16.3 (world avg. 15.7).
Marriage rate per 1,000 population (1995): 3.6.
Total fertility rate (avg. births per childbearing woman; 1996): 3.3.
Life expectancy at birth (1996): male 55.7 years; female 60.2 years.
Major causes of death per 100,000 population (1993–94): accidents and violence 221.9; diseases of the circulatory system 102.3; infectious and parasitic diseases 51.8; ill-defined conditions 424.0.

National economy

Budget (1995–96). Revenue: R119,957,000,000 (personal income taxes 42.2%, value-added taxes 27.3%, company income taxes 13.8%). Expenditures: R 152,573,000,000 (education 21.9%, interest on public debt 19.3%, health 10.2%, defense 7.2%).
Public debt (external, outstanding; 1996): U.S.$10,348,000,000.
Production (in R '000,000 except as noted). Agriculture, forestry, fishing (in value of production; 1995): poultry 4,327, beef 3,080, corn (maize) 2,825, temperate fruits 1,964, wheat 1,955, sugarcane 1,657, milk 1,577, potatoes 1,081, citrus fruits 988, grapes 966, sheep and goat meat 824, swine 509; roundwood (1995) 25,332,000 cu m; fish catch (1995) 575,177 metric tons. Mining and quarrying (in value of sales; 1995): gold 23,335; rough diamonds 16,431; coal 12,586; platinum-group metals 6,573; copper 1,679; iron ore 1,658; lime and limestone 693. Manufacturing (in U.S.$'000,000 value added; 1994): food products 2,734; iron and steel 2,303; transport equipment 2,082; metal products 1,588; nonelectrical machinery 1,566; beverages 1,531; refined petroleum 1,281. Energy production (consumption): electricity (kW-hr; 1994) 182,448,000,000 ([1995] 172,039,000,000); coal (metric tons; 1994) 182,496,000 (140,581,000[8]); crude petroleum (barrels; 1996) 3,650,000 ([1994] 125,000,-000[8]); petroleum products (metric tons; 1994) 16,425,000[8] (16,428,000[8]); natural gas (cu m; 1994): 1,896,000,000[8] (1,896,000,000[8]).
Tourism (1995): receipts U.S.$1,595,000,000; expenditures U.S.$1,749,000,000.
Household income and expenditure. Average household size (1994) 4.6; average annual income per household (1990–91)[5] R 16,814 (U.S.$6,500); expenditure (1992)[5]: food and beverages 35.8%, transportation 14.7%, household goods 10.0%, housing and energy 9.6%.
Population economically active (1994): total 14,297,048; activity rate of total population 35.3% (participation rates: over age 15, 55.6%; female 44.2%; unemployed [1997] *c.* 25%).

Price and earnings indexes (1990 = 100)

	1992	1993	1994	1995	1996	1997	1998[9]
Consumer price index	131.3	144.0	157.0	170.5	183.1	198.7	206.9
Monthly earnings index[10]	129.6	143.2	...	...	...	...	...

Gross national product (1996): U.S.$132,455,000,000 (U.S.$3,520 per capita).

Structure of gross domestic product and labour force

	1995 in value R '000,000[11]	1995 % of total value	1994 labour force	1994 % of labour force
Agriculture	18,779	4.4	1,277,346	8.9
Mining	33,305	7.7	277,176	1.9
Manufacturing	104,474	24.3	1,614,596	11.3
Construction	13,606	3.2	437,167	3.1
Public utilities	17,797	4.1	95,046	0.7
Transp. and commun.	32,691	7.6	520,789	3.6
Trade	70,094	16.3	1,675,448	11.7
Finance, real estate	56,877	13.2	587,331	4.1
Pub. admin., defense	65,463	15.2	3,055,753	21.4
Services	8,479	2.0		
Other	8,859	2.0	4,756,396[12]	33.3[12]
TOTAL	430,424	100.0	14,297,048	100.0

Land use (1994): forest 6.7%; pasture 66.7%; agriculture 10.8%; other 15.8%.

Foreign trade

Balance of trade (current prices)

	1992	1993	1994	1995	1996	1997
R '000,000	+13,917	+20,500	+13,753	+2,783	+10,578	+13,202
% of total	11.6%	14.8%	8.3%	1.4%	4.4%	4.8%

Imports (1995): R 98,614,000,000 (machinery and apparatus 31.9%, chemicals and chemical products 12.5%, motor vehicles 11.6%). *Major import sources:* Germany 15.9%; U.K. 11.5%; U.S. 10.9%; Japan 9.8%; Italy 4.5%.
Exports (1995): R 101,397,000,000 (gold 19.9%, base metals and metal products 15.4%, gem diamonds 9.8%, food 7.4%). *Major export destinations:* Italy 7.8%; Japan 7.3%; U.S. 6.6%; unspecified 27.9%.

Transport and communications

Transport. Railroads: route length (1995) 21,595 km; passenger-km (1992–93) 895,000,000[13]; metric ton-km cargo (1994–95) 95,260,000,000. Roads (1995): length 182,580 km (paved 33%). Vehicles (1995): passenger cars 3,810,000; trucks and buses 1,640,000. Air transport (1996)[14]: passenger-km 13,833,-000,000; metric ton-km cargo 539,977,000; airport (1996) 24.

Communications

Medium	date	unit	number	units per 1,000 persons
Daily newspapers	1995	circulation	1,201,000	29
Radio	1996	receivers	11,200,000	268
Television	1995	receivers	3,485,000	84
Telephones	1995	main lines	3,919,100	95
Cellular telephones	1995	subscribers	535,000	13
Facsimile machines	1995	units	75,000	1.8
Personal computers	1995	units	1,100,000	27

Education and health

Educational attainment (1994). Percentage of population age 25 and over having: no formal schooling 14.5%; primary/incomplete secondary 61.6%; secondary/incomplete higher 20.4%; complete higher 3.1%; other/unknown 0.4%. *Literacy* (1995): total population age 15 and over literate: 81.8%.

Education (1994)

	schools	teachers	students	student/ teacher ratio
Primary/Secondary	22,260	349,436	11,782,324	35.7
Voc., teacher tr.	187	10,807	140,531	13.0
Tertiary vocational	15	7,341[15]	151,410	18.7[15]
Higher	...	27,099	617,897	22.8

Health: physicians (1994) 26,452 (1 per 1,529 persons); hospital beds (1995) 172,292 (1 per 239 persons); infant mortality rate (1996) 52.4.
Food (1995): daily per capita caloric intake 2,890 (vegetable products 88%, animal products 12%); 118% of FAO recommended minimum.

Military

Total active duty personnel (1996): 137,900 (army 85.6%, navy 4.0%, air force 6.1%, intraservice medical service 4.3%). *Military expenditure as percentage of GNP* (1995): 2.2% (world 2.8%); per capita expenditure U.S.$71.

---

[1]All articles of permanent constitution announced in May 1996 were effective as of June 30, 1997. [2]Afrikaans; English; Ndebele; Pedi (North Sotho); Sotho (South Sotho); Swazi; Tsonga; Tswana (West Sotho); Venda; Xhosa; Zulu. [3]Preliminary; adjusted (rounded) final equals 40,580,000. [4]Projection(s) based on 1991 census. [5]Excludes formerly nominally independent Transkei, Venda, Bophuthatswana, and Ciskei (TVBC). [6]Population of urban areas. [7]The 1991 population of the Witwatersrand (including East Rand [1,379,000], Far East Rand [701,000], and West Rand [870,000] urban areas) is 4,866,000. [8]Includes Botswana, Lesotho, Namibia, and Swaziland. [9]April. [10]Mining only. [11]At factor cost. [12]Includes 100,320 not adequately defined and 4,656,076 unemployed. [13]Excludes suburban traffic. [14]SAA only. [15]1993.

Internet resources for further information:
• **Central Statistical Service**
  http://www.css.gov.za/index.htm
• **South African High Commission in Canada**
  http://www.southafrica.net/welcome.html

Spain

Official name: Reino de España
(Kingdom of Spain).
Form of government: constitutional
monarchy with two legislative
houses (Senate [257[1]]; Congress of
Deputies [350]).
Chief of state: King.
Head of government: Prime Minister.
Capital: Madrid.
Official languages: Castilian Spanish[2].
Monetary unit: 1 peseta (Pta) = 100
céntimos; valuation (Sept. 25, 1998)
1 U.S.$ = Ptas 141.88;
1 £ = Ptas 241.55.

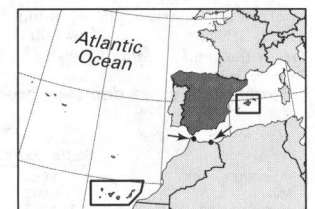

Area and population		area[2]		population
				1996[3]
Autonomous communities	Capitals	sq mi	sq km	estimate
Andalucía	Seville	33,822	87,599	7,234,873
Aragón	Zaragoza	18,425	47,720	1,187,546
Asturias	Oviedo	4,094	10,604	1,087,885
Baleares (Balearic Islands)	Palma de Mallorca	1,927	4,992	760,379
Canarias (Canary Islands)	Santa Cruz de Tenerife	2,875	7,447	1,606,534
Cantabria	Santander	2,504	5,321	527,437
Castilla-La Mancha	Toledo	30,680	79,461	1,712,529
Castilla y León	Valladolid	36,380	94,224	2,508,496
Cataluña	Barcelona	12,399	32,113	6,090,040
Ceuta	—	8	20	68,796
Extremadura	Mérida	16,075	41,634	1,070,244
Galicia	Santiago de Compostela	11,419	29,575	2,742,622
La Rioja	Logroño	1,948	5,045	264,941
Madrid	Madrid	3,100	8,028	5,022,289
Melilla	—	5	12	59,576
Murcia	Murcia	4,368	11,314	1,097,249
Navarra	Pamplona	4,012	10,391	520,574
País Vasco (Basque Country)	Vitoria (Gasteiz)	2,793	7,234	2,098,055
Valencia	Valencia	8,979	23,255	4,009,329
TOTAL		195,364[4, 5]	505,990[5]	39,669,394

Demography

Population (1998): 39,371,000[6].
Density (1998): persons per sq mi 201.3, persons per sq km 77.8.
Urban-rural (1990): urban 78.4%; rural 21.6%.
Sex distribution (1997): male 48.92%; female 51.08%.
Age breakdown (1997): under 15, 15.8%; 15–29, 24.1%; 30–44, 22.1%; 45–59, 16.8%; 60–69, 10.4%; 70 and over, 10.8%.
Population projection: (2000) 39,466,000; (2010) 39,917,000.
Doubling time: not applicable; doubling time exceeds 100 years.
Ethnolinguistic composition (1991): Spanish 74.4%; Catalan 16.9%; Galician 6.4%; Basque 1.6%; other 0.7%.
Religious affiliation (1995): Roman Catholic 66.7%; Muslim 1.2%; Protestant 0.8%; other 31.3%.
Major cities (1996)[3, 7]: Madrid 2,866,850; Barcelona 1,508,805; Valencia 746,683; Seville 697,487; Zaragoza 601,674.

Vital statistics

Birth rate per 1,000 population (1995): 9.2 (world avg. 25.0).
Death rate per 1,000 population (1995): 8.7 (world avg. 9.3).
Natural increase rate per 1,000 population (1995): 0.5 (world avg. 15.7).
Total fertility rate (avg. births per childbearing woman; 1995): 1.3.
Life expectancy at birth (1996): male 74.9 years; female 81.8 years.
Major causes of death per 100,000 population (1994): circulatory diseases 334.2; malignant neoplasms (cancers) 224.3; respiratory diseases 78.8.

National economy

Budget (1996)[8]. Revenue: Ptas 16,090,900,000,000 (direct taxes 46.8%; indirect taxes 38.9%, of which value-added tax on products 24.1%; other taxes on production 14.3%). Expenditures: Ptas 18,099,200,000,000 (public debt 19.1%; health 18.2%; education 5.9%; pensions 5.0%; defense 4.8%).
Tourism (1995): receipts U.S.$25,701,000,000; expenditures U.S.$4,540,000,000.
Gross national product (1996): U.S.$563,249,000,000 (U.S.$14,350 per capita).

Structure of gross domestic product and labour force				
	1996			
	in value Ptas '000,000	% of total value	labour force	% of labour force
Agriculture	2,582,800	3.5	1,310,600	8.2
Mining			78,900	0.5
Manufacturing	17,468,000	23.7	2,673,600	16.8
Public utilities			95,400	0.6
Construction	5,720,400	7.7	1,516,500	9.5
Transp. and commun.	...	...	803,900	5.0
Trade			3,307,100	20.8
Finance			1,217,900	7.6
Services	43,505,100	59.1		
Pub. admin., defense			3,390,600	21.3
Other	4,384,700[9]	6.0[9]	1,541,500[10]	9.7[10]
TOTAL	73,661,000	100.0	15,936,000	100.0

Production (metric tons except as noted). Agriculture, forestry, fishing (1996): barely 10,660,000, sugar beets 7,359,000, wheat 6,002,000, grapes 4,486,000, potatoes 4,032,000 corn (maize) 3,996,000, olives 2,856,000, tomatoes 2,780,000, oranges 2,154,000; livestock (number of live animals) 21,322,000

sheep, 18,000,000 pigs, 5,660,000 cattle, 2,465,000 goats; roundwood (1995) 15,121,000 cu m; fish catch (1995) 1,320,000. Mining and quarrying (metal content in metric tons; 1996): iron ore 1,269,000; zinc 140,000; lead 24,000. Manufacturing (value added in U.S.$'000; 1994): machinery and transport equipment 20,322,000; food products 11,072,000; chemical products 8,618,000; publishing products 6,082,000; wood products 3,208,000. Construction (1996): dwellings 311,038. Energy production (consumption): electricity (kW-hr; 1994) 161,502,000,000 (163,377,000,000); coal (metric tons; 1994) 29,556,000 (42,808,000); crude petroleum (barrels; 1994) 6,057,000 (407,793,000); petroleum products (metric tons; 1994) 42,227,000 (40,591,000); natural gas (cu m; 1994) 206,650,000 (7,754,694,000).
Public debt (1997): Ptas 45,417,300,000,000 (U.S.$310,000,000,000).
Population economically active (1996): total 15,936,000; activity rate of total population 40.6% (participation rates: ages [1995] 16–64, 60.7%; female 38.3%; unemployed 22.9%).

Price and earnings indexes (1990 = 100)							
	1991	1992	1993	1994	1995	1996	1997
Consumer price index	105.9	112.2	117.3	122.9	128.6	133.2	135.8
Monthly earnings index	108.2	116.5	124.4	124.4	136.2	143.4	149.3

Household income and expenditure. Average household size (1991) 3.4; income per household (1996) Ptas 2,964,843 (U.S.$23,408); expenditure (1995): housing 26.0%, food 24.0%, transportation 12.8%, clothing and footwear 7.4%, household goods and services 6.1%.

Foreign trade

Balance of trade (current prices)						
	1992	1993	1994	1995	1996	1997
Ptas '000,000	−3,546.9	−2,376.4	−2,559.7	−2,767.1	−2,504.5	−2,699.1
% of total	21.0%	13.2%	11.6%	10.8%	8.8%	8.1%

Imports (1996): Ptas 15,435,699,000,000 (machinery 12.1%; energy products 9.1%, of which crude petroleum 9.0%; transportation equipment 8.5%; agricultural products 7.9%). *Major import sources:* France 17.8%; Germany 14.8%; Italy 9.5%; U.K. 8.3%; Japan 2.8%.
Exports (1996): Ptas 12,931,008,000,000 (transport equipment 20.2%; agricultural products 12.8%; machinery 8.3%). *Major export destinations:* France 20.1%; Germany 14.5%; Italy 8.7%; U.K. 8.5%.

Transport and communications

Transport. Railroads (1995): route length 13,280 km; passenger-km 15,330,000,000; metric ton-km cargo 9,671,000,000. Roads (1995): length 343,197 km (paved 99%). Vehicles (1995): cars 14,212,257; trucks and buses 2,984,140. Merchant marine (1992): vessels 2,190; deadweight tonnage 5,077,275. Air transport (1995): passenger-km 34,043,765,000; metric ton-km cargo 3,763,516,000; airports (1997) with scheduled flights 25.

Communications				units
				per 1,000
Medium	date	unit	number	persons
Daily newspapers	1994	circulation	4,100,000	104
Radio	1996	receivers	12,000,000	306
Television	1995	receivers	19,200,000	490
Telephones	1995	main lines	15,095,400	385
Cellular telephones	1995	subscribers	965,700	25
Facsimile machines	1995	units	215,000	5.2
Personal computers	1995	units	3,200,000	82

Education and health

Educational attainment (1996). Percentage of economically active population age 16 and over having: no formal schooling 6.9%[11]; primary 28.0%; secondary 57.2%; higher 7.9%.

Education (1994–95)				student/
	schools	teachers	students	teacher ratio
Primary (age 6–11)	16,540[12]	132,566	2,364,910	17.8
Secondary (age 12–18)[13]	25,775[14]	299,056	4,744,829	15.9
Higher	1,415[14]	80,563	1,398,113	17.3

Health (1995): physicians 162,650 (1 per 241 persons); hospital beds (1991) 168,514 (1 per 234 persons); infant mortality rate 5.6.
Food (1995): daily per capita caloric intake 3,338 (vegetable products 73%, animal products 27%); 136% of FAO recommended minimum requirement.

Military

Total active duty personnel (1997): 197,500 (army 65.1%, navy 19.7%, air force 15.2%). *Military expenditure as percentage of GNP* (1995): 1.6% (world 2.8%); per capita expenditure U.S.$221.

---

[1]At the March 1996 elections, 208 seats were directly elected and 49 indirectly elected by the parliaments of the autonomous communities. [2]The constitution states that "Castilian is the Spanish official language of the State," but that "all other Spanish languages will also be official in the corresponding Autonomous Communities." [3]De jure population for January 1. [4]Detail does not add to total given because of rounding. [5]Includes other enclaves (*plazas de soberanía*). [6]Estimate based on 1991 census. [7]For municipios, which may contain rural population. [8]Preliminary. [9]Import taxes and value-added tax on products. [10]Includes 813,600 unemployed persons not previously employed. [11]Includes illiterate. [12]1993–94. [13]Includes vocational. [14]1992–93.

Internet resources for further information:
• **"Sí Spain" (Embassy of Spain, Ottawa, Canada)**
  http://www.DocuWeb.ca/SiSpain/
• **National Institute of Statistics http://www.ine.es/**

Sri Lanka

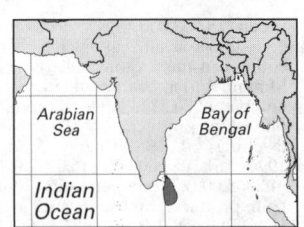

Official name: Śrī Lankā Prajātāntrika Samājavādī Janarajaya (Sinhala); Ilangai Jananayaka Socialisa Kudiarasu (Tamil) (Democratic Socialist Republic of Sri Lanka).
Form of government: unitary multiparty republic with one legislative house (Parliament [225]).
Head of state and government: President assisted by Prime Minister.
Capitals: Colombo (executive); Sri Jayewardenepura Kotte (Colombo suburb; legislative and judicial).
Official languages: Sinhala; Tamil.
Official religion: none.
Monetary unit: 1 Sri Lanka rupee (SL Rs) = 100 cents; valuation (Sept. 25, 1998) 1 U.S.$ = SL Rs 66.18; 1 £ = SL Rs 112.67.

Area and population

Districts	Capitals	area sq mi	area sq km	population 1994 estimate
Amparai	Amparai	1,705	4,415	512,000
Anuradhapura	Anuradhapura	2,772	7,179	750,000
Badulla	Badulla	1,104	2,861	735,000
Batticaloa	Batticaloa	1,102	2,854	443,000
Colombo	Colombo	270	699	2,062,000
Galle	Galle	638	1,652	983,000
Gampaha	Gampaha	536	1,387	1,568,000
Hambantota	Hambantota	1,007	2,609	537,000
Jaffna	Jaffna	396	1,025	896,000
Kalutara	Kalutara	617	1,598	969,000
Kandy	Kandy	749	1,940	1,286,000
Kegalle	Kegalle	654	1,693	763,000
Kilinochchi	Kilinochchi	494	1,279	110,000
Kurunegala	Kurunegala	1,859	4,816	1,481,000
Mannar	Mannar	771	1,996	140,000
Matale	Matale	770	1,993	434,000
Matara	Matara	495	1,283	810,000
Monaragala	Monaragala	2,177	5,639	367,000
Mullaitivu	Mullaitivu	1,010	2,617	98,000
Nuwara Eliya	Nuwara Eliya	672	1,741	541,000
Polonnaruwa	Polonnaruwa	1,271	3,293	336,000
Puttalam	Puttalam	1,186	3,072	626,000
Ratnapura	Ratnapura	1,264	3,275	972,000
Trincomalee	Trincomalee	1,053	2,727	327,000
Vavuniya	Vavuniya	759	1,967	119,000
TOTAL		25,332	65,610	17,865,000

Demography

Population (1998): 18,729,000.
Density (1998): persons per sq mi 739.3, persons per sq km 285.5.
Urban-rural (1997): urban 23.0%; rural 77.0%.
Sex distribution (1994): male 50.98%; female 49.02%.
Age breakdown (1994): under 15, 35.2%; 15–29, 29.7%; 30–44, 17.9%; 45–59, 10.6%; 60–74, 5.2%; 75 and over, 1.4%.
Population projection: (2000) 19,153,000; (2010) 21,258,000.
Doubling time: 58 years.
Ethnic composition (1991)[1]: Sinhalese 82.7%; Tamil 8.9%; Sri Lankan Moor 7.7%; other 0.7%.
Religious affiliation (1981): Buddhist 69.3%; Hindu 15.5%; Muslim 7.5%; Christian 7.6%; other 0.1%.
Major cities (1990): Colombo 615,000; Dehiwala–Mount Lavinia 196,000; Moratuwa 170,000; Jaffna 129,000; Sri Jayewardenepura Kotte 109,000.

Vital statistics

Birth rate per 1,000 population (1997): 17.9 (world avg. 25.0); (1986) legitimate 96.3%; illegitimate 3.7%.
Death rate per 1,000 population (1997): 5.9 (world avg. 9.3).
Natural increase rate per 1,000 population (1997): 12.0 (world avg. 15.7).
Total fertility rate (avg. births per childbearing woman; 1997): 2.1.
Marriage rate per 1,000 population (1992): 9.2.
Life expectancy at birth (1997): male 71.0 years; female 75.0 years.
Major causes of death per 100,000 population (1989): diseases of the circulatory system 47.8%; violence and poisoning 38.6%; malignant neoplasms 26.7.

National economy

Budget (1999). Revenue: SL Rs 148,206,000,000 (sales and turnover tax 27.5%, import duties 19.4%, excise taxes 14.8%, income taxes 11.6%, nontax revenue 10.5%). Expenditures: SL Rs 212,984,000,000 (current expenditure 79.7%, current expenditure 20.3%).
Public debt (external, outstanding; 1996): U.S.$6,818,000,000.
Tourism (1995): receipts U.S.$224,000,000; expenditures U.S.$186,000,000.
Production (metric tons except as noted). Agriculture, forestry, fishing (1996): rice 2,241,000, coconuts 2,000,000, sugarcane 1,273,000, plantains 560,000; livestock (number of live animals) 1,701,700 cattle, 764,200 buffalo, 591,100 goats; roundwood (1995) 9,624,700 cu m; fish catch (1995) 235,829. Mining and quarrying (1995): quartz stone 1,100,000; limestone 700,000; titanium concentrate 62,400; gemstones U.S.$61,000,000. Manufacturing (value added, in SL Rs '000,000; 1993): food, beverages, and tobacco 23,832; textiles and apparel 17,350; petrochemicals 5,264. Construction (units completed; 1993): residential 1,128; nonresidential 96. Energy production (consumption): electricity (kW-hr; 1994) 4,386,000,000 (4,386,000,000); crude petroleum (barrels; 1994) none (14,601,000); petroleum products (metric tons; 1994) 1,807,000 (1,647,000).
Gross national product (1996): U.S.$13,475,000,000 (U.S.$740 per capita).

Structure of gross domestic product and labour force

	1995 in value SL Rs '000,000	1995 % of total value	1995 labour force[1]	1995 % of labour force[1]
Agriculture	124,854	18.8	1,985,300	32.7
Mining	8,042	1.2	56,400	0.9
Manufacturing	116,048	17.5	864,000	14.2
Construction	48,440	7.3	300,400	5.0
Public utilities	14,663	2.2	24,700	0.4
Transp. and commun.	62,325	9.4	244,700	4.0
Trade	142,836	21.6	557,100	9.2
Finance	47,383	7.2	91,500	1.5
Pub. admin., defense Services	72,211	10.9	893,500	14.7
Other	25,562	3.9	1,057,500[2]	17.4[2]
TOTAL	662,364	100.0	6,075,100	100.0

Population economically active: total (1995) 6,102,154; activity rate 40.5% (participation rates: ages 15 and over, 54.9%; female 32.2%; unemployed 12.5%[1]).

Price and earnings indexes (1990 = 100)

	1991	1992	1993	1994	1995	1996	1997
Consumer price index	112.2	125.0	139.6	151.4	163.1	189.0	207.1
Average wage index[3]	111.7	128.4	155.4	158.8	160.7	175.6	187.9

Household income and expenditure (1992). Average household size (1994) 4.6[1]; income per household SL Rs 116,100 (U.S.$2,600); sources of income: wages 48.5%, property income and self-employment 41.8%, transfers 9.7%; expenditure: food 58.6%, transportation 16.0%, clothing 8.4%.

Foreign trade

Balance of trade (current prices)

	1991	1992	1993	1994	1995	1996
SL Rs '000,000	−29,612	−27,128	−36,037	−53,894	−44,594	−42,709
% of total	14.9%	11.0%	11.5%	14.5%	10.3%	8.6%

Imports (1995): SL Rs 272,201,000,000 (industrial supplies 54.6%, machinery and transport equipment 19.1%, food and live animals 11.1%, mineral fuels 7.9%). *Major import sources:* Japan 10.5%; India 9.8%; Singapore 5.2%.
Exports (1995): SL Rs 195,117,000,000 (clothing and accessories 48.6%, tea 12.6%, gems 6.3%, rubber products 4.0%, natural rubber 2.9%). *Major export destinations:* U.S. 35.5%; U.K. 9.1%; Germany 6.7%; Japan 5.3%.

Transport and communications

Transport. Railroads (1994): route length 1,493 km; passenger-km 3,264,000,000; metric ton-km cargo 144,000,000. Roads (1995): total length 102,600 km (paved 11%). Vehicles (1995): passenger cars 220,000; trucks and buses 248,900. Air transport (1996): passenger-km 3,868,000,000; metric ton-km cargo 159,054,000; airports (1996) 1.

Communications

Medium	date	unit	number	units per 1,000 persons
Daily newspapers	1994	circulation	450,000	25
Radio	1996	receivers	3,300,000	182
Television	1995	receivers	700,000	39
Telephones	1995	main lines	204,400	11
Cellular telephones	1995	subscribers	53,100	3.0
Facsimile machines	1995	units	11,000	0.6
Personal computers	1995	units	20,000	1.1

Education and health

Educational attainment (1981). Percentage of population age 25 and over having: no schooling 15.5%; less than complete primary education 12.1%; complete primary 52.3%; postprimary 14.7%; secondary 3.0%; higher 1.1%; unspecified 1.3%. *Literacy* (1995): percentage of population age 15 and over literate 90.2%; males literate 93.4%; females literate 87.2%.

Education (1994)

	schools	teachers	students	student/ teacher ratio
Primary (age 5–10)	9,648	70,108	1,960,495	28.0
Secondary (age 11–17)	5,771[4]	105,916	2,315,541	21.9
Voc., teacher tr.[5]	23	437	8,908	20.4
Higher	8[5]	1,937[5]	59,790	16.2[5]

Health (1993): physicians 3,713 (1 per 4,745 persons); hospital beds 48,963 (1 per 360 persons); infant mortality rate per 1,000 live births (1997) 15.
Food (1995): daily per capita caloric intake 2,334 (vegetable products 95%, animal products 5%); 102% of FAO recommended minimum.

Military

Total active duty personnel (1996): 112,300 (army 81.9%, navy 9.2%, air force 8.9%). *Military expenditure as percentage of GNP* (1994): 4.5% (world 3.0%); per capita expenditure U.S.$29.

[1]Excludes the Northern and Eastern provinces where Tamils are in the majority. [2]Mainly unemployed. [3]Agricultural minimum rates. [4]1992. [5]1991.

Internet resources for further information:
• Central Bank of Sri Lanka http://www.lanka.net/centralbank

Sudan, The

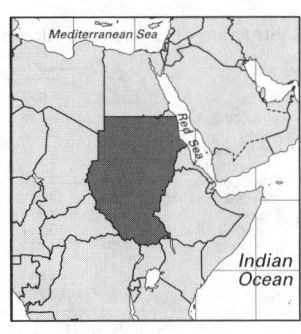

Official name: Jumhūrīyat as-Sūdān (Republic of the Sudan).
Form of government: Islamic military regime[1] with one legislative house (National Assembly [400][2]).
Head of state and government: President.
Capitals: Khartoum (executive); Omdurman (legislative).
Official language: Arabic.
Official religion: [3].
Monetary unit: 1 Sudanese dinar (Sd)[4]; valuation (Sept. 25, 1998) 1 U.S.$ = Sd 182.60; 1 £ = Sd 310.88.

Area and population

States[5]	Capitals	area sq mi	area sq km	population 1983 census
A'ālī an-Nīl (Upper Nile)	Malakāl	92,198	238,792	1,599,605
Baḥr al-Ghazāl (Bahr el-Ghazal)	Wāw	77,566	200,894	2,265,510
Dārfūr (Darfur)	al-Fāshir	194,404	508,684	3,093,699
al-Istiwā'īyah (Equatoria)	Juba	76,436	197,969	1,406,181
al-Khartūm (Khartoum)	Khartoum	10,874	28,165	1,802,299
Kurdufān (Kordofan)	al-Ubayyiḍ	146,817	380,255	3,093,294
ash-Shamālīyah (Northern)	ad-Dāmir	183,800	476,040	1,083,024
ash-Sharqīyah (Eastern)	Kassalā	128,987	334,074	2,208,209
al-Wusṭā (Central)	Wad Madanī	53,675	139,017	4,012,543
TOTAL		966,757[6]	2,503,890[6]	20,564,364[7]

Demography

Population (1998): 33,551,000.
Density (1998): persons per sq mi 34.7, persons per sq km 13.4.
Urban-rural (1995): urban 24.6%; rural 75.4%.
Sex distribution (1995): male 50.20%; female 49.80%.
Age breakdown (1995): under 15, 43.9%; 15–29, 27.0%; 30–44, 15.6%; 45–59, 8.8%; 60–74, 3.9%; 75 and over, 0.8%.
Population projection: (2000) 35,530,000; (2010) 46,573,000.
Doubling time: 23 years.
Ethnic composition (1983): Sudanese Arab 49.1%; Dinka 11.5%; Nuba 8.1%; Beja 6.4%; Nuer 4.9%; Azande 2.7%; Bari 2.5%; Fur 2.1%; other 12.7%.
Religious affiliation (1992): Sunnī Muslim c. 72%; traditional beliefs c. 17%; Christian c. 11%, of which Roman Catholic c. 7%.
Major cities (1993): Omdurman 1,267,077; Khartoum 924,505; Khartoum North 879,105; Port Sudan 305,385; Kassalā 234,270; Nyala 228,778.

Vital statistics

Birth rate per 1,000 population (1996): 41.1 (world avg. 25.0).
Death rate per 1,000 population (1996): 11.5 (world avg. 9.3).
Natural increase rate per 1,000 population (1996): 29.6 (world avg. 15.7).
Total fertility rate (avg. births per childbearing woman; 1996): 5.9.
Life expectancy at birth (1996): male 54.2 years; female 56.1 years.
Major causes of death per 100,000 population: n.a.

National economy

Budget (1996). Revenue: LSd 679,600,000,000[4] (import duties 20.5%, taxes on business profits 19.1%, nontax revenue 17.4%, excise duties 16.7%). Expenditures: LSd 2,377,100,000,000[4] (interest on debt 58.5%, current expenditure 31.9%, development expenditure 4.1%).
Public debt (external, outstanding; 1996): U.S.$9,369,000,000.
Tourism (1994): receipts U.S.$3,000,000; expenditures U.S.$30,000,000.
Production (metric tons except as noted). Agriculture, forestry, fishing (1996): sugarcane 4,900,000, sorghum 4,104,000, wheat 550,000, millet 491,000, peanuts (groundnuts) 430,000, seed cotton 325,000, cottonseed 210,000, sesame seeds 160,000, dates 145,000, cotton lint 106,000, gum arabic 40,000[8]; livestock (number of live animals) 23,500,000 cattle, 23,400,000 sheep, 16,900,000 goats, 2,950,000 camels; roundwood (1995) 25,409,000 cu m; fish catch (1995) 45,000. Mining and quarrying: salt (1994) 75,000; gold (1996) 96,000 troy oz. Manufacturing (1995): raw sugar 450,000; wheat flour 350,000; cement 199,000; vegetable oils 70,000; cattlehides and horsehides 38,000[9]; shoes 6,000,000 pairs. Construction: n.a. Energy production (consumption): electricity (kW-hr; 1994) 1,333,000,000 (1,333,000,000); coal, none (none); crude petroleum (barrels; 1994) none (7,601,000); petroleum products (metric tons; 1994) 864,000 (1,051,000); natural gas, none (none).
Gross national product (1996): U.S.$9,780,000,000 (U.S.$310 per capita).

Structure of gross domestic product and labour force

	1996 in value LSd '000,000[10]	1996 % of total value	1983 labour force[11]	1983 % of labour force[11]
Agriculture	3,659	42.0	4,028,705	63.5
Mining	72	0.8	6,534	0.1
Manufacturing	698	8.0	266,693	4.2
Construction	548	6.3	139,282	2.2
Public utilities	206	2.4	43,728	0.7
Transportation and communications	2,960	34.0	215,474	3.4
Trade and finance			314,676	5.0
Services			550,409	8.7
Pub. admin., defense	571	6.5		
Other			777,480[12]	12.2[12]
TOTAL	8,714	100.0	6,342,981	100.0

Population economically active (1993): total 8,866,000; activity rate of total population 32.3% (participation rates: ages 15–64, [1983] 57.4%; female 22.3%; unemployed c. 30.0%).

Price and earnings indexes (1991–92 = 100)

	1991–92	1992–93	1993–94	1994–95	1995–96	1996–97
Consumer price index[13, 14]	100.0	218.3	448.7	511.7	832.3	1,609.1[15]
Earnings index						

Household income and expenditure. Average household size: n.a.; income per household: n.a.[16]; expenditure (1983): food and beverages 63.6%, housing 11.5%, household goods 5.5%, clothing and footwear 5.3%.
Land use (1994): forested 18.1%; meadows and pastures 46.3%; agricultural and under permanent cultivation 5.5%; desert and other 30.1%.

Foreign trade

Balance of trade (current prices)

	1990–91	1991–92	1992–93	1993–94	1994–95	1995–96
U.S.$'000,000	−1,193	−941	−715	−463	−657	−673
% of total	63.6%	57.4%	50.3%	29.8%	42.5%	36.4%

Imports (1994–95): U.S.$1,101,000,000 (petroleum products 17.2%; foodstuffs 17.0%, of which wheat flour 3.9%; electrical machinery 13.6%; chemicals and chemical products 10.0%; transport equipment 8.7%). *Major import sources:* Saudi Arabia 13.5%; U.K. 12.1%; Egypt 5.8%; Germany 4.4%; U.S. 3.6%.
Exports (1994–95): U.S.$444,000,000 (cotton 18.7%; sheep and lambs 14.0%; sesame seeds 12.8%; gum arabic 11.6%; gold 8.0%; peanuts [groundnuts] 5.1%). *Major export destinations:* Saudi Arabia 19.7%; U.K. 9.7%; Italy 9.0%; China 7.5%; Japan 5.3%; Switzerland 4.7%.

Transport and communications

Transport. Railroads: route length (1995) 4,764 km; (1993) passenger-km 1,183,000,000; (1993) metric ton-km cargo 2,240,000,000[17]. Roads (1995): total length 11,610 km (paved 36%). Vehicles (1995): passenger cars 263,000; trucks and buses 47,800[18]. Air transport (1996)[19]: passenger-km 650,049,000; metric ton-km cargo 30,706,000; airports (1997) with scheduled flights 3.

Communications

Medium	date	unit	number	units per 1,000 persons
Daily newspapers	1995	circulation	650,000	21
Radio	1996	receivers	5,755,000	182
Television	1995	receivers	250,000	8.2
Telephones	1995	main lines	75,000	2.5
Facsimile machines	1995	units	5,800	0.2

Education and health

Educational attainment (1983). Percentage of population age 25 and over having: no formal schooling 76.7%; complete secondary 2.0%; higher 0.8%.
Literacy (1995): total population age 15 and over literate 7,280,000 (46.1%); males 4,540,000 (57.7%); females 2,740,000 (34.6%).

Education (1994–95)

	schools	teachers	students	student/ teacher ratio
Primary (age 7–12)	12,187	83,306	3,023,955	36.3
Secondary (age 13–18)[20]	2,578	29,208	683,982	23.4
Vocational	...	621	15,443	24.9
Higher[20]	24	1,943	54,345	28.0

Health: physicians (1994) 2,600[21] (1 per 11,300 persons); hospital beds (1986) 18,571 (1 per 1,222 persons); infant mortality rate (1996) 76.0.
Food (1995): daily per capita caloric intake 2,313 (vegetable products 82%, animal products 18%); 98% of FAO recommended minimum.

Military

Total active duty personnel (1996): 89,000 (army 95.5%, navy 1.1%, air force 3.4%). *Military expenditure as percentage of GNP* (1994): 6.6% (world 3.0%); per capita expenditure U.S.$15.

[1]The president (and military general) who was elected in March 1996 (and appointed himself president in 1989 after overthrowing a democratically elected government in a military coup) signed a new constitution into law on June 30, 1998. [2]Includes 8 nonelected seats filled by head of state for 8 local administrative units controlled by opposition forces in extreme southern Sudan. [3]Islamic law and custom are sources of national law per 1998 constitution. [4]The Sudanese dinar (introduced May 1992 at a value equal to 10 Sudanese pounds [LSd]) circulates in tandem with the Sudanese pound. [5]Local administrative reorganization into 26 new states was announced in February 1994 and confirmed in June 1998; area and population breakdown was not available in late 1998. [6]Including c. 50,000 sq mi (130,000 sq km) of inland water area. [7]Preliminary unadjusted 1993 census figure was 24,940,683, including an estimated 3,850,000 in the southern Sudan. [8]1994–95. [9]1992. [10]In constant prices of 1981–82 at factor cost. [11]Excludes nomads, the homeless, and institutionalized persons. [12]Includes 592,759 unemployed not previously employed. [13]Average of July 1–June 30 fiscal year. [14]For middle income residents of the Greater Khartoum area only. [15]September 1996 only. [16]Average annual income of paid worker (1992) U.S.$216. [17]Sections of the Sudan Railways were closed in 1995 because of insufficient funds. [18]Data unavailable for buses. [19]Sudan Airways only. [20]1991–92. [21]Estimated figure.

Internet resources for further information:
• **The Sudan Page (unofficial link)**
  http://www.sudan.net/

Suriname

Official name: Republiek Suriname (Republic of Suriname).
Form of government: multiparty republic with one legislative house (National Assembly [51]).
Head of state and government: President.
Capital: Paramaribo.
Official language: Dutch.
Official religion: none.
Monetary unit: 1 Suriname guilder (Sf) = 100 cents; valuation (Sept. 25, 1998) 1 U.S.$ = Sf 401.00; 1 £ = Sf 682.70.

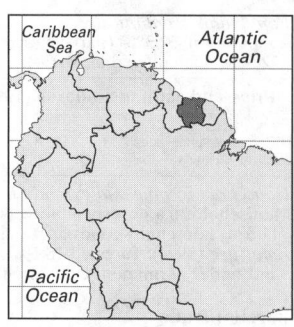

Area and population		area		population
				1980
Districts	**Capitals**	sq mi	sq km	census
Brokopondo	Brokopondo	2,843	7,364	6,621
Commewijne	Nieuw Amsterdam	908	2,353	20,063
Coronie	Totness	1,507	3,902	2,777
Marowijne	Albina	1,786	4,627	16,125
Nickerie	Nieuw Nickerie	2,067	5,353	32,690
Para	Onverwacht	2,082	5,393	12,827
Saramacca	Groningen	1,404	3,636	10,808
Sipaliwini	...	50,412	130,566	23,226
Wanica	Lelydorp	171	443	60,725
Town district				
Paramaribo	Paramaribo	71	183	167,798
TOTAL		63,251[1]	163,820[1]	355,240[2]

Demography

Population (1998): 418,000.
Density (1998): persons per sq mi 6.6, persons per sq km 2.6.
Urban-rural (1996): urban 51.0%; rural 49.0%.
Sex distribution (1996): male 49.54%; female 50.46%.
Age breakdown (1995): under 15, 35.2%; 15–29, 29.7%; 30–44, 19.0%; 45–59, 8.8%; 60–74, 5.9%; 75 and over, 1.4%.
Population projection: (2000) 425,000; (2010) 443,000.
Doubling time: 47 years.
Ethnic composition (1991): Suriname Creole 35.0%; Indo-Pakistani 33.0%; Javanese 16.0%; Bush Negro 10.0%; Amerindian 3.0%; other 3.0%.
Religious affiliation (1995): Hindu 27.4%; Roman Catholic 21.0%; Muslim 19.6%; Protestant (mostly Moravian) 16.4%; other 15.6%.
Major cities (1980): Paramaribo 200,970[3]; Nieuw Nickerie 6,078; Meerzorg 5,355; Marienburg 3,633.

Vital statistics

Birth rate per 1,000 population (1995): 21.5 (world avg. 25.0); legitimate n.a.; illegitimate n.a.
Death rate per 1,000 population (1995): 6.6 (world avg. 9.3).
Natural increase rate per 1,000 population (1995): 14.9 (world avg. 15.7).
Total fertility rate (avg. births per childbearing woman; 1997): 2.6.
Marriage rate per 1,000 population (1991): 4.9.
Divorce rate per 1,000 population (1991): 2.5.
Life expectancy at birth (1990–95): male 67.8 years; female 72.8 years.
Major causes of death per 100,000 population (1992): noncommunicable diseases 769.0; external and other causes 608.1; communicable and perinatal diseases 232.8; ill-defined diseases 279.0.

National economy

Budget (1995). Revenue: Sf 94,096,600,000 (grants 29.2%; corporate income taxes 26.6%; custom duties 13.4%; individual income taxes 9.4%; value-added taxes 6.8%). Expenditures: Sf 88,973,500,000 (current expenditures 87.2%, of which welfare and social services 3.6%, defense 2.7%, education 2.1%, debt service 2.0%, health 1.9%; capital expenditures 12.8%).
Production (metric tons except as noted). Agriculture, forestry, fishing (1997): rice 218,000, sugarcane 84,500, bananas 41,000, plantains 19,000, oranges 14,200, coconuts 11,000, watermelons 6,000, cassava 6,000, cucumbers 5,500, tomatoes 1,700, cabbage 1,400, grapefruit 900; livestock (number of live animals) 104,000 cattle, 20,000 pigs; roundwood (1996) 122,000 cu m; fish catch (1995) 13,000. Mining and quarrying (1996): bauxite 3,708,000; gold 9,645 troy oz[3]. Manufacturing (value of production at factor cost in Sf; 1993): food products 992,000,000; beverages 558,000,000; tobacco 369,000,000; chemical products 291,000,000; pottery and earthenware 258,000,000; wood products 180,000,000. Construction (value of building authorized; 1985): residential Sf 46,500,000; nonresidential Sf 8,100,000. Energy production (consumption): electricity (kW-hr; 1994) 1,683,000,000 (1,683,000,000); hard coal (metric tons) none (n.a.); crude petroleum (barrels; 1994) 1,686,000 (1,370,000); petroleum products (metric tons; 1992) none (461,000); natural gas, none (none).
Household income and expenditure. Average household size (1980) 3.9; income per household: n.a.; sources of income (1975): wages and salaries 74.6%, transfer payments 3.2%, other 22.2%; expenditure (1968–69): food and beverages 40.0%, household furnishings 12.3%, clothing and footwear 11.0%, transportation and communications 9.5%, recreation and education 8.4%, energy 6.9%, housing 4.4%, other 7.5%.
Land use (1994): forested 96.2%; meadows and pastures 0.1%; agricultural and other permanent cultivation 0.4%; other 3.3%.
Gross national product (1996): U.S.$433,000,000 (U.S.$1,000 per capita).

Structure of gross domestic product and labour force

	1994			
	in value Sf '000,000	% of total value	labour force	% of labour force
Agriculture, forestry	8,738.5	13.7	19,940[4]	20.3[4]
Mining	8,574.6	13.4	3,181	3.2
Manufacturing	6,548.9	10.3	4,432	4.5
Construction	2,360.3	3.7	1,656	1.7
Public utilities	2,885.2	4.5	1,288	1.3
Transp. and commun.	11,129.7	17.5	2,112	2.1
Trade[5]	12,877.3	20.2	4,383	4.5
Finance, real estate	13,257.3	20.8	1,954	2.0
Pub. admin., defense	3,441.7	5.4	38,552	39.2
Services	77.3	0.1	2,010	2.0
Other	−6,181.8[6]	−9.7[6]	18,732[7]	19.1[7]
TOTAL	63,709.1[8]	100.0[8]	98,240	100.0[8]

Public debt (external, outstanding; 1996): U.S.$216,500,000.
Population economically active (1994): total 98,240; activity rate of total population 24.3% (participation rates[9], [10]: ages 15–64, 56.0%; female 37.5%; unemployed 11.3%).

Price and earnings indexes (1990 = 100)						
	1991	1992	1993	1994	1995	1996	1997
Consumer price index	126.0	181.0	440.7	2,064.5	6,927.7	6,878.1	7,370.6
Earnings index	...	...	...	...	...	...	...

Tourism (1995): receipts from visitors U.S.$14,000,000; expenditures by nationals abroad U.S.$3,000,000[11].

Foreign trade

Balance of trade (current prices)					
	1991	1992	1993	1994	1995	1996
U.S.$'000,000	−117.9	−110.8	−77.2	−99.3	+38.3	+18.8
% of total	11.3%	10.2%	8.0%	20.4%	4.6%	2.2%

Imports (1994): U.S.$350,200,000 (fuels and lubricants 18.2%, machinery and transport equipment 13.3%, food and live animals 7.3%, home appliances 4.2%). *Major import sources:* United States 39.8%; The Netherlands 24.1%; Trinidad and Tobago 11.2%; Japan 3.3%; Brazil 3.0%.
Exports (1994): U.S.$339,800,000 (alumina 63.6%, shrimp and fish 9.7%, rice 9.6%, aluminum 9.3%, petroleum 3.0%, bananas 2.9%). *Major export destinations:* Norway 32.6%; The Netherlands 26.9%; United States 13.1%; Japan 6.6%; Brazil 6.3%; France 2.9%.

Transport and communications

Transport. Railroads (1991): length 187 mi, 301 km; passengers, not applicable; cargo, n.a. Roads (1995): total length 2,778 mi, 4,470 km (paved 26%). Vehicles (1995): passenger cars 44,300; trucks and buses 17,050. Merchant marine (1992): vessels (100 gross tons and over) 24; total deadweight tonnage 15,721. Air transport (1995)[12]: passenger-mi 548,885,000, passenger-km 883,347,000; short ton-mi cargo 17,684,000, metric ton-km cargo 25,818,000; airports (1997) with scheduled flights 3.

Communications				units per 1,000
Medium	date	unit	number	persons
Daily newspapers	1993	circulation	43,000	107
Radio	1993	receivers	290,300	719
Television	1994	receivers	59,000	146
Telephones	1995	main lines	53,200	130
Cellular telephones	1995	subscribers	3,700	9.0
Facsimile machines	1995	units	700	1.7

Education and health

Educational attainment: n.a. *Literacy* (1995): total population age 15 and over literate 271,000 (93.0%); males literate 137,000 (95.1%); females literate 134,000 (91.0%).

Education (1994–95)				student/
	schools	teachers	students	teacher ratio
Primary (age 6–11)	280	3,447	62,613	18.2
Secondary (age 12–18)	100	2,056	29,554	14.4
Voc., teacher tr.	64[13]	...	12,307	...
Higher[14]	1	155	1,478	9.5

Health: physicians (1990) 331 (1 per 1,222 persons); hospital beds (1989) 1,901 (1 per 212 persons); infant mortality rate per 1,000 live births (1994) 27.9.
Food (1995): daily per capita caloric intake 2,556 (vegetable products 87%, animal products 13%); 113% of FAO recommended minimum requirement.

Military

Total active duty personnel (1997): 1,800[15] (army 77.8%, navy 13.3%, air force 8.9%). *Military expenditure as percentage of GNP* (1995): 3.0% (world 2.8%); per capita expenditure U.S.$90.

---

[1]Area excludes 6,809 sq mi (17,635 sq km) of territory disputed with Guyana. [2]Detail does not add to total given because of computational discrepancies. [3]1993. [4]Derived value. [5]Includes hotels. [6]Indirect taxes less subsidies and imputed bank service charges. [7]Includes 11,300 unemployed. [8]Detail does not add to total given because of rounding. [9]Districts of Wanica and Paramaribo only. [10]1992. [11]1994. [12]SLM (Suriname Airways) only. [13]1988–89. [14]1995–96. [15]All services are part of the army.

Internet resources for further information:
• **Suriname Home Page http://www.sesrtcic.org/DIR-SUR/SURHOME.HTM**

Swaziland

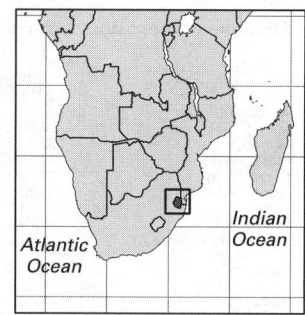

Official name: Umbuso weSwatini (Swazi); Kingdom of Swaziland (English).
Form of government[1]: monarchy with two legislative houses (Senate [30[2]]; House of Assembly [65[3]]).
Head of state and government: King, assisted by Prime Minister.
Capitals: Mbabane (administrative and judicial); Lozitha and Ludzidzini (royal); Lobamba (legislative).
Official languages: Swazi; English.
Official religion: none.
Monetary unit: 1 lilangeni[4] (plural emalangeni [E]) = 100 cents; valuation (Sept. 25, 1998) 1 U.S.$ = E 5.83; 1 £ = E 9.93.

Area and population		area		population
Districts	Capitals	sq mi	sq km	1986 census[5]
Hhohho	Mbabane	1,378	3,569	178,936
Lubombo	Siteki	2,296	5,947	153,958
Manzini	Manzini	1,571	4,068	192,596
Shiselweni	Nhlangano	1,459	3,780	155,569
TOTAL		6,704	17,364	681,059

Demography

Population (1998): 966,000.
Density (1998): persons per sq mi 144.1, persons per sq km 55.6.
Urban-rural (1991): urban 34.3%; rural (65.7%) 65.7%.
Sex distribution (1996): male 48.53% female 51.47%.
Age breakdown (1996): under 15, 45.7%; 15–29, 27.9%; 30–44, 14.9%; 45–59, 7.6%; 60–74, 3.3%; 75 and over, 0.6%.
Population projection: (2000) 1,004,000; (2010) 1,202,000.
Doubling time: 22 years.
Ethnic composition (1983): Swazi 84.3%; Zulu 9.9%; Tsonga 2.5%; Indian 0.8%; Pakistani 0.8%; Portuguese 0.2%; other 1.5%.
Religious affiliation (1995): Christian 66.7%, of which African indigenous 44.7%, Protestant 14.8%, Roman Catholic 5.3%; other (mostly traditional beliefs) 33.3%.
Major cities (1986): Manzini 52,000; Mbabane 38,290; Nhlangano 4,107; Piggs Peak 3,223; Siteki 2,271.

Vital statistics

Birth rate per 1,000 population (1996): 42.9 (world avg. 25.0).
Death rate per 1,000 population (1996): 10.6 (world avg. 9.3).
Natural increase rate per 1,000 population (1996): 32.3 (world avg. 15.7).
Total fertility rate (avg. births per childbearing woman; 1996): 6.0.
Life expectancy at birth (1996): male 53.2 years; female 61.4 years.
Major causes of death (1992)[6]: accidents and injuries 15.8%; infectious intestinal diseases 13.3%; tuberculosis 10.3%; malnutrition 6.2%; respiratory diseases 5.3%; circulatory diseases 5.0%; digestive diseases 4.6%.

National economy

Budget (1996–97). Revenue: E 1,648,600,000 (receipts from Customs Union of Southern Africa 51.7%; tax on income and profits 26.1%; sales tax 12.1%; foreign-aid grants 2.3%; property income 1.1%; fees, services, and fines 0.8%). Expenditures: E 1,861,100,000 (recurrent expenditure 80.3%, of which general administration 24.3%, education 16.9%, economic services 13.2%, justice and police 7.7%, health 6.1%, defense 5.9%).
Tourism (1995): receipts U.S.$35,000,000; expenditures U.S.$37,000,000.
Gross national product (1996): U.S.$1,122,000,000 (U.S.$1,210 per capita).

Structure of gross domestic product and labour force				
	1995–96		1986	
	in value E '000	% of total value	labour force	% of labour force
Agriculture	383,800	9.2	30,197	18.8
Mining	45,200	1.1	5,245	3.3
Manufacturing	1,092,600	26.3	14,742	9.2
Construction	157,100	3.8	7,661	4.8
Public utilities	68,100	1.6	1,315	0.8
Transp. and commun.	209,800	5.0	7,526	4.7
Trade	316,600	7.6	12,348	7.7
Finance	250,800	6.0	1,931	1.2
Pub. admin., defense	704,600	16.9	} 32,309	20.1
Services	67,600	1.7		
Other	864,800[7]	20.8[7]	47,081[8]	29.4[8]
TOTAL	4,161,000	100.0	160,355	100.0

Population economically active (1986): total 160,355; activity rate of total population 23.5% (participation rates: ages 15 and over, 44.1%; female 34.2%; unemployed 27.0%).

Price and earnings indexes (1990 = 100)							
	1990	1991	1992	1993	1994	1995	1996
Consumer price index	100.0	110.8	119.9	140.3	160.4	184.0	206.5
Earnings index[9]	100.0	113.2	136.6	154.7	177.3	...	...

Public debt (external, outstanding; 1996): U.S.$219,600,000.

Production (metric tons except as noted). Agriculture, forestry, fishing (1996): sugarcane 3,846,000, corn (maize) 135,600, grapefruit and pomelo 35,100, oranges 32,874, seed cotton 14,000, pineapples 8,000, roots and tubers 8,000 (of which potatoes 6,000, sweet potatoes 2,000), lint cotton 5,000, peanuts (groundnuts) 5,000; livestock (number of live animals) 646,000 cattle, 438,000 goats, 31,000 pigs, 27,000 sheep, 1,000,000 chickens; roundwood 1,424,000 cu m; fish catch (1995) 115. Mining and quarrying (1996): asbestos 26,000; diamonds 64,000 carats[10]. Manufacturing (value added in U.S.$'000; 1994): food and beverages 244,000, of which beverage processing 153,000; paper and paper products 35,000; textiles 19,000; printing and publishing products 18,000; clothing 7,000; metal and metal products 7,000. Construction (value in E; 1996)[11]: residential 34,100,000; nonresidential 17,500,000. Energy production (consumption): electricity (kW-hr; 1991) 387,000,000 (815,000,000); coal (metric tons; 1992) 100,220 (1989; 28,454); crude petroleum, n.a. (n.a.).
Household income and expenditure. Average household size (1986) 5.7; annual income per household (1985) E 332 (U.S.$151); sources of income (1985): wages and salaries 44.4%, self-employment 22.2%, transfers 12.2%, other 21.2%; expenditure (1985): food and beverages 33.5%, rent and fuel 13.4%, household durable goods 12.8%, transportation and communication 8.8%, clothing and footwear 6.0%, recreation 3.3%.

Foreign trade[12]

Balance of trade (current prices)						
	1991	1992	1993	1994	1995	1996
E '000,000	−340	−647.8	−615.8	−512.1	−533.6	−1,203
% of total	9.4%	15.1%	12.1%	8.4%	7.1%	−13.6%

Imports (1995): U.S.$907,700,000 (machinery and transport equipment 25.1%; manufactured items 17.5%; foodstuffs 16.4%; chemicals 13.2%; minerals, fuels, and lubricants 5.1%). *Major import sources* (1993): South Africa 81.7%; U.K. 2.5%; The Netherlands 0.4%; Switzerland 0.3%; France 0.1%.
Exports (1995): U.S.$798,000,000 (wood and wood products 18.4%; sugar 15.3%; refrigerators 6.6%; cotton yarn 6.0%; paper and paper products 2.3%; canned fruits 2.0%; citrus fruits 1.9%; asbestos 1.6%). *Major export destinations* (1991): South Africa 47.0%; U.S. 3.6%; U.K. 3.3%; Mozambique 2.4%; South Korea 2.2%; Zimbabwe 2.2%.

Transport and communications

Transport. Railroads (1995): length 187 mi, 301 km; passenger-mi 752,000,-000[12], passenger-km 1,210,000,000[13]; short ton-mi cargo 1,993,000,000[14], metric ton-km cargo 2,910,000,000[14]. Roads (1995): total length 2,377 mi, 3,825 km (paved 28%). Vehicles (1995): passenger cars 27,300; trucks and buses 26,340. Air transport (1995)[15]: passenger-mi 30,710,000, passenger-km 49,423,000; short ton-mi cargo 87,000, metric ton-km cargo 127,000; airports (1997) with scheduled flights 1.

Communications				units per 1,000 persons
Medium	date	unit	number	
Daily newspapers	1995	circulation	36,000	40
Radio	1995	receivers	117,000	129
Television	1995	receivers	90,000	96.0
Telephones	1995	main lines	19,800	21.0
Facsimile machines	1995	units	900	1.0

Education and health

Educational attainment (1986). Percentage of population age 25 and over having: no formal schooling 42.1%; some primary education 23.9%; complete primary 10.5%; some secondary 19.2%; complete secondary and higher 4.3%. *Literacy* (1995): total population age 15 and over literate 76.7%; males literate 78.0%; females literate 75.6%.

Education (1994)				
	schools	teachers	students	student/ teacher ratio
Primary (age 6–13)	535	5,887	192,599	32.7
Secondary (age 14–18)	165	2,872	52,571	18.3
Voc., teacher tr.[16]	5	228	2,958	13.0
Higher	1	190[16]	2,132	9.1[16]

Health: physicians (1990) 83 (1 per 9,265 persons); hospital beds (1984) 1,608 (1 per 396 persons); infant mortality rate per 1,000 live births (1996) 88.4.
Food (1995): daily per capita caloric intake 2,658 (vegetable products 90%, animal products 10%); 115% of FAO recommended minimum requirement.

Military

Total active duty personnel (1983): 2,657. *Military expenditure as percentage of GNP* (1995): 2.6% (world 2.8%); per capita expenditure U.S.$28.

[1]The Constitutional Review Committee announced by the King in July 1996 continued to prepare a new draft constitution in late 1998. [2]Includes 20 nonelective seats. [3]Includes 10 nonelective seats. [4]The lilangeni is at par with the South African rand. [5]Preliminary. [6]Percentage of deaths of known cause at government, mission, and private hospitals. [7]Includes indirect taxes less imputed bank service charges and subsidies. [8]Includes 43,925 unemployed. [9]Manufacturing sector only. [10]1994. [11]Urban areas under the jurisdiction of the Manzini and Mbabane town councils only. [12]Imports c.i.f.; exports f.o.b. [13]1988. [14]1991. [15]Royal Swazi National Airways only; international flights only. [16]1993–94.

Internet resources for further information:
• **Central Bank of Swaziland**
http://www.realnet.co.sz/cbs/cbs.html
• **Swaziland on the Internet**
http://www.realnet.co.sz/

Sweden

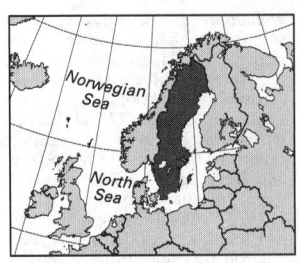

Official name: Konungariket Sverige
(Kingdom of Sweden).
Form of government: constitutional
monarchy and parliamentary
state with one legislative house
(Parliament [349]).
Chief of state: King.
Head of government: Prime Minister.
Capital: Stockholm.
Official language: Swedish.
Official religion: Church of Sweden
(Lutheran).
Monetary unit: 1 Swedish krona
(SKr) = 100 ore; valuation (Sept. 25,
1998) 1 U.S.$ = SKr 7.88;
1 £ = SKr 13.42.

Area and population

Counties	Capitals	area sq mi	area sq km	population 1997[1] estimate
Älvsborg	Vänersborg	4,400	11,395	448,074
Blekinge	Karlskrona	1,136	2,941	151,972
Dalarna	Falun	10,886	28,194	288,171
Gävleborg	Gävle	7,024	18,191	286,789
Göteborg och Bohus	Göteborg	1,985	5,141	775,638
Gotland	Visby	1,212	3,140	57,971
Halland	Halmstad	2,106	5,454	270,060
Jämtland	Östersund	19,090	49,443	134,561
Jönköping	Jönköping	3,839	9,944	311,765
Kalmar	Kalmar	4,313	11,170	241,896
Kronoberg	Växjö	3,266	8,458	179,655
Norrbotten	Luleå	38,191	98,913	264,320
Örebro	Örebro	3,289	8,519	275,855
Östergötland	Linköping	4,078	10,562	415,659
Skåne	Malmo	4,257	11,025	1,114,368
Skaraborg	Mariestad	3,065	7,937	278,263
Södermanland	Nyköping	2,340	6,060	257,383
Stockholm	Stockholm	2,505	6,488	1,744,330
Uppsala	Uppsala	2,698	6,989	289,153
Värmland	Karlstad	6,789	17,584	282,147
Västerbotten	Umeå	21,390	55,401	259,895
Västernorrland	Härnösand	8,370	21,678	256,587
Västmanland	Västerås	2,433	6,302	259,987
TOTAL LAND AREA		158,661[2]	410,929	
INLAND WATER		15,071	39,035	
TOTAL		173,732	449,964	8,844,499

Demography

Population (1998): 8,860,000.
Density (1998)[3]: persons per sq mi 55.8, persons per sq km 21.6.
Urban-rural (1996): urban 83.1%; rural 16.9%.
Sex distribution (1997[1]): male 49.41%; female 50.59%.
Age breakdown (1997[1]): under 15, 18.8%; 15–29, 19.0%; 30–44, 20.6%; 45–59, 19.6%; 60–74, 13.4%; 75 and over, 8.6%.
Population projection: (2000) 8,909,000; (2010) 9,084,000.
Ethnic composition (1997[1]): Swedish 89.3%; Finnish 2.3%; Yugoslavian 0.8%; Iranian 0.6%; Bosnian 0.5%; other 6.5%.
Religious affiliation (1995[1]): Church of Sweden 86.1% (nominally; about 30% nonpracticing); Roman Catholic 1.9%; Pentecostal 1.0%; other 11.0%.
Major cities (1997[1]): Stockholm 718,462; Göteborg 454,016; Malmö 248,007; Uppsala 184,507; Linköping 131,898.

Vital statistics

Birth rate per 1,000 population (1996): 10.8 (world avg. 25.0); (1995) legitimate 47.0%; illegitimate 53.0%.
Death rate per 1,000 population (1996): 10.6 (world avg. 9.3).
Natural increase rate per 1,000 population (1996): 0.2 (world avg. 15.7).
Total fertility rate (avg. births per childbearing woman; 1995): 1.7.
Marriage rate per 1,000 population (1996): 3.4.
Divorce rate per 1,000 population (1996): 2.4.
Life expectancy at birth (1991–95): male 75.6 years; female 81.0 years.
Major causes of death per 100,000 population (1994): heart disease 428.7; malignant neoplasms (cancers) 229.8; cerebrovascular disease 113.8.

National economy

Budget (1995–96). Revenue: SKr 816,978,000,000 (value-added and excise taxes 37.4%, social security 34.8%, income and capital gains taxes 15.1%, property taxes 3.2%). Expenditures: SKr 957,248,000,000 (health and social affairs 20.5%, debt service 12.9%, defense 4.7%, education 4.7%).
Public debt (1997): U.S.$153,400,000,000.
Production (metric tons except as noted). Agriculture, forestry, fishing (1996): sugar beets 2,430,000, barley 2,113,000, wheat 2,030,000, potatoes 1,211,000, oats 987,000; livestock (number of live animals) 2,348,800 pigs, 1,790,200 cattle, 469,000 sheep; roundwood (1995) 59,924,000 cu m; fish catch (1995) 395,721. Mining and quarrying (1996): iron ore 21,020,000; zinc 292,000; copper 269,000. Manufacturing (value added, in SKr '000,000; 1994): machinery and transport equipment 119,630; paper products 42,503; food 24,145; wood products 12,359; textiles and wearing apparel 3,767. Construction (dwellings completed; 1995): 12,678. Energy production (consumption): electricity (kW-hr; 1994) 142,889,000,000 (143,150,000,000); coal (metric tons; 1994) none (3,305,000); crude petroleum (barrels; 1994) 36,200 (128,773,000); petroleum products (metric tons; 1994) 16,616,000 (13,961,000); natural gas (cu m; 1994) none 763,223,000).
Gross national product (1996): U.S.$227,315,000,000 (U.S.$25,710 per capita).

Structure of gross domestic product and labour force

	1995 in value SKr '000,000	% of total value	labour force	% of labour force
Agriculture	34,770	2.4	124,000	2.9
Mining	4,525	0.3	8,000	0.2
Manufacturing	352,301	24.3	761,000	17.6
Public utilities	42,283	2.9	33,000	0.8
Construction	77,575	5.3	230,000	5.3
Transp. and commun.	94,824	6.5	261,000	6.0
Trade	169,339	11.6	609,000	14.1
Finance	343,791	23.6	415,000	9.6
Pub. admin., defense Services	392,817	27.0	1,506,000	34.9
Other	−58,806[4]	−4.0[4]	372,000[5]	8.6[5]
TOTAL	1,453,419	100.0[2]	4,319,000	100.0

Population economically active (1995): total 4,319,000; activity rate of total population 48.9% (participation rates: ages 16–64, 78.2%; female 47.9%; unemployed 7.7%).

Price and earnings indexes (1990 = 100)

	1991	1992	1993	1994	1995	1996	1997
Consumer price index	109.4	112.0	117.1	120.0	123.0	123.0	124.0
Hourly earnings index	105.0	110.0	113.0	118.0	123.0	132.0	137.0

Household income and expenditure. Average household size (1994) 2.1[6]; median income per household SKr 396,100 (U.S.$51,330); sources of income (1992): wages and salaries 58.9%, transfer payments 25.8%, self-employment 15.3%; expenditure (1995): housing and energy 29.6%, food 20.9%, transportation 16.1%, education and recreation 9.2%.
Tourism (1996): receipts U.S.$3,674,000,000; expenditures U.S.$6,236,800,000.
Land use (1994): forest 68.0%; pasture 1.4%; agriculture 6.8%, other 23.8%.

Foreign trade

Balance of trade (current prices)

	1992	1993	1994	1995	1996	1997
SKr '000,000	42,062	63,285	82,735	82,735	120,000	131,600
% of total	6.9%	8.9%	9.6%	8.1%	11.8%	11.6%

Imports (1996): SKr 447,600,000,000 (machinery and transport equipment 40.4%; chemicals 10.4%; food 6.6%). *Major import sources:* Germany 18.8%; U.K. 10.2%; Norway 7.8%; Denmark 7.5%; U.S. 5.8%.
Exports (1996): SKr 567,300,000,000 (machinery and transport equipment 47.4%, of which electrical machinery 17.2%; paper products 9.1%; chemicals 8.7%; iron and steel products 5.5%). *Major export destinations:* Germany 11.7%; U.K. 9.6%; Norway 8.4%; U.S. 8.3%; Denmark 6.3%.

Transport and communications

Transport. Railroads (1995): length 6,774 mi, 10,853 km; passenger-km 6,344,000,000; metric ton-km cargo 19,388,000,000. Roads (1996[1]): total length 84,419 mi, 136,223 km (paved 72%). Vehicles (1996[1]): passenger cars 3,630,762; trucks and buses 322,286. Merchant marine (1996[1]): vessels (100 gross tons and over) 430; total deadweight tonnage 2,881,000. Air transport (1994): passenger-km 8,426,647,000; metric ton-km cargo 249,528,000; airports (1995) 48.

Communications

Medium	date	unit	number	units per 1,000 persons
Daily newspapers	1995	circulation	4,544,000	515
Radio	1995	receivers	7,450,000	844
Television	1995	receivers	4,202,000	476
Telephones	1995	main lines	6,010,000	681
Cellular telephones	1995	subscribers	2,025,000	229.4
Facsimile machines	1995	units	329,000	37.3
Personal computers	1995	units	1,700,000	192.5

Education and health

Educational attainment (1995). Percentage of population age 16–64 having: primary education 30.7%; lower secondary education 32.2%; higher secondary 14.3%; some postsecondary 22.8%. *Literacy* (1995): virtually 100%.

Education (1994–95)

	schools	teachers	students	student/teacher ratio
Primary (age 7–12)	4,900	89,275	916,661	10.3
Secondary (age 13–18)	629	29,563	309,952	10.5
Higher	...	29,487	268,448	9.1

Health: physicians (1995) 23,000 (1 per 384 persons); hospital beds 45,537 (1 per 194 persons); infant mortality rate per 1,000 live births (1996) 3.5.
Food (1995): daily per capita caloric intake 3,117 (vegetable 65%, animal 35%).

Military

Total active duty personnel (1996): 62,600 (army 68.8%, navy 16.0%, air force 15.2%). *Military expenditure as percentage of GNP* (1995): 2.8% (world 2.8%); per capita expenditure U.S.$683.

[1]January 1. [2]Detail does not add to total given because of rounding. [3]Density based on land area only. [4]Includes statistical discrepancies less imputed bank service charges. [5]Includes 333,000 unemployed. [6]1990.

Internet resources for further information:
• Statistics Sweden http://www.scb.se/scbeng/keyeng.htm

Switzerland

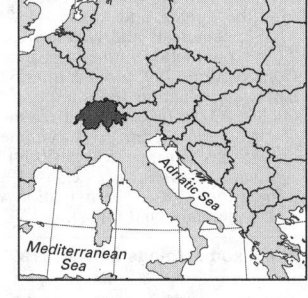

Official name: Confédération Suisse (French); Schweizerische Eidgenossenschaft (German); Confederazione Svizzera (Italian) (Swiss Confederation).
Form of government: federal state with two legislative houses (Council of States [46]; National Council [200]).
Head of state and government: President.
Capitals: Bern (administrative); Lausanne (judicial).
Official languages: French; German; Italian.
Official religion: none.
Monetary unit: 1 Swiss Franc (Sw F) = 100 centimes; valuation (Sept. 25, 1998) 1 U.S.$ = Sw F 1.38; 1 £ = Sw F 2.35.

Area and population

Cantons	Capitals	area[2] sq mi	area[2] sq km	population 1996[1] estimate
Aargau	Aarau	542	1,404	528,887
Appenzell Ausser-Rhoden[2]	Herisau	94	243	54,104
Appenzell Inner-Rhoden[2]	Appenzell	67	173	14,750
Basel-Landschaft[2]	Liestal	200	517	252,331
Basel-Stadt[2]	Basel	14	37	195,759
Bern	Bern	2,302	5,961	941,952
Fribourg	Fribourg	645	1,671	224,552
Genève	Geneva	109	282	395,466
Glarus	Glarus	264	685	39,410
Graubünden	Chur	2,743	7,105	185,063
Jura	Delémont	323	836	69,188
Luzern	Luzern	576	1,493	340,536
Neuchâtel	Neuchâtel	310	803	165,258
Nidwalden[2]	Stans	107	276	36,466
Obwalden[2]	Sarnen	189	490	31,310
Sankt Gallen	Sankt Gallen	782	2,026	442,350
Schaffhausen	Schaffhausen	115	299	74,035
Schwyz	Schwyz	351	908	122,409
Solothurn	Solothurn	305	791	239,264
Thurgau	Frauenfeld	383	991	223,372
Ticino	Bellinzona	1,086	2,812	305,199
Uri	Altdorf	416	1,077	35,876
Valais	Sion	2,017	5,225	271,291
Vaud	Lausanne	1,240	3,212	605,677
Zug	Zug	92	239	92,392
Zürich	Zürich	668	1,729	1,175,457
TOTAL		15,940	41,285	7,062,354[3]

Demography

Population (1998): 7,118,000.
Density (1998): persons per sq mi 446.5, persons per sq km 172.4.
Urban-rural (1996): urban 67.7%; rural 32.3%.
Sex distribution (1996): male 48.83%; female 51.17%.
Age breakdown (1996): under 15, 17.6%; 15–29, 19.8%; 30–44, 23.9%; 45–59, 19.1%; 60–74, 12.9%; 75 and over, 6.7%.
Population projection: (2000) 7,218,000; (2010) 7,438,000.
Linguistic composition (1990): German 63.6%; French 19.2%; Italian 7.6%; Spanish 1.7%; Portuguese 1.4%; Romansch 0.6%; other 5.9%.
Religious affiliation (1990): Roman Catholic 46.2%; Protestant 40.0%; Muslim 2.2%; Orthodox Christian 1.0%; Jewish 0.3%; other 10.3%.
Major cities (1996[1]): Zürich 343,869 (928,696[4]); Basel 174,007 (404,262[4]); Geneva 173,559 (446,464[4]); Bern 127,469 (320,045[4]); Lausanne 115,878.

Vital statistics

Birth rate per 1,000 population (1996): 11.7 (world avg. 25.0); (1995) legitimate 93.2%; illegitimate 6.8%.
Death rate per 1,000 population (1996): 8.9 (world avg. 9.3).
Natural increase rate per 1,000 population (1996): 2.8 (world avg. 15.7).
Total fertility rate (avg. births per childbearing woman; 1995): 1.5.
Marriage rate per 1,000 population (1995): 5.8.
Life expectancy at birth (1994–95): male 75.3 years; female 81.7 years.
Major causes of death per 100,000 population (1994): heart disease 256.3, of which ischemic 146.8, other 109.5; malignant neoplasms (cancers) 238.7.

National economy

Budget (1996)[5]. Revenue: Sw F 39,924,000,000 (turnover taxes 29.1%, direct federal taxes 23.5%, motor fuel fees 11.5%). Expenditures: Sw F 43,972,000,000 (social services 27.3%, transportation 14.3%, defense 12.9%).
National debt (end of year; 1997): Sw F 97,050,000,000.
Tourism (1995): receipts from visitors U.S.$9,459,000,000; expenditures by nationals abroad U.S.$7,713,000,000.
Production (metric tons except as noted). Agriculture, forestry, fishing (1996): milk (1995) 3,900,000, sugar beets 1,000,000, wheat 626,000, potatoes 610,000 barley 362,000, apples 262,000, grapes 155,000; livestock (number of live animals) 1,755,000 cattle, 1,580,000 pigs; roundwood (1994) 4,974,000 cu m; fish catch (1994) 2,716. Mining (1995): salt 400,000. Manufacturing (value added in Sw F '000,000; 1994): nonelectrical machinery and transport vehicles 13,570; chemical products 13,088; electrical goods, electronics, and optics 12,306; base metals and metal products 8,241. Construction (in Sw F '000,000; 1995): residential 20,855; nonresidential 25,821. Energy production (consumption): electricity (kW-hr; 1995) 60,358,000,000 ([1994] 53,793,000,000);

coal (metric tons; 1994) none (229,000); crude petroleum (barrels; 1994) none (34,796,000); petroleum products (metric tons; 1994) 4,694,000 (11,108,000); natural gas (cu m; 1994) 1,050,000 (2,374,000,000).
Gross national product (1996): U.S.$313,729,000,000 (U.S.$44,350 per capita).

Structure of gross domestic product and labour force

	1994 in value SwF '000,000	1994 % of total value	1995 labour force[6]	1995 % of labour force
Agriculture	9,230	2.6	154,000	3.9
Manufacturing	80,997	23.0	782,000	19.9
Mining	…	…	27,000	0.7
Public utilities	7,741	2.2		
Construction	24,749	7.0	286,000	7.3
Transp. and commun.	22,173	6.3	227,000	5.8
Trade	61,092	17.3	733,000	18.6
Finance, insurance[7]	84,744	24.0	485,000	12.3
Pub. admin., defense	45,647	12.9	160,000	4.0
Services	27,769	7.9	928,000	23.6
Other	−11,218[8]	−3.2[8]	154,000[9]	3.9[9]
TOTAL	352,924	100.0	3,936,000[10]	100.0

Population economically active (1995): total 3,936,000; activity rate of total population 55.9% (participation rates: age 15 and over [1993] 60.8%; female 40.7%; unemployed [1996] 4.7%).

Price and earnings indexes (1990 = 100)

	1992	1993	1994	1995	1996	1997	1998[11]
Consumer price index	110.1	113.8	114.7	116.8	117.8	118.3	118.2
Annual earnings index	111.9	114.8	116.6	117.6	…	…	…

Household income and expenditure (1993). Average household size 2.2; average income per household Sw F 70,700 (U.S.$47,850); sources of income: wages 62.9%, transfer payments 17.9%; expenditure: food 18.8%, housing 16.4%, transportation 11.8%, health care 11.6%.
Land use (1994): forested 31.6%; meadows and pastures 29.0%; agricultural and under permanent cultivation 11.0%; other 28.4%.

Foreign trade[12]

Balance of trade (current prices)

	1992	1993	1994	1995	1996	1997
Sw F '000,000	−591	+2,892	+2,934	+1,237	+2,207	+2,044
% of total	0.3%	1.7%	1.7%	0.7%	1.2%	1.0%

Imports (1996): Sw F 91,967,000,000 (machinery and electronics 22.6%; chemical products 14.7%; vehicles 12.2%; food products 9.0%). *Major import sources:* Germany 32.7%; France 12.0%; Italy 11.2%; U.S. 6.6%; U.K. 4.9%.
Exports (1996): Sw F 94,137,000,000 (machinery and electronics 29.8%; chemical products 27.6%; precision instruments, watches, and jewelry 15.6%; base metals and finished products 8.7%). *Major export destinations:* Germany 23.3%; France 9.4%; U.S. 9.0%; Italy 7.7%; U.K. 5.7%.

Transport and communications

Transport. Railroads: length (1994) 3,125 mi, 5,030 km; passenger-km (1995) 11,400,000,000[13]; metric ton-km cargo (1995) 8,156,000,000[13]. Roads (1995): total length 44,151 mi, 71,055 km. Vehicles (1995): passenger cars 3,229,169; trucks and buses 277,399. Air transport (1995)[14]: passenger-km 19,725,000,000; metric ton-km cargo 1,508,000,000; airports (1996) with scheduled flights 5.

Communications

Medium	date	unit	number	units per 1,000 persons
Daily newspapers	1994	circulation	2,920,000	418
Radio	1996	receivers	5,600,000	791
Television	1995	receivers	2,602,000	370
Telephones	1995	main lines	4,318,500	613
Cellular telephones	1995	subscribers	447,200	64
Facsimile machines	1995	units	197,000	28
Personal computers	1995	units	2,450,000	348

Education and health

Educational attainment (1993). Percentage of resident Swiss and resident alien population age 25–64 having: lower secondary education or less 18%; vocational 50%; upper secondary 11%; higher technical 13%; university 8%.
Health (1994): physicians 11,814[15] (1 per 592 persons); hospital beds 48,539 (1 per 144 persons); infant mortality rate per 1,000 live births (1995) 5.0.
Food (1992): daily per capita caloric intake 3,379 (vegetable products 62%, animal products 38%); 126% of FAO recommended minimum.

Military

Total active duty personnel (1996): 3,300[16]. *Military expenditure as percentage of GNP* (1994): 1.9% (world 3.0%); per capita expenditure U.S.$712.

[1]January 1. [2]Demicanton; functions as a full canton. [3]Includes 1,363,590 resident aliens. [4]Urban agglomeration. [5]Confederation-level only. [6]Per revised official definition of June 1, 1995. [7]Includes consulting services. [8]Import duties less imputed bank charges. [9]Unemployed. [10]Labour force includes 976,000 foreign workers. [11]May. [12]Imports c.i.f.; exports f.o.b. [13]Swiss Federal Railways. [14]Swissair only. [15]Hospital-based physicians with private practice. [16]Excludes 396,000 reservists.

Internet resources for further information:
• **Embassy of Switzerland (Washington, D.C.)**
  http://www.swissemb.org/
• **Swiss Federal Statistical Office http://www.admin.ch/bfs/eindex.htm**

Syria

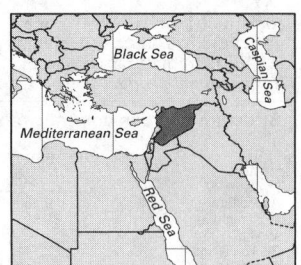

Official name: Al-Jumhūrīyah al-ʿArabīyah as-Sūrīyah (Syrian Arab Republic).
Form of government: unitary multiparty[1] republic with one legislative house (People's Council [250]).
Head of state and government: President.
Capital: Damascus.
Official language: Arabic.
Official religion: none[2].
Monetary unit: 1 Syrian pound (LS) = 100 piastres; valuation (Aug. 21, 1998) 1 U.S.$ = LS *c.* 52; 1 £ = LS *c.* 89[3].

Area and population		area		population
Governorates	**Capitals**	sq mi	sq km	1995 estimate
Darʿā	Darʿā	1,440	3,730	623,000
Dayr az-Zawr	Dayr az-Zawr	12,765	33,060	722,000
Dimashq	Damascus	6,962	18,032	1,730,000
Ḥalab	Aleppo	7,143	18,500	3,035,000
Ḥamāh	Ḥamāh	3,430	8,883	1,120,000
Al-Ḥasakah	Al-Ḥasakah	9,009	23,334	1,050,000
Ḥimṣ	Homs	16,302	42,223	1,247,000
Idlib	Idlib	2,354	6,097	922,000
Al-Lādhiqīyah	Latakia	887	2,297	766,000
Al-Qunayṭirah	Al-Qunayṭirah	719[4]	1,861[4]	50,000
Ar-Raqqah	Ar-Raqqah	7,574	19,616	566,000
As-Suwaydāʾ	As-Suwaydāʾ	2,143	5,550	270,000
Ṭarṭūs	Ṭarṭūs	730	1,892	596,000
Municipality				
Damascus	—	41	105	1,489,000
TOTAL		71,498[4]	185,180[4]	14,186,000

Demography

Population (1998): 15,335,000.
Density (1998): persons per sq mi 214.5, persons per sq km 82.8.
Urban-rural (1995): urban 52.4%; rural 47.6%.
Sex distribution (1995): male 50.71%; female 49.29%.
Age breakdown (1995): under 15, 44.7%; 15–29, 28.2%; 30–44, 14.8%; 45–59, 7.3%; 60 and over, 5.0%.
Population projection: (2000) 16,126,000; (2010) 20,468,000.
Doubling time: 21 years.
Ethnic composition (1992): Arab 90.0%; Kurdish 9.0%; other 1.0%.
Religious affiliation (1992): Muslim 86.0%, of which Sunnī 74.0%, ʿAlawite (Shīʿī) 12.0%; Christian 5.5%; Druze 3.0%; other 5.5%.
Major cities (1994): Aleppo 1,591,400; Damascus 1,549,932; Homs 644,204; Latakia 306,535; Ḥamāh 229,000.

Vital statistics

Birth rate per 1,000 population (1995): 40.0 (world avg. 25.0).
Death rate per 1,000 population (1995): 6.0 (world avg. 9.3).
Natural increase rate per 1,000 population (1995): 34.0 (world avg. 15.7).
Total fertility rate (avg. births per childbearing woman; 1995): 6.1.
Marriage rate per 1,000 population (1995)[5]: 8.4.
Life expectancy at birth (1994): male 68.4 years; female 71.3 years.
Major causes of death per 100,000 population (1989): n.a.; however, the leading causes of mortality among the total population were diseases of the circulatory system 39.6%, injuries and poisoning 9.1%, diseases of the nervous system 7.4%, diseases of the respiratory system 7.4%.

National economy

Budget (1995). Revenue: LS 125,718,000,000 (current revenues 81.3%, capital [development] revenues 18.7%). Expenditures: LS 162,040,000,000 (current expenditures 54.3%, capital [development] expenditures 45.7%).
Public debt (external, outstanding; 1996): U.S.$16,698,000,000.
Gross national product (1996): U.S.$16,808,000,000 (U.S.$1,160 per capita).

Structure of gross domestic product and labour force				
	1996[6]		1991	
	in value LS '000,000	% of total value	labour force	% of labour force
Agriculture	171,354	27.7	916,952	26.3
Mining	43,780	7.1	6,651	0.2
Manufacturing	35,212	5.7	456,162	13.1
Construction	27,633	4.5	340,779	9.8
Public utilities	5,041	0.8	8,422	0.2
Transp. and commun.	65,873	10.6	166,965	4.8
Trade	157,816	25.5	378,250	10.9
Finance	28,206	4.6	24,651	0.7
Pub. admin.	62,838	10.2 }	951,104	27.3
Services	12,072	1.9 }		
Other	8,441[7]	1.4[7]	235,432[8]	6.8[8]
TOTAL	618,266	100.0	3,485,368	100.0[9]

Production (metric tons except as noted). Agriculture, forestry, fishing (1997): wheat 4,300,000, barley 1,800,000, seed cotton 765,000, grapes 455,000, tomatoes 425,000, apples 240,000, eggplants 160,000; livestock (number of live animals) 13,609,000 sheep, 1,137,000 goats, 818,000 cattle; roundwood (1995) 54,600 cu m; fish catch (1994) 7,500. Mining and quarrying (1994): phosphate rock 1,600,000; gypsum 235,000; salt 130,000; marble blocks

18,000,000 cu m. Manufacturing (value of production in LS '000,000; 1994): food, beverages, and tobacco 48,395; textiles, wearing apparel, and leather 47,372; chemicals and chemical products 35,300; fabricated metal products 20,558; nonmetallic mineral products 13,750; wood and wood products 9,116. Construction (1993): residential 628,000 sq m; nonresidential 209,000 sq m. Energy production (consumption): electricity (kW-hr; 1994) 14,800,000,000 (14,800,000,000); crude petroleum (barrels; 1996) 220,825,000 ([1994] 85,-450,000); petroleum products (metric tons; 1994) 11,438,000 (10,044,000); natural gas (cu m; 1994) 2,050,160,000 (2,050,160,000).
Population economically active (1991); total 3,845,368; activity rate of total population 27.8% (participation rates: ages 15 and over, 49.0%; female 10.2%; unemployed 6.1%).

Price and earnings indexes (1990 = 100)							
	1991	1992	1993	1994	1995	1996	1997
Consumer price index	109.0	121.0	137.0	158.0	170.6	184.7	188.2
Earnings index[10]	107.9	140.8	152.2	...	...	...	...

Average household size (1986): 5.7; income per household: n.a.; sources of income: n.a.; expenditure (1987)[11]: food 58.8%, rent, fuel, and light 16.0%, clothing 7.5%, household goods 5.8%, transportation 2.4%, education and recreation 2.1%.
Tourism (1995): receipts U.S.$1,325,000,000; expenditures U.S.$398,000,000.
Land use (1994): steppe and pasture 45.2%; cultivable 30.1%; forested 2.6%; other 22.1%.

Foreign trade[12]

Balance of trade (current prices)						
	1991	1992	1993	1994	1995	1996
LS '000,000	+7,430	−4,458	−11,149	−21,550	−12,860	−15,500
% of total	10.7%	6.0%	13.6%	21.3%	13.8%	14.7%

Imports (1994): LS 61,370,000,000 (machinery and equipment 25.2%, food and beverages 15.7%, transportation equipment 12.0%, iron and steel 10.8%, chemicals and chemical products 8.5%, textiles 6.9%). *Major import sources:* Japan 10.1%; Italy 8.7%; Germany 8.5%; United States 5.8%; France 5.0%.
Exports (1994): LS 39,820,000,000 (crude petroleum and petroleum products 56.2%, fresh vegetables and fruits 10.7%, raw cotton 5.5%, textiles and fabrics 4.2%; live animals and meat 2.2%). *Major export destinations:* Italy 27.0%; France 12.4%; Lebanon 11.0%; Spain 6.8%; Saudi Arabia 5.5%.

Transport and communications

Transport. Railroads (1996): route length 1,766 km; passenger-km 498,000,-000[13]; metric ton-km cargo 1,285,000,000[13]. Roads (1995): total length 39,243 km (paved 71%). Vehicles (1995): passenger cars 229,084; trucks and buses 218,900. Air transport (1996): passenger-km 1,113,614,000; metric ton-km cargo 117,638,000; airports (1997) with scheduled flights 5.

Communications				units per 1,000
Medium	date	unit	number	persons
Daily newspapers	1994	circulation	261,000	19
Radio	1995	receivers	3,000,000	211
Television	1995	receivers	700,000	49
Telephones	1995	main lines	930,000	66
Facsimile machines	1995	units	5,000	0.4
Personal computers	1995	units	10,000	0.7

Education and health

Educational attainment (1984). Percentage of population age 10 and over having: no schooling 20.1%; knowledge of reading and writing 26.3%; primary education 29.3%; secondary 18.4%; certificate 3.3%; higher 2.7%. *Literacy* (1995): percentage of population age 15 and over literate 70.8%; males literate 85.7%; females literate 55.8%.

Education (1995–96)	schools	teachers	students	student/ teacher ratio
Primary (age 6–11)	10,564	113,530	2,672,960	23.5
Secondary (age 12–18)	2,526[14]	51,483[15]	846,778	16.4
Voc., teacher tr.	292[14]	12,200[15]	94,204	7.7
Higher[16]	4[14, 17]	4,869[14]	161,185	46.6[18]

Health (1995): physicians 15,391 (1 per 953 persons); hospital beds 17,623 (1 per 832 persons); infant mortality rate per 1,000 live births (1994) 29.6.
Food (1995): daily per capita caloric intake 3,296 (vegetable products 90%, animal products 10%); 133% of FAO recommended minimum requirement.

Military

Total active duty personnel (1997): 320,000 (army 67.2%, navy 1.6%, air force 31.2%). *Military expenditure as percentage of GNP* (1995): 7.2% (world 2.8%); per capita expenditure U.S.$236.

---

[1]Parties ideologically compatible with the Baʿth Party. [2]Islam is required to be the religion of the head of state and is the basis of the legal system. [3]Black market rate. [4]Includes territory in the Golan Heights recognized internationally as part of Syria. [5]Syrian Arabs only. [6]UN estimates. [7]Import duties less imputed bank service charge. [8]Unemployed. [9]Detail does not add to total given because of rounding. [10]Annual wages index in manufacturing industries. [11]Weights of consumer price index components for Damascus only. [12]Import figures are c.i.f. [13]1995. [14]1994–95. [15]Estimated or provisional. [16]University-level institutions only. [17]Government schools only. [18]1993–94.

Taiwan

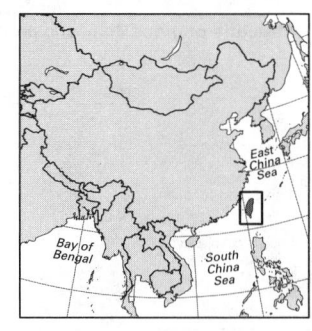

Official name: Chung-hua Min-kuo (Republic of China).
Form of government: multiparty republic with a National Assembly (334) and Legislative Yuan (225)[1].
Chief of state: President.
Head of government: Premier.
Capital: Taipei.
Official language: Mandarin Chinese.
Official religion: none.
Monetary unit: 1 New Taiwan dollar (NT$) = 100 cents; valuation (Sept. 25, 1998) 1 U.S.$ = NT$34.55; 1 £ = NT$58.82.

Area and population

Taiwan area Counties	Capitals	area sq mi	area sq km	population 1996 estimate
Chang-hua	Chang-hua	415	1,074	1,289,554
Chia-i	Chia-i	734	1,902	565,099
Hsin-chu	Hsin-chu	551	1,428	410,985
Hua-lien	Hua-lien	1,787	4,629	358,679
I-lan	I-lan	825	2,137	464,793
Kao-hsiung	Feng-shan	1,078	2,793	1,199,876
Miao-li	Miao-li	703	1,820	559,674
Nan-t'ou	Nan t'ou	1,585	4,106	545,370
P'eng-hu	Ma-kung	49	127	90,142
P'ing-tung	P'ing-tung	1,072	2,776	912,360
T'ai-chung	Feng-yuan	792	2,051	1,415,659
T'ai-nan	Hsin-ying	778	2,016	1,084,168
T'ai-pei	Pan-ch'iao	792	2,052	3,324,210
T'ai-tung	T'ai-tung	1,357	3,515	253,932
T'ao-yüan	T'ao-yüan	471	1,221	1,543,914
Yün-lin	Tou-liu	498	1,291	752,859
Municipalities				
Chia-i	—	23	60	262,300
Chi-lung	—	51	133	371,431
Hsin-chu	—	40	104	342,575
Kao-hsiung	—	59	154	1,428,694
T'ai-chung	—	63	163	864,363
T'ai-nan	—	68	176	709,440
Taipei	—	105	272	2,620,716
non-Taiwan area Counties[2]				
Kinmen (Quemoy) ⎱ Lienchiang (Matsu) ⎰	—	69	179	53,286
TOTAL		13,969[3]	36,179	21,424,079

Demography

Population (1998)[4]: 21,843,000.
Density (1998)[4]: persons per sq mi 1,563.7, persons per sq km 603.7.
Urban-rural (1991)[5]: urban 74.7%; rural 25.3%.
Sex distribution (1997[6])[5]: male 51.40%; female 48.60%.
Age breakdown (1996)[5]: under 15, 23.8%; 15–29, 26.5%; 30–44, 25.7%; 45–59, 13.0%; 60–69, 6.5%; 70 and over, 4.5%.
Population projection: (2000) 22,250,000; (2010) 24,399,000.
Major cities (1997[6])[5]: Taipei 2,595,699; Kao-hsiung 1,434,907; T'ai-chung 881,870; T'ai-nan 712,172; Chi-lung 374,874.

Vital statistics

Birth rate per 1,000 population (1997[6]): 14.7 (world avg. 25.0).
Death rate per 1,000 population (1997[6]): 6.1 (world avg. 9.3).
Natural increase rate per 1,000 population (1997[6]): 8.6 (world avg. 15.7).
Total fertility rate (avg. births per childbearing woman; 1995)[5]: 1.8.
Life expectancy at birth (1994): male 71.8 years; female 77.7 years.
Major causes of death per 100,000 population (1996)[5]: malignant neoplasms 130.2; cerebrovascular diseases 64.9; accidents and suicide 57.8; heart disease 52.5; diabetes 35.0; liver diseases 21.5; kidney diseases 16.5; pneumonia 14.9.

National economy

Budget (1995)[7]. Revenue: NT$2,102,737,000,000 (income taxes 15.2%, land tax 11.9%, business tax 10.2%, commodity tax 7.4%, surplus of public enterprises 6.7%, customs duties 5.5%). Expenditures: NT$2,074,929,000,000 (administration and defense 23.7%, economic development 21.1%).
Population economically active (1990): total 10,236,324; activity rate 50.5% (participation rates: ages 15–64, 72.5%; female 38.5%; unemployed [1997] 2.7%).

Price and earnings indexes (1990 = 100)[5]

	1991	1992	1993	1994	1995	1996	1997
Consumer price index	103.6	108.3	111.4	116.0	120.3	124.0	125.1
Monthly earnings index[8]	111.0	122.3	130.7	139.4	147.1	...	...

Production (metric tons except as noted). Agriculture, forestry, fishing (1996): sugarcane 4,190,000, rice 1,577,000, citrus fruits 463,710, corn (maize) 321,322[9], pineapples 274,113, sweet potatoes 204,000, bananas 140,997; livestock (number of live animals) 10,698,366 pigs, 318,404 goats, 164,825 cattle; timber 36,118 cu m; fish catch 1,231,834. Mining and quarrying (1990): silver 3,926 kg. Manufacturing (1996): cement 21,535,037; steel ingots 12,471,722; paperboard 3,209,458; fertilizers 2,197,742; polyester filament 1,199,470; polyvinyl chloride plastics 1,105,287; telephones 4,796,800 units; electronic calculators 2,951,086 units. Construction (1995): total residential and non-residential 46,221,000 sq m. Energy production (consumption): electricity (kW-hr; 1996) 124,973,000,000 (111,140,000,000); coal (metric tons; 1993)

328,000 ([[1992] 16,500,000]); crude petroleum (barrels; 1993) 400,000 ([[1992] 215,400]); natural gas (cu m; 1992) 767,000,000 (n.a.).
Gross national product (1998): U.S.$297,953,000,000 (U.S.$13,900 per capita).

Structure of gross domestic product and labour force[5]

	1996 in value NT$'000,000	% of total value	labour force[10]	% of labour force[10]
Agriculture	246,538	3.3	918,000	9.9
Mining	20,483	0.3	14,000	0.1
Manufacturing	2,104,338	28.1	2,422,000	26.0
Construction	359,927	4.8	928,000	10.0
Public utilities	188,298	2.5	35,000	0.4
Transp. and commun.	509,259	6.8	472,000	5.1
Trade	1,218,045	16.2	1,976,000	21.2
Finance	1,627,624	21.7	567,000	6.1
Pub. admin., defense	790,389	10.5 ⎱	1,736,000	18.6
Services	626,373	8.4 ⎰		
Other	−193,597[11]	−2.6[11]	242,000[12]	2.6[12]
TOTAL	7,497,677	100.0	9,310,000	100.0

Tourism (1995): receipts from visitors U.S.$3,286,000,000.
Household income and expenditure (1995). Average household size (1996) 3.6; income per household NT$965,890 (U.S.$36,470[13]); expenditure: food 27.1%, rent, fuel, and power 19.7%, education 17.5%, transportation 11.6%, health care 7.6%, clothing 4.7%, furniture 2.9%.

Foreign trade

Balance of trade (current prices)

	1992	1993	1994	1995	1996	1997
NT$'000,000	231,668	199,604	194,360	206,730	361,505	205,500
% of total	6.0%	4.7%	4.1%	3.6%	6.0%	3.0%

Imports (1996): NT$2,815,720,000,000 (electronic machinery 15.8%, nonelectrical machinery 10.9%, chemicals 10.7%, iron and steel 5.6%, crude petroleum 4.7%, road motor vehicles 4.4%). *Major import sources:* Japan 26.8%; U.S. 19.5%; Germany 4.9%; South Korea 4.1%; Malaysia 3.5%; Singapore 2.7%.
Exports (1996): NT$3,176,625,000,000 (nonelectrical machinery 24.3%, electrical machinery 21.5%, plastic articles 6.6%, synthetic fibres 5.0%, transportation equipment 4.5%). *Major export destinations:* U.S. 23.2%; Hong Kong 23.1%; Japan 11.8%; Singapore 3.9%; Germany 3.1%.

Transport and communications

Transport. Railroads (1996): track length 3,879 km; passenger-km 8,975,200,-000; metric ton-km cargo 1,584,800,000. Roads (1994): total length 19,038 km (paved 89%). Vehicles (1996): passenger cars 4,146,500; trucks and buses 799,600. Air transport (1996): passenger-km 40,603,500,000; metric ton-km cargo 3,567,900,000; airports (1996) 13.

Communications

Medium	date	unit	number	units per 1,000 persons
Daily newspapers	1988	circulation	4,000,000	202
Radio	1996	receivers	8,620,000	402
Television	1995	receivers	7,000,000	327
Telephones	1996	main lines	10,010,600	467
Cellular telephones	1996	subscribers	970,473	45.3
Facsimile machines	1995	units	430,000	20.2
Personal computers	1995	units	1,773,000	83.2

Education and health

Educational attainment (1995). Percentage of population age 25 and over having: no formal schooling 9.1%; less than complete primary education 6.9%; primary 23.9%; incomplete secondary 26.0%; secondary 20.5%; some college 8.2%; higher 5.4%. *Literacy* (1995): population age 15 and over literate 15,006,668 (93.7%); males 8,156,195 (97.6%); females 7,149,455 (90.2%).

Education (1995–96)

	schools	teachers	students	student/ teacher ratio
Primary (age 6–12)	2,523	87,934	1,971,439	22.4
Secondary (age 13–18)	920	76,562	1,412,201	18.4
Vocational	203	19,660	523,412	26.6
Higher	134	36,348	751,347	20.7

Health (1995): physicians 24,465 (1 per 867 persons); hospital beds 112,379 (1 per 189 persons); infant mortality rate per 1,000 live births 6.4.

Military

Total active duty personnel (1996): 376,000 (army 63.8%, navy 18.1%, air force 18.1%). *Military expenditure as percentage of GNP* (1995): 5.0% (world 2.8%); per capita expenditure U.S.$618.

[1]National Assembly functions as an electoral college or constituent body; the legislative branch is the formal lawmaking body. [2]The Nov. 7, 1992, constitutional reforms replaced the military administrations (established in 1949) on Quemoy and Matsu with civilian administrations. [3]Detail does not add to total given because of rounding. [4]Includes Quemoy and Matsu groups. [5]For Taiwan area only, excluding Quemoy and Matsu groups. [6]March. [7]General government. [8]In manufacturing. [9]1991. [10]Civilian employed persons only. [11]Import duties less imputed bank service charge. [12]Unemployed. [13]Based on the average exchange rate.

Internet resources for further information:
• The Republic of China Yearbook 1998
  http://www.gio.gov.tw/info/yb97/html/content.htm
• Directorate-General of Budget, Accounting and Statistics (Taiwan)
  http://www.dgbasey.gov.tw/english/dgbas_e0.htm

Tajikistan

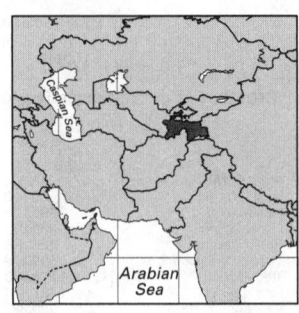

Official name: Jumhurii Tojikistan (Republic of Tajikistan).
Form of government: parliamentary republic with one legislative house (Supreme Council [181]).
Chief of state: President.
Head of government: Prime Minister.
Capital: Dushanbe.
Official language: Tajik (Tojik).
Official religion: none.
Monetary unit: 1 Tajik ruble;
  valuation (Oct. 2, 1998)
  1 U.S.$ = 754 Tajik rubles;
  1 £ = 1,284 Tajik rubles.

Area and population		area		population
				1991
Oblasts	**Capitals**	sq mi	sq km	estimate
Khujand	Khujand	10,100	26,100	1,635,900
Khatlon (Qŭrghonteppa)	Qŭrghonteppa	9,500	24,600	1,781,600
Autonomous oblast				
Badakhshoni Kuni				
(Gorno-Badakhshan)	Khorugh	24,600	63,700	167,100
City				
Dushanbe	—	100	300	591,900
Other[1]	—	11,000	28,400	1,181,800
TOTAL		55,300	143,100	5,358,300

Demography

Population (1997): 6,112,000.
Density (1997): persons per sq mi 110.5, persons per sq km 42.7.
Urban-rural (1995): urban 28.3%; rural 71.7%.
Sex distribution (1996): male 51.22%; female 48.78%.
Age breakdown (1989): under 15, 42.9%; 15–29, 28.1%; 30–44, 13.8%; 45–59, 9.0%; 60–74, 4.6%; 75 and over, 1.6%.
Population projection: (2000) 6,303,000; (2010) 7,497,000.
Doubling time: 35 years.
Ethnic composition (1991): Tajik 62.2%; Uzbek 23.1%; Russian 9.7%; Tatar 1.4%; Kyrgyz 1.3%; Ukrainian 0.7%; German 0.3%; other 1.3%.
Religious affiliation (1995): Sunnī Muslim 80.0%; Shī'ī Muslim 5.0%; Russian Orthodox 1.5%; Jewish 0.1%; other (mostly nonreligious) 13.4%.
Major cities (1989): Dushanbe 582,400; Khujand (formerly Leninabad) 164,500; Kŭlob 79,300; Qŭrghonteppa 58,400; Urateppa 47,700.

Vital statistics

Birth rate per 1,000 population (1996): 33.8 (1994; world avg. 25.0); (1994) legitimate 90.8%; illegitimate 9.2%.
Death rate per 1,000 population (1996): 8.4 (1994; world avg. 9.3).
Natural increase rate per 1,000 population (1996): 25.4 (1994; world avg. 15.7).
Total fertility rate (avg. births per childbearing woman; 1996): 4.4.
Marriage rate per 1,000 population (1994): 6.8.
Divorce rate per 1,000 population (1994): 0.8.
Life expectancy at birth (1995): male 64.4 years; female 70.4 years.
Major causes of death per 100,000 population (1993): diseases of the circulatory system 225.5; violence, poisoning, and accidents 184.0; diseases of the respiratory system 160.6; infectious and parasitic diseases 129.9; malignant neoplasms (cancers) 42.3; diseases of the digestive system 20.9.

National economy

Budget (1994). Revenue: 772,243,000,000 Tajik rubles (tax revenue 94.0%, of which domestic taxes 47.5%, income and profit taxes 35.8%, property taxes 8.7%; duties 7.5%; other 6.0%). Expenditures: 945,245,000,000 Tajik rubles (national economy 43.0%, social welfare and culture 30.0%, defense 4.0%).
Production (metric tons except as noted). Agriculture, forestry, fishing (1995): grain 206,200, vegetables 156,200, milk 76,100, eggs 31,100, potatoes 24,700; livestock (number of live animals) 2,930,000 sheep and goats, 1,147,000 cattle, 6,000 pigs, 1,200,000 poultry; roundwood, n.a.; fish catch (1995) 3,900. Mining and quarrying (1995): aluminum 500,000; lead 2,500; antimony 2,000. Manufacturing (value of production in '000,000 Tajik rubles; 1994): ferrous and nonferrous metals 604,705; textiles 496,481; energy 330,078; food products 163,559; machinery 77,331; chemical products 68,892; construction materials 66,306. Energy production (consumption): electricity (kW-hr; 1994) 17,000,000,000 (1993; 17,200,000,000); coal (metric tons; 1994) 150,000 (59,500); crude petroleum (barrels; 1994) 219,900 (1992; 279,000); petroleum products (metric tons; 1994) n.a. (305,500); natural gas (cu m; 1994) 40,000,000 (994,500).
Public debt (external, outstanding; 1996): U.S.$671,700,000.
Tourism: receipts from visitors, n.a.; expenditures by nationals abroad, n.a.
Population economically active (1995): total 1,783,000; activity rate of total population 30.7% (participation rates: ages 16–59 [male], 16–54 [female] 67.8%; female [1994] 38.0%; unemployed [1994] 27.0%).

Price and earnings indexes (1993 = 100)			
	1993	1994	1995
Consumer price index (Dec.)	100.0	107.2	1,428.8
Monthly earnings index	100.0	169.2	321.6

Gross national product (1996): U.S.$1,964,000,000 (U.S.$340 per capita).

Structure of gross domestic product and labour force

	1994			
	in value '000,000 Russian rubles	% of total value	labour force	% of labour force
Agriculture	326,040	19.0	1,004,800	50.7
Mining	} 595,219	34.7	205,400	10.4
Manufacturing				
Public utilities	...	...	26,900	1.4
Construction	206,527	12.0	104,900	5.3
Transp. and commun.	58,393	3.4	63,000	3.2
Trade	51,979	3.0	112,000	5.7
Finance	...	...	...	...
Public administration, defense	...	...	21,000	1.1
Services	56,933	3.3	299,500	15.1
Other	422,877[2]	24.6	146,100	7.4
TOTAL	1,717,968	100.0	1,983,600	100.0[3]

Household income and expenditure. Average household size (1989) 6.1; (1995) income per household: 18,744 Tajik rubles (U.S.$114); sources of income (1995): wages and salaries 34.5%, self-employment 34.0%, borrowing 2.4%, pension 2.0%, other 27.1%, expenditure: food 81.5%, clothing 10.2%, transport 2.5%, fuel 2.1%, other 3.7%.
Land use (1994): forest 3.8%; pasture 24.8%; agriculture 6.0%; other 65.4%.

Foreign trade

Balance of trade (current prices)			
	1993	1994	1995
U.S.$'000,000	−100.0	−400.0	+29.0
% of total	14.3%	33.0%	2.3%

Imports (1995): U.S.$628,000,000 (alumina 29.0%, petroleum products 13.0%, agricultural products 12.0%, natural gas 11.0%). *Major import sources* (1993): Uzbekistan 33.5%; Russia 24.4%; Turkmenistan 15.9%; Kazakstan 13.2%; Lithuania 5.5%; Ukraine 5.5%.
Exports (1995): U.S.$657,000,000 (aluminum 59.0%, cotton fibre 32.0%). *Major export destinations* (1993): Russia 42.0%; Uzbekistan 20.6%; Lithuania 12.4%; Kazakstan 9.2%; Ukraine 4.6%; Latvia 3.1%.

Transport and communications

Transport. Railroads (1995): length 294.5 mi, 474.0 km; (1990) passenger-mi 6,094,400,000, passenger-km 9,808,000,000; short ton-mi cargo 7,617,000,000, metric ton-km cargo 11,121,000,000. Roads (1994): total length (state roads) 8,098 mi, 13,034 km (paved 28%). Vehicles (1994): passenger cars 184,900; trucks and buses, 3,600. Merchant marine: vessels (100 gross tons and over) n.a.; total deadweight tonnage, n.a. Air transport (1989): passenger-mi 3,214,600,000, passenger-km 5,173,400,000; short ton-mi cargo 22,124,000, metric ton-km cargo 32,300,000; airports (1997) with scheduled flights 1.

Communications				units per 1,000
Medium	date	unit	number	persons
Daily newspapers	1994	circulation	80,000	13.7
Television	1995	receivers	1,500,000	259
Telephones	1995	main lines	262,700	45.3
Facsimile machines	1995	units	1,300	0.2

Education and health

Educational attainment (1989). Percentage of population age 25 and over having: primary education or no formal schooling 16.3%; some secondary 21.1%; completed secondary and some postsecondary 55.1%; higher 7.5%. *Literacy* (1989): percentage of total population age 15 and over literate 97.7%; males literate 98.8%; females literate 96.6%.

Education (1994–95)	schools	teachers	students	student/ teacher ratio
Primary (age 6–13)	} 3,400	84,000	1,289,000	15.3
Secondary (age 14–17)				
Voc., teacher tr.	75	...	35,000	...
Higher	...	...	10,000	...

Health (1995): physicians 13,084 (1 per 443 persons); hospital beds 50,637 (1 per 115 persons); infant mortality rate per 1,000 live births (1994) 42.7.
Food: daily per capita caloric intake (mid-1990s) 1,400 (vegetable products 88%, animal products 12%); 55% of FAO recommended minimum requirement.

Military

Total active duty personnel (1997): 7,000 (army 100%); more than 6,000 Russian troops remained in Tajikistan in late 1997. *Military expenditure as percentage of GNP* (1995): 1.0% (world 2.8%); per capita expenditure U.S.$36.

[1]No oblast-level administration. [2]Includes 91,587,000,000 rubles in undistributed GDP and 331,300,000,000 rubles indirect taxes. [3]Detail does not add to total given because of rounding.

Internet resources for further information:
• **Tajikistan Human Development Report 1996**
  http://www.undp.org/undp/rbec/nhdr/1996/tajikistan/
• **Tajikistan Resource Page**
  http://www.soros.org/tajkstan.html
• **Interactive Central Asia Resource Project: Tajikistan**
  http://www.rockbridge.net/personal/bichel/tajik.htp

Tanzania

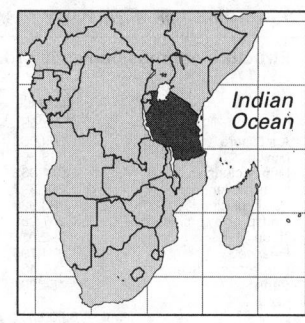

Official name: Jamhuri ya Muungano wa Tanzania (Swahili); United Republic of Tanzania (English).
Form of government: unitary multiparty republic with one legislative house (National Assembly [232[1]]).
Head of state and government: President.
Seat of government: Dar es Salaam[2] (Capital designate, Dodoma).
Official languages: Swahili; English.
Official religion: none.
Monetary unit: 1 Tanzania shilling (T Sh) = 100 cents; valuation (Sept. 25, 1998) 1 U.S.$ = T Sh 659.65; 1 £ = T Sh 1,123.05.

Area and population

Geographical Areas	Capitals	area sq mi	area sq km	population 1994 estimate
Mainland Tanzania (Tanganyika)[3]				
Arusha	Arusha	31,778	82,306	1,596,000
Dar es Salaam	—	538	1,393	1,606,000
Dodoma	Dodoma	15,950	41,311	1,461,000
Iringa	Iringa	21,955	56,864	1,427,000
Kagera	Bukoba	10,961	28,388	1,607,000
Kigoma	Kigoma	14,300	37,037	1,015,000
Kilimanjaro	Moshi	5,139	13,309	1,308,000
Lindi	Lindi	25,501	66,046	763,000
Mara	Musoma	7,555	19,566	1,146,000
Mbeya	Mbeya	23,301	60,350	1,742,000
Morogoro	Morogoro	27,336	70,799	1,483,000
Mtwara	Mtwara	6,451	16,707	1,050,000
Mwanza	Mwanza	7,564	19,592	2,217,000
Pwani (Coast)	Dar es Salaam	12,512	32,407	753,000
Rukwa	Sumbawanga	26,500	68,635	820,000
Ruvuma	Songea	24,517	63,498	924,000
Shinyanga	Shinyanga	19,607	50,781	2,092,000
Singida	Singida	19,051	49,341	934,000
Tabora	Tabora	29,402	76,151	1,223,000
Tanga	Tanga	10,351	26,808	1,546,000
Autonomous Territory				
Zanzibar and Pemba[4]				
Pemba	...	350	906	314,000
Zanzibar	Zanzibar	601	1,554	444,000
TOTAL LAND AREA		341,217[5]	883,749	
INLAND WATER		22,800	59,050	
TOTAL		364,017[6]	942,799[6]	27,471,000

Demography

Population (1998): 30,609,000.
Density (1998)[7]: persons per sq mi 83.9, persons per sq km 32.4.
Urban-rural (1995): urban 24.4%; rural 75.6%.
Sex distribution (1996): male 49.17%; female 50.83%.
Age breakdown (1996): under 15, 44.8%; 15–29, 28.6%; 30–44, 14.2%; 45–59, 7.8%; 60–74, 3.7%; 75 and over, 0.9%.
Population projection: (2000) 31,963,000; (2010) 39,390,000.
Doubling time: 29 years.
Ethnolinguistic composition (1987): Nyamwezi and Sukuma 21.1%; Swahili 8.8%; Hehet and Bena 6.9%; Haya 5.9%; Makonde 5.9%; Nyakyusa 5.4%; Chagga 4.9%; other 41.1%.
Religious affiliation (1984): Muslim 35%; animist 35%; Christian 30%.
Major cities (1988): Dar es Salaam 1,360,850; Mwanza 223,013; Dodoma 203,833; Tanga 187,155; Zanzibar 157,634.

Vital statistics

Birth rate per 1,000 population (1996): 41.0 (world avg. 25.0).
Death rate per 1,000 population (1996): 17.0 (world avg. 9.3).
Natural increase rate per 1,000 population (1996): 24.0 (world avg. 15.7).
Total fertility rate (avg. births per childbearing woman; 1996): 5.6.
Life expectancy at birth (1995): male 41.5 years; female 45.0 years.
Major causes of death per 100,000 population: n.a.; however, the major diseases include malaria, bilharziasis, tuberculosis, and sleeping sickness.

National economy

Budget (1996–97). Revenue: T Sh 564,000,000,000 (import duties 29.7%, sales and excise tax 25.0%, income tax 24.1%). Expenditures: T Sh 673,000,000,000 (public administration 27.4%, interest payments on debt 14.8%, other 57.8%).
Public debt (external, outstanding; 1996) U.S.$6,104,000,000.
Tourism (1995): receipts from visitors U.S.$259,000,000; expenditures by nationals abroad U.S.$360,000,000[8].
Production (metric tons except as noted). Agriculture (1996): cassava 5,912,000, corn (maize) 2,638,000, sugarcane 1,560,000, rice 681,000, bananas 631,000, plantains 631,000, sorghum 609,000, coconuts 375,000, sweet potatoes 358,000, millet 338,000, potatoes 245,000; livestock (number of live animals) 13,360,000 cattle, 9,682,000 goats, 3,955,000 sheep, 335,000 pigs, 27,000,000 chickens; roundwood (1995) 35,577,000 cu m; fish catch (1993) 345,000. Mining and quarrying (1994): gemstones (including emeralds, sapphires, and rubies) 33,000 kg; gold 3,370 kg; diamonds 15,700 carats. Manufacturing (1995): cement 796,000; fresh meat and poultry 291,000[9]; sugar 88,000; hides and skins 48,325[8]; soap 20,000[9]; wheat flour 3,000[10]; textiles 12,000,000 m. Construction: n.a. Energy production (consumption): elec-

tricity (kW-hr; 1994) 912,000,000 (912,000,000); coal (metric tons; 1994) 4,000 (4,000); crude petroleum (barrels; 1994) none (4,288,000); petroleum products (metric tons; 1994) 579,000 (657,000).
Gross national product (1996)[11]: U.S.$5,174,000,000 (U.S.$170 per capita).

Structure of gross domestic product and labour force

	1995 in value T Sh '000,000	1995 % of total value	1991 labour force	1991 % of labour force
Agriculture	1,209,622	50.7	10,540,000	80.3
Mining	29,526	1.2		
Manufacturing	142,576	6.0	614,000	4.7
Construction	75,245	3.2		
Public utilities	46,365	1.9		
Transp. and commun.	153,690	6.4		
Trade	315,273	13.2		
Finance	51,901	2.2	1,969,000	15.0
Pub. admin., defense	106,355	4.5		
Services				
Other	256,157	10.7	...	...
TOTAL	2,386,710	100.0	13,123,000	100.0

Population economically active (1994): total 13,852,000; activity rate 48.0% (participation rates [1991]: over age 10, 87.8%; female 40.0%).

Price index (1990 = 100)

	1991	1992	1993	1994	1995	1996	1997
Consumer price index	128.7	156.8	196.4	261.4	339.3	406.1	471.4

Household income and expenditure. Average household size (1988) 5.2; income per household: n.a.; sources of income: n.a.; expenditure (1994): food 64.2%, clothing 9.9%, housing 8.3%, energy 7.6%, transportation 4.1%.
Land use (1995): forested 37.0%; meadows and pastures 39.6%; agricultural and under permanent cultivation 4.2%; other 19.2%.

Foreign trade

Balance of trade (current prices)

	1992	1993	1994	1995	1996	1997
T Sh '000,000	−258,245	−342,654	−385,977	−433,525	−363,605	−379,905
% of total	51.0%	48.6%	42.1%	35.7%	29.2%	30.2%

Imports (1996): T Sh 804,949,000,000 (1995; machinery 31.3%, consumer goods 27.1%, chemicals 4.7%, food 2.3%). *Major import sources* (1995): U.K. 9.7%; Kenya 9.1%; Japan 7.2%; China 4.9%; India 4.7%.
Exports (1996): T Sh 441,344,000,000 (coffee 21.6%; cotton 18.2%, cashew nuts 9.7%, tobacco 4.1%). *Major export destinations* (1995): Germany 9.6%; Japan 8.5%; India 8.4%; U.K. 5.7%; Rwanda 5.0%; The Netherlands 5.2%.

Transport and communications

Transport. Railroads (1995): length 3,569 km; passenger-journeys 1,517,000[12]; metric ton-km cargo 1,160,000,000[12]. Roads (1995): length 88,100 km (paved 4.2%). Vehicles (1994): passenger cars 47,500; trucks and buses 38,000. Merchant marine (1992): vessels (100 gross tons and over) 43; deadweight tonnage 48,465. Air transport (1995)[13]: passenger-km 184,383,000; metric ton-km 2,904,000; airports (1997) with scheduled flights 11.

Communications

Medium	date	unit	number	units per 1,000 persons
Daily newspapers	1994	circulation	220,000	8.0
Radio	1995	receivers	565,200	20.0
Television	1995	receivers	80,000	2.8
Telephones	1995	main lines	90,300	3.2
Cellular telephones	1995	subscribers	3,500	0.1
Facsimile machines	1995	units	2,000	0.1

Education and health

Educational attainment (1978). Percentage of population age 10 and over having: no schooling 48.6%; some primary education 40.7%; completed primary 8.7%; secondary and higher 1.9%. *Literacy* (1995): percentage of population age 15 and over literate 67.8%; males 79.4%; females 56.8%.

Education (1994)[14]

	schools	teachers	students	student/ teacher ratio
Primary (age 7–13)	10,891	103,900	3,736,734[8]	...
Secondary (age 14–19)	491	10,612	180,899[8]	...
Teacher training	40	1,167[8]	15,824[8]	13.6
Higher	4[15]	1,206[15]	4,289	...

Health (1993): physicians 1,365 (1 per 20,511 persons); hospital beds 26,820 (1 per 1,000 persons); infant mortality rate (1995) 107.
Food (1995): daily per capita caloric intake 2,024 (vegetable products 93%, animal products 7%); 81% of FAO recommended minimum requirement.

Military

Total active duty personnel (1996): 34,600 (army 86.7%, navy 2.9%, air force 10.4%). *Military expenditure as percentage of GNP* (1995): 1.8% (world 3.0%); per capita expenditure U.S.$2.

[1]Includes 43 nonelective seats. [2]Government in process of being transferred from Dar es Salaam to Dodoma; legislative branch meets in Dodoma. [3]Internal government structure proposed in August 1993; not yet effective in mid-1998. [4]Has local internal government structure. [5]Detail does not add to total given because of rounding. [6]A recent survey indicates a total area of 364,901 sq mi (945,090 sq km). [7]Based on the total area of 364,901 sq mi. [8]1993. [9]1992. [10]1991. [11]Mainland Tanzania only. [12]Tanzanian Railways only; 1994. [13]Air Tanzania only. [14]Excludes Zanzibar and Pemba. [15]1989.

Thailand

Official name: Muang Thai, or Prathet Thai (Kingdom of Thailand).
Form of government: constitutional monarchy with two legislative houses (Senate [260][1]; House of Representatives [393]).
Chief of state: King.
Head of government: Prime Minister.
Capital: Bangkok.
Official language: Thai.
Official religion: Buddhism.
Monetary unit: 1 Thai baht (B) = 100 stangs; valuation (Sept. 25, 1998) 1 U.S.$ = B 38.85; 1 £ = B 66.14.

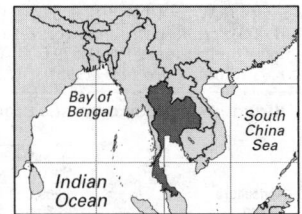

Area and population	area		population
Regions[2]	sq mi	sq km	1995 estimate[3]
Bangkok Metropolis	2,995	7,758	8,896,506
Central	6,407	16,594	2,877,458
Eastern	14,094	36,503	3,922,078
Northeastern	65,195	168,854	20,663,191
Northern	65,500	169,644	11,896,331
Southern	27,303	70,715	7,706,208
Western	16,621	43,047	3,498,610
TOTAL	198,115	513,115	59,460,382

Demography

Population (1998): 61,201,000[4].
Density (1998): persons per sq mi 308.9, persons per sq km 119.3.
Urban-rural (1995): urban 18.3%; rural 81.7%.
Sex distribution (1995): male 49.91%; female 50.09%.
Age breakdown (1996): under 15, 27.4%; 15–29, 28.4%; 30–44, 22.8%; 45–59, 13.2%; 60–74, 6.6%; 75 and over, 1.6%.
Population projection: (2000) 62,405,000; (2010) 67,597,000.
Doubling time: 67 years.
Ethnic composition (1983): Thai 79.5%, of which Siamese 52.6%; Lao 26.9%; Chinese 12.1%; Malay 3.7%; Khmer 2.7%; other 2.0%.
Religious affiliation (1992): Buddhist 94.8%; Muslim 4.0%; Christian 0.6%; other 0.6%.
Major cities (1991)[3]: Bangkok 5,620,591; Nonthaburi 264,201; Nakhon Ratchasima 202,503; Chiang Mai 161,541; Khon Kaen 131,478.

Vital statistics

Birth rate per 1,000 population (1997): 17.8 (world avg. 25.0).
Death rate per 1,000 population (1997): 7.4 (world avg. 9.3).
Natural increase rate per 1,000 population (1997): 10.4 (world avg. 15.7).
Total fertility rate (avg. births per childbearing woman; 1997): 2.0.
Marriage rate per 1,000 population (1995): 7.9.
Divorce rate per 1,000 population (1995): 0.9.
Life expectancy at birth (1997): male 67.0 years; female 72.0 years.
Major causes of death per 100,000 population (1993)[5]: accidents, homicide, and poisonings 13.7; diseases of the heart 10.7; malignant neoplasms (cancers) 9.1; hypertension and cerebrovascular disease 3.3; pneumonia and other lung diseases 2.8; diseases of the liver and the pancreas 2.6.

National economy

Budget (1995). Revenue: B 760,755,000,000 (taxes 91.7%; state enterprises 4.9%; sale of property and services 1.0%). Expenditures: B 643,283,000,000 (current expenditure 67.7%, of which goods and services 58.1%, transfer payments 9.6%; capital expenditure 32.3%, of which government capital formation 29.8%, transfer payments 2.3%).
Public debt (external, outstanding; 1996): U.S.$17,039,000,000.
Production (metric tons except as noted). Agriculture, forestry, fishing (1996): sugarcane 62,422,000, rice 21,800,000, tapioca 17,340,000[6], cassava 16,000,000, corn (maize) 4,361,000, natural rubber 2,257,000, pineapples 2,031,000, bananas 1,750,000, soybean 412,000, palm oil 400,000, tobacco 69,900; livestock (number of live animals) 8,000,000 cattle, 4,807,000 buffalo, 4,023,000 pigs, 110,000,000 chickens; roundwood (1995) 39,288,000 cu m; fish catch (1994) 3,432,000. Mining and quarrying (1995): limestone 45,559,000; gypsum 8,533,000; kaolin clay 461,000; zinc ore 135,198; fluorite 24,114; lead ore 22,786; tin concentrates 2,201. Manufacturing (1995): cement 33,445,000; refined sugar 5,201,800; synthetic fibre 540,800; galvanized iron sheet 370,000; tin plate 250,500; jute products 76,000. Construction (1990): residential 16,343,000 sq m; nonresidential 13,449,000 sq m. Energy production (consumption): electricity (kW-hr; 1994) 74,452,000,000 (75,278,000,000); coal (metric tons; 1994) 17,095,000 (17,198,000); crude petroleum (barrels; 1994) 9,583,000 (137,883,000); petroleum products (metric tons; 1994) 21,291,000 (28,850,000); natural gas (cu m; 1994) 9,513,000,000 (9,513,000,000).
Land use (1994): forested 29.0%; meadows and pastures 1.6%; agricultural and under permanent cultivation 40.0%; other 29.4%.
Population economically active (1995): total 31,347,900; activity rate of total population 53.0% (participation rates: over age 13, 69.8%; female 44.1%; unemployed 2.3%).

Price and earnings indexes (1990 = 100)							
	1991	1992	1993	1994	1995	1996	1997
Consumer price index	105.7	110.1	113.7	119.5	126.4	133.8	141.3
Monthly earnings index	116.8	132.8	144.7	133.8	...	...	...

Gross national product (1996): U.S.$177,476,000,000 (U.S.$2,960 per capita).

Structure of gross domestic product and labour force				
	1994		1995	
	in value B '000,000	% of total value	labour force[7]	% of labour force[7]
Agriculture	369,053	10.2	13,418,100	42.8
Mining	48,599	1.5	64,000	0.2
Manufacturing	1,014,952	28.2	4,839,500	15.4
Construction	267,999	7.5	2,649,100	8.5
Public utilities	83,923	2.3	194,000	0.6
Transp. and commun.	267,933	7.4	1,025,800	3.3
Trade	592,016	16.4	4,274,500	13.6
Finance	374,795	10.4		
Pub. admin., defense	127,436	3.5	4,142,800	13.2
Services	454,201	12.6		
Other	...	...	740,100[8]	2.4[8]
TOTAL	3,600,907	100.0	31,347,900	100.0

Household income and expenditure (1994). Average household size 3.8; average annual income per household B 99,912 (U.S.$3,973); sources of income: wages and salaries 41.2%, self-employment 30.2%, transfer payments 7.1%, other 21.5%; expenditure: food, tobacco, and beverages 36.5%, housing 21.9%, transportation and communications 14.8%, medical and personal care 6.0%, clothing 5.4%, education and recreation 4.0%, other 11.4%.
Tourism (1995): receipts from visitors U.S.$7,664,000,000; expenditures by nationals abroad U.S.$3,372,000,000.

Foreign trade[9]

Balance of trade (current prices)						
	1990	1991	1992	1993	1994	1995
U.S.$'000,000	−6,750	−5,990	−4,161	−4,297	−3,726	−7,968
% of total	12.9%	9.6%	6.1%	5.6%	4.0%	6.7%

Imports (1995): B 1,766,142,000,000 (electrical machinery 19.1%, nonelectrical machinery 18.9%, road vehicles 7.7%, iron and steel 7.1%, mineral fuels and lubricants 6.8%, organic chemicals 3.7%, plastics 3.4%). *Major import sources:* Japan 30.5%; U.S. 12.0%; Singapore 5.9%; Germany 5.3%; Taiwan 4.8%; Malaysia 4.6%; South Korea 3.5%.
Exports (1995): B 1,407,996,000,000 (electrical machinery 17.2%, nonelectrical machinery 14.0%, rubber products 5.8%, live fish 5.1%, garments 4.6%, plastics 4.4%, precious jewelry 3.9%, footwear 3.8%, cereals 3.5%). *Major export destinations:* U.S. 17.8%; Japan 16.8%; Singapore 14.0%; Hong Kong 5.2%; The Netherlands 3.2%; China 3.0%; Germany 2.9%.

Transport and communications

Transport. Railroads (1995[10]): route length 3,976 km; passenger-km 12,975,-000,000; metric ton-km cargo 3,242,000,000. Roads (1995): total length 62,000 km (paved 97%). Vehicles (1995): passenger cars 1,440,000; trucks and buses 2,969,000. Air transport (1996): passenger-km 29,226,000,000; metric ton-km cargo 1,320,300,000; airports (1996) with scheduled flights 25.

Communications				units per 1,000 persons
Medium	date	unit	number	
Daily newspapers	1994	circulation	2,766,000	47
Radio	1996	receivers	10,000,000	167
Television	1995	receivers	3,300,000	56
Telephones	1995	main lines	3,482,000	59
Cellular telephones	1995	subscribers	1,087,500	18
Facsimile machines	1995	units	60,000	1.0
Personal computers	1995	units	900,000	15

Education and health

Educational attainment (1990). Percentage of population age 25 and over having: no formal schooling 11.8%; primary education 71.3%; secondary 9.5%; postsecondary 6.6%; unknown 0.8%. *Literacy* (1995): total population age 15 and over literate 93.8%; males literate 96.0%; females literate 91.6%.

Education (1993)				student/ teacher ratio
	schools	teachers	students	
Primary (age 7–12)	34,412	445,542	8,583,525	19.3
Secondary (age 13–18)	2,318	107,025	2,118,767	19.8
Voc., teacher tr.	679	40,116	795,186	19.8
Higher	102	27,239	809,856	29.7

Health: physicians (1994) 14,098 (1 per 4,165 persons); hospital beds (1991) 93,852 (1 per 599 persons); infant mortality rate (1996) 32.0.
Food (1995): daily per capita caloric intake 2,296 (vegetable products 90%, animal products 10%); 103% of FAO recommended minimum requirement.

Military

Total active duty personnel (1996): 254,000 (army 59.1%, navy 25.2%, air force 15.7%). *Military expenditure as percentage of GNP* (1995): 2.5% (world 2.8%); per capita expenditure U.S.$68.

---

[1]All members are appointed by the prime minister. [2]Actual local administration is based on 76 provinces. [3]Based on registration records. [4]Based on 1990 census results, which are lower than the 1990 registration records estimate. [5]Percentage distribution. [6]1995. [7]February; economically active persons 13 years and over. [8]Mostly unemployed. [9]Import figures are f.o.b. in balance of trade and c.i.f. for commodities and trading partners. [10]Traffic data refer to fiscal year ending September 30.

Internet resources for further information:
• Thailand-WWW Virtual Library
  http://www.nectec.or.th/WWW-VL-Thailand.html

Togo

Official name: République Togolaise (Togolese Republic).
Form of government: multiparty republic[1] with one legislative body (National Assembly [81]).
Chief of state: President[1].
Head of government: Prime Minister.
Capital: Lomé.
Official language: French.
Official religion: none.
Monetary unit: 1 CFA franc (CFAF) = 100 centimes; valuation (Sept. 25, 1998) 1 U.S.$ = CFAF 560.38; 1 £ = CFAF 954.05.

Area and population

Regions Prefectures	Capitals	area sq mi	area sq km	population 1989 estimate
Centrale	Sokodé			339,000
Sotouboua	Sotouboua	2,892	7,491	162,500
Tchamba	Tchamba	1,214	3,143	54,500
Tchaoudjo	Sokodé	984	2,549	122,000
De la Kara	Kara			531,500
Assoli	Bafilo	362	938	41,000
Bassar	Bassar	2,444	6,330	152,000
Binah	Pagouda	180	465	61,000
Doufelgou	Niamtougou	432	1,120	75,000
Kéran	Kandé	419	1,085	49,500
Kozah	Kara	653	1,692	153,000
Des Plateaux	Atakpamé			810,500
Amou	Amlamé	773	2,003	98,500
Haho	Notsé	1,406	3,641	139,000
Kloto	Kpalimé	1,072	2,777	233,500
Ogou	Atakpamé	2,349	6,083	204,000
Wawa	Badou	954	2,471	135,500
Des Savanes	Dapaong			410,500
Oti	Sansanné-Mango	1,453	3,762	98,500
Tône	Dapaong	1,869	4,840	312,000
Maritime	Lomé			1,300,000[2]
Golfe	Lomé	133	345	560,000
Lacs	Aného	275	713	172,500
Vo	Vogan	290	750	125,000
Yoto	Tabligbo	483	1,250	187,000
Zio	Tsévié	1,288	3,337	255,000
TOTAL		21,925	56,785	3,391,500

Demography

Population (1998): 4,906,000.
Density (1998): persons per sq mi 223.8, persons per sq km 86.4.
Urban-rural (1995): urban 30.8%; rural 69.2%.
Sex distribution (1995): male 49.54%; female 50.46%.
Age breakdown (1995): under 15, 45.7%; 15–29, 25.9%; 30–44, 14.9%; 45–59, 8.5%; 60–74, 4.1%; 75 and over, 0.9%.
Population projection: (2000) 5,263,000; (2010) 7,401,000.
Doubling time: 22 years.
Ethnic composition (1981): Ewe-Adja 43.1%; Tem-Kabre 26.7%; Gurma 16.1%; Kebu-Akposo 3.8%; Ana-Ife (Yoruba) 3.2%; non-African 0.3%; other 6.8%.
Religious affiliation (1993): traditional beliefs 50%; Christian 35%, of which Roman Catholic 23%; Muslim 15%.
Major cities (1983): Lomé 366,476; Sokodé 48,098[2]; Kpalimé 27,669[2].

Vital statistics

Birth rate per 1,000 population (1990–95): 44.5 (world avg. 25.0).
Death rate per 1,000 population (1990–95): 12.8 (world avg. 9.3).
Natural increase rate per 1,000 population (1990–95): 31.7 (world avg. 15.7).
Total fertility rate (avg. births per childbearing woman; 1990–95): 6.6.
Life expectancy at birth (1990–95): male 53.2 years; female 56.8 years.
Morbidity (reported cases of illness; 1989): malaria 730,162; injury and trauma 218,949; diarrheal diseases 153,074; diseases of the respiratory system 90,061.

National economy

Budget (1995). Revenue: CFAF 97,100,000,000 (tax revenue 91.4%, of which taxes on international trade 37.3%, public enterprise taxes 18.6%; nontax revenue 8.6%). Expenditures: CFAF 147,200,000,000 (current expenditure 70.6%, of which education 16.2%, defense 10.5%, health 4.0%; development/unclassified expenditures 15.6%; debt service 13.9%).
Public debt (external, outstanding; 1996): U.S.$1,285,000,000.
Production (metric tons except as noted). Agriculture, forestry, fishing (1996): cassava 469,000, corn (maize) 414,000, yams 375,000, sorghum 144,000, cottonseed 140,000, millet 78,000, rice 59,000, pulses 34,000, peanuts (groundnuts) 42,000, bananas 16,000, coffee 16,000, coconuts 14,000, palm oil 14,000; livestock (number of live animals) 1,900,000 goats, 1,200,000 sheep, 850,000 pigs, 202,000 cattle, 6,000,000 chickens; roundwood (1995) 2,387,000 cu m; fish catch (1995) 13,723. Mining and quarrying (1995): phosphate rock 2,650,000; limestone is quarried for cement manufacture. Manufacturing (value added in CFAF '000,000; 1995): food products, beverages, and tobacco manufactures 36,393; nonmetallic manufactures 6,099; textiles, clothing, and leather 3,833; chemical products 3,625; paper, printing, and publishing 3,125; wood products 3,020; steel 330. Construction (value added in CFAF; 1995): 19,958,000,000. Energy production (consumption): electricity (kW-hr; 1994) 93,000,000 (408,000,000); petroleum products (metric tons; 1994) none (184,000).
Gross national product (1996): U.S.$1,278,000,000 (U.S.$300 per capita).

Structure of gross domestic product and labour force

	1995 in value CFAF '000,000,000	1995 % of total value	1994 labour force	1994 % of labour force
Agriculture	210.5	33.9	1,041,000	67.7
Mining	36.6	5.9		
Manufacturing	62.6	10.1	177,000	11.5
Construction	20.0	3.2		
Public utilities	23.7	3.8		
Transp. and commun.	39.7	6.4		
Trade and finance	131.6	21.2		
Pub. admin., defense	49.4	7.9	318,000	20.7
Services	47.4	7.6		
TOTAL	630.3[3]	100.0	1,538,000[4]	100.0[4]

Population economically active (1994): total 1,538,000; activity rate of total population 33.8% (participation rates over age 10, 50.7%; female 35.6%; unemployed 16–18%).

Price and earnings indexes (1990 = 100)

	1991	1992	1993	1994	1995	1996
Consumer price index	100.4	101.8	101.8	137.7	159.3	166.7
Hourly earnings index[5]	100.0	100.0	100.0	100.0	...	...

Household income and expenditure. Average household size (1980) 5.6; average annual income per household CFAF 102,000 (U.S.$452); sources of income: n.a.; expenditure (1987): food and beverages 45.9%, household durable goods 13.9%, clothing 11.4%, housing 5.9%, services 20.5%.
Tourism: receipts (1995) U.S.$8,000,000; expenditures (1994) U.S.$23,000,000.
Land use (1994): forested 16.5%; meadows and pastures 3.7%; agricultural and under permanent cultivation 44.7%; other 35.1%.

Foreign trade[6]

Balance of trade (current prices)

	1991	1992	1993	1994	1995
CFAF '000,000,000	−16.7	−21.8	−10.2	+7.8	+8.8
% of total	7.0%	11.2%	7.7%	3.2%	2.6%

Imports (1995): CFAF 177,300,000,000 (consumer goods 45.3%; capital equipment 23.2%; intermediate goods 21.0%; energy products 10.4%). *Major import sources* (1994): France 24.0%; Germany 9.9%; Côte d'Ivoire 6.3%.
Exports (1995): CFAF 173,200,000,000 (domestic exports 73.3%, of which cotton 29.8%, phosphates 23.8%, coffee 5.5%; reexports 26.7%). *Major export destinations* (1994): Canada 17.0%; Bolivia 7.6%; Indonesia 5.7%.

Transport and communications

Transport. Railroads (1995): route length 395 km; (1994) passenger-km 14,000,000; metric ton-km cargo 5,600,000. Roads (1995): total length 12,040 km (paved 14%). Vehicles (1994): passenger cars 67,936; trucks and buses 31,986. Merchant marine (1992): vessels (100 gross tons and over) 8; total deadweight tonnage 20,633. Air transport (1996)[7]: passenger-km 224,736,000; metric ton-km cargo 16,420,000; airports (1997) 2.

Communications

Medium	date	unit	number	units per 1,000 persons
Daily newspapers	1995	circulation	10,000	2.4
Radio	1995	receivers	880,000	212
Television	1995	receivers	150,000	36
Telephones	1995	main lines	21,700	5.2
Facsimile machines	1995	units	10,000	2.4

Education and health

Educational attainment (1981). Percentage of population age 25 and over having: no formal schooling 76.5%; primary education 13.5%; secondary 8.7%; higher 1.3%. *Literacy* (1995): total population age 15 and over literate 51.7%; males 67.0%; females 37.0%.

Education (1995–96)

	schools	teachers	students	student/ teacher ratio
Primary (age 6–11)	3,283	16,217	824,626	50.8
Secondary (age 12–18)	314[8]	4,736	161,672	34.1
Vocational	18[9]	586	7,631	13.0
Higher[10]	1	650	11,000	16.9

Health: physicians (1991) 319 (1 per 11,967 persons); hospital beds (1990) 5,307 (1 per 694 persons); infant mortality rate (1990–95) 85.
Food (1995): daily per capita caloric intake 1,754 (vegetable products 95%, animal products 5%); 76% of FAO recommended minimum requirement.

Military

Total active duty personnel (1997): 6,950 (army 93.5%, navy 2.9%, air force 3.6%). *Military expenditure as percentage of GNP* (1995): 2.3% (world 2.8%); per capita expenditure U.S.$6.

[1]Personal military-supported rule from 1967 continues under constitution approved by referendum in September 1992. [2]1981. [3]Total includes statistical discrepancy of CFAF 8,800,000,000. [4]Detail does not add to total given because of rounding. [5]January 1. [6]Import figures are f.o.b. in total and balance of trade and c.i.f. for commodities and trading partners. [7]Represents 1/11 of the traffic of Air Afrique, which is operated by 11 West African states. [8]1990. [9]1987. [10]University only; 1994–95.

Internet resources for further information:
• **République Togolaise: Accueil**
  http://www.republicoftogo.com/english/home.html

Tonga

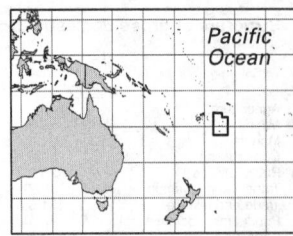

Official name: Pule'anga Fakatu'i 'o Tonga (Tongan); Kingdom of Tonga (English).
Form of government: constitutional monarchy with one legislative house (Legislative Assembly [30[1]]).
Head of state and government: King assisted by Privy Council.
Capital: Nuku'alofa.
Official languages: Tongan; English.
Official religion: none.
Monetary unit: 1 pa'anga[2] (T$) = 100 seniti; valuation (Sept. 25, 1998) 1 U.S.$ = T$1.70; 1 £ = T$2.89.

Area and population

Divisions		area		population
Districts	Capitals	sq mi	sq km	1986 census
'Eua	'Ohonua	33.7	87.4	4,393
'Eua Fo'ou		...	...	1,993
'Eua Motu'a		...	...	2,400
Ha'apai	Pangai	42.5	110.0	8,919
Foa		...	...	1,410
Ha'ano		...	...	891
Lulunga		...	...	1,584
Mu'omu'a		...	...	885
Pangai		...	...	2,850
'Uiha		...	...	1,299
Niuas	Hihifo	27.7	71.7	2,368
Niua Fo'ou		...	...	763
Niua Toputapu		...	...	1,605
Tongatapu	Nuku'alofa	100.6	260.5	63,794
Kolofo'ou		...	...	15,903
Kolomotu'a		...	...	13,115
Kolovai		...	...	4,031
Lapaha		...	...	7,005
Nukunuku		...	...	5,863
Tatakamotonga		...	...	6,773
Vaini		...	...	11,104
Vava'u	Neiafu	46.0	119.2	15,175
Hahake		...	...	2,299
Hihifo		...	...	2,093
Leimatu'a		...	...	2,884
Motu		...	...	1,384
Neiafu		...	...	5,268
Pangaimotu		...	...	1,247
TOTAL LAND AREA		278.1[3]	720.3[3]	
INLAND WATER		11.4	29.6	
TOTAL		289.5	749.9	94,649

Demography
Population (1998): 97,900.
Density (1998)[4]: persons per sq mi 352.0, persons per sq km 135.9.
Urban-rural (1997): urban 43.0%; rural 57.0%.
Sex distribution (1992): male 50.28%; female 49.72%.
Age breakdown (1986): under 15, 40.6%; 15–29, 29.0%; 30–44, 13.8%; 45–59, 10.2%; 60–74, 5.0%; 75 and over, 1.4%.
Population projection: (2000) 98,500; (2010) 101,000.
Doubling time: 33 years.
Ethnic composition (1986): Tongan 95.5%; part Tongan 2.8%; other 1.7%.
Religious affiliation (1998): Free Wesleyan 41.2%; Roman Catholic 15.8%; Mormon 13.6%.
Major cities (1986): Nuku'alofa 21,383; Neiafu 3,879; Haveluloto 3,070.

Vital statistics
Birth rate per 1,000 population (1997): 27.0 (world avg. 25.0).
Death rate per 1,000 population (1997): 5.8 (world avg. 9.3).
Natural increase rate per 1,000 population (1997): 21.2 (world avg. 15.7).
Total fertility rate (avg. births per childbearing woman; 1997): 3.4.
Marriage rate per 1,000 population (1992): 8.2.
Divorce rate per 1,000 population (1992): 1.1.
Life expectancy at birth (1997): male 68.0 years; female 72.0 years.
Major causes of death per 100,000 population (1993)[5]: circulatory diseases 58.1; nervous system diseases 51.0; senility 27.6; diabetes mellitus 17.3.

National economy
Budget (1996–97). Revenue: T$68,300,000 (foreign-trade taxes 41.6%, government services revenue 16.5%, direct taxes 12.0%, indirect taxes 10.7%, interest and rent 6.8%). Expenditures[6]: T$68,700,000 (education 17.8%, public works and communications 17.3%, general administration 14.4%, health 11.4%, law and order 10.5%, agriculture 9.0%).
Public debt (external, outstanding; 1996): U.S.$68,300,000.
Tourism (1995): receipts U.S.$11,000,000; expenditures (1993) U.S.$3,000,000.
Production (metric tons except as noted). Agriculture, forestry, fishing (1996): yams 31,000, cassava 28,000, taro 27,200, coconuts 24,500, fruits 12,500, vegetables 7,308, sweet potatoes 5,137, copra (1994) 2,000; livestock (number of live animals) 80,853 pigs, 13,939 goats, 11,400 horses, 9,318 cattle, 266,000 chickens; roundwood (1995) 4,600 cu m; fish catch (1995) 2,596. Mining and quarrying (1982): coral 150,000; sand 25,000. Manufacturing (output in T$'000,000; 1994): food products and beverages 7,766; chemical products 4,294; wood products 1,330; paper products 859; nonmetallic products 814; textile and wearing apparel 806. Construction (value in T$; 1984): residential 9,552,300; nonresidential 11,377,100. Energy production (consumption): electricity (kW-hr; 1994) 29,000,000 (29,000,000); petroleum (barrels; 1989) none (154,000); petroleum products (metric tons; 1994) n.a. (34,000).

Gross national product (1996): U.S.$175,000,000 (U.S.$1,790 per capita).

Structure of gross domestic product and labour force

	1995–96		1990	
	in value T$'000	% of total value	labour force	% of labour force
Agriculture	71,100	31.7	11,682	36.5
Mining	700	0.3		
Manufacturing	8,100	3.6 }	4,665	14.6
Construction	11,300	5.0	1,257	3.9
Public utilities	3,200	1.4	408	1.3
Transp. and commun.	14,600	6.5	1,821	5.7
Trade	26,400	11.8	2,597	8.1
Finance	25,200	11.3	1,188	3.7
Pub. admin., defense	30,000	13.4		
Services	10,500	4.7 }	7,052	22.0
Other	23,000	10.3	1,343	4.2
TOTAL	224,100	100.0	32,013	100.0

Population economically active (1993–94): total 36,665; activity rate 36.9% (participation rates: ages 10 and over 52.2%; female 42.9%; unemployed 11.8%).

Price and earnings indexes (1990 = 100)

	1991	1992	1993	1994	1995	1996	1997
Consumer price index	110.6	119.4	120.5	121.8	123.5	127.2	129.9
Quarterly earnings index[7]	114.3	124.6	...	...	...	...	...

Household income and expenditure. Average household size (1986) 6.3; income per household: n.a.; sources of income: n.a.; expenditure (1984)[8]: food 49.3%, household operations 13.3%, housing 10.5%, tobacco and beverages 7.0%, transportation 5.8%, clothing and footwear 5.6%.
Land use (1994): forest 11.1%; pasture 5.6%; agriculture 66.7%; other 16.6%.

Foreign trade[9]

Balance of trade (current prices)

	1991	1992	1993	1994	1995	1996
T$'000,000	−59.4	−67.7	−61.5	−72.8	−79.6	−78.2
% of total	63.0%	67.1%	56.8%	66.5%	68.3%	74.2%

Imports (1995–96): T$94,960,000 (food and live animals 28.7%, machinery and transport equipment 20.6%, basic manufactures 17.0%, mineral fuels 13.7%, chemicals 6.8%). *Major import sources:* New Zealand 36.1%; Australia 28.9%; U.S. 11.5%; Japan 8.0%; Fiji 7.2%.
Exports (1995–96): T$17,020,000 (squash 49.3%, fish 24.4%, vanilla beans 12.5%, root crops 5.5%). *Major export destinations:* Japan 51.8%; U.S. 27.7%; New Zealand 8.3%; Australia 4.0%; Fiji 1.5%.

Transport and communications
Transport. Railroads: none. Roads (1995): total length 674 km (paved 27%). Vehicles (1995): passenger cars 1,136, commercial vehicles 766. Merchant marine (1992): vessels (100 gross tons and over) 15; total deadweight tonnage 13,740. Air transport (1994): passenger-km 9,397,000; metric ton-km cargo 16,000; airports (1996) with scheduled flights 6.

Communications

Medium	date	unit	number	units per 1,000 persons
Daily newspapers	1994	circulation	7,000	70
Radio	1996	receivers	40,000	397
Television	1995	receivers	2,000	20
Telephones	1995	main lines	6,600	66

Education and health
Educational attainment (1986). Percentage of population age 25 and over having: complete primary 38.3%; lower secondary 30.3%; secondary 23.4%; postsecondary 4.9%; higher 1.0%; not stated 2.1%. *Literacy* (1976): total population age 15 and over literate 46,456 (92.8%); males 23,372 (92.9%); females 23,084 (92.8%).

Education (1994)

	schools	teachers	students	student/teacher ratio
Primary (age 6–11)	115	701	16,540	23.6
Secondary (age 12–18)	38	809	15,702	19.4
Voc., teacher tr.	9	65[10]	824	13.4[10]
Higher[11]	1	19	226	11.9

Health: physicians (1993) 45 (1 per 2,201 persons); hospital beds (1992) 307 (1 per 320 persons); infant mortality rate per 1,000 live births (1997) 15.
Food (1992): daily per capita caloric intake 2,946 (vegetable products 82%, animal products 18%); 129% of FAO recommended minimum requirement.

Military
Total active duty personnel (1991): Tonga has a national police (defense) force of about 300. *Military expenditure as percentage of GNP* (1989): 4.9% (world 4.9%); per capita expenditure U.S.$21.

[1]Includes 12 nonelective seats and 9 nobles elected by the 33 hereditary nobles of Tonga. [2]The pa'anga was pegged at par to the Australian dollar through Feb. 8, 1991, but beginning Feb. 11, 1991, it was linked to a weighted basket of foreign currencies. [3]Total includes 27.6 sq mi (71.5 sq km) of uninhabited islands. [4]Density is based on land area. [5]Reported inpatient deaths at all hospitals. [6]Excludes amortization of public debt and sinking funds. [7]In manufacturing. [8]Current weight of consumer price index components. [9]Import data used in computing balance of trade is c.i.f. [10]1990. [11]1992.

Internet resources for further information:
• Tonga Page http://user.cs.tu-berlin.de/~minibbjd/tonga/index.html

Trinidad and Tobago

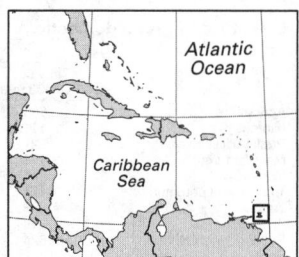

Official name: Republic of Trinidad and Tobago.
Form of government: multiparty republic with two legislative houses (Senate [31]; House of Representatives [36[1]]).
Chief of state: President.
Head of government: Prime Minister.
Capital: Port of Spain.
Official language: English.
Official religion: none.
Monetary unit: 1 Trinidad and Tobago dollar (TT$) = 100 cents; valuation (Sept. 25, 1998) 1 U.S.$ = TT$6.24; 1 £ = TT$10.62.

Area and population

Counties	Capitals	area sq mi	area sq km	population 1990 census
Caroni	Chaguanas	191.0	494.7	120,508
Nariva/Mayaro	Rio Claro	349.0	903.9	36,781
St. Andrew/St. David	Sangre Grande	360.0	932.4	62,944
St. George	Tunapuna	354.0	916.9	445,620
St. Patrick	Siparia	252.0	652.7	120,129
Victoria	Princes Town	315.0	815.9	210,833
Unitary State				
Tobago	Scarborough	116.0	300.4	50,282
Cities				
Port of Spain	—	4.0	10.4	50,878
San Fernando	—	3.0	7.8	30,092
Boroughs				
Arima	—	4.0	10.4	29,695
Chaguanas	—	23.0	59.6	56,601
Point Fortin	—	9.0	23.3	20,025
TOTAL		1,980.1[2]	5,128.4	1,234,388

Demography

Population (1998): 1,275,000.
Density (1998): persons per sq mi 643.9, persons per sq km 248.6.
Urban-rural (1995): urban 71.8%; rural 28.2%.
Sex distribution (1995): male 49.46%; female 50.54%.
Age breakdown (1995): under 15, 31.7%; 15–29, 26.6%; 30–44, 22.1%; 45–59, 11.5%; 60–74, 6.0%; 75 and over, 2.1%.
Population projection: (2000) 1,285,000; (2010) 1,333,000.
Doubling time: 74 years.
Ethnic composition (1990): East Indian 40.3%; black 39.6%; mixed 18.4%; white 0.6%; Chinese 0.4%; other/not stated 0.7%.
Religious affiliation (1990): six largest Protestant bodies 29.7%; Roman Catholic 29.4%; Hindu 23.7%; Muslim 5.9%; other 11.3%.
Major cities (1990): Chaguanas 56,601; Port of Spain 46,222[3]; San Fernando 30,115[4]; Arima 29,483[4]; Point Fortin 20,025; Scarborough 4,000.

Vital statistics

Birth rate per 1,000 population (1996): 16.3 (world avg. 25.0).
Death rate per 1,000 population (1996): 6.9 (world avg. 9.3).
Natural increase rate per 1,000 population (1996): 9.4 (world avg. 15.7).
Total fertility rate (avg. births per childbearing woman; 1996): 2.0.
Marriage rate per 1,000 population (1993): 5.6.
Divorce rate per 1,000 population (1993): 0.9.
Life expectancy at birth (1996): male 67.9 years; female 72.8 years.
Major causes of death per 100,000 population (1993): diseases of the circulatory system 270.0; accidents, violence, and homicide 110.3; malignant neoplasms (cancers) 86.4; diabetes mellitus 83.5.

National economy

Budget (1996). Revenue: TT$9,570,000,000 (company taxes 28.8%, of which petroleum sector 19.2%; individual income taxes 18.9%; value-added taxes 15.3%; nontax revenues 7.9%). Expenditures: TT$9,123,000,000 (current expenditures 94.3%; development expenditures 5.7%).
Tourism (1994): receipts from visitors U.S.$80,000,000; expenditures by nationals abroad U.S.$90,000,000.
Production (metric tons except as noted). Agriculture, forestry, fishing (1996): sugarcane 1,404,000, coconuts 20,000, oranges (1995) 14,906, rice 9,539, grapefruit and pomelo (1995) 7,297, bananas 6,000, cocoa 2,540, coffee 353; livestock (number of live animals) 59,000 goats, 45,000 pigs, 9,500,000 chickens; roundwood (1995) 67,600 cu m; fish catch (1994) 11,000. Mining and quarrying (1994): natural asphalt 21,000. Manufacturing (1996): anhydrous ammonia and urea (nitrogenous fertilizers) 2,674,200; methanol 1,358,000; steel billets 643,600; cement 617,100; steel wire rods 575,400; refined sugar 42,100; beer and stout 418,800 hectolitres; rum 78,000 hectolitres. Construction (authorized; 1993): residential 207,900 sq m; nonresidential 46,900 sq m. Energy production (consumption): electricity (kW-hr; 1995) 4,229,000,000 (1994; 3,978,000,000); coal, none (none) (none); crude petroleum (barrels; 1995) 41,493,000 (1994; 35,533,000); petroleum products (metric tons; 1994) 4,931,000 (1,268,000); natural gas (cu m; 1996) 9,033,000,000 (7,049,000,000).
Public debt (external, outstanding; 1996): U.S.$1,871,000,000.
Household income and expenditure. Average household size (1990) 4.1; average income per household (1988) TT$21,760 (U.S.$5,661); expenditure (1993): food, beverages, and tobacco 25.5%, housing 21.6%, transportation 15.2%, household furnishings 14.3%, clothing and footwear 10.4%.

Gross national product (1996): U.S.$5,017,000,000 (U.S.$3,870 per capita).

Structure of gross domestic product and labour force

	1996 in value TT$'000,000	1996 % of total value	1995 labour force	1995 % of labour force
Agriculture	688	2.1	50,600	9.7
Petroleum[5], natural gas, quarrying	8,747	26.7	21,100	4.0
Manufacturing[6]	2,698	8.2	53,800	10.3
Construction	2,762	8.4	71,200	13.7
Public utilities	545	1.7	7,300	1.4
Transp. and commun.	2,760	8.4	34,100	6.5
Trade	4,979	15.2	93,600	18.0
Finance, real estate	3,882	11.8	35,000	6.7
Pub. admin., defense	3,264	9.9 }	154,100	29.6
Services	1,917	5.8 }		
Other	569[7]	1.7[7]	500	0.1
TOTAL	32,811	100.0[2]	521,000[2]	100.0

Population economically active (1995): total 521,000; activity rate of total population 41.3% (participation rates: ages 15–64, 65.4%; female 37.2%; unemployed [1996] 16.3%).

Price and earnings indexes (1990 = 100)

	1991	1992	1993	1994	1995	1996	1997
Consumer price index	103.9	110.6	122.4	133.2	140.1	144.9	150.2
Weekly earnings index	100.1	103.0	104.6	109.9	111.1[8]	...	...

Land use (1994): forested 45.8%; meadows and pastures 2.1%; agricultural and under permanent cultivation 23.8%; other 28.3%.

Foreign trade[9]

Balance of trade (current prices)

	1992	1993	1994	1995	1996	1997
TT$'000,000	+2,495	+1,306	+4,354	+4,851	+2,147	−2,818
% of total	21.0%	8.0%	24.5%	20.4%	7.7%	8.1%

Imports (1995): TT$9,452,000,000 (nonelectrical machinery 25.5%, of which general industrial machinery 17.3%; food and live animals 14.2%; chemicals and chemical products 13.8%). Major import sources: United States 50.4%; United Kingdom 6.8%; Germany 6.2%; Canada 5.2%; Brazil 4.3%.
Exports (1995): TT$14,303,000,000 (refined petroleum 29.9%; crude petroleum 16.2%; anhydrous ammonia 10.8%; iron and steel 10.2%; methanol 8.7%; urea 3.9%). Major export destinations: United States 43.3%; Jamaica 8.4%; Guyana 3.1%; Barbados 3.1%; France 2.9%.

Transport and communications

Transport. Railroads: none. Roads (1995): total length 8,160 km (paved 51%). Vehicles (1994): passenger cars 123,500; trucks and buses 24,500. Air transport (1994): passenger-km 4,084,000,000; metric ton-km cargo 404,000,000; airports (1996) with scheduled flights 2.

Communications	date	unit	number	units per 1,000 persons
Medium				
Daily newspapers	1994	circulation	175,000	139
Radio	1996	receivers	550,000	433
Television	1995	receivers	250,000	198
Telephones	1995	main lines	209,300	166
Cellular telephones	1995	subscribers	5,600	4.4
Facsimile machines	1995	units	2,000	1.6
Personal computers	1995	units	25,000	20

Education and health

Educational attainment (1990). Percentage of population age 25 and over having: no formal schooling 4.5%; primary education 56.4%; secondary 32.1%; higher 3.4%; other/not stated 3.6%. Literacy (1995): total population age 15 and over literate 886,000 (97.9%).

Education (1993–94)

	schools	teachers	students	student/ teacher ratio
Primary (age 5–11)	475	7,210	195,013	27.0
Secondary (age 12–16)	101[10]	4,882[11]	100,609[11]	20.6[11]
Higher[12]	1	438	5,191	11.9

Health: physicians (1993) 1,051 (1 per 1,191 persons); hospital beds (1992) 3,653 (1 per 340 persons); infant mortality rate (1996) 18.2.
Food (1992): daily per capita caloric intake 2,585 (vegetable products 85%, animal products 15%); 107% of FAO recommended minimum requirement.

Military

Total active duty personnel (1996): 2,100 (army 66.7%, coast guard 33.3%). Military expenditure as percentage of GNP (1994): 1.7% (world 3.0%); per capita expenditure U.S.$60.

[1]Excludes speaker, who may be elected from outside the House of Representatives. [2]Detail does not add to total given because of rounding. [3]1994. [4]1991. [5]Includes refined petroleum. [6]Excludes refined petroleum. [7]Net of value-added taxes less imputed bank service charges. [8]Average of 2nd quarter. [9]Imports c.i.f.; exports f.o.b. [10]1992–93. [11]Excludes vocational. [12]University of the West Indies, St. Augustine campus only.

Internet resources for further information:
• Welcome to the Republic of Trinidad and Tobago
http://www.nisc.gov.tt/

Tunisia

Official name: Al-Jumhūrīyah at-Tūnisīyah (Republic of Tunisia).
Form of government: multiparty republic with one legislative house (Chamber of Deputies [163]).
Chief of state: President.
Head of government: Prime Minister.
Capital: Tunis.
Official language: Arabic.
Official religion: Islam.
Monetary unit: 1 dinar (D) = 1,000 millimes; valuation (Sept. 25, 1998) 1 U.S.\$ = D 1.09; 1 £ = D 1.85.

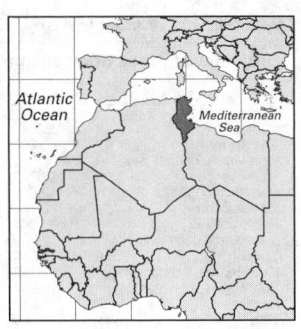

Area and population

Governorates	Capitals	area sq mi	area sq km	population 1994 census
Al-Ariānah	Al-Ariānah	602	1,558	570,700
Bājah	Bājah	1,374	3,558	306,500
Banzart	Bizerte (Banzart)	1,423	3,685	485,800
Bin ʿArūs	Bin ʿArūs	294	761	372,900
Jundūbah	Jundūbah	1,198	3,102	405,100
Al-Kāf	Al-Kāf	1,917	4,965	273,200
Madanīn	Madanīn	3,316	8,588	386,900
Al-Mahdīyah	Al-Mahdīyah	1,145	2,966	335,200
Al-Munastīr	Al-Munastīr	393	1,019	364,600
Nābul	Nābul	1,076	2,788	581,800
Qābis	Qābis	2,770	7,175	311,300
Qafsah	Qafsah	3,471	8,990	308,700
Al-Qasrayn	Al-Qasrayn	3,114	8,066	388,500
Al-Qayrawān	Al-Qayrawān	2,591	6,712	532,500
Qibilī	Qibilī	8,527	22,084	132,000
Safāqis	Safāqis	2,913	7,545	735,300
Sīdī Bū Zayd	Sīdī Bū Zayd	2,700	6,994	379,300
Siliānah	Siliānah	1,788	4,631	246,500
Sūsah	Sūsah	1,012	2,621	436,500
Tatāuīn	Tatāuīn	15,015	38,889	135,600
Tawzar	Tawzar	1,822	4,719	89,300
Tūnis	Tunis (Tūnis)	134	346	893,000
Zaghwān	Zaghwān	1,069	2,768	143,400
TOTAL		**63,378[1]**	**164,150[1]**	**8,814,500[2]**

Demography

Population (1998): 9,380,000.
Density (1998): persons per sq mi 148.0, persons per sq km 57.1.
Urban-rural (1994): urban 61.0%; rural 39.0%.
Sex distribution (1994): male 50.53%; female 49.47%.
Age breakdown (1994): under 15, 34.8%; 15–29, 28.5%; 30–44, 18.8%; 45–59, 9.6%; 60–74, 6.4%; 75 and over, 1.9%.
Ethnic composition (1983): Arab 98.2%; Berber 1.2%; French 0.2%; Italian 0.1%; other 0.3%.
Religious affiliation (1995): Sunnī Muslim 99.5%; Christian 0.3%; other 0.2%.
Major cities (commune; 1994): Tunis 674,100; Safāqis 230,900; Aryānah 152,700; Ettadhamen 149,200; Sūsah 125,000.

Vital statistics

Birth rate per 1,000 population (1995–2000): 23.9 (world avg. 25.0).
Death rate per 1,000 population (1995–2000): 5.9 (world avg. 9.3).
Natural increase rate per 1,000 population (1995–2000): 18.0 (world avg. 15.7).
Total fertility rate (avg. births per childbearing woman; 1995–2000): 2.9.
Marriage rate per 1,000 population (1995): 6.0.
Divorce rate per 1,000 population (1993–94): 0.9.
Life expectancy at birth (1995–2000): male 68.4 years; female 70.7 years.
Major causes of death per 100,000 population: n.a.; however, of approximately 12,000 deaths[3] for which a cause was reported in 1992, complications of pregnancy and childbirth represented 31.6%, circulatory diseases 22.4%, accidents and poisoning 14.9%, respiratory diseases 7.2%.

National economy

Budget (1996). Revenue: D 5,710,000,000 (tax revenue 83.0%, of which goods and services 32.5%, social security 16.8%, income tax 15.6%, import duties 13.3%; nontax revenue 15.8%; grants 0.7%; capital revenue 0.5%). Expenditures: D 6,484,000,000 (education 15.8%; economic services 15.7%; social security 13.7%; general public services 7.3%; health 6.0%; public order 5.8%; defense 5.0%).
Public debt (external, outstanding; 1996): U.S.\$8,689,000,000.
Production (metric tons except as noted). Agriculture, forestry, fishing (1996): wheat 2,018,000, olives 1,250,000, barley 834,000, tomatoes 700,000, watermelons 273,000, potatoes 270,000, sugar beets 306,000; livestock (number of live animals) 6,400,000 sheep, 1,250,000 goats, 700,000 cattle; roundwood (1995) 3,600,000 cu m; fish catch (1995) 84,000. Mining and quarrying (1995): phosphate rock 6,301,598; iron ore 224,949; zinc 80,446. Manufacturing (1995): cement 3,033,200; phosphoric acid 1,365,200; flour 473,600; crude steel 192,000[4]. Construction (1982): residential building authorized 2,679,000 sq m. Energy production (consumption): electricity (kW-hr; 1994) 6,714,000 (5,701,000); coal (metric tons; 1994) 9,000 (31,000); crude petroleum (barrels; 1994) 33,662,000 (12,994,000); petroleum products (metric tons; 1994) 1,591,000 (3,565,000); natural gas (cu m; 1994) 286,000,000 (786,000,000).
Land use (1994): forested 4.3%; meadows and pastures 20.0%; agricultural and under permanent cultivation 31.9%; other 43.8%.
Tourism (1995): receipts U.S.\$1,325,000,000; expenditures U.S.\$251,000,000.
Gross national product (1996): U.S.\$17,581,000,000 (U.S.\$1,930 per capita).

Structure of gross domestic product and labour force

	1996 in value D '000,000	1996 % of total value	1994 labour force	1994 % of labour force
Agriculture	2,630	13.9	501,000	21.6
Mining	111	0.6	} 36,800	1.6
Public utilities	927[5]	4.9[5]		
Manufacturing	3,453	18.2	455,700	19.6
Construction	874	4.6	305,800	13.2
Transp. and commun.	1,424	7.5	[6]	[6]
Trade	4,588	24.2	} 315,600	13.6
Finance	} 2,624	} 13.8		
Pub. admin., defense			} 667,100[6]	28.7[6]
Services				
Other	2,340[7]	12.3[7]	38,600	1.7
TOTAL	**18,971**	**100.0**	**2,320,600**	**100.0**

Population economically active (1989): total 2,360,000; activity rate of total population 28.8% (participation rates: ages 15–64, 42.2%; female 20.9%; unemployed 13.4%).

Price and earnings indexes (1990 = 100)

	1991	1992	1993	1994	1995	1996	1997
Consumer price index	108.2	114.5	119.0	124.7	132.5	137.4	142.4
Hourly earnings index[8]	101.6	105.5	113.3	...	...	...	...

Household income and expenditure. Average household size (1994) 5.2; income per household: n.a.; sources of income: n.a.; expenditure (1985): food and beverages 39.0%, household durable goods 11.2%, housing 10.7%, transportation 9.0%, recreation 7.1%, clothing and footwear 6.0%, energy 5.1%, health care 3.0%, education 1.8%, other 7.1%.

Foreign trade[9]

Balance of trade (current prices)

	1992	1993	1994	1995	1996	1997
D '000,000	−2,139.1	−2,419.1	−1,950.7	−2,291.2	−2,126.9	−2,608.1
% of total	23.2%	24.1%	17.2%	18.1%	16.5%	17.5%

Imports (1996): D 7,542,700,000 (1995; machinery and electrical equipment 35.0%, textiles 25.2%, food products 12.8%, chemical products 9.4%). *Major import sources* (1995): France 25.6%; Italy 15.4%; Germany 12.5%.
Exports (1996): D 5,372,000,000 (clothing and accessories 49.9%, machinery and electrical products 13.7%, phosphate products 9.0%, energy 8.4%). *Major export destinations* (1995): France 28.1%; Italy 18.7%; Germany 15.7%.

Transport and communications

Transport. Railroads (1994): route length 2,152 km; passenger-km 1,038,000,000; metric ton-km cargo 2,225,000,000. Roads (1995): total length 22,490 km (paved 79%). Vehicles (1995): passenger cars 248,000; trucks and buses 283,000. Air transport (1996)[10]: passenger-km 2,120,989,000; metric ton-km cargo 18,352,000; airports (1997) 5.

Communications

Medium	date	unit	number	units per 1,000 persons
Daily newspapers	1995	circulation	400,000	45
Radio	1996	receivers	1,700,000	188
Television	1995	receivers	1,400,000	156
Telephones	1995	main lines	521,700	58
Cellular telephones	1995	subscribers	3,200	0.4
Facsimile machines	1995	units	25,000	2.8
Personal computers	1995	units	60,000	6.7

Education and health

Educational attainment (1989). Percentage of population age 25 and over having: no formal schooling 54.9%; primary 26.9%; secondary 14.3%; higher 3.4%; unspecified 0.5%. *Literacy* (1995): total population age 15 and over literate 66.7%; males literate 78.6%; females literate 54.6%.

Education (1995–96)

	schools	teachers	students	student/ teacher ratio
Primary (age 6–11)	4,384	59,887	1,468,998	24.5
Secondary (age 12–18)	712[11]	41,885	794,394	19.0
Teacher tr. [12, 13]	...	237	3,839	16.2
Higher[14]	...	5,655	96,101	17.0

Health (1994): physicians 5,344 (1 per 1,640 persons); hospital beds 15,759 (1 per 556 persons); infant mortality rate (1995–2000) 37.0.
Food (1995): daily per capita caloric intake 3,187 (vegetable products 91%, animal products 9%); 133% of FAO recommended minimum requirement.

Military

Total active duty personnel (1997): 35,000 (army 77.1%, navy 12.9%, air force 10.0%). *Military expenditure as percentage of GNP* (1995): 2.0% (world 2.8%); per capita expenditure U.S.\$39.

[1]Total includes 3,714 sq mi (9,620 sq km) of territory that is not distributed by governorate. [2]Detail does not add to total given because of rounding. [3]Recorded deaths from urban areas only, including complete figures for Tunis. [4]1989. [5]Includes hydrocarbons. [6]Services includes transportation and communications. [7]Indirect taxes less subsidies. [8]Year-end; index refers to the *S.M.I.G.* (*salaire minimum interprofessionnel garanti*), a form of minimum professional wage. [9]Imports c.i.f. in balance of trade. [10]Tunis Air only. [11]1994–95. [12]1987–88. [13]Teacher training only. [14]1993–94.

Internet resources for further information:
• Tunisia Online http://www.tunisiaonline.com

Turkey

Official name: Türkiye Cumhuriyeti (Republic of Turkey).
Form of government: multiparty republic with one legislative house (Turkish Grand National Assembly [550]).
Chief of state: President.
Head of government: Prime Minister.
Capital: Ankara.
Official language: Turkish.
Official religion: none.
Monetary unit: 1 Turkish lira (LT) = 100 kurush; valuation (Sept. 25, 1998)
1 U.S.$ = LT 276,485;
1 £ = LT 470,716.

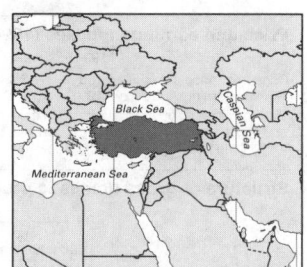

Area and population

Geographic regions[1]	area sq mi	area sq km	population 1990 census
Akdeniz kıyısı (Mediterranean Coast)	22,933	59,395	5,443,867
Batı Anadolu (West Anatolia)	29,742	77,031	3,864,661
Doğu Anadolu (East Anatolia)	68,074	180,180	6,867,415
Güneydoğu Anadolu (Southeast Anatolia)	15,347	35,880	2,699,776
İç Anadolu (Central Anatolia)	91,254	236,347	13,096,179
Karadeniz kıyısı (Black Sea Coast)	31,388	81,295	6,827,304
Marmara ve Ege kıyıları (Marmara and Aegean coasts)	33,035	85,560	11,698,384
Trakya (Thrace)	9,175	23,764	5,975,449
TOTAL	300,948	779,452	56,473,035

Demography

Population (1998): 64,567,000.
Density (1998): persons per sq mi 214.5, persons per sq km 82.8.
Urban-rural (1995): urban 68.8%; rural 31.2%.
Sex distribution (1995): male 50.57%; female 49.43%.
Age breakdown (1995): under 15, 32.3%; 15–29, 28.8%; 30–44, 20.3%; 45–59, 11.0%; 60–74, 6.4%; 75 and over, 1.2%.
Population projection: (2000) 66,618,000; (2010) 76,570,000.
Doubling time: 44 years.
Ethnic composition (1994): Turks (including Turkmen) 80–88%; Kurds 10–20%; Arabs 1.5%; others 0.3%.
Religious affiliation (1994): Sunnī Muslim c. 80.0%; Shī'ī Muslim c. 19.8%, of which nonorthodox Alevi c. 14.0%; Christian c. 0.2%.
Major cities (1995): Istanbul 7,774,169; Ankara 2,837,937; İzmir 2,017,699; Adana 1,066,544; Bursa 1,016,760; Gaziantep 730,435; Konya 584,785.

Vital statistics

Birth rate per 1,000 population (1996): 22.3 (world avg. 25.0).
Death rate per 1,000 population (1996): 5.5 (world avg. 9.3).
Natural increase rate per 1,000 population (1996): 16.8 (world avg. 15.7).
Total fertility rate (avg. births per childbearing woman; 1996): 2.6.
Marriage rate per 1,000 population (1993): 7.7.
Divorce rate per 1,000 population (1993): 0.5.
Life expectancy at birth (1996): male 69.5 years; female 74.4 years.
Major causes of death per 100,000 population (1993)[2]: diseases of the circulatory system 369; malignant neoplasms (cancers) 80; accidents and violence 33; infectious and parasitic diseases 24; ill-defined conditions 60.

National economy

Budget (1996). Revenue: LT 2,738,148,000,000,000 (indirect taxes 49.8%, direct taxes 32.3%, nontax revenue 16.2%). Expenditures: LT 3,955,888,000,000,000 (interest payments 37.9%, personnel 24.6%, investments 6.5%).
Tourism (1996): receipts from visitors U.S.$5,650,000,000; expenditures by nationals abroad U.S.$1,265,000,000.
Production (in '000 metric tons except as noted). Agriculture, forestry, fishing (1996): wheat 18,515, sugar beets 14,455, barley 8,000, potatoes 4,950, grapes 3,550, apples 2,100, seed cotton 2,089, corn (maize) 2,000, olives 1,500, cottonseed 1,200, cotton lint 802, sunflower seeds 780, oranges 700, lentils 615, apricots 460, hazelnuts 410, pears 410, tobacco 230, sultana raisins 179[3], tea 124, honey 69[3], attar of roses 800 kg[4]; livestock (number of live animals) 33,791,000 sheep, 11,789,000 cattle; roundwood (1995) 19,279,000 cu m; fish catch (1995) 652,193. Mining (1995): boron (concentrate) 1,200[5]; chromite 800[5]; bauxite 440; copper ore (metal content) 34.2. Manufacturing (1993)[6]: refined petroleum 5,450; textiles 4,150; food products 4,150; motor vehicles 3,200; iron and steel 2,600; bricks, cement, and tiles 1,950. Construction (approved; 1996): residential 56,863,000 sq m; nonresidential 18,047,000 sq m. Energy production (consumption): electricity (kW-hr; 1996) 94,863,-000,000 (94,787,000,000); hard coal (metric tons; 1996) 2,424,000 ([1994] 8,192,000); lignite (metric tons; 1996) 52,503,000 ([1994] 52,167,000); crude petroleum (barrels; 1996) 25,018,000 ([1994] 180,663,000); petroleum products (metric tons; 1994) 22,219,000 (25,417,000); natural gas (cu m; 1994) 184,500,000 (4,815,100,000).
Land use (1994): forested 26.2%; meadows and pastures 16.1%; agricultural and under permanent cultivation 36.1%; other 21.6%.
Household income and expenditure. Average household size (1993) 4.5; income per household (1987) LT 3,680,500 (U.S.$4,294); expenditure (1994): food, tobacco, and café expenditures 38.5%, housing 22.8%, clothing 9.0%.
Population economically active (1995)[7]: total 22,899,000; activity rate of total population 37.1% (participation rates: ages 15–64, 57.8%; female 30.4%; unemployed [1996] 5.8%).

Price and earnings indexes (1990 = 100)

	1992	1993	1994	1995	1996	1997	1998[8]
Consumer price index	282	469	967	1,819	3,281	6,093	10,138
Daily earnings index[9]	395	668	1,007	...	...	...	...

Gross national product (1996): U.S.$177,530,000,000 (U.S.$2,830 per capita).

Structure of gross domestic product and labour force

	1996 in value LT '000,000,000[10]	1996 % of total value	1995 labour force[7]	1995 % of labour force[7]
Agriculture	2,408,532	18.0	10,227,000	44.7
Mining	160,096	1.2	131,000	0.6
Manufacturing	2,417,651	18.0	2,948,000	12.9
Construction	764,339	5.7	1,228,000	5.4
Public utilities	393,968	2.9	111,000	0.5
Transp. and commun.	1,955,042	14.6	854,000	3.7
Trade	2,539,687	19.0	2,612,000	11.4
Finance, real estate	987,244	7.4	487,000	2.1
Pub. admin., defense	1,238,527	9.2	2,779,000	12.1
Services	533,546	4.0		
Other	—	—	1,522,000[11]	6.6[11]
TOTAL	13,398,632	100.0	22,899,000	100.0

Public debt (external, outstanding; 1996): U.S.$48,172,000,000.

Foreign trade[12]

Balance of trade (current prices)

	1992	1993	1994	1995	1996	1997
U.S.$'000,000	−8,156	−14,080	−5,164	−14,073	−19,382	−22,340
% of total	21.7%	31.4%	12.5%	24.5%	29.6%	29.9%

Imports (1996): U.S.$42,464,000,000 (nonelectrical machinery 19.3%; crude petroleum 8.1%; electrical and electronic equipment 7.0%; road vehicles and parts 6.2%; iron and steel 6.1%). *Major import sources:* Germany 17.6%; Italy 9.8%; United States 7.5%; France 6.3%; United Kingdom 5.8%.
Exports (1996): U.S.$23,082,000,000 (textiles and clothing 24.8%; iron and steel 7.6%; electrical and electronic machinery 5.7%; edible fruits 4.9%). *Major export destinations:* Germany 22.4%; United States 7.0%; Russia 6.4%; Italy 6.3%; United Kingdom 5.4%; France 4.5%.

Transport and communications

Transport. Railroads (1994): length 5,252 mi, 8,452 km; passenger-km 6,385,000,000; metric ton-km cargo 8,254,000,000. Roads (1995): total length 236,928 mi, 381,300 km (paved 23%). Vehicles (1995): passenger cars 3,231,562; trucks and buses 809,361. Air transport (1996)[13]: passenger-km 12,305,000,000; metric ton-km cargo 214,201,000; airports (1996) with scheduled flights 26.

Communications

Medium	date	unit	number	units per 1,000 persons
Daily newspapers	1994	circulation	2,679,000	44
Radio	1996	receivers	8,800,000	141
Television	1995	receivers	10,530,000	171
Telephones	1995	main lines	13,227,700	215
Cellular telephones	1995	subscribers	437,100	7.1
Facsimile machines	1995	units	99,100	1.6
Personal computers	1995	units	770,000	13

Education and health

Educational attainment (1993). Percentage of population age 25 and over having: no formal schooling 30.5%; incomplete primary education 6.6%; complete primary 40.4%; incomplete secondary 3.1%; complete secondary or higher 19.1%; unknown 0.3%. *Literacy* (1995): total population age 15 and over literate 33,605,000 (82.3%); males literate 19,191,000 (91.7%); females literate 14,414,000 (72.4%).

Education (1995–96)

	schools	teachers	students	student/ teacher ratio
Primary (age 6–10)	49,240	232,000	6,403,000	27.6
Secondary (age 11–16)	10,689	138,000	3,498,000	25.3
Voc., teacher tr.	3,678	71,000	1,309,000	18.4
Higher	817	50,000	1,161,000	23.2

Health: physicians (1995) 51,000[14] (1 per 1,200 persons); hospital beds (1994) 134,665 (1 per 450 persons); infant mortality rate (1996) 43.2.
Food (1995): daily per capita caloric intake 3,593 (vegetable products 89%, animal products 11%); 143% of FAO recommended minimum requirement.

Military

Total active duty personnel (1996): 639,000 (army 82.2%, navy 8.0%, air force 9.8%). *Military expenditure as percentage of GNP* (1994): 4.1% (world 3.0%); per capita expenditure U.S.$87.

---

[1]Administratively divided into 80 provinces as of 1998. [2]Projected rates based on about 35% of total deaths. [3]1995. [4]1993. [5]1994. [6]Value added in U.S.$'000,000. [7]Civilian population only. [8]April. [9]Based on June average. [10]At factor cost. [11]Unemployed. [12]Imports c.i.f.; exports f.o.b. [13]Turkish Airlines only. [14]Estimated figure.

Internet resources for further information:
• **Ministry of Foreign Affairs http://www.mfa.gov.tr/**
• **Republic of Turkey http://www.turkey.org/**
• **State Institute of Statistics http://www.die.gov.tr/**

Turkmenistan

Official name: Türkmenistan (Turkmenistan).
Form of government: unitary republic with one legislative body (Majlis [Parliament; 50]).
Head of state and government: President assisted by the People's Council[1].
Capital: Ashgabat (formerly Ashkhabad).
Official language: Turkmen.
Official religion: none.
Monetary unit: manat; valuation (Oct. 2, 1998) 1 U.S.$ = 5,200 manat; 1 £ = 8,853 manat.

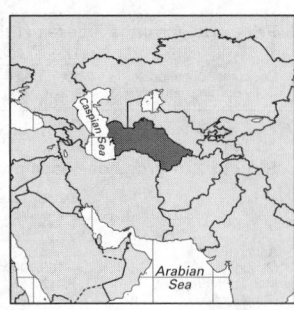

Area and population

Provinces	Capitals	area sq mi	area sq km	population 1996 estimate
Ahal	Ashgabat	37,500	97,100	677,700
Balkan	Nebitdag	53,500	138,600	389,700
Dashhowuz	Dashhowuz	28,100	72,700	956,500
Lebap	Chärjew	36,000	93,200	947,700
Mary	Mary	33,400	86,400	1,046,700
City				
Ashgabat	—	...	...	548,500
TOTAL		188,500[2]	488,100[2]	4,566,800

Demography

Population (1998): 4,731,000.
Density (1997): persons per sq mi 25.1, persons per sq km 9.7.
Urban-rural (1996): urban 44.8%; rural 55.2%.
Sex distribution (1996): male 49.59%; female 50.41%.
Age breakdown (1989): under 15, 40.5%; 15–29, 28.8%; 30–44, 15.5%; 45–59, 9.1%; 60–74, 4.7%; 75 and over, 1.4%.
Population projection: (2000) 4,905,000; (2010) 5,736,000.
Doubling time: 39 years.
Ethnic composition (1997): Turkmen 77.0%; Uzbek 9.2%; Russian 6.7%; Kazak 2.0%; Tatar 0.8%; other 4.3%.
Religious affiliation (1995): Muslim (mostly Sunnī) 87.0%; Russian Orthodox 2.4%; other (mostly nonreligious) 10.6%.
Major cities (1991): Ashgabat 416,400; Chärjew 166,400; Dashhowuz 117,000; Mary 94,900; Nebitdag 89,100.

Vital statistics

Birth rate per 1,000 population (1994): 32.1 (world avg. 25.0); legitimate 96.2%; illegitimate 3.8%.
Death rate per 1,000 population (1994): 7.9 (world avg. 9.3).
Natural increase rate per 1,000 population (1994): 24.2 (world avg. 15.7).
Total fertility rate (avg. births per childbearing woman; 1995): 4.0.
Marriage rate per 1,000 population (1994): 8.7.
Divorce rate per 1,000 population (1994): 1.5.
Life expectancy at birth (1994): male 61.5 years; female 68.5 years.
Major causes of death per 100,000 population (1994): diseases of the circulatory system 337.1; diseases of the respiratory system 150.3; infectious and parasitic diseases 75.7; accidents, poisoning, and violence 60.1; malignant neoplasms (cancers) 56.8; diseases of the digestive system 31.1.

National economy

Budget (1996). Revenue: 1,251,505,000,000 manat (value-added tax 35.0%, company profit tax 23.0%, social security tax 13.0%, natural resource tax 12.0%, other taxes 17.0%). Expenditures: 1,314,895,000,000 manat (capital investment 19.0%, social welfare 15.0%, education 13.0%, health 12.0%, defense 7.0%, price subsidies 4.0%, other expenditures 30.0%).
Public debt (external, outstanding; 1996): U.S.$538,200,000.
Production (metric tons except as noted). Agriculture, forestry, fishing (1996): vegetables 643,500, seed cotton 450,000, cereals 385,000, fruit 206,000; livestock (number of live animals) 6,574,000 sheep and goats, 1,199,000 cattle, 82,000 pigs, 3,500,000 poultry; roundwood (1990) 4,000,000 cu m; fish catch (1995) 40,013. Mining and quarrying (1995): sodium sulphate 400,000, sulfur 240,000. Manufacturing (value of production in '000,000 manat; 1994): ferrous and nonferrous metals 278; machinery and metalworks 223; food products 129; chemical products 90; construction materials 52; wood products 31. Construction (1994): 1,700,000 sq m. Energy production (consumption): electricity (kW-hr; 1994) 10,496,000,000 (7,846,000,000); coal (metric tons; 1994) none (none); crude petroleum (barrels; 1994) 30,053,000 (30,053,000); petroleum products (metric tons; 1994) 2,765,000 (2,765,000); natural gas (cu m; 1994) 30,891,000,000 (8,332,000,000).
Household income and expenditure. Average household size (1989) 5.6; income per household: 3,853 manat (U.S.$ equivalent, n.a.[3]); sources of income (1996): wages and salaries 70.6%, pensions and grants 20.9%, self-employment 2.3%[4], nonwage income of workers 1.1%; expenditure (1996): goods 26.8%, services 13.5%, taxes and other payments 9.4%.
Land use (1994): forested 8.2%; meadows and pastures 61.6%; agricultural and under permanent cultivation 3.0%; other 27.2%.
Population economically active (1996): total 1,680,000; activity rate of total population 36.8% (participation rates [1995]: ages 16–59 [male], 16–54 [female] 81.0%; female 41.0%; unemployed 3.0%[5]).

Price and earnings indexes (1994 = 100)[6]

	1994	1995	1996
Consumer price index	100	1,362	7,431
Monthly earnings index	100	739	6,334

Gross national product (at current market prices; 1995): U.S.$4,319,000,000 (U.S.$940 per capita)[3].

Structure of gross domestic product and labour force

	1995 in value '000,000 manat	1995 % of total value	1996 labour force	1996 % of labour force
Agriculture	325,156	30.3	746,000	44.4
Mining				
Manufacturing	559,761	52.2	165,000	9.8
Public utilities				
Construction	68,285	6.4	155,000	9.2
Transp. and commun.	26,199	2.4	83,000	4.9
Trade	31,796	3.0	106,700	6.4
Finance	...	...	8,000	0.5
Public administration, defense	...	...	25,000	1.5
Services	3,075	0.3	347,000	20.7
Other	57,639	5.4	44,000	2.6
TOTAL	1,071,911	100.0	1,680,000[2]	100.0

Tourism: n.a.

Foreign trade

Balance of trade (current prices)

	1994	1995	1996
U.S.$'000,000	+485	+536	+329
% of total	12.5%	15.4%	10.8%

Imports (1996): U.S.$1,532,000,000 (machinery and equipment 37.4%, food products 22.3%, chemicals 3.4%, medicines 2.5%). *Major import sources* (1995): U.S.$ 25.8%; Ukraine 17.4%; Turkey 13.1%; Russia 10.1%; Cyprus 3.9%.
Exports (1996): U.S.$1,691,000,000 (natural gas and oil products 69.2%, cotton 19.6%). *Major export destinations* (1995): Russia 62.5%; Switzerland 6.5%; Hong Kong 6.2%; Turkey 4.7%; Kazakstan 3.2%.

Transport and communications

Transport. Railroads (1995): length (1996) 1,317 mi, 2,120 km; passengers transported 1,773,000; short ton-mi cargo 6,004,000, metric ton-km cargo 8,766,000. Roads (1995): total length 8,451 mi, 13,600 km (paved 88.9%). Vehicles (1995): passenger cars 220,000; trucks and buses, 58,200. Merchant marine: vessels (100 gross tons and over) n.a.; total deadweight tonnage, n.a. Air transport (1989): passenger-mi 2,021,000,000, passenger-km 3,253,000,000; short ton-mi cargo 222,000,000, metric ton-km cargo 324,200,000; airports (1997) with scheduled flights 1.

Communications

Medium	date	unit	number	units per 1,000 persons
Radio	1995	receivers	850,000	189
Television	1995	receivers	850,000	189
Telephones	1995	main lines	320,000	71

Education and health

Educational attainment (1989). Percentage of population age 25 and over having: primary education or no formal schooling 13.6%; some secondary 21.3%; completed secondary and some postsecondary 56.8%; higher 8.3%. *Literacy* (1989): total population age 15 and over literate 3,453,000 (97.7%); males literate 1,714,000 (98.8%); females literate 1,739,000 (96.6%).

Education (1994–95)

	schools	teachers	students	student/ teacher ratio
Primary (age 6–13)	1,900	72,900	940,600	12.9
Secondary (age 14–17)				
Voc., teacher tr.	78	...	26,000	...
Higher	15	...	29,435[7]	...

Health (1995): physicians 13,500 (1 per 330 persons); hospital beds 46,000 (1 per 97 persons); (1994) infant mortality rate per 1,000 live births 46.4.

Military

Total active duty personnel (1997): 18,000 (100% army). *Military expenditure as percentage of GNP* (1995): 1.7% (world 2.8%); per capita expenditure U.S.$48.

---

[1]The People's Council is the ultimate representative organ of governmental supervision and is composed of the president, membership of the Majlis, elected members, and a variety of ex officio members of national, provincial, and local government. [2]Detail does not add to total given because of rounding. [3]Ruble-area GNP and exchange-rate data for this period are very speculative. [4]Mainly agricultural income. [5]Every Turkmen citizen is guaranteed employment, so that unemployment does not officially exist. However, the 1995 Household Survey indicates an unemployment rate of about 3 percent of the labour force (defined as those actively seeking employment but not employed as a proportion of the labour force). [6]December. [7]1995–96.

Internet resources for further information:
• **Turkmenistan Human Development Report 1996**
  http://www.undp.org/undp/rbec/nhdr/1996/turkmenistan/

Tuvalu

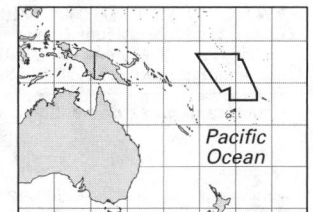

Pacific Ocean

Official name: Tuvalu.
Form of government: constitutional monarchy with one legislative house (Parliament [12]).
Chief of state: British Monarch, represented by Governor-General.
Head of government: Prime Minister.
Capital: government offices are at Vaiaku, Fongafale islet, of Funafuti atoll.
Official language: none.
Official religion: none.
Monetary units[1]: 1 Tuvalu dollar = 1 Australian dollar ($T = $A) = 100 Tuvalu and Australian cents; valuation (Sept. 25, 1998) 1 U.S.$ = $A 1.70; 1 £ = $A 2.89.

Area and population

Islands[2]	area		population
	sq mi	sq km	1991 census
Funafuti	1.08	2.79	3,172
Nanumaga	1.07	2.78	717
Nanumea	1.49	3.87	901
Niulakita	0.16	0.42	74
Niutao	0.98	2.53	889
Nui	1.09	2.83	661
Nukufetau	1.15	2.99	831
Nukulaelae	0.70	1.82	359
Vaitupu	2.16	5.60	1,280
TOTAL	9.90[3, 4]	25.63	8,884[5]

Demography

Population (1998): 10,400.
Density (1998): persons per sq mi 1,050.5, persons per sq km 405.8.
Urban-rural (1995): urban 46.0%; rural 54.0%.
Sex distribution (1997): male 48.59%; female 51.41%.
Age breakdown (1997): under 15, 35.7%; 15–29, 23.2%; 30–44, 23.4%; 45–59, 10.5%; 60–74, 6.1%; 75 and over, 1.1%.
Population projection: (2000) 10,700; (2010) 12,400.
Doubling time: 43 years.
Ethnic composition (1979): Tuvaluan (Polynesian) 91.2%; mixed (Polynesian/Micronesian/other) 7.2%; European 1.0%; other 0.6%.
Religious affiliation (1995): Church of Tuvalu (Congregational) 85.4%; Seventh-day Adventist 3.6%; Roman Catholic 1.4%; Jehovah's Witness 1.1%; Baha'i 1.0%; other 7.5%.
Major locality (1995): Fongafale, on Funafuti atoll, 4,000.

Vital statistics

Birth rate per 1,000 population (1997): 23.0 (world avg. 25.0); (1989) legitimate 82.2%; illegitimate 17.8%.
Death rate per 1,000 population (1997): 9.0 (world avg. 9.3).
Natural increase rate per 1,000 population (1997): 14.0 (world avg. 15.7).
Total fertility rate (avg. births per childbearing woman; 1997): 3.1.
Marriage rate per 1,000 population: n.a.
Divorce rate per 1,000 population: n.a.
Life expectancy at birth (1997): male 62.4 years; female 64.8 years.
Major causes of death per 100,000 population (1985): diseases of the digestive system 170.0; diseases of the circulatory system 150.0; diseases of the respiratory system 120.0; diseases of the nervous system 120.0; malignant neoplasms (cancers) 70.0; infectious and parasitic diseases 40.0; endocrine and metabolic disorders 20.0; ill-defined conditions 430.0; in 1992 the leading causes of death included liver diseases, meningitis, tuberculosis, and still and perinatal deaths; other health problems included acute respiratory infections, diarrhea, filariasis, conjunctivitis, fish poisoning, diabetes, rheumatism, and hypertension.

National economy

Budget (1995)[6]. Revenue: $A 4,400,000 (government charges and grants 49.0%; indirect taxes 34.0%; direct taxes 10.0%). Expenditures: $A 7,300,000 (1987; capital [development] expenditures 68.9%, of which marine transport 20.7%, education 13.0%, fisheries 5.6%, health 3.1%; current expenditures 31.1%).
Public debt (external; 1993): U.S.$6,000,000.
Gross national product (1996): U.S.$7,000,000 (U.S.$650 per capita).

Structure of gross domestic product and labour force

	1995		1991	
	in value[7] $A	% of total value	labour force	% of labour force
Agriculture, fishing, forestry	3,152,000	22.2	4,020	68.0
Mining	317,000	2.2	—	—
Manufacturing[8]	452,000	3.2	60	1.0
Construction	1,963,000	13.9	240	4.0
Public utilities	345,000	2.4	—	—
Transp. and commun.	599,000	4.2	60	1.0
Trade, hotels, and restaurants	2,043,000	14.4	240	4.0
Finance	1,390,000	9.8	—	—
Pub. admin., defense } Services	3,922,000	27.7	1,290	22.0
TOTAL	14,183,000	100.0	5,910	100.0

Production (metric tons except as noted). Agriculture[9], forestry, fishing (1997): coconuts 1,800, fruits 860, hens' eggs 12, other agricultural products include breadfruit, pulaka (taro), bananas, pandanus fruit, sweet potatoes, and pawpaws; livestock (number of live animals) 12,600 pigs[10]; forestry, n.a.; fish catch (1995) 1,460, of which (1993) tuna 15.0%. Mining and quarrying: n.a[11]. Manufacturing (1988): copra 90; handicrafts and baked goods are also important. Construction: n.a.; however, the main areas of construction activity are roadworks, coastal protection, government facilities, and water-related infrastructure projects. Energy production (consumption): electricity (kW-hr; 1992) 1,300,000 (1,300,000); coal, none (none); crude petroleum, none (n.a.); petroleum products, none (n.a.); natural gas, none (none).
Tourism (1993): receipts from visitors U.S.$300,000; expenditures by nationals abroad, n.a.
Population economically active (1991): total 5,910; activity rate of total population 65.3% (participation rates: ages 15–64, 85.5%; female [1979] 51.3%; unemployed [1979] 4.0%).

Price and earnings indexes (1990 = 100)

	1989	1990	1991	1992	1993	1994	1995
Consumer price index	96.4	100.0	106.4	108.7	110.3	111.9	113.6
Earnings index[12]	97.8	100.0	...	...	...	...	...

Household income and expenditure. Average household size (1979) 6.4; average annual income per household $A 2,575 (U.S.$2,044); sources of income (1987): agriculture and other 45.0%, cash economy only 38.0%, overseas remittances 17.0%; expenditure (1992)[13]: food 45.5%, housing and household operations 11.5%, transportation 10.5%, alcohol and tobacco 10.5%, clothing 7.5%, other 14.5%.
Land use (1987): agricultural and under permanent cultivation 73.6%[14]; scrub 16.1%; other 10.3%.

Foreign trade[15]

Balance of trade (current prices)

	1990	1991	1992	1993	1994	1995
$A '000	−5,909	−6,200	−6,595	−9,123	−9,498	−9,980
% of total	90.2%	86.8%	91.7%	93.3%	93.4%	93.5%

Imports (1995): U.S.$15,200,000 (1989; food 29.3%, manufactured goods 28.2%, petroleum and petroleum products 12.8%, machinery and transport equipment 12.2%, chemicals 7.1%, beverages and tobacco 3.9%). *Major import sources:* Fiji 65.8%; Australia 17.1%; New Zealand 3.9%; United Kingdom 3.3%; United States 2.0%; Germany 1.3%; The Netherlands 1.3%.
Exports (1995): U.S.$2,200,000 (1989; clothing and footwear 29.5%, copra 21.5%, fruits and vegetables 8.0%). *Major export destinations:* South Africa 63.6%; Colombia 9.1%; Belgium-Luxembourg 9.1%.

Transport and communications

Transport. Railroads: none. Roads (1995): total length 8 km (paved, none). Vehicles[16]: n.a. Merchant marine (1992): vessels (100 gross tons and over) 6; total deadweight tonnage 16,005. Air transport (1977): passenger arrivals (Funafuti) 1,443; cargo, n.a.; airports (1997) with scheduled flights 1.

Communications

Medium	date	unit	number	units per 1,000 persons
Radio	1995	receivers	3,000	320.0
Telephones	1994	main lines	113	11.5

Education and health

Educational attainment (1979). Percentage of population age 25 and over having: no formal schooling 0.4%; primary education 93.0%; secondary 6.1%; higher 0.5%. *Literacy* (1990): total population literate in Tuvaluan 8,593 (95.0%); literacy in English estimated at 45.0%.

Education (1991)

	schools	teachers[17]	students	student/ teacher ratio
Primary (age 5–11)	11	72	1,906[18]	...
Secondary (age 12–18)	1	21	314	...
Vocational	1	10	58	...
Higher	—	—	—	—

Health (1993): physicians 8 (1 per 1,152 persons); hospital beds (1990) 30 (1 per 302 persons); infant mortality rate per 1,000 live births (1997): 26.9.

Military

Total active duty personnel (1987): there is a police force numbering 32.

[1]The value of the Tuvalu dollar is pegged to the value of the Australian dollar, which is also legal currency in Tuvalu. [2]Local government councils have been established on all islands except Niulakita. [3]Another survey puts the area at 9.4 sq mi (24.4 sq km). [4]Detail does not add to total given because of rounding. [5]De facto population. [6]Estimated from 1995 gross national product. [7]At 1988 factor cost. [8]Including cottage industry. [9]Because of poor soil quality, only limited subsistence agriculture is possible on the islands. [10]Other livestock include goats. [11]Research into the mineral potential of Tuvalu's maritime exclusive economic zone (289,500 sq mi [750,000 sq km] of the Pacific Ocean) is currently being conducted by the South Pacific Geo-Science Commission. [12]Average minimum wage. [13]Weights of consumer price index components. [14]Capable of supporting coconut palms, pandanus, and breadfruit. [15]Exports and imports are f.o.b. [16]There are several cars, tractors, trailers, and light trucks on Funafuti; a few motorcycles are in use on most islands. [17]1990. [18]1994.

Internet resources for further information:
• Tuvalu http://www.emulateme.com/tuvalu.htm

Uganda

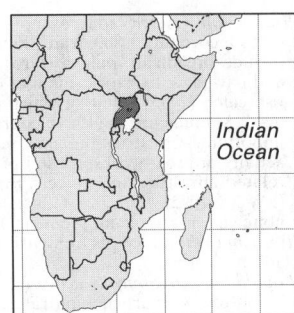

Official name: Republic of Uganda.
Form of government: republic with one legislative house (National Assembly [279[1]])[2].
Head of state and government: President.
Capital: Kampala.
Official language: English.
Official religion: none.
Monetary unit: 1 Uganda shilling (U Sh) = 100 cents; valuation (Sept. 25, 1998) 1 U.S.$ = U Sh 1,275; 1 £ = U Sh 2,171.

Area and population (1991 census)

Regions[3] Districts	area sq km	population	Regions[3] Districts	area sq km	population
Central			Arua	7,830	624,600
Kalangala	5,716	16,400	Gulu	11,735	338,700
Kampala	238	773,500	Kitgum	16,136	350,300
Kiboga	3,774	140,800	Kotido	13,208	190,700
Luwero	9,198	449,200	Lira	7,251	498,300
Masaka	10,611	831,300	Moroto	14,113	171,500
Mpigi	6,222	915,400	Moyo	5,006	178,500
Mubende	6,536	497,500	Nebbi	2,891	315,900
Mukono	14,242	816,200	Western		
Rakai	4,973	382,000	Bundibugyo	2,338	116,000
Eastern			Bushenyi	5,396	734,800
Iganga	13,113	944,000	Hoima	5,492	197,800
Jinja	734	284,900	Kabale	1,827	412,800
Kamuli	4,348	480,700	Kabarole	8,361	741,400
Kapchorwa	1,738	116,300	Kasese	3,205	343,000
Kumi	2,861	237,000	Kibaale	4,718	219,300
Mbale	2,546	706,600	Kisoro	662	184,900
Pallisa	1,919	356,000	Masindi	9,326	253,500
Soroti	10,060	430,900	Mbarara	10,839	929,600
Tororo	2,634	554,000	Ntungamo	...	...
Northern			Rukungiri	2,753	388,000
Apac	6,488	460,700	TOTAL	241,038[4]	16,582,700[5],[6]

Demography

Population (1998): 22,167,000.
Density (1998)[7]: persons per sq mi 291.4, persons per sq km 112.5.
Urban-rural (1995): urban 12.5%; rural 87.5%.
Sex distribution (1995): male 49.63%; female 50.37%.
Age breakdown (1995): under 15, 48.8%; 15–29, 26.5%; 30–44, 14.0%; 45-59, 6.9%; 60-74, 3.2%; 75 and over, 0.6%.
Population projection: (2000) 23,452,000; (2010) 31,768,000.
Doubling time: 24 years.
Ethnic composition (1983): Ganda 17.8%; Teso 8.9%; Nkole 8.2%; Soga 8.2%; Gisu 7.2%; Chiga 6.8%; Lango 6.0%; Rwanda 5.8%; other 31.1%.
Religious affiliation (1995): Christian 66%, of which Roman Catholic 33%, Protestant 33% (of which mostly Anglican); traditional beliefs 18%; Muslim 16%.
Major cities (1991): Kampala 773,500; Jinja 61,000; Mbale 53,600; Masaka 49,100; Gulu 42,800; Entebbe 41,600.

Vital statistics

Birth rate per 1,000 population (1990–95): 50.8 (world avg. 25.0).
Death rate per 1,000 population (1990–95): 21.8 (world avg. 9.3).
Natural increase rate per 1,000 population (1990–95): 29.0 (world avg. 15.7).
Total fertility rate (avg. births per childbearing woman; 1990–95): 7.3.
Life expectancy at birth (1990–95): male 43.6 years; female 46.2 years.

National economy

Budget (1995–96). Revenue: U Sh 875,400,000,000 (taxes 71.7%, of which customs duties 36.0%, sales taxes 25.9%, income taxes 13.2%; grants 28.3%). Expenditures: U Sh 992,000,000,000 (1994–95; current expenditures 54.4%, of which security 13.9%, education 6.4%, health 2.4%; capital expenditures 44.3%).
Public debt (external, outstanding; 1996): U.S.$3,151,000,000.
Tourism (1995): receipts from visitors U.S.$79,000,000; expenditures by nationals abroad U.S.$93,000,000.
Land use (1994): forest 31.5%; pasture 9.1%; agriculture 34.0%; other 25.4%.
Population economically active (1991): total 8,365,000; activity rate of total population 49.6% (participation rates: ages 15–64, 78.9%[8]; female 35.2%).

Price index (1990 = 100)

	1991	1992	1993	1994	1995	1996	1997
Consumer price index	128.0	195.0	207.0	227.0	247.0	264.0	283.0
Earnings index	...	...	...	...	...	...	...

Production (metric tons except as noted). Agriculture, forestry, fishing (1996): plantains 9,550,000, cassava 2,650,000, sweet potatoes 2,250,000, sugarcane 1,450,000, corn (maize) 939,000, millet 640,000, sorghum 405,000, potatoes 390,000, coffee 257,000, peanuts (groundnuts) 144,000, rice 83,000; livestock (number of live animals) 5,200,000 cattle, 3,500,000 goats, 1,900,000 sheep; roundwood (1995) 17,226,000 cu m; fish catch (1996) 231,600. Mining and quarrying (1996): gold 162,900 troy oz[9]. Manufacturing (1996): cement 149,100; sugar 78,500; soap 58,300; metal products 31,300; footwear 1,786,000 pairs; beer 642,000 hectolitres. Energy production (consumption): electricity

(kW-hr; 1994) 795,000,000 (681,000,000); coal (metric tons; 1994) none (none); crude petroleum (barrels; 1994) none (none); petroleum products (metric tons; 1994) none (319,000); natural gas (cu m; 1994) none (none).
Gross national product (1996): U.S.$5,826,000,000 (U.S.$300 per capita).

Structure of gross domestic product and labour force

	1995–96		1991	
	in value U Sh '000,000	% of total value	labour force	% of labour force
Agriculture	2,519,382	41.5	6,724,000	80.4
Mining	15,891	0.3		
Manufacturing	397,874	6.5	478,000	5.7
Construction	402,317	6.6		
Public utilities	65,167	1.1		
Transp. and commun.	213,856	3.5		
Trade	742,024	12.2		
Finance	410,500	6.8	1,163,000	13.9
Pub. admin., defense	248,231	4.1		
Services	293,394	4.8		
Other	768,398	12.6	...	...
TOTAL	6,077,035[5]	100.0	8,365,000	100.0

Household size. Average household size (1991) 4.8; income per household: n.a.; sources of income (1992–93)[10],[11]: wages and self-employment 86.4%; transfers 11.7%; rent 1.9%; expenditure (1992–93)[10]: food and beverages 64.0%; rent, energy, and services 18.3%; education 5.0%; health 4.2%.

Foreign trade

Balance of trade (current prices)

	1991	1992	1993	1994	1995	1996
U.S.$'000,000	–369.6	–278.6	–416.1	–463.8	–504.1	–627.7
% of total	51.3%	44.7%	57.0%	47.7%	31.9%	34.0%

Imports (1995–96): U.S.$1,218,000,000 (1995; machinery and transport equipment 32.3%, basic manufactures 11.0%, food and live animals 9.3%, chemicals 8.3%). *Major import sources* (1992): Kenya 22.6%; U.K. 10.0%; Japan 9.8%; Germany 5.5%; U.S. 4.8%.
Exports (1995–96): U.S.$590,300,000 (unroasted coffee 69.0%, cotton 2.2%, tea 2.1%). *Major export destinations* (1992): U.K. 20.7%; Belgium-Luxembourg 12.3%; Spain 9.2%; U.S. 8.1%; France 6.4%; Germany 4.3%.

Transport and communications

Transport. Railroads (1993): route length 1,241 km; passenger-km (1996) 28,000,000; metric ton-km cargo (1996) 187,000,000. Roads (1995): total length 26,800 km (paved 7.7%). Vehicles (1995): passenger cars 24,400; trucks and buses 25,300. Merchant marine (1992): vessels (100 gross tons and over) 2; total deadweight tonnage 8,600[12]. Air transport (1994): passenger-km 52,117,000; metric ton-km cargo 5,000,000; airports (1997) 1.

Communications

Medium	date	unit	number	units per 1,000 persons
Daily newspapers	1994	circulation	35,000	2.0
Radio	1997	receivers	10,000,000	485
Television	1995	receivers	500,000	27
Telephones	1995	main lines	43,200	2.3
Cellular telephones	1995	subscribers	1,700	0.1
Facsimile machines	1995	units	2,500	0.1
Personal computers	1995	units	10,000	0.5

Education and health

Educational attainment (1991). Percentage of population age 25 and over having: no formal schooling or less than one full year 46.9%; primary education 42.1%; secondary 10.5%; higher 0.5%. *Literacy* (1995): population age 15 and over literate 6,732,000 (61.8%); males literate 3,948,000 (73.7%); females literate 2,784,000 (50.2%).

Education (1995)

	schools	teachers	students	student/teacher ratio
Primary (age 5–11)[13]	8,531	76,111	2,912,473	38.3
Secondary (age 12–15)[13]	...	14,447	256,258	17.7
Voc., teacher tr. [13]	...	1,788	36,063	20.2
Higher[14]	...	2,029	27,586	13.6

Health (1989): physicians 774 (1 per 20,720 persons); hospital beds 20,136 (1 per 817 persons); infant mortality rate (1990–95) 122.0.
Food (1995): daily per capita caloric intake 2,268 (vegetable products 93%, animal products 7%); 97% of FAO recommended minimum requirement.

Military

Total active duty personnel (1997): 40,000–55,000[15]. *Military expenditure as percentage of GNP* (1995): 2.3% (world 2.8%); per capita U.S.$6.

[1]62 of 276 elected seats are allocated to special interest groups; all government ministers not elected to the National Assembly (3 in 1996) serve ex officio. [2]New constitution promulgated on Oct. 8, 1995. [3]Regions are geographical areas with no administrative function. [4]Includes water area of 43,989 sq km; Uganda's portion of Lake Victoria comprises 30,960 sq km. [5]Detail does not add to total given because of rounding. [6]Preliminary figure; final census total equals 16,671,705. [7]Based on land area only. [8]1985. [9]Export production only. [10]Based on first nationally representative household survey. [11]Highest quartile only. [12]1988. [13]Public sector only. [14]1994–95. [15]Breakdown by branch of service is unavailable.

Internet resources for further information:
• **Uganda National Information Center (unofficial web site) http://www.nic.ug/**

Ukraine

Official name: Ukrayina (Ukraine).
Form of government: unitary multiparty republic with a single legislative body (Supreme Council [450]).
Head of state: President.
Head of government: Prime Minister.
Capital: Kiev (Kyyiv).
Official language: Ukrainian.
Official religion: none.
Monetary unit: hryvnia (pl. hryvny)[1]; (no decimal unit); valuation (Sept. 25, 1998) free rate, 1 U.S.$ = 3.80 hryvny; 1 £ = 6.47 hryvny.

Area and population		area		population
				1996
Autonomous republic	Capitals	sq mi	sq km	estimate
Crimea (Krym)	Simferopol	10,400[2]	27,000[2]	2,205,600
Cities				
Kiev	—	[3]	[3]	2,638,700
Sevastopol	—	[2]	[2]	406,900
Provinces				
Cherkasy	Cherkasy	8,100	20,900	1,504,600
Chernihiv	Chernihiv	12,300	31,900	1,349,500
Chernivtsi	Chernivtsi	3,100	8,100	943,600
Dnipropetrovsk	Dnipropetrovsk	12,300	31,900	3,852,000
Donetsk	Donetsk	10,200	26,500	5,198,500
Ivano-Frankivsk	Ivano-Frankivsk	5,400	13,900	1,467,100
Kharkiv	Kharkiv	12,100	31,400	3,088,400
Kherson	Kherson	11,000	28,500	1,265,700
Khmelnytsky	Khmelnytsky	8,000	20,600	1,508,800
Kirovohrad	Kirovohrad	9,500	24,600	1,224,800
Kyyiv (Kiev)	Kiev	11,200[3]	28,900[3]	1,895,800
Luhansk	Luhansk	10,300	26,700	2,788,500
Lviv	Lviv	8,400	21,800	2,761,500
Mykolayiv	Mykolayiv	9,500	24,600	1,343,300
Odessa	Odessa	12,900	33,300	2,586,500
Poltava	Poltava	11,100	28,800	1,739,100
Rivne	Rivne	7,800	20,100	1,194,200
Sumy	Sumy	9,200	23,800	1,397,900
Ternopil	Ternopil	5,300	13,800	1,175,400
Vinnytsya	Vinnytsya	10,200	26,500	1,876,000
Volyn	Volodymyr-Volynsky	7,800	20,200	1,075,200
Zakarpatska	Uzhhorod	4,900	12,800	1,288,100
Zaporizhzhya	Zaporizhzhya	10,500	27,200	2,077,800
Zhytomyr	Zhytomyr	11,600	29,900	1,480,600
TOTAL		233,100	603,700	51,334,100

Demography

Population (1998): 50,302,000.
Density (1998): persons per sq mi 215.8, persons per sq km 83.3.
Urban-rural (1996): urban 67.9%; rural 32.1%.
Sex distribution (1994): male 46.45%; female 53.55%.
Age breakdown (1995): under 15, 19.5%; 15–29, 20.6%; 30–44, 22.3%; 45–59, 18.2%; 60–69, 10.3%; 70 and over, 9.1%.
Population projection: (2000) 49,516,000; (2010) 47,601,000.
Ethnic composition (1998): Ukrainian 64.7%; Russian 32.8%; Jewish 0.7%; Moldovan 0.6%; Tatar 0.4%; Belarusian 0.3%; other 0.5%.
Religious affiliation (1995): Ukrainian Orthodox (Russian patriarchy) 19.5%; Ukrainian Orthodox (Kiev patriarchy) 9.7%; Ukrainian Catholic (Uniate) 7.0%; Protestant 3.6%; other Orthodox 1.6%; Roman Catholic 1.2%; Jewish 0.9%; other (mostly nonreligious) 56.5%.
Major cities (1996): Kiev 2,630,200; Kharkiv 1,555,100; Dnipropetrovsk 1,147,200; Donetsk 1,088,200; Odessa 1,046,400.

Vital statistics

Birth rate per 1,000 population (1996): 9.1 (world avg. 25.0); (1993) legitimate 87.0%; illegitimate 13.0%.
Death rate per 1,000 population (1996): 15.2 (world avg. 9.3).
Natural increase rate per 1,000 population (1996): –6.1 (world avg. 15.7).
Life expectancy at birth (1994): male 62.0 years; female 73.0 years.
Major causes of death per 100,000 population (1995): circulatory diseases 874.0; neoplasms (cancers) 199.0; accidents 160.0; respiratory diseases 89.0.

National economy

Budget (1996). Revenue: 19,633,000,000 hryvny (value-added tax 20.9%, corporate tax 18.1%, income tax 8.8%, excise tax 2.2%, other 50%). Expenditures: 23,258,000,000 hryvny (social-cultural spending and education 34.9%; national economy 10.2%; defense 3.6%).
Public debt (external; 1996): U.S.$6,451,000,000.
Production (metric tons except as noted). Agriculture, forestry, fishing (1996): sugar beets 23,009,000, potatoes 18,410,000, wheat 13,547,000, barley 5,726,000, corn (maize) 1,837,000; livestock (number of live animals) 17,557,000 cattle, 13,144,000 pigs, 4,098,000 sheep and goats; roundwood (1993) 4,888,200 cu m; fish catch (1995) 607,707. Mining and quarrying (1995): iron ore 51,000,000; manganese 3,200,000. Manufacturing (value in '000 hryvny; 1994): metals 2,783,065; machinery 2,225,093; processed foods 1,285,328; chemicals 898,635. Construction (1996): residential 6,500,000 sq m. Energy production (consumption): electricity (kW-hr; 1994) 209,100,000,000 (208,100,000,000); coal (metric tons; 1994) 91,800,000 (94,267,000); crude petroleum (barrels; 1994) 30,786,000 (137,900,000); petroleum products 10,678,000 (12,180,000); natural gas (cu m; 1994) 18,600,000,000 (18,800,000,000).
Gross national product (1996)[4]: U.S.$60,904,000,000 (U.S.$1,200 per capita).

Structure of gross domestic product and labour force				
	1993		1995	
	in value '000,000 hryvny	% of total value	labour force	% of labour force
Agriculture	31,939	21.5	5,300,000	22.4
Mining	} 45,826	30.9	...	...
Manufacturing				
Public utilities	1,303	0.9	} 5,800,000	24.5
Construction	10,282	6.9	1,500,000	6.3
Transp. and commun.	17,425	11.8	1,400,000	5.9
Trade	16,482	11.1	1,600,000	6.8
Finance	17,784	12.0	200,000	0.8
Pub. admin., defense	5,304	3.6	700,000	3.0
Services	13,182	8.9	4,900,000	20.7
Other	–11,254[5]	–7.6[5]	2,427,000[6]	9.7[6]
TOTAL	148,273	100.0	23,627,000	100.0[7]

Population economically active (1995): total 23,627,000; activity rate of total population 46.0% (1993; participation rates: ages 16–59 [male], 15–64 [female] 82.4%; female [1994] 51.0%; unemployed [1997] 1.3%).

Price and earnings indexes (1993 = 100)				
	1993	1994	1995	1996
Consumer price index	100.0	991.2	4,725	8,519
Monthly earnings index	100.0	886.6	4,736	...

Household income and expenditure (1996). Average household size 3.0; income per household 4,968 hryvny[1]; sources of income (1995): wages and salaries 66.4%, sales of agricultural products 9.3%, subsidies 6.9%, pensions 6.5%, remuneration from abroad 5.3%; expenditures (1995): food and beverages 43.1%, consumer goods 27.5%, services 7.2%, housing 6.7%, taxes 6.2%.

Foreign trade

Balance of trade (current prices)				
	1994	1995	1996	1997
U.S.$'000,000	–2,572	–2,703	–4,296	–1,462
% of total	8.4%	8.7%	12.1%	17.5%

Imports (1996): U.S.$12,567,000,000 (1995; mineral commodities 55.2%; machinery 14.8%; chemicals 5.4%; nonferrous metals 4.8%; plastics, rubber, and products 3.6%). *Major import sources:* Russia 42.5%; Germany 6.7%.
Exports (1996): U.S.$13,413,000,000 (1995; ferrous metals 36.2%; machinery 11.8%; mineral commodities 10.6%; chemicals 9.7%; food 8.5%). *Major export destinations:* Russia 39.8%; China 5.3%.

Transport and communications

Transport. Railroads (1997): length 22,600 km; (1995) passenger-km 120,500,-000,000; metric ton-km cargo 518,500,000,000. Roads (1995): total length 172,257 km (paved 94.8%). Vehicles (1995): passenger cars 4,510,000. Air transport (1996): passenger-km 2,014,000,000; metric ton-km cargo 44,205,000; airports (1997) with scheduled flights 12.

Communications				units per 1,000
Medium	date	unit	number	persons
Daily newspapers	1995	circulation	6,083,000	118
Radio	1996	receivers	18,000,000	346
Television	1995	receivers	12,000,000	233
Telephones	1995	main lines	8,311,000	161
Cellular telephones	1995	subscribers	14,000	0.3
Facsimile machines	1995	units	1,500	0.03
Personal computers	1995	units	290,000	5.6

Education and health

Educational attainment (1989). Percentage of population age 15 and over having: some primary education 6.8%; completed primary 13.8%; some secondary 18.4%; completed secondary 31.1%; some postsecondary 19.5%; higher 10.4%. *Literacy* (1989): percentage of total population age 15 and over literate 98.4%; males literate 99.5%; females literate 97.4%.

Education (1995–96)				student/
	schools	teachers	students	teacher ratio
Primary (age 6–13)	} 21,900	576,000[8]	7,007,000	12.4[8]
Secondary (age 14–17)				
Voc., teacher tr.	782	...	618,000	...
Higher	255	...	922,800	...

Health (1995): physicians 230,000 (1 per 224 persons); hospital beds 639,000 (1 per 81 persons); infant mortality rate per 1,000 live births 14.5.

Military

Total active duty personnel (1997): 387,400 (army 41.7%, air force 32.1%, navy 4.1%, other 22.1%). *Military expenditure as percentage of GNP* (1995) 2.9% (world 2.8%); per capita expenditure U.S.$70.

[1]On Sept. 2, 1996, the karbovanets, a transitional currency, was replaced by the hryvnia at a 100,000-to-1 ratio. [2]Crimea includes area of Sevastopol. [3]Kyyiv includes area of Kiev (city). [4]Ruble-area GNP and exchange-rate data are very speculative. [5]Less imputed bank service charges, net indirect taxes, and taxes on production. [6]Includes 126,900 unemployed. [7]Detail does not add to total given because of rounding. [8]1994–95.

Internet resources for further information:
• **Welcome to the Parliament of Ukraine** http://www.rada.kiev.ua/
• **United Nations Office in Ukraine WWW Service** http://www.un.kiev.ua/

United Arab Emirates

Official name: Al-Imārāt al-ʿArabīyah al-Muttaḥidah (United Arab Emirates).
Form of government: federation of seven emirates with one appointive advisory body (Federal National Council [40[1]]).
Chief of state: President.
Head of government: Prime Minister.
Capital: Abu Dhabi.
Official language: Arabic.
Official religion: Islam.
Monetary unit: 1 U.A.E. dirham (Dh) = 100 fils; valuation (Sept. 25, 1998) 1 U.S.$ = Dh 3.67; 1 £ = Dh 6.25.

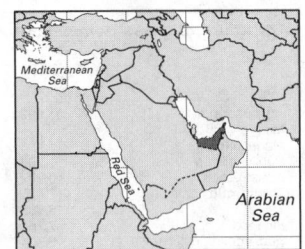

Area and population

Emirates	Capitals	area sq mi	area sq km	population 1995 census[2]
Abu Dhabi (Abū Ẓaby)	Abu Dhabi	28,210[3]	73,060[3]	928,360
ʿAjmān (Ajman)	ʿAjmān	100	260	118,812
Dubayy (Dubai)	Dubayy	1,510	3,900	674,101
Al-Fujayrah (Fujairah)	Al-Fujayrah	500	1,300	76,254
Ra's al-Khaymah (Ras al-Khaimah)	Ra's al-Khaymah	660	1,700	144,430
Ash-Shāriqah (Sharjah)	Ash-Shāriqah	1,000	2,600	400,339
Umm al-Qaywayn (Umm al-Qaiwain)	Umm al-Qaywayn	300	780	35,157
TOTAL		32,280	83,600	2,377,453

Demography

Population (1998): 2,744,000.
Density (1998): persons per sq mi 85.0, persons per sq km 32.8.
Urban-rural (1995): urban 84.0%; rural 16.0%.
Sex distribution (1995): male 66.45%; female 33.55%.
Age breakdown (1994): under 15, 34.3%; 15-29, 25.3%; 30-44, 30.6%; 45-59, 7.8%; 60-74, 1.5%; 75 and over, 0.5%.
Population projection: (2000) 2,844,000; (2010) 3,399,000.
Doubling time: 32 years.
Ethnic composition (1993): expatriates of Bangladesh, India, Pakistan, and Sri Lanka 45.0%; Arabs 25.0%, of which non-UAE Arabs (primaily Egyptians) 13.0%, UAE Arabs 12.0%; Iranians 17.0%; other Asians and Africans 8.0%; Europeans and North Americans 5.0%.
Religious affiliation (1995): Muslim 96.0% (Sunnī 80.0%, Shīʿī 16.0%); other (mostly Christian and Hindu) 4.0%.
Major cities (1989): Dubayy 585,189; Abu Dhabi 363,432; Al-ʿAyn 176,411; Ash-Shāriqah 125,000[4]; Ra's al-Khaymah 42,000[4].

Vital statistics

Birth rate per 1,000 population (1994): 25.0 (world avg. 25.0).
Death rate per 1,000 population (1994): 3.4 (world avg. 9.3).
Natural increase rate per 1,000 population (1994): 21.6 (world avg. 15.7).
Total fertility rate (avg. births per childbearing woman; 1994): 3.5.
Marriage rate per 1,000 population (1994): 3.2.
Life expectancy at birth (1994): male 69.2 years; female 75.2 years.
Major causes of death per 100,000 population (1989)[5]: accidents and poisoning 43.7; diseases of the circulatory system 34.3; malignant neoplasms (cancers) 13.7; respiratory diseases 8.1.

National economy

Budget (1996). Revenue: Dh 17,396,000,000 (1994; current [domestic] grants 79.5%; other sources 20.5%, of which nontax revenue 15.3%, tax revenue 5.2%). Expenditures: Dh 18,254,000,000 (1994; current expenditures 95.3%, of which defense 37.1%, education 17.2%, public safety 12.9%, health 7.3%, economic services 5.3%; cultural and religious affairs 3.2%).
Gross national product (1996): U.S.$44,370,000,000 (U.S.$17,400 per capita).

Structure of gross domestic product and labour force

	1996 in value Dh '000,000	1996 % of total value	1990 labour force	1990 % of labour force
Agriculture	3,703	2.4	43,100	6.3
Petroleum	53,572	34.7	10,000	1.5
Manufacturing	13,242	8.6	63,400	9.2
Construction	14,611	9.5	119,200	17.3
Public utilities	1,687	1.1	20,600	3.0
Transp. and commun.	8,696	5.6	71,700	10.4
Trade	19,323	12.5	101,400	14.7
Finance, real estate	20,357	13.2	18,800	2.7
Pub. admin., defense	17,547	11.4	241,300	35.0
Services	2,969[7]	1.9[7]		
Other	−1,423[8]	−0.9[8]	—	—
TOTAL	154,284	100.0	689,500	100.0[9]

Public debt: n.a.
Tourism (1995): total number of tourist arrivals 2,200,000.
Production (metric tons except as noted). Agriculture, forestry, fishing (1997): tomatoes 545,000, dates 245,000, cabbages 45,000, lemons and limes 21,000, pumpkins and squash 20,000, eggplants 16,983, cucumbers and gherkins 13,612, mangoes 9,500; livestock (number of live animals) 990,000 goats, 385,000 sheep, 160,000 camels, 70,000 cattle, 10,700,000 chickens; fish catch (1994) 108,000. Mining and quarrying (1994): sulfur 144,000; gypsum 100,000;

lime 45,000. Manufacturing (value of production in Dh '000,000; 1993): chemical products 13,086; fabricated metal products 2,234; food, beverages, and tobacco 2,122; nonmetallic mineral products 2,025; basic metal manufactures 1,992; textiles, clothing, and leather products 1,135. Energy production (consumption): electricity (kW-hr; 1994) 18,870,000,000 (18,870,000,000); crude petroleum (barrels; 1996) 803,000,000 ([1994] 73,722,000); petroleum products (metric tons; 1994) 14,710,000 (7,625,000); natural gas (cu m; 1996) 35,000,000,000 (27,800,000,000).
Population economically active (1992): total 733,500; activity rate of total population 36.9% (participation rates [1986]: ages 15–64, 76.7%; female 6.6%).

Price and earnings indexes (1990 = 100)

	1989	1990	1991	1992	1993	1994	1995
Consumer price index[10]	98.8	100.0	105.4	112.4	118.0	123.9	129.3
Earnings index	...	...	...	...	...	...	...

Household income and expenditure. Average household size (1986) 6.8; income per household: n.a.; sources of income: n.a.; expenditure (1991): rent, fuel, and light 23.9%, food 22.7%, transportation and communications 14.1%, durable household goods 11.6%, education, recreation, and entertainment 8.6%.
Land use (1994): forested, virtually none; meadows and pastures 2.4%; agricultural and under permanent cultivation 0.5%; built-on, wasteland, and other 97.1%.

Foreign trade

Balance of trade (current prices)

	1990	1991	1992	1993	1994	1995
U.S.$'000,000	+11,960	+10,471	+4,528	+3,755	−1,974	−1,000
% of total	34.1%	27.3%	10.1%	8.7%	4.9%	2.2%

Imports (1994): U.S.$23,883,000,000 (1993; machinery and transport equipment 38.4%, basic manufactures 24.8%, food and live animals 9.7%, chemicals 6.1%, crude minerals 1.6%, mineral fuels 1.4%). *Major import sources:* Japan 10.4%; United Kingdom 7.8%; Germany 7.5%; United States 7.3%; Italy 6.7%; South Korea 5.4%; India 4.9%; Hong Kong 4.5%; China 4.0%.
Exports (1994): U.S.$20,906,000,000 (1993; crude petroleum and refined petroleum 92.6%, manufactured goods 3.0%, machinery and transport equipment 0.8%, food and live animals 0.6%). *Major export destinations:* Japan 39.7%; India 5.3%; Oman 4.9%; South Korea 4.7%; Iran 4.6%; Singapore 3.8%; Thailand 2.7%; Hong Kong 2.4%; United States 2.1%.

Transport and communications

Transport. Railroads: none. Roads (1995): total length 2,952 mi, 4,750 km (paved 100%). Vehicles (1995): passenger cars 197,000; trucks and buses 49,150. Merchant marine (1992): vessels (100 gross tons and over) 276; total deadweight tonnage 1,491,728. Air transport (1996)[11]: passenger-mi 1,714,175,000, passenger-km 2,758,697,000; short ton-mi cargo 72,435,000, metric ton-km cargo 105,754,000; airports (1997) with scheduled flights 6.

Communications

Medium	date	unit	number	units per 1,000 persons
Daily newspapers	1994	circulation	300,000	135
Radio	1995	receivers	490,000	206
Television	1995	receivers	43,900	18
Telephones	1995	main lines	140,900	59
Cellular telephones	1995	subscribers	27,600	12
Facsimile machines	1995	units	5,700	2.4
Personal computers	1995	units	29,000	12

Education and health

Educational attainment (1975). Percentage of population age 25 and over having: no formal schooling 72.2%; primary education 5.2%; secondary 16.6%; higher 6.0%. *Literacy* (1995): total population age 15 and over literate 79.2%; males literate 78.9%; females literate 79.8%.

Education (1994–95)

	schools	teachers	students	student/ teacher ratio
Primary (age 6–11)	512[12]	15,449	262,628	17.0
Secondary (age 12–18)		12,388	158,625	12.0
Vocational	9[13]	189	1,215	6.4
Higher	4	510[14]	13,900	19.2[14]

Health (1994): physicians 4,095 (1 per 545 persons); hospital beds 6,193 (1 per 360 persons); infant mortality rate per 1,000 live births (1995) 16.6.
Food (1995): daily per capita caloric intake 3,361 (vegetable products 75%, animal products 25%); 139% of FAO recommended minimum requirement.

Military

Total active duty personnel (1997): 64,500 (army 91.5%, navy 2.3%, air force 6.2%). *Military expenditure as percentage of GDP* (1995): 4.8% (world 2.8%); per capita expenditure U.S.$643.

[1]All appointed seats. [2]Preliminary. [3]Approximate, based on reported total and on reported partial areas for smaller emirates. [4]1980. [5]Registered; Abu Dhabi Emirate only. [6]At current prices. [7]Services include domestic help. [8]Import duties less imputed bank service charges. [9]Detail does not add to total given because of rounding. [10]Abu Dhabi only. [11]One-fourth apportionment of international flights of Gulf Air. [12]1991–92. [13]1990–91. [14]1992–93.

Internet resources for further information:
• U.A.E. Home Page http://www.emirates.org/

United Kingdom

Official name: United Kingdom of
Great Britain and Northern Ireland.
Form of government: constitutional
monarchy with two legislative houses
(House of Lords [1,223]; House of
Commons [659]).
Chief of state: Sovereign.
Head of government: Prime Minister.
Capital: London.
Official language: English.
Official religion: Churches of England
and Scotland "established" (protected
by the state, but not "official")
in their respective countries; no
established church in Northern
Ireland or Wales.
Monetary unit: 1 pound sterling
(£) = 100 new pence; valuation
(Sept. 25, 1998) 1 £ = U.S.$1.70;
1 U.S.$ = £0.59.

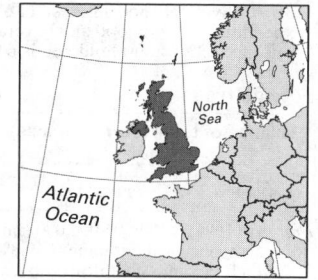

Place of birth (1991): U.K. 93.2% (52,721,000); foreign-born 6.8%, of which
India 1.5%, Ireland 1.1%, Caribbean 0.9%, Pakistan 0.9%, other 2.2%.
Mobility (1991)[6]. Population living in the same residence as 1990: 90.1%; different residence, same country (of Great Britain) 8.1%; different residence,
different country of Great Britain 1.2%; from outside Great Britain 0.6%.
Households (1994)[6]. Average household size 2.4; 1 person 27%, 2 persons 34%,
3 persons 16%, 4 persons 15%, 5 persons 6%, 6 or more persons 2%. Family
household: 16,900,000 (72.0%), nonfamily 6,600,000 (28.0%, of which 1-per-
son 12.0%).
Immigration (1995): permanent residents 245,000, from United States 11.0%,
Australia 8.6%, Bangladesh, India, and Sri Lanka 4.5%, New Zealand 4.1%,
South Africa 3.7%, Canada 3.3%, other 64.8%, of which EU 14.7%.

Vital statistics

Birth rate per 1,000 population (1996): 12.5 (world avg. 25.0); legitimate (1994)
68.0%; illegitimate 32.0%.
Death rate per 1,000 population (1996): 10.9 (world avg. 9.3).
Natural increase rate per 1,000 population (1996): 1.6 (world avg. 15.7).
Total fertility rate (avg. births per childbearing woman; 1994): 1.7.
Marriage rate per 1,000 population (1995): 5.5.
Divorce rate per 1,000 population (1995)[6]: 3.0.
Life expectancy at birth (1996): male 74.4 years; female 79.7 years.
Major causes of death per 100,000 population (1994): diseases of the circula-
tory system 473.3, of which ischemic heart disease 265.2, cerebrovascular dis-
ease 116.8; malignant neoplasms (cancers) 275.4; diseases of the respiratory
system 155.6, of which pneumonia 92.9; diseases of the digestive system 36.4;
diseases of the endocrine system 14.1, of which diabetes mellitus 11.2; diseases of the genitourinary system 13.4; suicide 7.5.

Social indicators

Educational attainment (1981). Percentage of population age 25 and over having: primary or secondary education only 89.7%; some postsecondary 4.8%;
bachelor's or equivalent degree 4.9%; higher university degree 0.6%.

Distribution of disposable Income (1994–95)

percentage of household income by quintile

1	2	3	4	5 (highest)
7.9	12.2	16.1	23.0	40.8

Quality of working life (1992). Average workweek (hours): male 43.3, female
30.2. Annual rate per 100,000 workers for: injury or accident 752.6; industrial diseases 1.3[7, 8]; death 1.5. Proportion of labour force (employed persons)
insured for damages or income loss resulting from: injury 100%; permanent
disability 100%; death 100%. Average days lost to labour stoppages per 1,000
employee workdays 1994: 0.05. Principal means of transport to work (1991;
London only): public transportation 81%, private automobile 15%, motor or
pedal cycle 2%, other 2%.
Access to services (1991)[6]. Proportion of households having access to: bath or
shower 98.7%; toilet 99.8%; central heating 81.1%.
Social participation. Eligible voters participating in last national election (May
1997): 71.3%. Population age 16 and over participating in voluntary work
(1987)[6]: 22%. Trade union membership in total workforce (1992) 32.0%.
Social deviance (1995)[6]. Offense rate per 100,000 population for: theft and handling stolen goods 4,944.2; burglary 2,431.0; violence against the person 406.2;
fraud and forgery 277.8; robbery 135.8; sexual offense 58.5. Incidence per
100,000 population of: registered drug addicts 36.5[9]; suicide 7.5.
Leisure (1994). Favourite leisure activities (hours weekly): watching television
17.1; listening to radio 10.3; reading 8.8, of which books 3.8, newspapers 3.3;
gardening 2.1.
Material well-being (1995). Households possessing: automobile 69.7%, telephone 92.4%, television receiver 98.3% (colour 95%)[10], refrigerator 98.5%,
central heating 85.3%, washing machine 90.9%, video recorder 79.2%.

National economy

Budget (1996–97). Revenue: £280,900,000,000 (income tax 33.5%, value-added
16.9%, social security contributions 16.6%). Expenditures: £308,500,000,000
(social security 24.9%, health 11.0%, debt interest 7.2%, defense 7.2%).
Tourism (1996): receipts U.S.$20,019,700,000; expenditures U.S.$25,046,100,-
000.
Land use (1994): forest 10.4%; pasture 45.9%; agriculture 24.8%; other 18.9%.
Total national debt (March 31, 1996): £374,636,000,000.
Gross national product (1996): U.S.$1,152,136,000,000 (U.S.$19,600 per capita).

Population (1995 estimate)

Countries[1]	population		population		population
England	48,903,400[2]	NW Somerset	183,800	Dumfries and	
Counties		Poole	138,900	Galloway	147,900
Bedfordshire	364,300	Portsmouth	189,900	Dundee City	151,000
Berkshire	783,200	Redcar and		East Ayrshire	124,000
Buckinghamshire	473,000	Cleveland	141,400	East Dumbarton-	
Cambridgeshire	693,900	Rutland	34,600	shire	110,000
Cheshire	978,100	South		East Lothian	86,800
Cornwall (includes		Gloucestershire	233,200	East Renfrewshire	86,800
Isles of Scilly)	482,700	Southampton	213,400	Falkirk	142,800
Cumbria	490,300	Stockton-on-Tees	178,100	Fife	351,600
Derbyshire	1,058,800	Stoke-on-Trent	254,300	Glasgow City	616,400
Dorset	378,900	Swindon	173,800	Highland	207,500
Durham	507,100	York	174,400	Inverclyde	89,400
East Sussex	482,800	**Metropolitan**		Midlothian	79,900
Essex	1,577,500	**Counties/Greater**		Moray	87,200
Gloucestershire	552,700	**London**		North Ayrshire	139,000
Hampshire	1,213,400	Greater London[4]	7,007,100	North Lanarkshire	326,800
Hereford and		Greater		Orkney Islands	19,700
Worcester	694,300	Manchester[4]	2,578,600	Perth and Kinross	130,700
Hertfordshire	1,011,200	Merseyside[4]	1,427,300	Renfrewshire	177,000
Kent	1,551,300	South Yorkshire[4]	1,304,000	Scottish Borders	105,300
Lancashire	1,426,000	Tyne and Wear[4]	1,130,900	Shetland Islands	23,100
Leicestershire	592,700	West Midlands[4]	2,637,000	South Ayrshire	114,000
Lincolnshire	611,800	West Yorkshire[4]	2,105,800	South Lanarkshire	307,500
Norfolk	772,400	Wales	2,916,800[2]	Stirling	81,600
North Yorkshire	556,200	**Unitary Districts**		West Dumbarton-	
Northamptonshire	599,300	Anglesey	67,200	shire	97,800
Northumberland	307,300	Blaenau Gwent	73,200	Western Isles	29,400
Nottinghamshire	1,031,900	Bridgend	130,700	West Lothian	148,200
Oxfordshire	598,400	Caerphilly	169,900	Northern Ireland	1,649,000
Shropshire	419,900	Cardiff	309,400	**Districts**	
Somerset	481,000	Carmarthenshire	169,500	Antrim	48,500
Staffordshire	802,100	Ceredigion	70,200	Ards	66,700
Suffolk	656,800	Conway	111,200	Armagh	52,500
Surrey	1,044,400	Denbighshire	91,600	Ballymena	57,500
Warwickshire	498,700	Flintshire	145,700	Ballymoney	24,600
West Sussex	731,500	Gwynedd	118,000	Banbridge	37,300
Wiltshire	416,800	Merthyr Tydfil	58,700	Belfast	296,700
Unitary Districts		Monmouthshire	85,600	Carrickfergus	34,900
Bath and		Neath and		Castlereagh	63,400
NE Somerset	164,600	Port Talbot	139,600	Coleraine	54,100
Bournemouth	160,900	Newport	137,200	Cookstown	31,300
Brighton and		Pembrokeshire	113,500	Craigavon	78,100
Hove	400,700	Powys	122,300	Derry	102,800
Bristol	400,700	Rhondda, Cynon,		Down	60,700
Darlington	100,600	Taff	239,000	Dungannon	46,800
Derby	231,900	Swansea	230,600	Fermanagh	54,700
East Riding of		Torfaen	90,400	Lame	30,000
Yorkshire	308,400	The Vale of		Limavady	30,900
Hartlepool	92,200	Glamorgan	118,800	Lisburn	106,000
Isle of Wight[3]	125,100	Wrexham	123,400	Magherafelt	37,000
Kingston upon		Scotland	5,136,600[5]	Moyle	14,800
Hull	268,600	**Unitary Districts**		Newry and Mourne	84,100
Leicester	295,700	Aberdeen City	219,100	Newtownabbey	78,600
Luton	181,400	Aberdeenshire	226,500	North Down	74,000
Middlesbrough	147,500	Angus	111,800	Omagh	46,900
Milton Keynes	192,900	Argyll and Bute	90,000	Strabane	36,100
NE Lincolnshire	160,100	City of Edinburgh	447,600	TOTAL	58,605,800
North Lincolnshire	152,100	Clackmannanshire	47,700		

Demography

Population (1998): 59,126,000.
Density (1998): persons per sq mi 627.3, persons per sq km 242.2.
Urban-rural (1996): urban 89.4%; rural 10.6%.
Sex distribution (1996): male 49.09%; female 50.91%.
Age breakdown (1996): under 15, 19.5%; 15–29, 20.1%; 30–44, 21.9%; 45–59,
18.0%; 60–74, 13.3%; 75 and over, 7.2%.
Population projection: (2000) 59,454,000; (2010) 60,800,000.
Ethnic composition (1992–94)[6]: white 93.7%; Asian Indian 1.8%; Pakistani
1.4%; Black 1.4%; other and not stated 1.6%.
Religious affiliation (1995): Christian 65.9%, of which Protestant 53.4%
(Anglican 43.5%, Presbyterian 4.5%, Methodist 2.2%), Roman Catholic
9.8%, Orthodox 1.0%, other Christian 1.7%; Muslim 2.6%; Hindu 0.6%; Sikh
0.5%; Jewish 0.5%; other/nonreligious 29.9%.
Major cities (1996): Greater London 7,074,300; Birmingham 1,020,600; Leeds
726,900; Glasgow 616,400; Sheffield 530,400; Bradford 483,400; Liverpool
468,000; Edinburgh 448,900; Manchester 430,800; Bristol 399,600; Kirklees
388,800; Wirral 329,200.

Structure of gross domestic product and labour force

	1996			
	in value £'000,000	% of total value	labour force	% of labour force
Agriculture	11,790	1.8	278,000	1.0
Mining[11]	18,068	2.8	268,000	1.0
Manufacturing	137,006	21.3	4,105,000	14.4
Construction	33,746	5.2	825,000	3.0
Public utilities	13,606	2.1	147,000	0.5
Transp. and commun.	54,056	8.4	1,315,000	4.7
Trade	93,091	14.5	3,749,000	13.4
Finance	164,282	25.6	984,000	3.5
Pub. admin., defense	120,120	18.7	5,798,000	20.7
Services	24,713	3.8	4,937,000	17.6
Other	−27,562[12]	−4.3[12]	5,653,000[13]	20.2[13]
TOTAL	642,916	100.0[2]	27,969,000	100.0

Production (metric tons except as noted). Agriculture, forestry, fishing (1996):
wheat 16,102,000, sugar beets 9,555,000, barley 7,784,000, potatoes 7,219,000,
rapeseed 1,448,000, carrots 630,000, oats 590,000, cabbage 574,000; livestock
(number of live animals) 41,530,000 sheep, 11,913,000 cattle, 7,496,000 pigs;

roundwood (1995) 8,229,000 cu m; fish catch (1995) 1,003,740. Mining and quarrying (1996): limestone 97,000,000; tin 1,920; lead 1,080. Manufacturing (value added in £'000,000; 1996): electrical and optical equipment 18,270; food and beverages 17,622; paper, printing, and publishing 16,214; chemicals and chemical products 15,819; metals and metal products 15,199; transport equipment 13,914; machinery and equipment 12,196; textiles and leather products 7,186. Construction (value in £; 1995)[6]: residential 7,135,000,000; nonresidential 13,877,000,000.

Financial aggregates

	1991	1992	1993	1994	1995	1996	1997
Exchange rate							
U.S. dollar per £	1.77	1.76	1.50	1.53	1.58	1.56	1.64
SDRs per £	1.31	1.10	1.08	1.07	1.04	1.18	1.22
International reserves (U.S.$)							
Total (excl. gold; '000,000,000)	41.89	36.64	36.78	41.01	42.02	39.90	32.32
SDRs ('000,000,000)	1.31	0.54	0.29	0.49	0.41	0.34	0.47
Reserve pos. in IMF ('000,000,000)	1.85	2.01	1.86	1.99	2.42	2.43	2.97
Foreign exchange ('000,000,000)	38.73	34.09	34.63	38.53	39.18	37.12	28.88
Gold ('000,000 fine troy oz)	18.89	18.61	18.45	18.44	18.43	18.43	18.42
% world reserves	2.0	2.0	2.0	2.0	2.0	2.0	2.1
Interest and prices							
Central bank discount (%)	...	...	...	...	...	...	...
Govt. bond yield (%) long term	9.92	9.12	7.87	8.05	8.26	8.10	7.09
Industrial share prices (1990 = 100)	109.8	114.7	131.7	141.5	147.3	166.9	188.9
Balance of payments (U.S.$'000,000)							
Balance of visible trade,	−17,990	−24,618	−20,570	−16,127	−18,266	−18,870	−20,540
Imports, f.o.b.	201,081	212,058	201,802	222,263	259,154	278,400	−299,810
Exports, f.o.b.	183,091	187,440	181,232	206,136	240,888	259,530	−279,270
Balance of invisibles	6,768	3,904	4,179	13,736	7,697	19,110	−28,560
Balance of payments, current account	−11,222	−20,714	−16,391	−2,391	−10,569	240	−7,920

Manufacturing, mining, and construction enterprises (1993)

	no. of enterprises	no. of employees	annual wages as a % of avg. of all wages	annual value added (£'000,000)
Manufacturing				
Food, beverages, and tobacco	9,463	554,700	...	16,559
Paper and paper products; printing and publishing	26,825	430,400	...	13,438
Electrical and data-processing equipment	13,902	512,800	...	13,209
Transport equipment	3,704	414,200	...	12,815
Chemical engineering	3,809	270,200	...	12,538
Machinery and equipment	11,636	387,500	...	9,391
Rubber and plastics	5,103	228,500	...	5,679
Metal manufacturing	3,524	144,400	...	4,197
Textiles	7,256	171,800	...	3,498
Clothing and footwear	8,119	211,800	...	2,716
Mineral-oil processing	148	13,100	...	1,618
Wood and wood products	7,767	73,600	...	1,292
Mining				
Extraction of coal, mineral oil, and natural gas	358	80,000[10]	...	10,261
Extraction of minerals other than fuels	921	30,200	...	1,090
Construction	199,363	1,016,000[10]	...	19,274

Retail trade enterprises (1992)

	no. of enterprises	no. of employees	weekly wage as a % of all wages	annual turnover (£'000,000)[14]
Food and grocery, of which	60,119	854,000	...	51,462
large grocery	71	579,000	...	40,837
other grocery	18,557	95,000	...	4,086
meats	12,149	58,000	...	2,523
Household goods, of which	45,532	299,000	...	20,881
electrical and musical goods	10,887	87,000	...	7,270
furniture	11,927	60,000	...	4,575
Drink, confectionery, and tobacco, of which	46,671	254,000	...	13,810
tobacco and confectionery	41,502	215,000	...	10,880
Clothing and footwear, of which	24,923	264,000	...	12,428
women's, girls', and infants' wear	13,624	102,000	...	4,771
footwear	3,098	67,000	...	2,589
men's and boys' wear	3,751	37,000	...	2,063
Pharmaceuticals	7,560	87,000	...	5,231

Energy production (consumption): electricity (kW-hr; 1994) 325,383,000,000 (342,270,000,000); coal (metric tons; 1994) 47,717,000 (80,582,000); crude petroleum (barrels; 1994) 888,454,000 (629,354,000); petroleum products (metric tons; 1994) 86,184,000 (75,021,000); natural gas (cu m; 1994) 76,680,000,000 (79,391,000,000).

Population economically active (1996): total 27,969,000, activity rate of total population 47.6% (participation rates: ages 15–64, 76.2%[8]; female 44.3%; unemployed 7.7%).

Price and earnings indexes (1990 = 100)

	1991	1992	1993	1994	1995	1996	1997
Consumer price index	105.9	109.8	111.5	114.3	118.2	121.1	124.9
Monthly earnings index	108.0	114.7	118.9	123.5	127.7	132.6	138.5

Household income and expenditure (1994–95). Average household size 2.4; average annual disposable income per household £15,762 (U.S.$22,937); sources of income (1995): wages and salaries 64.3%, social security benefits 13.7%, dividends and interest 11.6%, income from self-employment 8.6%; expenditure (1995): food and beverages 17.8%, transport and vehicles 15.8%, housing 14.2%, household goods 6.9%, clothing 5.8%, energy 3.6%.

Foreign trade

Balance of trade (current prices)

	1992	1993	1994	1995	1996	1997
£'000,000	−24,618	−20,570	−12,029	−10,621	−11,174	−11,529
% of total	6.2%	5.4%	4.3%	3.3%	3.2%	3.2%

Imports (1996): £184,305,000,000 (machinery and transport equipment 42.2%, of which electrical equipment 19.8%, road vehicles 11.2%; chemicals 10.0%, of which organic chemicals 2.6%, plastics 2.4%; food 7.9%; clothing and footwear 4.3%; petroleum and petroleum products 3.1%; textiles 2.8%; paper and paperboard 2.7%). *Major import sources:* Germany 14.7%; U.S. 12.4%; France 9.6%; The Netherlands 6.8%; Japan 4.9%; Italy 4.8%; Belgium-Luxembourg 4.7%; Ireland 3.9%; Switzerland 2.9%; Spain 2.7%.
Exports (1996): £166,340,000,000 (machinery and transport equipment 44.1%, of which electrical equipment 19.8%, road vehicles 8.6%; chemicals 13.3%, of which organic chemicals 3.1%; petroleum and petroleum products 6.2%; food 4.2%; professional and scientific 4.0%; iron and steel products 2.4%). *Major export destinations:* Germany 12.3%; U.S. 11.8%; France 10.2%; The Netherlands 8.0%; Ireland 5.2%; Belgium-Luxembourg 5.1%; Italy 4.8%; Spain 4.0%; Sweden 2.6%; Japan 2.5%; Switzerland 1.9%.

Transport and communications

Transport. Railroads (1995–96)[15]: length 23,518 mi[16], 37,849 km[16]; passenger-mi 18,154,000,000, passenger-km 29,216,000,000; ton-mi cargo 2,026,000,000, metric ton-km cargo 2,916,000,000[17]. Roads (1995): total length 228,042 mi, 366,999 km (paved 100%). Vehicles (1995)[6]: passenger cars 20,505,000, trucks and buses 2,712,000. Merchant marine (1992): vessels (over 100 gross tons) 1,631; total deadweight tonnage 4,355,063. Air transport (1996): passenger-mi 77,575,900,000, passenger-km 124,846,500,000; short ton-mi cargo 2,662,600,000, metric ton-km cargo 3,831,900,000; airports (1997) 57.

Communications

Medium	date	unit	number	units per 1,000 persons
Daily newspapers	1995	circulation	22,450,000	383
Radio	1995	receivers	70,000,000	1,194
Television	1995	receivers	35,800,000	612
Telephones	1995	main lines	29,408,700	502
Cellular telephones	1995	subscribers	5,735,800	309
Facsimile machines	1995	units	1,800,000	30.7
Personal computers	1995	units	10,900,000	186

Education and health

Literacy (1990): total population literate, virtually 100%[18].

Education (1994–95)[19]

	schools	teachers	students	student/teacher ratio
Primary (age 5–10) }	32,385	231,659	4,906,439	21.2
Secondary (age 11–19) }		228,187	3,779,262	16.6
Voc., teacher tr.	...	...	586,000[20]	...
Higher[21]	70	c. 48,000	c. 810,000	c. 17.0

Health (1993)[6]: physicians 92,474 (1 per 629 persons); hospital beds 283,814 (1 per 205 persons); infant mortality rate (1995) 6.2.
Food (1995): daily per capita caloric intake 3,149 (vegetable products 67%, animal products 33%); 125% of FAO recommended minimum requirement.

Military

Total active duty personnel (1996): 213,800 (army 52.5%, navy 21.0%, air force 26.5%). *Military expenditure as percentage of GNP* (1995): 3.0% (world 2.8%); per capita expenditure U.S.$572.

[1]As of April 1997, with the current continuing U.K. reorganization of first-order administrative units, England's former 46 counties (including 7 metropolitan counties) reorganized into 35 counties, 27 unitary districts, 6 metropolitan counties, and Greater London; Wales's former 8 counties reorganized into 22 unitary districts; Scotland's former 9 regions and 3 island councils organized into 32 unitary districts; Northern Ireland remained unchanged [2]Detail does not add to total given because of rounding. [3]Only unitary district with county status. [4]Geographic entity only; administrative functiions dispersed among local metropolitan authorities. [5]Detail does not add to total given because of source discrepancies. [6]Great Britain only. [7]Lung disease only. [8]1993. [9]1994. [10]1992. [11]Includes petroleum extraction. [12]Plus rent; less imputed bank service charges. [13]Includes 2,150,000 unemployed and 3,282,000 self-employed not distributed by sector and 221,000 military personnel. [14]Includes value-added taxes. [15]British Rail only. [16]1990. [17]Much of British Rail's freight business was sold during 1996. [18]A survey in 1986–87, however, put the number of functional illiterates at 9–12% of the adult population. [19]Public sector only. [20]1992–93. [21]Universities only.

Internet resources for further information:
• Office for National Statistics http://www.ons.gov.uk/ons.htm

United States

Official name: United States of
America.
Form of government: federal republic
with two legislative houses (Senate
[100]; House of Representatives
[435[1]]).
Head of state and government:
President.
Capital: Washington, D.C.
Official language: none.
Official religion: none.
Monetary unit: 1 dollar (U.S.$) = 100
cents; valuation (Sept. 25, 1998)
1 U.S.$ = £0.59; 1 £ = U.S.$1.70.

Major cities (1996): New York 7,380,906; Los Angeles 3,553,638; Chicago
2,721,547; Houston 1,744,058; Philadelphia 1,478,002; San Diego 1,171,121;
Phoenix 1,159,014; San Antonio 1,067,816; Dallas 1,053,292; Detroit
1,000,272.

Other principal cities (1996)

	population		population		population
Akron	221,886	Fresno	396,011	Omaha	364,253
Albuquerque	419,681	Honolulu	423,475	Pittsburgh	350,363
Anaheim	288,945	Indianapolis	746,737	Portland (Ore.)	480,824
Anchorage	250,505	Jacksonville	679,792	Raleigh	243,835
Arlington (Tex.)	294,816	Jersey City	229,039	Riverside	255,069
Atlanta	401,907	Kansas City (Mo.)	441,259	Sacramento	376,243
Aurora (Colo.)	252,341	Las Vegas	376,906	St. Louis	351,565
Austin	541,278	Lexington (Ky.)	239,942	St. Paul	259,606
Baltimore	675,401	Long Beach	421,904	St. Petersburg	235,988
Birmingham	258,543	Louisville	260,689	San Francisco	735,315
Boston	558,394	Memphis	596,725	San Jose	838,744
Buffalo	310,548	Mesa	344,764	Santa Ana	302,419
Charlotte	441,297	Miami	365,127	Seattle	524,704
Cincinnati	345,818	Milwaukee	590,503	Stockton	232,660
Cleveland	498,246	Minneapolis	358,785	Tampa	285,206
Colorado Springs	345,127	Nashville	511,263	Toledo	317,606
Columbus	657,053	New Orleans	476,625	Tucson	449,002
Corpus Christi	280,260	Newark	268,510	Tulsa	378,491
Denver	497,840	Norfolk	233,430	Virginia Beach	430,385
El Paso	599,865	Oakland	367,230	Washington, D.C.	543,213
Fort Worth	479,716	Oklahoma City	469,852	Wichita	320,395

Area and population

States	Capitals	area sq mi	area sq km	population 1997 estimate
Alabama	Montgomery	51,718	133,950	4,319,154
Alaska	Juneau	587,875	1,522,595	609,311
Arizona	Phoenix	114,006	295,275	4,554,966
Arkansas	Little Rock	53,182	137,741	2,522,819
California	Sacramento	158,647	410,895	32,268,301
Colorado	Denver	104,100	269,619	3,892,644
Connecticut	Hartford	5,006	12,966	3,269,858
Delaware	Dover	2,026	5,247	731,581
Florida	Tallahassee	58,680	151,981	14,653,945
Georgia	Atlanta	58,930	152,629	7,486,242
Hawaii	Honolulu	6,459	16,729	1,186,602
Idaho	Boise	83,574	216,456	1,210,232
Illinois	Springfield	57,918	150,008	11,895,849
Indiana	Indianapolis	36,420	94,328	5,864,108
Iowa	Des Moines	56,276	145,755	2,852,423
Kansas	Topeka	82,282	213,110	2,594,840
Kentucky	Frankfort	40,411	104,664	3,908,124
Louisiana	Baton Rouge	47,719	123,592	4,351,769
Maine	Augusta	33,128	85,801	1,242,051
Maryland	Annapolis	10,455	27,078	5,094,289
Massachusetts	Boston	8,262	21,399	6,117,520
Michigan	Lansing	96,705	250,466	9,773,892
Minnesota	St. Paul	86,943	225,182	4,685,549
Mississippi	Jackson	47,695	123,530	2,730,501
Missouri	Jefferson City	69,709	180,546	5,402,058
Montana	Helena	147,046	380,849	878,810
Nebraska	Lincoln	77,359	200,360	1,656,870
Nevada	Carson City	110,567	286,368	1,676,809
New Hampshire	Concord	9,283	24,043	1,172,709
New Jersey	Trenton	7,790	20,176	8,052,849
New Mexico	Santa Fe	121,598	314,939	1,729,751
New York	Albany	53,013	137,304	18,137,226
North Carolina	Raleigh	52,672	136,420	7,425,183
North Dakota	Bismarck	70,704	183,123	640,883
Ohio	Columbus	44,828	116,104	11,186,331
Oklahoma	Oklahoma City	69,903	181,049	3,317,091
Oregon	Salem	97,052	251,364	3,243,487
Pennsylvania	Harrisburg	45,759	118,516	12,019,661
Rhode Island	Providence	1,213	3,142	987,429
South Carolina	Columbia	31,117	80,593	3,760,181
South Dakota	Pierre	77,121	199,743	737,973
Tennessee	Nashville	42,145	109,155	5,368,198
Texas	Austin	266,873	691,201	19,439,337
Utah	Salt Lake City	84,904	219,901	2,059,148
Vermont	Montpelier	9,615	24,903	588,978
Virginia	Richmond	40,598	105,149	6,733,996
Washington	Olympia	68,126	176,446	5,610,362
West Virginia	Charleston	24,232	62,761	1,815,787
Wisconsin	Madison	65,500	169,645	5,169,677
Wyoming	Cheyenne	97,819	253,351	479,743
District				
Dist. of Columbia	—	68	176	528,964
TOTAL		3,675,031[2]	9,518,323[2]	267,636,061[3]

Demography

Population (1998)[3]: 270,262,000.
Density (1998)[3]: persons per sq mi 73.5, persons per sq km 28.4.
Urban-rural (1996): urban 76.4%; rural 23.6%.
Sex distribution (1996): male 48.93%; female 51.07%.
Age breakdown (1996): under 15, 21.8%; 15–29, 20.8%; 30–44, 24.4%; 45–59,
16.5%; 60–74, 10.8%; 75 and over, 5.7%.
Population projection: (2000) 274,894,000; (2010) 297,976,000.
Doubling time: not applicable; doubling time exceeds 100 years.
Population by race and Hispanic[4] origin (1996): non-Hispanic white 73.1%;
non-Hispanic black 12.0%; Hispanic 10.7%; Asian and Pacific Islander 3.5%;
American Indian and Eskimo 0.7%.
Religious affiliation (1995): Christian 85.3%, of which Protestant 57.9%,
Roman Catholic 21.0%, other Christian 6.4%; Jewish 2.1%; Muslim 1.9%;
nonreligious 8.7%; other 2.0%.
Mobility (1996). Population living in the same residence as in 1995: 84.0%; dif-
ferent residence, same county 10.0%; different county, same state 3.0%; different state 3.0%; moved from abroad 1.0%.
Households (1996). Total households 99,627,000 (married-couple families
53,567,000 [53.8%]). Average household size (1995) 2.6; 1 person 25.0%; 2
persons 32.1%, 3 persons 17.0%, 4 persons 15.5%, 5 or more persons 10.4%.
Family households: 69,594,000 (69.8%); nonfamily 30,033,000 (30.2%), of
which 1-person 82.9%.
Immigration (1995[5]): permanent immigrants admitted 720,500, from Mexico
12.5%, Philippines 7.1%, Vietnam 5.8%, Dominican Republic 5.3%, China
4.9%, India 4.8%, Cuba 2.5%, Ukraine 2.4%, Jamaica 2.3%, South Korea
2.2%, Russia 2.0%, Poland 1.9%, Haiti 1.8%, Canada 1.8%, United Kingdom
1.7%, El Salvador 1.6%, Colombia 1.5%. Refugee arrivals (1995[5]): 114,664.

Place of birth (1990): native-born 227,078,000 (91.3%); foreign-born 21,632,000
(8.7%), of which Mexico 4,447,000, Germany (East and West) 1,163,000,
Philippines 998,000, Canada 871,000, United Kingdom 765,000, Cuba 751,000,
South Korea 663,000, Italy 640,000, Vietnam 556,000, China 543,000, India
463,000, Japan 422,000, Poland 397,000, U.S.S.R. 337,000.

Vital statistics

Birth rate per 1,000 population (1996): 14.9 (world avg. 25.0); (1994) legitimate
67.4%; illegitimate 32.6%.
Death rate per 1,000 population (1996): 9.2 (world avg. 9.3).
Natural increase rate per 1,000 population (1996): 5.7 (world avg. 15.7).
Total fertility rate (avg. births per childbearing woman; 1996): 2.1.
Marriage rate per 1,000 population (1996): 8.8; median age at first marriage
(1991): men 26.3 years, women 24.1 years.
Divorce rate per 1,000 population (1996): 4.3
Life expectancy at birth (1995): white male 73.4 years, black and other male
67.5[6] years; white female 79.6 years, black and other female 75.8[6] years.
Major causes of death per 100,000 population (1997[7]): cardiovascular diseases
353.9, of which ischemic heart disease 177.3, cerebrovascular diseases 60.0,
atherosclerosis 10.0; malignant neoplasms (cancers) 202.4; diseases of the respiratory system 72.0, of which pneumonia 31.2; accidents and adverse effects
34.1, of which motor-vehicle accidents 16.5; diabetes mellitus 23.3; suicide
11.5; AIDS 10.6; chronic liver disease and cirrhosis 9.3.
Morbidity rates of infectious diseases per 100,000 population (1995): chlamydia
181.6; gonorrhea 149.3; chicken pox 45.8; AIDS 27.2; syphilis 26.2; salmonel-
losis 17.4; shigellosis 12.2; hepatitis A (infectious) 12.0; tuberculosis 8.7; lyme
disease 4.4.; hepatitis B (serum) 4.1; aseptic meningitis 3.4[6]; pertussis 1.9.
Incidence of chronic health conditions per 1,000 population (1994): chronic
sinusitis 133.9; arthritis 128.3; deformities or orthopedic impairments 119.2;
hypertension 108.3; hay fever 100.3; hearing impairment 85.9; heart conditions 85.5; asthma 55.9; chronic bronchitis 53.8; migraine 43.2.

Social indicators

Educational attainment (1996). Percentage of population age 25 and over having: some primary 9.3%; incomplete secondary 16.5%; secondary 35.1%;
some postsecondary 25.5%; 4-year higher degree or more 13.6%. Number of
earned degrees (1995): bachelor's degree 1,192,000; master's degree 405,000;
doctor's degree 43,000; first-professional degrees (in fields such as medicine,
theology, and law) 77,000.

Distribution of income (1995)

percentage of disposable household income by quintile

1	2	3	4	5 (highest)
4.8	10.4	16.0	23.0	46.5

Quality of working life (1996). Average workweek: 39.2 hours. Annual rate per
100,000 workers for (1995): injury or accident 2,720; death 4.0. Proportion of
labour force insured for damages or income loss resulting from: injury, permanent disability, and death (1988) 56.6%. Average days per 1,000 workdays
lost to labour stoppages (1996): 1.6. Average duration of journey to work
(1990): 22.4 minutes (private automobile 94.7%, of which drive alone 80.0%,
carpool 14.7%; take public transportation 5.3%). Rate per 1,000 employed
workers of discouraged workers (unemployed no longer seeking work; 1992):
6.9.
Access to services (1995). Proportion of occupied dwellings having access to:
electricity, virtually 100.0%; safe public water supply 99.4% (12.6% from
wells); public sewage collection 77.0%; septic tanks 22.8%.
Social participation. Eligible voters participating in last presidential election
(1996): 48.9%. Population age 18 and over participating in voluntary work
(1995): 48.8%. Trade-union membership in total workforce (1996): 14.5%.
Practicing religious population in total affiliated population (church attendance; 1987) once a week 47%; once in six months 67%; once a year 74%.
Social deviance (1995[7]). Offense rate per 100,000 population for: murder 8.2;
rape 37.1; robbery 221.0; aggravated assault 418.0; motor-vehicle theft 561.0;
burglary and housebreaking 988.0; larceny-theft 3,045.0; drug-abuse violation
434.2; drunkenness 200.2. Drug and substance users (population age 26 and
over; 1994): alcohol 41.2%; tobacco (cigarettes) 33.5%; marijuana 16.0%;

cocaine 0.4%; analgesics 1.3%; tranquilizers 0.2%; stimulants 0.4%; hallucinogens 1.2%; heroin, n.a. Rate per 100,000 population of suicide (1997): 11.5.

Crime rates per 100,000 population in metropolitan areas[8] (1995)

	violent crime				
	total	murder	rape	robbery	assault
Atlanta	3,646	45.5	109.1	1,301	2,191
Baltimore	3,018	45.6	95.9	1,594	1,282
Boston	1,738	17.4	68.8	653	998
Chicago	...	30.0	...	1,094	1,425
Dallas	1,532	26.5	81.8	566	858
Detroit	2,408	47.6	110.7	1,010	1,239
Houston	1,284	18.2	48.3	532	685
Los Angeles	2,034	24.5	45.9	840	1,124
Miami	3,413	29.0	52.3	1,499	1,833
Minneapolis	1,978	26.8	161.6	992	797
New York	1,573	16.1	32.4	810	715
Philadelphia	1,436	28.2	50.5	890	468
Pittsburgh	979	16.3	68.5	585	309
St. Louis	3,352	54.9	73.5	1,383	1,841
San Francisco	1,477	13.4	41.2	876	546
Washington, D.C.	2,662	65.2	52.7	1,239	1,305

	property crime			
	total	burglary	larceny	auto theft
Atlanta	13,421	2,898	8,464	2,066
Baltimore	10,300	2,326	6,405	1,569
Boston	7,755	1,211	4,722	1,822
Chicago	7,198	1,463	4,418	1,316
Dallas	7,932	1,603	4,709	1,620
Detroit	9,531	2,243	4,353	2,935
Houston	6,304	1,432	3,574	1,299
Los Angeles	5,646	1,192	3,120	1,333
Miami	12,210	2,607	7,271	2,332
Minneapolis	9,567	2,243	6,069	1,255
New York	4,503	1,010	2,501	993
Philadelphia	5,642	1,057	3,028	1,556
Pittsburgh	5,150	1,014	3,182	955
St. Louis	12,730	2,879	7,697	2,155
San Francisco	6,714	965	4,626	1,123
Washington, D.C.	9,505	1,838	5,827	1,840

Leisure (1992). Favourite leisure activities (percentage of total population age 18 and over that undertook activity at least once in the previous year): movie 59.0%, amusement park 50.0%, sports event 37.0%, live theatre 31.0%, art museum 27.0%; reading literature 54.0%, playing sports 39.0%.
Material well-being (1995). Occupied dwellings with householder possessing: automobile 84.9%[9]; telephone 93.9%; radio receiver 99.0%; television receiver 98.3%; air conditioner 68.4%[10]; washing machine 77.1%[10]; video-cassette recorder 81.0%; cable television 63.4%.
Recreational expenditures (1995): U.S.$401,700,000,000 (television and radio receivers, computers, and video equipment 23.2%; sports supplies 10.9%; nondurable toys and sports equipment 10.6%; golfing, bowling, and other participatory activities 9.2%; magazines and newspapers 6.3%; books and maps 5.2%; spectator amusements 5.0%, of which theatre and opera 2.2%, movies 1.4%, spectator sports 1.3%; flowers, seeds, and potted plants 3.5%).

National economy

Budget (1997). Revenue: U.S.$1,577,700,000 (individual income tax 46.4%, social-insurance taxes and contributions 34.1%, corporation income tax 11.8%, other 7.7%). Expenditures: U.S.$1,615,000,000,000 (social security and medicare 34.5%, defense 16.6%, interest on debt 15.2%, income security 14.4%, health 7.8%, other 11.5%).
Total national debt (1998): U.S.$5,516,800,000,000.

Manufacturing, mining, and construction enterprises (1995)

	no. of enter- prises[11]	no. of employees	hourly wages as a % of all wages	value added (U.S.$'000,000)
Manufacturing				
Chemical and related products	12,109	839,000	135.2	196,906
Food and related products	20,624	1,525,000	104.0	180,975
Electric and electronic machinery	15,962	1,534,000	101.1	173,920
Machinery, except electrical	52,135	1,926,000	114.9	172,945
Transportation equipment	10,500	1,523,000	144.7	172,926
Printing and publishing	...	1,534,000	...	125,936
Fabricated metal products	36,105	1,465,000	105.3	102,672
Instruments and related products	10,326	809,000	111.2	92,534
Paper and related products	6,342	630,000	125.5	79,836
Rubber and plastic products	14,515	1,018,000	95.8	73,023
Primary metals	6,771	688,000	127.8	69,594
Stone, clay, and glass products	16,166	503,000	108.4	42,424
Lumber and wood	33,982	741,000	88.9	40,937
Apparel and related products	22,872	950,100	66.3	39,519
Textile-mill products	6,412	606,800	81.8	32,705
Petroleum and coal products	2,254	110,000	167.5	31,580
Furniture and fixtures	11,613	514,000	85.6	26,238
Tobacco products	138	31,300	191.6	24,715
Leather and leather products	2,193	86,000	69.7	4,126
Miscellaneous manufacturing industries	16,544	397,000	87.2	25,672
Mining				
Oil and gas extraction	20,891[6]	320,700	127.9	79,700[6]
Coal mining	3,060[6]	105,300	159.9	17,283[6]
Nonmetallic, except fuels	5,804[6]	109,900	117.3	9,619[6]
Metal mining	1,023[6]	52,100	145.5	7,180[6]
Construction				
Special trade contractors	367,800[6]	3,383,500	134.6	122,422[6]
Heavy construction contractors	37,300[6]	814,200	129.5	49,066[6]
General contractors and operative builders	168,200[6]	1,251,100	123.4	63,743[6]

Gross national product (at current market prices; 1996): U.S.$7,567,100,000,000 (U.S.$28,495 per capita).

Gross domestic product and national income

(in U.S.$'000,000,000)

	1992	1993	1994	1995	1996
Gross domestic product	6,038.6	6,377.9	6,738.4	7,245.8	7,576.1
By type of expenditure					
Personal consumption expenditures	4,139.9	4,391.8	4,628.4	4,924.3	5,151.4
Durable goods	497.3	537.9	591.5	606.4	632.1
Nondurable goods	1,300.9	1,350.0	1,394.3	1,486.1	1,545.1
Services	2,341.6	2,503.9	2,642.7	2,831.6	2,974.3
Gross private domestic investment	796.5	891.7	1,032.9	1,066.3	1,117.0
Fixed investment	789.1	876.1	980.7	1,028.2	1,101.5
Changes in business inventories	7.3	15.6	52.2	33.7	15.4
Net exports of goods and services	−30.3	−65.3	−98.2	−114.2	−98.7
Exports	638.1	659.1	718.7	774.8	855.2
Imports	668.4	724.3	816.9	888.9	953.9
Government purchases of goods and services	1,131.8	1,158.1	1,175.3	1,260.7	1,406.4
Federal	448.8	443.4	437.3	472.7	523.1
State and local	313.8	714.6	738.0	788.8	...
By major type of product					
Goods output	2,312.8	2,421.9	2,584.7	2,697.4	2,799.8
Durable goods	977.9	1,047.9	1,153.6	1,179.8	1,232.3
Nondurable goods	1,334.9	1,374.0	1,431.1	1,517.6	1,567.5
Services	3,221.1	3,410.5	3,576.2	3,920.8	4,105.2
Structures	504.6	545.5	577.6	627.6	671.1
National income (incl. capital consumption adjustment)	4,836.6	5,140.3	5,458.4	5,799.2	6,164.2
By type of income					
Compensation of employees	3,582.0	3,772.2	4,004.6	4,209.1	4,448.5
Proprietors' income	414.3	321.0	473.7	478.3	3,630.1
Rental income of persons	−8.9	12.6	27.7	122.2	641.2
Corporate profits	407.2	466.6	542.7	588.6	670.2
Net interest	442.0	445.6	409.7	401.0	403.3
By industry division (excl. capital consumption adjustment)					
Agriculture, forestry, fishing	100.9	105.3	101.9	94.0	114.1
Mining and construction	251.3	268.1	278.5	301.2	325.9
Manufacturing	895.3	929.0	979.7	1,026.3	1,069.1
Durable	501.7	523.0	562.4	597.1	628.6
Nondurable	393.6	406.1	417.3	429.3	440.5
Transportation	151.0	161.8	177.5	189.4	196.5
Communications	103.7	107.4	113.4	136.6	148.5
Public utilities	101.5	106.9	116.5	125.0	126.5
Wholesale and retail trade	700.3	742.8	785.8	805.6	857.8
Finance, insurance, real estate	748.9	815.6	894.2	991.9	1,037.0
Services	1,085.8	1,171.0	1,254.4	1,335.9	1,441.1
Government and government enterprise	734.5	765.3	793.4	820.3	843.1
Other	7.3	0.2	−11.4	−7.0	−8.9

Structure of gross domestic product and labour force

	1994		1996	
	in value U.S.$'000,000,000	% of total value	labour force[12]	% of labour force[12]
Agriculture	117.3	1.7	3,443,000	2.6
Mining	90.1	1.3	569,000	0.4
Manufacturing	1,197.1	17.3	20,518,000	15.3
Construction	269.2	3.9	7,943,000	5.9
Public utilities	195.3	2.8	} 8,817,000	6.6
Transp. and commun.	411.1	5.9		
Trade	1,071.8	15.5	26,497,000	19.8
Finance	1,273.7	18.4	8,076,000	6.0
Public administration, defense	931.3	13.4	5,802,000	4.3
Services	1,342.7	19.4	45,043,000	33.6
Other	31.8[13]	0.4[13]	7,236,000[14]	5.4[14]
TOTAL	6,931.4	100.0	133,943,000[15]	100.0[15]

Business activity (1994): number of businesses 21,989,000 (sole proprietorships 73.5%, active corporations 19.7%, active partnerships 6.8%), of which services 9,488,000, wholesaling and retailing 4,213,000; business receipts $14,380,000,000,000 (active corporations 89.4%, sole proprietorships 5.5%, active partnerships 5.1%), of which wholesaling and retailing $4,343,000,-000,000, services $1,602,000,000,000; net profit $827,000,000,000 (active corporations 69.8%, sole proprietorships 20.2%, partnerships 10.0%), of which services $167,700,000,000, wholesaling and retailing $88,600,000,000. New business starts and business failures (1995): total number of new business starts 168,158; total failures 71,194, of which commercial service 21,850, retail trade 12,952; failure rate per 10,000 concerns 90.0; current liabilities of failed concerns $37,507,000,000; average liability $526,830. Business expenditures for new plant and equipment (1995): total $594,465,000,000, of which trade, services, and communications $244,829,000,000, manufacturing businesses $172,308,000,000 (durable goods 53.0%, nondurable goods 47.0%), public utilities $42,816,000,000, transportation $37,021,000,000, mining and construction $35,985,000.
Production. Agriculture, forestry, fishing (value of production/catch in U.S.$'000,000 except as noted; 1996): corn (maize) 24,853, soybeans 16,276, wheat 9,764, cotton lint 6,524, tobacco 2,938, potatoes 2,515, grapes 2,242, sorghum 2,053, oranges 1,895, apples 1,840, rice 1,612, lettuce 1,423, barley 1,091, sugar beets 1,071, almonds 1,048, peanuts (groundnuts) 964, cotton seed 934, tomatoes 879, sugarcane 860, strawberries 770, dry beans 680, onions 590, bell peppers 461, sunflower seeds 405, cantaloupes 401, broccoli 396, peaches 378, carrots 347, grapefruit 310, oats 309, pears 297, watermelon 276, lemons 252, cabbage 245; livestock (number of live animals; 1997) 101,209,000 cattle, 56,171,000 pigs, 8,303,000 sheep, 6,150,000 horses, 1,553,000,000 chickens; roundwood (1996) 495,305,000 cu m; fish and shellfish catch (1995) 3,770, of which fish 2,136 (including salmon 527, Alaska pollack 266), shellfish 1,634 (including shrimp 570, crabs 512). Mining (metal content in metric tons except as noted; 1996): iron 39,342,000; copper

1,910,000; zinc 620,000; lead 430,000; molybdenum 57,000; vanadium 2,700; mercury 550; silver 1,800,000 kg; gold 325,000 kg; helium 101,000,000 cu m. Quarrying (metric tons; 1996): crushed stone 1,300,000,000; sand and gravel 992,000,000; cement 75,000,000; clay 44,000,000; phosphate rock 43,000,000; common salt 40,000,000; gypsum 17,000,000; lime 18,900,000. Manufacturing (1995): motor vehicles 238,384; aircraft 104,858; meat products 94,072; industrial machinery 79,439; electronic components 73,642; pharmaceuticals 67,792; computer and office equipment 66,708; commercial printing 56,229; medical instruments 39,535; cigarettes 29,745; missiles and space vehicles 29,508; photographic equipment 22,119; household furniture 20,508; household appliances 18,633; ships and boats 15,249; toys and sporting goods 12,123; audio and video equipment 10,614. Construction (completed; 1996): private U.S.$427,776,000,000, of which residential U.S.$246,899,000,000, nonresidential U.S.$140,692,000,000; public U.S.$141,132,000,000.

Retail and wholesale trade and services (1996)

	no. of establish-ments[6]	no. of employees[16]	hourly wage as a % of all wages[16]	annual sales or receipts (U.S.$'000,000)
Retail trade	1,564,200	20,988,000	66.9	2,445,300
Automotive dealers	198,400	2,228,300	91.4	592,900
Food stores	182,500	3,376,600	70.5	423,300
General merchandise group stores	36,700	2,466,200	65.8	312,800
Eating and drinking places	449,100	7,432,500	46.6[17]	236,500
Gasoline service stations	99,300	647,100	60.5	155,000
Building materials, hardware, garden supply, and mobile home dealers	69,900	888,800	79.4	134,500
Furniture, home furnishings, equipment stores	114,500	937,900	88.4	133,500
Apparel and accessory stores	142,400	1,085,700	65.4	113,700
Drugstores and proprietary stores	45,700	607,800	77.5	90,700
Liquor stores	29,500	112,200		22,800
Wholesale trade	495,500[18]	6,367,000	107.7	2,420,700
Durable goods	313,500[18]	3,693,000	111.5	1,245,800
Professional and commercial equipment	46,800[18]	768,700	133.5	231,400
Motor vehicles, automotive equipment	47,300[18]	498,000	98.1	211,100
Machinery, equipment, and supplies	73,900[18]	774,300	112.5	187,300
Electrical goods	39,300[18]	477,400	116.2	173,800
Metals and minerals, except petroleum	11,200[18]	140,300	110.5	98,400
Lumber and other construction materials	19,500[18]	242,700	102.5	85,800
Hardware, plumbing, heating equipment and supplies	24,700[18]	290,600	105.8	70,500
Furniture and home furnishings	16,500[18]	149,600	97.7	43,600
Miscellaneous durable goods	34,300[18]	327,200	88.5	143,900
Nondurable goods	182,000[18]	2,674,000	102.3	1,174,900
Groceries and related products	42,900[18]	890,700	105.4	315,400
Petroleum and petroleum products	16,100[18]	166,400	96.6	177,800
Farm-products raw materials	11,600[18]	109,000	78.1	130,200
Drugs, drug proprietaries, and druggists' sundries	6,100[18]	197,100	128.2	102,900
Paper and paper products	19,700[18]	262,700	106.7	82,700
Apparel and accessories	19,600[18]	212,700	100.4	75,500
Beer, wine, and distilled alcoholic beverages	5,300[18]	155,900	116.3	56,400
Chemicals and allied products	14,200[18]	140,100	116.4	53,500
Miscellaneous nondurable goods	43,700[18]	539,800	84.5	180,500
Services[19]	2,342,300	33,106,000	98.4	1,826,200
Health	476,200	9,280,900	108.0	382,600
Business, except computer services	273,500	6,628,100	92.9	272,100
Computer and data-processing services	66,800	1,043,300	154.0	152,200
Legal services	161,600	946,200	140.0	114,400
Automotive repair, services, garages	178,400	1,031,200	86.4	98,300
Management and public relations	61,300	813,200	125.5	89,700
Hotels and motels	53,500	1,724,400	68.1	86,300
Amusement and recreation	90,800	1,720,600	73.2	77,400
Engineering services	42,600	579,000	154.7	76,600
Personal services	201,800	1,115,000	65.6	69,900
Motion pictures	42,700	601,700	121.8	58,100

Energy production (consumption): electricity (kW-hr; 1994) 3,268,250,000,000 (3,312,888,000,000); coal (metric tons; 1994) 937,580,000 (843,873,000); crude petroleum (barrels; 1994) 2,464,000,000 (5,024,000,000); petroleum products (metric tons; 1994) 704,201,000 (737,681,000); natural gas (cu m; 1994) 530,014,000,000 (592,209,000,000). Domestic production of energy by source (1994): coal 31.2%, natural gas 27.6%, crude petroleum 19.9%, other[20] 21.3%.

Energy consumption by source (1994): petroleum and petroleum products 38.8%, natural gas 24.0%, coal 22.0%, other[20] 15.2%; by end use: industrial 38.0%, residential and commercial 35.0%, transportation 26.5%.

Household income and expenditure. Average household size (1995) 2.6; average (median) annual income per household U.S.$34,076, of which average white household U.S.$35,766, average Hispanic[4] household U.S.$22,860, average black household U.S.$22,393; sources of income: wages and salaries 55.8%, transfer payments 16.5%, self-employment 7.9%, other 19.8%; expenditure: transportation 18.6%, housing 18.4%, food 14.0%, fuel and utilities 6.8%, household furnishings 5.9%, recreation 5.5%, health 5.4%, wearing apparel 5.3%, education 1.5%, other 18.6%.

Average annual expenditure of "consumer units" (households, plus individuals sharing households or budgets; 1995): total U.S.$32,277, of which housing U.S.$10,465, transportation U.S.$6,016, food U.S.$4,505, pensions and social

security U.S.$2,593, health care U.S.$1,732, clothing U.S.$1,704, other U.S.$5,262.

Selected household characteristics (1996). Total number of households 99,627,000, of which (by race) white 84.8%, black 11.6%, other 3.6%; in central cities 31.4%[6], in suburbs 46.3%[6], outside metropolitan areas 22.3%[6]; (by tenure[6]) owned 64,045,000 (64.7%), rented 34,946,000 (35.3%); family households 69,594,000, of which married couple 76.9%, female head with own children[21] under age 18, 11.0%, female head without own children[21] under 18, 7.0%; nonfamily households 30,033,000, of which female living alone 48.6%, male living alone 34.2%, other 17.2%.

Financial aggregates

	1991	1992	1993	1994	1995	1996	1997[22]
Exchange rate, U.S.$ per:							
£23	1.77	1.76	1.50	1.53	1.58	1.56	1.61
SDR[23]	1.37	1.41	1.40	1.43	1.52	1.45	1.36
International reserves (U.S.$)[24]							
Total (excl. gold; '000,000,000)	66.66	60.27	62.35	63.28	74.78	64.04	56.10
SDRs ('000,000,000)	11.24	8.50	9.02	10.04	11.04	10.31	10.00
Reserve pos. in IMF ('000,000,000)	9.49	11.76	11.80	12.03	14.65	15.43	14.04
Foreign exchange ('000,000,000)	45.93	40.01	41.53	41.22	49.10	38.29	32.06
Gold ('000,000 fine troy oz)	261.91	261.84	261.79	261.73	261.70	261.66	261.72
% world reserves	27.86	28.13	28.67	28.70	29.00	28.86	29.34
Interest and prices							
Central bank discount (%)[24]	3.50	3.00	3.00	4.75	5.25	5.00	5.00
Govt. bond yield (%)[23]	6.81	5.31	4.44	6.26	6.26	6.44	6.21
Industrial share prices[23] (1990 = 100)	114.1	125.5	132.3	138.0	164.1	202.7	280.9
Balance of payments (U.S.$'000,000,000)							
Balance of visible trade	−73.44	−96.14	−112.74	−164.33	−158.78	−189.25	...
Imports, f.o.b.	−489.40	−536.28	−580.51	−668.87	−743.52	−803.23	...
Exports, f.o.b.	415.96	440.14	467.77	504.54	584.71	613.98	...
Balance of invisibles	69.75	29.84	3.49	162.83	10.55	40.52	...
Balance of payments, current account	−3.69	−66.30	−109.25	−1.50	−148.23	−148.73	...

Population economically active (1996): total 133,943,000[12]; activity rate of total population 50.4% (participation rates: ages 15–64, 79.4%; female 48.8%; unemployed 5.4%).

Price and earnings indexes (1990 = 100)

	1991	1992	1993	1994	1995	1996	1997
Consumer price index	104.2	107.4	110.6	113.4	116.6	120.0	122.9
Hourly earnings index[25]	103.3	105.8	108.5	111.4	114.2	118.0	121.5

Average employee earnings

	average hourly earnings in U.S.$		average weekly earnings in U.S.$	
	July 1996	July 1997	July 1996	July 1997
Manufacturing				
Durable goods	13.35	13.63	556.70	571.10
Lumber and wood products	10.47	10.83	426.13	441.86
Furniture and fixtures	10.13	10.53	398.11	414.88
Stone, clay, and glass products	12.94	13.21	562.89	571.99
Primary metal industries	15.08	15.30	657.49	671.67
Fabricated metal products	12.51	12.68	520.42	528.76
Machinery, except electrical	13.55	14.01	574.52	599.63
Electrical and electronic equipment	12.26	12.70	497.78	524.51
Transportation equipment	17.29	17.26	738.28	730.10
Instruments and related products	13.18	13.55	540.38	556.91
Miscellaneous manufacturing	10.37	10.52	402.36	415.54
Nondurable goods	12.00	12.38	482.40	500.15
Food and kindred products	11.25	11.53	460.13	475.04
Tobacco manufactures	20.98	21.08	809.83	827.12[26]
Textile mill products	7.95	8.21	292.56	300.49
Apparel and other textile products	7.95	8.21	292.56	300.49
Paper and allied products	14.79	15.18	638.93	657.29
Printing and publishing	12.63	13.02	479.94	496.06
Chemicals and allied products	16.16	16.60	693.26	708.82
Petroleum and coal products	19.02	20.03	842.59	857.28
Rubber and miscellaneous plastics products	11.25	11.58	459.00	474.78
Leather and leather products	8.43	8.74	317.81	329.50
Nonmanufacturing				
Metal mining	17.28	17.71	753.41	782.78
Coal mining	18.65	19.00	813.14	830.30
Oil and gas extraction	14.80	15.47	651.20	685.32
Nonmetallic minerals, except fuels	13.88	14.34	673.18	698.36
Construction	15.51	15.59	617.30	641.20
Transportation and public utilities	17.67	17.78	848.16	878.33
Wholesale trade	12.82	13.36	488.44	513.02
Retail trade	7.93	8.26	233.14	244.50
Finance, insurance, and real estate	12.69	13.14	451.76	471.32
Hotels, motels, and tourist courts	7.96	8.38	249.15	261.46
Health services	12.84	13.25	418.58	438.58
Legal services	16.57	17.29	568.35	599.96
Miscellaneous services	15.99	16.50	574.04	570.90

Tourism (1996): receipts from visitors U.S.$84,133,000,000; expenditures by nationals abroad U.S.$68,976,000,000; number of foreign visitors (1995) 42,993,000 (13,668,000 from Canada, 9,610,000 from Mexico, 8,803,000 from Europe); number of nationals traveling abroad (1995) 47,419,000 (15,759,000 to Mexico, 12,920,000 to Canada).

Land use (1994): forested 32.3%; meadows and pastures 26.1%; agricultural and under permanent cultivation 20.5%; other 21.0%.

Foreign trade

Balance of trade (current prices)

	1992	1993	1994	1995	1996	1997
U.S.$'000,000,000	−84.5	−115.7	−151.3	−158.8	−189.2	−181.9
% of total	8.6%	11.1%	12.9%	12.0%	13.4%	−11.7

Imports (1996): U.S.$803,239,000,000 (machinery and transport equipment 44.6%, of which motor vehicles and parts 16.0%; office and data-processing machines 15.8%; petroleum and petroleum products 9.0%; wearing apparel 5.8%; food and live animals 4.4%; chemicals and related products 3.3%). *Major import sources:* Canada 19.8%; Japan 14.3%; Mexico 9.4%; China 6.4%; Germany 4.8%; Taiwan 3.7%; United Kingdom 3.6%; South Korea 2.8%; Singapore 2.5%; France 2.3%; Malaysia 2.2%; Italy 2.2%; Thailand 1.4%; Hong Kong 1.2%; Brazil 1.1%.

Exports (1996): U.S.$612,069,000,000 (machinery and transport equipment 46.6%, of which motor vehicles and parts 11.9%; chemicals and related products 7.2%; food and live animals 6.9%; scientific and precision equipment 3.0%). *Major export destinations:* Canada 22.0%; Japan 10.8%; Mexico 9.3%; United Kingdom 4.9%; South Korea 4.2%; Germany 3.8%; Taiwan 2.9%; The Netherlands 2.7%; Singapore 2.6%; France 2.4%; Hong Kong 2.3%; Belgium 2.1%.

Trade by commodity group (1995)

SITC Group	imports U.S.$'000,000	%	exports U.S.$'000,000	%
00 Food and live animals	29,318[27]	3.8[27]	42,223[27]	7.3[27]
01 Beverages and tobacco	5,674	0.7	8,086	1.4
02 Crude materials, excluding fuels	22,311	2.9	34,758	6.0
03 Mineral fuels, lubricants, and related materials	63,052	8.2	10,720	1.8
04 Animal and vegetable oils, fat, and waxes	27	27	27	27
05 Chemicals and related products, n.e.s.	41,346	5.4	60,220	10.4
06 Basic manufactures	94,767	12.3	54,444	9.4
07 Machinery and transport equipment	357,625	46.5	281,184	48.4
08 Miscellaneous manu-factured articles	129,077	16.8	62,106	10.7
09 Goods not classified by kind	26,204	3.4	26,793	4.6
TOTAL	770,822[28]	100.0	582,965[28]	100.0

Direction of trade (1996)

	imports U.S.$'000,000	%	exports U.S.$'000,000	%
Africa	19,460	2.4	10,584	1.7
South Africa	2,436	0.3	3,106	0.5
Other Africa	17,024	2.1	7,478	1.2
Americas	285,937	35.0	242,001	38.8
Canada	159,746	19.5	132,584	21.3
Caribbean countries and Central America	15,208	1.9	16,524	2.6
Mexico	74,111	9.1	56,761	9.1
South America	36,872	4.5	36,132	5.8
Asia	335,173	41.0[15]	208,383	33.4
China	54,409	6.6	11,978	1.9
Japan	117,963	14.4	67,536	10.8
Other Asia	162,801	19.9	128,869	20.7
Europe	171,713	21.0	149,085	23.9
EU	147,467	18.0	127,520	20.5
Russia	3,745	0.5	3,340	0.5
Other Europe	20,501	2.5	18,225	2.9
Oceania	5,916	0.7	13,872	2.2
Australia	4,127	0.5	11,992	1.9
Other Oceania	1,789	0.2	1,880	0.3
Other	−414	−0.1	−980	−0.2
TOTAL	817,785	100.0[15]	622,945	100.0[15]

Transport and communications

Transport. Railroads (1995): length[6] 137,900 mi, 222,000 km; passenger-mi 13,897,000,000, passenger-km 22,365,000,000; short ton-mi cargo 1,305,-685,000,000, metric ton-km cargo 1,906,268,000,000. Roads (1995): total length 3,912,226 mi, 6,296,130 km (paved 91.0%). Vehicles (1995): passenger cars 134,803,000; trucks and buses 66,727,000. Merchant marine (1996): vessels (1,000 gross tons and over) 509; total deadweight tonnage 18,585,000. Air transport (1995): passenger-mi 540,400,000,000, passenger-km 869,700,000,-000; short ton-mi cargo 14,568,400,000, metric ton-km cargo 21,269,500,000; localities (1996) with scheduled flights 834[29]. Certified route passenger/cargo air carriers (1992) 77; operating revenue (U.S.$'000,000; 1991) 74,942, of which domestic 56,119, international 18,823; operating expenses 76,669, of which domestic 56,596, international 20,073.

Intercity passenger and freight traffic by mode of transportation (1993)

	cargo traffic ('000,000,000 ton-mi)	% of nat'l total	passenger traffic ('000,000,000 passenger-mi)	% of nat'l total
Rail	1,183	38.1	14	0.7
Road	871	28.0	1,718	81.7
Inland water	467	15.1	—	—
Air	12	0.4	370	17.6
Petroleum pipeline	572	18.4	—	—
TOTAL	3,105	100.0	2,102	100.0

Communications

Medium	date	unit	number	units per 1,000 persons
Daily newspapers	1995	circulation	62,600,000	238
Radio	1994	receivers	558,440,000	2,122
Television	1995	receivers	204,100,000	776
Telephones	1995	main lines	164,624,400	626
Cellular telephones	1995	subscribers	33,785,700	128
Facsimile machines	1995	units	14,052,000	53
Personal computers	1995	units	23,012,250	87

Other communications media (1996)

Print	titles		titles
Books (new)	46,898	General interest	181
of which		History	151
Agriculture	443	Home economics	90
Art	1,511	Industrial arts	106
Biography	2,238	Journalism and commun.	90
Business	1,266	Labour and industrial	
Education	1,215	relations	70
Fiction	3,919	Law	273
General works	2,061	Library and information	
History	2,466	sciences	118
Home economics	1,027	Literature and language	158
Juvenile	4,291	Mathematics and science	238
Language	592	Medicine	182
Law	764	Philosophy and religion	130
Literature	2,412	Physical education and	
Medicine	2,866	recreation	151
Music	322	Political science	136
Philosophy, psychology	1,749	Psychology	138
Poetry, drama	1,119	Sociology and anthropology	149
Religion	2,725	Zoology	94
Science	2,576		
Sociology, economics	8,180	**Cinema**[16]	
Sports, recreation	1,198	Feature films	419
Technology	1,572		
Travel	386		traffic
Periodicals[9]	3,731	**Cellular telephones**	
of which		Number of	
Agriculture	153	subscribers	44,043,000
Business and economics	262		
Chemistry and physics	170		(pieces of mail)
Children's periodicals	78	**Post**	
Education	203	Mail	182,661,000,000
Engineering	265	Domestic	181,662,000,000
Fine and applied arts	145	International	999,000,000

Education and health

Literacy: studies in the late 1980s indicated that adult "functional" literacy may not exceed 85%.

Education (1995–96)

	schools	teachers	students	student/teacher ratio
Primary (age 5–13)[30]	} 85,393[31]	1,784,000	33,410,000	18.7
Secondary and vocational (age 14–17)		1,187,000	17,390,000	14.6
Higher, including teacher-training colleges	5,758[32]	833,000	14,210,000	17.1

Health (1995): doctors of medicine 720,300[33] (1 per 365 persons), of which office-based practice 427,300 (including specialties in internal medicine 17.0%, general and family practice 14.0%, pediatrics 7.9%, obstetrics and gynecology 6.8%, general surgery 5.6%, psychiatry 5.4%, anesthesiology 5.6%, orthopedics 4.0%, ophthalmology 4.3%); doctors of osteopathy 35,700; nurses 2,116,000 (1 per 124 persons); dentists 190,000 (1 per 1,385 persons); hospital beds 1,081,000 (1 per 243 persons), of which nonfederal 92.9% (community hospitals 80.8%, psychiatric 10.2%, long-term general and special 1.8%), federal 7.1%; infant mortality rate per 1,000 live births (1996) 7.2.

Food (1995): daily per capita caloric intake 3,603 (vegetable products 72%, animal products 28%); 136% of FAO recommended minimum requirement. Per capita consumption of major food groups (kilograms annually; 1995): milk 255.7; fresh fruits 123.2; cereal products 114.5; fresh vegetables 110.4; red meat 74.8; sweeteners 69.3; potatoes 58.7; poultry products 43.8; fats and oils 30.8; fish and shellfish 21.8.

Military

Total active duty personnel (1997): 1,447,600 (army 34.2%, navy 27.3%, air force 26.4%, marines 12.1%). *Military expenditure as percentage of GNP* (1995): 3.8% (world 2.8%); per capita expenditure U.S.$1,056. *Military aid* (1993): total $4,143,000,000 (Middle East 76.2%, of which Israel 43.4%, Egypt 31.4%; Europe 20.8%, of which Turkey 10.9%; Latin America 1.8%).

[1]Excludes 5 delegates having only committee voting privileges. [2]Total area per most recent official survey equals 3,675,267 sq mi (9,518,898 sq km); total area excluding U.S. share of Great Lakes is 3,615,215 sq mi (9,363,364 sq km). [3]Includes military personnel residing overseas. [4]Persons of Hispanic origin may be of any race. [5]Fiscal year ending September 30. [6]1994. [7]Data for 12-month period ending February 28. [8]Estimated crime rates include unreported crimes. [9]1988. [10]1993. [11]1987. [12]Excludes military personnel overseas. [13]Statistical discrepancy. [14]Unemployed. [15]Detail does not add to total given because of rounding. [16]1995. [17]Excludes tips. [18]1992. [19]Annual receipts for 1995. [20]Includes hydroelectric, nuclear, and geothermal power. [21]"Own children" includes adopted children and stepchildren. [22]September. [23]Period average. [24]End-of-year. [25]Manufacturing sector only. [26]June. [27]Animal and vegetable oils included in Food and live animals. [28]Detail does not add to total given because of statistical discrepancies in the data. [29]Includes 292 localities in Alaska. [30]Primary includes kindergarten. [31]1993–94. [32]1992–93. [33]646,000 professionally active.

Internet resources for further information:
• U.S. Census Bureau http://www.census.gov
• 1996 Statistical Abstract
   http://www.census.gov/prod/2/gen/96statab/96statab.html

Uruguay

Official name: República Oriental del Uruguay (Oriental Republic of Uruguay).
Form of government: republic with two legislative houses (Senate [31][1]; Chamber of Representatives [99]).
Head of state and government: President.
Capital: Montevideo.
Official language: Spanish.
Official religion: none.
Monetary unit: 1 peso uruguayo (Uruguayan peso)[2]; valuation (Sept. 25, 1998) 1 U.S.$ = Ur$10.87; 1 £ = Ur$18.51.

Area and population

Departments	Capitals	area sq mi	area sq km	population 1996 census
Artigas	Artigas	4,065	11,928	75,786
Canelones	Canelones	1,751	4,536	410,524
Cerro Largo	Melo	5,270	13,648	81,218
Colonia	Colonia del Sacramento	2,358	6,106	117,380
Durazno	Durazno	4,495	11,643	56,986
Flores	Trinidad	1,986	5,144	25,348
Florida	Florida	4,022	10,417	68,257
Lavalleja	Minas	3,867	10,016	60,618
Maldonado	Maldonado	1,851	4,793	113,884
Montevideo	Montevideo	205	530	1,378,705
Paysandú	Paysandú	5,375	13,922	107,706
Río Negro	Fray Bentos	3,584	9,282	48,730
Rivera	Rivera	3,618	9,370	97,959
Rocha	Rocha	4,074	10,551	71,492
Salto	Salto	5,468	14,163	115,244
San José	San José de Mayo	1,927	4,992	91,874
Soriano	Mercedes	3,478	9,008	83,741
Tacuarembó	Tacuarembó	5,961	15,438	84,078
Treinta y Tres	Treinta y Tres	3,679	9,529	49,846
TOTAL LAND AREA		67,574	175,016	
INLAND WATER		463	1,199	
TOTAL		68,037	176,215	3,139,376

Demography

Population (1998): 3,216,000.
Density (1998): persons per sq mi 47.3, persons per sq km 18.3.
Urban-rural (1996): urban 88.7%; rural 11.3%.
Sex distribution (1996): male 48.47%; female 51.53%.
Age breakdown (1995): under 15, 24.5%; 15–29, 23.7%; 30–44, 19.5%; 45–59, 15.3%; 60–74, 12.2%; 75 and over, 4.8%.
Population projection: (2000) 3,278,000; (2010) 3,524,000.
Doubling time: 91 years.
Ethnic composition (1990): white (mostly Spanish, Italian, or mixed Spanish-Italian) 86.0%; mestizo 8.0%; mulatto or black 6.0%.
Religious affiliation (1997): Roman Catholic 78.5%[3]; Protestant 4.5%; other Christian 3.5%; Jewish 0.9%; other 12.6%.
Major cities (1985): Montevideo (1996) 1,378,707; Salto 80,823; Paysandú 76,191; Las Piedras 58,288; Rivera 57,316.

Vital statistics

Birth rate per 1,000 population (1995): 17.8 (world avg. 25.0).
Death rate per 1,000 population (1995): 10.0 (world avg. 9.3).
Natural increase rate per 1,000 population (1995): 7.8 (world avg. 15.7).
Total fertility rate (avg. births per childbearing woman; 1994): 2.4.
Marriage rate per 1,000 population (1992): 6.2.
Divorce rate per 1,000 population (1992): 2.7.
Life expectancy at birth (1994): male 70.9 years; female 77.5 years.
Major causes of death per 100,000 population (1990): diseases of the circulatory system 378.4; malignant neoplasms 222.8; respiratory diseases 76.3.

National economy

Budget (1996). Revenue: Ur$29,157,875,000 (direct taxes 78.0%, receipts from foreign trade 5.4%). Expenditures: Ur$32,151,841,000 (1995; social security and welfare 60.8%, general public services 14.3%, capital investments 7.7%).
Public debt (external, outstanding; 1996): U.S.$4,097,000,000.
Tourism (1994): receipts U.S.$632,000,000; expenditures U.S.$190,000,000.
Production (metric tons except as noted). Agriculture, forestry, fishing (1996): rice 868,000, wheat 628,000, sugarcane 160,000, potatoes 145,000, oranges 133,000, corn (maize) 119,000, sunflower seed 112,000; livestock (number of live animals) 19,865,000 sheep, 10,677,000 cattle; roundwood (1995) 4,093,000 cu m; fish catch (1995) 120,737. Mining and quarrying (1995): hydraulic cement 1,000,000; gypsum 145,000. Manufacturing (value added in U.S.$'000,000; 1994): food products (excluding beverages) 792; beverages 393; chemicals and chemical products 313; textiles 253; tobacco products 170. Construction (approvals; 1994): residential 301,666 sq m; nonresidential 177,752 sq m. Energy production (consumption): electricity (kW-hr; 1994) 7,617,000,000 (5,957,000,000); crude petroleum, none (n.a.); petroleum products (metric tons; 1994) none (1,197,000).
Household income and expenditure. Avg. household size (1985) 3.3; avg. annual income per household (1985) NUr$266,261[2] (U.S.$2,625); sources of income[4]: wages 53.5%, self-employment 17.0%, transfer payments and other 29.5%; expenditure (1982–83)[5]: food 39.9%, housing 17.6%, transportation and communications 10.4%, health care 9.3%, clothing 7.0%.
Gross national product (1996): U.S.$18,464,000,000 (U.S.$5,760 per capita).

Structure of gross domestic product and labour force

	1996 in value Ur$'000[2]	1996 % of total value	1993 labour force	1993 % of labour force
Agriculture	15,057,460	10.0	47,700	3.8
Mining	248,752	0.2	2,100	0.2
Manufacturing	26,970,003	17.8	254,300	20.2
Construction	6,696,290	4.4	86,400	6.9
Public utilities	5,565,933	3.7	16,900	1.3
Transp. and commun.	10,401,852	6.9	67,900	5.4
Trade	18,695,930	12.4	231,300	18.3
Finance	13,000,875	8.6	68,400	5.4
Pub. admin., defense	14,706,486	9.7	455,800	36.1
Services	18,039,814	11.9		
Other	21,784,311[6]	14.4[6]	30,200[7]	2.4[7]
TOTAL	151,167,706	100.0	1,261,000	100.0

Population economically active (1994): total 1,307,600; activity rate 45.9% (participation rates: ages 14 and over, 58.1%; female 42.4%).

Price and earnings indexes (1990 = 100)

	1991	1992	1993	1994	1995	1996	1997
Consumer price index	202.0	340.2	524.3	758.9	1,079.5	1,385.4	1,660.0
Monthly earnings index[8]	212.0	363.7	588.1	858.3	1,185.5	1,364.5	...

Land use (1994): forested 5.3%; meadows and pastures 77.3%; agricultural and under permanent cultivation 7.5%; other 9.9%.

Foreign trade[9]

Balance of trade (current prices)

	1991	1992	1993	1994	1995	1996
U.S.$'000,000	+44.9	−248.9	−536.7	−732.2	−647.2	−773.4
% of total	1.4%	6.8%	14.0%	16.1%	13.4%	13.9%

Imports (1996): U.S.$3,322,798,000 (machinery and appliances 21.3%; chemical products 13.6%; mineral products 11.5%; transport equipment 11.2%; synthetic plastics, resins, and rubber 6.5%; processed foods 6.4%; textile products 5.8%). *Major import sources:* Brazil 22.4%; Argentina 20.8%; United States 12.0%; Italy 5.2%; France 3.5%; Spain 3.3%.
Exports (1996): U.S.$2,397,224,000 (live animals and live-animal products 26.3%; textiles and textile products 19.5%; vegetable products 17.0%; hides and skins 11.5%; processed foods 3.8%). *Major export destinations:* Brazil 34.7%; Argentina 11.3%; United States 7.0%; Germany 4.7%.

Transport and communications

Transport. Railroads: route length (1996) 2,073 km; metric ton-km cargo (1994) 189,000,000. Roads (1995): length 50,900 km (paved 14%). Vehicles (1995): passenger cars 444,835; trucks and buses 46,245. Air transport (1994): passenger-km 645,000,000; metric ton-km cargo 62,000,000; airports (1997) 1.

Communications

Medium	date	unit	number	units per 1,000 persons
Daily newspapers	1994	circulation	750,000	241
Radio	1996	receivers	1,850,000	586
Television	1995	receivers	600,000	191
Telephones	1995	main lines	622,000	198
Cellular telephones	1995	subscribers	40,000	13
Facsimile machines	1995	units	11,000	3.5
Personal computers	1995	units	70,000	22

Education and health

Educational attainment (1985). Percentage of population age 25 and over having: no formal schooling 7.5%; less than primary education 26.6%; primary 31.2%; secondary 19.9%; higher 14.8%. *Literacy* (1995 est.): population age 15 and over literate 97.3%; males 96.9%; females 97.7%.

Education (1994)

	schools	teachers	students	student/ teacher ratio
Primary (age 6–11)	2,423	16,821	337,889	20.1
Secondary (age 12–17)	348	20,061	184,083	9.2
Vocational	104	...	56,879	...
Higher	2	7,157	61,367	8.6

Health: physicians (1994) 11,241 (1 per 282 persons); hospital beds (1987) 14,133 (1 per 215 persons); infant mortality rate (1995) 19.6.
Food (1992): daily per capita caloric intake 2,750 (vegetable products 63%, animal products 37%); 103% of FAO recommended minimum requirement.

Military

Total active duty personnel (1997): 25,600 (army 68.8%, navy 19.5%, air force 11.7%). *Military expenditure as percentage of GNP* (1995): 2.4% (world 2.8%); per capita expenditure U.S.$131.

[1]Includes the vice president, who serves as ex officio presiding officer. [2]The peso uruguayo (Uruguayan peso [Ur$]) replaced the new Uruguayan peso (Nur$) on March 1, 1993, at the rate of 1 Uruguayan peso = 1,000 new Uruguayan pesos. [3]About 30–40% of Roman Catholics are estimated to be nonreligious. [4]Salaried employees only. [5]Weights of consumer price index components in Montevideo. [6]Includes indirect taxes less subsidies. [7]Includes unemployed not previously employed. [8]From urban areas only. [9]Import figures are f.o.b. in balance of trade.

Internet resources for further information:
• Embassy of Uruguay http://www.embassy.org/uruguay/
• Uruguay: Datos Estadísticos http://www.rau.edu.uy/web/rau/uruguay/generalidades/Uy.estad.htm

Uzbekistan

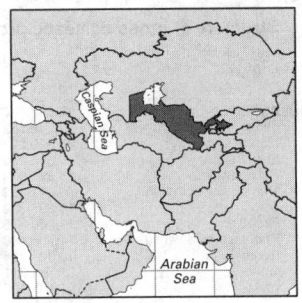

Official name: Ŭzbekiston Respublikasi (Republic of Uzbekistan).
Form of government: multiparty republic with a single legislative body (Supreme Assembly [250]).
Heads of state and government: President assisted by Prime Minister.
Capital: Tashkent (Toshkent).
Official language: Uzbek.
Official religion: none.
Monetary unit: sum[1] (plural sumy); valuation (Sept. 25, 1998) 1 U.S.$ = 300.00 sumy; 1 £ = 510.75 sumy.

Area and population

Autonomous Republic	Administrative centres	area sq mi	area sq km	population 1993 estimate
Qoraqalpoghiston	Nuqus	63,700	164,900	1,343,000
Provinces				
Andijon	Andijon	1,600	4,200	1,899,000
Bukhoro	Bukhara (Bukhoro)	15,200	39,400	1,262,000
Farghona	Fergana (Farghona)	2,700	7,100	2,338,000
Jizzakh	Jizzakh	7,900	20,500	831,000
Khorazm	Urganch	2,400	6,300	1,135,000
Namangan	Namangan	3,100	7,900	1,652,000
Nawoiy	Nawoiy	42,800	110,800	715,000
Qashqadaryo	Qarshi	11,000	28,400	1,812,000
Samarqand	Samarkand (Samarqand)	6,300	16,400	2,322,000
Sirdaryo	Guliston	2,000	5,100	600,000
Surkhondaryo	Termiz	8,000	20,800	1,437,000
Tashkent (Toshkent)	Tashkent (Toshkent)	6,000[1]	15,600[1]	2,236,000
City				
Tashkent (Toshkent)	—	1	1	2,121,000
TOTAL		172,700	447,400	21,703,000

Demography

Population (1998): 24,091,000.
Density (1998): persons per sq mi 139.5, persons per sq km 53.8.
Urban-rural (1996): urban 38.38%; rural 61.62%.
Sex distribution (1995): male 49.50%; female 50.50%.
Age breakdown (1989): under 15, 40.8%; 15–29, 28.4%; 30–44, 15.0%; 45–59, 9.3%; 60–74, 4.7%; 75 and over, 1.8%.
Population projection: (2000) 24,987,000; (2010) 28,723,000.
Ethnic composition (1995): Uzbek 75.8%; Russian 6.0%; Tajik 4.8%; Kazak 4.1%; Kyrgyz 0.9%; Ukrainian 0.6%; Turkmen 0.6%; other 7.2%.
Religious affiliation (1995): Muslim (mostly Sunnī) 88.0%; Russian Orthodox 1.0%; Jewish 0.2%; other (mostly nonreligious) 10.8%.
Major cities (1995): Tashkent 2,107,000; Samarkand 362,000; Namangan 362,000; Andijon 313,000; Bukhara 238,000.

Vital statistics

Birth rate per 1,000 population (1994): 29.5 (world avg. 25.0); (1994) legitimate 96.5%; illegitimate 3.5%.
Death rate per 1,000 population (1994): 6.7 (world avg. 9.3).
Natural increase rate per 1,000 population (1994): 22.8 (world avg. 15.7).
Total fertility rate (avg. births per childbearing woman; 1993): 3.8.
Marriage rate per 1,000 population (1994): 7.9.
Divorce rate per 1,000 population (1994): 1.1.
Life expectancy at birth (1994): male 66.0 years; female 72.0 years.
Major causes of death per 100,000 population (1993): diseases of the circulatory system 303.6; diseases of the respiratory system 115.0; accidents, poisoning, and violence 50.0; cancers 48.7; infectious and parasitic diseases 38.4; diseases of the digestive system 31.8; diseases of the nervous system 10.3; endocrine and metabolic disorders 10.3.

National economy

Budget (1995). Revenue: 89,914,000,000 sumy (taxes on income and profits 38.1%, excise taxes 27.6%, value-added tax 19.2%, property and land taxes 4.7%, other 10.4%). Expenditures: 100,262,000,000 sumy (social and cultural affairs 36.9%, investments 18.8%, national economy 13.3%, payments on interest 4.9%, administration 3.0%, other 23.1%).
Household income and expenditure (1995). Average household size (1989) 5.5; income per household 35,165 sumy (U.S.$1,040); sources of income: wages and salaries 63.0%, subsidies, grants, and nonwage income 34.9%, other 2.1%; expenditure: food and beverages 71%, clothing and footwear 14%, recreation 6%, household durables 4%, housing 3%.
Public debt (external, outstanding; 1996): U.S.$1,990,000,000.
Production (metric tons except as noted). Agriculture, forestry, fishing (1996): seed cotton 3,300,000, vegetables 2,916,000, fruit (except grapes) and berries 1,165,000, grapes 580,000, potatoes 490,000, rice 480,000, barley 230,000; livestock (number of live animals) 8,352,000 sheep, 5,204,000 cattle, 208,000 pigs, 13,000,000 chickens; roundwood (1990) 15,000 cu m; fish catch (1995) 26,312. Mining and quarrying (1995): copper 100,000; zinc 80,000; gold 85. Manufacturing (value of production in '000,000 sumy; 1993): textiles 987; machine building and metalworking equipment 519; ferrous and nonferrous metals 484; processed foods 429; construction materials 294; chemical products 270. Construction (1992): residential 7,000,000,000 sq m. Energy production (consumption): electricity (kW-hr; 1994) 47,800,000,000 (47,400,000,000); coal (metric tons; 1995) 3,045,000 (1994; 4,200,000); crude petroleum (barrels; 1994) 25,655,000 (43,980,000); petroleum products (met-

ric tons; 1994) 7,880,000 (7,880,000); natural gas (cu m; 1995) 48,600,000,000 (1994; 38,564,000,000).
Gross national product (1996): U.S.$23,490,000,000 (U.S.$1,010 per capita).

Structure of gross domestic product and labour force

	1995 in value '000,000 sumy	1995 % of total value	1995 labour force	1995 % of labour force
Agriculture	85,070	28.5	3,735,000	44.8
Manufacturing and mining	49,068	16.4	1,010,000	12.1
Construction	23,228	7.8	493,000	5.9
Transp. and commun.	25,119	8.4	218,000	2.6
Trade	16,821	5.6	566,000	6.8
Finance Pub. admin., defense	} 58,864	19.7	2,135,000	25.6
Services				
Other	40,360[2]	13.5[2]	188,000[3]	2.2[3]
TOTAL	298,530	100.0[4]	8,345,000	100.0

Population economically active (1995): total 8,345,000; activity rate of total population 36.8% (participation rates: ages 16–59 [male], 16–54 [female] 74.5%; female [1994] 43.0%; unemployed 2.2%).

Price and earnings indexes (1992 = 100)

	1991	1992	1993	1994	1995
Consumer price index	13.4	100.0	634.1	5,219	11,724
Monthly earnings index	11.8	100.0	1,196	10,791	41,952

Land use (1994): forested 2.9%; meadows and pastures 46.5%; agricultural and under permanent cultivation 10.1%; other 40.5%.

Foreign trade

Balance of trade (current prices)

	1992	1993	1994	1995
U.S.$'000,000	−39.1	+314.8	+26.1	−103.7
% of total	13.7%	11.5%	0.8%	3.1%

Imports (1996): U.S.$4,763,000,000 (1995; machinery and metalworking products 29.1%, chemical products 13.6%, ferrous and nonferrous metal products 12.4%, food products 5.5%, forestry and paper products 4.0%, light industrial products 2.9%). *Major import sources:* Russia 24.9%; Korea 11.8%; Germany 11.0%; U.S. 8.1%; Turkey 5.4%.
Exports (1996): U.S.$2,649,000,000 (1995; light industrial products 34.7%, oil and gas 15.1%, machine-building equipment 5.9%, food products 5.8%, electricity 5.4%). *Major export destinations:* Russia 22.4%; Italy 8.8%; Tajikistan 6.8%; China 5.1%; Ukraine 5.1%.

Transport and communications

Transport. Railroads (1996): length 3,380 km; (1995) passenger-km 2,500,000,000; (1995) metric ton-km cargo 16,907,000,000. Roads (1995): total length 84,400 km (paved 86%). Vehicles (1994): passenger cars 865,300; buses 14,500. Air transport (1995): passenger-km 3,000,000,000; metric ton-km cargo 105,000,000; airports (1996) with scheduled flights 9.

Communications

Medium	date	unit	number	units per 1,000 persons
Daily newspapers	1995	circulation	160,000	7.0
Television	1995	receivers	4,000,000	176
Telephones	1995	main lines	1,738,000	76
Cellular telephones	1995	subscribers	3,700	0.2
Facsimile machines	1995	units	1,900	0.1

Education and health

Educational attainment (1989). Percentage of population age 25 and over having: primary education or no formal schooling 13.3%; some secondary 19.8%; completed secondary and some postsecondary 57.7%; higher 9.2%. *Literacy* (1989): percentage of total population age 15 and over literate 97.2%; males literate 98.5%; females literate 96.0%.

Education (1995–96)

	schools	teachers	students	student/ teacher ratio
Primary (age 6–13) Secondary (age 14–17)	} 9,300	413,000	5,090,000	12.3
Voc., teacher tr.	252	22,164[5]	194,800	11.0[5]
Higher	58	...	192,100	...

Health (1995): physicians 76,000 (1 per 302 persons); hospital beds 192,000 (1 per 120 persons); infant mortality rate per 1,000 live births (1996) 25.7.

Military

Total active duty personnel (1997): 65,000 (army 69.2%, air force 6.2%, other 24.6%). *Military expenditure as percentage of GNP* (1995): 3.8% (world 2.8%); per capita expenditure U.S.$90.

---

[1]Tashkent province includes Tashkent City. [2]Includes value-added taxes: excise taxes plus net import taxes minus subsidies. [3]Unemployed. [4]Detail does not add to total given because of rounding. [5]1992–93.

Internet resources for further information:
• **Welcome to Uzbekistan** http://www.gov.uz/
• **Republic of Uzbekistan** http://www.uzbekistan.org/

Vanuatu

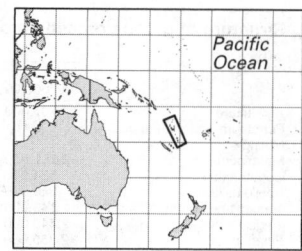

Official name: Ripablik blong Vanuatu (Bislama); République de Vanuatu (French); Republic of Vanuatu (English).
Form of government: republic with a single legislative house (Parliament [52]).
Chief of state: President.
Head of government: Prime Minister.
Capital: Vila.
Official languages: Bislama; French; English.
Official religion: none.
Monetary unit: vatu (VT); valuation (Sept. 25, 1998) 1 U.S.$ = VT 131.87; 1 £ = VT 224.51.

Area and population

Provinces	Capitals	area sq mi	area sq km	population 1989 census
Malampa	...	1,073	2,779	28,185
Penama	...	463	1,198	22,299
Sanma	...	1,640	4,248	25,581
Shefa	...	562	1,455	38,471
Tafea	...	628	1,627	22,423
Torba	...	341	882	5,985
TOTAL		4,707	12,190[1]	142,944

Demography

Population (1998): 182,000.
Density (1998): persons per sq mi 38.7, persons per sq km 14.9.
Urban-rural (1997): urban 20.0%; rural 80.0%.
Sex distribution (1989): male 51.60%; female 48.40%.
Age breakdown (1989)[2]: under 15, 45.5%; 15–29, 26.6%; 30–44, 15.2%; 45–59, 8.4%; 60–74, 3.7%; 75 and over, 0.6%.
Population projection: (2000) 192,000; (2010) 245,000.
Doubling time: 26 years.
Ethnic composition (1989): Ni-Vanuatu 97.9%; European 1.0%; other Pacific Islanders 0.4%; other 0.7%.
Religious affiliation (1989): Christian 77.2%, of which Presbyterian 35.8%, Roman Catholic 14.5%, Anglican 14.0%, Seventh-day Adventist 8.2%; Custom 4.6%; nonreligious 1.7%; unknown 4.0%; other 12.5%.
Major towns (1989): Vila (Port-Vila) 19,400; Luganville (Santo) 6,900.

Vital statistics

Birth rate per 1,000 population (1997): 33.0 (world avg. 25.0).
Death rate per 1,000 population (1997): 6.2 (world avg. 9.3).
Natural increase rate per 1,000 population (1997): 26.8 (world avg. 15.7).
Total fertility rate (avg. births per childbearing woman; 1997): 4.4.
Marriage rate per 1,000 population (1985): c. 7.4.
Divorce rate per 1,000 population (1985): less than 0.7.
Life expectancy at birth (1997): male 65.0 years; female 69.0 years.
Major causes of death per 100,000 population (1994)[3]: diseases of the circulatory system 39.0; diseases of the respiratory system 30.4; malignant neoplasms (cancers) 29.2; infectious and parasitic diseases 25.0; diseases of the digestive system 9.7.

National economy

Budget (1995). Revenue: VT 10,013,000,000 (foreign grants 35.5%, taxes on international trade 28.7%, taxes on goods and services 16.3%, nontax revenue 15.1%). Expenditures: VT 10,439,000,000 (current expenditure 67.4%, of which general public services 21.4%, education 12.7%, economic affairs and services 6.8%, health 5.7%, public order and safety 5.6%; development expenditure 32.6%).
Household income and expenditure (1985)[5]. Average household size (1989) 5.1; income per household U.S.$11,299; sources of income: wages and salaries 59.0%, self-employment 33.7%; expenditure (1990)[5, 6]: food and nonalcoholic beverages 30.5%, housing 20.7%, transportation 13.2%, health and recreation 12.3%, tobacco and alcohol 10.4%.
Production (metric tons except as noted). Agriculture, forestry, fishing (1996): coconuts 280,000, roots and tubers 50,000, copra (1994) 30,000, bananas 12,500, vegetables and melons 8,200, cacao beans 1,783, peanuts (groundnuts) 1,750, corn (maize) 700; livestock (number of live animals) 151,000 cattle, 60,000 pigs, 12,000 goats, 320,000 chickens; roundwood (1995) 63,200 cu m; fish catch (1995) 2,833. Mining and quarrying: small quantities of coral-reef limestone, crushed stone, sand, and gravel. Manufacturing (value added in VT '000,000; 1994): food, beverages, and tobacco 495; wood products 327; fabricated metal products 150; paper products 99; textiles, clothing, and leather 90; chemical, rubber, plastic, and nonmetallic products 83. Construction (approvals in Vila and Luganville; 1992): residential 20,386 sq m; nonresidential 19,876 sq m. Energy production (consumption): electricity (kW-hr; 1994) 29,000,000 (29,000,000); coal, none (none); crude petroleum, none (none); petroleum products (metric tons; 1994) none (20,000); natural gas, none (none).
Land use (1994): forested 75.0%; meadows and pastures 2.0%; agricultural 11.8%; other 11.2%.
Population economically active (1989): total 66,957; activity rate of total population 47.0% (participation rates: ages 15–64, 85.0%; female 46.3%; unemployed 0.5%).

Price and earnings indexes (1990 = 100)

	1991	1992	1993	1994	1995	1996	1997
Consumer price index	106.5	108.8	114.7	117.4	120.0	121.1	124.5
Earnings index	...	...	...	...	...	...	...

Gross national product (at current market prices; 1996): U.S.$224,000,000 (U.S.$1,290 per capita).

Structure of gross domestic product and labour force

	1995 in value VT '000,000	1995 % of total value	1989 labour force	1989 % of labour force
Agriculture	6,051	22.7	49,811	74.4
Mining	...	...	1	—
Manufacturing	1,386	5.2	891	1.3
Construction	1,721	6.4	1,302	1.9
Public utilities	462	1.7	109	0.2
Transportation and communications	2,247	8.4	1,031	1.5
Trade	8,611	32.2	2,713	4.1
Finance	1,918	7.2	646	1.0
Pub. admin., defense	3,089	11.6 }	7,892	11.8
Services	1,779	6.7 }		
Other	−550[4]	−2.1[4]	2,561	3.8
TOTAL	26,714	100.0	66,957	100.0

Public debt (external, outstanding; 1996): U.S.$42,100,000.
Tourism (1994): receipts from visitors U.S.$55,000,000; expenditures by nationals abroad U.S.$1,000,000.

Foreign trade[7]

Balance of trade (current prices)

	1991	1992	1993	1994	1995	1996
VT '000,000	−7,364	−6,689	−6,409	−7,493	−7,486	−7,520
% of total	67.0%	56.8%	53.7%	56.3%	54.1%	52.7%

Imports (1995): VT 10,659,000,000 (machinery and transport equipment 28.2%, basic manufactures 19.4%, food and live animals 15.0%, mineral fuels 8.0%, chemical products 6.6%, beverages and tobacco 3.5%). *Major import sources:* Australia 37.0%; New Zealand 12.0%; Japan 9.0%; France 6.0%; Fiji 6.0%.
Exports (1995): VT 3,173,000,000 (copra 34.7%, beef and veal 13.5%, timber 7.9%, squash and pumpkin 4.7%, cacao beans 4.0%). *Major export destinations*[8]: European Union 37.0%; Japan 24.0%; Australia 10.0%; Bangladesh 10.0%; New Caledonia 6.0%.

Transport and communications

Transport. Railroads: none. Roads (1995): total length 652 mi, 1,050 km (paved 24%). Vehicles (1994): passenger cars 4,000; trucks and buses 2,300. Merchant marine (1992): vessels (100 gross tons and over) 280; total deadweight tonnage 3,259,594. Air transport (1996): passenger-mi 93,000,000, passenger-km 150,000,000; short ton-mi cargo 845,000, metric ton-km 1,233,000; airports (1996) with scheduled flights 29.

Communications

Medium	date	unit	number	units per 1,000 persons
Radio	1996	receivers	55,000	319
Television	1993	receivers	2,000	13
Telephones	1995	main lines	4,200	25
Cellular telephones	1995	subscribers	100	0.6
Facsimile machines	1995	units	600	3.6

Education and health

Educational attainment (1989). Percentage of population age 6 and over having: no formal schooling or less than one year 22.3%; some primary education 52.6%; lower-level secondary 18.3%; upper-level secondary and higher 4.8%; not stated 2.0%. *Literacy* (1979): total population age 15 and over literate 32,120 (52.9%); males 18,550 (57.3%); females 13,570 (47.8%).

Education (1992)

	schools	teachers	students	student/ teacher ratio
Primary (age 6–11)[9]	272	852	26,267	30.8
Secondary (age 11–18)	21[10]	220	4,269	19.4
Voc., teacher tr.	...	...	444	...
Higher	1	...	124[11]	...

Health (1995): physicians 12 (1 per 14,025 persons); hospital beds 374 (1 per 450 persons); infant mortality rate per 1,000 live births (1997) 39.
Food (1995): daily per capita caloric intake 2,541 (vegetable products 85%, animal products 15%); 111% of FAO recommended minimum requirement.

Military

Total active duty personnel: Vanuatu has a paramilitary force of about 300.

[1]Detail does not add to total given because of rounding. [2]For indigenous population only. [3]Deaths reported to the Ministry of Health only. [4]Imputed bank service charges. [5]Vila and Luganville only. [6]Weights of consumer price index components. [7]Imports c.i.f.; exports f.o.b. [8]Destination of domestic exports only. [9]Excludes independent private schools. [10]1986. [11]1991.

Venezuela

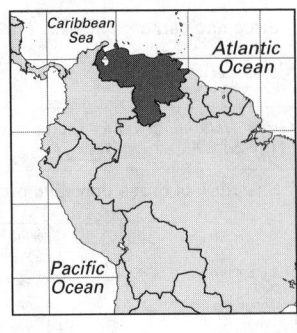

Official name: República de Venezuela (Republic of Venezuela).
Form of government: federal multiparty republic with two legislative houses (Senate [49[1, 2]; Chamber of Deputies [189[2]]).
Head of state and government: President.
Capital: Caracas.
Official language: Spanish.
Official religion: none.
Monetary unit: 1 bolívar (B, plural Bs) = 100 céntimos; valuation (Sept. 25, 1998) 1 U.S.$ = BS 580.25; 1 £ = Bs 987.88.

Area and population

States	Capitals	area sq mi	area sq km	population 1995 estimate
Amazonas	Puerto Ayacucho	67,900	175,750	66,668
Anzoátegui	Barcelona	16,700	43,300	1,028,097
Apure	San Fernando de Apure	29,500	76,500	376,220
Aragua	Maracay	2,708	7,014	1,335,303
Barinas	Barinas	13,600	35,200	516,789
Bolívar	Ciudad Bolívar	91,900	238,000	1,122,975
Carabobo	Valencia	1,795	4,650	1,807,542
Cojedes	San Carlos	5,700	14,800	226,684
Delta Amacuro	Tucupita	15,500	40,200	110,838
Falcón	Coro	9,600	24,800	684,062
Guárico	San Juan de Los Morros	25,091	64,986	585,418
Lara	Barquisimeto	7,600	19,800	1,423,683
Mérida	Mérida	4,400	11,300	686,709
Miranda	Los Teques	3,070	7,950	2,326,143
Monagas	Maturín	11,200	28,900	551,015
Nueva Esparta	La Asunción	440	1,150	325,909
Portuguesa	Guanare	5,900	15,200	719,473
Sucre	Cumaná	4,600	11,800	771,580
Táchira	San Cristóbal	4,300	11,100	944,259
Trujillo	Trujillo	2,900	7,400	549,878
Yaracuy	San Felipe	2,700	7,100	463,911
Zulia	Maracaibo	24,400	63,100	2,752,431
Other federal entities				
Dependencias Federales	—	50	120	...
Distrito Federal	Caracas	745	1,930	2,268,534
TOTAL		352,144[3]	912,050	21,644,121

Demography

Population (1998): 23,242,000.
Density (1998): persons per sq mi 66.0, persons per sq km 25.5.
Urban-rural (1992): urban 84.6%; rural 15.4%.
Sex distribution (1994): male 50.40%; female 49.60%.
Age breakdown (1992): under 15, 37.4%; 15–29, 28.0%; 30–44, 19.0%; 45–59, 9.7%; 60 and over, 5.9%.
Population projection: (2000) 24,170,000; (2010) 28,716,000.
Ethnic composition (1993): mestizo 67%; white 21%; black 10%; Indian 2%.
Religious affiliation (1996): Roman Catholic 92.7%; other 7.3%.
Major cities (1992): Caracas 1,964,846; Maracaibo (1990) 1,249,670; Valencia 1,034,033; Barquisimeto 692,599; Ciudad Guayana 523,578.

Vital statistics

Birth rate per 1,000 population (1996): 26.7 (world avg. 25.0); (1974) legitimate 47.0%; illegitimate 53.0%.
Death rate per 1,000 population (1996): 4.7 (world avg. 9.3).
Natural increase rate per 1,000 population (1996): 22.0 (world avg. 15.7).
Total fertility rate (avg. births per childbearing woman; 1996): 2.9.
Marriage rate per 1,000 population (1992): 5.4.
Divorce rate per 1,000 population (1992): 0.9.
Life expectancy at birth (1996): male 69.1 years; female 75.3 years.
Major causes of death per 100,000 population (1992): heart diseases 79.9; cancers 53.7; accidents 43.6; perinatal problems 33.0.

National economy

Budget (1994). Revenue: Bs 1,635,864,000,000 (tax revenues 78.3%, oil revenues 18.2%, nontax revenues 3.5%). Expenditures: Bs 1,627,732,000,000 (subsidies 32.0%, goods and services 29.9%, debt service 20.7%).
Public debt (external, outstanding; 1996): U.S.$28,452,000,000.
Tourism (1995): receipts U.S.$811,000,000; expenditures U.S.$1,865,000,000.
Land use (1994): forest 34.0%; pasture 20.2%; agriculture 4.4%; other 41.4%.
Production (metric tons except as noted). Agriculture, forestry, fishing (1996): sugarcane 6,844,000, bananas 1,365,000, corn (maize) 1,050,000, rice 733,000, plantains 516,086, oranges 493,028, sorghum 300,000, cassava 299,233; livestock (number of live animals) 14,584,500 cattle, 3,182,000 goats, 3,150,000 pigs, 100,000,000 chickens; roundwood (1995) 2,267,000 cu m; fish catch (1995) 504,791. Mining and quarrying (1996): iron ore 20,840,000; limestone 15,130,000; bauxite 5,600,000; gold 12,127 kg; diamonds 160,000 carats. Manufacturing (value added in 1990 U.S.$'000,000; 1994): petroleum refineries 2,718; food products 1,282; chemicals 1,163; beverages 760; transport equipment 691; iron and steel 458; nonferrous metals 386; metal products 382; tobacco 368; printing and publishing 294. Energy production (consumption): electricity (kW-hr; 1994) 73,116,000,000 (72,796,000,000); coal (metric tons; 1994) 4,741,000 (354,000); crude petroleum (barrels; 1994) 986,468,000 (380,271,000); petroleum products (metric tons; 1994) 54,575,000 (24,229,000); natural gas (cu m; 1994) 24,675,000,000 (24,675,000,000).
Gross national product (1996): U.S.$67,333,000,000 (U.S.$3,020 per capita).

Structure of gross domestic product and labour force

	1995 in value Bs '000,000	% of total value	1995 labour force	% of labour force
Agriculture	707,000	5.3	1,012,300	11.8
Petroleum and natural gas } Mining	1,927,000	14.5	73,000	0.9
Manufacturing	2,282,000	17.2	1,046,800	12.3
Construction	534,000	4.0	623,900	7.3
Public utilities	340,000	2.6	66,000	0.8
Transp. and commun.	1,143,000	8.6	477,400	5.6
Trade	2,449,000	18.5	1,738,800	20.3
Finance	2,355,000	17.8	434,900	5.1
Pub. admin., defense	588,000	4.4 }	2,186,600	25.6
Services	150,000	1.1 }		
Other	791,000	6.0	885,000[4]	10.4[4]
TOTAL	13,266,000	100.0	8,544,600[3]	100.0[3]

Population economically active (1995): total 8,544,600; activity rate 39.1% (participation rates: over age 15 (1993) 57.9%; female (1993) 31.2%; unemployed 10.2%).

Price and earnings indexes (1990 = 100)

	1991	1992	1993	1994	1995	1996	1997
Consumer price index	134.2	176.4	243.6	391.8	626.5	1,252.3	1,878.9

Household income and expenditure. Average household size (1990) 5.1; average annual income per household (1981) Bs 42,492 (U.S.$9,899); expenditure (1990): food 37.1%, housing 9.4%, clothing 8.3%, transportation and communications 5.1%, education and recreation 4.9%.

Foreign trade

Balance of trade (current prices)

	1991	1992	1993	1994	1995	1996
Bs '000,000	+286,500	+154,700	+274,600	+1,159,400	+1,407.7	+5,996.8
% of total	20.1%	9.3%	12.1%	32.7%	27.2%	44.3%

Imports (1995): U.S.$10,791,261,000 (processed industrial supplies 34.9%, machinery 24.7%, transport equipment 12.4%, manufactured consumer goods 11.6%, food products 11.2%). *Major import sources:* U.S. 42.6%; Colombia 7.6%; Germany 4.8%; Japan 4.4%; Canada 4.2%; Brazil 3.9%; Mexico 3.3%.
Exports (1995): U.S.$18,814,219,000 (crude petroleum and petroleum products 76.8%, basic metal manufactures 8.2%). *Major export destinations:* U.S. 51.3%; Brazil 9.0%; Colombia 7.6%; Netherlands Antilles 4.9%; Suriname 2.1%; Germany 1.8%; The Netherlands 1.7%; Japan 1.6%.

Transport and communications

Transport. Railroads (1994): length 627 km; passenger-km 31,400,000; metric ton-km cargo 46,800,000. Roads (1995): total length 89,700 km (paved 39%). Vehicles (1995): passenger cars 1,485,221; trucks and buses 511,809. Merchant marine (1992): vessels (over 100 gross tons) 271; total deadweight tonnage 1,355,419. Air transport (1994): passenger-km 7,372,000,000; metric ton-km cargo 210,300,000; airports (1997) with scheduled flights 20.

Communications

Medium	date	unit	number	units per 1,000 persons
Daily newspapers	1994	circulation	4,600,000	215
Radio	1996	receivers	8,300,000	372
Television	1995	receivers	4,000,000	183
Telephones	1995	main lines	2,463,200	113
Cellular telephones	1995	subscribers	400,000	18
Facsimile machines	1995	units	16,000	0.7
Personal computers	1995	units	370,000	17

Education and health

Educational attainment (1990). Percentage of population age 25 and over having: no formal schooling 23.5%; primary education or less 47.2%; some secondary and secondary 22.3%; postsecondary 7.0%. *Literacy* (1995 est.): total population age 15 and over literate 91.1%; males 91.8%; females 90.3%.

Education (1993–94)

	schools	teachers	students	student/ teacher ratio
Primary (age 7–12)	15,984[5]	185,748	4,217,283	22.7
Secondary (age 13–17)[6]	1,621[7]	33,692	311,209	9.2
Higher	99[8]	43,833[7]	550,783[7]	12.6[7]

Health (1992): physicians (1989) 32,616 (1 per 576 persons); hospital beds 52,786 (1 per 382 persons); infant mortality rate (1996) 16.8.
Food (1995): daily per capita caloric intake 2,442 (vegetable products 83%, animal products 17%); 99% of FAO recommended minimum.

Military

Total active duty personnel (1997): 79,000 (army 72.1%, navy 19.0%, air force 8.9%). *Military expenditure as percentage of GNP* (1995): 1.1% (world 2.8%); per capita expenditure U.S.$39.

[1]Includes three former presidents holding lifetime membership. [2]Based on preliminary information for November 1998 elections. [3]Detail does not add to total given because of rounding. [4]Mostly unemployed. [5]1992–93. [6]Includes vocational and teacher training. [7]1991–92. [8]1990–91.

Internet resources for further information:
- **Central Office of Statistics and Informatics http://www.ocei.gov.ve/**
- **Embassy of the Republic of Venezuela http://www.embassy.org/embassies/ve.html**

Vietnam

Official name: Cong Hoa Xa Hoi Chu
Nghia Viet Nam (Socialist Republic
of Vietnam).
Form of government: socialist republic
with one legislative house (National
Assembly [450]).
Head of state: President.
Head of government: Prime Minister.
Capital: Hanoi.
Official language: Vietnamese.
Official religion: none.
Monetary unit: 1 dong (D) = 10
hao = 100 xu; valuation (Sept. 25, 1998)
1 U.S.$ = D 13,904; 1 £ = D 23,672.

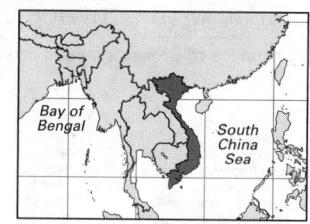

Area and population

Geographic Regions[1]	Principal cities	area		population
		sq mi	sq km	1993 estimate
Central Highlands	Da Lat	21,455	55,569	2,903,500
North Central Coast	Hue	19,763	51,187	9,516,900
Northeastern South Region	Ho Chi Minh City	9,066	23,481	8,692,900
North Mountains and Midlands	Thai Nguyen	39,749	102,949	12,109,300
Mekong River Delta	Long Xuyen	15,280	39,575	15,531,600
Red River Delta	Hanoi	4,810	12,457	13,808,800
South Central Coast	Da Nang	17,692	45,823	7,374,700
TOTAL		127,816[2]	331,041	70,982,500[3]

Demography

Population (1998): 76,236,000.
Density (1998): persons per sq mi 596.5, persons per sq km 230.3.
Urban-rural (1995): urban 20.8%; rural 79.2%.
Sex distribution (1997): male 49.03%; female 50.97%.
Age breakdown (1997): under 15, 35.5%; 15–29, 28.3%; 30–44, 20.2%; 45–59,
8.5%; 60–74, 5.8%; 75 and over, 1.7%.
Population projection: (2000): 78,350,000; (2010) 88,602,000.
Doubling time: 47 years.
Ethnic composition (1989): Vietnamese 87.1%; Tho (Tay) 1.8%; Chinese
(Hoa) 1.5%; Tai 1.5%; Khmer 1.4%; Muong 1.4%; Nung 1.1%; other 4.2%.
Religious affiliation (1995): Buddhist 66.7%; Christian 8.7%, of which Roman
Catholic 7.7%, Protestant 1.0%; Cao Dai (a New-Religionist group) 3.5%;
Hoa Hao (a New-Religionist group) 2.1%; other 19.0%.
Major cities (1992): Ho Chi Minh City 4,322,300[4]; Hanoi 2,154,900[4]; Haiphong
783,133; Da Nang 382,674; Buon Ma Thuot 282,095; Nha Trang 221,331; Hue
219,149; Can Tho 215,587.

Vital statistics

Birth rate per 1,000 population (1997): 22.0 (world avg. 25.0).
Death rate per 1,000 population (1997): 7.0 (world avg. 9.3).
Natural increase rate per 1,000 population (1997): 15.0 (world avg. 15.7).
Total fertility rate (avg. births per childbearing woman; 1996): 2.7.
Marriage rate per 1,000 population: n.a.
Divorce rate per 1,000 population: n.a.
Life expectancy at birth (1997): male 65.0 years; female 69.9 years.
Major causes of death per 100,000 population: n.a.

National economy

Budget (1996). Revenue: D 60,500,000,000,000 (tax revenue 86.7%, nontax
revenues 13.3%). Expenditures: D 66,417,000,000,000 (current expenditures
71.5%, of which social services 28.4%).
Public debt (external, outstanding; 1996): U.S.$22,344,000,000.
Gross national product (1996): U.S.$21,915,000,000[5] (U.S.$290 per capita[5]).

Structure of gross domestic product and labour force

	1995			
	in value D '000,000,000	% of total value	labour force	% of labour force
Agriculture, forestry, fishing	61,387	27.5	24,765,000	71.6
Mining, manufacturing }	67,075	30.1	3,395,000	9.8
Construction }			1,099,000	3.2
Transp. and commun.	8,747	3.9	568,000	1.6
Trade and restaurants	30,284	13.6	2,290,000	6.6
Finance, insurance	5,580	2.5	}	
Pub. admin. } Services }	22,600	10.1	1,431,000	4.1
Other	27,167[6]	12.2[6]	1,052,000	3.0
TOTAL	222,840	100.0[2]	34,600,000	100.0[2]

Tourism (1994): receipts from visitors U.S.$85,000,000; expenditures by nation-
als abroad, n.a.
Production (metric tons except as noted). Agriculture, forestry, fishing (1997):
rice 27,646,000, sugarcane 11,428,000, cassava 1,983,000, sweet potatoes
1,642,000, corn (maize) 1,641,000, bananas 1,300,000, coffee 400,000, oranges
380,000, natural rubber 181,000, cashews 110,000, pimento 74,000, tea 52,000;
livestock (number of live animals) 17,500,000 pigs, 3,700,000 cattle, 2,953,700
buffalo; roundwood (1995) 34,713,000 cu m, of which fuelwood 30,290,000 cu
m, industrial roundwood 4,423,000 cu m; fish catch (1995) 1,100,000, of which
marine fish 450,000, crustaceans 306,000, freshwater fish 287,000. Mining and
quarrying (1994): phosphate rock 470,000; gold 10,000 kg. Manufacturing
(1995): cement 5,828,000; fertilizers 931,000; raw sugar 517,000; crude steel
408,000; beer 5,120,000 hectolitres; garments 145,000,000 units; bicycles

236,000 units. Energy production (consumption): electricity (kW-hr; 1994)
12,020,000,000 (12,020,000,000); coal (metric tons; 1994) 5,600,000 (4,000,000);
crude petroleum (barrels; 1994) 50,282,000 (283,300); petroleum products
(metric tons; 1994) 38,000 (3,848,000); natural gas (cu m; 1995): 5,100,000
(5,100,000).
Population economically active (1989): total 30,521,019; activity rate 47.4%
(participation rates: ages 15–64, 79.9%; female 51.7%; unemployed 5.8%).
Household income and expenditure. Average household size (1989) 4.8; income
per household (1990)[7] D 577,008 (U.S.$93); sources of income: n.a.; expen-
diture (1990): food 62.4%, clothing 5.0%, household goods 4.6%, education
2.9%, housing 2.5%.
Land use (1994): forested 29.6%; meadows and pastures 1.0%; agricultural and
under permanent cultivation 21.5%; other 47.9%.

Foreign trade

Balance of trade (current prices)

	1991	1992	1993	1994	1995	1996
U.S.$'000,000	−294	−109	−939	−1,772	−5,983	−6,735
% of total	6.3%	1.8%	13.6%	17.9%	34.4%	32.7%

Imports (1996): U.S.$13,668,000,000 (1995; machinery and spare parts 28.9%,
petroleum products 8.6%, fertilizers 6.6%, motor scooters 5.0%, iron and
steel 4.6%). *Major import sources* (1996): Singapore 13.8%; South Korea
12.9%; Taiwan 9.5%; Japan 9.2%; France 6.0%.
Exports (1996): U.S.$6,933,000,000 (1995; crude petroleum 19.7%, coffee
10.9%, rice 9.5%, fish and fish products 8.3%, clothing 8.3%, rubber 3.1%).
Major export destinations (1996): Japan 26.4%; Germany 8.1%; Singapore
5.7%; France 4.9%; Australia 4.4%.

Transport and communications

Transport. Railroads (1995): length 1,619 mi, 2,605 km; passenger-mi
1,305,000,000[8], passenger-km 2,100,000,000[8]; short ton-mile cargo
727,000,000[8], metric ton-km cargo 1,062,000,000[8]. Roads (1995): total length
65,895 mi, 106,048 km (paved 26%). Vehicles (1994): passenger cars, trucks,
and buses 200,000. Air transport (1994): passenger-mi 130,000,000, passenger-km 209,000,000; short ton-mile cargo 13,000,000, metric ton-km cargo
19,000,000; airports (1997) with scheduled flights 12.

Communications

Medium	date	unit	number	units per 1,000 persons
Daily newspapers	1995	circulation	570,000	8.0
Radio	1995	receivers	7,800,000	106.0
Television	1995	receivers	3,200,000	43.0
Telephones	1996	main lines	1,050,000	14.2
Cellular telephones	1995	subscribers	14,600	0.2
Facsimile machines	1995	units	7,300	0.1
Personal computers	1996	units	100,000	1.4

Education and health

Educational attainment (1989). Percentage of population age 25 and over having: no formal education (illiterate) 16.6%; some primary 46.6%; complete
primary 23.5%; secondary 6.5%; postsecondary and higher 6.8%. *Literacy*
(1995): percentage of population age 15 and over literate 93.7%; males
96.5%; females 91.2%.

Education (1995–96)

	schools	teachers	students	student/ teacher ratio
Primary (age 7–12)	13,092[9, 10]	298,856	10,228,800	34.2
Secondary (age 13–18)[11]	6,298[10]	193,814	5,332,400	27.5
Vocational	451[10]	9,425	197,500	21.0
Higher	104[10]	22,750	297,900	13.1

Health (1994): physicians 29,700 (1 per 2,444 persons); hospital beds 191,000
(1 per 380 persons); infant mortality rate per 1,000 live births (1997) 37.0.
Food (1995): daily per capita caloric intake 2,463 (vegetable products 91%,
animal products 9%); 114% of FAO recommended minimum requirement.

Military

Total active duty personnel (1997): 492,000 (army 85.4%, navy 8.5%, air force
6.1%). *Military expenditure as percentage of GNP* (1995): 2.6% (world 2.8%);
per capita expenditure U.S.$7.

---

[1]Seven geographic regions are divided into 60 provinces as of the administrative reorganization of 1997. [2]Detail does not add to total given because of rounding. [3]Total
includes 1,044,800 persons not distributed in province and region estimates. [4]1993.
[5]Figure indicates the World Bank's nominal assessment of the Vietnamese economy.
[6]Includes housing and tourism. [7]Wage workers and government officials only. [8]1994.
[9]Includes 2,955 institutions that provide primary and first cycle of secondary education. [10]1993–94. [11]Includes first and second cycles of secondary education.

Internet resources for further information:
• **Vietnam Information http://www.batin.com.vn/**

Yemen

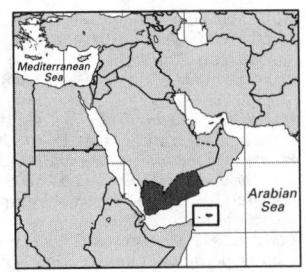

Official name: Al-Jumhūrīyah al-Yamanīyah (Republic of Yemen).
Form of government: multiparty republic with one legislative house (House of Representatives [301]).
Head of state: President[1].
Head of government: Prime Minister.
Capital: Ṣanʿāʾ.
Official language: Arabic.
Official religion: Islam.
Monetary unit: 1 Yemeni Rial (YRls) = 100 fils; valuation (Sept. 25, 1998): 1 U.S.$ = YRls 133.82, 1 £ = YRls 227.83.

Area and population		area		population
Governorates	**Capitals**	**sq mi**	**sq km**	**1994 census**
Northern Yemen				
Al-Baydāʾ	Al-Baydāʾ	4,310	11,170	509,265
Dhamār	Dhamār	3,430	8,870	1,050,346
Hajjah	Hajjah	3,700	9,590	1,262,590
Al-Hudaydah	Al-Hudaydah	5,240	13,580	1,749,944
Ibb	Ibb	2,480	6,430	1,959,313
Al-Jawf	Al-Jawf	...	...	157,096
Al-Maḥwīt	Al-Maḥwīt	830	2,160	403,465
Maʾrib	Maʾrib	15,400	39,890	167,388
Saʿdah	Saʿdah	4,950	12,810	486,059
Ṣanʿāʾ	Ṣanʿāʾ	7,840	20,310	1,910,286
Taʿizz	Taʿizz	4,020	10,420	2,205,947
Southern Yemen				
Abyān	Zinjibār	8,297	21,489	414,543
ʿAdan	Aden	2,695	6,980	562,162
Ḥaḍramawt	Al-Mukallā	59,991	155,376	870,025
Lahij	Lahij	4,928	12,766	634,652
Al-Mahrah	Al-Ghaydah	25,618	66,350	112,512
Shabwah	ʿAtāq	28,536	73,908	377,080
TOTAL		182,278[2, 3]	472,099[2]	14,832,673

Demography

Population (1998): 16,388,000.
Density (1998)[4]: persons per sq mi 76.5, persons per sq km 29.5.
Urban-rural (1994): urban 23.5%; rural 76.5%.
Sex distribution (1994): male 51.23%; female 48.77%.
Age breakdown (1994): under 15, 51.3%; 15–29, 22.9%; 30–44, 12.8%; 45–59, 7.7%; 60–74, 4.0%; 75 and over, 1.3%.
Population projection: (2000) 17,521,000; (2010) 24,794,000.
Doubling time: 21 years.
Ethnic composition (1986): predominantly Arab.
Religious affiliation (1980): Muslim 99.9%, of which Sunnī 53.0%, Shīʿī 46.9%; other 0.1%.
Major cities (1995): Ṣanʿāʾ 972,000; Aden 562,000; Taʿizz 290,107[5]; Al-Ḥudaydah 246,068[5]; Al-Mukallā 59,100[6].

Vital statistics

Birth rate per 1,000 population (1994): 45.1 (world avg. 25.0).
Death rate per 1,000 population (1994): 11.8 (world avg. 9.3).
Natural increase rate per 1,000 population (1994): 33.3 (world avg. 15.7).
Total fertility rate (avg. births per childbearing woman; 1994): 7.4.
Life expectancy at birth (1994): male 55.9 years; female 59.1 years.
Major causes of death per 100,000 population: n.a.; however, infant, child, and maternal mortality were very high (130, 190, and 100 per 1,000 live births, respectively).

National economy

Budget (1995). Revenue: YRls 87,951,000,000 (current revenue 75.7%, of which state property revenue 26.9%, international trade 18.4%, taxes on income and profits 15.6%; development revenue 19.7%; loans and grants 4.7%). Expenditures: YRls 124,140,409,000 (defense 25.2%; education 17.6%; public order and safety 8.1%; health 4.7%).
Production (metric tons except as noted). Agriculture, forestry, fishing (1997): sorghum 450,000, tomatoes 225,000, potatoes 185,000, wheat 170,000, grapes 153,000, watermelons 95,000, bananas 79,000, onions 68,000, papayas 57,500, millet 56,000; livestock (number of live animals) 4,000,000 sheep, 3,600,000 goats, 1,190,000 cattle, 500,000 asses, 180,000 camels, 3,000 horses, 21,900,000 chickens; roundwood (1995) 324,000 cu m; fish catch (1994) 86,811. Mining and quarrying (1994): salt 280,000; gypsum 80,000. Manufacturing (value of production in YRls '000,000; 1995): food, beverages, and tobacco 41,733.2; chemicals and chemical products 13,654.3; nonmetallic mineral products 7,539.6; paper products 2,601.8; basic metal industries 2,182.8; clothing, textiles, and leather 1,171.3; wood products 373.1. Construction: n.a. Energy production (consumption): electricity (kW-hr; 1994) 1,958,000,000 (1,958,000,000); coal, none (n.a.); crude petroleum (barrels; 1996) 135,050,000 ([1994] 25,945,000); petroleum products (metric tons; 1994) 3,330,000 (3,100,000).
Population economically active (1994): total 3,320,950; activity rate of total population 24.4% (participation rates: age 15 and over, 45.8%; female 18.2%; unemployed c. 50%).

Price index (1990 = 100)							
	1991	1992	1993	1994	1995	1996	1997
Consumer price index	136	176	236	344	537	699	737

Gross national product (1996): U.S.$6,016,000,000 (U.S.$380 per capita).

Structure of gross domestic product and labour force				
	1996		1986	
	in value Y Rls '000,000[7]	% of total value	labour force	% of labour force
Agriculture	132,945	23.9	1,151,348	56.3
Mining	91,941	16.6	11,771	0.6
Manufacturing	56,778	10.2	94,913	4.6
Public utilities	11,488	2.1	160,952	7.9
Construction	20,647	3.7	32,852	1.6
Transp. and commun.	39,254	7.1	107,611	5.3
Trade	79,724	14.4	248,979	12.2
Finance, real estate	31,306	5.6	8,757	0.4
Pub. admin., defense	79,218	14.3	226,054	11.1
Services	12,515	2.2	...	...
Other	−475[8]	−0.1[8]	...	...
TOTAL	555,341	100.0	2,043,237	100.0

Household income and expenditure. Average household size (1994) 6.7.
Tourism (1995): receipts U.S.$38,000,000; expenditures U.S.$76,000,000.
Public debt (external, outstanding; 1996): U.S.$5,622,000,000.
Land use (1994): forest 3.8%; pasture 30.4%; agriculture 2.9%; other 62.9%.

Foreign trade[9]

Balance of trade						
	1990	1991	1992	1993	1994	1995
U.S.$'000,000	−901.2	−1,517.3	−1,506.9	−1,508.7	−623.8	+242.8
% of total	38.8%	60.0%	77.4%	66.9%	25.1%	7.3%

Imports (1995): U.S.$1,537,800,000 (machinery and transport equipment 23.1%, basic manufactured goods 23.0%, food and live animals 22.1%, chemical products 8.2%, mineral fuels 7.9%, beverages and tobacco 2.1%). *Major import sources:* Arab countries 32.8%, of which Economic and Social Commission for Western Asia (ESCWA) countries 30.6%; Asia 28.1%, of which Japan 4.0%, India 1.6%; EC 23.2%; the Americas 11.6%, of which U.S. 7.7%.
Exports (1995): U.S.$1,780,600,000 (mineral fuels 95.3%, food and live animals 2.5%, crude minerals 1.2%). *Major export destinations:* Asia 85.4%, of which Japan 12.7%, India 0.1%; Arab countries 9.8%, of which ESCWA countries 9.1%; Africa 3.3%; EC 0.6%; the Americas 0.3%.

Transport and communications

Transport. Railroads: none. Roads (1995): total length 64,605 km (paved 7.9%). Vehicles (1995): passenger cars 229,084; trucks and buses 282,615. Merchant marine (1992): vessels (100 gross tons and over) 40; deadweight tonnage 13,653. Air transport (1994): passenger-km 1,183,000,000; metric ton-km cargo 119,000,000; airports (1997) with scheduled flights 11.

Communications				units per 1,000 persons
Medium	**date**	**unit**	**number**	
Daily newspapers	1994	circulation	230,000	16
Radio	1995	receivers	665,000	43
Television	1995	receivers	100,000	6.5
Telephones	1995	main lines	187,000	12
Cellular telephones	1995	subscribers	8,300	0.5
Facsimile machines	1995	units	2,000	0.1

Education and health

Educational attainment (1986)[10]. Percentage of population age 10 and over having: no formal schooling 74.2%; reading and writing ability 19.8%; primary education 4.0%; secondary education 0.6%; higher 0.6%; not specified 0.8%. *Literacy* (1994): percentage of total population age 15 and over literate 43.2%; males literate 68.6%; females literate 23.1%.

Education (1994–95)	schools	teachers	students	student/ teacher ratio
Primary (age 7–12)	11,013[11]	78,646[12]	2,493,017[12]	31.7[12]
Secondary (age 13–18)[12]	1,224	11,130	232,506	20.9
Voc., teacher tr.[12]	125	369	15,074	40.9
Higher[12]	2	1,991	90,826	45.6

Health (1995): physicians 3,220 (1 per 4,530 persons); hospital beds 9,169 (1 per 1,582 persons); infant mortality rate per 1,000 live births (1994) 80.9.
Food (1995): daily per capita caloric intake 2,025 (vegetable products 94%, animal products 6%); 84% of FAO recommended minimum requirement.

Military

Total active duty personnel (1997): 66,300 (army 92.0%, navy 2.7%, air force 5.3%). *Military expenditure as percentage of GNP* (1993): 15.7% (world 5.3%); per capita expenditure U.S.$100.

---

[1]Presidential Council assisting the President was abolished by a constitutional amendment of September 1994. [2]Yemeni territorial claims with regard to alignment of the long-undemarcated eastern boundary with Saudi Arabia (which increased Yemen's claimed total area to 214,300 sq mi [555,000 sq km]) were under negotiation with Saudi Arabia in 1996. [3]Detail does not add to total given because of rounding. [4]Based on the higher total area estimate of 214,300 sq mi (555,000 sq km). [5]1993. [6]1984. [7]In purchasers' value at current prices. [8]Includes import duties of 18.5 million Yemeni Rials less imputed bank service charges. [9]Imports are c.i.f. [10]Yemen Arab Republic only. [11]1993–94. [12]Public schools only, which comprise the vast majority of schools in Yemen.

Internet resources for further information:
• The Yemen Times http://www.yementimes.com
• Embassy of Yemen http://www.nusacc.org/yemen/

Yugoslavia

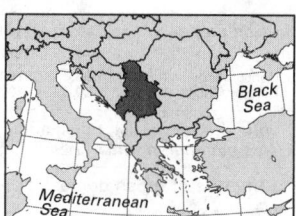

Official name: Savezna Republika Jugoslavija (Federal Republic of Yogoslavia).
Form of government: federal multiparty republic with two legislative houses (Chamber of Republics [40]; Chamber of Citizens [138]).
Chief of state: Federal President.
Head of government: Prime Minister.
Capital: Belgrade.
Official language: Serbian (Serbo-Croatian.
Official religion[1]: none.
Monetary unit[2]: 1 Yugoslav new dinar (second) = 100 paras; valuation (Sept. 25, 1998) 1 U.S.$ = 10.16 Yugoslav new dinars; 1 £ = 17.30 Yugoslav new dinars.

Area and population

Republics	Capitals	area sq mi	area sq km	population 1996 estimate
Montenegro	Podgorica	5,333	13,812	640,000
Serbia	Belgrade	21,609	55,968	5,800,000
Autonomous provinces[3]				
Kosovo and Metohia	Priština	4,203	10,887	2,151,000
Vojvodina	Novi Sad	8,304	21,506	1,983,000
TOTAL		39,449	102,173	10,574,000

Demography

Population (1998): 10,664,000.
Density (1998): persons per sq mi 270.3, persons per sq km 104.4.
Urban-rural (1991): urban 51.2%; rural 48.8%.
Sex distribution (1996): male 49.53%; female 50.47%.
Age breakdown (1991): under 15, 22.8%; 15–29, 21.6%; 30–44, 21.7%; 45–59, 17.1%; 60–74, 12.2%; 75 and over, 3.5%; unknown, 1.1%.
Population projection: (2000) 10,799,000; (2010) 11,171,000.
Doubling time: not applicable; doubling time exceeds 100 years.
Ethnic composition (1991): Serb 62.6%; Albanian 16.5%; Montenegrin 5.0%; multi-ethnic 3.4%; Hungarian 3.3%; Muslim 3.2%; Romany (Gypsy) 1.4%; Croat 1.1%; other 3.5%.
Religious affiliation (1995): Serbian Orthodox 62.6%; Muslim 19.0%; Roman Catholic 5.8%; other, mostly nonreligious 12.6%.
Major cities (1991): Belgrade 1,168,454; Novi Sad 179,626; Niš 175,391; Priština 155,499; Kragujevac 147,305; Podgorica 117,875.

Vital statistics

Birth rate per 1,000 population (1996): 12.9 (world avg. 25.0).
Death rate per 1,000 population (1996): 10.5 (world avg. 9.3).
Natural increase rate per 1,000 population (1996): 2.4 (world avg. 15.7).
Total fertility rate (avg. births per childbearing woman; 1995): 1.9.
Marriage rate per 1,000 population (1996): 5.4.
Divorce rate per 1,000 population (1996): 0.7.
Life expectancy at birth (1995): male 69.9 years; female 74.7 years.
Major causes of death per 100,000 population (1995): diseases of the circulatory system 573.6; malignant neoplasms (cancers) 167.6; accidents, violence, and poisoning 42.2; diseases of the respiratory system 40.9.

National economy

Budget (1997). Revenue: 28,745,000,000 Yugoslav new dinars (social security tax 39.1%, turnover tax 16.6%, income tax 16.5%). Expenditure: 28,745,000,000 Yugoslav new dinars (social security 39.1%, current transfers and other 60.9%).
Production (metric tons except as noted). Agriculture, forestry, fishing (1996): corn (maize) 5,367,000, sugar beets 2,418,000, wheat 1,507,000, grapes 433,000, sunflower seeds 390,000; livestock (number of live animals) 4,446,000 pigs, 2,656,000 sheep, 1,926,000 cattle, 26,457,000 poultry; roundwood 3,503,000 cu m; fish catch 7,461. Mining and quarrying: copper ore 20,206,000; lead-zinc ore 856,000; magnesite 89,000; aluminum and ingots 37,000; salt 21,646; asbestos ore 18,000; refined silver 69,000 kg. Manufacturing: wheat flour 798,000; crude steel 679,000; sulfuric acid 231,000; nitric acid 229,000; electrolytic copper 104,000; canned fruit 42,300; refined lead 30,000; welded pipes 25,000; rolled copper 16,800; medicines 14,600. Construction (residential units constructed; 1995): 11,847. Energy production (consumption): electricity (kW-hr; 1994) 35,328,000,000 (35,328,000,000); coal (metric tons; 1994) 38,351,000 (38,401,000); crude petroleum (barrels; 1994) 7,997,000 (10,222,000); petroleum products (metric tons; 1994) 781,000 (881,000); natural gas (cu m; 1994) 787,222,000 (1,630,200,000).
Population economically active (1996): total 3,232,000; activity rate 30.4% (1995; participation rates: over age 15, 59.0%; female 43.7%; (1996) unemployed 7.8%).

Price and earnings indexes (1991 = 100)

	1991	1992[4]	1993	1994	1995	1996
Consumer price index	100.0	9,026	222	103	179	192
Annual earnings index	100.0	151	211	158	205	187

Household income and expenditure. Average household size (1993) 3.9; income per household (1996) 20,073 Yugoslav new dinars (U.S.$3,515); sources of income (1996): wages and salaries 43.0%, pensions 15.7%, self-employment 13.5%, other 21.1%; expenditure (1996): food 47.1%, fuel and light 11.0%, beverages and tobacco 7.9%, clothing and footwear 6.5%, transportation and communications 5.3%, health care 4.7%, housing 2.7%.
Gross national product (1996): U.S.$20,039,000,000 (U.S.$1,900 per capita).

Structure of gross material product and labour force

	1996 in value '000,000 Yugoslav new dinars	% of total value	labour force	% of labour force
Agriculture	8,495.7	22.3	104,000	3.2
Mining	} 14,806.3	38.9	848,000	26.2
Manufacturing				
Construction	2,124.3	5.6	130,000	4.0
Public utilities	498.6	1.3	55,000	1.7
Transp. and commun.	3,045.4	8.0	142,000	4.4
Trade	5,421.2	14.2	469,000	14.5
Finance	...	...	...	...
Pub. admin., defense	} 2,045.5	5.4	665,000	20.6
Services				
Other	1,664.5	4.4	819,000[5]	25.3[5]
TOTAL	38,101.5[6]	100.0[6]	3,232,000	100.0[6]

Tourism (1994): receipts from visitors U.S.$31,000,000; expenditures, n.a.
Land use (1994): forested 17.3%; meadows and pastures 20.7%; agricultural and under permanent cultivation 40.0%; other 22.0%.

Foreign trade

Balance of trade (current prices)

	1987	1988	1988	1990	1991	1992
Din '000,000[7]	−1,431	−1,027	−1,716	−2,647	−1,356	−2,105
% of total	8.9%	6.3%	9.3%	12.3%	8.0%	20.8%

Imports (1996): Din 20,395,000,000 (manufactured goods 19.8%, machinery and transport equipment 19.4%, chemicals 14.3%, mineral fuels and lubricants 13.9%, food and live animals 12.2%). *Major import sources:* Germany 12.8%; Italy 10.6%; Russia 5.5%; Macedonia 5.2%.
Exports (1996): Din 9,156,000,000 (manufactured goods 33.1%, food and live animals 22.0%, machinery and transport equipment 12.2%, chemicals 9.1%). *Major export destinations:* Macedonia 11.5%; Russia 8.5%; Germany 8.0%; Greece 5.1%; Switzerland 4.5%.

Transport and communications

Transport. Railroads (1996): length 4,031 km; (1996) passenger-km 1,830,000,-000; metric ton-km cargo 2,062,000,000. Roads (1996): total length 49,620 km (paved 58.4%). Vehicles (1994): passenger cars 1,400,000; trucks and buses 132,000. Merchant marine (1992): fishing vessels 12. Air transport (1996): passenger-mi 598,000,000, passenger-km 963,000,000; short ton-mi cargo 3,371,000,000, metric ton-km cargo 4,921,000,000; airports (1997) 4.

Communications

Medium	date	unit	number	units per 1,000 persons
Daily newspapers	1995	circulation	1,363,000	256
Radio	1996	receivers	630,000	118
Television	1995	receivers	290,000	27
Telephones	1995	main lines	155,000	14
Facsimile machines	1995	units	10,000	0.9
Personal computers	1995	units	220,000	41

Education and health

Educational attainment (1991). Percentage of population age 15 and over having: less than full primary education 33.5%; primary 25.0%; secondary 32.2%; postsecondary and higher 9.3%. *Literacy* (1991): total population age 10 and over literate 93.0%; males literate 97.2%; females literate 88.9%.

Education (1995–96)

	schools	teachers	students	student/ teacher ratio
Primary (age 7–14)	4,441	51,728	914,532	17.7
Secondary (age 15–18)	570	26,954	352,346	13.1
Higher	93	10,544	131,689	12.5

Health (1995): physicians 21,313 (1 per 495 persons); hospital beds 56,107 (1 per 188 persons); infant mortality rate per 1,000 live births (1996) 14.3.
Food (1990)[8]: daily per capita caloric intake 3,545 (1988–90; vegetable products 93%, animal products 7%); 140% of FAO recommended minimum.

Military

Total active duty personnel (1997): 114,200 (army 78.8%, air force 14.6%, navy 6.6%). *Military expenditure as percentage of government expenditure* (1991): 3.9% (world 2.8%); per capita expenditure U.S.$167.

[1]Government gives "preferential treatment" to the Serbian Orthodox Church according to the U.S. Department of State, *Country Reports on Human Rights Practices for 1996.* [2]The Dinar, which had been fixed at 3.3 to the Deutsche Mark since November 1995, was set at a new rate of 6.0 on April 1, 1998. [3]The autonomous provinces are administratively part of the Republic of Serbia. [4]In new dinars after extreme hyperinflation. [5]Includes 819,000 unemployed. [6]Detail does not add to total given because of rounding. [7]In new dinars before extreme hyperinflation. [8]Data refer to Yugoslavia as constituted prior to 1991.

Internet resources for further information:
• **Federal Statistical Office of Yugoslavia** http://www.szs.sv.gov.yu/homee.htm
• **Federal Republic of Yugoslavia Official Web Site** http://www.gov.yu

Zambia

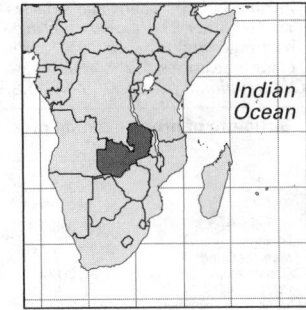

Official name: Republic of Zambia.
Form of government: multiparty republic with one legislative house (National Assembly [156[1]]).
Head of state and government: President.
Capital: Lusaka.
Official language: English.
Official religion: none[2].
Monetary unit: 1 Zambian kwacha (K) = 100 ngwee; valuation (Sept. 25, 1998) 1 U.S.$ = K 2,020; 1 £ = K 3,439.

Area and population

Provinces	Capitals	area sq mi	area sq km	population 1990 census
Central	Kabwe	36,446	94,395	725,611
Copperbelt	Ndola	12,096	31,328	1,579,542
Eastern	Chipata	26,682	69,106	973,818
Luapula	Mansa	19,524	50,567	526,705
Lusaka	Lusaka	8,454	21,896	1,207,980
North-Western	Solwezi	48,582	125,827	383,146
Northern	Kasama	57,076	147,826	867,795
Southern	Livingstone	32,928	85,283	946,353
Western	Mongu	48,798	126,386	607,497
TOTAL		290,586	752,614	7,818,447

Demography

Population (1998): 9,461,000.
Density (1998): persons per sq mi 32.6, persons per sq km 12.6.
Urban-rural (1995): urban 43.1%; rural 56.9%.
Sex distribution (1997): male 49.56%; female 50.44%.
Age breakdown (1997): under 15, 49.4%; 15–29, 28.0%; 30–44, 12.6%; 45–59, 6.2%; 60–74, 3.1%; 75 and over, 0.7%.
Population projection: (2000) 9,872,000; (2010) 12,150,000.
Doubling time: 24 years.
Ethnolinguistic composition (1990): Bemba peoples 39.7%; Maravi (Nyanja) peoples 20.1%; Tonga peoples 14.8%; North-Western peoples 8.8%; Barotze peoples 7.5%; Tumbuka peoples 3.7%; Mambwe peoples 3.4%; other 2.0%.
Religious affiliation (1995): Christian 47.8%, of which Protestant 22.9%, Roman Catholic 16.9%, African Christian 5.6%; traditional beliefs 27.0%; Muslim 1.0%; other 24.2%.
Major cities (1990): Lusaka 982,362 (metro. area, 1,400,000[3]); Ndola 376,311; Kitwe 348,571; Mufulira 175,025.

Vital statistics

Birth rate per 1,000 population (1997): 45.0 (world avg. 25.0); legitimate, n.a.; however, marriage is both early and universal, suggesting that legitimate births are a relatively high proportion of all births.
Death rate per 1,000 population (1997): 23.0 (world avg. 9.3).
Natural increase rate per 1,000 population (1997): 22.0 (world avg. 15.7).
Total fertility rate (avg. births per childbearing woman; 1997): 6.5.
Life expectancy at birth (1995): male 46.7 years; female 48.0 years.
Major causes of death per 100,000 population: n.a.; however, the major causes of morbidity are respiratory infections, diarrheal diseases, malaria, malnutrition, measles, AIDS, and accidents.

National economy

Budget (1997). Revenue: K 1,489,100,000,000 (1995; value-added and excise taxes 26.0%; customs duties 22.1%; grants 21.1%; personal income taxes 18.2%; company income taxes 5.2%). Expenditures: K 1,427,100,000,000 (1995; current expenditures 86.2%, of which debt service 34.7%, health 9.5%, education 9.4%, defense 5.3%; capital expenditures 13.8%).
Production (metric tons except as noted). Agriculture, forestry, fishing (1997): sugarcane 1,420,000, corn (maize) 963,000, cassava 540,000, fruits and vegetables 358,450 (of which onions 26,000, tomatoes 23,000, oranges 3,500), millet 61,000, wheat 60,000, sweet potatoes 52,000, peanuts (groundnuts) 50,000, seed cotton 35,000, sorghum 30,756, soybeans 29,292, sunflower seeds 7,983, tobacco 3,500; livestock (number of live animals) 2,600,000 cattle, 580,000 goats, 290,000 pigs, 65,000 sheep, 20,000,000 chickens; roundwood (1995) 14,613,000 cu m; fish catch (1995) 69,081. Mining and quarrying (1996)[4]: copper 307,071; zinc added 3,577; silver 8,676 kg; gold 2,926 troy oz. Manufacturing (value added in K '000,000; 1994): food products 39,765.1; beverages 36,596.5; chemicals and pharmaceuticals 32,141.5; textiles 15,358.5; tobacco 14,060.2; iron and steel, non-ferrous metals, and fabricated metal products 13,874.6. Construction (value added in K; 1995): 45,663,000,000. Energy production (consumption): electricity (kW-hr; 1994) 7,785,000,000 (6,305,000,000); coal (metric tons; 1994) 380,000 (375,000); crude petroleum (barrels; 1994) none (4,032,000); petroleum products (metric tons; 1994) 496,000 (435,000); natural gas, none (n.a.).
Household income and expenditure. Average household size (1990) 5.6; average annual income per household (1981) K 1,041 (U.S.$908); sources of income (1981): wages and salaries 94.0%, other 6.0%; expenditure (1977): food 37.7%, housing 11.0%, clothing 8.3%, transportation 4.3%, education 2.1%, health 1.0%.
Population economically active (1991): total 2,928,000; activity rate of total population 33.4% (participation rates: over age 10, 52.6%; female 29.6%; unemployed 17.4%[5]).

Price and earnings indexes (1990 = 100)

	1991	1992	1993	1994	1995	1996	1997
Consumer price index	193.2	519.8	1,497.4	2,300.4	3,086.8	4,515.2	5,635.4
Earnings index	120.6	110.9	74.8	...	...	...	...

Public debt (external, outstanding; 1996): U.S.$5,307,000,000.
Gross national product (1996): U.S.$3,363,000,000 (U.S.$360 per capita).

Structure of gross domestic product and labour force

	1995 in value K '000,000	1995 % of total value	1990 labour force	1990 % of labour force
Agriculture	581,164	16.5	1,872,000	68.9
Mining	318,438	9.0	56,800	2.1
Manufacturing	1,286,745	36.5	50,900	1.9
Construction	65,335	1.9	29,100	1.1
Public utilities	45,663	1.3	8,900	0.3
Transp. and commun.	172,969	4.9	25,600	0.9
Trade	338,513	9.6	30,700	1.1
Finance	251,767	7.1	24,200	0.9
Pub. admin., defense } Services	371,801	10.6	111,600	4.1
Other	89,328[6]	2.5[6]	506,100	18.6
TOTAL	3,521,723	100.0[7]	2,716,000[7]	100.0[7]

Tourism (1995): receipts from visitors U.S.$47,000,000; expenditures by nationals abroad U.S.$.56,000,000[8].
Land use (1994): forest 43.0%; pasture 40.4%; agriculture 7.1%; other 9.5%.

Foreign trade

Balance of trade (current prices)

	1991	1992	1993	1994	1995	1996
U.S.$'000,000	+420	−85	+202	+63	−88	+120
% of total	21.8%	5.3%	12.6%	3.0%	3.6%	6.3%

Imports (1996): U.S.$890,000,000 (1988; machinery and transport equipment 38.3%; basic manufactures 19.8%; chemicals 16.9%; mineral fuels, lubricants, and electricity 12.3%; food 3.8%). *Major import sources* (1995): South Africa 27.7%; United Kingdom 11.3%; Zimbabwe 9.2%; Japan 8.6%; United States 7.0%; India 4.9%; Germany 4.3%.
Exports (1996): U.S.$1,010,000,000 (1995; copper 70.6%; cobalt 11.3%). *Major export destinations* (1995): Japan 17.9%; Saudi Arabia 12.9%; Thailand 12.8%; Taiwan 7.2%; India 5.3%; Belgium-Luxembourg 5.0%; France 4.5%.

Transport and communications

Transport. Railroads (1995)[9]: length 791 mi, 1,273 km; passenger-mi 166,000,000, passenger-km 267,000,000; short ton-mi cargo 316,000,000, metric ton-km cargo 462,000,000. Roads (1995): total length 24,170 mi, 38,898 km (paved 18%). Vehicles (1995): passenger cars 142,000; trucks and buses 73,500. Merchant marine: vessels (100 gross tons and over) none. Air transport (1995)[10]: passenger arrivals and departures 294,000; metric ton cargo unloaded and loaded 6,900; airports (1997) with scheduled flights 4.

Communications

Medium	date	unit	number	units per 1,000 persons
Daily newspapers	1995	circulation	107,000	13.0
Radio	1995	receivers	800,000	99.0
Television	1995	receivers	260,000	32.0
Telephones	1995	main lines	76,800	8.2
Cellular telephones	1995	subscribers	1,800	0.2
Facsimile machines	1995	units	900	0.1

Education and health

Educational attainment (1993)[11]. Percentage of population age 14 and over having: no formal schooling 18.6%; some primary education 54.8%; some secondary 25.1%; higher 1.5%. *Literacy* (1995): population age 15 and over literate 3,890,000 (78.2%); males literate 2,060,000 (85.6%); females literate 1,830,000 (71.3%).

Education (1995)

	schools	teachers	students	student/teacher ratio
Primary (age 7–13)	3,883	38,528	1,506,349	39.1
Secondary (age 14–18)	480[12]	5,786[13]	199,081[14]	...
Voc., teacher tr.	26[12]	846[12]	7,982[15]	...
Higher	2[12]	481[14]	5,270[14]	11.0

Health: physicians (1993) 786 (1 per 10,917 persons); hospital beds (1989) 22,461 (1 per 349 persons); infant mortality rate per 1,000 live births (1997) 93.
Food (1995): daily per capita caloric intake 1,931 (vegetable products 95%, animal products 5%); 84% of FAO recommended minimum requirement.

Military

Total active duty personnel (1997): 21,600 (army 92.6%; navy, none; air force 7.4%). *Military expenditure as percentage of GNP* (1995): 2.8% (world 2.8%); per capita expenditure U.S.$11.

[1]Includes 5 nonelective seats. [2]Zambia was declared a Christian nation according to the preamble of a constitutional amendment in 1996. [3]1996 estimate; urban agglomeration. [4]The lead and zinc mines at Kabwe were closed in 1994. [5]1987. [6]Less imputed bank service charge. [7]Detail does not add to total given because of rounding. [8]1992. [9]Excludes Tanzania-Zambia Railway Authority (TAZARA) data. [10]Lusaka airport only. [11]Based on a sample survey of 35,502 persons. [12]1989. [13]1988. [14]1994. [15]1990.

Internet resources for further information:
• **Zambian National WWW Server (Zamnet)** http://www.zamnet.zm/

Zimbabwe

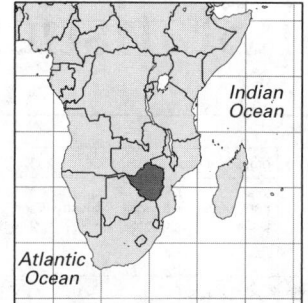

Official name: Republic of Zimbabwe.
Form of government: multiparty republic with one legislative house (House of Assembly [150[1]]).
Head of state and government: President.
Capital: Harare.
Official language: English.
Official religion: none.
Monetary unit: 1 Zimbabwe dollar (Z$) = 100 cents; valuation (Sept. 25, 1998) 1 U.S.$ = Z$31.75; 1 £ = Z$54.05.

Area and population

Provinces	Capitals	area sq mi	area sq km	population 1992 census[2]
Bulawayo	—	185	479	620,936
Harare	—	337	872	1,478,810
Manicaland	Mutare	14,077	36,459	1,537,676
Mashonaland Central	Bindura	10,945	28,347	857,318
Mashonaland East	Marondera	12,444	32,230	1,033,336
Mashonaland West	Chinhoyi	22,178	57,441	1,116,928
Masvingo	Masvingo	21,840	56,566	1,221,845
Matabeleland North	...	28,967	75,025	640,957
Matabeleland South	Gwanda	20,916	54,172	591,747
Midlands	Gweru	18,983	49,166	1,302,214
TOTAL		150,872	390,757	10,401,767

Demography

Population (1998): 11,044,000.
Density (1998): persons per sq mi 73.2, persons per sq km 28.3.
Urban-rural (1988): urban 26.4%; rural 73.6%.
Sex distribution (1992): male 48.80%; female 51.20%.
Age breakdown (1997): under 15, 43.6%; 15–29, 31.5%; 30–44, 13.8%; 45–59, 6.8%; 60–74, 3.4%; 75 and over, 0.9%.
Population projection: (2000) 11,272,000; (2010) 11,953,000.
Doubling time: 50 years.
Ethnolinguistic composition (1982): African 97.6%, of which Shona-speaking Bantu 70.8%, Ndebele-speaking Bantu 15.8%; European 2.0%; Asian 0.1%; other 0.3%.
Religious affiliation (1995): Christian 45.4%, of which Protestant (including Anglican) 23.5%, African indigenous 13.5%, Roman Catholic 7.0%; animist 40.5%; other 14.1%.
Major cities (1992): Harare 1,184,169; Bulawayo 620,936; Chitungwiza 274,035; Mutare 131,808; Gweru 124,735.

Vital statistics

Birth rate per 1,000 population (1997): 31.6 (world avg. 25.0).
Death rate per 1,000 population (1997): 19.0 (world avg. 9.3).
Natural increase rate per 1,000 population (1997): 12.6 (world avg. 15.7).
Total fertility rate (avg. births per childbearing woman; 1997): 3.9.
Life expectancy at birth (1992): male 58.0 years; female 62.0 years.
Major causes of death per 100,000 population (1990): infectious and parasitic diseases 64.7; accidents and poisoning 44.4; diseases of the circulatory system 40.9; diseases of the respiratory system 39.5; malignant neoplasms (cancers) 28.4; diseases of the digestive system 12.1; diseases of the nervous system 9.4; endocrine and metabolic disorders 4.9.

National economy

Budget (1996–97). Revenue: Z$23,350,355,000 (income tax 36.4%; sales tax 20.5%; customs duties 16.5%; excise tax 4.8%; revenue from investments and property 4.2%; stamp duties 1.0%). Expenditures: Z$30,173,080,000 (recurrent expenditures 85.8%, of which goods and services 46.4%, transfer payments 39.4%).
Population economically active (1992): total 3,600,000; activity rate of total population 34.6% (participation rates: over age 15, 63.4%; female 39.8%; unemployed 7.2%[3]).

Price and earnings indexes (1990 = 100)

	1991	1992	1993	1994	1995	1996	1997
Consumer price index	123.3	175.2	223.6	273.3	335.1	406.9	481.4
Earnings index	...	...	...	...	...	...	...

Production (metric tons except as noted). Agriculture, forestry, fishing (1996): sugarcane 2,826,000, corn (maize) 2,609,000, wheat 280,000, seed cotton 242,000, tobacco 209,000, cotton seed 153,000, cassava 150,000, vegetables (including melons) 147,000, millet 118,000, soybeans 110,000, sorghum 108,000, bananas 83,000, peanuts (groundnuts) 80,000; livestock (number of live animals) 5,436,000 cattle, 2,705,000 goats, 530,000 sheep, 267,000 pigs, 15,000,000 chickens; roundwood 8,102,000 cu m; fish catch (1993) 21,800 metric tons. Mining and quarrying (value of production in Z$; 1995): gold 2,567,100,000; nickel 738,900,000; asbestos 586,500,000; coal 557,100,000; chrome 197,400,000; copper 188,700,000. Manufacturing (value in Z$; 1993): foodstuffs 5,329,600,000; metals and metal products 4,107,100,000; chemicals and petroleum products 3,153,600,000; textiles 2,584,000,000; beverages and tobacco 2,523,400,000; clothing and footwear 1,394,600,000; transport equipment 1,387,500,000; paper, printing, and publishing 1,132,900,000; nonmetallic mineral products 740,200,000; wood and furniture 691,500,000; other manufactured goods 261,300,000. Construction (Z$; 1995): residential 794,054,000; commercial 248,794,000; industrial 136,358,000. Energy produc-

tion (consumption): electricity (kW-hr; 1994) 7,334,000,000 (9,050,000,000); coal (metric tons; 1994) 5,469,000 (5,614,000); crude petroleum, none (none); petroleum products (metric tons; 1994) none (1,051,000); natural gas, none (none).
Public debt (external, outstanding; 1996): U.S.$3,338,000,000.
Household income and expenditure. Average household size (1992) 4.8; income per household Z$1,689 (U.S.$2,628); sources of income: n.a.; expenditure (1990[4]): food, beverages, and tobacco 39.1%, housing 18.7%, clothing and footwear 9.8%, transportation 8.4%, education 7.6%, household durable goods 7.2%, health 2.8%, recreation 2.0%, other 4.4%.
Gross national product (1996): U.S.$6,815,000,000 (U.S.$610 per capita).

Structure of gross domestic product and labour force

	1994 in value Z$'000,000	1994 % of total value	1995 labour force[5]	1995 % of labour force[5]
Agriculture	4,004	10.1	334,000	26.9
Mining	2,739	6.9	59,000	4.7
Manufacturing	16,300	41.0	185,900	15.0
Construction	865	2.2	71,800	5.8
Public utilities	2,455	6.2	9,500	0.8
Transp. and commun.	2,125	5.3	50,900	4.1
Trade	4,357	10.9	100,600	8.2
Finance	1,973	5.0	21,100	1.7
Pub. admin., defense	902	2.3	406,800	32.8
Services	2,670	6.7		
Other	1,385[6]	3.4[6]	...	...
TOTAL	39,775	100.0	1,239,600	100.0

Tourism (1995): receipts U.S.$154,000,000; expenditures U.S.$106,000,000.

Foreign trade

Balance of trade (current prices)

	1990	1991	1992	1993	1994	1995
Z$'000,000	−296.8	−1,867.4	−2,475.6	−95.3	−522.8	−1,683.9
% of total	3.4%	14.4%	14.4%	0.5%	1.7%	4.4%

Imports (1996): Z$28,095,100,000 (machinery and transport equipment 38.7%, of which transport equipment 9.1%; manufactured goods 16.7%, of which textiles 2.6%, paper and paperboard 1.8%; fuels 10.4%, of which petroleum 9.7%). *Major import sources:* South Africa 38.3%; U.K. 7.9%; Japan 5.1%; U.S. 5.0%; Germany 4.9%; France 3.1%; Italy 2.5%; The Netherlands 1.8%.
Exports (1996)[7]: Z$24,209,300,000 (domestic exports 86.8%, of which tobacco 30.5%, gold sales 12.3%, ferroalloys 6.7%, nickel metal 3.2%, cotton 2.7%, asbestos 2.6%, cut flowers 1.4%, corn [maize] 1.2%). *Major export destinations:* U.K. 10.1%; South Africa 9.6%; Germany 7.9%; U.S. 6.7%; Japan 5.1%; Zambia 4.3%; Italy 4.3%; Botswana 4.0%; The Netherlands 3.8%.

Transport and communications

Transport. Railroads (1995): route length 1,714 mi, 2,759 km; passenger-mi 339,254,000, passenger-km 545,977,000; short ton-mi cargo 3,256,000, metric ton-km cargo 4,754,000. Roads (1995): total length 57,048 mi, 91,810 km (paved 19%). Vehicles (1995): passenger cars 492,000; trucks and buses 108,000. Merchant marine: none. Air transport (1995)[8]: passenger-mi 521,673,000, passenger-km 839,553,000; short ton-mi cargo 27,016,000, metric ton-km cargo 39,442,000; airports (1997) with scheduled flights 7.

Communications

Medium	date	unit	number	units per 1,000 persons
Daily newspapers	1995	circulation	192,000	17
Radio	1996	receivers	1,300,000	113
Television	1995	receivers	137,090	12
Telephones	1995	main lines	154,600	14
Facsimile machines	1995	units	10,000	0.9
Personal computers	1995	units	33,000	3.0

Education and health

Educational attainment (1986–87). Percentage of employed population age 15 and over having: no formal schooling 24.5%; primary 42.9%; secondary and tertiary 31.7%. *Literacy* (1995): percentage of total population age 15 and over literate 85.1%; males literate 90.4%; females literate 79.9%.

Education (1995)

	schools	teachers	students	student/teacher ratio
Primary (age 7–13)	4,633	63,475	2,655,564	41.8
Secondary (age 14–19)	1,535	27,320	711,094	26.0
Voc., teacher tr.[9]	25	1,479	27,431	18.5
Higher[10]	28[9]	3,581	46,492	13.0

Health: physicians (1993) 1,551 (1 per 6,909 persons); hospital beds (1996) 22,975 (1 per 501 persons); infant mortality rate (1997) 72.6.
Food (1995): daily per capita caloric intake 1,965 (vegetable products 92%, animal products 8%); 82% of FAO recommended minimum requirement.

Military

Total active duty personnel (1997): 39,000 (army 89.7%, air force 10.3%). *Military expenditure as percentage of GNP* (1995): 4.0% (world 2.8%); per capita expenditure U.S.$21.

---

[1]Includes 30 nonelective seats. [2]Preliminary results. [3]Does not take into consideration seasonal unemployment of communal workers; 1986–87. [4]Based on consumer price index. [5]Wage-earning workers only. [6]Less imputed bank service charges. [7]Excludes gold sales and reexports. [8]Air Zimbabwe only. [9]1992. [10]Includes postsecondary vocational and teacher training at the higher level.

Comparative National Statistics

World and regional summaries

region/bloc	area and population, 1998						gross national product, 1996						labour force, 1990		
	area		population			population projection, 2010	total ('000,000 U.S.$)	% agricul-ture	% industry	% ser-vices	growth rate, 1990–95	GNP per capita (U.S.$)	total ('000)	% male	% female
	square miles	square kilometres	total	per sq mi	per sq km										
World	52,432,420	135,799,290	5,898,075,000	112.5	43.4	6,810,084,000	29,584,168	5	33	62	1.3	5,610	2,353,806	63.8	36.2
Africa	11,716,640	30,346,090	755,919,000	64.5	24.9	988,065,000	489,179	18	33	49	–0.2	670	242,784	65.6	34.4
Central Africa	2,552,970	6,612,160	90,087,000	35.3	13.6	125,806,000	25,633	34	32	34	–5.2	310	26,428	64.7	35.3
East Africa	2,473,690	6,406,680	230,389,000	93.1	36.0	296,188,000	54,822	32	24	44	–0.3	240	85,082	58.8	41.2
North Africa	3,287,830	8,515,370	169,988,000	51.7	20.0	215,955,000	199,834	16	33	51	0.4	1,240	40,016	84.6	15.4
Southern Africa	1,032,300	2,673,660	48,961,000	47.4	18.3	54,635,000	142,750	5	39	56	–0.0	3,280	14,532	64.3	35.7
West Africa	2,369,850	6,138,220	216,494,000	91.4	35.3	295,481,000	66,140	37	23	40	0.4	310	76,726	63.8	36.2
Americas	16,243,910	42,071,480	794,888,000	48.9	18.9	910,340,000	9,823,314	3	27	69	1.3	12,560	293,723	66.5	33.5
Anglo-America[3]	8,301,330	21,500,350	301,064,000	36.3	14.0	333,174,000	8,006,510	2	26	72	1.2	27,110	135,438	58.7	41.3
Canada	3,849,670	9,970,610	30,677,000	8.0	3.1	35,065,000	569,899	3	32	66	0.6	19,020	13,360	60.2	39.8
United States	3,615,220	9,363,360	270,262,000	74.8	28.9	297,976,000	7,433,517	2	26	73	1.2	28,020	122,005	58.6	41.4
Latin America	7,942,580	20,571,130	493,824,000	62.2	24.0	577,166,000	1,816,804	10	33	57	2.0	3,730	158,285	73.1	26.9
Caribbean	90,750	234,980	35,840,000	394.9	152.5	40,306,000	90,559	8	35	57	3.0	2,490	13,813	66.9	33.1
Central America	202,240	523,820	33,771,000	167.0	64.5	43,186,000	49,533	19	21	60	1.9	1,4700	9,520	78.5	21.5
Mexico	756,070	1,958,200	95,830,000	126.7	48.9	112,891,000	341,718	6	24	70	–0.3	3,670	30,487	72.9	27.1
South America	6,893,520	17,854,130	328,383,000	47.6	18.4	380,783,000	1,334,994	11	35	54	2.6	4,120	104,465	73.6	26.4
Andean Group	2,110,470	5,466,100	120,682,000	57.2	22.1	146,131,000	300,071	9	35	56	3.0	2,550	34,715	75.6	24.4
Brazil	3,300,170	8,547,400	161,766,000	49.0	18.9	181,918,000	709,591	14	37	49	2.0	4,400	55,026	72.6	27.4
Other South America	1,482,880	3,840,630	45,935,000	31.0	12.0	52,734,000	325,332	7	31	63	3.7	7,260	14,724	72.4	27.6
Asia	12,319,360	31,906,780	3,589,233,000	291.3	112.5	4,143,646,000	9,068,770	8	39	52	2.8	2,610	1,464,452	64.5	35.5
Eastern Asia	4,546,910	11,776,540	1,468,405,000	322.9	124.7	1,578,859,000	7,018,717	5	41	54	2.7	4,900	775,590	57.4	42.6
China	3,696,100	9,572,900	1,242,980,000	336.3	129.8	1,341,848,000	906,079	21	48	31	11.0	750	669,693	56.7	43.3
Japan	145,880	377,820	126,398,000	866.5	334.5	127,657,000	5,149,185	2	40	58	1.2	40,940	62,202	62.1	37.9
South Korea	38,330	99,270	46,451,000	1,211.9	467.9	50,317,000	483,130	7	44	49	6.2	10,610	18,664	66.2	33.8
Other Eastern Asia	666,600	1,726,550	52,576,000	78.9	30.5	59,037,000	480,323	3	30	67	4.5	9,210	25,031	58.8	41.2
South Asia	1,939,850	5,021,590	1,319,854,000	680.7	262.8	1,596,894,000	476,953	29	28	44	3.3	380	411,136	77.4	22.6
India	1,222,240	3,165,600	984,004,000	805.1	310.8	1,182,171,000	357,759	29	29	41	3.8	380	322,944	74.8	25.2
Pakistan	307,370	796,100	141,900,000	461.7	172.8	176,400,000	63,567	23	23	54	1.1	480	33,698	87.5	12.5
Other South Asia	409,240	1,059,890	193,950,000	473.9	183.0	238,323,000	55,627	31	22	47	2.9	300	54,494	86.2	13.8
Southeast Asia	1,742,440	4,512,870	502,404,000	288.3	111.3	595,532,000	810,723	21	35	45	5.5	1,660	189,297	63.0	37.0
ASEAN	1,319,540	3,417,570	439,087,000	332.8	128.5	518,358,000	686,406	13	39	47	5.5	1,600	164,976	63.2	36.8
Non-ASEAN	422,900	1,095,300	63,317,000	149.7	57.8	77,174,000	124,317	60	10	30	3.3	2,050	24,321	62.2	37.8
Southwest Asia	4,091,160	10,595,780	298,570,000	73.0	28.2	372,361,000	762,377	13	37	50	1.0	2,620	88,429	69.4	30.6
Central Asia	1,545,790	4,003,400	55,422,000	35.9	13.8	63,470,000	54,472	21	32	48	–9.4	1,000	20,728	54.8	45.2
Gulf Cooperation Council	1,031,350	2,671,050	28,972,000	28.1	10.8	42,302,000	241,212	4	51	45	3.1	8,910	6,511	91.7	8.3
Iran	635,240	1,645,260	61,531,000	96.9	37.4	73,130,000	131,328	25	35	41	4.6	2,150	15,253	82.0	18.0
Other Southwest Asia	878,780	2,276,070	152,645,000	173.7	67.1	193,459,000	335,365	13	29	57	0.8	2,260	45,936	68.7	31.3
Europe	8,868,640	22,969,860	728,198,000	82.1	31.7	733,543,000	9,759,087	3	32	65	0.2	13,400	340,666	57.1	42.9
Eastern Europe	7,437,160	19,262,290	340,551,000	45.8	17.7	337,085,000	805,847	9	37	54	–6.2	2,350	171,080	50.6	49.4
Russia	6,592,800	17,075,400	146,861,000	22.3	8.6	143,918,000	356,030	7	36	57	–9.2	2,410	72,286	47.6	52.4
Ukraine	233,100	603,700	50,302,000	215.8	83.3	47,601,000	60,904	18	42	41	–13.5	1,200	25,401	48.0	52.0
Other Eastern Europe	611,260	1,583,190	143,338,000	234.6	90.6	145,566,000	388,913	10	37	53	–0.3	2,700	73,393	54.4	45.6
Western Europe	1,431,480	3,707,580	387,647,000	270.8	104.6	396,458,000	8,953,240	3	31	66	0.9	23,220	169,586	63.6	36.4
European Union (EU)	1,249,620	3,236,510	375,001,000	300.1	115.9	383,194,000	8,468,991	3	31	66	1.0	22,700	163,771	63.6	36.4
France	210,030	543,970	58,841,000	280.2	108.2	61,757,000	1,533,619	3	30	68	0.7	26,270	25,404	60.1	39.9
Germany	137,850	357,020	82,148,000	595.9	230.1	84,346,000	2,364,632	1	31	69	0.7	28,870	38,981	60.7	39.3
Italy	116,340	301,320	57,650,000	495.5	191.3	56,484,000	1,140,484	3	32	66	0.9	19,880	23,339	68.1	31.9
Spain	195,360	505,990	39,371,000	201.5	77.8	39,917,000	563,249	3	32	65	1.0	14,350	14,456	75.5	24.5
United Kingdom	94,250	244,110	59,126,000	627.3	242.2	60,800,000	1,152,136	2	32	66	1.5	19,600	27,766	61.4	38.6
Other EU	495,790	1,284,100	77,865,000	157.1	60.6	79,890,000	1,714,871	4	32	64	1.2	22,150	33,825	63.4	36.6
Non-EU	181,860	471,060	12,646,000	69.5	26.8	13,264,000	484,249	3	33	64	0.4	38,620	5,815	61.9	38.1
Oceania	3,283,860	8,505,080	29,837,000	9.1	3.5	34,490,000	443,819	4	29	66	2.6	15,310	12,181	63.0	37.0
Australia	2,966,200	7,682,300	18,725,000	6.3	2.4	21,018,000	367,802	3	30	67	2.7	20,090	7,963	61.9	38.1
Pacific Ocean Islands	317,670	822,780	11,112,000	35.0	13.5	13,472,000	76,017	10	26	64	1.9	7,110	4,218	65.0	35.0

[1]Refers only to the outstanding long-term external public and publicly guaranteed debt of the 136 countries that report under the World Bank's Debtor Reporting System (DRS).   [2]World total contains

Africa

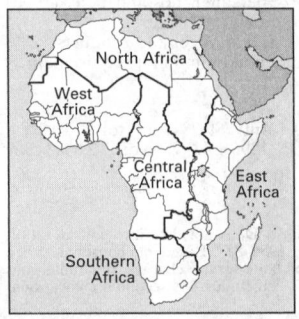

Americas

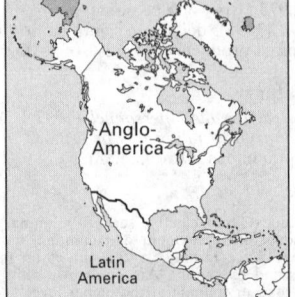

Asia

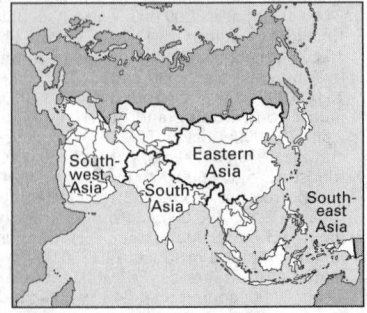

		economic indicators						social indicators (latest)								region/bloc
pop. per 1,000 ha of arable land, 1995	electricity consumption (kW-hr per capita), 1995	trade ('000,000 U.S.$), 1995			debt ('000,000 U.S.$), 1996[1]		life expectancy (years)		health			food (% FAO recommended minimum), 1995	literacy (%)		
		imports (c.i.f.)	exports[2] (f.o.b.)	balance[2]	total	% of GNP	male	female	pop. per doctor	infant mortality per 1,000 births	pop. having safe water (%)		male	female	
4,160	2,296	5,432,210	5,265,800[2]	−166,410[2]	1,332,228	24.0	64.1	68.4	710	56.4	67	116	83.7	71.0	World
4,040	509	136,690	119,120	−17,570	258,763	57.1	53.2	56.2	2,570	85.5	53	104	65.9	45.5	Africa
3,720	135	7,490	6,930	−560	37,412	146.0	50.4	53.6	12,820	91.9	31	86	77.7	56.4	Central Africa
5,110	138	20,930	16,820	−4,110	49,876	96.1	47.9	50.7	12,340	98.9	42	86	65.4	44.1	East Africa
4,350	684	52,340	46,890	−5,450	98,558	57.9	63.2	66.1	880	55.8	76	125	64.8	40.1	North Africa
2,840	3,992	30,830	26,390	−4,440	11,786	8.5	61.3	66.9	1,690	68.0	68	115	81.6	80.0	Southern Africa
3,510	127	25,110	22,080	−3,020	61,132	92.4	49.9	52.9	6,300	89.6	52	103	58.4	37.5	West Africa
2,070	6,053	1,317,370	1,240,170	−77,200	375,067	21.4	67.7	74.6	510	31.1	86	125	91.3	89.9	Americas
1,270	13,095	1,005,870	968,590	−37,280	—	—	72.8	79.1	370	7.4	91	134	96.1	95.7	Anglo-America[3]
650	17,047	187,040	171,440	−15,600	—	—	74.6	81.0	470	6.1	100	116	96.6	96.6	Canada
1,420	12,663	817,790	796,040	−21,740	—	—	72.6	78.9	370	7.5	90	136	95.7	95.3	United States
3,420	1,671	311,500	271,570	−39,920	375,067	21.4	64.7	71.7	660	39.8	82	118	87.8	85.6	Latin America
5,750	1,485	29,740	22,450	−7,290	10,245	37.3	68.5	72.9	480	48.9	73	104	83.8	83.0	Caribbean
4,660	608	33,030	31,810	−1,220	22,317	45.1	67.3	72.3	1,170	43.2	69	109	73.6	68.1	Central America
3,550	1,646	98,410	73,770	−24,640	93,438	27.3	69.5	75.5	620	31.0	87	135	91.8	87.4	Mexico
3,160	1,802	150,320	143,540	−6,780	249,067	18.7	62.5	70.4	670	41.9	83	115	88.4	87.0	South America
6,850	1,562	58,030	54,300	−3,720	85,244	28.4	67.9	73.3	870	31.8	82	107	92.6	88.7	Andean Group
2,910	1,954	58,910	53,940	−4,970	94,587	13.3	56.7	66.8	680	55.3	92	119	83.3	83.2	Brazil
1,510	1,877	33,390	35,300	+1,910	69,236	21.4	69.2	76.0	410	25.2	56	127	96.0	95.7	Other South America
7,320	1,095	1,600,280	1,478,430	−121,850	483,471	19.2	64.5	67.6	970	55.8	60	114	81.2	63.7	Asia
14,060	1,702	943,290	872,880	−70,410	102,734	11.3	69.1	73.1	620	34.5	53	117	91.4	77.0	Eastern Asia
13,100	839	138,820	157,600	+18,770	102,260	11.3	68.2	71.7	630	38.0	46	116	89.9	72.7	China
31,540	7,915	349,510	316,590	−32,920	—	—	77.0	83.6	540	4.2	95	123	100.0	100.0	Japan
25,100	4,567	150,370	129,140	−21,230	—	—	68.8	76.0	780	10.0	89	139	99.3	96.7	South Korea
13,750	4,153	304,590	269,550	−35,030	474	52.5	70.8	76.6	510	17.2	97	108	95.9	91.4	Other Eastern Asia
6,020	398	65,410	60,710	−4,700	122,919	26.1	59.3	60.5	2,330	74.3	63	106	62.4	35.5	South Asia
5,640	448	40,090	37,770	−2,330	74,406	20.8	59.1	60.3	2,170	71.1	63	108	65.5	37.7	India
6,170	441	12,150	11,530	−620	23,694	37.3	62.9	65.1	1,860	75.0	60	107	50.0	24.4	Pakistan
8,960	104	13,170	11,420	−1,750	24,819	49.7	57.7	58.3	5,300	87.9	68	92	53.5	30.9	Other South Asia
7,800	573	380,630	354,670	−25,960	152,142	21.4	64.0	68.0	2,530	48.3	62	118	91.8	83.3	Southeast Asia
8,880	644	375,850	350,320	−25,520	143,129	24.4	65.0	69.2	2,480	41.0	66	117	92.6	84.9	ASEAN
4,200	71	4,790	4,350	−440	9,013	7.3	57.0	60.2	2,970	86.0	35	119	86.0	71.6	Non-ASEAN
2,780	2,062	210,950	190,170	−20,790	105,676	24.6	65.7	70.1	590	47.1	83	123	86.7	72.4	Southwest Asia
1,390	2,837	11,800	11,760	−40	5,772	10.6	63.5	71.1	300	35.0	80	...	98.8	96.1	Central Asia
6,690	6,352	85,180	76,800	−8,380	2,646	20.1	70.6	74.0	620	22.4	91	118	73.8	55.8	Gulf Cooperation Council
3,530	1,190	13,780	12,480	−1,300	15,917	12.1	66.1	68.7	1,600	52.7	89	123	78.4	65.8	Iran
3,400	1,415	100,190	89,130	−11,070	81,341	35.3	65.3	69.8	650	53.6	79	125	87.8	68.1	Other Southwest Asia
2,430	5,558	2,289,900	2,272,610	−17,290	212,887	26.3	68.7	77.0	290	10.5	99	125	99.0	97.5	Europe
1,550	4,440	220,220	223,490	+3,270	212,742	26.4	62.6	73.3	280	16.1	98	117	99.1	96.6	Eastern Europe
1,130	5,661	43,320	56,910	+13,590	100,463	28.2	58.0	71.5	240	18.0	...	114	99.5	96.8	Russia
1,550	3,694	24,240	16,210	−8,040	6,451	10.6	63.6	74.0	220	14.1	97	...	99.5	97.4	Ukraine
2,510	3,449	152,660	150,380	−2,280	105,828	27.2	66.8	74.9	380	15.3	99	121	98.7	96.1	Other Eastern Europe
4,960	6,561	2,069,680	2,049,120	−20,560	145	4.3	74.0	80.4	310	5.6	100	131	98.9	98.2	Western Europe
4,890	6,295	1,951,430	1,919,590	−31,840	—	—	73.9	80.4	310	5.6	100	131	98.8	98.1	European Union (EU)
3,180	7,282	275,970	269,070	−6,910	—	—	73.7	81.8	360	4.9	100	142	98.9	98.7	France
6,900	6,615	445,020	438,920	−6,100	—	—	73.0	79.5	300	5.6	100	123	100.0	100.0	Germany
7,070	4,867	207,000	187,110	−19,900	—	—	74.1	80.5	190	6.0	100	137	97.8	96.4	Italy
2,570	4,312	121,870	115,130	−6,740	—	—	74.9	81.8	240	5.6	99	136	98.1	95.1	Spain
9,890	6,016	283,590	271,920	−11,670	—	—	74.4	79.7	640	6.2	100	125	100.0	100.0	United Kingdom
4,630	7,503	617,990	637,450	+19,460	—	—	74.2	80.1	340	5.6	100	131	97.9	97.2	Other EU
8,810	14,651	118,240	129,530	+11,290	145	4.3	75.1	81.2	310	4.9	100	121	99.9	99.9	Non-EU
570	7,524	87,970	75,410	−12,550	2,040	25.6	71.8	76.9	470	23.5	85	116	96.3	94.0	Oceania
370	9,706	67,670	57,590	−10,080	—	—	75.4	81.1	400	5.7	95	115	99.5	99.5	Australia
5,150	3,887	20,300	17,820	−2,480	2,040	25.6	65.8	69.6	710	40.4	65	116	89.8	82.7	Pacific Ocean Islands

U.S.$80,060,000,000 undistributable by continent or region. ³Anglo-America includes Canada, the United States, Greenland, Bermuda, and St. Pierre and Miquelon.

Europe
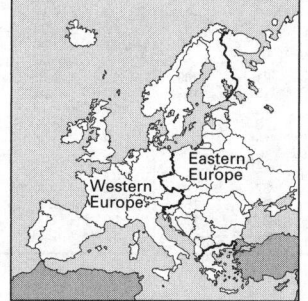

Eastern Europe

Oceania
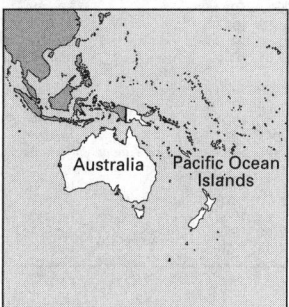

Government and international organizations

This table summarizes principal facts about the governments of the countries of the world, their branches and organs, the topmost layers of local government constituting each country's chief administrative subdivisions, and the participation of their central governments in the principal intergovernmental organizations of the world.

In this table "date of independence" may refer to a variety of circumstances. In the case of the newest countries, those that attained full independence after World War II, the date given is usually just what is implied by the heading—the date when the country, within its present borders, attained full sovereignty over both its internal and external affairs. In the case of longer established countries, the choice of a single date may be somewhat more complicated, and grounds for the use of several different dates often exist. The reader should refer to *Macropædia* and *Micropædia* articles on national histories and relevant historical acts. In cases of territorial annexation or dissolution, the date given here refers either to the final act of union of a state composed of smaller entities or to the final act of separation from a larger whole (*e.g.,* the separation of Bangladesh from Pakistan in 1971).

The date of the current, or last, constitution is in some ways a less complicated question, but governments sometimes do not, upon taking power, either adhere to existing constitutional forms or trouble to terminate the previous document and legitimize themselves by the installation of new constitutional forms. Often, however, the desire to legitimize extraconstitutional political activity by associating it with existing forms of long precedent leads to partial or incomplete modification, suspension, or abrogation of a constitution, so that the actual day-to-day conduct of government may be largely unrelated to the provisions of a constitution still theoretically in force. When a date in this column is given in italics, it refers to a document that has been suspended, abolished by extraconstitutional action, or modified extensively.

The characterizations adopted under "type of government" represent a compromise between the forms provided for by the national constitution and the more pragmatic language that a political scientist might adopt to describe these same systems. For an explanation of the application of these terms in the Britannica World Data, *see* the Glossary at page 533.

The positions denoted by the terms "chief of state" and "head of government" are usually those identified with those functions by the constitution. The duties of the chief of state may range from largely ceremonial responsibilities, with little or no authority over the day-to-day conduct of government, to complete executive authority as the effective head of government. In certain countries, an official of a political party or a revolutionary figure outside the constitutional structure may exercise the powers of both positions.

Membership in the legislative house(s) of each country as given here includes all elected or appointed members, as well as ex officio members (those who by virtue of some other office or title are members of the body), whether voting or nonvoting. The legislature of a country with a unicameral system is shown as the upper house in this table.

The number of administrative subdivisions for each country is listed down to the second level. A single country may, depending on its size, complexity, and historical antecedents, have as many as five levels of administrative subordination or it may have none at all. Each level of subordination may have several kinds of subdivisions.

Government and international organizations

country	date of independence[a]	date of current or last constitution[b]	type of government	executive branch[c] chief of state	head of government	legislative branch[d] upper house (members)	lower house (members)	admin. subdivisions first-order (number)	second-order (number)	seaward claims territorial (nautical miles)	fishing/economic (nautical miles)
Afghanistan	Aug. 19, 1919	—	Islamic emirate	——leader of the faithful[1]——		...	...	32	298	—	—
Albania	Nov. 28, 1912	Nov. 28, 1998	republic	president	prime minister	155	—	26	c. 200	12	2
Algeria	July 5, 1962	Dec. 7, 1996[4]	republic	president	prime minister	144	380	48	1,541	12	5
American Samoa		July 1, 1967	territory (U.S.)	U.S. president	governor	18	21	3	14	12	200
Andorra	Dec. 6, 1288	May 4, 1993	parl. coprincipality	[6]	head of govt.	28	—	7	...	—	—
Angola	Nov. 11, 1975	Aug. 27, 1992	republic	——president[7]——		220[8]	—	18	163	20	200
Antigua and Barbuda	Nov. 1, 1981	Nov. 1, 1981	constitutional monarchy	British monarch	prime minister	17[9]	17	30	—	12[10]	200[10]
Argentina	July 9, 1816	Aug. 24, 1994[11]	federal republic	——president[12]——		72	257	24	503	12	200
Armenia	Sept. 23, 1991	July 5, 1995[13]	republic	president	prime minister	190	—	11	...	—	—
Aruba		Jan. 1, 1986	overseas territory (Neth.)	Dutch monarch	[14]	21	—	...	...	12	200
Australia	Jan. 1, 1901	July 9, 1900	federal parl. state[16]	British monarch	prime minister	76	148	8	c. 900	12	200
Austria	Oct. 30, 1918	Oct. 1, 1920	federal state	president	chancellor	64	183	9	99	—	—
Azerbaijan	Aug. 30, 1991	Nov. 12, 1995[13]	federal republic	——president[7]——		124[17]	—	2	71	...	...
Bahamas, The	July 10, 1973	July 10, 1973	constitutional monarchy	British monarch	prime minister	16	40	...	21	12	200
Bahrain	Aug. 15, 1971	June 1973	monarchy (emirate)	emir	prime minister	40[19]	...	...	—	12	20
Bangladesh	March 26, 1971	Dec. 16, 1972	republic	president	prime minister	330	—	7	64	12	200
Barbados	Nov. 30, 1966	Nov. 30, 1966	constitutional monarchy	British monarch	prime minister	21	28	...	...	12	200
Belarus	Aug. 25, 1991	Nov. 27, 1996[21]	republic	——president[7]——		64[21]	110[21]	6	...	—	—
Belgium	Oct. 4, 1830	Feb. 17, 1994	fed. const. monarchy	monarch	prime minister	71[22]	150	23	589	12	20
Belize	Sept. 21, 1981	Sept. 21, 1981	constitutional monarchy	British monarch	prime minister	8	29	6	...	12[24]	200
Benin	Aug. 1, 1960	Dec. 2, 1990	republic	——president——		83	—	12	86	200	200
Bermuda	—	June 8, 1968	dependent territory (U.K.)	British monarch	[25]	11	40	11	—	12	200
Bhutan	March 24, 1910	—	[26]	——king[27]——		150	—	20	—	—	—
Bolivia	Aug. 6, 1825	Feb. 2, 1967	republic	——president——		27	130	9	112	—	—
Bosnia and Herzegovina	March 3, 1992	Dec. 14, 1995[28]	federal republic	[29]	[30]	15	42	2	135	...	...
Botswana	Sept. 30, 1966	Sept. 30, 1966	republic	——president——		15[19]	46	19	...	—	—
Brazil	Sept. 7, 1822	Oct. 5, 1988	federal republic	——president——		81	513	27	4,974	12	200
Brunei	Jan. 1, 1984	*Sept. 29, 1959*	monarchy (sultanate)	——sultan——		21[19]	—	4	...	12	200
Bulgaria	Oct. 5, 1908	July 12, 1991	republic	president	prime minister	240	—	9	255	12	200
Burkina Faso	Aug. 5, 1960	June 11, 1991	republic	president	prime minister	178[19]	111	30	109	—	—
Burundi	July 1, 1962	June 6, 1998[31]	republic[32]	——president[7]——		121	—	15	122	—	—
Cambodia	Nov. 9, 1953	Sept. 24, 1993	constitutional monarchy	king	prime minister	122	—	23	...	12	200
Cameroon	Jan. 1, 1960	Jan. 18, 1996	republic	president	prime minister	180	—	10	56	50	2
Canada	July 1, 1867	April 17, 1982	federal parl. state[16]	Canadian GG[33]	prime minister	104	301	12	...	12	200
Cape Verde	July 5, 1975	Sept. 25,1992	republic	president	prime minister	72	—	16	...	12[10]	200[10]
Central African Republic	Aug. 13, 1960	Jan. 14, 1995	republic	president	prime minister	109	—	17	69	—	—
Chad	Aug. 11, 1960	April 14, 1996	republic	president	prime minister	125	—	14	53	—	—
Chile	Sept. 18, 1810	March 11, 1981	republic	——president——		48	120	13	51	12	200
China	1523 BC	Dec. 4, 1982	people's republic	president	premier SC	2,979	—	31	334	12	2
Colombia	July 20, 1810	July 5, 1991	republic	——president——		102	161	26	1,011	12	200
Comoros	July 6, 1975	Sept. 13, 1997[34]	republic[32]	——president[7]——		—	—	...	...	12[10]	200[10]
Congo, Dem. Rep. of the	June 30, 1960	*April 9, 1994*	republic[32]	——president——		(738)	—	11	...	12	200
Congo, Rep. of the	Aug. 15, 1960	Nov. 3, 1997[35]	republic[32]	——president——		75	...	16	47	200	2
Costa Rica	Sept. 15, 1821	Nov. 9, 1949	republic	——president——		57	—	7	81	12	200
Côte d'Ivoire	Aug. 7, 1960	Oct. 31, 1960	republic	president	prime minister	175	—	16	58	12	200
Croatia	June 25, 1991	Dec. 22, 1990	republic	president	prime minister	68	127	21	489	12	...
Cuba	May 20, 1902	Feb. 24, 1976	socialist republic	——president——		601	—	15	169	12	200
Cyprus[37]	Aug. 16, 1960	Aug. 16, 1960	republic	——president——		56[38]	—	...	...	12	2
Czech Republic	Jan. 1, 1993	Jan. 1, 1993	republic	president	prime minister	81	200	8	81	—	—
Denmark	c. 800	June 5, 1953	constitutional monarchy	monarch	prime minister	179	—	16	275	3	200
Djibouti	June 27, 1977	Sept. 15, 1992	republic	——president——		65	—	5	...	12	200
Dominica	Nov. 3, 1978	Nov. 3, 1978	republic	president	prime minister	32	—	37	...	12	200
Dominican Republic	Feb. 27, 1844	Nov. 28, 1966	republic	——president——		30	149	30	160	6	200
Ecuador	May 24, 1822	Aug. 10, 1979	republic	——president——		125	—	21	193	200	200
Egypt	Feb. 28, 1922	Sept. 11, 1971	republic	president	prime minister	454	—	27	...	12[39]	200[39]

Finally, in the second half of the table are listed the memberships each country maintains in the principal international intergovernmental organizations of the world. This part of the table may also be utilized to provide a complete membership list for each of these organizations as of Dec. 1, 1998.

Notes for the column headings

a. The date may also be either that of the organization of the present form of government or the inception of the present administrative structure (federation, confederation, union, etc.).
b. Constitutions whose dates are in italic type had been wholly or substantially suspended or abolished as of late 1998.
c. For abbreviations used in this column see the list on the facing page.
d. When a legislative body has been adjourned or otherwise suspended, figures in parentheses indicate the number of members in the legislative body as provided for in constitution or law.
e. States contributing funds to or receiving aid from UNICEF in 1997.
f. 15 nations with judicial representation in ICJ in 1998.
g. Palestine (Liberation Organization) also a member.

International organizations, conventions

ACP	African, Caribbean, and Pacific (Lomé IV) convention
ADB	Asian Development Bank
APEC	Asia-Pacific Economic Cooperation Council
CARICOM	Caribbean Community and Common Market
EU	The European Union
ECOWAS	Economic Community of West African States
EEC	European Economic Community
FAO	Food and Agriculture Org.
GCC	Gulf Cooperation Council
I-ADB	Inter-American Development Bank
IAEA	International Atomic Energy Agency
IBRD	International Bank for Reconstruction and Development
ICAO	International Civil Aviation Org.
ICJ	International Court of Justice
IDA	International Development Association
IDB	Islamic Development Bank
IFC	International Finance Corporation
ILO	International Labour Org.
IMF	International Monetary Fund
IMO	International Maritime Org.
ITU	International Telecommunication Union
LAS	League of Arab States
OAS	Organization of American States
OAU	Organization of African Unity
OPEC	Organization of Petroleum Exporting Countries
SPC	South Pacific Commission
UNCTAD	United Nations Conference on Trade and Development
UNESCO	United Nations Educational Scientific and Cultural Org.
UNICEF	United Nations Children's Fund
UNIDO	United Nations Industrial Development Org.
UPU	Universal Postal Union
WHO	World Health Org.
WIPO	World Intellectual Property Org.
WMO	World Meteorological Org.
WTO	World Trade Org.

Abbreviations used in the executive-branch column

EC	Executive Council
FC	Federal Council
GG	Governor-General
GPC	General People's Committee
NDC	National Defense Commission
PC	People's Council
PNA	Palestine National Authority
PRC	Provisional Ruling Council
SC	State Council
SPDC	State Peace and Development Council

UN date	UNCTAD	UNICEF	ICJ	FAO	IAEA	IBRD	ICAO	IDA	IFC	ILO	IMF	IMO	ITU	UNESCO	UNIDO	UPU	WHO	WIPO	WMO	WTO	Common-wealth	EU	GCC	LAS	OAS	OAU	SPC	ACP	ADB	APEC	CARICOM	ECOWAS	EEC	I-ADB	IDB	OPEC	country
1946	●	●		●	●	●	●	●	●	●	●	●	●	●	●	●	●	●	●										●						●		Afghanistan
1955	●	●		●	●	●	●	●	●	●	●	●	●	●	●	●	●	●	●	●3															●		Albania
1962	●	●	●	●	●	●	●	●	●	●	●	●	●	●	●	●	●	●	●	●3				●		●									●	●	Algeria
—	●							●		●			●			●	●	●	●	●3							●										American Samoa
1993	●												●	●		●	●	●	●																		Andorra
1976	●	●		●		●	●	●	●	●	●	●	●	●	●	●	●	●	●		●					●		●									Angola
1981	●	●		●		●	●	●	●	●	●	●	●	●	●	●	●	●	●	●	●				●			●			●						Antigua and Barbuda
1945	●	●	●	●	●	●	●	●	●	●	●	●	●	●	●	●	●	●	●	●					●									●		Argentina
1992	●	●		●	●	●	●	●	●	●	●	●	●	●15		●	●	●	●	●3															●		Armenia
—													●	●																	●						Aruba
1945	●	●		●	●	●	●	●	●	●	●	●	●	●	●	●	●	●	●	●							●		●	●						Australia
1955	●	●		●	●	●	●	●	●	●	●	●	●	●	●	●	●	●	●	●		●							●				●	●		Austria
1992	●	●		●	●	●	●	●	●	●	●	●	●	●	●	●	●	●	●	●18									●						●		Azerbaijan
1973	●	●		●		●	●	●	●	●	●	●	●	●		●	●	●	●		●				●			●			●			●			Bahamas, The
1971	●	●		●		●	●	●	●	●	●	●	●	●	●	●	●	●	●				●	●											●		Bahrain
1974	●	●		●	●	●	●	●	●	●	●	●	●	●	●	●	●	●	●		●								●						●		Bangladesh
1966	●	●		●		●	●	●	●	●	●	●	●	●	●	●	●	●	●	●	●				●			●			●			●			Barbados
1945	●	●		●	●	●	●	●	●	●	●	●	●	●	●	●	●	●	●	●3															●		Belarus
1945	●	●		●	●	●	●	●	●	●	●	●	●	●	●	●	●	●	●	●		●							●				●	●			Belgium
1981	●	●		●		●	●	●	●	●	●	●	●	●		●	●	●	●		●				●						●			●			Belize
1960	●	●		●		●	●	●	●	●	●	●	●	●		●	●	●	●							●		●				●		●			Benin
—																																					Bermuda
1971	●	●		●		●	●	●	●	●	●	●	●	●	●	●	●	●	●	●3									●						●		Bhutan
1945	●	●		●	●	●	●	●	●	●	●	●	●	●	●	●	●	●	●						●									●			Bolivia
1992	●	●		●		●	●	●	●	●	●	●	●	●	●	●	●	●	●																●		Bosnia and Herzegovina
1966	●	●		●		●	●	●	●	●	●	●	●	●		●	●	●	●		●					●		●									Botswana
1945	●	●	●	●	●	●	●	●	●	●	●	●	●	●	●	●	●	●	●	●					●									●			Brazil
1984	●	●		●		●	●			●	●	●	●	●		●	●	●	●		●								●	●					●		Brunei
1955	●	●		●	●	●	●	●	●	●	●	●	●	●	●	●	●	●	●																		Bulgaria
1960	●	●		●		●	●	●	●	●	●	●	●	●	●	●	●	●	●							●		●				●		●			Burkina Faso
1962	●	●		●		●	●	●	●	●	●	●	●	●	●	●	●	●	●							●		●						●			Burundi
1955	●	●		●		●	●	●	●	●	●	●	●	●	●	●	●	●	●	●3									●						●		Cambodia
1960	●	●		●		●	●	●	●	●	●	●	●	●	●	●	●	●	●							●		●						●	●		Cameroon
1945	●	●		●	●	●	●	●	●	●	●	●	●	●	●	●	●	●	●	●					●				●	●				●			Canada
1975	●	●		●		●	●	●	●	●	●	●	●	●		●	●	●	●	●3						●		●				●			●		Cape Verde
1960	●	●		●		●	●	●	●	●	●	●	●	●		●	●	●	●							●		●						●			Central African Republic
1960	●	●		●		●	●	●	●	●	●	●	●	●		●	●	●	●							●		●						●	●		Chad
1945	●	●		●	●	●	●	●	●	●	●	●	●	●	●	●	●	●	●	●					●									●			Chile
1945	●	●	●	●	●	●	●	●	●	●	●	●	●	●	●	●	●	●	●	●3									●								China
1945	●	●		●		●	●	●	●	●	●	●	●	●	●	●	●	●	●						●									●			Colombia
1975	●	●		●		●	●	●	●	●	●	●	●	●		●	●	●	●					●		●		●							●		Comoros
1960	●	●		●		●	●	●	●	●	●	●	●	●	●	●	●	●	●							●		●						●			Congo, Dem. Rep. of the
1960	●	●		●		●	●	●	●	●	●	●	●	●	●	●	●	●	●							●		●						●			Congo, Rep. of the
1945	●	●		●		●	●	●	●	●	●	●	●	●	●	●	●	●	●						●									●			Costa Rica
1960	●	●		●		●	●	●	●	●	●	●	●	●		●	●	●	●							●		●				●		●			Côte d'Ivoire
1992	●	●		●	●	●	●	●	●	●	●	●	●	●	●	●	●	●	●	●18															●		Croatia
1945	●	●		●	●	●	●	●	●	●	●	●	●	●	●	●	●	●	●						●36												Cuba
1960	●	●		●	●	●	●	●	●	●	●	●	●	●	●	●	●	●	●		●												●15				Cyprus[37]
1993	●	●		●	●	●	●	●	●	●	●	●	●	●	●	●	●	●	●	●																	Czech Republic
1945	●	●		●	●	●	●	●	●	●	●	●	●	●	●	●	●	●	●	●		●											●	●			Denmark
1977	●	●		●		●	●	●	●	●	●	●	●	●		●	●	●	●					●		●		●						●	●		Djibouti
1978	●	●		●		●	●	●	●	●	●	●	●	●		●	●	●	●		●				●			●			●18			●			Dominica
1945	●	●		●		●	●	●	●	●	●	●	●	●		●	●	●	●						●									●			Dominican Republic
1945	●	●		●		●	●	●	●	●	●	●	●	●	●	●	●	●	●						●									●			Ecuador
1945	●	●		●	●	●	●	●	●	●	●	●	●	●	●	●	●	●	●					●		●									●	●	Egypt

Government and international organizations   (continued)

country	date of independence[a]	date of current or last constitution[b]	type of government	executive branch[c] chief of state	head of government	legislative branch[d] upper house (members)	lower house (members)	admin. subdivisions first-order (number)	second-order (number)	seaward claims territorial (nautical miles)	fishing/ economic (nautical miles)
El Salvador	Jan. 30, 1841	Dec. 20, 1983	republic	——————president——————		84	—	14	262	200	200
Equatorial Guinea	Oct. 12, 1968	Nov. 16, 1991[13]	republic	president	prime minister	80	—	7	18	12	200
Eritrea	May 24, 1993	May 23, 1997[40]	republic[32]	——————president——————		150	—	6	...	...	...
Estonia	Aug. 20, 1991	July 3, 1992	republic	president	prime minister	101	—	15	57	12	...
Ethiopia	c. 1000 BC	Aug. 21, 1995[41]	republic	president	prime minister	117	548	10	...	—	—
Faroe Islands	—	April 1, 1948	part of Danish realm	Danish monarch	[42]	32	—	7	50	3	200
Fiji	Oct. 10, 1970	July 27, 1998	republic	president	prime minister	34	70	4	15	12[10]	200[10]
Finland	Dec. 6, 1917	July 17, 1919[43]	republic	president	prime minister	200	—	6	20	12[44]	12
France	August 843	Oct. 4, 1958	republic	president	prime minister	321	577	22	96	12	200
French Guiana	—	Feb. 28, 1983	overseas dept. (Fr.)	French president	[45]	19	31	2	22	12	200
French Polynesia	—	Sept. 6, 1984	overseas territory (Fr.)	French president	[46]	41	—	5	48	12	200
Gabon	Aug. 17, 1960	March 26, 1991	republic	president	prime minister	91	120	9	37	12	200
Gambia, The	Feb. 18, 1965	Jan. 16, 1997	republic	——————president——————		49	—	7	45	12	200
Gaza Strip	—	May 4, 1994[47]	interim authority	——————chairman PNA——————		89	—	...	...	...	...
Georgia	April 9, 1991	Oct. 17, 1995	republic	——————president——————		235	—	13	67	...	...
Germany	May 5, 1955	May 23, 1949	federal republic	president	chancellor	69	672	16	29	12[39]	200
Ghana	March 6, 1957	Jan. 7, 1993	republic	——————president——————		200	—	10	110	12	200
Gibraltar	—	May 23, 1969	dependent territory (U.K.)	British monarch	governor	18	—	—	...	...	...
Greece	Feb. 3, 1830	June 11, 1975	republic	president	prime minister	300	—	53	...	6/10	2
Greenland	—	May 1, 1979	part of Danish realm	Danish monarch	[42]	31	—	18	...	3	200
Grenada	Feb. 7, 1974	Feb. 7, 1974	constitutional monarchy	British monarch	prime minister	13	15	9	...	12	200
Guadeloupe	—	Feb. 28, 1983	overseas dept. (Fr.)	French president	[45]	43	41	3	34	12	200
Guam	—	Aug. 1, 1950	territory (U.S.)	U.S. president	governor	21	—	...	...	12	...
Guatemala	Sept. 15, 1821	Jan. 14, 1986	republic	——————president——————		80	—	22	330	12	200
Guernsey	—	Jan. 1, 1949[43]	crown dependency (U.K.)	British monarch[48]	bailiff	59	—	1	2	...	...
Guinea	Oct. 2, 1958	Dec. 23, 1990[35]	republic	——————president[49]——————		114	—	8	...	12	200
Guinea-Bissau	Sept. 10, 1974	May 11, 1991	republic	president	prime minister	100	—	9	37	12	200
Guyana	May 26, 1966	Oct. 6, 1980	cooperative republic	——————president——————		65	—	10	71	12	200
Haiti	Jan. 1, 1804	March 29, 1987	republic	president	prime minister[50]	27	83	...	...	12	200
Honduras	Nov. 5, 1838	Jan. 20, 1982	republic	——————president——————		128	—	18	297	12	200
Hong Kong	—	April 4, 1990[51]	[52]	——————chief executive EC——————		60	—	3	...	12	2
Hungary	Nov. 16, 1918	Oct. 18, 1989[35]	republic	president	prime minister	386[53]	—	20	195	—	—
Iceland	June 17, 1944	June 17, 1944	republic	president	prime minister	63	—	165	—	12	200
India	Aug. 15, 1947	Jan. 26, 1950	federal republic	president	prime minister	245	545	32	506	12	200
Indonesia	Aug. 17, 1945	Aug. 17, 1945	republic	——————president——————		980	480	27	310	12[10]	200[10]
Iran	Oct. 7, 1906	Dec. 2–3, 1979	Islamic republic	——————president[54]——————		270	—	28	265	12	50[55]
Iraq	Oct. 3, 1932	Sept. 22, 1968[56]	republic	——————president——————		250	—	18	96	12	2
Ireland	Dec. 6, 1921	Dec. 29, 1937	republic	president	prime minister	60	166	32	86	12	200
Isle of Man	—	1961[43]	crown dependency (U.K.)	British monarch[48]	chief minister	11	24	...	—	12[57]	...
Israel	May 14, 1948	June 1950[43]	republic	president	prime minister	120	—	6	15	12	2
Italy	March 17, 1861	Jan. 1, 1948	republic	president	prime minister	326	630	20	102	12	2
Jamaica	Aug. 6, 1962	Aug. 6, 1962	constitutional monarchy	British monarch	prime minister	21	60	13	—	12	200
Japan	c. 660 BC	May 3, 1947	constitutional monarchy	emperor	prime minister	252	500	47	3,233	12[58]	200
Jersey	—	Jan. 1, 1949[43]	crown dependency (U.K.)	British monarch[48]	bailiff	58	—	—	—	3	...
Jordan	May 25, 1946	Jan. 8, 1952	constitutional monarchy	——————king[7]——————		40	80	12	...	3	2
Kazakstan	Dec. 16, 1991	Sept. 6, 1995	republic	——————president[7]——————		47	67	15[59]	...	—	—
Kenya	Dec. 12, 1963	Dec. 12, 1963	republic	——————president——————		224	—	8	...	12	200
Kiribati	July 12, 1979	July 12, 1979	republic	——————president——————		42	—	3	6	12[10]	200[10]
Korea, North	Sept. 9, 1948	April 19, 1992[60]	socialist republic	chairman NDC	premier	687	—	13	172	12	200
Korea, South	Aug. 15, 1948	Feb. 25, 1988	republic	——————president[7]——————		299	—	15	193	12[61]	12
Kuwait	June 19, 1961	Nov. 16, 1962	const. mon. (emirate)	——————emir[7]——————		64	—	—	—	12	2
Kyrgyzstan	Aug. 31, 1991	May 5, 1993	republic	——————president[7]——————		70	35	7	89	—	—
Laos	Oct. 23, 1953	Aug. 15, 1991	republic	president	prime minister	99	—	18	114	—	—
Latvia	Aug. 21, 1991	Nov. 7, 1922	republic	president	prime minister	100	—	33	...	12	...
Lebanon	Nov. 26, 1941	Sept. 21, 1990	republic	president	prime minister	128	—	6	c. 700	12	200
Lesotho	Oct. 4, 1966	April 2, 1993	constitutional monarchy	king	prime minister	33[19]	80	10	...	—	—
Liberia	July 26, 1847	Aug. 20, 1995[62]	republic	——————president——————		26	64	13	...	200	2
Libya	Dec. 24, 1951	March 2, 1977	socialist state[63]	leader[64]	sec. GPC	760	—	...	...	12[65]	2
Liechtenstein	July 12, 1806	Oct. 5, 1921	constitutional monarchy	prince	head of govt.	25	—	11	...	—	—
Lithuania	Sept. 6, 1991	Nov. 6, 1992	republic	president	prime minister	141	—	10	56	12	...
Luxembourg	May 10, 1867	Oct. 17, 1868	constitutional monarchy	grand duke	prime minister	21[19]	60	3	12	—	—
Macau	—	May 10, 1990	special terr. (Port.)[66]	——————governor——————		23	—	...	...	6	12
Macedonia	Nov. 17, 1991	Nov. 17, 1991	republic	president	prime minister	120	—	34	...	—	—
Madagascar	June 26, 1960	April 8, 1998	federal republic	——————president[7]——————		150	—	6	113	12	200
Malawi	July 6, 1964	May 18, 1994	republic	——————president——————		177	—	3	24	—	—
Malaysia	Aug. 31, 1957	Aug. 31, 1957	fed. const. monarchy	paramount ruler	prime minister	70	192	15	131	12	200
Maldives	July 26, 1965	Jan. 1, 1998	republic	——————president——————		48	—	21	...	12[10]	39
Mali	Sept. 22, 1960	Feb. 25, 1992	republic	president	prime minister	147	—	9	701	—	—
Malta	Sept. 21, 1964	Dec. 13, 1974	republic	president	prime minister	65	—	1	67	12	25
Marshall Islands	Dec. 22, 1990	May 1, 1979	republic	——————president——————		12[19]	33	24	—	12[10]	200
Martinique	—	Feb. 28, 1983	overseas dept. (Fr.)	French president	[45]	45	41	4	34	12	200
Mauritania	Nov. 28, 1960	July 21, 1991	republic	——————president[7]——————		56	79	13	53	12	200
Mauritius	March 12, 1968	March 12, 1992	republic	president	prime minister	66	—	11	...	12	200
Mayotte	—	Dec. 24, 1976	terr. collectivity (Fr.)	French president	[67]	19	—	19	...	12	200
Mexico	Sept. 16, 1810	Feb. 5, 1917	federal republic	——————president——————		128	500	32	2,378	12	200
Micronesia	Dec. 22, 1990	Jan. 1, 1981	federal republic	——————president——————		14	—	4	...	12	200
Moldova	Aug. 27, 1991	Aug. 27, 1994	republic	president	prime minister	101	—	2	50	—	—
Monaco	Feb. 2, 1861	Dec. 17, 1962	constitutional monarchy	prince	min. of state[68]	18	—	1	—	12	2
Mongolia	March 13, 1921	Feb. 12, 1992	republic	president	prime minister	76	—	22	299	—	—
Morocco	March 2, 1956	Oct. 7, 1996	constitutional monarchy	——————king[7]——————		270	325	16	...	12	200
Mozambique	June 25, 1975	Nov. 30, 1990	republic	——————president——————		250	—	11	112	12	200
Myanmar (Burma)	Jan. 4, 1948	Jan. 4, 1974	republic	——————chairman SPDC——————		(492)	—	14	58	12	200
Namibia	March 21, 1990	March 21, 1990	republic	president	prime minister	26	78	13	—	12	200
Nauru	Jan. 31, 1968	Jan. 31, 1968	republic	——————president——————		18	—	1	—	12	200
Nepal	Nov. 13, 1769	Nov. 9, 1990	constitutional monarchy	king	prime minister	60	205	14	75	—	—

membership in international organizations																																					country
United Nations (date of admission)	UN organs★ and affiliated intergovernmental organizations																				Commonwealth of Nations	regional multipurpose						economic									
	UNCTAD★	UNICEF★e	ICJ★f	FAO	IAEA	IBRD	ICAO	IDA	IFC	ILO	IMF	IMO	ITU	UNESCO	UNIDO	UPU	WHO	WIPO	WMO	WTO		EU	GCC	LAS9	OAS	OAU	SPC	ACP	ADB	APEC	CARICOM	ECOWAS	EEC	I-ADB	IDB9	OPEC	
1945	•	•		•	•	•	•	•	•	•	•	•	•	•	•	•	•	•	•	•					•									•			El Salvador
1968	•	•		•	•	•	•	•	•	•	•	•	•	•	•	•	•	•	•					•³		•		•									Equatorial Guinea
1993	•	•		•	•	•	•	•	•	•	•	•	•	•	•	•	•	•	•							•		•									Eritrea
1991	•	•		•	•	•	•	•	•	•	•	•	•	•	•	•	•	•	•	•18																	Estonia
1945	•	•		•	•	•	•	•	•	•	•	•	•	•	•	•	•	•	•	•18						•		•									Ethiopia
—													•			•	•	•	•	•	•						•		•		•						Faroe Islands
1970	•	•		•		•	•	•	•	•	•	•	•	•	•	•	•	•	•	•	•						•	•	•								Fiji
1955	•	•	•	•	•	•	•	•	•	•	•	•	•	•	•	•	•	•	•	•		•							•				•	•			Finland
1945	•	•		•	•	•	•	•	•	•	•	•	•	•	•	•	•	•	•	•		•					•						•	•			France
—																•																					French Guiana
—																•											•										French Polynesia
1960	•	•		•	•	•	•	•	•	•	•	•	•	•	•	•	•	•	•	•						•		•								•	Gabon
1965	•	•		•		•	•	•	•	•	•	•	•	•	•	•	•	•	•	•	•					•		•				•					Gambia, The
—																•																					Gaza Strip
1992	•	•		•	•	•	•	•	•	•	•	•	•	•	•	•	•	•	•	•18															•		Georgia
1973	•	•	•	•	•	•	•	•	•	•	•	•	•	•	•	•	•	•	•	•		•											•	•	•		Germany
1957	•	•		•	•	•	•	•	•	•	•	•	•	•	•	•	•	•	•	•	•					•		•				•					Ghana
—													•			•	•	•	•			•											•				Gibraltar
1945	•	•		•	•	•	•	•	•	•	•	•	•	•	•	•	•	•	•	•		•											•				Greece
—																•																					Greenland
1974	•	•		•		•	•	•	•	•	•		•	•		•	•		•	•	•				•			•			•						Grenada
—																•																					Guadeloupe
—																•											•										Guam
1945	•	•		•	•	•	•	•	•	•	•	•	•	•	•	•	•	•	•	•					•									•			Guatemala
—																•																					Guernsey
1958	•	•		•	•	•	•	•	•	•	•	•	•	•	•	•	•	•	•	•						•		•				•			•		Guinea
1974	•	•		•	•	•	•	•	•	•	•	•	•	•	•	•	•	•	•	•						•		•				•			•		Guinea-Bissau
1966	•	•		•	•	•	•	•	•	•	•	•	•	•	•	•	•	•	•	•	•				•			•			•			•			Guyana
1945	•	•		•	•	•	•	•	•	•	•	•	•	•	•	•	•	•	•	•					•			•						•			Haiti
1945	•	•		•	•	•	•	•	•	•	•	•	•	•	•	•	•	•	•	•					•									•			Honduras
—		•										•15				•	•	•	•	•	•								•	•							Hong Kong
1955	•	•	•	•	•	•	•	•	•	•	•	•	•	•	•	•	•	•	•	•																	Hungary
1946	•	•		•	•	•	•	•	•	•	•	•	•	•	•	•	•	•	•	•																	Iceland
1945	•	•		•	•	•	•	•	•	•	•	•	•	•	•	•	•	•	•	•	•								•	•							India
1950	•	•		•	•	•	•	•	•	•	•	•	•	•	•	•	•	•	•	•									•	•				•	•		Indonesia
1945	•	•		•	•	•	•	•	•	•	•	•	•	•	•	•	•	•	•										•					•	•	•	Iran
1945	•	•		•	•	•	•	•	•	•	•	•	•	•	•	•	•	•	•					•	•									•	•	•	Iraq
1955	•	•		•	•	•	•	•	•	•	•	•	•	•	•	•	•	•	•	•		•											•				Ireland
—																•																	•				Isle of Man
1949	•	•		•	•	•	•	•	•	•	•	•	•	•	•	•	•	•	•	•													•				Israel
1955	•	•		•	•	•	•	•	•	•	•	•	•	•	•	•	•	•	•	•		•											•	•			Italy
1962	•	•		•	•	•	•	•	•	•	•	•	•	•	•	•	•	•	•	•	•				•			•			•			•			Jamaica
1956	•	•	•	•	•	•	•	•	•	•	•	•	•	•	•	•	•	•	•	•					•				•	•			•				Japan
—																•																					Jersey
1955	•	•		•	•	•	•	•	•	•	•	•	•	•	•	•	•	•	•	•3				•											•		Jordan
1992	•	•		•	•	•	•	•	•	•	•	•	•	•	•	•	•	•	•	•18															•		Kazakstan
1963	•	•		•	•	•	•	•	•	•	•	•	•	•	•	•	•	•	•	•	•					•		•									Kenya
—		•		•									•			•	•		•								•		•								Kiribati
1991	•	•		•	•	•	•	•	•	•	•	•	•	•	•	•	•	•	•																		Korea, North
1991	•	•		•	•	•	•	•	•	•	•	•	•	•	•	•	•	•	•	•									•	•							Korea, South
1963	•	•		•	•	•	•	•	•	•	•	•	•	•	•	•	•	•	•	•			•	•										•	•		Kuwait
1992	•	•		•	•	•	•	•	•	•	•	•	•	•	•	•	•	•	•	•															•		Kyrgyzstan
1955	•	•		•	•	•	•	•	•	•	•	•	•	•	•	•	•	•	•	•18									•								Laos
1991	•	•		•	•	•	•	•	•	•	•	•	•	•	•	•	•	•	•	•18																	Latvia
1945	•	•		•	•	•	•	•	•	•	•	•	•	•	•	•	•	•	•					•											•		Lebanon
1966	•	•		•	•	•	•	•	•	•	•	•	•	•	•	•	•	•	•	•	•					•		•									Lesotho
1945	•	•		•	•	•	•	•	•	•	•	•	•	•	•	•	•	•	•	•						•		•									Liberia
1955	•	•		•	•	•	•	•	•	•	•	•	•	•	•	•	•	•	•	•18				•		•		•							•	•	Libya
1990	•	•		•										•		•	•18	•		•18																	Liechtenstein
1991	•	•		•	•	•	•	•	•	•	•	•	•	•	•	•	•	•	•	•18																	Lithuania
1945	•	•		•	•	•	•	•	•	•	•	•	•	•	•	•	•	•	•	•		•											•				Luxembourg
—												•15		•15		•				•																	Macau
1993	•	•		•	•	•	•	•	•	•	•	•	•	•	•	•	•	•	•	•18																	Macedonia
1960	•	•	•	•	•	•	•	•	•	•	•	•	•	•	•	•	•	•	•	•						•		•									Madagascar
1964	•	•		•	•	•	•	•	•	•	•	•	•	•	•	•	•	•	•	•	•					•		•									Malawi
1957	•	•		•	•	•	•	•	•	•	•	•	•	•	•	•	•	•	•	•	•								•	•					•		Malaysia
1965	•	•		•	•	•	•	•	•	•	•	•	•	•	•	•	•	•	•	•	•								•						•		Maldives
1960	•	•		•	•	•	•	•	•	•	•	•	•	•	•	•	•	•	•	•						•		•				•	•15		•		Mali
1964	•	•		•	•	•	•	•	•	•	•	•	•	•	•	•	•	•	•	•	•												•				Malta
1991	•	•		•									•			•	•		•								•		•								Marshall Islands
—																•																					Martinique
1961	•	•		•	•	•	•	•	•	•	•	•	•	•	•	•	•	•	•	•				•		•		•							•		Mauritania
1968	•	•		•	•	•	•	•	•	•	•	•	•	•	•	•	•	•	•	•	•					•		•									Mauritius
—		•														•																					Mayotte
1945	•	•		•	•	•	•	•	•	•	•	•	•	•	•	•	•	•	•	•					•					•		•3		•			Mexico
1991	•	•		•									•			•	•		•								•		•								Micronesia
1992	•	•		•	•	•	•	•	•	•	•	•	•	•	•	•	•	•	•	•3									•								Moldova
1993	•	•		•	•	•	•	•	•	•	•	•	•	•	•	•	•	•	•	•																	Monaco
1961	•	•		•	•	•	•	•	•	•	•	•	•	•	•	•	•	•	•	•					•				•								Mongolia
1956	•	•		•	•	•	•	•	•	•	•	•	•	•	•	•	•	•	•	•				•		•								•	•		Morocco
1975	•	•		•	•	•	•	•	•	•	•	•	•	•	•	•	•	•	•	•	•					•		•							•		Mozambique
1948	•	•	•	•	•	•	•	•	•	•	•	•	•	•	•	•	•	•	•	•									•								Myanmar (Burma)
1990	•	•		•	•	•	•	•3	•	•	•	•	•	•	•	•	•	•	•	•	•69					•		•							•		Namibia
—		•		•									•			•	•	•	•								•		•								Nauru
1955	•	•		•	•	•	•	•	•	•	•	•	•	•	•	•	•	•	•	•3									•								Nepal

Government and international organizations (continued)

country	date of independence[a]	date of current or last constitution[b]	type of government	executive branch[c]: chief of state	executive branch[c]: head of government	legislative branch[d]: upper house (members)	legislative branch[d]: lower house (members)	admin. subdivisions: first-order (number)	admin. subdivisions: second-order (number)	seaward claims: territorial (nautical miles)	seaward claims: fishing/economic (nautical miles)
Netherlands, The	March 30, 1814	Feb. 17, 1983	constitutional monarchy	monarch	prime minister	75	150	12	548	12	200
Netherlands Antilles	—	Dec. 29, 1954	overseas territory (Neth.)	Dutch monarch	[14]	22	—	5	—	12	200
New Caledonia	—	Nov. 9, 1988	overseas territory (Fr.)	French president	[70]	54	—	3	33	12	200
New Zealand	Sept. 26, 1907	June 30, 1852[43]	constitutional monarchy	British monarch	prime minister	120	—	12	74	12	200
Nicaragua	April 30, 1838	Jan. 9, 1987	republic	president		93	—	17	145	200	200
Niger	Aug. 3, 1960	May 22, 1996	republic	president[9]		83	—	8	38	—	—
Nigeria	Oct. 1, 1960	*Oct. 1, 1979*	federal republic	chairman PRC		(91)	(593)	37	990	30	200
Northern Mariana Is.	—	Jan. 9, 1978	commonwealth (U.S.)	U.S. president	governor	9	18	4	—	12	200
Norway	June 7, 1905	May 17, 1814	constitutional monarchy	king	prime minister	165	—	19	435	4	200
Oman	Dec. 20, 1951	Nov. 6, 1996[71]	monarchy (sultanate)	sultan		[72]	—	8[73]	...	12	200
Pakistan	Aug. 14, 1947	Aug. 14, 1973	federal Islamic republic	president	prime minister	87	217	16[74]	...	12	200
Palau	Oct. 1, 1994	Jan. 1, 1981	republic	president		14	16	16	—	3	200
Panama	Nov. 3, 1903	May 20, 1983[75]	republic	president[76]		72	—	12	67	200	[2]
Papua New Guinea	Sept. 16, 1975	Sept. 16, 1975	constitutional monarchy	British monarch	prime minister	109	—	20	267	12[10]	200[10]
Paraguay	May 14, 1811	June 22, 1992	republic	president		46	80	18	217	—	—
Peru	July 28, 1821	Dec. 29, 1993	republic	president		120	—	14/28[77]	194	200	200
Philippines	July 4, 1946	Feb. 11, 1987	republic	president		24	260[78]	16	92	...	200[10]
Poland	Nov. 10, 1918	Oct. 17, 1997	republic	president	prime minister	100	460	16	308	12	[79]
Portugal	*c.* 1140	April 25, 1976	republic	president	prime minister	230	—	20	305	12	200
Puerto Rico	—	July 25, 1952	commonwealth (U.S.)	U.S. president	governor	27[80]	51[80]	78	...	12	200
Qatar	Sept. 3, 1971	July 1970[56]	monarchy	emir[7]		35[19]	—	9	—	12	[81]
Réunion	—	Feb. 28, 1983	overseas dept. (Fr.)	French president	[45]	47	45	4	24	12	200
Romania	May 21, 1877	Dec. 13, 1991	republic	president	prime minister	143	343	41	2.687	12[39]	200[39]
Russia	Dec. 8, 1991	Dec. 24, 1993	federal republic	president	prime minister	178	450	89	1, 868	12	...
Rwanda	July 1, 1962	May 5, 1995[82]	republic[32]	president[83]		70	—	11	...	—	—
St. Kitts and Nevis	Sept. 19, 1983	Sept. 19, 1983	constitutional monarchy	British monarch	prime minister	15	—	1	—	12	200
St. Lucia	Feb. 22, 1979	Feb. 22, 1979	constitutional monarchy	British monarch	prime minister	11	17[9]	10	—	12	200
St. Vincent	Oct. 27, 1979	Oct. 27, 1979	constitutional monarchy	British monarch	prime minister	21	—	6	—	12	200
Samoa	Jan. 1, 1962	Oct. 28, 1960	[84]	head of state	prime minister	49	—	11	—	12	200
San Marino	855	Oct. 8, 1600	republic	captains-regent (2)		60	—	9	—	—	—
São Tomé and Príncipe	July 12, 1975	Sept. 10, 1990	republic	president	prime minister	55	—	1	6	12[10]	200[10]
Saudi Arabia	Sept. 23, 1932	[85]	monarchy	king		90[19]	—	13	103	12	[2]
Senegal	Aug. 20, 1960	March 7, 1963	republic	president	prime minister	140	—	10	30	12[39]	200[39]
Seychelles	June 29, 1976	June 21, 1993	republic	president		34	—	...	...	12	200
Sierra Leone	April 27, 1961	Oct. 1, 1991	republic	president		80	—	4	12	200	[2]
Singapore	Aug. 9, 1965	June 3, 1959[43]	republic	president	prime minister	90	—	—	—	3	12
Slovakia	Jan. 1, 1993	Jan. 1, 1993	republic	president	prime minister	150	—	8	79	—	—
Slovenia	June 25, 1991	Dec. 23, 1991	republic	president	prime minister	40	90	147	—	...	...
Solomon Islands	July 7, 1978	July 7, 1978	constitutional monarchy	British monarch	prime minister	50	—	10	...	12[10]	200[10]
Somalia	July 1, 1960	July 1, 1960	republic[86]	[87]		—	—	1	...	200	200
South Africa	May 31, 1910	June 30, 1997	republic	president		90	400	9	360	12	200
Spain	1492	Dec. 29, 1978	constitutional monarchy	king	prime minister	257	350	19	50	12	200[88]
Sri Lanka	Feb. 4, 1948	Sept. 7, 1978	republic	president		225	—	...	...	12	200
Sudan, The	Jan. 1, 1956	June 30, 1998	Islamic military regime	president		400	—	26	66	12	[2]
Suriname	Nov. 25, 1975	Nov. 25, 1987	republic	president		51	—	10	...	12	200
Swaziland	Sept. 6, 1968	*Sept. 6, 1968*	monarchy	king[7]		30[19]	65[19]	4	55	—	—
Sweden	before 836	Jan. 1, 1975	constitutional monarchy	king	prime minister	349	—	23	288	12	[20]
Switzerland	Sept. 22, 1499	May 29, 1874	federal state	president FC		46	200	26	2,929	—	—
Syria	April 17, 1946	March14, 1973	republic	president		250	—	14	47	35	[2]
Taiwan	Oct. 25, 1945	Dec. 25, 1947[43]	republic	president	premier	334	225	2	25	24	200
Tajikistan	Sept. 9, 1991	Nov. 6, 1994	republic	president	prime minister	181	—	4	...	—	—
Tanzania	Dec. 9, 1961	April 25, 1977	republic	president		275	—	1	22	12	200
Thailand	1350	Oct. 11, 1997	constitutional monarchy	king	prime minister	260	393	76	794	12	200
Togo	April 27, 1960	Sept. 27, 1992[13]	republic	president	prime minister	81	—	5	21	30	200
Tonga	June 4, 1970	Nov. 4, 1875	constitutional monarchy[89]	monarch[90]		30	—	2	23	12	200
Trinidad and Tobago	Aug. 31, 1962	July 27, 1976	republic	president	prime minister	31	36	12	124	12[10]	200[10]
Tunisia	March 20, 1956	June 1, 1959	republic	president	prime minister	163	—	23	254	12	[2]
Turkey	Oct. 29, 1923	Nov. 7, 1982	republic	president	prime minister	550	—	80	829	12[91]	[20]
Turkmenistan	Oct. 27, 1991	May 18, 1992	republic	president PC		50	—	6	...	—	—
Tuvalu	Oct. 1, 1978	Oct. 1, 1986	constitutional monarchy	British monarch	prime minister	12	—	8	—	12[10]	200[10]
Uganda	Oct. 9, 1962	Oct. 8, 1995	republic	president[7]		279	—	39	...	—	—
Ukraine	Aug. 24, 1991	June 28, 1996	republic	president	prime minister	450	—	27	485	12	200
United Arab Emirates	Dec. 2, 1971	Dec. 2, 1971	federation of emirates	president	prime minister	40[19]	—	7	—	12	200
United Kingdom	Dec. 6, 1921	[92]	constitutional monarchy	monarch	prime minister	1,223	659	211	...	12[57]	200
United States	July 4, 1776	March 4, 1789	federal republic	president		100	435	51	3,043	12	200
Uruguay	Aug. 25, 1828	Feb. 15, 1967	republic	president		31	99	19	...	200	200
Uzbekistan	Aug. 31, 1991	Dec. 8, 1992	republic	president[7]		250	—	14	162	...	...
Vanuatu	July 30, 1980	July 30, 1980	republic	president	prime minister	52	—	6	...	12[10]	200[10]
Venezuela	July 5, 1811	Jan. 23, 1961	federal republic	president		49	189	24	330	12	200
Vietnam	Sept. 2, 1945	April 15, 1992	socialist republic	president	prime minister	450	—	60	479	12	200
Virgin Islands (U.S.)	—	July 22, 1954	territory (U.S.)	U.S. president	governor	15	—	...	...	12	200
West Bank	—	May 4, 1994[47]	interim authority	chairman PNA		89	—	...	...	—	—
Western Sahara	—	—	annexure of Morocco	—	—	—	—	...	...	12	200
Yemen	December 1918	Sept. 29, 1994[75]	republic	president	prime minister	301	—	17	...	12	200
Yugoslavia	Dec. 1, 1918	April 27, 1992	federal republic	federal president	prime minister	40	138	2	29	...	...
Zambia	Oct. 24, 1964	May 28, 1996[4]	republic	president		156	—	9	57	—	—
Zimbabwe	April 18, 1980	April 18, 1980	republic	president		150	—	10	80	—	—

[1]Title of the supreme leader of the Taleban. [2]Territorial sea claim assumed to claim fishing/economic rights within the same zone. [3]Pending. [4]Date president signed new constitution. [5]Varies between 32 and 52 nautical miles. [6]President of France and Bishop of Urgell, Spain. [7]Assisted by the prime minister. [8]Includes 70 UNITA members expelled September 1998. [9]Excludes possible ex officio members. [10]Measured from claimed archipelagic baselines. [11]Promulgation date of significant amendments to July 9, 1853, constitution. [12]Assisted by the ministerial coordinator. [13]Date of referendum approving new constitution. [14]Executive responsibilities divided between (for The Netherlands) the governor and (locally) the prime minister. [15]Associate member. [16]Formally a constitutional monarchy. [17]Excludes one vacant seat reserved for Nagorno-Karabakh representative. [18]Observer status. [19]Body with limited or no legislative authority. [20]Defined by equidistant line. [21]Legal status is controversial. [22]Excludes children of the monarch serving ex officio from age 18. [23]10 provincial councils; 5 region/community councils. [24]3 nautical miles from the mouth of the Sarstoon River (southern boundary with Guatemala) to Ranguana Caye. [25]Executive responsibilities divided between (for the U.K.) the governor and (locally) the premier of the Cabinet. [26]Resembles a constitutional monarchy without a formal constitution. [27]Assisted by the Council of Ministers. [28]Date of international treaty confirming the existence of a single state. [29]Tripartite presidency. [30]Two co-chairmen assisted by the Council of Ministers. [31]Promulgation of transitional constitutional act. [32]Transitional government. [33]Governor-general can exercise all the powers of the reigning monarch of the Commonwealth. [34]Date of formation of State Transition Commission. [35]Transitional constitution. [36]Suspended membership. [37]Republic of Cyprus only. [38]Occupied seats only. [39]Zone defined by geographic coordinates. [40]Date new constitution approved by constituent assembly. [41]Date new republic was formally established. [42]Executive responsibilities divided between (for Denmark) the high commissioner and (locally) the prime minister. [43]Evolving body of constitutional law. [44]3 nautical miles in the Gulf of Finland. [45]Executive responsibilities divided among (for France) the prefect and (locally) the president of the General Council and the president of the Regional Council. [46]Executive responsibilities divided between (for France) the high commissioner and (locally) the president of the territorial government. [47]Date of agreement providing for Palestinian self-rule. [48]Represented by the lieutenant governor. [49]Assisted by extraconstitutional prime minister.

membership in international organizations

United Nations (date of admission)	UN organs★ and affiliated intergovernmental organizations																				Commonwealth of Nations	regional multipurpose						economic										country
	UNCTAD★	UNICEF★[e]	ICJ★[f]	FAO	IAEA	IBRD	ICAO	IDA	IFC	ILO	IMF	IMO	ITU	UNESCO	UNIDO	UPU	WHO	WIPO	WMO	WTO		EU	GCC	LAS[g]	OAS	OAU	SPC	ACP	ADB	APEC	CARICOM	ECOWAS	EEC	I-ADB	IDB[g]	OPEC	
1945	●	●	●	●	●	●	●	●	●	●	●	●	●	●	●	●	●	●	●	●		●							●				●	●			Netherlands, The
—														●15		●			●	●											●18						Netherlands Antilles
—																●			●								●										New Caledonia
1945	●	●		●	●	●	●	●	●	●	●	●	●	●	●	●	●	●	●	●	●						●		●	●							New Zealand
1945	●	●		●	●	●	●	●	●	●	●	●	●	●	●	●	●	●	●	●					●									●			Nicaragua
1960	●	●		●	●	●	●	●	●	●	●		●	●	●	●	●	●	●	●						●		●				●			●		Niger
1960	●	●		●	●	●	●	●	●	●	●	●	●	●	●	●	●	●	●	●	●					●		●				●				●	Nigeria
—																●											●										Northern Mariana Is.
1945	●	●		●	●	●	●	●	●	●	●	●	●	●	●	●	●	●	●	●									●					●			Norway
1971	●	●		●		●	●	●	●	●	●	●	●	●	●	●	●	●	●	●18			●	●											●		Oman
1947	●	●		●	●	●	●	●	●	●	●	●	●	●	●	●	●	●	●	●	●								●						●		Pakistan
1994		●				●	●		●		●					●	●										●										Palau
1945	●	●		●	●	●	●	●	●	●	●	●	●	●	●	●	●	●	●	●					●									●			Panama
1975	●	●		●		●	●	●	●	●	●	●	●	●	●	●	●	●	●	●	●						●	●	●	●							Papua New Guinea
1945	●	●		●	●	●	●	●	●	●	●	●	●	●	●	●	●	●	●	●					●									●			Paraguay
1945	●	●		●	●	●	●	●	●	●	●	●	●	●	●	●	●	●	●	●					●									●			Peru
1945	●	●		●	●	●	●	●	●	●	●	●	●	●	●	●	●	●	●	●									●	●							Philippines
1945	●	●		●	●	●	●	●	●	●	●	●	●	●	●	●	●	●	●	●																	Poland
1955	●	●		●	●	●	●	●	●	●	●	●	●	●	●	●	●	●	●	●		●											●	●			Portugal
—				●15												●	●15														●18						Puerto Rico
1971	●	●		●	●	●	●			●	●	●	●	●	●	●	●	●	●	●			●	●											●	●	Qatar
—																●																					Réunion
1955	●	●		●	●	●	●	●	●	●	●	●	●	●	●	●	●	●	●	●																	Romania
1991	●	●	●		●	●	●	●	●	●	●	●	●	●	●	●	●	●	●	●3										●3							Russia
1962	●	●		●		●	●	●	●	●	●		●	●	●	●	●	●	●	●						●		●									Rwanda
1983	●	●		●		●		●	●	●	●			●	●	●	●	●		●	●				●			●			●						St. Kitts and Nevis
1979	●	●		●		●	●	●	●	●	●	●	●	●	●	●	●	●	●	●	●				●			●			●						St. Lucia
1980	●	●		●		●	●	●		●	●	●	●	●	●	●	●	●		●	●				●			●			●						St. Vincent
1976	●	●		●		●	●	●	●		●	●	●	●		●	●		●	●18	●						●	●	●								Samoa
1992	●	●					●			●	●		●	●		●	●	●	●																		San Marino
1975	●	●		●		●	●	●		●	●	●	●	●	●	●	●	●	●	●3						●		●									São Tomé and Príncipe
1945	●	●		●	●	●	●	●	●	●	●	●	●	●	●	●	●	●	●	●3			●	●											●	●	Saudi Arabia
1960	●	●		●	●	●	●	●	●	●	●	●	●	●	●	●	●	●	●	●						●		●				●			●		Senegal
1976	●	●		●		●	●		●	●	●	●		●	●	●	●		●	●3	●					●		●									Seychelles
1961	●	●	●	●	●	●	●	●	●	●	●	●	●	●	●	●	●	●	●	●	●					●		●				●			●		Sierra Leone
1965	●	●			●	●	●		●	●	●	●	●			●	●	●	●	●	●								●	●							Singapore
1993	●	●		●	●	●	●	●	●	●	●	●	●	●	●	●	●	●	●	●																	Slovakia
1992	●	●		●	●	●	●	●	●	●	●	●	●	●	●	●	●	●	●	●														●			Slovenia
1978	●	●		●		●	●	●	●	●	●	●	●	●		●	●		●	●	●						●	●	●								Solomon Islands
1960	●	●		●		●	●	●	●	●	●	●	●	●	●	●	●	●	●	●18				●		●		●							●		Somalia
1945	●	●		●	●	●	●	●	●	●	●	●	●	●		●	●	●	●	●	●					●											South Africa
1955	●	●		●	●	●	●	●	●	●	●	●	●	●	●	●	●	●	●	●		●							●				●	●			Spain
1955	●	●	●	●	●	●	●	●	●	●	●	●	●	●	●	●	●	●	●	●	●								●								Sri Lanka
1956	●	●		●	●	●	●	●	●	●	●36	●	●	●	●	●	●	●	●	●18				●		●		●							●		Sudan, The
1975	●	●		●		●	●			●	●	●	●	●	●	●	●	●	●	●					●			●			●			●			Suriname
1968	●	●		●		●	●	●	●	●	●		●	●	●	●	●	●	●	●	●					●		●									Swaziland
1946	●	●		●	●	●	●	●	●	●	●	●	●	●	●	●	●	●	●	●		●							●				●	●			Sweden
—	●	●		●	●	●	●	●	●	●	●	●	●	●	●	●	●	●	●	●									●					●			Switzerland
1945	●	●		●	●	●	●	●	●	●	●	●	●	●	●	●	●		●					●											●		Syria
—																				●3									●	●							Taiwan
1992	●	●		●		●	●	●	●	●	●	●	●	●	●	●	●	●	●																●		Tajikistan
1961	●	●		●	●	●	●	●	●	●	●	●	●	●	●	●	●	●	●	●	●					●		●									Tanzania
1946	●	●		●	●	●	●	●	●	●	●	●	●	●	●	●	●	●	●	●									●	●							Thailand
1960	●	●		●		●	●	●	●	●	●	●	●	●	●	●	●	●	●	●						●		●				●					Togo
—	●	●		●		●	●	●	●		●		●	●	●	●	●			●18	●						●	●	●								Tonga
1962	●	●		●		●	●	●	●	●	●	●	●	●	●	●	●	●	●	●	●				●			●			●			●			Trinidad and Tobago
1956	●	●		●	●	●	●	●	●	●	●	●	●	●	●	●	●	●	●	●				●		●									●		Tunisia
1945	●	●		●	●	●	●	●	●	●	●	●	●	●	●	●	●	●	●	●									●				●15		●		Turkey
1992	●	●		●		●	●	●3	●	●	●	●	●	●		●	●	●	●																●		Turkmenistan
—		●											●	●	●	●	●				●69						●	●	●								Tuvalu
1962	●	●		●	●	●	●	●	●	●	●		●	●	●	●	●	●	●	●	●					●		●							●		Uganda
1945	●	●			●	●	●	●3	●	●	●	●	●	●	●	●	●	●	●	●3																	Ukraine
1971	●	●		●	●	●	●	●	●	●	●	●	●	●	●	●	●	●	●	●			●	●											●	●	United Arab Emirates
1945	●	●	●	●	●	●	●	●	●	●	●	●	●	●	●	●	●	●	●	●	●	●					●		●				●	●			United Kingdom
1945	●	●	●	●	●	●	●	●	●	●	●	●	●		●	●	●	●	●	●					●		●		●	●				●			United States
1945	●	●		●	●	●	●		●	●	●	●	●	●	●	●	●	●	●	●					●									●			Uruguay
1992	●	●			●	●	●	●	●	●	●		●	●	●	●	●	●	●	●18									●								Uzbekistan
1981	●	●		●		●	●	●	●		●	●	●	●	●	●	●		●	●18	●						●	●	●								Vanuatu
1945	●	●	●	●	●	●	●		●	●	●	●	●	●	●	●	●	●	●	●					●						●18			●		●	Venezuela
1977	●	●		●	●	●	●	●	●	●	●	●	●	●	●	●	●	●	●	●3									●	●3							Vietnam
—																●															●						Virgin Islands (U.S.)
—		●																																			West Bank
—																										●93											Western Sahara
1947	●	●		●	●	●	●	●	●	●	●	●	●	●	●	●	●	●	●	●18				●											●		Yemen
1945	●	●		●	●	●3	●3	●3		●		●	●	●	●	●	●	●	●	●18																	Yugoslavia
1964	●	●		●	●	●	●	●	●	●	●		●	●	●	●	●	●	●	●	●					●		●									Zambia
1980	●	●		●	●	●	●	●	●	●	●		●	●	●	●	●	●	●	●	●					●		●									Zimbabwe

50Office vacant from June 1997 through November 1998. 51Approval date for post-reversion Basic Law. 52Special administrative region (China). 53Excludes 13 seats set aside for ethnic minorities. 54Shares coexecutive authority with spiritual leader. 55Sea of Oman only; median line boundaries in Persian Gulf. 56Provisional constitution. 57Median line between the Isle of Man and the United Kingdom. 583 nautical miles in 5 straits. 59Excludes Baykonur city which is under Russian jurisdiction. 60Approval date by legislature; made public Nov. 23, 1993. 613 nautical miles in Korea Strait. 62Date of peace accord. 63Formally a *jamahiriya,* translated as "the masses of people"; in fact, a military dictatorship. 64De facto chief of state. 65Based on Gulf of Sidra closing line (32° 30′ N), in part. 66Macau will revert to Chinese sovereignty on Dec. 20, 1999. 67Executive responsibilities divided between (for France) the prefect and (locally) the president of the General Council. 68Under prince's authority. 69Special member. 70Executive responsibilities divided between (for France) the high commissioner and (locally) the president of the Territorial Congress. 71Basic law promulgated by sultan. 72Has 2 consultative bodies with advisory authority only. 733 governorates and 5 geographic regions. 74Includes federally administered tribal areas, excludes Jammu and Kashmir. 75Effective date of significant amendments. 76Assisted by vice presidents. 77Two concomitant administrative systems. 78Includes 43 vacant seats. 79Defined by international treaties. 80Excludes additional seats for both houses of the legislature to meet 1/3 total representation requirements for minority parties per constitution. 81Limits of continental shelf or median line boundaries. 82Date constitution adopted by transitional legislature. 83In conjunction with the vice president (minister of defense) and prime minister. 84Mixed political system approximating a constitutional monarchy. 85Royal decrees since March 1, 1992, provide a formal description of the king's governance. 86The internationally unrecognized Republic of Somaliland declared its independence from Somalia in 1991. 87No central government from 1991. 88Atlantic Ocean only. 89In practice resembles a system of monarchical absolutism. 90Assisted by Privy Council. 91Black Sea and Mediterranean Sea; 6 nautical miles in Aegean Sea. 92Based on evolving body of statutes and common law. 93Membership held by the Sahrawi Arab Democratic Republic.

Area and population

This table provides the area and population for each of the countries of the world and for all but the smallest political dependencies having a permanent civilian population. The data represent the latest published and unpublished data for both the surveyed area of the countries and their populations, the latter both as of a single year (1998) to provide the best comparability and as of the most recent census to provide the fullest comparison of certain demographic measures that are not always available between successive national censuses. The 1998 midyear estimates represent a combination of national, United Nations (UN) or other international organizations, and *Encyclopædia Britannica* estimates so as to give the best fit to available published series, to take account of unpublished information received via Internet, facsimile, or correspondence, and to incorporate the results of very recent censuses for which published analyses are not yet available.

One principal point to bear in mind when studying these statistics is that all of them, whatever degree of precision may be implied by the exactness of the numbers, are estimates—all of varying, and some of suspect, accuracy—even when they *contain* a very full enumeration. The United States—which has a long tradition both of census taking and of the use of the most sophisticated analytical tools in processing the data—is unable to determine within 2.1% (the estimated 1990 undercount) its total population nationally. And that is an *average* underenumeration. In states and larger cities, where enumeration of particular populations, both legal and illegal, is most difficult, the accuracy of the enumerated count may be off as much as 4% at a state level and as much as 10% for a single city. The high accuracy attained by census operations in China may approach 0.25% of rigorously maintained civil population registers. Other national census operations not so based, however, are inherently less accurate. For example, Ethiopia's first-ever census in 1984 resulted in figures that were 30% or more above prevailing estimates; Nigeria's 1991 census corrected decades of miscounts and was well below prevailing estimates. An undercount of 2–8% is more typical, but even census operations offering results of 30% or more above or below prevailing estimates can still represent well-founded benchmarks from which future planning may proceed. The editors have tried to take account of the range of variation and accuracy in published data, but it is difficult to establish a value for many sources of inaccuracy unless some country or agency has made a conscientious effort to establish both the relative accuracy (precision) of its estimate and the absolute magnitude of the quantity it is trying to measure—for example, the number of people in Cambodia who died at the hands of the Khmer Rouge. If a figure of 2,000,000 is adopted, what is its accuracy: ± 1%, 10%, 50%? Are the original data documentary or evidentiary, complete or incomplete, analytically biased or unbiased, in good agreement with other published data?

Many similar problems exist and in endless variations: What is the extent of southern European immigration to western Europe in search of jobs? How many refugees from Afghanistan, Liberia, Rwanda, or Burundi are there in surrounding countries? How many undocumented aliens are there in the United States? How many Palestinians are there in the Middle East (they are politically inconvenient to enumerate everywhere)? How many Amerindians exist (remain, preserving their original language and a mode of life unassimilated by the larger national culture) in the countries of South America? How many people have died or emigrated as a result of the civil violence in Central America?

Area and population

country	area			population (latest estimate)					population (latest census)				
	square miles	square kilo- metres	rank	total midyear 1998	rank	density		% annual growth rate 1993–98	census year	total	male (%)	female (%)	urban (%)
						per sq mi	per sq km						
Afghanistan	251,825	652,225	41	24,792,000	39	98.4	38.0	5.6	1979	13,051,358[1]	51.4	48.6	15.1
Albania	11,100	28,748	142	3,331,000	128	300.1	115.9	1.1	1989	3,182,417	51.5	48.5	35.7
Algeria	919,595	2,381,741	11	30,045,000	35	32.7	12.6	2.2	1987	23,038,942	49.9	50.1	49.7
American Samoa	77	199	205	62,100	206	806.5	312.1	3.2	1990	46,773	51.4	48.6	33.4
Andorra	181	468	193	65,200	203	360.2	139.3	0.6	1992[2]	61,599	53.1	46.9	62.5[3]
Angola	481,354	1,246,700	24	10,865,000	66	22.6	8.7	3.3	1970	5,673,046	52.1	47.9	14.2
Antigua and Barbuda	171	442	195	69,100	201	405.3	156.5	1.5	1991	63,896	48.2	51.8	36.2
Argentina	1,073,400	2,780,092	8	36,125,000	31	33.7	13.0	1.3	1991	32,615,528	48.9	51.1	88.4
Armenia	11,484	29,743	141	3,800,000	120	330.9	127.8	0.4	1989	3,287,677	49.3	50.7	67.8
Aruba	75	193	206	88,600	195	1,181.3	459.1	3.5	1991	66,687	49.2	50.8	...
Australia	2,966,200	7,682,300	6	18,725,000	51	6.3	2.4	1.2	1996	17,892,423	49.5	50.5	85.3[4]
Austria	32,378	83,859	115	8,070,000	84	249.2	96.2	0.2	1991	7,795,786	48.2	51.8	64.5
Azerbaijan	33,400	86,600	113	7,650,000	88	229.0	88.3	0.7	1989	7,037,867	48.7	51.3	53.8
Bahamas, The	5,382	13,939	158	293,000	174	54.4	21.0	1.7	1990	255,095	49.0	51.0	64.3
Bahrain	268	694	186	633,000	160	2,361.9	911.8	3.3	1991	508,037	57.9	42.1	88.4
Bangladesh	56,977	147,570	93	127,567,000	8	2,238.9	911.8	1.9	1991	111,455,185	51.4	48.6	20.2
Barbados	166	430	196	265,000	178	1,596.4	616.3	0.1	1990[5]	257,083	47.7	52.3	37.9[6]
Belarus	80,153	207,595	85	10,235,000	72	127.7	49.3	-0.2	1989	10,199,709	46.9	53.1	65.5
Belgium	11,787	30,528	139	10,208,000	73	866.0	334.4	0.2	1991	9,978,681	48.9	51.1	96.6[7]
Belize	8,867	22,965	150	235,000	179	26.5	10.2	2.7	1991	189,392	50.9	49.1	47.5
Benin	43,500	112,680	101	6,101,000	96	140.3	54.1	3.4	1992	4,855,349	48.7	51.3	39.6
Bermuda	21	54	212	62,100	205	2,957.1	1,150.0	0.6	1991[5]	58,460	48.5	51.5	100.0
Bhutan	18,150	47,000	131	633,000	161	34.9	13.5	2.6	...	...	50.6[6]	49.4[6]	5.3[6]
Bolivia	424,164	1,098,581	28	7,957,000	85	18.8	7.2	2.4	1992	6,420,792	49.4	50.6	57.5
Bosnia and Herzegovina	19,741	51,129	127	3,366,000	127	170.5	65.8	-3.8	1991	4,377,033	49.9	50.1	39.6
Botswana	224,607	581,730	47	1,448,000	146	6.4	2.5	1.3	1991	1,326,796	47.8	52.2	23.9
Brazil	3,300,171	8,547,404	5	161,766,000	5	49.0	18.9	1.4	1991	146,825,475	49.4	50.6	75.6
Brunei	2,226	5,765	167	315,000	173	141.5	54.6	2.6	1991	260,482	52.8	47.2	66.6
Bulgaria	42,855	110,994	103	8,273,000	83	193.0	74.5	-0.5	1992	8,487,317	49.1	50.9	67.2
Burkina Faso	105,946	274,400	73	11,266,000	63	106.3	41.1	2.8	1985[5]	7,964,705	48.1	51.9	11.7
Burundi	10,740	27,816	145	5,537,000	101	515.5	199.1	-0.3	1990[5]	5,292,793	48.6	51.4	6.3
Cambodia	70,238	181,916	89	10,751,000	68	153.1	59.1	2.5	1993	9,307,597	48.3	51.7	21.0[9]
Cameroon	183,569	475,442	53	15,029,000	59	81.9	31.6	2.9	1987	10,516,232	49.0	51.0	38.3
Canada	3,849,674	9,970,610	2	30,677,000	33	8.0	3.1	1.2	1996	28,846,761	49.3[4]	50.7[4]	77.9
Cape Verde	1,557	4,033	169	400,000	170	256.9	99.2	1.6	1990	341,491	47.3	52.7	44.1
Central African Republic	240,324	622,436	43	3,376,000	126	14.0	5.4	2.2	1988	2,688,426	49.1	50.9	36.5
Chad	495,755	1,284,000	21	7,360,000	90	14.8	5.7	2.8	1993	6,279,931	47.9	52.1	21.4
Chile	292,135	756,626	38	14,822,000	60	50.7	19.6	1.5	1992	13,348,401	49.1	50.9	83.5
China	3,696,100	9,572,900	3	1,242,980,000	1	336.3	129.8	1.1	1990	1,133,682,501	51.6	48.4	26.4
Colombia	440,762	1,141,568	26	37,685,000	30	85.5	33.0	1.8	1993	33,109,840	49.2	50.8	70.3[6]
Comoros	719	1,862	175	546,000	163	759.4	293.2	3.1	1991	446,817	49.5	50.5	28.5
Congo, Dem. Rep. of the	905,354	2,344,858	12	49,001,000	24	54.1	20.9	3.2	1984	29,671,407	49.2	50.8	29.1[9]
Congo, Rep. of the	132,047	342,000	63	2,658,000	134	20.1	7.8	2.3	1984[5]	1,909,248	48.7	51.3	52.0
Costa Rica	19,730	51,100	128	3,533,000	124	179.1	69.1	2.0	1984	2,416,809	50.0	50.0	43.9
Côte d'Ivoire	124,504	322,463	68	15,446,000	57	124.1	47.9	3.2	1988	10,815,694	51.1	48.9	39.0
Croatia	21,857	56,610	126	4,672,000	113	213.8	82.5	-0.1	1991	4,784,265	48.5	51.5	54.3
Cuba	42,804	110,861	104	11,116,000	64	259.7	100.3	0.5	1993	10,904,466	50.3	49.7	74.4
Cyprus[11]	3,572	9,251	164	861,000	155	241.0	93.1	1.4	1992[5, 12]	615,013	49.8	50.2	67.7
Czech Republic	30,450	78,866	117	10,302,000	71	338.3	130.6	-0.1	1991	10,302,215	48.5	51.5	75.2
Denmark	16,639	43,094	133	5,303,000	104	318.7	123.1	0.4	1996[2]	5,251,027	49.4	50.6	85.1[3]
Djibouti	8,950	23,200	149	652,000	159	72.8	28.1	2.7	1983	273,974	51.9	48.1	82.8[9]
Dominica	290	750	183	76,400	199	263.4	101.9	1.2	1991	71,183	49.8	50.2	...
Dominican Republic	18,792	48,671	130	7,883,000	87	419.5	162.0	1.7	1993	7,293,390	48.7	51.3	56.0
Ecuador	105,037	272,045	74	12,175,000	62	115.9	44.8	2.1	1990	9,648,189	49.7	50.3	55.4
Egypt	385,229	997,739	30	63,261,000	16	164.2	63.4	2.1	1996	61,452,382	51.2	48.8	44.6[9]

Still, much information is accurate, well founded, and updated regularly. The sources of these data are censuses; national population registers (cumulated periodically); registration of migration, births, deaths, and so on; sample surveys to establish demographic conditions; and the like.

The statistics provided for area and population by country are ranked, and the population densities based on those values are also provided. The population densities, for purposes of comparison within this table, are calculated on the bases of the 1998 midyear population estimate as shown and of total area of the country. Elsewhere in individual country presentations the reader may find densities calculated on more specific population figures and more specialized area bases: land area for Finland (because of its many lakes) or ice-free area for Greenland (most of which is ice cap). The data in this section conclude with the estimated average annual growth rate for the country (including both natural growth and net migration) during the five-year period, 1993–98.

In the section containing census data, information supplied includes the census total (usually de facto, the population actually present, rather than de jure, the population legally resident, who might be anywhere); the male-female breakdown; the proportion that is urban (according to the country's own definition); and finally an analysis of the age structure of the population by 15-year age groups. This last analysis may be particularly useful in distinguishing the type of population being recorded—young, fast-growing nations show a high proportion of people under 30 (most countries in sub-Saharan Africa and the Middle East have nearly one-half of their population under 15 years), while other nations (for example Sweden, which suffered no age-group losses in World War II) exhibit quite uniform proportions.

Finally, a section is provided giving the population of each country at 10-year intervals from 1940 to 2010. The data for years past represent the best available analysis of the published data by the country itself, by the demographers of the UN, or by the editors of Britannica. The projections for 2000 and 2010 similarly represent the best fit of available data through the mid-1990s with projected population structure and growth rates during the next two decades. The evidence of the last 25 years with respect to similar estimates published about 1970, however, shows how cloudy is the glass through which these numbers are read. In 1970 no respectable Western analyst would have imagined proposing that mainland China could achieve the degree of birth control that it apparently has since then (as evidenced by the results of 1982 and 1990 censuses); on the other hand, even the Chinese admit that their methods have been somewhat Draconian and that they have already seen some backlash in terms of higher birth rates among those who have so far postponed larger families. How much is "some" by 2000? Compound that problem with all the social, economic, political, and biological factors that can affect 217 countries' populations, and the difficulty facing the prospective compiler of such projections may be appreciated.

Specific data about the vital rates affecting the data in this table may be found in great detail in both the country statistical boxes in "The Nations of the World" section and in the *Vital statistics, marriage, family* table, beginning at page 778.

Percentages in this table for male and female population will always total 100.0, but percentages by age group may not, for reasons such as non-response on census forms, "don't know" responses (which are common in countries with poor birth registration systems), and the like.

age distribution (%)						population (by decade, '000s)						2000 projection	2010 projection	country
0–14	15–29	30–44	45–59	60–74	75 and over	1940	1950	1960	1970	1980	1990	2000 projection	2010 projection	
44.5	26.9	15.8	8.6	3.6	0.6	...	8,150	9,829	12,431	14,985	14,767	26,668	34,098	Afghanistan
33.0	28.9	18.5	11.7	5.9	1.9	1,088	1,227	1,623	2,157	2,699	3,273	3,401	3,784	Albania
43.9	28.0	13.9	8.4	4.2	1.6	7,688	8,956	10,800	14,330	18,666	25,022	31,345	37,943	Algeria
38.1	29.0	18.1	9.4	4.3	1.1	13	19	20	27	32	47	66	81	American Samoa
16.3	27.7	27.2	15.1	9.9	3.8	5	6	8	19	33	53	66	72	Andorra
41.7	23.2	17.0	7.4	3.8	1.0	3,738	4,118	4,797	5,606	6,794	8,430	11,487	14,932	Angola
30.4	27.8	20.5	10.2	7.7	3.4	34	45	55	66	69	64	89	93	Antigua and Barbuda
30.6	23.3	19.3	13.9	9.6	3.3	14,169	17,150	20,616	23,962	28,094	32,527	37,032	41,474	Argentina
30.3	25.7	20.8	13.6	6.4	3.2	1,320	1,354	1,867	2,520	3,067	3,545	3,827	3,796	Armenia
24.4	22.0	27.0	16.1	7.2	3.0	31	51	57	61	60	64	89	93	Aruba
22.1[4]	24.2[4]	23.4[4]	15.0[4]	11.1[4]	4.4[4]	7,079	8,219	10,315	12,552	14,741	17,065	19,117	21,018	Australia
17.4	23.7	21.6	17.2	13.4	6.7	6,684	6,935	7,048	7,447	7,549	7,718	8,080	8,115	Austria
32.8	29.7	16.8	12.8	5.7	2.2	3,274	2,896	3,895	5,172	6,165	7,159	7,749	8,202	Azerbaijan
32.2	30.8	19.7	10.6	5.0	1.8	70	79	110	170	210	256	302	343	Bahamas, The
31.7	28.4	28.2	8.0	3.1	0.6	90	110	149	210	334	503	660	780	Bahrain
41.5	25.2	16.2	8.1	4.3	1.1	41,259	45,646	54,622	67,403	88,077	110,118	131,199	153,084	Bangladesh
24.1	27.1	22.1	11.4	9.9	5.4	179	209	232	235	249	261	266	270	Barbados
23.0	22.4	20.6	18.0	11.5	4.5	9,046	7,745	8,190	9,040	9,650	10,260	10,178	10,227	Belarus
18.2	21.8	22.5	16.9	14.1	6.6	8,301	8,639	9,153	9,690	9,859	9,967	10,260	10,149	Belgium
43.9	27.9	14.9	7.2	4.4	1.6	56	68	90	120	146	189	248	307	Belize
48.3[8]	26.9[8]	13.3[8]	7.4[8]	3.2[8]	0.8[8]	...	1,673	2,055	2,620	3,444	4,676	6,517	8,955	Benin
19.5	24.0	26.8	16.4	—13.3—		31	37	43	53	55	59	63	67	Bermuda
40.6[6]	26.5[6]	17.1[6]	10.4[6]	4.6[6]	0.8[6]	...	...	...	...	...	518	662	821	Bhutan
41.2	26.2	16.8	8.9	—6.5—		2,508	2,714	3,351	4,212	5,355	6,573	8,329	10,229	Bolivia
23.5[7]	26.3[7]	22.6[7]	16.2[7]	8.9[7]	2.7[7]	...	2,662	3,240	3,703	4,107	4,360	3,592	3,737	Bosnia and Herzegovina
42.8	27.3	14.3	7.3	4.1	2.2	278	430	497	584	903	1,304	1,479	1,570	Botswana
34.7	28.1	19.3	10.6	5.7	1.6	41,525	53,444	72,594	95,847	118,617	143,581	165,562	181,918	Brazil
34.5	29.3	24.2	7.9	—4.1—		36	45	83	128	185	254	331	410	Brunei
20.5	19.2	—39.8—		—20.5—		6,344	7,251	7,867	8,490	8,862	8,718	8,179	7,926	Bulgaria
48.3	23.4	13.4	8.7	4.7	1.4	3,036	4,376	4,866	5,626	6,939	9,024	11,892	15,371	Burkina Faso
46.4	25.3	15.4	7.0	4.0	1.7	1,887	2,363	2,812	3,513	4,138	5,285	5,931	7,539	Burundi
47.0	—53.0—					3,400	4,346	5,433	6,938	6,498	8,695	11,207	13,433	Cambodia
46.4	24.5	14.6	8.7	4.1	1.6	...	4,888	5,609	6,727	8,761	11,894	15,892	20,632	Cameroon
20.9[4]	22.7[4]	25.1[4]	15.3[4]	11.3[4]	4.7[4]	11,693	13,737	17,909	21,324	24,593	27,791	31,472	35,065	Canada
45.0	27.3	11.4	8.0	5.5	2.9	181	146	197	269	296	349	411	464	Cape Verde
43.2	27.5	15.0	9.2	4.1	0.8	991	1,260	1,467	1,827	2,244	2,798	3,516	4,314	Central African Republic
48.1	24.6	14.7	7.2	4.2	1.3	2,351	2,608	3,042	3,733	4,507	5,889	7,760	10,055	Chad
29.4	27.3	21.2	12.2	7.2	2.5	5,063	6,082	7,608	9,496	11,147	13,100	15,211	17,010	Chile
27.7	31.0	20.7	12.1	6.9	1.7	530,000	556,613	667,070	818,316	981,242	1,133,683	1,263,098	1,341,848	China
33.1[10]	30.0[10]	20.6[10]	9.9[10]	5.2[10]	1.3[10]	9,097	11,946	15,939	21,360	26,525	32,596	38,905	44,741	Colombia
47.6[7]	27.0[7]	13.1[7]	7.7[7]	3.5[7]	1.0[7]	119	148	183	236	334	429	581	782	Comoros
47.3[9]	25.9[9]	14.1[9]	8.1[9]	3.8[9]	0.8[9]	10,370	13,569	16,462	21,395	28,129	37,978	51,988	70,276	Congo, Dem. Rep. of the
44.7	27.2	13.3	9.1	4.6	0.7	...	768	931	1,183	1,620	2,206	2,776	3,368	Congo, Rep. of the
37.9	31.5	15.8	9.2	4.4	1.2	619	862	1,236	1,731	2,246	2,994	3,673	4,333	Costa Rica
46.8	27.3	15.0	7.5	2.8	0.6	2,350	2,860	3,565	5,427	8,261	11,904	16,190	20,565	Côte d'Ivoire
19.4	20.7	22.7	18.3	12.9	4.5	...	3,851	4,140	4,411	4,588	4,754	4,681	4,634	Croatia
22.3	29.4	21.3	14.8	8.4	3.9	4,566	5,850	6,985	8,520	9,710	10,628	11,201	11,516	Cuba
25.4	22.0	22.3	15.4	10.2	4.7	413	494	573	615	631	757	882	1,000	Cyprus[11]
21.0	21.8	22.6	16.8	12.7	5.1	...	8,925	9,539	9,830	10,292	10,298	10,290	10,464	Czech Republic
17.5	20.8	22.0	19.9	12.7	7.0	3,832	4,271	4,581	4,929	5,123	5,141	5,340	5,506	Denmark
39.4	32.9	16.9	7.4	2.8	0.6	44	62	83	148	281	517	687	866	Djibouti
33.3	28.3	16.3	9.7	—11.8—		45	51	60	70	75	72	78	86	Dominica
36.5[10]	29.5[10]	18.4[10]	9.6[10]	4.8[10]	1.2[10]	1,759	2,353	3,231	4,423	5,697	6,902	8,142	9,503	Dominican Republic
38.8	28.5	17.3	9.0	4.7	1.7	2,546	3,307	4,421	5,958	8,123	10,264	12,646	14,899	Ecuador
36.9[13]	28.3[13]	18.4[13]	10.6[13]	4.9[13]	0.9[13]	16,942	20,461	26,085	33,329	40,546	53,051	65,627	77,345	Egypt

Area and population   (continued)

country	area square miles	square kilo-metres	rank	population (latest estimate) total midyear 1998	rank	density per sq mi	per sq km	% annual growth rate 1993–98	population (latest census) census year	total	male (%)	female (%)	urban (%)
El Salvador	8,124	21,041	151	5,752,000	98	708.0	273.4	1.6	1992	5,118,599	48.6	51.4	50.4
Equatorial Guinea	10,831	28,051	144	454,000	164	41.9	16.2	2.6	1983	300,060	48.8	51.2	28.2
Eritrea	46,774	121,144	118	3,842,000	118	82.1	31.7	3.7	1984	2,703,998	49.9	50.1	15.1
Estonia	17,462	45,227	132	1,447,000	147	82.9	32.0	–0.9	1989	1,572,916	46.9	53.1	71.6
Ethiopia	437,794	1,133,882	27	58,390,000	21	133.4	51.5	2.5	1984	39,480,954	50.0	50.0	9.9
Faroe Islands	540	1,399	177	44,300	209	82.0	31.7	–0.8	1996[2]	43,495	51.6	48.4	...
Fiji	7,055	18,272	155	793,000	156	112.4	43.4	1.0	1996	775,077	50.8	49.2	46.4
Finland	130,559	338,145	64	5,154,000	107	39.5	15.2	0.3	1990	4,998,478	48.5	51.5	79.7
France	210,026	543,965	49	58,841,000	20	280.2	108.2	0.4	1990	56,625,026	48.7	51.3	74.0
French Guiana	33,399	86,504	114	169,000	185	5.1	2.0	4.0	1990	114,808	52.1	47.9	79.4
French Polynesia	1,544	4,000	170	228,000	180	147.7	57.0	1.7	1996	219,521	52.1[15]	47.9[15]	55.0[15]
Gabon	103,347	267,667	76	1,208,000	150	11.7	4.5	1.5	1993	1,011,710	49.3	50.7	73.2
Gambia, The	4,127	10,689	162	1,292,000	148	313.1	120.9	3.6	1993	1,038,145	50.1	49.9	36.7
Gaza Strip	140	363	199	1,082,000	153	7,728.6	2,980.7	8.0	1995[2, 16]	1,054,000	50.9	49.1	...
Georgia	26,831	69,492	121	5,431,000	102	202.4	78.2	–0.0	1989	5,443,359	47.2	52.8	55.7
Germany	137,847	357,002	62	82,148,000	12	595.9	230.1	0.2	1987[17]	61,077,042	48.0	52.0	85.3[6]
Ghana	92,098	238,533	81	18,497,000	53	200.8	77.5	2.4	1984	12,296,081	49.3	50.7	32.0
Gibraltar	2.2	5.8	216	27,100	213	12,318.2	4,672.4	–1.0	1991[18]	26,703	51.0	49.0	...
Greece	50,949	131,957	96	10,543,000	70	206.9	79.9	0.3	1991	10,264,156	49.3	50.7	58.9
Greenland	836,330	2,166,086	14	56,200	208	0.1	0.0	0.3	1996[2]	55,863	53.4	46.6	81.1
Grenada	133	344	201	100,000	193	751.9	290.7	0.8	1991	95,597	48.8	51.2	33.5
Guadeloupe	687	1,780	176	434,000	165	631.7	243.8	1.2	1990	387,034	48.9	51.1	48.4
Guam	209	541	190	148,000	187	708.1	273.6	0.6	1990	133,152	53.3	46.7	38.2
Guatemala	42,042	108,889	105	10,802,000	67	256.9	99.2	2.7	1994	8,331,874	49.3	50.7	35.0
Guernsey	30	78	210	61,700	207	2,056.7	791.0	–0.0	1996[19]	58,681	48.1[4]	51.9[4]	...
Guinea	94,926	245,857	78	7,477,000	89	78.8	30.4	1.7	1996	7,164,823	48.8	51.2	29.6
Guinea-Bissau	13,948	36,125	137	1,206,000	151	86.5	33.4	2.4	1991	983,367	48.4	51.6	20.3[7]
Guyana	83,044	215,083	84	782,000	157	9.4	3.6	0.3	1980	758,619	49.5	50.5	35.4[9]
Haiti	10,695	27,700	146	6,781,000	93	634.0	244.8	1.4	1982	5,053,792	48.5	51.5	20.6
Honduras	43,433	112,492	102	5,919,000	97	136.3	52.6	2.8	1988	4,376,839	49.6	50.4	39.4
Hong Kong	422	1,092	179	6,660,000	94	15,797.0	6,099.5	2.4	1996[5]	6,218,000	50.0	50.0	100.0
Hungary	35,919	93,030	110	10,117,000	74	281.7	108.7	–0.3	1990	10,375,323	48.1	51.9	61.8
Iceland	39,699	102,819	106	276,000	176	7.0	2.7	0.9	1996[2]	269,735	50.1	49.9	91.9
India	1,222,243	3,165,596	7	984,004,000	2	805.1	310.8	1.8	1991	846,302,688	51.9	48.1	25.7
Indonesia	747,949	1,937,179	16	202,957,000	4	271.4	104.8	1.6	1990	179,378,946	49.9	50.1	30.9
Iran	635,238	1,645,258	18	61,531,000	17	96.9	37.4	1.4	1991[5]	55,473,189	51.5	48.5	57.3
Iraq	167,975	435,052	58	21,722,000	47	129.3	49.9	3.3	1997	22,017,983	51.4[20]	48.6[20]	74.5[9]
Ireland	27,137	70,285	120	3,647,000	123	134.4	51.9	0.4	1996	3,626,087	49.6	50.4	57.0
Isle of Man	221	572	189	72,600	200	328.5	126.9	0.6	1996[5]	71,714	48.5	51.5	51.1[4]
Israel[21, 22]	7,846	20,320	152	5,740,000	99	731.6	282.5	2.2	1995[5, 23]	5,643,500	49.8[24]	50.2[24]	86.9[24]
Italy	116,341	301,323	71	57,650,000	22	495.5	191.3	0.2	1991	57,103,833	48.6	51.4	67.1
Jamaica	4,244	10,991	161	2,254,000	135	601.8	232.4	1.0	1991	2,374,193	49.0	51.0	50.4
Japan	145,877	377,819	61	126,398,000	9	866.5	334.5	0.3	1995	125,570,246	49.0	51.0	78.1[9]
Jersey	45	116	209	85,600	196	1,902.2	737.9	0.3	1996	85,150	48.6	51.4	...
Jordan[25]	34,489	89,326	112	4,682,000	112	135.8	52.4	3.6	1994	4,095,579	52.2	47.8	78.6
Kazakstan	1,052,090	2,724,900	9	15,797,000	55	15.0	5.8	–1.4	1989	16,536,511	48.5	51.5	57.2
Kenya	224,961	582,646	46	28,337,000	36	126.0	48.6	1.7	1989	21,443,636	49.6	50.4	23.6[6]
Kiribati	313	811	181	84,000	197	268.4	103.6	1.9	1990	72,335	49.2	50.8	35.1
Korea, North	47,399	122,762	98	21,234,000	48	448.0	173.0	0.2	1993	21,213,378	48.7	51.3	58.9
Korea, South	38,328	99,268	108	46,451,000	26	1,211.9	467.9	1.0	1995[5]	44,608,726	50.2	49.8	81.0[9]
Kuwait	6,880	17,818	156	1,866.000	144	271.2	104.7	5.0	1995	1,575,983	58.0	42.0	97.0[9]
Kyrgyzstan	77,200	199,900	86	4,691,000	111	60.8	23.5	0.9	1989	4,290,442	48.9	51.1	38.2
Laos	91,429	236,800	83	5,261,000	105	57.5	22.2	2.9	1995	4,581,258	49.5	50.5	20.7[9]
Latvia	24,946	64,610	124	2,445,000	137	98.0	37.8	–1.1	1989	2,680,029	46.6	53.4	71.1
Lebanon	4,016	10,400	163	3,506,000	125	873.0	331.7	1.5	1970	2,126,325	50.8	49.2	60.1
Lesotho	11,720	30,355	140	2,090,000	140	178.3	68.9	2.2	1986[5]	1,577,536	48.2	51.8	16.0
Liberia	37,743	97,754	109	2,772,000	131	73.4	28.4	4.1	1984	2,101,628	50.6	49.4	38.8
Libya	678,400	1,757,000	17	5,691,000	100	8.4	3.2	3.2	1995[5]	4,404,986	50.8	49.2	85.3[9]
Liechtenstein	62	160	208	31,400	212	508.1	196.3	0.9	1980	25,215	49.6	50.4	...
Lithuania	25,213	65,301	123	3,704,000	122	146.9	56.7	–0.1	1989	3,689,779	47.4	52.6	68.0
Luxembourg	999	2,586	172	425,000	168	425.4	164.3	1.3	1991	384,634	49.0	51.0	85.9[7]
Macau	8.1	21.0	215	426,000	166	52,657.6	20,324.4	2.1	1991	339,464	48.5	51.5	97.0
Macedonia	9,928	25,713	148	2,023,000	141	203.8	78.7	0.5	1994	1,945,932	50.4	49.6	58.7
Madagascar	226,658	587,041	45	14,463,000	61	63.8	24.6	2.9	1993[5]	12,092,157	49.5	50.5	26.4[9]
Malawi	45,747	118,484	100	9,840,000	77	215.1	83.0	0.0	1987	7,988,507	48.4	51.6	10.7
Malaysia	127,311	329,733	66	22,083,000	44	173.5	67.0	2.5	1991	17,566,982	50.5	49.5	50.6
Maldives	115	298	203	270,000	177	2,347.8	906.0	3.0	1995	244,644	51.1	48.9	25.9[26]
Mali	482,077	1,248,574	23	10,109,000	75	21.0	8.1	3.0	1987	7,696,348	48.9	51.1	22.0
Malta	122	316	202	377,000	172	3,090.2	1,193.0	0.7	1995	378,132	49.4	50.6	85.3[27]
Marshall Islands	70	181	207	62,800	204	897.1	347.0	3.8	1988	43,380	51.1	48.9	64.5
Martinique	436	1,128	178	398,000	171	912.8	352.8	1.1	1990	359,579	48.4	51.6	80.5
Mauritania	398,000	1,030,700	29	2,511,000	136	6.3	2.4	2.7	1988	1,864,236	49.5	50.5	39.1
Mauritius	788	2,040	174	1,157,000	152	1,468.3	567.2	1.1	1990	1,056,827	49.9	50.1	39.3
Mayotte	145	375	198	134,000	189	924.1	357.3	4.9	1991	94,385	52.0	48.0	59.7[27]
Mexico	756,066	1,958,201	15	95,830,000	11	126.7	48.9	1.7	1990	81,249,645	49.1	50.9	71.3
Micronesia	271	701	185	108,000	192	398.8	154.0	0.9	1994	105,506	51.1	48.9	19.4[28]
Moldova	13,000	33,700	138	4,243,000	117	326.4	125.9	–0.5	1989	4,337,592	47.5	52.5	46.9
Monaco	0.75	1.95	217	32,000	211	42,666.7	16,410.3	0.7	1990	29,972	47.5	52.5	100.0
Mongolia	604,800	1,566,500	19	2,413,000	138	4.0	1.5	1.6	1989	2,043,100	48.9	51.1	57.1
Morocco	177,117	458,730	55	27,772,000	37	156.8	60.5	1.9	1994	25,821,571	49.7	50.3	51.7
Mozambique	313,661	812,379	35	18,641,000	52	59.4	22.9	4.4	1980	11,673,725	48.6	51.4	13.2
Myanmar (Burma)	261,228	676,577	40	47,305,000	25	181.1	69.9	1.7	1983	35,307,913	49.6	50.4	24.0
Namibia	318,580	825,118	34	1,622,000	145	5.1	2.0	1.7	1991	1,401,711	48.6	51.4	32.8
Nauru	8.2	21.2	214	10,500	216	1,280.5	495.3	1.2	1992	9,919	51.2	48.8	100.0
Nepal	56,827	147,181	94	21,959,000	45	386.4	149.2	2.6	1991	18,491,097	49.9	50.1	9.6

age distribution (%)						population (by decade, '000s)								country
0–14	15–29	30–44	45–59	60–74	75 and over	1940	1950	1960	1970	1980	1990	2000 projection	2010 projection	
38.7	28.7	16.0	9.2	5.4	1.9	1,550	1,940	2,574	3,583	4,527	5,041	5,925	6,850	El Salvador
41.7	25.1	15.7	11.2	5.3	1.0	...	211	244	270	256	369	478	615	Equatorial Guinea
46.1	23.0	15.9	8.9	4.4	1.6	...	1,403	1,612	2,153	2,555	2,945	4,142	5,737	Eritrea
22.2	21.4	21.0	18.5	11.7	5.1	1,054	1,101	1,216	1,365	1,473	1,571	1,421	1,351	Estonia
46.6	22.7	15.6	8.9	4.5	1.7	...	20,175	24,252	29,673	36,413	48,015	60,967	74,832	Ethiopia
24.4	—57.9—			—17.8—		27	31	35	39	44	48	44	44	Faroe Islands
38.2[14]	29.5[14]	17.8[14]	9.6[14]	3.8[14]	0.8[14]	218	289	394	520	634	738	811	912	Fiji
19.3	20.5	24.6	17.1	12.9	5.7	3,698	4,009	4,430	4,606	4,800	4,986	5,189	5,194	Finland
19.1	22.6	22.8	15.6	12.8	7.1	41,300	41,736	45,684	50,770	53,880	56,735	59,317	61,757	France
33.4	27.3	23.2	10.2	4.4	1.5	30	27	33	49	68	119	182	227	French Guiana
36.0[15]	29.7[15]	18.9[15]	10.4[15]	4.1[15]	0.9[15]	50	62	84	109	151	197	238	274	French Polynesia
33.8[10]	23.7[10]	17.0[10]	17.4[10]	6.9[10]	1.2[10]	...	416	446	514	808	1,078	1,244	1,445	Gabon
43.8	27.7	15.1	6.8	3.5	1.4	193	305	391	502	676	964	1,381	1,864	Gambia, The
50.3	25.8	13.1	6.2	3.7	0.9	...	...	...	370	456	630	1,176	1,781	Gaza Strip
24.8	24.1	19.2	17.5	10.8	3.6	3,612	3,527	4,160	4,708	5,075	5,460	5,432	5,234	Georgia
14.6	24.0	20.1	20.6	13.6	7.2	57,400	68,373	72,673	77,772	78,289	79,433	82,510	84,346	Germany
45.0	26.4	14.6	8.1	4.1	1.8	3,636	5,297	6,958	8,789	10,880	15,190	19,272	22,929	Ghana
19.6	21.3	22.6	18.2	12.9	5.3	14	23	24	26	30	31	27	27	Gibraltar
19.3	22.2	20.3	18.3	14.1	5.9	7,319	7,566	8,327	8,793	9,643	10,161	10,566	10,869	Greece
27.7	22.3	27.7	15.0	—7.4—		19	23	33	41	50	56	57	58	Greenland
42.5[7]	30.4[7]	12.9[7]	6.6[7]	5.5[7]	2.1[7]	71	76	90	95	89	95	102	120	Grenada
24.9	29.5	21.4	12.5	8.3	3.4	180	206	265	320	327	391	443	482	Guadeloupe
30.0	30.0	22.6	10.8	5.5	1.1	22	60	67	86	107	134	152	178	Guam
44.0	26.1	15.8	8.3	—5.8—		2,201	2,969	3,963	5,243	6,820	8,749	11,385	14,631	Guatemala
17.0[4]	23.3[4]	22.2[4]	16.8[4]	13.5[4]	7.2[4]	44	44	45	51	55	61	62	62	Guernsey
44.1[13]	26.5[13]	15.9[13]	9.0[13]	3.9[13]	0.6[13]	...	2,586	3,019	3,587	4,320	5,939	7,611	9,440	Guinea
43.9[7]	26.5[7]	16.1[7]	8.8[7]	3.7[7]	1.0[7]	341	573	617	620	789	998	1,263	1,579	Guinea-Bissau
40.8	30.5	14.0	8.8	4.4	1.2	344	428	560	714	759	759	787	803	Guyana
39.2	26.9	15.6	10.0	5.4	2.9	2,827	3,097	3,723	4,605	5,056	6,048	6,992	8,266	Haiti
46.8	25.8	14.4	7.9	3.8	1.4	1,146	1,390	1,873	2,553	3,316	4,681	6,206	7,370	Honduras
19.4[9]	22.7[9]	28.2[9]	14.7[9]	10.9[9]	4.1[9]	1,786	1,974	3,074	3,942	5,063	5,705	6,833	7,701	Hong Kong
21.3	19.4	22.5	17.9	13.4	5.6	9,280	9,338	9,984	10,337	10,693	10,365	10,047	9,845	Hungary
24.0	22.9	22.8	15.2	10.2	4.9	121	143	176	204	228	255	281	309	Iceland
36.0[7]	28.7[7]	18.5[7]	10.8[7]	5.1[7]	1.0[7]	317,000	369,880	445,857	555,042	690,462	850,558	1,017,645	1,182,171	India
36.6	28.3	18.1	10.6	5.2	1.1	70,500	75,449	92,701	119,467	146,449	178,302	209,342	237,973	Indonesia
44.3	26.6	15.1	8.2	4.8	0.8	14,000	16,913	21,554	28,359	38,783	54,134	63,328	73,130	Iran
45.2[20]	27.2[20]	14.2[20]	7.0[20]	3.7[20]	1.4[20]	3,745	5,163	6,822	9,413	13,233	18,135	23,151	31,152	Iraq
26.7	24.1	20.2	13.8	10.6	4.6	2,958	2,969	2,834	2,954	3,421	3,506	3,673	3,837	Ireland
17.3[4]	20.7[4]	20.4[4]	17.0[4]	15.3[4]	9.2[4]	52	55	49	52	64	69	73	73	Isle of Man
32.6[24]	26.4[24]	18.0[24]	12.3[24]	9.4[24]	3.1[24]	...	...	2,114	2,958	3,862	4,613	5,911	6,847	Israel[21, 22]
15.7[8]	23.6[8]	21.1[8]	18.5[8]	14.7[8]	6.4[8]	43,840	47,104	50,200	53,822	56,434	56,749	57,903	56,484	Italy
34.4	30.6	16.6	9.0	—9.4—		1,212	1,403	1,629	1,891	2,133	2,369	2,589	2,814	Jamaica
15.9	21.5	19.7	22.0	15.0	5.9	73,075	83,200	93,419	103,720	116,807	123,478	126,926	127,657	Japan
15.5[4]	24.9[4]	23.9[4]	17.0[4]	11.9[4]	6.8[4]	51	57	63	71	76	84	86	88	Jersey
42.2	31.4	13.8	8.1	—4.5—		...	1,095	1,384	1,795	2,183	3,306	5,025	6,715	Jordan[25]
31.9	26.3	19.4	13.2	6.9	2.3	6,148	6,703	9,996	13,110	14,940	16,742	15,768	16,158	Kazakstan
47.8	27.6	13.1	6.6	3.4	1.5	4,470	6,121	8,157	11,272	16,685	23,674	29,251	32,443	Kenya
40.3	27.5	17.3	9.2	4.8	0.9	29	33	41	49	58	72	87	95	Kiribati
29.5[10]	31.9[10]	21.3[10]	11.0[10]	5.0[10]	1.2[10]	...	9,471	10,392	13,912	17,114	20,019	21,688	23,505	Korea, North
23.0	27.6	25.7	14.5	7.4	1.9	...	21,147	25,142	32,976	38,124	42,869	47,386	50,317	Korea, South
40.4[9]	25.7[9]	22.5[9]	8.6[9]	2.2[9]	0.6[9]	...	145	292	748	1,358	2,141	2,017	2,712	Kuwait
37.5	27.0	16.3	10.9	6.2	2.1	1,528	1,740	2,173	2,965	3,631	4,395	4,797	5,356	Kyrgyzstan
45.4[9]	26.5[9]	14.9[9]	8.1[9]	4.2[9]	1.0[9]	1,075	1,886	2,309	2,845	3,293	4,191	5,557	7,168	Laos
21.4	21.7	20.3	19.2	12.0	5.3	1,886	1,949	2,129	2,374	2,544	2,671	2,394	2,214	Latvia
42.6	23.8	16.7	9.1	—7.7—		965	1,364	1,786	2,383	3,075	3,130	3,620	4,164	Lebanon
40.7	25.1	16.6	10.7	5.6	1.3	566	726	859	1,067	1,346	1,744	2,167	2,445	Lesotho
43.2	28.2	14.7	7.7	4.4	1.8	...	824	1,055	1,397	1,900	2,265	3,090	4,342	Liberia
45.4[9]	26.4[9]	14.7[9]	9.1[9]	3.7[9]	0.6[9]	900	961	1,338	2,056	3,119	4,338	6,122	8,708	Libya
23.0	26.5	24.1	14.1	9.2	3.1	11	14	16	21	26	29	32	35	Liechtenstein
22.6	23.8	20.0	17.9	10.9	4.8	2,925	2,567	2,779	3,148	3,439	3,722	3,702	3,639	Lithuania
17.3	21.5	23.8	17.5	12.8	7.1	296	296	314	339	364	382	433	462	Luxembourg
24.1	27.2	29.4	9.6	7.3	2.3	375	188	169	221	243	332	433	480	Macau
24.8	24.1	22.3	15.8	10.6	2.4	...	1,229	1,392	1,629	1,900	2,024	2,064	2,157	Macedonia
45.1[10]	26.8[10]	15.1[10]	7.7[10]	4.3[10]	1.0[10]	4,034	4,620	5,482	6,766	8,678	11,525	15,295	20,096	Madagascar
46.1	25.4	14.5	8.0	—6.0—		1,696	2,817	3,450	4,489	6,129	9,139	10,154	11,330	Malawi
36.7	27.6	20.0	9.9	4.6	1.2	...	6,187	7,908	10,466	13,764	17,857	23,036	27,940	Malaysia
46.9[26]	26.7[26]	12.3[26]	9.0[26]	4.0[26]	0.8[26]	81	82	106	128	155	215	285	364	Maldives
46.1	23.9	15.0	8.9	4.9	1.2	3,388	3,688	4,486	5,525	6,731	8,231	10,751	14,611	Mali
21.9	20.9	22.5	18.8	11.6	4.3	270	308	329	326	324	354	382	393	Malta
51.0	24.5	14.6	5.5	3.6	0.8	...	11	15	22	32	47	68	91	Marshall Islands
23.1	28.9	20.5	13.5	9.7	4.3	200	222	252	287	326	362	407	440	Martinique
44.1	26.6	15.0	8.1	4.7	1.4	666	960	1,057	1,227	1,550	1,979	2,660	3,582	Mauritania
29.7	28.9	22.3	10.9	6.6	1.6	428	479	662	829	966	1,059	1,169	1,298	Mauritius
47.0	27.4	15.0	6.5	3.0	1.2	16	17	25	35	52	89	148	241	Mayotte
38.3	29.4	16.6	8.9	4.5	1.7	19,815	27,737	36,945	50,596	67,570	83,226	98,881	112,891	Mexico
46.4[28]	26.8[28]	12.6[28]	8.5[28]	4.5[28]	1.1[28]	...	30	40	57	73	101	110	120	Micronesia
27.9	22.9	21.0	15.6	9.7	2.9	2,468	2,341	3,004	3,595	4,002	4,364	4,252	4,397	Moldova
12.3	16.7	21.2	20.4	17.9	10.8	20	18	21	24	27	30	32	33	Monaco
41.9	29.2	14.6	8.5	—5.8—		750	747	931	1,248	1,663	2,122	2,496	2,952	Mongolia
37.0[3]	29.6[3]	17.3[3]	9.2[3]	5.4[3]	1.5[3]	7,750	8,953	11,640	15,126	19,177	23,837	28,851	34,040	Morocco
46.4	23.9	15.6	8.6	4.0	1.2	...	6,250	7,472	9,304	12,103	14,056	19,614	24,809	Mozambique
38.6	28.7	15.5	10.9	5.2	1.1	...	19,488	22,836	27,386	33,766	41,068	48,852	56,573	Myanmar (Burma)
41.7	28.8	14.7	7.8	—6.9—		336	464	591	765	975	1,409	1,674	1,915	Namibia
41.8	25.0	20.7	8.2	—2.8—		3	3	4	7	8	9	11	11	Nauru
42.3	25.7	16.7	9.7	4.7	0.9	7,000	8,000	9,180	11,232	14,634	18,111	23,042	28,698	Nepal

Area and population　(continued)

country	area			population (latest estimate)					population (latest census)				
	square miles	square kilo- metres	rank	total midyear 1998	rank	density		% annual growth rate 1993–98	census year	total	male (%)	female (%)	urban (%)
						per sq mi	per sq km						
Netherlands, The	16,033	41,526	134	15,691,000	56	978.7	377.9	0.5	1996[2]	15,493,889	49.5	50.5	91.0
Netherlands Antilles	308	800	182	213,000	181	691.6	266.3	1.9	1992	189,474	47.9	52.1	...
New Caledonia	7,172	18,576	154	204,000	182	28.4	11.0	2.0	1996	196,836	51.2	48.8	59.4[29]
New Zealand	104,454	270,534	75	3,801,000	119	36.4	14.0	1.3	1996	3,681,546	49.1	50.9	85.0
Nicaragua	50,893	131,812	97	4,763,000	109	93.6	36.1	3.1	1995	4,357,099	49.3	50.7	54.4
Niger	489,000	1,267,000	22	9,672,000	79	19.8	7.6	3.0	1988[5]	7,228,552	49.5	50.5	15.3
Nigeria	356,669	923,768	32	110,532,000	10	309.9	119.7	3.1	1991	88,514,501	50.3	49.7	35.0[6]
Northern Mariana Islands	184	477	192	66,600	202	362.0	139.6	4.9	1990	43,345	52.6	47.4	28.0
Norway	125,004	323,758	67	4,429,000	116	35.4	13.7	0.5	1990	4,247,546	49.4	50.6	72.0
Oman	119,500	309,500	70	2,364,000	139	19.8	7.6	3.5	1993	2,018,074	58.4	41.6	71.7
Pakistan[30]	307,374	796,095	36	141,900,000	7	461.7	178.2	2.9	1981	84,253,644	52.5	47.5	28.3
Palau	188	488	191	18,100	215	96.3	37.1	2.1	1995	17,255	53.5	46.5	69.4[26]
Panama	29,157	75,517	118	2,767,000	132	94.9	36.6	1.8	1990	2,329,329	50.6	49.4	53.7
Papua New Guinea	178,704	462,840	54	4,600,000	114	25.7	9.9	2.3	1990[31]	3,607,954	52.7	47.3	15.2
Paraguay	157,048	406,752	59	5,223,000	106	33.3	12.8	2.7	1992	4,123,550	50.2	49.8	50.5
Peru	496,225	1,285,216	20	24,801,000	38	50.0	19.3	1.8	1993	22,639,443	49.7	50.3	70.1
Philippines	115,860	300,076	72	73,131,000	14	631.2	243.7	2.3	1995	68,616,536	50.4	49.6	48.6[26]
Poland	120,728	312,685	69	38,665,000	29	320.3	123.7	0.1	1988	37,878,641	48.7	51.3	61.2
Portugal	35,574	92,135	111	9,964,000	76	280.1	108.1	0.2	1991	9,862,540	48.2	51.8	48.2
Puerto Rico	3,515	9,104	165	3,786,000	121	1,077.1	415.9	0.9	1990	3,522,037	48.4	51.6	71.2
Qatar	4,416	11,437	160	579,000	162	131.1	50.6	1.9	1986	369,079	67.2	32.8	88.0[32]
Réunion	968	2,507	173	692,000	158	714.9	276.0	1.7	1990	597,828	49.2	50.8	73.4
Romania	91,699	237,500	82	22,491,000	42	245.3	94.7	-0.2	1992	22,760,449	49.1	50.9	54.4
Russia	6,592,800	17,075,400	1	146,861,000	6	22.3	8.6	-0.2	1989	147,400,537	46.9	53.1	73.6
Rwanda	10,169	26,338	147	7,965,000	86	782.4	302.1	0.6	1991	7,164,994	48.7	51.3	5.4
St. Kitts and Nevis	104	269	204	42,300	210	406.7	157.0	0.9	1991	40,618	49.1	50.9	48.9[6]
St. Lucia	238	617	188	151,000	186	634.5	244.7	1.4	1991	133,308	48.5	51.5	44.1[6]
St. Vincent and the Grenadines	150	389	197	113,000	191	751.8	290.3	0.6	1991	106,499	49.9	50.1	24.6
Samoa	1,093	2,831	171	171,000	184	156.5	60.4	1.0	1991	161,298	52.5	47.5	21.2
San Marino	24	61	211	26,100	214	1,104.5	426.5	1.6	1976	19,149	50.4	49.6	90.1[7]
São Tomé and Príncipe	386	1,001	180	136,000	188	352.3	135.9	1.8	1991	117,504	49.4	50.6	44.1[8]
Saudi Arabia	868,000	2,248,000	13	20,786,000	49	23.9	9.2	3.6	1992	16,929,294	55.9	44.1	77.3[6]
Senegal	75,951	196,712	87	9,723,000	78	128.0	49.4	3.4	1988	6,928,405	48.7	51.3	38.6
Seychelles	176	455	194	79,400	198	451.1	174.5	1.9	1996	75,304	49.7[20]	50.3[20]	35.5[20]
Sierra Leone	27,699	71,740	119	4,577,000	115	165.2	63.8	2.3	1985	3,517,530	49.6	50.4	31.8
Singapore	249	646	187	3,164,000	130	12,706.8	4,897.8	1.9	1990[5]	2,705,115	50.6	49.4	100.0
Slovakia	18,933	49,036	129	5,425,000	103	286.5	110.6	0.4	1991	5,268,935	48.9	51.1	56.8
Slovenia	7,821	20,256	153	1,985,000	142	253.8	98.0	-0.1	1991	1,974,839	48.5	51.5	48.9
Solomon Islands	10,954	28,370	143	426,000	167	38.9	15.0	3.7	1986	285,176	51.9	48.1	15.7
Somalia	246,000	637,000	42	6,842,000	92	27.8	10.7	2.5	1975	4,089,203	50.1	49.9	25.4
South Africa	470,693	1,219,090	25	42,835,000	27	91.0	35.1	1.6	1996	37,859,000	48.0	52.0	60.3[4]
Spain	195,364	505,990	51	39,371,000	28	201.5	77.8	0.1	1991	38,999,181	49.1	50.9	75.3
Sri Lanka	25,332	65,610	122	18,729,000	50	739.3	285.5	1.2	1981	14,848,364	50.8	49.2	21.5
Sudan, The	966,757	2,503,890	10	33,551,000	32	34.7	13.4	3.0	1993	24,940,683	50.2	49.8	31.3[9]
Suriname	63,251	163,820	92	418,000	169	6.6	2.6	0.7	1980	354,860	49.5	50.5	49.1[9]
Swaziland	6,704	17,364	157	966,000	154	144.1	55.6	1.1	1986	681,059	47.2	52.8	22.8
Sweden	173,732	449,964	56	8,860,000	82	51.0	19.7	0.3	1996[2]	8,837,496	49.4	50.6	83.9
Switzerland	15,940	41,285	135	7,118,000	91	446.5	172.4	0.5	1990[33]	6,873,687	49.3	50.7	68.9
Syria	71,498	185,180	88	15,335,000	58	214.5	82.8	2.7	1994	13,812,000	51.1[3]	48.9[3]	52.2[9]
Taiwan	13,969	36,179	136	21,843,000	46	1,563.7	603.7	0.9	1990[5]	20,393,628	52.1	47.9	74.5
Tajikistan	55,300	143,100	95	6,112,000	95	110.5	42.7	1.6	1989	5,108,576	49.7	50.3	32.6
Tanzania	364,901	945,090	31	30,609,000	34	83.9	32.4	2.5	1988	23,174,336	48.9	51.1	18.5
Thailand	198,115	513,115	50	61,201,000	18	308.9	119.3	1.1	1990	54,532,300	49.6	50.4	18.7
Togo	21,925	56,785	125	4,906,000	108	223.8	86.4	3.6	1981	2,719,567	48.7	51.3	15.2
Tonga	290	750	184	97,900	194	338.2	130.6	0.3	1996[5]	97,446	50.3[14]	49.7[14]	30.7[14]
Trinidad and Tobago	1,980	5,128	168	1,275,000	149	643.9	248.6	0.4	1990	1,234,388	50.1	49.9	64.8
Tunisia	63,378	164,150	91	9,380,000	81	148.0	57.1	1.6	1994	8,785,364	50.6	49.4	61.0
Turkey	300,948	779,452	37	64,567,000	15	214.5	82.8	1.7	1990	56,473,035	50.7	49.3	59.0
Turkmenistan	188,500	488,100	52	4,731,000	110	25.1	9.7	1.9	1995	4,483,251	49.6	50.4	46.0
Tuvalu	9.9	25.6	213	10,400	217	1,050.5	405.8	1.6	1991	9,043	48.4	51.6	42.5
Uganda	93,065	241,038	80	22,167,000	43	238.2	92.0	3.0	1991	16,671,705	49.1	50.9	11.3
Ukraine	233,100	603,700	44	50,302,000	23	215.8	83.3	-0.7	1989	51,706,746	46.3	53.7	66.9
United Arab Emirates	32,280	83,600	116	2,744,000	133	85.0	32.8	5.7	1995	2,377,700	66.5	33.5	84.0[9]
United Kingdom	94,251	244,110	79	59,126,000	19	627.3	242.3	0.3	1991[5]	56,467,000	48.4	51.6	89.1[16]
United States	3,615,215	9,363,364	4	270,262,000	3	74.8	28.9	0.9	1990[34]	248,709,873	48.7	51.3	75.2
Uruguay	68,037	176,215	90	3,216,000	129	47.3	18.3	0.8	1996	3,151,662	48.4	51.6	89.3
Uzbekistan	172,700	447,400	57	24,091,000	40	139.5	53.8	1.9	1989	19,905,158	49.3	50.7	40.7
Vanuatu	4,707	12,190	159	182,000	183	38.7	14.9	2.6	1989	142,630	51.6	48.4	17.7
Venezuela	352,144	912,050	33	23,242,000	41	66.0	25.5	2.1	1990	19,405,429	49.7	50.3	84.0
Vietnam	127,816	331,041	65	76,236,000	13	596.5	230.3	1.6	1989	64,411,713	48.7	51.3	20.1
Virgin Islands (U.S.)	136	352	200	118,000	190	867.6	335.2	1.4	1990	101,809	48.3	51.7	37.2
West Bank[35]	2,270	5,900	166	1,881,000	143	828.6	318.8	9.9	1995[2, 16]	1,707,000	51.2	48.8	...
Western Sahara	97,344	252,120	77	288,000	175	3.0	1.1	3.6	1994	252,146	...	...	90.7
Yemen	214,300	555,000	48	16,388,000	54	76.5	29.5	3.4	1994	14,587,807	51.2	48.8	23.5
Yugoslavia	39,449	102,173	107	10,664,000	69	270.3	104.4	0.3	1991	10,394,026	49.6	50.4	53.2[6]
Zambia	290,586	752,614	39	9,461,000	80	32.6	12.6	2.0	1990	7,818,447	49.2	50.8	42.0
Zimbabwe	150,872	390,757	60	11,044,000	65	73.2	28.3	0.9	1992	10,412,548	48.8	51.2	30.6

[1]Settled population only.　[2]Civil register; not a census.　[3]1994 estimate.　[4]1991 census.　[5]Data are for de jure population.　[6]1990 estimate.　[7]1991 estimate.　[8]1992 estimate.　[9]1995 estimate.
[10]1993 estimate.　[11]Except census, data are for the island of Cyprus.　[12]Republic of Cyprus only.　[13]1996 estimate.　[14]1986 census.　[15]1988 census.　[16]Projections from 1995 demographic survey.
[17]Former West Germany only.　[18]Excludes visitors, transients, and family members of British servicemen.　[19]Data exclude Alderney (population 2,297) and Sark (population 604).　[20]1987 census.
[21]Area figures exclude the West Bank, East Jerusalem, Gaza Strip, and Golan Heights.　[22]Population figures include the Golan Heights and East Jerusalem, and exclude Israelis in the West Bank and

age distribution (%)						population (by decade, '000s)						2000 projection	2010 projection	country
0–14	15–29	30–44	45–59	60–74	75 and over	1940	1950	1960	1970	1980	1990			
18.4	21.3	23.9	18.6	12.1	5.7	8,834	10,027	11,417	12,958	14,150	14,952	15,835	16,504	Netherlands, The
26.0	23.9	25.5	14.3	7.3	3.0	77	112	136	163	174	188	221	266	Netherlands Antilles
32.6[29]	28.6[29]	19.8[29]	12.1[29]	5.4[29]	1.6[29]	53	59	79	110	140	171	211	250	New Caledonia
23.2[4]	24.6[4]	22.4[4]	14.4[4]	10.9[4]	4.5[4]	1,637	1,909	2,377	2,820	3,144	3,363	3,878	4,225	New Zealand
45.1	27.5	15.0	7.2	3.7	1.4	825	1,098	1,493	2,053	2,776	3,740	5,045	6,429	Nicaragua
48.7	24.8	14.6	6.8	3.6	1.5	1,700	2,482	3,168	4,182	5,629	7,644	10,260	13,678	Niger
47.9[6]	21.9[6]	14.3[6]	9.0[6]	5.2[6]	1.6[6]	...	31,797	39,230	49,309	65,699	86,530	117,171	150,274	Nigeria
23.8	33.5	30.7	9.1	2.3	0.5	48	6	9	10	17	44	72	99	Northern Mariana Islands
18.8	22.9	22.1	15.1	13.9	7.2	2,973	3,265	3,581	3,877	4,086	4,241	4,468	4,658	Norway
41.0	25.5	21.9	7.8	2.9	0.9	...	489	597	774	1,175	1,773	2,533	3,520	Oman
44.5	23.9	15.4	9.3	5.3	1.6	28,300	39,513	49,955	65,706	85,299	112,857	147,140	176,400	Pakistan[30]
30.3[26]	27.8[26]	22.8[26]	10.5[26]	6.4[26]	2.2[26]	25	7	9	12	13	15	19	22	Palau
34.8	29.2	18.2	10.2	5.5	2.0	620	893	1,148	1,531	1,950	2,398	2,856	3,266	Panama
41.9	28.5	16.6	8.7	—3.2—		1,308	1,412	1,747	2,288	2,991	3,823	4,812	5,925	Papua New Guinea
40.1	27.6	18.7	8.3	4.2	1.1	1,111	1,351	1,774	2,351	3,136	4,219	5,496	6,980	Paraguay
37.0	28.6	17.7	9.8	—7.0—		6,784	7,632	9,931	13,193	17,295	21,307	25,662	30,506	Peru
39.6[26]	28.7[26]	17.3[26]	9.2[26]	4.2[26]	1.1[26]	16,459	20,988	27,561	36,850	48,286	60,937	76,320	91,851	Philippines
25.4	21.2	23.3	15.5	10.4	4.2	31,500	24,824	29,561	32,526	35,578	38,057	38,684	39,969	Poland
19.9[7]	23.7[7]	20.3[7]	16.9[7]	13.7[7]	5.3[7]	7,696	8,405	8,826	9,040	9,766	9,896	9,998	10,170	Portugal
27.2	25.1	20.4	14.1	9.2	4.0	1,878	2,218	2,360	2,721	3,204	3,528	3,836	4,120	Puerto Rico
27.8	29.3	32.3	8.6	1.6	0.4	...	47	59	151	229	484	599	693	Qatar
29.5	29.8	20.3	11.7	6.5	2.1	221	244	338	447	507	602	716	847	Réunion
22.4	22.9	20.8	17.1	—16.8—		15,907	16,311	18,403	20,253	22,201	23,207	22,374	22,371	Romania
23.1	22.0	21.9	17.6	11.2	4.2	110,098	105,018	119,906	130,392	138,660	148,292	145,905	143,918	Russia
45.6	28.6	12.4	8.4	3.9	0.9	1,910	2,429	3,083	3,813	5,170	7,161	8,337	9,881	Rwanda
36.9[7]	31.8[7]	14.5[7]	6.0[7]	6.9[7]	3.8[7]	43	49	51	46	44	40	43	50	St. Kitts and Nevis
36.8	29.4	16.3	8.7	6.3	2.5	70	79	86	101	122	134	154	172	St. Lucia
37.2	29.5	16.1	8.3	6.4	2.5	61	67	80	86	99	105	114	124	St. Vincent and the Grenadines
40.5	30.0	14.6	—6.0—		3.9	61	82	111	143	155	159	174	192	Samoa
24.4	23.0	19.9	17.4	11.4	3.9	10	13	15	19	21	23	27	32	San Marino
46.9	26.2	12.2	8.0	—6.7—		60	60	64	74	94	117	141	169	São Tomé and Príncipe
42.1[8]	22.8[8]	21.6[8]	9.9[8]	3.0[8]	0.6[8]	...	3,860	4,718	6,109	9,949	15,871	22,246	31,198	Saudi Arabia
47.5	26.1	13.6	7.8	—5.0—		1,857	2,654	3,270	4,318	5,640	7,408	10,390	14,362	Senegal
33.6[20]	30.3[20]	15.3[20]	10.7[20]	7.1[20]	2.9[20]	32	34	42	54	63	70	82	94	Seychelles
43.9[32]	25.6[32]	15.7[32]	9.6[32]	4.5[32]	0.7[32]	1,700	1,944	2,241	2,656	3,236	3,997	4,866	6,056	Sierra Leone
23.2	27.3	27.7	12.7	6.9	2.2	751	1,022	1,639	2,075	2,282	2,705	3,288	3,985	Singapore
25.0	22.7	22.8	14.6	10.7	4.2	3,553	3,463	3,994	4,528	4,984	5,298	5,466	5,676	Slovakia
20.0	22.4	23.7	17.4	11.9	4.6	1,450	1,467	1,580	1,727	1,901	1,998	1,982	2,004	Slovenia
47.3	25.7	13.9	8.1	—4.9—		94	104	125	163	230	319	459	600	Solomon Islands
45.6	24.9	15.5	7.4	—5.4—		...	2,438	2,956	3,667	5,791	6,675	7,434	10,132	Somalia
34.6[4]	28.5[4]	19.6[4]	10.8[4]	5.1[4]	1.4[4]	10,353	13,596	17,417	22,739	29,252	37,191	43,982	47,503	South Africa
19.1[7]	24.9[7]	20.1[7]	16.5[7]	13.7[7]	5.7[7]	25,757	27,868	30,303	33,779	37,636	38,798	39,466	39,917	Spain
35.3	29.6	17.9	10.6	5.2	1.4	5,972	7,678	9,889	12,514	14,747	16,993	19,153	21,258	Sri Lanka
43.0	27.0	16.4	9.3	3.7	0.6	...	8,051	10,589	13,788	19,064	26,628	35,530	46,573	Sudan, The
39.3	29.5	13.8	10.0	4.5	2.8	193	208	285	373	355	402	425	443	Suriname
47.3	26.6	13.4	7.4	3.4	1.3	154	277	352	455	607	840	1,004	1,202	Swaziland
18.8	19.3	20.4	19.4	13.6	8.4	6,371	7,041	7,498	8,081	8,310	8,559	8,909	9,084	Sweden
16.8	22.8	23.2	18.0	12.5	6.7	4,234	4,715	5,429	6,270	6,362	6,712	7,218	7,438	Switzerland
47.3[3]	27.8[3]	13.8[3]	6.7[3]	3.7[3]	0.8[3]	2,597	3,495	4,561	6,305	8,704	12,116	16,126	20,468	Syria
27.1	27.8	23.1	12.3	7.9	1.8	5,987	7,619	10,668	14,583	17,705	20,279	22,250	24,399	Taiwan
42.9	28.1	13.8	9.0	4.6	1.6	1,525	1,532	2,083	2,942	3,968	5,303	6,303	7,497	Tajikistan
47.2[6]	26.7[6]	14.2[6]	7.8[6]	3.3[6]	0.7[6]	...	8,909	10,876	14,038	18,689	24,886	31,963	39,390	Tanzania
28.8	30.4	21.2	12.3	5.7	1.6	15,296	20,010	26,392	35,037	46,538	56,096	62,405	67,597	Thailand
49.8	24.8	13.1	6.8	3.3	2.0	834	1,172	1,456	1,964	2,596	3,680	5,263	7,401	Togo
40.6[14]	29.0[14]	13.8[14]	10.1[14]	5.0[14]	1.4[14]	37	50	65	80	92	96	99	101	Tonga
33.5	27.2	19.9	10.7	6.4	2.3	503	668	828	941	1,082	1,227	1,285	1,333	Trinidad and Tobago
34.8	28.5	18.8	9.6	6.4	1.9	2,887	3,517	4,149	5,099	6,443	8,207	9,645	10,960	Tunisia
35.0	28.6	18.4	10.9	5.6	1.6	17,723	20,809	27,509	35,321	44,438	56,123	66,618	76,570	Turkey
40.5[29]	28.8[29]	15.5[29]	9.1[29]	4.7[29]	1.4[29]	1,302	1,211	1,594	2,189	2,860	3,668	4,905	5,736	Turkmenistan
34.6	24.0	20.7	11.3	—9.2—		4	5	5	6	8	9	11	12	Tuvalu
47.3	27.7	13.1	6.9	3.7	1.3	4,233	5,522	7,262	9,728	12,298	17,227	23,452	31,768	Uganda
21.5	21.0	20.6	18.5	10.7	7.7	41,340	36,906	42,783	47,317	50,034	51,892	49,516	47,601	Ukraine
34.9[9]	18.7[9]	31.6[9]	12.7[9]	1.9[9]	0.2[9]	...	70	90	223	1,042	1,844	2,844	3,399	United Arab Emirates
19.1	21.9	21.2	16.7	14.1	7.0	48,226	50,290	52,372	55,632	56,330	57,561	59,454	60,800	United Kingdom
21.5	23.4	23.9	14.4	11.5	5.3	132,594	152,271	180,671	204,879	227,726	249,949	274,894	297,976	United States
24.4[13]	23.8[13]	19.3[13]	15.2[13]	12.3[13]	4.9[13]	1,974	2,194	2,531	2,824	2,914	3,041	3,278	3,524	Uruguay
40.8	28.4	15.0	9.3	4.7	1.8	6,551	6,314	8,559	11,973	15,977	20,515	24,987	28,723	Uzbekistan
45.5	26.6	15.2	8.4	3.7	0.6	43	52	65	86	115	147	192	245	Vanuatu
38.3	28.1	18.6	9.3	4.5	1.2	3,740	5,094	7,579	10,721	15,091	19,502	24,170	28,716	Venezuela
39.0	28.7	16.0	9.1	5.6	1.6	...	25,587	31,955	42,978	54,234	66,314	78,350	88,602	Vietnam
28.9	23.7	22.0	16.0	7.3	2.2	25	27	32	63	100	104	121	132	Virgin Islands (U.S.)
44.6	28.4	14.0	7.4	4.4	1.2	...	...	...	608	733	1,011	2,002	2,736	West Bank[35]
...	...	...	...	...	...	...	14	32	76	155	214	306	386	Western Sahara
47.6[3]	28.7[3]	11.9[3]	7.4[3]	3.6[3]	0.7[3]	...	4,461	5,483	6,628	8,527	12,023	17,521	24,794	Yemen
22.8	21.6	21.7	17.1	12.2	3.5	...	7,131	8,050	8,910	9,842	10,529	10,799	11,171	Yugoslavia
47.3	28.2	12.9	7.3	3.5	0.7	1,484	2,553	3,254	4,247	5,638	7,957	9,872	12,150	Zambia
45.1	28.4	14.0	7.3	3.9	1.2	1,940	2,853	4,011	5,515	7,298	9,958	11,272	11,953	Zimbabwe

Gaza Strip. [23]Includes East Jerusalem and Israelis in the West Bank, Gaza Strip, and Golan Heights. [24]1983 census. [25]Excludes the West Bank. [26]1990 census. [27]1985 census. [28]1980 census. [29]1989 census. [30]Excludes Afghan refugees (1997; 1.2 million) and the area (32,323 sq mi [83,716 sq km]) and population (1997; 3.9 million) of Pakistani-occupied Jammu and Kashmir. [31]Excludes an estimated 155,000 persons in North Solomons province and five remote census districts. [32]1985 estimate. [33]Includes resident aliens; excludes seasonal workers. [34]Excludes 515,000 armed forces overseas. [35]Excludes East Jerusalem.

Major cities and national capitals

The following table lists the principal cities or municipalities (those exceeding 100,000 in population [75,000 for Anglo-America]) of the countries of the world, together with figures for each national capital (indicated by a ★), regardless of size.

Most of the populations given refer to a so-called city proper, that is, a legally defined, incorporated, or chartered area defined by administrative boundaries and by national or state law. Some data, however, refer to the municipality, or commune, similar to the medieval city-state in that the city is governed together with its immediately adjoining, economically dependent areas, whether urban or rural in nature. Some countries define no other demographic or legal entities within such communes or municipalities, but many identify a centre, seat, head (*cabecera*), or locality that corresponds to the most densely populated, compact, contiguous core of the municipality. Because the amount of work involved in carefully defining these "centres" may be considerable, the necessary resources usually exist only at the time of a national census (generally 5 or 10 years apart). Between censuses, therefore, it may be possible only to track the growth of the municipality as a whole. Thus, in order to provide the most up-to-date data for cities in this table, figures referring to municipalities or communes may be given (identified by the abbreviation "MU"), even though the country itself may define a smaller, more closely knit city proper. Specific identification of municipalities is provided in this table *only* when the country also publishes data for a more narrowly defined city proper; it is *not* provided when the sole published figure is the municipality, whether or not this is the proper local administrative term for the entity.

Problems also exist in the identification of cities in terms of named legal entities. There is, for example, a single municipality *(commune)* named Brussel (Brussels) at the centre of the Brussels agglomeration in Belgium; the *commune* numbers only about 136,000 population, while the agglomeration, which is understood by most people to constitute the city, numbers nearly a million. Both are shown so as to apprise the reader of the existence of a problem.

For certain countries, more than one form of the name of the city is given, usually to permit recognition of recent place name changes or of *forms* of the place name likely to be encountered in press stories if the title of the city's entry in the *Encyclopædia Britannica* is spelled according to a different romanization or spelling policy. Chinese names, for example, are given first in their Wade-Giles spelling (the scholarly system used by Britannica) and then, parenthetically, in their Pinyin spelling, the official Chinese system now encountered in press reports, official documents and maps, and in the *Britannica Book of the Year.*

Sources for this data were usually the national census and statistical abstracts of the countries concerned, supplemented by the Internet and correspondence with most national statistical offices to solicit unpublished data.

Major cities and national capitals

country / city	population
Afghanistan (early 1990s est.)	
Herāt	186,800
★ Kābul	700,000[1]
Kandahār (Qandahār)	237,500
Mazār-e Sharīf	127,800
Albania (1995 est.)	
★ Tiranë	270,000
Algeria (1987)	
★ Algiers	2,168,000[2]
Annaba	222,518
Batna	181,601
Béchar	107,311
Bejaïa	114,534
Biskra	128,280
Blida (el-Boulaida)	127,284
Constantine (Qacentina)	440,842
Mostaganem	114,037
Oran (Wahran)	609,823
Sétif	170,182
Sidi bel Abbès	152,778
Skikda	128,747
Tébessa	107,559
Tlemcen (Tilimsen)	107,632
American Samoa (1990)	
★ Fagatogo (legislative and judicial)	2,323[3]
★ Utulei (executive)	930[3]
Andorra (1995 est.)	
★ Andorra la Vella	21,984
Angola (1993 est.)	
Huambo	400,000
★ Luanda	2,081,000[2]
Lubango	105,000[4]
Antigua and Barbuda (1991)	
★ Saint John's	22,342
Argentina (1991)	
Avellaneda	346,620[5]
Bahía Blanca	260,096
★ Buenos Aires	2,988,006[2, 5]
Catamarca	110,269
Comodoro Rivadavia	124,104
Concordia	116,485
Córdoba	1,208,713[5]
Corrientes	258,103
Formosa	148,074
General San Martín	407,506[5]
La Matanza	1,111,811
La Plata	642,979[5]
La Rioja	103,727
Lanús	466,755[5]
Lomas de Zamora	572,769[5]
Mar del Plata	512,880
Mendoza	773,113[5]
Morón	641,541[5]
Neuquén	243,803[5]
Paraná	211,936[5]
Posadas	210,755[5]
Quilmes	509,445[5]
Resistencia	292,350[5]
Río Cuarto	138,853[5]
Rosario	1,118,984[5]
Salta	370,904[5]
San Fernando	132,626[5]
San Isidro	299,022[5]
San Juan	352,691[5]
San Luis	110,136
San Miguel de Tucumán	622,324[5]
San Nicolás de los Arroyos	119,302
San Salvador de Jujuy	180,102[5]
Santa Fe	406,388[5]
Santiago del Estero La Banda	263,471
Vicente López	289,142[5]
Armenia (1995 est.)	
Gyumri (Kumayri; Leninakan)	120,000[6]
★ Yerevan	1,248,700
Aruba (1996 est.)	
★ Oranjestad	21,000
Australia (1995 est.)	
Adelaide	1,081,000[7]
Bankstown	162,600[8]
Blacktown	228,400[8]
Brisbane	1,489,100[7]
Cairns	100,900
Campbelltown	149,100[8]
★ Canberra	303,700[7]
Canterbury	134,500[8]
Fairfield	186,100[8]
Geelong	152,600[9]
Gold Coast-Tweed	326,900[9]
Gosford	142,150[8]
Hobart	194,700[7]
Keilor	114,639[8]
Knox	132,686[8]
Lake Macquarie	175,510[8]
Liverpool	106,750[8]
Melbourne	3,218,100[7]
Moorabbin	100,389[8]
Newcastle	466,000[9]
Parramatta	137,450[8]
Penrith	163,500[8]
Perth	1,262,600[7]
Randwick	117,600[8]
Stirling	178,734[1]
Sydney	3,772,700[7]
Townsville	124,900[9]
Wanneroo	190,965[1]
Wollongong	253,600[9]
Austria (1991)	
Graz	237,810
Innsbruck	118,112
Linz	203,044
Salzburg	143,978
★ Vienna	1,560,471[10]
Azerbaijan (1995 est.)	
★ Baku (Baky)	1,739,900
Gäncä (Gyandzha)	292,500
Sumqayit (Sumgait)	270,000
Bahamas, The (1990)	
★ Nassau	172,196[11]
Bahrain (1995 est.)	
★ Al-Manāmah	148,000
Bangladesh (1991)	
Barisāl	188,000
Bogra	130,000
Brāhmanbāria	125,000
Chittagong	1,599,000
Comilla	156,000
★ Dhākā (Dacca)	3,839,000
Dinājpur	138,000
Gāzipur	104,000
Jamālpur	111,000
Jessore	154,000
Khulna	731,000
Mymensingh	202,000
Naogaon	110,000
Nārāyanganj	296,000
Narsinghdi	106,000
Nawābganj (Nowābgonj)	141,000
Pābna	112,000
Rājshāhi	318,000
Rangpur	207,000
Saidpur	105,000
Savar	115,000
Sirājganj	108,000
Sylhet	109,000
Tangail	114,000
Tongi	181,000
Barbados (1990)	
★ Bridgetown	6,070
Belarus (1996 est.)	
Baranovichi (Baranavichy)	172,000
Bobruysk (Babrujsk)	227,100
Borisov (Barysau)	153,000
Brest (Bierascie)	293,000
Gomel (Homiel)	512,000
Grodno (Horadnia)	301,000
Lida	101,000
★ Minsk	1,700,000
Mogilyov (Mahilou)	367,000
Mozyr (Mazyr)	108,000
Orsha (Vorsha)	134,000
Pinsk	130,000
Soligorsk	101,000
Vitebsk (Viciebsk)	365,000
Belgium (1996 est.)	
Antwerp	455,852
Brugge (Bruges)	115,815
★ Brussels	136,424[12]
Agglomeration	948,122
Charleroi	205,591
Ghent	226,464
Liège (Luik)	190,525
Namur	105,059
Belize (1996 est.)	
★ Belmopan	6,490
Benin (1994 est.)	
Abomey-Calavi	125,565[13]
★ Cotonou (official)	750,000
Djougou	132,000
Parakou	120,000
★ Porto-Novo (de facto)	200,000
Bermuda (1995 est.)	
★ Hamilton	1,100
Bhutan (1993 est.)	
Paro	3,000[14]
★ Thimphu	30,340
Bolivia (1993 est.)	
Cochabamba	448,756
El Alto	446,189
★ La Paz (administrative)	784,976
Oruro	201,831
Potosí	123,327
Santa Cruz	767,260
★ Sucre (judicial)	144,994
Bosnia and Herzegovina (1991)	
Banja Luka	143,079
★ Sarajevo	250,000[2]
Botswana (1995 est.)	
★ Gaborone	182,000
Brazil (1991)	
Alvorada	132,582
Americana	153,592
Anápolis	222,400
Aracaju	401,676
Araçatuba	145,751
Arapiraca	124,790
Araraquara	101,302
Barra Mansa	145,112
Bauru	254,211
Belém	765,476
Belo Horizonte	1,529,566
Betim	152,846
Blumenau	185,200
Boa Vista	118,928
★ Brasília	1,492,542
Cachoeiro de Itapemirim	112,099
Campina Grande	298,331
Campinas	748,076
Campo Grande	516,403
Campos	275,508
Canoas	269,234
Carapicuíba	207,264
Caruaru	180,654
Cascavel	175,294
Caxias do Sul	262,983
Colombo	105,464
Contagem	195,705
Cuiabá	252,784
Curitiba	841,882
Diadema	305,068
Divinópolis	141,984
Dourados	116,754
Duque de Caxias	325,903
Embu	155,851
Feira de Santana	340,034
Florianópolis	191,664
Fortaleza	743,335
Foz do Iguaçu	186,362
Franca	227,613
Goiânia	912,136
Governador Valadares	210,396
Gravataí	166,954
Guarapuava	107,046
Guarulhos	544,698
Ilhéus	135,117
Imperatriz	209,970
Ipatinga	120,025
Itabuna	170,434
Itajaí	114,558
Itapevi	107,983
Itaquaquecetuba	164,665
Jaboatão	217,905
Jacareí	143,468
Jequié	114,542
João Pessoa	497,306
Joinville	326,208
Juàzeiro do Norte	163,527
Juiz de Fora	377,538
Jundiaí	253,177
Lages	137,169
Limeira	177,016
Londrina	355,062
Luziânia	194,128
Macapá	146,523
Maceió	554,727
Manaus	1,005,634
Marabá	102,364
Maracanaú	133,206
Marília	144,906
Maringá	225,516
Mauá	294,631
Mogi das Cruzes	125,992
Montes Claros	223,046
Mossoró	117,020
Natal	459,827
Nilópolis	104,671
Niterói	400,586
Nova Friburgo	111,020
Nova Iguaçu	562,062
Novo Hamburgo	199,479
Olinda	341,059
Osasco	566,949
Parnaíba	105,131
Passo Fundo	135,158
Pelotas	260,510
Petrolina	123,857
Petrópolis	164,849
Piracicaba	223,170
Poços de Caldas	104,800
Ponta Grossa	219,648
Porto Alegre	1,237,223
Porto Velho	226,198
Presidente Prudente	157,618
Recife	1,296,995
Ribeirão Prêto	416,186
Rio Branco	167,457
Rio Claro	130,364
Rio de Janeiro	5,473,909
Rio Grande	157,608
Salvador	2,070,296
Santa Bárbara d'Oeste	140,208
Santa Maria	193,294
Santarém	168,153
Santo André	518,272
Santos	415,554
São Bernardo do Campo	550,030
São Caetano do Sul	149,203
São Carlos	100,502
São Gonçalo	296,021
São João de Meriti	220,742
São José do Rio Prêto	263,454
São José dos Campos	385,879
São Leopoldo	160,228
São Luís	164,334
São Paulo	9,393,753
São Vicente	268,467
Sapucaia do Sul	104,626
Sete Lagoas	137,537
Sorocaba	348,952
Susano (Suzano)	110,414
Taboão da Serra	159,894
Taubaté	185,790
Teresina	556,073
Uberaba	198,565
Uberlândia	354,710
Uruguaiana	103,160
Vila Velha	263,897
Vitória	258,243
Vitória da Conquista	179,868
Volta Redonda	219,988
Brunei (1991)	
★ Bandar Seri Begawan	21,484
Bulgaria (1996 est.)	
Burgas	199,470
Dobrich	103,532
Pleven	125,029
Plovdiv	344,326
Ruse	168,051
Sliven	107,011
★ Sofia	1,116,823
Stara Zagora	149,666
Varna	301,421

country city	population
Burkina Faso (1993 est.)	
Bobo Dioulasso	300,000
Koudougou	105,000
★ Ouagadougou	690,000
Burundi (1994 est.)	
★ Bujumbura	300,000
Gitega	101,827[15]
Cambodia (1994 est.)	
★ Phnom Penh	920,000
Cameroon (1992 est.)	
Bafoussam	120,000
Bamenda	110,690[16]
Douala	1,200,000
Garoua	160,000
Maroua	140,000
★ Yaoundé	800,000
Canada (1991)	
Brampton	234,445
Brantford	81,997
Burlington	129,575
Burnaby	158,858
Calgary	710,677
Cambridge	92,772
Coquitlam	84,021
Delta	88,978
East York	102,696
Edmonton	616,741
Etobicoke	309,993
Gatineau	92,284
Gloucester	101,677
Guelph	87,976
Halifax	114,455
Hamilton	318,499
Kelowna	75,950
Kitchener	168,282
Laval	314,398
London	303,165
Longueuil	129,874
Markham	153,811
Mississauga	463,388
Montreal	1,017,666
Montreal-Nord	85,516
Nepean	107,627
Niagara Falls	75,399
North York	562,564
Oakville	114,670
Oshawa	129,344
★ Ottawa	313,987
Quebec	167,517
Regina	179,178
Richmond	126,624
Richmond Hill	80,142
Saanich	95,577
Saint Catharines	129,300
Saint John's	95,770
Saskatoon	186,058
Sault Sainte Marie	81,476
Scarborough	524,598
Sherbrooke	76,429
Sudbury	92,884
Surrey	245,173
Thunder Bay	113,746
Toronto	635,395
Vancouver	471,844
Vaughan	111,359
Windsor	191,435
Winnipeg	616,790
York	140,525
Cape Verde (1995 est.)	
★ Praia	68,000
Central African Republic (1995 est.)	
★ Bangui	553,000
Chad (1993; MU)	
Abéché	187,936
Bongor	196,713
Doba	185,461
Moundou	282,103
★ N'Djamena	530,965
Sarh	193,753
Chile (1995 est.; MU)	
Antofagasta	236,730
Arica	173,336
Calama	120,602[1]
Chillán	157,083
Concepción	350,268
Copiapó	100,946[13]
Coquimbo	122,872[13]
Curicó	103,919[13]
Iquique	152,592
La Serena	117,983
Los Angeles	142,136[13]
Osorno	123,055
Puente Alto	318,898
Puerto Montt	122,399
Punta Arenas	117,206
Quilpué	110,340
Rancagua	193,755
San Bernardo	206,315
★ Santiago (administrative)	5,076,808
Talca	169,448
Talcahuano	260,915
Temuco	239,340
Valdivia	119,431
★ Valparaíso (legislative)	282,168
Viña del Mar	322,220
China (1990 est.)[17]	
A-ch'eng (Acheng)	197,595
A-k'o-su (Aksu)	164,092
An-ch'ing (Anqing)	250,718
An-k'ang (Ankang)	142,170
An-shan (Anshan)	1,500,000[18,19]
An-shun (Anshun)	174,142
An-ta (Anda)	136,446
An-yang (Anyang)	420,332
Canton (Guangzhou)	3,580,000[20]
Chan-chiang (Zhanjiang)	400,997
Ch'ang-chi (Changji)	132,260
Chang-chia-k'ou (Zhangjiakou)	529,136
Ch'ang-chih (Changzhi)	317,144
Ch'ang-chou (Changzhou)	531,470
Chang-chou (Zhangzhou)	181,424
Ch'ang-ch'un (Changchun)	2,110,000[20]
Ch'ang-sha (Changsha)	1,330,000[20]
Ch'ang-shu (Changshu)	181,805
Ch'ang-te (Changde)	301,276
Chao-ch'ing (Zhaoqing)	194,784
Ch'ao-chou (Chaozhou)	313,469
Ch'ao-hsien (Chaoxian)	123,676
Chao-tung (Zhaodong)	179,976
Ch'ao-yang (Chaoyang)	222,394
Chen-chiang (Zhenjiang)	368,316
Cheng-chou (Zhengzhou)	1,710,000[20]
Ch'eng-te (Chengde)	246,799
Ch'eng-tu (Chengdu)	2,810,000[20]
Chi-an (Ji'an)	148,583
Chi-hsi (Jixi)	683,885
Chi-lin (Jilin)	1,270,000[20]
Chi-nan (Jinan)	2,320,000[20]
Chi-ning (Jining) (*Inner Mongolia*)	163,552
Chi-ning (Jining) (*Shantung*)	265,248
Ch'i-t'ai-ho (Qitaihe)	214,957
Ch'i-tung (Qidong)	126,872
Chia-hsing (Jiaxing)	211,526
Chia-mu-ssu (Jiamusi)	493,409
Chiang-men (Jiangmen)	230,587
Chiang-yin (Jiangyin)	213,659
Chiang-yu (Jiangyou)	175,753
Chiao-hsien (Jiaoxian)	153,364
Chiao-nan (Jiaonan)	121,397
Chiao-tso (Jiaozuo)	409,100
Ch'ien-chiang (Qianjiang)	205,504
Ch'ih-feng (Chifeng)	350,077
Chin-ch'ang (Jinchang)	105,287
Chin-ch'eng (Jincheng)	136,396
Chin-chou (Jinzhou)	569,518
Ch'in-chou (Qinzhou)	114,586
Chin-hsi (Jinxi)	357,052
Chin-hua (Jinhua)	144,280
Ch'in-huang-tao (Qinhuangdao)	364,972
Ch'ing-chou (Qingzhou)	128,258
Ch'ing-tao (Qingdao)	2,060,000[20]
Ching-te-chen (Jingdezhen)	281,183
Ch'ing-yüan (Qingyuan)	164,641
Chiu-chiang (Jiujiang)	291,187
Chiu-t'ai (Jiutai)	180,130
Chou-k'ou (Zhoukou)	146,288
Chou-shan (Zhoushan)	156,317
Chu-ch'eng (Zhucheng)	102,134
Ch'ü-ching (Qujing)	178,669
Ch'u-chou (Quzhou)	112,373
Chu-chou (Zhuzhou)	409,924
Chu-hai (Zhuhai)	164,747
Ch'u-hsien (Chuxian)	125,341
Chu-ma-tien (Zhumadian)	123,232
Ch'üan-chou (Quanzhou)	185,154
Chung-shan (Zhongshan)	278,829
Chungking (Chongqing)	2,980,000[20]
Feng-ch'eng (Fengcheng)	193,784
Fo-shan (Foshan)	303,160
Fu-chin (Fujin)	103,104
Fu-chou (Fuzhou) (*Fukien*)	874,809
Fu-chou (Fuzhou) (*Kiangsi*)	1,290,000[20]
Fu-hsin (Fuxin)	635,473
Fu-ling (Fuling)	173,878
Fu-shun (Fushun)	1,350,000[20]
Fu-yang (Fuyang)	179,572
Fu-yü (Fuyu)	192,981
Ha-mi (Hami)	161,315
Hai-ch'eng (Haicheng)	205,560
Hai-k'ou (Haikou)	280,153
Hai-la-erh (Hailar)	180,650
Hai-lun (Kailun)	133,565
Hai-ning (Haining)	100,478
Han-chung (Hanzhong)	169,930
Han-tan (Handan)	1,110,000[20]
Hang-chou (Hangzhou)	1,340,000[20]
Harbin	2,830,000[20]
Heng-shui (Hengshui)	104,269
Heng-yang (Hengyang)	487,148
Ho-fei (Hefei)	1,000,000[20]
Ho-kang (Hegang)	522,747
Ho-pi (Hebi)	212,976
Ho-tse (Heze)	189,293
Ho-yuan (Heyuan)	120,101
Hsi-ch'ang (Xichang)	134,419
Hsi-ning (Xining)	551,776
Hsia-men (Xiamen)	368,786
Hsiang-fan (Xiangfan)	410,407
Hsiang-t'an (Xiangtan)	441,968
Hsiao-kan (Xiaogan)	166,280
Hsiao-shan (Xiaoshan)	162,930
Hsien-ning (Xianning)	136,811
Hsien-t'ao (Xiantao)	222,884
Hsien-yang (Xianyang)	352,125
Hsin-hsiang (Xinxiang)	473,762
Hsin-t'ai (Xintai)	281,248
Hsin-yang (Xinyang)	192,509
Hsin-yu (Xinyu)	173,524
Hsing-ch'eng (Xingcheng)	102,384
Hsing-huz (Xinghua)	161,910
Hsing-t'ai (Xingtai)	302,789
Hsü-ch'ang (Xuchang)	208,815
Hsü-chou (Xuzhou)	805,695
Hsuan-ch'eng (Xuancheng)	112,673
Hu-chou (Huzhou)	218,071
Hu-ho-hao-t'e (Hohhot)	652,534
Hua-tien (Huadian)	175,873
Huai-an (Huai'an)	131,149
Huai-hua (Huaihua)	126,785
Huai-nan (Huainan)	1,200,000[20]
Huai-pei (Huaibei)	366,549
Huai-yin (Huaiyin)	239,675
Huang-shan (Huangshan)	102,628
Huang-shih (Huangshi)	457,601
Hui-chou (Huizhou)	161,023
Hun-chiang (Hunjiang)	482,043
Hung-hu (Honghu)	190,772
I-ch'ang (Yichang)	371,601
I-cheng (Yizheng)	109,268
I-ch'un (Yichun)	795,789
I-ch'un (Yichun) (*Kiangsi*)	151,585
I-hsing (Yixing)	200,824
I-ning (Yining)	177,193
I-pin (Yibin)	241,019
I-yang (Yiyang)	185,818
Jen-ch'iu (Renqiu)	114,256
Jih-chao (Rizhao)	185,048
Jui-an (Rui'an)	156,468
K'ai-feng (Kaifeng)	507,763
K'ai-li (Kaili)	113,958
K'ai-yuan (Kaiyuan)	124,219
Kan-chou (Ganzhou)	220,129
Kashgar (Kashi)	174,570
Ko-chiu (Gejiu)	214,294
K'o-la-ma-i (Karamay)	197,602
K'u-erh-le (Korla)	159,344
Kuang-shui (Guangshui)	102,770
Kuang-yüan (Guangyuan)	182,241
Kuei-hsien (Guixian)	114,025
Kuei-lin (Guilin)	364,130
K'uei-t'un (Kuitun)	118,553
Kuei-yang (Guiyang)	1,530,000[20]
K'un-ming (Kunming)	1,520,000[20]
K'un-shan (Kunshan)	102,052
Kung-chu-ling (Gongzhuling)	226,569
Lai-chou (Laizhou)	198,664
Lai-wu (Laiwu)	246,833
Lai-yang (Laiyang)	137,080
Lan-chou (Lanzhou)	1,510,000[20]
Lang-fang (Langfang)	148,105
Lao-ho-k'ou (Laohekou)	123,366
Le-shan (Leshan)	341,128
Lei-yang (Leiyang)	130,115
Leng-shui-chiang (Lengshuijiang)	137,994
Lhasa	106,885
Li-ling (Liling)	108,504
Li-yang (Liyang)	109,520
Liang-ch'eng (Liangcheng)	156,307
Liao-ch'eng (Liaocheng)	207,844
Liao-yang (Liaoyang)	492,559
Liao-yüan (Liaoyuan)	354,141
Lien-yüan (Lianyuan)	118,858
Lien-yün-kang (Lianyungang)	354,139
Lin-ch'ing (Linqing)	123,958
Lin-fen (Linfen)	187,309
Lin-ho (Linhe)	133,183
Lin-i (Linyi)	324,720
Liu-chou (Liuzhou)	609,320
Liu-p'an-shui (Liupanshui)	363,954
Lo-ho (Luohe)	126,438
Lo-yang (Luoyang)	1,190,000[20]
Long-yen (Longyan)	134,481
Lou-ti (Loudi)	128,418
Lu-an (Lu'an)	144,248
Lu-chou (Luzhou)	262,892
Lung-ching (Longjing)	139,417
Lung-k'ou (Longkou)	148,362
Ma-an-shan (Ma'anshan)	305,421
Man-chou-li (Manzhouli)	120,023
Mao-ming (Maoming)	178,683
Mei-ho-k'ou (Meihekou)	209,038
Mei-hsien (Meixian)	132,156
Mi-shan (Mishan)	132,744
Mien-yang (Mianyang)	262,947
Mu-tan-chiang (Mudanjiang)	571,705
Nan-ch'ang (Nanchang)	1,350,000[20]
Nan-ch'ung (Nanchong)	180,273
Nan-ning (Nanning)	1,070,000[20]
Nan-p'ing (Nanping)	195,064
Nan-t'ung (Nantong)	343,341
Nan-yang (Nanyang)	243,303
Nanking (Nanjing)	2,500,000[20]
Nei-chiang (Neijiang)	256,012
Ning-po (Ningbo)	1,090,000[20]
O-ch'eng (Echeng)	190,123
Pai-ch'eng (Baicheng)	217,987
Pai-yin (Baiyin)	204,970
P'an-chih-hua (Panzhihua) (Tu-k'ou [Dukou])	415,466
P'an-shan (Panshan)	362,773
Pang-pu (Bengbu)	449,245
Pao-chi (Baoji)	337,765
Pao-ting (Baoding)	483,155
Pao-t'ou (Baotou)	1,200,000[20]
Pei-an (Bei'an)	204,899
Pei-hai (Beihai)	112,673
Pei-p'iao (Beipiao)	194,301
★ Peking (Beijing)	7,000,000[20]
Pen-hsi (Benxi)	768,778
Pin-chou (Binzhou)	133,555
P'ing-hsiang (Pingxiang)	425,579
P'ing-ting-shan (Pingdingshan)	410,775
P'ing-tu (Pingdu)	150,123
Po-chou (Bozhou)	106,346
P'u-ch'i (Puqi)	117,264
P'u-yang (Puyang)	175,988
San-men-hsia (Sanmenxia)	120,523
San-ming (Sanming)	160,691
San-ya (Sanya)	102,820
Sha-shih (Shashi)	281,352
Shan-t'ou (Shantou)	578,630
Shan-wei (Shanwei)	107,847
Shao-hsing (Shaoxing)	179,818
Shao-kuan (Shaoguan)	350,043
Shao-yang (Shaoyang)	247,227
Shang-chih (Shangzhi)	215,373
Shang-ch'iu (Shangqiu)	164,880
Shang-jao (Shangrao)	132,455
Shanghai	7,830,000[20]
Shen-chen (Shenzhen)	350,727
Shen-yang (Shenyang)	4,540,000[20]
Shih-chia-chuang (Shijiazhuang)	1,320,000[20]
Shih-ho-tzu (Shihezi)	299,676
Shih-shou (Shishou)	104,571
Shih-tsui-shan (Shizuishan)	257,862
Shih-yen (Shiyan)	273,786
Shuang-ch'eng (Shuangcheng)	142,659
Shuang-ya-shan (Shuangyashan)	386,081
Sian (Xi'an)	2,760,000[20]
Ssu-p'ing (Siping)	317,223
Su-ch'ien (Suqian)	105,021
Su-chou (Suzhou) (*Anhwei*)	151,862
Su-chou (Suzhou) (*Kiangsu*)	706,450
Sui-hua (Suihua)	227,881
Sui-ning (Suining)	146,086
Ta-an (Da'an)	138,963
Ta-ch'ing (Daqing)	657,297
Ta-hsien (Daxian)	188,101
Ta-li (Dali)	136,554
Ta-lien (Dalian)	2,400,000[20]
Ta-t'ung (Datong)	1,110,000[20]
T'ai-an (Tai'an)	350,696
T'ai-chou (Taizhou)	152,442
T'ai-yüan (Taiyuan)	1,960,000[20]
Tan-chiang (Danjiang)	103,211
Tan-tung (Dandong)	523,699
Tan-yang (Danyang)	169,603
T'ang-shan (Tangshan)	1,500,000
T'ao-nan (Taonan)	150,168
Te-chou (Dezhou)	195,485
Te-yang (Deyang)	182,488
T'eng-hsien (Tengxian)	315,083
T'ieh-fa (Tiefa)	131,807
T'ieh-li (Tieli)	265,683
T'ieh-ling (Tieling)	254,842
T'ien-men (Tianmen)	186,332
T'ien-shui (Tianshui)	244,974
Tientsin (Tianjin)	5,770,000[20]
Tsa-lan-t'un (Zalantun)	130,031
Ts'ang-chou (Cangzhou)	242,708
Tsao-chuang (Zaozhuang)	380,846
Tsao-yang (Zaoyang)	162,198
Tsitsihar (Qiqihar)	1,380,000[20]
Tsun-i (Zunyi)	261,862
Tu-chiang-yen (Dujiangyan)	123,357
Tu-yun (Duyun)	132,971
Tun-hua (Dunhua)	235,100
T'ung-ch'uan (Tongchuan)	280,657
T'ung-hua (Tonghua)	324,600
Tung-kuan (Dongguan)	308,669
T'ung-liao (Tongliao)	255,129
T'ung-ling (Tongling)	228,017
Tung-t'ai (Dongtai)	192,247
Tung-ying (Dongying)	281,728
Tz'u-hsi (Cixi)	107,329
Tzu-hsing (Zixing)	110,048
Tzu-kung (Zigong)	393,184
Tzu-po (Zibo)	2,460,000[20]
Wa-fang-tien (Wafangdian)	251,733
Wan-hsien (Wanxian)	156,823
Wei-fang (Weifang)	428,522
Wei-hai (Weihai)	128,888
Wei-nan (Weinan)	140,169
Wen-chou (Wenzhou)	401,871
Wen-teng (Wendeng)	133,910
Wu-chou (Wuzhou)	210,452
Wu-hai (Wuhai)	264,081
Wu-han (Wuhan)	3,750,000[20]
Wu-hsi (Wuxi)	826,833
Wu-hu (Wuhu)	425,740
Wu-lan-hao-t'e (Ulanhot)	159,538
Wu-lu-mu-ch'i (Ürümqi)	1,160,000[20]
Wu-wei (Wuwei)	133,101
Ya-k'o-she (Yakeshi)	377,869
Yang-chiang (Yangjiang)	215,196
Yang-chou (Yangzhou)	312,892
Yang-ch'üan (Yangquan)	362,268
Yen-an (Yan'an)	113,277
Yen-ch'eng (Yancheng)	296,831
Yen-chi (Yanji)	230,892
Yen-t'ai (Yantai)	452,127
Yin-ch'uan (Yinchuan)	356,652
Ying-k'ou (Yingkou)	421,589
Yü-lin (Yulin)	144,467
Yü-men (Yumen)	109,234
Yü-shu (Yushu)	131,861
Yü-tz'u (Yuci)	191,356
Yu-yao (Yuyao)	114,065
Yüan-chiang (Yuanjiang)	107,004
Yüeh-yang (Yueyang)	302,800
Yun-ch'eng (Yuncheng)	108,359
Yung-an (Yong'an)	111,762
Colombia (1997 est.)	
Armenia	283,842
Barrancabermeja	180,653[2]
Barranquilla	1,157,826
Bello	304,819[2]
Bucaramanga	508,240
Buenaventura	266,988[2]
Cali	1,985,906

Major cities and national capitals (continued)

country / city	population
Cartagena	812,595
Cartago	117,166[2]
Ciénaga	144,340[2]
Cúcuta	589,196
Dosquebradas	163,599[2]
Envigado	109,240[2]
Florencia	114,848
Floridablanca	246,834[2]
Ibagué	419,883
Itagüí	169,374[2]
Magangué	104,496[2]
Malambo	112,289[2]
Manizales	358,194
Medellín	1,970,691
Montería	327,249
Neiva	305,625
Palmira	256,823[2]
Pasto	362,227
Pereira	434,267
Popayán	218,057
Quibdó	123,102
Ríohacha	114,608
Santa Marta	343,038
★ Santafé de Bogotá, D.C.	6,004,782
Sincelejo	213,916
Soacha	266,817[2]
Soledad	264,583[2]
Tuluá	138,124[2]
Tumaco	114,802[2]
Tunja	118,406
Turbo	127,045[2]
Valledupar	296,624
Villavicencio	299,296
Comoros (1991)	
★ Moroni	30,000
Congo, Dem. Rep. of the (1994 est.)	
Boma	135,284
Bukavu	201,569
Butembo	109,406
Goma	109,094
Kalemi	101,309
Kananga	393,030
Kikwit	182,142
★ Kinshasa	4,655,313
Kisangani	417,517
Kolwezi	417,810
Likasi	299,118
Lubumbashi	851,381
Matadi	172,730
Mbanadaka	169,841
Mbuji-Mayi	806,475
Mwene-Ditu	137,459
Tshikapa	180,860
Uvira	115,590
Congo, Rep. of the (1992 est.)	
★ Brazzaville	937,579
Pointe-Noire	576,206
Costa Rica (1997 est.)	
★ San José	329,154[21]
Côte d'Ivoire (1995 est.)	
★ Abidjan (de facto; legislative)	2,500,000[18]
Bouaké	330,000
Daloa	123,000
Korhogo	109,445[22]
★ Yamoussoukro (de jure; administrative)	110,000
Croatia (1991)	
Osijek	129,792
Rijeka	167,964
Split	200,459
★ Zagreb	867,717
Cuba (1994 est.)	
Bayamo	137,663
Camagüey	293,961
Cienfuegos	132,038
Guantánamo	207,796
★ Havana	2,241,000[2]
Holguín	242,085
Las Tunas	126,930
Manzanillo	107,650[23]
Matanzas	123,843
Pinar del Río	128,570
Santa Clara	205,400
Santiago de Cuba	440,084
Cyprus (1994 est.)	
Limassol	143,400
★ Nicosia (Lefkosia)	186,400[24]
Czech Republic (1996 est.)	
Brno	388,899
Hradec Králové	100,528
Liberec	100,604
Olomouc	104,845
Ostrava	324,813
Plzen	171,249
★ Prague	1,209,855
Denmark (1996 est.; MU)	
Ålborg	159,980
Århus	279,759
★ Copenhagen	1,362,264[19]
Odense	183,564
Djibouti (1995 est.)	
★ Djibouti	383,000
Dominica (1991)	
★ Roseau	15,853
Dominican Republic (1993)	
La Romana	132,834
San Francisco de Macorís	129,943
San Pedro de Macorís	123,987
Santiago	364,859
★ Santo Domingo	1,555,656[25]
Ecuador (1997 est.)	
Ambato	160,302
Cuenca	255,028
Duran	135,675
Esmeraldas	117,722
Guayaquil	1,973,880
Ibarra	119,243
Loja	117,365
Machala	197,350
Manta	156,981
Milagro	119,371
Portoviejo	167,956
Quevedo	120,640
★ Quito	1,487,513
Riobamba	117,270
Santo Domingo	183,219
Egypt (1992 est.)	
Alexandria	3,700,000[18,19]
Aswān	220,000
Asyūṭ	321,000
Banhā	136,000
Banī Suwayf	179,000
Būr Sa'īd (Port Said)	460,000[8]
★ Cairo	9,900,000[18,19]
Damanhūr	222,000
al-Fayyūm	250,000
Hulwan (Helwan)	352,300[26]
Al-Ismā'īlīyah	255,000
Al-Jīzah (Giza)	2,144,000
Kafr ad-Dawwar	226,000
Kafr ash-Shaykh	102,910[27]
Al-Maḥallah al-Kubrā	408,000
Al-Manṣūrah	371,000
Al-Minyā	208,000
Qinā	141,000
Sawhāj	156,000
Shibīn al-Kawm	158,000
Shubrā al-Khaymah	834,000
As-Suways (Suez)	388,000
Ṭanṭā	380,000
Al-Uqṣur (Luxor)	155,000[8]
Az-Zaqāzīq	287,000
El Salvador (1992; MU)	
Apopa	100,763
Delgado	104,790
Mejicanos	145,000[19]
Nueva San Salvador	116,575
San Miguel	182,817
★ San Salvador	422,570
Santa Ana	202,337
Soyapango	251,811[19]
Equatorial Guinea (1991 est.)	
★ Malabo	58,040
Eritrea (1995 est.)	
★ Asmara	431,000
Estonia (1996 est.)	
★ Tallinn	427,500
Tartu	103,400
Ethiopia (1994)	
★ Addis Ababa	2,112,737
Dire Dawa	164,851
Gonder	112,249
Harer	131,139
Nazret	127,842
Faroe Islands (1996 est.)	
★ Tórshavn	15,272
Fiji (1996)	
★ Suva	167,421[28]
Finland (1997 est.; MU)	
Espoo	196,260
★ Helsinki	532,053
Oulu	111,556
Tampere	186,026
Turku	166,929
Vantaa	168,778
France (1990)	
Aix-en-Provence	126,854
Amiens	136,234
Angers	146,163
Besançon	119,194
Bordeaux	213,274
Boulogne-Billancourt	101,971
Brest	153,099
Caen	115,624
Clermont-Ferrand	140,167
Dijon	151,636
Grenoble	153,973
Le Havre	197,219
Le Mans	148,465
Lille	178,301
Limoges	136,407
Lyon	422,444
Marseille	807,726
Metz	123,920
Montpellier	210,866
Mulhouse	109,905
Nancy	102,410
Nantes	252,029
Nice	345,674
Nîmes	133,607
Orléans	107,965
★ Paris	2,175,200
Perpignan	108,049
Reims	185,164
Rennes	203,533
Rouen	105,470
Saint-Étienne	201,569
Strasbourg	255,937
Toulon	170,167
Toulouse	365,933
Tours	133,403
Villeurbanne	119,848
French Guiana (1995 est.)	
★ Cayenne	45,000
French Polynesia (1988)	
★ Papeete	23,555
Gabon (1993)	
★ Libreville	362,386
Gambia, The (1993)	
★ Banjul	42,407
Serekunda	102,600[29]
Gaza Strip (early 1990s est.)	
Gaza (Ghazzah)	293,000
Khan Younis	160,463
Rafah	101,926
Georgia (1994 est.)	
Bat'umi (Batumi)	137,100
K'ut'aisi (Kutaisi)	240,600
Rust'avi (Rustavi)	155,500
Sukhumi	112,000[1]
★ T'bilisi (Tbilisi)	1,253,100
Germany (1996 est.)	
Aachen	247,923
Augsburg	259,699
Bergisch Gladbach	105,478
Berlin	3,471,418
Bielefeld	324,066
Bochum	400,395
★ Bonn	291,431
Bottrop	120,642
Braunschweig	252,544
Bremen	549,357
Bremerhaven	130,400
Chemnitz	266,737
Cologne (Köln)	965,697
Cottbus	123,214
Darmstadt	138,980
Dortmund	598,840
Dresden	469,110
Duisburg	535,250
Düsseldorf	571,030
Erfurt	211,108
Erlangen	101,406
Essen	614,861
Frankfurt am Main	650,055
Freiburg im Breisgau	199,273
Fürth	108,418
Gelsenkirchen	291,164
Gera	123,555
Göttingen	126,253
Hagen	212,003
Halle	282,784
Hamburg	1,707,901
Hamm	183,408
Hannover	523,147
Heidelberg	138,781
Heilbronn	121,509
Herne	179,897
Hildesheim	106,101
Ingolstadt	111,979
Jena	101,061
Kaiserslautern	102,002
Karlsruhe	275,690
Kassel	201,573
Kiel	246,033
Koblenz	109,219
Krefeld	249,606
Leipzig	470,778
Leverkusen	162,252
Lübeck	216,986
Ludwigshafen	167,369
Magdeburg	257,656
Mainz	183,720
Mannheim	311,292
Moers	107,095
Mönchengladbach	266,702
Mülheim an der Ruhr	176,530
Munich (München)	1,236,370
Münster	265,061
Neuss	148,796
Nürnberg	492,425
Oberhausen	224,397
Offenbach am Main	116,533
Oldenburg	151,382
Osnabrück	168,618
Paderborn	133,717
Pforzheim	118,763
Potsdam	136,619
Recklinghausen	127,216
Regensburg	125,836
Remscheid	122,260
Reutlingen	108,565
Rostock	227,535
Saarbrücken	187,032
Salzgitter	117,713
Schwerin	114,688
Siegen	111,398
Solingen	165,735
Stuttgart	585,604
Ulm	115,721
Wiesbaden	267,122
Witten	104,754
Wolfsburg	126,331
Wuppertal	381,884
Würzburg	127,295
Zwickau	102,563
Ghana (1988 est.)	
★ Accra	1,781,100[19, 23]
Kumasi	385,192
Sekondi-Takoradi	103,653
Tamale	151,069
Tema	109,975
Gibraltar (1997 est.)	
★ Gibraltar	27,100[30]
Greece (1991)	
★ Athens	748,110
Iráklion	117,167
Kallithéa	110,738
Larissa	113,426
Pátrai (Patras)	155,180
Peristérion	145,854
Piraiévs (Piraeus)	169,622
Thessaloníki	377,951
Greenland (1996 est.)	
★ Nuuk (Godthåb)	12,882
Grenada (1991)	
★ Saint George's	4,621
Guadeloupe (1990)	
★ Basse-Terre	14,107
Guam (1995 est.)	
★ Agana	2,000
Guatemala (1995 est.; MU)	
★ Guatemala City	1,167,495
Mixco	436,668
Villa Nueva	165,567
Guernsey (1991)	
★ St. Peter Port	16,648
Guinea (1995 est.)	
★ Conakry	1,508,000
Guinea-Bissau (1995 est.)	
★ Bissau	233,000
Guyana (1995 est.)	
★ Georgetown	254,000
Haiti (1995 est.)	
Cap-Haïtien	100,638
Carrefour	277,662
Delmas	232,142
★ Port-au-Prince	846,247
Honduras (1995 est.; MU)	
San Pedro Sula	383,900
★ Tegucigalpa	813,900[31]
Hong Kong (1997 est.)	
Hong Kong	6,491,000[30]
Hungary (1997 est.)	
★ Budapest	1,885,000
Debrecen	210,000
Győr	127,000
Kecskemét	105,000
Miskolc	178,000
Nyíregyháza	113,000
Pécs	161,000
Szeged	166,000
Székesfehérvár	106,000
Iceland (1996 est.)	
★ Reykjavík	105,487
India (1991)	
Abohar	107,163
Ādoni	136,182
Agartala	157,358
Āgra	891,790
Ahmadābād	2,876,710
Ahmadnagar	181,339
Āizawl	155,240
Ajmer	402,700
Akola	328,034
Alandur	125,244
Alappuzha (Alleppey)	174,666
Alībāg	328,640
Alīgarh	480,520
Allahābād	792,858
Alwar	205,086
Ambāla	119,338
Ambattur	215,424
Amrāvati	421,576
Amritsar	708,835
Amroha	137,061
Anand	110,266
Anantapur	174,924
Āra (Arrah)	157,082
Āsānsol	262,188
Āvadi	183,215
Baharampur	115,144
Bahraich	135,400
Bally	184,474
Bālurghāt	119,796
Bangalore	2,660,088
Bānkura	114,876
Barāhanagar	224,821
Bārāsat	102,660
Barddhamān (Burdwān)	245,079
Bareilly	587,211
Barrackpore	133,265
Basīrhāt	101,409
Bathinda (Bhatinda)	159,042
Beāwar	105,363
Belgaum	326,399
Bellary	245,391
Bhāgalpur	253,225
Bharatpur	148,519
Bharūch (Broach)	133,102
Bhātpāra	304,952
Bhāvnagar	402,338
Bhilainagar	395,360
Bhīlwāra	183,965
Bhīmavaram	121,314
Bhind	109,755
Bhiwandi	379,070
Bhiwāni	121,629
Bhopāl	1,062,771
Bhubaneshwar	411,542
Bhuj	102,176
Bhusāwal	145,143
Bīd (Bhīr)	112,434
Bīdar	108,016
Bidhān Nagar	100,048
Bihār Sharīf	201,323
Bijāpur	186,939
Bīkaner	416,289
Bilāspur	179,833
Bokāro	333,683
Brahmapur	210,418
Budaun	116,695
Bulandshahr	127,201
Burhānpur	172,710
Burnpur	174,933
Calcutta	4,399,819
Chāmpdānī	101,067
Chandannagar	120,378
Chandīgarh	504,094
Chandrapur	226,105
Chennai (Madras)	3,841,396
Chhapra	136,877
Chittoor	133,462
Coimbatore	816,321
Cuddalore	144,561
Cuddapah	121,463
Cuttack	403,418
Darbhanga	218,391
Dāvangere	266,082
Dehra Dūn	270,159
Delhi	7,206,704
Dewās	164,364
Dhānbād	151,789
Dhūle (Dhūlia)	278,317
Dibrugarh	120,127
Dindigul	182,447
Durg	150,645
Durgāpur	425,836
Elūru	212,866
Erode	159,232
Etāwah	124,072
Faizābād	124,437
Farīdābād	617,717
Farrukhābād-cum-Fatehgarh	194,567
Fatehpur	117,675
Fīrozābād	215,128
Gadag-Betigeri	134,051
Gāndhīdhām	104,585
Gāndhīnagar	123,359
Gangānagar	161,482
Gaya	291,675
Ghāziābād	454,156
Gondia	109,470
Gorakhpur	505,566
Gudivāda	101,656
Gulbarga	304,099
Guna	100,490
Guntakal	107,592
Guntūr	471,051
Gurgaon	121,486
Guwāhāti (Gauhāti)	584,342
Gwalior	690,765
Hābra	100,223

country / city	population
Haldīa	100,347
Haldwāni-cum-Kāthgodam	104,195
Hālisahar	114,028
Hāora (Howrah)	950,435
Hāpur	146,262
Haridwār (Hardwār)	147,305
Hāthras	113,285
Hindupur	104,651
Hisār (Hissār)	172,677
Hoshiārpur	122,705
Hubli-Dhārwād	648,298
Hugli-Chunchura	151,806
Hyderābād	3,145,939
Ichalkaranji	214,950
Imphāl	198,535
Indore	1,091,674
Ingrāj Bāzār	139,204
Jabalpur	741,927
Jaipur	1,458,183
Jalandhar (Jullundur)	509,510
Jalgaon	242,193
Jālna	174,985
Jammu	206,135[14]
Jāmnagar	341,637
Jamshedpur	478,950
Jaunpur	136,062
Jhānsi	300,850
Jodhpur	666,279
Jūnāgadh	130,484
Kākināda	279,980
Kalyān	1,014,557
Kāmārhāti	266,889
Kānchipuram	144,955
Kānchrāpāra	100,194
Kānpur	1,874,409
Karīmnagar	148,583
Karnāl	173,751
Katihār	135,436
Khammam	127,992
Khandwa	143,133
Kharagpur	177,989
Kochi (Cochin)	564,589
Kolhāpur	406,370
Kollam (Quilon)	139,852
Kota	537,371
Kozhikode (Calicut)	419,831
Krishnanagar	121,110
Kukatpalle	186,963
Kulti-Barākar	108,518
Kumbakonam	139,483
Kurnool	236,800
Lālbāhādur Nagar	155,514
Lātūr	197,408
Lucknow	1,619,115
Ludhiāna	1,042,740
Machilīpatnam (Masulipatam)	159,110
Madurai	940,989
Mahbūbnagar	116,833
Mālegaon	342,595
Mālkājgiri	127,178
Mandya	120,265
Mangalore	273,304
Māngo	108,100
Mathura	226,691
Maunāth Bhanjan	136,697
Medinīpur (Midnāpore)	125,498
Meerut	753,778
Mira-Bhayandar	175,605
Miraj	121,593
Mirzāpur-cum-Vindhyāchal	169,336
Modinagar	101,660
Moga	108,304
Morādābād	429,214
Morena	147,124
Mumbāi (Bombay)	9,925,891[19]
Munger (Monghyr)	150,112
Murwāra (Katni)	163,431
Muzaffarnagar	240,609
Muzaffarpur	241,107
Mysore	480,692
Nadiād	167,051
Nāgercoil	190,084
Nāgpur	1,624,752
Naihāti	132,701
Nānded (Nānder)	275,083
Nandyāl	119,813
Nāshik (Nāsik)	656,925
Navadwīp	125,037
Navsāri	126,089
Nellore	316,606
New Bombay	307,724
★ New Delhi	301,297
Neyveli	118,080
Nizāmābād	241,034
Noida	146,514
North Barrackpore	100,606
North Dum Dum	149,965
Ongole	100,836
Pālghāt (Palakkad)	123,289
Pāli	136,842
Pallavaram	111,866
Pānihāti	275,990
Pānīpat	191,212
Parbhani	190,255
Pathānkot	123,930
Patiāla	238,368
Patna	917,243
Pīlībhīt	106,605
Pimpri-Chinchwad	517,083
Pondicherry	203,065
Porbandar	116,671
Proddatūr	133,914
Pune	1,566,651
Puri	125,199
Pūrnia (Pūrnea)	114,912
Qutubullapur	106,591
Rāe Bareli	129,904
Rāichūr	157,551
Rāiganj	151,045
Raipur	438,639
Rāj Nāndgaon	125,371
Rājahmundry	324,851
Rājapālaiyam	114,202
Rājkot	559,407
Rāmagundam	214,384
Rāmpur	243,742
Rānchi	599,306
Ratlām	183,375
Raurkela Steel Township	215,509
Rewa	128,981
Rishra	102,815
Rohtak	216,096
Sāgar	195,346
Sahāranpur	374,945
Salem	366,712
Sambalpur	131,138
Sambhal	150,869
Sāngli	193,197
Satna	156,630
Shāhjahānpur	237,713
Shāmbājinagar (Aurangābād)	573,272
Shāntipur	109,956
Shiliguri (Silīguri)	216,950
Shillong	131,719
Shimoga	179,258
Shivpuri	108,277
Sholāpur (Solapur)	604,215
Shrīrāmpur	137,028
Sīkar	148,272
Silchar	115,483
Sirsa	112,841
Sitāpur	121,842
Sonīpat (Sonepat)	143,922
South Dum Dum	232,811
Srīnagar	586,038[14]
Sūrat	1,498,817
Surendranagar	106,110
Tāmbaram	107,187
Tenāli	143,726
Thalassery (Tellicherry)	103,579
Thāne (Thāna)	803,389
Thanjāvūr	202,013
Thiruvananthapuram (Trivandrum)	524,006
Tiruchchirāppalli	387,223
Trunelveli	135,825
Tirupati	174,369
Tirupper (tiruppūr)	235,661
Tiruvannāmalai	109,196
Tiruvottiyūr	168,642
Titāgarh	114,085
Tonk	100,079
Tumkūr	138,903
Tuticorin	199,854
Udaipur	308,571
Ujjain	362,266
Ulhāsnagar	369,077
Uluberia	155,172
Unnāo	107,425
Uttarpāra-Kotrung	101,268
Vadodara (Baroda)	1,031,346
Vārānasi (Benares)	929,270
Vellore	175,061
Vijayawāda	701,827
Vishākhapatnam	752,037
Vizianagaram	160,359
Warangal	447,657
Wardha	102,985
Yamunanagar	144,346
Yavatmāl (Yeotmāl)	108,578
Indonesia (1995 est.)	
Ambon	313,100
Balikpapan	416,200
Banda Aceh	291,300
Bandar Lampung	458,215[15]
Bandung	2,368,200
Banjarmasin	534,600
Batam	168,200
Bengkulu	262,100
Binjai	206,800
Blitar	122,600
Bitung	107,100
Bogor	285,000
Cilacap	113,893[32]
Cimahi	105,940[32]
Cirebon	262,300
Denpasar	435,000
Gorontalo	132,900
★ Jakarta	9,160,500
Jambi	410,400
Jayapura	180,400
Jember	140,105[32]
Kediri	261,300
Madiun	106,600
Magelang	123,100
Malang	763,400
Manado	398,900
Mataram	306,600
Medan	1,909,700
Mojokerto	170,900
Padang	721,500
Palangkaraya	148,700
Palembang	1,352,300
Pangkai Pinang	124,000
Pare Pare	109,700
Pasuruan	162,800
Pekalongan	341,400
Pekanbaru	558,200
Pematangsiantar	230,900
Pontianak	449,100
Probolinggo	190,100
Purwokerto	105,395[32]
Salatiga	103,000
Samarinda	536,100
Semarang	1,366,500
Sukabumi	125,400
Sumba	355,073[32]
Surabaya	2,701,300
Surakarta	516,500
Tangerang	1,198,300
Tanjung Balai	114,700
Tanjung Karang-Telukbetung	284,275[32]
Tasikmalaya	165,297[32]
Tebing Tinggi	129,300
Tegal	313,400
Ujung Pandang	1,091,800
Yogyakarta	419,500
Iran (1994 est.)	
Ahvāz	828,380
Āmol	154,796
Arāk	378,597
Ardabīl	329,869
Bābol	152,536
Bandar 'Abbās	383,515
Bandar-e Būshehr	140,615
Bīrjand	114,944
Bojnūrd	125,661
Borūjerd	212,056
Dezfūl	202,004
Eṣfahān (Isfahan)	1,220,595
Gonbad-e Kavus	102,768[12]
Gorgān	178,080
Hamadān	406,070
Īlām	136,759
Islāmshahr (Eslāmshahr)	239,716
Karaj	588,287
Kāshān	166,080
Kermān	349,626
Kermānshāh (Bākhtarān)	665,636
Khomeynīshahr	127,415
Khorramābād	277,370
Khorramshahr	197,241[12]
Khvoy	153,473
Malāyer	149,774
Marāgheh	128,717
Mehrshahr	413,299
Mashhad (Meshed)	1,964,489
Masjed-e Soleymān	109,224
Najafābād	182,028
Neyshābūr	154,511
Orūmīyeh	396,392
Qā'emshahr	133,216
Qazvīn	298,705
Qom	780,453
Rājaishahr	192,912
Rasht	374,475
Sabzevār	160,755
Sanandaj	271,314
Sārī	185,899
Shīrāz	1,042,801
Sīrjān	120,224
Tabrīz	1,166,203
★ Tehrān	6,750,043
Yazd	306,268
Zāhedān	419,886
Zanjān	280,691
Iraq (1987)	
Al-'Amārah	208,797
★ Baghdad	4,400,000[18,19]
Ba'qūbah	114,516[33]
Al-Baṣrah	406,296
Al-Ḥillah	268,834
Dīwanīyah	196,519
Irbīl	485,968
Karbalā'	296,705
Karkūk	418,624
Al-Kūt	183,183
Mosul	664,221
An-Najaf	309,010
An-Nāṣirīyah	265,937
Ar-Ramādī	192,556
As-Sulaymānīyah	364,096
Ireland (1996)	
Cork	127,092[34]
★ Dublin	480,996[34]
Isle of Man (1996)	
★ Douglas	23,487
Israel (1997 est.)	
Ashdod	137,100
Bat Yam	140,800
Beersheba (Be'er Sheva')	156,500
Bene Beraq	130,500
Haifa (Ḥefa)	255,300
Ḥolon	163,900
★ Jerusalem (Yerushalayim, Al-Quds)	591,400
Netanya	148,400
Petaḥ Tiqwa	153,100
Ramat Gan	121,700
Rishon LeẒiyyon	165,300
Tel Aviv–Yafo	355,900
Italy (1996 est.; MU)	
Bari	336,560
Bergamo	116,990
Bologna	386,491
Brescia	190,208
Cagliari	174,543
Catania	341,623
Ferrara	135,135
Florence (Firenze)	383,594
Foggia	156,032
Forlì	108,017
Genoa (Genova)	659,116
Latina	110,233
Lecce	100,046
Livorno	164,569
Messina	263,092
Milan (Milano)	1,306,494
Modena	174,518
Monza	119,658
Naples (Napoli)	1,050,234
Novara	102,219
Padua (Padova)	212,731
Palermo	689,301
Parma	167,516
Perugia	151,118
Pescara	118,764
Prato	167,991
Ravenna	137,216
Reggio di Calabria	179,623
Reggio nell'Emilia	135,406
Rimini	129,598
★ Rome (Roma)	2,654,187
Salerno	143,863
Sassari	121,639
Siracusa (Syracuse)	127,448
Taranto	212,650
Terni	108,435
Trento	103,181
Trieste	223,611
Turin (Torino)	923,106
Venice (Venezia)	298,915
Verona	254,145
Vicenza	107,786
Jamaica (1991)	
★ Kingston	103,771[35]
Japan (1995)	
Abiko	124,255
Ageo	206,099
Aizuwakamatsu	119,632
Akashi	287,613
Akishima	107,289
Akita	312,035
Amagasaki	488,574
Anjō	149,459
Aomori	294,165
Asahikawa	360,569
Asaka	110,793
Ashikaga	165,830
Atsugi	208,622
Beppu	128,251
Chiba	856,882
Chigasaki	212,944
Chōfu	198,524
Daitō	128,840
Ebetsu	115,491
Ebina	113,416
Fuchu	216,202
Fuji	229,189
Fujieda	124,822
Fujinomiya	119,536
Fujisawa	368,636
Fukaya	100,271
Fukui	255,601
Fukuoka	1,284,741
Fukushima	285,745
Fukuyama	374,510
Funabashi	540,814
Gifu	407,145
Habikino	117,728
Hachinohe	242,657
Hachiōji	503,320
Hadano	164,703
Hakodate	298,868
Hamamatsu	561,568
Handa	106,451
Higashi-Hiroshima	113,935
Higashi-Kurume	111,076
Higashi-Murayama	135,115
Higashi-Ōsaka	517,228
Hikone	103,508
Himeji	470,986
Hino	166,429
Hirakata	400,130
Hiratsuka	253,818
Hirosaki	177,971
Hiroshima	1,108,868
Hitachi	199,241
Hōfu	118,802
Hoya	100,259
Ibaraki	258,237
Ichihara	277,080
Ichikawa	440,527
Ichinomiya	267,359
Iida	106,774
Ikeda	104,292
Ikoma	106,727
Imabari	120,215
Iruma	144,401
Ise	102,631
Isesaki	120,235
Ishinomaki	121,209
Itami	188,436
Iwaki	360,497
Iwakuni	107,386
Iwatsuki	109,551
Izumi	157,301
Joetsu	132,202
Kadoma	140,507
Kagoshima	546,294
Kakamigahara	131,955
Kakogawa	260,558
Kamakura	170,319
Kanazawa	453,977
Kariya	125,307
Kashihara	121,987
Kashiwa	317,752
Kasugai	277,579
Kasukabe	200,130
Kawachi-Nagano	117,082
Kawagoe	323,345
Kawaguchi	448,801
Kawanishi	144,539
Kawasaki	1,202,811
Kiryū	120,375
Kisarazu	123,499
Kishiwada	194,820
Kita-Kyūshū	1,019,562
Kitami	110,449
Kobe	1,423,830
Kochi	322,077
Kodaira	173,032
Kofu	201,123
Koganei	109,275
Kokubunji	105,781
Komaki	137,163
Komatsu	107,964
Koriyama	326,831
Koshigaya	298,285
Kumagaya	156,395
Kumamoto	650,322
Kurashiki	422,824
Kure	209,477
Kurume	234,433
Kusatsu	101,827
Kushiro	199,325
Kuwana	103,049
Kyōto	1,463,601
Machida	360,418
Maebashi	284,780
Matsubara	134,457
Matsudo	461,489
Matsue	147,414
Matsumoto	205,532
Matsusaka	122,449
Matsuyama	460,870
Minō	127,540
Misato	133,601
Mishima	107,890
Mitaka	165,739
Mito	246,350
Miyakonojō	132,712
Miyazaki	300,054
Moriguchi	157,290
Morioka	286,478
Muroran	109,767
Musashino	135,026
Nagano	358,512
Nagaoka	190,470
Nagareyama	146,250
Nagasaki	438,724
Nagoya	2,152,258
Naha	301,928
Nara	359,234
Narashino	152,884
Neyagawa	258,440
Niigata	494,785
Niihama	127,916
Niiza	144,735
Nishinomiya	390,388
Nobeoka	126,628
Noda	119,791
Numazu	212,245
Obihiro	171,714
Odawara	200,092
Ōgaki	149,758
Ōita	426,981
Okayama	616,056
Okazaki	322,615

Major cities and national capitals (continued)

country city	population
Okinawa	115,342
Ōme	137,208
Ōmiya	433,768
Ōmuta	145,085
Ōsaka	2,602,352
Ōta	143,067
Ōtaru	157,024
Ōtsu	276,331
Oyama	150,114
Saga	171,219
Sagamihara	570,594
Sakai	802,965
Sakata	101,224
Sakura	162,624
Sapporo	1,756,968
Sasebo	244,879
Sayama	162,232
Sendai	971,263
Seto	129,396
Shimizu	240,172
Shimonoseki	259,791
Shizuoka	474,089
Sōka	217,912
Suita	342,794
Suzuka	179,795
Tachikawa	157,892
Tajimi	101,274
Takamatsu	330,997
Takaoka	173,612
Takarazuka	202,547
Takasaki	238,132
Takatsuki	362,259
Tama	148,127
Tokorozawa	320,448
Tokushima	268,712
Tokuyama	108,675
★ Tokyo	7,966,195
Tomakomai	169,324
Tondabayashi	121,690
Tottori	146,336
Toyama	325,303
Toyohashi	352,913
Toyokawa	114,379
Toyonaka	398,912
Toyota	341,038
Tsu	163,309
Tsuchiura	132,246
Tsukuba	156,009
Tsuruoka	100,538
Ube	175,113
Ueda	123,282
Uji	184,829
Urawa	453,300
Urayasu	123,660
Utsunomiya	435,446
Wakayama	393,951
Yachiyo	154,507
Yaizu	115,932
Yamagata	254,485
Yamaguchi	135,581
Yamato	203,920
Yao	276,658
Yatsushiro	107,708
Yokkaichi	285,777
Yokohama	3,307,408
Yokosuka	432,202
Yonago	134,769
Zama	118,146
Jersey (1996)	
★ St. Helier	27,523
Jordan (1994)	
★ Amman	963,490
Irbid	208,201
Al-Mafraq	109,841[19]
Ar-Ruṣayfah	131,130
As-Salṭ	187,014[19]
Az-Zarqāʾ	344,524
Kazakstan (1995 est.)	
★ Almaty (Alma-Ata)	1,150,500
★ Aqmola (Akmola; Tselinograd)	280,200
Aqtaū (Aktau; Shevchenko)	151,300
Aqtöbe (Aktyubinsk)	258,900
Atyraū (Guryev)	146,900
Auliye-Ata (Dzhambul)	310,600
Ekibastuz	141,100
Kökshetaū (Kokchetav)	141,400
Oral (Uralsk)	219,100
Öskemen (Ust-Kamenogorsk)	326,300
Pavlodar	340,700
Petropavl (Petropavlovsk)	239,000
Qaraghandy (Karaganda)	573,700
Qostanay (Kustanay)	232,100
Qyzylord (Kzyl-Orda)	162,000
Rūdny	125,700
Semey (Semipalatinsk)	320,200
Shymkent (Shimkent; Chimkent)	397,600
Taldyqorghan (Taldy-Kurgan)	116,100
Temirtaū	206,100
Zhezqazghan (Zhezkazgan; Dzhezkazgan)	108,700
Kenya (1991 est.)	
Kisumu	201,100
Mombasa	600,000
★ Nairobi	2,000,000
Nakuru	124,200
Kiribati (1990)	
★ Bairiki	2,226
Korea, North (1987 est.)	
Anju	186,000
Ch'ŏngjin	520,000
Haeju	195,000
Hamhŭng-Hungnam	701,000
Hŭich'ŏn	163,000
Kaesŏng	120,000
Kanggye	211,000
Kimch'aek (Songjin)	179,000
Kusŏng	177,000
Namp'o	370,000
★ P'yŏngyang	2,500,000[18,19]
Sinp'o	158,000
Sinŭiju	289,000
Sunch'ŏn	356,000
Tanch'ŏn	284,000
Tŏkch'ŏn	217,000
Wŏnsan	274,000
Korea, South (1995)	
Andong	188,452
Ansan	510,317
Anyang	590,996
Asan	154,635
Ch'angwŏn	481,678
Chech'ŏn	137,065
Cheju	258,509
Chinhae	125,997
Chinju	329,913
Ch'ŏnan	330,509
Ch'ŏngju	531,195
Chŏng-ŭp	139,084
Chŏnju	563,406
Ch'unch'ŏn	235,067
Ch'ungju	205,131
Hanam	115,805
Iksan	322,749
Inch'ŏn	2,307,618
Iri	203,382
Kangnŭng	220,430
Kimch'ŏn	146,996
Kimhae	256,270
Kimje	115,430
Kŏje	147,551
Kongju	131,220
Koyang	518,269
Kumi	311,488
Kunp'o	235,194
Kunsan	266,517
Kuri	142,299
Kwangju	1,257,504
Kwangmyŏng	350,902
Kwangyang	122,061
Kyŏngju	273,819
Kyŏngsan	173,762
Masan	441,358
Miryang	121,502
Mokp'o	247,524
Naju	107,831
Namwon	103,538
Namyangju	228,931
P'ohang	508,983
Poryŏng	122,631
Puch'ŏn	779,476
Pusan	3,813,814
P'yŏngt'aek	312,938
Sach'ŏn	113,492
Sangju	124,136
★ Seoul (Sŏul)	10,229,262
Shihŭng	133,411
Sŏngnam	869,243
Sŏsan	134,758
Sunch'ŏn	249,241
Suwŏn	755,502
Taegu	2,449,139
Taejŏn	1,272,143
Tongyŏng	131,716
Ŭijŏngbu	276,255
Ŭiwang	108,761
Ulsan	967,394
Wŏnju	237,423
Yŏngch'ŏn	113,510
Yŏngju	131,090
Yŏsu	183,557
Kuwait (1995)	
As-Sālimīyah	130,215
★ Kuwait (Al-Kuwayt)	28,859
Qalīb ash-Shuyūkh	102,178
Kyrgyzstan (1995 est.)	
★ Bishkek (Frunze)	589,800[18]
Osh	218,300
Laos (1996 est.; MU)	
★ Vientiane (Viangchan)	531,800
Latvia (1996 est.)	
Daugavpils	118,500
★ Rīga	826,100
Lebanon (1991 est.)	
★ Beirut (Bayrūt)	1,900,000[18,19]
Jūniyah	100,000
an-Nabaṭīyah	100,000[33]
Sidon (Ṣaydā)	100,000[33]
Tripoli (Ṭarābulus)	240,000
Zaḥlah	200,000[33]
Lesotho (1995 est.)	
★ Maseru	297,000[19]
Liberia (1995 est.)	
★ Monrovia	962,000[19]
Libya (1988 est.)	
Banghāzī	446,250
Misrātah	121,669
★ Tripoli (Ṭarābulus)	591,062
Liechtenstein (1997 est.)	
★ Vaduz	5,017
Lithuania (1996 est.)	
Kaunas	410,800
Klaipėda	201,500
Panevėžys	132,300
Šiauliai	146,500
★ Vilnius	573,200
Luxembourg (1997 est.)	
★ Luxembourg	78,300
Macau (1995 est.)	
★ Macau (Santo Nome de Deus)	424,000
Macedonia (1994; MU)	
Bitola	106,012
Giostivar	108,189
Kumanovo	126,543
★ Skopje (Skopije)	541,280
Tetovo	174,748
Madagascar (1993)	
★ Antananarivo	1,052,835
Antsirabe	120,239
Mahajanga	100,807
Toamasina	127,441
Malaŵi (1994 est.)	
★ Blantyre (executive; judicial)	446,800[36]
★ Lilongwe (ministerial; financial)	395,500
★ Zomba (legislative)	62,700
Malaysia (1991)	
Alor Setar	124,412
George Town (Pinang)	219,603
Ipoh	382,853
Johor Baharu	328,436
Kelang	243,355
Kota Baharu	219,582
Kota Kinabalu	208,484
★ Kuala Lumpur	1,145,342
Kuala Terengganu	228,119
Kuantan	199,484
Kuching	148,059
Melaka	296,897
Petaling Jaya	254,350
Port Kelang	192,080
Sandakan	125,841
Seloyang Baru	124,228
Seremban	182,869
Shah Alam	102,019
Sibu	126,381
Taiping	183,261
Tawau	244,765
Maldives (1995 est.)	
★ Male'	62,973
Mali (1995 est.)	
★ Bamako	800,000
Malta (1996 est.)	
★ Valletta	9,128
Marshall Is. (1995 est.)	
★ Majuro	28,000
Martinique (1995 est.)	
★ Fort-de-France	104,000
Mauritania (1995 est.)	
★ Nouakchott	735,000
Mauritius (1995 est.)	
★ Port Louis	145,584
Mayotte (1991; MU)	
★ Mamoudzou	20,274
★ Dzaoudzi	8,268
Mexico (1990)	
Acapulco	515,374
Aguascalientes	440,425
Atizapán de Zaragoza (Ciudad López Mateos)	315,059
Campeche	150,518
Cancún	167,730
Celaya	214,856
Chihuahua	516,153
Ciudad Apodaca	103,364
Ciudad Madero	160,331
Ciudad Obregón	219,980
Ciudad Santa Catarina	162,707
Ciudad Victoria	194,996
Coatzacoalcos	198,817
Colima	106,967
Córdoba	130,695
Cuautla	110,242
Cuernavaca	279,187
Culiacán	415,046
Durango	348,036
Ensenada	169,426
Gómez Palacio	164,092
Guadalajara	1,650,042
Guadalupe	535,332
Hermosillo	406,417
Heroica Nogales	105,873
Irapuato	265,042
Juárez	789,522
La Paz	137,641
León	758,279
Los Mochis	162,659
Matamoros	266,055
Mazatlán	262,705
Mérida	523,422
Mexicali	438,377
★ Mexico City	9,815,795
Minatitlán	142,060
Monclova	177,792
Monterrey	1,068,996
Morelia	428,486
Nezahualcóyotl	1,255,456
Nuevo Laredo	218,413
Oaxaca	212,818
Orizaba	114,216
Pachuca	174,013
Poza Rica	151,739
Puebla	1,007,170
Querétaro	385,503
Reynosa	265,663
Salamanca	123,190
Saltillo	420,947
San Luis Potosí	488,238
San Nicolás de los Garza	436,603
San Pedro Garza García	113,017
Soledad de Graciano Sanchez	123,943
Tampico	272,690
Tapachula	138,858
Tehuacán	139,450
Tepic	206,967
Tijuana	698,752
Tlaquepaque	328,031
Toluca	327,865
Tonala	151,190
Torreón	439,436
Tuxtla	289,626
Uruapan	187,623
Veracruz	438,821
Villahermosa	261,231
Xalapa (Jalapa) Enríquez	279,451
Zacatecas	100,051
Zamora de Hidalgo	109,751
Zapopan	668,323
Micronesia	
★ Palikir	—
Moldova (1993 est.)	
Bălţi (Beltsy)	156,081
★ Chişinău (Kishinyov)	657,775
Tighina (Bendery)	128,881
Tiraspol	184,852
Monaco (1997 est.)	
★ Monaco	31,900[30]
Mongolia (1997 est.)	
★ Ulaanbaatar (Ulan Bator)	627,300
Morocco (1994; MU)	
Agadir	155,244
Agdal	129,914
Ain-Chock	165,907
Ain-Sebaa	139,323
Al-Fida	109,565
Al-Idrissia	110,861
Al-Ismailia	117,989
Ben-Msick	195,753
Beni-Mellal	140,212
Bouchentouf	140,370
Casablanca	523,279[37]
El-Jadida	119,083
El-Youssoufia	195,208
Fes-Medina	263,828
Hay Mohammadi	174,635
Kenitra Saknia	150,113
Khouribga	152,090
Ksar el-Kebir	107,065
Marrakech	621,914[37]
Meknès	188,224[37]
Mohammedia	170,083
Moulay Rachid	167,909
Nador	112,450
Ouad Ennachef Sidi Maafa	112,840
Oujda Sidi Ziane	146,142
★ Rabat	623,457[38]
Safi	364,648[37]
Salé	504,420
Sidi Bernoussi	153,118
Sidi Moumen	107,825
Sidi Othmane	183,195
Sidi Youssef-Ben Ali	118,770
Tanger	521,735[37]
Temara	126,303
Tétouan	277,516
Zouagha	262,429
Mozambique (1991 est.)	
Beira	298,847
Chimoio	108,818
★ Maputo (Lourenço Marques)	931,591
Matala	337,239
Nacala	125,208
Nampula	250,473
Quelimane	146,206
Tete	112,221
Myanmar (Burma) (1983)	
Bassein (Pathein)	144,096
Mandalay	532,949
Monywa	106,843
Moulmein (Mawlamyine)	219,961
Pegu (Bago)	150,528
Sittwe (Akyab)	107,621
Taunggye	108,231
★ Yangôn (Rangoon)	4,000,000[18,19]
Namibia (1995 est.)	
★ Windhoek	190,000
Nauru (1983)	
★ Yaren	559
Nepal (1993 est.; MU)	
Bhaktapur (Bhādgāon)	130,000
Birātnagar	132,000
★ Kāthmāndu	535,000
Lalitpur (Patan)	190,000
Netherlands, The (1996 est.)	
Almere	112,704
Amersfoort	114,884
★ Amsterdam (capital)	718,119
Apeldoorn	150,915
Arnhem	135,026
Breda	130,033
Dordrecht	116,196
Eindhoven	197,374
Enschede	147,832
Groningen	169,627
Haarlem	147,617
Haarlemmermeer	106,095
Leiden	116,224
Maastricht	118,518
Nijmegen	147,600
Rotterdam	592,745
's-Hertogenbosch	125,044
★ The Hague (seat of government)	442,503
Tilburg	164,380
Utrecht	234,254
Zaanstad	133,817
Zoetermeer	106,581
Zwolle	100,835
Netherlands Antilles (1995 est.)	
★ Willemstad	119,000
New Caledonia (1989)	
★ Nouméa	65,110
New Zealand (1996)	
Auckland	353,670
Christchurch	313,969
Dunedin	121,100[2]
Hamilton	106,700[2]
Manukau	254,577
North Shore	170,913
Waitakere	147,500[2]
★ Wellington	158,275
Nicaragua (1995)	
León	123,865
★ Managua	864,201
Niger (1994 est.)	
★ Niamey	420,000
Zinder	100,000
Nigeria (1996 est.)[39]	
Aba	298,900
Abeokuta	427,400
★ Abuja (capital designate)	350,100[40]
Ado-Ekiti	359,400
Agege	105,000
Akure	162,300
Awka	111,200
Benin City	229,400
Bida	125,500
Calabar	174,400
Deba Habe	138,600
Ede	307,100
Effon-Alaiye	153,100
Ejigbo	105,900
Enugu	316,100
Epe	101,000
Gombe	107,800
Gusau	158,000
Ibadan	1,432,000
Ife	296,800
Igboho	106,800

country / city	population
Ijebu-Ode	156,400
Ikare	140,800
Ikerre	244,600
Ikire	123,300
Ikirun	181,400
Ikorodu	184,900
Ila	264,000
Ilawe-Ekiti	184,500
Ilegbo	101,600
Ilesha	378,400
Ilobu	199,000
Ilorin	475,800
Inisa	119,800
Ise-Ekiti	103,400
Iseyin	217,300
Iwo	362,000
Jos	206,300
Kaduna	342,200
Kano	674,100
Katsina	206,500
Kumo	148,000
Lafia	122,500
★ Lagos	1,518,000
Maiduguri	320,000
Makurdi	123,100
Minna	136,900
Mushin	333,200
Offa	197,200
Ogbomosho	730,000
Oka	142,900
Ondo	173,600
Onitsha	371,900
Oshogbo	476,800
Owo	183,500
Oyo	256,400
Port Harcourt	410,000
Sapele	139,200
Shagamu	117,200
Shaki	174,500
Shomolu	147,700
Sokoto	204,900
Ugep	102,600
Warri	126,100
Zaria	379,200
Northern Mariana Is. (1990)	
★ Saipan	38,896
Norway (1997 est.; MU)	
Bergen	224,130
★ Oslo	493,973
Stavanger	105,573
Trondheim	144,599
Oman (1993)	
★ Muscat	51,969
Pakistan (1981)	
Bahāwalpur	180,263
Chiniot	105,559
Dera Ghāzi Khān	102,007
Faisalābād (Lyallpur)	1,104,209
Gujrānwāla	658,753
Gujrāt	155,058
Hyderābād	751,529
★ Islamābād	204,364
Jhang	195,558
Jhelum	106,462
Karāchi	5,208,132
Kasūr	155,523
Lahore	2,952,689
Lahore Cantonment	237,000
Lārkāna	123,890
Mardān	147,977
Mīrpur khās	124,371
Multān	730,070
Nawābshāh	102,139
Okāra	153,483
Peshāwar	566,248
Quetta	285,719
Rahīm Yār Khān	119,036
Rāwalpindi	794,843
Sāhiwāl	150,954
Sargodha	291,362
Sheikhūpura	141,168
Siālkot	302,009
Sukkur	190,551
Wāh Cantonment	122,335
Palau (1995 est.)	
Koror	12,000
Panama (1995 est.)	
Colón	137,825[10]
★ Panama City	452,041
San Miguelito	290,919
Papua New Guinea (1990)	
★ Port Moresby (National Capital District)	193,242
Paraguay (1992)	
★ Asunción	502,426
Ciudad del Este	133,893
San Lorenzo	133,311
Peru (1993)	
Arequipa	619,156
Ayacucho	105,918
Callao	615,046
Chiclayo	411,536
Chimbote	268,979
Chincha Alta	110,016
Cusco	255,568
Huancayo	258,209
Huánuco	118,814
Ica	161,406
Iquitos	274,759
Juliaca	142,576
★ Lima	421,570[23]
Metro Lima-Callao	5,706,127
Piura	277,964
Pucallpa	172,286
Sullana	147,361
Tacna	174,336
Trujillo	509,312
Philippines (1994 est.)	
Angeles	276,545
Bacolod	343,048
Bago	139,771
Baguio	169,565
Batangas	190,627
Butuan	244,900
Cabanatuan	185,728
Cadiz	143,299
Cagayan de Oro	413,689
Calbayog	130,321
Caloocan	642,670
Cavite	103,422
Cebu	688,196
Cotabato	112,934
Dagupan	116,936
Davao	960,910
General Santos	279,343
Gingoog	111,326
Iligan	209,639
Iloilo	302,200
Lapu-Lapu	141,009
Las Piñas	380,482
Legaspi	125,128
Lipa	159,769
Lucena	161,049
Makati	453,000[15]
Malabon	277,000[15]
Mandaluyong	247,000[15]
Mandaue	212,987
★ Manila	1,894,667[20]
Metro Manila	8,594,150
Marikina	308,000[15]
Muntilupa	275,056
Naga	102,545
Navotas	187,000[15]
Olongapo	208,633
Ormoc	142,092
Pagadian	113,905
Parañaque	308,000[15]
Pasay	388,129
Pasig	395,000[15]
★ Quezon City	1,676,644[41]
Roxas	111,649
San Carlos (*Negros Occidental*)	106,000[15]
San Carlos (*Pangasinan*)	123,473
San Juan del Monte	127,000[15]
San Pablo	163,297
Silay	140,175
Tacloban	153,068
Tagig	267,000[15]
Toledo	125,978
Valenzuela	340,000[15]
Zamboanga	464,466
Poland (1996 est.)	
Białystok	277,800
Bielsko-Biała	180,700
Bydgoszcz	386,100
Bytom	227,600
Chorzów	125,800
Czestochowa	259,500
Dąbrowa Górnicza	130,900
Elbląg	128,700
Gdańsk	462,800
Gdynia	251,400
Gliwice	214,000
Gorzów Wielkopolski	124,900
Grudziadz	102,900
Jastrzębie-Zdrój	103,500
Kalisz	106,800
Katowice	354,200
Kielce	213,700
Koszalin	111,700
Kraków	745,400
Legnica	108,000
Łódź	825,600
Lublin	353,300
Olsztyn	167,400
Opole	130,600
Płock	126,900
Poznań	581,800
Radom	232,300
Ruda Śląska	166,300
Rybnik	144,300
Rzeszów	160,300
Słupsk	102,700
Sosnowiec	249,000
Szczecin	419,300
Tarnów	121,500
Toruń	204,300
Tychy	133,900
Wałbrzych	139,600
★ Warsaw (Warszawa)	1,638,300
Włocławek	123,100
Wrocław	642,700
Zabrze	201,600
Zielona Góra	116,100
Portugal (1991)	
★ Lisbon	677,790
Porto	310,600
Puerto Rico (1996 est.; MU)	
Arecibo	100,755
Bayamón	231,845
Caguas	140,114
Carolina	188,427
Guaynabo	104,927
Mayaguez	100,937
Ponce	189,988
★ San Juan	433,705
Qatar (1993 est.)	
★ Doha	339,471
Réunion (1994 est.)	
★ Saint-Denis	104,454
Romania (1994 est.)	
Arad	187,876
Bacău	207,730
Baia Mare	149,975
Botoşani	128,322
Brăila	235,763
Braşov	324,210
★ Bucharest	2,060,551
Buzău	149,610
Cluj-Napoca	326,017
Constanţa	348,575
Craiova	306,825
Drobeta-Turnu Severin	118,383
Focşani	100,900
Galaţi	326,728
Iaşi	339,889
Oradea	221,885
Piatra Neamţ	125,622
Piteşti	184,171
Ploieşti	254,136
Râmnicu Vâlcea	114,286
Satu Mare	131,431
Sibiu	170,528
Suceava	117,314
Timişoara	327,830
Tirgu Mureş	166,315
Russia (1995 est.)	
Abakan	161,000
Achinsk	123,000
Almetyevsk	138,000
Angarsk	267,000
Anzhero-Sudzhensk	101,000
Arkhangelsk	374,000
Armavir	164,000
Arzamas	112,000
Astrakhan	486,000
Balakovo	206,000
Balashikha	136,000
Barnaul	596,000
Belgorod	322,000
Berezniki	184,000
Biysk	228,000
Blagoveshchensk	214,000
Bratsk	257,000
Bryansk	462,000
Cheboksary	450,000
Chelyabinsk	1,100,000[18]
Cherepovets	320,000
Cherkessk	119,000
Chita	322,000
Dimitrovgrad	135,000
Dzerzhinsk	285,000
Elektrostal	150,000
Engels	186,000
Glazov	107,000
Grozny (Dzhokhar)	364,000[1]
Irkutsk	585,000
Ivanovo	474,000
Izhevsk	654,000
Kaliningrad	419,000
Kaliningrad (*Moscow oblast*)	134,000
Kaluga	347,000
Kamensk-Uralsky	197,000
Kamyshin	128,000
Kansk	109,000
Kazan	1,100,000[18]
Kemerovo	503,000
Khabarovsk	618,000
Khimki	134,000
Kineshma	103,000
Kirov	464,000
Kiselyovsk	116,000
Kislovodsk	120,000
Kolomna	154,000
Kolpino	143,000
Komsomolsk-na-Amure	309,000
Kostroma	285,000
Kovrov	162,000
Krasnodar	646,000
Krasnoyarsk	869,000
Kurgan	363,000
Kursk	442,000
Kuznetsk	100,000
Leninsk-Kuznetsky	121,000
Lipetsk	474,000
Lyubertsy	166,000
Magadan	128,000
Magnitogorsk	427,000
Makhachkala	339,000
Maykop	165,000
Mezhdurechensk	105,000
Miass	167,000
Michurinsk	108,000
★ Moscow	8,400,000[18]
Murmansk	407,000
Murom	126,000
Mytishchi	152,000
Naberezhnye Chelny (Brezhnev)	526,000
Nakhodka	163,000
Nalchik	239,000
Neftekamsk	117,000
Nevinnomyssk	131,000
Nikolo-Beryozovka (Neftekamsk)	117,000
Nizhnekamsk	210,000
Nizhnevartovsk	238,000
Nizhny Novgorod (Gorky)	1,400,000[18]
Nizhny Tagil	409,000
Noginsk	119,000
Norilsk	159,000
Novgorod	233,000
Novocheboksarsk	123,000
Novocherkassk	190,000
Novokuybyshevsk	115,000
Novokuznetsk	572,000
Novomoskovsk (*Tula oblast*)	144,000
Novorossiysk	202,000
Novoshakhtinsk	107,000
Novosibirsk	1,400,000[18]
Novotroitsk	110,000
Obninsk	108,000
Odintsovo	129,000
Oktyabrsky	110,000
Omsk	1,200,000[18]
Orekhovo-Zuyevo	126,000
Orenburg	532,000
Orsk	275,000
Oryol	348,000
Penza	534,000
Perm	1,000,000[18]
Pervouralsk	137,000
Petropavlovsk-Kamchatsky	210,000
Petrozavodsk	280,000
Podolsk	202,000
Prokopyevsk	253,000
Pskov	207,000
Pyatigorsk	133,000
Rostov-na-Donu	1,000,000[18]
Rubtsovsk	170,000
Ryazan	536,000
Rybinsk (Andropov)	248,000
Saint Petersburg (Leningrad)	4,200,000[18]
Salavat	156,000
Samara (Kuybyshev)	1,200,000[18]
Saransk	320,000
Sarapul	109,000
Saratov	895,000
Sergiev Posad (Zagorsk)	114,000
Serov	100,000
Serpukhov	139,000
Severodvinsk	241,000
Seversk	110,000
Shakhty	230,000
Shchyolkovo	108,000
Simbirsk (Ulyanovsk)	678,000
Smolensk	355,000
Sochi	355,000
Solikamsk	108,000
Stary Oskol	198,000
Stavropol	342,000
Sterlitamak	259,000
Surgut	263,000
Syktyvkar	229,000
Syzran	177,000
Taganrog	292,000
Tambov	316,000
Tolyatti	702,000
Tomsk	470,000
Tula	532,000
Tver (Kalinin)	455,000
Tyumen	494,000
Ufa	1,100,000[18]
Ukhta	106,000
Ulan-Ude	366,000
Usolye-Sibirskoye	106,000
Ussuriysk	162,000
Ust-Ilimsk	110,000
Velikiye Luki	116,000
Vladikavkaz (Ordzhonikidze)	312,000
Vladimir	339,000
Vladivostok	632,000
Volgodonsk	183,000
Volgograd	1,003,000
Vologda	299,000
Volzhsky	288,000
Vorkuta	104,000
Voronezh	908,000
Votkinsk	104,000
Yakutsk	192,000
Yaroslavl	629,000
Yekaterinburg (Sverdlovsk)	1,300,000[18]
Yelets	119,000
Yoshkar-Ola	251,000
Yuzhno-Sakhalinsk	160,000
Zelenodolysk	101,000
Zelenograd	191,000
Zlatoust	203,000
Rwanda (1991)	
★ Kigali	232,733
St. Kitts and Nevis (1994 est.)	
★ Basseterre	12,605
St. Lucia (1992 est.)	
★ Castries	13,615[42]
St. Vincent and the Grenadines (1991)	
★ Kingstown	15,466
Samoa (1995 est.)	
★ Apia	33,000
San Marino (1996 est.)	
★ San Marino	2,316
São Tomé and Príncipe (1991)	
★ São Tomé	43,420
Saudi Arabia (1991 est.)	
Ad-Dammām	350,000
Jiddah	1,500,000
Mecca (Makkah)	630,000
Medina (Al-Madinah)	400,000
★ Riyadh (Ar-Riyad)	2,800,000[18, 19]
Aṭ-Ṭā'if	410,000
Senegal (1995 est.)	
★ Dakar	1,500,000
Kaolack	181,000
Mboure	106,046[8]
Rufisque	138,837[8]
St.-Louis	179,000
Thiès	319,000
Ziguinchor	161,680[8]
Seychelles (1993 est.)	
★ Victoria	25,000
Sierra Leone (1990 est.)	
★ Freetown	669,000[19]
Singapore (1997 est.)[30]	
★ Singapore	3,104,000
Slovakia (1996 est.)	
★ Bratislava	452,053
Košice	240,915
Slovenia (1996 est.)	
★ Ljubljana	269,621
Maribor	134,289
Solomon Islands (1996 est.)	
★ Honiara	43,643
Somalia (1995 est.)	
★ Mogadishu	997,000
South Africa (1991)	
Alexandra	124,586
Benoni	113,501
★ Bloemfontein (judicial)	126,867
Boksburg	119,890
Botshabelo	177,926
★ Cape Town (legislative)	854,616
Carletonville	118,699
Daveyton	151,659
Diepmeadow	241,099
Durban	715,669
East London	102,325
Evaton	201,026
Germiston	134,005
Ibhayi	257,054
Johannesburg	712,507
Kathlehong (Katlehong)	201,785
Kempton Park	106,606
Khayelitsa	189,586
Kwamashu (Kwa Mashu)	156,679
Lekoa	217,582
Mamelodi	154,845
Manguang (Mangaung)	125,545
Mdantsane	242,823
Ntuzuma	102,310
Pietermaritzburg	156,473
Port Elizabeth	303,353
★ Pretoria (executive)	525,583
Roodepoort	162,632
Sandton	101,197
Soshanguve	146,334
Soweto	596,632
Tembisa	209,238
Umlazi	299,275

Major cities and national capitals (continued)

country city	population
Spain (1995 est.; MU)	
Albacete	143,779
Alcalá de Henares	166,925
Alcorcón	143,532
Algeciras	104,216
Alicante	276,526
Almería	169,509
Badajoz	132,154
Badalona	217,983
Barakaldo	102,561
Barcelona	1,614,571
Bilbao	370,997
Burgos	166,732
Cádiz	154,511
Cartagena	180,553
Castellón de la Plana	139,889
Córdoba	323,138
Coruña, La	254,822
Donostia (San Sebastián)	178,470
Elche (Elx)	192,424
Fuenlabrada	160,573
Getafe	144,662
Gijón	270,867
Granada	272,738
Hospitalet de Llobregat	262,501
Huelva	145,712
Jaén	113,141
Jerez de la Frontera	191,394
Laguna, La	127,743
Leganés	178,321
León	147,780
Lleida (Lérida)	114,367
Logroño	125,456
★ Madrid	3,029,734
Málaga	532,425
Mataró	102,137
Móstoles	199,411
Murcia	344,904
Ourense (Orense)	110,796
Oviedo	202,421
Palma (de Mallorca)	318,030
Palmas de Gran Canaria, Las (Is. Canarias)	373,772
Pamplona	181,776
Sabadell	188,386
Salamanca	167,316
Santa Coloma de Gramanet	129,751
Santa Cruz de Tenerife	204,948
Santander	194,837
Sevilla (Seville)	719,588
Tarragona	114,931
Terrassa	162,327
Valencia	763,299
Valladolid	334,820
Vigo	290,582
Vitoria (Gasteiz)	215,049
Zaragoza (Saragossa)	607,899
Sri Lanka (1990 est.)	
★ Colombo (administrative)	645,000[2]
Dehiwala-Mount Lavinia	196,000
Jaffna	129,000
Kandy	104,000
Moratuwa	170,000
★ Sri Jayawardenepura Kotte (legislative and judicial)	109,000[43]
Sudan, The (1993)	
Juba	114,980
Kassalā	234,270
★ Khartoum (executive)	924,505
Khartoum North	879,105
Nyala	228,778
★ Omdurman (legislative)	1,267,077
Port Sudan	305,385
al-Qaḍārif	189,384
al-Ubayyiḍ	228,096
Wad Madanī	218,714
Wāw	116,000[44]
Suriname (1993 est.)	
★ Paramaribo	200,970
Swaziland (1990 est.)	
★ Lobamba (legislative)	...
★ Lozitha (royal)	...
★ Ludzidzini (royal)	...
★ Mbabane (administrative)	47,000
Sweden (1997 est.; MU)	
Göteborg	454,016
Helsingborg	114,866
Jönköping	115,636
Linköping	131,898
Malmö	248,007
Norrköping	123,531
Örebro	120,774
★ Stockholm	718,462
Umeå	102,487
Uppsala	184,507
Västerås	124,084
Switzerland (1996 est.)	
Basel (Bâle)	174,007
★ Bern (Berne)	127,469
Geneva (Genève)	173,549
Lausanne	115,878
Zürich	343,869
Syria (1994 est.)	
Aleppo (Ḥalab)	1,591,400
★ Damascus (Dimashq)	1,549,000
Dar'ā	180,093
Dayr az-Zawr	174,085
Dūmā	131,158
Ḥamāh	229,000[10]
Al-Ḥasakah	106,000[10]
Homs (Ḥims)	644,204
Jaramānah	138,469
Latakia (al-Ladhiqiyah)	306,535
Al-Qāmishlī	151,000[10]
Ar-Raqqah	219,016
Ṭarṭūs	136,812
Taiwan (1997 est.)	
Chang-hua	221,090[8]
Chi-lung (Keelung)	374,874
Chia-i	263,549
Chung-ho	387,123[2]
Chung-li	295,825[2]
Feng-shan (Kao-hsiung-hsien)	301,374[2]
Féng-yüan	157,548[2]
Hsin-chu	346,979
Hsin-chuang	328,758[2]
Hsin-tien	248,822[2]
Hua-lien	107,824[2]
Kao-hsiung	1,434,907
Pan-ch-'iao (T'ai-pei-hsien)	539,115[2]
P'ing-tung	214,728[2]
San-chu'ung	382,880[2]
T'ai-chung	881,870
T'ai-nan	712,172
T'ai-tung	109,189[2]
★ Taipei (T'ai-pei)	2,595,699
T'ao-yuan	260,680[2]
Yung-ho	241,104[2]
Tajikistan (1994 est.)	
★ Dushanbe	524,000
Khujand (Khudzhand; Leninabad)	164,500[20]
Tanzania (1988)	
Arusha	134,708
★ Dar es Salaam	1,360,850
★ Dodoma (legislative)	203,833
Mbeya	152,844
Morogoro	117,760
Mwanza	223,013
Shinyanga	100,724
Tanga	187,155
Zanzibar	157,634
Thailand (1993 est.)	
★ Bangkok	5,584,963[18]
Chiang Mai	170,397
Hat Yai	148,632
Nakhon Ratchasima	188,171
Nonthaburi	261,335
Ubon Ratchathani	105,936
Togo (1990 est.)	
★ Lomé	513,000[19]
Tonga (1990 est.)	
★ Nuku'alofa	34,000
Trinidad and Tobago (1995 est.)	
★ Port-of-Spain	52,000
Tunisia (1994)	
Aryānah	152,700
Ettadhamen	149,200
Kairouan	102,600
Ṣafāqis (Sfax)	230,900
Sūsah	125,000
★ Tunis	674,100
Turkey (1995 est.)	
Adana	1,066,544
Adapazari	186,000[8]
Adıyaman	129,919
Afyan	102,997
★ Ankara	2,837,937
Antakya	137,200[8]
Antalya	502,269
Aydın	123,163
Balıkesir	189,702
Batman	186,178
Bursa	1,016,760
Çorum	136,736
Denizli	239,698
Diyarbakır	448,145
Edirne	117,331
Elaziğ	224,781
Erzurum	247,585
Eskişehir	455,285
Gaziantep	730,435
Gebze	231,052
Hatay	138,998
İçel	532,774
İskenderun	153,871
Isparta	121,663
Istanbul	7,774,169
İzmir	2,017,699
İzmit	275,800[8]
Kahramanmaraş	242,491
Karabük	114,698
Kayseri	463,759
Kilis	107,605
Kırıkkale	154,764
Kocaeli	205,762
Konya	584,785
Kütahya	141,450
Malatya	314,539
Manisa	191,287
Mersin	523,000[8]
Ordu	123,782
Osmaniye	140,257
Sakarya	185,187
Samsun	330,360
Sivas	243,432
Sultanbeyli	169,999
Tarsus	229,518
Trabzon	143,573
Urfa (Şanlıurfa)	362,598
Uşak	121,972
Van	197,679
Zonguldak	113,627
Turkmenistan (1995 est.)	
★ Ashkhabad (Ashgabat)	536,000
Chărjew (Chardzhev; Chardzhou)	166,400[20]
Dashhowuz (Dashkhovuz; Tashauz)	117,000[20]
Tuvalu (1995 est.)	
★ Funafuti	4,000
Uganda (1995 est.)	
★ Kampala	954,000
Ukraine (1996 est.)	
Alchevsk	124,000
Berdyansk	135,000
Bila Tserkva (Belaya Tserkov)	216,000
Cherkasy (Cherkassy)	312,000
Chernihiv (Chernigov)	312,000
Chernivtsi (Chernovtsy)	261,000
Dniprodzerzhynsk (Dneprodzerzhinsk)	281,000
Dnipropetrovsk (Dnepropetrovsk)	1,147,000
Donetsk	1,088,000
Horlivka (Gorlovka)	322,000
Ivano-Frankivsk (Ivano-Frankovsk)	237,000
Kamyanets-Podilsky (Kamenets-Podolsky)	108,000
Kerch	175,000
Kharkiv (Kharkov)	1,555,000
Kherson	363,000
Khmelnytsky (Khmelnitsky)	259,000
★ Kiev (Kyyiv)	2,630,000
Kirovohrad	276,000
Kostyantynivka (Konstantinovka)	102,000
Kramatorsk	197,000
Krasny Luch	109,000
Kremenchuk (Kremenchug)	246,000
Kryvy Rih (Krivoy Rog)	720,000
Luhansk (Voroshilovgrad)	487,000
Lutsk	219,000
Lviv (Lvov)	802,000
Lysychansk (Lisichansk)	123,000
Makiyivka (Makeyevka)	409,000
Mariupol (Zhdanov)	510,000
Melitopol	174,000
Mykolayiv (Nikolayev)	508,000
Nikopol	157,000
Odesa (Odessa)	1,046,000
Oleksandriya (Aleksandriya)	103,000
Pavlohrad	134,000
Poltava	321,000
Rivne (Rovno)	246,000
Sevastopol	365,000
Severodonetsk	132,000
Simferopol	348,000
Slovyansk (Slavyansk)	133,000
Stakhanov	109,000
Sumy	304,000
Ternopil (Ternopol)	235,000
Uzhhorod	126,000
Vinnytsya (Vinnitsa)	388,000
Yenakiyeve (Yenakiyevo)	114,000
Yevpatoriya	115,000
Zaporizhzhya (Zaporozhye)	882,000
Zhytomyr (Zhitomir)	301,000
United Arab Emirates (1989 est.)	
★ Abu Dhabi (Abū Ẓaby)	363,432
Al-'Ayn	176,441
Dubai (Dubayy)	585,189
Sharjah (Ash-Shāriqah)	125,123[25]
United Kingdom (1995 est.)[45]	
Aberdeen	219,100
Aylesbury	152,000[8]
Barnsley	226,700
Basildon	162,100[8]
Basingstoke/Deane	147,200[8]
Bedford	137,000[8]
Belfast	296,700
Beverley	118,000[8]
Birmingham	1,017,500
Blackburn	140,100[8]
Blackpool	154,000[8]
Bolton	265,400
Bournemouth	160,100[8]
Bracknell	104,600[8]
Bradford	482,700
Braintree	123,600[8]
Brighton	154,900[8]
Bristol	400,700
Bury	182,200[8]
Cambridge	113,000[8]
Canterbury	133,900[8]
Cardiff	302,700
Carlisle	103,300[8]
Chelmsford	155,800[8]
Cheltenham	106,800[8]
Chester	120,600[8]
Chesterfield	101,100[8]
Chichester	103,100[8]
Colchester	149,600[8]
Coventry	303,600
Crewe/Nantwich	111,400[8]
Darlington	100,600[8]
Derby	231,900
Doncaster	292,900
Dover	106,900[8]
Dudley	312,500
Dundee	167,600
Eastleigh	110,800[8]
Edinburgh	447,600
Elmbridge	119,700[8]
Epping Forest	118,900[8]
Exeter	104,500[8]
Fareham	101,800[8]
Gateshead	201,800
Glasgow	674,800
Gloucester	104,700[8]
Guildford	126,200[8]
Harrogate	148,400[8]
Havant	119,400[8]
Horsham	114,300[8]
Huntingdon	149,900[8]
Ipswich	114,100[8]
King's Lynn/West Norfolk	131,000[8]
Kingston upon Hull	268,600
Kirklees	387,700
Knowsley	154,000[8]
Lancaster	135,000[8]
Leeds	725,000
Leicester	295,700
Liverpool	470,800
★ London	7,007,100
Luton	180,800[8]
Macclesfield	151,500[8]
Maidstone	138,500[8]
Manchester	432,600
Mansfield	102,100[8]
Middlesbrough	146,900[8]
Milton Keynes	188,400[8]
Newbury	141,600[8]
Newcastle under Lyme	123,100[8]
Newcastle upon Tyne	283,100
Newport	137,400[8]
Northampton	187,600[8]
Norwich	127,800[8]
Nottingham	283,800
Nuneaton/Bedworth	119,100[8]
Oldham	220,000
Oxford	132,800[8]
Peterborough	158,700
Plymouth	257,500
Poole	138,100[8]
Portsmouth	189,300[8]
Preston	133,100[8]
Reading	138,500[8]
Reigate/Banstead	118,300[8]
Renfrew	203,100
Rhymney Valley	104,300[8]
Rochdale	207,600
Rochester upon Medway	145,500[8]
Rotherham	255,800
St. Albans	128,700[8]
St. Helens	181,000[8]
Salford	230,500
Salisbury	110,000[8]
Sandwell	293,700
Scarborough	108,700[8]
Sefton	291,000
Sevenoaks	109,900[8]
Sheffield	528,500
Slough	104,900[8]
Solihull	202,900
Southampton	213,500
Southend-on-Sea	169,900[8]
Stafford	122,500[8]
Stockport	290,600
Stockton-on-Tees	178,200[8]
Stoke-on-Trent	254,300
Stratford-on-Avon	109,500[8]
Stroud	106,300[8]
Sunderland	295,800
Swale	117,200[8]
Swansea	188,800[8]
Tameside	221,500
Tonbridge/Malling	102,800[8]
Trafford	218,300
Tunbridge Wells	102,700[8]
Wakefield	317,100
Walsall	262,800
Warrington	186,700[8]
Warwick	119,800[8]
Wigan	309,800
Winchester	101,800[8]
Windsor/Maidenhead	137,800[8]
Wirral	331,500
Wokingham	141,700[8]
Wolverhampton	244,300
Wrexham Maelor	117,400[8]
Wycombe	162,600[8]
York	104,100[8]
United States (1996 est.)	
Abilene (*Texas*)	108,476
Akron (*Ohio*)	216,882
Alameda (*Calif.*)	76,042
Albany (*Ga.*)	78,591
Albany (*N.Y.*)	103,564
Albuquerque (*N.M.*)	419,681
Alexandria (*Va.*)	117,586
Alhambra (*Calif.*)	83,644
Allentown (*Pa.*)	102,211
Amarillo (*Texas*)	169,588
Anaheim (*Calif.*)	288,945
Anchorage (*Alaska*)	250,505
Antioch (*Calif.*)	76,293
Ann Arbor (*Mich.*)	108,758
Arlington (*Texas*)	294,816
Arlington (*Va.*)	175,334[46]
Arlington Heights (*Ill.*)	76,740
Arvada (*Colo.*)	96,340
Atlanta (*Ga.*)	401,907
Aurora (*Colo.*)	252,341
Aurora (*Ill.*)	116,405
Austin (*Texas*)	541,278
Bakersfield (*Calif.*)	205,508
Baltimore (*Md.*)	675,401
Baton Rouge (*La.*)	215,882
Beaumont (*Texas*)	111,224
Bellevue (*Wash.*)	92,267
Berkeley (*Calif.*)	103,243
Billings (*Mont.*)	91,195
Birmingham (*Ala.*)	258,543
Bloomington (*Minn.*)	86,664
Boise City (*Idaho*)	152,737
Boston (*Mass.*)	558,394
Boulder (*Colo.*)	90,928
Bridgeport (*Conn.*)	137,990
Brockton (*Mass.*)	92,324
Brownsville (*Texas*)	132,091
Buffalo (*N.Y.*)	310,548
Burbank (*Calif.*)	96,579
Cambridge (*Mass.*)	93,707
Camden (*N.J.*)	84,844
Canton (*Ohio*)	81,079
Cape Coral (*Fla.*)	88,053
Carrollton (*Texas*)	96,757
Carson (*Calif.*)	86,516
Cedar Rapids (*Iowa*)	113,482
Chandler (*Ariz.*)	142,918
Charlotte (*N.C.*)	441,297
Chattanooga (*Tenn.*)	150,425
Chesapeake (*Va.*)	192,342
Chicago (*Ill.*)	2,721,547
Chula Vista (*Calif.*)	151,963
Cincinnati (*Ohio*)	345,818
Clarksville (*Tenn.*)	94,879
Clearwater (*Fla.*)	100,132

[1]1993 estimate. [2]1995 estimate. [3]Eight villages, including Fagatogo, Utulei, and Pago Pago, are collectively known as Pago Pago (1990 census pop. 10,559). [4]1984 estimate. [5]Population of municipality. [6]1989 census. [7]Population of the statistical division containing the city. [8]1994 estimate. [9]Statistical district. [10]1992 estimate. [11]Population cited is for New Providence Island. [12]1991 census. [13]1992 census. [14]1982 estimate. [15]1990 census. [16]1987 census. [17]Excludes the agricultural population of the named civil division. [18]1996 estimate. [19]Population refers to widest officially defined agglomeration or metropolitan area. [20]1991 estimate. [21]San José canton. [22]1988 census. [23]Mid-1990s estimate. [24]Excludes population of Lefkosia (Turkish-occupied Nicosia), estimated at 37,400 in 1985. [25]Population of the urban area of the National district. [26]1986 estimate. [27]1986 census. [28]Urban centre of Suva. [29]1983 census. [30]No separate areas within the state are

country city	population
Cleveland (*Ohio*)	498,246
Colorado Springs (*Colo.*)	345,127
Columbia (*Mo.*)	76,756
Columbia (*S.C.*)	112,773
Columbus (*Ga.*)	182,828
Columbus (*Ohio*)	657,053
Compton (*Calif.*)	91,700
Concord (*Calif.*)	114,850
Coral Springs (*Fla.*)	105,275
Corona (*Calif.*)	100,208
Corpus Christi (*Texas*)	280,260
Costa Mesa (*Calif.*)	100,938
Dallas (*Texas*)	1,053,292
Daly City (*Calif.*)	97,649
Davenport (*Iowa*)	97,010
Dayton (*Ohio*)	172,947
Dearborn (*Mich.*)	91,418
Decatur (*Ill.*)	81,369
Denver (*Colo.*)	497,840
Des Moines (*Iowa*)	193,422
Detroit (*Mich.*)	1,000,272
Downey (*Calif.*)	93,073
Duluth (*Minn.*)	83,699
Durham (*N.C.*)	149,799
El Cajon (*Calif.*)	92,057
El Monte (*Calif.*)	110,026
El Paso (*Texas*)	599,865
Elgin (*Ill.*)	86,034
Elizabeth (*N.J.*)	110,149
Erie (*Pa.*)	105,270
Escondido (*Calif.*)	116,184
Eugene (*Ore.*)	123,718
Evansville (*Ind.*)	123,456
Everett (*Wash.*)	81,028
Fairfield (*Calif.*)	85,610
Fall River (*Mass.*)	90,865
Fargo (*N.D.*)	83,778
Farmington Hills (*Mich.*)	79,918
Fayetteville (*N.C.*)	79,631
Flint (*Mich.*)	134,881
Fontana (*Calif.*)	104,124
Fort Collins (*Colo.*)	104,196
Fort Lauderdale (*Fla.*)	151,805
Fort Wayne (*Ind.*)	184,783
Fort Worth (*Texas*)	479,716
Fremont (*Calif.*)	187,800
Fresno (*Calif.*)	396,011
Fullerton (*Calif.*)	120,188
Gainesville (*Fla.*)	87,295
Garden Grove (*Calif.*)	149,208
Garland (*Texas*)	190,055
Gary (*Ind.*)	110,975
Glendale (*Ariz.*)	182,219
Glendale (*Calif.*)	184,321
Grand Prairie (*Texas*)	109,231
Grand Rapids (*Mich.*)	188,242
Green Bay (*Wis.*)	102,076
Greensboro (*N.C.*)	195,426
Gresham (*Ore.*)	81,583
Hammond (*Ind.*)	80,081
Hampton (*Va.*)	138,757
Hartford (*Conn.*)	133,086
Hayward (*Calif.*)	121,631
Henderson (*Nev.*)	122,339
Hialeah (*Fla.*)	204,684
Hollywood (*Fla.*)	127,894
Honolulu (*Ha.*)	423,475
Houston (*Texas*)	1,744,058
Huntington Beach (*Calif.*)	190,751
Huntsville (*Ala.*)	170,424
Independence (*Mo.*)	110,303
Indianapolis (*Ind.*)	746,737
Inglewood (*Calif.*)	111,040
Irvine (*Calif.*)	127,873
Irving (*Texas*)	176,993
Jackson (*Miss.*)	192,923
Jacksonville (*Fla.*)	679,792
Jersey City (*N.J.*)	229,039
Joliet (*Ill.*)	86,749
Kalamazoo (*Mich.*)	77,460
Kansas City (*Kan.*)	142,654
Kansas City (*Mo.*)	441,259
Kenosha (*Wis.*)	86,888
Killeen (*Texas*)	78,022
Knoxville (*Tenn.*)	167,535
Lafayette (*La.*)	104,899
Lakewood (*Calif.*)	75,462
Lakewood (*Colo.*)	134,999
Lancaster (*Calif.*)	115,675
Lansing (*Mich.*)	125,736
Laredo (*Texas*)	164,899
Las Vegas (*Nev.*)	376,906
Lawton (*Okla.*)	82,582
Lexington-Fayette (*Ky.*)	239,942
Lincoln (*Neb.*)	209,192
Little Rock (*Ark.*)	175,752
Livonia (*Mich.*)	105,099
Long Beach (*Calif.*)	421,904
Los Angeles (*Calif.*)	3,553,638
Louisville (*Ky.*)	260,689
Lowell (*Mass.*)	100,973
Lubbock (*Texas*)	193,565
Lynn (*Mass.*)	80,563
McAllen (*Texas*)	103,352
Macon (*Ga.*)	113,352
Madison (*Wis.*)	197,630
Manchester (*N.H.*)	100,967
Memphis (*Tenn.*)	596,725
Mesa (*Ariz.*)	344,764
Mesquite (*Texas*)	111,947
Miami (*Fla.*)	365,127
Miami Beach (*Fla.*)	94,540
Midland (*Texas*)	97,162
Milwaukee (*Wis.*)	590,503
Minneapolis (*Minn.*)	358,785
Mission Viejo (*Calif.*)	84,689
Mobile (*Ala.*)	202,581
Modesto (*Calif.*)	178,559
Montgomery (*Ala.*)	196,363
Moreno Valley (*Calif.*)	140,932
Naperville (*Ill.*)	107,001
Nashua (*N.H.*)	81,094
Nashville-Davidson (*Tenn.*)	511,263
New Bedford (*Mass.*)	96,903
New Haven (*Conn.*)	124,665
New Orleans (*La.*)	476,625
New York City (*N.Y.*)	7,380,906
Newark (*N.J.*)	268,510
Newport News (*Va.*)	176,122
Newton (*Mass.*)	80,238
Norfolk (*Va.*)	233,430
Norman (*Okla.*)	90,228
North Las Vegas (*Nev.*)	78,659
Norwalk (*Calif.*)	100,209
Norwalk (*Conn.*)	77,977
Oakland (*Calif.*)	367,230
Oceanside (*Calif.*)	145,941
Odessa (*Texas*)	90,883
Oklahoma City (*Okla.*)	469,852
Olathe (*Kan.*)	78,666
Omaha (*Neb.*)	364,253
Ontario (*Calif.*)	144,854
Orange (*Calif.*)	119,890
Orem (*Utah*)	79,736
Orlando (*Fla.*)	173,902
Overland Park (*Kan.*)	131,053
Oxnard (*Calif.*)	151,009
Palmdale (*Calif.*)	106,540
Parma (*Ohio*)	85,006
Pasadena (*Calif.*)	134,116
Pasadena (*Texas*)	131,620
Paterson (*N.J.*)	150,270
Pembroke Pines (*Fla.*)	100,662
Peoria (*Ariz.*)	76,045
Peoria (*Ill.*)	112,306
Philadelphia (*Pa.*)	1,478,002
Phoenix (*Ariz.*)	1,159,014
Pittsburgh (*Pa.*)	350,363
Plano (*Texas*)	192,280
Plantation (*Fla.*)	78,674
Pomona (*Calif.*)	134,706
Port St. Lucie (*Fla.*)	75,532
Portland (*Ore.*)	480,824
Portsmouth (*Va.*)	101,308
Providence (*R.I.*)	152,558
Provo (*Utah*)	99,606
Pueblo (*Colo.*)	99,406
Quincy (*Mass.*)	85,532
Racine (*Wis.*)	82,572
Raleigh (*N.C.*)	243,835
Rancho Cucamonga (*Calif.*)	116,613
Reading (*Pa.*)	75,723
Redding (*Calif.*)	76,616
Reno (*Nev.*)	155,499
Rialto (*Calif.*)	82,320
Richardson (*Texas*)	81,133
Richmond (*Calif.*)	91,018
Richmond (*Va.*)	198,267
Riverside (*Calif.*)	255,069
Roanoke (*Va.*)	95,548
Rochester (*Minn.*)	75,638
Rochester (*N.Y.*)	221,594
Rockford (*Ill.*)	143,531
Sacramento (*Calif.*)	376,243
St. Louis (*Mo.*)	351,565
St. Paul (*Minn.*)	259,606
St. Petersburg (*Fla.*)	235,988
Salem (*Ore.*)	122,566
Salinas (*Calif.*)	111,757
Salt Lake City (*Utah*)	172,575
San Angelo (*Texas*)	88,098
San Antonio (*Texas*)	1,067,816
San Bernardino (*Calif.*)	183,474
San Buenaventura (Ventura) (*Calif.*)	97,205
San Diego (*Calif.*)	1,171,121
San Francisco (*Calif.*)	735,315
San Jose (*Calif.*)	838,744
San Mateo (*Calif.*)	90,161
Sandy (*Utah*)	94,593
Santa Ana (*Calif.*)	302,419
Santa Barbara (*Calif.*)	86,154
Santa Clara (*Calif.*)	98,726
Santa Clarita (*Calif.*)	125,153
Santa Monica (*Calif.*)	88,471
Santa Rosa (*Calif.*)	121,879
Savannah (*Ga.*)	136,262
Scottsdale (*Ariz.*)	179,012
Scranton (*Pa.*)	77,189
Seattle (*Wash.*)	524,704
Shreveport (*La.*)	191,558
Simi Valley (*Calif.*)	106,974
Sioux City (*Iowa*)	83,791
Sioux Falls (*S.D.*)	113,223
South Bend (*Ind.*)	102,100
South Gate (*Calif.*)	88,125
Southfield (*Mich.*)	76,184
Spokane (*Wash.*)	186,562
Springfield (*Ill.*)	112,921
Springfield (*Mass.*)	149,948
Springfield (*Mo.*)	143,407
Stamford (*Conn.*)	110,056
Sterling Heights (*Mich.*)	118,698
Stockton (*Calif.*)	232,660
Sunnyvale (*Calif.*)	125,156
Sunrise (*Fla.*)	77,592
Syracuse (*N.Y.*)	155,865
Tacoma (*Wash.*)	179,114
Tallahassee (*Fla.*)	136,812
Tampa (*Fla.*)	285,206
Tempe (*Ariz.*)	162,701
Thousand Oaks (*Calif.*)	113,368
Toledo (*Ohio*)	317,606
Topeka (*Kan.*)	119,658
Torrance (*Calif.*)	136,183
Trenton (*N.J.*)	85,437
Troy (*Mich.*)	79,120
Tucson (*Ariz.*)	449,002
Tulsa (*Okla.*)	378,491
Tuscaloosa (*Ala.*)	82,379
Tyler (*Texas*)	82,185
Vacaville (*Calif.*)	81,355
Vallejo (*Calif.*)	109,593
Virginia Beach (*Va.*)	430,385
Visalia (*Calif.*)	87,737
Vista (*Calif.*)	78,494
Waco (*Texas*)	108,412
Warren (*Mich.*)	138,078
Warwick (*R.I.*)	84,514
★ Washington, D.C.	543,213
Waterbury (*Conn.*)	106,412
West Covina (*Calif.*)	101,526
West Palm Beach (*Fla.*)	79,305
West Valley City (*Utah*)	99,136
Westland (*Mich.*)	90,798
Westminster (*Calif.*)	82,425
Westminster (*Colo.*)	93,115
Whittier (*Calif.*)	78,740
Whichita (*Kan.*)	320,395
Wichita Falls (*Texas*)	100,138
Winston-Salem (*N.C.*)	153,541
Worcester (*Mass.*)	166,350
Yonkers (*N.Y.*)	190,316
Youngstown (*Ohio*)	87,405
Uruguay (1996)	
★ Montevideo	1,378,707
Uzbekistan (1993 est.)	
Andijon (Andizhan)	313,000
Angren	132,000[1]
Bukhoro (Bukhara)	238,000
Chirchiq (Chirchik)	156,000[1]
Farghona (Fergana)	191,000[1]
Jizzakh (Dzhizak)	116,000[1]
Marghilon (Margilan)	129,000[1]
Namangan	362,000
Nawoiy (Navoi)	115,000[1]
Nukus	185,000[1]
Olmaliq (Almalyk)	116,000[1]
Qarshi (Karshi)	177,000[1]
Quqon (Kokand)	184,000[1]
Samarqand (Samarkand)	362,000
★ Tashkent (Toshkent)	2,107,000
Urganch (Urgench)	135,000[1]
Vanuatu (1996 est.)	
★ Vila	31,800
Venezuela (1990)	
Acarigua	116,551
Barcelona	221,792
Barinas	153,630
Barquisimeto	625,450
Baruta	182,941[19]
Cabimas	165,755[19]
★ Caracas	1,822,465
Catia la Mar	100,104
Ciudad Bolívar	253,112[10]
Ciudad Guayana (San Felix de Guayana)	523,578[10]
Coro	137,040[10]
Cumaná	232,228[10]
Guacara	100,766
Guarenas	152,612[10]
Los Teques	162,145[10]
Maracaibo	1,249,670
Maracay	384,782[10]
Maturín	233,279[10]
Mérida	188,063[10]
Petare	379,338[10]
Puerto Cabello	143,765[10]
Puerto La Cruz	155,731
San Cristóbal	238,670[10]
Santa Ana de Coro	124,506
Turmero	195,711[10]
Valencia	1,034,033[10]
Valera	107,236[10]
Vietnam (1992 est.)	
Bien Hoa	97,094[6]
Buon Ma Thuot	282,095
Cam Pha	209,086
Cam Ranh	114,041[6]
Can Tho	215,587
Da Lat	106,409
Da Nang	382,674
Haiphong	783,133
★ Hanoi	2,154,900[1]
Ho Chi Minh City (Saigon)	4,322,300[1]
Hong Gai	127,484
Hue	219,149
Long Xuyen	132,681
My Tho	108,404
Nam Dinh	171,699
Nha Trang	221,331
Phan Thiet	114,236[6]
Qui Nhon	163,385
Rach Gia	141,132
Thai Nguyen	127,643
Vinh	112,455
Vung Tau	145,145
Virgin Islands (U.S.) (1990)	
★ Charlotte Amalie	12,331
West Bank (1987 est.)	
Nābulus	106,944
★ —	—
Western Sahara (1994)	
★ Laayoune (El Aaiún)	136,950
Yemen (1995 est.)[19]	
Aden	562,000
Al-Ḥudaydah	246,068[1]
Al-Mukallā	154,360
★ Ṣan'ā'	972,000
Ta'izz	290,107[1]
Yugoslavia (1991)	
★ Belgrade (Beograd)	1,168,454
Kragujevac	147,305
Niš	175,391
Novi Sad	179,626
Podgorica (Titograd)	117,875
Priština	155,499
Subotica	100,386
Zambia (1990)	
Chingola	167,954
Kabwe	166,519
Kitwe	338,207
Luanshya	146,275
★ Lusaka	982,362
Mufulira	152,944
Ndola	376,311
Zimbabwe (1992)	
Bulawayo	620,936
Chitungwiza	274,035
Gweru	124,735
★ Harare	1,184,169
Mount Darwin	164,362
Mutare	131,808

distinguished administratively as cities. [31]Population includes Comayagüela. [32]1980 census, adjusted for consistent bounding of localities. [33]1985 estimate. [34]County borough. [35]City of Kingston is coextensive with Kingston parish. [36]Population includes Limbe. [37]Includes adjoining municipalities. [38]Population of prefecture. [39]Projections based on a repudiated census taken in 1963. A 1991 census suggests that the 1963 census had overestimated Nigeria's population by as much as 70 percent. [40]Federal Capital territory. [41]National government centre. [42]Urban area. [43]Population refers to Kotte only. [44]1980 estimate. [45]Population of local authority areas. [46]Census-designated place (CDP).

Language

This table presents estimated data on the principal language communities of the countries of the world. The countries, and the principal languages (occasionally, language families) represented in each, are listed alphabetically. A bullet (●) indicates those languages that are official in each country. The sum of the estimates equals the 1998 population of the country given in the "Area and population" table.

The estimates represent, so far as national data collection systems permit, the distribution of mother tongues (a mother tongue being the language spoken first and, usually, most fluently by an individual). Many countries do not collect any official data whatever on language use, and published estimates not based on census or survey data usually span a substantial range of uncertainty. The editors have adopted the best-founded distribution in the published literature (indicating uncertainty by the degree of rounding shown) but have also adjusted or interpolated using data not part of the base estimate(s). Such adjustments have not been made to account for large-scale refugee movements, as these are of a temporary nature.

A variety of approaches have been used to approximate mother-tongue distribution when census data were unavailabe. Some countries collect data on ethnic or "national" groups only; for such countries ethnic distribution often had to be assumed to conform roughly to the distribution of language communities. This approach, however, should be viewed with caution, because a minority population is not always free to educate its children in its own language and because better economic opportunities often draw minority group members into the majority-language community. For some countries, a given individual may be visible in national statistics only as a passport-holder of a foreign country, however long he may remain resident. Such persons, often guest workers, have sometimes had to be assumed to be speakers of the principal language of their home country. For other countries, the language mosaic may be so complex, the language communities so minute in size, scholarly study so inadequate, or the census base so obsolete that it was possible only to assign percentages to entire groups, or families, of related languages, despite their mutual unintelligibility (Papuan and Melanesian languages in Papua New Guinea, for instance). For some countries in the Americas, so few speakers of any single indigenous language remain that it was necessary to combine these groups as *Amerindian* so as to give a fair impression of their aggregate size within their respective countries.

No systematic attempt has been made to account for populations that may legitimately be described as bilingual, unless the country itself collects data on that basis, as does Bolivia or the Comoros, for example. Where a nonindigenous official or excolonial language constitutes a lingua franca of the country, however, speakers of the language as a second tongue are shown in italics, even though very few may speak it as a mother tongue. No comprehensive effort has been made to distinguish between dialect communities *usually* classified as belonging to the same language, though such distinctions were possible for some countries—*e.g.*, between French and Occitan (the dialect of southern France) or among the various dialects of Chinese.

In giving the names of Bantu languages, grammatical particles specific to a language's autonym (name for itself) have been omitted (the form *Rwanda* is used here, for example, rather than *kinyaRwanda* and *Tswana* instead of *seTswana*). Parenthetical alternatives are given for a number of languages that differ markedly from the name of the people speaking them (such as Kurukh, spoken by the Oraon tribes of India) or that may be combined with other groups sometimes distinguishable in national data but appearing here under the name of the largest member—*e.g.*, "Tamil (and other Indian languages)" combining data on South Asian Indian populations in Singapore. The term *creole* as used here refers to distinguishable dialectal communities related to a national, official, or former colonial language (such as the French creole that survives in Mauritius from the end of French rule in 1810).

Internet resources for further information:
- *Ethnologue* (13th ed.; Summer Institute of Linguistics)
  http://www.sil.org/ethnologue
- Joshua Project 2000—People's List (Christian interfaith missionary database identifying some 2,000 ethnolinguistic groups)
  http://www.ad2000.org/peoples/index.htm
- U.S. Census Bureau: http://www.census.gov/ftp/pub/ipc/www/idbconf.html (especially tables 57 and 59)
- Living Languages of the Americas (Summer Institute of Linguistics)
  http://www.sil.org/lla

Language

Major languages by country	Number of speakers
Afghanistan[1]	
Indo-Aryan languages	
Pashai	150,000
Iranian languages	
Balochi	230,000
● Dari (Persian)	
Chahar Aimak	700,000
Hazāra	2,190,000
Tajik	5,060,000
Nūristāni group	190,000
Pamir group	150,000
● Pashto	12,990,000
Turkic languages	
Turkmen	480,000
Uzbek	2,190,000
Other	470,000
Albania[1]	
● Albanian	3,263,000
Greek	62,000
Macedonian	5,000
Other	1,000
Algeria	
● Arabic	25,840,000
Berber	4,210,000
English	...
French	*6,000,000*
American Samoa	
● English	2,000
English (lingua franca)	*61,000*
● Samoan	56,000
Tongan	2,000
Other	2,000
Andorra[2]	
● Catalan (Andorran)	20,000
French	4,000
Portuguese	7,000
Spanish	30,000
Other	3,000
Angola[1]	
Ambo (Ovambo)	260,000
Chokwe	460,000
Herero	80,000
Kongo	1,430,000
Luchazi	260,000
Luimbe-Nganguela	590,000
Lunda	130,000
Luvale (Luena)	390,000
Mbunda	130,000
Mbundu	2,350,000
Nyaneka-Nkhumbi	590,000
Ovimbundu (Umbundu)	4,040,000
● Portuguese	*3,800,000*
Other	170,000

Major languages by country	Number of speakers
Antigua and Barbuda	
● English	*69,000*
English/English Creole	66,000
Other	3,000
Argentina	
Amerindian languages	110,000
Italian	630,000
● Spanish	34,980,000
Other	400,000
Armenia	
● Armenian	3,550,000
Azerbaijani (Azeri)	100,000
Other	150,000
Aruba	
● Dutch	5,000
English	8,000
Papiamento	68,000
Spanish	7,000
Other	1,000
Australia	
Aboriginal languages	50,000
Arabic	182,000
Cantonese	214,000
Dutch	45,000
● English	15,204,000
English (lingua franca)	*18,100,000*
French	43,000
German	109,000
Greek	292,000
Hungarian	29,000
Indonesian Malay	29,000
Italian	414,000
Macedonian	77,000
Maltese	50,000
Mandarin	98,000
Pilipino (Filipino)	76,000
Polish	69,000
Portuguese	27,000
Russian	34,000
Serbo-Croatian	115,000
Spanish	98,000
Turkish	48,000
Vietnamese	151,000
Other/not stated	1,273,000
Austria	
Czech	19,000
● German	7,424,000
Hungarian	34,000
Polish	19,000
Romanian	17,000
Serbo-Croatian	175,000
Slovene	30,000
Turkish	123,000
Other	229,000

Major languages by country	Number of speakers
Azerbaijan	
Armenian	150,000
● Azerbaijani (Azeri)	6,810,000
Lezgi (Lezgian)	170,000
Russian	230,000
Other	290,000
Bahamas, The	
● English	...
English/English Creole	260,000
French (Haitian) Creole	30,000
Bahrain[2]	
● Arabic	430,000
English	...
Other	200,000
Bangladesh[1]	
● Bengali	124,670,000
Chakmā	470,000
English	*3,300,000*
Gāro	110,000
Khāsī	100,000
Marma (Magh)	240,000
Mro	40,000
Santhālī	90,000
Tripurī	90,000
Other	1,750,000
Barbados	
Bajan (English Creole)	252,000
● English	...
Other	13,000
Belarus	
● Belarusian	6,720,000
Polish	60,000
● Russian	3,270,000
Ukrainian	130,000
Other	60,000
Belgium[2, 3]	
Arabic	160,000
● Dutch (Flemish; Netherlandic)	6,050,000
● French (Walloon)	3,340,000
● German	90,000
Italian	250,000
Spanish	50,000
Turkish	90,000
Other	180,000
Belize	
● English	119,000
English Creole (lingua franca)	*180,000*
Garifuna (Black Carib)	16,000
German	3,000
Mayan languages	23,000

Major languages by country	Number of speakers
Spanish	74,000
Spanish (lingua franca)	*130,000*
Benin[1]	
Adja	680,000
Aizo (Ouidah)	530,000
Bariba	530,000
Dendi	130,000
Djougou	180,000
Fon	2,430,000
● French	*600,000*
Fula (Fulani)	340,000
Somba (Ditamari)	400,000
Yoruba (Nago)	740,000
Other	150,000
Bermuda	
● English	62,000
Bhutan[1]	
Assamese	90,000
● Dzongkha (Bhutiā)	320,000
Nepālī (Hindī)	220,000
Bolivia	
● Aymara	250,000
Guaraní	10,000
● Quechua	650,000
● Spanish	3,320,000
Spanish-Amerindian (multilingual), of which	3,660,000
Spanish-Aymara	*1,570,000*
Spanish-Guaraní	30,000
Spanish-Quechua	*2,060,000*
Other	60,000
Bosnia and Herzegovina	
● Serbo-Croatian (Bosnian)	3,340,000
Other	30,000
Botswana[1]	
● English (lingua franca)	*580,000*
Khoekhoe (Hottentot)	36,000
Ndebele	19,000
San (Bushman)	50,000
Shona	180,000
Tswana	1,093,000
Tswana (lingua franca)	*1,160,000*
Other	71,000
Brazil[1]	
Amerindian languages	280,000
German	890,000
Italian	680,000
Japanese	610,000
● Portuguese	157,800,000
Other	1,500,000

Major languages by country	Number of speakers
Brunei	
Chinese	29,000
English	10,000
● Malay	143,000
Malay-Chinese	3,000
Malay-English	91,000
English-Chinese	7,000
Malay-Chinese-English	12,000
Other	17,000
Bulgaria[1]	
● Bulgarian	6,880,000
Macedonian	210,000
Romany	310,000
Turkish	780,000
Other	100,000
Burkina Faso[4]	
Dogon	40,000
French	30,000
● French (lingua franca)	*4,600,000*
Fula (Fulani)	1,090,000
Gur (Voltaic) languages	
Bwamu	240,000
Gouin (Cerma)	60,000
Grusi (Gurunsi) group	
Ko	20,000
Lyele	270,000
Nuni	130,000
Sissala	10,000
Lobi	210,000
Mossi (Moore) group	
Dagara	350,000
Gurma	640,000
Kusaal	20,000
Mossi (Moore)	5,625,000
Senufo group	
Minianka	–
Senufo	160,000
Kru languages	
Seme (Siamou)	20,000
Mande languages	
Bobo	250,000
Busansi (Bisa)	400,000
Dyula (Jula)	300,000
Marka	190,000
Samo	260,000
Tamashek (Tuareg)	100,000
Other	800,000
Burundi[1]	
● French	*520,000*
● Rundi	5,430,000
Hutu	4,570,000
Tutsi	800,000
Twa	60,000
Other[5]	110,000

Major languages by country	Number of speakers
Cambodia[1]	
Cham	250,000
Chinese	330,000
● Khmer	9,520,000
Vietnamese	590,000
Other[6]	50,000
Cameroon[1]	
Chadic languages	
Buwal	290,000
Hausa	180,000
Kotoko	160,000
Mandara (Wandala)	850,000
Masana (Masa)	590,000
● English	7,500,000
● French	4,500,000
Niger-Congo languages	
Adamawa-Ubangi languages	
Baya (Gbaya)	180,000
Chamba	360,000
Mbum	200,000
Atlantic languages	
Fula (Fulani)	1,440,000
Benue-Congo languages	
Bamileke (Medumba)-Widikum (Mogha-mo)-Bamum (Mum)	2,790,000
Basa (Bassa)	160,000
Duala	1,640,000
Fang (Pangwe)-Beti-Bulu	2,950,000
Ibibio (Efik)	20,000
Igbo	80,000
Jukun	100,000
Lundu	410,000
Maka	740,000
Tikar	1,120,000
Tiv	390,000
Wute	50,000
Saharan languages	
Kanuri	50,000
Semitic languages	
Arabic	150,000
Other	120,000
Canada	
● English	18,655,000
● French	7,362,000
English-French	245,000
English-other	454,000
French-other	52,000
English-French-other	34,000
Aboriginal (Amerindian and Eskimo [Inuktitut]) languages	221,000
Arabic	49,000
Chinese	322,000
Czech	28,000
Danish	25,000
Dutch	150,000
Finnish	31,000
German	531,000
Greek	135,000
Hungarian	83,000
Italian	552,000
Pilipino (Filipino)	52,000
Polish	150,000
Portuguese	187,000
Punjābī	77,000
Russian	31,000
Serbo-Croatian	49,000
Spanish	101,000
Ukrainian	252,000
Vietnamese	49,000
Yiddish	28,000
Other	773,000
Cape Verde	
Crioulo (Portuguese Creole)	400,000
● Portuguese	...
Central African Republic	
Banda	790,000
● French	800,000
Gbaya (Baya)	800,000
Mandjia	500,000
Mbum	210,000
Ngbaka	260,000
Nzakara	50,000
● Sango (lingua franca)	3,000,000
Sara	220,000
Zande (Azande)	70,000
Other	480,000
Chad[1]	
● Arabic	1,920,000
Daju (Dagu)	170,000
● French	2,200,000
Hausa	170,000
Kanuri	170,000
Kotoko	150,000
Masa	170,000
Masalit, Maba, and Mimi	460,000
Mbum	480,000
Mubi	310,000
Sara, Bagirmi, and Kreish	2,240,000
Tama	460,000
Teda (Tubu)	540,000
Other	120,000
Chile[1]	
Araucanian (Mapuche)	1,420,000
Aymara	70,000
Rapa Nui	34,000
● Spanish	13,290,000
China[1]	
Achang	30,000
Bulang (Blang)	90,000
Ch'iang (Qiang)	220,000
Chinese (Han)	1,142,990,000
Cantonese (Yüeh [Yue])	57,000,000
Hakka	42,000,000
Hsiang (Xiang)	55,000,000
Kan (Gan)	27,000,000
● Mandarin	817,000,000
Min	47,000,000
Wu	97,000,000
Ching-p'o (Jingpo)	130,000
Chuang (Zhuang)	16,980,000
Daghur (Daur)	130,000
Evenk (Ewenki)	30,000
Gelo	480,000
Hani (Woni)	1,370,000
Hui	9,430,000
Kazak	1,220,000
Korean	2,110,000
Kyrgyz	160,000
Lahu	450,000
Li	1,220,000
Lisu	630,000
Manchu	10,770,000
Maonan	80,000
Miao	8,110,000
Mongol	5,270,000
Mulam	180,000
Na-hsi (Naxi)	300,000
Nu	30,000
Pai (Bai)	1,750,000
Pumi	30,000
Puyi (Chung-chia)	2,790,000
Salar	100,000
She	690,000
Shui	380,000
Sibo (Xibe)	190,000
Tai (Dai)	1,120,000
Tajik	40,000
Tibetan	5,040,000
Tu (Monguor)	210,000
T'u-chia (Tujia)	6,250,000
Tung (Dong)	2,760,000
Tung-hsiang (Dongxiang)	410,000
Uighur	7,910,000
Wa (Va)	390,000
Yao	2,340,000
Yi	7,210,000
Other	980,000
Colombia[1]	
Amerindian languages	320,000
Arawakan	40,000
Cariban	20,000
Chibchan	160,000
Other	100,000
English Creole	50,000
● Spanish	37,320,000
Comoros	
● Arabic	...
● Comorian	410,000
Comorian-French	70,000
Comorian-Malagasy	30,000
Comorian-Arabic	9,000
Comorian-Swahili	3,000
Comorian-French-other	21,000
● French	110,000
Other	3,000
Congo, Dem. Rep. of the[1]	
Boa	1,150,000
Chokwe	900,000
● French	3,800,000
Kongo	7,860,000
Kongo (lingua franca)	15,000,000
Lingala (lingua franca)	34,000,000
Luba	8,810,000
Lugbara	790,000
Mongo	6,610,000
Ngala and Bangi	2,830,000
Rundi	1,890,000
Rwanda	5,030,000
Swahili (lingua franca)	24,000,000
Teke	1,340,000
Zande (Azande)	2,990,000
Other	8,810,000
Congo, Rep. of the[1]	
Bobangi	30,000
● French	1,400,000
Kongo	1,370,000
Kota	20,000
Lingala (lingua franca)	...
Maka	50,000
Mbete	130,000
Mboshi	310,000
Monokutuba (lingua franca)	1,600,000
Punu	80,000
Sango	70,000
Teke	460,000
Other	140,000
Costa Rica	
Chibchan languages	10,000
Bribrí	6,000
Cabécar	4,000
Chinese	7,000
English Creole	71,000
● Spanish	3,445,000
Côte d'Ivoire[1]	
Akan (including Baule and Anyi)	4,640,000
● French	7,700,000
Gur ([Voltaic] including Senufo and Lobi)	1,810,000
Kru (including Bete)	1,620,000
Malinke (including Dyula and Bambara)	1,770,000
Southern Mande (including Dan and Guro)	1,190,000
Other (non-Ivoirian population)	4,420,000
Croatia	
● Serbo-Croatian (Croatian)	4,490,000
Other	190,000
Cuba	
● Spanish	11,116,000
Cyprus (island)[1]	
● Greek	640,000
● Turkish	190,000
Other	30,000
Czech Republic[1]	
Bulgarian	3,000
● Czech	8,363,000
German	48,000
Greek	3,000
Hungarian	20,000
Moravian	1,326,000
Polish	60,000
Romanian	1,000
Romany	33,000
Russian	5,000
Ruthenian	2,000
Silesian	44,000
Slovak	315,000
Ukrainian	8,000
Other	70,000
Denmark[2]	
Arabic	24,000
● Danish	5,010,000
English	24,000
German	27,000
Iranian languages	10,000
Norwegian	15,000
South Slavic languages	24,000
Swedish	18,000
Turkish	26,000
Other	126,000
Djibouti[1]	
Afar	230,000
● Arabic	70,000
● French	100,000
Somali	290,000
Gadaboursi	...
Issa	...
Issaq	...
Other	60,000
Dominica	
● English	...
English Creole	76,000
French Creole	69,000
Dominican Republic	
French (Haitian) Creole	160,000
● Spanish	7,730,000
Ecuador	
Quechuan (and other Amerindian languages)	850,000
● Spanish	11,320,000
Egypt[1]	
● Arabic	62,500,000
Other	760,000
El Salvador	
● Spanish	5,752,000
Equatorial Guinea[1]	
Bubi	50,000
Fang	380,000
● French	...
Krio (English Creole)	...
● Spanish	...
Other	30,000
Eritrea	
Cushitic languages	
Afar	160,000
Bilin	120,000
Hadareb (Beja)	150,000
Saho	120,000
Nilotic languages	
Kunama	110,000
Nara	80,000
Semitic languages	
Arabic (Rashaida)	10,000
Tigré	1,220,000
Tigrinya	1,880,000
Estonia[1]	
Belarusian	20,000
● Estonian	940,000
Finnish	10,000
Russian	410,000
Ukrainian	40,000
Other	30,000
Ethiopia[1]	
Amharic	17,540,000
Gurage	2,740,000
Oromo (Oromifa)	18,110,000
Sidamo	1,870,000
Somali	2,360,000
Tigrinya	4,200,000
Walaita	1,620,000
Other	9,960,000
Faroe Islands	
● Danish	...
● Faroese	44,000
Fiji[1]	
● English	160,000
Fijian	403,000
Hindī	347,000
Other	44,000
Finland	
Estonian	9,000
Finnish	4,786,000
Russian	18,000
Sami (Lapp)	2,000
Swedish	295,000
Other	44,000
France	
Arabic[7]	1,490,000
English[7]	80,000
● French[7, 8, 9]	55,100,000
Basque	80,000
Breton	500,000
Catalan (Rousillonais)	260,000
Corsican	260,000
Dutch (Flemish)	90,000
German (Alsatian)	1,510,000
Occitan	920,000
Italian[7]	260,000
Polish[7]	50,000
Portuguese[7]	680,000
Spanish[7]	220,000
Turkish[7]	210,000
Other[7]	750,000
French Guiana	
Amerindian languages	3,000
● French	...
French/French Creoles	159,000
Other	7,000
French Polynesia[10]	
Chinese	13,000
● French	184,000
Polynesian languages	208,000
● Tahitian	...
Other	45,000
Gabon[1]	
Fang	430,000
● French	1,000,000
Kota	40,000
Mbete	170,000
Mpongwe (Myene)	180,000
Punu, Sira, Nzebi	200,000
Teke	20,000
Other	160,000
Gambia, The[1]	
● English	...
Gambians	
Aku (Krio)	8,000
Atlantic languages	
Diola (Jola)	119,000
Fula (Fulani)	209,000
Manjak	21,000
Serer	31,000
Wolof	163,000
Mande languages	
Bambara	9,000
Malinke	440,000
Soninke	99,000
Other	16,000
non-Gambians	178,000
Gaza Strip	
Arabic	1,076,000
Hebrew	6,000
Georgia	
Abkhaz	90,000
Armenian	370,000
Azerbaijani (Azeri)	300,000
● Georgian (Kartuli)	3,880,000
Ossetian	130,000
Russian	480,000
Other	170,000
Germany[2]	
● German	74,830,000
Greek	360,000
Italian	590,000
Polish	280,000
South Slavic languages	1,360,000
Turkish	2,050,000
Kurdish	400,000
Other	2,680,000
Ghana[1]	
Akan	9,700,000
● English	1,290,000
Ewe	2,200,000
Ga-Adangme	1,440,000
Gurma	620,000
Hausa (lingua franca)	11,100,000
Mole-Dagbani (Moore)	2,930,000
Yoruba	250,000
Other	1,370,000
Gibraltar[2]	
Arabic	2,000
● English	24,000
Spanish	...
Other	1,000
Greece	
● Greek	10,380,000
Turkish	90,000
Other	60,000
Greenland[2]	
● Danish	7,000
● Greenlandic	49,000
Grenada	
● English	...
English/English Creole	100,000
Guadeloupe	
● French	...
French/French Creole	413,000
Other	21,000
Guam	
● Chamorro	43,000
Chinese	2,000
Chuukese (Trukese)	2,000
● English	55,000
English (lingua franca)	147,000
Japanese	3,000
Korean	5,000
Palauan	2,000
Philippine languages	30,000
Other	6,000
Guatemala	
Garifuna (Black Carib)	20,000
Mayan languages	3,790,000
Cakchiquel	970,000
Kekchí	520,000
Mam	300,000
Quiché	1,100,000
● Spanish	6,990,000
Guernsey	
● English	62,000
French	...
Guinea[1]	
Atlantic languages	
Basari-Konyagi	90,000
Fula (Fulani)	2,890,000
Kissi	450,000
Other	230,000
● French	700,000
Mande languages	
Kpelle	350,000
Loma	170,000
Malinke	1,730,000
Susu	820,000
Yalunka	220,000
Other	520,000
Other	10,000
Guinea-Bissau	
Balante	175,000
Crioulo (Portuguese Creole)	51,000
Crioulo-Portuguese	27,000
Crioulo-other (except Portuguese)	360,000
French	120,000
Fula(Fulani)	200,000
Malinke	83,000
Mandyako	60,000
Pepel	33,000
● Portuguese	—
Portuguese-other (except Crioulo)	97,000
Other	118,000
Guyana	
Amerindian languages	
Arawakan	11,000
Cariban	17,000

Language (continued)

Major languages by country	Number of speakers
● English	…
English/English Creoles	749,000
Haiti	
● French	*1,400,000*
French-Haitian (French) Creole	6,780,000
● Haitian (French) Creole	…
Honduras	
English Creole	11,000
Garifuna (Black Carib)	74,000
Miskito	10,000
● Spanish	5,752,000
Other	71,000
Hong Kong	
Chinese	
● Cantonese	5,905,000
Cantonese (lingua franca)	*6,380,000*
Chiu Chau	93,000
Fukien (Min)	127,000
Hakka	107,000
Putonghua (Mandarin)	74,000
Putonghua (lingua franca)	*1,210,000*
Sze Yap	27,000
● English	147,000
English (lingua franca)	*2,100,000*
Japanese	13,000
Pilipino (Filipino)	7,000
Other	161,000
Hungary	
German	40,000
● Hungarian	9,970,000
Romanian	10,000
Romany	50,000
Serbo-Croatian	20,000
Slovak	10,000
Other	20,000
Iceland[2]	
● Icelandic	264,000
Other	12,000
India	
Austroasiatic languages	
Ho	1,100,000
Khaṛiā	260,000
Khāsī	1,060,000
Korkū	540,000
Muṇḍā	480,000
Muṇḍārī	1,000,000
Santhālī	6,070,000
Savara (Sora)	320,000
Other Austroasiatic	210,000
Dravidian languages	
Goṇḍī	2,470,000
Kannaḍa	38,080,000
Khond	260,000
Koyā	320,000
Kui	750,000
Kurukh (Oraon)	1,660,000
Malayālam	35,320,000
Tamil	61,630,000
Telugu	76,760,000
Tuḷu	1,810,000
Other Dravidian	630,000
English	210,000
● English (lingua franca)	*187,000,000*
Hamito-Semitic languages	
Arabic	30,000
Indo-Iranian (Indo-Aryan) languages	
Assamese	15,210,000
Bengali	80,920,000
Bhīlī (Bhilodī)	6,480,000
Barel	*540,000*
Bhilālī	*550,000*
Gujarātī	47,290,000
Halabī	620,000
● Hindī	392,150,000
Awadhi	*560,000*
Baghelkhaṇḍī	*1,610,000*
Bāgrī	*690,000*
Banjārī	*1,030,000*
Bhojpurī	26,860,000
Bundelkhaṇḍī	*1,930,000*
Chhattīsgaṛhī	*12,320,000*
Dhundhāri	*1,120,000*
Gaṛhwālī	*2,180,000*
Hāṛautī	*1,440,000*
Haryānvi	*420,000*
Hindī	*271,410,000*
Kangri	*570,000*
Khorthā (Khottā)	*1,220,000*
Kumaunī	*2,000,000*
Lamanī (Banjārī)	*2,390,000*
Magahī (Magadhī)	*12,290,000*
Maithilī	*9,030,000*
Mālvī	*3,450,000*
Maṇḍealī	*510,000*
Mārwārī	*5,430,000*
Mewārī	*2,460,000*
Nagpurī	*900,000*
Nīmāḍī	*1,650,000*
Pahāṛī	*2,540,000*
Rājasthānī	*15,500,000*
Sadānī (Sadrī)	*1,820,000*
Surgujiā	*1,220,000*
Surjapurī	*430,000*
Other Hindī dialects	*7,170,000*
Hindī (lingua franca)	*649,400,000*
Kashmirī	4,580,000
Khandeshī	1,130,000
Koṅkanī	2,050,000
Lahnda	30,000
Marāṭhī	72,650,000
Nepālī (Gorkhalī)	2,420,000
Oṛiyā	32,630,000
Punjābī	27,180,000
Sanskrit	60,000
Sindhī	2,470,000
Kachchhī	*660,000*
Urdū	50,470,000
Sino-Tibetan languages	
Ādi	180,000
Āngami	110,000
Āo	200,000
Bodo/Boro	1,420,000
Dimasa	100,000
Gāro	790,000
Karbi/Makir	430,000
Konyak	160,000
Lotha	100,000
Lushai (Mizo)	630,000
Manipurī (Meithei)	1,480,000
Miri/Mishing	450,000
Nissī/Dafla	200,000
Rabha	160,000
Sema	190,000
Tangkhul	120,000
Thado	130,000
Tripurī	810,000
Kokbarak	600,000
Other Sino-Tibetan languages	2,350,000
Other	5,130,000
Indonesia	
Balinese	3,370,000
Banjarese	3,550,000
Batak	4,510,000
Buginese	4,470,000
● Indonesian (Malay)	24,580,000
Javanese	80,030,000
Madurese	8,790,000
Minangkabau	4,790,000
Sundanese	32,010,000
Other	36,880,000
Iran[1]	
Armenian	300,000
Iranian languages	
Bakhtyārī (Lurī)	1,030,000
Balochi	1,400,000
● Farsī (Persian)	28,080,000
Farsī (lingua franca)	*50,900,000*
Gīlakī	3,250,000
Kurdish	5,620,000
Lurī	2,660,000
Māzandarānī	2,220,000
Other	1,340,000
Semitic languages	
Arabic	1,330,000
Other	150,000
Turkic languages	
Afshari	700,000
Azerbaijani (Azeri)	10,340,000
Qashqa'i	780,000
Shahsavani	370,000
Turkish (mostly Pishagchi, Bayat, and Qajar)	440,000
Turkmen	960,000
Other	120,000
Other	460,000
Iraq[1]	
● Arabic	16,750,000
Assyrian	180,000
Azerbaijani (Azeri)	370,000
Kurdish	4,120,000
Persian	180,000
Other	130,000
Ireland	
● English	3,590,000
● Irish[11]	60,000
Irish	*1,190,000*
Isle of Man	
● English	73,000
Israel[12]	
● Arabic	1,030,000
● Hebrew	3,620,000
Russian	520,000
Other	570,000
Italy[1]	
Albanian	120,000
Catalan	30,000
French	310,000
German	310,000
Greek	40,000
● Italian	54,230,000
Rhaetian	740,000
Friulian	710,000
Ladin	20,000
Romany	110,000
Sardinian	1,530,000
Slovene	120,000
Other	130,000
Jamaica	
● English	…
English/English Creoles	2,400,000
Hindī and other Indian languages	50,000
Other	100,000
Japan[2]	
Ainu	15,000
Chinese	240,000
English	80,000
● Japanese	125,280,000
Korean	660,000
Philippine languages	80,000
Other	40,000
Jersey	
● English	86,000
French	…
Jersey Norman French	*6,000*
Jordan[1]	
● Arabic	4,590,000
Armenian	50,000
Kabardian (Circassian)	50,000
Kazakstan[1]	
Azerbaijani (Azeri)	100,000
Belarusian	160,000
German	480,000
● Kazak	7,260,000
Korean	100,000
Russian	5,490,000
Tatar	300,000
Uighur	180,000
Ukrainian	780,000
Uzbek	360,000
Other	580,000
Kenya[1]	
Bantu languages	
Bajun (Rajun)	70,000
Basuba	110,000
Embu	330,000
Gusii (Kisii)	1,750,000
Kamba	3,190,000
Kikuyu	5,920,000
Kuria	160,000
Luhya	3,920,000
Mbere	110,000
Meru	1,550,000
Nyika (Mijikenda)	1,350,000
Pokomo	70,000
Swahili	10,000
● Swahili (lingua franca)	*18,000,000*
Taita	280,000
Cushitic languages	
Oromo languages	
Boran	130,000
Gabbra	60,000
Gurreh	150,000
Orma	60,000
Somali languages	
Degodia	170,000
Ogaden	50,000
Somali	290,000
● English (lingua franca)	*2,600,000*
Nilotic languages	
Kalenjin	3,050,000
Luo	3,620,000
Masai	440,000
Sambur	140,000
Teso	240,000
Turkana	380,000
Semitic languages	
Arabic	70,000
Other	630,000
Kiribati[1]	
● English	*21,000*
Kiribati (Gilbertese)	83,100
Tuvaluan (Ellice)	400
Other	500
Korea, North[1]	
Chinese	30,000
● Korean	21,200,000
Korea, South[1]	
Chinese	50,000
● Korean	46,400,000
Kuwait	
● Arabic	1,460,000
Other	410,000
Kyrgyzstan[1]	
Azerbaijani (Azeri)	20,000
German	30,000
Kazak	40,000
● Kyrgyz	2,800,000
Russian	760,000
Tajik	40,000
Tatar	60,000
Ukrainian	80,000
Uzbek	660,000
Other	210,000
Laos[1]	
● Lao-Lum (Lao)	3,520,000
Lao-Soung (Miao [Hmong] and Man [Yao])	280,000
Lao-Tai (Tai)	410,000
Lao-Theung (Mon-Khmer)	870,000
Other[13]	180,000
Latvia[1]	
Belarusian	100,000
● Latvian	1,350,000
Lithuanian	30,000
Polish	50,000
Russian	800,000
Ukrainian	70,000
Other	50,000
Lebanon[1]	
● Arabic	3,260,000
Armenian	210,000
French	*840,000*
Other	40,000
Lesotho[1]	
● English	*500,000*
● Sotho	1,780,000
Zulu	310,000
Liberia[1]	
Atlantic (Mel) languages	
Gola	110,000
Kissi	112,000
● English	*550,000*
Krio (English Creole)	*2,500,000*
Kru languages	
Bassa	384,000
Belle	14,000
De (Dewoin, Dey)	10,000
Grebo	248,000
Krahn	105,000
Kru (Krumen)	203,000
Mande (Northern) languages	
Gbandi	78,000
Kpelle	538,000
Loma	157,000
Malinke (Mandingo)	141,000
Mende	22,000
Vai	99,000
Mande (Southern) languages	
Gio (Dan)	217,000
Mano	197,000
Other	137,000
Libya	
● Arabic	5,460,000
Berber	60,000
Other[14]	170,000
Liechtenstein[2]	
● German	27,900
Italian	800
Turkish	800
Other	1,900
Lithuania[1]	
Belarusian	50,000
● Lithuanian	3,020,000
Polish	260,000
Russian	300,000
Ukrainian	40,000
Other	30,000
Luxembourg[2]	
Belgian	13,000
Dutch	4,000
English	4,000
French	16,000
German	10,000
Italian	20,000
Luxemburgian	280,000
Portuguese	54,000
Other	24,000
Macau	
Chinese	
● Cantonese (Yüeh [Yue])	370,000
Mandarin	5,000
Other Chinese languages	40,000
English	2,000
● Portuguese	10,000
Other	5,000
Macedonia[1]	
Albanian	463,000
● Macedonian	1,346,000
Romany	46,000
Serbo-Croatian	41,000
Turkish	81,000
Vlach	9,000
Other	38,000
Madagascar[1]	
French	*2,200,000*
Malagasy	14,310,000
Other	150,000
Malaŵi[1]	
Chewa (Maravi)	5,740,000
● English	*510,000*
Lomwe	1,810,000
Ngoni	660,000
Yao	1,300,000
Other	340,000
Malaysia	
Bajau	140,000
Chinese	1,280,000
Chinese-others	720,000
Dusun	230,000
English	110,000
English-others	250,000
English (lingua franca)	*6,700,000*
Iban	530,000
Iban-others	90,000
● Malay	9,520,000
Malay-others	3,380,000
Tamil	860,000
Tamil-others	10,000
Other	4,970,000
Maldives	
● Divehi (Maldivian)	270,000
Mali[1]	
Afro-Asiatic languages	
Berber languages	
Tamashek (Tuareg)	740,000
Semitic languages	
Arabic (Mauri)	160,000
● French	*1,000,000*
Niger-Congo languages	
Atlantic languages	
Fula (Fulani) and Tukulor	1,410,000
Dogon	400,000
Gur (Voltaic) languages	
Bwa (Bobo)	240,000
Mossi (Moore)	40,000
Senufo and Minianka	1,210,000
Mande languages	
Bambara	3,220,000
Bambara (lingua franca)	*8,100,000*
Bobo Fing	10,000
Dyula (Jula)	300,000
Malinke, Khasonke, and Wasulunka	670,000
Samo (Duun)	70,000
Soninke	890,000
Nilo-Saharan languages	
Songhai	720,000
Other	20,000
Malta[1]	
● English	8,000
● Maltese	361,000
Other	8,000
Marshall Islands[2]	
● English	*62,800*
● Marshallese	60,800
Other	2,000
Martinique	
● French	…
French/French Creole	385,000
Other	13,000
Mauritania[1]	
● Arabic	…
French	*250,000*
Fula (Fulani)	30,000
Ḥassānīyah Arabic	2,050,000
Soninke	70,000
Tukulor	130,000
Wolof	170,000
Zenaga	30,000
Other	30,000
Mauritius	
Bhojpurī	221,000
Bhojpurī-other	24,000
Chinese	4,000
● English	2,000
French	40,000
French Creole	714,000
French Creole-other	103,000
Hindī	14,000
Marāṭhī	8,000
Tamil	9,000
Telugu	7,000
Urdū	7,000
Other	3,000
Mayotte[15]	
● Arabic	…
Mahorais (local dialect of Comorian Swahili)	117,000
Other Comorian Swahili dialects	52,000
Malagasy	45,000
● French	56,000
Other	9,000
Mexico	
Amerindian languages	7,560,000
Amuzgo	40,000

Major languages by country	Number of speakers
Aztec (Nahuatl)	1,720,000
Chatino	40,000
Chinantec	160,000
Chocho	20,000
Chol	190,000
Chontal	50,000
Cora	20,000
Cuicatec	20,000
Huastec	170,000
Huave	20,000
Huichol	30,000
Kanjobal	20,000
Mame	20,000
Mayo	50,000
Mazahua	190,000
Mazatec	240,000
Mixe	130,000
Mixtec	550,000
Otomí	410,000
Popoluca	50,000
Purepecha	130,000
Tarahumara	80,000
Tepehua	10,000
Tepehuan	30,000
Tlapanec	100,000
Tojolabal	50,000
Totonac	300,000
Trique	20,000
Tzeltal	380,000
Tzotzil	340,000
Yaqui	20,000
Yucatec (Mayan)	1,020,000
Zapotec	560,000
Zoque	60,000
Other	340,000
● Spanish	88,270,000
Spanish-Amerindian languages	*6,150,000*
Micronesia	
Chuukese (Trukese)	44,900
English	500
Kosraean	7,900
Mortlockese	8,200
Palauan	400
Pohnpeian	25,600
Woleaian	4,000
Yapese	6,300
Other	10,200
Moldova	
Bulgarian	70,000
Gagauz	140,000
● Romanian (Moldovan)	2,630,000
Russian	98,000
Ukrainian	360,000
Other	60,000
Monaco[2]	
English	2,000
● French	13,000
Italian	5,000
Monegasque	5,000
Other	6,000
Mongolia[1]	
Bayad	46,000
Buryat	41,000
Darhat	17,000
Dariganga	34,000
Dörbet	65,000
Dzakhchin	27,000
Kazak	142,000
● Khalkha (Mongolian)	1,901,000
Khalkha (lingua franca)	*2,160,000*
Ould	10,000
Torgut	12,000
Tuvan (Uryankhai)	24,000
Other	94,000
Morocco	
● Arabic	18,050,000
Berber	9,160,000
French	*11,100,000*
Other	560,000
Mozambique	
Chopi	530,000
Chuabo	1,060,000
Koti	70,000
Kunda	10,000
Lomwe	1,450,000
Makonde	360,000
Makua	5,180,000
Marendje	640,000
Mwani	80,000
Ngulu	20,000
Nguni	
Swazi	20,000
Zulu	10,000
Nsenga	40,000
Nyanja	620,000
Nyungwe	420,000
Phimbi	20,000
● Portuguese	230,000
Portuguese (lingua franca)	*5,030,000*
Ronga	680,000
Sena	1,740,000
Shona	1,220,000
Swahili	10,000
Tonga	360,000
Tsonga	2,310,000
Tswa	1,110,000
Yao	310,000
Other	120,000
Myanmar (Burma)[1]	
● Burmese	32,620,000
Burmese (lingua franca)	*37,800,000*
Chin	1,030,000
Kachin (Ching-p'o)	640,000
Karen	2,940,000
Kayah	190,000
Mon	1,140,000
Rakhine (Arakanese)	2,130,000
Shan	4,010,000
Other	2,590,000
Namibia	
Afrikaans	153,000
Caprivi	76,000
● English	13,000
English (lingua franca)	*310,000*
German	15,000
Herero	130,000
Kavango (Okavango)	157,000
Nama	202,000
Ovambo (Ambo [Kwanyama])	822,000
San (Bushman)	31,000
Tswana	7,000
Other	16,000
Nauru	
Chinese	900
English	800
English (lingua franca)	*10,400*
Kiribati (Gilbertese)	1,900
Nauruan	6,000
Tuvaluan (Ellice)	900
Nepal	
Austroasiatic (Munda) languages	
Santhālī	40,000
English	*6,500,000*
Indo-Aryan languages	
Bengali	30,000
Bhojpurī	1,640,000
Dhanwar	30,000
Hindī	200,000
Hindī (Awadhī dialect)	440,000
Maithilī	2,600,000
● Nepālī (Eastern Pahāṛī)	10,050,000
Rājbanśī	100,000
Tharu	1,180,000
Urdū	240,000
Tibeto-Burman languages	
Bhutiā (Sherpa)	140,000
Chepang	30,000
Gurung	270,000
Limbū	300,000
Magar	510,000
Newārī	820,000
Rai and Kirāntī	520,000
Tamāng	1,070,000
Thakali	10,000
Thami	20,000
Other	700,000
Netherlands, The[2]	
Arabic	140,000
● Dutch	15,007,000
Dutch and Frisian	*590,000*
Turkish	128,000
Other	416,000
Netherlands Antilles	
● Dutch	...
English	17,000
Papiamento	183,000
Other	13,000
New Caledonia[1]	
● French	70,000
Indonesian	5,000
Melanesian languages	92,000
Polynesian languages (mostly Wallisian)	24,000
Vietnamese	3,000
Other	10,000
New Zealand	
● English	3,309,000
English-Māori	148,000
● Māori	13,000
Other	331,000
Nicaragua	
English Creole	27,000
Misumalpan languages	
Miskito	78,000
Sumo	8,000
● Spanish	4,648,000
Other	2,000
Niger[1]	
Atlantic languages	
Fula (Fulani)	940,000
Berber languages	
Tamashek (Tuareg)	1,000,000
Chadic languages	
Hausa	5,120,000
Hausa (lingua franca)	*6,800,000*
● French	*1,500,000*
Gur (Voltaic) languages	
Gurma	30,000
Saharan languages	
Kanuri	430,000
Teda (Tubu)	40,000
Semitic languages	
Arabic	30,000
Songhai and Zerma	2,050,000
Other	20,000
Nigeria[1]	
Arabic	300,000
Bura	1,700,000
Edo	3,700,000
● English/English Creole (lingua franca)	*50,000,000*
Fula (Fulani)	12,400,000
Hausa	23,600,000
Hausa (lingua franca)	*55,000,000*
Ibibio	6,200,000
Igbo (Ibo)	19,900,000
Ijo (Ijaw)	2,000,000
Kanuri	4,600,000
Nupe	1,400,000
Tiv	2,500,000
Yoruba	23,600,000
Other	8,600,000
Northern Mariana Islands	
Carolinian	3,200
Chamorro	19,900
Chinese	4,700
Chuukese (Trukese)	1,500
● English	3,200
English (lingua franca)	*60,300*
Japanese	1,300
Korean	4,300
Palauan	2,300
Philippine languages	22,700
Other	3,300
Norway[2]	
Danish	18,000
English	24,000
● Norwegian	4,276,000
Swedish	12,000
Other	99,000
Oman	
● Arabic (Omani)	1,810,000
Other	550,000
Pakistan	
Balochī	4,270,000
Brāhūī	1,700,000
English (lingua franca)	*16,000,000*
Pashto	18,650,000
Punjābī	
Punjābī	68,350,000
Hindko	3,450,000
Sindhī	
Saraikī	13,950,000
Sindhī	16,700,000
● Urdū	10,780,000
Other	4,040,000
Palau	
Chinese	300
● English	600
English (lingua franca)	*18,000*
● Palauan	14,900
Philippine languages	1,700
Other	700
Panama	
Amerindian languages	
Bokotá	4,000
Chibchan	
Cuna	56,000
Guaymí	147,000
Teribe	2,000
Chocó	
Embera	17,000
Waunana	3,000
Arabic	15,000
Chinese	8,000
English	...
English Creoles	387,000
● Spanish	2,125,000
Papua New Guinea[1]	
● English	*70,000*
Melanesian languages	920,000
Motu	*150,000*
Papuan languages	3,590,000
Tok Pisin (English Creole)	*2,990,000*
Other	90,000
Paraguay	
German	45,000
● Guaraní	2,096,000
Guaraní-Spanish	2,540,000
Portuguese	165,000
● Spanish	339,000
Other	38,000
Peru	
Amerindian languages	
● Aymara	570,000
● Quechua	4,080,000
Other	170,000
● Spanish	19,790,000
Other	200,000
Philippines	
Aklanon	530,000
Bantoanon	70,000
Bicol	4,160,000
Bilaan	40,000
Bontoc	60,000
Butuanon	70,000
Cebuano	17,020,000
Chavacano	450,000
Chinese	70,000
Davaweno (Mansaka)	500,000
● English (lingua franca)	*38,000,000*
Hiligaynon	6,660,000
Ibaloi (Nabaloi)	120,000
Ibanag	270,000
Ifugao	200,000
Ilocano	6,810,000
Ilongot	110,000
Kalinga	120,000
Kankanai	280,000
Kinaray-a (Hamtikanon)	460,000
Maguindanao	1,060,000
Manobo	490,000
Maranao	930,000
Masbateño	500,000
Palawano	80,000
Pampango	2,180,000
Pangasinan	1,320,000
● Pilipino (Filipino; Tagalog)	21,420,000
Romblon	230,000
Samal	460,000
Sambal	190,000
Subanon	300,000
Surigaonon	530,000
Tau Sug	840,000
Tboli	100,000
Tinggian	70,000
Tiruray	70,000
Waray-Waray	2,790,000
Yakan	140,000
Other	1,440,000
Poland	
Belarusian	190,000
German	500,000
● Polish	37,740,000
Ukrainian	230,000
Portugal[2]	
● Portuguese	9,870,000
Other	100,000
Puerto Rico	
● English	19,000
● Spanish	1,943,000
Spanish-English	1,775,000
Other	48,000
Qatar[2]	
● Arabic	230,000
Other[16]	350,000
Réunion	
Chinese	20,000
Comorian	20,000
● French	*210,000*
French Creole	630,000
Malagasy	10,000
Tamil	*130,000*
Other	10,000
Romania	
Bulgarian	9,000
Czech	5,000
German	97,000
Hungarian	1,616,000
Polish	3,000
● Romanian	20,394,000
Romany (Tigani)	164,000
Russian	31,000
Serbo-Croatian	33,000
Slovak	18,000
Tatar	22,000
Turkish	27,000
Ukrainian	63,000
Other	5,000
Russia	
Adyghian	120,000
Armenian	360,000
Avar	530,000
Azerbaijani (Azeri)	280,000
Bashkir	980,000
Belarusian	440,000
Buryat	360,000
Chechen	890,000
Chuvash	1,370,000
Dargin	350,000
Georgian (Kartuli)	90,000
German	350,000
Ingush	210,000
Kabardian	380,000
Kalmyk	150,000
Karachay	150,000
Kazak	560,000
Komi-Permyak	100,000
Komi-Zyryan	240,000
Kumyk	270,000
Lak	100,000
Lezgi (Lezgian)	240,000
Mari	530,000
Mordvin	740,000
Ossetian	370,000
Romanian	120,000
Romany	130,000
● Russian	127,170,000
Tabasaran	90,000
Tatar	4,720,000
Tuvan	200,000
Udmurt	510,000
Ukrainian	1,870,000
Uzbek	100,000
Yakut	360,000
Other	1,450,000
Rwanda	
● English	...
● French	*600,000*
● Rwanda	7,956,000
St. Kitts and Nevis	
● English	...
English/English Creole	42,000
St. Lucia	
● English	30,000
English/French Creole	121,000
St. Vincent and the Grenadines	
● English	...
English/English Creole	112,000
Other	1,000
Samoa	
● English	1,000
● Samoan	81,000
Samoan-English	89,000
San Marino[1]	
● Italian (Romagnolo)	26,100
São Tomé and Príncipe	
Crioulo (Portuguese Creole)	117,000
English	...
French	1,000
● Portuguese	...
Other	17,000
Saudi Arabia[1]	
● Arabic	19,750,000
Other	1,040,000
Senegal	
● French	*3,400,000*
Senegalese	
Bambara	90,000
Diola	480,000
Fula (Fulani)-Tukulor	2,110,000
Malinke (Mandingo)	360,000
Serer	1,220,000
Soninke	130,000
Wolof	4,680,000
Wolof (lingua franca)	*7,800,000*
Other	430,000
non-Senegalese	220,000
Seychelles	
English	3,000
English (lingua franca)	*28,000*
French	1,000
French (lingua franca)	*75,000*
Seselwa (French Creole)	73,000
Other	3,000
Sierra Leone[1]	
Atlantic languages	
Bullom-Sherbro	170,000
Fula (Fulani)	170,000
Kissi	110,000
Limba	380,000
Temne	1,450,000
● English	*700,000*
Krio (English Creole [lingua franca])	*4,400,000*
Mande languages	
Kono-Vai	240,000
Kuranko	160,000
Mende	1,580,000
Susu	70,000
Yalunka	160,000
Other	80,000
Singapore[1]	
Chinese	2,441,000
● English	*1,183,000*
● Malay	446,000

Language (continued)

Major languages by country	Number of speakers
● Mandarin Chinese	*1,371,000*
● Tamil (and other Indian languages)	235,000
Other	42,000
Slovakia[1]	
Czech, Moravian, and Silesian	59,000
German	5,000
Hungarian	574,000
Polish	3,000
Romany	86,000
Russian	2,000
Ruthenian and Ukrainian	32,000
● Slovak	4,649,000
Other	14,000
Slovenia	
Hungarian	9,000
Serbo-Croatian	157,000
● Slovene	1,774,000
Other	75,000
Solomon Islands[1]	
● English	*9,000*
Melanesian languages	365,000
Papuan languages	36,000
Polynesian languages	16,000
Solomon Island Pidgin (English Creole)	*149,000*
Other	9,000
Somalia[1]	
● Arabic	...
English	...
● Somali	6,730,000
Other	120,000
South Africa	
● Afrikaans	6,470,000
Afrikaans/English	90,000
● English	3,900,000
Nguni	
● Ndebele	640,000
● Swazi	1,110,000
● Xhosa	7,500,000
● Zulu	9,600,000
Sotho	
● North Sotho (Pedi)	4,200,000
● South Sotho	2,960,000
● Tswana (Western Sotho)	3,080,000
● Tsonga	1,800,000
● Venda	730,000
Other	770,000
Spain	
Basque (Euskera)	620,000
● Castilian Spanish	29,290,000
Catalan (Català)	6,650,000
Galician (Gallego)	2,520,000
Other	300,000
Sri Lanka	
English	10,000
English-Sinhala	1,030,000
English-Sinhala-Tamil	680,000
English-Tamil	210,000
● Sinhala	11,300,000
Sinhala-Tamil	1,750,000
● Tamil	3,680,000
Other	60,000
Sudan, The[1]	
● Arabic	16,560,000
Bari	830,000
Beja	2,140,000
Dinka	3,870,000
Fur	690,000
Lotuko	490,000
Nubian languages	2,720,000
Nuer	1,650,000
Shilluk	580,000
Zande (Azande)	910,000
Other	3,120,000
Suriname	
● Dutch	*110,000*
English/English Creole	*400,000*
Sranantonga	170,000
Sranantonga-other	170,000
Other (mostly Hindī, Javanese, and Saramacca)	80,000
Swaziland[1]	
● English	*40,000*
● Swazi	870,000
Zulu	20,000
Other	70,000
Sweden[2]	
Arabic	68,000
Danish	41,000
English	32,000
Finnish	209,000
German	45,000
Iranian languages	49,000
Norwegian	46,000
Polish	39,000
South Slavic languages	116,000
Spanish	56,000
● Swedish	7,933,000
Turkish	29,000
Other	197,000
Switzerland	
● French	1,370,000
● German	4,530,000
● Italian	540,000
Romansch	40,000
Other	640,000
Syria[1]	
● Arabic	13,800,000
Kurdish	1,380,000
Other	150,000
Taiwan	
Austronesian languages	
Ami	136,000
Atayal	87,000
Bunun	41,000
Paiwan	67,000
Puyuma	10,000
Rukai	10,000
Saisiyat	6,000
Tsou	7,000
Yami	4,000
Chinese languages	
Hakka	2,400,000
● Mandarin	4,390,000
Min (South Fukien)	14,570,000
Other	110,000
Tajikistan	
Russian	590,000
● Tajik (Tojik)	3,800,000
Uzbek	1,410,000
Other	300,000
Tanzania[1]	
Chaga (Chagga), Pare	1,500,000
● English	*3,300,000*
Gogo	1,200,000
Ha	1,050,000
Haya	1,800,000
Hehet	2,100,000
Iramba	870,000
Luguru	1,500,000
Luo	250,000
Makonde	1,800,000
Masai	300,000
Ngoni	400,000
Nyakusa	1,650,000
Nyamwesi (Sukuma)	6,460,000
Shambala	1,310,000
● Swahili	2,700,000
Swahili (lingua franca)	*28,000,000*
Tatoga	230,000
Yao	750,000
Other	4,710,000
Thailand[1]	
Chinese	7,420,000
Karen	220,000
Malay	2,230,000
Mon-Khmer languages	
Khmer	780,000
Kuy	650,000
Other	210,000
Thai languages	
Lao	16,460,000
● Thai (Siamese)	32,170,000
Other	420,000
Other	630,000
Togo[1]	
Atlantic (Mel) languages	
Fula (Fulani)	67,000
Benue-Congo languages	
Ana (Ana-Ife)	123,000
Nago	13,000
Yoruba	9,000
Chadic languages	
Hausa	13,000
● French	*2,500,000*
Gur (Voltaic) languages	
Basari	86,000
Chakossi (Akan)	58,000
Chamba	47,000
Dye (Gangam)	46,000
Gurma	167,000
Kabre	676,000
Konkomba	69,000
Kotokoli (Tem)	282,000
Moba	264,000
Mossi (Moore)	13,000
Namba (Lamba)	149,000
Naudemba (Losso)	201,000
Tamberma	27,000
Yanga	14,000
Kwa languages	
Adja (Aja)	153,000
Adele	10,000
Ahlo	9,000
Akposo	131,000
Ane (Basila)	278,000
Anlo	4,000
Anyaga	10,000
Ewe	1,138,000
Fon	49,000
Hwe	6,000
Kebu	56,000
Kpessi	4,000
Peda-Hula (Pla)	20,000
Watyi (Ouatchi)	505,000
Other	208,000
Tonga	
● English	*29,000*
● Tongan	96,000
Other	2,000
Trinidad and Tobago	
● English	...
English Creole[17]	36,000
Hindī	44,000
Trinidad English	1,199,000
● Other	3,000
Tunisia	
● Arabic	6,560,000
Arabic-French	2,460,000
Arabic-French-English	300,000
Arabic-other	10,000
Other-no Arabic	30,000
Other	30,000
Turkey[1]	
Arabic	880,000
Kurdish[18]	6,840,000
● Turkish	56,540,000
Other	300,000
Turkmenistan[1]	
Armenian	36,000
Azerbaijani (Azeri)	39,000
Balochi	39,000
Kazak	93,000
Russian	318,000
Tatar	39,000
● Turkmen	3,627,000
Ukrainian	25,000
Uzbek	434,000
Other	82,000
Tuvalu	
English	...
Kiribati (Gilbertese)	800
Tuvaluan (Ellice)	9,600
Uganda[1]	
Bantu languages	
Amba	80,000
Ganda (Luganda)	4,010,000
Gisu (Masaba)	1,000,000
Gwere	370,000
Kiga (Chiga)	1,850,000
Konjo	480,000
Nkole (Nyankole and Hororo)	2,370,000
Nyole	300,000
Nyoro	660,000
Ruli	90,000
Rundi	140,000
Rwanda	710,000
Samia	300,000
Soga	1,820,000
Swahili (lingua franca)	*7,800,000*
Toro	650,000
Central Sudanic languages	
Lugbara	1,050,000
Madi	170,000
Ndo	220,000
● English	*2,400,000*
Nilotic languages	
Acholi	980,000
Alur	530,000
Kakwa	120,000
Karamojong	460,000
Kumam	150,000
Lango	1,300,000
Padhola	330,000
Sebei (Kupsabiny)	150,000
Teso	1,330,000
Other (mostly Gujarātī and Hindī)	550,000
Ukraine	
Belarusian	150,000
Bulgarian	160,000
Hungarian	150,000
Polish	30,000
Romanian	330,000
Russian	16,520,000
● Ukrainian	32,530,000
Other	430,000
United Arab Emirates[2]	
● Arabic	1,150,000
Other[16]	1,590,000
United Kingdom	
● English	57,520,000
Scots-Gaelic	80,000
Welsh	560,000
Other	960,000
United States	
Amharic	40,000
Arabic	420,000
Armenian	180,000
Bengali	40,000
Cajun	40,000
Chinese (including Formosan)	1,520,000
Czech	110,000
Danish	40,000
Dutch	170,000
English	232,910,000
English (lingua franca)	*262,000,000*
Finnish	60,000
French	2,000,000
French Creole (mostly Haitian)	220,000
German	1,810,000
Greek	460,000
Gujarātī	120,000
Hebrew	170,000
Hindī (including Urdū)	390,000
Hungarian	170,000
Ilocano	50,000
Italian	1,530,000
Japanese	500,000
Korean	730,000
Kru (Gullah)	80,000
Lithuanian	70,000
Malayālam	40,000
Miao (Hmong)	100,000
Mon-Khmer (mostly Cambodian)	150,000
Navajo	170,000
Norwegian	90,000
Pennsylvania Dutch	100,000
Persian	240,000
Polish	850,000
Portuguese	500,000
Punjābī	60,000
Romanian	80,000
Russian	280,000
Samoan	40,000
Serbo-Croatian	140,000
Slovak	90,000
Spanish	20,340,000
Swedish	90,000
Syriac	40,000
Tagalog	990,000
Thai (including Laotian)	240,000
Turkish	50,000
Ukrainian	110,000
Vietnamese	590,000
Yiddish	250,000
Other	800,000
Uruguay	
● Spanish	3,080,000
Other	140,000
Uzbekistan	
Crimean Tatar	210,000
Karakalpak	470,000
Kazak	910,000
Korean	120,000
Kyrgyz	170,000
Russian	2,620,000
Tajik	1,070,000
Tatar	450,000
Turkish	120,000
Turkmen	130,000
Ukrainian	90,000
● Uzbek	17,180,000
Other	530,000
Vanuatu[19]	
● Bislama (English Creole)	120,000
● English	60,000
● French	30,000
Other	2,000
Venezuela	
Amerindian languages	
Goajiro	80,000
Warrau (Warao)	30,000
Other	110,000
● Spanish	22,510,000
Other	500,000
Vietnam[1]	
Bahnar	160,000
Cham	110,000
Chinese (Hoa)	1,070,000
French	*370,000*
Hre	110,000
Jarai	290,000
Khmer	1,060,000
Koho	110,000
Man (Mien, or Yao)	560,000
Miao (Meo, or Hmong)	660,000
Mnong	80,000
Muong	1,080,000
Nung	840,000
Rade (Rhadé)	230,000
Roglai	80,000
San Chay (Cao Lan)	140,000
San Diu	110,000
Sedang	110,000
Stieng	60,000
Tai	1,240,000
Tho (Tay)	1,410,000
● Vietnamese	66,200,000
Other	150,000
Virgin Islands (U.S.)	
● English	96,000
French	3,000
Spanish	16,000
Other	3,000
West Bank[20]	
Arabic	1,740,000
Hebrew	150,000
Western Sahara	
Arabic	288,000
Yemen[1]	
● Arabic	16,000,000
Other	300,000
Yugoslavia[1]	
Albanian	1,760,000
Hungarian	350,000
Macedonian	50,000
Romanian	40,000
Romany	150,000
● Serbo-Croatian (Serbian)	8,020,000
Serbo-Croatian (lingua franca)	*10,100,000*
Slovak	70,000
Vlach	20,000
Other	200,000
Zambia[21]	
Bemba group	
Bemba	2,810,000
Bemba (lingua franca)	*4,900,000*
Bisa	110,000
Lala	230,000
Lamba	210,000
Other	400,000
● English	100,000
English (lingua franca)	*1,800,000*
Lozi (Barotse) group	
Lozi (Barotse)	710,000
Other	100,000
Mambwe group	
Lungu	70,000
Mambwe	110,000
Mwanga (Winawanga)	130,000
Other	10,000
North-Western group	
Kaonde	220,000
Lunda	190,000
Luvale (Luena)	170,000
Other	260,000
Nyanja (Maravi) group	
Chewa	540,000
Ngoni	160,000
Nsenga	410,000
Nyanja (Maravi)	740,000
Nyanja (lingua franca)	*2,500,000*
Other	60,000
Tonga (Ila-Tonga) group	
Ila	90,000
Lenje	150,000
Tonga	1,040,000
Other	120,000
Tumbuka group	
Senga	70,000
Tumbuka	270,000
Other	10,000
Other	90,000
Zimbabwe	
● English	250,000
English (linguafranca)	*5,200,000*
Ndebele (Nguni)	1,790,000
Nyanja	250,000
Shona	7,970,000
Other	790,000

[1]Figures given represent ethnolinguistic groups. [2]Data refer to nationality (usually resident aliens holding foreign passports). [3]Data are partly based on place of residence. [4]Majority of population speak Moore (language of the Mossi); Dyula is language of commerce. [5]Swahili also spoken. [6]English and French also spoken. [7]Based on "nationality" at 1982 census. [8]Includes naturalized citizens. [9]French is the universal language throughout France; traditional dialects and minority languages are retained regionally in the approximate numbers shown, however. [10]Data reflect multilingualism; 1998 population estimate is 228,000. [11]Refers to Irish speakers in Gaeltacht areas. [12]Includes the population of the Golan Heights and East Jerusalem; excludes the Israeli population in the West Bank and Gaza Strip. [13]English and French also spoken. [14]English and Italian also spoken. [15]Data reflect ability to speak the language, not mother tongue; 1998 population estimate is 134,000. [16]Mostly Pakistanis, Indians, and Iranians. [17]Spoken on Tobago only. [18]Other estimates of the Kurdish population range from 6 percent to 20–25 percent. [19]Data reflect multilingualism; 1998 population is 182,000. [20]Excludes East Jerusalem. [21]Groups are officially defined geographic divisions; elements comprising them are named by language.

Religion

The following table presents statistics on religious affiliation for each of the countries of the world. An assessment was made for each country of the available data on distribution of religious communities within the total population; the best available figures, whether originating as census data, membership figures of the churches concerned, or estimates by external analysts in the absence of reliable local data, were applied as percentages to the estimated 1998 midyear population of the country to obtain the data shown below.

Several concepts govern the nature of the available data, each useful separately but none the basis of any standard of international practice in the collection of such data. The word "affiliation" was used above to describe the nature of the relationship joining the religious bodies named and the populations shown. This term implies some sort of formal, usually documentary, connection between the religion and the individual (a baptismal certificate, a child being assigned the religion of its parents on a census form, maintenance of one's name on the tax rolls of a state religion, etc.) but says nothing about the nature of the individual's personal religious practice, in that the individual may have lapsed, never been confirmed as an adult, joined another religion, or may have joined an organization that is formally atheist.

The user of these statistics should be careful to note that not only does the nature of the affiliation (with an organized religion) differ greatly from country to country, but the social context of religious practice does also. A country in which a single religion has long been predominant will often show more than 90% of its population to be *affiliated*, while in actual fact, no more than 10% may actually *practice* that religion on a regular basis. Such a situation often leads to undercounting of minority religions (where someone [head of household, communicant, child] is counted at all), blurring of distinctions seen to be significant elsewhere (a Hindu country may not distinguish Protestant [or even Christian] denominations; a Christian country may not distinguish among its Muslim or Buddhist citizens), or double-counting in countries where an individual may conscientiously practice more than one "religion" at a time.

Until 1989 communist countries had for long consciously attempted to ignore, suppress, or render invisible religious practice within their borders. Countries with large numbers of adherents of traditional, often animist, religions and belief systems usually have little or no formal methodology for defining the nature of local religious practice. On the other hand, countries with strong missionary traditions, or good census organizations, or few religious sensitivities may have very good, detailed, and meaningful data.

The most comprehensive works available are DAVID B. BARRETT (ed.), *World Christian Encyclopedia* (1982); and PETER BRIERLEY, *World Churches Handbook* (1997).

Religion

Religious affiliation	1998 population	Religious affiliation	1998 population	Religious affiliation	1998 population	Religious affiliation	1998 population	Religious affiliation	1998 population
Afghanistan		**Azerbaijan**		**Botswana**		**Chad**		other (mostly	
Sunnī Muslim	20,830,000	Shīʿī Muslim	5,000,000	African Christian	400,000	Muslim	3,960,000	Christian)	30,000
Shīʿī Muslim	3,720,000	Sunnī Muslim	2,140,000	Protestant	180,000	Roman Catholic	1,500,000		
other	250,000	other	510,000	Roman Catholic	60,000	Protestant	1,060,000	**Czech Republic**	
				other (mostly		traditional beliefs	540,000	Roman Catholic	4,020,000
Albania		**Bahamas, The**		traditional beliefs)	810,000	other	300,000	Evangelical Church of	
Muslim	2,330,000	Protestant	133,000					Czech Brethren	200,000
Albanian Orthodox	240,000	Roman Catholic	49,000	**Brazil**		**Chile**		Czechoslovak Hussite	180,000
Roman Catholic	170,000	Anglican	32,000	Roman Catholic		Roman Catholic	11,370,000	Silesian Evangelical	30,000
other	590,000	other	79,000	(including syncretic		Evangelical Protestant	1,840,000	Eastern Orthodox	20,000
				Afro-Catholic cults		other	1,610,000	atheist and	
Algeria		**Bahrain**		having Spiritist				nonreligious	4,110,000
Sunnī Muslim	29,910,000	Shīʿī Muslim	390,000	beliefs and rituals)	117,000,000	**China**		other	1,740,000
Ibādīyah Muslim	110,000	Sunnī Muslim	130,000	Evangelical Protestant	37,500,000	nonreligious	644,000,000		
other	20,000	other	110,000	other	7,300,000	Chinese folk-		**Denmark**	
						religionist	250,000,000	Evangelical Lutheran	4,590,000
American Samoa		**Bangladesh**		**Brunei**		atheist	149,000,000	other	720,000
Congregational	35,000	Muslim	112,650,000	Muslim	212,000	Buddhist	105,000,000		
Roman Catholic	13,000	Hindu	13,410,000	other	103,000	Christian	75,000,000	**Djibouti**	
other	14,000	other	1,510,000			Muslim	18,000,000	Sunnī Muslim	634,000
				Bulgaria		traditional beliefs	1,000,000	Christian	18,000
Andorra		**Barbados**		Bulgarian Orthodox	3,020,000				
Roman Catholic	60,000	Anglican	87,000	Muslim (mostly		**Colombia**		**Dominica**	
other	5,000	Protestant	79,000	Sunnī)	1,080,000	Roman Catholic	34,640,000	Roman Catholic	54,000
		Roman Catholic	12,000	other	4,170,000	other	3,050,000	Protestant	13,000
Angola		other	57,000					other	9,000
Roman Catholic	5,510,000			**Burkina Faso**		**Comoros**			
Protestant	1,590,000	**Belarus**		Muslim	5,630,000	Sunnī Muslim	542,000	**Dominican Republic**	
African Christian	470,000	Belarusian		traditional beliefs	4,510,000	Christian	4,000	Roman Catholic	6,450,000
other (mostly		Orthodox	3,230,000	Christian	1,130,000			Protestant	510,000
traditional beliefs)	3,300,000	Roman Catholic	1,820,000			**Congo, Dem. Rep. of the**		other	920,000
		other	5,180,000	**Burundi**		Roman Catholic	20,090,000		
Antigua and Barbuda				Roman Catholic	3,600,000	Protestant	15,480,000	**Ecuador**	
Protestant	29,000	**Belgium**		nonreligious	1,030,000	African Christian	6,550,000	Roman Catholic	11,260,000
Anglican	22,000	Roman Catholic	8,980,000	other (mostly		traditional beliefs	5,240,000	other	920,000
Roman Catholic	7,000	other	1,230,000	Protestant)	910,000	Muslim	690,000		
other	11,000					other	1,640,000	**Egypt**	
		Belize		**Cambodia**				Sunnī Muslim	56,300,000
Argentina		Roman Catholic	136,000	Buddhist	10,210,000	**Congo, Rep. of the**		Coptic Orthodox[1]	6,330,000
Roman Catholic	31,690,000	Protestant	64,000	Muslim	230,000	Roman Catholic	1,090,000	Protestant	630,000
Protestant	2,710,000	Anglican	16,000	other	310,000	traditional beliefs	870,000		
Muslim	540,000	other	19,000			Protestant	640,000	**El Salvador**	
Jewish	260,000			**Cameroon**		Muslim	60,000	Roman Catholic	4,500,000
other	930,000	**Benin**		Roman Catholic	5,220,000			Protestant	990,000
		Voodoo		traditional beliefs	3,900,000	**Costa Rica**		other	260,000
Armenia		(traditional beliefs)	3,780,000	Muslim	3,280,000	Roman Catholic	3,040,000		
Armenian Apostolic		Roman Catholic	1,280,000	Protestant	2,630,000	other	490,000	**Equatorial Guinea**	
(Orthodox)	2,450,000	Muslim	730,000					Roman Catholic	420,000
other	1,350,000	other	310,000	**Canada**		**Côte d'Ivoire**		other	30,000
				Roman Catholic	13,860,000	Muslim	5,970,000		
Aruba		**Bermuda**		Protestant	8,530,000	Roman Catholic	3,210,000	**Eritrea**	
Roman Catholic	63,000	Anglican	23,000	Anglican	2,460,000	traditional beliefs	2,630,000	Muslim	2,660,000
other	26,000	Methodist	10,000	Eastern Orthodox	440,000	nonreligious	2,070,000	Eritrean Orthodox	1,180,000
		Roman Catholic	9,000	Jewish	360,000	Protestant	820,000		
Australia		other	20,000	Muslim	280,000	other	750,000	**Estonia**	
Roman Catholic	5,060,000			Buddhist	180,000			Estonian Orthodox	280,000
Anglican	4,120,000			Hindu	180,000	**Croatia**		Evangelical Lutheran	200,000
Uniting Church	1,410,000	**Bhutan**		Sikh	170,000	Roman Catholic	3,370,000	other	970,000
Presbyterian	710,000	Lamaistic Buddhist	470,000	nonreligious	3,840,000	Serbian Orthodox	660,000		
other Protestant	1,360,000	Hindu	160,000	other	770,000	Sunnī Muslim	60,000	**Ethiopia**	
Orthodox	520,000					Protestant	30,000	Ethiopian Orthodox	19,940,000
nonreligious	3,110,000	**Bolivia**		**Cape Verde**		other	550,000	other Christian	4,820,000
other	2,440,000	Roman Catholic	7,040,000	Roman Catholic	384,000			Muslim (mostly	
		Protestant	720,000	Protestant	16,000	**Cuba**		Sunnī)	17,570,000
Austria		other	200,000			Roman Catholic	4,390,000	traditional beliefs	7,120,000
Roman Catholic	6,060,000			**Central African Republic**		other (mostly non-		other	8,940,000
Protestant (mostly		**Bosnia and Herzegovina**		Protestant	860,000	religious and atheist)	6,730,000		
Lutheran)	430,000	Sunnī Muslim	1,350,000	traditional beliefs	810,000			**Faroe Islands**	
atheist and		Serbian Orthodox	960,000	Roman Catholic	570,000	**Cyprus**		Evangelical Lutheran	36,000
nonreligious	690,000	Roman Catholic	460,000	Muslim	510,000	Greek Orthodox	640,000	other	8,000
other	890,000	other	600,000	other	630,000	Muslim (mostly			
						Sunnī)	190,000		

Religion (continued)

Religious affiliation	1998 population
Fiji	
Christian (mostly Methodist and Roman Catholic)	418,000
Hindu	302,000
Muslim	62,000
other	8,000
Finland	
Evangelical Lutheran	4,410,000
other	740,000
France	
Roman Catholic	44,860,000
nonreligious	6,260,000
Muslim	3,240,000
atheist	2,000,000
Protestant	1,080,000
Jewish	610,000
other	790,000
French Guiana	
Roman Catholic	92,000
other	77,000
French Polynesia	
Protestant	114,000
Roman Catholic	90,000
other	24,000
Gabon	
Roman Catholic	600,000
traditional beliefs	230,000
Protestant	220,000
other	160,000
Gambia, The	
Muslim (mostly Sunnī)	1,230,000
other	60,000
Gaza Strip	
Muslim (mostly Sunnī)	1,068,000
other	14,000
Georgia	
Georgian Orthodox	1,990,000
Sunnī Muslim	600,000
Armenian Apostolic (Orthodox)	300,000
Russian Orthodox	140,000
other (mostly nonreligious)	2,400,000
Germany	
Protestant (mostly Evangelical Lutheran)	35,160,000
Roman Catholic	27,870,000
Muslim	1,750,000
other (mostly nonreligious)	17,370,000
Ghana	
African Christian	5,430,000
Protestant	3,710,000
traditional beliefs	3,250,000
Roman Catholic	2,720,000
Muslim	2,660,000
other	730,000
Gibraltar	
Roman Catholic	21,000
other	6,000
Greece	
Greek Orthodox	9,670,000
Muslim	140,000
other	730,000
Greenland	
Evangelical Lutheran	55,000
other	1,000
Grenada	
Roman Catholic	53,000
Anglican	14,000
other	33,000
Guadeloupe	
Roman Catholic	350,000
other	80,000
Guam	
Roman Catholic	111,000
Protestant	18,000
other	19,000
Guatemala	
Roman Catholic	8,200,000
Evangelical Protestant	2,350,000
other	250,000

Religious affiliation	1998 population
Guernsey	
Anglican	40,000
other	22,000
Guinea	
Muslim	6,500,000
traditional beliefs	340,000
Christian	320,000
other	320,000
Guinea-Bissau	
traditional beliefs	780,000
Muslim	360,000
Christian	60,000
Guyana	
Hindu	266,000
Protestant	147,000
Roman Catholic	90,000
Muslim	70,000
Anglican	67,000
other	142,000
Haiti	
Roman Catholic	4,650,000
Protestant	1,550,000
other	580,000
Honduras	
Roman Catholic	5,130,000
Evangelical Protestant	610,000
other	180,000
Hong Kong	
Buddhist and Taoist	4,920,000
Protestant	290,000
Roman Catholic	280,000
other	1,170,000
Hungary	
Roman Catholic	6,380,000
Protestant	2,580,000
other (mostly nonreligious and atheist)	1,160,000
Iceland	
Evangelical Lutheran	250,000
other	26,000
India	
Hindu	800,000,000
Sunnī Muslim	89,000,000
Shī'ī Muslim	30,000,000
Sikh	19,000,000
Protestant	11,000,000
Roman Catholic	10,000,000
Buddhist	7,000,000
Jain	4,000,000
Zoroastrian (Parsi)	80,000
other	14,000,000
Indonesia	
Muslim	177,000,000
Protestant	12,260,000
Roman Catholic	7,270,000
Hindu	3,710,000
Buddhist	2,090,000
other	630,000
Iran	
Shī'ī Muslim	57,490,000
Sunnī Muslim	3,480,000
other	560,000
Iraq	
Shī'ī Muslim	13,580,000
Sunnī Muslim	7,490,000
other (mostly Christian)	650,000
Ireland	
Roman Catholic	3,340,000
other	310,000
Isle of Man	
Anglican	45,000
other	28,000
Israel	
Jewish[2]	4,620,000
Muslim (mostly Sunnī)	840,000
other	280,000
Italy	
Roman Catholic	47,120,000
Muslim	700,000
other (mostly nonreligious and atheist)	9,830,000
Jamaica	
Protestant	1,000,000

Religious affiliation	1998 population
Roman Catholic	270,000
Anglican	100,000
other	1,180,000
Japan	
Shintoist[3]	117,620,000
Buddhist[3]	88,000,000
Christian	1,460,000
other	10,190,000
Jersey	
Anglican	53,000
Roman Catholic	20,000
other	13,000
Jordan	
Sunnī Muslim	4,520,000
Christian	160,000
Kazakstan	
Muslim (mostly Sunnī)	7,430,000
Russian Orthodox	1,290,000
Protestant	340,000
other (mostly nonreligious)	6,740,000
Kenya	
traditional beliefs	8,580,000
Protestant	8,000,000
Roman Catholic	5,530,000
African Christian	2,230,000
Muslim	1,700,000
Anglican	1,580,000
other	720,000
Kiribati	
Roman Catholic	45,000
Congregational	33,000
other	6,000
Korea, North	
atheist and nonreligious	14,500,000
traditional beliefs	3,310,000
Ch'öndogyo	2,950,000
other	470,000
Korea, South	
nonreligious	23,270,000
Buddhist	11,310,000
Protestant	8,440,000
Roman Catholic	2,740,000
Confucian	190,000
Wonbulgyo	140,000
Ch'öndogyo	50,000
other	500,000
Kuwait	
Sunnī Muslim	840,000
Shī'ī Muslim	560,000
other Muslim	190,000
other (mostly Christian and Hindu)	280,000
Kyrgyzstan	
Muslim (mostly Sunnī)	3,280,000
Russian Orthodox	260,000
other (mostly nonreligious)	1,150,000
Laos	
Buddhist	3,040,000
traditional beliefs	1,770,000
other	450,000
Latvia	
Roman Catholic	363,000
Evangelical Lutheran	358,000
Russian Orthodox	187,000
other (mostly nonreligious)	1,537,000
Lebanon	
Shī'ī Muslim	1,190,000
Sunnī Muslim	750,000
Maronite Catholic	670,000
Druze	250,000
Greek Orthodox	210,000
Armenian Apostolic (Orthodox)	180,000
Greek Catholic (Melchite)	160,000
other	100,000
Lesotho	
Roman Catholic	820,000
traditional beliefs	630,000
Protestant	290,000
African Christian	240,000
Anglican	110,000
Liberia	
Christian	1,880,000

Religious affiliation	1998 population
traditional beliefs	510,000
Muslim	380,000
Libya	
Sunnī Muslim	5,520,000
other	170,000
Liechtenstein	
Roman Catholic	25,000
other	6,000
Lithuania	
Roman Catholic	2,670,000
Russian Orthodox	90,000
other (mostly nonreligious)	940,000
Luxembourg	
Roman Catholic	400,000
other	20,000
Macau	
nonreligious	259,000
Buddhist	71,000
other	96,000
Macedonia	
Serbian (Macedonian) Orthodox	1,100,000
Sunnī Muslim	610,000
other	310,000
Madagascar	
traditional beliefs	7,520,000
Roman Catholic	3,080,000
Protestant	2,850,000
Muslim	1,010,000
Malaŵi	
Protestant (mostly Presbyterian)	2,020,000
Muslim	1,970,000
Roman Catholic	1,770,000
traditional beliefs	980,000
African Christian	970,000
other	2,130,000
Malaysia	
Muslim	11,680,000
Buddhist	3,820,000
Chinese folk religionist	2,560,000
Hindu	1,550,000
Christian	1,410,000
other	1,060,000
Maldives	
Sunnī Muslim	270,000
Mali	
Muslim	9,100,000
traditional beliefs	910,000
Christian	100,000
Malta	
Roman Catholic	352,000
other	25,000
Marshall Islands	
Protestant	39,000
Roman Catholic	5,000
other	19,000
Martinique	
Roman Catholic	340,000
other	60,000
Mauritania	
Sunnī Muslim	2,500,000
other	10,000
Mauritius	
Hindu	590,000
Roman Catholic	320,000
Muslim	190,000
other	60,000
Mayotte	
Sunnī Muslim	130,000
Christian	4,000
Mexico	
Roman Catholic	86,620,000
Protestant	3,670,000
other Christian	1,740,000
other (mostly nonreligious)	3,800,000
Micronesia	
Roman Catholic	44,000
Protestant	40,000
other	24,000

Religious affiliation	1998 population
Moldova	
Romanian Orthodox	1,480,000
Russian (Moldovan) Orthodox	400,000
other (mostly nonreligious)	2,360,000
Monaco	
Roman Catholic	26,000
other	6,000
Mongolia	
Tantric Buddhist (Lamaist)	2,320,000
Muslim	100,000
Morocco	
Muslim (mostly Sunnī)	27,730,000
other	50,000
Mozambique	
traditional beliefs	8,760,000
Muslim	5,260,000
Roman Catholic	2,150,000
Protestant	1,710,000
other	760,000
Myanmar (Burma)	
Buddhist	42,310,000
Christian	2,320,000
Muslim	1,810,000
traditional beliefs	540,000
Hindu	240,000
other	80,000
Namibia	
Protestant (mostly Lutheran and Dutch Reformed)	834,000
Roman Catholic	268,000
African Christian	114,000
Anglican	90,000
other	316,000
Nauru	
Protestant	5,300
Roman Catholic	2,900
other	2,300
Nepal	
Hindu	19,000,000
Buddhist	1,710,000
Muslim	780,000
other	470,000
Netherlands, The	
Roman Catholic	5,020,000
Dutch Reformed Church (NHK)	2,350,000
Reformed Churches	1,260,000
Muslim	680,000
nonreligious	5,960,000
other	420,000
Netherlands Antilles	
Roman Catholic	157,000
other	56,000
New Caledonia	
Roman Catholic	125,000
Protestant	30,000
other	49,000
New Zealand	
Anglican	660,000
Roman Catholic	500,000
Presbyterian	480,000
Methodist	130,000
Baptist	60,000
Ratana	40,000
Mormon	40,000
nonreligious	940,000
other	1,030,000
Nicaragua	
Roman Catholic	3,480,000
Protestant	790,000
other (mostly nonreligious)	490,000
Niger	
Sunnī Muslim	8,580,000
traditional beliefs	1,060,000
other	30,000
Nigeria	
Muslim	47,500,000
traditional beliefs	21,000,000
Protestant	16,500,000
Roman Catholic	9,000,000
African Christian	7,400,000
Anglican	5,700,000
other	3,400,000

Religious affiliation	1998 population
Northern Mariana Islands	
Roman Catholic	40,000
other	27,000
Norway	
Evangelical Lutheran (Church of Norway)	3,910,000
other	520,000
Oman	
Ibāḍīyah Muslim	1,740,000
Sunnī Muslim	340,000
Hindu	180,000
Christian	90,000
other	10,000
Pakistan	
Sunnī Muslim	106,430,000
Shīʿī Muslim	28,380,000
Christian	2,840,000
Hindu	2,550,000
other	1,700,000
Palau	
Roman Catholic	7,000
Modekne	5,000
Protestant	5,000
other	1,000
Panama	
Roman Catholic	2,220,000
Protestant	400,000
other	150,000
Papua New Guinea	
Protestant	2,760,000
Roman Catholic	1,300,000
Anglican	180,000
other	360,000
Paraguay	
Roman Catholic	4,620,000
Protestant	260,000
other	200,000
Peru	
Roman Catholic	22,030,000
Protestant	1,640,000
other (mostly non-religious)	1,130,000
Philippines	
Roman Catholic	60,640,000
Protestant	3,970,000
Muslim	3,340,000
Aglipayan	1,920,000
Church of Christ (Iglesia ni Cristo)	1,710,000
other	1,550,000
Poland	
Roman Catholic	35,060,000
Polish Orthodox	550,000
other (mostly non-religious)	3,060,000
Portugal	
Roman Catholic	9,190,000
other	780,000
Puerto Rico	
Roman Catholic	2,450,000
Protestant	1,070,000
other	270,000
Qatar	
Muslim (mostly Sunnī)	550,000
other	29,000
Réunion	
Roman Catholic	650,000
other (mostly Muslim)	40,000
Romania	
Romanian Orthodox	19,530,000
Roman Catholic	1,150,000
other	1,820,000
Russia	
Russian Orthodox	23,980,000
Muslim	14,690,000
Protestant	1,340,000
Jewish	600,000
other (mostly non-religious)	106,250,000
Rwanda	
Roman Catholic	5,170,000
traditional beliefs	1,990,000
Protestant	720,000
Muslim	80,000
St. Kitts and Nevis	
Anglican	14,000
Methodist	12,000
other	16,000
St. Lucia	
Roman Catholic	119,000
other	32,000
St. Vincent and the Grenadines	
Anglican	47,000
Methodist	24,000
Roman Catholic	13,000
other	29,000
Samoa	
Mormon	44,000
Congregational	42,000
Roman Catholic	36,000
Methodist	21,000
other	28,000
San Marino	
Roman Catholic	23,000
other	3,000
São Tomé and Príncipe	
Roman Catholic	122,000
Protestant	14,000
Saudi Arabia	
Sunnī Muslim	19,400,000
Shīʿī Muslim	690,000
Christian	610,000
other	80,000
Senegal	
Sunnī Muslim	8,950,000
traditional beliefs	580,000
Christian	190,000
Seychelles	
Roman Catholic	69,000
other	10,000
Sierra Leone	
Sunnī Muslim	2,750,000
traditional beliefs	1,370,000
Christian	460,000
Singapore	
Buddhist and Taoist	1,705,000
Muslim	472,000
Protestant	277,000
Roman Catholic	130,000
Hindu	103,000
nonreligious	457,000
other	19,000
Slovakia	
Roman Catholic	3,270,000
Slovak Evangelical	340,000
atheist	530,000
other	1,290,000
Slovenia	
Roman Catholic	1,640,000
other	340,000
Solomon Islands	
Protestant	178,000
Anglican	144,000
Roman Catholic	82,000
other	22,000
Somalia	
Sunnī Muslim	6,830,000
other	10,000
South Africa[4]	
Christian	23,080,000
Protestant	11,370,000
Dutch (Afrikaans) Reformed Churches	4,080,000
other Protestant	7,290,000
Methodist	2,030,000
Presbyterian	450,000
United Congregational	430,000
Lutheran	860,000
Apostolic Faith Mission of South Africa	450,000
New Apostolic Church	160,000
other Apostolic	480,000
Baptist	280,000
Pentecostal Protestant	80,000
African Protestant Church	30,000
Full Gospel	230,000
Pentecostal	20,000
Salvation Army	40,000
Seventh-day Adventist	90,000
Swiss	50,000
Assemblies of God	170,000
other	1,430,000
Roman Catholic	2,630,000
Anglican	1,320,000
Greek Orthodox	30,000
black independent churches	7,720,000
Zion Christian Church	1,700,000
other	6,020,000
Mormon	10,000
Hindu	440,000
Muslim	380,000
Jewish	80,000
other beliefs	30,000
nonreligious	420,000
not stated	10,320,000
Spain	
Roman Catholic	26,270,000
Muslim	450,000
other (mostly non-religious)	12,650,000
Sri Lanka	
Buddhist	12,980,000
Hindu	2,900,000
Muslim	1,410,000
Roman Catholic	1,290,000
other	150,000
Sudan, The	
Sunnī Muslim	24,490,000
traditional beliefs	5,600,000
Christian	3,050,000
other	410,000
Suriname	
Hindu	114,000
Roman Catholic	88,000
Muslim	82,000
Protestant	68,000
other	66,000
Swaziland	
Christian	640,000
other (mostly traditional beliefs)	330,000
Sweden	
Church of Sweden (Lutheran)	7,660,000
other	1,200,000
Switzerland	
Roman Catholic	3,280,000
Protestant	2,850,000
other	990,000
Syria	
Sunnī Muslim	11,350,000
Shīʿī Muslim	1,840,000
Christian	840,000
Druze	460,000
other	850,000
Taiwan	
nonreligious	10,430,000
Buddhist	4,990,000
Taoist	3,950,000
I Kuan Tao	970,000
Protestant	430,000
Roman Catholic	310,000
Tien Te Chiao	210,000
Tien Ti Chiao	190,000
Confucianism (Li)	140,000
Hsuan Yuan Chiao	140,000
Muslim	50,000
Shinto (Tenrikyo)	20,000
Baha'i	20,000
Tajikistan	
Sunnī Muslim	4,890,000
Shīʿī Muslim	310,000
Russian Orthodox	90,000
other (mostly nonreligious)	820,000
Tanzania	
Muslim	10,710,000
traditional beliefs	10,710,000
Christian	9,180,000
Thailand	
Buddhist	58,020,000
Muslim	2,470,000
Christian	340,000
other	370,000
Togo	
traditional beliefs	2,880,000
Roman Catholic	1,050,000
Sunnī Muslim	590,000
Protestant	330,000
other	60,000
Tonga	
Free Wesleyan	42,000
Roman Catholic	16,000
other	40,000
Trinidad and Tobago	
Roman Catholic	375,000
Hindu	303,000
Protestant	240,000
Anglican	139,000
Muslim	74,000
other	144,000
Tunisia	
Sunnī Muslim	9,330,000
other	50,000
Turkey	
Muslim (mostly Sunnī)	64,410,000
other	160,000
Turkmenistan	
Muslim (mostly Sunnī)	4,120,000
Russian Orthodox	110,000
other (mostly nonreligious)	500,000
Tuvalu	
Congregational	8,900
other	1,500
Uganda	
Roman Catholic	7,320,000
Anglican	7,320,000
traditional beliefs	3,990,000
Muslim (mostly Sunnī)	3,550,000
Ukraine	
Ukrainian Orthodox (Russian patriarchy)	9,790,000
Ukrainian Orthodox (Kiev patriarchy)	4,900,000
Ukrainian Autocephalous Orthodox	340,000
Ukrainian Catholic (Uniate)	3,520,000
Protestant	1,790,000
Roman Catholic	590,000
Jewish	440,000
other (mostly nonreligious)	28,930,000
United Arab Emirates	
Sunnī Muslim	2,200,000
Shīʿī Muslim	410,000
other	100,000
United Kingdom	
Christian	38,980,000
Anglican	24,930,000
Protestant	5,890,000
Roman Catholic	5,760,000
Eastern Orthodox	580,000
other Christian	1,030,000
Muslim	830,000
Hindu	410,000
Jewish	300,000
Sikh	240,000
other (mostly non-religious and atheist)	28,240,000
United States	
Christian (professing)	230,720,000
Christian (affiliated)	198,150,000
Protestant	121,720,000
Roman Catholic	60,150,000
Eastern Orthodox	5,700,000
Anglican	2,380,000
other Christian	11,540,000
multiply affiliated Christians	-3,340,000
Christian (unaffiliated)	32,580,000
nonreligious	23,670,000
Jewish	5,580,000
Muslim	3,810,000
Buddhist	1,890,000
atheist	880,000
Hindu	810,000
Baha'i	690,000
New-Religionist	610,000
Sikh	190,000
other	1,400,000
Uruguay	
Roman Catholic	2,520,000
Protestant	140,000
other	560,000
Uzbekistan	
Muslim (mostly Sunnī)	21,200,000
Russian Orthodox	240,000
other (mostly nonreligious)	2,650,000
Vanuatu	
Presbyterian	65,000
Roman Catholic	26,000
Anglican	25,000
other	66,000
Venezuela	
Roman Catholic	21,550,000
other	1,690,000
Vietnam	
Buddhist	50,820,000
Roman Catholic	5,890,000
New-Religionist	
Cao Dai	2,680,000
Hoa Hao	1,610,000
other	15,240,000
Virgin Islands (U.S.)	
Protestant	54,000
Roman Catholic	40,000
other	24,000
West Bank	
Muslim (mostly Sunnī)	1,540,000
Jewish[5]	190,000
Christian and other	150,000
Western Sahara	
Sunnī Muslim	288,000
Yemen	
Muslim (mostly Sunnī)	16,370,000
other	20,000
Yugoslavia	
Serbian Orthodox	6,670,000
Sunnī Muslim	2,030,000
Roman Catholic	620,000
other (mostly nonreligious)	1,350,000
Zambia	
traditional beliefs	2,550,000
Protestant	2,170,000
Roman Catholic	1,600,000
other	3,080,000
Zimbabwe	
traditional beliefs	4,470,000
Protestant	2,340,000
African Christian	1,490,000
Roman Catholic	770,000
other	1,970,000

[1]Official 1986 census figure is 5.9 percent. [2]Includes the Golan Heights and East Jerusalem; excludes the West Bank and Gaza Strip. [3]Many Japanese practice both Shintoism and Buddhism. [4]Excludes the former black independent states of Bophuthatswana, Ciskei, Transkei, and Venda, in which there are about 5,960,000 Christians and 2,140,000 practicers of traditional beliefs. [5]Excludes East Jerusalem.

Vital statistics, marriage, family

This table provides some of the basic measures of the factors that influence the size, direction, and rates of population change within a country. The accuracy of these data depends on the effectiveness of each respective national system for registering vital and civil events (birth, death, marriage, etc.) and on the sophistication of the analysis that can be brought to bear upon the data so compiled.

Data on birth rates, for example, depend not only on the completeness of registration of births in a particular country but also on the conditions under which those data are collected: Do all births take place in a hospital? Are the births reported comparably in all parts of the country? Are the records of the births tabulated at a central location in a timely way with an effort to eliminate inconsistent reporting of birth events, perinatal mortality, etc.? Similar difficulties attach to death rates but with the added need to identify "cause of death." Even in a developed country such identifications are often left to nonmedical personnel, and in a developing country with, say, only one physician for every 10,000 population, there will be too few physicians to perform autopsies to assess accurately the cause of death after the fact and also too few to provide ongoing care at a level where records would permit inference about cause of death based on prior condition or diagnosis.

Calculating natural increase, which at its most basic is simply the difference between the birth and death rates, may be affected by the differing degrees of completeness of birth and death registration for a given country. The total fertility rate may be understood as the average number of children that would be borne per woman if all childbearing women lived to the end of their childbearing years and bore children at each age at the average rate for that age. Calculating a meaningful fertility rate requires

analysis of changing age structure of the female population over time, changing mortality rates among mothers and their infants, and changing medical practice at births, each improvement of natural survivorship or medical support leading to greater numbers of live-born children and greater numbers of children who survive their first year (the basis for measurement of infant mortality, another basic indicator of demographic conditions and trends within a population).

As indicated above, data for causes of death are not only particularly difficult to obtain, since many countries are not well equipped to collect the data, but also difficult to assess, as their accuracy may be suspect and their meaning may be subject to varying interpretation. Take the case of a citizen of a less developed country who dies of what is clearly a lung infection: Was the death complicated by chronic malnutrition, itself complicated by a parasitic infestation, these last two together so weakening the subject that he died of an infection that he might have survived had his general health been better? Similarly, in a developed country: Someone may die from what is identified in an autopsy as a cerebrovascular accident, but if that accident occurred in a vascular system that was weakened by diabetes, what was the actual cause of death? Statistics on causes of death seek to identify the "underlying" cause (that which sets the final train of events leading to death in motion) but often must settle for the most proximate cause or symptom. Even this kind of analysis may be misleading for those charged with interpreting the data with a view to ordering health-care priorities for a particular country. The eight groups of causes of death utilized here include most, but not all, of the detailed causes classified by the World Health Organization and would not, thus, aggregate to the country's crude death rate for the same year. Among the

Vital statistics, marriage, family

country	vital rates						causes of death (rate per 100,000 population)								
	year	birth rate per 1,000 population	death rate per 1,000 population	infant mortality rate per 1,000 live births	rate of natural increase per 1,000 population	total fertility rate	year	infectious and parasitic diseases	malignant neoplasms (cancers)	endocrine and metabolic disorders	diseases of the nervous system	diseases of the circulatory system	diseases of the respiratory system	diseases of the digestive system	accidents, poisoning, and violence
Afghanistan	1997	43.0	18.0	146.7	25.0	6.1	...	...	...	...	...	...	...	...	...
Albania	1996	16.6	4.7	32.0[2]	11.9	20.4	1993	10.8	53.8	5.1	24.1	187.0	84.5	16.5	41.7
Algeria	1996	28.5	5.9	48.7	22.6	3.6	...	...	...	...	...	...	...	...	...
American Samoa	1993	37.8	4.2	11.0	33.6	5.44	1990	16.4[5]	46.8	16.4[6]	...	131.1[7]	65.6[8]	...	58.5
Andorra	1995	11.0	3.4	7.7	7.6	1.7	...	...	...	...	...	...	...	...	...
Angola	1995–2000	47.7	18.7	124.0	29.0	6.7	...	...	...	...	...	...	...	...	...
Antigua and Barbuda	1995	20.9	6.7	17.2[9]	14.2	1.7[9]	1988	14.0	44.5	25.4	7.6	237.5	44.5	15.2	5.1
Argentina	1995–2000	19.9	7.9	22.0	12.0	2.6	1991	27.3	143.0	26.3	13.7	337.3	49.0	33.5	51.6
Armenia	1995–2000	13.3	7.5	25.0	5.8	1.7	1993	11.0	93.8	21.6[12]	4.9[12]	369.7	51.4	27.8	62.8
Aruba	1995	17.4	6.2	9.6[13]	11.2	1.8[14]	1991	9.8	124.9	47.7	4.2	189.5	30.9	23.9	11.2
Australia	1996	14.1	6.9	5.7	7.2	1.8	1995	6.0	190.0	23.0	17.0	296.0	52.0	21.0	41.0
Austria	1996	10.8	9.9	5.0	0.9	1.5	1995	2.1	243.5	25.1	15.9	539.9	47.6	25.1	60.8
Azerbaijan	1995–2000	19.2	6.6	33.0	12.6	2.3	1994	28.8	67.4	12.8	12.0	336.3	98.8	8.1	106.4
Bahamas, The	1995	22.5	5.9	19.0	16.6	2.0	1990	18.0	80.4	72.2	11.0	126.3	52.2	29.0	40.8
Bahrain	1995–2000	21.0	3.6	18.0	17.4	3.0	1991	2.8	32.3	16.8	3.8	86.6	27.7	10.2	19.0
Bangladesh	1997	26.8	12.2	79.0	14.6	3.2	...	...	...	...	...	...	...	...	...
Barbados	1996	13.3	9.1	14.2	4.2	1.8	1992	19.0	178.5	120.2	17.1	366.8	39.9	28.9	40.3
Belarus	1996	9.3	13.0	12.6	–3.7	1.7[15]	1993	8.0	184.5	9.0[16]	14.7	624.7	69.7	8.9	132.6
Belgium	1996	11.4	10.4	5.6	1.0	1.6[17]	1990	11.1	270.1	23.1	38.0	398.9	88.1	38.8	65.1
Belize	1996	32.8	5.7	33.9	27.1	4.2	1990	...	52.4	37.0[6]	...	164.0	57.1	32.8	92.6[19]
Benin	1996	46.0	13.0	103.0	33.0	6.6	...	...	...	...	...	...	...	...	...
Bermuda	1992	15.1	7.4	8.8	7.7	1.8[13]	1990	...	181.5	...	...	344.4	25.2	...	38.6
Bhutan	1997	41.3	13.9	105.0	27.4	5.9	...	...	...	...	...	...	...	...	...
Bolivia	1995–2000	33.2	9.1	66.0	20.4	4.4	...	...	...	...	...	...	...	...	...
Bosnia and Herzegovina	1995	6.5	15.5	43.2	–9.0	1.0	1989	9.9	122.6[21]	12.6	11.9	344.1	29.0	29.2	47.1
Botswana	1991–95	37.1	6.6	39.0[15]	30.5	4.5[9]	...	...	...	...	...	...	...	...	...
Brazil	1996	20.8	9.2	55.3	11.6	2.3	1994[22]	41	94	45[16]	9	238	79	36	104
Brunei	1997	23.3	3.0	9.0	20.3	2.9	1986	5.3	27.0	...	...	80.0	23.4	...	39.8
Bulgaria	1996	8.6	14.0	15.6	–5.4	1.2[23]	1995	7.3	192.4	27.3	8.0	869.8	66.0	42.8	66.0
Burkina Faso	1996	47.0	20.0	117.8	27.0	6.8	...	...	...	...	...	...	...	...	...
Burundi	1996	42.7	17.8	104.8	24.9	6.5	...	...	...	...	...	...	...	...	...
Cambodia	1997	43.0	15.0	106.0	28.0	5.8	...	...	...	...	...	...	...	...	...
Cameroon	1995–2000	39.3	11.9	58.0	27.4	5.3	...	...	...	...	...	...	...	...	...
Canada	1996	12.5	7.2	6.1[23]	5.3	1.7[15]	1993	10.9	196.7	22.2	19.9	274.4	62.8	26.3	47.2
Cape Verde	1995–2000	31.9	7.1	41.0	24.8	3.6	1980	153.7	43.8	20.6	16.5	135.8	72.3	27.7	30.1
Central African Republic	1997	39.2	17.0	108.0	22.2	5.2	...	...	...	...	...	...	...	...	...
Chad	1995–2000	41.6	17.3	115.0	24.3	5.5	...	...	...	...	...	...	...	...	...
Chile	1995	19.7	5.5	11.1	14.2	2.3	1993	15.1	111.5	16.2	8.0	157.4	64.9	34.2	66.1
China	1995–2000	16.2	7.1	38	9.1	1.8	1994[24]	15.2	117.7	17.2[16]	4.4	206.4	125.3	25.3	56.6
Colombia	1996	25.9	5.9	26.9[23]	20.0	2.9	1991	18.3	62.9	12.5	7.4	144.7	37.9	16.7	132.3
Comoros	1996	45.8	10.3	75.3	35.5	6.7	...	...	...	...	...	...	...	...	...
Congo, Dem. Rep. of the	1995–2000	44.9	13.5	89.0	31.4	6.2	...	...	...	...	...	...	...	...	...
Congo, Rep. of the	1995–2000	42.5	14.6	90	27.9	5.9	...	...	...	...	...	...	...	...	...
Costa Rica	1995	23.8	4.2	13.3	19.6	2.8	1994	9.7	80.0	12.6	8.5	126.6	40.6	24.6	49.7
Côte d'Ivoire	1995–2000	37.2	13.8	86	23.4	5.1	...	...	...	...	...	...	...	...	...
Croatia	1995	10.5	10.6	8.9	–0.1	1.5[18]	1994	8.6	216.1	20.6	8.2	517.4	46.0	50.1	77.8
Cuba	1996	13.5	7.2	8.0	6.3	1.8[20]	1990	9.4	128.7	23.3	10.6	294.7	58.0	26.3	79.9
Cyprus	1995	15.4	7.7	4.9	7.7	2.1	...	...	...	...	...	...	...	...	...
Czech Republic	1996	8.8	10.9	6.0	–2.1	1.4[23]	1995	2.4	277.1	10.8	9.0	638.4	49.1	41.9	82.3
Denmark	1996	12.9	11.6	5.7	1.3	1.8	1994	9.8	296.6	21.3	14.5	471.3	95.6	50.3	70.8

lesser causes excluded by the present classification are: benign neoplasms; nutritional disorders; anemias; mental disorders; kidney and genito-urinary diseases not classifiable under the main groups; maternal deaths (for which data *are* provided, however, in the "Health services" table); diseases of the skin and musculoskeletal systems; congenital and perinatal conditions; and general senility and other ill-defined (ill-diagnosed) conditions, a kind of "other" category.

Expectation of life is probably the most accurate single measure of the quality of life in a given society. It summarizes in a single number all of the natural and social stresses that operate upon individuals in that society. The number may range from as few as 40 years of life in the least developed countries to as much as 80 years for women in the most developed nations. The lost potential in the years separating those two numbers is prodigious, regardless of how the loss arises—wars and civil violence, poor public health services, or poor individual health practice in matters of nutrition, exercise, stress management, and so on.

Data on marriages and marriage rates probably are less meaningful in terms of international comparisons than some of the measures mentioned above because the number, timing, and kinds of social relationships that substitute for marriage depend on many kinds of social variables—income, degree of social control, heterogeneity of the society (race, class, language communities), or level of development of civil administration (if one must travel for a day or more to obtain a legal civil ceremony, one may forgo it). Nevertheless, the data for a single country say specific things about local practice in terms of the age at which a man or woman typically marries, and the overall rate will at least define the number of legal civil marriages, though it cannot say anything about other, less formal arrangements

(here the figure for the legitimacy rate for children in the next section may identify some of the societies in which economics or social constraints may operate to limit the number of marriages that are actually confirmed on civil registers). The available data usually include both first marriages and remarriages after annulment, divorce, widowhood, or the like.

The data for families provide information about the average size of a family unit (individuals related by blood or civil register) and the average number of children under a specified age (set here at 15 to provide a consistent measure of social minority internationally, though legal minority depends on the laws of each country). When well-defined family data are not collected as part of a country's national census or vital statistics surveys, data for households have been substituted on the assumption that most households worldwide represent families in some conventional sense. But increasing numbers of households worldwide are composed of unrelated individuals (unmarried heterosexual couples, aged [or younger] groups sharing limited [often fixed] incomes for reasons of economy, or homosexual couples). Such arrangements do not yet represent great numbers overall. Increasing numbers of census programs, however, even in developing countries, are making more adequate provision for distinguishing these nontraditional, often nonfamily households.

Internet resources for further information:
- World Health Organization (World)
  http://www.who.ch/
- Pan American Health Organization (the Americas)
  http://www.paho.org
- National Center for Health Statistics (U.S.)
  http://www.cdc.gov/nchswww/nchshome.htm

expectation of life at birth (latest year)		nuptiality, family, and family planning														country
		marriages			age at marriage (latest)						families (F), households (H) (latest)					
		year	total number	rate per 1,000 population	groom (percent)			bride (percent)			families (households)		children		induced abortions	
male	female				19 and under	20–29	30 and over	19 and under	20–29	30 and over	total ('000)	size	number under age 15	percent legiti-mate	number	ratio per 100 live births	
46.4	45.2	...	...	...	...	...	...	...	...	...	H 2,110	H 6.2	H 2.8[1]	...	...	...	Afghanistan
68.0	74.0	1991	24,853	7.6	1.5	80.4	18.1	24.0	71.4	4.6	F 675	F 4.7	F 1.6	...	...	...	Albania
67.2	69.5	1993	153,137	5.7	0.7[3]	67.1[3]	32.2[3]	29.8[3]	61.4[3]	8.8[3]	H 3,824	H 6.9	H 3.0	...	...	...	Algeria
69.0	74.0	1990	370	7.8	...	...	...	...	...	...	H 7	H 7.0	H 2.7	72.0	...	...	American Samoa
75.6	81.7	1994	132	2.0	...	...	...	...	...	...					...	...	Andorra
44.9	48.1	...	...	...	...	...	...	...	...	...		H 4.8			...	...	Angola
71.5	75.8	1988	382	4.9	1.0[10]	37.4[11]	61.6	3.7[10]	52.4[11]	43.9	H 18	H 3.2	H 1.2	23.4	...	...	Antigua and Barbuda
69.6	76.8	1983	177,010	6.0	5.6	71.5	22.9	26.0	58.6	15.4	H 10,097	H 3.2	H 1.0	67.5	...	...	Argentina
67.2	74.0	1994	17,300	4.6	5.0	73.8	21.2	39.3	49.9	10.8	H 559	H 4.7	H 1.8	87.7	27,958	39.6	Armenia
71.1	77.1	1992	566	7.9	...	...	...	...	...	...	H 19	H 3.6		63.2	...	...	Aruba
75.4	81.1	1996	109,386	6.0	0.7	54.5	44.8	3.6	63.6	32.8	H 6,636	H 2.6	H 0.6	75.0	...	...	Australia
73.5	80.1	1994	43,284	5.4	1.2	55.1	43.7	5.3	64.9	29.8	H 3,131	H 2.5	H 0.5	75.2	...	...	Austria
66.5	74.5	1994	47,386	6.4	1.2[13]	80.4[13]	18.4[13]	24.8[13]	63.9[13]	11.3[13]	H 1,381	H 4.8	H 1.7	97.5	42,134	23.2	Azerbaijan
68.0	77.2	1994	2,506	9.2	19.0[12]	53.0[12]	27.7[12]	34.0[12]	48.3[12]	17.1[12]	H 68	H 3.9		44.7	...	...	Bahamas, The
71.1	75.3	1994	2,973	5.3	2.2	63.8	34.0	25.8	56.2	18.0	H 67	H 6.5	H 2.2	...	...	...	Bahrain
58.0	58.0	1995	1,320,000	10.2	...	...	...	...	...	...	H 19,980	H 5.6		...	...	...	Bangladesh
71.6	77.2	1993	2,310	8.5	0.1	40.2	59.7	1.4	53.6	44.9	H 67	H 3.5	H 1.5	26.9	723	19.6	Barbados
66.0	75.7	1993	82,326	7.9	6.5	71.5	22.0	30.7	51.3	18.0	H 2,796	H 3.2	H 0.8	91.0	85,685	73.0	Belarus
73.0	79.8	1994	51,962	5.1	0.7[18]	64.9[18]	34.4[18]	4.9[18]	69.5[18]	25.6[18]	F 3,613	F 2.7	F 0.5	88.7	...	...	Belgium
66.6	70.6	1994	1,347	5.3	6.5	57.2	36.3	24.2	51.6	24.2	H 38	H 4.9	H 2.2	41.6	990	15.1	Belize
50.7	54.7	1980–85	...	12.8	...	...	...	...	...	...		H 5.9		...	...	...	Benin
73.0	79.0	1992	909	15.1	0.2[20]	37.4[20]	62.4[20]	1.5[20]	49.4[20]	49.1[20]	H 22	H 2.6	H 0.5	63.9	92	11.0	Bermuda
51.0	53.0	...	...	...	...	...	...	...	...	...		H 5.4		...	...	...	Bhutan
59.8	63.2	1980	26,990	4.8	8.3	75.1	16.6	26.1	55.4	18.5	H 1,655	H 3.8	H 1.6	80.9	...	...	Bolivia
72.1	77.7	1990	31,449	7.0	2.1	75.2	22.7	28.5	59.2	12.3	H 1,203	H 3.6	H 1.1	...	...	...	Bosnia and Herzegovina
59.5	65.6	1986	1,638	1.5	—	33.0	67.0	5.0	69.2	25.8	H 125	H 5.7	H 2.0	28.8	17	0.1	Botswana
56.7	66.8	1994	763,129	5.0	7.5[12]	70.6[12]	21.9[12]	32.4[12]	54.7[12]	12.9[12]	F 39,768	F 3.7	1.2	...	...	...	Brazil
73.0	78.0	1993	1,971	7.1	10.6[12]	50.1[12]	39.3[12]	11.4[12]	54.7[12]	33.9[12]	H 45	H 5.8	H 2.0	99.6	...	...	Brunei
67.1	74.9	1996	...	4.3	4.8[18]	75.9[18]	19.3[18]	34.8[18]	54.5[18]	10.7[18]	H 2,795	H 3.0	...	74.3	107,416	127.3	Bulgaria
43.5	42.9	...	...	...	...	...	...	...	...	...		H 6.2		...	...	...	Burkina Faso
44.3	47.3	...	...	...	...	...	...	...	...	...		H 4.6		...	...	...	Burundi
52.0	55.0	...	...	...	...	...	...	...	...	...		H 5.6		...	...	...	Cambodia
54.5	57.2	...	...	...	...	...	...	...	...	...		H 5.2		...	...	...	Cameroon
74.7	81.7	1993	159,316	5.5	0.9	52.1	47.0	3.9	60.2	35.9	H 10,018	H 2.7	H 0.6	83.8	99,971	25.7	Canada
65.5	67.5	1992	1,360	3.8	2.3[14]	62.4[14]	35.3[14]	17.0[14]	61.1[14]	21.9[14]	F 59	F 5.1	...	55.2	...	...	Cape Verde
44.7	48.3	...	...	...	...	...	...	...	...	...		H 4.7		...	...	...	Central African Republic
46.3	49.3	...	...	...	...	...	...	...	...	...		H 3.9		...	...	...	Chad
71.8	77.8	1994	91,555	6.5	5.8	68.8	25.4	19.9	62.4	17.7	H 3,537	H 3.8	...	61.9	67	—	Chile
68.2	71.7	1994	9,290,027	7.8	...	...	...	...	...	...	H 278.6[25]	H 4.1	H 1.1	...	10,500,000	47.7	China
65.4	73.4	1986	70,350	2.3	4.0	64.1	31.5	22.3	58.5	19.0	F 4,772	F 5.4	F 2.5	75.2	...	...	Colombia
56.4	61.0	...	...	...	...	...	...	...	...	...		H 5.6		...	...	...	Comoros
51.3	54.5	...	...	...	...	...	...	...	...	...		H 6.0		...	...	...	Congo, Dem. Rep. of the
48.6	53.4	...	...	...	...	...	...	...	...	...	H 326	H 4.7	H 2.0	...	...	...	Congo, Rep. of the
71.9	77.5	1995	23,564	7.1	7.3[15]	61.5[15]	31.2[15]	26.6[15]	52.1[15]	21.3[15]	H 772	H 4.1	...	53.4	...	...	Costa Rica
50.0	52.2	...	...	...	...	...	...	...	...	...		H 5.4		...	...	...	Côte d'Ivoire
68.6	76.0	1994	23,966	5.0	1.4[15]	67.2[15]	31.4[15]	15.7[15]	66.2[15]	18.1[15]	H 1,544	H 3.1	H 0.6	...	...	...	Croatia
73.9	77.6	1991	161,160	15	6.3	54.1	39.6	18.8	51.0	30.2	F 2,860	F 3.7	H 1.6	99.6	124,059	71.3	Cuba
75.3	79.8	1994	6,097	9.6	0.6	61.0	38.4	11.0	64.7	24.3	H 160	H 3.5	H 1.1	99.6	...	...	Cyprus
70.0	76.9	1996	53,896	5.2	5.1	66.4	28.5	19.8	61.3	18.9	H 3,557	H 2.9	...	84.4	61,590	64.1	Czech Republic
72.6	77.8	1995	34,970	6.7	0.3[15]	37.4[15]	62.3[15]	1.9[15]	48.6[15]	49.5[15]	H 2,027	H 2.2	...	53.5	17,598	25.2	Denmark

Vital statistics, marriage, family   (continued)

country	year	birth rate per 1,000 population	death rate per 1,000 population	infant mortality rate per 1,000 live births	rate of natural increase per 1,000 population	total fertility rate	year	infectious and parasitic diseases	malignant neoplasms (cancers)	endocrine and metabolic disorders	diseases of the nervous system	diseases of the circulatory system	diseases of the respiratory system	diseases of the digestive system	accidents, poisoning, and violence
Djibouti	1996	38.6	15.0	106.0	23.6	5.4	...	...	...	...	...	...	...	...	...
Dominica	1996	18.4	5.3	9.6	13.1	1.9	1990	37.5	116.6	51.4	9.7	273.5	43.0	20.8	18.0
Dominican Republic	1996	23.5	5.7	47.7	17.8	2.7	1985[26]	85	45	15[6]	7[27]	165	41	25	56
Ecuador	1995	15.8	4.4	30.5	11.4	11.4[15]	1992	52.0	50.0	11.8[6]	1.9[27]	93.1	40.6	13.2	66.7
Egypt	1997	27.8	8.6	71.0	19.2	3.5	1987	98.9	22.0	9.1	13.6	314.4	140.7	45.8	39.1
El Salvador	1996	27.7	6.6	31.5	21.1	3.2	1991[29]	43	49	17	12	120	43	38	140
Equatorial Guinea	1995–2000	40.8	16.2	107.0	24.6	5.5	...	...	...	...	...	...	...	...	...
Eritrea	1995–2000	39.8	14.7	98.0	25.1	5.3	...	...	...	...	...	...	...	...	...
Estonia	1996	9.0	12.9	10.5	–3.9	1.3[23]	1994	11.3	218.1	10.1	13.6	815.7	44.3	34.5	233.1
Ethiopia	1995–2000	48.2	16.2	107.0	32.0	7.0	...	...	...	...	...	...	...	...	...
Faroe Islands	1996	15.4	9.0	8.5[4]	6.4	2.7[20]	1992	4.3	191.3	14.9[6]	...	352.8	59.5	14.9	57.4
Fiji	1997	22.7	4.6	20.0	18.1	2.8	1987	18.2	35.5	27.3[6]	2.4[27]	153.4	31.7	15.5	32.2
Finland	1996	11.8	9.6	3.9	2.2	1.7	1994	7.0	192.3	12.0	18.0	448.6	71.8	36.3	85.0
France	1996	12.6	9.2	4.9	3.4	1.7[23]	1993	12.6	247.5	27.6	20.1	302.0	70.0	45.4	81.0
French Guiana	1993	29.2	4.1	15.4	25.1	3.7[4]	1989	61.7	58.1	16.3	10.9	114.3	20.9	13.6	98.0
French Polynesia	1996	21.0	4.5	10.2	16.5	3.9[20]	1986–92	22.0	83.0	12.0	12.0	118.0	35.0	14.0	69.0
Gabon	1995–2000	37.6	14.3	85.0	23.3	5.4	...	...	...	...	...	...	...	...	...
Gambia, The	1995–2000	39.9	17.4	122.0	22.5	5.2	...	...	...	...	...	...	...	...	...
Gaza Strip	1995–2000	46.7	5.3	37.0	41.4	8.0	...	...	...	...	...	...	...	...	...
Georgia	1996	9.9	6.4	17.4	3.5	2.2[15]	1990	12.7	100.8	14.6	4.3	548.4	43.3	8.5	56.1
Germany	1995	9.3	10.7	5.6	–1.4	1.3[15]	1994	7.3	260.2	33.6	16.9	527.4	64.7	52.5	50.1
Ghana	1995–2000	38.2	10.4	73.0	27.8	5.3	...	...	...	...	...	...	...	...	...
Gibraltar	1996	16.5	8.3	5.7[4]	8.2	2.8[4]	1987	17.0	203.9	...	—	601.4	34.0	23.8	3.4
Greece	1996	9.7	9.6	8.1	0.1	1.4[18]	1994	6.4	206.7	10.3	11.7	478.5	52.0	24.3	42.4
Greenland	1994	20.7	8.0	13.0	12.7	2.9[12]	1993	27.1	186.3	...	...	188.2	47.0	12.7	152.0
Grenada	1996	21.3	7.9	14.3	13.4	3.8[23]	1987	9.6	82.8	57.3	7.4	264.3	45.6	38.2	...
Guadeloupe	1995–2000	18.5	6.5	8.0	12.0	2.1	1990	20.8[14]	121.2	23.0[14]	12.3[14]	186.8	30.5	29.7	72.9
Guam	1995	24.0	4.0	8.0	20.0	3.1	1994	1.4	60.0	26.5[6]	6.8	141.8	27.9	1.4	64.1
Guatemala	1994	35.4	7.5	53.9	27.9	4.8	1984	211.5	29.8	29.6	9.0	57.2	145.7	21.7	52.0
Guernsey	1996	11.2	10.4	7.6	0.8	1.6[13]	1996	5.3	282.3	15.9	15.9	441.1	150.0	49.4	24.7
Guinea	1995–2000	48.2	18.4	124.0	29.8	6.6	...	...	...	...	...	...	...	...	...
Guinea-Bissau	1995–2000	40.3	20.6	132.0	19.7	5.4	...	...	...	...	...	...	...	...	...
Guyana	1996	19.0	9.5	51.4	9.5	2.2	1984	19.3	37.1	33.3	11.6	202.5	39.8	74.0	56.5
Haiti	1996	33.5	15.5	105.1	18.0	4.8	...	...	...	...	...	...	...	...	...
Honduras	1993	35.8	6.4	47.2	29.4	4.9	1983	46.6	12.4	5.3	7.8	48.4	26.3	16.7	42.2
Hong Kong	1996	10.0	4.9	4.1	5.1	1.1[23]	1996	17.9	156.1	9.1	4.3	131.3	96.6	21.6	26.2
Hungary	1996	10.4	14.1	10.9	–3.7	1.6[23]	1994	8.2	318.7	20.6	12.3	722.9	67.0	117.6	115.6
Iceland	1995	16.0	7.2	4.6[33]	8.8	2.1	1994	4.1	166.5	5.3	14.7	300.4	80.1	15.8	35.7
India	1996	25.9	9.6	71.1	16.3	3.2	...	...	...	...	...	...	...	...	...
Indonesia	1997	22.4	7.9	51.0	14.5	2.6	...	...	...	...	...	...	...	...	...
Iran	1996	33.7	6.6	52.7	27.1	4.7	1990[35]	34	61	12[16]	26	304	48	24	108
Iraq	1994	34.1	9.8	91.9	24.3	4.9[9]	...	...	...	...	...	...	...	...	...
Ireland	1996	13.9	8.7	5.9[15]	5.2	1.8	1994	4.8	205.6	11.6	...	392.1	66.8	...	62.2
Isle of Man	1996	11.4	13.2	5.7[3]	–1.8	1.8[13]	1994	107.9	217.4	8.6[6]	—	552.7	204.4	20.2	95.0
Israel	1996	21.2	6.0	5.8	15.2	2.9	1993	9.6	137.6	20.3	10.0	268.8	32.0	18.9	36.7
Italy	1996	9.2	9.5	6.0	–0.3	1.2	1993	3.6	270.5	...	29.2	423.7	56.2	49.8	49.8
Jamaica	1995	23.2	5.0	28.6	18.2	3.0	1991	8.1	84.1	51.3	7.5	189.5	30.2	14.1	8.4
Japan	1995	9.5	7.4	4.2[15]	2.1	1.4	1994	12.7	196.4	11.5	6.2	239.1	94.7	32.1	49.1
Jersey	1991	12.5	9.9	6.0[13]	2.6	1.3[13]	...	...	...	...	...	...	...	...	...
Jordan	1995	32.9	3.0	34.0[15]	29.9	5.9[23]	...	...	...	...	...	...	...	...	...
Kazakstan	1995	16.7	10.2	27.9	6.5	2.5[15]	1994	30.3	133.5	10.6	9.0	456.6	87.4	30.3	125.0
Kenya	1996	32.4	10.8	55.2	21.6	4.3	...	...	...	...	...	...	...	...	...
Kiribati	1994	31.0	11.0	54.0[9]	20.0	3.3[36]	...	...	...	...	...	...	...	...	...
Korea, North	1996	22.5	5.3	23.0	17.2	2.3	1986	19.4	69.0	3.0[16]	6.5	224.9	46.7	51.6	38.2
Korea, South	1997	15.1	6.4	10.0[9]	8.7	1.7	1994	12.8	110.3	17.6	5.3	155.0	25.2	39.6	72.0
Kuwait	1995	24.3	2.2	11.1	22.1	3.7[15]	1994	5.8	22.6	6.6	6.0	76.5	11.9	3.8	35.2
Kyrgyzstan	1995	26.0	8.2	27.7	17.8	3.1[15]	1994	32.9	67.3	7.9	9.0	333.0	132.4	11.0	96.3
Laos	1997	44.3	13.7	87.0	30.6	6.2	...	...	...	...	...	...	...	...	...
Latvia	1996	7.9	13.8	15.9	–5.9	1.4[15]	1994	19.9	220.1	12.2	9.4	915.9	51.7	24.8	233.8
Lebanon	1994	24.9	4.3	28.0	20.6	2.9	...	...	...	...	...	...	...	...	...
Lesotho	1995–2000	35.4	10.6	72.0	24.8	4.9	...	...	...	...	...	...	...	...	...
Liberia	1995–2000	47.5	15.3	153.0	32.2	6.3	...	...	...	...	...	...	...	...	...
Libya	1995–2000	40.0	6.9	56.0	33.1	5.9	...	...	...	...	...	...	...	...	...
Liechtenstein	1995	11.7	6.7	5.5	5.0	1.5	1994	23.0	134.6	...	6.6	328.2	36.1	26.3	36.1
Lithuania	1996	10.6	11.6	10.1	–1.0	2.0[13]	1994	14.5	200.7	7.7	10.3	654.3	49.2	29.8	185.9
Luxembourg	1996	13.7	9.4	4.9	4.3	1.7	1994	8.9	234.5	18.8	13.6	391.1	68.4	44.8	62.7
Macau	1995	14.1	3.2	5.6	10.9	1.6[4]	1995	9.4	76.6	6.8	1.6	119.5	28.0	14.1	23.3
Macedonia	1995	14.9	7.6	22.7	7.3	2.2[15]	1993	12.9	6.2	16.4	4.7	385.8	34.5	14.8	35.3
Madagascar	1995–2000	41.1	9.9	77.0	31.2	5.7	...	...	...	...	...	...	...	...	...
Malawi	1996	41.6	24.5	139.9	17.1	5.9	1986[37]	711	27	25	60	50	265	34	78
Malaysia	1997	25.6	4.8	11.0	20.8	3.3	1994	15.4	20.4	4.2	1.0	54.0	7.9	7.5	29.0
Maldives	1997	41.8	7.6	50.0	34.2	6.8	1988	31.3	—	—	—	170.1	66.2	—	9.9
Mali	1995–2000	47.4	17.1	149.0	30.3	6.6	...	...	...	...	...	...	...	...	...
Malta	1996	12.2	7.5	10.5	4.7	1.8	1994	4.3	187.8	23.6	9.0	324.2	63.6	32.6	25.5
Marshall Islands	1996	26.1	4.0	26.0	22.1	7.0[18]	1993[38]	169.9	68.4	...	—	155.1	105.1	63.3	36.7
Martinique	1995–2000	16.8	7.1	7.0	9.7	2.0	1990	22.0	135.5	30.7	10.7[28]	208.0	34.2	31.3	54.8
Mauritania	1996	46.9	15.2	81.7	31.7	6.8	...	...	...	...	...	...	...	...	...
Mauritius	1995	18.3	6.7	19.7	11.6	2.1	1995	13.7	60.2	25.8	5.8	288.6	63.4	35.6	49.9
Mayotte	1991	43.7	6.0	38.0	37.7	6.8[13]	...	...	...	...	...	...	...	...	...
Mexico	1995	30.4	4.8	17.5	25.6	3.7[20]	1993	26.4	49.9	42.8	6.8	100.7	45.2	41.4	64.6
Micronesia	1997	35.0	8.0	49.0	27.0	5.1	1984	20.4	27.1	6.8	4.5	53.2	47.5	5.7	23.8
Moldova	1996	12.3	11.8	20.4	0.5	2.1[15]	1994	16.1	138.0	12.0	11.5	504.4	72.6	112.2	112.8
Monaco	1988	22.9	18.5	9.0[13]	4.4	1.2[13]	...	...	...	...	...	...	...	...	...
Mongolia	1996	22.0	7.6	40.5	14.4	4.5[15]	...	...	...	...	...	...	...	...	...
Morocco	1995–2000	25.3	6.7	51.0	18.6	3.1	1992	10.2	14.0	12.2	4.9	35.5	9.5	7.9	19.2

expectation of life at birth (latest year)		nuptiality, family, and family planning															country
		marriages			age at marriage (latest)						families (F), households (H) (latest)						
					groom (percent)			bride (percent)			families (households)		children		induced abortions		
male	female	year	total number	rate per 1,000 population	19 and under	20–29	30 and over	19 and under	20–29	30 and over	total ('000)	size	number under age 15	percent legitimate	number	ratio per 100 live births	
48.7	52.0	...															Djibouti
74.5	80.4	1990	228	3.3	...	41.2	58.8	3.1	58.3	38.6	H 19	H 5.6	H 2.2	96.8	...	...	Dominica
66.9	71.3	1992	25,351	3.6	8.0[28]	63.0[28]	29.0[28]	29.7[28]	51.0[28]	19.3[28]	H 1,804	H 3.9		32.8	562	0.5	Dominican Republic
67.5	72.6	1993	68,193	6.2	12.6	63.9	23.5	33.4	52.3	14.3		H 4.1		67.9	...	...	Ecuador
65.4	69.5	1993	479,000	8.3	3.8[20]	61.0[20]	35.2[20]	34.4[20]	52.9[20]	12.7[20]	H 9,733	H 4.9	H 2.1	100.0	...	...	Egypt
65.5	72.4	1992	23,084	4.2	6.6	54.8	38.6	21.5	51.4	27.1	H 1,092	H 4.8		30.6	...	...	El Salvador
48.4	51.6											H 4.5					Equatorial Guinea
49.1	52.1	1992	68									30					Eritrea
65.0	75.0	1995	6,852	4.5	5.3[15]	53.7[15]	41.0[15]	17.2[15]	47.8[15]	35.0[15]	H 427	H 3.1	H 0.8	66.1	28,403	157.7	Estonia
48.4	51.6	...										H 4.5[30]					Ethiopia
72.8	79.6	1990	203	4.3	1.0[31]	68.8[31]	30.2[31]	8.8[31]	70.7[31]	20.5[31]	F 14	F 3.0	F 0.9	57.5	26	3.3	Faroe Islands
70.0	78.0	1988	6,892	9.6	6.6[31]	68.7[31]	24.7[31]	31.0[31]	55.8[31]	13.2[31]	F 97	F 6.0	F 2.5	82.7	...	...	Fiji
72.8	80.2	1995	23,737	4.6	1.1[15]	52.7[15]	46.2[15]	4.0[15]	61.1[15]	34.9[15]	F 2,270	F 2.2		66.9	10,013	15.4	Finland
73.7	81.8	1996	279,690	4.8	0.2[15]	55.7[15]	44.1[15]	2.0[15]	66.0[15]	32.0[15]	H 20,899	H 2.6	H 1.0	63.9	162,902	21.5	France
63.4	69.7	1992	716	5.3	...			...			H 33	H 3.4	H 1.2	20.3	388	16.8	French Guiana
68.4	72.8	1994	1,263	5.9	11.3[31,32]	75.8[31,32]	12.9[31,32]	41.5[31,32]	52.5[31,32]	6.0[31,32]	H 40	H 4.7	H 1.7	37.2	...	...	French Polynesia
53.8	57.2	...									H 136	H 4.0					Gabon
45.4	48.7	...										H 8.3					Gambia, The
66.2	69.3	...															Gaza Strip
68.9	76.5	1993	24,105	4.9	5.7[13]	66.2[13]	28.1[13]	27.8[13]	55.7[13]	16.5[13]	H 1,244	H 4.1	H 1.1	82.3	68,883	75.6	Georgia
72.5	79.0	1995	428,650	5.2	0.6[15]	49.4[15]	50.0[15]	3.6[15]	60.8[15]	35.6[15]	H 36,230	H 2.2	H 0.3	86.6	103,586	13.5	Germany
56.2	59.9	...									H 2,355	H 4.9	H 2.2				Ghana
73.4	80.4	1994	697	5.2							H 8	H 3.2	H 0.7	97.1	...	...	Gibraltar
74.6	79.8	1995	62,000	5.9	1.0[15]	54.5[15]	44.5[15]	10.7[15]	68.7[15]	20.6[15]	H 2,990	H 2.6	H 0.7	97.1	11,977	11.5	Greece
60.7	68.4	1991	451	8.1	1.1	44.6	54.3	2.7	59.6	37.7	F 31	F 1.8	F 0.5	28.0	962	80.7	Greenland
68.2	73.2	1991		4.3							H 24	H 3.7	H 2.2				Grenada
72.1	78.8	1992	1,880	4.7	0.5[4]	51.4[4]	48.0[4]	7.2[4]	61.4[4]	31.4[4]	H 112	H 3.4	H 0.9	39.3	561	8.7	Guadeloupe
73.0	79.0	1994	1,596	10.9	3.0[12]	55.5[12]	41.5[12]	9.2[12]	59.3[12]	31.5[12]	H 31	H 4.0	H 1.3	41.3	...	...	Guam
61.9	67.1	1993	46,789	4.7	15.9[14]	55.7[14]	28.4[14]	41.5[14]	38.0[14]	20.5[14]	H 1,806	H 5.2		34.8	...	...	Guatemala
		1996	340	5.8	...			...			H 21	H 2.6	H 0.5	73.2	...	...	Guernsey
46.0	47.0	...									H 1,064	H 4.7	H 2.2				Guinea
42.4	45.2	...									H 124	H 4.1	H 2.8	11.3			Guinea-Bissau
57.2	62.8	...									H 150	H 5.1	H 2.1				Guyana
47.3	51.3	...									H 1,147	H 4.4	H 1.8				Haiti
64.8	69.2	1983	19,875	4.9	7.7	65.1	27.2	27.9	58.5	13.6	H 463	H 5.7	H 2.8		...	...	Honduras
75.9	81.5	1996	37,045	5.9	0.9[15]	46.0[15]	53.1[15]	3.7[15]	66.3[15]	30.0[15]	H 1,840	H 3.2		94.5	17,600	25.2	Hong Kong
64.8	74.2	1995	54,000	5.3	4.2	65.2	24.6	19.6	64.3	16.1	F 3,058	F 2.9	F 0.8	81.5	74,491	64.4	Hungary
76.5	80.6	1995	1,238	4.6	0.2	44.3	56.5	2.3	55.5	42.2	H 85	H 2.9	H 1.3	39.1	775	17.4	Iceland
59.1	60.3	...									H 151,033	H 5.6	H 2.4		581,215	...	India
63.0	66.0	1992–93[34]	1,423,774	7.6	...			...			H 39,695	H 4.5	H 1.8		...	...	Indonesia
66.1	68.7	1993	460,888	7.9	...			...			H 9,759	H 5.1	H 2.2		...	...	Iran
57.3	60.4	1992	144,055	7.8							H 1,873	H 8.9	H 4.1		...	...	Iraq
72.3	77.9	1995	15,623	4.4	0.8[12]	67.4[12]	31.8[12]	2.4[12]	78.5[12]	19.1[12]	H 541	H 3.3	H 1.3	77.8	...	...	Ireland
		1994	452	6.5	0.4	42.7	56.9	2.2	54.0	43.8				76.1	...	...	Isle of Man
75.1	78.5	1995	33,365	6.4	3.5[18]	73.7[18]	22.8[18]	22.0[18]	67.4[18]	10.6[18]	H 1,355	H 3.7	H 1.1	98.5	17,164	15.3	Israel
74.1	80.5	1996	274,621	4.7	0.6	62.6	36.8	6.2	74.6	19.2	F 19,766	F 2.6	F 0.5	90.2	124,334	23.6	Italy
74.4	75.8	1994	15,171	6.1							H 554	H 4.2	H 1.4	14.9	...	...	Jamaica
76.4	82.8	1995		6.4	1.3	61.7	37.0	3.1	78.6	18.3	H 43,447	H 2.8		99.0	364,350	29.4	Japan
											H 29	H 2.6	H 0.4	88.1	313	29.2	Jersey
64.4	69.9	1992	37,216	8.0	5.2	72.4	22.4	39.2	54.3	6.5	H 11,891	H 6.1	H 3.4				Jordan
63.2	72.7	1993	146,161	8.6	7.7	74.1	18.2	35.6	51.3	13.1	H 3,824	H 4.0	H 1.4	87.6	206,877	65.4	Kazakstan
54.2	54.6	...									H 1,938	H 6.2	H 2.7		...	...	Kenya
62.0	67.0	1988	352	5.2							H 11	H 6.6	H 2.5				Kiribati
69.0	75.0	1987	188,007	9.3							H 4,054	H 4.8	H 1.7		...	...	Korea, North
69.0	76.0	1994	304,146	6.8	0.3	69.4	30.3	1.9	87.4	10.7	H 12,961	H 3.7	H 1.0	99.5	...	...	Korea, South
74.4	79.0	1993	11,418	7.8	6.1[12]	72.2[12]	21.7[12]	35.9[12]	53.3[12]	10.8[12]	H 246	H 7.4	H 1.6	100.0	...	...	Kuwait
63.9	72.6	1994	26,097	5.8	6.3	79.3	14.4	40.6	50.1	9.3	H 856	H 4.2	H 1.9	83.2	31,389	28.5	Kyrgyzstan
51.0	54.0	...										H 6.0					Laos
64.2	74.6	1995	11,072	4.4	6.5[15]	64.9[15]	28.8[15]	19.8[15]	56.1[15]	24.1[15]	H 732	H 3.1	H 0.8	73.6	26,795	110.5	Latvia
72.5	77.9	...									H 405	H 5.3	H 2.2				Lebanon
58.0	63.0	...									H 330	H 4.8	H 2.0				Lesotho
50.0	53.0	...									H 474	H 5.0					Liberia
63.9	67.5	...									F 383	F 5.4	F 2.9				Libya
66.5	79.5	1994	202	13.1	...	54.5	44.5	0.0	66.3	29.2	H 8	H 3.0	H 0.7	85.3	...	...	Liechtenstein
65.3	76.1	1995	22,150	6.0	8.4[18]	70.7[18]	20.9[18]	27.9[18]	55.0[18]	17.1[18]	H 1,000	H 3.2	H 0.8	93.3	42,023	89.9	Lithuania
72.6	79.1	1993	2,379	6.3	1.1	53.2	45.7	4.9	65.0	30.1	H 145	H 2.6	H 0.5	87.3	...	...	Luxembourg
68.1	71.8	1995	2,146	5.1	0.7	43.6	55.7	3.0	65.0	32.0	H 99	H 3.5	H 0.9	99.3	...	...	Macau
70.1	74.4	1994	15,736	7.6	5.1	75.4	19.5	27.7	62.5	9.8	H 468	H 3.8	H 1.3	91.5	18,754	57.9	Macedonia
57.0	60.0	...									H 1,709	H 4.7	H 2.0		...	...	Madagascar
35.9	36.5	...										H 4.3					Malawi
70.0	74.0	...									H 3,580	H 4.9					Malaysia
65.0	63.0	1995	4,998	19.7	13.7[18]	58.2[18]	29.1[18]	...				H 7.2					Maldives
46.4	49.7	1987	33,646	4.4	0.1	1.4	98.5	...			H 1,364	H 5.6					Mali
74.9	79.5	1995	2,203	6.2	2.3	73.4	24.3	9.4	76.3	14.3	H 76	H 3.3	H 1.2	95.8	...	...	Malta
61.9	65.0	...									H 5	H 8.7					Marshall Islands
73.7	80.3	1993	1,555	4.2	0.1[12]	46.8[12]	53.1[12]	3.3[12]	61.5[12]	35.2[12]	H 107	H 3.3	H 0.8	34.1	1,753	30.6	Martinique
46.1	52.1	...									H 246	H 5.0					Mauritania
66.5	74.0	1995	10,430	9.5	1.9[15]	59.9[15]	38.2[15]	25.5[15]	55.9[15]	18.6[15]	F 155	F 5.3	F 2.0	72.8	...	...	Mauritius
54.0	58.0	...									H 19	H 4.9	H 2.3	89.2	...	...	Mayotte
66.5	73.1	1994	671,640	7.2	15.7	65.2	19.1	34.6	53.7	11.7	H 17,152	H 5.1	H 2.0	72.5	...	...	Mexico
72.0	72.0	...									H 11	H 7.0					Micronesia
67.9	71.5	1993	39,469	9.1	5.9[4]	74.6[4]	19.5[4]	37.6[4]	46.9[4]	15.5[4]	H 1,144	H 3.4	H 1.1	89.6	52,003	74.7	Moldova
72.0	80.0	1987		7.5							H 14	H 2.2	H 0.3	96.8	...	...	Monaco
60.0	63.5	1989	16,100	7.8							F 428	F 4.8					Mongolia
64.8	68.5	...									H 2,819	H 5.8	H 2.5				Morocco

Vital statistics, marriage, family (continued)

country	vital rates						causes of death (rate per 100,000 population)								
	year	birth rate per 1,000 population	death rate per 1,000 population	infant mortality rate per 1,000 live births	rate of natural increase per 1,000 population	total fertility rate	year	infectious and parasitic diseases	malignant neoplasms (cancers)	endocrine and metabolic disorders	diseases of the nervous system	diseases of the circulatory system	diseases of the respiratory system	diseases of the digestive system	accidents, poisoning, and violence
Mozambique	1995–2000	42.5	17.5	110.0	25.0	6.1	...	...	...	...	...	...	...	...	...
Myanmar (Burma)	1997	27.4	9.9	79.0	17.5	3.3	...	...	...	...	...	...	...	...	...
Namibia	1995–2000	35.9	11.8	60.0	24.1	4.9	...	...	...	...	...	...	...	...	...
Nauru	1997	18.8	4.5	26.0[9]	14.3	2.5[13]	1976–81[39]	33.0	38.0	24.0	13.0	89.0	16.0	53.0	116.0
Nepal	1997	36.6	11.2	83.0	25.4	5.0	...	...	...	...	...	...	...	...	...
Netherlands, The	1995	12.3	8.8	5.1[9]	3.5	1.5	1994	6.7	237.1	28.9	14.6	335.9	73.7	32.6	34.3
Netherlands Antilles	1995	18.3	6.7	6.3[13]	12.5	2.2[12]	1995[40]	16.7	149.0	61.7	9.9	71.6	40.8	21.4	47.6
New Caledonia	1995	22.7	5.5	7.8	17.2	2.9[15]	1992	19.3	129.0	10.8	9.1	115.3	45.4	15.3	80.7
New Zealand	1995	16.3	7.9	6.7	8.4	2.0[15]	1993	4.1	205.1	19.5	13.0	346.7	78.2	21.2	50.3
Nicaragua	1996	33.8	6.0	45.8	27.8	4.0	1991[41]	100	56	18	13	142	73	34	93
Niger	1996	54.5	24.6	117.6	29.9	7.4	...	...	...	...	...	...	...	...	...
Nigeria	1990–95	45.4	15.4	84.2	30.0	6.4	...	...	...	...	...	...	...	...	...
Northern Mariana Islands	1992	29.0	3.0	9.0[2]	26.0	2.4[20]	1987	18.7	70.2[21]	23.4	14.0	135.7	70.2	9.4	145.1
Norway	1996	13.9	10.1	4.1[23]	3.5	1.9[23]	1993	7.4	237.0	17.0	17.6	483.7	125.8	29.8	56.5
Oman	1990–95	43.7	4.8	28.2[9]	38.9	6.9	...	...	...	...	...	...	...	...	...
Pakistan	1997	36.4	7.9	75.0	28.5	5.1	...	...	...	...	...	...	...	...	...
Palau	1997	22.0	8.0	21.0	14.0	3.2	1993	43.6	136.9	...	...	192.9	43.6	...	112.0
Panama	1996	22.5	5.2	25.3	17.3	2.6	1994	18.3	57.3[21]	14.2[6]	1.9[27]	118.4	24.0	7.5	58.0
Papua New Guinea	1997	32.4	10.0	62.0	22.4	4.7	...	...	...	...	...	...	...	...	...
Paraguay	1995–2000	31.3	5.4	39.0	25.9	4.2	1993[43]	33	53	22	8	162	38	17	45
Peru	1995–2000	24.9	6.4	50.1	18.5	3.0	1989[41]	85	73	19	11	115	100	36	67
Philippines	1997	28.7	5.8	36.0	22.9	3.7	1991	65.9	35.2	17.9	124.9	82.2	20.5	20.5	71.8
Poland	1995	12.0	10.1	14.0	1.9	2.1[4]	1994	6.8	198.0	15.2	7.9	512.7	32.7	32.8	75.4
Portugal	1996	11.5	10.8	6.9	0.3	1.4	1994	8.5	193.6	41.2	9.4	431.2	71.5	44.5	57.2
Puerto Rico	1996	17.2	7.9	11.5[15]	9.3	2.0[23]	1993	59.4	122.2	66.7	19.2	242.3	80.5	43.9	34.1
Qatar	1990–95	19.9	3.4	20.0	16.5	4.1	1992	3.4	21.4[21]	7.3[20]	2.6	59.9	7.5	3.4	36.0
Réunion	1996	19.6	5.4	7.3	14.2	2.3	1993	14.9	99.7	22.5	16.0	170.1	41.5	59.5[45]	65.3
Romania	1995	10.4	12.0	21.2	–1.6	2.2[13]	1992	12.4	163.4	11.7	8.2	707.7	94.0	57.9	74.3
Russia	1995	9.3	15.0	18.0	–5.7	1.4	1995	21.0	203.0	11.0[15]	10.9[15]	784.0	75.0	46.0	234.0
Rwanda	1995–2000	42.8	19.7	125.0	23.1	6.0	...	...	...	...	...	...	...	...	...
St. Kitts and Nevis	1995	19.4	9.4	25.1	10.0	2.6[15]	1985	50.0	95.5	20.5[6]	11.4	443.2	81.8	25.0	29.5
St. Lucia	1995	25.2	5.9	18.0	19.3	2.5[15]	1992	31.1	64.4	22.4	5.8	205.6	48.5	21.0	34.7
St. Vincent and the Grenadines	1994	23.3	6.7	14.1	16.6	2.1[12]	1994	44.7	94.0	68.5	14.6	239.2	44.7	21.0	39.3
Samoa	1997	26.7	6.0	60.0	20.7	3.8	1992[38]	3.1	11.2	9.9	3.1	24.2	9.9	6.8	2.5
San Marino	1996	11.1	6.8	7.1[46]	4.3	1.5[23]	1991–95	...	229.4	2.4[6]	...	324.8	10.7	...	45.2
São Tomé and Príncipe	1995	34.9	8.7	62.1	26.2	4.4	1987	240.7	19.6	5.3[6]	2.7[27]	143.5	86.5	15.2	14.3
Saudi Arabia	1995–2000	34.3	4.2	23.0	30.1	5.9	...	...	...	...	...	...	...	...	...
Senegal	1996	45.5	11.8	64.0	33.7	6.3	...	...	...	...	...	...	...	...	...
Seychelles	1997	20.0	7.0	17.0	13.0	2.0	1994	43.3	128.6	16.2	16.2	288.4	98.8	39.3	43.3
Sierra Leone	1990–95	49.1	25.1	166.0	24.0	6.5	...	...	...	...	...	...	...	...	...
Singapore	1996	16.0	5.1	3.8	10.9	1.7	1994	12.5	128.2	12.8	2.4	186.2	87.4	13.4	37.5
Slovakia	1996	11.2	9.5	10.2	1.6	1.5	1995	3.4	206.5	13.7	4.4	541.1	67.9	42.1	67.9
Slovenia	1996	9.3	4.8	5.5[23]	4.5	1.3[23]	1995	4.4	235.6	28.8	8.5	408.1	74.7	56.7	87.6
Solomon Islands	1997	36.2	4.1	23.0	32.1	5.0	...	...	...	...	...	...	...	...	...
Somalia	1995–2000	50.0	16.9	112.0	33.1	7.0	...	...	...	...	...	...	...	...	...
South Africa	1996	27.4	11.1	52.4	16.3	3.3	1993	42.4	48.0	19.1	7.7	91.2	38.2	12.4	99.3
Spain	1995	9.2	8.7	5.6	0.5	1.3	1994	10.3	224.3	39.1	15.1	334.2	78.8	47.0	41.1
Sri Lanka	1997	17.9	5.9	15.0	12.0	2.1	1989	26.0	26.7	8.4	36.9	101.4	31.1	17.4	135.7
Sudan, The	1995–2000	33.7	11.7	71.0	22.0	4.6	...	...	...	...	...	...	...	...	...
Suriname	1995	21.3	6.6	30.2	14.7	2.7	1992[47]	40	68	40	11	193	37	32	71
Swaziland	1996	42.9	10.6	88.4	32.3	6.0	...	...	...	...	...	...	...	...	...
Sweden	1996	10.8	10.6	3.5	0.2	1.7	1994	7.5	229.8	21.9	...	514.8	78.9	...	32.6
Switzerland	1997	11.7	8.9	5.0[23]	2.8	1.5[23]	1994	16.3	238.7	23.3[16]	18.1	381.5	64.2	27.1	69.3
Syria	1995	40.0	6.0	29.6	34.0	6.1	1981[29]	22	12	7	13	86	19	8	27
Taiwan	1997	14.7	6.1	6.4[23]	8.6	1.8[23]	1992	...	101.5	23.7[6]	...	140.1[18]	24.3[47]	18.2[48]	63.7[48]
Tajikistan	1994	28.2	7.0	42.4	21.2	4.5	1993	128.3	40.7	8.8[4, 16]	7.9[4]	222.8	158.7	20.7	181.3
Tanzania	1996	41.0	17.0	107.0	24.0	5.6	...	...	...	...	...	...	...	...	...
Thailand	1996	17.8	7.4	32.0	10.4	2.0	1991	...	162.0	...	...	250.0	55.0	73.0	104.0
Togo	1995–2000	41.2	14.9	86.0	26.3	6.1	...	...	...	...	...	...	...	...	...
Tonga	1997	27.0	5.8	15.0	21.2	3.4	1992	16.3	54.9	15.2	6.1	158.5	31.5	18.3	4.1
Trinidad and Tobago	1996	16.3	6.9	18.2	9.4	2.0	1993	31.1	86.4	83.5[6]	2.8[27]	270.0	34.3	12.3	56.1
Tunisia	1995–2000	23.9	5.9	37.0	18.0	2.9	...	...	...	...	...	...	...	...	...
Turkey	1996	22.3	5.5	43.2	16.8	2.6	1993[48]	24	80	9[6]	2[15]	369	19	10	33
Turkmenistan	1994	33.0	7.0	45.0	26.0	4.1	1994	75.7	55.4	11.2	7.6	337.2	150.3	7.6	60.1
Tuvalu	1997	27.0	9.0	41.0	18.0	5.3	1985	40.0	70.0	20.0	120.0	150.0	120.0	170.0	...
Uganda	1995–2000	51.1	21.0	113.0	30.1	7.1	...	...	...	...	...	...	...	...	...
Ukraine	1996	13.0	10.5	14.1	2.5	1.7[15]	1993	14.5	198.9	8.2[12, 16]	8.9[12]	782.6	81.3	38.3	131.2
United Arab Emirates	1995–2000	18.7	2.9	15.0	15.8	3.5	...	...	...	...	...	...	...	...	...
United Kingdom	1996	12.5	10.9	6.2[23]	1.6	1.7[15]	1994	6.2	275.4	14.1	17.2	473.3	155.6	36.4	32.8
United States	1996	14.7	8.8	7.5	5.9	2.0[4]	1996	25.1[49]	204.5	23.2[6]	0.2[27]	355.1	70.6[50]	13.6	54.4
Uruguay	1995	17.8	10.0	19.6	7.8	2.4[15]	1990	16.0	222.8	25.5	16.2	378.4	76.3	39.1	61.7
Uzbekistan	1994	33.0	6.0	35.0	27.0	4.0	1993	38.0	48.2	9.4[12]	8.9[12]	300.3	113.8	31.4	49.5
Vanuatu	1997	33.0	6.2	39.0	26.8	4.4	1994[38]	25.0	29.2	9.1	5.5	39.0	30.4	9.7	9.1
Venezuela	1996	26.7	4.7	16.8	22.0	3.1[15]	1989	30.0	51.1	18.6	7.4	115.0	29.0	18.8	61.4
Vietnam	1997	25.6	7.0	38.0	18.6	3.2	1979	48.0	54.0	...	...	123.8	...	...	...
Virgin Islands (U.S.)	1993	24.3	5.5	12.3	18.8	2.6[13]	1989	10.8	78.9	36.5[5]	—	232.7	14.8[50]	12.8	56.2
West Bank	1994	46.0	7.0	40.0	39.0	5.7	...	...	...	...	...	...	...	...	...
Western Sahara	1995–2000	31.4	8.6	64.0	22.8	4.0	...	...	...	...	...	...	...	...	...
Yemen	1995–2000	47.7	10.4	80.0	37.3	7.6	...	...	...	...	...	...	...	...	...
Yugoslavia	1996	13.0	10.5	14.1	2.5	1.9[23]	1995	9.0	167.7[21]	23.8	10.1	573.7	40.9	28.3	42.2
Zambia	1995–2000	42.4	18.0	103	24.4	5.5	...	...	...	...	...	...	...	...	...
Zimbabwe	1997	31.6	19.0	62.3	12.6	3.9	1990	64.7	28.4	4.9	9.4	40.8	39.5	12.1	44.9

[1]Excludes nomadic tribes. [2]1995–2000. [3]1986. [4]1991. [5]Septicemia only. [6]Diabetes mellitus only. [7]Cerebrovascular disease and heart disease only. [8]Chronic obstructive pulmonary diseases, pneumonia, and influenza only. [9]1996. [10]Under 21 years of age. [11]21–29 years of age. [12]1992. [13]1989. [14]1988. [15]1994. [16]Includes nutritional disorders. [17]1990–95. [18]1993. [19]Accidents only. [20]1990. [21]Includes benign neoplasms (cancers). [22]Projected rates based on about 67 percent of the total deaths. [23]1995. [24]Results based on a sample population of about 100,000. [25]Millions of households. [26]Projected rates based on about 60 percent of the total deaths. [27]Meningitis only. [28]1985. [29]Projected rates based on about 75 percent of the total deaths. [30]Ethiopia

Column groups: **expectation of life at birth (latest year)**: male, female · **nuptiality, family, and family planning** — *marriages*: year, total number, rate per 1,000 population; *age at marriage (latest)* — groom (percent): 19 and under / 20–29 / 30 and over, bride (percent): 19 and under / 20–29 / 30 and over; *families (F), households (H) (latest)* — families (households): total ('000) / size, children: number under age 15 / percent legitimate, induced abortions: number / ratio per 100 live births · **country**

male	female	year	total number	rate per 1,000 pop.	groom 19 and under	groom 20–29	groom 30 and over	bride 19 and under	bride 20–29	bride 30 and over	families total ('000)	size	children no. under age 15	percent legitimate	abortions number	ratio per 100 live births	country
45.5	48.4	...	...	...	...	...	...	...	...	...	F 1,860	F 4.4	F 2.0	73.1	...	...	Mozambique
58.0	62.0	...	...	...	...	...	...	...	...	...		H 5.6	...	...	...	...	Myanmar (Burma)
54.7	56.6											H 5.2					Namibia
64.0	69.0	1976	43	6.1	...	...	...	...	...	...	H 1	H 8.0	H 2.6	...	...	...	Nauru
57.0	57.0										H 3,345	H 5.6	H 2.3				Nepal
74.6	80.4	1995	81,469	5.3	0.3	51.8	47.9	1.9	64.5	33.6	H 6,185	H 2.4	H 0.4	84.5	20,811	10.6	Netherlands, The
71.8	77.7	1995	1,056	5.2	...	...	...	...	...	...	H 41	H 3.7	H 2.1	51.6	...	...	Netherlands Antilles
69.0	76.0	1993	896	5.0	0.1	45.4[14]	54.5[14]	5.0[14]	61.3[14]	33.7[14]	...	H 4.1		48.1			New Caledonia
73.4	79.1	1994	21,858	6.2	0.8	50.6	48.6	3.2	60.8	36.0	H 1,178	H 2.9	H 0.7	63.3	11,460	19.3	New Zealand
63.4	68.1	1991	13,122	3.3	18.1[10,28]	—81.9[28,42]—		48.2[10,28]	—51.8[28,42]—		H 752	H 5.8	...	...			Nicaragua
41.1	40.2	...	...	...	...	...	...	...	...	...	H 1,130	H 6.4					Niger
53.5	55.9										H 21,283	H 4.7					Nigeria
59.0	64.0	1987	685	31.2	2.5	50.2	47.3	5.7	70.4	23.9	H 7	H 4.6	H 1.5	53.9			Northern Mariana Islands
74.9	80.6	1994	20,605	4.8	0.6[12]	53.7[12]	45.7[12]	3.2[12]	67.6[12]	29.2[12]	H 1,864	H 2.3		52.4	14,909	25.0	Norway
67.7	71.8											H 8.0					Oman
63.0	65.0	...	...	...	...	...	...	...	...	...		H 6.3					Pakistan
69.1	73.0																Palau
71.0	76.5	1994	13,523	5.6	2.5[18]	52.0[18]	45.5[18]	11.9[18]	55.2[18]	32.9[18]	H 524	H 4.4	H 1.5	25.5			Panama
57.0	59.0	...	...	...							H 674	H 4.6					Papua New Guinea
67.5	72.0	1992	16,042	3.6	4.2	64.8	31.0	3.4	50.2	19.4	H 868	H 4.7	1.9	68.7			Paraguay
65.9	70.9	1993	90,000	4.1	5.5[44]	60.4[44]	34.1[44]	25.9[44]	51.4[44]	22.6[44]	F 3,099	F 5.1		57.8			Peru
66.0	70.0	1992	454,155	6.9	5.3	67.2	27.5	18.9	64.0	17.1	F 9,566	F 5.7	F 2.4	93.9	2,315		Philippines
67.5	76.1	1994	208,900	5.4	3.7	76.6	19.7	19.4	67.6	13.0	F 9,435	F 3.6	F 0.9	95.0	874	0.2	Poland
71.3	78.6	1996	63,700	6.4	4.0[18]	7.9[18]	17.0[18]	18.0[18]	71.0[18]	11.0[18]	H 3,150	H 3.1	H 0.8	85.5			Portugal
69.6	78.5	1994	33,200	9.0	9.9	54.5	35.6	21.1	50.3	28.6	H 1,005	H 3.6	H 1.0	59.6			Puerto Rico
68.8	74.2	1994	1,495	2.8	3.7	69.0	27.3	26.6	62.0	11.4	H 61	H 6.4		19.2			Qatar
71.7	78.0	1996	3,313	4.9	1.2[20]	65.2[20]	33.6[20]	12.5[20]	66.8[20]	20.7[20]	H 185	H 3.5		44.1			Réunion
69.3	75.4	1995	153,943	6.8	3.0[15]	76.2[15]	20.8[15]	29.4[15]	58.3[15]	12.3[15]	H 7,115	H 3.1			530,191	214.9	Romania
58.0	72.0	1995	1,074,900	7.3	9.7[15]	79.4[15]	10.9[15]	41.0[15]	51.6[15]	7.4[15]	H 40,426	H 3.2	H 0.8	85.4	2,481,493	176.2	Russia
40.8	43.4	1982	14,313	2.6	...	...	...	...	...	...	H 1,509	H 4.7	2.3	94.9	...	...	Rwanda
63.0	69.0	...	...	...	...	...	...	...	...	...	H 12	H 3.7	H 1.4	19.2			St. Kitts and Nevis
67.0	72.0	1992	436	3.2	0.8[13]	34.4[13]	64.8[13]	3.5[13]	45.1[13]	51.4[13]	H 33	H 4.0	H 2.0	14.2			St. Lucia
71.0	74.0	1994	458	4.2	1.0[12]	37.0[12]	62.0[12]	4.8[12]	46.3[12]	48.9[12]	H 27	H 3.9	H 2.0				St. Vincent and the Grenadines
67.0	71.0	1993	759	4.7	0.5	51.0	48.5	8.0	65.0	27.0	F 20	F 7.8	H 3.8	43.5			Samoa
77.2	85.3	1989	169	7.4	0.6	75.1	24.3	5.3	85.3	9.5	H 9	H 2.6	H 0.4	95.2			San Marino
61.8	65.6	...	...	...	...	...	...	...	...	...	...	H 4.0		9.8	...	...	São Tomé and Príncipe
69.9	73.4	...									H 1,513	H 6.6					Saudi Arabia
53.7	59.3	...										H 8.7					Senegal
66.0	73.0	1994	937	12.7	2.0	45.8	42.2	11.2	51.5	29.6	H 13	H 4.8	H 1.9	27.2	387	22.8	Seychelles
41.4	44.6											H 6.6					Sierra Leone
74.4	78.9	1996	24,106	7.9	0.5[23]	56.4[23]	43.1[23]	3.7[23]	74.7[23]	21.6[23]	H 662	H 4.2	H 1.3	...	15,690	31.7	Singapore
68.8	76.7	1996	27,489	5.1	6.9[15]	76.2[15]	16.9[15]	30.5[15]	59.5[15]	10.0[15]		H 4.0		86.0	34,883	52.6	Slovakia
70.3	77.8	1995	8,245	4.2	0.6	64.9	34.5	6.6	73.6	19.8	H 637	H 3.1		70.2	11,324	58.1	Slovenia
69.0	74.0	...	...	...							H	H 5.8					Solomon Islands
47.4	50.6											H 4.9					Somalia
55.7	60.2	1995	148,148	3.6	...	...	...	...	...	...	H 8,688	H 4.6		75.9			South Africa
74.9	81.8	1995	187,049	4.8	1.8[4]	71.5[4]	26.7[4]	8.2[4]	76.7[4]	15.1[4]	F 10,665	F 3.5		89.5			Spain
71.0	75.0	1992	152,154	9.2	0.6	67.0	32.4	15.7	70.9	13.4	H 3,282	H 4.6		96.3			Sri Lanka
53.6	56.4	...									H 3,471	H 5.3					Sudan, The
67.2	72.4	1993	1,944	4.7								H 3.9					Suriname
53.2	61.4	1989	...	4.3	...	...	...	...	...	...	H 122	H 5.7			1,145		Swaziland
75.6	81.0	1996	33,484	3.4	0.3	40.5	59.2	1.5	54.0	44.5	H 3,670	H 2.1	H 0.5	47.0	32,293	28.8	Sweden
75.3	81.7	1995	40,820	5.8	0.3	45.1	54.6	2.1	60.7	37.2	H 3,250	H 2.2	0.4	93.2			Switzerland
68.4	71.3	1993	114,979	8.6	...	...	...	...	...	...	F 1,151	F 6.2	F 2.4				Syria
71.8	77.7	1996	169,096	7.8	1.5[20]	62.3[20]	36.2[20]	6.0[20]	77.7[20]	16.3[20]	H 5,964	H 3.6	H 1.0	97.2			Taiwan
65.7	71.5	1993	53,946	9.6	2.1	86.8	11.1	39.0	54.3	6.7	H 799	H 6.1	H 2.7	93.0	40,078	21.5	Tajikistan
41.5	45.0	...									H 3,435	H 5.2	H 2.3				Tanzania
67.0	72.0	1995	470,751	7.9							H 15,551	H 3.8					Thailand
48.8	51.5	1979	...	2.3							H 479	H 5.6					Togo
68.0	72.0	1992	806	8.2							F 15	F 6.3	F 2.7	80.6			Tonga
67.9	72.8	1993	7,012	5.6	5.7	59.1	35.2	23.5	52.4	24.1	H 301	H 4.1	H 1.3		9	—	Trinidad and Tobago
68.4	70.7	1995	52,203	6.0	...	60.5[12]	39.5[12]	24.7[12]	62.7[12]	20.2[12]	H 1,703	H 5.1	H 1.9	99.8	23,300	10.9	Tunisia
69.5	74.4	1993	460,002	7.7	6.5	76.4	17.1	33.6	58.3	8.2		H 4.5					Turkey
61.4	68.6	1993	42,106	10.7	3.0[13]	87.4[13]	9.6[13]	16.1[13]	77.1[13]	6.8[13]	H 598	H 6.4	H 2.4	96.5	39,068	31.3	Turkmenistan
64.0	70.0	...	...	...							H 1	H 6.4	H 2.2	82.2			Tuvalu
40.4	42.3	...									H 2,766	H 4.8					Uganda
65.3	74.7	1993	427,882	8.2	8.3	67.5	24.2	37.2	43.2	19.6	H 14,507	H 3.2	H 0.8	89.2	957,022	159.5	Ukraine
73.9	76.5	1991	...	2.7							H 247	H 6.8					United Arab Emirates
74.4	79.7	1995	282,900	5.5	1.1[18]	53.9[18]	45.0[18]	4.1[18]	61.6[18]	34.3[18]	H 29,533	H 2.4	H 1.7	68.0	169,964	22.6	United Kingdom
72.0	78.9	1996	2,324,000	8.8	4.3[20]	51.8[20]	43.9[20]	10.9[20]	55.8[20]	35.3[20]	H 96,391	H 2.6	F 1.0	70.5	1,388,937	33.8	United States
70.9	77.5	1992	54,754	6.2	7.2[20]	59.8[20]	33.0[20]	23.6[20]	52.3[20]	24.1[20]	H 863	H 3.3	H 0.9	73.8			Uruguay
65.1	71.8	1994	176,300	7.8	2.3[18]	87.4[18]	10.3[18]	37.9[18]	55.2[18]	6.9[18]	H 3,415	H 5.5	H 2.4	95.8	226,276	33.8	Uzbekistan
65.0	69.0	...									H 28	H 5.1	H 2.2		113	2.4	Vanuatu
70.1	76.0	1992	108,955	5.4	10.7[4]	61.3[4]	28.0[4]	30.4[4]	51.7[4]	17.9[4]	H 2,707	H 5.3	H 2.2	47.0			Venezuela
66.0	69.0	...									H 12,958[51]	H 4.8[51]	H 1.9[51]				Vietnam
66.7	70.7	1993	3,646	35.1	0.4	33.6	66.0	1.9	45.9	52.2	H 32	H 3.1	H 1.0	38.4			Virgin Islands (U.S.)
65.7	67.5	...															West Bank
59.8	63.1	...															Western Sahara
57.4	58.4	...									H 1,848	H 5.6					Yemen
69.1	74.3	1995	60,325	5.7	2.3	64.5	33.2	18.7	63.5	17.8	H 2,870	H 3.6	H 0.9				Yugoslavia
42.2	43.7	...									H 1,370	H 4.8	H 2.1				Zambia
58.0	62.0	...									H 2,166	H 4.4	1.1	95.8			Zimbabwe

includes Eritrea. [31]1987. [32]First marriages only. [33]1993–95. [34]Muslims only. [35]Projected rates based on about 20 percent of the total deaths. [36]1997. [37]Projected rates based on about 10 percent of the total deaths. [38]Registered deaths only. [39]Average annual rates for the period. [40]Includes Aruba. [41]Projected rates based on about 45 percent of the total deaths. [42]Over 21 years of age. [43]Reporting areas only (constituting about 75 percent of the total population). [44]1982. [45]Includes all deaths associated with alcoholism. [46]1990–94. [47]Projected rates based on about 70 percent of the total deaths. [48]Projected rates based on about 35 percent of the total deaths. [49]Of which AIDS, 11.8. [50]Bronchitis, pneumonia, and influenza only. [51]Private households only.

National product and accounts

This table furnishes, for most of the countries of the world, breakdowns of (1) gross national product (GNP)—its global and per capita values, purchasing power parity (PPP), and growth rates (1990–96), (2) principal industrial and accounting components of gross domestic product (GDP), and (3) principal elements of each country's balance of payments, including international goods trade, invisibles, and tourism payments.

Measures of national output. The two most commonly used measures of national output are GDP and GNP. Each of these measures represents an aggregate value of goods and services produced by a specific country. The GDP, the more basic of these, is a measure of the total value of goods and services produced entirely within a given country. The GNP, the more comprehensive value, is composed of both domestic production (GDP) and the net income from current (short-term) transactions with other countries. When the income received from other countries is greater than payments to them, a country's GNP is greater than its GDP. In theory, if all national accounts could be equilibrated, the global summation of GDP would equal GNP.

In the first section of the table, data are provided for the nominal and real GNP. ("Nominal" refers to value in current prices for the year indicated and is distinguished from a "real" valuation, which is one adjusted to eliminate the effect of recent inflation [most often] or, occasionally, of deflation between two given dates.) Both the total and per capita values of this product are denominated in U.S. dollars for ease of comparison, as is a new value for GNP per capita adjusted for purchasing power parity.

The latter is a concept that provides a better approximation of the ability of equivalent values of two (or more) national currencies to purchase comparable quantities of goods and services in their respective domestic markets and may differ substantially from two otherwise equal GNP per capita values based solely on currency exchange rates. Beside these are given figures for average annual growth of total and per capita real GNP. GNP per capita provides a rough measure of annual national income per person, but values should be compared cautiously, as they are subject to a number of distortions, notably of exchange rate, but also of purchasing power parity and in the existence of elements of national production that do not enter the monetary economy in such a way as to be visible to fiscal authorities (e.g., food, clothing, or housing produced and consumed within families or communal groups or services exchanged). For reasons of comparability, the majority of the data in this section are taken from the World Bank's *The World Bank Atlas* (annual).

The internal structure of the national product. GDP/GNP values allow comparison of the relative size of national economies, but further information is provided when these aggregates are analyzed according to their industrial sectors of origin, component kinds of expenditure, and cost components.

The distribution of GDP for ten industrial sectors, usually compiled from national sources, is aggregated into three major industrial groups:

1. The primary sector, composed of agriculture (including forestry and fishing) and mineral production (including fossil fuels).

National product and accounts

country	gross national product (GNP), 1996						origin of gross domestic product (GDP) by economic sector, 1994 (%)										
	nominal ('000,000 U.S.$)	per capita		average annual growth rates, 1990–96			primary		secondary			tertiary					other
		nominal (U.S.$)	purchasing power parity (PPP; U.S.$)	real GNP (%)	population (%)	real GNP per capita (%)	agriculture	mining	manufacturing	construction	public utilities	transp., communications	trade	financial svcs.	other svcs.	government	
Afghanistan	18,131[1]	800[1]	...	...	...	...	48[2]	3	26[2,3]	10[2]	3	4[2]	10[2]	2[2]			—
Albania	2,705	820	...	2.2	0.0	2.2	55	3	13[3]	9	3	3	19				—
Algeria	43,726	1,520	4,620	−1.9	2.3	−4.2	10	23	9	12	—	33		13			—
American Samoa	253	4,300	...	...	...	...	...	...	...	...	...	...	...	...	...	...	—
Andorra	1,155[1]	18,000[1]	...	...	...	...	...	...	...	...	...	...	...	...	...	...	—
Angola	2,972	270	1,030	−5.6	3.1	−8.7	12	51	3	2	—	2	10	19			—
Antigua and Barbuda	482	7,330	8,660	2.0	0.4	1.6	4	1	2	9	4	20	25	15	7	18	−5
Argentina	295,131	8,380	9,530	3.9	1.3	2.6	6[5]	25	22[5]	5[5]	2[5]	5[5]	15[5]	17[5]	26[5]		—
Armenia	2,387	630	2,160	−15.0	1.0	−16.0	43	3	29[3]	7	3	1	4	15			—
Aruba	1,470[1]	16,010[1]	...	...	...	...	...	...	...	...	...	...	...	...	...	...	...
Australia	367,802	20,090	19,870	2.7	1.2	1.5	3	4	16	7	3	9	19	22	14	4	−1
Austria	226,510	28,110	21,650	0.9	0.7	0.2	2	9	24[9]	8	3	6	16	19	5	14	3
Azerbaijan	3,642	480	1,490	−18.7	1.0	−19.7	30	3	25[3]	4	3	7	34				—
Bahamas, The	3,391	11,940	...	...	...	...	1	15	17	6	2	11	11	19	5	19	−6
Bahrain	4,693	7,840	...	...	...	...	1	15	15	6	3	11	8	22	5	20	−7
Bangladesh	31,217	260	1,010	2.7	1.6	1.1	30	9	10[9]	6	2	12	8	2	24	5	—
Barbados	1,735	6,560	...	4	1	6	4	3	8	27	14	4	15				16
Belarus	22,452	2,070	4,380	−8.6	0.1	−8.7	16	3	45[3]	9	3	5	9	8	7	2	—
Belgium	268,633	26,440	22,390	1.2	0.3	0.9	2	—	22	5	2	8	13[11]	18[11]	7		5
Belize	600	2,700	4,170	0.7	2.7	−2.0	19	—	14	7	4	11	17	11	6	13	−4
Benin	1,998	350	1,230	1.9	2.9	−1.0	33	9	8[9]	4	1	8	20	11		9	5
Bermuda	2,126	34,670	...	...	...	...	...	...	...	...	...	...	...	...	...	...	...
Bhutan	282	390	...	2.0	2.9	−0.9	38	1	10	12	7	7	8	6	9		3
Bolivia	6,302	830	2,860	1.8	2.4	−0.6	16[10]	10[10]	14[10]	4[10]	2[10]	11[10]	11[10]	11[10]	7[10]	9[10]	6[10]
Bosnia and Herzegovina	799[1,10]	300[1,10]	...	...	...	...	...	...	...	...	...	...	...	...	...	...	...
Botswana	4,381	3,020	5,580	9.0	3.0	6.0	5	35	4	5	3	3	16	5	3	22	−9
Brazil	709,591	4,400	6,340	2.0	1.4	0.6	14	1	23	8	6	6	7	9	25	10	−3
Brunei	7,546	25,160	...	...	...	...	3	9	4[19]	5	1	4	8	8	32		−3
Bulgaria	9,924	1,190	4,280	−1.8	−0.7	−1.1	12	9	29[9]	5	12	7	11	15[12]	20		2
Burkina Faso	2,410	230	950	−0.1	2.8	−2.9	30	9	18[9]	5	1	4	18	20			4
Burundi	1,066	170	590	−6.4	2.6	−9.0	47	1[13]	11	4	13	4	4	2		15	11
Cambodia	3,088	300	...	2.9	2.8	0.1	51	—	5	8	1	3	15	13		4	—
Cameroon	8,356	610	1,760	−3.8	2.9	−6.7	39	9	10	2	2	24				13	2
Canada	569,899	19,020	21,380	0.6	1.3	−0.7	3[10]	4[10]	19[10]	5[10]	3[10]	9[10]	12[10]	16[10]	22[10]	6[10]	—
Cape Verde	393	1,010	2,640	−16.7	2.2	−18.9	18[2]	—	6[2]	18[2]	3[2]	11[2]	21[2]	3[2]	12	7[2]	13[2]
Central African Republic	1,024	310	1,430	−1.7	2.2	−3.9	53	6	7	4	—	3	12	5		10	—
Chad	1,035	160	880	−1.7	2.5	−4.2	21	—	6	1	—	12		5			55
Chile	70,060	4,860	11,700	6.4	1.6	4.8	8	8	17	6	3	8	17	17	7	3	7
China	906,079	750	3,330	11.0	1.1	9.9	21	3	41[3]	6	3	6	9	17			—
Colombia	80,174	2,140	6,720	3.0	1.8	1.2	13	4	19	6	3	10	33				—
Comoros	228	450	1,770	−1.8	2.6	−4.4	39[10]	...	4[10]	7[10]	1[10]	4[10]	27[10]	14	3[10]	14[10,14]	—
Congo, Dem. Rep. of the	5,727	130	790	−10.4	3.2	−13.6	58	5	5	2	2	3	16	6		3	1
Congo, Rep. of the	1,813	670	1,410	−4.3	2.9	−7.2	11	33	8	2	1	8	12	8		14	3
Costa Rica	9,081	2,640	6,470	2.4	2.1	0.3	16	—	19[9]	3	4	5	20	11	7	14	—
Côte d'Ivoire	9,434	660	1,580	0.2	3.1	−2.8	31	—	18	2		8	18	8		10	5
Croatia	18,130	3,800	4,290	2.2	0.0	2.2	11	9	28[9]	2	—	4	16	8	30		—
Cuba	16,308[1]	1,480[1]	...	...	...	...	...	...	...	...	...	...	...	...	...	...	...
Cyprus[15]	8,926	13,720	...	...	...	...	5	—	13	9	2	8	19	16	7	13	7
Czech Republic	48,861	4,740	10,870	0.9	−0.1	1.0	5[2]	4	28[2,4]	4[2]	6[2]	6[2]	8[2]	29[2]			13[2]
Denmark	168,917	32,100	22,120	2.1	0.4	1.7	4	1	19	5	2	10	14	19	5	22	−2
Djibouti	485[1]	790[1]	...	...	...	...	3[10]	—	5[10]	5[10]	8[10]	15[10]	15[10]	9[10]	4[10]	23[10]	12[10]
Dominica	228	3,090	4,390	2.3	0.3	2.0	17	1	6	7	4	15	12	12	1	16	9
Dominican Republic	12,765	1,600	4,390	3.1	1.9	1.2	13	2	18	9	2	10	18	10	8	9	—
Ecuador	17,531	1,500	4,730	0.8	2.2	−1.4	17	15	15	3	1	9	15	12	6	7	1
Egypt	64,275	1,080	2,860	2.2	2.0	0.2	15	9	25[9]	5	2	10	17	7			13

2. The secondary sector, composed of manufacturing, construction, and public utilities.
3. The tertiary sector, which includes transportation and communications, trade (wholesale and retail), restaurants and hotels, financial services (including banking, real estate, insurance, and business services), other services (community, social, and personal), and government services.

Percentages in this section of the table may not add to 100 because the value of each economic sector is calculated as a percentage of the total GDP, which may contain adjustments such as import duties and bank service charges that are not distributed by sector.

There are three major domestic components of GDP expenditure: private consumption (analyzed in greater detail in the "Household budgets and consumption" table), government spending, and gross domestic investment. The fourth, nondomestic, component of GDP expenditure is net foreign trade; values are given for both exports (a positive value) and imports (a negative value, representing obligations to other countries). The sum of these five percentages, excluding statistical discrepancies and rounding, should be 100% of the GDP.

The structure of GDP as accounted by cost components here comprises four general categories: indirect taxes (excise or value-added taxes), net of subsidies; consumption of fixed capital (depreciation); and two income categories: (a) compensation of employees (salaries, wages, etc.) and (b) net operating surplus ("profits," interests, rent, etc.).

Balance of payments (external account transactions). The external account records the sum (net) of all economic transactions of a current nature between one country and the rest of the world. The account shows a country's net of overseas receipts and obligations, including not only the trade of goods and merchandise but also such invisible items as services, interest and dividends, short- and long-term investments, tourism, transfers to or from overseas residents, etc. Each transaction gives rise either to a foreign claim for payment, recorded as a deficit (*e.g.*, from imports, capital outflows), or a foreign obligation to pay, recorded as a surplus (*e.g.*, from exports, capital inflows) or a domestic claim on another country. Any international transaction automatically creates a deficit in the balance of payments of one country and a surplus in that of another. Values are given in U.S. dollars for comparability.

Tourist trade. Net income or expenditure from tourism (in U.S. dollars for comparability) is often a significant element in a country's balance of payments. Receipts from foreign nationals reflect payments for goods and services from foreign currency resources by tourists in the given country. Expenditures by nationals abroad are also payments for goods and services, but in this case made by the residents of the given country as tourists abroad. The majority of the data in this section are compiled by the World Tourism Organization.

gross domestic product (GDP) by type of expenditure, 1994 (%)					cost components of gross domestic product (GDP), 1994 (%)				balance of payments, 1996 (current external transactions; '000,000 U.S.$)			tourist trade, 1995 ('000,000 U.S.$)		country
consumption		gross domestic invest-ment	foreign trade		indirect taxes net of subsidies	consump-tion of fixed capital	compen-sation of employ-ees	net operating surplus	net transfers		current balance of payments	receipts from foreign nationals	expendi-tures by nationals abroad	
private	govern-ment		exports	imports					goods, merchan-dise	invisibles				
...	...	...	...	...	...	...	...	...	...	...	...	1[4]	1[4]	Afghanistan
—170[5]—		10[5]	12[5]	-92[5]	...	13[4]	62[4]	25[4]	-678.3	571.0	-107.3	7	5	Albania
56	17	32	24	-28	...	...	...	...	4,100	-2,900	1,200	27	135	Algeria
...	...	...	...	...	...	...	...	...	...	...	...	10[6]	...	American Samoa
...	...	...	...	...	...	...	...	...	...	...	...	...	...	Andorra
56	34	14	66	-70	7[4]	7	39[4]	54[4,7]	2,879	-3,485	-606	13[8]	66[3]	Angola
53	21	24	106	-104	15	—85—			-262.6	22.8	39.8	329	24[8]	Antigua and Barbuda
—82—		20	7	-9	...	...	...	...	1,622	-5,752	-4,130	4,306	2,067	Argentina
87[2]	16[2]	9[2]	44[2]	-57[2]	...	...	...	...	-469.2	-177.7	-291.5	...	...	Armenia
62	16	27	36	-41	...	...	...	...	-307.7	238.6	-69.1	521	73	Aruba
62	18	22	19	-20	12	15	49	24	-891	-14,979	-15,870	7,100	4,604	Australia
55	19	26	37	-37	14	13	52	22	-7,786	3,796	-3,990	14,618	11,687	Austria
69	24	21	58	-71	3	25	24	48	...	...	...	146	70	Azerbaijan
76[2]	15[2]	21[2]	44[2]	-56[2]	14[5]	7	52[5]	34[5,7]	-990.0	744.2	-245.8	1,346	213	Bahamas, The
30	25	26	107	-88	3[2]	17[2]	44[2]	35[2]	768.6[10]	-211.6[10]	557.0[10]	288	163	Bahrain
78	14	14	12	-18	7	—93—			-2,254.9	1,004.0	-1,250.9	23	229	Bangladesh
64	20	13	49	-47	16	—84—			-456.2	559.2	103.0	680	52[3]	Barbados
63	21	29	72	-85	9[2]	20[2]	49[2]	22[2]	-1,335.8	426.5	-909.3	...	...	Belarus
63	15	18	72	-67	10	9	53	27	9,146	5,241	14,387	5,719	9,215	Belgium
66	17	23	53	-59	15[5]	6[5]	—78[5]—		-66.1[10]	48.9[10]	-17.2[10]	78	21	Belize
78	12	20	31	-41	...	...	...	...	-64.8[8]	101.2[8]	36.4[8]	27	6[8]	Benin
69	13	12	61	-55	...	...	...	...	-502	627	125	488	140[3]	Bermuda
53	18	45	31	-47	4	9	—87—		-26.7[10]	-21.5[10]	-48.2[10]	5	...	Bhutan
75	14	16	23	-28	...	...	...	...	-309.8	-92.8	-402.6	146	148	Bolivia
...	...	...	...	...	...	...	...	...	...	...	...	...	...	Bosnia and Herzegovina
43	31	26	51	-51	10[2]	13[2]	31[2]	45[2]	791.3	-182.7	608.6	162	145	Botswana
63	15	21	9	-7	14	—86—			-3,157[10]	-14,979[10]	-18,136[10]	2,171	4,245	Brazil
...	...	...	...	...	...	...	...	...	...	...	...	...	...	Brunei
71	16	13	43	-44	6[2]	13[2]	52[2]	27[2]	188	-172	16	473	195	Bulgaria
78	16	22	14	-30	4	—96—			-128.7[8]	143.6[8]	14.9[8]	22	23[8]	Burkina Faso
84	16	13	12	-25	11	—89—			-59.8	33.4	-26.4	1	25	Burundi
83	11	19	11	-25	...	...	...	...	-428.4	130.6	-297.8	100	8	Cambodia
72	8	16	28	-23	2	—98—			608.2	-278.0	330.2	47[2]	225[2]	Cameroon
60	20	19	33	-33	13	13	55	19	30,062	-27,254	2,808	8,012	10,220	Canada
82	24	42	—-48—		13[2]	—87[2]—			-223.8[10]	185.1[10]	-38.8[10]	10	12	Cape Verde
76	15	13	22	27	6	—94—			15.3[8]	-40.0[8]	-24.7[8]	6[2]	43[8]	Central African Republic
87	14	16	22	-39	...	...	...	...	-76.8[8]	39.1[8]	-37.7[8]	36[8]	26[8]	Chad
62	9	27	28	-27	...	...	...	...	-1,146	-1,775	-2,921	990	774	Chile
51[2]	9[2]	41[2]	24[2]	-25[2]	...	...	...	...	19,535	-12,292	7,243	8,733	3,688	China
69	13	22	16	-20	10[5]	7	39[5]	51[5,7]	-2,133	-2,621	-4,754	851	822	Colombia
80	22	19	14	-35	...	...	...	...	-42.8	23.9	-18.9	8[5]	6[5]	Comoros
86	8	3	13	-10	...	...	...	...	643[8]	-1,058[8]	-415[8]	6[2]	16[2]	Congo, Dem. Rep. of the
55	22	51	64	-93	...	...	...	...	62.9	-1,096.8	-1,033.9	4	39	Congo, Rep. of the
60	17	27	39	-43	13[2]	22	50[2]	35[2]	-473.5[10]	330.5[10]	-143.0[10]	660	312	Costa Rica
65	13	12	44	-33	...	...	...	...	1,859.8	-2,063.3	-203.5	72	159	Côte d'Ivoire
71	27	3	—-1—		11[4]	13[4]	62[4]	14[4]	-2,497.3	1,045.1	-1,452.2	1,584	771	Croatia
...	...	...	...	...	...	...	...	...	...	...	...	1,100	...	Cuba
60	17	24	49	-49	7	11	—83—		-2,085.5[10]	1,872.9[10]	-212.6[10]	1,783	293	Cyprus[15]
58	22	20	52	-53	...	...	...	...	-5,877	1,578	-4,299	2,875	1,630	Czech Republic
54	26	15	35	-29	14[2]	10[2]	54[2]	23[2]	7,313	-5,393	1,920	3,672	4,280	Denmark
71	38	12	47	-67	13	—87—			-171.5[10]	148.5[10]	-23.0[10]	13[2]	72	Djibouti
71	23	24	—-17—		16	—84—			-47.8	7.8	-39.9	33	5	Dominica
75	5	23	24	-27	12[2]	6[2]	—82[2]—		-1,764.5	1,654.4	-110.1	1,604	85	Dominican Republic
69	9	19	27	-24	12[2]	7	14[2]	74[2,7]	1,402	-1,109	293	255	235	Ecuador
75	10	20	23	-28	4[2]	4[2]	27[2]	64[2]	-8,390	8,198	-192	2,800	1,278	Egypt

National product and accounts (continued)

country	gross national product (GNP), 1996 nominal ('000,000 U.S.$)	per capita nominal (U.S.$)	per capita purchasing power parity (PPP; U.S.$)	real GNP (%)	population (%)	real GNP per capita (%)	agriculture	mining	manufacturing	construction	public utilities	transp., communications	trade	financial svcs.	other svcs.	government	other
El Salvador	9,868	1,700	2,790	3.5	2.4	1.1	14	—	21	4	1	18	17	12	18	6	—
Equatorial Guinea	217	530	2,690	15.9	2.6	13.3	47	9	21[9]	5	3	2	9	2	3	5	2
Eritrea	807	220	...	...	...	...	18	—	12	4	1	13	28	4	3	10	7
Estonia	4,509	3,080	4,660	-4.9	-1.2	-3.7	9	2	17	6	3	9	19	8	8	4	16
Ethiopia	6,042	100	500	2.0	2.2	-0.2	54	4	8[4]	3	1	5	10	8	4	7	—
Faroe Islands	838[1]	19,210[1]	...	...	...	...	15[2]	—	13[2]	4[2]	12	9[2]	11[2]	7[2]	24[2]	16[2]	-10[2]
Fiji	1,983	2,470	4,070	0.6	1.5	-0.9	22	—	12	3	1	15	21	12	—16—		-3
Finland	119,086	23,240	18,260	-0.2	0.5	-0.7	5	—	25	5	3	9	11	19	3	20	-1
France	1,533,619	26,270	21,510	0.7	0.5	0.2	3	1	20	5	3	6	14[16]	6	18[16]	19	6
French Guiana	1,543[10]	10,580[10]	...	...	...	...	10[6]	3	11[3,6]	16[6]	3	17[6]	16[6]	—30[6]—			
French Polynesia	3,418	14,910	...	...	...	...	5[4]	—	7[4]	6[4]	2[4]	17	23[4]	—29[4,17]—		29[4]	-1[4]
Gabon	4,444	3,950	6,300	-1.2	2.6	-3.8	9	45	5	4	2	5	7	1	10	11	—
Gambia, The	401[1]	330[1]	...	...	...	...	21	—	6	4	1	18	17	6	4	11	13
Gaza Strip	1,065[1]	1,100[1]	...	...	...	...	13	—	10	8	2	5	15	23	8	16	—
Georgia	4,590	850	1,810	-19.3	-0.2	-19.1	29	3	21[3]	5	3	9	6	—29—			—
Germany	2,364,632	28,870	21,110	0.7	0.5	0.2	1	2[13]	23	5	13	5	8	13	19	9	16
Ghana	6,223	360	1,790	1.5	2.7	-1.2	47	2	9	3	2	4	19	4	—9—		
Gibraltar	205[1,2]	6,600[1,2]	...	...	...	...	...	...	...	...	...	...	...	...	...	...	...
Greece	120,021	11,460	12,730	1.3	0.5	0.8	15	1	15	6	3	7	14	3	10	19	8
Greenland	893[1,10]	15,500[1,10]	...	...	...	...	...	...	...	...	...	...	...	...	...	...	...
Grenada	285	2,880	4,340	0.6	1.4	-0.8	12	—	6	7	4	23	21	13	3	17	-6
Guadeloupe	3,706[1,10]	9,200[1,10]	...	...	...	...	...	...	...	...	...	...	...	...	...	...	...
Guam	2,993	19,600	...	...	...	...	...	...	...	...	...	...	...	...	...	...	...
Guatemala	16,018	1,470	3,820	0.5	2.9	-2.4	24	—	14	2	3	9	24	9	6	8	—
Guernsey[18]	1,531[5]	26,000[5]	...	...	...	...	...	...	...	...	...	...	...	...	...	...	...
Guinea	3,804	560	1,720	1.9	2.7	-0.8	24	19	5	7	—	5	—26—		6	5	3
Guinea-Bissau	270	250	1,030	0.5	2.1	-1.6	52	3	11[3]	4	3	2	25	—1—		4	1
Guyana	582	690	2,280	10.4	0.9	9.5	31	18	10[19]	3	19	4	4	6	1	7	16
Haiti	2,282	310	1,130	-6.9	2.1	-9.0	41	—	11	2	1	1	11	—12—		20	1
Honduras	4,012	660	2,130	1.2	3.0	-1.8	24	2	18	6	3	5	10	15	10	7	—
Hong Kong	153,288	24,290	24,260	3.7	1.7	2.0	—	—	9	5	2	9	26	25	—15—		10
Hungary	44,274	4,340	6,730	-0.6	-0.3	-0.3	6	9	20[9]	5	3	8	11	18	—19—		10
Iceland	7,175	26,580	21,710	0.5	1.0	-0.5	9[10]	—	13[10]	6[10]	3[10]	6[10]	10[10]	15[10]		14[10]	18[10]
India	357,759	380	1,580	3.8	1.8	2.0	31	2	17	6	3	8	13	9	6	5	—
Indonesia	213,384	1,080	3,310	5.9	1.7	4.2	17	8	24	7	1	7	17	7	6	5	—
Iran	131,328	2,150	...	...	...	...	21	19	13	3	1	6	15	9	2	10	-1
Iraq	1,382[1]	65[1]	...	...	...	...	35[5]	—	9[5]	4[5]	—	10[5]	26[5]	8[5]	—12[5]—		-5[5]
Ireland	62,040	17,110	16,750	5.1	0.6	4.5	9	20	38[20]	20	20	—16—		—31—		6	—
Isle of Man	780[1,10]	10,800[1,10]	...	...	...	...	2[6]	—	12[6]	8[6]	3[6]	9[6]	21	27[6]	33[6,21]	6[6]	—
Israel	90,310	15,870	18,100	3.2	3.3	-0.1	3[5]	9	22[5,9]	8[5]	2[5]	8[5]	10[5]	25[5]	4[5]	23[5]	-5[5]
Italy	1,140,484	19,880	19,890	0.9	0.2	0.7	3	9	21[9]	5	6	6	18	14	14	12	1
Jamaica	4,066	1,600	3,450	0.9	1.0	-0.1	10	8	20	13	2	9	25	14	5	4	-9
Japan	5,149,185	40,940	23,420	1.2	0.3	0.9	2[10]	—	25[10]	10[10]	3[10]	7[10]	13[10,11]	18[10]	19[10,11]	8[10]	-4[10]
Jersey	2,198[1,8]	25,920[1,8]	...	...	...	...	5[4]	—	—24—			—93[4]—					
Jordan	7,088	1,650	3,570	4.0	5.1	-1.1	8	3	14	7	2	16	10	17	4	19	-1
Kazakstan	22,213	1,350	3,230	-10.3	-0.3	-10.0	12	3	26[3]	9	3	8	8	—37—			—
Kenya	8,661	320	1,130	-0.5	2.6	-3.1	29	—	11	5	1	8	15	19	—12—		—
Kiribati	75	920	...	...	...	...	23	—	1	2	2	12	16	4	—29—		12
Korea, North	19,361[1]	900[1]	...	...	...	...	...	...	...	...	...	...	...	...	...	...	...
Korea, South	483,130	10,610	13,080	6.2	1.0	5.2	7	—	29	11	2	8	13	17	6	6	—
Kuwait	35,901	20,470	...	...	...	...	—	39	11	5	4	7	12	—25—			-1
Kyrgyzstan	2,486	550	1,970	-12.7	0.7	-13.4	38	3	21[3]	3	3	4	10	5	—12—		6
Laos	1,895	400	1,250	3.9	2.6	1.3	56	—	13	3	2	5	9	—5—			2
Latvia	5,730	2,300	3,650	-10.1	-1.2	-8.9	6	9	15[9]	5	3	15	7	5	33	10	—
Lebanon	12,118	2,970	6,060	5.4	1.9	3.5	8	—	12	5	5	3	26	13	8	18	—
Lesotho	1,331	660	2,380	0.9	2.1	-1.2	11	—	14	22	2	3	9	12	3	12	14
Liberia	2,510[1,10]	1,100[1,10]	...	...	...	...	...	...	...	...	...	...	...	...	...	...	...
Libya	34,159[1,10]	6,570[1,10]	...	...	...	...	7[5]	25[5]	8[5]	13[5]	2[5]	6[5]	9[5]	12[5]	7[5]	10[5]	—
Liechtenstein	714[1]	123,000[1]	...	...	...	...	...	...	...	...	...	...	...	...	...	...	...
Lithuania	8,455	2,280	4,390	-6.0	-0.1	-5.9	15[2]	9	26[2,9]	7[2]	5[2]	8[2]	17[2]	6[2]	5[2]	7[2]	5[2]
Luxembourg	18,850	45,360	34,480	0.1	1.4	-1.3	1[6]	—	24[6]	7[6]	2[6]	7[6]	16[6]	14[6]	15[6]	15[6]	-2[6]
Macau	7,313[1]	17,600[1]	...	...	...	...	...	...	...	...	...	...	...	...	...	...	...
Macedonia	1,956	990	...	-8.5	0.7	-9.2	19	9	38[9]	6	—	4	25	—7—			5
Madagascar	3,428	250	900	-2.0	2.7	-4.7	37	9	—13[9]—			—41—				5	5
Malawi	1,832	180	690	-0.2	2.7	-2.9	31	—	14	4	3	5	12	11	5	16	-2
Malaysia	89,800	4,370	10,390	6.1	2.3	3.8	15	7	31	4	2	7	12	11	2	10	-2
Maldives	277	1,080	3,140	4.1	2.9	1.2	8	2	6[19]	9	19	7	19	40	—9—		
Mali	2,422	240	710	-0.2	2.8	-3.0	41[10]	3[10]	6[10]	5[10]	1[10]	4[10]	19[10]	1[10]	7[10]	6[10]	6[10]
Malta	3,344	8,980	...	...	...	...	3	22	24	3[22]	8	7	—39—			16	—
Marshall Islands	96	1,600	...	...	...	...	16	—	1	10	2	5	19	17	—27—		2
Martinique	3,942[1,10]	10,000[1,10]	...	...	...	...	...	...	...	...	...	...	...	...	...	...	...
Mauritania	1,089	470	1,810	1.7	2.5	-0.8	23	10	10	—8—		6	14	—7—		11	11
Mauritius	4,205	3,710	9,000	3.6	1.2	2.4	9	—	24	8	2	12	18	11	6	11	—
Mayotte	54[8]	600[8]	...	...	...	...	...	...	...	...	...	...	...	...	...	...	...
Mexico	341,718	3,670	7,660	-0.3	1.8	-2.1	7	3	22	6	2	8	25	12	—17—		-2
Micronesia	203	1,860	...	-1.3	2.1	-3.4	...	...	...	...	...	...	...	...	...	...	...
Moldova	2,542	590	1,440	-16.8	-0.1	-16.7	48	9	24[9]	2	1	1	4	—20—			
Monaco	793[1]	25,000[1]	...	...	...	...	...	...	...	...	...	...	...	...	...	...	...
Mongolia	902	360	1,820	-2.3	2.1	-4.4	34	9	32[9]	2	—	4	14	—13—			1
Morocco	34,936	1,290	3,320	0.2	1.9	-1.7	19	2	17	4	8	6	20	...	12	12	
Mozambique	1,472	80	500	2.6	4.0	-1.4	31[2]	—	8[2]	11[2]	2[2]	15[2]	10[2]	—23[2]—			—
Myanmar (Burma)	119,334	2,610	...	...	...	...	61	1	8	1	—	2	22	—5—			
Namibia	3,569	2,250	5,390	1.6	2.6	-1.0	14	16	9	3	1	5	10	12	1	26	3
Nauru	81	7,210	...	...	...	...	...	...	...	...	...	...	...	...	...	...	...
Nepal	4,710	210	1,090	2.3	2.7	-0.4	42	1	9	11	1	7	5	10	—9—		4

private	govern-ment	gross domestic invest-ment	exports	imports	indirect taxes net of subsidies	consump-tion of fixed capital	compen-sation of employ-ees	net operating surplus	goods, merchan-dise	invisibles	current balance of payments	receipts from foreign nationals	expendi-tures by nationals abroad	country
87	8	20	20	−35	6[5]	4[5]	—90[5]—		−1,197.4	1,097.6	−99.8	75	72	El Salvador
59	16	25	55	−55	...	...	...		−116.7	−227.3	−334.0	...	...	Equatorial Guinea
...	...	...	...	...	10	...	90		418.4	287.7	130.7	...	...	Eritrea
59	23	29	80	−91	12[2]	12[2]	50[2]	25[2]	−1,057.7	610.4	−447.3	353	90	Estonia
84	11	15	12	−22	...	...	...		−817.3	647.3	−170.0	36	25	Ethiopia
49[2]	34[2]	4[2]	44[2]	−32[2]	...	...	...		51.6[10]	94.4[10]	146.0[10]	...	...	Faroe Islands
67[2]	20[2]	15[2]	56[2]	−59[2]	13[2]	7[2]	34[2]	46[2]	−182.4	192.6	10.2	312	55	Fiji
56	22	15	36	−29	11	17	51	20	11,035	−6,245	4,790	1,716	2,383	Finland
60	20	18	23	−21	13	13	52	23	15,099	5,412	20,511	27,527	16,328	France
...	...	...	...	...	8[5]	7	61[5]	31[5,7]						French Guiana
60[4]	40[4]	21[4]	9[4]	−31[4]	...	...	97					260	...	French Polynesia
31	17	27	65	−40	3	—97—			1,744.4[10]	−1,644.6[10]	99.8[10]	4	112	Gabon
79	18	16	44	−57	16	—84—			−98.4	50.7	−47.7	23	16	Gambia, The
149[5]	16[5]	41[5]	19[5]	−84[5]	...	...	...		...	...	...	...	...	Gaza Strip
89[2]	9[2]	32[2]	36[2]	−66[2]	...	...	...		...	...	...	...	...	Georgia
57	19	23	23	−22	12[2]	13[2]	54[2]	21[2]	71,210	−84,280	−13,070	16,221	50,675	Germany
85	11	16	27	−39	...	...	...		−366.0	42.2	−323.8	233	20[8]	Ghana
...	...	...	...	...	...	...	90[2]		...	...	...	...	...	Gibraltar
74	14	21	17	−26	14[2]	9[2]	36[2]	41[2]	−15,505	10,951	−4,554	4,106	1,322	Greece
...	...	...	...	...	...	...	...		...	...	...	...	...	Greenland
50	19	36	50	−55	16	—84—			−122.6	64.6	−57.9	58	4	Grenada
...	...	...	...	...	11[5]	7	78[5]	11[5,7]	...	...	...	458	...	Guadeloupe
...	...	...	...	...	...	...	...		...	...	...	950[2]	...	Guam
86	6	16	18	−25	6[4]	2[4]	—92[4]—		−643.4	191.9	−451.5	277	174	Guatemala
...	...	...	...	...	...	...	...		...	...	...	146[2]	...	Guernsey[18]
82	9	14	20	−24	...	...	...		111.2	−288.5	−177.3	1	21	Guinea
88	9	22	19	−38	...	...	...		−35.4[10]	−6.0[10]	−41.5[10]	...	...	Guinea-Bissau
64	18	32	108	−122	16	—84—			−40.8[10]	−94.0[10]	−134.8[10]	47	21	Guyana
101	6	2	4	−12	1	—99—			−416.1	278.4	−137.7	81	35	Haiti
63	10	38	39	−50	14[2]	6[2]	48[2]	32[2]	−141.4[10]	−59.5[10]	−200.9[10]	80	57	Honduras
59	8	32	140	−138	6[2]	7	47[2]	46[2,7]				9,604	...	Hong Kong
72	13	21	29	−35	16[2]	7	54[2]	34[2,7]	−2,652	963	−1,689	1,723	1,070	Hungary
59	21	15	36	−31	17[2]	13[2]	50[2]	14[2]	206.0[10]	−155.0[10]	51.0[10]	167	282	Iceland
65[2]	12[2]	23[2]	12[2]	−12[2]	10[2]	10[2]	—80[2]—		−9,462	4,163	−5,299	2,574	470[5]	India
57	8	32	26	−24	7[2]	5[2]	—88[2]—		5,948	−13,611	−7,663	5,228	2,172	Indonesia
56	13	24	25	−18	2[4]	15[4]	—84[4]—		7,402	−2,170	5,232	160	862[2]	Iran
48[6]	35[6]	19[6]	3[6]	−5[6]	−7[6]	10[6]	45[6]	52[6]	...	...	...	55[4]	...	Iraq
60	16	14	72	−63	10[2]	9[2]	50[2]	31[2]	15,194	−13,792	1,402	2,688	2,030	Ireland
...	...	...	...	...	...	...	...		...	...	...	...	...	Isle of Man
64	28	24	33	−48	17[2]	14[2]	49[2]	20[2]	−7,969	912	−7,057	2,784	3,148	Israel
63	17	17	23	−20	10[2]	12[2]	44[2]	34[2]	60,821	−19,781	41,040	27,451	12,419	Italy
64	12	31	58	−66	...	...	...		−1,489	1,231	−258	1,069	148	Jamaica
59	10	29	9	−7	7	16	56	21	83,560	−17,680	65,880	3,226	36,792	Japan
...	...	...	...	...	...	...	...		...	...	...	526[4]	...	Jersey
66	24	35	50	−74	16	11	38	35	−2,001.1	1,779.2	−221.9	696	420	Jordan
43[2]	14[2]	49[2]	33[2]	−39[2]	...	...	...		−326.3	−426.1	−752.4	...	...	Kazakstan
62	15	20	38	−34	15[2]	7	35[2]	50[2,7]	−510.3	343.9	−166.4	454	135	Kenya
...	...	...	...	...	12	—88—			...	...	...	1	3[8]	Kiribati
...	...	...	...	...	...	...	...		...	...	...	...	...	Korea, North
54	11	36	30	−31	11[2]	10[2]	47[2]	31[2]	−15,306	−7,755	−23,061	5,587	5,903	Korea, South
41	34	16	51	−43	...	...	...		7,034	−261	6,773	107	2,322	Kuwait
66	20	20	33	−39	6	—94—			−251.7	−173.0	−424.7	5	6	Kyrgyzstan
90[6]	10[6]	13[6]	13[6]	−25[6]	2	—98—			−320.9	−43.6	−364.5	51	30	Laos
52[2]	22[2]	9[2]	73[2]	−57[2]	13	12	46	29	−927	512	−415	20	24	Latvia
110[4]	44[4]	10[4]	32[4]	−96[4]	...	...	...		...	...	...	672[8]	...	Lebanon
89	19	84	21	−114	18	—82—			−666.7[8]	774.8[8]	108.1[8]	17[8]	7[8]	Lesotho
58[4]	13[4]	10[4]	42[4]	−23[4]	...	...	...		...	...	...	...	...	Liberia
34[6]	27[6]	22[6]	46[6]	−28[6]	...	...	...		...	...	...	7[8]	154[5]	Libya
...	...	...	...	...	...	...	...		...	...	...	...	...	Liechtenstein
76[2]	13[2]	18[2]	71[2]	−78[2]	10[5]	2[5]	39[5]	50[5]	−896.2	173.6	−722.6	124	138	Lithuania
49	11	19	94	−73	16[5]	11[5]	66[5]	8[5]	−1,599[8]	3,512[8]	1,913[8]	290[4]	...	Luxembourg
30	8	33	69	−39	...	...	...		...	...	...	3,117	117	Macau
57	6	42	44	−49	11[2]	7	67[2]	22[2,7]	−316.5	28.4	−288.1	19	24[8]	Macedonia
90	7	11	22	−30	...	...	...		−120	−171	−291	60	59	Madagascar
69	23	13	30	−35	7	—93—			−276.4[8]	−173.2[8]	−499.6[8]	6	15[8]	Malawi
50	13	39	90	−91	14[5]	—86[5]—			−100[10]	−7,262[10]	−7,362[10]	3,910	1,737[8]	Malaysia
49[4]	22[4]	19[4]	62[4]	−53[4]	...	...	...		−173.8	183.0	9.2	210	32[8]	Maldives
88	13	25	22	−48	4	—96—			−101.9[8]	−62.5[8]	−164.4[8]	17	56	Mali
61	21	30	97	−110	11	6	46	38	−755.4	397.6	−357.8	606	184	Malta
...	...	...	...	...	4[6]	4[6]	70[6]	22[6]	−50.7[8]	54.6[8]	3.9[8]	2[8]	...	Marshall Islands
...	...	...	...	...	10[5]	7	71[5]	19[5,7]				384	...	Martinique
83	10	16	42	−51	...	...	...		183.8[10]	−161.7[10]	22.1[10]	15[4]	31[4]	Mauritania
64	12	32	57	−66	15	7	42	43[7]	−294.6	311.7	17.1	430	159	Mauritius
47[4]	92[4]	3[4]	—42[4]—		...	...	...		...	...	...	...	...	Mayotte
70	12	23	13	−18	9	11	29	50	6,531	−8,454	−192.3	6,164	3,153	Mexico
—162—		—	34	−96	...	...	...		−112.0[8]	109.5[8]	−2.5[8]	...	...	Micronesia
51	20	35	—6—		...	...	...		−254.1	−45.9	−300.0	57	56	Moldova
...	...	...	...	...	...	...	...		...	...	...	...	...	Monaco
66[2]	18[2]	19[2]	63[2]	−66[2]	23	22[4]	39[4]	40[4,23]	25.3[10]	13.6[10]	38.9[10]	...	...	Mongolia
67	17	21	21	−27	...	...	...		−2,111	1,484	−627	1,163	302	Morocco
66	20	70	23	−79	...	...	...		−478.3	119.4	−358.9	...	...	Mozambique
—88—		12	1	−2	3	3	46	48	−737[8]	563[8]	−174[8]	38	165	Myanmar (Burma)
49	31	24	54	−59	16[2]	7	46[2]	38[2,7]	24.9	110.2	85.3	263	82	Namibia
...	...	...	...	...	...	...	...		...	...	...	...	...	Nauru
77	8	22	24	−32	6	—94—			−1,105.9	779.3	−326.6	117	136	Nepal

National product and accounts (continued)

country	gross national product (GNP), 1996						origin of gross domestic product (GDP) by economic sector, 1994 (%)										
	nominal ('000,000 U.S.$)	per capita		average annual growth rates, 1990–96			primary		secondary			tertiary					other
		nominal (U.S.$)	purchasing power parity (PPP; U.S.$)	real GNP (%)	popu-lation (%)	real GNP per capita (%)	agri-culture	mining	manu-factur-ing	con-struc-tion	public util-ities	transp., commu-nications	trade	finan-cial svcs.	other svcs.	govern-ment	
Netherlands, The	402,565	25,940	20,850	1.8	0.6	1.2	4	3	19	6	2	7	16	——48——			−4
Netherlands Antilles	2,388[1]	11,610[1]	...	...	...	...	...	...	...	...	...	...	...	...			...
New Caledonia	3,017	15,330	...	...	...	...	2[4]	4[4]	13[4]	6[4]	3[4]	6[4]	23[4]	——20[4]——		25[4]	−2[4]
New Zealand	57,135	15,720	16,500	1.7	1.3	0.4	9[2]	1[2]	18[2]	3[2]	3[2]	8[2]	15[2]	22[2]	6[2]	11[2]	4[2]
Nicaragua	1,705	380	1,760	−0.2	3.1	−3.3	33	1	16	3	1	4	24	5	6	7	—
Niger	1,879	200	920	−2.3	3.3	−5.6	43	4	7	2	2	5	——15——		10	11	1
Nigeria	27,599	240	870	1.2	2.9	−1.7	39	27	6	1	—	3	16	4	—	2	—
Northern Mariana Is.	550	8,730	...	...	...	...	...	...	...	...	...	...	...	...			...
Norway	151,198	34,510	23,220	3.7	0.5	3.2	3[6]	15[6]	13[6]	4[6]	4[6]	9[6]	11[6]	9[6]	10[6]	16[6]	6[6]
Oman	13,135	5,950	...	...	...	...	3	38	5	4	1	5	15	4	12	18	−6
Pakistan	63,567	480	1,600	1.1	2.9	−1.8	23	—	16	3	3	9	14	7	7	7	10
Palau	145[1]	8,810[1]	...	...	...	...	...	...	...	...	...	...	...	...			...
Panama	8,249	3,080	7,060	3.6	1.8	1.8	10[2]	—	8[2]	6[2]	4[2]	20[2]	13[2]	19[2]	9[2]	13[2]	−3[2]
Papua New Guinea	5,049	1,150	2,820	5.0	2.3	2.7	27	26	8	4	1	5	8	1	——15——		5
Paraguay	9,179	1,850	3,480	−1.5	2.7	−4.2	26	—	15	5	5	5	27	——13——		5	—
Peru	58,671	2,420	4,410	4.8	2.0	2.8	14[10]	8[10]	22[10]	9[10]	2[10]	7[10]	18[10]	14[10]	——5[10]——		—
Philippines	83,298	1,160	3,550	1.0	2.3	−1.3	22	1	25	6	3	6	15	10	——12——		—
Poland	124,682	3,230	6,000	3.3	0.2	3.1	6	9	29[9]	6	4	6	14	7	13	4	11
Portugal	100,934	10,160	13,450	1.5	0.1	1.4	6[4]	9	29[4, 9]	8[4]	3[4]	6[4]	17[4]	9[4]	8[4]	13[4]	—
Puerto Rico	31,600[1]	8,200[1]	...	...	...	...	1	22	42	2[22]	2[4]	8[24]	14	13	11	10	−1
Qatar	6,473	11,600	...	...	...	...	1	31	13	5	1	4	7	12	——27——		—
Réunion	2,864[1, 10]	4,300[1, 10]	...	...	...	...	4[5]	—	9[5]	6[5]	4[5]	6[5]	18[5]	21[5]	——32[5]——		—
Romania	36,191	1,600	4,580	0.1	−0.4	0.5	20	3	32[3]	6	3	10	12	——17——			3
Russia	356,030	2,410	4,190	−9.2	−0.1	−9.1	7	3	29[3]	8	3	13	16	14	10	5	—
Rwanda	1,268	190	630	−8.2	−0.6	−7.6	40	9	14[9]	3	1	3	20	——8——		6	5
St. Kitts	240	5,870	7,310	3.5	−0.5	4.0	6	—	11	12	2	15	24	12	4	19	−5
St. Lucia	553	3,500	4,920	2.8	1.0	1.8	8	1	5	7	4	14	22	14	3	12	10
St. Vincent	264	2,370	4,160	2.4	0.7	1.7	9	—	8	10	4	18	15	9	2	15	11
Samoa	200	1,170	...	0.1	1.2	−1.1	42	—	12	2	7	3	11	...	11	13	—
San Marino	607[1, 8]	24,700[1, 8]	...	...	...	...	...	...	...	...	...	...	...	...			—
São Tomé and Príncipe	45	330	...	−1.7	2.7	−4.4	25	—	5[19]	14	19	——19——		6	8	22	—
Saudi Arabia	129,186[1]	6,660[1]	...	...	...	...	6[2]	35[2]	8[2]	8[2]	—	7[2]	7[2]	6[2]	2[2]	20[2]	2[2]
Senegal	4,856	570	1,650	−0.6	2.5	−3.1	22	9	13[9]	3	2	10	——21——		——29——		—
Seychelles	526	6,850	...	1.5	1.5	0.0	4	9	11[9]	8	1	28	8	9	2	14	16
Sierra Leone	925	200	510	−3.9	2.4	−6.3	39	17	9	2	—	9	14	2	2	3	4
Singapore	92,987	30,550	26,910	6.6	2.0	4.6	—	—	28	7	2	15	18	27	——10——		−6
Slovakia	18,206	3,410	7,460	−1.2	0.2	−1.4	8	9	25[9]	5	6	10	16	9	10	11	—
Slovenia	18,390	9,240	12,110	4.4	−0.1	4.5	5[5]	25	30[5]	4[5]	2[5]	7[5]	13[5]	13[5]	14[5]	4[5]	7[5]
Solomon Islands	349	900	2,250	1.3	3.3	−2.0	33	—	4	2	2	6	9	5	——24——		17
Somalia	4,582[1, 10]	500[1, 10]	...	...	...	...	65[6]	—	4[6]	4[6]	1[6]	6[6]	9[6]	3[6]	2[6]	6[6]	−1[6]
South Africa	132,455	3,520	7,450	−0.2	1.7	−1.9	5	9	23	3	4	8	16	17	2	15	−2
Spain	563,249	14,350	15,290	1.0	0.2	0.8	3	3	23[3]	8	3	——60——					—
Sri Lanka	13,475	740	2,290	3.4	1.2	2.2	24	2	15	7	—	——52——					—
Sudan, The	27,131[1]	860[1]	...	...	...	...	37	—	9	5	2	——37——			8		—
Suriname	433	1,000	2,630	−0.3	1.1	−1.4	14	13	10	4	5	17	20	21	—	5	−10
Swaziland	1,122	1,210	3,320	−1.2	3.1	−4.3	10	2	29	3	1	5	7	5	5	18	16
Sweden	227,315	25,710	18,770	−0.2	0.5	−0.7	2	—	22	6	3	7	11	25	——28——		−5
Switzerland	313,729	44,350	26,340	−1.0	0.9	−1.9	3[5]	9	23[5, 9]	7[5]	2[5]	6[5]	17[5]	25[5]	——21[5]——		−4[5]
Syria	16,808	1,160	3,020	4.3	3.0	1.3	29	7	5	4	1	9	29	4	2	10	1
Taiwan	297,953	13,900	...	4.9	0.9	4.0	4	—	29	5	3	7	15	21	7	11	−1
Tajikistan	1,964	340	900	−18.5	1.9	−20.4	19	3	35[3]	12	3	5	1	——9——			19
Tanzania	5,174	170	...	−0.2	3.0	−3.2	50	1	7	5	2	7	13	9	——4——		2
Thailand	177,476	2,960	6,700	6.7	1.3	5.4	10	1	28	7	2	7	16	10	——16——		—
Togo	1,278	300	1,650	−3.9	3.0	−6.9	34	5	9	3	4	6	22	——7——		9	22
Tonga	175	1,790	...	2.0	0.2	1.8	33	9	4[9]	4	...	12	12	...	——12——		22
Trinidad and Tobago	5,017	3,870	6,100	0.1	0.8	−0.7	2	27	9	7	2	9	14	13	6	10	1
Tunisia	17,581	1,930	4,550	1.3	1.9	−0.6	13	4	18	4	2	8	27	——14——			10
Turkey	177,530	2,830	6,060	1.7	1.8	−0.1	16	1	20	7	3	15	19	6	4	10	—
Turkmenistan	4,319	940	2,010	−13.1	3.8	−16.9	9	66	7	5	1	2	3	1	——2——		3
Tuvalu	7	650	...	...	...	...	22	2	3	14	2	4	14	10	——28——		—
Uganda	5,826	300	1,030	4.0	3.2	0.8	45	—	6	5	1	4	11	6	9	4	9
Ukraine	60,904	1,200	2,230	−13.5	−0.4	−13.1	22[2]	9	31[2, 9]	7[2]	1[2]	12[2]	11[2]	12[2]	9[2]	4[2]	−8[2]
United Arab Emirates	44,620[1]	17,500[1]	...	...	...	...	3	33	8	10	2	6	11	12	3	12	−2
United Kingdom	1,152,136	19,600	19,960	1.5	0.3	1.2	2	2	21	5	3	8	14	27	4	19	−5
United States	7,433,517	28,020	28,020	1.2	1.0	0.2	2[2]	1[2]	18[2]	4[2]	3[2]	6[2]	16[2]	19[2]	20[2]	12[2]	—
Uruguay	18,464	5,760	7,760	3.8	0.6	3.2	9	—	18	5	—	7	15	10	12	10	14
Uzbekistan	23,490	1,010	2,450	−5.6	2.1	−7.7	28[10]	3	16[3, 10]	8[10]	3	8[10]	6[10]	——20[10]——			14[10]
Vanuatu	224	1,290	3,020	−1.1	2.7	−3.8	22	—	5	6	2	8	34	13	1	12	−2
Venezuela	67,333	3,020	8,130	−0.3	2.2	−2.5	5[2]	22[2]	16[2]	7[2]	2[2]	5[2]	14[2]	——19[2]——		8[2]	2[2]
Vietnam	21,915	290	1,570	6.2	2.2	4.0	29	9	——30[9]——			4	14	——11——			11
Virgin Islands (U.S.)	1,246[1, 25]	11,740[1, 25]	...	...	...	...	...	...	...	...	...	...	...	...			...
West Bank	2,726[1]	1,600[1]	...	...	...	...	14	1	14	10	—	8	17	18	7	11	...
Western Sahara	601[1, 6]	300[1, 6]	...	...	...	...	...	...	...	...	...	...	...	...			...
Yemen	6,016	380	790	−2.2	4.7	−6.9	18	10	13	3	1	11	14	6	1	20	3
Yugoslavia	19,881[1, 10]	2,000[1, 10]	...	...	...	...	23[10]	9	41[9, 10]	7[10]	—	7[10]	16[10]	——11[10]——			4[10]
Zambia	3,363	360	860	−4.8	2.8	−7.6	26	8	30	3	1	4	12	6	——8——		3
Zimbabwe	6,815	610	2,200	−1.1	2.4	−3.5	10	7	41	2	6	5	11	5	2	7	3

[1]Gross domestic product (GDP).   [2]1993.   [3]Manufacturing includes mining and public utilities.   [4]1990.   [5]1992.   [6]1991.   [7]Net operating surplus includes consumption of fixed capital.   [8]1994.
[9]Manufacturing includes mining.   [10]1995.   [11]Services includes restaurants and hotels.   [12]Finance includes public utilities.   [13]Mining includes public utilities.   [14]Government includes finance, insurance.
[15]Republic of Cyprus only.   [16]Services includes hotels.   [17]Services includes transportation, communications.   [18]Excludes Alderney and Sark.   [19]Manufacturing includes public utilities.

gross domestic product (GDP) by type of expenditure, 1994(%)					cost components of gross domestic product (GDP), 1994 (%)				balance of payments, 1996 (current external transactions; '000,000 U.S.$)			tourist trade, 1995 ('000,000 U.S.$)		country
consumption		gross domestic invest-ment	foreign trade		indirect taxes net of subsidies	consump-tion of fixed capital	compen-sation of employ-ees	net operating surplus	net transfers		current balance of payments	receipts from foreign nationals	expendi-tures by nationals abroad	
private	govern-ment		exports	imports					goods, merchan-dise	invisibles				
60	14	20	51	−46	10	12	52	26	19,968	446	20,414	5,762	11,455	Netherlands,The
...	...	...	...	...					−964.4[10]	1,050.9[10]	86.5[10]	639[8]	...	Netherlands Antilles
...	...	...	...	...	8[5]	10[5]	51[5]	30[5]				102[8]	...	New Caledonia
62	15	21	32	−30	14	10	43	33	493	−4,441	−3,948	2,163	1,283	New Zealand
86	16	25	24	−52	...	...	...	...	−377.4	−119.3	−496.7	50	40	Nicaragua
82	16	10	16	−25	1	— 99 —			−17.6[10]	−134.1[10]	−151.7[10]	15	21	Niger
82	3	9	24	−19	1	2	9	88	8,482	−5,390	3,092	54	144[8]	Nigeria
...												655		Northern Mariana Is.
50	21	23	38	−32	11[2]	15[2]	51[2]	23[2]	13,917	−2,671	11,246	2,386	4,221	Norway
42	31	17	49	−40	23	7	33[5]	67[5, 7, 23]	2,954	−3,219	−265	92	47	Oman
71	12	19	16	−19	10	6	— 84 —		−2,878[10]	−455[10]	−3,333[10]	114	449	Pakistan
...	...	...	...	...										Palau
60	15	28	100	−104	...	7	41	42	−629.8	569.5	−60.3	310	128	Panama
52[2]	21[2]	19[2]	49[2]	−40[2]	11[6]	12[6]	37[6]	40[6]	1,016.6	−703.4	313.2	60	75	Papua New Guinea
88	7	23	34	−53	7[5]	8[5]	30[5]	56[5]	−1,276.7[8]	527.9[8]	−748.8[8]	213	181	Paraguay
74	7	22	11	−14	7[6]	4[6]	20[6]	69[6]	−2,000	−1,607	−3,607	520	302	Peru
72	10	23	33	−39	10	11	26	53	−11,342	7,389	−3,953	2,450	422	Philippines
64	19	16	24	−23	15	7	44	40[7]	−7,287	4,023	−3,264	6,700	5,500	Poland
68	19	25	25	−36	12	4	48	36	−1,664	715	−949	4,402	2,155	Portugal
63	14	17	69	−63	5	7	40	49	...	...	...	1,826	833	Puerto Rico
32[2]	34[2]	19[2]	46[2]	−31[2]	1[2]	12[2]	36[2]	52[2]	...	...	...	...	...	Qatar
79[5]	29[5]	27[5]	4[5]	−39[5]	9[5]	7	59[5]	31[5, 7]				157[5]	...	Réunion
62	27	11	— 1 —		5[2]	7	36[2]	59[2, 7]	−2,470	−109	−2,579	574	695	Romania
47	23	26	28	−23	11	20	38	30	22,826	−11,427	11,399	4,312	11,599	Russia
147	8	3	6	−64	5	— 95 —			−148.4	149.1	0.7	2[2]	17[5]	Rwanda
49[2]	25[2]	39[2]	— −13[2] —		13[5]	— 87[5] —			−89.6	24.9	−64.7	65	5	St. Kitts
67	15	24	65	−71	16	— 84 —			−184.4	104.0	−80.3	268	23[8]	St. Lucia
71	20	33	41	−65	16	— 84 —			−65.9	46.4	−19.5	57	3	St. Vincent
...	...	...	...	...	...	...	...	...	−80.8	93.1	12.3	36	3	Samoa
61	17	25	275	−278	...	...	...	...	−235.9[8]	288.9[8]	53.0[8]	...	...	San Marino
84	33	41	25	−83	...	...	...	...	−14.7	19.6	4.9	1[4]	2[4]	São Tomé and Príncipe
43	27	20	40	−30	2[2]	9[2]	30[2]	60[2]	31,345	−31,130	215	1,884[4]	...	Saudi Arabia
78	12	15	35	−40	...	...	...	...	−249.6[10]	192.1[10]	−57.5[10]	130	75	Senegal
53[2]	30[2]	29[2]	54[2]	−65[2]	22[6]	11[6]	38[6]	29[6]	−158.9	138.8	−20.1	100	24	Seychelles
70	11	8	31	−20	8[4]	6[4]	14[4]	73[4]	−126.7[10]	0.2[10]	−126.5[10]	6	2	Sierra Leone
42	8	32	— 17 —		...	...	...	...	2,281	12,002	14,283	8,212	5,134	Singapore
50	22	23	65	−59	13[6]	14[6]	48[6]	25[6]	−2,283	193	−2,090	620	330	Slovakia
54	20	21	61	−56	13[2]	17[2]	61[2]	9[2]	−881.6	920.6	39.0	1,079	413	Slovenia
...	...	...	...	...	...	...	...	...	...	...	...	65[5]	11[6]	Solomon Islands
75[4]	9[4]	20[4]	1[4]	−5[4]	...	...	...	...	...	...	...	...	...	Somalia
60	21	18	23	−22	11	14	54	22	2,030	−4,063	−2,033	1,595	1,749	South Africa
63	17	20	22	−22	8	12	45	36	−14,912	16,668	1,756	25,701	4,540	Spain
75	10	27	34	−46	14[2]	5[2]	44[2]	37[2]	−776.9	124.4	−652.5	224	186	Sri Lanka
71[6]	18[6]	17[6]	5[6]	−10[6]	...	...	...	...	−719.2	−107.6	−826.8	3[2]	33[5]	Sudan, The
61	23	21	120	−125	7[5]	11[5]	45[5]	36[5]	123.0[10]	−50.1[10]	72.9[10]	14	3[8]	Suriname
65	27	18	105	−115	...	...	...	...	−76.9	86.2	9.3	35	37	Swaziland
54	27	14	37	−32	10[2]	14[2]	59[2]	16[2]	18,636	−12,744	5,892	3,447	5,422	Sweden
59	14	22	36	−32	5	10	63	22	1,836	18,634	20,470	9,364	7,636	Switzerland
70	14	30	30	−45	−9[2]	4[2]	— 106[2] —		−218	503	285	1,325	398	Syria
59	15	24	44	−42	11	9	53	27	17,568	−6,541	11,027	3,286	8,457	Taiwan
...	...	...	...	...	19	— 81 —			...	...	...	...	...	Tajikistan
92	7	28	25	−52	9	3	8	80	−449.0	−61.9	−510.9	259	360	Tanzania
53	9	42	37	−42	12[2]	11[2]	26[2]	51[2]	−9,488	−5,204	−14,692	7,664	3,372	Thailand
78	12	14	31	−35	...	...	...	...	−37.1[8]	−19.7[8]	−56.8[8]	8	23[8]	Togo
...	...	...	...	...	14	— 86 —			...	...	...	11	1[2]	Tonga
57	15	13	44	−28	10[2]	11[2]	50[2]	29[2]	587.7[10]	−293.9[10]	293.8[10]	73	79	Trinidad and Tobago
56	24	23	40	−43	...	...	...	...	−1,804	1,268	−536	1,325	251	Tunisia
66	12	21	21	−20	9	5	— 86 —		−9,632	8,182	−1,450	4,957	912	Turkey
44[2]	23[2]	46[2]	— −13[2] —		...	...	...	...	485[8]	−401[8]	84[8]	...	...	Turkmenistan
...	...	...	...	...	...	...	...	...	...	...	...	0.3[2]	...	Tuvalu
84	9	13	11	−17	9	— 91 —			−352.1	101.5	−250.6	79	93	Uganda
59	9	35	35	−39	−5[6]	15[6]	77[6]	13[6]	−4,296	3,111	−1,185	...	...	Ukraine
54	18	27	70	−68	−1[2]	15[2]	24[2]	62[2]	...	...	...	...	...	United Arab Emirates
64	21	15	26	−27	13[2]	10[2]	56[2]	20[2]	−19,470	19,020	−450	19,073	24,737	United Kingdom
68	16	17	10	−12	8[2]	12[2]	61[2]	19[2]	−189,250	40,520	−148,730	61,137	45,855	United States
74	13	15	21	−22	19[5]	7	44[5]	37[5, 7]	−702.9	407.3	−295.6	611	236	Uruguay
58[2]	25[2]	15[2]	— −3[2] —		−1[5]	3[5]	65[5]	33[5]	...	...	...	...	...	Uzbekistan
51	29	30	49	−60	...	...	...	...	−51.2[10]	32.9[10]	−18.3[10]	58	5	Vanuatu
72	7	13	30	−22	7	8	34	51	13,756	−4,932	8,824	811	1,865	Venezuela
70[2]	16[2]	19[2]	28[2]	−33[2]	...	...	...	...	−900[8]	−66[8]	−966[8]	854[4]	...	Vietnam
...	...	...	...	...	...	...	...	...	...	...	...	821	...	Virgin Islands (U.S.)
...														West Bank
...														Western Sahara
68[2]	29[2]	20[2]	15[2]	−32[2]	11[2]	5[2]	— 84[2] —		−11.0[10]	193.7[10]	182.7[10]	38	76	Yemen
...					6	17	46	31	...	...	...	42	...	Yugoslavia
66	19	14	22	−20	7[4]	9[4]	57[4]	26[4]	...	...	...	47	56[5]	Zambia
63	18	18	40	−40	10[6]	— 90[6] —			157.6[8]	−582.5[8]	−424.9[8]	154	106	Zimbabwe

[20]Manufacturing includes mining, construction, and public utilities. [21]Services includes trade. [22]Construction includes mining. [23]Net operating surplus includes indirect taxes net of subsidies. [24]Transportation includes public utilities. [25]1987.

Employment and labour

This table provides international comparisons of the world's national labour forces—giving their size; composition by demographic component and employment status; and structure by industry.

The table focuses on the concept of "economically active population," which the International Labour Organisation (ILO) defines as persons of all ages who are either employed or looking for work. In general, the economically active population does not include students, persons occupied solely in domestic duties, retired persons, persons living entirely on their own means, and persons wholly dependent on others. Persons engaged in illegal economic activities—smugglers, prostitutes, drug dealers, bootleggers, black marketeers, and others—also fall outside the purview of the ILO definition. Countries differ markedly in their treatment, as part of the labour force, of such groups as members of the armed forces, inmates of institutions, the unemployed (both persons seeking their first job and those previously employed), seasonal and international migrant workers, and persons engaged in informal, subsistence, or part-time economic activities. Some countries include all or most of these groups among the economically active, while others may treat the same groups as inactive.

Three principal structural comparisons of the economically active total are given in the first part of the table: (1) participation rate, or the proportion of the economically active who possess some particular character-istic, is given for women and for those of working age (usually ages 15 to 64), (2) activity rate, the proportion of the total population who *are* economically active, is given for both sexes and as a total, and (3) employment status, usually (and here) grouped as employers, self-employed, employees, family workers (usually unpaid), and others.

Each of these measures indicates certain characteristics in a given national labour market; none should be interpreted in isolation, however, as the meaning of each is influenced by a variety of factors—demographic structure and change, social or religious customs, educational opportunity, sexual differentiation in employment patterns, degree of technological development, and the like. Participation and activity rates, for example, may be high in a particular country because it possesses an older population with few children, hence a higher proportion of working age, or, because, despite a young population with many below working age, the economy attracts eligible immigrant workers, themselves almost exclusively of working age. At the same time, low activity and participation rates might be characteristic of a country having a young population with poor employment possibilities or of a country with a good job market distorted by the presence of large numbers of "guest" or contract workers who are not part of the domestic labour force. An illiterate woman in a strongly sex-differentiated labour force is likely to begin and end as a family or

Employment and labour

country	year	economically active population										distribution by economic sector			
		total ('000)	participation rate (%)		activity rate (%)			employment status (%)				agriculture, forestry, fishing		manufacturing; mining, quarrying; public utilities	
			female	ages 15–64	total	male	female	employers, self-employed	employees	unpaid family workers	other	number ('000)	% of econ. active	number ('000)	% of econ. active
Afghanistan	1979	3,941	7.9	49.1	30.3	54.2	4.9	52.2	33.8	14.0	—	2,369	60.1	494	12.5
Albania	1994	1,340	47.0[3]	92.0[3,4]	57.4[3]	60.8[3]	54.0[3]	...	...	...	...	534	39.9	84[5]	6.3[5]
Algeria	1987	5,341	9.2	44.3	23.6	42.4	4.4	16.8	61.7	2.6	18.9	725	13.6	622	11.6
American Samoa	1990	14.2	41.1	52.6[8]	30.4	34.8	25.7	2.1	92.6	0.2	5.1	0.3	2.3	4.8	33.7
Andorra	1989	25	45.6	74.3	55.1	...	...	...	...	...	...	0.3	1.2	2.7	11.0
Angola	1991	4,166	38.4	60.1[10]	40.3	50.4	30.4	...	...	...	...	2,892	69.4	438[11]	10.5[11]
Antigua and Barbuda	1991	26.8	45.6	69.7	45.1	50.9	39.6	12.1	82.8	0.7	4.4	1.0	3.9	1.9	7.3
Argentina	1995	14,345	36.7	64.5	41.5	53.5	29.9	28.0[13]	60.4[13]	5.0[13]	6.6[13]	1,201[14]	12.0[14]	2,136[14]	21.3[14]
Armenia	1994	1,618	...	74.5[16]	43.1	...	...	7.0	86.4	0.3	6.3	538	33.3	323	20.0
Aruba	1991	31.1	42.5	67.1	46.7	54.5	39.0	7.0	86.4	0.3	6.3	0.2	0.5	2.3	7.3
Australia	1995–96[18]	9,066	42.9	73.3[19]	49.9	57.2	42.6	13.4	77.2	0.8	8.6	422	4.7	1,278	14.1
Austria	1994[18]	3,881	42.8	70.8	48.3	57.0	40.1	9.7[20]	87.4[20]	3.0[20]	—	273	7.0	898	23.1
Azerbaijan	1994	2,698	...	64.4[16,20]	36.2	...	...	...	...	...	...	1,011	37.5	466	17.3
Bahamas, The	1994	139	47.5	77.8	50.7	54.8	46.8	11.6[22]	85.1[22]	0.3[22]	3.0[22]	6.9	5.0	7.3	5.3
Bahrain	1991	226	17.5	66.8	44.6	63.5	18.5	5.1	88.5	0.1	6.3	5	2.3	33	14.6
Bangladesh	1990–91[18]	51,155	39.3	76.9	46.0	54.2	38.9	26.3	11.5	46.2	16.0	33,033	65.1	5,980	11.7
Barbados	1995[18]	137	49.5	79.9	51.8	54.6	49.1	8.8[24]	76.4[24]	0.2[24]	14.6[24]	6.3	4.6	15.6	11.4
Belarus	1994	4,798	...	77.7[16]	46.5	...	...	...	...	...	...	917	19.1	1,365	28.4
Belgium	1992	4,237	42.3	51.5[25]	42.2	49.8	34.9	12.7	72.4	3.4	11.5	95	2.2	788	18.6
Belize	1996	75.5	30.8	58.5[26]	34.1	47.2	21.0	26.2[20]	59.2[20]	4.9[20]	9.8[20]	18.3[13]	31.4[13]	7.0[13]	12.0[13]
Benin	1992	2,085	42.6	73.4	43.0	50.6	35.7	58.4	5.3	30.5	5.8	1,148	55.0	162	7.8
Bermuda	1995	34.1	50.0	63.5[13]	55.8	57.4	54.4	9.7[13]	84.0[13]	0.1[13]	6.2[13]	0.5	1.5	1.4	4.2
Bhutan	...	...	...	...	...	...	...	...	...	...	...	...	...	...	...
Bolivia	1992	2,530	38.2	64.0	39.4	48.7	30.4	41.2	31.5	7.1	20.2	984	38.9	281	11.1
Bosnia and Herzegovina	1990[5]	1,026	36.9	...	22.7	...	...	...	...	...	...	39	3.8	519	50.5
Botswana	1991[18]	441	38.5	59.4	33.3	42.8	24.5	6.5	62.5	17.1	13.9	98	22.1	47	10.7
Brazil	1993[18]	70,965	39.6	68.2[25]	47.9	59.2	37.1	26.3[22]	62.3[22]	7.7[22]	3.7[22]	18,254	25.7	9,486	13.4
Brunei	1991	112	32.9	67.6	43.0	54.6	30.0	3.5	91.4	0.4	4.7	2.2	1.9	11.6	10.4
Bulgaria	1995	3,738	48.4[28]	68.8[28]	46.3[28]	48.7[28]	44.1[28]	8.4	75.9	0.9	14.8	783	20.9	1,003	26.8
Burkina Faso	1991	4,679	49.4	83.9[25]	50.9	52.7	49.2	...	...	...	...	4,294	91.8	58	1.2
Burundi	1990	2,780	52.6	91.4	52.5	51.2	53.8	62.8	5.1	30.3	1.8	2,574	92.6	37	1.3
Cambodia	1993	4,010	55.8	86.2	43.1	39.5	46.4	...	...	...	...	2,454[14]	74.4[14]	220[11,14]	6.7[11,14]
Cameroon	1991	4,740	33.2	58.9[10]	40.0	53.9	26.3	60.2[22]	14.6[22]	18.0[22]	7.1[22]	2,856	60.3	628[11]	13.2[11]
Canada	1995[18]	14,928	45.1	74.7	50.4	55.9	45.0	9.6[20]	89.0[20]	0.5[20]	0.9[20]	554	3.7	2,375	15.9
Cape Verde	1990	121	37.1	64.3	35.3	46.9	24.9	24.7	53.7	2.0	19.6	29.9	24.8	6.8	5.7
Central African Republic	1988	1,187	46.8	78.3	48.2	52.2	44.3	75.3	8.0	8.1	8.6	881	74.2	31	2.6
Chad	1991	2,016	18.2	51.6[10]	35.3	56.5	14.7	...	...	...	...	1,489	73.9	149[11]	7.4[11]
Chile	1995[18]	5,274	32.4	58.6	37.8	52.1	24.0	26.4[19]	64.6[19]	3.2[19]	5.8[19]	810	15.4	983	18.6
China	1990	657,290	44.9	85.0	57.9	61.8	53.7	...	...	...	...	467,926	71.2	87,275	13.3
Colombia	1985	9,558	32.8	49.4[29]	34.3	46.6	22.3	...	...	...	...	2,412[14]	28.5[14]	1,231[14]	14.5[14]
Comoros	1991	215	40.0	57.8[10]	44.4	53.7	35.2	47.6[14]	25.6[14]	— 26.8[14] —		171	79.4	14[11]	6.5[11]
Congo, Dem. Rep. of the	1991	13,848	35.2	64.2[10]	36.1	47.2	25.2	...	...	...	...	9,021	65.1	2,200[11]	15.9[11]
Congo, Rep. of the	1984	563	45.6	54.0	29.5	33.0	26.2	64.3	31.4	1.2	3.1	294	52.2	50	8.8
Costa Rica	1995	1,232	30.5	57.0[19,25]	36.9	50.8	22.8	24.0[19]	72.2[19]	3.3[19]	0.6[19]	261	21.2	218	17.7
Côte d'Ivoire	1988	4,263	32.3	66.6	39.4	52.2	26.0	...	...	...	...	2,628	61.6	100	2.3
Croatia	1991	2,040	42.9	65.2	45.3	53.9	37.4	12.7	73.7	2.0	11.6	341	16.7	571	28.0
Cuba	1988	4,570	36.1	56.9[25]	44.2	56.2	32.1	5.7[30]	94.1[30]	0.2[30]	—	791[30]	22.3[30]	668[30]	18.9[30]
Cyprus[31,32]	1995	303	38.6	71.5	47.0	57.8	36.2	18.7[28]	73.1[28]	6.1[28]	2.1[28]	31	10.1	48	15.9
Czech Republic	1995	5,283	46.2	77.9[13]	51.1	56.6	46.0	12.7	83.4	0.5	3.4	342	6.5	1,733	32.8
Denmark	1995	2,812	45.3	79.1	53.4	59.2	47.8	8.8	84.2	—	7.0	123	4.4	582	20.7
Djibouti	1991	282	40.8	70.4[10]	61.5	74.1	50.3	...	...	...	...	212	75.2	31[11]	11.0[11]
Dominica	1991	26.4	34.5	62.4	38.0	50.0	26.1	29.2[33]	50.6[33]	1.9[33]	18.3[33]	7.3	27.9	2.3	8.8
Dominican Republic	1981	1,915	28.9	53.6	33.9	48.1	19.7	36.5	51.3	3.3	8.9	420	22.0	243	12.7
Ecuador	1990	3,360	26.4	55.7	34.8	51.5	18.3	45.7	42.5	4.4	7.4	1,036	30.8	404	12.0
Egypt	1994[18]	17,572	23.0	50.9	30.4	45.9	14.2	24.7[28]	50.0[28]	16.4[28]	9.0[28]	5,365	30.5	2,274	12.9
El Salvador	1995	2,136	37.1	62.9	39.1	51.4	27.8	31.7	48.2	8.0	12.1	585	27.4	412	19.3
Equatorial Guinea	1983	103	35.7	66.7	39.2	52.5	26.9	29.0	16.0	29.9	25.1	59.4	57.9	1.8	1.8
Eritrea	...	...	...	...	...	...	...	...	...	...	...	...	...	...	...
Estonia	1994	730[34]	47.6[34]	71.8[34]	48.9[34]	54.9[34]	43.7[34]	4.8	85.2	0.8	9.2	92	12.9	182	25.5
Ethiopia	1995	24,606	41.1	72.2	43.3	50.3	36.5	58.5[35]	6.5[35]	34.0[35]	1.0[35]	21,605	87.8	419	1.7

traditional agricultural worker. Loss of working-age men to war, civil violence, or emigration for job opportunities may also affect the structure of a particular labour market.

The distribution of the economically active population by employment status reveals that a large percentage of economically active persons in some less developed countries falls under the heading "employers, self-employed." This occurs because the countries involved have poor, largely agrarian economies in which the average worker is a farmer who tills his own small plot of land. In countries with well-developed economies, "employees" will usually constitute the largest portion of the economically active.

Caution should be exercised when using the economically active data to make intercountry comparisons, as countries often differ in their choices of classification schemes, definitions, and coverage of groups and in their methods of collection and tabulation of data. The population base containing the economically active population, for example, may range, in developing countries, from age 9 or 10 with no upper limit to, in developed countries, age 18 or 19 upward to a usual retirement age of from 55 to 65, with sometimes a different range for each sex. Data on female labour-force participation, in particular, often lack comparability. In many less developed countries, particularly those dominated by the Islamic faith,

a cultural bias favouring traditional roles for women results in the undercounting of economically active women. In other less developed countries, particularly those in which subsistence workers are deemed economically active, the role of women may be overstated.

The second major section of the table provides data on the distribution by economic (also conventionally called industrial) sector of the economically active population. The data usually include such groups as unpaid family workers, members of the armed forces, and the unemployed, the last distributed by industry as far as possible.

The categorization of industrial sectors is based on the divisions listed in the *International Standard Industrial Classification of All Economic Activities*. The "other" category includes persons whose activities were not adequately defined and the unemployed who were not distributable by industrial sector.

A substantial part of the data presented in this table is summarized from various issues of the ILO's *Year Book of Labour Statistics*, which compiles its statistics both from official publications and from information submitted directly by national census and labour authorities. The editors have supplemented and updated ILO statistical data with information from Britannica's holdings of relevant official publications and from direct correspondence with national authorities.

construction		transportation, communications		trade, hotels, restaurants		finance, real estate		public administration, defense		services		other		country
number ('000)	% of econ. active	number ('000)	% of econ. active	number ('000)	% of econ. active	number ('000)	% of econ. active	number ('000)	% of econ. active	number ('000)	% of econ. active	number ('000)	% of econ. active	
51	1.3	66	1.6	138	3.5	1	1	1	1	749[1]	19.0[1]	78[2]	2.0[2]	Afghanistan
33[5]	2.5[5]	19[5]	1.4[5]	3[5]	0.2[5]	3[5]	0.2[5]	16[5]	1.2[5]	145[5]	10.8[5]	505[6]	37.7[6]	Albania
690	12.9	216	4.1	391	7.3	143	2.7	7	7	1,180[7]	22.1[7]	1,374	25.7	Algeria
1.2	8.3	0.8	5.5	1.8	13.0	0.3	2.1	1.4	10.0	2.8	19.8	0.7[9]	5.1[9]	American Samoa
2.9	11.8	...	...	6.0	24.2	1.3	5.4	2.6	10.3	4.1	16.7	0.1	0.5	Andorra
11	11	12	12	12	12	12	12	12	12	836[12]	20.1[12]	—	—	Angola
3.1	11.6	2.4	9.0	8.5	31.9	1.5	5.4	7	7	6.4[7]	23.9[7]	1.9	7.0	Antigua and Barbuda
1,003[14]	10.0[14]	460[14]	4.6[14]	1,702[14]	17.0[14]	396[14]	3.9[14]	7	7	2,399[7,14]	23.9[7,14]	736[14,15]	7.3[14,15]	Argentina
108	6.7	49	30.0	65	4.0	29	1.8	30	1.9	350	21.6	126[17]	7.8[17]	Armenia
3.2	10.4	2.3	7.5	11.0	35.4	2.4	7.8	7	7	8.6[7]	27.7[7]	1.1[17]	3.5[17]	Aruba
600	6.6	547	6.0	2,107	23.2	1,111	12.3	379	4.2	1,844	20.3	779[17]	8.6[17]	Australia
372	9.6	251	6.5	810	20.9	355	9.1	7	7	912[7]	23.5[7]	10	0.3	Austria
200	7.4	180	6.7	169	6.3	11	0.4	7	7	589[7]	21.8[7]	712[17]	2.6[17]	Azerbaijan
11.6	8.3	11.2	8.1	44.2	31.8	12.9	9.3	10.7	7.7	29.7	21.4	4.5[23]	3.2[23]	Bahamas, The
27	11.8	14	6.1	30	13.2	17	7.6	41	18.1	43	19.0	16[17]	7.3[17]	Bahrain
525	1.0	1,611	3.1	4,285	8.4	296	0.6	7	7	1,909[7]	3.7[7]	3,245[21]	6.3[21]	Bangladesh
12.2	8.9	5.9	4.3	35.3	25.8	8.4	6.1	7	7	48.8[7]	35.7[7]	4.3[2]	3.1[2]	Barbados
370	7.7	318	6.6	459	9.6	97	2.0	90	1.9	952	19.8	230[21]	4.8[21]	Belarus
245	5.8	257	6.1	634	15.0	342	8.1	7	7	1,393[7]	32.9[7]	484[17]	11.4[17]	Belgium
4.1[13]	7.0[13]	2.9[13]	5.0[13]	10.0[13]	17.2[13]	1.8[13]	3.1[13]	5.4[13]	9.2[13]	6.0[13]	10.3[13]	2.8[13]	4.8[13]	Belize
52	2.5	53	2.5	433	20.7	3	0.1	7	7	165[7]	7.9[7]	71[21]	3.4[21]	Benin
1.7	5.0	2.2	6.4	10.8	31.6	5.2	15.3	7	7	12.3[7]	35.9[7]	—	—	Bermuda
...	...	...	...	...	...	...	...	...	...	...	...	...	...	Bhutan
129	5.1	117	4.6	232	9.2	54	2.1	59	2.3	350	13.8	323[15]	12.7[15]	Bolivia
75	7.3	69	6.7	131	12.8	39	3.8	7	7	155[7]	15.1[7]	—	—	Bosnia and Herzegovina
58	13.2	11	2.6	35	8.0	13	3.0	7	7	107[7]	24.2[7]	72[17]	16.2[17]	Botswana
4,289	6.0	2,284	3.2	8,475[27]	11.9[27]	1,389	2.0	7	7	22,392[7,27]	31.6[7,27]	4,395[9]	6.2[9]	Brazil
14.1	12.6	5.4	4.8	15.4	13.8	5.8	5.2	7	7	52.1[7]	46.6[7]	5.3[17]	4.7[17]	Brunei
188	5.0	251	6.7	357	9.5	51	1.4	76	2.0	532	14.2	497[17]	13.3[17]	Bulgaria
11	0.2	1.5	0.3	120	2.6	2	—	7	7	112[7]	2.4[7]	67[17]	1.4[17]	Burkina Faso
20	0.7	9	0.3	26	0.9	2.0	0.1	7	7	85[7]	3.1[7]	27[17]	1.0[17]	Burundi
11	11	12	12	12	12	12	12	12	12	625[2,14]	18.9[1,14]	—	—	Cambodia
11	11	12	12	12	12	12	12	12	12	1,256[12]	26.5[12]	—	—	Cameroon
724	4.9	890	6.0	3,168	21.2	1,676	11.2	810	5.4	3,308	22.2	1,422[9]	9.5[9]	Canada
22.7	18.8	6.1	5.1	12.7	10.6	0.8	0.7	7	7	17.4[7]	14.4[7]	24.1	20.0	Cape Verde
6	0.5	7	0.6	92	7.8	0.7	0.1	7	7	70[7]	5.9[7]	100[17]	8.5[17]	Central African Republic
11	11	12	12	12	12	12	12	12	12	377[12]	18.7[12]	—	—	Chad
411	7.8	401	7.6	974	18.5	340	6.4	7	7	1,323[7]	25.1[7]	34[15]	0.6[15]	Chile
11,890	1.8	11,814	1.8	25,631	3.9	8,268	1.3	7	7	34,053[7]	5.2[7]	10,434	1.6	China
242[14]	2.9[14]	353[14]	4.2[14]	1,262[14]	14.9[14]	278[14]	3.3[14]	7	7	1,998[7,14]	23.6[7,14]	691[14,15]	8.2[14,15]	Colombia
11	11	12	12	12	12	12	12	12	12	30[12]	14.1[12]	—	—	Comoros
11	11	12	12	12	12	12	12	12	12	2,627[12]	19.0[12]	—	—	Congo, Dem. Rep. of the
25	4.5	29	5.1	67	11.8	3	0.5	7	7	85[7]	15.1[7]	10	2.0	Congo, Rep. of the
80	6.5	64	5.2	239	19.4	52	4.2	7	7	298[7]	24.2[7]	19[15]	1.6[15]	Costa Rica
85	2.0	118	2.8	530	12.4	1	1	1	1	591[1]	13.9[1]	210[2]	4.9[2]	Côte d'Ivoire
93	4.5	112	5.5	223	10.9	58	2.8	104	5.1	204	10.0	329[17]	16.1[17]	Croatia
313[30]	8.8[30]	249[30]	7.0[30]	306[30]	8.6[30]	1	1	1	1	1,086[1,30]	30.7[1,30]	128[30]	3.6[30]	Cuba
26	8.7	19	6.2	77	25.4	23	7.6	7	7	65[7]	21.6[7]	13	4.4	Cyprus[30,31]
479	9.1	396	7.5	835	15.8	353	6.7	277	5.2	823	15.6	44[23]	0.8[23]	Czech Republic
175	6.2	197	7.0	471	16.8	279	10.0	167	6.0	803	28.5	15[23]	0.5[23]	Denmark
11	11	12	12	12	12	12	12	12	12	39[12]	13.8[12]	—	—	Djibouti
2.8	10.7	1.2	4.6	3.7	13.9	0.8	3.1	1.5	5.8	3.4	13.1	3.2[17]	12.3[17]	Dominica
81	4.3	40	2.1	192	10.0	22	1.2	7	7	363[7]	18.9[7]	553[15]	28.9[15]	Dominican Republic
197	5.9	131	3.9	477	14.2	81	2.4	7	7	838[7]	24.9[7]	196[15]	5.8[15]	Ecuador
1,037	5.9	849	4.8	1,581	9.0	297	1.7	7	7	3,919[7]	22.3[7]	2,250[23]	12.8[23]	Egypt
147	6.9	86	4.0	414	19.4	28	1.3	7	7	433[7]	20.2[7]	32[2]	1.5[2]	El Salvador
1.9	1.9	1.8	1.7	3.1	3.0	0.4	0.4	7	7	8.4[7]	8.2[7]	25.8[17]	25.2[17]	Equatorial Guinea
...	...	...	...	...	...	...	...	...	...	...	...	...	...	Eritrea
53	7.5	63	8.8	114	16.0	39	5.5	38	5.3	124	17.4	9[23]	1.2[23]	Estonia
61	0.2	103	0.4	936	3.8	19	0.1	7	7	1,252[7]	5.1[7]	210[2]	0.9[2]	Ethiopia

Employment and labour (continued)

country	year	economically active population — total ('000)	participation rate (%) female	participation rate (%) ages 15–64	activity rate (%) total	activity rate (%) male	activity rate (%) female	employment status (%) employers, self-employed	employment status (%) employees	employment status (%) unpaid family workers	employment status (%) other	distribution by economic sector — agriculture, forestry, fishing number ('000)	% of econ. active	manufacturing; mining, quarrying; public utilities number ('000)	% of econ. active
Faroe Islands	1977	17.6	27.2	64.0	41.9	58.2	23.9	11.9	86.1	...	2.0	3.3	18.8	3.9	21.9
Fiji	1986	241	21.2	56.0	33.7	52.4	14.5	33.6	42.2	16.3	7.9	106	44.1	22	9.0
Finland	1995	2,521	47.0	73.5	49.4	53.7	45.2	12.7[19]	83.3[19]	0.6[19]	3.4[19]	176	7.0	517	20.5
France	1994[18]	25,871	44.9	67.7	44.8	50.6	39.2	10.2	77.4	—	12.4	1,048	4.1	4,432	17.4
French Guiana	1990	48.8	38.2	67.3	42.5	50.5	33.9	10.6	62.7	2.5	24.2	4.2	8.6	3.1	6.4
French Polynesia	1988	75	37.1	64.8	39.9	48.2	30.9	13.0	55.0	4.0	28.0	7.6	10.0	5.4	7.2
Gabon	1991	504	36.9	56.0[10]	43.9	53.9	30.7	...	...	...	...	338	67.1	71[11]	14.1[11]
Gambia, The	1983	326	46.3	78.2	47.3	51.1	43.6	0.5	78.0	14.3	7.1	240	73.7	9	2.9
Gaza Strip	1996	173	9.0	36.3[25]	18.0	32.0	3.2	15.7	46.8	6.7	30.8	9.0	5.2	17.0[36]	9.8[36]
Georgia	1993	1,920	...	58.1[16, 28]	35.7	...	...	...	...	...	...	562	29.3	303	15.8
Germany	1995	40,083	42.8	71.9	49.1	57.8	40.9	8.3	80.4	1.2	10.1	1,334	3.3	10,956	27.3
Ghana	1984	5,580	51.2	82.5[25]	45.4	44.9	45.8	67.7	15.7	12.2	4.4	3,311	59.3	631	11.3
Gibraltar	1994	12.9	38.0	66.9[13, 25]	47.5	58.7	36.2	6.6[30]	89.7[30]	...	3.6[30]	—	—	0.7	5.7
Greece	1995[18]	4,249	38.1	60.7	41.5	53.3	30.5	30.4	48.5	11.1	10.0	788	18.6	703	16.5
Greenland	1976	21.4	33.4	63.5[25]	43.1	53.0	31.4	12.6	82.5	0.4	4.5	3.2	15.1	3.3	15.3
Grenada	1988	38.9	48.6	72.7[35]	39.9	42.9	37.2	16.0[30]	64.2[30]	0.8[30]	19.0[30]	5.6	14.3	3.3	8.6
Guadeloupe	1990	172	45.5	66.4	44.5	49.6	39.7	13.2	53.7	2.0	31.1	8.4	4.9	9.6	5.6
Guam	1990	61.1	37.4	75.7[8]	49.7	58.4	39.7	2.4	94.4	0.1	3.1	0.5	0.8	3.5	5.3
Guatemala	1989[18]	2,898	25.5	59.1	33.5	50.8	16.7	32.7	47.6	16.2	3.5	1,416	48.9	405	14.0
Guernsey[38]	1991	30.2	43.2	74.2	51.2	60.6	42.6	13.7	86.3	—	—	2.4	7.8	2.4	7.9
Guinea	1983	1,823	39.4	63.5	39.1	48.7	30.1	36.2	15.6	37.6	10.6	1,424	78.1	27	1.5
Guinea-Bissau	1991	464	40.5	67.1[10]	45.9	56.2	36.1	...	...	...	...	362	78.0	21[11]	4.5[11]
Guyana	1992–93	278	34.1	61.8	38.8	51.9	26.0	14.3[14]	63.8[14]	1.9[14]	20.0[14]	50[14]	20.4[14]	41[14]	16.8[14]
Haiti	1990	2,679	40.0	64.8	41.1	50.3	32.3	59.1	16.5	10.4	14.0	1,535	57.3	178	6.6
Honduras	1995[18]	1,866	29.9	59.4[25]	35.0	49.7	20.7	36.5[28]	48.7[28]	10.7[28]	4.1[28]	680	36.5	346	18.6
Hong Kong	1995[18]	3,068	37.9	70.0	50.8	62.2	39.1	9.9[19]	87.4[19]	0.7[19]	1.9[19]	17	0.5	591	19.3
Hungary	1995[18]	4,095	43.6	58.6	40.1	47.3	33.5	10.6	76.8	1.0	11.5	336	8.2	1,100	26.9
Iceland	1995	149.0	46.7	81.9	55.6	59.2	52.1	17.2	76.6	1.1	4.8	14.1	9.5	26.7	17.9
India	1991	314,131	28.6	60.7[25, 30]	37.5	51.6	22.3	8.8[30]	16.3[30]	3.6[30]	71.3[30]	191,341	60.9	30,423	9.7
Indonesia	1995	86,361	38.2[28]	67.0[28]	42.9[28]	53.1[28]	32.7[28]	42.7	33.0	17.1	7.2	35,233	40.8	10,987	12.7
Iran	1991	14,737	11.1	46.8	26.4	45.6	6.0	39.7	45.4	2.3	12.6	3,205	21.8	2,243	15.2
Iraq	1988	4,127	12.0	45.3	24.7	42.3	6.1	25.4[39]	59.5[39]	11.4[39]	3.7[39]	477	11.6	439	10.6
Ireland	1995	1,443	37.8	61.6	40.3	50.6	30.2	18.1	68.5	1.2	12.1	150	10.4	293	20.3
Isle of Man	1991	33.2	42.3	73.2	47.6	56.9	38.9	15.8	80.1	—	4.1	1.2	3.7	3.9	11.6
Israel	1995[18]	2,100	43.2	53.8[25]	37.9	43.4	32.5	13.8	79.3	0.6	6.3	57	2.7	424	20.2
Italy	1994[18]	22,680	36.9	57.4	40.1	52.1	28.8	21.4	62.8	4.0	11.8	1,573	6.9	4,837	21.3
Jamaica	1994	1,091	47.4	72.0[40]	43.6	46.8	40.6	32.7	49.5	2.0	15.8	218	20.0	107	9.8
Japan	1995	66,660	40.5	71.5	53.2	64.6	42.3	12.0[19]	78.8[19]	6.1[19]	3.1[19]	3,670	5.5	15,330	23.0
Jersey	1991	47.5	43.2	66.9[25]	56.5	66.1	47.5	12.6	84.0	...	3.4	2.2	4.7	3.8	8.0
Jordan	1993	859	11.4[42]	43.2[42]	22.2	...	...	22.8[43]	67.2[43]	0.8[43]	9.2[43]	55	6.4	97	11.3
Kazakstan	1995	6,976	...	71.8[16, 20]	40.8	...	...	...	...	...	...	1,442	20.7	1,372	19.7
Kenya	1991	10,260	39.4	64.4[10]	39.0	47.4	30.7	...	...	...	...	7,857	76.6	816[11]	8.0[11]
Kiribati	1990	32.6	46.4	75.6[25]	45.1	48.9	41.4	71.9	25.3	...	2.8	23.1	71.0	0.9	2.8
Korea, North	1985	9,084	46.0	75.3	44.6	48.6	40.6	...	...	...	...	3,726[24]	44.1[24]	2,790[11, 24]	33.0[11, 24]
Korea, South	1995[18]	20,797	40.2	62.0[25]	46.4	55.2	37.5	27.4	61.2	9.3	2.0	2,544	12.2	4,937	23.7
Kuwait	1995	746	26.1	61.5[42]	47.4	60.4	29.4	3.9[42]	94.1[42]	0.1[42]	1.9[42]	9[42]	1.3[42]	69[42]	9.4[42]
Kyrgyzstan	1995	1,691	...	...	37.5	...	...	...	...	...	...	378	22.3	162	9.6
Laos	1985	2,014	45.3	84.2	48.9	53.1	44.6	...	...	...	...	1,393[14]	75.7[14]	130[11, 14]	7.1[11, 14]
Latvia	1995	1,272	49.1	...	50.8	...	...	...	...	...	...	220	17.3	228	17.9
Lebanon	1988	904	16.6	44.0	26.5	43.9	8.9	...	...	...	...	132[44]	19.1[44]	131[44]	18.9[44]
Lesotho	1986	504	27.0	44.0	31.6	47.3	16.7	16.8	55.7	20.5	7.0	131	25.9	142	28.2
Liberia	1984	704	41.0	56.3	33.5	39.1	27.8	59.1	21.6	14.4	5.0	481	68.3	31	4.4
Libya	1991	1,169	9.3	37.1[10]	24.8	42.9	4.9	...	...	...	...	129	11.0	372[11]	31.8[11]
Liechtenstein	1996	16.2	40.3	71.3	52.0	63.7	40.8	6.4	90.8	0.1	2.7	0.3	2.0	4.9	30.2
Lithuania	1994	1,937	...	81.8[16, 20]	52.1	...	...	...	...	...	...	390	20.1	378	19.5
Luxembourg	1991[45]	168	36.5	62.5	43.5	56.4	31.2	9.2	85.3	1.1	4.4	5	3.2	26	15.8
Macau	1995[18]	187.1	43.2	64.0	44.1	51.7	36.9	10.5	84.6	1.2	3.7	0.5	0.2	43.0	23.0
Macedonia	1993	937	...	...	45.2	...	...	...	...	...	...	215	22.9	168	17.9
Madagascar	1991	5,311	39.3	63.9[10]	42.8	52.4	33.0	...	...	...	...	4,043	76.1	632[11]	11.9[11]
Malawi	1987	3,458	51.0	89.4	43.3	43.9	42.8	4.9	16.2	77.6	1.3	2,968	85.8	114	3.3
Malaysia	1995[18]	7,869	33.9	57.3[13]	35.1[13]	47.3[13]	22.6[13]	21.1[20]	71.4[20]	7.5[20]	—	1,527	19.4	1,861	23.6
Maldives	1990	56.4	19.9	50.2	26.5	41.3	10.8	39.7	49.3	4.5	6.5	14.1	25.0	9.4	16.6
Mali	1987	3,438	37.4	67.4	44.7	57.2	32.7	35.4	5.2	57.6	1.8	2,803	81.5	191	5.6
Malta	1990	132	25.4	47.4[13]	37.2	56.1	18.7	14.1[48]	77.4[48]	...	8.5[48]	3	2.5	38	28.8
Marshall Islands	1988	11.5	30.1	54.1[28]	26.5	37.7	14.8	21.6	58.9	7.1	12.5	2.2	18.7	1.0	9.0
Martinique	1990	165	47.5	68.1	45.9	49.8	42.2	9.5	56.9	1.5	32.1	8.4	5.1	9.7	5.9
Mauritania	1991	638	22.3	45.5[10]	30.8	48.1	13.8	...	...	...	...	410	64.3	70[11]	11.0[11]
Mauritius[49]	1993	463	35.2	68.0	44.5	57.9	31.2	12.2[22]	80.1[22]	1.9[22]	5.9[22]	81	17.5	146	31.5
Mayotte	1991	27.3	29.4	56.4	28.9	39.2	17.7	12.0	42.9	7.3	37.8	3.1	11.4	1.3	4.7
Mexico	1995	35,558	32.1	61.8	39.4	54.5	24.9	30.1[20]	53.8[20]	13.6[20]	2.6[20]	8,453	23.8	5,628	15.8
Micronesia	1990	30.5	29.8[14]	60.6	30.3	...	...	2.7[14]	74.4[14]	0.1[14]	22.7[14]	12.7	41.5	1.6	5.2
Moldova	1994	1,699	...	68.7[16]	39.1	...	...	...	...	...	...	767	45.1	232	13.7
Monaco	1990	12.6	39.7	...	42.0	53.2	31.8	17.4	75.1	0.3	7.2	—	0.3	2.7	21.8
Mongolia	1993	845	47.2[33]	77.9[33, 51]	39.3[33]	41.6[33]	37.1[33]	...	...	...	...	300	35.5	124	14.7
Morocco	1982	5,999	19.7	48.9	29.3	47.1	11.6	27.1	40.5	17.6	14.8	2,352	39.2	1,016	16.9
Mozambique	1980	5,671	52.4	87.3[25]	48.6	47.6	49.5	...	...	...	...	4,755	83.8	347	6.1
Myanmar (Burma)	1994[18]	17,358	35.3[48]	64.2[48]	40.2[48]	52.4[48]	28.2[48]	41.4[48]	27.4[48]	30.2[48]	1.0[48]	11,551	66.5	1,354	7.8
Namibia	1991	494	43.6	61.3	35.2	39.9	30.5	17.8	49.1	17.9	15.2	190	38.5	41	8.2
Nauru	1977	2.2	...	...	30.5	...	...	...	...	...	...	...	...	...	...
Nepal	1991	7,340	40.4	57.0[10]	40.0	47.8	32.2	75.8	21.4	2.3	0.4	5,962	81.2	164	2.2
Netherlands, The	1995	7,358	41.5	70.1	47.5	56.2	39.0	9.9	81.8	1.1	7.1	244	3.3	1,134	15.4
Netherlands Antilles	1992	87.8	45.1	68.6	46.3	53.1	40.1	...	...	...	...	0.5	0.6	8.4	9.6
New Caledonia	1989	66	37.5	70.7[53]	40.2	49.1	30.8	16.3	64.3	1.6	17.8	7.8	11.8	6.2	9.3
New Zealand	1995[18]	1,742	44.1	74.7	48.7	55.2	42.1	18.2[20]	71.3[20]	1.0[20]	9.5[20]	169	9.7	330	18.9
Nicaragua	1995	1,459	33.2[13]	51.6[10, 20]	35.2	...	...	...	...	...	...	457	31.4	183	12.5

construction		transportation, communications		trade, hotels, restaurants		finance, real estate		public administration, defense		services		other		country
number ('000)	% of econ. active	number ('000)	% of econ. active	number ('000)	% of econ. active	number ('000)	% of econ. active	number ('000)	% of econ. active	number ('000)	% of econ. active	number ('000)	% of econ. active	
2.0	11.1	1.9	11.1	2.1	11.9	0.3	1.9	[7]	[7]	3.5[7]	20.1[7]	0.6	3.2	Faroe Islands
12	4.9	13	5.5	26	10.8	6	2.5	[7]	[7]	37[7]	15.2[7]	20[17]	8.2[17]	Fiji
174	6.9	177	7.0	353	14.0	198	7.9	[7]	[7]	832[7]	33.0[7]	96[23]	3.8[23]	Finland
1,443	5.7	1,397	5.5	3,716	14.6	2,340	9.2	[7]	[7]	7,733[7]	30.3[7]	3,376[17]	13.2[17]	France
4.4	9.1	1.9	3.8	4.2	8.5	1.7	3.5	[7]	[7]	17.5[7]	35.9[7]	11.8[9]	24.2[9]	French Guiana
5.5	7.4	2.8	3.7	10.3	13.7	1.2	1.5	[7]	[7]	21.5[7]	28.6[7]	21.1[17]	28.0[17]	French Polynesia
[11]	[11]	[12]	[12]	[12]	[12]	[12]	[12]	[12]	[12]	951[12]	18.8[12]	—	—	Gabon
4	1.3	8	2.5	17	5.1	5	1.4	8	2.5	9	2.9	25	7.7	Gambia, The
17.8	10.3	5.7	3.3	20.8	12.0	[1]	[1]	[1]	[1]	49.3[1, 36]	28.5[1, 36]	53.3[9]	30.8[9]	Gaza Strip
125	6.5	107	5.6	117	6.1	20	1.0	49	2.6	479	24.9	158[17]	8.2[17]	Georgia
3,756	9.4	2,218	5.5	6,916	17.3	3,685	9.2	3,362	8.4	7,623	19.0	235[2]	0.6[2]	Germany
65	1.2	123	2.2	792	14.2	27	0.5	98	1.7	376	6.7	158[9]	2.8[9]	Ghana
1.2	9.6	0.9	7.4	3.2	24.7	1.6	12.4	1.9	14.8	3.3	25.5	—	—	Gibraltar
273	6.4	266	6.3	906	21.3	250	5.9	279	6.6	573	13.5	210[23]	4.9[23]	Greece
3.1	14.6	1.8	8.6	2.7	12.6	0.3	1.6	[7]	[7]	6.3[7]	29.5[7]	0.6	2.8	Greenland
3.5	9.1	1.7	4.4	5.4	13.9	0.8	2.0	[7]	[7]	5.9[7]	15.3[7]	12.7[17]	32.5[17]	Grenada
14.0	8.1	7.0	4.0	15.0	8.7	2.8	1.6	[7]	[7]	60.8[7]	35.2[7]	54.9[17]	31.8[17]	Guadeloupe
8.0	12.1	4.5	6.8	11.5	17.5	3.9	6.0	17.7	26.7	14.5	21.9	2.0[9]	3.1[9]	Guam
114	3.9	72	2.5	375	12.9	38	1.3	[7]	[7]	417[7]	14.4[7]	60[17]	2.1[17]	Guatemala
3.2	10.5	1.4	4.5	7.4	24.6	5.8	19.3	1.9	6.4	5.3	17.7	0.4	1.3	Guernsey[38]
9	0.5	29	1.6	37	2.0	4	0.2	[7]	[7]	138[7]	7.5[7]	156	8.5	Guinea
[11]	[11]	[12]	[12]	[12]	[12]	[12]	[12]	[12]	[12]	81[12]	17.5[12]	—	—	Guinea-Bissau
7[14]	2.8[14]	9[14]	3.8[14]	15[14]	6.2[14]	3[14]	1.2[14]	30[14]	12.1[14]	29[14]	11.9[14]	61[14, 17]	24.7[14, 17]	Guyana
28	1.0	21	0.8	353	13.2	5	0.2	[7]	[7]	155[7]	5.8[7]	404[17]	15.1[17]	Haiti
107	5.7	60	3.2	300	16.1	37	2.0	[7]	[7]	317[7]	17.0[7]	18[17]	1.0[17]	Honduras
252	8.2	347	11.3	869	28.3	355	11.6	[7]	[7]	626[7]	20.4[7]	12[2]	0.4[2]	Hong Kong
261	6.4	342	8.4	637	15.6	225	5.5	334	8.2	793	19.4	68[23]	1.7[23]	Hungary
10.3	6.9	9.6	6.4	24.8	16.6	13.5	9.1	6.3	4.2	41.8	28.1	1.9[23]	1.3[23]	Iceland
5,543	1.8	8,108	2.6	21,296	6.8	[1]	[1]	[1]	[1]	29,312[1]	9.3[1]	28,199	9.0	India
3,768	4.4	3,458	4.0	13,884	16.1	658	0.8	[7]	[7]	12,122[7]	14.0[7]	6,251[9]	7.2[9]	Indonesia
1,372	9.3	762	5.2	1,238	8.4	195	1.3	[7]	[7]	3,518[7]	23.9[7]	2,203[17]	14.9[17]	Iran
461	11.2	266	6.4	282	6.8	42	1.0	[7]	[7]	2,160[7]	52.3[7]	—	—	Iraq
101	7.0	81	5.6	272	18.8	120	8.3	74	5.1	283	19.6	69[15]	4.8[15]	Ireland
3.4	10.3	2.4	7.3	6.1	18.4	4.4	13.1	[7]	[7]	10.4[7]	31.4[7]	1.4[9]	4.1[9]	Isle of Man
141	6.7	115	5.5	330	15.7	244	11.6	107	5.1	533	25.4	149[17]	7.1[17]	Israel
1,641	7.2	1,080	4.8	4,221	18.6	1,514	6.7	[7]	[7]	5,134[7]	22.6[7]	2,676[9]	11.8[9]	Italy
66	6.1	40	3.7	196	17.9	47	4.3	[7]	[7]	237[7]	21.7[7]	180[17]	16.5[17]	Jamaica
6,750	10.1	4,130	6.2	14,790[41]	22.2[41]	5,550	8.3	[7]	[7]	15,190[7, 41]	22.8[7, 41]	1,240[17]	1.9[17]	Japan
4.4	9.3	2.4	5.0	6.8	14.4	7.4	15.6	3.1	6.5	15.7	33.1	1.6[17]	3.4[17]	Jersey
60	7.0	58	6.7	130	15.1	25	2.9	[7]	[7]	435[7]	50.6[7]	—	—	Jordan
364	5.2	507	7.3	1,035	14.8	334	4.8	[7]	[7]	1,664[7]	23.9[7]	258[17]	3.7[17]	Kazakstan
[11]	[11]	[12]	[12]	[12]	[12]	[12]	[12]	[12]	[12]	1,587[12]	15.5[12]	—	—	Kenya
0.3	1.0	0.9	2.8	1.3	4.1	0.4	1.4	2.1	6.5	2.3	7.0	1.1[17]	3.4[17]	Kiribati
[11]	[11]	[12]	[12]	[12]	[12]	[12]	[12]	[12]	[12]	1,939[12, 24]	22.9[12, 24]	—	—	Korea, North
1,934	9.3	1,082	5.2	5,445	26.2	1,655	8.0	647	3.1	2,390	11.5	165[2]	0.8[2]	Korea, South
115[42]	15.7[42]	38[42]	5.2[42]	83[42]	11.4[42]	22[42]	3.0[42]	[7]	[7]	384[7, 42]	52.6[7, 42]	112[, 42]	1.5[2, 42]	Kuwait
77	4.6	86	5.1	112	6.6	17	1.0	58	3.4	610	36.1	191[21]	11.3[21]	Kyrgyzstan
[11]	[11]	[12]	[12]	[12]	[12]	[12]	[12]	[12]	[12]	316[12, 14]	17.2[12, 14]	—	—	Laos
71	5.6	105	8.3	191	15.0	77	6.1	56	4.4	241	18.9	83	6.5	Latvia
43[44]	6.2[44]	48[44]	7.0[44]	115[44]	16.5[44]	24[44]	3.5[44]	[7]	[7]	200[7, 44]	28.8[7, 44]	—	—	Lebanon
28	5.5	8	1.6	24	4.7	2	0.5	[7]	[7]	157[7]	31.1[7]	13	2.6	Lesotho
4	0.6	14	2.0	47	6.7	[1]	[1]	[1]	[1]	63[1]	9.0[1]	64[17]	9.1[17]	Liberia
[11]	[11]	[12]	[12]	[12]	[12]	[12]	[12]	[12]	[12]	668[12]	57.1[12]	—	—	Libya
1.1	7.0	0.5	3.2	2.4	14.8	1.3	7.8	1.0	6.4	4.1	25.4	0.6[17]	3.4[17]	Liechtenstein
111	5.7	92	4.7	246	12.7	63	3.3	60	3.1	335	17.3	262[9]	13.5[9]	Lithuania
14	8.4	11	6.3	29	17.5	15	9.2	21	12.8	31	18.7	14[21]	8.1[21]	Luxembourg
18.6	9.9	10.4	5.6	47.3	25.3	11.4	6.1	[7]	[7]	55.4[7]	29.6[7]	0.3	0.1	Macau
37	3.9	21	2.3	54	5.8	20	2.2	15	1.6	69	7.4	338[46]	36.1[46]	Macedonia
[11]	[11]	[12]	[12]	[12]	[12]	[12]	[12]	[12]	[12]	636[12]	12.0[12]	—	—	Madagascar
46	1.4	25	0.7	94	2.7	6	0.2	[7]	[7]	147[7]	4.3[7]	57	1.7	Malaẅi
611	7.8	359	4.6	1,371	17.4	364	4.6	[7]	[7]	1,552[7]	19.7[7]	224[9]	2.8[9]	Malaysia
3.2	5.6	5.3	9.4	8.9	15.7	1.1	1.9	[7]	[7]	11.8[7]	21.0[7]	2.7[47]	4.7[47]	Maldives
13	0.4	6	0.2	159	4.6	0.3	—	75	2.2	84	2.4	107	3.1	Mali
6	4.4	9	6.9	13	9.8	5	3.7	[7]	[7]	53[7]	40.0[7]	5[9]	3.8[9]	Malta
1.1	9.4	0.5	4.7	1.4	12.1	0.8	7.3	[7]	[7]	3.1[7]	26.4[7]	1.4[17]	12.5[17]	Marshall Islands
9.3	5.6	6.7	4.0	14.0	8.5	3.0	1.8	[7]	[7]	59.1[7]	35.8[7]	54.8[17]	33.2[17]	Martinique
[11]	[11]	[12]	[12]	[12]	[12]	[12]	[12]	[12]	[12]	158[12]	24.8[12]	—	—	Mauritania
24	5.2	32	6.9	61	13.2	11	2.4	[7]	[7]	94[7]	20.3[7]	14[17]	3.1[17]	Mauritius[49]
3.1	11.4	1.5	5.4	2.0	7.2	0.1	0.4	[7]	[7]	5.7[7]	21.0[7]	10.5[17]	38.4[17]	Mayotte
2,033	5.7	1,528	4.3	8,015	22.5	1,183	3.3	[7]	[7]	8,030[7]	22.6[7]	688[17]	1.9[17]	Mexico
1.8	6.1	[50]	[50]	[50]	[50]	[50]	[50]	6.3	20.8	3.7[50]	12.1[50]	4.1[9]	13.5[9]	Micronesia
91	5.4	73	4.3	107	6.3	20	1.2	32	1.9	344	20.2	33[17]	1.9[17]	Moldova
0.7	5.3	....	....	2.5	20.2	1.0	8.0	2.8	22.4	1.9	14.9	0.9[21]	7.1[21]	Monaco
33	3.9	38	4.4	62	7.3	[1]	[1]	[1]	[1]	123[1]	14.5[1]	166[21]	19.7[21]	Mongolia
437	7.3	141	2.3	498	8.3	[52]	[52]	533	8.9	474[52]	7.9[52]	548[2]	9.1[2]	Morocco
42	0.7	7.7	1.4	112	2.0	[1]	[1]	[1]	[1]	243[1]	4.3[1]	95[9]	1.7[9]	Mozambique
292	1.7	420	2.4	1,450	8.4	1,264	7.3	[7]	[7]	486[7]	2.8[7]	541[9]	3.1[9]	Myanmar (Burma)
19	3.8	9	1.9	38	7.7	9	1.7	[7]	[7]	67[7]	1.2[7]	183[17]	37.1[17]	Namibia
....	....	....	....	....	....	....	....	[7]		....	....	....	....	Nauru
36	0.5	51	0.7	256	3.5	20	0.3	[7]	[7]	752[7]	10.3[7]	98	1.3	Nepal
406	5.5	406	5.5	1,342	18.2	880	12.0	529	7.2	1,650	22.4	762[17]	10.4[17]	Netherlands, The
6.5	7.4	5.0	5.7	20.9	23.8	8.2	9.3	[7]	[7]	24.8[7]	28.2[7]	13.4[9]	15.3[9]	Netherlands Antilles
4.5	6.8	3.1	4.7	9.5	14.3	2.5	3.8	[7]	[7]	22.0[7]	33.4[7]	13.5[9]	16.0[9]	New Caledonia
106	6.1	103	5.9	368	21.1	179	10.3	[7]	[7]	460[7]	26.4[7]	29[15]	1.7[15]	New Zealand
32	2.2	32	2.2	201	13.8	16	1.1	79	5.4	195	13.4	265[9]	18.2[9]	Nicaragua

Employment and labour   (continued)

country	year	economically active population										distribution by economic sector			
		total ('000)	participation rate (%)		activity rate (%)			employment status (%)				agriculture, forestry, fishing		manufacturing; mining, quarrying; public utilities	
			female	ages 15–64	total	male	female	employers, self-employed	employees	unpaid family workers	other	number ('000)	% of econ. active	number ('000)	% of econ. active
Niger	1988[54]	2,316	20.4	55.2	31.9	51.1	13.0	51.4	5.0	40.3	3.3	1,764	76.2	73	3.1
Nigeria	1986[18]	30,766	33.3	58.8	31.1	41.1	20.9	64.6	18.8	10.7	5.9	13,259	43.1	1,401	4.6
Northern Mariana Islands	1990	26.6	43.2	83.6[8]	61.3	66.2	55.9	1.4	96.1	0.2	2.3	0.6	2.3	6.0	22.5
Norway	1995	2,186	45.7	77.3[8]	50.2	55.1	45.3	8.1[19]	85.3[19]	0.9[19]	5.7[19]	109	5.0	363	16.6
Oman	1993	705	9.7	60.9	34.9	54.0	8.1	5.2	91.0	0.1	3.7	64	9.1	79	11.3
Pakistan	1993–94[18]	34,726	15.4	50.2	27.9	45.7	8.9	41.2[55]	32.4[55]	20.2[55]	6.2[55]	16,535	47.6	3,677	10.6
Palau	1990	6.1	36.9	64.1[8]	40.2	47.1	32.1	2.5	89.5	0.2	7.8	0.4	7.1	0.2	3.0
Panama	1994	967	34.3	60.7[25]	37.5	48.6	26.0	24.1	59.1	2.8	14.0	171	17.7	115	11.9
Papua New Guinea	1980[56]	733	39.8	35.2[10]	24.6	28.3	20.5	72.7	26.4	—	0.9	564	77.0	21	2.9
Paraguay	1982	1,039	19.7	57.5	34.3	54.8	13.6	43.1	37.7	9.2	9.9	446	42.9	129	12.4
Peru	1995	8,906	34.7	60.9	37.8	49.8	26.1	39.8[30]	41.8[30]	8.4[30]	10.0[30]	2,693[20]	32.5[20]	1,091[20]	13.2[20]
Philippines	1995[18]	28,040	37.4	67.3	...	...	...	36.2[19]	41.7[19]	13.7[19]	8.4[19]	11,323	40.4	2,769	9.9
Poland	1995[18]	17,004	45.9	66.9	44.0	48.9	39.3	20.1	61.6	5.1	13.1	3,355	19.7	4,436	26.1
Portugal	1993[18]	4,806[19]	44.6[19]	67.8[19]	48.8[19]	56.4[19]	41.9[19]	23.1	74.2	1.8	0.9	528	11.2	1,173	24.9
Puerto Rico	1995[18]	1,228	39.4	52.9[8]	32.2	40.1	24.8	13.6	85.2	0.7	0.6	42	3.4	220	17.9
Qatar	1988	293	11.2	80.8	53.7	77.3	22.2	1.8[44]	97.7[44]	—	0.5[44]	4.5	1.6	22.0	7.5
Réunion	1990[018]	234	41.1	60.3	39.1	46.8	31.6	8.4	53.1	1.1	37.4	11	4.8	11	4.8
Romania	1995	12,120	46.3	72.6	53.4	58.5	48.5	22.8	55.8	13.4	8.0	4,581	37.8	3,302	27.2
Russia	1994	73,655	...	...	49.8	...	...	...	...	...	...	11,029	15.0	18,126	24.6
Rwanda	1991	3,649	47.5	79.1[10]	50.2	53.3	47.2	...	...	...	...	3,313	90.8	129[11]	3.5[11]
St. Kitts and Nevis	1980	17.1	41.0	69.5	39.5	48.4	31.2	9.7	78.5	0.4	11.4	4.5	26.1	3.8	22.3
St. Lucia	1991	53.1	40.3	67.6	39.9	49.1	31.2	21.0[14]	55.8[14]	1.6[14]	21.6[14]	11.6	21.8	7.5	14.0
St. Vincent	1991	41.7	35.9	67.5	39.1	50.3	28.0	18.2	59.6	2.1	20.1	8.4	20.1	3.5	8.4
Samoa	1986	45.6	18.8	48.6[30]	29.0	44.5	11.6	21.1[30]	43.5[30]	35.0[30]	0.4[30]	29.0	63.6	2.4	5.4
San Marino	1995	16.8	39.3	76.4	57.2	66.1	47.4	15.3	77.1	0.3	7.3	0.2	1.5	5.3	31.3
São Tomé and Príncipe	1991	35	33.6	59.1	30.1	40.5	20.0	25.8	68.6	0.7	4.9	13.6	38.4	1.8	5.0
Saudi Arabia	1988	5,369	3.6	59.1	36.3	54.9	3.6	...	...	...	...	192	3.6	595	11.1
Senegal	1991	3,249	39.1	64.2[10]	42.6	52.6	32.9	...	...	...	...	2,543	78.3	228[11]	7.0[11]
Seychelles	1994[57]	28.1	...	...	38.9	...	...	...	...	...	...	2.2	7.7	4.6[11]	16.4[11]
Sierra Leone	1991	1,532	32.4	53.3[10]	35.9	49.4	22.8	...	...	...	...	945	61.7	275[11]	18.0[11]
Singapore	1995[18]	1,748	38.7	68.7	58.5	71.4	45.5	10.6	85.5	1.2	2.7	4	0.2	414	23.7
Slovakia	1995[18]	2,481	44.9	68.9	46.2	52.3	40.5	5.6	80.4	0.1	13.9	224	9.0	692	27.9
Slovenia	1995	952	46.2	67.9	47.9	53.1	42.9	11.3	77.0	4.3	7.4	94	9.9	363	38.1
Solomon Islands	1993[58]	29.6	25.6[44]	24.9[44,59]	13.7[44]	19.7[44]	7.3[44]	29.6[44]	68.6[44]	—	1.8[44]	8.1	27.4	3.1	10.4
Somalia	1991	3,215	40.5	64.3[10]	40.9	51.1	31.0	...	...	...	...	2,275	70.8	336[11]	10.5[11]
South Africa[60]	1991	11,624	39.4	69.3[53]	37.5	45.5	29.5	7.0	74.8	...	18.2	1,224	10.5	2,361	20.3
Spain	1995[18]	15,625	38.3	60.7[8]	40.2	50.7	30.1	16.7	57.2	2.9	23.1	1,351	8.6	2,864	18.3
Sri Lanka	1995	6,115	33.3	54.9[25]	40.5	54.8	26.6	24.9	54.2	7.8	13.1	1,985	32.5	945	15.5
Sudan, The	1983[54]	6,343	29.1	57.4	35.1	50.0	20.4	...	...	...	...	4,029	63.5	317	5.0
Suriname	1994[61]	89.8	35.1	52.3	45.2	59.4	31.4	...	...	...	...	4.8	5.3	10.7	11.9
Swaziland	1991	326	39.0	62.3[10]	39.8	49.5	30.3	...	...	...	...	215	66.0	39[11]	12.0[11]
Sweden	1995	4,319	47.9	78.2[8]	48.9	51.6	46.3	9.9	82.0	0.4	7.7	132	3.1	841	19.5
Switzerland	1995[18,45]	3,860	43.2	66.7[25]	55.0	64.0	46.4	12.8[19]	84.3[19]	2.9[19]	—	154	4.0	809	21.0
Syria	1991[18]	3,485	18.0	46.7[44]	27.8	44.6	10.2	31.0	49.3	13.0	6.7	917	26.3	471	13.5
Taiwan	1996[18]	9,310	39.2	58.4[25]	43.4	51.3	35.0	21.7	67.5	8.1	2.6	918	9.9	2,471	26.5
Tajikistan	1994	1,984	...	63.5[16,20]	34.4	...	...	...	...	...	...	1,005	50.7	205	10.4
Tanzania	1991	13,123	40.0	87.8[10]	46.0	48.9	43.2	...	...	...	...	10,540	80.3	614[11]	4.7[11]
Thailand	1995[18,62]	33,002	45.6	74.4[25,63]	55.5	60.5	50.5	31.2[63]	40.3[63]	19.5[63]	9.1[63]	16,991[64]	51.5[64]	4,365	13.2
Togo	1991	1,432	36.2	58.8[10]	40.0	51.8	28.5	70.3[30]	10.4[30]	11.3[30]	8.0[30]	991	69.2	161[11]	11.2[11]
Tonga	1990	32.0	33.0	57.0	33.6	45.2	22.0	33.7	45.4	16.8	4.1	11.7	36.5	5.1	15.8
Trinidad and Tobago	1995	521	37.2	65.4	41.3	52.4	30.4	17.8	61.3	2.7	18.3	51	9.7	82	15.8
Tunisia	1989	2,361	20.9	50.6	29.8	46.5	12.7	20.9	54.9	7.4	16.8	510	21.6	418	17.7
Turkey	1995[18]	22,899	30.4	57.0	37.1	51.0	23.0	27.6[20]	41.5[20]	27.7[20]	3.2[20]	10,477	45.8	3,397	14.8
Turkmenistan	1996	1,680	40.0	71.9[16]	36.1	43.9	28.5	...	...	...	...	746	44.4	165	9.8
Tuvalu	1991	5.9	51.3[43]	85.5	65.3	...	...	0.3[43]	22.2[43]	— 77.5[43] —		4.2	68.0	0.1	2.0
Uganda	1991	8,365	40.8	67.3[10]	43.6	52.2	35.2	...	...	...	...	6,724	80.4	478[11]	5.7[11]
Ukraine	1994	22,270	...	...	43.5	...	...	...	...	...	...	4,821	21.6	6,249	28.1
United Arab Emirates	1990	690	10.4[42]	69.0[42]	47.0[42]	67.6[42]	12.9[42]	6.8[14]	92.7[14]	0.1[14]	0.5[14]	43	6.3	94	13.6
United Kingdom	1993	28,271	43.8	76.2	49.4	56.8	42.3	11.2	76.7	0.5	11.6	522	1.8	5,775	20.4
United States	1995[18]	132,304	46.0	79.1[53]	50.1	55.4	46.2	8.3[19]	91.0[19]	0.1[19]	0.5[19]	3,866	2.9	23,750	18.0
Uruguay	1995[65]	1,344	42.8	70.4[40]	46.8	57.0	37.8	22.9[28]	72.3[28]	2.3[28]	2.5[28]	62	4.6	261	19.4
Uzbekistan	1994	8,235	...	...	37.3	...	...	...	...	...	...	3,754	45.6	1,225	14.9
Vanuatu	1989	67.0	46.3	85.0	47.0	49.0	44.9	...	...	...	...	49.8	74.4	1.0	1.5
Venezuela	1995[18]	8,611	33.6	64.0	39.4	52.0	26.6	30.2[20]	61.8[20]	1.7[20]	6.3[20]	1,043	12.1	1,344	15.6
Vietnam	1989	30,521	51.7	79.9	47.4	47.0	47.7	...	...	...	...	20,471	67.1	3,390	11.1
Virgin Islands (U.S.)	1990[18]	47.4	47.8	70.3	46.6	50.3	43.1	7.6	85.5	0.2	6.7	0.6	1.2	3.7	7.8
West Bank	1996	356.9	16.1	42.2[25]	22.7	37.7	7.4	24.5	49.0	8.1	18.5	41.3	11.6	51.8[36]	14.5[36]
Western Sahara	...	...	...	...	...	...	...	...	...	...	...	...	...	...	...
Yemen	1988	3,029	31.6	52.6	26.4	36.8	16.4	...	...	...	...	2,152	71.1	129	4.3
Yugoslavia	1996	3,182	43.4[19]	58.7[25,34]	30.1	...	...	...	...	...	...	104	3.3	903	28.4
Zambia	1991	2,928	29.6	52.6[10]	33.4	47.4	19.6	22.9[14]	42.5[14]	3.6[14]	31.0[14]	2,010	68.6	333[11]	11.4[11]
Zimbabwe	1992	3,601	39.6	63.4	34.6	42.8	26.7	24.1	43.9	9.2	22.8	2,110[67]	64.7[67]	179[67]	5.5[67]

[1]Services includes finance, real estate and public administration, defense. [2]Unemployed, not previously employed only. [3]Includes emigrant workers (352,000). [4]Ages 15–59 (male) and 15–54 (female). [5]State sector only. [6]Includes nonagricultural private sector (241,000) and unemployed (261,000). [7]Services includes public administration, defense. [8]Ages 16–64. [9]Unemployed only. [10]Over age 10. [11]Manufacturing; mining, quarrying; public utilities includes construction. [12]Services includes transportation, communications; trade, hotels, restaurants; finance, real estate; and public administration, defense. [13]1991. [14]1980. [15]Includes unemployed, not previously employed. [16]Ages 16–59 (male) and 16–54 (female). [17]Mostly unemployed. [18]Excludes all or some classes or elements of the military. [19]1994. [20]1993. [21]Includes unemployed. [22]1990. [23]Mostly unemployed, not previously employed. [24]1982. [25]Over age 15. [26]Ages 14–64. [27]Services includes restaurants and hotels. [28]1992. [29]Over age 12. [30]1981. [31]Republic of Cyprus only. [32]1993 population economically active for Turkish Republic of Northern Cyprus is 75,947. [33]1989. [34]1995.

construction		transportation, communications		trade, hotels, restaurants		finance, real estate		public administration, defense		services		other		country
number ('000)	% of econ. active	number ('000)	% of econ. active	number ('000)	% of econ. active	number ('000)	% of econ. active	number ('000)	% of econ. active	number ('000)	% of econ. active	number ('000)	% of econ. active	
14	0.6	15	0.6	209	9.0	2	0.1	[7]	[7]	123[7]	5.3[7]	117[21]	5.0[21]	Niger
546	1.8	1,112	3.6	7,417	24.1	120	0.4	[7]	[7]	4,902[7]	15.9[7]	2,009[17]	6.5[17]	Nigeria
5.8	21.7	1.4	5.3	5.3	19.8	1.0	3.8	1.4	5.3	4.5	16.9	0.6[9]	2.3[9]	Northern Mariana Islands
131	6.0	174	8.0	369	16.9	164	7.5	150	6.9	671	30.7	56[23]	2.6[23]	Norway
108	15.3	25	3.5	104	14.8	17	2.5	166	23.5	111	15.8	30[23]	4.3[23]	Oman
2,166	6.2	1,651	4.8	4,237	12.2	259	0.7	[7]	[7]	4,638[7]	13.4[7]	1,542[23]	4.4[23]	Pakistan
0.9	14.2	0.4	6.6	1.1	18.7	0.2	2.9	0.8	13.7	1.6	26.1	0.5[9]	7.8[9]	Palau
63	6.5	66	6.8	199	20.6	50	5.2	67	6.9	192	19.8	44[23]	4.6[23]	Panama
22	2.9	1.7	2.4	25	3.4	4	0.6	[7]	[7]	777	10.5[7]	2	0.2	Papua New Guinea
70	6.7	31	2.9	86	8.3	18	1.7	[7]	[7]	174[7]	16.8[7]	86[15]	8.3[15]	Paraguay
308[20]	3.7[20]	364[20]	4.4[20]	1,352[20]	16.3[20]	197[20]	2.4[20]	[7]	[7]	2,287[7,20]	27.6[7,20]	—	—	Peru
1,239	4.4	1,489	5.3	3,745[27]	13.4[27]	551	2.0	[7]	[7]	4,559[7,27]	16.3[7,27]	2,363[17]	8.4[17]	Philippines
1,126	6.6	940	5.5	2,430	14.3	690	4.1	793	4.7	2,723	16.0	511[23]	3.0[23]	Poland
384	8.2	216	4.6	923	19.6	312	6.6	[7]	[7]	1,137[7]	24.1[7]	42[2]	0.9[2]	Portugal
84	6.8	42	3.4	250	20.4	34	2.8	[7]	[7]	550[7]	44.8[7]	7	0.6	Puerto Rico
64.2	22.0	11.9	4.1	34.2	11.7	6.2	2.1	[7]	[7]	149.6[7]	51.1[7]	—	—	Qatar
17	7.1	7	3.1	18	7.7	3	1.3	[7]	[7]	79[7]	33.9[7]	87[17]	37.4[17]	Réunion
521	4.3	584	4.8	807	6.7	249	2.1	572	4.7	1,018	8.4	486[23]	4.0[23]	Romania
6,274	8.5	5,354	7.3	5,788	7.9	3,755	5.1	1,450	2.0	16,688	22.7	5,171[9]	7.0[9]	Russia
[11]	[11]	[12]	[12]	[12]	[12]	[12]	[12]	[12]	[12]	207[12]	5.7[12]	—	—	Rwanda
0.4	2.5	0.3	1.6	1.3	7.3	0.8	4.7	1.0	5.7	2.9	17.0	2.2[17]	12.8[17]	St. Kitts and Nevis
5.0	9.3	2.7	5.0	11.1	20.8	1.9	3.6	[7]	[7]	9.2[7]	17.2[7]	4.3	8.2	St. Lucia
3.5	8.5	2.3	5.5	6.5	15.7	1.4	3.4	[7]	[7]	7.7[7]	18.5[7]	8.3[9]	20.0[9]	St. Vincent
0.1	0.1	1.5	3.3	1.7	3.7	0.8	1.8	[7]	[7]	9.4[7]	20.7[7]	0.6	1.4	Samoa
1.4	8.6	0.3	1.9	2.6	15.7	1.1	6.8	2.0	12.1	2.5	14.9	1.2[21]	7.2[21]	San Marino
2.9	8.1	2.2	6.2	4.5	12.6	0.2	0.5	[7]	[7]	8.0[7]	22.5[7]	2.4	6.7	São Tomé and Príncipe
1,181	22.0	321	6.0	964	18.0	151	2.8	[7]	[7]	1,965[7]	36.6[7]	—	—	Saudi Arabia
[11]	[11]	[12]	[12]	[12]	[12]	[12]	[12]	[12]	[12]	477[12]	14.7[12]	—	—	Senegal
[11]	[11]	3.4	12.2	5.2	18.6	1.0	3.4	2.6	9.1	5.6	20.0	3.6[17]	12.6[17]	Seychelles
[11]	[11]	[12]	[12]	[12]	[12]	[12]	[12]	[12]	[12]	312[12]	20.4[12]	—	—	Sierra Leone
113	6.4	183	10.5	344	19.7	253	14.5	100	5.7	289	16.5	47[9]	2.7[9]	Singapore
227	9.1	177	7.1	331	13.3	134	5.4	146	5.9	426	17.2	126[15]	5.1[15]	Slovakia
50	5.3	54	5.7	145	15.2	56	5.9	39	4.1	131	13.8	19[23]	2.0[23]	Slovenia
1.0	3.3	1.7	5.8	3.4	11.5	1.1	3.9	4.3	14.6	6.8	23.1	—	—	Solomon Islands
[11]	[11]	[12]	[12]	[12]	[12]	[12]	[12]	[12]	[12]	604[12]	18.8[12]	—	—	Somalia
526	4.5	497	4.3	1,358	11.7	504	4.3	[7]	[7]	2,641[7]	22.7[7]	2,513[17]	21.6[17]	South Africa[60]
1,474	9.4	797	5.1	3,289	21.1	1,119	7.2	844	5.4	2,374	15.2	1,514[23]	9.7[23]	Spain
300	4.9	245	4.0	557	9.1	92	1.5	[7]	[7]	894[7]	14.6[7]	1,098[17]	17.9[17]	Sri Lanka
139	2.2	215	3.4	294	4.6	21	0.3	[7]	[7]	550[7]	8.7[7]	777[23]	12.3[23]	Sudan, The
4.2	4.6	5.1	5.6	11.4	12.7	3.5	3.9	[7]	[7]	35.7[7]	39.7[7]	14.6[17]	16.3[17]	Suriname
[11]	[11]	[12]	[12]	[12]	[12]	[12]	[12]	[12]	[12]	72[12]	20.1[12]	—	—	Swaziland
266	6.2	272	6.3	639	14.8	471	10.9	205	4.7	1,330	30.8	21	0.5	Sweden
286	7.4	227	5.9	733	19.0	485	12.6	[7]	[7]	1,088[7]	28.2[7]	77	2.0	Switzerland
341	9.8	167	4.8	378	10.9	25	0.7	[7]	[7]	951[7]	27.3[7]	235[9]	6.8[9]	Syria
928	10.0	472	5.1	1,976	21.2	567	6.1	324	3.5	1,412	15.2	242[9]	2.6[9]	Taiwan
105	5.3	63	3.2	112	5.6	52[52]	52[52]	21	1.1	326[52]	16.5[52]	146[17]	7.4[17]	Tajikistan
[11]	[11]	[12]	[12]	[12]	[12]	[12]	[12]	[12]	[12]	1,969[12]	15.0[12]	—	—	Tanzania
1,857	5.6	977	3.0	4,104	12.4	[1]	[1]	[1]	[1]	4,104[1]	12.4[1]	603[17]	1.8[17]	Thailand
[11]	[11]	[12]	[12]	[12]	[12]	[12]	[12]	[12]	[12]	280[12]	19.6[12]	—	—	Togo
1.3	3.9	1.8	5.7	2.6	8.1	1.2	3.7	[7]	[7]	7.1[7]	22.0[7]	1.3[9]	4.2[9]	Tonga
71	13.7	44	8.4	84	16.1	35	6.7	[7]	[7]	154[7]	29.6[7]	1	0.1	Trinidad and Tobago
248	10.5	96	4.1	217	9.2	15	0.7	[7]	[7]	444[7]	18.8[7]	412[17]	17.5[17]	Tunisia
1,379	6.0	892	3.9	2,776	12.1	519	2.3	[7]	[7]	2,892[7]	12.6[7]	567[2]	2.5[2]	Turkey
155	9.2	83	4.9	107	6.4	55	3.3	25	1.5	300	17.9	44	2.6	Turkmenistan
0.2	4.0	0.1	1.0	0.2	4.0	—	—	[7]	[7]	1.3[7]	22.0[7]	—	—	Tuvalu
[11]	[11]	[12]	[12]	[12]	[12]	[12]	[12]	[12]	[12]	1,163[12]	13.9[12]	—	—	Uganda
1,640	7.4	1,491	6.7	1,629	7.3	176	0.8	681	3.1	5,023	22.6	560[21]	2.5[21]	Ukraine
119	17.3	72	10.4	101	14.7	19	2.7	[7]	[7]	241[7]	35.0[7]	—	—	United Arab Emirates
1,679	5.9	1,626	5.8	5,031	17.8	3,210	11.4	[7]	[7]	7,214[7]	25.5[7]	3,214[17]	11.4[17]	United Kingdom
8,478	6.4	7,527	5.7	27,804[41]	21.0[41]	14,462	10.9	[7]	[7]	45,805[7,41]	34.6[7,41]	612[23]	0.5[23]	United States
98	7.3	73	5.4	261	19.4	79	5.9	[7]	[7]	479[7]	35.7[7]	33[2]	2.4[2]	Uruguay
550	6.7	330	4.0	501	6.1	29	0.4	90	1.1	1,690	20.5	66	0.8	Uzbekistan
1.3	1.9	1.0	1.5	2.7	4.1	0.6	1.0	[7]	[7]	7.9[7]	11.8[7]	2.6	3.8	Vanuatu
753	8.7	524	6.1	1,894	22.0	488	5.7	[7]	[7]	2,353[7]	27.3[7]	220[23]	2.6[23]	Venezuela
581	1.9	576	1.9	1,880	6.2	90	0.3	305	1.0	1,374	4.5	1,854[17]	6.1[17]	Vietnam
5.7	12.0	3.7	7.8	10.3	21.8	3.6	7.7	5.1	10.8	7.8	16.4	6.9	14.6	Virgin Islands (U.S.)
60.8	17.0	15.7	4.4	52.6	14.8	[1]	[1]	[1]	[1]	68.6[1,36]	19.2[1,36]	66.0[9]	18.5[9]	West Bank
...	...	...	...	...	...	...	...	...	...	...	...	...	...	Western Sahara
178	5.9	90	3.0	84	2.8	4	0.1	[7]	[7]	391[7]	12.9[7]	—	—	Yemen
130	4.1	142	4.5	557[66]	17.5[66]	77	2.4	92	2.9	356	11.2	819[9]	25.7[9]	Yugoslavia
[11]	[11]	[12]	[12]	[12]	[12]	[12]	[12]	[12]	[12]	585[12]	20.0[12]	—	—	Zambia
51[67]	1.6[67]	76[67]	2.3[67]	128[67]	3.9[67]	24[67]	0.7[67]	[7]	[7]	397[7,67]	12.2[7,67]	277[17,67]	8.5[17,67]	Zimbabwe

[35]1984. [36]Services includes public utilities. [37]Ages 15–65. [38]Excludes Alderney and Sark. [39]1977. [40]Ages 14–64. [41]Services includes hotels. [42]1988. [43]1979. [44]1986. [45]Excludes foreign border workers. [46]Includes unemployed, emigrant workers, and employees in private nonagricultural sector. [47]Includes unemployed, previously employed. [48]1983. [49]Island of Mauritius only. [50]Services includes transportation, communications; trade, hotels, restaurants; and finance, real estate. [51]Ages 16–59. [52]Services includes finance, real estate. [53]Ages 20–64. [54]Excludes nomadic population. [55]1992–93. [56]Citizens over age 10 involved in money-raising activities only. [57]Excludes domestic workers (private households), self-employed, and family workers. [58]Wage earners only. [59]Over age 14. [60]Excludes the former black independent states of Bophuthatswana, Ciskei, Transkei, and Venda. [61]Districts of Wanica and Paramaribo only. [62]August survey. [63]1994; February survey. [64]Includes seasonally inactive labour force (51,600). [65]Urban areas only. [66]Includes arts and crafts and owners and employees of private shops. [67]1986–87.

Agriculture and land use

This table provides data on the structure of national agricultural sectors from the perspective of farms and farmland use. The data are taken mainly from national agricultural censuses and surveys, supplemented by reports of the United Nations Food and Agriculture Organization's (FAO's) *World Census of Agriculture* (WCA). Many of these national censuses, of course, are taken under guidelines established by the FAO for the *World Census of Agriculture* programs (the 1990 census was the fifth and included national censuses taken during the decade 1986–95). Some 120 countries participated in the 1990 census. WCA 2000 commenced in 1996 and represents a continuing cooperative effort by FAO member countries to collect agricultural data within a general framework that permits international harmonization of concepts and definitions; transfer of technical expertise; and increased effectiveness in the collection, analysis, publication, and policy-related use of such statistics.

All agricultural statistics are subject to methodological problems, including errors or biases arising from such factors as incomplete or inaccurate lists of holdings, ambiguous questions, respondents who inadvertently or willfully give inaccurate information, failure to record data for all parts of fragmented holdings, respondents' misunderstandings of the definitions of land use and cropping methods, or a failure to report livestock temporarily absent from the holding on public or common pasture land or in transit. Frequently, subjects studied, classificational schemes, and definitions vary from the FAO guidelines (economic planners need different information

about a commercial, high-technology, multicrop agricultural sector than they do for a family-subsistence, low-technology, one-crop sector). When a complete census of agriculture is impossible, a sample survey may be taken. This is a limited census of a predetermined number of carefully screened holdings. From these results, nationwide projections may be prepared.

With respect to the first section of the table, number and size of farms, many countries impose a minimum size limit for holdings that may be covered in their census reports, and this cutoff, if not sufficiently low, can result in a substantial undercount of smaller holdings; conversely Soviet-bloc nations formerly published statistics only on state collective or cooperative farms and excluded production from privately held plots of land, even though these often represented a significant fraction of agricultural output.

The land tenure statistics classify farms (a single parcel of land, or holding, or a group of holdings operated as a single farm) according to the rights under which the farmer holds the land or operates enterprise represented by the farm. Owner-operated includes two types of ownership: outright ownership in which the holder has title and has the right to determine use and transfer of the land; and ownerlike possession in which the holder lacks the legal title but uses it under perpetual lease, hereditary tenure, or leases of 30 years or more with nominal, or no, rent. Farms classed as owner-operated are divided into individual and family, corporate or state, and socialized or collective proprietorships. Rented includes sharecropping; communal/tribal includes types of customary or traditional

Agriculture and land use

country	farms (latest census of agriculture)[a]															
	year	number of farms ('000)	size of holding								tenure (% of farms)					
			average (ha)	size class (%)							owner-operated			rented (including share-croppers)	tribal/ communal	other[b]
				under 1ha	1–5 ha	5–10 ha	10–20 ha	20–50 ha	50–200 ha	over 200 ha	individual/ family	corporate/ state	socialized/ collective			
Afghanistan	1994	126[1]	3.5[1]	44.8[1]	35.2[1]			—20.0[1]—			55.1[1]	—	—	25.1[1]	—	19.8[1]
Albania	1990	0.5[3]	1,182[2,3]						...	...	100.0[4]	—	—	—	—	—
Algeria	1987	899[6]	6.2[6]	1.1[6]	12.7[6]	15.8[6]	21.7[6]	25.6[6]	18.0[6]	5.1[6]	...	...	...	...	...	...
American Samoa	1990	1.1	2.9	44.7[8]	40.0[9]	—13.8[10]—			—1.5[11]—		93.9	—	—	2.2	—	3.9
Andorra	—	—	—													
Angola	1970–71	1,067	3.9	3.3	13.5	9.3	11.3	13.7	19.2	29.7	80.5	1.1	—	—	18.2	0.2
Antigua and Barbuda	1984	2.3	2.1	61.7	33.8	2.9	0.6	0.6	0.4	—	32.1[14]	—22.9[14]—		40.5[14]	—	4.5[14]
Argentina	1988	421	469	—15.1—		8.4	14.0[15]	12.0[16]	25.1	25.5	85.1[14]	—	—	8.3[14]	—	6.6[14]
Armenia	1996	316[18]	1[18]	...	...	...	...	...	...	...	...	...	...	...	...	...
Aruba	...	...	...	...	...	...	...	...	...	...	...	...	...	...	...	...
Australia	1994–95	150	3,710[7]	—15.7—					9.2[19]	75.1[20]	...	...	...	...	...	...
Austria	1993	267	26.4[24]	3.3[24]	32.2[24]	17.8[24]	20.0[24]	21.5[24]	4.6[24]	0.6[24]	38.9[24]	1.5[24]	—	59.5[24]	...	0.1[24]
Azerbaijan	1996	3.2[18]	19[18]								...	...	...	...	...	...
Bahamas, The	1994	1.8	8.5	43.6[25,26]	34.5[27]	9.7	6.2	2.3	—3.7—		25.7	—	—	20.1	39.7	14.5
Bahrain	1980	0.8	4.4	19.4	52.9	17.4	8.2	2.0	—0.1—		37.9	0.1	—	62.0	—	—
Bangladesh	1983–84	10,045	0.9	70.3	27.0[28]	2.5[29]	—0.2[30]—				62.8	...	...	1.4	...	35.8
Barbados	1989	17.2	95.8[33]	95.0[25]	3.9	0.3	0.2	0.1	0.3	0.2	76.2[14]	—	—	7.5[14]	—16.3[14]—	
Belarus	1996	3.0[18]	20[18]	...	...	...	...	...	...	...	52.1	13.1	34.8	—	—	—
Belgium	1995	73	16.5	13.9	24.1	14.8	19.1	22.1	—6.0—		33.4[14]	...	...	65.7[14]	—	0.9[14]
Belize	1996	11.0[36]	26.7[36]	9.3[36]	15.2[36]	—56.3[36]—			—19.2[36]—		43.6[17]	56.4[17]	—	...	...	...
Benin	1992	408	...	...	...	...	...	...	...	...	...	...	...	...	...	...
Bermuda	1990	0.08[37]	3.1[37]	...	...	...	...	...	...	...	...	...	...	...	...	...
Bhutan	1984	160	0.8	51.3[8,38]	42.9[9,38]	—5.8[38,39]—					...	...	...	...	...	...
Bolivia	1996	519	72.1	27.1	41.1	11.8	6.6	6.0	4.8	2.6	78.0	—	—	2.0	4.1	15.9
Bosnia and Herzegovina[18]	1981	540	...	34.5	48.9	13.7	2.3	—0.6—			100.0	—	—	—	—	—
Botswana	1990	90.3[40]	5.0	9.1	56.1	26.9	—7.9—				—	0.4	—	—	99.6	—
Brazil	1985	5,835	64.5	11.3	28.6	13.2	14.0	15.6	12.4	4.9	63.2	—	—	17.9	—	18.9[42]
Brunei	1964	6.3	2.6	44.1[8]	40.4[9]	—15.5[39]—					52.3	1.0	—	22.0	—	24.7
Bulgaria	1991	2.2[44,45]	2,467[44,45]	...	...	...	...	...	...	...	19.0[46]	40.0[46]	41.0[46,47]	—	—	—
Burkina Faso	1984	1,860	4.8	...	...	...	...	...	...	...	...	...	...	...	...	...
Burundi	1983	...	...	...	...	...	...	...	...	...	...	...	...	...	...	...
Cambodia	1962[49]	840	3.6	30.7	54.9	10.4	3.4	—0.6—			...	...	...	...	...	...
Cameroon	1973	926	1.6	42.7	53.8	3.2	0.3	—	—	—	2.4	—	—	5.2	59.5	32.9
Canada	1996	277[50]	246[50]	1.4[8]	3.5[9]	—24.2[51]—			—70.9[52]—		—	—63.5[14]—		36.5[14]	—	—
Cape Verde	1988	32.2	1.3	...	...	...	...	...	...	...	...	...	...	...	...	...
Central African Republic	1980	283[17]	1.7[17]	32.2[17]	65.2[17]	2.6[17]	—	—	—	—	0.3[14]	—	—	0.1[14]	98.6[14]	1.0[14]
Chad	1973	366	2.6	19.7	69.5	10.0	—0.8—		—	—	...	...	...	...	...	...
Chile	1983–84	306[55]	94.1[55]	16.0[55]	32.5[55]	13.4[55]	12.3[55]	11.8[55]	9.2[55]	4.8[55]	—	—84.0—		7.2	—8.8—	
China	1987	1,650	...	...	...	...	...	...	...	...	—	10.0[57]	90.0[57]	—	—	—
Colombia	1988	1,548	26.3[57]	19.2[27]	32.4	15.0	11.8	10.8	8.8	2.0	77.6	—	—	5.6	3.7	13.1
Comoros	1982	...	...	...	...	...	...	...	...	...	...	...	...	...	...	...
Congo, Dem. Rep. of the	1990	4,480	2.3	86.7	—13.3—			—	—	—	19.7	...	...	2.7	69.5	8.1
Congo, Rep. of the	1986	143[6]	1.46	37.3[6]	62.2[6]	0.5[6]	—	—	—	—	91.7[14]	8.3[14]	—	...	...	...
Costa Rica	1973	82	38.3	23.3	25.5	11.2	10.8	15.2	10.7	3.3	97.9	1.7	—	0.1	—	0.3
Côte d'Ivoire	1975	550	5.0	9.5	54.4	24.9	9.4	1.7	0.1	—	...	...	...	...	...	...
Croatia[58]	1981	569	...	31.6	51.1	14.7	2.3	—0.3—			100.0	—	—	—	—	—
Cuba	1988	1.8[45]	1,047[45]	...	...	...	...	...	...	...	—	—79.0—		9.4	—	11.6[59]
Cyprus	1985	48.0	3.8	24.4	56.8	15.0	2.9	—0.9—			—	—	—	—	—	—
Czech Republic[60]	1995	26.9[61]	...	—31.0—		19.0	18.0	13.6	8.2	10.2	51.2	—	45.1[47]	—	—	3.7
Denmark	1995[63]	68.8	35.9[64]	—3.1—		16.5	21.7	33.8	—24.9—		—	—64.4[3]—		—35.6[3]—		
Djibouti	1988–89	1.2	0.4	*c.* 100	...	...	...	...	...	...	...	...	...	...	...	...
Dominica	1995	10.1	2.5	72.2[65]	—26.4[66]—			—	—1.4—		76.0	...	...	5.6	5.6	12.8
Dominican Republic	1981	385	6.3	16.0	65.7	8.5	5.4	2.6	1.5	0.3	53.2	18.5	4.5	1.6	—	22.2
Ecuador[17]	1991	517	15.4	27.8	38.8	10.6	8.0	8.2	5.6	1.0	70.3	0.3	—	7.7	7.4	14.3
Egypt	1990	3,896	0.7[37]	95.8[67]	2.3[68]	—1.9[69]—					...	...	...	...	...	...

arrangements in which title or goods do not change hands. "Other" usually includes farms operated on several parcels of land and held under multiple forms of tenure.

Statistics on types of farms by commodities produced refer to FAO categories. The terms "mainly crops" and "mainly livestock" indicate that more than half of the for-sale production was that indicated.

The section on technology provides some measures of the role modern technology plays in the farm activities of each country (although, of course, irrigation may employ technology developed in ancient times). Ratios referred to area mean area of "arable" (cultivated and cultivable) land, roughly "cropland," less area of permanent crops (see below).

The classification of farmland by economic use is also subject to differing treatment internationally. For purposes of this table, "cropland" comprises: (1) land under temporary crops (those requiring replanting after each harvest), (2) land under permanent crops (those *not* requiring replanting, including tree, bush and shrub, and vine crops), and (3) land temporarily (less than five years) fallow (unused, but capable of being returned to cultivation with no special preparation). "Meadows and pastures" includes land (both permanent and temporary use) whose principal purpose is the raising of animal fodder or forage. "Woodland and forest" includes both natural and planted tracts of timber (*e.g.*, plantings of Christmas trees), whether harvested or not. "Other" comprises: (1) mixed and multiple use lands, (2) residue of farmland holdings not classifiable according to cate-

gories listed above (including areas of farm buildings, roads, ornamental gardens, watercourses and flooded land, wasteland, etc.), (3) land not classified by respondents in census, or (4) detail not distinguishable as one of the categories above by reason of its summarization in a published source. When "cropland" is indicated to compose 100 percent of farmland, it should usually be understood to mean only that woodland, pasture, etc., were not part of the published data, rather than that those classes of land use do not exist.

Measurements of area are given in hectares (ha; 1 hectare is equal to 2.471 acres). A kilogram (kg) is equal to 2.205 pounds (1 kg/ha = 0.89 lb/ac). The following notes further define the column headings:

a. All properties used wholly or partly for agricultural production. A property need not have agricultural land to be considered a farm; piggeries, hatcheries, and poultry batteries are farms because they engage in agricultural production, *i.e.*, raise livestock and produce livestock products.

b. All forms of tenure not included in the preceding categories. Includes land operated by schools, religious bodies, squatters, seasonally by nomads, and built-on, waste, and similar types of alienation.

... Not available, or no agricultural census or survey ever taken.

— None, less than half the smallest unit shown or not applicable.

Internet resources for further information:

• Food and Agriculture Organization (Agricultural World Census Programme) gopher://faov02.FAO.ORG:70/11gopher_root:[fao]

activity (% of farms)			technology (latest)				farmland use									country
							land in farms		land use (%)							
									cropland				mead-	wood-	other	
mainly crops	mainly live- stock	mixed/ other	tractors (per 1,000 ha)	electric- ity (% of farms having)	irriga- tion (% of land irrig.)	artificial fertilizer (kg/ha)	total ('000 ha)	% of total land area	perma- nent crops	tempo- rary crops	fallow	total crop- land	ows and pastures	land and forest		
...	...	...	0.1		35	7	38,054[2]	58.4[2]	1.8	46.3	51.9	19.9	75.4	4.7	—	Afghanistan
48.9[5]	51.1[5]	—	15.6	...	61	158	1,126[2]	41.1[2]	17.8	—82.2—		24.0[4]	15.0[4]	36.0[4]	25.0[4]	Albania
...	...	...	13.2	...	7	13	39,640	16.6	6.9[7]	55.2[7]	37.9[7]	20.4[7]	77.2[7]	...	2.4[7]	Algeria
55.7[5]	44.3[5]	—	15.0	38.5	...	...	3.2	16.4	—88.7—		11.3	71.4	5.3	...	23.3	American Samoa
...	...	...	...	...	...	...	...	2.0	...	...	...	2.2	55.6	22.2	20.0	Andorra
...	...	...	3.4	...	89[12]	7	3,500[13]	2.8[13]	36.8	63.2	—	1.7	82.0	...	16.3	Angola
32.9	44.1	23.0	30.0	...	...	...	2.5	5.7	26.0	57.1	16.9	62.6	36.0	—1.4—		Antigua and Barbuda
10.6[17]	78.9[17]	10.5[17]	11.2	...	7	4	177,437	64.8	4.8	71.5	23.7	15.4	56.4	21.3	6.9	Argentina
...	...	...	33.1	...	59		1,261[2]	44.7[2]	12.6	84.3	3.1	30.8	61.5	—	7.7	Armenia
...	...	...	...	...	...	...	...	...	...	...	...	...	...	...	...	Aruba
26.7[21]	58.9	14.4[22]	6.8	...	5	28	463,100	60.3	1.1	—98.9—		4.0	8.0	...	88.0[23]	Australia
59.8[24]	—	40.2[24]	242	...	0.3	201	7,563	91.4	—100.0—			19.7	26.1	43.4	10.8	Austria
...	...	...	20.6	...	62		4,200[2]	48.5[2]	28.9	63.9	7.2	37.2	53.5	—	9.3	Azerbaijan
...	...	...	13.3	...	10[12]		20.3	2.0	50.0	17.8	32.2	38.5	11.0	28.3	22.2	Bahamas, The
...	...	...	...	21.3	100	333	3.5	5.2	50.7	49.3		45.9	...	...	54.1	Bahrain
91.3[31]	8.7[31]	—	0.6	...	35	98	9,137[32]	70.2[32]	—88.2[32]—		11.8[32]	89.5[32]	—10.5[32]—			Bangladesh
...	...	...	38.0	...	6	91	21.6	50.2	3.0	82.9	14.1	78.7	8.9	0.6	11.8	Barbados
73.2	26.8		19.9	...	2	119.0	9,346	45.0	...	...	...	64.5	33.3	...	2.2	Belarus
97.5[34]	2.5[35]	—	144	...	0.1	496	1,392	45.6	1.2	98.4	0.4	51.9	45.2	0.5	2.4	Belgium
...	...	...	25.6	...	4	88	233[17]	10.0[17]	13.1[17]	81.1[17]	5.8[17]	36.5[17]	11.5[17]	36.1[17]	11.5[17]	Belize
...	...	...	0.1	...	0.7	2	3,300	29.3	...	...	...	100.0	—	—	—	Benin
...	...	...	9.0	...	...	...	2.4	4.4	18.6	72.9	8.5	91.1	8.9	—	...	Bermuda
...	...	...	...	...	34	1	156	3.4	11.7	—88.3—		100.0	—	—	—	Bhutan
...	...	...	2.5	...	5	3	22,670	20.6	3.6	96.4	—	5.0	47.4	41.6	6.0	Bolivia
...	...	...	48.3	...	0.3		2,525[24]	49.4[24]	8.9[24]	70.9[24]	20.2[24]	44.2[24]	55.4[24]	...	0.4[24]	Bosnia and Herzegovina[18]
13.6[37]	27.9[37]	58.5[37]	14.3	...	0.2	1	343[41]	5.9[41]	—100.0[41]—			83.5[41]	...	...	16.5[41]	Botswana
80.0[43]	16.2[43]	3.8[43]	17.0	4.1[43]	7	43	376,287	44.5	18.2[41]	66.9[41]	14.9[41]	15.8[41]	47.8[41]	24.2[41]	12.2[41]	Brazil
...	...	...	24.0	...	33	57	16.4	2.8	78.0	22.0	—	54.8	0.1	16.4	28.7	Brunei
48.8[48]	46.9[48]	4.3[48]	9.2	...	20	195	6,164[2]	55.8[2]	4.3[48]	—95.7[48]—		76.1[48]	23.9[48]	...	...	Bulgaria
...	...	...	0.04	...	0.7	6	9,565[2]	35.0[2]	...	...	...	...	...	...	...	Burkina Faso
...	...	...	0.2	...	1.4	4	2,170[2]	84.5[2]	—73.8—		26.2	56.7	37.7	5.6	...	Burundi
...	...	...	0.4	...	4	1	2,984	16.5	94.9	3.5	1.6	96.1	...	3.9	...	Cambodia
...	...	...	0.1	...	0.3	6[3]	1,490	3.3	...	...	...	100.0	—	—	—	Cameroon
43.9	42.9	13.2	16.3	...	1.6	47	68,057	7.4	—82.1—		17.9	60.5	—39.5—			Canada
...	...	...	0.4	...	7	—	41	10.2	20.8[53]	79.2[53]	...	100.0[53]	—	—	—	Cape Verde
...	...	...	0.1	...	...	2	491	0.8	11.8	88.2	—	100.0	—	—	—	Central African Republic
...	...	...	0.05	...	0.4	2	23,877[54]	45.8[54]	50.0[54]	—50.0[54]—		23.7[54]	76.3[54]	...	...	Chad
...	...	...	10.4	...	32	69	8,746[56]	11.7[56]	26.5[56]	59.5[56]	14.0[56]	15.3[56]	52.4[56]	...	32.3[56]	Chile
...	...	...	7.7	...	53	261	166,902	17.4	4.1	—95.9—		100.0	—	...	—	China
...	...	...	9.4	...	19	101	36,034	34.7	47.3	34.6	18.1	14.7	48.5	14.0	22.8	Colombia
...	...	...	...	...	...	...	100	44.8	56.4	—43.6—		100.0	—	—	—	Comoros
92.3	—7.7—		0.3	...	0.1	1	7,900[13]	3.5[13]	7.7	—92.3—		70.6	20.1	2.0	7.3	Congo, Dem. Rep. of the
6.2[5]	93.8[5]	—	4.8	...	0.7	3	226	0.7	14.8	85.2	—	100.0	—	—	—	Congo, Rep. of the
...	...	...	24.6	...	44	203	2,870	56.2	42.2	57.8	—	15.7	49.9	22.9	11.5	Costa Rica
...	...	...	1.5	...	3	11	2,753	8.6	65.9	34.1	—	100.0	—	—	—	Côte d'Ivoire
...	...	...	3.6	...	0.3	...	3,220	57.0	8.8	81.8	9.4	50.4	48.5	—	1.1	Croatia[58]
...	...	...	30.0	...	35	199	8,679	78.3	...	...	...	33.9	32.1	31.9	2.1	Cuba
51.5[5, 46]	37.0[5, 46]	11.5[5, 46]	137	...	40	144	210	35.6	34.7	54.3	11.0	74.9	—	—25.1—		Cyprus
43.5[5]	56.5[5]	—	21.1	100.0	0.8	97	4,280[62]	55.4[62]	0.9[62]	—99.1[62]—		74.1[62]	21.1[62]	—4.8[62]—		Czech Republic[60]
49.1	27.9	23.0	61.8	...	19	255	2,726	64.2	0.7	92.7	7.3	70.7	29.3	...	...	Denmark
...	...	...	...	...	...	...	1	0.5	...	6.8	...	100.0	—	—	—	Djibouti
...	...	...	12.9	...	...	259	23[2]	30.7[2]	91.0	7.1	1.9	61.7	...	28.3	10.0	Dominica
44.0	56.0		2.4	60.0	25	50	2,412	49.8	38.0	40.2	21.8	34.1	51.6	13.0	1.3	Dominican Republic
67.8	12.4	19.8	5.5	...	34	29	7,954[30]	30.5[30]	50.1[30]	20.7[30]	29.2[30]	34.7[30]	62.0[30]	—3.3[30]—		Ecuador[17]
...	...	...	25.1	...	112	384	5,216[2, 4]	5.2[2, 4]	7.3[4]	92.7[4]	...	100.0[4]	—	—	—	Egypt

Agriculture and land use   (continued)

country	year	number of farms ('000)	average (ha)	size of holding — size class (%) under 1ha	1–5 ha	5–10 ha	10–20 ha	20–50 ha	50–200 ha	over 200 ha	tenure (% of farms) — owner-operated individual/ family	corporate/ state	socialized/ collective	rented (including share-croppers)	tribal/ com-munal	other[b]
El Salvador	1970–71	271	5.4	48.9	37.9	5.8	3.4	2.6	1.2	0.2	41.5	—	—	28.2	6.3	24.0
Equatorial Guinea	...	...	...	...	...	...	...	...	...	...	...	...	...	...	...	...
Eritrea	—	—	...	...	...	...	...	...	...	...	...	...	...	...	...	...
Estonia[18]	1994	10.4	...	—8.0[4]—		12.8[4]	27.8[4]	42.2[4]	—9.2[4]—		93.5[4]	...	—6.5[4]—	...	...	...
Ethiopia[70]	1994–95[71]	6,092[71]	1.3[71]	49.9[31]	46.5[31]	3.4[31]	0.2[31]	—	—	—	98.4[31]	1.6[31]				
Faroe Islands	...	...	...	...	...	...	...	...	...	...	...	...	...	...	...	...
Fiji	1991	95	4.2[72]	43.3	31.4	13.3	6.6	3.3	1.5[19]	0.6[20]	15.8	0.4	—	49.5	32.2	2.1
Finland	1995[74]	170	12.8[24]	—	31.9	20.1	22.8	21.3	—3.9—		—84.5[46]—			15.5[46]	—	—
France	1995	735[48]	26.6[41]	—36.7—			25.7[75]	10.5[76]	—27.1—		45.0[35]			55.0[35]	—	—
French Guiana	1993	3.9	4.6	16.2	72.3	6.0	2.1	—3.4—			17.0[2]			57.2[2]		25.8[2]
French Polynesia	1987	5.6	...	37.7	—62.3—						36.5			6.3	...	57.2
Gabon	1975	71	1.0	68.0	—32.0—		—	—	—		81.8			0.3	5.3	12.6
Gambia, The	1989–90	...	...	...	...	...	...	...	...	...	...	...	...	...	...	...
Gaza Strip	1968	...	...	...	...	...	...	...	...	...	...	...	...	...	...	...
Georgia	1990	17.0[18,56]	...	...	...	...	...	...	...	...	...	...	...	...	...	...
Germany	1995[74]	581	28.0[56]	15.8[65]	15.7[78]	15.2	18.2	23.0	—12.1—		89.1	—	—	10.9	—	...
Ghana	1970	805	3.2	36.6	48.7	9.0	3.9	1.8	—	—	...			...		
Gibraltar	—	—	...	...	...	...	...	...	...	...	...	...	...	...	...	...
Greece	1991	862	0.8	26.8[79]	50.6	14.4	6.2	—2.0—			79.9			18.7	...	1.4
Greenland	—	...	...	...	...	...	...	...	...	...	...	...	...	...	...	...
Grenada	1995	8	1.7	88.3[65]	6.9[80]	3.3[81]	0.7	0.4[82]	—0.4[83]—		—73.2—			14.1		12.7
Guadeloupe	1993	14	2.8	34.6	52.1	10.0	2.4	—0.9—			57.7[2,14]			18.8[2,14]		23.5[2,14]
Guam	1997	0.2[56]	4.0	58.8[8]	17.6[9]	—19.6[10]—		—4.0[11]—			53.8			30.1		16.1[84]
Guatemala	1979	600	6.8	39.7[85]	49.8[86]	—8.2[87]—			—2.3[88]—		—74.0[89]—			6.3[89]	5.8[89]	13.9[89]
Guernsey	1993	0.08[9]	16.2[64]	6.7[17]	24.0[17]	23.1[17]	—46.2[17]—				32.4[3,14]			67.6[3,14]		
Guinea	1989[2]	431	2.4[90]	—95.4—		4.0	—0.6—				9.0	...	...	12.4	73.3	5.3
Guinea-Bissau	1988	84	3.0[1]	13.4[1]	73.3[1]	10.0[1]	3.0[1]	0.3[1]	—	—	...	...	...	...	...	...
Guyana	1993	25[91]	...	—90.0—		—10.0—		—	—		...	90.0		...		10.0
Haiti	1987	667	1.4[57]	61.8	36.6	1.5	0.1	—	—		93.4	—		5.9	—	0.7
Honduras	1992–93	318	13.5	25.2	46.5	11.0	7.2	6.3	3.1	0.7	39.9	23.1		16.6		20.4
Hong Kong	1986	11	0.3	97.5	2.3	0.1	—0.2—				—9.0—			77.0		14.0
Hungary	1996	3.2[4,47]	...	90.0[64]	—9.9[64]—		—0.1[64]—				51.9[48]	17.6[48]	3.5[48]	—	—	—
Iceland	1981	7.0	...	15.7	9.3	11.7	23.7	35.8	—3.8—		...	...	...	...	...	...
India	1990–91	105,300	1.6	59.0	32.2	7.2	—1.6—				94.1	—	—	0.5	—	5.4
Indonesia	1993	21,737	1.0	70.8	27.8	1.2	—0.2—				74.8[44]	—[6]	—[6]	3.2[6]	—[6]	22.0[6]
Iran	1988	3,326	...	26.8	39.3	17.1	10.9	4.8	1.0	0.1	...	...	...	...	...	...
Iraq	1979	470	13.3	25.9[93]	27.6[94]	23.2[95]	11.5[96]	9.4	1.9[97]	0.5[98]	52.5[12]	...	...	40.9[12]	...	6.6[12]
Ireland	1995	153	27.7	0.9	10.3	14.1	28.3	34.8	11.1	0.5	95.9	0.4	—	3.7	—	—
Isle of Man	1992	0.8	59.7	—26.7[99]—			16.2[100]	17.0[82]	12.4[101]	27.7[102]	72.4[44]	—	—	27.6[44]	—	—
Israel	1981	52	11.3	26.5	57.6	8.3	4.0	2.0	—1.6—		84.0	—	1.4	—	—	14.6
Italy	1990	2,941	7.5[32]	33.0[32]	43.0[32]	11.7[32]	6.7[32]	3.8[32]	—1.8[32]—		88.0	—	—	3.1	—	8.9
Jamaica	1978–79	184	2.9	32.5[103]	60.7[104]	4.8[81]	0.9	0.4[82]	0.3[101]	0.4[102]	99.5[35]	0.2[35]		—		0.3[35]
Japan	1995	3,444	1.2	24.5	53.5	13.9	—8.1—				—76.5—			—23.5—		
Jersey	1990	0.6	11.1	—45.0[105]—		16.4[106]	19.6[107]	—19.0[108]—			31.4[37]			68.6[37]		
Jordan	1983	57	6.3	25.3	44.6	15.6	8.6	4.5	1.3	0.1	80.5			13.1	0.3	6.1
Kazakstan	1996	30.8[18]	412[18]	...	...	...	...	...	...	...	...	...	...	...	...	...
Kenya	1976–79[112]	2,750	2.5	65.5	27.3	2.7[113]	—4.5[114]—				...	...	...	...	...	...
Kiribati	...	...	...	...	...	...	...	...	...	...	...	...	...	...	...	...
Korea, North	...	...	...	...	...	...	...	...	...	...	...	...	...	...	...	...
Korea, South	1995[2]	1,500[91]	3.7[91]	59.2[25]	—40.8—						82.5[24,43]	—	—	17.4[24,43]		0.1[24,43]
Kuwait	1994–95	2.6	2.4[115]	48.6[43]	25.4[43]	10.2[43]	8.7[43]	4.0[43]	3.1[43]	—	95.3[7]	...				4.7[7]
Kyrgyzstan	1996	23.2[18]	86[18]	...	...	...	...	...	...	...	100.0[46]	...				...
Laos	1983	...	...	...	...	...	...	...	...	...	...	...	...	...	...	...
Latvia	1993	64.3[18,46]	16.5[18,56]	...	...	...	...	...	...	...	64.0[46]	2.0[46]	17.0[46,47]	...	...	17.0[46]
Lebanon	1970	143	4.3	47.7	—44.5—		—6.5—		1.2	0.1	...	...	...	...	...	...
Lesotho	1989–90	229	1.5	46.8	49.6	—3.6—					87.0			10.0		3.0
Liberia	1971[116]	122	3.0	52.8	31.0	12.0	—3.7—		—0.5—		40.0[14]			—	43.3[14]	16.7[14]
Libya	1987	176	14.0	8.2	37.5	24.7	17.3	9.8	—2.5—		...	...	...	...	...	...
Liechtenstein	1995	0.40	8.7[24]	—63.1—			5.0	12.2	—19.7—		31.7[24]			24.5[24]		43.8[24]
Lithuania	1994	5.9[18,56]	16[18,56]	...	...	...	...	...	...	...	—57.2[24]—			—42.8[24]—		
Luxembourg	1996	3.1	41.3	14.3[65]	10.2	8.3	8.3	20.7	—38.2—		50.1[24]			49.4[24]		0.5[24]
Macau	...	...	...	...	...	...	...	...	...	...	...	...	...	...	...	...
Macedonia[58]	1981	176	1.3	46.7	45.2	6.7	1.2	—0.2—			100.0	—	—	—	—	—
Madagascar	1984–85	1,453	1.3	54.4	44.2	1.0	0.2	0.1	—0.1—		—87.3[14]—			4.9[14]		7.8[14]
Malawi	1980–81[112]	1,136	1.2	54.9	40.1[119]	—5.0[120]—					...	...	...	...	...	...
Malaysia	1990[112,121]	920	2.2	...	...	...	...	...	...	...	53.2[43]	18.2[43]		19.6[43]		9.0[43]
Maldives	1985	...	...	...	...	...	...	...	...	...	...	...	...	...	...	...
Mali	1982–83	562	4.0	20.1	54.1	17.4	—8.4—				96.8[123]	3.2	—	—	—	—
Malta	1982–83	12	1.1	67.8	30.0	2.0	—0.2—				16.0			70.4		13.6[59]
Marshall Islands	—	...	...	...	...	...	...	...	...	...	...	...	...	...	...	...
Martinique[2]	1993	10.2	2.3	54.1	37.0	4.9	2.0	—2.0—			65.3[14]			22.5[14]	...	12.2[14]
Mauritania	1984–85	100	2.0	49.2	41.0[28]	7.0[81]	2.0	0.5[82]	—0.3[83]—		68.4			4.4	10.4	16.8
Mauritius	1980	32.5	1.1	61.3	36.2	1.9	0.3	0.2	—0.1—		95.8	—		4.2	—	—
Mayotte	1987	5.9[117]	1.7[109]	...	...	...	...	...	...	...	...	...	...	...	...	...
Mexico	1991	4,408[125]	50	23.5[43]	39.4[43]	21.1[43]	8.8[43]	2.7[43]	2.9[43]	1.6[43]	—95.8—			1.1	—	3.1
Micronesia	...	...	...	...	...	...	...	...	...	...	...	...	...	...	...	...
Moldova	1996	16.1[18]	3[18,48]	...	...	...	...	...	...	...	—	30.8	55.2	—	—	14.0
Monaco	...	...	...	...	...	...	...	...	...	...	...	...	...	...	...	...
Mongolia	1985	0.3	385,000	...	...	...	...	...	...	...	—	16.0	84.0	—	—	...
Morocco	1996	1,900[109]	3.9[109]	29.8[6]	44.0[6]	14.9[6]	7.7[6]	3.0[6]	—0.6[6]—		...	...	...	...	...	...
Mozambique	1973	1,605	3.1	...	...	...	...	0.2	0.1	—				99.7	—	
Myanmar (Burma)	1992–93	2,925	2.3	53.6[65]	27.8[80]	15.2[127]	3.3[100]	—0.1[111]—			...	...	...	...	...	...
Namibia	1989	6.3[128]	...	...	...	...	...	...	...	...	45.0	—	—	55.0	—	...
Nauru	...	...	...	...	...	...	...	...	...	...	...	...	...	...	...	...
Nepal	1992	2,736	1.1[38]	69.8[25]	28.7	1.2	—0.3—				82.6	—	—	1.8	—	15.6

activity (% of farms)			technology (latest)				farmland use — land in farms		farmland use — land use (%) — cropland				meadows and pastures	woodland and forest	other	country
mainly crops	mainly livestock	mixed/other	tractors (per 1,000 ha)	electricity (% of farms having)	irrigation (% of land irrig.)	artificial fertilizer (kg/ha)	total ('000 ha)	% of total land area	permanent crops	temporary crops	fallow	total cropland				
95.3	4.7	—	6.1	...	21	106	1,340[2]	64.7[2]	25.0	58.6	16.4	44.9	38.2	11.6	5.3	El Salvador
...	...	...	0.8	...	...	...	...	...	...	...	...	...	...	...	...	Equatorial Guinea
...	...	...	1.9	...	6	...	362	3.6	...	...	...	...	...	...	...	Eritrea
...	...	...	13.3	...	...	...	252.3	22.7	...	...	...	44.0	10.0	34.0	12.0	Estonia[18]
16.5[71]	2.0[71]	81.5[71]	0.3	...	2	7	7,042[71]	6.4[71]	6.9[71]	82.0[71]	11.1[71]	87.0[71]	8.7[71]	0.8[71]	3.5[71]	Ethiopia[70]
																Faroe Islands
26.5	29.3	44.2[73]	38.9	100.0	2	96[72]	260[13]	14.2[13]	...	...	...	37.8	34.0	19.1	9.1	Fiji
52.3[46]	—47.6[46]—		88.7	100.0	3	210	12,966	42.6	1.4	78.5	20.1	19.4	0.8	60.1	19.7	Finland
37.3[24,77]	38.7[24]	24.0[24]	78.6	...	8	319	30,059	54.7	7.6	81.3	11.1	51.5	35.1	—13.4—		France
...	...	...	35.0	...	20	64	23.8[2]	0.3[2]	9.1[2,48]	80.7[2,48]	10.2[2,48]	43.5[2,48]	46.8[2,48]	—9.7[2,48]—		French Guiana
...	...	...	31.2	...	19.4	33	36.8	10.4	90.0	7.1	2.9	62.0	8.5	1.9	27.6	French Polynesia
...	...	...	5.1	...	1	3	73.0	0.3	...	...	...	...	...	...	...	Gabon
...	...	...	0.3	...	1	11	172[13]	17.2[13]	...	100.0	...	100.0	...	...	...	Gambia, The
...	...	...	83.3	...	133	...	16.5[56]	50.0[56]	68.8[56]	31.2[56]	...	100.0	—	—	—	Gaza Strip
...	...	...	22.9	...	59	...	3,011	43.2	36.4	—63.6—		36.6	63.4	—	—	Georgia
...	...	...	110.1	...	4	384	17,344	49.7	1.7	—98.3—		68.2	30.4	—1.4—		Germany
...	...	...	1.5	...	0.2	3	2,574	10.8	61.4	38.6	—	100.0	...	...	...	Ghana
...	...	...	...	...	...	4	...	...	...	...	...	...	...	...	...	Gibraltar
69.2	1.1	29.7	93.8	...	55	175	3,351	26.0	32.5	63.5	4.0	90.1	9.9	...	...	Greece
...	c. 100		...	...	...	...	...	...	...	...	...	...	...	...	...	Greenland
...	...	...	6.0	...	...	...	12.5	36.8	...	...	...	...	...	...	...	Grenada
...	...	...	38.6	...	14	307	53.6[2]	31.7[2]	13.1[2,48]	79.8[2,48]	7.1[2,48]	52.3[2,48]	45.5[2,48]	—2.2[2,48]—		Guadeloupe
38.2	29.6	32.2	181.5	...	20.7	...	0.8	1.4	—51.0—		49.0	71.6	9.5	6.5	12.4	Guam
...	...	...	3.2	...	9	66	4,510[2]	41.6[2]	27.6	—72.4—		42.0	27.3	27.2	3.5	Guatemala
28.1[34]	71.9	...	...	...	...	...	2	27.6	—	100.0		12.3	87.7	...	...	Guernsey
...	...	...	0.5	...	15	1	727	3.0	...	...	...	...	...	...	...	Guinea
...	...	...	0.1	...	6	3	96[2]	3.4[2]	...	...	...	...	...	...	...	Guinea-Bissau
...	...	...	7.6	...	27	33	10,652	26.2	...	...	...	8.4	91.6	...	...	Guyana
...	...	...	0.4	...	13	4	1,405[2]	51.0[2]	...	...	...	33.5	18.0	1.5	47.0	Haiti
...	...	...	2.9	...	4	18	3,337	29.8	23.8	33.7	42.5	41.7	45.9	10.9	1.5	Honduras
56.3	37.3	6.4	0.7	...	33	100.0[37]	8.0[2]	8.1[2]	7.4	37.0	55.6	...	...	...	...	Hong Kong
55.0[5]	31.0[5]	14.0[5]	7.6	...	4	231	8,017	86.2	4.1	95.9	—	58.8	14.3	22.0	4.9	Hungary
...	...	...	1,667	87.0[53]	...	2,529	...	...	...	...	...	...	...	...	...	Iceland
...	...	...	7.6	...	29	75	165,600	55.7	—84.4[92]—		15.6[92]	97.9[92]	—2.1[92]—			India
86.8[6]	—6	13.2[6]	3.2	...	27	110	51,050	28.2	—77.8[46]—		22.2[46]	61.1[46]	3.7[46]	18.9[46]	16.6[46]	Indonesia
...	...	...	7.1	...	44	80	104,900[38]	63.8[38]	6.4	62.4	31.2	10.2	89.8	...	...	Iran
87.9	11.2	0.9	5.8	...	46	39	5,750[13]	13.1	3.0	62.4	34.6	87.2	0.7	0.2	11.9	Iraq
2.9	93.2	3.9	127	...	...	741	5,692	82.6	65.1[48]	—	34.9[48]	9.1[48]	—90.9[48]—			Ireland
...	...	...	...	...	...	...	47	81.4	3.4	—96.6—		11.3	88.7	...	...	Isle of Man
...	...	...	73.2	...	55	252	435[13]	21.1[13]	25.0[56]	—75.0[56]—		81.5[56]	—18.5[56]—			Israel
81.2	13.2	5.6	176	...	32	151	22,702	75.3	25.5	—74.5—		48.1	18.2	24.7	9.0	Italy
...	...	...	19.9	...	23	116	476[2]	44.0[2]	22.2[35]	72.2[35]	5.6[35]	41.3[35]	21.6[35]	13.5[35]	23.6[35]	Jamaica
90.0	1.9	8.1	513	...	70	414	5,038	13.4	10.3	—89.7—		82.6	9.9	—7.5—		Japan
85.1[109]	14.9[109]	—	...	...	...	...	6.5	56.2	—98.9—		1.1	63.4	—36.6—			Jersey
58.2[110,111]	14.9[110,111]	26.9[110,111]	24.2	1.5	20	63	405	4.5	13.3	63.0	23.7	87.7	1.0	0.3	11.0	Jordan
...	...	...	6.0	...	6	19	179,800	66.2	1.2	—98.8—		19.3	80.6	—	0.1	Kazakhstan
...	...	...	3.5	...	2	48	6,922	11.9	11.5	—88.5—		71.0	23.8	1.9	3.3	Kenya
...	...	...	...	...	...	...	...	...	...	...	...	...	...	...	...	Kiribati
...	...	...	44.2	...	86	407	...	...	...	...	...	...	...	...	...	Korea, North
75.0[5]	25.0[5]	—	42.6	...	71	454	1,985[2]	20.1[2]	6.7	—93.3—		100.0	—	—	—	Korea, South
38.9[7]	61.1[7]	—	20.0	100.0	100	167	7.9	0.4	20.6[7]	79.4[7]	—	70.0[7]	—30.0[7]—			Kuwait
...	...	...	16.4	...	71	...	10,100	50.9	6.1	90.9	3.0	13.9	86.1	—	—	Kyrgyzstan
...	...	...	1.1	...	18	2	1,700[2]	7.4[2]	2.3	—97.7—		52.4	47.6	—31.5[48]—		Laos
...	...	...	32.5	...	...	...	2,540	39.3	...	...	...	68.5[48]	...	...	...	Latvia
77.0[110]	8.1[110]	14.9[110]	13.9	...	41	79	316[2]	30.9[2]	36.7[41]	39.7[41]	23.6[41]	100.0[41]				Lebanon
56.0[5]	3.0[5]	41.0[5]	5.8	...	0.9	14	320[13]	10.5[13]	...	...	...	76.4	...	...	23.6	Lesotho
...	...	...	2.6	...	2	7	375	3.9	66.2[117]	33.8[117]	—	98.3[117]	...	1.7[117]	...	Liberia
...	...	...	18.7	...	26	39	15,470[2]	8.8[2]	—28.7—		71.3	49.5	11.7	...	38.8	Libya
23.9[37]	61.6[37]	14.5[37]	112	...	...	...	4,013	24.0[13]	1.1[24]	—98.9[24]—		39.9[24]	57.5[24]	1.1[24]	1.5[24]	Liechtenstein
...	...	...	28.6	...	...	...	3,519	54.3	38.3	60.9	0.8	76.2	13.5	—10.3—		Lithuania
25.3[118]	57.7	17.0	134	...	...	...	136	53.3	—97.9—		2.1	42.9	48.9	6.3	1.9	Luxembourg
...	...	...	...	...	...	...	...	...	...	...	...	...	...	...	...	Macau
...	...	...	77.3	...	11	...	1,320	51.3	9.3	65.4	25.3	46.4	52.4	—	1.2	Macedonia[58]
...	...	...	1.1	...	42	2	3,105[13]	5.3[13]	15.4	84.6	—	100.0	—	—	—	Madagascar
22.1	...	77.9	0.8	...	2	23	1,700[13]	18.1[13]	0.2	99.8	—	94.8	...	5.2	...	Malawi
...	...	...	21.4[122]	...	33[122]	170[122]	7,604[13]	23.1[13]	84.8[37]	15.2[37]	—	100.0[37]	...	...	...	Malaysia
...	...	...	...	...	...	...	19	63.5	...	...	...	...	...	...	...	Maldives
...	...	...	0.3	...	3	9	2,503[13]	2.0[13]	—	100.0	—	100.0	...	...	...	Mali
...	...	...	37.5	...	8	39	13.0	40.6	5.0	—95.0—		87.5	—12.5—			Malta
...	...	...	...	...	...	...	...	...	...	...	...	...	...	...	...	Marshall Islands
...	...	...	117	...	50	945	32.3[2]	30.5[2]	59.9[2,48]	36.5[2,48]	3.6[2,48]	54.4[2,48]	37.4[2,48]	—8.2[2,48]—		Martinique[2]
...	...	...	1.6	...	24	12	208[2]	0.2[2]	—	56.2	43.8	100.0	...	...	...	Mauritania
...	...	...	3.7	...	19[46]	304	90[46]	44.3[46]	4.2[124]	95.8[124]	—	90.0[124]	—10.0[124]—			Mauritius
...	...	...	...	...	...	...	14.6	39.0	33.3	66.7	—	100.0	...	...	...	Mayotte
83.9	12.9	3.2	7.4	...	26	70	99,229[2]	52.0[2]	6.3	58.1	35.6	16.5	53.3	14.2	16.0	Mexico
61.4[5]	15.7[5]	22.9[5]	7.4	45	0	...	5.8	12.2	—9.3—		90.7	32.9	30.2	—36.9—		Micronesia
67.4[5,46]	32.6[5,46]	—	30.5	...	18	...	2,614[2]	79.3[2]	26.5[56]	—73.5[56]—		68.0[56]	12.0[56]	—	20.0[56]	Moldova
...	...	...	...	...	...	...	...	...	...	...	...	...	...	...	...	Monaco
13.6[5,46]	86.4[5,46]	—	8.4	...	6	12	118,470[2]	75.6[2]	...	66.8	33.2	0.9	99.1	...	...	Mongolia
...	...	...	4.9	...	15	36	9,291[65,126]	20.8[65,126]	7.2[65,123]	73.3[65,126]	19.5[65,126]	100.0[65,126]	—	—	—	Morocco
...	...	...	1.9	...	4	1	13,626	17.8	—44.9—		55.1	55.0	45.0	...	...	Mozambique
93.3	6.7	—	1.2	...	14	8	6,887	10.5	3.3	93.3	3.4	99.7	...	...	0.3	Myanmar (Burma)
1.3[5]	94.4[5]	4.3[5]	4.8	...	0.9	...	662[13]	0.8[13]	0.3	—99.7—		100.0	...	...	...	Namibia
...	...	...	...	...	...	...	...	...	...	...	...	...	...	...	...	Nauru
...	...	...	2.0	...	37	25	2,599	19.0	1.7	97.1	1.2	90.6	1.4	4.2	3.8	Nepal

Agriculture and land use (continued)

country	farms (latest census of agriculture)[a]															
	year	number of farms ('000)	size of holding								tenure (% of farms)					
			average (ha)	size class (%)							owner-operated			rented (including share-croppers)	tribal/ com-munal	other[b]
				under 1ha	1–5 ha	5–10 ha	10–20 ha	20–50 ha	50–200 ha	over 200 ha	individual/ family	corporate/ state	socialized/ collective			
Netherlands, The	1996[63]	110[129]	15.5[35]	9.1	23.9	15.8	18.1	26.5	—6.6—		—31.5[14, 35]—		—	12.2[14, 35]	—	56.3[14, 35]
Netherlands Antilles	…	…	…	…	…	…	…	…	…	…	…	…	…	…	…	…
New Caledonia	1991	10.3	23[130]	71.2[65, 130]	13.8[78, 130]	3.7[130]	2.3[130]	2.5[130]	3.8[130]	2.7[130]	…	…	…	…	84.5	15.5
New Zealand	1995	68.8	241	—12.6—		9.1	8.8	14.8	31.2	23.5	85.7[37]	10.9[37]	—	—	—	3.4[37]
Nicaragua	1991	…	…	—26.2[90]—				—30.6[90]—		43.2[90]	64.4[14, 38]	—35.6[14, 38]—		—	—	—
Niger	1980[2]	699	4.9	3.8	54.1	37.8	—4.3—				…	…	…	…	…	…
Nigeria	1993–94	…	…	92.0	7.8	0.2	—	—	—	—	—56.0—			9.0	—35.0—	
Northern Mariana Is.	1997	0.1[24]	49.1	26.1[133]	35.3[134]	—24.4[10]—		—14.2—			56.3	…	…	23.5	…	20.2
Norway	1995[63]	83.2[135]	10.2[3]	—28.7—		24.2	29.7	16.0	—1.4—		—65.4[3]—			34.6[3]	—	—
Oman	1992–93	95	1.6	71.0	24.3	3.8	0.5	0.3	0.1	—	99.3	—	—	0.4	—	0.3
Pakistan	1990	5,071	9.3	27.0	54.0	12.2	4.7	—2.1—			68.8	—	—	—31.2—		
Palau[136]	1989	0.3	…	…	…	…	…	…	…	…	79.1[14]	—	—	12.7[14]	8.2[14]	—
Panama	1991	214	13.8	46.7	24.8	7.6	7.1	7.7	5.3	0.8	28.6	—	—	1.4	—	70.0[42]
Papua New Guinea	1985[137]	0.8	483	—26.8[63]—					28.3[87]	44.9[87]	26.9[14]	71.0[14]	—	2.1[14]	—	—
Paraguay	1991	307	88[117]	7.3	31.0	22.3	22.1	10.5	4.0	2.8	52.4	—	—	7.4	—	40.2[42]
Peru	1994	1,574	9.5	24.1	47.7	13.2	6.7	5.5	—2.8—		75.5	—	—	0.8	6.8	16.9
Philippines	1991	4,610	2.2	22.7	63.3	10.5	—3.5—				58.3	—	—	27.4	—	14.3
Poland[18]	1994	2,030	7.6	21.7[65]	32.8[78]	26.7	11.0[138]	—7.8[139]—			78.3[4, 14]	13.9[4, 14]	3.3[4, 14]	—	—	4.5[4, 14]
Portugal[4]	1995	489	10.5	24.9	53.2	—17.0—		3.0	—1.9—		92.0	—	—	—8.0—		
Puerto Rico	1997	22[56]	14.5	—5.1[140]—		7.5[141]	14.3[142]	14.2[143]	—58.9[83]—		—79.5—		—	10.6	—	9.9
Qatar	1990	0.8	7.0	20.5	41.8	18.0	12.6	5.8	—1.3—		…	…	…	…	…	…
Réunion[2]	1993	12.6	4.1	37.7	41.8	14.9	4.0	—1.6—			46.1[6]	—	—	22.5[6]	—	31.4[6]
Romania	1996	3.6[45]	3,900[45]	…	…	…	…	…	…	…	51.0[14]	14.0	35.0[47]	…	…	—
Russia	1996	280[18]	43[18]	…	…	…	…	…	…	…	45.0[48]	55.0[48]	—	—	—	—
Rwanda	1984	1,112	1.2	56.8	26.8[144]	—16.4[145]—					50.9	—	—	1.4	—	47.7[59]
St. Kitts and Nevis	1987	3.4	…	90.1[26]	8.7[27]	0.5[29]	—0.7—				82.0[14]	—	—	7.7[14]	—	10.3[42]
St. Lucia	1996	12	2.0	76.9[65]	11.4[80]	5.9[81]	1.9	1.3[82]	1.2[101]	1.4[102]	72.0	—	—	15.5	—	12.5
St. Vincent	1988	9	1.8[146]	78.4[25]	18.6[28]	2.0[81]	0.4[147]	—0.6—			53.8	—	—	12.3	—	33.9[42]
Samoa	1989	11	6.1	…	…	…	…	…	…	…	0.1	…	…	2.6[14]	94.2[14]	3.2[14]
San Marino	1975	0.7	7.0	21.3	47.8	—24.7—		5.1	—1.1—		39.9[14]	15.5[14]	—	29.9[14]	—	14.7[14]
São Tomé and Príncipe	1989	13.8	8.7[148]	88.5[148]	9.8[148]	0.7[148]	0.2[148]	0.2[148]	0.2[148]	0.4[148]	77.2[148]	—	—	20.5[148]	—	2.3[148]
Saudi Arabia	1982–83	212	10.1	36.6	35.8	11.3	8.2	5.0	2.6	0.5	85.9	—	—	2.6	—	11.5
Senegal	1976	362	7.0	—99.4—					—0.6—		…	…	0.6	…	…	99.4
Seychelles	1993	0.9[149]	…	…	…	…	…	…	…	…	98.9	—1.1—		—	—	—
Sierra Leone	1971	286	1.8	38.8	55.0	—6.1—		—0.1—			93.6	—	—	6.4	—	—
Singapore	1973	16	0.8	77.4	22.2	0.3	—0.1—				7.4	—	—	88.8	—	3.8
Slovakia	1994	10	245	—52.4—		12.6	9.8	6.8	—18.4—		77.6	2.2	9.9	—10.3—		
Slovenia	1991	157	…	28.4	36.0	18.0	—17.6—				93.0[14, 46]	7.0[14, 46]	—	—	—	—
Solomon Islands	1975[112]	92	1.0	…	…	…	…	…	…	…	—	—	—	—	100.0	—
Somalia	1984	198	3.6	…	…	…	…	…	…	…	99.9	0.1	—	—	—	—
South Africa[152]	1996	62[153]	1,319	—0.8[105]—		1.5	1.9	6.4	13.7	75.7	89.6[84]	…	…	…	…	10.4
Spain	1989	2,285	19.0	27.7	36.6	13.2	9.5	6.8	3.9	2.3	72.5	…	…	19.8	—7.7—	
Sri Lanka	1982	1,817	1.1	77.5[8]	—22.2[155]—		0.1[156]	0.1[82]	—0.1[83]—		59.0[157]	27.2[157]	—	8.2[157]	—	5.6[157]
Sudan, The	1982	…	…	…	…	…	…	…	…	…	22.3	2.2	—	28.0	42.0	5.5
Suriname	1981	22	7.5	21.9[33]	61.2[33]	11.1[33]	3.6[33]	1.6[33]	0.3[33]	0.3[33]	20.2[33]	0.9[33]	—	49.5[33]	—	29.4[33]
Swaziland[158]	1992–93	0.4	51	41.2	29.5	10.3	6.1	—12.9—			84.4[32]	—	—	—15.6[32]—		
Sweden	1996	90	29.5[24]	…	16.3	19.7	20.7	25.6	—17.7—		46.4	—	—	14.5	—	39.1[59]
Switzerland	1990	108	9.9	21.7	19.0	17.4	29.1	12.3	0.5	—	59.1[14, 160]	—	—	39.9[14, 160]	—	1.0[14, 160]
Syria	1994	444	8.9	16.7	36.8[28]	22.8[81]	13.1	8.5	2.0[161]	0.1[162]	65.8[14, 123]	1.8[14]	32.4[14]	…	—	—
Taiwan	1994	808[91]	1.1[91]	72.6[3]	27.4[3]	…	…	…	…	…	83.5	—	—	3.8	—	12.7
Tajikistan	1995	2.8[91]	7.0[91]	…	…	…	…	…	…	…	…	…	…	…	…	…
Tanzania	1993–94	5,440	0.5	70.1	28.8	1.0	—0.1—				49.0[163]	—	—	3.0	38.2	9.8
Thailand	1993	5,647	3.4	19.7	67.5[164]	—12.8[165]—					77.4	—	—	7.3	—	15.3[84]
Togo	1982–83	263	1.5	48.8	38.6[119]	—12.6[120]—					70.7[14]	—	—	21.1[14]	8.2[14]	—
Tonga	1985	10.1	3.3	18.9	67.9	12.7	—	0.5	—	—	—97.2—			—	—	2.8
Trinidad and Tobago	1987	30.6	4.3	35.1	50.7	9.6	4.1	—	0.4	0.1	52.1	—	—	36.5	—	11.4
Tunisia	1988	376	13.6	—45.7—		20.6	17.9	11.4	—4.4—		…	…	…	…	…	…
Turkey	1991	4,068	…	16.0[167]	51.1	18.0	9.7	4.4	—0.8—		95.9	—	—	1.1	—	3.0
Turkmenistan	1996	1.0[18]	6[18]	…	…	…	…	…	…	…	3.3[3, 48]	—96.7[3, 48]—		…	…	…
Tuvalu	1976	1.5	1.7	…	…	…	…	…	…	…	99.9	…	…	…	0.1	—
Uganda	1991	1,704	3.9	49.2	41.5	5.7	—3.6—				13.2[14]	—	—	—	17.3[14]	69.5[14, 42]
Ukraine	1996	34.8[18]	23[18]	…	…	…	…	…	…	…	…	…	…	…	…	…
United Arab Emirates	1986–87	17.9	2.3	45.4	38.8[168]	—15.8[169]—					…	…	…	…	…	…
United Kingdom	1995	242[56]	107.3[56, 170]	5.6[56, 65]	8.4[56, 66]	11.9[56]	15.2[56]	24.7[56]	28.0[56]	6.2[56]	—74.3[171]—		—	25.7[171]	—	—
United States	1992	2,073[172]	190[172]	—8.6[104]—		—20.1[10]—		30.3[173]	22.2[174]	18.8[175]	57.7	…	—	11.3	—	31.0[84]
Uruguay	1990	55	280.5[124]	—	8.2	12.1	13.2	16.5	23.3	26.7	—59.1[41]—		—	17.3[41]	—	23.6[41]
Uzbekistan[18]	1996	18.1	15	…	…	…	…	…	…	…	9.0	55.0	35.0	—1.0—		
Vanuatu[176]	1993	22	6.9[130]	…	…	…	…	…	…	…	65.3[41]	34.7[41]	—	…	…	…
Venezuela	1984–85	381	82.0	8.3	36.3	15.7	13.0	10.4	9.3	7.0	61.5[57]	…	—	6.1[57]	…	32.4[57]
Vietnam	1991	31[45]	28.0[2]	…	…	…	…	…	…	…	—	—100.0—		—	—	—
Virgin Islands (U.S.)	1997	0.3[44]	27.0[44]	30.0[44, 177]	30.3[44, 178]	12.0[44]	13.9[44]	6.0[44]	3.7[44, 179]	4.1[44, 180]	75.3[44]	…	—	8.6[44]	—	16.1[44]
West Bank	1965	55	3.4	49.8	34.4	10.6	4.0	1.0	0.2	0.0	71.6	—	—	6.4	—	22.0
Western Sahara	1983	…	…	…	…	…	…	…	…	…	…	…	…	…	…	…
Yemen[181]	1977–83	591	2.3	57.5	30.9	7.4	3.3	0.8	0.1	—	90.3[14]	—	—	9.4[14]	—	0.3[14]
Yugoslavia	1991	1,176	…	24.7	48.8	19.9	4.4	—2.2—			83.0	—17.0—		—	—	—
Zambia	1990	520	3.1[57]	—92.2—		—7.4—		—0.4—			99.9	0.1	—	—	—	—
Zimbabwe[184]	1996	1,000[48]	38.7[17]	—16.7[17, 99]—			—82.6[17, 185]—		—0.7[17, 20]—		—2.0[17]—		—	—	98.0[17]	—

[1]1967. [2]Cultivated area only. [3]1989. [4]1993. [5]Based on value of output by sector. [6]1973. [7]1991–92. [8]Less than 1.6 ha. [9]1.6 to 4.0 ha. [10]4.0 to 20 ha. [11]20 ha or more. [12]Percentage of farms having irrigation. [13]Arable and permanent crops only. [14]Based on area, not number, of holdings. [15]10 to 25 ha. [16]25 to 50 ha. [17]1974. [18]Private farms only. [19]50 to 100 ha. [20]100 ha or more. [21]Includes fruits and vegetables. [22]Includes houseplants and cut flowers. [23]Includes fallow and grazing lands. [24]1990. [25]Includes holdings without land. [26]Less than 1.2 ha. [27]1.2 to 4.0 ha. [28]1.0 to 4.0 ha. [29]4.0 to 10.1 ha. [30]10.1 ha or more. [31]1977. [32]1990–91. [33]1969. [34]Includes mixed/other activity. [35]1988. [36]1984–85. [37]1985. [38]1982. [39]4.0 ha or more. [40]Includes about 21,000 farms without land; distribution by size refers to traditional farms with land only. [41]1980. [42]More than one-half squatters. [43]1970. [44]1987. [45]State farms and cooperatives only. [46]1994. [47]Agricultural cooperatives only. [48]1995. [49]Precollectivization. [50]Includes Christmas tree farms, which were enumerated for the first time in the 1996 agricultural census. [51]4.0 to 52.2 ha. [52]52.2 ha and over. [53]Irrigated land only. [54]1968. [55]1975–76. [56]1992. [57]1971. [58]Holdings and tenure refer to private plots only; size and tenure 1990. [59]Owned and rented holdings. [60]Data for Czech Republic exclude Slovakia unless otherwise noted. [61]Number of units reported in the census. [62]1996. [63]Arable area only. [64]1991. [65]Less than 2.0 ha. [66]2.0 to 20 ha. [67]2.1 ha or less. [68]2.1 to 4.2 ha. [69]4.2 ha or more. [70]Data for Ethiopia include Eritrea, unless otherwise stated. [71]Excludes Eritrea, Tigray, Asab, Ogaden, and regions and nomadic areas. [72]1978–79. [73]Includes 28 percent under forests. [74]Excludes holdings of less than 1.0 ha. [75]10 to 35 ha. [76]35 to 50 ha. [77]Includes fruit-growing and viticulture. [78]2.0 to 5.0 ha. [79]Excludes 1.1 percent of holdings with no agricultural land. [80]2.0 to 4.0 ha. [81]4.0 to 10 ha. [82]20 to 40 ha. [83]40 ha or more. [84]Includes part-owners. [85]Less than 0.7 ha. [86]0.7 to 7.1 ha. [87]7.1 to 45 ha. [88]45 ha or more. [89]Excludes holdings of 0.04 ha (500 sq m) or less. [90]1984. [91]Farm households only. [92]1986–87. [93]Less than 2.5 ha. [94]2.5 to 7.5 ha. [95]7.5 to 12.5 ha. [96]12.5 to 20 ha. [97]50 to 250 ha. [98]250 ha or more. [99]Less than 8.0 ha. [100]8.0 to 20 ha. [101]40 to 61 ha. [102]61 ha or more. [103]Less than 0.4 ha. [104]0.4 to 4.0 ha. [105]Less than 4.5 ha. [106]4.5 to 9.0 ha. [107]9.0 to 18 ha.

activity (% of farms)			technology (latest)				farmland use									country
							land in farms		land use (%)							
									cropland							
mainly crops	mainly livestock	mixed/ other	tractors (per 1,000 ha)	electricity (% of farms having)	irrigation (% of land irrig.)	artificial fertilizer (kg/ha)	total ('000 ha)	% of total land area	permanent crops	temporary crops	fallow	total cropland	meadows and pastures	woodland and forest	other	
32.2	57.3	10.5	198	…	61	628	1,982	58.4	— 99.4 —		0.6	46.9	53.1	—	—	Netherlands, The
…	…	…	2.5	…	…	…	…	…	…	…	…	…	…	…	…	Netherlands Antilles
…	…	…	200	…	…	60	314	17.2	39.9	— 60.1 —		4.8	68.2	10.6	16.4	New Caledonia
25.3	73.6	1.1	197	…	74	741	16,578	61.9	— 80.1[46] —		19.9[46]	1.9[46]	80.1[46]	9.0[46, 131]	9.0[46, 132]	New Zealand
52.7[5, 46]	38.0[5, 46]	9.3[5, 46]	2.4	…	8	28	5,651	47.7	…	…	…	…	…	…	…	Nicaragua
…	…	…	0.05	…	2	1	3,605[13]	2.8[13]	…	…	…	…	…	…	…	Niger
— 94.0 —		6.0	0.4	…	0.8	12	32,700[13]	35.9[13]	— 20.0 —		80.0	31.4	27.5	41.1	…	Nigeria
64.3[5]	35.7[5]	—	22	45	…	…	5.8	12.2	…	…	…	32.9	30.2	— 36.9 —		Northern Mariana Is.
24.3[5]	70.6[5]	5.1[5]	164	…	11	242	1,026[2]	3.3[2]	— 95.7 —		4.3	42.7	— 57.3 —			Norway
28.0	34.0	38.0	9.4	…	92	83	106	0.4	68.5	31.5	—	59.1	— 40.9 —			Oman
…	…	…	13.6	…	82	91	22,150	28.7	— 76.9 —		23.1	95.4	— 4.6 —			Pakistan
…	…	…	2.2	…	…	…	…	…	— 78.5 —		21.5	43.3	— 56.7 —			Palau[136]
88.1	11.9	—	10.1	0.5[57]	6	58	2,942	39.5	23.7	41.3	35.0	22.2	50.0	24.1	3.7	Panama
…	…	…	28.5	…	…	40	415[13]	0.9[13]	100.0	—	—	33.7	26.4	…	39.9	Papua New Guinea
33.0[117]	— 67.0[117] —		7.5	…	3	9	23,818	59.9	1.9	85.5	12.6	19.1	43.1	32.8	5.0	Paraguay
4.9	93.0	2.1	3.5	6.5	45	41	14,893	11.6	24.1	75.9	—	27.1	47.5	19.8	5.6	Peru
98.2	1.5	0.3	2.1	…	29	67	9,190[13]	30.8[13]	57.5	42.5	—	86.3	6.8	— 6.9 —		Philippines
53.8[5]	46.2[5]	—	91.7	…	0.7	219	18,648	61.3	1.9	— 98.1 —		78.3	21.7	…	…	Poland[18]
66.7	19.4	13.9	68.2	…	29	73	4,822	52.4	28.0	50.1	21.9	56.0	18.9	18.3	6.8	Portugal[4]
61.0[5]	33.4[5]	5.6[5]	126.7	…	118	…	325	36.7	— 78.9 —		21.1	33.3	50.1	9.4	7.2	Puerto Rico
50.4[5]	49.6[5]	—	8.6	…	100	200	8.0[13]	0.7[13]	25.2	74.8	—	100.0	—	—	—	Qatar
…	…	…	38.9	…	27	282	59.7	23.9	3.8[48]	92.0[48]	4.2[48]	71.1[48]	21.5[48]	— 7.4[48] —		Réunion[2]
…	…	…	17.3	…	33	133	14,797[2]	64.2[2]	6.0	94.0	—	67.2	32.8	—	—	Romania
52.1	47.9	—	8.8	…	4	17	209,600	12.4	— 86.4[48] —		13.6[48]	60.9[48]	37.5[48]	—	1.6[48]	Russia
…	…	…	0.1	…	0.5	1	1,170[13]	47.4[13]	— 85.6 —		14.4	63.7	10.6	5.2	20.5	Rwanda
…	…	…	27.0	…	…	…	8.9	24.7	17.3	70.7	12.0	65.5	18.3	10.9	5.3	St. Kitts and Nevis
25.0[17]	— 75.0[17] —		17.4	…	20	…	21	34.4	68.5[17]	— 31.5[17] —		57.9[17]	10.2[17]	26.4[17]	5.5[17]	St. Lucia
…	…	…	20.0	…	25	…	12	30.8	64.3	16.1	19.6	84.2	…	12.3	3.5	St. Vincent
…	…	…	1.4	…	…	…	67	23.7	71.2[111]	28.8[111]	—	93.8[111]	6.2[111]	…	…	Samoa
…	…	…	…	…	…	…	4.7	76.5	60.9	6.5	32.6	69.2	6.0	8.2	16.6	San Marino
…	…	…	62.5	…	…	…	55	72.4	94.9	— 5.1 —		54.3	— 45.7 —			São Tomé and Príncipe
…	…	…	0.6	…	12	398	2,135	1.0	4.1	18.7	77.2	88.5	— 11.5 —			Saudi Arabia
…	…	…	0.2	…	3	2	8,050	41.8	0.1	— 99.9 —		22.4	77.6	…	…	Senegal
1.8[150]	32.4	65.8[151]	40.0	…	…	…	7.0[2]	15.6[2]	89.6	— 10.4 —		100.0	—	—	—	Seychelles
50.3	— 49.7 —		1.1	…	6	1	2,740[2]	38.3[2]	20.7	— 79.3 —		19.3	80.7	…	…	Sierra Leone
12.5	6.2	81.3	65.0	…	100	5,600	5.6[90]	9.0[90]	75.0	25.0	—	66.7	…	33.3	…	Singapore
50.0	28.4	21.6	22.1	…	5.4	45[48]	2,446	49.9	3.2	92.1	4.7	60.5[48]	34.2[48]	— 5.3[48] —		Slovakia
50.7	11.9	37.4	214	…	0.8	270[48]	739	36.7	12.7[48]	54.6[48]	32.7[48]	21.2[48]	24.4[48]	54.2[48]	0.2[48]	Slovenia
43.4	— 56.6 —		…	…	…	…	96[2]	3.4[2]	40.0	45.2	14.8	100.0	—	—	—	Solomon Islands
20.0	60.0	20.0	1.8	…	20	3	…	…	…	…	…	…	…	…	…	Somalia
26.2	52.5	21.3[154]	10.2	…	10	59	94,557[2]	77.4[2]	…	…	…	12.5[35]	83.7[35]	2.1[35]	1.7[35]	South Africa[152]
…	…	…	50.6	…	23	101	30,816[2]	61.7[2]	— 79.4 —		20.6	48.9	34.3	16.8	—	Spain
…	…	…	36.3	…	61	111	2,323[2]	35.9[2]	56.4	43.6	—	86.0	1.0	2.7	10.3	Sri Lanka
…	…	…	0.8	…	15	4	31,500	13.3	0.8	88.7	10.5	23.8	76.2	…	…	Sudan, The
33.0[33]	12.5[33]	54.5[33]	23.3	…	105	26	165	1.0	15.0	53.0	32.0	40.4	23.1	19.1	17.4	Suriname
45.8[130]	25.3[130]	28.9[130, 131]	21.6	…	36	46	527	30.6	6.3	70.8	22.9	10.2	57.2	17.9	14.7	Swaziland[158]
15.3	39.0	45.7[159]	61.3	…	4	127	8,134	19.8	— 90.4 —		9.6	34.6	5.5	50.1	9.8	Sweden
58.0	— 42.0 —		278	…	6	430	1,071	27.1	6.2	93.8	—	31.2	68.1	—	0.7	Switzerland
…	…	…	16.1	…	22	46	5,527[13]	30.1[13]	— 83.2[4] —		16.8[4]	32.1[4]	44.4[4]	3.2[4]	20.3[4]	Syria
41.9[3]	30.3[3]	27.8[3]	…	…	38	400[109]	2,827	78.5	27.5[3]	72.5[3]	—	31.7[3]	…	65.7[3]	2.4[3]	Taiwan
66.3[46]	33.7[46]	—	36.6	…	88	…	4,300	30.1	43.1	56.6	0.3	20.9	76.7	—	2.4	Tajikistan
65.0	0.4	35.0	2.2	…	5	9	7,545[146]	8.5[146]	19.1[146]	72.5[146]	8.4[146]	49.8[146]	10.2[146]	24.7[146]	15.3[146]	Tanzania
…	…	…	6.9	…	27	36	19,002	37.2	17.2	— 82.8 —		93.8	…	2.7	3.5	Thailand
…	…	…	0.2	…	0.3	8	406	7.1	17.3[31]	— 82.7[31] —		71.0[31]	29.0[31]	…	…	Togo
…	—	…	6.8	…	…	2	48[13]	66.7[13]	— 62.7 —		37.3	81.2	6.7	10.2	1.9	Tonga
63.7[166]	— 36.3[166] —		35.3	40.7	29	57	133[2]	25.9[2]	55.9	— 44.1 —		62.3	4.4	6.1	27.2	Trinidad and Tobago
…	…	…	9.2	…	13	20	10,040[56]	64.6[56]	— 87.1[56] —		12.9[56]	74.5[56]	25.5[56]	…	…	Tunisia
—	3.6[24]	96.4[24]	30.9	…	17	64	23,896	31.0	11.1[46]	69.9[46]	19.0[46]	91.5	3.9	0.8	3.8	Turkey
…	…	…	35.7	…	93	…	35,200	74.9	…	…	…	3.7	96.0	—	0.3	Turkmenistan
…	…	…	…	…	…	…	…	…	…	…	…	…	…	…	…	Tuvalu
…	…	…	0.9	…	0.2	…	3,683	15.3	29.8[148]	70.2[148]	—	100.0[148]	—	—	—	Uganda
47.9[5, 46]	52.1[5, 46]	—	13.1	…	8	…	40,400	69.7	7.7	88.2	4.1	80.9	16.3	—	2.8	Ukraine
…	…	…	5.7	…	17	120	39.0[13]	0.5[13]	64.8[109]	18.2[109]	17.0[109]	97.6[109]	…	1.3[109]	1.1[109]	United Arab Emirates
…	…	…	84.1	…	2	376	18,406	76.2	0.8[46]	98.5[46]	0.7[46]	32.3[46]	60.0[46]	— 7.7[46] —		United Kingdom
44.8	55.2	—	25.9	68.8	12	99	393,471[172]	41.1[172]	— 88.5 —		11.5	46.0	43.5	7.8	2.7	United States
37.1[41]	58.7[41]	4.2[41]	26.2	…	11	54	15,682	88.4	6.6	— 93.4 —		4.3	— 95.7 —			Uruguay
…	…	…	41.5	…	98	…	26,200	63.2	43.9	— 56.1 —		16.8	80.5	—	2.7	Uzbekistan[18]
92.2[130]	7.2[130]	0.6[130]	3.8	…	…	…	183	15.0	62.5[130]	3.0[130]	34.5[130]	84.9[130]	15.1[130]	…	…	Vanuatu[176]
27.6	9.0	63.4	15.2	…	6	138	31,278	34.3	19.0[57]	59.0[57]	22.0[57]	13.2[57]	57.0[57]	22.8[57]	7.0[57]	Venezuela
74.5[5]	25.5[5]	—	6.3	…	31	82	9,060	27.4	7.4	— 92.6 —		100.0	…	…	…	Vietnam
48.3[44]	40.8[44]	10.9[44]	15.6	15.6	…	…	7.2	21.2	18.3[44]	13.7[44]	68.0[44]	10.7[44]	75.3[44]	10.3[44]	3.7[44]	Virgin Islands (U.S.)
61.9[5, 46]	38.1[5, 46]	—	14.1[38]	…	5	…	185[41]	31.4[41]	62.2[41]	37.8[41]	—	100.0[41]	—	—	—	West Bank
…	…	…	…	…	…	…	5,002[2]	18.8[2]	—	—	—	—	100.0	…	…	Western Sahara
35.5[14, 182]	56.9[14, 182]	7.6[14, 182]	3.8	…	33	12	1,545[13]	2.9[13]	6.7	69.7	23.6	98.8	…	…	1.2	Yemen[181]
12.7[33, 183]	— 87.3[33, 183] —		111	…	2	221	6,243	61.2	8.6[46]	88.8[46]	2.6[46]	65.4[46]	33.9[46]	—	0.7[46]	Yugoslavia
15.8[57]	9.7[57]	74.5[57]	1.1	…	0.9	15	938	1.3	4.5[57]	— 95.5 —		14.2[57]	38.1[57]	…	47.7[57]	Zambia
74.2[5, 48]	25.8[5, 48]	—	7.1	…	4	53	32,800	84.8	2.5[17]	— 97.5 —		34.5[17]	65.5[17]	…	…	Zimbabwe[184]

[108]18 ha or more. [109]1978. [110]Commercial farms only. [111]1975. [112] Excludes large commercial farms. [113]5.0 to 8.0 ha. [114]8.0 ha or more. [115]1985–86. [116]Excludes temporary rangeland available for agricultural use to subsistence farms. [117]1981. [118]Three-fourths under horticulture and viticulture. [119]1.0 to 3.0 ha. [120]3.0 ha or more. [121]West Malaysia except as noted. [122]Malaysia. [123]Includes some rented farms. [124]1986. [125]Farms in rural areas only. [126]1993–94. [127]4.0 to 8.0 ha. [128]Commercial farms owned mostly by whites. [129]Includes agricultural and horticultural farms. [130]1983–84. [131]Includes timber plantations. [132]Includes conservation planting and plantations of native trees. [133]Less than 0.8 ha. [134]0.8 to 4.0 ha. [135]Excludes holdings of less than 0.5 ha. [136]Partial data. [137]Large holdings only; tenure data 1983. [138]10 to 15 ha. [139]15 ha or more. [140]1.0 to 3.9 ha. [141]3.9 to 7.5 ha. [142]7.5 to 19.3 ha. [143]19.3 to 39 ha. [144]1.0 to 2.0 ha. [145]2.0 ha or more. [146]1972. [147]10.0 to 20.1 ha. [148]1964. [149]Includes 700 part-time farmers. [150]Includes root crops. [151]Includes fruits, vegetables, coconuts, and cinnamon. [152]Data excludes Transkei, Bophuthatswana, Venda, and Ciskei states. [153]Total indicates white commercial farmers, of which 60 percent have viable farming units. [154]Includes horticulture. [155]1.2 to 12 ha. [156]12 to 20 ha. [157]1988–89. [158]Includes individual-tenured farms and large estates. [159]Includes 38 percent of small farms not identified by activity. [160]Data excludes tenure of communal grazing lands. [161]50 to 300 ha. [162]300 ha or more. [163]Includes 5 percent multiple tenure. [164]1.0 to 6.4 ha. [165]6.4 ha or more. [166]1963. [167]Excludes approximately 102,000 holdings without land. [168]1.0 to 7.5 ha. [169]7.5 ha or more. [170]Full-time operations only. [171]Excludes Northern Ireland. [172]July 1995. [173]20 to 72 ha. [174]72 to 202 ha. [175]202 ha or more. [176]Tanna Island only. [177]Less than 3.0 ha. [178]3.0 to 10 ha. [179]100 to 260 ha. [180]260 ha or more. [181]Former Yemen Arab Republic only. [182]1976. [183]Data refer to Yugoslavia as constituted prior to 1991. [184]Total number of farms includes resettlement schemes and commercial land holdings. [185]8.0 to 100 ha.

Crops and livestock

This table provides comparative data for selected categories of agricultural production for the countries of the world. The data are taken mainly from the United Nations Food and Agriculture Organization's (FAO) annual *Production Yearbook* and the online FAOSTAT statistics database (http://apps.fao.org/default.htm).

The FAO depends largely on questionnaires supplied to each country for its statistics, but, where no official or semiofficial responses are returned, the FAO makes estimates, using incomplete, unofficial, or other similarly limited data. And, although the FAO provides standardized guidelines upon which many nations have organized their data collection systems and methods, persistent, often traditional, variations in standards of coverage, methodology, and reporting periods reduce the comparability of statistics that *can* be supplied on such forms. FAO data are based on calendar-year periods; that is, data for any particular crop refer to the calendar year in which the harvest (or the bulk of the harvest) occurred.

In spite of the often tragic food shortages in a number of countries in recent years, worldwide agricultural production is probably more often underreported than overreported. Many countries do not report complete domestic production. Some countries, for example, report only crops that are sold commercially and ignore subsistence crops produced for family or communal consumption, or barter; others may limit reporting to production for export only, to holdings above a certain size, or represent a sampling only.

Methodological problems attach to much smaller elements of the agricultural whole, however. The FAO's cereals statistics relate, ideally, to weight or volume of crops harvested for dry grain (excluding cereal crops used for grazing, harvested for hay, or harvested green for food, feed, or silage). Some countries, however, collect the basic data they report to the FAO on sown or cultivated areas instead and calculate production statistics from estimates of yield. Millet and sorghum, which in many European and North American countries are used primarily as livestock or poultry feed, may be reportable by such countries as animal fodder only, while elsewhere many nations use the same grains for human consumption and report them as cereals. Statistics for tropical fruits are frequently not compiled by producing countries, and coverage is not uniform, with some countries reporting only commercial fruits and others including those consumed for

Crops and livestock

country	grains production ('000 metric tons) 1989–91 average	grains production 1997	grains yield (kg/hectare) 1989–91 average	grains yield 1997	roots and tubers[a] production ('000 metric tons) 1989–91 average	roots and tubers production 1997	roots and tubers yield (kg/hectare) 1989–91 average	roots and tubers yield 1997	pulses[b] production ('000 metric tons) 1989–91 average	pulses production 1997	pulses yield (kg/hectare) 1989–91 average	pulses yield 1997	fruits[c] production ('000 metric tons) 1989–91 average	fruits production 1997	vegetables[d] production ('000 metric tons) 1989–91 average	vegetables production 1997
Afghanistan	2,754	3,683	1,200	1,348	217	235	16,291	16,786	32	35	913	946	647	615	466	492
Albania	792	628	2,609	2,813	88	135	8,409	11,345	20	23	729	785	154	105	377	449
Algeria	2,482	870	823	780	962	948	9,173	14,104	49	28	424	346	1,055	1,152	1,782	2,379
American Samoa	...	...	...	...	2	2	3,721	3,361	...	...	...	...	1	1	...	...
Andorra	...	...	...	...	...	...	...	...	...	...	...	...	...	...	...	...
Angola	313	461	350	570	1,818	2,547	3,914	4,611	35	66	273	376	414	441	250	256
Antigua and Barbuda	—	45	1,921	1,607	—	—	5,171	4,811	...	...	...	...	9	8	2	2
Argentina	19,938	35,343	2,341	3,307	2,296	2,775	18,240	20,495	244	350	1,089	1,260	5,977	6,184	2,798	3,143
Armenia	282[1]	326	1,500[1]	1,766	365[1]	379	12,080[1]	11,492	3[1]	5	1,714[1]	1,924	237[1]	242	444[1]	365
Aruba	...	...	...	...	...	...	...	...	...	...	...	...	...	...	...	...
Australia	21,390	30,262	1,665	1,926	1,127	1,315	28,301	33,382	1,530	2,120	1,025	1,022	2,361	2,654	1,525	1,757
Austria	5,115	4,994	5,443	5,903	810	690	24,907	29,392	119	98	3,555	2,933	944	902	455	392
Azerbaijan	1,130[1]	1,059	1,733[1]	1,732	153[1]	224	8,179[1]	8,421	...	9	...	4,095	803[1]	393	771[1]	974
Bahamas, The	1	—	1,522	1,740	1	1	6,900	7,305	1	—	1,199	718	12	24	27	21
Bahrain	—	—	...	...	—	—	14,112	16,000	—	—	836	1,091	20	22	10	12
Bangladesh	28,032	29,703	2,530	2,706	1,643	1,914	9,744	10,801	512	518	699	765	1,331	1,394	1,332	1,532
Barbados	2	2	2,656	2,500	6	7	9,271	8,998	1	1	1,261	1,254	3	3	7	12
Belarus	6,749[1]	5,733	2,610[1]	2,335	9,623[1]	6,942	12,975[1]	9,917	235[1]	337	1,335[1]	1,937	561[1]	365	917[1]	1,176
Belgium[2]	2,236	2,527	6,094	7,497	1,838	2,300	37,421	38,333	18	14	4,062	4,759	371	570	1,479	1,631
Belize	28	54	1,640	2,121	4	3	21,838	21,765	3	3	763	821	134	301	5	5
Benin	566	891	860	1,133	2,102	3,395	10,356	10,356	60	84	552	709	160	161	211	289
Bermuda	...	...	...	...	1	1	20,985	20,706	...	...	...	...	—	—	3	3
Bhutan	102	112	1,062	1,097	52	56	9,910	10,750	2	2	800	800	64	64	9	10
Bolivia	882	1,277	1,416	1,658	1,219	1,295	6,192	6,359	31	27	1,079	1,047	782	952	374	495
Bosnia and Herzegovina	1,176[1]	297	3,230[1]	2,121	230[1]	188	4,672[1]	6,267	19[1]	15	1,086[1]	1,216	130[1]	86	533[1]	566
Botswana	60	31	308	253	7	10	5,385	6,250	17	14	556	393	11	10	16	15
Brazil	37,705	47,288	1,868	2,455	27,247	27,709	12,574	12,810	2,471	2,948	473	602	30,184	38,026	5,590	6,445
Brunei	1	1	1,793	2,222	1	2	3,344	4,261	...	...	...	...	5	5	8	9
Bulgaria	8,872	6,289	4,121	3,026	495	320	11,987	8,000	89	29	1,021	520	1,576	1,130	1,754	1,215
Burkina Faso	1,975	2,015	717	705	79	63	5,830	5,864	60	66	815	825	71	73	229	254
Burundi	283	310	1,299	1,498	1,429	1,297	6,843	6,386	333	300	1,014	937	1,675	1,372	210	210
Cambodia	2,591	3,479	1,431	1,761	105	125	5,366	5,120	13	14	500	514	239	299	472	455
Cameroon	892	1,126	1,182	1,208	2,070	2,435	5,293	5,637	68	97	517	656	1,846	2,213	451	493
Canada	53,016	49,643	2,467	2,589	2,903	4,050	24,683	27,000	628	2,313	1,587	1,802	751	750	1,993	2,067
Cape Verde	10	10	287	333	17	6	9,102	10,159	5	3	380	71	14	15	8	21
Central African Republic	103	149	845	1,021	816	1,010	3,551	3,734	16	28	941	966	196	235	60	73
Chad	665	979	565	649	648	596	4,812	4,130	36	44	566	601	108	100	74	101
Chile	2,997	2,872	3,862	4,500	858	1,311	14,315	16,069	128	74	1,141	1,231	2,596	3,677	1,943	2,374
China	388,969	445,765	4,208	4,865	141,227	164,862	14,976	16,280	5,589	4,203	1,364	1,377	21,729	52,602	114,949	237,136
Colombia	4,090	3,219	2,471	2,822	4,120	4,937	11,558	12,873	167	140	691	992	4,880	5,866	1,598	1,293
Comoros	19	21	1,289	1,313	58	65	5,230	5,804	7	9	838	864	54	60	4	5
Congo, Dem. Rep. of the	1,480	1,443	803	740	19,525	17,665	7,940	7,437	191	219	609	592	3,309	3,527	558	614
Congo, Rep. of the	26	20	885	799	724	861	6,745	7,121	9	10	792	805	168	181	42	47
Costa Rica	262	235	2,775	2,659	152	249	20,865	22,042	34	22	524	576	2,119	3,108	126	198
Côte d'Ivoire	1,239	1,963	884	1,175	4,334	5,095	5,751	5,810	8	8	667	667	1,598	2,084	450	541
Croatia	2,562[1]	3,179	4,128[1]	5,014	517[1]	620	8,085[1]	9,812	22[1]	24	1,914[1]	2,096	539[1]	565	259[1]	354
Cuba	543	391	2,383	2,102	823	840	5,099	5,891	27	18	363	340	1,402	902	582	345
Cyprus	107	148	1,901	2,731	187	182	22,328	22,521	2	1	967	1,471	368	283	125	139
Czech Republic	6,622[3]	6,990	4,101[3]	4,137	1,652[3]	1,402	19,261[3]	19,300	175[3]	105	2,371[3]	2,036	496[3]	485	541[3]	539
Denmark	9,211	9,475	5,887	6,173	1,394	1,545	36,010	42,917	481	402	4,303	4,727	88	48	304	307
Djibouti	—	—	1,524	1,625	...	...	...	...	...	...	...	...	...	...	22	22
Dominica	—	—	1,354	1,308	23	24	9,298	10,326	—	—	450	400	85	98	6	6
Dominican Republic	523	575	3,737	4,271	310	200	7,262	6,123	92	55	974	956	1,561	1,335	252	399
Ecuador	1,422	1,815	1,718	1,680	500	642	6,596	7,101	40	57	489	632	4,446	6,988	357	369
Egypt	12,667	17,492	5,526	6,668	1,904	2,077	21,762	14,839	423	537	2,511	3,013	4,456	5,951	9,249	12,201
El Salvador	785	764	1,840	1,717	38	93	15,090	17,140	55	67	802	805	290	232	146	125
Equatorial Guinea	...	...	...	...	77	85	2,898	2,576	...	...	...	...	16	16	...	...
Eritrea	175[3]	130	740[3]	447	109[3]	110	2,804[3]	2,828	36[3]	33	545[3]	529	4[3]	5	30[3]	30
Estonia	638[1]	651	1,665[1]	2,031	590[1]	437	13,743[1]	12,415	11[1]	11	1,452[1]	1,279	33[1]	28	75[1]	58
Ethiopia	7,783[3]	8,381	1,409[3]	1,066	2,000[3]	2,054	3,659[3]	3,698	978[3]	1,138	890[3]	892	228[3]	229	568[3]	583

subsistence as well. Figures on wild fruits and berries are seldom included in national reports at all. FAO vegetable statistics include vegetables and melons grown for human consumption only. Some countries do not make this distinction in their reports, and some exclude the production of kitchen gardens and small family plots, although in certain countries, such small-scale production may account for 20 to 40 percent of total output.

Livestock statistics may be distorted by the timing of country reports. Ireland, for example, takes a livestock enumeration in December that is reported the following year and that appears low against data for otherwise comparable countries because of the slaughter and export of animals at the close of the grazing season. It balances this, however, with a June enumeration, when numbers tend to be high. Milk production as defined by the FAO includes whole fresh milk, excluding milk sucked by young animals but including amounts fed by farmers or ranchers to livestock, but national practices vary. Certain countries do not distinguish between milk cows and other cattle, so that yield per dairy cow must be estimated. Some countries do not report egg production statistics (here given of metric tons), and external estimates must be based on the numbers of chickens

and reported or assumed egg-laying rates. Other countries report egg production by number, and this must be converted to weight, using conversion factors specific to the makeup by species of national poultry flocks.

Metric system units used in the table may be converted to English system units as follow:

    metric tons × 1.1023 = short tons
    kilograms × 2.2046 = pounds
    kilograms per hectare × 0.8922 = pounds per acre

The notes that follow, keyed by references in the table headings, provide further definitional information.

a. Includes such crops as potatoes and cassava.
b. Includes beans and peas harvested for dry grain only. Does not include green beans and green peas.
c. Excludes melons.
d. Includes melons, green beans, and green peas.
e. From milk cows only.
f. From chickens only.

livestock												country
cattle		sheep		hogs		chickens		milke				eggsf	
stock ('000 head)		stock ('000 head)		stock ('000 head)		stock ('000 head)		production ('000 metric tons)		yield (kg/animal)		production (metric tons)	
1989–91 average	1997	1989–91 average	1997	1989–91 average	1997	1989–91 average	1997	1989–91 average	1997	1989–91 average	1996	1989–91 average	1997	
1,500	1,500	14,173	14,300	...	...	7,073	7,200	300	300	395	395	14,300	18,300	Afghanistan
657	850	1,645	2,500	183	100	4,864	4,300	403	840	1,384	1,829	15,033	15,072	Albania
1,366	1,255	17,302	16,755	5	6	73,000	132,000	595	580	940	946	120,000	110,000	Algeria
—	—	—	—	11	11	34	37	—	—	...	...	30	30	American Samoa
...		...		...		...		...		...		...		Andorra
3,117	3,556	240	250	802	830	6,117	6,550	151	175	483	491	3,900	4,300	Angola
16	16	13	12	2	2	87	90	6	6	936	968	173	150	Antigua and Barbuda
52,633	51,696	28,139	17,295	2,633	3,200	42,333	55,000	6,375	9,405	2,621	3,989	298,453	256,030	Argentina
5221	510	8581	566	1301	55	3,2091	2,800	3941	415	...	1,482	11,2421	10,700	Armenia
...		1	—	1	—	50	—	...		...		...		Aruba
23,086	26,354	165,046	123,333	2,617	2,684	55,991	72,059	6,514	9,304	3,945	4,582	186,667	155,000	Australia
2,546	2,198	284	384	3,762	3,680	13,738	13,950	3,344	3,034	3,805	4,429	94,284	100,000	Austria
1,7261	1,828	4,7141	5,195	841	22	21,2671	13,200	7981	854	...	1,201	37,3331	26,500	Azerbaijan
4	1	39	6	12	5	1,733	3,500	1	1	1,000	1,000	500	950	Bahamas, The
14	12	21	18	...	...	553	700	19	14	2,602	2,564	2,800	2,950	Bahrain
23,173	23,962	871	1,158	...	...	90,253	152,875	741	770	206	206	56,936	104,000	Bangladesh
28	23	40	41	29	30	3,437	3,400	14	9	1,784	1,670	1,511	792	Barbados
6,2161	4,855	3321	155	4,3971	3,715	47,5731	39,800	5,6601	4,850	...	2,424	193,2001	194,000	Belarus
3,264	3,284	174	155	6,439	7,313	35,000	43,000	3,875	3,700	4,313	4,811	168,171	205,200	Belgium2
51	60	4	3	26	23	987	1,400	7	7	1,159	1,045	1,284	1,581	Belize
1,037	1,400	869	605	479	600	23,333	27,000	16	20	130	130	17,940	19,800	Benin
1	1	...	...	1	1	75	45	1	1	2,901	3,857	472	280	Bermuda
402	435	49	59	69	75	250	310	29	29	257	257	317	380	Bhutan
5,542	6,238	7,573	8,232	2,160	2,569	23,697	57,785	113	200	1,399	1,419	47,333	68,000	Bolivia
4381	260	5181	276	4041	60	5,1671	3,870	3031	202	...	1,298	17,8331	7,100	Bosnia and Herzegovina
2,694	2,300	317	240	16	3	2,080	1,400	113	98	350	350	1,860	1,278	Botswana
147,797	163,000	20,061	18,000	33,643	35,800	557,282	892,000	15,004	19,100	780	841	1,244,227	1,415,350	Brazil
2	2	...	...	17	5	2,254	3,000	...		...		3,083	3,400	Brunei
1,548	582	8,226	3,020	4,219	1,500	34,167	15,127	1,999	1,000	3,370	2,830	129,127	87,752	Bulgaria
3,937	4,522	5,049	6,207	510	587	17,028	20,517	101	157	156	175	15,283	17,000	Burkina Faso
431	400	352	330	92	80	4,000	4,000	33	32	350	350	3,040	3,040	Burundi
2,178	2,900	...	...	1,601	2,151	8,565	11,412	17	19	170	170	8,667	10,450	Cambodia
4,660	4,900	3,407	3,800	1,344	1,410	17,333	20,000	116	125	500	500	11,867	13,000	Cameroon
11,165	13,341	595	628	10,505	11,483	110,000	139,000	7,915	7,800	5,800	6,255	319,848	336,290	Canada
18	22	6	9	115	560	505	430	1	6	447	449	495	520	Cape Verde
2,589	2,926	134	191	430	596	2,772	3,718	46	60	224	229	1,314	1,386	Central African Republic
4,298	5,079	1,926	2,585	14	19	3,950	4,700	116	123	270	270	3,555	4,230	Chad
3,402	4,142	4,803	3,710	1,144	1,722	32,000	68,000	1,353	2,050	1,862	1,911	95,761	95,000	Chile
79,282	116,459	112,299	132,691	360,247	468,055	2,120,630	3,010,535	4,410	6,946	1,562	1,476	6,698,453	17,214,440	China
24,383	27,945	2,547	2,416	2,627	2,480	53,333	110,000	3,897	5,408	963	1,020	236,933	315,950	Colombia
47	50	13	20	...	...	392	440	4	4	500	500	632	720	Comoros
1,535	1,100	934	1,020	1,050	1,183	28,623	25,000	8	7	851	854	8,143	8,500	Congo, Dem. Rep. of the
65	75	104	115	49	45	1,650	1,950	1	1	500	500	1,170	1,170	Congo, Rep. of the
2,181	1,529	3	3	270	300	14,000	16,500	431	595	1,308	1,306	18,976	27,147	Costa Rica
1,101	1,312	1,137	1,347	361	271	24,333	31,059	18	23	150	165	12,693	16,000	Côte d'Ivoire
5661	451	5021	452	1,2641	1,175	11,6651	9,984	6431	400	...	1,897	51,1671	51,000	Croatia
4,922	4,650	385	310	2,184	1,500	27,876	19,000	1,100	920	1,866	1,756	109,506	64,000	Cuba
50	71	300	252	281	400	2,625	3,500	98	133	4,746	4,659	7,942	9,210	Cyprus
2,2343	1,866	2053	121	4,1793	4,080	25,5743	26,489	3,2073	2,703	...	4,156	154,2263	166,115	Czech Republic
2,227	2,030	103	170	9,390	11,100	15,808	19,224	4,710	4,431	6,227	6,736	82,800	85,100	Denmark
188	190	433	470	...	...	...	...	7	7	350	350	...	...	Djibouti
9	13	7	8	4	5	129	190	5	6	902	910	155	225	Dominica
2,283	2,481	115	135	543	960	31,227	42,952	345	390	1,701	1,708	38,864	47,954	Dominican Republic
4,351	5,150	1,417	1,933	2,213	2,708	51,901	64,736	1,529	1,929	2,092	2,296	51,471	57,000	Ecuador
2,771	3,120	3,310	4,291	24	28	34,555	85,000	974	1,324	689	677	143,817	163,000	Egypt
1,213	1,177	5	5	305	316	5,200	5,049	268	368	999	967	45,612	46,426	El Salvador
5	5	35	36	5	5	228	245	...		...		175	190	Equatorial Guinea
1,290	1,320	1,5203	1,530	...	...	4,3003	4,300	303	31	...	196	5,9343	5,934	Eritrea
5951	348	1161	42	5881	315	3,9651	2,900	8341	717	...	3,939	22,4871	18,480	Estonia
29,5753	29,900	21,7003	21,850	203	23	54,2003	55,000	7383	740	...	209	73,3703	73,830	Ethiopia

Crops and livestock (continued)

country	grains				roots and tubers[a]				pulses[b]				fruits[c]		vegetables[d]	
	production ('000 metric tons)		yield (kg/hectare)		production ('000 metric tons)		yield (kg/hectare)		production ('000 metric tons)		yield (kg/hectare)		production ('000 metric tons)		production ('000 metric tons)	
	1989–91 average	1997	1989–91 average	1997	1989–91 average	1997	1989–91 average	1997	1989–91 average	1997	1989–91 average	1997	1989–91 average	1997	1989–91 average	1997
Faroe Islands	...	...	...	...	1	2	13,677	13,636	...	...	...	...	...	...	...	...
Fiji	30	19	2,289	2,064	36	90	3,739	13,588	...	...	773	1,000	13	12	9	17
Finland	3,845	3,808	3,360	3,392	845	754	20,656	22,714	14	13	2,549	2,183	90	93	205	249
France	57,683	63,428	6,240	6,889	5,213	6,686	29,853	38,872	3,310	3,121	4,735	4,960	10,560	10,979	7,441	7,927
French Guiana	22	31	4,199	3,407	32	21	10,178	8,400	...	...	...	...	7	16	9	21
French Polynesia	...	...	...	...	13	16	12,273	11,923	...	...	...	...	8	7	7	6
Gabon	22	32	1,563	1,728	376	416	5,409	5,616	—	—	639	667	256	283	30	34
Gambia, The	99	104	1,076	950	6	6	3,000	3,000	4	4	267	267	4	4	8	8
Gaza Strip	1	1	510	529	23	35	22,624	21,875	...	...	...	...	168	137	140	158
Georgia	457[1]	657	1,823[1]	1,664	223[1]	380	10,300[1]	13,571	...	...	...	...	745[1]	793	1,205[1]	595
Germany	37,910	45,487	5,534	6,477	14,057	12,067	27,747	34,978	267	236	2,750	2,915	4,652	3,874	3,806	3,394
Ghana	1,155	1,790	1,074	1,403	5,504	11,096	7,000	11,264	18	20	102	100	1,149	2,049	416	513
Gibraltar	...	...	...	...	...	...	...	...	...	...	...	...	...	...	...	...
Greece	5,504	4,725	3,741	3,615	1,065	887	20,131	18,522	51	44	1,511	1,678	3,987	3,715	3,965	4,254
Greenland	...	...	...	...	...	...	...	...	...	...	...	...	...	...	...	...
Grenada	—	—	1,000	1,000	4	4	5,206	5,227	1	1	1,094	1,139	24	14	2	2
Guadeloupe	...	...	...	...	20	17	9,649	8,732	—	—	577	756	129	157	24	25
Guam	...	...	2,000	2,000	2	2	14,904	14,904	...	...	...	...	2	2	4	5
Guatemala	1,410	1,223	1,943	1,911	61	73	4,899	5,582	119	118	848	805	838	1,175	380	542
Guernsey	...	...	...	...	...	...	...	...	...	...	...	...	...	...	...	...
Guinea	632	908	1,052	1,260	578	947	7,320	6,839	60	60	857	857	856	988	420	420
Guinea-Bissau	165	193	1,556	1,480	67	60	6,953	6,977	2	2	960	600	64	60	20	20
Guyana	213	541	3,115	4,015	31	51	7,045	10,646	1	1	612	591	67	60	12	13
Haiti	405	388	996	917	770	770	3,785	3,802	92	82	634	675	1,005	868	283	214
Honduras	671	758	1,409	1,576	30	34	8,836	9,351	81	55	767	662	1,404	1,440	197	317
Hong Kong	—	—	1,667	—	—	—	22,000	33,750	...	...	...	...	4	4	116	85
Hungary	14,592	14,160	5,173	4,797	1,230	1,049	16,713	16,651	347	112	2,251	1,820	2,184	1,600	2,041	1,558
Iceland	...	...	...	...	9	7	9,553	9,155	...	...	...	...	—	—	2	2
India	195,478	225,274	1,911	2,257	21,280	26,393	15,906	17,307	13,427	14,520	567	596	30,505	37,189	59,320	54,967
Indonesia	51,258	58,579	3,814	4,062	19,150	18,100	11,616	11,678	455	872	1,322	1,605	6,493	7,205	4,558	5,346
Iran	12,973	15,897	1,377	1,856	2,387	3,284	17,383	19,404	398	567	584	570	7,088	10,596	7,630	9,277
Iraq	2,541	2,211	927	799	196	400	15,980	15,686	19	37	995	1,148	1,507	1,545	2,855	2,948
Ireland	1,950	1,944	6,374	6,381	577	472	25,060	23,600	8	19	4,798	4,524	24	21	235	221
Isle of Man	...	...	...	...	...	...	...	...	...	...	...	...	...	...	...	...
Israel	234	121	2,222	1,583	209	278	32,359	38,480	9	9	1,276	1,181	1,711	1,409	1,263	1,507
Italy	17,921	19,720	4,005	4,716	2,340	2,045	19,637	23,173	221	144	1,430	1,672	17,569	15,667	14,436	14,056
Jamaica	3	3	1,232	1,066	225	308	12,534	16,318	6	5	898	1,089	383	416	108	181
Japan	13,946	13,326	5,645	6,064	5,539	5,045	25,459	26,935	145	133	1,670	1,833	4,838	4,474	14,457	13,571
Jersey	...	...	...	...	...	...	...	...	...	...	...	...	...	...	...	...
Jordan	105	101	1,040	1,006	59	107	23,167	24,943	4	5	740	699	233	353	634	1,262
Kazakstan	22,521[1]	12,379	1,040[1]	793	2,303[1]	1,472	9,742[1]	8,350	96[1]	35	782[1]	683	160[1]	127	1,096[1]	1,082
Kenya	2,893	2,768	1,567	1,430	1,536	2,007	8,200	7,483	219	240	312	343	888	1,031	624	656
Kiribati	...	...	...	...	7	8	7,449	8,020	...	...	...	...	5	6	4	5
Korea, North	5,955	3,479	3,784	2,599	2,543	961	13,338	11,230	325	270	922	844	1,304	1,300	4,344	3,324
Korea, South	8,412	7,814	5,891	6,631	940	685	21,156	20,842	45	35	1,134	1,098	2,027	2,606	9,768	10,806
Kuwait	2	2	4,568	5,085	2	1	19,476	17,059	...	...	...	...	1	2	84	83
Kyrgyzstan	1,339[1]	1,821	2,271[1]	2,947	321[1]	678	12,190[1]	13,560	...	...	...	...	97[1]	129	291[1]	347
Laos	1,433	1,740	2,269	2,843	265	215	8,011	8,921	36	14	1,870	929	130	173	87	125
Latvia	1,072[1]	1,028	1,739[1]	2,140	1,161[1]	843	13,147[1]	12,116	6[1]	8	1,480[1]	1,766	73[1]	29	256[1]	144
Lebanon	82	96	1,995	2,464	249	356	18,708	24,306	28	42	1,631	2,066	1,222	1,285	798	1,214
Lesotho	170	206	805	978	45	90	15,319	16,364	9	18	481	750	18	15	24	22
Liberia	225	95	1,032	1,267	432	272	7,327	6,904	3	1	517	500	130	137	73	76
Libya	297	322	676	685	141	135	7,704	7,297	12	12	1,113	1,121	287	250	708	623
Liechtenstein	...	...	...	...	...	...	...	...	...	...	...	...	...	—	...	...
Lithuania	2,319[1]	2,873	1,974[1]	2,377	1,316[1]	1,830	11,213[1]	14,592	30[1]	43	1,239[1]	1,676	145[1]	267	306[1]	400
Luxembourg[2]	...	...	...	...	...	...	...	...	...	...	...	...	...	...	...	...
Macau	...	...	...	...	7	...	13,394	...	1	...	...	...	—	...	1	...
Macedonia	583[1]	596	2,453[1]	2,696	127[1]	157	9,534[1]	10,861	29[1]	28	1,348[1]	1,323	342[1]	347	462[1]	525
Madagascar	2,545	2,742	1,919	2,000	3,155	3,368	6,562	6,442	59	82	876	853	790	844	328	353
Malawi	1,560	1,349	1,104	965	506	580	4,294	4,681	268	280	589	587	485	501	252	241
Malaysia	2,014	2,018	2,890	2,959	497	488	9,683	9,512	...	...	...	...	1,115	1,101	334	459
Maldives	—	—	1,125	4,400	7	7	5,108	4,738	—	—	633	688	9	9	20	24
Mali	2,114	2,202	879	1,094	28	28	4,772	4,978	57	71	224	216	15	52	255	318
Malta	9	7	3,517	3,500	17	32	13,181	25,600	1	1	2,341	2,667	12	16	53	75
Marshall Islands	...	...	...	...	...	...	...	...	...	...	...	...	...	...	...	...
Martinique	...	...	...	...	23	18	11,540	9,902	...	1	...	...	273	335	24	28
Mauritania	131	122	831	633	6	6	1,933	2,115	28	34	385	330	19	38	9	9
Mauritius	2	—	3,885	5,272	19	19	18,733	21,859	1	2	708	773	8	11	42	73
Mayotte	...	...	...	...	...	...	...	...	...	...	...	...	...	...	...	...
Mexico	23,553	28,157	2,350	2,652	1,302	1,428	15,957	21,172	1,290	1,205	646	670	9,216	11,983	5,925	6,867
Micronesia	...	...	...	...	...	...	...	...	...	...	...	...	...	...	...	...
Moldova	2,274[1]	3,172	3,019[1]	3,294	504[1]	392	7,989[1]	6,331	107[1]	58	1,537[1]	1,377	1,562[1]	1,426	689[1]	513
Monaco	...	...	...	...	...	...	...	...	...	...	...	...	...	...	...	...
Mongolia	719	240	1,104	859	128	55	10,613	7,205	3	1	708	667	—	—	41	24
Morocco	7,457	4,102	1,346	835	975	1,197	17,347	18,015	386	212	790	581	2,306	2,472	2,942	3,390
Mozambique	629	1,531	403	821	3,944	5,475	4,136	5,435	87	153	301	389	368	369	197	173
Myanmar (Burma)	14,109	18,208	2,737	2,896	214	322	8,594	9,893	432	1,188	677	702	957	1,090	2,160	2,488
Namibia	103	172	745	487	197	240	8,194	8,571	7	8	1,062	1,096	10	10	8	9
Nauru	...	...	...	...	...	...	...	...	...	...	...	...	...	...	...	...
Nepal	5,685	6,402	1,887	1,953	826	1,142	7,401	8,111	168	231	597	699	457	428	962	1,357
Netherlands, The	1,327	1,565	6,909	7,764	6,947	7,973	40,168	44,319	85	14	4,109	3,111	506	652	3,455	3,748
Netherlands Antilles	...	...	...	...	...	...	...	...	...	...	...	...	...	...	...	...
New Caledonia	1	2	1,837	5,778	21	21	6,023	5,957	—	—	393	600	4	2	4	3
New Zealand	783	1,034	5,028	5,451	277	443	26,817	30,343	61	63	2,262	1,667	794	1,027	506	736
Nicaragua	453	676	1,483	1,783	77	82	11,790	11,431	69	90	621	648	304	250	54	59

livestock														country
cattle		sheep		hogs		chickens		milk[e]		yield		eggs[f]		
stock ('000 head)		stock ('000 head)		stock ('000 head)		stock ('000 head)		production ('000 metric tons)		(kg/animal)		production (metric tons)		
1989–91 average	1997	1989–91 average	1997	1989–91 average	1997	1989–91 average	1997	1989–91 average	1997	1989–91 average	1996	1989–91 average	1997	
2	2	67	68	...	...	...	...	...	...	...	...	...	...	Faroe Islands
274	360	—	8	88	125	2,600	3,700	58	56	1,705	1,692	2,494	2,835	Fiji
1,352	1,150	59	103	1,322	1,394	5,583	5,230	2,712	2,463	5,666	6,090	72,967	66,700	Finland
21,407	20,664	11,196	10,463	12,233	14,976	198,306	231,489	26,334	24,243	4,797	5,494	903,413	975,400	France
15	9	4	3	9	11	202	190	—	—	...	...	250	423	French Guiana
8	9	—	—	33	42	100	100	2	1	2,207	1,778	1,347	1,670	French Polynesia
30	39	161	173	160	208	2,217	2,700	1	1	250	250	1,500	1,750	Gabon
333	346	127	182	11	14	558	740	7	7	175	175	820	585	Gambia, The
3	3	24	24	...	...	2,633	3,600	7	8	4,000	4,000	4,867	8,000	Gaza Strip
1,051[1]	1,008	1,160[1]	580	525[1]	333	15,113[1]	14,000	450[1]	550	...	1,000	12,717[1]	18,000	Georgia
20,048	15,760	3,824	2,324	33,350	24,283	116,263	102,731	30,976	28,702	4,931	5,427	989,467	847,000	Germany
1,159	1,150	2,199	2,100	495	395	9,682	13,300	23	24	130	130	12,278	13,780	Ghana
...	...	...	...	...	...	...	...	...	...	...	...	...	...	Gibraltar
651	542	8,684	9,244	1,002	904	27,213	28,500	646	750	2,523	3,450	132,343	115,446	Greece
...	...	21	22	...	...	...	...	...	...	...	...	...	...	Greenland
4	4	11	13	3	5	260	280	1	1	...	800	920	920	Grenada
70	80	4	3	28	15	311	160	1	—	506	...	1,412	1,540	Guadeloupe
—	—	...	...	4	4	170	200	...	...	...	...	367	700	Guam
2,052	1,769	432	551	602	802	14,633	23,000	312	321	680	845	66,051	108,880	Guatemala
...	...	...	...	...	...	...	...	...	...	...	...	...	...	Guernsey
1,491	2,200	429	610	24	45	5,800	7,000	42	55	185	185	14,035	7,770	Guinea
412	475	239	255	290	310	807	850	12	12	170	170	580	612	Guinea-Bissau
138	220	129	130	42	20	2,000	11,500	19	13	840	828	8,600	6,800	Guyana
1,067	1,270	86	161	330	600	5,167	3,800	25	37	250	249	3,583	3,750	Haiti
2,412	2,200	10	13	589	600	9,436	17,000	346	524	911	1,190	27,923	39,644	Honduras
2	2	—	—	296	109	5,678	3,000	2	—	...	...	1,497	900	Hong Kong
1,619	909	2,050	872	7,996	5,289	50,950	27,827	2,733	1,912	4,977	5,000	253,631	167,400	Hungary
75	73	540	450	18	42	450	186	112	105	3,509	3,459	2,647	2,195	Iceland
191,897	209,084	43,706	56,472	11,193	15,419	400,000	342,500	26,333	34,500	880	1,000	1,229,333	1,611,000	India
10,390	12,148	6,008	7,963	7,231	8,638	560,093	1,195,000	335	446	1,094	1,335	383,000	644,100	Indonesia
7,382	8,600	44,754	52,000	—	—	161,667	210,000	2,480	3,897	1,014	1,180	310,000	486,000	Iran
1,416	1,300	7,804	6,584	...	...	58,500	48,000	297	200	734	690	64,450	45,000	Iraq
5,923	6,757	5,523	5,391	1,125	1,665	8,697	11,491	5,376	5,256	3,849	4,491	32,733	25,900	Ireland
...	...	...	...	...	...	...	...	...	...	...	...	...	...	Isle of Man
340	375	383	350	122	165	22,733	22,000	964	1,124	8,783	9,105	104,663	92,400	Israel
8,541	7,240	11,088	10,920	9,150	8,090	133,000	138,000	10,893	10,200	3,724	4,925	686,867	720,000	Italy
382	400	2	2	192	180	7,167	9,000	51	53	1,000	1,000	25,833	28,000	Jamaica
4,772	4,749	30	16	11,673	9,809	337,667	309,000	8,169	8,645	5,825	6,257	2,446,228	2,566,607	Japan
...	...	...	...	...	...	...	...	...	...	...	...	...	...	Jersey
35	90	1,660	2,000	...	...	52,300	78,000	60	115	2,485	3,000	32,420	50,000	Jordan
9,336[1]	5,425	33,688[1]	13,000	2,610[1]	1,036	50,400[1]	15,296	5,327[1]	3,295	...	1,236	176,667[1]	70,000	Kazakstan
13,583	13,414	6,447	5,800	103	108	24,667	28,900	2,297	2,300	497	491	41,440	48,480	Kenya
...	...	...	...	9	10	259	300	...	...	...	...	124	140	Kiribati
1,293	1,150	385	355	3,215	3,100	20,767	14,000	88	80	2,379	2,250	144,333	130,000	Korea, North
2,149	3,396	3	2	4,792	7,096	70,336	88,251	1,752	1,984	5,944	6,369	398,578	477,967	Korea, South
14	21	197	405	...	...	16,982	28,000	21	40	3,226	2,258	6,390	9,300	Kuwait
1,124[1]	848	8,261[1]	3,545	257[1]	88	9,867[1]	2,000	918[1]	911	...	1,000	22,000[1]	8,800	Kyrgyzstan
853	1,186	...	...	1,397	1,900	8,165	11,660	9	6	200	200	32,500	7,500	Laos
1,068[1]	509	154[1]	56	865[1]	460	5,397[1]	3,000	1,212[1]	986	...	2,951	25,033[1]	26,000	Latvia
65	75	222	315	46	59	21,638	25,500	94	158	2,826	2,604	55,167	30,000	Lebanon
550	590	1,450	1,200	62	70	967	1,500	24	26	290	290	826	1,260	Lesotho
38	36	222	210	123	120	3,800	3,500	1	1	130	130	3,904	3,600	Liberia
238	160	5,100	4,500	...	...	15,867	17,000	99	98	1,202	1,214	33,917	35,250	Libya
6	6	3	3	3	3	...	...	13	12	4,645	4,444	...	...	Liechtenstein
1,761[1]	1,054	52[1]	28	1,579[1]	1,128	10,860[1]	7,775	2,128[1]	1,889	...	3,072	41,167[1]	41,500	Lithuania
...	...	...	...	...	...	450	420	...	...	...	...	638	650	Luxembourg[2]
...	...	...	...	...	...	...	...	...	...	...	...	...	...	Macau
282[1]	295	2,425[1]	1,814	176[1]	192	4,458[1]	3,361	127[1]	138	...	1,430	25,653[1]	20,900	Macedonia
10,254	10,331	719	760	1,431	1,662	13,062	16,500	476	485	273	276	15,050	13,100	Madagascar
862	710	179	101	236	230	11,500	14,200	37	33	460	457	11,203	18,400	Malawi
677	725	212	255	2,577	3,400	62,377	110,000	29	33	470	417	287,400	360,000	Malaysia
...	...	...	...	...	...	...	...	...	...	...	...	...	...	Maldives
5,007	5,725	6,072	5,950	59	65	22,000	24,000	123	140	245	245	11,880	11,880	Mali
21	21	6	16	101	69	867	820	24	41	3,851	4,767	6,800	6,450	Malta
...	...	...	...	...	...	...	...	...	...	...	...	...	...	Marshall Islands
37	30	46	42	39	33	347	250	2	2	756	764	1,214	1,500	Martinique
1,350	1,312	5,067	6,199	...	...	3,800	3,900	97	109	350	350	4,250	4,590	Mauritania
34	37	7	7	12	18	2,200	3,200	25	25	2,500	2,500	4,200	4,900	Mauritius
...	...	...	...	...	...	...	...	...	...	...	...	...	...	Mayotte
32,194	26,900	5,862	5,500	15,715	15,020	240,218	393,000	6,336	8,091	992	1,251	1,066,065	1,328,935	Mexico
...	14	...	32	...	...	...	185	...	...	...	...	...	175	Micronesia
962[1]	646	1,300[1]	1,264	1,468[1]	950	17,767[1]	13,000	998[1]	645	...	1,936	35,833[1]	31,000	Moldova
...	...	...	...	...	...	...	...	...	...	...	...	...	...	Monaco
2,694	3,476	14,266	13,561	166	24	351	58	271	314	352	398	1,669	280	Mongolia
3,284	2,590	13,528	17,580	9	10	71,200	100,000	955	950	521	567	170,800	200,000	Morocco
1,373	1,290	120	122	167	175	21,833	23,000	63	59	170	170	11,333	12,000	Mozambique
9,269	10,303	275	357	2,355	3,358	23,989	33,074	422	468	245	245	35,208	54,218	Myanmar (Burma)
2,104	2,055	3,289	2,429	18	17	1,717	2,400	70	73	411	421	1,306	1,780	Namibia
...	...	...	...	3	3	5	5	...	...	...	...	16	16	Nauru
6,274	7,025	903	870	571	724	8,233	15,577	252	310	366	378	16,133	20,300	Nepal
4,918	4,366	1,663	1,674	13,747	14,253	92,050	93,106	11,198	11,100	6,040	6,581	644,480	555,000	Netherlands, The
1	1	6	7	3	2	125	135	—	—	1,278	1,250	432	510	Netherlands Antilles
122	110	3	4	37	38	317	260	4	3	600	600	1,367	1,400	New Caledonia
7,987	8,924	57,861	47,394	404	417	9,067	12,000	7,572	11,052	2,835	3,047	45,507	42,000	New Zealand
1,693	1,712	4	4	565	420	4,533	7,900	162	209	797	798	25,500	28,658	Nicaragua

Crops and livestock (continued)

country	grains production ('000 metric tons) 1989–91 average	1997	grains yield (kg/hectare) 1989–91 average	1997	roots and tubers[a] production ('000 metric tons) 1989–91 average	1997	roots and tubers yield (kg/hectare) 1989–91 average	1997	pulses[b] production ('000 metric tons) 1989–91 average	1997	pulses yield (kg/hectare) 1989–91 average	1997	fruits[c] production ('000 metric tons) 1989–91 average	1997	vegetables[d] production ('000 metric tons) 1989–91 average	1997
Niger	1,902	2,225	310	335	248	263	7,689	7,450	330	428	133	162	44	47	274	264
Nigeria	18,100	21,945	1,139	1,190	34,383	51,950	10,031	10,084	1,421	1,700	734	497	6,595	7,150	5,017	6,040
Northern Mariana Islands	...	...	...	...	...	...	...	...	...	...	...	...	...	...	...	...
Norway	1,410	1,294	3,943	3,869	452	400	24,246	22,240	—	—	...	...	122	108	182	172
Oman	5	6	2,124	2,173	5	6	25,208	21,923	...	...	...	...	184	210	155	173
Pakistan	21,038	25,041	1,784	2,034	1,052	1,362	11,467	12,370	719	1,025	483	591	3,931	5,389	3,165	4,622
Palau	...	...	...	...	...	...	...	...	...	...	...	...	...	...	...	...
Panama	336	328	1,884	2,143	66	83	5,901	7,151	9	11	526	495	1,225	1,024	65	104
Papua New Guinea	3	10	1,761	4,085	1,254	895	7,224	5,326	2	2	500	528	1,076	947	357	370
Paraguay	859	1,575	1,844	2,411	3,471	3,235	15,074	14,046	49	75	859	924	522	512	264	270
Peru	2,003	2,579	2,492	2,770	2,302	3,708	8,112	9,424	105	135	882	898	1,891	3,084	910	1,632
Philippines	14,350	15,601	2,018	2,375	2,716	2,873	6,876	6,659	36	40	792	786	6,250	9,825	4,143	5,061
Poland	27,594	25,399	3,231	2,854	33,247	20,776	18,350	15,903	635	277	1,857	1,885	1,793	2,884	5,797	5,116
Portugal	1,673	1,496	2,012	2,069	1,258	1,071	10,097	12,624	69	37	300	190	2,221	1,667	2,019	1,943
Puerto Rico	—	1	7,462	8,127	28	9	6,499	11,248	2	—	569	609	258	179	43	31
Qatar	3	4	2,910	3,114	—	—	9,611	10,833	...	...	...	...	8	16	30	43
Réunion	12	17	5,590	6,724	15	11	11,006	8,792	1	1	1,429	741	46	36	45	60
Romania	18,286	22,096	3,084	3,497	3,159	3,206	10,517	12,572	149	75	889	1,462	2,295	2,596	3,215	3,062
Russia	92,890[1]	86,803	1,612[1]	1,627	36,603[1]	37,040	10,673[1]	11,049	2,880[1]	1,576	1,383[1]	1,273	2,989[1]	3,095	10,411[1]	11,796
Rwanda	299	220	1,234	1,212	1,631	1,397	6,275	6,251	216	128	777	619	2,912	2,303	131	120
St. Kitts and Nevis	...	...	...	...	1	1	3,688	3,006	—	—	1,000	1,000	1	2	—	1
St. Lucia	—	—	699	714	11	11	4,179	3,938	—	—	2,133	2,500	176	114	1	1
St. Vincent and the Grenadines	1	1	3,348	3,910	21	14	4,917	5,342	—	—	1,000	1,000	78	61	3	4
Samoa	...	...	...	...	41	41	5,002	6,164	...	...	...	...	51	43	1	1
San Marino	...	...	...	...	...	...	...	...	...	...	...	...	...	...	...	...
São Tomé and Príncipe	3	4	2,015	2,177	6	15	7,346	6,740	...	...	...	...	10	17	3	6
Saudi Arabia	4,214	2,440	4,177	4,099	59	250	19,157	14,706	7	8	1,832	1,857	832	1,039	1,987	2,400
Senegal	996	783	823	704	67	49	4,009	3,277	19	33	337	377	105	138	129	408
Seychelles	...	...	...	...	...	...	5,000	5,000	...	...	...	...	2	2	2	2
Sierra Leone	566	467	1,225	1,205	139	363	5,220	4,503	38	42	652	676	163	159	189	182
Singapore	...	...	...	...	—	—	13,933	10,000	...	...	...	...	1	—	8	5
Slovakia	3,494[3]	3,774	4,068[3]	4,391	566[3]	504	13,232[3]	15,518	161[3]	98	2,313[3]	2,509	285[3]	280	528[3]	573
Slovenia	486[1]	541	4,131[1]	5,608	379[1]	495	13,756[1]	22,500	7[1]	5	777[1]	787	255[1]	242	77[1]	110
Solomon Islands	...	...	...	...	107	117	17,595	17,747	2	2	1,175	1,000	15	15	6	6
Somalia	497	284	715	403	50	57	10,421	10,000	13	13	312	236	284	215	65	73
South Africa	12,237	13,076	1,956	2,022	1,334	1,640	16,535	21,722	135	82	1,269	1,000	3,903	4,141	1,885	2,104
Spain	19,306	19,354	2,489	2,782	5,337	3,447	19,448	20,420	238	391	755	639	13,490	14,730	10,966	10,808
Sri Lanka	2,370	2,277	2,924	3,270	547	410	8,845	8,366	50	40	780	760	743	812	578	618
Sudan, The	2,755	4,706	505	536	138	166	2,674	2,691	103	168	1,064	1,252	758	910	903	1,064
Suriname	229	229	3,770	4,577	3	6	11,900	15,048	—	—	690	727	75	67	26	26
Swaziland	127	110	1,401	1,761	9	8	1,665	1,930	5	7	569	968	144	96	13	10
Sweden	5,677	5,986	4,594	4,815	1,132	1,214	32,977	35,397	91	169	2,494	4,362	188	115	261	272
Switzerland	1,331	1,228	6,352	6,659	731	761	37,867	42,044	8	13	4,267	4,156	625	455	308	324
Syria	2,598	4,324	668	1,266	407	266	17,543	14,797	131	190	577	742	1,353	1,626	1,691	1,798
Taiwan	...	...	...	...	...	...	...	...	...	...	...	...	...	...	...	...
Tajikistan	256[1]	468	944[1]	1,281	151[1]	115	12,215[1]	11,500	7[1]	6	742[1]	556	248[1]	271	623[1]	655
Tanzania	4,142	3,533	1,390	1,174	8,167	6,290	8,824	7,811	437	375	501	527	2,094	1,761	1,099	1,022
Thailand	23,624	26,541	2,149	2,307	21,776	18,294	14,245	15,000	476	333	794	739	6,164	7,223	2,514	2,641
Togo	505	709	809	919	913	1,275	7,992	7,043	22	53	202	292	48	49	152	159
Tonga	...	...	...	...	99	92	6,551	10,008	...	...	...	...	15	13	20	7
Trinidad and Tobago	17	15	2,816	3,635	10	12	9,645	10,336	3	4	1,458	2,568	62	76	16	22
Tunisia	1,611	1,056	1,115	923	205	327	12,592	14,730	73	72	663	792	670	810	1,477	1,720
Turkey	28,283	29,677	2,065	2,100	4,321	5,001	22,388	23,582	1,946	1,694	885	938	9,117	9,622	17,963	21,256
Turkmenistan	1,038[1]	595	2,870[1]	1,553	32[1]	28	4,750[1]	7,000	...	...	...	...	158[1]	220	539[1]	673
Tuvalu	...	...	...	...	—	—	—	—	...	...	...	...	1	1	...	...
Uganda	1,597	1,625	1,483	1,218	5,360	4,545	6,335	4,903	493	351	774	441	8,384	9,941	404	488
Ukraine	37,208[1]	34,395	2,957[1]	2,490	19,129[1]	16,701	12,040[1]	10,590	2,840[1]	1,075	2,300[1]	1,556	2,597[1]	2,510	5,750[1]	5,785
United Arab Emirates	7	7	5,383	7,845	4	5	19,300	21,429	...	...	...	...	205	304	270	835
United Kingdom	22,644	23,515	6,168	6,714	6,333	7,123	35,916	43,042	750	674	3,425	3,802	514	278	3,747	3,278
United States	292,060	342,512	4,582	5,297	18,530	21,731	32,018	37,605	1,621	1,734	1,832	1,962	25,392	32,172	30,808	34,965
Uruguay	1,237	2,214	2,414	3,437	215	200	7,514	12,500	6	6	986	981	391	521	117	148
Uzbekistan	2,281[1]	3,370	1,714[1]	1,776	468[1]	510	10,083[1]	10,200	...	...	...	...	985[1]	1,169	3,760[1]	3,064
Vanuatu	1	1	515	539	49	50	10,072	10,000	...	...	...	...	18	19	8	8
Venezuela	1,989	2,413	2,423	3,465	682	887	8,686	9,811	57	35	585	645	2,579	2,771	498	1,141
Vietnam	20,013	29,292	3,060	3,776	4,758	3,926	7,432	7,322	187	210	639	667	4,009	3,848	3,625	4,508
Virgin Islands (U.S.)	...	...	...	...	...	...	...	...	...	...	...	...	—	—	...	...
West Bank	...	30	...	...	...	17	...	...	...	2	...	...	...	153	...	228
Western Sahara	...	2	...	774	...	...	...	...	...	...	...	...	...	...	...	...
Yemen	693	646	871	897	153	196	12,223	12,720	64	66	1,424	1,157	314	471	536	526
Yugoslavia	7,613[1]	10,303	3,102[1]	4,277	766[1]	904	6,928[1]	8,071	100[1]	142	1,438[1]	1,804	1,391[1]	1,855	1,045[1]	1,353
Zambia	1,467	1,125	1,569	1,494	573	811	5,388	6,509	15	13	629	447	105	98	274	260
Zimbabwe	2,391	2,673	1,488	1,230	127	192	4,792	4,603	50	48	694	678	170	184	153	145

livestock														country
cattle		sheep		hogs		chickens		milk[e]				eggs[f]		
stock ('000 head)		stock ('000 head)		stock ('000 head)		stock ('000 head)		production ('000 metric tons)		yield (kg/animal)		production (metric tons)		
1989–91 average	1997	1989–91 average	1997	1989–91 average	1997	1989–91 average	1997	1989–91 average	1997	1989–91 average	1996	1989–91 average	1997	
1,712	2,089	3,100	4,097	37	39	17,833	20,000	140	168	393	400	8,500	9,180	Niger
14,650	19,610	12,477	14,000	3,558	7,600	122,120	126,000	350	380	239	233	313,000	350,000	Nigeria
...	...	...	...	...	...	...	...	...	...	...	...	...	...	Northern Mariana Islands
959	998	2,202	2,524	696	768	3,663	3,656	1,944	1,844	5,757	5,619	51,046	49,000	Norway
137	146	141	155	...	...	2,500	3,000	18	19	420	420	5,850	6,300	Oman
17,677	17,917	25,703	30,532	...	...	77,767	110,000	3,525	4,540	842	1,010	210,867	284,400	Pakistan
...	...	...	...	...	...	...	...	...	...	...	...	...	...	Palau
1,401	1,362	...	...	228	244	7,668	10,000	129	156	1,162	1,230	11,117	15,000	Panama
103	87	4	6	997	1,500	2,883	3,500	—	—	—	—	2,950	3,900	Papua New Guinea
7,985	9,794	422	387	2,443	2,525	15,065	14,835	224	352	1,904	1,899	34,883	47,000	Paraguay
4,126	4,560	12,484	13,108	2,417	2,481	62,406	81,968	788	948	1,323	1,636	103,800	149,400	Peru
1,644	2,266	30	30	7,968	9,752	76,853	134,963	14	20	1,036	1,029	276,000	428,000	Philippines
9,875	7,307	3,934	491	20,056	18,135	58,196	53,285	15,560	12,123	3,260	3,362	410,255	425,943	Poland
1,355	1,285	5,531	6,300	2,531	2,365	19,667	27,000	1,500	1,770	3,734	4,098	85,400	101,225	Portugal
595	388	7	8	204	175	11,241	11,643	396	357	4,233	4,100	16,690	15,143	Puerto Rico
10	14	126	200	...	...	2,932	3,850	3	11	1,490	1,491	3,270	3,600	Qatar
20	26	2	2	88	87	6,916	10,500	7	14	627	524	4,117	4,700	Réunion
6,029	3,435	15,236	9,662	12,675	8,235	120,969	78,478	3,450	5,126	1,867	2,429	354,367	247,650	Romania
51,939[1]	35,800	46,998[1]	21,710	31,820[1]	19,500	582,667[1]	415,000	45,088[1]	34,100	...	1,960	2,233,333[1]	1,700,000	Russia
592	465	387	250	117	80	1,292	1,400	85	80	579	727	1,787	2,000	Rwanda
4	4	14	9	2	5	56	60	...	...	...	...	347	300	St. Kitts and Nevis
12	12	16	12	12	15	223	260	1	1	1,396	1,563	528	460	St. Lucia
6	6	13	13	10	9	205	200	1	1	1,351	1,414	627	640	St. Vincent and the Grenadines
24	26	...	...	186	179	356	350	1	1	1,000	1,000	192	200	Samoa
...	...	...	...	...	...	...	...	...	...	...	...	...	...	San Marino
4	4	2	3	3	2	124	270	—	—	...	...	175	280	São Tomé and Príncipe
195	200	6,370	8,042	...	...	76,000	95,000	274	458	6,254	6,863	113,005	130,000	Saudi Arabia
2,616	2,913	3,500	4,239	295	320	19,667	44,100	98	105	360	360	14,767	32,500	Senegal
2	2	...	...	18	18	293	500	—	—	...	...	1,760	2,100	Seychelles
333	400	271	350	50	50	5,900	6,000	17	17	250	250	6,785	6,900	Sierra Leone
—	—	—	—	300	190	2,500	2,000	...	...	...	...	16,543	16,693	Singapore
1,030[3]	892	412[3]	419	2,162[3]	1,985	13,321[3]	13,000	1,206[3]	1,116	...	3,552	79,549[3]	88,000	Slovakia
488[1]	484	23[1]	28	574[1]	559	10,420[1]	8,550	569[1]	567	...	2,742	19,712[1]	24,200	Slovenia
11	10	...	...	53	55	144	145	1	1	650	650	288	300	Solomon Islands
3,967	5,200	12,117	13,500	9	9	2,833	3,000	435	560	403	412	2,267	2,400	Somalia
12,920	13,667	32,060	29,187	1,480	1,617	46,000	59,000	2,426	2,720	2,637	2,576	213,362	285,000	South Africa
5,125	5,914	23,800	23,981	16,720	19,269	75,000	126,000	6,100	6,108	3,728	4,724	649,413	589,400	Spain
1,690	1,644	25	11	88	85	8,630	9,300	172	213	271	320	46,033	48,470	Sri Lanka
20,593	22,250	20,179	24,500	...	...	32,371	40,000	2,252	2,928	480	480	33,212	41,000	Sudan, The
91	107	9	9	29	21	7,625	2,700	17	16	1,832	1,565	3,033	3,000	Suriname
712	658	24	27	23	32	1,133	990	42	37	274	300	315	350	Swaziland
1,704	1,784	408	470	2,243	2,338	11,433	11,000	3,401	3,276	6,097	6,947	116,333	109,000	Sweden
1,845	1,755	392	442	1,793	1,550	5,912	6,251	3,892	3,867	4,954	5,156	37,833	38,200	Switzerland
786	857	14,571	13,829	1	1	14,405	18,825	782	1,009	2,314	2,322	75,133	113,650	Syria
157	165[4]	...	...	8,813	10,509[4]	80,119	101,838[4]	204	318[4]	4,349	4,802[4]	...	...	Taiwan
1,238[1]	1,082	2,110[1]	1,663	49[1]	2	4,029[1]	1,000	472[1]	350	...	731	14,667[1]	3,300	Tajikistan
13,047	14,163	3,551	3,955	320	335	20,567	26,000	516	600	169	180	41,167	52,000	Tanzania
5,513	7,500	161	60	4,766	4,209	107,858	135,000	137	300	1,659	2,208	430,033	489,000	Thailand
247	264	1,164	1,379	617	850	6,070	6,448	8	8	225	225	5,558	6,325	Togo
11	9	...	...	94	81	221	266	—	—	...	...	287	280	Tonga
55	38	14	12	53	34	9,500	11,500	11	10	1,593	1,504	9,167	9,500	Trinidad and Tobago
626	701	5,935	6,293	6	6	39,367	35,567	393	613	1,420	1,483	52,250	64,000	Tunisia
12,037	11,700	43,195	33,072	10	30	73,181	152,957	8,183	8,914	1,352	1,501	369,080	630,000	Turkey
962[1]	959	5,793[1]	5,400	203[1]	40	6,900[1]	3,000	565[1]	725	...	2,940	14,933[1]	14,300	Turkmenistan
...	...	...	...	12	13	29	27	...	...	...	...	12	12	Tuvalu
4,777	5,363	1,350	1,950	797	940	18,667	22,422	418	469	350	350	14,933	18,000	Uganda
22,597[1]	15,313	6,658[1]	2,193	16,437[1]	11,236	180,352[1]	105,000	18,363[1]	13,607	...	2,198	664,865[1]	491,303	Ukraine
49	75	255	385	...	...	6,733	10,700	5	8	210	212	9,877	12,500	United Arab Emirates
11,980	11,609	29,241	42,559	7,519	7,992	124,076	130,939	14,976	14,163	5,206	6,630	616,334	645,120	United Kingdom
96,316	101,460	11,384	7,937	54,557	56,171	1,333,000	1,553,000	66,423	71,500	6,672	7,483	4,004,766	4,567,000	United States
9,019	10,557	25,359	18,187	217	270	7,900	11,500	1,006	1,411	1,604	1,801	21,933	31,890	Uruguay
5,273[1]	5,217	8,681[1]	8,700	524[1]	200	26,867[1]	13,000	3,622[1]	3,088	...	1,817	96,833[1]	57,000	Uzbekistan
124	151	...	...	59	60	306	320	2	3	202	203	312	280	Vanuatu
13,311	15,049	551	820	2,801	3,200	59,890	130,000	1,518	1,475	1,285	1,214	118,562	163,810	Venezuela
3,153	3,905	...	...	12,225	17,636	77,228	112,000	38	48	800	800	97,133	155,000	Vietnam
8	8	3	3	3	3	30	35	2	2	2,725	2,703	120	160	Virgin Islands (U.S.)
...	12	...	352	...	...	...	...	...	27	...	...	...	15,000	West Bank
...	...	...	29	...	...	...	...	...	...	...	...	...	...	Western Sahara
1,154	1,201	3,682	4,267	...	...	16,385	25,200	152	162	600	600	17,612	25,500	Yemen
1,925[1]	1,899	2,701[1]	2,566	3,876[1]	4,216	21,920[1]	24,287	1,841[1]	2,000	...	1,836	96,833[1]	81,500	Yugoslavia
2,845	2,600	59	65	296	290	16,033	20,000	77	70	300	300	25,653	32,000	Zambia
6,147	5,400	584	530	300	270	12,000	15,500	609	600	454	439	15,500	19,800	Zimbabwe

[1]1992–94 average. [2]Belgium includes Luxembourg. [3]1993–95 average. [4]1995.

Extractive industries

Extractive industries are generally defined as those exploiting in situ natural resources and include such activities as mining, forestry, fisheries, and agriculture; the definition is often confined, however, to nonrenewable resources only. For the purposes of this table, agriculture is excluded; it is covered in the two tables immediately preceding.

Extractive industries are divided here into three parts: mining, forestry, and fisheries. These major headings are each divided into two main subheadings, one that treats production and one that treats foreign trade. The production sections are presented in terms of volume except for mining, and the trade sections are presented in terms of U.S. dollars. Volume of production data usually imply output of primary (unprocessed) raw materials only, but, because of the way national statistical information is reported, the data may occasionally include some processed and manufactured materials as well, since these are often indistinguishably associated with the extractive process (sulfur from petroleum extraction, cured or treated lumber, or "processed" fish). This is also the case in the trade sections, where individual national trade nomenclatures may not distinguish some processed and manufactured goods from unprocessed raw materials.

Mining. In the absence of a single international source publication or standard of practice for reporting volume or value of mineral production, single-country sources predominantly have been used to compile mining production figures, supplemented by U.S. Bureau of Mines data, by the United Nations' *National Accounts Statistics* (annual; 2 parts), and by industry sources, especially *Mining Journal's Mining Annual Review*. Each

country has its own methods of classifying mining data, which do not always accord with the principal mineral production categories adopted in this table—namely, "metals," "nonmetals," and "energy." The available data have therefore been adjusted to accord better with the definition of each group. Included in the "metal" category are all ferrous and nonferrous metallic ores, concentrates, and scrap; the "nonmetal" group includes all nonmetallic minerals (stone, clay, precious gems, etc.) except the mineral fuels; the last group, "energy," is composed predominantly of the natural hydrocarbon fuels, though it may also include manufactured gas.

The contribution (value) of each national mineral sector to its country's gross domestic product is given, as is the distribution by group of that contribution (to gross domestic product and to foreign trade), although statistics regarding the value of mineral production are less readily available in country sources than those regarding trade or volume of minerals produced. Figures for value added by mineral output, though not always available, were sought first, as they provide the most consistent standard to compare the importance of minerals both within a particular national economy and among national mineral sectors worldwide. Where value added to the gross domestic product was not available, gross value of production or sales was substituted and the exception footnoted. Figures for value of production are reported here in millions of U.S. dollars to permit comparisons to be made from country to country. Comparisons can also be made as to the relative importance of each mineral group within a given country.

Extractive industries

country	mining														
	% of GDP, 1995	mineral production (value added)				trade (value)									
		year	total ('000,000 U.S.$)	by kind (%)			year	exports				imports			
				metals[a]	non-metals[b]	energy[c]		total ('000,000 U.S.$)	by kind (%)			total ('000,000 U.S.$)	by kind (%)		
									metals[a]	non-metals[b]	energy[c]		metals[a]	non-metals[b]	energy[c]
Afghanistan	...	1988[1]	16.2	—	17.7	82.3	1995	0.5	—	100.0	—	—	—	—	—
Albania	...	1994[1]	81.4	46.1	0.8	53.1	1995	8.6	99.7	0.3	—	—	—	—	—
Algeria	25.7	1995	10,628.8	—— 0.5 ——		99.5	1995	7,156.6	—	0.3	99.7	54.7	23.7	2.2	74.1
American Samoa	...	1995	...	—	100.0	—	...	...	...	...	...	...	...	...	...
Andorra	...	...	...	...	...	...	1992	0.3	—	100.0	—	7.8	—	100.0	...
Angola	52.1[2]	1994	2,610.9	—	2.0	98.0	1995	2,788.0	—	3.7	96.3	—	—	—	—
Antigua and Barbuda	1.5	1995	7.6	—	100.0	—	1991	—	—	—	—	—	—	—	—
Argentina	1.7[3]	1993	4,383.3	2.7[4]	3.9[4]	93.4[4]	1995	1,688.1	—	1.2	98.8	563.9	44.1	8.8	47.2
Armenia	...	1995	...	—— 100.0 ——			1993	5.4	—	100.0	—	—	—	—	—
Aruba	...	1995	...	—	100.0	—	1991	0.4	31.2	68.8	—	0.5	—	97.9	2.1
Australia	4.4[2]	1994–95	14,150.8	37.5[5]	7.1[5]	55.4[5]	1995	14,129.4	40.7	4.1	55.2	2,245.8	5.9	10.3	83.8
Austria	0.4	1994	515.1	—	39.3	60.7	1995	501.4	41.3	58.3	0.5	2,316.4[2]	18.7[2]	11.1[2]	70.2[2]
Azerbaijan	...	...	...	...	...	...	1995	24.5	100.0	—	—	—	—	—	—
Bahamas, The	...	1995	...	—	100.0	—	1995	252.7	8.1	79.1	12.8	10.8	62.2	—	37.8
Bahrain	15.1[2]	1994	763.8	—	3.9[6]	96.1[6]	1995	2,471.1	0.6	—	99.3	1,372.7	3.0	0.1	96.9
Bangladesh	—	1995	5.2[7]	—	—— 100.0[7] ——		1995	0.6	100.0	—	—	207.0	0.9	9.1	90.0
Barbados	0.6	1995	10.4[7]	—	—— 100.0[8] ——		1995	3.2	—	100.0	—	7.2	—	44.5	55.5
Belarus	0.1[6]	1992	2.0	—	—— 100.0 ——		1995	18.8	35.4	4.5	60.1	65.1	0.6	99.4	—
Belgium	0.2[2]	1994	541.0	—	—— 100.0 ——		1995[9]	12,480.1	6.6	91.2	2.1	19,724.5	15.1	56.8	28.1
Belize	0.6	1995	3.5	—	100.0	—	1995	—	—	—	—	3.1	—	21.5	78.5
Benin	0.7	1995	14.4[10]	—	—— 100.0[10] ——		1995	—	—	—	—	—	—	—	—
Bermuda	...	...	...	...	...	...	1995	0.0	—	100.0	—	0.3	—	100.0	—
Bhutan	1.9	1995	6.0	—	—— 100.0 ——		1995	—	—	—	—	2.26	—	39.7[6]	60.3[6]
Bolivia	5.3	1995	369.6	—— 58.1[3] ——		41.9[3]	1995	336.0	71.5	1.0	27.5	26.6	82.7	17.3	—
Bosnia and Herzegovina	...	...	...	...	...	...	...	...	...	...	...	...	...	...	...
Botswana	35.5	1995	1,478.7	11.4[2]	88.0[2]	0.7[2]	[11]	...	...	...	...	...	...	...	...
Brazil	1.0	1995	7,171.9	...	...	...	1995	3,049.2	91.6	8.4	...	4,107.9[2]	12.0[2]	4.3[2]	83.8[2]
Brunei	57.9[2]	1994	1,437.7	—— 3.0 ——		97.0	1995	1,970.2	—	—	100.0	31.6[2]	—	100.0[2]	—
Bulgaria	...	1991[1]	582.1	24.6	28.2	47.2	1995	96.1	85.2	14.8	—	1,044.5	5.5	0.3	94.2
Burkina Faso	0.9[3]	1992	28.4	—— 100.0 ——			1991	0.6	—	100.0	—	3.2[4]	—	100.0[4]	—
Burundi	0.6	1994	5.4	...	...	...	1993	—	—	—	—	1.2	—	100.0	—
Cambodia	0.2	1995	4.4	—	100.0	—	...	...	...	...	...	...	...	...	...
Cameroon	7.3	1995	681.6	—	100.0	—	1995	303.4	—	—	100.0	153.9[12]	84.3[12]	8.6[12]	7.1[12]
Canada	4.4	1990	25,411.4	24.6	6.4	69.0	1995	18,899.6	19.4	4.8	75.8	7,688.7	32.4	7.2	60.5
Cape Verde	0.3[12]	1991	0.8	—	100.0	—	1994	0.0	—	100.0	—	1.5	—	—	100.0
Central African Republic	5.8	1995	65.5[13]	—— 100.0[13] ——		—	1995	78.6	—	100.0	—	...	...	...	...
Chad	0.5[12]	1991	5.0	—	100.0	—	...	...	...	...	...	...	...	...	...
Chile	8.0[2]	1994	2,440.0	...	...	...	1995	2,564.2	97.5	2.5	—	1,315.1	12.2	2.9	84.9
China	2.7[12]	1991	9,885.2	10.7	11.8	77.5	1995	4,888.9	3.0	30.6	66.4	6,304.0	48.5	5.7	45.7
Colombia	5.1	1995	4,045.4	...	...	...	1995	2,685.0	0.1	17.0	82.9	85.7	31.9	68.1	—
Comoros	—	1995	...	—	100.0	—	1994	—	—	—	—	—	—	—	—
Congo, Dem. Rep. of the	4.3	1995	226.5	—— 100.0 ——		—	1995	302.7	—	84.5	15.5	3.4	—	100.0	—
Congo, Rep. of the	32.8[15]	1995	659.9[15]	—	32.2	67.8	1995	906.3	—	32.2	67.8	2.7	—	100.0	—
Costa Rica	...	1990	3.8	12.8	87.2	—	1995	6.9	100.0	—	—	73.9	—	13.1	86.9
Côte d'Ivoire	0.2[2]	1994	13.3	...	...	...	1995	73.8	—	100.0	—	2.6	—	—	100.0
Croatia	...	1991	119.7	1.3	71.3	27.4	1995	57.3	37.8	23.4	38.8	775.4	0.3	6.5	93.1
Cuba	...	...	...	...	...	...	1995	342.3	100.0	—	—	13.0	—	100.0	—
Cyprus	0.3[16]	1995[16]	23.7	—	100.0	—	1995[16]	14.7	62.7	37.3	—	116.8	—	13.8	86.2
Czech Republic	...	1995[1]	1,050.3	—— 8.4 ——		91.6	1995	739.9	21.3	11.8	67.0	1,927.7	15.2	5.4	79.5
Denmark	0.9	1995	1,289.7	—	14.5[6]	85.5[6]	1995	990.2	24.8	9.3	65.9	932.2	7.4	16.7	75.9
Djibouti	—	1995	...	—	100.0	—	1992	—	—	—	—	—	—	—	—
Dominica	0.7	1995	1.5	—	100.0	—	1991	0.2	—	100.0	—	1.6	—	21.1	78.9
Dominican Republic	2.8	1995	126.0	...	...	...	1994	2.6	—	100.0	—	0.0	—	100.0	—
Ecuador	10.5	1995	1,883.6	—— 6.8[3] ——		93.2[3]	1995	1,247.0	0.3	0.1	99.7	92.4	—	15.2	84.8
Egypt	9.8[2]	1994	5,151.3	—— 1.0 ——		99.0	1995	738.4	—	2.6	97.4	264.3	46.6	15.7	37.7

Since the data for value of mineral production are obtained mostly from country sources, there is some variation (from a standard calendar year) in the time periods to which the data refer. In addition, the time period for which production data are available does not always correspond with the year for which mineral trade data are available.

The Standard International Trade Classification (SITC), Revision 3, was used to determine the commodity groupings for foreign trade statistics. The actual trade data for these groups is taken largely from the United Nations' *International Trade Statistics Yearbook* (2 vol.) and national sources.

Forestry. Data for the production and trade sections of forestry are based on the Food and Agriculture Organization (FAO) of the United Nations' *Yearbook of Forest Products.* Production of roundwood (all wood obtained in removals from forests) is the principal indicator of the volume of each country's forestry sector; this total is broken down further (as percentages of the roundwood total) into its principal components: fuelwood and charcoal, and industrial roundwood. The latter group was further divided to show its principal component, sawlogs and veneer; lesser categories of industrial roundwood could not be shown for reasons of space. These included pitprops (used in mining, a principal consumer of wood) and pulpwood (used in papermaking and plastics). Value of trade in forest products is given for both imports and exports, although exports alone tend to be the significant indicator for producing countries, while imports of wood are rarely a significant fraction of the trade of most importing countries.

Fisheries. Data for nominal (live weight) catches of fish, crustaceans, mollusks, etc., in all fishing areas (marine areas and inland waters) are taken from the FAO *Yearbook of Fishery Statistics (Catches and Landings).* Total catch figures are given in metric tons; the catches in inland waters and marine areas are given as percentages of the total catch, as are the main kinds of catch—fish, crustaceans, and mollusks. The total catch figures exclude marine mammals, such as whales and seals; and such aquatic animal products as corals, sponges, and pearls; but include frogs, turtles, and jellyfish. The subtotals by kind of catch, however, exclude the last group, which do not belong taxonomically to the fish, crustacean, or mollusk groups.

Figures for trade in fishery products (including processed products and preparations like oils, meals, and animal feeding stuffs) are taken from the FAO's *Yearbook of Fishery Statistics (Commodities).* Value figures for trade in fish products are given for both imports and exports.

The following notes further define the column headings:
a. Includes ferrous and nonferrous metallic ores, concentrates, and scraps, such as iron ore, bauxite and alumina, copper, zinc, gold (except unwrought or semimanufactured), lead, or uranium.
b. Includes natural fertilizers; stone, sand, and aggregate; and pearls, precious and semiprecious stones, worked and unworked.
c. Includes hydrocarbon solids, liquids, and gases.
1 cubic metre = 35.3147 cubic feet
1 metric ton = 1.1023 short tons

forestry, 1995						fisheries, 1994								country
production of roundwood				trade (value, '000 U.S.$)		catch (nominal)						trade (value, '000 U.S.$)		
total ('000 cubic metres)	fuelwood, charcoal (%)	industrial roundwood (%)		exports	imports	total ('000 metric tons)	by source (%)		by kind of catch (%)			exports	imports	
		total	sawlogs, veneer				marine	inland	fish	crustaceans	mollusks			
7,680	78.0	22.0	11.1	234	240	1.3	—	100.0	100.0	—	—	—	...	Afghanistan
409	84.5	15.5	15.5	6,177	6,823	3.2	59.7	40.3	87.9	0.5	11.6	1,770	430	Albania
2,517	84.5	15.5	1.6	366	453,252	135.4	99.7	0.3	97.3	2.0	0.7	2,362	9,130	Algeria
...	...	...	...	—	302	0.04	100.0	—	100.0	—	—	...	...	American Samoa
...	...	...	...	444	6,383	—	—	100.0	100.0	—	—	...	...	Andorra
7,005	85.8	14.2	0.9	877	5,282	77.9	91.0	9.0	97.2	2.6	0.2	7,165	23,510	Angola
...	...	...	...	246	4,604	0.6	100.0	—	77.2	11.0	11.8	420	1,940	Antigua and Barbuda
11,792	45.5	54.5	20.9	280,956	575,009	949.3	98.7	1.3	76.9	1.7	21.4	728,091	66,805	Argentina
...	...	...	...	17	42	4.1	—	100.0	100.0	—	—	...	555	Armenia
...	...	...	...	6	7,321	0.3	100.0	—	100.0	—	—	20	7,430	Aruba
22,458	12.9	87.1	42.7	737,797	1,814,759	210.5	95.5	4.5	61.5	18.6	19.9	758,011	428,116	Australia
14,405	21.2	78.8	56.1	3,360,990	1,986,551	4.6	—	100.0	99.9	0.1	—	5,424	192,874	Austria
...	...	...	...	409	663	35.0	—	100.0	100.0	—	—	480	900	Azerbaijan
117	—	100.0	14.5	436	24,271	10.0	100.0	—	16.3	78.4	5.3	48,160	7,300	Bahamas, The
—	—	—	—	411	33,281	7.6	100.0	—	70.5	28.2	1.3	3,240	5,570	Bahrain
32,044	97.7	2.3	0.9	118	59,102	1,090.6	25.6	74.4	90.5	9.4	—	239,550	160	Bangladesh
5	—	100.0	100.0	2,033	18,433	2.6	100.0	—	100.0	—	—	349	6,891	Barbados
10,015	8.1	91.9	39.1	40,487	3,296	14.5	—	100.0	100.0	—	—	2,030	9,000	Belarus
4,185[9]	13.1[9]	86.9[9]	60.9[9]	2,790,723[9]	4,066,241[9]	34.6	97.6	2.4	92.7	5.1	2.2	320,421[9]	920,918[9]	Belgium
188	67.2	32.8	32.8	3,703	3,849	1.9	99.9	0.1	9.4	79.6	11.0	13,253	707	Belize
5,899	94.6	5.4	0.8	813	1,484	37.0	21.6	78.4	81.2	18.8	—	390	8,300	Benin
...	...	...	...	822	9,004	0.4	100.0	—	97.4	2.6	—	...	9,250	Bermuda
1,399	96.8	3.2	1.3	66	1,511	0.3	—	100.0	100.0	—	—	...	...	Bhutan
2,567	49.6	50.4	34.7	79,717	25,237	6.0	—	100.0	100.0	—	—	138	2,790	Bolivia
5,379[4]	...	...	...	366	336	2.4	—	100.0	100.0	—	—	...	4,700	Bosnia and Herzegovina
1,584	93.8	6.2	—	...	...	2.0	—	100.0	100.0	—	—	11	5,222	Botswana
285,295	70.3	29.7	16.7	3,547,061	1,217,981	820.0	73.2	26.8	89.6	9.7	0.7	178,548	261,453	Brazil
295	26.8	73.2	69.8	482	28,101	4.5	99.6	0.4	70.8	28.4	0.8	520	6,590	Brunei
2,856	31.0	69.0	30.7	38,522	43,116	22.0	56.1	43.9	95.5	—	4.5	12,175	9,890	Bulgaria
10,033	95.5	4.5	—	193	943	8.0	—	100.0	100.0	—	—	...	2,956	Burkina Faso
4,969	97.8	2.2	0.9	227	1,024	23.1	—	100.0	100.0	—	—	230	906	Burundi
7,765	86.6	13.4	5.3	171,139	1,827	103.2	29.6	70.4	90.7	7.9	1.4	14,225	...	Cambodia
15,710	78.8	21.2	15.6	329,114	24,117	66.0	65.2	34.8	99.2	0.8	—	2,060	20,600	Cameroon
186,195	3.2	96.8	75.8	27,786,860	2,952,518	1,010.6	96.4	3.6	69.1	16.0	14.8	2,182,078	913,404	Canada
...	...	...	...	77	3,619	5.9	100.0	—	99.2	0.8	—	2,350	350	Cape Verde
3,864	84.1	15.9	8.4	29,165	271	13.0	—	100.0	100.0	—	—	—	890	Central African Republic
4,531	85.6	14.4	0.3	573	4,895	80.0	—	100.0	100.0	—	—	—	...	Chad
31,365	31.8	68.2	31.9	2,060,239	136,535	7,841.0	99.7	0.3	97.7	0.4	1.4	1,303,974	27,574	Chile
300,360[14]	67.9[14]	32.1[14]	16.9[14]	1,499,458[14]	7,209,168[14]	20,718.9	56.3	43.7	73.9	9.2	16.4	2,320,125	855,706	China
20,491	86.8	13.2	8.3	30,415	286,103	122.7	57.9	42.1	90.1	9.7	0.2	259,259	95,962	Colombia
...	...	...	...	426	2,033	13.5	100.0	—	99.9	0.1	—	...	915	Comoros
47,189	92.9	7.1	0.6	54,904	4,169	194.0	2.1	97.9	100.0	—	—	...	33,820	Congo, Dem. Rep. of the
3,830	61.5	38.5	16.6	126,638	717	37.0	48.7	51.3	99.3	0.7	—	5,761	21,726	Congo, Rep. of the
4,806	69.9	30.1	25.0	20,409	148,114	20.8	80.2	19.8	70.3	28.4	0.8	104,864	23,985	Costa Rica
14,782	78.4	21.6	15.5	354,713	26,960	74.1	78.8	21.2	98.4	1.6	—	134,361	157,267	Côte d'Ivoire
2,670	33.7	66.3	47.7	248,365	176,564	21.4	77.8	22.0	90.3	3.5	6.2	50,256	25,199	Croatia
3,152	80.6	19.4	6.1	349	28,666	87.7	76.8	23.2	75.2	16.2	8.3	103,359	18,672	Cuba
54	31.4	68.6	46.0	1,662	122,883	3.1	97.2	2.8	77.4	0.2	22.4	2,319	30,243	Cyprus
12,906	6.6	93.4	45.3	731,059	410,900	21.8	—	100.0	100.0	—	—	24,478	69,636	Czech Republic
2,288	21.5	78.5	38.2	534,520	1,587,591	1,886.9	98.1	1.9	93.7	0.9	5.4	2,359,034	1,415,239	Denmark
—	—	—	—	992	1,190	0.3	100.0	—	100.0	—	—	100	1,130	Djibouti
...	...	...	...	41	3,077	0.9	99.7	0.3	99.8	0.2	—	...	1,470	Dominica
982	99.4	0.6	0.4	1,972	134,461	25.9	75.1	24.9	72.2	9.5	18.3	960	32,250	Dominican Republic
10,361	50.2	49.8	43.4	66,525	230,310	339.9	99.6	0.4	69.7	29.5	0.8	723,691	9,454	Ecuador
2,698	95.4	4.6	—	12,658	965,005	305.7	27.9	72.1	96.4	3.1	0.5	4,120	91,818	Egypt

Extractive industries (continued)

country	% of GDP, 1995	mineral production (value added) year	total ('000,000 U.S.$)	metals[a] (%)	non-metals[b] (%)	energy[c] (%)	trade (value) year	exports total ('000,000 U.S.$)	exports metals[a] (%)	exports non-metals[b] (%)	exports energy[c] (%)	imports total ('000,000 U.S.$)	imports metals[a] (%)	imports non-metals[b] (%)	imports energy[c] (%)
El Salvador	0.4	1994	40.3	100.0	—	—	1995	—	—	—	—	135.5[2]	1.8[2]	5.4[2]	92.8[2]
Equatorial Guinea	20.2[2]	1994	26.0	—	—	100.0	1990	—	—	—	—	2.1	—	100.0	—
Eritrea	0.1	1995	0.3	—	100.0	—	...	...	...	...	...	...	...	...	...
Estonia	1.6	1995	58.3	—	—	100.0	1995	135.7	59.2	17.7	23.0	11.0	—	100.0	—
Ethiopia	0.3[2]	1994	13.9	100.0	—	—	1993	—	—	—	—	72.3	—	1.3	98.7
Faroe Islands	0.1[2]	1994	0.9	...	...	...	1994	—	—	—	—	1.5	—	100.0	—
Fiji	0.2[2]	1994	1.7	...	...	...	1994	0.8	100.0	—	—	5.8	—	41.4	58.6
Finland	0.3	1995	424.1	18.1[2]	81.9[2]	—	1995	209.1	49.1	47.3	3.7	2,900.1	25.8	10.2	64.0
France	0.8	1995	11,521.0	3.0[6]	21.2[6]	75.8[6]	1995	2,604.6	52.9	33.1	13.9	17,183.1	11.5	6.6	81.9
French Guiana	...	1995	...	100.0	—	—	1995	—	—	—	—	—	—	—	—
French Polynesia	...	...	...	...	...	...	1995	169.8	—	100.0	—	...	...	...	...
Gabon	37.4	1995	1,214.1	8.1	—	91.9	1995	2,224.1	7.8	—	92.2	3.8[2]	—	100.0[2]	—
Gambia, The	—	1995	...	—	100.0	—	1994	—	—	—	—	7.4	—	—	100.0
Gaza Strip	...	...	...	...	...	...	...	...	...	...	...	...	...	...	...
Georgia	...	...	...	...	...	...	1995	29.2	100.0	—	—	29.5[3]	—	100.0[3]	...
Germany	...	1989[17]	11,803.2	0.6	20.0	79.4	1995	5,194.2	51.7	28.4	19.9	27,778.6	18.4	7.3	74.3
Ghana	1.7	1995	109.8	100.0	—	—	1995	335.8	12.2	87.8	—	4.9	100.0	—	—
Gibraltar	...	...	...	...	...	...	...	...	...	...	...	...	...	...	...
Greece	1.0	1995	922.1	13.6[4]	34.6[4]	51.8[4]	1995	306.6	47.3	35.0	17.7	1,637.3[2]	3.1[2]	3.6[2]	93.3[2]
Greenland	—	1995	...	...	...	...	1995	—	—	—	—	1.2	—	100.0	—
Grenada	0.5	1995	1.4	—	100.0	—	1991	—	—	—	—	1.6	—	11.2	88.8
Guadeloupe	...	1995	...	—	100.0	—	1995	0.9	100.0	—	—	58.0	—	—	100.0
Guam	...	1995	...	—	100.0	—	...	...	...	...	...	...	...	...	...
Guatemala	0.4	...	...	...	...	...	1995	39.0	—	15.8	84.2	149.5	—	—	100.0
Guernsey	...	...	...	...	...	...	...	...	...	...	...	...	...	...	...
Guinea	19.1[2]	1994	336.5[19]	100.0[19]	—	—	1995	416.7	78.7	21.3	—	—	—	—	—
Guinea-Bissau	—	1995	...	—	100.0	—	...	...	...	...	...	...	...	...	...
Guyana	19.4	1995	105.8	100.0	—	—	1995	78.1	99.2	0.8	—	...	...	...	...
Haiti	—	1994	0.2	—	100.0	—	1994	—	—	—	—	...	...	...	...
Honduras	1.8	1995	69.2	100.0	—	—	1995	2.3	100.0	—	—	9.0	—	37.1	62.9
Hong Kong	—	1995	34.7	—	100.0	—	1995	2,256.6	28.4	71.0	0.6	4,923.7	14.3	77.9	7.7
Hungary	0.9[3]	1993	335.0	4.8[20]	4.3[20]	90.9[20]	1995	250.6	90.3	2.6	7.1	232.2	33.3	25.2	41.5
Iceland	...	1995	26.7	—	100.0	—	1995	26.7	24.9	75.1	—	71.0	75.5	16.4	8.1
India	1.8	1995	6,065.9	7.6[21]	12.9[21]	79.5[21]	1995	6,397.4	14.1	85.9	0.1	6,805.9[2]	11.0[2]	29.9[2]	59.1[2]
Indonesia	8.4	1995	16,919.4[8]	...	...	...	1995	12,212.9	15.4	1.1	83.5	2,193.5	24.7	13.8	61.5
Iran	19.2[22]	1994–95	14,341.5	—	2.5	97.5	1995	18,525.9	1.0	0.4	98.6	1,271.4	17.5	7.5	75.0
Iraq	0.4[6]	1992	739.9	...	...	...	1995	451.0	—	—	100.0	...	...	...	...
Ireland	...	1989	512.1[23]	30.3	68.7	1.0[23]	1995	502.6	74.3	13.4	12.3	700.3	19.3	13.3	67.4
Isle of Man	...	1995	...	—	100.0	—	...	...	...	...	...	...	...	...	...
Israel	...	1990	352.6	...	...	...	1995	6,122.1	0.5	98.0	1.6	6,823.9	—	77.3	22.7
Italy	...	1989	2,554.5	3.4	25.2	71.4	1995	501.2	56.1	32.5	11.5	14,946.6	19.4	9.7	70.9
Jamaica	6.4	1995	271.4	99.2[12]	0.8[12]	—	1995	539.5	100.0	—	—	...	...	...	...
Japan	0.2[2]	1994	10,047.9	...	...	...	1995	875.1	41.2	57.9	0.9	61,982.7	15.2	8.5	76.3
Jersey	...	...	...	...	...	...	...	...	...	...	...	...	...	...	...
Jordan	3.5	1995	194.7	—	100.0	—	1995	343.4	5.2	94.8	—	416.2	0.5	8.8	90.7
Kazakstan	...	...	...	...	...	...	1995	263.4	9.7	—	90.3	...	...	...	...
Kenya	0.2	1995	14.1	100.0	—	—	1995	7.1	—	100.0	—	17.8[3]	11.9[3]	21.1[3]	67.0[3]
Kiribati	—	1995	—	...	...	...	1992	—	—	—	—	...	...	...	...
Korea, North	...	...	...	...	...	...	1995	57.0	22.6	46.0	31.4	1,004.0	5.0	4.8	90.2
Korea, South	0.3	1995	1,103.6	2.5[2]	72.1[2]	25.4[2]	1995	236.0	20.7	56.6	22.7	18,969.2	17.1	3.7	79.3
Kuwait	39.5	1995	10,513.4	—	—	100.0	1995	12,258.4	0.3	—	99.7	30.6	—	100.0	—
Kyrgyzstan	...	...	...	...	...	...	1995	...	...	...	...	...	...	...	...
Laos	0.2	1995	3.6	100.0	—	—	...	...	...	...	...	...	...	...	...
Latvia	0.2	1991	30.9	—	—	100.0	1995	11.4	61.0	—	39.0	109.4	—	6.2	93.8
Lebanon	—	1995	...	—	100.0	—	1995	75.5	34.0	66.0	—	53.0	—	100.0	—
Lesotho	0.1[2]	1994	0.8	—	100.0	—	[11]	...	...	...	...	...	...	...	...
Liberia	3.0[4]	1989	122.3[24]	100.0[24]	—	—	1995	244.6	—	100.0	—	...	...	...	...
Libya	25.4[6]	1992	7,212.2[8]	—	—	100.0[8]	1995	9,451.2	—	—	100.0	70.4	80.2	19.8	—
Liechtenstein	...	...	...	...	...	...	...	...	...	...	...	...	...	...	...
Lithuania	...	...	...	...	...	...	1995	221.9	85.8	—	14.2	194.9[2]	—	13.4[2]	86.6[2]
Luxembourg	0.3[12]	1991	29.2	—	100.0	—	[9]	...	...	...	...	...	...	...	...
Macau	...	1991	1.8	—	100.0	—	1995	...	...	...	...	16.9	—	25.6	74.4
Macedonia	...	...	...	...	...	...	1994	20.9	69.1	30.9	—	151.2[3]	5.0[3]	9.1[3]	85.9[3]
Madagascar	0.3[12]	1991	8.1	100.0	—	—	1995	28.4	44.8	55.2	—	...	...	...	...
Malawi	1.0[2]	1994	12.8	...	...	...	1991	—	—	—	—	6.6	—	100.0	—
Malaysia	7.3	1995	6,103.8	2.1[4]	2.4[4]	95.5[4]	1995	4,473.0	3.6	3.1	93.3	1,284.1	41.8	31.3	26.8
Maldives	1.7	1995	3.3	—	100.0	—	1991	—	—	—	—	—	—	—	—
Mali	3.1	1995	68.4	100.0	—	—	1995	19.4	—	100.0	—	—	—	—	—
Malta	...	1992	6.7	—	100.0	—	1995	3.5	97.9	2.1	—	17.7[3]	—	52.1[3]	47.9[3]
Marshall Islands	0.3	1995	0.3	—	100.0	—	...	...	...	...	...	...	...	...	...
Martinique	...	1995	...	—	100.0	—	1995	4.1	19.4	38.3	42.3	102.5	—	—	100.0
Mauritania	10.1[2]	1994	104.1	100.0	—	—	1995	280.2	100.0	—	—	...	...	...	...
Mauritius	0.1	1995	4.9	—	100.0	—	1995	27.5	—	100.0	—	46.6	—	71.5	28.5
Mayotte	...	...	...	...	...	...	...	...	...	...	...	...	...	...	...
Mexico	1.7[26]	1996	5,526.5	...	...	...	1995	8,519.5	7.5	3.3	89.2	1,005.5	34.0	32.5	33.5
Micronesia	—	—	—	—	—	—	1994	—	—	—	—	...	...	...	...
Moldova	...	1995	...	—	100.0	—	1995	18.6	100.0	—	—	162.7	2.7	2.2	95.1
Monaco	...	...	...	...	...	...	...	...	...	...	...	...	...	...	...
Mongolia	...	...	...	...	...	...	1995	132.8	100.0	—	—	...	...	...	...
Morocco	1.8	1995	574.2	...	...	...	1995	473.6	30.9	69.1	—	1,248.1	—	17.0	83.0
Mozambique	0.4	1995[1]	8.2[1]	100.0	—	—	1994	2.4	100.0	—	—	—	—	—	—
Myanmar (Burma)	0.5	1995	497.4	...	...	...	1995	65.1	0.2	99.8	—	—	—	—	—
Namibia	11.2	1995	302.4	100.0	—	—	[11]	...	...	...	...	...	...	...	...
Nauru	...	1995	...	—	100.0	—	1995	140.8	—	100.0	—	...	...	...	...
Nepal	0.5	1995	20.6	100.0	—	—	1995	—	—	—	—	4.6	100.0	—	—

forestry, 1995						fisheries, 1994								country
production of roundwood				trade (value, '000 U.S.$)		catch (nominal)						trade (value, '000 U.S.$)		
total ('000 cubic metres)	fuelwood, charcoal (%)	industrial roundwood (%)		exports	imports	total ('000 metric tons)	by source (%)		by kind of catch (%)			exports	imports	
		total	sawlogs, veneer				marine	inland	fish	crustaceans	mollusks			
6,804	97.9	2.1	1.3	5,470	70,410	13.1	64.0	36.0	58.3	35.4	6.3	31,314	5,841	El Salvador
811	55.1	44.9	44.9	35,876	998	3.7	89.2	10.8	84.3	11.4	3.8	...	1,970	Equatorial Guinea
...	...	...	...	...	...	3.0	100.0	—	100.0	—	—	...	...	Eritrea
3,730	15.4	84.6	38.4	191,694	51,680	124.1	98.3	1.7	99.2	0.8	—	101,212	13,539	Estonia
47,337	96.4	3.6	0.1	800	3,444	5.3	—	100.0	100.0	—	—	...	200	Ethiopia
...	...	...	...	221	4,162	249.9	100.0	—	94.8	3.7	1.5	311,816	13,464	Faroe Islands
598	6.2	93.8	42.6	37,385	20,930	32.0	90.2	9.8	83.5	1.8	13.7	38,606	18,147	Fiji
50,217	8.2	91.8	45.5	11,967,800	981,472	167.2	69.8	30.2	99.9	0.1	—	20,129	140,725	Finland
46,345	22.6	77.4	46.8	5,850,807	8,197,550	838.3	93.0	7.0	65.3	2.5	32.2	909,734	2,796,719	France
132	54.4	45.6	38.8	2,581	2,424	7.5	100.0	—	43.8	56.2	—	36,255	4,502	French Guiana
...	...	...	...	3	16,541	8.6	99.9	0.1	99.2	0.8	—	732	8,689	French Polynesia
4,882	59.2	40.8	40.8	387,948	2,251	24.4	89.7	10.3	97.0	2.7	0.3	1,780	8,382	Gabon
1,221	90.8	9.2	8.7	212	682	22.3	89.2	10.8	97.0	2.7	0.3	3,061	202	Gambia, The
...	...	...	...	...	...	...	...	...	...	...	...	...	...	Gaza Strip
...	...	...	...	308	303	35.0	92.2	7.8	99.9	—	0.1	...	830	Georgia
38,970	9.7	90.3	53.1	7,716,631	10,857,540	270.8	82.1	17.9	91.6	6.2	2.2	772,731	2,580,349	Germany
26,473	95.2	4.8	4.5	275,773	11,132	336.3	83.7	16.3	98.6	0.7	0.7	30,738	10,986	Ghana
...	...	...	...	268	827	—	100.0	—	100.0	—	—	...	...	Gibraltar
2,306	57.2	42.8	32.3	50,315	414,230	223.1	92.8	7.2	83.6	2.0	14.4	148,276	167,645	Greece
—	—	—	—	141	7,179	112.6	100.0	—	27.2	71.0	1.8	267,058	3,455	Greenland
...	...	...	...	—	6,244	1.6	100.0	—	95.7	1.8	0.1	135	2,310	Grenada
15	98.0	2.0	2.0	153	40,069	8.7	99.7	0.3	92.1	2.0	5.8	230	25,182	Guadeloupe
...	...	...	...	14	2,378	0.7	70.6	29.4	96.9	3.1	—	...	...	Guam
14,123	94.4	5.6	5.3	26,781	131,704	11.6	61.0	39.0	45.6	54.2	0.2	31,365	7,954	Guatemala
...	...	...	...	...	...	[18]	[18]	[18]	[18]	[18]	[18]	...	...	Guernsey
4,788	86.7	13.3	3.6	4,236	2,506	44.0	90.0	10.0	96.1	1.4	2.5	8,110	4,800	Guinea
579	72.9	27.1	6.9	3,991	186	5.3	95.2	4.8	79.6	20.2	0.2	740	400	Guinea-Bissau
508	7.8	92.2	88.0	38,823	1,283	46.4	98.3	1.7	83.9	16.1	—	16,129	...	Guyana
6,417	96.3	3.7	3.5	18	16,099	5.2	90.4	9.6	75.6	17.1	7.3	1,970	3,350	Haiti
6,459	90.9	9.1	8.8	21,005	81,151	23.2	98.6	1.4	25.8	49.9	24.3	87,421	4,590	Honduras
19[2]	100.0[2]	—	—	784,330[2]	2,804,335[2]	220.1	99.9	0.1	87.6	4.3	8.1	677,371	1,642,105	Hong Kong
4,415	46.0	54.0	29.5	161,228	400,627	24.0	—	100.0	100.0	—	—	8,892	40,985	Hungary
—	—			1,907	58,593	1,560.2	99.9	0.1	94.4	5.0	0.5	1,264,615	25,209	Iceland
299,163	91.7	8.3	6.1	34,516	357,944	4,540.2	65.4	34.6	89.3	8.6	2.1	1,125,440	6,618	India
185,895	81.4	18.6	16.9	4,727,553	847,879	3,954.2	75.1	24.9	87.2	9.5	2.3	1,583,416	120,674	Indonesia
7,463	34.3	65.7	5.2	994	224,399	314.3	63.4	36.6	97.3	2.2	0.5	52,885	21,780	Iran
161	68.9	31.1	12.4	159	439	22.0	18.2	81.8	100.0	—	—	...	...	Iraq
2,204	2.9	97.1	62.2	223,590	729,008	314.1	98.6	1.4	88.9	4.3	6.8	286,050	76,661	Ireland
...	...	...	...	...	...	3.6	100.0	—	26.6	2.2	71.2	...	...	Isle of Man
113	11.5	88.5	31.9	18,337	508,219	20.4	18.5	81.5	98.7	1.0	0.3	9,246	112,923	Israel
9,802	54.4	45.6	25.9	2,874,407	8,637,262	547.3	89.5	10.5	59.8	4.8	35.3	289,873	2,257,462	Italy
577	92.6	7.4	7.2	859	102,116	24.0	68.2	31.8	98.2	1.6	0.2	13,340	31,560	Jamaica
23,257	1.5	98.5	70.9	1,781,177	19,485,870	7,363.3	97.7	2.3	75.9	2.2	20.2	742,972	16,140,465	Japan
...	...	...	...	...	...	4.3[18]	100.0[18]	—[18]	11.0[18]	49.8[18]	39.2[18]	...	...	Jersey
11	63.6	36.4	—	8,258	177,093	0.1	2.3	97.7	100.0	—	—	810	19,772	Jordan
...	...	...	...	390	2,997	45.6	—	100.0	100.0	—	—	8,175	2,950	Kazakhstan
41,696	95.4	4.6	1.1	791	21,110	203.5	2.9	97.1	99.6	0.3	0.1	22,534	2,966	Kenya
...	...	...	...	...	769	29.0	100.0	—	85.3	0.7	14.0	1,329	338	Kiribati
4,923	87.8	12.2	12.2	6,406	46,597	1,800.0	93.7	6.3	96.2	0.7	3.1	62,390	1,430	Korea, North
6,485	69.3	30.7	16.4	1,210,245	4,972,032	2,700.0	98.9	1.1	63.9	5.2	28.6	1,411,052	718,451	Korea, South
...	...	...	...	1,846	78,115	7.8	100.0	—	73.0	27.0	—	3,011	15,270	Kuwait
...	...	...	...	18	66	0.3	—	100.0	100.0	—	—	...	425	Kyrgyzstan
5,508	81.9	18.1	15.9	70,427	1,108	35.0	—	100.0	100.0	—	—	...	170	Laos
6,907	17.6	82.4	42.0	277,228	105,647	138.7	99.2	0.8	95.3	0.2	4.5	54,288	12,058	Latvia
515	98.6	1.4	1.4	871	91,756	2.4	90.9	9.1	98.0	1.0	1.0	...	...	Lebanon
709	100.0	—	—	...	...	0.04	—	100.0	100.0	—	—	11	11	Lesotho
6,267	84.3	15.7	12.8	68,080	325	7.7	48.2	51.8	98.0	1.9	0.1	908	1,672	Liberia
651	82.3	17.7	9.7	177	45,083	8.5	98.9	1.1	99.5	0.5	—	31,260	13,680	Libya
...	...	...	...	...	...	...	...	...	...	...	...	25	25	Liechtenstein
5,499	18.3	81.7	38.9	170,809	62,960	51.0	94.0	6.0	91.9	1.7	6.4	18,157	22,571	Lithuania
[9]	[9]	[9]	[9]	[9]	[9]	...	...	...	...	...	...	[9]	[9]	Luxembourg
...	...	...	...	4,244	23,269	1.9	100.0	—	66.6	29.7	3.7	4,314	16,376	Macau
151	—	100.0	95.4	25,243	37,663	1.2	—	100.0	100.0	—	—	130	7,778	Macedonia
10,893	96.0	4.0	0.9	3,962	10,258	104.8	71.3	28.7	84.5	13.3	0.5	103,656	11,005	Madagascar
10,475	94.9	5.1	1.2	2,043	8,057	58.8	—	100.0	100.0	—	—	215	917	Malawi
45,573	21.5	78.5	75.0	4,225,865	987,386	1,173.5	97.9	2.1	76.8	9.6	12.7	324,857	304,258	Malaysia
...	...	...	...	28	4,220	104.1	100.0	—	99.8	—	0.1	36,503	...	Maldives
6,540	93.6	6.4	0.2	172	1,556	63.0	—	100.0	100.0	—	—	410	660	Mali
...	...	...	...	—	68,823	1.8	100.0	—	99.5	0.2	0.3	6,869	14,606	Malta
...	...	...	...	...	1,923	0.3	100.0	—	100.0	—	—	690	250	Marshall Islands
12	83.3	16.7	16.7	136	22,872	5.9	98.2	1.8	97.1	2.6	—	161	34,196	Martinique
14	57.1	42.9	7.1	137	711	85.0	94.1	5.9	54.7	0.6	44.7	154,528	800	Mauritania
12	50.0	50.0	33.3	291	50,145	19.0	99.5	0.5	97.6	0.5	1.9	30,391	29,329	Mauritius
...	...	...	...	...	...	0.5	100.0	—	100.0	—	—	...	...	Mayotte
22,474	73.0	27.0	21.0	230,102	1,366,614	1,260.0	86.1	13.9	85.7	7.7	6.5	480,872	158,627	Mexico
...	...	...	...	...	2,110	1.7	99.8	0.2	97.8	1.2	0.9	440	5,700	Micronesia
...	...	...	...	3,492	19,314	4.8	—	100.0	100.0	—	—	195	2,537	Moldova
...	...	...	...	...	...	0.003	100.0	—	100.0	—	—	...	...	Monaco
541	69.6	30.4	30.4	4,186	773	0.1	—	100.0	100.0	—	—	...	1,840	Mongolia
2,346	61.8	38.2	10.5	102,852	445,905	750.1	99.8	0.2	87.8	1.1	11.1	620,451	7,044	Morocco
18,390	94.2	5.8	0.4	2,968	4,033	30.0	84.3	15.7	59.0	40.2	0.8	74,040	11,682	Mozambique
23,281	87.8	12.2	6.2	307,303	11,366	824.5	72.8	27.2	99.2	0.8	—	102,710	...	Myanmar (Burma)
[27]	[27]	[27]	[27]	[27]	[27]	300.9	99.7	0.3	99.8	0.1	0.1	11	11	Namibia
...	...	...	...	50	205	0.5	100.0	—	100.0	—	—	...	...	Nauru
20,822	97.0	3.0	3.0	185	2,230	17.0	—	100.0	100.0	—	—	...	...	Nepal

Extractive industries   (continued)

country	mining % of GDP, 1995	mineral production (value added) year	total ('000,000 U.S.$)	by kind (%) metals[a]	non-metals[b]	energy[c]	trade (value) year	exports total ('000,000 U.S.$)	by kind (%) metals[a]	non-metals[b]	energy[c]	imports total ('000,000 U.S.$)	by kind (%) metals[a]	non-metals[b]	energy[c]
Netherlands, The	2.7	1995	9,620.1	—	5.5[6]	94.5[6]	1995	6,350.8	22.5	8.1	69.5	11,696.7	14.3	7.4	78.3
Netherlands Antilles	...	1994	...	—	100.0	—	1995	283.3	—	55.3	44.7	840.2	—	0.4	99.6
New Caledonia	10.4[4]	1990	262.4	100.0	—	—	1995	175.3	100.0	—	—	5.0	—	—	100.0
New Zealand	1.4[28]	1993–94	621.0	— 29.8 —		70.2	1995	264.5	15.3	6.1	78.6	782.9	18.8	15.4	65.8
Nicaragua	0.6	1995	11.3	82.2[12]	17.8[12]	—	1995	3.8	100.0	—	—	140.3	—	—	100.0
Niger	3.5[2]	1994	62.5	— 100.0 —		—	1995	233.3[2]	100.0[2]	—	—	5.0	—	100.0	—
Nigeria	16.8	1995	11,361.0	—	0.8	99.2	1995	11,131.5	—	—	100.0	19.9	1.5	98.5	—
Northern Mariana Islands	...	...	...	...	...	...	...	...	...	...	...	...	...	...	...
Norway	11.3	1995	16,446.5	0.4[12]	1.2[12]	98.4[12]	1995	18,502.9	0.8	1.2	97.9	1,779.3	73.8	11.7	14.5
Oman	38.5	1995	5,300.9	—	0.7[2]	99.3[2]	1995	4,611.9	—	0.1	99.9	80.0	82.0	18.0	—
Pakistan	0.5	1995	284.4	...	2.3	...	1995	45.3	—	2.3	97.7	794.2	13.8	4.3	82.0
Palau	...	...	...	...	...	...	...	...	...	...	...	...	...	...	...
Panama	0.1	1995	8.6	— 100.0 —		—	1994	7.3	100.0	—	—	1,390.1	0.5	4.4	95.1
Papua New Guinea	19.5[3]	1993	944.9	100.0	—	—	1995	1,123.1	48.0	—	52.0	66.7	2.8	15.5	81.6
Paraguay	0.3	1995	25.6	—	100.0	—	1994	...	...	...	...	...	...	...	...
Peru	9.6[3]	1991	1,098.1	— 52.9[30] —		47.1	1995	1,013.5	86.1	0.1	13.9	354.2	0.1	—	99.9
Philippines	0.9	1995	668.9	67.3[6]	29.1[6]	3.6[6]	1995	402.0	70.5	2.6	26.9	2,863.2	14.4	5.2	80.4
Poland	4.2	1995	4,964.0	17.9[4]	17.6[4]	64.5[4]	1995	1,519.7	6.2	12.8	81.0	2,636.2	14.8	7.1	78.0
Portugal	0.9[3]	1993	704.2	—	100.0	—	1995	450.1	72.3	27.7	—	2,294.3	1.4	6.4	92.2
Puerto Rico	0.1[21]	1992–93	31.0	—	100.0	—	...	...	...	...	...	...	...	...	...
Qatar	32.5	1995	2,445.1[8]	...	0.1	99.9	1995	3,000.3	—	0.1	99.9	51.3[2]	75.3[2]	24.7[2]	—
Réunion	...	1995	...	—	100.0	—	1995	0.9	100.0	—	—	15.0	—	—	100.0
Romania	...	1991	1,315.6	1.7	7.8	90.5	1994	44.0	64.9	35.1	—	1,723.1	9.7	3.7	86.6
Russia	...	...	...	...	...	...	1995	26,969.2	7.4	5.3	87.3	560.0	60.2	16.9	23.0
Rwanda	—	1995	0.3	...	...	...	...	...	...	...	...	...	...	...	...
St. Kitts and Nevis	0.3	1995	0.6	—	100.0	—	1991	—	—	—	—	—	—	—	—
St. Lucia	0.6	1995	3.1	—	100.0	—	1991	—	—	—	—	5.0	—	61.5	38.5
St. Vincent	0.3	1995	0.8	—	100.0	—	1993	—	—	—	—	1.7	—	19.3	80.7
Samoa	—	1995	—	...	...	...	...	...	...	...	...	...	...	...	...
San Marino	...	...	...	...	...	...	...	...	...	...	...	...	...	...	...
São Tomé and Príncipe	—	1995	—	—	100.0	—	...	...	...	...	...	...	...	...	...
Saudi Arabia	33.1[2]	1994	39,809.9	— 1.4 —		98.6	1995	32,557.4	0.4	0.4	99.2	96.4	79.9	20.1	—
Senegal	0.7[6]	1992	42.3	—	100.0	—	1995	51.5	—	100.0	—	21.8	—	100.0	—
Seychelles	...	1995	...	—	100.0	—	1994	—	—	—	—	0.7	—	100.0	—
Sierra Leone	16.8[22]	1994–95	117.7	— 100.0 —		—	1995	16.7	25.4	74.6	—	0.6	—	100.0	—
Singapore	—	1995	25.6	—	100.0	—	1995	669.7	42.8	35.0	22.2	7,248.2	1.6	8.8	89.5
Slovakia	...	...	...	...	...	...	1995	139.5	52.8	38.6	8.6	1,374.4[2]	10.9[2]	2.7[2]	86.4[2]
Slovenia	1.2	1995	195.1	0.7[12]	15.2[12]	84.1[12]	1995	0.2	—	—	100.0	381.8	30.5	17.1	52.4
Solomon Islands	0.1	1995	...	— 100.0 —		—	1994	...	...	...	...	...	...	...	...
Somalia	0.2[12]	1991	1.0	—	100.0	—	...	...	...	...	...	...	...	...	...
South Africa	7.7	1995	9,182.3	...	...	...	1995[11]	5,537.0	24.2	46.5	29.3	3,274.7	5.7	12.5	81.8
Spain	...	1990	3,786.9	8.6	32.3	59.1	1995	647.5	39.9	54.5	5.6	10,444.7	19.8	4.5	75.7
Sri Lanka	1.2	1995	157.3[33]	— 100.0[33] —			1995	176.3	5.2	94.8	—	271.1	—	40.0	60.0
Sudan, The	0.8[26]	1996	95.4	...	...	...	...	...	...	...	...	...	...	...	...
Suriname	13.4	1994	63.9[34]	...	...	...	1995	449.5	100.0	—	—	14.5[6]	—	45.9[6]	54.1[6]
Swaziland	1.0[35]	1995–96	10.6	...	...	...	1995[11]	...	...	...	...	...	...	...	...
Sweden	0.3	1995	634.3	55.2[6]	44.8[6]	—	1995	1,046.2	80.2	15.6	4.2	2,836.6	14.9	8.5	76.6
Switzerland	...	1995	...	—	100.0	—	1995	2,297.2	12.0	87.5	0.4	3,264.2	2.0	65.4	32.5
Syria	6.6[2]	1994	2,594.1[10]	— 100.0[10] —			1995	2,675.5	—	1.4	98.6	44.9[2]	30.9[2]	16.3[2]	52.9[2]
Taiwan	0.3	1995	791.6	—	79.6	20.4	1995	843.7	...	...	...	8,035.8	— 35.8 —		64.2
Tajikistan	...	...	...	...	...	...	1995	1.9	100.0	—	—	...	...	...	...
Tanzania	1.1[12]	1991	22.0	...	...	...	1995	—	—	—	—	3.4	—	100.0	—
Thailand	1.3	1995	2,231.6	1.3[12]	36.2[12]	62.5[12]	1995	1,553.6	3.5	86.7	9.9	4,536.3	7.0	27.9	65.1
Togo	5.9	1995	73.3	—	100.0	—	1995	62.4	—	100.0	—	0.9	—	40.3	59.7
Tonga	0.3	1995	0.4	—	100.0	—	1994	0.1	—	100.0	—	...	...	...	...
Trinidad and Tobago	26.8	1995	1,300.8[8]	— 100.0[8] —			1995	452.3	—	—	100.0	75.8	86.4	13.6	—
Tunisia	4.1	1995	704.5	...	...	...	1995	457.9	7.7	9.8	82.5	466.7	0.2	31.3	68.5
Turkey	1.3	1995	1,882.4	10.6[4]	19.9[4]	69.5[4]	1995	453.1	42.7	54.9	2.3	5,548.5	22.0	2.1	75.9
Turkmenistan	...	1995	...	— 100.0[8] —			1995	26.1	—	2.0	98.0	...	...	...	...
Tuvalu	0.9	1995	0.1	—	100.0	—	...	...	...	...	...	...	...	...	...
Uganda	0.3[35]	1995–96	15.8	— 100.0 —		—	1994	...	...	...	...	...	...	...	...
Ukraine	...	...	...	...	...	...	1995	1,311.8	70.7	9.2	20.1	473.5	27.3	17.8	55.0
United Arab Emirates	33.4[2]	1994	12,269.1	—	0.5[3]	99.5[3]	1995	13,815.3	0.8	0.5	98.6	214.3	38.2	61.8	—
United Kingdom	2.4	1995	23,006.6	—	30.6	62.6	1995	17,479.3	6.8	30.6	62.6	13,736.7	17.1	37.1	45.8
United States	1.4[3]	1993	89,400.0	6.2[12]	7.7[12]	86.1[12]	1995	13,962.7	40.1	29.0	31.0	63,642.5	6.8	12.8	80.4
Uruguay	0.2	1995	30.8	—	100.0	—	1995	...	...	...	...	195.8	—	4.1	95.9
Uzbekistan	...	...	...	...	...	...	1995	4.0	—	100.0	—	—	—	—	—
Vanuatu	...	1995	...	—	100.0	—	1993	...	...	...	...	0.6	—	—	100.0
Venezuela	14.5	1995	9,156.9	3.0[6]	1.5[6]	95.5[6]	1995	8,842.6	1.5	0.2	98.3	123.7	39.7	60.3	—
Vietnam	...	1989	1,062.9	...	...	...	1995	823.1	0.1	—	99.9	10.8	—	100.0	—
Virgin Islands (U.S.)	...	1995	...	—	100.0	—	...	...	...	...	...	...	...	...	...
West Bank	...	...	...	...	...	...	...	...	...	...	...	...	...	...	...
Western Sahara	...	...	...	...	...	...	...	...	...	...	...	...	...	...	...
Yemen	9.8[2]	1994	1,788.2[10]	— 100.0[10] —			1995	1,502.8	—	—	100.0	208.4	—	—	100.0
Yugoslavia	9.5[2]	1994	981.7	12.0	3.1	84.9	1995	3.7	100.0	—	—	335.9	—	19.0	81.0
Zambia	9.0	1995	371.5	...	...	...	1995	12.9	—	100.0	—	1.7	100.0	—	—
Zimbabwe	6.9[2]	1994	336.1	...	...	...	1995	124.0	18.9	79.7	1.4	37.2	63.0	37.0	—

[1]Gross value of production (output). [2]1994. [3]1993. [4]1990. [5]1988–89. [6]1992. [7]Mostly natural gas. [8]Mostly crude petroleum and natural gas. [9]Belgium includes Luxembourg. [10]Mostly crude petroleum. [11]South Africa includes Botswana, Lesotho, Namibia, and Swaziland. [12]1991. [13]Mostly diamonds, some gold. [14]China includes Taiwan. [15]Petroleum sector only. [16]Republic of Cyprus only. [17]Data refer to former West Germany only. [18]Jersey includes Guernsey. [19]Mostly bauxite and diamonds. [20]1989. [21]1992–93. [22]1994–95. [23]Excludes crude petroleum and natural gas.

forestry, 1995						fisheries, 1994								country
production of roundwood				trade (value, '000 U.S.$)		catch (nominal)						trade (value '000 U.S.$)		
total ('000 cubic metres)	fuelwood, charcoal (%)	industrial roundwood (%)		exports	imports	total ('000 metric tons)	by source (%)		by kind of catch (%)			exports	imports	
		total	sawlogs, veneer				marine	inland	fish	crusta-ceans	mollusks			
1,103	15.3	84.7	46.9	3,017,387	5,163,185	526.1	99.7	0.3	70.5	1.9	27.6	1,614,368	1,430,696	Netherlands, The
...	...	...	...	256	21,052	1.1	100.0	—	100.0	—	—	148	7,672	Netherlands Antilles
5	—	100.0	58.3	47	10,925	3.9	100.0	—	58.1	18.7	2.5	8,179	6,275	New Caledonia
17,155	0.3	99.7	64.9	1,634,147	317,853	493.2	99.7	0.3	77.5	0.9	21.4	691,733	40,315	New Zealand
3,809	96.1	3.9	3.9	15,321	6,566	12.3	93.3	6.7	32.6	67.4	—	53,081	1,319	Nicaragua
5,866	93.8	6.2	—	258	696	2.2	—	100.0	100.0	—	—	740	1,830	Niger
111,049	92.6	7.4	5.4	12,134	50,961	282.1	58.3	41.7	95.5	4.5	—	26,420	159,378	Nigeria
...	...	...	...		51	0.1	100.0	—	99.3	0.7	—	20	...	Northern Mariana Islands
9,035	5.2	94.8	50.5	2,179,431	1,158,851	2,551.5	100.0	—	98.1	1.6	0.3	2,718,132	322,087	Norway
...	...	...	...	1,309	53,484	118.6	100.0	—	96.9	0.9	2.2	49,467	4,646	Oman
29,665	94.8	5.2	3.7	1,000	154,902	551.9	75.8	24.2	93.3	5.5	1.2	153,265	152	Pakistan
...	...	...	...	990	1,123	1.5	100.0	—	98.6	1.1	0.1	...	195	Palau
1,070	89.0	11.0	5.4	17,696	76,273	165.4	99.7	0.3	88.5	10.6	0.9	106,293[29]	11,161[29]	Panama
8,772	63.1	36.9	34.9	536,220	5,501	27.0	48.1	51.9	91.6	6.2	—	11,131	44,150	Papua New Guinea
10,401	62.7	37.3	32.8	98,071	27,536	13.9	—	100.0	100.0	—	—	519	2,505	Paraguay
12,580	84.9	15.1	15.0	23,430	140,552	11,587.3	99.6	0.4	98.1	0.1	1.8	979,502	2,201	Peru
39,857	91.7	8.3	1.2	91,323	983,218	2,276.2	74.2	25.8	82.5	6.9	10.5	533,087	108,193	Philippines
19,334	14.0	86.0	46.8	690,120	745,372	460.2	88.7	11.3	97.7	1.7	0.6	117,992	154,180	Poland
9,448	6.3	93.7	44.3	1,732,571	1,145,268	253.9	99.1	0.9	91.3	0.6	8.1	203,123	669,888	Portugal
...	...	...	...	...	...	2.2	85.9	14.1	77.8	15.9	6.3	[31]	[31]	Puerto Rico
...	...	...	...	192	10,333	5.1	100.0	—	98.3	1.0	0.7	35	3,980	Qatar
36	85.9	14.1	11.6	846	69,029	4.5	99.9	0.1	89.8	10.1	—	13,477	38,478	Réunion
12,856	22.1	77.9	33.2	276,616	127,614	42.7	27.3	72.7	100.0	—	—	1,847	21,848	Romania
109,552	26.3	73.7	44.8	3,230,725	150,569	3,780.5	92.2	7.8	96.6	1.3	2.0	1,191,192	61,225	Russia
5,660	95.3	4.7	1.1	239	1,003	3.5	—	100.0	100.0	—	—	...	270	Rwanda
...	...	...	...	33	1,797	0.2	100.0	—	90.1	—	9.9	180[32]	1,260[32]	St. Kitts and Nevis
...	...	...	...	—	11,692	0.9	100.0	—	98.3	1.7	—	5	3,290	St. Lucia
...	...	...	...	14	6,578	1.7	100.0	—	93.7	—	6.3	654	680	St. Vincent
131	53.4	46.6	44.3	158	1,724	1.5	100.0	—	98.0	0.5	1.5	35	3,960	Samoa
...	...	...	...	...	...	—	—	100.0	100.0	—	—	...	...	San Marino
9	—	100.0	100.0	189	144	3.0	100.0	—	99.2	0.1	0.7	...	240	São Tomé and Príncipe
...	...	...	...	21,400	880,421	58.0	94.2	5.8	89.9	9.5	0.6	2,485	52,135	Saudi Arabia
5,219	86.2	13.8	0.8	94	20,464	388.0	92.8	7.2	94.7	1.0	4.3	113,292	11,970	Senegal
...	...	...	...	99	1,416	5.4	100.0	—	95.4	3.3	1.3	21,694	7,954	Seychelles
3,328	96.3	3.7	0.1	400	895	63.9	76.5	23.5	96.4	2.0	1.6	14,000	3,420	Sierra Leone
120	100.0	—	—	746,738	1,234,403	13.7	99.8	0.2	68.4	11.6	20.0	563,502	619,595	Singapore
5,323	8.2	91.8	39.6	364,343	149,467	3.5	—	100.0	100.0	—	—	2,049	33,222	Slovakia
1,944	12.1	87.9	53.8	351,567	346,489	3.1	67.8	32.2	100.0	—	—	6,227	23,321	Slovenia
872	15.8	84.2	84.2	115,219	833	49.2	100.0	—	98.7	—	0.2	28,189	200	Solomon Islands
8,794	98.8	1.2	0.3	29	172	16.3	98.2	1.8	93.8	2.5	3.7	5,680	80	Somalia
25,332[27]	28.2[27]	71.8[27]	21.4[27]	991,506[27]	564,285[27]	521.1	99.6	0.4	97.7	0.4	1.9	255,996[11]	134,565[11]	South Africa
15,121	17.9	82.1	36.8	1,617,660	3,826,287	1,380.0	97.6	2.4	77.7	2.5	19.8	1,021,015	2,638,697	Spain
9,625	92.7	7.3	0.6	6,182	101,826	224.0	94.6	5.4	96.3	3.6	0.1	31,896	32,074	Sri Lanka
25,410	90.7	9.3	—	488	7,150	44.2	9.0	91.0	100.0	—	—	190	2,560	Sudan, The
122	15.6	84.4	81.1	2,893	2,406	14.5	99.0	1.0	98.4	1.6	—	3,470	500	Suriname
1,424	39.3	60.7	18.3	59,665	—	0.1	—	100.0	100.0	—	—	11	11	Swaziland
59,924	6.4	93.6	52.6	10,849,980	1,588,361	394.2	98.7	1.3	98.6	0.9	0.5	160,941	448,661	Sweden
4,748	17.5	82.5	69.6	1,912,101	2,856,728	2.7	—	100.0	100.0	—	—	5,536[25]	390,403[25]	Switzerland
55	36.8	63.2	29.3	182	97,049	7.3	21.2	78.8	98.9	1.1	—	105	1,452	Syria
48	25.3	74.7	...	...	...	1,286.8	80.3	19.7	...	...	...	...	...	Taiwan
...	...	...	...	24	101	3.8	—	100.0	100.0	—	—	...	150	Tajikistan
36,747	94.1	5.9	0.9	5,870	3,520	342.9	12.5	87.5	98.8	0.6	0.1	19,118	230	Tanzania
39,288	92.9	7.1	0.1	552,939	2,458,975	3,432.0	91.5	8.5	78.0	13.0	8.5	4,190,036	815,616	Thailand
2,401	90.0	10.0	1.5	390	4,158	13.2	91.3	8.7	99.9	—	0.1	600	13,550	Togo
5	—	100.0	100.0		1,953	2.5	100.0	—	96.8	3.2	—	2,987	542	Tonga
68	32.5	67.5	63.6	1,891	56,529	11.0	100.0	—	87.7	12.3	—	8,813	5,124	Trinidad and Tobago
3,562	94.2	5.8	0.6	17,824	239,453	86.6	97.7	0.3	87.2	3.2	9.6	80,048	7,619	Tunisia
19,279	44.3	55.7	28.4	103,735	891,085	604.1	91.3	8.7	91.2	0.7	7.8	70,705	38,149	Turkey
...	...	...	...	92	784	38.0	—	100.0	100.0	—	—	300	305	Turkmenistan
...	...	...	...	—	323	0.6	100.0	—	100.0	—	—	389	...	Tuvalu
17,226	86.7	13.3	0.9	33	3,317	213.1	—	100.0	100.0	—	—	12,263	...	Uganda
...	...	...	...	15,622	22,660	310.7	81.4	18.6	92.6	2.8	4.6	114,850	16,360	Ukraine
...	...	...	...	14,849	273,975	108.0	100.0	—	99.9	0.1	—	16,774	24,279	United Arab Emirates
8,299	3.1	96.9	48.1	1,713,905	8,083,620	953.9	98.1	1.9	88.6	4.9	6.5	1,180,158	1,880,350	United Kingdom
503,413	18.8	81.2	46.9	18,715,270	22,516,470	5,940.7	94.9	5.1	78.0	6.7	14.8	3,229,585[31]	7,043,431[31]	United States
4,093	74.5	25.5	19.2	41,799	60,480	120.7	99.2	0.8	97.3	0.7	2.0	82,445	6,815	Uruguay
...	...	...	...	166	654	17.7	—	100.0	100.0	—	—	500	...	Uzbekistan
63	38.0	62.0	62.0	1,785	368	2.8	100.0	—	63.8	13.6	21.2	60	1,150	Vanuatu
2,267	39.7	60.3	55.8	69,923	415,279	424.0	94.4	5.6	86.0	4.9	9.1	99,067	14,916	Venezuela
34,913	87.3	12.7	6.9	62,087	95,403	1,150.0	75.0	25.0	66.8	27.8	5.4	452,380	...	Vietnam
...	...	...	...	...	...	0.9	100.0	—	87.2	8.7	4.1	...	...	Virgin Islands (U.S.)
...	...	...	...	...	...	...	...	...	...	...	...	...	...	West Bank
...	...	...	...	...	...	...	—	—	—	—	—	...	...	Western Sahara
324	100.0	—	—	245	48,698	82.8	98.9	1.1	98.2	1.3	0.4	102,550	5,958	Yemen
1,320	3.8	96.2	82.6	20,892	8,843	6.8	3.9	96.1	99.6	0.1	0.3	...	...	Yugoslavia
14,613	92.1	7.9	4.1	2,198	4,483	70.1	—	100.0	100.0	—	—	66	1,561	Zambia
8,102	77.4	22.6	6.5	28,407	27,545	20.3	—	100.0	100.0	—	—	270	7,665	Zimbabwe

[24]Mostly iron ore.   [25]Switzerland includes Liechtenstein.   [26]1996.   [27]South Africa includes Namibia.   [28]1993–94.   [29]Excludes the Free Zone of Colón and the Canal Zone.   [30]Includes coal mining.   [31]United States includes Puerto Rico.   [32]Includes Anguilla.   [33]Mostly precious and semiprecious stones.   [34]Mostly bauxite.   [35]1995–96.

Manufacturing industries

This table provides a summary of manufacturing activity by industrial sector for the countries of the world, providing figures for total manufacturing value added, as well as the percentage contribution of 29 major branches of manufacturing activity to the gross domestic product. U.S. dollar figures for total value added by manufacturing are given but should be used with caution because of uncertainties with respect to national accounting methods; purchasing power parities; preferential price structures and exchange rates; labour costs; and costs for material inputs influenced by "most favored" international trade agreements, barter, and the like.

Manufacturing activity is classified here according to a modification of the International Standard Industrial Classification (ISIC), revision 2, published by the United Nations. A summary of the 2-, 3-, and 4-digit ISIC codes (groups) defining these 29 sectors follows, providing definitional detail beyond that possible in the column headings.

The collection and publication of national manufacturing data is usually carried out by one of three methods: a full census of manufacturing (usually done every 5 to 10 years for a given country), a periodic survey of manufacturing (usually taken at annual or other regular intervals between censuses), and the onetime sample survey (often limited in geographic, sectoral, or size-of-enterprise coverage). The full census is, naturally, the most complete, but, since up to 10 years may elapse between such censuses, it has sometimes been necessary to substitute a survey of more recent date but less complete coverage. In addition to national sources, data published by the United Nations Industrial Development Organization (UNIDO), especially its *International Yearbook of Industrial Statistics* and *Industrial Development Global Report;* occasional publications of the International Monetary Fund (IMF); and other sources have been used.

ISIC code(s)	Products manufactured
31	Food, beverages, and tobacco
311 + 312	food including prepared animal feeds
313	alcoholic and nonalcoholic beverages
314	tobacco manufactures
32	Textiles, wearing apparel, and leather goods
321	spinning of textile fibres, weaving and finishing of textiles, knitted articles, carpets, rope, etc.
322	wearing apparel (including leather clothing; excluding knitted articles and footwear)
323 + 324	leather products (including footwear; excluding wearing apparel), leather substitutes, and fur products

Manufacturing industries

country	year	total manufac- turing value added ('000,000 U.S.$)	(31) food	bever- ages	tobacco manufac- tures	(32) textiles (exc. wearing apparel)	wearing apparel	leather and fur products	(33) wood products (exc. furniture)	wood furniture	(34) paper, paper products	printing and pub- lishing	(35) industrial chemi- cals	paints, soaps, etc.	drugs and medicines
			(311 + 312)	(313)	(314)	(321)	(322)	(323 + 324)	(331)	(332)	(341)	(342)	(351)	(352 exc. 3522)	(3522)
Afghanistan	1988–89[1]	435	18.3	1.9	—	8.0	0.4	16.7	—0.5—		0.9	4.9	4.8	0.2	2.7
Albania	1993[2]	224	42.5	0.9	3.7	4.6	2.0	2.3	2.1	1.3	0.2	1.3	1.7	0.9	—
Algeria	1994	4,084	16.8	3.5	4.5	3.2	2.7	1.0	1.9	0.9	2.3	0.3	0.3	—2.2—	
American Samoa	1993[3, 4]	326	99.5[5]	...	...	...	...	...	...	...	...	...	...	...	...
Andorra	1992[6]	38	2.3	9.0	0.1	0.3	30.2	0.9	—0.6—		—0.3—		1.0	1.8	0.1
Angola	1989	319	20.0	—12.2—		—11.6—			—3.7—		—0.3—		9.1[7]	[7]	[7]
Antigua and Barbuda	1995	8.4	...	...	...	...	...	...	...	...	...	...	...	...	...
Argentina	1993[9]	29,622	16.0	6.0	6.2	4.4	2.4	2.4	1.2	1.2[10]	2.0	5.1	2.2	3.6	3.8
Armenia	1994	368	4.1	15.7	2.2	12.4	18.6	...	1.6	1.9	0.3	0.3	5.4	—0.8—	
Aruba	...	...	...	...	...	...	...	...	...	...	...	...	...	...	...
Australia	1992–93	47,563	15.7	3.8	0.7	2.9	2.2	0.7	3.1	1.9	2.8	9.7	3.4	2.8	2.1
Austria	1994[9]	33,371	7.7	3.6	4.7	3.7	1.2	0.7	2.4	4.2	4.0	3.7	3.7	1.7	2.0
Azerbaijan	1994[2]	512	21.4	1.6	1.3	14.7	—	0.8	0.3	0.2		0.2	5.4	0.4	0.1
Bahamas, The	1992[3]	95	7.4	38.9	—	0.3	3.6	—	—	3.5	...	10.0	...	22.0	...
Bahrain	1992[2]	1,730	6.8	1.2	—	—	4.8	0.2	0.1	5.0	0.5	3.0	4.4	0.2	0.1
Bangladesh	1991–92[9, 11]	1,899	12.7	0.6	12.2	23.5	10.2	3.9	0.7	0.1	2.9	1.2	5.6	4.5	5.8
Barbados	1993[9]	95[12]	26.8[12]	—19.6—		0.6[13]	2.6	[13]	—0.6—		—11.0—		14.4[14]	—3.0—	
Belarus	1994[2, 3, 15]	3,006	16.2			7.0	2.1	2.6	—5.4[16]—			[16]	16.3[17]	[7]	[7]
Belgium	1994	44,163	14.9	1.6	0.8	4.7	2.4	0.5	1.0	3.7	2.1	4.5	10.8	—3.4—	
Belize	1992[9]	59	45.9	7.5	3.9	—3.8—			5.5	2.7	1.1	1.5	—14.1—		
Benin	1990	59	20.6	13.1	—	3.2	5.5	6.9	3.6	5.2		2.5	—9.5—		
Bermuda	1990	173	...	...	...	...	...	...	...	...	...	...	...	...	...
Bhutan	1989[9]	21	6.0	10.1	—	—5.6—			18.1	2.7	0.4	1.0	21.5	—1.7—	
Bolivia	1994[9, 19]	880	20.4	10.9	2.8	3.0	0.5	1.3	2.1	0.2	0.5	1.8	0.3	0.8	1.8
Bosnia and Herzegovina	1991	4,021	9.1	2.6	1.7	5.9	4.5	3.3	6.3	4.2	3.9	1.4	5.5	—4.1—	
Botswana	1994	186	32.8	12.9	—	11.2	2.2	2.7	1.6	1.6	2.7	2.7	1.1	—1.6—	
Brazil	1994	154,425	12.6	1.5	1.3	4.6	2.9	2.3	0.7	0.7	3.4	2.2	7.1	—10.1—	
Brunei	1991	305	...	...	...	...	...	...	...	...	...	...	...	...	...
Bulgaria	1994	5,889	6.6	2.3	2.1	4.1	2.4	2.2	1.1	0.9	0.8	1.3	34.1[20]	—3.8—	
Burkina Faso	1994	131	48.5	16.1	0.8	14.6	1.5	4.6	—	1.5		0.8	0.8	...	...
Burundi	1994	94	55.8	21.0	5.2	8.4	1.1	—	1.1	1.1	—	1.1	—1.1—		
Cambodia	1994	128	...	...	...	...	...	...	...	...	...	...	...	...	...
Cameroon	1994	470	11.5	18.9	1.1	7.6	0.2	0.2	16.4	0.6	1.5	0.6	1.9	—1.5—	
Canada	1993[9]	103,690	11.9	3.2	0.9	2.7	2.1	0.4	5.9	1.7	5.9	6.4	3.7	3.4	2.5
Cape Verde	1990	14	33.1	0.6	26.8	...	8.0	2.0	...	...	...	9.2	...	...	...
Central African Republic	1990	27	29.8	13.9	25.4	−25.0	−3.7	−0.5	25.6	1.9	—	5.9	4.1	—8.9—	
Chad	1994[3]	98	...	...	...	18.8[21]			...	...	...	...	...	...	...
Chile	1993[9, 22]	11,841	19.6	5.1	3.7	3.2	2.4	1.8	3.5	0.7	5.7	3.2	3.5	4.9	3.0
China	1995	146,612	5.8	2.9	5.0	7.3	2.8	1.6	1.5	0.5	1.9	1.0	—9.4—		2.2
Colombia	1994	10,846	19.1	10.8	0.5	7.0	3.6	1.9	0.7	0.4	3.8	3.1	6.4	—9.0—	
Comoros	1995	9.9	...	...	—	...	...	...	...	...	...	...	...	...	...
Congo, Dem. Rep. of the	1990	808	86.7	5.4	1.9	0.6	0.2	0.6	0.1	0.2	—	0.1	0.9	—0.1—	
Congo, Rep. of the	1994	75	27.4	26.0	6.8	1.4	1.4	1.4	4.1	2.7	1.4	1.4	4.1	—4.1—	
Costa Rica	1994[9]	1,285	29.5	14.4	2.0	2.3	3.7	1.1	1.9	1.3	3.2	3.8	3.5	4.4	4.4
Côte d'Ivoire	1994	1,022	28.3	4.1	0.4	10.2	0.7	0.8	7.2	—	0.3	1.2	2.5	—3.8—	
Croatia	1994	5,227	11.1	3.7	3.6	5.5	5.0	2.2	3.6	2.7	2.2	3.2	3.4	—6.9—	
Cuba	1994	5,560[23]	15.7	5.4	39.8	3.5	1.8	1.4	1.0	0.8	0.2	1.2	1.9	—7.9—	
Cyprus[24]	1994	899	15.1	9.3	7.0	3.5	10.0	3.6	5.4	4.7	2.3	4.9	0.6	3.7	1.4
Czech Republic	1995[25]	9,896	—13.9—			—6.2—		1.5	—1.6—		—5.3—		—6.8—		
Denmark	1994	26,633	18.6	3.6	1.0	2.4	1.0	0.4	2.0	2.7	2.7	6.6	5.3	—7.1—	
Djibouti	1995	23	...	...	—	...	...	...	...	...	...	...	...	...	...
Dominica	1995	13	...	...	...	...	...	...	...	...	...	...	...	—3.4—	
Dominican Republic	1990	1,298	31.9	13.8	5.2	3.5	1.2	3.0	0.2	1.5	2.9	1.7	1.6	—3.4—	
Ecuador	1994[9, 11]	3,095	11.8	2.8	0.2	3.3	0.4	0.4	0.8	0.4	0.9	1.7	1.3	0.7	29.1
Egypt	1992–93[28, 29]	5,486	10.7	1.5	2.0	9.7	1.0	1.5	0.4	0.3	2.4	1.5	4.4	1.5	2.4
El Salvador	1994	521	15.9	4.0	5.0	8.6	5.4	1.9	...	1.1	4.2	5.2	2.9	—17.5—	
Equatorial Guinea	1990[2]	1.9	27.6	4.1	...	...	2.6	...	...	49.3	...	1.2	...	—13.8—	
Eritrea	1993[2]	58	16.7	22.7	1.3	—5.7—		9.8	...	...	—6.1—		...	—17.7—	
Estonia	1994[2, 3]	1,254	35.0[30]	6.7	[30]	5.6	3.9	1.7	5.7	5.4	0.8	3.0	9.2[31]	[31]	[31]
Ethiopia[32]	1992	529	18.3	24.6	8.5	10.8	1.5	4.7	0.9	0.7	0.7	1.9	0.2	—2.3—	

ISIC code(s)		Products manufactured
33		Wood and wood products
	331	sawlogs, wood products (excluding furniture), cane products, and cork products
	332	wood furniture
34		Paper and paper products, printing and publishing
	341	wood pulp, paper, and paper products
	342	printing, publishing, and bookbinding
35		Chemicals and chemical, petroleum, coal, rubber, and plastic products
	351	basic industrial chemicals (including fertilizers, pesticides, and synthetic fibres)
	352 minus 3522	chemical products not elsewhere specified (including paints, varnishes, and soaps and other toiletries)
	3522	drugs and medicines
	353 + 354	refined petroleum and derivatives of petroleum and coal
	355	rubber products
	356	plastic products (excluding synthetic fibres)
36		Glass, ceramic, and nonmetallic mineral products
	361 + 362	pottery, china, glass, and glass products
	369	bricks, tiles, cement, cement products, plaster products, etc.

ISIC code(s)		Products manufactured
37		Basic metals
	371	iron and steel
	372	nonferrous basic metals and processed nickel and cobalt
38		Fabricated metal products, machinery and equipment
	381	fabricated metal products (including cutlery, hand tools, fixtures, and structural metal products)
	382 minus 3825	nonelectrical machinery and apparatus not elsewhere specified
	3825	office, computing, and accounting machinery
	383 minus 3832	electrical machinery and apparatus not elsewhere specified
	3832	radio, television, and communications equipment (including electronic parts)
	384 minus 3843	transport equipment not elsewhere specified
	3843	motor vehicles (excluding motorcycles)
	385	professional and scientific equipment; photographic and optical goods; watches and clocks
39		Other manufactured goods
	390	jewelry, musical instruments, sporting goods, artists' equipment, toys, etc.

			(36)				(37)		(38)									(39)	country
refined petroleum and products	rubber products	plastic products	pottery, china, and glass	bricks, tiles, cement, etc.		iron and steel	non-ferrous metals	fabricated metal products	nonelec-trical mach-inery	office equip., com-puters	electrical equip.	radio, tele-vision	transport equip. exc. motor vehicles	motor vehicles	profes-sional equip.		jewelry, musical instru-ments	
(353 + 354)	(355)	(356)	(361 + 362)	(369)		(371)	(372)	(381)	(382 exc. 3825)	(3825)	(383 exc. 3832)	(3832)	(384 exc. 3843)	(3843)	(385)		(390)	
—	—	2.1	1.1			0.4	—	—	—	—	—	—	—	0.1	—		37.1	Afghanistan
21.6	—	1.2	0.1	7.9		2.5	—	1.2	0.7	—	0.5	0.7	—	—	0.1		—	Albania
3.7	0.4	0.8	1.2	8.8		14.5	0.8	12.0	2.0		5.6		8.2		1.3		1.2	Algeria
...	...	...	...	...		...	...	...	...		...		...		...		...	American Samoa
—	0.3	0.4	0.6	0.3		1.7	0.2	0.5	3.8		4.3		21.1		9.1		2.9	Andorra
20.0	7	7	11.3			1.9		5.0					4.7		8		0.3[8]	Angola
...	...	...	...	...		...	...	...	...		...		...		...		...	Antigua and Barbuda
9.1	0.9	3.0	1.2	2.4		2.4	0.8	4.6	5.6	0.2	2.2	1.4	0.6	7.6	0.7		0.8	Argentina
0.5	0.3	1.1	0.5	2.2		0.3	3.2	0.5	3.2		10.5		0.3		3.2		10.8	Armenia
...	...	...	...	...		...	...	...	...		...		...		...		...	Aruba
2.5	0.9	3.5	2.0	3.3		4.4	4.2	7.8	4.1	0.6	3.8	1.9	2.5	4.8	1.1		0.8	Australia
1.8	1.0	2.2	2.2	5.2		4.7	1.1	8.5	9.8		10.4	2.7	0.9	4.7	0.7		0.8	Austria
34.9	0.5	1.1	0.4	2.2		1.1	1.8	2.2	4.4		4.1	—	0.5	—	—		0.5	Azerbaijan
...	...	...	...	7.0		2.6	—	—	—	—	—	—	—	—	...		...	Bahamas, The
11.2	—	1.1		5.7		2.4	36.0	2.4	—	—	6.0	—	3.6	—	0.1		5.2	Bahrain
0.4	0.5	0.4	1.0	1.7		3.6	0.1	1.2	0.4	—	1.2	0.5	0.8	3.7	—		0.6	Bangladesh
14	14	14	2.3			—	—	9.0			8.3		1.6		—		0.2	Barbados
7.6	7	7	5.5			3.0		—			26.8				—		...	Belarus
1.0	0.6	4.6	2.4	2.3		4.6	1.8	6.2	8.8		6.6		8.2		1.1		1.4	Belgium
—	—	0.3[17]	17	6.2		—	—	2.0	—	—	0.1	—	4.2	—	—		1.1	Belize
—	—	—	0.5	24.6		—	—	4.8	—	—	—	—	—	—	—		—	Benin
...	—	—	29.0			...	...	...	...		...		...		...		...	Bermuda
...	0.7	2.2				...	...	...	1.0[18]								18	Bhutan
38.1	—	0.8	0.5	6.0		0.2	3.0	0.9	0.1		0.3	0.1	—	0.3	0.1		3.2	Bolivia
2.3	0.3	1.3	0.5	3.2		5.5	3.4	10.8	5.0		3.3		8.6		2.6		0.7	Bosnia and Herzegovina
—	0.5	0.5	—	—		—	—	3.2	1.1		0.5		1.1		—		19.9	Botswana
3.2	1.1	2.2	1.0	3.7		5.7	1.7	3.9	7.5		8.0		10.4		0.8		1.4	Brazil
20	0.7	0.8	2.1	1.6		12.1	2.5	3.6	3.8		3.3		3.3		...		...	Brunei
—	0.8	0.8	—	—		0.8	—	—	—	—	0.8	—	1.5	—	—		6.2	Bulgaria
																		Burkina Faso
—	—	—	—	1.1		—	—	2.1	—	—	—	—	—	—	—		—	Burundi
...	...	...	...	...		...	...	...	...		...		...		...		...	Cambodia
6.8	0.8	14.0	1.1	1.5		8.1	3.2	0.6	0.2		0.6		—		...		1.1	Cameroon
1.9	1.6	2.8	0.6	2.0		3.2	2.6	4.7	5.8	1.0	2.5	3.9	3.7	10.8	0.8		1.4	Canada
...	...	...	...	...		...	...	...	...		...		20.1		...		0.2	Cape Verde
—	—	—	—	—		—	—	0.9	—	—	0.2	—	4.8	—	—		7.7	Central African Republic
—	—	—	—	—		—	—	—	...		...		...		—		—	Chad
8.2	1.1	2.7	0.9	4.1		2.4	10.3	4.1	1.8		1.4	0.2	1.0	1.1	0.2		0.2	Chile
4.6	1.1	1.8	7.3			8.6	2.5	3.1	9.1		4.9	5.2	6.6		1.0		2.2	China
3.2	1.7	3.5	2.3	4.7		4.1	0.5	3.2	1.7		3.3		3.8		0.7		1.0	Colombia
—	—	—	—	—		—	—	—	—	—	—	—	—	—	—		—	Comoros
0.1	—	—	—	0.2		—	—	0.4	0.3		0.2		0.5		—		1.5	Congo, Dem. Rep. of the
—	1.4	—	—	1.4		...	—	6.8	1.4		2.7		4.1		—		—	Congo, Rep. of the
2.6	1.5	4.0	1.2	3.3		...	0.1	2.4	1.7		1.3	4.3	1.2	0.5	...		0.4	Costa Rica
20.8	1.4	—	0.1	2.0		0.2	0.1	5.3	—	—	0.3	—	7.2	—	...		3.1	Côte d'Ivoire
3.6	0.4	1.6	1.6	3.9		2.7	0.9	4.7	5.8		6.9		8.1		0.4		0.3	Croatia
...	2.4	2.1	0.5	2.0		0.6	0.9	1.6	1.7		0.9		3.5		0.2		3.0	Cuba
1.1	0.4	3.2	0.5	9.4		—	—	6.5	2.9		1.3	—	0.4	0.7	0.1		2.0	Cyprus[24]
4.3	2.9		7.3			18.7[26]		26	12.1		7.2[27]		8.1		27		4.2	Czech Republic
1.5	0.4	2.9	0.7	3.6		1.1	0.3	8.2	12.9		4.9		4.9		2.6		2.6	Denmark
—	—	...	—	—		—	—	...	—	—	—	—	—	—	...		...	Djibouti
—	—	—	—	...		—	—	—	—	—	—	—	—	—	—		—	Dominica
16.2	0.8	1.6	0.7	3.5		1.8	0.2	3.7	0.5		0.8		0.1		0.2		0.2	Dominican Republic
32.3	0.9	1.8	0.6	3.2		1.1	0.2	2.4	0.1	—	1.7	0.2	—	1.3	0.2		0.2	Ecuador
32.1	0.3	1.5	0.8	6.8		3.5	1.4	5.6	1.7	—	2.8	0.8	1.4	1.6	0.2		0.2	Egypt
12.1	1.0	3.8	—	3.1		0.6	—	2.1	0.4		3.6		0.2		0.6		0.8	El Salvador
...	...	...	...	0.8		—	—	0.6	—	—	...	...	...	...	...		...	Equatorial Guinea
—	—	—	8.3			11.7[26]		26	—	—	—	—	—	—	—		—	Eritrea
31	1.3		5.7			...	—	3.8	3.1		2.2	0.3	5.0		0.9		0.3	Estonia
16.6	1.1	1.3	0.2	2.1		0.6	—	1.7	—	—	1.3	—	—	—	—		—	Ethiopia[32]

Manufacturing industries (continued)

country	year	total manufacturing value added ('000,000 U.S.$)	(31) food (311 + 312)	beverages (313)	tobacco manufactures (314)	(32) textiles (exc. wearing apparel) (321)	wearing apparel (322)	leather and fur products (323 + 324)	(33) wood products (exc. furniture) (331)	wood furniture (332)	(34) paper, paper products (341)	printing and publishing (342)	(35) industrial chemicals (351)	paints, soaps, etc. (352 exc. 3522)	drugs and medicines (3522)
Faroe Islands	1990[3, 28]	120	69.3[33]	...	...	...	...	1.0	7.2	2.8	3.7	4.4	...	5.8	...
Fiji	1992[9]	156	38.5	—10.1—		—13.6—		1.0	...	...	...	...	...	...	...
Finland	1994	20,972	9.2	1.7	0.5	1.5	1.0	0.5	6.6	1.3	18.1	6.5	4.2	2.0	1.1
France	1994[9]	254,935	10.4	2.4	1.2	2.6	2.0	0.9	1.7	1.6	2.3	6.0	3.3	—5.9—	
French Guiana	1991[11]	45	...	...	...	—[35]—			—38.2[35]—				...	...	...
French Polynesia	1993[3]	214	—27.2—			...	...	—	...	...	...	...	3.4	—1.7—	
Gabon	1994	174	9.2	6.9	5.7	1.2	1.7	—	17.8	2.3	1.2	1.7	...	...	...
Gambia, The	1990	22	58.1	5.3	—	4.1	—	0.1	...	6.3	...	3.8		—2.0—	
Gaza Strip	1994	50	...	...	...	...	...	...	...	...	...	...	...	...	...
Georgia	1992	150	...	...	...	...	...	...	...	...	...	...	...	...	...
Germany	1994[37]	596,225	—8.8—		2.5	1.6	1.1	0.3	—3.0—		2.5	2.1	—11.7—		
Ghana	1993[9, 37]	610	8.4	9.1	18.1	4.6	—0.5—		15.2	0.8	1.8	1.3	0.9	—8.9—	
Gibraltar	...	...	...	...	...	...	...	...	...	...	...	...	...	...	...
Greece	1992[11, 28]	10,660	17.0	5.9	3.6	10.2	5.3	1.7	1.8	1.0	3.0	3.2	2.2	4.9	2.4
Greenland	1991	27	...	...	...	...	...	...	...	...	...	...	...	...	...
Grenada	1995[2, 39]	19	29.1	55.2	2.4	—	...	...	...	...	7.0	...	...	6.3	...
Guadeloupe	1993[40]	77	...	...	...	...	...	...	...	...	...	...	...	...	...
Guam	1986	9.1	...	...	...	...	...	...	...	...	...	...	...	...	...
Guatemala	1993[2, 9, 37]	3,674	38.4	12.9	3.2	9.4	0.9	1.2	0.6	0.2	1.8	1.6	1.6	4.4	4.2
Guernsey	1993[4]	61	—5.1—			—1.5—			...	...	...	17.6	...	—	7.8
Guinea	1994	83	...	...	...	...	...	...	...	...	...	...	—	...	...
Guinea-Bissau	1991	16	...	...	...	...	...	...	...	...	...	...	...	...	...
Guyana	1995[41]	20	...	...	...	...	...	...	...	...	...	...	...	...	...
Haiti	1994–95[3]	73	40.0	4.7	5.8	—7.7—			...	...	...	...		—10.1—	
Honduras	1994[9, 42]	526	28.3	17.1	5.5	2.1	13.1	1.0	4.8	1.5	2.7	2.2	0.4	2.9	0.9
Hong Kong	1994	11,198	4.7	2.1	1.6	13.4	15.6	0.4	0.3	0.2	2.3	11.5	—2.4—		
Hungary	1994	8,062	—19.0—		0.7	3.0	4.4	1.9	2.8	2.8[43]	1.8	4.6	—10.5—		
Iceland	1993[9]	795	49.9	2.0	—	1.9	1.6	0.8	0.2	4.2	1.2	9.3	1.5	2.4	—
India	1992–93[28, 44]	22,176	8.3	1.0	2.1	10.1	1.6	0.9	0.3	—	1.9	1.7	10.4	4.2	3.8
Indonesia	1994[28, 37]	27,701	8.8	1.0	10.4	13.5	3.8	4.1	7.8	1.0	3.2	1.4	4.7	2.1	2.2
Iran	1994	5,839	12.9	2.2	0.9	10.9	0.3	1.0	0.7	0.3	1.6	0.9	4.8	—5.4—	
Iraq	1994	606	9.7	3.1	1.2	3.3	1.2	3.6	—	0.2	3.3	1.3	13.0	—1.0—	
Ireland	1990[45]	14,780	20.5	5.4	1.1	2.3	1.4	0.3	1.2	0.6	1.3	3.8	2.8	1.4	12.6
Isle of Man	1990–91[3, 28]	98	—15.7—			...	...	...	...	...	...	...	...	...	...
Israel	1993[9, 42]	10,624	10.3	—1.5—		3.4	4.5	0.7	1.3	1.5	2.2	5.3	5.0	—6.2—	
Italy	1991[37]	146,179	7.4	1.3	0.4	7.2	3.8	2.5	1.1	2.1	2.7	4.4	3.6	2.8	—
Jamaica	1995	819	20.1	15.4[46]	10.3	—6.6—		0.7	0.2	2.6	—3.8—		9.7[7]	[7]	[7]
Japan	1993[48]	1,140,051	8.7	1.2	0.3	2.8	1.3	0.3	1.6	0.9	2.6	5.7	4.3	2.7	5.3
Jersey	1991	45	...	...	...	...	...	...	...	...	...	...	...	...	...
Jordan	1994[9]	987	11.3	5.3	12.5	2.8	2.5	1.1	1.2	2.7	3.5	2.1	5.7	2.7	5.3
Kazakstan	1994[2, 3, 15]	6,867	14.9	...	...	3.1	1.0	0.6	—1.3[16]—		—16—		4.6[7]	[7]	[7]
Kenya	1994[28]	703[49]	32.4	9.7	1.5	5.7	1.8	1.4	1.8	0.8[10]	4.4	2.6	1.9	—6.6—	
Kiribati	1992	0.68	...	...	—	...	...	...	...	...	...	...	...	...	...
Korea, North	...	...	...	...	...	...	...	...	...	...	...	...	...	...	...
Korea, South	1994[9, 42]	161,226	—7.7—		1.7	6.3	3.3	1.8	0.9	2.5	2.4	2.7	—9.8—		
Kuwait	1993[9]	2,232	5.3	1.9	—	1.1	5.3	0.2	0.5	2.2	1.1	1.0	2.8	1.0	—
Kyrgyzstan	1994[2]	452	25.3	1.9	4.5	26.7	3.1	1.5	0.4	0.8	—	0.5	—	0.1	0.1
Laos	1990[2]	66	4.5	7.4	16.3	—	5.1	0.3	40.1	5.0	—	1.2	—4.0—		
Latvia	1994[28]	714	27.0	10.6	0.5	5.7	3.2	1.7	7.8	2.9	0.5	3.4	1.9	1.9	1.0
Lebanon	1994	870	...	...	...	...	...	...	...	...	...	...	...	...	...
Lesotho	1994[3]	128	—52.9—			—30.5—		2.0	—2.8—		...	3.0	...	—2.2—	
Liberia	1985[2, 9, 37]	64	10.8	42.7	...	...	...	0.3	—	4.5	0.6	1.3	0.4	—7.2—	
Libya	1994	784	4.6	2.3	9.8	3.8	0.6	8.8	0.9	0.3	0.4	1.0	6.9	—6.1—	
Liechtenstein	...	...	...	...	...	...	...	...	...	...	...	...	...	...	...
Lithuania	1994[2]	2,667	25.1	5.9	1.3	8.0	3.5	1.7	4.0	2.0	1.4	1.4	4.2	0.4	0.6
Luxembourg	1994	2,035	5.4	3.2	0.7	6.5	0.6	...	0.4	0.5	2.6	3.2	6.7	—4.8—	
Macau	1994[9]	448	2.2	0.6	0.3	18.9	52.1	2.4	0.2	0.8	0.5	3.1	—0.5—		0.4
Macedonia	1994	768	2.2	8.8	12.7	6.8	11.7	3.5	0.8	2.9	1.3	1.5	5.9	—3.7—	
Madagascar	1994	121	14.5	10.5	0.8	34.7	3.2	2.4	0.8	0.8	4.0	1.6	—	—6.5—	
Malawi	1994	92	20.9	7.7	5.5	13.2	1.1	2.2	1.1	1.1	—	6.6	5.5	—17.6—	
Malaysia	1993[28]	16,287	8.0	0.9	1.0	3.1	2.3	0.2	7.6	1.2	1.6	2.7	8.0	1.9	0.3
Maldives	1994	11[52]	...	...	—	—	...	—	0.1	—	0.4	0.8	0.8	—0.7—	
Mali	1990	96	18.4	1.2	13.1	36.5	10.3	0.1	0.1	—	0.4	0.8	0.5	—3.6[53]—	
Malta	1993	499	10.3	9.2	1.0	2.6	13.5	3.6	0.5	5.4	1.4	9.3	...	...	...
Marshall Islands	1995[3]	2.7	3.7[55]	...	...	...	...	...	...	...	...	...	...	...	...
Martinique	1993	145	...	...	...	...	...	...	...	...	...	...	6.0		—18.8—
Mauritania	1993	35	—42.9—			...	...	...	...	...	...	...	...	...	...
Mauritius	1993[9, 57]	658	15.8	10.2	5.1	3.4	40.9	1.2	0.6	1.2	0.9	2.5	2.1	2.1	0.1
Mayotte	1992	...	...	...	...	...	...	...	...	...	...	...	...	...	...
Mexico	1994	49,208	14.8	6.5	1.7	4.6	1.9	1.5	1.2	0.9	2.7	2.9	6.4	—7.3—	
Micronesia	1992	2.2[4]	[58]	...	...	...	91.0	...	...	...	...	...	...	1.6[58]	...
Moldova	1995[2, 3, 59]	254	—58.1—			1.9	1.6	1.3	—3.3[16]—		—16—		0.3[7]	[7]	[7]
Monaco	...	...	...	...	...	...	...	...	...	...	...	...	...	...	...
Mongolia	1994[3, 9, 11]	86	22.6	2.7	—	25.0	3.5	6.8	3.4	0.1	—1.0—		...	—1.2—	
Morocco	1994	4,165	7.3	14.1	6.0	9.9	8.1	1.3	1.7	0.4	3.0	0.8	11.1	—0.5—	
Mozambique	1995[2]	238	32.5	16.2	2.2	9.7	3.8	0.1	6.3	0.2	1.5	...	—5.4—		
Myanmar (Burma)	1993	858[49]	14.8	20.4	4.6	26.4	...	...	1.9	0.7	5.7	...	0.2	2.0	1.6
Namibia	1994[3]	234	63.6[60]	...	...	...	...	...	...	...	...	...	...	...	...
Nauru	1989	...	...	...	...	...	...	...	...	...	...	...	...	...	...
Nepal	1993–94[3, 9, 11]	356	18.4	7.3	9.6	17.8	12.7	3.4	1.8	0.9	1.4	1.1	...	4.1	0.3
Netherlands, The	1993[9, 37]	43,948	15.0	3.8	4.7	2.1	0.5	0.3	1.1	0.9	3.5	8.3	7.8	3.3	2.3
Netherlands Antilles	1993	101	...	...	...	...	...	...	...	...	...	...	...	...	...
New Caledonia	1992[3]	341[13]	—15.4—			...	...	...	...	...	...	...	...	...	...
New Zealand	1994	8,251	25.6	3.0	0.6	3.0	2.3	1.2	4.8	1.9	7.6	7.7	3.5	—3.1—	
Nicaragua	1994	653	23.2	27.2	7.8	6.1	2.7	3.4	0.9	0.2	0.2	2.3	2.0	—6.9—	

refined petroleum and products (353 + 354)	rubber products (355)	plastic products (356)	pottery, china, and glass (361 + 362)	bricks, tiles, cement, etc. (369)	iron and steel (371)	non-ferrous metals (372)	fabricated metal products (381)	nonelectrical machinery (382 exc. 3825)	office equip., computers (3825)	electrical equip. (383 exc. 3832)	radio, television (3832)	transport equip. exc. motor vehicles (384 exc. 3843)	motor vehicles (3843)	professional equip. (385)	jewelry, musical instruments (390)	country
...	...	...	...	...	...	...	...	...	...	...	...	...	...	...	...	Faroe Islands
—	0.5	1.6	—	4.0[34]	...	—	4.3	0.8				0.6	0.4	—	0.7	Fiji
2.5	0.6	2.5	0.9	2.2	4.9	1.4	4.4	10.5	0.6	3.3	5.2	2.9	1.3	1.5	1.2	Finland
6.4	1.4	3.2	1.1	2.9	2.5	1.9	8.0	7.6		10.0		11.4		1.5	1.8	France
...	...	...	61.8[36]		36		36								...	French Guiana
							35.4								...	French Polynesia
10.3	—	—	0.6	5.7	1.7	1.7	9.2	1.2		5.2		7.5		0.6	3.5	Gabon
—	1.3	—	—	0.9	...	...	3.5	—	—	—	—	—	—	—	14.6	Gambia, The
...	...	...	...	...	...	...	...	...	...	...	...	...	...	...	...	Gaza Strip
...	...	...	...	...	...	...	...	...	...	...	...	...	...	...	...	Georgia
5.2	1.1	3.5	1.3	3.5	3.1	1.0	7.5	11.4	1.2	13.2		1.2	11.2	1.5	0.6	Germany
8.1	0.6	2.6	4.4		0.7	8.2	3.4	0.3		1.5		0.6[38]		—	38	Ghana
...	...	...	...	...	...	...	...	...	...	...	...	...	...	...	...	Gibraltar
5.5	0.7	3.1	1.0	6.0	1.9	2.7	4.7	1.6	—	3.4	1.6	3.8	1.2	0.2	0.5	Greece
...	...	...	...	...	...	...	...	...	...	...	...	...	...	...	...	Greenland
—	...	...	—	...	...	...	...	...	...	...	...	...	...	...	...	Grenada
...	...	...	...	...	...	...	...	...	...	...	...	...	...	...	...	Guadeloupe
—	...	...	—	...	...	...	...	...	...	...	...	...	...	...	...	Guam
3.2	1.6	4.3	0.8	3.7	1.9	—	1.5	0.5	—	0.8	0.1	0.3	0.1	0.3	0.5	Guatemala
—	—	10.9	—	1.9	...	...	7.4		—	40.3	3.0	—	—		4.6	Guernsey
...	...	...	...	...	...	...	...	...	...	...	...	...	...	...	...	Guinea
...	—	—	...	...	...	...	...	...	...	...	...	...	...	...	...	Guinea-Bissau
—	—	—	...	3.6	...	...	...	...	...	...	...	...	...	...	...	Guyana
...	...	...	...	...	...	...	20.0	...	...	...	...	...	...	...	...	Haiti
0.2	1.0	2.8	0.1	6.6	0.5	0.2	3.5	0.7	—	0.9	0.1	—	0.2	0.1	0.7	Honduras
0.1	0.1	2.9	1.7		0.8		5.6	7.6	4.1	1.1	9.4	4.1		4.1	3.9	Hong Kong
9.8	3.3		4.9		2.5		6.3	6.6	0.3	4.3	2.2	0.9	3.8	3.6	43	Hungary
—		3.2	0.5	3.8	1.7	2.2	7.4	—	—	—	2.5	—	—		3.7	Iceland
5.6	2.1	1.3	0.6	3.9	8.2	2.8	2.3	7.4	1.1	5.7	2.7	3.6	5.0	0.7	0.7	India
0.1	2.0	1.9	1.5	2.4	5.8	1.2	3.5	1.3	—	1.8	2.2	5.6	5.8	0.2	0.7	Indonesia
0.6	2.1	1.6	1.7	7.7	15.2	3.6	4.5	3.9		7.9		8.1		0.7	0.4	Iran
24.1	0.7	1.6	0.7	16.5	4.0	—	4.6	2.1		4.3		0.5		—		Iraq
0.2	0.8	2.2	1.2	3.8	0.6	0.1	3.2	2.6	11.2	2.9	9.5	1.5	0.6	4.1	0.9	Ireland
...	...	...	...	...	...	...	...	...	...	...	...	...	...	...	...	Isle of Man
—	0.7	5.4	0.6	3.7	1.3	0.6	11.4	3.0		29.9		6.0		1.3	1.2	Israel
1.8	1.6	3.4	3.1	3.1	4.9	1.2	5.9	13.0	1.0	7.5	2.9	3.1	6.1	1.2	1.0	Italy
9.5	7	7	5.9		47		15.0[47]								0.2	Jamaica
1.4	1.3	3.7	1.2	3.1	4.7	1.2	7.5	9.5	3.0	6.5	7.8	1.6	9.1	1.3	1.6	Japan
...	...	...	...	...	...	...	...	...	...	...	...	...	...	...	...	Jersey
4.4	0.1	3.9	0.2	16.9	2.4	1.8	4.6	2.0	—	2.1	—	—	2.3	0.1	0.5	Jordan
27.0	7	7	5.1		29.5		9.0								...	Kazakstan
0.8	2.9	3.3	0.5	3.7	...	...	6.4	0.6		5.7		3.7		8	1.8[8]	Kenya
—	—	—	...	...	...	...	—	—	—	—	...	—	—	...	...	Kiribati
...	...	...	...	...	...	...	...	...	...	...	...	...	...	...	...	Korea, North
3.1	3.8		5.0		6.8		5.2	8.0	1.0	3.1	12.4	3.7	7.8	8	1.1[8]	Korea, South
57.2	—	1.7	0.6	4.7	1.1	—	5.0	2.6	—	1.5	—	2.1	0.2	—	0.9	Kuwait
0.4	0.1	0.2	3.0	6.0	—	9.0	2.6	6.4	0.1	5.1	—	—	1.3	0.9		Kyrgyzstan
—	0.5		0.1	3.8	—	—	10.8	0.5		0.2		—	—		0.1	Laos
0.1	0.1	0.9	1.2	2.4	2.7	—	1.8	5.3	0.2	3.6	2.3	6.3	2.0	0.4	2.6[50]	Latvia
...	...	...	...	...	...	...	...	...	...	...	...	...	...	...	...	Lebanon
...	...	...	3.3		1.5	...	...	...	...	...	...	...	...	...	...	Lesotho
—	—	0.6	0.2	20.7	—	...	9.5	0.3		0.7		...	...	...	—	Liberia
26.1	...	0.9	0.3	22.6	—	—	0.5	...	...	...	...	...	...	...	4.1	Libya
...	...	...	...	...	...	...	...	...	...	...	...	...	...	...	...	Liechtenstein
19.7	—	0.4	0.5	4.1	0.4	—	1.3	5.0	0.2	1.1	3.3	2.3	0.2	1.1	0.9[50]	Lithuania
0.1	6.1	3.6	3.5	8.3	16.8	3.4	11.1	7.3		3.5		0.6		1.0	0.1	Luxembourg
—	51	0.5	51	4.3	...	...	2.0	0.1	—	2.3		0.8		...	7.9	Macau
4.7	0.1	1.9	1.7	1.0	3.4	0.8	6.8	1.8		7.3		7.0		0.3	1.4	Macedonia
7.3	0.8	1.6	0.8	2.4	—	—	3.2	2.2		1.6		1.6		—	0.8	Madagascar
...	...	4.4	—	6.6	—	—	3.3	2.2				1.1		...	...	Malawi
1.5	4.5	3.4	0.9	3.9	2.9	0.7	4.3	4.1	0.9	4.3	22.9	1.8	2.9	1.1	1.1	Malaysia
—	—	...	—	1.3	—	...	...	...	...	...	...	...	...	...	...	Maldives
0.7	0.3	0.4	—	1.3	—	54	6.2	0.5		1.7		6.5		—	...	Mali
53	3.4	2.6	0.5	3.4	—	54	4.0[54]	2.0		4.5	8.8	1.1	0.3	3.4	5.1	Malta
...	...	...	...	...	...	...	...	...	...	...	...	...	...	...	14.8[56]	Marshall Islands
...	...	...	...	16.8	...	...	15.5	...	...	...	...	...	...	...	...	Martinique
—	0.3	1.2	0.1	3.5	1.0		2.4	0.2		0.8	0.2	0.1	0.2	1.3	2.7	Mauritius
—	—	...	—	...	—	54	...	...	...	...	...	...	...	...	...	Mauritania
—	—	...	—	...	—	...	...	...	...	...	...	...	...	...	...	Mayotte
10.8	2.0	1.8	1.9	1.8	4.2	0.8	4.1	3.3		3.2		10.1		1.7	1.9	Mexico
...	...	...	...	...	...	...	...	...	...	...	...	...	...	...	7.4	Micronesia
...	7	7	...	4.5	...	...	13.9								...	Moldova
...	...	...	...	...	...	...	...	...	...	...	...	...	...	...	...	Monaco
0.1	—	—	0.1	5.2	—	...	2.0	...	...	...	...	...	...	0.1	...	Mongolia
8.8	1.7	1.2	0.3	8.0	1.3	0.6	5.1	1.7		3.2		3.6		0.2	0.1	Morocco
3.0	4.1	0.6	6.8		2.4	0.3	1.3	0.2		1.1		2.1		—	0.2	Mozambique
—	0.5	0.2	—	0.5	6.1	7.0	0.2	...	...	0.7	—	—	1.5	...	5.0	Myanmar (Burma)
...	...	...	...	...	...	...	...	...	...	...	...	...	...	...	...	Namibia
...	...	...	...	...	...	...	...	...	...	...	...	...	...	...	...	Nauru
...	1.1	1.8	51	8.2	2.0	...	4.3	...	...	2.3	0.4	...	...	51	0.8	Nepal
2.3	0.6	3.1	1.6	2.4	3.9		6.7	8.3		11.4		4.8		0.9	0.4	Netherlands, The
...	...	...	...	...	...	...	...	...	...	...	...	...	...	...	...	Netherlands Antilles
...	...	...	...	...	...	43.2	...	...	...	...	...	...	...	...	...	New Caledonia
1.8	0.9	3.3	1.3	2.1	1.7	2.0	7.6	4.9		4.1		4.4		0.4	1.2	New Zealand
7.3	0.7	1.8	0.2	1.5	0.2	—	4.0	0.3		0.6		0.3		—	0.2	Nicaragua

Manufacturing industries (continued)

country	year	total manufac- turing value added ('000,000 U.S.$)	(31) food (311 + 312)	bever- ages (313)	tobacco manufac- tures (314)	(32) textiles (exc. wearing apparel) (321)	wearing apparel (322)	leather and fur products (323 + 324)	(33) wood products (exc. furniture) (331)	wood furniture (332)	(34) paper, paper products (341)	printing and pub- lishing (342)	(35) industrial chemi- cals (351)	paints, soaps, etc. (352 exc. 3522)	drugs and medicines (3522)
Niger	1993	153	—6.7—			—1.1—		...	—61—		...	0.9	—4.8—		
Nigeria	1994	3,165	16.9	15.3	1.8	11.2		2.9	0.5	0.8	3.4	3.2	0.3	—11.2—	
Northern Mariana Islands	1987[1, 3]	58	—3.3—			26.0	—62.7[62]		...	...	...	1.3	...	...	...
Norway	1994[11]	13,472	12.3	—9.3—		1.3	0.4	0.2	3.9	2.1[10]	4.8	9.9	6.1	1.2	1.8
Oman	1993	669	—10.6—		...	1.9[13]	2.9	13	1.2	3.5[43]	1.0	1.5	—4.3—		
Pakistan	1994	5,719	16.7	1.9	10.1	16.8	2.0	1.4	0.3	0.1	1.0	0.9	6.9	—7.2—	
Palau	1992	12	...	...	...	...	...	...	...	...	...	...	...	...	...
Panama	1995	694	43.5	10.0	3.6	0.8	2.6	1.1	1.4	1.3	4.0	2.8	1.4	—5.5—	...
Papua New Guinea	1989	451	48.4	13.1	4.9	—	0.4	—	11.6	2.0	1.1	2.4	1.1	—1.1—	
Paraguay	1994	782	30.9	9.7	0.8	7.3	0.3	5.5	18.2	1.7	—	4.4	0.8	—0.8—	
Peru	1994	6,895	14.9	12.0	0.9	7.9	1.1	0.6	0.6	0.5	1.1	2.9	2.8	—7.0—	
Philippines	1992[9]	10,548	17.2	9.1	5.0	3.5	5.8	0.6	1.3	0.8	2.4	1.4	3.6	6.3	5.1
Poland	1994	22,523	—20.6—		3.8	3.7	4.6	1.7	3.6	3.7	1.6	3.6	—18.1—		
Portugal	1994[9]	17,025	8.2	2.5	4.7	9.7	7.0	4.5	3.6	1.8	3.6	4.1	1.7	1.9	1.5
Puerto Rico	1992[3]	22,737	4.6	11.6	...	0.5	4.0	1.0	...	0.5	0.8	1.4	2.7	1.9	43.9
Qatar	1994[9]	810	3.4	0.5	...	0.3	—6.2—		0.9	1.8	0.1	3.2	29.6	—0.4—	
Réunion	1994	371	34.5	12.3		—0.5—			—3.8—		5.0[64]	6.3	...	—3.7—	
Romania	1993[65]	6,651	19.6	6.8	0.9	5.9	3.4	2.6	3.3	3.1	1.1	0.7	3.5	2.4	1.0
Russia	1994	54,512[49]	15.3	1.3	0.3	2.4	1.5	1.0	1.7	1.0	1.6	0.8	6.9	1.2	0.9
Rwanda	1990	178	29.1	18.1	11.2	...	...	...	4.4	0.9	1.0	1.3	9.0	—	—
St. Kitts and Nevis	1994[28]	19	...	...	...	...	...	...	...	...	...	...	...	...	...
St. Lucia	1995[2, 39]	46	10.0	—27.6—		2.4	7.2	...	...	...	40.8	...	...	...	...
St. Vincent	1988[3, 28]	14	24.9	—25.4—		—10.1—			—1.9—		—5.3—		...	...	...
Samoa	1990	15	36.0	25.5	19.2	—	...	—	10.7	—	...	...	...	8.6	
San Marino	...	...	...	...	...	...	...	...	...	...	...	...	...	...	...
São Tomé and Príncipe	1993[2]	4.6	26.3	20.7	—	—	26.3	—	—15.1—		—	1.2	—	6.6	—
Saudi Arabia	1994	6,780	5.9	0.5	0.3	0.4	0.1	0.1	0.2	0.6	2.3	1.0	39.3	—1.9—	
Senegal	1994[9]	310[68]	41.7[68]	2.9	3.8	5.1	—	—	0.2	0.1	1.2	1.5	16.7	4.8	1.8
Seychelles	1989	26	—79.6—			—0.6—			—2.1—		—6.0—		—4.1—		
Sierra Leone	1993[9]	92	37.0	21.6	10.5	—	1.0	0.1	0.3	1.2	0.2	2.2	—20.2—		
Singapore	1994[11, 28]	20,593	2.5	1.0	0.7	0.3	1.2	0.2	0.2	0.6	1.5	4.7	3.7	1.4	3.5
Slovakia	1994[3]	2,720	9.7[49]	3.0	...	3.1[49]	3.5	2.1	2.3	1.7	4.5	2.5	5.1	1.2	2.4
Slovenia	1994[9]	4,837	12.6	2.1	0.5	3.6	4.0	3.8	3.0	5.1	6.2	3.9	8.1	—4.5—	
Solomon Islands	1994	7.8	...	...	...	...	...	...	...	...	...	...	...	...	...
Somalia	1990	36	21.6	6.3	37.5	10.5	0.8	2.0	—	7.3	-0.6	0.3	0.4	—5.1—	
South Africa	1994	25,669	10.6	6.0	0.4	3.4	2.9	1.3	1.4	1.1	4.8	3.5	4.9	—4.9—	
Spain	1992[28, 42]	94,549	13.2	4.4	1.2	3.3	2.7	1.3	2.3	1.9	2.3	5.3	3.3	3.4	3.4
Sri Lanka	1993[9, 42]	1,267	14.8	12.4	11.8	8.3	20.1	1.9	0.6	0.2	2.5	1.1	0.9	4.5	0.3
Sudan, The	1990	1,179	40.0	3.0	16.7	11.9	0.4	5.4	0.2	0.2	2.1	6.4	0.7	—2.2—	
Suriname	1992[2, 28, 39]	700	33.4	22.3	12.3	...	1.5	1.6	8.7	1.4	0.7	1.6	...	—8.3—	
Swaziland	1994	344	26.3	44.2		5.5	2.0	0.3	1.2	1.2	10.1	5.2	—	—0.3—	
Sweden	1994[11, 28]	35,125	7.2	1.2	0.5	1.0	0.2	0.1	4.9	1.1	9.8	5.8	3.9	1.8	5.4
Switzerland	1994	60,111	8.1	1.4	0.8	1.8	1.0	0.5	4.6	3.0	1.9	7.4	7.4	—5.9—	
Syria	1994	2,990	13.1	2.3	7.4	25.5	1.5	2.6	2.0	5.3	0.4	0.7	0.3	—2.0—	
Taiwan	1995	73,210	—7.3—		1.5	5.8	2.2	0.7	0.6	0.9	2.1	1.2	9.0	—2.0—	
Tajikistan	1994[2, 3]	862	19.4	1.0	1.1	27.5	1.8	0.3	0.3	0.2	...	0.2	3.4	0.2	...
Tanzania	1994	101	10.9	5.9	10.9	16.8	1.0	2.0	2.0	1.0	3.9	3.0	14.8	—2.0—	
Thailand	1991[9, 11]	65,413	4.1	2.3	2.9	3.1	5.0	1.4	0.6	0.4	0.2	33.9	1.5	0.7	0.6
Togo	1994[3]	90	—65.3—			—6.7—			—6.5—		—4.7—		—6.4—		
Tonga	1994[2, 9]	13	—45.1—			1.1	1.5	2.0	1.3	69	69	5.0	—	—24.9—	
Trinidad and Tobago	1993	593	17.3	9.6	6.2	0.3	1.4	0.3	0.5	0.7	2.3	3.6	21.1	3.0	0.1
Tunisia	1993[3, 9]	3,696	9.8	3.3	6.5	7.1	13.1	3.4	—5.1—		—2.2—		2.6	2.7	0.5
Turkey	1993[9, 72]	40,159	10.3	2.9	3.5	10.3	3.6	0.5	0.8	0.4	1.5	2.2	3.7	2.9	3.0
Turkmenistan	1992[2, 3, 15]	801	13.3	...	...	18.9	1.2	0.4	—0.3[16]—		—16—		3.2[7]	7	7
Tuvalu	1994[28]	0.31	...	...	...	—	—	—	—	—	...	...	...	—	—
Uganda	1989	155	42.8	11.9	8.9	8.0	1.3	1.5	0.1	4.0	0.9	1.4	0.3	0.7	5.1
Ukraine	1994[2, 3, 28]	28,630	24.3	1.8	0.1	3.2[49]	0.9	1.4	0.7	1.2	0.6	0.3	6.3[49]	1.0[49]	0.5
United Arab Emirates	1993[2]	6,621	—8.7—			—4.7—			—2.8—		—2.8—		—53.8—		
United Kingdom	1993[28]	169,348	11.0	2.6	1.1	3.1	1.9	0.8	1.1	2.1[10]	3.1	8.8	4.1	3.4	3.6
United States	1994	1,598,464	8.8	2.0	1.4	2.7	1.8	0.3	2.5	1.6	4.0	7.5	5.2	2.9	3.5
Uruguay	1993[9, 42]	2,962	24.0	12.6	5.6	8.3	3.7	2.6	0.6	0.6	2.1	4.9	1.9	—8.4—	
Uzbekistan	1992[2, 3, 15]	2,147	12.6	...	...	21.4	3.1	1.9	—1.3[16]		—16—		5.4[7]	7	7
Vanuatu	1993[3]	10	—44.5—			—3.8—			—22.5—		5.3	...	—9.2[73]—		
Venezuela	1993[3, 42]	11,292	11.8	7.1	3.4	1.7	-1.3	2.1	0.3	0.8	2.3	2.8	5.1	3.6	2.4
Vietnam	1995[2, 3]	5,472	—33.4—			7.2	2.6	1.0	3.7	...	2.3	1.1	9.3[74]	74	74
Virgin Islands (U.S.)	...[51]	...	...	...	...	...	...	...	...	...	...	...	...	...	...
West Bank	1994	132	...	...	...	...	...	...	...	...	...	...	...	...	...
Western Sahara	...	...	...	...	...	...	...	...	...	...	...	...	...	...	...
Yemen	1994[2, 76]	3,541	—64.0—			—1.7—			—0.6—		—8.5—		—13.2—		
Yugoslavia	1994[3]	4,506	19.5	5.7	4.7	3.1	5.3	2.9	1.0	3.2	2.0	2.0	3.6	—9.2—	
Zambia	1994[9, 11]	305	19.5	18.0	6.9	7.5	1.2	0.8	3.4	1.1	1.0	2.4	5.0	9.0	1.8
Zimbabwe	1993–94[28]	1,479	20.3	13.0	4.7	8.4	3.1	2.9	2.3	1.0	2.5	3.5	4.0[77]	1.3	1.7

[1]Gross output in value of sales. [2]Gross output of production. [3]Complete ISIC detail is not available. [4]Value of manufactured exports. [5]Canned tuna and salmon. [6]Value of manufactured exports (excluding duty-free reexports). [7]351 includes 352, 355, and 356. [8]390 includes 385. [9]In producer's prices. [10]Includes metal furniture. [11]Establishments employing 10 or more persons. [12]Excludes sugar refining. [13]321 includes 323 + 324. [14]351 includes 353 + 354, 355, and 356. [15]Includes extraction of petroleum, natural gas, metals, and nonmetals. [16]33 includes 34. [17]355 and 356 includes 361 + 362. [18]38 includes 39. [19]Establishments employing 15 or more persons. [20]351 includes 353 + 354. [21]Cotton fibre only. [22]Establishments employing 50 or more persons. [23]Excludes petroleum refining. [24]Republic of Cyprus only. [25]Establishments employing 100 or more persons. [26]37 includes 381. [27]383 includes 385. [28]In factor values. [29]Private establishments employing 10 or more persons, and all public establishments. [30]311 + 312 includes 314. [31]351 includes 352, 353, and 354. [32]Ethiopia includes Eritrea. [33]Processed fish only. [34]369 includes 371. [35]33 includes 32. [36]36 includes 37 and 38. [37]Establishments employing 20 or more persons. [38]384 includes 390. [39]Selected industries only. [40]Establishments employing six or more persons; excludes food and beverages. [41]Excludes sugar and rice manufacturing; includes public utilities. [42]Establishments employing five or more persons. [43]332 includes 390. [44]Establishments with

refined petroleum and products (353+354)	rubber products (355)	plastic products (356)	(36) pottery, china, and glass (361+362)	bricks, tiles, cement, etc. (369)	(37) iron and steel (371)	non-ferrous metals (372)	(38) fabricated metal products (381)	nonelectrical machinery (382 exc. 3825)	office equip., computers (3825)	electrical equip. (383 exc. 3832)	radio, television (3832)	transport equip. exc. motor vehicles (384 exc. 3843)	motor vehicles (3843)	professional equip. (385)	(39) jewelry, musical instruments (390)	country
—	...	...	...	1.3	0.2[61]		...								85.0[56]	Niger
1.1	1.8	2.7	0.4	5.6	1.1	1.8	5.0	1.1		2.0		9.6		—	0.3	Nigeria
...	[62]	[62]	4.9		...	...	...	...	...	...	...	...	...	...	...	Northern Mariana Islands
1.6	0.2	1.8	0.8	2.4	2.4	5.5	4.3	6.7	0.4	3.5	1.8	11.7[63]	1.1	1.7	0.8	Norway
34.8	1.8		15.4		3.8		5.4	11.1		...	...	0.1	0.7	...	[43]	Oman
6.7	0.8	0.5	1.0	8.6	7.2	—	0.9	1.8		3.1		3.5		0.3	0.3	Pakistan
...	...	...	...	...	...	...	...	...	...	...	...	...	...	...	...	Palau
5.8	0.2	4.1	0.6	4.8	1.2	0.4	2.2	—	...	0.9	—	1.2	0.2	0.1	0.3	Panama
—	—	0.4	0.7	1.6	...	1.3	6.7	1.3		0.7		2.4		...	...	Papua New Guinea
5.2	—	1.8	0.5	2.9	—	1.3	1.3	0.3		0.1		0.6		0.1	5.5	Paraguay
21.0	0.7	2.2	1.0	3.7	1.5	7.7	2.9	1.4		1.8		1.8		0.3	1.7	Peru
7.5	2.4	1.8	1.4	3.2	3.6	0.7	1.6	1.1	0.1	3.0	6.6	2.4	1.3	0.2	1.0	Philippines
			5.3		5.0		5.1	7.3	0.2	2.7	1.5	6.3		1.2	0.3	Poland
12.8	0.6	1.5	3.6	5.2	0.8	0.5	6.0	3.4	0.1	3.3	2.4	1.6	1.9	0.5	1.0	Portugal
0.5	0.1	1.0	0.3	1.1	...	...	1.4	1.1	2.1	3.2	4.3	—	0.4	5.7	0.9	Puerto Rico
31.3	...	0.9	7.4		10.8	...	3.0								0.2	Qatar
...	...	[64]	...	16.8	...	...	12.2	5.0							—	Réunion
5.7	1.9	1.5	6.6		5.2	0.5	4.7	8.9	0.2	1.3	1.9	2.7	3.0	1.1	0.5	Romania
5.1	1.2	0.5	0.9	6.1	8.6	7.9	1.7	12.1	0.6	2.6	[51]	3.0[66]	6.5	1.6	1.5	Russia
				11.7			10.3	0.9		0.8		1.4			...	Rwanda
...	...	...	...	...	...	...	...	...	...	...	...	...	...	...	...	St. Kitts and Nevis
...	...	...	...	...	...	...	...	...	...	12.0		...	...	...	...	St. Lucia
...	...	0.4	...	...	...	...	6.6[67]	...	...	[67]	[67]	...	...	...	...	St. Vincent
...	...	...	...	...	...	...	...	...	...	...	...	...	...	...	...	Samoa
...	...	...	...	...	...	...	...	...	...	...	...	...	...	...	...	San Marino
—	—	—	3.8		—	—	—	—		—		—		—	...	São Tomé and Príncipe
13.9	0.1	3.0	0.6	12.3	7.6	0.4	5.3	1.1		1.9		0.6		—	0.6	Saudi Arabia
5.5	—	2.2	...	6.5	—	—	3.5	0.2	...	...	...	1.5	0.8	...	...	Senegal
...	...	...	5.2		...	...	...	2.4						...	—	Seychelles
...	...	...	3.5		...	...	2.1	...	...	...	...	...	...	...	0.1	Sierra Leone
6.1	0.3	2.8	0.4	1.6	0.5	0.3	6.5	5.6	20.7	4.0	20.1	7.0	0.3	1.8	0.5	Singapore
6.7	2.1	2.0	2.5	3.9	9.5[49]	1.5[49]	3.7[49]	5.9[49]	0.2	2.5	1.5	1.2[49]	1.3	1.7	0.6[49]	Slovakia
0.2	1.6	1.7	4.1		9.7	0.3	4.8	6.0		8.2		3.9		1.8	0.4	Slovenia
—	—	—	—	3.0	—	—	1.1	—	...	—		0.9		—	1.7	Solomon Islands
1.6	—	0.5	—	3.0	—	—	1.1	—	...	—		0.9		—	1.7	Somalia
5.8	1.4	2.6	1.5	3.4	9.0	3.4	6.2	6.1		4.6		8.1		1.0	1.7	South Africa
2.8	1.8	3.0	1.7	5.0	3.3	1.2	6.3	5.9	0.3	4.1	1.8	2.9	10.5	0.5	1.0	Spain
1.4	4.2	1.4	1.8	2.9	1.1	0.2	1.3	0.9	0.2	1.1	0.1	1.6	0.3	—	2.1	Sri Lanka
1.3	0.8	1.2	0.1	0.5	0.1	0.7	2.6	0.1		1.2		2.1		—	0.1	Sudan, The
...	0.7	0.6	5.3		...	...	...	...	...	...	...	0.9		0.2	0.5	Suriname
...	...	...	0.3	0.9	...	...	2.0	0.3		0.3		...		—	—	Swaziland
1.2	0.7	1.4	0.7	1.6	4.8	1.3	7.7	11.9	0.8	3.1	5.6	2.7	10.5	2.8	0.3	Sweden
2.0	0.8	2.3	1.7	2.7	1.2	1.9	6.4	12.8		16.9		1.7		5.4	0.4	Switzerland
7.0	1.3	1.0	2.1	6.8	...	1.9	10.9	2.3		2.7		0.4		—	0.5	Syria
8.2	1.1	5.1	4.3		7.8		6.8	4.5		18.7		7.5		0.9	0.8	Taiwan
...	0.1	—	0.3	5.0	...	31.8	0.2	1.0		1.0		...	0.6	...	0.1	Tajikistan
4.0	1.0	1.0	—	5.9	2.0	2.0	3.9	1.0		2.0		3.0		—	—	Tanzania
7.9	1.6	0.3	0.9	3.5	1.7	0.5	1.7	10.3	0.1	1.5	5.6	0.2	5.8	0.2	1.5	Thailand
...	...	...	6.5		0.3	...	2.8	...	...	...	...	...	...	...	...	Togo
—	—	—	4.7		—	—	3.8	—		—		4.1		—	6.4[69]	Tonga
11.0	0.6	0.6	1.9	4.3	7.5	—	2.0	—		1.2	0.5	0.3	0.9	[8]	2.8[8]	Trinidad and Tobago
20.2	0.9	1.3[70]	2.9	6.4	1.6	3.3[71]	[71]	0.4		2.8		—	—	...	...	Tunisia
13.6	1.8	1.3	2.8	4.9	6.5	1.0	3.0	4.3	0.8	2.5	3.2	1.0	8.0	0.4	0.2	Turkey
55.7	[7]	[7]	4.0		0.1		...	...	...	...	...	...	...	...	...	Turkmenistan
—	—	—	—	...	—	—	—	—		—		—		—	—	Tuvalu
—	0.2	—	—	2.5	3.0	—	4.7	0.7	—	1.3	0.5	—	0.1	—	—	Uganda
7.5	1.1	0.2	0.9	5.1	18.5	1.3	4.6	5.7	0.2	2.1[49]		3.4[49]	2.0	0.7[49]	0.4[49]	Ukraine
...	...	...	8.3		8.2		9.2								1.4	United Arab Emirates
2.1	1.2	3.8	1.5	1.7	2.1	1.7	6.7	8.3	1.9	3.7	3.0	5.1	6.3	3.1	1.1	United Kingdom
1.8	1.2	3.2	0.9	1.6	2.2	1.6	6.0	7.9	2.1	3.4	5.7	4.5	6.4	5.8	1.5	United States
3.0	1.2	2.9	1.6	2.3	0.9	0.4	3.6	1.2		2.8		3.5		0.7	0.6	Uruguay
12.4	[7]	[7]	5.4		12.2		13.2								...	Uzbekistan
					12.0[26]		[26]	...	...	...	...	...	...	...	...	Vanuatu
26.3	1.6	1.9	1.8	3.2	4.3	3.9	3.7	1.8	0.1	1.8	0.3	0.1	6.3	0.4	0.4	Venezuela
17.4[75]	[74]	...	1.2	8.7	1.5	0.7	1.8	...	...	...	2.1	...	...	...	...	Vietnam
...	...	...	...	...	...	...	...	...	...	...	...	...	...	...	...	Virgin Islands (U.S.)
...	...	...	...	...	...	...	...	...	...	...	...	...	...	...	...	West Bank
...	...	...	...	...	...	...	...	...	...	...	...	...	...	...	...	Western Sahara
—	2.8	...	10.5		1.5		8.6	3.9		6.3		5.7		...	—	Yemen
...	...	...	5.1		2.0	2.7	...	...	...	...	...	...	...	...	...	Yugoslavia
3.8	1.8	1.3	-0.2	3.3	1.3	0.1	5.4	4.7		0.6				—	0.1	Zambia
[77]	2.3	1.3	0.6	2.5	9.5	0.6	5.1	1.0		2.9	0.3	0.4	4.2	0.1	0.5	Zimbabwe

electric power and employing 10 or more workers and all establishments employing 20 or more workers. [45]Establishments employing three or more persons. [46]Includes refined sugar and molasses. [47]738 includes 37. [48]Establishments employing four or more persons. [49]Sum of available data. [50]Includes recycled waste and scrap. [51]Data withheld for reasons of confidentiality. [52]Includes public utilities. [53]352 Includes 353 + 354. [54]381 includes 372. [55]Processed copra only. [56]Traditional sector handicrafts. [57]All establishments employing 10 or more persons and smaller establishments with an annual output of production of more than U.S.$56,000. [58]Coconut soap includes coconut oil. [59]Excludes Transdniester area and city of Tighina (Bendery). [60]Fish and meat processing. [61]37 includes 33. [62]322 and 323 + 324 includes 355 + 356. [63]Includes petroleum platforms (6.5% of total). [64]341 includes 356. [65]State enterprises only; state enterprises account for about 80% of all industrial output. [66]Excludes shipbuilding and aircraft. [67]381 includes 383. [68]Excludes fish processing. [69]939 includes 332 and 341. [70]Includes synthetic fibres. [71]372 includes 381. [72]Private establishments employing 25 or more persons, and all public establishments. [73]35 includes 36. [74]351 includes 352 and 355. [75]Includes crude petroleum production. [76]Conversion to U.S. dollars based on official exchange rate. [77]351 includes 353 + 354.

Energy

This table provides data about the commercial energy supplies (reserves, production, consumption, and trade) of the various countries of the world, together with data about oil pipeline networks and traffic. Many of the data and concepts used in this table are adapted from the United Nations' *Energy Statistics Yearbook*.

Electricity. Total installed electrical power capacity comprises the sum of the rated power capacities of all main and auxiliary generators in a country. "Total installed capacity" (kW) is multiplied by 8,760 hours per year to yield "Total production capacity" (kW-hr).

Production of electricity comprises the total gross production of electricity by publicly or privately owned enterprises and also that generated by industrial establishments for their own use, but usually excludes consumption by the utility itself. Measured in millions of kilowatt-hours (kW-hr), annual production of electricity ranges generally between 50% and 60% of total production capacity. The data are further analyzed by type of generation: fossil fuels, hydroelectric power, and nuclear fuel.

The great majority of the world's electrical and other energy needs are met by the burning of fossil hydrocarbon solids, liquids, and gases, either for thermal generation of electricity or in internal combustion engines. Many renewable and nontraditional sources of energy are being developed worldwide (wood, biogenic gases and liquids, tidal, wave, and wind power, geothermal and photothermal [solar] energy, and so on), but collectively these sources are still negligible in the world's total energy consumption. For this reason only hydroelectric and nuclear generation are considered here separately with fossil fuels.

Trade in electrical energy refers to the transfer of generated electrical output via an international grid. Total electricity consumption (residential and nonresidential) is equal to total electricity requirements less transformation and distribution losses.

Coal. The term coal, as used in the table, comprises all grades of anthracite, bituminous, subbituminous, and lignite that have acquired or may in the future, by reason of new technology or changed market prices, acquire an economic value. These types of coal may be differentiated according to heat content (density) and content of impurities. Most coal reserve data are based on proven recoverable reserves only, of all grades of coal. Exceptions are footnoted, with proven in-place reserves reported only when recoverable reserves are unknown. Production figures include deposits removed from both surface and underground workings as well as quantities used by the producers themselves or issued to the miners. Wastes recovered from mines or nearby preparation plants are excluded from production figures.

Natural gas. This term refers to any combustible gas (usually chiefly methane) of natural origin from underground sources. The data for production cover, to the extent possible, gas obtained from gas fields,

Energy

country	electricity												coal		
	installed capacity, 1995 ('000 kW)	production, 1995		power source, 1995			trade, 1995		consumption				reserves, latest ('000,000 metric tons)	production 1995 ('000 metric tons)	consumption, 1995 ('000 metric tons)
		capacity ('000,000 kW-hr)	amount ('000,000 kW-hr)	fossil fuel (%)	hydro-power (%)	nuclear fuel (%)	exports ('000,000 kW-hr)	imports ('000,000 kW-hr)	amount, 1995 ('000,000 kW-hr)	per capita, 1995 (kW-hr)	resi-dential 1994 (%)	non-resi-dential 1994 (%)			
Afghanistan	494	4,327	625	33.4	66.6	—	—	120	745	38	...	...	66	5	5
Albania	1,892	16,574	4,414	4.8	95.2	—	74	139	4,479	1,324	...	...	15[1]	130	130
Algeria	6,007	52,621	19,714	99.0	1.0	—	491	218	19,441	692	28.8	71.2	43	22	1,222
American Samoa	33	289	110	100.0	—	—	—	—	110	2,037	...	...	—	—	—
Andorra	...	...	...	...	...	...	...	...	...	...	...	...	—	—	...
Angola	617	5,405	1,870	25.9	74.1	—	—	—	1,870	173	...	...	...	—	—
Antigua and Barbuda	26	228	98	100.0	—	—	—	—	98	1,485	...	...	...	...	...
Argentina	19,610	171,784	67,169	45.8	41.8	12.4	220	2,342	69,291	1,993	41.4	58.6	130	305	1,677
Armenia	3,583	31,387	5,561	60.0	34.5	5.5	...	13	5,574	1,535	...	...	...	...	7
Aruba	90	788	463	100.0	—	—	—	—	463	6,614	...	...	...	...	...
Australia	39,693	347,711	173,404	90.6	9.4	—	—	—	173,404	9,706	...	...	90,940	241,806	102,490
Austria	17,440	152,774	56,587	32.0	68.0	—	9,757	7,287	54,117	6,727	...	...	31	1,297	5,050
Azerbaijan	5,239	45,894	17,000	90.6	9.4	—	250	450	17,200	2,284	...	...	...	...	6
Bahamas, The	401	3,513	1,028	100.0	—	—	—	—	1,028	3,685	...	...	—	—	—
Bahrain	1,080	9,461	4,750	100.0	—	—	—	—	4,750	8,528	...	...	—	—	—
Bangladesh	3,284	28,768	11,689	96.8	3.2	—	—	—	11,689	99	50.7	49.3	1,054[1]	...	...
Barbados	140	1,226	613	100.0	—	—	—	—	613	2,349	32.7	67.3	...	...	...
Belarus	7,390	64,736	24,918	99.9	0.1	—	2,907	10,066	32,077	3,099	...	...	...	—	1,125
Belgium	14,916	130,664	74,428	42.8	1.7	55.5	5,326	9,398	78,500	7,752	...	...	410	637	12,589
Belize	25	219	148	100.0	—	—	—	—	148	695	89.4	10.6	...	—	—
Benin	15	131	6	100.0	—	—	—	263	269	50	78.7	21.3	...	—	—
Bermuda	146	1,279	521	100.0	—	—	—	—	521	8,270	...	...	...	—	—
Bhutan	366	3,206	1,717	0.4	99.6	—	1,475	4	246	139	...	...	...	2	22
Bolivia	805	7,052	3,020	43.0	57	—	3	13	3,030	409	51.6	48.4	1	—	—
Bosnia and Herzegovina	2,407	21,085	2,203	35.5	64.5	—	182	387	2,408	675	...	...	...	1,640	1,640
Botswana	5	5	522[5, 11]	5	5	5	5	825[5]	5	5	41.0	59.0	3,500	5	5
Brazil	59,036	517,155	275,399	6.9	92.2	0.9	—	35,352	310,751	1,954	47.2	52.8	2,845	5,173	16,916
Brunei	473	4,143	1,560	100.0	—	—	—	—	1,560	5,324	56.6	43.4	...	—	—
Bulgaria	12,087	105,882	41,789	53.2	5.5	41.3	2,121	1,961	41,629	4,892	50.4	49.6	2,710	30,830	34,299
Burkina Faso	78	683	220	65.9	34.1	—	—	—	220	21	...	...	...	—	—
Burundi	43	377	120	1.7	98.3	—	—	29	149	25	73.7	26.3	...	...	...
Cambodia	35	307	194	61.9	38.1	—	—	—	194	19	...	...	...	—	—
Cameroon	627	5,493	2,746	3.1	96.9	—	—	—	2,746	208	...	...	...	1	1
Canada	113,340	992,858	537,114	21.2	61.6	17.2	43,321	7,428	501,221	17,047	...	...	8,623	74,942	52,464
Cape Verde	7	61	39	100.0	—	—	—	—	39	101	...	...	...	—	—
Central African Republic	43	377	102	20.6	79.4	—	—	—	102	31	...	...	4	—	—
Chad	29	254	89	100.0	—	—	—	—	89	14	...	...	...	—	—
Chile	5,954	52,157	29,906	38.4	61.6	—	—	—	29,906	2,105	34.5	65.5	1,181	1,078	3,431
China	204,100	1,787,916	1,007,726	79.8	18.9	1.3	4,200	2,000	1,005,526	839	27.3	72.7	114,500	1,360,730	1,327,220
Colombia	10,758	94,240	45,303	24.4	75.6	—	—	316	45,619	1,274	71.9	28.1	4,539	26,020	6,273
Comoros	5	44	16	87.5	12.5	—	—	—	16	26	...	...	...	—	—
Congo, Dem. Rep. of the	3,193	27,971	5,920	0.3	99.7	—	1,080	58	4,898	108	24.6	75.4	88	95	140
Congo, Rep. of the	118	1,034	435	0.7	99.3	—	—	112	547	211	...	...	...	...	...
Costa Rica	1,165	10,205	4,840	15.5	74.8	9.7[7]	151	179	4,868	1,422	77.6	22.4	...	...	...
Côte d'Ivoire	1,173	10,275	1,913	42.2	57.8	—	—	—	1,913	140	33.0	67.0	...	...	...
Croatia	3,633	31,825	8,863	40.6	59.4	—	886	5,382	13,359	2,965	62.6	37.4	39	108	807
Cuba	3,988	34,935	11,189	99.0	1.0	—	—	—	11,189	1,021	52.5	47.5	...	—	157
Cyprus	699	6,123	2,473	100.0	—	—	—	—	2,473	3,319	80.4	19.6	...	—	20
Czech Republic	13,852	121,344	60,847	74.8	2.8	22.4	5,900	3,100	58,047	5,656	...	...	5,142	70,947	61,117
Denmark	11,144	97,621	36,790	96.7	0.1	3.2[7]	4,806	4,012	35,996	6,892	...	...	...	—	10,918
Djibouti	85	745	184	100.0	—	—	—	—	184	306	...	...	...	—	—
Dominica	8	70	37	48.6	51.4	—	—	—	37	521	...	...	...	—	—
Dominican Republic	1,450	12,702	6,506	69.4	30.6	—	—	—	6,506	832	74.3	25.7	...	—	111
Ecuador	2,539	22,242	8,349	19.2	80.8	—	—	—	8,349	729	71.6	28.4	24	—	—
Egypt	16,015	140,291	48,864	77.9	22.1	—	—	—	48,864	787	76.7	23.3	53	—	1,540

petroleum fields, or coal mines that is actually collected and marketed. (Much natural gas in Middle Eastern and North African oil fields is flared [burned] because it is often not economical to capture and market it.) Manufactured gas is generally a by-product of industrial operations such as gasworks, coke ovens, and blast furnaces. It is usually burned at the point of production and rarely enters the marketplace. Production of manufactured gas is, therefore, only reported as a percentage of domestic gas consumption.

Crude petroleum. Crude petroleum is the liquid product obtained from oil wells; the term also includes shale oil, tar sand extract, and field or lease condensate. Production and consumption data in the table refer, so far as possible, to the same year so that the relationship between national production and consumption patterns can be clearly seen; both are given in barrels.

Proven reserves are that oil remaining underground in known fields whose existence has been "proved" by the evaluation of nearby producing wells or by seismic tests in sedimentary strata known to contain crude petroleum, and that is judged recoverable within the limits of present technology and economic conditions (prices). The published proven reserve figures do not necessarily reflect the true reserves of a country, because government authorities or corporations often have political or economic motives for withholding or altering such data.

The estimated exhaustion rate of petroleum reserves is an extrapolated ratio of published proven reserves to the current rate of withdrawal/production. Present world published proven reserves will last about 40 to 45 years at the present rate of withdrawal, but there are large country-to-country variations above or below the average.

Data on petroleum and refined product pipelines are provided because of the great importance to both domestic and international energy markets of this means of bringing these energy sources from their production or transportation points to refineries, intermediate consumption and distribution points, and final consumers. Their traffic may represent a very significant fraction of the total movement of goods within a country. Available data for petroleum pipelines are often incomplete and their basis varies internationally, some countries reporting only international shipments, others reporting domestic shipments of 50 kilometres or more, and so on.

For data in the hydrocarbons portions of the table (coal, natural gas, and petroleum), extensive use has been made of a variety of international sources, such as those of the United Nations, the International Energy Agency (of the Organization for Economic Cooperation and Development), the World Energy Council (in its *World Energy Resources* [triennial]); the U.S. Department of Energy (especially its *International Energy Annual*); and of various industry surveys, such as those published by the *International Petroleum Encyclopedia* and *World Oil*.

natural gas						crude petroleum							country
published proven reserves, 1997 ('000,000,-000 cu m)	production		consumption			reserves, 1997		produc-tion, 1996 ('000,000 barrels)	consump-tion, 1995 ('000,000 barrels)	refining capacity, 1997 ('000 barrels per day)	pipelines (latest)		
	natural gas, 1995 ('000,000 cu m)	manufac-tured gas, 1995 (% of total gas con-sumption)	amount, 1995 ('000,000 cu m)	resi-dential, 1990 (%)	non-resi-dential, 1990 (%)	published proven ('000,000 barrels)	years to exhaust proven reserves				length (km)	traffic ('000,000 metric ton-km)	
99	294	...	168	...	...	...	...	—	—	—	...	...	Afghanistan
2	136	...	12	...	...	165	55	3	3	40	200	...	Albania
3,690	51,817	21.7	24,262	...	...	9,200	31	298	164	465	6,910	...	Algeria
...	...	...	...	...	...	...	...	—	—	—	...	...	American Samoa
...	...	...	...	...	...	...	...	—	—	—	—	—	Andorra
48	561	10.9	168	...	...	5,412	21	258	11	32	179	...	Angola
...	...	...	...	...	...	...	...	—	—	—	—	—	Antigua and Barbuda
619	17,336	10.4	32,954	49.2	50.8	2,386	9	275	163	665	6,990	...	Argentina
...	...	...	1,038	...	...	...	...	—	1	...	—	—	Armenia
...	...	...	...	...	...	...	...	—	2	...	—	—	Aruba
550	29,554	32.0	17,164	...	...	1,800	9	195	205	771	3,000	...	Australia
22	1,475	12.5	8,516	...	...	76	10	8	61	210	725	6,701	Austria
100	3,896	1.1	6,153	...	...	3,300[2]	38[2]	190	74	442	1,760	1,705	Azerbaijan
...	...	—	...	...	...	...	...	—	—	—	—	—	Bahamas, The
147	5,250	5.0	6,768	...	...	210	6	38	91	249	72	...	Bahrain
288	7,365	0.3	7,712	34.2	65.8	5	10	0.5	10	31	—	—	Bangladesh
0.1	17	6.2	26	62.6	37.4	2	5	0.4	2	4	—	—	Barbados
...	262[3]	1.9	12,329	...	...	...	...	37	97	473	2,570	—	Belarus
—	1.4[3]	18.4	15,513	...	...	...	...	—	192[4]	630	1,328	1,168	Belgium
...	...	...	...	...	...	...	...	—	—	—	—	—	Belize
1.2	...	...	...	...	...	29	41	0.7	—	—	—	—	Benin
...	...	...	...	...	...	...	...	—	—	—	—	—	Bermuda
...	...	...	...	...	...	...	...	—	—	—	—	—	Bhutan
128	3,279	16.5	1,597	—	100.0	132	12	11	10	48	2,380	...	Bolivia
...	—	...	275	...	...	...	...	—	15[2]	...	174	—	Bosnia and Herzegovina
...	...	5	...	...	...	—	...	—	5	—	—	—	Botswana
154	2,880	54.6	4,404	—	100.0	4,800	17	285	452	1,256	5,804	...	Brazil
399	9,922	0.7	2,450	...	...	1,350	25	55	2	9	553	...	Brunei
4	11	14.4	5,465	...	...	15	38	0.4	59	300	718	259	Bulgaria
...	...	...	...	...	...	...	...	—	—	—	—	—	Burkina Faso
...	...	...	...	...	...	...	...	—	—	—	—	—	Burundi
...	...	...	...	...	...	...	...	—	—	—	—	—	Cambodia
110	—	100.0	...	...	...	400	12	33	9	42	—	—	Cameroon
1,929	175,897	22.9	79,260	...	...	4,894	7	664	492	1,852	23,564	99,908	Canada
...	...	...	...	...	...	...	...	—	—	—	—	—	Cape Verde
...	...	...	...	...	...	...	...	—	—	—	—	—	Central African Republic
...	...	...	...	...	...	...	...	—	—	—	—	—	Chad
102	1,164	34.7	1,808	23.4	76.6	300	100	3	58	192	1,540	...	Chile
1,171	17,300	52.9	17,917	12.2	87.8	24,000	21	1,141	1,068	2,867	10,800	61,200	China
234	4,437	27.1	4,745	12.8	87.2	2,800	12	227	98	249	4,935	...	Colombia
...	...	...	...	...	...	...	...	—	—	—	—	—	Comoros
1	—	...	—	—	—	187	17	11	0.4	17	390	...	Congo, Dem. Rep. of the
91	2[6]	58.3	3	...	...	1,506	20	74	3	21	25	...	Congo, Rep. of the
...	—	5.5	—	—	—	...	...	—	4	15	176	...	Costa Rica
23	—	60.0	—	—	—	100	14	7	25	64	—	—	Côte d'Ivoire
22	1,869	25.1	2,306	...	...	55	5	12	37	294	690	89	Croatia
3	...	84.7	41	3.4	96.6	100	10	10	40	301	—	—	Cuba
—	—	63.8	—	—	—	...	...	—	6	26	—	—	Cyprus
4	290	24.5	7,964	...	...	6	9	0.7	43	187	—	—	Czech Republic
109	4,936	14.7	3,597	...	...	957	13	75	74	189	688	2,212	Denmark
...	...	...	...	...	...	—	...	—	—	—	—	—	Djibouti
...	...	...	...	...	...	...	...	—	—	—	—	—	Dominica
...	...	11.6	...	...	...	—	...	—	15	50	104	...	Dominican Republic
105	102	33.0	212	—	—	2,115	15	141	53	148	2,158	...	Ecuador
576	12,233	10.1	13,573	5.3	94.7	3,696	11	337	192	546	1,767	...	Egypt

Energy (continued)

country	electricity installed capacity, 1995 ('000 kW)	production, 1995 capacity ('000,000 kW-hr)	production, 1995 amount ('000,000 kW-hr)	power source, 1995 fossil fuel (%)	hydro-power (%)	nuclear fuel (%)	trade, 1995 exports ('000,000 kW-hr)	imports ('000,000 kW-hr)	consumption amount, 1995 ('000,000 kW-hr)	per capita, 1995 (kW-hr)	residential, 1994 (%)	non-residential, 1994 (%)	coal reserves, latest ('000,000 metric tons)	production, 1995 ('000 metric tons)	consumption, 1995 ('000 metric tons)
El Salvador	751	6,579	3,405	23.8	60.1	16.1[7]	65	30	3,370	595	66.2	33.8	...	—	—
Equatorial Guinea	5	44	20	90.0	10.0	—	—	—	20	50	...	...	...	—	—
Eritrea	...	...	...	...	...	...	...	...	...	...	...	...	...	...	...
Estonia	3,287	28,794	7,607	99.9	0.1	—	1,005	245	6,847	4,601	53.4	46.6	...	13,310	15,523
Ethiopia	464	4,065	1,328	7.8	87.0	5.2[7]	—	—	1,328	24	34.9	65.1	11	—	—
Faroe Islands	92	806	175	56.0	43.4	0.6	—	—	175	3,723	...	...	...	—	20
Fiji	200	1,752	544	21.1	78.9	—	—	—	544	694	25.7	74.3	...	—	—
Finland	14,427	126,381	63,885	49.7	20.2	30.1	279	7,253	70,859	13,875	...	...	...	—	6,540
France	107,619[9]	942,672[9]	493,177[9]	8.0[9]	15.4[9]	76.6[9]	72,701[9]	2,860[9]	423,336[9]	7,282[9]	...	...	139	9,045[9]	23,273[9]
French Guiana	165	1,445	450	100.0	—	—	—	—	450	3,061	...	...	...	—	—
French Polynesia	89	780	349	63.9	36.1	—	—	—	349	1,594	...	...	...	—	—
Gabon	310	2,716	940	22.9	77.1	—	—	—	940	874	52.6	47.4	...	—	—
Gambia, The	29	254	74	100.0	—	—	—	—	74	67	...	...	...	—	—
Gaza Strip	...	...	...	...	...	...	...	...	...	...	...	...	...	—	—
Georgia	4,558	39,928	6,800	30.7	69.3	—	180	950	7,570	1,389	...	...	...	40	250
Germany	115,428	1,011,149	534,902	66.6	4.5	28.9	34,911	39,735	539,726	6,615	...	...	67,300	251,615	269,035
Ghana	1,187	10,398	6,159	0.7	99.3	—	228	4	5,935	342	45.0	55.0	...	—	3
Gibraltar	30	263	88	100.0	—	—	—	—	88	3,143	...	...	...	—	—
Greece	8,942	78,332	41,551	90.8	9.1	0.1	593	1,390	42,348	4,051	...	...	3,000	57,662	58,422
Greenland	106	929	257	100.0	—	—	—	—	257	4,431	...	...	183	...	...
Grenada	9	79	71	100.0	—	—	—	—	71	772	88.1	11.9	...	—	—
Guadeloupe	388	3,399	1,014	100.0	—	—	—	—	1,014	2,392	...	...	...	—	—
Guam	302	2,646	825	100.0	—	—	—	—	825	5,500	...	...	...	—	—
Guatemala	766	6,710	3,229	32.8	67.2	—	—	—	3,229	304	66.1	33.9	...	—	...
Guernsey	...	...	227[2]	100.0[2]	...	...	...	...	227[2]	4,997[2]	...	...	...	—	...
Guinea	176	1,542	543	64.8	35.2	—	—	—	543	74	...	...	...	—	—
Guinea-Bissau	11	96	43	100.0	—	—	—	—	43	40	...	...	...	—	—
Guyana	114	999	318	98.4	1.6	—	—	16	334	402	...	...	...	—	—
Haiti	153	1,340	407	59.5	40.5	—	—	—	407	57	56.9	43.1	13[1]	—	—
Honduras	305	2,672	2,742	12.4	87.6	—	...	4	2,746	486	64.3	35.7	21[1]	...	...
Hong Kong	10,096	88,441	27,916	100.0	—	—	1,483	7,546	33,979	5,549	...	...	...	—	9,109
Hungary	7,012	61,425	34,017	58.3	0.5	41.2	776	3,181	36,422	3,604	61.3	38.7	4,461	14,588	15,230
Iceland	1,081	9,470	4,981	0.2	94.0	5.8[7]	—	—	4,981	18,517	...	...	...	—	65
India	93,755	821,294	414,622	81.0	17.3	1.7	130	1,675	416,167	448	52.2	47.8	69,947	287,682	297,527
Indonesia	20,296	177,793	68,804	82.2	15.1	2.7[7]	—	—	68,804	348	37.7	62.3	32,063	36,104	13,824
Iran	26,257	230,011	81,330	90.7	9.3	—	—	—	81,330	1,190	...	...	193	1,000	1,320
Iraq	9,500	83,220	29,000	98.0	2.0	—	—	—	29,000	1,443	...	...	—	—	—
Ireland	4,399	38,535	17,878	94.4	5.4	0.2[7]	35	20	17,863	5,038	...	...	14	1	2,441
Isle of Man	...	...	...	...	...	...	...	...	...	...	...	...	...	...	...
Israel	4,480	39,245	29,100	99.9	0.1	—	310	—	28,790	5,211	70.3	29.7	...	—	6,118
Italy	65,821[10]	576,592[10]	241,111[10]	81.2[10]	17.4[10]	1.4[7,10]	1,235[10]	38,662[10]	278,538[10]	4,867[10]	...	...	34	380[10]	17,850[10]
Jamaica	1,182	10,354	5,829	97.9	2.1	—	—	—	5,829	2,362	56.3	43.7	...	—	55
Japan	226,996	1,988,485	989,965	61.0	9.2	29.8	—	—	989,965	7,915	...	...	821	6,277	129,281
Jersey	...	...	440[2]	...	...	...	...	...	440[2]	6,579[2]	...	...	...	...	...
Jordan	1,126	9,864	5,616	99.7	0.3	—	—	—	5,616	1,045	64.9	35.1	...	...	...
Kazakstan	18,958	166,072	66,659	87.5	12.5	—	12,702	19,539	73,496	4,370	...	...	25,000	87,011	75,213
Kenya	809	7,087	3,747	8.9	83.3	7.8[7]	—	172	3,919	144	39.0	61.0	...	—	94
Kiribati	2	18	7	100.0	—	—	—	—	7	90	...	...	...	—	—
Korea, North	9,500	83,220	36,000	36.1	63.9	—	—	—	36,000	1,629	...	...	600	97,000	98,900
Korea, South	35,355	309,710	205,102	64.6	2.7	32.7	—	—	205,102	4,567	37.0	63.0	183	5,720	47,043
Kuwait	6,988	61,215	24,126	100.0	—	—	—	—	24,126	14,267	93.2	6.8	...	—	—
Kyrgyzstan	3,694	32,359	12,349	10.0	90.0	—	8,355	6,987	10,981	2,462	...	...	812	743	1,071
Laos	256	2,243	908	4.7	95.3	—	640	27	295	60	...	...	—	1	1
Latvia	2,066	18,098	3,979	26.2	73.8	—	391	2,647	6,235	2,459	58.9	41.1	—	—	252
Lebanon	1,220	10,687	5,573	86.9	13.1	—	—	—	5,573	1,852	...	...	...	—	185
Lesotho	5	5	5	5	5	5	5	5	5	5	...	...	...	5	5
Liberia	332	2,908	486	63.4	36.6	—	—	—	486	229	...	...	...	...	...
Libya	4,600	40,296	18,000	100.0	—	—	—	—	18,000	3,329	...	...	—	—	5
Liechtenstein	11	11	11	11	11	11	11	11	11	11	...	...	...	—	11
Lithuania	6,335	55,495	13,898	9.5	5.4	85.1	7,948	5,270	11,220	3,003	...	...	...	—	372
Luxembourg	1,257	11,011	1,240	33.3	66.7	—	743	5,746	6,243	15,339	...	...	...	—	227
Macau	312	2,733	1,272	100.0	—	—	3	180	1,449	3,370	82.8	17.2	...	—	—
Macedonia	1,494	13,087	6,114	86.9	13.1	—	—	—	6,114	2,836	...	...	...	7,249	7,435
Madagascar	220	1,927	611	42.2	57.8	—	—	—	611	41	32.2	67.8	1,075[1]	—	14
Malawi	185	1,621	803	2.4	97.6	—	—	—	803	83	65.2	34.8	2	—	17
Malaysia	10,600	92,856	46,632	83.9	16.1	—	25	2	46,609	2,314	45.3	54.7	4	112	2,373
Maldives	17	149	57	100.0	—	—	—	—	57	224	...	...	—	—	—
Mali	87	762	290	22.4	77.6	—	—	—	290	27	...	...	—	—	—
Malta	250	2,190	1,512	100.0	—	—	—	—	1,512	4,120	...	...	—	—	300
Marshall Islands	...	...	...	...	...	...	...	...	...	...	...	...	...	...	...
Martinique	115	1,007	905	100.0	—	—	—	—	905	2,382	...	...	...	...	...
Mauritania	105	920	152	81.6	18.4	—	—	—	152	67	...	...	...	...	6
Mauritius	364	3,189	1,120	87.9	12.1	—	—	—	1,120	1,003	65.2	34.8	...	—	66
Mayotte	11[3]	96[3]	27[3]	100.0[3]	—	—	—	—	32	276	...	...	...	...	...
Mexico	44,257	387,691	150,820	72.1	19.4	8.5[7]	1,862	1,081	150,039	1,646	29.7	70.3	1,211	8,886	10,942
Micronesia	...	...	...	...	...	...	...	...	...	...	...	...	...	—	...
Moldova	2,635	23,083	8,392	96.7	3.3	—	5,100	5,600	8,892	2,004	...	...	...	—	1,315
Monaco	9	9	9	9	9	9	9	9	9	9	...	...	...	9	9
Mongolia	901	7,893	2,629	100.0	—	—	—	381	3,010	1,222	...	...	24,000[1]	4,871	4,701
Morocco	3,795	33,244	11,724	94.8	5.2	—	—	1,000	12,724	480	51.0	49.0	45	649	2,336
Mozambique	2,383	20,875	563	91.1	8.9	—	—	601	1,164	67	...	...	240	38	56
Myanmar (Burma)	1,344	11,773	3,780	59.6	40.4	—	—	—	3,780	84	59.6	40.4	2.3	79	80
Namibia	5	5	5	5	5	5	5	5	5	5	...	...	...	5	5
Nauru	10	88	32	100.0	—	—	—	—	32	2,909	...	...	...	...	...
Nepal	292	2,558	1,007	3.3	96.7	—	42	110	1,075	50	58.5	41.5	...	—	118

natural gas — published proven reserves, 1997 ('000,000,000 cu m)	production — natural gas, 1995 ('000,000 cu m)	production — manufactured gas, 1995 (% of total gas consumption)	consumption — amount, 1995 ('000,000 cu m)	consumption — residential, 1990 (%)	consumption — non-residential, 1990 (%)	crude petroleum reserves, 1997 — published proven ('000,000 barrels)	years to exhaust proven reserves	production, 1996 ('000,000 barrels)	consumption, 1995 ('000,000 barrels)	refining capacity, 1997 ('000 barrels per day)	pipelines length (km)	pipelines traffic ('000,000 metric ton-km)	country
—	—	26.3	—	—	—	...	...	—	5	21	—	—	El Salvador
37	...	...	...	...	...	12	4	3	0.01	—	—	—	Equatorial Guinea
...	...	...	...	...	...	...	...	...	...	18	—	—	Eritrea
...	...	4.1[8]	625	...	...	—	—	—	...	...	—	—	Estonia
25	—	100.0	—	...	...	0.4	...	—	6	—	—	—	Ethiopia
...	...	...	...	—	—	...	...	—	—	—	—	—	Faroe Islands
...	...	...	...	...	...	...	...	—	—	—	—	—	Fiji
...	—	27.6	3,551	...	...	...	...	—	63	200	—	—	Finland
19	3,395	19.3[9]	36,800[9]	...	...	117	7	16	585[9]	1,786	7,546	22,501	France
...	...	...	...	...	...	...	...	...	...	...	—	—	French Guiana
...	...	...	...	...	...	...	...	—	—	—	—	—	French Polynesia
14	102	9.7[3]	825	19.7	80.3	1,340	10	135	7	17	284	...	Gabon
...	...	...	...	...	...	...	...	—	—	—	—	—	Gambia, The
...	...	...	...	...	...	...	...	—	—	—	—	—	Gaza Strip
...	45[6]	...	3,080	...	...	...	...	3.0	3	106	670	...	Georgia
329	18,998	16.3	101,053	...	...	385	18	21	745	2,108	7,590	13,872	Germany
6	—	94.8	—	—	—	17	9	2	7	27	—	—	Ghana
...	...	...	...	...	...	...	...	—	—	—	—	—	Gibraltar
8	119	102.3	51	...	...	12	4	3	107	396	573	...	Greece
...	...	...	...	...	...	...	...	—	—	—	—	—	Greenland
...	...	...	...	...	...	...	...	—	—	—	—	—	Grenada
...	...	...	...	...	...	...	...	—	—	—	—	—	Guadeloupe
...	...	...	...	...	...	...	...	—	—	—	—	—	Guam
0.3	8	6.8	11	...	...	200	40	5	8	20	275	...	Guatemala
...	...	...	...	...	...	...	...	—	—	—	—	—	Guernsey
24[2]	...	...	...	...	...	...	...	—	—	—	—	—	Guinea
...	...	...	...	...	...	...	...	—	—	—	—	—	Guinea-Bissau
...	...	...	...	...	...	...	...	—	—	—	—	—	Guyana
...	...	...	...	...	...	...	...	—	—	—	—	—	Haiti
—	—	30.7[2]	—	—	—	...	...	—	3[2]	14	—	—	Honduras
...	—	79.4	—	—	—	...	...	—	—	—	—	—	Hong Kong
94	5,479	7.8	10,590	...	...	120	11	11	51	232	1,204	2,607	Hungary
...	...	...	...	...	...	...	...	—	—	—	—	—	Iceland
685	19,595	14.6	19,073	53.7	46.3	4,333	18	235	477	1,086	5,692	...	India
2,046	61,864	14.9	26,322	—	100.0	4,980	9	553	308	805	2,961	...	Indonesia
21,000	31,857	9.6	42,687	—	...	93,000	69	1,341	348	1,242	9,800	...	Iran
3,341	3,426	44.5	3,143	...	...	112,000	511	219	208	348	5,075	—	Iraq
11	2,500	3.0	2,629	...	...	—	—	—	16	65	—	—	Ireland
—	—	—	...	...	...	...	...	—	—	—	—	—	Isle of Man
0.3	23	110.6	22	—	100.0	4	100	0.04	89	220	998	...	Israel
297	20,499	13.3[10]	54,540[10]	...	...	685	19	37	539[10]	2,262	3,851	11,348	Italy
—	—	30.0	—	—	—	...	...	—	7	36	10	—	Jamaica
30	2,192	41.6	58,995	...	...	50	10	5	1,610	4,989	406	...	Japan
...	...	...	...	...	...	...	...	—	—	—	—	—	Jersey
6	294	73.2	—	...	...	0.3	8	0.04	23	100	209	...	Jordan
1,800	5,500	...	12,476	...	...	...	...	169	69	427	4,350	22,300	Kazakhstan
—	—	103.2	—	...	...	...	...	—	12	86	483	...	Kenya
...	...	...	...	...	...	...	...	—	—	—	—	—	Kiribati
—	...	33.9	...	...	...	...	...	—	16	71	37	...	Korea, North
—	...	...	9,884	...	...	...	...	—	632	2,211	455	...	Korea, South
1,498	5,975	44.5	9,074	25.0	75.0	96,500	128	752	289	824	917	...	Kuwait
...	34[3]	...	768	...	...	...	...	0.7	0.5	10	—	—	Kyrgyzstan
...	...	...	—	...	...	...	...	—	...	...	136	...	Laos
...	—	...	1,084	...	...	...	...	—	...	...	1,530	...	Latvia
—	...	2.7[8]	...	...	...	...	...	—	3[8]	38	72	...	Lebanon
...	—	5	...	...	...	...	...	—	5	—	—	—	Lesotho
—	—	...	...	...	...	...	...	—	—	15	—	—	Liberia
1,311	6,298	19.5	4,822	...	...	29,500	58	512	113	348	4,826	...	Libya
...	...	[11]	[11]	...	...	...	...	—	[11]	—	—	—	Liechtenstein
...	—	8.4	2,192	...	...	...	...	1.2	23	240	105	...	Lithuania
...	—	31.1	650	...	...	...	...	—	4	—	48	...	Luxembourg
...	...	...	...	...	...	...	...	—	—	—	—	—	Macau
...	—	5.6	269[8]	...	...	...	...	—	0.9	51	—	—	Macedonia
2	—	33.6	—	...	...	...	...	—	1.4	15	—	—	Madagascar
...	—	—	...	...	...	...	...	—	—	—	—	—	Malawi
2,271	26,193	9.4	15,866	6.6	93.4	4,000	17	237	116	330	1,307	...	Malaysia
...	...	...	...	...	...	...	...	—	—	—	—	—	Maldives
...	...	...	...	...	...	...	...	—	—	—	—	—	Mali
...	...	—	...	...	...	...	...	—	—	—	—	—	Malta
...	...	...	...	...	...	...	...	—	—	—	—	—	Marshall Islands
—	—	153.9	...	...	...	...	...	—	6	16	—	—	Martinique
...	...	88.1	...	...	...	...	...	—	7	—	—	—	Mauritania
...	...	...	...	...	...	...	...	—	—	—	—	—	Mauritius
...	...	...	...	...	...	...	...	—	—	—	—	—	Mayotte
1,916	38,454	26.1	28,399	...	...	48,796	47	1,042	475	1,520	38,350	...	Mexico
...	...	...	...	...	...	...	...	—	—	—	—	—	Micronesia
...	—	...	2,517	...	...	...	...	—	...	...	—	—	Moldova
...	...	[9]	[9]	...	...	...	...	—	[9]	—	—	—	Monaco
...	...	...	...	...	...	...	...	—	—	—	—	—	Mongolia
1.1	17	25.3	25	—	100.0	1.2	30	0.04	47	156	362	...	Morocco
57	...	...	...	...	...	...	...	—	—	—	595	...	Mozambique
311	1,430	0.8	1,453	...	...	50	10	5	7	32	1,343	...	Myanmar (Burma)
85	—	5	...	...	...	...	...	—	5	—	—	—	Namibia
...	...	...	...	...	...	...	...	—	—	—	—	—	Nauru
...	—	—	...	—	—	...	...	—	—	—	—	—	Nepal

Energy (continued)

country	electricity installed capacity, 1995 ('000 kW)	production, 1995 capacity ('000,000 kW-hr)	amount ('000,000 kW-hr)	power source, 1995 fossil fuel (%)	hydro-power (%)	nuclear fuel (%)	trade, 1995 exports ('000,000 kW-hr)	imports ('000,000 kW-hr)	consumption amount, 1995 ('000,000 kW-hr)	per capita, 1995 (kW-hr)	resi-dential, 1994 (%)	non-resi-dential, 1994 (%)	coal reserves, latest ('000,000 metric tons)	pro-duction, 1995 ('000 metric tons)	con-sump-tion, 1995 ('000 metric tons)
Netherlands, The	19,012	166,545	80,832	94.5	0.1	5.4	586	11,979	92,225	5,957	...	...	497	—	14,689
Netherlands Antilles	220	1,927	1,470	100.0	—	—	—	—	1,470	7,577	...	...	...	...	...
New Caledonia	253	2,216	1,175	70.6	29.4	—	—	—	1,175	6,492	...	...	2	—	165
New Zealand	7,520	65,875	34,375	14.6	79.3	6.1[7]	—	—	34,375	9,653	...	...	117	3,517	2,667
Nicaragua	457	4,003	1,713	50.4	19.3	30.3[7]	87	73	1,699	412	79.3	20.7	...	...	...
Niger	63	552	175	100.0	—	—	—	195	370	40	49.2	50.8	70	173	173
Nigeria	5,881	51,518	14,810	59.5	40.5	—	...	—	14,810	133	...	...	190	50	50
Northern Mariana Islands	114[2]	999[2]	...	...	...	...	...	...	...	...	...	...	...	...	...
Norway	27,674	242,424	123,136	0.6	99.4	—	8,563	2,201	116,774	26,956	...	...	4	292	1,019
Oman	1,744	15,277	8,258	100.0	—	—	—	—	8,258	3,742	...	...	...	...	...
Pakistan	14,025	122,859	60,155	61.2	38.0	0.8	—	—	60,155	441	66.1	33.9	734	3,043	4,139
Palau	62	543	208	85.6	14.4	—	—	—	208	856	...	...	—	—	—
Panama	957	8,383	3,519	31.3	68.3	—	122	209	3,606	1,371	83.2	16.8	...	—	54
Papua New Guinea	490	4,292	1,790	72.3	27.7	—	—	—	1,790	416	28.0	72.0	...	...	1
Paraguay	6,533	57,229	41,630	0.1	99.9	—	37,939	1	3,692	765	68.9	31.1	...	...	...
Peru	3,831	33,560	16,759	17.8	82.2	—	—	—	16,759	712	...	...	1,060	143	473
Philippines	7,722	67,645	33,426	62.7	19.5	17.8[7]	—	—	33,426	493	56.9	43.1	263	1,321	2,566
Poland	29,465	258,113	139,006	97.2	2.8	—	7,157	4,356	136,205	3,533	38.9	61.1	42,100	200,713	168,963
Portugal	9,378	82,151	33,263	74.4	25.4	0.2	1,741	2,655	34,177	3,482	...	...	36	147[3]	5,801
Puerto Rico	4,575	40,077	19,033	98.2	1.8	—	—	—	19,033	5,143	...	...	...	—	...
Qatar	1,365	11,957	5,738	100.0	—	—	—	—	5,738	10,471	83.7	16.3	...	...	...
Réunion	299	2,619	1,128	55.5	44.5	—	—	—	1,128	1,722	...	...	...	...	...
Romania	22,276	195,138	59,266	71.8	28.2	—	456	755	59,565	2,621	25.7	74.3	3,118	41,121	45,700
Russia	210,857	1,847,101	860,026	67.8	20.6	11.6	37,982	18,377	840,421	5,661	37.7	62.3	241,000[12]	326,828	321,455
Rwanda	34	298	164	2.4	97.6	—	3	14	175	34	...	...	...	...	...
St. Kitts and Nevis	16	140	86	100.0	—	—	—	—	86	2,098	...	...	...	...	...
St. Lucia	22	193	113	100.0	—	—	—	—	113	796	...	...	...	...	...
St. Vincent and the Grenadines	14	123	65	67.7	32.3	—	—	—	65	580	...	...	...	...	...
Samoa	19	166	65	61.5	38.5	—	—	—	65	394	...	...	...	...	...
San Marino	10	10	10	10	10	10	10	10	10	10	...	...	...	10	10
São Tomé and Príncipe	6	53	15	46.7	53.3	—	—	—	15	113	...	...	—	—	—
Saudi Arabia	20,934	183,382	99,833	100.0	—	—	—	—	99,833	5,469	...	...	—	—	—
Senegal	231	2,024	774	100.0	—	—	—	—	774	93	...	...	—	—	—
Seychelles	28	245	128	100.0	—	—	—	—	128	1,753	32.0	68.0	—	—	—
Sierra Leone	126	1,104	241	100.0	—	—	—	—	241	57	...	...	...	...	...
Singapore	4,513	39,534	22,057	100.0	—	—	—	—	22,057	6,630	...	...	...	—	1
Slovakia	7,115	62,327	25,240	32.1	18.4	49.5	2,105	1,280	24,415	4,574	...	...	228	2,310	11,308
Slovenia	2,518	22,058	12,648	36.6	25.6	37.8	2,392	740	10,996	5,712	...	...	...	4,884	5,239
Solomon Islands	12	105	32	100.0	—	—	—	—	32	85	...	...	—	—	—
Somalia	70	613	272	100.0	—	—	—	—	272	29	...	...	—	—	—
South Africa	35,897[5]	314,458[5]	190,515[5]	94.5[5]	0.4[5]	5.1[5]	1,600[5]	60	188,975[5]	3,992[5]	49.1[5]	50.9[5]	55,333	197,001[5]	143,001[5]
Spain	45,764	400,893	166,380	51.9	14.8	33.3	3,147	7,633	170,866	4,312	...	...	1,450	28,403	42,640
Sri Lanka	1,555	13,622	4,800	6.0	94.0	—	—	—	4,800	268	60.2	39.8	...	—	1[2]
Sudan, The	500	4,380	1,331	29.0	71.0	—	—	—	1,331	50	...	...	...	—	...
Suriname	425	3,723	1,614	20.8	79.2	—	—	—	1,614	3,780	...	...	...	—	...
Swaziland	5	5	5	5	5	5	5	5	5	5	...	...	1,115	5	5
Sweden	33,623	294,537	147,035	6.8	45.6	47.6	9,421	7,720	145,334	16,538	...	...	1	...	3,495
Switzerland	16,657[11]	145,915[11]	63,080[11]	3.5[11]	57.0[11]	39.5[11]	26,690[11]	19,419[11]	55,809[11]	7,754[11]	...	...	—	—	127[11]
Syria	4,330	37,931	15,300	83.6	16.4	—	—	—	15,300	1,077	...	...	—	—	—
Taiwan	21,898	191,826	117,859	63.7	7.5	28.8	—	—	105,368	4,946	...	...	99	235	...
Tajikistan	4,443	38,921	14,760	3.9	96.1	—	5,600	4,800	13,960	2,395	...	...	...	30	30
Tanzania	543	4,757	1,738	13.1	86.9	—	—	—	1,738	58	...	...	200	5	5
Thailand	17,544	153,685	83,660	92.0	8.0	—	79	699	84,280	1,447	53.7	46.3	999	18,421	20,825
Togo	34	298	93	93.5	6.5	—	—	315	408	100	...	...	—	—	—
Tonga	7	61	29	100.0	—	—	—	—	29	296	...	...	—	—	—
Trinidad and Tobago	1,150	10,074	4,229	100.0	—	—	—	—	4,229	3,286	36.7	63.3	—	—	—
Tunisia	1,736	15,207	7,589	99.5	0.5	—	140	171	7,620	848	15.6	84.4	—	—	1
Turkey	20,953	183,548	81,734	56.4	43.5	0.1[7]	696	—	81,038	1,332	...	...	7,148	55,073	60,891
Turkmenistan	3,950	34,602	9,800	99.9	0.1	—	3,000	980	7,780	1,909	...	...	...	...	...
Tuvalu	...	...	...	...	...	...	...	...	...	...	...	...	...	...	...
Uganda	162	1,419	792	0.9	99.1	—	115	—	677	34	...	...	...	—	—
Ukraine	54,243	475,169	194,000	66.1	6.4	27.5	18,300	15,500	191,200	3,694	...	...	...	83,600	97,200
United Arab Emirates	5,390	47,216	19,070	100.0	—	—	—	—	19,070	8,629	...	...	...	—	—
United Kingdom	70,213	615,066	334,454	71.3	2.0	26.7	23	16,336	350,767	6,016	...	...	2,500	52,630	76,196
United States	764,876	6,700,314	3,345,314	70.1	9.2	20.7	8,275	45,323	3,382,362	12,663	...	...	240,558	937,099	853,332
Uruguay	2,052	17,976	7,650	2.0	98.0	—	302	188	7,536	2,365	67.2	32.8	...	—	...
Uzbekistan	11,422	100,057	47,200	85.0	15.0	—	14,900	14,500	46,800	2,056	...	...	...	3,100	3,475
Vanuatu	11	96	30	100.0	—	—	—	—	30	178	...	...	—	—	—
Venezuela	19,975	174,981	74,886	25.7	74.3	—	134	—	74,752	3,422	45.7	54.3	417	4,640	346
Vietnam	4,500	39,420	14,867	12.9	83.0	4.1[7]	—	—	14,867	201	...	...	150	7,452	4,252
Virgin Islands (U.S.)	323	2,829	1,071	100.0	—	—	—	—	1,071	10,200	...	...	—	—	250
West Bank	...	...	...	...	...	...	...	...	...	...	...	...	...	...	...
Western Sahara	56	491	87	100.0	—	—	—	—	87	351	...	...	...	...	...
Yemen	810	7,096	1,980	100.0	—	—	—	—	1,980	132	...	...	—	—	—
Yugoslavia	11,779	103,184	37,176	69.8	30.2	—	—	—	37,176	3,627	...	...	16,570[13]	40,010	40,070
Zambia	2,436	21,339	7,790	0.5	99.5	—	1,500	20	6,310	781	31.7	68.3	55	360	355
Zimbabwe	2,148	18,816	8,275	71.3	28.7	—	...	2,075	10,350	925	52.8	47.2	734	2,120	2,190

natural gas						crude petroleum							country
published proven reserves, 1997 ('000,000,-000 cu m)	production		consumption			reserves, 1997		produc-tion, 1996 ('000,000 barrels)	consump-tion, 1995 ('000,000 barrels)	refining capacity, 1997 ('000 barrels per day)	pipelines (latest)		
	natural gas, 1995 ('000,000 cu m)	manufac-tured gas, 1995 (% of total gas con-sumption)	amount, 1995 ('000,000 cu m)	resi-dential, 1990 (%)	non-resi-dential, 1990 (%)	published proven ('000,000 barrels)	years to exhaust proven reserves				length (km)	traffic ('000,000 metric ton-km)	
1,815	78,778	18.4	50,100	...	...	88	4	22	385	1,187	1,383	5,503	Netherlands, The
—		117.3		...	...	...	...	—	99	525	—	—	Netherlands Antilles
...	...		...	...	...	...	...	—			—	—	New Caledonia
68	4,763	6.8	4,209	...	...	135	10	13	35	91	160	...	New Zealand
—		70.9		...	—	...	...	—	5	17	56	...	Nicaragua
...			—	—		...	...	—			—	—	Niger
2,965	4,131	1.4	4,460	—	100.0	15,521	21	735	65	433	5,042	...	Nigeria
...	...		...	...	...	—		...	...				Northern Mariana Islands
1,352	27,663	36.8	3,865	...	...	11,234	10	1,126	93	307	53	11,019	Norway
850	4,361	3.8	2,355	...	...	5,138	16	322	26	85	1,300	...	Oman
623	17,840	1.0	16,839	41.5	58.5	208	10	20	47	137	1,135	...	Pakistan
—	—		—	...	...	...	...	—					Palau
—	—	24.7	60	—	—	...	...	—	9	60	130	...	Panama
42	99	...	82	—	—	275	7	39	0.6	—	—		Papua New Guinea
—		1.5	...	...	...	...	...	—	2	8	—	—	Paraguay
200	1,303	40.5	213	61.4	38.6	808	18	44	62	182	800	...	Peru
109	—	53.6		—	—	213	533	0.4	114	323	357	...	Philippines
149	4,593	27.4	13,206	...	...	40	20	2	100	352	2,346	11,932	Poland
—	—	57.1	...	...	...	...	...	—	94	304	80	...	Portugal
—		146.7	...	...	...	...	...	—	45	134	—	—	Puerto Rico
7,079	13,499	11.4	13,599	—	100.0	3,700	21	175	22	58	235	...	Qatar
...				...	...	...	...	—			—	—	Réunion
396	21,300	10.9	20,299	...	...	1,606	32	50	116	559	4,229	2,558	Romania
48,334	582,988	7.4	394,964	...	...	155,146	71	2,183	1,367	6,733	63,000	1,899,000	Russia
57	...	—	0.2	...	...	...	...	—			—	—	Rwanda
...	...	...	...	...	...	...	...	—	—	—	—	—	St. Kitts and Nevis
...	...	...	...	...	...	...	...	—	—	—	—	—	St. Lucia
...	...	...	...	...	...	...	...	—	—	—	—	—	St. Vincent and the Grenadines
...	...	...	...	...	...	...	...	...	...	...	—	—	Samoa
...		[10]	[10]	...	...	...	...	—	[10]		—	—	San Marino
...	...	...	...	...	...	...	...	—			—	—	São Tomé and Príncipe
5,355	37,718	49.1	40,339	...	...	261,500	88	3,039	589	1,651	6,550	...	Saudi Arabia
...		13.7	...	...	...	...	...	—	6	17	—	—	Senegal
...	...		...	...	...	...	...	—			—	—	Seychelles
—	...		...	...	...	...	...	—	2	10	—	—	Sierra Leone
...	...	344.4		—	—	...	...	—	425	1,157	—	—	Singapore
15	241[3]	14.2	5,641	...	...	9	23	0.4	34	115	...	...	Slovakia
4	11[3]	...	800	...	...	7	700	0.01	3	12	290	128	Slovenia
...	—		...	...	...	...	...	—	...	10	—	—	Solomon Islands
6	...	...	...	...	...	...	...	—	...	10	15	...	Somalia
25	—	56.5[5]	1,845	...	...	27	7	4	136[5]	414	2,679	...	South Africa
17	178	32.7	8,879	...	...	30	5	6	415	1,296	2,059	5,266	Spain
—	—	45.4	...	...	...	...	...	—	14	48	62	...	Sri Lanka
85	—	58.3	...	...	...	300	600	0.5	8	22	815	...	Sudan, The
—	...	...	...	...	...	74	25	3	1.4	—	—	—	Suriname
—	—	[5]	...	...	...	...	...	—	[5]		—	—	Swaziland
—	—	35.2	811	...	...	...	...	—	124	427	—	—	Sweden
—	—	13.1[11]	2,681[11]	...	...	...	...	...	33[11]	132	314	1,265	Switzerland
235	4,412	12.8	2,306	...	...	2,500	11	220	86	246	1,819	...	Syria
76	841	...		...	...	4	10	0.4	...	770	615	...	Taiwan
...	34[3]	...	1,923	...	...	...	...	0.7	1	...	—	—	Tajikistan
21	—	100.0		...	...	...	...	...	4	16	982	...	Tanzania
202	10,477	17.6	9,438	—	100.0	295	13	22	165	558	67	...	Thailand
...	...	...	...	...	...	...	...	...	...	—	—	—	Togo
...						...	...	...			—	—	Tonga
350	6,071	8.0	6,172	1.8	98.2	551	12	47	38	245	1,051	...	Trinidad and Tobago
68	337	6.5	1,685	9.1	90.9	308	10	32	14	34	883	...	Tunisia
9	201	26.1	6,520	...	...	260	10	25	186	683	4,059	2,994	Turkey
2,900	30,100	...	8,265	...	...	3,000	94	32	29	237	250	...	Turkmenistan
...	...		...	...	...	...	...	...	...	—	—	—	Tuvalu
...	...	...	...	...	...	...	...	—			—	—	Uganda
1,100	16,900	0.6	89,647	...	...	...	...	25	125	1,246	3,930	38,402	Ukraine
5,686	25,429	22.9	22,639	...	...	93,800	116	809	74	213	830	...	United Arab Emirates
700	71,144	13.1	82,694	...	...	4,517	5	961	612	1,941	3,926	10,388	United Kingdom
4,676	559,261	14.7	616,183	...	...	22,351	9	2,364	5,171	15,459	276,000	843,586	United States
—	—	55.9		...	...	...	...	—	10	40	—	—	Uruguay
1,900	45,300	...	34,976	...	...	...	...	63	51	175	290	200	Uzbekistan
...	...	...	...	...	...	...	...	—	...	—	—	—	Vanuatu
4,010	25,406	13.9	36,677	9.1	90.9	64,878	60	1,079	379	1,177	6,850	...	Venezuela
142	697	...	5	...	...	600	10	62	0.3	—	150	...	Vietnam
—	—	112.0	...	...	...	...	...	...	118	545	—	—	Virgin Islands (U.S.)
...	...		...	...	...	...	...	...			—	—	West Bank
...	...		...	...	...	...	...	...			—	—	Western Sahara
479	...	100.0		...	...	4,000	33	123	35	120	676	...	Yemen
45	765	1.0	1,855	...	...	78	11	7	10	167	545	...	Yugoslavia
—	—	100.0	—	—	—	...	...	...	4	25	1,724	...	Zambia
...	—	94.3	...	...	...	...	...	...	...	—	212	...	Zimbabwe

[1] Estimated reserves in place. [2] 1992. [3] 1994. [4] Belgium includes Luxembourg. [5] South Africa includes Botswana, Lesotho, Namibia, and Swaziland. [6] 1991. [7] Geothermally generated electricity. [8] 1993. [9] France includes Monaco. [10] Italy includes San Marino. [11] Switzerland includes Liechtenstein. [12] Data refer to former U.S.S.R. [13] Data refer to Yugoslavia as constituted prior to 1991.

Transportation

This table presents data on the transportation infrastructure of the various countries and dependencies of the world and on their commercial passenger and cargo traffic. Most states have roads and airports, with services corresponding to the prevailing level of economic development. A number of states, however, lack railroads or inland waterways because of either geographic constraints or lack of development capital and technical expertise. Pipelines, one of the oldest means of bulk transport if aqueducts are considered, are today among the most narrowly developed transportation modes worldwide for shipment of bulk materials. Because the principal contemporary application of pipeline technology is to facilitate the shipment of hydrocarbon liquids and gases, coverage of pipelines will be found in the "Energy" table. It is, however, also true that pipelines now find increasing application for slurries of coal or other raw materials.

While the United Nations' *Statistical Yearbook* and *Monthly Bulletin of Statistics* provide much data on infrastructure and traffic and have established basic definitions and classifications for transportation statistics, the number of countries covered is limited. Several commercial publications maintain substantial databases and publishing programs for their particular areas of interest: highway and vehicle statistics are provided by the International Road Federation's annual *World Road Statistics;* the International Union of Railway's *International Railway Statistics* and Jane's *World Railways* provide similar data for railways; Lloyd's *Register of Shipping Statistical Tables* summarizes the world's merchant marine; the

Official Airline Guide, the International Civil Aviation Organization's *Digest of Statistics: Commercial Air Carriers,* and the International Air Transport Association's *World Air Transport Statistics* have also been used to supplement and update data collected by the UN. Because several of these agencies are commercially or insurance-oriented, their data tend to be more complete, accurate, and timely than those of intergovernmental organizations, which depend on periodic responses to questionnaires or publication of results in official sources. All of these international sources have been extensively supplemented by national statistical sources to provide additional data. Such diversity of sources, however, imposes limitations on the comparability of the statistics from country to country because the basis and completeness of data collection and the frequency and timeliness of analysis and publication may vary greatly. Data shown in italic are from 1992 or earlier.

The categories adopted in the table also have special problems of comparability. Total road length is subject to wide international variation of interpretation, as "roads" can mean anything from mere tracks to highly developed highways. Each country also has individual classifications that differ according to climate, availability of road-building materials, traffic patterns, administrative responsibility, and so on. "Paved roads," by contrast, is a much more tightly definable category, but the proportion of paved to total roads may be distorted by the less comparable total road statistics. Automobile and truck and bus fleet statistics, which are usually

Transportation

country	roads and motor vehicles (latest)								railroads (latest)					
	roads			motor vehicles			cargo		track length		traffic			
	length		paved (percent)	automobiles	trucks and buses	persons per vehicle	short ton-mi ('000,000)	metric ton-km ('000,000)	mi	km	passengers		cargo	
	mi	km									passenger-mi ('000,000)	passenger-km ('000,000)	short ton-mi ('000,000)	metric ton-km ('000,000)
Afghanistan	13,000	21,000	13	31,000	34,000	332	*1,993*	*2,910*	16	25	—	—	—	—
Albania	9,631	15,500	30	58,682	34,441	34	55	80	419	674	139	223	0.3	0.5
Algeria	63,643	102,424	69	871,000	566,000	20	*9,589*	*14,000*	2,965[2]	4,772[2]	1,568	2,524	1,644	2,400
American Samoa	217	350	43	4,628	489	11	...	...	—	—	—	—	—	—
Andorra	167	269	74	35,941	4,186	1.6	...	...	—	—	—	—	—	—
Angola	45,128	72,626	25	197,000	26,000	52	...	...	*1,739[2]*	*2,798[2]*	*203*	*326*	*1,178*	*1,720*
Antigua and Barbuda	721	1,161	33	13,588	1,342	4.3	...	...	—	—	—	—	—	—
Argentina	134,278	216,100	29	4,665,329	1,181,569	5.9	...	...	21,015[2]	33,821[2]	4,014	6,460	5,214	7,613
Armenia	4,797	7,720	97	1,590	5,950	499	53	78	515	829	196	316	3,345	4,884
Aruba	*236*	*380*	100	35,679	935	2.2	...	...	—	—	—	—	—	—
Australia	556,145	895,030	39	8,370,000	2,640,300	1.6	*60,416*	*88,206*	22,385[2, 8]	36,026[2, 8]	7,152	11,510	67,593	98,684
Austria	80,792	130,023	100	3,593,588	300,042	2.1	7,362	10,749	3,524	5,672	6,509[8]	10,476[8]	9,526[8]	13,908[8]
Azerbaijan	35,897	57,770	94	289,000	88,800	20	1,190	1,740	1,305	2,100	516	830	1,055	1,540
Bahamas, The	1,522	2,450	57	46,089	11,858	4.7	...	...	—	—	—	—	—	—
Bahrain	1,762	2,835	75	141,901	29,584	3.4	...	...	—	—	—	—	—	—
Bangladesh	104,709	168,513	9	82,198	104,860	634	...	...	1,681[2]	2,706[2]	2,508	4,037	521	760
Barbados	1,000	1,610	95	43,711	10,583	4.9	...	...	—	—	—	—	—	—
Belarus	32,030	51,547	99	955,526	9,289	11	6,534	9,539	3,480	5,600	7,770	12,505	17,473	25,510
Belgium	88,579	142,555	97	4,339,231	431,376	2.1	18,800	27,500	2,093[2]	3,368[2]	4,199	6,757	5,334	7,787
Belize	1,721	2,770	19	10,667	6,108	12	...	...	—	—	—	—	—	—
Benin	5,257	8,460	31	22,200	12,400	160	...	...	359	578	66	107	173	253
Bermuda	149	240	100	20,700	4,000	2.5	...	...	—	—	—	—	—	—
Bhutan	1,998	3,216	*79*	*2,590*	*1,367*	348	...	...	—	—	—	—	—	—
Bolivia	34,478	55,487	5	213,666	133,984	21	*1,133*	*1,654*	2,295[2]	3,694[2]	216.8	348.9	521.9	761.9
Bosnia and Herzegovina	13,153	21,168	54	438,080	50,578	8.9	*2,708*	*3,954*	634	1,021	*344*	*554*	*1,333*	*1,946*
Botswana	11,388	18,327	25	27,058	42,696	20	...	...	603	971	53	86	1,171	1,710
Brazil	1,205,000	1,939,000	9	12,000,000	3,160,689	10	*178,359*	*260,400*	18,578[2]	29,899[2]	9,009	14,498	93,455	136,442
Brunei	1,527	2,457	59	141,371	16,557	1.9	...	...	12[15]	19[15]	—	—	...	...
Bulgaria	23,190	37,320	92	1,647,571	204,950	4.5	6,510	9,510	4,043	6,507	3,147	5,065	5,171	7,549
Burkina Faso	7,771	12,506	16	16,800	17,222	304	...	...	386[2]	622[2]	126	202	31	45
Burundi	8,997	14,480	7	16,800	15,000	186	...	...	—	—	—	—	—	—
Cambodia	7,643	12,300	34	42,210	9,005	197	1,360	1,990	380	612	*33.6*	*54.0*	*6.9*	*10.0*
Cameroon	21,300	34,300	13	92,200	60,000	91	*175*	*255*	686[2]	1,104[2]	247	398	405	592
Canada	634,400	1,021,000	35	14,280,000	3,895,600	1.6	*29,033*	*42,388*	44,182	71,104	889	1,430	185,641	271,032
Cape Verde	680	1,095	78	6,479	2,099	43	...	...	—	—	—	—	—	—
Central African Republic	14,795	23,810	2	9,500	7,000	195	62	90	—	—	—	—	—	—
Chad	20,319	32,700	1	9,630	14,360	265	580	850	—	—	—	—	—	—
Chile	49,550	79,750	14	888,645	469,142	10	...	...	4,084[2]	6,572[2]	428	689	1,595	2,329
China	718,931	1,157,009	90	4,179,000	5,213,270	128	321,570	469,490	45,319	72,934	220,319	354,570	881,539	1,287,025
Colombia	66,238	106,600	12	1,150,000	550,000	21	*4,265*	*6,227*	2,007[2]	3,230[2]	*9.6*	*15.5*	*166.4*	*242.9*
Comoros	544	875	76	7,080	4,870	41	...	...	—	—	—	—	—	—
Congo, Dem. Rep. of the	95,708	154,027	...	762,000	550,000	33	...	...	*3,162*	*5,088*	*360[16]*	*580[16]*	*1,258[16]*	*1,836[16]*
Congo, Rep. of the	7,929	12,760	10	36,100	15,600	48	*46*	*67*	494	795	141	227	152	222
Costa Rica	22,121	35,600	17	259,000	132,940	8.5	2,000	2,900	590[2]	950[2]	3.7	5.9	45.8	66.8
Côte d'Ivoire	31,168	50,160	10	271,000	150,000	34	...	...	405[2]	651[2]	117[19]	189[19]	182[19]	266[19]
Croatia	16,732	26,928	81	710,910	77,394	6.0	394	575	1,676	2,699	598	962	1,071	1,563
Cuba	16,839	27,100	56	20,000	33,000	205	*2,482*	*3,623*	3,033	4,881	*1,880*	*3,025*	*937*	*1,368*
Cyprus	6,307	10,150	57	219,749	103,852	2.6	...	...	—	—	—	—	—	—
Czech Republic	77,528	124,770	13	3,113,476	204,238	3.1	14,167	20,684	5,860	9,430	4,985	8,023	17,439	25,468
Denmark	44,378	71,420	100	1,729,405	288,464	2.6	7,300	10,600	1,780	2,865	3,004	4,834	1,360	1,985
Djibouti	1,796	2,890	13	8,550	1,870	56	...	...	*66*	*106*	173	279	187	273
Dominica	475	765	50	2,770	2,839	13	...	...	—	—	—	—	—	—
Dominican Republic	7,643	12,300	49	209,000	141,400	21	...	...	1,083[2]	1,743[2]	...	...	...	...
Ecuador	26,785	43,106	18	395,000	58,650	25	2,315	3,380	600[2]	966[2]	17	27	6	9
Egypt	36,000[23]	58,000[23]	78[23]	1,280,000	423,300	35	21,500	31,400	2,989	4,810	29,821	47,992	1,600	2,336

based upon registration, are relatively accurate, though some countries round off figures, and unregistered vehicles may cause substantial undercount. There is also inconsistent classification of vehicle types; in some countries a vehicle may serve variously as an automobile, a truck, or a bus, or even as all three on certain occasions. Relatively few countries collect and maintain commercial road traffic statistics.

Data on national railway systems are generally given for railway track length rather than the length of routes, which may be multitracked. Siding tracks usually are not included, but some countries fail to distinguish them. The United States data include only class 1 railways, which account for about 94 percent of total track length. Passenger traffic is usually calculated from tickets sold to fare-paying passengers. Such statistics are subject to distortion if there are large numbers of nonpaying passengers, such as military personnel, or if season tickets are sold and not all the allowed journeys are utilized. Railway cargo traffic is calculated by weight hauled multiplied by the length of the journey. Changes in freight load during the journey should be accounted for but sometimes are not, leading to discrepancies.

Merchant fleet and tonnage statistics collected by Lloyd's registry service for vessels over 100 gross tons are quite accurate. Cargo statistics, however, reflect the port and customs requirements of each country and the reporting rules of each country's merchant marine authority (although these, increasingly, reflect the recommendations of the International Maritime Organization); often, however, they are only estimates based on customs declarations and the count of vessels entered and cleared. Even when these elements are reported consistently, further uncertainties may be introduced because of ballast, bunkers, ships' stores, or transshipped goods included in the data.

Airport data are based on scheduled flights reported in the commercial Official Airline Guide and are both reliable and current. The comparability of civil air traffic statistics suffers from differing characteristics of the air transportation systems of different countries; data for an entire country may be two to three years behind those for a single airport.

Outside of Europe, where standardization of data on inland waterways is necessitated by the volume of international traffic, comparability of national data declines markedly. Calculations as to both the length of a country's waterway system (or route length of river, lake, and coastal traffic) and the makeup of its stock of commercially significant vessels (those for which data will be collected) are largely determined by the nature and use of the country's hydrographic net—its seasonality, relief profile, depth, access to potential markets—and inevitably differ widely from country to country. Data for coastal or island states may refer to scheduled coastwise or interisland traffic.

merchant marine (latest)		international cargo (latest)		air	traffic (latest)				canals and inland waterways (latest)				country
fleet (vessels over 100 gross tons)	total dead-weight tonnage ('000)	loaded metric tons ('000)	off-loaded metric tons ('000)	airports with scheduled flights, 1996	passengers passenger-mi ('000,000)	passenger-km ('000,000)	cargo short ton-mi ('000,000)	metric ton-km ('000,000)	length mi	km	cargo short ton-mi ('000,000)	metric ton-km ('000,000)	
—	—	—	—	3	122[1]	197[1]	7.5[1]	11[1]	750	1,200	...	...	Afghanistan
24	81.0	1,065	664	1	...	...	...	...	27	43	24	35	Albania
149	1,093.4	57,607	14,284	28	1,643[3]	2,644[3]	10.1[3]	14.8[3]	...	...	...	...	Algeria
3	0.1	380	581	3	—	—	—	—	...	...	...	...	American Samoa
—	—	—	—	—	—	—	—	—	—	—	—	—	Andorra
113	123.5	23,288	1,261	17[4]	589[5]	948[5]	77[5]	113[5]	805	1,295	...	...	Angola
292	997.4	28	113	2	140	225	14	20	...	...	...	...	Antigua and Barbuda
423	1,173.1	55,572	17,316	39[4]	7,323[6]	11,785[6]	911[6]	1,330[6]	6,800	11,000	19,326	28,215	Argentina
...	...	...	...	14	3,453	5,557	34	49	...	...	...	...	Armenia
7	7	...	...	1	...	...	...	...	...	...	...	...	Aruba
695	3,857.3	13,536	22,740	400	44,687	71,917	1,257	1,836	5,200	8,368	66,439	97,000	Australia
26	208.5	1,311	5,122	6	4,701	7,566	120.3	175.6	277	446	1,247	1,820	Austria
				1	1,259	2,026	34	49			3,600	5,300	Azerbaijan
1,061	33,081.7	5,920	5,705	23	119	191	0.01	0.02	...	...	...	...	Bahamas, The
87	192.5	13,285	3,512	1	1,714[9]	2,759[9]	72.5[9]	105.8[9]	...	...	...	...	Bahrain
301	566.8	1,848	10,608	8[4]	1,763	2,838	82	121	5,000	8,046	...	...	Bangladesh
37	84.0	206	538	1	93[10]	149[10]	0.8[11]	1.1[11]	...	...	...	...	Barbados
...	18,373.0	...	...	2	864	1,390	7	10	...	...	91	133	Belarus
232	218.5	291,540	292,476	2	5,599	9,011	221.9	323.9	1,269	2,043	14,600	21,300	Belgium
32	45.7	178	241	9[4]	...	...	...	...	513	825	...	...	Belize
12	0.2	339	1,738	1[4]	139.6[12]	224.7[12]	11.2[12]	16.4[12]	...	...	...	...	Benin
94	5,206.5	130	470	1	...	...	...	...	...	...	...	...	Bermuda
—	—	—	—	1[4]	29	46	...	...	—	—	—	—	Bhutan
1	15.8	...	...	14[4]	912	1,468	31.7	46.2	6,214	10,000	90	132	Bolivia
...	...	...	...	1	...	...	...	...	...	...	...	...	Bosnia and Herzegovina
—	—	—	—	4	36.3[13]	58.4[13]	0.3[13]	0.5[13]	...	...	...	...	Botswana
635	9,348.3	168,026	52,570	139[4]	22,471	36,164	1,118	1,632	31,069	50,000	56,030	81,803	Brazil
51	349.7	13,554	1,325	1	1,685	2,712	74	108	130	209	...	...	Brunei
222	1,938.2	5,290	20,080	3	1,765	2,840	24.1	35.2	292	470	502	733	Bulgaria
—	—	—	—	2	134.9	217.2	23.4	34.2	...	...	...	...	Burkina Faso
1	0.4	35	188	1[4]	1.2	2.0	...	...	...	...	...	...	Burundi
3	3.8	11	95	8[4]	...	...	...	...	2,300	3,700	51	75	Cambodia
47	39.8	1,260	2,328	5	196	315	27	39	1,299	2,090	...	...	Cameroon
1,185	2,896.8	176,667	83,287	301	35,364	56,913	4,824	7,043	1,860	3,000	...	...	Canada
42	30.9	144	299	9[4]	106	171	13.2	19.2	...	...	...	...	Cape Verde
—	—	53	126	1[4]	139.6[12]	224.7[12]	11.2[12]	16.4[12]	500	800	161	235	Central African Republic
—	—	—	—	4	138	223	10.5	15.3	1,240	2,000	...	...	Chad
392	854.9	21,768	13,464	23[4]	3,935	6,333	923	1,348	450	725	5,629	8,218	Chile
2,390	20,658.0	105,852	101,688	113	42,334	68,130	1,527	2,230	68,700	110,562	1,202,226	1,755,220	China
101	403.0	159,084	456,636	43[4]	2,837	4,565	662	966	8,900	14,300	7,038	10,276	Colombia
6	3.6	12	107	2[4]	1.9	3.0	...	...	...	...	...	...	Comoros
27	30.7	2,395	1,453	12	135[17]	218[17]	29[17]	42[17]	9,300	15,000	678	990	Congo, Dem. Rep. of the
22	10.8	8,987	736	5	139[12]	223[12]	10.5	15.3	696	1,120	...	...	Congo, Rep. of the
24	8.4	2,643	4,054	14	1,135[18]	1,827[18]	30.0[18]	43.8[18]	454	730	...	...	Costa Rica
51	98.6	4,173	7,228	11	139[20]	223[20]	10.5[20]	15.3[20]	609	980	...	...	Côte d'Ivoire
203	140.9	3,948	7,776	5	306	492	2.4	3.5	488	785	160	230	Croatia
393	924.6	8,092	15,440	14	1,648	2,652	31.2	45.6	149	240	2,085	3,044	Cuba
1,416	36,198.1	2,232	5,028	2	1,588	2,556	26	38	...	...	...	...	Cyprus
22[21]	446.2[21]	...	...	2	1,469	2,364	16.0	23.4	295	475	221	322	Czech Republic
456	7,589.1	20,284	37,314	13	3,340[22]	5,376[22]	117[22]	171[22]	259	417	1,100	1,600	Denmark
10	4.1	414	958	1	42	67	4	6	...	...	...	...	Djibouti
7	3.2	103	181	2	...	...	...	...	...	...	...	...	Dominica
28	10.4	2,550	4,182	7[4]	145	234	1.7	2.5	...	...	...	...	Dominican Republic
154	504.1	11,783	1,958	14	876	1,410	111	162	932	1,500	...	...	Ecuador
444	1,685.2	14,808	22,860	11[4]	5,432	8,742	136	198	2,175	3,500	580	850	Egypt

Transportation   (continued)

country	roads and motor vehicles (latest)								railroads (latest)					
	roads			motor vehicles			cargo		track length		traffic			
	length		paved (percent)	automobiles	trucks and buses	persons per vehicle	short ton-mi ('000,000)	metric ton-km ('000,000)	mi	km	passengers		cargo	
	mi	km									passenger-mi ('000,000)	passenger-km ('000,000)	short ton-mi ('000,000)	metric ton-km ('000,000)
El Salvador	7,655	12,320	14	102,000	159,700	21	...	...	349[2]	562[2]	3.4	5.5	20.3	29.6
Equatorial Guinea	1,667	2,682	19	6,500	4,000	37	...	...	—	—	—	—	—	—
Eritrea	2,442	3,930	21	5,350	...	...	...	...	...	...	...	...	...	...
Estonia	9,316	14,992	54	383,444	72,607	3.3	1,061	1,549	636	1,024	262	421	2,634	3,846
Ethiopia	17,622	28,360	15	45,559	20,462	842	...	...	486[24]	782[24]	172	277	86	126
Faroe Islands	285	458	...	11,528	2,895	3.0	...	...	—	—	—	—	—	—
Fiji	3,200	5,100	20	49,712	33,928	9.4	...	...	370[15]	595[15]	...	...	...	...
Finland	48,294	77,722	63	1,900,855	260,115	2.4	15,900	23,200	3,641[2]	5,859[2]	1,626	2,616	6,551	9,564
France	504,987	812,700	92	25,100,000	5,005,000	1.9	104,500	152,500	19,847[2]	31,940[2]	34,467	55,470	32,466	47,400
French Guiana	706	1,137	40	27,700	10,400	3.5	...	...	—	—	—	—	—	—
French Polynesia	584	940	42	38,900	16,500	3.9	...	...	—	—	—	—	—	—
Gabon	4,743	7,633	8	23,800	15,700	29	...	...	415	668	21	34	126	184
Gambia, The	1,640	2,640	35	7,950	8,240	72	...	...	—	—	—	—	—	—
Gaza Strip	...	...	...	21,206	4,639	29	...	...	—	—	—	—	—	—
Georgia	13,049	21,000	94	441,828	50,220	11	67	98	983	1,583	792	1,274	705	1,030
Germany	404,325	650,700	99	40,499,442	2,336,760	1.9	138,975	202,900	54,994	88,504	39,830	64,100	45,649	66,646
Ghana	23,339	37,561	25	86,200	130,000	80	873	1,275	592[2]	953[2]	73.1	117.7	93.9	137.1
Gibraltar	27	43	100	18,404	1,064	1.4	...	...	—	—	—	—	—	—
Greece	72,350	116,440	92	2,204,761	908,423	3.4	11,400	16,700	1,537[2]	2,474[2]	869	1,399	210	307
Greenland	50	80	...	1,944	1,039	19	...	...	—	—	—	—	—	—
Grenada	700	1,127	51	4,739	3,068	12	...	...	—	—	—	—	—	—
Guadeloupe	2,000	3,200	80	94,700	36,000	3.1	...	...	—	—	—	—	—	—
Guam	550	885	76	74,728	30,739	1.4	...	...	—	—	—	—	—	—
Guatemala	7,950	12,795	28	102,000	96,800	52	...	...	549[2]	884[2]	7.8	12.5	32.3	47.2
Guernsey	...	...	...	33,037	7,522	1.6	...	...	—	—	—	—	—	—
Guinea	18,809	30,270	16	13,700	19,300	217	...	...	411[2]	662[2]	25.8	41.5	5.0	7.3
Guinea-Bissau	2,703	4,350	10	6,300	4,900	100	...	...	—	—	—	—	—	—
Guyana	4,859	7,820	7	24,000	9,000	22	...	...	116[15]	187[15]	...	...	...	...
Haiti	2,535	4,080	24	32,000	21,000	121	...	...	—	—	—	—	—	—
Honduras	9,383	15,100	20	81,439	170,006	22	...	...	614	988	4.8	7.7	20.7	30.2
Hong Kong	1,083	1,743	100	325,131	142,446	13	...	...	21	34	2,231	3,591	68	99
Hungary	18,640	29,999	93	2,264,165	322,000	3.9	495	723	8,190	13,181	5,814	9,358	5,200	7,600
Iceland	7,691	12,378	25	124,909	16,623	1.9	318	464	—	—	—	—	—	—
India	1,248,700	2,009,600	50	2,720,000	2,207,000	190	144,000	210,000	38,935[2]	62,660[2]	198,500	319,400	173,268	252,967
Indonesia	234,900	372,414	47	2,107,299	2,024,702	47	17,000	25,000	4,090	6,583	9,895	15,924	2,679	3,912
Iran	98,200	158,000	59	1,630,000	609,000	26	46,750	68,250	4,527[2]	7,286[2]	3,990	6,422	6,249	9,124
Iraq	28,900	46,500	86	672,000	368,000	20	...	...	1,263[2]	2,032[2]	973	1,566	1,129	1,649
Ireland	57,377	92,340	94	990,384	155,153	3.1	3,519	5,138	1,210[2]	1,947[2]	828	1,332	392	573
Isle of Man	357	574	58	38,917	4,925	1.6	...	...	37[2]	59[2]	...	...	...	...
Israel	9,134	14,700	100	1,121,730	272,593	3.9	...	...	379[2]	610[2]	166	267	805	1,176
Italy	195,334	314,360	100	31,700,000	5,127,000	1.6	138,000	202,000	9,944	16,003	30,882	49,700	28,499	41,608
Jamaica	11,600	18,600	71	86,791	41,312	19	...	...	129[2]	208[2]	12.1	19.5	1.7	2.5
Japan	706,091	1,136,346	73	44,680,000	21,934,000	1.9	188,000	274,000	12,511	20,134	248,584	400,058	17,193	25,101
Jersey	...	...	...	58,491	9,922	1.3	...	...	—	—	—	—	—	—
Jordan	4,194	6,750	100	167,828	82,516	16	19,133	27,934	421[2]	677[2]	3.7	6.0	915	1,336
Kazakstan	98,583	158,655	68	1,030,000	516,000	11	9	13	13,422	21,600	1,355	2,180	661	965
Kenya	39,558	63,663	14	271,000	75,900	80	134	196	1,885[2]	3,034[2]	288	464	899	1,312
Kiribati	407	655	5	307	130	147	...	...	—	—	—	—	—	—
Korea, North	18,600	30,000	6	248,000	...	...	...	...	5,302	8,533	2,100	3,400	6,200	9,100
Korea, South	46,127	74,235	76	6,006,290	2,462,611	5.3	36,100	52,700	4,072	6,554	18,201	29,292	9,478	13,838
Kuwait	2,704	4,360	81	545,000	155,000	2.4	...	...	—	—	—	—	—	—
Kyrgyzstan	11,533	18,560	91	164,000	...	...	555	811	249	400	81.5	131.2	394	575
Laos	11,280	18,153	14	17,200	6,020	208	16	23	—	—	—	—	—	—
Latvia	40,198	64,693	18	379,895	90,184	5.3	1,200	1,700	1,499	2,413	734	1,182	8,502	12,412
Lebanon	3,951	6,359	95	1,197,521	84,736	2.9	...	...	138	222	5.3	8.6	29	42
Lesotho	3,079	4,955	18	11,100	22,200	58	...	...	1.6	2.6	...	...	...	...
Liberia	6,400	10,300	6	10,300	28,300	59	...	...	306[2]	493[2]	...	...	137[15]	200[15]
Libya	50,704	81,600	57	592,000	312,000	5.8	...	...	12	19	—	—	—	—
Liechtenstein	201	323	...	18,820	1,949	1.5	...	...	—	—	—	—	—	—
Lithuania	38,178	61,442	86	718,469	118,474	4.4	3,534	5,160	1,862	2,996	702	1,130	5,264	7,685
Luxembourg	3,206	5,160	99	231,666	25,529	1.6	164	239	171[2]	275[2]	176	284	388	566
Macau	80	130	100	41,403	3,803	9.2	...	...	—	—	—	—	—	—
Macedonia	5,302	8,532	63	285,907	29,197	6.2	807	1,178	573	922	40	65	116	170
Madagascar	30,967	49,837	12	58,100	15,340	181	220	321	640[2]	1,030[2]	29	46	64	93
Malawi	17,324	27,880	18	25,400	28,900	174	—	—	490[2]	789[2]	11.8	19.0	38.9	56.8
Malaysia	58,393	93,975	75	2,588,641	465,940	6.8	...	...	1,113	1,791	798[33]	1,284[33]	970[33]	1,416[33]
Maldives	...	...	...	938	1,117	123	...	...	—	—	—	—	—	—
Mali	9,181	14,776	12	24,700	17,100	224	...	...	398[2]	641[2]	304.2	489.5	187.2	273.3
Malta	997	1,604	94	173,259	41,849	1.7	...	...	—	—	—	—	—	—
Marshall Islands	...	...	...	1,418	193	34	...	...	—	—	—	—	—	—
Martinique	1,286	2,069	75	135,269	7,328	2.3	...	...	—	—	—	—	—	—
Mauritania	4,700	7,600	11	17,300	9,210	85	...	...	437[2]	704[2]	...	...	4,719	6,890
Mauritius	1,138	1,831	93	37,766	10,625	23	...	...	—	—	—	—	—	—
Mayotte	195	284	39	1,528		40	...	...	—	—	—	—	—	—
Mexico	188,886	303,983	36	8,449,969	3,950,456	7.2	107,000	156,000	16,432[2]	26,445[2]	2,382	3,833	24,042	35,100
Micronesia	140	226	17	...	...	...	...	...	—	—	—	—	—	—
Moldova	7,617	12,259	87	165,941	69,069	18	579	845	746	1,200	633	1,019	2,147	3,134
Monaco	27	43	100	20,715	2,702	1.3	...	...	1	2	...	...	...	...
Mongolia	6,947	11,180	11	21,200	33,420	42	183.8	268.4	1,294	2,083	516	830	1.4	2.1
Morocco	37,601	60,513	50	1,030,000	273,100	20	1,288	1,880	1,099[2]	1,768[2]	951	1,531	3,165	4,621
Mozambique	18,523	29,810	19	84,000	26,800	155	...	...	1,940	3,123	194	312	612	893
Myanmar (Burma)	17,100	27,600	12	44,000	42,000	525	71	103.7	3,144	5,060	3,041	4,894	603	880
Namibia	25,134	40,450	13	62,500	66,500	13	...	...	1,480	2,382	1,248	2,008	741	1,082
Nauru	17	28	79	1,448		6.3	...	...	3[15]	5[15]	...	...	4.7	6.8
Nepal	4,691	7,550	41	4,949	3,363	2,259	984	1,437	63[2]	101[2]	...	...	...	...

merchant marine (latest)				air						canals and inland waterways (latest)				country
fleet (vessels over 100 gross tons)	total dead-weight tonnage ('000)	international cargo (latest)		airports with sched-uled flights, 1996	traffic (latest)					length		cargo		
		loaded metric tons ('000)	off-loaded metric tons ('000)		passengers		cargo			mi	km	short ton-mi ('000,000)	metric ton-km ('000,000)	
					passenger-mi ('000,000)	passenger-km ('000,000)	short ton-mi ('000,000)	metric ton-km ('000,000)						
15	...	221	1,023	1[4]	1,229	1,978	9.8	14.3	...	...	...	...	...	El Salvador
3	6.7	110	64	1[4]	4	7	0.7	1.0	...	...	...	...	...	Equatorial Guinea
...	...	...	...	2	...	...	...	...	...	...	...	...	...	Eritrea
234	680.4	11,460	3,996	3	67	108	0.4	0.6	311	500	0.7	1	...	Estonia
27	84.3	592	3,120	31	1,142	1,838	77	112	...	...	...	...	...	Ethiopia
191	59.8	130	367	1	...	...	...	...	...	...	...	...	...	Faroe Islands
64	60.4	568	625	13[4]	742	1,195	51.6	75.4	126	203	...	...	...	Fiji
263	989.3	33,336	36,948	24	6,654	10,709	165.3	241.3	4,148	6,675	2,500	3,600	...	Finland
729	4,981.0	55,296	177,696	61	41,942[25]	67,500[25]	7,740[25]	11,300[25]	9,278	14,932	3,800	5,600	...	France
7	0.7	69	481	8	...	...	...	...	286	460	...	...	...	French Guiana
41	16.5	15	666	36	...	...	...	...	...	...	...	...	...	French Polynesia
29	30.2	12,828	212	23	354	570	56	82	994	1,600	...	...	...	Gabon
11	2.0	185	240	1	31	50	3	5	250	400	...	...	...	Gambia, The
—	—	...	...	—	...	...	...	...	—	—	...	...	...	Gaza Strip
54	1,108	...	...	1[4]	3,291	5,296	...	...	...	...	17,561	25,638	...	Georgia
1,375	6,832.3	71,028	128,448	40	39,409	63,423	8,611	12,572	4,686	7,541	39,425	57,559	...	Germany
155	131.0	2,424	2,904	1	407	655	20	30	803	1,293	75	110	...	Ghana
49	1,136.1	5	400	1	...	...	...	...	—	—	...	...	...	Gibraltar
1,872	45,276.6	21,087	33,048	36[4]	4,937	7,945	80	117	50	80	585	854	...	Greece
82	17.2	298	288	5	16.3	26.3	0.23	0.34	...	...	...	...	...	Greenland
3	0.5	21	193	2[4]	...	...	...	...	...	...	...	...	...	Grenada
20	4.4	431	1,933	6	...	...	...	...	...	...	...	...	...	Guadeloupe
5	0.1	195	1,524	1	...	...	...	...	...	...	...	...	...	Guam
8	0.4	2,096	3,822	2	239	384	14	21	162	260	...	...	...	Guatemala
—	...	...	...	1[4]	...	...	...	...	...	...	...	...	...	Guernsey
23	1.7	16,760	734	2	20.4	32.8	0.9	1.2	805	1,295	...	...	...	Guinea
19	1.8	46	283	2[4]	3.7	6.0	0.7	1.0	...	...	...	...	...	Guinea-Bissau
82	13.5	1,730	673	1	139	224	16	23	3,700	6,000	...	...	...	Guyana
4	0.4	170	704	2[4]	...	...	...	...	60	100	...	...	...	Haiti
966	1,437.3	1,316	1,002	8	180[26]	289[26]	26[26]	38[26]	289	465	...	...	...	Honduras
387	11,688.6	41,512[27]	87,106[27]	1[4]	...	...	...	...	...	...	...	...	...	Hong Kong
15	93.2	...	...	1[4]	1,716	2,762	22.5	32.9	1,008	1,622	569	831	...	Hungary
394	114.9	1,162	1,733	24	1,850	2,977	36.2	52.9	...	...	58	84	...	Iceland
888	10,365.9	53,220	75,000	66	12,563	20,219	437.9	639.3	10,054	16,180	202,000	295,000	...	India
2,014	3,130.2	216,396	64,656	81	8,904	14,330	415.6	606.8	13,409	21,579	17,000	25,000	...	Indonesia
403	8,345.3	113,207	16,719	19	3,808	6,128	75.1	109.6	562	904	...	...	...	Iran
131	1,578.8	97,830	8,638	...	976	1,570	37.4	54.6	631	1,015	...	...	...	Iraq
189	208.6	6,367	17,637	9	3,186	5,127	70	102	...	...	...	...	...	Ireland
101	2,836.5	6	203	1	115.5	185.9	0.2	0.3	...	...	...	...	...	Isle of Man
58	723.4	10,656	19,608	7	7,430[28]	11,957[28]	815[28]	1,190[28]	...	...	...	...	...	Israel
1,966	7,149.5	51,420	222,060	34[4]	18,429[29]	29,659[29]	914.3[29]	1,335[29]	1,500	2,400	59	86	...	Italy
12	16.2	8,802	5,285	4[4]	1,204[30]	1,938[30]	136[30]	199[30]	...	...	...	...	...	Jamaica
7,165	22,000	114,756	782,916	73	80,959	130,292	4,487	6,551	1,100	1,770	155,000	227,000	...	Japan
—	—	...	...	1	...	...	...	...	...	...	...	...	...	Jersey
5	113.6	7,392	4,608	2[4]	2,731	4,395	181.6	265.2	...	...	19,202	28,035	...	Jordan
...	...	...	...	6	2,858	4,600	68	100	2,487	4,002	123	180	...	Kazakstan
29	11.6	1,596	3,228	13	1,142[31]	1,838[31]	32.7[31]	47.8[31]	...	...	...	...	...	Kenya
7	2.7	15	26	17	6	10	0.5	0.8	3	5	...	...	...	Kiribati
100	951.2	635	5,520	1[4]	52.2	84.0	1.4	2.0	1,400	2,253	...	...	...	Korea, North
2,138	11,724.9	74,736	273,672	14	30,139	48,504	3,924	5,729	1,000	1,609	48,600	70,900	...	Korea, South
209	3,188.5	51,400	4,522	1[4]	3,184	5,124	225.8	329.7	...	...	...	...	...	Kuwait
...	...	...	...	2[4]	2,739	4,408	44.7	65.2	...	...	6	9	...	Kyrgyzstan
1	1.5	—	—	11	29	46	3	5	2,850	4,587	68	99	...	Laos
261	1,436.9	36,012	2,448	1	187.3	301.5	3.6	5.2	186	300	311	454	...	Latvia
163	438.2	152	1,150	1[4]	1,174	1,889	32	46	...	...	...	...	...	Lebanon
—	—	—	—	1[4]	3.9	6.2	0.4	0.6	—	—	—	—	...	Lesotho
1,672	97,374.0	21,653	1,608	1	4.3	7.0	0.7	1.0	—	—	—	...	...	Liberia
150	1,223.6	62,491	7,808	12	247.6[32]	398.5[32]	0.3[32]	0.4[32]	—	—	...	...	...	Libya
—	—	—	—	—	...	...	...	...	—	...	...	...	...	Liechtenstein
52	373.9	10,092	2,628	3	219	352	23	34	373	600	12	18	...	Lithuania
54	2,603.6	—	—	1[4]	79.5	232	606.9	886.1	23	37	232	338	...	Luxembourg
6	0.1	755	3,935	—	—	—	—	—	...	...	...	...	...	Macau
...	...	...	...	2[4]	181.7	292.4	20	29	...	...	...	...	...	Macedonia
85	82.1	540	984	19	409	659	58	85	...	...	...	...	...	Madagascar
1	0.3	...	...	5[4]	180	289	19	28	891	1,434	0.5	0.7	...	Malawi
552	2,916.3	23,472	44,184	39[4]	14,017	22,558	795	1,160	4,534	7,296	...	...	...	Malaysia
44	79.0	27	78	5[4]	4.8	7.0	...	...	...	...	...	...	...	Maldives
—	—	—	—	9[4]	139.6	224.7	11.2	16.4	1,128	1,815	18	27	...	Mali
889	17,073.2	309	1,781	1	1,070	1,723	9.4	13.7	...	...	...	...	...	Malta
35	4,182.4	29	123	23	30	49	7	10	...	...	...	...	...	Marshall Islands
6	1.1	768	1,524	2	...	...	...	...	...	...	...	...	...	Martinique
126	23.9	10,400	724	9[4]	139.6	224.7	11.2	16.4	...	...	...	...	...	Mauritania
35	152.2	834	2,419	1[4]	2,115	3,404	93.4	136.3	...	...	...	...	...	Mauritius
1	1.1	—	—	1	...	...	...	...	...	...	...	...	...	Mayotte
635	1,495.3	139,776	61,956	83	12,902	20,764	1,348	1,968	1,800	2,900	...	...	...	Mexico
17	6.9	...	...	6	...	...	...	...	...	...	...	...	...	Micronesia
...	...	...	...	1	1,461	2,352	13.0	19.0	263	424	172	251	...	Moldova
1	...	...	...	1	—	—	...	...	...	...	...	...	...	Monaco
—	—	—	—	1	305	491	31	45	247	397	613	895	...	Mongolia
492	586.2	19,476	21,120	12	2,992	4,815	268	391	...	...	...	...	...	Morocco
107	31.6	2,800	3,400	7[4]	239	384	6	9	2,330	3,750	...	...	...	Mozambique
144	1,354.0	2,040	3,624	19	272	439	2.2	3.2	7,954	12,800	240	351	...	Myanmar (Burma)
30	5.9	1,132	644	13	470	756	16	23	...	...	...	...	...	Namibia
2	5.8	1,650	59	1	128[34]	206[34]	14[34]	20[34]	...	...	...	...	...	Nauru
—	—	...	...	24	478	769	63.8	93.1	...	...	...	...	...	Nepal

Transportation (continued)

country	roads and motor vehicles (latest)								railroads (latest)					
	roads			motor vehicles			cargo		track length		traffic			
	length		paved (per-cent)	auto-mobiles	trucks and buses	persons per vehicle	short ton-mi ('000,000)	metric ton-km ('000,000)	mi	km	passengers		cargo	
	mi	km									passenger-mi ('000,000)	passenger-km ('000,000)	short ton-mi ('000,000)	metric ton-km ('000,000)
Netherlands, The	77,090	124,064	91	5,740,000	680,000	2.4	16,000	24,000	1,702	2,739	8,685	13,977	2,121	3,097
Netherlands Antilles	368	592	51	69,321	21,194	2.2	...	...	—	—	—	—	—	—
New Caledonia	3,580	5,762	22	58,500	22,600	2.3	...	...	—	—	—	—	—	—
New Zealand	57,081	91,864	73	1,650,112	351,494	1.8	...	...	2,433	3,915	285	458	2,277	3,324
Nicaragua	10,654	17,146	10	72,413	68,090	31	...	...	—	—	—	—	—	—
Niger	6,129	9,863	9	37,500	14,100	171	1,044	1,524	—	—	—	—	—	—
Nigeria	20,387	32,810	83	663,000	68,300	134	...	...	2,178	3,505	345	555	1.5	2.2
Northern Mariana Islands	307	494	27	12,113	6,479	3.0	...	...	—	—	—	—	—	—
Norway	56,086	90,262	74	1,684,664	382,017	2.1	6,575	9,600	2,485[2]	3,999[2]	1,479	2,381	1,860	2,715
Oman	19,160	30,830	20	202,741	108,600	6.8	...	...	—	—	—	—	—	—
Pakistan	123,585	198,891	55	955,098	225,829	107	2,723	3,976	5,453[2]	8,775[2]	10,908	17,555	3,877	5,661
Palau	40	64	59	—4,271—		3.8	...	...	...	...	...	...	...	...
Panama	6,706	10,792	34	140,900	79,000	12	...	...	220[2]	354[2]	...	...	0.5	0.7
Papua New Guinea	12,263	19,736	6	13,000	32,000	93	...	...	—	—	—	—	—	—
Paraguay	17,956	28,900	9	174,212	76,565	18	...	...	274[2]	441[2]	1.9	3.0	3.8	5.5
Peru	44,400	71,400	11	505,766	338,871	28	...	...	1,318[2]	2,121[2]	102.7	165.3	605.8	884.4
Philippines	100,062	161,035	17	609,000	221,900	82	...	...	557[2]	897[2]	43	70	1.0	1.5
Poland	231,447	372,479	65	7,517,266	1,472,278	4.3	49,042	71,600	14,904	23,986	16,550	26,635	47,341	69,116
Portugal	42,708	68,732	88	2,560,000	219,696	3.6	7,665	11,190	1,909[2]	3,072[2]	3,025	4,869	1,382	2,018
Puerto Rico	14,379	23,140	87	1,432,000	229,000	2.2	...	...	—	—	—	—	—	—
Qatar	752	1,210	90	125,700	63,800	3.0	...	...	—	—	—	—	—	—
Réunion	1,711	2,754	79	157,700	38,600	3.4	...	...	—	—	—	—	—	—
Romania	95,175	153,170	51	2,197,477	385,111	8.8	13,526	19,748	7,062	11,365	11,731	18,880	18,617	27,180
Russia	590,000	949,000	79	10,499,000	407,000	14	987	1,441	94,400	152,000	163,900	263,800	704	1,028
Rwanda	9,050	14,565	10	11,900	15,900	216	140	200	—	—	—	—	—	—
St. Kitts and Nevis	193	310	43	4,000	700	10	...	...	—	—	—	—	—	—
St. Lucia	500	805	56	10,000	9,200	7.3	...	...	—	—	—	—	—	—
St. Vincent and the Grenadines	634	1,020	31	5,473	2,878	13	...	...	—	—	—	—	—	—
Samoa	485	781	42	1,068	1,169	74	...	...	—	—	—	—	—	—
San Marino	147	237	...	23,561	4,013	0.9	...	...	—	—	—	—	—	—
São Tomé and Príncipe	193	310	68	3,810	1,470	25	...	...	—	—	—	—	—	—
Saudi Arabia	98,798	159,000	43	1,710,000	1,172,600	6.2	57,859	84,473	864[2]	1,390[2]	86	139	559	816
Senegal	9,060	14,580	29	80,600	32,410	78	375	547	562	904	128	206	476	695
Seychelles	214	345	80	5,100	2,000	11	...	...	—	—	—	—	—	—
Sierra Leone	7,254	11,674	11	20,860	11,014	141	36	53	52	84	...	...	...	...
Singapore	1,886	3,035	97	384,450	139,113	5.8	...	...	52	83	33	33	33	33
Slovakia	11,103	17,869	...	1,015,794	97,516	4.8	3,533	5,158	2,277	3,665	2,611	4,202	9,366	13,674
Slovenia	9,158	14,739	79	698,211	40,206	2.7	1,190	1,740	746	1,201	370	595	1,973	2,881
Solomon Islands	826	1,330	2	2,052	2,574	75	...	...	—	—	—	—	—	—
Somalia	14,300	23,000	12	11,800	12,200	278	...	...	—	—	—	—	—	—
South Africa	113,450	182,580	33	3,810,000	1,640,000	7.6	1,053	1,538	13,418[2]	21,595[2]	556	895	65,248	95,260
Spain	213,252	343,197	99	14,212,257	2,984,140	2.3	53,914	78,713	8,252[2]	13,280[2]	9,526	15,330	6,624	9,671
Sri Lanka	63,753	102,600	11	220,000	248,900	39	2,617	3,821	928[2]	1,493[2]	2,028	3,264	99	144
Sudan, The	7,214	11,610	36	263,000	47,800	98	...	...	2,960[2]	4,764[2]	735	1,183	1,534	2,240
Suriname	2,778	4,470	26	44,300	17,050	7.0	...	...	187	301	...	...	...	...
Swaziland	2,377	3,825	28	27,300	26,340	18	...	...	187	301	752	1,210	1,993	2,910
Sweden	84,645	136,223	72	3,630,760	322,286	2.2	20,800	30,400	6,744	10,853	3,942	6,344	13,280	19,388
Switzerland	44,151	71,055	96	3,229,169	277,399	2.0	7,108	10,378	3,125	5,030	7,084	11,400	5,586	8,156
Syria	24,384	39,243	71	134,000	218,900	40	1,075	1,570	1,097[2]	1,766[2]	531	855	751	1,097
Taiwan	11,830	19,038	89	4,146,500	799,600	4.3	9,326	13,616	2,410	3,879	5,577	8,975	1,086	1,585
Tajikistan	8,000	13,000	93	184,900	3,600	30	3,518	5,136	300	500	6,094	9,808	7,617	11,121
Tanzania	54,743	88,100	4	47,500	38,000	323	...	...	2,218	3,569	2,324	3,740	1,021	1,490
Thailand	38,000	62,000	97	1,440,000	2,969,000	13	...	...	2,471[2]	3,976[2]	8,062	12,975	2,221	3,242
Togo	4,672	7,519	32	74,662	33,061	41	...	...	245[2]	395[2]	9	14	3.8	5.6
Tonga	419	674	27	1,136	766	53	...	...	—	—	—	—	—	—
Trinidad and Tobago	5,070	8,160	51	123,500	24,500	8.5	...	...	—	—	—	—	—	—
Tunisia	13,975	22,490	79	248,000	283,000	17	678	990	1,337[2]	2,152[2]	636	1,038	1,524	2,225
Turkey	236,928	381,300	23	3,231,562	809,361	15	67,017	97,843	5,252	8,452	3,967	6,385	5,654	8,254
Turkmenistan	14,600	23,500	81	170,600	...	...	3,283	4,793	1,359	2,187	1,300	2,100	13,600	19,800
Tuvalu	5	8	—	...	...	...	...	...	...	...	...	...	...	...
Uganda	16,653	26,800	8	24,400	25,300	397	...	...	771[2]	1,241[2]	17	28	128	187
Ukraine	107,035	172,257	95	4,510,000	...	...	15,800	23,100	14,100	22,700	42,900	69,100	85,600	125,000
United Arab Emirates	2,952	4,750	100	197,000	49,150	9.7	...	...	—	—	—	—	—	—
United Kingdom	228,042	366,999	100	20,505,000	2,712,000	2.5	105,000	153,000	23,518[46]	37,849[46]	18,154	29,216	1,997	2,916
United States	3,912,226	6,296,130	91	134,803,000	66,727,000	1.3	1,096,000	1,600,000	137,900	222,000	13,897	22,365	1,305,685	1,906,268
Uruguay	31,600	50,900	14	444,835	46,245	6.4	500	730	1,288[2]	2,073[2]	87.4	140.6	129	189
Uzbekistan	48,715	78,400	86	865,300	14,500	25	15,037	21,954	2,100	3,380	3,300	5,200	48,400	70,600
Vanuatu	652	1,050	24	4,000	2,300	26	...	...	—	—	—	—	—	—
Venezuela	55,737	89,700	39	1,485,221	511,809	11	...	...	390[2]	627[2]	19.5	31.4	32.1	46.8
Vietnam	65,895	106,048	26	...	...	...	1,462	2,134	1,619	2,605	1,305	2,100	727	1,062
Virgin Islands (U.S.)	532	856	100	47,255	14,868	1.6	...	...	—	—	—	—	—	—
West Bank	...	...	...	69,200	20,723	13	...	...	—	—	—	—	—	—
Western Sahara	3,900	6,200	23	6,284	424	20	...	...	...	...	...	...	...	...
Yemen	40,144	64,605	8	229,084	282,615	31	...	...	—	—	—	—	—	—
Yugoslavia	30,832	49,620	58	1,400,000	132,000	6.9	14,929[49]	21,796[49]	2,505	4,031	1,137	1,830	1,412	2,062
Zambia	24,170	38,898	18	142,000	73,500	44	...	...	791	1,273	166	267	316	462
Zimbabwe	57,048	91,810	19	492,000	108,000	19	...	...	1,714[2]	2,759[2]	339	546	3.2	4.7

[1]Ariana Afghan Airlines only. [2]Route length. [3]Air Algérie International flights only. [4]1997. [5]TAAG airline only. [6]Aerolineas Argentinas only. [7]Included in Netherlands Antilles. [8]Government railways only. [9]Portion of Gulf Air traffic. [10]Caribbean Airways only. [11]Caribbean Air Cargo only. [12]Air Afrique only. [13]Air Botswana only. [14]1995. [15]For industrial purposes only. [16]Zaire National Railways only. [17]Air Zaire only. [18]LASCA only. [19]Traffic between Ouagadougou, Burkina Faso, and Abidjan, Côte d'Ivoire. [20]Air Ivoire only. [21]Data refer to former Czechoslovakia. [22]Including SAS international and domestic traffic. [23]National roads only. [24]Includes 62 mi (100 km) of the Chemin de Fer Djibouti-Éthiopien (CDE) in Djibouti. [25]Air France and UTA only. [26]TAN and SAHSA

| merchant marine (latest) | | | | air | | | | | canals and inland waterways (latest) | | | | country |
fleet (vessels over 100 gross tons)	total dead-weight tonnage ('000)	international cargo (latest) loaded metric tons ('000)	off-loaded metric tons ('000)	airports with scheduled flights, 1996	traffic (latest) passengers passenger-mi ('000,000)	passenger-km ('000,000)	cargo short ton-mi ('000,000)	metric ton-km ('000,000)	length mi	km	cargo short ton-mi ('000,000)	metric ton-km ('000,000)	
399	2,874	84,816	293,304	6	28,292	45,531	2,490	3,635	3,939	6,340	5,100	7,500	Netherlands, The
154[35]	1,053.6[35]	18,560	18,715	5	234[36]	377[36]	1.2[36]	1.8[36]	...	...	...	...	Netherlands Antilles
17	18.1	1,040	930	10	145[37]	233[37]	3.4[37]	4.9[37]	...	...	...	...	New Caledonia
139	279.8	19,692	11,604	36[4]	11,090	17,848	444	648	1,000	1,609	1,503	2,195	New Zealand
25	1.3	320	1,629	10[4]	44.8	72.2	4.8	7.0	1,379	2,220	...	...	Nicaragua
—	—	—	—	6	139.6	224.7	11.2	16.4	186	300	13	19	Niger
271	733.3	86,993	11,346	12	612	985	7.9	11.5	5,328	8,575	...	...	Nigeria
2	0.9	33	205	3	...	...	...	...	...	...	...	...	Northern Mariana Islands
1,597	20,834	152,604	22,776	50	5,439[22]	8,753[22]	639[22]	933[22]	980	1,577	5,920	8,650	Norway
26	11.7	33,843	2,492	6[4]	1,714[9]	2,759[9]	72.4[9]	105.8[9]	...	...	...	...	Oman
73	513.8	5,625	17,526	34	6,911	11,123	290	423	...	...	...	...	Pakistan
4	...	—	64	1	...	...	...	...	...	...	...	...	Palau
5,217	79,255.6	116,844	84,312	10	542	872	6.4	9.3	497	800	...	...	Panama
87	40.9	2,463	1,784	129	458.8	738.4	56.4	82.4	6,798	10,940	...	...	Papua New Guinea
38	38.5	...	...	5[4]	767	1,235	8.0	11.7	1,900	3,100	...	...	Paraguay
623	615.6	10,197	5,077	27	1,535	2,470	177	259	5,300	8,600	...	...	Peru
1,499	13,807.1	12,864	34,128	21	7,987[38]	12,854[38]	225.2[38]	328.8[38]	2,000	3,219	...	...	Philippines
644	4,314.3	30,823	17,247	8[4]	2,879	4,633	51	74	2,484	3,997	600	876	Poland
332	1,129.3	9,672	37,260	16[4]	4,957	7,978	143.6	209.7	510	820	...	...	Portugal
13	...	...	...	7[4]	...	...	...	...	...	...	...	...	Puerto Rico
65	635.6	18,145	2,588	1[4]	1,714[9]	2,759[9]	72.4[9]	105.8[9]	...	...	...	...	Qatar
7	33.5	399	1,975	1	...	...	...	...	...	...	...	...	Réunion
439	4,845.5	14,676	21,684	12	1,126	1,812	10.8	15.7	1,071	1,724	2,128	3,107	Romania
4,543	16,592.3	14,124	1,428	58	44,600	71,700	1,200	1,800	62,800	101,000	96	140	Russia
—	—	—	—	3	1.2	2.0	...	...	...	...	...	...	Rwanda
1	0.6	24	36	2	...	...	...	...	...	...	...	...	St. Kitts and Nevis
7	2.1	150	234	2	...	...	...	...	...	...	...	...	St. Lucia
881	7,044.2	80	140	4	...	...	...	...	...	...	...	...	St. Vincent and the Grenadines
7	6.5	12	192	3[4]	...	...	...	...	...	...	...	...	Samoa
—	—	—	—	—	—	—	—	—	—	—	—	—	San Marino
4	2.3	16	45	2	5	8	0.7	1.0	...	...	...	...	São Tomé and Príncipe
301	1,361.7	214,070	46,437	25[4]	11,500	18,501	613	895	...	...	...	...	Saudi Arabia
183	27.5	1,739	2,959	7	139.6[32]	224.7[32]	11.2[32]	16.4[32]	557	897	...	...	Senegal
9	3.3	11	348	2[4]	389	626	48	70	...	...	...	...	Seychelles
62	18.4	2,310	589	1[4]	68[39]	110[39]	1.4[39]	2.0[39]	500	800	447	652	Sierra Leone
946	14,929.2	134,592	179,568	1[4]	33,330	53,640	2,871	4,191	...	...	...	...	Singapore
...	...	...	...	2	37.5	60.3	3.8	5.6	107	172	1,005	1,468	Slovakia
13	346.5	137	2,204	1	382	614	2.3	3.7	...	...	12,175	17,775	Slovenia
33	5.0	278	349	21[4]	40[40]	65[40]	3	5	...	...	...	...	Solomon Islands
28	18.5	324	1,007	1[4]	81	131	3.0	5.0	...	...	...	...	Somalia
219	282.5	114,331	22,203	24	8,595[41]	13,833[41]	370[41]	540[41]	...	...	...	...	South Africa
2,190	5,077.3	49,860	147,804	25	21,154	34,044	2,578	3,764	649	1,045	21,836[42]	31,880[42]	Spain
66	472.6	5,892	9,588	1	2,403	3,868	109	159	267	430	...	...	Sri Lanka
16	62.2	1,543	4,300	3[4]	404[43]	650[43]	21[43]	31[43]	3,300	5,310	...	...	Sudan, The
24	15.7	1,595	1,265	3[4]	54[44]	88[44]	18[44]	26[44]	746	1,200	...	...	Suriname
—	—	—	—	1	30.7	49.4	0.09	0.1	—	—	...	...	Swaziland
430	2,881	52,812	63,912	48	5,236[22]	8,427[22]	171[22]	250[22]	1,275	2,052	5,600	8,200	Sweden
24	602.8	...	...	5	12,257	19,725	1.033	1,508	40	65	127	186	Switzerland
94	210.4	1,788	4,512	5	692	1,114	81	118	541	870	...	...	Syria
649	9,241.3	156,230	263,938	13	25,230	40,604	2,444	3,568	...	234	...	341	Taiwan
...	...	...	...	1[4]	1,386	2,231	140	205	...	...	...	...	Tajikistan
43	48.5	1,249	2,721	11[4]	114	184	2.0	2.9	...	...	...	...	Tanzania
351	1,194.5	21,192	40,152	25	18,160	29,226	904	1,320	2,300	3,701	...	...	Thailand
8	20.6	148	709	1	134	215	23	34	31	50	...	...	Togo
15	13.7	15	104	6	5.8	9.4	0.01	0.01	...	...	...	...	Tonga
53	17.5	9,622	10,961	2	2,538	4,084	277	404	...	...	...	...	Trinidad and Tobago
77	443.3	6,888	11,136	5	1,338	2,154	139.5	203.6	...	...	...	...	Tunisia
880	7,114.3	22,956	61,728	26	7,646[45]	12,305[45]	146.7[45]	214.2[45]	750	1,200	209	305	Turkey
...	...	...	...	1	971	1,562	98	143	...	...	...	...	Turkmenistan
6	16.0	...	...	1	...	...	...	...	...	...	...	...	Tuvalu
2	8.6	...	...	1[4]	32.4	52.1	3	5	...	...	...	...	Uganda
...	...	34,200	...	20	1,775	2,857	210	306	1,039	1,672	2,658	3,880	Ukraine
276	1,491.7	88,153	9,595	6	1,714[9]	2,759[9]	72.5[9]	105.8[9]	...	...	...	...	United Arab Emirates
1,631	4,355	177,228	178,572	57[4]	77,576	124,847	2,625	3,832	1,990	3,200	34,400	50,200	United Kingdom
509	18,585	388,716[47]	602,436[47]	83[4]	540,400	869,700	14,568	21,270	25,482	41,009	807,700	1,179,000	United States
93	172.5	710[48]	1,450[48]	1[4]	401	645	42	62	1,000	1,600	...	...	Uruguay
...	...	...	...	9	3,017	4,855	306	447	...	...	...	...	Uzbekistan
280	3,259.6	80	55	29	93	150	0.8	1.2	...	...	...	...	Vanuatu
271	1,355.4	101,435	17,932	20[4]	4,581	7,372	144	210	4,400	7,100	...	...	Venezuela
230	872.8	303	1,510	12	130	209	13	19	11,000	17,702	1,339	1,955	Vietnam
1	...	105.5	648.3	4	...	...	...	...	...	...	...	...	Virgin Islands (U.S.)
—	—	—	—	—	...	...	...	...	...	...	...	...	West Bank
—	—	40	15	1	...	...	...	...	...	...	...	...	Western Sahara
40	13.7	1,936	7,829	11	735	1,183	82	119	...	...	...	...	Yemen
462[49]	5,173.1[49]	288	1,212	4	598	963	3,371	4,921	1,616[49]	2,600[49]	3,430[49]	5,007[49]	Yugoslavia
—	—	—	—	4	192	308	6.8	9.9	1,398	2,250	...	...	Zambia
—	—	—	—	7	522	840	27	39	...	...	...	...	Zimbabwe

airlines only. [27]Includes transshipments. [28]El Al only. [29]Alitalia only. [30]Air Jamaica only. [31]Kenya Airways only. [32]International traffic only. [33]Peninsular Malaysia and Singapore. [34]Air Nauru only. [35]Includes Aruba. [36]Antillean Airlines only. [37]Air Caledonie only. [38]Philippine Air Lines only. [39]Sierra Leone Airlines international traffic only. [40]Solair only. [41]SAA only. [42]Coastal shipping only. [43]Sudan Airways only. [44]Suriname Airways only. [45]Turkish Airlines only. [46]British Railways only; excludes Northern Ireland. [47]Includes Puerto Rico. [48]Port of Montevideo only. [49]Data refer to Yugoslavia as constituted prior to 1991.

Communications

Virtually all the states of the world have a variety of communications media and services available to their citizens: book, periodical, and newspaper publishing (although only daily papers are included in this table); postal services; and telecommunication systems: radio and television broadcasting, telephones (fixed and mobile), facsimile (fax) machines, personal computers (PCs), and access to the Internet. Unfortunately, the availability of information about these services often runs behind the capabilities of the services themselves. Certain countries publish no official information; others publish data analyzed according to a variety of fiscal, calendar, religious, or other years; still others, while they possess such data almost simultaneously with the end of the business or calendar year, may not see them published except in company or parastatal reports of limited distribution. Even when such data are published in national statistical summaries, it may be only after a delay of up to several years.

The data also differ in their completeness and reliability. Figures for book production, for example, generally include all works published in separate bindings except advertising works, timetables, telephone directories, price

lists, catalogs of businesses or exhibitions, musical scores, maps, atlases, and the like. The figures include government publications, school texts, theses, offprints, series works, and illustrated works, even those consisting principally of illustrations. Figures refer to works actually published during the year of survey, usually by a registered publisher, and deposited for copyright. A book is defined as a work of 49 or more pages; a work published simultaneously in more than one country is counted as having been published in each. A periodical is a publication issued at regular or stated intervals and, in Unesco's usage, directed to the general public. Newspaper statistics are especially difficult to collect and compare. Newspapers continually are founded, cease publication, merge, or change frequency of publication. Data on circulation are often incomplete, slow to be aggregated at the national level, or regarded as proprietary. In some countries no daily newspaper exists.

Post office statistics are compiled mainly from the Universal Postal Union's annual summary *Statistique des services postaux*. Postal services, unlike the other media discussed earlier, tend most often to be operated by

Communications

| country | publishing (latest) | | | | | | | postal services | | | | telecommunications | |
| | books | | periodicals | | daily newspapers | | | post offices, 1995 | | | | radio, 1996 | |
	number of titles	number of copies ('000)	number of titles	number of copies ('000)	number	total circulation ('000)	circulation per 1,000 persons	number	persons per office	pieces of mail handled ('000,000)	pieces handled per person	receivers (all types; '000)	receivers per 1,000 persons
Afghanistan	—	—	...	...	15	216	11	352	61,300	...	...	...	...
Albania	...	...	143	3,477	3	185	54	698	4,600	3.5	1.0	550	157
Algeria	323	...	48	803	6	1,250	46	3,145	8,950	564	20	3,500	125
American Samoa	...	...	...	...	1	2.8	51	...	...	—	—	...	...
Andorra	57	...	...	...	3	4.0	63	...	...	...	...	10	5.7
Angola	...	...	...	...	4	117	11	62	162,000	2.6	0.2	450	39
Antigua and Barbuda	...	...	...	...	1	6.0	94	...	—	—	—	50	778
Argentina	9,065	48,882	...	...	187	4,705	138	5,676	6,100	420	12	21,500	637
Armenia	224	1,739	40	5,064	7	80	23	...	...	1.8	0.5	...	...
Aruba	...	...	...	...	14	52	757	4.0	20,500	...	...	40	571
Australia	10,835	...	...	...	69	4,600	255	3,954	4,560	4,556	252	21,000	1,152
Austria	7,987	...	2,481	...	23	3,736	465	2,634	3,050	3,627	425	4,710	584
Azerbaijan	375	5,557	49	801	3	210	28	1,857	4,040	7.5	1.0	...	...
Bahamas, The	...	...	...	...	3	35	126	136	2,040	611[1]	216[1]	80	282
Bahrain	...	...	26	73	3	70	128	12	48,100	72[2]	122[2]	320	542
Bangladesh	...	...	...	...	51	710	6.0	...	...	261	2.2	8,000	67
Barbados	...	...	...	...	2	41	159	17	15,500	18	68	300	1,132
Belarus	3,346	80,606	155	3,765	10	1,899	187	3,894[2]	2,650[2]	6.7[4]	0.7[4]	3,200	311
Belgium	...	...	13,706	...	32	3,231	321	1,635	6,200	3,557	352	5,000	500
Belize	70	—	...	...	4	23.5	0.5	113	1,900	3.8	18	30	140
Benin	84	42	...	...	1	12	2	159	34,700	8.4	1.5	400	73
Bermuda	...	...	...	...	1	16	254	14	4,350	15	240	80	1,311
Bhutan	...	...	...	...	...	...	...	103	7,990	1.9	1.2	23	28
Bolivia	...	...	...	...	11	500	69	159	46,600	21	2.8	4,250	553
Bosnia and Herzegovina	...	...	...	...	2	518	131	159	21,800	0.5	0.1	840	263
Botswana	...	...	14	177	...	42.1	29.0	193	7,520	36	25	300	206
Brazil	21,574	104,397	...	...	317	7,200	45	10,905	14,300	5,564[5]	365[5]	55,000	340
Brunei	45	...	15	132	1	20	71	6.0	48,700	13	45	125	417
Bulgaria	5,925	42,746	745	3,097	17	1,179	141	3,579	2,340	156	193[3,5]	3,920	437
Burkina Faso	...	...	37	24	1	176[6]	1.6[6]	667	157,000[7]	14[7]	1.5[7]	513	48
Burundi	...	...	...	...	1	20	3.0	272[2]	219,000[2]	7.6[2]	1.3[2]	300	47
Cambodia	...	...	...	...	...	...	...	30	328,000	11[8]	1.1[8]	1,500	150
Cameroon	...	...	...	...	1	50	4.0	261	53,100	5.3	0.4	1,500	115
Canada	22,208	...	1,400	37,108	107	5,500	189	18,607[2]	1,590[2]	10,715[5,8]	370[5,8]	22,600	803
Cape Verde	...	...	...	...	...	...	...	55	6,930	1.7	4.5	57	135
Central African Republic	...	...	...	...	1	2.0	1.0	31	104,000	...	...	180	55
Chad	...	...	...	...	1	2.0	0.4	342[2]	200,000[2]	7.9[2]	1.3[2]	1,310	240
Chile	1,820	...	417	3,450	32	1,411	99	587	24,200	294[2]	21[2]	4,400	317
China	100,951	5,945	6,486	205,060	38	27,790	23	69,003	17,500	7,955[9]	6.5[9]	215,950	178
Colombia	...	...	...	...	46	2,200	64	1,655	21,207	136	3.9	5,400	150
Comoros	...	...	...	...	...	...	...	36[8]	13,611[8]	0.9[8]	1.5[8]	61	97
Congo, Dem. Rep. of the	64	535	...	...	9	112	3.0	304	144,000	...	...	3,480	81
Congo, Rep. of the	...	...	3	34	6	19	8.0	114	2,170	1.8	0.7	240	95
Costa Rica	963	...	...	...	5	333	102	...	...	288[8]	8.5[9]	760	224
Côte d'Ivoire	...	...	...	...	1	90	7.0	364	38,900	46	3.2	1,600	110
Croatia	2,671	...	352	6,357	6	2,600	575	1,190	4,010	262	58	1,100	230
Cuba	932	4,610	160	2,797	17	1,315	120	1,545[8]	7,150[8]	288[8]	2.6[8]	...	...
Cyprus	1,040	1,530	37	167	15	81	110	738	1,130	58	79	210	288
Czech Republic	9,309	...	1,168	81,387	23	2,259	219	3,511	2,940	729	71	9,100	884
Denmark	11,973	...	205	7,838	51	1,610	308	64	81,800	1,828	350	5,200	988
Djibouti	...	...	7	6.0	...	...	...	10	58,600	16	28	35	61
Dominica	...	...	...	...	...	—	—	131[2]	566[2]	2.9[2]	42[2]	65	875
Dominican Republic	...	...	...	...	11	264	35	215	35,000	9.8[1]	1.3[1]	1,180	154
Ecuador	11	40	199	...	24	808	72	267	42,900	18	1.6	3,240	277
Egypt	3,108	108,042	266	1,815	17	3,949	64	7,197	8,280	309	5.2	16,450	265
El Salvador	...	...	...	...	6	284	53	297	18,500	21	3.6	2,080	373
Equatorial Guinea	...	...	...	...	...	1.0	2.5	23[2]	18,300[2]	...	...	200	488
Eritrea	106	420	...	...	...	...	...	35	95,300	1.8	0.5	...	...
Estonia	2,291	8,592	470	...	4	373	242	582	2,550	49	32	...	...
Ethiopia	...	...	...	...	4	81	10	570	97,500	29	0.5	9,000	167

a single national service, to cover a country completely, and to record traffic data according to broadly similar schemes (although the details of *classes* of mail handled may differ). Some countries do not enumerate domestic traffic or may record only international traffic requiring handling charges.

Data for some kinds of telecommunications apparatus are relatively easy to collect; telephones, for example, must be installed, and service recorded so that it may be charged. But in most countries the other types of apparatus mentioned above may be purchased by anyone and used whenever desired. As a result, data on distribution and use of these types of apparatus may be collected in a variety of ways—on the basis of numbers of subscribers, licenses issued, periodic sample surveys, trade data, census or housing surveys, or private consumer surveys. Data on broadcast media refer to receivers; data on telephones to "main lines," or the lines connecting a subscriber's apparatus (fixed or mobile) to the public, switched net. Information on fax machines and PCs is estimated only, as noted above. Internet "hosts" refers to the number of computers directly connected to the worldwide network.

The *Statistical Yearbook* of Unesco contains extensive data on book, periodical, and newspaper publishing, and on radio and television broadcasting that have been collected from standardized questionnaires. The quality and recency of its data, however, depend on the completion and timely return of each questionnaire by national authorities. The commercially published annual *World Radio TV Handbook* (Andrew G. Sennitt, editor) is a valuable source of information on broadcast media and has complete and timely coverage. It depends on data received from broadcasters, but, because some do not respond, local correspondents and monitors are used in many countries, and some unconfirmed or unofficial data are included as estimates. The statistics on telecommunication apparatus and computers are derived mainly from the UN-affiliated International Telecommunication Union's *World Telecommunication Development Report* (annual).

... Not available.

— None, nil, or not applicable.

television, 1995		telephones, 1995		cellular phones, 1995		fax, 1995		personal computers, 1995		Internet hosts, 1995	country
receivers (all types; '000)	receivers per 1,000 persons	main lines ('000)	per 1,000 persons	cellular subscriptions ('000)	subscriptions per 1,000 persons	receivers ('000)	receivers per 1,000 persons	units ('000)	units per 1,000 persons	connections per 1,000,000 persons	
180	10	29	1.4	—	—	0.6	...	...	...	—	Afghanistan
300	89	42	12	—	—	0.6	—	...	...	10	Albania
1,945	71	1,176	42	4.7	0.2	5.2	0.2	85	3.0	0.6	Algeria
...	...	...	...	...	...	...	...	...	...	...	American Samoa
22	360	30	438	2.8	42	1.3	20	...	...	147	Andorra
550	51	60	5.6	2.0	0.2	...	...	...	...	—	Angola
27	419	20	311	...	...	...	...	...	...	2,424	Antigua and Barbuda
12,000	347	5,532	160	341	9.9	50	1.4	850	25	154	Argentina
900	241	583	155	—	—	0.3	0.1	...	...	46	Armenia
33	471	27	390	1.7	25	0.5	6.9	...	...	—	Aruba
11,565	641	9,200	510	2,305	128	475	26	4,979	276	17,146	Australia
4,000	497	3,749	466	384	48	285	35	1,000	124	6,623	Austria
1,600	212	640	85	6.0	0.8	2.5	0.1	...	...	2.1	Azerbaijan
65	233	77	277	2.4	8.6	0.5	1.8	...	...	989	Bahamas, The
255	442	141	242	28	48	5.7	9.9	29	50	244	Bahrain
850	7.0	287	2.4	2.5	2.1	4.0	3.3	...	...	—	Bangladesh
75	284	90	345	4.6	18	1.8	6.8	15	58	7.7	Barbados
2,700	265	1,968	190	5.9	0.6	8.9	0.9	...	...	2.2	Belarus
4,700	464	4,632	458	235	23	165	16	1,400	138	3,024	Belgium
36	167	29	134	1.2	5.7	0.5	2.3	6.0	28	4.6	Belize
400	73	28	5.2	1.1	0.2	0.8	0.1	...	...	—	Benin
...	...	...	...	...	...	0.3	0.4	...	...	...	Bermuda
...	...	5.2	6.3	—	—	...	...	...	...	—	Bhutan
1,500	202	348	47	7.2	1.0	...	...	...	...	8.9	Bolivia
385	111	238	69	—	—	...	...	...	...	—	Bosnia and Herzegovina
35	24	60	41	—	—	3.1	2.1	...	...	—	Botswana
45,000	278	12,083	78	1,286	8.2	200	1.3	2,000	13	124	Brazil
173	609	68	240	36	126	2.0	6.8	8.0	29	549	Brunei
3,011	359	2,563	306	21	2.5	15	1.8	180	22	126	Bulgaria
46	4.4	30	2.9	...	...	...	...	...	...	—	Burkina Faso
40	7.0	17	2.7	0.3	0.1	0.1	0.02	...	...	—	Burundi
80	8.0	5.4	0.5	15	1.5	0.6	0.1	...	...	—	Cambodia
960	75	60	4.5	2.8	0.2	...	...	...	...	—	Cameroon
18,917	647	17,457	590	2,590	88	525	18	5,700	193	12,595	Canada
1.0	3.0	22	55	—	—	0.5	1.3	...	...	—	Cape Verde
17	5.0	7.8	2.3	0.1	—	0.2	0.1	...	...	—	Central African Republic
11	2.0	5.3	0.8	—	—	0.2	0.03	...	...	—	Chad
4,000	280	1,885	132	197	14	15	1.1	540	38	632	Chile
300,000	247	40,706	34	3,629	3.0	270	0.2	2,600	2.1	1.8	China
7,314	188	3,873	100	275	7.1	100	2.6	630	16	58	Colombia
2.0	5.0	4.5	8.2	—	—	0.1	0.2	...	...	324	Comoros
1,800	41	36	0.8	10	0.2	5.0	0.1	...	...	—	Congo, Dem. Rep. of the
42	17	21	8.1	—	—	0.1	0.04	...	...	...	Congo, Rep. of the
750	220	557	167	19	5.6	2.2	0.7	...	...	439	Costa Rica
790	59	116	8.1	—	—	...	...	...	...	0.2	Côte d'Ivoire
1,100	230	1,287	269	34	7.1	38	8.0	100	21	515	Croatia
2,200	200	353	32	1.9	0.2	0.4	0.04	...	...	0.1	Cuba
105	143	347	474	45	61	7.0	9.3	30	41	532	Cyprus
4,200	406	2,444	237	49	4.7	74	7.1	550	53	2,115	Czech Republic
2,800	536	3,203	612	822	157	250	48	1,416	270	9,670	Denmark
42	73	7.6	13	—	—	0.1	0.2	1.0	1.7	10	Djibouti
10	141	18	240	—	—	0.3	4.0	...	...	521	Dominica
680	87	569	76	33	4.4	2.5	0.3	...	...	18	Dominican Republic
1,700	148	748	65	50	4.3	30	2.6	45	3.9	44	Ecuador
7,400	126	2,716	46	14	0.2	3.5	0.05	235	4.1	10	Egypt
1,300	241	285	53	14	2.5	...	...	...	...	4.3	El Salvador
37	92	2.5	6.3	—	—	0.1	0.3	...	...	—	Equatorial Guinea
22	6.0	17	4.8	—	—	0.8	0.2	...	...	—	Eritrea
610	411	412	277	31	21	13	8.7	10	6.7	2,782	Estonia
230	4.2	143	2.5	—	—	1.4	0.02	...	...	0.02	Ethiopia

Communications (continued)

country	publishing (latest) books number of titles	books number of copies ('000)	periodicals number of titles	periodicals number of copies ('000)	daily newspapers number	daily newspapers total circulation ('000)	daily newspapers circulation per 1,000 persons	postal services post offices, 1995 number	persons per office	pieces of mail handled ('000,000)	pieces handled per person	telecommunications radio, 1996 receivers (all types; '000)	receivers per 1,000 persons
Faroe Islands	...	...	...	...	...	...	...	43	1,010	10	198	21	447
Fiji	401	2,256	...	...	1	35	45	261	2,930	24[7]	31[7]	450	574
Finland	12,539	...	5,711	...	56	2,368	464	1,791	2,850	1,143[5]	224[5]	4,950	966
France	45,311	1,041	2,672	120,018	118	13,685	237	16,919[2]	3,440[2]	24,391	419	50,000	862
French Guiana	...	...	...	...	1	2.0	11	...	...	...	...	71	486
French Polynesia	...	...	...	...	4	24	112	97	2,250	21[2]	95[2]	105	488
Gabon	...	...	...	...	1	20	16	60	19,300	5.7	4.3	155	119
Gambia, The	21	20	10	885	2	2.0	2.0	...	...	...	...	150	125
Gaza Strip	...	...	...	...	...	...	...	...	...	...	...	...	...
Georgia	314	1,131	...	...	...	...	...	...	...	1,025[2,4]	188[2,4]	...	...
Germany	70,643	...	9,010	395,036	411	25,757	317	17,172	4,760	19,963	244	150,000	1,875
Ghana	28	...	121	774	4	310	18	1,001	17,300	121	6.9	1,300	76
Gibraltar	...	...	...	...	2	6.0	214	3.0	9,040	6.4	214	17	573
Greece	...	...	...	...	168	1,622	156	1,266	8,260	368[5]	35[5]	4,200	400
Greenland	...	...	...	...	...	...	...	75	744	7.2	120	22	374
Grenada	...	...	...	...	1[10]	4.0[10]	45[10]	58[2]	1,680[2]	...	...	45	489
Guadeloupe	...	...	...	...	1	35	83	...	...	...	...	85	208
Guam	...	...	...	...	1	25	170	...	...	...	...	274	1,827
Guatemala	...	...	...	...	5	240	23	540[2]	19,700[2]	79[2]	7.7[2]	570	52
Guernsey	...	...	...	...	...	...	...	15	4,120	15[9]	251[9]	...	...
Guinea	...	...	3	5.0	...	...	...	83	86,300	9.5	1.4	230	35
Guinea-Bissau	...	...	...	...	1	6.0	6.0	26	43,300	311[11]	0.3[11]	40	36
Guyana	33	508	...	...	2	45	63	85	8,950	4.4[4]	5.3[4]	380	454
Haiti	...	...	...	...	4	45	7.1	121	53,200	8.6[4]	1.2[4]	270	41
Honduras	22	80	...	...	5	240	44	435	12,700	35	5.9	1,910	354
Hong Kong	...	...	598	...	43	2,951[12]	479[12]	123	50,000	1,151	187	3,700	586
Hungary	10,108	75,645	1,203	14,927	27	2,321	228	3,230	3,170	1,187	116	6,250	590
Iceland	1,429	...	938	384	5	137	515	...	...	...	...	197	733
India	11,460	...	...	...	...	...	...	152,792	6,130	13,751	15	111,000	121
Indonesia	6,303	...	117	3,985	56	3,800	20	8,146	23,800	775	4.0	26,000	132
Iran	10,753	26,275	318	6,166	12	1,200	20	10,539	5,700	223	3.3	13,000	213
Iraq	...	...	...	...	4	532	27	...	...	62	3.1	13,000	630
Ireland	...	...	...	...	8	600	170	1,934	1,860	614	172	...	...
Isle of Man	...	...	...	...	...	...	...	35	2,040	205[5,8]	2815[5,8]	...	...
Israel	4,608	9,368	...	...	34	1,534	281	663	8,160	505	92	2,250	481
Italy	32,673	289,100	9,951	80,469	74	5,985	105	14,142	4,050	5,691	100	46,350	801
Jamaica	...	...	...	...	3	160	66	793	3,140	70	28	1,859	747
Japan	35,496	316,725	2,926	...	121	71,924	576	24,587	5,090	24,651	197	100,000	801
Jersey	...	...	...	...	...	...	...	23[8]	3,700[8]	50[8]	594[8]	...	...
Jordan	500	...	31	43	4	250	48	1,007	4,190	61	11	980	234
Kazakstan	1,148	18,999	...	...	...	...	...	4,355	3,810	201	0.01	...	...
Kenya	...	...	...	...	5	358	13	1,061	26,000	386	12	3,000	103
Kiribati	...	...	...	...	...	...	...	247[7]	3,310[7]	353[7]	4.7[7]	6.4	79
Korea, North	...	...	...	...	11	5,000	213	...	...	...	...	4.7	0.2
Korea, South	34,204	160,305	...	...	62	18,000	405	3,437	13,000	3,432[9]	77[9]	42,000	928
Kuwait	196	...	...	...	9	655	387	...	...	99[8]	68[8]	1,000	591
Kyrgyzstan	328	1,875	...	...	3	53	11	918	4,920	525	115	...	...
Laos	64	136	...	...	3	14	3.0	417	11,600	1.4	0.3	575	121
Latvia	1,677	10,835	213	1,660	22	589	228	1,019	2,470	23	9.0	1,396	547
Lebanon	...	...	...	...	16	500	135	...	...	...	...	2,247	601
Lesotho	...	...	...	...	2	14	7.0	155	12,500	74	36	1,100	569
Liberia	...	...	...	...	8	35	14	...	...	...	...	600	275
Libya	...	...	...	...	4	70	13	383[2]	13,700[2]	28[2]	5.8[2]	1,000	190
Liechtenstein	...	...	...	...	2	18	581	...	...	177	0.6[7]	...	...
Lithuania	2,885	19,627	269	...	16	506	136	1,009	3,680	39	10	1,420	381
Luxembourg	681	...	508	...	5	154	384	106	3,860	155	378	240	586
Macau	...	...	16	...	9	250	591	13	34,500	16	37	250	591
Macedonia	672	2,918	74	347	3	44	21	...	...	...	...	350	179
Madagascar	114	287	55	108	7	60	4.5	816	16,300	39	2.6	2,300	173
Malawi	243	10	...	...	1	25	2.6	307	30,800	96	10	1,060	112
Malaysia	4,050	17,424	25	996	44	2,800	142	1,475	14,000	1,051	52	9,500	476
Maldives	...	...	...	...	2	3.0	12	362	700	2.4	9.6	25	99
Mali	...	...	...	...	2	40	4.4	124	75,600	4.1	0.4	1,600	176
Malta	417	...	359	...	3	54	145	50[2]	7,420[2]	136[2]	373[2]	95	260
Marshall Islands	...	...	...	...	...	...	...	...	...	...	...	...	...
Martinique	...	...	...	...	1	32	84	...	...	...	...	71	187
Mauritania	...	...	...	...	1	1.0	0.5	60	37,700	617	0.3	1,000	444
Mauritius	84	100	62	...	6	75	68	103	10,900	43	38	400	353
Mayotte	...	...	...	...	...	...	...	...	...	...	...	50	427
Mexico	...	...	158	13,097	309	10,420	113	7,382	12,300	948	10	21,000	230
Micronesia	...	...	...	...	...	...	...	...	...	...	...	70	667
Moldova	797	5,850	76	196	4	106	24	1,307	3,320	57	13	1,556	358
Monaco	...	...	3	38	1	8.0	263	...	...	...	...	30	987
Mongolia	285	959	45	6,361	1	207	88	358[2]	6,430[2]	2.3[2]	1.8[2]	280	121
Morocco	354	1,380	...	...	13	344	13	...	...	...	...	5,100	194
Mozambique	...	...	...	...	2	81	5.0	425	40,400	8.8	0.5	620	36
Myanmar (Burma)	3,660	...	...	...	5	1,032	23	1,206	37,400	88	1.9	3,300	72
Namibia	...	...	...	...	4	153	93	86	18,900	29[2,5]	18[2,5]	230	136
Nauru	...	...	...	...	...	...	...	25	406	...	...	6.0	577
Nepal	...	...	...	...	28	162	8.0	2,874[2]	7,080[2]	104[2]	4.9[2]	625	29
Netherlands, The	34,067	...	367	19,283	46	4,600	299	2,009	7,690	...	...	12,000	775
Netherlands Antilles	...	...	...	...	6	53	260	...	...	...	...	206	1,009
New Caledonia	...	...	...	...	3	23	123	57	3,280	24	131	92	495
New Zealand	...	...	...	...	31	1,050	297	...	...	...	...	3,100	866
Nicaragua	...	...	...	...	4	130	30	202[2]	21,600[2]	112[2,4]	2.6[2,4]	925	222

television, 1995		telephones, 1995		cellular phones, 1995		fax, 1995		personal computers, 1995		Internet hosts, 1995	country
receivers (all types; '000)	receivers per 1,000 persons	main lines ('000)	per 1,000 persons	cellular subscriptions ('000)	subscriptions per 1,000 persons	receivers ('000)	receivers per 1,000 persons	units ('000)	units per 1,000 persons	connections per 1,000,000 persons	
...	...	...	...	...	...	...	...	...	...	...	Faroe Islands
70	89	65	83	2.2	2.8	3.0	3.8	...	...	66	Fiji
2,650	519	2,796	547	1,018	199	132	26	930	182	42,229	Finland
33,600	579	32,400	558	1,379	24	1,900	33	7,800	134	2,604	France
25	170	41	288	—	—	...	...	...	...	—	French Guiana
39	177	47	219	—	—	0.9	4.1	...	...	—	French Polynesia
100	76	32	24	4.0	3.0	0.4	0.4	6.0	4.5	—	Gabon
...	...	19	17	1.4	1.3	1.0	0.6	...	...	—	Gambia, The
...	...	...	...	...	...	...	...	...	...	...	Gaza Strip
1,200	220	554	103	0.2	0.04	0.5	0.1	...	...	11	Georgia
45,000	550	40,400	494	3,750	46	1,447	18	13,500	165	5,794	Germany
265	16	60	3.5	6.2	0.4	4.5	0.3	20	1.2	0.4	Ghana
											Gibraltar
4,630	442	5,163	493	273	26	15	1.5	350	33	740	Greece
...	...	...	...	...	...	...	...	...	...	...	Greenland
15	158	23	255	0.4	4.4	0.3	3.1	...	...	—	Grenada
112	262	159	378	...	...	3.4	8.1	...	...	—	Guadeloupe
95	648	69	461	5.0	33	...	...	...	...	367	Guam
1,300	122	290	27	30	2.8	10	0.9	30	2.8	2.5	Guatemala
...	...	42	689	2.4	39	0.7	11	...	...	...	Guernsey
500	76	11	1.6	1.0	0.1	0.2	0.03	1.0	0.2	0.3	Guinea
...	...	9.4	8.8	—	—	0.5	0.5	...	...	—	Guinea-Bissau
35	42	45	63	1.2	1.6	...	...	...	...	—	Guyana
35	5.0	60	8.4	—	—	—	...	—	...	—	Haiti
450	80	161	29	—	—	...	...	...	...	—	Honduras
2,092	359	3,508	556	798	129	285	46	720	116	2,858	Hong Kong
4,530	444	1,893	185	265	26	45	4.4	400	39	1,546	Hungary
120	447	149	556	31	116	4.1	15	55	206	31,007	Iceland
57,000	61	11,978	13	136	0.1	50	0.1	1,200	1.3	0.9	India
28,000	147	3,291	17	219	1.1	85	0.4	730	3.7	12	Indonesia
9,000	134	5,090	85	9.2	0.2	30	0.5	...	...	4.0	Iran
1,450	74	675	33	—	—	...	...	...	...	—	Iraq
1,370	382	1,310	365	158	44	80	22	520	145	3,747	Ireland
...	...	...	...	...	...	...	...	...	...	...	Isle of Man
1,700	303	2,343	418	300	54	140	25	540	100	5,260	Israel
25,000	436	24,854	433	3,864	67	202	3.5	4,800	84	1,280	Italy
773	306	292	116	45	18	0.6	...	...	...	65	Jamaica
77,500	619	61,106	488	10,204	82	8,000	64	19,100	153	2,151	Japan
...	...	59	687	4.4	51	0.7	8.0	...	...	...	Jersey
740	175	317	73	12	2.6	32	7.3	35	8.0	4.4	Jordan
4,578	275	1,963	118	4.6	0.3	2.9	0.2	...	...	11	Kazakhstan
462	18	240	9.0	2.3	0.1	3.8	0.1	18	0.7	0.6	Kenya
2.0	25	2.0	26	—	—	0.2	2.5	...	...	—	Kiribati
2,700	115	1,100	46	—	—	3.0	0.1	...	...	—	Korea, North
14,400	321	18,600	415	1,641	37	375	8.4	5,420	121	653	Korea, South
630	373	382	226	118	70	35	21	95	56	729	Kuwait
1,110	247	357	77	—	—	...	...	...	...	—	Kyrgyzstan
35	7.0	20	4.1	1.5	0.3	0.5	0.1	...	...	—	Laos
1,213	482	705	280	15	6.0	0.9	0.3	20	7.9	525	Latvia
1,075	291	330	89	120	30	3.0	0.8	50	13	22	Lebanon
13	7.0	18	9.0	—	—	0.6	0.3	...	...	—	Lesotho
54	25	4.5	2.1	—	—	...	...	...	...	—	Liberia
720	138	318	59	—	—	...	...	...	...	—	Libya
...	...	...	...	...	...	...	...	...	...	...	Liechtenstein
1,350	364	941	254	15	4.0	3.8	1.0	24	6.5	123	Lithuania
242	593	222	550	—	—	—	—	—	—	4,608	Luxembourg
48	113	153	361	37	86	7.3	17	40	94	153	Macau
350	179	349	179	—	—	1.8	0.8	...	...	42	Macedonia
320	24	33	2.4	—	—	...	...	...	...	—	Madagascar
...	...	34	3.6	0.4	0.04	1.1	0.1	...	...	—	Malawi
4,500	226	3,332	166	873	43	58	3.0	800	40	...	Malaysia
10	40	14	57	—	—	3.5	14	3.0	12	—	Maldives
110	12	17	1.7	—	—	...	...	...	...	—	Mali
167	448	171	459	11	29	3.2	8.6	30	81	231	Malta
...	...	...	...	...	...	...	...	...	...	...	Marshall Islands
53	137	148	381	12	31	20	52	36	93	—	Martinique
132	58	9.2	4.1	—	—	0.3	0.1	...	...	—	Mauritania
210	187	148	131	12	10	20	18	36	32	—	Mauritius
...	0.6	5.3	48	—	—	...	...	...	...	—	Mayotte
17,600	192	8,801	96	642	7.0	180	2.1	2,400	26	...	Mexico
2.0	21	7.9	74	—	—	0.3	2.9	...	...	—	Micronesia
1,300	300	567	131	—	—	0.6	0.1	9.0	2.1	1.2	Moldova
...	...	...	...	...	...	...	...	...	...	...	Monaco
143	59	78	32	—	—	2.2	0.9	...	...	—	Mongolia
3,800	145	1,158	43	1.6	0.1	7.5	0.3	45	1.7	8.6	Morocco
51	3.0	60	3.4	—	—	7.2	0.4	...	...	—	Mozambique
3,450	76	147	3.3	2.1	0.04	1.4	0.03	...	...	—	Myanmar (Burma)
45	29	79	51	3.5	2.3	...	...	...	...	7.1	Namibia
...	...	...	...	...	...	...	...	...	...	...	Nauru
60	3.0	77	3.6	—	—	0.6	0.03	...	...	0.9	Nepal
7,650	495	8,120	525	513	33	500	32	3,100	200	11,110	Netherlands, The
65	325	75	374	12	59	...	...	...	...	...	Netherlands Antilles
71	380	44	236	0.8	4.5	2.2	12	...	...	5.4	New Caledonia
1,818	506	1,719	479	388	108	65	18	800	223	14,923	New Zealand
700	170	97	23	4.4	1.1	...	...	...	...	34	Nicaragua

Communications (continued)

country	publishing (latest) books number of titles	books number of copies ('000)	periodicals number of titles	periodicals number of copies ('000)	daily newspapers number	daily newspapers total circulation ('000)	daily newspapers circulation per 1,000 persons	postal services post offices, 1995 number	persons per office	pieces of mail handled ('000,000)	pieces handled per person	telecommunications radio, 1996 receivers (all types; '000)	receivers per 1,000 persons
Niger	...	...	...	...	4	11	1.3	66	134,000	3.9	0.4	440	48
Nigeria	1,562	...	...	...	27	1,950	18	3,639	26,900	812	7.3	17,200[13]	170[13]
Northern Mariana Islands	...	...	...	...	...	...	...	...	...	...	...	11	190
Norway	6,846	...	8,017	...	83	2,170	498	2,356	1,850	2,176	499	3,342	767
Oman	24	25	15	...	4	63	30	90	23,400	32[2,5]	15[2,5]	900	416
Pakistan	124	714	...	...	273	2,840	22	13,320	9,750	257[5]	2.0[5]	10,200	76
Palau	...	...	...	...	...	...	...	...	...	...	...	9.0	536
Panama	...	...	...	...	7	160	62	343	7,670	10	3.9	527	200
Papua New Guinea	...	...	...	...	2	65	15	108[14]	39,800[14]	39[14]	10[14]	300	72
Paraguay	152	...	...	...	5	203	42	321	15,000	5.0	1.0	700	144
Peru	1,993	...	...	...	48	2,000	86	836[2]	28,100[2]	22	0.9	5,300	225
Philippines	1,233	...	1,570	9,468	42	4,286	65	3,023[2]	22,600[2]	1,108[2]	16[2]	8,300	116
Poland	10,874	98,612	3,999	77,735	66	5,404	141	7,853	4,920	1,217	32	16,300	421
Portugal	6,667	26,942	984	10,208	23	404	41	6,638	1,490	1,009[9]	93[9]	2,220	224
Puerto Rico	...	...	...	...	3	670	184	...	...	...	...	2,480	666
Qatar	371	184	12	157	4	80	138	30	18,600	20[4]	36[4]	180	311
Réunion	69	...	...	...	3	55	83	...	...	...	...	170	265
Romania	4,074	50,230	987	...	69	6,800	297	5,243	4,330	292	13	4,500	198
Russia	30,390	594,323	2,592	918,218	17	39,301	267	45,594	3,250	7,110[5]	48[5]	...	...
Rwanda	...	...	15	101	1	0.5	0.1	1.0[2]	6,018,000[2]	...	...	...	...
St. Kitts and Nevis	...	...	10	44	...	...	...	7.0	5,630	2.4	59	4.5	110
St. Lucia	...	...	...	...	...	...	...	...	...	...	...	100	699
St. Vincent and the Grenadines	...	...	...	...	...	...	...	41	2,680	...	...	65	565
Samoa	...	...	...	...	...	...	...	38	4,360	998	5,871	...	...
San Marino	...	...	18	11	5	1.3	0.5	10	2,488	...	...	13	522
São Tomé and Príncipe	...	...	...	...	...	...	...	10[2]	13,100[2]	0.3	0.02	31	237
Saudi Arabia	...	...	471	...	19	950	54	1,282	13,900	896	50	3,800	213
Senegal	...	...	...	...	3	48	6.0	131	61,100	6.7[9]	0.7[9]	...	...
Seychelles	...	...	...	...	1	3.0	40	5.0	15,000	4.5	64	50	667
Sierra Leone	...	...	...	...	1	10	2.2	54	85,000	1.1	0.2	1,000	221
Singapore	...	...	...	...	8	1,015	340	1,163	2,570	646	216	822	275
Slovakia	3,481	6,139	424	8,725	21	1.363	256	1,731	3,100	526	98	630	118
Slovenia	2,906	...	784	...	6	360	183	515	3,860	267	135	630	320
Solomon Islands	...	...	...	...	...	...	...	140	2,730	4.3	11	45	117
Somalia	...	...	...	...	1	9.0	1.0	...	...	...	...	300	41
South Africa	4,574	37,561	11	2,149	17	1,346	33	...	...	2,452	59	11,200	273
Spain	44,261	180,081	...	...	148	4,100	104	4,527	8,660	4,295	110	12,000	304
Sri Lanka	2,929	15,337	...	...	9	450	25	4,138	4,440	486	26	3,300	182
Sudan, The	...	...	...	...	5	620	23	411	74,300	5.3[8]	0.2[8]	5,755	193
Suriname	...	...	...	...	3	43	103	...	...	...	...	262	609
Swaziland	...	...	...	...	3	12	14	65	14,900	25	27	500	550
Sweden	13,822	...	4,272	...	94	4,544	515	1,745	5,060	4,533	513	7,450	844
Switzerland	15,378	...	60	4,561	80	2,920	415	3,674	1,920	4,230[7]	601[7]	5,600	791
Syria	598	...	...	...	8	261	18	650	21,800	17	1.2	3,000	207
Taiwan	...	...	...	...	...	4,000	188	...	...	...	...	8,620	402
Tajikistan	231	2,561	22	50	2	80	13	736	7,930	9.2	1.6	...	...
Tanzania	...	...	...	...	3	220	8.0	525	54,400	22	0.2	3,500	123
Thailand	7,626	...	1,522	...	35	2,766	47	4,264[2]	13,900[2]	1,228	21	10,000	167
Togo	...	...	...	...	1	10	2.0	50	88,200	4.1	1.0	720	170
Tonga	...	...	...	...	1	7.0	73	1.8[8]	55,600[8]	4.0[8]	40[8]	40	400
Trinidad and Tobago	26	30	...	...	4	175	135	243	5,190	30	23	550	433
Tunisia	539	94	...	...	7	403	46	955	9,390	117	13	1,700	193
Turkey	4,473	...	3,554	...	57	2,679	44	31,122	1,970	1,482	24	8,800	141
Turkmenistan	565	6,604	...	...	...	...	...	...	...	...	...	850	189
Tuvalu	...	...	...	...	...	...	...	...	...	...	...	3.0	319
Uganda	314	2,229	26	158	2	35	2.0	306	64,500	18	1.0	10,000	507
Ukraine	5,002	87,567	321	3,491	90	6,083	118	16,421	3,140	591	11	18,000	349
United Arab Emirates	293	5,117	80	922	8	300	126	180	13,200	162	70	490	206
United Kingdom	95,015	...	...	...	103	20,372	351	...	...	...	...	65,400	1,109
United States	51,863	...	11,593	...	1,548	59,305	228	49,906	5,300	178,970	0.7	520,000	1,976
Uruguay	...	...	...	...	32	750	237	295	10,600	15	4.7	1,850	591
Uzbekistan	1,340	44,033	70	2,032	4	160	7.0	...	...	...	...	...	...
Vanuatu	...	...	...	...	...	...	...	...	...	...	...	55	327
Venezuela	3,660	8,180	...	...	89	4,600	215	444	49,200	93	4.3	8,300	383
Vietnam	5,581	83,000	...	...	4	570	8.0	...	...	...	...	7,000	95
Virgin Islands (U.S.)	...	...	...	...	2	26	267	9[2]	10,800	3.6[4]	0.2[4]	100	1,029
West Bank	...	...	...	...	...	...	...	...	...	...	...	...	...
Western Sahara	...	...	...	...	...	...	...	...	...	...	...	...	...
Yemen	...	...	...	...	3	230	17	451	34,000	6.8	0.5	665	48
Yugoslavia	2,799	11,905	395	...	9	966	90	1,569[7]	6,722[7]	0.21[15]	0.02[15]	2,692	256
Zambia	...	...	...	...	...	...	...	203	44,200	26	2.8	1,300	139
Zimbabwe	232	...	28	680	2	192	17	280	39,900	298	26	1,300	113

television, 1995 receivers (all types; '000)	television, 1995 receivers per 1,000 persons	telephones, 1995 main lines ('000)	telephones, 1995 main lines per 1,000 persons	cellular phones, 1995 cellular subscriptions ('000)	cellular phones, 1995 subscriptions per 1,000 persons	fax, 1995 receivers ('000)	fax, 1995 receivers per 1,000 persons	personal computers, 1995 units ('000)	personal computers, 1995 units per 1,000 persons	Internet hosts, 1995 connections per 1,000,000 persons	country
200	23	13	1.5	—	—	300	33	...	...	—	Niger
4,000	38	405	3.6	13	0.1	...	...	440	4.1	...	Nigeria
											Northern Mariana Islands
2,450	561	2,431	558	1,013	232	130	30	1,193	273	19,289	Norway
132	61	170	79	8.1	3.7	1.6	0.7	28	13	...	Oman
2,800	22	2,127	16	43	0.3	159	1.2	155	1.2	0.1	Pakistan
...	...	...	...	...	...	...	...	...	...	...	Palau
610	229	304	116	—	—	—	—	...	...	56	Panama
700	163	44	10	—	—	0.8	0.2	...	...	—	Papua New Guinea
710	144	167	34	16	3.2	1.7	0.4	...	...	—	Paraguay
2,350	100	1,109	47	74	3.1	15	0.6	140	5.9	35	Peru
9,000	129	1,787	25	493	6.9	35	0.5	770	11	26	Philippines
15,765	408	5,729	148	75	1.9	55	1.4	1,100	29	598	Poland
...	...	3,586	362	341	34	35	3.4	600	61	1,187	Portugal
1,160	311	1,196	321	171	48	543	146	...	...	23	Puerto Rico
...	...	123	212	19	33	9.4	16	30	52	11	Qatar
135	205	219	329	...	...	1.9	2.9	...	...	—	Réunion
4,580	201	2,968	131	9.1	0.4	21	0.9	120	5.3	77	Romania
56,244	380	25,019	170	89	0.6	31	0.2	2,600	18	149	Russia
10	1.7	15	2.5	—	—	0.5	0.1	...	...	—	Rwanda
...	...	...	...	...	...	...	...	...	...	...	St. Kitts and Nevis
...	...	...	...	...	...	...	...	...	...	...	St. Lucia
...	...	...	...	...	...	...	...	...	...	...	St. Vincent and the Grenadines
7.0	38	7.8	46	—	—	0.4	2.4	...	...	...	Samoa
...	...	...	...	...	...	...	...	...	...	...	San Marino
...	...	2.5	19	—	—	0.2	1.5	...	...	—	São Tomé and Príncipe
4,600	257	1,719	96	16	0.9	75	4.4	600	35	1.5	Saudi Arabia
290	37	82	9.8	0.1	0.01	...	...	60	7.2	0.7	Senegal
14	184	14	187	0.3	4.3	0.6	8.0	...	...	—	Seychelles
73	16	17	3.7	—	—	1.0	0.2	...	...	—	Sierra Leone
650	218	1,429	478	292	98	56	19	515	172	7,624	Singapore
1,157	216	1,119	208	12	2.3	45	8.4	220	41	543	Slovakia
745	374	615	309	157	14	80	41	95	48	2,948	Slovenia
6.0	16	6.5	17	0.2	0.6	0.8	2.1	...	...	24	Solomon Islands
118	13	15	1.7	—	—	...	118[1]	...	...	—	Somalia
4,200	101	3,919	95	535	13	75	1.8	1,100	27	1,165	South Africa
19,200	490	15,095	385	966	25	215	5.2	3,200	82	1,018	Spain
1,200	66	204	11	53	3.0	11	0.6	20	1.1	0.3	Sri Lanka
2,300	76	75	2.7	—	—	5.8	0.2	...	...	—	Sudan, The
80	186	53	123	3.7	8.6	0.3	0.7	...	...	—	Suriname
90	96	20	21	—	—	0.9	1.0	...	...	1.1	Swaziland
4,202	476	6,010	681	2,025	229	329	37	1,700	193	16,405	Sweden
2,602	370	4,319	613	447	64	197	28	2,450	348	11,383	Switzerland
1,300	89	930	63	—	—	5.0	0.3	10	0.7	—	Syria
7,000	327	10,011	467	970	45	430	20	1,773	83	1,207	Taiwan
1,500	258	263	45	—	—	1.3	0.2	...	...	—	Tajikistan
450	16	90	3.0	3.5	0.1	0.1	...	...	...	—	Tanzania
13,500	227	3,482	59	1,088	18	60	1.0	900	15	68	Thailand
50	12	22	5.2	—	—	10	2.4	...	...	—	Togo
2.0	20	6.6	67	0.1	1.2	0.2	2.0	...	...	10	Tonga
415	328	209	166	5.6	4.4	2.6	1.6	25	20	42	Trinidad and Tobago
1,400	156	523	58	3.2	0.4	25	2.8	60	6.7	8.8	Tunisia
15,000	240	13,228	215	437	7.1	99	1.6	770	13	85	Turkey
850	189	320	71	—	—	...	...	...	...	...	Turkmenistan
...	...	...	...	...	...	...	...	...	...	...	Tuvalu
500	26	43	2.3	1.7	0.1	2.5	—	10	0.5	3.1	Uganda
12,000	233	8,311	161	14	0.3	1.5	0.03	290	5.6	45	Ukraine
500	26	672	283	129	54	25	11	115	48	154	United Arab Emirates
35,800	61	29,409	502	5,736	98	1,800	31	10,900	186	7,513	United Kingdom
204,100	78	164,624	626	33,786	128	14,052	54	86,300	328	23,012	United States
970	310	622	199	40	13	11	3.5	70	22	346	Uruguay
4,000	176	1,738	76	3.7	0.2	1.9	0.1	...	...	1.5	Uzbekistan
2.0	12	42	250	0.1	0.7	0.6	3.6	...	...	—	Vanuatu
4,000	180	2,463	111	400	18	16	0.8	370	17	52	Venezuela
12,000	163	775	11	24	0.3	15	0.1	30	0.4	—	Vietnam
...	...	58	597	...	...	...	32	...	...	—	Virgin Islands (U.S.)
...	...	80	63	20	16	...	...	...	...	...	West Bank
...	...	...	...	...	...	...	...	...	...	...	Western Sahara
3,900	243	187	12	8.3	0.5	2.0	0.1	...	...	—	Yemen
1,800	170	2,017	192	—	—	15	1.4	125	12	—	Yugoslavia
600	64	77	8.2	1.5	0.2	0.6	0.1	...	...	7.3	Zambia
290	27	155	14	—	—	10	0.9	33	3.0	8.5	Zimbabwe

[1]1985. [2]1994. [3]Letters dispatched only. [4]Foreign-dispatched and foreign-received only. [5]Domestic only. [6]Circulation for 3 newspapers only. [7]1992. [8]1993. [9]Domestic and foreign-dispatched only. [10]1980. [11]Foreign-received only. [12]Circulation for 32 newspapers only. [13]1995. [14]1991. [15]Letters only.

Trade: external

The following table presents comparative data on the international, or foreign, trade of the countries of the world. The table analyzes data for both imports and exports in two ways: (1) into several major commodity groups defined in accordance with the United Nations system called the Standard International Trade Classification (SITC) and (2) by direction of trade for each country with major world trading blocs and partners. These commodity groupings are defined by the SITC code numbers beneath the column headings. The single-digit numbers represent broad SITC categories (in the SITC, called "sections"); the double-digit numbers represent subcategories ("divisions") of the single-digit categories (27 is a subcategory of 2); the three-digit number is a subcategory ("group") of the double-digit (667 is a subcategory of 66). Where a plus or minus sign is used before one of these SITC numbers, the SITC category or subcategory is being added to or subtracted from the aggregate implied by the total of the preceding sections. The SITC commodity aggregations used here are listed in the table at the end of this headnote. The full SITC commodity breakdown—some 3,118 basic headings—is presented in the 1986 United Nations publication *Standard International Trade Classification, Revision 3.*

The SITC was developed by the United Nations through its Statistical Commission as an outgrowth of the need for a standard system of aggregating commodities of external trade to provide international comparability of foreign trade statistics. The United Nations Statistical Commission has defined external merchandise trade as "all goods whose movement into or out of the customs area of a country compiling the statistics adds to or subtracts from the material resources of the country." Goods passing through a country for transport only are excluded, but goods entering for reexport, or deposited (as in a bonded warehouse, or free trade area) for reimport, are included. Statistics in this table refer only to goods and exclude purely financial transactions that are covered in the "Finance" and "National product and accounts" tables. Gold for fabrication (*e.g.*, as jewelry) is included; monetary and reserve gold are excluded.

For purposes of comparability of data, total value of imports and exports is given in this table in U.S. dollars. Conversions from currencies other than U.S. dollars are determined according to the average market rates for the year for which data are supplied; these are mainly as calculated by the International Monetary Fund (IMF) or other official sources. The commodity categories are given in terms of percentages of the total value of the country's import or export trade (with the exclusions noted above). Value is based on transaction value: for imports, the value at which the goods were purchased by the importer plus the cost of transportation and insurance to the frontier of the importing country (c.i.f. [cost, insurance,

Trade: external

country	year	imports total value ('000,000 U.S.$)	Standard International Trade Classification (SITC) categories (%)							direction of trade (%)				
			food and agricultural raw materials (0 + 1 + 2 − 27 − 28 + 4)	mineral ores and concentrates (27 + 28 + 667)	fuels and other energy (3)	manufactured goods				from European Union (EU)[b]	from United States	from Eastern Europe[c]	from Japan	from all other[d]
						total[a] (5 + 6 − 667 + 7 + 8 + 9)	of which chemicals and related products (5)	of which machinery and transport equipment (7)	of which other[a] (6 − 667 + 8 + 9)					
Afghanistan	1991[1]	936.4	15.0	—[2]	0.4	84.6[3]	2.1	48.2	34.3[3]	4.8[4]	0.2[4]	59.9[4, 5]	7.9[4]	27.2[4]
Albania	1994	601.0	25.7[6]	—24.5[6]—		49.8[6]	9.3[6]	31.0[6]	9.5[6]	67.9[7]	0.2	9.9	—	22.0
Algeria	1995	9,830.6	32.6	0.3	1.1	66.0	11.3	30.5	24.1	59.3	13.2	2.5	3.4	21.6
American Samoa	1993[8]	427.5	63.1	...	8.1	28.8[3]	0.2	5.5	23.1	0.2[9]	73.4[9]	—[9]	8.5[9]	17.9[9]
Andorra	1995	1,055.5	30.6	0.9	3.5	65.0	10.0	21.9	33.1	85.7	4.2	0.1	3.4	6.6
Angola	1993	2,041.9	—32.4[2, 6]—		0.7[6]	66.9[3, 6]	10.6[6]	25.0[6]	31.3[3, 6]	79.7[4]	7.2	0.9[4]	2.2	10.0[4]
Antigua and Barbuda	1991	245.9	—17.8[2]—		9.9	72.3[3]	6.2	26.8	39.3[3]	41.3[11]	29.5[11]	—[11]	—[11]	29.2[11]
Argentina	1995	20,121.7	7.5	1.5	4.2	86.8	17.8	44.5	24.4	29.9	20.9	1.1	3.5	44.6
Armenia	1995	673.9	33.6	—42.6—		23.8	8.8	8.3	6.7	13.2	17.0	22.6	—	47.2
Aruba	1991	486.9	23.3	0.1	0.4	76.2	8.7	27.6	39.9	16.7	57.3	—	3.4	22.6
Australia	1996	65,427.0	6.3	0.4[2]	6.2	87.1[3]	11.6	47.0	28.6[3]	24.9	23.0	0.2	13.0	39.0
Austria	1995	65,662.5	9.3	1.5	4.5	84.6	10.6	36.7	37.4	75.5	3.1	6.4	1.7	13.3
Azerbaijan	1995	667.6	42.3	—15.1—		42.6	10.9	17.9	13.8	12.7	2.0	24.4	0.2	60.7
Bahamas, The	1990	2,919.9	8.6	—	65.2	26.2	5.3	8.3	12.7	5.9	36.2	0.25	0.5	57.3
Bahrain	1995	3,624.8	—13.3[2]—		38.1	48.5[3]	8.7	16.2	23.6[3]	19.7	8.2	0.2	4.1	67.8
Bangladesh	1993[12]	2,708.8	40.6	4.6	9.6	45.3	9.2	13.6	22.5	11.1	5.2	1.3	6.7	75.8
Barbados	1995	766.0	20.6	0.5	8.5	70.4	12.2	26.8	31.4	17.1	40.7	0.2	6.7	35.2
Belarus	1995	5,563.6	11.8	—36.1—		52.1	14.8	17.0	20.3	16.7	1.7	74.8	0.4	6.4
Belgium[13]	1995	150,624.7	13.2	9.4	6.1	71.3	13.7	26.1	31.5	74.5	5.6	2.1	2.6	15.1
Belize	1995	258.3	19.4	0.3	11.5	68.9	10.7	25.8	32.3	15.5	54.1	—	1.3	29.0
Benin	1991	408.0	—32.9[2]—		11.6	55.5[3]	7.5	13.7	34.4[3]	30.6	4.5	0.7	2.4	61.8
Bermuda	1993	588.9	20.5	0.1[2]	5.8	73.6[3]	13.9	23.3	36.3[3]	10.1[7]	70.2	—	5.4	14.3
Bhutan	1992	128.0	15.0	0.7	8.1	76.2	4.9	46.2	25.1	25.5	0.8	—	10.8	62.9[17]
Bolivia	1995	1,396.3	11.2	1.9	4.5	82.4	13.7	46.3	22.4	19.6	22.3	0.5	12.3	45.3
Bosnia and Herzegovina	1996	1,879.0[4]	...	...	31.6[6]	...	...	...	...	35.8[4]	3.4[4]	8.6[4]	0.1[4]	52.2[4]
Botswana	1994	1,636.6	21.1	2.7	5.7	70.5	7.7	29.6	33.2	7.5	1.9	0.1	2.1	88.5[20]
Brazil	1995	53,736.7	13.4	1.6	12.1	72.9	15.2	39.2	18.6	27.9	23.7	1.0	5.1	42.3
Brunei	1993	1,820.5	9.9	0.5	0.8	88.8	4.4	49.6	34.8	25.7	25.1	17.1	9.4	22.7
Bulgaria	1995	5,125.0	11.0	2.7	27.0	59.3	12.8	19.3	27.2	37.2	2.1	36.2	0.8	23.7
Burkina Faso	1991	536.0	—25.6[2]—		11.6	62.8[3]	18.5	20.8	23.5[3]	40.4	4.9	0.3	4.2	50.1
Burundi	1993	204.5	13.0	0.6	12.4	74.0	14.1	21.3	38.6	45.4	1.8	0.4	9.2	43.3
Cambodia	1993	403.9	17.2[22]	...	11.7	...	6.5[22]	17.0[22]	...	9.2[4]	4.5[4]	2.5[4]	12.2[4]	71.6[4]
Cameroon	1996	1,204.3	16.2	3.2	15.7	64.9	14.6	27.6	22.7	53.4	8.5	1.8	5.0	31.3
Canada	1996	171,007.2	7.3	1.8	4.3	86.6	8.4	51.1	27.1	9.8	67.6	0.4	4.5	17.8
Cape Verde	1994	210.1	32.8	—	3.6	63.6	5.1	36.0	22.5	75.0	2.3	0.7	5.0	17.0
Central African Republic	1995	265.5	25.5	0.3	8.7	65.6	8.0	42.2	15.3	43.5	1.8	—	19.7	34.9
Chad	1992	243.0	25.1[25]	1.4[15, 25]	1.6[25]	71.8[16, 25]	15.1[25]	20.7[25]	36.0[16, 25]	46.5[4]	2.5[4]	0.4[4]	1.6[4]	49.0[4]
Chile	1995	14,903.1	8.4	1.3	9.0	81.3	12.2	42.3	26.8	15.9	25.5	0.2	6.8	51.6
China	1995	132,083.5	12.2	2.6	3.9	81.3	12.9	39.9	28.6	16.1	12.2	3.7	22.0	46.1
Colombia	1995	13,863.1	11.9	0.6	2.8	84.7	18.1	37.4	29.2	18.5	33.8	1.3	8.9	37.5
Comoros	1994	52.8	27.8[22]	...	11.6	60.6	1.4[22]	7.4[22]	51.9	40.0[7]	—[4]	1.9[4]	5.7[4]	52.4[4]
Congo, Dem. Rep. of the	1992	420.0	—20.0[11]—		13.8[11]	66.2[11]	4.4[11]	45.5[11]	16.3[11]	57.9[4]	4.9[4]	0.8[4]	2.7[4]	33.7[4]
Congo, Rep. of the	1994	408.4	27.1	0.7	1.2	71.0	13.8	28.5	28.7	54.0	10.0	0.2	2.6	33.3
Costa Rica	1994	3,029.7	11.6	0.3	9.1	79.0	18.2	29.4	31.4	11.3	44.3	0.55	5.5	38.3
Côte d'Ivoire	1992	2,447.0[4]	—23.7[26]—		21.3[26]	55.0[26]	14.8[26]	16.4[26]	23.8[26]	56.0[4]	3.9[4]	0.1[4]	3.8[4]	36.2[4]
Croatia	1996	7,787.8	13.1	0.8	11.0	75.1	10.9	27.3	36.8	59.4	2.7	10.5	1.3	26.1
Cuba	1992	2,185.0	14.9[26]	0.5[2, 26]	32.4[26]	52.2[3, 26]	6.2[26]	27.5[26]	18.5[3, 26]	30.0[4]	—[4]	9.0[4]	1.0[4]	60.0[4]
Cyprus	1996	3,982.5	25.5	0.4	8.5	65.6	7.8	24.3	33.5	48.6	16.8	5.5	6.0	23.1
Czech Republic	1995	20,915.0	10.9	1.9	9.4	77.8	13.2	35.1	29.4	56.4	3.7	27.3	1.7	10.9
Denmark	1995	41,626.4	15.6	0.5	3.4	80.4	11.6	33.2	35.7	68.7	4.7	3.7	2.7	20.3
Djibouti	1991	214.4	38.3	0.2	9.1	52.3	6.0	15.5	30.8	46.6	3.7	0.75	7.2	41.8
Dominica	1991	109.6	27.6	0.3	7.9	64.2	12.0	21.6	30.5	21.2	31.4	0.3	5.6	41.5
Dominican Republic	1994	2,626.4	13.7[27]	0.3[27]	35.2[27]	50.7[27]	11.7[27]	23.2[27]	15.9[27]	2.0[4]	37.4[4]	—[4]	1.5[4]	59.1[4]
Ecuador	1995	4,195.2	10.4	0.4	5.9	83.3	17.6	40.1	25.6	15.3	30.7	0.4	8.6	44.9
Egypt	1995	11,739.0	35.4	1.4	1.2	61.9	13.2	25.3	23.4	38.9	18.8	7.1	2.7	32.5

and freight] valuation); for exports, the value at which the goods were sold by the exporter, including the cost of transportation and insurance to bring the goods onto the transporting vehicle at the frontier of the exporting country (f.o.b. [free-on-board] valuation).

The largest part of the information presented here comes from the United Nations' *Commodity Trade Statistics* (microfiche format) and *International Trade Statistics Yearbook*. These sources, however, cannot always provide the most recent data for all countries listed in this table and must be supplemented by national and regional information. In some cases where the original data were only available for an alternative trade classification, an approximation has been made of the SITC commodity groupings.

The notes that follow further define the column headings.
a. Also includes any unallocated commodities.
b. EU of 15 countries (Austria, Belgium, Denmark, Finland, France, Germany, Greece, Ireland, Italy, Luxembourg, The Netherlands, Portugal, Spain, Sweden, and the United Kingdom).
c. Includes Albania, Bulgaria, Czech Republic, Hungary, Poland, Romania, Slovakia, and European republics of the former U.S.S.R. (Belarus, Estonia, Latvia, Lithuania, Moldova, Russia, and Ukraine).
d. May include value of trade shown as not available (...) in any of the four preceding columns. May include any unspecified areas or countries.

... Not available.
— None, less than 0.05%, or not applicable.
Detail may not add to 100.0 or indicated subtotals because of rounding.

SITC category codes

code	description
0	food and live animals
1	beverages and tobacco
2	crude materials, inedible, except fuels
27	crude fertilizers and crude minerals (excluding coal, petroleum, and precious stones)
28	metalliferous ores and metal scrap
3	mineral fuels, lubricants, and related materials (including coal, petroleum, natural gas, and electric current)
4	animal and vegetable oils, fats, and waxes
5	chemicals and related products not elsewhere specified
6	manufactured goods classified chiefly by material
667	pearls, precious and semiprecious stones, unworked or worked
7	machinery and transport equipment
8	miscellaneous manufactured articles
9	commodities and transactions not classified elsewhere

total value ('000,000 U.S.$)	food and agricultural raw materials (0+1+2 −27−28 +4)	mineral ores and concentrates (27+28 +667)	fuels and other energy (3)	manuf. total[a] (5+6 −667 +7+8 +9)	of which chemicals and related products (5)	of which machinery and transport equipment (7)	of which other[a] (6−667 +8+9)	to European Union (EU)[b]	to United States	to Eastern Europe[c]	to Japan	to all other[d]	country
235.1	63.0[2]		...	37.0[3]	...	...	...	7.3[4]	0.5[4]	70.2[4,5]	0.3[4]	21.8[4]	Afghanistan
141.3	37.9[6]	46.8[6]		15.3[6]	1.5[6]	0.8[6]	13.0[6]	76.2[7]	11.1	1.3	1.4	10.0	Albania
8,555.5	1.2	0.4	95.2	3.2	1.2	0.4	1.6	64.8	16.7	2.7	0.7	15.1	Algeria
488.2	100.0	—		—	—	—	—	—[10]	100.0[10]	—[10]	—[10]	—[10]	American Samoa
48.9	8.1	1.1	0.2	90.6	5.5	40.2	44.9	99.6	—	0.1	—	0.3	Andorra
3,178.9	0.1	1.1	98.6	0.2[4]	—	—	0.2[4]	25.3[4]	64.4	0.5[4]	1.3	8.5[4]	Angola
39.8	4.4[2]		25.0	70.6[3]	7.1	30.2	33.3[3]	15.0[11]	15.4[11]	—[11]	—[11]	69.5[11]	Antigua and Barbuda
20,962.6	54.1	0.2	10.3	35.3	6.4	10.9	18.0	21.4	8.6	0.7	2.2	67.2	Argentina
270.9	5.1	—	43.7	51.2	9.3	18.6	23.2	17.8	0.2	33.3	—	48.7	Armenia
37.5	12.6	1.0	3.1	83.3	3.8	11.9	67.5	6.7	9.7	—	—	83.6	Aruba
60,534.0	29.3	11.8[2]	16.8	42.0[3]	3.9	12.8	25.3[3]	10.8	6.4	0.4	20.1	62.2	Australia
57,141.5	8.0	1.0	0.9	90.1	8.8	39.6	41.7	58.6	2.8	11.1	1.2	26.2	Austria
547.4	7.1	51.8		41.2	6.1	8.0	27.1	17.2	0.2	26.9	—	55.7	Azerbaijan
2,592.6	4.9		73.5	21.5	19.9	0.6	1.0	2.6	93.8	—	0.6	3.0	Bahamas, The
4,092.1	2.4[2]		60.0	37.6[3]	5.0	1.3	31.3[3]	4.0[4]	3.2[4]	—	8.2[4]	84.6[4]	Bahrain
2,137.6	16.0	0.1	0.9	83.1	2.4	0.1	80.6	37.4	35.0	1.6	2.6	23.4	Bangladesh
237.5	29.9	1.7	14.4	54.0	13.9	19.8	20.4	20.5	16.0	—	0.6	62.8	Barbados
4,706.8	8.9	13.0		78.1	19.1	29.3	29.7	12.2	1.2	75.1	—	11.5	Belarus
165,173.1	11.6	7.4	2.7	78.4	16.1	27.3	35.0	71.2	3.7	2.3	1.3	21.4	Belgium[13]
161.7	81.9	0.2	3.2	14.8	0.2	3.0	11.6	51.4	36.6	—	0.1	12.0	Belize
43.0	63.5[2]		29.0	7.5[3]	1.0	2.8	3.8[3]	18.6	18.7	—	0.4	62.3	Benin
35.3	5.6[14]	3.1[14,15]	45.6[14]	45.8[14,16]	9.5[14]	18.5[14]	17.8[14,16]	27.0[14]	62.3[14]	—[14]	—[14]	10.6[14]	Bermuda
67.1	34.3	3.1	22.1[18]	40.5	21.5	—	18.9	0.1	—	—	—	99.9[19]	Bhutan
1,181.4	27.8	20.6	12.9	38.6	1.1	3.2	34.3	25.9	27.8	0.1	0.3	45.9	Bolivia
171.0[4]	...	...	...	...	9.4[6]	20.8[6]	...	45.6[4]	5.3[4]	2.3[4]	1.2[4]	45.6[4]	Bosnia and Herzegovina
1,848.8	7.1	75.8	—	17.1	1.0	7.4	8.7	28.8	0.7	—	—	70.5[21]	Botswana
46,505.4	33.7	6.6	0.9	58.9	6.6	19.0	33.3	27.8	18.9	2.1	6.7	44.5	Brazil
2,093.9	—	—	99.7	0.3	—	—	0.3	—	0.4	—	74.8	24.8	Brunei
5,184.4	24.4	1.4	6.1	68.2	16.9	11.3	39.9	37.7	3.0	19.5	0.3	39.5	Bulgaria
105.4	83.5	0.5	—	16.0	0.1	1.0	14.9	36.2	0.3	—	1.8	61.6	Burkina Faso
68.7	85.1	—	—	14.9	1.4	—	13.4	63.8[4]	2.0[4]	—[4]	0.7[4]	33.6[4]	Burundi
219.1[23]	88.9[24]	...	...	...	...	...	...	15.5[4]	0.5[4]	0.5[4]	37.6[4]	45.9[4]	Cambodia
1,757.9	49.5	0.1	36.2	14.3	1.1	1.1	12.1	77.4	2.3	0.2	0.8	19.3	Cameroon
201,573.7	15.6	2.2	10.2	72.0	5.7	39.0	27.3	5.7	81.6	0.3	3.8	8.6	Canada
5.0[24]	50.6	0.6	—	48.9	0.1	2.2	46.6	98.3	0.1	—	—	1.6	Cape Verde
119.5	24.0	63.5	0.8	11.7	0.4	8.8	2.5	90.7	0.2	—	0.8	8.3	Central African Republic
261.0	88.2	—	—	11.9	6.5	3.1	2.3	42.9	0.8	0.8	7.3	48.2	Chad
15,901.1	37.2	16.1	0.2	46.4	3.5	1.8	41.1	22.0	13.4	0.5	17.9	46.3	Chile
148,779.6	10.1	1.1	3.6	85.2	6.1	21.1	58.0	12.9	16.6	2.0	19.1	49.4	China
10,327.8	35.1	4.7	24.4	35.7	7.9	5.6	22.2	25.5	34.3	0.5	3.5	36.2	Colombia
11.4	70.2	—	—	29.8	19.9	—	10.0	52.5[7]	28.7	—	0.9	18.8	Comoros
506.0	13.1	58.5[2,15]	11.1	17.3[3,16]	0.2	1.2	15.9[3,16]	58.7	15.7[4]	4.5	6.5	14.6[4]	Congo, Dem. Rep. of the
948.5	13.4	1.1	83.4	2.2	—	0.4	1.8	35.9	42.1	—	0.3	21.7	Congo, Rep. of the
2,217.5	66.3	0.3	0.6	32.8	6.3	3.3	23.2	28.2	43.4	0.2[5]	0.9	27.2	Costa Rica
3,105.0	68.2	0.3[2,15]	15.4	16.1[3,16]	3.3	2.0	10.9[3,16]	56.6	5.7	8.0	1.1	28.6	Côte d'Ivoire
4,511.7	16.1	0.7	9.2	73.9	14.3	21.4	38.3	51.0	2.0	7.9	—	39.0	Croatia
3,860.0	82.2	8.4[2,15]	4.8	4.6[3,16]	2.7	0.6	1.3[3,16]	11.0[4]	—	76.2[5]	2.7	10.1	Cuba
1,391.0	57.4	1.2	4.4	37.0	6.0	11.1	19.9	28.4	0.7	36.3	0.1	34.5	Cyprus
17,099.1	11.6	1.4	5.3	81.8	10.3	25.4	46.1	55.2	1.8	30.0	0.5	12.5	Czech Republic
47,221.8	27.8	0.7	2.7	68.9	10.0	26.0	32.9	59.9	3.7	4.3	3.5	28.6	Denmark
17.3	32.5	—	—	67.5	0.4	8.3	58.7	62.6	0.8	—	0.9	35.7	Djibouti
54.2	67.2	0.4	—	32.4	23.7	4.2	4.4	61.2	5.2	—	—	33.6	Dominica
2,007.8	20.7	0.1	—	79.2[28]	2.6	11.6	65.1[28]	8.6	83.6	—	0.8	6.9	Dominican Republic
4,361.5	54.8	0.2	35.1	10.0	1.2	2.0	6.8	19.3	42.5	2.7	2.7	32.7	Ecuador
3,444.1	16.0	0.6	37.3	46.1	5.8	0.6	39.6	45.8	15.2	2.7	1.3	35.0	Egypt

Trade: external (continued)

country	year	imports												
		total value ('000,000 U.S.$)	Standard International Trade Classification (SITC) categories (%)							direction of trade (%)				
			food and agricultural raw materials (0 + 1 + 2 − 27 − 28 + 4)	mineral ores and concentrates (27 + 28 + 667)	fuels and other energy (3)	manufactured goods				from European Union (EU)[b]	from United States	from Eastern Europe[c]	from Japan	from all other[d]
						total[a] (5 + 6 − 667 + 7 + 8 + 9)	of which chemicals and related products (5)	of which machinery and transport equipment (7)	of which other[a] (6 − 667 + 8 + 9)					
El Salvador	1994	2,261.8	17.8	0.7	9.5	72.1	16.9	30.8	24.4	10.6	41.5	0.5	6.3	41.1
Equatorial Guinea	1990	61.6	13.5	3.4	7.7	75.4	3.9	58.2	13.3	31.5	39.9	—	0.3[4]	28.3
Eritrea	1995	423.6	—21.3[2]—		1.9	76.8[3]	6.0	45.2	25.6[3]	27.2[7]	5.9	...		66.9
Estonia	1996	3,197.2	17.0	—10.0—		72.9	13.6	29.4	29.9	64.8	2.3	21.7	2.0	9.2
Ethiopia	1993	771.6	17.4	0.1	21.6	60.9	13.8	26.8	20.3	39.3	9.5	—	4.1	47.2
Faroe Islands	1994	238.2	30.7	0.6	11.8	56.8	8.5	19.8	28.5	67.5	1.4	3.6	2.0	25.5
Fiji	1994	830.5	15.9	0.3	11.2	72.5	7.3	30.9	34.3	3.9	14.8	0.1	8.0	73.3
Finland	1996	30,904.9	9.2	4.0	10.5	76.2	11.3	39.2	25.7	58.5	7.3	10.2	5.2	18.8
France[31]	1995	273,387.4	13.3	1.1	6.8	78.8	12.5	35.4	30.8	63.9	7.8	2.4	3.5	22.4
French Guiana	1995	783.3	18.8	0.1	5.3	75.8	8.0	42.2	25.6	76.9	3.3	0.5	1.4	17.9
French Polynesia	1994	880.7	20.4[32]	0.2[32]	5.4[32]	74.1[32]	6.4[32]	35.9[32]	31.8[32]	44.8[7]	13.9	—	4.0	37.3
Gabon	1994	680.8	17.9	0.5	2.3	79.2	10.2	44.5	24.5	67.6	11.8	0.3	5.3[4]	15.0
Gambia, The	1995[12]	141.3	—35.3[2]—		14.4	50.3[3]	5.6	20.3	24.5[3]	47.3	5.2	0.7	3.5	43.3
Gaza Strip	1994	339.3	...	...	...	...	...	...	...	...	...	...	...	100.0[33]
Georgia	1995	379.0	32.3	—52.7—		15.0	4.0	5.8	5.3	13.4	4.7	30.0	0.2	51.6
Germany	1995	443,223.8	12.5	1.6	6.4	79.5	9.4	34.4	35.7	54.7	7.1	8.3	5.5	24.4
Ghana	1992	2,145.4	12.5	3.1	17.4	66.9	11.1	33.6	22.2	43.6	10.2	1.4	6.6	38.2
Gibraltar	1995	436.0[37]	—24.4[2, 32]—		20.7[32]	54.9[3, 32]	4.3[32]	21.4[32]	29.2[3, 32]	75.7	...	...	1.9	22.4
Greece	1995	25,926.8	18.5	0.6	7.2	73.7	13.2	27.4	33.1	69.9	3.2	6.6	2.6	17.6
Greenland	1995	421.1	15.4	0.3	5.8	78.5	4.3	24.6	49.7	83.2	2.4	0.2	3.3	10.9
Grenada	1991	117.2	28.4	0.2	7.4	64.1	8.5	24.2	31.3	19.8	32.2	0.1	7.1	40.8
Guadeloupe	1995	1,901.3	22.6	0.3	5.8	71.3	9.5	32.0	29.8	77.8	3.3	0.3	2.2	16.5
Guam	1983	610.7	16.9	0.1	46.9	36.2	2.3	19.1	14.8	...	23.4	...	19.9	56.6
Guatemala	1995	3,292.5	13.4	0.3	12.4	73.9	17.2	31.5	25.2	10.4	44.9	1.0[5]	3.7	40.0
Guernsey[39]	...		...	...	...	...	...	...	...	...	...	...	...	...
Guinea	1994	687.0	10.8	...	9.9	...	...	22.3	...	54.3[4]	8.0[4]	0.7[4]	3.8[4]	33.2[4]
Guinea-Bissau	1994	63.5	31.7	...	9.9	58.4	...	33.1	...	44.8[4]	48.1[4]	—[4]	2.6[4]	4.5[4]
Guyana	1993	483.8	9.0	...	16.7	74.3	5.1	44.5	24.7	21.9[4]	27.9[4]	0.4[4]	18.2[4]	31.6[4]
Haiti	1993[8]	226.0	—46.6[2]—		28.4	25.1[3]	6.9	5.4	12.8	18.1[4]	57.9[4]	...	4.8[4]	19.3[4]
Honduras	1995	1,727.5	13.7	0.2	11.5	74.6	17.3	29.1	28.2	14.5	46.6	0.4[5]	3.4	35.0
Hong Kong	1996	201,164.5	7.1	2.1	2.2	88.6	6.8	36.5	45.3	11.0	7.8	0.4	13.4	67.5
Hungary	1995	15,466.3	8.8	0.9[2]	11.6	78.6[3]	14.3	30.7	33.6[3]	61.5	3.1	21.8	2.2	11.3
Iceland	1995	1,751.4	13.3	3.7	7.2	75.7	9.3	32.4	34.0	59.8	8.4	4.8	4.4	22.6
India	1995[1]	28,654.8	10.3	9.7	23.8	56.2	14.7	19.0	22.5	26.2	10.1	3.2	7.1	53.5
Indonesia	1995	40,628.7	15.0	2.1	7.4	75.5	15.4	40.1	20.0	20.1	11.7	1.6[5]	22.7	43.9
Iran	1992	30,712.1	—11.4[2]—		1.3	87.4[3]	9.8	50.3	27.3[3]	49.8	2.7	3.0[5]	12.0	32.5
Iraq	1990	4,833.9	—31.5[2]—		0.4	68.1[3]	8.8	30.3	28.9[3]	45.7[4]	10.8[4]	3.0[4]	4.6[4]	35.9[4]
Ireland	1996	35,767.7	9.5	0.6	3.7	86.2	12.3	42.1	31.9	56.5	15.5	0.7	5.4	21.9
Isle of Man[39]	...		...	...	...	...	...	...	...	...	...	...	...	...
Israel	1995	29,579.0	8.2	17.1	5.9	68.8	9.4	34.0	25.5	52.3	18.6	1.9	3.3	23.9
Italy[40]	1996	206,965.5	16.3	1.9	8.4	73.4	13.0	30.2	30.3	60.8	4.9	5.6	1.9	26.7
Jamaica	1996	2,916.4	16.2	0.2[2]	15.2	68.4[3]	10.1	26.7	31.7[3]	11.2	51.9	0.5	5.6	30.8
Japan	1996	349,186.1	21.0	3.8	17.4	57.9	6.5	24.4	26.9	14.1	22.8	1.3	—	61.7
Jersey	1980	537.1	23.9	0.4	9.3	66.5	6.5	24.8	35.2	84.9[41]	...	...	...	15.1
Jordan	1995	3,722.7	22.7	1.1	12.9	63.4	12.3	24.5	26.5	33.2	9.3	4.6	3.5	49.4
Kazakstan	1995	3,781.0	12.3	—29.3—		58.4	11.9	27.1	19.4	13.4	1.9	56.7	0.2	27.8
Kenya	1993	1,695.9	16.2	0.4	14.9	68.5	20.7	26.9	20.9	41.9	8.3	0.7[5]	8.4	40.7
Kiribati	1994	26.4	42.4	0.3	9.3	47.9	6.4	17.4	24.1	0.8	9.6	—	6.7	82.9
Korea, North	1996	2,238.0[4]	...	...	...	...	...	...	...	10.3[4]	—[4]	33.9[4]	11.1[4]	44.6[4]
Korea, South	1996	150,334.3	10.4	2.4	16.2	71.0	8.8	36.4	25.8	14.1	22.2	1.5	20.9	41.3
Kuwait	1995	7,789.8	16.6	0.4	0.5	82.4	7.3	41.2	33.9	38.1	16.1	0.9	9.4	35.6
Kyrgyzstan	1995	522.3	19.9	—37.5—		42.6	7.4	17.9	17.3	6.4	3.7	25.8	1.4	62.8
Laos	1994	564.1	18.6	8.3[2]	3.8	69.3	...	25.9	43.4	8.0[4]	0.9	0.3[4]	11.8	79.0
Latvia	1995	1,817.5	12.2	0.4	21.2	66.2	12.7	25.4	28.2	49.9	1.9	41.9	0.6	5.8
Lebanon	1994	5,990.0	21.7	—13.3—		65.0	10.2	27.0	27.8	49.1[4]	9.3	4.6[4]	4.2	32.8[4]
Lesotho	1992	977.0	23.2[43]	0.4[43]	8.7[43]	67.8[43]	7.4[43]	16.7[43]	43.7[43]	4.8	...	—[4]	—[4]	95.2[44]
Liberia	1992	5,760.0[4]	—19.8[2, 32]—		20.3[32]	59.9[3, 32]	5.6[32]	30.2[32]	24.1[3, 32]	22.6[4]	0.6[4]	0.8[4]	28.3[4]	47.7[4]
Libya	1991	5,357.5	25.7	0.3	0.4	73.7	7.6	33.8	32.2	62.6	1.3	0.9[5]	3.3	31.9
Liechtenstein	1995	906.4	3.8	0.3[2]	1.1	94.8[3]	4.6	33.9	56.3[3]	...	...	...	...	...
Lithuania	1996	4,558.8	15.6	1.9	18.0	64.5	12.2	25.8	26.6	39.8	2.6	46.1	1.2	10.4
Luxembourg	1995	9,861.5	12.6	—9.8—		77.6	14.2	28.1	35.3	91.1	3.3	...	1.2	4.3
Macau	1995	2,018.6	16.7	0.2	5.1	78.0	4.5	18.9	54.6	14.7	7.4	0.3	10.5	67.1
Macedonia	1994	1,484.1	24.4	1.5[2]	10.8	63.3[3]	13.3	19.7	30.4[3]	38.2	3.3	24.6	0.9	33.1
Madagascar	1995	549.5	18.1	0.3	14.0	67.7	13.0	25.7	28.9	50.6	3.8	0.7[5]	6.0	39.0
Malawi	1991	647.4	8.6	1.0	10.9	79.5	20.0	33.1	26.3	35.6	3.3	0.1	7.4	53.7
Malaysia	1995	77,292.3	6.0	1.2	2.2	90.5	7.1	59.9	23.5	15.3	16.4	0.5	27.5	40.3
Maldives	1993	191.4	31.5	2.8	12.8	52.9	7.5	22.2	23.2	7.9	1.0	0.4	3.9	86.9
Mali	1990	601.8	26.2	0.9	19.5	53.5	10.7	22.2	20.6	46.8	4.8	1.3[5]	4.3	42.9
Malta	1996	2,803.0	—12.0[2]—		5.4	82.6[3]	7.4	48.2	27.0[3]	68.5	6.6	1.3	3.2	20.1
Marshall Islands	1995	75.1	34.5	1.0[4]	30.0	34.5	2.6	12.8	19.2	...	51.1	...	7.4	41.5
Martinique	1995	1,969.8	20.4	0.2	7.5	71.9	10.3	32.4	29.2	76.8	2.9	0.2	2.2	17.9
Mauritania	1992	600.0[4]	30.6[32]	...	7.0[32]	62.4[32]	...	51.0[32]	11.4[32]	58.4[4]	11.2[4]	1.8[4]	3.8[4]	24.7[4]
Mauritius	1995	2,022.8	19.7	1.8	6.9	71.6	7.7	19.2	44.7	36.3	...	0.5	4.7	58.5
Mayotte	1996	144.3	—23.7—		4.6	71.7	11.0	35.1	25.6	74.0[14, 46]	...	...	3.3[14]	22.7[14]
Mexico	1995	73,993.0	8.8	0.9	2.1	88.2	10.0	42.9	35.3	9.4	74.3	0.2	5.0	11.0
Micronesia	1994	129.1	—24.7[2]—		14.3	61.0[3]	4.4	13.5	43.1[3]	...	32.9	...	32.0	35.1
Moldova	1995	840.7	10.7	1.0	45.9	42.4	9.2	15.2	17.9	13.7	1.3	80.2	0.2	4.7
Monaco	...		...	...	...	...	...	...	...	...	...	...	...	...
Mongolia	1995	415.3	9.3	—20.0—		70.7	10.4	35.7	24.6	9.5	3.5	53.3	10.9	22.8
Morocco	1995	8,551.5	25.9	2.6	13.7	57.8	11.9	23.3	22.6	56.1	6.5	7.8	1.5	28.1
Mozambique	1994	544.0	19.2	0.3	14.1	66.4	13.5	35.5	17.4	33.0	4.1	—	8.4	54.5
Myanmar (Burma)	1995[1]	1,419.3	—16.2[2]—		3.4	80.4[3]	7.3	31.8	41.2[3]	4.4	1.2	0.3	23.6	70.6
Namibia	1994	1,374.3	23.8	1.1[2]	4.2	70.9[3]	7.1	31.4	32.5[3]	4.5	0.9	—	1.3	93.3[47]
Nauru	1991[48]	17.8	—24.2[2]—		4.8	70.9[3]	2.1	23.4[22]	45.4[3]	...	...	...	...	...
Nepal	1995[12]	855.9	14.1	0.5	13.7	71.6	8.1	13.4	50.1	10.6	1.0	1.0	7.5	79.9

total value ('000,000 U.S.$)	food and agricultural raw materials (0+1+2−27−28+4)	mineral ores and concentrates (27+28+667)	fuels and other energy (3)	manufactured goods total[a] (5+6−667+7+8+9)	of which chemicals and related products (5)	of which machinery and transport equipment (7)	of which other[a] (6−667+8+9)	to European Union (EU)[b]	to United States	to Eastern Europe[c]	to Japan	to all other[d]	country
812.7	52.2	0.1	0.5	47.1	12.3	3.0	31.8	25.0	22.6	—	0.8	51.6	El Salvador
61.7	48.6	—	—	51.4	0.1	39.8[29]	11.5	47.2	...	—	—	52.8	Equatorial Guinea
86.0	—59.8—		...	40.2	2.5	3.8	34.0	2.7[7]	...	...	...	97.3[30]	Eritrea
2,074.1	27.2	—7.5		65.3	11.0	19.8	34.6	51.1	2.2	39.3	0.7	6.6	Estonia
201.7	95.3	—	4.0	0.7	0.1	—	0.6	41.6	9.2	0.3	19.0	29.9	Ethiopia
321.3	96.8			3.2	0.1	2.5	0.6	88.0	2.9	0.1	2.7	6.3	Faroe Islands
544.5	49.3	0.1	7.4	43.2	1.0	8.0	34.3	20.3	17.9	—	6.8	55.0	Fiji
40,556.5	9.9	0.6	3.1	86.4	6.2	38.4	41.9	52.7	7.9	12.8	2.6	24.1	Finland
284,045.7	15.6	0.8	2.3	81.3	12.8	39.7	28.8	63.5	5.9	2.2	2.0	26.5	France[31]
158.2	33.6	0.1	0.2	66.1	1.4	33.0	31.7	77.6	1.0	—	—	21.3	French Guiana
226.2	5.9[32]	31.3[32]	—[32]	62.8[32]	1.6[32]	38.6[32]	22.6[32]	32.7[7]	8.4	—	45.8	13.1	French Polynesia
1,040.9	19.8	7.5	70.4	2.3	0.8	0.5	1.0	49.4	6.5	—	8.0[4]	36.1	Gabon
21.5	—78.8[2]—		—	21.2[3]	1.6	2.5	17.1	57.1[4]	3.6[4]	—[4]	—[4]	39.3[4]	Gambia, The
49.4	...	...	...	...	...	...	...	...	...	...	...	100.0[34]	Gaza Strip
154.4	25.9	—14.5—		59.5	9.7	6.8	43.1	5.6	0.4	39.4	0.1	54.5	Georgia
508,508.5	6.1	0.8	0.9	92.1	13.5	49.6	29.1	57.1	7.5	7.4	2.6	25.5	Germany
1,234.4	37.7	6.2	5.4	50.6	0.2	1.2	49.3[35]	30.3	2.6	1.1	1.8	64.2[36]	Ghana
116.2[37]	—8.2[2, 32]		51.5[32]	40.3[3, 32]	2.8[32]	18.1[32]	19.4[3, 32]	22.2[7, 32]	...	...	...	77.8[38]	Gibraltar
10,954.6	33.9	2.4	6.5	57.1	4.9	8.0	44.2	60.7	3.1	13.5	0.8	22.0	Greece
363.6	95.7	—	0.8	3.5	—	0.3	3.2	93.3	0.6	—	4.6	1.4	Greenland
20.1	77.0	—		23.0	4.5	2.1	16.4	44.1	14.2	—	2.6	39.2	Grenada
162.0	52.3	0.6	—	47.0	1.1	36.5	9.4	77.0	3.4	—	—	19.6	Guadeloupe
39.2	23.5	2.7	3.5	70.3	5.6	11.5	53.2	...	24.9	...	4.8	70.4	Guam
1,935.5	69.3	0.4	2.0	28.2	10.9	1.8	15.5	15.7	31.3	0.5[5]	2.8	49.7	Guatemala
...	...	...	...	...	...	...	...	...	...	...	...	...	Guernsey[39]
625.9	12.2[22]	66.3	—	21.5	...	...	...	63.4[4]	15.1[4]	8.3[4]	1.3[4]	11.9[4]	Guinea
33.2	95.2	...	—	4.8	...	...	...	52.2[4]	—[4]	—[4]	2.9[4]	44.9[4]	Guinea-Bissau
404.0	43.5[22]	47.3[22]	—	9.2	...	...	...	35.9[4]	22.8[4]	—[4]	2.1[4]	39.9[4]	Guyana
74.3	14.1	—	—	86.0	1.7	14.0	70.3	12.4[4]	78.8[4]	—[4]	0.8[4]	8.0[4]	Haiti
656.0	90.2	0.4	—	9.4	1.7	0.7	7.0	36.3	42.7	0.4	6.7	13.8	Honduras
180,801.9	4.3	1.2	1.1	93.4	5.9	32.2	55.3	14.8	21.2	0.6	6.5	56.8	Hong Kong
12,867.0	24.0	1.6[2]	3.2	71.1[3]	11.8	25.6	33.7[3]	62.8	3.2	19.2	0.6	14.2	Hungary
1,802.5	76.1	1.5	—	22.4	0.7	5.1	16.6	62.7	12.4	0.9	11.3	12.7	Iceland
26,330.0	16.7	18.5	1.9	62.8	8.2	7.2	47.5	27.9	19.1	3.9	7.7	41.5	India
45,418.0	18.0	4.4	25.3	52.2	3.4	8.4	40.4	14.9	13.9	0.7[5]	27.1	43.4	Indonesia
19,868.0	7.8	1.9[2, 15]	80.9	9.3[3, 16]	0.2	0.5	8.6[3, 16]	39.8	0.8	10.4[5]	13.5	35.5	Iran
6,659.0	0.8	0.3[15]	96.8	2.1[16]	1.2	0.2	0.7[16]	26.6[4]	33.6[4]	6.8[4, 5]	9.5[4]	23.5[4]	Iraq
48,153.2	16.6	1.0	0.4	82.1	22.3	34.8	25.0	68.6	9.4	1.8	2.9	17.4	Ireland
...	...	...	...	...	...	...	...	...	...	...	...	...	Isle of Man[39]
19,046.0	7.3	31.0	0.5	61.2	14.6	28.4	18.2	32.2	30.1	3.3	6.9	27.4	Israel
250,830.3	7.2	0.3	1.2	91.3	7.8	38.4	45.1	55.5	7.4	5.8	2.2	29.1	Italy[40]
1,386.9	23.7	49.7[2]	0.4	26.2[3]	3.4	2.3	20.5[3]	30.8	36.8	1.9	2.3	28.3	Jamaica
410,947.0	1.1	0.3	0.5	98.2	7.0	69.5	21.6	15.4	27.5	0.5	—	56.7	Japan
209.2	27.6	4.3[42]	—	68.0	1.2	31.1	35.7	67.3[41]	...	...	...	32.7	Jersey
1,782.0	24.1	19.4	—	56.5	27.0	13.1	16.4	8.0	3.9	1.3	1.1	85.7	Jordan
4,974.4	11.5	—28.0—		60.4	10.3	4.0	46.1	21.6	0.9	51.3	—	26.1	Kazakstan
1,391.9	58.1	2.7	9.3	30.0	4.3	1.4	24.3	36.2	3.5	0.1[5]	0.9	59.4	Kenya
5.2	91.8	—	—	8.2	—	—	8.2	4.4	12.1	–	0.1	83.4	Kiribati
1,095.0[4]	...	...	...	...	...	...	...	9.3[4]	—[4]	30.2[4]	24.2[4]	36.3[4]	Korea, North
129,714.6	3.4	0.1	3.0	93.5	7.1	52.1	34.3	11.9	16.9	3.0	12.2	56.0	Korea, South
12,944.4	0.3	0.3	94.7	4.7	2.0	1.4	1.3	11.7[4]	10.3[4]	—[4]	19.4[4]	58.5[4]	Kuwait
408.9	29.4	—11.8—		58.8	6.6	9.2	43.0	9.5	1.0	31.4	0.1	58.0	Kyrgyzstan
300.4	37.1	...	8.4	54.6	...	16.9	37.7	19.3[4]	3.2	3.2[4]	0.6	73.6	Laos
1,303.8	37.4	0.7	1.7	60.1	6.9	16.3	36.9	44.0	1.3	47.7	0.3	6.6	Latvia
572.7	19.6	—10.5—		69.9	9.1	11.5	49.3	17.0[4]	3.7	4.9[4]	0.7	73.7[4]	Lebanon
109.1	14.8	1.3	—	83.9	0.5	10.2	73.2	22.7	23.0[4]	—	—	54.3[4]	Lesotho
389.0	32.4	33.7[2, 15]	2.6	31.3[3, 16]	—	26.0	5.3[3, 16]	66.8	11.4[4]	1.5	—	20.3[4]	Liberia
11,211.7	0.7	—	95.4	3.9	3.4	—	0.5	86.2	—	1.6	—	12.2	Libya
1,817.7	4.4	—[2]	0.1	95.5[3]	8.1	46.9	40.5[3]	45.7[45]	...	...	—	54.3	Liechtenstein
3,354.9	22.5	2.3	14.9	60.4	12.8	19.0	28.7	32.9	0.8	58.3	0.5	7.5	Lithuania
7,743.0	7.2	—1.5—		91.3	18.6	19.8	52.9	85.5	3.1	...	0.6	10.8	Luxembourg
2,017.3	4.0	—	—	95.9	1.1	4.4	90.5	31.4	41.2	—	1.3	26.1	Macau
1,086.3	21.1	1.9[2]	0.1	76.8[3]	4.4	12.3	60.2[3]	33.6	3.6	35.0	—	27.7	Macedoni
359.9	73.5	7.9	4.0	14.6	2.1	0.9	11.6	59.9	6.6	0.9[5]	6.2	26.4	Madagascar
472.4	96.4	—	—	3.6	0.3	0.2	3.1	47.3	15.0	—	12.0	25.7	Malawi
74,120.1	15.7	0.4	7.0	76.9	3.1	55.1	18.7	14.2	20.7	0.3	12.7	52.1	Malaysia
34.4	83.7	0.2	—	16.1	0.1	—	16.0	31.3	11.3	—	4.1	53.3	Maldives
330.3	98.4	—	—	1.6	—	0.9	0.8	26.0	0.6[4]	—	0.9[4]	72.5	Mali
1,748.3	—3.5[2]—		2.7	93.8[3]	2.9	60.1	30.8[3]	57.1	13.3	1.0	2.9	25.7	Malta
23.1	71.0			29.0	—	—	29.0	...	80.0[4]	...	...	20.0[4]	Marshall Islands
241.9	62.3	1.0	17.8	18.9	2.1	13.0	3.8	78.0	2.6	—	—	19.3	Martinique
471.0	48.2	48.6[2, 15]	1.9	1.3[3, 16]	—	—	1.3[3, 16]	58.2	4.5	10.8[5]	20.4	6.1	Mauritania
1,555.8	29.6	2.0	—	68.4	0.8	2.3	65.3	87.3	—	0.1	0.6	12.0	Mauritius
8.2	21.3[24]	—[24]	—[24]	78.7[24]	78.7[24]	—[24]	—[24]	70.0[14, 46]	...	...	...	30.0[14]	Mayotte
79,488.6	9.0	1.2	10.3	79.5	4.9	52.4	22.2	4.2	83.7	—	1.2	10.8	Mexico
78.2	96.9	—	—	3.1	...	...	...	...	3.5	...	72.7	23.8	Micronesia
745.5	73.5	2.7	0.9	22.9	1.4	7.9	13.7	11.6	1.1	80.5	—	6.8	Moldova
...	...	...	...	...	...	...	...	...	...	...	...	...	Monaco[31]
473.3	4.8	—65.5—		29.7	0.3	3.1	26.2	12.9	5.5	16.6	9.9	55.2	Mongolia
4,728.1	34.8	10.0	2.2	53.0	20.8	3.2	28.9	62.1	3.4	1.5	7.7	25.4	Morocco
164.0	75.9	1.8	9.0	13.4	0.1	3.3	10.0	34.7	8.4	—	14.7	42.2	Mozambique
920.7	—78.9[2]—		0.9	20.2[3]	...	0.4	19.7[3]	1.9	5.1	0.7[4]	4.8	87.5	Myanmar (Burma)
1,321.4	47.0	50.1	—	2.8	...	...	...	...	3.0[4, 10]	...	—[4, 10]	97.0[4, 10]	Namibia
28.9	—	99.4	—	0.6	—	—	0.6	...	...	...	...	...	Nauru
286.3	1.1	—	—	98.9	—	0.2	98.6	57.1	36.0	0.1	0.5	6.2	Nepal

Trade: external   (continued)

country	year	imports total value ('000,000 U.S.$)	Standard International Trade Classification (SITC) categories (%)							direction of trade (%)				
			food and agricultural raw materials (0 + 1 + 2 − 27 − 28 + 4)	mineral ores and concentrates (27 + 28 + 667)	fuels and other energy (3)	manufactured goods total[a] (5 + 6 − 667 + 7 + 8 + 9)	of which chemicals and related products (5)	of which machinery and transport equipment (7)	of which other[a] (6 − 667 + 8 + 9)	from European Union (EU)[b]	from United States	from Eastern Europe[c]	from Japan	from all other[d]
Netherlands, The	1996	160,896.3	15.8	1.4	8.9	73.9	11.7	34.4	27.8	58.8	8.4	2.9	3.8	26.1
Netherlands Antilles	1992	1,868.3	9.1	0.1	58.8	32.0	3.7	13.7	14.7	11.7	17.0	0.1	2.2	69.0
New Caledonia	1994	842.2	— 21.0[2] —		10.2	68.7[3]	7.4	33.0	28.3[3]	43.7	4.6	—	4.8	47.0
New Zealand	1995	13,957.7	8.6	1.9	5.3	84.1	13.1	42.2	28.9	21.6	18.7	0.1	13.9	45.7
Nicaragua	1995	1,009.2	18.8	0.3	17.9	63.0	17.5	23.1	22.4	10.1	30.2	1.0	5.0	53.8
Niger	1991	355.3	25.7	2.1	9.4	62.7	9.6	13.6	39.5	39.6	5.1	0.3	6.6	48.4
Nigeria	1992	8,839.3	7.6	0.9	0.4	91.0	13.9	54.2	22.9	62.8	8.5	0.8[5]	6.3	21.7
Northern Mariana Islands	1991	392.2	19.3	—	20.9	59.8	2.3	22.2	35.3	...	18.2	...	16.6	65.2
Norway	1996	34,309.2	9.1	4.8	4.5	81.6	9.1	39.2	33.3	70.8	6.5	3.3	3.9	15.6
Oman	1995	4,248.6	20.6	1.9	1.5	76.0	6.8	39.4	29.8	27.9	6.5	0.4	15.8	49.5
Pakistan	1995	11,703.6	23.0	1.2	16.1	59.7	17.0	28.9	13.8	23.5	9.3	2.5	10.7	53.9
Palau	1984	25.1[50]	28.9	0.1[2]	0.9[50]	70.0[3]	4.0	24.5	41.5[3]	—	41.8	—	38.2	20.0
Panama[51]	1995	3,799.0	14.4	1.2	63.5	20.9	6.6	2.4	11.9	5.6	34.8	0.5	0.5	58.5
Papua New Guinea	1993	1,298.6	18.8[6]	0.3[6]	6.8[6]	74.1[6]	7.0[6]	38.3[6]	28.8[6]	4.0	3.9	0.9	14.5	76.7
Paraguay	1995	3,135.9	18.7	0.2	6.5	74.6	9.0	42.3	23.2	11.0	12.5	0.1	8.7	67.7
Peru	1995	9,224.0	15.4	0.4	8.8	75.4	13.2	39.2	23.1	17.9	25.2	0.7	7.0	49.3
Philippines	1995	28,487.4	10.5	2.0	9.2	78.3	9.2	32.5	36.6	10.7	18.9	1.9	22.1	46.4
Poland	1995	28,929.9	12.9	2.0	9.1	76.0	15.0	30.0	31.0	64.8	3.8	14.7	1.7	15.0
Portugal	1996	34,121.9	16.5	0.6	7.8	75.2	10.1	36.3	28.8	75.7	3.2	1.4	2.2	17.5
Puerto Rico	1992[12]	15,387.3	17.3	0.3	10.6	71.8	25.4	21.8	24.7	4.8	68.1	0.1	3.7	23.2
Qatar	1994	1,927.4	15.8	2.7	0.6	80.8	7.0	39.7	34.2	33.9	10.6	1.4[5]	13.4	40.8
Réunion	1995	2,711.1	21.5	0.2	4.7	73.6	10.7	29.8	33.1	80.1	0.6	0.1	2.1	17.2
Romania	1996	11,435.3	9.5	2.8	20.9	66.8	10.0	25.6	31.2	51.5	3.7	20.4	0.9	23.6
Russia	1995	46,680.0	28.8	— 7.0 —		64.2	10.9	29.5	23.8	37.9	5.7	30.1	1.6	24.7
Rwanda	1990	291.1	18.2	1.9	15.3	64.6	10.2	16.1	38.3	44.6	1.2	1.4[5]	7.7	45.1
St. Kitts and Nevis	1990	110.7	21.2	0.1	5.0	73.7	7.3	29.4	37.0	18.0	43.6	—	3.7	34.7
St. Lucia	1993	300.3	— 26.8[2] —		7.6	65.6[3]	9.1	22.8	33.6[3]	19.1	37.3	—	5.6	38.0
St. Vincent and the Grenadines	1994	129.9	25.7	0.4[2]	6.3	67.6[3]	11.1	20.6	35.9[3]	24.8	35.1	0.3	2.8	37.1
Samoa	1993	130.9	21.6	0.6[2]	8.4	69.4[3]	5.0	37.0	27.4[3]	4.3	8.3	—	15.9	71.5
San Marino[40]	...	...	...	...	...	...	...	...	...	...	...	...	...	...
São Tomé and Príncipe	1994	30.4	21.5[22]	...	7.2	71.3	...	40.2	31.1	53.8[7]	25.0[4]	...	5.5	15.7[4]
Saudi Arabia	1994	23,343.5	14.0	0.9	0.2	84.8	8.7	40.1	36.1	34.7	21.3	0.6	11.7	31.6
Senegal	1993	1,139.2	35.3	1.4	9.1	54.2	11.8	22.2	20.3	57.1	5.2	1.5[5]	3.6	32.6
Seychelles	1994	206.5	22.7	0.3	15.6	61.4	6.9	23.2	31.4	35.1	3.8	—	3.3	57.8
Sierra Leone	1994	149.9	— 41.7[2] —		18.5	39.8[3]	7.3	18.0	14.5[3]	47.0[4]	10.0[4]	2.2[4]	5.6[4]	35.2[4]
Singapore	1996	131,480.2	5.1	0.7	9.3	84.8	5.9	57.9	21.0	14.5	16.4	0.3	18.2	50.7
Slovakia	1994	6,611.0	11.0	2.8	19.3	66.9	13.2	27.8	25.9	33.5	2.8	54.2	1.2	8.3
Slovenia	1995	9,491.7	12.4	1.9	6.6	79.1	12.1	33.8	33.3	68.8	3.1	10.1	1.7	16.4
Solomon Islands	1994	170.6	— 16.2[2] —		8.2	75.6[3]	5.2	38.0	32.5[3]	2.8	2.8	—	17.1	77.4
Somalia	1992	228.0[4]	30.3[43]	0.2[43]	4.6[43]	64.9[43]	5.1[43]	37.1[43]	22.7[43]	27.2[4]	10.1[4]	—[4]	0.7[4]	62.0[4]
South Africa[55]	1995	27,737.0	8.7	2.2	10.2	79.0	12.1	43.9	23.0	44.5	11.8	0.5	9.9	33.4
Spain	1996	121,255.4	14.9	2.1	9.1	73.9	11.8	37.3	24.8	66.3	6.2	2.2	2.8	22.5
Sri Lanka	1995	2,833.2	15.0	3.9	7.9	73.2	9.9	19.8	43.5	18.2	3.5	0.9	10.2	67.1
Sudan, The	1994	1,161.5	— 22.4[2] —		20.6	57.0[3]	9.0	26.2	21.8[3]	32.8	3.5	3.7	2.1	57.8
Suriname	1992	639.8	8.5	1.0	13.5	76.9	12.8	38.7	25.4	22.5	39.7	—	15.6	22.2
Swaziland	1994	962.6	21.8[1]	0.4[1]	10.3[1]	67.4[1]	10.2[1]	26.7[1]	30.6[1]	7.6[1]	0.6[1]	—[1]	0.9[1]	90.9[1, 57]
Sweden	1996	63,986.8	8.8	1.3	7.4	82.4	10.3	41.8	30.2	69.1	6.0	3.7	2.5	18.7
Switzerland[58]	1995	79,365.3	8.4	2.8	2.9	85.8	14.6	33.4	37.8	79.6	6.4	1.5	3.2	9.4
Syria	1995	4,708.8	20.0	0.5	1.1	78.4	10.2	31.6	36.7	34.4	6.8	10.8	4.4	43.7
Taiwan	1996	102,554.4	8.8	1.1	8.1	82.1	13.1	39.6	29.3	16.2	19.5	1.5	26.9	35.9
Tajikistan	1995	799.2	7.9	— 74.6 —		17.5	1.6	11.5	4.4	25.4	3.2	18.9	—	52.6
Tanzania	1990	1,021.5	5.4	1.5	10.3	82.8	9.8	45.6	27.4	58.2	1.6	0.8[5]	7.7	31.8
Thailand	1995	71,387.4	7.9	2.2	6.7	83.2	10.5	47.5	25.2	16.0	12.0	2.3	30.5	39.2
Togo	1994	222.0	24.4[10]	0.7[10]	9.8[10]	65.1[10]	11.9[10]	28.3[10]	25.0[10]	53.1	5.5	0.6	3.5	37.3
Tonga	1994	69.1	34.4	0.5	12.1	53.0	8.3	17.0	27.7	1.0	8.2	—	6.7	84.1
Trinidad and Tobago	1994	1,136.2	20.5	5.6	0.6	73.2	13.7	29.8	29.7	16.2	48.3	0.3	4.6	30.6
Tunisia	1996	7,698.2	13.1	1.7	8.4	76.8	9.2	27.3	40.3	72.4	4.2	3.3	2.1	18.1
Turkey	1995	35,707.5	12.6	3.8	12.9	70.7	15.0	32.2	23.6	47.2	10.4	11.4	3.9	27.0
Turkmenistan	1995	1,364.0	27.0	— 6.3 —		66.6	11.3	17.9	37.4	10.9	3.9	39.7	0.5	44.9
Tuvalu	1994	17.6	36.1[10]	0.1[2, 10]	14.6[10]	49.2[3, 10]	6.8[10]	13.9[10]	28.5[3, 10]	...	0.6	—	1.7	97.7
Uganda	1992	524.4	13.0	1.5[2]	13.4	72.0[3]	8.3	32.2	31.5[3]	29.7	4.8	—	9.9	55.6
Ukraine	1995	11,335.5	4.9	— 56.0 —		39.1	9.1	17.4	12.6	16.4	2.6	61.4	0.1	19.5
United Arab Emirates	1992	17,410.0	11.6	0.7	1.7	86.1	5.5	35.1	45.4	33.5	8.9	0.5	16.6	40.5
United Kingdom[39]	1996	287,528.6	12.2	2.9	3.8	81.1	10.1	42.1	28.9	54.1	12.5	2.0	4.9	26.5
United States[59]	1996	817,627.2	7.0	1.6	9.4	82.0	5.7	45.2	31.1	18.0	—	0.9	14.4	66.7
Uruguay	1995	2,865.7	14.4	0.3	10.1	75.2	15.3	34.5	25.4	20.9	9.9	0.5	2.6	66.2
Uzbekistan	1995	2,892.7	19.3	— 2.7 —		78.0	9.0	43.1	25.9	17.7	1.1	36.9	1.5	42.8
Vanuatu	1993	73.5	22.2	0.2	9.3	68.3	6.6	29.8	31.9	8.5	1.1	—	8.1	82.3
Venezuela	1995	10,791.3	18.8	1.2	1.1	79.0	16.4	37.0	25.6	17.9	42.6	0.3	4.4	34.8
Vietnam	1993	3,924.0	— 9.4[2, 10] —		22.9[10]	67.8[3, 10]	16.3[10]	26.1[10]	25.4[3, 10]	10.4	0.1	4.8	11.5	73.2
Virgin Islands (U.S.)	1995	3,200.3	...	...	68.6[54]	...	...	...	...	...	32.7	...	...	...
West Bank	1994	102.5[61]	...	...	...	...	...	...	...	...	...	...	...	...
Western Sahara	...	...	...	...	...	...	...	...	...	...	...	...	...	...
Yemen	1994	2,087.4	39.3	0.3[2]	5.2	55.3[3]	7.7	20.5	27.0[3]	30.0	9.0	1.4[5]	4.5	55.1
Yugoslavia	1991	5,548.6	12.4	1.3	19.0	67.4	13.7	22.7	31.0	46.5[4]	4.2	24.5[5]	2.3	22.6
Zambia	1990	1,237.7	3.7	1.1[2]	15.2	79.9[3]	12.6	47.0	20.3[3]	38.7	10.1	0.1	6.7	44.4
Zimbabwe	1995	2,726.2	7.9	1.4	9.0	81.8	13.7	41.7	26.4	25.1	4.5	0.4	7.3	62.7

[1]Year ending March.   [2]Excluding precious stones, etc. (667).   [3]Including precious stones, etc. (667).   [4]Estimate.   [5]Including also Asian republics of the former U.S.S.R.   [6]1990.   [7]Main countries only.   [8]Year ending September 30.   [9]Percentage of the total excluding fish imports for the cannery (52.1% of the overall total), and government purchases (0.1%).   [10]1991.   [11]1987.   [12]Year ending June 30.   [13]Figures for Belgium-Luxembourg Economic Union (Luxembourg is also shown separately).   [14]1992.   [15]Excluding metals.   [16]Excluding metals.   [17]Includes 52.6% from India.   [18]Mainly electricity.   [19]Includes 83.8% to India.   [20]Includes 77.7% from South Africa.   [21]Includes 48.7% to Switzerland.   [22]Main items only.   [23]Includes 82.8% for reexports.   [24]Domestic exports only.   [25]1980.   [26]1989.   [27]1985.   [28]Includes 9.1% for ferronickel.   [29]Includes 38.7% for ships and boats.   [30]Includes 63.3% for Ethiopia.   [31]Figures for France include Monaco.   [32]1988.   [33]Includes 82.4% from Israel.   [34]Includes 69.2% to Israel and 25.1% to Jordan.   [35]Includes 42.5% for nonmonetary gold.   [36]Includes 41.5% to Switzerland.   [37]Excluding petroleum products.   [38]Includes 51.5% for ships' bunkers.   [39]Figures for United Kingdom include Guernsey, Isle of Man, and Jersey (data for Jersey is also shown separately).   [40]Figures for Italy include San Marino.   [41]United Kingdom only.   [42]Including

exports total value ('000,000 U.S.$)	food and agricultural raw materials (0 + 1 + 2 − 27 − 28 + 4)	mineral ores and concentrates (27 + 28 + 667)	fuels and other energy (3)	manufactured goods total[a] (5 + 6 − 667 + 7 + 8 + 9)	of which chemicals and related products (5)	of which machinery and transport equipment (7)	of which other[a] (6 − 667 + 8 + 9)	to European Union (EU)[b]	to United States	to Eastern Europe[c]	to Japan	to all other[d]	country
177,369.4	22.7	0.9	8.2	68.2	15.5	28.5	24.1	71.3	3.1	2.8	1.0	21.8	Netherlands, The
1,558.9	3.0	0.8	91.2	5.0	0.9	3.0	1.0	8.1	25.0	—	3.1	63.8	Netherlands Antilles
354.8	—	31.1	—	68.9	—	—	68.9[49]	45.0	4.8	—	27.1	23.1	New Caledonia
13,745.4	60.4	0.5	1.6	37.5	7.6	8.6	21.3	16.0	10.0	0.9	16.2	56.9	New Zealand
509.2	76.5	0.8	0.6	22.2	1.2	6.1	14.9	31.8	42.1	0.1	1.4	24.7	Nicaragua
311.9	22.4	74.8	0.8	2.0	0.1	1.2	0.7	56.4	0.1	—	18.8	24.7	Niger
11,886.5	1.8	—	97.6	0.7	—	—	0.6	46.9	44.1	—	—	9.0	Nigeria
263.0	—	—	—	100.0	—	—	100.0	—	100.0	—	—	—	Northern Mariana Islands
48,955.0	8.9	0.8	54.7	35.6	2.9	11.1	21.7	76.9	7.4	1.9	1.8	12.0	Norway
5,917.4	5.1	0.4	78.6	15.9	0.4	9.6	5.9	0.9	2.8	0.1	28.5	67.7	Oman
8,157.9	15.6	0.2	1.0	83.2	0.7	0.5	82.0	30.5	15.1	0.6	6.8	47.1	Pakistan
0.5	69.1	—	—	30.9	—	—	30.9	—	8.0	—	58.8	33.2	Palau
1,202.5	82.3	1.2	11.9	4.6	1.1	—	3.5	52.9	29.8	0.4	0.1	16.8	Panama[51]
2,624.6	26.8	19.5	30.6	23.1[52]	—	2.5	20.6[52]	12.1	4.0	—	21.4	62.5	Papua New Guinea
819.6	85.8	—	0.1	14.1	1.8	0.4	12.0	20.4	3.8	—	0.1	75.8	Paraguay
5,575.1	31.3	16.2	4.9	47.6	2.2	0.6	44.8	30.5	17.2	0.6	8.4	43.2	Peru
17,447.2	14.1	1.8	1.5	82.7	2.0	22.2	58.5	17.7	36.2	0.1	15.5	30.4	Philippines
22,863.3	13.3	1.3	8.1	77.4	7.8	21.1	48.5	70.1	2.7	17.0	0.2	9.9	Poland
23,185.6	10.6	1.5	2.4	85.5	4.6	30.6	50.3	79.5	4.7	1.2	0.8	13.8	Portugal
21,051.2	15.8	0.1	2.6	81.5	43.7	21.7	16.2	5.1	87.5	—	0.2	7.2	Puerto Rico
3,212.9	0.5	0.2	73.8	25.4	15.9	1.4	8.1	1.9[4]	2.5[4]	—[4]	55.6[4]	40.0[4]	Qatar
208.7	78.6	0.5	0.2	20.7	1.7	12.7	6.2	79.9	0.6	—	6.1	13.4	Réunion
8,084.5	12.0	0.3	7.4	80.3	9.8	13.6	56.9	56.6	2.4	8.7	0.5	31.9	Romania
79,910.0	6.1	—— 48.5 ——		45.5	9.8	9.9	25.8	32.6	5.7	27.2	4.5	30.0	Russia
131.9	72.8	3.9		23.3[53]	—	—	23.3[53]	64.1[4]	6.1[4]	—[4]	1.9[4]	27.9[4]	Rwanda
27.7	32.8	—	—	67.2	0.3	46.2	20.7	21.4	50.9	—	—	27.7	St. Kitts and Nevis
119.7	56.4	—	—	43.6	1.3	8.6	33.8	53.2	27.0	—	0.1	19.7	St. Lucia
50.4	75.0	0.2[2]	0.1	24.7[3]	0.8	12.3	11.7[3]	33.0	9.3	—	0.1	57.6	St. Vincent and the Grenadines
17.5	32.7	...	...	67.3	...	...	...	...	3.2	—	—	96.8	Samoa
...	...	...	...	...	...	...	...	...	...	...	...	...	San Marino[40]
6.5	76.9[22]	...	...	...	...	...	...	88.8[7]	1.9[4]	...	0.5[4]	8.8[4]	São Tomé and Príncipe
42,584.0	1.1[54]	0.3[54]	91.1[54]	7.5[54]	5.2[54]	0.9[54]	1.3[54]	22.6	18.5	—	16.0	42.9	Saudi Arabia
605.1	41.4	11.0	14.5	33.2	17.2	6.5	9.5	40.3	2.0	—	1.7	55.9	Senegal
51.8	46.7	0.1	45.9	7.3	0.1	2.7	4.4	42.5	4.0	—	0.6	53.0	Seychelles
115.8	4.8	84.2	...	11.0	...	...	...	51.0[4]	28.0[4]	1.1[4]	1.7[4]	18.2[4]	Sierra Leone
125,153.1	4.5	0.5	7.9	87.2	5.6	65.9	15.6	13.0	18.4	0.9	8.2	59.4	Singapore
6,690.2	9.3	1.5	4.6	84.6	12.9	19.0	52.6	35.0	1.6	52.8	0.1	10.5	Slovakia
8,315.8	5.7	0.2	1.2	92.9	10.5	31.4	51.0	67.0	3.1	9.7	0.3	19.9	Slovenia
142.2	—— 98.8[2] ——		...	1.2[3]	—	—	1.2[3]	24.4	0.1	—	41.1	34.4	Solomon Islands
44.0	95.4	2.3	—	2.3	—	—	2.3	52.3	—	—	—	47.7	Somalia
27,339.9	12.3	14.3	8.1	65.4	7.7	8.8	48.9	28.3	6.6	0.7	5.8	58.6[56]	South Africa[55]
100,955.5	16.9	0.7	2.5	79.9	8.0	42.7	29.2	71.3	4.2	2.2	1.2	21.1	Spain
2,391.4	22.8	7.4	0.9	68.9	0.8	3.2	64.9	31.4	36.3	2.8	5.2	24.3	Sri Lanka
523.9	87.4[14]	5.3[14]	—[14]	7.2[14]	—[14]	—[14]	7.2[14]	29.8	3.4	0.1	4.5	62.2	Sudan, The
357.1	18.1	67.6	1.3	13.0	—	0.1	12.9	47.5	10.7	—	5.3	36.5	Suriname
751.8	69.1[24]	3.3[24]	0.9[24]	26.7[24]	1.4[24]	8.3[24]	17.1[24]	19.8[24]	3.1[24]	—[24]	0.7[24]	76.4[24]	Swaziland
82,880.5	7.6	1.2	2.1	89.1	6.8	44.4	37.9	56.1	8.5	4.0	3.3	28.1	Sweden
80,454.9	3.7	2.8	0.1	93.3	25.7	31.6	36.1	60.6	8.5	2.4	3.9	24.6	Switzerland[58]
3,969.9	18.6	0.6	62.5	18.2	0.8	0.8	16.8	57.0	0.9	6.1	0.2	35.8	Syria
115,724.0	4.1	0.1	0.9	94.9	8.6	50.8	35.5	13.6	23.2	0.5	11.8	50.9	Taiwan
748.6	0.6	—— 16.5 ——		82.9	—	0.6	82.2	46.3	2.0	21.3	1.1	29.4	Tajikistan
416.1	82.0	1.0	2.0	15.1	1.0	2.2	11.8	40.5	6.8	0.7[5]	3.9	48.2	Tanzania
56,743.2	24.6	2.5	0.7	72.1	4.4	33.7	34.0	15.1	17.9	2.1	16.8	48.1	Thailand
162.2	57.7[54]	32.8[54]	0.3[54]	9.2[54]	1.2[54]	3.4[54]	4.6[54]	19.6	0.1	2.5	—	77.7	Togo
14.0	93.0	0.4	—	6.6	0.4	1.8	4.4	0.4	23.7	—	50.8	25.1	Tonga
1,960.4	8.2	0.1	49.2	42.6	26.7	1.7	14.2	7.7	46.4	—	0.2	45.7	Trinidad and Tobago
5,517.4	8.1	1.5	10.5	79.9	12.7	9.8	57.4	80.1	1.4	0.5	0.3	17.7	Tunisia
21,598.7	21.0	2.1	1.3	75.6	4.1	11.1	60.4	51.3	7.0	11.8	0.8	29.1	Turkey
1,880.7	0.6	—— 72.6 ——		26.8	0.6	0.2	26.0	7.6	1.7	29.7	8.8	52.2	Turkmenistan
0.7	92.2[26]	—[26]	—[26]	7.8[26]	—[26]	—[26]	7.8[26]	42.9[7]	...	...	...	57.1	Tuvalu
171.4	95.2	—	3.0	1.8	—	0.9	0.9	63.8	8.1	—	0.6	27.5	Uganda
11,566.5	15.0	—— 11.2 ——		73.9	12.5	18.2	43.2	12.5	4.8	56.8	0.6	25.3	Ukraine
24,756.0	0.3	0.1	96.6	3.0	0.2	0.2	2.6	7.0[4]	3.2[24]	0.1[4]	35.7[4]	53.9[4]	United Arab Emirates
261,950.2	7.8	2.7	6.5	83.1	13.3	44.1	25.6	57.0	11.8	2.5	2.5	26.1	United Kingdom[39]
622,784.3	13.2	1.4	2.0	83.5	10.1	49.2	24.2	20.5	—	1.0	10.8	67.6	United States[59]
2,116.5	59.3	0.3	0.9	39.4	5.6	5.9	27.9	21.0	5.9	0.3	0.3	72.0	Uruguay
3,109.0	2.5	—— 14.8 ——		82.7	2.8	2.4	77.4	18.6	0.4	24.3	0.1	56.7	Uzbekistan
17.6	83.2	0.1	—	16.7	—	2.0	14.7	31.6	0.2	—	29.1	39.0	Vanuatu
18,914.2	3.0	0.8	77.0	19.2	4.2	2.8	12.2	9.1	51.0	0.2	1.5	38.1	Venezuela
2,985.2	—— 48.9[2, 10] ——		35.6[10]	15.5[3, 10]	0.7[10]	0.1[10]	14.7[3, 10]	7.2	—	5.4	31.4	56.0	Vietnam
3,026.3	...	...	83.3[54, 60]	...	...	...	...	...	92.7	...	...	...	Virgin Islands (U.S.)
22.6[62]	...	...	...	...	...	...	...	...	...	...	...	...	West Bank
...	...	...	...	...	...	...	...	...	...	...	...	...	Western Sahara
933.9	9.6	0.2[2]	89.0	1.2[3]	0.5	—	0.7[3]	6.8	12.3	1.3[5]	13.3	66.4	Yemen
4,704.1	15.9	0.6	4.4	79.1	9.1	19.6	50.3	54.6[4]	4.5	29.1[5]	0.2	11.6	Yugoslavia
1,049.2	3.4	89.0[2, 15]	—	7.5[3, 16]	—	0.2	7.3[3, 16]	30.6	1.6	—	31.0	36.8	Zambia
1,895.5	50.2	6.1	1.3	42.4	2.6	2.7	37.2	40.3	4.7	1.6	7.9	45.4	Zimbabwe

coins. [43]1986. [44]Includes 83.8% from rest of Customs Union of Southern Africa. [45]Including also Iceland and Norway. [46]France only. [47]Includes 85.0% from South Africa. [48]Based on trade with Australia and New Zealand only. [49]Includes 58.8% for ferroalloys. [50]Excluding bulk imports of fuels. [51]Including trade with the former Canal Zone. [52]Includes 19.7% for nonmonetary gold. [53]Includes 19.8% for nonmonetary gold. [54]1993. [55]Figures for South Africa refer to the Customs Union of Southern Africa (includes South Africa, Botswana, Lesotho, Namibia, and Swaziland, also shown separately). [56]Including unspecified destinations of 21.2%. [57]Includes 87.7% from South Africa; these imports may have had their origin from other countries. [58]Figures for Switzerland include Liechtenstein also shown separately. [59]Figures for United States include American Samoa, Guam, Puerto Rico, and Virgin Islands (U.S.), also shown comparative. [60]Exports of refined petroleum to United States only. [61]Excluding imports from Israel (90.9% in 1987). [62]Excluding exports to Israel (70.3% in 1987).

Trade: domestic

The following table presents data relating to domestic wholesale and retail trade for the countries of the world. The section on wholesale trade is based for the most part on establishments (service points from which a business enterprise operates [see note a]) engaged primarily in selling goods to retailers and distributors for resale or to purchasers who buy for business and farm uses. The retail trade section is based on businesses engaged in selling merchandise for personal or household consumption; restaurants are, when possible, included, hotels excluded.

The data presented here are based on information from a variety of country and international sources. The country sources include statistical abstracts, correspondence, annual reports, and censuses of business and trade.

Because there is no single published source or common international methodology for the compilation of data on wholesale and retail trade, nor a single current year on which, by common agreement, the various national reports would be based, allowance must be made for variations in the meaning and recency of the information provided for any single country and for its comparability internationally. Variations occur in part because of the ways in which countries define wholesale and retail trade; the conventional free-enterprise distinction between wholesale and retail activity (of a single enterprise or an entire national trade sector) may not exist in the business practice of some countries. Variations also exist in the kind and level of detail reported. For example, countries may design surveys differently according to the size (number of employees, sales, surface area) of establishments surveyed, their profitability, or other less direct criteria, such as ownership or

location. The depth of analysis to which the data are subjected may also vary. The structure of a national trade sector is also affected by the degree of government involvement, which may range from total control of wholesale distribution in some socialist countries to partial involvement in some strategic sectors, or to relative noninvolvement in fully private trade sectors of capitalist countries. In some smaller countries data may refer to a single trading enterprise.

At the table's extreme left, preceding the year to which the trade data refer, the combined value of the country's wholesale and retail trade as a percentage of gross domestic product or net material product is given. Unless otherwise noted, GDP data include restaurants and exclude hotels.

Both the wholesale and retail sections of the table provide similar detail: establishments or outlets, employees, sales, and certain derived values for relationships among these measures; the retail section provides an additional breakdown of sales by an end-use classification of retail sales outlets.

Although all sales figures are given in U.S. dollars, the comparability of these dollar figures may differ considerably; for instance, the purchasing power of various national currencies in domestic transactions may bear only a distant relationship to the exchange rate of the same currency in international transactions, especially for countries having nonconvertible currencies. The price of goods may also vary, depending on the degree to which they are subject to direct subsidies and artificial cost controls such as tax, investment, or free-trade preferences by a central government seeking to influence social or economic conditions.

Trade: domestic

country	domestic trade as percentage of GDP, 1994	year	wholesale trade					retail trade		
			establish-ments[a]	employees[b]	sales[c] (U.S.$'000,000)	employees per establishment	sales per establishment (U.S.$'000)	outlets[a]	employees[b]	sales[c] (U.S.$'000,000)
Afghanistan	9.8	1981–82	...	1	...	...	...	...	126,100[1]	...
Albania	4.6[2]	1990	...	1	...	...	...	11,741[3]	62,000[1]	1,570[3]
Algeria	17.8[4]	1986	...	1	...	...	...	3,600[5, 6]	390,990[1, 7, 8]	16,200
American Samoa	...	1990	177	255	...	1.4	...	583	1,495	...
Andorra	19.4[9]	1988	...	...	...	...	...	592[10]	7,227	...
Angola	6.1[11]	1973	1	...	...	...	...	29,138[1]	...	...
Antigua and Barbuda	24.7[7]	1980	25	350	...	14.0	...	199	1,000	23[12]
Argentina	15.4[13]	1985	54,452	351,087[14]	1,113	6.4[14]	20,435	500,342	1,055,071[14]	1,003
Armenia	2.2	1990	...	1	...	...	...	...	88,100[1]	...
Aruba	37.2[7, 15]	1990	...	723	...	...	...	...	5,700	...
Australia	19.0[7, 16]	1991–92	15,514	153,092	44,553	9.9	2,872	209,909	1,290,173	107,230
Austria	15.8	1995	17,149[4]	184,000	90,070	10.2[4]	3,526[4]	33,601[4]	252,000	47,912
Azerbaijan	2.2[17]	...	...	...	...	...	...	...	...	...
Bahamas, The[18]	23.0[13]	1980	23	1,066	143	46.3	6,235	132	4,059	460[19]
Bahrain	8.5	1983	1	1	...	...	1	255[1]	12,551[1]	1,601
Bangladesh	7.9[7, 20]	1985	...	1	...	...	...	271,000	3,610,000[1]	5,500[19]
Barbados	26.8[7, 9]	1990	...	1	...	...	...	1,911[21]	20,800[1]	264[12]
Belarus	12.6[9]	1994	1	1	1	...	...	30,300[1]	459,200[1]	654[1]
Belgium	14.1[17]	1984	60,589	160,600	65,110	2.6	1,075	135,534	193,500	20,957
Belize	17.2[7]	1983	...	1	...	...	...	...	4,558[1]	33[20]
Benin	20.0[22]	1979	...	...	...	...	...	170[5]	1,910[14, 19]	150[12]
Bermuda	32.8[23]	1985	60[23]	820	...	...	...	310[5, 23]	4,342[14]	116[24, 25]
Bhutan	7.8[7]	1982	...	1	...	...	...	...	9,000[1, 3, 14]	...
Bolivia	10.7[9]	1992	4,820	21,814	...	4.5	...	64,136	122,892	1,570[19]
Bosnia and Herzegovina	13.9[4]	1990	...	1	18,469[4]	...	...	...	130,914[1]	18,065[4]
Botswana	15.7[16]	1983–84	205	3,500	494[12]	...	...	1,660	10,700	165[12]
Brazil	7.0	1990	45,278	652,054	22,706	14.1	501	680,634	4,102,638	39,312
Brunei	8.4[9]	1986	1	1	...	1	...	833[1, 26]	4,261[1, 26]	...
Bulgaria	10.6	1995	...	...	2,923	...	...	88,115	...	6,020
Burkina Faso	11.8	1975	...	...	...	...	...	...	19,354[1, 14]	...
Burundi	3.3[9]	1986	...	...	...	...	...	...	...	210
Cambodia	14.8	...	...	...	...	...	...	...	...	...
Cameroon	11.7[11]	1980	...	...	...	...	...	1,312[5]	13,776[14, 19]	1,430[19]
Canada	12.1[9]	1995	...	1	232,900[4]	...	...	...	2,428,000[1, 2]	150,200
Cape Verde	28.0[11]	1980	...	1	...	...	...	...	3,930[1]	...
Central African Republic	11.6	1989	113	302	...	2.7	...	14,543	23,078	230
Chad	29.5[4]	1983	...	1	1	...	...	1,661[1, 5, 28]	497[1]
Chile	17.0	1983	561[5]	15,300[5]	2,312[5]	27.2[5]	4,121[5]	1,125[19, 24]	21,700[19, 24]	1,403[19, 24]
China	9.0	1995	14,961,000	41,515,693[14]	196,241	2.8[14]	16	15,779,970[14]	37,051,765	246,905
Colombia	10.4	1985	...	...	...	...	...	1,110[31]	49,000[31]	8,600[19]
Comoros	27.0[7]	1980	...	1	...	...	...	...	1,873[1, 5]	...
Congo, Dem. Rep. of the	16.7[9]	1981	...	...	...	...	...	3,036[5]	33,398[5]	3,300[12]
Congo, Rep. of the	11.9[9]	1984	...	1	...	...	...	...	13,240[1]	...
Costa Rica	20.3	1975	3323[2]	4,073[32]	35[32]	12.3[32]	104[32]	9,713	26,486	475[33]
Côte d'Ivoire	27.1	1981	...	...	...	...	...	2,023[5]	16,720[5]	1,800[19]
Croatia	12.0	1994[34]	1,155	6,461	4,015	5.5	3,476	16,959	48,615	3,734
Cuba	20.1[4, 35]	1989	...	...	15,174	...	...	56,916[36]	230,000[8, 14]	8,124
Cyprus	19.4[1]	1993	1,559[25]	14,137	443	5.3[25]	720[25]	8,474[25]	39,676	1,102
Czech Republic	8.3[17]	1990[37]	63,110[36]	251,000[36]	40,083[36]	4.0[36]	635[36]	62,667[4]	258,127	21,235
Denmark	13.9	1992	32,432	176,205	73,937	5.4	2,280	40,733	210,015	32,145
Djibouti	15.5[9]	1985	28	371[15]	...	...	...	431	1,877[15]	...
Dominica	15.0[7, 9]	1989	...	1	...	...	...	...	3,700[1]	79[19]
Dominican Republic	18.5[9]	1983	670	...	3,136	...	4,681	11,220[15]	...	1,259[15]
Ecuador	14.8	1990	426	18,014	139	42.3	326	554	20,168	102
Egypt	17.0[16]	1983–84	2,552	45,500[14]	4,492	18.0[14]	1,760	2,545	55,800[14]	29,700[19]

The data on distribution of retail sales by kind of consumer goods may have their origin in several different types of data or analysis. One country may aggregate sales data by kind of establishment only (this may be perfectly satisfactory in a country of small, independent outlets); another may aggregate data directly by kind of goods (most easily done in a country with well-developed statistical, tax-reporting, and commercial systems). Other countries may find it impolitic to publish data that reflect the poverty of their distribution network or their supply of consumer goods and may aggregate or publish data for only a few sectors: food or nonfood goods, for example. For countries with only a few trading enterprises in a particular sector, detail must often be withheld to preserve the confidentiality of individual businesses.

The notes that follow further define the column headings.

a. The number of establishments or outlets refers to economic units that operate at a single physical location in one principal kind of activity, whether singly owned or part of a multiunit firm. Such units are not necessarily identical with a company or enterprise.

b. Number of employees refers to full-time and part-time paid workers, including salaried managers and officers; it usually excludes owner-operators, partners, vendors, and unpaid relatives.

c. Total sales (also called turnover) includes the value of merchandise sold for cash or credit; amounts received from customers for layaway purchases; receipts from rental or leasing of vehicles, equipment, tools, instruments, etc.; receipts for delivery, installation, maintenance, repair, alteration, storage, and other services.

d. Outlets engaged primarily in the sale of food and nonalcoholic beverages, such as grocery stores, meat and fish markets, and bakeries.

e. Outlets engaged primarily in the sale of clothing and shoes; also includes outlets that sell accessory items, such as millinery, furs, and leather goods.

f. Outlets engaged primarily in the sale of home furnishings, including furniture, draperies, floor coverings, household appliances, and home entertainment equipment.

g. Outlets that primarily serve food and drink, including restaurants, lunchrooms, cafeterias, social caterers, refreshment places, contract feeders, ice cream parlours, and bars and taverns.

h. Outlets engaged primarily in the sale of pharmaceuticals, cosmetics, and perfumes.

i. Outlets engaged primarily in the sale of building materials, hardware, garden supplies, paint, electrical supplies, and farm equipment.

j. Outlets engaged primarily in the sale of motor vehicles, motorcycles, bicycles, and tires, batteries, and other automotive supplies and parts; includes service stations.

k. Outlets engaged in the sale of multiple lines of merchandise, such as department stores, variety stores, and rural general stores.

l. Miscellaneous specialized outlets such as those engaged primarily in the sale of liquors, sporting goods, books, jewelry, photographic and optical goods, gifts, flowers, tobacco products, home fuels, and newspapers.

retail trade (continued)

food[d]	clothing, shoes[e]	home furnishings[f]	eating, drinking[g]	drugs, pharmaceuticals[h]	building materials[i]	automobile parts[j]	general merchandise[k]	other[l]	employees per outlet	sales per outlet (U.S.$'000)	population per outlet	country
...	...	...	...	...	...	...	...	...	...	...	277[3]	Afghanistan
62.4				37.6					...	134[3]	...	Albania
...	...	...	...	...	...	...	...	...	5.0[5,6]	...	5,146[5,6]	Algeria
...	...	...	...	...	...	...	...	...	...	...	81	American Samoa
...	...	...	...	...	...	...	...	...	3.8[10]	...	39[10]	Andorra
...	...	...	...	...	...	...	...	...	...	...	...	Angola
15.5	13.3	7.1	5.4	4.3	7.8	13.7	10.1	22.8	5.0	100	378	Antigua and Barbuda
									2.1[14]	2,004	61	Argentina
...	...	...	...	...	...	...	...	...	...	...	...	Armenia
...	...	...	...	...	...	...	...	...	...	...	...	Aruba
28.9	3.6	8.9	3.7	2.9	2.4	31.9	7.9	10.7	6.1	511	82.8	Australia
31.0	12.2	6.9	...	6.7	1.9	17.3	4.3	19.7	7.1[4]	857[4]	227[4]	Austria
...	...	...	...	...	...	...	...	...	...	...	...	Azerbaijan
24.4[15]	7.7[15]	7.1[15]	—	3.7[15]	8.4[15]	30.1[15]	7.6[15]	11.0[15]	30.8	1,881	1,026	Bahamas, The[18]
...	...	...	...	...	...	...	...	...	49.2[1]	...	1,507[1]	Bahrain
...	...	...	...	...	...	...	...	...	...	...	...	Bangladesh
...	...	...	...	...	...	...	...	...	...	...	130[21]	Barbados
...	...	...	...	...	...	...	...	...	15.2[1]	2,157[1]	341	Belarus
35.1				64.9					1.4	155	73	Belgium
...	...	...	...	...	...	...	...	...	...	...	...	Belize
...	...	...	...	...	...	...	...	...	11.3[14,19]	...	19,871[19]	Benin
...	...	...	...	...	...	...	...	...	11.0[12,24]	...	178[5,23]	Bermuda
...	...	...	...	...	...	...	...	...	...	...	...	Bhutan
...	...	...	...	...	...	...	...	...	1.9	...	107	Bolivia
...	...	...	...	...	...	...	...	...	...	...	...	Bosnia and Herzegovina
...	...	...	...	...	...	...	...	...	6.4	99	604	Botswana
11.1	12.1	...	...	4.2	8.4	31.4	15.4	17.4	6.0	55	213	Brazil
...	...	...	...	...	...	...	...	...	5.1[1,26]	...	279[1,26]	Brunei
44.1	17.3	5.1	—	6.2	1.2	16.8	[27]	9.3[27]	...	68	...	Bulgaria
...	...	...	...	...	...	...	...	...	...	...	...	Burkina Faso
...	...	...	...	...	...	...	...	...	...	...	...	Burundi
...	...	...	...	...	...	...	...	...	...	...	...	Cambodia
...	...	...	...	...	...	...	...	...	10.5[5,14]	...	6,481[15]	Cameroon
25.5	6.0	5.1	...	5.6	...	35.7	16.7	5.4	...	...	...	Canada
...	...	...	...	...	...	...	...	...	...	...	...	Cape Verde
...	...	...	...	...	...	...	...	...	1.6	16	187	Central African Republic
...	...	...	...	...	...	...	...	...	...	...	...	Chad
28.3[15]	29	5.0[15]	1.6[15]	5.4[15]	4.7[15]	18.0[15]	17.1[15,29]	19.9[15]	19.3[19,24]	1,247[19,24]	10,210[19,24]	Chile
57.3[30]	16.0[30]			26.7[30]					2.3[14]	16	76	China
...	...	...	...	...	...	...	...	...	44.1[31]	1,522[31]	...	Colombia
...	...	...	...	...	...	...	...	...	...	...	...	Comoros
...	...	...	...	...	...	...	...	...	11.0[5]	...	9,676[5]	Congo, Dem. Rep. of the
...	...	...	...	...	...	...	...	...	...	...	...	Congo, Rep. of the
37.7	13.5	6.9	...	8.2	7.0	15.1	5.9	5.7	2.7	59	202	Costa Rica
...	...	...	...	...	...	...	...	...	8.3[5]	...	4,257[5]	Côte d'Ivoire
25.2	5.5	1.6	...	—	3.2	19.1	28.5	16.9	2.9	220	282	Croatia
35.8	17.2	9.9	...	5.3	0.8	5.1	...	25.9	4.0[8,14]	184[36]	177[36]	Cuba
10.2	8.2	...	43.7	2.4	3.1	14.9	...	17.5	1.0[25]	124[25]	77[25]	Cyprus
42.9	15.1	12.8	...	3.6	2.9	10.0	...	12.7	4.2[4]	362[4]	249[4]	Czech Republic
47.1	5.6	3.4	...	3.2	3.1	17.7	1.4	18.5	5.2	789	127	Denmark
...	...	...	...	...	...	...	...	...	...	...	998	Djibouti
...	...	...	...	...	...	...	...	...	...	...	...	Dominica
...	...	...	...	...	...	...	...	...	...	112[15]	519[15]	Dominican Republic
26.3	2.0	11.5	3.9	1.6	7.2	38.2	6.2	3.1	36.4	184	18,520	Ecuador
...	...	...	...	...	...	...	...	...	21.9[14]	1,278	17,756	Egypt

Trade: domestic (continued)

country	domestic trade as percentage of GDP, 1994	year	wholesale trade establishments[a]	employees[b]	sales[c] (U.S.$'000,000)	employees per establishment	sales per establishment (U.S.$'000)	retail trade outlets[a]	employees[b]	sales[c] (U.S.$'000,000)
El Salvador	16.5	1983	396	6,400	1,038	16.2	2,621	1,416	10,700	485
Equatorial Guinea	9.2	1983	...	36	...	...	...	...	2,701	...
Eritrea	19.7[9]	[39]	...	...	...	...	...	...	...	...
Estonia	18.6	1994	17,629	...	1,357	...	77	821	70,000[2]	807
Ethiopia	10.17, 20	1984[39]	375[5, 42]	3,200[5, 42]	...	8.5[5, 42]	...	7,416[5, 42]	17,100[5, 42]	273
Faroe Islands	13.1[13]	1987	78	1	19	...	241	430	1,484[1, 7, 33]	38
Fiji	20.5[7]	1993	276	2,914	102	10.6	370	1,315	7,335	151
Finland	11.3	1995	9,367[43]	80,394[43]	49,376	8.6[43]	4,946[43]	37,303[13]	137,609[13]	31,842
France	14.31, 9	1992	88,371	912,131	399,844	10.3	4,525	363,701	1,615,700	320,274
French Guiana	16.3[11]	1995	339	858	1,770	2.5	355	1,517	2,720	425
French Polynesia	17.7[17]	1986	1	1	...	...	...	947[1]	5,038[1]	...
Gabon	7.5	1982	...	1	...	...	...	...	12,683[1, 14, 23]	...
Gambia, The	16.6[16]	1983	...	1	...	...	...	...	16,551[1]	...
Gaza Strip	...	1986	...	1	...	...	...	...	13,400[1]	...
Georgia	2.7[13]	1988	...	1	...	...	...	...	172,400[1]	...
Germany	7.6	1993	194,381	1,544,085	674,247	7.9	3,469	487,320	2,727,312	406,188
Ghana	19.2	1983	460[44]	1,100[44]	115[44]	2.4[44]	250[44]	1,500	16,000	252[19]
Gibraltar	...	1991	...	737	...	...	...	...	1,835	...
Greece	13.5	1988	31,032	115,979	...	3.7	...	184,821	388,132	12,263[45]
Greenland	8.0[21]	1992	...	1	139	...	...	...	2,214[1, 8]	211
Grenada	21.17, 16	1988	...	1	1	...	...	...	5,421[1]	6[1, 12]
Guadeloupe	19.64, 7	1993	696	3,538	6,008	7.0	1,524	4,004	11,061	7,467
Guam	51.5[15]	1992	169	2,045	1	12.1	1	768	12,060	1,400[1]
Guatemala	24.3	1989	...	1	...	...	...	88,200[15]	374,690[1]	1,200[19]
Guernsey	...	1991	...	642	...	...	...	...	2,573	...
Guinea	26.0[22]	1979	...	1	...	...	...	...	12,808[44]	...
Guinea-Bissau	25.87, 11	1979	1	1	...	...	...	685[1, 44]	5,085[1]	44[1, 26]
Guyana	4.4	1980	...	1	...	...	...	147[5]	14,690[1]	93[12]
Haiti	10.9[20]	1983	...	1	...	...	...	653[5, 46]	303,353[1]	500[19]
Honduras	10.3	1991	...	1	...	...	...	...	156,500[1]	401[12]
Hong Kong	25.5	1994	21,712	61,951	23,100	2.8	1,064	58,362	162,760	33,112
Hungary	11.4	1994	206[15]	122,600[15]	13,121[23]	595[23]	...	217,861	467,400	19,470
Iceland	10.4[9]	1992	1,509[12, 47]	5,132[23]	598[33, 47]	...	...	1,680	7,774[48]	825
India	13.4[16]	1980	1	1	...	...	...	3,132,000[1, 24]	3,615,000[1, 24]	108,300[12]
Indonesia	16.6	1980	1	1	1	1	1	54,632[1]	85,400[1]	3,451[1]
Iran	15.4[16]	1986–87	118,698	1	2,429[50]	...	133[50]	634,084	521,708[1, 51]	37,350
Iraq	25.6[13]	1987–88[26]	1,942	3,902	130	2.0	67	108,460	165,594	7,077
Ireland	17.17, 17	1988	3,972	39,101	11,420	9.8	2,875	31,699	89,680	10,952
Isle of Man	10.5[52]	1991	...	851	...	...	...	...	2,993	...
Israel	10.4[13]	1988	17,967	67,300	16,875	3.8	939	43,844	103,100	10,763
Italy	18.4[7]	1983	...	1	...	...	...	1,033,725	1,369,200[1]	122,978
Jamaica	27.77, 9	1991	...	1	...	...	...	10,150[33]	173,500[1]	1,457[12]
Japan	12.5	1994	429,302	4,581,372	5,272,000	10.7	12,280	1,499,948[24]	7,384,177[24]	1,321,000[24]
Jersey	...	1986	...	855	...	...	...	...	7,046	...
Jordan	10.5[9]	1993	508	3,292	405	6.5	798	35,866	81,656	1,766
Kazakstan	8.9[17]	1991	...	...	...	...	...	42,168	484,800	...
Kenya	14.9	1990	2,097	21,266	...	10.1	...	4,316	36,300	...
Kiribati	14.1[13]	1987	...	1	...	...	...	30	1,127[1, 36]	3.8
Korea, North	...	...	...	...	...	...	...	...	...	...
Korea, South	12.6	1994	118,471	603,093	91,480	5.1	772	758,953	1,548,297	79,850
Kuwait	7.67, 9	1992	2,426	21,934	647	9.0	267	11,541	60,506	508
Kyrgyzstan	10.1	1992	...	1	...	...	...	...	92,900[1, 46]	138
Laos	8.2[9]	1990	...	...	...	...	...	15,000	...	576
Latvia	7.0	1994	...	...	...	...	...	7,214[11]	95,300[11]	986
Lebanon	25.6	1986	...	1	...	...	...	...	114,706[1]	1,662[14]
Lesotho	8.6		...	...	...	...	...	...	46,850[1]	115[19]
Liberia	5.3[4]	1984	...	1	...	...	...	...	...	...
Libya	9.0[13]	1973	1,126	4,148[14]	...	3.7[14]	...	26,825	44,605[14]	9,205[12]
Liechtenstein	...	1975	67	216	...	3.2	...	228	740	...
Lithuania	17.2[17]	1992	...	1	...	...	...	6,425	127,400[1]	236
Luxembourg	16.4[11]	1994	2,125	10,980	7,864	5.2	3,700	3,204	17,495	4,617
Macau	...	1991	...	1	...	...	...	...	47,706[1]	...
Macedonia	24.7	1990	...	1	9,522[4]	...	...	...	65,593[1, 4]	9,238[6]
Madagascar	10.9[11]	1976	1,104	...	...	...	...	1,570	...	696[23]
Malawi	11.5	1984	439	23,000	522	52	1,189	500	8,600	127
Malaysia	12.4	1980	19,663	116,200	15,461	5.9	786	95,993	73,000	8,200[19]
Maldives	19.1[7]	1990	...	1	...	...	...	...	8,884[1]	5[19]
Mali	19.37, 9	1979	...	1	...	...	...	...	5,200[1]	...
Malta	14.37, 11	1983	3	1	1.0	...	333	4[21]	11,936[1, 5]	2.3
Marshall Islands	19.2[7]	1988	...	1	...	...	...	...	1,394[1]	...
Martinique	21.97, 11	1993	700	3,680	7,957	5.2	2,007	4,137	16,313	2,109
Mauritania	14.2[22]	1971[15]	23	100	102	4.3	4,445	59	700	103
Mauritius	17.8[7]	1986	1	1	...	1	...	207[1, 5, 7]	10,107[1, 5, 7]	164[1, 5, 7]
Mayotte	...	1983	1	1	1	...	1	41[1]	597[1, 8]	271[1]
Mexico	25.5	1988	36,512	1	23,506	...	644	713,315	3,875,100[1, 2]	39,810
Micronesia	12.7[17]	1980	...	348[14]	...	...	...	...	489[7, 14]	...
Moldova	5.8	1990	...	1	...	...	...	...	148,000[1]	...
Monaco	...	1975	...	273	...	...	...	...	1,439	...
Mongolia	17.6[9]	1983[1, 55]	...	1	...	...	...	4,828	21,100	1,235[36]
Morocco	19.8	1972	...	...	...	...	...	4,000[5]	20,000[5]	5,750[19]
Mozambique	10.4[17]	1980	...	1	...	...	...	...	63,058[1]	...
Myanmar (Burma)	22.3[20]	1983	...	1	...	...	...	...	1,405,000[1, 56]	2,116
Namibia	10.1[7]	1977	222	5,035	377	22.7	1,698	1,248	7,569	254
Nauru	...	...	...	...	...	...	...	...	...	...
Nepal	4.7[16]	1983	...	1	...	...	...	...	119,000[1, 14, 23]	736

retail trade (continued)

percentage breakdown of sales

food[d]	clothing, shoes[e]	home furnishings[f]	eating, drinking[g]	drugs, pharmaceuticals[h]	building materials[i]	automobile parts[j]	general merchandise[k]	other[l]	employees per outlet	sales per outlet (U.S.$'000)	population per outlet	country
11.9[6,38]	7.6[6,38]	16.2[6,38]	...	7.9[6,38]	6.3[6,38]	12.4[6,38]	28.2[6,38]	9.5[6,38]	7.6	342	3,336	El Salvador
...	...	...	...	...	...	...	...	...	...	...	...	Equatorial Guinea
...	...	...	...	...	...	...	...	...	...	...	...	Eritrea
46.0	10.1	6.8[40]	...	[41]	[40]	13.1	18.2	5.8[41]	...	984	1,826	Estonia
15.9	45.2	...	...	...	7.9	9.8	10.5	10.7	2.3[5,42]	275[5,42]	55,200[5,42]	Ethiopia
...	...	...	...	...	...	...	...	...	...	89	109	Faroe Islands
11.9[11]	10.2[11]	7.6[11]	8.5[11]	2.6[11]	12.3[11]	9.6[11]	36.1[11]	1.2[11]	5.6	115	573	Fiji
31.6	6.0	6.0	...	4.6	5.4	27.9	11.2	7.3	3.7[13]	940[13]	135[13]	Finland
38.2	15.7	17.6	...	6.4	...	6.1	6.3	9.7	4.4	881	158	France
...	...	...	...	...	...	...	...	...	3.1	2,419	155	French Guiana
...	...	...	...	...	...	...	...	...	5.3[1]	...	188[1]	French Polynesia
50.5	9.6	...	...	...	33.8	6.1	...	...	...	...	...	Gabon
...	...	...	...	...	...	...	...	...	...	...	...	Gambia, The
...	...	...	...	...	...	...	...	...	...	...	...	Gaza Strip
...	...	...	...	...	...	...	...	...	...	...	...	Georgia
35.2	12.7	12.0	...	8.4	4.1	...	18.9	8.7	5.6	834	166	Germany
...	...	...	...	...	...	...	...	...	1.1	108[44]	7,993	Ghana
...	...	...	...	...	...	...	...	...	...	...	...	Gibraltar
60.0[45]	18.1[45]	9.5[45]	...	...	...	...	...	12.4[45]	2.1	...	54	Greece
...	...	...	...	...	...	...	...	...	...	...	...	Greenland
...	...	...	...	...	...	...	...	...	...	...	...	Grenada
44.8[11]	13.4[11]	19.6[11]	...	7.1[11]	...	...	...	15.1[11]	2.8	337	102	Guadeloupe
11.6[8]	10.9[8]	4.9[8]	8.0[8]	0.3[8]	5.2[8]	26.9[8]	3.3[8]	28.9[8]	15.7	1,494[1]	181	Guam
...	...	...	...	...	...	...	...	...	...	...	83[15]	Guatemala
...	...	...	...	...	...	...	...	...	...	...	...	Guernsey
...	...	...	...	...	...	...	...	...	...	...	...	Guinea
...	...	...	...	...	...	...	...	...	0.8[1,44]	...	1,080[1,44]	Guinea-Bissau
9.7	18.9	13.8	4.5	2.8	17.7	18.6	...	14.0	...	743	5,884	Guyana
...	...	...	...	...	...	...	...	...	...	...	7,034[5,46]	Haiti
...	...	...	...	...	...	...	...	...	...	...	...	Honduras
18.8[17]	13.6[17]	...	...	...	...	11.5[17]	...	56.1[17]	2.8	567	103	Hong Kong
11.4	5.2	7.6	6.8	2.1	13.6	19.1	23.4	10.8	2.1	89	47	Hungary
62.6[49]	8.8	...	...	...	...	...	[49]	28.6	4.6[48]	825	155	Iceland
...	...	...	...	...	...	...	...	...	1.2[1,24]	...	219[1,24]	India
...	...	...	...	...	...	...	...	...	1.6[1]	63[1]	2,681[1]	Indonesia
...	...	...	...	...	...	...	...	...	...	59	78	Iran
...	...	...	...	...	...	...	...	...	1.5	20	158	Iraq
40.6	9.1	1.4	10.4	2.9	5.1	21.6	2.8	6.1	2.8	345	112	Ireland
...	...	...	...	...	...	...	...	...	...	...	...	Isle of Man
35.4	12.2	20.0	...	...	...	...	6.2	26.2	2.4	245	103	Israel
50.8	15.1	...	...	3.4	...	...	...	30.7	...	119	55	Italy
...	...	...	...	...	...	...	...	...	...	...	214[33]	Jamaica
30.5	10.0	4.8	—	[53]	[53]	11.4	15.0	28.3[53]	4.9[24]	880[24]	83[24]	Japan
...	...	...	...	...	...	...	...	...	...	...	...	Jersey
23.5	12.6	11.2	—	1.5	9.2	22.9	12.5	6.6	2.3	49	109	Jordan
...	...	...	...	...	...	...	...	...	11.5	...	400	Kazakstan
...	...	...	...	...	...	...	...	...	8.4	...	6,003	Kenya
...	...	...	...	...	...	...	...	...	...	127	2,226	Kiribati
...	...	...	...	...	...	...	...	...	...	...	...	Korea, North
29.7	17.8	13.7	—	4.5	2.9	...	12.0	19.4	2.0	105	58	Korea, South
18.4[49]	14.5	17.3	...	2.6	6.5	16.4	[49]	24.3	5.2	150	123	Kuwait
...	...	...	...	...	...	...	...	...	...	...	...	Kyrgyzstan
...	...	...	...	...	...	...	...	...	...	38	278	Laos
53.9	9.1	2.1	8.1	...	1.2	...	...	25.6	13.2[11]	2,831[11]	373[11]	Latvia
...	...	...	...	...	...	...	...	...	...	...	...	Lebanon
...	...	...	...	...	...	...	...	...	...	...	...	Lesotho
...	...	...	...	...	...	...	...	...	...	...	...	Liberia
...	...	...	...	...	...	...	...	...	1.7[14]	...	84	Libya
...	...	...	...	...	...	...	...	...	3.2	...	105	Liechtenstein
59.2	10.9	3.7	...	...	1.3	0.8	...	24.1	19.8[1]	38	584	Lithuania
26.8	8.5	10.1	...	3.0	...	42.6	...	9.1	5.4	1,441	126	Luxembourg
...	...	...	...	...	...	...	...	...	...	...	...	Macau
...	...	...	...	...	...	...	...	...	...	...	...	Macedonia
...	...	...	...	...	...	...	...	...	...	...	4,977	Madagascar
...	...	...	...	...	...	...	...	...	17.2	254	14,196	Malawi
32.9[54]	7.3[54]	10.8[54]	...	2.5[54]	1.1[54]	33.3[54]	4.4[54]	7.7[54]	0.8	64	143	Malaysia
...	...	...	...	...	...	...	...	...	...	...	...	Maldives
...	...	...	...	...	...	...	...	...	...	...	...	Mali
...	...	...	...	...	...	...	...	...	...	578[5]	83,378[5]	Malta
...	...	...	...	...	...	...	...	...	...	...	...	Marshall Islands
...	...	...	...	...	...	...	...	...	3.9	510	91	Martinique
...	...	...	...	...	...	...	...	...	11.9	1,742	20,300	Mauritania
...	...	...	...	...	...	...	...	...	48.8[1,5,7]	792[1,5,7]	4,976[1,5,7]	Mauritius
...	...	...	...	...	...	...	...	...	...	652[1]	1,477[1]	Mayotte
33.8	...	...	...	...	37.0	23.7	...	5.8	...	59	113	Mexico
...	...	...	...	...	...	...	...	...	...	...	...	Micronesia
...	...	...	...	...	...	...	...	...	...	...	...	Moldova
...	...	...	...	...	...	...	...	...	...	...	...	Monaco
...	...	...	...	...	...	...	...	...	4.3	225	372	Mongolia
...	...	...	...	...	...	...	...	...	5.0[5]	...	c. 4,000[5]	Morocco
...	...	...	...	...	...	...	...	...	...	...	...	Mozambique
...	...	...	...	...	...	...	...	...	...	...	...	Myanmar (Burma)
31.4	11.9	5.3	...	2.8	1.7	...	41.9	5.0	5.9	196	713	Namibia
...	...	...	...	...	...	...	...	...	...	...	...	Nauru
...	...	...	...	...	...	...	...	...	...	...	...	Nepal

Trade: domestic (continued)

country	domestic trade as percentage of GDP, 1994	year	wholesale trade					retail trade		
			establish-ments[a]	employees[b]	sales[c] (U.S.$'000,000)	employees per establishment	sales per establishment (U.S.$'000)	outlets[a]	employees[b]	sales[c] (U.S.$'000,000)
Netherlands, The	15.6	1994	55,500	344,000[13]	180,165	6.8[13]	3,246	86,500	482,500[13]	64,121
Netherlands Antilles	21.8[2]	1988	...	1	...	...	...	...	15,890[1]	149[14]
New Caledonia	31.0[2]	1991	...	1	...	...	...	1,023	4,995[1]	...
New Zealand	14.7[7, 57]	1996	8,263[58]	76,664[58]	16,295[58]	9.3[58]	1,972[58]	29,961[24, 58]	116,301[24, 58]	6,399
Nicaragua	24.2	1987	...	1	...	...	...	20,610[15]	94,600[1]	790[19]
Niger	18.5[7, 17, 22]		...	...	...	...	...	...	...	...
Nigeria	16.4[7]	1983[5]	154	16,000	2,220	104	14,415	421	20,000	2,202
Northern Mariana Islands	...	1987	28	187	49	6.7	1,777	383	2,304	155
Norway	11.0[7, 11]	1992	18,390	101,385[48]	56,056	5.5[48]	3,048	40,154	121,677[48]	31,264
Oman	15.4[7]	1990	1	1	...	...	...	25,840[1, 4, 7]	87,500[1]	2,449[12]
Pakistan	14.4[7, 16]	1983	...	...	...	...	...	276,701[46]	501,773[14, 46]	12,848
Palau	20.0[36]	1984	...	124	...	...	...	...	133	...
Panama	12.7[17]	1982[60]	560	13,115	1,491	23.4	2,662	7,561	15,765[5]	1,334
Papua New Guinea	8.0[17]	1985	...	1	...	...	...	...	25,100[1, 33]	669[7]
Paraguay	30.4[7, 17]	1982	...	1	...	...	...	...	85,961[1]	2,645[19]
Peru	16.9[17]	1973	4,210	34,100	2,163	8.1	514	103,010	72,200	8,500[19]
Philippines	15.3	1981	20,642	122,717	4,538	5.9	220	279,968	241,872	4,836
Poland	14.1	1994	...	...	15,945[17]	...	...	785,000	984,883	57,467
Portugal	17.4[2]	1983	4,522	135,400[14]	9,260	29.9[14]	2,048	4,889	74,400[14]	3,057
Puerto Rico	14.5	1991	1,876	34,571	7,365[36]	18.4	3,165[36]	9,164	106,239	7,206[36]
Qatar	7.0	1990	134	3,801	85	28.4	636	4,956	18,238	1,048[43]
Réunion	17.9[7, 13]	1992	1,313	6,732	2,664	5.1	203	3,506	12,927	2,114
Romania	11.7	1989	...	...	...	...	...	82,035	465,200	19,926
Russia	15.7	1992	...	...	...	...	...	319,500	3,135,000	18,771
Rwanda	19.4[7]	1978	...	1	...	...	...	...	8,014[1, 7]	350[19]
St. Kitts and Nevis	23.9[7]	1984	...	1	...	...	...	...	940[1]	...
St. Lucia	24.6[17]	1980	...	1	...	...	...	...	4,770[1, 7, 14]	...
St. Vincent	17.5[7]		...	...	...	...	...	...	...	...
Samoa	8.3[17]	1986	...	1	...	...	...	...	842[1]	...
San Marino	...	1994	209	1	...	...	...	1,126	2,531[1]	...
São Tomé and Príncipe	10.0[4]	1981	...	1	...	...	...	...	1,994[1]	...
Saudi Arabia	7.0[17]	1991[24]	4,460	31,481[14]	1,354	7.1[14]	304	80,266	174,187[14]	2,292
Senegal	27.4[13]	1987	97[5]	1,843[5]	...	19[5]	...	289[5]	4,964[5]	664[12]
Seychelles	12.3[9]	1989	1	1	...	1	...	243[1]	1,301[1]	...
Sierra Leone	13.8[7, 20]	1983–84	...	1	...	...	...	...	7,211[1]	177[12]
Singapore	17.6[7]	1992	24,820	158,993	132,480	6.4	5,338	17,798[24]	78,152[24]	12,058[24]
Slovakia	16.2	1992	...	...	...	...	...	5,590	24,638	1,313
Slovenia	12.9[13]	1995	909	27,000	5,814	29.7	6,396	6,972	35,472	5,955
Solomon Islands	9.6[11]	1991	...	1	...	...	...	405[19]	2,849[1]	139[19]
Somalia	9.3[11]		...	...	...	...	...	...	...	...
South Africa	16.1	1991	...	...	46,541	...	...	58,100[33]	373,200[33]	35,592
Spain	20.5[7, 36]	1984	40,000[21]	...	...	...	...	710,865[21]	1,400,000[21]	54,777
Sri Lanka	21.4[7, 17]	1983[5]	190	15,000	1	78.9	...	1,348	44,300	1,116[1, 25]
Sudan, The	12.8[4]	1981	...	...	...	...	...	...	...	3,278
Suriname	20.2	1985	...	1	...	...	...	13,000[61]	12,840[1]	110[19]
Swaziland	6.7[7]	1984	67	1,000	...	14.9	...	656	3,700	23[21]
Sweden	11.1	1993	31,960[25]	167,800[25]	37,518[25]	5.2[25]	1,174[25]	58,497	248,208[13]	30,159
Switzerland	17.5[13]	1991	22,094	176,857	...	8.0	...	55,080	245,443	23,620[25]
Syria	28.7	1983	2,827[46]	...	...	...	...	75,865[46]	110,000[14, 46]	7,330[19]
Taiwan	16.1[7, 9]	1987	55,654[12]	169,100	7,572[36]	2.9[12]	101[12]	355,760[12]	181,200	14,291[36]
Tajikistan	4.0		...	1	...	...	...	...	145,400[1]	...
Tanzania	14.0[7]	1983	...	...	...	...	...	1,620[5]	16,524[5]	3,975[19]
Thailand	16.6[17]	1988	16,740	139,252	14,535	8.3	868	260,030	280,886	13,683
Togo	21.2[9, 22]	1980	...	1	...	...	...	181[5]	1,815[5]	112
Tonga	12.4[20]	1976	...	14[14]	...	...	...	...	654[14]	...
Trinidad and Tobago	14.3[7]	1977	124	6,786	509	54.7	4,102	370	15,986	1,670[19]
Tunisia	27.3[7]	1984	...	1	...	...	...	...	153,860[1, 36]	2,814
Turkey	18.5	1991	53,122	250,671	72,071	4.7	1,357	444,803	586,416	63,621
Turkmenistan	3.4	1990	...	1	...	...	...	...	90,000[1]	4,150
Tuvalu	14.2[7]	1979	...	1	...	...	...	...	113[1, 14]	...
Uganda	12.6[16]	1977	226	4,100	...	18.1	...	251	3,200	5,285[24]
Ukraine	11.1[7]	1991	...	1	...	...	...	...	1,753,000[1, 2]	70,800
United Arab Emirates	11.0	1983	1	1	...	1	...	13,906[1, 7, 44]	121,278[1, 44]	5,910[19]
United Kingdom	14.0[9]	1994[63]	117,771	800,000	382,905	6.8	3,251	289,996	2,379,000	202,030
United States	15.8[17]	1992	495,457	5,791,401	3,249,874	11.7	6,559	1,526,215	18,407,453	1,894,880
Uruguay	14.5	1988	...	1	...	...	...	52,954[1, 7]	161,285[1, 7]	5,397[24, 25]
Uzbekistan	5.6	1991	...	1	...	...	...	...	462,000[1]	...
Vanuatu	30.9[17]	1983[51]	18	187[14]	...	10.4[14]	...	256	1,439[14]	...
Venezuela	13.6[17]	1979	...	...	...	...	...	...	161,596	12,345[19]
Vietnam	13.6	1990	...	...	...	...	...	25,723	419,400	4,414
Virgin Islands (U.S.)	...	1987	84	1,322	211	15.7	2,509	1,311	8,529	703
West Bank	...	1986	...	1	...	...	...	...	23,000[1]	...
Western Sahara	...		...	...	...	...	...	...	...	...
Yemen[64]	14.3	1986	...	1	...	...	...	...	201,606[1]	2,195[13]
Yugoslavia	16.3[9, 35]	1992	5,723	17,693	8,671	3.1	1,515	51,159	125,348	8,958
Zambia	9.6[9]	1974	494[5]	15,500[5]	977[5]	31.4[5]	1,978[5]	1,636[5]	13,700[5]	768[12]
Zimbabwe	10.9	1990	...	1	...	...	...	...	95,400[1]	693[36]

[1]Retail-trade data include wholesale trade. [2]1990. [3]Excludes retail-trade network of the agricultural cooperatives. [4]1989. [5]Data refer to larger establishments only. [6]1971. [7]Includes hotels.
[8]1987. [9]1995. [10]1972. [11]1991. [12]1983. [13]1992. [14]All persons engaged, including proprietors. [15]1982. [16]1994–95. [17]1993. [18]Data refer to New Providence Island only. [19]1986. [20]1993–94.
[21]1979. [22]Includes finance. [23]1981. [24]Excludes restaurants (eating and drinking establishments). [25]1984. [26]Privately owned establishments only. [27]Other includes general merchandise. [28]1976.
[29]General merchandise includes clothing and shoes. [30]1994. [31]For major cities only. [32]Wholesale selling directly to the public only. [33]1980. [34]Data exclude pharmacies. [35]Percentage of net
material product. [36]1985. [37]Data refer to former Czechoslovakia. [38]Selected outlets in urban areas only. [39]Ethiopia includes Eritrea. [40]Home furnishings includes building materials. [41]Other

retail trade (continued)

percentage breakdown of sales									employees per outlet	sales per outlet (U.S.$'000)	population per outlet	country
food[d]	clothing, shoes[e]	home furnishings[f]	eating, drinking[g]	drugs, pharma-ceuticals[h]	building materials[i]	automobile parts[i]	general merchandise[k]	other[l]				
40.3	11.4	6.8	...	3.2	———————38.3———————				5.9[12]	741	180	Netherlands, The
...	...	...	...	...	...	...	...	...				Netherlands Antilles
											169	New Caledonia
20.8	4.3	6.2	14.9	2.8	1.9	32.3	4.9	11.9	3.9[24,58]	346[24,58]	106[24,58]	New Zealand
...											143[15]	Nicaragua
									47.5	5,230	226,615	Niger
27.0	[59]	2.3	8.8	...	7.2	[59]	4.7	50.0[59]	6.0	406	56	Nigeria
34.9	9.9	7.3	...	...	4.8	27.0	4.0	12.1	3.0[48]	779	107	Norway
											561[1,4,7]	Oman
64.0	12.0	4.0	...	...	...	...	...	20.0	1.8[14,46]	...	273[46]	Pakistan
												Palau
									13.9[5]	176	270	Panama
...	...	...	7.1[7]	...	...	26.0	...	66.9				Papua New Guinea
...	...	...	...	...	...	...	...	...				Paraguay
									0.7	20	145	Peru
25.4	12.3	6.7	...	...	11.3	29.5	...	14.8	0.9	17	177	Philippines
37.4	6.1	2.8	...	...	...	27.8	...	25.9	1.3	73	49	Poland
21.5[45]	14.1[45]	11.2[45]	...	3.3[45]	5.6[45]	35.2[45]	——9.1[45]——		15.3[14]	625	2,047	Portugal
30.5[15]	9.9[15]	4.5[15]	7.5[15]	4.3[15]	5.9[15]	23.2[15]	8.9[15]	5.3[15]	11.6	201[36]	387	Puerto Rico
9.0[43]	9.6[43]	13.2[43]	...	2.7[43]	7.2[43]	29.7[43]	9.1[43]	19.5[43]	3.7	177[10]	98	Qatar
54.4	11.5	17.8	6.9	...	...	...	...	9.4	3.7	603	178	Réunion
30.0[33]	10.0[33]	5.9[33]	25.0[33]	1.6[33]	0.8[33]	...	...	26.7[33]	5.7	243	282	Romania
...	...	...	...	...	...	...	...	...	9.8	59	563	Russia
...	...	...	...	...	...	...	...	...	...	...	...	Rwanda
...	...	...	...	...	...	...	...	...	...	...	...	St. Kitts and Nevis
...	...	...	...	...	...	...	...	...	...	...	...	St. Lucia
...	...	...	...	...	...	...	...	...	...	...	...	St. Vincent
...	...	...	...	...	...	...	...	...	...	...	...	Samoa
									2.2[1]	...	21.8[1]	San Marino
												São Tomé and Príncipe
...	...	...	...	...	...	...	...	...	2.2[14]	29	201	Saudi Arabia
...	...	...	...	...	...	...	...	...	17.2[5]	...	23,430[5]	Senegal
...	...	...	...	...	...	...	...	...	54[1]	...	285[1]	Seychelles
...	...	...	...	...	...	...	...	...	...	...	...	Sierra Leone
17.7[49]	20.4	11.6	...	...	...	24.2	[49]	26.1	4.4	677	158	Singapore
42.1	7.7	9.3	...	1.9	0.8	3.7	1.7	32.8	1.4	235	948	Slovakia
14.8	4.8	1.1	...	4.4	1.5	26.3	35.0	12.1	5.1	854	285	Slovenia
...	...	...	...	...	...	...	...	...				Solomon Islands
...	...	...	...	...	...	...	...	...				Somalia
35.0	13.9	8.1	...	3.3	...	18.7	4.5	16.5	6.4[33]	383[33]	c. 540[33]	South Africa
39.2	10.5	16.7	...	...	...	4.2	...	29.4	2.0[21]	119[21]	52[21]	Spain
...	...	...	...	...	...	...	...	...	32.9	...	11,436	Sri Lanka
...	...	...	...	...	...	...	...	...	...	...	...	Sudan, The
...	...	...	...	...	...	...	...	...	...	...	...	Suriname
52.5[21]	25.1[19]	22.4[19]	...	...	...	...	...	...	5.6	...	969	Swaziland
35.5[13]	——9.3[13]——		...	...	...	...	...	55.2[13]	3.5[13]	515	149	Sweden
46.4[25]	13.5[25]	...	...	4.0[25]	...	...	...	36.1[25]	4.5	...	123	Switzerland
16.0	2.5	...	...	3.5	12.3	39.5[62]	3.5	22.7	1.4[14,46]	...	97[46]	Syria
21.5[23]	3.2[23]	8.8[23]	...	4.1[23]	3.1[23]	8.7[23]	3.1[23]	47.5[23]	0.3[12]	33[12]	52[12]	Taiwan
...	...	...	...	...	...	...	...	...				Tajikistan
...	...	...	...	...	...	...	...	...	10.0[5]	...	12,600[5]	Tanzania
10.5	3.4	4.6	...	1.0	7.2	43.2	12.4	17.7	1.1	53	209	Thailand
...	...	...	...	...	...	...	...	...	10.0[5]	...	15,600[5]	Togo
...	...	...	...	...	...	...	...	...	...	...	...	Tonga
18.6	...	8.5	2.7	...	10.7	28.2	15.3	15.9	43.2	1,467	2,798	Trinidad and Tobago
...	...	...	...	...	...	...	...	...				Tunisia
15.0[2]	10.6[2]	15.5[2]	3.8[2]	2.8[2]	2.9[2]	27.3[2]	10.6[2]	11.5[2]	1.3	143	129	Turkey
...	...	...	...	...	...	...	...	...	...	...	...	Turkmenistan
...	...	...	...	...	...	...	...	...	...	...	...	Tuvalu
									12.7	...	47,200	Uganda
...	...	...	...	...	...	...	...	...	...	...	...	Ukraine
											49[1,7,44]	United Arab Emirates
45.3	14.4	7.7	...	3.7	3.2	...	6.4	19.3	8.2	697	201	United Kingdom
19.5	5.4	4.9	10.3	4.1	5.2	28.0	12.9	9.7	12.1	1,242	165	United States
...	...	...	...	...	...	...	...	...	3.0[1,7]	...	...	Uruguay
...	...	...	...	...	...	...	...	...				Uzbekistan
...	...	...	...	...	...	...	...	...	5.6[14]	...	484	Vanuatu
50.2	10.1	7.6	...	...	...	5.0	...	27.1				Venezuela
									16.6	171	2,575	Vietnam
17.6	7.9	6.4	12.0	2.3	4.8	11.4	1.9	35.7	6.5	536	81	Virgin Islands (U.S.)
...	...	...	...	...	...	...	...	...				West Bank
...	...	...	...	...	...	...	...	...				Western Sahara
...	...	...	...	...	...	...	...	...				Yemen[64]
									2.5	175	205	Yugoslavia
									8.4[5]	359[5]	2,873[5]	Zambia
...	...	...	...	...	...	...	...	...	...	...	...	Zimbabwe

includes drugs, pharmaceuticals. [42]Excludes Addis Ababa and Asmera. [43]1988. [44]1977. [45]1978. [46]1975. [47]Excludes fuels, automobiles, alcohol and tobacco, and building materials. [48]Full-time equivalents. [49]Food includes general merchandise. [50]1972. [51]Urban establishments only. [52]1990–91. [53]Other includes drugs, pharmaceuticals, and building materials. [54]Peninsular Malaysia only. [55]State- and cooperative-owned establishments, including public catering. [56]1989–90. [57]1992–93. [58]1982–83. [59]Other includes clothing, shoes, and automobile parts. [60]Excludes Colón Free Zone. [61]1973. [62]Other includes machinery, transport equipment, and petroleum products. [63]Great Britain only. [64]Data refer to former Yemen Arab Republic only.

Finance

This table presents major statistical aggregates comprising national financial structure or constituting a basis for certain international financial comparisons. It includes such data as international reserves, money supply, central banking activity and discount rates, commercial (or "deposit money") banking activity, and external indebtedness of the central government. The country models are broadly similar and permit comparison of internal structure and external position at a high level of generalization.

One of the principal financial criteria of the relative economic position of a country is the size of its international reserves. International reserves as represented in this table comprise the sum of a country's (1) reserve position in the International Monetary Fund (IMF), a quota subscribed in the country's own currency, constituting a level up to which transactions may be effected within the IMF system, (2) holdings of foreign exchange, (3) holdings of gold, and (4) holdings of Special Drawing Rights (SDRs; an unconditional credit allocation, within a quota system set by the IMF, of currency needed by a country to maintain stability of foreign exchange transactions or markets). At appropriate accounting intervals these four elements are valued in a single unit of account (the SDR) and summed. The portion of this reserve total comprised by foreign exchange is very significant as an indication of the country's international liquidity (ability to pay its debts immediately in hard, or convertible, currencies). The ratio of external debt to total reserves, however, is less susceptible of interpretation in isolation: a low ratio, for example, may characterize the situation of a country with little need to borrow or of one with substantial debt but also the means to repay it. Much higher ratios, on the other hand, may be manageable, despite small reserves, if a country's export earnings are also high.

The section on money supply for the country, both as a total and as a per capita amount, refers to one particular measure of money in circulation: M1, the sum of money in private sector demand deposit accounts and outside banks in circulation; it is distinguished from a broader measure of supply, M2, which is roughly M1 plus "quasi-money" (the time, savings, and foreign-currency deposits of residents).

The section of the table outlining banking activity and the principal monetary aggregates encompasses both central bank authorities and commercial (deposit) banks. For both, the principal component aggregates are grouped under assets and liabilities. For certain countries, the four principal aggregates under assets and liabilities do not comprise the entire total, and the percentages shown, therefore, may add to less than 100% (occasionally more, when the net of other liabilities [capital, reserves, undistributed profits, checks, and other transit items] is negative, reducing the total against which these percentages are calculated). The items excluded by the choice of categories are the least significant worldwide but may be important locally; they include such items as quasi-money, money seasonally adjusted, unused bank overdrafts, and so on. In the case of the central bank authority, data are also provided for the central bank discount rate, generally the controlling interest rate for banking and commercial activity in the country.

Finance

country	international reserves, 1997[a]			money supply, 1996[b]		central bank authority, 1996[b]								
						assets (%)				liabilities (%)				central bank
	total ('000,000 SDRs)	% foreign exchange	ratio of external debt to total reserves, 1995[b]	stock ('000,000,000 national currency)	M1 per capita	claims on government	claims on private sector	claims on banks	claims on foreign assets	reserve money	government deposits	foreign liabilities	capital accounts	discount rate, 1998[a]
Afghanistan	...	...	...	...	...	...	...	...	...	...	...	...	...	...
Albania	202	98.0	2.3	90.4	27,600	46.7	—	3.0	50.3	54.2	2.9	32.5	13.5	32.0
Algeria	4,835	95.9	13.3	520.3[3]	18,300[3]	44.8[3]	—	34.7[3]	20.5[3]	46.9[3]	1.8[3]	17.7[3]	—	...
American Samoa	...	...	...	...	...	...	...	...	...	...	...	...	...	...
Andorra	...	...	...	...	...	...	...	...	...	...	...	...	...	...
Angola	...	...	...	...	...	...	...	...	...	...	...	...	...	...
Antigua and Barbuda	32	100.0	...	0.255	3,960	17.6	—	0.6	81.8	100.0	...	—	...	7.0[4]
Argentina	14,335	97.4	4.3	19.076	540	15.6	—	45.5	38.9	27.7	4.4	12.4	8.0	5.79[5]
Armenia	...	...	...	...	...	...	...	...	...	...	...	...	...	65.10
Aruba	135	97.0	...	0.447	5,330	—	—	—	100.0	63.9	23.2	—	15.4	9.5
Australia	10,511	94.0	...	95.650	5,200	57.5	—	—	42.5	75.7	7.9	0.1	—	5.0[4]
Austria	15,221	93.6	...	401.9	49,800	3.3	—	14.5	82.3	69.5	0.1	—	35.8	2.50
Azerbaijan	...	...	...	...	...	...	...	...	...	...	...	...	...	12
Bahamas, The	220	97.3	...	0.445	1,560	47.8	—	1.1	51.1	71.1	3.3	—	28.4	6.50
Bahrain	1,045	94.0	...	0.291	480	—	—	—	100.0	32.2	32.9	3.3	48.6	5.3[6]
Bangladesh	1,226	96.9	6.6	141.676	1,140	23.6[1]	—	27.8	48.6	72.2	—	5.9	4.4	8.00
Barbados	249	100.0	1.7	0.627	2,370	12.2	—	1.3	86.5	67.1	34.1	7.1	4.8	9.00
Belarus	...	...	...	15,708.4	1,519,000	37.6[1]	0.5	29.4	32.4	53.2	4.7	28.4	6.0	50.0
Belgium	12,610	87.3	...	1,439.2	141,000	9.2	—	15.4	75.4	49.9	0.1	0.5	5.1	2.75
Belize	43	90.7	5.9	0.164	730	47.3	—	2.7	49.9	51.1	28.2	1.5	8.2	12.00
Benin	184	98.9	7.6	161.7[3]	28,800[3]	30.0	—	1.4	68.6	35.8	25.9	40.5	—	...
Bermuda	...	...	...	...	...	...	...	...	...	...	...	...	...	...
Bhutan	119	99.2	0.7	2.074	2,440	—	...	5.6	94.4	43.1	6.0	4.5	—	8.0[6, 7]
Bolivia	781	91.2	6.3	4.759	620	27.6[1]	—	25.6	46.8	27.9	30.9	27.0	23.4	12.39[4]
Bosnia and Herzegovina	...	...	...	...	...	...	...	...	...	...	...	...	...	...
Botswana	3,961	98.8	0.1	0.951	640	—	—	—	100.0	12.5	39.6	—	33.3	11.75
Brazil	41,445	99.7	1.9	39.591	250	16.7[1]	—	41.0	42.3	30.1	15.2	2.1	2.5	21.61
Brunei	...	...	...	...	...	...	...	...	...	...	...	...	...	...
Bulgaria	...	...	...	...	...	...	...	...	...	...	...	...	...	2.22[5]
Burkina Faso	238	96.2	3.3	213.7[3]	20,400[3]	25.7	—	1.9	72.4	62.7	16.2	19.5	—	...
Burundi	103	93.2	5.2	43.644	7,280	17.2[2]	2.2	13.8	66.8	36.4	10.1	9.1	24.2	...
Cambodia	...	...	...	328.926	32,100	22.6	—	1.0	76.4	47.7	8.7	19.9	21.3	7.9[6]
Cameroon	27	50.0[7]	1,355.7	319.2[3]	22,700[3]	92.1[3]	—	5.8[3]	2.1[3]	40.2[3]	15.4[3]	96.2[3]	0.7[3]	8.60[7]
Canada	15,315	88.6	...	155.8	5,170	9.3	—	—	90.7	97.3	—	—	—	5.0
Cape Verde	...	...	...	13.001	33,300	45.5[1]	9.8	5.1	39.6	93.0	—	0.5	24.8	5.00[6]
Central African Republic	165[7]	100.0[7]	3.6	111.2[3]	34,300[3]	23.8[3]	—	1.0[3]	75.1[3]	65.1[3]	1.0[3]	11.1[3]	0.5[3]	8.60[7]
Chad	123[7]	100.0[7]	5.9	85.3[3]	12,400[3]	39.4[3]	—	0.8[3]	59.8[3]	59.2[3]	8.5[3]	19.2[3]	1.3[3]	8.60[7]
Chile	11,928	99.2	0.5	2,686.7	185,000	28.2[1]	1.7	16.7	53.4	78.4	14.9	—	2.0	12.55[6]
China	88,926	98.0	1.2	3,066.3	2,510	6.0	2.5	55.4	36.2	101.7	4.6	—	1.5	9.00
Colombia	7,173	95.9	1.6	9,937.3	277,000	9.4[1]	—	3.9	86.7	62.8	2.1	3.0	27.4	38.7[7]
Comoros	...	...	4.2	13.341	23,000	15.1	—	—	84.9	52.3	7.3	5.9	36.9	...
Congo, Dem. Rep. of the	457	97.8[7]	64.7	1,889.0[3]	42,400[3]	5.4[1, 3]	1.9[3]	24.7[3]	68.1[3]	47.6[3]	1.8[3]	326.2[3]	66.9[3]	...
Congo, Rep. of the	837	98.8[7]	83.3	134.9[3]	52,800[3]	69.5[3]	—	3.7[3]	26.8[3]	80.1[3]	13.7[3]	8.8[3]	1.2[3]	8.60[7]
Costa Rica	825	98.9	3.0	166.9	48,600	55.2[1]	—	8.4	36.4	68.0	20.0	43.9	22.7	32.00
Côte d'Ivoire	634	99.7	22.4	944.5[3]	63,900[3]	48.6	—	15.5	35.9	61.8	5.5	29.4	—	...
Croatia	...	...	...	10.683	2,240	1.7	—	1.6	96.7	66.2	4.2	8.8	14.3	5.90
Cuba	...	...	...	...	...	...	...	...	...	...	...	...	...	...
Cyprus[8]	911	95.5	...	0.654	1,000	43.1	—	0.5	58.3	55.1	24.9	1.9	—	7.00
Czech Republic	8,659	99.2	0.7	451.6	43,800	0.8[1]	—	17.4	81.8	81.1	9.5	9.1	5.9	13.00
Denmark	11,301	94.5	...	325.5	61,700	9.1	3.6	36.5	50.8	56.3	18.6	1.0	—	3.75
Djibouti	52	100.0	3.0	35.925	58,600	—	—	0.3	99.7	72.8	2.1	—	12.6	...
Dominica	18	100.0	3.8	0.097	1,310	19.1	—	—	80.9	96.1	0.9	2.9	—	6.4[4]
Dominican Republic	263	99.6	9.7	20.884	2,760	22.3[1]	—	25.3	52.3	160.7	—	128.1	-25.1	17.29[5]
Ecuador	1,662	98.0	7.3	5,349.5	453,000	6.8[1]	0.3	11.0	81.9	49.2	28.7	13.3	21.9	44.13
Egypt	13,260	98.2	1.9	44.521	720	37.4[1]	—	11.6	50.9	42.6	22.3	32.7	—	12.25

The largest share of assets in the case of both central and commercial banks is usually either claims on government and government agencies or foreign assets and holdings, though some of the latter, such as the large outstanding loans to socialist and less developed countries, have become the chief liabilities. The chief liability of a central bank is usually reserve money (the currency and notes issued by the bank). When government deposits represent a substantial share, budgetary surpluses have usually been deposited by the central government. Large foreign liabilities imply extensive foreign investment. Among the deposit money banks, loans to the private sector normally represent the largest share of assets and savings deposits the largest share of liabilities.

Because the majority of the world's countries are in the less developed bloc, and because their principal financial concern is often external debt and its service, data are given for outstanding external public and publicly guaranteed long-term debt rather than for total public debt, which is the major concern in the developed countries. For comparability, the data are given in U.S. dollars. The volume of debt by itself does not create external payment problems. If the country's external debt service (interest payments plus principal repayment) needs can be met by a strong, dependable export market, by export of services, or, occasionally, by direct remittances from abroad (by residents working abroad and sending wages home in foreign currencies, for example), no debt problem need exist. Countries whose debt service ratio (total debt service as a percent of exports of goods and services) is relatively high, however, must often base their external borrowing policy on mainte-

nance of domestic conditions of strict efficiency and, sometimes, austerity. The failure to adhere to such policies may lead to eventual crises of financial liquidity, deflation, and slower growth.

Ideally, the data presented here should be obtained by utilizing a single international methodology to provide a universally comparable set of international statistics. No international agency, however, can collect such data for all countries because of differences, both overall and in detail, in national definitions of financial aggregates, in accounting methodology, and in the completeness with which it is possible to survey a country's financial activity. The greater part of the data presented in the table comes from the IMF's *International Financial Statistics* and the World Bank's *Global Development Finance* (formerly *World Debt Tables*). These sources are supplemented by other recent data from national, regional, or other international sources. In a few cases the desired data are negligible or unavailable, as noted.

Detailed percentages may not add to 100.0 because of rounding, statistical discrepancy, or nonaccounting of negligible quantities.
— None, less than half the last significant figure, or not applicable.
... Not available.
a. Latest month.
b. Year-end.

deposit money banks, 1996[b]										external public debt outstanding (long-term, disbursed only), 1996							country
assets (%)				liabilities						total ('000,000 U.S.$)	creditors (%)		debt service				
loans to government	loans to private sector	reserves	foreign assets	deposits ('000,000,000 national currency)	composition (%)						official	private	total ('000,000 U.S.$)	repayment (%)		debt service ratio (%)	
					demand depos.	savings depos.	govt. depos.	foreign liabilities						principal	interest		
71.1[1]	5.3	6.3	17.3	205.2	20.8	31.3[2]	39.0	0.6		672.5	55.4	44.6	23.1	20.6	79.4	2.4	Afghanistan
80.2[1, 3]	14.4[3]	0.8[3]	4.6[3]	717.6[3]	29.4[3]	38.8[3]	8.1[3]	20.0[3]		30,808	57.9	42.1	3,991	48.4	51.6	26.2	Albania
...	...	...	...	...	...	...	...	...		...	...	...	...	...	...	...	Algeria
...	...	...	...	...	...	...	...	...		...	...	...	...	...	...	...	American Samoa
																	Andorra
...	...	...	...	...	...	...	...	...		9,400	31.3	68.7	645	76.7	23.3	12.4	Angola
14.6[1]	63.9	7.0	14.5	1.340	14.0	56.4[2]	5.3	15.4		...	...	...	...	...	...	...	Antigua and Barbuda
22.0[1]	63.4	2.8	11.8	84.950	8.6	50.2[2]	3.6	18.6		63,392	31.9	68.1	8,620	53.3	46.7	27.2	Argentina
...	...	...	...	...	...	...	...	...		434.1	100.0	—	45.8	81.9	18.1	10.0	Armenia
3.4	63.9	8.8	23.8	1.754	19.7	48.7	0.9	19.5		...	...	...	...	...	...	...	Aruba
7.6[1, 3]	85.5[3]	1.4[3]	5.4[3]	415.513[3]	15.6[3]	52.1[3]	0.8[3]	16.0[3]		...	...	...	...	...	...	...	Australia
20.4[1, 3]	54.7[3]	1.8[3]	23.0[3]	4,075.7[3]	6.0[3]	43.5[3]	1.9[3]	24.6[3]		...	...	...	...	...	...	...	Austria
...	...	...	...	...	...	...	...	...		244.9	100.0	—	4.3	—	100.0	...	Azerbaijan
17.8[1]	88.7	5.3	−11.9	2.219	15.7	71.2[2]	2.7	...		...	...	...	...	...	...	...	Bahamas, The
3.3	25.3	30.0	41.4	3.301	5.7	34.7	15.4	14.7		...	...	...	...	...	...	...	Bahrain
19.8[1]	61.9	11.4	7.0	468.212	15.7	74.0	7.9	3.6		15,403	98.6	1.4	595	66.1	33.9	10.1	Bangladesh
26.8	46.1	7.1	20.0	3.419	10.8	56.8[2]	7.2	23.5		381.6	56.3	43.7	61.7	56.4	43.6	1.0	Barbados
33.0[1]	36.1	16.3	14.6	34,919.9	26.5	33.2[2]	8.2	6.3		665	54.3	45.7	94	61.7	38.3	1.9	Belarus
29.6[1]	29.2	1.1	40.0	21,407.6	5.6	25.8[2]	0.3	43.9		...	...	...	...	...	...	...	Belgium
6.5[1]	73.3	8.4	11.8	0.652	15.2	64.6[2]	4.3	12.7		252.3	79.9	20.1	37.7	71.4	28.6	12.2	Belize
14.9[3]	30.0[3]	11.9[3]	43.2[3]	271.7[3]	39.7[3]	31.6[3]	12.5[3]	9.0[3]		1,449	99.7	0.3	39	61.5	38.5	6.2	Benin
...	...	...	...	8.475[3]	...	...	...	...		...	...	...	...	...	...	...	Bermuda
11.8[1]	15.1	42.0	31.1	4.962	33.3	29.5[2]	9.3	—		86.3	94.7	5.3	5.8	72.4	27.6	5.3	Bhutan
6.9	81.4	8.8	2.8	21.178	14.0	53.6[2]	0.5	13.7		4,238	99.0	1.0	304	51.0	49.0	22.8	Bolivia
...	...	...	...	...	...	...	...	...		—	—	—	—	—	—	—	Bosnia and Herzegovina
2.0[1]	47.7	37.8	12.5	3.621	19.4	60.6	1.1	4.2		606.5	94.1	5.9	149.5	49.4	50.6	4.8	Botswana
20.7[1]	61.1	12.3	5.9	327.431	3.7	50.4	4.8	15.8		94,587	27.7	72.3	12,812	55.4	44.6	21.0	Brazil
...	...	...	...	...	...	...	...	...		...	...	...	...	...	...	...	Brunei
...	...	...	...	...	...	...	...	...		8,138	32.5	67.5	933	50.2	49.8	14.9	Bulgaria
11.0[3]	31.8[3]	7.1[3]	50.1[3]	248.2[3]	32.9[3]	28.6[3]	24.7[3]	11.6[3]		1,160	99.6	0.4	45	66.7	33.3	10.0	Burkina Faso
18.2[1]	65.2	3.0	13.7	57.491	31.5	28.5	—	4.3		1,081	99.9	0.1	21	57.1	42.9	37.5	Burundi
0.5[1]	38.6	15.9	45.1	1,125.724	2.6	51.8[2]	0.4	14.4		2,023	99.5	0.5	8	50.0	50.0	1.0	Cambodia
32.3[1, 3]	53.4[3]	5.3[3]	9.0[3]	711.9[3]	30.1[3]	46.3[3]	13.2[3]	5.6[3]		8,001	89.8	10.2	459	49.9	50.1	20.5	Cameroon
13.0[1]	73.0	0.7	13.3	728.7	17.4	47.8[2]	0.6	15.6		...	...	...	...	...	...	...	Canada
34.0[1]	37.1	18.8	10.2	27.806	35.8	50.7[2]	6.9	1.0		202.4	94.2	5.8	5.5	57.3	42.7	2.8	Cape Verde
29.7[1, 3]	57.4[3]	5.1[3]	7.8[3]	40.4[3]	30.4[3]	22.2[3]	17.9[3]	9.6[3]		844.3	98.5	1.5	5.2	34.6	65.4	2.5	Central African Republic
26.5[1, 3]	47.8[3]	17.3[3]	8.4[3]	58.2[3]	35.6[3]	13.5[3]	18.6[3]	14.6[3]		913.7	98.1	1.9	22.9	44.5	55.5	7.2	Chad
1.3[1]	93.1	4.3	1.3	17,298.8	10.6	53.9[2]	4.0	8.9		4,890	55.6	44.4	3,495	84.7	15.3	18.0	Chile
2.2	76.1	16.6	5.1	8,355.1	22.5	54.4	—	5.6		102,260	38.6	61.4	14,891	68.9	31.1	8.2	China
9.5[1]	77.7	10.9	1.9	25,156.9	20.8	36.4[2]	5.8	10.6		14,814	43.9	56.1	2,861	70.5	29.5	18.3	Colombia
3.4	54.0	41.5	1.0	12.238	38.0	50.4	−0.3	0.1		192.9	100.0	—	1.4	57.1	42.9	2.3	Comoros
1.7[1, 3]	23.9[3]	4.4[3]	70.0[3]	1,466.0[3]	12.8[3]	43.0[2, 3]	—	16.9[3]		9,262	90.7	9.3	—	—	—	...	Congo, Dem. Rep. of the
27.9[1, 3]	56.6[3]	4.8[3]	10.6[3]	152.9[3]	32.2[3]	15.9[3]	7.2[3]	9.3[3]		4,665	81.4	18.6	320	43.7	56.3	20.2	Congo, Rep. of the
11.8[1]	41.4	40.0	6.9	796.9	9.3	76.6[2]	0.4	5.6		2,889	77.9	22.1	502	64.8	35.2	12.1	Costa Rica
23.2[3]	62.4[3]	3.6[3]	10.8[3]	1,600.8[3]	30.7[3]	30.3[3]	11.4[3]	12.3[3]		11,367	77.3	29.7	850	61.2	38.8	16.5	Côte d'Ivoire
27.9[1]	46.7	6.7	18.6	67.222	10.4	37.3[2]	2.6	18.5		3,101	49.0	51.0	250	59.6	40.4	3.0	Croatia
...	...	...	...	...	...	...	...	...		...	...	...	...	...	...	...	Cuba
11.3	57.3	7.5	24.0	6.403	6.0	54.5	0.6	31.7		...	...	...	...	...	...	...	Cyprus[8]
26.0[1]	54.4	9.8	9.8	1,615.1	19.7	41.1[2]	5.5	15.3		12,017	11.1	88.9	1,978	68.5	31.5	6.4	Czech Republic
8.6	49.0	5.2	37.2	996.6	28.8	29.7	—	24.0		...	...	...	...	...	...	...	Denmark
0.8[1]	54.8	0.9	43.5	70.864	26.4	32.7	0.8	22.4		226.2	99.9	0.1	10.4	76.0	24.0	5.0	Djibouti
16.2[1]	59.0	7.6	17.2	0.610	11.1	56.2[2]	7.9	15.6		94.0	100.0	—	5.2	60.6	39.4	4.1	Dominica
9.8[1]	68.9	16.5	4.8	51.177	21.9	53.1	5.1	7.7		3,515	82.0	18.0	335	51.6	48.4	8.6	Dominican Republic
3.4	79.4	8.3	8.9	22,319.4	13.3	65.2[2]	—	13.8		12,435	41.1	58.9	1,058	46.5	53.5	18.2	Ecuador
36.1[1]	36.6	11.9	15.4	235.802	7.6	57.6[2]	5.8	2.6		28,918	95.3	4.7	1,890	44.7	55.3	9.5	Egypt

Finance (continued)

country	international reserves, 1997[a]			money supply, 1996[b]		central bank authority, 1996[b]								central bank discount rate, 1998[a]
	total ('000,000 SDRs)	% foreign exchange	ratio of external debt to total reserves, 1995[b]	stock ('000,000,000 national currency)	M1 per capita	assets (%)				liabilities (%)				
						claims on government	claims on private sector	claims on banks	claims on foreign assets	reserve money	government deposits	foreign liabilities	capital accounts	
El Salvador	744	94.4	2.6	9.898	1,760	30.5[1]	—	18.4	51.0	69.9	6.4	10.0	10.4	10.00[6]
Equatorial Guinea	...	...	...	9.5[3]	22,300[3]	99.9[3]	—	—	0.1[3]	50.0[3]	0.4[3]	61.4[3]	1.7[3]	...
Eritrea	...	...	...	...	...	...	...	...	...	...	...	...	...	...
Estonia	447	100.0	0.3	10.786	7,310	—	0.2	1.7	98.0	76.3	—	12.5	25.0	6.45[5]
Ethiopia	421	98.1	6.4	9.273	160	59.7	—	3.6	36.7	51.9	13.6	12.0	9.0	3.55[4, 9]
Faroe Islands	...	...	...	...	...	...	...	...	...	...	...	...	...	...
Fiji	257	93.0	0.5	0.456	590	—	—	—	100.0	42.0	7.9	...	7.2	2.50
Finland	7,470	93.5	...	204.834	39,900	3.0	3.8	20.7	72.4	61.2	—	1.5	10.5	4.00
France	23,732	77.5	...	1,811.0	31,000	11.0	3.4	27.1	58.5	59.7	3.8	0.8	36.2	3.30[10]
French Guiana	...	...	...	4.621	30,700	...	...	...	...	...	...	...	...	...
French Polynesia	...	...	...	71.742	319,000	...	...	...	...	...	...	...	...	...
Gabon	105[7]	100.0[7]	27.6	219.1[3]	188,000[3]	56.4[3]	—	2.1[3]	41.5[3]	70.0[3]	6.9[3]	26.4[3]	0.7[3]	8.60[7]
Gambia, The	74	97.3	3.6	0.453	370	20.6[1]	—	—	79.4	30.6	53.0	15.9	6.4	14.00
Gaza Strip	...	...	...	...	...	...	...	...	...	...	...	...	...	...
Georgia	...	...	...	...	...	...	...	...	...	...	...	...	...	...
Germany	61,518	86.6	...	879.8	10,700	6.3	—	59.2	34.6	86.0	0.1	4.1	—	2.5
Ghana	640	95.3	6.4	1,215.7	67,900	50.8[1]	—	0.6	48.6	29.2	5.9	39.1	—	45.00
Gibraltar	...	...	...	...	...	...	...	...	...	...	...	...	...	...
Greece	11,205	97.9	...	3,839.8[3]	366,000[3]	40.2	—	3.6	56.2	44.3	6.7	24.6	—	14.5
Greenland	...	...	...	...	...	...	...	...	...	...	...	...	...	...
Grenada	27	100.0	2.6	0.148	1,510	17.6	—	—	82.4	99.5	0.5	—	—	6.5[4]
Guadeloupe	...	...	...	7.283	16,900	...	...	...	...	...	...	...	...	...
Guam	...	...	...	...	...	...	...	...	...	...	...	...	...	...
Guatemala	769	97.8	3.5	8.822	800	37.8[1]	—	10.5	51.6	347.5	101.4	15.5	7.3	5.1[6]
Guernsey	...	...	...	...	...	...	...	...	...	...	...	...	...	...
Guinea	...	...	...	274.125[3]	37,200[3]	62.0[1,3]	—	1.7[3]	36.3[3]	36.5[3]	46.0[3]	18.2[3]	10.2[3]	15.0
Guinea-Bissau	12	100.0	40.8	709.3	609,000	48.8[1]	6.5	—	44.7	70.0	31.5	100.0	−164.6	35.0[9]
Guyana	232	100.0	6.6	17.531	24,700	68.0[1]	—	—	32.0	14.3	20.8	60.0	1.8	10.5
Haiti	90	100.0	7.0	5.740	870	66.1[1]	1.6	0.7	31.6	64.3	16.1	13.4	8.0	20.10[4]
Honduras	366	99.7	15.1	6.053	1,050	20.9[1]	0.9	20.3	57.9	77.0	32.5	106.2	30.7	12.2[6]
Hong Kong	...	...	...	217.840	34,000	...	...	...	...	...	...	...	...	7.0
Hungary	6,173	99.0	2.0	1,030.5	101,000	36.2[3]	0.1[3]	9.7[3]	53.9[3]	48.6[3]	13.2[3]	99.8[3]	1.8[3]	...
Iceland	299	96.0	...	42.472	157,000	26.6	0.9	3.6	68.9	36.3	18.0	27.7	—	6.8
India	18,963	96.5	4.3	2,124.5	2,210	58.1	—	5.6	36.2	81.3	—	2.4	6.8	9.00
Indonesia	14,759	97.3	4.7	51,652.0	261,000	...	...	...	...	...	...	...	...	20.00
Iran	...	...	...	45,865.0	743,000	74.0[1]	—	2.5	23.5	50.4	15.7	4.2	1.2	...
Iraq	...	...	...	...	...	...	...	...	...	...	...	...	...	...
Ireland	5,472	93.7	...	5.361[3]	1,480[3]	2.6	—	—	97.4	65.2	23.1	—	16.2	6.75
Isle of Man	...	...	...	...	...	...	...	...	...	...	...	...	...	...
Israel	12,868	100.0	...	16.716[3]	3,080[3]	26.5[3]	—	11.0[3]	62.5[3]	47.7[3]	47.3[3]	1.8[3]	—	12.6[4]
Italy	32,752	89.1	...	602,150.0	10,480,000	...	...	...	...	...	...	...	...	5.00
Jamaica	590	99.7	5.0	33.548	13,300	40.4	—	—	59.6	65.5	73.4	4.2	4.0	27.99[4]
Japan	160,146	95.6	...	181,150.0	1,440,000	53.3	—	16.9	29.8	98.5	13.0	—	—	0.50
Jersey	...	...	...	...	...	...	...	...	...	...	...	...	...	...
Jordan	1,198	96.9	3.4	1.533	340	29.2	—	—	70.8	68.0	10.2	...	...	7.75
Kazakstan	1,113	71.3	2.3	...	...	25.2[3]	0.2[3]	6.7[3]	67.9[3]	42.5[3]	9.4[3]	20.1[3]	40.1[3]	18.50
Kenya	668	97.8	16.5	78.999	2,770	54.8	—	—	45.2	79.3	26.2	17.8	1.8	32.90
Kiribati	...	...	...	...	...	...	...	...	...	...	...	...	...	...
Korea, North	...	...	...	...	...	...	...	...	...	...	...	...	...	...
Korea, South	24,555	97.7	...	39,542.0	870,000	4.2[1]	—	44.6	51.2	47.0	12.2	0.1	—	5.0
Kuwait	2,460	88.4	...	1.243	580	3.6	—	—	96.4	42.9	23.0	—	16.3	7.50
Kyrgyzstan	...	...	...	...	...	...	...	...	...	...	...	...	...	50.0
Laos	...	...	...	75.558	15,000	6.3[1]	5.8	21.8	66.1	43.5	27.0	26.1	10.5	35.00[9]
Latvia	...	...	...	0.420	170	5.0	—	4.5	90.5	74.8	7.4	16.1	4.6	4.00
Lebanon	5,645	93.7	0.3	1,753.4	459,000	0.4	2.2	1.3	96.1	37.2	23.8	0.6	2.1	30.00
Lesotho	420	99.0	1.3	0.633	320	6.9	—	—	93.1	14.4	68.0	7.0	3.4	15.60
Liberia	...	...	...	...	...	...	...	...	...	...	...	...	...	6.60[6]
Libya	...	...	...	6.324	1,140	59.2	8.1	—	32.6	63.0	10.5	—	...	...
Liechtenstein	...	...	...	...	...	...	...	...	...	...	...	...	...	...
Lithuania	...	...	...	3.643	980	—	—	4.2	95.8	71.8	1.9	31.5	—	5.32[5]
Luxembourg	59	30.5	...	111.4	267,000	36.1	—	7.5	56.4	42.9	24.8	6.8	32.3	3.25[6]
Macau	...	...	...	...	...	...	...	...	...	...	...	...	...	...
Macedonia	...	...	...	...	...	...	...	...	...	...	...	...	...	8.90
Madagascar	182	100.0	34.0	2,167.7	156,000	55.3[1]	—	4.9	39.8	65.7	23.2	24.6	1.3	9.0
Malawi	107	97.2	18.0	2.743	260	19.7[1]	—	3.4	76.8	74.2	20.0	14.8	10.9	23.00[7]
Malaysia	18,946	96.5	0.7	63.594[3]	3,130[3]	2.9[3]	0.8[3]	9.2[3]	87.1[3]	65.5[3]	11.4[3]	—	—	10.59[5]
Maldives	69	98.6	3.1	1.059	4,010	52.1[1]	—	0.1	47.8	63.6	7.8	10.0	5.5	6.80[5]
Mali	297	96.6	8.8	198.2[3]	31,900[3]	25.4	—	—	74.6	51.1	19.7	26.2	—	6.25[9]
Malta	1,076	93.2	0.1	0.490	1,310	11.6	—	—	88.4	76.5	5.2	—	—	5.5
Marshall Islands	...	...	...	...	...	...	...	...	...	...	...	...	...	...
Martinique	...	...	...	6.937[3]	17,700[3]	...	...	...	...	...	...	...	...	...
Mauritania	118	99.2	25.3	16.227	6,840	41.5[1]	1.8	5.8	50.9	25.3	74.6	74.3	9.8	...
Mauritius	606	94.7	1.4	9.830	8,640	5.2	—	2.5	92.2	64.8	1.4	0.1	2.5	10.53
Mayotte	...	...	...	1.133	9,100	...	...	...	...	...	...	...	...	...
Mexico	17,135	98.7	5.6	206.166	2,210	−3.9	—	8.2	95.7	69.5	—	73.0	2.3	23.24[5]
Micronesia	...	...	...	...	...	...	...	...	...	...	...	...	...	...
Moldova	204	99.0	1.9	0.995	230	21.1	0.1	15.4	63.3	36.4	5.4	50.3	4.1	21.0[10]
Monaco	...	...	...	...	...	...	...	...	...	...	...	...	...	...
Mongolia	73	91.8	3.7	73.807	31,400	34.1	—	2.0	63.9	59.9	9.8	48.4	17.9	37.5
Morocco	2,993	98.1	5.9	143.818	5,330	29.5	14.0	1.9	54.5	88.5	1.3	0.9	—	7.50[5]
Mozambique	...	...	...	...	...	...	...	...	...	...	...	...	...	...
Myanmar (Burma)	136	93.4	9.4	...	...	...	...	...	...	...	...	...	...	12.50[6]
Namibia	...	...	...	2.800	1,640	48.3	—	—	51.7	28.4	9.1	46.0	—	16.00
Nauru	...	...	...	...	...	...	...	...	...	...	...	...	...	...
Nepal	...	...	3.9	35.540	1,680	40.3	1.5	2.9	55.3	56.1	12.2	5.6	26.3	9.00

deposit money banks, 1996[b] — assets (%) loans to govern-ment	loans to private sector	re-serves	foreign assets	liabilities — deposits ('000,000,000 national currency)	composition (%) demand depos.	savings depos.	govt. depos.	foreign liabilities	external public debt outstanding (long-term, disbursed only), 1996 — total ('000,000 U.S.$)	creditors (%) offi-cial	private	debt service — total ('000,000 U.S.$)	repayment (%) princi-pal	inter-est	debt service ratio (%)	country
3.3	71.8	22.7	2.2	40.909	12.2	64.9[2]	3.9	8.5	2,297	94.5	5.5	278	62.8	37.2	8.4	El Salvador
11.0[1,3]	38.6[3]	22.1[3]	28.3[3]	8.8[3]	31.0[3]	23.3[3]	10.0[3]	19.8[3]	222.2	92.8	7.2	3.3	68.2	31.8	1.8	Equatorial Guinea
...	...	...	...	...	...	...	...	...	45.9	100.0	—	—	—	—	—	Eritrea
7.6[1]	60.9	10.2	21.3	18.855	34.5	17.9[2]	17.8	20.1	216.5	74.9	25.1	21.1	53.8	46.2	0.6	Estonia
16.9	57.4	7.9	17.8	15.467	25.0	43.3	4.8	9.5	9,483	96.3	3.7	346	84.4	15.6	42.0	Ethiopia
...	...	...	...	...	...	...	...	...	...	...	...	...	...	...	...	Faroe Islands
13.0[1]	67.6	13.1	6.3	1.724	19.1	59.9	1.2	10.0	146.5	99.8	0.2	28.6	68.5	31.5	2.1	Fiji
5.8	65.7	4.8	23.7	529.488	36.1	19.8	3.8	22.7	...	...	...	...	...	...	...	Finland
13.5	55.2	0.4	30.9	11,591.0	13.4	30.9	—	30.2	...	...	...	...	...	...	...	France
...	...	...	...	...	...	...	...	...	...	...	...	...	...	...	...	French Guiana
...	...	...	...	...	...	...	...	...	...	...	...	...	...	...	...	French Polynesia
38.6[1,3]	46.9[3]	6.1[3]	8.4[3]	442.0[3]	26.7[3]	31.6[3]	3.5[3]	8.9[3]	3,874	96.3	3.7	357	36.1	63.9	10.5	Gabon
39.8[1]	40.8	15.3	4.1	0.837	23.7	61.4	—	7.4	412.0	100.0	—	20.1	73.4	26.6	8.9	Gambia, The
...	...	...	...	...	...	...	...	...	...	...	...	...	...	...	...	Gaza Strip
...	...	...	...	...	...	...	...	...	1,100	90.9	9.1	7	14.3	85.7	...	Georgia
19.5[1]	63.0	1.5	16.0	5,893.5	10.7	25.1	4.2	12.9	...	...	...	...	...	...	...	Germany
6.0[1]	31.3	30.7	32.0	2,177.8	22.1	26.9	4.8	29.4	4,684	90.4	9.6	294	65.0	35.0	16.5	Ghana
...	...	...	...	...	...	...	...	...	...	...	...	...	...	...	...	Gibraltar
31.8[1,3]	31.9[3]	24.9[3]	11.4[3]	18,630.7[3]	8.4[3]	46.1[3]	—	36.5[3]	...	...	...	...	...	...	...	Greece
...	...	...	...	...	...	...	...	...	...	...	...	...	...	...	...	Greenland
9.0[1]	62.9	7.4	20.8	0.804	11.8	62.8[2]	5.1	17.0	99.6	93.0	7.0	8.1	72.8	27.2	...	Grenada
...	...	...	...	...	...	...	...	...	...	...	...	...	...	...	...	Guadeloupe
...	...	...	...	...	...	...	...	...	...	...	...	...	...	...	...	Guam
7.5	69.0	21.4	2.2	22.403	20.6	39.3	0.9	10.0	2,766	78.4	21.6	287	60.1	39.9	8.9	Guatemala
...	...	...	...	...	...	...	...	...	...	...	...	...	...	...	...	Guernsey
9.1[1,3]	54.9[3]	8.6[3]	27.4[3]	330.610[3]	31.5[3]	19.6[2,3]	5.0[3]	24.1[3]	2,981	96.7	3.3	101	57.4	42.6	13.0	Guinea
0.5[1]	31.2	15.4	52.9	1,104.1	26.5	37.2[2]	3.3	23.6	856.2	99.9	0.1	9.6	58.3	41.7	41.7	Guinea-Bissau
25.5[1]	53.3	15.7	5.5	68.529	11.0	65.2[2]	4.3	5.3	1,370	95.4	4.6	78	62.8	37.2	...	Guyana
0.1	50.5	34.5	14.9	11.483	19.1	78.4	0.5	0.6	836.1	100.0	—	20.7	52.2	47.8	10.8	Haiti
5.3[1]	66.4	11.9	16.3	16.547	18.6	52.7[2]	2.0	12.0	3,855	91.5	8.5	445	67.1	32.9	22.7	Honduras
...	...	...	...	7,906.0	...	...	...	...	...	...	...	...	...	...	...	Hong Kong
24.6[1,3]	38.5[3]	32.9[3]	4.0[3]	3,241.6[3]	17.9[3]	40.6[2,3]	0.4[3]	12.4[3]	18,423	18.7	81.3	6,376	75.8	24.2	31.3	Hungary
5.5	86.8	4.9	2.9	272.621	13.6	51.0	—	15.6	...	...	...	...	...	...	...	Iceland
30.0	58.9	11.1	—	5,056.1	15.3	78.2	—	—	74,406	71.6	28.4	10,661	65.7	34.3	20.3	India
...	...	...	...	...	...	...	...	...	60,108	76.8	23.2	11,664	69.0	31.0	20.0	Indonesia
2.3	51.8	36.4	9.5	79,286.0	42.4	62.3	—	5.9	15,917	80.5	19.5	3,025	73.0	27.0	...	Iran
...	...	...	...	...	...	...	...	...	...	...	...	...	...	...	...	Iraq
10.5[3]	61.5[3]	3.2[3]	24.9[3]	25.667[3]	11.3[3]	58.5[3]	0.6[3]	20.3[3]	...	...	...	...	...	...	...	Ireland
...	...	...	...	...	...	...	...	...	...	...	...	...	...	...	...	Isle of Man
21.7	61.5	5.1	11.8	357.555	3.4	60.7	7.7	13.7	...	...	...	...	...	...	...	Israel
...	...	...	...	...	...	...	...	...	...	...	...	...	...	...	...	Italy
20.8[1]	45.0	20.3	13.9	116.334	19.6	53.5	5.8	11.1	3,183	89.4	10.6	560	67.3	32.7	14.8	Jamaica
9.0[1]	76.1	1.2	13.8	756,960.0	18.4	49.3	—	10.6	...	...	...	...	...	...	...	Japan
...	...	...	...	...	...	...	...	...	...	...	...	...	...	...	...	Jersey
3.2	44.9	24.8	27.0	7.465	7.7	43.0	8.5	29.4	7,137	76.5	23.5	579	51.1	48.9	10.9	Jordan
4.3[3]	60.0[3]	12.3[3]	23.5[3]	120.060[3]	— 53.2[3] —		4.5[3]	22.1[3]	1,932	67.0	33.0	246	62.2	37.8	3.5	Kazakstan
17.5[1]	58.2	15.4	8.9	275.670	15.6	57.9[2]	1.4	7.8	5,647	89.8	10.2	645	67.0	33.0	21.2	Kenya
...	...	...	...	...	...	...	...	...	...	...	...	...	...	...	...	Kiribati
...	...	...	...	...	...	...	...	...	...	...	...	...	...	...	...	Korea, North
2.4	69.6	14.0	14.0	204,487.0	11.8	19.0[2]	8.0	17.8	...	...	...	...	...	...	...	Korea, South
47.3	30.6	1.2	20.9	10.366	8.6	58.7	3.6	7.3	...	...	...	...	...	...	...	Kuwait
...	...	...	...	...	...	...	...	...	640.3	94.8	5.2	43.7	74.6	25.4	7.9	Kyrgyzstan
17.5[1]	37.9	15.9	28.8	373.746	8.7	45.3[2]	5.8	12.5	2,186	100.0	—	25	76.0	22.0	5.4	Laos
17.1[1]	20.0	7.1	55.9	1.016	15.4	22.7[2]	2.8	46.7	298.0	77.0	23.0	30.8	44.2	55.8	1.1	Latvia
33.6	35.4	12.2	18.7	35,844.1	1.6	75.1[2]	0.8	12.9	1,933	32.6	67.4	216	32.2	67.8	4.6	Lebanon
15.4[1]	47.6	17.5	19.5	1.403	39.1	49.4	2.8	4.3	611.6	94.4	5.6	32.3	57.1	42.9	5.4	Lesotho
...	...	...	...	...	...	...	...	...	1,110	82.1	17.9	—	—	...	...	Liberia
—	53.2	43.2	3.6	6.062	57.9	33.5	5.6	1.3	...	...	...	...	...	...	...	Libya
...	...	...	...	...	...	...	...	...	...	...	...	...	...	...	...	Liechtenstein
15.6[1]	57.1	9.4	18.0	6.425	27.0	30.5[2]	19.8	12.5	792	53.0	47.0	75	71.3	28.7	1.8	Lithuania
0.1[1]	3.4	—	96.5	16,465.8	0.5	3.7	0.4	80.8	...	...	...	...	...	...	...	Luxembourg
...	...	...	...	...	...	...	...	...	...	...	...	...	...	...	...	Macau
...	...	...	...	...	...	...	...	...	863	82.9	17.1	44	56.8	43.2	3.3	Macedonia
6.3	48.1	27.3	18.3	3,270.6	40.9	26.8	5.0	4.9	3,589	97.8	2.2	55	68.2	31.8	6.7	Madagascar
36.2[1]	23.9	30.6	9.3	5.928	25.6	51.4[2]	7.9	2.7	2,092	100.0	—	68	59.6	40.4	14.3	Malawi
4.2[3]	83.3[3]	8.3[3]	4.2[3]	245.064[3]	14.8[3]	54.9[3]	1.7[3]	6.5[3]	15,701	26.9	73.1	4,170	78.2	21.8	4.4	Malaysia
7.4[1]	36.1	43.3	13.2	1.988	27.8	39.5	4.5	7.6	162.6	93.2	6.8	11.3	67.3	32.7	2.9	Maldives
7.8[3]	52.7[3]	6.9[3]	32.5[3]	247.0[3]	36.6[3]	22.8[3]	20.6[3]	20.3[3]	2,766	100.0	—	106	44.8	55.2	16.4	Mali
8.1	45.6	4.0	42.4	2.434	3.6	58.1	—	34.5	145.1	89.3	10.7	16.9	68.9	31.1	0.5	Malta
...	...	...	...	...	...	...	...	...	...	...	...	...	...	...	...	Marshall Islands
...	...	...	...	...	...	...	...	...	...	...	...	...	...	...	...	Martinique
5.9	74.3	11.5	8.3	46.584	23.6	18.2	7.4	10.8	2,073	99.0	1.0	106	72.6	27.4	19.0	Mauritania
23.7	57.8	10.5	7.9	59.892	8.0	80.8	0.5	1.8	1,152	53.4	46.6	139	52.5	47.5	5.1	Mauritius
...	...	...	...	...	...	...	...	...	...	...	...	...	...	...	...	Mayotte
2.4[1]	61.5	29.9	6.3	770.964	16.7	65.9[2]	-13.3	18.3	93,438	30.7	69.3	26,726	76.0	24.0	23.2	Mexico
...	...	...	...	...	...	...	...	...	...	...	...	...	...	...	...	Micronesia
51.2[1]	35.0	2.1	11.7	1.717	15.3	25.4[2]	1.6	14.2	559.5	84.2	15.8	37.9	35.8	64.2	4.1	Moldova
...	...	...	...	...	...	...	...	...	...	...	...	...	...	...	...	Monaco
14.2[1]	46.0	5.4	34.4	125.891	17.9	61.8[2]	17.9	6.8	474.0	88.9	11.1	37.1	79.8	20.2	7.5	Mongolia
32.0	58.3	6.0	3.7	156.494	55.8	35.1	—	2.9	20,774	74.0	26.0	3,101	58.4	41.6	27.1	Morocco
...	...	...	...	...	...	...	...	...	5,433	99.5	0.5	134	47.8	52.2	24.8	Mozambique
...	...	...	...	...	...	...	...	...	4,804	92.4	7.6	157	88.9	11.1	...	Myanmar (Burma)
6.9	84.5	3.4	5.2	6.700	37.6	48.5[2]	1.2	4.4	...	...	...	...	...	...	...	Namibia
...	...	...	...	...	...	...	...	...	...	...	...	...	...	...	...	Nauru
10.4[1]	66.6	9.3	13.8	89.956	9.7	65.3	—	5.6	2,349	98.3	1.7	76	60.5	39.5	6.8	Nepal

Finance (continued)

country	international reserves, 1997[a]			money supply, 1996[b]		central bank authority, 1996[b]								central bank discount rate, 1998[a]
	total ('000,000 SDRs)	% foreign exchange	ratio of external debt to total reserves, 1995[b]	stock ('000,000,000 national currency)	M1 per capita	assets (%)				liabilities (%)				
						claims on government	claims on private sector	claims on banks	claims on foreign assets	reserve money	government deposits	foreign liabilities	capital accounts	
Netherlands, The	20,460	86.7	...	193.9	12,500	5.4	—	19.3	75.3	60.2	17.3	—	—	2.75[10]
Netherlands Antilles	138	86.2	...	0.893	4,210	10.6	—	—	89.4	63.0	5.7	3.1	30.3	6.00
New Caledonia	...	...	...	62.453[3]	325,000[3]	...	...	...	...	...	...	...	...	...
New Zealand	3,308	96.4	...	33.865	9,310	23.5	—	9.8	66.7	14.8	67.5	3.2	—	9.40
Nicaragua	...	...	...	1.330[3]	320[3]	89.9[1]	—	1.5	8.6	11.6	1.2	97.3	1.2	8.8[6]
Niger	66	83.3	14.5	100.2[3]	11,200[3]	50.7	—	4.1	45.2	65.9	7.2	22.3	—	6.25[9]
Nigeria	5,564	99.6	19.4	200.325[3]	2,020[3]	86.1[1, 3]	0.7[3]	5.9[3]	7.3[3]	30.4[3]	39.6[3]	12.1[3]	16.4[3]	13.50
Northern Mariana Islands	...	...	...	...	...	...	...	...	...	...	...	...	...	...
Norway	20,538	95.7	...	392.7	89,400	5.2	—	0.1	94.7	29.8	55.1	—	—	6.50
Oman	1,211	95.7	2.2	0.503	230	5.7	—	—	94.3	39.4	3.8	—	32.4	7.30[6]
Pakistan	913	92.1	12.9	528.011	3,920	70.1	—	15.7	14.3	74.1	6.6	17.0	—	13.25[5]
Palau	...	...	...	...	...	...	...	...	...	...	...	...	...	...
Panama	1,337	98.8	5.0	0.841	310	52.3[1]	12.3	—	35.4	10.9	76.4	11.8	17.4	6.72[6]
Papua New Guinea	407	99.3	6.2	1.065	240	42.7	—	—	57.3	35.5	61.2	4.9	8.9	14.50[4]
Paraguay	595	84.9	1.4	1,715.6	342,000	29.0[1]	0.3	20.6	50.2	47.7	12.1	3.9	8.0	11.80[6]
Peru	7,578	99.5	2.3	8.986	370	2.4[1]	—	-4.6	102.2	48.3	33.5	14.7	2.3	18.0
Philippines	7,600	96.8	4.6	233.1	3,210	42.8[1]	—	2.5	54.6	45.5	22.6	19.1	5.3	12.89
Poland	13,996	99.2	2.8	49.338	1,270	16.7[1]	—	14.7	68.6	44.8	8.0	0.9	0.5	24.5[9]
Portugal	11,692	92.5	...	4,885.6	492,000	6.6[1]	—	7.3	86.1	35.9	13.9	0.2	8.2	4.70
Puerto Rico	...	...	...	...	...	...	...	...	...	...	...	...	...	...
Qatar	...	...	...	3.885	6,290	16.0	—	6.2	77.8	66.4	3.4	—	36.5	...
Réunion	...	...	...	11.497	17,000	...	...	...	...	...	...	...	...	...
Romania	1,747	90.8	2.3	10,747.5	476,000	25.0	—	45.7	29.3	46.7	17.8	40.5	—	40.0[10]
Russia	11,895	95.4	6.7	197,449.0	1,340,000	61.2[1]	0.3	3.7	34.8	54.1	5.0	23.3	23.1	75.1[5]
Rwanda	145	84.1	...	45.423	6,230	52.2[1]	0.4	0.2	47.2	48.7	22.9	24.8	19.1	11.13
St. Kitts and Nevis	28	100.0	1.6	0.089	2,250	4.3	—	—	95.7	97.3	2.7	—	—	6.5[4]
St. Lucia	43	97.7	1.8	0.246	1,660	13.5	—	—	86.4	97.3	2.7	—	—	7.0[4]
St. Vincent and the Grenadines	19	94.7	2.9	0.115	1,030	9.9	—	—	90.1	93.3	6.7	—	—	6.5[4]
Samoa	45	93.3	2.9	0.061	360	—	—	—	100.0	55.9	42.1	—	—	5.5[6]
San Marino	...	...	...	...	...	...	...	...	...	...	...	...	...	...
São Tomé and Príncipe	...	...	...	...	...	...	...	...	...	...	...	...	...	55.0
Saudi Arabia	6,826	82.6	...	132.9	7,090	...	...	...	...	...	...	...	...	6.07[6]
Senegal	256	95.7	11.7	316.8[3]	35,400[3]	59.5	—	0.8	39.7	44.1	7.1	60.0	—	6.25[9]
Seychelles	19	100.0	5.6	0.450	5,870	88.9	—	—	11.1	87.5	1.7	—	1.6	9.49[4]
Sierra Leone	24	79.2	28.3	53.208	11,100	93.3[1]	0.2	0.3	6.1	9.8	0.5	50.1	42.7	6.00[6]
Singapore	57,861	99.6	...	27.040	8,800	—	—	—	100.0	16.9	47.8	—	—	6.25[5]
Slovakia	2,181	97.4	1.0	173.350	32,100	16.6[1]	—	20.0	63.4	45.6	9.9	29.2	5.1	8.80
Slovenia	...	...	...	202.4	103,000	4.3	—	4.4	91.3	32.3	6.2	0.1	12.0	10.00
Solomon Islands	21	100.0	6.1	0.198	490	39.7[1]	—	—	60.3	50.6	1.9	1.2	35.3	6.00[4]
Somalia	...	...	...	...	...	...	...	...	...	...	...	...	...	...
South Africa	2,828	95.3	...	147.664	3,500	40.7	—	30.3	29.4	71.4	24.4	11.4	—	20.21
Spain	46,232	95.8	...	20,600.0	524,000	19.8	—	28.7	51.5	60.0	17.6	—	10.3	4.25
Sri Lanka	1,277	98.2	3.4	78.202	4,320	33.2	—	1.4	65.3	53.6	2.2	29.0	16.0	17.00
Sudan, The	75[7]	100.0[7]	59.8	404.6[3]	13,000[3]	78.7[1, 3]	—	0.8[3]	20.4[3]	84.9[3]	—	534.4[3]	1.0[3]	...
Suriname	74	82.4	...	56.967	135,000	10.6	0.1	—	89.3	79.8	14.2	1.9	7.4	15.00[5, 9]
Swaziland	209	95.7	0.8	0.423	420	—	—	2.7	97.3	20.8	56.2	6.9	3.7	16.75
Sweden	10,431	92.0	...	...	...	28.3	—	4.6	67.1	54.7	—	2.0	—	2.50
Switzerland	28,130	85.7	...	128.2	18,100	7.4	—	4.0	88.6	56.6	1.5	—	—	1.00
Syria	...	...	...	...	...	...	...	...	...	...	...	...	...	...
Taiwan	...	...	...	3,426.1	159,000	0.1	—	14.6	85.4	51.0	4.6	—	—	5.00[7]
Tajikistan	...	...	...	...	...	...	...	...	...	...	...	...	...	...
Tanzania	331	97.0	22.5	462.1	15,800	52.6	—	1.0	46.5	59.0	14.5	89.4	—	15.80
Thailand	22,679	98.0	0.5	423.5	7,020	4.2	—	8.0	87.8	40.1	31.0	—	31.6	12.50
Togo	80	100.0	9.9	131.2[3]	29,200[3]	45.8	—	5.0	49.2	63.4	5.7	31.7	—	6.25[9]
Tonga	22	90.9	2.4	0.023	230	14.1	—	—	85.9	56.2	4.1	—	6.4	5.50[6]
Trinidad and Tobago	386	99.2	4.9	4.161	3,270	12.6	—	5.5	82.0	50.0	19.8	5.1	32.7	13.00
Tunisia	1,121	97.2	5.5	4.109	450	4.7	—	8.1	87.2	103.2	11.6	11.4	6.1	6.88[5]
Turkey	11,697	98.6	4.0	882,290.0	14,000,000	29.3[1]	—	2.5	68.3	32.7	7.6	46.9	3.8	74.19[10]
Turkmenistan	...	...	...	...	...	...	...	...	...	...	...	...	...	...
Tuvalu	...	...	...	...	...	...	...	...	...	...	...	...	...	...
Uganda	414	99.8	6.6	460.797	22,600	69.6[1]	0.1	0.4	29.9	18.4	73.4	24.1	7.8	14.75
Ukraine	1,364	97.6	6.3	6.316	120	57.3[1]	—	7.9	34.8	45.9	2.0	40.1	8.6	51.00
United Arab Emirates	6,455	95.6	...	22.266	8,870	—	—	0.2	99.8	65.9	28.1	0.2	5.6	...
United Kingdom	26,372	90.3	...	...	...	54.0	—	—	46.0	48.8	—	52.0	—	7.19[5]
United States	50,117	47.3	...	1,237.5	4,640	84.7	—	—	15.3	97.1	6.1	—	—	5.00
Uruguay	918	91.5	3.1	9.530	3,010	42.4[1]	0.3	16.0	41.3	45.2	31.8	21.5	—	81.1
Uzbekistan	...	...	...	...	...	...	...	...	...	...	...	...	...	...
Vanuatu	27	88.9	0.9	6.528	37,500	13.0[1]	1.9	1.7	83.4	60.0	29.8	0.3	11.2	9.97[5]
Venezuela	9,921	92.6	4.1	3,349.4	149,000	16.1[1]	—	13.4	70.4	24.7	9.6	16.2	21.9	60.00
Vietnam	...	...	...	...	...	...	...	...	...	...	...	...	...	...
Virgin Islands (U.S.)	...	...	...	...	...	...	...	...	...	...	...	...	...	...
West Bank	...	...	...	...	...	...	...	...	...	...	...	...	...	...
Western Sahara	...	...	...	...	...	...	...	...	...	...	...	...	...	...
Yemen	786	96.8	8.9	156.579	9,300	60.7[1]	—	—	39.3	57.7	12.5	13.4	1.8	...
Yugoslavia	...	...	...	...	...	...	...	...	...	...	...	...	...	...
Zambia	...	...	...	227.9[3]	25,100[3]	90.1[3]	0.6[3]	—	9.3[3]	5.7[3]	25.8[3]	65.8[3]	—	17.20
Zimbabwe	343	91.3	5.3	13.875	1,220	74.9[1]	—	—	25.1	20.1	74.4	16.4	—	31.50

deposit money banks, 1996[b]									external public debt outstanding (long-term, disbursed only), 1996							country
assets (%)				liabilities					total ('000,000 U.S.$)	creditors (%)		debt service				
loans to government	loans to private sector	reserves	foreign assets	deposits ('000,000,000 national currency)	composition (%)					official	private	total ('000,000 U.S.$)	repayment (%)		debt service ratio (%)	
					demand depos.	savings depos.	govt. depos.	foreign liabilities					principal	interest		
10.9[1]	55.7	0.3	33.2	1,254.9	12.4	29.7[2]	—	34.1	...	...	...	...	...	...	...	Netherlands, The
5.0[1]	68.3	5.0	21.7	3.296	20.4	50.7[2]	1.8	21.7	...	...	...	...	...	...	...	Netherlands Antilles
...	...	...	...	...	...	...	...	...	...	...	...	...	...	...	...	New Caledonia
2.6	90.3	3.1	4.1	97.868	33.0	48.5[2]	—	24.1	...	...	...	...	...	...	...	New Zealand
0.5[1,3]	77.0[3]	16.8[3]	5.7[3]	6.749[3]	7.0[3]	54.8[2,3]	9.3[3]	3.7[3]	5,122	91.1	8.9	211	58.8	41.2	23.1	Nicaragua
15.0[3]	50.5[3]	10.0[3]	24.5[3]	83.1[3]	46.3[3]	40.5[3]	23.2[3]	26.5[3]	1,350	100.0	—	15	60.0	40.0	4.6	Niger
8.4[1,3]	57.7[3]	8.8[3]	25.0[3]	305.420[3]	28.0[3]	36.4[2,3]	1.2[3]	1.0[3]	25,431	73.3	26.7	2,433	57.9	42.1	15.5	Nigeria
...	...	...	...	...	...	...	...	...	...	...	...	...	...	...	...	Northern Mariana Islands
12.3[1]	77.3	3.4	7.1	829.4	42.3	20.1[2]	4.5	15.4	...	...	...	...	...	...	...	Norway
8.2[1]	71.3	4.0	16.5	2.195	12.4	51.5	9.6	11.4	2,646	26.2	73.8	719	79.3	20.7	9.4	Oman
32.9	53.1	7.9	6.1	1,013.676	26.6	44.2	4.7	14.5	23,694	94.8	5.2	2,251	65.1	34.9	18.9	Pakistan
...	...	...	...	...	...	...	...	...	...	...	...	...	...	...	...	Palau
1.0	28.3	...	70.7	21.917	3.5	20.4	—	63.7	5,136	20.8	79.2	803	51.2	48.8	9.0	Panama
42.0	47.4	4.5	6.1	2.610	26.5	54.0	6.4	1.2	1,522	88.8	11.2	245	70.0	30.0	8.2	Papua New Guinea
1.3[1]	67.5	20.4	10.9	6,855.5	9.9	55.3	15.8	5.9	1,377	94.9	5.1	186	68.3	31.7	4.3	Paraguay
3.0[1]	62.7	22.5	11.8	45.510	12.4	55.1[2]	10.5	10.4	20,415	73.2	26.8	2,385	48.9	51.1	28.8	Peru
15.0[1]	64.5	8.2	12.3	1,743.0	5.5	54.5[2]	3.0	21.7	27,937	71.7	28.3	4,446	65.6	34.4	10.5	Philippines
43.0[1]	32.9	13.9	10.3	170.650	15.1	50.2[2]	4.6	4.5	39,217	77.8	22.2	2,158	37.2	62.8	5.4	Poland
18.8[1]	50.1	7.6	23.6	24,711.4	16.2	34.1	3.2	34.4	...	...	...	...	...	...	...	Portugal
...	...	...	...	...	...	...	...	...	...	...	...	...	...	...	...	Puerto Rico
38.9[1]	31.6	2.6	26.9	32.427	7.7	48.6[2]	11.7	11.5	...	...	...	...	...	...	...	Qatar
74.7[1]	—	10.6	14.7	44,581.2	13.4	42.6[2]	5.0	11.2	6,456	62.6	37.4	679	50.2	49.8	7.0	Romania
45.2[1]	30.9	9.5	14.4	511,065.0	18.1	33.2[2]	2.4	11.9	100,463	62.4	37.6	6,010	40.0	60.0	5.6	Russia
7.6[1]	42.3	20.4	29.7	67.859	36.8	37.8	16.1	2.0	977	99.9	0.1	16	59.4	40.6	17.6	Rwanda
23.2[1]	46.9	5.8	24.1	0.995	5.7	39.7	19.6	24.5	56.3	92.9	7.1	5.9	67.8	32.2	4.2	St. Kitts and Nevis
8.6[1]	78.2	7.4	5.9	1.386	12.6	52.8[2]	15.4	15.6	122.0	99.9	0.1	11.6	54.3	45.7	7.9	St. Lucia
14.5[1]	60.3	7.4	17.8	0.684	12.8	47.0[2]	20.6	14.0	86.2	94.4	5.6	8.0	66.9	33.1	4.7	St. Vincent and the Grenadines
2.5[1]	61.4	29.0	7.0	0.187	21.3	61.7	4.4	4.4	162.8	100.0		4.7	66.0	34.0	3.8	Samoa
...	...	...	...	...	...	...	...	...	...	...	...	...	...	...	...	San Marino
...	...	...	...	...	...	...	...	...	229.5	100.0	—	2.7	48.1	51.9	20.6	São Tomé and Príncipe
25.4[1]	38.3	3.5	32.9	322.9	27.8	38.9[2]	...	11.9	...	...	...	...	...	...	...	Saudi Arabia
11.7[3]	67.5[3]	5.9[3]	14.9[3]	526.7[3]	30.4[3]	35.0[3]	25.9[3]	12.3[3]	3,103	99.5	0.5	213	50.7	49.3	12.4	Senegal
62.5[1]	14.3	32.4	5.1	1.890	15.0	49.7	4.7	4.5	138.1	78.5	21.5	14.9	69.5	30.5	4.2	Seychelles
29.0[1]	33.4	9.3	28.3	63.808	24.5	50.2	3.3	—	892	99.1	0.9	54	81.5	18.5	48.2	Sierra Leone
8.2	59.7	3.7	28.3	213.016	7.9	39.9	3.2	36.4	...	...	...	...	...	...	...	Singapore
35.4[1]	40.2	8.1	16.4	489.833	26.4	48.3[2]	5.2	14.1	3,891	16.3	83.7	925	71.7	28.3	8.3	Slovakia
19.9[1]	44.6	13.0	22.5	1,606.2	8.3	48.2[2]	9.1	12.1	2,038	37.1	62.9	499	79.1	20.9	4.6	Slovenia
47.5[1]	37.4	11.6	3.5	0.343	40.3	57.1	2.3	4.2	97.9	95.7	4.3	4.6	67.4	32.6	2.0	Solomon Islands
...	...	...	...	...	...	...	...	...	1,918	98.1	1.9	3	—	100.0	...	Somalia
6.4	89.3	2.7	1.6	426.242	30.7	38.9	5.3	10.4	10,348	—	100.0	2,235	70.2	29.8	6.5	South Africa
24.2[1]	55.3	3.3	17.2	99,075.0	12.8	37.9	1.6	16.3	...	...	...	...	...	...	...	Spain
12.6[1]	64.2	13.7	9.5	300.672	11.8	58.2[2]	4.3	17.8	6,818	93.4	6.6	343	61.8	38.2	5.8	Sri Lanka
0.4[3]	34.3[3]	21.0[3]	44.3[3]	381.2[3]	40.9[3]	67.5[3]	0.8[3]	7.4[3]	9,369	83.0	17.0	—	—	—	...	Sudan, The
0.8	40.6	17.1	41.6	112.220	22.4	46.9	0.3	26.9	...	...	...	...	...	...	...	Suriname
3.9	55.8	11.4	28.9	1.743	19.1	54.6	5.8	13.6	219.6	100.0	—	32.8	64.2	35.8	2.9	Swaziland
7.4	57.0	0.7	34.9	1,639.4	—44.7[2]—		0.1	39.0	...	...	...	...	...	...	...	Sweden
5.1	59.3	1.1	34.5	1,025.0	9.1	36.5	—	29.4	...	...	...	...	...	...	...	Switzerland
55.6[1,3]	21.1[3]	9.8[3]	13.5[3]	297.516[3]	27.3[3]	27.1[3]	2.8[3]	0.9[3]	16,698	93.1	6.9	124	61.7	38.3	1.9	Syria
12.8[1,3]	75.4[3]	8.0[3]	3.8[3]	13,589.9[3]	19.5[3]	63.7[3]	5.0[3]	4.1[3]	...	...	...	...	...	...	...	Taiwan
...	...	...	...	...	...	...	...	...	671.7	89.9	10.1	0.3	—	100.0	...	Tajikistan
43.6[1]	17.7	11.1	27.6	657.6	31.1	57.3[2]	3.1	0.7	6,104	94.0	6.0	228	57.5	42.5	16.5	Tanzania
2.3[1]	91.3	3.1	3.4	5,369.2	2.0	61.5	3.3	23.3	17,039	62.3	37.7	2,159	59.7	40.3	2.9	Thailand
5.8[3]	62.2[3]	6.0[3]	26.0[3]	209.6[3]	26.9[3]	32.8[3]	17.8[3]	17.8[3]	1,285	96.1	3.9	42	46.4	53.6	8.1	Togo
8.5[1]	54.6	35.3	1.5	0.111	14.5	49.3	10.1	0.7	68.3	84.9	15.1	4.0	82.5	17.5	4.8	Tonga
16.8[1]	59.0	13.9	10.4	17.104	17.5	55.4	2.6	3.6	1,871	46.6	53.4	403	60.0	40.0	13.3	Trinidad and Tobago
2.6	85.3	6.9	5.2	10.993	21.6	43.1	—	17.6	8,689	78.1	21.9	1,338	62.6	37.4	14.9	Tunisia
22.7[1]	50.8	10.7	15.8	6,439,550.0	8.7	70.0[2]	6.1	13.5	48,172	31.6	68.4	8,372	65.1	34.9	16.6	Turkey
...	...	...	...	...	...	...	...	...	538.2	24.9	75.1	167.5	84.3	15.7	9.9	Turkmenistan
...	...	...	...	...	...	...	...	...	...	...	...	...	...	...	...	Tuvalu
19.4[1]	42.7	16.2	21.7	677.602	33.9	30.2	7.1	20.7	3,151	97.5	2.5	95	60.0	40.0	12.7	Uganda
60.3[1]	12.0	9.0	18.8	9.469	23.8	30.5[2]	8.4	6.7	6,451	69.5	30.5	1,072	67.2	32.8	5.2	Ukraine
8.6[1]	45.1	7.4	38.9	180.199	8.6	35.9	5.6	20.5	...	...	...	...	...	...	...	United Arab Emirates
1.2[1]	51.3	0.4	47.1	1,775.7	—44.2[2]—		—	47.5	...	...	...	...	...	...	...	United Kingdom
10.5[1]	85.5	1.8	2.1	5,971.2	14.0	54.6	0.5	5.4	...	...	...	...	...	...	...	United States
6.4[1]	43.3	12.8	37.6	101.408	4.1	44.7[2]	2.6	34.1	4,097	35.9	64.1	549	52.0	48.0	12.9	Uruguay
...	...	...	...	...	...	...	...	...	1,990	61.7	38.3	278	66.5	33.5	7.8	Uzbekistan
1.5[1]	28.1	5.2	65.2	34.885	14.0	71.3[2]	—	9.0	42.1	99.3	0.7	1.6	59.4	40.6	1.2	Vanuatu
17.2[1]	41.5	34.9	6.4	5,856.2	33.6	42.4[2]	4.5	1.9	28,452	14.3	85.7	3,112	41.5	58.5	11.6	Venezuela
...	...	...	...	...	...	...	...	...	22,344	93.0	7.0	251	60.2	39.8	2.5	Vietnam
...	...	...	...	...	...	...	...	...	...	...	...	...	...	...	...	Virgin Islands (U.S.)
...	...	...	...	...	...	...	...	...	...	...	...	...	...	...	...	West Bank
...	...	...	...	...	...	...	...	...	...	...	...	...	...	...	...	Western Sahara
6.9[1]	16.7	44.7	31.7	133.914	20.4	66.2[2]	0.1	19.9	5,622	69.4	30.6	79	73.4	26.6	2.2	Yemen
...	...	...	...	...	...	...	...	...	8,480	51.2	48.8	—	—	—	...	Yugoslavia
30.5[1]	40.3	7.2	21.9	868.9	18.8	52.3[2]	5.7	1.7	5,307	97.5	2.5	309	64.7	35.3	23.4	Zambia
24.5[1]	54.8	10.9	9.8	33.100	34.1	24.6	3.3	27.1	3,338	82.8	17.2	483	66.5	33.5	15.5	Zimbabwe

[1]Includes claims on nonfinancial government (public) enterprises and/or local governments. [2]Includes foreign currency deposits. [3]1995. [4]Treasury bill rate. [5]Money market rate. [6]Short-term deposit rate. [7]1996. [8]Republic of Cyprus only. [9]1997. [10]Interbank rate.

Housing and construction

The present table summarizes data about the housing stock and the construction industries of the countries of the world. The principal focus is on the elements that are most comparable internationally: the age of the housing (by decade, so far as possible), the legal tenure of the householder, construction of exterior walls, principal physical amenities, sanitary arrangements, and the amount of space both absolutely (total area of the average dwelling in square metres [1 square metre equals 1.20 square yards, or 10.76 square feet]) and relatively (persons per room). The data on construction characterize the industry in terms of: (1) the portion of national gross domestic product (GDP) represented by each country's construction industry, (2) the number of new dwelling units constructed annually, their area, and the rate (in years) required to replace the total national stock of dwellings shown on the extreme left of the table, and (3) for nonresidential construction, the number of buildings or portions of buildings built for nonresidential purposes and their area in square metres.

Because housing patterns differ greatly from country to country, the portion of each country's housing stock for which data are compared was defined as specifically as possible. In general, the numbers refer to permanent, private dwelling units that are usually occupied year-round, whether or not actually occupied on the date of the housing census or survey. That definition implies the exclusion of certain housing that is often part of national housing censuses: vacation homes, second homes occupied less than half the year, collective or communal dwellings, and so on. The housing unit to which the data on tenure refer may be either the individual dwelling or the household, according to the reporting practice of the country concerned.

The data are collected mostly from national housing censuses and surveys. The majority of countries combine the housing census with the population census at five- to ten-year intervals. Some countries, however, can conduct a meaningful housing census only in the capital city or in the few largest cities; others may be able to collect and process data for only a few of the most important housing characteristics even when national coverage is complete. These choices may be dictated by the lack of funding to collect data for the entire country or by the perception, particularly in a tropical, rural country where adequate dwellings can be built by hand, that no urgent housing problem exists. These choices may be complex, however, as

Housing and construction

country	year	dwelling units[a]	median age[b] (years)	1949 or earlier	1950–59	1960–69	1970–79	1980 or later	owned	rented	collective, vacant, other	traditional materials	sawn/ framed wood	masonry or cement	other
Afghanistan	1979	2,260,000[1]	...	...	...	...	...	...	55.2	23.5	21.3	...	...	...	...
Albania	1989	674,633[3]	22.6	20.0[4]	14.3[5]	19.0[6]	24.3[7]	22.4[8]	91.2	8.8	—	...	...	...	...
Algeria	1987	3,050,812	...	—51.4[10]—		6.4[11]	18.6	23.6	64.1	22.6	13.3	...	...	...	...
American Samoa	1990	6,959	13.9	4.4	7.5	21.9	22.7	43.5	74.2	20.8	5.1	3.3	52.9	42.5	1.3
Andorra	1990	17,881	18.1	18.0	5.7	20.8	—55.5—		—86.0—		14.0	...	...	...	...
Angola	...	...	...	...	...	...	...	...	...	...	...	...	...	...	...
Antigua and Barbuda	1991	18,476	18.1	—39.6—		11.3	16.3	32.8	64.6	29.3	6.1	0.1	49.6	49.2	1.1
Argentina	1991	8,515,441[17]	21.6[18]	24.0[18]	17.3[18]	22.0[18]	18.3[18]	18.4[18]	78.0	16.0	6.0	6.1[18]	6.7[18]	84.2[18]	3.0[18]
Armenia	1989	559,000[19]	...	...	...	...	...	...	...	...	...	...	...	...	...
Aruba	1991	19,224	27.7	—46.8—		11.2	15.7	26.3	70.6	26.7	2.7	—	7.7	90.6	1.7
Australia	1994	6,677,900	26.1[20]	37.9[20]	10.4[20]	18.6[20]	—33.1[20]—		70.1	27.6	2.3	—	16.0	73.0	11.0
Austria	1991	3,393,271	33.8	33.0[28]	14.7[29]	18.1[6]	18.5[7]	15.7[8]	50.0	38.7	11.3	—	5.1[30]	81.9[30]	13.0[30]
Azerbaijan	1994	1,473,100	...	—15.0—			18.0	67.0	65.3	34.7	—	...	...	...	...
Bahamas, The	1980	54,308	30.7	—54.7—		25.6	—19.7—		51.4	37.4	11.2	4.0[32]	32.3	54.7	9.0
Bahrain	1991	83,470	15.2[20]	58.3[20]	14.5[20]	—27.2[20]—			51.3	38.2	10.5	—	—	93.6[20]	6.4[20]
Bangladesh	1991	19,020,489	...	...	...	...	...	...	86.3	6.5	7.2	78.9	2.4	8.0	10.7
Barbados	1990	75,211	19.1	—48.6—			22.9	28.5	76.1	20.4	3.5	0.2	61.2[34]	35.4	3.2
Belarus	1994	3,679,600	...	...	...	...	...	...	...	...	...	...	...	...	...
Belgium	1991	3,748,165	...	37.0[28]	21.5[35]	13.1[36]	18.5[7]	9.9[8]	64.5	34.2	1.3	...	...	...	...
Belize	1991	37,658	...			26.3	17.8	55.9	65.9	22.8	11.3	5.1	65.6	24.8	4.5
Benin	1992	832,526	...	...	...	...	...	...	76.8[37]	10.1[37]	13.1[37]	75.4	—24.6—		
Bermuda	1991	22,061	...	—56.0—		15.8	12.0	16.2	43.4	52.4	4.2	—	1.7[18,34]	95.1[18]	3.2[18]
Bhutan	...	...	...	...	...	...	...	...	...	...	...	...	...	...	...
Bolivia	1992	1,614,995	...	...	...	...	...	...	65.5	19.8	14.7	72.3[38]	2.3[38]	21.1[38]	4.2[38]
Bosnia and Herzegovina	1991	1,203,000	...	...	...	...	...	...	...	...	...	...	...	...	...
Botswana	1991	276,209	...	...	...	...	...	...	59.2	22.9	17.9	48.7	—	49.3	2.0
Brazil	1991	34,734,715	...	...	...	...	...	...	69.8	16.4	13.8	...	...	...	...
Brunei	1991	40,351	...	...	...	...	...	...	83.8[20]	11.8[20]	4.4[20]	0.2[20]	54.8[20]	36.5[20]	8.5[20]
Bulgaria	1995	3,419,937	...	24.8[28,33]	29.0[29,33]	20.0[6,33]	15.4[7,33]	10.8[8,33]	72.7	16.4[27]	10.9[27]	...	...	...	...
Burkina Faso	1985	1,274,546	...	...	...	...	...	...	...	...	...	...	...	...	...
Burundi	1979	938,000[40]	...	...	...	...	...	...	98.7	1.1	0.2	...	...	...	...
Cambodia	...	...	...	...	...	...	...	...	...	...	...	...	...	...	...
Cameroon	1987	1,787,835[19]	...	...	...	...	...	...	74.0	18.0	8.0	66.0	13.0	17.0	4.0
Canada	1991	10,018,625	10.5	20.3[28]	20.0[29]	19.4[6]	—40.3[42]—		62.6	37.1	0.3	...	...	...	...
Cape Verde	1990	67,619	...	—73.6—			26.4		...	15.4[18]		36.1	—	60.1	3.8
Central African Republic	1988	519,314	...	...	...	...	...	...	88.2	—11.8—		71.7	—28.3—		
Chad	1993	1,228,862	...	...	...	...	...	...	85.0	8.4	6.6	88.6	—11.4—		
Chile	1992	3,369,849	20.4[41]	—46.2[41]—		21.1[41]	—32.7[41]—		68.3	24.6	7.1	14.0	53.1	31.9	1.0
China	1990	276,947,962	...	...	...	...	...	...	18.5[2,41]	81.5[2,41]	—	16.7	7.0	75.6	0.7
Colombia	1985	5,824,857	20.6[43]	54.6[43]	26.2[43]	19.2[43]	—	—	67.6	23.6	8.8	...	...	...	...
Comoros	1980	81,791	...	5.3	7.7	21.3	—63.7—		87.4	3.1	9.5	73.5	1.8	16.9	7.8
Congo, Dem. Rep. of the	1984	5,669,600[19]	...	...	...	...	...	...	47.4[43,44]	38.3[43,44]	14.3[43,44]	52.4[43]	—45.5[43]—		2.1[43]
Congo, Rep. of the	1984	363,140[19]	...	...	...	...	...	...	61.4	24.1	14.5	10.5	15.9	54.9	18.7
Costa Rica	1984	500,788	...	...	...	...	...	...	65.8	20.7	13.5	1.1	60.1	35.6	3.2
Côte d'Ivoire	1985	1,798,799[19]	...	...	...	...	...	...	...	...	...	...	...	...	...
Croatia	1991	1,575,644	...	...	...	...	...	...	64.0	35.4	0.6	...	...	...	...
Cuba	1981	2,363,364	24.6	—44.5—		21.6	—25.6—		...	...	...	3.8	33.2	61.5	1.4
Cyprus	1992	185,459	22.8[41]	—39.9[41]—		15.4[41]	—44.7[41]—		60.0[41]	16.5[41]	23.5[41]	11.9[41]	—	87.6[41]	0.5[41]
Czech Republic	1991	3,705,691	42.4	41.7[28]	10.2[29]	14.5[6]	19.6[7]	14.0[8]	44.7[18]	41.7[18]	13.6[18]	—	32.0[47]	67.1	0.9
Denmark	1995	2,426,503	36.9[9]	43.2	9.8	16.1	17.8	13.1	52.4	45.4	2.2	...	...	...	...
Djibouti	1982	25,000[43]	27.6	...	...	...	...	...	...	...	...	—	73.0[48]	22.5	4.5
Dominica	1991	19,374[19]	18.6	—36.2—		11.6	12.8	31.8	71.9	19.7	8.4	—	50.5	48.4	1.1
Dominican Republic	1981	1,125,785[17]	...	...	...	...	...	...	72.0	17.0	11.0	31.1	31.3	31.4	6.2
Ecuador	1990	2,111,121	...	...	...	...	...	...	68.1	22.6	9.3	32.2	9.3	57.7	0.8
Egypt	1986	9,732,728	...	—37.1[2]—		—62.9[2]—			64.0	27.2	8.8	...	...	...	...
El Salvador	1992	1,236,866	...	...	...	...	...	...	69.6	17.9	12.5	39.8	2.9	52.6	4.7
Equatorial Guinea	...	...	...	...	...	...	...	...	...	...	...	...	...	...	...
Eritrea	...	...	...	...	...	...	...	...	...	...	...	...	...	...	...
Estonia	1995	618,300	24.5	15.0[28]	12.8[29]	22.9[6]	25.5[7]	23.8[8]	18.3[39]	81.5[39]	0.2[39]	—	18.2[39]	77.4[39]	4.4[39]
Ethiopia	1984	9,300,000	...	...	...	...	...	...	48.8[2]	47.2[2]	4.0[2]	89.5	—	5.9	4.6
Faroe Islands	1977	11,172[27]	32.5	—60.1—		21.8	—15.0—		84.5	9.9	5.6	—	43.9	53.5	2.6
Fiji	1986	124,098	...	...	...	...	...	...	75.5	11.1	13.4	9.0	26.4	29.8	34.8
Finland	1994	2,331,406	17.1	—25.5—		14.6	23.3	36.6	73.7	24.7	1.6	14.0[27,30]	81.8[27,30]	—4.2[27,30]—	
France	1992	22,130,800	19.1[54]	36.8[55]	—19.8[56]—		28.8[57]	15.1[58]	53.8	39.2	7.0	...	...	...	...
French Guiana	1990	38,324	...	—38.7[60]—			21.5[61]	39.8[62]	41.3	—58.7—		29.4	—70.6—		

planners are always aware that much housing physically inadequate to protect dwellers from the elements, is disadvantageously placed in relation to tainted or disease-infested water supply or to the outfall of unprocessed sewage, or is built of materials (mud, skins, thatch, etc.) that may harbour pests or disease. In the developed countries, median age and the distribution of physical amenities provide strong indicators of the quality and availability of housing.

The data for the construction industry refer to the most recent year in which a broad range of countries could be surveyed.

The broadest indication of total activity in a national construction industry is its contribution to the national gross domestic product, since that figure, in addition to construction of buildings, also includes civil engineering projects, such as dams, roads and other transportation infrastructure, recreational facilities, irrigation and land reclamation works, and the like. The scope of the data relating to construction of buildings may be limited in several respects. It may be confined to activity capable of being surveyed in the modern or urban sectors only, may be limited to private new construction only or to government and government-financed

activity only, or may refer to construction mortgaged or financed through certain organizations only. Depending on national data-collection systems, it usually excludes remodeling of old premises but may include extensions or enlargements of existing buildings. The data for new construction are usually of two principal types: authorized new construction or certification after construction that newly built structures meet building and fire codes and the like. Data for construction completed are naturally more meaningful but are not available for every country, necessitating the substitution of authorized construction data, which are usually available only for areas regulated by certain types of governmental authorities.

The following notes further define the column headings:
a. Data refer to permanent, private dwelling units that are usually occupied year-round, whether or not occupied on the census date.
b. Data are estimates unless specifically provided by a country source.
c. Data may be either for dwellings or for households, depending on country reporting practice.
d. Data may be either for construction completed or for construction authorized, depending on country reporting practice.

Column groupings — physical amenities (percent): piped water / electricity / inside toilet or WC. sewage disposal (percent): closed public sewer or septic tank / open public sewer / other. space[b]: average area (sq m) / rooms per dwelling unit / persons per room. construction industry (1994) — percent of GDP; new residential[d]: total no. of dwellings / floor area ('000 sq m) / years to replace nat'l stock; new nonresidential[d]: number of units / floor area ('000 sq m).

piped water	electricity	inside toilet or WC	closed public sewer or septic tank	open public sewer	other	average area (sq m)	rooms per dwelling unit	persons per room	percent of GDP	total no. of dwellings	floor area ('000 sq m)	years to replace nat'l stock	number of units	floor area ('000 sq m)	country
25.3[2]	66.5[2]	5.5[2]	5.5	77.9	16.6	...	5.5	2.1	9.8	...	...	...	...	...	Afghanistan
44.6	...	29.9	...	...	...	35.7	1.8	2.6	9.5	12,428[9]	...	54.3	...	...	Albania
87.4	72.7	68.9	52.4	19.1	28.5	...	2.9	2.6	11.3[12]	71,433[13]	...	42.6	...	...	Algeria
96.2	94.4	93.4	68.5	—31.5—		...	4.5	1.6	...	223[14]	...	31.2	...	...	American Samoa
—	...	...	...	...	...	...	...	...	...	...	212[15]	...	...	15	Andorra
...	...	...	...	...	...	...	...	...	1.6	...	...	...	...	...	Angola
91.5	...	...	53.0	...	...	...	3.6	0.9	9.3	764[16]	...	20.2	...	...	Antigua and Barbuda
77.4	93.5	95.1[18]	77.1[18]	—22.9[18]—		...	3.9[18]	1.3[18]	6.7	37,272	7,091	228.4	10,405	3,942	Argentina
...	...	...	...	...	...	...	...	...	6.7	3.040	282	183.9	...	...	Armenia
97.9	98.7[20]	89.2[20]	...	...	...	...	5.2	0.7	8.2[21]	402[14]	...	47.8	...	...	Aruba
97.1[22]	98.4[23]	92.2[20]	99.0[20]	—1.0[20]—		...	5.1[20]	0.6[20]	6.9[24]	167,953[25]	11,170[26]	39.8	23,340[27]	13,727[26]	Australia
95.0[20]	...	88.7	94.3[20]	—	5.7[20]	85.0	4.3[16]	0.6[16]	7.9	48,851	4,616	69.5	...	...	Austria
88.4[31]	...	...	87.4[31]	...	...	...	...	...	3.5	9,400	779	156.7	...	...	Azerbaijan
83.0[33]	77.9	...	63.2	2.2	34.6	...	4.0	1.2	3.0[21]	733[15,30]	...	...	15	...	Bahamas, The
92.8	97.1	78.2	99.8	...	0.2	...	4.2	1.4	6.0	3,066[14]	...	27.2	...	...	Bahrain
56.8[20]	14.3	12.5	1.5[20]	—98.5[20]—		...	2.0[20]	2.9[20]	5.9[25]	300,900[14]	...	49.1	...	...	Bangladesh
94.0	92.6	66.2	66.8	0.4	32.8	...	4.3	0.8	3.8	2,116[16]	...	...	...	...	Barbados
78.4[33]	...	76.7[33]	...	...	...	52.3	...	...	8.7	50,900	3,403	48.6	1,127	1,125	Belarus
99.6	100.0	91.9	...	...	...	86.3	4.3	0.6	5.3	35,600	32,600	105.3	8,323	7,915	Belgium
54.9	67.2	34.7	34.7	—65.3—		...	...	...	7.4	742[14]	...	40.0	...	...	Belize
...	...	...	...	...	...	...	3.2	1.0	4.5	17,011[14]	...	54.8	...	...	Benin
97.4[18]	...	96.7[18]	96.7[18]	—3.3[18]—		...	3.2[18]	0.7[18]	...	193	...	114.3	...	...	Bermuda
...	...	...	...	...	...	...	...	...	11.9	...	...	...	...	...	Bhutan
57.5	55.5	42.8	42.8	—57.2—		...	...	...	4.2	34,258[14]	...	47.1	...	...	Bolivia
66.2[39]	94.2[39]	53.2[39]	...	...	...	56.0[39]	4.0[20]	1.0[20]	...	26,568[9]	...	48.9	...	...	Bosnia and Herzegovina
77.0	5.4[20]	25.4[20]	8.6[20]	20.4[20]	71.0[20]	...	2.5	1.9	5.0[25]	...	...	...	...	...	Botswana
73.6	90.0[33]	...	58.7[33]	—41.3[33]—		...	5.1[18]	0.9[18]	7.7	865,825[14]	...	42.7	...	...	Brazil
90.3[20]	64.2[20]	94.2[20]	57.4[20]	—42.6[20]—		...	4.2[20]	1.6[20]	5.4	1,168[14]	...	34.6	...	...	Brunei
100	99.9[27]	...	90.4	—9.6—		63.7	2.9	0.9	6.4	8,669	727	394.5	7,024	2,217	Bulgaria
...	...	...	...	...	...	...	...	...	5.3	28,133[14]	...	45.3	...	...	Burkina Faso
11.0	0.6	...	1.6	—98.4—		37.2[41]	2.4[41]	0.6[41]	4.7	...	...	...	...	...	Burundi
...	...	...	...	...	...	...	...	1.2	7.6	...	...	...	...	...	Cambodia
32.0	22.0	7.0	2.2	70.4	27.6	...	4.1	1.2	5.3[9]	37,862[14]	...	47.2	...	...	Cameroon
99.9	100.0	99.5	98.9[29]	—1.1[17]—		...	5.7[17]	0.5[17]	5.3	205,391[14]	...	48.8	14,846[27]	...	Canada
16.2	24.9	25.1	—3.4[18]—		96.6[18]	...	1.8[18]	2.8[18]	20.0[9]	861	...	78.5	...	...	Cape Verde
...	...	...	...	...	...	...	...	...	4.1	...	...	...	...	...	Central African Republic
...	...	...	...	...	...	...	...	...	0.5	...	...	...	...	...	Chad
88.2	90.2	70.3	69.9	0.3	29.4	...	4.4	1.0	5.5	118,630	7,044	28.4	...	2,880	Chile
89.4[2,13]	...	25.2[2,13]	47.0[2,13]	—53.0[2,13]—		37.0[13]	2.2[13]	1.8[13]	6.4	...	323,830	...	...	...	China
70.5	78.5	77.9	69.6	—30.4—		...	3.3	1.6	6.3	10,705	9,436[33]	...	3,678	...	Colombia
12.9	5.7	...	2.1	—97.9—		33.7	2.5	2.1	6.3[12]	807[14]	...	89.2	...	...	Comoros
...	...	...	...	...	...	...	...	...	2.0	...	...	...	...	...	Congo, Dem. Rep. of the
30.5	8.8	16.6	—86.2[2]—		13.8[2]	...	3.7[2]	1.7[2]	1.7[12]	...	...	...	...	...	Congo, Rep. of the
86.9	97.3	...	66.5	—33.5—		...	4.0	1.4	2.7	...	1,914[39]	...	2,868[27]	178[27]	Costa Rica
23.0	39.6	23.9	—68.5—		31.5	88.0	...	...	1.9[12]	50,674[14]	...	35.5	...	...	Côte d'Ivoire
86.2	98.6	80.3	80.8	—19.2—		70.4	2.8	1.1	2.1	9,700	819	162.4	1,419	1,476	Croatia
74.1	82.9	45.2	60.9	9.3	30.1	...	4.1	1.0	9.3[39,45]	25,344[38]	1,800[38]	93.2	469[27]	1,803[27]	Cuba
100.0[41]	98.1[41]	74.5[41]	95.6[41]	—4.4[41]—		...	4.6[41]	0.8[41]	9.1	8,400	1,496	22.1	...	1,632[46]	Cyprus
96.9	100.0	88.5	98.1	—1.9—		70.5	2.7	1.0	5.9	18,162	1,039	204.0	...	...	Czech Republic
100.0	100.0	97.1	98.6[20]	—1.4[20]—		107.8[9]	3.7	0.6	5.5	12,932	1,311	186.6	...	3,080	Denmark
45.0	58.0	82.0	26.0	23.0	51.0	...	1.9	6.9	4.8[12]	...	54[39]	...	26[13]	13.7[13]	Djibouti
87.4	...	36.8	36.8	—63.2—		...	3.3	1.1	6.7	188[14]	...	103.1	...	...	Dominica
64.4	...	14.1	...	...	...	...	...	...	9.5	3,234	1,225	—	...	...	Dominican Republic
62.7	77.7	49.6	39.5	25.1	35.4	...	2.8	1.7	2.5	42,204[14]	...	50.0	...	...	Ecuador
73.1	87.0	...	...	...	...	...	3.3	1.5	5.1[49]	160,613[26]	...	60.6	...	...	Egypt
46.4	69.3	39.7	39.7	—60.3—		...	1.5[50]	3.3[50]	3.7	694	341[27]	...	271	0.7[27]	El Salvador
...	...	...	...	...	...	...	...	...	4.7	...	...	...	...	...	Equatorial Guinea
...	...	...	...	...	...	...	...	...	...	...	...	...	...	...	Eritrea
93.8	99.9	89.6	...	...	...	34.5[39]	2.5[39]	0.9[39]	5.5	1,953	159.2	316.6	346	242	Estonia
67.9[2]	...	55.2[2]	...	...	...	...	1.9	2.4	2.9[49]	...	260[51]	...	92[52]	63.3[51]	Ethiopia
99.7	99.5	95.0	89.7	8.1	2.2	...	5.5	1.1	3.3	223[21]	...	50.1	...	...	Faroe Islands
73.7	48.5	56.0	35.4[53]	—64.6[53]—		...	3.3	1.8	3.3	1,356	108	91.5	...	60	Fiji
94.0	95.9[27,30]	96.3	97.3	—2.7—		75.1	3.6	0.6	5.3	26,731	2,168	87.2	29,083	3,298	Finland
99.9	...	95.8	73.8[59]	—26.2[59]—		75.8[33]	3.8	0.7	4.9	356,000	...	60.5	...	34,548	France
77.0	86.7	62.0	34.3[41]	—65.7[41]—		...	2.8	1.2	9.3[39]	2,023	...	18.9	...	64	French Guiana

Housing and construction (continued)

country	year	dwelling units[a]	median age[b] (years)	1949 or earlier	1950–59	1960–69	1970–79	1980 or later	owned	rented	collective, vacant, other	traditional materials	sawn/ framed wood	masonry or cement	other
				colspan decade built (percent)					colspan tenure[c] (percent)			colspan construction of exterior walls (percent)			
French Polynesia	1988	39,513	10.8	—11.3—		16.0	27.6	45.1	68.5	21.2	10.3	36.9	15.8	45.2	2.2
Gabon	1967	15,886[43]	...	...	...	...	...	...	—87.0—		13.0	...	...	...	...
Gambia, The	1983	202,199	...	...	...	...	63.9	21.9	14.2				82.9	—	12.9	4.2
Gaza Strip	1992	66,819[44]	23.0	4.7	31.2	14.3	25.8	23.9	89.1[27,63]	7.6[27,63]	3.3[27,63]	—	—	96.0	4.0
Georgia	1989	1,244,000[19]	...	...	...	...	...	...	...	...	...	...	...	...	...
Germany	1993	34,988,753	39.4	32.9[55]	—62.4[64]—			4.7[65]	38.8	61.2	—	...	...	...	...
Ghana	1992	3,320,000[19]	...	...	...	...	...	...	37.0	19.6	43.4	62.6	1.3	33.6	2.5
Gibraltar	1991	7,604[17]	25.0	37.3[66]	16.7[67]	15.6[68]	23.0[69]	7.4[58]	15.2	84.8	—	...	...	...	...
Greece	1991	3,167,152	29.2[20]	30.2[20,28]	27.4[20,29]	20.7[6,20]	—21.5[20]—		75.7	20.4	3.9	...	...	...	...
Greenland	1997	19,847	10.2	11.9[22]	18.8[22]	46.5[22]	—22.8[22]—		39.3[22]	—60.7[27]—		...	...	...	...
Grenada	1991	21,974	...	—49.1[70]—			20.7[71]	30.2[58]	78.7	13.8	7.5		68.5	30.2	1.3
Guadeloupe	1990	112,478	...						62.6	—37.4—		29.5		—70.5—	
Guam	1990	35,223	15.8	2.3	7.1	19.2	41.5	29.9	45.6	54.4	—	0.0	5.1	85.8	9.1
Guatemala	1981	1,259,598	12.5	—62.0—		10.0	—28.0—		64.7	11.3	24.0	55.6	21.1	19.3	4.0
Guernsey	1991	21,215[17]	...	...	...	...	...	...	68.4	31.6		...	...	...	...
Guinea	1983	716,378	...	...	...	...			81.3	10.6	8.1	26.2	...	12.7	61.1
Guinea-Bissau	1979	123,936	...	...	...	...			...	...	...	95.7	0.1	2.3	1.9
Guyana	1980	149,734[19]	17.6	—43.5—		19.4	—37.1—		57.2	27.3	15.5	1.8	85.6	6.6	6.0
Haiti	1987	1,164,136	...	—75.9—			—24.1—		73.2	4.5	22.3	37.0	57.4	5.4	0.2
Honduras	1988	809,263	12.1[72]	—38.9[72]—		—37.8[72,73]—		—23.3[72,74]—	71.8[72]	16.5[72]	12.7[72]	61.0[72]	26.4[72]	11.7[72]	0.9[72]
Hong Kong	1994	1,735,500	...	—48.1[20]—		13.6[20]	—38.3[20]—		45.1	50.1	4.8	21.8	14.6	63.6	—
Hungary	1995	3,971,000	16.4	32.9[1,28]	11.8[1,77]	14.9[1]	23.2[1]	17.2[1]	75.9	23.7	0.4	...	...	71.9[78]	...
Iceland	1984	70,777	25.6	—46.0—		—54.1—			70.3[78]	—29.7[78]—		...	...	...	...
India	1991	195,024,357	...	...	...	...	...	...	86.3	11.8	1.9	87.7	1.5	2.0	8.7
Indonesia	1993	42,016,761[24]	...	...	...	...	...	...	87.0[76]	5.0[76]	8.0[76]	...	...	...	...
Iran	1986	8,211,375	...	—82.5[22]—			—17.5[22]—		77.0	12.2	9.8	28.8	0.7	69.2	1.3
Iraq	1987	1,759,176	...	...	...	...	...	...	65.3[19]	18.1[19]	16.6[19]	...	...	...	...
Ireland	1991	1,006,506	47.2[20]	—48.2[80]—		11.7[6]	22.4[7]	18.2[8]	80.2	16.8	3.0	...	...	...	...
Isle of Man	1991	27,316	...	...	...	...	...	...	66.5	32.5	1.0	...	...	...	...
Israel	1983	1,104,270	...	9.5[81]	—90.5[82]—				74.3	23.1	2.6	...	...	...	...
Italy	1991	25,028,522	32.2	30.8[28]	19.7[35]	27.5[83]	—22.0[42]—		53.6	20.0	26.4	7.1	28.4	54.4	10.1
Jamaica	1982	517,297[19]	17.0	—33.6—		28.8	—39.6—		46.7	32.6	20.7	—	68.1	—31.9—	
Japan	1993	40,835,000	16.5	5.4[85]	10.9[86]	13.4[6]	31.5[7]	38.8[8]	59.8	38.5	1.7	...	...	...	...
Jersey	1991	32,463	...	...	...	...	...	...	49.6	48.0	2.4	...	...	...	...
Jordan	1994	683,000	...	...	...	...	...	...	59.7	38.8	1.5	...	...	...	...
Kazakhstan	1993	4,410,000	...	...	...	...	...	...	...	...	...	...	...	...	...
Kenya	1989	4,352,751[19]	...	...	...	...	...	...	68.2[50]	17.9[50]	13.9[50]	64.4[50]	—35.6[50]—		
Kiribati	1990	11,301[19]	...	...	...	...	...	...	...	...	...	...	...	...	...
Korea, North	1987	4,054,027[19]	...	...	...	...	...	...	...	...	...	...	...	...	...
Korea, South	1995	9,204,929	13.1[1]	5.6	4.0	6.3	14.9	69.2	74.9	22.5	2.6	7.8[1]	18.9[1]	73.0[1]	0.3[1]
Kuwait	1995	251,682	14.5[18]	—12.2[18]—		38.8[18]	—34.5[18]—		38.2[27]	53.6[27]	8.2[27]	46.5[30]	...	36.5[30]	17.0[30]
Kyrgyzstan	1989	856,000[19]	...	...	...	...	...	...	...	...	...	...	...	...	...
Laos	1985	601,797[88]	...	...	...	...	...	...	...	...	...	...	...	...	...
Latvia	1994	953,000	...	—37.1[89]—		17.7[6]	22.0[7]	23.1[8]	40.8	59.2	—	...	...	...	...
Lebanon	1970	483,908[17]	...	30.1[90]	40.2[91]	29.4[6]	—		...	...	...	...	...	...	...
Lesotho	1986	312,655[19]	...	...	...	...	...	...	87.1	8.2	4.7	...	...	...	...
Liberia	1974[43]	263,333	...	...	...	...	...	...	...	...	...	...	...	...	...
Libya	1984	569,679	...	23.9[30]	14.4[30]	20.4[30]	—41.3[30]—		62.5[75]	28.0[75]	9.5[75]	...	...	...	...
Liechtenstein	1990	10,386[17]	29.4[30]	...	...	...	...	...	53.6	41.7	4.7	...	...	...	...
Lithuania	1994	1,225,800	...	...	...	...	...	...	87.1	12.9		...	...	...	...
Luxembourg	1991	144,683	33.1	34.5[28]	17.6[29]	12.5[6]	17.8[7]	17.6[8]	66.1	28.3	5.6	...	...	...	...
Macau	1991	89,193	...	6.9[28]	11.6[29]	21.2[6]	23.4[7]	41.8[8]	65.9	32.0	2.1	—	0.5[92]	99.3[92]	0.2[92]
Macedonia	1991	511,300	...	...	...	...	...	...	63.2	18.4	18.4	...	...	...	...
Madagascar	1993	2,688,951[19]	...	...	...	...	...	...	39.6	—60.4—		51.6	3.1	44.4	0.9
Malawi	1987	1,859,572[19]	...	...	...	...	...	...	...	...	...	...	...	...	...
Malaysia	1991	3,447,597	...	...	...	...	...	...	63.4[18]	25.0[18]	11.6[18]	53.8	2.7	41.1	2.4
Maldives	1990	37,114	11.6	15.1	7.9	13.7	21.7	41.6	96.4	3.6	—	75.9	8.5	10.3	5.3
Mali	1987	1,364,079[19]	...	...	...	...	...	...	84.2	8.5	7.3	93.0[44]	...		
Malta	1985	101,509	...	—81.8[94]—		18.2[95]			53.9	43.0	3.1			92.9[44]	0.2[144]
Marshall Islands	1980[96]	4,923[38]	...	6.4	13.3	24.7	—55.5—		60.0	33.0	7.0	10.7	63.5	15.9	9.9
Martinique	1990	106,536	19.0	—54.5[60]—		17.9[61]	—27.6[58]—		60.9	32.5	6.6	20.4[41]	—79.6[41]—		
Mauritania	1977	246,462[19]	...	...	...	...	...	...	75.9	15.2	8.9	—	4.2[52]	66.8[52]	28.9[52]
Mauritius	1990	236,885	...	—19.7[52]—		24.3[52,97]	—56.0[52,98]—		77.8	14.8	7.3	50.4	—48.2—		1.4
Mayotte	1991	19,227	...						77.9	14.6	7.5	...	...	...	...
Mexico	1990	16,197,802	...	—51.4[18]—		15.4[18]	—33.2[18]—		77.9	14.6	7.5	19.0	8.1	69.5	3.4
Micronesia	1980	11,562	...	3.8	5.2	21.3	—69.7—		51.8	39.2	9.0	6.0	41.8	14.6	37.6
Moldova	1994	1,112,800	...	...	...	...	...	...	...	...	...	...	...	...	...
Monaco	1990	16,122	30.0	39.5[55]	13.0[99]	19.7[100]	27.8[61]	—	23.3	60.5	16.2	...	...	...	...
Mongolia	1969	242,000	...	...	...	...	...	...	100.0			...	...	...	...
Morocco	1994	4,444,271[19]	...	...	...	...	...	...	69.3[27]	22.1[27]	8.6[27]	24.5[47]	—73.5[41]—		1.8[41]
Mozambique	1980	2,712,439[19]	...	...	...	...	...	...	...	...	...	86.5	2.3	8.3	2.9
Myanmar (Burma)	1983	6,750,884	...	...	...	...	...	...	...	...	...	80.3	14.8	3.2	1.7
Namibia	1991	254,389	...	...	...	...	...	...	69.2	16.9	13.9	52.0	—	36.2	11.8
Nauru	1977	508[102]	...	—88.6[102]—			—11.4[102]—		11.0[103]	80.6[103]	8.4[103]	—76.8—		10.7	12.6
Nepal	1996	2,585,154[19]	...	...	...	...	...	...	93.8	2.2	4.0	...	...	...	...
Netherlands, The	1995	6,195,100	27.5	25.7	11.0	16.8	20.4	26.1	47.6[96]	52.4[96]	—	...	...	...	...
Netherlands Antilles	1992	57,608	14.0	—28.4—		13.6	21.3	36.7	59.8	36.7	—	—	18.3[20]	78.8[20]	2.9[20]
New Caledonia	1989	40,266	...	—19.3—		—80.7—			56.4	29.7	13.9	6.4	11.7	61.7	20.2
New Zealand	1991	1,185,396	...	—64.1[20]—		19.2[20]	—16.2[20]—		72.4	22.7	4.9	30.8[76]	45.6[76]	21.8[76]	1.8[76]
Nicaragua	1995	794,093	...	...	...	...	...	...	64.4[76]	20.3[76]	15.3[76]	...	...	...	...
Niger	1988	1,163,424[19]	...	...	...	...	...	...	77.3	6.3	16.4	83.0	—17.0—		
Nigeria	1982[43]	...	...	...	...	...	...	...	37.0	46.0	17.0	29.0	—	71.0	—
Northern Mariana Islands	1990	8,210	...	1.0	2.5	6.4	13.3	76.8	39.5	56.6	3.9	0.0	13.5	66.5	20.0
Norway	1990	1,769,000	25.3	44.1[28]	20.6[29]	17.8[6]	20.7[7]	16.0[8]	80.3	—19.7—		...	...	...	...
Oman	1993	344,846	...	...	...	...	...	...	61.6	21.7	16.7	...	...	...	...

piped water	electricity	inside toilet or WC	closed public sewer or septic tank	open public sewer	other	average area (sq m)	rooms per dwelling unit	persons per room	percent of GDP	total no. of dwellings	floor area ('000 sq m)	years to replace nat'l stock	number of units	floor area ('000 sq m)	country
92.5	91.0	78.9	2.0[53]	67.0[53]	31.0[53]	...	3.8	1.3	6.1[1]	834	...	47.4	1,329	...	French Polynesia
...	50.5	...	...	...	...	...	3.0	1.3	3.9	...	...	...	...	...	Gabon
21.9	...	...	...	...	...	...	2.0	2.0	5.0	...	...	...	...	...	Gambia, The
97.2[27]	97.6	98.4	...	...	...	...	2.6[27]	2.5[27]	18.2[9]	1,247[13]	180[13]	53.6	...	31.1[13]	Gaza Strip
...	...	...	...	...	...	...	...	...	5.5	...	1,005[18]	...	...	...	Georgia
100.0	99.7	98.3	97.1[18]	—2.9[18]—		82.3	4.3	0.5	5.1	641,958	56,098	54.5	38,025	37,215	Germany
36.0	28.5	7.0	...	...	...	23.7	1.9[39]	2.4	3.3	...	...	...	...	...	Ghana
96.7[20]	100.0[20]	99.2	100.0[20]	—	—	...	3.3	1.1	...	66[14]	...	115.2	...	...	Gibraltar
96.4	99.2	87.5	56.6	—43.4—		138.4[17]	3.9	0.8	6.3	80,607	9,386	57.8	49,435	14,915	Greece
62.7[22]	84.2[22]	39.1[22]	39.1[22]	—60.9[22]—		64.7	2.9	1.1	8.5[21]	251	...	79.1	...	...	Greenland
88.1	...	36.1	36.1	—63.9—		...	2.9[20]	1.6[20]	7.0	...	...	...	...	...	Grenada
83.2	89.4	78.2	24.6[41]	—75.4[41]—		...	3.7	0.9	7.4[39]	676[39]	358	166.4	...	160	Guadeloupe
99.2	98.4	97.0	97.0	—3.0—		...	5.0	0.8	7.9[41]	697	...	50.5	500[13]	...	Guam
52.0	37.0	14.3	20.1	3.4	76.5	...	2.4	2.2	2.1	...	495[15,39]	...	...	15	Guatemala
96.5[22]	...	98.3	68.9	—31.1—		...	5.5	0.5	...	311[14]	...	68.2	...	...	Guernsey
11.9	12.5	...	...	...	...	...	...	...	6.9	...	...	...	...	...	Guinea
3.7	3.9	...	4.2	—95.8—		...	1.4	4.5	4.1	...	...	...	...	...	Guinea-Bissau
38.1	69.0	29.0	10.4	—89.6—		...	2.9	1.8	3.6	...	...	...	...	...	Guyana
5.8	21.9	45.8	2.0[41]	—98.0[41]—		...	2.3	2.1	2.9	...	...	...	...	...	Haiti
55.0[18]	25.0[18]	13.0[18]	14.4[18]	—85.6[18]—		...	2.4[18]	2.3[18]	6.4	1,442[54]	214[16]	...	148[16]	98[16]	Honduras
85.7[20]	...	69.2[75]	65.4[75]	—34.6[75]—		53.2[76]	3.1[75]	2.8[75]	4.9	56,042	1,250	31.0	1,391	1,638	Hong Kong
84.1	98.8[23]	75.1	84.6	—15.4—		52.3	2.6	1.0	4.9	20,947	2,040	...	1,026[33]	1,590[33]	Hungary
99.1[23]	94.6[23]	93.6[23]	86.5[23]	—13.5[23]—		...	4.8[78]	0.9[78]	6.8	1,718	746	41.2	531	945[26]	Iceland
32.3	42.4	23.7	...	...	...	...	2.2	2.7	5.8[25]	5,206,944[14]	...	37.5	...	...	India
14.7	55.2	51.5	24.7	—75.3—		59.0	3.3	1.7[79]	7.4	107,269	...	...	...	...	Indonesia
74.6	84.1	43.6	...	...	...	60.0[22]	2.8	1.8	3.3[49]	129,181[79]	28,608[79]	—	...	...	Iran
...	...	90.3	...	...	...	...	5.9	1.5	2.8[9]	...	4,558[9]	...	11,799[27]	410[9]	Iraq
94.8[20]	94.7[76]	96.4	72.3[76]	—27.7[76]—		...	5.2	0.6	5.0[13]	25,735	2,913	36.3	5,344	1,735	Ireland
...	...	99.5	...	...	...	...	...	0.4[20]	9.8[13]	168[13]	...	162.6	...	...	Isle of Man
96.5[76]	96.5[76]	98.8	99.0[72]	—1.0[72]—		...	3.0	1.2	7.6[9]	33,820	4,880	32.7	...	1,464	Israel
99.1	99.0[20]	97.4	95.7[22]	—4.3[22]—		94.1	4.3	0.7	5.1	166,236	14,961	150.6	21,377	...	Italy
76.9	48.6	35.2	...	...	...	...	2.4[37]	4.3	12.6	7,950	...	65.1	...	6,998[84]	Jamaica
94.0[52]	...	74.7	61.2[52]	—38.8[52]—		89.2[38]	4.9[38]	0.7[38]	10.3	1,688,700	156,800	24.2	...	81,260	Japan
80.8	...	93.0[22]	98.0	—2.0—		...	4.7	0.5	...	354[13]	...	91.7	...	...	Jersey
95.8	93.9	55.4[23]	54.5	—84.3—		...	3.2	...	7.4	4,200	4,206[15]	—	820[16]	15	Jordan
50.0	...	...	...	—41.0—		...	...	...	9.6	65,000	3,432	67.8	...	...	Kazakstan
...	...	...	...	...	...	...	...	...	5.3	...	828[9,15]	...	85[16]	15	Kenya
33.1	23.7[58]	53.3	...	...	...	...	...	...	2.2	190[14]	...	59.5	...	...	Kiribati
...	...	...	...	...	...	...	...	...	...	...	...	...	...	...	Korea, North
82.9[87]	49.9[23]	75.1	...	...	...	58.9	3.1	1.1	11.4	622,854	63,387	14.8	68,215	52,834	Korea, South
53.9[18]	99.5[18]	...	35.9[18]	—64.1[18]—		...	4.3[18]	1.8[18]	3.4	2,287[14]	713	110.0	1,459	102	Kuwait
...	...	...	...	...	...	...	...	...	3.4	5,000	405	171.2	...	...	Kyrgyzstan
...	...	...	...	...	...	...	...	...	3.4	...	...	...	...	...	Laos
78.3	100.0[9]	74.0	...	...	...	55.4	...	...	4.5	3,300	174	288.8	...	...	Latvia
...	93.4	82.9	...	...	...	...	...	...	5.2	...	...	...	...	...	Lebanon
31.9	2.2	2.5	2.5	—97.5—		...	2.2	2.4	21.9	7,081[14]	...	44.2	...	...	Lesotho
...	...	...	...	...	...	...	2.3[27]	1.7	2.2[39]	...	...	...	...	...	Liberia
70.1[75]	72.1[75]	40.6[75]	40.6[75]	—59.4[75]—		...	3.3[75]	1.8[75]	11.8[9]	...	...	...	...	...	Libya
96.5	96.6	86.7	90.2	—9.8—		102.0	4.5	0.6	...	197[14]	...	52.7	...	...	Liechtenstein
59.5	...	...	...	...	...	58.3	2.5	...	8.7	6,900	590	177.6	385	280	Lithuania
99.4	...	99.4	93.0[92]	—7.0[92]—		114.2	5.4[18]	0.5[18]	7.9	2,744	1,931[26]	52.7	282	1,964[26]	Luxembourg
98.0	99.8	97.9	...	...	...	...	3.1	1.3	...	9,553	1,141[15]	9.3	327	15	Macau
81.8	96.4[39]	61.4	...	...	...	68.6[39]	...	...	6.4	4,830	348	105.9	310	53	Macedonia
...	...	...	...	...	...	...	...	...	1.2[9]	...	...	...	...	...	Madagascar
23.6	22.8[18]	33.4[18]	33.0[44]	—67.0[44]—		...	1.9	1.7	4.2	...	...	...	...	...	Malawi
65.0[18]	64.4[18]	...	56.4[18]	4.4[18]	39.2[18]	...	2.3[92,93]	2.6[92,93]	4.1	...	8,809[16]	...	...	960[16]	Malaysia
...	53.4[27]	...	43.2	—56.8—		...	4.4	1.5	9.1	95[14]	...	34.5	...	...	Maldives
3.8	3.6	1.3	...	...	...	...	2.6	2.2	3.6[52]	10,025[14]	...	136.1	...	...	Mali
98.0	98.0	98.8	98.0	15.4[44]	6.1[44]	...	3.2[44]	1.3[44]	3.4	3,420	...	29.7	2,024[33]	...	Malta
49.8[38]	56.0[38]	43.7[38]	28.6	—71.4—		...	...	...	10.4	132	...	37.4	...	...	Marshall Islands
94.1	90.2	89.0	41.8[41]	—58.2[41]—		...	3.7	0.9	5.2[21]	6,893	113	15.5	...	...	Martinique
...	...	...	...	...	...	...	...	...	9.2[12]	...	...	...	...	...	Mauritania
94.7	96.2	63.3	63.3	—36.7—		...	3.6[52]	1.4[52]	7.6	4,592[14]	1,108	51.6	682	371	Mauritius
42.5	32.2	6.7	54.4	—45.6—		...	2.2	2.2	...	616[16]	...	21.3[16]	...	...	Mayotte
79.4	87.5	45.0[18]	60.9	2.7	36.4	...	3.4	1.5	5.5	412,319[14]	...	39.3	...	...	Mexico
40.0	28.3	...	8.0	—92.0—		...	...	...	...	...	...	...	...	...	Micronesia
74.9	100.0	71.6	46.0	—54.0—		61.7	...	...	9.9	7,500	...	148.4	158	86	Moldova
100.0	100.0	96.2	98.4[59]	—1.6[59]—		...	2.8	0.8	...	187[14]	...	86.2	...	...	Monaco
0.3	47.5	...	...	...	...	...	...	...	2.4[101]	...	112[9]	...	...	176[17]	Mongolia
32.1[27]	37.8[27]	52.5[27]	...	...	...	...	2.7[41]	2.2[41]	4.2	57,281	7,070	...	2,229	998	Morocco
12.7	4.2	...	...	...	...	...	...	...	10.6	...	...	...	...	...	Mozambique
...	...	...	...	...	...	...	...	...	1.7[49]	1,193[51]	...	...	1,483[51]	...	Myanmar (Burma)
49.8	24.2	30.9	...	...	...	...	3.6	1.4	2.7	...	...	...	...	...	Namibia
...	49.2	...	...	...	...	...	3.6[103]	1.6[103]	...	...	...	...	...	...	Nauru
32.8	14.1	21.6	9.2	—90.8—		56.1	3.0	1.9	10.4[49]	...	...	...	...	...	Nepal
100.0	98.0	100.0	90.0[13]	—10.0[13]—		...	4.1[27]	0.7[27]	5.7	87,369	...	70.9	13,034	13,625	Netherlands, The
79.6[20]	96.9[20]	82.0[20]	...	...	...	...	4.2[20]	1.0[20]	6.6[33]	547[9]	...	150.2[9]	361[33]	...	Netherlands Antilles
90.1	85.3	70.9	76.7	—23.3—		...	3.3	1.2	4.9[38]	942[33]	46[16]	46.8	1[54]	...	New Caledonia
92.7[76]	...	97.1[76]	...	...	...	...	5.6	0.5	3.1	22,540	3,700	52.6	...	2,568	New Zealand
27.9[76]	40.9[76]	19.3[76]	19.2[76]	—80.8[76]—		...	2.2[76]	2.1[76]	2.8	17,489[14]	...	41.3	...	...	Nicaragua
15.5	4.3	1.2	...	...	...	...	...	...	1.9	...	...	...	...	...	Niger
24.7	33.7	3.5	...	...	...	...	1.4	1.1	1.1	...	...	...	...	...	Nigeria
91.0	94.1[18]	79.5	81.7	—18.3—		...	3.6	1.1	...	469[14]	...	17.5	...	...	Northern Mariana Islands
97.5[92]	...	94.6	86.8[92]	—13.2[18]—		103.5	4.1	0.6	3.3	17,836	2,453	99.2	14,860	2,404	Norway
35.8	86.3	76.1	...	...	...	...	...	2.9	2.0	1,043[16]	...	...	266[16]	...	Oman

Housing and construction (continued)

country	housing stock			1949 or earlier	1950–59	1960–69	1970–79	1980 or later	owned	rented	collective, vacant, other	traditional materials	sawn/framed wood	masonry or cement	other
	year	dwelling units[a]	median age[b] (years)	decade built (percent)					tenure[c] (percent)			construction of exterior walls (percent)			
Pakistan[104]	1980	12,597,000	17.2	17.0[90]	36.7[105]	24.9[106]	21.3[107]	—	78.4	7.7	13.9	49.2	2.4	41.4	7.1
Palau	1990	3,312	12.8	2.1	6.0	16.8	30.6	44.5	76.4	23.6	—	0.0	27.9	26.5	45.6
Panama	1990[108]	524,284[17]	18.0[18]	47.4[18]	12.8[18]	18.1[18]	—21.7[18]—		75.5	15.7	8.8	16.9	—81.2—		1.9
Papua New Guinea	1980	556,519[19]	...				—60.0[59]—		40.0[59]	—60.0[59]—		...	...	...	...
Paraguay	1982	868,284[21]	21.1	—56.0—		17.0	—27.0—		80.4	10.5	9.1	21.5	29.7	47.6	1.2
Peru	1993	4,427,517	...	—30.9[20]—		—69.1[20]—			82.0	11.0	7.0	55.7	7.0	35.7	1.6
Philippines	1990	11,395,304	...	—78.5[92]—		—21.5[92]—			83.0	8.0	9.0	35.3	27.3	33.5	3.9
Poland	1988	11,967,021	...	35.0[85]	—33.7[110]—		—31.3[111]—		35.2	64.3	0.9	—14.1[50]—		—85.9[50]—	
Portugal	1991	3,059,300	33.7[20]	—38.3[80]—		16.9[6]	21.2[7]	22.6[8]	64.7	35.3	—	—	0.7[20]	61.0[20]	38.3[20]
Puerto Rico	1990	1,188,985	18.0	9.0	12.8	22.9	29.5	25.8	72.1	27.9	—		15.1	83.6	1.3
Qatar	1986	64,543	...	...	...	...	...	...	21.9	72.0	6.1	...	...	...	...
Réunion	1994	184,500[17]	14.3[1]	—47.6[60]—	...	19.9[61]	—32.5[58]—		50.3	38.9	10.8	23.9	12.5	—63.7—	
Romania	1992	7,632,000	...	...	...	19.9	14.2	...	78.6	20.8	0.6	...	...	...	...
Russia	1994	52,123,000	...	...	...	...	...	...	...	...	...	...	...	...	...
Rwanda	1978	1,055,950[19]	...	...	...	...	...	...	95.3	1.7	3.0	88.6	7.9	1.3	2.2
St. Kitts and Nevis	1980	11,615[19]	24.2	—63.5—		17.9	—14.7—		54.7	29.5	15.8	—	76.2	21.3	2.5
St. Lucia	1991	33,079	13.5	—17.0—		12.4	26.0	44.6	72.4	26.8	0.8	—	53.4	46.1	0.5
St. Vincent and the Grenadines	1980	27,110	...	—	...	...	...	...	72.1	16.0	11.9	—	53.8	42.9	3.3
Samoa	1981	33,402	...	...	...	...	...	...	80.1	2.0	17.9	62.3	24.4	8.6	4.7
San Marino	1991	8,518	...	...	...	...	...	...	73.5[37]	21.9[37]	4.6[37]	...	...	...	...
São Tomé and Príncipe	1981	27,449[19]	...	...	...	...	...	...	...	...	...	2.2	67.2	25.7	4.9
Saudi Arabia	...	...	...	...	...	...	...	...	...	...	...	...	...	...	...
Senegal	1955[43,115]	13,000	...						—84.6—		15.4	...	...	...	...
Seychelles	1987	15,050	...	...	...	...	...	...	63.7	25.1	11.2	1.0	40.0	52.0	7.0
Sierra Leone	1985	486,550	...	...	...	...	...	...	75.2	20.7	4.1	64.6	...	26.2	9.2
Singapore	1990	744,203	...	—63.2[18]—		—36.8[18]—			87.5	—12.5—		4.7[18]	—95.3[18]—		
Slovakia	1991	1,617,829	26.9	17.1[28]	17.3[29]	20.3[6]	25.4[7]	19.9[8]	...	...	...	—	38.0[47]	61.4	0.6
Slovenia	1991	640,000	...	—35.3[80]—		18.2[6]	25.7[7]	19.4[8]	60.2	39.8	—	...	...	...	...
Solomon Islands	1986	43,842[19]	...	...	...	...	...	...	27.4[22]	43.0[22]	29.6[22]	...	...	...	...
Somalia	...	...	...	...	...	...	...	...	...	...	...	...	...	...	...
South Africa	1991	3,599,518	18.6[92]	40.6[92]	24.2[92]	35.2[92]	—	—	54.5	34.0	11.5	...	...	...	...
Spain	1991	11,736,000	39.4[16]	19.5[28]	14.3[29]	23.7[6]	27.2[7]	15.1[8]	67.5	14.9	17.6	...	...	...	...
Sri Lanka	1981	2,811,406	...	...	...	...	...	...	69.4	10.1	20.5	...	...	...	...
Sudan, The	1983		...	...	...	...	...	...	86.2	8.1	5.7	76.5	4.4	16.7	2.4
Suriname	1980	77,744	...	—52.4—		—47.6—			...	...	...	38.9[116]	—61.1[116]—		
Swaziland	1986	122,369	...	...	...	...	...	...	...	...	...	65.9	—34.1—		
Sweden	1990	3,830,037	20.0	33.2	14.2	22.4	22.2	10.6	55.9	40.0	4.1	...	...	...	...
Switzerland	1990	2,800,953	28.5	33.2[90]	15.9[91]	19.4[6]	17.2[7]	14.3[8]	31.3	66.5	2.2	...	...	...	...
Syria	1987	1,836,195	...	—91.3[92]—			—8.7[92]—		81.6[92]	15.5[92]	2.8[92]	...	...	...	...
Taiwan	1990	4,237,174[17]	17.2	6.1[28]	6.7[29]	15.8[6]	42.6[7]	28.8[8]	78.5	12.8	8.7	...	...	...	...
Tajikistan	1989	799,000[19]	...	...	...	...	...	...	...	...	...	...	...	...	...
Tanzania	1978	3,554,793	...	—17.0—		—83.0—			75.4	19.4	5.2	83.0	—	16.3	0.7
Thailand	1990	12,305,197[19]	...	22.0[92]	25.0[92]	53.0[92]	—	—	86.0	11.2	2.8	8.4	68.2	22.3	1.1
Togo	1981	462,694	...	...	...	...	...	...	...	...	...	...	...	...	...
Tonga	1986	15,091	22.5	—59.4[117]—		20.3[118]	—20.3[119]—		82.0	3.5	14.5	35.1[22]	45.4[22]	15.3[22]	4.2[22]
Trinidad and Tobago	1990	271,871	15.3	—41.6—			17.9	40.5	64.6[18]	34.0[18]	1.4[18]	1.0	28.1	70.0[34]	0.9
Tunisia	1984	1,703,279[96]	...	...	...	...	...	...	78.9	12.6	8.5	...	—28.8—	—71.2—	
Turkey	1994	13,341,000	8.4[16]	16.2[117]	6.2[120]	19.6[106]	—58.0[108]—		77.2	12.0	10.8	...	...	...	...
Turkmenistan	1989	598,000[19]	...	...	...	...	...	...	...	...	...	...	...	...	...
Tuvalu	1979	1,079	...	...	...	...	...	...	81.6	12.1	6.6	64.9	4.2	31.0	—
Uganda	1991	3,434,177	...	...	...	...	...	...	...	...	...	...	...	...	...
Ukraine	1989	14,057,000[19]	...	...	...	...	...	...	...	...	...	...	...	...	...
United Arab Emirates	1980	153,009	15.0	0.8	1.3	11.4	—86.5—		36.2	45.2	18.6	2.9	7.3	87.3	2.5
United Kingdom[122]	1991	21,897,322	32.6[20]	54.0[20]	13.0[20]	16.6[20]	—16.4[20]—		66.4	33.6	—	...	...	...	...
United States	1995	106,403,000	28.0	27.4	12.4	14.4	21.6	23.7	59.7	32.1	8.2	...	...	...	...
Uruguay	1985	852,400	...	...	...	...	...	...	57.6	23.2	19.2	...	...	...	...
Uzbekistan	1989	3,415,000[19]	...	...	...	...	...	...	...	...	...	...	...	...	...
Vanuatu	1979	28,252[19,39]	...	...	...	...	...	...	40.9[43]	25.7[43]	33.4[43]	61.4	7.7	13.6	17.2
Venezuela	1990	3,534,507	...	...	...	...	...	...	75.8	13.9	10.3	14.6	0.5	84.9	—
Vietnam	1989	12,958,041[19]	...	...	...	...	...	...	...	...	...	...	...	...	...
Virgin Islands (U.S.)	1990	39,290	14.7	10.0[18]	8.9[18]	42.7[18]	—38.4[18]—		44.6	55.4	—	...	...	...	...
West Bank	1992	119,165[44]	12.2	8.0	12.7	24.6	26.2	28.6	86.2[63]	11.5[63]	2.3[63]	23.0	—	75.3	1.7
Western Sahara	1994	46,120	...	...	...	...	...	...	32.2[30]	62.3[30]	5.5[30]	...	...	...	...
Yemen[123]	1988[124]	1,701,203	...	...	...	...	...	...	83.9	5.2	10.9	...	...	...	...
Yugoslavia	1993	3,039,000	...	...	...	...	...	...	...	...	...	...	...	...	...
Zambia	1990	1,327,098[19]	...	...	...	...	...	...	78.8[125]	21.1[125]	...	...	...	...	...
Zimbabwe	1992	2,163,289[19]	...	...	...	...	...	...	58.3	39.1	2.6	55.9[125,126]	—44.1[125,126]—		

[1]1990. [2]Urban only. [3]Data refer to "apartments," approximately equal in numbers to families, or households. [4]1950 and earlier. [5]1951–60. [6]1961–70. [7]1971–80. [8]1981 and later. [9]1991. [10]1962 and earlier. [11]1963–69. [12]Includes public utilities. [13]1987. [14]Average annual gain in housing stock/households during intercensal interval ending year indicated at extreme left. [15] Residential includes nonresidential. [16]1986. [17]Occupied dwellings only. [18]1980. [19]Data refer to households. [20]1981. [21]1992. [22]1976. [23]Minimum. [24]1992–93. [25]1994–95. [26]1990–91. [27]1985. [28]1945 and earlier. [29]1946–60. [30]Data refer to buildings. [31]Public, state, and cooperative-owned dwellings only. [32]Stucco. [33]1993. [34]Includes wood and brick, and wood and concrete. [35]1946–61. [36]1962–70. [37]1979. [38]1988. [39]1989. [40]Data refer to compound dwellings. [41]1982. [42]1971 and later. [43]Capital city only. [44]1967. [45]Percentage of net material product. [46]Volume enclosed in cubic metres. [47]Includes prefabricated units. [48]Includes corrugated steel. [49]1993–94. [50]1978. [51]1987–88. [52]1983. [53]1977. [54]1984. [55]1948 and earlier. [56]1949–67. [57]1967–81. [58]1982 and later. [59]1975. [60]1974 and earlier. [61]1975–82. [62]1983 and later. [63]Excludes refugee camps. [64]1949–87. [65]1988 and later. [66]1952 and earlier. [67]1953–62. [68]1963–72. [69]1973–81. [70]1975 and earlier.

physical amenities (percent)			sewage disposal (percent)			space[b]			construction industry (1994)						country
									percent of GDP	new residential[d]			new nonresidential[d]		
piped water	electricity	inside toilet or WC	closed public sewer or septic tank	open public sewer	other	average area (sq m)	rooms per dwelling unit	persons per room		total no. of dwellings	floor area ('000 sq m)	years to replace nat'l stock	number of units	floor area ('000 sq m)	
20.3	30.6	25.1	...	...	...	...	1.9	3.3	3.5[49]	...	...	...	...	...	Pakistan[104]
87.9	87.5	46.3	44.3	—55.7—		...	2.6	1.8	7.5[21]	85[14]	...	33.8	...	...	Palau
80.7	72.8	74.3[18]	44.2	—55.8—		...	2.8	1.6	4.2	7,110	...	73.7	517	...	Panama
50.0	56.0	40.0	...			...	...	...	4.0	...	...	...	...	...	Papua New Guinea
...	...	26.4				...	2.2[109]	2.4[109]	5.4	...	61[27]	...	2,715[13]	365[13]	Paraguay
46.7	54.9	35.7	40.0	22.2	37.8	42.4[20]	2.6[20]	2.0[20]	8.5	97,533[14]	...	45.4	...	1,546	Peru
38.8	55.1	35.0[18]	67.6	14.4	18.0	...	2.4	2.3[109]	5.5	263,729[14]	3,862[33]	43.2	6,425[33]	3,693[33]	Philippines
84.3	96.2[50]	68.9	67.0[50]	—33.0[50]—		55.6[54]	3.2	1.0	6.3	76,100	6,735	157.5	30,949	...	Poland
90.6	99.4	91.8	75.5[20]	—24.5[20]—		...	5.0[34]	0.8	7.5[1]	62,000	...	49.3	4,292[33]	1,772[21]	Portugal
95.6	97.4[49]	94.7	95.7	4.3		...	4.8[18]	0.8[18]	2.2[112]	10,212[21]	1,872[21]	82.8	900[27]	41.0[27]	Puerto Rico
...	93.2	...	—50.5—		49.5	...	4.9	1.3	4.9	12,240[33]	391[16]	58.9	1,416[33]	168[16]	Qatar
95.0	98.0	80.0	52.4[41]	—47.6[41]—		86.0	3.7	0.9	6.2[1]	7,627	...	24.2	...	...	Réunion
51.4	48.6[113]	44.9	12.2[113]	—87.8[113]—		...	2.6	1.4	6.0	36,700	2,683	208.0	...	...	Romania
68.4	...	63.7	...			...	...	...	7.7	611,000	39,200	85.3	...	...	Russia
...						...			2.8	435[54]	60[20]	...	63[54]	34[20]	Rwanda
46.3	57.5	33.5	31.8[46]	—68.2[46]—		...	3.0	1.1	11.9	171[14]	...	68.0	...	...	St. Kitts and Nevis
64.7	72.9	35.7	35.7	—64.3—		...	3.4	1.2	8.2	752[14]	...	44.0	61[21]	41[21]	St. Lucia
95.0[52]	...	...	22.0[52]	—78.0[52]—		...	2.8	1.8	12.4	...	...	...	...	...	St. Vincent and the Grenadines
80.7	37.7	71.0	16.6	—83.4—		...	...	...	1.8	132[27]	...	...	118[27]	...	Samoa
100.0	100.0	100.0	98.3[37]	—1.7[37]—		...	3.8	0.7	...	145[114]	...	58.7	123[114]	...	San Marino
22.3	22.0	9.2	9.8	—90.2—		...	2.2	1.8	13.8	225[14]	...	122.0	...	...	São Tomé and Príncipe
...	...	...	...			...	...	...	8.6[21]	...	16,078[9]	...	2,205[9]	...	Saudi Arabia
44.1	23.1	...	...			...	2.3	1.5	3.4	584[21]	338[21]	...	22[21]	18[21]	Senegal
77.0	75.8	95.0	33.1[53]	—66.9[53]—		...	4.1	1.1	9.4	...	...	...	...	...	Seychelles
15.9	8.3	7.3	13.1	66.2	20.7	...	...	...	2.2[25]	...	...	...	...	...	Sierra Leone
90.6[92]	98.3[18]	63.6[92]	63.6[92]	—36.4[92]—		...	1.8[92]	2.5[92]	7.1	42,702[14]	4,303[33]	17.4	1,991[9]	2,730[33]	Singapore
91.8	...	80.1	87.6	—12.4—		71.7	2.9	1.1	5.2	6,710	760	241.1	...	...	Slovakia
97.4[21]	99.5[21]	89.9	...			103.1[33]	3.0	1.0	4.6[18]	5,500	589	116.4	1,571[33]	520[33]	Slovenia
92.7[22]	79.6[22]	89.2	89.2[22]	—10.8[22]—		10.8[22]	2.3[22]	2.0[22]	5.4	...	...	...	...	...	Solomon Islands
...	...	...				...	...	...	3.8[9]	...	...	...	...	...	Somalia
66.4	55.9	54.9	...			...	3.4[92]	...	3.2	29,587	4,266	...	1,686	2,437	South Africa
98.7	99.2	97.1	87.9[18]	—12.1[18]—		86.6	4.4[92]	...	8.0	219,511	...	53.5	...	...	Spain
18.2	14.9	4.7	4.7	—95.3—		18.6[92]	2.5	2.1	7.3	59,637[16]	...	47.2[16]	...	...	Sri Lanka
29.4	9.9	70.2[2,113]	2.6[2,113]	—97.4[2,113]—		...	2.2[113]	2.5[113]	6.7	...	...	...	...	...	Sudan, The
62.9	82.0	40.4	19.6[116]	—80.4[116]—		...	2.1	1.9	3.7	...	355[27,46]	...	161[27]	...	Suriname
42.5	11.6	21.4	...			...	...	...	2.7	...	...	...	...	...	Swaziland
99.0[27]	96.2[18]	98.0	96.3[18]	—3.7[18]—		...	3.4	0.6	5.8	21,630	...	177.1	...	3,818[54]	Sweden
100.0[18]	...	93.3[18]	92.2[16]	—	7.8[18]	93.0	3.7	0.6	7.0	47,107	...	59.5	8,109[16]	...	Switzerland
40.2[52]	41.7[52]	...	36.0[52]	—64.0[52]—		93.0	3.0	2.0	4.1	24,297[21]	2,977[21]	33.0[13]	...	1,147[2]	Syria
79.4[18]	99.7[18]	94.2[18]	69.3[18]	...		30.5	4.1	1.2	5.3	...	47,533[15,33]	...	...	15	Taiwan
60[9,87]	...	...	50	—50—		51.4	...	...	16.1	...	400[33]	...	...	...	Tajikistan
37.2	6.3	...	...			...	2.5	1.9	4.7	...	...	...	...	...	Tanzania
29.7	89.7	40.9[23]	40.9[22]	9.8[22]	49.3[22]	...	1.6	2.7	7.5	...	16,343[9]	...	...	13,499[9]	Thailand
4.1[78]	10.3[78]	...	...	—100.0[78]—		...	1.8	3.4	3.0	...	...	...	...	...	Togo
61.3[22]	20.9[22]	42.3[22]	11.2[22]	—88.8[22]—		...	...	...	5.1[49]	...	...	...	...	...	Tonga
64.3[18]	83.3[18]	41.1[18]	41.0[18]	—59.0[18]—		...	3.3[18]	1.4[18]	7.5	1,012	208	14.9	38	48	Trinidad and Tobago
26.4	63.4	43.3	69.2[39]	—30.8[39]—		...	1.9	2.4	4.1	34,566[13]	...	43.8	...	...	Tunisia
68.0	56.8	70.6	42.0	52.0	6.0	...	2.4[27]	2.2[92]	6.8	245,449	19,693	54.4	4,533	17,336	Turkey
...	...	...	...			...	...	...	4.7	...	20,754[15,21]	...	...	15	Turkmenistan
65.4	7.4	37.3	...			...	...	...	13.9	...	...	...	...	...	Tuvalu
...	...	...	...			...	...	...	6.0[49]	...	...	...	65[109]	26.8[109]	Uganda
...	...	...	...			...	...	...	10.0[9]	...	14,454[9]	...	...	...	Ukraine
30.9[121]	24.2[121]	84.5	...			...	2.8	1.8	9.8	...	...	...	...	...	United Arab Emirates
...	...	99.8	...			...	5.0	0.5	5.4	182,438	...	120.0	...	...	United Kingdom[122]
86.8	96.9[1]	98.9[1]	99.8	—0.2—		156.7	5.5	0.5	5.8	1,284,000[33]	210,640	82.9	...	106,340	United States
89.3	84.7	73.3	...	92.0		...	3.4	1.7	5.3	...	274	...	84	70	Uruguay
...	...	...	...			...	...	...	7.2	...	7,000	...	...	...	Uzbekistan
39.2[39]	14.2	27.5[39]	...			...	...	...	5.6	574[14]	...	49.2	...	15.3[16]	Vanuatu
86.2	89.8	84.4[20]	80.2	—19.8—		...	4.2	1.3	4.9	91,666[16]	4,904[16]	29.5	678[16]	1,067[16]	Venezuela
...	...	...	...			...	...	...	6.8	298,073[14]	...	43.5	53[54]	59.3[54]	Vietnam
96.3[18]	98.1[18]	86.0[18]	93.6[18]	—6.4[18]—		...	4.3	0.6	...	574[14]	...	68.4	262[18]	...	Virgin Islands (U.S.)
75.2[7]	75.3	98.4	...			...	2.4[27]	2.7[27]	14.1[13]	5,740[9]	730[9]	20.8	...	175.8[9]	West Bank
78.5	95.3	...	...			...	4.5	1.2	4.4[39]	2,213[14]	...	20.8	...	...	Western Sahara
5.7[59]	4.6[59]	...	...			...	2.0[59]	2.8[59]	5.0[21]	...	1,988[27]	...	...	...	Yemen[123]
79.1	98.0	61.2	...			57.6[9]	2.8	1.3	7.8	17,442	...	179.1	40[33]	256	Yugoslavia
12.4[125]	27.5[78]	15.1[125]	...	...	82.3[125]	...	1.9[125]	2.6[125]	2.6	...	...	...	...	...	Zambia
39.1	28.2	37.0	...			...	2.8[125]	1.9[125]	2.2	...	...	...	...	...	Zimbabwe

[71]1976-81. [72]1974. [73]1969-78. [74]1979 and later. [75]1973. [76]1971. [77]1946-59. [78]1960. [79]Urban only. [80]1960 and earlier. [81]1947 and earlier. [82]1948-83. [83]1961-71. [84]Factory space only. [85]1944 and earlier. [86]1945-60. [87]Data refer to persons. [88]Data refer to families. [89]1960 and earlier. [90]1946 and earlier. [91]1947-60. [92]1970. [93]Peninsular Malaysia only. [94]1957 and earlier. [95]1958-67. [96]1994. [97]1960-68. [98]1969 and later. [99]1949-61. [100]1962-74. [101]Percentage of net material product. [102]Dwellings of indigenous population only. [103]1961. [104]Excludes Islāmābād, North-West Frontier, and federally administered tribal areas. [105]1947-65. [106]1966-75. [107]1976 and later. [108]Excludes areas under U.S. military control in the provinces of Colón and Panamá. [109]1972. [110]1945-70. [111]1971 and later. [112]Includes mining. [113]1966. [114]1995. [115]European-style dwellings only. [116]1964. [117]1955 and earlier. [118]1956-66. [119]1967 and later. [120]1956-65. [121]1968. [122]Excludes Northern Ireland. [123]Former Yemen Arab Republic only. [124]Total of 1986 and 1988 censuses. [125]1969. [126]Bantu dwellings only.

Household budgets and consumption

This table provides international data on household income, on the consumption expenditure of households for goods and services, and on the principal object of such expenditure (in most countries), food consumption (by kind). For purposes of this compilation, income comprises pretax monetary payments and payment in kind. The first part of the table provides data on distribution of income by households and by sources of income; the second part analyzes the largest portion of income use—consumption expenditure. Such expenditure is defined as the purchase of goods and services to satisfy current wants and needs. This definition excludes income expended on taxes, debts, savings and investments, and insurance policies. The third and last part of the table focuses on food, which usually, and often by a wide margin, represents the largest share of consumer spending worldwide. The data provided include daily available calories per capita and consumption of major food groups.

For both sources of income and consumption expenditure, the primary basis of analysis for most countries is the household, an economic unit that can be as small as a single person or as large as an extended family. For some of the countries that do not compile information by household, the table provides data on personal income and personal expenditure—i.e., the income and expenditure of all the individuals constituting a society's households. When no expenditure data at all is available, the table reports the weights of each major class of goods and services making up a given country's consumer (or retail) price index (CPI). The weighting of the components of the CPI usually reflects household spending patterns within the country or its principal urban or rural areas.

The data on distribution of income show, collectively for an entire country, the proportion of total income earned (occasionally, expended) by households constituting the lowest quintile and highest decile (poorest 20% and wealthiest 10%) within the country. These figures show the degree to which either group represents a disproportionate share of poverty or wealth.

The data on sources of income illuminate patterns of economic structure in the gaining of an income. They indicate, for example, that in poor, agrarian countries income often derives largely from self-employment (usually farming) or that in industrial countries, with well-developed systems of salaried employment and social welfare, income derives mainly from wages and salaries and secondarily from transfer payments (see note a). Because household sizes and numbers of income earners vary so greatly internationally, and because the frequency and methodology of household and CPI surveys do not permit single-year comparisons for more than a few countries at once, no summary of total household income or expenditure was possible. Instead, U.S. dollar figures are supplied for per capita private final consumption expenditure (for a single, recent year) that are more comparable internationally and refer to the same date. The figures on distribution of consumption expenditure by end use reveal patterns of personal and family use of disposable income and indicate, inter alia, that in developing countries, food may absorb 50% or more of disposable income, while in the larger household budgets of the developed countries, by contrast, food purchases may account for only 20–30% of spending. Each category of expenditure betrays similar complexities of local habit, necessity, and aspiration.

The reader should exercise caution when using these data to make intercountry comparisons. Most of the information comes from single-country surveys, which ofter differ markedly in their coverage of economically or demographically stratified groups, in sample design, or in the methods

Household budgets and consumption

country	income (latest)						consumption expenditure						
	percent received by		by source (percent)				per capita private final, U.S.$ 1995	by kind or end use (percent of household or personal budget; latest)					
	lowest 20% of households	highest 10% of households	wages, salaries	self-employment	transfer payments[a]	other[b]		food[c]	housing[d]	clothing[e]	health care	energy, water	education
Afghanistan	...	...	20.7	28.0	8.2	43.1	...	33.9	3.0	...	1.1	0.7	...
Albania	...	...	53.0	4.0	11.5	31.5	680	...	...	...	...	...	...
Algeria	6.9[1]	31.5[1]	43.1	38.3	18.6	1.8	810	52.3	6.7[2]	8.6	2.8	[2]	[3]
American Samoa	...	...	...	...	...	...	1,880[4]	32.9	20.4[5]	5.2	...	...	...
Andorra	...	...	...	...	...	...	...	...	...	...	...	...	...
Angola	...	...	...	...	...	...	370	74.1[6]	10.2[2,6]	5.5[6]	1.8[6]	[2,6]	2.7[6]
Antigua and Barbuda	...	...	...	...	...	...	4,050	42.9	23.3	7.5	...	5.5	...
Argentina	4.4	35.2	53.9	31.5	1.5	12.7	6,620	40.1	9.3	8.0	7.9	9.0	2.6
Armenia	...	...	24.5	13.6[7]	5.5	56.4	360	47.3	...	17.4	...	...	...
Aruba	...	...	...	...	...	...	11,190	26.9	9.9	8.4	2.9	8.5	1.9
Australia	3.8	28.0	72.7	7.5	13.0	6.8	12,040	18.7	18.5	5.6	7.1	2.2	1.6
Austria	4.0	28.7	55.7	[8]	24.4	19.9[8]	16,020	28.1	14.5	8.5	5.8	4.0	0.4
Azerbaijan	...	...	70.2	10.8[7]	19.0	—	460	42.2	—	13.6	4.8	—	
Bahamas, The	3.6	32.1	...	...	...	...	3,950[9]	13.8	32.8	5.9	4.4	...	5.3
Bahrain	...	...	...	...	...	...	2,240	32.4	21.2	5.9	2.3	2.2	2.3
Bangladesh	9.4[1]	23.7[1]	18.7	48.3	7.5	25.5	170[10]	63.3	8.8	5.9	1.1	8.4	1.2
Barbados	7.0	44.0[11]	...	...	...	...	4,860	45.8	16.8	5.1	3.8	5.2	[3]
Belarus	11.1[12]	19.4[12]	47.1	7.3[9]	45.6	—	610	29.0	2.7	...	...	...	...
Belgium	7.9[13]	21.5[13]	49.6	10.9	20.7	18.8	16,550	18.3	11.4	7.0	10.5	6.2	[3]
Belize	...	...	84.1	—15.9—			1,780	34.0	9.0	8.8	1.6	9.1	2.3
Benin	8.0	39.0	26.3	—73.7—			240	37.0	10.0	14.0	5.0	2.0	4.0
Bermuda	7.2	24.7	65.3	9.0	3.3	22.4	12,690[14]	14.6	27.7	4.9	7.6	3.3	3.8
Bhutan	...	...	...	...	...	...	170	72.3	...	21.2	...	3.7	...
Bolivia	5.6[12]	31.7[12]	53.2	12.0	18.2	16.6	690	46.6	7.8	5.1	2.1	4.7	0.3
Bosnia and Herzegovina	...	...	...	...	...	...	1,890[15]	44.7	1.6	8.3	3.4	7.8	[3]
Botswana	3.7	42.9	73.3	15.4	10.8	0.4	1,030	39.5[16]	11.8	5.6	2.3	2.5	4.9
Brazil	2.1[12]	51.3[12]	62.4	14.7	10.9	12.0	4,420	25.3	21.3[2]	12.9	9.1	[2]	[3]
Brunei	...	...	...	...	...	...	...	45.1	2.6	6.1	...	2.4	[3]
Bulgaria	8.3[12]	24.7[12]	34.7	23.6[7]	14.8	—	1,470	47.0	4.1	7.4	3.2	4.3	[3]
Burkina Faso	...	...	...	...	...	...	220	38.7[6]	5.1[6]	4.4[6]	5.2[6]	13.7[6]	[3]
Burundi	...	...	...	...	...	...	190	59.6[6]	4.4[6]	11.1[6]	...	5.8[6]	...
Cambodia	...	...	...	...	...	...	280	...	...	...	...	...	...
Cameroon	...	...	41.4	52.6	3.0	3.0	570	49.1	18.0[2]	7.6	8.6	[2]	...
Canada	5.7	24.1	57.0	13.7	20.7	8.6	11,460	13.4	24.5[2]	5.3	4.7	[2]	3.1
Cape Verde	...	...	...	...	...	...	920	60.0	8.5	2.5	0.5	4.9	[19]
Central African Republic	...	...	...	...	...	...	350	70.5[6]	0.6[6]	9.5[6]	1.0[6]	6.5[6]	...
Chad	8.0	30.0	...	...	...	...	170	45.3[6]	...	3.5[6]	11.9[6]	5.8[6]	...
Chile	3.5[12]	46.1[12]	—75.1—		12.0	12.9	2,940	27.9	15.2	22.5	...	...	...
China	5.5[13]	30.9[13]	21.6	72.2	—6.2—		260	49.9[16,20]	6.8[20]	13.7[20]	2.9[20]	...	2.3[20]
Colombia	3.6[12]	39.5[12]	45.1	35.4	14.2	5.3	1,540	45.0	7.8	4.5	6.4	2.2	1.7
Comoros	...	...	25.6	64.5	8.7	1.2	350	67.3	2.3	11.6	3.2	3.8	[3]
Congo, Dem. Rep. of the	...	...	...	...	...	...	190	61.7	11.5[2]	9.7	2.6	[2]	[3]
Congo, Rep. of the	7.0	43.5	...	...	...	...	870	37.0	6.0	6.0	6.0	3.0	8.0
Costa Rica	4.0[12]	34.1[12]	61.0	22.6	9.6	6.8	1,600	39.1	12.1[2]	9.4	3.7	[2]	[3]
Côte d'Ivoire	6.8[1]	28.5[1]	44.9	49.9	—5.2—		480	48.0	7.8	10.0	0.7	8.5	...
Croatia	...	...	40.2	40.8	12.1	6.9	3,790	37.8	2.9	8.6	4.3	7.6	[3]
Cuba	...	...	57.3	—42.7—			1,510[9]	26.7	...	...	...	2.5	...
Cyprus	7.9[20]	...	76.3	5.9	14.4	3.4	8,300	22.7	5.5	10.0	3.1	1.3	1.4
Czech Republic	10.5[12,21]	23.5[12,21]	—66.7—		27.6	5.7	2,620	26.7	5.5[2]	7.3	[22]	[2]	...
Denmark	3.5	25.6	63.3	14.6	25.9	-3.8	17,730	17.9	22.9	5.2	2.2	6.1	1.9
Djibouti	...	...	51.6	36.0	10.5	1.9	590	50.3	6.4	1.7	2.4	13.1	...
Dominica	...	...	...	...	...	...	2,110	43.1	16.1	6.5	...	5.4	...
Dominican Republic	4.2[12]	39.6[12]	41.7	31.8	1.5	25.0	1,150	46.0	10.0	3.0	8.0	5.0	3.0
Ecuador	5.4[1]	37.6[1]	17.4	76.9	3.6	2.1	1,040	36.1	9.0	10.1	4.2	3.3	[19]
Egypt	8.7[1]	26.7[1]	...	...	...	...	740	50.2	10.5[2]	10.9	2.7	[2]	[3]

employed for collection, classification, and tabulation of data. Further, the reference period of the data varies greatly; while a significant portion of the data is from 1980 or later, information for some countries dates from the 1970s. This older information is typeset in italic. Finally, intercountry comparisons of annual personal consumption expenditure may be misleading because of the distortions of price and purchasing power present when converting a national currency unit into U.S. dollars.

The table's food consumption data include total daily available calories per capita (food supply), which amounts to domestic production and imports minus exports, animal feed, and nonfood uses, and a percentage breakdown of the major food groups that make up food supply.

The data for daily available calories per capita provide a measure of the nutritional adequacy of each nation's food supply. The following list, based on estimates from the United Nations Food and Agriculture Organization (FAO), indicates the regional variation in recommended daily minimum nutritional requirements, which are defined by factors such as climatic ambience, physical activity, and average body weight: Africa (2,320 calories), formerly Centrally Planned Asia (2,300 calories), Far East (2,240 calories), Latin America (2,360 calories), Near East (2,440 calories).

The breakdown of diet by food groups describes the character of a nation's food supply. A typical breakdown for a low-income country might show a diet with heavy intake of vegetable foods, such as cereals, potatoes, or cassava. In the high-income countries, a relatively larger portion of total calories derives from animal products (meat, eggs, and milk). The reader should note that these data refer to total national *supply* and often do not reflect the differences that may exist within a single country.

In compiling this table, Britannica editors rely on both numerous national reports and principal secondary sources such as the World Bank's *World Development Report* (annual), the International Labour Organisation's *Sources and Methods: Labour Statistics vol. 1 Consumer Price Indices* (3rd ed.), the UN's *Yearbook of National Accounts Statistics* (annual) and *National Accounts Statistics: Compendium of Income Distribution Statistics,* and the FAO's *Food Balance Sheet 1995 and Compendium of Food Consumption Statistics from Household Surveys in Developing Countries* (2 vol.).

The following terms further define the column headings:
a. Includes pensions, family allowances, unemployment payments, remittances from abroad, and social security and related benefits.
b. Includes interest and dividends, rents and royalties, and all other income not reported under the three preceding categories.
c. Includes alcoholic and nonalcoholic beverages and meals away from home when identifiable. Excludes tobacco except as noted.
d. Rent, maintenance of dwellings, and taxes only; excludes energy and water (heat, light, power, and water) and household durables (furniture, appliances, utensils, and household operations), shown separately.
e. Includes footwear.
f. Furniture, appliances, and utensils; usually includes expenditure on household operation.
g. Includes expenditure on cultural activities other than education.
h. May include data not shown separately in preceding categories, including meals away from home (*see* note c).
i. Represents pure fats and oils only.
j. Consists mainly of peas, beans, and lentils; spices; stimulants; alcoholic beverages (when combined with "other"); sugars and honey; and nuts and oilseeds.

transportation, communications	household durable goods[f]	recreation[g]	personal effects, other[h]	daily available calories per capita	cereals	potatoes, cassava	meat, poultry	fish	eggs, milk	fruits, vegetables	fats, oils[i]	other[j]	country
													food consumption, 1995 — percent of total calories derived from:
...	...	...	61.3	...	...	...	...	...	...	...	...	...	Afghanistan
12.0	4.5	4.6[3]	8.5	2,324	38.6	1.8	8.7	—	22.9	5.8	10.2	11.9	Albania
17.8	5	1.1	22.6	3,042	59.3	1.5	3.0	0.3	5.1	3.8	16.9	10.3	Algeria
...	...	...	...	...	...	...	...	...	...	...	...	...	American Samoa
...	...	...	...	...	...	...	...	...	...	...	...	...	Andorra
3.9[6]	...	...	1.8[6]	1,927	28.1	35.3	3.6	1.2	1.7	3.3	10.8	15.9	Angola
10.0	...	...	10.8	2,406	26.7	1.0	14.5	4.4	11.0	7.2	16.0	19.2	Antigua and Barbuda
11.6	...	7.5	5.9	3,110	30.6	3.7	16.3	0.4	10.2	4.2	14.8	19.8	Argentina
...	6.6	...	28.7	...	...	...	...	...	...	...	...	...	Armenia
15.5	9.1	3.1	11.9	...	...	...	...	...	...	...	...	...	Aruba
15.1	7.0	7.5	16.7	3,068	24.6	3.0	15.3	1.0	14.2	5.5	11.9	24.4	Australia
16.3	7.8	7.1	7.5	3,417	22.2	3.3	13.4	0.7	12.0	6.0	20.7	21.6	Austria
5.1	6.5	0.7	27.1	...	...	...	...	...	...	...	...	...	Azerbaijan
14.8	8.9	4.9	9.2	2,498	29.0	1.5	17.5	1.7	7.3	7.9	9.6	25.5	Bahamas, The
8.5	9.8	6.4	9.0	...	...	...	...	...	...	...	...	...	Bahrain
0.9	...	...	10.4	2,017	82.4	1.4	0.8	0.8	1.4	1.1	5.8	6.2	Bangladesh
10.5	8.1	4.8[3]	—	3,207	28.1	4.2	13.7	1.8	6.3	4.6	13.7	27.5	Barbados
...	...	...	68.3	...	...	...	...	...	...	...	...	...	Belarus
13.4	10.6	6.8[3]	15.8	3,530	21.2	5.4	9.9	1.2	9.3	6.3	26.2	20.5	Belgium
13.7	8.0	...	9.4	2,791	31.2	1.6	8.2	0.4	8.8	7.5	11.1	31.2	Belize
14.0	5.0	...	9.0	2,405	35.1	37.2	2.3	0.8	0.9	2.8	5.4	15.6	Benin
7.3	16.6	10.8	3.4	3,050	27.0	1.8	13.9	2.0	7.6	10.3	14.7	22.8	Bermuda
...	0.7	...	2.1	...	...	...	...	...	...	...	...	...	Bhutan
17.7	9.7	2.7	3.3	2,192	44.4	7.0	10.4	0.1	3.1	7.5	9.9	17.5	Bolivia
6.0	4.1	3.5[3]	2.3	...	...	...	...	...	...	...	...	...	Bosnia and Herzegovina
13.1	13.8	3.1	3.4	2,153	52.9	1.6	5.9	0.6	8.1	2.6	7.5	20.9	Botswana
15.0	...	...	16.4	2,834	31.4	5.5	9.4	0.3	7.5	5.2	13.1	27.6	Brazil
17.2	8.3	8.9[3]	9.4	2,849	43.6	1.2	14.2	1.0	6.1	4.6	7.4	22.0	Brunei
6.6	4.0	3.0[3]	21.5[17]	2,907	40.3	1.9	9.0	0.1	9.6	6.3	15.6	17.2	Bulgaria
18.6[6]	3.0[6]	2.3[3, 6]	9.0[6]	2,250	75.6	0.7	2.4	0.1	1.4	1.0	4.1	14.7	Burkina Faso
...	6.0[6]	...	13.1[6, 18]	1,749	17.0	27.4	1.3	0.4	0.7	9.9	1.3	41.9	Burundi
...	...	...	...	2,012	81.2	1.7	4.2	0.8	0.6	2.9	3.9	4.6	Cambodia
13.0	...	2.4	1.3	2,214	42.4	16.0	3.3	0.7	1.4	13.7	7.9	14.5	Cameroon
14.3	8.8	8.0	17.9	3,093	22.1	3.5	11.5	1.1	9.7	6.7	19.8	25.6	Canada
8.8	6.9	19	7.9[19]	3,031	48.6	1.9	7.5	0.8	4.5	2.6	17.1	16.9	Cape Verde
4.1[6]	0.8[6]	1.3[6]	5.7[6]	1,885	21.3	31.5	6.3	0.4	1.5	6.5	16.1	16.4	Central African Republic
...	...	...	33.5[6]	1,913	54.0	12.1	2.7	0.6	2.5	1.9	6.2	20.0	Chad
6.4	...	...	28.0	2,769	39.4	3.6	11.8	2.0	7.0	6.0	10.8	19.3	Chile
4.7[20]	5.3[20]	2.4[20]	12.0[20]	2,741	57.6	5.5	13.6	0.8	2.4	4.9	6.3	8.9	China
18.5	5.7	...	8.2	2,758	32.5	7.4	6.8	0.3	7.7	7.6	10.8	26.9	Colombia
2.2	3.0	2.5[3]	4.1	1,850	44.3	15.4	1.9	3.0	1.1	8.3	9.4	16.6	Comoros
5.9	4.8	3.8[3]	—	1,879	16.6	55.3	1.9	0.5	0.1	7.8	6.7	11.2	Congo, Dem. Rep. of the
15.0	4.0	...	15.0	2,141	22.3	39.3	3.4	2.7	1.1	7.5	11.6	12.2	Congo, Rep. of the
11.6	10.9	4.4[3]	8.8	2,865	34.4	1.3	6.7	0.3	9.3	5.8	13.6	28.6	Costa Rica
12.2	3.4	...	9.4	2,517	41.5	26.1	2.0	1.0	0.8	10.0	7.4	11.3	Côte d'Ivoire
9.3	4.5	4.1[3]	1.5	2,413	30.2	7.0	5.9	0.2	12.0	6.8	12.8	24.9	Croatia
5.4	...	...	65.4	2,291	36.5	5.9	5.3	0.6	7.9	4.0	13.1	26.8	Cuba
15.6	10.5	6.3	23.6	3,708	24.1	2.1	20.6	0.8	12.5	6.4	15.3	18.2	Cyprus
3.1	4.5	0.8[22]	52.7	3,175	26.7	4.7	11.7	0.4	10.6	4.3	19.4	22.2	Czech Republic
15.5	6.1	8.3	13.9	3,704	21.7	3.2	22.5	2.1	9.1	3.8	15.4	22.2	Denmark
...	1.5	...	24.6	1,831	48.6	0.3	5.1	0.2	6.0	1.8	15.7	22.3	Djibouti
11.6	6.0	...	11.3	3,032	27.2	7.8	9.9	1.6	9.1	9.8	8.6	26.0	Dominica
4.0	8.0	...	13.0	2,323	31.4	3.2	7.3	0.7	6.4	10.2	16.0	24.8	Dominican Republic
12.8	5.5	19	19.0[19]	2,436	32.4	3.0	6.4	0.7	7.0	9.4	22.7	18.3	Ecuador
4.7	5.0	3.3[3]	12.7	3,327	66.3	1.6	2.4	0.4	1.8	6.2	7.7	13.7	Egypt

Household budgets and consumption (continued)

country	income (latest)						consumption expenditure						
	percent received by		by source (percent)				per capita private final, U.S.$ 1995	by kind or end use (percent of household or personal budget; latest)					
	lowest 20% of households	highest 10% of households	wages, salaries	self-employment	transfer payments[a]	other[b]		food[c]	housing[d]	clothing[e]	health care	energy, water	education
El Salvador	5.5[13]	29.5[13]	...	...	...	...	1,520	37.0[20]	12.1[20]	6.7[20]	4.2[20]	3.6[20]	3.7[20]
Equatorial Guinea	...	...	57.0[6]	42.0[6]	—	1.0[6]	310	62.0[6]	...	10.0[6]	6.0[6]	...	...
Eritrea[23]	...	...	...	...	...	...	170	...	...	...	...	...	...
Estonia	6.6[12]	31.3[12]	53.0	5.7	12.8	28.5	1,390	41.0	9.6	8.4	[22]	6.5	3.1
Ethiopia[23]	8.6[1]	27.5[1]	0.2	79.5	—	20.3	87	49.0	7.0	6.0	3.0	7.0	4.0
Faroe Islands	...	...	88.3	11.7	—	—	...	40.9	11.0	8.0	...	18.9	...
Fiji	3.7	37.8	81.5	9.1	...	9.4	1,430[11]	34.7	15.6[2]	9.3	2.4	[2]	[3]
Finland	3.7	26.9	70.3	7.4	9.7	12.6	13,260	22.5	16.9	5.0	4.8	4.6	[3]
France	5.6	26.1	51.1	14.1	27.5	7.3	15,810	17.4	16.2	6.1	9.8	3.8	0.7
French Guiana	...	...	74.6		—25.4—		...	30.0[16]	16.1[2]	6.7	4.4	[2]	[3]
French Polynesia	...	...	61.9	18.5	16.6	3.0	4,310[24]	39.6	9.7	6.3	1.0	8.1	1.0
Gabon	3.3	54.4	...	...	...	...	4,060	54.7[6,16,25]	13.0[6,25]	17.5[6,25]	1.9[6,25]	...	...
Gambia, The	...	...	...	...	...	...	330	58.0[26]	5.1[26]	17.5[26]	...	5.4[26]	...
Gaza Strip	...	...	...	...	...	...	910[27]	...	...	...	...	...	...
Georgia	...	...	34.5	21.6[7]	21.7	22.0	430	38.3	...	14.8	...	0.3	...
Germany	7.0[28]	24.4[28]	57.9	[8]	21.3	20.8[8]	16,850	19.0	16.9	7.9	3.5	4.1	[3]
Ghana	7.9[1]	27.3[1]	41.6[29]	47.1[29]	—	11.3[29]	290	57.4	11.5[2]	14.3	1.3	[2]	[3]
Gibraltar	...	...	...	...	...	...	...	39.1[16]	12.6	11.0	...	...	...
Greece	...	...	34.0	22.8	17.0	26.2	8,140	29.9	14.1	6.5	3.1	3.3	0.5
Greenland	...	...	...	...	...	...	11,110	30.1	10.0	7.7	0.3	5.4	...
Grenada	...	...	...	...	...	...	1,650	40.7[16]	11.9	5.2	[30]	3.9	[3]
Guadeloupe	...	...	78.9	13.7	7.4	—	4,080[27]	31.6[16]	11.3[2]	9.3	4.6	[2]	[3]
Guam	...	...	...	...	...	...	...	24.1	28.6	10.6	4.8	...	...
Guatemala	2.1[12]	46.6[12]	...	...	...	...	1,180	64.4	16.0[2]	3.1	0.6	[2]	0.3
Guernsey	...	...	...	...	...	...	...	23.7	12.1	7.5	...	8.2	...
Guinea	3.0[1]	31.7[1]	...	...	...	...	510	61.5	7.3[2]	7.9	11.1	[2]	...
Guinea-Bissau	2.1[1]	42.4[1]	...	...	...	...	230	...	...	...	...	...	...
Guyana	4.0	40.0[11]	73.0	...	6.3	20.7	...	42.5[16]	21.4	8.6	...	5.2	[3]
Haiti	...	...	...	...	...	...	320	51.1[16]	4.3	8.7	2.2	...	[3]
Honduras	3.8[12]	41.9[12]	58.3	[8]	1.8	39.9[8]	450	44.4	22.4[2]	9.1	7.0	[2]	[3]
Hong Kong	5.4[21]	31.3[21]	—55.0—		19.2	5.8	13,880	15.1	15.7[2]	21.3	5.0	[2]	0.5
Hungary	9.5[1]	22.6[1]	73.1	2.7	10.2	14.0	4,270	38.1	5.7	7.4	1.5	6.1	0.7
Iceland	4.7	27.3					15,850	31.3	16.0	7.5	2.3	2.9	1.3
India	8.5[1]	28.4[1]	42.2	39.7	—18.1—		210	52.2	6.1[31]	10.0	2.4	4.7[31]	1.8
Indonesia	8.7[1]	25.6[1]	42.1	41.5	2.5	13.9	640	47.5[20]	20.1[2,20]	5.5[20]	...	...	...
Iran	3.8	41.7	37.4[20]	30.5[20]	—32.1[20]—		1,040	42.6[16]	24.9[2]	11.8	3.9	[2]	[3]
Iraq	2.1	...	23.9	33.9	23.0	18.6	1,710[14]	50.2	19.9[2]	10.6	1.6	[2]	[3]
Ireland	4.6	26.5	58.6	13.3	19.9	8.2	9,650	30.5	7.1	7.4	3.2	6.1	2.4
Isle of Man	6.4	26.6	64.1	6.6	16.9	12.4	...	31.0	7.9	7.0	...	11.0	...
Israel	8.4	23.1	63.4[20,25]	14.6[20,25]	18.9[20,25]	3.1[20,25]	9,930	23.8	19.8	5.3	6.2	2.4	2.9
Italy	6.8	25.3	41.7	25.9	20.3	12.1	11,860	19.5	10.0	9.8	6.7	3.8	0.7
Jamaica	5.8[1]	31.9[1]	63.6	13.9	14.0	8.5	1,770	35.7	5.7	4.6	2.8	4.9	0.2
Japan	10.9	31.6[1]	59.3	11.1	19.5	10.1	24,670	22.6	6.7	6.0	2.7	5.6	5.3
Jersey	...	...	...	...	...	...	...	28.3	14.9	8.3	...	6.5	...
Jordan	5.9[1]	34.7[1]	51.4	11.1	13.7	23.8	1,020	40.6	15.8	6.7	2.2	5.0	3.5
Kazakstan	7.5[12]	24.9[12]	67.7	5.8[7]	16.9	9.6	1,290	29.6	2.6	...	...	...	...
Kenya	3.4	47.7	...	...	...	...	220	46.5	10.0	7.7	2.2	2.6	1.0
Kiribati	...	...	69.7	21.4	6.0	2.9	370[4]	50.0[16]	7.5[2,5]	8.0	...	[2]	...
Korea, North	...	...	...	...	...	...	...	46.5[32]	0.6[32]	29.9[32]	...	3.3[32]	...
Korea, South	7.4	27.6	53.8	25.1	13.1	8.0	5,390	29.7	4.1	7.7	5.0	4.0	14.2
Kuwait	...	...	53.8	20.8	—25.4—		...	28.1[16]	15.5	8.1	0.7	9.6	[3]
Kyrgyzstan	3.0	57.0[11]	67.3		—32.7—		670	33.5	2.2	...	...	...	...
Laos	9.6[1]	26.4[1]	...	...	...	...	140[9]	...	...	...	...	...	...
Latvia	9.6[12]	22.1[12]	67.0	5.4[7]	17.4	10.2	2,400	51.6	...	...	...	...	...
Lebanon	5.0	45.0	27.9	...	3.0	69.1	3,010	42.8[6]	16.8[6]	8.6[6]	7.2[6]	4.5[6]	3.9[6]
Lesotho	2.8[1]	43.4[1]	22.4	27.8	44.7	5.1	530	48.0[20]	10.1	16.4	...	...	...
Liberia	5.0	73.0[11]	...	...	...	...	330[9]	34.4[6]	14.9[6]	13.8[6]	...	5.0[6]	...
Libya	10.1	...	...	...	...	...	2,330[9]	37.2[16]	32.2[2]	6.9	3.3	[2]	[3]
Liechtenstein	...	...	92.9[33]	7.1[33]	...	...	...	21.3[16]	18.0	6.6	7.7	4.4	[3]
Lithuania	8.1[12]	28.0[12]	66.4	9.7	18.7	5.2	1,910	50.3	...	...	...	...	...
Luxembourg	10.0	34.0[11]	67.1	4.8	28.1	...	15,140[34]	12.8	13.7	5.9	7.3	6.1	[3]
Macau	...	...	65.0	18.1	7.0	9.9	5,480	39.2[16]	17.5	6.8	4.0	5.2	[3]
Macedonia	...	...	57.7	17.2	16.2	9.0	1,010	40.6	1.9	7.8	3.0	7.8	[3]
Madagascar	5.8[1]	34.9[1]	58.8[6,35]	14.1[6,35]	—	27.1[6,35]	220	59.0	6.0	6.0	2.0	6.0	4.0
Malawi	10.4	40.1	83.3	6.0	—	11.7	109	30.0	4.0	9.0	4.0	5.0	10.0
Malaysia	4.6[12]	37.9[12]	...	...	...	...	2,090	28.7	10.2[2]	4.3	2.5	[2]	0.6
Maldives	...	...	...	...	...	...	270[9]	57.4	1.6	8.0	2.5	...	...
Mali	...	...	...	...	...	...	200	57.0	2.0	6.0	2.0	6.0	4.0
Malta	...	...	63.8	19.3	—	16.9	5,380	31.2	3.5	7.6	3.5	2.0	0.4
Marshall Islands	...	...	...	...	...	...	...	57.7	15.6[2,5]	12.0	...	[2]	...
Martinique	...	...	80.0	...	...	20.0	4,840[6]	32.1[16]	10.6[2]	8.0	5.2	[2]	[3]
Mauritania	3.6[1]	30.4[1]	...	...	...	...	470	73.1	2.5	8.1	0.9	7.7	0.4
Mauritius	4.0	46.7	51.7	29.0	11.2	8.1	2,290	41.9	8.8	8.4	3.0	6.4	2.9
Mayotte	...	...	...	...	...	...	...	42.2	...	31.5	...	6.8	...
Mexico	4.1[1]	39.2[1]	61.5	29.1	7.8	1.6	2,110	36.6[16]	13.3[2]	8.4	3.4	[2]	[3]
Micronesia	...	...	51.8	23.0	2.1	23.1	...	73.5	...	...	...	...	...
Moldova	6.9[12]	25.8[12]	41.2	10.4	15.3	33.1	220	...	...	...	...	...	...
Monaco	...	...	...	...	...	...	...	...	...	...	...	...	...
Mongolia	...	...	72.1	9.5[7]	9.7	8.7	230	39.1	5.9[2]	23.4	0.5	[2]	2.9
Morocco	6.6[1]	30.5[1]	...	...	...	...	900	38.0	7.0	11.0	5.0	2.0	8.0
Mozambique	...	...	51.6	—48.4—			57	74.6	11.7	3.7	0.8	...	[3]
Myanmar (Burma)	8.0	40.0[11]	...	...	...	...	750[34]	49.1[6]	10.4[6]	15.3[6]	2.4[6]	4.0[6]	5.9[6]
Namibia	...	...	67.1	27.5	5.4	...	1,050	...	...	...	...	...	...
Nauru	...	...	...	...	...	...	...	...	...	...	...	...	...
Nepal	7.6[1]	29.8[1]	25.1	63.4	—11.5—		170	61.2	17.3	11.7	3.7	...	[3]

transpor-tation, com-munications	household durable goods[f]	recrea-tion[g]	personal effects, other[h]	food consumption, 1995									country
				daily available calories per capita	percent of total calories derived from:								
					cereals	potatoes, cassava	meat, poultry	fish	eggs, milk	fruits, vegeta-bles	fats, oils[i]	other[j]	
10.2[20]	5.7[20]	4.3[20]	12.5[20]	2,577	55.9	2.0	2.7	0.2	6.0	3.2	7.7	22.4	El Salvador
...	...	...	22.0[6]	...									Equatorial Guinea
...	...	...	...	...									Eritrea[23]
9.2	2.3	5.0[22]	15.0	...									Estonia
8.0	2.0	...	14.0	...									Ethiopia[23]
...	6.6	...	14.6										Faroe Islands
13.8	9.3	4.3[3]	10.6	3,078	38.1	5.6	8.8	2.0	3.9	1.7	17.2	22.7	Fiji
14.8	6.3	9.5[3]	15.6	3,022	21.2	4.3	16.4	2.1	16.1	4.1	14.2	21.4	Finland
16.1	7.7	6.9	15.3	3,588	23.7	3.6	15.9	1.1	12.7	5.3	19.4	18.2	France
17.5	7.9	6.2[3]	11.2	2,818	32.4	7.9	13.2	2.1	7.5	7.0	10.5	19.3	French Guiana
16.4	4.4	4.0	9.5	2,906	33.6	4.6	14.2	2.6	6.7	3.8	13.2	21.3	French Polynesia
6.3[6,25]	...	...	6.6[6,25]	2,511	26.0	20.3	8.2	2.7	2.1	16.3	7.6	16.8	Gabon
...	...	...	14.0[26]	2,157	53.5	0.8	1.4	1.6	1.5	1.3	13.0	26.9	Gambia, The
...	...	...	...	...									Gaza Strip
...	5.9	...	40.7	...									Georgia
17.8	9.4	10.6[3]	10.8	3,265	20.9	4.2	11.3	0.9	10.4	5.7	22.1	24.5	Germany
3.3	3.8	3.9[3]	4.5	2,622	28.4	45.6	1.4	1.9	0.2	8.9	5.6	8.0	Ghana
13.3	10.0	...	14.0	...									Gibraltar
17.5	6.9	5.2	13.0	3,561	29.0	4.2	8.7	1.1	10.8	9.1	20.4	16.7	Greece
8.0	9.2	15.5	13.8	...									Greenland
9.1	13.7	4.6[3]	10.9[30]	2,713	27.9	2.4	7.6	3.1	9.7	8.1	13.3	28.0	Grenada
20.5	9.3	4.7[3]	8.7	2,732	37.8	2.6	10.8	2.6	8.5	8.4	13.1	16.1	Guadeloupe
18.0	...	5.1	8.8	...									Guam
7.0	5.0	0.9	2.7	2,300	60.3	0.4	2.8	0.1	3.8	2.6	5.2	24.9	Guatemala
15.7	8.3	...	24.7	...									Guernsey
5.1	2.9	4.1	0.1	2,161	46.7	13.3	0.9	0.6	1.1	13.1	13.9	10.3	Guinea
...	...	...	...	2,433	63.2	6.2	4.5	0.4	1.4	3.7	14.7	5.8	Guinea-Bissau
4.8	2.9	6.4[3]	8.2	2,460	50.1	4.6	4.4	3.0	4.7	4.4	4.5	24.4	Guyana
7.6	9.2	5.3[3]	11.6	...									Haiti
3.0	8.3	2.4[3]	3.1	2,359	48.5	0.3	2.7	—	6.8	6.7	12.5	22.5	Honduras
8.4	17.5	8.1	8.4	3,285	31.1	1.6	20.3	3.0	5.2	4.7	17.9	16.2	Hong Kong
15.2	8.8	5.9	10.6	3,302	27.0	3.4	10.5	0.2	8.6	4.0	23.1	23.0	Hungary
14.5	7.6	9.6	7.0	3,159	24.1	3.0	14.4	6.1	13.9	4.0	10.4	24.3	Iceland
10.6	3.1	1.8	5.7	2,388	62.1	1.8	0.9	0.3	4.6	3.7	8.2	18.6	India
...	2.9[20]	...	24.0	2,732	63.7	6.2	2.3	1.2	0.7	2.5	8.4	15.0	Indonesia
5.0	6.4	1.7[3]	3.7	2,955	59.2	2.6	3.5	0.3	3.4	8.0	11.2	11.8	Iran
6.5	6.7	0.8[3]	3.7	2,268	51.2	1.4	1.6	0.1	1.6	8.6	27.4	8.1	Iraq
14.0	7.2	8.9	13.1	3,638	27.3	6.0	12.8	0.9	12.1	3.7	16.2	21.1	Ireland
14.9	5.7	...	22.5	...									Isle of Man
12.9	10.8	4.3	11.6	3,271	34.2	2.3	8.3	0.9	8.7	9.0	16.8	19.7	Israel
13.2	9.5	8.4	18.4	3,458	33.0	2.0	11.6	1.1	8.6	7.0	20.9	15.8	Italy
12.4	5.5	2.1	26.1	2,647	32.8	11.0	6.4	1.2	5.8	6.6	9.7	26.5	Jamaica
11.0	3.7	9.5	26.9	2,887	40.0	2.4	6.2	6.3	6.6	4.6	11.0	22.9	Japan
13.9	7.1	...	21.0	...									Jersey
11.2	6.1	4.0	4.9	2,734	47.0	1.5	5.4	0.3	4.6	5.5	16.1	19.6	Jordan
...	...	...	67.8	...									Kazakstan
8.4	9.4	3.1	9.1	1,991	52.9	7.7	3.8	0.5	7.0	3.1	9.3	15.6	Kenya
8.0	5	...	26.5	2,772	36.2	8.5	5.3	5.1	1.3	4.8	7.9	30.9	Kiribati
...	3.8[32]	—	15.9	2,360	62.1	5.4	3.7	3.3	1.2	6.2	5.7	12.4	Korea, North
11.3	5.0	— 19.0 —		3,268	47.6	0.9	8.6	2.8	2.0	6.7	10.3	21.1	Korea, South
13.7	11.2	5.2[3]	7.9	3,160	35.6	1.3	11.0	0.5	10.5	7.7	13.8	19.7	Kuwait
...	...	...	64.3	...									Kyrgyzstan
...	...	...	...	2,117	75.6	4.2	3.5	0.6	1.7	2.3	2.1	9.9	Laos
...	...	...	54.8	...									Latvia
5.4[6]	2.6[6]	1.9[6]	6.3[6]	3,270	34.6	3.6	4.6	—	5.8	14.2	15.7	21.3	Lebanon
4.7	11.9	...	8.8	1,972	73.2	4.8	4.4	0.4	1.4	1.6	3.7	10.5	Lesotho
...	6.1[6]	...	25.8[6]	...									Liberia
9.4	4.6	8.5[3]	2.5	3,126	47.8	1.5	4.0	0.3	4.6	5.5	23.2	13.1	Libya
13.3	5.8	16.3[3]	6.6	...									Liechtenstein
...	...	...	49.7	...									Lithuania
19.1	10.8	4.2[3]	20.1	3,530	21.2	5.4	9.9	1.2	9.3	6.3	26.2	20.5	Luxembourg
8.2	3.0	8.8[3]	7.3	3,094	37.7	0.6	14.8	2.0	4.6	4.8	17.7	17.8	Macau
6.5	4.2	3.3[3]	1.8	2,340	44.1	3.3	8.6	0.2	6.0	7.8	9.8	20.2	Macedonia
4.0	1.0	...	12.0	2,009	55.8	20.9	5.2	0.6	2.9	3.5	3.9	7.2	Madagascar
10.0	3.0	...	25.0	2,038	68.4	4.3	1.3	0.6	0.6	4.9	3.4	16.5	Malawi
20.9	7.7	11.0	14.1	2,807	40.3	2.4	9.6	1.5	6.2	3.8	13.1	23.1	Malaysia
2.6	17.0	5.9[3]	5.0	2,485	41.3	3.5	1.8	10.9	4.2	5.7	5.7	26.9	Maldives
10.0	1.0	...	12.0	2,149	76.1	0.3	3.8	0.6	4.1	0.8	7.4	7.0	Mali
16.4	9.9	7.1	18.4	3,387	29.0	3.7	8.9	1.2	11.0	7.9	13.7	24.5	Malta
...	5	...	14.7	...									Marshall Islands
20.7	9.4	5.4[3]	8.6	2,865	30.0	4.2	12.1	2.9	8.5	11.0	8.7	22.5	Martinique
2.0	1.2	4.0	0.1	2,592	53.6	0.4	4.2	0.9	11.1	2.4	11.9	15.4	Mauritania
10.0	6.4	—	12.2	2,943	45.8	1.3	4.6	2.0	7.6	2.5	16.7	19.5	Mauritius
5.1	8.8	...	5.6	...									Mayotte
10.0	11.8	5.5[3]	11.0	3,136	46.2	0.8	7.5	0.6	5.9	4.1	11.0	23.9	Mexico
...	...	...	26.5	...									Micronesia
...	...	...	...	...									Moldova
...	...	...	...	...									Monaco
3.5	8.0	0.4	16.2	1,897	46.4	1.2	26.3	0.1	9.0	0.5	5.9	10.6	Mongolia
8.0	5.0	...	16.0	3,157	62.6	1.2	2.7	0.5	2.0	4.3	12.3	14.4	Morocco
...	...	1.4[3]	7.9	1,678	41.8	35.6	1.7	0.2	0.7	1.5	9.7	8.8	Mozambique
3.8[6]	0.5[6]	1.1[6]	7.5[6]	2,752	77.6	0.4	1.8	0.9	1.1	2.3	8.9	7.2	Myanmar (Burma)
...	...	...	...	2,107	48.6	13.9	5.6	0.6	3.4	1.9	5.1	20.9	Namibia
...	...	...	...	...									Nauru
1.2	...	2.9[3]	2.0	2,367	77.9	2.9	1.4	—	3.2	2.6	5.5	6.5	Nepal

Household budgets and consumption   (continued)

country	income (latest)						consumption expenditure						
	percent received by		by source (percent)				per capita private final, U.S.$ 1995	by kind or end use (percent of household or personal budget; latest)					
	lowest 20% of households	highest 10% of households	wages, salaries	self-employment	transfer payments[a]	other[b]		food[c]	housing[d]	clothing[e]	health care	energy, water	education
Netherlands, The	8.2	21.9	48.2	10.7	29.1	12.0	15,290	13.6	14.9	7.1	12.9	3.1	0.7
Netherlands Antilles	...	...	...	...	...	...	6,050[10]	24.4[36]	10.4[36]	8.7[36]	2.2[36]	8.3[36]	1.2[36]
New Caledonia	...	...	68.2	18.1	13.7	...	5,410[37]	25.9	23.3[2,5]	3.5	3.2	[2]	...
New Zealand	5.1[21]	28.7[21]	65.8	9.8	15.2	9.1	10,300	20.0	19.4	4.4	2.9	3.2	1.5
Nicaragua	4.2[1,38]	39.8[1,11]	...	...	...	...	360	...	...	...	...	...	...
Niger	7.5[1]	29.3[1]	...	...	...	...	210	50.5	19.1[5]	7.3	...	...	...
Nigeria	4.0[1]	31.3[1,11]	30.2[20]	46.3[20]	0.9[20]	22.6[20]	350[39]	48.0	3.0	5.0	3.0	1.0	4.0
Northern Mariana Islands	...	...	...	...	...	...	...	49.2[16]	19.5[2,5]	9.1	[22]	[2]	...
Norway	2.6	26.6	58.8	9.9	24.2	7.1	16,570	23.5	13.7	7.0	5.4	6.2	0.6
Oman	...	...	...	...	...	...	3,000	40.6	24.6	5.1	2.4	3.2	[3]
Pakistan	8.4[1]	25.2[1]	22.0	56.0	22.0		300	37.0	11.0	6.0	1.0	5.0	1.0
Palau	...	...	63.7	7.4	18.5	10.4	...	...	...	...	...	...	...
Panama	2.0[12]	42.2[12]	60.8[6]	12.8[6]	13.2[6]	13.2[6]	1,570	34.9	12.6[2]	5.1	3.5	[2]	[3]
Papua New Guinea	...	...	57.3	[8]	1.1	41.6[8]	1,140	40.9	12.5[5]	6.2	...	4.9	...
Paraguay	6.0	46.0[11]	33.9	[8]	2.5	63.6[8]	1,590	48.7	16.4	9.7	3.4	—	1.5
Peru	4.9[1]	34.3[1]	31.2	65.1	3.7	...	1,820	44.1[16]	6.8[2]	10.1	2.7	[2]	[3]
Philippines	6.5[1]	32.1[1]	45.7	42.5	3.4	8.4	800	56.8	4.1[2]	3.9	...	[2]	[3]
Poland	9.3[1]	22.1[1]	34.0	4.3	20.7	41.0	1,940	41.2	2.8	10.9	8.1	1.0	[3]
Portugal	5.2	33.4	46.4	[8]	21.8	31.8[8]	6,860	34.8	2.0	10.3	4.5	3.0	1.4
Puerto Rico	3.2	34.7	56.3	6.4	29.5	7.8	5,640[10]	20.6	11.8[2]	7.4	11.6	[2]	3.1
Qatar	...	...	80.8	5.6	...	13.6	3,600[4]	24.5	35.1[5]	9.1	1.0	1.9	4.3
Réunion	3.1[21]	51.4[21]	68.9	[8]	16.0	15.1[8]	4,820[37]	22.4	11.8	7.9	2.2	2.2	[3]
Romania	9.2[12]	20.2[12]	62.6		37.4		1,570	51.1	16.4[2,5]	15.7	1.2	[2]	[3]
Russia	3.7[1]	38.7[1]	68.5	6.4	15.7	12.1	1,180	34.8	2.7	22.3	...	...	...
Rwanda	9.7[1]	24.2[1]	10.4[38]	47.7[38]	13.9[38]	28.0[8]	130	32.1[38]	13.1[38]	9.4[38]	1.3[38]	1.2[38]	[38]
St. Kitts and Nevis	...	...	...	...	...	...	2,480[34]	55.6[16]	7.6	7.5	...	6.6	...
St. Lucia	...	...	...	...	...	...	...	49.6[16]	13.5	6.5	2.3	4.5	[3]
St. Vincent and the Grenadines	...	...	...	...	...	...	1,700	59.8	6.3	7.7	...	6.2	...
Samoa	...	...	49.4	22.8	...	27.8	710[1]	58.8	5.1[5]	4.2	...	5.0	...
San Marino	...	...	...	...	...	...	...	22.1	20.9[2]	8.0	2.6	[2]	[3]
São Tomé and Príncipe	...	...	...	...	...	...	270	...	...	...	...	...	...
Saudi Arabia	...	...	...	...	48.4[6]		2,980	52.2[20,40]	17.2[20,40]	6.6[20,40]	2.1[20,40]	1.8[20,40]	1.1[20,40]
Senegal	3.5[1]	42.8[1]	51.6[6]		48.4[6]		380	49.0	7.0	11.0	2.0	4.0	6.0
Seychelles	4.1	35.6	77.2	3.8	3.2	15.8	3,410[39]	53.9	13.6	4.2	0.4	9.1	...
Sierra Leone	5.6	37.8	27.9	61.6	10.5		190	63.8	5.8[2]	7.3	4.5	[2]	[3]
Singapore	5.1	33.5	81.2	16.8	2.0		11,710	18.7	10.2[2]	7.1	4.6	[2]	1.4
Slovakia	11.9[12]	18.2[11,12]	76.7	[8]	8.7	14.4[8]	1,580	26.8	7.6[2]	8.9	...	[2]	[3]
Slovenia	9.5[12]	23.8[12]	52.4	13.0	23.4	11.2	5,460	30.8	18.3	8.5	5.0	7.3	[3]
Solomon Islands	...	...	74.1	25.9			820[4]	46.8	21.9[2,5]	5.7	[22]	[2]	...
Somalia	...	...	...	...	...	...	171	62.3[6,16]	15.3[6]	5.6[6]	...	4.3[6]	...
South Africa	3.3[1]	47.3[1,11]	73.6	[8]	4.9	21.5[8]	1,970	29.3	12.6[2]	7.5	4.5	[2]	1.4
Spain	8.3[13]	21.8[13]	48.5	27.5	19.5	4.5	8,840	21.6[16]	12.6[2]	8.6	4.7	[2]	[3]
Sri Lanka	8.9[1]	25.2[1]	48.5	[8]	9.7	41.8[8]	520	48.0	1.9	10.1	1.8	3.3	0.8
Sudan, The	4.0	34.6	...	...	...	...	1,050[41]	63.6	11.5	5.3	4.1	3.8	[3]
Suriname	9.3	...	74.6	...	3.2	22.2	5,960[10]	39.9[6]	4.4[6]	11.0[6]	3.6[6]	6.9[6]	2.6[6]
Swaziland	2.8	54.5	44.4	22.2	12.2	21.2	500	33.5[16]	13.4[2]	6.0	1.8	[2]	[3]
Sweden	5.3	18.6	58.9	9.7	25.8	5.6	13,680	21.3	19.9	8.6	3.2	4.9	0.1
Switzerland	6.0[42]	27.0[42]	63.6	[8]	16.5	19.9[8]	26,060	27.0[16]	13.1	4.4	9.9	7.7	[3]
Syria	6.0	...	40.7	...	25.1	34.2	2,210	58.8[16]	16.0[2]	7.5	...	[2]	[3]
Taiwan	7.1	25.5	64.5	19.7	4.5	11.3	12,230	26.8	22.5	5.6	7.8	3.0	5.6
Tajikistan	...	...	64.3	5.6[9]	30.1	—	340	65.3	...	...	...	...	...
Tanzania	6.9[1]	30.2[1]	28.1	34.2	3.5	34.2	150	66.7	8.3	9.9	1.3	7.6	...
Thailand	5.6[1]	37.1[1]	36.4	45.0	0.9	17.7	1,540	29.0	6.3	11.6	8.0	1.7	0.5
Togo	8.0	30.5	...	...	...	...	210	42.5[6]	13.4[2,6]	11.5[6]	5.0[6]	[2,6]	[3,6]
Tonga	...	...	...	...	...	...	...	49.3	10.5	5.6	0.3	2.7	...
Trinidad and Tobago	2.6	33.6	...	...	...	...	2,050	25.5[16]	21.6	10.4	[19]	...	1.5
Tunisia	5.9[1]	30.7[1]	...	...	...	...	1,260	39.0	10.7	6.0	3.0	5.1	1.8
Turkey	11.9	39.0[11]	24.1	51.4	10.8	13.7	1,940	38.5	22.8[2]	9.0	2.6	[2]	1.4
Turkmenistan	6.7[12]	26.9[12]	56.6	26.0[7]	14.4	3.0	570[10]	...	...	...	...	...	...
Tuvalu	...	...	17.9	76.1		6.0	...	45.5	11.5[5]	7.5	...	...	...
Uganda	6.8[1]	33.4[1]	...	...	...	...	260	57.1[6,16]	...	5.5[6]	...	7.3[6]	...
Ukraine	9.5[12]	20.8[12]	66.4	9.3	13.4	10.9	490	41.3	1.7	...	...	...	...
United Arab Emirates	...	...	...	...	...	...	7,940	24.1	23.7	9.1	1.1	1.2	3.9
United Kingdom	4.6[13]	27.8[13]	66.2	9.8	13.9	11.0	12,020	17.1	21.7	6.0	...	4.6	...
United States	4.2	28.5[11]	64.4	9.0	19.3	7.3	18,840	15.4	14.9	6.9	17.0	3.5	2.2
Uruguay	6.0[13,18]	29.3[13,18]	53.5	17.0	29.5		4,140	39.9	17.6[2]	7.0	9.3	[2]	1.3
Uzbekistan	...	...	59.8	18.5	21.7	...	950	...	...	...	...	...	...
Vanuatu	...	...	59.0	33.7	7.3		680	30.5[16]	29.0[2,5]	4.7	[22]	[2]	...
Venezuela	3.6[12]	42.7[12]	...	...	...	...	2,490	30.4	11.5	10.6	2.9	3.0	0.8
Vietnam	7.8[1]	29.0[1,11]	17.2	64.6	17.6	0.5	280	62.4	2.5	5.0	...	...	2.9
Virgin Islands (U.S.)	...	...	65.7	2.6	13.0	12.7	...	25.3[43]	24.9[43]	5.4[43]	...	6.5[43]	...
West Bank	...	...	...	...	...	...	1,380[27]	...	...	...	...	...	...
Western Sahara	...	...	...	...	...	...	...	...	...	...	...	...	...
Yemen	...	...	...	...	...	...	310	61.0[44]	13.2[44]	...	1.1[44]	6.1[44]	...
Yugoslavia	5.3[12,45]	27.4[12,45]	41.7	15.8	12.7	29.8	2,480[41]	51.6	1.4	7.4	5.2	8.4	[3]
Zambia	3.9[1]	31.3[1]	79.9	17.8	1.3	1.0	220	36.0	7.0	10.0	8.0	4.0	14.0
Zimbabwe	4.0[1]	46.9[1]	92.0	1.0	...	7.0	580	30.1[16]	6.5	10.3	7.1	8.9	6.0

[1]Data refer to expenditure by fractiles of persons. [2]Housing includes energy, water. [3]Recreation includes education. [4]1988. [5]Housing includes household durable goods. [6]Capital city only. [7]Agricultural self-employment only. [8]Other includes self-employment. [9]1989. [10]1993. [11]Highest 20%. [12]Data refer to income shares by fractiles of persons. [13]Based on posttax income. [14]1985. [15]1990. [16]Includes tobacco. [17]1988–90. [18]Includes wage taxes. [19]Personal effects, other includes education and recreation. [20]Urban areas only. [21]Based on posttax per capita income. [22]Recreation includes health care. [23]Ethiopia includes Eritrea, except consumption expenditure. [24]1984. [25]Wage-earners only. [26]Low-income population in Banjul and Kombo St. Mary

| transportation, communications | household durable goods[f] | recreation[g] | personal effects, other[h] | food consumption, 1995 | | | | | | | | | country |
| | | | | daily available calories per capita | percent of total calories derived from: | | | | | | | | |
					cereals	potatoes, cassava	meat, poultry	fish	eggs, milk	fruits, vegetables	fats, oils[i]	other[j]	
13.3	7.1	9.7	17.6	3,230	16.7	5.0	13.4	1.2	14.5	6.5	17.8	25.0	Netherlands, The
19.5[36]	10.0[36]	4.2[36]	10.1[36]	2,759	31.6	4.2	15.5	1.5	9.1	5.4	13.2	19.6	Netherlands Antilles
16.1	[5]	6.7	21.3	2,867	35.5	5.9	11.3	1.3	9.6	3.8	15.8	16.8	New Caledonia
17.1	10.9	——— 20.6 ———		3,379	23.2	3.0	15.9	0.8	10.5	6.9	14.6	25.0	New Zealand
...	...	...	...	2,311	50.7	1.5	2.6	0.1	4.3	2.4	11.3	27.0	Nicaragua
...	[5]	...	23.1	2,136	71.0	3.6	2.5	—	2.2	1.6	4.6	14.3	Niger
3.0	6.0	...	27.0	2,508	42.1	24.3	1.8	0.4	0.6	4.5	13.6	12.6	Nigeria
8.3	[5]	13.9[22]	—	...	...	...	...	...	...	...	...	...	Northern Mariana Islands
12.8	6.9	8.8	15.1	3,274	27.2	4.5	11.1	3.5	12.6	5.2	17.1	18.7	Norway
8.9	7.1	4.1[3]	4.0	...	...	...	...	...	...	...	...	...	Oman
13.0	5.0	...	21.0	2,475	55.2	0.8	2.7	0.2	8.0	2.9	15.6	14.7	Pakistan
...	...	...	...	...	...	...	...	...	...	...	...	...	Palau
15.1	8.4	11.7[3]	8.7	2,490	41.7	1.8	6.8	1.1	8.0	5.7	14.5	20.4	Panama
13.0	[5]	...	22.5	2,323	29.1	26.6	6.6	2.2	0.7	17.3	7.7	9.8	Papua New Guinea
4.5	6.2	2.3	7.3	2,560	26.5	15.5	13.2	0.3	6.2	4.7	11.0	22.6	Paraguay
7.3	7.5	7.6[3]	13.9	2,277	40.1	9.0	5.5	1.5	4.5	6.8	11.7	20.9	Peru
5.0	12.8	...	17.3	2,395	51.4	4.1	8.2	3.2	2.0	6.6	6.9	17.6	Philippines
8.9	8.3	15.0[3]	3.8	3,307	35.6	7.7	10.6	0.8	9.0	4.1	15.6	16.7	Poland
15.4	8.6	4.4	15.6	3,639	28.3	7.6	10.1	2.4	7.6	6.5	18.2	19.2	Portugal
11.8	11.2	7.9	14.7	...	...	...	...	...	...	...	...	...	Puerto Rico
13.0	[5]	——— 11.1 ———		...	...	...	...	...	...	...	...	...	Qatar
24.9	6.0	10.1[3]	12.5	3,308	41.4	1.7	11.9	1.5	5.2	5.0	9.8	23.5	Réunion
6.6	[5]	4.5[3]	4.5	3,166	49.1	4.1	7.0	0.2	11.2	4.8	9.7	13.8	Romania
...	9.4	...	30.8	2,926	42.2	7.6	9.3	1.3	9.2	3.2	10.5	16.6	Russia
1.7[38]	5.3[38]	0.4[38]	35.5[38]	...	...	...	...	...	...	...	...	...	Rwanda
4.3	9.4	...	9.0	2,234	27.7	2.4	11.2	3.5	7.9	3.4	14.7	29.2	St. Kitts and Nevis
6.3	5.8	3.2[3]	8.3	2,801	33.3	5.4	15.4	1.5	8.2	9.0	5.8	21.5	St. Lucia
3.7	6.6	...	9.7	2,427	34.4	8.0	10.1	1.3	4.6	5.1	8.1	28.5	St. Vincent and the Grenadines
9.0	[5]	...	17.9	...	...	...	...	...	...	...	...	...	Samoa
17.6	7.2	7.1[3]	14.5	...	...	...	...	...	...	...	...	...	San Marino
...	...	...	...	2,156	40.4	8.3	1.8	1.6	0.8	8.0	11.6	27.4	São Tomé and Príncipe
4.5[20, 40]	5.9[20, 40]	...	8.6[20, 40]	2,746	50.7	1.6	7.3	0.4	4.1	10.6	12.4	12.8	Saudi Arabia
5.0	2.0	...	12.0	2,416	55.2	1.0	3.6	2.1	2.3	1.1	16.8	17.8	Senegal
6.4	6.6	1.4	4.4	2,428	39.9	1.1	5.1	4.9	5.7	5.1	13.2	25.1	Seychelles
4.4	3.9	3.8[3]	4.8	2,029	53.5	8.9	1.1	1.8	0.7	3.2	18.1	12.8	Sierra Leone
13.8	8.9	13.1	23.3	...	...	...	...	...	...	...	...	...	Singapore
...	3.9	...	26.2	2,892	30.9	5.9	8.4	—	9.2	4.1	16.1	25.2	Slovakia
12.7	3.3	6.1[3]	8.0	3,396	32.2	7.8	11.8	0.3	10.0	5.0	17.5	15.4	Slovenia
9.9	[5]	[22]	15.7	2,131	35.9	34.4	3.2	2.2	0.7	2.7	3.2	17.8	Solomon Islands
...	...	...	12.1[6]	...	...	...	...	...	...	...	...	...	Somalia
16.7	10.0	6.3	11.7	2,890	54.3	1.9	7.1	0.5	3.8	2.3	12.8	17.3	South Africa
15.3	7.1	7.0[3]	23.1	3,338	22.8	5.5	13.4	2.1	9.4	6.6	22.1	18.2	Spain
17.0	3.9	2.4	10.8	2,334	58.7	2.0	0.9	1.4	2.8	4.2	1.8	28.3	Sri Lanka
1.5	5.5	0.7[3]	4.0	2,313	58.5	0.6	4.5	0.1	12.6	2.8	7.7	13.1	Sudan, The
9.5[6]	12.3[6]	5.8[6]	4.0[6]	2,556	51.1	2.3	5.2	1.4	5.9	7.2	7.9	19.0	Suriname
8.8	12.8	3.3[3]	20.4	2,658	47.0	1.2	5.8	—	3.8	2.4	5.6	34.3	Swaziland
15.7	6.6	10.9	8.8	3,117	23.9	3.8	9.3	2.4	15.1	4.7	20.6	20.1	Sweden
12.9	5.1	9.8[3]	10.1	3,220	22.0	3.0	15.5	0.8	12.8	5.6	18.0	22.4	Switzerland
2.4	5.8	2.1[3]	7.4	3,296	55.7	1.2	3.1	—	5.3	5.3	13.2	16.1	Syria
10.7	2.2	1.1[3]	4.7	...	...	...	...	...	...	...	...	...	Taiwan
...	...	...	34.7	...	...	...	...	...	...	...	...	...	Tajikistan
4.1	1.4	0.7	—	2,024	49.4	20.1	2.6	1.0	2.2	5.0	6.1	13.6	Tanzania
12.9	10.9	4.2	14.9	2,296	51.0	1.0	4.6	2.1	2.6	6.1	6.5	26.1	Thailand
9.5[6]	4.4[6]	5.1[3, 6]	8.6[6]	1,754	42.7	31.1	3.1	1.0	0.9	2.1	10.8	8.4	Togo
5.8	10.6	0.5	14.7	...	...	...	...	...	...	...	...	...	Tonga
15.2	14.3	[19]	6.2[19]	2,566	37.3	2.7	5.0	0.6	6.6	3.8	14.8	29.3	Trinidad and Tobago
9.0	11.2	7.1	7.1	3,187	50.3	1.7	2.9	0.5	4.9	6.0	19.4	14.4	Tunisia
8.8	9.0	5.6	2.3	3,593	49.5	3.3	2.4	0.4	7.4	8.2	13.8	14.9	Turkey
...	...	...	...	...	...	...	...	...	...	...	...	...	Turkmenistan
10.5	[5]	...	25.0	...	...	...	...	...	...	...	...	...	Tuvalu
5.9[6]	...	...	24.2[6]	2,268	21.0	22.0	3.1	0.8	1.8	24.2	2.9	24.3	Uganda
...	6.8	6.3[3]	43.9	...	...	...	...	...	...	...	...	...	Ukraine
14.1	11.6	4.7	6.5	3,361	34.1	1.6	12.0	1.0	9.3	14.1	10.6	17.5	United Arab Emirates
15.1	8.0	15.9	11.6	3,149	22.6	6.3	14.1	1.0	11.6	5.0	19.0	20.5	United Kingdom
13.9	1.5	5.8	18.9	3,603	23.5	2.8	12.0	0.8	11.6	5.2	18.4	25.6	United States
10.4	6.3	3.1	5.1	2,826	28.5	3.2	22.6	0.4	14.4	3.5	10.3	17.1	Uruguay
...	...	...	...	...	...	...	...	...	...	...	...	...	Uzbekistan
13.2	[5]	12.3[22]	10.3	2,542	17.9	28.0	9.5	1.5	1.8	7.0	12.2	22.0	Vanuatu
7.1	4.5	2.7	26.4	2,442	37.6	2.8	7.9	1.3	6.5	7.4	15.3	21.3	Venezuela
...	4.6	...	22.6	2,463	73.1	5.0	6.5	1.0	0.6	4.0	2.8	6.9	Vietnam
11.7[43]	4.3[43]	...	21.9[43]	...	...	...	...	...	...	...	...	...	Virgin Islands (U.S.)
...	...	...	...	...	...	...	...	...	...	...	...	...	West Bank
...	...	...	...	...	...	...	...	...	...	...	...	...	Western Sahara
1.9[44]	3.0[44]	...	13.7[44]	2,025	66.7	1.1	3.0	0.6	1.7	3.4	10.2	13.2	Yemen
5.7	1.6	2.4[3]	16.3	3,134	35.8	2.4	11.1	0.1	10.2	4.9	19.4	16.0	Yugoslavia
5.0	1.0	...	15.0	1,931	66.7	10.4	2.8	0.8	1.3	1.7	3.4	12.9	Zambia
1.1	12.9	0.6	16.5	1,965	58.9	2.2	1.8	0.2	2.3	1.1	11.9	21.5	Zimbabwe

only.   [27]1986.   [28]Former West Germany only.   [29]Urban areas of Eastern region only.   [30]Personal effects, other includes health care.   [31]Housing includes water.   [32]Workers and clerical workers only.   [33]Earned income only.   [34]1992.   [35]Malagasy households only.   [36]Curaçao only.   [37]1987.   [38]Rural areas only.   [39]1994.   [40]Middle-income population only.   [41]1991.   [42]Excludes transfer payments and property income.   [43]St. Thomas only.   [44]Data refer to former Yemen Arab Republic.   [45]Data refer to former Socialist Federal Republic of Yugoslavia.

Health services

The provision of health services in most countries is both a principal determinant of the quality of life and a large and growing sector of the national economy. This table summarizes the basic indicators of health personnel; hospitals, by kind and utilization; mortality rates that are most indicative of general health services; external controls on health (adequacy of food supply and availability of safe drinking water); and sources and amounts of expenditure on health care. Each datum refers more or less directly to the availability or use of a particular health service in a country, and, while each may be a representative measure at a national level, each may also conceal considerable differences in availability of the particular service to different segments of a population or regions of a country. In the United States, for example, the availability of physicians ranges from about one per 730 persons in the least well-served states to one per 260 in the best-served, with a rate of one per 150 in the national capital. In addition, even when trained personnel exist and facilities have been created, limited financial resources at the national or local level may leave facilities underserved; or lack of good transportation may prevent those most in need from reaching a clinic or hospital that could help them.

Definitions and limits of data have been made as consistent as possible in the compilation of this table. For example, despite wide variation worldwide in the nature of the qualifying or certifying process that permits an individual to represent himself as a physician, organizations such as the World Health Organization (WHO) try to maintain more specific international standards for training and qualification. International statistics presented here for "physicians" refer to persons qualified according to WHO standards and exclude traditional health practitioners, whatever the local custom with regard to the designation "doctor." Statistics for health personnel in this table uniformly include all those actually working in the health service field, whether in the actual provision of services or in teaching, administration, research, or other tasks. One group of practitioners for whom this type of guideline works less well is that of midwives, whose training and qualifications vary enormously from country to country but who must be included, as they represent, after nurses, perhaps the largest and most important category of health auxiliary worldwide. The statistics here refer to those midwives working in some kind of institutional setting (a hospital, clinic, community health-care centre, or the like) and exclude rural noninstitutional midwives and traditional birth attendants.

Hospitals also differ considerably worldwide in terms of staffing and services. In this tabulation, the term hospital refers generally to a permanent facility offering inpatient services and/or nursing care and staffed by at least one physician. Establishments offering only outpatient or custodial care are excluded. These statistics are broken down into data for general hospitals (those providing care in more than one specialty), specialized facilities (with care in only one specialty), local medical centres, and rural health-care centres; the last two generally refer to institutions that provide a more limited range of medical or nursing care, often less than full-time. Hospital data are further analyzed into three categories of administrative classification: public, private nonprofit, and private for profit. Statistics on number of beds refer to beds that are maintained and staffed on a full-time basis for a succession of inpatients to whom care is provided.

Data on hospital utilization refer to institutions defined as above. Admission and discharge, the two principal points at which statistics are normally collected, are the basis for the data on the amount and distribution of care by kind of facility. The data on numbers of patients exclude babies born during a maternal confinement but include persons who die before being discharged. The bed-occupancy and average length-of-stay statistics depend on the concept of a "patient-day," which is the annual total of daily censuses of inpatients. The bed-occupancy rate is the ratio of total patient-days to potential days based on the number of beds; the average length-of-stay rate is the ratio of total patient-days to total admissions.

Health services

country	health personnel							hospitals		kinds (%)				ownership (%)			hospital beds per 10,000 pop.
	year	physicians	dentists	nurses	pharmacists	midwives	population per physician	year	number	general	specialized	medical centres	rural	government	private nonprofit	private for profit	
Afghanistan	1991	2,233	267	1,451	510	388	6,701	1988–93	...	...	...	...	...	...	...	...	3
Albania	1990	4,467	1,099	6,801[1]	772[2]	9,936[2]	729	1989	895	— 17.9 —		— 82.1 —		100.0	—	—	57
Algeria	1994	25,796	7,763	...	3,425	...	1,066	1990[3]	181	...	...	...	...	...	...	...	19[4]
American Samoa	1991	26	7[6]	140[6]	2[6]	1[6]	1,885	1990	1	100.0	...	—	—	100.0	—	—	27
Andorra	1994	132	...	...	...	...	491	1992	1	100.0	...	—	—	100.0	—	—	18[7]
Angola	1990	662	10	9,334	...	...	15,136	1990	58	...	...	...	...	...	...	...	12
Antigua and Barbuda	1992	59	13	179	13	...	1,083	1991	2	50.0	50.0	—	—	100.0	—	—	58[1]
Argentina	1992	88,800	21,900[10]	18,000[6]	...	...	376	1992	...	...	...	...	...	...	...	...	44
Armenia	1995	19,000[11]	[11]	34,900[4,12]	...	[12]	198[11]	1994	183	...	...	...	...	100.0	—	—	82
Aruba	1992	74	19	515	13	3	936	1992	2	50.0	—	50.0	—	100.0	—	—	44
Australia	1995–96	45,800	9,100	160,500	12,900	...	400	1990	1,071[8]	...	...	...	...	65.5[8]	— 34.5[8] —		89[7,13]
Austria	1995	27,869	3,687	...	2,068[14]	1,030	289	1995	330	37.6	62.4	—	—	...	...	...	93
Azerbaijan	1995	29,300[11]	[11]	70,100[4,12]	...	[12]	256[11]	1994	787	...	...	...	...	100.0	—	—	96
Bahamas, The	1992	373	58	1,067	52[15]	...	709	1995	5	60.0	20.0	20.0	—	60.0	— 40.0 —		40
Bahrain	1993	482	40	1,608	101	...	1,115	1991	12	58.3	42.7	—	—	75.0	16.7	8.3	28[7]
Bangladesh	1994	24,911	812	9,630	7,485[15]	7,713	4,759	1994	919	69.5	— 30.5 —			...	...	...	3
Barbados	1992	312	38	889	138	377	842	1992	10	70.0	30.0	—	—	80.0	—	20.0	75
Belarus	1995	45,000[11]	[11]	117,000[12]	...	[12]	222[11]	1995	880	...	...	...	...	100.0	—	—	122
Belgium	1996	38,363	6,983	...	13,926	...	264	1993	363	80.4	19.6	—	—	38.6	61.4	—	76
Belize	1995	139	12[7]	300[7]	177	233[7]	1,546	1993	7	...	...	...	...	100.0	—	—	29
Benin	1993	363	16[6]	1,236	86[6]	453[6]	14,216	1993	...	...	...	...	...	...	...	...	2
Bermuda	1995	100	22	553	27	...	609	1995	2	50.0	50.0	—	—	...	...	...	43
Bhutan	1994	100	9[15]	233[15]	5[15]	70[15]	8,000	1996	27	...	...	...	...	...	...	...	12[4]
Bolivia	1993	3,392	1,643[1]	1,869	...	...	2,083	1995	336	10.7	8.9	23.5	56.8	...	...	...	107
Bosnia and Herzegovina	1996	4,500	550	11,900	...	...	703	1989	...	...	...	...	...	...	...	...	46
Botswana	1994	339	...	3,329	...	...	4,395	1994	30	53.3	3.3	43.3	—	...	...	...	23
Brazil	1993	222,658	160,000	...	57,047[1]	...	681	1993	6,372	— 100.0 —				...	...	...	34
Brunei	1995	251	38	1,288	15	278	1,164	1995	10	90.0	—	—	10.0	90.0	— 10.0 —		33
Bulgaria	1996	29,529	5,467	51,269	1,736	6,576	283	1996	289	— 79.2 —		20.8	—	...	...	...	103
Burkina Faso	1991[16]	341	19	2,627	113	339	27,158	1993	78	— 14.1 —		85.9	—	100.0	—	—	5[10]
Burundi	1993	354	9[15]	1,270	55[15]	...	17,153	1993	...	...	...	...	...	100.0	—	—	7
Cambodia	1993	5,642	36[1]	9,950	262[1]	3,235	11,650	1988[3]	188	...	...	...	...	100.0	—	—	16
Cameroon	1989	945	55	6,053	206	...	11,848	1988	629	— 27.0 —		— 73.0 —		72.3	— 27.7 —		27
Canada	1995	63,700[13]	14,621[10]	262,288[10]	22,112[15]	...	465[13]	1989	1,079	81.8	16.6	1.6	—	95.8	—	4.2	54[4]
Cape Verde	1988	112	...	205	9	...	2,931	1987	75	6.7	...	93.3	—	100.0	—	—	15
Central African Republic	1992	157	8[15]	1,353[15]	22[15]	166[15]	18,660	1988	133	— 21.1 —		— 78.9 —		79.7	— 20.3 —		15
Chad	1993	217	5[6]	878	10	130	27,765	1993	...	...	...	...	...	...	...	...	7
Chile	1994	16,000	5,200[7]	5,653[7]	230[7,16]	1,924[7,16]	875	1994	198	...	...	...	...	89.4	— 10.6 —		31
China	1995	1,918,000[11,17]	[11]	1,125,000	418,000	49,000	633[17]	1995	67,807	15.5	6.3	— 78.2 —		100.0	—	—	24
Colombia	1992	36,551	13,815	46,376	...	...	914	1989	947	...	...	...	...	...	...	...	14
Comoros	1993	77	6[15]	155[15]	6[15]	86[15]	6,600	1989	...	...	...	...	...	...	...	...	25
Congo, Dem. Rep. of the	1990	2,469	41	27,601	59	...	15,584	1986	400	...	...	...	...	52.5	— 47.5 —		21
Congo, Rep. of the	1990	613	35	1,624	175	498	4,028	1990	...	...	...	...	...	...	...	...	33
Costa Rica	1996	4,422	1,332	2,600	1,254	...	763	1996	33	...	...	...	...	87.9	—	12.1	18
Côte d'Ivoire	1990	2,020	219	3,691	135	1,533	5,931	1989	...	...	...	...	...	...	...	...	8
Croatia	1994	9,138	1,798	...	1,598	...	524	1994	84	38.1	61.9	—	—	...	...	...	59
Cuba	1992	46,860	8,057	73,943	...	...	231	1992	244	...	...	...	...	100.0	—	—	65[7]
Cyprus[18]	1993	1,455	498	2,536	423	120	433	1993[19]	110	39.1	58.2	—	2.7	10.0	0.9	89.1	52
Czech Republic	1995	32,195	6,267	...	4,032	...	321	1995	299	69.2	30.8	—	—	72.6	— 27.4 —		89
Denmark	1994	14,497	5,088	63,841	...	1,038	358	1992	163	42.9	57.1	—	—	42.9	57.1	—	35

Bed-occupancy rates may exceed 100% because stays of partial days are counted as full days.

Two measures that give health planners and policy makers an excellent indication of the level of ordinary health care are those for mortality of children under age five and for maternal mortality. The former reflects the probability of a newborn infant dying before age five. The latter refers to deaths attributable to delivery or complications of pregnancy, childbirth, the puerperium (the period immediately following birth), or abortion. A principal source for the former data was WHO's *The World Health Report* (annual) and for the latter, the UN Development Programme's *Human Development Report* (annual).

Levels of nutrition and access to safe drinking water are two of the most basic limitations imposed by the physical environment in which health-care activities take place. The nutritional data are based on reported levels of food supply (whether or not actually consumed), referred to the recommendations of the United Nations' Food and Agriculture Organization for the necessary daily intake (in calories) for a moderately active person of average size in a climate of a particular kind (fewer calories are needed in a hot climate) to remain in average *good* health. Excess intake in the many developed countries ranges to more than 40% above the minimum required to maintain health (the excess usually being construed to diminish, rather than raise, health). The range of deficiency is less dramatic numerically but far more critical to the countries in which deficiencies are chronic, because the deficiencies lead to overall poor health (raising health service needs and costs), to decreased productivity in nearly every area of national economic life, and to the loss of social and economic potential through early mortality. By "safe" water is meant only water that has no substantial quantities of chemical or biological pollutants—*i.e.*, quantities sufficient to cause "immediate" health problems. Data refer to the proportion of persons having "reasonable access" to an "adequate" supply of water within a "convenient" distance of the person's dwelling, as these concepts are interpreted locally.

The data on health care expenditure were excerpted from a joint effort by the WHO and the World Bank to create better analytical tools by which the interrelations among health policy, health care delivery systems, and human health might be examined against the more general frameworks of government operations, resource allocation, and development process. First published in the World Bank's *World Development Report 1993: Investing in Health* and, the following year, in the World Health Organization's *Global Comparative Assessments in the Health Sector* (edited by C.J.L. Murray and A.D. Lopez), the database and underlying methodology are expected to provide a continuing basis for international comparisons and policy analysis. The first two of ten volumes of the final results appeared in 1996 as *The Global Burden of Disease* and *Global Health Statistics* by the same editors.

Expenditures were tabulated for direct preventative and curative activities and for public health and public education programs having direct impact on health status—family planning, nutrition, and health education—but not more indirect programs like environmental, waste removal, or relief activities. Public, parastatal (semipublic, *e.g.*, social security institutions), international aid, and household expenditure reports and surveys were utilized to build up a comprehensive picture of national, regional, and world patterns of health care expenditures and investment that could not have been assembled from any single type of source. For reasons of space, public and parastatal are combined as the former.

Internet resources for further information:
● Most Recent Values of W.H.O. Global Health-For-All Indicators (for personnel and general indicators)
http://www.who.ch/programmes/hst/hsp/a/country.htm
No comparable source exists for hospitals.

admissions or discharges					bed occu-pancy rate (%)	aver-age length of stay (days)	mortality		popu-lation with access to safe water 1994–95 (%)	food supply (% of FAO require-ment) 1995	total health expenditures, 1990					country
rate per 10,000 pop.	by kinds of hospital (%)						under age 5 per 1,000 live newborn 1996	maternal mortality per 100,000 live births 1990			as percent of GDP	per capita (U.S.$)	by source (percent)			
	general	special-ized	medical centres	rural									public	private	inter-national aid	
...	...	...	...	...	...	...	248	...	10	...	...	...	...	...	...	Afghanistan
...	...	...	...	...	...	...	38	65	...	96	4.00	26	84.0	16.0	—	Albania
400	...	...	...	...	49.3	5	54	160	78[5]	127	6.95	149	76.9	23.0	0.1	Algeria
965	100.0	—	—	—	38.4	4	...	...	...	...	...	...	...	...	...	American Samoa
...	...	...	...	...	...	...	...	...	...	...	...	...	...	...	...	Andorra
238	...	...	...	...	44.5[8]	16[8]	179	1,500	32	82	...	...	...	...	...	Angola
63[8]	...	...	...	...	49.9[8]	7[8]	22[9]	...	95	102	4.55	241	59.1	37.3	3.6	Antigua and Barbuda
520[3]	...	...	...	...	51.9[3]	8[3]	25	100	64	132	4.21	137	60.1	39.7	0.2	Argentina
...	...	...	...	...	...	...	23	50	...	...	4.17	152	59.8	40.2	—	Armenia
...	...	...	...	...	92.2	...	...	...	...	...	...	...	...	...	...	Aruba
...	...	...	...	...	...	14[7]	8	9	95	115	7.67	1,294	69.6	30.4	...	Australia
2,710	...	...	...	...	79.4	10	8	10	100[5]	130	8.38	1,711	66.4	33.6	—	Austria
...	...	...	...	...	...	...	37	22	...	...	4.27	99	61.2	38.8	...	Azerbaijan
822[3, 10]	...	...	...	...	83.7[3, 10]	8[3, 10]	24	...	97[5]	103	...	...	...	...	...	Bahamas, The
...	...	...	...	...	...	...	23	...	100[5]	...	4.62	324	63.0	36.9	0.1	Bahrain
853[2]	...	...	...	...	...	...	144	850	83	87	3.19	6	24.8	56.7	18.5	Bangladesh
810	93.5	6.5	—	—	88.3	32	15	...	100[5]	133	5.04	323	64.3	33.8	1.9	Barbados
...	...	...	...	...	...	...	19	37	...	...	3.19	157	68.7	31.3	—	Belarus
1,963	96.0	4.0	—	—	84.4	12	7	10	100[5]	134	7.50	1,449	82.5	17.5	—	Belgium
...	...	...	...	...	...	...	37	...	82	123	5.88	23	48.4	41.0	10.7	Belize
...	...	...	...	...	...	...	158	990	70	105	4.32	19	26.3	36.4	37.3	Benin
1,370	97.0	3.0	—	—	73.9	9	...	...	...	121	...	...	...	...	...	Bermuda
...	...	...	...	...	...	...	145	1,600	21	...	5.05	10	41.1	30.4	28.5	Bhutan
252[10]	...	...	...	...	45.9[10]	5[10]	88	650	60	92	4.01	25	39.9	39.6	20.5	Bolivia
529[8]	...	...	...	...	82.4[8]	11[8]	20	...	...	...	...	...	...	...	...	Bosnia and Herzegovina
...	...	...	...	...	93.1[6]	...	57	250	70	93	6.19	139	61.8	21.6	16.5	Botswana
970	...	...	...	...	...	7[4]	69	220	92	119	4.20	146	65.7	33.9	0.4	Brazil
...	...	...	...	...	...	...	13	...	90[5]	127	...	...	...	...	...	Brunei
...	...	...	...	...	...	...	18	27	99[5]	116	5.36	121	81.4	18.6	—	Bulgaria
...	...	...	...	...	...	...	186	930	78[5]	95	8.46	7	9.8	17.9	72.3	Burkina Faso
...	...	...	...	...	...	...	143	1,300	58	75	3.28	30	42.4	48.3	9.3	Burundi
...	...	...	...	...	...	...	137	900	13	91	...	...	...	...	...	Cambodia
...	...	...	...	...	...	...	109	550	41	95	2.62	27	26.4	61.7	11.9	Cameroon
...	...	...	...	14	...	...	8	6	100	116	9.05	1,945	74.1	25.9	—	Canada
...	...	...	...	...	...	...	60	...	51[5]	129	6.32	64	20.7	25.5	53.7	Cape Verde
...	...	...	...	...	...	...	149	700	18[5]	83	4.19	18	26.5	37.5	36.0	Central African Republic
...	...	...	...	...	...	...	172	1,500	29	80	6.22	12	27.6	24.7	47.7	Chad
749[3]	...	...	...	...	69.9[3]	7[3]	17	65	96	113	4.73	100	70.1	29.1	0.7	Chile
418	— 60.4 —		— 39.6 —		66.9	15	43	95	46	116	3.51	11	58.5	40.9	0.6	China
614	41.4	16.7	— 41.9 —		57.2	6	40	100	96	119	3.98	51	44.0	54.4	1.6	Colombia
...	...	...	...	...	...	...	111	...	48[5]	79	5.40	28	46.3	29.2	24.5	Comoros
...	...	...	...	...	...	...	131	870	25	85	2.38	5	8.5	64.8	26.7	Congo, Dem. Rep. of the
...	...	...	...	...	...	...	133	890	60	96	3.99	50	47.1	40.7	12.1	Congo, Rep. of the
958[10]	...	...	...	...	78.2[10]	6[10]	14	60	100	128	6.51	132	73.6	25.2	1.2	Costa Rica
...	...	...	...	...	...	...	137	810	82	109	3.35	28	48.7	47.9	3.4	Côte d'Ivoire
1,278	81.9	18.1	—	—	81.6	14	16	...	96	95	...	...	...	...	...	Croatia
1,376[10]	...	...	...	...	...	...	13	95	94	99	...	...	...	...	...	Cuba
747[3]	...	...	...	...	75.7[3]	7[3]	9	...	100[5]	150	3.96	64	62.9	26.8	10.3	Cyprus[18]
2,035	96.5	3.5	—	—	79.0	13	10	15	100[5]	129	5.94[20]	169[20]	84.9[20]	15.1[20]	...	Czech Republic
1,253	92.9	7.1	—	—	80.4	8	8	9	100	138	6.30	1,588	84.2	15.8	—	Denmark

Health services (continued)

country	health personnel							hospitals		kinds (%)				ownership (%)			hospital beds per 10,000 pop.
	year	physicians	dentists	nurses	pharmacists	midwives	population per physician	year	number	general	specialized	medical centres	rural	government	private non-profit	private for profit	
Djibouti	1989	97	10	...	14	...	5,258	1993	8	—25.0—		—75.0—		100.0	...	...	27[6]
Dominica	1994	23	6	265	27	...	3,200	1994	53	1.9	—	—	98.1	100.0	...	—	25
Dominican Republic	1992	11,130	1,898	6,035	115[4]	...	671	1992[3]	723	—7.9—		—92.1—		...	...	...	12[4]
Ecuador	1993	12,149	1,524	4,215[1]	906	667[1]	904	1992	429	16.1	6.1	—77.8—		...	...	...	16
Egypt	1996	129,000	15,150[1]	...	34,700[1]	...	472	1991	6,418	5.1		—94.9—		...	...	...	19[4]
El Salvador	1993	4,525	1,182	5,094	...	1,940[10]	1,219	1993	78	...	...	...	...	61.5	1.3	37.2	17
Equatorial Guinea	1990	99	...	154	...	55	3,532	1988	...	...	...	...	...	...	...	...	29
Eritrea	1993	68	...	488	...	33	46,200	1993	10	...	...	...	...	...	...	...	9
Estonia	1994	4,680	820	7,302	930[10]	710	319	1994	107	...	...	...	...	96.3	—3.7—		84
Ethiopia	1988	1,466	...	3,496	364	...	30,195	1986–87	86	...	...	...	...	...	...	...	3
Faroe Islands	1994	81	40	385	10	19	550	1994	3	33.3	—	—	66.7	100.0	...	...	64
Fiji	1994	426	40	1,631	...	...	1,829	1994	25	...	...	...	...	...	...	...	22
Finland	1995	13,771	4,696	131,829	584[14]	3,975	371	1994[8]	380	...	...	...	...	...	...	...	98
France	1994	160,235	39,284	330,943	53,085	11,957	361	1993	3,810		—91.7—		8.3	27.7	—72.3—		118
French Guiana	1994	213	38	495	47	40	669	1993	...	...	...	...	...	...	...	...	56
French Polynesia	1993	353	81	586	47	54	595	1988	34[10]	...	...	...	...	...	...	...	48
Gabon	1989	448	32	759	71	240	2,504	1988	27	...	...	...	...	...	...	...	51
Gambia, The	1991	61	...	430[6]	...	...	14,536	1994	13	15.4	—	—84.6—		83.3	—16.7—		7[3]
Gaza Strip	1993[21]	...	...	...	...	...	...	1995	6	...	...	...	...	83.3	—16.7—		9
Georgia	1994	29,900[11]	11	64,100[12, 15]	...	12	182[11]	1994	422[15]	...	...	...	...	100.0[15]	...	...	105
Germany	1995	273,880	60,616	708,000[1, 12]	44,696	12	298	1993	2,354	...	...	...	...	49.2	36.0	14.8	77
Ghana	1995[16]	753	396	11,808[6]	67[6]	1,736[6]	22,970	1991	121	90.9	9.1	—	—	60.3	—39.7—		16[4]
Gibraltar	1994	29	...	302[10]	...	...	951	1994	2	50.0	50.0	—	—	100.0	—	—	88
Greece	1994	40,487	10,865	34,314[7, 22]	8,147[14]	1,916[7, 22]	258	1993	368	47.8	52.2	—	—	...	...	...	50
Greenland	1995	83	31	539	10[10]	17[10]	672	1990	16	6.3	—	—	93.7	100.0	...	...	75
Grenada	1995	64	8	365	28[15]	36[15]	1,523	1991[8]	3	100.0	—	—	—	100.0	—	—	38
Guadeloupe	1993	590	119	1,470	206	108	692	1991	30[6]	...	...	...	...	56.7[6]	—43.3[6]—		80
Guam	1986	147	...	594[12]	...	12	823	...	...	...	...	...	...	...	...	...	...
Guatemala	1992	7,601	1,065[2]	14,401	...	...	1,282	1985	...	...	...	...	...	...	...	...	16[6]
Guernsey	1993	79	...	...	...	...	804	1993	1	100.0	—	—	—	100.0	—	—	...
Guinea	1991	920	...	...	197	371	6,448	1988	38	—100.0—		...	...	100.0	...	...	6
Guinea-Bissau	1986	274	13	...	12	...	3,245	1993	16	...	...	...	...	62.5	—37.5—		13
Guyana	1993	244	34	681	22	172[6]	3,148	1994	30	...	...	...	...	83.3	—16.7—		30
Haiti	1994	641	95	2,725	...	...	9,846	1994	50	...	...	...	...	...	...	...	10
Honduras	1993	3,803	622	6,288	975	...	1,358	1994	61	...	...	...	...	47.5	—52.5—		9
Hong Kong	1996	9,196	1,654	36,395	1,067	20	686	1995	88	...	...	...	...	78.4	—21.6—		47
Hungary	1995	37,420	5,069	54,792	2,024[14]	2,414	273	1995	...	...	...	...	...	...	...	...	91
Iceland	1995	797	273	1,952	176	194	335	1992	26	88.5	11.5	—	—	...	...	...	105
India	1993[23]	410,875[1]	19,523	449,351	...	...	2,173[1]	1991	15,067	...	...	...	...	55.0	—45.0—		7[7]
Indonesia	1994	28,989	...	138,816[12]	3,988[14]	12	6,570	1994	1,039	...	...	...	...	...	...	...	6
Iran	1994	37,000	6,080[7]	48,639[10, 12]	4,185[7]	12	1,600	1992	653	...	...	...	...	70.9	—29.1—		15[9]
Iraq	1993	8,787	1,656	13,206[10]	1,561	...	2,181	1993	185	...	...	...	...	...	...	...	14
Ireland	1995	6,200[13]	...	...	...	...	580[13]	1994[3, 8]	63	100.0	—	—	—	100.0	—	—	33
Isle of Man	1988	86	...	...	...	...	745	1986	3	33.3	33.3	—	33.3	100.0	—	—	...
Israel	1993	24,344	6,956	...	4,127	...	214	1995	259	18.5	81.5	—	—	12.0	51.7	36.3	61
Italy	1992	296,385	10,814[6]	170,409[6]	53,948[6]	...	193	1994	1,874	88.3	11.7	—	—	57.4	—42.6—		65
Jamaica	1995	1,589[1]	270[1]	1,836[16]	37[16]	250[16]	1,541[1]	1992	30	80.0	20.0	—	—	80.0	—20.0—		22[3]
Japan	1995	230,519	81,055	891,021	176,871	23,048	542	1993	9,844	88.9	11.1	—	—	73.4	—26.6—		135
Jersey	1995	95	...	4,309[2]	...	...	895	1990	6	16.7	83.3	—	—	100.0	—	—	88
Jordan	1996	7,322	2,180	4,304[9]	3,265	861[9]	607	1994	63	...	...	...	...	42.9	—57.1—		18[24]
Kazakhstan	1995	62,290	7,075[1]	213,320[1]	8,722[1]	16,280[1]	265	1996	1,805[10]	...	...	...	...	100.0[10]	...	...	86
Kenya	1994	4,558	630	27,143[7]	605[7]	...	5,954	1993	877	—35.1—		—64.9—		...	...	...	14
Kiribati	1993	10	...	147	...	...	7,687	1990	1	...	...	...	...	...	...	...	40
Korea, North	1993	61,200	...	...	...	...	370	1989	...	...	...	...	...	...	...	...	135
Korea, South	1995	57,188	13,681	120,415	43,269	8,352	784	1995[22]	...	63.6[25]	36.4[25]	...	...	...	...	...	34
Kuwait	1995	3,077	437	8,337	969	19	549	1995	24	...	...	10.9	...	66.7	...	33.3	31
Kyrgyzstan	1995	15,000	1,100	42,300	1,122[4]	3,414[1]	301	1994	396	89.1	—	—	...	100.0	—	—	99
Laos	1990	1,173	...	5,593[12]	...	12	3,555	1990	1,074	0.7	—	—99.3—		100.0	—	—	25
Latvia	1994	7,714	968	12,559	292	981	330	1994	170	51.2	4.1	28.8	15.9	97.6	2.4	—	121
Lebanon	1995	6,987	3,100	3,500	2,369	...	529	1995	153	...	...	...	...	10.5	—89.5—		22
Lesotho	1993	136	...	874[15]	60[15]	...	14,306	1987	22	90.9	9.1	—	—	54.5	45.5	—	15
Liberia	1985	89	5	908	...	443	24,600	1988	92	—37.0—		—63.0—		...	...	...	...
Libya	1989–91	4,749	686	13,849	...	...	690	1990	...	...	...	...	...	...	...	...	41
Liechtenstein	1995	32	12	...	2	...	966	1989	1	...	...	...	...	...	...	...	35
Lithuania	1995	14,737	1,742	29,259	3,203	1,829	252	1995	195	...	...	...	...	100.0	...	...	92
Luxembourg	1995	908	203[7]	...	336[7]	143[7]	454	1994	34	50.0	50.0	—	—	...	...	...	109
Macau	1995	467	22	861	41	...	876	1994	30	6.7	—	93.3	—	46.7	—53.3—		22
Macedonia	1995	4,516	1,087[4]	5,638[5]	357[4]	1,436[7]	432	1994	62	27.4	24.2	—48.4—		100.0	—	—	56
Madagascar	1990	1,392	89	3,124	19	1,703	8,628	1990	...	...	...	...	...	...	...	...	9
Malawi	1989	186	...	284	5	...	49,118	1987	395	12.2	0.8	—87.0—		59.2	—40.8—		16
Malaysia	1995	9,608	1,750	34,996[4]	...	5,500[4]	2,153	1995	315	...	...	...	...	37.5	—62.5—		20
Maldives	1995	100	...	281	134	461	2,533	1994	5	20.0	—	80.0	—	100.0	—	—	8
Mali	1993	483	13[27]	1,674	57[27]	321[27]	18,376	1987	...	...	...	...	...	...	...	...	4
Malta	1996	925	122	4,000	648	200	403	1996	7	...	...	...	...	71.4	—28.6—		57
Marshall Islands	1995	17	4	124	...	4[10]	3,269	1995	2	100.0	—	—	—	100.0	—	—	19
Martinique	1994	652	112	1,460	225	129	588	1993	...	...	...	...	...	...	...	...	77
Mauritania	1991	135	20	819	6	141	14,259	1990	16	...	...	...	...	100.0	...	...	7
Mauritius	1995	960	152	2,629[12, 16]	223	12	1,169	1994	23	73.9	17.4	8.7	—	60.9	4.3	34.8	28[3]
Mayotte	1985	9	1	51	1	2	7,427	1991	2	100.0	—	—	—	100.0	—	—	11
Mexico	1994	146,021	5,612[16]	166,644[16]	...	...	623	1993	1,539	...	...	...	...	53.9	—46.1—		10
Micronesia	1994	45	7[7]	230[7]	77	...	2,311	1993	4	100.0	—	—	—	100.0	...	...	31
Moldova	1994	17,400[11]	11	48,400[12]	...	12	251[11]	1994	339	...	...	...	...	100.0	...	...	125
Monaco	1995	186	22	293[6]	...	8[6]	169	1995	1	100.0	—	—	—	100.0	...	...	163
Mongolia	1993	5,911	299	9,183	1,113	...	376	1993	475	...	...	...	...	...	...	...	105
Morocco	1994	8,838	1,204	13,358[7]	2,470	87[15]	2,923	1993[28]	201	48.8	—	51.2	—	100.0	...	...	10

rate per 10,000 pop.	general	special-ized	medical centres	rural	bed occu-pancy rate (%)	aver-age length of stay (days)	under age 5 per 1,000 live newborn 1996	maternal mortality per 100,000 live births 1990	popu-lation with access to safe water 1994–95 (%)	food supply (% of FAO require-ment) 1995	as percent of GDP	per capita (U.S.$)	public	private	inter-national aid	country
...	...	...	...	...	...	...	164	...	90[5]	79	...	...	...	...	...	Djibouti
1,026	...	...	...	...	94.6	8	21[9]	...	77[5]	125	8.06	192	65.1	20.4	14.5	Dominica
470	...	...	...	...	...	...	46	110	79	103	3.72	38	52.7	43.3	4.0	Dominican Republic
518	...	...	...	...	57.5	7	57	150	70	106	4.14	44	55.9	37.3	6.8	Ecuador
...	...	...	...	...	...	...	70	170	84	133	2.61	28	30.3	62.0	7.7	Egypt
...	...	...	...	...	54.9[1, 3]	61[1, 3]	64	300	62	113	5.86	58	29.7	55.6	14.7	El Salvador
...	...	...	...	...	...	...	167	...	95[5]	...	7.60	28	36.6	20.7	42.7	Equatorial Guinea
...	...	...	...	...	...	...	146	1,400	...	...	...	...	...	...	...	Eritrea
1,773	76.7	21.5	—	1.8	83.7	14	19	41	...	...	3.62	228	53.0	47.0	—	Estonia
...	...	...	...	...	...	...	170	1,400	27	...	3.80	4	41.3	39.9	18.8	Ethiopia
...	...	...	...	...	86.4	...	...	...	...	...	...	...	...	...	...	Faroe Islands
...	...	...	...	...	...	...	23	...	77[5]	135	3.76	70	54.9	38.3	6.9	Fiji
2,322	...	...	...	...	70.9	11	6	11	100	112	7.82	2,046	83.3	16.7	—	Finland
2,345	...	...	...	...	...	...	9	15	100	142	9.40	1,869	74.2	25.8	—	France
1,714	...	...	...	...	70.3	8	...	...	...	125	...	...	...	...	...	French Guiana
...	...	...	...	...	...	...	...	...	...	127	...	...	...	...	...	French Polynesia
...	...	...	...	...	...	...	130	500	67	107	4.10	164	52.7	40.9	6.4	Gabon
...	...	...	...	...	...	...	190	1,100	61	91	7.53	22	28.3	20.7	51.0	Gambia, The
752	...	...	...	...	74.9	3	...	...	...	...	...	...	...	...	...	Gaza Strip
...	...	...	...	...	...	...	21	33	...	...	4.45	152	62.5	37.5	—	Georgia
1,812	...	...	...	...	82.8	13	7	22	100[5]	123	8.73	1,511	72.7	27.3	—	Germany
...	...	...	...	...	...	...	111	740	56	114	3.50	15	35.0	51.8	13.2	Ghana
1,730	...	...	...	...	40.6	8	...	...	...	...	...	...	...	...	...	Gibraltar
1,389	79.6	20.4	—	—	66.3	9	10	10	99[5]	142	5.39	359	76.0	24.0	—	Greece
2,450	29.2	—	—	70.8	69.4	8	...	...	...	...	...	...	...	...	...	Greenland
774	100.0	—	—	—	59.1	7	33[9]	...	85[5]	112	5.96	133	68.8	27.8	3.5	Grenada
2,136	...	...	...	...	82.3	11	...	...	...	113	...	...	...	...	...	Guadeloupe
...	...	...	...	...	...	...	...	...	...	...	...	...	...	...	...	Guam
284	...	...	...	...	57.7	9	67	200	64	105	3.70	27	44.2	43.2	12.6	Guatemala
1,100	100.0	—	—	—	...	...	...	...	...	...	...	...	...	...	...	Guernsey
...	...	...	...	...	...	...	196	1,600	49	94	3.90	17	39.7	40.3	20.0	Guinea
...	...	...	...	...	...	...	203	910	57	105	8.15	16	31.3	18.9	49.8	Guinea-Bissau
...	...	...	...	...	...	...	60	...	65[5]	108	10.37	42	40.7	15.1	44.2	Guyana
...	...	...	...	...	...	...	104	1,000	28	...	6.99	27	26.3	54.8	19.0	Haiti
459[7]	...	...	...	...	...	...	50	220	70	104	4.54	52	56.7	35.7	7.7	Honduras
1,811	...	...	...	...	...	...	6[9]	7	100[5]	143	5.69	687	19.5	80.5	0.0	Hong Kong
2,346	...	...	...	...	76.3	11	17	30	94	126	5.95	185	84.4	15.6	—	Hungary
2,828	94.0	6.0	—	—	86.5	12	4	...	100[5]	119	8.34	1,884	87.5	12.5	—	Iceland
...	...	...	...	...	...	...	99	570	63	108	6.00	21	20.0	78.4	1.6	India
...	...	...	...	...	...	...	63	650	63	126	2.01	12	25.6	66.7	7.7	Indonesia
...	...	...	...	...	...	...	59	120	89	123	2.54	244	56.9	43.1	0.0	Iran
645[15]	...	...	...	...	42.4[15]	4[15]	59	310	45	94	...	...	...	...	...	Iraq
1,465	100.0	—	—	—	79.8	7	7	10	100[5]	145	7.22	876	81.1	18.9	—	Ireland
...	...	...	...	...	...	...	...	...	...	...	...	...	...	...	...	Isle of Man
1,979	...	...	...	...	91.2	10	9	7	99	127	4.20	480	49.3	50.6	0.1	Israel
1,599	93.0	7.0	—	—	72.7	11	9	12	100[5]	137	7.54	1,449	77.7	22.3	—	Italy
550[3]	81.7[3]	18.3[3]	—	—	63.8[3, 8]	6[3, 8]	20	120	70	118	5.04	83	57.4	33.2	9.5	Jamaica
...	...	...	...	...	...	...	6	18	95	123	6.45	1.538	74.5	25.5	—	Japan
1,718	84.0	16.0	—	—	...	...	...	...	...	...	...	...	...	...	...	Jersey
478[3]	...	...	...	...	68.1[3]	4[3]	39	150	89	111	3.77	55	36.9	52.3	10.8	Jordan
...	...	...	...	...	...	...	31	80	...	...	4.44	154	62.3	37.7	—	Kazakstan
...	...	...	...	...	...	...	106	650	49	86	4.33	16	40.0	37.9	22.1	Kenya
...	...	...	...	...	...	...	78[4]	...	99[5]	122	...	...	...	...	...	Kiribati
...	...	...	...	...	...	...	26	70	100	101	...	...	...	...	...	Korea, North
629	97.5	2.5	—	—	65.5	13	13	130	89	139	6.61	365	40.9	58.9	0.2	Korea, South
950[3, 4]	72.2[3, 4]	27.8[3, 4]	—	—	64.9[3, 4]	7[3, 4]	16	29	100[5]	131	4.86	541	64.2	35.6	0.1	Kuwait
1,775	95.5	—	4.5	—	75.6	15	39	110	75	...	4.97	118	66.7	33.3	—	Kyrgyzstan
...	...	...	...	...	...	...	143	650	41	95	2.53	5	17.4	60.7	21.9	Laos
2,106	78.4	4.6	13.8	3.2	78.7	16	20	40	...	...	3.87	220	56.1	43.9	—	Latvia
...	...	...	...	...	...	...	36	300	100[5]	132	...	...	...	...	...	Lebanon
221[8]	...	...	...	...	...	...	81	610	57	86	8.32	26	38.3	26.5	35.2	Lesotho
...	...	...	...	...	...	...	151	...	40[5]	...	8.24	4	19.9	11.8	68.3	Liberia
...	...	...	...	...	...	...	80	220	30	132	...	...	...	...	...	Libya
...	...	...	...	...	...	...	...	...	...	...	...	...	...	...	...	Liechtenstein
2,001	...	...	...	...	74.4	15	17	36	...	...	3.58	159	72.0	28.0	—	Lithuania
1,941	94.6	5.4	—	—	75.0	16	8	...	100[5]	134	6.56	1,662	91.4	8.6	—	Luxembourg
329	...	...	...	...	64.4	16	...	...	...	135	...	...	...	...	...	Macau
995	67.2	6.1	—26.7—		68.5	14	37	...	...	92	...	...	...	...	...	Macedonia
...	...	...	...	...	...	...	121	490	32	89	2.56	7	29.0	49.6	21.4	Madagascar
...	...	...	...	...	...	...	212	560	54	88	4.98	11	35.0	41.7	23.3	Malawi
717[3, 6]	...	...	...	...	71.4[7, 26]	47, 26	22	80	90	126	2.96	71	44.0	55.8	0.2	Malaysia
256[7, 26]	...	...	...	...	...	...	68	...	88[5]	112	...	...	...	...	...	Maldives
...	...	...	...	...	...	...	184	1,200	44	91	5.19	15	24.9	46.7	28.4	Mali
...	...	...	...	...	...	...	11	...	100[5]	137	5.38	349	68.3	31.7	0.0	Malta
...	...	...	...	...	...	...	92[4]	...	31[5]	...	...	...	...	...	...	Marshall Islands
2,092	...	...	...	...	73.7	10	...	...	...	118	...	...	...	...	...	Martinique
...	...	...	...	...	...	...	142	930	72	112	3.80	18	28.5	41.5	30.0	Mauritania
1,446[3]	...	...	...	...	74.6[3]	5[3]	17	120	100	130	4.40	100	47.8	39.0	13.3	Mauritius
...	...	...	...	...	...	...	...	...	...	...	...	...	...	...	...	Mayotte
403[3, 10]	...	...	...	...	64.7[3, 10]	5[3, 10]	40	110	87	135	3.17	89	49.3	49.8	0.9	Mexico
...	...	...	...	...	...	...	29[4]	...	100[5]	...	...	...	...	...	...	Micronesia
...	...	...	...	...	...	...	28	60	...	...	3.91	143	74.4	25.6	—	Moldova
...	...	...	...	...	...	...	...	...	...	...	...	...	...	...	...	Monaco
...	...	...	...	...	...	...	68	65	54	78	6.63	58	83.0	15.1	1.9	Mongolia
255	...	...	...	...	63.8	8	76	610	59	130	2.55	26	33.6	63.3	3.1	Morocco

Health services (continued)

country	health personnel							hospitals									
	year	physicians	dentists	nurses	pharmacists	midwives	population per physician	year	number	kinds (%)				ownership (%)			hospital beds per 10,000 pop.
										general	specialized	medical centres	rural	government	private non-profit	private for profit	
Mozambique	1990	387	108	3,533	353	1,139	36,320	1990	238	4.2	0.8	— 95.0 —		100.0		—	8[7]
Myanmar (Burma)	1995	12,950	860	9,851	...	8,143	3,485	1995	710	...	...	...	...	...	...	—	6
Namibia	1992	324	51	4,471	91[10]	...	4,594	1992	47	...	...	...	...	91.5	— 8.5 —		45[10]
Nauru	...	...	...	...	...	...	...	...	...	...	...	...	...	...	...	...	...
Nepal	1995	1,478	45	5,015[12]	18	[12]	13,777	1995	84	...	...	...	...	...	...	...	2
Netherlands, The	1995	37,493	7,328	124,000[7]	2,484	1,276	412	1995	231	64.1	35.9	—	—	...	...	...	55
Netherlands Antilles	1996	314	67	1,441	37	10	669	1996	12	33.3	41.7	25.0	—	...	...	...	70
New Caledonia	1994	358	97	669	78	52	513	1990	8	12.5	12.5	75.0	—	62.5	— 37.5 —		62
New Zealand	1995	11,889	1,959	45,107[12]	3,532	[12]	301	1994	330	...	...	...	...	38.2	— 61.8 —		68
Nicaragua	1994	2,577	321	2,144	...	...	1,566	1994	56	46.4	7.1	46.4	—	...	...	...	11
Niger	1993	237	5[15]	2,213	29[15]	457[15]	35,141	1987	...	...	...	...	...	...	...	...	5
Nigeria	1993	21,739	1,335	80,186	6,474[1]	62,386	4,257	1985	11,588	6.6	0.5	— 92.9 —		81.4	— 18.6 —		7[9]
Northern Mariana Islands	1986	23	4	103	2	2	1,324	1988	1	100.0	—	—	—	100.0	—	—	19
Norway	1996	15,368	5,222	68,308	...	...	285	1994	...	...	...	...	...	...	...	...	51
Oman	1995[16]	2,476	152[7]	6,036	370	...	852	1995	53	...	...	...	...	...	...	...	21
Pakistan	1995	69,694	2,753	22,531	3,772[1]	20,869	1,863	1994	10,667	— 7.6 —		— 92.4 —		...	...	...	6
Palau	1990	10	...	84	...	...	1,518	1986	1	...	...	...	...	...	...	...	50
Panama	1995	3,074	656	2,823	115[6]	...	856	1995	59	...	...	...	...	...	...	...	27
Papua New Guinea	1993	736	...	2,614	...	...	5,584	1993	...	...	...	...	...	...	...	...	34
Paraguay	1993	3,341	1,160[1]	4,558[1]	...	...	1,406	1993	...	...	...	...	...	...	...	...	12
Peru	1992	23,771	7,945	15,026	5,940[10]	3,520[10]	944	1992	427	...	...	...	...	56.7	— 43.3 —		17
Philippines	1993	78,445	1,614[16]	14,853[16]	...	12,339[16]	849	1992	1,723	96.5	3.1	0.5	—	36.4	— 63.6 —		11
Poland	1996	88,523	17,619	210,425	19,450	24,445	436	1995	753	93.6	6.4	—	—	...	...	...	63
Portugal	1993	24,499	1,509	30,975	5,950	...	403	1993	335	43.0	18.8	38.2	—	74.3	14.7	11.0	42
Puerto Rico	1989	6,269	902	19,666	2,111	120	558	1994	72	83.3	8.3	8.3	—	36.1	30.6	33.3	26
Qatar	1995[16]	715	88	1,834	187	...	787	1995	4	25.0	75.0	—	—	100.0	—	—	18
Réunion	1996	1,164	295	2,785	266[14]	164	571	1995	...	...	...	...	...	69.6[25]	— 30.4[25] —		44
Romania	1994[16]	41,827	6,163	...	6,432[6]	...	544	1994	...	...	...	...	...	...	...	...	77
Russia	1995	630,000	47,100[4]	1,008,800[4]	7,300[4]	117,200[4]	235	1995	12,265	37.4	17.2	—	45.4	99.8	— 0.2 —		119
Rwanda	1989	272	7	835	25	...	24,697	1985[3]	220	— 13.6 —		— 86.4 —		100.0	—	—	9[6]
St. Kitts and Nevis	1992	39	8	260	14	...	1,057	1992	4	50.0	— 50.0 —			...	...	...	67
St. Lucia	1992	64	6	256	...	...	2,235	1992	4	25.0	25.0	—	50.0	...	...	...	37
St. Vincent	1992	40	6	224	27[10]	...	2,708	1992	9	...	...	...	...	77.8	— 22.2 —		44
Samoa	1992	60	7	298	6	...	2,682	1992	36	2.8	—	—	97.2	100.0	—	—	34
San Marino	1987	60	...	...	...	...	375	1987	...	...	...	...	...	...	...	...	66
São Tomé and Príncipe	1989	61	5	223	1	54	1,881	...	...	...	...	...	...	...	...	...	...
Saudi Arabia	1995	29,227	...	61,246	...	...	612	1995	279	...	...	...	...	74.2	— 25.8 —		23
Senegal	1992	520	58[27]	...	200[27]	474[27]	14,825	1992	17	...	...	...	...	...	...	...	10
Seychelles	1996	84	9	346	4	...	906	1996	7	14.3	14.3	71.4	—	100.0	—	—	54
Sierra Leone	1992	404	...	...	...	...	10,832	1988	219	— 25.6 —		— 74.4 —		...	...	...	10
Singapore	1996	4,661	835	13,193	858	487	653	1996	24	...	...	...	...	41.7	— 58.3 —		35
Slovakia	1995	14,447	2,236[4]	...	322[14]	...	371	1991	111	72.1	27.9	—	...	100.0	—	—	92[9]
Slovenia	1990	4,086	1,194[9]	...	1,019	...	489	1995	24	54.2	45.8	—	—	...	...	...	57
Solomon Islands	1990	52	...	447	...	...	6,154	1986	8	100.0	—	—	—	75.0	25.0	—	53
Somalia	1986	450	2	1,834	180	556	13,315	1988	...	...	...	...	...	...	...	...	7
South Africa	1994	26,452	4,029	158,538	9,447	...	1,529	1995	698	...	...	...	...	66.8	— 33.2 —		42
Spain	1995	162,089	13,242	161,852	40,323	6,105	241	1991	813	...	...	...	...	42.4	— 57.6 —		42
Sri Lanka	1993[16]	3,713	333[6]	11,818	520[6]	5,030[6]	4,745	1993[3]	426	...	...	...	...	100.0	—	—	28
Sudan, The	1994	2,600	...	...	...	...	11,300	1986	...	...	...	...	...	...	...	...	8
Suriname	1994	251	...	995[1]	...	...	1,685	1989	...	...	...	...	...	...	...	...	33[4]
Swaziland	1990	83	7	1,264	13	...	9,265	1986	24	— 41.7 —		— 58.3 —		...	...	...	...
Sweden	1995	23,000	4,700	91,400[12]	5,945	[12]	382	1994	...	...	...	...	...	...	...	...	52
Switzerland	1994	21,680[13]	4,400[1]	...	1,591[14]	...	323[13]	1994	...	...	...	...	...	...	...	...	69
Syria	1995	15,391	8,025	23,151	5,919	6,063	922	1993	264	...	...	...	...	20.5	— 79.5 —		11
Taiwan	1996	27,782	7,332	61,494	19,667	774	775	1995	787	...	...	...	...	12.1	— 87.9 —		53
Tajikistan	1994	13,084	926	38,852	709	1,027	439	1994	449	...	...	...	...	98.2	— 1.8 —		88
Tanzania	1993	1,365	...	...	...	...	20,511	1993	173[10]	...	...	...	...	...	...	...	10
Thailand	1994	14,098	2,984	94,103	5,575	10,342	4,165	1992	1,097	92.9	7.1	—	—	73.7	— 26.3 —		17
Togo	1991	319	22	1,187	65	222	11,270	1990	...	...	...	...	...	...	...	...	16
Tonga	1993	45	9	292	...	...	2,139	1993	4	...	...	...	...	...	...	...	28
Trinidad and Tobago	1995	1,183	134	2,260[7, 12]	534	[12]	1,067	1992	...	...	...	...	...	...	...	...	29
Tunisia	1994	5,344	1,004	12,195	1,685	...	1,640	1994[3]	163	— 13.5 —		— 86.5 —		100.0	—	—	18
Turkey	1994	65,832	11,457	56,280	18,366	36,263[7]	917	1994	982	75.3	8.8	— 15.9 —		84.3	— 15.7 —		22
Turkmenistan	1994	14,100[11]	[11]	43,000[12]	...	[12]	320[11]	1994	398	...	...	...	...	100.0	—	—	115
Tuvalu	1993	8	2[1]	39	...	...	1,152	1985	8	11.1	—	—	88.9	100.0	—	—	36
Uganda	1993	840	...	2,782	...	...	22,399	1989	81	...	...	...	...	...	...	...	12
Ukraine	1995	230,000[11]	[11]	598,000[12]	...	[12]	224[11]	1995	3,900	...	...	...	...	100.0	—	—	130
United Arab Emirates	1994	4,095	563	8,506	686[10]	...	545	1994	47	...	...	...	...	70.2	— 29.2 —		28
United Kingdom	1994	91,100[13]	...	284,578[6]	37,832[15]	24,801[6]	641[13]	1994	...	...	...	...	...	...	...	...	49[13]
United States	1995	720,300	190,000[4]	2,044,000[4]	184,000	3,000	365	1995	6,580[7]	82.1[7]	17.9[7]	—	—	31.1[7]	51.2[7]	17.7[7]	41
Uruguay	1994	11,241	3,740	2,139	922	554	282	1993	112	...	...	...	...	61.6	— 38.4 —		45
Uzbekistan	1995	76,200	4,300[4]	249,600	1,700[4]	20,100[4]	299	1995	192	...	...	...	...	100.0	—	—	84
Vanuatu	1995	12	3	259	6	33	14,025	1995	90	5.6	—	21.1	73.3	100.0	—	—	22
Venezuela	1992	32,616	7,945	52,260	5,615	...	626	1992	610	...	...	...	...	37.0	— 63.0 —		26
Vietnam	1994	29,700	...	53,700[7]	6,500[7]	12,000[7]	2,411	1994	12,500	...	...	...	...	...	...	...	27
Virgin Islands (U.S.)	1985	167	...	...	...	...	622	1985	...	...	...	...	...	...	...	...	49
West Bank	1993[21]	1,344	445	2,279	149	56	1,536	1995	17	...	...	...	...	52.9	— 47.1 —		9
Western Sahara	1994	100	...	...	24	...	2,504	...	...	...	...	...	...	...	...	...	...
Yemen	1994	2,785	167	5,772	295	385	4,549	1994	81	...	...	...	...	...	...	...	7
Yugoslavia	1995	21,313	4,075	...	2,016	...	495	1995	...	...	...	...	...	...	...	...	52
Zambia	1990	713	26	1,503	24	311	11,414	1987	965	8.2	0.3	19.0	72.5	80.9	19.1	—	29[7]
Zimbabwe	1993	1,551	194	22,590	411	2,894	6,909	1993[3]	1,378	0.9	2.6	83.7	12.7	100.0	—	—	19[9]

[1]1992. [2]1987. [3]Government hospitals only. [4]1994. [5]Data refer to a period other than 1994–95, differ from the standard definition, or refer to only part of the country. [6]1989. [7]1993. [8]General hospitals only. [9]1995. [10]1991. [11]Physicians includes dentists. [12]Nurses includes midwives. [13]OECD estimate. [14]Number of pharmacies. [15]1990. [16]Government-employed health personnel only. [17]Includes doctors of traditional Chinese medicine (359,000 in 1995). [18]Republic of Cyprus only. [19]Excludes psychiatric hospitals. [20]Data refer to former Czechoslovakia. [21]West Bank includes Gaza Strip. [22]General and

admissions or discharges					bed occu-pancy rate (%)	aver-age length of stay (days)	mortality		popu-lation with access to safe water 1994–95 (%)	food supply (% of FAO require-ment) 1995	total health expenditures, 1990					country
rate per 10,000 pop.	by kinds of hospital (%)						under age 5 per 1,000 live newborn 1996	maternal mortality per 100,000 live births 1990			as percent of GDP	per capita (U.S.$)	by source (percent)			
	general	special-ized	medical centres	rural									public	private	inter-national aid	
...	...	...	...	...	...	...	176	1,500	28	72	5.86	5	21.0	25.7	53.3	Mozambique
...	...	...	...	...	...	...	95	580	39	127	...	...	...	...	...	Myanmar (Burma)
...	...	...	...	...	...	...	91	370	57	92	3.92	45	47.8	41.3	10.9	Namibia
...	...	...	...	...	...	...	...	...	...	...	...	...	...	...	...	Nauru
...	...	...	...	...	...	...	122	1,500	48	108	4.54	7	23.0	51.7	25.4	Nepal
1,060	97.2	2.8	—	—	77.2	15	8	12	100	120	8.03	1,501	72.6	27.4	—	Netherlands, The
...	...	...	...	...	...	...	...	...	...	114	...	...	...	...	...	Netherlands Antilles
1,165[8]	...	...	...	...	84.8[8]	8[8]	...	...	...	126	...	...	...	...	...	New Caledonia
1,379[3]	...	...	...	...	60.7[3]	8[3]	10	25	100[5]	128	7.37	925	81.7	18.3	20.6	New Zealand
769	—76.2—		23.8		...	...	66	160	57	103	8.61	34	56.9	22.5	20.6	Nicaragua
...	...	...	...	...	...	...	182	1,200	57	91	4.98	16	24.5	31.3	34.1	Niger
...	...	...	...	...	...	...	146	1,000	43	106	2.72	10	36.5	57.4	6.1	Nigeria
1,550	100.0	—	—		54.7	4	...	...	...	...	...	...	...	...	...	Northern Mariana Islands
1,515	96.4	3.6	—	—	83.0	10	9	6	100	122	7.35	1,835	95.7	4.3	—	Norway
...	...	...	...	...	...	...	32	190	56	...	4.22	209	59.5	40.1	0.5	Oman
...	...	...	...	...	...	...	104	340	60	107	3.48	12	47.4	47.1	5.5	Pakistan
...	...	...	...	...	...	...	35[4]	...	...	146	...	...	...	...	...	Palau
1,112	...	...	...	...	61.8	6	28	55	82	108	7.13	142	72.6	23.1	4.3	Panama
...	...	...	...	...	...	...	82	930	31	102	4.44	37	59.1	36.1	4.8	Papua New Guinea
...	...	...	...	...	...	...	47	160	8	111	2.97	35	35.1	58.2	6.7	Paraguay
...	...	...	...	...	...	...	71	280	60	97	3.21	61	56.1	41.7	2.2	Peru
538	...	...	...	...	62.1	5	45	280	84	106	2.15	16	46.7	46.4	6.9	Philippines
1,288[1]	96.0[1]	4.0[1]	—		72.5[1]	14[1]	18	19	100[5]	126	5.07	84	80.3	19.7	—	Poland
1,146	86.3	10.5	3.2	—	74.5	10	11	15	100[5]	149	6.99	383	61.7	38.3	—	Portugal
1,101	94.0	4.3	1.7	—	63.1	5	...	...	...	...	...	...	...	...	...	Puerto Rico
...	...	...	...	...	71.7[1,29]	71[1,29]	23	...	100[5]	...	4.73	630	63.0	36.9	0.0	Qatar
1,951[4]	...	...	...	...	79.8[4]	74	...	...	...	146	...	...	...	...	...	Réunion
...	...	...	...	...	...	...	30	130	100[5]	119	3.87	58	61.4	38.6	—	Romania
2,150	...	...	...	...	83.2	17	27	75	...	114	3.02	159	66.8	33.2	—	Russia
85	...	...	...	...	42.8[22]	7[22]	161	1,300	66[5]	...	3.44	10	15.0	45.2	39.8	Rwanda
1,068[8]	...	...	...	...	49.3[8]	9[8]	40[9]	...	100[5]	92	5.99	212	58.1	27.8	14.1	St. Kitts and Nevis
890[22]	...	...	...	...	...	...	22[9]	...	...	116	7.18	169	75.6	23.0	1.4	St. Lucia
776[8]	...	...	...	...	67.9[8]	6[8]	23[9]	...	...	100	5.69	102	68.5	28.8	2.7	St. Vincent
894	70.8	—	—	29.2	32.9	5	71	...	90[5]	...	2.94	20	6.1	54.2	39.7	Samoa
...	...	...	...	...	...	...	...	...	100[5]	...	...	...	...	...	...	San Marino
...	...	...	...	...	...	...	81[9]	...	70[5]	92	9.22	38	28.8	17.0	54.2	São Tomé and Príncipe
...	...	...	...	...	...	...	30	130	93	113	4.76	260	64.3	35.7	0.0	Saudi Arabia
...	...	...	...	...	...	...	157	1,200	50[5]	102	3.66	29	45.1	38.0	16.9	Senegal
1,744[30]	...	...	...	...	76.4[30]	6[30]	20[9]	...	97[5]	104	6.03	289	50.2	28.0	21.9	Seychelles
...	...	...	...	...	...	...	242	1,800	34[5]	88	2.43	4	19.6	30.9	49.5	Sierra Leone
1,127	...	...	...	...	73.1[4]	8[4]	9	10	100	...	1.87	215	58.3	41.6	0.1	Singapore
1,679	94.9	5.1	—	—	73.2	14	14	...	...	117	...	...	...	...	...	Slovakia
1,565	...	...	...	...	79.4	11	12	13	...	134	...	...	...	...	...	Slovenia
...	...	...	...	...	...	...	29	...	...	93	2.18	117	43.2	50.5	6.3	Solomon Islands
...	...	...	...	...	...	...	176	...	...	...	1.51	8	7.3	41.1	51.6	Somalia
...	...	...	...	...	...	...	73	230	70[5]	118	5.56	77	57.5	42.5	0.0	South Africa
997	...	...	...	...	76.7	12	8	7	99	136	6.59	831	78.4	21.6	—	Spain
1,464[15]	...	...	...	...	...	...	19	140	57	105	3.74	18	40.4	51.1	8.6	Sri Lanka
...	...	...	...	...	...	...	112	660	77	98	3.33	34	11.0	84.5	4.5	Sudan, The
766[31]	...	...	...	...	68.8[31]	10[31]	26	...	72[5]	113	2.88	93	37.9	58.0	4.1	Suriname
...	...	...	...	...	...	...	99	...	43[5]	115	7.22	64	43.6	22.2	34.2	Swaziland
1,906	...	...	...	...	82.2	8	6	7	100[5]	116	8.79	2,343	89.3	10.7	—	Sweden
...	...	...	...	...	...	...	7	6	100	120	7.52	2,520	68.5	31.5	—	Switzerland
352[3]	...	...	...	...	75.5[3]	3[3]	43	180	87	133	2.07	41	16.6	79.4	4.0	Syria
...	...	...	...	...	...	...	8[9]	8	...	...	4.30	323	53.0	47.0	0.0	Taiwan
1,492	...	...	...	...	70.2	15	56	130	...	...	5.98	100	72.6	27.4	—	Tajikistan
...	...	...	...	...	...	...	126	770	49	87	4.73	4	14.4	31.6	54.0	Tanzania
...	...	...	...	...	...	...	43	200	81	103	4.98	72	20.4	78.7	0.9	Thailand
...	...	...	...	...	...	...	118	640	67	76	4.10	18	40.4	38.5	21.2	Togo
622[1]	...	...	...	...	56.2[1]	10[1]	24[4]	...	100[5]	...	6.46	63	60.3	25.0	14.8	Tonga
1,114[3,8]	...	...	...	...	70.7[3,8]	6[3,8]	17	90	82	106	4.54	180	62.4	36.9	0.6	Trinidad and Tobago
...	...	...	...	...	...	...	49	170	86	133	4.91	76	63.8	33.3	3.0	Tunisia
568[15]	...	...	...	...	...	...	65	180	92	143	3.94	76	36.2	63.3	0.5	Turkey
...	...	...	...	...	...	...	66	55	85	...	4.99	125	66.4	33.2	0.4	Turkmenistan
1,368	40.9	—	—	59.1	51.5[8]	12.2[8]	56[4]	...	100[5]	...	2.66	472	34.0	66.0	0.1	Tuvalu
...	...	...	...	...	...	...	172	1,200	42	97	3.40	8	13.3	53.0	33.7	Uganda
...	...	...	...	...	...	...	21	50	97	...	3.30	131	69.7	30.3	—	Ukraine
...	...	...	...	...	...	...	19	26	98	139	2.66	472	34.0	66.0	0.1	United Arab Emirates
...	...	...	...	...	...	...	8	9	100	125	6.11	1,039	84.9	15.1	—	United Kingdom
1,176[32]	...	...	...	...	62.8[32]	7[32]	9	12	90	136	12.71	2,765	44.1	55.9	—	United States
442[3,4]	...	...	...	...	76.3[3,4]	16[3,4]	20	85	34	106	4.62	123	53.8	44.8	1.4	Uruguay
...	...	...	...	...	...	...	47	55	...	...	5.90	116	72.1	27.9	—	Uzbekistan
567	...	...	...	...	41.9	6	48	...	72[5]	111	5.68	67	51.5	25.7	22.8	Vanuatu
601[3]	...	...	...	...	69.7[3]	6[3]	25	120	88	99	3.60	88	54.2	45.6	0.1	Venezuela
...	...	...	...	...	...	...	56	160	38	114	2.11	3	39.3	47.4	13.3	Vietnam
...	...	...	...	...	...	...	...	...	...	...	...	...	...	...	...	Virgin Islands (U.S.)
711	...	...	...	...	80.9	4	...	...	...	...	...	...	...	...	...	West Bank
...	...	...	...	...	...	...	...	...	...	...	...	...	...	...	...	Western Sahara
...	...	...	...	...	...	...	155	1,400	52	84	3.19	20	34.7	54.1	11.3	Yemen
1,117	...	...	...	...	71.6	12	...	...	...	123	5.11[33]	264[33]	80.4[33]	19.6[33]	—	Yugoslavia
1,249	—75.7—		24.3		68.5	7	140	940	47	84	3.16	17	65.4	30.6	4.1	Zambia
546	...	...	...	...	69.8	7	103	570	74	82	6.23	39	40.3	48.7	11.0	Zimbabwe

specialized hospitals only. [23]Registered personnel; all may not be present and working in the country. [24]1996. [25]Based on bed ownership. [26]Central Hospital only. [27]1988. [28]Public sector only. [29]Hamad General Hospital only. [30]Victoria Hospital only. [31]Paramaribo hospitals (1,213 beds) only. [32]5,194 community hospitals only. [33]Data refer to the former Socialist Federal Republic of Yugoslavia.

Social protection

This table summarizes three principal areas of social protective activity for the countries of the world: social security, crime and law enforcement, and military affairs. Because the administrative structure, financing, manning, and scope of institutions and programmed tasks in these fields vary so greatly from country to country, no well-accepted or well-documented body of statistical comparisons exists in international convention to permit objective assessment of any of these subjects, either from the perspective of a single country or internationally. The data provided within any single subject area do, however, represent the most consistent approach to problems of international comparison found in the published literature for that field.

The provision of social security programs to answer specific social needs, for example, is summarized simply in terms of the existence or nonexistence of a specific type of benefit program because of the great complexity of national programs in terms of eligibility, coverage, term, age limits, financing, payments, and so on. Activities connected with a particular type of benefit often take place at more than one governmental level, through more than one agency at the same level, or through a mixture of public and private institutions. The data shown here are summarized from the U.S. Social Security Administration's *Social Security Programs Throughout the World* (biennial). A bullet symbol (●) indicates that a country has at least one program within the defined area; in some cases it may have several. A blank space indicates that no program existed providing the benefit shown; ellipses [...] indicate that no information was available as to whether a program existed.

Data given for social security expenditure as a percentage of total central governmental expenditure are taken from the International Monetary Fund's *Government Finance Statistics Yearbook,* which provides the most comparable analytic series on the consolidated accounts of central governments, governmentally administered social security funds, and independent national agencies, all usually separate accounting entities, through which these services may be provided in a given country.

Data on the finances of social security programs are taken in large part from the International Labour Office's *The Cost of Social Security* (triennial), supplemented by national data sources.

Figures for criminal offenses known to police, usually excluding civil offenses and minor traffic violations, are taken in part from Interpol's *International Crime Statistics* (annual) and a variety of national sources. Statistics are usually based on the number of offenses reported to police, not the number of offenders apprehended or tried in courts. Attempted offenses are counted as the offense that was attempted. A person identified as having committed multiple offenses is counted only under the most serious offense. Murder refers to all acts involving the voluntary taking of life, including infanticide, but excluding abortion, or involuntary acts such as those normally classified as manslaughter. Assault includes "serious," or aggravated, assault—that involving injury, endangering life, or perpetrated with the use of a dangerous instrument; Burglary involves theft from the premises of another; although Interpol statistics are reported as "breaking and entering," national data may not always distinguish cases of forcible

Social protection

country	old-age, invalidity, death[a]	sickness and maternity[b]	work injury[c]	unemployment[d]	family allowances[e]	expenditures, 1994 (% of total central govt.)[f]	year	receipts total ('000,000 natl. cur.)	insured persons (%)	employers (%)	government (%)	other (%)	expenditures total ('000,000 natl. cur.)	benefits (%)	administration (%)	other (%)
Afghanistan	●	●	●		●	...	...	...	...	...	...	...	...	...	...	...
Albania	●	●	●		●	21.7	1990	967.0	—	—	88.8	11.2	1,440.0	99.5	0.5	...
Algeria	●	●	●	●	●	...	1990	27,700.0	...	...	...	...	28,748.0	61.8	30.6	7.6
American Samoa	●	...	●	...	...	...	1990	...	...	...	...	...	13.0	100.0	—	—
Andorra	●	●	●		●	...	1993	11,832.2	...	...	...	...	7,937.2	90.2	4.6	5.2
Angola	...	...	...	...	...	...	...	...	...	...	...	...	...	...	...	...
Antigua and Barbuda	●	●	●		●	...	1983	13.0	29.2	48.7	—	22.1	4.2	66.1	33.9	—
Argentina	●	●	●	●	●	50.7[9]	1989	1,015,837.0	28.8	45.0	16.6	9.6	989,009.0	95.0	5.0	—
Armenia	●	●	●	●	●	...	...	...	...	...	...	...	...	...	...	...
Aruba	●	...	●	...	...	11	1992	66.3	...	...	...	...	60.4	...	...	...
Australia	●	●	●	●	●	33.9	1989	28,525.6	1.9	7.8	88.4	1.9	28,880.4	98.7	1.0	0.3
Austria	●	●	●	●	●	46.4	1989	425,417.0	30.1	45.9	21.1	2.9	412,134.0	96.5	2.3	1.2
Azerbaijan	●	●	●	●		...	...	...	...	...	...	...	...	...	...	...
Bahamas, The	●	●	●		●	4.1[12]	1989	95.9	22.9	38.5	2.1	36.5	43.5	71.1	27.2	1.7
Bahrain	●		●			3.9	1989	39.6	12.3	40.2	—	47.5	9.7	69.8	20.9	9.3
Bangladesh		●	●			9.8[13]	1989	73.6	12.4	37.5	2.4	47.7	34.1	94.0	6.0	—
Barbados	●	●	●	●		19.8[6,14]	1989	191.7	38.0	40.8	1.5	19.7	149.1	93.5	5.8	0.7
Belarus	●	●	●	●	●	11.0[9,14]	1986	3,199.0	—	—	93.2	6.8	3,199.0	100.0	—	—
Belgium	●	●	●	●	●	42.3[6]	1986	1,347,070.0	24.4	39.7	31.6	4.3	1,322,636.0	94.5	4.3	1.2
Belize	●	●	●			4.6	1989	15.3	8.9	53.2	—	38.0	3.9	56.7	43.3	—
Benin	●		●		●	8.7[17]	1989	3,551.9	16.8	81.4	—	1.8	4,500.9	69.3	28.1	2.6
Bermuda	●			●		...	...	...	...	...	...	...	...	...	...	...
Bhutan	...	...	...	...	...	0.5[9]	1990	...	...	...	...	...	26.0[18]	...	...	...
Bolivia	●	●	●		●	14.6	1989	346.6	29.3	47.7	11.2	11.8	340.2	84.9	14.3	0.8
Bosnia and Herzegovina	●	●	●	●	●	...	...	...	...	...	...	...	...	...	...	...
Botswana			●			3.8[12]	1993	—	...	...	...	...	148.3[18]	...	...	...
Brazil	●	●	●	●	●	27.1[12]	1989	71,847.0	24.4	51.0	20.0	4.6	68,957.0	61.9	18.6	19.5
Brunei	●		...		...	...	1984	...	...	...	...	...	39.5	...	...	...
Bulgaria	●	●	●	●		28.0	1989	6,016.8	—	71.4	28.1	0.5	6,000.1	96.6	3.3	0.1
Burkina Faso	●		●		●	0.1[19]	1989	8,816.5	15.6	62.9	—	21.5	4,975.3	69.5	30.4	0.1
Burundi	●		●		●	0.7[14,20]	1989	1,991.5	31.6	47.6	—	20.8	1,563.9	74.8	16.8	8.4
Cambodia	...		...		●	...	...	...	...	...	...	...	...	...	...	...
Cameroon	●		●		●	1.0[12]	1989	41,331.8	13.1	64.8	—	22.1	41,332.0	70.6	28.8	0.6
Canada	●	●	●	●	●	39.8	1989	130,306.6	9.9	15.6	64.4	10.1	115,764.2	96.9	2.5	0.6
Cape Verde	●	●	●		●	...	1989	697.7	26.5	58.5	—	15.0	316.7	82.4	16.1	1.5
Central African Republic	●		●		●	6.2[4]	1989	3,604.0	8.4	76.0	—	15.6	3,247.0	64.6	32.9	2.5
Chad	●		●		●	1.9[14,21]	1989	1,172.8	12.6	77.6	—	9.8	634.5	43.0	51.4	5.6
Chile	●	●	●	●	●	33.3	1989	1,186,056.0	32.8	2.7	37.9	26.6	798,770.0	83.9	14.7	1.4
China	●	●	●	●		0.1	1989	57,446.2	—	99.4	—	0.6	54,654	98.4	0.6	1.0
Colombia	●	●	●		●	7.8	1989	294,438.0	24.8	56.0	0.2	19.0	257,455.0	85.5	11.5	3.0
Comoros	...		●	...		...	1983	40.7	100.0	—	—	—	54.3	17.4	62.3	20.3
Congo, Dem. Rep. of the	●		●		●	1.1[12]	1986	1,238.3	28.6	60.2	—	11.2	1,044.2	27.9	72.1	—
Congo, Rep. of the	●	●	●		●	0.4[14,24]	1983	15,272.8	12.1	80.2	—	7.7	7,256.7	66.6	21.3	12.1
Costa Rica	●	●	●		●	17.7	1989	36,407.3	33.2	44.4	1.2	21.2	31,049.8	89.0	4.1	6.9
Côte d'Ivoire	●	●	●		●	3.6[4,14]	1989	27,288.4	19.3	75.4	—	5.3	20,593.5	100.0	—	—
Croatia	●	●	●	●	●	30.5	...	...	...	...	...	...	...	...	...	...
Cuba	●	●	●			...	1989	2,284.8	—	37.4	62.6	...	2,284.8	96.7	...	3.3
Cyprus[25]	●	●	●	●	●	23.2	1989	217.5	24.7	40.3	17.3	17.7	117.7	98.4	1.6	—
Czech Republic	●	●	●	●	●	28.2	1989[26]	132,748.0	—	3.9	96.1	—	132,748.0	99.7	0.3	—
Denmark	●	●	●	●	●	43.2	1989	225,965.6	4.3	5.0	88.2	2.5	218,258.2	97.0	3.0	—
Djibouti	●	...	...	...	●	6.2[27]	1979	1,352.2	...	...	...	...	1,115.7	...	...	...
Dominica	●	●	●			1.4[14,17]	1986	12.3	22.6	50.9	—	26.5	4.4	68.0	32.0	—
Dominican Republic	●	●	●			3.8	1986	77.9	20.1	72.9	—	6.8	74.3	75.9	24.1	—
Ecuador	●	●	●			1.9[3]	1988	71,286.0	37.0	50.0	—	13.0	52,032.4	86.0	14.0	—
Egypt	●	●	●	●		11.0[12]	1989	2,443.5	22.8	41.0	2.0	34.2	1,685.6	93.4	6.6	—

entry. Automobile theft excludes brief use of a car without the owner's permission, "joyriding," and implies intent to deprive the owner of the vehicle permanently. Criminal offense data for certain countries refer to cases disposed of in court, rather than to complaints. Police manpower figures refer, for the most part, to full-time, paid professional staff, excluding clerical support and volunteer staff. Personnel in military service who perform police functions are presumed to be employed in their principal activity, military service.

The figures for military manpower refer to full-time, active-duty military service and exclude reserve, militia, paramilitary, and similar organizations. Because of the difficulties attached to the analysis of data on military manpower and budgets (including problems such as data withheld on national security grounds, or the publication of budgetary data specifically intended to hide actual expenditure, or the complexity of long-term financing of purchases of military matériel [how much was actually spent as opposed to what was committed, offset by nonmilitary transfers, etc.]), extensive use is made of the principal international analytic tools: publications such as those of the International Institute for Strategic Studies (*The Military Balance* and *Strategic Survey*) and the U.S. Arms Control and Disarmament Agency (*World Military Expenditures and Arms Transfers*), both annuals.

The data on military expenditures are from the sources identified above, as well as from the IMF's *Government Finance Statistics Yearbook* and country statistical publications.

The following notes further define the column headings:

a. Programs providing cash payments for *each* of the three types of long-term benefit indicated to persons (1) exceeding a specified working age (usually 50–65, often 5 years earlier for women) who are qualified by a term of covered employment, (2) partially or fully incapacitated for their usual employment by injury or illness, and (3) qualified by their status as spouse, cohabitant, or dependent minor of a qualified person who dies.
b. Programs providing cash payments (jointly, or alternatively, medical services as well) to occupationally qualified persons for *both* of the short-term benefits indicated: (1) illness and (2) maternity.
c. Programs providing cash or medical services to employment-qualified persons who become temporarily or permanently incapacitated (fully or partially) by work-related injury or illness.
d. Programs providing term-limited cash compensation (usually 40–75% of average earnings) to persons qualified by previous employment (of six months minimum, typically) for periods of involuntary unemployment.
e. Programs providing cash payments to families or mothers to mitigate the cost of raising children and to encourage the formation of larger families.
f. Includes welfare.
g. A police officer is a full-time, paid professional, performing domestic security functions. Data include administrative staff but exclude clerical employees, volunteers, and members of paramilitary groups.
h. Includes all active-duty personnel, regular and conscript, performing national security functions. Excludes reserves, paramilitary forces, border patrols, and gendarmeries.

crime and law enforcement (latest) offenses reported to the police per 100,000 population					population per police officer[g]	military protection manpower, 1997[h]		expenditure, 1995				arms trade, 1995 ('000,000 U.S.$)		country
total	personal murder	assault	property burglary	automobile theft		total ('000)	per 1,000 population	total '000,000	per capita	% of central government expenditure	% of GDP or GNP	imports	exports	
...	...	...	...	...	540[1]	2	2	408[3]	24[4]	64.4[4]	9.1[4]	20	0	Afghanistan
...	...	...	...	...	550	5	5	157[6]	56[6]	11.3[6]	4.1[6]	0	0	Albania
584	1.0	19.7	39.7	8.5	840	124.0	4.2	1,238	43	6.9	3.2	230	0	Algeria
3,006	8.0	494.0	588.0	6.0	460	—	7	—	—	—	—	...	...	American Samoa
2,795	1.6	36.5	796.8	111.1	220	—	—	...	...	...	...	...	...	Andorra
31	3.4	6.1	...	...	14[8]	110.5	10.4	225	22	...	3.0	90	0	Angola
4,977	4.7	475.0	1,984.4	35.9	120	0.2	2.3	...	...	...	...	...	...	Antigua and Barbuda
186.2	0.3	0.6	1.5	19.9	1,270	73.0	2.1	4,684	137	27.0[10]	1.7	40	70	Argentina
160.4	5.4	3.4	...	2.1	...	58.6	15.5	79	23	...	0.9	30	0	Armenia
5,461	1.2	180.0	451.3	202.5	...	—	7	—	—	—	—	...	...	Aruba
6,279	1.8	560.3	2,131.9	703	453	57.4	3.1	8,401	465	8.8	2.5	930	50	Australia
6,314	2.5	2.5	1,128.2	31.8	470	45.5	5.6	2,106	264	2.2[9]	0.9	120	0	Austria
247	8.1	5.6	8.4	4.1	...	66.7	8.8	304	40	3.8[9]	2.8	0	0	Azerbaijan
6,752	17.6	115.7	1,336.5	...	125	0.9	3.0	9[4]	40[4]	2.5[4]	0.5[4]	...	...	Bahamas, The
1,714	1.8	547.1	86.7	8.2	180	11.0	17.7	273	473	14.8	5.4	40	0	Bahrain
64	1.9	3.6	4.6	0.6	2,560	121.0	1.0	502	4.0	9.9[12]	1.7	60	0	Bangladesh
4,337	6.8	170.8	1,267.2	34.2	280	0.6	2.3	13	50	2.3	0.8	0	0	Barbados
650	2.9	7.0	...	...	...	80.0	7.7	...	...	...	...	0	170	Belarus
5,769	3.1	33.0	1,529.5	310.7	640	44.5	4.4	4,449	439	3.5[10]	1.7	340	130	Belgium
...	33.2[15]	275.6[16]	833.6	...	290	1.1	4.6	9	41	5.0	1.6	0	0	Belize
125	0.9	37.9	3.4	1.3	3,250	4.8	0.8	24	4	8.6[12]	1.2	0	0	Benin
8,871	5.1	221.7	1,949.2	...	370	—	7	—	—	—	—	...	...	Bermuda
...	...	...	...	...	...	4.0[13]	3.1[13]	...	...	...	...	0	0	Bhutan
...	...	...	...	...	...	33.5	4.3	132	19	9.5	2.3	10	0	Bolivia
402	2.5	2.6	...	...	...	40.0	12.8	...	...	...	...	270	0	Bosnia and Herzegovina
8,281	12.7	431.9	1.9	73.1	750	7.5	5.0	225	155	12.7	5.3	0	0	Botswana
116	...	...	...	...	...	314.7	2.0	10,900	68	3.9	1.7	170	10	Brazil
1,148	1.5	2.7	133.1	42.7	100	5.0	16.2	269	919	20.1[3]	6.0	5	0	Brunei
2,522	5.9	38.6	1,174.9	208.0	...	75.8	9.1	1,073	125	6.3	2.8	0	150	Bulgaria
41	0.2	4.1	—	—	...	10.0	0.9	68	7	12.0[12]	2.9	0	0	Burkina Faso
87	3.3	7.4	...	...	...	18.5	3.1	46	8	24.8	4.4	0	0	Burundi
...	...	...	...	...	1,980	140.5	13.5	90	9	16.7[10]	3.1	20	0	Cambodia
11	0.1	0.1	1.2	0.2	1,170	13.1	0.9	102[10]	8[10]	10.2[12]	1.9[10]	10	0	Cameroon
10,351	5.2	769.1	1,326.2	545.9	8,640	61.6	2.0	9,077	319	7.1[10]	1.7	210	280	Canada
...	...	...	...	...	110	1.1	2.8	4	9	1.3[12]	1.0	0	0	Cape Verde
135	1.6	22.8	2.7	...	2,740[1]	5.0	1.5	30[10]	10[10]	6.6[6]	3.2[10]	0	0	Central African Republic
...	...	...	...	...	990	25.4	3.5	34	5	9.7[9]	3.1	10	0	Chad
1,086	11.0	96.3	...	13.1	470	94.3	6.5	2,243	158	17.5	3.8	380	0	Chile
128	0.2	5.2	45.2	6.9	1,360[22]	2,840.0	2.3	63,510	53	18.5	2.3	725	625	China
641	81.9	110.5	...	32.4	420	146.3	4.0	2,000	55	16.2	2.6	60	0	Colombia
...	...	...	...	...	960	...	23	...	...	...	...	...	...	Comoros
...	...	...	...	...	910	—	—	17	0	3.7	0.3	0	0	Congo, Dem. Rep. of the
32	1.5	4.7	0.2	0.2	870	10.0	3.9	48	19	11.13	2.9	10	0	Congo, Rep. of the
868	5.3	11.1	232.4	23.1	480	—	—	50	15	2.7	0.6	0	0	Costa Rica
67	2.5	73.1	19.5	11.9	4,640	8.4	0.6	98	7	4.2[12]	1.1	0	0	Côte d'Ivoire
1,334	7.4	23.2	379.8	20.9	...	58.0	12.1	...	...	...	...	110	0	Croatia
...	...	...	...	...	650	53.0	4.7	350	32	...	1.6	0	0	Cuba
689	1.9	17.7	203.3	3.0	180	10.0	13.0	495	672	17.1	5.8	50	0	Cyprus[25]
1,911[26]	2.0[26]	89.4[26]	621.5[26]	95.7[26]	640[26]	44.0	4.3	2,368	229	6.6	2.3	0	120	Czech Republic
10,525	4.9	190.1	2,046.3	663.3	600	32.9	6.2	3,118	596	4.1	1.8	80	20	Denmark
402	4.4	12.4	40.0	16.0	...	9.6	15.4	22	52	13.9[12]	4.5	0	0	Djibouti
1,956	4.2	25.2	1,078.1	33.6	300	28	28	...	...	...	...	...	...	Dominica
946	11.9	30.8	154.0	24.8	580	24.5	3.1	122	16	6.8	1.1	10	0	Dominican Republic
466	10.5	32.9	94.4	36.5	260	57.1	4.8	611	54	18.3	3.7	260	0	Ecuador
3,693	1.6	0.7	...	3.1	580	450.0	7.2	2,653	43	13.7	5.7	1,900	0	Egypt

Social protection (continued)

country	old-age, invalidity, death[a]	sickness and maternity[b]	work injury[c]	unemployment[d]	family allowances[e]	expenditures, 1994 (% of total central govt.)[f]	year	receipts total ('000,000 natl. cur.)	insured persons (%)	employers (%)	government (%)	other (%)	expenditures total ('000,000 natl. cur.)	benefits (%)	administration (%)	other (%)
El Salvador	•	•	•	—	—	7.3[12]	1989	465.3	27.1	51.7	—	21.2	368.3	78.1	21.9	—
Equatorial Guinea	•	•	•	—	•	...	1989	141.0	7.1	92.9	—	—	134.0	49.3	50.7	—
Eritrea[30]	...	...	...	...	...	...	...	...	...	...	...	...	...	...	...	...
Estonia	•	•	•	•	•	30.0	...	90.1	...	...	...	...	...	...	...	...
Ethiopia[30]	•	...	•	...	•	6.9[9]	1989	190.9	32.8	65.3	—	1.9	153.7	98.3	1.7	—
Faroe Islands	•	...	•	...	...	...	...	...	...	...	...	...	...	...	...	...
Fiji	•	...	•	...	...	4.7	1989	153.5	20.9	33.8	0.8	44.5	75.47	95.3	4.7	...
Finland	•	•	•	•	•	44.4	1989	118,589.0	7.7	41.1	44.0	7.2	106,235	96.3	3.7	—
France	•	•	•	•	•	39.3[12]	1989	1,700,202.0	77.7	—	20.4	1.9	1,669,096.0	95.5	3.7	0.8
French Guiana	•	...	•	...	•	...	1991	1,071.5	...	...	...	...	997.1	...	...	...
French Polynesia	•	...	•	...	•	...	1990	19,268.0	...	...	...	...	17,832.0	...	...	...
Gabon	•	...	•	...	•	...	1989	3,415.0	—	44.3	29.3	26.4	2,737.0	55.2	44.8	...
Gambia, The	•	...	•	...		3.0[3]	1982	—	...	...	...	...	5.6	...	...	...
Gaza Strip	...	...	...	...	...	...	...	...	...	...	...	...	...	...	...	...
Georgia	•	•	•	...	•	...	...	...	...	...	...	...	...	...	...	...
Germany	•	•	•	•	•	45.3[19]	1989[33]	522,172.0	36.9	34.3	26.1	2.7	507,604.0	97.1	2.8	0.1
Ghana	•	...	•	...		7.1[12]	1989	17,920.8	21.1	52.9	—	26.0	4,147.7	13.3	64.0	22.7
Gibraltar	•	•	•	•	•	...	...	...	...	...	...	...	...	...	...	...
Greece	•	•	•	•	•	13.4[12]	1989	1,314,421.0	24.9	38.4	30.8	5.9	1,349,693.0	92.5	7.5	—
Greenland	...	...	...	...	...	...	...	...	...	...	...	...	...	...	...	...
Grenada	•	•			•	7.6	1989	24.1	20.1	60.3	3.2	16.3	13.5	93.1	6.9	—
Guadeloupe	•	...	•	...	•	...	1994	2,607.3	...	...	...	...	5,883.4	...	...	...
Guam	•	...	...	...	...	...	1989	...	...	...	...	...	7.3	...	...	...
Guatemala	•	•	•	...		5.2[6]	1989	348.5	29.1	54.8	—	16.1	279.7	82.7	14.6	2.7
Guernsey	•	•	•	•	•	...	1993	66,369	—44.3—		45.5	10.2	62,458	94.2	5.8	...
Guinea	•	•	•	...	•	...	1989	3,387.0	0.4	90.3	—	9.3	1,108.1	54.9	45.1	—
Guinea-Bissau	...	•	...	...	•	8.8[12]	1986	138.0	22.8	63.4	10.3	3.8	61.9	59.6	40.4	—
Guyana	•	•	•	...		3.7[14,34]	1994	1,070.8	...	...	...	...	1,373.7	...	...	...
Haiti	•	...	•	...		5.1[14]	1977	60.5	—26.6—		69.9	3.5	52.4	92.7	7.3	—
Honduras	•	•	•	...		4.5[14,17]	1986	166.2	23.9	40.8	3.3	32.0	76.8	84.6	15.4	—
Hong Kong	•	...	•	...	•	...	1995–96	...	...	...	...	...	13,267.7	74.9	25.1	—
Hungary	•	•	•	•	•	27.7[3]	1994	798,000.0	—	—	—	—	737,000.0	—	—	—
Iceland	•	•	•	•	•[36]	22.5	1994	10,840	...	...	...	...	80,819.0	97.8	2.2	—
India	•	...	•	...		...	1989	43,913.8	23.8	27.7	5.3	43.2	13,775.8	90.0	8.2	1.8
Indonesia	•	...	•	...		5.3	1989	239,477.0	50.7	49.3	—	—	181,499.0	12.3	15.8	71.9
Iran	•	...	•	...	•	10.3	1986	346,460.0	83.2	0.1	8.2	8.5	167,879.0	43.4	6.3	50.0
Iraq	•	•	•	...		...	1977	107.8	9.9	55.6	21.9	12.6	71.0	94.0	2.4	3.6
Ireland	•	•	•	•	•	27.6[12]	1989	4,627.5	16.3	24.8	57.7	1.2	4,612.9	95.2	4.7	0.1
Isle of Man	•	•	•	•	•	37.0[14,38]	1985	...	...	...	...	...	14.4	...	...	...
Israel	•	•	•	•	•	24.5	1989	13,851.1	31.1	27.7	35.0	6.2	13,593.3	81.7	15.4	2.9
Italy	•	•	•	•	•	38.0[14,39]	1989	278,383.0	16.5	51.4	30.0	2.1	100,251.0	89.3	2.0	8.7
Jamaica	•	...	•	...	•	3.2[14,20]	1989	374.3	11.5	13.6	43.8	31.1	273.6	92.6	7.4	—
Japan	•	•	•	•	•	36.8[12]	1989	59,571,299.0	27.4		24.4	16.6	46,684,159.0	94.3	1.7	4.0
Jersey	•	•	•	...		9.5[12,14]	1991	60.9	—63.8—		23.4	12.8	52.8	...	...	...
Jordan	•	•	•	...		14.3	1986	53.6	28.7	55.3	—	16.0	9.5	77.4	14.0	8.6
Kazakstan	•	•	•	•	•	...	...	...	...	...	...	...	...	...	...	...
Kenya	•	...	•	...		0.1[12]	1989	4,262.0	18.2	13.7	10.0	58.1	1,857.8	53.8	46.1	0.1
Kiribati	•	...	...	...	...	...	...	...	...	...	...	...	...	...	...	...
Korea, North	...	•	•	...	...	...	...	...	...	...	...	...	...	...	...	...
Korea, South	•	...	•	...		9.9[12]	1995	4,981,400.0	60.3	—	—	—	7,862,000.0	...	...	...
Kuwait	•	...			•	16.6	1989	445.8	7.1	13.2	54.3	25.4	206.5	97.0	3.0	—
Kyrgyzstan	•	•	•	•	•	...	...	...	...	...	...	...	...	...	...	...
Laos	...	•	...	...	...	...	...	...	...	...	...	...	...	...	...	...
Latvia	•	...	•	•	•	36.7	...	...	...	...	...	...	...	...	...	...
Lebanon	•	•	•	...		...	...	...	...	...	...	...	...	...	...	...
Lesotho	...	...	•	...		1.19	1992	—	...	...	...	...	12.0[18]	...	...	...
Liberia	•	•	•	...		1.0[14,39]	1983	2.9	—	69.0	13.8	17.2	2.6	54.4	45.6	—
Libya	•	•	•	...	•	...	1989	314.3	21.6	25.4	50.2	2.8	260.0	77.5	19.5	3.0
Liechtenstein	•	•	•	•	•	...	...	...	...	...	...	...	...	...	...	...
Lithuania	•	•	•	•	•	35.6	...	...	...	...	...	...	24,981.7	...	...	...
Luxembourg	•	•	•	•	•	51.1	1989	72,471.8	24.2	34.6	34.4	6.8	65,214.4	97.2	2.4	0.4
Macau	•	...			•	...	1995	168.0	...	...	...	...	146.1	...	...	...
Macedonia	•	•	•	•	•	...	1995	20,785	...	...	...	...	...	...	...	...
Madagascar	•	...	•	...	•	1.9	1989	15,229.0	22.2	77.8	—	—	14,542.0	81.2	18.8	...
Malawi	•	...	•	...		0.1[39]	1986	...	...	...	...	...	5.4	...	...	...
Malaysia	•	...	•	...		6.6	1989	7,958.7	20.7	40.2	—	39.1	2,826.5	97.0	3.0	—
Maldives	...	...	...	...	...	3.2	1990	—	...	...	...	...	7.1	...	...	...
Mali	•	...	•	...	•	3.0[14,39]	1986	8,128.8	16.6	74.3	—	9.1	7,924.6	63.7	34.7	1.6
Malta	•	•	•	•	•	33.6	1989	82.2	26.1	31.6	42.3	—	110.7	92.5	7.5	—
Marshall Islands	...	...	...	...	...	...	...	...	...	...	...	...	...	...	...	...
Martinique	...	...	...	...	...	...	1994	3,503.2	...	...	...	...	6,187.8	...	...	...
Mauritania	•	...	•	...	•	3.7[14,17]	1989	808.4	1.5	90.4	—	8.1	735.2	63.5	31.2	5.3
Mauritius	•	...	•	...	•	16.6	1989	1,733.5	2.9	47.9	31.7	17.5	1,072.7	95.2	3.0	1.8
Mayotte	...	...	...	...	...	...	...	...	...	...	...	...	...	...	...	...
Mexico	•	•	•	...		22.8	1989	16,011,795.0	20.9	54.8	12.9	11.4	14,562,293.0	79.9	15.5	4.6
Micronesia	...	...	...	...	...	...	...	...	...	...	...	...	...	...	...	...
Moldova	...	•	•	...	•	...	...	...	...	...	...	...	...	...	...	...
Monaco	...	...	...	...	...	...	...	...	...	...	...	...	...	...	...	...
Mongolia	•	•	•	...	•	21.6	1989	2,431.6	—	—	20.8	79.2	2,304.6	100.0	—	—
Morocco	•	•	•	...	•	5.9[9]	1989	4,660.5	20.6	47.5	12.9	19.0	3,040.7	94.8	5.0	0.2
Mozambique	•	...	...	...		...	1986	228.2	—	86.2	13.7	0.1	145.0	100.0	—	—
Myanmar (Burma)	•	...	•	...		3.6	1986	44.3	19.9	59.6	18.5	2.0	35.9	51.5	15.6	32.9
Namibia	•	...	•	...		6.8[14,19]	...	...	...	...	...	...	...	...	...	...
Nauru	•	...	•	...		...	...	...	...	...	...	...	...	...	...	...
Nepal	•	...	•	...		0.7[13,14]	1985	—	...	...	...	...	59.3	...	...	...

crime and law enforcement (latest) — offenses reported to the police per 100,000 population					population per police officer[g]	military protection — manpower, 1997[h]		expenditure, 1995				arms trade, 1995 ('000,000 U.S.$)		country
total	personal — murder	assault	property — burglary	automobile theft		total ('000)	per 1,000 population	total '000,000	per capita	% of central government expenditure	% of GDP or GNP	imports	exports	
...	...	...	...	...	1,000	28.4	5.0	101	18	7.4	1.1	20	0	El Salvador
...	...	...	...	...	190	1.3	3.0	2	6	21.0[29]	1.6	0	0	Equatorial Guinea
...	...	...	...	...	...	[31]	[31]	...	...	...	...	0	0	Eritrea[30]
2,383	24.3	29.3	1,160.7	169.1	...	3.5	2.4	118	80	2.9[10]	1.1	5	0	Estonia
263	16.4	49.9	6.3	2.3	1,100	[32]	[32]	118	2	9.2	2.2	0	0	Ethiopia[30]
...	...	...	...	...	407	—	[7]	—	—	—	—	...	...	Faroe Islands
2,518	11.5	51.3	463.7	51.7	407	3.6	4.6	32	42	6.0	1.7	20	0	Fiji
14,799	0.6	40.0	1,934.9	53.2	640	31.0	6.0	2,381	467	5.1	2.0	30	0	Finland
6,733	4.7	98.8	812.6	667.0	630	380.8	6.5	47,770	826	6.6	3.1	150	2,200	France
8,936	27.2	178.7	1,367.3	150.6	...	—	[7]	—	—	—	—	...	...	French Guiana
1,799	0.9	98.9	232.7	...	...	—	[7]	—	—	—	—	...	...	French Polynesia
114	1.4	17.9	2.3	7.5	1,290	4.7	3.9	104	90	9.6[12]	2.6	0	0	Gabon
89	0.4	10.6	5.6	...	3,310	0.8	0.6	15	13	16.2	4.6	0	0	Gambia, The
4,355	...	...	...	...	...	—	—	...	...	...	...	...	...	Gaza Strip
325	10.7	107.8	40.7	1.5	...	—	—	194	37	2.4[9]	2.4	10	0	Georgia
8,038	4.6	108.2	1,927.1	260.1	...	347.1	4.2	41,160	496	5.0	1.9	310	1,200	Germany
942	2.1	387.4	5.4	...	620	7.0	0.4	87	5	5.8[12]	1.4	0	0	Ghana
18,316	3.7[15]	3,213	5,250	...	170	—	[7]	—	—	—	—	...	...	Gibraltar
2,956	2.6	78.7	330.2	100.3	380	162.3	15.4	5,056	482	10.8	5.5	825	0	Greece
9,360	18.1	845.0	1,883.5	...	340	—	[7]	—	—	—	—	...	...	Greenland
8,543	7.8	98.9	582.2	...	230	[28]	[28]	...	...	...	...	...	...	Grenada
5,793	13.2	215.2	821.5	453.9	...	—	[7]	...	...	...	...	...	...	Guadeloupe
10,080	7.9	169.3	634.2	333.6	...	—	[7]	...	...	...	...	...	...	Guam
510	27.4	77.1	27.9	58.1	670	40.7	3.6	191	17	14.2	1.3	5	0	Guatemala
...	...	...	...	...	...	—	[7]	—	—	—	—	...	...	Guernsey
18.4	0.5	0.7	0.7	0.1	1,140	9.7	1.3	51	7	7.0[9]	1.5	5	0	Guinea
129	0.5	8.7	4.0	0.2	...	7.3	6.2	7	6	7.6[12]	2.8	0	0	Guinea-Bissau
3,682	4.5	40.2	242.6	32.2	190	1.6	2.1	7	10	3.0	1.3	0	0	Guyana
701	...	...	...	...	400	[35]	[35]	59	9	21.6	2.9	0	0	Haiti
...	9.4	7.7	...	3.3	1,040	18.8	3.2	51	9	8.7	1.4	10	0	Honduras
1,449	1.6	118.8	222.8	38.9	221	—	[7]	—	—	—	—	...	...	Hong Kong
3,789	4.3	79.3	767.4	51.1	710	49.1	4.8	961	95	4.6	1.5	30	20	Hungary
1,550	0.9	64.3	704.8	112.8	940	—	—	—	—	—	—	0	0	Iceland
594	4.6	...	15.6	...	820	1,145.0	1.2	7,831	8	12.7	2.4	410	5	India
60	0.8	5.1	24.8	8.0	1,119	284.0	1.4	3,398	17	8.9	1.8	170	10	Indonesia
76.6	0.5	47.7	...	...	...	518.0	8.3	4,191	65	13.6[10]	2.6	270	290	Iran
197	7.1	34.7	...	...	140	387.5	17.4	9,007[19]	528[19]	50.8[37]	74.9[19]	0	0	Iraq
2,834	1.2	13.3	859.7	44.3	310	12.7	3.5	689	193	3.4	1.3	0	0	Ireland
2,867	0.7	12.3	921.4	60.6	...	—	[7]	—	—	—	—	...	...	Isle of Man
5,191	2.1	267.2	817.2	479.5	210	175.0	31.0	8,734	1,646	21.1	9.6	340	775	Israel
3,828	4.7	36.8	...	532.8	680	325.2	5.7	19,380	338	3.9[10]	1.8	110	150	Italy
1,723	27.6	552.1	267.7	9.9	430	3.3	1.3	28	11	1.4	0.8	0	0	Jamaica
1,490	1.0	14.4	198.1	27.8	480	235.6	1.9	50,240	401	4.2[12]	1.0	625	20	Japan
...	...	...	...	...	...	—	[7]	—	—	—	—	...	...	Jersey
751	2.0	19.1	43.4	28.5	630	130.0	28.7	481	117	21.7	7.7	70	0	Jordan
815	...	...	...	...	...	35.1	2.1	426	25	...	0.9	280	20	Kazakstan
484	6.4	54.1	76.9	9.7	1,500	24.2	0.8	173	6	6.2	2.3	10	0	Kenya
261	5.1	11.6	38.6	...	330	—	—	...	...	...	...	...	...	Kiribati
...	...	...	...	...	460	1,055.0	43.4	6,000	255	40.7[39]	28.6	100	40	Korea, North
1,029	1.4	410.5	6.7	...	506	672.0	14.7	14,410	320	13.6	3.4	1,100	60	Korea, South
1,171	1.7	46.5	75.9	18.2	80	15.3	7.0	3,488	1,919	25.2	11.6	900	0	Kuwait
987	10.4[40]	12.6	482.4	...	...	12.2	2.7	57[10]	13[10]	1.1[9]	0.7[10]	0	10	Kyrgyzstan
...	...	...	...	...	280	29.0	5.7	72	15	21.3[4]	4.2	0	0	Laos
1,597	14.6	27.8	390.4	109.2	...	4.5	1.8	74	29	4.3[10]	0.9	5	0	Latvia
657	4.3	28.4	1.2	13.8	530	55.1	14.3	410	111	9.7[10]	3.7	40	0	Lebanon
1,885	33.9	170.6	221.5	...	1,130	2.0	1.0	28	15	2.5	1.9	0	0	Lesotho
...	...	...	...	...	1,570	[41]	[41]	45	21	13.3[6]	4.8[6]	0	0	Liberia
951	1.3	4.9	...	...	...	65.0	11.5	1,999	381	28.0[6]	6.0	0	0	Libya
...	...	114.3	614.3	153.6	660	—	[42]	—	—	—	—	...	...	Liechtenstein
1,199	6.9	9.1	325.2	28.1	...	5.3	1.4	78	21	2.1	0.5	5	0	Lithuania
6,933	13.2	291.7	855.2	275.5	829	0.8	1.9	142	348	1.9	0.7	0	0	Luxembourg
1,491	3.8	67.3	250.5	172.8	...	—	[7]	...	...	...	...	...	...	Macau
944	3.9	46.4	...	35.1	...	15.4	7.8	63	30	...	3.3	0	0	Macedonia
112	0.6	12.0	0.7	0.1	2,900	21.0	1.5	28	2	5.0	0.9	5	0	Madagascar
850	3.1	82.2	13.1	...	1,670	5.0	0.5	21	2	3.9[9]	1.6	0	0	Malawi
454	2.1	14.4	108.7	12.4	760	111.5	5.3	2,444	125	12.4	3.0	750	40	Malaysia
2,353	1.9	3.3	36.1	...	35,710	—	—	...	...	...	...	...	...	Maldives
33	—	1.1	3.9	...	160	7.4	0.7	43	5	9.4[9]	1.8	0	0	Mali
1,841	3.0	35.2	1,079.2	243.9	230	2.0	5.2	32	87	2.0[10]	1.1	0	0	Malta
2,273	...	...	...	...	400	—	[43]	—	...	...	...	...	...	Marshall Islands
6,305	5.8	184.9	641.2	192.8	...	—	[7]	—	...	...	...	...	...	Martinique
225	1.8	38	2.5	9.1	710	15.7	6.5	33	15	9.3[10]	3.2	5	0	Mauritania
3,430	3.2	11.2	85.9	...	240	—	—	14	12	1.6	0.4	0	0	Mauritius
...	...	...	...	...	...	—	[7]	—	...	...	...	...	...	Mayotte
108	7.3	30.2	...	...	...	175.0	1.9	2,321	25	5.1	1.0	20	20	Mexico
...	...	...	...	...	...	—	[43]	—	...	...	...	...	...	Micronesia
858	8.8	13.4	...	...	...	11.0	2.5	222	50	...	2.1	0	40	Moldova
4,277	...	63.4	407.1	126.8	...	...	...	...	...	...	...	...	...	Monaco
823	19.0	22.8	204.5	...	120	9.0	3.8	20	8	7.0	2.4	0	0	Mongolia
366	1.4	6.7	...	...	840	196.3	7.2	1,375	47	13.8[10]	4.3	50	0	Morocco
166	4.2	9.2	45.9	...	...	[44]	[44]	69	4	16.6[9]	5.4	0	0	Mozambique
309	4.1	31.2	0.1	0.1	650	429.0	9.2	1,833	41	37.5	3.9	140	0	Myanmar (Burma)
3,359	72.4	657.8	793.0	115.4	...	5.7	3.3	...	...	...	—	5	0	Namibia
...	25.0	400.0	100.0	...	110	—	—	...	...	...	...	...	...	Nauru
44	2.5	1.1	0.8	...	1,000	46.0	2.1	42	2	5.8	0.9	0	0	Nepal

Social protection (continued)

country	social security															
	programs available, 1997					expenditures, 1994 (% of total central govt.)[f]	finances									
							year	receipts					expenditures			
	old-age, invalidity, death[a]	sickness and maternity[b]	work injury[c]	unemployment[d]	family allowance[e]			total ('000,000 natl. cur.)	insured persons (%)	employers (%)	government (%)	other (%)	total ('000,000 natl. cur.)	benefits (%)	administration (%)	other (%)
Netherlands, The	●	●	●	●	●	37.2	1989	154,427.0	37.3	30.3	19.0	13.4	135,609.0	96.9	3.1	—
Netherlands Antilles	●	...	●	...	...	38.1[11]	1995	210.2	100.0	—	—	—	190.2	...	...	...
New Caledonia	...	...	●	...	●	...	1987	15,834.0	...	...	...	...	14,598.0	...	...	...
New Zealand	●	●	●	●	●	38.0	1989	14,266.0	1.0	4.7	92.5	1.8	14,372.3	95.6	2.8	1.6
Nicaragua	●	●	●	...	●	14.9	1989	647,454.8	13.5	49.1	7.6	29.8	452,038.6	82.4	17.6	—
Niger	●	...	●	...	●	1.7[29]	1989	5,634.9	9.4	90.6	—	—	3,804.2	62.5	...	37.5
Nigeria	●	...	●	...	...	2.5[47]	1989	54.0	50.0	50.0	—	—	22.6	42.5	57.5	...
Northern Mariana Islands	●	...	●	...	...											
Norway	●	●	●	●	●	36.7	1989	158,105.0	18.3	31.4	46.6	3.7	131,578.2	98.7	1.3	...
Oman	●	...	...	...	...	3.2	1995	—	...	...	...	...	62.2[18]	...	...	...
Pakistan	●	●	●	...	...	0.2[14, 48]	1989	9,321.4	1.3	8.0	84.3	6.4	8,092.0	97.4	1.2	1.4
Palau	●	...	...	...	...											
Panama	●	●	●	...	...	21.4	1989	496.7	31.0	39.5	7.1	22.4	452.8	94.0	4.8	1.2
Papua New Guinea	●	...	●	...	...	0.7	1983	45.0	40.5	32.1	8.0	19.4	9.4	82.3	9.7	8.0
Paraguay	●	●	●	...	...	16.2[12]	1993	49,272.0[39]	...	...	...	...	249,819.0	...	...	...
Peru	●	●	●	...	...	0.2[14, 34]	1989	1,363,280.6	30.2	65.1	4.7	—	1,435,134.1	78.5	21.5	...
Philippines	●	●	●	...	...	2.9[12]	1989	19,213.6	22.2	32.3	...	45.5	7,878.3	87.3	12.3	—
Poland	●	●	●	●	●	...	1989	11,572,248.0	2.1	70.2	25.1	2.6	11,452,165.0	98.8	1.2	—
Portugal	●	●	●	●	●	27.3[3]	1989	833,442.5	31.3	50.1	13.4	5.2	756,410.8	94.6	4.2	1.2
Puerto Rico	●	●	●	●	...	...	1980	...	...	...	...	...	1,041.3	100.0	...	—
Qatar	...	...	...	...	...	...	1986	80.0	—	—	100.0	—	80.0	100.0	—	—
Réunion	...	...	...	...	●	...	1994	...	...	...	...	...	11,030.7	...	...	...
Romania	●	●	●	●	●	28.8	1989	90,561.2	—	48.9	51.1	—	90,561.2	100.0	...	...
Russia	●	●	●	●	●	28.5										
Rwanda	●	...	●	...	...	2.9[37]	1989	2,350.0	23.9	39.8	—	36.3	965.8	60.8	39.2	...
St. Kitts and Nevis	●	●	●	...	...	9.4[49]	1989	14.3	...	...	...	...	7.9	...	...	...
St. Lucia	●	●	●	...	...	...	1986	14.6	28.6	28.6	—	42.8	3.4	61.4	38.6	...
St. Vincent and the Grenadines	●	●	●	...	...	7.7	1989	...	...	...	...	...	...	...	...	...
Samoa	●	...	●	...	...	...	...	—	...	...	...	...	—	...	...	...
San Marino	●	●	●	●	...	...	1983	51,673.0	12.0	48.7	36.1	3.2	46,179.0	95.7	3.7	0.6
São Tomé and Príncipe	●	...	●	...	...	...	1986	46.4	37.7	56.3	—	6.0	23.7	100.0	—	—
Saudi Arabia	●	...	●	...	...	...	1989	1,761.4	26.8	73.2	—	—	4,292.9	100.0	—	—
Senegal	●	●	●	...	●	2.6[14, 19]	1989	17,202.0	—	47.6	51.4	1.0	15,371.0	84.6	11.1	4.3
Seychelles	●	●	●	...	...	12.8	1983	69.1	30.1	60.2	—	9.7	42.7	69.6	4.9	25.5
Sierra Leone	●	...	●	...	...	2.3[3]	1990	...	...	...	...	...	153.00	100.00	...	...
Singapore	●	...	●	...	...	2.9	1989	7,531.9	49.1	35.3	0.1	15.6	5,045.8	78.0	0.6	21.4
Slovakia	●	●	●	●	●	...	1995	44,603	18.5	66.4	10.6	0.5	28,673	...	...	...
Slovenia	●	●	●	●	●	...										
Solomon Islands	●	...	●	...	...	0.7[14, 39]	1989	20.9	27.8	41.1	—	31.1	17.4	89.7	10.3	—
Somalia	●	...	●	...	...	1.7[47]										
South Africa	●	●	●	●	...	...	1994	2,034	—	100.0	—	—	2,260.0	...	...	...
Spain	●	●	●	●	●	39.6[12]	1989	8,320,972.0	15.9	53.9	27.9	2.3	8,038,090.0	94.3	2.6	3.1
Sri Lanka	●	●	●	...	...	16.7	1989	15,399.9	22.0	24.4	29.1	24.5	5,819.0	98.5	1.3	0.2
Sudan, The	●	...	●	...	...	0.4[6, 14]	1989	62.0	24.9	0.5	—	74.6	14.7	37.5	62.5	...
Suriname	●	...	...	...	...	6.0[14, 48]	1989	73.0	24.7	75.3	—	—	70.6	100.0	—	—
Swaziland	●	...	●	...	...	0.4[12]	1986	10.7	31.4	31.4	—	37.2	3.9	45.8	54.2	—
Sweden	●	●	●	●	●	48.2	1989	446,909.7	2.8	37.9	50.8	8.5	439,997.3	93.7	3.3	3.0
Switzerland	●	●	●	●	●	48.2[12]	1989	45,800.1	45.6	22.6	25.9	5.9	41,745.7	91.5	3.0	5.5
Syria	●	...	●	...	...	2.1	1989	3,147.9	30.4	60.9	...	5.6	1,455.9	95.7	4.2	0.1
Taiwan	●	●	●	...	...	13.8[3]										
Tajikistan	●	●	●	●	●	...										
Tanzania	●	...	●	...	...	0.5[13]	1989	3,275.8	25.9	25.9	—	48.2	2,780.7	5.8	14.1	80.1
Thailand	●	●	●	...	...	3.5	1989	654.0	—	60.2	—	39.8	260.0	88.2	11.8	—
Togo	●	●	●	...	●	6.5[14, 49]	1989	10,162.0	8.1	61.5	—	30.4	5,844.0	77.5	22.5	—
Tonga						0.8[19]										
Trinidad and Tobago	●	●	●	...	●	5.3[14, 27]	1989	584.9	12.0	24.1	39.7	24.2	438.4	85.6	11.1	3.3
Tunisia	●	●	●	...	●	14.3[13]	1989	325.3	36.9	63.1	—	—	358.3	90.0[20]	6.1[20]	3.9[20]
Turkey	●	●	●	...	...	3.9	1989	12,075,809.0	28.5	32.9	22.8	15.8	10,241,427.0	97.2	2.2	0.6
Turkmenistan	●	●	●	...	...	...										
Tuvalu	●	...	...	...	...	...	1981	...	...	...	...	...	0.1	67.6	32.4	—
Uganda	●	...	●	...	...	2.1[14, 48]	1989	265.9	32.1	64.3	1.1	2.5	145.0	0.3	76.8	22.9
Ukraine	●	●	●	●	●	...	1989	20,350.0	...	...	...	...	20,350.0	100.0	—	...
United Arab Emirates	...	...	...	...	...	3.4	1989	182.2	17.3	6.2	0.5	76.0	182.2	100.0	—	...
United Kingdom	●	●	●	●	●	31.3	1989	92,157.0	18.1	24.9	52.9	4.1	88,294.0	93.8	3.3	2.9
United States	●	●	●	●	●	29.2	1989	804,909.0	25.5	33.9	28.8	11.8	627,653.0	95.5	3.3	1.2
Uruguay	●	●	●	●	●	60.6	1989	535,507.0	31.4	37.3	26.0	5.3	548,591.0	93.6	5.4	1.0
Uzbekistan	●	●	●	●	●	...										
Vanuatu	●	...	...	...	...	0.9[14, 48]										
Venezuela	●	●	●	●	...	6.9[48]	1986	7,457.6	21.3	40.7	12.7	25.3	6,355.7	86.1	14.9	—
Vietnam	●	...	●	...	...	...										
Virgin Islands (U.S.)	●	...	●	●	●	...										
West Bank	...	...	...	...	...	...										
Western Sahara	...	...	...	...	...	...										
Yemen	●	...	●	...	...	...										
Yugoslavia	●	●	●	●	●	6.0[57]	1986[57]	2,777,651.0	63.3	32.2	3.4	1.1	2,732,679.0	90.3	1.9	7.8
Zambia	●	...	●	...	...	3.9	1986	179.2	28.4	28.4	—	43.2	67.7	40.6	59.4	—
Zimbabwe	●	...	●	...	...	3.4[6]	1983	167.0	25.9	7.6	64.2	2.3	112.2	93.7	6.2	0.1

[1]Rural areas only. [2]The bulk of the national armed forces disintegrated after the fall of the central government in April 1992, with only the northern corps retaining its integrity. [3]1990. [4]1984. [5]The Albanian forces have not been reconstituted since the civil unrest of early 1997. [6]1989. [7]Political dependency; defense is the responsibility of the administering country. [8]Includes civilian militia. [9]1992. [10]1994. [11]Netherlands Antilles includes Aruba. [12]1993. [13]1985. [14]Social security only. [15]Includes manslaughter. [16]Includes rape. [17]1979. [18]Includes welfare. [19]1991. [20]1977. [21]1976. [22]Local officers only. [23]Military defense is the responsibility of France. [24]1971. [25]Republic of Cyprus only. [26]Data refer to former Czechoslovakia. [27]1981. [28]Paramilitary unit of country participating in the U.S.-sponsored Regional Security System, a defense pact among eastern Caribbean countries. [29]1980. [30]Ethiopia includes Eritrea except in arms trade. [31]Demobilization of some Eritrean forces began in late 1993. Estimated strength of these forces is currently about 46,000. [32]Following the declaration of independence by Eritrea in May 1993, estimated strength of Ethiopian forces is currently about 100,000. [33]Former West Germany. [34]1983. [35]In 1994 the military government of Haiti was replaced by a civilian administration. Both the armed forces and police have been

	crime and law enforcement (latest)				military protection									country
	offenses reported to the police per 100,000 population				population per police officer[g]	manpower, 1997[h]		expenditure, 1995				arms trade, 1995 ('000,000 U.S.$)		
total	personal		property			total ('000)	per 1,000 population	total '000,000	per capita	% of central government expenditure	% of GDP or GNP	imports	exports	
	murder	assault	burglary	automobile theft										
10,181	24.9	191.8	3,803.0	316.8	510	52.8	3.4	8,012	518	4.4	2.1	220	230	Netherlands, The
5,574[45]	...	396	3,455	...	330	—	[7]	—	—	—	—	...	...	Netherlands Antilles
...	...	...	...	...	...	...	[7]	...	...	...	...	...	...	New Caledonia
13,854	3.9	546.3	2,352.9	788.6	630	9.6	2.6	740	211	3.3	1.3	40	5	New Zealand
1,069	25.6	203.8	110.7	...	90[8]	17.0	3.9	34	8	5.3	2.2	0	40	Nicaragua
32	0.2	2.5	1.0	0.1	2,350[46]	5.3	0.6	21	2	7.9	1.2	0	0	Niger
312	...	...	...	...	1,140	77.0	0.7	324[10]	3[10]	5.0[10]	0.8[10]	10	0	Nigeria
245	3.8	92.6	73.7	20.8	...	...	[7]	...	...	...	...	...	...	Northern Mariana Islands
9,187	1.0	—	95.0	516.6	660	33.6	7.6	3,508	804	6.5[10]	2.7	140	20	Norway
198	0.8	1.1	...	...	430	43.5	19.2	1,735	822	33.9	16.7	460	0	Oman
247	6.4	0.1	9.1	4.1	720	587.0	4.3	3,740	30	25.3	6.1	480	20	Pakistan
...	...	...	323.0	...	...	—	[43]	—	—	—	—	...	...	Palau
380	13.9	21.9	...	77.7	180	—	—	—	—	—	—	0	0	Panama
766	8.6	66.7	63	22.0	720	4.3	1.0	107	25	5.6	1.4	0	0	Papua New Guinea
313	15.6	62.2	105.1	50.3	310	20.2	4.0	121	23	7.3	1.4	0	0	Paraguay
1,178	9.3	104.3	87.0	22.7	730	125.0	5.1	989	41	9.3	1.7	280	0	Peru
230	30.1	41.8	...	1.2	1,160	110.5	1.5	1,151	16	8.5	1.5	90	0	Philippines
2,351	3.1	71.8	789.5	109.0	370	241.8	6.2	4,887	127	5.4	2.3	90	40	Poland
988	4.2	1.7	186.9	65.8	660	59.3	6.0	2,690	273	5.9[10]	2.6	90	0	Portugal
3,182	26.8	174.8	853.0	482.9	380	—	[7]	—	—	—	—	...	...	Puerto Rico
775	1.8	41.7	40.8	10.5	...	11.8	19.0	330	617	9.4	4.4	50	0	Qatar
2,097	7.8	123.1	181.3	137.9	220	—	[7]	—	—	—	—	...	...	Réunion
1,039	3.3	4.7	133.2	9.5	...	227.0	10.1	2,520	115	11.2	2.5	0	20	Romania
1,779	21.8	45.8	262.3	55.2	...	1,240.0	8.4	76,000	513	38.1[10]	11.4	0	3,300	Russia
14,550	12,500	25.0	12.5	12.5	4,650	55.0	7.1	118	20	23.3[12]	5.2	0	0	Rwanda
15,468	...	...	...	...	300	[28]	[28]	...	...	...	...	...	...	St. Kitts and Nevis
4,386	17.0	1,193.0	778.0	...	430	[28]	[28]	...	...	...	...	...	...	St. Lucia
3,977	10.3	986.9	...	...	250	[28]	[28]	...	...	...	...	...	...	St. Vincent and the Grenadines
...	...	...	...	...	...	—	[50]	...	...	...	...	...	...	Samoa
...	4.1	...	...	...	...	...	...	...	...	...	...	...	...	San Marino
558	4.0	...	...	...	400	—	—	1[29]	7[29]	2.5[29]	1.6[29]	0	0	São Tomé and Príncipe
131	0.9	17.2	...	28.5	280	105.5	5.5	17,210	919	41.5	13.5	8,600	40	Saudi Arabia
190	1.4	44.7	2.0	...	730	13.4	1.4	76	9	13.7[9]	1.6	5	0	Senegal
4,517	2.7	698.7	1,058.9	...	120	0.2	2.6	8[4]	124[4]	7.4[4]	5.6[4]	...	...	Seychelles
...	...	...	...	...	600	[51]	[51]	41	9	28.9	6.1	0	0	Sierra Leone
1,367	1.7	4.9	83.9	7.2	230	70.0	22.6	3,970	1,191	24.0	4.7	200	30	Singapore
2,571	2.4	158.1	629.8	170.6	...	35.8	6.6	577	108	6.8	3.0	290	70	Slovakia
2,210	4.9	20.9	526.4	25.1	...	9.6	4.9	344	176	3.5	1.5	30	5	Slovenia
...	...	...	...	...	620	—	—	...	...	...	...	0	0	Solomon Islands
144	1.5	8.0	31.2	...	540	[52]	[52]	8[12]	1[12]	30.0[48]	0.9[12]	...	...	Somalia
...	...	...	...	...	870	79.4	1.9	2,895	71	6.7	2.2	250	100	South Africa
2,287	2.6	23.5	555.4	253.0	580	197.5	5.0	8,652	221	5.6	1.6	675	80	Spain
280	8.2	10.8	54.7	...	860	115.3	6.3	585	32	15.7	4.6	160	0	Sri Lanka
1,565	4.2	40.5	0.4	3.4	740	79.7	2.4	882[9]	32[9]	175.4[9]	17.1[9]	100	0	Sudan, The
17,819	7.6	1,824.4	...	...	...	1.4	3.3	39	90	5.3[3]	3.0	0	0	Suriname
4,853	88.1	589.1	941.4	71.4	610	—	—	27	28	7.0	2.6	0	0	Swaziland
12,982	4.5	42.5	1,615.1	658.9	330	53.4	6.0	6,042	683	5.8	2.8	10	310	Sweden
4,326.8	2.3	52.9	973.0	1,247.4	640	3.3	0.5	5,034	703	6.0[12]	1.6	20	100	Switzerland
89	1.4	7.0	21.2	2.9	1,970	320.0	21.3	3,563	236	60.3[19]	7.2	20	0	Syria
799	8.2	...	...	124.9	720	376.0	17.4	13,140	618	34.9	5.0	1,200	10	Taiwan
317	2.5	4.6	...	...	...	7.0	1.2	209	36	...	3.7	0	10	Tajikistan
1,250	6.4	0.5	97.3	0.9	1,330	34.6	1.2	69	2	8.4	1.8	0	0	Tanzania
351	7.7	25.4	9.9	3.3	530	266.0	4.4	4,014	69	15.2	2.5	1,100	0	Thailand
11	...	...	...	...	1,970	7.0	1.2	28	7	10.2	2.3	0	0	Togo
2,100	...	...	...	...	330	—	[50]	—	—	—	—	...	...	Tonga
1,382	11.7	56.7	567.0	86.4	280	2.1	1.6	82	64	4.0[10]	1.7	0	0	Trinidad and Tobago
1,240	2.1	134.0	143.6	11.1	340	35.0	3.8	345	39	6.3[12]	2.0	40	0	Tunisia
339	3.6	24.2	...	17.0	1,570	639.0	10.0	6,606	108	17.6	4.0	700	60	Turkey
...	...	...	...	—	...	[53]	[53]	196	48	3.7[9]	4.1	30	0	Turkmenistan
...	...	...	...	...	290	...	...	...	...	...	...	...	...	Tuvalu
140	9.5	15.6	15.1	5.3	1,090	[54]	[54]	126	6	13.3	2.3	0	0	Uganda
1,096	8.8	32.3	...	42.3	...	387.4	7.6	3,588	70	7.8	2.9	0	0	Ukraine
1,496	1.1	1.7	10.5	...	140	35.0	13.6	1,880	643	38.4	4.8	875	10	United Arab Emirates
9,880[55]	2.5[55]	362.1[55]	2,404.4[55]	1,147.3[55]	350	213.8	3.6	33,400	572	7.2	3.0	190	5,200	United Kingdom
5,374	9.0	430.2	1,041.8	591.2	318	1,447.6	5.4	277,800	1,056	17.4	3.8	1,000	15,600	United States
6,806	4.1	169.6	56.9	...	170	25.6	8.0	410	127	7.3	2.4	5	0	Uruguay
334	5.5	4.5	40.9	5.9	...	49.0	2.1	2,062	90	...	3.8	0	10	Uzbekistan
...	...	...	...	...	450	—	—	...	...	...	...	...	...	Vanuatu
1,106	22.1	152.2	358.2	239.4	320	79.0	3.5	854	40	6.3	1.1	90	0	Venezuela
...	...	...	...	...	...	492.0	6.5	544	7	10.9	2.6	200	0	Vietnam
10,441	22.3	1,943.2	3,183.7	954	240	—	[7]	—	—	—	—	...	...	Virgin Islands (U.S.)
2,226	...	...	...	...	...	...	...	...	...	...	...	...	...	West Bank
...	...	...	...	...	...	—	[7]	...	...	...	...	...	...	Western Sahara
170[56]	...	...	...	...	1,940	66.3	4.0	2,082[10]	147[10]	14.5[10]	14.1[10]	140	0	Yemen
1,268	...	...	...	...	140[53]	114.2	10.7	3,608[19,57]	158[19,57]	55.0[3,57]	3.9[19,57]	0	0	Yugoslavia
666	9.8	9.5	153.5	9.6	540	21.6	2.3	102	11	12.6	2.8	0	0	Zambia
2,160	5.0	193.6	445.3	9.1	750	39.0	3.4	220	20	10.5[10]	3.9	0	0	Zimbabwe

disbanded and an Interim Public Security Force of about 3,000 has been formed.   [36]Coverage is through tax system.   [37]1982.   [38]1988–89.   [39]1988.   [40]Includes attempted murders.   [41]All militias agreed to disarm and demobilize under a transitional plan negotiated in 1996.   [42]Military defense is the responsibility of Switzerland.   [43]Military defense is the responsibility of the United States.   [44]Forces are estimated between 5,100–6,100.   [45]Curaçao only.   [46]Includes paramilitary forces.   [47]1978.   [48]1986.   [49]1987.   [50]Military defense is the responsibility of New Zealand.   [51]Following the civil war of May–June 1997, the armed forces were reorganized. An exact figure is not known.   [52]Following the 1991 revolution, no national armed forces have yet been formed.   [53]Forces estimated between 19,000–21,000.   [54]Forces estimated between 40,000–50,000.   [55]England and Wales.   [56]Former Yemen Arab Republic.   [57]Data refer to Yugoslavia as constituted prior to 1991.

Education

This table presents international data on education analyzed to provide maximum comparability among the different educational systems in use among the nations of the world. The principal data are, naturally, numbers of schools, teachers, and students, arranged by four principal levels of education—the first (primary); general second level (secondary); vocational second level; and third level (higher). Whenever possible, data referring to preprimary education programs have been excluded from this compilation. The ratio of students to teachers is calculated for each level. These data are supplemented at each level by a figure for enrollment ratio, an indicator of each country's achieved capability to educate the total number of children potentially educable in the age group usually represented by that level. At the first and second levels this is given as a net enrollment ratio and at the third level as a gross enrollment ratio. Two additional comparative measures are given at the third level: students per 100,000 population and proportion (percentage) of adults age 25 and over who have achieved some level of higher or post-secondary education. Data in this last group are confined as far as possible to those who have completed their educations and are no longer in school. No enrollment ratio is provided for vocational training at the second level because of the great variation worldwide in the academic level at which vocational training takes place, in the need of countries to encourage or direct students into vocational programs (to support national development), and, most particularly, in the age range of students who normally constitute a national vocational system (some will be as young as 14, having just completed a primary cycle; others will be much older).

At each level of education, differences in national statistical practice, in national educational structure, public-private institutional mix, training and deployment of teachers, and timing of cycles of enrollment or completion

of particular grades or standards all contribute to the problems of comparability among national educational systems.

Reporting the number of schools in a country is not simply a matter of counting permanent red-brick buildings with classrooms in them. Often the resources of a less developed country are such that temporary or outdoor facilities are all that can be afforded, while in a developed but sparsely settled country students might have to travel 80 km (50 mi) a day to find a classroom with 20 students of the same age, leading to the institution of measures such as traveling teachers, radio or televisual instruction at home under the supervision of parents, or similar systems. According to UNESCO definitions, therefore, a "school" is defined only as "a body of students . . . organized to receive instruction."

Such difficulties also limit the comparability of statistics on numbers of teachers, with the further complications that many at any level must work part-time, or that the institutions in which they work may perform a mixture of functions that do not break down into the tidy categories required by a table of this sort. In certain countries teacher training is confined to higher education, in others as a vocational form of secondary training, and so on. For purposes of this table, teacher training at the secondary level has been treated as vocational education. At the higher level, teacher training is classified as one more specialization in higher education itself.

The number of students may conceal great variation in what each country defines as a particular educational "level." Many countries do, indeed, have a primary system composed grades 1 through 6 (or 1 through 8) that passes students on to some kind of postprimary education. But the age of intake, the ability of parents to send their children or to permit them to finish that level, or the need to withdraw the children seasonally

Education

country	year	first level (primary)					general second level (secondary)					vocational second level[a]	
		schools	teachers[c]	students[d]	student/ teacher ratio	net enroll-ment ratio[b]	schools	teachers[c]	students[d]	student/ teacher ratio	net enroll-ment ratio[b]	schools	teachers[c]
Afghanistan	1995	1,753[1]	20,055[2]	1,312,197	...	29	819[3]	17,548[2, 4]	512,815[4]	...	...	33[1]	4
Albania	1993	1,777	32,098	535,713	16.7	96	476	4,149	73,259	17.7	...	466[6]	7,390[6]
Algeria	1996	17,186	169,010	4,617,000	27.3	95	3,954	150,397	2,544,864	16.9	56	...	...
American Samoa	1992	30	524	7,884	15.0	...	7[3]	245	3,483	14.2	...	1	21
Andorra	1997	12		5,424	...	...	6		2,655	...	...	...	...
Angola	1991	...	31,062	990,155	31.9	...	...	5,138[6]	166,812	30.2[6]	...	...	566[6]
Antigua and Barbuda	1995	43[8]	439	11,506	26.2	...	12[8]	277	4,294	15.5	...	1	16
Argentina	1995	25,448	286,885	5,126,307	17.9	...	7,239[4]	233,564[4]	2,238,091[4]	9.6[4]	...	4	4
Armenia	1995	1,400[9]	54,000[2, 9]	574,500[9]	11.0[2, 9]	...	9	9	9	9	...	692[9]	...
Aruba	1993	32	331	7,139	21.6	...	10	183	3,247	17.7	...	14	225
Australia	1995	9,865[9]	202,401[9]	3,109,337[9]	15.4[9]	98	9	9	9	9	89	...	...
Austria	1996	4,557[10]	65,977[10]	649,994[10]	9.9[10]	100	693[4]	39,553[4]	295,473[4]	7.5[4]	90	4	4
Azerbaijan	1995	4,502[9]	156,000[9]	1,486,000[9]	9.5[9]	...	9	9	9	9	...	78	...
Bahamas, The	1994	115	1,581	33,343	21.1	95	...	1,775	28,363	16.0	87	...	...
Bahrain	1995	124	3,536[12]	72,329	...	100	...	2,305[12]	48,944	...	85	...	820[12]
Bangladesh	1994	66,168	242,252	15,185,000	62.7	62	11,019	135,217	4,884,000	36.1	20	152	1,857
Barbados	1992	106	1,553	26,662	17.2	78	33[6]	1,406[6]	21,259[6]	15.1[6]	75	...	...
Belarus	1996	4,900[9]	127,000[9]	1,561,000[9]	12.3[9]	95	9	9	9	9	...	149	...
Belgium	1994	4,453	72,589[1, 13]	731,527	...	98	1,950	110,599[8]	796,914	...	98	304[1]	...
Belize	1997	245	1,939[7]	52,994	25.9[7]	99	30	740[7]	10,648	13.7[7]	36	...	...
Benin	1994	2,889	12,343	602,069	48.8	59	145	2,384	97,480	40.9	...	14	283
Bermuda	1995	24[6]	294	5,793	19.7	...	12[6]	198	3,610	18.2	classrooms	...	...
Bhutan	1990	235[1]	1,859[1]	56,773[1]	30.5[1]	...	31	662	15,984	24.1	...	8	149
Bolivia	1991	...	51,763	1,278,775	24.7	91	...	12,434[4]	219,232[4]	17.6[4]	29	...	4
Bosnia and Herzegovina	1991	2,205	23,369	539,875	23.1	98	238	9,030	172,063	19.1	...	...	...
Botswana	1994	669	11,726	310,050	26.4	96	188	4,712	86,684	18.4	45	45	966
Brazil	1994	195,545	1,335,270	31,101,662	23.3	90	13,449	295,542	4,510,199	15.3	19	...	...
Brunei	1995	170[13]	3,380[13]	55,241[13]	16.3[13]	91	37	2,157	27,801	12.9	68	6	370
Bulgaria	1996	3,325[9]	70,763[9]	963,582[9]	13.6[9]	97	9	9	9	9	75	535	19,141
Burkina Faso	1994	2,971	10,300	600,032	58.2	31	173[8]	3,346	116,033	34.7	7	228[8]	639
Burundi	1993	1,418	10,400	651,086	62.6	52	113[14]	2,562	55,713	21.7	5	...	...
Cambodia	1995	4,539[1]	37,827	1,703,316	45.0	...	440[1]	16,349	297,555	18.2	...	65[1]	2,618[1]
Cameroon	1995	6,801	40,970	1,896,722	46.3	...	...	14,917	459,068	30.8	...	...	5,885
Canada	1995	12,700	148,724	2,413,126	16.2	95	3,324	133,358	2,469,552	18.5	92	...	...
Cape Verde	1994	370[14]	2,657	78,173	29.4	100	...	438	11,808	27.0	22	...	94[16]
Central African Republic	1991	930	4,004	308,409	77.0	54	46[4]	845[4]	46,989[4]	55.6[4]	...	4	4
Chad	1995	2,447	9,404[17]	591,784[17]	62.9[17]	...	66[3]	2,046	82,559	40.4	...	...	157
Chile	1994	8,323	78,813	2,119,737	26.9	86	...	50,187[4]	664,498[4]	13.2[4]	55	...	4
China	1995	849,123	6,539,000	159,064,000	24.3	99	81,020	3,334,000	53,710,000	16.1	...	14,196	549,000
Colombia	1994	46,707	170,526	4,327,507	25.4	85	8,161	141,484	2,879,681	20.3	50	...	...
Comoros	1994	275	1,737[12]	77,837	43.0[12]	53	...	613[8]	17,474	25.5[8]	...	...	...
Congo, Dem. Rep. of the	1995	14,885	121,054	5,417,506	44.8	61	4,276[1, 4]	59,325[1, 4]	640,298[2]	22.6[1, 4]	23	4	4
Congo, Rep. of the	1996	1,612	7,060	497,305	70.4	...	...	5,710	189,381	33.2	...	...	1,463
Costa Rica	1995	3,544	15,806[2]	508,923	31.4[2]	92	285	...	207,231	...	43	...	...
Côte d'Ivoire	1995	7,185	36,058	1,609,929	44.6	47	...	9,505	463,810	48.8	...	...	1,424
Croatia	1995	1,928	24,194	431,795	17.8	82	482	15,269	196,740	12.9	66	3	79
Cuba	1996	9,864	90,565	1,074,153	11.9	99	2,175[6]	46,722	460,438	9.8	59	618[6]	27,267
Cyprus[18]	1995	383	3,498	64,884	18.5	96	107	3,832	53,738	14.0	93	11	509
Czech Republic	1996	4,212	63,019	1,004,565	15.9	98	361	10,903	133,093	12.2	88	832	18,458
Denmark	1995	2,536	58,500[2]	605,798	10.4[2]	99	153	11,000[2]	75,793	6.8[2]	86	237	12,000[2]

for agricultural work all make even a simple enrollment figure difficult to assess in isolation. All of these difficulties are compounded when a country has instruction in more than one language or when its educational establishment is so small that higher, sometimes even secondary, education cannot take place within the country. Enrollment figures in this table may, therefore, include students enrolled outside the country.

Student-teacher ratio, however, usually provides a good measure of the ratio of trained educators to the enrolled educable. In general, at each level of education both students and teachers have been counted on the basis of full-time enrollment or employment, or full-time equivalent when country statistics permit. At the primary and secondary levels, net enrollment ratio is the ratio of the number of children within the usual age group for a particular level who are actually enrolled to the total number of children in that age group (× 100). This ratio is usually less than (occasionally, equal to) 100 and is the most accurate measure of the completeness of enrollment at that particular level. It is not always, however, the best indication of utilization of teaching staff and facilities. Utilization, provided here for higher education only, is best seen in a gross enrollment ratio, which compares total enrollment (of all ages) to the population within the normal age limits for that level. For a country with substantial adult literacy or general educational programs, the difference may be striking: typically, for a less developed country, even one with a good net enrollment ratio of 90 to 95, the gross enrollment ratio may by 20%, 25%, even 30% higher, indicating the heavy use made by the country of facilities and teachers at that level.

Literacy data provided here have been compiled as far as possible from data for the population age 15 and over for the best comparability inter-

nationally. Standards as to what constitutes literacy may also differ markedly; sometimes completion of a certain number of years of school is taken to constitute literacy; elsewhere it may mean only the ability to read or write at a minimal level testable by a census taker; in other countries studies have been undertaken to distinguish among degrees of functional literacy. When a country reports an official 100% (or near) literacy rate, it should usually be viewed with caution, as separate studies of "functional" literacy for such a country may indicate 10%, 20%, or even higher rates of inability to read, or write, effectively. Substantial use has been made of UNESCO literacy estimates, both for some of the least developed countries (where the statistical base is poorest) and for some of the most fully developed, where literacy is no longer perceived as a problem, thus no longer in need of monitoring.

Finally, the data provided for public expenditure on education are complete in that they include all levels of public expenditure (national, state, local) but are incomplete for certain countries in that they do not include data for private expenditure; in some countries this fraction of the educational establishment may be of significant size. Occasionally data for external aid to education may be included in addition to domestic expenditure.

The following notes further define the column headings:
a. Usually includes teacher training at the second level.
b. Latest.
c. Full-time.
d. Full-time; may include students registered in foreign schools.

third level (higher)								literacy[b]				public expenditure on education (percent of GNP)[b]	country
students[d]	student/ teacher ratio	institutions	teachers[c]	students[d]	student/ teacher ratio	gross enroll-ment ratio[b]	students per 100,000 popula-tion[b]	percent of population age 25 and over with post-secondary education[b]	over age	total (%)	male (%)	female (%)	
4	...	5[3,5]	444[6]	9,367[6]	21.1[6]	1.8	165	...	15	31.5	47.2	15.0	...	Afghanistan
138,000[6]	18.7[6]	8[6]	1,774	30,185	17.0	9.6	899	...	10	91.8	95.5	88.0	3.4	Albania
...	...	...	14,475[7]	233,019[7]	16.1[7]	10.9	1,126	...	15	61.6	73.9	49.0	5.6	Algeria
160	7.6	2	...	...	...	...	...	22.6	15	95.9	95.6	96.3	...	American Samoa
...	...	—	—	—	—	...	...	...	15	100.0	100.0	100.0	...	Andorra
19,687	...	1	439	6,534	14.9	0.7	71	...	15	41.7	55.6	28.5	4.9	Angola
46	2.9	...	...	...	...	...	...	...	15	90.0	...	...	Antigua and Barbuda
4	4	1,705	118,695	926,793	7.8	38.1	3,116	12.0	15	96.2	96.2	96.2	4.5	Argentina
25,200[2]	...	14	...	36,500	...	41.8	3,225	...	15	98.8	99.4	98.1	7.2	Armenia
2,594	11.5	1	16	88	5.5	...	...	7.0	15	95.0	...	...	4.5	Aruba
917,801	...	95[3]	25,916[3]	604,177	...	71.7	5,401	...	15	99.5	...	...	5.6	Australia
4	4	447	14,322[7]	222,095	15.9[7]	44.8	2,933	...	15	100.0	100.0	100.0	5.5	Austria
73,000	...	23	...	89,100	...	19.8	1,619	...	15	97.3	98.9	95.9	3.0	Azerbaijan
...	...	1[1,11]	300[1,11]	3,201[1,11]	...	...	...	13.5	15	98.2	98.5	98.0	4.0	Bahamas, The
7,113	...	...	655[2]	7,676[2]	11.7[2]	20.2	1,445	10.3	15	85.2	89.1	79.4	4.8	Bahrain
29,923	16.1	1,268	36,000	1,032,635	28.7	4.4	399	...	15	38.1	49.4	26.1	2.3	Bangladesh
...	...	1[6]	153[6]	1,314[6]	8.6[6]	28.1	2,501	...	15	97.4	98.0	96.8	7.2	Barbados
122,400	...	59	16,900[2]	197,400	10.5[2]	42.6	3,031	...	15	97.9	99.4	96.6	5.6	Belarus
155,192[1]	...	21[1]	...	123,320[1]	...	49.1	3,206	...	15	100.0	100.0	100.0	5.7	Belgium
...	...	11	...	2,469	...	...	...	6.6	14	70.3	...	...	6.1	Belize
4,873	17.2	16	602	9,964	16.5	2.6	208	1.3	15	37.0	48.7	25.8	3.1	Benin
...	...	1	56[6]	512	8.9[6]	...	...	18.4	15	96.9	96.7	97.0	3.7	Bermuda
1,822	12.2	2	57	519	9.1	...	...	...	15	42.2	56.2	28.1	2.7	Bhutan
4	4	...	4,261[8]	109,503[8]	25.7[8]	22.2	2,154	9.9	15	83.1	90.5	76.0	6.6	Bolivia
...	...	44	2,802	37,541	13.4	...	...	...	10	85.5	96.5	76.6	...	Bosnia and Herzegovina
6,373	6.6	1	507	5,062	10.0	4.1	403	1.4	15	69.8	80.5	59.9	9.6	Botswana
...	...	851	155,776	1,661,034	10.7	11.3	1,094	...	15	83.3	83.3	83.2	4.6	Brazil
1,966	5.3	4	325	1,606	4.9	6.6	518	...	15	87.8	92.5	82.5	3.1	Brunei
213,337	11.1	88	25,339	248,571	9.8	39.4	2,942	15.0	15	97.9	98.7	97.1	4.2	Bulgaria
8,808	13.8	9[8]	571	8,815	15.4	1.1	93	...	15	19.2	29.5	9.2	3.6	Burkina Faso
...	...	8	556	4,256	7.6	0.9	74	0.6	15	35.3	49.3	22.5	2.8	Burundi
16,350	...	9[1]	784	11,652	14.9	1.6	119	...	15	65.3	79.7	53.4	...	Cambodia
91,779	15.6	...	1,086[14]	33,177[14]	30.5[14]	3.3	289	...	15	63.4	75.0	52.1	2.9	Cameroon
...	...	265[15]	64,100[2]	1,209,386[15]	14.4[2]	102.9	6,984	21.4	15	96.6	...	...	7.3	Canada
2,289	...	...	...	...	...	...	...	...	15	71.6	81.4	63.8	4.4	Cape Verde
4	4	1[5,8]	139[5,8]	2,923[5,8]	21.0[5,8]	1.4	131	2.0	15	60.0	68.5	52.4	2.5	Central African Republic
3,277	20.9	4[3]	311	3,049	9.8	0.8	70	...	15	48.1	62.1	34.7	2.2	Chad
4	4	...	18,084[1,5]	315,653[1]	...	30.3	2,412	12.3	15	95.2	95.4	95.0	2.9	Chile
8,205,000	14.9	1,054	401,000	2,906,000	7.2	5.7	461	2.0	15	81.5	89.9	72.7	2.3	China
...	...	...	54,164[8]	510,649[8]	9.4[8]	17.2	1,643	...	15	91.3	91.2	91.4	3.5	Colombia
163	...	...	...	400	...	0.6	...	...	15	57.3	64.2	50.4	3.9	Comoros
701,148[2]	4	...	...	93,266	...	2.3	212	...	15	77.3	86.6	67.7	...	Congo, Dem. Rep. of the
25,269	17.3	...	656[8]	13,806[8]	21.0[8]	5.3	582	...	15	74.9	83.1	67.2	5.9	Congo, Rep. of the
...	...	29	...	79,959	...	31.9	2,919	...	15	94.8	94.7	95.0	4.5	Costa Rica
11,037	7.8	...	...	51,215[2]	...	4.4	396	8.7	15	40.1	49.9	30.0	4.7	Côte d'Ivoire
2,660	33.7	61	5,814	77,525	13.3	28.3	1,917	6.4	15	96.7	98.8	94.8	5.3	Croatia
244,253	9.0	35[6]	22,967	122,346	5.3	12.7	1,116	...	15	95.7	96.2	95.3	6.6	Cuba
4,066	8.0	32	648	7,765	12.0	20.0	1,069	17.0	15	95.2	97.8	92.8	4.4	Cyprus[18]
229,909	12.5	23	12,892	139,774	10.8	20.8	1,741	8.5	15	100.0	100.0	100.0	6.1	Czech Republic
168,417	13.6[2]	158	8,000[2]	155,661	19.5[2]	45.0	3,261	18.9	...	100.0	100.0	100.0	8.3	Denmark

Education (continued)

country	year	first level (primary)					general second level (secondary)					vocational second level[a]	
		schools	teachers[c]	students[d]	student/ teacher ratio	net enroll-ment ratio[b]	schools	teachers[c]	students[d]	student/ teacher ratio	net enroll-ment ratio[b]	schools	teachers[c]
Djibouti	1997	81[7]	1,005[7]	33,960	...	32	26[4,14]	628[4,7]	11,628[4]	...	...	4	4
Dominica	1995	64	641[1]	12,627	29.8[1]	...	13[1]	1	6,493	1	...	...	...
Dominican Republic	1995	4,001	42,135	1,462,722	34.7	81	...	10,757	240,441	22.4	22	...	1,297
Ecuador	1993	...	63,347	1,986,753	31.4	92	...	62,630[4]	813,557[4]	13.0[4]	...	...	4
Egypt	1996	16,188	302,916	7,470,437	24.7	89	7,307[2]	235,313	4,242,245	24.7	65	1,351[2]	133,794
El Salvador	1993	3,961	26,259[12]	1,042,256	39.7[12]	79	...	...	29,527	...	21	...	...
Equatorial Guinea	1994	781	1,381	75,751	54.9	...	...	466	14,511	31.1	...	...	122
Eritrea	1996	537	5,828	241,725	41.5	31	86[1]	2,031	78,902	38.8	15	4[1]	133
Estonia	1995	741[9]	15,453[9]	218,600[9]	14.1[9]	94	9	9	9	9	77	84	1,585
Ethiopia	1995	9,276	83,113	2,722,192	32.8	24	...	22,779	747,142	32.8	...	...	826
Faroe Islands	1994	62[19]	...	6,895[19]	...	...	6[20]	...	1,017[20]	...	...	9	...
Fiji	1992	693	4,644	145,630	31.4	99	142	3,045	60,237	19.8	...	45	625
Finland	1996	4,474	...	588,162	...	99	477	...	134,851	...	93	520	21,245[7]
France	1995	41,244	301,699[13]	4,012,600	...	99	11,212[4]	454,000[2,4]	5,737,458[2,4]	12.6[2,4]	92	4	...
French Guiana	1996	78[2]	802	17,006	21.2	...	22[14]	875	13,585	15.5	...	...	210
French Polynesia	1995	278	2,949	48,160	16.3	100	38	1,745	25,541	14.6	61	...	...
Gabon	1995	1,105	4,709	247,018	52.5	...	...	1,897	56,457	29.8	...	...	485
Gambia, The	1994	250	3,158	105,471	33.4	55	32[4]	1,126[4]	27,120[4]	24.1[4]	18	4	...
Gaza Strip	1997	339[9]	7,941[9]	281,255[9]	35.4[9]	...	9	9	9	9	...	...	...
Georgia	1994	3,378[9]	...	815,000[9]	...	82	9	...	9	...	71	...	...
Germany	1996	17,910	199,623	3,634,342	18.2	100	17,711	402,472	5,822,242	14	88	9,245	107,548
Ghana	1992	11,056	66,068	1,796,490	27.2	...	5,540	43,367	816,578	18.8	...	57[6]	422[6]
Gibraltar	1995	21[9]	305[9]	2,936	16.3[9]	...	9	...	1,805	9	...	1	29[3]
Greece	1993	7,634	37,549	745,666	19.9	98	2,988	45,794	700,488	15.3	85	695	14,349
Greenland	1997	88[9]	1,021[9]	9,056	10.5[9]	...	9	...	1,649	...	...	...	...
Grenada	1995	57	849	23,256	27.4	...	19	381	7,260	19.1	...	...	...
Guadeloupe	1994	344	3,167	38,092	12.0	...	84[4]	3,834[4]	51,366[4]	13.4[4]	...	4	4
Guam	1993	36[6]	898	16,816	18.7	...	24[6]	758	17,531	23.1	...	3[6]	370[6]
Guatemala	1993	10,770	44,220	1,393,921	31.5	...	1,274[14]	20,942[4]	334,383[4]	16.0[4]	...	626[14]	4
Guernsey	1993	22[8]	236	4,697	19.9	...	8[8]	276	3,642	13.2	...	...	...
Guinea	1996	3,237	11,875	584,161	49.2	37	...	4,690	127,517	27.2	...	...	1,302[1]
Guinea-Bissau	1988	...	...	100,369[7]	...	...	...	...	5,505	...	...	...	107
Guyana	1995	423[6]	3,453	100,806	29.2	90	93[6]	1,828	67,039	36.7	66	8[6]	176[6]
Haiti	1993	6,111[8]	27,607	787,553	28.5	26	630[4,8]	10,174[4]	193,624[4]	19.0[4]	...	4	4
Honduras	1995	8,186	28,978	1,008,092	34.8	90	661[4]	12,480[4]	184,589[4]	14.8[4]	21	4	4
Hong Kong	1997	856	19,710[17]	466,507	23.7[17]	91	498	22,777[17]	477,708	21.2[17]	71	9	...
Hungary	1997	3,765	83,658	966,000	11.5	93	980	29,462	361,400	12.3	73	363	5,292
Iceland	1997	205	3,549	42,212	11.9	...	35	1,454	17,970	12.4	...	...	...
India	1996	590,421	1,740,736	109,734,292	63.0	...	265,869	2,657,985	63,521,637	23.9	...	...	...
Indonesia	1995	149,464	1,172,640	26,200,023	22.3	97	27,177	595,962	8,864,001	14.9	42	3,502[2]	102,114[2]
Iran	1995	61,889	311,531[2]	9,745,600	31.7[2]	...	18,445[6]	228,869	7,284,611	31.8	...	...	20,418
Iraq	1995	8,035	132,030	2,977,800	22.6	79	2,635	48,961	1,062,204	21.7	37	310	9,903
Ireland	1995	3,319	20,901	491,256	23.5	100	452	12,635	225,490	17.8	85	327	8,019
Isle of Man	1992	32[3]	...	5,550	...	...	7[3]	...	4,458	...	...	1[3]	...
Israel	1997	1,937[17]	57,618[17]	691,800	...	...	797[17]	39,093[1]	478,900	...	...	435[17]	17,141[1]
Italy	1996	20,442	289,055	2,825,838	9.8	97	9,278	214,861	1,907,024	8.9	...	7,888	313,001
Jamaica	1995	788[8]	11,283	319,298	28.3	100	126	8,377	207,035	24.7	64	18	950
Japan	1995	24,548	431,000	8,371,000	19.4	100	16,775	552,000	9,296,000	16.8	96	6,679[14]	53,000[14]
Jersey	1990	32	...	5,794	...	...	14	...	4,405	...	...	1	...
Jordan	1994	2,482	48,158	1,036,079	21.5	89	741	4,597	93,773	20.4	42	54	2,553
Kazakstan	1996	8,700[9]	262,000[9]	3,060,000[9]	11.7[9]	...	9	9	9	9	...	3,504[7]	...
Kenya	1993	15,804	173,002	5,428,600	31.4	...	2,639	31,657	517,577	16.3	...	63	...
Kiribati	1993	92	537	16,316	30.4	...	9[6]	179	3,152	17.6	...	6[6]	40
Korea, North	1987	6,122	138,945	1,543,000	11.1	...	...	111,000	2,468,000	22.2	...	...	...
Korea, South	1996	5,732	137,912	3,800,540	27.6	99	3,790	157,731	3,683,857	23.4	96	797	44,163
Kuwait	1996	251	9,414	140,979	15.0	65	409	18,700	204,194	10.9	54	36	717
Kyrgyzstan	1996	1,885	24,086	473,077	19.7	97	1,474[2]	38,915	498,849	12.8	...	53[2]	3,371
Laos	1996	7,591	24,600	724,100	29.4	68	750[6]	35,100	886,500	25.3	18	139[3]	1,600
Latvia	1997	643	23,779[17]	98,694	...	84	376	41,029[17]	235,952	...	78	128	9,576[17]
Lebanon	1995	2,100[8]	...	365,174	...	...	...	...	277,646	...	...	275	6,065
Lesotho	1995	1,234	7,433	366,935	49.4	65	187	2,597	61,615	23.7	16	9[2]	225[2]
Liberia	1987	...	...	...	...	...	...	...	...	...	...	...	...
Libya	1993	...	103,791	1,254,242	12.1	97	...	14,941[8]	181,368[8]	12.1[8]	...	...	7,072[8]
Liechtenstein	1997	14	144	1,998	13.9	...	8	164	1,887	11.5	...	2[7]	247[7]
Lithuania	1996	2,361[9]	47,000[9]	562,000[9]	12.0[9]	...	9	9	9	9	80	106	4,671
Luxembourg	1995	...	1,732[12]	26,867[12]	15.5[12]	...	...	1,686	9,012	5.3	53	...	2,904[16]
Macau	1995	61	1,482	45,153	30.5	81	25[4]	1,205[4]	21,813[4]	18.1[4]	53	4	4
Macedonia	1995	1,050	13,102[2]	258,955	19.9[2]	85	95	4,520[2,4]	77,754[4]	16.5[2,4]	51	4	4
Madagascar	1994	13,624	37,676	1,504,668	39.9	...	1,142[3]	15,118	298,241	19.7	...	...	1,484[14]
Malawi	1995	3,425	45,775	2,860,819	62.5	69	94[6]	1,096[6]	48,332	26.8[6]	2	13[6]	250[6]
Malaysia	1996	7,049	144,937	2,843,663	19.6	91	1,427	86,891	1,694,243	19.5	...	101	6,044
Maldives	1992	134	...	45,333	...	25	...	...	15,933	...	...	...	...
Mali	1996	1,996	8,738	608,444	69.6	25	307[8]	4,549	112,670	24.8	5	...	...
Malta	1996	111	1,990	35,479	17.8	100	59	2,679	29,907	20.9	84	22	541
Marshall Islands	1995	103	669	13,355	20.0	...	12	144	2,400	16.7	...	...	...
Martinique	1994	276	3,251	33,532	10.3	...	76[4]	3,736[4]	47,172[4]	12.6[4]	...	4	4
Mauritania	1994	1,635	5,181[7]	268,216[7]	51.8[7]	60	56[8]	1,776	43,861	24.7	...	5[8]	162
Mauritius	1995	279	6,381	122,895	19.3	96	123	4,375	91,401	20.8	...	19[8]	...
Mayotte	1993	88[6]	555	21,579	38.9	...	5	246	3,973	16.2	...	2[6]	17[6]
Mexico	1995	91,857	507,669	14,572,202	28.7	100	22,255	256,831	4,493,173	17.5	45	6,571[1]	77,347[1]
Micronesia	1988	177	...	25,139	...	...	16	...	5,385	...	...	...	...
Moldova	1996	1,700[9]	14,209	320,055	22.5	...	9	33,752[4]	412,679	...	...	64	4
Monaco	1996	7	102	1,893	18.6	...	...	196	2,387	12.2	...	...	91
Mongolia	1996	650[9]	7,088	176,036	24.8	80	9	12,323	227,811	18.5	...	...	495
Morocco	1995	4,740	102,163	2,895,737	28.3	72	1,172	73,726	1,247,608	16.9	57	562[8,16]	2,951[16]

students[d]	student/ teacher ratio	third level (higher)				gross enrollment ratio[b]	students per 100,000 population[b]	percent of population age 25 and over with post-secondary education[b]	literacy[b]				public expenditure on education (percent of GNP)[b]	country
		institutions	teachers[c]	students[d]	student/ teacher ratio				over age	total (%)	male (%)	female (%)		
4	4	1[14]	13[14]	130[17]	...	0.2	22	...	15	46.2	60.3	32.7	3.8	Djibouti
...	...	2[1]	34[1]	484[1]	14.2[1]	...	...	...	15	90.0	...	...	5.5	Dominica
22,795	17.6	7[2,5]	5,091[2,5]	73,461[2,5]	14.4[2,5]	...	...	...	15	82.1	82.0	82.2	1.9	Dominican Republic
4	4	...	12,856[6]	206,541[16]	16.1[6]	20.0	2,012	12.7	15	90.1	92.0	88.2	3.4	Ecuador
1,900,406	14.2	125	38,828[2,5]	696,988[7]	...	18.1	1,674	4.6	15	51.4	63.6	38.8	5.6	Egypt
88,588	...	...	4,643[5]	77,359[5]	16.7[5]	17.7	2,031	6.3	15	74.1	77.4	71.3	2.2	El Salvador
2,105	17.3	...	58	578	10.0	...	164	...	15	78.5	89.6	68.1	1.8	Equatorial Guinea
1,246	9.4	1[2]	144[2]	2,032[2]	14.1[2]	1.1	102	...	...	20.0	...	...	1.9	Eritrea
27,806	17.5	22	...	23,169	...	38.1	2,670	13.7	15	99.7	99.9	99.6	6.9	Estonia
9,103	11.0	...	1,937	32,671	16.9	0.7	60	...	15	35.5	45.5	25.3	4.7	Ethiopia
2,090	...	1[14]	20[14]	91[14]	4.6[14]	...	...	...	15	99.0	99.0	99.0	...	Faroe Islands
7,283	11.6	...	277[14]	7,908[14]	28.5[14]	11.9	757	4.5	15	91.6	93.8	89.3	5.4	Fiji
199,200	9.5[7]	21	7,790[7]	133,359	16.4[7]	66.9	4,033	18.3	15	100.0	100.0	100.0	7.6	Finland
4	4	1,062[3]	52,663[2]	2,107,600	...	49.6	3,617	11.4	...	98.8	98.9	98.7	5.9	France
2,404	11.4	1[1]	...	324[1]	...	...	...	...	15	83.0	83.6	82.3	...	French Guiana
...	...	4[3]	70[3]	701[3]	10.3	1.4	...	...	15	95.0	94.9	95.0	...	French Polynesia
9,261	19.1	2[5,8]	299[5,8]	3,000[5,8]	10.0[5,8]	19.1	449	...	15	63.2	73.7	53.3	3.2	Gabon
4	4	...	155	1,591	10.3	1.7	148	...	15	38.6	52.8	24.9	5.5	Gambia, The
...	...	5	717	20,153	28.1	...	...	...	...	...	...	...	...	Gaza Strip
29,300	...	19	...	93,000	...	38.1	2,845	...	15	99.5	99.7	99.4	5.2	Georgia
2,435,753	22.6	335	152,401	1,838,456	12.1	42.7	2,635	19.9[21]	15	100.0	100.0	100.0	4.7	Germany
13,232[6]	31.4[6]	166	700[6]	9,274[6]	13.2[6]	1.4	127	...	15	64.5	75.9	53.5	3.1	Ghana
772	...	—	—	—	—	...	...	...	15	99.0	99.0	99.0	...	Gibraltar
190,443	13.3	17[8]	9,124[8]	115,284[8]	12.6[8]	38.1	2,846	8.7	15	95.2	97.7	93.0	3.7	Greece
...	...	...	...	...	...	...	...	...	15	100.0	100.0	100.0	...	Greenland
...	...	1[2]	66[2]	651[2]	9.9[2]	...	...	...	15	85.0	...	...	4.7	Grenada
4	...	1	121	4,673	38.6	...	...	...	15	90.1	89.7	90.5	...	Guadeloupe
3,788[6]	10.2[6]	1[3]	192[6]	2,385[6]	12.4[6]	...	...	39.9	15	99.0	99.0	99.0	...	Guam
4	4	5[3]	4,346[3]	69,532[3]	16.0[3]	8.1	755	...	15	55.6	62.5	48.6	1.7	Guatemala
...	...	...	...	...	...	...	...	...	15	100.0	100.0	100.0	...	Guernsey
9,278[1]	7.1[1]	...	805[1,5]	6,245[1,5]	7.8[1,5]	1.1	93	...	15	35.9	49.9	21.9	1.8	Guinea
825	7.7	...	...	404	...	...	...	...	15	54.9	68.0	42.5	...	Guinea-Bissau
5,388[6]	30.6[6]	...	492[2]	8,257[2]	16.8[2]	8.6	846	...	15	98.1	98.6	97.5	4.1	Guyana
4	4	2[17,22]	777[17,22]	11,546[17,22]	14.9[17,22]	...	...	0.7	15	45.0	48.0	42.2	1.5	Haiti
4	4	8	3,676	54,293	14.8	10.0	985	...	15	72.7	72.6	72.7	3.9	Honduras
48,837	...	17	...	87,411	...	21.9	1,635	10.6	15	92.2	96.0	88.2	2.8	Hong Kong
143,800	27.2	89	19,426	141,900	7.3	19.1	1,522	10.1	15	98.9	99.2	98.6	6.6	Hungary
...	...	14	508	7,972	15.7	35.2	2,658	...	15	100.0	100.0	100.0	5.0	Iceland
...	...	8,407[2]	286,000[2]	5,007,000[2]	17.5[2]	6.4	601	...	15	52.0	65.5	37.7	3.5	India
1,405,220	13.8	1,236	150,607	2,229,796	14.8	11.1	1,167	2.3	15	83.8	89.6	78.0	...	Indonesia
368,218	18.0	...	36,366	478,455	13.2	14.8	1,533	...	15	72.1	78.4	65.8	4.0	Iran
135,711	13.7	12	11,847	201,984	17.0	...	...	...	15	58.0	70.7	45.0	...	Iraq
146,050	18.2	29	4,889	88,925	18.2	37.0	3,443	14.6	15	100.0	100.0	100.0	6.3	Ireland
425[14]	...	...	...	...	...	...	...	...	...	...	...	...	...	Isle of Man
142,900	...	7	7,829[7]	101,700[17]	...	41.1	3,598	...	15	95.6	97.7	93.6	6.6	Israel
2,661,760	8.5	48[5,7]	58,874[5,7]	1,601,873[5,7]	27.2[5,7]	40.6	3,134	...	15	97.1	97.8	96.4	4.9	Italy
15,898	16.7	15[3]	...	24,200	...	6.0	677	...	15	85.0	80.8	89.1	8.2	Jamaica
1,242,000[14]	23.4[14]	1,223	162,000	3,101,000	19.1	40.3	3,139	20.7	15	100.0	100.0	100.0	3.8	Japan
...	...	...	...	...	...	...	...	...	15	100.0	100.0	100.0	...	Jersey
30,052	11.8	55[3]	4,280	85,934	20.1	24.5	2,136	...	15	86.6	93.4	79.4	6.3	Jordan
984,300[7]	...	69[7]	...	267,000[7]	...	32.7	2,807	12.4	15	97.5	99.1	96.1	4.5	Kazakhstan
29,593	...	14	4,392[5,14]	88,180	8.1[5,14]	1.6	143	...	15	78.1	86.3	70.0	7.4	Kenya
297	7.4	—	—	—	—	...	...	...	15	90.0	...	...	6.3	Kiribati
220,000	...	281	27,000	390,000	14.4	...	...	...	15	95.0	...	...	...	Korea, North
950,173	21.5	802	60,883	2,056,370	33.8	52.0	4,955	21.1	15	98.0	99.3	96.7	3.7	Korea, South
3,604	5.0	1	960	16,767	17.5	25.4	2,247	12.7	15	78.6	82.2	74.9	5.6	Kuwait
32,005	9.5	23[2]	3,691	49,744	13.5	12.2	1,115	...	15	97.0	98.6	95.5	6.8	Kyrgyzstan
9,400	5.9	9[6]	1,300	7,800	6.0	1.5	134	...	15	56.6	69.4	44.4	2.4	Laos
43,170	...	28	...	55,434	...	25.7	1,737	13.4	15	99.5	99.8	99.2	6.3	Latvia
45,776	7.5	20	7,173	79,029	11.0	27.0	2,712	...	15	92.4	94.7	90.3	2.0	Lebanon
2,326[2]	10.3[2]	1[2]	492[2]	4,001[2]	8.1[2]	2.4	221	...	15	71.3	81.1	62.3	5.9	Lesotho
...	...	...	472	5,095	10.8	...	...	...	15	38.3	53.9	22.4	...	Liberia
94,961[8]	10.8[8]	10[3]	...	72,899[8]	...	16.4	1,358	...	15	76.2	87.9	63.0	...	Libya
2,515[7]	10.2[7]	...	...	...	...	...	...	...	15	100.0	100.0	100.0	...	Liechtenstein
49,000	10.5	15	...	54,000	...	28.2	2,023	12.6	15	99.5	99.6	99.3	6.1	Lithuania
16,909	5.7[16]	1	200	1,100	5.5	...	...	10.8	15	100.0	100.0	100.0	...	Luxembourg
4	4	12	663	6,145	9.3	26.4	1,995	5.9	15	89.5	94.1	85.3	...	Macau
4	4	44	2,320[2]	27,340	11.8[2]	17.5	1,372	...	10	89.1	94.2	83.8	5.5	Macedonia
17,419[14]	11.7[14]	5[3]	855[8]	42,681[8]	49.9[8]	3.4	316	...	15	80.2	87.7	72.9	1.9	Madagascar
1,080	14.7[6]	4[6]	235[6]	7,308[2]	11.4[6]	0.8	76	0.4	15	56.4	71.9	41.8	5.7	Malawi
47,770	7.9	48	12,247	191,290	15.6	10.6	971	...	15	83.5	89.1	78.1	5.3	Malaysia
452	...	—	—	—	—	...	...	...	15	93.2	93.3	93.0	8.4	Maldives
...	...	7[14]	701[14]	6,703[14]	9.6[14]	0.8	73	...	15	31.0	39.4	23.1	2.2	Mali
4,539	8.4	1[1]	284[1]	3,679[1]	13.0[1]	21.8	1,595	...	15	96.2	95.9	...	5.2	Malta
...	...	...	...	...	...	...	...	...	15	91.2	92.4	90.0	...	Marshall Islands
4	4	1	99	4,486	45.3	...	...	...	15	92.5	91.8	93.2	...	Martinique
1,949	12.0	4	727[7,23]	2,850[7,23]	39.6[7,23]	4.1	393	1.3	15	37.7	49.6	26.3	5.0	Mauritania
2,052[1]	...	2	526[14]	2,344	7.7[14]	6.3	564	1.9	15	82.9	87.1	78.8	4.3	Mauritius
839	23.1[6]	—	—	—	—	...	...	...	15	91.9	...	...	...	Mayotte
1,076,700[1]	13.9[1]	10,341	319,551	3,763,938	11.8	14.3	1,586	9.2	15	89.6	91.8	87.4	5.3	Mexico
...	...	...	...	...	...	...	...	...	15	76.7	67.0	87.2	...	Micronesia
27,943	...	20	8,846	87,700	9.9	25.0	1,976	11.3	15	96.7	98.6	94.4	6.1	Moldova
520	5.7	...	...	...	...	...	...	...	15	...	...	...	...	Monaco
7,987	16.1	127	1,341[8]	13,800[7]	...	15.2	1,569	...	15	82.9	88.6	77.2	5.6	Mongolia
17,585[16]	6.0[16]	50[1]	6,877[1]	230,012[1]	33.4[1]	11.3	1,075	...	15	43.7	56.6	31.0	4.9	Morocco

Education (continued)

country	year	first level (primary)					general second level (secondary)					vocational second level[a]	
		schools	teachers[c]	students[d]	student/teacher ratio	net enrollment ratio[b]	schools	teachers[c]	students[d]	student/teacher ratio	net enrollment ratio[b]	schools	teachers[c]
Mozambique	1995	4,167	24,575	1,415,428	57.6	40	239[2]	4,376	165,868	37.9	6	31[2]	1,239
Myanmar (Burma)	1995	35,856	169,748	5,711,202	33.6	...	2,916	71,904	1,779,503	24.7	...	103	2,462
Namibia	1994	933	10,912[8]	366,666	32.0[8]	92	114	2,534[6]	101,838	29.3[6]	36	17	140[3]
Nauru	1989	3	61	1,367	22.4	...	2	34	629	18.5	...	1	3
Nepal	1995	22,157	85,621	3,191,600	37.3	...	7,582[4]	30,637[4]	944,500[4]	30.8[4]	...	4	4
Netherlands, The	1996	7,411	99,031[14]	1,477,000	15.7[14]	99	1,124	89,370[14]	868,000	7.7[14]	84	218	18,613[14]
Netherlands Antilles	1993	85	1,059	22,735	21.5	...	27	617	8,801	14.3	...	30	439
New Caledonia	1992	280	1,758	34,591	19.7	98	46	1,669[4, 14]	15,664	13.1[4, 14]	72	16	4
New Zealand	1996	2,397[24]	23,379[24]	455,671[24]	19.5[24]	100	339	15,246	227,934	14.9	93	30	5,314
Nicaragua	1994	4,993	20,626	765,972	37.1	83	451[4]	5,356[4]	211,606[4]	39.5[4]	27	4	4
Niger	1994	2,656	12,216	414,296	33.9	25	105[6]	2,219[1]	88,810	35.1[1]	6	7[6]	175[1]
Nigeria	1995	38,649	435,210	16,191,000	37.2	...	6,074	152,596	4,451,000	29.2	...	4	15,738[3]
Northern Mariana Islands	1989	18	240	4,882	20.3	...	9[4]	163[4]	2,075[4]	12.7[4]	...	4	4
Norway	1995	3,308	37,640	470,936	12.5	99	746[4]	21,197[4]	226,983[4]	10.7[4]	94	4	4
Oman	1994	415	11,158	297,209	26.6	71	128[6]	9,188	160,654	17.5	56	25[6]	342
Pakistan	1996	115,744	337,400	11,484,000	34.0	...	20,243	281,700	4,819,000	17.1	...	687	7,459
Palau	1993	...	...	2,635	...	...	...	...	1,021	...	...	...	...
Panama	1995	2,845	14,998	362,142	24.1	91	339[4]	11,627[4]	216,217[4]	18.6[4]	51	4	4
Papua New Guinea	1995	2,790	13,652	525,995	38.5	...	135[6]	2,415[6]	68,818	24.1[8]	...	117[6]	878[8]
Paraguay	1995	5,318	34,580	835,089	24.1	89	1,102[4]	20,793[2, 4]	235,914[4]	10.3[2, 4]	33	4	4
Peru	1995	46,652	176,173	4,822,423	27.4	91	8,085	104,476	2,023,830	19.4	53	2,425	12,293
Philippines	1995	35,671	324,418	10,903,529	33.6	100	5,880[2]	131,831[4]	4,762,877[4]	36.1[4]	60	1,261[8]	4
Poland	1996	19,823	323,500	5,104,200	15.8	97	1,705	34,700	683,000	19.7	83	8,887	88,700
Portugal	1994	12,069	73,221	910,650	12.4	100	663	69,095[4]	749,838	11.3[4]	78	214	4
Puerto Rico	1986	1,542	18,359	427,582	23.3	...	395	13,612	334,661	24.6	...	52	...
Qatar	1995[12]	169	5,853	52,130	8.9	80	123[2]	3,738	36,964	9.9	70	3[2]	120
Réunion	1995	345	...	73,702[17]	...	...	104[4]	4,591[2]	71,694[17]	16.3[2]	...	4	1,108[2]
Romania	1995	13,963[19]	168,702[19]	2,532,169[19]	15.0[19]	92	1,276[20]	60,514[20]	757,673[20]	12.5[20]	73	1,530	9,360
Russia	1996	70,200[9]	1,705,000[9]	22,000,000[9]	12.9[9]	100	9	9	9	9	...	2,612	4
Rwanda	1992	1,710	18,937	1,104,902	58.3	76	...	3,413[4]	94,586[4]	27.7[4]	8	...	4
St. Kitts and Nevis	1995	31[2]	366[2]	7,101[2]	19.4[2]	...	7	326	4,541	13.9	...	...	...
St. Lucia	1993	88	1,204	32,545	27.0	...	14	524	9,550	18.2	...	1	34
St. Vincent and the Grenadines	1994	65	1,080	21,386	19.8	...	21[8]	395	9,870	25.0	...	2[8]	49
Samoa	1989	...	...	37,833	...	99	...	...	...	...	45	...	...
San Marino	1996	14	217	1,134	5.2	...	3	134	771	5.8	...	...	44[2]
São Tomé and Príncipe	1989	64	559	19,822	35.5	...	...	318	7,446	23.4	...	...	...
Saudi Arabia	1996	11,217	169,321	2,248,122	13.3	62	6,346[7]	105,056	1,375,753	13.1	48	293[7]	4,473
Senegal	1993	2,454	12,711	738,550	58.1	54	359	5,509	182,140	33.1	...	19	182
Seychelles	1997	27[7]	633	9,825	15.5	...	20[2]	440	6,548	14.9	...	1[2]	134
Sierra Leone	1993	1,643	10,595	267,425	25.2	...	167	4,313	70,900	16.4	...	44	709
Singapore	1995	199	10,356	261,648	25.3	...	178	9,777	203,662	20.8	...	11	1,382
Slovakia	1996	2,485	39,224	661,082	16.7	...	190	5,457	76,380	14.0	...	364	9,558
Slovenia	1995	850	15,471	210,989	13.6	100	224	9,748	102,117	10.5	...	...	...
Solomon Islands	1994	520	2,510	73,120	29.1	...	23	618	7,981	12.9	...	1	...
Somalia	1987	1,125	8,208	171,830	20.9	...	82	2,109	42,764	20.3	...	21	498
South Africa	1994	22,260[9]	349,436[9]	11,782,324[9]	35.7[9]	96	9	9	9	9	52	187	10,807
Spain	1995	16,540[2]	132,566	2,364,910	17.8	100	25,775[1, 4]	299,056[4]	4,744,829[4]	15.9[4]	94	4	4
Sri Lanka	1994	9,648	70,108	1,960,495	28.0	...	5,771[8]	105,916	2,315,541	21.9	...	231[4]	437[14]
Sudan, The	1995	12,187	83,306	3,023,955	36.3	54	2,578[8]	29,208[8]	683,982[8]	23.4[8]	...	64[3]	621
Suriname	1995	280	3,447	62,613	18.2	...	100	2,056	29,554	14.4	...	...	...
Swaziland	1994	535	5,887	192,599	32.7	95	165	2,872	52,571	18.3	...	5	228
Sweden	1995	4,900	89,275	916,661	10.3	100	629	29,563	309,952	10.5	96	...	...
Switzerland	1996	...	...	452,789	...	100	...	...	369,036	...	79	...	...
Syria	1996	10,564	113,530	2,672,960	23.5	91	2,526[7]	51,483	846,778	16.4	39	292[7]	12,200
Taiwan	1996	2,523	87,934	1,971,439	22.4	...	920	76,562	1,412,201	18.4	...	203	19,660
Tajikistan	1995	3,400[9]	84,000[9]	1,289,000[9]	15.3[9]	...	9	9	9	9	...	75	4
Tanzania	1994[25]	10,892	101,816	3,736,734[1]	36.7[1]	48	491	10,612	180,899[1]	18.9[1]	...	40	1,167[1]
Thailand	1993	34,412	445,542	8,583,525	19.3	...	2,318	107,025	2,118,767	19.8	...	679	40,116
Togo	1996	3,283	16,217	824,626	50.8	85	...	4,736	161,672	34.1	18	...	586[7]
Tonga	1994	115	701	16,540	23.6	...	38	809	15,702	19.4	...	9	65[6]
Trinidad and Tobago	1994	475	7,210	195,013	27.0	88	...	4,844[4]	100,609[4]	20.6[4]	64	...	4
Tunisia	1996	4,384	59,887	1,468,998	24.5	97	712[7]	41,885	794,394	19.0	...	...	...
Turkey	1996	49,240	232,000	6,403,000	27.6	96	10,689	138,000	3,498,000	25.3	50	3,678	71,000
Turkmenistan	1995	1,900[9]	72,900[9]	940,600[9]	12.9[9]	...	9	9	9	9	...	78	...
Tuvalu	1991	11	72[6]	1,906[2]	...	...	1	21[6]	314	...	...	1	10[6]
Uganda	1995[12]	8,531	76,111	2,912,473	38.3	...	...	14,447	256,258	17.7	...	...	1,788
Ukraine	1996	21,900[9]	576,000[7, 9]	7,007,000[9]	12.4[7, 9]	...	9	9	9	9	...	782	...
United Arab Emirates	1995	512[8, 9]	15,449	262,628	17.0	83	9	12,388	158,625	12.0	71	9[14]	189
United Kingdom	1995	32,385[9]	231,659	4,906,439	21.2	100	9	228,187	3,779,262	16.6	92	...	...
United States	1996	85,393[2, 9]	1,784,000[26]	33,410,000[26]	18.7[26]	96	9	1,187,000	17,390,000	14.6	89	...	...
Uruguay	1994	2,423	16,821	337,889	20.1	95	348	20,061	184,083	9.2	...	104	4
Uzbekistan	1996	9,300[9]	413,000[9]	5,090,000[9]	12.3[9]	...	9	9	9	9	...	252	22,164[1]
Vanuatu	1992	272	852	26,267	30.8	...	...	220	4,269	19.4	17	4	4
Venezuela	1994	15,894[1]	185,748	4,217,283	22.7	88	1,621[4, 8]	33,692[4]	311,209[4]	9.2[4]	20	4	4
Vietnam	1996	13,092[2]	298,856	10,228,800	34.2	...	6,298[2]	193,814	5,332,400	27.5	...	451[2]	9,425
Virgin Islands (U.S.)	1993[12]	62	790	14,544	18.4	...	...	541[14]	12,502	17.2[14]	...	—	—
West Bank	1997	1,193[9]	15,912[9]	431,565[9]	27.1[9]	...	9	9	9	9	...	...	...
Western Sahara	1995[12]	40	925	32,257	34.9	...	13	1,267	10,541	8.3	...	...	...
Yemen	1995[12]	11,013[2]	78,646	2,493,017	31.7	...	1,224	11,130	232,506	20.9	...	125	369
Yugoslavia	1996	4,441	51,728	914,532	17.7	69	570	26,954	352,346	13.1	62	...	...
Zambia	1995	3,883	38,528	1,506,349	39.1	75	...	...	199,081[2]	...	16	...	4
Zimbabwe	1995	4,633	63,475	2,655,564	41.8	...	1,535	27,320	711,094	26.0	...	258[8]	1,479[8]

[1]1993. [2]1994. [3]1989. [4]General second level includes vocational second level. [5]Universities only. [6]1990. [7]1995. [8]1992. [9]First level includes general second level. [10]First level includes lower second level. [11]College of the Bahamas only. [12]Public schools only. [13]Includes preschool. [14]1991. [15]1997. [16]Excludes teacher training. [17]1996. [18]Republic of Cyprus only.

students[d]	student/teacher ratio	institutions	teachers[c]	students[d]	student/teacher ratio	gross enrollment ratio[b]	students per 100,000 population[b]	percent of population age 25 and over with post-secondary education[b]	over age	total (%)	male (%)	female (%)	public expenditure on education (percent of GNP)[b]	country
		third level (higher)							literacy[b]					
19,313	15.6	3[2]	833[2]	7,000	...	0.5	41	...	15	40.1	57.7	23.3	6.3	Mozambique
25,374	10.3	51	9,147	309,446	33.8	5.4	564	...	15	83.1	88.7	77.7	1.3	Myanmar (Burma)
1,503	11.9[3]	7	213[14]	6,523	11.8[14]	8.1	738	4.0	15	75.8	77.8	74.0	9.4	Namibia
30	10.0	1	...	200	...	...	...	...	15	99.0	...	...	...	Nauru
[4]	[4]	3[1]	4,925[14]	99,300	22.4[14]	5.2	501	2.5	15	27.5	40.9	14.0	2.9	Nepal
519,000	28.0[14]	20	...	408,000	...	48.9	3,485	...	15	100.0	100.0	100.0	5.3	Netherlands, The
5,817	13.3	2	51	734	14.4	...	...	8.8	15	93.8	94.2	93.4	...	Netherlands Antilles
7,543	[4]	6	141[3]	1,207[6]	9.9[3]	...	...	7.5	15	57.9	57.4	58.3	...	New Caledonia
107,736	20.3	75	5,982[5]	105,690[5]	17.7[5]	58.2	4,603	39.1	15	100.0	100.0	100.0	6.7	New Zealand
[4]	[4]	10	2,005	22,120	11.0	9.4	947	...	15	65.7	64.6	66.6	3.9	Nicaragua
2,110	12.1[1]	2	315	4,060	12.9	...	55	...	15	13.6	20.9	6.6	3.1	Niger
391,583[3]	24.9[3]	31	12,103	228,000	18.8	4.1	367	...	15	57.1	67.3	47.3	...	Nigeria
[4]	[4]	1	102	1,097	10.8	...	...	...	15	96.3	96.9	95.6	...	Northern Mariana Islands
[4]	[4]	89	10,366	169,306	16.3	54.5	4,009	17.9	15	100.0	100.0	100.0	8.3	Norway
2,350	6.9	5[6]	732[6]	7,322[8]	...	4.7	334	...	15	58.8	71.1	46.2	4.4	Oman
94,000	12.6	888	33,654	953,659	28.3	3.0	291	2.5	15	37.8	50.0	24.4	2.7	Pakistan
...	...	...	...	509	...	...	...	...	15	97.6	98.3	96.6	...	Palau
[4]	[4]	9	4,689	76,839	16.4	30.0	2,921	13.2	15	90.8	91.4	90.2	5.2	Panama
9,941	12.9[8]	26	...	13,663	...	3.2	318	...	15	72.2	81.0	62.7	...	Papua New Guinea
[4]	[4]	2	742[1]	39,694	40.9[1]	10.3	931	...	15	92.1	93.5	90.6	2.9	Paraguay
270,576	22.0	886	49,249	714,512	14.5	31.1	3,268	20.4	15	88.7	94.5	83.0	3.8	Peru
[4]	[4]	975[2]	56,880[14]	1,582,820[2]	23.7[14]	27.4	2,760	18.7	15	94.6	95.0	94.3	2.2	Philippines
1,729,300	19.5	179	71,300	794,600	11.1	27.4	1,946	7.9	15	98.7	99.2	98.3	4.6	Poland
28,627	[4]	273	30,998[1]	236,537	6.9[1]	34.0	3,003	7.7	15	89.6	92.5	87.0	5.4	Portugal
149,191	...	45	9,045	156,818	17.3	...	...	...	18	89.7	89.6	89.7	...	Puerto Rico
671	5.6	1	637	7,794	12.2	27.4	1,509	13.3	15	79.4	79.2	79.9	3.4	Qatar
15,055	12.4[2]	1[5]	242[5]	8,058[5]	33.3[5]	...	...	...	15	78.2	75.9	80.3	...	Réunion
345,394	36.9	63	20,452	255,162	12.5	18.3	1,483	6.9	15	96.7	98.5	95.0	3.0	Romania
1,923,000	...	569	...	2,655,000	...	42.9	2,998	15.1	15	98.0	99.5	96.8	4.1	Russia
[4]	[4]	...	646[3]	3,454	5.2[3]	0.6	...	...	15	60.5	69.8	51.6	3.7	Rwanda
...	...	1[1]	51[1]	394[1]	7.7[1]	...	...	...	15	90.9	90.0	90.0	3.3	St. Kitts and Nevis
808	23.7	1	389	870	2.4	...	...	...	15	82.0	...	...	9.9	St. Lucia
414	8.4	...	...	...	...	...	...	...	15	96.0	...	...	6.9	St. Vincent and the Grenadines
...	...	...	...	...	...	...	...	...	15	100.0	100.0	100.0	4.2	Samoa
428	6.2[2]	...	...	...	...	...	...	...	15	99.1	99.4	98.8	...	San Marino
289	...	...	...	...	...	...	...	...	15	54.2	70.2	39.1	...	São Tomé and Príncipe
49,032	11.0	777	18,039[7]	233,710[7]	13.0[7]	15.3	1,316	...	15	62.8	71.5	50.2	5.5	Saudi Arabia
7,301	40.1	2[5,7]	784[5,7]	16,733[5,7]	21.3[5,7]	3.4	297	...	15	33.1	43.0	23.2	3.6	Senegal
1,338	10.0	...	...	...	...	...	...	4.6	15	84.2	82.9	85.7	7.5	Seychelles
7,756	10.9	2[14]	257[14]	2,571[14]	10.0[14]	1.3	119	...	15	31.4	45.4	18.2	0.9	Sierra Leone
9,476	6.9	7	6,902	83,914	12.2	33.7	2,522	4.7	15	89.1	95.1	83.0	3.0	Singapore
119,853	12.5	14	8,014	74,322	9.3	20.2	1,715	9.5	15	100.0	100.0	100.0	5.1	Slovakia
...	...	28	2,783[2]	45,951[17]	14.5[2]	31.9	2,387	10.4	15	100.0	100.0	100.0	5.8	Slovenia
...	...	1	...	...	...	...	...	...	15	54.1	62.4	44.9	3.8	Solomon Islands
4,809	9.7	1	...	1,692	...	...	...	...	15	24.0	36.0	14.0	...	Somalia
140,531	13.0	...	27,099	617,897	22.8	17.3	1,524	1.5	15	81.8	81.9	81.7	6.8	South Africa
[4]	[4]	1,415[8]	80,563	1,398,113	17.3	46.1	3,858	8.4	15	96.5	98.1	95.1	5.0	Spain
8,908[14]	20.4[14]	8[14]	1,937[14]	59,790	16.2[14]	5.1	474	...	15	90.2	93.4	87.2	3.1	Sri Lanka
15,443	24.9	24[8]	1,943[8]	54,345[8]	28.0[8]	3.0	272	...	15	46.1	57.7	34.6	...	Sudan, The
12,307[1]	...	1[1]	155[1]	1,478[1]	9.5[1]	...	1,124	...	15	93.0	95.1	91.0	3.5	Suriname
2,958	13.0	1	190	2,132	11.2	5.1	543	3.3	15	76.7	78.0	75.6	8.1	Swaziland
...	...	...	29,487	268,448	9.1	42.5	2,810	21.7	15	100.0	100.0	100.0	8.0	Sweden
191,696	...	...	...	148,024	...	31.8	2,085	...	15	100.0	100.0	100.0	5.5	Switzerland
94,204	7.7	...	4,869[5,7]	161,185[5]	...	17.9	1,760	...	15	70.8	85.7	55.8	4.3	Syria
523,412	26.6	134	36,348	751,347	20.7	...	...	...	15	94.0	97.6	90.2	5.2	Taiwan
35,000	...	...	...	10,000	...	20.3	1,890	11.7	15	97.7	98.8	96.6	8.6	Tajikistan
15,824[1]	13.6[1]	4[3]	1,206[3]	4,289	4.4[3]	0.5	43	...	15	67.8	79.4	56.8	3.7	Tanzania
795,186	19.8	102	27,239	809,856	29.7	20.1	2,096	...	15	93.8	96.0	91.6	4.2	Thailand
7,631[7]	13.0[7]	1[5]	...	11,172	...	3.2	281	...	15	51.7	67.0	37.0	5.6	Togo
824	13.4[6]	1[8]	19[8]	226[8]	11.9[8]	...	...	2.8	15	92.8	92.9	92.8	4.7	Tonga
[4]	[4]	1	438	5,191	11.9	7.7	705	...	15	97.9	98.8	97.0	4.5	Trinidad and Tobago
...	...	...	5,655[2]	96,101[2]	17.0[2]	12.9	1,253	...	15	66.7	78.6	54.6	6.8	Tunisia
1,309,000	18.4	817	50,000	1,161,000	23.2	18.2	1,960	...	15	82.3	91.7	72.4	3.4	Turkey
26,000	...	15	...	29,435[17]	...	21.8	2,072	...	15	97.7	98.8	96.6	4.0	Turkmenistan
58	...	—	—	—	—	...	...	...	15	95.0	...	...	...	Tuvalu
36,063	20.2	...	2,029	27,586	13.6	1.5	142	0.5	15	61.8	73.7	50.2	1.9	Uganda
618,000	...	255	...	922,800	...	40.6	2,977	...	15	98.4	99.5	97.4	7.7	Ukraine
1,215	6.4	4	510[1]	13,900	19.2[1]	8.8	521	...	15	79.2	78.9	79.8	1.8	United Arab Emirates
586,000[1]	...	...	48,000[5]	810,000[5]	17.0[5]	48.3	3,126	...	15	100.0	100.0	100.0	5.5	United Kingdom
...	...	5,758[1]	833,000	14,210,000	17.1	81.1	5,398	46.5	15	95.5	95.7	95.3	5.3	United States
56,879	...	2	7,157	61,367	8.6	27.3	2,179	8.1	15	97.3	96.9	97.7	2.8	Uruguay
194,800	11.0[1]	58	...	192,100	...	31.7	2,938	...	15	97.2	98.5	96.0	9.5	Uzbekistan
444	...	1	...	124[14]	...	...	...	...	15	52.9	57.3	47.8	4.9	Vanuatu
[4]	[4]	99[14]	43,833[8]	550,783[8]	12.6[8]	28.5	2,820	11.8	15	91.1	91.8	90.3	5.2	Venezuela
197,500	21.0	104[2]	22,750	297,900	13.1	4.1	404	2.6	15	93.7	96.5	91.2	2.7	Vietnam
—	—	1	266	2,924	11.0	...	...	...	...	...	...	...	...	Virgin Islands (U.S.)
...	...	22	1,598	30,622	19.2	...	...	...	...	...	...	...	...	West Bank
1,222	...	...	—	...	...	...	...	...	...	...	...	...	...	Western Sahara
15,074	40.9	2	1,991	90,826	45.6	4.3	407	...	15	43.2	68.6	23.1	7.5	Yemen
...	...	93	10,544	131,689	12.5	21.1	1,556	...	15	93.3	97.6	89.2	...	Yugoslavia
7,982[14]	...	...	481[2]	5,270[2]	11.0[2]	2.5	241	1.5	15	78.2	85.6	71.3	1.8	Zambia
27,431[8]	18.5[8]	28[8]	3,581	46,492	13.0	6.9	679	4.9	15	85.1	90.4	79.9	8.5	Zimbabwe

[19]Includes lower second level.   [20]Upper second level only.   [21]Former West Germany only.   [22]Port-au-Prince universities only.   [23]University of Nouakchott only.   [24]Includes schools that provide both first and second level education.   [25]Mainland Tanzania only.   [26]First level includes kindergarten.

BIBLIOGRAPHY AND SOURCES

The following list indicates the principal documentary sources used in the compilation of *Britannica World Data*. It is by no means a complete list, either for international or for national sources, but is indicative more of the range of materials to which reference has been made in preparing this compilation.

While *Britannica World Data* has long been based primarily on print sources, many rare in North American library collections, the burgeoning resources of the Internet can be accessed from any appropriately equipped personal computer (PC). At this writing, some 60 national statistical offices had Internet sites and there were also sites for central banks, national information offices, individual ministries, and the like.

Because of the relative ease of access to these sites for PC users, uniform resource locators (URLs) for mainly official sites have been added to both country statements (at the end, in boldface) and individual Comparative National Statistics tables (at the end of the headnote) when a source providing comparable international data existed. Many sites exist that are narrower in coverage or less official and that may also serve the reader (on-line newspapers; full texts of national constitutions; business and bank sites) but space permitted the listing of only the top national and intergovernmental sites. Sites that are wholly or predominantly in a language other than English are so identified.

International Statistical Sources

Asian Development Bank. *Asian Development Outlook* (annual); *Key Indicators of Developing Member Countries of ADB* (annual).
Billboard Books. *World Radio TV Handbook* (annual).
Caribbean Development Bank. *Annual Report*.
Christian Research. *World Churches Handbook* (1997).
Comité Monétaire de la Zone Franc. *La Zone Franc: Rapport* (annual).
Commonwealth of Independent States. *Demographic Yearbook; Sodruzhestvo Nezavizimykh Gosudarstv v 19** godu; Strany-Chleny SNG: Statistichesky Yezhegodnik (Member States of the CIS: Statistical Yearbook).*
Eastern Caribbean Central Bank. *Report and Statement of Accounts* (annual).
Europa Publications Ltd. *Africa South of the Sahara* (annual); *The Europa Year Book* (2 vol.); *The Far East and Australasia* (annual); *The Middle East and North Africa* (annual).
Food and Agriculture Organization. *Food Balance Sheets; Production Yearbook; Trade Yearbook; World Census of Agriculture* (decennial); *Yearbook of Fishery Statistics* (2 vol.); *Yearbook of Forest Products*.
Her Majesty's Stationery Office. *The Commonwealth Yearbook*.
Instituts d'Émission d'Outre-Mer et des Départements d'Outre-Mer (France). *Bulletin trimestriel* (quarterly); *Rapport annuel*.
Inter-American Development Bank. *Economic and Social Progress in Latin America* (annual).
Inter-Parliamentary Union. *Chronicle of Parliamentary Elections and Developments* (annual); *World Directory of Parliaments* (annual).

International Air Transport Association. *World Air Transport Statistics* (annual).
International Bank for Reconstruction and Development/The World Bank. *Statistical Handbook 19**: States of the Former USSR* (annual); *World Bank Atlas* (annual); *Global Development Finance* (2 vol.; annual); *World Development Report* (annual).
International Civil Aviation Organization. *Civil Aviation Statistics of the World* (annual); *Digest of Statistics*.
International Institute for Strategic Studies. *The Military Balance* (annual).
International Labour Organisation. *Year Book of Labour Statistics; The Cost of Social Security: Basic Tables* (triennial).
International Monetary Fund. *Annual Report on Exchange Arrangements and Exchange Restrictions; Direction of Trade Statistics Yearbook; Government Finance Statistics Yearbook; IMF Staff Country Reports* (irreg.); *International Financial Statistics* (monthly, with yearbook).
International Road Federation. *World Road Statistics* (annual).
International Telecommunication Union. *World Telecommunication Development Report* (irreg.).
Jane's Publishing Co., Ltd. *Jane's World Railways* (annual).
Keesing's Worldwide LLC. *Keesing's Record of World Events* (monthly except August).
Macmillan Press Ltd. *The Statesman's Year-Book*.
Middle East Economic Digest Ltd. *Middle East Economic Digest* (semimonthly).
Mining Journal, Ltd. *Mining Annual Review* (2 vol.).
Organization for Economic Cooperation and Development. *Economic Surveys* (annual); *Financing and External Debt of Developing Countries* (annual).
Oxford University Press. *World Christian Encyclopedia* (David B. Barrett, ed. [1982]).
Pan American Health Organization. *Health Conditions in the Americas* (2 vol.; quadrennial).
PennWell Publishing Co. *International Petroleum Encyclopedia* (annual).
Reed Travel Group. *OAG Desktop Guide—Worldwide* (monthly).
René Moreux et Cie. *Marchés tropicaux & Méditerranéens* (weekly).
United Nations (UN). *Demographic Yearbook; Energy Balances and Electricity Profiles* (biennial); *Industrial Commodities Statistics Yearbook; Energy Statistics Yearbook; International Trade Statistics Yearbook* (2 vol.); *Monthly Bulletin of Statistics; Population Studies* (irreg.); *National Accounts Statistics* (2 parts; annual); *Population and Vital Statistics Report* (quarterly); *Statistical Yearbook; World Population Prospects 19*** (biennial).
UN: Economic Commission for Africa. *African Socio-Economic Indicators* (annual); *African Statistical Yearbook* (2 vol. in 4 parts); *Demographic and Related Socio-Economic Data Sheets for ECA Member States* (irreg.); *Economic and Social Survey of Africa* (annual).
UN: Economic Commission for Europe. *Annual Bulletin of Housing and Building Statistics for Europe; Annual Bulletin of Transport Statistics for Europe.*
UN: Economic Commission for Latin America. *Economic Survey of Latin America and the Caribbean* (2 vol.; annual); *Statistical Yearbook for Latin America and the Caribbean.*
UN: Economic and Social Commission for Asia and the Pacific. *Statistical Indicators for Asia and the Pacific* (quarterly); *Statistical Yearbook for Asia and the Pacific.*
UN: Economic and Social Commission for Western Asia. *Demographic and Related Socio-Economic Data Sheets* (irreg.); *National Accounts Studies of the ESCWA Region* (irreg.); *The Population Situation in the ESCWA Region* (irreg.); *Prices and Financial Statistics in the ESCWA Region* (irreg.); *Statistical Abstract of the Region of the Economic and Social Commission for Western Asia* (annual).
UN: Educational, Scientific, and Cultural Organization. *Statistical Yearbook.*

United Nations Development Programme. *Human Development Report* (annual); *National Human Development Report series* (irreg.).
United Nations Industrial Development Organization. *Industrial Development Review Series* (irreg.); *Industrial Development: Global Report* (annual); *International Yearbook of Industrial Statistics.*
United States: Central Intelligence Agency, *The World Factbook* (annual); Dept. of Commerce, *World Population Profile* (biennial); Dept. of Health and Human Services, *Social Security Programs Throughout the World* (biennial); Dept. of Interior, *Minerals Yearbook* (3 vol. in 6 parts); Dept. of State, *Background Notes* (irreg.).
World Energy Conference. *Survey of Energy Resources* (triennial).
World Health Organization. *World Health Statistics Annual; World Health Statistics Quarterly.*
World Tourism Organization. *Compendium of Tourism Statistics* (annual); *World Tourism Statistics* (2 vol.; annual).

National Statistical Sources

Afghanistan. *Afghanistan Rehabilitation Strategy: Action Plan* (6 vol.; 1993); *Preliminary Results of the First Afghan Population Census (1979).*
Albania. *Albanian Human Development Report 1996* (UNDP); *IMF Economic Reviews: Albania* (1994); *Population and Housing Census 1989; Statistical Yearbook of Albania.*
Algeria. *Annuaire statistique; Recensement général de la population et de l'habitat, 1987.*
American Samoa. *American Samoa Statistical Digest* (annual); *1990 Census of Population and Housing.*
Andorra. *Estadístiques* (annual); *Recull Estadístic General de la Població Andorra 90.*
Angola. *Angola—Recent Economic Developments* (IMF Staff Country Report [1995]); *Perfil estatístico de Angola* (annual).
Antigua. *Antigua and Barbuda—Statistical Annex* (IMF Staff Country Report [1996]); *Statistical Yearbook; 1991 Population and Housing Census.*
Argentina. *Anuario estadístico de la República Argentina; Censo nacional de población y vivienda, 1991; Encuesta permanente de hogares* (irreg.).
Armenia. *Armenia Human Development Report* (UNDP; 1996); *Economic Reviews: Armenia* (IMF [irreg.]); *Statisticheskii Yezhegodnik Armenii* (Statistical Yearbook of Armenia).
Aruba. *Statistical Yearbook; Third Population and Housing Census October 6, 1991.*
Australia. *Monthly Summary of Statistics, Australia; Social Indicators* (annual); *Year Book Australia; 1991 Census of Population and Housing.*
Austria. *Grosszählung 1991* (General Census 1991). *Sozialstatistische Daten* (irreg.); *Statistisches Jahrbuch für die Republik Österreich.*
Azerbaijan. *Azerbaijan—Recent Economic Developments* (IMF Staff Country Report [1997]); *Azerbaijan Human Development Report* (UNDP; 1996); *Statistical Yearbook of Azerbaijan.*
Bahamas, The. *Census of Population and Housing 1990; Statistical Abstract* (annual).
Bahrain. *Statistical Abstract* (annual); *The Population, Housing, Buildings and Establishments Census—1991.*
Bangladesh. *Bangladesh Population Census, 1991; Statistical Yearbook of Bangladesh.*
Barbados. *Barbados Economic Report* (annual); *Monthly Digest of Statistics; 1993–2000 Development Plan.*
Belarus. *Economic Reviews: Belarus* (IMF [irreg.]); *Narodnoye Khozyaystvo Respubliki Belarus: Statisticheskiy Yezhegodnik* (National Economy of the Republic of Belarus: Statistical Yearbook).
Belgium. *Annuaire statistique de la Belgique; Recensement de la population et des logements au 1er mars 1991.*
Belize. *Abstract of Statistics* (annual); *Belize Economic Survey* (annual); *Belize—Statistical Appendix* (IMF Staff Country Report [1997]);

886

Development Plan 1990–94; Labour Force Survey (1993); *1991 Population Census: Major Findings.*

Benin. *Annuaire statistique; Recensement général de la population et de l'habitation* (1992).

Bermuda. *Bermuda Digest of Statistics* (annual); *Report of the Manpower Survey* (annual); *The 1991 Census of Population and Housing.*

Bhutan. *Bhutan—Selected Issues* (IMF Staff Country Report [1997]); *Statistical Yearbook of Bhutan.*

Bolivia. *Anuario Estadístico; Censo Nacional de población y vivienda 1992; Compendio Estadístico* (annual); *Estadísticas Socio-económicas* (annual); *Resumen estadístico* (annual).

Botswana. *National Development Plan 7, 1991– 1997; 1991 Population and Housing Census.*

Brazil. *Anuário Estatístico do Brasil; Censo Demografico 1991.*

Brunei. *Brunei Statistical Yearbook; Summary Tables of the Population Census 1991.*

Bulgaria. *Prebroyavaneto na naselenieto kŭm 4.12.1985 godina* (Census of Population of Dec. 4, 1985); *Naselenie* (Population; annual); *Statisticheskii godishnik na Republika Bŭlgariya* (Statistical Yearbook of the Republic of Bulgaria).

Burkina Faso. *Annuaire Statistique; Burkina Faso —Statistical Tables* (IMF Staff Country Report [1997]); *Recensement général de la population du 10 au 20 decembre 1985.*

Burundi. *Annuaire statistique; Recensement général de la population, 1990.*

Cambodia. *Cambodia: A Country Study* (1990); *Intersectoral Basic Needs Assessment Mission to Cambodia* (UNESCO; 1991); *Report of the Kampuchea Needs Assessment Study* (UNDP; 1989).

Cameroon. *Cameroon—Selected Issues and Statistical Appendix* (IMF Staff Country Report [1996]); *Recensement général de la population et de l'habitat 1987.*

Canada. *Canada Year Book* (biennial); *Census Canada 1991: Population.*

Cape Verde. *Boletím Anual de Estatística; Cape Verde—Recent Economic Developments* (IMF Staff Country Report [1996]); *I.º Recenseamento Geral da População e Habitação—1990.*

Central African Republic. *Annuaire statistique; Central African Republic—Recent Economic Developments* (IMF Staff Country Report [1997]); *Recensement général de la population 1988.*

Chad. *Annuaire statistique; Chad: A Country Study* (1990); *Chad—Background Issues and Statistical Update* (IMF Staff Country Report [1995]).

Chile. *Chile XVI censo nacional de población y V de vivienda, 22 de abril 1992; Compendio estadístico* (annual).

China, People's Republic of. *People's Republic of China Year-Book; Statistical Yearbook of China; 10 Percent Sampling Tabulation on the 1990 Population Census of the People's Republic of China.*

Colombia. *Colombia estadística* (2 vol.; annual); *XV Censo nacional de población y IV de vivienda* (1985).

Comoros. *Comoros—Recent Economic Developments* (IMF Staff Country Report [1996]); *Recensement général de la population et de l'habitat 15 septembre 1980.*

Congo, Dem. Rep. of the (Zaire). *Annuaire statistique* (irreg.); *Recensement Scientifique de la Population du 1er juillet 1984.*

Congo, Rep. of the. *Annuaire statistique; Recensement Général de la Population et de l'Habitat de 1984.*

Costa Rica. *Anuario estadístico; Censo de Población 1984; Plan Nacional de Desarrollo, 1986–90* (2 vol.).

Côte d'Ivoire. *Côte d'Ivoire—Statistical Annex* (IMF Staff Country Report [1996]); *Recensement général de la population et de l'habitat 1988.*

Croatia. *Census of Population, Households, Dwellings and Farms 31st March 1991; Statistical Yearbook.*

Cuba. *Anuario estadístico; Censo de población y viviendas, 1981.*

Cyprus. *Census of Industrial Production* (annual); *Census of Population 1992; Economic Report* (annual); *Statistical Abstract* (annual).

Czech Republic. *Statistická ročenka České Republiky* (Statistical Yearbook of the Czech Republic).

Denmark. *Folke- og boligtaellingen, 1981* (Population and Housing Census); *Statistisk årbog* (Statistical Yearbook).

Djibouti. *Annuaire statistique de Djibouti.*

Dominica. *Dominica—Recent Economic Developments* (IMF Staff Country Report [1997]); *Population and Housing Census 1991; Statistical Digest* (irreg.).

Dominican Republic. *Cifras Dominicanas* (irreg.); *VI Censo nacional de población y vivienda, 1981.*

Ecuador. *Serie estadística* (quinquennial); *Censo de población* (V) *y de vivienda* (IV) *1990.*

Egypt. *Population, Housing, and Establishment Census, 1986; Statistical Yearbook.*

El Salvador. *Censos Nacionales: V Censo de Población y IV de Vivienda* (1992); *El Salvador en cifras* (annual); *Indicadores Económicos y Sociales* (annual); *Plan de Desarrollo Economico y Social 1989–1994.*

Equatorial Guinea. *Censos Nacionales, I de Población y I de Vivienda—4 al 17 de Julio de 1983; Equatorial Guinea—Background Appendices and Recent Economic Developments* (IMF Staff Country Reports [1995 and 1996]); *Guinea en cifras* (irreg.).

Eritrea. *Eritrea—Recent Economic Developments* (IMF Staff Country Report [1996]); *Ethiopia and Eritrea: A Documentary Study* (1993).

Estonia. *Eesti Statistika Aastaraamat* (Estonia Statistical Yearbook); *Estonian Human Development Report* (annual).

Ethiopia. *Ethiopia 1984 Population and Housing Census; Ethiopia Statistical Abstract* (annual).

Faroe Islands. *Rigsombudsmanden på Færøerne: Beretning* (annual).

Fiji. *Annual Employment Survey; Census of Industries* (annual); *Current Economic Statistics* (quarterly); *1986 Census of the Population.*

Finland. *Annual Statistics of Agriculture; Economic Survey* (annual); *Population Census 1990; Statistical Yearbook of Finland.*

France. *Annuaire statistique de la France; Données sociales* (triennial); *Recensement général de la population de 1990; Tableaux de l'Economie Française* (annual).

French Guiana. *Recensement général de la population de 1990: logements-population-emplois, 973: Guyane; Tableaux economiques regionaux: Guyane* (biennial).

French Polynesia. *Résultats du Recensement Général de la Population de la Polynésie Française, du 6 Septembre 1988; Tableaux de l'economie polynesienne* (irreg.); *Te avei'a: Bulletin d'information statistique* (monthly).

Gabon. *Gabon: Poste d'Expansion Economique à Libreville* (1995); *Situation économique, financière et sociale de la République Gabonaise* (annual).

Gambia, The. *Statistical Abstract* (annual?); *The Gambia—Recent Economic Developments* (IMF Staff Country Report [1995]).

Gaza Strip. *Judaea, Samaria, and Gaza Area Statistics Quarterly; Palestinian Statistical Abstract* (annual).

Georgia. *Georgia—Recent Economic Developments* (IMF Staff Country Report [1997]); *Narodnoye Khozyaystvo Gruzinskoy SSR* (National Economy of the Georgian S.S.R. [annual]).

Germany. *Statistisches Jahrbuch für die Bundesrepublik Deutschland; Volkszählung vom 25. Mai 1987* (Census of Population).

Ghana. *Ghana—Selected Issues and Statistical Annex* (IMF [1996]); *Population Census of Ghana, 1984; Quarterly Digest of Statistics.*

Gibraltar. *Abstract of Statistics* (annual); *Census of Gibraltar, 1991.*

Greece. *Recensement de la population et des habitations, 1991; Statistical Yearbook of Greece.*

Greenland. *Grønland* (annual); *Grønlands befolkning* (Greenland Population [annual]).

Grenada. *Abstract of Statistics* (annual); *Grenada— Statistical Appendix* (IMF Staff Country Report [1996]). *1991 Population and Housing Census.*

Guadeloupe. *Recensement général de la population de 1990: logements-population-emplois, 971: Guadeloupe; Tableaux economiques regionaux: Guadeloupe* (biennial).

Guam. *Guam Annual Economic Review; Census '90: Guam.*

Guatemala. *Anuario Estadística; Censos nacionales, 1981: IX de población—IV de habitación.*

Guernsey. *Guernsey Census 1991; Statistical Digest* (annual).

Guinea. *Guinea—Background Paper* (IMF Staff Country Report [1996]).

Guinea-Bissau. *Guinea-Bissau—Recent Economic Developments* (IMF Staff Country Report [1996]); *Recenseamento Geral da População e da Habitação, 16 de Abril de 1979.*

Guyana. *Annual Statistical Abstract; Guyana: From Economic Recovery to Sustained Growth* (1993); *Guyana and Belize: Country Studies* (1993).

Haiti. *Dominican Republic and Haiti: Country Studies* (1991); *Haiti—Statistical Annex* (IMF Staff Country Report [1996]). *Résultats préliminaires du recensement général* (Septembre 1982).

Honduras. *Anuario estadístico; Censo nacional de Población y Vivienda, 1988; Honduras—Statistical Appendix* (IMF Staff Country Report [1997]); *Honduras en cifras* (annual).

Hong Kong. *Annual Digest of Statistics; Hong Kong* (annual); *Hong Kong 1991 Population Census; Hong Kong Social and Economic Trends* (biennial).

Hungary. *Statisztikai évkönyv* (Statistical Yearbook); *1990, Évi népszámlálás* (Census of Population).

Iceland. *Hagtidhindi* (monthly); *Landshagir* (Statistical Yearbook of Iceland [annual]); *Utanrikisverslun* (External Trade [annual]).

India. *Census of India, 1991; Economic Survey* (annual); *India: A Reference Annual; Statistical Abstract* (annual).

Indonesia. *Indonesia: An Official Handbook* (irreg.); *Hasil Sensus penduduk Indonesia, 1990* (Census of Population); *Statistical Yearbook of Indonesia.*

Iran. *Multi-Round Population Survey 1991; National Census of Population and Housing, October 1986; A Statistical Reflection of the Islamic Republic of Iran* (annual); *Iran Statistical Yearbook.*

Iraq. *Iraq: A Country Study* (1990); *Annual Abstract of Statistics.*

Ireland. *Census of Population of Ireland, 1991; National Income and Expenditure* (annual); *Statistical Abstract* (annual).

Isle of Man. *Census Report 1991; Isle of Man Digest of Economic and Social Statistics* (annual).

Israel. *1995 Census of Population and Housing; Statistical Abstract* (annual).

Italy. *Statistica agrarie; Statistiche demografiche* (4 parts); *Statistiche dell'istruzione; Annuario statistico Italiano; 13º Censimento generale della popolazione e delle Abìtazioni 20 Ottobre 1991.*

Jamaica. *Economic and Social Survey* (annual); *Statistical Abstract* (annual); *Statistical Yearbook of Jamaica.*

Japan. *Japan Statistical Yearbook; Statistical Indicators on Social Life* (annual); *1995 Population Census of Japan.*

Jersey. *Report of the Census for 1991; Statistical Digest* (annual).

Jordan. *Population and Housing Census 1994; Family Expenditure Survey* (1980); *National Accounts* (irreg.); *Statistical Yearbook.*

Kazakstan. *Economic Reviews: Kazakhstan* (IMF [irreg.]); *Statistical Yearbook; Statistichesky Yezhegodnik* (Statistical Yearbook).

Kenya. *Economic Survey* (annual); *Population Census 1989; Statistical Abstract* (annual).

Kiribati. *Annual Abstract of Statistics; Kiribati Population Census 1990.*

Korea, North. *North Korea: A Country Study* (1994); *The Population of North Korea* (1990).

Korea, South. *Korea Statistical Yearbook; Social Indicators in Korea* (annual); *1995 Population and Housing Census.*

Kuwait. *Annual Statistical Abstract; General Census of Population and Housing and Buildings 1985.*

Kyrgyzstan. *Economic Reviews: Kyrgyz Republic* (IMF [irreg.]); *Statistichesky Yezhegodnik Kyrgyzstana* (Statistical Yearbook of Kyrgyzstan).

Laos. *Lao People's Democratic Republic—Recent Economic Developments* (IMF Staff Country Report [1996]).

Latvia. *Latvia: The Transition to a Market Economy* (1993); *Statistical Yearbook of Latvia.*

Lebanon. *Lebanon: A Country Study* (1989).

Lesotho. *Lesotho—Recent Economic Developments* (IMF Staff Country Report [1996]); *Statistical Yearbook; 1986 Population Census.*

Liberia. *Economic Survey* (annual); *1974 Census of Population and Housing.*

Libya. *The Five-Year Development Plan 1981–85; Libya Population Census, 1973.*

Liechtenstein. *Statistisches Jahrbuch; Volkszählung, 2 Dezember 1980* (Census of Population).

Lithuania. *Lietuvos Statistikos Metraštis* (Lithuanian Statistical Yearbook); *Lithuania: The Transition to a Market Economy* (1993).

Luxembourg. *Annuaire statistique; Bulletin du STATEC* (monthly); *Recensement général de la population du 31 mars 1991.*

Macau. *Anuário Estatístico; XIII Recenseamento Geral da População, 1991.*

Macedonia. *Former Yugoslav Republic of Macedonia—Statistical Appendix* (IMF Staff Country Report [1997]); *Statistical Yearbook of the Republic of Macedonia.*

Madagascar. *Madagascar—Selected Issues and Statistical Annex* (IMF Staff Country Report [1996]); *Recensement général de la population et de l'habitat, aout 1993; Situation économique* (annual).

Malaŵi. *Malaŵi Population and Housing Census, 1987; Malawi Statistical Yearbook; Malawi Yearbook.*

Malaysia. *Population and Housing Census of Malaysia 1991; Yearbook of Statistics.*

Maldives. *National Development Plan 1991–1993; Population and Housing Census of Maldives 1990; Statistical Year Book of Maldives.*

Mali. *Annuaire statistique du Mali; Recensement general de la population et de l'habitat* (du 1er au 14 avril 1987).

Malta. *Annual Abstract of Statistics; Quarterly Digest of Statistics.*
Marshall Islands. *Marshall Islands Statistical Abstract* (annual).
Martinique. *Recensement de la population de 1990: logements-population-emplois, 972: Martinique; Tableaux economiques regionaux: Martinique* (biennial).
Mauritania. *Annuaire Statistique; Mauritania—Statistical Appendix* (IMF Staff Country Report [1997]).
Mauritius. *Annual Digest of Statistics; 1990 Housing and Population Census of Mauritius.*
Mayotte. *Bulletin Trimestriel* (quarterly) and *Rapport Annuel* (Institut d'Emission, France); *Recensement général de la population de la Collectivité territoriale de Mayotte: août 1991.*
Mexico. *Anuario estadístico; XI Censo general de población y vivienda, 1990; Informe de Gobierno: Estadístico* (annual).
Micronesia. *Micronesia—Recent Economic Developments* (IMF Staff Country Report [1996]); *Second National Development Plan 1992–1996.*
Moldova. *Economic Reviews: Moldova* (IMF [irreg.]); *Republica Moldova in Cifre* (annual); *1996 National Human Development Report: Republic of Moldova* (UNDP).
Mongolia. *Mongolia—Background Material* (IMF Staff Country Report [1996]); *National Economy of the MPR for 70 years: 1921–91* (1991; quinquennial); *The Mongolian People's Republic: Towards a Market Economy* (1991).
Morocco. *Annuaire statistique du Maroc; Recensement général de la population et de l'habitat de 1994.*
Mozambique. *Anuário Estatístico; Mozambique—Recent Economic Developments* (IMF Staff Country Report [1996]); *1º Recenseamento Geral da População, 1980.*
Myanmar (Burma). *Myanmar—Recent Economic Developments* (IMF Staff Country Report [1997]); *Report to the Pyithu Hluttaw on the Financial, Social, and Economic Conditions for 19**** (annual); *Statistical Abstract* (irreg.); *1983 Population Census.*
Namibia. *1991 Population and Housing Census; Statistical/Economic Review* (annual).
Nepal. *Economic Survey* (annual); *Population Monograph of Nepal* (1995); *The Seventh Plan (1985–90); Statistical Pocket Book* (irreg.); *Statistical Yearbook of Nepal.*
Netherlands, The. *Statistical Yearbook of the Netherlands; 14e Algemene volkstelling, 28 februari 1971* (14th General Population Census).
Netherlands Antilles. *Netherlands Antilles—Recent Economic Developments* (IMF Staff Country Report [1997]); *Tweede Algemene Volks- en Woningtelling Nederlandse Antillen: toestand per 1 Februari 1981; Statistical Yearbook of the Netherlands Antilles.*
New Caledonia. *Annuaire statistique; Recensement de la population de la Nouvelle-Calédonie au 4 avril 1989; Tableaux de l'economie Caledonienne* (annual).
New Zealand. *1991 New Zealand Census of Population and Dwellings; New Zealand Official Yearbook.*
Nicaragua. *Censos Nacionales 1995; Compendio Estadístico* (annual); *Nicaragua—Recent Economic Developments* (IMF Staff Country Report [1996]).
Niger. *Annuaire statistique; Niger—Background Paper* (IMF Staff Country Report [1996]); *Plan de developpement economique et social du Niger 1987–91; 2ème Recensement général de la population 1988.*
Nigeria. *Annual Abstract of Statistics; Nigeria: A Country Study* (1992); *Nigeria—Statistical Appendix* (IMF Staff Country Report [1997]).
Norway. *Folke- og boligtelling 1990* (Population and Housing Census); *Industristatistikk* (annual); *Statistisk årbok* (Statistical Yearbook).
Oman. *General Census of Population, Housing, and Establishments* (1993); *Statistical Year Book; Fourth Five-Year Development Plan (1991–1995).*
Pakistan. *Economic Survey* (annual); *Eighth Five Year Plan* (1993–98); *Pakistan Statistical Yearbook; Population Census of Pakistan, 1981.*
Palau. *Abstract of Statistics* (annual); *Census '90.*
Panama. *Indicadores económicos y sociales* (annual); *Censos nacionales de 1990: IX de población y V de vivienda, 13 de mayo de 1990; Panama en cifras* (annual); *Situación económica: Cuentas nacionales* (annual); *Situación económica: Industria* (annual).
Papua New Guinea. *Papua New Guinea—Statistical Appendix* (IMF Staff Country Report [1997]); *Summary of Statistics* (annual); *1990 National Population Census.*
Paraguay. *Anuario estadístico del Paraguay; Censo nacional de población y viviendas, 1992.*
Peru. *Censos nacionales; IX de población: IV de vivienda, 11 de julio de 1993; Compendio estadístico* (3 vol.; annual); *Informe estadístico* (annual).
Philippines. *Philippine Statistical Yearbook; Philippine Yearbook; 1990 Census of Population and Housing.*
Poland. *Narodowy spis powszechny 1988* (Census of Population); *Rocznik statystyczny* (Statistical Yearbook).
Portugal. *Anuário Estatístico; XIII Recenseamento Geral da População: III Recenseamento Geral da Habitação, 1991.*
Puerto Rico. *Estadísticas socioeconomicas* (annual); *Informe económico al gobernador* (Economic Report to the Governor [annual]); *1990 Census of Population and Housing* (U.S.).
Qatar. *Annual Statistical Abstract; Economic Survey of Qatar* (annual); *Qatar Year Book.*
Réunion. *Recensement général de la population de 1990: logements-population-emploi, 974; Réunion; Tableau Economique de la Réunion* (biennial).
Romania. *Anuarul statistic al României; Population and Housing Census January 7, 1992.*
Russia. *Demograficheskiy Yezhegodnik Rossii* (Demographic Yearbook of Russia; [annual]); *Rossiysky Statistichesky Yezhegodnik* (Russian Statistical Yearbook).
Rwanda. *Bulletin de Statistique: Supplement Annuel; Recensement General de la Population et de l'Habitat 1991.*
St. Kitts and Nevis. *Annual Digest of Statistics; St. Christopher and Nevis—Recent Economic Developments* (IMF Staff Country Report [1995]).
St. Lucia. *Annual Statistical Digest; St. Lucia—Recent Economic Developments* (IMF Staff Country Report [1996]).
St. Vincent and the Grenadines. *Digest of Statistics* (annual); *Population and Housing Census 1991.*
Samoa (Western Samoa). *Annual Statistical Abstract; Census of Population and Housing, 1981; Seventh Development Plan 1992–1994; Western Samoa—Recent Economic Developments* (IMF Staff Country Report [1997]).
San Marino. *Bollettino di Statistica* (quarterly); *5 Censimento generale della popolazione* (1979).
São Tomé and Príncipe. *1º Recenseamento Geral da População e da Habitação 1981; Sao Tome—Select Issues and Statistical Appendix* (IMF Staff Country Report [1996]).
Saudi Arabia. *The Statistical Indicator* (annual); *Statistical Yearbook.*
Senegal. *Recensement de la Population et de l'Habitat 1988; Situation économique du Senegal* (annual).
Seychelles. *National Development Plan, 1990–94* (2 vol.); *Statistical Abstract* (annual); *1987 Census Report.*
Sierra Leone. *Sierra Leone—Statistical Annex* (IMF Staff Country Report [1996]).
Singapore. *Census of Population, 1990; Singapore Yearbook; Yearbook of Statistics Singapore.*
Slovakia. *Sčítanie L'udu, Domov a Bytov 1991* (Census of Population, Housing, and Families 1991); *Statistical Yearbook of the Slovak Republic.*
Slovenia. *Statistični Letopis Republike Slovenija* (Statistical Yearbook of the Republic of Slovenia).
Solomon Islands. *Solomon Islands 1986 Population Census; Statistical Bulletin* (irreg.).
Somalia. *Statistical Abstract* (annual).
South Africa. *1991 Population Census; South Africa: Official Yearbook of the Republic of South Africa; South African Statistics* (biennial).
Spain. *Anuario estadístico; Censo de población de 1991.*
Sri Lanka. *Census of Population and Housing, 1981; Sri Lanka Year Book; Statistical Pocketbook of the Democratic Socialist Republic of Sri Lanka* (annual).
Sudan, The. *Sudan: A Country Study* (1992); *Third Population Census, 1983.*
Suriname. *General Population Census 1980; Statistisch Jaarboek van Suriname; Suriname—Statistical Annex* (IMF Staff Country Report [1996]).
Swaziland. *Annual Statistical Bulletin; Report on the 1986 Swaziland Population Census; Swaziland—Recent Economic Developments* (IMF Staff Country Report [1997]).
Sweden. *Folk- och bostadsräkningen, 1990* (Population and Housing Census); *Statistisk årsbok för Sverige* (Statistical Abstract of Sweden [annual]).
Switzerland. *Recensement fédéral de la population, 1990; Statistisches Jahrbuch* (Statistical Yearbook).
Syria. *General Census of Housing and Inhabitants, 1981; Statistical Abstract* (annual).
Taiwan. *Industry of Free China* (monthly); *The Republic of China Yearbook; Social Indicators of the Republic of China* (annual); *Statistical Abstract* (annual); *Statistical Yearbook of the Republic of China; Taiwan Statistical Data Book* (annual); *1990 Census of Population and Housing.*
Tajikistan. *Economic Reviews: Tajikistan* (IMF [irreg.]); *Narodnoye Khozyaystvo Tadzhikskoy SSR* (National Economy of the Tadzhik S.S.R. [annual]).
Tanzania. *Tanzania—Selected Issues and Statistical Appendix* (IMF Staff Country Report [1996]); *Tanzania in Figures* (annual); *Tanzania Statistical Abstract* (irreg.); *1978 Population Census.*
Thailand. *Report of the Industrial Survey, Whole Kingdom* (biennial); *Report of the Labor Force Survey: Whole Kingdom* (three issues annually); *Statistical Handbook of Thailand* (annual); *Statistical Yearbook; 1990 Population and Housing Census.*
Togo. *Annuaire statistique du Togo; Eurostat Country Profile: Togo* (1991); *Recensement Général de la Population et de l'Habitat 1981; Togo—Statistical Annex* (IMF Staff Country Report [1996]).
Tonga. *Population Census, 1986; Sixth Development Plan 1991–95; Tonga—Recent Economic Developments* (IMF Staff Country Report [1997]).
Trinidad and Tobago. *Annual Statistical Digest; 1990 Population and Housing Census.*
Tunisia. *Annuaire statistique de la Tunisie; Recensement général de la population et des logements, 30 mars 1984.*
Turkey. *1990 Genel Nüfus Sayımı* (1990 Census of Population); *Türkiye İstatistik Yilliği* (Statistical Yearbook of Turkey).
Turkmenistan. *Turkmenistan—Recent Economic Developments* (IMF Staff Country Report [1996]); *Turkmenistan Human Development Report* (UNDP [1996]); *Turkmenistan v tsifrakh* (Turkmenistan in figures [annual]).
Tuvalu. *1992–94 Medium-Term Economic Framework Programme.*
Uganda. *Uganda: A Country Study; Uganda—Background Paper* (IMF Staff Country Report [1995]).
Ukraine. *Statistichniy Shchorichnik Ukraini za 19*** *rik* (Statistical Yearbook of Ukraine for the year 19**); *Ukraine—Recent Economic Developments* (IMF Staff Country Report [1996]); *Ukraine Human Development Report* (UNDP [1996]).
United Arab Emirates. *Statistical Yearbook* (Abu Dhabi).
United Kingdom. *Annual Abstract of Statistics; Britain: An Official Handbook* (annual); *Census 1991; General Household Survey* series (individual titles vary; annual); *United Kingdom National Accounts.*
United States. *Agricultural Statistics* (annual); *Annual Energy Review; Current Population Reports; Digest of Education Statistics* (annual); *Minerals Yearbook* (3 vol. in 6 parts); *National Transportation Statistics* (annual); *Statistical Abstract* (annual); *U.S. Exports: SIC-Based Products* (annual); *U.S. Imports: SIC-Based Products* (annual); *Vital and Health Statistics* (series 1–20); *1992 Census of Agriculture; 1992 Census of Construction Industries; 1992 Census of Manufacturing; 1992 Census of Retail Trade; 1992 Census of Service Industries; 1992 Census of Wholesale Trade; 1990 Census of Population and Housing.*
Uruguay. *Anuario Estadístico; Censo General: VI de población: IV de viviendas, Octubre 1985.*
Uzbekistan. *Narodnoye Khozyaystvo Respubliki Uzbekistan v 19*** *g.* (National Economy of Uzbekistan in the Year 19** [annual]); *Republic of Uzbekistan; Uzbekistan—Selected Issues and Statistical Appendix* (IMF Staff Country Report [1996]).
Vanuatu. *National Population Census 1989; Second National Development Plan 1987–1991* (2 vol.); *Vanuatu Statistical Yearbook.*
Venezuela. *Anuario estadístico; Censo General de la Población y Vivienda 1990; Encuesta de hogares por muestreo* (annual); *Encuesta industrial* (annual).
Vietnam. *Nien Giam Thong Ke* (Statistical Yearbook); *Tong Dieu Tra Dan So Viet Nam—1989* (*Vietnam Population Census—1989*); *Vietnam—Recent Economic Development* and *Selected Issues* (IMF Staff Country Report [1996]).
Virgin Islands of the United States. *1990 Census of Population and Housing* (U.S.).
West Bank. *Judaea, Samaria, and Gaza Area Statistics Quarterly; Palestinian Statistical Abstract* (annual).
Western Sahara. *Recensement General de la Population et de l'Habitat* (1994 [Morocco]).
Yemen. *Country Presentation: Republic of Yemen* (1990); *The Yemens: Country Studies* (1986).
Yugoslavia. *Popis stanovištva, domaćinstava, stanova i poljoprivrednih gazdinstava 1991 godine* (Census of Population, Households, Housing, and Agricultural Holdings 1991); *Statistički godišnjak Jugoslavije* (Statistical Yearbook of Yugoslavia).
Zambia. *National Development Plan, 1989–93; Zambia—Statistical Annex* (IMF Staff Country Report [1996]); *1990 Census of Population, Housing, Agriculture.*
Zimbabwe. *Population Census 1992; Statistical Yearbook* (irreg.).

Aalto / American 889

Index

This index covers both *Britannica Book of the Year* (cumulative for 10 years) and *Britannica World Data.*

Entries in dark type are titles of articles in the *Book of the Year;* **an accompanying year in dark type gives the year the reference appears, and the accompanying page number** in light type **shows where the article appears. References for previous years are preceded by the year in dark type. For example, "Architecture 99:**139; **98:**136; **97:**137; **96:**117; **95:**104; **94:**99; **93:**100; **92:**98; **91:**127; **90:**146**" indicates that the article "Architecture" appeared every year from 1990 through 1999. Other references that appear with a page number but without a year refer to references from the current yearbook.**

Indented entries in light type that follow dark-type article titles refer by page number to other places in the text where the subject of the article is discussed. Light-type entries that are not indented refer by page number to subjects that are not themselves article titles. Names of people covered in biographies and obituaries are followed by the abbreviation "(biog.)" or "(obit.)" with the year in dark type and a page number in light type, *e.g.,* Bombeck, Erma Louise (obit.) **97:**94, or Clinton, Bill, *or* William Jefferson Clinton (biogs.) **99:**68; **97:**70; **94:**37; **93:**37. In cases where a person has both a biography and an obituary, the words appear as subentries under the main entry and are alphabetized accordingly,

e.g.:

Amis, Sir Kingsley William
  biography **92:**33
  obituary **96:**73

References to illustrations are by page number and are preceded by the abbreviation *il.*

The index uses word-by-word alphabetization (treating a word as one or more characters separated by a space from the next word). Names beginning with "Mc" and "Mac" are alphabetized as "Mac"; "St." is treated as "Saint."

A

Aalto, Alvar 140
Abacha, Sani 477, *il.* 30
  biography **98:**65
  Commonwealth of Nations 388
  human rights 319
  Nigeria 230
  obituary 90
ABB: *see* Asea Brown Boveri
Abbott, George Francis (obit.) **96:**73
ABC: *see* American Bowling Congress; American Broadcasting Corporation
'Abd al-Wahab, Muhammad (obit.) **92:**54
Abdul, Paula (biog.) **91:**64
Abdul Rahman (obit.) **91:**86
Abe Kobo, *or* Abe Kimifusa (obit.) **94:**54
Abernathy, Ralph David (obit.) **91:**86
Abiola, Moshood Kashimawo Olawale 388, 478
  human rights 319
  obituary 90
Abkhazia (region, Georgia), refugees 303, *il.* 303
aborigine people: *see* Australian Aborigine; Native American peoples
abortion
  court decisions 230
  Portugal 484, *il.* 484
  Roman Catholic Church 311, 496
  Spain 496
  United States 517
Abrahams, William Miller (obit.) 90
Abramovic, Marina 147
Abravanel, Maurice (obit.) **94:**54
ABT: *see* American Ballet Theatre
Abu Rishah, 'Umar (obit.) **91:**86
Abu Seif, Salah (obit.) **97:**91
Abubakar, Abdulsalam
  biography 65
  Commonwealth of Nations 388
  human rights 319
  Nigeria 230
Abzug, Bella, *or* Bella Savitzky (obit.) 90, *il.* 90
Academy Awards, *or* Oscars (Los Angeles, California) *table* 295
  fashion 223
accelerator mass spectrometry, *or* AMS 138
accessory units, senior citizen housing 320
acquired immune deficiency syndrome: *see* AIDS
Acquisitions and Cross-Servicing Agreement, Japan-U.S. 457
action figures (dolls), retailing 167
Acton, Sir Harold Mario Mitchell (obit.) **95:**60
Acuff, Roy Claxton (obit.) **93:**54
Ad tuendam fidem (pastoral letter) 311
Adamkus, Valdas V. 467
  biography 65, *il.* 65
Adams, Bryan (biog.) **93:**33
Adams, Diana (obit.) **94:**54
Adams, Gerry (biog.) **95:**39
Adams, John Coolidge (biog.) **98:**65
Adams, Michael 337
Adams, Scott (biog.) **96:**52
Adamson, George (obit.) **90:**103
Adansonia digitata: see baobab tree
Addison, John Mervyn (obit.) 90
Adelie penguin, *or Pygoscelis adeliae* 217
Ademola, Sir Adetokunbo Adegboyega (obit.) **94:**54
Aden: *see* Yemen, People's Democratic Republic of
Aden-Abyan Islamic Army 522
Adidas America, footwear 159
adipic acid 261
Adler, Stella (obit.) **93:**54
Admiral's Cup (sailing) *table* 365
"Adriatico" (Nigro) 253
ADRs: *see* American Depository Receipts
advanced ceramics 170
advanced composites 171
Advanced Composition Explorer (satellite) 266
Advanced Photo System, *or* APS 175
"adventurers' grand slam" 394
Advertising 157, *il.* 157
  magazine 276
  pharmaceutical 174
aerial sports **94:**278; **93:**279; **92:**305; **91:**305; **90:**321
Aerospace 158
  mergers 437
  military affairs 278
  see also Aviation
Afanasyev, Viktor Grigoryevich (obit.) **95:**60
AFC: *see* American Football Conference
Afewerke, Issayas, *or* Isaias Afwerki (biog.) **92:**33
affirmative action (U.S. education) 211, *il.* 211
Afghanistan 99:399; **98:**389; **97:**388; **96:**366; **95:**367; **94:**402; **93:**402; **92:**401; **91:**428; **90:**447
  disasters
    aviation 58
    natural 59, 60, *il.* 187
  education 210, *il.* 399
  human rights 230, 319, *il.* 319
  Iran 451
  literature 258
  military affairs 278
  refugees 302
  special reports **94:**377; **93:**233
  terrorism 231
  Turkmenistan 507
  United States 516
  U.S. missile strike 158
  Uzbekistan 519
  see also WORLD DATA
'Aflaq, Michel (obit.) **90:**103
AFPs: *see* private pension fund administrators
Africa Cup (assoc. football) 415
African affairs **94:**352; **93:**354; **92:**348; **91:**378; **90:**399
  agricultural and tourist zone 498
  AIDS deaths 226
  anthropology 134
  business and industry
    airline 378
    cotton 179
    mining 174
  Clinton visit and U.S. policy (spotlight) 441
  economic affairs 191, 196
    external debt 200
  El Niño 126
  ethnic conflict 229
  food emergencies 125
  military affairs 283
    armed forces, strength *table* 280–281
  motion pictures 299
  population trends 301
  refugees 301
  religion 305, 309, 310
  special report **92:**349
  see also Middle Eastern and North African affairs; individual countries by name
African-American people: *see* black American
African Development Bank, Republic of the Congo 427
"African Jungle Picture" (art by Dial) *il.* 149
African lions, *or Leo leo* 238
African National Congress, *or* ANC (pol. party, S. Africa) 494
African rock python 217
African Unity, Organization of, *or* OAU
  mediation efforts 415
    Anjouan secession 426
    Eritrea-Ethiopia 434
  summit 415
African wild dog, *or Lycaon pictus* 238, *il.* 238
Afro-American people: *see* black American
Afwerki, Isaias: *see* Afewerke, Issayas
Aga Khan Award for Architecture 140
Agassi, Andre 361
age, population average 300
Agency for International Development, *or* AID, Dominican Republic 431
Agfa (Belgian company)
  photography 175
  printing 176
"aging-in-place," senior citizen housing 321
Agnew, Spiro Theodore (obit.) **97:**91
Agriculture and Food Supplies 99:124; **98:**123; **97:**123; **96:**103; **95:**90; **94:**83; **93:**83; **92:**83; **91:**113; **90:**129
  Africa, regional zone 498
  archaeology 137
  Bolivia 409, *il.* 409
  crop destruction/loss
    Bangladesh 406
    Bolivia 409
    China *il.* 422
    Cuba 428
    El Niño (spotlight) 481
    Ethiopia 434
    Fiji 435
    Honduras 446
    Netherlands, The 476
    Philippines 483
  Dominica 431
  drug resistance 224, 228
  food-aid relief *il.* 36
  Jordan 458
  Kazakstan 458
  Mali 469
  Morocco 473
  Russia 488
  special reports **99:**132; **92:**167; **90:**140
  Tonga 504
  Uganda 507
  United States 518
  Zimbabwe 523
  see also WORLD DATA; and individual countries by name
Agrio River (Spain) mining waste spill 214
Aguilar Manzo, Luis, *or* The Wild Rooster (obit.) **98:**90
agunahs (Judaism) 312
Ahern, Bertie 452
Ai Qing, *or* Jiang Haicheng (obit.) **97:**91
AID: *see* Agency for International Development
aid: *see* relief aid
AIDS, *or* acquired immune deficiency syndrome 226
  population trends 301
  prostitution and sex slavery 319
  special reports **95:**278; **94:**263
  television programming 273
Aikman, Troy Kenneth (biog.) **97:**65
Ailey, Alvin (obit.) **90:**103
AIOC: *see* Azerbaijan International Operating Co.
Air France 436
air pollution 215
  see also pollution; water pollution
air turbulence (aviation) 158
Airbus Industrie (European company) 158
aircraft, *or* airlines: *see* Aerospace; Aviation
airport architecture 139
AIS: *see* Army of Islamic Salvation
Ajit, *or* Hamid Ali Khan (obit.) 90
Akalaitis, JoAnne (biog.) **92:**33
"Akameshijūyataki shinjūmisui" (Kurumatani) 259
Akashi, Yasushi (biog.) **93:**33
Akashi Kaikyo Bridge (Japan) 141, 144, *il.* 141
Akayesu, Jean Paul 232, *il.* 42
Ake, Claude (obit.) **97:**91
Akebono (biog.) **94:**33
Akhromeyev, Sergey Fedorovich (obit.) **92:**54
Akii-Bua, John (obit.) **98:**90
Akzo Nobel (paint company) 174
Al-Muhtadee Billah, Prince *il.* 40
al-: *see under* substantive word, *e.g.,* Hariri, Rafiq al- (Arab. lang.)
Alabama (state, U.S.) church-state relations 518
Alagna, Roberto (biog.) **97:**65
Alam, Shahidul 153
Alameda Corridor project (Long Beach, California) 379
Alaska (state, U.S.)
  marijuana 517
  marriage ban 518
  oil production 393
Alaskan North Slope Project Sponsor Agreement (pipeline project) 394
Albania 99:399; **98:**394; **97:**388; **96:**366; **95:**367; **94:**421; **93:**424; **92:**418; **91:**468; **90:**485
  Greece 443
  Majko, Prime Minister *il.* 45
  new flag *illus.* **93:**345
  refugees *il.* 303
  see also WORLD DATA
Albanian people
  food emergencies 125
  Macedonia 468
  Yugoslavia 387, 400, 522, *il.* 523
Albert, Prince (Monaco) 473
Albert II (biog.) **94:**33
Alberts, Bruce (biog.) **95:**39
Albertson's Inc. (U.S.) 176, *il.* 176
Albrecht, *or* Prince Albert Luitpold Ferdinand Michael, duke of Bavaria (obit.) **97:**91
Albright, Josephine Patterson (obit.) **97:**91
Albright, Madeleine *il.* 505
  ASEAN Regional Forum 390
  biography **98:**65
  Iran 451
  Japan 457
  Malaysia 469
  Papua New Guinea 480
Alcayaga, María Lucia: *see* Beltrán, Lola
"Alcobas de palacio" (Loret de Mola) **97:**248
alcohol consumption
  in birds 240
  student 211
  warning labels 226
Alea, Tomás Gutiérrez (obit.) **97:**91
Alepoudhelis, Odysseus: *see* Elytis, Odysseus
Alfaro, Emilio (obit.) 90
Alfredsson, Helen 355
ALFs: *see* assisted living facilities
Alfvén, Hannes Olof Gésta (obit.) **96:**73
Algeria 99:400; **98:**394; **97:**389; **96:**367; **95:**368; **94:**379; **93:**380; **92:**378; **91:**404; **90:**424
  literature 259
  Morocco 473
  murder protest *il.* 400
  Spain 496
  see also WORLD DATA
Ali Mahdi, Muhammad 494
Aliyev, Heydar (biog.) **94:**33
alien species, environmental invasion 217
All-England Championships (badminton) 325
All-England (Wimbledon) Tennis Championships 372
Allchurch, Ivor John (obit.) **98:**90
Allen, George Herbert (obit.) **91:**86
Allen, Sir George Oswald Browning (obit.) **90:**103
Allen, Joan *il.* 296
Allen, Mel, *or* Melvin Allen Israel (obit.) **97:**91
Allende, Isabel 254
  biography **96:**52
Alliance for Freedom, *or* Freedom Alliance (pol. party, It.) **97:**436
Alliance pipeline construction project 379
Allin, the Right Rev. John Maury 306
  obituary 90
Allison, Davey (obit.) **94:**54
Allison, Fran (obit.) **90:**103
Allison, Luther (obit.) **98:**90
Almeida Theatre Company (London, England) 291
Almendros, Nestor (obit.) **93:**54
Almodóvar, Pedro (biog.) **91:**64
alpine skiing 366, *table* 359
  1998 Winter Olympics *table* 359
Alsgaard, Thomas 366
Alsop, Joseph Wright (obit.) **90:**103
Alstrom (multinational company) 164
alternative energy 166
alternative medicine 227
  special report **98:**228
alternative sports (special report) **98:**320
Altman, Sidney (biog.) **90:**81
Alton, John, *or* Aldan Jacko (obit.) **97:**91
aluminum
  materials 172
  mining 173
Alzado, Lyle (obit.) **93:**54
Alzheimer's disease 228
Amanpour, Christiane (biog.) **97:**65
amateur radio 274
Amato, Giuliano (biog.) **93:**33
Amazon rain forest *il.* 25
Amazon.com (Web site) 177, 277
Ambartsumian, Viktor Amazaspovich (obit.) **97:**91
amber, fossils in 239
Ambler, Eric (obit.) 90
Amboseli Park (Kenya) (special report) 180, *il.* 181
Ambystoma talpoideum: see mole salamander
Ameche, Don (obit.) **94:**54
Amedeo (Brunei company) 414
America Online, *or* AOL (U.S. company) 183
American Apparel Manufacturers Association 158
American Ballet Theatre, *or* ABT 288
American Basketball League 329
American Bottling Co. (U.S.) 131
American Bowling Congress, *or* ABC 333
American Broadcasting Corporation, *or* ABC (U.S.) 267
American Classical Music Hall of Fame and Museum 285
American Episcopal Church 305, 306
American Family Publishers 207, 276, 518
American Football Conference, *or* AFC 351, *il.* 351
American Girls (doll collection) 168
American Home Products (U.S. company) 175
American Indian people: *see* Native American peoples
American League (major league baseball) 326
"American Pastoral" (Roth) 277
American Samoa (U.S. territory) 392
American Stock Exchange, *or* Amex 201
American Stores (U.S.) 176, *il.* 176

C

F

G

M

N

V